Contemporary Authors

Contemporary Authors

A BIO-BIBLIOGRAPHICAL GUIDE TO CURRENT AUTHORS AND THEIR WORKS

CLARE D. KINSMAN
MARY ANN TENNENHOUSE

Editors

volumes 9-12

first revision

GALE RESEARCH COMPANY • THE BOOK TOWER • DETROIT, MICHIGAN 48226

CONTEMPORARY AUTHORS

Published By
Gale Research Company, The Book Tower, Detroit, Michigan 48226
Each Year's Volumes Are Cumulated and Revised About Five Years Later

Frederick G. Ruffner, *Publisher*   James M. Ethridge, *Editorial Director*

Clare D. Kinsman and Mary Ann Tennenhouse, *Co-Editors*
Sandra Bunnell and Roberta Dahlberg, *Associate Editors*
Cynthia R. Fadool, Phyllis Carmel Mendelson,
and Alexander James Roman, *Assistant Editors*
Laura Bryant, *Operations Supervisor*
Daphne Cox, *Production Manager*

EDITORIAL ASSISTANTS

Norma Sawaya, Shirley Seip

Library of Congress Card Number 62-52046
ISBN 0-8103-0002-8

PREFACE

Contemporary Authors

VOLUME 9-12, FIRST REVISION

This volume represents a complete revision and a consolidation into one alphabet of biographical material which originally appeared in *Contemporary Authors*, volumes 9-10, published in 1964, and volumes 11-12, published in 1965. The revised material is up-to-date, in most cases, through late 1973.

In preparing the revision, the following are the major steps which have been taken:

1) Every sketch has been submitted to the author concerned, if he is still living, and all changes requested which were within the scope and purpose of *Contemporary Authors* have been made.

2) If an author has failed to submit changes or to approve his sketch as still correct, the editors have attempted to verify present address, present position, and the bibliography. A symbol (†) has been used to indicate those sketches appearing in this revision which have not been personally verified by their subjects.

3) Additional research has been done on the bibliographies of many authors, both to pick up publications which were not included in the previous versions of their sketches and to assure that all recent works have been included.

4) "Sidelights" have been added to many listings for prominent authors whose sketches did not include this material previously, and "Sidelights" for numerous other authors have been revised substantially.

As a result of these editorial procedures, the amount of new material in this volume is very substantial, and, even after the deletions described below, the revised volume contains 994 pages, 57 more pages of text than did the two original volumes.

Series of Permanent Volumes Established
for Retired and Deceased Authors

Beginning with this revision, a series of Permanent Volumes is being established as an adjunct to *Contemporary Authors*, in order to avoid reprinting in the future the sketches of authors which will normally not require further change.

Therefore, the editors are omitting from this revision and from future revisions two classes of authors—first, persons now deceased, and second, persons who are approaching or who have passed normal retirement age and who have not reported in revising their listings that they have published books recently or have work in progress.

Authors at retirement age and without recent works who nevertheless have books still in print would usually be retained in the revised regular volumes, in the expectation that they may produce additional work.

Cumulative Index Should Always be Consulted

As always, the cumulative index published in alternate volumes of *CA* will continue to be the user's guide to the location of an individual author's listing. Authors not included in this revision, *all of whom will be included in the first Permanent Volume,* will be indicated in the cumulative index as having appeared in specific original volumes of *CA*, and as having their finally revised sketches listed in Permanent Volume 1.

The editors believe that this revision plan will prove to be not only convenient but economical, as well, since it removes from the revision cycle material which no longer needs periodic review and reprinting. As always, suggestions from users on revisions or any other aspect of *CA* will be welcomed.

CONTEMPORARY AUTHORS

ABBOTT, May L(aura) 1916-

PERSONAL: Born March 10, 1916, in London England, daughter of Charles William and Laura (Winteringham) Cox; married Frank Abbott, 1939 (killed in military action); married I. Henry Bate (a journalist), 1949. *Education:* Attended Manor House, Surrey, England, and Pensionnat de la Mere de Dieu, Tournai, Belgium. *Home:* 48 Berwyn Rd., Richmond, Surrey, England. *Agent:* Winant, Towers Ltd., 1 Furnival St., London E.C.4, England.

CAREER: Owned and operated literary competition agency, 1938-39; free-lance journalist, 1939-40; journalist on newspapers in Bedfordshire, England, 1941, 1942-46; *Daily Telegraph,* London, England, reporter, 1946-55; *Woman's Sunday Mirror,* London, England, 1955-61, news editor, later feature writer, broadcaster, and author, free-lance journalist, 1961—. *Home and Country* Magazine, London, England, deputy editor, 1970—. Part-time volunteer nursing service, 1939-45. *Member:* National Union of Journalists, Wig and Pen Club (London).

WRITINGS: Working with Animals, Bodley Head, 1962, Evans Brothers, 1967; (contributor) *Eve and Oil,* British Petroleum Co. Ltd., 1964; *Me and the Bee: The Battles of a Bumbling Beekeeper,* Hammond, 1965; *Careers in Art and Design,* Bodley Head, 1969, International Publications Service, 1971. Contributor of articles to *Punch, Today, Woman's Mirror, Trio, Motor, Autocar, Times, Daily Telegraph, Guardian, Sunday Telegraph, News of the World,* and other magazines and newspapers. Script writer for radio programs.

SIDELIGHTS: Me and the Bee was recording in "Talking Books for the Blind," in 1967. *Avocational interests:* Painting, beekeeping.

*   *   *

ABBOTT, R(obert) Tucker 1919-

PERSONAL: Born September 28, 1919, in Watertown, Mass.; son of Charles Matthew (a manufacturer) and Frances (Tucker) Abbott; married Mary M. Sisler, February 18, 1946 (died, 1964); married Sue Sweeney Darwin, January 8, 1966; children: (first marriage) Robert T., Jr., Carolyn Tucker, Cynthia Douglas. *Education:* Harvard University, B.S., 1946; George Washington University, M.S., 1953, Ph.D., 1955. *Religion:* Episcopalian. *Home:* 8044 Crittenden St., Philadelphia, Pa. 19118. *Office:* Delaware Museum of Natural History, Greenville, Del. 19807.

CAREER: U.S. National Museum, Washington, D.C., assistant curator, division of mollusks, 1946-49, associate curator, 1949-54; Academy of Natural Sciences of Philadelphia, Philadelphia, Pa., research scientist and holder of Pilsbry Chair, 1954-69; Delaware Museum of Natural History, Greenville, assistant director (malacology), 1969—. Member of ten scientific expeditions in search of marine life, in the Philippines, Zanzibar, Thailand, Australia, the Marianas, Hawaii, Bermuda, West Indies, Fiji, Samoa. Member of board of directors, Natural Sciences Foundation, 1956-63. Member of board of trustees, Bermuda Biological Life Station. *Military service:* U.S. Navy Reserve, 1942-46; became lieutenant. *Member:* American Association for the Advancement of Science (life fellow), American Malacological Union (life member; president, 1959), Australian Malacological Society (patron, 1960—), Philadelphia Shell Club (founder; president, 1955-56), honorary member of other shell clubs, Sons of the American Revolution, Harvard Club of Philadelphia.

WRITINGS: Handbook of Medically Important Mollusks of the Orient and Western Pacific, Museum of Comparative Zoology, Harvard University, 1948; (contributor) *A Manual of Tropical Medicine,* Saunders, 1954; *American Seashells,* Van Nostrand, 1954; *Introducing Sea Shells: A Colorful Guide for the Beginning Collector,* Van Nostrand, 1955; *Shells,* National Audubon Society, 1958; *The Marine Mollusks of Grand Cayman Island, British West Indies* (monograph), Academy of Natural Sciences (Philadelphia), 1958; *The Genus Strombus in the Indo-Pacific,* Academy of Natural Sciences, 1960; *How to Know the American Marine Shells,* Signet Books, 1961; (with Germaine L. Warmke) *Caribbean Seashells,* Livingston, 1961; *Sea Shells of the World,* Golden Press, 1962; (with R.J.L. Wagner) *Van Nostrand's Standard Catalog of Shells,* Van Nostrand, 1964, 2nd edition, 1967; *Shells,* Doubleday, 1966; *Venom Apparatus and Geographical Distribution of Conus Gloriamaris* (pamphlet), Academy of Natural Sciences, 1967; *Seashells of North America: A Guide to Field Identification,* Golden Press, 1968; (with Hugh and Marguerite Stix) *The Shell: Five Hundred Years of Inspired Design,* Abrams, 1968; (editor) *Swainson's Exotic Conchology;* Delaware Museum of Natural History and Van Nostrand, 1968. Writer of other reports on mollusks issued by Museum of Comparative Zoology, Harvard University, Smithsonian Institution, and Raffles Museum, Singapore. Contributor to *World Book Encyclopedia, Encyclopedia Americana, Grolier's Encyclopedia* and other encyclopedias. Contributor to *Natural History, Science Digest, Science Counselor.* Editor-in-chief, *Nautilus* and *Indo-Pacifica Mollusca;* associate editor, *Johnsonia,* 1941—.

WORK IN PROGRESS: Monographs on marine mollusks; revision of *American Seashells*, for Van Nostrand; *The New Shell Book*, for Macmillan; *Kingdom of the Seashell*.

*   *   *

ABBOTT, Walter M(atthew) 1923-

PERSONAL: Born December 2, 1923, in Somerville, Mass.; son of Walter Perkins and Rose Genevieve (O'Byrne) Abbott. *Education:* Boston College, A.B., 1947, M.A., 1948; Oxford University, postgraduate study, 1948-51; Weston College, S.T.L., 1957. *Home and office:* 64 Via dei Corridori, 00 193, Rome, Italy.

CAREER: Roman Catholic priest of the Society of Jesus (Jesuit). Weston College, Weston, Mass., lecturer in Greek philosophy, 1952-57, founder and first managing editor of *New Testament Abstracts*, 1956-57; *America* (Catholic weekly review), New York, N.Y., assistant editor, 1958-59, associate editor, 1959-66; John LaFarge Institute, New York, N.Y., director, 1964-66; assistant to Cardinal Augustin Bea, 1966-68; Vatican Department of Common Bible Work, Rome, Italy, director, 1968—. Lecturer, and radio and television speaker. *Member:* Catholic Biblical Association of America, American Philological Association, Catholic Institute of the Press.

WRITINGS: The Bible—Road to Unity, America Press, 1961; *New Vocations for Catholics*, America Press, 1961; *Twelve Council Fathers*, Macmillan, 1963; (editor) *The Documents of Vatican II*, Herder & Herder, 1966; (with Arthur Gilbert, R.C. Hunt, and J. Carter Swaim) *The Bible Reader: An Interfaith Interpretation*, Bruce, 1969.

SIDELIGHTS: Abbott has been an advocate of a common Bible for English-speaking Christians since 1959, resulting in the drafting of *The Bible Reader* by a rabbi, a Presbyterian minister, a Methodist layman, and a Catholic priest.

*   *   *

ABELL, George O(gden) 1927-

PERSONAL: Born March 1, 1927, in Los Angeles, Calif.; son of Theodore Curtis (a Unitarian minister) and Ann (Ogden) Abell; married Lois Everson, June 16, 1951; married Phyllis Fox (an artist), March 10, 1972; children: (first marriage) Anthony Alan, Jonathan Edward. *Education:* California Institute of Technology, B.S., 1951, M.S., 1952, Ph.D., 1957. *Office:* Department of Astronomy, University of California, Los Angeles, Calif. 90024.

CAREER: National Geographic Society, Palomar Observatory Sky Survey, observer, 1953-56; University of California, Los Angeles, associate professor, 1956-67, professor of astronomy and chairman of the department, 1967—. Lecturer Griffith Observatory, 1953-57. Mount Wilson and Palomar Observatories, guest investigator 1957—. Thacher School, Ojai, Calif., academic director of summer science program for gifted high school seniors, 1960-67. Guest Max-Planck Institute fuer Physik und Astrophysik, 1966-67. *Miliary service:* U.S. Army Air Corps, 1945-46; became sergeant. *Member:* International Astronomical Union, American Astronomical Society, Astronomical Society of Pacific (president, 1968-70), American Association for the Advancement of Science.

WRITINGS: (Contributor) Stars and Galaxies, Prentice-Hall, 1962; (contributor) *Problems of Extragalactic Research*, Macmillan, 1962; (contributor with Rudolph L. Minkowski) K.A. Strand, editor, *Basic Astronomical Data*, University of Chicago Press, 1963; *Exploration of the Universe*, Holt, 1964, 2nd edition, 1969. Contributor of about fifty articles to professional journals.

WORK IN PROGRESS: Research on rich clusters of galaxies, their distribution in space, their membership, and dynamics.

AVOCATIONAL INTERESTS: Collecting old operatic and lieder phonograph records dating from 1900.

*   *   *

ABELSON, Raziel A. 1921-

PERSONAL: Born June 24, 1921, in New York, N.Y.; son of Alter (a rabbi) and Anna (Schwartz) Abelson; married Ulrike Koenigsfeld, August 24, 1947; children: Gabriel. *Education:* Brooklyn College (now Brooklyn College of the City University of New York), student, 1938-40; University of Chicago, M.A., 1950; New York University, Ph.D., 1957. *Politics:* Socialist. *Religion:* Jewish. *Home:* 80 LaSalle St., New York, N.Y. 10027. *Office:* New York University, Bronx, N.Y. 10053.

CAREER: New York University, Bronx, N.Y., 1956—, now professor of philosophy. Lecturer at Hunter College of the City University of New York, and Columbia College; visiting professor at University of Hawaii, 1965. *Wartime service:* U.S. Maritime Service, radio officer, 1942-46; became lieutenant j.g. *Member:* American Philosophical Association, American Psychological Association, Mathematical Association of America, American Association of University Professors. *Awards, honors:* Carnegie Foundation fellowship in law and philosophy, 1962, American Council of Learned Societies grant-in-aid, 1968.

WRITINGS: Ethics and Metaethics: Readings in Ethical Philosophy, St. Martin's, 1963. Contributor of articles to encyclopedias and anthologies, and of essays and reviews to philosophical periodicals.

WORK IN PROGRESS: A book on philosophy and psychology.

AVOCATIONAL INTERESTS: Literature, tennis, automobile mechanics, child psychology.

*   *   *

ABRAHAMS, Roger D. 1933-

PERSONAL: Born June 12, 1933, in Philadelphia, Pa.; son of Robert D. and Florence (Kohn) Abrahams; married Mary Rodman, February 16, 1959; children: Rodman David, Lisa. *Education:* Swarthmore College, B.A., 1955; Columbia University, M.A., 1958; University of Pennsylvania, Ph.B., 1961. *Residence:* Austin, Tex.

CAREER: University of Texas, Austin, instructor, 1960-63, assistant professor, 1963-66, associate professor, 1966-69, professor of English and anthropology, 1969—, associate director, Center for Intercultural Studies in Folklore and Oral History, 1968-69, director, African and Afro-American Research Institute, 1969—. Visiting faculty member, Folklore Institute, Indiana University, 1967; Andersen Professor of American Studies, Carleton College, 1969. Member of Social Science Research Council Committee on Afro-American Societies and Cultures; member of Texas Education Agency Consulting Committee on Confluence of Texas Cultures. *Member:* International Society for Folk Narrative Research, American Folklore Society. *Awards, honors:* John Simon Guggenheim fellow, 1965-66; National Institute of Mental Health fellow, 1968; American Folklore Society fellow, 1970.

WRITINGS: Deep Down in the Jungle: Negro Narrative Folklore from the Streets of Philadelphia, Folklore Associates, 1964, revised edition, Aldine, 1970; *The Shaping of Folklore Traditions in the British West Indies*, University of Texas (Austin), c.1967; (with George Foss) *Anglo-American Folksong Style*, Prentice-Hall, 1968; (editor) *Jump Rope Rhymes: A Dictionary*, University of Texas

Press for American Folklore Society, 1969; *Positively Black*, Prentice-Hall, 1970; (editor) *Singer and Her Songs: Almeda Riddle's Book of Ballads*, Louisana State University Press, 1970. Author of fourteen book chapters or introductions, fifty articles in professional journals, primarily in folklore and Afro-American studies.

WORK IN PROGRESS: An Afro-American folklore bibliography, with John Szwed; *Counting-Out Rhymes: A Dictionary*, with Lois Rankin, for University of Texas Press; *West Indian Sea Shanties*, for American Folklore Society; an ethnography of communication of a peasant village in St. Vincent, West Indies; and a book of folk plays from Nevis and St. Kitts, West Indies.

* * *

ACKERMAN, James S(loss) 1919-

PERSONAL: Born November 8, 1919, in San Francisco, Calif., married Mildred Rosenbaum, 1947; children: three. *Education:* Yale University, A.B., 1941; New York University, M.A., 1947, Ph.D., 1952. *Home:* 12 Coolidge Hill Rd., Cambridge, Mass. 02138. *Office:* Department of Art, Harvard University, Cambridge, Mass. 02138.

CAREER: Yale University, New Haven, Conn., instructor, 1948; American Academy in Rome, Rome, Italy, research fellow, 1949-52; University of California, Berkeley, assistant professor, 1952-56, associate professor, 1956-59, professor of architecture and art, 1959-60; Harvard University, Cambridge, Mass., professor of fine arts, 1960—, chairman of department, 1963—. Visiting lecturer, Harvard University, 1958-59. Visiting fellow, Council of the Humanities, Princeton University, 1960-61. Member of art committee, Massachusetts Institute of Technology, 1963—; trustee, American Academy in Rome, 1963—. *Military service:* U.S. Army, Signal Intelligence Service, 1942-45. *Member:* American Academy of Arts and Sciences (fellow), Society of Architectural Historians (former director), Renaissance Society of America (member of council), Society of Aesthetics, College Art Association. *Awards, honors:* Fulbright fellow, 1950-51; L.H.D., Kenyon College, 1961; Alice Davis Hitchcock Award, Society of Architectural Historians and Charles Rufus Morey Award, College Art Association, 1961, for *The Architecture of Michelangelo.*

WRITINGS: *The Cortile del Belvedere*, Biblioteca Apostolica Vaticana (Vatican City), 1954; (author of notes and addenda with Roy Flamm) *Notes and Addenda Relative to a Collection of Photographs of a Group of California Buildings Photographed by Roy Flamm*, [San Francisco], 1957; *The Architecture of Michelangelo*, Viking, 1961, revised edition, Zwemmer, 1964, Viking, 1967; (contributor) Hedley Howell Rhys, editor, *Seventeenth Century Science and the Arts*, Princeton University Press, 1961; (with Rhys Carpenter) *Art and Archaeology*, Prentice-Hall, 1963; (with Wolfgang Lota) *Vignoliana*, J.J. Augustin, c.1965; *Palladio*, Penguin, 1966; *Palladio's Villas*, J.J. Augustin, 1967; *The Arts on Campus: The Necessity for Change*, edited by Margaret Mahoney, New York Graphic Society, 1970. Contributor to *Encyclopaedia Britannica, Architectural Review, Atlantic, Marsyas, Rendiconti della Pontificia Accademia di Archeologia, Renaissance News*, and other journals. *Art Bulletin*, editor-in-chief, 1956-60, chairman of editorial committee, 1963—.

BIOGRAPHICAL/CRITICAL SOURCES: *New Statesman*, July 28, 1967.

* * *

ADAMS, Hazard 1926-

PERSONAL: Born February 15, 1926, in Cleveland, Ohio; son of Robert Simeon (a headmaster) and Mary Leone (Thurness) Adams; married Diana Violet White, September 17, 1949; children: Charles Simeon, Perry White. *Education:* University of Washington, Seattle, student, 1943, M.A., 1949, Ph.D., 1953; Princeton University, A.B., 1948. *Residence:* Newport Beach, Calif. *Office address:* Office of the Vice-Chancellor, Academic Affairs, University of California, Irvine, Calif.

CAREER: Cornell University, Ithaca, N.Y., instructor, 1952-56; University of Texas, Austin, assistant professor of English, 1956-59; Michigan State University, East Lansing, associate professor, 1959-62, professor of English, 1962-64; University of California, Irvine, professor and chairman of department of English, 1964-69, dean of School of Humanities, 1970-72, vice-chancellor of academic affairs, 1972—. Washington University, St. Louis, visiting professor, 1959; Trinity College, Dublin, Fulbright research scholar and lecturer, 1962-63. *Military service:* U.S. Marine Corps, 1943-45, 1951; became first lieutenant. *Member:* Modern Language Association, American Society for Aesthetics.

WRITINGS: (Editor) *Poems by Robert Simeon Adams*, Bobbs-Merrill, 1952; *Blake and Yeats: The Contrary Vision*, Cornell University Press, 1955; *The Contexts of Poetry*, Little, Brown, 1963; *William Blake: A Reading of the Shorter Poems*, University of Washington Press, 1963; (editor) *Poetry: An Introductory Anthology*, Little, Brown, 1968; *The Horses of Instruction* (novel), Harcourt, 1968; (with Carl Hartman) *Fiction as Process*, Dodd, 1968; *The Interests of Criticism: An Introduction to Literary Theory*, Harcourt, 1969; (editor and author of notes and commentary) William Blake, *Jerusalem: Selected Poems and Prose*, Holt, 1970; *The Truth About Dragons: An Anti-Romance* (novel), Harcourt, 1971; (editor) *Critical Theory Since Plato*, Harcourt, 1971; *Lady Gregory*, Bucknell, 1973. Contributor to *Poetry Northwest, Accent, Poetry, Modern Fiction Studies, Critique*, and other professional journals. Member of editorial board, *Blake Studies, Studies in Romanticism.*

SIDELIGHTS: "My own interest in writing dates back a long way," Adams told *Library Journal*, "—to early childhood, when my father was writing poetry, and to third grade, when I had a teacher who encouraged all of us to write, and even published us. Poetry, I thought, was my game—after baseball, that is! But then there was a hiatus until one year at Princeton when I ruined my grade average writing in great secrecy a novel, of which, I am glad to say, not a scrap remains. After that, I turned to criticism and a scholarly career, but with an interest mainly in poetry, and particularly that of William Blake." *William Blake: A Reading of the Shorter Poems* has been called a "superb study" by a reviewer for the *Virginia Quarterly Review*. A *Yale Review* writer states that Adams "writes with a fine sense of the broad tradition of mythopoetic poetry from the Bible to Yeats," and that *Blake and Yeats: The Contrary Vision* "is the best study we have of Yeats's debt to Blake."

Adams's interest in Blake prompted his wife to suggest that he "read Joyce Cary's *The Horse's Mouth;* it had a lot of Blake in it, and besides it was a fine novel. I tried, but as is often the case with me and really great novels, I didn't take to it the first time. In fact, I failed to finish it. But a few months later I tried again and persisted with it, went on to read all of Cary, and finally published a number of articles on him. The manner of his trilogies, in which the narrative is mixed up and there are several speakers, interested me.... A phrase that appears several times in Blake ('They became what they beheld') stuck in my mind, and I concluded that I'd write a novel in which the people *make* their realities, construct the past in a certain way, which is, for them, the only way. My people are what their imaginations make of events." Adams arrived at the title of his novel, *The Horses of In-*

struction, in this way: "It seemed to me as I constructed these people that what each of them accomplishes in the realm of spirit, in building themselves, no matter how idiosyncratically, comes from their struggling energetically against some preconceived notion of how they must or ought to act. The abstract model of what the so-called 'given' world wishes them to be is what Blake calls a horse of instruction. Inside each of my people, however, is a contrary to this, called by Blake a tiger of wrath. To make tradition and the external useful, wrath is necessary. If it isn't expressed in some useful way, then it will take destructive forms. It always needs something to struggle against, however, just as a good sonnet wars with its own form. That is what my novel is all about."

Thomas Lask notes that Adams is not only well acquainted with the workings of the academic community, but that he is really too well acquainted, because, Lask believes, there is too much "academic trivia" included in the book. He would rather that Adams had concentrated on one of the characters, Hastings, whom he finds unusual. A reviewer for the *Virginia Quarterly Review* writes that, in the novel, "action, dialogue, and drama are minimized throughout, for the author leans heavily upon straight narration by each of the major participants to gain whatever variety and impetus the tale may display. Lightness of mood brightens many pages and gives the book an air of restrained academic gaiety.'

The Truth About Dragons is a novel of a different sort. Martin Levin states that Adams "mingles myth and reality with a playfulness that disguises the sharp edges of his humor." A *Virginia Quarterly Review* writer credits Adams for his "skill in weaving substance from shadow as his tale effortlessly unfolds and comes to its ingenious and acceptable conclusion."

BIOGRAPHICAL/CRITICAL SOURCES: Yale Review, June, 1964; *Virginia Quarterly Review,* summer, 1964, winter, 1969, summer, 1971; *Library Journal,* June 1, 1968; *New York Times,* October 12, 1968; *Writer,* November, 1969; *New York Times Book Review,* March 28, 1971.

*   *   *

ADAMS, Kramer A.   1920-

PERSONAL: Born April 26, 1920, in Sacramento, Calif.; son of David Arden (a newspaperman) and Phyllis (Kramer) Adams; married Mary Ethel Starbeck, October 2, 1942; children: Kent Kramer, Hillary Hawthorne. *Education:* Sacramento City College, student, 1938-41; attended University of California, 1941. *Politics:* Republican. *Religion:* Protestant. *Home:* 1333 Gough St., San Francsico, Calif. 94109.

CAREER: Started as newspaper reporter, then radio news editor, Sacramento, Calif.; War Assets Administration, site-sales advertising manager, San Francisco, Calif., 1946-47; California Department of Fish and Game, Sacramento, public information officer, 1947-54; Weyerhaeuser Co., Tacoma, Wash., publicity manager, 1954-62; American Forest Product Industries, San Francisco, Calif., district manager, 1962-65; California Redwood Association, San Francisco, conservation director, 1965—. Pacific Northwest International Writers Conference, trustee, 1957-62. *Military service:* California National Guard, 1937-40. U.S. Army, Infantry, 1941-43; became captain. California National Guard Reserve, 1950-52.

MEMBER: Outdoor Writers Association of America (director, 1950-60; vice-president, 1960-62), Izaak Walton League (secretary of Portland chapter, 1956-57; Oregon division chairman, 1958; national committee chairman, 1961), Forest History Society (director and treasurer, 1970—), University of California Alumni Association.

Awards, honors: Rounce and Coffen Club Award for *Covered Bridges of the West,* 1963.

WRITINGS: Logging Railroads of the West, Superior, 1961; *Covered Bridges of the West: A History and Illustrated Guide,* Howell-North Books, 1963; *The Redwoods,* Popular Library, 1969. Regular contributor to *Forest History.* Editor, *Outdoor California,* 1952-54; supervising editor, *Weyerhaeuser Magazine* and *Weyerhaeuser News,* 1960-61.

WORK IN PROGRESS: Highball Days, a history of the western timber industry.

*   *   *

ADLER, Max K(urt)   1905-

PERSONAL: Born June 12, 1905, in Pilsen, Czechoslovakia; son of Rudolf (a businessman) and Selma (Wiener) Adler; married Janka Steiner, January 4, 1932; children: Eric. *Education:* University of Vienna, Dr.rer.pol., 1932; University of London, B.Sc. (Economics), 1947. *Home:* 793 Finchley Rd., London N.W. 11, England.

CAREER: Started in market research with family firm, Joseph Adler & Sons, Pilsen, Czechoslovakia; continued in same field in London, England, as manager of market research departments of Osborne-Peacock Co. Ltd. for two years, Odhams Press Ltd. for eight years, Hoover Ltd. for three years, and Standard Telephone & Cables Ltd. for three years; with General Electric Co. Ltd., London, England, as adviser to board on market research; Institute of Marketing, director of studies and business consultant, 1968—. Lecturer, University of London Extra-Mural Department for more than twenty-five years. *Member:* European Society of Market and Opinion Research, Royal Statistical Society, British Sociological Society, British Market Research Society, Association of Scientific Workers. *Awards, honors:* Silver medal, European Society of Marketing and Opinion Research (one of three medals given in the twenty-five years of the society's existence).

WRITINGS: A Short Course in Market Research, C.E. Fisher & Co., 1951; *Modern Market Research: A Guide for Business Executives,* Crosby Lockwood, 1956, Philosophical Library, 1957; *A Short Guide to Market Research in Europe,* Crosby Lockwood, 1962; *Directory of British Market Research Organisations and Services,* Crosby Lockwood, 1965, 2nd edition, 1967; *Lectures in Market Research,* edited by Jacqueline Marrian, International Publications Service, 1965; *Business Languages of the World,* Marketing House Publishers, 1966; *Marketing and Market Research,* Crosby Lockwood, 1967; (editor) *Leading Cases in Market Research,* International Publications Service, 1971. Author of several hundred articles and papers on marketing, market research, economics, and politics. Editor, *European Marketing Review.*

WORK IN PROGRESS: General Sociology; research on sociology of language; research in bilingualism, pidgins, Creoles, Lingua Francas, and the dying languages of Europe.

SIDELIGHTS: Adler speaks most European languages; his books have been translated into German, French, Dutch, Spanish, Italian, and Portuguese.

*   *   *

ADLER, William   1929-
   (Bill Adler, Jay David)

PERSONAL: Born May 14, 1929, in New York, N.Y.; son of William J. (a display man) and Belle Adler; married Gloria Goodman, February 26, 1956; children: William, Diane. *Education:* Attended Brooklyn College (now Brooklyn College of City University of New

York), 1947-51. *Home:* 110 East End Ave., New York, N.Y. 10028.

CAREER: Full-time writer. Member of New York City Youth Board. *Military service:* U.S. Army, 1951-53; became corporal. *Member:* Radio and Television Executives Society (former member of board of governors).

WRITINGS—Under name Bill Adler: (With Irving Settel) *Congratulations, It's Your Birthday!*, Citadel, 1959; (with Settel) *Congratulations, You're a Grandparent!*, Citadel, 1959; (with Settel) *Congratulations, You're Married!*, Citadel, 1959; (with Bob Reisner) *Western on Wry*, Citadel, 1960; (with Reisner) *What Goes on Here?*, Citadel, 1963; *Pope Paul in the United States: His Mission for Peace on Earth, October 4, 1965*, Hawthorn, 1965; (with Arnie Kogen) *What to Name Your Jewish Baby*, Dutton, 1966; (with Ross Sayre) *Medicare and You*, New American Library, 1966; *Speaker's Complete Library of Wit and Humor*, Parker Publishing, 1970.

Editor under name Bill Adler: *Letters from Camp*, Chilton, 1961; *Boys Are Very Funny People*, Morrow, 1962; *Kids' Letters to President Kennedy*, Morrow, 1962; *Love Letters to the Beatles*, Putnam, 1964; *Dear President Johnson*, Morrow, 1964; *The Kennedy Wit*, Citadel, 1964 (published in England as *The Wit of President Kennedy*, Frewin Publishers, 1964); *John F. Kennedy and the Young People of America*, McKay, 1965; *Love Letters to the Mets*, Simon & Schuster, 1965; *Sir Winston Churchill, The Churchill Wit*, Coward, 1965; *Lyndon B. Johnson, The Johnson Humor*, Simon & Schuster, 1965; *More Kennedy Wit*, Citadel, 1965; *The Common Sense Wisdom of Three First Ladies*, Citadel, 1966; *Dear Beatles*, Wonder Books, 1966; *Dear Internal Revenue*, Doubleday, 1966; *Dear 007*, Simon & Schuster, 1966; *Dear Senator Kennedy*, Dodd, 1966; *Kids' Letters to the F.B.I.*, Prentice-Hall, 1966; *Letters to Smokey Bear*, Wonder Books, 1966; *More Letters from Camp*, New American Library, 1966; with Ross Sayre) *The Pope John Album: His Life, His Family, His Career, His Words*, Hawthorn, 1966; *Presidential Wit from Washington to Johnson*, Trident, 1966; Adlai E. Stevenson, *The Stevenson Wit*, Doubleday, 1966; *Letters from Vietnam*, Dutton, 1967; *Letters to the Air Force on UFOs*, Dell, 1967; *Letters to the Editor*, Doubleday, 1967; Billy Graham and others, *My Favorite Funny Story*, Four Winds, 1967; *Washington—A Reader: The National Capitol as Seen Through the Eyes of Thomas Jefferson and Others*, Meredith, 1967; (and author of introduction) *The Washington Wits*, Macmillan, 1967; Billy Graham, *The Wit and Wisdom of Billy Graham*, Random House, 1967; *Children's Letters to Santa Claus*, Simon & Schuster, 1967; John F. Kennedy, *The Complete Kennedy Wit*, Citadel, 1967; *Prescription: Laughter—An Anthology of Medical Merriment*, Harcourt, 1968; *Funniest Stories for Grownups Only*, Citadel, 1968; *Israel: A Reader*, Chilton, 1968; *The Wit and Wisdom of Bishop Fulton J. Sheen*, Prentice-Hall, 1968; *Bridge Players Write the Funniest Letters*, Doubleday, 1968; *Dear Dating Computer*, Bobbs-Merrill, 1968; *Dear Rabbi*, Morrow, 1968; (with Catherine J. Greene) *The Wall Street Reader*, World Publishing, 1970; *Funny Letters from Famous People*, Four Winds, 1970; *Hip Kids' Letters from Camp*, Morrow, 1971; *Kids' Letters to Spiro Agnew*, Geis, 1971; *Letters to Wall Street*, World Publishing, 1971; (with Greene) *Profits in Real Estate: A Reader*, World Publishing, 1971; *Letters to the Obstetrician*, St. Martin's, 1972.

Editor under pseudonym Jay David: *The Flying Saucer Reader*, New American Library, 1967; *The Kennedy Reader*, Bobbs-Merrill, 1967; *Growing Up Black*, Morrow, 1968; *Letters from Israel: The Making of a Nation, 1948-1968*, introduction by Leon Uris, Coward, 1968; *The Weight of the Evidence: The Warren Report and Its Critics*, Meredith, 1968; *Growing Up Jewish*, Morrow,

1969; *Flying Saucers Have Arrived!*, World Publishing, 1970; (with Mel Watkins) *To Be A Black Woman: Portraits in Fact and Fiction*, Morrow, 1971; (with Greene) *Black Roots: An Anthology*, Lothrop, 1971; (with Helise Harrington) *Growing Up African*, Morrow, 1971; (with Elaine Crane) *Living Black in White America*, Morrow, 1971; *Black Joy*, Cowles, 1971; (with Crane) *The Black Soldier: From the American Revolution to Vietnam*, Morrow, 1971; *Black Defiance: Black Profiles in Courage*, Morrow, 1972. Writer for the "Candid Camera" and "Tex and Jinx" television programs.

BIOGRAPHICAL/CRITICAL SOURCES: Saturday Review, April 19, 1967; *Books*, September, 1967; *Best Sellers*, September 15, 1967, January 1, 1970; *Library Journal*, March 1, 1970; *Show Business*, March 28, 1970.

* * *

AHMANN, Mathew H(all) 1931-

PERSONAL: Born September 10, 1931, in St. Cloud, Minn.; son of Norbert Theodore (a dentist) and Clotilde (Hall) Ahmann; married Margaret Cunningham, September 18, 1954; children: Elizabeth, Thomas, Teresa, Timothy, Ruth, Katherine. *Education:* St. John's University, Collegeville, Minn., B.A., 1952; University of Chicago, graduate study in sociology, 1953-54. *Religion:* Roman Catholic. *Home:* 7134 Oakridge Dr., San Antonio, Tex. 78229. *Office:* Archdiocese of San Antonio, P.O. Box 13190, San Antonio, Tex. 78213.

CAREER: Chicago Department of Welfare, Chicago, Ill. social worker, 1954-56; *Today* magazine, Chicago, Ill., business and circulation manager, 1956-57; Catholic Interracial Council, Chicago, Ill., field representative, 1957-59, assistant and acting director, 1959-60; National Catholic Conference for Interracial Justice, Chicago, Ill., executive director, 1960-69; Archdiocese of San Antonio, Commission on Church and Society, San Antonio, Tex., executive director, 1969—. Organizer and executive secretary, National Conference on Religion and Race, 1962-63; Catholic chairman of the March on Washington, August 28, 1963. Member of board of governors, Center for Research and Education in American Liberties, Columbia University; member of board, Workers Defense League. Trustee, Sperry Fund. *Member:* American Civil Liberties Union, National Association of Intergroup Relations Officials, National Association for the Advancement of Colored People, National Committee on Tithing and Investment (sponsor); National Committee for Free Elections in Mississippi, National Committee for the Mississippi Challenge. *Awards, honors:* National Mass Media Brotherhood Book Award, National Conference of Christians and Jews, 1964, for *Race: Challenge to Religion*.

WRITINGS: (Editor) *The New Negro*, Fides, 1961; (editor) *Race: Challenge to Religion*, Regnery, 1963; (editor with Margaret Roach) *The Church and the Urban Crisis*, Divine Word Publications, 1967. Contributor to *Commonweal, America*, and other magazines. Member of editorial advisory board, *Integrated Education*.

SIDELIGHTS: Among his interests Ahmann lists theology, relationship of religion to society, social problems, family life, and war and peace.

BIOGRAPHICAL/CRITICAL SOURCES: Today, fall, 1964.

* * *

AIKEN, Joan 1924-

PERSONAL: Born September 4, 1924, in Rye, Sussex, England; daughter of Conrad Potter (a poet) and Jessie (MacDonald) Aiken; married Ronald George Brown, July 7, 1945 (deceased); children: John Sebastian, Elizabeth Delano. *Education:* Attended Wychwood School, Oxford,

England, 1936-41. *Politics:* Liberal. *Religion:* Agnostic. *Home:* White Hart House, High St., Petworth, Sussex, England. *Agent:* Brandt & Brandt, 101 Park Ave., New York, N.Y. 10017.

CAREER: Was associated with British Broadcasting Corp., 1942-43, United Nations Information Office, London, England, 1943-49, *Argosy* Magazine, 1955-60, J. Walter Thompson Advertising Agency, 1961; full-time writer, 1961—. *Awards, honors: Guardian* award, and runner-up for Carnegie Award, 1969, for *The Whispering Mountain;* Mystery Writers of America award, 1972, for *Night Fall.*

WRITINGS—Juvenile: *All You've Ever Wanted,* J. Cape, 1953, also published in *All and More* (see below); *More Than You Bargained For,* J. Cape, 1955, Abelard, 1957, also published in *All and More* (see below); *The Kingdom and the Cave,* Abelard, 1960; *The Wolves of Willoughby Chase,* J. Cape, 1962, Doubleday, 1963; *Black Hearts in Battersea,* Doubleday, 1964; *Nightbirds on Nantucket,* Doubleday, 1966; *The Whispering Mountain,* J. Cape, 1968, Doubleday, 1969; *A Necklace of Raindrops, and Other Stories,* J. Cape, 1968, Doubleday, 1969; *Armitage, Armitage, Fly Away Home,* Doubleday, 1968; *A Small Pinch of Weather, and Other Stories,* J. Cape, 1969; *Night Fall,* Macmillan, 1969, Holt, 1971; *Smoke From Cromwell's Time, and Other Stories,* Doubleday, 1970; *The Cuckoo Tree,* Doubleday, 1971; *The Kingdom Under the Sea,* J. Cape, 1971; *All and More* (short stories; originally published as *All You've Wanted,* J. Cape, 1953, and *More Than You Bargained For,* J. Cape, 1955), J. Cape, 1971; *Winterthing: A Child's Play,* Holt, 1972.

Adult books: *The Silence of Herondale,* Doubleday, 1964; *The Fortune Hunters,* Doubleday, 1965; *Beware of the Bouquet,* Doubleday, 1966 (published in England as *Trouble with Product X,* Gollancz, 1966); *Dark Interval,* Doubleday, 1967 (published in England as *Hate Begins at Home,* Gollancz, 1967); *The Ribs of Death,* Gollancz, 1967, published in America as *The Crystal Crow,* Doubleday, 1968; *The Windscreen Weepers, and Other Tales of Horror and Suspense,* Gollancz, 1969, published in America as *Green Flash, and Other Takes of Horror, Suspense, and Fantasy,* Holt, 1971; *The Embroidered Sunset,* 1970; *Nightly Deadshade,* Macmillan, 1971; *Died on a Rainy Sunday,* Holt, 1972; *A Cluster of Separate Sparks,* Doubleday, 1972.

Contributor of short stories to *Argosy, Everywoman, John Bull, Vogue, Good Housekeeping, Housewife, Vanity Fair, New Statesman, Woman's Own, Woman's Journal,* and of reviews to *History Today.*

WORK IN PROGRESS: A new thriller.

SIDELIGHTS: Miss Aiken writes: "Widowed at 30 with two small children, I have not had much time or money for hobbies or travel. My chief pleasures are reading, meeting friends, painting, gardening, listening to classical music. Vocational interests are cooking and housewifery. I write to please myself and amuse my children; would like to learn the guitar, travel extensively, and read Gibbon's *Decline and Fall* when there is more time.

"I always intended to be a writer; when I was five I went to the village store and spent two shillings (a huge sum then) on a large, thick writing-block in which to write poems, stories, and thoughts, as they occurred. It lasted for years (I still have it) and when it was finished I bought another and then another. I used to tell stories to my younger brother to beguile the boring parts of walks. My first work was published when I was 17—a story broadcast on the B.B.C. children's hour. In my children's books I write the sort of thing I should have liked to read myself when I was young, and am helped by comments and criticisms from my own children who read each work as it goes along."

Miss Aiken states that she makes little distinction between the process of writing for children and that for adults. "I enjoy *writing.* At least I suppose I must, or I wouldn't keep on doing something so utterly consuming and exhausting. While I am at work on one kind of piece I am feverishly longing and planning to write something else in a different idiom, so as to use another set of muscles. Thinking back over my children's books and my adult thrillers (if thrillers are adult) I honestly can't recall any difference at all in the actual writing process. . . . If ever I find myself writing anything, even a letter of thanks for a packet of deckle-edged paper napkins with shiny embossed holly-sprigs in primary colours, with less than the total care and skill I can command, I shall take this as a sign that I have written enough, and shall turn to some other profession."

The Wolves of Willoughby Close has been bought for filming by Alan Pakula.

BIOGRAPHICAL/CRITICAL SOURCES: Books and Bookmen, January, 1969, May, 1969; *Times Literary Supplement,* January, 1969; *Variety,* October 1, 1969; *Book World,* November 9, 1969; *Saturday Review,* April 17, 1971; Best Sellers, July 15, 1971.

*   *   *

ALDERFER, Harold F(reed)   1903-

PERSONAL: Born February 1, 1903, in Souderton, Pa.; son of Henry A. and Lydia M. Freed; married Ella F. Rohrbach, September 2, 1925; children: Johanna (Mrs. William Harris), Henrietta (Mrs. Alan Helffrich, Jr.), Marianna. *Education:* Bluffton College, A.B., 1922; Syracuse University, A.M., 1926, Ph.D., 1928. *Address:* R.D. 3, Mechanicsburg, Pa.

CAREER: Teacher and principal, then superintendent of schools, Marion, S.D., 1922-25; Pennsylvania State University, University Park, started as assistant professor, 1928, professor of political science, 1935-59, professor emeritus, 1959—, head of political science department, 1954-56, founder and executive secretary of Institute of Local Government, 1936-57. University of Pennsylvania, Philadelphia, lecturer in political science and public administration, 1938-39, 1941-45, 1958-69. Lewis Stevens Professor of Public Affairs, Lincoln University, 1964-65. U.S. Economic Cooperation Administration, local government specialist stationed in Athens, Greece, 1950-52; Urban Renewal Administration, assistant commissioner for operations, 1956-57; International Cooperation Administration, local government consultant, Philippines, 1959, Iran, 1961; United Nations, public administration specialist in Egypt and the Middle East, 1962-63. Commonwealth of Pennsylvania, director of bureau of municipal affairs, Department of Internal Affairs, 1944-50, and first deputy superintendent of public instruction, 1957-62.

MEMBER: American Political Science Association, American Society for Public Administration, American Municipal Association (vice-president, 1948). *Awards, honors:* Commander, Order of the Phoenix (Greece), 1952; LL.D., Parsons College, 1954; annual award for outstanding achievement in public administration, Central Pennsylvania Chapter, American Society for Public Administration, 1960.

WRITINGS: Facts on Greek Local Government, U.S. Economic Cooperation Administration, 1951; *American Local Government and Administration,* Macmillan, 1956; *I Like Greece,* Bald Eagle Press, 1956; *Professional Licensing in Pennsylvania,* University of Pennsylvania, 1962; *Pennsylvania Government, Views, Reviews and Previews,* Local Government Service, 1962; *Local Government in Developing Countries,* McGraw, 1964; *A Bibliography of African Government, 1950-64,* Lincoln University, 1964, 2nd revised edition published as *A*

Bibliography of African Government, 1950-1966, Lincoln University Press, 1967; *Pennsylvania Government Today: Fourteen Thumbnail Sketches,* Local Government Service, 1965; *A Citizen's Guide to Pennsylvania Local Government,* Commonwealth of Pennsylvania, Department of Community Affairs, 1967; *Public Administration in the Newer Nations,* Praeger, 1967; *Pennsylvania Government for the Seventies,* Local Government Service, 1971.

Co-author: *County Government Costs in Pennsylvania,* Department of Agriculture Economics, Pennsylvania State College, 1933; (with Jacob Tanger) *Pennsylvania Government, State and Local,* Pennsylvania Book Service, 1933, 2nd edition, 1950; (with A.S. Sukel) *American Citizenship for Pennsylvania,* Pennsylvania Book Service, 1935, 2nd edition, 1953; *Pennsylvania Local Government Survey,* University of Pennsylvania Press, 1935; (with R.M. Sigmond) *Presidential Elections by Pennsylvania Counties, 1920-1940,* Institute of Local Government, Pennsylvania State College, 1941; (with Sukel) *American Government for Pennsylvanians,* Pennsylvania Book Service, 1945, revised edition, 1955; (with F.B.H. Luhrs) *Gubernatorial Elections by Pennsylvania Counties, 1922-42,* Pennsylvania Municipal Publications, 1946; (with Louise M. Young) *Know Pennsylvania: Your State and Local Government,* Pennsylvania Book Service, 1964, revised edition, 1951; (with Luhrs) *Registration in Pennsylvania Elections, 1925-1946,* Pennsylvania Municipal Publications, 1948; (with M. Fathalla El Khatib and Moustafa Ahmed Fahmy) *Local Government in the United Arab Republic,* Institute of Public Administration (Cairo), 1963; (with Henry D. Harral) *Constitutional and Legal Limitations Affecting Local Government in Pennsylvania,* Better Government Associates for Pennsylvania Department of Community Affairs, 1968.

Contributor of more than thirty articles to *Pennsylvania History, Better Roads, American City, Pennsylvania Medical Journal, American Political Science Review,* and other government and political science journals. Author of research and survey reports. Editor and publisher, *Commonwealth, the Magazine for Pennsylvania* (monthly), 1947-54. Editor and co-founder of four Pennsylvania local government journals, 1936-56.

WORK IN PROGRESS: A book, tentatively titled, *Political Philosophy of a Pennsylvanian.*

* * *

ALDERSON, William T(homas), Jr.   1926-

PERSONAL: Born May 8, 1926, in Schenectady, N.Y.; son of William Thomas and Helen (Knowlton) Alderson; married Sylvia Caldwell Farrell, September 14, 1953; children: William Thomas III, Virginia Ann, Rebecca Louise. *Education:* Tulane University, student, 1944-45; Colgate University, A.B., 1947; Vanderbilt University, M.A., 1949, Ph.D., 1952. *Religion:* Methodist. *Home:* 124 Taggart Ave., Nashville, Tenn. 37205. *Office:* American Association for State and Local History, 1315 Eighth Ave. S., Nashville, Tenn. 37203.

CAREER: Tennessee State Library and Archives, Nashville, senior archivist, 1952-57; Tennessee Historical Commission, Nashville, executive secretary, 1957-61; Tennessee State Library and Archives, assistant state librarian and archivist, 1959-61, state librarian and archivist, 1961-64; American Association for State and Local History, Nashville, Tenn., director, 1964—. Member of board of directors, American Heritage Publishing Co., 1965—; Tennessee Historical Commission, chairman, 1961-64; member of advisory board, Historic American Buildings Survey, 1967-71; Tennessee Conference on Historic Preservation, co-founder; member of advisory board, National Museum Art, Smithsonian Institution, 1971—. *Military service:* U.S. Navy, 1943-46. *Member:* Society of American Archivists (fellow; member of council, 1963—), American Association of Museums, Organization of American Historians (vice-president, 1969-71), American Association for State and Local History (member of council, 1959-64), American Records Management Association (chapter president, 1963-64), Southern Historical Association, Tennessee Association of Museums (vice-president, 1964; president, 1965-67), Tennessee Historical Society, Nashville Rose Society (vice-president, 1969-71), Rotary International (president, 1963). *Awards, honors:* Award of Merit, American Association for State and Local History, 1959, for *Tennessee Historical Markers,* and 1966, for *Landmarks of Tennessee History.*

WRITINGS: Tennessee Historical Markers, Tennessee Historical Commission, 1958, 2nd edition (with Robert McBride), 1962; (with Robert H. White) *A Guide to the Study and Reading of Tennessee History,* Tennessee Historical Commission, 1959; (with H. Glyn Thomas) *Historic Sites in Tennessee,* Tennessee Historical Commission, 1963; (editor with McBride) *Landmarks of Tennessee History,* Tennessee Historical Commission, 1965; *Tennessee: A Student's Guide to Localized History,* Teachers College Press, 1966. Contributor to *Encyclopaedia Britannica, Western Historical Quarterly, Journal of Southern History, American Archivist.* Editor, *Tennessee Historical Quarterly,* 1956-65, *History News* (publication of American Association for State and Local History), 1964—.

WORK IN PROGRESS: Interpretation of Historic House Museums.

AVOCATIONAL INTERESTS: Photography, travel, leather work.

* * *

ALDRIDGE, Richard Boughton   1930-

PERSONAL: Born November 12, 1930, in New York, N.Y.; son of Albert H. (a physician) and Nancy (Symington) Aldridge; married Josephine Haskell (an artist and author of children's books), October, 1958; children: Abigail Nancy. *Education:* Amherst College, B.A., 1952; Oxford University, M.A., 1957. *Home:* Sebasco Estates, Me. 04565.

CAREER: National Security Agency, Washington, D.C., research analyst, 1952-53; Doubleday & Co., Inc., New York, N.Y., staff member, 1957-58; Morse High School, Bath, Me., member of English department, 1958—, chairman, 1962-69; Hyde School, Bath, Me., teacher, 1970—. *Military service:* U.S. Army Counterintelligence Corps, 1953-55. *Awards, honors:* Fulbright fellowships to Oxford, 1955-57.

WRITINGS: An Apology Both Ways, Indiana University Press, 1957; *Down Through the Clouds, the Sea,* Golden Quill, 1963; (editor) *Maine Lines: 101 Contemporary Poems About Maine,* Lippincott, 1970; (with wife, Josephine Aldridge) *Reasons and Raisins,* Parnassus, 1971.

BIOGRAPHICAL/CRITICAL SOURCES: Library Journal, July, 1970.

* * *

ALEGRIA, Fernando   1918-

PERSONAL: Born September 26, 1918, in Santiago, Chile; son of Santiago Alegria Toro and Julia Alfaro; married Carmen Letona Melendez, January 29, 1943; children: Carmen, Daniel, Andres, Isabel. *Education:* University of Chile, Professor of Spanish, 1939; Bowling Green State University, M.A., 1941; University of California, Berkeley, Ph.D., 1947. *Home:* 55 Arlmonte Dr., Berkeley, Calif. 94707. *Office:* Stanford University, Stanford, Calif. 94305.

CAREER: Bowling Green State University, Bowling Green, Ohio, instructor in Spanish, Extension Division, 1940-41; University of California, Berkeley, instructor, 1947-49, assistant professor, 1949-55, associate professor, 1955-63, professor of Spanish, 1964-67; Stanford University, Stanford, Calif., professor of Spanish, 1967—. *Member:* Instituto Internacional de Literatura Iberoamericana, American Association of Teachers of Spanish, Sociedad de Escritores (Chile). *Awards, honors:* Guggenheim fellow, 1947-48; Latin American Prize of Literature for *Lautaro, joven libertador de Arauco,* 1943; Premio Atenea and Premio Municipal (both Chile), for *Caballo de copas.*

WRITINGS: Recabarren, Antares, 1938; Ideas esteticas de la poesia moderna, Multitud, 1939; Leyenda de la ciudad perdida, Zig-Zag, 1942; Lautaro, joven libertador de Arauco (juvenile fiction), Zig-Zag, 1943, 5th edition, 1965; Ensayo sobre cinco temas de Thomas Mann, Funes, 1949; Camaleon, Ediapsa, 1951; La Poesia chilena: Origenes y desarollo del siglo XVI al XIX, University of California Press, 1954; Walt Whitman en Hispanoamerica, Studium, 1954; El Poeta que se volvio gusano, Cuadernos Americanos, 1956; Caballo de copas, Zig-Zag, 1957, 2nd edition, 1961, translation by Carlos Lozano published in America as My Horse Gonzalez, Las Americas, 1964; Breve historia de la novela hispanoamericana, Studium, 1959, 2nd edition published as Historia de la novela hispanoamericana, De Andrea, 1965; El Cataclismo (short stories), Nascimento, 1960; Las Noches del cazador, Zig-Zag, 1961; Las Fronteras del realismo: Literatura chilena del siglo XX, Zig-Zag, 1962, 2nd edition published as La Literatura chilena del siglo XX, 1967; (editor) Novelistas contemporaneos hispanoamericanos, Heath, 1964; Manana los guerreros (novel), Zig-Zag, 1964; Viva Chile M!, Editorial Universitaria (Santiago), 1965; (editor and translator) Rene Marill, Historia de la novela moderna, Union Tipografica Editorial Hispano Americana, 1966; Genio y figura de Gabriela Mistral, Editorial Universitaria de Buenos Aires, 1966; La Novela hispano-americana, siglo XX, Centro Editor de America Latina, 1967; (translator with others) Nicanor Parra, Poems and Antipoems, edited by Miller Williams, New Directions, 1967; Los Dias contados (novel), Siglo XXI, 1968; Ten Pastoral Psalms (poetry; bilingual edition; English versions by Bernardo Garcia and Matthew Zion), Kayak, 1968; Como un arbol rojo, Editora Santiago, 1968; La Maraton del Palomo (short stories), Centro Editor de America Latina, 1968; Los Mejores cuentos de Fernando Alegria, edited, with a prologue, by Alfonso Calderon, Zig-Zag, 1968; La Literatura chilena contemporanea, Centro Editor de America Latina, 1969; Instructions for Undressing the Human Race (poem; bilingual edition; English version by Matthew Zion and Lennart Bruce), Kayak, 1969; Amerika, Editorial Universitaria, 1970.

BIOGRAPHICAL/CRITICAL SOURCES: Chicago Review, Number 1, 1968, January-February, 1971; Carleton Miscellany, Number 3, 1969; Poetry, March, 1970; Books Abroad, winter, 1970.

*   *   *

ALEXANDER, John A(leck)   1912-

PERSONAL: Born November 21, 1912, in Coumani, Elis, Greece; son of Aleck J. and Panayota Toumblaris) Alexander; married Eclecte Tsiropoulou, November 19, 1950; children: Patricia, Effie. Education: Emory University, B.A., 1934, M.A., 1935; Washington University, St. Louis, Mo., postgraduate study, 1935-36; Johns Hopkins University, Ph.D., 1939. Religion: Greek Orthodox. Home: 1284 Citadel Dr. N.E., Atlanta, Ga. 30324.

CAREER: St. Bonaventure University, Olean, N.Y., assistant professor of classical languages and civilization,

1941-42; Georgia State College, Atlanta, assistant professor, 1947-49, associate professor, 1949-54, professor of history, 1954—, head of department of history, 1955—. Staff member of Johns Hopkins University archaeological expedition to Olynthus, Greece, 1938. *Military service:* U.S. Army, 1942-46; intelligence officer, Allied Force Headquarters in Africa, Italy; became captain. *Member:* Archaeological Institute of America (Atlanta society, vice-president, 1955-56, member of executive committee, 1958—), University Center in Georgia (history section vice-chairman, 1962-63, chairman, 1963-64), American Historical Association, American Philological Association, Classical Association of Middle West and South, Southern Historical Association, American Legion.

WRITINGS: Potidaea: Its History and Remains, University of Georgia Press, 1963; Yugoslavia Before the Roman Conquest, Praeger, 1972. Contributor to American Journal of Philology and other periodicals.

WORK IN PROGRESS: Cassandreia: Its History and Remains, a monograph about the city in northern Greece founded on the site of Potidaea.

SIDELIGHTS: Alexander is competent in classical languages, modern Greek, Italian, and French.

*   *   *

ALEXANDER, Mary Jean McCutcheon

PERSONAL: Born September 18, in Mount Vernon, Iowa; daughter of Lloyd Allan (a newspaper editor and publisher) and Mary Washburn McCutcheon. Education: Cornell College, Mount Vernon, Iowa, B.A., 1929; Parsons School of Design, graduate, 1935; University of Iowa, M.A., 1966. Home: 106 East 60th St., New York, N.Y. 10022.

CAREER: Interior designer, 1936—. University of Iowa, part-time teacher of interior design, 1964-65; teacher of interior design classes at Parsons School of Design, Pratt Institute, San Jose State College, and University of Tennessee. Painter. Member: American Institute of Interior Designers (former chairman of national committee on education), Authors Guild, Decorators Club of New York (past president).

WRITINGS: Decorating Begins with You, Doubleday, 1958; Decorating Made Simple, Doubleday, 1964; Decorative Ornament and Design, Tudor, 1965; Home Design: A Positive Guide, New American Library, 1971; Designing Interior Environment, Harcourt, 1972.

*   *   *

ALEXANDER, Sidney   1912-

PERSONAL: Born March 6, 1912, in New York, N.Y.; son of David (a businessman) and Sadie (Breslau) Alexander; married Frances Rosenbaum, January 19, 1936. Education: Columbia University, B.S., 1934, graduate study, 1934-35; New School for Social Research, graduate study, 1946-48; University of Florence, Certificate of Merit in Italian Studies, 1949. Home: Via Ugo Foscola 34, Florence, Italy. Agent: Mavis McIntosh, McIntosh, McKee & Dodds, 30 East 60th St., New York, N.Y. 10022.

CAREER: Welfare Department, New York, N.Y., social investigator, 1935-41; Office of War Information, Washington, D.C., editor on overseas news staff, 1943; Reporter Magazine, New York, N.Y., consultant, 1947-48; United Nations, New York, N.Y., English editor of Journal of the United Nations, 1952; Italian Air Ministry, Rome, Italy, English instructor, 1953-54; School for Interpreters, Rome, English instructor, 1954; Fairleigh Dickinson University, Rutherford, N.J., instructor in English, 1955-56; New School for Social Research, New York, N.Y., instructor in English, 1955-58; Hunter College (now Hunter College of City University of New York), New York, N.Y., instructor in English, 1957-58; *Diogenes Magazine*, New York, N.Y., translator, 1962-64; Syracuse University, Syracuse, N.Y., associate professor of fine arts, 1963—, Villa Mercede, Florence, Italy, writing workshop, 1962—. English instructor, Lenox Hill Hospital, 1958; conductor of novel workshop, New York City Writers Conference, 1958; guest lecturer at America Italy Society, 1958, Sarah Lawrence College in Florence, 1960-61, Stanford University in Florence, 1960-61, 1962-63, 1965, Syracuse University in Florence, 1961, and Villa Mercede, 1961. *Military service:* U.S. Army Air Corps, public relations, 1943-46.

MEMBER: American Association of University Professors. *Awards, honors:* Maxwell Anderson Award for dramatic composition in verse, Stanford University, honorable mention, 1938, for "The Third Great Fool," first prize, 1948, for "Salem Story"; *Charm Magazine* short story contest, second prize, 1944, first prize, 1945; grants from Ministry of Foreign Affairs, Government of Italy, 1958, 1959, 1960; grant from Max Ascoli Foundation, 1958-59; Syracuse University faculty research grant, 1965; translation prize, P.E.N., 1970, for *The History of Italy.*

WRITINGS: The Man on the Queue (poetry and verse plays), Press of J.A. Decker, 1941; (translator) Valery, *The Marine Cemetery*, [Italy], 1949; *Tightrope in the Dark* (poetry), Press of J.A. Decker, 1949; *The Celluloid Asylum* (novel), Bobbs-Merrill, 1951; *Michelangelo, the Florentine* (novel), Random House, 1957; (translator) *The House in Milan*, Harcourt, 1963; (editor and translator with wife, Frances Alexander) *The Berenson Collection*, Ricordi, 1964; *My Beard to Heaven* (novel), Mario Casalini, c.1965; *The Hand of Michelangelo* (novel), Mario Casalini, 1966, Twayne, 1967; (editor and translator) Francesco Guicciardini, *The History of Italy*, Macmillan, 1969.

Plays: "The Great Third Fool," first produced in 1938; "The Hawk and the Flesh" (radio play), first broadcast by WNYC, 1939; "Salem Story" (radio play), first broadcast by WNYC, 1940; "Giles Corey" (based on "Salem Story"), first produced Off-Broadway, 1948.

Represented in several anthologies, including *The Poetry of Flight*, edited by Selden Rodman, Duell, Sloan & Pearce, 1941, *Accent Anthology: Selections from Accent, a Quarterly of New Literature, 1940-1945*, edited by Kerker Quinn and Charles Shattuck, Harcourt, 1946, *Best American Short Stories, 1944, 1948*, edited by Martha Foley, Houghton, 1945, 1949, *The Poetry of the Negro, 1746-1949*, edited by Langston Hughes and A.W. Bontemps, Doubleday, 1949, *Modern Poetry*, edited by Paul Engle and Warren Carrier, Scott, Foresman, 1955, and *The Short Story*, edited by James B. Hall and Joseph Langland, Macmillan, 1956. Writer for radio and films. Contributor to *Collier's Encyclopedia, Reporter* and other publications in the United States and abroad.

SIDELIGHTS: In a review of *The Hand of Michelangelo*, Orville Prescott writes: "Like the mills of the gods, which grind slowly but grind exceeding small, Mr. Alexander writes with loving care and a sort of stately grandeur. Steeped in the lore of the time, he is well qualified to write a biography of his hero. He has preferred to write it as fiction, probably because that method allows him to speculate about the gaps in the record, and to interpret the torments and travails of the artist's spirit."

BIOGRAPHICAL/CRITICAL SOURCES: Milton Allen Kaplan, *Radio and Poetry*, Columbia University Press, 1949; *Reporter*, May 4, 1967; *New York Times Book Review*, September 9, 1967.

ALEXANDER, Thomas W(illiamson), Jr. 1930-

PERSONAL: Born October 16, 1930, in Asheville, N.C.; son of Thomas Williamson (a forester and farmer) and Judith (Barksdale) Alexander; married Martha Jane Duvall (a journalist), September 30, 1961; children: Ames Barksdale. *Education:* University of North Carolina, B.A., 1953; New York University, M.A., 1957; Columbia University, postgraduate study, 1963-64. *Home:* 81 Chester Pl., Englewood, N.J. 07631. *Agent:* Ann Elmo Agency, Inc., 52 Vanderbilt Ave., New York, N.Y. 10017.

CAREER: Columbus Ledger, Columbus, Ga., reporter, 1953-54; *Richmond News Leader*, Richmond, Va., reporter, 1956-58; *Life*, New York, N.Y., reporter, 1959-62; Time Inc., Books Division, New York, N.Y., writer, 1963—. *Military service:* U.S. Army, 1954-56.

WRITINGS: Project Apollo: Man to the Moon, Harper, 1964. Contributor to *Esquire, Saturday Evening Post, Fortune*, and other magazines.

WORK IN PROGRESS: Scientific and technical articles for magazines.†

* * *

ALLEGRO, John Marco 1923-

PERSONAL: Born February 17, 1923, in London, England; son of John Marco and Mabel Jessie (Perry) Allegro; married Joan Ruby Lawrence, June 17, 1948; children: Judith Anne, John Mark. *Education:* University of Manchester, B.A. (first class honors), 1952, M.A., 1953; Oxford University, graduate student, 1952-53. *Home:* Craigmore, Ballasalla, Isle of Man, U.K. *Agent:* (Lectures) Foyles Lecture Agency, 125 Charing Cross Rd., London W.C.2, England.

CAREER: University of Manchester, Manchester, England, special lecturer in comparative Semitic philology, 1954-60, lecturer in Hebrew, 1960-62, lecturer in Old Testament and intertestamental studies, 1962-70; free-lance scholar and writer, 1970—. Organizer and leader of archaeological expeditions to Judaean wilderness, 1959—; British member of international team editing Dead Sea scrolls in Jordan, 1953—; adviser on Dead Sea scrolls to Jordanian Government. Lecturer on radio and television and to clubs and societies. *Military service:* Royal Navy, 1941-46. *Member:* Society for Old Testament Study, Glasgow University Oriental Society.

WRITINGS: The Dead Sea Scrolls, Penguin, 1956, 3rd edition, revised, 1959; (with D.N. Freedman) *The People of the Dead Sea Scrolls*, Doubleday, 1958; *The Treasure of the Copper Scroll: The Opening and Decipherment of the Most Mysterious of the Dead Sea Scrolls*, Doubleday, 1960, revised edition, Doubleday-Anchor, 1964; *The Dead Sea Scrolls: A Reappraisal*, Penguin, 1964; *Search in the Desert*, Doubleday, 1964; *The Shapira Affair*, Doubleday, 1965; (with A.A. Anderson) *Discoveries in the Judaean Desert of Jordan V: Qumran Cave 4, I*, Oxford University Press, 1968; *The Sacred Mushroom and the Cross: A Study of the Nature and Origins of Christianity within the Fertility Cults of the Ancient Near East*, Doubleday, 1970; *The End of a Road*, MacGibbon & Kee, 1970, Dial, 1971; *The Chosen People*, Doubleday, 1971. Also author, with Roy Plomley, of a play, "The Lively Oracles," and of a film strip, "The Dead Sea Scrolls," 1960; writer, narrator, and producer of television film, "Search in the Kidron," 1963.

WORK IN PROGRESS: Folk Tales and Songs from the Bible, a new translation of biblical stories, etc.

SIDELIGHTS: The Sacred Mushroom and the Cross, ostensibly a scholarly, philological work, has caused Allegro to be the subject of controversy. The thesis of the book, as stated by the *Newsweek* reviewer, is that: "All religion ... grew from fertility cults that imagine a heavenly god's sperm raining down on a womb-like earth. In many early cults, he says, wisdom and the divinity itself were sought in visionary states induced by hallucinogenic mushrooms. . . . Such cults did, in fact, exist in Central Asia and still linger in Mexico, and Allegro argues that they were also the origin of ancient paganism, Judaism, Christianity, and Islam."

Although critics have been nearly unaminous in their rejection of Allegro's book, it has nonetheless enjoyed enormous popularity in both England and America. Critical opinion ranges from polite skepticism to overt horror. Christopher Booker writes: "I am sure Mr. Allegro is sincere about all this, and I am not in a position to question the soundness of his philology (although I would suggest that some of his readings do seem a little arbitrary)." The *Times Literary Supplement* reviewer simply dismisses the book as "one long gush of phallic drivel." The *Newsweek* reviewer expresses Allegro's position in the scholarly world since the publication of *The Sacred Mushroom and the Cross:* "But as Allegro moved from agnosticism to outright doubt as to the historical existence of Jesus, he got into sharp skirmishes with Biblical scholars. And with his new book, he has set himself up against the entire scholarly establishment."

BIOGRAPHICAL/CRITICAL SOURCES: J. H. Jacques, *The Mushroom and the Bride,* Citadel, 1970; J. C. King, *A Christian View of the Mushroom Myth,* Hodder & Stoughton, 1970; *Observer Review,* May 17, 1970; *Spectator,* May 23, 1970; *Times Literary Supplement,* May 28, 1970; *Show,* August 20, 1970; *Newsweek,* August 31, 1970; *Christian Century,* August 26, 1970, January 13, 1971; *Washington Post,* September 1, 1970.

*   *   *

ALLEN, Edith Beavers 1920-

PERSONAL: Born February 15, 1920, in Berwind, W. Va.; daughter of Charles Thomas and Bertha (Belcher) Beavers; married Vivian C. Allen, July 18, 1935; children: Fred Kent, Dwight Mason. *Education:* Educated in West Virginia schools. *Religion:* Baptist. *Home:* 904 Sevard Ave., Clearwater, Fla. 33516; and P.O. Box 432, Elfers, Fla. 33573.

CAREER: Waitress and saleswoman in own business, Tazewell, Va.; variously secretary, manager of gift shop, real estate broker and saleswoman, Clearwater, Fla. Sunday school teacher of junior girls, 1959—. *Member:* Epsilon Sigma Alpha.

WRITINGS: New Testament Bible Games: 100 Games Related to the New Testament, Zondervan, 1963; *Better Bible Games,* Baker Book, 1969; *Bridal Showers,* Zondervan, 1969; *Get in the Game,* Baker Book, 1971; *Bible Symbol Puzzles,* Zondervan, 1971. Contributor to *Home Life.*

WORK IN PROGRESS: Complete Bible Games; research on everyday life in Holy Land; *Diary of Mexico;* another game book; and *Inspirational Names.*

*   *   *

ALLEN, Jack 1914-

PERSONAL: Born June 18, 1914, in Prestonsburg, Ky.; son of Edward L. (a lawyer) and Anna (Mayo) Allen; married Cherry Falls, August 16, 1941; children: David E., Robert L., Edward L. *Education:* Eastern Kentucky State College, A.B., 1935; George Peabody College for Teachers, M.A., 1935, Ph.D., 1941. *Politics:* Democrat. *Religion:* Presbyterian. *Home:* 3705 Hilldale Dr., Nashville, Tenn. 37215. *Office:* George Peabody College for Teachers, Nashville, Tenn. 37203.

CAREER: Kentucky public schools, social studies teacher, 1935-37; Eastern Kentucky State College, Rich-

mond, teacher in history department, 1940-42, and 1946; George Peabody College for Teachers, Nashville, associate professor, 1946-52, professor of history, 1952—, chairman of department of history and political science, 1954—, chairman of division of social science, 1963—. Visiting professor, University of Colorado. Social studies consultant to Republic of Korea; consultant to local school systems in United States. *Military service:* U.S. Navy, 1942-45; became lieutenant. *Member:* National Council for Social Studies (board of directors, 1951-62; president, 1958), American Council on Education, Education Policies Committee (advisory council), American Viewpoint Society (advisory board), Phi Delta Kappa, Kappa Delta Pi, Pi Gamma Mu, Pi Omega Pi. *Awards, honors:* Alumnus of the Year, Eastern Kentucky State College, 1960; award of merit, American Association for State and Local History, for *Pen and Sword: The Life and Journals of Randal W. McGavock.*

WRITINGS: (Editor) *The Teacher of the Social Studies,* National Council for Social Studies, 1952; (with F.P. Wirth) *This Government of Ours,* American Book Co., 1952; (with Clarence Stegmeir) *Civics,* American Book Co., 1956; (with Hershel Gower) *Pen and Sword: The Life and Journals of Randal W. McGavock,* Tennessee Historical Commission, 1960; *A Charter for Social Studies in Korea,* Republic of Korea, Ministry of Education, 1961; (with others) *Social Studies and the National Interest,* National Council for Social Studies, 1962; (contributor) *The Problems and Promise of American Democracy,* McGraw, 1964; (with John L. Betts) *History: U.S.A.,* American Book Co., 1967, 2nd edition, 1971; *Documents: U.S.A.,* American Book Co., 1967; *The American Public School,* McGraw, 1969; (contributor) *Contemporary Issues in American Democracy,* McGraw, 1969; (with Betts) *U.S.A.: History and Documents,* two volumes, American Book Co., 1971.

With Adelene Howland; all published by Prentice-Hall: *Canada,* 1964, *The Americas,* 1964, *Latin America,* 1964, *Western Europe,* 1964, *Soviet Union and Eastern Europe,* 1965, *Africa South of the Sahara,* 1965, *Pacific Lands and Antarctica,* 1965, *Southwest and North Africa,* 1965, *The United States of America,* 1966, *The Earth and Our States,* 1966, *Nations Around the Globe,* 1966, *Eastern and Southern Asia,* 1966, *Nations of Other Lands,* 1966, *The United States and Canada,* 1966.

Author of workbooks and teacher's manuals; contributor to professional journals. Member of publications committee, National Council for Social Studies, 1949-52; member of editorial board, Civic Education Serivce, 1957-60; member of advisory board, *Issues Today,* 1970—.

WORK IN PROGRESS: A high school text in citizenship; elementary school materials for social studies.

*   *   *

ALLEN, Jerry 1911-

PERSONAL: Born October 12, 1911, in Benton, Wis.; daughter of James Edward and Susannah (Thompson) Allen. *Education:* University of Wisconsin, B.A.; Columbia University, M.S. *Politics:* Democrat. *Religion:* Protestant. *Agent:* McIntosh & Otis, Inc., 18 East 41st St., New York, N.Y. 10017.

CAREER: Reporter and department editor for *New York Herald Tribune,* New York, N.Y., and Paris, France, 1931-33, for Reuters News Agency, London, England, 1933-38; National Broadcasting Co., broadcaster, Paris, France, 1939-40; editorial assistant to Raymond Gram Swing, New York, N.Y., and Washington, D.C., 1940-43; U.S. Office of War Information, and U.S. Department of State, Washington, D.C., head of news desk, 1943-47; now free-lance writer. *Member:* Authors Guild, Authors League, Theta Sigma Phi. *Awards, honors:* Fellow, Bread Loaf Writers' Conference, 1954; Sorbonne honor, 1967, for research on Conrad; silver medal, Academie de Marine, 1969, for *The Sea Years of Joseph Conrad;* National Institute of Arts and Letters grant, 1969.

WRITINGS: Hearth in the Snow, Wilfred Funk, 1952; *The Adventures of Mark Twain* (biography), Little, Brown, 1954; *The Thunder and the Sunshine: Biography of Joseph Conrad,* Putnam, 1958; *The Sea Years of Joseph Conrad* (biography), Doubleday, 1965; (editor and author of introduction) *Great Short Works of Joseph Conrad,* Harper, 1966; (editor and author of introduction) *Great Short Works of Herman Melville,* Harper, 1966; (editor and author of introduction) Herman Melville, *Moby Dick,* Harper, 1966; (editor and author of introduction) Oscar Wilde, *The Picture of Dorian Gray,* Harper, 1966. Contributor of articles to *National Geographic, Reader's Digest, Good Housekeeping, Columbia University Forum,* and other periodicals; also contributor of columns and articles to British and American newspapers.

WORK IN PROGRESS: The Jeddah Case (history), for Doubleday; *Mark Twain at Home* (memoir); a volume of autobiography; and a novel, *A Tale of Pleasing Woe,* publication by Doubleday expected in 1974-75.

AVOCATIONAL INTERESTS: Travel, reading, and outdoor life.

BIOGRAPHICAL/CRITICAL SOURCES: Punch, July 5, 1967.

*   *   *

ALLEN, M(arion) C.   1914-
(Sam Allen)

PERSONAL: Born December 12, 1914, in Spartanburg, S.C.; son of Albert Mayfield and Caroline Mae (Rogers) Allen; married Eleanor Earl Burt (a music teacher), July 31, 1943; children: Marian Carol, Burt Mayfield, Robert William, Mary Louise. *Education:* Furman University, A.B., 1937; Yale University, B.D., 1940; Hartford Seminary Foundation, graduate study; University of Kansas, M.A., 1960. *Politics:* Democrat. *Home:* 441 Nebraska St., Lawrence, Kan. 66044. *Office:* First Baptist Church, 801 Kentucky St., Lawrence, Kan. 66044.

CAREER: Baptist minister in Bristol, Conn., 1940-47, Beaufort, S.C., 1947-50, Clemson, S.C., 1950-56; Clemson College, Clemson, S.C., instructor in religion, 1952-56; First Baptist Church, Lawrence, Kan., minister, 1956—. University of Kansas, teacher of English, 1958-61, research associate in modern American drama, 1962—. President, Lawrence Council of Churches, 1960-63. Vice-chairman, Lawrence advisory curriculum board in public education, 1960-62. *Member:* Pi Gamma Mu, Masons, Lions Club, Hand and Torch.

WRITINGS: (Under pseudonym Sam Allen) *A Voice Not Our Own,* Judson, 1963; (editor) Val Haining Wilson, *The Springs of Learning: A Collection of Articles and Addresses,* Skidmore College, 1969. Contributor to religious journals. Columnist, *Pulpit Digest,* 1949-58.

WORK IN PROGRESS: The Light and the Mirror, sermons based on modern dramas.

*   *   *

ALLEN, R. Earl   1922-

PERSONAL: Born May 26, 1922, in Fort Worth, Tex.; son of James Roy (a carpenter) and Mary Ellen (Coker) Allen; married December 25, 1941 (wife's maiden name Lovelace); children: James Todd, Joy Earline. *Education:* Howard Payne College, B.A., 1946; Hardin College, B.S., 1947; further study, Southwestern Baptist Theological Seminary; Howard Payne College,

D.D., 1953. *Home:* 2523 Prairie, Fort Worth, Tex. 76106.

CAREER: Baptist minister, currently pastor of Rosen Heights Baptist Church, Fort Worth, Tex. Southern Baptist Convention, member of Home Mission board of directors; Baptist Convention of Texas, former member of executive board and of Christian education commission; Tarrant Baptist Association, former chairman of executive board; Trustee, Howard Payne College.

WRITINGS: Bible Paradoxes, Revell, 1963; *Memorial Messages,* Broadman, 1964; (compiler) *Pastor Minister in Time of Death: Bibliography,* 1964; *Trials, Tragedies, and Triumph*s, Revell, 1965; *Christian Comfort: Three Messages of Consolation for the Difficulties of Life,* Broadman, 1965; *Strength from Shadows,* Broadman, 1967; *The Sign of the Star,* Broadman, 1968; *Silent Saturday,* Baker Book, 1968. Anthologized in *Best Sermons of 1966-68,* edited by G.P. Butter, Simon & Schuster, 1968.

*   *   *

ALLEN, Roach Van   1917-

PERSONAL: Born September 24, 1917, in Lockney, Tex.; son of James Brice (a teacher) and Myrtle (Roach) Allen; married Pauline Claryce Whitten, May 23, 1943; children: Lynda Kay, Larry Van, Elva Claryce. *Education:* West Texas State University, B.A., 1938, M.A., 1941; University of Texas, Ed.D., 1948. *Politics:* Democrat. *Religion:* Presbyterian. *Home:* 5515 Via Entrada, Tucson, Ariz. 85718. *Office:* College of Education, University of Arizona, Tucson, Ariz. 85721.

CAREER: Canyon (Tex.) Public Schools, elementary teacher, 1939-41; Southern Methodist University, Dallas, Tex., director of elementary teacher education, 1949-53; Harlingen (Tex.) Public Schools, director of curriculum, 1953-55; San Diego County (Calif.) Department of Education, director of curriculum coordination, 1955-63; University of Arizona, Tucson, professor of elementary education, 1963—. Consultant on reading research projects. *Military service:* U.S. Army, 1941-46; became captain. *Member:* Association for Childhood Education International (research committee, 1961-63; public board chairman, 1968-70), International Reading Association (San Diego County branch president, 1962-63), American Association of Elementary Kindergarten Nursery Educators, Association for Supervision and Curriculum Development (state president, 1951-52), National Education Association (life member), Arizona Education Association, Arizona State Reading Council (president), Phi Delta Kappa, Tucson Art Gallery Association.

WRITINGS: (With Gertrude Keller) *Preparing Your Child for School,* Compton, 1959; *Beginning Writing Experiences,* Department of Education, San Diego County, 1960; (with Helen Darrow) *Independent Activities for Creative Learning,* Teachers College Press, 1961; *Language Experiences in the Kindergarten,* Department of Education, San Diego County, 1962; (with Dorris M. Lee) *Learning to Read through Experience,* Appleton, 1963; *Attitudes and the Art of Teaching Reading,* National Education Association, 1965; (with wife, Claryce Allen) *Language Experiences in Reading,* Levels I, II and III, Encyclopaedia Britannica Press, 1966-67; (with C. Allen) *Language Experiences in Early Childhood,* Encyclopaedia Britannica Press, 1969. Author of scripts for "Magic Moments," a series of twenty films, Encyclopaedia Britannica Educational Corp., 1969. Contributor to reading conference yearbooks, including *Teaching Young Children to Read,* published by U.S. Office of Education, and author of approximately 100 articles published in journals and magazines. Member of editorial board, *Childhood Education,* 1964-66.

WORK IN PROGRESS: Research in teaching reading in first grade and in teaching children with language handicaps.

AVOCATIONAL INTERESTS: Arts and crafts, music.

*   *   *

ALMAN, David 1919-
(Emily David, a joint pseudonym)

PERSONAL: Born March 19, 1919, in New York, N.Y.; son of Gabriel and Ethel (Friedberg) Alman; married Emily Arnow (an associate professor of sociology and a writer), August 1, 1940; children: Michelle, Jennifer. Home: 15 Ainsworth Ave., East Brunswick, N.J. 08816. Agent: Barthold Fles Literary Agency, 507 Fifth Ave., New York, N.Y. 10017.

CAREER: Mainly a free-lance writer until 1957; Smith, Kline & French Laboratories, Philadelphia, Pa., film producer, 1957-69; Science & Medicine Co., Inc., film producer, 1970—.

WRITINGS: The Hourglass, Simon & Schuster, 1947; Well of Compassion, Simon & Schuster, 1948; World Full of Strangers, Doubleday, 1949; (with wife, Emily Alman) Prisoner on Our Conscience, Committee to Secure Justice for Morton Sobell, c.1956; Conquest: A Book about Scientists, Their Inquiries and Achievements, Doubleday, 1963; Generations, Regnery, 1971. Also author, with wife, Emily Alman, under joint pseudonym Emily David, of a film, "The 91st Day," 1963.

WORK IN PROGRESS: Several books and plays.

*   *   *

ALONSO, William 1933-

PERSONAL: Born January 29, 1933, in Buenos Aires, Argentina; son of Amado (a professor) and Joan (Cann-Evans) Alonso; married Mary Ellen Peters (in visual studies), May 9, 1959. Education: Harvard University, A.B., 1954, Masters of City Planning, 1956; University of Pennsylvania, Ph.D., 1959. Home: 52 Oakvale Ave., Berkeley, Calif. 94705. Office: Department of City and Regional Planning, University of California, Berkeley, Calif. 94720.

CAREER: Harvard University, Cambridge, Mass., assistant professor, 1959-64, associate professor of regional planning, 1964-67, director of Center for Urban Studies, 1963-67; University of California, Berkeley, professor of regional planning, 1967—. Private practice as consultant on city and regional planning and development; consultant to Ford Foundation. Member: Regional Science Association, Phi Beta Kappa.

WRITINGS: Location and Land Use: Toward a General Theory of Land Rent, Harvard University Press, 1964; (editor with John Friedmann) Regional Development and Planning: A Reader, M.I.T. Press, 1964; (contributor) K.S. Lynn, editor, The Professions in America, Houghton, 1965.

Monographs: Location, Primacy and Regional Economic Development, Harvard University, 1966; A Reformulation of Classical Location Theory and Its Relation to Rent Theory, Harvard University, 1967; Aspects of Regional Planning and Theory in the United States, Institute of Urban and Regional Development, University of California (Berkeley), 1968; Beyond the Inter-disciplinary Approach to Planning, Institute of Urban and Regional Development, University of California, 1968; Equity and Its Relation to Efficiency in Urbanization, Institute of Urban and Regional Development, University of California, 1968; Industrial Location and Regional Policy in Economic Development, Institute of Urban and Regional Development, University of California, 1968.

Contributor of articles on urban topics to scholarly journals. Editor, Papers and Proceedings of Regional Science Association, 1957, Journal of Regional Science, 1958-59.

WORK IN PROGRESS: Research on national patterns and policies of urbanization.

*   *   *

ALSOP, Mary O'Hara 1885-
(Mary O'Hara)

PERSONAL: Resumed maiden name legally in 1947; born July 10, 1885, in Cape May Point, N.J.; daughter of Reese Fell (an Episcopal clergyman) and Mary Lee (Spring) Alsop; married Kent Kane Parrot, 1905 (divorced); married Helge Sture-Vasa, 1922 (divorced, 1947); children: (first marriage) Mary O'Hara (deceased), Kent Kane, Jr. Education: Educated privately in United States and studied languages and music during European travel. Religion: Roman Catholic (convert). Home: 5506 Grove Street, Chevy Chase, Md. 20015.

CAREER: Author and composer. Grew up in Brooklyn Heights, N.Y.; moved to California after first marriage and subsequently became a screen writer; lived in Wyoming during her second marriage, writing there the three classics about the range country; returned to the East to make her home there in 1948.

WRITINGS: Let Us Say Grace, Christopher, 1930; My Friend Flicka, Lippincott, 1941, annotated edition, edited by A.H. Lass, Lippincott, 1944; Thunderhead, Lippincott, 1943; Green Grass of Wyoming, Lippincott, 1946; The Son of Adam Wyngate, McKay, 1952; Novel-in-the-Making (autobiographical), McKay, 1954; Wyoming Summer, Doubleday, 1963; The Catch Colt (folk musical; produced at Catholic University of America and at Lincoln Theatre, Cheyenne, Wyo.) Dramatists Play Service, 1964; A Musical in the Making, Markane Publishing, 1966.

Composer (for piano) of "Esperan" (1943), "May God Keep You" (1946), and others.

SIDELIGHTS: Critical praise was lavished on My Friend Flicka when it appeared in 1941. Marianne Hauser wrote that reading the story "makes you smell the grass and feel the coolness of the wind.... [It has] the delightful, radiant touch of a fairy tale. And yet this is a very real book." The warm, human story of a boy and his colt has become a classic, translated into a great number of languages, and beloved by children throughout the world. Subsequent stories of ranch life confirmed Miss O'Hara's success with her subject. When the author wrote The Son of Adam Wyngate she was projecting some of the religious philosophies which reflected her personal exploration into the life of the spirit, but, in 1963, resurrection of her sixteen-year old diary, issued as Wyoming Summer, reemphasized her special talent for depicting western life for man and his animals, and opened vistas into her own personality and life.

My Friend Flicka was filmed by 20th Century Fox in 1943, followed by its sequel, Thunderhead, Son of Flicka, in 1945. Green Grass of Wyoming was filmed by 20th Century Fox in 1948. An ABC-TV series was based on My Friend Flicka in 1957.

BIOGRAPHICAL/CRITICAL SOURCES: Mary (Alsop) Sture-Vasa, Novel-in-the-Making, McKay, 1954; Mary O'Hara, Wyoming Summer, Doubleday, 1963; New York Times, August 24, 1941, October 27, 1946; Saturday Review, November 1, 1941, May 17, 1952, September 16, 1954; Catholic World, December 1943; Yale Review, Winter, 1944; Kirkus, August 15, 1946; Time, March 31, 1952; Library Journal, September 15, 1954; Best Sellers, March 15, 1963; Christian Science Monitor, March 7, 1963.

ALTHOLZ, Josef L(ewis) 1933-

PERSONAL: Born August 14, 1933, in New York, N.Y.; son of Carl Hyman (an attorney) and Rae (Huberfeld) Altholz. *Education:* Cornell University, B.A., 1954; Columbia University, M.A., 1955, Ph.D., 1960. *Politics:* Democrat. *Religion:* Jewish.

CAREER: University of Minnesota, Minneapolis, instructor, 1959-61, assistant professor, 1961-64, associate professor, 1964-67, professor of history, 1967—. Visiting professor of history, University of Wisconsin, 1970-71. *Military service:* U.S. Army, 1955-57; became first lieutenant. *Member:* American Historical Association, American Catholic Historical Association, American Society of Church History, American Jewish Historical Society, Conference on British Studies, American Committee for Irish Studies, American Association of University Professors. *Awards, honors:* Guggenheim fellow, 1964-65.

WRITINGS: The Liberal Catholic Movement in England: The "Rambler" and Its Contributors, Burns & Oates, 1962; *The Churches in the Nineteenth Century,* Bobbs, 1967; (compiler) *Victorian England, 1837-1901,* Cambridge University Press, 1970; (editor with D.M. Elrath) *Correspondence of Lord Alton and Richard Simpson,* volume I, Cambridge University Press, 1971. Contributor to *Victorian Studies, Catholic Historical Review,* and other journals. Associate editor, *Wellesley Index to Victorian Periodicals.*

*   *   *

AMATORA, Sister Mary (Delphine Fleury)

EDUCATION: Indiana University, B.S., 1937; Purdue University, M.S., 1938, Ph.D., 1942. *Home and office:* 3012 Summit St., Oakland, Calif. 94609.

CAREER: Roman Catholic religious, member of Order of St. Francis, with name in religion, Sister Mary Amatora. St. Francis College, Lafayette, Ind., instructor in psychology and education, 1937-42, director of student teaching, 1938-42, assistant professor, 1942-44; St. Francis College, Fort Wayne Ind., professor of psychology, 1944—, research professor of psychology, 1948—, director of psychological clinic, 1954-70; University of California, Berkeley, member of faculty, 1970—. St. Elizabeth School of Nursing, Lafayette, Ind., consultant in education and psychology, 1948-54. Lecturer throughout United States and Mexico. *Member:* American Psychological Association (fellow), American Catholic Psychological Association (board), Society for Research in Child Development, American Educational Research Association, American Association for Advancement of Science, National Education Association, Association for Higher Education, Fort Wayne-Lima Psychological Association (president), Sigma Xi, Delta Epsilon Sigma.

WRITINGS: The Queen's Heart of Gold, Pageant, 1957; *The Queen's Portrait,* Academy Guild Press, 1961. Also author of *The Queen's Way, The Queen's Secret, Diagnostic Teacher-Rating Scale,* and *Personality Rating Scale.*

Author of more than one hundred research studies and other articles published in professional journals, including *Journal of Experimental Education, Journal of Social Psychology,* and *Journal of Genetic Psychology,* and of more than four hundred other articles in fifty religious magazines. Weekly newspaper columnist for five years. Associate editor, *Education,* 1949—; abstractor for *Psychological Abstracts.*

WORK IN PROGRESS: Studies on children's and adolescents' interest, family life, interpersonal relationships in the classroom, teacher-pupil relationships.

AVOCATIONAL INTERESTS: Music, art.

AMBLER, Eric 1909-
(Eliot Reed, a joint pseudonym)

PERSONAL: Born June 28, 1909, in London, England; son of Alfred Percy and Amy Madeline (Andrews) Ambler; married Louise Crombie, October 5, 1939 (divorced May, 1958); married Joan Harrison, October 11, 1958. *Education:* University of London, engineering student, 1924-27. *Home:* 10640 Taranto Way, Los Angeles, Calif. 90024. *Agent:* Peter Janson-Smith Ltd., 2 Caxton St., London, S.W.1, England.

CAREER: Engineering apprentice, London, England, 1927-28; actor briefly, then advertising copywriter, 1928-37; professional writer, 1937—. Producer of several films, including "October Man," 1947. *Military service:* British Army, Artillery, 1940-46; served in North Africa and Italy; later assistant director of Army Kinematography, War Office; lieutenant colonel; awarded Bronze Star. *Member:* Authors League of America, Writers Guild of America, West (council member, 1961-64), Academy of Motion Picture Arts and Sciences, Garrick Club (London). *Awards, honors:* Crime Writers Association Award, 1959, for *A Passage of Arms,* runner up, 1962, for *The Light of Day,* best crime novel, 1967, for *Dirty Story;* Mystery Writers Association Edgar Award for best mystery novel, 1963, for *The Light of Day.*

WRITINGS—Novels, except as indicated: *The Dark Frontier,* Hodder & Stoughton, 1936; *Uncommon Danger,* Hodder & Stoughton, 1937, published in America as *Background to Danger,* Knopf, 1937; *Cause for Alarm* (although the character Zaleshoff appears both in this novel and in *Uncommon Danger,* the novels are otherwise unconnected), Hodder & Stoughton, 1938, Knopf, 1939; *Epitaph for a Spy,* Hodder & Stoughton, 1938, published in America with a new footnote by Ambler, Knopf, 1952, reissued in England with a new preface by Ambler, Bodley Head, 1966; *The Mask of Dimitrios,* Hodder & Stoughton, 1939, published in America as *A Coffin for Dimitrios,* Knopf, 1939; *Journey Into Fear* (originally announced as *The Passenger for Modano*), Knopf, 1940; *Intrigue* (contains *Journey Into Fear, Coffin for Dimitrios, Cause for Alarm,* and *Background to Danger*), introduction by Alfred Hitchcock, Knopf, 1943 (English edition, with same cover title, includes *The Mask of Dimitrios, Journey Into Fear,* and *Judgment on Deltchev,* Hodder & Stoughton, 1965); *Eric Ambler's Double Decker* (two complete novels), World Publishing, 1945; *Judgment on Deltchev,* Knopf, 1951; *The Schirmer Inheritance,* Knopf, 1953; *The Night-Comers,* Heinemann, 1956, published in America as *State of Siege,* Knopf, 1956; *A Passage of Arms,* Heinemann, 1959, Knopf, 1960; *The Light of Day,* Heinemann, 1962, Knopf, 1963; *The Ability to Kill, and Other Pieces* (essays). Bodley Head, 1963; *A Kind of Anger,* Atheneum, 1964; (editor, author of introduction, and contributor of one of the seven stories) *To Catch a Spy: An Anthology of Favourite Spy Stories,* Bodley Head, 1964, Atheneum, 1965; *The Intriguers: A Second Omnibus* (contains *A Passage of Arms, State of Siege, The Schirmer Inheritance,* and *Judgment on Deltchev*), Knopf, 1965; *Dirty Story: A Further Account of the Life and Adventures of Arthur Abdel Simpson* (sequel to *The Light of Day;* Literary Guild alternate selection), Atheneum, 1967; *The Intercom Conspiracy,* Atheneum, 1969; (contributor of essay) Dorothy Salisbury Davis, editor, *Crime Without Murder: An Anthology of Stories by the Mystery Writers of America,* Scribner, 1970; *The Levanter,* Atheneum, 1972.

With Charles Rodda, under joint pseudonym Eliot Reed; all novels: *Skytip,* Doubleday, 1950; *Tender to Danger,* Doubleday, 1951 (published in England as *Tender to Moonlight,* Hodder & Stoughton, 1952); *The Maras Affair,* Doubleday, 1953; *Charter to Danger,* Collins, 1954; *Passport to Panic,* Collins, 1958.

Screenplays: (with Peter Ustinov) "The Way Ahead," filmed by 20th Century-Fox, 1944; "United States" (U.S. Army documentary), 1945; "The October Man," Eagle Lion, 1947; "Highly Dangerous," Lippert Productions, 1951; "The Magic Box," J. Arthur Rank Organization, 1952; "Encore," Paramount, 1952; "The Promoter," Universal, 1952; "Shoot First," United Artists, 1953; "The Cruel Sea" (from the novel by Nicholas Monsarrat), Universal, 1953; "Lease of Life," Italian Films Export, 1955; "The Purple Plain," United Artists, 1955; "Yangtse Incident," 1957; "A Night to Remember," Lopert, 1958; "The Wreck of the Mary Deare," M-G-M, 1959; "Love, Hate, Love" (written for television), ABC "Movie of the Week," 1970. Ambler also provided the idea for the television series, "Checkmate," 1961-62.

Contributor of articles and stories to newspapers and magazines.

SIDELIGHTS: "Between 1936 and 1940 Mr. Eric Ambler published six books. During these years, and still more in the eleven years that elapsed before the publication of his next story, he acquired the sort of reputation that has about it almost a legendary nature," Julian Symons writes. "These six books were very well-written thrillers, with a background of spying and international politics. Yes: but they had some other quality about them, they were very intimately linked with their period, the time of the Left Book Club and the Popular Front. Writers of spy stories, from John Buchan onwards, have almost always been staunch right wingers, proudly unaware of political subtleties: Mr. Ambler seemed to many readers refreshingly aware of the world's changed political climate." Ambler uses real countries and incidents in his books, and this lends to the believability of his stories. Most thrillers of merit are involved with the theme of a man being chased or hunted in some way, and their writers are strongly interested in some part of the hunt. "Mr. Ambler was fascinated by foreign cities, the mechanics of travel, and obscure plots to overthrow governments," Symons comments. "It is said that this preoccupation with frontiers, passports, and methods of travelling from one place to another in the Balkans was based upon a very slender basis of experience. So much the more credit to Mr. Ambler if that is true, for making his background sketches of Istanbul and Sofia, Belgrade and Milan so convincing. He has adroitly heightened the seemingly realistic, yet curiously exotic, effect of these descriptions by using as narrator an impatient or slightly stupid Englishman—the engineer Graham in *Journey into Fear,* the crime novelist Latimer in *The Mask of Dimitrios,* the journalist Kenton in *Uncommon Danger.*" Ambler is also known for keeping track of all the diverse parts of his stories, pulling everything together. All of the details, the statements that make the books so real, as Symons says, "are written in a casually factual manner that is Mr. Ambler's hallmark."

George Grella has called Ambler "One of those authors who [has] successfully bridged the gap between the prewar and contemporary novel of espionage." He believes that Ambler "occupies an enviable position in the field of suspense literature. Along with Somerset Maugham and Graham Greene, he changed the spy novel from the jolly-good-fellows, sporting tale of hearty English Fascism to a sophisticated examination of the methods and moralities of modern international intrigue.... The consistently high level of his achievement and the durability of his appeal derive from the unique Ambler touch. His style and viewpoint are urbane and ironic; he maintains the disenchanted, liberal political views which were innovative in a form previously dominated by a provincial, upper-class vision—the world through a monocle." Ambler has successfully made the jump to postwar suspense

fiction, but in his novels of the fifties Symons senses that Ambler is "at a loss for an attitude."

He notes that this is especially apparent in *Judgment on Deltchev* and *The Schirmer Inheritance,* and again in *State of Siege,* which, he says, "is certainly his best book since the war." James Sandoe comments on *State of Siege:* "If as a thriller it is admirably taut, as a novel it is admirably articulated, its observation of men acute and its view of a political event lucid and dispassionate." Anthony Boucher finds the book "less a novel than a coldly illuminating textbook on a political and military strategy."

"Ambler has changed a trifle over the years," Boucher states, especially in *The Light of Day* and *A Kind of Anger.* His anti-heroes are even more anti, and he is shifting from espionage to a more private form of international malefaction." The main character in *The Light of Day* is definitely an anti-hero. A *New Yorker* writer describes him as "middle-aged, sickly, and afraid of heights. [He is] a sneak thief, a pimp, and a pornographer who calls himself a tourist guide. . . . And yet such is Mr. Ambler's skill that from the moment this poor creature comes cringing into view, we follow his struggles for survival with an interest that develops into something very close to liking." This man, Arthur Abdel Simpson, is encountered again in *Dirty Story.* Grella states that "the dirty story of the title refers to more than the sordid but engaging history of . . . Simpson. It also describes the actions of Ambler's favorite targets—the industrial cartels he has frequently attacked as manipulators of men and nations since his early, anti-Fascist novels.... The protagonists quest for formal identity in a world dominated by business ethics makes the novel a characteristically ironic comment on espionage—an account of the rude awakening of a squalid, frightened little man who has the decency to be outraged by criminals far worse but infinitely more respectable than he." Dick Adler comments on Simpson: "Ambler has managed to personify the survival instinct that exists in varying degrees in most of us, and few readers will come away from *Dirty Story* without a small shock of self-recognition."

With his most recent novels Ambler seems to have changed again with the times, and with his characters and events he is right up to the minute, just as he always has been. He is, as Melvin Maddocks says, "one of those writers so good at his specialty that he has only his younger self . . . to compete against."

Ambler continues to do just that. The editor in *The Intercom Conspiracy* has been welcomed by A.L. Rosenzweig as "one of those men at the end of their tether that grand master Ambler has been portraying so formidably well for more than thirty years." A *New Yorker* writer calls *The Levanter* "one of the best—if not the best—of Mr. Ambler's postwar thrillers." A *New York Times Book Review* writer states that "Ambler is a superb technician. Anything but avant-garde, he is descended from Maugham and certain Edwardian stylists." More importantly, Ambler continues in his *own* tradition.

Journey into Fear, with a screenplay by Joseph Cotten and Orson Welles, was filmed by RKO, 1942, and was adapted for television and produced on "Climax!," 1956; *Background to Danger* was filmed by Warner Bros., 1943; *A Coffin for Dimitrios* was filmed as "The Mask of Dimitrios" by Warner Bros., 1944; *Epitaph for a Spy* was filmed as "Hotel Reserve" by RKO, 1946; *Odd Man Out* was filmed by Universal, 1947; *The Light of Day* was filmed as "The Man in the Middle" by United Artists, title changed before release to "Topkapi," 1964.

A repository for Ambler's manuscripts has been established at the library of Boston University.

BIOGRAPHICAL/CRITICAL SOURCES: New York *Times,* August 8, 1937, January 29, 1939, September 23, 1956, September 16, 1969; *Saturday Review,* January 28, 1939; *Books,* October 22, 1939, April, 1970; *Atlantic,* January, 1941; *Spectctor,* July 19, 1940, February 28, 1970; *New York Herald Tribune Book Review,* March 23, 1952, August 2, 1953, September 16, 1956; *Commonweal,* August 7, 1953; *Times Literary Supplement,* July 20, 1956; *New Yorker,* March 2, 1963; November 21, 1964, July 15, 1972; *New York Times Book Review,* October 18, 1964, October 8, 1967, September 21, 1969, July 16, 1972; Julian Symons, *Critical Occasions,* Hamish Hamilton, 1966; *Publishers Weekly,* July 24, 1967; *National Observer,* October 16, 1967, September 22, 1969; *Book World,* January 14, 1968, July 20, 1969, September 14, 1969; *Best Sellers,* September 15, 1969; *Christian Science Monitor,* October 2, 1969, July 12, 1972; *Punch,* March, 1970.

*   *   *

AMIS, Kingsley (William)   1922-
(Robert Markham)

PERSONAL: Born April 16, 1922, in London, England; son of William Robert (an office clerk) and Rosa Annie (Lucas) Amis; married Hilary Ann Bardwell, 1948 (divorced, 1965); married Elizabeth Jane Howard (a novelist), 1965; children: (first marriage) Philip Nicol William, Martin Louis, Sally Myfanwy. *Education:* St. John's College, Oxford, M.A. (first class honors in English), 1947. *Home:* 108 Maida Vale, London W.9, England. *Agent:* A.D. Peters Ltd., 10 Buckingham St., London W.C.2, England.

CAREER: University College of Swansea, Swansea, Glamorganshire, Wales, lecturer in English, 1949-61; Peterhouse, Cambridge University, Cambridge, England, fellow, 1961-63; writer. Visiting fellow in creative writing, Princeton University, 1958-58; visiting professor of English, Vanderbilt University, 1967-68. *Military service:* British Army, 1942-45; became lieutenant. *Member:* Authors' Club (London), British Channel Yacht Club. *Awards, honors:* Somerset Maugham Award, 1955, for *Lucky Jim.*

WRITINGS—Novels: *Lucky Jim,* Doubleday, 1954 (though title page of first printing reads 1953), edited and abridged by K.W. Swan, Longmans, 1963; *That Uncertain Feeling,* Gollancz, 1955, Harcourt, 1956; *I Like It Here,* Harcourt, 1958; *Take a Girl Like You,* Gollancz, 1960, Harcourt, 1961; *One Fat Englishman,* Gollancz, 1963, Harcourt, 1964; (with Robert Conquest) *The Egyptologists,* J. Cape, 1965, Random House, 1966; *The Anti-Death League,* Harcourt, 1966; (under pseudonym Robert Markham) *Colonel Sun: A James Bond Adventure,* Harper, 1968; *I Want It Now,* J. Cape, 1968; Harcourt, 1969; *The Green Man,* J. Cape, 1969, Harcourt, 1970; *Girl, 20,* J. Cape, 1971, Harcourt, 1972.

Poetry: *A Frame of Mind,* School of Art, Reading University, 1953; *Kingsley Amis,* Fantasy Press, 1954; *A Case of Samples: Poems, 1946-1956,* Gollancz, 1956, Harcourt, 1957; (with Dom Moraes and Peter Porter) *Penguin Modern Poets 2,* Penguin, 1962; *The Evans Country,* Fantasy Press, 1962; *A Look Round the Estate: Poems 1957-1967,* J. Cape, 1967, Harcourt, 1968.

Contributor: *Winter's Tales 1,* St. Martin's, 1955; Robert Conquest, editor, *New Lines: An Anthology,* Macmillan (London), 1956, St. Martin's, 1957.

Editor: (With James Michie) *Oxford Poetry, 1949,* Basil Blackwell, 1949; *Spectrum 1: A Science Fiction Anthology,* Gollancz, 1961, Harcourt, 1962; (with Conquest) *Spectrum 2,* Gollancz, 1962, Harcourt, 1963; (with Conquest) *Spectrum 3,* Gollancz, 1963, Harcourt, 1964; (with Conquest) *Spectrum 4,* Harcourt, 1965; (with Conquest) *Spectrum 5,* Gollancz, 1966, Harcourt, 1967, *Tennyson,* Penguin, 1973.

Other: *Socialism and the Intellectuals,* Fabian Society (London), 1957; (author of introduction) Oscar Wilde, *Essays and Poems,* Norton, 1959; *New Maps of Hell: A Survey of Science Fiction,* Harcourt, 1960; *My Enemy's Enemy* (short stories), Gollancz, 1962, Harcourt, 1963; *The James Bond Dossier,* New American Library, 1965; *Lucky Jim's Politics,* Conservative Political Centre (London), 1968; *What Became of Jane Austen? and Other Questions* (essays), J. Cape, 1970, Harcourt, 1971. Author of a science fiction radio play, "Something Strange," and of a television play, "A Question about Hell." Represented in anthologies, including *New Poets of England and America,* edited by Donald Hall and others, Meridian, 1957, 2nd edition, 1962, *Poet's Choice,* edited by Paul Engle and Joseph Langland, Dial, 1962, and *The Modern Poets,* edited by Malcolm Brinnin and Bill Read, McGraw, 1963.

Contributor to *Spectator, Encounter, New Statesman, London Magazine,* and other periodicals.

WORK IN PROGRESS: A book on detective fiction; spy fiction, etc.

SIDELIGHTS: "We record with deep regret the death of Baron Amis in the microfilm library of his home in Nassau.... Born in 1922, Amis rose to immediate success with his brilliant first novel, *Lucky Jim,* the film rights of which soon freed him from the heavy responsibility of struggling for further literary recognition, as his subsequent books testified. During the 1960's, Amis grew less and less *terrible* as he grew more and more *enfant,* finally becoming, at the same moment, both a Conservative and Robert Markham, the pseudonym under which he began producing a lucrative range of new James Bond thrillers.... He became, in quick succession, Harold Robbins, Barbara Cartland, Godfrey Winn, [and] Mao Tse-Tung...."

This fictitious obituary, which appeared in *Punch,* in 1968, exemplifies the difficulty Kingsley Amis has encountered with critics in recent years. When *Lucky Jim* first appeared, Patricia Hodgart called it "a brilliantly and a preposterously funny book," Walter Allen found Amis a "novelist of formidable and uncomfortable talent," and Edmund Fuller praised the novel as "written with the cool detached, sardonic style which is the trademark of the British satirical novelist ... [and] is funny in something approaching the Wodehouse vein, but it cuts a bit deeper." Amis's later works have generally been poorly received. His more recent novels are termed "amusing," but are found to be lacking in commitment and ideal. James Gindin states that, while Amis shows an "enormous verbal facility," he lacks "the richness and force that derive from some form of commitment or commentary. The flatness of the pure and uncommitted comedy, its satisfaction with simple reflection, may often become repetitious and dull." "What Amis has done," Frederick R. Karl asserts, "is to take the superficial incidents and characters and make them the center of the novel, as though even farcical comedy can proceed this way."

Amis admits that he finds it difficult to take adverse criticism gracefully. He told a *Book World* interviewer: "To say I didn't like your book is like saying I just met your son and I didn't like him—I didn't like his manners or the way he looked." He also feels that the critics misread his intentions. "I don't think critics will say," Amis told *CA,* "... that I primarily want to write funny books."

Some of the critics' harshness may be due to a change in Amis's political viewpoints. Though originally categorized as one of the "angries," Amis has since disavowed the use of polemic in his fiction. In an open letter to London Magazine, Amis declared that while "political wickedness and folly is as valid a subject for the novelist, etc., as any other kind, ... full-time political commitment—'the writer as polemicist'—is not for me. Not at the moment: 'one's instinct as an artist' is more important."

When Gildrose Productions, the firm to which the "James Bond" copyright was sold after Ian Fleming's death, awarded the first non-Fleming sequel to Amis, the literary world received the news with a mixture of apprehension and interest. Earlier, Amis had done an analysis of the nature of Fleming's hero in *The James Bond Dossier;* thus it appeared logical that Amis would become the successor to Bond's creator. The critics, however, have been mixed in their reactions to *Colonel Sun.* S.K. Oberbeck believes that "although Amis faithfully uses the usual Fleming script, ... the changes he has wrought on Bond's essential character throw the formula askew.... In humanizing Bond ... Amis somehow deprives him of the very ingredients that made his barely believable adventures so rewarding...." Clara Siggins, however, states that Amis has "produced an exciting narrative with the expertise and verve of Fleming himself...."

Amis's recent reviews have not been entirely unfavorable. L.E. Sissman writes that "Amis is especially good ... on shabbiness and shabby gentility; on pretensions, particularly lower-middle-class ones; and on all kinds of cant and sham, for which he has an X-ray eye. But he is best and most original on the subject of sex, to which he brings the faultless eye and ear of a handsome man who has been there himself. His women possess real dimension of a kind not often seen since Fitzgerald...." R.G.G. Price defends Amis's recent works by pointing out that "Amis has suffered a good deal from admirers who insist on seeing him as a cultural portent or a satirist of the voice of the Left or, now, of the Right.... He is an intelligent poet and critic, an effective journalist and a straightforward, honest writer of fiction which is both entertaining and firmly committed to traditional moral values."

Lucky Jim was filmed in 1958; *That Uncertain Feeling* in 1962, under the title "Only Two Can Play"; *Take a Girl Like You* was released in 1970 by Columbia Pictures; *I Want It Now* is currently being produced by Stanley Donen for National General Productions. In 1968, Amis appeared in the movie "Tell Me Lies."

AVOCATIONAL INTERESTS: Music (jazz, Mozart), thrillers, television, science fiction.

BIOGRAPHICAL/CRITICAL SOURCES—Books: Kenneth Allsop, *The Angry Decade,* P. Owen, 1958; Gene Feldman and Max Gartenberg, editors, *The Beat Generation and the Angry Young Men,* Citadel, 1958; James Gindin, *Postwar British Fiction,* University of California Press, 1962; Frederick R. Karl, *The Contemporary English Novel,* Farrar, Straus, 1962; Howard Nemerov, *Poetry and Fiction: Essays,* Rutgers University Press, 1963; William Van O'Connor, *The New University Wits and the End of Modernism,* Southern Illinois University Press, 1963; Charles Shapiro, editor, *Contemporary British Novelists,* Southern Illinois University Press, 1965; Edmund Wilson, *The Bit Between My Teeth: A Literary Chronicle of 1950-1965,* Farrar, Straus, 1965; David Lodge, *Language of Fiction,* Columbia University Press, 1966; Brigid Brophy, *Don't Never Forget,* Holt, 1967; Rubin Rabinovitz, *The Reaction Against Experiment in the English Novel, 1950-1960,* Columbia University Press, 1967.

Articles: *Spectator,* January 29, 1954, September 2, 1955, January 17, 1958, October 11, 1969; *New Statesman,* January 30, 1954, August 20, 1955, January 18, 1958, November 28, 1963, July 7, 1967, December 1, 1967, October 11, 1968; *Nation,* January 30, 1954, August 20, 1955, April 28, 1969, May 5, 1969, October 5, 1970; *New York Times,* January 31, 1954, February 26, 1956, February 23, 1958, April 25, 1967, April 25, 1968, March 12, 1969, August 17, 1970; *Manchester Guardian,* February 2, 1954, August 23, 1955, November 30, 1956; *Times Literary Supplement,* February 12, 1954, September 16, 1955, January 17, 1958, September 21, 1962, November 23, 1967, March 28, 1968; *Saturday Review,* February 20, 1954, February 25, 1956, March 8, 1958, April 6, 1963, April 5, 1969; *New Yorker,* March 6, 1954, March 24, 1956, March 24, 1958, April 26, 1969, September 13, 1969; *Atlantic,* April, 1956, April, 1958, July, 1965, June, 1968, June, 1970; *Christian Science Monitor,* January 16, 1958; *Commonweal,* March 21, 1958; *New Republic,* March 24, 1958, September 19, 1970; *Wilson Library Bulletin,* May, 1958, May, 1965; *New York Times Book Review,* April 28, 1963, July 25, 1965, April 28, 1968, May 19, 1968, March 23, 1968; *Newsweek,* March 2, 1964, May 8, 1967, May 6, 1968, September 14, 1970; *Books and Bookmen,* December, 1965, July, 1968, January, 1969, September, 1969; *Critique,* spring-summer, 1966; *New York Review of Books,* October 6, 1966, August 1, 1968; *Listener,* November 9, 1967, January 11, 1968, November 26, 1970; *Observer Review,* November 12, 1967, October 6, 1968; *London Magazine,* January, 1968, August, 1968, October, 1968, January, 1970; *Punch,* April 24, 1968, August 28, 1968, October 12, 1968, October 22, 1969, November 18, 1970; *Life,* May 3, 1968, March 14, 1969; *Book World,* May 5, 1968, August 8, 1968, October 20, 1968; *Best Sellers,* May 15, 1968, April 1, 1969; *Poetry Review,* spring, 1968; *National Review,* June 18, 1968, June 3, 1969, August 25, 1970; *Poetry,* July, 1969; *National Observer,* September 15, 1969; *Yale Review,* autumn, 1969; *Library Journal,* July, 1970; *Time,* August 31, 1970; *New Leader,* September 21, 1970; *Bookseller,* November 11, 1970.

*   *   *

AMMONS, (Archie) R. 1926-

PERSONAL: Born February 18, 1926, in Whiteville, N.C.; son of Willie M. and Lucy Della (McKee) Ammons; married Phyllis Plumbo, November 26, 1949; children: John Randolph. *Education:* Wake Forest College (now University), B.S., 1949; University of California, Berkeley, studies in English, 1950-52. *Office:* Cornell University, Ithaca, N.Y. 14850.

CAREER: Frederich & Dimmock, Inc., Atlantic City, N.J., executive vice-president, 1952-61; Cornell University, Ithaca, N.Y., teacher of creative writing, 1964—. *Military service:* U.S. Naval Reserve, 1944-46; served in South Pacific. *Awards, honors:* Scholarship in poetry, Bread Loaf Writers' Conference, 1961; John Simon Guggenheim fellowship, 1966; American Academy of Arts and Letters traveling fellowship, 1967; Levinson Prize, 1970; D.Litt., Wake Forest University, 1972.

WRITINGS—Poetry: Ommateum, Dorrance, 1955; *Expressions of Sea Level,* Ohio State University Press, 1964; *Corsons Inlet,* Cornell University Press, 1965; *Tape for the Turn of the Year,* Cornell University Press, 1965; *Northfield Poems,* Cornell University Press, 1966; *Selected Poems,* Cornell University Press, 1968; *Uplands,* Norton, 1970; *Briefings,* Norton, 1971; *Collected Poems, 1951-1971,* Norton, 1972. Contributor to *Hudson Review, Poetry, Carleton Miscellany,* and other periodicals. Poetry editor, *Nation,* 1963.

SIDELIGHTS: Although they may see very different qualities in Ammons's work, many critics believe him to be one of the best contemporary poets. "Like true art songs, [his] poems are brief without being small," Thomas Lask comments. "They have weight and solidity, a resonance and compactness that have nothing to do with size. They also have a certain hardness of outlook because the poet refuses to be sentimental or self-illusory about what he sees. . . .What he sees he renders fully without retouching. He stays away from the vast and the grand, finding all he needs in small objects thoroughly observed and truly rendered." Daniel Hoffman emphasizes the use of Nature in Ammons's work. "The poems of A.R. Ammons take their shapes the way water flows, moving with quick runs or slow eddies along an unspoiled landscape in which is revealed the immanence of a spiritual force greater than any found in the industrial world they avoid describing. His enterprise is founded on an implied Emersonian division of experience into Nature and the Soul; and indeed, Mr. Ammons places himself in the transcendentalist tradition, sometimes echoing familiar lines from Emerson, Whitman and Dickinson."

Lawrence Lieberman believes that the language Ammons uses has "a spiritualizing power. The poetry glides with a lingering, light-fingered savoriness over the shades, tones, and hues of sensory experience. Ammons's language, disciplined by attending to the minutest motion in nature with the intensest caring for the 'lowliest' forms of life, exhibits a precision and a quality of quiet spiritual rejoicing that carries over from his eye to his verbal ear. He has won his way through to an imperishable quiet at the heart of words, and he has infused more of this quality, this quietness . . . into his poetry than is to be found in the work of any poet now writing."

BIOGRAPHICAL/CRITICAL SOURCES: Book Week, February 20, 1966; *Nation,* April 24, 1967, January 18, 1971; *Hudson Review,* summer, 1967; *Prairie Schooner,* fall, 1967; *Contemporary Literature,* winter, 1968; *Poetry,* April, 1969; *New York Times Book Review,* December 14, 1969; *Time,* July 12, 1971; *New York Times,* November 10, 1972.

* * *

ANCKARSVARD, Karin Inez Maria 1915-

PERSONAL: Surname is pronounced *ank*-er-sord; born August 10, 1915, in Stockholm, Sweden; daughter of Oscar Emil (a doctor of medicine) and Iris (Forssling) Olson; married Carl M. Cosswa Anckarsvard, January 20, 1940; children: Marie Christine (Mrs. Reinhold Fahlbeck), Marie Cecile, Marie Madeleine, Mikael, Carl Henrik. *Education:* Attended Oxford University, 1934-35; commercial college degree, Stockholm, Sweden, 1936. *Politics:* Conservative. *Religion:* Roman Catholic. *Home:* Skandiavagen 13, Djursholm, Sweden.

CAREER: Secretary of Sveriges Yngre Lakares, 1936-40. *Member:* Catholic Women's League of Sweden (president), Association of Sweden's Authors of Children's Books, Association of Sweden's Authors, Conservative Women's League. *Awards, honors:* Bonnier's childrens' book award, 1958; Ungdomsnytt's Stip.; Swedish State Stip., 1960; Children's Book Choice award, 1963, for *Doktorns pojk.*

WRITINGS: Bonifacius den groene, Bonniers, 1952, translation by C.M. Anckarsvard and K.H. Beales published as *Bonifacius the Green,* Abelard, 1962; *Tag Fast magistern!,* Bonniers, 1955, translation by Annabelle MacMillan published as *The Mysterious Schoolmaster,* Harcourt, 1959; *Tag Fast spoket!,* Bonniers, 1955, translation by MacMillan published as *The Robber Ghost,* Harcourt, 1961; *Tag Fast snoegubben!,* Bonniers, 1957, translation by MacMillan published as *Madcap Mystery,* Harcourt, 1962; *Bonifacius och Lill-Bonnie,* Bonniers, 1958, translation by C.M. Anckarsvard and Beales published as *Bonifacius and Little Bonnie,* Abelard, 1963; *Varfor just krabat?,* Bonniers, 1958, translation by MacMillan published as *Rider By Night,* Harcourt, 1960;

Liten roman om Eva, Bonniers, 1959, translation by MacMillan published as *Springtime for Eva,* Harcourt, 1961; *Foeraeldrafritt med faster lava,* Bonniers, 1960, translation by MacMillan published as *Aunt Vinnie's Invasion,* Harcourt, 1962; *De Sex och faster lava,* Bonniers, 1962, translation by MacMillan published as *Aunt Vinnie's Victorious Six,* Harcourt, 1964; *Jag Vantar pa fransiska,* Bonniers, 1962; *Doktorns pojk,* Bonniers, 1963, translation by MacMillan published as *The Doctor's Boy,* Harcourt, 1965; *Gatan med ringen,* Bonniers, 1965, translation by MacMillan published as *The Riddle of the Ring,* Harcourt, 1966; *Svenssons pojk,* Bonniers, 1966, translation by MacMillan published as *Struggle at Soltuna,* Harcourt, 1968; *Riktiga djuroch naesten riktiga,* Bonnier, 1967. Contributor to *Expressea* (Swedish daily newspaper).†

BIOGRAPHICAL/CRITICAL SOURCES: New York Times Book Review, May 9, 1965.

* * *

ANDERSEN, Wayne V. 1928-

PERSONAL: Born July 7, 1928, in Sioux City, Iowa; son of Henry Vesti and Anna Marie (Steinhagen) Andersen; married Ebba Stoll-Andersen, 1951; married second wife, Phyllis Sutton, July 17, 1968; children: (first marriage) Maja, Mark Vesti. *Education:* University of California, Berkeley, B.A., 1958; Columbia University, M.A., 1961, Ph.D., 1964. *Agent:* Julian Bach, 3 East 48th St., New York, N.Y. 10017.

CAREER: Walker Art Center, Minneapolis, Minn., senior curator, 1961-62; William Bayard Cutting traveling fellow, Paris, France, 1962-63; Ford Foundation fellow in humanities, 1963-64; Massachusetts Institute of Technology, Cambridge, 1964—, began as associate professor, now professor of art history. Fellow, Belgian-American Commission for Relief in Belgium, summer, 1963. Visiting professor, Harvard University, summer, 1967, Columbia University, summer, 1968, Yale University, spring, 1969. Art consultant, Boston Redevelopment Authority, 1968-71. *Military service:* U.S. Army, 1946-48. *Member:* College Art Association of America.

WRITINGS: The Sculpture of Herbert Ferber, Walker Art Center, 1962; *Seven Montreal Painters,* M.I.T. Press, 1968; *Cezanne's Portrait Drawings: A Study in Evolution of His Graphic Style,* M.I.T. Press, 1970; *Takis: Evidence of the Unseen,* Cambridge University Press, 1970; *Gaughin's Paradise Lost,* Viking, 1971. Contributor to *Burlington Magazine* (London), *Art International* (Zurich), *Master Drawings,* and other art periodicals.

WORK IN PROGRESS: Cezanne and the Eternal Feminine: A Study in Nineteenth Century Symbolism.

* * *

ANDERSON, Charles W(illiam) 1934-

PERSONAL: Born June 28, 1934, in Manitowoc, Wis.; son of Herbert F. and Ruth (Krause) Anderson; married Jean Wood (a computer programmer), June 5, 1955. *Education:* Grinnell College, B.A., 1955; Johns Hopkins University, M.A., 1957; University of Wisconsin, Ph.D., 1960. *Politics:* Independent Democrat. *Religion:* Lutheran. *Home:* 1304 Nishishin Trail, Monona, Wis. 53716. *Office:* Department of Political Science, University of Wisconsin, Madison, Wis. 53706.

CAREER: University of Wisconsin, Madison, 1960—, now professor of political science. External consultant, U.S. Department of State, American Council of Learned Societies—Social Science Research Council Joint Committee on Latin America. *Member:* American Political Science Association.

WRITINGS: The Relocation of the Wisconsin School for Boys: A Case Study in Public Administration, Bureau of Government, University Extension Division, University of Wisconsin, 1961; (with William P. Glade, Jr.) The Political Economy of Mexico, University of Wisconsin Press, 1963; Toward a Theory of Latin American Politics, Graduate Center for Latin American Studies, Vanderbilt University, 1964; (with Fred R. Von der Mehden and Crawford Young) Issues of Political Development, Prentice-Hall, 1967; Politics and Economic Change in Latin America: The Governing of Restless Nations, Van Nostrand, 1967; The Political Economy of Modern Spain: Policy-Making in an Authoritarian System, University of Wisconsin Press, 1970. Contributor of articles to professional journals.

SIDELIGHTS: In a review of Politics and Economic Change in Latin America: The Governing of Restless Nations, J. Bernard Burnham writes: "Keeping his eyes firmly fastened on what is, rather than what ought to be, Anderson points out that the politics of development, like any other sort of politics, remain the art of the possible. In addition, he makes a convincing case for asking the economists to consider the political side before they go off proposing grandiose economic development plans."

BIOGRAPHICAL/CRITICAL SOURCES: National Review, July 11, 1967.

*   *   *

ANDERSON, Frank J(ohn)   1919-

PERSONAL: Born January 29, 1919, in Chicago, Ill.; son of Charles Emil (a stationary engineer) and Alida (Solomon) Anderson; married Jeanette Rioux, February 17, 1944; children: Maria Alida. Education: Attended University of Connecticut, New London, 1947-48; Indiana University, A.B., 1950; Syracuse University, M.S., in library science, 1951. Politics: Independent Democrat. Home: 111 West Wilson, Salina, Kan. 67401. Office: Library, Kansas Wesleyan University, Salina, Kan. 67401.

CAREER: Kansas Wesleyan University, Salina, librarian and professor of library science, 1952-56; East Chicago Public Library, East Chicago, Ind., head of Baring Avenue branch, 1956-57; General Dynamics Corp., Groton, Conn., director of Submarine Library, 1957-60; Kansas Wesleyan University, Salina, librarian and professor of library science, 1960—. Owner of Kitemaug Press, a publishing firm dealing with out-of-print books, with specialty in submarine literature. Military service: U.S. Naval Reserve, 1946-54; on active duty in Submarine Service, 1943-45, 1951-52; became torpedoman second class. Member: U.S. Submarine Veterans of World War II (national historian, 1957-60), Special Libraries Association, American Association of University Professors (chapter secretary, 1963-64), Mountain Plains Library Association (vice-president, 1964), Kansas Library Association, Salina Society of Art (vice-president, 1962-63; president, 1963-64), Beta Phi Mu.

WRITINGS: (With others) Complete Book of Submarines, World Publishing, 1958; A Manual of Library Practice, Prepared for the Use of the USN Submarine School, General Dynamics, 1959; Staff Manual for Student Assistants of the Memorial Library of Kansas Wesleyan University, Kansas Wesleyan University, 1961; Submarines, Submariners, Submarining: A Checklist of the Submarine Books in the English Language, Principally of the Twentieth Century, Shoe String, 1963; The Bradford Collection of Torpedo Memorabilia, Kitemaug Press, 1963; (editor) Henry Larcom Abbot, Beginning of Modern Submarine Warfare Under Captain Lieutenant David Bushell, Archon Books, 1966; Saint Arithmeticus, Kitemaug Press, 1967. Contributor to Collier's Encyclopedia, Library Journal, Wilson Library Bulletin, Books Abroad, and

other publications. Former editor, Kernels, Livres and Chaff.

WORK IN PROGRESS: Bio-bibliographical research on Richard Bissell; a humorous anthology regarding library work, tentatively titled The Librarian's Home Companion.

AVOCATIONAL INTERESTS: Refurbishing his forty-year-old house and travel.†

*   *   *

ANDERSON, Hugh   1920-

PERSONAL: Born May 18, 1920, in Galston, Ayrshire, Scotland; son of Hugh (an insurance manager) and Jean (Muir) Anderson; married June 25, 1945 (wife's maiden name, Torbit); children: Gordon Torbit (deceased), Kenneth Muir, Louise Nancy. Education: University of Glasgow, M.A., 1941, B.D., 1944, Ph.D., 1949. Home: 5 Comiston Springs Ave., Edinburgh 10, Scotland. Office: New College, The Mound, University of Edinburgh, Edinburgh, Scotland.

CAREER: Presbyterian minister; University of Glasgow, Glasgow, Scotland, lecturer in Hebrew, 1946-51; Trinity Church, Glasgow, minister, 1951-57; Trinity College, Glasgow, A.B. Bruce Lecturer in New Testament, 1954-57; Duke University, Durham, N.C., professor of Biblical criticism and theology; currently professor of New Testament language, literature, and theology, University of Edinburgh, Edinburgh, Scotland. Military service: British Army, chaplain in Near East, 1944-46. Member: Glasgow University Oriental Society, Society for New Testament Studies, Society of Biblical Literature and Exegesis, Rotary Club (Durham, N.C.). Awards, honors: D.D., University of Glasgow, 1970.

WRITINGS: (With Robert Dobbie) Psalms I-XLI and Amos and Hosea, St. Andrew Press, 1954; Historians of Israel, Abingdon, 1962; Jesus and Christian Origins: A Commentary on Modern Viewpoints, Oxford University Press, 1964; (editor) The New Testament in Historical and Contemporary Perspective: Essays in Memory of G.H.C. Macgregor, Basil Blackwell, 1965; Jesus, Prentice-Hall, 1967; Lutheranism in the Southeastern States, 1860-1886: A Social History, Mouton & Co., 1969; (contributor) Bible Commentary, Abingdon, 1971. Contributor of articles to Scottish Journal of Theology, Expository Times, Religion in Life, Interpretation, and other publications.

WORK IN PROGRESS: A book, Life Beyond Death in Intertestamental Judaism; commentary on Mark's Gospel for The New Century Bible.

AVOCATIONAL INTERESTS: Golf and soccer.

*   *   *

ANDERSON, James E(lliott)   1933-

PERSONAL: Born July 6, 1933, in Galva, Ill.; son of Albin C. (a farmer) and Amy (Nelson) Anderson; married Alberta Hedstrom, June 21, 1953; children: Carrie, Elise, Joel. Education: University of Illinois, student, 1950-52; Illinois State Normal University, student, 1952-53; Southwest Texas State College, B.S., 1955; University of Texas, Ph.D., 1960. Politics: Democratic. Office: Department of Political Science, University of Houston, 3801 Cullen Blvd., Houston, Tex. 77004.

CAREER: Wake Forest College, Winston-Salem, N.C., instructor, 1959-60, assistant professor, 1960-64, associate professor of political science, 1964-66; University of Houston, Houston, Tex., associate professor, 1966-69, professor of political science, 1969—. Member: American Association of University Professors, American Political Science Association, Policy Studies Organization, Southern Political Science Association, Southwestern Political Science Association.

WRITINGS: The Emergence of the Modern Regulatory State, Public Affairs Press, 1962; Politics and the Economy, Little, Brown, 1966; (compiler) Politics and Economic Policy-Making: Selected Readings, Addison-Wesley, 1970; (with others) Texas Politics: An Introduction, Harper, 1971. Contributor to professional journals.

WORK IN PROGRESS: Public Policy Making: Decisions and Their Implementation.

* * *

ANDERSON, James Norman Dalrymple 1908-

PERSONAL: Born September 29, 1908, in Aldeburgh, Suffolk, England; son of William Dalrymple Anderson (a merchant); married Patricia Hope Givan, May 31, 1933; children: Hazel Patricia (Mrs. John Trapnell), Sheila Janet, Hugh Ronald. Education: St. Lawrence College, Ramsgate, England, student, 1922-27; Trinity College, Cambridge, B.A. (first class honors in Law Tripos), 1930, LL.B. (first class honors), 1931, M.A., 1934, LL.D., 1955. Politics: Independent. Religion: Church of England. Home: 12, Constable Close, London N.W.11, England. Office: Institute of Advanced Legal Studies, 25 Russell Sq., London W.C.1, England.

CAREER: Missionary in Egypt, 1932-40; School of Oriental and African Studies, University of London, London, England, lecturer, 1947-50, reader, 1951-53, professor of Oriental laws and head of Department of Law, 1954—, director of Institute of Advanced Legal Studies, 1959-64, dean of Faculties of Law, 1964-68. Council of Legal Education, Gray's Inn, London, England, lecturer in Muhammedan Law, 1953—. Visiting professor at Princeton University and New York University, 1958, and at Harvard University, 1965. Member of Native Law Advisory Panel, and honorary member, Louisiana State Law Institute. Military service: British Army, 1940-46; became colonel; member of the British Empire, 1943, Officer of the British Empire, 1945, Lybian Order of Independence, 1959. Member: International African Law Association, (vice-president), Royal African Society, Royal Asiatic Society, Royal Central Asian Society, British Academy (fellow), Association of British Orientalists, International Committee of Comparative Law, United Kingdom National Committee of Comparative Law, International Academy of Comparative Law, Society of Public Teachers of Law (president, 1968-69).

WRITINGS: (Editor and contributor) The World's Religions, Intervarsity, 1950; Islamic Law in Africa, H.M.S.O., 1955, Barnes & Noble, 1970; Islamic Law in the Modern World, New York University Press, 1959; The Maliki Law of Homicide, [Zaria, Nigeria], 1959; (editor and contributor) Changing Law in Developing Countries, Praeger, 1963; The Adaptation of Muslim Law in Sub-Saharan Africa, African Studies Center, University of California (Los Angeles), 1963; (editor and contributor) Family Law in Asia and Africa, Praeger, 1968; Into the World: The Need and Limits of Christian Involvement, Church Pastoral Aid Society (London), 1968; Christianity: The Witness of History, Tyndale Press, 1969; Christianity and Comparative Religion, Tyndale Press, 1970. Contributor of articles to learned periodicals.

SIDELIGHTS: Anderson has traveled extensively in Africa and the Arab world.

* * *

ANDERSON, Jessica (Margaret) Queale

PERSONAL: Born in Gayndah, Queensland, Australia; daughter of Charles James (a stock inspector) and Alice (Hibbert) Queale; married Leonard Culbert Anderson, March 12, 1954; children: (former marriage) Laura Rae McGill. Education: Attended public schools in Brisbane, Queensland, Australia. Home: 46 William St., Hornsby, Sydney, New South Wales, Australia.

MEMBER: Society of Authors (London), Australian Society of Authors.

WRITINGS: An Ordinary Lunacy (novel), Macmillan (London), 1963, Scribner, 1964; The Last Man's Head (novel), Macmillan (London), 1970. Contributor to Australian and English magazines and to Australian radio prior to 1960.

WORK IN PROGRESS: Tirra Lirra by the River, a short novel.

SIDELIGHTS: Author of a widely reviewed first novel, Mrs. Anderson explains her late start at serious writing: "Literature has always been my strongest and most abiding interest. I am absorbed in it still, but fortunately have lost the exaggerated respect that I once felt for it, and which delayed for many years my own attempt to write."

Like other authors and artists of Australia, she feels drawn to London and Europe (as the center of things), but says that "some return, as I did, feeling that Australia is inescapable, . . . though never at home away from the place, nor ever quite at home in it. . . ."

* * *

ANDERSON, M(ary) D(esiree) 1902-

PERSONAL: Born October 28, 1902, in Cambridge, England; daughter of Sir Hugh Kerr Anderson (Master of Gonville and Caius College, Cambridge) and Jessie (Innes) Anderson; married Sir Trenchard Cox (formerly director of Victoria and Albert Museum), November 14, 1935. Education: Privately educated. Religion: Church of England. Home: 33 Queen's Gate Gardens, London S.W. 7, England.

MEMBER: Society of Antiquaries (fellow), Royal Archaeological Institute.

WRITINGS: The Medieval Carver, Macmillan, 1935; Animal Carvings in British Churches, Macmillan, 1938; Design for a Journey, Cambridge University Press, 1940, Macmillan, 1941; British Women at War, J. Murray, 1941; Bow Bells Are Silent (war poems), Williams & Norgate, 1943; Looking for History in British Churches, Morrow, 1951; The Choir Stalls of Lincoln Minister, Friends of Lincoln Cathedral, 1951, 2nd edition, 1967; Misericords: Medieval Life in English Woodcarvings, Penguin, 1954; The Imagery of British Churches, J. Murray, 1955; Drama and Imagery in English Churches, Cambridge University Press (London), 1963, Cambridge University Press (New York), 1964; A Saint at Stake: The Strange Death of William of Norwich, 1144, Fernhill, 1964; History by the Highway, Faber, 1967, Transatlantic, 1968; The Changeling Niobid (novel), Chatto & Windus, 1969; History and Imagery in British Churches, J. Murray, 1971. Contributor to Archaeologia, Times Educational Supplement, Countryman, and other periodicals.

WORK IN PROGRESS: Papers on matters connected with medieval iconography.

SIDELIGHTS: Miss Anderson told CA: "[I] am particularly concerned with the interrelation of literature and art, and the way in which church imagery illustrates the popular mentality of the Middle Ages." She has traveled extensively in Europe and in parts of the United States.

BIOGRAPHICAL/CRITICAL SOURCES: Spectator, November 22, 1969.

ANDERSON, Margaret Bartlett 1922-
(Mrs. James C. Bentley)

PERSONAL: Born December 22, 1922, in Boulder, Colo.; daughter of John Thomas (an editor and publisher) and Margaret (Abbott) Bartlett; married Samuel T.D. Anderson, December 24, 1948 (divorced, 1965); married James C. Bentley (a retired naval officer), July, 1967; children: (first marriage) Bartlett Eric, Katherine Rebecca, David Larz, Deborah Winthrop, Christopher Radcliff, Maria Marshall. *Education:* Wellesley College, A.B., 1944; additional study at University of Chicago, University of California, Berkeley, Wesleyan University, Middletown, Conn., 1946-48, and San Francisco State College, 1965-66. *Politics:* Democrat. *Religion:* Protestant. *Home:* 3144 Browns Valley Rd., Napa, Calif. 94558.

CAREER: Author and Journalist, editorial assistant, 1947; California Department of Public Welfare, Shasta County, social worker, 1948; presently teaching at high school in Napa, Calif. *Military service:* U.S. Naval Reserve, 1944-46; became lieutenant junior grade. *Member:* National Association of Teachers of English, California Teachers Association, Wellesley Alumni Association.

WRITINGS: Robert Frost and John Bartlett, Holt, 1963; (contributor) Mitzie Green, editor, *Teaching Strategies and Classroom Realities,* Prentice-Hall, 1971. Contributor to *Parents' Magazine* and *Wellesley Alumni Magazine.*

WORK IN PROGRESS: Research on contemporary fiction.

*   *   *

ANDERSON, Robert T(homas) 1926-

PERSONAL: Born December 27, 1926, in Alameda, Calif.; son of Victor Thomas and Stella (Hansen) Anderson; married Barbara Gallatin (an anthropologist), August 20, 1955; children: Andrea, Robin, Scott. *Education:* University of California, Berkeley, B.A., 1949, M.A., 1953, Ph.D., 1956; University of Copenhagen, certificate of advanced study, 1951; Sorbonne, University of Paris, D.U.P., 1959. *Office:* Mills College, Oakland, Calif. 94613.

CAREER: University of Washington, Seattle, acting assistant professor of anthropology, 1959-60; Mills College, Oakland, Calif., associate professor of anthropology and sociology, 1960-67, Edward Hohfeld Professor of Anthropology, 1967—. University of California, Berkeley, summer assistant professor, 1961, visiting professor, 1966-67. *Military service:* U.S. Navy, 1946-48. *Member:* American Anthropological Association, American Sociological Association.

WRITINGS: Acculturation and Indigenous Economy as Factors in Lapp Cultural Change (monograph), University of Alaska, 1958; (with wife, Barbara G. Anderson) *The Vanishing Village: A Danish Maritime Community,* University of Washington Press, 1964; (with Barbara G. Anderson) *Bus Stop for Paris,* Doubleday, 1965; *Traditional Europe: A Study in Anthropology and History,* Wadsworth, 1970; *Anthropology: A Perspective on Man,* Wadsworth, 1971; *Denmark: Medieval Kingdom, Developing Nation, Modern State,* Schenkman, 1971. Contributor to professional journals.

WORK IN PROGRESS: The Anthropology of Europe, for Goodyear Publishing.

ANDREWS, F(rank) Michael 1916-

PERSONAL: Born March 4, 1916, in Central City, Pa.; son of Frank and Libra (Testa) Andrews; married Helen Wilma Baker, December 30, 1940; children: Judith Lynn (Mrs. Stanley Thomas III), Connee Jean (Mrs. Larry Dolin), Michael Curtis. *Education:* Attended Juniata College, 1935-37; University of Kansas, B.F.A., 1940,

M.S., 1948; Ohio State University, Ph.D., 1952. *Home:* 6657 Woodchuck Hill Rd., Jamesville, N.Y. 13078. *Office:* Department of Synaesthetic Education, Syracuse University, Syracuse, N.Y. 13210.

CAREER: Teacher in public schools in Lawrence, Kan. and Hayes, Kan., 1940-42; instructor at University of Kansas, Lawrence, 1946-48, Ohio State University, Columbus, 1948-50; University of Southern California, Los Angeles, assistant professor of art education, 1950-52; University of Wisconsin, Madison, assistant professor of art education, 1952-55; Syracuse University, Syracuse, N.Y., professor of art education, 1955—, chairman of department of synaesthetic education, 1970—. Lecturer at art assemblies, congresses, and other institutions in U.S., Canada, Japan, and Europe. Work as sculptor has been exhibited throughout the country; sculpture and photography exhibited at one-man show at Fine Arts Festival, Cortland, N.Y., 1961. Member of advisory board, Marcy State Hospital. *Military service:* U.S. Army Air Forces, 1942-46; became first lieutenant. *Member:* International Society for Education Through Art, National Association for Humanities Education, National Committee on Art Education (council of directors), National Art Education Association, Eastern Arts Association (secretary, 1962-64; vice-president, 1964-66; president, 1966-68), American Association of University Professors, Kansas Art Teachers Association (president, 1947-49), California Art Teachers Association (vice-president, 1951-52), New York State Art Teachers Association. *Awards, honors:* Wichita Decorative Arts and Ceramic Exhibition award for ceramic sculpture, 1949; Columbus Art League Sculpture award, 1950; Sculpture House award, 1953; Wisconsin Salon of Art award, 1954.

WRITINGS: Aesthetic Form and Education, Syracuse University Press, 1958; *Sound Seminars,* McGraw, 1960; (editor) *Creativity and Psychological Health,* Syracuse University Press, 1961; *Creative Print-making, for Schools and Camp Programs,* Prentice-Hall, 1964; *Creative Education: The Liberation of Man,* Syracuse University Press, 1965; *Sculpture and Ideas,* Prentice-Hall, 1966; (with others) *Synaesthetic Education,* Syracuse University Press, 1971.

"Growing with Art" series, all with Maud Ellsworth, published by Singer in 1950, revised in 1960: *Fun to Begin, Learning to Talk a New Way, Seeing and Doing, Discovering Where We Live, Exploration and Making, Art Where We Live, Adventure at Your Elbow,* and *Everybody's Business.* Contributor of articles to *Art Education Journal, School Arts,* and other education journals. Consulting editor, *Journal of Creative Behavior.*

WORK IN PROGRESS: Synasthesia, for Syracuse University Press.

*   *   *

ANDREWS, Ralph W(arren) 1897-

PERSONAL: Born January 12, 1897, in Denver, Colo.; son of Lyman E. (a salesman) and Helen E. (Bronson) Andrews; married Margaret G. Stone, October 25, 1927; children: Murray McN., Lee E. (Mrs. Thomas C. Wright). *Education:* Attended University of Minnesota. *Home:* 2405 South 122nd St., Seattle, Wash. 98168.

CAREER: Worked as a saw salesman; short story writer, 1923-45; copywriter and account executive for four advertising agencies in Los Angeles, Calif., and Seattle, Wash., 1925-41, 1950-55; U.S. Army, civilian employment as port historian at Seattle (Wash.) Port of Embarkation and personnel work at Pasco, Wash., 1941-45; copywriter and author, 1945-50, 1955—. Trustee and former vice-president, friends of Seattle Public Library. *Member:* Jefferson Park Lawn and Sailing Club (vice-president). *Awards, honors:* Seattle Historical Society award, 1955, for best book by Seattle author; Governor's Certificate of Recognition, 1966.

WRITINGS—All published by Superior, except as indicated: This Was Logging, 1954; Glory Days of Logging, 1955; (with Harry A. Kirwin) This Was Seafaring, 1956; This Was Sawmilling, 1957; Redwood Classic, 1958; (with A.K. Larssen) Fish and Ships, 1959; Heroes of the Western Woods, Dutton, 1959; Indian Primitive, 1960; Curtis' Western Indians, 1962; Indians as the Westerners Knew Them, 1963; The Seattle I Saw, 1964; Picture Gallery Pioneers, 1964; Photographers of the Frontier West: Their Lives and Works, 1875 to 1915, 1965; Historic Fires of the West, 1966; Timber: Toil and Trouble in the Big Woods, 1968; Indian Leaders Who Helped Shape America, 1971.

SIDELIGHTS: Andrews' interest in lumbering developed from early days as a saw salesman; in recent years he has gone out with harvest crews, thoroughly covered western states and British Columbia doing research on timber and Indians.

*   *   *

ANDREWS, Wayne 1913-
(Montagu O'Reilly)

PERSONAL: Born September 5, 1913, in Kenilworth, Ill.; son of Emory Cobb (a businessman) and Helen (Armstrong) Andrews; married Elizabeth Anderson Hodges, June 12, 1948; children: Elizabeth Waties. Education: Lawrenceville School, student, 1927-32; Harvard University, A.B., 1936; Columbia University, graduate student, 1946-48, Ph.D., 1955. Politics: Democrat. Religion: Episcopalian. Home: 521 Neff Rd., Grosse Pointe, Mich. 48230. Office: Archives of American Art, 5200 Woodward Ave., Detroit, Mich. 48202.

CAREER: New York Historical Society, New York, N.Y., curator of manuscripts, 1948-56; Charles Scribner's Sons, New York, N.Y., editor, trade department, 1956-63; Wayne State University, Detroit, Mich., Archives of American Art Professor, 1964—. Architectural photographer. Member: Societe Chateaubriand (Paris).

WRITINGS: The Vanderbilt Legend, Harcourt, 1941; Battle for Chicago, Harcourt, 1946; (under pseudonym Montagu O'Reilly) Who Has Been Tampering with These Pianos?, New Directions, 1948; Architecture, Ambition and Americans: A Social History of American Architecture, Harper, 1955; (editor) Best Short Stories of Edith Wharton, Scribner, 1958; (editor) Theodore Roosevelt, Autobiography, Scribner, 1958; Architecture in America, Atheneum, 1960; (editor with Thomas W. Cochran) Concise Dictionary of American History, Scribner, 1962; Germaine: A Portrait of Madame de Stael, Atheneum, 1963; Architecture in Michigan: A Representative Photographic Survey, edited by Ralph Busick, Wayne State University Press, 1967; Architecture in Chicago and Mid-America: A Photographic History, Atheneum, 1968; Architecture in New York: A Photographic History, Atheneum, 1969; Siegfried's Curse: The German Journey from Nietzsche to Hesse, Athenaeum, 1972.

WORK IN PROGRESS: History of art and architecture in France in the eighteenth century, completion expected in 1975.

BIOGRAPHICAL/CRITICAL SOURCES: Book World, October 13, 1968.

*   *   *

ANDREWS, William Linton 1886-
(Edith Settle)

PERSONAL: Born May 27, 1886, in Hull, England; son of William and Jean Leslie (Carnie) Andrews; married Gertrude Douglas, September 13, 1915 (died March 23, 1958). Education: Studied at Christ's Hospital in London and later in West Horsham, Sussex, England. Politics: Conservative. Religion: Church of England. Home: 1 Grosvenor Mount, Leeds LS6 2DX, England. Office: Yorkshire Post, Albion St., Leeds 1, England.

CAREER: Started as journalist in Hull, England; freelance writer, Paris, France, 1907-08; journalist in Dundee, Scotland, 1911-14; Daily Mail, London, England, sub-editor, 1919-23; Leeds Mercury, Leeds, England, editor 1923-39; Yorkshire Post, Leeds, editor, 1939-60. Former director, Yorkshire Conservative Newspaper Co. Ltd., Yorkshire Evening Post Printing Co. Ltd., Yorkshire Radio and Television Co. Ltd., Leeds Musical Festival Ltd., and Bronte Parsonage Museum. Chairman, Press Council, 1955-59. Has lectured in British, North American, and Italian cities, and made four hundred radio and television appearances. Military service: Black Watch, 1914-19; became second lieutenant. Member: Institute of Journalists (president, 1946), Guild of British Newspaper Editors (president, 1952-53), Bronte Society (chairman, 1940—). Awards, honors: Medaille d'Argent de la Reconnaissance, 1947; knighted, 1954; Doctor of Laws, University of Leeds, 1955; D. Litt., Emerson College.

WRITINGS: The Haunting Years: The Commentaries of a War Territorial, Hutchinson, 1930; (with A.P. Maguire) Wayside Pageant: The Old Country Tells Her Secrets, Heath Cranton, 1933; Yorkshire Folk: Memories of a Journalist, Heath Cranton. 1935; (under pseudonym Edith Settle) My Editor Says, Pitman, 1937; (contributor) James Marchant, editor, Has the Church Failed?, Odhams, 1947; (contributor) James Marchant, editor, If I Had My Time Again, Odhams, 1950, Wm. H. Wise, 1951; (editor) British Newspapers, British Council, 1952; (editor) The Yorkshire Post: Two Centuries, Yorkshire Post, 1954; Englands Presserad (in Danish), Berlingske Tidende, 1955, translation published as Britain's Press Council, Berlingske Forlag, 1955; Newspaper English: Its Vices and Virtues, [Leeds], 1959; The Press and Its Freedom: An Inquiry, Yorkshire Post, 1960; Problems of an Editor: A Study in Newspaper Trends, Oxford University Press, 1962; Linton Andrews: The Autobiography of a Journalist, Benn, 1964; (with H.A. Taylor) Lords and Laborers of the Press, Southern Illinois University Press, 1970. Contributor of articles to many newspapers. Former editor, Bronte Society Transactions.

WORK IN PROGRESS: Press Council history; Bronte criticism; a book on Yorkshire.

*   *   *

ANDRIST, Ralph K. 1914-

PERSONAL: Born January 11, 1914, in Crookston, Minn.; son of John J. (a railroadman) and Mary (Knutson) Andrist; married Vivian Margaret Witt, February 22, 1941; children: Jill, Mary G., Melissa E. Education: University of Minnesota, B.A., 1937. Politics: Democrat. Home: Chichester Rd., New Canaan, Conn. 06840.

CAREER: Radio Station WCCO, Minneapolis, Minn., news editor, 1945-48; Better Homes and Gardens, Des Moines, Iowa, garden editor, 1948-50; Crusade for Freedom, New York, N.Y., press publicity director, 1951-52; Episcopal Church Foundation (fund-raising), New York, N.Y., associate director, 1952-60; free-lance writer, 1961—. Member, New Canaan (Conn.) Democrate Town Committee, 1955-59. Military service: U.S. Naval Reserve, 1942-45; became lieutenant; awarded Bronze Star. Member: Sigma Delta Chi, Phi Beta Kappa. Awards, honors: Award of National Conference of Christians and Jews; Variety plaque award; Heywood Broun Award for radio documentary series on prejudice; Peabody Award for radio documentary series on juvenile delinquency.

WRITINGS—Juveniles; all published by American Heritage Press, except as indicated: *The California Gold Rush*, 1961; *Steamboats on the Mississippi*, 1962; *Heroes of Polar Exploration*, 1962; *Andrew Jackson, Soldier and Statesman*, 1963; *The Erie Canal*, 1964; *The Long Death: The Last Days of the Plains Indians*, Macmillan, 1964; *To the Pacific with Lewis and Clark*, 1967; (editor) Francis Russell, *The American Heritage History of the Confident Years*, 1969; (editor) *The American Heritage History of the Making of the Nation [1783-1960]*, 1969; (author of text) Ray Brosseau, compiler, *Looking Forward: Life in the Twentieth Century as Predicted in the Pages of American Magazines from 1895-1905*, 1970. Contributor to *American Heritage* and *Reader's Digest;* ghost writer of two books for U.S. government officials.

SIDELIGHTS: About his transition to full-time writer, Andrist says: "I was sick of commuting, sick of working for someone else, I had wanted all my life to write, and was at an age where I had to put up or shut up. So far, I have not regretted taking the plunge." Wolper Productions is making a documentary based on *The Long Death: The Last Days of the Plains Indians.*

BIOGRAPHICAL/CRITICAL SOURCES: *Christian Science Monitor*, November 2, 1967; *Book World*, November 5, 1967; *New York Times Book Review*, February 4, 1968.

* * *

ANSON, Peter Frederick 1889-

PERSONAL: Born August 22, 1889, in Portsmouth, Hampshire, England; son of Charles E. (an admiral, Royal Navy) and Evelyn (Ross) Anson. *Education:* Attended Architectural Association School, London, England. *Religion:* Roman Catholic. *Residence:* Caldey Island, South Wales. *Agent:* Curtis Brown Ltd., 13 King St., Covent Garden, London WC2E 8HU, England.

CAREER: Artist and writer. *Member:* Society of Marine Artists (founder member).

WRITINGS: (Self-illustrated) *The Pilgrim's Guide to Franciscan Italy*, Sands & Co., 1927; (self-illustrated) *Fishing Boats and Fisher Folk on the East Coast of Scotland*, Dutton, 1930; (self-illustrated) *Mariners of Brittany*, Dutton, 1931; *A Pilgrim Artist in Palestine*, Ouseley, 1931, Dutton, 1932; (self-illustrated) *Fishermen and Fishing Ways*, Harrap, 1932; (self-illustrated) *The Quest of Solitude*, Dent, 1932, Dutton, 1933, reissued as *The Call of the Desert: The Solitary Life in the Christian Church*, S.P.C.K., 1964; *The Pilgrim's Sketch Books*, Burns & Oates, 1934; (illustrator) Sir David Blair, *A Last Medley of Memories*, Edward Arnold, 1936; (self-illustrated) *The Catholic Church in Modern Scotland, 1560-1937*, Burns & Oates, 1937; (self-illustrated) *The Caravan Pilgrim*, Heath Cranton, 1938; *The Sea Fisheries of Scotland: Are They Doomed?*, Oliver & Boyd, 1939.

(Self-illustrated) *The Benedictines of Caldey*, Burns & Oates, 1940; *How to Draw Ships*, Studio Ltd., 1941, revised edition, 1955; *British Sea Fishermen*, Hastings House, 1944; (self-illustrated) *Harbour Head: Maritime Memories*, Gifford, 1944; *A Roving Recluse: More Memories*, Mercier Press, 1946, Newman Bookshop, 1947; *The Sea Apostolate in Ireland*, Irish Messenger Office, 1946; *The Apostleship of the Sea in England and Wales*, Catholic Truth Society, 1946; *Churches: Their Plan and Furnishing*, edited by Thomas F. Croft-Fraser and H.A. Reinhold, Bruce, 1948; *The Church and the Sailor: A Survey of the Sea Apostolate, Past and Present*, Gifford,

1948; *The Religious Orders and Congregations of Great Britain and Ireland*, Stanbrook Abbey Press, 1949.

Scots Fisherfolk, Banffshire Journal for Saltire Society, 1950; *Christ and the Sailor: A Study of Maritime Incidents in the New Testament*, Burns & Oates, 1954, American Library Guild, 1956; *The Call of the Cloister: Religious Communities and Kindred Bodies in the Anglican Communion*, Macmillan, 1955, 4th edition, revised and edited by A.W. Campbell, S.P.C.K., 1964; *Banff and Macduff*, Mearns Publications, 1956; (with Cecily Hallack) *These Made Peace: Studies in the Lives of the Beatified and Canonized Members of the Third Order of St. Francis of Assisi*, St. Anthony Guild Press, 1957; *The Hermit of Cat Island: The Life of Fra Jerome Hawes*, Kenedy, 1957; *Abbot Extraordinary: A Memoir of Aelred Carlyle, Monk and Missionary, 1874-1955*, Faith Press, 1958, Sheed, 1959.

Fashions in Church Furnishings, 1840-1940, Macmillan, 1960, 2nd edition, British Book Centre, 1966; (editor) *The Brothers of Braemore*, Taplinger, 1960; *A Monastery in Moray: The Story of Pluscarden Priory 1930-1948*, S.P.C.K., 1960; (with Iris Conlay) *The Art of the Church*, Hawthorn, 1964; *Bishops at Large*, Faber, 1964, October House, 1965; *The Building of Churches*, Hawthorn, 1964; *Fisher Folklore: Old Customs, Taboos and Superstitions Among Fisher Folk*, Faith Press, 1965; *Life on Low Shore: Memories of 20 Years Among Fisher Folk at Macduff, Banffshire 1938-1958*, Banffshire Journal, 1969; (self-illustrated) *Underground Catholicism in Scotland*, Standard Press (Montrose), 1970. Contributor to *Fishing News*, and to religious and architectural journals.

* * *

ANTON, Rita (Kenter) 1920-

PERSONAL: Born April 5, 1920, in Sioux City, Iowa; daughter of George Joseph (a clerk) and Loretta (Kelly) Kenter; married Alfred John Anton (a broker), June 21, 1941; children: Ann (Mrs. P. Jirousek), Alfred, Loretta (Mrs. Edward Ivory), Barbara, William. *Education:* Special courses at Loyola University, Chicago, Ill., and Wright City College. *Religion:* Roman Catholic. *Home:* 926 North Linden Ave., Oak Park, Ill. 60302.

CAREER: Director, Nevett Fund of America (organization to support missionary work of Rev. Albert Nevett, S.J., in India).

WRITINGS: *Pleasant Company Accepted* (autobiography), Doubleday, 1964. Contributor to periodicals.

WORK IN PROGRESS: Writings of family interest in a humorous vein.

AVOCATIONAL INTERESTS: Music, gardening, and poetry.

* * *

APPLEBAUM, William 1906-

PERSONAL: Born April 24, 1906, in Pruzana, Russia; son of Lipa (a merchant) and Esther (Volk) Applebaum; married Berenice Milgroom, September, 1960. *Education:* University of Minnesota, A.B., 1931, graduate study, 1932-33; University of Cincinnati, graduate study, 1931-32. *Religion:* Jewish. *Home:* 29 Tobey Rd., Belmont, Mass. 02178. *Office:* Harvard Business School, Soldiers Field, Boston, Mass. 02163.

CAREER: Kroger Co., Cincinnati, Ohio, market research analyst, 1933-35, chief of market research department,

1935-38; Stop & Shop, Inc., Boston, Mass., director of marketing research department, 1938-42, 1945-47, director of planning and coordination, 1948, assistant general manager, 1949-53, director, 1949—; Harvard Graduate School of Business Administration, Boston, Mass., visiting consultant on food distribution, 1954-60, lecturer on food distribution and comparative marketing, 1960-68, lecturer emeritus, 1968—. Director, Hannaford Brothers Co., Portland, Me., 1960—, Chatham Super Markets, Inc., Warren, Mich., 1969—. Consultant to Research and Development Board, National Security Council, 1948-52; member of advisory committees of U.S. Department of Agriculture and of Super Market Institute. Marketing consultant, 1954—. Member of committees for various local, state, national, and foreign agencies. *Military service:* U.S. Marine Corps Reserve, on active duty in Office of Strategic Services, 1942-45; became captain; received Bronze Star Medal; inactive service, 1945-57; became major.

MEMBER: American Marketing Association (president, New England chapter, 1946-47; director, 1956-58; chairman of publications policy and review board, 1958-59), American Statistical Association, Association of American Geographers, American Geographical Society, Regional Science Association, American Association for the Advancement of Science (fellow), Food Distribution Research Society, Super Market Institute (honorary), Eta Mu Pi. *Awards, honors:* American Marketing Association National Award, 1950; Association of American Geographers citation of merit, 1959.

WRITINGS: The Secondary Commercial Centers of Cincinnati, two volumes, Institute of Industrial Research, University of Cincinnati, 1932; (with Richard F. Spears) *Shopping Habits of Super Market Customers,* Marketing Research Department, Stop & Shop, 1947; *The Super Market Industry Speaks,* Super Market Institute, 1949; *A Plan for Cooperative Marketing Research in the Food Distribution Industry,* Super Market Institute, 1954; *What Price Success?,* Hannaford Bros. Co., 1955; (with Bernard L. Schapker) *A Quarter Century of Change in Cincinnati Business Centers,* Cincinnati Enquirer, 1956; (with Schapker) *Atlas of Business Centers: Cincinnati-Hamilton County, Ohio, 1955,* American Marketing Association, 1956; (with Richard H. Moulton) *An Exploration into the Reasons Why Super Markets Add and Discontinue Items,* McCall Publishing, 1956; (with Malcom P. McNair and Walter J. Salmon) *Cases in Food Distribution,* Irwin, 1964; (with Salmon, Robert D. Buzzell, Richard F. Vancil, and John D. Glover) *Product Profitability Measurement and Merchandizing Decisions,* Division of Research, Harvard Business School, 1965; *Patterns of Food Distribution in a Metropolis,* Super Market Institute, 1966; (with Ray Goldberg) *Brand Strategy in United States Food Marketing* [and] *Dynamic Brand Strategies* (the former by Applebaum, the latter by Goldberg), Division of Research, Graduate School of Business Administration, Harvard University, 1967; *Private Brands: Basic Consideration* (pamphlet), Institute of Food Distribution, 1968; *Store Location Strategy Cases,* Addison-Wesley, 1968; (with Robert Minichiello) *Teachers Manual: Store Location Strategy Cases,* Addison-Wesley, 1968; *Super Marketing: The Past, the Present, a Projection,* Super Market Institute, 1969; (with Milton P. Brown and Salmon) *Strategy Problems of Mass Retailers and Wholesalers,* Irwin, 1970; *Shopping Center Strategy,* International Council of Shopping Centers, 1970; *Hardware Retailing Strategy Cases,* Russell R. Mueller Retail Hardware Research Foundation, 1971.

Contributor: H.G. Wales and R. Ferber, editors, *Marketing Research: Selected Literature,* W.C. Brown, 1952; *American Geography: Inventory and Prospect,* Syracuse University Press, 1954; *Social Science for Industry,* Stanford Research Institute, 1956; *New Directions in Food Retailing,* University of Pittsburgh Press, 1957; *The Frontiers of Marketing Thought and Science,* American Marketing Association, 1957; *How to Make a Profit in a Highly Competitive Industry,* Super Market Institute, 1957; *Store Location and Development Studies,* Clark University, 1961; *Store Location Research for the Food Industry,* National American Wholesale Grocers Association, 1961; *Guideposts for Decision Makers,* Super Market Institute, 1961; *On the Threshold: Action and Promise in Creative Teamwork,* National American Wholesale Grocer's Association, 1965; Curt Kornblau, editor, *Guide to Store Location Research with Emphasis on Super Markets,* Addison-Wesley, 1968.

Editor of four other Super Market Institute publications, 1947-48. Contributor to *Annals of the Association of American Geographers,* 1961, and to marketing surveys and reports. Author of more than fifty articles published in *Professional Geographer, Chain Store Age, Economic Geography,* and other journals. Member of editorial board, *Journal of Marketing,* 1943-44, *Journal of Retailing,* 1965—.

*   *   *

ARBUTHNOT, May Hill   1884-1969

PERSONAL: Born August 17, 1884, in Mason City, Iowa; daughter of Frank and Mary Elizabeth (Seville) Hill; married Charles C. Arbuthnot, December 17, 1932 (deceased). *Education:* University of Chicago, Ph.B., 1922; Columbia University, M.A., 1924. *Politics:* Republican. *Religion:* Episcopalian. *Home:* 2300 Overlook Rd., Cleveland, Ohio 44106.

CAREER: Teacher, 1912, 1921-22; Cleveland Kindergarten-Primary Training School, Cleveland, Ohio, teacher, 1922-27, continuing on staff when school became affiliated with Western Reserve University (now Case Western Reserve University), 1927, until retirement as associate professor of education at Western Reserve, 1949; full-time writer and lecturer. *Member:* Phi Beta Kappa, Pi Lambda Theta. *Awards, honors:* Constance Lindsey Skinner Medal, National Association of Book Women of America, 1960, for distinguished contribution to field of books; L.H.D., Western Reserve University, 1961; Regina Medal, Catholic Library Association, 1964, for distinguished contribution to children's literature.

WRITINGS—All published by Scott, Foresman, except as indicated: *Children and Books,* 1947, 4th revised edition, 1972; (with others) *Children's Books Too Good to Miss,* Press of Western Reserve University, 1948, 6th edition, 1971; (compiler) *Time for Poetry* (student's edition), 1951, revised edition, 1959; (with William Scott Gray) *Basic Readers,* 1951 edition, 1951; (compiler with S.L. Root) *Time for Poetry: A Representative Collection of Poetry for Children* (teacher's edition), 1952, 3rd edition, 1967; (compiler) *Time for Fairy Tales Old and New: A Representative Collection of Folk Tales, Myths, Epics, Fables, and Modern Fanciful Tales for Children,* 1952, revised edition (with Mark Taylor) published in two volumes as *Time for Old Magic: A Representative Collection of Folk Tales, Fables, Myths, and Epics,* 1970, and *Time for New Magic: A Representative Collection of Modern Fanciful Stories for Children,* 1971; (editor) *Time for True Tales and Almost True: A Representative Collection of Realistic Stories for Children,* 1953, 2nd revised edition (with Dorothy M. Broderick) published in two volumes as *Time for Stories of the Past and Present,*

1968, and *Time for Biography: A Representative Collection of Biographies for Children*, 1969; (compiler) *The Arbuthnot Anthology of Children's Literature* (contains *Time for Poetry, Time for Fairy Tales Old and New*, and *Time for True Tales and Almost True)*, 1953, 2nd edition, revised, Lothrop, 1971; *Children's Reading in the Home*, 1969; (compiler with Evelyn L. Wenzel) *Time for Discovery; Informational Books*, 1971. Review editor of children's books for both *Childhood Education* and *Elementary English*, for ten years.

SIDELIGHTS: While discussing her criteria for judging good books for children in *Children and Books*, Mrs. Arbuthnot added a cautionary note: "Two facts we need to keep constantly before us: a book is a good book for children only when they enjoy it; a book is a poor book for children, even when adults rate it a classic, if children are unable to read it or are bored by its content."

In June, 1969, Scott, Foresman established the "May Hill Arbuthnot Honor Lectureship" to be given annually "in perpetuity." The lectureship is to be administered by the Children's Services Division of the American Library Association. The first lecture was given April, 1970, at Case Western Reserve University, by Margery Fisher.

BIOGRAPHICAL/CRITICAL SOURCES: Charlotte Huck and D.A. Young, *Children's Literature in the Elementary School*, Holt, 1961; *The Children's Bookshelf*, Child Study Association of America, Bantam, 1965; Nancy Larrick, *A Parent's Guide to Children's Books*, 3rd edition, Doubleday, 1969.

(Died October 2, 1969)

*   *   *

ARCHER, Jules   1915-

PERSONAL: Born January 27, 1915, in New York, N.Y.; married Eleanor McMahon, May 2, 1942; children: Michael, Dane, Kerry. *Education:* College of the City of New York (now City College of the City University of New York), diploma in advertising. *Politics:* Independent. *Residence:* Pine Plains, N.Y. *Agent:* Edith Margolis, Lenniger Literary Agency, 437 Fifth Ave., New York, N.Y. 10036.

CAREER: Publicity and advertising copywriter for Universal Pictures and other companies, prior to World War II; free-lance writer, 1940—. Consultant to *World Book Encyclopedia*. *Military service:* U.S. Air Force, World War II; served in Pacific with 5th Air Force, and as war correspondent.

WRITINGS: I Sell What I Write, Fell, 1950; (with Shailer Upton Lawton) *Sexual Conduct of the Teen-Ager*, Greenberg, 1951; (with Abel Green and Joe Laurie) *Show Biz*, Holt, 1951; *Front-Line General: Douglas MacArthur*, Messner, 1963; *Twentieth Century Caesar: Benito Mussolini*, Messner, 1964; *What Should Parents Expect from Children?* (pamphlet), Public Affairs Committee (New York), 1964; *Man of Steel: Joseph Stalin*, Messner, 1965; *Fighting Journalist: Horace Greeley*, Messner, 1966; *Battlefield President: Dwight D. Eisenhower*, Messner, 1967; *World Citizen: Woodrow Wilson*, Messner, 1967; *The Dictators*, Hawthorn, 1967; *Laws That Changed America*, Criterion, 1968; *Red Rebel: Tito of Yugoslavia*, Messner, 1968; *Science Explorer: Roy Chapman Andrews*, Messner, 1968; *The Unpopular Ones*, Crowell-Collier, 1968; *African Firebrand: Kenyatta of Kenya*, Messner, 1969; *Angry Abolitionist: William Lloyd Garrison*, Messner, 1969; *Achieve Executive Success, Avoid Family Failure*, Grosset, 1969, reissued as *The*

Executive Success, Universal Library, 1970; *The Extremists: Gadflies of American Society*, Hawthorn, 1969; *Indian Foe, Indian Friend*, Crowell-Collier, 1969; *Colossus of Europe: Metternich*, Messner, 1970; *Thorn in Our Flesh: Castro's Cuba*, Cowles, 1970; *Hawks, Doves and the Eagle*, Hawthorn, 1970; *Congo: The Birth of a New Nation*, Messner, 1970; *The Philippines' Fight for Freedom*, Crowell-Collier, 1970; *Treason in America: Disloyalty Versus Dissent*, Hawthorn, 1971; *1968: Year of Crisis*, Messner, 1971; *Our Exasperating Friends: The French*, Four Winds, 1971; *Ho Chi Minh: Legend of Hanoi*, Crowell-Collier, 1971; *Revolution in Our Time*, Messner, 1971.

Contributor of short stories and articles to *Good Housekeeping, Cosmopolitan, Look, Esquire, Playboy, This Week, Pageant, Family Circle*, and other magazines.

SIDELIGHTS: Archer's stories and articles have been adapted for television, translated into twelve languages, and reprinted by U.S. Department of State for distribution overseas.

BIOGRAPHICAL/CRITICAL SOURCES: Best Sellers, May 1, 1967, January 1, 1968, December 1, 1968, September 1, 1969, May 1, 1970, June 1, 1970, April 15, 1971; *Young Readers' Review*, May, 1968, October, 1968, December, 1968; *New York Times Book Review*, November 3, 1968; *Commonweal*, May 23, 1969; *Book World*, April 12, 1970; *Library Journal*, May 15, 1970, June 15, 1970, September, 1970.

*   *   *

ARCHIBALD, Joseph S(topford)   1898-
   (Joe Archibald)

PERSONAL: Born September 2, 1898, in Newington, N.H.; son of Alexander and Angelina (Stopford) Archibald; married Dorothy Allison Fenton, November 9, 1927. *Education:* Attended Chicago Academy of Fine Arts, eighteen months. *Politics:* Independent. *Religion:* Episcopalian. *Home and office:* 48 Windsor Rd., Port Chester, N.Y. 10573. *Agent:* Lurton Blassingame, 60 East 42nd St., New York, N.Y. 10017.

CAREER: McClure Newspaper Syndicate, New York, N.Y., sport cartoonist during 1920's; *New York Graphic*, New York, N.Y., creator of first story cartoon strip, "Saga of Steve West," 1928-29; editorial art director for Magazine Publishers, Inc., Pines Publications, and Better Publications, Inc., 1949-54; free-lance writer. American Theatre Wing, trick cartoonist entertaining military personnel at air and naval bases in United States, West Indies, Far East, Pacific islands, and in U.S. Army and Navy hospitals, 1940-45; field director in European Theater Operations, American Red Cross, 1945. Guest performer as cartoonist on national television programs. Chapter president and Westchester County publicity director, American Cancer Society. *Military service:* U.S. Navy, 1918-19. *Member:* Authors League of America, National Cartoonist Society, Rotary (honorary), American Legion.

WRITINGS: Touchdown Glory, Westminster, 1949; *Hold That Line!*, Macrae, 1950; *Inside Tackle*, Macrae, 1951; *Block That Kick*, Macrae, 1953; *Fighting Coach*, Macrae, 1954; *Double Play Rookie*, Macrae, 1955; *Fullback Fury*, Macrae, 1955; *Aviation Cadet*, Longmans, Green, 1955; *Full Count*, Macrae, 1956; *Go, Navy, Go*, Macrae, 1956; *Circus Catch*, Macrae, 1957; *Mister Slingshot*, Macrae, Fight, Macrae, 1958; *The Billy Martin Story*, Messner, 1957; *Catcher's Choice*, Macrae, 1958; *Fight, Team,*

1959; *Bonus Kid,* Macrae, 1959; *Falcons to the Fight,* Macrae, 1959.

The Richie Ashburn Story, Messner, 1960; *First Base Hustler,* Macrae, 1960; *Backfield Twins,* Macrae, 1960; *Jet Flier,* Longmans, Green, 1960; *Crazy Legs McBain,* Macrae, 1961; *Outfield Orphan,* Macrae, 1961; (with Pauline Innis) *Hurricane Fighters,* McKay, 1962; *Red-Dog Center,* Macrae, 1962; *Windmill Pilot,* McKay, 1963; *Big League Busher,* Macrae, 1963; *Hard-Nosed Halfback,* Macrae, 1963; *The Smoker Eaters,* McKay, 1965; *Special Forces Trooper,* McKay, 1967.

Under name Joe Archibald: *Riders of the Shadows,* Dodge Publishing Co., 1938; *Bedtime Tories; or, Where There's a Wilkie, There's a Way,* House of Field, 1940; *Rebel Halfback,* Westminster, 1947; *Shortstop on Wheels,* Macrae, 1962; *Quarterback & Son,* Macrae, 1964; *The Easy Out,* Macrae, 1965; *Southpaw Speed,* Macrae, 1965; *West Point Wingback,* Macrae, 1965; *Commander of the Flying Tigers: Claire Lee Chennault,* Messner, 1966; *The Long Pass,* Macrae, 1966; *Right Field Rookie,* Macrae, 1967; *The Scrambler,* Macrae, 1967; *Fast Break Fury,* Macrae, 1968; *Mitt Maverick,* Macrae, 1968; *Two Time Rookie,* Macrae, 1969; *Pro Coach,* Macrae, 1969; *Baseball Talk for Beginners,* Messner, 1969; *Back Court Commando,* Macrae, 1970; *Powerback,* Macrae, 1970; *Payoff Pitch,* Macrae, 1971; *Phantom Blitz,* Macrae, 1972; *Right Field Runt,* Macrae, 1972. Author of short stories and novelettes.

WORK IN PROGRESS: A baseball instruction book for Follett.

SIDELIGHTS: Archibald writes: "I do not believe that there is a more rewarding profession in this world than being a writer. A cartoonist draws a funny picture that is almost immediately forgotten. An author's words are preserved in the Library of Congress and are read over and over again by youngsters a long time after he has gone. I do not consider it a glamorous profession; it has never built up my ego, for after all there are thousands of writers in the United States. It is my contention that 'somebody up there' has been more than kind to me, blessing me with two talents."

* * *

ARESTY, Esther B (radford)

PERSONAL: Born in Syracuse, N.Y.; daughter of Jacob and Bertha (Levin) Bradford; married Jules Aresty (a retailer), June 24, 1936; children: Robert, Jane. *Education:* DePaul University, student, 1929-31. *Home:* 32 Hilvista Blvd., Trenton, N.J. 08618.

CAREER: Radio Station WJJD, Chicago, Ill., commentator, 1931-35; Mandel Brothers (department store), Chicago, Ill., advertising manager, 1934-36; retailer, freelance fashion consultant, radio writer, and author, 1936—. Trenton Community Foundation, president, 1962; member of board. of governors of Florence Crittenton Home, Mercer County Child Guidance Center, Union Industrial Home. *Member:* Authors League of America, Women's National Book Association.

WRITINGS: The Grand Venture, Bobbs, Merrill, 1963; *The Delectable Past: The Joys of the Table,* Simon & Schuster, 1964; *The Best Behavior: The Course of Good Manners—from Antiquity to the Present—as Seen Through Courtesy and Etiquette Books,* Simon & Schuster, 1970. Contributor to children's magazines.

WORK IN PROGRESS: A Cookbook History, for Hawthorn.

AVOCATIONAL INTERESTS: Collecting rare cookbooks, music, and painting.

* * *

ARLOTT, (Leslie Thomas) John 1914-

PERSONAL: Born December 25, 1914, in Basingstoke, Hampshire, England; son of William John and Nellie Jenvey (Clarke) Arlott; married Dawn Rees; married second wife, Valerie France, July 18, 1960; children: (first marriage) Timothy Mark John; (second marriage) Robert Francis John. *Education:* Attended schools in Basingstoke, Hampshire, England. *Politics:* Liberal. *Home:* The Old Sun, Alresford, Hampshire, England.

CAREER: Clerk in town planning office and in hospital, Basingstoke, Hampshire, England, 1931-34: Southampton County Borough Police, Hampshire, England, 1934-54, began as detective, became sergeant; British Broadcasting Corp., London, England, producer of literary programs, 1945-51, instructor in training school, 1951-53, regular broadcaster on cricket, 1946-67; *The Guardian,* London, cricket correspondent, 1966—. Liberal candidate for Parliament, Epping Division, 1951, 1955. Wine and food correspondent for *Evening News,* London, 1951-55, for *News-Chronicle,* 1955-58; Association football correspondent for *Guardian,* 1956-58, for *Observer,* 1958—. Writer and commentator for television topographical film series, "ABC of the South"; member of "Any Questions" panel. *Member:* Cricketers Association (president, 1968—).

WRITINGS: (Compiler with G. Rostrevor Hamilton) *Landmarks: A Book of Topographical Verse for England and Wales,* Cambridge University Press, 1943; *Of Period and Place* (poems), J. Cape, 1944; *Clausentum* (sonnets), J. Cape, 1946; *Indian Summer: An Account of the Cricket Tour in England, 1946,* Longmans, Green, 1947; *Gone to the Cricket,* Longmans, Green, 1948; (compiler and author of introduction) *First Time in America: A Selection of Poems Never Before Published in the U.S.A.,* Duell, Sloan & Pearce, 1948; *How to Watch Cricket,* Sporting Handbooks, 1948; (editor) *From Hambledon to Lord's: The Classics of Cricket,* Christopher Johnson, 1948; (with others) *Day & Mason Cricket Annual, 1949: A New Annual on Cricket,* Day, Mason & Ford, 1949; *Gone to the Test Match: Primarily an Account of the Test Series of 1948,* Longmans, Green, 1949; (with Wilfred Wooler and Maurice Edelston) *Wickets, Tries and Goals: Review of Plays and Players in Modern Cricket, Rugby and Soccer,* Low, 1949; *Concerning Cricket: Studies of the Plays and Players,* Longmans, Green, 1949; (editor) William Denison and James Pycroft, *The Middle Ages of Cricket,* Christopher Johnson, 1949.

Gone with the Cricketers, Longmans, Green, 1950; *Cricket,* Cambridge University Press, 1950; (editor and author of introduction) *Cricket in the Counties: Studies of the First-class Counties in Action,* Saturn Press, 1950; *Maurice Tate,* Phoenix House, 1951; *Concerning Soccer,* Longmans, Green, 1952; *The Echoing Green: Cricket Studies,* Longmans, Green, 1952; (with others) *Elizabeth Crowned Queen: The Pictorial Record of the Coronation,* Crown, 1953; *Death on the Road* (poetry), Barrie & Rockliff, 1953; *Test Match Diary,* Barrie & Rockliff, 1953; (editor and author of introduction) John Speed, *England: A Coloured Facsimile of the Maps and Tests from The Theatre of the Empire of Great Britaine,* Phoenix House, 1953-54; (author of introduction) James John Corbett, *The Roar of the Crowd: The Rise and Fall of a Champion,* Phoenix House, 1954; *Australian Test Journal: A Diary of the Test Matches, Australia vs. England, 1954-55,* Phoenix House, 1955; *The Picture of Cricket,* Penguin, 1955; *Alletson's Innings,* Epworth, 1957; (with H.S. Altham, E.D.R. Eagar, and Roy Webber) *History of Hampshire Cricket,* Phoenix House, 1957; *English Cheeses of the South and West,* Harrap, 1958; *Cricket*

Journal 1, Heinemann, 1958; *Cricket Journal 2,* Heinemann, 1959; *Attention!,* Newman Neame, 1959.

Cricket Journal 3: Cricket on Trial, Heinemann, 1960; *Cricket Journal 4: The Australian Challenge,* Heinemann, 1961; *Crime and Punishment,* Newman Neame, 1961; *Rothman's Jubilee History of Cricket, 1890-1965,* Weidenfeld & Nicolson, 1965; *World Cup '66,* Eyre & Spottiswoode, 1966; *Vintage Summer: 1947,* Eyre & Spottiswoode, 1967; (contributor) Hugh McIlvanney, *Cricket: The Great Ones,* Pelham Books, 1967; (with Arthur Daley) *Pageantry of Sport, from the Age of Chivalry to the Age of Victoria,* Hawthorn, 1968; (editor) *Cricket: The Great Bowlers,* Pelham Books, 1968; (editor) *Soccer: The Great Ones,* Pelham Books, 1968; (contributor) Oliver Stallybrass, editor, *Aspects of E.M. Forster: Essays and Recollections Written for His Ninetieth Birthday,* Harcourt, 1969; (compiler with Neville Cardus) *The Noblest Game: A Book of Fine Cricket Prints,* Harrap, 1969.

Fred, Eyre & Spottiswoode, 1971. Also author of a pamphlet, *The Problem of Infantile Paralysis,* published by the Infantile Paralysis Fellowship.

AVOCATIONAL INTERESTS: Collecting cricketana, engraved glass, topographical books illustrated with aquatints, Gladstoniana; fishing, golf, eating, and talking.

BIOGRAPHICAL/CRITICAL SOURCES: Book World, January 12, 1969.

*   *   *

ARMSTRONG, Ann Seidel 1917-

PERSONAL: Born October 8, 1917, in River Forest, Ill.; daughter of Emory P. and Hildegard (Erbsmehl) Seidel; married John M. Armstrong (a manufacturing executive), June 20, 1942; children: John, Jr., David, Paul, Daniel, Margaret, Thomas, Mary, Ellen. *Education:* Radcliffe College, A.B., 1938; University of Chicago, M.A., 1939. *Politics:* Republican. *Religion:* Roman Catholic. *Home:* 176 West Saint Charles Rd., Elmhurst, Ill. 60126.

CAREER: Teacher of Latin, Centralia, Ill., 1940-42; teacher of English and creative writing, 1967—.

WRITINGS: Remember No More, Bruce, 1963; *The Story of a Parish,* Immaculate Conception Parish (Elmhurst), 1966.

WORK IN PROGRESS: In a Man's Voice, a contemporary novel; *Interlude in Tunis,* a novel about a recent discovery of third century scrolls.

*   *   *

ARMSTRONG, Douglas Albert 1920-
(Albert Douglas, Rex Windsor, Tribune)

PERSONAL: Born March 22, 1920, in Windsor, Berkshire, England; son of Albert William and Kathleen Ruth (Magee) Armstrong; married Elizabeth Wettle, May 17, 1957. *Education:* Attended schools in Windsor, England. *Home and office:* North Lodge, Shurlock Row, Berkshire, England.

CAREER: Author and journalist. *Member:* Guild of Motoring Writers (chairman, 1961), British Racing Drivers' Club (associate), United Motor Sports Club, Wig and Pen Club (London; life).

WRITINGS: Editor with Roy Pearl) *Formula III Year Books, 1953-54,* Pearl, Cooper, 1953; *A.B.C. of British Motor Cycles,* Ian Allan, 1954; (under pseudonym Albert Douglas) *A.B.C. of British Sports Cars,* Ian Allan, 1955, reissued as *ABC Sports Cars,* Ian Allen, 1956; *The Motoring Annual,* Ian Allan, 1955; *The World's Racing Cars and Sports Cars,* Macdonald & Co., 1958, Doubleday, 1959; (English editor) *Automobile Year, 1963-64, 1964-65,* Bentley Publishing, 1963-64, Foulis & Co., 1965; (edi-

tor) *Automobile Year, 1967-68, 1968-69,* Walter R. Haessner & Associates, 1968, Edita, 1969. Contributor to *Sports Cars Illustrated* (now *Car and Driver*), *Motoring, Ici Renault, Town, Motor Industry,* and other motoring publications in Britain and abroad, as well as to British newspapers. Contributor under pseudonym Tribune to *Modern Motoring and Travel;* former British correspondent for *Motor Life* (United States). Founder-editor of British monthlies, *Cars Illustrated* and *Motor-Cyclist Illustrated;* London editor of *Modern Motor* (Australia), *Teknikens Varld* (Sweden); former contributing editor of *Scooter Weekly;* former editor of *Motor Racing.*†

*   *   *

ARMSTRONG, Gregory T(imon) 1933-

PERSONAL: Born December 23, 1933, in Evanston, Ill.; son of John R. (in industrial advertising) and Clara (Carlson) Armstrong; married Edna Stagg, May 11, 1957; children: Edna Louisa, Elizabeth Stagg. *Education:* Wesleyan University, B.A., 1955; McCormick Theological Seminary, B.D., 1958; University of Heidelberg, Dr. Theol., 1961. *Home and office address:* P.O. Box AY, Sweet Briar, Va. 24595.

CAREER: Ordained Presbyterian minister, 1961; McCormick Theological Seminary, Chicago, Ill., instructor in church history, 1961-62; Vanderbilt Divinity School, Nashville, Tenn., assistant professor of church history, 1962-68; Sweet Briar College, Sweet Briar, Va., associate professor of religion, 1968—. *Member:* American Historical Association, American Association of University Professors, American Society of Church History, American Catholic Historical Association, American Academy of Religion, Phi Beta Kappa. *Awards, honors:* American Council of Learned Societies study fellowship, 1965-66.

WRITINGS: Die Genesis in der Alten Kirche, Mohr, 1962; (contributor) Frank N. Magill, editor, *Masterpieces of Christian Literature,* Harper, 1963; *Imperial Church Building and Church State Relations,* American Society of Church History, 1967. Contributor to *Britannica Junior Encyclopaedia,* 1965—, and of articles and reviews to religious journals.

WORK IN PROGRESS: A monograph on Constantine's Churches.

SIDELIGHTS: Armstrong is competent in German, French, Latin, Biblical Greek, and Hebrew.

*   *   *

ARMSTRONG, William M(artin) 1919-

PERSONAL: Born January 14, 1919, in Peoria, Ill.; son of Haskell R. and Lilian (Nofsinger) Armstrong; married Norma Campbell, April 17, 1943 (divorced, 1970); children: Lois Lee, Dean, Bruce. *Education:* Bradley University, A.B., 1948; Louisiana State University, A.M., 1949; Stanford University, Ph.D., 1954. *Politics:* Democrat. *Religion:* Unitarian. *Home:* 150 Maple St., Potsdam, N.Y. 13676.

CAREER: Stanford University, Palo Alto, Calif., instructor in history, 1949-50, 1951-53; Eastern Illinois University, Charleston, assistant professor of history, 1954-56; Washington College, Chestertown, Md., head of history department, 1956-59; Alma College, Alma, Mich., associate professor of history, 1961-65; Clarkson College of Technology, Potsdam, N.Y., professor of history, 1965—. Fulbright lecturer in American history, University of Helsinki, 1963-64; summer visiting professor at Long Island University, 1961, Brooklyn College of the City University of New York, 1963, and City College of the City University of New York, 1964. *Military service:* U.S. Army, Infantry, 1941-46; became first lieutenant; received Combat Infantry Badge and Bronze Star. *Member:*

American Historical Association, American Civil Liberties Union, American Association of University Professors, Organization of American Historians. *Awards, honors:* Research grants from American Philosophical Society, 1956, 1958, National Endowment for the Humanities, 1967.

WRITINGS: E.L. Godkin and American Foreign Policy, 1865-1900, Twayne, 1957. Contributor of articles and reviews to journals.

WORK IN PROGRESS: A biography of E.L. Godkin.

* * *

ARMYTAGE, Walter Harry Green 1915-

PERSONAL: Born November 22, 1915, in Kimberley, South Africa; son of Walter Green and Harriet Jane May (Harry) Armytage; married Lucy Frances (a university teacher), May 28, 1947; children: John Russell. *Education:* Downing College, Cambridge, first class honors in historical tripos, 1937, certificate in education, 1938, M.A., 1941. *Religion:* Church of England *Home:* 3 The Green, Totley, Sheffield, England. *Office:* University of Sheffield, Sheffield 10, England.

CAREER: University of Sheffield, Sheffield, England, professor of education, 1946—. University of Michigan, Ann Arbor, visiting professor, 1955, 1959, 1961, 1963; University of Wales, Bangor, Ballard-Matthews Lecturer, 1963. *Military service:* London Irish Rifles; became captain; mentioned in dispatches.

WRITINGS: A.J. Mundella: The Liberal Background of the Labour Movement, Benn, 1951; (with E.C. Mack) *Thomas Hughes: The Life of the Author of "Tom Brown's Schooldays,"* Benn, 1952; *Civic Universities: Aspects of a British Tradition,* De Graff, 1955; *Sir Richard Gregory: His Life and Work,* Macmillan, 1957; *A Social History of Engineering,* Faber, 1961, M.I.T. Press, 1966, 3rd edition, Faber, 1970; *Heavens Below: Utopian Experiments in England, 1560-1960,* Routledge & Kegan Paul, 1962; *Four Hundred Years of English Education,* Cambridge University Press, 1964, 2nd edition, 1970; *The Rise of the Technocrats: A Social History,* Routledge & Kegan Paul, 1965; *The American Influence on English Education,* Humanities, 1967; *The French Influence on English Education,* Humanities, 1968; *Yesterday's Tomorrows: A Historical Survey of Future Societies,* Routledge & Kegan Paul, 1968; *The German Influence on English Education,* Humanities, 1969; *The Russian Influence on English Education,* Humanities, 1969; *Looking North: Influence and Inference from Sweden in English Education,* Arthur Mellows Memorial Trust, 1969. Member of editorial board of *British Journal of Educational Studies, International Journal of Social Psychiatry.*

BIOGRAPHICAL/CRITICAL SOURCES: Observer Review, May 12, 1968.

* * *

ARNHEIM, Daniel D(avid) 1930-

PERSONAL: Born February 9, 1930, in Los Angeles, Calif.; son of Herbert G. (a salesman) and Ruth (Kennedy) Arnheim; married Helene Buys, September 1, 1951; children: Craig Steven, Karen Durrell, Mark Lawence. *Education:* Pepperdine College, B.A., 1952; Los Angeles State College of Applied Arts and Sciences (now California State University), M.A., 1954; postgraduate study at University of Southern California, 1960-62; Springfield College, Ph.D., 1964. *Religion:* Protestant.

CAREER: Certified corrective therapist. Teacher in secondary school in California prior to 1959; Long Beach State College, Long Beach, Calif., 1959—, began as associate professor, now professor of physical education, head athletic trainer, and director of Institute for Sensory Mo-

tor Development, on leave as doctoral teaching fellow at Springfield College, Springfield, Mass., 1964-65. Director of therapeutic physical education, California State University at Long Beach; consultant in area of motor development. *Military service:* U.S. Army Reserve, physical reconditioning officer, 1953—; became captain. *Member:* American College of Sports Medicine (fellow), Association for Physical and Mental Rehabilitation, American Association for Health, Physical Education and Recreation.

WRITINGS: (With Carl E. Klafs) *Modern Principles of Athletic Training,* Mosby, 1963, 2nd edition, 1969; (contributor) *The Coaching Clinic,* Prentice-Hall, 1963; (with David Auxter and Walter Crowe) *Principles and Methods of Adapted Physical Education,* Mosby, 1969; (with Robert Pistolesi) *Developing Movement Behavior in Children: A Balanced Approach to Elementary Physical Education,* Mosby, 1973.

* * *

ARNOLD, Armin H. 1931-

PERSONAL: Born September 1, 1931, in Zug, Switzerland. *Education:* Kant Gymnasium, Zurich, Switzerland, B.A., 1951; University of Fribourg, Lic. es Lettres, 1953, Docteur es Lettres, 1956; additional study at University of Zurich, 1953-54, and University of London, 1955-57. *Politics:* Conservative. *Religion:* Roman Catholic. *Office:* Department of German, McGill University, Montreal, Quebec, Canada.

CAREER: Supported self as professional jazz musician during years of study; University of Fribourg, Fribourg, Switzerland, instructor, 1956-57; College of Fahrwangen, Switzerland, headmaster, 1957-59; University of Alberta, Edmonton, assistant professor of German, 1959-61; McGill University, Montreal, Quebec, assistant professor, 1961-64, associate professor, 1964-65, professor of German and chairman of the department, 1965—.

WRITINGS: D.H. Lawrence and America, Linden Press, 1958, Philosophical Library, 1959; *Heinrich Heine in England and America,* International Publications, 1959; *James Joyce,* Colloquium-Verlag, 1963, revised and translated edition (with Judy Young), Ungar, 1969; *D.H. Lawrence and German Literature, with Two Hitherto Unknown Essays,* Manfield Book Mart, 1963; (editor) D.H. Lawrence, *The Symbolic Meaning: The Uncollected Versions of Studies in Classic American Literature,* Centaur Press, 1962, Viking, 1964; *G.B. Shaw,* Colloquium-Verlag, 1965; *Die Literatur des Expressionismus: Sprachliche und theomatische Quellen,* Kohlhammer, 1966; *Felix Steumpers Abenteuer und Streiche,* Francke (Bern), 1967; (editor) *Kanadische Erzahler der Gegenwart,* Manesse, 1967; *Friedrich Durrenmatt,* Colloquium-Verlag, 1969.

* * *

ARNOLD, Richard 1912-
(Coch-y-Bonddhu)

PERSONAL: Born November 7, 1912, in Corstorphine, Scotland; son of Richard (an engineer) and Margaret Marjorie (Sinclair) Arnold; married Trudy Feith, August 13, 1949; children: David James. *Education:* Attended Manchester Grammar School, Manchester, England. *Religion:* Roman Catholic. *Home:* 4 Albermarle Road, Saint Ives, Huntingdonshire, England. *Office:* Institute of Physics and the Physical Society, 47 Belgrave Sq., London S.W.1, England.

CAREER: Wilson Meats Ltd. (branch of Wilson Meats, Inc., Chicago, Ill.), London, England, assistant sales manager, 1953-59; Millard Bros. Ltd. (guns and fishing tackle), London, sales manager, 1959-60; Institute of Physics and The Physical Society, London, accountant, 1961-65; Steel Sheet Information and Development Association, publicity officer, 1965-69; in own practice as publicity consultant, 1965—. *Military service:* British Army, with Expeditionary Force to Dunkirk, 1939-40, Commandos, 1940-44, Royal Scots Fusiliers, 1944-46. *Member:* Muzzle Loaders Association of Great Britain (founder).

WRITINGS: The Shoreshooter, Seeley Service, 1953; *Come Shooting with Me,* Muller, 1953, Sportshelf, 1956; *Come Sea Fishing with Me,* Muller, 1954, Sportshelf, 1956; *The True Book About the Commandos,* Muller, 1954, Sportshelf, 1958; *The Shooter's Handbook: Gun Care, Minor Gunsmithing, Handloading of Cartridges, Making Decoys, the Law Relating to Firearms and Kindred Matters,* Sweetman, 1955, 3rd revised edition, Kaye & Ward, 1971; *Pigeon Shooting,* Faber, 1956, 2nd edition, 1966; *Making and Repairing Fishing Tackle,* W. & G. Foyle, 1956; *Rifle Shooting,* W. & G. Foyle, 1957; *The True Book About David Livingstone,* Muller, 1957, published in America as *The True Story of David Livingstone, Explorer,* Childrens Press, 1964; (contributor) Jack Thorndike, editor, *Sea Fishing with the Experts,* Allen & Unwin, 1957; *The Complete Sea Angler,* Kaye & Ward, 1957, Sportshelf, 1958, revised edition published as *Modern Sea Angling,* Kaye & Ward, 1970; *Automatic and Repeating Shotguns,* Kaye & Ward, 1958, A.S. Barnes, 1960; *The Book of the .22: A Complete Manual for the .22 Rifleman and the Pistoleer,* A.S. Barnes, 1962; *Modern Camping,* Kaye & Ward, 1963; *The Angler's Handbook,* Arthur Barker, 1967; *Fishing,* Pan Books, 1967; *The Book of Angling,* Arthur Barker, 1969; *Clay Pigeon Shooting,* Kaye & Ward, 1973. Contributor of articles to *Angling Times, Field Sports, Shooting Times, Country Sportsman, Hobbies, Motor Cycle News, Lilliput,* and other magazines, mainly in outdoor field.

WORK IN PROGRESS: Your Book of Sea Fishing, Faber, publication expected in 1972.

AVOCATIONAL INTERESTS: All aspects of sports, including ice figure and dance skating, roller skating, foil and sabre fencing, fresh and salt water fishing, sailing, ballroom dancing, and Scottish dancing; natural history and the countryside; photography, including film processing.

*   *   *

ARNOW, Harriette Louisa Simpson   1908-

PERSONAL: Born July 7, 1908, in Wayne County, Ky.; daughter of Elias Thomas (a teacher, farmer, and oil well driller) and Mollie Jane (a teacher; maiden name, Denney) Simpson; married Harold B. Arnow (publicity director for Michigan Heart Association), 1939; children: Marcella Jane, Thomas Louis. *Education:* Berea College, student, 1924-26; University of Louisville, B.S., 1931. *Residence:* Ann Arbor, Mich.

CAREER: Author. *Member:* Authors Guild, American Civil Liberties Union, Women's International League for Peace and Freedom, Mid-Western Writers, Ann Arbor Women for Peace. *Awards, honors:* Friends of American Writers award, an honorary degree from Albion College, Berea College Centennial award, *Woman's Home Companion* Silver Distaff award for "unique contribution by a woman to American life," all 1955, all for *The Dollmaker;* commendation from Tennessee Historical Commission and award of merit of American Association for State and Local History, both 1961, both for *Seedtime on the Cumberland; Tennessee Historical Quarterly* prize for best article of the year, 1962.

WRITINGS: Mountain Path (novel), Covici-Friede, 1936; *Hunter's Horn* (novel), Macmillan, 1949; *The Dollmaker* (novel), Macmillan, 1954; *Seedtime on the Cumberland* (nonfiction), Macmillan, 1960; *Flowering of the Cumberland* (nonfiction), Macmillan, 1963; *The Weedkiller's Daughter* (novel), Knopf, 1970. Author of short stories in the 1930's, two of them anthologized in *O. Henry Memorial Award Prize Stories.* Contributor of articles and reviews to magazines.

SIDELIGHTS: A regionalist (transplanted), Mrs. Arnow writes: "I still hope to be able to give most of my time to writing. Life in exurbia has been a sore trial both in the amount of time and mind that must go into such a complicated way of life, and the loss of casual contacts with people—housewife writers have little time for social lives."

BIOGRAPHICAL/CRITICAL SOURCES: New York Times, May 28, 1949; *Commonweal,* June 10, 1949; *New York Herald Tribune,* April 25, 1954; *New Yorker,* May 1, 1954; *Library Journal,* June 15, 1960, December 1, 1963, April 15, 1970; *Christian Science Monitor,* November 20, 1963; *Saturday Review,* November 23, 1963; *New York Times Book Review,* March 22, 1970.†

*   *   *

ARONSON, Theo   1930-

PERSONAL: Born November 13, 1930, in Kirkwood, South Africa; son of Philip (a businessman) and Hannah (Wilson) Aronson. *Education:* Studied at Grey College, Port Elizabeth, South Africa, 1943-46, and University of Cape Town, 1947-50. *Religion:* Church of England. *Agent:* Laurence Pollinger Ltd., 18 Maddox St., Mayfair, London W1R 0EU, England. *Home:* Gum Tree Cottage, Teubes Rd., Kommetjie, South Africa.

CAREER: J. Walter Thompson Co. Ltd. (advertising agency), advertising designer and art director at offices in London, England, in Nairobi, Kenya, and in Cape Town, Johannesburg, Durban, and Port Elizabeth, South Africa, 1952-64; full-time writer, 1964—.

WRITINGS: The Golden Bees: The Story of the Bonapartes, New York Graphic Society, 1964; *Royal Vendetta: The Crown of Spain, 1829-1965,* Bobbs-Merrill, 1966; *Defiant Dynasty: The Coburgs of Belgium,* Bobbs-Merrill, 1968 (published in England as *The Coburgs of Belguim,* Cassell, 1969); *The Fall of the Third Napoleon,* Bobbs-Merrill, 1970; *The Kaisers,* Bobbs-Merrill, 1971; *Queen Victoria and the Bonapartes,* Bobbs-Merrill, 1972.

AVOCATIONAL INTERESTS: Art, architecture, and especially history of the nineteenth century.

BIOGRAPHICAL/CRITICAL   SOURCES: Punch, March 12, 1969; *Times Literary Supplement,* July 24, 1969; *Books and Bookmen,* December, 1969, April, 1970; *Spectator,* February 28, 1970; *Library Journal,* March 1, 1970.

*   *   *

ARRABAL, (Fernando)   1932-

PERSONAL: Born August 11, 1932, in Melilla, Morocco; son of Fernando and Carmen (Teran) Arrabal Ruiz; married Luce Moreau (a professeur agrege, University of Paris, Sorbonne), January 2, 1958; children: a daughter. *Education:* Studied law at University of Madrid, received license de droit. *Home:* 32 boulevard de Strasbourg, Paris 10, France. *Agent:* S.A.C.D., 9 rue Ballu, Paris 9, France.

CAREER: Writer. Moved to France in 1954. *Awards, honors:* Lugne Poe theatre prize, 1966; Societe des Auteurs prize, 1966; Grand Prix du Theatre, 1967, for *L'Architecte et l'empereur d'Assyrie;* Black Humor Prize (Paris), 1969.

WRITINGS—Plays: Theatre, two volumes, R. Julliard, Volume I inculdes: "Oraison" (produced under title "Orison" in New York at Cafe 4, September, 1968), "Les

Deux Bourreaux" (one-act; produced under title "The Two Executioners" Off-Off-Broadway at The Extension, December, 1967), "Fando et Lis" (one-act; produced Off-Broadway, May, 1967), and "Le Cimetiere des voitures" (two-act; first produced in Paris at Theatre des Arts, December 19, 1967; also produced Off-Broadway at Cafe LaMama under title, "Automobile Graveyard"), 1958, translation of Volume I by Barbara Wright published as *Four Plays: Orison* [and] *The Two Executioners* [and] *Frando and Lis* [and] *The Car Cemetery*, J. Calder, 1962, Volume I published as *Theater I*, C. Bourgois, 1968, Volume II includes: "Guernica" (one-act; produced Off-Broadway at Barbizon-Plaza Theatre, April 30, 1969), "Le Labyrinthe" (first produced in Paris, 1967; produced under title "Labyrinthe" in Waltham, Mass. at Brandeis University, August, 1968), "Le Tricycle" (one-act; produced under title "The Tricycle" in New York by the Inner Theatre Troupe, January 9, 1970), "Pique-nique en campagne" (produced under title "Picnic on the Battlefield" Off-Broadway at St. Clement's Church, September 8, 1967), and "La Bicyclette du condamne," 1961, translation of Volume II by Wright published as *Plays* (includes "Guernica," "The Labyrinth," The Tricycle," "Picnic on the Battlefield," and "The Condemned Man's Bicycle"), Calder & Boyars, 1967, Volume II published as *Theatre II*, C. Bourgois, 1968.

The Automobile Graveyard (Le Cimitiere [sic] *des voitures), a Play in Two Acts, and The Two Executioners (Les Deux Bourreaux), a Melodrama in One Act*, translated by Richard Howard, Grove, 1960; *Theatre III* (includes "La Communion solennelle" [one-act; first produced in Paris at Theatre de Poche-Montparnasse, July 8, 1966], "Les Amours impossibles" [first produced in Paris at Theatre de Poche-Montparnasse, July 8, 1966], "Une Chevre sur le nuage," "La Jeunesse illustree," and "Dieu est-il devenue fou?"), R. Julliard, 1965; *Theatre V* (includes "Theatre Panique" [seven short plays] and "L'Architecte et l'empereur d'Assyrie" [two-act; first produced in Paris at Theatre Montparnasse, spring, 1967; produced under title "The Architect and the Emperor of Assyria," in San Francisco by The American Conservatory Theater, 1968; produced under English title in London at Old Vic, February 3, 1971]), C. Bourgois, 1967; *Theatre 1969*, C. Bourgois, 1969, Volume I: *La Contestation*, Volume II: *Le Grand Guignol; Theatre IV* (includes "Le Lai de Barabbas" and "Concert dans un oeuf"), C. Bourgois, 1969; *Theatre VI* (includes "Le Jardin des delices" [title means "The Garden of Delights"; first produced in Paris at Theatre Antoine, November, 1969], "Bestialite erotique," and "Une Torture nommee Dostoievsky"), C. Bourgois, 1969; *Theatre VII; Theatre de guerilla* (includes "Et ils passerent des menottes aux fleurs" [one-act; produced in Paris, winter, 1970; produced under title "And They Put Handcuffs on the Flowers," Off-Off-Broadway at The Extension, October, 1971] and "L'Aurore rouge et noire" [first produced in Brussels at Theatre de Poche, January, 1969]), C. Bourgois, 1969; *Guernica and Other Plays* (includes "The Labyrinth," "The Tricycle," and "Picnic on the Battlefield"), translated by Wright, Grove, 1969; *The Architect and the Emperor of Assyria*, translated by Everard d'Harnoncourt and Adele Shank, Grove, 1969.

*Theatre VIII: Deux Operas paniques (*includes "Ars Amandi" and "Dieu tente par les mathematiques"), C. Bourgois, 1970; *Theatre 1970: Theatre en marge*, C. Bourgois, 1970; *The Architect and the Emperor of Assyria* [and] *The Grand Ceremonial* (translation of "Le Grand Ceremonial"; produced in Hamburg under title "Nacht der Puppen" ["Night of the Dolls"], spring, 1969) [and] *The Solemn Communion*, translated by Jean Benedetti and John Calder, Calder & Boyars, 1970; *L'Architecte et l'empereur d'Assyrie* [and] *Theatre de guerilla* [including] *Et ils passerent des menottes aux fleurs* [and]

L'Aurore rouge et noire, Union Generale d'Editions, 1971; *Theatre IX*, C. Bourgois, [?].

Other: *Baal Babylone* (novel), R. Julliard, 1959, translation by Richard Howard published as *Baal Babylon*, Grove, 1961; *L'Enterrement de la sardine* (novel), R. Julliard, 1961, new edition, C. Bourgois, 1970, translation by Patrick Bowles published as *The Burial of the Sardine*, Calder & Boyars, 1966; *Le Pierre de la folie* ("livre panique"), R. Julliard, 1963; *Arrabal Celebrando la Ceremonia de la Confusion* (novel), Alfaguara (Madrid), 1966, published in Paris as *Fete et rite de la confusion*, Le Terrain Vague, 1967; (author of text) Fernando Botero, *Botero: peintures, pastels, fusains* (art collection), Galerie Claude Bernard, 1969; (author of text) Antonio Saura, *Peintures sur papier de Saura* (catalog of an art exhibit), Galerie Stadler, c.1969; (with others) *La Revolution surrealista a traves de Andre Breton*, Monte Avila (Caracas), 1970; *Baal Babylon* [and] *Viva la muerte* (title means "Long Live Death"; original screenplay, produced in 1971), with preface by Dominique Sevrain, C. Bourgois, 1971; *Lettre au General Franco* (complete text of a letter sent by Arrabal to Franco in 1971), Union Generale d'Editions, 1972.

Unpublished plays: "Orchestration theatrale" (a play without words), produced in 1959; "La Princesse" (one-act), first produced in Paris at Theatre de Poche-Montparnasse, summer, 1966; "Revolution-Imagination," first produced in Brussels at Theatre de Poche, winter, 1969; "Ceremony for a Murdered Black," produced Off-Broadway at St. Clement's Church, November, 1972; "La Couronnement"; "The Thousand Year War."

Plays are represented in anthologies, including *Panorama du theatre: Theatre de la derision*, edited by Jacques Benay and Reinhard Kuhn, Appleton, 1967, and in periodicals, including *Drama Review* and *Daily Bulletin*. Contributor to *Les Lettres Nouvelles, Evergreen Review, A.B.C.* (Madrid), *Panic* (Spain), and other publications.

WORK IN PROGRESS: A play about Gilles de Rais, a fifteenth century French figure.

SIDELIGHTS: Although Arrabal writes in French and lives in Paris, his early years were spent in post-Civil War Spain where, according to Genevieve Serreau in the preface to *Theatre*, Volume II, he grew up "a witness, as was all of his generation, to the final crushing of liberties, to the terrorism of a church reestablished on repressive rights, to the torpor of a humiliated people." He believes, according to Mme. Serreau, that "half-crushed under the yoke of familial and social prohibitions, the solitary 'little man,' ever endowed with an incredible desire for hope, attempts by laughter to purge himself of fear. On this basis, a work is born."

Having much in common with the Theatre of the Absurd, exemplified in the works of Beckett, Ionesco, Artaud, and others, Arrabal's "panic theatre" is an elaboration of, or variation on the absurd. He explains that the term "panic theatre" is based on his faith in the god Pan, and also on the use of "pan-" to mean all-encompassing.

His plays are unfixed in time or space, and present a world where all things are possible and valid. Except for murder, which Arrabal says, in a *New York Times* interview, is the "one irreparable act," all things are possible onstage. His characters, Mme. Serreau writes, "pass their time in a no-man's-land on the edge of the adult world." They engage in nightmarish tortures and cruelties, and seem to be unaffected by the "adult" world's structures and restrictive morality.

Some critics have suggested that Arrabal shocks his audiences for the sake of shock alone, although this criticism is by no means unanimous or unqualified. Edith Oliver says that "Arrabal is a writer for whom shock-tactics appear to be second nature, but although I have often been put off in the past by his Hispanic relish for blood and pain and religiosity, I have always valued him as a savage jester with a streak of wild, original, blasphemous impudence."

Arrabal observed, in an *Evergreen Review* interview, "I'm not trying to deliberately offend people. And at times even I am shocked at what I write." "I do not write for shock," he told the *New York Times,* "but what I write is an imitation of nature and of the senses. I write plays in order to live more intensely."

Arrabal has written sixty plays, nearly forty of them published. Regardless of whether they are published or performed, his works invite controversy. His plays have never been performed in Spain (partly for political reasons), and he is regularly attacked by the French press for "obscenity and blasphemy." "The Thousand Year War" was prevented from being shown at France's Avignon Festival in 1970, while in the winter of that same year, three of his plays were shown simultaneously in Paris.

He has directed two American productions of "And They Put Handcuffs on the Flowers," a film version of his novel, *Baal Babylone* (in production in 1970), and a film based on his screenplay, "Viva la muerte," produced in 1971.

"Fando y Lis" was filmed in Mexico by Alexandro Jodrowsky in 1969, "The Great Ceremonial" was produced by Pierre-Alain Jolivet in 1969, and the American film rights to "The Garden of Delights" were sold to Audubon Films in 1971.

AVOCATIONAL INTERESTS: Painting.

BIOGRAPHICAL/CRITICAL SOURCES: Genevieve Serreau, preface to *Theatre,* Volume II, Julliard, 1961; *Les Lettres Nouvelles,* November, 1958 (translated in *Evergreen Review,* November-Decmber, 1969); *Evergreen Review,* November-December, 1960, October, 1969; *New Yorker,* November 25, 1961, April 15, 1967, January 20, 1968, November 29, 1969, October 30, 1971; *Commonweal,* December 8, 1961; *Yale French Studies,* spring-summer, 1962; *Saturday Review,* April 23, 1966, May 6, 1967; *Village Voice,* May 18, 1967; *Le Table Ronde,* May, 1967; *Drama Review,* fall, 1968; *New York Times,* September 22, 1968, August 9, 1970, May 10, 1972; Alain Schifres, *Entretiens avec Arrabal,* P. Belfond, 1969; Bernard Gille, *Fernando Arrabal,* Seghers, 1970; *Vogue,* March 15, 1970; *Books Abroad,* spring, 1970, summer, 1970; *Nation,* November 29, 1971; *America,* June 10, 1972; *New Republic,* June 24, 1972.†

*   *   *

ARROWSMITH, William Ayres 1924-

PERSONAL: Born April 13, 1924, in Orange, N.J.; son of William Weed and Dorothy (Ayres) Arrowsmith; married Jean Reiser, January 10, 1945; children: Nancy, Beth. *Education:* Princeton University, B.A., 1947, Ph.D., 1954; Oxford University, B.A., 1951, M.A., 1958. *Politics:* Liberal Democrat. *Home and office address:* R.D. 1, Bristol, Vt. 05443.

CAREER: Princeton University, Princeton, N.J., instructor in classics, 1951-53; Wesleyan University, Middletown, Conn., instructor in classics and humanities, 1953-54; University of California, Riverside, assistant professor of classics and humanities, 1954-56; University of Texas, Austin, associate professor, 1958-59, professor of classics, 1959-70, university professor of arts and letters, 1966-70; educational consultant and professor-at-large, 1970—. Honor professor, University of Michigan, summer, 1962; faculty member, Bread Loaf School of English, summers, 1964-67; visiting professor of humanities, Massachusetts

Institute of Technology, 1971. Consultant, Ford Foundation, 1970-71, Leadership Training Institute, 1970-71. *Military service:* U.S. Army, Military Intelligence (Japanese), 1943-46. *Member:* P.E.N., National Humanities Faculty, Center for Advanced Studies (fellow), Battelle Memorial Center (fellow). *Awards, honors:* Woodrow Wilson fellowship, 1947-48; Rhodes Scholar, 1948-51; Prix de Rome research fellowship, 1956-57; Guggenheim fellow, 1957-58; Phi Beta Kappa visiting scholar, 1964-65; Longview Award for criticism, 1961; Morris L. Ernst Award for excellence in teaching, 1962; Piper Professor, 1966, for "outstanding academic achievement"; LL.D., Loyola University (Chicago), 1968; D.Lit. Hum., St. Michael's College, 1968; D.Litt., Westminster College, 1969, Dartmouth College, 1970.

WRITINGS: (Translator) Petronius, *The Satyricon,* University of Michigan Press, 1959; (translator) Homer, *Thetis and Achilles,* privately printed, 1959; (contributing translator) *The Complete Greek Tragedies,* University of Chicago Press, 1960; (editor) *The Image of Italy,* University of Texas Press, 1961; (translator) Aristophanes, *The Birds,* University of Michigan Press, 1961; (editor with Robert Shattuck) *The Craft and Context of Translation: A Critical Symposium,* University of Texas Press, 1961; (translator) Aristophanes, *The Clouds,* University of Michigan Press, 1962; (editor and translator) *Six Modern Italian Novellas,* Pocket Books, 1964; (translator with D.S. Carne Ross) Cesare Pavese, *Dialogues with Leuco,* University of Michigan Press, 1965; (editor, and translator with Douglas Parker) Aristophanes, *Three Comedies,* University of Michigan Press, 1969; (editor) Aristophanes, *Four Comedies,* University of Michigan Press, 1969. Founding editor, *Chimera,* 1942-44; editor, *Hudson Review,* 1948-60, *Arion,* 1962—, *Delos,* 1967-69; advisory editor, *Mosaic,* 1968—.

WORK IN PROGRESS: Editing *The Complete Greek Tragedies,* for Atheneum; a translation of Nietzsche's *Wir Philologen;* a collection of educational essays entitled *The Future of Teaching;* editing, with commentary, a collection of American Indian speeches and interviews, for Knopf.

SIDELIGHTS: Arrowsmith is competent in Greek, Latin, Italian, and has some competence in French and German. *Avocational interests:* Walking in Vermont and exploring Greece and Southern Italy.

*   *   *

ARTHOS, John 1908-

PERSONAL: Born July 18, 1908, in Wilmington, Del.; son of James (a businessman) and Norma (Bennett) Arthos; married Martha Ennen, July 3, 1924; children: Lydie, John, James, Maria, Martha. *Education:* Dartmouth College, A.B., 1930; Harvard University, M.A., 1933, Ph.D., 1937. *Office:* 2636 Haven Hall, Ann Arbor, Mich. 48104.

CAREER: University of Michigan, Ann Arbor, instructor, 1938-42, assistant professor, 1942-48, associate professor, 1948-54, professor of English, 1954—. Fulbright research professor at University of Florence, 1949-50; visiting professor at University of Washington, summer, 1963; research professor, University of Rome. University chairman of Ann Arbor Community Fund; member of Mayor's Committee for the Preservation of Ann Arbor. *Military service:* U.S. Army, 1942-45; became sergeant; awarded Bronze Star. *Member:* Modern Language Association of America, Renaissance Society of America, Michigan Academy of Science, Arts, and Letters. *Awards, honors:* Sheldon Traveling fellowship, 1937-38; Guggenheim fellowship, 1956-57; American Council of Learned Societies fellowship, 1963-64.

WRITINGS: *Minturno to the Appenines*, U.S. Army, 1945; *The Language of Natural Description in Eighteenth Century Poetry*, University of Michigan Press, 1949; *On a Mask Presented at Ludlow Castle*, University of Michigan Press, 1954; *On the Poetry of Spenser and the Form of Romances*, Allen & Unwin, 1956; *Dante, Michelangelo and Milton*, Humanities, 1963; *The Art of Shakespeare*, Barnes & Noble, 1964; (editor) Shakespeare, *Love's Labor's Lost*, New American Library, 1965; (editor with R.C. Flanagan) *The Life of Adam by G.B. Loredane*, Scholars' Facsimiles, 1967; (contributor) C.A. Patrides, editor, *Approaches to Paradise Lost: The York Tercetary Lectures*, Edward Arnold, 1968; *Milton and the Italian Cities*, Barnes & Noble, 1968; (editor) *Selected Poetry of John Dryden*, New American Library, 1970; *Shakespeare: The Early Writing*, Rowman & Littlefield, 1972. Contributor to *Atlantic, Essays in Criticism, Shakespeare Quarterly, Isis, Anglia, American Literature*, and other periodicals. Advisory editor, *Studies in English Literature*.

WORK IN PROGRESS: A book on Keats, Leopardi, and Hugh; a book on Shakespeare and Petrarch.

SIDELIGHTS: Arthos has lived in Italy and has traveled widely in the Mediterranean. He is interested in the literature of travel in Italy and Greece.

BIOGRAPHICAL/CRITICAL SOURCES: *Times Literary Supplement*, July 25, 1968.

* * *

ARTHUR, Ruth M(abel) 1905-

PERSONAL: Born May 26, 1905, in Glasgow, Scotland; daughter of Allan (an electrical contractor) and Ruth M. (Johnston) Arthur; married Frederick N. Huggins (a lawyer), September 2, 1932; children: two sons, four daughters. *Education:* Froebel Training College, diploma, 1926. *Religion:* Church of Scotland. *Home:* 46 Victoria Ave., Seranage, Dorsetshire, England. *Agent:* Curtis Brown Ltd., 60 East 56th St., New York, N.Y. 10022; and Curtis Brown Ltd., 73 King St., Covent Garden, London WC2E 8HU, England.

CAREER: Kindergarten teacher in Glasgow, Scotland, 1927-30, in Loughton, Essex, England, 1930-32; writer of stories for children and novels for teen-agers. *Member:* Society of Authors, National Book League, Children's Writers Group.

WRITINGS: *Carolina's Holiday*, Harrap, 1956; *The Daisy Cow*, Harrap, 1957; *Carolina's Golden Bird*, Harrap, 1958; *A Cottage for Rosemary*, Harrap, 1959; *Carolina and Roberto*, Harrap, 1960; *Dragon Summer*, Hutchinson, 1962, Atheneum, 1963; *Carolina and the Sea Horse, and Other Stories*, Harrap, 1963; *My Daughter, Nicola*, Atheneum, 1965; *A Candle in Her Room*, Atheneum, 1966; *Requiem for a Princess*, Atheneum, 1967; *Portrait of Margarita*, Atheneum, 1968; *The Whistling Boy*, Atheneum, 1969; *The Saracen Lamp*, Atheneum, 1970; *The Little Dark Thorn*, Atheneum, 1971.

AVOCATIONAL INTERESTS: Theatre, music, cooking, country living, and travel, especially in Italy and the Swiss Alps.

BIOGRAPHICAL/CRITICAL SOURCES: *Young Readers' Review*, May, 1966, June, 1968; *Christian Science Monitor*, August 3, 1967, July 17, 1969; *Times Literary Supplement*, October 16, 1969, July 20, 1970; *Library Journal*, October 15, 1970.

* * *

ASH, David W(ilfred) 1923-

PERSONAL: Born June 6, 1923, in Des Moines, Iowa; son of James Wesley (a contractor) and Carrie (Way) Ash; married Martha Peters, August 19, 1945; children: Sheryl Elizabeth, Robert Wesley, Richard David, Susan Louise. *Education:* University of Iowa, student, 1941-42; Simpson College, Indianola, Iowa, A.B., 1945; Garrett Theological Seminary, B.D., 1948. *Politics:* Democrat. *Home:* 206 Fifth Ave., Decorah, Iowa 52101. *Office:* First Methodist Church, Court and West Broadway, Decorah, Iowa 52101.

CAREER: Ordained elder in Methodist Church, 1948; associate minister in Ames, Iowa, 1948-50, minister in Minburn, Iowa, 1950-53, Nevada, Iowa, 1953-58, Clarinda, Iowa, 1958-62; Willard Street Methodist Church, Ottumwa, Iowa, minister, 1962-70; First Methodist Church, Decorah, Iowa, minister, 1970—. Iowa Conference of Methodist Church, director of youth work, 1948-60, district director of general church work, 1962-70; certified laboratory school leader. *Member:* Masons.

WRITINGS—With wife, Martha Ash: *Being Christian in Your Personal Life*, Cokesbury, 1952; *Junior Highs and the M.Y.F.*, Cokesbury, 1953, revised edition, 1963. Writer of teaching helps for junior high church workers, 1946—. Contributor to denominational magazines.

* * *

ASHCRAFT, Allan Coleman 1928-

PERSONAL: Born August 19, 1928, in San Antonio, Tex.; son of Allan C. and Vivian (Martindale) Ashcraft; married Nena A. Harris (a pediatrician), September 6, 1958; children: Ann, Allan III. *Education:* Texas A. & M. University, B.A., 1950; Columbia University, M.A., 1951, Ph.D., 1960. *Religion:* Protestant. *Home:* 201 Elm St., Bryan, Tex. 77801. *Office:* History Department, Texas A. & M. University, College Station, Tex. 77840.

CAREER: Texas A & M. University, College Station, assistant professor, 1956-64, associate professor of history, 1964—. Texas Civil War Centennial Advisory Committee, member of executive committee. *Military service:* U.S. Air Force, 1946-47; U.S. Army, 1951-53; became lieutenant; received Bronze Star. U.S. Army Reserve; currently major. *Member:* Southern Historical Association, Reserve Officers Association, Phi Kappa Phi. *Awards, honors:* Award of Merit from Texas State Civil War Centennial Committee for *Texas and the Civil War;* Standard Oil Foundation award, 1966-67, for distinguished teaching; Gamma Sigma Delta award of merit for teaching, 1968.

WRITINGS: *Texas and the Civil War: A Resume History*, Texas Historical Survey Committee, 1962. Contributor of articles to *Texas Military History*, and to other military and state historical journals.

WORK IN PROGRESS: *History of the Confederate Department of the Trans-Mississippi West in the Civil War*.

* * *

ASINOF, Eliot 1919-

PERSONAL: Surname is pronounced *Ace*-in-of; born July 13, 1919, in New York, N.Y.; son of Max and Rose (Tager) Asinof; married Jocelyn Brando (an actress), April 11, 1950 (divorced); children: Martin. *Education:* Swarthmore College, A.B., 1940. *Home:* 255 West End Ave., New York, N.Y. 10023.

CAREER: Professional baseball player with minor league teams owned by Philadelphia Phillies, 1939-41; salesman in men's clothing business in eastern U.S., 1947-50; free-lance writer, 1950—. *Military service:* U.S. Army Air Forces, 1942-46; became first lieutenant.

WRITINGS: *Man on Spikes*, McGraw, 1955; *Eight Men Out: The Black Sox and the 1919 World Series*, Holt, 1963; *The Bedfellow*, Simon & Schuster, 1968; *Seven Days to Sunday: Crisis Week with the New York Foot-*

ball Giants, Simon & Schuster, 1968; *The Name of the Game is Murder: An Inner Sanctum Mystery,* Simon & Schuster; 1968; *People Versus Blutcher: Black Men and White Law in Bedford-Stuyvesant,* Viking, 1970, revised edition, Ace Books, 1971; *Craig and Joan: Two Lives for Peace,* Viking, 1971. Writer of television dramas and documentaries, motion picture scripts, and magazine articles.

WORK IN PROGRESS: A novel.

SIDELIGHTS: In a review of *People Versus Blutcher,* John Leonard states that Asinof "doesn't merely assert the innocence of Laurence Blutcher; he creates a world in which that innocence is as necessary as weather or darkness. He reduces the whole heave, moan, fat and statistical overkill of sociology to one individual, particularizing the victim so skillfully that he becomes one's relative, one's brother."

BIOGRAPHICAL/CRITICAL SOURCES: New York Times Book Review, January 26, 1969; *New York,* June 29, 1970; *New York Times,* July 30, 1970; *Washington Post,* September 14, 1970; *New York Review of Books,* November 5, 1970; *Variety,* April 28, 1971.

*   *   *

ATKINS, John (Alfred) 1916-

PERSONAL: Born May 26, 1916, in Carshalton, Surrey, England; son of Frank Periam (a broker) and Bertha (Lovell) Atkins; married Dorothy Grey. *Education:* University of Bristol, B.A. (honors), 1938. *Politics:* Liberal Socialist. *Religion:* Agnostic. *Home:* Mill Lane, Birch Green, Colchester, Essex, England. *Agent:* David Higham Associates Ltd., 5-8 Lower John St., London W1R 4HA, England. *Office:* Zaklad Filologii Angielskiej, Universytet Lodzki, Jaracza 43, Lodz, Poland.

CAREER: Mass Observation, London, England, interviewer, 1939-41; *Tribune,* London, literary editor, 1942-44; Workers' Educational Association, Bristol, England, district organizer, 1948-51; Sudan Government, Ministry of Education, Khartoum, teacher, 1951-55, 1958-68; University of Lodz, Lodz, Poland, teacher, 1970—. Rural District Councilor, Dorchester, 1950. *Military service:* Royal Artillery, 1944-46. *Member:* P.E.N. International, Society of Authors.

WRITINGS: Cat on Hot Bricks (novel), Macdonald & Co., 1948; *The Art of Ernest Hemingway: His Works and His Personality,* Nevill, 1952, reissued with new introduction, Spring Books, 1964; *George Orwell: A Literary and Biographical Study,* J. Calder, 1953, Ungar, 1965, new edition, J. Calder, 1971; *Arthur Koestler,* Spearman, 1954; *Rain and the River* (novel), Putnam, 1954; *Aldous Huxley: A Literary Study,* J. Calder, 1955, Ungar, 1965, revised edition, J. Calder, 1967, Orion Press, 1968; *Tomorrow Revealed,* Spearman, 1955; *Graham Greene,* J. Calder, 1956, revised edition, 1966, Humanities, 1967; (with J.B. Pick) *A Land Fit for Eros* (novel), Arco, 1956; (contributor) R.O. Evans, editor, *Graham Greene: Some Critical Considerations,* University Press of Kentucky, 1963; *Sex in Literature: The Erotic Impulse,* Calder & Boyars, 1970; *Nine Novelists in Search of Society,* Calder & Boyars, 1971. Contributor to *Penguin New Writing* and other collections, and to *Adelphi, Life and Letters Today,* and other periodicals. Compiler of weekly radio magazine in English for European service of Radio Omdurman.

WORK IN PROGRESS: Sex in Literature: The Classical Experience, for Calder & Boyars.

BIOGRAPHICAL/CRITICAL SOURCES: Book World, July 14, 1968; *Christian Science Monitor,* July 18, 1968; *Virginia Quarterly Review,* spring, 1969.

AUDEN, W(ystan) H(ugh) 1907-1973

PERSONAL: Born February 21, 1907, in York, England; came to the United States, 1939, became U.S. citizen, April, 1946; son of George Augustus (a medical officer) and Constance Rosalie (a nurse; maiden name, Bicknell) Auden; married Erica Mann (a writer; daughter of Thomas Mann), 1935, in order to provide her with a British passport, later divorced. *Education:* Attended Gresham's School, Holt; Christ Church, Oxford, 1925-28, went up as Exhibitioner. *Religion:* Episcopal. *Home:* All Souls College, Oxford University, Oxford, England, and No. 6 Hinterholz, Kirschstetten, St. Poelten, Austria. *Agent:* Curtis Brown Ltd., 347 Madison Ave., New York, N.Y. 10017.

CAREER: Larchfield Academy, Helensburgh, Scotland, and Downs School, Colwall, near Malvern, England, schoolmaster, 1930-35; with Rupert Doone, Robert Medley, and others, founded the Group Theatre, 1932; worked with General Post Office film unit, 1935, collaborating on such films as "Night Mail" and "Coal-Face"; made trip to Iceland with Louis MacNeice, 1936; went to Spain as stretcher-bearer for Loyalists during Spanish Revolution, 1937; made trip to China with Christopher Isherwood, 1938; taught at St. Mark's School, Southborough, Mass., 1939-40; faculty member of American Writers League Writers School, 1939; taught at New School for Social Research, 1940-41, 1946-47; faculty member, University of Michigan, 1941-42, Swarthmore College, 1942-45, Bryn Mawr College, 1943-45, Bennington College, 1946, Barnard College, 1947; with Lionel Trilling and Jacques Barzun, founded The Reader's Subscription Book Club, 1951, associated with Club until 1959, wrote occasionally for its publication, *The Griffin,* 1951-58; Smith College, Northampton, Mass., W.A. Neilson Research Professor, 1953; Oxford University, Oxford, England, professor of poetry, 1956-61; with Jacques Barzun and Lionel Trilling, established the Mid-Century Book Society, 1959, wrote occasionally for its periodical, *The Mid-Century,* 1959-63.

MEMBER: American Academy of Arts and Letters, 1954-73. *Awards, honors:* King's Gold Medal for poetry, 1937; Guggenheim fellowships, 1942, 1945; Award of Merit Medal, American Academy of Arts and Letters, 1945; Pulitzer Prize in Poetry, 1948, for *The Age of Anxiety;* Bollingen Prize in Poetry, 1954; National Book Award, 1956, for *The Shield of Achilles;* Feltrinelli Prize (Rome), 1957; Alexander Droutzkoy Memorial Award, 1959; shared Guiness Poetry Award (Ireland) with Robert Lowell and Edith Sitwell, 1959; honored on Chicago Poetry Day, 1960; Honorary Student (Fellow), Christ College, Oxford, 1962-73; Austrian State Prize for European Literature, 1966; National Medal for Literature of National Book Committee, 1967, for total contributions to literature; Gold Medal of National Institute of Arts and Letters, 1968.

WRITINGS—Poems: Poems, hand printed by Stephen Spender, Oxford, 1928, Faber, 1930, 2nd edition, 1933, Random House, 1934, revised edition, Faber, 1960, revised, with new foreword by Stephen Spender, for Elliston Poetry Foundation of University of Cincinnati, 1965; *The Orators: An English Study* (poems and prose), Faber, 1932, revised edition, with new forward, Random House, 1967; *Look, Stranger!,* Faber, 1936 published in America as *On This Island,* Random House, 1937; *Spain,* Faber, 1937; (with Louis MacNeice) *Letters From Iceland,* Random House 1937, revised edition, 1969; *Selected Poems,* Faber, 1938; (with Christopher Isherwood) *Journey to a War,* Random House, 1939; *Another Time,* Random House, 1940; *Some Poems,* Random House, 1940; *Three Songs for St. Cecilia's Day,* privately printed, 1941; *The Double Man,* Random House, 1941 (published in England as *New Year Letter,* Faber, 1941); *For the*

Time Being, Random House, 1944, Faber, 1958; The Collected Poetry of W.H. Auden, Random House, 1945; The Age of Anxiety: A Baroque Eclogue, (performed Off-Broadway at the Attic Theatre, New York, March 18, 1954, Random House, 1947; Collected Shorter Poems, 1930-1944, Faber, 1950; Nones, Random House, 1951; Mountains, Faber, 1954; The Shield of Achilles, Random House, 1955; The Old Man's Road, Voyages Press, 1956; A Gobble Poem ("snatched from the notebooks of W.H. Auden, and now believed to be in the Morgan Library"), [London], 1957; Selected Poetry, Modern Library, 1959, 2nd edition, Vintage, 1971; Homage to Clio, Random House, 1960; W.H. Auden, A Selection, with notes and critical essay by Richard Hoggart, Hutchinson, 1961; About the House, Random House, 1965; The Platonic Blow, [New York], 1965; Collected Shorter Poems, 1927-1957, Faber, 1966, Random House, 1967; Portraits, Apiary Press, 1966; Marginalia, Ibex Press, 1966; Selected Poems, Faber, 1968; Two Songs, Phoenix Book Shop, 1968; Collected Longer Poems, Faber, 1968, Random House, 1969; City Without Walls and Other Poems, Random House, 1969; Academic Graffiti, Faber, 1971, Random House, 1972; (with Leif Sjoeberg) Selected Poems, Pantheon, 1972; Epistle to a Godson and Other Poems, Random House, 1972.

Personal recollections: A Certain World: A Commonplace Book (an annotated personal anthology, ". . . a sort of autobiography."), Viking, 1970.

Drama: The Dance of Death, Faber, 1933, 2nd edition, 1935; (with Isherwood) The Dog Beneath the Skin; or, Where is Francis?, Faber, 1935 (also see below); (with Isherwood) A Tragedy in Two Acts: The Ascent of F6, Faber, 1936, 2nd edition, 1957 published in America as The Ascent of F6, Random House, 1937, 2nd edition, 1956 (also see below); (with Isherwood) On the Frontier, A Melodrama in Three Acts, Random House, 1938 (previous two plays appeared in one volume, The Ascent of F6, and On the Frontier, Faber, 1958); (with Isherwood) Two Great Plays (The Dog Beneath the Skin and The Ascent of F6), Random House, 1959. Also author of "The Dark Valley," original radio play, with songs by Benjamin Britten, performed by CBS-Radio, New York, in 1940, at the time of the fall of France (all original material reported lost and untraceable), and commentary for "Runner," a film produced by the National Film Board of Canada.

Critical and expository prose: (With T.C. Worley) Education, Today and Tomorrow, Hogarth, 1939; Address on Henry James (booklet), [New York], 1947; The Enchafed Flood: The Romantic Iconography of the Sea, Random House, 1950; Making, Knowing and Judging, Clarendon Press, 1956; The Dyer's Hand, and Other Essays (criticism), Random House, 1962; Louis MacNeice (memorial address), Faber, 1963; Shakespeare, Fuenf Aufsaetze, [Frankfurt am Main], 1964; Secondary Worlds (T.S. Eliot Memorial Lectures at University of Kent, 1967), Faber, 1968, Random House, 1969; Forewords and Afterwords, Random House, 1973.

Editor: (With Charles Plumb) Oxford Poetry, 1926, Basil Blackwell, 1926; (with C. Day Lewis) Oxford Poetry, 1927, Appleton, 1927; (with John Garrett) The Poet's Tongue, G. Bell, 1935; (with Arthur Elton) "The March of Time" series, number I, Mechanics, Longmans, Green, 1936; (with introduction) Oxford Book of Light Verse, Oxford University Press, 1938; (with introduction) A Selection of the Poems of Alfred Lord Tennyson; Doubleday, 1944; Tennyson, Selections From Poems, Phoenix House, 1946; (with introduction) Henry James, American Scene, Scribner, 1946; (with introduction) John Betjeman, Slick But Not Streamlined, Doubleday, 1947; (with introduction) The Portable Greek Reader, Viking, 1948; (with introduction) Edgar Allan Poe, Selected

Prose and Poetry, Rinehart, 1950, revised edition, 1957; (with Norman Holmes Pearson) "Poets of the English Language," Volume I, Medieval and Renaissance Poets; Langland to Spenser, Volume II, Elizabethan and Jacobean Poets; Marlowe to Marvell, Volume III, Restoration and Augustan Poets; Milton to Goldsmith, Volume IV, Romantic Poets; Blake to Poe, Volume V, Victorian and Edwardian Poets; Tennyson to Yeats, Viking, 1950; (with introduction) The Living Thoughts of Keirkegaard, McKay, 1952; (with introduction) Kierkegaard, Cassell, 1955; (with Chester Kallman and Noah Greenberg) An Elizabethan Song Book: Lute Songs, Madrigals, and Rounds, Doubleday, 1956 reissued as An Anthology of Elizabethan Lute Songs, Madrigals & Rounds, Norton, 1970; (with introduction) Selected Writings of Sydney Smith, Farrar, Straus, 1956; (with introduction) The Criterion Book of Modern American Verse, Criterion, 1956 (published in England as The Faber Book of Modern American Verse, Faber, 1956); Van Gogh, A Self Portrait (selected letters), New York Graphic Society, 1961; Joseph Jacobs, The Pied Piper, and Other Fairy Tales, Macmillan, 1963; (with Louis Kronenberger) The Viking Book of Aphorisms, Viking, 1963 (published in England as The Faber Book of Aphorisms, Faber, 1964); Walter de la Mare, A Choice of de la Mare's Verse, Faber, 1963; Selected Poems of Louis MacNeice, Faber, 1964; (with introduction) Nineteenth Century British Minor Poets, Dial, 1966 (published in England as Nineteenth Century Minor Poets, Faber, 1967); (with John Lawlor) To Nevill Coghill From Friends, Faber, 1966; Selected Poetry and Prose of George Gordon Lord Byron, New American Library, 1966; Louis MacNeice, Persons From Porlock and Other Plays for Radio, BBC Publications, 1969; G.K. Chesterton: A Selection From His Non-Fictional Prose, Faber, 1970. Editor and author of foreword, "Yale Series of Younger Poets," 1947 through 1959; also editor, with others, of "The Looking Glass Library," a series of children's books.

Contributor: Clifton Fadiman, editor, I Believe, Simon & Schuster, 1939, revised edition, G. Allen, 1941; Donald A. Stauffer, editor, The Intent of the Critic, Princeton University Press, 1941; Poets at Works, Harcourt, 1948; Marvin Halvorsen, editor, Religious Drama, Peter Smith, Volume I, 1957; Igor Stravinsky, Memories and Commentaries (letters), Faber, 1960; Raymond Mortimer, compiler, The Seven Deadly Sins, Sunday Times Publications, 1962; Norman Davis and C.C. Wrenn, editors, English and Medieval Studies, (tribute to J.R.R. Tolkien), Allen & Unwin, 1962; A.Ostroff, editor, The Contemporary Poet as Artist and Critic, Little, Brown, 1964; Eric W. White, editor, Poems by W.H. Auden and Others, Poetry Book Society, 1966; C.B. Cox and A.E. Dyson, editors, Word in the Desert, Oxford University Press, 1968; G.F. Kennan, editor, Democracy and the Student Left, Little, Brown, 1968.

Author of introduction or afterword: (With others) Robert Frost, Selected Poems of Robert Frost, Cape, 1936; Baudelaire, Intimate Journals, Methuen, 1949; Charles Williams, The Descent of the Dove, Meridian Books, 1956; Iwan Goll, Jean Sans Terre, Yoseloff, 1958; Francis Fergusson, editor, Romeo and Juliet, Dell, 1958; Phyllis McGinley, Times Three: Selected Poems from Three Decades, Viking, 1960; Henrik Ibsen, Brand, Anchor, 1960; Konstantinos P. Kabaphes, The Complete Poems of Cavafy, Harcourt, 1961; M.F.K. Fisher, The Art of Eating, Faber, 1963; William Burto, editor, Shakespeare: The Sonnets, New American Library, 1964; Anne Fremantle, editor, The Protestant Mystics, Little, Brown, 1964; Oscar Wilde, De Profundis and The Ballad of Reading Gaol, Avon, 1964; B.C. Bloomfield, W.H. Auden: A Bibliography, University Press of Virginia, 1964; Sister Mary Immaculate, The Tree and the Master:

An Anthology of Literature on the Cross of Christ, Random House, 1965; V.S. Yanovsky, *No Man's Time,* Weybright & Talley, 1967; George MacDonald, *The Golden Key,* Farrar, Strauss, 1967; G. Handley-Taylor and T.d'A. Smith, compilers, *Cecil Day Lewis, The Poet Laureate,* St. James Press, 1968; Eugen Rosenblock-Huessy, *I Am an Impure Thinker,* Argo Books, 1970.

Translator: Ernest Toller, *No More Peace* (lyrics), Farrar & Rinehart, 1937; (with others) *Adam Mickiewicz, 1798-1855: Selected Poems,* Noonday Press, 1956; (with Kallman) Mozart, *The Magic Flute* (libretto), Random House, 1956; Jean Cocteau, *The Knights of the Round Table,* 1957; (with others) Bertolt Brecht, "The Caucasian Chalk Circle," in *Bertolt Brecht Plays,* Volume I, Methuen, 1960; St. John Perse (pseudonym of Alexis Saint-Leger Leger), *On Poetry,* Pantheon, 1961, also published in *Two Addresses* (see below); (with Elizabeth Mayer) Goethe, *Italian Journey,* Pantheon, 1962; (with others) Mozart, *Great Operas of Mozart,* Grossett, 1962; (with Leif Sjoeberg, and author of foreword) Dag Hammarskjoeld, *Markings,* Knopf, 1964; St. John Perse, *Two Addresses,* Pantheon, 1966; (with others, and author of foreword) Andrei Voznesenski, *Antiworlds,* Basic Books, 1966, bilingual edition, including additional Voznesenski work, published as *Antiworlds, and the Fifth Ace,* 1967; (with Paul Beekman Taylor) *Voeluspa: The Song of the Sybil,* Windhover Press, 1968; (with Taylor) *The Elder Edda: A Selection,* Random House, 1969; St. John Perse, *Collected Poems,* Princeton University Press, 1971.

Librettos and lyrics: *Our Hunting Fathers,* music by Benjamin Britten, Boosey & Hawkes, 1936; *Fish in the Unruffled Lakes,* music by Britten, Boosey & Hawkes, 1937; *On This Island,* music by Britten, Boosey & Hawkes, 1937; *Night Mail,* 1937; *Two Ballads,* Boosey & Hawkes, 1937; *Now Through the Night's Caressing Grip,* music by Britten, Boosey & Hawkes, 1938; *Ballad of Heroes,* music by Britten, Boosey & Hawkes, 1939; *Hymn to St. Cecilia for S.S.A.T.B.,* music by Britten, Boosey & Hawkes, 1942; *For the Time Being: A Christmas Oratorio,* music by Marvin David Levy, [New York], 1944 (first performed at Carnegie Hall, New York, December 7, 1959); (with Kallman) *The Rake's Progress,* by Igor Stravinski, Boosey & Hawkes, 1951; (with Noah Greenberg) *The Play of Daniel: A Thirteenth Century Musical Drama,* Oxford University Press, 1959; *Five Poems,* music by Lennox Berkeley, J.&W. Chester, 1960 (performed in New York, March, 1959); (with Kallman) *Elegy for Young Lovers,* music by Hans Werner Henze, Schott (Mainz), 1961; *The Twelve: Anthem for the Feast Day of Any Apostle,* music by Sir William Walton, Oxford University Press, 1966; (with Kallman) *The Bassarids,* music by H. W. Henze (based on Euripides' "The Bacchae"; performed in German translation at Salzburg Festival, 1966; first performed in America by Sante Fe, New Mexico, Opera, August, 1968), Schott, 1966. Author of unpublished librettos, including "Paul Bunyan," for music by Benjamin Britten, performed at Columbia University, New York, 1941, John Webster's "The Duchess," on which he collaborated with Bertolt Brecht and H.R. Hays, performed in New York, 1946, and, with Kallman, "Delia, Or a Masque of Night" (appeared in *Botteghe Oscure,* 1953). With Kallman, translated the Brecht-Weill ballet cantata, "The Seven Deadly Sins," performed at New York City Center, 1959. With others, wrote text for "Time Cycle, for Soprano and Orchestra," performed by New York Philharmonic, directed by Leonard Bernstein, at Carnegie Hall, New York, October 21, 1960. With Kallman, wrote English version of Mozart's opera "Don Giovanni," performed on NBC-TV, 1961, published by G. Schirmer. With Kallman, adapted "Arcifanfano, King of Fools" for its first performance since 1778, held at Town Hall, New York, November, 1965. Composed narrative for "The Ballad of Barnaby," based on Anatole France's

version of "Our Lady's Juggler," for music written by students of Wykeham Rise School under the direction of Charles Turner, first performed at St. John's Episcopal Church, Washington, Conn., May, 1969. With Kallman, wrote libretto for adaptation of William Shakespeare's "Love's Labour Lost," for music by Nicholas Nabokov, first performed at 25th Edinburgh International Festival, Scotland, 1971.

Contributor to *Botteghe Oscure, Poetry, New Verse, New Republic, The Griffin, Trace, Listener, Times Literary Supplement, New Statesman, Mid-Century, Texas Quarterly, Nation, New York Times Book Review, Atlantic, Spectator, Kenyon Review, Reporter, Horn Book, New Yorker, Harper's, Mademoiselle, Partisan Review, Christian Scholar, Encounter, Vogue, Tulane Drama Review, Esquire, Delos, New York Review of Books, Quest,* and other publications.

WORK IN PROGRESS: La Gran Tenda Verde, with Chester Kallman.

SIDELIGHTS: Auden is, writes Monroe K. Spears, "more like Dryden ... than like most modern poets: he is a kind of maverick and extremely unofficial Anglo-American laureate, and, appropriately, writes much occasional verse. Like Dryden, he was much reproached for changes of faith and allegiance, and like him outmoded such reproaches by the tenacity and obvious sincerity of his convictions.... Auden, like Dryden, writes much for music.... If one superimposes on the figure of Dryden that of Lord Byron, to contribute audacity, rebelliousness, comic vigor and cosmopolitan sophistication; and then adds the spectre of Coleridge to bring in magic and the supernatural, an affinity with Germany and a concern for abstruse questions of aesthetics and theology, the composite image is close to Auden."

This intellectual maverick once lived in Birmingham, England, which left him with an interest in industrial centers such as Manchester, Detroit, and Pittsburgh, and with man in an urban environment. Four of his uncles and both of his grandfathers were Anglican ministers, and his fascination with the rites of the church is evident. His poetry is rooted in the tradition of English poetry—from Anglo-Saxon and Middle English verse, through Langland, Pope, Hopkins, and Eliot. He admires Dante, Yeats, German poetry (notably Rilke), German theater (especially Brecht), and German cabaret songs. The psychological aspects of his writings derive from Freud and Groddeck, through such writers as John Layard, Andre Gide, and D.H. Lawrence. During the Forties he came under the intellectual influence of Soren Kierkegaard and Reinhold Niebuhr.

He has said that he first began writing poetry in 1922, at the suggestion of a friend. During the Thirties his interests were social; he bemoaned, for example, Britain's becoming a nation of "aspirins and weak tea." A *Times Literary Supplement* writer recently said: "The Auden of those distant years [the 1930s] shows in the mind now as a kind of Yorkshire Shelley, outspoken, not notably introspective, with a keen eye for all that was old, mad, blind, despicable and, especially, dying in prewar England; but a man at the same time full of romantic self-concern and wild hope...." Before his arrival in the United States he attracted American literary revolutionaries "chiefly by his power of invention, which inspired others to make inventions of their own: to emulate rather than imitate," writes Malcolm Cowley. Moreover, he captured as perhaps no one else did the spirit of an age. Robert Lowell says of him: "He's made the period immortal, of waiting for the war. Auden's glory is that he caught all those things with much greater power than any of the people in his group."

The New Statesman has called him "the outstanding American poet of his generation. He thinks, and is intelligent, and chooses—but as one who distrusts the intellect, and who has analysed the docile imbecilities of the intellectuals. To all this should be added quite strong doses of pleasure in shocking, of wild buffoonery, of affectionate good nature, of deliberated virtue; and a liking for mystification and elaboration, combined with a hatred for significances that don't, according to given rules, 'work out'." Joseph Warren Beach believes that "when it comes to subject matter and thought, [Auden] has the ... distinction of being perhaps the most representative of poets in his time writing in the English language.... No poet of our time has covered more ground, or ground more favorable to the growth of speculations suited to the felt needs of the time. He is to poetry what Aldous Huxley is to prose."

In 1967, Chad Walsh assessed Auden's poetry as "the work of a craftsman.... At the service of a formidable and well-stocked mind.... He has the analytical power, the precision, the ability to break a question down into its elements, to find new ways of putting familiar things together. There is hardly an Auden poem that does not bespeak, and speak to, the brain at work.... He is the poet of conscience, of moral sensitivity. He has been peculiarly open to the horrors, the despairs, the tentative hopes of more than four decades; he has opened himself to them and they are in him and in his poetry, not in the raw, unprocessed outcries that make such a poetic mishmash of most civil rights and Vietnam poems, but in genuine poems that have truly gestated." In the same vein, in 1970, Daniel Hoffman writes: "Auden doesn't succumb to the imitative fallacy and gibber at the window because the house is on fire. If the times be mad, need the poet be irrational therefore? What Auden has perfected is the technical skill that embraces all states of feeling, all modes of thought, and renders them intelligible."

Recently, in reviewing *Epistle To a Godson*, Webster Schott said: "Auden even named the time for us. 'The Age of Anxiety,' he called it in 1948. Auden was our poet-seer, all that recently, as he had been for a decade earlier. Auden felt and said all the right things—the true things then—because he had been into or on the edge of the essential movements, experienced the large moral shocks crucial to his era. [Now] the world out there exists for Auden. But he will not participate.... Two or three earlier books ... took us into the narrower world Auden began inhabiting in the late 1950s. *Epistle* . . . slams the door shut." Victor Howes, however, does a different 'summing up,' and sees Auden as "more than just another writer. He is a classic in his time. From a distance he can be mistaken for a small institution. Over twenty of his books are in print. He is the subject of several book-length studies and scores of articles. His poetry is widely anthologized and frequently found in college textbooks. Graduate seminars are devoted to his work. It is almost enough to turn off the Now Generation forever. Which is too bad. For Auden has been to a lot of places the Now Generation has been and he has visited some of the stations where they have yet to arrive."

Auden believed that poetry was "a game of knowledge"; it consisted of playing with words and being bound by certain rules. Yet the game involved knowledge. "Poetry," wrote Auden, "is not magic. In so far as poetry or any of the arts, can be said to have an ulterior purpose, it is, by telling the truth, to disenchant and disintoxicate." The concern of the poet lies not in "personalities or psychology or progress or news—the extreme opposite of poetry is the daily paper. What moves him to write are his encounters with the sacred in nature, in human beings, nothing else." Poetry, moreover, has a moral function. In the introduction to *The Poet's Tongue*, 1935,

Auden wrote: "Poetry [is concerned] with extending our knowledge of good and evil, perhaps making the necessity for action more urgent and its nature more clear, but only leading us to the point where it is possible for us to make a rational and moral choice." Auden has affirmed that "Art is not enough." Art is, in fact, of two kinds: escape art, and parable art, the latter capable of teaching man to unlearn hatred and learn love.

Spears calls Auden "supreme among modern poets as a writer of songs." His particular passion was opera librettos, perhaps because, as Spears suggests, the librettist does not need to worry about probability. He can indulge in fantasy, Auden's avowed and continuing interest. He once said: "No good opera plot can be sensible for people do not sing when they are feeling sensible."

In *Letters From Iceland* Auden includes this autobiographical verse: "My head looks like an egg upon a plate; / My nose is not too bad, but isn't straight; / I have no proper eyebrows, and my eyes / Are far too close together to look nice. . . ." He was considered to be a gifted mimic and a born entertainer, capable of delightful impersonations which rivalled the charm of his light verse, and was reported to have written off-color poems for his friends. The *New Statesman* has described his personal life thus: "In New York Auden lives quietly, seeing a few friends, one of whom, until his death in the summer of 1971, was the theologian Reinhold Niebuhr.... His reading is mostly history: Merovingian, Roman, early British. He is also interested in geography, geology and mineralogy. His bedside reading is Tolkien, and Saintsbury's *History of English Literature*. He has a Siamese cat. The order of his poetry grows out of an untidiness in his rooms which must rival that of Beethoven." In 1971, Auden and the famed cellist and composer, Pablo Casals, collaborated on a hymn, the subject of which was world peace. In 1972, Auden left what the *Village Voice* described as "the hazards of the East Village for the tranquility of Oxford," where he settled into the quiet of a 'grace and favor' living.

Auden may be heard reading on the Caedmon recording, "W.H. Auden Reading His Poems," 1954, the Columbia recording, with New York Pro Musica Antiqua, "An Evening of Elizabethan Verse and Its Music," 1955, and the Spoken Arts recordings, "W.H. Auden Reads a Selection of His Poems," 1960, and "W.H. Auden," 1968.

Leonard Bernstein's "The Age of Anxiety, Symphony No. 2 for Piano and Orchestra" was inspired by Auden's collection of poetry.

BIOGRAPHICAL/CRITICAL SOURCES—Books: Francis Scarfe, *Auden and After*, Routledge, 1942; Richard Hoggart, *Auden: An Introductory Essay*, Yale University Press, 1951; James Albert Pike, editor, *Modern Canterbury Pilgrims*, Morehouse, 1956; Joseph Warren Beach, *The Making of the Auden Canon*, University of Minnesota Press, 1957; Edward Callan, *An Annotated Check List of the Works of W.H. Auden*, A. Swallow, 1958; Louis Untermeyer, *Lives of the Poets*, Simon & Schuster, 1959; Monroe K. Spears, *The Poetry of W.H. Auden: The Disenchanted Island*, Oxford University Press, 1963; B.C. Bloomfield, *W.H. Auden: A Bibliography*, University Press of Virginia, 1964; J.G. Blair, *The Poetic Art of W.H. Auden*, Princeton University Press, 1965; Herbert Greenberg, *Quest for the Necessary: W.H. Auden and the Dilemma of Divided Consciousness*, Harvard University Press, 1969; G. Nelson, *Changes of Heart: A Study of the Poetry of W.H. Auden*, University of California Press, 1969; J.M. Replogle, *Auden's Poetry*, Methuen, 1969, University of Washington Press, 1971; G.T.W. Wright, *W.H. Auden*, Twayne, 1969; G.W. Bahlke, *The Later Auden*, Rutgers University Press, 1970; J.D. Brophy, *W.H. Auden,* Columbia University Press, 1970; D. Davidson, *W.H. Auden,* Evans, 1970; J. Fuller, *A Raader's Guide to W.H. Auden,* Thames, 1970.

Articles: *New Statesman,* January 28, 1956, June 9, 1956, July 19, 1958, December 13, 1968, September 26, 1969; *New Republic,* April 23, 1956; *New Yorker,* August 4, 1956; *Philological Quarterly,* January, 1960; *Time,* May 3, 1960, January 26, 1970, July 6, 1970; *Twentieth Century,* September, 1960; *Poetry,* March, 1961; *London Magazine,* January, 1961, March, 1968, October, 1969; *Reporter,* January 31, 1963; *Times Literary Supplement,* June 7, 1963, January 23, 1969; *Atlantic,* August, 1966, July, 1967, May, 1970; *Listener,* March 17, 1966; *Virginia Quarterly Review,* spring, 1966, spring, 1969; *Shenandoah,* winter, 1967; *Book World,* November 19, 1967; *New York Times Book Review,* February 15, 1968, March 18, 1973; *Hudson Review,* spring, 1968; *Holiday,* June, 1969; *Punch,* October 1, 1969; *Christian Science Monitor,* January 8, 1970; *Commonweal,* November 27, 1970; *Comparative Literature,* spring, 1970; *Harper's,* April, 1970; *Life,* June 30, 1970; *Nation,* February 9, 1970; *New York Times,* January 24, 1970; *Observer,* June 28, 1970, May 2, 1971; *Twentieth Century Literature,* January, 1970; *Yale Review,* autumn, 1970; *Village Voice,* February 10, 1972; *Choice,* April, 1972; *Book World,* November, 26, 1972.

(Died, September 28, 1973)

*   *   *

AUER, J(ohn) Jeffery   1913-

PERSONAL: Born May 8, 1913, in Aurora, Ill.; son of John J. (an accountant) and Marie (Jeffery) Auer; married Eleanor R. Richmond, June 25, 1938; children: John J., Jane H., Judy R. *Education:* Wabash College, A.B., 1934; University of Wisconsin, M.A., 1935, Ph.D., 1947. *Politics:* Democrat. *Religion:* Unitarian. *Home:* 1105 Southdowns Dr., Bloomington, Ind. 47403. *Office:* Department of Speech and Theatre, Indiana University, Bloomington, Ind. 47405.

CAREER: Hanover College, Hanover, Ind., instructor in speech, 1935-37; Oberlin College, Oberlin, Ohio, chairman of department of speech, 1937-52; University of Virginia, Charlottesville, chairman of department of speech and drama, 1952-58; Indiana University, Bloomington, chairman of department of speech and theatre, 1958—. *Military service:* U.S. Naval Reserve, 1943-45; became lieutenant junior grade. *Member:* Speech Communication Association of America (president, 1965).

WRITINGS: (With Henry Lee Ewbank) *Discussion and Debate,* revised edition, Appleton, 1951; (with Ewbank) *Handbook for Discussion Leaders,* revised edition, Harper, 1954; *Essentials of Parliamentary Procedure,* 3rd edition, Appleton, 1959; *An Introduction to Research in Speech,* Harper, 1959; (editor) *Anti-Slavery and Disunion, 1858-1861: Studies in the Rhetoric of Compromise and Conflict,* Harper, 1963; (with Jon Eisenson and John V. Irwin) *The Psychology of Communication,* Appleton, 1963; *Speech Communication,* Appleton, 1967; (editor) *The Rhetoric of Our Times,* Appleton, 1969. *Speech Monographs,* editor, 1954-56, contributing editor, 1956—.

WORK IN PROGRESS: A college textbook on public speaking; a biography of Thomas Corwin; two volumes of essays on teaching speech in elementary and secondary schools.

*   *   *

AUERBACH, Marjorie (Hoffberg)

PERSONAL: Born in New York, N.Y.; daughter of Irving M. (an optometrist) and Martha (Baer) Hoffberg: married Leon Auerbach (an advertising art director),

June 27, 1954. *Education:* University of Wisconsin, B.S., 1952; attended Cooper Union, 1952-54; attended Art Students League. *Home:* 340 Riverside Dr., New York, N.Y. 10025.

CAREER: Esquire, New York, N.Y., designer, 1954-55; free-lance illustrator of book jackets, record album covers, textbooks, New York, N.Y., 1955—. *Member:* American Institute of Graphic Arts.

WRITINGS—Self-Illustrated: *Seven Uncles Come to Dinner,* Knopf, 1963; *King Lavra and the Barber,* Knopf, 1964.

Illustrator: Alejandro Arratia and C.D. Hamilton, editors, *Diez Cuentos Hispanoamericanos,* Oxford University Press, 1958; Helen Jill Fletcher, *The First Book of Bells,* F. Watts, 1959; Cathleen Schurr, *Cats Have Kittens, Do Gloves Have Mittens?,* Knopf, 1962; Elizabeth Jane Coatsworth, *The Place,* Holt, 1966; Betty Miles, *A Day of Autumn,* Knopf, 1967; Betty Miles, *A Day of Spring,* Knopf, 1970.

AVOCATIONAL INTERESTS: Travel and foreign films.†

*   *   *

AVERY, Gillian (Elise)   1926-

PERSONAL: Born September 30, 1926; daughter of Norman Bates (an estate agent) and Grace Elise (Dunn) Avery; married Anthony Oliver John Cockshut (a university lecturer and writer), August 25, 1952; children: Ursula Mary Elise. *Education:* Attended schools in England. *Religion:* Anglican. *Home:* 32 Charlbury Rd., Oxford, England.

CAREER: Writer.

WRITINGS: The Warden's Niece, Collins, 1957, Penguin, 1963; *Trespassers at Charlcote,* Collins, 1958; *James Without Thomas,* Collins, 1959; *The Elephant War,* Collins, 1960, Holt, 1971; *To Tame A Sister,* Collins, 1961, Van Nostrand, 1964; *Mrs. Ewing,* Bodley Head, 1961, Walck, 1964; *The Greatest Gresham,* Collins, 1962; *The Peacock House,* Collins, 1963; *The Italian Spring,* Collins, 1964, Holt, 1972; (with Angela Bull) *Nineteenth Century Children: Heroes and Heroines in English Children's Stories,* Hodder & Stoughton, 1965; *Call of the Valley,* Collins, 1966, Holt, 1968; (with others) *The Eleanor Farjeon Book,* Hamish Hamilton, 1966; (contributor) Caroline Hillier, editor, *Winter's Tales for Children No. 2,* Macmillan, 1966; (author of introduction) *The Life and Adventures of Lady Anne,* Gollancz, 1969; *Victorian People in Life and Literature,* Holt, 1970; (with others) *Authors' Choice: Stories,* Hamish Hamilton, 1970, Crowell, 1971; *A Likely Lad,* Holt, 1971; *Ellen's Birthday,* Hamish Hamilton, 1971; *Ellen and the Queen,* Hamish Hamilton, 1971; *Jemima and the Welsh Rabbit,* Hamish Hamilton, 1972; (with others) *Allsorts 5,* Macmillan, 1972; (with others) *Rudyard Kipling,* Weidenfeld & Nicolson, 1972.

Editor: *The Sapphire Treasury of Stories for Boys and Girls,* Gollancz, 1960; *In the Window-Seat: A Selection of Victorian Stories,* Oxford University Press, 1960, Van Nostrand, 1965; (and author of introduction) *Unforgettable Journeys,* F. Watts, 1965; *School Remembered: An Anthology for Young Adults,* Gollancz, 1967, Funk, 1968; *The Hole in the Wall, and Other Stories,* Oxford University Press, 1968; (and author of introduction) *Victoria-Bess, and Others,* Gollancz, 1968, published in America as *Victorian Doll Stories,* Schocken, 1969; *Red Letter Days,* Hamish Hamilton, 1971. Author of introductions to reissues of Victorian children's novels.

SIDELIGHTS: In a review of *Victorian People in Life and Literature,* Helen MacGregor writes: "Other books will no doubt be written about the period but I do not think there can be a better one than this. It is a book to buy and to keep, combining as it does erudition and entertainment. So wide is the author's range of reading, so well-balanced her comments, so lucid her writing that *Victorian People* combines the best points of an accurate social history, a guide to good reading, a fascinating picture book, and 'a good book to read.' "

BIOGRAPHICAL/CRITICAL SOURCES: *New Statesman,* November 3, 1967; *Young Readers' Review,* April, 1968; *Best Sellers,* April 1, 1968; December 15, 1971; *Books and Bookmen,* May, 1968, October, 1970; *Book World,* June 2, 1968; *Library Journal,* July, 1968; *New Yorker,* December 14, 1968.

*   *   *

AYRAULT, Evelyn West   1922-

PERSONAL: Surname is pronounced *A*-row; born March 3, 1922, in Buffalo, N.Y.; daughter of John (a military instructor) and Evelyn (West) Ayrault. *Education:* Columbia University, student, 1943; Florida State College for Women (now part of Florida State University), B.S., 1945; University of Chicago, M.A., 1947. *Politics:* Republican. *Religion:* Episcopalian. *Home and office:* 336 West Ninth St., Erie, Pa. 16502. *Agent:* Paul R. Reynolds & Son, 599 Fifth Ave., New York, N.Y. 10017.

CAREER: Certified to practice psychology in New York State, 1961, and in the State of Pennsylvania, 1969; Crippled Children School, Jamestown, N.D., chief psychologist and assistant principal, 1947-48; Special Education Department, Sharon Public School District, Sharon, Pa., psychologist and teacher, 1948-50; Medical College of Virginia, Richmond, chief psychologist and instructor in departments of physical medicine and physical therapy, 1950-52; United Cerebral Palsy Association, Miami, Fla., director of psychological services, 1952-54; in private practice as psychologist, lecturer and consultant to community health agencies and hospitals, New York, N.Y., 1955-68, in Erie, Pa., 1968—. *Member:* American Psychological Association, Council for Exceptional Children, New York State Psychological Association, Pennsylvania Psychological Association, Psi Chi.

WRITINGS: Take One Step (autobiography), Doubleday, 1963; *You Can Raise Your Handicapped Child,* preface by Margaret Mead, Putnam, 1964; *Helping the Handicapped Teenager Mature,* Association Press, 1971.

WORK IN PROGRESS: Psychological Habilitation of the Handicapped; research on the development of a tool to counsel nonspeaking persons with severe cerebral palsy.

SIDELIGHTS: Miss Ayrault has risen above a physical handicap (cerebral palsy) to live an independent life, earn a living, lecture, ride horseback, and type her own manuscripts. *Avocational interests:* The theatre, and reading biographies.

*   *   *

BACH, Richard David   1936-

PERSONAL: Born June 23, 1936, in Oak Park, Ill.; son of Roland R. (an American Red Cross chapter manager) and Ruth (Shaw) Bach; married Bette Jeanne Franks, October 15, 1957 (divorced, 1971); children: Kristel Louise, Robert Allen, Erica Lynn, James, Jonathan, Beth. *Education:* Attended Long Beach State College, one year. *Residence:* Bridgehampton, Long Island, New York. *Agent:* Kenneth Littauer, Littauer & Wilkinson, 500 Fifth Ave., New York, N.Y. 10036.

CAREER: U.S. Air Force, pilot, 1956-59, 1961-62, becoming captain; *Flying* (magazine), Beverly Hills, Calif., associate editor, 1961-64; now technical and free-lance writer.

WRITINGS: Stranger to the Ground, Harper, 1963; *Biplane,* prelude by Ray Bradbury, Harper, 1966; *Nothing by Chance: A Gypsy Pilot's Adventures in Modern America,* Morrow, 1969; *Jonathan Livingston Seagull,* Macmillan, 1970. Contributor of about one hundred articles, most of them about flying, to *Flying, Air Facts, Argosy, Holiday, Writer,* and other magazines.

WORK IN PROGRESS: Screenplay of *Jonathan Livingston Seagull;* a nonfiction book; a novel.

SIDELIGHTS: A direct descendant of Johann Sebastian Bach and a enthusiast of aviation (Bach once had his family car repossessed while he still owned an airplane), Richard Bach has said that *Jonathan Livingston Seagull* is the result of a vision. "I realized," he said in a *Life* interview, "that I was meant to write it all down, not just watch it." Midway through the writing of the book the vision disappeared, and was not to return for several years. Then, he reports, "this strange visionesque thing picked up just where it had left off. And there was the end of the story."

The enormous popularity of the book sometimes leads Bach to wish that he had written it under a pseudonym. He has been deluged with mail from readers wishing to know the underlying metaphysical philosophy behind the story of the seagull who deviates from the behavior of his flock. Paul S. Nathan mentions that "Buddhists ... say the story of the seagull who strives for perfection in flying, and progresses through different states of being in his quest, perfectly captures the spirit of Buddhism." A bishop denounced the book as being an example of the sin of pride. A group of reformed alcoholics use it for inspiration. Timothy Foote reports that "a columnist, dismissing the whole thing as 'half-baked fantasy,' offered its success as proof that America's brains are addled." Bach's own interpretation of the book: "Find out what you love to do, and do your darndest to make it happen." His close friend Ray Bradbury describes it as "a great Rorschach test. You read your own mystical principles into it." However, Bach still asserts that he is not really the author of the book, and any analysis on his part is supposition. "If I'd written the book myself," he says, "I could say what it meant. But I didn't so I can't."

As proof of that fact that he did not really write *Jonathan Livingston Seagull,* Bach points to the differences in style between it and his earlier books. Foote writes: "His normal style is highly personal and full of description. As a parable, *Jonathan* is little more than a narrative skeleton supporting a number of inspirational and philosophic assertions. Bach also points out that he disagrees entirely with Jonathan's decision to abandon the pursuit of private perfection in favor of returning to the dumb old Flock and encouraging its members toward higher wisdom. 'Self-sacrifice,' says Bach, 'is a word I cannot stand.' "

Foote describes Bach as a "big, slope-shouldered, rawwristed man, [who] wears a bushy mustache, a crinkly smile and a slightly bemused expression. He has a remarkable gift for saying tentatively, and with disarming humor, things that ought to sound pretentious or phony or both, but instead convince and captivate his listeners. The result is that after meeting Bach, even the veriest cynic is likely to find himself shamelessly rooting for *Jonathan Livingston Seagull* and curiously willing to forgive the book its literary trespasses."

Bach is now working on a plan to open a school that will combine flying and a graduate seminar for people who want to use aviation as, in Foote's words, "a gateway to joy and wisdom. Only Bach could think up such a thing," Foote concludes. "But if the track record means anything, it will probably become the most sought-after place of higher learning since applications to

Harvard and Yale began to sag. Whether his book raises tingles at the back of your neck or curdles your vichysoisse, it is hard not to believe that somebody up there loves Richard Bach. Maybe even the Great Gull himself."

BIOGRAPHICAL/CRITICAL SOURCES: Publishers Weekly, October 18, 1971; Life, March 3, 1972; Book World, April 23, 1972; Time, November 13, 1972.†

*   *   *

BAER, Eleanora A(gnes) 1907-

PERSONAL: Born December 22, 1907, in Springfield, Mo.; daughter of Oliver L. and Agnes (Robineau) Baer. Education: Attended St. Louis Library School, 1928-29; Fontbonne College, A.B., 1931; St. Louis University, M.Ed., 1944; attended Washington University, summer, 1954; University of Wisconsin, M.S. in L.S., 1961. Home: 1359 McCutcheon, Brentwood, Mo. 63144.

CAREER: St. Louis Public Library, St. Louis, Mo., library assistant, 1925-26; Fontbonne College, St. Louis, Mo., librarian 1929-46, instructor in education, summer, 1944; St. Louis University Library, St. Louis, Mo., assistant librarian 1946-52; University City Public Library, University City, Mo., part-time library assistant, 1952-60; Clayton High School, Clayton, Mo., librarian, 1953-67; Clayton (Mo.) School District, library coordinator, 1967—. Member: American Association of University Women, American Library Association, Catholic Library Association, National Education Association, Beta Phi Mu, Delta Epsilon Sigma.

WRITINGS: Titles in Series, (handbook for librarians and students), Scarecrow, volume 1, 1953, volume 2, 1957, volume 3, 1960, 2nd edition, two volumes, 1964, 1st supplement to 2nd edition, 1967, 2nd supplement to 2nd edition, 1970. Contributor to Journal of Higher Education, Journal of Educational Research, and Missouri Historical Review.

WORK IN PROGRESS: Preparing another supplement to Titles in Series.

*   *   *

BAER, Max Frank 1912-

PERSONAL: Born November 10, 1912, in Frankfurt, Germany; son of Bernard and Erna (Hoelzel) Baer. Education: Student at University of Notre Dame, 1930-31, 1932-34, and at University of Arizona, 1934; Creighton University, LL.B. and J.D., 1937; Columbia University, M.A., 1942; George Washington University, Ed.D., 1947. Home: 4201 Cathedral Ave. N.W., Washington, D.C. 20016. Office: B'nai B'rith, 1640 Rhode Island Ave. N.W., Washington, D.C. 20036.

CAREER: Aleph Zadik Aleph of B'nai B'rith, Omaha, Neb., assistant executive secretary, 1934-37; B'nai B'rith, Washington, D.C., national director of vocational service, 1938-54, national director of youth organization, 1948—. Visiting lecturer at Catholic University of America, George Washington University, Bucknell University, and Marquette University. Consultant to U.S. Bureau of Employment Security, and to Board of Hearings and Appeals of Social Security Administration. Member: National Vocational Guidance Association (president of District of Columbia chapter, 1946-47; national president, 1951-52), American Group Psychotherapy Association, National Association of Social Workers, National Education Association, National Conference of Jewish Communal Workers, American Personnel and Guidance Association, American Psychological Association, Academy of Certified Social Workers, Phi Delta Kappa.

WRITINGS: (With Edward C. Roeber) Occupational Information: Its Nature and Use, Science Research Associates, 1951, 3rd edition published as Occupational Information: The Dynamics of Its Nature and Use, 1964. Regular contributor to Personnel and Guidance Journal, 1943-69. Founding editor, Vocational Guidance Quarterly; editor, Your Future Occupation, 1957-66.

*   *   *

BAER, Werner 1931-

PERSONAL: Born December 14, 1931, in Offenbach, Germany; son of Richard (a physician) and Grete (Herz) Baer. Education: Queens College (now Queens College of City University of New York), B.A., 1953; Harvard University, M.A., 1955, Ph.D., 1958. Religion: Jewish. Home: 3415 West End Ave., Apt. #1108, Nashville, Tenn. 37203. Office: Department of Economics, Vanderbilt University, Nashville, Tenn. 37235.

CAREER: Harvard University, Cambridge, Mass., instructor in economics, 1958-61; Yale University, New Haven, Conn., assistant professor of economics, 1961-65; Vanderbilt University, Nashville, Tenn., associate professor, 1965-69, professor of economics, 1969—. Member: American Economic Association, Royal Economic Society, Latin American Studies Association, Southern Economic Association.

WRITINGS: The Puerto Rican Economy and United States Economic Fluctuations, Social Science Research Center, University of Puerto Rico, 1962; (editor with Isaac Kerstenetzky) Inflation and Growth in Latin America, Irwin, 1964; Industrialization and Economic Development in Brazil, Irwin, 1965; The Development of the Brazilian Steel Industry, Vanderbilt University Press, 1969. Contributor of articles and reviews to Economica, Yale Review, Public Policy, Business History Review, American Economic Review, Economic Development and Cultural Change, Latin American Research Review, and other professional periodicals.

*   *   *

BAERG, Harry J(ohn) 1909-

PERSONAL: Surname is pronounced Berg; born May 17, 1909, in Waldheim, Saskatchewan; became American citizen, 1965; son of John George (a farmer) and Helena (Nickel) Baerg; married Ida May Wentworth (an elementary teacher), February 29, 1944; children: Coral Anne, Willard Wentworth, Nadene Lenore. Education: Walla Walla College, B.A., 1947. Religion: Seventh-Day Adventist. Home: 311 Elm Ave., Takoma Park, Md. 20012. Office: Review & Herald Publishing Association, 6856 Eastern Ave., Washington, D.C. 20012.

CAREER: Free-lance writer and illustrator, 1947-56; Review & Herald Publishing Association, Washington, D.C., book and periodical illustrator, 1956-68, art director, 1968—. Illustrator of over fifty books besides his own. Columbia Union College, evening school instructor. Military service: U.S. Army, Saddler in Veterinary Corps and artist in headquarters unit, 1942-45.

WRITINGS—All self-illustrated: Bright Eyes: The Story of a Wild Duckling, Southern Publishing, 1952; Gray Ghosts, Southern Publishing, 1952; How to Know the Western Trees, W.C. Brown, 1955, revised edition, 1971; Chipmunk Willie, Review & Herald, 1958; Humpy the Moose, Review & Herald, 1963; Benny the Beaver, Review & Herald, 1964; Tico the Coyote, Review & Herald, 1970; Kari the Elephant, Review & Herald, 1970; Billy the Buck, Review & Herald, 1970; Winnie the White Heron, Review & Herald, 1972. Author and illustrator of some fifty articles, mainly on natural history subjects, for youth and farm magazines. Wrote and drew weekly animal biography series for youth papers, 1950-60.

WORK IN PROGRESS: Our Father's World, for Review & Herald.

SIDELIGHTS: Much of Baerg's illustrating (also for books written by others) has been in the natural history field, on subjects pursued and researched over a large part of North America. His work includes about one-hundred fifty full-color paintings for bird, fish, and mammal guides.

* * *

BAGDIKIAN, Ben Haig 1920-

PERSONAL: Surname is accented on second syllable; born January 30, 1920, in Marash, Turkey; came to United States in 1920; son of Aram Theodore (a minister) and Daisy (Uvezian) Bagdikian; married Elizabeth S. Ogasapian, October 2, 1942; children: Christopher, Frederick. Education: Clark University, Worcester, Mass., A.B., 1941. Politics: Democrat. Religion: Unitarian. Office: National Press Building, Washington, D.C. 20004.

CAREER: Springfield Morning Union, Springfield, Mass., general reporter, 1941-42; Periodical House, Inc. (magazine publishers), New York, N.Y., associate editor, 1946; Providence Journal, Providence, R.I., correspondent, 1947-61; Saturday Evening Post, New York, N.Y., contributing writer, 1962-67; Rand News Media Study Project, director, 1968-69; Washington Post, Washington, D.C., assistant managing editor, 1970—. Trustee, Clark University, 1964—. Military service: U.S. Army Air Corps and U.S. Air Force, navigator, 1942-45; became first lieutenant. Member: Urban League, American Civil Liberties Union, Overseas Writers, Authors League of America, National Press Club. Awards, honors: George Foster Peabody Award, 1951, for articles analyzing American commentators; Odgen Reid Foundation fellow, 1956; Sydney Hillman Foundation award, 1956, for study of internal security system; Brotherhood award, National Conference of Christians and Jews, 1958, for articles on race relations; Guggenheim fellow, 1961; L.H.D., Brown University, 1961; D.Litt., Clark University, 1963.

WRITINGS: (Editor) Man's Contracting World in an Expanding Universe, Brown University Bookstore, 1960; (contributor) Lester Tanzer, editor, The Kennedy Circle, Luce, 1961; In the Midst of Plenty: The Poor in America, Beacon Press, 1964; (contributor) Frederick T.C. Yu, editor, Behavioral Sciences and the Mass Media, Russell Sage, 1968; (contributor) Charles V. Daly, editor, The Media and the Cities, Center for Policy Study, University of Chicago, 1968; The Information Machines: Their Impact on Men and the Media, Harper, 1971; The Effete Conspiracy: And Other Crimes by the Press, Harper, 1972; (with Leon Dash) The Shame of the Prisons, Pocket Books, 1972.

Pamphlets: Pitchmen of the Press; The Newsmagazines, Promotion Department, Providence Journal Co., 1958; The Principal Instrument of Freedom, Phi Beta Kappa Society, 1961; (with James Rhea) We Went South; What Price Security?; Atomic Age, 1945—?. Contributor to Atlantic, New Republic, New York Times Magazine, Coronet, and Columbia Journalism Review.

BIOGRAPHICAL/CRITICAL SOURCES: Washington Post, February 24, 1971; New York Times, February 26, 1971; Saturday Review, March 13, 1971; New Republic, May 1, 1971.

* * *

BAHM, Archie J(ohn) 1907-

PERSONAL: Surname rhymes with game; born August 21, 1907, in Imlay City, Mich.; son of John Samuel (a builder) and Lena (Kohn) Bahm; married Luna Parks Bachelor (an instructor in mathematics), February 13, 1930; children: Raymond John, Elaine Lucia (Mrs. Arthur L. Fox). Education: Taylor University, student,

1925-26; Albion College, A.B., 1929; University of Michigan, M.A., 1930, Ph.D., 1933. Politics: Democrat. Religion: Humanist. Home: 1915 Las Lomas Rd. N.E., Albuquerque, N.M. 87106.

CAREER: Royal Oak Daily Tribune, Royal Oak, Mich., staff reporter, summers, 1927 and 1928; Texas Technological College, Lubbock, instructor, 1934-37, assistant professor, 1937-41, associate professor of philosophy and sociology, 1941-46; University of Denver, Denver, Colo., associate professor of philosophy, 1946-48; University of New Mexico, Albuquerque, professor of philosophy, 1948—, acting chairman of department, 1954-55, 1964-65. Visiting lecturer in philosophy, University of Rangoon, 1955-56, and University of Rhode Island, 1964.

MEMBER: International Metaphysical Society (founding member, 1968), American Philosophical Association, Metaphysical Society of America, American Society for Aesthetics, Society for the Study of Process Philosophers, Indian Congress of Philosophy (life member), American Association of University Professors, Southwestern Philosophical Society (organizer, 1935; vice-president, 1946-1947; president, 1948), Mountain-Plains Philosophical Conference (organizer, 1947; chairman, 1953-54; member of executive committee, 1960-61), New Mexico Philosophical Society (organizer, 1949; president, 1949-50; secretary-treasurer for three terms), Phi Beta Kappa, Phi Kappa Phi, Phi Sigma Tau. Member of Tenth, Eleventh, Thirteenth, and Fourteenth International Congresses of Philosophy. Awards, honors: Fulbright research scholar at University of Rangoon, 1955-56, and at Benares Hindu University, 1962-63; Humanist of the Year award, American Humanist Association (Albuquerque chapter), 1963.

WRITINGS: (Contributor) Elmer Pendell, editor, Society Under Analysis, Catell Press, 1942; Philosophy: An Introduction, Wiley, 1953; (editor and translator) Lao Tzu, Tao Teh King, Ungar, 1958; Philosophy of the Buddha, Rider & Co., 1958, Harper, 1959; What Makes Acts Right?, Christopher, 1958; Logic for Beginners, Student Outlines, 1960; Types of Intuition (monograph), University of New Mexico Press, 1961; Yoga: Union with the Ultimate (new version of the ancient sutras of Patanjali), Ungar, 1961; The World's Living Religions, Dell, 1964; Yoga for Business Executives and Professional People, Citadel, 1965, reissued as Executive Yoga, Paperback Library, 1970 (published in England as Yoga for Business Executives, Stanley Paul, 1967); The Heart of Confucius: Interpretations of "Genuine Living" and "Great Wisdom" (includes 16 Ming Dynasty Confucian prints), Walker & Co., 1969 (published in Japan as The Heart of Confucius, Weatherhill, 1969); Bhagavad Gita: The Wisdom of Krishna, Somaiya Publications Pvt. Ltd. (Bombay), 1970; Polarity, Dialectic, and Organicity, C.C Thomas, 1970.

Editor and publisher of biennial Directory of American Philosophers, 1962—. Contributor to Dictionary of Philosophy, Philosophical Library, 1942. Contributor of numerous articles and reviews to Scientific Monthly, Personalist, Journal of Philosophy, International Philosophical Quarterly, Journal of Aesthetics and Art Criticism, Darshana International, Democracy and World Peace, Review of Metaphysics, Philosophy Today, and other philosophy journals and periodicals. Contributing editor, Philosophic Abstracts, 1940-50; associate editor, Humanist, 1950-53; editor, Oriental Philosophy Newsletter, 1950-51; news editor, Philosophy East and West, 1951-62; member of advisory board, Indian Journal of Philosophic Studies, 1963-64; associate editor, Journal of Thought, 1967—.

WORK IN PROGRESS: Ethics as a Behavioral Science; Interdependence: and Metaphysics.

SIDELIGHTS: Bahm has traveled extensively in the Middle and Far East. Some of his books and articles have been translated into Tamil, Japanese, and other languages, and two books have been reproduced for the blind, *Philosophy: An Introduction* on records, and *The World's Living Religions* on magnetic tape.

BIOGRAPHICAL/CRITICAL SOURCES: Free Mind, November, 1960.

* * *

BAILEY, Hugh C(oleman) 1929-

PERSONAL: Born July 2, 1929, in Berry, Ala.; son of Coleman Costello (a railway agent) and Susie (Jenkins) Bailey; married Ahleida Joan Seeyer, November 17, 1962; children: Debra Jane, Laura Joan. *Education:* Howard College (now Samford University), A.B., 1950; University of Alabama, M.A., 1951, Ph.D., 1954. *Religion:* Episcopalian. *Home:* 1801 Windsor Blvd., Birmingham, Ala. 35209. *Office:* Department of History, Samford University, 800 Lakeshore Dr., Birmingham, Ala. 35209.

CAREER: Samford University, Birmingham, Ala., instructor, 1953-54, assistant professor, 1954-56, associate professor, 1956-59, professor of history, 1959—, chairman, department of history and political science, 1967-70, dean, Howard College of Arts and Sciences, 1970—. *Member:* American Historical Association, Southern Historical Association, Alabama Historical Association, Pi Gamma Mu (national trustee-at-large). *Awards, honors:* Guggenheim fellow, 1963-64.

WRITINGS: John Williams Walker: A Study in the Political, Social and Cultural Life of the Old Southwest, University of Alabama Press, 1964; *Americanism vs. Communism,* American-Southern Publishing Co., 1964; *Hinton Rowan Helper: Abolitionist-Racist,* University of Alabama Press, 1965; *Edgar Gardner Murphy: Gentle Progressive,* University of Miami Press, 1968; *Liberalism in the New South: Southern Social Reformers and the Progressive Movement,* University of Miami Press, 1969.

WORK IN PROGRESS: Heralds of Reform; a biography of Alexander J. McKelway.

* * *

BAILY, Nathan A(riel) 1920-

PERSONAL: Born July 19, 1920, in New York, N.Y.; son of Saul (a rabbi and cantor) and Eleanor (Mintz) Baily; married Judith Bernstein, June 20, 1946; children: Alan Eric, Lawrence Joel. *Education:* City College of the City University of New York, B.S., 1940, fellow, 1940-42, Greenfield fellow, 1942; Columbia University, M.A., 1941, Ph.D., 1946. *Religion:* Hebrew. *Home:* 5516 Greystone St., Chevy Chase, Md. 20015. *Office:* Postal Rate Commission, Washington, D.C. 20260.

CAREER: Teacher at City College of the City University of New York, 1942-46, and Fashion Institute of Technology and Design; senior editor and economic analyst, Research Institute of America, 1944-45; Office of Price Administration, price economist, 1946-47; American University, Washington, D.C., 1947-70, began as assistant professor, became professor of business administration, founding dean of School of Business Administration, 1955-70; member of Postal Rate Commission, Washington, D.C., 1970—. Management consultant to government agencies, business firms, and professional associations. Middle Atlantic Association of Colleges of Business Administration, secretary-treasurer, 1963-64, president, 1964-65; trustee, Council on Opportunities in Selling.

MEMBER: American Economic Association, American Society of Association Executives, American Institute of Management (honorary), American Wholesalers (board), National Advisory Council on Economic Education, American Association of University Professors, Chamber of Commerce of the U.S. (board), Washington Society

of Investment Analysts (charter member), Washington Mutual Investors Fund (board), Washington Sales Executives Club (board, 1962-63), Friends of United States of Latin America (board), Phi Beta Kappa, Rho Epsilon, Pi Sigma Epsilon. *Awards, honors:* Fellowships from Danforth Foundation, Volker Fund, E.I. Dupont de Nemours, Swift & Co.

WRITINGS: (Editor) *Marketing Profitably under the Robinson-Patman Act,* Public Affairs Press, 1963. Contributor to *Business Perspectives* and other professional journals. Contributing editor, *Modern Securities Services.*

* * *

BAIRD, Alexander (John) 1925-

PERSONAL: Born September 28, 1925, in Liverpool, England; son of Samuel Alexander and Emma (Macdonald) Baird; married Eileen Mary Kerruish, July 31, 1954; children: Katharine Mary, Christina Jane. *Education:* Emmanuel College, Cambridge, M.A., 1953; University College, London, Ph.D., 1970. *Religion:* Anglo-Catholic. *Home:* 303 Elm Tree Ct., St. John's Wood, London N.W. 8, England. *Agent:* Bolt & Watson Ltd., Chandos House, Buckingham Gate, London S.W. 1, England. *Office:* c/o University of London, Institute of Education, London W.C. 1, England.

CAREER: University of Hiroshima, Hiroshima, Japan, lecturer in English language and literature, 1959-62; Central Institute of English, Hyderabad, India, lecturer in phonetics, 1963-65; University of London, Institute of Education, London, England, lecturer in education and English as a foreign language, 1965—. *Military service:* Royal Air Force, 1943-47. *Member:* International P.E.N.

WRITINGS: The Micky-Hunters, Heinemann, 1957; *The Unique Sensation,* Heinemann, 1959; *Poems* (Poetry Book Society choice), Chatto & Windus, 1963; (contributor) Eugene Fodor and Robert C. Fisher, editors, *Fodor's Guide to Japan and East Asia,* McKay, 1963 (published in England as *Japan and East Asia: A Definitive Handbook of the Far East and Southeast Asia,* MacGibbon & Kee, 1963). Poetry anthologized in *New Poems, 1960,* edited by Anthony Cronin and others, Hutchinson, 1960, Transatlantic, 1961, and *New Poems, 1962,* edited by Lawrence Durrell, Hutchinson, 1962. Author of short stories for British Broadcasting Corp. Contributor to *Listener, Times Literary Supplement, London Magazine, Texas Quarterly, Encounter, Transatlantic Review, English Language Teaching, Journal of English Teaching* (Japan), *Levende Talen* (Netherlands), and *Teaching English* (New Delhi).

WORK IN PROGRESS: A volume of new poems; a novel; books on English prosody, and on the teaching of English literature overseas.

AVOCATIONAL INTERESTS: Ornithology.

* * *

BAKER, Betty D(oreen Flook) 1916-
(Elizabeth Renier)

PERSONAL: Born November 22, 1916, in Bristol, England; daughter of Leonard Joseph and Edith (Bath) Flook; married Frank Edward Baker (deceased). *Education:* Attended The Collegiate School and Merchant Venturers College, Bristol, England. *Religion:* Church of England. *Home:* Inchcoulter Cottage, 15 Douglas Ave., Exmouth, Devonshire, England.

CAREER: Doctor's secretary. Volunteer helper, Family Planning Association, 1958-62. *Wartime service:* Voluntary Aid Detachment, Red Cross, attached to Royal Army Medical Corps, 1940-42. *Member:* Romantic Novelists' Association, Royal Society for the Protection of Birds, Shoreham Ornithological Society, Bognor Regis

Natural Science Society, Sussex Naturalists Trust, West Sussex Writers Club. *Awards, honors:* Pauline Warwick Award from Romantic Novelists' Association, and scholarship to Writers Summer School, both for *The Generous Vine*, 1961.

WRITINGS—Novels, all under pseudonym Elizabeth Renier: *The Generous Vine*, Hurst & Blackett, 1962, Ace Books, 1972; *The House of Water*, Hurst & Blackett, 1963, Ace Books, 1972; *Blade of Justice*, Hurst & Blackett, 1965, Ace Books, 1972; *If This Be Treason*, Hurst & Blackett, 1965, published in America as *If This Be Love*, Ace Books, 1971; *Valley of the Nightingales*, Hurst & Blackett, 1966; *A Singing in the Woods*, Hurst & Blackett, 1966, Ace Books, 1972; *Prelude to Freedom*, Hurst & Blackett, 1967, published in America as *Prelude to Love*, Ace Books, 1972; *The House of Granite*, Hurst & Blackett, 1968, Ace Books, 1971; *By Sun and Candlestick*, Hurst & Blackett, 1968, Ace Books, 1973; *Tomorrow Comes the Sun*, Hurst & Blackett, 1969, Ace Books, 1971; *The Spanish Doll*, Hurst & Blackett, 1970, Ace Books, 1972; *Valley of Secrets*, Hurst & Blackett, 1970, Ace Books, 1972; *Woman From the Sea*, Ace Books, 1972. Contributor of short stories to *Woman's Story, Sincerely, John O'London's*, British Broadcasting Corp. radio, and of serials to *Woman's Realm*.

WORK IN PROGRESS: Historical novel with Dartmoor background.

AVOCATIONAL INTERESTS: Natural history, gardening, music, and working with deprived children.

*   *   *

BAKER, Denys Val   1917-

PERSONAL: Born October 24, 1917, in Poppleton, Yorkshire, England; son of Valentine Henry and Dilys (Eames) Baker; married Jess Margaret Bryan (a self-employed potter), January 28, 1948; children: Martin, Gillian, Jane, Stephen, Demelza, Genevieve. *Politics:* Pacifist. *Home:* St. Christophers, Porthmeur Rd., St. Ives, Cornwall, England.

CAREER: Writer on British daily and trade newspapers, 1935-41; free-lance writer, 1941—. *Member:* Society of Authors, West Country Writers Association.

WRITINGS: Selected Stories, Staples, 1944; *Worlds Without End* (short stories), Sylvan Press, 1945; *The White Rock* (novel), Sylvan Press, 1945, Appleton, 1947; *The More We Are Together* (novel), Low, 1947; *The Return of Uncle Walter, and Other Stories*, Low, 1948; *The Widening Mirror* (novel), Low, 1949.

(Author of introduction) *Paintings from Cornwall*, Cornish Library, 1950; *Britain Discovers Herself*, Christopher Johnson, 1950; *How to Be an Author*, Harvill Press, 1952; *The Title's My Own* (novel), Bles, 1955; *A Journey with Love* (novel), Brideshead, 1955; *Strange Fulfillment* (short stories), Pyramid Press, 1958; (with wife, Jess Baker) *The Pottery Book: An Introduction to an Individual Art and Craft*, Cassell, 1959; *Britain's Art Colony by Sea*, George Ronald, 1959.

The Minack Theatre, George Ronald, 1960; *How to Be a Parent*, Boardman & Co., 1960; *Pottery Today*, Oxford University Press, 1961; *The Sea's in the Kitchen*, Phoenix House, 1962; *The Door Is Always Open*, Phoenix House, 1963; *The Young Potter: A How-It-Is-Done Book of Pottery*, Warne, 1963; *The Flameswallower, and Other Stories from Cornwall*, J.H. Locke, 1963; *Cornwall for the Cornish*, Porthmoor Press, 1964; (contributor) James E. Turner, editor, *Thy Neighbor's Wife: Twelve Original Variations on a Theme*, Cassell, 1964; *The Strange and the Damned* (short stories), Pyramid Press, 1964; *We'll Go Around the World Tomorrow*, Baker Publishers,

1965; *To Sea with Sam*, Baker Publishers, 1967; *Adventures Before Fifty*, Baker Publishers, 1969.

The Face in the Mirror, Arkham House, 1971.

Editor: *Little Reviews, 1914-1943*, Allen & Unwin, 1943; *Little Reviews Anthology*, Volume I, Allen & Unwin, 1943, Volume II-IV, Eyre & Spottiswoode, 1945, 1946, 1948, Volume V, Methuen, 1949; *Writing Today*, Staples, Volume I (with Peter Ratazzi), 1943, Volumes II-IV, 1944-46; *International Short Stories*, two volumes, W.H. Allen, 1944-45; *Modern Short Stories*, Staples, 1944; *Voyage: An Anthology of Selected Stories*, Sylvan Press, 1945; *Writers of Today*, two volumes, Sidgwick & Jackson, 1946-48; *Modern British Writing*, Vanguard, 1947; *One and All: A Selection of Stories from Cornwall*, Museum Press, 1951. Contributor of short stories to *Argosy, Pick of Todays Stories, Esquire, Town and Country, Chicago Review, Western Review, Good Housekeeping, Home, Evening News, Evening Standard, Punch*, and other publications; author of nearly one hundred stories broadcast on British Broadcasting Corp. programs.

WORK IN PROGRESS: Short stories; continuing autobiographical books.

AVOCATIONAL INTERESTS: Surfing and boating.

*   *   *

BAKER, Frank   1910-

PERSONAL: Born April 15, 1910, in Hull, Yorkshire, England; son of Frank (a locomotive engineer) and Annie Elizabeth (Moore) Baker; married Ellen Eliza Levitt, August 11, 1937; children: Margaret (Mrs. Alan Whitehead), Enid (Mrs. Dyson Hickingbotham), Peter. *Education:* University College of Hull, B.A. (external degree of University of London; honors), 1931; University of Manchester, B.D., 1934; University of Nottingham, Ph.D., 1952. *Home:* 1505 Pinecrest Rd., Durham, N.C. 27705. *Office:* Divinity School, Duke University, Durham, N.C. 27706.

CAREER: Minister of British Methodist Church doing pastoral work in seven circuits in England, twice as minister in charge, 1934-59; Municipal Training College, Hull, England, lecturer in charge of religious education, 1958-59; South Holderness County Secondary School, Preston, Yorkshire, England, assistant master of religious education, 1959-60; Duke University, Durham, N.C., 1960—, now professor of English church history in department of religion and in Divinity School. Member, World Methodist Council, 1944-60; British Methodist Church, member of ministerial training committee, 1950-60, secretary of archives commission, 1955-60. Member of court, University of Hull, 1955-60. *Member:* World Methodist Historical Society (executive, 1970—), Wesley Historical Society (registrar, 1943-49; secretary, 1949-60; life), Royal Historical Society (life), International Methodist Historical Society (joint secretary, 1947-60), American Society of Church History. *Awards, honors:* Eayrs Essay Prize, Methodist Church of Great Britain, first prize, 1936, 1942, 1948, second prize, 1941, 1947; fellow in Methodist history, 1956; St. George's gold medalist, 1969.

WRITINGS: Treasure in Earthen Vessels (four-act play), Epworth, 1937; *Sidelights on Sixty Years*, Keighley Methodist Church, 1941; *A Charge to Keep: An Introduction to the People Called Methodists*, Epworth, 1947, 2nd edition, 1954; *Thomas Coke: The St. Paul of Methodism*, Cargate, 1947; *Charles Wesley as Revealed by His Letters*, Epworth, 1948; *The Relations Between the Society of Friends and Early Methodism*, Epworth, 1949.

The Methodist Pilgrim in England, Epworth, 1951, 2nd edition, 1961; *The Story of Cleethorpes and the Contribu-*

tion of Methodism Through Two Hundred Years, Trinity Methodist Church (Cleethorpes), 1953; *Methodism and the Love Feast,* Macmillan (New York), 1957; *The Story of Methodism in Newland,* Trustees of the Newland Methodist Church, 1958; *John Cennick (1718-1755): A Handlist of His Writings,* Wesley Historical Society, 1958.

(Editor and author of introduction) *Representative Verse of Charles Wesley,* Epworth, 1962, Abingdon, 1963, revised edition published as *Charles Wesley's Verse: An Introduction,* Epworth, 1964; *William Grimshaw, 1708-1763,* Epworth, 1963; (editor with George Walton Williams) *John Wesley's First Hymn-Book,* Dalcho Historical Society, 1964; (compiler) *A Union Catalogue of Publications of John and Charles Wesley,* Divinity School, Duke University, 1966; *John Wesley and the Church of England,* Abingdon, 1970. Contributor to *Encyclopaedia Britannica, Chambers's Encyclopaedia,* and about two hundred articles to *London Quarterly Review* and other religious, learned, and popular periodicals.

WORK IN PROGRESS: Letters of John and Charles Wesley; a biography of Sarah Wesley; a biography of Captain Thomas Webb; a bibliography of the writings of the Wesleys, in preparation for the definitive edition of the writings of John Wesley, for Oxford University Press.

SIDELIGHTS: His collection of seventeen thousand items on the lives of the Wesleys and early British Methodism has been purchased by Duke University. *Avocational interests:* Tennis, badminton, table tennis, music, word puzzles, and carpentry.

*   *   *

BAKER, Paul R(aymond)   1927-

PERSONAL: Born September 28, 1927, in Everett, Wash.; son of Loren R. (a factory manager) and Alma (Ball) Baker. *Education:* Stanford University, A.B., 1949; Columbia University, M.A., 1951; Harvard University, Ph.D., 1960. *Politics:* Independent. *Office:* Department of History, University of Oregon, Eugene, Ore. 97403.

CAREER: Encyclopedia Americana, New York, N.Y., staff writer and editor, 1952-55; California Institute of Technology, Pasadena, 1960-63, began as instructor, became assistant professor of history; University of California, Riverside, lecturer in history, 1963-64; University of Oregon, Eugene, lecturer in history, 1964—. *Member:* American Historical Association, American Studies Association, American Association of University Professors, Phi Beta Kappa.

WRITINGS: (Editor) Frances Wright D'Arusmont, *Views of Society and Manners in America,* Harvard University Press, 1963; *The Fortunate Pilgrims: Americans in Italy, 1800-1860,* Harvard University Press, 1964; (editor) *The Atomic Bomb: The Great Decision,* Holt, 1968. Contributor to *Encyclopedia Americana, Americana Annual, Keats-Shelley Journal,* and *Engineering and Science.*

WORK IN PROGRESS: Research in field of early nineteenth-century American social and intellectual history.

*   *   *

BALABKINS, Nicholas (W.)   1926-

PERSONAL: Born July 17, 1926, in Daugavpils, Latvia; son of Joseph (a farmer) and Anna (Sheleskina) Balabkins. *Education:* Georg-August University, Dipl. Rer. Pol., 1949; Rutgers University, M.A., 1953, Ph.D., 1956. *Religion:* Greek-Orthodox. *Home:* 252 Uncas St., Bethlehem, Pa. 18015. *Office:* Economics Department, Lehigh University, Bethlehem, Pa. 18015.

CAREER: Lehigh University, Bethlehem, Pa., associate professor, 1957-66, professor of economics, 1966—. *Mili-*

tary service: German Army, Latvian Division, 1944-45. *Member:* American Economic Association, American Association of University Professors.

WRITINGS: Germany Under Direct Controls: Economic Aspects of Industrial Disarmament, 1945-1948, Rutgers University Press, 1964; *West German Reparations to Israel,* Rutgers University Press, 1971. Contributor of articles to *World Affairs Quarterly, Kyklos, Business Horizons, South African Journal of Economics, Il Politico,* and *Zeitschrift fuer die Gesamte Staatswissenschaft.*

*   *   *

BALDWIN, Michael   1930-
(Michael Jesse)

PERSONAL: Born May 1, 1930, in Gravesend, Kent, England; son of Harold Jesse and Elizabeth (Crittenden) Baldwin; married Jean Margaret Bruce, May 22, 1954; children: Matthew, Adam. *Education:* St. Edmund Hall, Oxford, B.A., 1953, research student, 1954-55. *Home:* 18 Sydney Rd., Richmond, Surrey, England. *Agent:* Brandt & Brandt, 101 Park Ave., New York, N.Y. 10017; and A.M. Heath & Co., Dover St., London, W.1, England.

CAREER: St. Paul's College, Cheltenham, England, lecturer, 1955; St. Clement Danes Grammar School, London, England, assistant master, 1956-59; Whitelands College, London, senior lecturer, 1959—. Member of advisory committee, *Daily Mirror* children's literary competition. *Military service:* British Army, National Service, 1949-50; became sergeant. Territorial Army, 1950-61; became lieutenant, Royal Artillery. *Member:* Association of School Magazines (member, national advisory committee).

WRITINGS: The Silent Mirror (poems), Fortune Press, 1953; *Voyage from Spring* (poems), Routledge & Kegan Paul, 1957; *Poetry Without Tears* (educational), Routledge & Kegan Paul, 1959.

Grandad with Snails (autobiographical), Routledge & Kegan Paul, 1960; *A World of Men* (novel), Secker & Warburg, 1962; *Death on a Live Wire, and On Stepping from a Sixth-Storey Window* (poems), Longmans, Green, 1962; (editor) *Poems by Children, 1950-1961* (educational), Dufour, 1962; (editor) *Billy the Kid, an Anthology of Tough Verse* (educational), Hutchinson, 1963; *Miraclejack* (novel), Secker & Warburg, 1963, Holt, 1967; *In Step with a Goat* (autobiographical), Hodder & Stoughton, 1963; *A Mouthful of Gold* (novel), Secker & Warburg, 1964; *Sebastian and Other Voices,* Secker & Warburg, 1966; *How Chas. Egget Lost His Way in a Creation Myth* (poems), Secker & Warburg, 1967; *The Great Cham,* Secker & Warburg, 1967; *Underneath, and Other Situations* (stories), Secker & Warburg, 1968; (with Terry Atkinson) *22 Sentences: The French Army,* Art & Language Press, 1968; (with Atkinson) *Hot, Warm, Cool, Cold,* Art & Language Press, 1969.

There's a War On, Hodder & Stoughton, 1970; *The Cellar; A Fable,* Hodder & Stoughton, 1972. Author of screenplay, "Miraclejack," based on his novel. Author of a number of dramatic broadcasts.

SIDELIGHTS: Reviewing *Miraclejack,* Peter Buitenhuis writes: "The idea of the story is good; its execution is breathtaking. Baldwin's style is at once terse and poetic. It achieves masterpieces of understatement and splendors of imagery at the same time. His metaphors are reminiscent of the extravagant early phase of Dylan Thomas...." Gillian Tindall is enthusiatic about Baldwin's shorter works. "Michael Baldwin's stories are ... consciously ingenious, carefully planned virtuoso performances by a serious writer who knows just what he wants to do. His settings are designedly those of action: a coal-mine, the building trade, the army. I can't think of another writer who conveys the intricate preoccupations and jokes of these traditionally masculine worlds without ever once resorting to a consciously plainman tone in order to do so. Yet perhaps it is this ability of illuminating specialised areas of life without appearing to be involved in them himself that makes Michael Baldwin a slightly sinister writer. He puts distance between himself and his subjects: one story verges on poetry, another is a kind of Gothic comedy, in several apocalyptic judgment seems hovering over the next page, and in one the world ticks to an end in the style of a shooting script."

The same tone in Baldwin's prose is found in his verse. Philip Callow writes: "Michael Baldwin doesn't want poetry that sings, he wants it rheumy, rusty; and it has to rasp. There are as many definitions of poetry as there are blades of grass, but perhaps most poets would agree that a poem is life in concentrated form. These poems are more than concentrated—they are bursting at the seams, splitting at the shoulders, spewing at the mouth. And each time there's an oil slick of ugliness to remind us that the world's a very nasty place but it's all there is at the moment, and it's our own sick mugs we're looking at. Make poetry from that. So, as I see it, these extraordinary buckets slopping over with images, witty and gruesome, gay and grave are poems in the very teeth of that 'contemporary urban existence' of the birth, and its indifference to poetry. . . . Elsewhere he is fast and lusty and apocalyptic and satiric, sometimes all at once, and I began to long for some silence around the words, as you need space in paintings. But that's not his style. He's an awakener, a bull-roarer, and a very talented one."

Baldwin has broadcast extensively for the British Broadcasting Corporation, particularly to schools. He is interested in music, jazz, anything to do with live theatre, and creative writing by children. His favorite occupations are drinking and eating.

A Mouthful of Gold has been made into a film.

BIOGRAPHICAL/CRITICAL SOURCES: *Books and Bookmen*, September, 1963, August, 1967; *New York Times Book Review*, April 16, 1967; *Book Week*, May 7, 1967; *Times Literary Supplement*, September 14, 1967; *Punch*, January 3, 1968; *Listener*, January 4, 1968, May 23, 1968; *New Yorker*, May 11, 1968; *Observer Review*, May 19, 1968.†

*　*　*

BALFOUR, Michael (Leonard) Graham   1908-

PERSONAL: Born November 22, 1908, in Oxford, England; son of Sir Graham (a writer and administrator) and Rhoda (Brooke) Balfour; married Grizel Wilson, June 28, 1934; children: Alison (Mrs. Francis Holmes A. Court), Rosanne, Corinna. *Education:* Attended Rugby School, 1922-27, Balliol College, Oxford, 1927-32. *Politics:* Independent. *Religion:* Church of England. *Home:* 17 Redington Rd., London N.W.3, England.

CAREER: Magdalen College, Oxford University, Oxford, England, lecturer in politics, 1932-36; Royal Institute of International Affairs, London, England, research secretary, 1936-39; British government, principal, Ministry of Information, London, 1939-42, with Foreign Office, London, 1942-44; Supreme Headquarters, Allied Expeditionary Forces, Paris, France, deputy chief of intelligence in Psychological Warfare Division (as civilian), 1944-46; British Control Commission for Germany, Berlin, director of Information Services Branch, 1945-47; Board of Trade, London, England, chief information officer, 1947-64. *Awards, honors:* Commander, Order of the British Empire, 1963.

WRITINGS: (Contributor as secretary and drafter to research group) *Nationalism*, Royal Institute of International Affairs, 1939; *States and Mind: Reflections on Their Interaction in History*, Cresset, 1953; (with John Mair) *Four-Power Control in Germany and Austria, 1945-46*, Oxford University Press, 1956; *The Kaiser and His Times*, Houghton, 1964; *West Germany*, Praeger, 1968. Contributor of articles to *Times* (London).

WORK IN PROGRESS: Research on British history.

BIOGRAPHICAL/CRITICAL SOURCES: *Library Journal*, June 1, 1968.

*　*　*

BALL, Robert Hamilton   1902-

PERSONAL: Born May 21, 1902, in New York, N.Y.; son of George Martin (a physician) and Flora C. (Hill) Ball; married Esther M. Smith, June 26, 1928; children: Marcia Merrill (Mrs. Benjamin R. Carson). *Education:* Princeton University, A.B., 1923, A.M., 1924, Ph.D., 1928. *Home:* 11 North Washington St., Port Washington, N.Y. 11050. *Office:* Department of English, Queens College of the City University of New York, 6530 Kissena Blvd., Flushing, N.Y. 11367.

CAREER: Princeton University, Princeton, N.J., instructor, 1927-31, assistant professor of English and dramatic art, 1931-39, curator of William Seymour Theatre Collection, 1936-39; Queen's College (now Queens College of the City University of New York), Flushing, N.Y., assistant professor, 1939-43, associate professor, 1944-51, professor of English, 1951-71, professor emeritus, 1971—, chairman of department, 1941-47, 1960-64, chairman of Arts Division, 1949-55. Founder of chair and first professor of American literature at University of Ankara, 1955-56; visiting professor at New York University, University of Colorado, and University of California, Los Angeles. Consultant to Middle States Association of Colleges and Secondary Schools, to New York State Department of Education, and to various publishers. Member of Art Advisory Council, Port Washington, 1961—.

MEMBER: International Federation for Theatre Research, Modern Language Association of America, Shakespeare Association of America, Modern Humanities Research Association (member of American executive committee), Theatre Library Association (past chairman of theatre documents board; past member of executive board), American Society for Theatre Research (past program chairman; member of executive committee), American Association of University Professors (past chapter president), Malone Society (England). *Awards, honors:* Guggenheim fellow, 1946-47; Rockefeller Foundation grant, 1955-56.

WRITINGS: *The Amazing Career of Sir Giles Overreach, Being the Life and Adventures of a Nefarious Scoundrel Who for Three Centuries Pursued His Sinister Designs in Almost All the Theatres of the British Isles and America, the Whole Comprising a History of the Stage*, Princeton University Press, 1939; (editor) *The Plays of Henry C. DeMille*, Princeton University Press, 1940; (with Thomas Mare Parrott) *A Short View of Elizabethan Drama: Together with Some Account of Its Principal Playwrights and the Conditions Under Which It Was Produced*, Scribner, 1943, revised edition, 1960; (editor) *Cagdas Amerikan siirleri: Antologie*, Guezel (Ankara), 1956; (with Walter Parker Bowman) *Theatre Language: A Dictionary of Terms in English of the Drama and Stage*, Theatre Arts, 1961; *Shakespeare on Silent Film: A Strange Eventful History*, Theatre Arts, 1968. Member of advisory board, *America's Lost Plays*, twenty volumes, Princeton University Press, 1939-42. Contributor to *Encyclopedia Americana*, *Collier's Encyclopedia*, *Random House Dictionary of the English Language*, *Shakespeare Encyclopedia*, and to journals, including *Theatre Survey, Pacific Spectator, Quarterly of Film, Radio, and Television, University of Colorado Studies,* and *Modern Language Notes.*

WORK IN PROGRESS: An article on Shakespeare and George Chapman; articles and book on Shakespeare on sound film.

SIDELIGHTS: Ball is competent in varying degrees in French, German, Italian, Latin, and Turkish.

*   *   *

BANKS, Richard L.   1920-

PERSONAL: Born January 17, 1920, in St. Louis, Mo.; son of Richard C. (a steel engineer) and Ethel (Perkins) Banks; married Edythe Mellicker, June, 1941; children: Bar John. *Education:* University of Colorado, B.A., 1942; Sorbonne, University of Paris, Docteur de la Universite, 1951. *Home and office:* 15 rue de Remusat, Paris 16e, France.

CAREER: Free-lance writer, 1950-60; Columbia Films, Hollywood, Calif., story scout in Paris, France, 1961-62; University of Maryland, College Park, professor of French culture courses in Overseas Program, Paris, France, 1962-67; Universite de Rouen, Rouen, France, Charge de Cours, Modern American Novels, 1970—. *Military service:* U.S. Army, Signal Corps, 1942-46; served in Film and Photographic Division of Supreme Headquarters, Allied Expeditionary Forces; became first lieutenant.

WRITINGS: The Beaver Hunters, St. Martin's, 1964; *Essays in Fiction,* Merlin, 1968. Editor, *Parnassus* (Paris literary magazine).

WORK IN PROGRESS: Research in Sumerian ethnology; literary criticism; western novels; and novels on France and America.

AVOCATIONAL INTERESTS: Sumerian studies, and European and American prehistory.

BANY, Mary A.   1913-

PERSONAL: Born June 24, 1913, in Corvallis, Ore.; daughter of Frank A. and Grace (Houck) Bany. *Education:* Oregon College of Education, elementary teaching credential, 1936; University of Oregon, B.S., 1942; Los Angeles State College (now California State University at Los Angeles), M.A., 1953; University of Southern California, Ed.D., 1960. *Office:* California State University, Los Angeles, Calif. 90032.

CAREER: Elementary school teacher in Salem, Ore., 1936-45, elementary and high school teacher in Alhambra, Calif., 1945-55; California State University, Los Angeles, member of elementary education faculty, 1955-63, chairman of department of elementary education, 1963—. *Member:* National Education Association (life), American Association of University Professors, National Council of Teachers of English, National Council for Social Studies, National Society for Study of Education, American Council of Education (past chapter president), Association for Student Teaching, Southern California Council on Children's Literature, Phi Beta Sigma, Pi Lambda Theta, Delta Kappa Gamma.

WRITINGS: (With Lois V. Johnson) *Classroom Group Behavior: Group Dynamics in Education,* Macmillan, 1964; (with Johnson) *Classroom Management: Theory and Skill Training,* Macmillan, 1970. Contributor of articles to education journals and encyclopedias.

*   *   *

BARBOUR, Philip L(emont)   1898-

PERSONAL: Born December 21, 1898, in Louisville, Ky.; son of Philip Foster (a pediatrician) and Jessie (a

poet; maiden name, Lemont) Barbour; divorced. *Education:* Studies at Columbia University, 1914-17, Cornell University, 1917-19. *Home:* The Arn, The Old Road, Newtown, Conn. 06470.

CAREER: Sometime newspaperman in New York, N.Y., and in Italy; World Wide Broadcasting Foundation, Boston, Mass., director of inter-American broadcasts, 1937-38; National Broadcasting Co., New York, N.Y., foreign press and station relations, 1938-41; U.S. Coordinator of Inter-American Affairs, New York, N.Y., principal radio program officer, 1941-42; U.S. Military Government, Berlin Sector, Germany, chief of political intelligence section, 1946-48; Radio Free Europe, New York, N.Y., educational coordinator, 1949-52; full-time writer, 1952—. *Military service:* U.S. Army, 1942-46; became captain. *Member:* American Oriental Society (life), Mediaeval Academy of America (life), Renaissance Society of America, American Name Society, Ateneo de Caracas (Venezuela; honorary), Hakluyt Society (London), Navy Records Society (London). *Awards, honors:* Citation of Honor, Society of Colonial Wars, 1965, for *The Three Worlds of Captain John Smith;* Award of Merit, American Association for State and Local History, 1970, for *The Jamestown Voyages Under the First Charter, 1606-1609.*

WRITINGS: Kleine Geschichte der westlichen Welt, Karl H. Henssel Verlag, 1948; (translator and annotator) Alexander Pushkin, *Boris Godunov,* Columbia University Press, 1953; (editor and contributor) Warner F. Gookin, *Bartholomew Gosnold: Discoverer and Planter,* Archon Books, 1963; (contributor) *Literature as a Mode of Travel,* New York Public Library, 1963; *Toponymy in the Service of Biography,* University of California Press, 1964; *The Three Worlds of Captain John Smith,* Houghton, 1964; *Dimitry, Called the Pretender: Tsar and Great Prince of All Russia, 1605-1606,* Houghton, 1966; (editor) *The Jamestown Voyages Under the First Charter, 1606-1609,* two volumes, Cambridge University Press for Hakluyt Society, 1969; *Pocahontas and Her World,* Houghton, 1970. Editor and narrator for recordings, "The Jamestown Saga," Caedmon Records, 1969, and "The Pilgrim Saga," Caedmon Records, 1971. Contributor of articles to *Annals* of the American Academy of Political and Social Science, *William and Mary Quarterly, Virginia Magazine of History and Biography, Mariner's Mirror* (London), *Huntington Library Quarterly,* and other publications.

WORK IN PROGRESS: A fully annotated edition of Captain John Smith's complete works.

SIDELIGHTS: Barbour is competent in Spanish, Italian, French, Portuguese, German, Russian, and Latin.

BIOGRAPHICAL/CRITICAL SOURCES: New Yorker, June 13, 1970; *Virginia Quarterly Review,* autumn, 1970.

*   *   *

BARCLAY, Harold B.   1924-

PERSONAL: Born January 3, 1924, in Newton, Mass.; son of Harold Glenburn and Mabel (Barton) Barclay; married Jane Lepore, August 26, 1953; children: Alan, Alison. *Education:* Boston University, B.A. (cum laude), 1952; Cornell University, M.A., 1954, Ph.D., 1961. *Religion:* Society of Friends. *Home:* 11581 University Ave., Edmonton, Alberta, Canada.

CAREER: American University at Cairo, Cairo, Egypt, instructor in anthropology, 1956-59, conductor of anthropological research in Sudan, 1959-60; Knox College, Galesburg, Ill., assistant professor of anthropology, 1960-63; University of Oregon, Eugene, assistant professor of anthropology, 1963-66; University of Alberta, Edmonton, associate professor, 1966-71, professor of anthropology, 1971—, acting chairman of department, 1967-68. *Member:*

American Anthropological Association (fellow), Phi Beta Kappa.

WRITINGS: Buurri al Lamaab: A Suburban Village in the Sudan, Cornell University Press, 1964. Also author of monograph on an Egyptian village.

Contributor: Louise Sweet, editor, The Central Middle East, Human Relations Area Files, 1968; Brigham Young Card, editor, Perspectives on Regions and Regionalism, University of Alberta, 1969; J.J. Mahar, H. Orenstein, and M.D. Zamore, editors, On Culture, University of Philippines Press, 1971; J.L. Elliott, editor, Minority Canadians, Prentice-Hall, 1971; K. Ishwaran, editor, The Canadian Family, Holt, 1971. Contributor of articles to Muslim World.

WORK IN PROGRESS: Research on "utopian" communities.

* * *

BARKER, A(udrey) L(illian) 1918-

PERSONAL: Born April 13, 1918, in England; daughter of Harry (an engineer) and Elsie A. (Dutton) Barker. Education: Attended county secondary school in England. Address: c/o Hogarth Press Ltd., 40-42 William IV St., London W.C. 2, England.

CAREER: British Broadcasting Corp., London, England, secretary, now part-time; free-lance writer. Member: Society of Authors, Royal Society of Literature (fellow). Awards, honors: Atlantic award in Literature, 1946; Somerset Maugham award for Innocents, 1947; Cheltenham Festival Literary award, 1962.

WRITINGS: Innocents: Variations on a Theme (short stories), Hogarth, 1947, Scribner, 1948; Apology for a Hero, Scribner, 1950; Novelette, with Other Stories, Scribner, 1951; The Joy-Ride and After, Hogarth, 1963; Scribner, 1964; Lost Upon the Roundabouts (short stories), Hogarth, 1964; A Case Examined (novel), Hogarth, 1965; The Middling: Chapters in the Life of Ellie Toms, Hogarth, 1967; John Brown's Body, Hogarth, 1969; Femina Real (short stories), Hogarth, 1971. Author of television play, "Pringle."

WORK IN PROGRESS: A novel.

BIOGRAPHICAL/CRITICAL SOURCES: Listener, October 26, 1967; Observer Review, October 29, 1967; Times Literary Supplement, November 2, 1967; Books and Bookmen, January, 1970.

* * *

BARKER, George Granville 1913-

PERSONAL: Born February 26, 1913, in Essex, England; son of George and Marion Frances (Taaffe) Barker; married first wife, Elizabeth, 1942; married second wife, Elspeth Langlands, January 10, 1964; children: Raffaella-Flora, Alescander, Roderick, Samuel. Education: Attended Marlborough School, 1920-27, Regents Street Polytechnic, 1927-30. Politics: None. Religion: Roman Catholic. Home: Bintry House, 1 Itteringham, Aylsham, Norfolk, England. Agent: John Johnson, 3 Albemarle St., London, England.

CAREER: Writer. Professor of English literature, Imperial Tohoku University, Sendai, Japan, 1939-41; visiting professor of English literature, State University of New York at Buffalo, 1965-66. Awards, honors: Guiness Prize; Borestone Mountain Poetry award; Levinson Prize, Poetry Magazine, 1965.

WRITINGS: Thirty Preliminary Poems, Archer Press, 1933; Alanna Autumnal, Wishart & Co., 1933; Janus (stories), Faber, 1935; Poems, Faber, 1935; Calamiterror (poems), Faber, 1937.

Lament and Triumph (poems), Faber, 1940; Selected Poems, Macmillan, 1941; Sacred and Secular Elegies, New Directions, 1943; Eros in Dogma (poems), Faber, 1944; Love Poems, Dial, 1947.

News of the World (poems), Faber, 1950; The Dead Seagull (novel), Lehmann, 1950, Farrar, Straus, 1951; The True Confession of George Barker (poem), Fore Publications, 1950, New American Library, 1964; A Vision of Beasts and Gods, Faber, 1954; Collected Poems, 1930-1955, Faber, 1957, Criterion, 1958; Two Plays, Faber, 1958.

The View from a Blind I (poems), Faber, 1962; (with Martin Bell and Charles Causley) Penguin Modern Poets Number Three, Penguin, 1962; (author of foreword) Alfred, Lord Tennyson, Idylls of the King, and a Selection of Poems, New American Library, 1962; Collected Poems, 1930-1965, October House, 1965; Dreams of a Summer Night (poems), Faber, 1966; The Golden Chains, Faber, 1968; Runes and Rhymes and Tunes and Chimes, Faber, 1969.

Essays, Macgibbon & Kee, 1970; To Aylsham Fair (poems), Faber, 1970; Poems of People and Places, Faber, 1971; The Alphabetical Zoo, Faber, 1972.

BIOGRAPHICAL/CRITICAL SOURCES: Saturday Review, December 25, 1965; Times Literary Supplement, April 14, 1966, April 16, 1970; Punch, March 27, 1968; London Magazine, May, 1968; Sewanee Review, summer, 1968; Martha Fodaski, George Barker, Twayne, 1969; New Statesman, September 25, 1970.

* * *

BARKER, Will 1913-
(Doug Demarest)

PERSONAL: Born March 25, 1913, in Troy, N.Y.; son of William, Jr. (manufacturer, president of William Barker Co.) and Florence (Herring) Barker. Education: Attended New York University. Politics: "Republican, more or less." Religion: Episcopalian. Home and office: 1601 Argonne Pl., Washington, D.C. 20009. Agent: Marie F. Rodell, 141 East 55th St., New York, N.Y. 10022.

CAREER: U.S. Department of Interior, Fish and Wildlife Service, Washington, D.C., writer and editor, 1949-54; free-lance writer, 1955—. Editorial consultant, Robert B. Luce, Inc., 1962-63. Copywriter, G. S. Schirmer, Inc. (music publisher), New York, N.Y. Lecturer at Montana State University Writers' Conference, 1958, Fredonia State Teachers College, 1960, and Georgetown University Writer's Institute, 1961. Photographer-illustrator of own work. Actor in community theatre, Washington, D.C. area. Member of publicity staff, District of Columbia Action Committee for School Libraries, 1960-61. Military service: U.S. Army Air Forces, 1942-43.

MEMBER: American Museum of Natural History (associate), National Wildlife Federation (associate), Children's Book Guild of Washington, D.C. (secretary, 1960-61; program director, 1961-62). Awards, honors: National Wildlife Federation citation for work in conservation education, twice.

WRITINGS: Familiar Animals of America (Outdoor Life Book Club selection), Harper, 1956; Winter-Sleeping Wildlife, Harper, 1958; Familiar Insects of America, Harper, 1960; Wildlife in America's History, Luce, 1962; Familiar Reptiles and Amphibians of America, Harper, 1964; Fresh-Water Friends and Foes, Acropolis Books, 1966, 2nd edition, 1967.

Contributor: The Illustrated Library of Natural Sciences, Simon & Schuster, 1958; Nila Banton Smith and others, editors, Time for Adventure, Bobbs-Merrill, 1960; Nila Banton Smith and others, editors, Beyond the Horizon,

Bobbs-Merrill, 1960. Author of produced one-act play, "First Make Mad." Author and editor of circulars, leaflets, papers, and brochures for U.S. Fish and Wildlife Service. Contributor of nature column to *Science News Letter;* regular contributor to *American Forests,* and to *American Junior Red Cross News* and *American Junior Red Cross Journal,* 1956—; also contributor of articles, features, and verse to *American Field, Ford Times, Natural History, Science Digest, Sports Afield, Sports Illustrated, Kansas City Star, Milwaukee Journal,* and other magazines and newspapers; contributor to *Book of Knowledge.*

SIDELIGHTS: *Fifty Years of Children's Books,* published by National Council of Teachers of English, lists *Winter-Sleeping Wildlife* as one of 250 most significant books for children in fifty-year period, 1910-60.

* * *

BARKER, William P(ierson) 1927-

PERSONAL: Born February 14, 1927, in Pittsburgh, Pa.; son of John Bryant and Blair (Jessop) Barker; married Elsie Jean Cotton, June 28, 1950; children: John Bryant II, Ellen Cotton. *Education:* Haverford College, B.A., 1947; University of Edinburgh, graduate student, 1947-48; Pittsburgh Theological Seminary, B.D., 1950. *Home:* 2621 Walnut St., Allentown, Pa. 18104. *Office:* First Presbyterian Church, 3231 Tilghman St., Allentown, Pa. 18104.

CAREER: Minister, United Presbyterian Church in the U.S.A.; Bower Hill Community Church, Pittsburgh, Pa., pastor, 1950-68; Pittsburgh Theological Seminary, Pittsburgh, Pa., director of continuing education and alumni relations, 1968-72; First Presbyterian Church, Allentown, Pa., senior pastor, 1972—. Director of summer work camp in Puerto Rico, 1963.

WRITINGS—All published by Revell: *Twelve Who Were Chosen: The Disciples of Jesus,* 1958; *Saints in Aprons and Overalls: Friends of Paul,* 1959; *Kings in Shirtsleeves: Men Who Ruled Israel,* 1961; *Personalities Around Jesus,* 1964; *As Matthew Saw the Master,* 1964; *Everyone in the Bible,* 1966; *They Stood Boldly: Men and Women in the Book of Acts,* 1967; *Who's Who in Church History,* 1969; *Saints and Swingers: The Under-Thirties in the Bible,* 1971; *Women and the Liberator,* 1972.

* * *

BARKIN, Solomon 1907-

PERSONAL: Born December 2, 1907, in New York, N.Y.; son of Julian and Lillian (Kroll) Barkin; married Elaine Rappaport, April 21, 1940; children: David, Roger, Amy. *Education:* College of the City of New York (now City College of the City University of New York), B.S., 1928; Columbia University, M.A., 1929, postgraduate study, 1932-33; Harvard University, Wertheim fellow in industrial relations, 1948-49. *Politics:* Democrat. *Religion:* Jewish. *Home:* Long Hill Rd., Leverett, Mass. 01054. *Office:* Department of Economics, University of Massachusetts, Amherst, Mass. 01002.

CAREER: College of the City of New York, New York, N.Y., instructor, 1928-31; New York State Commission on Old Age Security, assistant director of research, 1929-30, of continuation committee, 1930-33; National Recovery Administration, assistant director of labor advisory board, 1933-35, of labor studies section, 1935-36; U.S. Department of Commerce, Division of Industrial Economics, chief of labor section, 1936-37; Textile Workers Union of America, New York, N.Y., director of research, 1937-63; Organization of Economic Cooperation and Development, Paris, France, deputy to director, 1963-68; University of Massachusetts, Amherst, professor of economics and research associate of the Labor Center, 1968—. Adjunct professor of industrial relations, Columbia University, Graduate School of Business. U.S. posts include vice-chairman of committee on research of President's Conference on Industrial Safety, member of labor research advisory council, Department of Labor. Vice-president, Joint Council on Economic Education; director, League for Industrial Democracy. Trustee, National Council on Aging, and National Planning Association.

MEMBER: Gerontological Society (fellow), Inter-Union Institute (chairman of board), Industrial Relations Research Association (president, 1964), American Statistical Association, Council on Foreign Relations, American Economic Association, Phi Beta Kappa. *Awards, honors:* Citations for contribution to economic education, Joint Council for Economic Education, 1958; honors award, *Journal of Political Economy,* 1972.

WRITINGS: *Old Age Security,* J.B. Lyon, 1930; *The Older Workers in Industry: A Study of New York State Manufacturing Industries,* J.P. Lyon, 1933; *N.R.A. Policies,* U.S. Government Printing Office, 1933; *Substandard Conditions of Living,* Textile Workers Union of America, 1944; *Toward Fairer Federal Labor Standards: Questions and Answers on Improving the Fair Labor Standards Act of 1938,* Committee on the Revision of Fair Labor Standards Act, C.I.O., 1948; (with Franklin G. Bishop) *Air Conditioning in Textile Mills: The Case for Temperature and Humidity Control to Provide Comfort, Health, Safety, and Optimum Production,* Textile Workers Union of America, 1948; (with Bishop) *Work-Duty Charts for Textile Operations: A Checklist of Job Content and Equipment,* Textile Workers Union of America, 1951; (with Bishop and Sumner Shapiro) *Textile Workers' Job Primer,* Volume I, Textile Workers Union of America, 1953; (editor with others) *Research in Industrial Human Relations,* Harper, 1957; *Automation and the Community,* Research Department, Textile Workers Union of America, 1960; *The Decline of the Labor Movement, and What Can Be Done About It,* Center for the Study of Democratic Institutions, 1961; (editor with Albert Blum) *The Crisis in the American Trade-Union Movement,* American Academy of Political and Social Science, 1963; (with others) *Manpower Policies and Problems in the Netherlands,* Organization of Economic Cooperation and Development (Paris), 1967; (editor and contributor) *Technical Change and Manpower Planning: Coordination at Enterprise Level,* Office of Economic Cooperation and Development, 1967; (editor) *The Role of Trade Unionism in Independent Developing Countries,* Office of Economic Cooperation and Development, 1967; (editor with others, and contributor) *International Labor,* Harper, 1968; (editor and contributor) *Flexibility of Retirement Age,* Office of Economic Cooperation and Development, 1971; *Manpower Policy in Norway,* Office of Economic Development and Cooperation, 1972. Contributor to economics and industrial journals. Member of board of editors, *Arbitration Journal.*

WORK IN PROGRESS: *Comparative Manpower Systems: Crossroads in Industrial Relations in the Western World.*

* * *

BARKSDALE, Hiram C(ollier) 1921-

PERSONAL: Born December 4, 1921, in Sandersville, Ga.; son of William Henry (an educator) and Maude (Smith) Barksdale; married Jeanne Epp, July 22, 1950; children: Hiram C., Jr., Beverly J., Sally B., A. Andrew. *Education:* University of Georgia, B.B.A., 1948; New York University, M.S., 1949, Ph.D., 1955. *Home:* 340 Cedar Creek Dr., Athens, Ga. 30601. *Office:* Marketing

Department, University of Georgia, Athens, Ga. 30601.

CAREER: Advertising Research Foundation, New York, N.Y., project manager, 1952-56, assistant to the president, 1956-60; New York University, New York, N.Y., associate professor, 1956-60, professor and chairman of marketing department, 1960-65; University of Georgia, Athens, professor, 1965—, chairman of marketing department, 1968—. Consultant to business and legal firms. Market Research Council, member. *Military service:* U.S. Army, 1943-46. *Member:* American Marketing Association, American Association for the Advancement of Science, Institute of Management Sciences, Society for the History of Technology, World Future Society, Phi Beta Kappa, Beta Gamma Sigma.

WRITINGS: The Use of Survey Research Findings as Legal Evidence, Printers' Ink Books, 1957; *Problems in Marketing Research: In-Basket Simulation,* Holt, 1963; (editor) *Marketing in Progress: Patterns and Potentials,* Holt, 1964; (editor) *Marketing—Change and Exchange: Readings from "Fortune,"* Holt, 1964; (editor with William Weilbacher) *Marketing Research: Selected Readings with Analytical Commentaries,* Ronald, 1966.

*   *   *

BARLOW, Frank   1911-

PERSONAL: Born April 19, 1911, in Stoke-on-Trent, England; son of Percy Hawthorn (a schoolmaster) and Margaret Julia (Wilkinson) Barlow; married July 1, 1936; children: John Francis, Michael Edward. *Education:* St. John's College, Oxford, B.A., 1933, M.A., D.Phil., 1937. *Home:* Middle Court Hall, Kenton, Exeter, Devonshire, England. *Office:* Queen's Building, Queen's Dr., Exeter, England.

CAREER: University College, University of London, London, England, assistant lecturer, 1936-40; University College of the South-West, Exeter, England, lecturer, 1946-53, reader, 1949-53; University of Exeter, Exeter, professor of history, 1953—, dean of faculty of arts, 1955-59, deputy vice-chancellor, 1961-63. *Military service:* British Army, 1941-46; became major. *Member:* British Academy (fellow), Royal Society of Literature (fellow), Royal Historical Society (fellow; member of council, 1960-63).

WRITINGS: (Editor) *The Letters of Arnulf of Lisieux,* Royal Historical Society, 1939; (editor) *Durham Annals and Documents of the Thirteenth Century,* Surtees Society, 1945; *Durham Jurisdictional Peculiars,* Oxford University Press, 1950; *The Feudal Kingdom of England, 1042-1216,* Longmans, Green, 1955, 2nd edition, McKay, 1961, 3rd edition, Longmans, Green, 1972; (editor, translator, and author of introduction and notes) *The Life of King Edward, Who Rests at Westminster,* Oxford University Press, 1962; *The English Church, 1000-1066: A Constitutional History,* Shoe String, 1963; *William I and the Norman Conquest,* English Universities Press, 1965, Collier, 1967; *Edward the Confessor and the Norman Conquest,* Historical Association, 1966; (editor) *Exeter and Its Region,* University of Exeter, 1969; *Edward the Confessor,* University of California Press, 1970.

BIOGRAPHICAL/CRITICAL SOURCES: Observer Review, November 15, 1970; *Books and Bookmen,* February, 1971.

*   *   *

BARMANN, Lawrence Francis   1932-

PERSONAL: Born June 9, 1932, in Maryville, Mo.; son of Francis L. (a merchant) and Weber (LaMar) Barmann. *Education:* St. Louis University, B.A., 1956, Ph.L., 1957, S.T.L., 1964; Fordham University, M.A., 1960; Princeton University, doctoral study, 1965-66; Cambridge

University, Ph.D., 1970. *Home:* 221 North Grand Blvd., St. Louis, Mo. 63103.

CAREER: Ordained Roman Catholic priest, 1963; member of Society of Jesus; St. Louis University High School, St. Louis, Mo., teacher of history, and advanced placement program to honors seniors, 1957-59; St. Mary's College, St. Mary's Kan., teacher of church history, 1963-64; St. Louis University, St. Louis, Mo., now assistant professor of history.

WRITINGS: (Editor and author of introduction) John Henry Newman, *Newman at St. Mary's: A Selection of the Parochial and Plain Sermons,* Newman, 1962; (editor) John Henry Newman, *Reflections on God and Self,* Herder, 1965; *Baron Friedrich von Huegel and the Modernist Crisis in England,* Cambridge University Press, 1971. Contributor of articles to historical, philosophical, and theological journals.

WORK IN PROGRESS: Editing complete correspondence of Baron Friedrich von Huegel, with Norman Kemp Smith, under a research grant from the American Philosophical Society of Philadelphia.

*   *   *

BARNARD, (James) Alan   1928-

PERSONAL: Born November 6, 1928, in Mildura, New South Wales, Australia; son of Colin (a research botanist) and Joyce (Deane) Barnard; married Patricia Brockbank, December 30, 1949; children: Jill Amanda, Matthew Alan. *Education:* University of Sydney, B.Ec., 1950; graduate study at University of London and University of Leeds, 1954; Australian National University, Ph.D., 1956. *Home:* 18 Godfrey St., Campbell, Australian Capital Territory, Australia. *Office address:* Australian National University, Box 4 G.P.O., Canberra, Australian Capital Territory, Australia.

CAREER: Canberra University College, Canberra, Australian Capital Territory, Australia, lecturer in economic history, 1955-57; Australian National University, Canberra, research fellow, 1957-60, fellow, 1960-63, senior fellow, 1963-70, professorial fellow in economic history, 1970—. *Member:* Economic History Society, Economic History Association.

WRITINGS: The Australian Wool Market, 1840-1900, Melbourne University Press for Australian National University, 1958; *Visions and Profits: Studies in the Business Career of Thomas Sutcliffe Mort,* Cambridge University Press, 1961; *Thomas Sutcliffe Mort,* Oxford University Press, 1962; (editor) *The Simple Fleece: Studies in the Australian Wool Industry,* Cambridge University Press, 1962; (contributor) R.O. Slatyer and R.A. Perry, editors, *Arid Lands of Australia,* Australian National University Press, 1969. Contributor of articles to learned journals. Member of editorial board, *Business Archives and History* (Sydney).

WORK IN PROGRESS: A history of Goldsbrough, Mort & Co. Ltd., Australian wool-broking and pastoral finance company.

*   *   *

BARNES, Djuna   1892-
(Lydia Steptoe)

PERSONAL: Born June 12, 1892, in Cornwall-on-Hudson, N.Y., daughter of Wald and Elizabeth (Chappell) Barnes (father, Henry Budington, changed his name to Wald Barnes). *Education:* Privately educated; studied art at Pratt Institute and Art Students League. *Home:* 5 Patchin Place, New York, N.Y. 10011.

CAREER: Reporter, illustrator, special feature writer for magazines and newspapers, 1913-31. Full-time writer,

1931—. Trustee, New York committee, Dag Hammarskjoeld Foundation. *Member:* National Institute of Arts and Letters, Authors Guild, League of Dramatists (England).

WRITINGS: The Book of Repulsive Women, Bruno Chap Book, 1915; (self-illustrated) *A Book* (short stories, short plays, poems, and drawings), Boni & Liveright, 1923, new edition, with three new stories added, published as *A Night Among the Horses,* Liveright, 1929; (self-illustrated) *Ryder* (novel), Liveright, 1928; (self-illustrated) *The Ladies' Almanack,* published anonymously, privately printed at Dijon, France, 1928, reprinted, Harper, 1972; *Nightwood* (novel), with introduction by T.S. Eliot, Faber, 1936, Harcourt, 1937, 2nd edition, Faber, 1950, New Directions, 1961; *The Antiphon* (play in verse), Farrar, Straus & Cudahy, 1958 (produced at Royal Theatre, Stockholm, February, 1961, from a translation by Dag Hammarskjoeld and Karl Ragner Gierow); *Spillway* (short stories), Faber, 1962; *Selected Works: Spillway, The Antiphon, Nightwood,* Farrar, Straus & Cudahy, 1962. Plays: "Three From the Earth," "An Irish Triangle," "Kurzy of the Sea" (all one act), produced by Provincetown Players, 1919-20; "The Dove," produced at Studio Theatre 1926. Contributor to *Little Review, Dial, All-Story Magazine, Smart Set, Vanity Fair* and other publications, under pseudonym, Lydia Steptoe. Represented in prose and poetry anthologies.

SIDELIGHTS: Reviews were not wholly in praise of Barnes' early work. Some described her writing as "not comfortable or pleasant," as having "unintelligibilities. . . . although she attains a momentary but genuine power." In 1923 Burton Rascoe wrote: "In escaping the commonplace, the platitude, the cliche, and the formula she has retreated so far into ironic and disillusioned disdain that she has seemingly nothing left but a will for acrid observation and grim absurdities." He continued, however, "Her book is one of the curiosities of modern American letters, and it has unusual qualities which make it something more than a curiosity. For one thing it is intelligently entertaining." Peter Quennell called *Nightwood* "not only a strangely original but an extremely moral work," and said: "She shows remarkable fertility of invention, a very uncommon skill in the management of words." Mark Van Doren wrote of the same book: "For brilliance and formal beauty few novels of any age can compare with [this]. But one must also say how desperate it is. . . . The point is that Miss Barnes has strained rather than enriched our sensibilities." Upon the appearance of her only published play, the *Times Literary Supplement* reviewer observed: "*The Antiphon,* because of its uncompromising bitterness and its equally uncompromising language, is even less likely than *Nightwood* to prove popular, but it is probably that there will always be one or two eccentrics who think that it gives its author the first place among women who have written verse in the English language."

Sylvia Beach in *Shakespeare and Company,* writes that Miss Barnes "was not one to cry her wares." Her writing is considered difficult, and is unknown by the general reading public. There is, however, an audience of avant gardists who credit her (as does T.S. Eliot in his introduction to *Nightwood)* with "the great achievement of a style, the beauty of phrasing, the brilliance of wit and characterization, and a quality of horror and doom very nearly related to that of Elizabethan tragedy." "To say [as Eliot does] that *Nightwood* will appeal primarily to readers of poetry does not mean that it is not a novel, but that it is so good a novel that only sensibilities trained on poetry can wholly appreciate it." Rose C. Feld once wrote: "If genius is perfection wrought out of anguish and pain and intellectual flagellation, then Djuna Barnes's novel *Nightwood* is a book of genius. . . . No

gayety and no light falls upon her pattern, which is not to say that her pages are devoid of laughter or humor. For humor she has in abundance but it runs deep in hidden places and the laughter it evokes is tragic. . . . Her prose is lyrical to a degree where it seems of another age and another world but at the same time it does not lose kinship with the earthiness of humans." Edwin Muir calls *The Antiphon* "one of the greatest things that has been written in our time," adding, "Miss Barnes's prose is the only prose by a living writer which can be compared with that of Joyce, and in one point it is superior to his: in its richness in exact and vivid imagery."

She spent a great deal of time in Paris, has lived in London, and traveled extensively. *Nightwood* has been translated into Dutch, Swedish, French, Italian, Spanish, and German.

BIOGRAPHICAL/CRITICAL SOURCES: New York Herald Tribune Book Section, October 14, 1923, March 7, 1937, April 29, 1962; *Nation,* January 2, 1924, April 3, 1937; *Saturday Review,* November 17, 1928; *New Statesman,* October 17, 1936; Edwin Muir, *The Present Age,* Cresset Press, 1939; *Times Literary Supplement,* April 4, 1958; Sylvia Beach, *Shakespeare and Company,* Harcourt, 1959; *Kirkus,* October 15, 1961; *Berkeley Daily Gazette,* March 31, 1961; *Time,* April 20, 1962; *Atlantic,* May, 1962; *Chapel Hill Weekly,* September 9, 1962; Joseph Frank, *The Widening Gyre,* Rutgers University Press, 1963; *Critique,* Spring, 1964.†

*   *   *

BARNES, James A(nderson) 1898-

PERSONAL: Born November 17, 1898, in Prentiss, Ky.; son of Joseph Franklin (a farmer) and Emma (Brown) Barnes; married Elinor Shafer, January 14, 1928 (died, 1957); married Doris Engstrom, Aug. 8, 1968. *Education:* Kentucky State Teachers College (now Western Kentucky State University), B.A., 1924; University of Wisconsin, M.A., 1925, Ph.D., 1928. *Politics:* Democrat. *Religion:* Methodist. *Home:* 5989 S.W. 80th St., Miami, Fla. 33143.

CAREER: State University of South Dakota, Vermillion, assistant professor, 1928-29; Temple University, Philadelphia, instructor, 1930-32, associate professor, 1932-46, became professor of history, 1946; currently professor emeritus. Historian, U.S. War Department, Army Service Forces, 1942-45. Visiting professor at University of Pennsylvania, 1948-49, and University of Miami, 1955, 1966; visiting professor, summers, at University of Kentucky, 1929, University of Texas, 1936, 1941, University of North Carolina, 1937, and University of Pennsylvania, 1946, 1948. Deviser of early microfilm reading machine similar to present commercial reader. Introduced miniature camera (35 mm) as portable copying instrument. Member of board of directors, Pennsylvania Historical Foundation. *Military service:* U.S. Army, American Expeditionary Forces, World War I; became sergeant.

MEMBER: American Historical Association, Society of American Historians (charter), American Association for State and Local History, American Economic History Association, Western History Society (charter), Mississippi Valley Historical Association (former member of executive committee), Pennsylvania Historical Association (president, 1960-63), Philadelphia Lincoln-Civil War Society, Rotary. *Awards, honors:* Brookings Institution fellow, 1929-30; Social Science Research Council fellow, 1932-33, and grant-in-aid, 1937; Hayes Memorial Foundation, grant-in-aid, 1940.

WRITINGS: John G. Carlisle: Financial Statesman, Dodd, 1931, Peter Smith, 1967; *The Wealth of the American People: A History of Their Economic Life,* Prentice-Hall, 1949; (editor with wife, Elinor Barnes) *Naval Surgeon: Blockading the South, 1862-1866,* Indiana University Press, 1963; (editor with E. Barnes) *Naval Surgeon: Revolt in Japan, 1868-1869,* Indiana University Press, 1963.

Contributor: *Leica Manual; The United States, 1865-1900; Annual Guide to Historical Literature;* James Truslow Adams, *Dictionary of American History,* Supplement I, 1961, Supplement II, 1973. Contributor of reviews and articles to historical journals. *Pennsylvania History,* book review editor, 1937-41, editor-in-chief, 1941-45; member of editorial board of Hayes Memorial Foundation, 1941-46; also former member of editorial board of Mississippi Valley Historical Association.

WORK IN PROGRESS: Documentary History of American Economic Development; Origins of American Discontent.

AVOCATIONAL INTERESTS: Travel, photography, gardening, and orchid growing.

*   *   *

BARNES, James J(ohn)   1931-

PERSONAL: Born November 16, 1931, in St. Paul, Minn.; son of Harry George (a businessman) and Bertha (Blaul) Barnes; married Patience Plummer, July 9, 1955; children: Jennifer Chase, Geoffrey Prescott. *Education:* Amherst College, B.A., 1954; New College, Oxford, B.A., 1956, M.A., 1961; Harvard University, Ph.D., 1960. *Religion:* Protestant Episcopal. *Home:* 7 Locust Hill, Crawfordsville, Ind. 47933. *Office:* Department of History, Wabash College, Crawfordsville, Ind. 47933.

CAREER: Wabash College, Crawfordsville, Ind., assistant professor, 1962-67, associate professor of history, 1968—. Crawfordsville Human Relations Council, member. *Member:* American Historical Association, American Rhodes Scholars, Bibliographical Society (Great Britain), History Association and Economic History Society (both Great Britain), Society for Religion in Higher Education, Phi Beta Kappa. *Awards, honors:* Rhodes Scholar, 1954-56; grants from Social Science Research Council, 1962 and 1970, American Philosophical Society, 1964 and 1968, and American Council of Learned Societies, 1964.

WRITINGS: Free Trade in Books: A Study of the London Book Trade Since 1800, Oxford University Press, 1964.

WORK IN PROGRESS: The Efforts to Secure an Anglo-American Copyright Agreement in the Mid-19th Century.

AVOCATIONAL INTERESTS: Folk singing, accompanying self on guitar, cycling, and horseback riding.

*   *   *

BARNITT, Nedda Lemmon
(N.B. Lamont, Nedda Lamont)

PERSONAL: Born in Brighton, England. *Home:* 1610 South West St., Falls Church, Va. 22042. *Agent:* Ruth D. Champenois, Caldwell, N.J. 07006.

CAREER: Novelist.

WRITINGS: (Under pseudonym Nedda Lamont) *The Shining Mountain,* Hutchinson, 1956; (under pseudonym Nedda Lamont) *The Beauty Makers,* Dutton, 1958; (under pseudonym N.B. Lamont) *Erika,* Cassell, 1959; (under pseudonym N.B. Lamont) *No Wider Than the Heart,* Doubleday, 1961; (under pseudonym N.B. Lamont) *The Island,* Cassell, 1961.

WORK IN PROGRESS: The Golden Ring, a novel.

BARON, Samuel H(askell)   1921-

PERSONAL: Born May 24, 1921, in New York, N.Y.; son of James (a clothier) and Dinah (Bader) Baron; married M. Virginia Wilson; children: Sheila, Carla, Laura. *Education:* Cornell University, B.S., 1942; Columbia University, M.A., 1948, Ph.D., 1952. *Home:* 8888 Cliffridge Ave., La Jolla, Calif. 92037. *Office:* University of California, La Jolla, Calif. 92037.

CAREER: University of Tennessee, Knoxville, instructor in history, 1948-50, 1951-53; Grinnell College, Grinnell, Iowa, assistant professor, 1956-57, associate professor, 1957-63, professor of history, 1963-66; University of California, San Diego, professor, 1966—. Visiting lecturer in history, Northwestern University, 1953-54; visiting assistant professor of history, University of Missouri, 1954-55, University of Nebraska, 1955-56. *Military service:* U.S. Army, 1942-46; became captain. *Member:* American Historical Association, American Association for the Advancement of Slavic Studies, American Association of University Professors (national council member, 1963-65), American Civil Liberties Union. *Awards, honors:* Harvard fellowship in East Asian studies; grants from Social Science Research Council, American Council of Learned Societies, and Guggenheim Foundation.

WRITINGS: Plekhanov, the Father of Russian Marxism, Stanford University Press, 1963; (editor and translator) Adam Olearius, *The Travels of Olearius in Seventeenth Century Russia,* Stanford University Press, 1967.

WORK IN PROGRESS: The Failure of Capitalist Development in Russia, publication expected in 1974.

*   *   *

BARR, Donald   1921-

PERSONAL: Born August 2, 1921, in New York, N.Y.; son of Pelham (an economist) and Estelle (a psychologist; maiden name, de Young) Barr; married Mary Margaret Ahern (a college teacher), April 22, 1946; children: Christopher James, William Pelham, Hilary Benedict Thomas, Stephen Matthew. *Education:* Columbia University, A.B., 1941, M.A., 1951. *Politics:* Republican. *Home:* 445 Riverside Dr., New York, N.Y. 10027. *Office:* Dalton School, 108 East 89th St., New York, N.Y. 10028.

CAREER: Columbia University, New York, N.Y., instructor in English, 1946-56, assistant to dean, School of Engineering 1956-59, assistant dean, Faculty of Engineering and Applied Science, 1959-64, former director of Science Honors Program; Dalton School, New York, N.Y., headmaster, 1964—. Associate program director, National Science Foundation, 1963-64. Member, New York County Republican Committee, 1952-63. *Military service:* U.S. Army, 1943-45; served in Office of Strategic Services, 1945. *Member:* American Association for the Advancement of Science, Authors League of America.

WRITINGS: The How and Why Wonder Book of Atomic Energy, Grosset, 1961; *The How and Why Wonder Book of Primitive Man,* Grosset, 1961; (contributor) Nona Balakian and Charles Simmons, editors, *The Creative Present: Notes on Contemporary American Fiction,* Doubleday, 1963; *The How and Why Wonder Book of Building,* Grosset, 1964; *Arithmetic for Billy Goats,* Harcourt, 1966; (with Darlene Geis and Martin L. Keen) *The Wonders of Prehistoric Life,* Grosset, 1966; *Who Pushed Humpty Dumpty?: Dilemmas in American Education Today,* Atheneum, 1971. Contributor of articles and reviews to *Saturday Review, Columbia University Forum, Commonweal, New York Times Book Review, Columbia Engineering Quarterly,* and other periodicals. Editor, "Intermediate Science Series," Holt; member of editorial board, *Nature and Science.*

SIDELIGHTS: Barr, who is alternately described as a conservative and iconoclastic educator, believes in both rigid discipline and internal motivation for students. He rejects mass testing, saying: "Everywhere schools and colleges ignore and starve the youngster's desire to learn; they find and exploit his desire to *pass*." He adds: "What youngsers, even adolescents, need to see is not a system grinding out decisions but a man making moral choices. How else will they learn to become men and to make moral choices?"

Barr also advocates strong control by parents. In *Who Pushed Humpty Dumpty?: Dilemmas in American Education Today,* Barr writes: "We offer very little resistance to our children. We tend to withhold reality from them by behaving as if there were no such notion as *earning* things. We thus keep them ignorant of the fundamental concept of human society, the concept of reciprocity ... we feel that we are being gratuitously mean if we make a child wait for satisfaction we could just as easily grant at once. But it is by waiting that children learn what time is."

Jerrold K. Footlick comments on Barr's philosophy: ". . . He is not content merely to comment; he reports what works for him and recommends specific approaches in such areas as reading, mathematics and science. And now that the awesome educational reforms of the past decade are being retrospectively viewed with growing skepticism, men like Donald Barr will be heard from with greater frequency. It is no more possible to reach a conclusion on their wisdom now than it was possible to judge the progressives in the 1920s or the reformers in the '60s. But for those who fear that education has become too undisciplined, Barr's manifesto will provide an arsenal of thought and a manual of action. His book is by turns pedantic and stubborn, charming and daring. And a lot of it makes sense."

BIOGRAPHICAL/CRITICAL SOURCES: Newsweek, September 27, 1971.†

*   *   *

BARREN, Charles   1913-
(Thomas Rainham)

PERSONAL: Born December 21, 1913, in London, England; son of Thomas Bearman and Ada Boone (Winfield) Barren; married Vera Dace, November 21, 1936; children: Melvyn, Stuart, Dianne. *Education:* Attended West Ham Technical College and Forest Training College. *Politics:* Independent. *Religion:* Church of England. *Home:* 1 Broomhill Rd., Goodmayes, Ilford, Essex, England.

CAREER: Held various teaching posts; lecturer in English and liberal studies at South East Essex Technical College and School of Art, Dagenham, Essex, England; Northeast London Polytechnic, lecturer in department of applied philosophy. Warden of various youth and community centers; chairman, NELP Science Fiction Foundation. *Military service:* British Army, 1940-46.

WRITINGS: (Under pseudonym Thomas Rainham) *Too Late to Mend,* Hurst & Blackett, 1957; *The Stunted Tree,* R. Hale, 1958; *The Seed of Evil,* R. Hale, 1958; *The Unmastered,* R. Hale, 1959; *Greenbury Hill,* R. Hale, 1960; *Eighty North,* R. Hale, 1960; *Jamestown,* R. Hale, 1961; (ghost and amanuensis for Frederick Barnardo) *An Active Life,* Bodley Head, 1963; (with R.C. Abel) *Trivana One,* Panther, 1966; *English for Overseas Students,* three books, Macmillan, 1967-68; (with Sol Scriden) *Tomorrow's Immortals,* Transcription Books, 1972. Contributor of articles, short stories, and poems to magazines. Editor-in-chief, *Foundation.*

WORK IN PROGRESS: Realism in Science Fiction, with D.P. Smith.

AVOCATIONAL INTERESTS: All sports except blood sports; the arts, particularly the theatre.

BIOGRAPHICAL/CRITICAL SOURCES: Books and Bookmen, May, 1961.

*   *   *

BARROSSE, Thomas   1926-

PERSONAL: Accent in surname is on second syllable, rhymes with "cross"; born June 3, 1926, in New Orleans, La.; son of Thomas Oakley (an automobile salesman) and Rosalie (Points) Barrosse. *Education:* University of Notre Dame, B.A., 1947; Pontifical Gregorian University, Rome, Italy, S.T.L., 1951; Pontifical Biblical Institute, Rome, Italy, S.S.L., 1953. *Home and office:* Holy Cross Novitiate, Bennington, Vt. 05201.

CAREER: Roman Catholic priest of Holy Cross order (C.S.C.); research in Near East, 1954, and Rome, Italy, 1954-56; University of Notre Dame, South Bend, Ind., lecturer in theology, 1956-57; Holy Cross College, Washington, D.C., professor of Scripture and dean of studies, 1957-66; Catholic University of America, Washington, D.C., lecturer in theology, 1961-62; International College of Holy Cross order, Rome, Italy, staff member, 1966-69; Holy Cross Novitiate, Bennington, Vt., director, 1969—. *Member:* Catholic Biblical Association of America, Society for New Testament Study (England), North American Josephology Society.

WRITINGS: (With Sister Jane Marie Murray) *God and His People* (high school religion text), Fides, 1958, abridged edition published as *God's People,* edited by Vincent J. Giese, 1960; (with Sister Jane Marie Murray) *Christ in the World* (high school religion text), Fides, 1960, abridged edition published as *Christ and His Church,* edited by Giese, 1961; *God Speaks to Men: Understanding the Bible,* Fides, 1960, revised and enlarged edition, 1964; *God Exists: The Biblical Record of God's Self-Revelation,* University of Notre Dame Press, 1963; *Christianity: Mystery of Love,* Fides, 1964; *Moreau: Portrait of a Founder,* Fides, 1969.

Contributor: Robert S. Pelton, editor, *Proceedings of the Institute for Local Superiors, 1963,* University of Notre Dame Press, 1964; *The Challenge of the Council: Person, Parish, World,* Liturgical Conference, 1964; *Studies in Salvation History,* Prentice-Hall, 1964; Sister M. Rosalie Ryan, editor, *Contemporary New Testament Studies,* Liturgical Press, 1965; *Reappraisal: Prelude to Change,* Maryknoll Publications, 1965. Author of pamphlets and monographs. Contributor to *Yearbook of Liturgical Studies, New Catholic Encyclopedia,* and *Catholic Youth Encyclopedia;* contributor of reviews and articles to theological and popular journals. Former member of editorial board, *Catholic Biblical Quarterly* and *Yearbook of Liturgical Studies.*

WORK IN PROGRESS: A Brief Commentary on the Fourth Gospel.

*   *   *

BARROW, Rhoda Catharine (Kitto)   1910-

PERSONAL: Born August 23, 1910, in St. Mawgan, Cornwall, England; daughter of John Vivian (librarian of the House of Commons) and Nettie Catherine (Ryves) Kitto. *Education:* Attended St. Albans High School, Hertfordshire, and Kerr Saunders College, London, England. *Home:* April Cottage, Chalfont Heights, Chalfont St. Peter, Buckinghamshire, England.

CAREER: Bridge teacher and writer. *Member:* International Bridge Press Association (assistant secretary and bulletin editor), English Bridge Union Teachers' Training Scheme (secretary), American Bridge Teachers' Association, London Duplicate Bridge Club, and other bridge organizations.

WRITINGS: Acol-ite's Quiz, Allen & Unwin, 1970; (with Eric Jannersten) *Cards on the Table,* Allen & Unwin, in press.

With Ben Cohen: *Acol Without Tears,* Allen & Unwin, 1962, 2nd edition published in America as *Bidding Better Bridge: Acol for Americans,* A.S. Barnes, 1965, 2nd edition revised, 1967; *Basic Acol,* Allen & Unwin, 1962; *Your Lead, Partner,* Allen & Unwin, 1963, published in America as *Opening Leads to Better Bridge,* A.S. Barnes, 1964; *Acol Quiz,* Allen & Unwin, 1963; *The ABC of Contract Bridge,* Anthony Blond, 1964, A.S. Barnes, 1965; *Contract Bridge,* Collins, 1965; *Calling a Spade a Spade; or, Acol in Action,* Anthony Blond, 1965, A.S. Barnes, 1966; *Conventions Made Clear: A Handbook for Contract Bridge Players,* Anthony Blond, 1966; *All About Acol,* Allen & Unwin, 1969.

Editor, with Ben Cohen, of *The Bridge Players' Encyclopedia,* international edition, Hamlyn, 1966. Compiler and distributor of the annual *Acol Player's Diary.* Contributor of regular columns to *Buckinghamshire Advertiser, Windsor, Slough & Eton Express, Brighton Herald, Bridge Magazine,* and other periodicals.

* * *

BARRY, Katharina Watjen 1936-

PERSONAL: Born March 31, 1936, in Berlin, Germany; daughter of Heinrich Eduard (a lawyer) and Irene (Sarre) Watjen; married Robert E. Barry, December 28, 1958; children: John Eduard, Christopher Luis. *Education:* Attended school in Zurich, Switzerland. *Religion:* Roman Catholic. *Home:* "Driftwood," Cliff Ave., Newport, R.I. 02840.

AWARDS, HONORS: A Is for Anything was listed among fifty best books of the year 1962, American Institute of Graphic Arts.

WRITINGS: (Self-illustrated) *A Is for Anything: An ABC Book of Pictures and Rhymes,* Harcourt, 1961; *A Bug to Hug,* Harcourt, 1964; (illustrator) Sesyle Joslin, *There Is a Bull on My Balcony,* Harcourt, 1966.

* * *

BARTRUM, Douglas A(lbert) 1907-

PERSONAL: Born June 28, 1907, in Marlow, Buckinghamshire, England; son of George and Maud Bartrum. *Education:* Attended High Wycombe Technical School. *Home:* Sunnyside, Bovingdon Green, Marlow, Buckinghamshire, England.

WRITINGS: Shrubs and Trees for Your Garden, W. & G. Foyle, 1955; *Climbing Plants for Your Garden,* Dover, 1956; *Rhododendrons and Magnolias,* Gifford, 1957; *Hydrangeas and Viburnums,* Gifford, 1958; *Lilac and Laburnum,* Gifford, 1959; *Climbing Plants and Some Wall Shrubs,* Gifford, 1959, revised edition, Branford, 1968; *Magnolias and Camellias,* W. & G. Foyle, 1959; *Foliage Plants for Your Garden,* W. & G. Foyle, 1961, Sportshelf, 1963; *Colour and Contrast in the Garden,* Gifford, 1962; *The Gourmet's Garden,* Faber, 1964, International Publications Service, 1971; *Rhododendrons and Azaleas,* W. & G. Foyle, 1964, Sportshelf, 1965; *Evergreens for Your Garden,* Gifford, 1967; *Water in Your Garden,* Branford, 1968; *From Garden to Kitchen,* Gifford, 1969; *Exotic Plants for the Home,* Gifford, 1970.

WORK IN PROGRESS: A book on the fundamentals of music criticism.

BASSET, Bernard 1909-

PERSONAL: Born March 21, 1909, in London, England; son of Hugh Fortescue and Bessie Lee (Cooper) Basset. *Education:* Attended Stonyhurst College; Campion Hall, Oxford, M.A. (first class honors), 1937; Heythorp College, theological student, 1931-35, 1938-42. *Home:* The Presbytery, 1 Albert Rd., Bournemouth, Hampshire, England.

CAREER: Roman Catholic priest of Jesuit order; Stonyhurst College, Blackburn, England, and Beaumont College, Windsor, England, lecturer in history, 1937-38, 1942-46; associated with Royal Air Force moral leadership courses, 1945-49; Roman Catholic Sodality Organisation, national secretary, 1950-62; Southwell House, Hampstead, London, England, superior, 1954-62; currently lecturer in history and religion, preacher attached to Jesuit church in Bournemouth, Hampshire, England, and organizer of Catholic youth work. Lecturer on two U.S. tours, 1959, 1961. Attached to Vatican Radio for first session of Vatican Council; represented *Catholic Herald,* London, at Eucharistic Congress in Bombay, India, 1964.

WRITINGS: Blessed Edmund Campion (verses), Burns & Oates, 1936; *Mr. Brice Lets Us Down and Other Stories,* Catholic Truth Society, 1939; *A Secret Service Agent and Other Stories,* Catholic Truth Society, 1940; *O.K. and Other Stories,* Catholic Truth Society, 1941; *Margery and Me* (short stories), David Organ, 1945; *The Seven Deadly Virtues, and Other Stories,* David Organ, 1947; *Farm Street,* David Organ, 1949.

Two Hundred Gospel Questions and Enquiries, Sheed, 1959; *We Neurotics: A Handbook for the Half-Mad,* Academy Guild Press, 1962; (with Vincent Whelan) *Youth and You: A Guide to Youth Work,* Catholic Social Guild, 1962; *Best of Both Worlds: A Guide to Holiness in the Suburbs,* Burns & Oates, 1963, Academy Guild Press, 1964; *Priest in the Piazza: Goal Line Tribute to a Council,* Academy Guild Press, 1963 (published in England as *Priest in the Piazza: Touchline Tribute to a Council,* Burns & Oates, 1963); *The Noonday Devil: Spiritual Support in Middle Age,* Academy Guild Press, 1964; *Priest in the Presbytery: A Psycho-ecclesiastical Extravaganza,* Burns & Oates, 1964, Herder & Herder, 1966; *Born for Friendship: The Spirit of Sir Thomas More,* Sheed, 1965; *Priest in Paradise: With God to Illinois,* Herder & Herder, 1966; *The English Jesuits from Campion to Martindale,* Burns & Oates, 1967, Herder & Herder, 1968; *We Agnostics: On the Tightrope to Eternity,* Herder & Herder, 1968.

How to Be Really With It: Guide to the Good Life, Doubleday, 1970 (published in England as *The Good Life Guide: Saints, Snobs and Sanity,* Sheed, 1971); *Let's Start Praying Again: Field Work in Meditation,* Herder & Herder, 1972.

SIDELIGHTS: Basset was once described in the English press as "the only Catholic priest writer who manages to have his tongue in his cheek and the bit between his teeth."

* * *

BASSETT, William Travis 1923-

PERSONAL: Born September 19, 1923; son of Homer Travis and Aileen (Lemon) Bassett; married Eva Campbell, May 18, 1952; children: Randall K., Melanie Ann. *Education:* Baylor University, A.B., 1948; Southern Baptist Theological Seminary, B.D., 1951, Th.M., 1960. *Home address:* Route 2, East Bend, N.C. 27018.

CAREER: Minister of Southern Baptist Church; pastor in Owentry, Ky., 1949-51; North Carolina Baptist Hospital, Winston-Salem, chaplain, 1951-52; pastor in Mocksville, N.C., 1954-56; Evon Baptist Church, East

Bend, N.D., pastor, 1959—. President, Yadkin Baptist Pastors' Conference, 1962. *Military service:* U.S. Navy, 1940-46; became yeoman first class. U.S. Naval Reserve, chaplain, 1952-62; served on active duty, 1952-54, 1956-58; retired for disability, as lieutenant, 1962.

WRITINGS: Counseling the Childless Couple, Prentice-Hall, 1963.

WORK IN PROGRESS: A study of the theology of mental health and illness.

AVOCATIONAL INTERESTS: Writing, bowling, tennis, and coin collecting.

BIOGRAPHICAL/CRITICAL SOURCES: The Fighting Men of Texas, Volume IV, Historical Publishing Co., 1948.

*   *   *

BATTIN, R(osabell) Ray   1925-

PERSONAL: Born May 25, 1925, in Rock Creek, Ohio; daughter of Harry Walter (a broker) and Sophia (Boldt) Ray; married Tom C. Battin (a professor), August 27, 1949. *Education:* Kent State University, student, 1944-45; University of Denver, A.B., 1948; University of Michigan, M.S., 1950; University of Miami, Coral Gables, Fla., postgraduate study, 1957; University of Florida, Ph.D., 1959. *Religion:* Unitarian. *Home:* 2130 Willowick, Houston, Tex. 77035. *Office:* 3931 Essex Lane, Houston, Tex. 77027.

CAREER: Speech and hearing clinician at universities and schools in Denver, Colo., Ann Arbor, Mich., and Gainesville, Fla., 1949-54; Houston Speech and Hearing Center, Houston, Tex., audiologist, 1954-56; Hedgecroft Hospital and Rehabilitation Center, Houston, Tex., director of department of communicative disorders, 1955-59; licensed psychologist, State of Texas; private practice as speech pathologist, audiologist, and clinical psychologist, Houston, Tex., 1959—. University of Houston, instructor in speech, 1956-59; University of Texas, School of Medicine, clinical instructor in department of surgery, 1963—. *Member:* International Association of Logopedics and Phoniatrics, American Psychological Association, American Speech and Hearing Association (fellow), Texas Psychological Association, Texas Speech and Hearing Association, Houston Psychological Association, Sigma Alpha Eta.

WRITINGS: A Study of the Comparative Effectiveness of Two Methods of Presenting to Parents Information Relative to Speech and Language Development in the Preschool Child, University of Florida, 1959; (with C. Olaf Haug) *Speech and Language Delay: A Home Training Program,* C.C Thomas, 1964, 2nd edition, 1968. Contributor to professional journals; book reviewer in speech and hearing for *Players* and *CEA Critic.*

WORK IN PROGRESS: A book on articulation disorders; *The Dysynchronous Child,* with Irvin Kraft.

*   *   *

BAUER, E. Charles   1916-

PERSONAL: Born May 7, 1916, in Rochester, N.Y.; son of Jacob P. (a grocer) and Jessie (Shoemaker) Bauer. *Education:* Studied at Aquinas Institute of Rochester, 1930-34, St. Andrew's Minor Seminary, 1934-36; St. Bernard's Theological Seminary, B.A., 1938, graduate study, 1938-42. *Home:* 529 Church St., Newark, N.Y. 14513.

CAREER: Ordained a Roman Catholic priest, 1942. Assistant pastor of churches in Rochester, N.Y., 1942-59; Newark State School for the Mentally Retarded, Newark, N.Y., Catholic chaplain, 1959-71; Newark Diocesan Coordinator for Special Education, 1971—. Deanery director, Rochester Diocesan Sodality Union, 1946-51. *Member:* National Association of Catholic Chaplains, National Association for Retarded Children, National Apostolate to the Mentally Retarded, American Association on Mental Deficiency.

WRITINGS: A Graphichism of Christian Doctrine, Queen's Work, 1958; *Retarded Children Are People,* Bruce, 1964; *Instant Theology,* Catholic Information Society, 1964; *Institutions are People* (documentary on life in a state school), John Day, 1966; *Instant Homilies* (150 sermons preached to the retarded), Concordia, 1971. Author of four musical plays for amateur groups; contributor of articles to several periodicals.

WORK IN PROGRESS: A novel based on retardation, *Small World—A Fantasy.*

*   *   *

BAUER, Erwin A.   1919-
(Ken Bourbon, Nat Franklin, Tom Hardin, Charles W. North, Barney Peters)

PERSONAL: Born August 22, 1919, in Cincinnati, Ohio; son of Adam John (a safety engineer) and Louise (Volz) Bauer; married Doris Parker, April 26, 1941; children: Parker, Robert. *Education:* Studied at the University of Cincinnati for three years. *Home and office:* 1720 Grace Lane, Columbus, Ohio 43220.

CAREER: Free-lance writer specializing in outdoor travel and adventure; illustrates own work (average fifty feature stories annually) with photographs. Public relations consultant for outdoor industries. *Military service:* U.S. Army, World War II and Korean Conflict; became first lieutenant; received Purple Heart and Croix de Guerre. *Member:* Society of Magazine Writers, American Society of Travel Writers, Ohio Outdoor Writers Association (former president). *Awards, honors:* Awards from Ohio Outdoor Writers Association for best magazine articles by an Ohio writer, 1949, 1950, 1962, and for best photos, 1965, 1966, 1968, and 1969.

WRITINGS: Bass in America: The Haunts, Habits, and Other Secrets of One of the World's Finest Fresh-Water Game Fish, includes photographs by Bauer and David Goodnow, Simon & Schuster, 1955; *The Bass Fisherman's Bible,* Doubleday, 1961; *The Salt-Water Fisherman's Bible,* Doubleday, 1962; *Complete Book of Outdoor Photography,* Popular Science, 1964, reissued as *Outdoor Photography,* Harper, 1965; *The Duck Hunter's Bible,* Doubleday, 1965; (with George Laycock) *The New Archery Handbook,* Fawcett, 1965; (with Laycock) *Hunting with Bow and Arrow,* Arco, 1966; *My Adventures with African Animals,* includes photographs by Bauer, Norton, 1968; *The Sportsman on Wheels,* Popular Science, 1969; (illustrator) Charles F. Waterman, *The Hunter's World,* includes photographs by Bauer and others, Random House, 1970; *Treasury of Big Game Animals,* Harper, 1972.

SIDELIGHTS: Bauer has visited fifty-seven countries in carrying out feature assignments. *Avocational interests:* Camping, climbing, exploration, hunting, nature, boating, dogs, ecology, and environment.

*   *   *

BAUGHMAN, Ray Edward   1925-

PERSONAL: Surname is pronounced *Bow*-man; born November 9, 1925, in Hutchinson, Kan.; son of Francis Edward and Ethel (Freese) Baughman; married Irma Lou Smith, April 18, 1949; children: Bryan Lee, Craig Allen, Ann Elaine. *Education:* Attended Kansas State College (now Kansas State University), 1943-44, and Halbert School of Photography, 1946-47; Dallas Bible Institute and Bible College, B.A., 1960, Th.B., 1963. *Home:* 1316 Chamberlain, Irving, Tex. 75060.

CAREER: Worked on a newspaper in Perry, Okla., and as operator of a portrait studio there before studying for the Baptist ministry; Dallas Bible Institute and Bible College, Dallas, Tex., director of Institute's correspondence school and director of Christian journalism department in day school, 1959—; Paris Bible Church, Paris, Tex., pastor, 1962—. Military service: U.S. Army, Armored Forces, 1944-46; served in Europe.

WRITINGS: The Abundant Life, Moody, 1959; Do You Know?, Dallas Bible Institute, 1959; Bible History Visualized, Moody, 1963; How to Hunt for Bible Treasure, Emmaus Bible School, 1964; The Kingdom of God Visualized, Moody, 1972. Reporter-photographer, Battle Star (Army newspaper), 1946; editor, Dallas Bible Institute News, 1956—.

WORK IN PROGRESS: How to Edit Small Publications, slanted to Christian churches and organizations; Publicity for the Christian Organization; Galatians Visualized; The Life of Christ Visualized; research on contemporary problems of the church.

SIDELIGHTS: Baughman illustrates some of his work with line drawings. Avocational interests: Camping, hunting, fishing, electronics, woodworking, mechanics, reading, and cooking.

*   *   *

BAUMAN, H(erman) Carl 1913-

PERSONAL: Born April 1, 1913, in New York, N.Y.; son of Jacob L. and Rose (Grummer) Bauman; married Ruth Berg, November 29, 1936; children: Elaine Marilyn (Mrs. Martin R. Rosen), Steven Michael. Education: Cooper Union, B.S. in Electrical Engineering, 1936; New York University, B.E.E., 1939. Home: 821 Albemarle St., Wyckoff, N.J. 07481. Office: Engineering and Construction Division, American Cyanamid Co., Berdan Ave., Wayne, N.J. 07470.

CAREER: Registered professional engineer in New York, New Jersey, and Louisiana; J. Sterling-Getchell, director of product research, 1935-40; Chemical Construction Corp., New York, N.Y., 1940-45, 1954-56, started as junior engineer, became assistant manager of cost and estimating department; American Cyanamid Co., New York, N.Y., chief electrical engineer, 1945-52, assistant head of general engineering department, 1952-53, manager of cost engineering at Wayne (N.J.) administrative offices, 1956—. Holder of two industrial patents. Member, Industrial and Engineering Chemistry Advisory Board, 1962-65.

MEMBER: National Society of Professional Engineers (director, 1961; vice-chairman, northeast region of professional engineers in industry committee, 1962-65), American Association of Cost Engineers (president, 1966-67), Institute of Electrical and Electronics Engineers, New York State Society of Professional Engineers (president, Kings County chapter, 1955-56), Eta Kappa Nu. Awards, honors: Citation from New York University, 1955, for significant achievement and distinction; award of merit, American Association of Cost Engineers, 1966.

WRITINGS: Fundamentals of Cost Engineering in the Chemical Industry, Reinhold, 1964. Contributor to Chemical Engineers' Handbook. Contributor of more than forty articles and reviews to engineering and technical journals.

*   *   *

BAUMGARTNER, John Stanley 1924-

PERSONAL: Born May 2, 1924, in Hampton, Iowa; son of Ralph Wesley (an insurance and real estate agent) and Winifred (Inglis) Baumgartner. Education: U.S. Military Academy, B.S., 1946; Harvard University, M.B.A., 1955. Home: 10843 Gothic Ave., Granada Hills, Calif. 91344.

CAREER: U.S. Army, career service in Signal Corps, 1946-59; commissioned second lieutenant, 1946, became major and senior parachutist. Formerly senior staff administrator at Hughes Aircraft Corp., Culver City, Calif.; now management consultant in private practice in Granada Hills, Calif., and part-time assistant professor at University of Southern California.

WRITINGS: Project Management, Irwin, 1963; (with Robert Q. Parsons) Anatomy of a Merger: How to Sell Your Company, Prentice-Hall, 1970; The Lonely Warriers: Case for the Military-Industrial Complex, Nash Publishing, 1970.

WORK IN PROGRESS: A book, The Competitive Organization.

BIOGRAPHICAL/CRITICAL SOURCES: New York Times Book Review, May 24, 1970; Library Journal, July, 1970.

*   *   *

BAUMRIN, Bernard H(erbert) 1934-
(Stefan Baumrin, Stefan Bernard)

PERSONAL: Born January 7, 1934, in New York, N.Y.; son of David (a corporate executive head) and Regina (Zuckerberg) Baumrin; married Judith Anne Marti (a psychologist), December 20, 1953; children: Seth Nathan, Jeanne. Education: Student at Marietta College, 1951-52, New York University, 1952-53; Ohio State University, A.B., 1956; Johns Hopkins University, Ph.D., 1960; Washington University, law student, 1965-67; Columbia University, J.D., 1970. Religion: Jewish. Home: 590 West End Ave., New York, N.Y. 10024; and Christiantown, West Tisbury, Mass. 02575. Office: Lehman College of the City University of New York, Bedford Blvd. W., Bronx, N.Y. 10468; and Graduate School, City University of New York, 33 West 42nd St., New York, N.Y. 10036.

CAREER: Teacher at private schools in Ohio, 1953-54, 1958; Johns Hopkins University, Baltimore, Md., director of forensics, 1957-59; Marti School, Dayton, Ohio, acting headmaster, 1958, 1959; University of Delaware, Newark, assistant professor of philosophy, 1961-64; Washington University, St. Louis, Mo., assistant professor of philosophy, 1964-67; Hunter College of the City University of New York, New York, N.Y., associate professor of philosophy, 1967-68; Lehman College of the City University of New York, Bronx, N.Y., associate professor of philosophy, 1968—. Visiting instructor in philosophy, Butler University, 1960-61; visiting assistant professor of philosophy, Antioch College, 1961. Member of executive board, Jewish Community Centers Association, 1965-66; member of executive committee, City University of New York Doctoral Faculty in Philosophy.

MEMBER: American Philosophical Association, Mind Association, Philosophy of Science Association, Society of Ancient Greek Philosophy, American Association for the Advancement of Science, American Association of University Professors (chairman, academic freedom and tenure committee, University of Delaware, 1961-64; member of executive board, Washington University, 1966-67), American Civil Liberties Union (member of executive board, St. Louis chapter, 1966-67).

WRITINGS: (Editor) Philosophy of Science: The Delaware Seminar, two volumes, Interscience, 1963; (author of introduction) L.A. Selby-Bigge, editor, British Moralists, Bobbs-Merrill, 1964, (with others) The Politics of Escalation in Viet Nam: A Citizens' White Paper, Beacon Press, 1966; (editor) Hobbes' Leviathan: Interpretation and Criticism, Wadsworth, 1969. Contributor to

Journal of Philosophy, Concept, New Scholasticism, American Philosophical Quarterly, Journal of the History of Philosophy, Proceedings of the XIV International Congress of Philosophy, and other journals. Member of editorial board, Metaphilosophy and Columbia Survey of Human Rights Law.

WORK IN PROGRESS: The Logical Foundations of Ethics; Moral Foundations of the Law; The British Intuitionist Tradition.

AVOCATIONAL INTERESTS: Travel and chess.

BIOGRAPHICAL/CRITICAL SOURCES: Nation, May, 1966.

*   *   *

BAUR, John E(dward)   1922-

PERSONAL: Born February 19, 1922, in Chicago, Ill.; son of Edward Sebastian and Mary Louise (Evans) Baur. Education: Los Angeles City College, A.A., 1944; University of California, Los Angeles, B.A. (with honors), 1945, M.A., 1947, Ph.D., 1951. Politics: Republican. Religion: Methodist. Home: 7616 Lexington Ave., Los Angeles, Calif. 90046. Office: History Department, San Fernando Valley State College, 18111 Nordhoff St., Northridge, Calif. 91324.

CAREER: University of California, Los Angeles, editorial assistant, Pacific Historical Review, 1949-53, instructor in history, 1954, 1957-67; Los Angeles County Museum of History and Science, Los Angeles, Calif., museum educational specialist in history, 1954-64, conductor of history workshop for gifted senior high school students, 1960-64, San Fernando Valley State College, Northridge, Calif., associate professor of history, 1968—. Former historical researcher for business and individuals, 1950—. Member: American Historical Association, Conference of Latin Americanists, Western History Association, California Historical Society. Awards, honors: Frederic Bancroft Award for best article of year in Journal of Negro History, 1947.

WRITINGS: (Contributor) J.W. Caughey, editor, Rushing for Gold, University of California Press, 1949; The Health Seekers of Southern California, 1870-1900, Huntington Library, 1959; Christmas on the American Frontier, 1800-1900, Caxton, 1961; Dogs on the Frontier, Naylor, 1964; (contributor) R.D. Delmatier, editor, The Rumble of California Politics, Wiley, 1970. Contributor to "Mountain Man" biography series, Arthur Clark, 1964—. Contributor to Encyclopaedia Britannica, and of more than thirty-five articles to magazines and historical journals. Member of board of editors, Southern California Quarterly, 1962—.

WORK IN PROGRESS: A biography of John Percival Jones of Nevada.

AVOCATIONAL INTERESTS: Philately, numismatics, photography, and mineralogy.

*   *   *

BAXTER, Eric P(eter)   1913-

PERSONAL: Born October 29, 1913, in Lowestoft, Suffolk, England; son of Peter (a builder) and Julia (Folley) Baxter; married Joan Olive Seville (a schoolmistress), April 16, 1949; children: Neil, Robin. Education: Goldsmiths' College, London, England, student, 1932-34; College of Preceptors, associate, 1937, licentiate, 1949. Home: 137 Brighton Rd., Purley, Surrey, England.

CAREER: Schoolmaster at various primary schools in Croydon, Surrey, England, 1934—. Military service: British Army, Royal Artillery, 1940-45; attached to North German Coal Control; became captain. Member: National Union of Teachers, Independent Order of Foresters.

WRITINGS—All juveniles: The Study Book of Coal, Bodley Head, 1959; The Study Book of Water Supply, Bodley Head, 1959; The Study Book of Oil, Bodley Head, 1960; The Study Book of Gas, Dufour, 1961; The Study Book of Ships, Bodley Head, 1963; The Study Book of Railways, Bodley Head, 1964; The Study Book of Safety at Sea, Bodley Head, 1969.

*   *   *

BEAGLE, Peter S(oyer)   1939-

PERSONAL: Born April 20, 1939, in New York, N.Y.; son of Simon and Rebecca (Soyer) Beagle; married Enid Nordeen, May 8, 1964; stepchildren: Vicki, Kalisa, Daniel. Education: University of Pittsburgh, B.A., 1959; Stanford University, graduate study, 1960-61. Agent: McIntosh & Otis, Inc., 18 East 41st St., New York, N.Y. 10017.

CAREER: Writer.

WRITINGS: A Fine and Private Place (novel), Viking, 1960; I See By My Outfit, Viking, 1965; The Last Unicorn, (novel), Viking, 1968 (published in England as The Last Unicorn: A Fantastic Tale, Bodley Head, 1968); The California Feeling, Doubleday, 1969.

SIDELIGHTS: Combining fantasy and reality, Peter S. Beagle has generally found favor with critics. Granville Hicks writes of A Fine and Private Place: "Fable though it is, A Fine and Private Place has one of the virtues of the realistic novel: the ability to create characters.... [It] may not be a work of the first importance, but it seems to me quite as important as many solemn and pretentious novels I have read. Beagle neatly avoids those pitfalls of the fantasist: sentimentality, coyness, and an air of profundity. He persuades the reader to play his game of make-believe, and then rewards him with an admirably sustained performance." Edmund Fuller sees in Beagle's work "wit, charm and individuality—with a sense of style and structure notable in a first novel." Orville Prescott adds: "Beagle is not an imitator. His story is original. His combination of wistful melancholy and tart humor is his own. And his smooth, precise, graceful prose, bright with wit and sparkling with imaginative phrases, is entirely personal...."

The Last Unicorn has been equally well received, critics again citing as its virtues originality expression and believable characterization. Harold Jaffe writes: "Inevitably, critics have compared The Last Unicorn to Tolkien's The Lord of the Rings. Beagle's book is less ambitious, yet it comes closer to poetry. While Tolkien's fine energy was largely directed at keeping the plot rolling, Beagle is interested in texture as much as structure: he meanders, embroiders, occasionally fusses too much with his palette, but usually manages to imbue his characters and situations with an incandescence as bright as the supernal glow of his unicorn's horn."

Other reviewers agree that while Beagle's work may be compared fairly to those of Lewis Carroll and Tolkien, his writing is distinctive and original. Hicks describes The Last Unicorn as "rich not only in comic bits but also in passages of uncommon beauty. Beagle is a true magician with words, a master of prose and a deft practitioner in verse. He has been compared, not unreasonably, with Lewis Carroll and J.R.R. Tolkien, but he stands squarely and triumphantly on his own feet." Norman Stein asserts that the book "fulfills the vogue of questing literature, enriched with 'lore,' arcane, occult, new-minted. It may refresh palates jaded by pornography and paradox.... [It] is neither quite fairy tale, myth, dream or nightmare. But Peter S. Beagle is much too original and gifted to be contained by familiar forms."

Beagle told *CA:* "I play the guitar and sing, to make up to my children for refusing to buy a television set, and I love to read, walk, swim, and look at newspapers every fourth day to see if Warren Spahn won."

BIOGRAPHICAL/CRITICAL SOURCES: Saturday Review, May 28, 1960, March 30, 1968; *New York Herald Tribune Book Review,* May 29, 1960; *San Francisco Chronicle,* June 2, 1960; *New York Times Book Review,* June 5, 1960, March 24, 1968; *Christian Century,* August 31, 1960; *Best Sellers,* April 1, 1968; *Book World,* April 7, 1968; *Commonweal,* June 28, 1968; *Virginia Quarterly Review,* summer, 1968; *Books and Bookmen,* October, 1968.†

* * *

BEAL, Anthony (Ridley) 1925-

PERSONAL: Born February 28, 1925, in Edgware, Middlesex, England; son of Harold Giveen and Nesta (Baker) Beal; married Rosemary Howarth, November 15, 1948; children: Sarah Rosemary, Kate Elizabeth, Emma Mary. *Education:* Attended Haberdashers' Aske's Hampstead School; Cambridge University, B.A., 1947, M.A., 1950. *Home:* 24 Loom Lane, Radlett, Hertfordshire, England. *Office:* Heinemann Educational Books Ltd., 48 Charles St., London W. 1, England.

CAREER: Eastbourne Training College, Eastbourne, England, lecturer in English, 1949; William Heinemann Ltd. (publishers), London, England, editor, 1949-61; Heinemann Educational Books Ltd., London, England, deputy managing director, 1961—. *Military service:* Royal Navy, 1943-46. *Member:* Savile Club (London).

WRITINGS: (Editor) D.H. Lawrence, *Selected Literary Criticism,* Viking, 1956; *D.H. Lawrence,* Grove, 1961; (editor and author of introduction) D.H. Lawrence, *Sons and Lovers,* Heinemann Educational Books, 1963.

* * *

BEARCE, George D(onham) 1922-

PERSONAL: Born November 5, 1922, in New York, N.Y.; son of George D. (a business executive) and Katherine (Wells) Bearce; married Jeana Dale (an artist), June 25, 1955; children: Barbara Emily. *Education:* University of Maine, A.B., 1943; Harvard University, law student, 1946-47; University of Wisconsin, M.A., 1949, Ph.D., 1952. *Religion:* Protestant. *Home:* Mere Point Rd., Brunswick, Me. 04011.

CAREER: Kalamazoo College, Kalamazoo, Mich., instructor in history, 1952-54; Bowdoin College, Brunswick, Me., assistant professor, 1954-61, 1962-63, associate professor of history, 1963—. Fulbright lecturer, Osmania University, Hyderabad, India, 1961-62. *Military service:* U.S. Army, Ordnance, 1943-46; served in European theater; became captain. *Member:* American Historical Association, Conference on Asian History (secretary-treasurer, 1962—), Conference on British History, Association for Asian Studies, American Political Science Association, American Association of University Professors, Northern New England Historians (chairman, 1958), Phi Beta Kappa, Phi Kappa Phi. *Awards, honors:* American Council of Learned Societies grant for twenty-sixth Oriental Congress; Fulbright grant, 1961; Watumull Prize, American Historical Association, 1962, for *British Attitudes Towards India, 1784-1858.*

WRITINGS: British Attitudes Towards India, 1784-1858, Oxford University Press, 1961; (with Stuart C. Welch, Jr.) *Painting in British India, 1757-1857,* Bowdoin College Press, 1963; (contributor) R. N. Iyer, editor, *The Glass Curtain Between Asia and Europe: A Symposium on the Historical Encounters and the Changing Attitudes of the People of the East and West,* Oxford University Press, 1965. Contributor to historical journals in United States and India.

WORK IN PROGRESS: The British and Their Concept of Empire in India; The Culture of India in Transition, 1740-1840.

SIDELIGHTS: Bearce has traveled extensively, studying culture and monuments of south Asia and medieval western Europe in connection with teaching. He is competent in Latin, French, and Italian, and knows some Urdu and German.

* * *

BEASLEY, M. Robert 1918-

PERSONAL: Born June 24, 1918, in Washington, D.C.; son of William H. and Sue D. Beasley; married Betty Marie Amundson, December 19, 1959; children: (previous marriage) one. *Education:* Attended Baltimore Institute of Engineering, 1939-40, University of Kansas, 1954-56. *Home address:* P.O. Box 14066, Detroit, Mich. 48214.

CAREER: Free-lance writer, 1938—. Henry Ford Museum and Greenfield Village, Dearborn, Mich., press relations manager, 1963; Dearborn Guide Newspapers, Dearborn, Mich., managing editor, 1963—. Public relations consultant, Studebaker Corp., Detroit, Mich., 1959-62. Assignment work for numerous national advertising and public relations agencies. *Military service:* U.S. Army, Counterintelligence Corps, 1942-45. *Awards, honors:* Freedoms Foundation Award, 1959; International Lions Award for work with blind, 1962.

WRITINGS: Fell's Guide to Buying, Building and Financing a Home, Fell, 1963; *Protect Yourself,* Macrae Smith, 1964. Contributor to *American Home, Better Homes and Gardens, Popular Mechanics, Popular Science, Mechanix Illustrated, True, Catholic Digest, Motor Trend,* and other magazines. Writer of booklets for industrial and business concerns on variety of subjects, including safety, home maintenance, churches, public service, and crime prevention.

* * *

BEASLEY, Rex 1925-

PERSONAL: Born April 20, 1925, in Joplin, Mo.; son of Theodore P. (an insurance executive) and Beulah (Porter) Beasley; married Jane Sanford, September 28, 1962; children: Robert Reagan, Victoria Ann, Ronny. *Education:* Attended Texas Christian University and Southern Methodist University. *Religion:* Disciples of Christ. *Home:* 3785 West Bay Circle, Dallas, Tex. 75214. *Office:* Republic National Life Insurance Co., P.O. Box 6210, Dallas Tex. 75222.

CAREER: Republic National Life Insurance Co., Dallas, Tex., now senior vice-president and vice-chairman of the board. *Member:* Authors Guild, Dallas Athletic Club. *Awards, honors:* George Washington Honor Medal of Valley Forge Freedoms Foundation and Award of Excellence of Life Advertisers Association, both for "Great Men of History" magazine series.

WRITINGS: Edison, Chilton, 1964. Author of a play, "Splendor of Three," and of "Great Men of History" monthly magazine series. Contributor of editorial essays to magazines.

WORK IN PROGRESS: The Golden Mask: Shakespeare.

AVOCATIONAL INTERESTS: Painting, photography, and stereo high fidelity.†

* * *

BEATTY, Jerome, Jr. 1918-

PERSONAL: Born December 9, 1918, in New Rochelle, N.Y. *Education:* Dartmouth College, B.A., 1939. *Home address:* Box 168, Waquoit, Mass. 02536.

CAREER: Newark News, Newark, N.J., reporter, 1940-43; *Coronet,* New York, N.Y., associate editor, 1946-49; *Pageant,* New York, N.Y., associate editor, 1949-52; *Collier's,* New York, N.Y., staff writer, 1952-57; free-lance writer, 1957—. *Military service:* U.S. Army, 1943-46; interpreter attached to Chinese Army.

WRITINGS: I Married a Barracks Bag, Kaw River Press, 1944; *Sex Rears Its Lovely Head,* Bantam, 1956; (compiler) *The Saturday Review Gallery,* introduction by John T. Winterich, Simon & Schuster, 1959; *Show Me the Way to Go Home: The Commuter Story,* Crowell, 1959; *Matthew Looney's Voyage to the Earth: A Space Story* (juvenile), W.R. Scott, 1961; *Have You Ever Wondered?,* Macfadden, 1962; *Bob Fulton's Amazing Soda Pop Stretcher: An International Spy Story* (juvenile), W.R. Scott, 1963; *The Girls We Leave Behind: A Terribly Scientific Study of American Women at Home,* Doubleday, 1963; *The Clambake Mutiny: An Undersea Story* (juvenile), W.R. Scott, 1964; *One O'Clock in the Button Factory,* Macmillan, 1964; *Matthew Looney's Invasion of the Earth* (juvenile), W.R. Scott, 1965; (editor) *Daniel Weston Hall, Arctic Rovings* (juvenile), W.R. Scott, 1968; *Matthew Looney in the Outback: A Space Story* (juvenile), W.R. Scott, 1969; *Sheriff Stonehead and the Teenage Termites* (juvenile), W.R. Scott, 1970; *Blockade!,* Doubleday, 1971; (compiler) *Double Take,* cartoons by Terence Parkes, Greene, 1971. Contributor to *Esquire, Redbook,* and other magazines. Contributing editor, *Saturday Review.*

BIOGRAPHICAL/CRITICAL SOURCES: Library Journal, July, 1969, May 15, 1970; *Book World,* September 7, 1969.

*   *   *

BEAULAC, Willard L(eon)   1899-

PERSONAL: Surname is pronounced *Bow*-lack; born July 25, 1899, in Pawtucket, R.I.; son of Sylvester Clinton (a machinist) and Lena E. (Jarvis) Beaulac; married Catherine H.A. Green, February 25, 1935; children: Noel Jeanne (Mrs. Ronald Peters), Joan Caroll (Mrs. Alexander Zachor), Nancy Anne (Mrs. Albert McChristy III), Willard Leon, Jr. *Education:* Brown University, student, 1916-18; Georgetown University, Bachelor of Foreign Service, 1921. *Home:* 1810 St. Marks Pl., Fairfax, Va. 22030.

CAREER: U.S. Department of State, career Foreign Service officer, serving in Central and South American countries much of the period, 1921-41; ambassador to Paraguay, 1944-47, to Colombia, 1947-51, to Cuba, 1951-53, to Chile, 1953-56, to Argentina, 1956-60; National War College, Washington, D.C., deputy commandant for foreign affairs, 1960-62; writer and lecturer on Latin America, 1962—. Diplomat in residence and visiting professor, Southern Illinois University, Carbondale, 1966-69; visiting professor of political science, Ball State University, Muncie, Ind., 1969—. *Military service:* U.S. Navy, 1918-19. *Member:* Metropolitan Club (Washington, D.C.). *Awards, honors:* LL.D., Georgetown University, 1951.

WRITINGS: Career Ambassador, Macmillan, 1951; *Economic Trends in Latin America,* U.S. Industrial College of the Armed Forces, 1964; *Career Diplomat: A Career in the Foreign Service of the United States,* Macmillan, 1964; (with others) *Dominican Action, 1965: Intervention or Cooperation?,* Center for Strategic Studies, Georgetown University, 1966; *A Diplomat Looks at Aid to Latin America,* Southern Illinois University Press, 1970.

BIOGRAPHICAL/CRITICAL SOURCES: Library Journal, July, 1970.

BEAUMAN, E(ric) Bentley

PERSONAL: Born in London, England; son of Martin Bentley and Estelle (Beddington) Beauman; married Katharine Miller Jones; children: Christopher Burgoyne. *Education:* Attended Malvern College and University of Geneva. *Home:* 59 Chester Row, London S.W.1, England.

CAREER: Royal Air Force, pilot, 1914-38, served in Air Ministry, 1938-51; became wing commander; mentioned in dispatches; Royal United Service Institution, Whitehall, London, England, librarian, 1952-57. *Member:* Royal Air Force Mountaineering Association (vice-president, 1951—), Ski Club of Great Britain (chairman, touring committee, 1952-53), Alpine Club (honorary librarian, 1947-53), Alpine Ski Club (president, 1933-35), Royal Air Force Club, Army and Navy Club, Society of Authors.

WRITINGS: The Art of Constantinople, Phaidon, 1936; (editor) *The Airmen Speak,* Doubleday, 1941 (published in England as *Winged Words: Our Airmen Speak for Themselves,* Heinemann, 1941); (with Cecil Day Lewis) *We Speak from the Air,* Ministry of Information, 1942; (with Lewis) *Over to You,* Ministry of Information, 1943; *The Boys Country Book,* Collins, 1955, 2nd edition, 1961. Contributor of articles to *Times, Field, Daily Telegraph, New York Times,* and to *Dictionary of National Biography* and *Encyclopaedia Britannica.*

WORK IN PROGRESS: Writing on mountaineering, skiing, and holiday resorts.

SIDELIGHTS: Beauman participated in Kamet Expedition in the Himalayas, 1931, and in the first crossing of the Coast Range of British Columbia, 1934.†

*   *   *

BEAUVOIR, Simone (Lucie Ernestine Marie) de   1908-

PERSONAL: Born January 9, 1908, in Paris, France; daughter of Georges Bertrand (an advocate to the Court of Appeal, Paris) and Francoise (Brasseur) de Beauvoir. *Education:* Attended Institut normal catholique Adelina-Desir, Paris, and Institution Sainte-Marie de Neuilly-sur-Seine; Sorbonne, University of Paris, licencie es lettres, agrege des lettres (philosophy), 1929. *Home:* 11 bis rue Schoelcher, Paris 14e, France.

CAREER: Teacher of philosophy at Lycee Montgrand, Marseilles, 1931-33, at Lycee Jeanne d'Arc, Rouen, France, 1933-37, at Lycee Moliere and Lycee Camille-See, both Paris, France, 1938-43; full-time writer, 1943—; editor, with Jean Paul Sartre, of *Les Temps Modernes,* 1945—. Made a lecture tour of America on a grant from the French government, 1947. *Member:* International War Crimes Tribunal. *Awards, honors:* Prix Goncourt, 1945, for *Les Mandarins;* L.L.D. from Cambridge University.

WRITINGS: L'Invitee (novel), Gallimard, 1943, translation by Yvonne Moyse and Roger Senhouse published as *She Came to Stay,* Secker & Warburg, 1949, World Publishing, 1954; *Pyrrhus et Cineas* (nonfiction), Gallimard, 1944; *Les Bouches inutiles* (play in two acts; title means "The Useless Mouths"), Gallimard, 1945; *Le Sang des autres* (novel), Gallimard, 1945, translation by Senhouse and Moyse published as *The Blood of Others,* Knopf, 1948; *Tous les hommes sont mortels* (novel), Gallimard, 1946, translation by Leonard M. Friedman published as *All Men are Mortal,* World Publishing, 1955; *Pour une morale de l'ambiguite,* Gallimard, 1947, translation by Bernard Frechtman published as *The Ethics of Ambiguity,* Philosophical Library, 1949; *L'Amerique au jour le jour* (diary), P. Morihien, 1948, translation by Patrick Dudley published as *America Day by Day,* Duckworth,

1952, Grove, 1953; *L'existentialisme et la sagesse des nations*, Nagel, 1948; *Le Deuxieme sexe*, two volumes, Gallimard, 1949, translation by H.M. Parshley published as *The Second Sex*, Knopf, 1953 (Volume I published in England as *A History of Sex*, New English Library, 1961, reissued as *Nature of the Second Sex*, 1963); *Faut-il bruler Sade?* (essay; originally published in *Les Temps Modernes*), translation by Annette Michelson published as *The Marquis de Sade*, Grove, 1953 (published in England as *Must We Burn De Sade?*, Nevill, 1953); *Les Mandarins* (novel), Gallimard, 1954, translation by Friedman published as *The Mandarins*, World Publishing, 1956; *Privileges* (essays, including *Faut-il bruler Sade?*), Gallimard, 1955; *La Longue marche; essai sur la Chine*, Gallimard, 1957, translation by Austryn Wainhouse published as *The Long March*, World Publishing, 1958; *Memoires d'une jeune fille rangee* (autobiography), Gallimard, 1958, translation by James Kirkup published as *Memoirs of a Dutiful Daughter*, World Publishing, 1959; *Brigitte Bardot and the Lolita Syndrome*, translated by Frechtman, Reynal, 1960, with foreward by George Amberg, Arno, 1972; *La Force de l'age* (autobiography), Gallimard, 1960, translation by Peter Green published as *The Prime of Life*, World Publishing, 1962; (with Gisele Halimi) *Djamila Boupacha*, Gallimard, 1962, translation by Green published under same title, Macmillan, 1962; *La Force des choses* (autobiography), Gallimard, 1963, translation by Richard Howard published as *The Force of Circumstance*, Putnam, 1965; *Une Mort tres douce* (autobiography), Gallimard, 1964, translation by Patrick O'Brian published as *A Very Easy Death*, Putnam, 1966; (author of introduction) Charles Perrault, *Bluebeard and Other Fairy Tales of Charles Perrault*, Macmillan, 1964; (author of preface) Violette Leduc, *La Batarde*, Gallimard, 1964; (author of preface) Jean-Francois Steiner, *Treblinka*, Simon & Schuster, 1967; *Les Belles Images* (novel), Gallimard, 1966, translation by O'Brian published under same title, Putnam, 1968; *La Femme Rompue* (3 novellas), Gallimard, 1968, translation by O'Brian published as *The Woman Destroyed*, Putnam, 1969; *La Vieillesse*, Gallimard, 1970, translation by O'Brian published in America as *The Coming of Age*, Putnam, 1972 (published in England as *Old Age*, Weidenfeld & Nicolson, 1972); *Toute Compte fait* (autobiography; title means "All Accounting Made"), Gallimard, 1972.

SIDELIGHTS: On the distaff side of French Existentialism, Mlle de Beauvoir has no peers. Associated intellectually and personally with Jean-Paul Sartre since her early twenties, she has helped him to reshape the intellectual climate of the time. Once irritated, as was Sartre, by the label "existentialism" that became attached to their writings, she later wrote: "I had written my novels before I had even encountered the term Existentialist; my inspiration came from my own experience, not from a system. But our protests were in vain. In the end, we took the epithet that everyone used for us and used it for our own purposes."

Bernard Kalb once remarked that Mlle de Beauvoir is "a major existentialist, not merely a dulcet-voiced carbon-copy of Sartre." *The Ethics of Ambiguity* has proved a valuable complement to Sartre's *L'Etre et le neant*. Victor Brombert maintains that "*Le Sang des autres* is no doubt, of all the Existentialist novels, the one to focus most sharply on the problem of involvement, giving it its neatest artistic formulation."

With the publication of *The Mandarins*, a roman a clef, she achieved widespread recognition. Again, for *Memoirs of a Dutiful Daughter*, her autobiography from a Catholic childhood to the Sorbonne and her friendship with Sartre, she received critical acclaim. V.S. Pritchett wrote: "Like George Eliot, with whose life and development she has some things in common, Mlle Simone de Beauvoir is a singularly ungenial writer of brilliant intelligence and stern moral curiosity.... I do not remember having read a girl's adolescent life being done before, with anything like Mlle de Beauvoir's pleasant precision. . . . The best parts of this book recall the precision of Santayana's autobiography which, in a different way, is one of the best analyses of religious and family claustrophobia ever written."

The Long March, an account of a trip to Communist China, has been severely criticized, generally for being overly partisan and subjective. Charles Rolo remarked: "All I can say with certainty is that her effusions are for the most part a suffocating bore. She is probably the most long-winded woman writer currently in business and definitely the most humorless."

The Second Sex, a work Philip Wylie called "one of the few great books of our era," is a monumental, scholarly, brilliant, and angry account of the secondary position accorded to women throughout history by the myths, environment, and social traditions forged and controlled by men. Woman has been, in effect, deprived of her essential human dignity as a free and independent being. Mlle de Beauvoir did not begin from this position. She recently reported in *Harper's:* "I had never had any feeling of inferiority; no one had ever said to me, 'You think that way because you're a woman'; my femininity had never been irksome to me in any way." Sartre's comment—"All the same, you weren't brought up in the same way as a boy would have been; you should look into it further"—became the genesis of *The Second Sex*.

Today she says: "*The Second Sex* is possibly the book that has brought me the greatest satisfaction out of all those I have written." The book, however, also aroused controversy, and indignant comments came in from some readers. "I received—some signed and some anonymous—epigrams, epistles, satires, admonitions, and exhortations addressed to me by, for example, 'some very active members of the First Sex.' Unsatisfied, frigid, priapic, nymphomaniac, lesbian, a hundred times aborted, I was everything, even an unmarried mother.... Many men declared I had no right to discuss women because I hadn't given birth; and they? . . . The Right could only detest my book, which Rome naturally put on the Index. . . . I devoted a chapter to the problem of abortion; Sartre had already written about it in *The Age of Reason*, and I myself in *The Blood of Others*; people were always rushing into the office of *Les Temps Modernes* asking the secretary for addresses. She got so irritated by it that one day she designed a poster: 'We do it on the premises, ourselves.' "

The approach of old age and death, the loss of love and life are recurring themes in her work. Madeleine Cobeil quoted de Beauvoir as saying: "I've always been haunted by the passing of time and by the fact that death keeps closing in on us." In *La Vieillesse* this theme is treated from a sociological standpoint. She told Steve Saler, in a *Newsweek* interview: "Society treats an old man as less than a man, as a *sous-homme*." She still has hopes for her dream of "complete reform of society," to solve, too, these problems of the aged. Mlle de Beauvoir explains, however, "Many of the things I wrote about do not apply to me. I hope to live to the end of my days."

The Mandarins was filmed by 20th Century-Fox in 1969. *The Second Sex* has been translated into nineteen languages, and has sold nearly a half million copies.

BIOGRAPHICAL/CRITICAL SOURCES: Fontaine, October, 1945; M. Merleau Ponty, *Sens et non-sens*, Nagel, 1948; *Yale French Studies*, I, i, 1948; *Le Monde*, March 20, 1948; Henri Peyre, *The Contemporary French Novel*, Oxford University Press, 1955; *New York Times Book Review*, May 18, 1958, June 7, 1959, March 3, 1968; *At-*

lantic, June, 1958; *Nation*, June 8, 1958, June 27, 1959; *Catholic World*, August, 1958; G. Gennari, *Simone de Beauvoir*, Editions Universitaires, 1959; *Times Literary Supplement*, June 5, 1959, May 5, 1966, March 30, 1967; *New Statesman*, June 6, 1959, January 5, 1968; Mary McCarthy, *On the Contrary*, Farrar, Straus, 1961; Victor Brombert, *The Intellectual Hero*, Lippincott, 1961; G. Hourdin, *Simone de Beauvoir*, Cerf, 1963; *L'Express*, November 7, 1963; *Harper's*, November and December, 1964; *Paris Review*, Spring-Summer, 1965; *Commentary*, August, 1965; *Canadian Forum*, October, 1965; *Time*, March 20, 1966, May 22, 1972; *Book World*, February 2, 1969; *London Magazine*, April, 1969; *Newsweek*, February 9, 1970; *New York Times Magazine*, July 11, 1971; *New York Review of Books*, July 20, 1972; E. Marks, *Simone de Beauvoir: Encounter with Death*, Rutgers University Press, 1973.

* * *

BECK, Henry G(abriel) J(ustin)   1914-

PERSONAL: Born June 9, 1914, in New York, N.Y.; son of Henry Joseph and Ellen Frances (Dempsey) Beck. *Education:* St. Peter's College, Jersey City, N.J., student, 1930-32; Seton Hall University, B.A., 1934; Gregorian University, Th.L., 1938, D.ec.Hist., 1948. *Office:* Department of History, Seton Hall University, South Orange, N.J. 07079.

CAREER: Roman Catholic priest; named papal chamberlain with title of very reverend monsignor, 1958; Immaculate Conception Seminary, Darlington, Ramsey, N.J., professor of church history, 1940—; Catholic Archdiocese of Newark, Newark, N.J., historian, 1961—. Lecturer on historical and ecclesiastical subjects. *Member:* American Historical Association, American Catholic Historical Association, American Society of Church History, Federation Historique de Provence, Societe d'Histoire Ecclesiastique de la France. *Awards, honors:* Gold Medal, 1948, for doctoral dissertation from Pope Pius XII.

WRITINGS: The Pastoral Care of Souls in South-East France during the Sixth Century, Gregorian University Press, 1950; *The Centennial History of the Immaculate Conception Seminary, Darlington, N.J.*, Seton Hall University Press, 1962. Contributor to *Encyclopaedia Britannica*, *Encyclopedia Americana*, *American Historical Review*, *Speculum*, *American Ecclesiastical Review*, and other publications. Area editor in medieval history, *New Catholic Encyclopedia*.

WORK IN PROGRESS: Pope Nicholas I, for Newman; thirty articles for the *New Catholic Encyclopedia.†*

* * *

BECKWITH, John Gordon   1918-

PERSONAL: Born December 2, 1918, in Southend, England; son of John Frederick and Winifred Mary (Cullabine) Beckwith. *Education:* Attended Ampleforth College, York; Exeter College, Oxford, B.A. (history), M.A., 1947. *Religion:* Roman Catholic. *Home:* Flat 6, 77 Ladbroke Grove, London W. 11, England. *Office:* Victoria and Albert Museum, South Kensington, London S.W. 7, England.

CAREER: Victoria and Albert Museum, London, England, began as assistant keeper in 1948, now deputy keeper, department of architecture and sculpture. Tours for British Council in Germany, 1957, and the Middle East, 1960. Visiting professor, Harvard University, 1964, University of Missouri, 1968. *Military service:* British Army, Infantry, 1939-45; became captain. *Member:* Centre International d'Etudes des Textiles Anciens, Lyon.

WRITINGS: The Art of Constantinople: An Introduction to Byzantine Art, Phaidon, 1961, 2nd edition, 1968;

Coptic Sculpture, 300-1300, Tiranti, 1963; *Early Medieval Art*, Praeger, 1964 (published in England as *Early Medieval Art: Carolingian, Ottonian, Romanesque*, Thames & Hudson, 1964); *Early Christian and Byzantine Art*, Penguin, 1970; *Ivory Carvings in Early Medieval England*, New York Graphic Society, 1973.

Victoria and Albert Museum monographs, all published by H.M.S.O.: *The Andrews Diptych*, 1958; *Caskets from Cordoba*, 1960; *The Veroli Casket*, 1962; *The Basilewsky Situla*, 1963; *The Adoration of the Magi in Whalebone*, 1966. Contributor to art journals and *Times Literary Supplement*.

* * *

BEDAU, Hugo Adam   1926-

PERSONAL: Born September 23, 1926, in Portland, Ore.; married Jan Mastin, January 19, 1952; children: Lauren, Mark, Paul, Guy. *Education:* University of Redlands, B.A. (summa cum laude), 1949; Boston University, M.A., 1951; Harvard University, A.M., 1953, Ph.D., 1961. *Office:* Department of Philosophy, Tufts University, Medford, Mass. 02155.

CAREER: Dartmouth College, Hanover, N.H., instructor, 1953-54; Princeton University, Princeton, N.J., lecturer, 1954-61; Reed College, Portland, Ore., associate professor of philosophy, 1962-66; Tufts University, Medford, Mass., professor of philosophy, 1966—. *Military service:* U.S. Naval Reserve, 1944-46. *Member:* American League for Abolition of Capital Punishment (president, 1969—), American Civil Liberties Union, American Philosophical Association, American Society of Political and Legal Philosophy, American Association of University Professors, Northwest Conference on Philosophy (president, 1965), Society for Philosophy and Public Affairs. *Awards, honors:* Danforth teacher grant, 1957-58; Carnegie fellow in law and philosophy, Harvard University, 1961-62.

WRITINGS: (Co-author) *Nomos VI: Justice*, Atherton, 1963; (editor) *The Death Penalty in America* (anthology), Doubleday-Anchor, 1964, 2nd edition, 1967; *Capital Punishment in Oregon, 1903-64* (originally published in *Oregon Law Review*, December, 1965), [Eugene], 1965; *Death Sentences in New Jersey, 1907-1960* (originally published in *Rutgers Law Review*, fall, 1964), [New Brunswick], c.1965; (co-author) *Nomos IX: Equality*, Atherton, 1967; (editor) *Civil Disobedience: Theory and Practice*, Pegasus, 1969; (editor) *Justice and Equality*, Prentice-Hall, 1971. Contributor of essays and reviews to *Nation*, *New Leader*, *Christian Century*, *Philosophical Review*, *Journal of Philosophy*, *Philosophy of Science*, and other periodicals.

WORK IN PROGRESS: Editing text and commentary on John Locke's second treatise of government; editing classic and recent writings on human rights.

AVOCATIONAL INTERESTS: Swimming, tennis, hiking, and camping.

BIOGRAPHICAL/CRITICAL SOURCES: Library Journal, May 15, 1969.

* * *

BEDFORD, Henry F(rederick)   1931-

PERSONAL: Born June 21, 1931, in Oskaloosa, Iowa; son of Henry Ward (an educator) and Mary Louise (Bates) Bedford; married Kennetha McKinley, June 21, 1952; children: Henry Ward II, William McKinley, Jeffrey Clark, Caroline Elizabeth. *Education:* Amherst College, B.A., 1952; University of Wisconsin, M.A., 1953; University of Massachusetts, Ph.D., 1965. *Home:* 4 Gill St., Exeter, N.H. 03833.

CAREER: Bedford Gas., Inc., Burlington, Vt., vice-president and treasurer, 1955-57; Phillips Exeter Academy, Exeter, N.H., teacher in history department, 1957-66, chairman of history department, 1966-69, dean of the faculty, 1969—. Military service: U.S. Army, 1953-55. Member: New England Historical Association (member of executive committee), Organization of American Historians, American Historical Association, Phi Beta Kappa.

WRITINGS: The Union Divides: Politics and Slavery, 1850-1861, Macmillan, 1963; Socialism and the Workers in Massachusetts, 1886-1912, University of Massachusetts Press, 1966; From Versailles to Nuremberg, Macmillan, 1969; (contributor) H.H. Quint, D. Albertson, and M. Cantor, editors, Main Problems in American History, two volumes, Dorsey, 1969. Contributor of articles to Labor History, South Carolina Magazine of History, and Proceedings of the Essex Institute.

WORK IN PROGRESS: A Brief History of the United States, to be published by Harcourt.

*   *   *

BEDFORD, Sybille 1911-

PERSONAL: Born 1911, in Charlottenburg, Germany; married Walter Bedford. Education: Privately educated. Address: c/o Messrs. Coutts & Co., 440 Strand, London W.C. 2, England.

CAREER: Writer. Member: Society of Authors, P.E.N., Royal Society of Literature (fellow).

WRITINGS: The Sudden View: A Mexican Journey (travel book), Gollancz, 1953, Harper, 1954, revised edition, Atheneum, 1963 (also published in England as A Visit to Don Otavio: A Traveller's Tale From Mexico, Collins, 1960); A Legacy (novel), Weidenfeld & Nicolson, 1956, Simon & Schuster, 1957; The Best We Can Do: An Account of the Trial of John Bodkin Adams, Collins, 1958, published in America as The Trial of Dr. Adams, Simon & Schuster, 1959; The Faces of Justice: A Traveller's Report, Simon & Schuster, 1961; A Favourite of the Gods (novel), Simon & Schuster, 1963; A Compass Error (novel), Collins, 1968, Knopf, 1969. Contributor to Horizon, Encounter, Harper's Bazaar, Vogue, Decision, Esquire, Chimera, Spectator, Life, New York Review of Books, Observer, and other publications.

WORK IN PROGRESS: The authorized biography of Aldous Huxley.

SIDELIGHTS: Mrs. Bedford's novels have been variously described as "elegant" and "witty," "irrelevant and mannered." This divergence of critical opinion is largely due to her use of the aristocracy and upper classes as the prevailing milieus of her fiction. While she is highly praised by such persons as Nancy Mitford, Evelyn Waugh, and Aldous Huxley, many critics consider her later novels anachronistic. John Wain believes that "what is portrayed isn't interesting enough or strong enough to be called a civilization; it is merely a bundle of habits and attitudes, a soap-bubble blown up by the movement of international capital and fashion."

Although some may dislike the topics and setting of her work, critics generally agree that Mrs. Bedford has an unquestionably graceful and lucid style of writing. Paul Pickrel compares her writing to "late Impressionist painting, full of sunlight and flowers and figured carpets and ladies in large hats. Her special talent lies in the ability to manipulate that brilliant surface to reveal something a good deal more substantial, even sinister, beneath." Granville Hicks believes that she has an unerring instinct for portraying human beings in their moments of strength and weakness. "Miss Bedford has wisdom. . . . If she knows anything, she knows that human beings are not simple, that always there is a mystery within a mystery. A constant awareness of human absurdity is balanced by a noble tenderness. . . . However she acquired her experience, she has learned how to use it to excellent literary effect. England at the moment has many gifted women writers, and Sybille Bedford is not far down on the list."

BIOGRAPHICAL/CRITICAL SOURCES: Times Literary Supplement, March 13, 1953, April 20, 1956, October 24, 1968; Nation, March 28, 1953, March 31, 1956, May 4, 1963; New York Herald Tribune Book Review, January 10, 1954, February 3, 1957; New York Times, January 17, 1954, February 3, 1957; Spectator, April 13, 1956, November 14, 1958, May 26, 1961, October 25, 1968; Christian Science Monitor, January 31, 1957, October 21, 1969; Saturday Review, February 9, 1957, March 16, 1963; Atlantic, March, 1957, April, 1969; Manchester Guardian, March 27, 1957; New Yorker, April 27, 1957; New Statesman, January 17, 1959, May 26, 1961, October 18, 1968; New Republic, June 26, 1961; Encounter, March, 1963; Harper's, April, 1963, April, 1969; American Scholar, summer, 1965; Observer Review, October 13, 1968; Listener, November, 1968; Washington Post, December 11, 1968; New York Times Book Review, March 23, 1969; Best Sellers, April 1, 1969; New York Review of Books, April 24, 1969.

*   *   *

BEECH, George T(homas) 1931-

PERSONAL: Born November 9, 1931, in Lansing, Mich.; son of John L. (an engineer) and Lilian (Woods) Beech; married Beatrice Hibbard (a librarian), June 19, 1954; children: Valerie Lynn, Rebecca Anne. Education: Michigan State University, B.A., 1954; studied at University of Freiburg, 1954-55, University of Poitiers, 1958-59; Johns Hopkins University, Ph.D., 1960. Office: History Department, Western Michigan University, Kalamazoo, Mich. 49001.

CAREER: University of Massachusetts, Amherst, instructor in history, 1959-60; Western Michigan University, Kalamazoo, professor of medieval history, 1960—. Member: American Historical Association, Medieval Academy of America. Awards, honors: Fulbright grant, 1954-55; Fulbright research scholar in France, 1966-67.

WRITINGS: A Rural Society in Medieval France: The Gatine of Poitou in the 11th and 12th Centuries, Johns Hopkins Press, 1964. Contributor to Studies in Medieval Culture.

WORK IN PROGRESS: Further research into social and economic history of the medieval French province of Poitou.

*   *   *

BEIER, Ulli 1922-

PERSONAL: Born July 30, 1922, in Glowitz, Germany; son of Hugo and Martha (Bartel) Beier; married Susanne Wenger (a painter), September 13, 1950. Education: University of London, B.A. (with honors), 1948.

CAREER: University of Ibadan, Ibadan, Nigeria, associate professor in department of extra-mural studies and instructor in English, 1950-68; left Nigeria to take a teaching post in Papua, New Guinea, 1968. Member: Mbari Clubs of Ibadan and Oshogbo, Nigeria (founder and chairman).

WRITINGS: The Story of Sacred Wood Carvings from One Small Yoruba Town (booklet), edited by D.W. Macrow, Nigeria Magazine (Marina, Lagos), 1957; A Year of Sacred Festivals in One Yoruba Town, edited by Macrow, Nigeria Magazine, 1959; Art in Nigeria, 1960, Cambridge University Press, 1960; Yoruba: Plastiken eines afrikanischen Volkes (catalog of an art exhibit held at Kunsthalle am Steubenplatz, Darmstadt, June 3-July

15, 1962), translated from the English by Irmgard Schmiele, [Darmstadt], 1962; *African Mud Sculpture,* Cambridge University Press, 1963; *Yemi Bisiri, a Yoruba Brass Caster,* Mbari Publications (Ibadan, Nigeria), 1963; *Contemporary Art in Africa,* Praeger, 1968; (with Albert M. Kiki) *Ten Thousand Years in a Lifetime: A New Guinea Autobiography,* Praeger, 1968; (with Kiki) *Hohao,* Tri-Ocean, 1970; (author of introductory essay) (Contemporary New Guinea Art (catalog of an exhibit held January 16-February 28, 1971), Otis Art Institute (Los Angeles), 1971; (with Paul Cox) *Home of Man,* Tri-Ocean, 1971.

Editor: E.A. Olunlade, *Ede: A Short History,* Ministry of Education, Nigeria, 1961; (with Gerald Moore) *Modern Poetry from Africa,* Penguin, 1963, revised and enlarged edition, 1966; *"Black Orpheus": An Anthology of African and Afro-American Prose,* Longmans of Nigeria, 1964, published in America as *"Black Orpheus": An Anthology of New African and Afro-American Stories,* McGraw, 1965; *The Origin of Life and Death: African Creation Myths,* Heinemann, 1966; (and compiler) *Introduction to African Literature: An Anthology of Critical Writing from "Black Orpheus",* Northwestern University Press, 1967; (and author of introduction and notes) *Three Nigerian Plays* (includes "Moremi," by Duro Lapido, "The Scheme," by Wale Ogunyemi, and "Born With Fire On His Head," by Obotunde Ijimere), Longmans of Nigeria, 1967, Humanities, 1967; (with Bakare Gbadamosi) *Not Even God Is Ripe Enough,* Heinemann, 1968, Humanities, 1969; *Political Spider: An Anthology of Stories from "Black Orpheus",* Africana Publishing, 1969; *Anthology of South Pacific Third World Poetry,* Unicorn Press, 1972.

Translator: (And compiler, with Gbadamosi) *Yoruba Poetry* (published as a special issue of *Black Orpheus*), Ministry of Education, Nigeria, 1959; (and compiler, with Gbadamosi) *The Moon Cannot Fight: Yoruba Children's Poetry,* Mbari Publications, c.1960; Jean Joseph Rabearivelo, *Twenty-Four Poems,* Mbari Publications, 1962; Duro Lapido, *Three Yoruba Plays,* Mbari Publications, 1964; (and editor) Obotunde Ijimere, *The Imprisonment of Obatala, and Other Plays,* Heinemann, 1966; (and compiler and editor) *African Poetry: An Anthology of Traditional African Poems* (contains illustrations by wife, Susanne Wenger), Cambridge University Press, 1966; (and editor, with Gbadamosi) *Ijala: Animal Songs by Yoruba Hunters,* Papua Pocket Poets (Port Moresby, New Guinea), 1967; W.A. Braasem, compiler, *Luo Zaho* (Indonesian poetry), [Port Moresby], 1967; *Only Dust: Three Modern Indonesian Poets* (selections from the work of Basuki Gunawan, Chairil Anwar, and Joke Muljono), [Port Moresby], 1969; (and compiler and editor) *Yoruba Poetry: An Anthology of Traditional Poems* (not the same as *Yoruba Poetry* or *African Poetry: An Anthology;* with illustrations by Wenger), Cambridge University Press, 1970. Contributor of articles, reviews, and translations to *Black Orpheus* under various pseudonyms, including Sangodare Akanji and Omidiji Aragbabalu. Co-founder and member of editorial board of Mbari Publications; founder of *Black Orpheus,* and editor, 1957-68.

SIDELIGHTS: In an article for *Books Abroad* tracing the development of *Black Orpheus,* Bernth Lindfors writes that "Beier, a German living in Nigeria, was inspired to begin [the journal] after attending the first World Congress of Black Writers and Artists organized by *Presence Africaine,* a Paris-based literary journal, in September, 1956." He writes that Jean-Paul Sartre had coined the phrase "Black Orpheus" in an essay comparing the Negro search for his native land and identity to the descent of Orpheus into Hades to reclaim Eurydice from Pluto. As Lindfors points out, this journal "would

help the African writer to discover himself and to rediscover his past in the great traditions of oral literature." At the time *Black Orpheus* was founded, Nigerian literature was non-existent, and Beier was forced to rely on translations from French-African Writers for the first few issues. The Nigerian Ministry of Education was the publisher of the first twelve issues of the journal, and contributors were not paid. After Longmans of Nigeria took over publication, however, the Congress of Cultural Freedom provided funds for paying writers, and *Black Orpheus* became a powerful source of stimulation to African authors and poets, especially in Nigeria. The Journal soon gained an international reputation for literary innovation and excellence, bringing to African literature a prolific and exciting period of activity which continues, although Beier left the magazine to assume a teaching post in Papau four years ago. Lindfors believes that Beier, more than any other individual, was responsible for the reputation and longevity of the journal. "He was its architect, coordinating engineer, mason, day laborer, and workhorse; in ten years ... he wrote twenty-two articles, fifty reviews, and forty translations for *Black Orpheus,* many of them breaking new ground in unexplored regions of the arts. Today, on the foundations he laid, *Black Orpheus* looms as a landmark in African literary history, a monument to Negro creativity. It is also a monument to Ulli Beier, the man who made it so."

Also well known for their translations from Yoruba into English, Beier and his fellow translators have won praise from the *Times Literary Supplement* because they "have wisely put accurate translation first and have eschewed English metrical forms.... Almost invariably, they have observed the literary necessity for live language and have often achieved telling rhythmic effects—though inevitably less strongly then in their originals.... The imagery is a source of constant delight." In a review of *Yoruba Poetry: An Anthology of Traditional Poems,* Louis Barron remarks: "A tonal language, with few vowel sounds and a limited range of consonants, yet marvelously complex, Yoruba, unlike English, can be communicated across relatively long distances or carried by drums that accurately imitate speech melody and rhythm. Since it is impossible to render Yoruba into an English equivalent, the literary translations ... have been created to convey the feeling and mood rather than the literal meaning of Yoruba poetry to the poetry lover."

The significance of Beier's work to the Western literary world is mentioned by Arthur Lerner in a review of *Introduction to African Literature: An Anthology of Critical Writing from "Black Orpheus":* "The concern here is with African and Afro-American literature and oral tradition.... Since African studies are also becoming of major concern in American higher institutions of learning, this excellent book should strike home. The genres represented include poetry, the novel, and drama, and offer many clear pointers into other forms of writing, while the carefully selected bibliography will prove most helpful to scholars in the field."

BIOGRAPHICAL/CRITICAL SOURCES: Saturday Review, August 10, 1963; *Times Literary Supplement,* February 6, 1964, July 28, 1966, June 20, 1968; *American Anthropologist,* April, 1964; *Books Abroad,* autumn, 1967, autumn, 1968, winter, 1969, autumn, 1970; *Poetry,* January, 1968.†

*   *   *

BELFRAGE, Cedric   1904-

PERSONAL: Last syllable of surname is pronounced as in "beverage"; born November 8, 1904, in London, England; son of Sidney Henning (a physician) and Grace (Powley) Belfrage; married Mary Bernick; children: Sally, Nicholas, Anne. *Education:* Attended Gresham's

School and Corpus Christi College, Cambridge. *Politics:* Socialist. *Home:* Apdo. 630, Cuernavaca, Morelos, Mexico.

CAREER: Hollywood correspondent for British publications, *New York Herald Tribune,* and *New York Sun,* 1927-30; went to London as public relations man for Samuel Goldwyn, 1930, remained as film and theatre critic, waterfront coverer, and roving correspondent for London *Sunday* and *Daily Express;* returned to United States, 1936; *National Guardian,* New York, N.Y., founder and editor, 1948-55; ruled subversive by McCarthy Committee in 1953, twice apprehended by U.S. Immigration and Naturalization Service, and deported to England, 1955; editor-in-exile of *National Guardian* and reporter for various overseas left-wing journals from Europe, Middle East, Africa, Soviet Asia, China, India, Cuba, and South America, 1955-67; settled in Mexico, 1963. *Wartime service:* British Intelligence, New York, 1941-43; Psychological Warfare Division of SHAEF, France, 1944, Germany (reconstruction of press), 1945. *Awards, honors:* Guggenheim fellow, 1947; Louis M. Rabinowitz Foundation award, 1968.

WRITINGS: Away From It All, Simon & Schuster, 1937; *Promised Land,* Gollancz, 1938; *Let My People Go,* Gollancz, 1940, published in America as *South of God,* Modern Age, 1941; *They All Hold Swords,* Modern Age, 1941; *A Faith to Free the People,* Dryden Press, 1944; *Abide With Me,* Sloane, 1948; *Seeds of Destruction,* Cameron & Kahn, 1954; *The Frightened Giant,* Secker & Warburg, 1957; *My Master Columbus,* Doubleday, 1961; *The Man at the Door with the Gun,* Monthly Review, 1963; *La Inquisicion democratica* (originally written in English as *The American Inquisition,* but published in Spanish), Siglo Veintiuno (Mexico), 1971.

* * *

BELSHAW, Cyril S(hirley) 1921-

PERSONAL: Born December 3, 1921, in Waddington, New Zealand; son of Horace (a professor of economics) and Marion L. (McHardie) Belshaw; married Betty Joy Sweetman, March 8, 1943; children: Diana Marion, Adrian William. *Education:* University of New Zealand, B.A., 1943, M.A., 1945; London School of Economics and Political Science, Ph.D., 1949. *Home:* 5749 Chancellor Blvd., Vancouver 8, British Columbia, Canada. *Office:* University of British Columbia, Vancouver 8, British Columbia, Canada.

CAREER: Colonial Service, British Solomon Islands, administrative officer, 1943-46; British Air Ministry, London, England, senior scientific officer, 1949; Australian National University, Canberra, research fellow, 1950-53; University of British Columbia, Vancouver, Canada, assistant professor, 1953-56, associate professor, 1956-61, professor of anthropology, 1961—, senator, 1963-72, head of anthropology and sociology, 1966—. United Nations, consultant on social affairs, 1962-63, member of UNESCO expert group on social prerequisites to economic growth, 1963, and of group on contribution of social sciences to development, 1969; member of ECOSOC team to study contribution of UN family's technical assistance in Thailand, 1965. President, Vancouver Institute, 1961; vice-chairman, Canadian University Service Overseas, 1961-62. *Military service:* New Zealand Territorial Forces, served in Pacific, 1940-43; Defence Force, British Solomon Islands, 1943-46; became captain.

MEMBER: Royal Society of Canada (fellow, 1968—), Royal Economic Society, American Anthropological Association (member of executive board, 1969-70), American Ethnological Society, Society for International Development, Society for Applied Anthropology, Royal Anthropological Institute, Association of Social Anthropologists of the British Commonwealth, Canadian Institute of International Affairs, Canadian Sociology and Anthropology Association, Canadian Social Science Research Council (vice-president, 1968-71), Pacific Science Association (chairman, Anthropology and Social Sciences Standing Committee, 1967—), University Club (Vancouver; director, 1963-66). *Awards, honors:* John Simon Guggenheim fellow; fellow, United Nations Research Institute for Social Development, Geneva, 1965-66.

WRITINGS: Island Administration in the Southwest Pacific, Royal Institute of International Affairs, 1950; *Changing Melanesia: Social Economics of Changing Contact,* Oxford University Press, 1954; *In Search of Wealth: A Study of the Emergence of Commercial Operations in the Melanesian Society of Southeastern Papua,* American Anthropological Association, 1955; *Small Scale Industry for the South Pacific* (technical paper), South Pacific Commission, 1956; *A Study of Recreation in North Vancouver,* Community Chest and Council of Greater Vancouver, 1956; *The Great Village: The Economic and Social Welfare of Hanuabada, an Urban Community in Papua,* Routledge & Kegan Paul, 1957; (with H.B. Hawthorn and S. Jamieson) *The Indians of British Columbia,* University of California Press, 1958; *Under the Ivi Tree: Society and Economic Growth in Rural Fiji,* University of California Press, 1964; *Anatomy of a University,* Publications Centre, University of British Columbia, 1964; *Traditional Exchange and Modern Markets,* Prentice-Hall, 1965; *The Conditions of Social Performance: An Exploratory Theory,* Routledge & Kegan Paul, 1970. Contributor to anthropological and related journals. Member of international editorial committee, *Ethnography,* 1961-63; member of editorial committee, *Pacific Affairs.*

SIDELIGHTS: Belshaw's field work in anthropology has covered most of the island groups of Oceania. *Avocational interests:* Gardening, music, travel.

* * *

BEMIS, Samuel Flagg 1891-1973

PERSONAL: Born October 20, 1891, in Worcester, Mass.; son of Charles Harris (a newspaperman) and Flora Bemis; married Ruth M. Steele, June 20, 1919; children: Barbara (Mrs. Peter K. Bloch). *Education:* Clark University, A.B., 1912, A.M., 1913; Harvard University, A.M., 1915, Ph.D., 1916. *Politics:* Independent. *Religion:* Unitarian. *Home:* 120 Ogden St., New Haven, Conn. 06511. *Office:* 241 H.G.S., Yale University, New Haven, Conn. 06520.

CAREER: Colorado College, Colorado Springs, instructor in history, 1917-18, associate professor, 1918-20; Whitman College, Walla Walla, Wash., professor of history, 1920-23; Carnegie Institution of Washington, research associate, 1923-24; George Washington University, Washington, D.C., professor of history, 1924-34; Library of Congress, Washington, D.C., director of European mission, 1927-29; Harvard University, Cambridge, Mass., lecturer, 1934-35; Yale University, New Haven, Conn., professor of diplomatic history and inter-American relations, 1935-60, professor emeritus, 1960-73. Carnegie Visiting Professor to Latin American universities, 1937-38, to Cuba, 1945, 1956. *Member:* American Historical Association (president, 1961), American Antiquarian Society, Massachusetts Historical Society, other historical organizations. *Awards, honors:* Knights of Columbus award for best book on American history by a college teacher, 1923, for *Jay's Treaty;* Pulitzer Prize in History, 1927, for *Pinckney's Treaty;* Pulitzer Prize in Biography, 1950, for *John Quincy Adams and the Foundations of American Foreign Policy;* D.H.L., Clark University, 1937, Yale University, 1963; Doctor of Letters, Williams College, 1953.

WRITINGS: *The United States and the Abortive Armed Neutrality of 1794,* Macmillan, 1918; *Jay's Treaty: A Study in Commerce and Diplomacy,* Macmillan, 1923, 2nd revised edition, Yale University Press, 1962; *Pinckney's Treaty: A Study of America's Advantage from Europe's Distress, 1783-1900,* John Hopkins Press, 1926, revised edition, Yale University Press, 1960; (editor and contributor) *The American Secretaries of State and Their Diplomacy,* Volumes I-X, Knopf, 1927-29, Volumes XI-XV, Cooper Square, 1963-66; *The Hussey-Cumberland Mission and American Independence: An Essay in the Diplomacy of the American Revolution,* Princeton University Press, 1931, Peter Smith, 1968; (with Grace Gardner Griffin) *Guide to the Diplomatic History of the United States, 1775-1921,* U.S. Government Printing Office, 1935; *The Diplomacy of the American Revolution,* Appleton, 1935; *A Diplomatic History of the United States,* Holt, 1936, 5th edition, 1965.

Early Diplomatic Missions from Buenos Aires to the United States, 1811-1824, American Antiquarian Society, 1940; *The Latin American Policy of the United States,* Harcourt, 1943; *John Quincy Adams and the Foundations of American Foreign Policy,* Knopf, 1949; *The United States as a World Power: A Diplomatic History, 1900-1950* (originally published as part three of *A Diplomatic History of the United States*), Holt, 1950, revised edition, 1955; *John Quincy Adams and the Union,* Knopf, 1956; *A Short History of American Foreign Policy and Diplomacy,* Holt, 1959; *American Foreign Policy and the Blessings of Liberty, and Other Essays,* Yale University Press, 1962.

SIDELIGHTS: Bemis' interests included European and Inter-American relationships, countries, peoples, and languages.

BIOGRAPHICAL/CRITICAL SOURCES: *American Scholar,* summer, 1965.†

(Died September 26, 1973)

*   *   *

BENDA, Harry J(indrich)   1919-

PERSONAL: Born October 28, 1919, in Liberec, Czechoslovakia; son of Robert and Elizabeth (Frank) Benda; married Eva S. Bloch, April 13, 1950; children: Peter M., Susan R. *Education:* Victoria University College, Wellington, New Zealand, B.A., 1950; University of New Zealand, M.A. (first class honors), 1952; Cornell University, Ph.D., 1954. *Home:* 141 Ridgewood Ave., Hamden, Conn. 06517. *Office:* Department of History, Yale University, New Haven, Conn.

CAREER: Cornell University, Ithaca, N.Y., instructor in government, 1953-54; University of Rochester, Rochester, N.Y., assistant professor of history, 1955-59; Yale University, New Haven, Conn., associate professor of history, 1959-66, professor of history, 1966—. Visiting lecturer, Foreign Service Institute; writer. *Member:* American Historical Association, Association for Asian Studies (member of board of directors, 1967-70), Asia Society, Indonesia Council, Council on Foreign Relations. *Awards, honors:* Guggenheim fellowship, 1961-62.

WRITINGS: (With Vera M. Dean and Warren S. Hunsberger) *The Nature of the Non-Western World,* Mentor Press, 1957; *The Crescent and the Rising Sun: Indonesian Islam Under the Japanese Occupation, 1942-45,* W. van Hoeve, 1958; (editor and author of introduction with Ruth T. McVey) *The Communist Uprisings of 1926-1927 in Indonesia: Key Documents,* Modern Indonesia Project, Cornell University, 1960; (editor with James K. Irikura and Koichi Kishi) *Japanese Military Administration in Indonesia,* translation by Irikura, Margaret W. Broekhuysen, and Imam J. Pamoedjo, Yale University Southeast Studies, 1965; (contributor) Grant K.

Goodman, compiler, *Imperial Japan and Asia: A Reassessment,* Columbia University East Asian Institute, 1967; (compiler with John A. Larkin) *The World of Southeast Asia,* Harper, 1968; (with John S. Bastin) *A History of Modern Southeast Asia: Colonialism, Nationalism and Decolonization,* Prentice-Hall, 1968; (contributor) P.M. Holt and others, editors, *Cambridge History of Islam,* Cambridge University Press, 1971. Contributor of articles to professional journals. Assistant editor, *Journal of Asian Studies,* 1962-65.

WORK IN PROGRESS: A monograph on the Islamic roots of the Java War, 1825-30; a book on Batavia as a colonial capital, 1870-1942, completion expected in 1975.

SIDELIGHTS: Benda's interest in Southeast Asia is the result of seven years' residence there, including two years as a Japanese prisoner. He is fluent in Dutch and Indonesian, and knows German, Czech, and some French.

*   *   *

BENDINER, Robert   1909-

PERSONAL: Surname is pronounced Ben-*deen*-er; born December 15, 1909, in Pittsburgh, Pa.; son of William and Lillian (Schwartz) Bendiner; married Kathryn Rosenberg (a theatre project coordinator), December 24, 1934; children: David, William, Margaret. *Education:* Attended City College of New York (now City College of the City University of New York), evening sessions, 1928-33. *Home:* 45 Central Parkway, Huntington, N.Y. 11743. *Office: New York Times,* Editorial Board, 229 West 43rd St., New York, N.Y. 10036.

CAREER: *Nation,* New York, N.Y., managing editor, 1937-44, associate editor, 1946-50; free-lance writer, 1951-69; *Reporter,* New York, NY., contributing editor, 1956-60; *New Statesman,* London, England, American correspondent, 1959-61; *New York Times,* New York, N.Y., member of editorial board, 1968—. Lecturer at Wellesley Summer Institute for Social Progress, 1946-53, Salzburg Seminar in American Studies, 1956. *Military service:* U.S. Army, correspondent for *Yank,* 1944-45; served as sergeant. *Member:* Society of Magazine Writers (vice-president, 1958; president, 1964), National Press Club (Washington), Coffee House Club. *Awards, honors:* Benjamin Franklin Magazine Award, University of Illinois, 1955; School Bell Award, National Education Association, 1960; Guggenheim fellow, 1962-63.

WRITINGS: *The Riddle of the State Department,* Farrar & Rinehart, 1942; *White House Fever: An Innocent's Guide to Principles and Practices, Respectable and Otherwise, Behind the Election of American Presidents,* Harcourt, 1960; *Obstacle Course on Capitol Hill,* McGraw, 1964; *Just Around the Corner: A Highly Selective History of the Thirties,* Harper, 1967; *The Politics of Schools: A Crisis in Self-Government,* Harper, 1969; (editor with Daniel Aaron) *The Strenuous Decade: A Social and Intellectual Record of the 1930's,* Doubleday-Anchor, 1970. Also author of "The Man in the Middle—the State Legislator," a television documentary in the National Broadcasting Co. "White Paper" series, 1961. Member of editorial board, *New York Times,* 1969—.

SIDELIGHTS: Bendiner is "one of the best magazine reporters around," according to Gerald Weales of *Reporter.* *"Just Around the Corner,* like his idea of the 1930's," writes Weales, "is neither one thing nor another, neither narrative history nor cultural description, neither personal reminiscence nor objective reporting. It is a little of all of them. . . . [The book] does not pretend to be a contribution to our knowledge of the 1930's. It is simply one man's portrait of the decade, to be read for pleasure and—if possible—profit." Unlike most accounts of the Depression years, which tend to be either overly sentimental or unbearably grim, Bendiner's narrative is "free-swinging" and "amiable." Paraphrasing Bendiner himself, Saul Maloff points out that "Bendiner arrived at the Depression better prepared than most. His father had gone bankrupt in 1922; so by the time the rest of the country was catching up, he had had 'experience in the ways of genteel poverty.' The experience stood Bendiner in good stead: his view is neither jaundiced nor tearful, but jaunty and zestful."

A political reporter who began as office boy at *World Tomorrow,* spent a few months on the staff of *New Masses,* and became managing editor of *Nation* at 27, Bendiner has also written an analysis of American school boards which Ivor Kraft, among others, considers "the best book of its kind now available." According to Diane Ravitch of *New Leader,* Bendiner spent two years studying school boards under a Carnegie Corporation grant. "In less skilled hands," she writes, "the result might have been a ponderous technical report that concluded with the usual trumpet blast of dire warnings. Fortunately Bendiner . . . is an excellent writer and reporter with a keen eye; his book is devoid of the jargon and rhetoric which mars much writing concerning education."

Bendiner told *CA* that he has become "extremely interested in environmental matters in recent years; I have made a number of interesting trips in this connection—from the Beaufort Sea on the Arctic ice shelf to 'gator holes in the Everglades, including a 200-mile helicopter journey over England and Wales . . . Finding these investigations both more fruitful and more interesting than the political coverage that preoccupied me for most of my journalistic career."

BIOGRAPHICAL/CRITICAL SOURCES: Book Week, April 23, 1967; *New York Times Book Review,* May, 1967, December 14, 1969; *Newsweek,* May 8, 1967; *Atlantic,* June, 1967; *Reporter,* August 10, 1967; *Library Journal,* December 1, 1969; *New Leader,* January 19, 1970; *Nation,* February 16, 1970.

* * *

BENET, Laura 1884-

PERSONAL: Born June 13, 1884, at Fort Hamilton, Brooklyn, N.Y.; daughter of James Walker (an army officer) and Frances Neill (Rose) Benet. *Education:* Emma Willard School, graduate, 1903; Vassar College, A.B., 1907. *Politics:* Democrat. *Religion:* Protestant Episcopal, *Home:* Hotel Van Rensselaer, 15 East 11th St., New York, N.Y. 10003.

CAREER: Spring Street Settlement, New York, N.Y., settlement worker, 1913-16; Red Cross Sanitary Commission, Augusta, Ga., inspector, World War I; St. Bartholomew's Mission, New York, N.Y., visitor, 1924-25; *New York Evening Post,* New York, N.Y., assistant editor of book page, 1926-28; *New York Sun,* New York, N.Y., assistant to book page editor, 1928-29; writer, 1930—. *New York Times,* New York, N.Y., substitute review editor, 1930. Air raid warden during World War II. *Member:* Poetry Society of America, P.E.N., Women Poets, Craftsman Group, Pen and Brush Club (honorary). *Awards, honors:* Prizes for poetry from *Lyric* and *Voices;* D.Litt., Moravian College, 1967.

WRITINGS: Fairy Bread (poems), Thomas Seltzer, 1921; *Noah's Dove* (poems), Doubleday, 1929; *Goods and Chattels* (fantasies in prose), Doubleday, 1930; *Basket for a Fair* (poems), Doubleday, 1934; *The Boy Shelley,* Dodd, 1937; *The Hidden Valley* (juvenile), Dodd, 1938; *Enchanting Jenny Lind,* Dodd, 1939; *Roxana Rampant* (girl's novel), Dodd, 1940; *Young Edgar Allan Poe,* Dodd, 1941; *Caleb's Luck,* Grosset, 1942; *Come Slowly, Eden* (novel about Emily Dickinson), Dodd, 1942; *Washington Irving, Explorer of American Legend,* Dodd, 1944; *Is Morning Sure?* (poems), Odyssey, 1947; *Thackeray, of*

the Great Heart and Humorous Pen, Dodd, 1947; *Barnum's First Circus, and Other Stories,* 1949.

Famous American Poets, Dodd, 1950; *Coleridge, Poet of Wild Enchantment,* Dodd, 1952; (author of biographical introduction) *Tales by Edgar Allan Poe,* Dodd, 1952; (author of biographical introduction) *Thackeray's Henry Esmond,* Heritage, 1952; *Stanley, Invincible Explorer,* Dodd, 1955; *In Love with Time* (poems), Wake-Brook, 1959; *Famous American Humorists,* Dodd, 1959; *Famous Poets for Young People,* Dodd, 1964; *Famous English and American Essayists,* Dodd, 1966; *Famous Storytellers for Young People,* Dodd, 1968; *Famous New England Authors,* Dodd, 1970.

WORK IN PROGRESS: A new book of poems.

* * *

BENHAM, Leslie 1922-

PERSONAL: Surname is pronounced *Ben*-am; born April 29, 1922, in Galt, Ontario; son of William Charles and Mabel (Hays) Benham; married Lois Irene Dakin, July 31, 1950; children: a daughter. *Education:* Attended Galt Collegiate Institute and Vocational School. *Religion:* Presbyterian. *Home:* 14 Hillcrest Dr., Galt, Ontario, Canada.

CAREER: Babcock-Wilcox, Ltd., Galt, Ontario, 1947—, now order supervisor, service parts sales. *Military service:* Royal Canadian Air Force, aero engine mechanic, 1942-45; became leading aircraftsman. *Member:* Colour Photographic Association of Canada (president of affiliated Galt Camera Club, 1959-60).

WRITINGS: (With wife, Lois Benham) *The Heroine of Long Point* (juvenile), St. Martin's, 1963. Contributor of articles on travel and nature to newspapers.

AVOCATIONAL INTERESTS: Photography, music, and oil painting.

BIOGRAPHICAL/CRITICAL SOURCES: Canadiana, April, 1963.

* * *

BENHAM, Lois (Dakin) 1924-

PERSONAL: Born March 19, 1924, in Galt, Ontario; daughter of Harry (a plumber and electrician) and Alice E. (Atkinson) Dakin; married Leslie Benham, July 31, 1950; children: one daughter. *Education:* Attended Galt Collegiate Institute and Vocational School; McMaster University, B.A. (with honors), 1946; Canada Business College, summer course, 1946. *Religion:* Presbyterian. *Home:* 14 Hillcrest Dr., Galt, Ontario, Canada.

CAREER: McMaster University, Hamilton, Ontario, secretary to director of extension courses, 1946-48; secretary in local business firm, Galt, Ontario, 1948-50. *Member:* Colour Photographic Association of Canada (member of affiliated Galt Camera Club). *Awards, honors:* Ribbons and acceptances in Canadian photographic competitions.

WRITINGS: (With husband, Leslie Benham) *The Heroine of Long Point,* St. Martin's, 1963. Co-author of travel and nature articles published in newspapers.

AVOCATIONAL INTERESTS: Photography (particularly tabletops and nature), music, and oil painting.

BIOGRAPHICAL/CRITICAL SOURCES: Canadiana, April, 1963.

* * *

BENJAMIN, Claude (Max Edward Pohlman) 1911-
(Max Edwards, Marion E. George)

PERSONAL: Born October 17, 1911, in Bloomington, Ind.; son of Augustus Grote (a physician) and Kathleen

(Black) Pohlman; married Harriet Witbeck, August 1, 1945; children: Kathleen, Edward. *Education:* St. Louis University, B.S., 1930, M.D., 1934. *Agent:* Ben Benjamin, c/o Ashley-Steiner-Famous Artists, Inc., Beverly Hills, Calif. *Office:* 2200 West Third St., Los Angeles, Calif. 90057.

CAREER: Physician specializing in ear, nose and throat; University of Southern California, Los Angeles, member of faculty of department of surgery. *Military service:* U.S. Navy, Medical Corps, 1940-46; held prisoner at Bilibid in Philippines; became captain. *Member:* Dramatists Guild.

WRITINGS: The Medical Itch, Obolensky, 1964. Author of three-act plays under pseudonym Marion E. George: "Bilibid," produced at Pasadena Playhouse, 1964; (with Clyde Binyon) "The Soft Touch" (comedy), under option by George Abbott. Contributor to medical journals.

WORK IN PROGRESS: A farce in three acts, "What's the Matter with Walter?"

SIDELIGHTS: Benjamin uses a pseudonym for plays because patients are uneasy about doctor-writers. "Especially doctors who write comedy," he adds.

* * *

BENKO, Stephen 1924-

PERSONAL: Born June 13, 1924, in Budapest, Hungary; came to United States, 1952; son of Stephen (a minister) and Vilma (Nemeth) Benko; married Brigitte Staehelin, January, 1953; children: Evelyn, Catherine, Stephen, Suzanne. *Education:* Theological Academy, Budapest, Hungary, B.D., 1947; University of Zurich, graduate study, 1947-48; University of Basel, Ph.D., 1951; Yale University, research fellow, 1953-54; Temple University, postgraduate study, 1968. *Home:* 563 West Stuart, Fresno, Calif. 93704. *Office:* Department of History, California State University, Fresno, Calif. 93710.

CAREER: Temple University, Philadelphia, Pa., instructor, 1956-60; Conwell School of Theology, Philadelphia, Pa., professor of biblical history, 1960-69; California State University, Fresno, professor of ancient history, 1969—. *Member:* American Historical Association, American Philological Society, American Society of Church History, Society of Biblical Literature and Exegesis.

WRITINGS: Sanctorum Communio: Eine dogmengeschichtliche Untersuchung ueber das Symbolglied, University of Basel, 1951, translation by David L. Scheidt published as *The Meaning of Sanctorum Communio,* Allenson, 1964; *Protestants, Catholics and Mary,* Judson, 1968; *My Lord Speaks,* Judson, 1970; (editor with J.J. O'Rourke) *The Catacombs and the Colosseum: The Early Roman Empire as Background of Primitive Christianity,* Judson, 1971 (published in England as *The Early Church,* Oliphant, 1972).

Contributor: *OIKONOMIA: Heilsgeschichte als Thema der Theologie,* Reich, 1967; *Gottesreich und Menschenreich,* Helbing & Lichtenhahn, 1969; (contributor to English translation) Walter Bauer, *Orthodoxy and Heresy in Earliest Christianity,* edited by Robert Kraft and Gerhard Krodel, Fortress, 1971. Contributor of numerous articles to religious and scholarly journals, including *Theologische Zeitschrift, Lutheran Quarterly,* and *Evangelium Vilagszolgalat;* contributor of reviews to *Church History, Christian Century, Journal of Biblical Literature, Westminster Bookman, Voice,* and other periodicals.

WORK IN PROGRESS: Studies in ancient history and primitive Christianity.

SIDELIGHTS: Benko speaks English, German, and Hungarian, and reads Latin, Greek, French, and Hebrew.

BENKOVITZ, Miriam J (eanette) 1911-

PERSONAL: Born November 16, 1911, in Chattanooga, Tenn.; daughter of Jake (a merchant) and Josephine (Bloomstein) Benkovitz. *Education:* Vanderbilt University, B.A., 1932; Peabody College, M.A., 1942; Yale University, M.A, 1947, Ph.D., 1951. *Home:* 17 Ten Springs Dr., Saratoga Springs, N.Y. 12866. *Agent:* Gunther Stuhlmann, 60 Irving Pl., New York, N.Y. 10003. *Office:* Department of English, Skidmore College, Saratoga Springs, NY. 12866.

CAREER: Skidmore College, Saratoga Springs, N.Y. 1946—, began as assistant professor, professor of English, 1962—. Visiting professor, State University of New York at Albany, 1969. Partner, Saratoga Travel Bureau, Saratoga Springs, N.Y. *Member:* Modern Language Association of America (member of delegate assembly, 1971-74), Bibliographical Society of America, American Association of University Women, Manuscript Society.

WRITINGS: (Editor and author of introduction) Madame d'Arblay, *Edwy and Elgiva,* edited by Fanny Burney, Shoe String, 1957; *A Bibliography of Ronald Firbank,* Hart-Davis, 1963, Oxford University Press, 1964; (contributor) H.D. Ford, editor, *Nancy Cunard: Brave Poet, Indomitable Rebel, 1896-1965,* Chilton, 1968; *Ronald Firbank: A Biography,* Knopf, 1969; (editor) *A Passionate Prodigality: Letters from Richard Aldington to Alan Bird,* New York Public Library, 1973. Author of introductions to reprints of short pieces by Ronald Firbank, published by Enitharmon Press and Albondocani Press; contributor to various journals.

WORK IN PROGRESS: Frederick Rolfe Barco Corvo: A Biography, publication by Knopf expected in 1974; with Norman T. Gates, *A Checklist of Richard Aldington's Letters,* 1974.

SIDELIGHTS: In a review of *Ronald Firbank: A Biography,* Edward M. Potoker writes: ". . . Miriam Benkovitz has produced a work of art. She shows Firbank romping through the mauve decade, enduring World War I with disapproval but forbearance, and trying to remain enchanted, or at least engaged, with the disenchanting Twenties. He would have admired her sense of drama, her 'staging.' Most important, Ronald Firbank here emerges as a revolutionary writer, just as Oscar Wilde has come to be recognized as a revolutionary critic." The *New Yorker* reviewer adds: "Her biography follows Firbank almost day by day, and at its best has the qualities of Firbank's own fiction: style, wit, and an enormous gossipy interest."

AVOCATIONAL INTERESTS: Collecting first and special editions of twentieth-century English writers, their manuscripts, and letters.

BIOGRAPHICAL/CRITICAL SOURCES: New York Times Book Review, May 11, 1969; *Atlantic,* June, 1969; *Newsweek,* June 2, 1969; *Saturday Review,* June 7, 1969; *New Yorker,* August 2, 1969; *Spectator,* January 31, 1970; *Books and Bookmen,* April, 1970; *London Magazine,* June, 1970; *Carleton Miscellany,* winter, 1970.

* * *

BENNETT, Charles E (dward) 1910-

PERSONAL: Born December 2, 1910, in Canton, N.Y.; son of Walter James (a U.S. meteorologist) and Roberta (Broadhurst) Bennett; married Dorothy Jean Fay, April 6, 1953; children: Bruce C., Charles E., Jr., James F., Lucinda Fay. *Education:* University of Florida, B.A. and Jur.D., 1934. *Politics:* Democrat. *Religion:* Disciples of Christ. *Home:* 2130 Riverside Ave., Jacksonville, Fla. *Office:* 2113 Rayburn Bldg., Washington, D.C.

CAREER: Admitted to Florida bar, 1934. Lawyer in Jacksonville, Fla. as associate of Knight, Adair, Cooper &

Osborne, 1934-38, and in private practice, 1938-48. Representative, Florida State Legislature, 1941; representative in U.S. Congress from Florida's Second District, 1949—. *Military service:* U.S. Army, Infantry, 1942-47; served in New Guinea and with guerilla forces in Philippines; became captain; received Silver Star, Bronze Star, Combat Infantryman Badge, Philippine Legion of Honor and Gold Cross for gallantry in action. *Member:* Jacksonville Junior Chamber of Commerce (president, 1938). *Awards, honors:* H.H.D. from University of Tampa, 1950; Freedoms Foundation awards, 1951, 1956; Junior Chamber of Commerce good government award, 1952.

WRITINGS: Laudonniere and Fort Caroline: History and Documents, University of Florida Press, 1964; (compiler) *Settlement of Florida,* University of Florida Press, 1968; *Southernmost Battlefields of the Revolution,* Blair Press, 1970; (contributor) John B. Anderson, editor, *Congress and Conscience,* Lippincott, 1970. Contributor of articles to *Encyclopedia Americana, Nation's Business,* and historical journals.

WORK IN PROGRESS: Compiling rare sixteenth-century material for book tentatively titled *Three Voyages;* a book on World War II experiences, *Coconuts and Combat Too;* and a book on the American Revolution tentatively titled *General Robert Howe and His Order Books.*

* * *

BENNETT, Jack Arthur Walter 1911-

PERSONAL: Born February 28, 1911, in Auckland, New Zealand; son of Ernest and Alexandra (Corrall) Bennett; married Gwyneth Mary Nicholas, March 29, 1951; children: Edmund Piers, Charles Anslem. *Education:* University College, Auckland, New Zealand, M.A., 1933; Merton College, Oxford University, B.A., 1935, M.A., D.Phil. 1938. *Politics:* Liberal. *Religion:* Roman Catholic. *Home:* Westgates, Ferry Hinksey, Oxford, England. *Office:* Magdalen College, Oxford, England.

CAREER: The Queen's College, Oxford University, Oxford, England, research fellow, 1938-46; British Information Service, New York, N.Y., acting director, 1940-45; Magdalen College, Oxford University, fellow and tutor, 1947-64; Oxford University, lecturer in English literature, 1949-64; Cambridge University, Cambridge, England, professor of mediaeval and Renaissance English, Fellow of Magdalene College, 1964—. *Member:* Early English Text Society (council, 1956—).

WRITINGS: (Editor) Geoffrey Chaucer, *The Knight's Tale,* Harrap, 1954, 2nd edition, 1958; (editor with H.R. Trevor-Roper) Richard Corbett, *Poems,* Clarendon Press, 1955; (editor) *Devotional Pieces in Verse and Prose from Ms. Arundel 285 and Ms. Harleian 6919,* Scottish Text Society, 1955; *The Parlement of Foules: An Interpretation,* Clarendon Press, 1957; (editor) Walter Oakeshott and others, *Essays on Malory,* Oxford University Press, 1963; *The Humane Medievalist* (inaugural lecture), Cambridge University Press, 1965; (editor with G.V. Smithers) *Early Middle English Verse and Prose,* Clarendon Press, 1966, 2nd edition, 1968; *Chaucer's Book of Fame: An Exposition of "The House of Fame",* Oxford University Press, 1968; (editor) *Selections from John Gower,* Oxford University Press, 1968. Contributor to *Times Literary Supplement, Listener, Landfall* (New Zealand), and to learned journals. Editor of "Clarendon Medieval and Tudor Series," and of *Medium Aevum,* 1955—.

WORK IN PROGRESS: Editing Chaucer's *The House of Fame;* a commentary on *Piers Plowman;* a volume in "Oxford History of English Literature" series.

BIOGRAPHICAL/CRITICAL SOURCES: Times Literary Supplement, January 12, 1967, July 25, 1968; *Virginia Quarterly Review,* spring, 1969.

BENNETT, Marion T(insley) 1914-

PERSONAL: Born June 6, 1914, in Buffalo, Mo.; son of Philip Allen (a congressman) and Bertha (Tinsley) Bennett; married June Young, April 27, 1941; children: Ann, William Philip. *Education:* Southwest Missouri State College, A.B., 1935; Washington University, St. Louis, Mo., LL.B., 1938. *Politics:* Republican. *Religion:* Methodist. *Home:* 3715 Cardiff Rd., Chevy Chase, Md. 20015.

CAREER: Admitted to Missouri bar, 1938, to bar of U.S. Supreme Court, 1944; private practice of law, Springfield, Mo., 1938-43; U.S. Congress, representative from Sixth Missouri District, 1943-49; U.S. Court of Claims, Washington, D.C., commissioner (trial judge), 1949—, chief trial commissioner, 1964—. Consultant to congressional committees on immigration law and the administration of justice. Public speaker on legal and political problems. *Military service:* U.S. Air Force Ready Reserve; now colonel. *Member:* American Bar Association, Federal Bar Association (national council, 1960—), District of Columbia Bar Association, Reserve Officers Association, Judge Advocates Association, National Lawyers Club, National Exchange Club, Delta Theta Phi. *Awards, honors:* Award of Merit, American Academy of Public Affairs, 1964, for *American Immigration Policies: A History.*

WRITINGS: American Immigration Policies: A History, Public Affairs Press, 1963; *Private Claims and Congressional References* (originally published in USAF Jag Law Review, December, 1967), U.S. Government Printing Office, 1968. Contributor to *Annals* of American Academy of Political and Social Science, to *Federal Bar Journal,* and to law journals and reviews.

WORK IN PROGRESS: Further research in public law, with emphasis on immigration, and tax and contract law.

SIDELIGHTS: Bennett followed his father to Congress, was the youngest member of the House when he took his seat. As a Court of Claims trial judge he acts on suits for money damages against the United States.

* * *

BENNETT, Norman Robert 1932-

PERSONAL: Born October 31, 1932, in Marlboro, Mass.; son of Norman (a shoe worker) and Viola (Belmore) Bennett; married Ruth Roberts (a university teacher), December 31, 1954. *Education:* Tufts University, A.B. (magna cum laude), 1954; Princeton University, graduate student, 1954-55; Fletcher School of Law and Diplomacy, M.A., 1956; Boston University, Ph.D., 1961. *Politics:* Independent. *Religion:* None. *Office:* African Studies Center, 10 Lenox St., Brookline, Mass. 02146.

CAREER: Boston University, Boston, Mass., instructor, 1960-63, assistant professor, 1963-67, associate professor, 1967-70, professor of history, 1970—. Smith-Mundt Visiting Professor at Kivukoni College, Tanganyika, 1962-63. *Member:* American Historical Association, African Studies Association (chairman of archives committee, 1961-63), British Institute of Archaeology and History in East Africa, Tanzania Society, Uganda Society, Kenya Historical Society. *Awards, honors:* Ford Foundation fellowship, 1958-60; American Philosophical Society award, 1966.

WRITINGS: (Compiler) *Discovering Africa: Source Materials on the Opening of a Great Continent* (exhibition held at Chenery Library, Boston University, October 1-30, 1961), [Boston], 1961; *Studies in East African History,* Boston University Press, 1963; (editor with George E. Brooks, Jr.) *New England Merchants in Africa: A History Through Documents, 1802 to 1865,* Boston University Press, 1965; (editor with Creighton Gabel) *Reconstructing African Culture History,* Boston University Press, 1967; (editor) *Leadership in Eastern Africa: Six*

Political Biographies, Boston University Press, 1968; (compiler) *A Study Guide for Tunisia,* African Studies Center, Boston University, 1968; (compiler) *A Study Guide for Morocco,* African Studies Center, Boston University, 1968; (editor with Daniel F. McCall and Jeffrey Butler) *Eastern African History,* published for the African Studies Center of Boston University by Praeger, 1969; (editor with McCall and Butler) *Western African History,* published for the African Studies Center of Boston University by Praeger, 1969; *From Zanzibar to Ujiji,* African Studies Center, Boston University, 1969; (editor) *Stanley's Despatches to the New York Herald, 1871-1872, 1874-1877,* Boston University Press, 1970; *Miramba of Tanzania,* Oxford University Press, 1971; (editor with Marguerite Minsaker) *The Central African Journal of Lovell J. Proctor, 1860-1864,* African Studies Center, Boston University, 1971; (editor with McCall) *Aspects of West African Islam,* African Studies Center, Boston University, 1971. Contributor to *Tanganyika Notes and Records, Journal of African History, African Studies Bulletin,* Essex Institute *Historical Collections, African Affairs,* and other history and education journals. Editor, *African Studies Bulletin,* 1967-70, *International Journal of African Historical Studies,* 1968—.

WORK IN PROGRESS: Arab versus European in Nineteenth Century East Africa; Americans in East Africa; Africa and Europe.

*   *   *

BENSEN, Donald R.   **1927-**

PERSONAL: Born October 3, 1927, in Brooklyn, N.Y.; son of Roynold (a machine distributor) and Dorothy (Thatcher) Bensen; married Anne McCurdy, October 11, 1957; children: Nicholas. *Education:* Columbia University, A.B., 1950. *Home:* 152 Colabaugh Pond Rd., Croton-on-Hudson, N.Y. 10520.

CAREER: Wilfred Funk, Inc. (publisher), New York, N.Y., production manager, 1951-52; Peoples Book Club, New York, N.Y., assistant editor, 1952-56; Pyramid Books, New York, N.Y., editor, 1957-68; Berkley Publishing Corp., New York, N.Y., executive editor, 1968-70; Beagle Books, New York, N.Y., editor-in-chief, 1970—. *Military service:* U.S. Army, 1946-47.

WRITINGS—Editor: *The Unknown,* Pyramid Books, 1963; *The Unknown Five,* Pyramid Books, 1964. Contributor of verse and fiction to *Ellery Queen's Mystery Magazine.*

*   *   *

BENTLEY, Howard Beebe   **1925-**

PERSONAL: Born October 8, 1925, in Norfolk, Mass.; son of Oliver Daniel Howard (an engineer) and Dorothy (Beebe) Bentley. *Education:* Principia College, B.A., 1947; Simmons College, M.S. in Library Science. *Office:* Time, Inc., Time-Life Building, New York, N.Y. 10020.

CAREER: Time, Inc, New York, N.Y., librarian, 1959—. *Member:* American Documentation Institute, American Recorder Society, Special Libraries Association (chairman of planning, building, and housing section, 1963-64).

WRITINGS: Building Construction Information Sources, Gale, 1964. Contributor to *Library Journal.*

AVOCATIONAL INTERESTS: Sailboating and music.

*   *   *

BENWARD, Bruce (Charles)   **1921-**

PERSONAL: Born June 29, 1921, in Churubusco, Ind.; son of Charles Arthur (a druggist) and Maude (Jones) Benward; married Mary Gene Aishe, July 4, 1942; children: Cynthia, Tamara, Nadia. *Education:* Indiana University, B.Mus., 1942, M.Mus., 1932; University of Rochester, Ph.D., 1951. *Home:* 5602 Hammersley Rd., Madison, Wis. 53711. *Office:* School of Music, University of Wisconsin, Madison, Wis. 53706.

CAREER: University of Idaho, Moscow, instructor in music, 1945-46; University of Arkansas, Fayetteville, chairman of music department, 1946-65; University of Wisconsin, Madison, professor of music and chairman of School of Music, 1965—. *Member:* National Association of Schools of Music (chairman, Southwest Division), National Association of Music Executives of State Universities, Music Teachers National Association, American Musicological Society, American Association of University Professors, Rotary Club.

WRITINGS: Teacher's Dictation Manual in Ear Training (includes workbook), W.C. Brown, 1961, 2nd edition, 1969; *College Ear Training Applied* (records), W.C. Brown, 1961; (with Barbara Seagrave) *Practical Beginning Theory,* W.C. Brown, 1963, revised edition, 1966; (with Seagrave) *Teacher's Key for Practical Beginning Theory* (includes recordings), W.C. Brown, 1963; *Sight-singing Complete,* W.C. Brown, 1965, 2nd edition, 1972; *Teacher's Dictation Manual in Advanced Ear Training and Sightsinging,* W.C. Brown, 1969; *Workbook in Advanced Ear Training and Sightsinging* (12 tape recordings), W.C. Brown, 1969, 2nd edition with two additional tape recordings, 1969.

*   *   *

BERCZELLER, Richard   **1902-**

PERSONAL: Born February 4, 1902, in Sopron, Hungary; son of Adolf and Sidonie (Kohn) Berczeller; married Maria Frances Unger, March 27, 1931; children: Peter Hanns. *Education:* University of Vienna, M.D., 1926. *Home and office:* 242 East 19th St., New York, N.Y. 10003. *Agent:* Robert Lantz-Candida Donadio, Inc., 111 West 57th St., New York, N.Y. 10019.

CAREER: Physician, practicing in Austria, 1926-1938, in France, 1938-41, in New York, N.Y., 1941—. Member of attending staff, Beth Israel Hospital, New York, N.Y. *Member:* American Medical Association, New York County Medical Society, Medical Society of the State of New York, Alumni Association of Beth Israel Hospital. *Awards, honors:* Golden Cross of Merit, Republic of Australia.

WRITINGS: Displaced Doctor, Odyssey, 1964 (published in England as *Doctors of All Trades,* M. Joseph, 1965); *Time Was* (autobiography), Viking, 1971. Contributor of stories to *New Yorker.*

WORK IN PROGRESS: Memoirs from World War I to 1921; magazine stories.

BIOGRAPHICAL/CRITICAL SOURCES: Atlantic, April, 1971; *Best Sellers,* April 15, 1971.

*   *   *

BERENSON, Conrad   **1930-**

PERSONAL: Born June 17, 1930, in Brooklyn, N.Y.; son Samuel Arthur (a lawyer) and Elizabeth (Stollerman) Berenson. *Education:* College of City of New York (now City College of the City University of New York), B.Ch.E., 1952; Columbia University, M.S., 1953; New York University, M.B.A., 1959, Ph.D., 1962. *Office:* Bernard M. Baruch College of the City University of New York, 17 Lexington Ave., New York, N.Y. 10010.

CAREER: American Cyanamid Co., chemical engineer and project leader, 1953-59; City College, and Bernard M. Baruch College of the City University of New York, New York, N.Y., professor of marketing, Editor of Corporate Publications' Chemical Executives' Reports. Executive director, Research Foundation of The City University of New York, 1964-69. Consultant in marketing, management, and engineering. *Member:* American Institute of Chemical Engineers (chairman of Group 6, 1962-67), American Marketing Association, American Association of University Professors, Sigma Xi, Phi Lambda Upsilon, Pi Sigma Epsilon. *Award, honors:* Ford Foundation fellowship, 1959-61.

WRITINGS: (With Edward M. Mazze) *How to Organize for International Marketing in the Chemical Industry,* Corporate Publications, 1962; *Product Abandonment in the Chemical Industry,* Corporate Publications, 1962; (editor and contributor) *Administration of the Chemical Enterprise,* Interscience, 1963 (editor) *The Chemical Industry: Viewpoints and Perspectives,* Interscience, 1963; *How to Increase the Profitability of the Product Line,* Corporate Publications, 1964; (with Henry O. Ruhnke) *Job Descriptions of Production and Research Personnel in the Chemical Process Industries,* Corporate Publications, 1964; (with Ruhnke) *Job Descriptions: How to Write and Use Them,* Personnel Journal, 1967; (with R.R. Colton) *Research and Report Writing for Business and Economics,* Random House, 1971; (with Henry Eilbert) *Social Dynamics of Marketing,* Random House, 1973. Contributor to business and engineering periodicals. Consulting editor and columnist, *Laboratory Management* and *Detergent Age.* Technical editor, *Chemical Purchasing.*

* * *

BERGER, Carl 1925-

PERSONAL: Born January 28, 1925, in Chicago, Ill.; son of Fred and Rae (Greenberg) Berger. *Education:* University of Iowa, B.A., 1949; Drake University, M.A., 1952; George Washington University, postgraduate study, 1957-58. *Home:* 1301 South Scott St., Arlington, Va. 22204.

CAREER: Des Moines Register, Des Moines, Iowa, reporter, 1949-53; U.S. Army, civilian historian in Japan, 1953-55; American University, Special Operations Research Office, Washington, D.C., writer-analyst, 1957-59; Office of Air Force History, Washington, D.C., civilian historian, 1959—. *Military service:* U.S. Army, 1943-46; became sergeant. U.S. Army Reserve, 1949-53; became first lieutenant. *Member:* American Historical Association, Air Force Historical Foundation, Air Force Association, Phi Beta Kappa. *Awards, honors:* U.S. Air Force Commendation for meritorious civilian service, 1962, 1964, 1969.

WRITINGS: The Korea Knot: A Military-Political History, University of Pennsylvania Press, 1957, 2nd edition, 1964; *An Introduction to Wartime Leaflets,* Special Operations Research Office, American University, 1959; (with Howard C. Reese and Charles A. Feder) *A Psychological Operations Bibliography,* Special Operations Research Office, American University, 1960; *History of the 1st Missile Division,* Vandenberg Air Force Base, 1960; *Broadsides and Bayonets: The Propaganda War of the American Revolution,* University of Pennsylvania Press, 1961; *B-29: The Superfortress,* Ballantine, 1970.

WORK IN PROGRESS: A book on Andrew Jackson and the American frontier.

* * *

BERGIN, Thomas Goddard 1904-

PERSONAL: Born November 17, 1904, in New Haven, Conn.; son of Thomas Joseph and Irvinea (Goddard) Bergin; married Florence T. Bullen, December 30, 1929; children: Winifred Mandeville (Mrs. Boyd Hart), Jennifer Mandeville (Mrs. Peter Von Mayrhauser) *Education:* Yale University, B.A., 1925, Ph.D., 1929. *Home:* 48 Wyndybrook Lane, Madison, Conn. 06443. *Office:* Dept.

of Romance Languages, Yale University, New Haven, Conn. 06520.

CAREER: Yale University, New Haven, Conn., instructor in Italian, 1925-30; Western Reserve University, Mather College, Cleveland, Ohio, associate professor of Spanish and Italian, 1930-35; State University of New York, College of Education at Albany, professor of Romance languages, 1935-41; Cornell University, Ithaca, N.Y., professor of Romance languages and curator of Fiske Dante-Petrarch collections, 1941-48, chairman of division of literature and acting chairman of department of English, 1946-48; Yale University, professor of Romance languages, 1948-68, Benjamin F. Barge Professor of Romance Languages, 1949-57, Sterling Professor of Romance Languages, 1958—, chairman of department of Italian and Spanish, 1949-58, master of Timothy Dwight College, 1953-68. *Military service:* U.S. Army, 1943-46; became lieutenant colonel; served with Allied Commission in Italy; received Bronze Star, Order of British Empire, Order of Crown of Italy, Order of Sts. Maurice and Lazarus (Italy); special commendation from School of Military Government.

MEMBER: Modern Language Association of America, American Association of Teachers of Italian (president, 1947), Mediaeval Academy of America, American Association of University Professors (president of Yale chapter, 1951-52), Dante Society, Renaissance Society, P.E.N., Phi Beta Kappa, Graduates Club, Lawn Club, Mory's, Elizabeth Club, Yale Club, Cornell Club (New York), Savile Club (London). *Awards, honors:* Fulbright scholar in Italy, 155-56; Litt. D. from Hofstra College, 1958; L.H.D. from Fairfield University, 1956; Order of Civic Merit (Italy), 1970.

WRITINGS: Giovanni Vergi, Yale University Press, 1931; (editor) *Modern Italian Short Stories,* Heath, 1938, revised and enlarged edition, 1959.

Luciano Zuccoli, ritratto umbertino, Societa Editrice del Libro Italiano (Rome), 1940; (editor with Raymond Thompson Hill) *Anthology of the Provencal Troubadours,* Yale University Press, 1941; (editor and author of introduction with Theodore Andersson) *French Plays: Brieux, Hervieu, Miroeau,* American Book Co., 1941; (with George Irving Dale) *Spanish Grammar,* Ronald, 1943; (translator with Max Harold Fisch) *The Autobiography of G.B. Vico,* Cornell University Press, 1944; *Parco Grifeo* (poems), privately printed, 1946; (editor and translator) Machiavelli, *The Prince,* Appleton, 1947; (editor and translator) Dante, *Inferno,* Appleton, 1948; (translator with Fisch) Vico, *The New Science of G.B. Vico,* Cornell University Press, 1948, revised translation with new introduction, Doubleday, 1961; (contributor) *Humanities for Our Times,* University of Kansas Press, 1949.

(Editor and translator) Dante, *Purgatory,* Appleton, 1953; (editor and translator) Dante, *Paradise,* Appleton, 1954; (author of introduction and various translations) *Lyric Poetry of the Italian Renaissance,* edited by Levi Robert Lind, Yale University Press, 1954; (editor) Shakespeare, *The Taming of the Shrew,* Yale University Press, 1954; (editor and translator) Dante, *Divine Comedy,* Appleton, 1955; (translator) Guillaume IX, *The Poems of William of Poitou,* [New Haven], 1955; (editor) Petrarch, *Rhymes: A Selection of Translations,* Oliver & Boyd, 1955; (editor) Raimbaut de Vaqueiras, *Liriche,* Sansoni (Florence), 1956; *Il Canto IX del "Paradiso,"* A. Signorelli (Rome), 1959.

Almanac for Academics, Yale University Press, 1960; *The Pressure Is Mine,* Printers to Timothy Dwight, 1960; (translator with Sergio Pacifici) Salvatore Quasimodo, *The Poet and the Politician,* Southern Illinois University Press, 1964; (translator) *Italian Sampler: An Anthology of Italian Verse,* M. Casalini (Montreal), 1964;

(editor) Bertran de Born, *Liriche,* [Varese], 1964; *Master Pieces from the Files of T.G.B.,* edited by Thomas K. Swing and A. Bartlett Giamatti, Timothy Dwight College Press, 1964; *Dante,* Orion Press, 1965 (published in England as *An Approach to Dante,* Bodley Head, 1965); (editor with Ernest Hatch Wilkins) *A Concordance to "The Divine Comedy" of Dante Alighieri,* Belknap Press, 1965; (editor) Petrarch, *Sonnets,* Heritage Press, 1966; (editor) Petrarch, *Selected Sonnets, Odes, and Letters,* Appleton, 1966; (editor) *From Time to Eternity: Essays on Dante's "Divine Comedy,"* Yale University Press, 1967; *Perspectives on "The Divine Comedy"* (essays), Rutgers University Press, 1967; *A Diversity of Dante,* Rutgers University Press, 1969; *Cervantes: His Life, His Times, His Works,* McGraw, 1969; *Dante: His Life, His Times, His Works.* McGraw, 1969; (translator) Ugo Foscolo, *On Sepulchres,* Bethany Press, 1971; *Invito alla Divina Commedia,* Adriatica editrice, 1971.

Petrarch, Twayne, 1970; *Dante's "Divine Comedy,"* Prentice-Hall, 1971.

Also contributor to several anthologies, and to *Columbia Dictionary of Modern European Literature,* 1957, *Collier's Encyclopedia, Enciclopedia Bompiani;* contributor of articles to *Saturday Review, New York Times, New York Herald Tribune, Speculum, Yale Review, Virginia Quarterly Review,* and other scholarly journals. Former member of editorial board of Modern Language Association of America; member of editorial board, *Italian Quarterly;* consulting editor, *Books Abroad.*

WORK IN PROGRESS: Studies in old Provencal and Italian.

SIDELIGHTS: Bergin's studies of Dante have been praised not only for their scholarly workmanship, but also for their lucid, direct presentation. William John Roscelli praises Bergin's style of writing as "simple and direct, infused with warmth and admiration for the subject." Morris Bishop believes that Bergin avoids the esoteric quality which marks most scholarly literary critics. "Imagination stirs imagination; the reader is moved to join the great journey through the other world."

BIOGRAPHICAL/CRITICAL SOURCES: Book Week, February 14, 1965; *New York Times Book Review,* March 14, 1965; *Christian Science Monitor,* April 20, 1965; *Saturday Review,* May 8, 1965; *National Review,* July 13, 1965; *Yale Review,* October, 1965; *Virginia Quarterly Review,* autumn, 1965; *Times Literary Supplement,* December 2, 1965; *New York Review of Books,* February 17, 1966; *Library Journal,* April 15, 1967, May 15, 1969; *Choice,* June, 1966, March, 1968, December, 1969; *Newsweek,* December 15, 1969; *Atlantic,* February, 1970; *Books Abroad,* autumn, 1970.

*   *   *

BERMONT, Hubert Ingram   1924-

PERSONAL: Born May 2, 1924, in New York, N.Y.; son of George J. (a music teacher) and Naomi (Horowitz) Bermont; married Arynne Abeles (a radio public relations director), March 9, 1947 (divorced, 1967); married Shelly Langston (a child photographer), February, 1971; children: Sheldon. *Education:* New York University, B.A. *Politics:* Conservative. *Religion:* Jewish. *Home:* 2560 36th St. N.W., Washington, D.C. 20007. *Office:* 1317 F St. N.W., Washington, D.C. 20004.

CAREER: Brentano's (book stores), executive director of branch stores, 1957-67; heads own book industry consultation firm, 1967—. *Military service:* U.S. Army, 1942-46; received Purple Heart. *Member:* American Booksellers Association.

WRITINGS: Psychoanalysis Is a Great Big Help, Stein & Day, 1963; *Have You Read a Good Book Lately?,* Stein & Day, 1964; *Mine Son, the Sam-u-rai,* Pocket Books, 1965; (author of text) Shelley Langston, *The Child,* Simon & Schuster, 1965; (author of text) Shelley Langston, *All God's Children,* Stein & Day, 1968; (author of text) Shelley Langston, *The Mother,* Simon & Schuster, 1968; (with Robert M. Artz) *New Approaches to Financing Parks and Recreation,* Acropolis, 1970; (with David S. Thomas) *Getting Published: The Complete Guide for the Non-Fiction Writer,* Fleet Press, 1972.

WORK IN PROGRESS: Two humorous books for Stein & Day; *The Mile-High Mind,* the philosophy of Frank Lloyd Wright; and a first play.

*   *   *

BERMOSK, Loretta Sue   1918-

PERSONAL: Born July 17, 1918, in Johnstown, Pa.; daughter of Frank J. and Mary E. Bermosk. *Education:* St. Francis Hospital School of Nursing, Pittsburgh, Pa., R.N., 1939; New York University, B.S.N.Ed., 1949; University of Pittsburgh, M.Litt. in Psychiatric Nursing Education, 1952; University of California, "Research in Social Psychiatry" certificate, 1965. *Politics:* Democrat. *Religion:* Roman Catholic. *Home:* 1602 Mikahala Way, Honolulu, Hawaii 96816.

CAREER: University of Michigan, School of Nursing, Ann Arbor, 1952-59, began as instructor, became assistant professor; University of Arizona, College of Nursnig, Tucson, associate professor, 1959-63; University of Hawaii, Honolulu, School of Nursing, associate professor and chairman of graduate programs, 1965—. Consultant in mental health-psychiatric nursing to World Health Organization, 1970—. *Military service:* U.S. Army Nurse Corps, 1941-46; became captain. *Member:* National League for Nursing, American Nurses Association, Mental Health Association, International Transactional Analysis Association, Hawaii Mental Health Association.

WRITINGS: (With Mary Jane Mordan) *Interviewing in Nursing,* Macmillan, 1964.

Contributor: *Concepts of the Behavioral Sciences in Basic Nursing Education,* National League for Nursing, 1958; *Suggested Core Curriculum for Pre-Service Education of Practical Nurses and Psychiatric Attendant Nurses,* Michigan League for Nursing, 1959; *Suggestions for Experimentation in the Education of Psychiatric Aides,* National League for Nursing, 1959; *Education and Supervision in Mental Health and Psychiatric Nursing,* National League for Nursing, 1963.

WORK IN PROGRESS: Critical Incidents in Nursing, with Raymond Corsini, to be published by Saunders.

*   *   *

BERNAL y GARCIA y PIMENTEL, Ignacio   1910-

PERSONAL: Born February 13, 1910, in Mexico City, Mexico; son of Rafael and Rafaela (Garcia Pimentel) Bernal; married Sofia Verea (an artist), October 14, 1944; children: Ignacio, Rafaela, Carlos, Concepcion. *Education:* Attended Escuela Libre de Derecho; Escuela Nacional de Antropologia, Mexico, M.A., 1946; Universidad Nacional Autonoma de Mexico, Ph.D., 1949. *Religion:* Catholic. *Home:* Tres Picos 65, Mexico 5, D.F. *Office:* Museo Nacional de Antropologia, Calzada de la Milla, Mexico 5, D.F.

CAREER: Mexican Government, cultural counselor of Mexican Embassy in Paris, France, and permanent delegate to UNESCO, 1955-56; Universidad Nacional Autonoma de Mexico, Mexico City, Mexico, professor of archaeology, 1948—; Instituto Nacional de Antropologia e Historia, Mexico City, director, Departamento de Monumentos Prehispanicos, 1956-58, subdirector general, 1958-68, director general, 1968-70, director, Proyecto Teotihuacan, 1962-64; Museo Nacional de Antropologia, Mexico City, director, 1962-68, 1970—. Visiting professor at Universities of Texas, Paris, Puerto Rico, California, Oregon, London, Arizona, and California, and Miami and Harvard Universities, and at Colegio de Mexico.

MEMBER: Academia Mexicana de la Historia, Society for American Archaeology (president, 1969-70), American Anthropological Association (fellow), American Academy of Arts and Sciences (foreign honorary fellow), Royal Anthropological Society of Great Britain and Ireland (fellow), El Colegio Nacional de Mexico, British Academy. *Awards, honors:* Order of Orange-Nassau (Netherlands); Legion of Honor (France): Order of Merit (Italy); Officer of the Belgian Crown (Belgium); Order of Merit (Germany; Royal Order of Danebrog (Denmark); National Science Award, Mexico; H.H.D., University of Americas; L.H.D., University of California, Berkeley; LL.D., St. Mary's University.

WRITINGS: Compendio de arte mesoamericano, Enciclopedia Mexicana de Arte, 1950; (with Alfonso Caso) *Urnas de Oaxaca,* Instituto Nacional de Antropologia e Historia (Mexico), 1952; *Introduccion a la arqueologia,* prologue by Alfonso Caso, Fondo de Cultura Economica (Mexico), 1952; *Mesoamerica: Periodo indigena,* Instituto Panamericano de Geografia e Historia, 1953; (with G. Reichel-Dolmatoff) *Mesoamerica y Colombia* (supplement to *Mesoamerica: Periodo indigena),* Instituto Panamericano de Geografia e Historia, 1953; (with Roman Pina Chan) *Official Guide to the Mayan Hall, Instituto Nacional de Antropologia e Historia,* translated by Pablo Martinez del Rio, Instituto Nacional de Antropologia e Historia, 1957; *Guia de Oaxaca, Monte Alban y Mitla,* Instituto Nacional de Antropologia e Historia, 1957, translation by Pablo Martinez del Rio Published as *Monte Alban [y] Mitla: Official Guide,* 1958; *Exploraciones en Cuilapan de Guerrero, 1902-1954,* Departamento de Monumentos Prehispanicos, Instituto Nacional de Antropologia e Historia, 1958; (with Jacques Soustelle) *Pinturas mexicanas precolombinas,* UNESCO, 1958, English translation published as *Mexico: Pre-hispanic Paintings,* New York Graphic Society, 1958; *Tenochtitlan en una isla,* Instituto Nacional de Antropologia e Historia, 1959, transslation by Willis Barnstone published as *Mexico Before Cortez: Art, History, Legend,* Doubleday, 1963; (with Leslie A. White) *Correspondencia de Adolfo F. Bandelier* (includes "La Interpretacion Morgan-Bandelier de la sociedad azteca," by White, and "Correspondencia Bandelier-Garcia Icazbalceta," edited, with a prologue and notes, by Bernal), Instituto Nacional de Antropologia e Historia, 1960; (with Bernard Villaret) *Arts anciens du Mexique: Architecture et sculpture,* Le Temps (Paris), 1962; *Bibliografia de arqueologia y etnografia: Mesoamerica y Norte de Mexico, 1514-1960,* Instituto Nacional de Antropologia e Historia, 1962; (author of introduction) *Mexican Wall Paintings of the Maya and Aztec Periods,* New American Library, 1963; *Teotihuacan: Descubrimientos, reconstrucciones,* Instituto Nacional de Antropologia e Historia, 1963; *Mexican Art,* [Tokyo], 1964; *Alte Kunst Mexikes,* Mexican Embassy (Cologne), 1966; *Museo Nacional de Antropologia de Mexico: Arqueologia,* Aguilar (Mexico), 1967, 2nd edition, 1969; (with Alfonso Caso and Jorge R. Acosta) *La Ceramica de Monte Alban,* Instituto Nacional de Antropologia e Historia, 1967; *La Presencia olmeca en Oaxaca* (pamphlet), Museo Nacional de Antropologia e Historia, 1967; *El Mundo olmeca,* Editorial Porrua (Mexico), 1968, translation by Doris Heyden and Fernando Horcasitas published as *The Olmec World,* University of California Press, 1969; (author of introduction) Pedro Ramirez Vazquez and others, *El Museo Nacional de Antropologia: Arte, arquitectura, arqueologia, etnografia,* Editorial Tlaloc (Mexico), 1968, translation by Mary

Jean Labadie and Aza Zatz published as *The National Museum of Anthropology, Mexico: Art, Architecture, Archaeology, Ethnography,* Abrams, 1968; (with Roman Pina Chan and Fernando Camara Barbachano) *Mexico: 3000 Years of Art and Life, As Seen in the National Museum of Anthropology, Mexico City,* photographs by Irmgard Groth, translated by Carolyn B. Czitrom, Abrams, 1968 (published in England as *The Mexican National Museum of Anthropology,* Thames & Hudson, 1968); *Ancient Mexico in Colour,* photographs by Irmgard Groth, McGraw, 1968; *Yugos de la coleccion del Museo Nacional de Antropologia,* Corpus Antiquitatum Americanensium, 1970; *Cien obras maestras del Museo Nacional de Antropologia,* J. Bolea (Mexico), 1969, bilingual edition published as *One Hundred Masterpieces of the Mexican National Museum of Anthropology,* 1970; (with Pedro Ramirez Vazquez and Otto Schoendube) *Coleccion arqueologica mexicana de Licio Lagos,* Ediciones Lito Offset Fersa (Mexico), 1970, 2nd edition, 1971; (with Paul Gendrop) *Arte precolombina dell'America Centrale,* Sansoni (Rome), 1971. Editor, *Tlalocan* (journal of Mexican source material).

Contributor: *Esplendor del Mexico antiguo,* 1959; Jesse D. Jennings and Edward Norbeck, editors, *Prehistoric Man in the New World,* University of Chicago Press, 1964; John Paddock, editor, *Ancient Oaxaca: Discoveries in Mexican Archaeology and History,* Stanford University Press, 1966; Arnold Toynbee, editor, *Cities of Destiny,* McGraw, 1967; Daniel P. Biebuyck, editor, *Tradition and Creativity in Tribal Art,* University of California Press, 1969. Contributor to *Handbook of Middle American Indians,* published by University of Texas Press, to proceedings of congresses and conferences, and to periodicals, including *Revista Mexicana de Estudios Antropologicos, Cuadernos Americanos, Estudios de Cultura Nahuatl,* and *Archaeology.*

WORK IN PROGRESS: Two books, *The Ballplayers at Dainzu* and *El Palacio de los Seis Patios en Yagul.*

* * *

BERWICK, Jean Shepherd 1929-

PERSONAL: Born September 3, 1929; daughter of Otis Floyd (a bank vice-president) and Dorothy (Steelman) Shepherd; married Keith B. Berwick (an assistant professor of American history), May 3, 1952; married second husband, Donald Meyer; children: (first marriage) Rebecca, Sarah, Jeffery, Rachel. *Education:* Syracuse University, B.F.A., 1951; Art Institute of Chicago, graduate study, 1955-56. *Politics:* Democrat. *Religion:* Presbyterian. *Home:* Norwich Rd., East Haddam, Conn. 06423.

CAREER: Free-lance illustrator of children's books and textbooks.

WRITINGS: (Self-illustrated) *Arthur and the Golden Guinea,* Golden Gate, 1963.

WORK IN PROGRESS: Children's books with historical settings and background.

SIDELIGHTS: Mrs. Berwick gathered material for her book, and others underway, in Williamsburg (Va.) sources during a year's residence there.

* * *

BETHELL, Jean (Frankenberry) 1922-

PERSONAL: Surname is pronounced *Beth*-ell; born February 12, 1922, in Sharon, Pa.; daughter of Thomas Howard (an electrical engineer) and Helen (a teacher; maiden name, Rogers) Frankenberry; married Frederick L. Bethell (a construction superintendent), August 19, 1955. *Education:* Purdue University, B.S., 1943. *Home:* Massapequa, Long Island, N.Y. 11758.

CAREER: National Broadcasting Co., New York, N.Y., writer for "Dave Garroway Show," 1950-52; Batten, Barton, Durstine and Osborn (advertising firm), New York, N.Y., copywriter, 1953; Benton & Bowles (advertising firm), New York, N.Y., copywriter, 1954-55; Wieboldt Stores, Inc., Chicago, Ill., advertising copy chief, 1956; Edward H. Weiss Advertising, Chicago, Ill., copywriter, 1957. *Member:* Pi Beta Phi.

WRITINGS: Herman and Katnip, Wonder Books, 1961; *Baby Huey,* Wonder Books, 1961; *The Monkey in the Rocket,* Grosset, 1962; *Barney Beagle,* Wonder Books, 1962; *Barney Beagle Plays Baseball,* Grosset, 1963; *The Clumsy Cowboy,* Wonder Books, 1963; *Ollie Bakes a Cake,* Wonder Books, 1964; *A Trick on Deputy Dawg,* Wonder Books, 1964; *How and Why Book of Famous Scientists,* Grosset, 1964; *Muskie and His Friends,* Wonder Books, 1964; *The Tale of Two Ducklings,* Wonder Books, 1964; *Luno the Soaring Stallion,* Wonder Books, 1964; *When I Grow Up,* Wonder Books, 1964; *Barbie Goes to a Party,* Grosset, 1964; *Barbie the Baby-Sitter,* Wonder Books, 1964; *Barbie Adventures to Read Aloud,* Wonder Books, 1964; *Barney Beagle and the Cat,* Grosset, 1965; *Hooray for Henry,* Grosset, 1965; *Petey, the Peanut Man,* Grosset, 1965; *When I Grow Up,* Grosset, 1965; *How to Care for Your Dog,* Four Winds, 1967; *Barney Beagle Goes Camping,* Grosset, 1970.

BIOGRAPHICAL/CRITICAL SOURCES: New York Times Book Review, May 9, 1965, November 5, 1967.

*   *   *

BETJEMAN, John   1906-
(Epsilon, Richard J. Farren)

PERSONAL: Born 1906, in London, England; son of Ernest E. Betjamin (a merchant and manufacturer); married Penelope Valentine Hester Chetwode, 1933; children: Paul, Candida. *Education:* Attended Marlborough, and Magdalen College, Oxford. *Religion:* Church of England. *Home:* The Mead, Wantage, Berkshire, England.

CAREER: After leaving school taught cricket and English at a London school; worked as an insurance broker; was member of staff of *Architectural Review;* was film critic for London *Evening Standard;* United Kingdom press attache, Dublin, Ireland, 1941-42; held a post with the British Admiralty, London, 1944; served with British Council, 1944-46. In October, 1972, Queen Elizabeth II appointed him Poet Laureate of England succeeding C. Day Lewis. Member of Royal Fine Arts Commission; governor of Pusey House. *Member:* Royal Society of Literature (fellow, companion of literature, 1968), Royal Institute of British Architects (honorary associate), Athenaeum, Beefsteak Club, Kildare Street Club (Dublin). *Awards, honors:* Heinemann Award, 1948, for *Selected Poems;* Foyle Poetry Prize, 1955, for *A Few Late Chrysanthemums,* and 1959, for *Collected Poems;* Russell Loins Memorial Fund award, 1956; Duff Cooper Prize, for *Collected Poems;* Queen's gold medal for poetry, 1960, for *Collected Poems;* Commander, Order of the British Empire, 1960, Knight of the British Empire, 1969; D.Litt., University of Reading, University of Birmingham; LL.D., Aberdeen University.

WRITINGS: Mount Zion, or, in Touch with the Infinite, James Press, 1931; *Ghastly Good Taste, or, A Depressing Story of the Rise and Fall of English Architecture,* Chapman & Hall, 1933, St. Martins, 1972; (editor) *Shell Guide to Cornwall,* Architectural Press, 1934, later published as *Cornwall Illustrated,* Architectural Press, 1935, revised edition published as *Cornwall,* Faber, 1965; (editor) *Devon Shell Guide,* Architectural Press, 1936, revised edition, Faber, 1955; *Continual Dew: A Little Book of Bourgeois Verse,* J. Murray, 1937; *An Oxford University Chest,* illustrated by L. Moholy-Nagy and others, J.

Miles, 1938; (under pseudonym Epsilon) *Sir John Piers* (poems; pamphlet), Westmeath Examiner (Mullingar, Ireland), c.1938; *Antiquarian Prejudice,* Hogarth, 1939.

Old Lights for New Chancels: Verses Topographical and Amatory, J. Murray, 1940; (author of introduction) Henry J. Newbolt, *Selected Poems,* Nelson, 1940; *Vintage London,* Collins, 1942; *English Cities and Small Towns,* Collins, 1943; *John Piper,* Penguin, 1944; (compiler with Geoffrey Taylor) *English, Scottish, and Welsh Landscape, 1700-c.1860,* Muller, 1944; *New Bats in Old Belfries* (poems), J. Murray, 1945; *Slick But Not Streamlined* (poems and short pieces), selected with an introduction by W.H. Auden, Doubleday, 1947; (editor) *Watergate Children's Classics,* Watergate Classics (London), 1947; *Selected Poems,* compiled with an introduction by John Sparrow, J. Murray, 1948; (editor, with Piper) *Murray's Berkshire Guide,* J. Murray, 1949.

St. Katherine's Church, Chiselhampton, Oxfordshire: Verses Turned in Aid of a Public Subscription Towards the Restoration of the Church of St. Katherine, Chiselhampton, c.1950; (contributor) *Studies in the History of Swindon,* [Swindon], 1950; (with Piper) *Shropshire,* Faber, 1951; *The English Scene* (contains reading list by L. Russell Muirhead), Cambridge University Press for the National Book League, 1951; *First and Last Loves,* J. Murray, 1952, Soccer, 1962; (contributor) *Gala Day London,* Harvill, 1953; *A Few Late Chrysanthemums* (poems), J. Murray, 1954, Transatlantic, 1954; *Poems in the Porch,* S.P.C.K., 1956; *The English Town in the Last Hundred Years,* Cambridge University Press, 1956; (author of introduction) William Purcell, *Onward Christian Soldier,* Longmans, 1957; (editor) *An American's Guide to English Parish Churches, Including the Isle of Man,* McDowell, Obolensky, 1958 (published in England as *Collins Guide to English Parish Churches,* Collins, 1958, revised edition, 1959, subsequent revised editions published as *Collins Pocket Guide to English Parish Churches,* Collins, Volume I: *The North,* 1968, Volume II: *The South,* 1968; (compiler, with Taylor) *English Love Poems,* Faber, 1957; *Collected Poems,* compiled with an introduction by the Earl of Birkenhead, Houghton, 1959, 2nd edition, J. Murray, 1962, 3rd edition, 1970; (editor) *Altar and Pew: Church of England Verses,* Hulton, 1959; *Poems,* Hulton, 1959.

(Editor) Charles T. Turner, *A Hundred Sonnets,* Hart-Davis, 1960; *Poems,* Vista Books, 1960; (under pseudonym Richard M. Farren) *Ground Plan to Skyline,* Newman Neame, 1960; *Summoned by Bells* (autobiography in verse), Houghton, 1960; (author of introduction) Charles Tennyson Turner, *A Hundred Sonnets,* Hart-Davis, 1960, Dufour, 1961; *A Ring of Bells,* selected with an introduction by Irene Slade, J. Murray, 1962, Houghton, 1963; (editor) *Cornwall,* Faber, 1964; (with Basil Fulford Lowther Clarke) *English Churches,* London House & Markwell, 1964; (contributor) *Moments of Truth* (poetry; 292 copies), privately printed, [London], 1965; *High and Low* (poems), J. Murray, Houghton, 1967; *First and Last Loves,* J. Murray, 1969; (author of introduction and commentaries) *Victorian and Edwardian London from Old Photographs,* Studio, 1969.

(Contributor) Greater London Council, Historic Buildings Board, *Do You Care About Historic Buildings?,* [London], 1970; (contributor) *The Twelfth Man* (in honor of Prince Philip's 50th birthday), Cassell, 1971; *A Pictorial History of English Architecture,* Macmillan, 1972; *London's Historic Railway Stations,* Transatlantic, 1972; (with J.S. Gay) *Victorian and Edwardian Brighton from Old Photographs,* Batsford, 1972. Also editor with Geoffrey Taylor of *An Anthology of Landscape Verse.*

SIDELIGHTS: Betjeman has been called a "poet of nostalgia." Jocelyn Brooke writes: "... modern 'progress' is anathema to him, he loathes 'processed' food, plastics, vita-glass, the Welfare State and (one may infer) democracy, though fortunately for us is still able to laugh at them." His technique is not original, though his sensibility is highly so. He can be "lyrically funny." Again Miss Brooke notes: "Perhaps he can best be described as a writer who uses the medium of light verse for a serious purpose: not merely as a vehicle for satire or social commentary, but as a means of expressing a peculiar and specialized form of aesthetic emotion, in which nostalgia and humour are about equally blended."

"As his commentators generally observe," Ralph J. Mills points out, "John Betjeman is a phenomenon in contemporary English literature, a truly popular poet. The sudden fame won by his *Collected Poems* ... which sold about 100,000 copies, brought him a wide reputation and made him quickly into a public personality." Betjeman, although popular, is admired by such poets and critics as W.H. Auden, and Edmund Wilson. Mills says: "Certainly it is very rare in our day to see much accord between distinguished critics and poets on the one hand and the general public on the other; but the very complexity of Betjeman's personality and feelings beneath the skillful though apparently simple surface of his verse probably unites, in whatever different kinds of levels of appreciation, the otherwise remote members of his audience." Mills says that Betjeman is a "topographical poet," in the sense that his poems, which describe some action or event, take place in a particular location, which he describes in great detail. Mills says that "there is further wide attraction in the fact that his poetry is literal and descriptive rather than symbolic; social rather than private; nostalgic—though balanced by humor and occasional irony, as well as a pervasive lightness of touch; beautifully and precisely evocative of place, period, and the moods they generate. And the manner of his poetry is musically graceful and various in form." Although Betjeman has named Eliot, Aldous Huxley, and the Sitwells as influences on his poems, "the clearest and strongest line of descent in his writing, Mills states, "leads back to 18th and 19th century poets such as Cowper, Crabbe, Tennyson, Dowson, Hardy; the Irish poets Tom Moore and William Allingham; and a host of lesser figures."

Architect as well as poet, Betjeman has been aptly praised by W.H. Auden (in the introduction to *Slick But Not Streamlined*) as a topophil, whose poetry is concerned with actual places, to whom "a branch railroad is as valuable as a Roman wall, a neo-Tudor teashop as interesting as a Gothic cathedral." He adds: "Topophilia . . . cannot survive at velocities greater than that of a somewhat rusty bicycle. (Hence, Betjeman's obsession with that vehicle.)" Betjeman is passionately involved in projects to preserve buildings of architectural or historical interest. He told Willa Petschek that he is even more interested "in saving groups of buildings of towns that can be ruined by 'a single frightful store that looks like a drive-in movie. The only way to prevent more and more ugly buildings going up,' he has said, 'is to draw people's attention to what's good in all periods.' " Betjeman has made numerous appearances on television to promote preservation of his various causes, and has, as Miss Petschek says, "become a cherished national cult." He champions his causes in his poetry as well, as he writes lovingly of the places of his childhood, and buildings and monuments in danger of destruction. Miss Petschek says: "Betjeman's approach to architecture (which he values second only to poetry) enabled him to recognize the 'living force' of 19th-century buildings, especially the Victorian Gothic. Partly through his verse and topographical writings, his guidebooks, poetry readings and TV appearances, but also through his warmth and peculiar genius for imparting enthusiasm for everything from rood

screens to ladies' legs, he has made the public accept a rapid reversal in taste."

Mills writes: "The detailed recreation of the past in *Summoned by Bells*, as well as in briefer poems, is evidence of an almost Proustian memory in Betjeman, who confirms this by saying in the poem that 'Childhood is measured out by sounds and smells/And sights, before the dark of reason grows.' Indeed, his richest imaginative resources seem to lie in the lost worlds of his childhood and early youth, their emerging interests and passionate attachments; they are restored and transformed in his poems. But the same past, of course, harbors the origins of the poet's melancholy, guilt, sense of evil, fear of pain and death, and apparent need for a kind of overmastering love; his authentic religious convictions do not develop, however, until quite a bit later ... the elements in life which hold profound significance and value for him—except his mature Anglican faith—that is to say, his love for poetry and will to be a poet; his sensitive awareness of landscape; his passion for churches, railways, towns, and architecture: all those materials on which his writing thrives initially appealed to him in his youth." Betjeman says in *Summoned by Bells*: "For myself/I knew as soon as I could read and write/That I must be a poet." And so he has ordered his life. His father wanted him to join the family business, but Betjeman could not, he was a poet. This decision caused a strain in the family about which Betjeman has had some guilt ever since.

Collected Poems, which brought Betjeman into the limelight, was enthusiastically received by the critics, but not by all of them. T.J. Ross wrote: "Though his ear is as flawless as Tennyson's and his effects sometimes as remarkable, Betjeman creates a world which, unlike the Victorian's, is a miniature." Ross believes that when Betjeman involved the reader completely with his subject "the result is poor." Only when he keep the reader at a distance does he bring his work up to the level of "first-rate minor art." Thom Gunn calls Betjaman's treatment of the middle class "entirely superficial." A *Times Literary Supplement* reviewer wrote: "Whether or not all Mr. Betjeman's verse is poetry, all his poetry is verse, and in this it is a pleasant change from the shapeless and unarticulated matter. . . . offered us by so many of his contemporaries. For Mr. Betjeman is a born versifier, ingenious and endlessly original; his echoes of Tennyson and Crabb, Praed and Father Prout, are never mere *pastiche*; and he is always attentive to the sound of his words, the run of his lines, the shape of his stanzas." Louise Bogan had high praise for Betjeman. "Since the early thirties, [he] has been producing light verse in which very close to but not crossing the line of parody, he has revived a whole set of emotional attitudes that can only be called Victorian.... His verse forms, elaborately varied, reproduce an entire set of neglected Victorian techniques, which he manipulates with the utmost dexterity and taste. His diction and his observation are delightfully fresh and original. And it is a pleasure to let down our defenses and be swept along by his anapaestic lines, with their bouncing unstressed syllables, and to meet no imperfect or false rhymes in the process; to recognize sentiment so delicately shaded, so sincerely felt, that it becomes immediately acceptable even to our modern sensibilities, grown used to the harsh, the violent, and the horrifying. We often, however, come upon a poem that brings us up short, to experience a melancholy, an irony that is close to Hardy or pathos that is timeless. ... However light his means, his purpose is never trivial."

"John Betjeman has been described," Miss Petschek writes, "as looking like a highly intelligent muffin: a small, plump, rumpled man with luminous, soft eyes, a chubby face topped by wisps of white hair and imparting a distinct air of absent-mindedness. He has an eager manner, a kind of old-fashioned courtesy and a sudden, schoolboy laugh which crumples his face like a paper bag." Betjeman owns a waistcoat which once belonged to Henry James. He told Miss Petschek: "Of course, I only wear it for weddings and funerals." In 1957 Miss Petschek wrote: "[Betjeman's] doll's house study is a jumble of books: old copies of verse, typography and ecclesiology and files of correspondence. The walls are covered with red William Morris wallpaper and pictures by Rossetti, John Piper and Sargent. In the corner a 17th-century clock chimes brassily every quarter hour and the telephone rings continually."

Norman writes that "after a miserable and pestered home life [Betjeman] found Oxford 'too delightful'; he lounged about in a shantung tie and took lavender-perfumed baths, so much so that C.S. Lewis, his tutor, thought him 'a pretentious playboy.' . . . His great love was the revival of the Gothic style in Victorian architecture. Sometimes, driving a car, he would take both hands from the wheel and yell, 'Phew! Gothic.' " Peter Bull tells of an afternoon that he and his Teddy Bear, Theodore, were invited to lunch by Betjeman and Archibald Ormsby-Gore, his "Teddy Bear companion for nearly sixty years," of whom Betjeman spoke in *Summoned by Bells.* Bull discovered that Archibald "had Baptist leanings and disapproved strongly of drinking and smoking. This had led to a certain amount of disagreement with Mr. Betjeman, . . . But the two of them get along rather famously on the whole. . . . Baptist or Protestant, Mr. Ormsby-Gore has tremendous personality—not very surprisingly, I suppose,—and he has to keep up with his friend Mr. Betjeman, who is one of the most beloved and revered wits in Britain. . . . In the 1968 Summer Academy Exhibition in London an extraordinary picture by Jann Haworth showed [Betjeman] in triplicate as a Teddy Bear, his face at different angles surrounded by fur. The work was called "A Valentine to John Betjeman."

Betjeman confided to Norman that "All his life . . . he's felt ruin 'very close'; yet the occasional depressions in his poems must not be interpreted as a desperate man's thought. . . . Betjeman says: 'It's a tone of voice—good old English melancholy like Hardy, Hood and Tennyson—solid village gloom.' "

Donald Swann has set some of Betjeman's poems to music.

BIOGRAPHICAL/CRITICAL SOURCES: W.H. Auden's introduction to *Slick But Not Streamlined,* Doubleday, 1947; Gladys Stern, *And Did He Stop and Speak to You,* Regnery, 1958; *Times Literary Supplement,* December 12, 1958, November 10, 1966, May 21, 1970; *Time,* February 2, 1959, December 5, 1960, October 23, 1972, December 4, 1972; *New Yorker,* April 18, 1959, September 2, 1967, May 23, 1970; *Newsweek,* November 28, 1960; *Spectator,* December 2, 1960, April 18, 1970; *New Statesman,* December 3, 1960, January 6, 1961, October 3, 1969; *New York Herald Tribune Lively Arts,* December 4, 1960; *Christian Century,* February 22, 1961, June 5, 1963; *Commonweal,* March 3, 1961; Jocelyn Brooke, *Ronald Firbank and John Betjeman,* Longmans, Green, 1962; *Listener,* January 26, 1967; *London Magazine,* March, 1967; *Books and Bookmen,* May, 1967; *New York Review of Books,* May 18, 1967; *New York Times Magazine,* August 13, 1967; *Poetry Review,* summer, 1967; *New York Times Book Review,* September 24, 1967, December 7, 1969; *Book World,* September 15, 1968; *Descant,* spring, 1969; Peter Bull, *The Teddy Bear Book,* Random House, 1970; *Punch,* April 29, 1970.

BETOCCHI, Carlo 1899-

PERSONAL: Born January 23, 1899, in Turin, Italy; son of Alessandro (a railroad technician) and Ernesta (Ermini) Betocchi; married Emilia de Palma, November 27, 1913; children: Marcello, Silvia. *Education:* Istituto Tecnico Galileo Galilei di Firenze, licenziato (in surveying), 1915. *Religion:* Catholic. *Home:* Borgo Pinti, 61, Florence 50121, Italy.

CAREER: Worked for many years until 1952 as surveyor and engineer in construction, shipyards, and mines in northern Italy and in France. Served as professore di lettere Italiane at Conservatorio Musicale Liugi Cherubini, Florence, Italy. Adviser on poetry for Casa Editrice Vallecchi; servizi culturali, Radio-Televisione-Italiana. *Military service:* Italian Army, 1917-20; served at Caporetto and in Libya; became infantry lieutenant. *Member:* European Community of Writers, P.E.N., Sindacato degli Scrittori Italiani (consigliere), Accademia Cherubini di Firenze. *Awards, honors:* Premio Viareggio for poetry (also called Premio Versilia), 1955; Premio Citta di Firenze, Gold Medal Dante Alighieri for poetry, 1961; Premio Montefeltro for all his literary work, 1961; Premio Feltrinelli of the Accademia Nazionale dei Lincei, 1967, for poetry.

WRITINGS: Realta vince il sogno (poetry), Edizioni del Frontespizio (Florence), 1932, Vallecchi (Florence), 1943; *Altre poesie,* Vallecchi, 1939; *Notizie di prosa e poesia,* Vallecchi, 1947; (editor and compiler) *Festa d'amore: Le Piu belle poesie d'amore di tutti i tempi e di tutti i paesi* (poetry anthology), Vallecchi, 1952; *Un Ponte nella pianura* (poetry), Schwarz (Milan), 1953; (editor) *Festa d'amore: Le Piu belle lettere d'amore di tutti i tempi e di tutti i paesi* (prose anthology), Vallecchi, 1954; *Poesie, 1930-1954,* Vallecchi, 1955; (contributor) *L'Otto-Novecento,* Sansoni (Florence), 1957; *Cuore di primavera* (fiction), Rebellato (Padua), 1959; *Il Vetturale di Cosenza; ovvero, Viaggio meridionale* (poetry), Edizioni Salentina di Pajano (Lecce), 1959; *L'Estate di San Martino* (poetry), Mondadori (Milan), 1961, 2nd edition, 1962; (author of introduction, with Giovanni Carandente) Joaquin Vaquero Turcios, *Trenta tavole dalla "Divina commedia",* Ferrajolo (Rome), 1963; *Poems* (bilingual edition), translated by I.L. Salomon, Clarke & Way, 1964; *Sparsi pel monto,* Rebellato, 1965; *Vino di Ciociaria,* S. de Luca (Rome), 1965; (author of introduction) Gianni Vagnetti, *La Strozzina, Firenze,* Vallecchi, 1966; *Un Passo, un altro passo* (poetry), Mondadori, 1967; *L'Anno di Caporetto* (personal war narratives), Il Saggiatore (Milan), 1967; *Collodi, Pinocchio, Firenze,* Industria Tipografica Fiorentina, 1968; *Due poesie inedite di Carlo Betocchi,* Galleria Pananti (Florence), 1969; (author of introductory text) *Firenze di Treccani: 25 Opere di Ernesto Treccani,* L'Indiano (Florence), c.1971.

Co-founder in 1923, of *Calendario dei pensieri e delle pratiche solari;* co-founder, in 1929, and editor of *Il Frontespizio;* editor of *L'Approdo letterario,* numbers 14-15, 1961; editor for literary program, "L'Approdo," on Italian Radio (R.A.I.), 1958—. Work included in several poetry anthologies; contributor to various Italian periodicals; translator from the French.

WORK IN PROGRESS: Enlarged edition of *Poesie, 1930-1954,* for Mondadori, to be entitled *Prime e ultimissime.*

SIDELIGHTS: As a young man, Betocchi became interested in associating the practical attitudes of the technical field with the humanistic delights of belles-lettres. He believes that the inspiration for his poetry is profoundly Italian and Catholic. Sidney Alexander in the *New York Times Book Review* describes him as "a poet of distillations, of swift winged flights, with an almost feminine distrust and avoidance of the explicit." Betocchi told *CA* that in the field of poetry he admires above all the *spirito* of English poetry. He has traveled often in France.

BIOGRAPHICAL/CRITICAL SOURCES: Oreste Macri, *Esemplari del sentimento poetico contemporaneo,* Vallecchi, 1941; Carlo Bo, *Nuovi studi,* Vallecchi, 1946; Maria Serafina Mazza, *Not For Art's Sake: The Story of Il Frontespezio,* King's Crown Press, 1948; Piero Bargellini, *Il Novecento,* Vallecchi, 1950; Oreste Macri, *Caratteri e figure della poesia contemporanea,* Vallecchi, 1956; Giuseppe de Robertis, *Scrittori del Novecento,* Le Monnier, 1958; *New York Times Book Review,* April 12, 1964; Gianni Pozza, *La Poesia italiana del '900,* Einaudi, 1965; *La Religione di serra,* Vallecchi, 1967; *Prosa e narrativadei contemporanei,* Studium, 1967; *Books Abroad,* autumn, 1968; *Un Po' id poesia,* Vallecchi, 1968; Gianfranco Contini, *Letteratura dell 'Italia unita,* Sansoni, 1968; *Nuova Antologia,* March 19, 1969; *Il Castoro,* September, 1971.

* * *

BEUM, Robert (Lawrence) 1929-
(Robert Lawrence)

PERSONAL: Surname is pronounced *bee*-um; born August 20, 1929, in Mount Vernon, Ohio; son of Robert Francis and Florence (Draper) Beum; married Phyllis Ann Fisher, July 10, 1954; children: Valerie, Elaine, Paul. *Education:* Ohio State University, B.A., 1952, M.A., 1958; University of Nebraska, postgraduate study, 1958-62. *Politics:* Republican. *Religion:* Episcopalian. *Office:* Department of English, University of Prince Edward Island, Charlottetown, Prince Edward Island, Canada DO 665.

CAREER: University of Nebraska, Lincoln, instructor, 1959-62; Creighton University, Omaha, Neb., assistant professor of English, 1962-64; Nebraska Wesleyan University, Lincoln, assistant professor of English, 1964-67; University of Prince Edward Island, Charlottetown, member of English faculty, 1967-70; University of Lethbridge, Lethbridge, Alberta, member of English faculty, 1970-71; University of Prince Edward Island, member of English faculty, 1971—. *Member:* Renaissance English Text Society, Milton Society of America.

WRITINGS: (Under pseudonym Robert Lawrence) *The Ninth Hour* (poems), Exposition, 1948; *Orpheus and Other Poems,* Odyssey, 1959; (with Maxine Cassen and Felix Stefanile) *9 x 3,* Hearse Press, c.1962; *Poems and Epigrams,* Regnery, 1964; (with Karl Shapiro) *A Prosody Handbook,* Harper, 1965; (editor) *Edmund Spenser: Epithalamion,* C.E. Merrill, 1968; *The Poetic Art of William Butler Yeats,* Ungar, 1969; (compiler with J.W. Sire) *Papers on Literature: Models and Methods,* Holt, 1970. Poetry anthologized in *Lyric and Longer Poems,* edited by A.H. Humble, Macmillan (Canada), 1960. Poems recorded for national archives, Library of Congress, 1960. Contributor of poetry to *Atlantic,* articles and criticism to journals in United States, Canada, and Europe. Former assistant editor, *Golden Goose;* former associate editor, *Prairie Schooner.*

WORK IN PROGRESS: W.B. Yeats and Women.

BIOGRAPHICAL/CRITICAL SOURCES: Library Journal, July, 1969.

* * *

BEVERIDGE, Oscar Maltman 1913-

PERSONAL: Born May 7, 1913, in Houston, Tex.; son of Ewart A. and Minnette (Maltman) Beveridge; married Dorothy H. Magor (vice-president of Beveridge Organization, Inc.), June 8, 1940; children: Bonnie M. *Education:* Amherst College, B.A., 1934; New York Univer-

sity, M.B.A., 1940. Home: 4100 Marine Dr., Chicago, Ill. 60603. *Office:* Beveridge Organization, Inc., 39 South LaSalle St., Chicago, Ill. 60603.

CAREER: Economics Statistics, Inc., New York, N.Y., economist and statistician, 1934-38; Carl Byoir & Associates (public relations), New York, N.Y., successively research director, production manager, and account executive, 1938-48; Booz, Allen & Hamilton (management consultants), Chicago, Ill., director of public relations, 1948-54; Beveridge Organization, Inc. (public relations consultants), Chicago, Ill., president, 1955—. *New York Journal of Commerce,* industrial news editor, 1942. Chicago Heart Association, member of board of governors, 1958-64, and chairman of public relations committee. *Military service:* U.S. Naval Reserve, public information officer, World War II. *Member:* Public Relations Society of America, Chicago Press Club, Amherst Club of Chicago; Lake Shore Club and Mid-Day Club (both Chicago).

WRITINGS: Financial Public Relations: Tested Techniques for Communicating with Financial Publics, McGraw, 1963. Contributor of articles to several periodicals.

* * *

BEVLIN, Marjorie Elliott 1917-

PERSONAL: Born May 9, 1917, in The Dalles, Ore.; daughter of John Arthur (a highway engineer) and Bess (Cornelius) Elliott; married Ervin William Bevlin (now a college professor), January 8, 1948; children: Kathleen Anne, Jennifer Jane. *Education:* University of Washington, Seattle, student, 1936-37; University of Colorado, B.F.A., 1938; New York University, retailing fellow, M.S. (with honors), 1939. *Home:* 12 Cactus Dr., La Junta, Colo. *Office:* Otero Junior College, La Junta, Colo.

CAREER: Gibbs and Cox, Inc., New York, N.Y., engineering draftsman, 1942-43; Otero Junior College, La Junta, Colo., chairman of fine arts, 1956—. Painter, with work exhibited in New York and Europe and at three one-man shows. *Member:* National Association of Women Artists, Delta Phi Delta (chapter vice-president, 1937-38).

WRITINGS: Design through Discovery, Holt, 1963, 2nd edition, 1970; *Drawing: The Artistic Process,* Holt, 1972. Contributor to *Junior College Journal.*

AVOCATIONAL INTERESTS: Horseback riding, travel.

* * *

BEYER, Werner William 1911-

PERSONAL: Born March 22, 1911, in LaPorte, Ind.; son of F.E.W. (a bookseller) and Martha L. Beyer; married Ruth Katherine Bibos, November 19, 1954; children: Tanya Elena, Mary Deirdre. *Education:* Columbia University, A.B. (with special honors), 1934, M.A., 1936, Ph.D., 1945. *Politics:* Independent. *Religion:* Presbyterian *Home:* 6455 East 96th St., Indianapolis, Ind. 46250. *Office:* Butler University, Indianapolis, Ind. 46208.

CAREER: Englewood School for Boys, Englewood, N.J., teacher, 1936-41; Drew University, Madison, N.J., instructor, 1943-45; Rutgers University, New Brunswick, N.J., assistant professor, 1945-48; Butler University, Indianapolis, Ind., associate professor, 1948-50, professor of English, 1950-66, Rebecca Clifton Reade Professor and head of department, 1967—. Visiting assistant professor, Columbia University, 1948; visiting professor, Indiana University, 1964-65. *Member:* Modern Language Association of America, College English Association, American Association of University Professors, Phi Kappa Phi.

WRITINGS: The Prestige of C.M. Wieland in England, Columbia University Library, 1936; *Keats and the*

Daemon King, Oxford University Press, 1947; *The Enchanted Forest,* Barnes & Noble, 1963; "Bibliography" for *The World in Literature,* 4 volumes, Scott, Foresman, 1967; (editor and author of introduction) *Oberon,* translated by William Sotheby, Scolar Press, in press. Contributor of articles to *Review of English Studies, Encounter, Notes and Queries, PMLA, Modern Philology,* and other journals.

WORK IN PROGRESS: An essay on a forgotten eighteenth-century "worthy"; editing a world literature anthology.

AVOCATIONAL INTERESTS: Music, art, travel, hiking, camping, swimming, canoeing, and golf.

* * *

BIDNEY, David   1908-

PERSONAL: Born September 25, 1908, in Russia; son of Samuel (a merchant) and Miriam (Guissman) Bidney; married Evelyn Breslin (a physician), August 20, 1940; children: Martin Paul, Rena Naomi. *Education:* University of Toronto, B.A. (honors), 1928, M.A., 1929; Yale University, Ph.D., 1932. *Office:* Department of Anthropology, Indiana University, Bloomington, Ind.

CAREER: Yale University, New Haven, Conn., Sterling Research Fellow in Philosophy, 1939-40, acting instructor, 1940-42; Wenner-Gren Foundation for Anthropological Research, New York, N.Y., research associate, 1942-50; Indiana University, 1950—, started as associate professor, now professor of anthropology and of philosophy of education. *Member:* American Philosophical Association, American Anthropological Association (fellow), American Folklore Society, Royal Anthropological Institute of Great Britain (fellow). *Awards, honors:* Guggenheim fellow, 1950; Ford International fellowship for research in Middle East, 1964.

WRITINGS: The Psychology and Ethics of Spinoza: A Study in the History and Logic of Ideas, Yale University Press, 1940, 2nd edition, Russell, 1962; *Theoretical Anthropology,* Columbia University Press, 1953, 2nd edition, Schocken, 1967; (editor) *The Concept of Freedom in Anthropology,* Humanities, 1963; (author of introduction) *Earlier Philosophical Writings: "The Cartesian Principles" and "Thoughts on Metaphysics" by Baruch Spinoza,* translation by Frank A. Hayes, Bobbs-Merrill, 1963; (contributor) G. Tagliacozzo and H.V. White, editors, *Giambattista Vico: An International Symposium,* Johns Hopkins Press, 1969.

WORK IN PROGRESS: Research in evolutionary and educational anthropology.

* * *

BIEN, Peter (Adolph)   1930-

PERSONAL: Surname is pronounced Bean; born May 28, 1930, in New York, N.Y.; son of Adolph F. (a pediatrician) and Harriet (Honigsberg) Bien; married Chrysanthi Yiannakou, July 17, 1955; children: Leander Thomas, Alexander Dimitrios, Daphne Madelaine. *Education:* Deerfield Academy, student, 1947-48; Harvard University, student, 1948-50; Haverford College, B.A., 1952; Columbia University, M.A., 1957, Ph.D., 1961; University of Bristol, postgraduate study, 1958-59. *Politics:* Democrat. *Religion:* Society of Friends (Quaker). *Home address:* Box 32, Riparius, N.Y. 12862. *Office:* Department of English, Dartmouth College, Hanover, N.H. 03755.

CAREER: Greek-American Cultural Institute, Salonika, Greece, teacher of English, 1955; American Language Center, Columbia University, New York, N.Y., teacher of English, 1957-61; Dartmouth College, Hanover, N.H., assistant professor of English, 1961—. *Member:* Modern Language Association of America, Modern Greek Studies Association.

WRITINGS: (Translator) Nikos Kazantzakis, *The Last Temptation of Christ,* Simon & Schuster, 1960; (translator) Kazantzakis, *St. Francis,* Simon & Schuster, 1962; *L.P. Hartley,* Pennsylvania State University Press, 1963; *Constantine Cavafy,* Columbia University Press, 1964; (translator) Kazantzakis, *Report to Greco,* Simon & Schuster, 1965; *Kazantzakis and the Linguistic Revolution in Greek Literature,* Princeton University Press, 1972; *Nikos Kazantzakis,* Columbia University Press, 1972; (editor with Edmund Keeley) *Modern Greek Writers,* Princeton University Press, 1972; (with John Rassias and wife, Chrysanthi Bien) *Demotic Greek,* University Press of New England, 1972.

AVOCATIONAL INTERESTS: Playing piano, house construction, and maintaining a farm.

* * *

BIENSTOCK, Myron Joseph   1922-
(Mike Bienstock)

PERSONAL: Born November 25, 1922, in New York, N.Y.; son of Samuel and Jennie (Brand) Bienstock; married Edith Regina Landau, May 28, 1950; children: Samuel Jonathan, Matthew Robert. *Education:* University of Miami, Coral Gables, Fla., A.B., 1948; New York University, graduate study. *Home:* 57 Upper Pitt St., Kirribilli, New South Wales 2061, Australia. *Office:* Hanimex Pty. Ltd., Old Pittwater Rd., Brookvale, N.S.W. 2100, Australia.

CAREER: Popular Electronics, New York, N.Y., associate editor, 1948-49; Yashica, Inc., Woodside, N.Y., advertising director, 1950—. Merchandising Services director, Han. Mex Pty. Ltd. Boy Scouts of America, communications examiner for Nassau County, 1952—.

WRITINGS: Radio and Television: How They Work, Rider, 1963. Contributor of articles to electronics and photographic publications.

SIDELIGHTS: Bienstock travels extensively in Japan and Europe. *Avocational interests:* Photography.

BIOGRAPHICAL/CRITICAL SOURCES: Long Island Press, November 24, 1963.

* * *

BIGGE, Morris L.   1908-

PERSONAL: Born December 20, 1908, in Stockton, Kan.; son of George William (a livestock dealer) and Luella (Slusser) Bigge; married Ada June Merriam, April 16, 1932; children: June Lee. *Education:* Washburn Municipal University, A.B., 1931; University of Michigan, M.S., 1938; University of Kansas, Ph.D., 1951. *Home:* 2235 East Brown Ave., Fresno, Calif. 93703. *Office:* Fresno State College, Fresno, Calif. 93710.

CAREER: High school teacher in Topeka, Kan., 1931-44; Washburn Municipal University, Topeka, Kan., assistant professor of education and psychology, and dean of students, 1946-50; Fresno State College, Fresno, Calif., 1950—, now professor of educational foundations. *Military service:* U.S. Army, 1944-46. *Member:* National Education Association, Philosophy of Education Society (fellow), American Psychological Education Association, Far Western Philosophy of Education Society (president, 1956-57), California Teachers Association, Kappa Delta Pi, Phi Delta Kappa, Pi Gamma Mu.

WRITINGS: (With Maurice P. Hunt) *Psychological Foundations of Education: An Introduction to Human Development and Learning,* Harper, 1962, 2nd edition, 1968; *Learning Theories for Teachers,* Harper, 1964, 2nd edition, 1971; *Positive Relativism: An Emergent Educational Philosophy,* Harper, 1971. Contributor to educational and educational psychology journals.

BILLIAS, George Athan 1919-

PERSONAL: Born June 26, 1919, in Lynn, Mass.; son of Athan O. and Grace (Papadakis) Billias; married Joyce Ann Baldwin, December 30, 1948; children: Stephen Woolman, Athan David, Nancy Susan. *Education:* Bates College, A.B. (magna cum laude), 1948; Columbia University, M.A., 1949, Ph.D., 1958. *Politics:* Democrat. *Home:* 50 Midland St., Worcester, Mass. 01602. *Office:* Department of History, Clark University, Worcester, Mass. 01610.

CAREER: University of Maine, Orono, associate professor of history, 1954-62; Clark University, Worcester, Mass., associate professor of history, 1962—. *Military service:* U.S. Army, Medical Corps, 1941-45; became first lieutenant; received Combat Medical Badge and Bronze Star. *Member:* Manuscript Society, American Historical Association, Organization of American Historians Phi Beta Kappa. *Awards, honors:* Guggenheim fellow, 1961-62; American Council of Learned Societies fellowship, 1968-69; National Endowment of the Humanities award, 1970-71.

WRITINGS: The Massachusetts Land Bankers of 1740, University of Maine, 1959; *General John Glover and His Marblehead Mariners*, Holt, 1960; (editor) *George Washington's Generals*, Morrow, 1964; (editor) *The American Revolution: How Revolutionary Was It?*, Holt, 1965, 2nd edition, 1972; (editor) *Law and Authority in Colonial America: Selected Essays*, Barre, 1965; (editor with Gerald N. Grob) *Interpretations of American History: Patterns and Perspectives*, two volumes, Free Press, 1967, 2nd edition, 1972; (editor) *George Washington's Opponents: British Generals and Admirals in the American Revolution*, Morrow, 1969; (editor) *The Federalists: Realists or Ideologues?*, Heath, 1970; (editor with Grob) *American History: Retrospect and Prospect*, Free Press, 1971; (editor with Thomas Balch) *The Examination of Joseph Galloway, Esq., by a Committee of the House of Commons*, Gregg, 1972; (editor with Charles K. Bolton) *Letters of Hugh, Earl of Percy, from Boston and New York, 1774-1776*, Gregg, 1972; (editor with Worthington C. Ford) *General Orders Issued by Major-General Israel Putnam*, Gregg, 1972; (editor with Victor H. Palsits) *Minutes of the Commissioners for Detecting and Defeating Conspiracies in the State of New York*, Gregg, 1972; (editor with William O. Raymond) *The Winslow Papers*, Gregg, 1972; (editor with Alden T. Vaughan) *Perspectives on Early American History: Essays in Honor of Richard B. Morris*, Harper, 1973.

WORK IN PROGRESS: Biography of Elbridge Gerry.

BIOGRAPHICAL/CRITICAL SOURCES: New York Times Book Review, April 6, 1969; *New England Quarterly*, December, 1969.

*   *   *

BIRD, Richard (Miller) 1938-

PERSONAL: Born August 22, 1938, in Fredericton, New Brunswick, Canada; son of Robert Bruce (a sales manager) and Annie (Miller) Bird; married Marcia Abbey, May 10, 1958; children: Paul, Marta, Abbey. *Education:* University of King's College, Halifax, Nova Scotia, Canada, B.A., 1958; Columbia University, M.A., 1959, Ph.D., 1961; London School of Economics and Political Science, University of London, postgraduate study, 1960-61.

CAREER: Harvard University, Cambridge, Mass., instructor in economics, 1961-63; lecturer, 1966-68; Columbia University, New York, N.Y., research associate in economics, 1963-64; Harvard University Development Advisory Service, adviser to government on fiscal policy, Bogota, Colombia, 1964-66; University of Toronto, Toronto, Ontario, associate professor, 1968-70, professor of economics, 1970—. *Member:* American Economic Association, Royal Economic Society, International Institute of Public Finance, Canadian Political Science Association, Canadian Tax Foundation. *Awards, honors:* Canada Council awards.

WRITINGS: (Editor with Oliver Oldman) Readings on Taxation in Developing Countries, Johns Hopkins Press, 1964, revised edition, 1967; *COMECON and Economic Integration in the Soviet Bloc* (originally published in *Quarterly Review of Economics and Business*, winter, 1964), Research Program in International Economic Integration, Columbia University, 1964; *The Possibility of Fiscal Harmonization in the Communist Bloc* (originally published in *Public Finance*, Number 3, 1964), Research Program in International Economic Integration, Columbia University, 1964; *The Need for Regional Policy in a Common Market* (originally published in *Scottish Journal of Political Economy*, Volume 12), Research Program in International Economic Integration, Columbia University, 1965; *Sales Tax and the Carter Report*, CCH Canadian, 1967; (co-author) *Financing Urban Development in Mexico City*, Harvard University Press, 1967; (compiler with Juan M. Teran) *Bibliography on Taxation in Developing Countries*, Harvard Law School, 1968; (with Oldman) *Tax Research and Tax Reform in Latin America: A Survey and Commentary*, Center for International Affairs, Harvard University, 1968; *Taxation and Development: Lessons from Colombian Experience*, Harvard University Press, 1970; *The Growth of Government Spending in Canada*, Canadian Tax Foundation, 1970. Also author of technical papers on taxation; contributor of articles to economics and business periodicals.

WORK IN PROGRESS: A book on earmarked taxes and benefit financing, for ECD.

*   *   *

BISCHOF, Ledford Julius 1914-

PERSONAL: Born July 20, 1914, in Chicago, Ill.; son of Richard Charles and Augusta (Krohn) Bischof; married Elizabeth Barbara Krell (now a teacher), December 25, 1941; children: Barbara Jane. *Education:* Northern Illinois University, B.Sc.Ed., 1941; Southern Illinois University, M.Sc.Ed., 1947; attended Syracuse University, 47-48; Indiana University, Ed.D., 1950. *Politics:* Independent. *Religion:* Protestant. *Home:* 593 Normal Rd., De Kalb, Ill. 60115. *Office:* Psychology Department, Northern Illinois University, De Kalb, Ill. 60115.

CAREER: American Steel and Wire Co., Chicago, Ill., sales correspondent, 1933-37; Southern Illinois University, Carbondale, assistant dean of men and Veterans' Administration vocational counselor, 1946-47, associate professor and counselor, 1950-54; Syracuse University, Syracuse, N.Y., psychological counselor, 1947-48; Northern Illinois University, De Kalb, professor of psychology, 1954—. Has private practice in psychology and serves as vocational consultant to the U.S. Department of Labor. *Military service:* U.S. Army, 1941-46; served as psychologist; became first lieutenant; vocational expert with Quartermaster Corps, 1944-46.

MEMBER: American Psychological Association, Midwestern Psychological Association, Illinois Psychological Association, International Council of Psychologists (fellow), American Personnel and Guidance Association, National Vocational Guidance Association (professional member), National Education Association, American Association of University Professors, Psi Chi, Cliffdwellers Club.

WRITINGS: Intelligence: Statistical Conceptions of Its Nature, Doubleday, 1954; *Interpreting Personality Theories*, Harper, 1964, 2nd edition, 1970; *Adult Psychology*,

Harper, 1969. Contributor of numerous articles to *American Psychologist* and other journals.

WORK IN PROGRESS: A book, *Child Psychology.*

SIDELIGHTS: Bischof lived a year in India and traveled extensively in Europe, studying with Anna Freud and Dr. C.J. Jung. He was invited to speak at the First International Congress of Psychodrama, Sorbonne, Paris, September, 1964. He also writes plays for local little theatre production.

* * *

BJERRE, Jens 1921-

PERSONAL: Surname pronounced to rhyme with *Pierre;* born March 16, 1921, in Maribo, Denmark; son of Markus (a managing director) and Ingeborg (Kjellerup) Bjerre; married Ketty Larsen, June 24, 1950; children: Lisbeth Elaine. *Education:* Attended high school and college in Skive, Denmark. *Home:* 10 Fennevangen, Gentofte, Denmark. *Agent:* Joan Daves, 145 East 49th St., New York, N.Y. 10017; (lectures) Martin A. Forrest, 80 Boylston St., Boston, Mass. 02116.

CAREER: Journalist in Denmark, 1937-45; *Aftenbladet,* Copenhagen, Denmark, political editor, 1945-46; correspondent in Paris and London, 1946-47; free-lance writer and film producer, 1948—. Lecturer at International Anthropological Congress, Moscow, 1964; public lecturer on regular tours in United States; conductor of expeditions to remote lands for museums and universities. *Member:* Writers Association of Denmark, Royal Geographical Society (London), Adventurers Club (Denmark). *Awards, honors:* Tenth International Film Festival award, Edinburgh, for documentary, "The Last Cannibals."

WRITINGS: Blandt menneskeaedere pa Ny Guinea, C. Andersen (Copenhagen), revised edition, 1967, translation of first edition by Estrid Bannister published as *The Last Cannibals* (Outdoor Book Club selection), Morrow, 1957; *Kalahari: Atomtidens Stenalder,* C. Andersen, 1958, transation by Estrid Banister published as *Kalahuri* (Outdoor Life Book Club selection), Hill & Wang, 1960; *Gensyn med stenalderen,* C. Andersen, 1963; *Savage New Guinea,* Hill & Wang, 1964. Contributor to *Life, Reader's Digest, True,* and to European magazines; contributor of articles on anthropology and ethnology to several scientific publications.

SIDELIGHTS: Books have been translated into twelve languages, with sales of Russian edition of *Kalahari* reaching a million copies.

* * *

BLACHFORD, George 1913-

PERSONAL: Born October 3, 1913, in England; son of Alfred and Elsie (Ades) Blachford; married Jean May Thompson, April 20, 1942; children: Richard Ades, Penelope Ann, Deborah Jean. *Education:* Loughborough College, diploma (first class honors). *Home:* 8 Hodgson Crescent, Leeds LS17 8PG, England. *Office:* Wyggeston School, University Rd., Leicester, England.

CAREER: Lockheed Hydraulic Brake Co., Leamington Spa, Warwickshire, England, head of Leicester training school, 1940-45; Army Correspondence College, London, England, senior tutor in handicrafts, 1945-54; Shropshire Education Committee, Shropshire, England, handicraft adviser, 1948-54; Nottingham Education Committee, Nottingham, England, handicrafts inspector, 1954-55; Wyggeston School, Leicester, England, handicrafts teacher, 1955—. Former examiner in handicrafts to University of London, Cambridge University, Northern and Southern Joint University Boards, and City and Guilds of London Institute. *Member:* Institution of Production Engineers (associate), Royal Aeronautical Association (associate), College of Handicraft, Toastmasters International (Leicester).

WRITINGS: (With Robert Hugh Grant) *Craftsmanship in Wood,* Warne, 1939; (with J.A.F. Divine) *Pottery Craft,* Warne, 1939; (with Divine) *Stained Glass Craft,* Warne, 1940; (with Grant) *A First Course in Practical Drawing,* four books, Warne, 1947; *Metalwork in Theory and Practice,* Christophers, 1958; *A History of Handicraft Teaching,* Christophers, 1961.

AVOCATIONAL INTERESTS: Camping, mountaineering, and heraldry.†

* * *

BLACK, E(dward) L(oring) 1915-

PERSONAL: Born May 3, 1915, in Sutton Coldfield, England; son of William (a park keeper) and Charlotte (Daniels) Black; married Edith Olivia Stradling Davies (now a secretary), December 28, 1938; children: Antony. *Education:* St. Catharine's College, Cambridge University, B.A., 1936, M.A., 1944; University of Manchester, M.Ed., 1953. *Politics:* Labour Party. *Religion:* Church of England, *Home:* 10 St. John's Park, Aldbrough, St. John, Yorkshire, England.

CAREER: Grammar school teacher, Leeds, England, 1936-46; Loughborough Teachers Training College, Loughborough, England, lecturer in English, 1946-50; University of Manchester, Manchester, England, lecturer in education, 1950-61; Mercer House (teachers' training college), Melbourne, Australia, vice-principal, 1962; Northicote School, Wolverhampton, England, senior English master, 1963; Poulton-le-Fylde Teachers' Training College, Lancashire, England, principal English lecturer, 1963-67; Middleton St. George College of Education, principal, 1967—. *Military service:* Royal Air Force, 1940-45; became flight lieutenant.

WRITINGS: (With Alec Henry Lawley) *Precis and Comprehension Practice,* University of London Press, 1953; (with Edward Rudolf Wood) *First Year English,* Blackie & Son, 1961; (with Wood) *Second Year English,* Blackie & Son, 1961; (with Wood) *Third Year English,* Blackie & Son, 1962; (with Wood) *Fourth Year English.,* Blackie & Son, 1962; *Manual of Instructions for Comprehension Test for Training College Students,* National Foundation for Educational Research, 1962; (with Wood) *Fifth Year English,* Blackie & Son, 1963, revised edition, 1969.

Editor: (With Alec Henry Lawley) *Sporting Scenes,* Metheun, 1956; (with John Pearce Parry) *Youth on the Prow: A Prose Anthology,* Allen & Unwin, 1956; (with Parry) *Aspects of the Short Story,* J. Murray, 1956; (with Parry) *Starting Work: A Prose Anthology,* Pitman, 1957; (with A.E.G. Roberts) *Animal Stories of Today,* Harrap, 1957; *Recent Short Stories,* Odhams, 1960; *Schooldays: A Prose Anthology,* Pitman, 1964; *Nine Modern Poets: An Anthology,* Macmillan, 1966; (and author of commentary) Cecil Scott Forester, *Death to the French,* Bodley Head, 1967; *Passport to Poetry,* Cassell, 1968; *1914-18 in Poetry,* University of London Press, 1971. Contributor to professional and academic journals in England.

WORK IN PROGRESS: A biography of Captain Bligh.

* * *

BLACK, Eugene (Charlton) 1927-

PERSONAL: Born December 15, 1927, in Boston, Mass.; son of Knox Charlton (a physicist) and Margaret Kirkley (Henely) Black; married Anne Galt Kirby, November 10, 1948; children: Alexander Charlton, Rebecca Galt, Andrew Gavin. *Education:* College of William and Mary, A.B., 1948; Harvard University,

A.M., 1954, Ph.D., 1958. *Politics:* Democrat. *Religion:* Episcopalian. *Home:* 22 Lathrop Rd., Wellesley, Mass. 02181. *Office:* Brandeis University, Waltham, Mass. 02154.

CAREER: Brandeis University, Waltham, Mass., instructor, 1958-60, assistant professor, 1960-63, associate dean of faculty, 1963-64, associate professor, 1963-68, professor of history, 1968—, Leff Professor of History, 1970—, chairman, Department of History, 1970—. *Military service:* U.S. Air Force, 1948-53; became captain, received battle star for Korean service. *Member:* American Historical Association, Academy of Political Science, Conference on British Studies, Economic History Society (United Kingdom), Historical Association (United Kingdom), American Association of University Professors, American Civil Liberties Union, National Association for the Advancement of Colored People, Downeaster Belgian Sheepdog Club, Belgian Sheepdog Club of America.

WRITINGS: The Association: British Extraparliamentary Political Organization, 1769-1793, Harvard University Press, 1963; (editor) *Posture of Europe, 1815-1940: Readings in European Intellectual History,* Dorsey, 1964; (editor) *European Political History, 1815-1870: Aspects of Liberalism,* Harper, 1967; (editor with Leonard Williams Levy) *British Politics in the Nineteenth Century,* Harper, 1969; (editor with Arthur J. Slavin) *Thomas Cromwell on Church and Commonwealth: Selected Letters,* Harper, 1969; (editor) *Victorian Culture and Society,* Harper, 1971. General editor with Levy of 50-volume "Documentary History of Western Civilization" series. Contributor to *Review of Politics, Journal of Modern History,* and *William and Mary Quarterly;* contributor of articles to professional journals and newspapers.

WORK IN PROGRESS: The Public Intervenes, a two- or three-volume study of evolution of British extraparliamentary political organization, 1793-1950; *Revolution and Modernization,* an analytical history of Europe from 1789 to the present, for Heath.

*   *   *

BLACK, Ian Stuart   1915-

PERSONAL: Born March 21, 1915, in London, England; son of Stuart and Hilda (Robertson) Black; married Winifred Williamson, February 2, 1931; children: Isobel Anne, Moray, Alison, Alan. *Education:* University of Manchester, B.A. (with honors). *Politics:* Liberal. *Religion:* Church of Scotland. *Home:* "Burwood," Rotherfield, Sussex, England.

CAREER: Rank Organisation, Pinewood Studios, London, England, script writer, 1946-49; Associated Television, London, England, story editor, 1958-64; Granada Television, London, England, story editor, 1964-65; writer for British and European films, 1965—. Company director of Isby Enterprises Ltd. and Telewriters Ltd. *Military service:* Royal Air Force, intelligence officer, 1941-46; became flying officer. *Member:* British Screenwriters Guild (honorary secretary, 1956-58).

WRITINGS: In the Wake of a Stranger, Dakers, 1953; *The Passionate City,* Viking, 1958; *The Yellow Flag,* Hutchinson, 1959; *Love in Four Countries,* Hutchinson, 1961; *The High Bright Sun* (novel), Hutchinson, 1962.

Plays: *We Must Kill Tony* (three-act comedy), Samuel French, 1952; "Shooting Party" (three-act comedy), first produced on theatrical tour in England, 1966, produced at Devonshire Park, Eastbourne, October 12, 1970. Author of several unpublished plays recently produced on television, including "The Trial of Mary, Queen of Scots," "Ransom for a Pretty Girl," "Wildcat," "The Dummy Run," and "Sunday Collection." Author of

screenplay of his novel, "The High Bright Sun," for Rank Organization, 1965; adaptor of Sir Walter Scott's "Red Gauntlet" for television production. Story editor of about 150 television films and author of about 80 television scripts. Occasional contributor to *Guardian.*

WORK IN PROGRESS: A novel; a television series.

AVOCATIONAL INTERESTS: Literature, criticism, travel, sport, art, and money.

*   *   *

BLACK, Joseph E.   1921-

PERSONAL: Born September 14, 1921, in Blanding, Utah; son of Henry G. and Louise (Brown) Black; married Gertrude Nelson (a teacher), September 9, 1950; children: Burton K., Jo Lynne, Carol, Sandra. *Education:* Utah State University, B.A., 1947; Northwestern University, M.A., 1948, Ph.D., 1950. *Home:* 3 Heathcote Rd., Scarsdale, N.Y. 10583. *Office:* 111 West 50th St., New York, N.Y. 10020.

CAREER: Lovell High School, Lovell, Wyo., teacher, 946-47; Miami University, Oxford, Ohio, assistant professor, 1950-54, associate professor, 1954-57, professor of political science and chairman of the department, 1957-63; University of Ibadan, Ibadan, Nigeria, professor of political science and dean of faculty of social sciences, 1963-65; Rockefeller Foundation, New York, N.Y., director of humanities and social science division, 1965—. Visiting professor of international relations, University of East Africa, Kampala, Uganda, 1963. Former consultant on African affairs, Rockefeller Foundation; member of board of directors, Cincinnati Council on World Affairs, 1951-54. *Military service:* U.S. Army Air Forces, World War II; received Presidential Citation. *Member:* American Political Science Association.

WRITINGS: The United Nations Charter: Problems of Review and Revision, University of Cincinnati Press, 1955; (editor with Kenneth W. Thompson) *Foreign Policies in a World of Change,* Harper, 1963.

WORK IN PROGRESS: A study of political change in Nigeria.†

*   *   *

BLACKER, Carmen Elizabeth   1924-

PERSONAL: Born July 13, 1924, in London, England; daughter of Carlos Paton (a psychiatrist) and Helen (Pilkington) Blacker. *Education:* School of Oriental and African Studies, University of London, B.A. (honors in Japanese), 1947, Ph.D., 1957; Somerville College, Oxford, B.A. (honors), 1948, M.A., 1949; postgraduate study at Radcliffe College, 1950-51, and Keio University, 1951-53. *Religion:* Buddhist. *Home:* 62 Grange Rd., Cambridge, England.

CAREER: Cambridge University, Cambridge, England, lecturer in Japanese, 1955—. *Member:* Folklore Society; Japan Society, Buddhist Society, Sherlock Holmes Society (all London).

WRITINGS: The Japanese Enlightenment: A Study of the Writings of Fukuzawa Yukichi, Cambridge University Press, 1964; (contributor) Donald H. Shively, editor, *Tradition and Modernization in Japanese Culture* Princeton University Press, 1971. Contributor of articles to *Asian Folklore Studies,* and other journals.

WORK IN PROGRESS: A study of cults in Japan with reference to Japanese Shamanism; a volume of Japanese short stories translated from eighteenth-century sources.†

*   *   *

BLACKING, John (Anthony Randoll)   1928-

PERSONAL: Born October 22, 1928, in Guilford, England; son of William (an architect) and Margaret

(Waymouth) Blacking; married Paula Gebers, October 30, 1932; children: Caroline (deceased), Jessica, Fiona (deceased), Laura Valentine. *Education:* Attended Sherborne School, 1942-47; King's College, Cambridge, B.A. (honors in social anthropology), 1953, M.A., 1957, Ph.D., 1965. *Politics:* Socialist. *Religion:* Church of England. *Home:* 18, Cleaver Park, Belfast BT9 5HX, Northern Ireland. *Agent:* Curtis Brown Ltd., 575 Madison Ave., New York, N.Y. 10022. *Office:* Department of Social Anthropology, Queen's University of Belfast, Belfast, Northern Ireland.

CAREER: International Library of African Music, Roodepoort, South Africa, musicologist, 1954-57; field work on anthropological scholarship in northern Transvaal, 1956-58; University of the Witwatersrand, Johannesburg, South Africa, lecturer in social anthropology and African administration, and honorary lecturer in music, 1959-65, professor of social anthropology and chairman of African Studies Programme, 1966-69; Queen's University of Belfast, Belfast, Northern Ireland, professor of social anthropology, 1970—. Visiting professor of anthropology, Western Michigan University, 1971; John Dang Professor, University of Washington, 1971. *Military service:* British Army, commissioned in Coldstream Guards, 1948-49; served in Malayan jungle. *Member:* Royal Anthropological Institute (fellow), Association of Social Anthropologists of the British Commonwealth. *Awards, honors:* D.Litt., Cambridge University, 1972.

WRITINGS: Black Background: The Childhood of a South African Girl, Abelard, 1964; (editor with Phillip V. Tobias) Antonio de Almeida, *Bushmen and Other Non-Bantu Peoples of Angola: Three Lectures,* Witwatersrand University Press, 1965; *Venda Children's Songs: A Study in Ethnomusicological Analysis,* Witwatersrand University Press, 1967; *Process and Product in Human Society,* Witwatersrand University Press, 1969; *How Musical Is Man?,* University of Washington Press, 1973. "Music from Petauke," Album I, a long-playing record issued by Ethnic Folkways Library, 1962, Album II, 1965, Album III, in press. Contributor to scientific journals.

WORK IN PROGRESS: Continuing ethnomusicological and anthropological research.

SIDELIGHTS: Blacking told *CA:* "I have no hobbies in the true sense of the word, as everything I do is related to my single interest in re-assessing the value of human institutions. [But] I enjoy . . . gardening, playing the piano, conducting a choir, and composing music." He speaks and writes French, Malay, and Venda and is learning Irish.

*   *   *

BLACKMORE, Peter   1909-

PERSONAL: Born March 19, 1909, in Clevedon, Somerset, England; son of Charles Henry and Elizabeth (Grattan) Blackmore. *Education:* Educated in English schools. *Home:* Green End, Sandon, Buntingford, Hertfordshire, England. *Agent:* Margery Vosper Ltd., 53A Shaftesbury Ave., London W.1, England.

CAREER: Became actor on leaving school at seventeen, training in repertory theatres in England, later playing in London productions; started writing in 1938, and after success of first play, *Lot's Wife,* decided to make writing a full-time profession. *Wartime service:* National Fire Service, London, England, throughout World War II; became senior company officer.

WRITINGS—Plays: Lot's Wife (three-act comedy; first produced on West End at Whitehall Theatre, June 10, 1938), Samuel French, 1939; "Not So Fast My Pretty!" (three-act comedy), first produced in London at the "Q" Theatre, 1945; *The Blue Goose* (three-act comedy; first produced on West End at London Gateway Theatre, December 24, 1950), Samuel French, 1941; *Miranda* (three-act comedy; first produced on West End at Embassy Theatre, June 10, 1947), Baker's Plays, 1948; *Down Came a Blackbird* (three-act comedy; first produced on West End at Savoy Theatre, October, 1954), H.W.F. Deane, 1954; *Mad About Men, a New Comedy About Miranda* (three-act; first produced on West End at Embassy Theatre, 1955), Baker's Plays, 1956; *Mock Orange* (three-act comedy; first produced in Worthing, England at Royal Theatre, 1959), Baker's Plays, 1960; "Tapetenwechsel" (three-act comedy), first produced in Berlin at Berliner Theatre, August 4, 1969; "The Morning After" (three-act comedy), first produced in Windsor at Royal Theatre, June 29, 1970.

Novels: *Pinch of Salt* (based on his play, Lot's Wife), Comyns, 1945; *Fickle Moment,* Putnam, 1948; *The Blue Goose* (adapted from his play), Ward, Lock, 1951.

Screenplays: (Adapter) "Miranda," Gainsborough, 1948; (adapter) "Mad About Men," Gainsborough, 1954; (author of original script) "Child's Play," Group Three, 1954; "All for Mary," United Artists, 1955; "Simon and Laura," United Artists, 1956; "Up in the World," Rank Organisation, 1956; (author of original script) "Just My Luck," Rank Organisation, 1957; "After the Ball," British Lion, 1957; (author of original script) "Make Mine a Million," British Lion, 1959; (author of dialogue) "Make Mine Mink," Continental, 1960; "Mrs. Gibbon's Boys," British Lion, 1962; (author of original script) "Time Gentlemen Please," Group Three.

SIDELIGHTS: Blackmore lives in a half-timbered Tudor farmhouse in a hamlet in Hertfordshire, and wanders far afield—generally traveling by freighter. He did research in Egypt before writing *Down Came a Blackbird,* and has visited the United States and traveled in Southeast Asia and the Far East. His favorite spot is Positano in southern Italy.

*   *   *

BLACKOFF, Edward M.   1934-

PERSONAL: Born July 1, 1934, in New York, N.Y.; son of Robert (a businessman) and Lily Ann (Reich) Blackoff; married Choy Lin Yau (an actress), October 24, 1961; children: Jeffrey, Lisa, Cara. *Education:* Attended Boston University, Florida Southern College, and Columbia University. *Politics:* Non-partisan. *Home:* 120 East 36th St., New York, N.Y. 10016.

CAREER: Blackmoor Agency (employment), New Rochelle, N.Y., and Huntington, N.Y., president, 1959—; Eurplace Associates, Inc., and Business Coordinating Holding Corp., London, England, and New Rochelle, N.Y., president, 1960—; The Roundabout (night club), New Rochelle, N.Y., president, 1963—; *Today's Model* (magazine), New York, N.Y., president, 1964—. A director of three employment agencies in United States and England. *Military service:* U.S. Army and U.S. Army Reserve, 1957-63; became sergeant.

WRITINGS: How to Solve Your Servant Problem: A Practical Guide to Finding, Hiring, Training, and (Alas!) Firing the Servant in Your Home, Stein & Day, 1963.

AVOCATIONAL INTERESTS: Stamp collecting and travel.

*   *   *

BLACKWELL, Leslie   1885-

PERSONAL: Born February 27, 1885, in Sydney, Australia. *Education:* University of Cape Town, B.A., LL.B. *Home:* 10 Cumbury Court, Kenilworth, Cape Town, South Africa.

CAREER: Union Parliament, South Africa, member, 1915-43; Supreme Court of South Africa, judge, 1943-55. *Military service:* World War I and II; awarded Military Cross, mentioned in dispatches; became major.

WRITINGS: Trading Under the Laws of the Union of South Africa, U.S. Government Printing Office, 1924; *African Occasions: Reminiscences of Thirty Years of Bar, Bench, and Politics in South Africa,* Hutchinson, 1938; *Farewell to Parliament: More Reminiscences of Bench, Bar, Parliament and Travel,* Shuter & Shooter (Pietermaritzburg), 1946; (with Henry John May) *This Is South Africa,* Shuter & Shooter, 1947; *Are Judges Human?,* Bailey Bros. & Swinfen, 1962; (with Brian Reginald Bamford) *Newspaper Law of South Africa,* Juta, 1963; *Murder, Mystery and the Law,* Howard Timmins, 1963; *Of Judges and Justice,* Howard Timmins, 1965; *Death Cell at Darlinghurst,* John Long, 1970; *Blackwell Remembers,* Howard Timmins, 1971. Extensive contributions to newspapers.

BIOGRAPHICAL/CRITICAL SOURCES: Books and Bookmen, June, 1970.†

* * *

BLAIR, (Robert) Dike 1919-

PERSONAL: Born April 9, 1919, in New Castle, Pa.; son of George Dike, Jr. and Hazel (Slingluff) Blair; married Reba Blizzard, June 5, 1943; children: Ann, Susan, Kate. *Education:* Williams College, B.A., 1940. *Office:* Vermont Book Shop, 38 Main St., Middlebury, Vt. 05753.

CAREER: Owner of Vermont Book Shops, Middlebury and Waitsfield, Vt., 1949—, of Vermont Books (publishing subsidiary), 1952—. Middlebury Inn, member of board of directors. *Military service:* U.S. Army, 1941-45.

WRITINGS: Books and Bedlam, Vermont Books, 1962.

* * *

BLAKE, Robert Norman William 1916-

PERSONAL: Born December 23, 1916, in Norfolk, England; son of William Joseph and Norah Lindley (Daynes) Blake; married Patricia Waters, August 22, 1953; children: Deborah, Letitia, Victoria. *Education:* Attended Norwich School, 1926-35; Magdalen College, Oxford, M.A. (first class honors), 1938. *Politics:* Conservative. *Religion:* Church of England. *Home:* Riverview House, Brundall, Norfolk, England. *Office:* Queen's College, Oxford, England.

CAREER: Christ Church, Oxford University, Oxford, England, student (fellow) in politics, 1947-68, university lecturer and senior proctor, 1959-60; Queen's College, Oxford University, provost, 1968—. Conservative member, Oxford City Council, 1957-64. *Military service:* British Army, Royal Artillery, 1940-46; became captain; taken prisoner of war but escaped from Italy, 1943; mentioned in dispatches. *Member:* Athenaeum Club, United Oxford and Cambridge Club, Brookes's Club. *Awards, honors:* Created life peer, 1971.

WRITINGS: (Editor) *The Private Papers of Douglas Haig,* Eyre & Spottiswoode, 1952, Verry, 1965; *The Unknown Prime Minister: The Life and Times of Andrew Bonar Law, 1858-1923,* Eyre & Spottiswoode, 1955, published in America as *Unrepentant Tory: The Life and Times of Andrew Bonar Law, 1858-1923, Prime Minister of the United Kingdom,* St. Martin's, 1956; *Esto Perpetua: The Norwich Union Life Insurance Society,* Norwich Union Life Insurance Society, 1958; (contributor) John Raymond, editor, *The Baldwin Age,* Eyre & Spottiswoode, 1960, Dufour, 1961; *Disraeli,* Eyre & Spottiswoode, 1966, St. Martin's, 1967; (with others) *Conservatism Today: Four Personal Points of View,* Conservative Political Centre, 1966; (contributor) Jeremy Murray-Brown, editor, *The Monarchy and Its Future,* Allen & Unwin, 1969; *The Conservative Party from Peel to Churchill,* Eyre & Spottiswoode, 1970, St. Martin's, 1971. Regular Contributor of book reviews to *Sunday Times;* occasional contributor to *Spectator;* regular article in *Illustrated London News,* 1964—.

WORK IN PROGRESS: History of Southern Rhodesia 1890-1965, completion expected in 1974.

SIDELIGHTS: Blake's biography of Disraeli has been highly praised by the critics for its objectivity, clarity, scholarship, and illuminating style of writing. John Clive lauds Blake for being both historian and political analyst. "Not only does Mr. Blake tell the story of Disraeli's life and political career on the basis of all the relevant primary sources . . . he [also] conceives his role to be that of judge as well as chronicler. When he comes to deal with the important junctures of Disraeli's personal and official biography, he does not rest content with merely relating the facts, but invariably supplies his own considered estimate of how these crises serve to illuminate his character and historical significance." Other critics appreciate the way in which Blake separates the myths from the facts of Disraeli's life. William Waldegrave writes: "Mr. Blake strips away much of the spurious mythology and shows us a Disraeli with no consistent 'vision of Empire,' no real concern with social reform or a Tory democracy . . . and whose great virtues of courage and intellect did not prevent much shadiness in his early life. But Mr. Blake, with consummate literary skill and painstaking scholarship, reveals a far more fascinating figure—Disraeli the man, not the myth."

Other critics believe that in *Disraeli,* Blake has written one of the more impressive works in that field. Gertrude Himmelfarb describes the book as "one of the great political biographies of our time. It is an impressive work of scholarship based on a wealth of archival material that is not only original but significantly original. . . . It is consistently thoughtful; the scholarship is never used as a substitute for mind or, as more often happens, as an occasion for self-exhibition. And it is—a still rarer quality in academia—consistently lucid, straightforward, candid, unpretentious." Barbara Gelpi concludes: "Blake's biography is . . . a model of the genre. The scholarship is impeccable, the recognition of previous work in the field courteous and detailed, and the breadth of knowledge about both domestic and foreign affairs awesome, while at the same time his style remains easy, frank, and charming. It is a book without 'cant,' either scholarly, social, or political; and one feels for that reason that Disraeli, as Blake presents him, would have liked it immensely."

BIOGRAPHICAL/CRITICAL SOURCES: New York Times Book Review, March 5, 1967; *National Review,* March 7, 1967; *Christian Science Monitor,* March 9, 1967; *Best Sellers,* March 15, 1967; *Book Week,* March 19, 1967; *Time,* March 24, 1967; *New Yorker,* April 1, 1967; *New York Review of Books,* April 6, 1967; *Commonweal,* April 14, 1967; *New Republic,* April 15, 1967; *Harper's,* May, 1967; *Virginia Quarterly Review,* summer, 1967; *Yale Review,* summer, 1967.

* * *

BLAKELEY, Thomas J(ohn) 1931-

PERSONAL: Born June 14, 1931, in Cleveland, Ohio; son of Thomas Jefferson and Elizabeth (Lecso) Blakeley; married Janet Stone, August 16, 1957; children: Mary Elizabeth, Damian Andrew, Timothy William. *Education:* Sacred Heart College, Detroit, Mich., B.A., 1953; University of Fribourg, Ph.D., 1960. *Religion:* Roman Catholic. *Home:* 16 Fairmount Way, Quincy, Mass. 02169. *Office:* Boston College, Chestnut Hill, Mass. 02167.

CAREER: University of Fribourg, Fribourg, Switzerland, chief research assistant and director of studies at Institute of East-European Studies, 1960-64; Boston College, Boston, Mass., associate professor, 1964-69, professor of philosophy, 1969—, now director of Russian philosophical studies program. *Military service:* U.S. Army, 1953-55. *Member:* Fribourg Philosophical Society (secretary, 1963-64).

WRITINGS: (Compiler, and editor with Joseph M. Bochenski) *Bibliographie der sovietischen Philosophie,* four volumes, Reidel, 1959-63; *Soviet Scholasticism,* Humanities, 1961; (editor with J.M. Bochenski) *Innocentius M. Bochenski, Studies in Soviet Thought,* Volume I, Humanities, 1961; *Soviet Theory of Knowledge,* Humanities, 1964; *Soviet Philosophy: A General Introduction to Contemporary Soviet Thought,* Humanities, 1964; (translator) Helmut Fleischer, *Short Handbook of Communist Ideology,* Reidel, 1965; (translator) Guy Planty-Bonjour, *The Categories of Dialectical Materialism: Contemporary Soviet Ontology,* Praeger, 1967; (translator) Peter P. Kirschenbaum, *Information and Reflections, on Some Problems of Cybernetics and How Contemporary Dialectical Materialism Copes with Them,* Humanities, 1970. Contributor of more than thirty articles and reviews to learned journals. *Studies in Soviet Thought,* managing editor, 1961-64, editor, 1969—.

WORK IN PROGRESS: *Soviet Scientific Atheism.*

*   *   *

BLAMIRES, Harry   1916-

PERSONAL: Born November 6, 1916, in England; son of Tom (a food merchant) and Clara (Size) Blamires; married Nancy Bowles, December 26, 1940; children: Gabriel, Alcuin, Cyprian, Benedict, Fabian. *Education:* University College, Oxford, M.A., 1939. *Religion:* Anglican. *Home:* 11 Worthy Lane, Winchester, Hampshire, England.

CAREER: King Alfred's College, Winchester, Hampshire, England, principal lecturer in English, 1948—.

WRITINGS: *Repair the Ruins: Reflections on Educational Matters from the Christian Point of View,* Bles, 1950; *English in Education,* Bles, 1951; *The Devil's Hunting-Grounds: A Fantasy,* Longmans, Green, 1954; *Cold War in Hell* (novel), Longmans, Green, 1955; *Blessing Unbounded: A Vision,* Longmans, Green, 1955; *The Faith and Modern Error: An Essay on the Christian Message in the Twentieth Century,* Macmillan (New York), 1956; *The Will and the Way: A Study of Divine Providence and Vocation,* Macmillan (New York), 1957; *The Kirkbride Conversations: Six Dialogues of the Christian Faith,* Morehouse, 1958; *Kirkbride and Company,* S.P.C.K., 1959; *The Offering of Man,* Church Literature Association, 1959, Morehouse, 1960.

The Christian Mind, Seabury, 1963; *The Tyranny of Time: A Defence of Dogmatism,* Morehouse, 1965 (published in England as *A Defence of Dogmatism,* S.P.C.K., 1965); *The Bloomsday Book: A Guide Through Joyce's "Ulysses,"* Barnes & Noble, 1966; *Word Unheard: A Guide Through Eliot's "Four Quartets,"* Methuen, 1969, Barnes & Noble, 1970; *Milton's Creation: A Guide Through "Paradise Lost,"* Methuen, 1971.

BIOGRAPHICAL/CRITICAL SOURCES: *Library Journal,* May 15, 1970.

*   *   *

BLANDFORD, Percy William   1912-

PERSONAL: Born October 26, 1912, in Bristol, England; son of John J. (a grocer) and Annie (Hunt) Blandford; married Ivy E. Harris, July 27, 1938; children: Peter. *Education:* Attended Temple Technical School, Bristol, England. *Home:* Quinton House, Newbold-on-Stour, Stratford-on-Avon, Warwickshire, England.

CAREER: John Lysaght, Bristol, England, engineering apprentice, 1928-35; Bristol Education Committee, Bristol, England, teacher of engineering subjects, 1935-37; Royal Air Force, technical writer, 1940-46; Middlesex Education Committee, Middlesex, England, teacher of engineering subjects, 1937-40, 1946-51; now boat designer and freelance writer. Member of Boy Scouts Association for forty years, now Sea Scout commissioner for Warwickshire and scoutmaster; also leader of annual national Scout canoe cruise, 1947—. *Member:* Institute of Journalists, Royal Institution ol Naval Architects (associate), College of Craft Education, Little Ship Club. *Awards, honors:* Bar to Silver Acorn, Boy Scouts Association.

WRITINGS: *Netmaking for Seamen,* Brown, Son & Ferguson, 1941, 3rd edition, 1961; *Handicraft in Scrap Materials,* Hutchinson, 1942; *Workshop Practice Simplified,* Pitman, 1943; (with H.C.B. Mackey) *1,000 Questions and Answers for Aero-Engine Mechanics,* Hutchinson, 1943; *Practical Aircraft Rigging,* Hutchinson, 1944; *1,000 Questions and Answers for Practical Engineers,* Hutchinson, 1944; *Canoeing To-day: A Fascinating Pastime Fully Explained,* Vawser & Wiles, 1946, 2nd edition, 1949; *Plastics in Handicraft,* Chapman & Hall, 1948; *Amateur Plastic Work,* Handicraft Supplies, 1948; *Rope Splicing,* Brown, Son & Ferguson, 1950; *Boat Building,* W. & G. Foyle, 1953; *Metal Turning,* Muller, 1953; *Wood Carving,* W. & G. Foyle, 1953; *Wood Turning,* W. & G. Foyle, 1953; *Model Boat Construction,* Muller, 1954; *Scouting on the Water,* Jenkins, 1955; *Home Power Tools,* Popular Handicrafts, 1956; (editor) Charles L. Spencer, *Knots, Splices and Fancy Work* (includes *Knots, Bends, and Splices* by J.N. Jutsum), 5th edition (Blandford was not associated with earlier editions), Brown, Son & Ferguson, 1956, Arc Books, 1965; *Scout Mapping,* Brown, Son & Ferguson, 1956, 2nd edition, 1960; *Working in Plastics,* Popular Handicrafts, 1956; *Canoeing,* W. & G. Foyle, 1957; *Tackle Canoeing This Way,* Stanley Paul, 1961, new edition, 1969; *Canoes and Canoeing,* Lutterworth, 1962, Norton, 1968; *Your Book of Knots,* Faber, 1962; *Building and Sailing Catamarans,* W. & G. Foyle, 1963; *Small Boats and Sailing,* Lutterworth, 1963; *Tackle Trailer Boating This Way,* Stanley Paul, 1963; *Camping,* Collins, 1964; *Holidays Afloat,* Lutterworth, 1964; *Projects on Water,* Boy Scouts Association, 1964; *The Art of Sailing,* Evans Brothers, 1965, St. Martins, 1972; *Working in Canvas,* Brown, Son & Ferguson, 1965; *Build Your Own Boat,* Stanley Paul, 1966, Sportshelf, 1967; *Canoeing Waters,* includes maps and diagrams by Blandford, Lutterworth, 1966; *Sailing Boat Recognition,* Ian Allen, 1970; *South Eastern England,* Constable, 1971. Contributor of about three thousand articles to magazines in England and the United States, including *Small Boat, Practical Boat Owner, Popular Camping, Waterkampioen,* and *Rudder.*

WORK IN PROGRESS: A series of five regional sailing guides for Constable; *Lightweight Boating,* to be published by W. & G. Foyle; *Sailing Dinghies of the World,* for Ian Allen; and *Practical Boatman,* for Stanley Paul.

SIDELIGHTS: Blandford has built about one hundred boats in thirty years. He illustrates his books and articles with his own black and white line drawings and photographs.

*   *   *

BLAU, Joseph L(eon)   1909-

PERSONAL: Surname rhymes with *now;* born May 6, 1909, in Brooklyn, N.Y., son of Joel (a rabbi) and Rachel (Woolf) Blau; married Eleanor Weslock, June 23, 1940; children: Rachel Maia (Mrs Robert St. Cyr DuPlessis), Judith Leona (Mrs. Richard S. Katz*). Educa-

tion: Columbia University, A.B., 1931, A.M., 1933, Ph.D., 1944. *Office:* Columbia University, 116th St. and Broadway, New York, N.Y. 10027.

CAREER: New York (N.Y.) secondary schools, teacher of English, 1932-46; Columbia University, New York, N.Y., lecturer, 1944-47, associate in philosophy, 1947-48, assistant professor of philosophy, 1948-57, associate professor of philosophy, 1957-63, professor of religion, 1963—, chairman, Department of Religion, 1966-68. Visiting professor of philosophy at University of Arkansas, 1950-51, California Institute of Technology, 1961-62, Vassar College, 1969, and Hunter College, 1970-71. Institute for Ethical Studies of New York Society for Ethical Culture, director, 1960-62. *Member:* American Council of Learned Societies (history of religion committee lecturer, 1964-65), American Association of University Professors, American Society for the Study of Religion (executive board, 1962-65), American Philosophic Association, American Studies Association (founder of New York branch; council, 1960-62), American Academy for Jewish Research, American Jewish Historical Society, Conference on Jewish Social Studies (executive secretary, 1946-47; director, 1963—), Society for the Scientific Study of Religion, Association for Jewish studies.

WRITINGS: The Christian Interpretation of the Cabala in 'the Renaissance, Columbia University Press, 1944; *Men and Movements in American Philosophy,* Prentice-Hall, 1952; *The Story of Jewish Philosophy,* Random House, 1962; (with Nathan Glazer and others) *The Characteristics of American Jews,* Jewish Education Committee Press, 1965; *Modern Varieties of Judaism,* Columbia University Press, 1966; *Reform Judaism: A Historical Perspective,* Ktav, 1972.

Editor: *American Philosophic Addresses, 1700-1900,* Columbia University Press, 1946; *Social Theories of Jacksonian Democracy: Representative Writings of the Period 1825-1850,* Hafner, 1947; *Cornerstones of Religious Freedom in America,* Beacon Press, 1949, revised and enlarged edition, Harper, 1964; (with Salo Wittmayer Baron) *Judaism: Post Biblical and Talmudic Period,* Liberal Arts Press, 1954; (with others) *Essays on Jewish Life and Thought,* Columbia University Press, 1959; Francis Wayland, *Elements of Moral Science,* Belknap Press, 1963; William James, *Pragmatism and Other Essays,* Washington Square, 1963: (with Baron) *The Jews of the United States, 1790-1840: A Documentary History,* three volumes, Columbia University Press, 1963; Kaufmann Kohler, *Jewish Theology,* Ktav, 1968.

Contributor of some fifty articles to scholarly journals. Editorial secretary of "Library of Religion," American Council of Learned Societies; chairman of editorial committee of Columbia University "Studies in the Humanities"; member of editorial board of *Review of Religion;* book editor of *Journal of Philosophy;* member of editorial board, *Jewish Social Studies.*

WORK IN PROGRESS: Research in the history of modern Judaism, history of American philosophy, and relation of science and religion in nineteenth-century United States.

* * *

BLAUW, Johannes 1912-

PERSONAL: Born July 10, 1912, in Hilversum, Netherlands; son of Pieter Wilhelmus and Elisabeth (Loef) Blauw; married Anthonia C. van de Walter, November 25, 1937; children: Elizabeth, Hendrik, Pieter Wilhelmus, Adriana Cornelia, Anthoma Clasina. *Education:* Free University, Amsterdam, Netherlands, Theologiae Doctor, 1950. *Home:* 8 Beyerincklaan 8, Hilversum, Netherlands.

CAREER: Reformed Churches, Netherlands, minister, 1937-47; Netherlands Missionary Council, secretary, 1947-62; Free University, Amsterdam, Netherlands, professor of religions, 1962—.

WRITINGS: Goden en mensen: Plaats en betekenis van de heidenen in de heilige schrift, J. Niemeijer, 1950; *Gezanten van de Hemel,* Bosche Heuning Baarn, 1954; *Op Sterke wieken: Wat het nederlandsch bijbelgenootschap is en wil zijn,* Boekencentrum, 1957; *De Andere wereld,* J.H. Kok, 1958; *De Weg der zencing,* J.H. Kok, 1960; *Het Geding om de wereld,* N.C.S.V., 1961; *Gottes Werk in dieser Welt: Grundzuege einer biblischen Theologie der Mission* (originally written in Dutch, but published in German), C. Kaiser, 1961, translation published as *The Missionary Nature of the Church: A Survey of the Biblical Theology of Mission,* McGraw, 1962; *Religie en inter-religie,* J.H. Kok, 1962.

* * *

BLAXLAND, W(illiam) Gregory 1918-

PERSONAL: Born December 7, 1918, in Norwich, Norfolk, England; son of A.J. (a surgeon) and Anna Marion (Andrews) Blaxland; married Elizabeth Finn, October 14, 1953; children: Henry, Lucy. *Education:* Attended Charterhouse School, 1932-37, Royal Military College at Sandhurst, 1938-39. *Religion:* Church of England. *Home:* Lower Heppington, Street End, Canterbury, Kent, England.

CAREER: British Army, regular officer, Infantry, 1939-55; retired as major after being disabled by poliomyelitis. *Member:* United Service Club, Mounted Infantry Club, Band of Brothers.

WRITINGS: Tom Glasse and the East Kent Hunt, privately printed, 1958; *The Home Counties Brigade: Its Members and Their Integration,* privately printed, 1960; *The Story of the Queen's Own Buffs, The Royal Kent Regiment,* privately printed, 1963; *J.H. Thomas: A Life for Unity,* Muller, 1964; *Objective Egypt,* Muller, 1966, reissued as *Egypt and Sinai: Eternal Battleground,* Funk, 1968; *The Farewell Years,* Queen's Own Buff Office, 1967; *Amiens, 1918,* Muller, 1968; *A Guide to the Queen's Regiment,* privately printed, 1970; *The Regiments Depart: A History of the British Army, 1945-70,* Kimber, 1971. Contributor of articles to *Sunday Express, Country Life, Field, Punch.* Editor, *Baily's Hunting Directory,* 1961-64.

* * *

BLEHL, Vincent Ferrer 1921-

PERSONAL: Surname rhymes with *male;* born July 31, 1921, in Brooklyn, N.Y.; son of Louis F. (a controller) and Mary (Allen) Blehl. *Education:* Woodstock College, AB., 1945, Ph.L., 1946, St.L., 1953; Fordham University, M.A., 1951; Harvard University, Ph.D., 1959. *Home and office:* Fordham University, New York, N.Y. 10458.

CAREER: Roman Catholic priest, member of Society of Jesus; University of Scranton, Scranton, Pa., instructor in English, 1946-48; Canisius College, Buffalo, N.Y., assistant professor of English, 1959-62; Fordham University, Bronx, N.Y., associate professor, 1962-67, professor of English, 1967—, co-director of Center of Newman Studies. Lecturer on Newman in United States and abroad. *Member:* Modern Language Association of America, Conference on Christianity and Literature. *Awards, honors:* Two research grants from American Philosophical Society.

WRITINGS—Editor: (With C. Stephen Dessain) *The Letters and Diaries of John Henry Newman,* Nelson, Volume 13, 1963, Volume 14, 1964; *The Essential Newman,* New American Library, 1963; (and author of introduction) *Realizations: Newman's Own Selection of His Parochial and Plain Sermons,* Darton, Longman & Todd, 1964; (with Francis X. Connolly) *Newman's Apologia:*

A Classic Reconsidered (symposium on the *Apologia,* Fordham University, 1963), Harcourt, 1964; *Cardinal Newman's Best Plain Sermons,* foreword by Muriel Spark, Herder & Herder, 1964. Editorial consultant, *Thought* (quarterly magazine, Fordham University).

Contributor of articles on Newman and on contemporary subjects to *Thought, Month* (London), *America, Dublin Review, Personalist, Comparative Literature Studies, Downside Review.*

WORK IN PROGRESS: A bibliography of editions of John Henry Newman's works; a book on Newman's Christian humanism.

SIDELIGHTS: Blehl spent three years in research at archives in London and Birmingham, England, and in Dublin and Rome. *Avocational interests:* Modern art, classical music.

* * *

BLISTEIN, Elmer M(ilton) 1920-

PERSONAL: Born September 17, 1920, in Pawtucket, R.I.; son of Philip and Lena (Melnick) Blistein; married Sophia Schaffer, November 27, 1946; children: Adam Dara, David Schaffer. *Education:* Brown University, A.B., 1942, A.M., 1947, Ph.D., 1953. *Politics:* Independent Democrat. *Religion:* Jewish. *Home:* 99 Alumni Ave., Providence, R.I. 02906. *Office:* English Department, Brown University, Providence, R.I. 02912.

CAREER: Brown University, Providence, R.I., 1942, 1946—, now professor of English. Pawtucket (R.I.) School Committee, member, 1954-58. *Military service:* U.S. Army, 1942-45. *Member:* Modern Language Association of America, American Arbitration Association, Renaissance Society of America, Malone Society, Phi Beta Kappa. *Awards, honors:* Franklin J. Meine Award, Sut Society, for *Comedy in Action.*

WRITINGS: (With E.A. Bloom and C.H. Philbrick) *The Order of Poetry,* Odyssey, 1961; (with Bloom and Philbrick) *The Variety of Poetry,* Odyssey, 1964; *Comedy in Action,* Duke University Press, 1964; (editor) *George Peel's "David and Bethsabe,"* Yale University Press, 1970; (editor) *The Drama of the Renaissance: Essays for Leicester Bradner,* Brown University Press, 1970.

WORK IN PROGRESS: A book on Shakespearean comedy; a book on the technique of dramatic analysis, for Odyssey.

* * *

BLITCH, Fleming Lee 1933-

PERSONAL: Born December 19, 1933, in St. Augustine, Fla.; son of Loonis and Jean (Fleming) Blitch. *Education:* University of Florida, B.A., 1955, M.A., 1959. *Home address:* P.O. Box 144, Oxford, Ohio. 45056. *Office:* Box 56, Upham Hall, Miami University, Oxford, Ohio 45056.

CAREER: Washington State University, Pullman, instructor in English, 1959-61; Miami University, Oxford, Ohio, instructor in English, 1962—. Part-time instructor in English, Western College for Women, Oxford, Ohio, 1962-63. *Awards, honors:* Children's Book Club fellowship to Bread Loaf Writers' Conference, 1963.

WRITINGS: The Amazing Adventures of Peter Grunt, Gentleman Pig of Yatapalachee County, Florida: His Thrilling Adventures, His Daring Ideas, His Narrow Escapes, Lippincott, 1963; *The Last Dragon,* Lippincott, 1964.

WORK IN PROGRESS: A sequel to *The Amazing Adventures of Peter Grunt;* an adult novel.†

BLOOD, Jerome W. 1926-

PERSONAL: Born February 1, 1926, in Syracuse, N.Y.; son of William H. and Bernadette (Plouffe) Blood; married Alice M. McGuirk August 19, 1961. *Education:* St. Bernard's Seminary and College, Rochester, N.Y., B.A., 1947; Fordham University, M.A., 1956; Columbia University, M.A., 1959. *Home:* 15 Half Moon Lane, Tarrytown, N.Y. 10591. *Office:* IBM, 590 Madison Ave., New York, N.Y. 10022.

CAREER: American Management Association, New York, N.Y., editor, 1959-67; Macmillan Co., New York, N.Y., editor, 1967-70; IBM, New York, N.Y., management education employee, 1970—.

WRITINGS—Editor; all published by American Management Association: *Optimum Use of Engineering Talent,* 1961, *The Management of Scientific Talent,* 1963, (with Elmo J. Miller) *Modern Maintenance Management,* 1963, *Investor Relations: The Company and Its Owners,* 1963, *The Personnel Job in a Changing World,* 1964, *Management Looks at Africa,* 1966, *Utilizing Research and Development By-Products,* 1967.

* * *

BLOOM, Alan (Herbert Vawser) 1906-

PERSONAL: Born November 19, 1906, in Over, Cambridgeshire, England; son of Charles Herbert and Katherine (Whitworth) Bloom; married second wife, Flora Elisabeth Mackintosh, October 30, 1956; children: (first marriage) Bridget, Robert, Adrian; (second marriage) Anthea, Jenny. *Education:* Attended schools in England. *Politics:* Liberal. *Religion:* Quaker. *Home:* Bressingham Hall, near Diss, Norfolk, England. *Office:* Blooms Nurseries Ltd., and Bressingham Steam Museum, both in Bressingham, Norfolk, England.

CAREER: Blooms Nurseries Ltd., Bressingham, Norfolk, England, managing director, 1936—. *Member:* Royal Horticultural Society, Royal Agricultural Society, Horticultural Trades Association, Society of Authors, County Landowners Association, various steam engine preservation societies.

WRITINGS: The Farm in the Fens, Faber, 1944; *The Fens,* R. Hale, 1953; *Hardy Perennials,* Faber, 1957; *The Skaters of the Fens,* Heffer, 1958; *Perennials for Trouble-Free Gardening,* Faber, 1959; *Alpines for Trouble-Free Gardening,* Faber, 1960, Branford, 1961; *The Bressingham Story,* Faber, 1963; *Hardy Plants of Distinction,* Collingridge, 1965; *Moisture Gardening: Hardy Perennials in Their Natural Environment,* Faber, 1966, Branford, 1967; *Alpine Plants of Distinction,* Collingridge, 1968; *Selected Garden Plants,* Jarrolds, 1968; *Selected Fen Plants in Colour,* Jarrolds, 1969; *Steam Engines at Bressingham: The Story of a Live Steam Museum,* Faber, 1970; *Hardy Garden Plants: Sachet Floral,* Faber, 1971; *Perennials for Your Garden,* Floraprint, 1971; *The Best Hardy Perennials,* Faber, 1972. Contributor of articles to gardening journals, *Reader's Digest Gardening Guides,* and railway magazines.

AVOCATIONAL INTERESTS: Collecting and restoring steam engines. Bloom told *CA:* "This hobby has now become the most comprehensive steam museum in the U.K., with over 30 road and rail locomotovies. . . . Some famous express locomotives are on permanent loan to the museum."

* * *

BLOOM, Samuel William 1921-

PERSONAL: Born September 18, 1921, in Reading, Pa.; son of Hyman (a businessman) and Esther (Knoblauch) Bloom; married Anne Rubinfeld (now a psychologist), January 11, 1948; children: Jonathan, Jessica. *Education:* University of Pennsylvania, A.B., 1943; New School for

Social Research, M.A., 1950; University of Wisconsin, Ph.D., 1956. *Politics:* Democrat. *Religion:* Jewish. *Home:* 170 East 83rd St., New York, N.Y. 10028. *Office:* Mt. Sinai School of Medicine, 19 East 98th St., New York, N.Y. 10029.

CAREER: Bennington College, Bennington, Vt., instructor in social science, 1951-53; Baylor University, College of Medicine, Houston, Tex., assistant professor of sociology, department of psychiatry, 1956-62; State University of New York, Downstate Medical Center, Brooklyn, 1962-68, began as associate professor of sociology in administration, became professor of sociology in psychiatry, research consultant, Psychiatric Treatment Research Center, 1963-68; City University of New York, Mt. Sinai School of Medicine, New York, N.Y., professor of sociology and community medicine, 1968—. Visiting professor of sociology at Bryn Mawr College, and lecturer in sociology and psychiatry at School of Medicine, University of Pennsylvania, 1961-62; visiting professor at Queens College, 1957, University of Houston, 1959. Consultant in sociology to Veterans Administration Hospital, Houston, Tex., 1959-63, to Texas Institute for Rehabilitation and Research, 1960-62. *Military service:* U.S. Army Air Forces, 1943-46; became staff sergeant.

MEMBER: American Sociological Association (fellow; secretary-treasurer of section on medical sociology, 1959-62, chairman-elect of section, 1962), American Association for the Advancement of Science, Association of American Medical Colleges, Alpha Kappa Delta.

WRITINGS: (Contributor) E. Gartly Jaco, editor, *Patients, Physicians and Illness,* Free Press of Glencoe, 1958; *The Doctor and His Patient: A Sociological Interpretation,* Russell Sage, 1963; (contributor) Harold Lief and others, editors, *The Psychological Basis of Medical Practice,* Harper, 1963; (contributor) H. Leideman and David Shapiro, editors, *Psychobiological Approaches to Social Behavior,* Stanford University Press, 1964; *The Medical School as a Social System,* Milbank Memorial Fund Quarterly, 1972. Contributor of articles and reviews to professional journals. Member of advisory board, *Bulletin on Sociology and the Practice of Medicine,* 1961-63; associate editor, *Journal of Health and Social Behavior,* 1966-68; associate editor, *Milbank Memorial Fund Quarterly,* 1969—.

WORK IN PROGRESS: The Sociology of Mental Disorder, to be published by McGraw.

*   *   *

BLOOMFIELD, B(arry) C(ambray) 1931-

PERSONAL: Born June 1, 1931, in London, England; son of Clifford Wilson (a dental technician) and Eileen (Cambray) Bloomfield; married Valerie Philpot (now a librarian), December 28, 1958. *Education:* University College, University of Exeter, B.A., 1952; University College, University of London, Diploma in Librarianship, 1955; Birkbeck College, University of London, M.A., 1961. *Office:* School of Oriental and African Studies, University of London, London WCIE 7HP, England.

CAREER: College of St. Mark and St. John, London, England, librarian, 1956-61; London School of Economics and Political Science, University of London, London, England, assistant librarian, 1961-63; School of Oriental and African Studies, University of London, deputy librarian, 1963—. *Military service:* British Army, 1952-54; became sergeant. *Member:* Library Association, Bibliographical Society, Cambridge Bibliographical Society, Virginia Bibliographical Society.

WRITINGS: English Poetry in the '30's: A Short Title List, Library, College of St. Mark and St. John, 1959; *New Verse in the '30's* (bibliography), Library Association, 1960; (editor) *The Autobiography of Sir James Kay Shuttleworth,* University of London Institute of Education Press, 1964; *W.H. Auden: A Bibliography: The Early Years Through 1955,* foreword by W.H. Auden, University Press of Virginia, 1964, 2nd edition (with Edward Mendelson), 1973; (with wife, Valerie J. Bloomfield, and J.D. Pearson) *Theses on Africa,* Heffer, 1964; (compiler with Malcolm D. McKee) *Africa in the Contemporary World,* National Book League, 1967; (compiler) *Theses on Asia,* Cass, 1967. Contributor to *British Journal of Educational Studies.*

WORK IN PROGRESS: Compiling an index to British little magazines in the '30's.

*   *   *

BLUM, Henrik L(eo) 1915-

PERSONAL: Born November 11, 1915, in San Francisco, Calif.; son of Haiman and Pauline Blum; married Marian Haas Ehrich, December 24, 1938. *Education:* University of California, Berkeley, B.S., 1937; University of California, San Francisco, M.D., 1942; postdoctoral study at Johns Hopkins University, 1945, and Stanford University, 1947; Harvard University, M.P.H., 1948. *Home:* 450 Muller Rd., Walnut Creek, Calif. 94598. *Office:* Department of City Planning, University of California, Berkeley, Calif. 94720.

CAREER: Stanford University, Stanford, Calif., associate in medicine, 1962—; University of California, Berkeley, clinical professor of public health, 1963—. Health officer, Contra Costa County, Calif., 1950—. National Institute of Mental Health, member of Committee on Social and Physical Environment Variables as Determinants of Mental Health and of Special Grants Review Committee; senior assistant surgeon, U.S. Public Health Service. *Member:* American Public Health Association (chairman of chronic disease and rehabilitation committee; member of technical development board), American Medical Association, American College of Preventive Medicine, California Medical Association, Northern California Public Health Association, Alameda-Contra Costa Medical Association. *Awards, honors:* Western States Tuberculosis award, 1961; World Health Organization fellowship grant, 1962, to study multipurpose workers in four countries.

WRITINGS: (With Henry B. Peters and Jerome W. Bettman) *Vision for Elementary Schools: The Orinda Study,* University of California Press, 1959; (with Alvin R. Leonard) *Public Administration—A Public Health Viewpoint,* Macmillan, 1963.

WORK IN PROGRESS: Multipurpose home visitor research project; a study of periodic health appraisals.†

*   *   *

BOALCH, Donald (Howard) 1914-

PERSONAL: Born October 25, 1914, in London, England; son of Herbert W. Boalch (a schoolmaster); married Helen Coppock, February, 1948; children: Julia Katharine, Stephen Gregory. *Education:* Attended St. Paul's School, London, England, 1927-33; Corpus Christi College, Cambridge, B.A., 1936, M.A., 1940. *Home:* 4 Hill Top Rd., Oxford, England. *Office:* Bodleian Library, Oxford, England.

CAREER: School of Oriental and African Studies, University of London, London, England, library assistant, 1941-47; British Museum, London, England, assistant keeper in department of oriental antiquities, 1947-48; Rothamsted Experimental Station (agricultural research), Harpenden, England, librarian, 1950-62; Bodleian Library, Oxford, England, keeper of scientific books, 1962—. *Member:* Society of Antiquaries (London), Galpin Society, Plainsong and Mediaeval Music Society.

WRITINGS: (Editor) *Two-Part Canzonets of Thomas Morley*, Ronald, 1950; *The Manor of Rothamsted* (history, 1212-1952), Rothamsted Experimental Station, 1953; (editor) *Fifty Years of Farming* (reminiscences of James Keith, 1879-1953), Faber, 1954; *Catalogue of Serial Publications in the Rothamsted Library* (entomology, insecticides, mycology), Rothamsted Experimental Station, 1956; *Makers of the Harpsichord and Clavichord, 1440-1840*, Macmillan, 1956, 2nd edition, Oxford University Press, 1972; (contributor) *Prints and Paintings of British Farm Livestock, 1780-1910* (includes a record of the Rothamsted Collection by Boalch), Rothamsted Experimental Station, 1958; *World Directory of Agricultural Libraries and Documentation Centres*, International Association of Agricultural Librarians and Documentalists, 1960; (editor) *Current Agricultural Serials: A World List of Serials in Agriculture and Related Subjects (Excluding Forestry and Fisheries) Current in 1964*, two volumes, Alden Press, 1965; (editor) *Union List of Serials in the Science Area, Stage 1*, Oxford University Bodleian Library, 1968.

* * *

BOARDMAN, Eunice 1926-

PERSONAL: Born January 27, 1926, in Rock Island County, Ill.; daughter of G. Hollister (a farmer) and Anna (Feaster) Boardman. *Education:* Cornell College, Mount Vernon, Iowa, B.M.E., 1947; Columbia University, M.M.E., 1951; University of Illinois, Ed.D., 1964. *Politics:* Democrat. *Religion:* Unitarian. *Home:* 3527 East 15th St., Wichita, Kan. 67208.

CAREER: Music specialist in public schools in Iowa, 1947-55; Northern Illinois University, De Kalb, instructor in music education, 1955-56; Wichita State University, Wichita, Kan., professor of music education, 1956—. Director, Southwestern Institute for Music in Contemporary Education, 1967-69. *Member:* Music Educators National Conference, Music Teachers National Association, Mu Phi Epsilon, Pi Kappa Lambda.

WRITINGS: (With Bjornar Bergethon) *Musical Growth in the Elementary Schools*, Holt, 1963, revised edition, 1970; (with Beth Landis, and editor) *Exploring Music* (elementary music textbook series), Holt, 1966.

WORK IN PROGRESS: Revising *Exploring Music*.

* * *

BOAZ, Martha (Terosse)

PERSONAL: Born in Stuart, Va.; daughter of James Robert (a county official for the Internal Revenue) and Kate (Gilley) Boaz. *Education:* Madison College, B.S., 1935; George Peabody College, B.S. in L.S., 1937; University of Michigan, M.A. in L.S., 1950, Ph.D., 1955. *Politics:* Independent. *Home:* 1849 Campus Rd., Los Angeles, Calif. 90007. *Office:* University of Southern California, Los Angeles, Calif. 90007.

CAREER: Bridgewater High School, Bridgewater, Va., librarian and critic teacher, 1935-37; Jeffersontown High School, Jeffersontown, Ky., librarian and teacher, 1937-40; Madison College, Harrisonburg, Va., assistant librarian, 1940-49; University of Tennessee, Knoxville, associate professor, 1950-51; University of Michigan, Ann Arbor, instructor, 1951-52; University of Southern California, Los Angeles, 1953—, began as associate professor, now professor and dean. *Member:* American Library Association, Association of American Library Schools (president, 1961-63), American Documentation Institute (president, Southern California chapter, 1962), California Library Association (president, 1962), Beta Phi Mu (president, 1962).

WRITINGS: (Compiler) *Quest for Truth*, two volumes (Volume 2 entitled "The Continuing Quest"), Scarecrow,

1957; (editor) *A Living Library*, University of Southern California Press, 1957; (with Leroy Merrit and Kenneth Tisdee) *Reviews in Library Book Selection*, Wayne State University Press, 1958; (editor) *Modern Trends in Documentation* (proceedings of symposium held at University of Southern California, April, 1958), Pergamon, 1959; (with Edwin Castagna) *The Ontario Public Library: A Survey*, [Ontario, Calif.], 1959; *Fervent and Full of Gifts: The Life of Althea Warren*, Scarecrow, 1961; *Strength Through Cooperation in Southern California Libraries: A Survey*, [Los Angeles], 1965; *New Directions in Library Service: A Cooperative Library System for Southern California*, Los Angeles Public Library, 1966; *Concepts of Service for the Port Angeles Public Library: A Study with Recommendations*, [Los Angeles], 1967.

WORK IN PROGRESS: Continuing a survey of metropolitan libraries in Southern California.

AVOCATIONAL INTERESTS: Creative writing, theatre, and travel.

* * *

BOCK, Frederick 1916-

PERSONAL: Born 1916, in Newton, Iowa; son of Conrad W. and Mary (Ramer) Bock. *Education:* State University of Iowa, B.A., 1937. *Religion:* Congregational. *Residence:* Newton, Iowa.

CAREER: *Poetry* magazine, Chicago, Ill., assistant editor, 1955-60. Poet. *Member:* Phi Beta Kappa.

WRITINGS: *The Fountains of Regardlessness* (poetry), Macmillan, 1961. Contributor to *Poetry, Poetry Northwest, Chelsea, Kenyon Review*, and *New Yorker*.

WORK IN PROGRESS: *The Mountains of Odds Come Even*, a new collection of poetry.

* * *

BODENHAM, Hilda Morris 1901-
(Hilda Boden, Pauline Welch)

PERSONAL: Born September 17, 1901, in Staffordshire, England; daughter of Thomas (a master tinsmith) and Mary (Draper) Morris; married Robert John William Bodenham (former justice of peace, headmaster, borough councillor), September 2, 1922; children: Gillian Bredon Newton, Patricia Clee Dussek, Roger Mynd. *Education:* Attended King Edward's School, Birmingham, England. *Politics:* Conservative. *Religion:* Church of England. *Home:* The Lee, Nolton Haven, Haverfordwest, Wales.

CAREER: Writer. *Member:* Haverfordwest Soroptimist Club (secretary), Girl Guides.

WRITINGS—All under pseudonym Hilda Boden: *Pony Trek*, Macmillan, 1948; *Family Affair: A Midland Chronicle*, Blue Book, 1948.

Bridge Club, Ronald, 1952; *One More Pony*, A. & C. Black, 1952, Macmillan, 1953; *Marlows at Newgale*, Brockhampton, 1956; *Marlow Wins a Prize*, Brockhampton, 1957; *Marlow Digs for Treasure*, Brockhampton, 1958; *Two Lost Emeralds*, Abelard, 1958; *Marlows into Danger*, Brockhampton, 1959.

Joanna's Special Pony, Burke, 1960; *Marlows at Castle Cliff*, McKay, 1960; *Noel and the Donkey*, Burke, 1960; *Marlows and the Regatta*, Brockhampton, 1961; *Faraway Farm*, McKay, 1961; *Joanna Rides the Hills*, Burke, 1961; *Noel's Happy Day*, Burke, 1961; *The House by the Sea*, McKay, 1962; *Marlow's Irish Holiday*, Brockhampton, 1962; *Noel's Christmas Holiday*, Burke, 1962; *Foxes in the Valley*, McKay, 1963; *Noel, the Brave*, Burke, 1963; *Marlow's Pigeon Post*, Brockhampton, 1963; *Water Wheel, Turn!*, McKay, 1964; *Pony Girl*, Lutterworth, 1964; *Noel, the Explorer*, Burke, 1965; (with Sheila Chapman) *Pony Adventure*, Burke, 1965; *Highland Holiday*, McKay,

1965; *Job for Noel*, Burke, 1966; *Peter and Pippin*, Wheaton, 1966; *The Mystery of Castle Croome*, McKay, 1966; *Wonderful Penny Stamp*, Burke, 1968; *The Mystery of Island Keep*, McKay, 1968; *Canal House*, Burke, 1969, *Storm Over Wales*, McKay, 1969.

Ward of the King, Collins, 1970; *The Severnside Mystery*, McKay, 1970; *Pedro Visits the Country*, Burke, 1970. Contributor to *Punch*, *Times* (London), *Homes and Gardens*, *Spectator*, and other magazines.

WORK IN PROGRESS: *Marlows in Town*, for Brockhampton; a book of illustrated rhymes for children.

AVOCATIONAL INTERESTS: Watercolor sketching, gardening, local archaeology.

* * *

BOEWE, Charles (Ernst) 1924-

PERSONAL: Born March 11, 1924, in West Salem, Ill; son of Fred Ernst and Susan (Wolters) Boewe; married Mary Catherine Scurrah, June 17, 1950; children: Abigail Ann, Emily Jane. *Education:* Attended University of Illinois 1942; Syracuse University, A.B., 1947, M.A., 1949; University of Wisconsin, Ph.D., 1955. *Office:* United States Educational Foundation, 83 N.I. Lines, Saddar, Karachi-3, West Pakistan.

CAREER: Syracuse University, Syracuse, N.Y., instructor in English, 1949-51; Lehigh University, Bethlehem, Pa., instructor in English, 1955-56; University of Pennsylvania, Philadelphia, assistant professor of English, 1958-64; Fulbright Foundation, Karachi, Pakistan, executive secretary, 1964—. Consultant to American Studies Advisory Committee, Committee on International Exchange of Persons, and Conference Board of Associated Research Councils, 1962-64; consultant to Wemyss Foundation, 1963—. *Military service:* U.S. Army, 1943-46. *Member:* Modern Language Association of America, American Studies Association (executive secretary, 1962-63). *Awards, honors:* Carnegie post-doctoral fellow in American Studies at University of Pennsylvania, 1956-58; Fulbright senior lecturer in Norway, 1960-61.

WRITINGS: (Editor and author of introduction) Constantine Samuel Rafinesque, *The World; or, Instability*, Scholars' Facsimiles and Reprints, 1956; (editor with Roy F. Nichols) *Both Human and Humane: The Humanities and Social Sciences in Graduate Education*, University of Pennsylvania Press, 1960; *Prairie Albion: An English Settlement in Pioneer Illinois*, Southern Illinois University Press, 1962. Contributor of scholarly articles to *American Literature*, *New England Quarterly*, and other professional journals; contributor of other articles, poems, and book reviews to *Atlantic*, *Saturday Review*, *Nation*, *Prairie Schooner*, *Audubon*, *Landscape*, *Names*, and other periodicals.

WORK IN PROGRESS: A study of the Norwegian-American novelist Ole Edvart Rolvaag for "U.S. Authors" series; editing letters of C.S. Rafinesque for American Philosophical Society; a book on the humanities in the university; a novel set in Norway.

* * *

BOHANNAN, Paul (James) 1920-

PERSONAL: Born March 5, 1920, in Lincoln, Neb.; son of Hillory (an engineer) and Hazel (Truex) Bohannan; married Laura Smith (a professor and author), May 15, 1943; children: Denis Michael. *Education:* University of Arizona, B.A. (with highest distinction), 1947; Oxford University, B.Sc., 1949, D.Phil., 1951; Chicago Institute for Psychoanalysis, postgraduate study, 1967-71. *Politics:* "Fiercely Independent." *Religion:* "Apathetically Agnostic." *Office:* Northwestern University, Evanston, Ill. 60201.

CAREER: Oxford University, Oxford, England, university lecturer in social anthropology, 1951-56; Princeton University, Princeton, N.J., 1956-59, began as visiting lecturer in social anthropology, became Jonathan Edwards Preceptor and assistant professor, then associate professor of anthropology; Northwestern University, Evanston, Ill., professor of anthropology, 1959—, Stanley G. Harris Professor of Social Science, 1968—. National Academy of Sciences, executive director of Human Environments in Central Africa Project, 1958-60. Did field work among Tiv in central Nigeria, 1949-53, Wanga of Nyanza Province, Kenya, 1955, and American middle class divorced, 1964—. *Military service:* U.S. Army Security Agency, ral Sciences, 1963-64.

MEMBER: American Anthropological Association, African Studies Association (vice-president, 1962-63; president, 1963-64), American Academy of Arts and Sciences, Social Science Research Council (director, 1960-63), Royal Anthropological Institute, American Association of Rhodes Scholars, Phi Beta Kappa, Phi Beta Phi, Sigma Xi (associate). *Awards, honors:* Rhodes Scholar, 1947-49, 1950-51; grants from Social Science Research Council, Wenner-Gren Foundation, Colonial Social Science Research Council, and government of Nigeria for field work in Nigeria, 1949-53; August Vollmer Award of American Criminological Society for *African Homicide and Suicide;* 1960; fellow, Center for Advanced Study in the Behavioral Sciences, 1963-64; senior postdoctoral fellow, National Science Foundation, 1967-68; Meville J. Herskovits Award, African Studies Association, 1969, for *TIV Economy.*

WRITINGS: (With wife, Laura Bohannan) *The Tiv of Central Nigeria*, International African Institute, 1953; *Tiv Farm and Settlement*, H.M.S.O., 1954; *Justice and Judgement Among the Tiv*, published for International African Institute by Oxford University Press, 1958; *Three Source Notebooks in TIV Ethnology*, Human Relations Area Files, 1958; (editor and contributor) *African Homicide and Suicide*, Princeton University Press, 1960; (with Alan J. Pifer and William O. Jones) *Africa in Transition*, University of Arizona Press, 1961; (editor with George Dalton) *Markets in Africa* (symposium), Northwestern University Press, 1962, eight selected essays also published separately as *Markets in Africa: Eight Subsistence Economies in Transition*, Doubleday-Anchor 1965; *Social Anthropology*, Holt, 1963; *Africa and Africans*, Natural History Press, 1964, 2nd edition (with Philip Curtin), 1971 (published in England as *African Outline: A General Introduction*, Penguin, 1966); (editor and author of introduction) Edward Burnett Tylor, *Researches into the Early History of Mankind and the Development of Civilization* (edited from 3rd edition), University of Chicago Press, 1964; (editor) Lewis H. Morgan, *Houses and House-Life of the American Aborigines*, University of Chicago Press, 1965; *Anthropology*, Purdue University, c.1966; (with Laura Bohannan) *A Source Notebook in Tiv History and Political Organization*, Human Relations Area Files, 1966; (with Laura Bohannan) *A Source Notebook in Tiv Subsistence, Technology and Economics*, Human Relations Area Files, 1966; (with Laura Bohannan) *A Source Notebook in the Tiv Life Cycle*, Human Relations Area Files, 1966; (editor) *Law and Warfare: Studies in the Anthropology of Conflict*, Natural History Press, 1967; (editor with Fred Plog) *Beyond the Frontier: Social Process and Cultural Change*, Natural History Press, 1967; (editor with John Middleton) *Marriage, Family and Residence*, Natural History Press, 1968; (editor with Middleton) *Kinship and Social Organization*, Natural History Press, 1968; (with Laura Bohannan) *Tiv Economy*, Northwestern University Press, 1968; (with Laura Bohannan) *Five Source Notebooks on Tiv Religion*, Human Relations Area Files, 1969; *Love, Sex and Being Human: A Book About the Human Con-*

dition for Young People, Doubleday, 1969; (editor and contributor) *Divorce and After,* Doubleday, 1970.

Contributor: Ruth Nanda Anshen, editor, *The Family in Africa,* 2nd edition, Harper, 1959; Kurt H. Wolff, editor, *Emile Durkheim, 1858-1917,* Ohio State University Press, 1960, reissued as *Essays on Sociology and Philosophy: With Appraisals of Durkheim's Life and Thought,* Harper, 1964; Marian W. Smith, editor, *The Artist in Tribal Society,* Routledge & Kegan Paul, 1961; *The Kennecott Lecture Series, 1960-61,* University of Arizona Press, 1961; Daniel Biebuyck, editor, *Land Tenure in Africa,* International African Institute, 1963; Melville J. Herskovits and Michell Harwitz, editors, *Economic Transition in Africa,* Northwestern University Press, 1964; Sol Tax, editor, *Horizons of Anthropology,* Aldine, 1964; (author of commentary) Henry Williamson, *Hustler!,* edited by Lincoln Keiser, Doubleday, 1965; James L. Gibbs, Jr., *Twelve African Tribes,* Holt, 1965; Douglas Fraser, editor, *The Many Faces of Primitive Art,* Prentice-Hall, 1966; Seymour M. Farber and Roger H.L. Wilson, editors, *Teen-Age Marriage and Divorce,* Diablo, 1967; Marvin E. Wolfgang, editor, *Studies in Homicide,* Harper, 1967; Laura Nader, editor, *Law in Culture and Society,* Aldine, 1969; Donald J. Mulvihill and Melvin M. Tumin, editors, *Crimes of Violence* (Volume 13 of a staff report, National Commission on the Causes and Prevention of Violence), U.S. Government Printing Office, c.1970; Francis L.K. Hsu, *Kinship and Society,* Aldine, 1971.

Contributor to *Encyclopedia Americana, Encyclopaedia Britannica, Grolier's Encyclopedia, World Book, American Educator Encyclopedia.* Contributor of other articles on African topics to *Africa, Man, Listener, World Digest, Journal of Economic History, Current Anthropology, Natural History,* other anthropology journals; reviewer for some of these same periodicals and for *New York Times Book Review, Nature,* and *Times Literary Supplement.*

WORK IN PROGRESS: The Renegotiated Marriage, for Doubleday; a study of divorce in cross-cultural perspective; *Man's Inhumanity,* a study of the psychic and social dimensions of cannibalism, rape, homicide, child abuse, capital punishment, feuds and warfare, with some asides on peacemaking and face-saving; *The American Experiment,* with Henry F. Graff.

SIDELIGHTS: Bohannan is probably best known to anthropologists and sociologists for his field work among African tribes, which resulted in several published studies, many of them written in collaboration with his wife. Recently, however, Bohannan has become more familiar to the lay public as an author and editor of books dealing with Western middle class concepts of marriage, family, household, and divorce. *Love, Sex and Being Human* is, according to Lois Fox Ruby in a review for *Library Journal,* "an outstanding title, far more comprehensive than and superior to current books for teenagers on sex and love." Miss Ruby is especially appreciative of the fact that the book is "personal, clear, sensitive, understanding, non-preachy. . . . Dr. Bohanan assumes that 'young people are mature enough that they can learn what their own morality is.' "

Divorce and After includes a history of divorce laws and analyses of the social problems accompanying divorce in America as contrasted to other cultures. "The entire book," writes Emily M. Brown for the *Washington Post,* "goes far below the surface stereotypes in looking at divorce—not an easy thing to do when stereotypes have always predominated the thinking in this area—and Bohannan's own articles are among the best. . . . [The book] is good reading, yet accurate and scholarly—a tough combination to pull off, but he has done it."

BIOGRAPHICAL/CRITICAL SOURCES: Choice, March, 1969; *Library Journal,* May 15, 1969, July, 1970; *American Anthropologist,* October, 1969; *Washington Post,* September 4, 1970.

*   *   *

BOLAND, (Bertram) John 1913-

PERSONAL: Born February 12, 1913, in Birmingham, England; son of Albert Edward (a manufacturer) and Elizabeth (Mills) Boland; married Philippa Carver (now her husband's secretary), May 29, 1952. *Education:* Privately educated. *Politics:* Independent. *Religion:* Agnostic. *Home and office:* The Red House, Mardens Hill, Crowborough, Sussex, England.

CAREER: Employed variously as a farm worker, laborer, deckhand, lumberjack, railroad worker, factory hand, and salesman, 1930-38; manufacturers' agent, selling advertising signs and automobile components, 1946-55; full-time author, 1956—. Formed own film company, John Boland Productions Limited, 1964. Writers' Summer School, chairman, 1958-60. *Military service:* British Army, Royal Artillery, 1939-45. *Member:* Writers' Guild of Great Britain (chairman, associates branch, 1960-61; chairman, radio committee, 1966-70), Crime Writers Association (chairman, 1963), Mystery Writers of America. *Awards, honors:* Writers' Guild of Great Britain "Zita," 1968, for best radio drama of the year.

WRITINGS: White August, Arcadia House, 1955; *No Refuge,* M. Joseph, 1956; *Queer Fish,* T.V. Boardman, 1958; *The League of Gentlemen,* T.V. Boardman, 1958; *Mysterious Way,* T.V. Boardman, 1959; *Operation Red Carpet: A Novel of Menace,* T.V. Boardman, 1959; *Bitter Fortune,* T.V. Boardman, 1959; *The Midas Touch,* T.V. Boardman, 1960; *Negative Value,* T.V. Boardman, 1960; *The Golden Fleece: A Slightly-Criminous Novel,* T.V. Boardman, 1961; *Inside Job,* T.V. Boardman, 1961; *The Gentlemen Reform,* T.V. Boardman, 1961, Macmillan, 1964; *Vendetta,* T.V. Boardman, 1961; *The Gentlemen at Large,* T.V. Boardman, 1962; *Fatal Error,* T.V. Boardman, 1962; *Counterpol,* Harrap, 1963, Walker & Co., 1965; *The Catch,* Harrap, 1964, Holt, 1966; *Counterpol in Paris,* Harrap, 1964, Walker & Co,. 1965; *The Good Citizens,* Harrap, 1965; *The Disposal Unit,* Harrap, 1966; *The Gusher,* Harrap, 1967; *Painted Lady,* Cassell, 1967; *Breakdown,* Cassell, 1968; *The Fourth Grave,* Cassell, 1969; *The Shakespeare Curse,* Cassell, 1969; *Kidnap,* Cassell, 1970; *The Big Job,* Cassell, 1970.

Nonfiction: *New Writers' Guide to Free-Lance Journalism,* T.V. Boardman, 1960; *New Writers' Guide to Short Story Writing,* T.V. Boardman, 1960.

Film scripts: "The Golden Fleece," "The Stone Desert," "The Good Citizens." Also author of television scripts, "The Fifth Victim" and "The Smoke Boys," and of more han three hundred and fifty short stories, radio plays, and a number of articles.

AVOCATIONAL INTERESTS: Gardening (Boland lives in a hundred-year-old cottage with an acre of garden on the edge of Ashdown Forest), good talk, good food, wine.

*   *   *

BOLAND, Charles Michael 1917-

PERSONAL: Born October 27, 1917, in Wilkes-Barre, Pa.; son of Michael Charles Boland (an engineer); married Jeanne Elizabeth Stickler (a bookshop manager), June 6, 1941; children: Barry Michael, Christopher Charles, Brian Windsor. *Education:* Attended Philadelphia Museum College of Art, 1933-37. *Politics:* Independent. *Home and office:* 143 Blackburn Ave., Lands Downe, Pa. 19050.

CAREER: Commercial illustrator, 1937-46; television writer, director, and producer in Philadelphia, Pa., 1946-51, doing thirteen shows weekly at one period; moved on to New York, N.Y., 1951, to write television commercials for McCann-Erickson, and later worked for Biow Co., Benton & Bowles, and Parkson Inc., and Ted Bates, 1951-63; left advertising twice to write as free lance, more recently in 1963; owner of Books from Bolands, New Canaan, Conn., publisher-editor of *Old Bow Window Literary Gazette and Belletristic Bugle* (monthly), conductor of twice-weekly radio program, "Boland on Books," Station WMMM, Westport, Conn., and writer of twice-weekly newspaper column on books, 1963—. Creative television consultant for small advertising agencies.

WRITINGS: *Iceland and Greenland,* Doubleday, 1959; (self-illustrated) *They All Discovered America,* Doubleday, 1961; *Careers and Opportunities in Advertising,* Dutton, 1964; (editor) *The Vikings,* American Heritage, 1964. Contributor to marine section of *New Grolier Encyclopedia;* former contributing editor, *Rudder.*

WORK IN PROGRESS: A book dealing with a Greek myth; a book on lighthouses; a novel.†

* * *

BOLES, Paul Darcy 1919-

PERSONAL: Born March 5, 1919, in Auburn, Ind.; son of Ernest Glendon and Gwendolyn (Marsden) Boles; married Dorothy Flory, December 25, 1941; children: Shawn Michael, Patric Laurence, Terence Ross. *Education:* Privately educated. *Politics:* Democrat. *Religion:* Episcopalian. *Home:* 4009 Wieuca Rd. N.E., Atlanta, Ga. 30342. *Agent:* Fox Chase Agency, Inc., Lincoln Bldg., 60 East 42nd St., New York, N.Y. 10017.

CAREER: Writer, with advertising companies and as free lance. Lay reader, Episcopal Church. *Awards, honors:* Friends of American Writers $1,000 award, 1959, for *Parton's Island;* University of Indiana Writers Conference award, 1969, for *A Million Guitars and Other Stories;* Georgia Writers' Association Literary Achievement award for fiction, 1969.

WRITINGS: *The Streak* (novel), Macmillan, 1953; *The Beggars in the Sun* (novel), Macmillan, 1954; *Glenport, Illinois* (novel), Macmillan, 1956; *Deadline* (novel), Macmillan, 1957; (contributor) Granville Hicks, editor, *The Living Novel: A Symposium,* Macmillan, 1957; (self-illustrated) *Parton's Island* (novel), Macmillan, 1958; *A Million Guitars and Other Stories,* Little, Brown, 1967; *I Thought You Were a Unicorn and Other Stories,* Little, Brown, 1971. Also author of a screenplay, "Altamaha Diary," as yet unpublished or produced, and a screenplay of *Parton's Island.* Short stories are anthologized in *Best Post Short Stories, 1957,* edited by Ben Hibbs, Random House, 1958, *Seventeen's Stories,* edited by Babette Rosmond, Lippincott, 1958, and *Best Post Short Stories, 1961,* Doubleday, 1961. Contributor of short stories to *Ladies' Home Journal, Cosmopolitan, Playboy, Cavalier,* and to magazines in France, Germany, England, and Sweden; contributor of essays to *Writer* and *Writer's Digest,* and of reviews to *Saturday Review.*

WORK IN PROGRESS: A novel based on the Altamaha; short stories; motion picture scripts.

SIDELIGHTS: In a review of *A Million Guitars and Other Stories,* Max Steele writes: "Paul Darcy Boles writes truly funny stories.... He is, of course, a professional writer in the good sense of the word. His stories have tremendous vitality. They have humor; there is sadness mixed with the laughter and the result is sometimes a lyrical pathos."

In an article in *The Writer,* Boles describes his feelings about the art of the short story. "A short story begins with you, within you, deeper than the flesh. Funny or tragic coming to you in one flash of thought or remembrance—or mined out of your depth, inch by inch, like a golden body coming out of the dark earth—it represents, more than any object which could possibly be manufactured, a triumph of exploration and discovery.

"Short stories are born—in joy, in pain, in eagerness, in need. Long after Marshall McLuhan and his electronic word-spasms are dust, men will be reading and pondering short stories, reading them with the eye of the spirit, the ear of the Word. From the experimental to the traditional, and back, they will change form again and again. What they will forever have in common is this: They will always be swift and living bridges from the writer to the reader. In the reader's passage across these bridges of words, he will be entertained, instructed, shocked, exalted; if the short story is worthy, the reader will have changed, become more aware—he will, somehow, be a wiser human being than he was before he crossed the bridge."

Boles adds: "Like everyone who thinks and feels, I worry about the world, the gift of life in the world, the international loss of delight in the world, and the need for wise and thorough change and leadership, which starts with the individual vision, and must start now or never."

BIOGRAPHICAL/CRITICAL SOURCES: *Atlanta Magazine,* September, 1963; *Best Sellers,* September 1, 1968, August 15, 1971; *New York Times Book Review,* November 3, 1968; *Book World,* January 12, 1969; *Writer,* March, 1971.

* * *

BOLLES, (Edmund) Blair 1911-

PERSONAL: Born February 26, 1911, in St. Louis, Mo.; son of Stephen and Zoe Papin (Blair) Bolles; married Mona Dugas, April 19, 1941; children: Blair, DeVallon, Zoe, Harry Peck. *Education:* Phillips Exeter Academy, student, 1926-29; Yale University, student, 1929-30, 1931-32. *Religion:* Roman Catholic. *Home:* 4831 Linnean Ave., Washington, D.C. 20008. *Agent:* Willis Kingsley Wing, 24 East 38th St., New York, N.Y. 10016. *Office:* Colt Industries, Inc., 1801 K St. N.W., Washington, D.C. 20006.

CAREER: Reporter, school teacher, and advertising writer, 1934-35; *Washington Star,* Washington, D.C., reporter, diplomatic correspondent, 1935-44; Foreign Policy Association, Washington, D.C., director of Washington bureau, 1944-51, Washington correspondent, 1951-53; *France Actuelle,* U.S. editor, 1952-53; *Toledo Blade,* Toledo, Ohio, European correspondent, 1953-56, associate editor, 1957-59; Fairbanks, Morse & Co., Chicago, Ill., and Washington, D.C., vice-president for government relations, 1959-66; Colt Industries, Inc., Washington, D.C., vice president in International Department, 1966-68, in Government Relations Department, 1968—. United Nations Food and Agriculture Organization, consultant, 1946. *Member:* American Geographical Society, American Association for Advancement of Science, National Press Club, Sigma Delta Chi, Yale Club (New York), Cosmos Club (Washington, D.C.), International Club (Washington, D.C.).

WRITINGS: (With Duncan Aikman) *America's Chance of Peace,* Doubleday, 1939; *Oil: An Economic Key to Peace,* Foreign Policy Association, 1944; *Congress and Foreign Policy,* Foreign Policy Association, 1945; *Pillars of the United Nations: International Economic and Social Agencies,* Foreign Policy Association, 1945; *Roosevelt's Foreign Policy,* Foreign Policy Association, 1945; *World Nutrition and Agrarian Stability: Proposals for a Food Board,* Foreign Policy Association, 1946; *Influence of Armed Forces on U.S. Foreign Policy,* Foreign Policy Association, 1936; *Who Makes Our Foreign Policy?,* Foreign Policy Association, 1947, 2nd edition, 1951; *Reorganization of the State Department,* Foreign Policy Association, 1947; (with Ona K.D. Ringwood) *Arctic Diplomacy,* Foreign Policy Association, 1948: *Bipartisanshin in American Foreign Policy,* Foreign Policy Association, 1948; (with Vera Micheles Dean) *North Atlantic Defense Pact: Background Pros and Cons,* Foreign Policy Association, 1949; (contributor) Virginia McLean Thompson, *Empire's End in Southeast Asia,* Foreign/ Policy Association, 1949; *Military Establishment of the United States,* Foreign Policy Association, 1949; (contributor) Charles L. Walker, *Man and Food: The Lost Equation?,* Foreign Policy Association, 1949; *American Policy Abroad,* Canadian Association for Adult Education, 1949.

United States Military Policy, Foreign Policy Association, 1950; *Switzerland: Oasis of Free Enterprise,* Foreign Policy Association, 1950; *Tyrant from Illinois: Uncle Joe Cannon's Experiment with Personal Power,* Norton, 1951; (contributor) Francis D. Scott, *Scandinavia Today,* Foreigh Policy Association, 1951; *How to Get Rich in Washington: Rich Men's Division of the Welfare State,* Norton, 1952; (with Francis O. Wilsox) *The Armed Road to Peace: An Analysis of NATO [and] Bipartisanship and the North Atlantic Treaty* (the former by Bolles, the latter by Wilcox), Foreign Policy Association, 1952; *The Big Change in Europe,* Norton, 1958; *Men of Good Intentions: Crisis of the American Presidency,* Doubleday, 1960 (published in England as *Corruption in Washington; or, Men of Good Intentions,* Gollanez, 1960).

Contributor to magazines and newspapers, 1936—, including articles on foreign affairs to North America Newspaper Alliance, other articles to *Toronto Star Weekly, New York Times, St. Louis Post-Dispatch, Harper's, Reader's Digest, American Historical Association Journal.*

WORK IN PROGRESS: A book on peopling of the desert, for Little, Brown.

SIDELIGHTS: Bolles told *CA:* "I like to write but making a living gets in the way. As writer was interested in observation of politics until age fifty; now am interested in the human condition."

*   *   *

BOLTON, Kenneth (Ewart)   1914-

PERSONAL: Born March 15, 1941, in Worcestershire, England; son of James William and Eliza Laura (Flower) Bolton; married Joyce Millicent, 1950 (divorced); married second wife, Doris, 1968; children: (first marriage) Stephen Paul. *Education:* Attended King Edward's School, Stourbridge, England. *Politics:* Liberal. *Home:* P.O. Box 30080, Nairobi, Kenya, Africa. *Office: East African Standard,* Standard St., Nairobi, Kenya, Africa.

CAREER: British Army, Royal Horse Artillery, 1938-53, retiring as lieutenant colonel; served in western desert, North Africa, Sicily, and Italy; wounded in action three times. Journalist, beginning as articled pupil on weekly paper, and working on editorial staffs of *County Express, Birmington Gazette, Evening Despatch, Daily Mail,* and *News Chronicle* in England; *East African Standard,* Nairobi, Kenya, Africa, editor, 1956—. Director of East African Standard Newspapers Ltd. and Newspaper Services Ltd., Nairobi. Radio and television broadcaster. *Member:* Commonwealth Press Union (Great Britain; overseas member of council), Royal Society of Arts (fellow), East African Guild of Editors (founder president, 1962), East African Gunners Association (chairman, 1961), Nairobi Club, Harlequins Football Club. *Awards, honors*—Military: Military Cross, commendation for

gallantry in action, mentioned in dispatches twice. Civilian: Order of British Empire for services to journalism in Kenya: Commonwealth award in journalism, Royal Society of Arts; Silver medal, Mexico Olympics Committee.

WRITINGS: History of the 11th (H.A.C.) Regiment, Royal Horse Artillery in the Second World War, H.A.C., 1946; *The Lion and the Lily: A Guide to Kenya,* Bles, 1962, revised edition published as *Harambee Country: A Guide to Kenya,* Bles, 1970, International Publications Service, 1971; *The Saturday Essays: Being a Collection of 50 Essays of an Exile Living in Kenya,* East African Standard, 1962. Contributor to *Baltimore Sun.*

AVOCATIONAL INTERESTS: Watching rugby football and gardening.

*   *   *

BOLTON, Maisie Sharman   1915-
    (Maisie Sharman, Miriam Sharman, Stratford Davis)

PERSONAL: Born February 6, 1915, in Glasgow, Scotland; daughter of Jacob (a tailor) and Celia (Ognall) Sharman; married Kenneth Bolton (a farmer), June 25, 1951. *Education:* University of Glasgow, M.A. *Home:* Upper Kiln Farm, Bragenham, Leighton Buzzard, Bedfordshire, England. *Agent:* Lom (Management) Ltd., 6A Maddox St., London W.1, England.

CAREER: Bee Bee Biscuits Ltd., London, England, secretary, 1934-38; British National Films, London, England, secretary and film-script writer, 1938-40; free-lance filmscript writer, 1940-46; Prebendal School, Aylesbury, England, teacher, 1947-50; free-lance writer, 1950—. *Member:* National Book League, Society of Authors, Crime Writers' Association. *Awards, honors:* Second prize, Ellery Queen contest, 1967, for short story, "Battle of Wits."

WRITINGS—Under pseudonym Stratford Davis: *Death in Seven Hours,* Melrose, 1952; *No Tears Are Shed,* Melrose, 1952; *The Troubled Mind,* Melrose, 1953; *One Man's Secret,* T.V. Boardman, 1956; *His Father's Ghost,* Abelard, 1963.

Under pseudonym Miriam Sharman: *Death Pays All Debts,* Gollancz, 1965; *Seeds of Violence,* Gollancz, 1966; *The Face of Danger,* Gollancz, 1967; *Law of Probability,* Macdonald & Co., 1971.

Television plays: "An Inch from the Heart," 1957; "Late Harvest," 1960. Author, with Stephen Clarkson, of stage version of her novel, *No Tears Are Shed.* Also author of film scripts "Death Goes to School," adapted from *Death in Seven Hours,* and "Man in the Shadow," adapted from *One Man's Secret.* Contributor of short stories to *Ellery Queen's Mystery Magazine, Edgar Wallace Mystery Magazine,* and *Alfred Hitchcock Mystery Magazine;* contributor to *Best Underworld Stories,* Faber, 1969.

WORK IN PROGRESS: Television plays; suspense novel.

AVOCATIONAL INTERESTS: Cooking and baking, the theatre, books, music, country walks.

BIOGRAPHICAL/CRITICAL SOURCES: Everywoman, (Odham), July, 1958; *Scottish Field,* October, 1960.

*   *   *

BONHAM, Frank   1914-

PERSONAL: Born February 25, 1914, in Los Angeles, Calif.; son of Alfred B. and Cecil (Thompson) Bonham; married Gloria Bailey (a schoolteacher), November 26, 1938; children: David, Bruce, Keith. *Education:* Glendale Junior College (now Glendale College), student. *Politics:* Independent. *Home:* 8302 Sugarman Dr., La Jolla, Calif.

CAREER: Self-employed writer. Military service: U.S. Army, 1942-43. Member: Writers Guild of America, West, CRASH, Inc. (Community Resources and Self-Help; board of directors), Physical Fitness Council, San Diego YMCA. Awards, honors: Mystery Writers of America Edgar Award runner-up, 1967, for Mystery of the Red Tide.

WRITINGS: Lost Stage Valley, Simon & Schuster, 1948; Bold Passage, Simon & Schuster, 1950; Snaketrack, Simon & Schuster, 1952; Blood on the Land, Ballantine, 1952; Outcast of Crooked River, Hodder & Stoughton, 1953; Night Raid, Ballantine, 1954; The Feud at Spanish Ford, Ballantine, 1954; Border Guns, Muller, 1956; Last Stage West, Dell, 1957; Tough Country, Dell, 1958; Hardrock, Ballantine, 1958; One for Sleep, Gold Medal, 1960; The Skin Game, Gold Medal, 1961; Trago . . . , Dell, 1962; By Her Own Hand, Monarch, 1963; Cast a Long Shadow, Monarch, 1964; Defiance Mountain, Popular Library, 1964; Rawhide Guns, Popular Library, 1964; Logan's Choice, Fawcett, 1964.

Youth books: Burma Rifles: A Story of Merrill's Marauders, Crowell, 1960; War Beneath the Sea, Crowell, 1962; Deepwater Challenge, Crowell, 1963; The Loud, Resounding Sea, Crowell, 1963; Honor Bound, Crowell, 1963; Speedway Contender, Crowell, 1964; Durango Street, Dutton, 1965; Mystery of the Red Tide, Dutton, 1966; Mystery in Little Tokyo, Dutton, 1966; The Ghost Front, Dutton, 1968; Mystery of the Fat Cat, Dutton, 1968; The Nitty Gritty, Dutton, 1968; The Vagabundos, Dutton, 1969; Viva Chicano, Dutton, 1970; Cool Cat, Dutton, 1971; Chief, Dutton, 1971; The Friends of the Loony Lake Monster, Dutton, 1972; Hey Big Spender!, Dutton, 1972.

Author of television scripts for "Wells Fargo," "Restless Gun," "Shotgun Slade," and "Death Valley Days" series. Contributor of approximately five hundred short stories, novels, and novelettes to magazines, including Saturday Evening Post serials, short stories to McCall's, American, and to mystery and western magazines. Selections from youth novels included in many anthologies.

SIDELIGHTS: Several of Bonham's novels for young people have focused on minority youth in America and the problems they encounter in the ghetto. He has said that "although Durango Street was written with a general audience in mind, I soon learned that it was of special interest to this neglected black audience. . . . Delinquency is a field of special interest to me, as it is closely related to ghetto and barrio problems. I attend meetings at a San Diego parolee house where a dozen young men and boys on parole from Youth Anthority prisons live and attempt to aid one another in finding acceptable ways of handling their problems. Most of my material is drawn from life. My story characters are real people transmuted by merging with other characters, and by sheer imagination." Avocational interests: Skin-diving, camping in Baja California, stories about dolphins, classical music.

BIOGRAPHICAL/CRITICAL SOURCES: New York Times Book Review, April 14, 1968, August 25, 1968; Book World, May 5, 1968, October 6, 1968; Commonweal, May 24, 1968; Young Readers' Review, September, 1968, November, 1968, October, 1969; Children's Book World, November 3, 1968; Saturday Review, August 16, 1969; Library Journal, July, 1970.

*　　*　　*

BONHAM-CARTER, Victor 1913-

PERSONAL: Born December 13, 1913, in Bearsted, Kent, England; son of General Sir Charles and Lady Madge (Fisher) Bonham-Carter; married Audrey Stogdon, July 22, 1938; children: Graeme Francis, Thomas Hugh. Edu-

cation: Attended Winchester College; Magdalene College, Cambridge University, M.A., 1935. Politics: Liberal. Religion: Anglican. Home: 84 Drayton Gardens, London W.8, England. Agent: Curtis Brown Ltd., 13 King St., London W.C. 2, England. Office: Society of Authors, 84 Drayton Gardens, London S.W. 10, England; and The Royal Literary Fund, 11 Ludgate Hill, London E.C.4, England.

CAREER: Free-lance writer; Society of Authors, London, England, planning officer, 1963—. Military service: British Army, 1939-45; received war service medals and Belgian Order of Leopold. Member: Authors Club (London).

WRITINGS: Billy the Bumblebee, Hammond, 1946; A Posy of Wildflowers, Wingate, 1946; Can Country Life Survive?, Bureau of Current Affairs (London), 1946; The Village Has a Future, Bureau of Current Affairs, 1948; The English Village, Penguin, 1952; (editor) Bryanston Miscellany, Bryanston School, 1958; (with William Burnless Curry) Dartington Hall: The History of an Experiment, Cornell University Press, 1958; Farming the Land, Routledge & Kegan Paul, 1959; In a Liberal Tradition: A Social Biography, 1700-1950, Constable, 1960; Exploring Parish Churches, Routledge & Kegan Paul, 1961; Soldier True: The Life and Times of Field-Marshall Sir William Robertson, 1860-1933, Muller, 1963, published in America as The Strategy of Victory: The Life and Times of the Master Strategist of World War I: Field-Marshal Sir William Robertson, Holt, 1964; Surgeon in the Crimea, Constable, 1969; The Survival of the English Countryside, Hodder & Stoughton, 1971. Contributor of articles to Countryman, Country Life, Farmers Weekly, Spectator, Sphere, Times Literary Supplement, and of radio scripts to British Broadcasting Corp.

WORK IN PROGRESS: A history of the Authors Society.

*　　*　　*

BONK, Wallace J. 1923-

PERSONAL: Born March 13, 1923, in Two Rivers, Wis.; married Joyce Johnson (a librarian), October 26, 1948. Education: Attended University of Wisconsin, 1941-43; University of Minnesota, B.A., 1942, M.A., 1949; University of Michigan, A.M. in L.S., 1954, Ph.D., 1956. Home: 2002 Shadford Rd., Ann Arbor, Mich. 48104. Office: School of Library Science, University of Michigan, Ann Arbor, Mich. 48104.

CAREER: East Texas State College (now East Texas State University), Commerce, assistant professor of English, 1949-52; University of Michigan, Ann Arbor, member of department of library science, 1954—, chairman of department, 1964-67. Military service: U.S. Army, 1943-6. Member: American Library Association, Association of American Library Schools, Michigan Library Association.

WRITINGS: The Public Library: Democratic or Equalitarian Institution?, Department of Library Science, Kent State University, 1956; Michigan's First Bookstore: A Study of Books Sold in the Detroit Book Store, 1817-1828, Department of Library Science, University of Michigan, 1957; (with Mary Duncan Carter) The Library as a Public Service Institution, Department of Library Science, University of Michigan, 1957, revised edition, 1962; (with Carter) Building Library Collections, Scarecrow, 1959, 3rd edition, 1969; Composite List of the Titles Taught in Basic Reference by 25 of the Accredited Library Schools, [Ann Arbor], 1960; Composite Lists of Titles in the Humanities and Social Sciences Courses in Certain of the Accredited Library Schools, Department of Library Science, University of Michigan, 1961; (with Carter) Bibliography and Book Selection, Department of Library Science, University of Michigan, 1961; A Crown

Garland of Ungolden Roses, Westpost House, 1962; *Use of Basic Reference Sources in Libraries,* Department of Library Science, University of Michigan, 1963.

AVOCATIONAL INTERESTS: Private hand press printing, two-piano playing, and collecting nineteenth-century editions of Jane Austen's novels.

*   *   *

BONNER, Gerald 1926-

PERSONAL: Born June 18, 1926, in London, England; son of Frederick John and Constance Emily (Hatch) Bonner. *Education:* Wadham College, Oxford University, B.A., 1952, M.A., 1956. *Politics:* Socialist. *Religion:* Anglican. *Home:* 39 Mount View Rd., London N. 4, England.

CAREER: British Museum, Department of Manuscripts, London, England, cataloguer, and interpreter of medieval and other manuscripts, specializing in Greek and Latin documents, 1953—. Member of council, Fellowship of St. Alban and St. Sergius. *Military service:* British Army, King's Dragoon Guards, 1944-48; served in Middle East and Palestine; became lieutenant.

WRITINGS: The Warfare of Christ, Morehouse, 1962; *St. Augustine of Hippo: Life and Controversies,* S.C.M. Press, 1963, Westminster, 1964; *Saint Bede in the Tradition of Western Apocalyptic Commentary* (Jarrow Lecture, 1966), J. & P. Bealls, 1966. Contributor of articles and reviews to learned journals and religious publications.

WORK IN PROGRESS: A study of the concept of deification in Christian theology, with special reference to the Latin Fathers; research for Volume II of St. Augustine, on his philosophy and theology.

AVOCATIONAL INTERESTS: The dead languages, especially Latin; wine, especially German; and reading military history.

*   *   *

BONNER, James Calvin 1904-

PERSONAL: Born June 16, 1904, in Heard County, Ga.; son of William Allen (a farmer) and Sara Amanda (Moore) Bonner; married Ida Munro (now a librarian), November 23, 1936; children: Page Munro (Mrs. Warren Craghead), James C., Jr. *Education:* University of Georgia, A.B.J., 1926, M.A., 1936; University of North Carolina, Ph.D., 1943. *Politics:* Democrat. *Religion:* Episcopalian. *Home:* 120 South Jackson St., Milledgeville, Ga. 31061.` *Office:* Hall, Russell/Georgia College, Milledgeville, Ga.

CAREER: High school principal, then headmaster of public agricultural school in Georgia, 1926-33; West Georgia College, Carrollton, instructor, then assistant professor of social science, 1933-41; Randolph-Macon Woman's College, Lynchburg, Va., adjunct professor of history, 1942-44; Woman's College of Georgia, Milledgeville, professor of history and chairman of department of social studies, 1944—. Visiting professor at Emory University, 1952. Georgia Council for the Social Studies, president, 1945. *Member:* American Historical Association, Southern Historical Association, Georgia Historical Society, Agricultural History Society (executive council, 1948-50), Old Capital Historical Society (president, 1958-60), Pi Gamma Mu (governor, Georgia province, 1960—). *Awards, honors:* West Georgia College Founders award, 1945; Southern fellowship grant, 1958; research grant, American Association for State and Local History, 1961; Distinguished Service Award, Georgia College, 1970.

WRITINGS: (Author and editor with Lucien E. Roberts) *Studies in Georgia History and Government,* University of Georgia Press, 1940; (editor) Sarah Frances Williams, *Plantation Experiences of a New York Woman* (originally published in *North Carolina Historical Review,* July-October, 1956), (N.C.) State Department of Archives and History, 1956; *The Georgia Story,* Harlow Publishing, 1958, 2nd edition, 1961; (contributor) Horace Montgomery, editor, *Georgians in Profile,* University of Georgia Press, 1958; *A Short History of Heard County,* privately printed, 1958, revised edition, Woman's College of Georgia, 1962, 2nd revised edition, Georgia College, 1967; (editor) Anna Maria Cook, *The Journal of a Milledgeville Girl, 1861-1867,* University of Georgia Press, 1964; *The Migration Pattern of the Descendants of Thomas Bonner,* [Milledgeville], 1964; *A History of Georgia Agriculture, 1732-1860,* University of Georgia Press, 1964; (contributor) Arthur Link and Rembert W. Patrick, editors, *Writing Southern History,* Louisiana State University Press, 1965; *Georgia: A Student's Guide to Localized History* (juvenile), Teachers College Press, 1965; *Georgia's Last Frontier,* University of Georgia Press, 1972.

Contributor to *Encyclopaedia Britannica, American Historical Review, Journal of Southern History, Agricultural History, Georgia Review,* and other historical publications. Editorial board member. *Journal of Social History,* 1950-54, *Agricultural History,* 1963-65.

WORK IN PROGRESS: Research on the history of Milledgeville, Ga.

AVOCATIONAL INTERESTS: Architecture and historical buildings (used hand-made brick from historical structures to build his own eight-room house in plantation classical style).

*   *   *

BONNER, Thomas N(eville) 1923-

PERSONAL: Born May 28, 1923, in Rochester, N.Y.; son of John Neville and Mary (McGowan) Bonner; married Joan Compton, October 12, 1947; children: Phillip, Diana. *Education:* University of Rochester, B.A., 1947, M.A., 1948; Northwestern University, Ph.D., 1952. *Politics:* Democrat. *Religion:* Unitarian. *Home:* 821 Dunore Dr., Cincinnati, Ohio 45220.

CAREER: William Woods College, Fulton, Mo., academic dean. 1951-54; University of Mainz, Mainz, Germany, Fulbright lecturer in American civilization, 1954-55; Municipal University of Omaha, Omaha, Neb., professor of history and head of social science department, 1955-62; U.S. Congress, Washington. D.C., legislative assistant to Senator McGovern, 1962-63; University of Cincinnati. Cincinnati, Ohio, head of history department, 1963-68, provost and vice president, 1967—. Salzburg Seminar in American Studies, lecturer, 1955. *Military service:* U.S. Army, Signal Intelligence in European theater, 1943-46. *Member:* American Historical Association, Royal Historical Society, Mississippi Valley Historical Association, American Association of University Professors (president, Omaha branch, 1957-59, Cincinnati branch, 1965-66), English-Speaking Union (president, Omaha branch, 1957-58), Veterans of Foreign Wars, Fraternal Order of Eagles, Phi Beta Kappa, Phi Alpha Theta, Pi Gamma Mu. *Awards, honors:* Grant, Fund for the Advancement of Education, 1957-58; Guggenheim fellow, 1959-60, 1964-65.

WRITINGS: Medicine in Chicago, 1850-1950: A Chapter in the Social and Scientific Development of a City, American Historical Research Center, 1957; *The Kansas Doctor: A Century of Pioneering,* University of Kansas Press, 1959; (translator from the German, and editor) Jacob H. Schiel. *Journey Through the Rocky Mountains and the Humboldt Mountains to the Pacific Ocean,* University of Oklahoma Press, 1959; (with Duane W. Hill and George L. Wilber) *The Contemporary World: The*

Social Sciences in Historical Perspective, Prentice-Hall, 1960; (co-author) *Education: The Challenge Ahead,* Norton, 1962; *American Doctors and German Universities, 1870-1914: A Chapter in International Intellectual Relations,* University of Nebraska Press, 1963; *Our Recent Past: American Civilization in the Twentieth Century,* Prentice-Hall, 1963. Contributor of more than a dozen articles to *Social Studies, Bulletin of the History of Medicine, Historian, Journal of Higher Education,* and other periodicals, and of some fifty book reviews to educational journals.

WORK IN PROGRESS: A history of the American home front during World War II, for Prentice-Hall.

* * *

BONNEY, H(anning) Orrin 1903-

PERSONAL: Born May 14, 1903, in Idaho Springs, Colo.; son of Rufus Choate (a gold mines manager and railroad agent) and Cliftonia (Hanning) Bonney; married Ethel Craik, June 4, 1928 (divorced, 1955); married Lorraine Gagnon (a writer), June 5, 1955; children: (first marriage) Roger. *Education:* University of Colorado, LL.B., 1926, J.D., 1968. *Politics:* Democrat. *Religion:* Presbyterian. *Home:* 625 East 14th, Houston, Tex. 77008; and Kelly, Wyo. 83011. *Office:* 627 East 14th St., Houston, Tex. 77008.

CAREER: Admitted to Texas bar, 1926; assistant county probate judge, Houston, Tex., 1926-30; private practice of law, Houston, Tex., 1930-33; Mathes, Bonney & Clawson (attorneys), Houston, Tex., partner, 1933-51; private practice, Houston, Tex., 1951—. President-director, Sunrise Place Co., Houston, Tex., 1939-52; secretary, Texas Water Wells, Inc., 1943—; director and vice-president, Erwin Realty Co. *Wartime service:* U.S. Army, military analyst in Quartermaster General's Office, 1944-45.

MEMBER: American Alpine Club (central vice-president, 1953-55), Outdoor Writers Association of America, Sierra Club (leader of wilderness studies; chairman of Lone Star chapter, 1967-70; chairman of Gulf Coast regional committee, 1972), Texas Bar Association, Harris County Bar Association, Scribblers Club (president, 1959-60), Junior Chamber of Commerce (Houston), Delta Sigma Phi, Masons. *Awards, honors:* Wyoming Historical Society annual award, 1967, for *Guide to Wyoming Mountain and Wilderness Areas.*

WRITINGS—With wife, Lorraine G. Bonney: *Guide to Wyoming Mountains and Wilderness Areas,* Sage Books, 1960, 3rd revised edition, Swallow Press, 1972; *Bonney's Guide: Jackson's Hole and Grand Teton National Park: The Most Historical Valley in the Rocky Mountains,* privately printed, 1961, reissued as *Bonney's Guide: Grand Teton National Park and Jackson's Hole: The Most Historical Valley in the Rocky Mountains,* 1966; *Field Book: The Wind River Range, Including Bridger, Glacier, and Popo Agie Wilderness Areas, and Wind River Reservation,* Sage Books, 1962, 2nd revised edition, privately printed, 1968; *The Teton Range and Gros Ventre Range: The Complete Guide to All Climbing Routes and Back Country,* Sage Books, 1963, 2nd edition, Swallow Press, 1972; *Field Book: The Absaroka Range, Yellowstone Park, Including North Absaroka, South Absaroka, Stratified, and Teton Wilderness Areas,* Sage Books, 1963, 2nd revised edition, Swallow Press, 1972; *Battle Drums and Geysers: The Life and Journals of Lt. Gustavus Cheyney Doane, Soldier and Explorer of the Yellowstone and Snake River Regions,* Sage Books, 1970; *Field Book: The Big Horn Range,* Swallow Press, 1972. Contributor to newspapers and mountaineering journals.

WORK IN PROGRESS: History of Jackson's Hole; Guide to Big Bend National Park; Early Colorado Mining Days and R.C. Bonney; Beginnings of Teton Climbing; Fort Ellis: Hot Spot in the West; The War Party; Canoe Guide to Texas Rivers.

SIDELIGHTS: Bonney has been a leader of mountain climbing expeditions in the United States, Mexico, Canada, and Europe; he made the first ascents of peaks in the Wind River range of Wyoming in 1939, 1940, and 1941. He is active in conservation in Texas, working especially on trails for hiking and preservation of parts of scenic rivers.

* * *

BONNOR, William (Bowen) 1920-

PERSONAL: Born September 13, 1920, in London, England; son of William George (a government official) and Hilda (Blum) Bonnor; married Jean Stott (now a government official), August 14, 1953; children: Helen, Richard. *Education:* University of London, B.Sc. (first class honors), Ph.D., D.Sc. *Politics:* Conservative. *Religion:* Atheist. *Home:* 64 Hornton St., London W.8, England. *Office:* Queen Elizabeth College, London W.8, England.

CAREER: Physical chemist prior to 1949; University of Liverpool, Liverpool, England, lecturer in mathematics, 199-57; University of London, London, England, reader in mathematics, 1957-61, professor of mathematics, 1962—. *Member:* Royal Astronomical Society (fellow).

WRITINGS: (With H. Bondi, R.A. Lyttleton, and G.J. Whitrow) *Rival Theories of Cosmology,* Oxford University Press, 1960; *The Mystery of the Expending Universe,* Macmillan, 1964; *The Status of General Relativity,* Hodgson, 1969. Contributor to learned journals in astrophysics, relativity, and other branches of physics.

SIDELIGHTS: Bonnor writes to *CA:* "I think that physics is the most important—indeed the only—means we have of finding out the origins and fundamentals of our universe, and this is what interests me most about it. I believe that as science advances religion necessarily recedes, and this is a process I wish to encourage, because I consider that, on the whole, the influence of religion is malign."

* * *

BOOKER, Simeon Saunders 1918-

PERSONAL: Born August 27, 1918, in Baltimore, Md.; son of Simeon Saunders (a Young Men's Christian Association secretary) and Roberta (Waring) Booker; married Thelma Cunningham; children: Theresa, Simeon, Jr., James. *Education:* Virginia Union University, A.B., 1942; Cleveland College, graduate study; Harvard University, Nieman Fellow, 1950-51. *Religion:* Baptist. *Home:* 4405 Campbell Dr., Washington, D.C. 20023. *Office:* Johnson Publishing Co., 1426 G St. N.W., Washington, D.C. 20005.

CAREER: Johnson Publishing Co., Inc., Washington, D.C., chief of Washington bureau.

WRITINGS: Black Man's America, Prentice-Hall, 1964; *Susie King Taylor, Civil War Nurse,* McGraw, 1969.

* * *

BOOTH, John E(rlanger) 1919-

PERSONAL: Born August 23, 1919, in New York, N.Y.; married, wife's name, Janet P.; children: Douglas G. *Education:* Attended Lawrenceville School and Columbia University. *Home:* 4 Ploughman's Bush, Riverdale, N.Y. 11901. *Agent:* Curtis Brown Ltd., 60 East 56th St., New York, N.Y. 10022. *Office:* Twentieth Century Fund, 41 East 70th St., New York, N.Y. 10021.

CAREER: New York Times, New York, N.Y., member of staff of Sunday edition, 1939-49; with U.S. Department of State and U.S. Economic Cooperation Administration, 1949-53; Twentieth Century Fund (endowed foundation for research and education), New York, N.Y. associate director, 1953—. *Member:* Drama Desk, Overseas Press Club, Foreign Press Association.

WRITINGS: (Editor with Lewis Funke) *Actors Talk about Acting: Fourteen Interviews with Stars of the Theatre,* Random House, 1961. Contributor to *New York Times, Harper's, Theatre Arts, Show,* and *Reader's Digest.*

* * *

BORDEN, Morton 1925-

PERSONAL: Born November 23, 1925, in Newark, N.J.; son of Samuel (a dress cutter) and Flora (Pistriech) Borden; married Estelle Schachter, December 24, 1954 (died, 1966); married Penelope A. Torgenrud, January 16, 1970; children: Jess, Sally, Lucy, Kate. *Education:* City University of New York, B.S., 1948; New York University, M.A., 1949; Columbia University, Ph.D., 1953. *Home:* 1018 Monte Dr., Santa Barbara, Calif. 93105. *Office:* University of California, Santa Barbara, Calif. 93106.

CAREER: Ohio State University, Columbus, instructor in history, 1953-57; Montana State University, Missoula, assistant professor history, 1957-58, associate professor, 1958-64, professor of history, 1964-65; University of California, Santa Barbara, professor of history, 1965—. *Military service:* U.S. Army Air Forces, 1944-46. *Member:* American Historical Association.

WRITINGS: The Federalism of James A. Bayard, Columbia University Press, 1954; (editor) *America's Ten Greatest Presidents,* Rand McNally, 1961, 2nd edition published as *America's Eleven Greatest Presidents,* 1971; (editor and author of introduction) *The Antifederalist Papers,* Michigan State University Press, 1965; *Parties and Politics in the Early Republic, 1789-1815,* Crowell, 1967; (editor) *George Washington,* Prentice-Hall, 1969; (with others) *The American Profile,* Heath, 1970; (editor with Penn Borden) *The American Tory,* Prentice-Hall, 1972; (editor) *Voices of the American Past: Readings in American History,* Heath, 1972.

* * *

BORER, Mary (Irene) Cathcart 1906-

PERSONAL: Born February 3, 1906, in London, England; daughter of Archibald James (a hospital secretary) and Florence Mary (Edmonds) Borer; married Oliver Myers (an archaeologist; divorced). *Education:* University College, University of London, B.Sc., 1928. *Politics:* Conservative. *Religion:* Church of England. *Home:* Robin Hill, Station Rd., Tring, Herts, England. *Agent:* Donald Coperman, Ltd., 157 Temple Chambers, Temple Ave., London E.C. 4, England.

CAREER: Wellcome Historical Medical Museum, London, England, senior research assistant, ethnological department, 1928-35; Egypt Exploration Society's archaeological expedition to Luxor, Egypt, artist and registrar, 1935-38; British National Films, London, England, scenario writer, 1939-42; Gaumont-British Instructional Films, London, England, scenario writer of propaganda films for British Council and Ministry of Information, 1942-44; Rank Organization, London, England, script editor and writer, children's film department, 1944-51; full-time, free-lance script writer for television and children's films, and author of books, 1951—.

WRITINGS—Books for children: Kilango, Pitman, 1936; *Taha, the Egyptian,* Pitman, 1937; *The Highcroft Mystery,* Warne. 1938: *The House with the Blue Door,* Pitman, 1939; *The Valley of the White Lake,* Warne, 1947; *Bush Christmas,* Pitman, 1948; *The First Term at Northwood,* Pitman, 1948; *Two Thousand Years Ago,* Pitman, 1948; *The Little Ballerina,* Pitman, 1949; *The Secret Tunnel,* Pitman, 1950; *Distant Hills,* Pitman, 1951; *The Last Load,* Pitman, 1951; *Trapped by the Terror,* Pitman, 1951; *The Mysterious Poacher,* Pitman, 1951; *The Lone Climber,* Pitman, 1951; *The Mystery of the Snakeskin Belt,* Pitman, 1951; *The Birthday Present,* Harrap, 1954; *The Baobab Tree,* Warne, 1955; *The Dog and the Diamonds,* Nelson, 1956; *The Dragons Remembered,* Brockhampton Press, 1956; *The Quest of the Golden Eagle,* Nelson, 1957; *Sophie and the Countess,* Watts, 1960; *Famous Rogues,* Longmans, Green, 1966.

Books for teen-agers: *People Like Us: A Social History of Britain,* M. Joseph, 1960; *Citizenship: Its Rights and Responsibilities,* International Publications Service, 1962; *The City of London: Its History, Institutions and Commercial Activities,* Pitman, 1962; *Mankind in the Making: An Introduction to European Prehistory,* Warne, 1962; *Women Who Made History,* Warne, 1963; *People of Medieval England,* International Publications Service, 1966; *People of Tudor England,* International Publications Service, 1966; *People of Stuart England,* International Publications Service, 1968; *England's Markets: The Story of Britain's Main Channels of Trade,* Abelard, 1968; *People of Georgian England,* International Publications Service, 1969; *People of Victorian and Edwardian England,* Macdonald & Co., 1969; *What Became of the Mamelukes?,* Wheaton, 1969; *Agincourt,* Lutterworth, 1970; *The Boer War,* Lutterworth, 1971; *The First World War,* Macmillan, 1971; *Liverpool,* Longmans, Green, 1971.

For general reading: *Africa: A Short History of the Peoples of Africa,* Museum Press, 1963, Soccer, 1964; *Covent Garden,* Abelard, 1967; *Britain—Twentieth Century: The Story of Social Conditions,* Warne, 1967; *A Visitor's Guide to Britain,* Fontana, 1971.

Stage plays: (With Arnold Ridley) *Tabitha* (first produced in London, 1956), Samuel French, 1956; (with Ridley) "Shadows of the Sands," produced in Northhampton, 1956; *Sophie and the Countess* (juvenile), Cassell, 1968; *The Man in the Green Cloak* (juvenile), Cassell, 1968. Television plays: "The Poachers," 1956; "The Secret of the Nubian Tomb," 1961. Also writer of a television serial for children, play adaptations, educational and Sunday break programs for commercial television and for British Broadcasting Corp. radio.

WORK IN PROGRESS: Royal Kensington, to be published by Abelard; *Chelsea: The Growth of a Village,* for Frewin; and a book on hotels for Lutterworth.

SIDELIGHTS: Miss Borer told *CA:* "The idea for my first children's book, *Kilango,* about a Kikuyu boy in East Africa, came to me when I was working amongst the ethnographical material in the Wellcome Museum. It was successful and is, in fact, still in print and selling, twenty-seven years later. When I went to Egypt it was not difficult to follow it up with two more books of adventure in and around Luxor."

Regarding the background for her present vocation, Miss Borer comments: "Towards the end of the war, conditions for children in London were at their worst. Many who had been evacuated to the country, on the outbreak of hostilities, had come back. Fathers were away, mothers working; schools were disorganized and under-staffed and there was not nearly enough discipline. The Odean and Gaumont Saturday morning cinema clubs were re-opened and managers complained that the children were badly in need of some form of moral training. The comptroller of the Odean group suggested that a one-reeler film be made, showing that stealing by finding was as bad as any other kind of stealing, and I was asked to write the script. When it was shown, the effect was astonishing. Managers reported that their cinemas had come to look like lost property offices with all the things children found and brought to them. It was the effect of this film, which today would seem unbelievably corny, which made me realize how we have wasted and misused the enormous potential of the screen. I have for long advocated the harmfulness of indoctrinating children (or adults either, for that matter) with scenes of crime and violence. Much has been said and written about the harmful effects of television on morals and outlook, but very little about the *good* it could do. It obviously *does* have an effect, so why not a good one instead of a bad one?"

BIOGRAPHICAL/CRITICAL SOURCES: Times Literary Supplement, October 16, 1969; *Library Journal,* March 15, 1971.

* * *

BORNEMAN, Ernest 1915-
  (Cameron McCabe)

PERSONAL: Born April 12, 1915, in Berlin, Germany; son of Curt and Hertha (Blochert) Borneman; married Eva Geisel (now in public relations); children: Stephen. *Education:* Studied at University of Berlin, 1931-33, School of Oriental and African Studies, University of London, 1933-35, Emmanuel College, Cambridge University, 1935-37. *Politics:* Liberal. *Home:* A 4612, Scharten, Austria.

CAREER: National Film Board of Canada, Ottawa, Ontario, Canada, head of foreign language production, 1941-45, head of international distribution, 1945-47; UNESCO, Paris, France, head of film division, 1947-49; Granada Television Network, London and Manchester, England, head of script department, 1955-58; British Film Institute, London, England, head of programming, 1959-60; Freies Fernsehen, Frankfurt, Germany, controller of programs and productions, 1960-62; head of literary agency, Ebohouse, 1963-72. Radio work includes some sixty talks on jazz and folk music of Caribbean, West Africa, and South America (using own recordings), in England, Germany, Denmark; panelist on British Broadcasting Corp. shows, "Musician Meets Critic," "Jazz for Moderns," and "Jazz Forum." Member of board of directors of London firms of Half Moon Productions Ltd., Screen Playwrights Ltd., Himalaya Films Ltd., Peter Cheyney Ltd. *Member:* Latin American Music Society (chairman, 1955—), Association of Cinema and Television Technicians, Screen Writers' Association, Society for Ethnomusicology.

WRITINGS: (Under pseudonym Cameron McCabe) *The Face on the Cutting Room Floor,* Gollancz, 1937; *A Love Story,* Jarrolds, 1941; *A Critic Looks at Jazz* (originally published as a serial, "An Anthropologist Looks at Jazz" in *Record Changer*), Jazz Music Books, 1946; *Tremolo,* Harper, 1948; *Tomorrow is Now: The Adventures of Welfare Willy in Search of a Soul,* Neville Spearman, 1959; *Something Wrong,* Four Square, 1961; *The Compromisers,* Deutsch, 1962; *The Man Who Loved Women: A Landscape with Nudes,* Coward, 1968.

Writings in German: *Lexikon der Liebe,* two volumes, List, 1968; *Sex im Volksmund,* Rowohlt, 1971; *Das Sexualverhalten der Alten Griechen,* Kindler, 1972; *Das Sexualverhalten der Alten Roemer,* Kinder, 1972.

Stage plays: "The Girl on the Highway," and "The Windows of Heaven."

Motion pictures and feature-length documentaries: "Ulysses," 1949; (with Guy Elmes) "The Flanagan Boy," 1950; (with Elmes) "Bang! You're Dead," 1954; "Face the Music" (musical), 1954; "Double Jeopardy," produced by Republic, 1956; (with Ranveer Singh) "The

Long Duel," 1959. Contributor, in one capacity or another, to about two hundred other features, documentaries, and shorts filmed in Canada, United States, and Europe.

Television plays and films: "Tremolo," 1950; "Four O'Clock in the Morning Blues," 1954; scripts in "Orient Express," "Sailor of Fortune," "Fabian of Scotland Yard," "Aggie," and "Slim Callaghan" series; (translator and adapter) "Hedda Gabler," 1957; (adapter from radio play) "Sorry Wrong Number," 1957; (adapter) "Break-Up," 1957; (adapter) "Don't Destroy Me," 1957; (adapter) "The Lie," 1957; (with John Hopkins) "After the Party," 1957. Contributor, in one capacity or another, to about seventy other television and radio shows.

Columnist, "Tropicana" in *Melody Maker,* "The Latin Touch" in *Record Review;* other columns in *Variety, Down Beat, Record Changer, Jazz Record;* jazz critic and columnist, *Sunday Dispatch,* 1957-58. Contributor of more than one thousand articles to scientific and popular music press; contributor of two hundred other articles and short stories to magazines, screen and television periodicals, including *Reader's Digest, Harper's Bazaar, Holiday, Esquire, Playboy,* and *Times Literary Supplement.*

WORK IN PROGRESS: History of American Negro music.

SIDELIGHTS: Borneman worked his way through school playing in a jazz band, studied comparative musicology, and has collected folk music and jazz on four continents. *Avocational interests:* Painting, conversation, "the other sex."

BIOGRAPHICAL/CRITICAL SOURCES: Library Journal, June 1, 1968; *New York Times Book Review,* June 9, 1968.

* * *

BOTSFORD, Keith 1928-

PERSONAL: Born March 29, 1928, in Brussels, Belgium; son of Willard Hudson and Carolina (Romani) Botsford; married Ann Winchester (a painter), December, 1949; children: Aubrey, Clarissa, Giannardrea, Joshua, Flora. *Education:* Attended Yale University, 1944-46, A.M., 1950; State University of Iowa, A.B., 1949.

CAREER: Taught Romance languages and comparative literature for eleven years at State University of Iowa, Yale University, Bard College, and University of Puerto Rico; former assistant producer, Shakespeare Festival, Stratford, Conn.; former assistant editor, CBS-TV's "Seven Lively Arts"; traveled in Latin America on three-year study-grant, 1962-65, was Latin-American correspondent during this time for *Encounter,* London, *New Leader,* New York, and other periodicals; University of Texas, Austin, executive director of National Translation Center, 1966.

WRITINGS: The Master Race, Wingate, 1955; *The Eighth-Best Dressed Man in the World,* Harcourt, 1958; *Benvenuto,* Hutchinson, 1960; *The March Man,* Viking, 1964; *Dominguen: The Passionale of Spain's Greatest Bullfighter,* Quadrangle, 1972; (translator from the French) Jules Michelet, *History of the French Revolution,* nine volumes, Livingston, 1972. Editor, *Yale Poetry Review,* 1944-47, *Poetry, New York,* 1948-51, *Noble Savage* (with Saul Bellow), 1958-61, *Locations* (with Bellow, Harold Rosenberg, and Thomas B. Hess), 1970—. Contributor to *Encounter, Commentary, New Leader, Western Review, Saturday Review, New York Times Magazine, Texas Quarterly, Quarterly Review of Literature,* and other publications.

WORK IN PROGRESS: Movements I, essays on North and South America, for Viking; general editor, "XXth Century Thought," a series of volumes containing selections from the political and social thought of representative twentieth-century thinkers; editor, with Octavio Paz, Jorge Luis Borges, Francisco Giner de los Rios, Robert Lowell, and Alastair Reid, of anthology of twentieth-century poetry in Latin America; *Ozanne,* a novel for Viking.

BIOGRAPHICAL/CRITICAL SOURCES: New York Times Book Review, April 26, 1964; *Commonweal,* July 3, 1964; *Virginia Quarterly Review,* summer, 1964.†

* * *

BOTTOMORE, (Thomas) B(urton) 1920-

PERSONAL: Born April 8, 1920, in Nottingham, England; son of Thomas Joseph (a civil servant) and Margaret (Bacon) Bottomore; married Mary Greasley, January 30, 1953; children: Katherine, Stephen, Eleanor. *Education:* University of London, B.Sc., 1943, M.Sc., 1949. *Politics:* Socialist. *Religion:* Humanist. *Home:* Cherry Tree Cottage, East End Lane, Ditchling, Sussex, England. *Office:* University of Sussex, Brighton, Sussex, England.

CAREER: London School of Economics, University of London, London, England, reader in sociology, 1952-64; Simon Fraser University, Vancouver, Canada, professor of sociology and head of department of political science, sociology and anthropology, 1965-67; University of Sussex, Brighton, England, professor of sociology, 1968—. *Military service:* British Army, Sherwood Foresters, 1943-47; staff captain at General Headquarters, India, 1945-46. *Member:* International Sociological Association (executive secretary, 1953-59; vice-president, 1970), British Sociological Association (president, 1969-71), Mind Association, Royal Institute of Philosophy, Aristotelian Society. *Awards, honors:* Rockefeller Foundation fellow at University of Paris, 1951-52.

WRITINGS: Classes in Modern Society, Ampersand, 1955, 2nd edition, Allen & Unwin, 1966, Pantheon, 1966; (translator of texts, and editor, with Maximilien Rubel) *Karl Marx: Selected Writings in Sociology and Social Philosophy,* Watts, 1956; (translator with wife, Mary Bottomore) Raymond Claude Ferdinand Aron, *German Sociology,* Heinemann, 1957; *Sociology: A Guide to Problems and Literature,* Allen & Unwin, 1962, Prentice-Hall, 1963, 2nd edition, Pantheon, 1971; (editor and translator) *Karl Marx: Early Writings,* Watts, 1963, McGraw, 1964; *Elites and Society,* Watts, 1964, Basic Books, 1965; *Social Criticism in North America* (series of radio talks first broadcast over CBC program, "Ideas," March-May, 1966), Canadian Broadcasting Corp., 1966, revised and enlarged edition published as *Critics of Society: Radical Thought in North America,* Allen & Unwin, 1967, Pantheon, 1968, new edition with additional chapter, Allen & Unwin, 1969. Contributor to *Encyclopaedia Britannica, Encyclopaedia Universalis, New York Review of Books,* and to sociological and philosophical journals in Britain, France, Italy, Yugoslavia, and other countries. Editor, *Current Sociology,* 1953-62; English editor, *European Journal of Sociology,* 1960—.

WORK IN PROGRESS: Sociology as Social Criticism, for Allen & Unwin; *Karl Marx,* for the "Makers of Modern Social Science" series published by Prentice-Hall; and *Political Sociology,* for Hutchinson's University Library.

SIDELIGHTS: According to Staughton Lynd of *Commonweal,* "T.B. Bottomore is a British sociologist known to many American readers through his selections from the early writings of Karl Marx. . . . [His] newest book, *Critics of Society* . . . surveys the course of American radical thought in the twentieth century, from Progressive pragmatism (Beard, Dewey and their colleagues) through the literary radicalism of the 1930's (Dos Passos, for instance) to Mills, Riesman and the New Left." Christo-

pher Lasch notes that "Bottomore's judgments, delivered matter-of-factly and without the stridency so often associated with books about American radicalism, seem consistently sound. None of them is novel or startling in itself. Nor do they have the force of arguments richly elaborated and supported by a mass of historical data . . . . In any case the material covered by Bottomore is thoroughly familiar. The value of his book is that the point of view is not. It is a point of view, however, to which Americans need very badly to be exposed. For one thing, [Bottomore's residence in Canada] . . . gives him a healthy distance from the subject; more important, it makes him aware, as many Americans are not, of the degree to which political ideas in the New World have necessarily derived from Europe, specifically from the classic social theorists of the nineteenth century."

AVOCATIONAL INTERESTS: Literature, especially French and English of the nineteenth and twentieth centuries; current politics, riding, swimming, walking.

* * *

BOULLE, Pierre (Francois Marie-Louis) 1912-

PERSONAL: Born February 20, 1912, in Avignon, France; son of Eugene and Therese (Seguin) Boulle. *Education:* Ecole superieure d'Electricite, license es sciences, engineering diploma. *Religion:* Catholic. *Home:* 18 rue Duret, Paris 16, France.

CAREER: Engineer in France, 1933-35; rubber planter in Malaya, 1936-48; full-time writer, 1949—. *Military service:* French Army, World War II; sent to Malaya, 1941, joined Free French forces there and became secret agent, using name Peter John Rule, and posing as a Mauritius-born Englishman; fought in Burma, China, and Indochina; taken prisoner and subsequently escaped in 1944; returned to France; awarded French Legion d'Honneur, Croix de Guerre, Medaille de la Resistance. *Awards, honors:* Prix Sainte-Beuve, 1952, for *Le Pont de la riviere Kwai;* Grand Prix de la Nouvelle, 1953, for *Contes de l'absurde.*

WRITINGS: William Conrad (novel), Julliard, 1950, translation by Xan Fielding published as *Not the Glory,* Vanguard, 1955 (published in England as *William Conrad,* Secker & Warburg, 1955, published as *Spy Converted,* Collins, 1960); *Le Sacrilege malais,* Julliard, 1951, translation by Fielding published as *S.O.P.H.I.A.,* Vanguard, 1959 (published in England as *Sacrilege in Malaya,* Secker & Warburg, 1959): *Le pont de la riviere Kwai* (novel), Julliard, 1952, translation by Fielding published as *The Bridge Over the River Kwai,* Vanguard, 1954 (published in England as *The Bridge On the River Kwai,* Secker & Warburg, 1954, French language edition with foreword by Boulle, edited by Georges Joyaux, Scribner, 1963; *Contes de l'absurde* (stories; contains "L'Hallucination," "Une Nuit interminable," "Le Poids d'un sonnet," "Le Regne des sages," "Le Parfait robot"), Julliard, 1953, translation by Fielding and Elisabeth Abbott published as *Time Out of Mind, and Other Stories,* Vanguard, 1966; *La Face* (novel), Julliard, 1953, translation by Fielding published as *Face of a Hero,* Vanguard, 1956 (published in England as *Saving Face,* Secker & Warburg, 1956); *Le Cas du procureur Berthier* (story), Les Oeuvres Libres, 1953; *Le Poids d'un sonnet,* Les Oeuvres Libres, 1953; *Le Proces chinois* (novel), Les Oeuvres Libres, 1954; *Le Bourreau* (novel), Julliard, 1954, translation by Fielding published as *The Executioner,* Vanguard, 1961 (published in England as *The Chinese Executioner,* Secker & Warburg, 1962); *L'Epreuve des hommes blancs* (novel), Julliard, 1955, translation by Fielding published as *Test,* Vanguard, 1957 (published in England as *White Man's Test,* Secker & Warburg, 1957); *E=MC²* (published with *Contes de l'absurde* as *Contes* de l'absurde [suivi de] E=MC²), Julliard, 1957; *Les Voies de salut* (novel), Julliard, 1958, translation by Richard Howard published as *The Other Side of the Coin,* Vanguard, 1968; "The Bridge on the River Kwai" (screenplay based on his own novel; produced by Horizon Pictures, 1958); *Walt Disney's Siam* (screenplay), Nouvelles Editions (Lausanne), 1958; *Un Metier de Seigneur* (novel), Julliard, 1960, translation by Fielding published as *A Noble Profession,* Vanguard, 1960, published in England as *For a Noble Cause* Secker & Warburg, 1961; *William Conrad* (play), Les Oeuvres Libres, 1962; *La Planete des singes* (novel), Julliard, 1963, translation by Fielding published as *Planet of the Apes,* Vanguard, 1963 (published in England as *Monkey Planet,* Secker & Warburg, 1964); *Le Jardin de Kanashima,* Julliard, 1964, translation published as *Garden on the Moon,* Vanguard, 1965; *Histoires charitables* (short stories; contains "Le Saint enigmatique," "L'Homme qui ramassait les epingles," "Histoire du bon petit ecrivain," "I'Arme diabolique," "Le Compte a rebours," "L'Homme qui haisait les machines"), Julliard, 1964; *Aux Sources de la riviere Kwai,* Julliard, 1966, translation by Fielding published as *My Own River Kwai,* Vanguard, 1967 (published in England as *The Source of the River Kwai,* Secker & Warburg, 1967); *Le Photographe* (novel), Julliard, 1967, translation by Fielding published as *The Photographer,* Vanguard, 1968 (published in England as *An Impartial Eye,* Secker & Warburg, 1968); *L'Etrange Croisade de l'empereur Frederic II,* Flammarion, 1968; *Quia absurdum (sur la terre comme au ciel),* Julliard, 1970, translation by Elizabeth Abbott published as *Because It Is Absurd (on Earth as in Heaven),* Vanguard, 1971; *Les Jeux de l'esprit* (novel), Julliard, 1971; *Ears of the Jungle* (novel), translated by Michael Dobry and Linda Cole, Vanguard, 1972.

SIDELIGHTS: Boulle's life as a rubber planter in Malaysia and his war experiences have had a definite effect on his writing. In *My Own River Kwai* he recounts his experiences as a secret agent during the war. He calls these experiences "eventful, often absurd adventures." During this time he learned much about several different types of Asians, many of whom have provided him with material for his novels and stories. Ladislas Farago calls *My Own River Kwai* "a sensibly and sensitively, modestly and charmingly written account" of his wartime experiences. Boulle is known for what Henri Peyre calls "absorbing stories of adventure and love, with some philosophical implications."

Boulle became well-known with *The Bridge Over the River Kwai,* in which, according to Peyre, the "portrayal of the muddle-headed officer was especially well-drawn," Praised not only for this main character, Boulle was also praised for his creation of "a situation that is simultaneously droll, pathetic, and appalling," C.J. Rolo stated. Boulle has been compared to Conrad and Kipling, and in this book such resemblances are evident.

William Conrad, his first novel, was also very well-received. Taliaferro Boatwright commented: "It is a penetrating, ironic, but deeply sympathetic study of the British national character." In fact, most of Boulle's novels have been about such "English" characters. *S.O.P.H.I.A.* is about "a young engineer's experiences in an exotic, faintly hostile microcosm," John Lord writes "[The book] is actually a highly artful exposition of the character of a corporation in terms of the young man's initial infatuation with it, growing knowledge of its caprices, and final, grudgingly respectful disillusionments, as he comes to know himself better." Although the young engineer in this book is French, Boulle's concerns are really "English," encompassing the changes in the rubber industry in Malaya from management by the pioneers to the takeover by large companies, which he does not see as necessarily good.

Boulle is known to have an ironic sense of humor, which comes through in his books. This humor is chiefly philosophical, and is considered well-illustrated in *The Chinese Executioner.* Max Cosman describes Boulle's concern: "In a world where evil is the norm, a good man is a criminal when he does good. [The book] is, however, much more serious than that. Indeed, it raises an issue as ancient as history, no less than that of mankind's terrifying inability to recognize its true benefactors while they are alive." Isabel Quigley calls the book "a quirky and at times near-brilliant little piece of satire in the form of an everlasting dialogue about death, life, and Chinamen."

In some of his more recent books Boulle has been using science fiction in an allegorical manner, such as in *Planet of the Apes,* the book upon which the popular film is based. A *Time* reviewer says: "The meaning of Boulle's cheerful parable is not a mocking warning but an observation: human dignity is both precarious and precious; too often it is based on pride in achievements that can be matched by clever mimics of what has been done before. Like the Red Queen, Western man has to keep running if he is to keep his place as the lord of creation." *Garden on the Moon* is also a science fiction novel of sorts, and is considered more realistic, since it is about the moon race. P.J. Henniker-Heaton comments: "Anything that Pierre Boulle writes has several dimensions of depth. This book is a commentary on nationalism's total irrelevance in an interplanetary age—at least its almost total irrelevance."

Planet of the Apes, adapted by Rod Serling and Michael Wilson, was filmed by 20th Century Fox, 1968; two additional films, "Beneath the Planet of the Apes," originally titled "Planet of the Apes Revisited," 1970, and "Escape from the Planet of the Apes," 1971, were releasd by 20th Century Fox. *Garden on the Moon* has been purchased for filming.

BIOGRAPHICAL/CRITICAL SOURCES: Spectator, April 9, 1954, December 11, 1959; *New Statesman & Nation,* April 10, 1954; *Chicago Sunday Tribune,* October 3, 1954, September 25, 1955; *Atlantic,* November, 1954, November, 1955; *New York Herald Tribune Book Review,* September 25, 1955, November 17, 1957, October 26, 1958, January 10, 1960; *Saturday Review,* October 8, 1955, January 7, 1960, December 3, 1960, November 18, 1967, December 7, 1968; *Times Literary Supplement,* October 12, 1956, February 9, 1962, October 21, 1965, June 8, 1967; *Manchester Guardian,* October 16, 1956; *New Yorker,* October 20, 1956, November 23, 1968; *New York Times Book Review,* October 23, 1960, March 7, 1965, October 15, 1967; *Booklist,* December 15, 1961; *Guardian,* February 2, 1962; *Time,* November 8, 1963; *Christian Science Monitor,* March 4, 1965, December 9, 1967; Henri Peyre, *French Novelists of Today,* Oxford University Press, 1967; *L'Express,* April 3-9, 1967; *Harper's,* December, 1967; *National Review,* November 19, 1968; *Critic,* April, 1969; *New York Times,* November 30, 1972.†

*   *   *

BOURKE, Vernon J(oseph) 1907-

PERSONAL: Born February 17, 1907, in North Bay, Ontario, Canada; became U.S. citizen in 1943; son of Joseph Walter (a prison warden) and Therese (Trudeau) Bourke; married Janet Leahy (now a social worker), June 12, 1947; children: Jane (Mrs. Ray Luckhaupt), Thomas, Nancy (Mrs. Vernal Beckmann). *Education:* St. Michael's College, University of Toronto, B.A., 1928; Institute of Mediaeval Studies, University of Toronto, M.A., 1929, Ph.D., 1937. *Religion:* Catholic. *Office:* St. Louis University, St. Louis, Mo. 63103.

CAREER: St. Michael's College, University of Toronto, Toronto, Ontario, lecturer in philosophy, 1928-31;

St. Louis University, St. Louis, Mo., 1931—, started as instructor, now professor of philosophy. Annual Aquinas Lecturer at some twenty-five centers in United States and Canada. Advisory editor, Musurgia Publishing Co., 1947-50, Macmillan Co., 1951—. *Member:* World Union of Catholic Philosophical Societies (president, 1963—), Mediaeval Academy of America, American Philosophical Association, American Catholic Philosophical Association (president, 1949'; representative at International Congress of Philosophy at Brussels, 1953, Venice, 1958, Mexico City, 1963), American Association of University Professors, Societe Philosophique de Louvain. *Awards, honors:* Aquinas Medal, 1963.

WRITINGS: Augustine's Quest of Wisdom: Life and Philosophy of the Bishop of Hippo, Bruce, 1945; *Thomistic Bibliography, 1920-1940,* St. Louis University Press, 1945; *St. Thomas and the Greek Moralists* (Aquinas Lecture, spring, 1947), Marquette University Press, 1947; (editor) Thomas Aquinas, *Opera omnia,* Musurgia, 1948-50; *Ethics: A Textbook in Moral Philosophy,* Macmillan, 1951, new edition, 1966; (translator) *Confessions of St. Augustine,* Catholic University of America Press, 1953; *St. Thomas on the Truth of the Catholic Faith,* Book III, Doubleday, 1956; *The Pocket Aquinas,* Washington Square, 1960; *Natural Law, Thomism—and Professor Nielsen* (originally published in *Natural Law Forum,* Volume 5, 1960), Notre Dame Law School, 1961; *Will in Western Thought: An Historical–Critical Survey,* Sheed, 1964; *Augustine's View of Reality*, Villanova University Press, 1964; (editor and translator) *The Essential Augustine,* Mentor Books, 1964; *Aquinas' Search for Wisdom,* Bruce, 1965; *Ethics,* Macmillan, 1966; *Ethics in Crisis,* Bruce, 1966; (contributor) J.E. Biechler, editor, *Law for Liberty,* Helicon, 1967; (contributor) *Melanges a la memoire de Charles De Koninck,* Presses de l'Universite Laval, 1968; *History of Ethics,* Doubleday, Volume I: *Graeco–Roman to Early Modern Ethics,* 1968, Volume II: *Modern and Contemporary Times,* 1968; (contributor) R.Z. Apostol, editor, *Human Values in a Secular World,* Humanities, 1970.

Contributor of articles on medieval philosophy and ethics to *Collier's Encyclopedia, Runes' Dictionary of Philosophy, New Catholic Encyclopedia, Encyclopedia of Philosophy,* and *Dictionary of Ethics.*

BIOGRAPHICAL/CRITICAL SOURCES: Commonweal, April 30, 1965, November 8, 1968; *Choice,* November, 1968.

*   *   *

BOURNE, Charles P.   1931-

PERSONAL: Born September 2, 1931, in San Francisco, Calif.; son of Frank Percy and Edith (Dunlap) Bourne; married Elizabeth Scheidtmann, August 15, 1953; children: Glen Wade, Holly Ann. *Education:* University of California, Berkeley, B.S. in E.E., 1957; Stanford University, M.S. in I.E., 1962. *Office:* Charles Bourne and Associates, Menlo Park, Calif.

CAREER: Stanford Research Institute, Menlo Park, Calif., research engineer, 1957-66; Information General Corp., Palo Alto, Calif., 1966-70; head of Charles Bourne and Associates, Menlo Park, Calif., 1970—. University of California School of Librarianship, lecturer, 1962-65. *Military service:* U.S. Marine Corps, 1950-51. *Member:* American Society for Information Science (past president), Institute of Electrical and Electronic Engineers, Association for Computing Machinery. *Awards, honors:* Annual award of merit, American Documentation Institute, 1965.

WRITINGS: A Bibliography on the Mechanization of Information Retrieval, Stanford Research Institute, 1958, annual supplements, 1959-62; (with Donald F. Ford) *The Historical Development, and Predicted State-of-the-Art of the General-Purpose Digital Computer,* Stanford Research Institute, c.1960; (contributor) *Information Systems Workshop: The Designer's Responsibility and His Methodology,* Spartan Books, 1962; (with Ford, G.D. Peterson, and B. Lefkowitz) *Requirements, Criteria, and Measures of Performance of Information Storage and Retrieval Systems,* Stanford Research Institute, 1962; *Research on Computer Augmented Information Management* (technical documentary report), Office of Technical Services, U.S. Department of Commerce, 1963; *Methods of Information Handling,* Wiley, 1963; (with Glen Densmore) *A Cost Analysis and Utilization Study of the Stanford University Library System,* Stanford University, 1965. Contributor to *American Documentation, Information and Control,* and to other technical journals and proceedings. Member of editorial or advisory boards for a book series on information sciences, published by Wiley, and for Chemical Abstracts Service, the *Encyclopedia for Library and Information Sciences, Documentation Abstracts,* and the *Annual Review of Information Science and Technology.*

*   *   *

BOWEN, Robert O.   1920-

PERSONAL: Born May 7, 1920, in Bridgeport, Conn.; son of Charles A. (a builder) and Irene (Johnson) Bowen; married second wife, Naomi L. Misumi, August 31, 1968. *Education:* Junior College of Connecticut, student, 1945-46; University of Alabama, B.A., 1948, M.A., 1950; University College of North Wales, postgraduate study, 1952-53. *Politics:* Conservative. *Religion:* Church of Jesus Christ of Latter-Day Saints. *Agent:* Sterling Lord Agency, 660 Madison Ave., New York, N.Y. 10021. *Office:* North Employment Agency, 440 West 5th Ave., Anchorage, Alaska 99501.

CAREER: U.S. Navy, 1937-45, became machinist's mate; writer, 1950—, and sometime professional mountain climber, carpenter, stevedore, teacher of creative writing courses, and lecturer at writers' workshops; Colonial Press, Northport, Ala., editor, 1960—. *Member:* Authors Guild, Modern Language Association of America, Phi Beta Kappa, Montana Institute of the Arts, Alaska Press Club, Mountaineering Club of Alaska.

*WRITINGS—*Fiction: *The Weight of the Cross,* Knopf, 1951; *Bamboo,* Knopf, 1953; *Sidestreet,* Knopf, 1954; *Marlow the Master and other Stories,* Colonial Press, 1963.

Nonfiction: (Editor) *Practical Prose Studies: A Critical Anthology of Contemporary American Prose Readings for the College Freshman,* Knopf, 1956; *The New Professors* (essays), Holt, 1960; *The Truth About Communism,* Colonial Press, 1962; *Marlow the Master and Other Stories,* Colonial Press, c.1963; *The College Style Manual,* Colonial Press, 1963; (editor with Robert A. Charles) *Alaska Literary Directory,* Alaska Methodist University, 1964; *An Alaskan Dictionary,* Nooshnik Press, 1965.

Librettist, "The Christmas Child," performed by Helena (Mont.) Civic Symphony, 1960. Stories anthologized in *Best American Short Stories.* Contributor of stories, essays, reviews, and poems to *Holiday, National Review, Contact, Saturday Review,* other periodicals and newspapers

*   *   *

BOWEN-JUDD, Sara (Hutton)   1922-
(Sara Woods)

PERSONAL: Born March 7, 1922, in Bradford, Yorkshire, England; daughter of Francis Burton and Sara Roberta (Woods) Hutton; married Anthony George Bowen-Judd (an electronics engineer), April 25, 1946.

Education: Attended Convent of Sacred Heart, Filey, Yorkshire, England. *Religion:* Roman Catholic. *Home:* Maplewood Cottage, Francklyn St., Halifax, Nova Scotia, Canada.

CAREER: Worked in a bank and as a solicitor's clerk in London, England, during World War II; pig breeder, 1948-54; Rotol Ltd., Gloucester, England, assistant to company secretary, 1954-58; St. Mary's University, Halifax, Nova Scotia, Canada, registrar, 1958-64. *Member:* Society of Authors (England), Authors League of America, Mystery Writers of America, Crime Writers Association (England).

WRITINGS—Crime novels under pseudonym Sara Woods: *Malice Domestic,* Collins, 1962; *Bloody Instructions,* Harper, 1962; *The Third Encounter,* Harper 1963 (published in England as *The Taste of Fears,* Collins, 1963); *Error of the Moon,* Collins, 1963; *Trusted Like the Fox,* Collins, 1964, Harper, 1965; *This Little Measure,* Collins, 1964; *The Windy Side of the Law,* Harper, 1965; *Though I Know She Lies,* Collins, 1965, Holt, 1972; *Enter Certain Murderers,* Harper, 1966; *Let's Choose Executors,* Collins, 1966, Harper, 1967; *And Shame the Devil,* Collins, 1967, Holt, 1972; *The Case Is Altered,* Harper, 1967; *Past Praying For,* Harper, 1968; *Knives Have Edges,* Collins, 1968, Holt, 1970; *Tarry and Be Hanged,* Collins, 1969, Holt, 1971; *An Improbable Fiction,* Collins, 1970, Holt, 1971; *Serpent's Tooth,* Collins, 1971, Holt, 1973; *The Knavish Crows,* Collins, 1971; *They Love Not Poison,* Macmillan, 1972; *Yet She Must Die,* Holt, 1973. Contributor of short stories to English newspapers.

WORK IN PROGRESS: Another novel.

SIDELIGHTS: Mrs. Bowen-Judd writes crime novels with legal background about ordinary people in extraordinary circumstances, having the theory that ordinary people can provide quite enough oddity and interest in their characters, without invading the realms of morbid psychology. *Bloody Instructions* has been published in German, Dutch, Finnish, Swedish, Norwegian, and French editions; other books have been published in German, Dutch, Italian, and Spanish. *Avocational interests:* Reading, especially history; walking, music, talking to friends, country living, and having time to "stand and stare."

BIOGRAPHICAL/CRITICAL SOURCES: Times Literary Supplement, December 21, 1967; *New York Times Book Review,* February 11, 1968, December 8, 1968; *Christian Science Monitor,* December 5, 1968; *Book World,* December 29, 1968.

* * *

BOWETT, Derek William 1927-

PERSONAL: Born April 20, 1927, in Manchester, England; son of Arnold William (a company director) and Marion (Wood) Bowett; married Betty Northall, 1953; children: Richard, Adam, Louise. *Education:* Downing College, Cambridge University, M.A., LL.B., 1951; University of Manchester, Ph.D., 1956. *Home:* Queens' College, Cambridge, England.

CAREER: Barrister, Middle Temple, London, England; University of Manchester, Manchester, England, lecturer in law, 1951-60; Cambridge University, Cambridge, England, lecturer in law, 1960—, fellow of Queen's College, 1960-70, president of Queen's College, 1970—. United Nations, New York, N.Y., member of legal office, 1957-59; member of General Counsel of UNRWA, 1966-68.

WRITINGS: Self-Defence in International Law, Praeger, 1958; *The Law of International Institutions,* Praeger, 1963, 2nd edition, Methuen, 1965, revised edition, Stevens, 1970; (with G.P. Barton and others) *United Nations Forces: A Legal Study of United Nations Practice,* Stevens, 1964, reissued as *United Nations Forces: A Legal Study,* Praeger, 1965; *The Law of the Sea,* Oceana, 1967; *The Law of the Area,* Oceana, 1967. Contributor to law reviews and journals.

* * *

BOWMAN, David J. 1919-

PERSONAL: Born May 20, 1919, in Oak Park, Ill; son of John Francis (a hotelman) and Winifred (Smith) Bowman. *Education:* Loyola University, Chicago, Ill., A.B., 1942, M.A., 1948; Gregorian University, Rome, Italy, S.T.D., 1954. *Politics:* Democrat. *Home:* Faber Hall, Fordham University, Bronx, N.Y. 10458. *Office:* National Council of Churches, 475 Riverside Dr., Room 832, New York, N.Y. 10027.

CAREER: Entered Society of Jesus (Jesuits), 1937, ordained Roman Catholic priest, 1950; St. Ignatius High School, Cleveland, Ohio, teacher, 1944-47; West Baden College, West Baden Springs, Ind., professor of theology, 1954-60; Catholic University of America, Washington, D.C., assistant professor, department of religious education, 1960-65, head of undergraduate program in religious education, 1962-64; Loyola University, Chicago, Ill., assistant professor of theology, 1966; Fordham University, New York, N.Y., associate professor of theology, 1966—; National Council of Churches, New York, N.Y., assistant director, Department of Faith and Order, 1966-68, Associate for Ecumenical Relations, Division of Christian Life and Missions, 1969, special assistant to the general secretary for Ecumenical Services, 1969—, assistant director, Commission on Regional and Local Ecumenism, 1970—. Visiting lecturer in Catholic theology, State University of Iowa, 1959. *Member:* Catholic Theological Society of America, College Theology Society (board of directors, 1956-58), Catholic Biblical Association, Religious Education Association, Liturgical Conference.

WRITINGS: The Word Made Flesh, Prentice-Hall, 1963. Contributor to *New Catholic Encyclopedia.* Editor, *Magister* (bulletin of College Theology Society), 1956-59.

WORK IN PROGRESS: Research on ecumenical developments today, especially Roman Catholic relations with conciliar and other agencies.

AVOCATIONAL INTERESTS: Watching sports, swimming.

* * *

BOWMAN, John S(tewart) 1931-

PERSONAL: Born May 30, 1931, in Cambridge, Mass.; son of John Russell (a teacher) and Anne (Stewart) Bowman; married second wife, Francesca Di Pietro (a social worker), February 11, 1967, children: (second marriage) Michela Ann. *Education:* Harvard University, B.A., 1953; attended Trinity College, Cambridge, 1953-54, University of Munich, 1958-59. *Home:* 305 East 10th St., New York, N.Y. 10009. *Agent:* McIntosh & Otis, Inc., 18 East 41st St., New York, N.Y. 10017.

CAREER: New England Opera Theatre, Boston, Mass., production assistant, 1957; University of Maryland overseas program, Athens and Crete, Greece, English instructor, 1960; *Natural History,* New York, N.Y., associate editor, 1961-62; Grolier, Inc. (encyclopedia publisher), New York, N.Y., associate editor, 1962-63; free-lance writer, 1963—. *Military service:* U.S. Army, 1954-56. *Member:* Phi Beta Kappa.

WRITINGS: Crete, Secker & Warburg, 1962, published in America as *A Guide to Crete,* Pantheon, 1963, revised and expanded edition published as *The Travelers' Guide to Crete,* Bobbs, 1969; *Early Civilizations,* Golden Press,

1966; *The Age of Enlightenment,* Golden Press, 1966; *On Guard: Living Things Defend Themselves,* Doubleday, 1969; *The Quest for Atlantis,* Doubleday, 1971; (editor) *A Book of Islands* (anthology), Doubleday, 1971; *Early Peoples of the Mediterranean,* Abrams, 1973; *The Worlds of Galileo,* Abrams in press. Contributor to *New Yorker, Drama Survey, Nature and Science,* and *Interplay.*

WORK IN PROGRESS: Books on archeology, commedia dell'arte, and works of fiction.

SIDELIGHTS: Bowman has lived and traveled extensively in England, France, Germany, Italy, Spain, and Greece; he manages solid French, passable German, and traveler's Italian and Greek. *Avocational interests:* Archeology, particularly of the Mediterranean; the theatre, particularly the commedia dell'arte.

* * *

BOYCE, Ronald R(eed) 1931-

PERSONAL: Born January 7, 1931, in Los Angeles, Calif.; son of Reed S. and Martha Fern (Puzey) Boyce; married Norma Rae Loraas, May 6, 1955; children: Renaye Noreen, Susan Annette. *Education:* University of Utah, B.S., 1956, M.S., 1957; University of Washington, Ph.D., 1960. *Office:* Department of Geography, University of Washington, Seattle, Wash. 98105.

CAREER: Western Washington State College, Bellingham, instructor in geography, 1959; Washington University, St. Louis, Mo., research associate, 1960-61; University of Illinois, Urbana, assistant professor of planning and director of Wabash Basin Study, 1961-63; University of Iowa, Iowa City, associate professor of geography and research associate, Bureau of Economic and Business Research, 1963-65; University of Washington, Seattle, professor of geography, 1965—. *Member:* Association of American Geographers, American Geographical Society, American Institute of Planners, American Association of University Professors, Regional Science Association (chairman, West Lakes Division, 1961), Sigma Xi, Omicron Delta Epsilon.

WRITINGS: (With Edgar M. Horwood) *Studies of the Central Business District and Urban Freeway Development,* University of Washington Press, 1959; (with Blair T. Bower) *Changing Industrial Patterns in Metropolitan St. Louis and the Demand and Supply of Industrial Land to 1980,* Meramec Basin Research Project, Washington University, 1961; (with E.L. Ullman and Donald J. Volk) *The Meramec Basin Research Project Report,* three volumes, Washington University Press, 1962; (with Seymour Z. Mann) *Urbanism in Illinois: Its Nature, Importance, and Problems,* Public Affairs Research Bureau, Southern Illinois University, 1964; (editor) *Regional Development and the Wabash Basin,* University of Illinois Press, 1964. Contributor of about twenty articles and reviews to scientific and geographical periodicals.

WORK IN PROGRESS: Urban Spatial Structure, for Wiley.

* * *

BOYD, Maurice 1921-

PERSONAL: Born April 3, 1921, in Guthrie, Ky.; son of Charles Hayden (a merchant) and Lorena (Shelton) Boyd; married Shirley Mereness, March 5, 1944; children: James, Robert, Chris, Thomas. *Education:* University of Missouri, B.A., 1943; University of Michigan, M.A., 1948, Ph.D., 1951. *Religion:* Protestant. *Home:* 4025 Glenwood Dr., Fort Worth, Tex. *Office:* Department of History, Texas Christian University, Fort Worth, Tex. 76129.

CAREER: Bradley University, Peoria, Ill., associate professor of history, 1950-56, director of general education,

1953-56; University of Florida, Gainesville, professor of social science and humanities, 1956-64, chairman of social science department, 1957-61; Texas Christian University, Fort Worth, professor of history, 1964—. Volunteer boys' recreational assistant and Little League coach. *Member:* Association of General and Liberal Education, American Historical Association, Southwestern Social Science Association, Organization of American Historians, Phi Alpha Theta, Pi Sigma Alpha.

WRITINGS: Cardinal Quiroga: Inquisitor General of Spain, W.C. Brown, 1954; *Eight Tarascan Legends,* University of Florida Press, 1958; (with Donald E. Worcester) *American Civilization: An Introduction to the Social Sciences,* Allyn & Bacon, 1964, 2nd edition, 1968; *William Knox and Abraham Lincoln: The Story of a Poetic Legacy,* Sage Books, 1966 (also published as introduction to *The Lonely Hearth: The Songs of Israel, Harp of Zion, and Other Poems,* by William Knox, Sage Books, 1966); (compiler with Worcester) *Contemporary America: Issues and Problems,* Allyn & Bacon, 1968; *Tarascan Myths and Legends: A Rich and Imaginative "History" of the Tarascans,* Texas Christian University Press, 1969.

WORK IN PROGRESS: Alonzo Sanchez Coello, the King's Painter, to be published by Porria; *Western Culture and Civilization,* for Canfield.

AVOCATIONAL INTERESTS: Fishing, boating, camping, and touring America.

* * *

BRADFORD, William C(astle) 1910-

PERSONAL: Born July 31, 1910, in Itta Bena, Miss.; son of Calvin Pendall and Tenna (Castle) Bradford; married Edith Ann Wiles, 1936; children: Barbara, Calvin. *Education:* Syracuse University, B.S., 1932, M.A., 1944; Harvard University, A.M., 1946, Ph.D., 1947. *Home:* 1110 Michigan Ave., Evanston, Ill. *Office:* Northwestern University, Evanston, Ill.

CAREER: Syracuse University, Syracuse, N.Y., instructor, 1942-44; Harvard University, Cambridge, Mass., assistant dean, 1944-47; Northwestern University, Evanston, Ill., assistant professor, 1947-49, associate professor, 1949-53, professor of business economics, 1953—, associate dean of faculties, 1963—. *Member:* American Economics Association, Comparative and International Education Society, Illinois Council on Economic Education (executive director), Navy League, Beta Gamma Sigma, Delta Sigma Pi. *Awards, honors:* Navy Distinguished Public Service award for NROTC program development.

WRITINGS: Business Economics, Irwin, 1951, 4th edition, 1970.

* * *

BRAMALL, Eric 1927-

PERSONAL: Born July 8, 1927, in Cheshire, England; son of Howard (an engineer) and Clare H. (Scase) Bramall. *Education:* Attended grammar schools in England. *Home:* The Mews House, Penrhyn Bay, Llandudno, Caernarvonshire, Wales. *Office:* Harlequin Puppet Theatre, Rhos-on-Sea, Colwyn Bay, Denbighshire, Wales.

CAREER: Eric Bramall Marionettes, founder, director, puppeteer, 1946—; Harlequin Puppet Theatre, Denbighshire, Wales, director, 1958—; Harlequin Puppet Films, producer, 1963—. Writer. Director of Britain's first International Puppet Festival at Colwyn Bay, Wales, 1963. Cabaret artiste with tours in Britain and Europe; presents regular weekly show on British Broadcasting Corp. Television in Wales, and has done five series for Yorkshire Television, broadcast all over Britain, New Zealand, and

Australia. *Member.* Royal Society of Arts, Royal Cambrian Academician (honorary).

WRITINGS: Making a Start with Marionettes, G. Bell, 1960; *Puppet Plays and Playwriting,* G. Bell, 1961; (with Christopher C. Somerville) *Expert Puppet Technique: A Manual of Production for Puppeteers,* Faber, 1963, Plays, 1966. Contributor of articles to *Connoisseur, ·Studio, Homes and Gardens, House Beautiful, Coming Events in Britain, Drama,* and *Apollo,* and of an article on collecting puppets to Volume III of *Concise Encyclopaedia of Antiques.*

WORK IN PROGRESS: A book of memoirs on his 25 years as a professional puppeteer.

AVOCATIONAL INTERESTS: Painting, collecting antiques, collecting puppets from all over the world.

* * *

BRAMS, Stanley Howard 1910-

PERSONAL: Born May 14, 1910, in Greenville, Mich.; son of Samuel S. (a salesman) and Fredericka (Fixel) Brams; married Jane Osborne Shannon, August 4, 1945; married Jane Martens Cummings, May 10, 1967; children: (first marriage) John, James. *Education:* Columbia University, student, 1928-31. *Home:* 3060 Glouchester Ave., Troy, Mich. 48084. *Office: Labor Trends,* 805-7 New Center Building, Detroit, Mich. 48202.

CAREER: Iron Age, Philadelphia, Pa., Detroit editor, 1940-46; McGraw-Hill Publishing Co., New York, N.Y., Detroit bureau manager, 1946-53; *Labor Trends,* Detroit, Mich., publisher, 1946—; Press Relations Newswire, Detroit, Mich., president, 1960—. *Member:* Industrial Relations Research Association (president, Detroit chapter, 1957-58), Society of Automotive Engineers, Engineering Society of Detroit, Economic Club of Detroit, Society of Older Graduates (Columbia University).

WRITINGS: (Contributor) *Understanding Collective Bargaining,* American Management Association, 1958; (editor) *Who's Who Among Automotive Executives,* Trends Publishing Co., 1964. Contributor of articles on automotive, labor, and other subjects to *New Yorker, Family Weekly, Town Journal, New York Times Sunday Magazine,* other periodicals and newspapers.

* * *

BRAMWELL, James Guy 1911-
(James Byrom)

PERSONAL: Born July 25, 1911; son of Charles Guy (a soldier) and Joan (Gilkison) Bramwell; divorced; children: Teresa Clare Bramwell Davison. *Education:* Balliol College, Oxford, B.A. (honors). *Home:* Mas Castaly, St. Jacques-de-Crasse, Alps-Maritimes, France. *Agent:* David Higham Associates, 76 Dean St., London W.1, England.

CAREER: London Mercury, London, England, editorial staff, 1934-36; British Council, member, 1946-51. Lecturer in English, Helsinki University.

WRITINGS: They Need No Candle, and Other Poems, Cranley & Day, 1932; *Beyond the Sunrise, and Other Poems,* Heinemann, 1934; *Going West* (novel), Cobden-Sanderson, 1935, Harper, 1936; *Lost Atlantis* (essay), Cobden-Sanderson, 1937, Harper, 1938; *Highland View,* R. Hale, 1940; *Sauna* (poetry), Caseg Press, 1949.

Under pseudonym James Byrom: *The Iron Gates,* R. Hale, 1936; *The Unfinished Man* (autobiography), Chatto & Windus, 1957; *Or Be He Dead* (novel), Chatto & Windus, 1958, Penguin (Baltimore), 1964; *Take Only as Directed* (novel), Chatto & Windus, 1959; *Thou Shouldst Be Living,* Heinemann, 1964; *The Olive Mill,* Heinemann, 1966.

WORK IN PROGRESS: A novel.†

BRANDON, Frances Sweeney 1916-

PERSONAL: Born June 23, 1916, in Nashville, Tenn.; daughter of Howell Fields (a school administrator) and Eustatia (Ellis) Sweeney; married Charles Morris Brandon (associate professor of art at Middle Tennessee State College), December 25, 1940; children: Stacia Ruth, Carl Morris. *Education:* Middle Tennessee State College, B.S., 1939; Peabody College for Teachers, M.A., 1959. *Politics:* Liberal. *Religion:* Methodist. *Home:* Route #1, Christiana, Tenn. 37037.

CAREER: Primary teacher in metropolitan Nashville (Tenn.) schools, 1948-60, 1961-64; teacher in Murfreesboro (Tenn.) schools, 1960-61. Restricted radiophone operator in Louisville, Ky., 1945-46; has done educational television programs. Executive secretary, Rutherford County (Tenn.) chapter of American Red Cross. *Member:* National Education Association (life member), American Childhood Education Association, Eastern Star.

WRITINGS: Rosie the Rock Hound, Abingdon, 1963; *Lonnie and the Flicker Family,* Macmillan, 1968. Contribuor to *Progressive Farmer,* education journals.

WORK IN PROGRESS: Juvenile books; short stories; adult drama.

AVOCATIONAL INTERESTS: Raising and training Pekingese and poodles; music, playing piano, cooking, theatre.

* * *

BRANT, Irving (Newton) 1885-

PERSONAL: Born January 17, 1885, in Walker, Iowa; son of David (a newspaper editor) and Ruth (Hurd) Brant; married Hazeldean Toof, September 3, 1913; children: Ruth (Mrs. Jack Davis), Robin (Mrs. Kenneth Lodewick). *Education:* State University of Iowa, B.A., 1909. *Politics:* Democrat. *Home and office:* 1575 Ferry St., Eugene, Ore. 97401.

CAREER: Iowa City Republican, Iowa City, Iowa, reporter, later managing editor, 1909-14; *Clinton Herald,* Clinton, Iowa, editor, 1914-15; *Des Moines Register and Tribune,* Des Moines, Iowa, associate editor, 1915-18; *St. Louis Star,* St. Louis, Mo., editorial writer, later editorial page editor, 1918-23; *St. Louis Star-Times,* St. Louis, Mo., editorial page editor, 1930-38, contributing editor, 1938-41; *Chicago Sun,* Chicago, Ill., editorial writer, 1941-43, foreign correspondent, 1945. Free-lance writer and researcher, 1923-30; full-time professional writer, 1945—. University of Virginia, Charlottesville, visiting scholar in history and political science, 1963-64; University of Oregon, Eugene, visiting professor, 1966. Director of National Public Housing Conference, New York, N.Y., 1935-44; U.S. Public Works Administration, consultant, 1938-40. Emergency Conservation Committee, New York, N.Y., treasurer, 1931-61. *Member:* Institute of Early American History and Culture (council, 1959-61), Society of American Historians, Overseas Writers (Washington, D.C.), American Civil Liberties Union, Delta Sigma Rho. *Awards, honors:* E.B. MacNaughton Civil Liberties Award, American Civil Liberties Union (Ore.), 1971.

WRITINGS: Dollars and Sense, John Day, 1933; *Storm Over the Constitution,* Bobbs-Merrill, 1936, reissued with a new introduction, 1963; *James Madison,* six volumes, Bobbs-Merrill, Volume 1: *The Virginia Revolutionist,* 1941, Volume 2: *The Nationalist, 1780-87,* 1948, Volume 3: *Father of the Constitution, 1787-1800,* 1950, Volume 4: *Secretary of State, 1800-1809,* 1953, Volume 5: *The President, 1809-1812,* 1956, Volume 6: *Commander in Chief, 1812-36,* 1961, one-volume condensation of entire study published as *The Fourth President: A Life of James Madison,* Bobbs-Merrill, 1970; *Road to Peace and Freedom,*

Bobbs-Merrill, 1943; *The New Poland,* International Universities Press, 1946 (published in England as *New Life in Poland,* Dobson, 1946); *Friendly Cove* (historical novel), Bobbs-Merrill, 1963; *The Free, Or Not So Free, Air of Pennsylvania,* Dickinson College, 1964; *The Books of James Madison, with Some Comments on the Reading of FDR and JFK* (address given at Tracy W. McGregor Library, 1964), University of Virginia, 1965; *The Bill of Rights: Its Origin and Meaning,* Bobbs-Merrill, 1965; *The Constitution and the Right to Know* (Harold L. Cross lecture given at University of Missouri, December 4, 1967), University of Missouri, 1967; *James Madison and American Nationalism,* Van Nostrand, 1968; *Impeachment: Trials and Errors,* Knopf, 1972.

Contributor: Joseph F. Guffy, *How Liberal is Justice Hughes?* (includes articles from *New Republic* by Brant), U.S. Government Printing Office, 1937; Harold L. Ickes, compiler, *Freedom of the Press Today,* Vanguard, 1941; Bruce Bliven and A. G. Mazerik, editors, *What the Informed Citizen Needs to Know,* Duell, 1945; W. Melville Jones, editor, *Chief Justice John Marshall: A Reappraisal,* Cornell University Press, 1956; Earl Schenck Miers, editor, *The American Story,* Channel Press, 1956; John A. Garraty, editor, *The Unforgettable Americans,* Channel Press, 1960; Edmond Cahn, editor, *The Great Rights,* Macmillan, 1963; Robert B. Luce, editor, *The Faces of Five Decades,* Simon & Schuster, 1964; (author of introduction) Fowler V. Harper, *Justice Rutledge and the Bright Constellation,* Bobbs-Merrill, 1965; John A. Garraty, editor, *Historical Viewpoints,* Volume 1 (to 1877), Harper, 1970; Arthur Schlesinger, Jr., editor, *A History of American Presidential Elections,* Chelsea House, 1971.

Frequent contributor of articles to *New Republic,* and occasional contributor to law reviews, historical magazines, and encyclopedias. Writer of many pamphlets on conservation of wildlife and scenic areas published by Emergency Conservation Commission; author of a survey and report to Secretary of the Interior in 1938, on which basis President Roosevelt enlarged Olympic National Park in 1940.

SIDELIGHTS: Brant started research in 1937 for the Madison biography, and worked on it for the next 23 years. He goes to original sources for all of his writings, mainly because he believes that it is virtually impossible to separate fact from error in conflicting secondary materials *without* going to the sources. His major aim in historical writing: "To bring the past to the aid of the present and future."

A venture into fiction, *Friendly Cove,* was called "an exciting quickie" by one reviewer because it was written and published so soon after completion of the Madison biography. Brant had spent two years of research on the historical background for the "quickie" in 1928-29, but didn't have time to write it until 33 years later. His outdoor interests are shared by his wife—hiking, canoeing, motor camping with tent (Brant has camped in 47 states, Canada, and Mexico), and mountain climbing ("now decidedly limited and non-rugged").

BIOGRAPHICAL/CRITICAL SOURCES: Saturday Review, April 8, 1953; *Library Journal,* March 15, 1970.

*   *   *

BRAUN, Richard Emil   1934-

PERSONAL: Born November 22, 1934, in Detroit, Mich.; son of Max Meyer (a lawyer) and Muriel (Barsook) Braun. *Education:* University of Michigan, A.B., 1956, A.M., 1957; University of Texas, Ph.D., 1969. *Office:* Department of Classics, University of Alberta, Edmonton, Alberta, Canada.

CAREER: University of Alberta, Edmonton, Alberta, associate professor of classics, 1962—. *Member:* American Philological Association.

WRITINGS: Companions to Your Doom (poetry), New Fresco, 1961; *Children Passing* (poetry), University of Texas Press, 1962; (editor and author of introduction) Decimus Junius Juvenalis, *Satires,* University of Michigan Press, 1965; *Bad Land* (poetry), Jargon, 1969; (editor and translator) Sophocles, *Antigone,* Atheneum, 1971; *The Foreclosure: Poems,* University of Illinois Press, 1972. Contributor to *Poetry, Arion, Beloit Poetry Journal, Carolina Quarterly, Antioch Review, Saturday Review, Texas Quarterly, Tamarack Review, Minnesota Review, Prism, Contact, Accent, New York Times,* and other publications.

WORK IN PROGRESS: A translation of Euripides' *Rhesus,* for Atheneum; several books of poetry.

AVOCATIONAL INTERESTS: Violin literature, weightlifting, and English literature.

BIOGRAPHICAL/CRITICAL SOURCES: Texas Quarterly, spring, 1962; Kenneth Hopkins, *A Trip to Texas,* Macdonald & Co., 1962.

*   *   *

BRAY, Allen Farris III   1926-

PERSONAL: Born January 4, 1926, in Taunton, Mass.; son of Allen Farris, Jr. and Beulah Chace (Dudley) Bray; married Janet Marilyn Powell, 1948; married second wife, Alison L. Stave, June 18, 1971; children: (first marriage) Allen Gardiner, Jayne Allison. *Education:* Trinity College, Hartford, Conn., A.B., 1949; Virginia Theological Seminary, B.D., 1952; Washington School of Psychiatry, graduate study, 1952-54; Seabury-Western Theological Seminary, S.T.M., 1961. *Home and office:* The Bishop Whipple Schools, Faribault, Minn. 55021.

CAREER: Ordained to Episcopal ministry, December 20, 1952; St. John's Parish, Accokeek, Md., rector, 1952-54; Trinity College, Hartford, Conn., acting chaplain, 1954-56; Culver Military Academy, Culver, Ind., chaplain and director of religious activities, 1958-67; St. James School, Faribault, Minn., headmaster, 1968-71; The Bishop Whipple Schools, Faribault, Minn., vice-rector, 1971-72, rector and headmaster, 1972—. Cathedral of Our Merciful Saviour, Faribault, Minn., canon, 1968—. Member of department of Christian education, Episcopal Diocese of Washington, 1952-54; member of committee on college work, Episcopal Diocese of Connecticut, 1954-56; member of church pension fund committee, Diocese of Minnesota. Trustee, Council for Religion in Independent Schools, 1963—. Director, Constance Bultman Wilson Center for Education and Psychiatry. *Military service:* U.S. Marine Corps., 1943-46; received Asiatic-Pacific theater ribbon with battle star. U.S. Navy, Chaplain Corps., active duty, 1956-58. U.S. Naval Reserve, Chaplain Corps., 1958—; now commander. *Member:* National Association of Independent Schools, National Association of Episcopal Schools (member of board of governors), Religious Education Association, Military Chaplains Association, Anglican Society, Aircraft Owners' and Pilots Association, National Pilots' Association, Independent Schools Association of Central States (director; member of finance committee), Indiana Society of Chicago, Faribault Concert Association (director), American Legion, Lions International.

WRITINGS: The Return to Self-Concern, Westminster, 1964; (contributor) Kendig B. Cully, editor, *The Episcopal Church in Education,* Morehouse, 1966. Contributor to *Westminster Dictionary of Christian Education,* 1963. Contributor of reviews to *Findings, Westminster Bookman,* and other publications.

WORK IN PROGRESS: The Seeking of Good.

AVOCATIONAL INTERESTS: Photography, sailing, and riding.

* * *

BRAYBROOKE, David 1924-

PERSONAL: Born October 18, 1924, in Hackettstown, N.J.; son of Walter Leonard (a civil engineer) and Netta Rose (Foyle) Braybrooke; married Alice Boyd Noble, December 31, 1948; children: Nicholas, Geoffrey, Elizabeth Page. *Education:* Hobart College, student, 1941-43; Harvard University, B.A., 1948; Cornell University, M.A., 1951, Ph.D., 1953; Oxford University, postgraduate study, 1952-53, postdoctoral study, 1959-60. *Politics:* Independent. *Home:* 6045 Fraser St., Halifax, Nova Scotia, Canada. *Office:* Arts and Administration Building, Room 364, Dalhousie University, Halifax, Nova Scotia, Canada.

CAREER: Hobart College (now Hobart and William Smith Colleges), Geneva, N.Y., instructor in history and literature, 1948-50; instructor in philosophy at University of Michigan, Ann Arbor, 1953-54, Bowdoin College, Brunswick, Me., 1954-56; Yale University, New Haven, Conn., assistant professor of philosophy, 1956-63; Dalhousie University, Halifax, Nova Scotia, associate professor, of philosophy and politics, 1963-65, professor, 1965—. Social Science Research Council, research assistant, Committee on the Study of Political Behavior, summers, 1957, 1958; Bridgeport Engineering Institute, part-time dean of liberal arts, 1961-63; Wesleyan University, external examiner, College of Social Studies, 1961-64, 1967, 1970. Visiting professor of philosophy, University of Pittsburgh, 1965, 1966, University of Toronto, 1966-67. Member of Academic Advisory Panel to the Canada Council, 1968-71. Town Democratic Committee, Guilford, Conn., chairman, 1961-62. *Military service:* U.S. Army, 1943-46.

MEMBER: American Philosophical Association, American Society for Political and Legal Philosophy, Canadian Philosophical Association, Canadian Association of University Teachers (member-at-large, national executive committee, 1970-71), National Committee for Sane Nuclear Policy (acting chairman of New Haven branch, 1963), Phi Beta Kappa. *Awards, honors:* Rockefeller Foundation grant in legal and political philosophy, Oxford University, 1959-60; Guggenheim fellow, 1962-63.

WRITINGS: (With Charles E. Lindblom) *A Strategy of Decision: Policy Evaluation as a Social Process,* Free Press, 1963; (editor) *Philosophical Problems of the Social Sciences,* Macmillan, 1965; *Three Tests for Democracy: Personal Rights, Human Welfare, Collective Preference,* Random House, 1968.

Contributor: Carl J. Friedrich, editor, *The Public Interest,* Atherton, 1962; Nelson W. Polsby, Robert A. Dentler, and Paul A. Smith, editors, *Politics and Social Life,* Houghton, 1963; Nicholas Rescher, editor, *Studies in Moral Philosophy,* Basil Blackwell and University of Pittsburgh, 1968; Kurt Baier and Nicholas Rescher, *Values and the Future,* Free Press, 1969; Howard E. Kiefer and Milton K. Munitz, editors, *Mind, Science, and History,* State University of New York Press, 1970. Contributor of articles and reviews to *Analysis, Ethics, Journal of Philosophy, Philosophical Review, Review of Metaphysics, Dialogue, American Philosophical Quarterly, History and Theory, Social Research,* and other journals. Member of board of editors, *American Political Science Review,* 1970—.

WORK IN PROGRESS: Essays on the logical processing, transformation, and disposition of political issues, on preferences and mistakes in preferences, and on vagueness and the character of empirical concepts.

* * *

BRELAND, Osmond P(hilip) 1910-

PERSONAL: Born September 17, 1910, in Decatur, Miss.; son of Oscar Phillips (a minister) and Lida (Adams) Breland; married Virginia Nell Ellington, August 4, 1931; children: Osmond P., Jr., William Michael. *Education:* Mississippi State University, B.S., 1931; Indiana University, Ph.D., 1936. *Home:* 3604 Meredith St., Austin, Tex. 78703. *Office:* Department of Zoology, University of Texas, Austin, Tex. 78712.

CAREER: North Dakota State University, Fargo, instructor in zoology, 1936-38; University of Texas, Austin, assistant professor, 1938-43, associate professor, 1946-50, professor of zoology, 1950—. *Military service:* U.S. Army, Medical Department Sanitary Corps, 1943-46; became captain. U.S. Army Reserve; became lieutenant colonel. *Member:* American Society of Zoologists, Entomological Society of America, American Mosquito Control Association, Sigma Xi.

WRITINGS: Manual of Comparative Anatomy, McGraw, 1943, 2nd edition, 1953; *Animal Facts and Fallacies,* Harper, 1948; (with Addison E. Lee) *Laboratory Studies in Biology,* Harper, 1954, 3rd edition, 1971; *Principles of Biology,* Harper, 1954, revised edition (with W. Gordon Whaley and others), 1964; *Animal Friends and Foes,* Harper, 1957; *Animal Life and Lore,* Harper, 1963, revised edition, 1972; (with Lee) *Biology in the Laboratory,* Harper, 1965. Contributor to *Natural History, Science Digest, Pageant, Audubon, Frontiers,* and to professional journals.

* * *

BRELIS, Dean 1924-

PERSONAL: Born April 1, 1924, in Newport, R.I.; son of Christopher and Mary (Phillips) Brelis; married Nancy Burns, December 10, 1949; married second wife, Isabel O'Donnell, June 5, 1967; married third wife, Mary Anne Weaver, March 21, 1973; children: (first marriage) Doron, Jane, Tia, Matthew. *Education:* Harvard University, A.B., 1949. *Home:* 27 West 44th St., New York, N.Y. 10036. *Agent:* Harold Ober Associates, Inc, 40 East 49th St., New York, N.Y. 10017. *Office:* Valaoritou, 9B, Athens, 134, Greece.

CAREER: Boston Globe, Boston, Mass., reporter 1946-49; Time-Life, Inc., New York, N.Y., correspondent, 1949-54; Harvard College and Radcliffe College, Cambridge, Mass., instructor, 1958-63; National Broadcasting Co., New York, N.Y., foreign correspondent in Middle East, North Africa, Cyprus, Vietnam, 1963-70; Columbia Broadcasting System, special correspondent to Greece, 1970—. *Military service:* U.S. Army, Office of Strategic Services, 1942-45; received battlefield commission as second lieutenant; awarded Bronze Star, Presidential Unit Citation, and Bronze Arrowhead. *Member:* P.E.N., Authors Guild, Dramatists Guild, Signet Society, Harvard Club (New York). *Awards, honors:* Nieman fellow, 1958-59; Overseas Press Club award, 1964, for best radio reporting from abroad; Emmy award for distinguished television news reporting, "Odyssey House," 1970.

WRITINGS:. The Mission, Random House, 1958; *Shalom,* Little, Brown, 1959; *Run, Dig or Stay?: A Search for an Answer to the Shelter Question,* Beacon Press, 1962; *My New-Found Land,* Houghton, 1963; (with William R. Peers) *Behind the Burma Road: The Story of America's Most Successful Guerilla Force,* Little, Brown, 1963; *The Face of South Vietnam,* Houghton, 1967.

WORK IN PROGRESS: A novel.

BRENNER, Barbara Johnes 1925-

PERSONAL: Born June 26, 1925, in Brooklyn, N.Y.; daughter of Robert Lawrence (a real estate broker) and Marguerite (Furboter) Johnes; married Fred Brenner (an illustrator), March 16, 1947; children: Mark, Carl. Education: Seton Hall College, student, 1942-43; extension courses at Rutgers University, 1944-46. Politics: Independent. Home: 11 Richard Dr., West Nyack, N.Y. 10960.

CAREER: Prudential Insurance Co., copywriter, 1942-46; free-lance artist's agent, 1946-52; free-lance writer, mainly of juveniles, 1957—. Committee for a Sane Nuclear Policy, county chairman, 1960-61. Member: Authors Guild. Awards, honors: N.Y. Herald Tribune Children's Spring Book Festival honor book award, 1961, for Barto Takes the Subway; Book World Spring Book Festival honor book award, 1970, for A Snake-Lover's Diary.

WRITINGS—All juveniles, unless otherwise noted; several illustrated by her husband, Fred Brenner: Somebody's Slippers, Somebody's Shoes, W.R. Scott, 1957; Barto Takes the Subway, Knopf, 1961; A Bird in the Family (Junior Literary Guild selection), W.R. Scott, 1962; Amy's Doll, Knopf, 1963; The Five Pennies, Knopf, 1963; Careers and Opportunities in Fashion (young adult book), Dutton, 1964; Beef Stew, Knopf, 1965; The Flying Patchwork Quilt, Knopf, 1965; Mr. Tall and Mr. Small, W.R. Scott, 1966; Nicky's Sister, Knopf, 1966; Summer of the Houseboat, Knopf, 1968; Faces, photographs by George Ancona, Dutton, 1970; A Snake-Lover's Diary, W.R. Scott, 1970; A Year in the Life of Rosie Bernard, Harper, 1971; Is It Bigger Than a Sparrow?: A Box for Young Bird Watchers, Knopf, 1972; Bodies, Dutton, 1973; If You Were an Ant, Harper, 1973. Author of the book and lyrics of a musical play for children, "Ostrich Feathers," first produced Off-Broadway in 1965.

WORK IN PROGRESS: Stories for the Bank Street Readers, to be published by Bank Street College and Houghton.

SIDELIGHTS: Mrs. Brenner told CA: "There are so many things that make life worth living: . . . among them love, children, writing, reading, and watching birds (in that order). I'd rather write plays than anything but its too all-consuming for my life right now." Avocational interests: Travel, gardening.

BIOGRAPHICAL/CRITICAL SOURCES: Young Readers' Review, April, 1966; Library Journal, July, 1968; May 15, 1970; Book World, July 28, 1968.

*   *   *

BRESLOVE, David 1891-

PERSONAL: Born October 10, 1891, in Toronto, Ontario, Canada; married Deborah Lasersohn, December 27, 1922; children: Harold. Education: University of Toronto, B.A. (honors), 1941, M.A., 1915; studied at Ontario College of Education, 1916. Home: 19 Lawrence Ave. W., Toronto, Ontario, Canada.

CAREER: High school teacher of classics in Ontario, 1916-1957; Lawrence Park Collegiate Institute, Toronto, Ontario, head of department of classics, 1936-57. Military service: Canadian Army, Infantry, 1918. Member: Ontario Educational Association (president of classical section), Ontario Classical Association (vice-president), Classical Association of Middle West (vice-president for Ontario), Toronto Classical Club (president). Awards, honors: Her Majesty's Coronation medal, 1953.

WRITINGS: (With K.P.R. Neville, Jolliffe, and Dale) A Book of Latin Poetry, Macmillan (Canada), 1931; (with Neville, Dale, and Tracy) A Book of Latin Prose, Macmillan (Canada), 1935; (with Dale) First Latin Lessons, Copp, 1936; Latin Composition for Grade 13, Gage, 1947; (with Cameron, King, Toll, and Tracy) Latin Prose Selections, Thomas Nelson, 1948; (with Cameron, King, Toll, and Tracy) Latin Poetry Selections, Thomas Nelson, 1948; (with Arthur G. Hooper) Latin for Canadian Schools, Copp, 1958; (with Hooper and Tracy) A Latin Reader for Canadian Schools, Copp, 1959; (with Hooper and May S. Hambly) Our Latin Heritage, Copp, Volume I, 1961, Volume II, 1962, Volume III, 1965; (with Hooper and Mary A. Barrett) Latin: Our Living Heritage, two volumes, Merrill, 1962, revised edition, 1969; Teacher's Guide and Answer Key (for Latin: Our Living Heritage), Merrill, 1963; (with Hooper and Hambly) Latin for Canadian Schools—A New Approach, Copp, 1967; Test Booklets Spirit Editions Nos. 1, 3, and 28, (for Latin: Our Living Heritage), Merrill, 1970.

*   *   *

BRETT, Grace Neff 1900-

PERSONAL: Born February 11, 1900, in Chicago, Ill.; daughter of George Gottlieb (a teacher) and Sophia (Bach) Neff; married Gilbert James Brett (a writer, editor, and radio moderator), July 15, 1942. Education: University of Illinois, B.A.; writing courses at Northwestern University and Columbia University. Home: 3927 North Frontier Ave., Chicago, Ill. 60613.

CAREER: Writer; lecturer on books, art, and related subjects. Member: Children's Reading Round Table, Society of Midland Authors, Matrix, Chicago Women's Literary Club, Theta Sigma Phi, Alpha Delta Kappa (honorary).

WRITINGS: Squiffy the Skunk, Rand McNally, 1953; The Runaway, Follett, 1958; That Willy and Wally, A. Whitman, 1964; The Picture Story and Biography of Tom Paine, Follett, 1965; Hatsy Catsy: The Cat That Loved Hats, Denison, 1969. Contributor of articles to American People's Encyclopedia, Chicago Tribune, and trade journals.

WORK IN PROGRESS: An adult novel about a musical family.

AVOCATIONAL INTERESTS: Photography, gardening, house furnishings, and fashion designing.

BIOGRAPHICAL/CRITICAL SOURCES: Christian Science Monitor, March 10, 1943; Ladies' Home Journal, October, 1943; Chicago Tribune, March 29, 1953, Milwaukee Journal, November 13, 1958.

*   *   *

BRETT, Mary Elizabeth
(Molly Brett)

PERSONAL: Born in Croydon, Surrey, England; daughter of J.V. (an insurance manager) and Mary Gould (Latham) Brett. Education: Educated in English schools. Politics: Conservative. Religion: Church of England. Home: Chimes Cottage, Horsell Vale, Woking, Surrey, England.

CAREER: Illustrator; author of stories for children. Member: Women's Institute, Woking Art Society, Guildford Art Society, Society of Authors, Horsell Women's Fellowship, Tuesday Lunch Club.

WRITINGS—Under pseudonym Molly Brett, all self-illustrated: The Little Garden, Warne, 1936; The Story of a Toy Car, Warne, 1938, revised edition, 1960; Drummer Boy Duckling, Muller, 1945; Follow Me Round the Farm (picture book), Raphael Tuck & Sons, 1947; Mr. Turkey Runs Away, Brockhampton Press, 1947; Puppy Schooldays, Brockhampton Press, 1948; Master Bunny *the Baker's Boy,* Brockhampton Press, 1950; *The Japanese Garden,* Warne, 1959; *Robin Finds Christmas,* Medici Society, 1961; *Tom Tit Moves House,* Medici Society, 1962; *A Surprise for Dumpy,* Medici Society, 1965; *The Untidy Little Hedgehog,* Medici Society, 1967; *The Forgotten Bear,* Medici Society; *Two in a Tent,* Medici Society; *Flip Flop's Secret,* Medici Society; *Paddy Gets Into Mischief,* Medici Society, 1972. Contributor of short stories to Amalgamated Press publications.

WORK IN PROGRESS: Jiggy's Treasure Hunt.

AVOCATIONAL INTERESTS: Gardening and sketching.

BIOGRAPHICAL/CRITICAL SOURCES: Woking Opinion, August 11, 1954; *Art Bulletin,* autumn, 1954, summer, 1955.

*   *   *

BREWER, James H. Fitzgerald 1916-

PERSONAL: Born November 20, 1916, in Baltimore, Md.; son of Stephen R. (a civil engineer) and Mary H. (Fitzgerald) Brewer; married Kathryn Elizabeth Burns, December 26, 1945; children: James H. Fitzgerald II, Mary Anne. *Education:* LaSalle College, B.A. (cum laude), 1938; Niagara University, M.A., 1939; postgraduate study at University of Minnesota, 1942-45; George Washington University, Ph.D., 1967. *Politics:* Independent Democrat. *Religion:* Roman Catholic. *Office:* Anne Arundel Community College, Arnold, Md. 21012.

CAREER: U.S. Naval Academy, Annapolis, Md., associate professor of European history, 1947-61; Johns Hopkins University, McCoy College, Baltimore, Md., lecturer in European history, 1947-61; Agency for International Development, Washington, D.C., chief of policy information, 1961-62; Loyola Evening College of Baltimore, Baltimore, Md., professorial lecturer in history, 1950—; Anne Arundel Community College, Arnold, Md., chairman of social sciences division, 1962—. *Military service:* U.S. Naval Reserve, active duty, 1940. U.S. Marine Corps Reserve, active duty, 1941. *Member:* American Historical Association, Baker Street Irregulars (Six Napoleons of Baltimore branch).

WRITINGS: History of the 175th Infantry Regiment, Maryland National Guard, 1774-1954, Maryland Historical Society, 1955; (contributor) *The Old Line State,* edited by Morris L. Radoff, Historical Records Society, 1957, 2nd edition, 1971; (author of preface) Arthur H. Furnia, *The Diplomacy of Appeasement,* University Press of Washington, D.C., 1960; *Politics in the French Army: The Aftermath of the Dreyfus Case, 1899-1905.* Contributor to *America.*

*   *   *

BRICKHILL, Paul Chester Jerome 1916-

PERSONAL: Born December 20, 1916, in Melbourne, Australia; son of George Russell and Victoria (Bradshaw) Brickhill; married Margaret Olive, April 22, 1950 (divorced, 1964); children: Timothy Paul, Tempe Melinda. *Education:* Attended University of Sydney. *Religion:* Church of England. *Agent:* Paul R. Reynolds Inc., 599 Fifth Ave., New York, N.Y. 10017; John Farquharson Ltd., 15 Red Lion Sq., London W.C. 1, England.

CAREER: Sydney Sun, Sydney, Australia, journalist, 1935-40; foreign correspondent in Europe and U.S.A., 1945-47; left journalism field to write books, 1949. *Military service:* Royal Australian Air Force, fighter pilot, 1940-46; became flight lieutenant (captain); was wounded in action twice and held prisoner of war in Germany for two years. *Member:* R.A.F. Club (London).

WRITINGS: (With Conrad Norton) *Escape to Danger,* Faber, 1946; *The Great Escape,* Norton, 1950; *The Dam Busters,* foreword by Lord Tedder, Evans Brothers, 1951, Ballantine, 1965; *Escape or Die* (authentic stories of the R.A.F. Escaping Society), Norton, 1952; *Reach for the Sky: The Story of Douglas Bader, Legless Ace of the Battle of Britain,* Norton, 1954 (published in England as *Reach for the Sky: The Story of Douglas Bader,* Collins, 1954, abridged edition, 1956, young peoples' edition, 1957); *The Deadline,* Collins, 1962, published in America as *War of Nerves,* Morrow, 1963.

SIDELIGHTS: Four of Brickhill's books have been made into films, two of which received Hollywood plaques as "Best Film of the Month." All his books have been extensively serialised on radio and television. The Rank Organization filmed *Reach for the Sky* in 1957. The film version of *The Great Escape,* produced in 1963 by United Artists, won a Writers Guild nomination for best-written American drama, 1963. *Avocational interests:* Golf, squash.

BIOGRAPHICAL/CRITICAL SOURCES: Young Readers' Review, October, 1966.

*   *   *

BRIDENBAUGH, Carl 1903-

PERSONAL: Surname is pronounced *Bry*-den-baw; born August 10, 1903, in Philadelphia, Pa; son of Charles Herbert (a manufacturer) and Mabel (Corbin) Bridenbaugh; married Jessica Hill, 1931 (died, 1943); married Roberta Herriott, June 17, 1944. *Education:* Dartmouth College, B.S., 1925; University of Pennsylvania, graduate study, 1925-27; Harvard University, A.M., 1930, Ph.D., 1936. *Office:* Department of History, Brown University, Providence, R.I. 02912.

CAREER: Meadowbrook School, Meadowbrook, Pa., French and history master, 1925-26; Episcopal Academy, Overbrook, Pa., first form master, 1926-27; Massachusetts Institute of Technology, Cambridge, instructor in English and history, 1927-29, 1930-34, assistant professor of history, 1934-38; Brown University, Providence, R.I., associate professor of American history, 1938-42; Institute of Early American History and Culture, Williamsburg, Va., first director and organizer, 1945-50; University of California, Berkeley, Margaret Byrne Professor of American History, 1950-62; Brown University, Providence, first University Professor, 1962—. U.S. Department of State specialist in India, 1956; consultant on American civilization, U.S. National Commission for UNESCO, 1957-60; member, Historical American Buildings Survey, 1957-62; member of advisory board, Society for Preservation of American Musical Heritage, 1960—; member, Commission on the Humanities, 1963—. *Military service:* U.S. Naval Reserve, 1942-45; became lieutenant commander.

MEMBER: Royal Historical Society (fellow), American Historical Association (president, 1962), American Philosophical Society, American Academy of Arts and Sciences, American Antiquarian Society, Massachusetts Historical Society, Colonial Society of Massachusetts, Providence Art Club. *Awards, honors:* Fellow, Center for Advanced Study in the Behavioral Sciences, 1956-57; Justin Winsor Prize, American Historical Association, 1937, for *Cities in the Wilderness;* Certificate of Award of Merit, American Association for State and Local History, 1952, for *Myths and Realities;* Commonwealth Club of California nonfiction award, Citation of Honour, Society of Colonial Wars in the State of New York, and citation of National Society of Colonial Dames of America, all for *Cities in Revolt,* 1955; Litt.D., Dartmouth College, 1958; A.M. ad eundem, Brown University, 1963.

WRITINGS: Cities in the Wilderness: The First Century of Urban Life in America 1625-1742, Ronald, 1938, second edition, Knopf, 1955; (with wife, Jessica Bridenbaugh) *Rebels and Gentlemen: Philadelphia in the Age of Franklin,* Reynal, 1942; *Peter Harrison, First Ameri-*

can Architect, University of North Carolina Press, 1949; *The Colonial Craftsman* (Anson G. Phelps Lectures), New York University Press, 1950; *Seat of Empire: The Political Role of Eighteenth-Century Williamsburg*, Colonial Williamsburg, 1950, revised edition, 1958; *Myths and Realities: Societies of the Colonial South* (Walter L. Fleming Lectures), Louisiana Sta'e University Press, 1952; *Cities in Revolt: Urban Life in America, 1743-1776*, Knopf, 1955; *Mitre and Sceptre: Transatlantic Faiths, Ideas, Personalities and Politics, 1689-1776*, Oxford University Press (New York), 1962; (author of foreword) William Gerold, *College Hill: A Photographic Study of Brown University*, Brown University Press, 1965; *Vexed and Troubled Englishmen, 1590-1642*, Oxford University Press, 1968; (with wife, Roberta Bridenbaugh) *No Peace Beyond the Line: The English in the Carribbean, 1642-1690*, Oxford University Press, 1972.

Editor and author of introduction: Nathaniel Beverly Tucker, *The Partisan Leader*, Knopf, 1933; Patrick M'Robert, *A Tour through Part of the North Provinces of America: Being a Series of Letters Wrote on the Spot, in the Years 1774 and 1775*, Historical Society of Pennsylvania, 1935; *Gentlemen's Progress: The Itinerarium of Dr. Alexander Hamilton, 1744*, University of North Carolina Press, 1948.

Contributor of book reviews to *New York Times*, *New York Herald Tribune*, learned journals, other newspapers. Member of board of editors, *New England Quarterly*, 1950—.

WORK IN PROGRESS: Multi-volume history with working title of *American People in the Colonial Period.*

SIDELIGHTS: In a review of *Vexed and Troubled Englishmen, 1590-1642*, Alden T. Vaughan states: ". . . Bridenbaugh offers . . . a brilliantly detailed insight into everyday England. His book is studded with apt quotations from a wide range of sources—plays, poetry and songs, as well as the usual diaries and public records—including much that the author has ferreted out of manuscript collections on both sides of the Atlantic. . . . Through a skillful use of these and similar sources Bridenbaugh makes clear, as no previous scholar has, the depth and pervasiveness of unrest that lurked below the surface of Jacobean England."

BIOGRAPHICAL/CRITICAL SOURCES: Washington Post, April 23, 1968; *New York Review of Books*, May 9, 1968; *New York Times Book Review*, June 16, 1968; *Virginia Quarterly Review*, spring, 1969; *Yale Review*, winter, 1969.†

*   *   *

BRIDGEMAN, William Barton   1916-

PERSONAL: Born June 25, 1916, in Ottumwa, Iowa; son of Willard and Lillian Bridgeman; married Jacqueline Hazard (an author), May 31, 1957; children: Christopher. *Education:* Educated at Pasadena Junior College and University of California, Los Angeles. *Politics:* Republican. *Religion:* Vedanta. *Home:* 665 Bienveneda, Pacific Palisades, Calif. 90272. *Agent:* Mitchell Hamilburg, Beverly Hills, Calif.

CAREER: Douglas Aircraft, Santa Monica, Calif., test pilot, 1948-60. *Military service:* U.S. Navy Air Corps, 1941-47; became lieutenant commander; received Purple Heart, Presidential Unit Citation, Distinguished Flying Cross, twice, five Air Medals. *Member:* Society of Experimental Test Pilots (charter member). *Awards, honors:* Citation of Honor, Air Force Association, 1952; Octave Chanute Award, 1953; Flying Tiger award, 1954.

WRITINGS: (With wife, Jacqueline Hazard) *The Lonely Sky*, Holt, 1955.

WORK IN PROGRESS: With Jacqueline Hazard, *The Tender Edge.*

SIDELIGHTS: A pioneer of the jet age, Bridgeman was the first civilian to probe beyond the sound barrier. He flew "Skyrocket," the second rocket-powered experimental aircraft in the world, and for three years, 1951-54, held the world altitude and speed record in a piloted aircraft.

BIOGRAPHICAL/CRITICAL SOURCES: Time, April 27, 1953.

*   *   *

BRIGGS, Katharine Mary   1898-

PERSONAL: Born November 8, 1898, in London, England; daughter of Ernest Edward (an artist) and Mary (Cooper) Briggs. *Education:* Studied at Lansdowne House: Lady Margaret Hall, Oxford University, M.A., 1923, Ph.D., 1952. *Religion:* Episcopalian. *Home:* The Barn House, Burford, Oxford, England. *Agent:* A.P. Watt & Son, 26 Bedford Row, London WC1R 2HL, England.

CAREER: Headed an amateur touring company for about fifteen years, produced plays in the Air Force, and wrote and produced plays locally in Perthshire and Oxfordshire, England; free-lance writer. *Military service:* Women's Auxiliary Air Force, 1941-45. *Member:* Folk-Lore Society, Bibliographical Society, Historical Association, American Folklore Society, English Folk Dance and Song Society. *Awards, honors:* D.Litt., Oxford University, 1969.

WRITINGS: *The Legend of Maiden-Hair*, Stockwell, 1915; *The Garrulous Lady* (dramatic sketch), Golden Vista, 1931; *The Lisles of Ellingham*, Alden Press, 1935; *A History of 75 Years*, Henry Briggs & Son, 1935; *The Witches' Ride*, Capricornus, 1937; *Stories Arranged for Mime*, Capricornus, 1937; *The Fugitive* (one-act play), Capricornus, 1938; *The Peacemaker* (one-act play), Capricornus, 1938; *The Prince, the Fox and the Dragon*, Capricornus, 1938; (with Winifred and Elspeth Briggs) *Whispers: An Experiment in Lino Cuts* (poems), Capricornus, 1940; *The Castilians*, Alden Press, 1949; *Lady in the Dark* (play), Capricornus, 1950; (with others) *The Twelve Days of Christmas*, Capricornus, 1952; *The Personnel of Fairyland: A Short Account of the Fairy People of Great Britain for Those Who Tell Stories to Children*, Alden Press, 1953, Bentley, 1954; *Hobberdy Dick*, Eyre & Spottiswoode, 1955; *Mime for Guides and Brownies*, Girl Guides Association, 1955; *Dunkeld and Birnam Guide*, Alden Press, 1956; *The Anatomy of Puck: An Examination of Fairy Beliefs Among Shakespeare's Contemporaries and Successors*, Routledge & Kegan Paul, 1959; *Pale Hecate's Team: An Examination of the Beliefs on Witchcraft and Magic Among Shakespeare's Contemporaries and His Immediate Successors*, Humanities, 1962; (contributor) *Bruder Grimm Gedenken*, Elwert Verlag, 1963; *Kate Crackernuts*, Alden Press, 1963; (contributor) Allardyce Nicoll, editor, *Shakespeare Survey, 1964*, Cambridge University Press, 1964; (editor with Ruth Lyndall Tongue) *Folktales of England*, University of Chicago Press, 1965; (editor) Ruth Lyndall Tongue, *Somerset Folklore*, Folk-Lore Society, 1965; *The Fairies in English Tradition and Literature*, University of Chicago Press, 1967 (published in England as *The Fairies in Tradition and Literature*, Routledge & Kegan Paul, 1967); *A Dictionary of British Folktales in the English Language*, four volumes, Indiana University Press, Part A: *Folk-Tales*, two volumes, 1970 (published in England as *Folk Narratives*, Routledge & Kegan Paul, 1970), Part B: *Folk Legends*, two volumes, 1971. Contributor to *Guider* and *Folklore.*

SIDELIGHTS: The Fairies in English Tradition and Literature continues the "historic survey" of the little people

Dr. Briggs began with *The Personnel of Fairyland* and furthered in *The Anatomy of Puck*. Geoffrey Gorer of *The Listener* calls her story "a useful source-book," but adds that "nowhere does she make clear that she is dealing with two different traditions. One aspect of beliefs about fairies is concerned with a quasi-human group of people. . . . The second aspect . . . deals with the supernatural, tiny people who may represent the spirits of the dead or some other mythological abstraction." A reviewer for the *Times Literary Supplement* agrees that "this should have been two books," dealing separately with the themes of literature and living tradition. B.A. Botkin calls "the first two sections . . . a contribution to folklore, written with the love, learning, and imaginative and social insight that make the English such good social historians and folklorists." He quotes Dr. Briggs' preface, in which she states her interest in fairies from a purely scientific point of view: " 'As in my earlier books, I have had no special ax to grind. This is not an attempt to prove that fairies are real. . . . I am agnostic on the subject.' "

A Dictionary of British Folktales in the English Language is a gigantic, four-volume work based on the F.J. Norton collection of folktales, and "drawn on a tremendous number of other sources to divide British folktales into fables, exempla, fairy tales, jocular tales, novelle, and nursery tales," according to Jerome Cushman of the University of California, Los Angeles. Tales originally recorded in obscure dialects have been translated. "Such industry," writes Bernard Levin, "even if it had nothing else to mark it, would alone make the reader suspect that Miss Briggs is in reality the Witch of Fraddam . . . who 'betook herself to Kynance Cove and there raised the Devil by her incantations, and pledged her soul to him in return for the aid he promised.' If so, this must be one of the few occasions on which he has delivered the goods. For the book is a monument not only to patience and learning, but to much more: to the almost unimaginable richness of Britain's legends. . . . There are four centuries of records in her book, and they cover legends from at least 20—indeed, some of these tales, in origin, must be as old as language, and possibly older; Britain owes Miss Briggs much."

BIOGRAPHICAL/CRITICAL SOURCES: Times Literary Supplement, August 17, 1967, July 23, 1970; *Listener,* August 31, 1967; *Books Abroad,* winter, 1967; *Carleton Miscellany,* fall, 1968; *Library Journal,* October 7, 1970; *Observer Review,* May 16, 1971.

*　　*　　*

BROCK, Peter (de Beauvoir) 1920-

PERSONAL: Born January 30, 1920, in Guernsey, Channel Islands; son of Leslie Evelyn (an engineer) and Norah (Mockler) Brock; married Carmen Williamson, December 31, 1958. *Education:* Oxford University, B.A. and M.A., 1948, D.Phil, 1954; University of Cracow, Ph.D., 1950. *Office:* Department of History, University of Toronto, Toronto, Ontario, Canada.

CAREER: Member of history department faculty, University of Toronto, Toronto, Ontario, 1957-58, University of Alberta, Edmonton, 1958-61, Columbia University, New York, N.Y., 1961-66, University of Toronto, 1966—. Visiting lecturer in history, Smith College, 1960-61. *Member:* American Association for the Advancement of Slavic Studies, Canadian Association of Slavists. *Awards, honors:* Guggenheim fellow, 1961.

WRITINGS: W zaraniu Ruchu Ludowego (originally written in English but published in Polish), Polskie Stronnictwo Ludowe, 1956; *The Political and Social Doctrines of the Unity of Czech Brethren in the Fifteenth and Early Sixteenth Centuries,* Mouton & Co., 1957; *Z dziejow Wielkiej Emigracji w Anglii* (essays on the Polish Great Emigration in England; originally written in English but published in Polish), translation. by A. Slosarczyk, Ksiazka i Wiedza, 1958; (editor) *Geneza Ludu Polskiego w Anglii,* B. Swiderski, 1962; *Pacifism in the United States: From the Colonial Era to the First World War,* Princeton University Press, 1968, Chapters 10-17 published separately as *Radical Pacifists in Antebellum America,* Princeton University Press, 1968, Chapters 1-3, 5, 8, 18, and 21 published separately as *Pioneers of the Peaceable Kingdom,* Princeton University Press, 1970; *Twentieth-Century Pacifism,* Van Nostrand, 1970; (editor with H. Gordon Skilling) *The Czech Renascence of the Nineteenth Century: Essays in Honour of Otakar Odlozilik,* University of Toronto Press, 1970; *Pacifism in Europe to 1914,* Princeton University Press, 1972. Contributor of articles to *Canadian Slavonic Papers, English Historical Review, Slavonic and East European Review,* and other historical periodicals.

WORK IN PROGRESS: A monograph, *History of Pacifism in Europe to 1914;* a social history of partitioned Poland.

SIDELIGHTS: Several reviewers, including Charles A. Barker and Charles Chatfield, have commented on the timeliness of *Pacifism in the United States,* although the book only covers the colonial era to World War I. Barker, in a review for *Virginia Quarterly Review,* writes that "its length and its detailed factuality make [the book] demanding on the reader. Yet these qualities are right, not wrong nor even overdone. Time and again the facts and ideas presented seem stunningly relevant to the Vietnam War, to larger American policy, and to world policy—to what the nations are now about—even though no fact in the book comes chronologically close." Martin E. Marty agrees that Brock has covered his subject so thoroughly that "for years [no one else] will have to follow the pacifists' trail as he has done." Chatfield believes the book is "as relevant as it is monumental because it illumines the dilemmas involved in the questions of principle that have faced pacifists in America: the relation of personal commitment and community standards (sect or society), the relative attraction of opposing values (peace and order or peace and justice), the relative authority of the individual and society, and the limits of coercive force. . . . Peter Brock—whatever his personal convictions may be—joins Merle Curti, Devere Allen, Rufus Jones and others who in banking its fires have made pacifism more readily available."

BIOGRAPHICAL/CRITICAL SOURCES: Library Journal, February 1, 1969; *Christian Century,* April 2, 1969; *New York Times Book Review,* April 6, 1969; *Virginia Quarterly Review,* winter, 1969; *Canadian Forum,* February, 1971.

*　　*　　*

BROEHL, Wayne G(ottlieb), Jr. 1922-

PERSONAL: Born August 11, 1922, in Peoria, Ill.; son of Wayne G. and Dimple (Rush) Broehl; married Jean Kirby, August 4, 1944; children: David Robert, James Richard, Michael Kirby. *Education:* University of Illinois, B.S., 1947; University of Chicago, M.B.A., 1950; Indiana University, D.B.A., 1954. *Home:* 6 Kingsford Rd., Hanover, N.H. 03755.

CAREER: Bradley University College of Commerce, Peoria, Ill., assistant professor and assistant dean, 1948-51; Dartmouth College, Amos Tuck School of Business Administration, Hanover, N.H., assistant professor, 1954-57, professor of business, 1957—. Visiting professor at University College, Dublin, Ireland, 1960-61. *Member:* American Economic Association, Economic History Association, American Historical Association, Academy of Management, Beta Gamma Sigma, Beta Theta Pi.

WRITINGS: Trucks, Trouble and Triumph: The Norwalk Truck Line Co., Prentice-Hall, 1954; Precision Valley: the Machine Tool Companies of Springfield, Vermont, Prentice-Hall, 1959; (editor with Lawrence L. Waters) Administering the Going Concern, Prentice-Hall, 1962; The Molly Maguires (on labour relations in the anthracite fields of eastern Pennsylvania in the 1870's, Harvard University Press, 1964; (with Robert Le Fevre Shurter and J.P. Williamson) Business Research and Report Writing, McGraw, 1965; Hospital Policy Decisions: Process and Action, Putnam, 1966; The International Basic Economy Corporation, National Planning Association, 1968.

*   *   *

BROEKEL, Rainer Lothar   1923-
(Ray Broekel)

PERSONAL: First syllable of surname rhymes with "rock"; born March 24, 1923, in Dresden, Germany; son of Eugene (a horticulturist) and Hedwig (Hartmann) Broekel; married Margaret McNeely, May 6, 1944; children: Peggy Rae, Randall Ray. Education: Illinois College, Jacksonville, B.A., 1948; graduate study at Stanford University, 1948-50, and Wesleyan University, 1955. Religion: Episcopalian. Home: 6 Edge St., Ipswich, Mass. 01938. Office: Addison-Wesley Publishing Co., Reading, Mass. 01867.

CAREER: Junior high school science teacher in Murrayville and Jacksonville, Ill., 1950-56; Junior Museum, Jacksonville, Ill., director, 1954-56; Wesleyan University, Middletown, Conn., member of department of school services, 1956-64; American Education Publications, Middletown, Conn., science supervisor of "My Weekly Reader" Publications, 1956-66; Silver Burdett Co., Morristown, N.J., senior editor, 1966; Addison-Wesley Publishing Co., Reading, Mass., managing editor of juvenile division, 1966—. Military service: U.S. Army Air Forces, 1943-46.

WRITINGS—Under name Ray Broekel: The True Book of Tropical Fishes, Childrens Press, 1956, reissued as The Junior True Book of Tropical Fishes, Muller, 1959; You and the Science of Plants, Animals, and the Earth, Childrens Press, 1956; You and the Sciences of Mankind, Childrens Press, 1956; "I Have a Green Nose," Said Zanzibar, Seale, 1963; Rodney Bounced Too Much on Monday, Seale, 1964; Pangborn, the Peanut Bear, and His Tummy-Drum, Seale, 1965; Hugo the Huge, Doubleday, 1968; The Saga of Sweet Basil, Doubleday, 1970. Contributor of over 1,000 stories and articles to children's magazines and other periodicals.

WORK IN PROGRESS: Arthur and the Old Oak Tree, for Doubleday; The Shrew: Its Life and Times; The Bucklin Kohlrabi Theory.

*   *   *

BROGAN, Phil(ip) F(rancis)   1896-

PERSONAL: Born March 23, 1896, in The Dalles, Ore.; son of John Curran and Grace (Curran) Brogan; married Louise E. Berning, July 4, 1925; children: John Philip. Education: University of Oregon, B.S., 1923. Politics: Republican. Home: 1426 Harmon, Bend, Ore. 97701.

CAREER: Bulletin, Bend, Ore., reporter, 1923-30, city editor, 1930-45, managing editor, 1945-53, associate editor, 1953—. Volunteer weather observer. Chairman, Oregon Geographic Names Board. Military service: U.S. Navy, World War I. Member: American Meteor Society (Northwest director), Sigma Delta Chi, Sigma Upsilon. Awards, honors: Thomas Jefferson Award, 1960, for volunteer work in weather field; Oregon Academy of Science citation for scientific writings in geology, astron-

omy, and paleontology; University of Oregon outstanding citizen award, 1963.

WRITINGS: East of the Cascades, edited by L.K. Phillips, Binfords, 1964. Contributor of science articles to Oregonian and other daily newspapers.

*   *   *

BRONSTEIN, Arthur J.   1914-

PERSONAL: Born March 15, 1914, in Baltimore, Md.; married Elsa Meltzer (a public school teacher in New York, N.Y.), May 15, 1941; children: Nancy, Nabby. Education: College of City of New York (now City College of City University of New York), B.A., 1934; Columbia University, M.A., 1936; New York University, Ph.D., 1949. Home: 36 Brokaw Lane, Great Neck, N.Y. Office: Graduate Center, City University of New York, New York, N.Y. 10036.

CAREER: Ohio University, Athens, instructor in speech, 1936-37; Queens College of the City University of New York, Flushing, N.Y., 1938-68, started as tutor, became professor of speech; Herbert H. Lehman College of the City University of New York, New York, N.Y., executive officer, doctoral program in speech, 1969—. Collier's Encyclopedia, pronunciation consultant; member of editorial advisory staff, American College Dictionary and The Random House Dictionary. Military service: U.S. Army, Adjutant General's Office and Army Air Forces, 1942-46; became captain. Member: International Linguistics Association, Linguistic Society of America, American Dialects Society, Speech Association of America, Modern Language Association, American Speech and Hearing Association.

WRITINGS: The Pronunciation of American English: An Introduction to Phonetics, Appleton, 1960; (with Beatrice F. Jacoby) Your Speech and Voice, Random House, 1967; (co-editor) Essays in Honor of Claude M. Wise, Standard (Hannibal), 1970. Contributor to professional and scholarly journals.

WORK IN PROGRESS: A study of vocal qualifiers; a study on phonetic and phonemic symbolization; reading problems and linguistics; a biographical dictionary in speech and linguistics.

*   *   *

BROOK, (George) Leslie   1910-

PERSONAL: Born March 6, 1910, in Shepley, Huddersfield, England; son of Willie and Lillie (Townend) Brook; married Stella Maguire, January 4, 1949. Education: University of Leeds, B.A., 1931, Ph.D., 1935. Home: 26 Chandos Rd. S., Manchester M21 1TF, England. Office: Department of English, The University, Manchester M13 9 PL, England.

CAREER: University of Manchester, Manchester, England, assistant lecturer in English, 1932-37, lecturer, 1937-45, professor of English language, 1945-51, professor of English language and medieval English literature, 1951—, dean of faculty of arts, 1956-57, pro-vice-chancellor, 1962—. Visiting professor at University of California, Los Angeles, 1951. Member: Modern Language Association of America (life), Bibliographical Society, Cambridge Bibliographical Society, Manchester Bibliographical Society (chairman, 1963-66), Lancashire Dialect Society (treasurer, 1963—), Yorkshire Dialect Society, Malone Society.

WRITINGS: An English Phonetic Reader, Manchester University Press, 1935; Notes on Some English Sound-Changes, Titus Wilson, 1935, revised edition, 1947, reissued as English Sound-Changes, Manchester University Press, 1957, revised edition, 1965; (editor) The Harley Lyrics (Middle English lyrics of Ms. Harley 2253), Manchester University Press, 1948, 3rd edition, Barnes & Noble, 1964; *An Introduction to Old English,* Manchester University Press, 1955, 2nd edition, 1962; *A History of the English Language,* Essential Books, 1958; *English Dialects,* Deutsch, 1963, 2nd edition, 1965; (editor with C.S. Lewis) *Selections from Layamon's Brut,* Oxford University Press, 1963; (editor with R.F. Leslie) *Layamon's Brut,* Volume I, Early English Text Society, 1963; *The Modern University,* Transatlantic, 1965; *The Language of Dickens,* Deutsch, 1970. General editor, "Old and Middle English Texts" series, Manchester University Press, 1958—; editor, *Journal* of Lancashire Dialect Society, 1961-64. Contributor to *Bulletin* of John Rylands Library, Manchester University.

WORK IN PROGRESS: Editing, with R.F. Leslie, Volumes II and III of *Layamon's Brut,* for Early English Text Society.

*　　*　　*

BROOKE, Maxey 1913-

PERSONAL: Born June 2, 1913, in Muskogee, Okla.; son of Lonnie Day and Laura (Maxey) Brooke; married Genęva Cowan, February 17, 1945; children: Linda, James. *Education:* University of Oklahoma, B.S., 1935. *Politics:* Uncommitted (registered Democrat). *Religion:* Methodist. *Home:* 912 Old Ocean Ave., Sweeny, Tex. 77480. *Agent:* Joe Madachy, Box 35, Kent, Ohio 44240. *Office:* Phillips Petroleum Co., Sweeny, Tex. 77480.

CAREER: During early years held jobs as dishwasher, cook, truck driver, welder, surveyor, doodle-bug, and pipe liner; Midland Gasoline Co., Conroe, Tex., chemist, 1936-39; Gulf Coast Petroleum Laboratory, Houston, Tex., chemist, 1939-40; Jefferson Lake Sulfur Co., Brazoria, Tex., chemist, 1940-47; Phillips Petroleum Co., Sweeny, Tex., chemist, 1947—. Holder of sixteen patents. Boy Scouts of America, district chairman; Brazoria County United Fund, member of board of directors. *Military service:* U.S. Army, 1945-46; became captain. *Member:* National Association of Corrosion Engineers, American Chemical Society, Water Pollution Control Federation, American Mathematics Association, Fibonacci Association, Masons. *Awards, honors:* Southwest Writers Conference Award for best humorous story, 1958; Silver Beaver Award, Boy Scouts of America, 1962.

WRITINGS: (With Kenneth Kraige McKelvey) *The Industrial Cooling Tower,* Elsevier, 1959; *150 Puzzles in Crypt-Arithmetic,* Dover, 1963; *Fun for the Money* (puzzles and games with coins) Scribner, 1963, reissued as *Coin Games and Puzzles,* Dover, 1973; *The Sweeny Story,* [Sweeny] c.1967; *Tricks, Games and Puzzles with Matches,* Dover, 1973. Staff member, *Chemical Abstracts;* abstractor, *Fibonacci Quarterly;* editorial consultant, American Public Health Association. Author of seventy-five technical articles and occasional short stories appearing in periodicals.

WORK IN PROGRESS: Corrosion Inhibitions, to be published by Gulf Publishing; *The Puzzlesmiths,* a history of puzzles; *Statistics for Process Engineers; The First Three Hundred Years,* a church hisory; *Iscariot,* a novel.

AVOCATIONAL INTERESTS: Theory of numbers.

*　　*　　*

BROOKS, Peter W(right) 1920-

PERSONAL: Born January 8, 1920, in Teddington, Middlesex, England; son of Douglas Charles Morris and Beryl (Anderson) Brooks; married Patricia Graham Thomson; children: Nigel George, Hilary Naomi Beryl. *Education:* Attended English Preparatory School and Chillon College, Montreux, Vaud, Switzerland, 1927-37; City and Guilds College, London, B.S. in Engineering, and associate of City and Guilds Institute, 1947. *Politics:*

Conservative. *Religion:* Church of England. *Home:* The Pightle, Ford, near Aylesbury, Buckinghamshire, England; and 5 Cumberland Court, Cumberland St., London S.W.1, England. *Agent:* A.M. Heath & Co. Ltd., 35 Dover St., London W.1, England. *Office:* British Aircraft Corp., Brooklands Rd., Weybridge, Surrey, England.

CAREER: Temple Press Ltd., London, England, member of editorial staff of *Aeroplane* and *Aeroplane Spotter,* 1940-41; *Manchester Evening News,* Manchester, England, air correspondent, 1941; Ministry of Civil Aviation, London, England, technical officer, 1947-50; British European Airways, London, England, 1950-61, started as assistant to chief executive, became fleet planning manager; Beagle Aircraft Ltd., started as deputy managing director, became joint managing director in London, Shoreham, and Leicester, England, 1961-68; British Aircraft Corp., Weybridge, England, manager, International Collaboration, 1968—. Business Aviation Ltd., technical consultant. Lecturer on air transport. Licensed pilot, 1938—; received A, B, and C gliding certificates, 1939, Silver C soaring badge, 1951, helicopter rating, 1960, instrument rating, 1969. *Military service:* Royal Navy, Fleet Air Arm, 1941-46; became lieutenant. *Member:* Royal Aeronautical Society (fellow), Institute of Transport, Air League (council), Royal Aero Club.

WRITINGS: (With B.S. Shenstone and K.G. Wilkinson) *The World's Sailplanes,* Organisation Scientifique et Technique Internationale du Vol a Voile, 1958; (contributor) *History of Technology,* Oxford University Press, 1958; *The Modern Airliner: Its Origins and Development,* Putnam, 1961; *The World's Airliners,* Putnam, 1962. Author of aircraft recognition books, Temple Press, 1941-42; contributor to *Collier's Encyclopedia, Chambers' Encyclopaedia.* Contributor of more than one hundred articles to *Aeroplane, Flight, Engineer,* other aviation journals, and to *Manchester Evening News.*

WORK IN PROGRESS: Cierva's Autogiros; Flying the Pup and Bulldog; History of Aircraft Development; Economics of Aircraft Manufacture; History of Rigid Airships.

*　　*　　*

BROOK-SHEPHERD, (Fred) Gordon 1918-

PERSONAL: Born March 24, 1918, in England; son of Alfred (an architect) and Doreen (Pearson) Brook-Shepherd; married Baroness Sochor, June, 1948; children: Clive Anthony, Nicola. *Education:* Cambridge University, B.A. (first class honors), 1939. *Politics:* Leftwing Conservative. *Religion:* Church of England. *Home:* 5 South Ter., Knightsbridge, London S.W. 7, England. *Agent:* Brandt & Brandt, 101 Park Ave., New York, N.Y. 10017. *Office: Sunday Telegraph,* 135 Fleet St., London E.C.4, England.

CAREER: Daily Telegraph, London, England, foreign correspondent, 1949-60; *Sunday Telegraph,* London, England, diplomatic editor, 1960-65, assistant editor, 1965—. *Military service:* British Army, General Staff, World War II; became lieutenant colonel. *Member:* Royal Central Asian Society, Royal Institute of International Affairs, P.E.N.; Travellers Club and Roehampton Club (both London).

WRITINGS: Russia's Danubian Empire, Praeger, 1954; *The Austrian Odyssey,* St. Martin's, 1957; (with Kurt Peter Karfeld) *Austria in Color* (includes text by Brook-Shepherd), Oesterreichische Staatsdruckerei, 1957; *Where the Lion Trod,* St. Martin's, 1960; *Dollfuss* (biography), St. Martin's, 1961, reissued as *Prelude to Infamy: The Story of Chancellor Dollfuss of Austria,* Obolensky, 1962; *The Anschluss,* Lippincott, 1963 (published in England as *Anschluss: The Rape of Austria,* Macmillan, 1963); *Eagle and Unicorn* (novel), Weidenfeld & Nicolson, 1966, published in America as *The Eferding Diaries,* Lippincott, 1967; *The Last Hapsburg,* Weybright & Talley, 1968; *Between Two Flags,* Putnam, 1973. Contributor to *Holiday, Atlantic Monthly, Esquire,* and other periodicals.

WORK IN PROGRESS: Research in Royal Archives in Windsor Castle.

AVOCATIONAL INTERESTS: Shooting, fishing, skiing, tennis, music.

BIOGRAPHICAL/CRITICAL SOURCES: New York Times Book Review, February 5, 1967; *Best Sellers,* April 1, 1969.

* * *

BROPHY, Liam 1910-

PERSONAL: Born 1910, in Dublin, Ireland; son of John and Elizabeth (Martin) Brophy; married Beda Herbert (a teacher), April, 1946; children: John, Don, Colm, Miriam. *Education:* Catholic University of Louvain, Ph.D., 1938. *Politics:* "Fine Gael." *Religion:* Catholic. *Home:* Umbria, 39 Anglesea Rd., Ballsbridge, Dublin 4, Ireland. *Office:* Office of Public Works, St. Stephen's Green, Dublin, Ireland.

CAREER: Civil servant, Dublin, Ireland, currently in Office of Public Works. Writer. *Member:* Catholic Poetry Society of America. *Awards, honors:* Named to Gallery of Living Catholic Authors.

WRITINGS: Canticles and Chorus: Flights of Franciscan Fancy (poetry), Franciscan Printery, 1956; *The Ardent General: The Career of Baron Geramb from Camp and Court to Trappist Cloister,* Clonmore & Reynolds, 1957; *Echoes of Assisi,* Franciscan Herald, 1958; *So Great a Lover,* Franciscan Herald, 1960; *The Marvelous Doctor: Friar Roger Bacon,* Franciscan Herald, 1963; *Brother Dante,* Franciscan Herald, 1964; *Mariner at the Gates* (a life of Columbus), Franciscan Herald, 1965. Also author of *The Relief of Distress,* an official history of the Irish Famine from state records. Contributor of essays and articles to *Katholischen Soziallexikons* and to periodicals in Ireland, England, United States, Canada, and Australia. Associate editor of *Apostle* and *Social Justice Review.*

WORK IN PROGRESS: A life of Giotto, *Rainbow at Morn; Random Sheaf,* gleanings of a Catholic journalist.

* * *

BROWN, B(artley) Frank 1917-

PERSONAL: Born March 2, 1917, in Dublin, Ga.; son of Bartley Frank and Martha Brown; married Wanda Jean Thomann; children: Barbara Jean, Cassandra Martha. *Education:* Young Harris College, student, 1934-36; University of Georgia, A.B., 1938; Marshall College, M.A., 1949; University of Florida, Ed.D., 1951. *Home:* 244 Michigan Ave., Indialantic, Fla. 32903. *Office:* Melbourne High School, Melbourne, Fla.

CAREER: Melbourne High School, Melbourne, Fla., principal, 1951—; Rollins College, Winter Park, Fla., faculty member, 1958—. Member, advanced placement committee of College Entrance Examination Board, President Johnson's Panel for Research and Educational Development, and advisory council of Aerospace Education Foundation. Studied European schools in connection with U.S. Office of Education survey, 1962. Lecturer on problems of education in thirty-four states, and Canada. Consultant to White House during administration of John F. Kennedy. *Military service:* U.S. Navy, 1943-45. *Member:* National Association of Secondary School Principals (member of curriculum committee), Southern Association of Colleges and Secondary Schools (member of govern-

ing board of project for development of educational opportunities for Negro youth). *Awards, honors:* Avirett Memorial Award of leadership and World Society Foundation, 1964.

WRITINGS: Florida's Beautiful Crotons, American Codiaeum Society, 1960; *The Nongraded High School,* Prentice-Hall, 1963; *The Appropriate Placement School: A Sophisticated Non-graded Curriculum,* Parker Publishing, 1965.

BIOGRAPHICAL/CRITICAL SOURCES: Saturday Review, January 18, 1964; *New York Herald Tribune,* April 19, 1964.

* * *

BROWN, Camille 1917-

PERSONAL: Born August 11, 1917, in Colorado Springs, Colo.; daughter of Elmer Erle (a mineralogist) and Camilus (O'Brien) Brown. *Education:* University of Wyoming, B.S., 1943; University of Michigan, M.P.H., 1945; Columbia University, Ed.D., 1952. *Politics:* Democrat. *Home:* 247 North Bowling Green Way, Los Angeles, Calif. 90049. *Office:* Physical Education Department, University of California, Los Angeles, Calif. 90024.

CAREER: Elementary school teacher, secondary school physical education teacher, Shoshoni and Laramie, Wyo., 1938-43; Kingston High School, Kingston, N.Y., physical education teacher, 1943-44; State College of New York (now State University College at Cortland), Cortland, instructor in health and physical education, 1945-47, assistant professor, 1948-50; University of Michigan, Ann Arbor, lecturer in physical education, 1951; University of California, Los Angeles, 1951—, began as assistant professor, now professor of physical education.

WRITINGS: (With Kimball Wiles and Rosalind Cassidy) *Supervision in Physical Education,* Prentice-Hall, 1956; (with Marjorie Latchow) *The Evaluation Process in Health Education, Physical Education and Recreation,* Prentice-Hall, 1962; (with Cassidy) *Theory in Physical Education: A Guide to Program Change,* Lea & Febiger, 1963.

* * *

BROWN, Edgar S., Jr. 1922-

PERSONAL: Born August 11, 1922, in Allentown, Pa.; son of Edgar S. and Hilda Helen (Merkle) Brown; married Marjorie T. Nicklarz; children: John Thomas III, Christine Anne. *Education:* Muhlenberg College, A.B., 1943; Lutheran Theological Seminary, Mount Airy, Pa., B.D., 1945; Divinity School of Protestant Episcopal Church, Philadelphia, Pa., Th.M., 1950, Th.D., 1954. *Home address:* R.D. 3, Box 308B, Selinsgrove, Pa. 17870. *Office:* Susquehanna University, Selinsgrove, Pa. 17870.

CAREER: Lutheran minister, Grace Church, Pottstown, Pa., 1949-55; United Lutheran Church in America, executive director of department of worship, 1955-62; Lutheran Church of America, director of commission on worship; Susquehanna University, Selinsgrove, Pa., assistant professor of religion and philosophy. *Military service:* U.S. Navy, chaplain, 1945-48.

WRITINGS: Symbols and Terms of the Church, Muhlenberg Press, 1958; *Living the Liturgy,* Muhlenberg Press, 1961; *Understanding the Service,* edited by Frank W. Klos, Lutheran Church Press, 1966; (editor) *Liturgical Reconnaissance,* Fortress, 1968. Contributor to religious journals.

BIOGRAPHICAL/CRITICAL SOURCES: New York Times Book Review, November 17, 1968; *New York Times,* May 15, 1971.

BROWN, Gerald Saxon 1911-

PERSONAL: Born February 25, 1911, in Port Maitland, Nova Scotia, Canada; son of George Cann (a merchant) and Catherine (Nickerson) Brown; married Dorothy Lorraine Meyer, June 14, 1941; children: Catherine Ruth. *Education:* Acadia University, B.A., 1932, M.A., 1937; University of Minnesota, Ph.D., 1948. *Politics:* Democrat. *Religion:* Presbyterian. *Home:* 1720 Hanover Rd., Ann Arbor, Mich. 48103.

CAREER: University of Michigan, Ann Arbor, instructor in history, 1946-50, assistant professor, 1950-55, associate professor, 1955-60, professor of Canadian and British history, 1960—. *Military service:* Royal Canadian Air Force, 1942-46. *Member:* American Historical Association, Canadian Historical Association, American Association of University Professors.

WRITINGS: (With Hugh L. Keenleyside) *Canada and the United States: Some Aspects of Their Historical Relations,* 2nd revised and enlarged edition, Knopf, 1952; (editor) *Reflections on a Pamphlet Entitled "A Letter to the Right Hon. Lord Vic. H—e",* University of Michigan Press, 1959; (editor with Sidney Fine) *The American Past: Conflicting Interpretations of the Great Issues,* two volumes, Macmillan, 1961, 3rd edition, 1970; *The American Secretary: The Colonial Policy of Lord George Germain, 1775-1778,* University of Michigan Press, 1963. Contributor of articles and reviews to *William and Mary Quarterly, Michigan Quarterly,* and *Proceedings* of Michigan Academy, and to historical journals.

WORK IN PROGRESS: The Prime Ministership: Style and Life Stories, 1874-1906.

AVOCATIONAL INTERESTS: Golf.

* * *

BROWN, Gwilym Slater 1928-

PERSONAL: Born February 17, 1928; son of William Slater (an author) and Susan (Jenkins) Brown; married Joyce Skeyhill, February 7, 1953; children: Kristin, Jason. *Education:* Harvard University, B.A., 1951. *Office:* Time, Inc., Rockefeller Center, New York, N.Y. 10020.

CAREER: Sports Illustrated, New York, N.Y., associate editor, 1954—. *Member:* New York Newspaper Guild.

WRITINGS: (With Tony Lema) *Golfer's Gold: An Inside View of the Pro Tour,* Little, Brown, 1964.

WORK IN PROGRESS: A Novel about the life of a professional tournament golfer, using this relatively narrow field to apply a larger theme.

AVOCATIONAL INTERESTS: Theatre, literature, education, sports, and travel.

* * *

BROWN, Ivor (John Carnegie) 1891-

PERSONAL: Born April 25, 1891, in Penang (now part of Federation of Malaya); son of William (a doctor) and Jean (Carnegie) Brown; married Irene Hentschel (a director of plays), January 4, 1916. *Education:* Attended Cheltenham College; Balliol College, Oxford, B.A. (with first class honors). *Politics:* "Capricious." *Religion:* Agnostic. *Home and office:* 20 Christchurch Hill, London N.W. 3, England. *Agent:* A.D. Peters, 10 Buckingham St., Adelphi, London W.C. 2, England.

CAREER: Author, 1915—. Entered Home Civil Service in 1913, resigned to take up career in journalism. *Manchester Guardian* (now *Guardian*), Manchester, England, drama critic, leader writer, and general journalist, 1921-35; drama critic for *Saturday Review,* 1923-30, *The Observer,* 1929-54, *Week End Review,* 1930-34, *Sketch,* 1935-39, *Punch,* 1940-42, all in London, England. Editor of *The Observer,* 1942-48, associate editor and honorary director, 1948-54; editor of *Theatre,* 1954-55; editor of *Drama,* 1956—. Liverpool University, Liverpool, England, Shute lecturer in Art of the Theatre, 1926; president of Critics' Circle, London, 1934-35; Royal Society of Literature, professor of drama, 1939; Council for Encouragement of Music and the Arts, director of drama, 1940-42; British Drama League, chairman, 1954-65; governor of Old Vic and Shakespeare Memorial Theatres. Commentator for British Broadcasting Corp. radio. *Member:* Authors' Society; Royal and Ancient Golf Club of St. Andrews; Garrick and Savile Clubs (both London). *Awards, honors:* Knight of Dannebrog (Denmark), 1949; LL.D., University of St. Andrews, 1950; D.Litt., University of Aberdeen, 1950; Institute of Journalists fellow, 1951.

WRITINGS: Years of Plenty (novel), Secker, 1915, Doran, 1916; *Security,* Secker, 1916.

English Political Theory, Methuen, 1920, 2nd edition, 1929; *Lighting-Up Time,* Cobden-Sanderson, 1920; *The Meaning of Democracy,* Cobden-Sanderson, 1920, revised edition, Duckworth, 1950; *H.G. Wells,* Nisbet & Co., 1923, 2nd edition, 1929; *Smithfield Preserv'd; or, The Divill, a Vegetarian* (interlude from quarto of 1925; produced by Critics' Circle at a private party in London, June 30, 1925), Samuel French (acting edition), 1925, privately printed for A.G. Leonard (Chicago), 1926; *Masques and Phases,* Cobden-Sanderson, 1926; *First Player: The Origin of Drama,* G. Howe, 1927; *Parties of the Play,* Benn, 1928; *Essays of To-day and Yesterday,* Harrap, 1929; *Now on View* (essays), Methuen, 1929; *Art and Everyman,* Benn, 1929.

Brown Studies (essays), Eyre & Spottiswoode, 1930; *Puck, Our Peke,* Routledge, 1931; (with others) *A London Symphony,* London Committee of International Illumination Congress, 1931; *Marine Parade,* Gollancz, 1932; *I Commit to the Flames!* (essays), Hamish Hamilton, 1934; *Master Sanguine, Who Always Believed What He Was Told,* Hamish Hamilton, 1934, Harper, 1935; *The Heart of England,* foreword by J.B. Priestley, Scribner, 1935, 3rd edition, Batsford, 1951; *The Great and the Goods,* Hamish Hamilton, 1937; *I Made You Possible: A Play for the Girls of To-day in One Act,* Samuel French, 1937; (with George Fearon) *This Shakespeare Industry: Amazing Monument,* Harper, 1939 (published in England as *Amazing Monument: A Short History of the Shakespeare Industry,* Heinemann, 1939), reissued as *Amazing Monument: A Short History of the Shakespeare Industry,* Kennikat, 1970; (with Fearon) *The Shakespeares [and] The Birthplace* (the former by Brown, the latter by Fearon), Edward Fox, 1939; *Life Within Reason,* Nicholson & Watson, 1939; *Down on the Farm* (one-act play), Samuel French, 1939.

(Contributor) James Lees-Milne, editor, *The National Trust: A Record of Fifty Years' Achievement,* Batsford, 1945; *The Old Vic "King Lear"* (critical review), Curtain Press, 1946; *William's Other Anne* (play), Samuel French, 1947; (with others) *Britain's Heritage: The Achievement of the National Trust, 1895-1945,* introduction by G.M. Trevelyan, Batsford, 1948; (author of introduction) *"Observer" Profiles,* Wingate, 1948; *Shakespeare* (biography), Doubleday, 1949, 2nd edition, revised and abridged, Collins, 1957, special edition, Time, Inc., 1962.

(Editor) *Shakespeare Memorial Theatre: A Photographic Record,* photographs by Angus McBean, Volume 1: *1948-50,* includes a foreword by Brown and Anthony Quayle, Reinhardt & Evans, 1951, Volume 2: *1951-53,* includes a critical analysis by Brown, Max Reinhardt, 1953, Volume 3: *1954-56,* includes a critical analysis by Brown, Max Reinhardt, 1956, Theatre Arts, 1957, Volume 4: *1957-59,* Max Reinhardt, 1959, Theatre Arts, 1960; *Winter in London,* Collins, 1951, Doubleday, 1952; (author of introduction) J.B. Priestley, *The Priestley Companion;* Penguin and Heinemann, 1951; *Summer in Scotland,* Collins, 1952, Macmillan, 1953; (compiler) *The Bedside "Guardian"* (selections from the *Manchester Guardian*), Collins, Volume 1, 1951-52, Volume 2, 1952-53, Volume 3, 1953-54, Volume 4, 1954-55; (author of introduction) *The Complete Works of William Shakespeare,* four volumes, Nonesuch Press, 1953; (with Christopher Fry) *The Approach to Dramatic Criticism [and] An Experience of Critics* (the former by Brown, and others, the latter by Fry), edited by Kaye Webb, prologue by Alec Guinness, Oxford University Press, 1953; *The Way of My World* (autobiography), Collins, 1954; (author of introduction) William Shakespeare, *Othello,* Folio Society (London), 1955; *Balmoral: The History of a Home,* Collins, 1955; *Pictures on the Wall* (one-act ghost play), Samuel French, 1955; *Emily's Night* (one-act play), Samuel French, 1957; *Dark Ladies,* Collins, 1957; *J.B. Priestley* (booklet; special issue of *British Book News*), Longmans, Green, 1957, revised edition, 1964; *William Shakespeare* (juvenile), Thomas Nelson, 1958; (editor) *A Book of England* (anthology), Collins, 1958; (author of introduction and notes on illustrations) *Royal Homes in Colour,* photographs by A.F. Kersting and others, Batsford, 1958.

London, Newnes, 1960, Macmillan, 1961; *Shakespeare in His Time,* Thomas Nelson, 1960; (editor) *A Book of London* (anthology), Collins, 1961; (with Ralph Dutton) *Stately Homes in Colour* (single-volume edition of *Royal Homes in Colour,* by Brown, and *English Country Houses in Colour,* by Dutton), Batsford, 1961; *Mind Your Language!,* Bodley Head, 1962, Dufour, 1964; *Look at Theatres,* Hamish Hamilton, 1962; (compiler) *A Book of Marriage,* Hamish Hamilton, 1963; *How Shakespeare Spent the Day,* Bodley Head, 1963, Hill & Wang, 1964; *Dickens in His Time,* Thomas Nelson, 1963; *Shakespeare and His World,* Walck, 1964; *What Is a Play?* Macdonald & Co., 1964; *London: An Illustrated History,* Studio Vista, 1965; *Shaw in His Time,* Thomas Nelson, 1965; *Dr. Johnson and His World,* Lutterworth, 1965, Walck, 1966; *Jane Austen and Her World,* Lutterworth, 1966, Walck, 1967; *William Shakespeare* (not the same as the two previous biographies), Morgan-Grampian, Books, 1968, A.S. Barnes, 1969; *The Women in Shakespeare's Life,* Bodley Head, 1968, Coward, 1969.

Dickens and His World, Walck, 1970; *W. Somerset Maugham,* International Textbook Co., 1970, A.S. Barnes, 1970; (compiler and author of introduction) Robert Louis Stevenson, *Home from the Sea* (poems), Bodley Head, 1970; (compiler) *Charles Dickens, 1812-1870* (facsimile documents, broadsheets, and essays), Jackdaws, 1970; *Shakespeare and the Actors,* Bodley Head, 1970, Coward, 1971; *Old and Young: A Personal Summing Up,* Bodley Head, 1971.

"Word-anthology" series: *A Word in Your Ear,* J. Cape, 1942; *Just Another Word,* J. Cape, 1943; *Book of Words* (comprising *A Word in Your Ear* and *Just Another Word*), J. Cape, 1944, published in America as *A Word in Your Ear; and, Just Another Word,* foreword by J. Donald Adams, Dutton, 1945; *I Give You My Word,* J. Cape, 1945, *Say the Word,* J. Cape, 1947, preceding two books published in America as single volume, *I Give You My Word [and] Say the Word,* with an introduction by Adams, Dutton, 1948; *No Idle Words,* J. Cape, 1948, *Having the Last Word,* J. Cape, 1950, preceding two books published in America as single volume, *No Idle Words [and] Having the Last Word,* with an introduction by Adams, Dutton, 1951; *I Break My Word,* J. Cape, 1951; *A Word in Edgeways,* J. Cape, 1953; *Chosen Words,* J. Cape, 1955; *Words in Our Time,* J. Cape, 1958; *Words in Season,* Hart-Davis, 1961; *A Ring of Words,* Bodley Head, 1967, Transatlantic, 1972; *A Rhap-*

sody of Words, Bodley Head, 1969, Transatlantic, 1972; *Random Words,* Bodley Head, 1971.

Also author of *Journalism in Our Time* (oration delivered by Brown during the 37th Foundation Week of University College Union Society), [London], 1933, and of essays on dramatic criticism, Shakespeare, and poetic drama, published in *Transactions* of the Royal Society of Literature.

SIDELIGHTS: Brown has said that he began his literary career when he learned to spell, and that he still has a book he wrote and illustrated at the age of five. Although he has always written about the theatre, he has never really specialized, preferring to practice journalism and authorship in several different forms. He has been known as an essayist, novelist, journalist, playwright, and drama critic, as well as a "word-collector" whose research and speculations have added much to the English language treasury of verbal meanings. A reviewer for the *Times Literary Supplement* wrote that "such guardians of English usage as Mr. Ivor Brown are much needed now and his onset against slipshod speech, pretentious writing and bureaucratic jargon should be taken to heart by everybody." In a review of *Mind Your Language!,* the *New York Times Book Review* writer found "the burden of Mr. Brown's message on simplicity and verbiage, on cliches and on the vitamin-rich qualities of slang in nourishing language . . . admirable in every way."

Brown's witty and imaginative approach to language has been carried over to his novels about English authors, which could be called social surveys of specific eras rather than histories, literary critiques, or biographies. Although he offers little which is new in the way of interpretation, he documents the periods of his subjects (e.g., Jane Austen, Charles Dickens, Samuel Johnson) through detailed analyses of their lives and times, augmenting the text with carefully selected, annotated photographs. *Jane Austen and Her World* is a description of the actual world in which she lived, rather than the narrow one of which she wrote. Contemporary drawings, fashion, furniture, and architecture share pages with the social, political, economic, and cultural flavor of her environment. Similarly, Brown fills in the background of *Shaw in His Time* with Shaw's stated opinions on the politics, economics, religion, theatre, education, and status of women of his day. A *Times Literary Supplement* reviewer of the book noted that "Brown's judgments on every aspect of Shaw's prodigious achievement are valid in the light of his own keen participation in its circumstances.... It is the measure of Mr. Brown's advocacy that he proves beyond any doubt that G.B.S. played a leading serio-comic role in the blood and thunder melodrama of his time."

A meticulous and scholarly writer in any genre of his choice, Brown is perhaps best known for his ventures into Shakespeareana. *The Women in Shakespeare's Life* is his latest contribution to an ever-widening field of historical (and conjectural) literature about Will Shakespeare and his family. A *New Yorker* reviewer writes that "this is Mr. Brown's fourth book on Shakespeare, and there is not enough material for it. . . . [His] two serious arguments are that the women in Shakespeare's family were more literate than has been held, and that his marriage was not that bad. His candidate for 'Mr. W.H.' is Pembroke, and for the Dark Lady is Mary Fitton, but he has no new evidence." "Although the index is inadequate, the bibliography a mild wave of the hand," James Sandoe recommends *The Women in Shakespeare's Life* to all libraries; "the popular library for its beguiling charm and lucidity and the academic library because so charmingly expressed and carefully considered a judgment has a weight that does not need footnotes.... It is a book that should lead readers contentedly to more of Mr. Brown's beguiling books." Donald Tyerman, who spent "the eleven most fruitful months of my journalistic life serving [Brown] . . . during the war," insists that Brown's latest book, *Old and Young,* "is really a precis and reassembly of the autobiography Ivor Brown wrote 17 years ago.... Here, lucid and downright as he always was, in print anyway, is the moody and merry and melancholy, the kindly, clubbable, convivial and curmudgeonly, tolerant and cantankerous, patient and exasperated, outspoken and circumspect, always loyal ,and occasionally resentful Ivor Brown we salute with affection."

BIOGRAPHICAL/CRITICAL SOURCES: Times Literary Supplement, June 1, 1962, January 27, 1966; *New York Times Book Review,* April 26, 1964, January 24, 1965, May 7, 1967; *Young Readers' Review,* April, 1967; *Books and Bookmen,* December, 1967; *Observer Review,* June 30, 1968, April 25, 1971; *Plays and Players,* October, 1968; *Library Journal,* March 15, 1969; *New Yorker,* March 29, 1969; *Books and Bookmen,* August, 1970; *Bookmen's Weekly,* August 2-9, 1971.

* * *

BROWN, John Mason 1900-1969

PERSONAL: Born July 3, 1900, in Louisville, Ky.; son of John Mason (a lawyer) and Carrie (Ferguson) Brown; married Catherine Screven Meredith, February 11, 1933; children: Preston, Meredith Mason. *Education:* Harvard University, A.B. (cum laude), 1923. *Home:* 17 East 89th St., New York, N.Y.

CAREER: Theatre Arts Monthly, New York, N.Y., associate editor and drama critic, 1924-28; *New York Evening Post,* New York, N.Y., drama critic, 1929-41; *New York World Telegram,* New York, N.Y., drama critic, 1941-42; *Saturday Review,* New York, N.Y. associate editor, 1944-45, author of column, "Seeing Things," 1944-64, editor-at-large, 1955-69. American Laboratory Theater, staff lecturer, 1925-31; teacher of courses on the theater at University of Montana, summers of 1923, 1929, 1931, at Yale University, 1932, at Bread Loaf Writers' Conference, Middlebury College, summers of 1935, 1936, and at Harvard University, summers of 1937-40. Public lecturer throughout United States, beginning in 1928. Conductor of Columbia Broadcasting System program, "Of Men and Books," 1944-47, American Broadcasting Co. television program, "Critic-at-Large," 1948-49; panelist on Columbia Broadcasting System television program, "The Last Word," 1957-59. Book-of-the-Month Club judge, 1956-69. Harvard College, overseer, 1949-55; trustee of Metropolitan Museum of Art, 1951-56, of New York Society Library, 1950-69, and of Recordings for the Blind. *Military service:* U.S. Naval Reserve, lieutenant, 1942-44; served on staff of Vice-Admiral Alan G. Kirk during invasions of Sicily and Normandy; received Bronze Star.

MEMBER: New York Drama Critics Circle (president, 1941-42, 1945-49), P.E.N. (president, 1947-48), National Institute of Arts and Letters, Pulitzer Prize Drama Jury (until resignation in 1963), Council on Foreign Relations, Century Association, Phi Beta Kappa, Harvard Club. *Awards, honors:* L.H.D., Williams College, 1941; D.Litt., University of Montana, 1942, Clark University, 1947, University of Louisville, 1948, Hofstra College, 1954, Long Island University, 1963.

WRITINGS: The Modern Theater in Revolt, Norton, 1929; *Upstage: The American Theatre in Performance,* Norton, 1930; (editor with Montrose Moses) *American Theatre as Seen by Its Critics,* Norton, 1934; *Letters from Greenroom Ghosts,* Viking, 1934; *The Art of Playgoing,* Norton, 1936; *Two on the Aisle,* Norton, 1938; (with others) *George Pierce Baker, a Memorial,* Dramatists, 1939.

Broadway in Review, Norton, 1940; *Insides Out,* Dodd, 1942; *Accustomed as I Am,* Norton, 1942; *To All Hands,* McGraw, 1943; *Many a Watchful Night,* McGraw, 1944; *Seeing Things,* McGraw, 1946; *Seeing More Things,* Whittlesey House, 1948; *Beyond the Present,* Ampersand, 1948; *Morning Faces,* Whittlesey House, 1949; (editor) *The Portable Charles Lamb,* Viking, 1949.

Still Seeing Things, McGraw, 1950; *As They Appear,* McGraw, 1952; *Daniel Boone, the Opening of the Wilderness,* Random, 1952; *Through These Men,* Harper, 1956; (editor) *Ladies' Home Journal Treasury,* Simon & Schuster, 1956; *Dramatis Personae,* (contains complete text of *The Modern Theatre in Revolt*), Viking, 1963; *The Worlds of Robert E. Sherwood: Mirror to His Times, 1896-1939,* Harper, 1965.

Author of introduction: Hiram K. Moderwell, *The Theater of Today,* Dodd, 1927; Bennett A. Cerf and V.H. Cartmell, editors, *Sixteen Famous British Plays,* Garden City Publishers, 1942; Margaret Webster, *Shakespeare Without Tears,* McGraw, 1942; Joseph Hennessey, editor, *The Portable Woollcott,* 1946.

SIDELIGHTS: As a critic John Mason Brown had an enthusiastic following, and an immense popularity as a lecturer. His fellow critics were at times divided as to his precise merits. George Freedley called his selected critical writings, *Dramatis Personae,* "one of the great theater books of this century." Yet John Simon said of the same collection: "What is most lacking is discrimination." At the time of Brown's death, Norman Cousins wrote: "He was first of all a man of taste, a presiding fact about his criticism that everyone connected with the theater came to recognize and respect. . . . His writings in [*The Saturday Review*] widened progressively until they embraced the world of the creative arts as a whole . . . combining the public interest in the topical with the critic's interest in the generic and the historical."

BIOGRAPHICAL/CRITICAL SOURCES: New Yorker, October 18 and 25, 1952; Loring Holmes Dodd, *Celebrities at Our Hearthside,* 1959; *Library Journal,* June 1, 1963; *New York Times Book Review,* July 14, 1963, September 19, 1965; *Atlantic,* September, 1965; *New York Times,* March 17, 1969; *Washington Post,* March 17, 1969; *Variety,* March 19, 1969; *Time,* March 28, 1969; *Saturday Review,* March 29, 1969; *Newsweek,* March 31, 1969.

(Died March 16, 1969)

* * *

BROWN, Leslie H(ilton) 1917-

PERSONAL: Born August 25, 1917, in Coonoor, South India; son of Charles Hilton (an author) and Margaret (Gordon) Brown; married Barbara Elisabeth Jackson, August 10, 1958; children: Charles Hilton. *Education:* Attended schools in India, and Oundle School ·in England; University of St. Andrews, B.Sc. (honors); Cambridge University and Imperial College of Tropical Agriculture, Trinidad, West Indies, associateship of Imperial College. *Home:* Mbagathi Ridge, Karen, Kenya. *Office:* Box 24916, Karen, Kenya.

CAREER: British Colonial Agricultural Service, 1940-63, serving in Nigeria as agricultural officer, 1940-45, in Kenya as agricultural officer, 1946-54, assistant director of agriculture, 1954-56, deputy director, 1956-60, chief agriculturist, 1960-63. Writer and consultant for IBRD, FAO, UNESCO, Ford Foundation, and other organizations, 1963—. *Member:* British Ornithologists' Union, South African Ornithological Society, Bombay Natural History Society, Indian Wild Life Society (life), Fauna Preservation Society, East African Natural History Society (past president), East African Wild Life Society (member of council).

WRITINGS: Outlaw of the Air, Bles, 1939; Birds and I, M. Joseph, 1947; Eagles, M. Joseph, 1955, Arco, 1970; The Mystery of the Flamingos, Country Life, 1959, new edition, Collins, 1972; Ethiopian Episode, Country Life, 1965; Africa: A Natural History, Random House, 1965; Mobil Handbook of Conservation, Ethiopia, Ethiopian Tourist Organization, c.1966; (with Dean Amadon) Eagles, Hawks, and Falcons of the World, two volumes, Country Life, 1968, McGraw, 1969; African Birds of Prey, Houghton, 1971; East African Mountains and Lakes, East African Publishing (Nairobi), 1971, International Publications Service, 1973; (with E.K. Urban) A Checklist of Ethiopian Ponds, Addis Ababa University Press, 1971; The Life of the African Plains, McGraw, 1972. Contributor of articles to Ibis, Field, Audubon Magazine, Country Life, Journal of the East African Natural History Society, East African Agricultural Journal, and other periodicals.

WORK IN PROGRESS: The Life of African Savannas, to be published by McGraw; East African Coasts and Reefs, for East African Publishing; British Birds of Prey, a New Naturalist monograph for Collins; and several research projects, notably on pesticide incidence in East African lakes.

AVOCATIONAL INTERESTS: Mountaineering, trout fishing, outdoor sports, photography; good food, good books, and wine.

BIOGRAPHICAL/CRITICAL SOURCES: Library Journal, July, 1969; New York Times Book Review, August 31, 1969; Natural History, November, 1969.

*   *   *

BROWN, Milton Perry, Jr.   1928-

PERSONAL: Born June 5, 1928, in Bessemer, Ala.; son of Milton Perry (an accountant) and Elaine (Hood) Brown; married Anne Marie Cochran, April 1, 1950; children: Marie Moore, George Milton. Education: Birmingham-Southern College, B.A., 1950; State University of Iowa, graduate study, 1950-51; Louisville Presbyterian Theological Seminary, B.D., 1954; Duke University, Ph.D., 1959. Home: 2725 Woodland Hills, Memphis, Tenn. 38127. Office: Southwestern at Memphis, Memphis, Tenn. 38112.

CAREER: Ordained minister in Presbyterian Church; pastor of church in Bardstown, Ky., 1953-55; Duke Divinity School, Durham, N.C., instructor in Hellenistic Greek, 1955-58; Washington and Lee University, Lexington, Va., chaplain and assistant professor of religion, 1958-60; Southwestern at Memphis, Memphis, Tenn., 1960—, began as assistant professor, now professor of Bible. Supply pastor of church in Sanford, N.C., 1956-58, and occasionally of other churches. Member: National Association of Biblical Instructors, Society of Biblical Literature and Exegesis, American Association of University Professors, Phi Beta Kappa, Omicron Delta Kappa, Eta Sigma Phi, Kappa Alpha.

WRITINGS: The Authentic Writings of Ignatius: A Study of Linguistic Criteria, Duke University Press, 1963; (contributor) B.L. Daniels and M.J. Suggs, editors, Studies in the History and Text of the New Testament, University of Utah Press, 1967.

WORK IN PROGRESS: A research paper on the function of the amanuensis in New Testament epistolography.

*   *   *

BROWN, Neville (George)   1932-

PERSONAL: Born April 8, 1932, in Watlington, Oxfordshire, England; son of Harold (a businessman) and Nel-honors degree in economics, 1954; New College, Oxford, lie (Jones) Brown. Education: University College, London,

honors degree in history, 1957. Home: Hill Rd., Watlington, Oxfordshire, England. Agent: A.D. Peters, 10 Buckingham St., London W.C.2, England. Office: The Department of Politics, University of Birmingham, Birmingham 15, England.

CAREER: Royal Military Academy, Sandhurst, England, lecturer in international affairs and military history, 1960-62; Institute for Strategic Studies, London, England, research associate, 1962-64; free-lance writer, 1964-65; University of Birmingham, Birmingham, England, lecturer, 1965-71, senior lecturer in international politics, 1971—. Military service: Royal Navy, Fleet Air Arm, meteorological branch, 1957-60; became lieutenant. Member: Royal Meteorological Society (fellow).

WRITINGS: Strategic Mobility Deadlock, published for Institute for Strategic Studies by Chatto & Windus, 1963, and by Praeger, 1964; (with W.F. Gutteridge) The African Military Balance, Institute for Strategic Studies, 1964; Britain in NATO, Fabian Society, 1964; Nuclear War: The Impending Strategic Deadlock, Pall Mall, 1964, Praeger, 1965; Britain and World Security, Fabian Society, 1966; (with Donald Cameron Watt and Frank Spencer) A History of the World in the Twentieth Century (Part I, 1899-1918, by Watt, Part II, 1918-1945, by Spencer, and Part III, 1945-1968, by Brown), Hodder & Stoughton, 1966; (with others) Has Israel Really Won?, Fabian Society, 1967; Arms Without Empire: British Defence Role in the Modern World, Penguin, 1967; (with others) Defence in a New Setting, Fabian Society, 1968; British Arms and Strategy, 1970-80, Royal United Service Institution, 1969.

BIOGRAPHICAL/CRITICAL SOURCES: Times Literary Supplement, February 15, 1968.

*   *   *

BROWN, Richard H(olbrook)   1927-

PERSONAL: Born September 25, 1927, in Boston, Mass.; son of Joseph Richard and Sylvia (Cook) Brown. Education: Yale University, B.A., 1949, M.A., 1952, Ph.D., 1955. Home: 900 North Lake Shore Dr., Chicago, Ill. 60611. Office: Newberry Library, 60 West Walton St., Chicago, Ill. 60610.

CAREER: University of Massachusetts, Amherst, instructor, later assistant professor of history, 1955-62; Northern Illinois University, DeKalb, associate professor of history, 1962-64; Committee on the Study of History, Hampshire College, and Chicago, Ill., staff director, 1964—. Member: American Historical Association, Organization of American Historians (chairman, Committee on History in the Schools and Colleges), University Club (Pittsburgh), Elizabethan Club (Yale). Awards, honors: Andrew Mellon fellowship in history, University of Pittsburgh, 1960-61.

WRITINGS: The Hero and the People: The Meaning of Jacksonian Democracy, Macmillan, 1964; The Missouri Compromise: Political Statesmanship or Unwise Evasion?, Heath, 1964. Co-editor, "New Dimensions in American History" series, Heath, 1964-68. Co-editor, Amherst Project, Addison-Wesley series in history, 1969—.

WORK IN PROGRESS: As contributing historian, a book on the nature of "history," with Peter Schraq.

*   *   *

BROWN, Roger H(amilton)   1931-

PERSONAL: Born September 7, 1931, in Cleveland, Ohio; son of Percy Whiting (an investment broker) and Helen (Hurd) Brown; married Christine Hodgdon, December 18, 1954; children: Matthew Whiting, Jennifer Lynam. Education: Harvard University, A.B., 1953, A.M., 1954, Ph.D., 1960. Politics: Democrat. Home:

3249 O St. N.W., Washington, D.C. 20007. *Office:* Department of History, American University, Washington, D.C. 20016.

CAREER: Social Science Research Council, New York, N.Y., research fellow, 1958-59; Dartmouth College, Hanover, N.H., instructor, 1960-62, assistant professor of history, 1962-64; Harvard University, Cambridge, Mass., research fellow, Center for the Study of History of Liberty in America, 1964-65; American University, Washington, D.C., associate professor, 1965-70, professor of history, 1971—. *Member:* American Historical Association, Organization of American Historians, American Association of University Professors. *Awards, honors:* Guggenheim fellow, 1970-71.

WRITINGS: The Struggle for the Indian Stream Territory, Western Reserve University Press, 1955; *The Republic in Peril: 1812,* Columbia University Press, 1964.

WORK IN PROGRESS: The Early Federalists.

* * *

BROWN, Wilfred (Banks Duncan) 1908-

PERSONAL: Born November 29, 1908, in Greenock, Scotland; son of Peter (a wholesaler) and Emily Janet (Skinner) Brown; married Marjorie Skinner, September 29, 1939; children: Richard, Michael, Angus. *Education:* Attended Rossal School. *Politics:* Labour. *Home:* 23 Prince Albert Rd., London N.W.1 75T, England.

CAREER: Glacier Metal Co. Ltd., Wembley, England, started as clerk, 1931, sales manager, 1934-39, managing director and chairman, 1939-65. Pro-chancellor, Brunel University. Privy councillor. *Member:* British Institute of Management (fellow). *Awards, honors:* Member of Order of British Empire.

WRITINGS: (With Winifred Raphael) *Managers, Men and Morale,* Macdonald & Evans, 1948; *Some Problems of a Factory: An Analysis of Industrial Institutions,* Institute of Personnel Management, c.1952; *Exploration in Management,* Wiley, 1960 (published in England as *Exploration in Management: A Description of the Glacier Metal Company's Concepts and Methods of Organization and Management,* Heinemann, 1960); *Piece-Work Abandoned: The Effect of Wage Incentive Systems on Managerial Authority,* Heinemann, 1963; *Product Analysis Pricing: A Method for Setting Policies for the Delegation of Pricing Decisions and the Control of Expense and Profitability,* Heinemann, 1964; (with Elliott Jaques) *Glacier Project Papers: Some Essays on Organization and Management from the Glacier Project Research,* Heinemann, 1965; (with Jaques) *Organization,* Heinemann, 1971; *Inflation: A Possible Solution,* privately printed, 1971.

BIOGRAPHICAL/CRITICAL. SOURCES: Investors Chronicle, February, 1959; *New Scientist,* October 19, 1961; *Scottish Field,* April, 1963.

* * *

BROWN, Zenith J. 1898-
(Leslie Ford, David Frome)

PERSONAL: Born December 8, 1898, in Smith River, Calif.; daughter of Milnor (an Episcopalian clergyman) and Mary Frances (Watkins) Jones; married Ford Keeler Brown (a college professor), 1918; children: Janet Calvert. *Education:* University of Washington, Seattle, A.B., 1921. *Home:* 235 King George St., Annapolis, Md. 21401. *Agent:* Brandt & Brandt, 101 Park Ave., New York, N.Y. 10017.

CAREER: Writer of detective novels, 1929—.

WRITINGS—Under pseudonym David Frome: *The Murder of an Old Man,* Methuen, 1929; *In at the Death,* Skeffington, 1929, Longmans, Green, (New York), 1930;

The Hammersmith Murders, Doubleday, 1930; *The Strange Death of Martin Green,* Doubleday, 1931 (published in England as *The Murder on the Sixth Hole,* Methuen, 1931); *Two Against Scotland Yard,* Farrar & Rinehart, 1931; *The Man from Scotland Yard,* Farrar & Rinehart, 1932; *The By-Pass Murder,* Longmans, Green, 1932; *The Eel Pie Murders,* Farrar & Rinehart, 1933 (published in England as *Eel Pie Mystery,* Longmans, Green, 1933); *Scotland Yard Can Wait,* Farrar & Rinehart, 1933 (published in England as "*That's Your Man, Inspector*", Longmans, Green, 1934); *Mr. Simpson Finds a Body,* Longmans, Green, 1933; *Mr. Pinkerton Finds a Body,* Farrar & Rinehart, 1934 (published in England as *The Body in the Turl,* Longmans, Green, 1935); *Mr. Pinkerton Goes to Scotland Yard,* Farrar & Rinehart, 1934 (published in England as *Arsenic in Richmond,* Longmans, Green, 1934); *Mr. Pinkerton and Inspector Bull: A New Scotland Yard Omnibus* (includes *Mr. Pinkerton Solves the Eel Pie Murders, Mr. Pinkerton Goes to Scotland Yard,* and *Mr. Pinkerton Finds a Body),* Farrar & Rinehart, 1934; *Mr. Pinkerton Grows a Beard,* Farrar & Rinehart, 1935 (published in England as *The Body in Bedford Square,* Longmans, Green, 1935); *Mr. Pinkerton: A Scotland Yard Omnibus* (includes *The Hammersmith Murders, Two Against Scotland Yard,* and *The Man from Scotland Yard),* Farrar & Rinehart, 1935; *Mr. Pinkerton Has the Clue,* Farrar & Rinehart, 1936 (abbreviated version published in *American Magazine* as "*Mr. Pinkerton is Present*"); *The Black Envelope: Mr. Pinkerton Again!,* Farrar & Rinehart, 1937 (published in England as *The Guilt is Plain: Mr. Pinkerton's Adventure at Brighton,* Longmans, Green, 1938); *Mr. Pinkerton: A Scotland Yard Omnibus* (includes *Two Against Scotland Yard* and *The Man from Scotland Yard),* Grosset, 1938; *Mr. Pinkerton at the Old Angel,* Farrar & Rinehart, 1939 (adapted version published in *American Magazine* as "*Visitor in the Night*"); *Homicide House: Mr. Pinkerton Returns,* Rinehart, 1950; *Murder on the Square: Mr. Pinkerton Returns,* R. Hale, 1951.

Under pseudonym Leslie Ford: *The Sound of Footsteps,* Doubleday, 1931 (published in England as *Footsteps on the Stairs,* Gollancz, 1931); *By the Watchman's Clock,* Farrar & Rinehart, 1932; *Murder in Maryland,* Farrar & Rinehart, 1932; *The Clue of the Judas Tree,* Farrar & Rinehart, 1933; *The Strangled Witness,* Farrar & Rinehart, 1934; *Burn Forever,* Farrar & Rinehart, 1935 (published in England as *Mountain Madness,* Hutchinson, 1935); *Ill Met by Moonlight,* Farrar & Rinehart, 1937; *The Simple Way of Poison,* Farrar & Rinehart, 1937; *Three Bright Pebbles,* Farrar & Rinehart, 1938; *False to Any Man,* Scribner, 1939 (published in England as *Snow-White Murder,* Collins, 1940); *Reno Rendezvous,* Farrar & Rinehart, 1939 (published in England as *Mr. Cromwell is Dead,* Collins, 1939); *The Town Cried Murder,* Scribner, 1939; *The Road to Folly,* Scribner, 1940; *Old Lover's Ghost,* Scribner, 1940; *The Murder of a Fifth Columnist,* Scribner, 1941 (published in England as *A Capital Crime,* Collins, 1941); *Murder with Southern Hospitality,* Scribner, 1942 (published in England as *Murder Down South,* Collins, 1942); *Murder in the O.P.M.,* Scribner, 1942 (published in England as *Priority Murder,* Collins, 1943); *Siren in the Night,* Scribner, 1943; *All for the Love of a Lady,* Scribner, 1944 (published in England as *Crack of Dawn,* Collins, 1945); *The Philadelphia Murder Story,* Scribner, 1945; *Honolulu Story,* Scribner, 1946 (published in England as *Honolulu Murder Story,* Collins, 1947); *The Woman in Black,* Scribner, 1947; *The Devil's Stronghold,* Scribner, 1948; *Date with Death,* Scribner, 1949 (originally announced as "Late Date—Annapolis"; published in England as *Shot in the Dark,* Collins, 1949); *Murder is the Pay-Off,* Scribner, 1951; *The Bahamas Murder Case,* Scribner, 1952; *Washington Whispers Murder,* Scribner, 1953 (published in England as *The Lying Jade,* Collins, 1953); *In-*

vitation to Murder, Scribner, 1954; *Murder Comes to Eden,* Scribner, 1955; *The Girl from the Mimosa Club,* Scribner, 1957 (also published in a single volume with *A Shadow in the Wild,* by Whit Masterson, and *Method in Madness,* by Doris Miles Disney, Walter J. Black, 1957); *Trial by Ambush,* Scribner, 1962 (published in England as *Trial for Ambush,* Collins, 1962).

SIDELIGHTS: Although it would appear from her Scotland Yard stories that Mrs. Brown had roots in England, she is descended from early Maryland settlers, was born in California, and spent her childhood in Washington State. Mr. Pinkerton and Inspector Bull, the protagonists of the David Frome mysteries, evolved from a stay in England where her husband was doing some advanced study; their American counterparts (of sorts), Colonel Primrose and Sergeant Buck of the Leslie Ford stories, followed shortly.

Their creator says that "mystery fiction is written to entertain, not to instruct. I don't regard it as 'literature' or of lasting value." Her books have appeared in nine languages, and continue to be reissued in paperback editions at the rate of half a dozen a year. Most of the Leslie Ford stories also ran as serials in magazines, notably in the *Saturday Evening Post.*

* * *

BROWNLEE, W(illiam) H(ugh)   1917-

PERSONAL: Born February 17, 1917, in Sylvia, Kan.; son of Hugh Leeman (a farmer) and Hazel (Stevenson) Brownlee; married Sarah Louis Dunn, August 12, 1948; children: Linda Louise, Mary Elizabeth, Hugh William, David Jenus, Martha Maude. *Education:* Sterling College, A.B., 1939; Pittsburgh-Xenia Theological Seminary, Th.B., 1942, Th.M., 1946; Duke University, Ph.D., 1947; American School of Oriental Research, Jerusalem, Palestine, postdoctoral study, 1947-48; Palestine Archaeological Museum, study in scrollery, 1962. *Home:* 1534 Wells Ave., Claremont, Calif. 91711. *Office:* Claremont Graduate School, Claremont, Calif. 91711.

CAREER: Presbyterian minister. Pastor in Newton, Kan., 1942-44; Duke University, Durham, N.C., instructor in religion at Trinity College, 1948-50, assistant professor, then associate professor of Old Testament at Divinity School, 1950-59; Claremont Graduate School, Claremont, Calif., professor of religion, 1959—. James W. Richard Lecturer in Christian Religion, University of Virginia, 1958. Explorer in part of Sinai Desert, 1948; participated in excavations of Bethel, Jordan, 1960, and Tell er Ras, Jordan, 1966 and 1968. *Member:* Society of Biblical Literature, American Schools of Oriental Research, National Academy of Religion, Archaeological Institute of America, World Affairs Council. *Awards, honors:* D.D. from Sterling College, 1960; research fellowship, American Council of Learned Societies and American Association of Theological Schools, 1961-62; research fellowship, American Philosophical Society, 1966.

WRITINGS: (With Millar Burrows and J.C. Trever) *The Dead Sea Scrolls of St. Mark's Monastery,* American School of Oriental Research, Volume I, 1950, Volume II, 1951; (editor and translator) *The Dead Sea Manual of Discipline,* American School of Oriental Research, 1951, supplemental studies, numbers 10-12, 1951; *The Dead Sea Habakkuk Midrash and the Targum of Jonathan,* Duke Divinity School, 1953; *The Text of Habakkuk in the Ancient Commentary from Qumran,* Society of Biblical Literature, 1959; *Recovering the Authentic Core of Ezekiel's Visions,* [Claremont] 1961; *The Meaning of the Qumran Scrolls for the Bible, with Special Attention to the Book of Isaiah,* Oxford University Press, 1964; (contributor) *Interpreter's One-Volume Commentary on the Bible,* Abingdon, 1971. Contributor of about fifty articles to professional journals.

WORK IN PROGRESS: The Qumran Bible Commentaries for the E.J. Brill series, "Studies on the Texts of the Desert of Judah"; *"Philistine" Manuscripts from Palestine,* to be published by Johns Hopkins Press.

SIDELIGHTS: Brownlee participated in the first study of the Dead Sea Scrolls while a fellow at the American School of Oriental Research, Jerusalem, 1947-48, and translated the first two scrolls; he also discovered the "Philistine" manuscripts in 1966.

BIOGRAPHICAL/CRITICAL SOURCES: Duke Divinity School Bulletin, November, 1956.

* * *

BROYLES, J(ohn) Allen   1934-

PERSONAL: Born January 13, 1934, in Johnson City, Tenn.; son of Joseph Warren (a college president) and Edith (Allen) Broyles; married Dolores Pettit, June 2, 1956; children: Marianne Aweagon. *Education:* University of Redlands, A.B., 1956; Boston University, S.T.B., 1959, Ph.D., 1963. *Politics:* Democrat. *Office:* Department of Religion, Oklahoma City University, Oklahoma City, Okla. 73106.

CAREER: Methodist minister. Pastor of churches in Boothbay Harbor, Me., 1962-65, Orono, Me., 1965-68, and Winchester, Mass., 1968-70; Oklahoma City University, Oklahoma City, Okla., assistant professor of religion and social ethics and chairman of department of religion, 1970—. President, Boothbay Region Ministers Association, 1962-65; chairman, Maine Council of Churches, Department of Social Education and Action; chairman of trustees, University of Maine Christian Association. *Member:* American Sociological Association, National Association for the Advancement of Colored People, Kiwanis Club.

WRITINGS: The John Birch Society: Anatomy of a Protest, Beacon Press, 1964, revised edition, 1966; (contributor) Walter M. Gerson, editor, *Social Problems in a Changing World: A Comparative Reader,* Crowell, 1969. Contributor of articles to *Journal of Social Issues.*

WORK IN PROGRESS: An introduction to Christian social ethics for the lay reader.

* * *

BRUCCOLI, Matthew J(oseph)   1931-

PERSONAL: Born August 21, 1931, in New York, N.Y.; son of Joseph M. and Mary (Gervasi) Bruccoli; married Arlyn S. Firkins, 1957; children: Mary. *Education:* Yale University, B.A., 1953; University of Virginia, M.A., 1956, Ph.D., 1961. *Home:* 113 East Lane Ave., Columbus, Ohio 43201.

CAREER: Ohio State University, Columbus, assistant professor, 1961-63, associate professor of English, 1963—, and associate textual editor of the "Centenary Hawthorne." *Member:* Bibliographical Society of America, Bibliographical Society of the University of Virginia, Yale Club of New York, Grolier Club.

WRITINGS: (With Frances Joan Brewer) *James Branch Cabell,* two volumes, University of Virginia Press, 1957; *Notes on the Cabell Collection at the University of Virginia,* University of Virginia Press, 1957; *Twentieth-Century Books,* University of Illinois Library School, 1959; *The Composition of "Tender Is the Night": A Study of the Manuscripts,* University of Pittsburgh Press, 1963; *Material for a Centenary Edition of "Tender Is the Night,"* University of Virginia Press, 1963; *F. Scott Fitzgerald: Collector's Handlist,* Fitzgerald Newsletter, 1964; (author of textual notes) Zelda Fitzgerald, *Save Me the Waltz,* Southern Illinois University Press, 1967; *Raymond Chandler: A Checklist,* Kent State University Press, 1968; *Profile of F. Scott Fitzgerald,* C.E. Merrill,

1971; *Kenneth Millar/Ross Macdonald: A Checklist,* Gale, 1971; *John O'Hara: A Checklist,* Random House, 1972.

Editor: (With A.K. Davis and others) *More Traditional Ballads of Virginia,* University of North Carolina Press, 1960; Henry James, *The American,* Houghton, 1962; (and author of introduction and notes) Jack London, *The Sea-Wolf,* Houghton, 1964; *The Profession of Authorship in America, 1800-1870: The Papers of William Charvat,* Ohio State University Press, 1968; *Fitzgerald/Hemmingway Annual, 1969,* Microcard Editions, 1969; *Ernest Hemingway, Cub Reporter: Kansas City Stories,* University of Pittsburgh Press, 1970; (with Jackson R. Bryer) *F. Scott Fitzgerald in His Own Time: A Miscellany,* Kent State University Press, 1971; (with Jennifer M. Atkinson) *As Ever, Scott Fitz—Letters Between F. Scott Fitzgerald and His Literary Agent Harold Ober, 1919-1940,* Lippincott, 1972; *F. Scott Fitzgerald: A Descriptive Bibliography,* University of Pittsburgh Press, 1972; (with C. Frazer Clark, Jr.) *Hemingway at Auction,* Gale, 1972. Editor and publisher, *Fitzgerald Newsletter,* 1958—.

BIOGRAPHICAL/CRITICAL SOURCES: Virginia Quarterly Review, spring, 1969, autumn, 1970; *South Atlantic Quarterly,* summer, 1969; *Library Journal,* January 15, 1970; *New York Times,* April 7, 1970; *Detroit News,* June 11, 1972.

* * *

BRUMMITT, Wyatt B. 1897-

PERSONAL: Born January 19, 1897, in Fort Smith, Ark.; son of Dan B. (an editor) and Stella (Wyatt) Brummitt; married Esther Petrie, December 23, 1926; children: Jane (Mrs. Robert Rush), Dan W. *Education:* Northwestern University, student, 1915-17; Columbia University, B.Litt., 1921. *Politics:* "A bit left of center." *Religion:* Protestant. *Home:* 215 Westbrook Rd., Pittsford, N.Y. 14534; and 2320 Forrest Rd., Winter Park, Fla. 32789.

CAREER: Eastman Kodak Co., Rochester, N.Y., manager of amateur picture-making advertising, 1934-58, manager of historical projects, 1958-68. Rochester Community Chest, promotional consultant, 1958-62; Pittsford Community Library, board member, 1962-66; Advertising Council of Rochester, board member, 1963-66. *Military service:* U.S. Army, 1917-18. *Member:* Sigma Delta Chi.

WRITINGS: (With Thomas H. Miller) *This Is Photography: Its Means and Ends,* Doubleday, 1946, revised edition, 1959; (with Herbert Zim) *Photography: A Golden Handbook,* Simon & Schuster, 1956, revised edition, 1964; *Kites,* Golden Press, 1971. Contributor of articles and fiction to newspapers and periodicals.

AVOCATIONAL INTERESTS: Hobbies range from kite flying to architecture and wood turning.

* * *

BRUSTEIN, Robert S(andford) 1927-

PERSONAL: Born April 21, 1927, in New York, N.Y.; son of Max (a businessman) and Blanche (Haft) Brustein; married Norma Ofstrock, March 25, 1962; children: Phillip (stepson), Daniel Anton. *Education:* Attended High School of Music and Art and Columbia Grammar School, New York, N.Y.; U.S. Merchant Marine Academy, cadet midshipman, 1945-47; Amherst College, B.A., 1948; Yale University, graduate study in drama, 1948-49; Columbia University, M.A., 1950, Ph.D., 1957; University of Nottingham, postgraduate study, 1953-55. *Home:* 10 St. Roman Ter., New Haven, Conn. *Office:* Yale University School of Drama, New Haven, Conn.

CAREER: Appeared in some seventy roles in summer and winter stock and on television, 1950-57; Cornell University, Ithaca, N.Y., instructor, 1955-56; Vassar College, Poughkeepsie, N.Y., instructor in drama, 1956-57; Columbia University, New York, N.Y., lecturer in drama, 1957-58, assistant professor, 1958-63, associate professor, 1963-64, professor of English, 1964-66; Yale University, New Haven, Conn., dean of School of Drama, 1966—. *New Republic,* drama critic, 1959—; *New York Review of Books,* cultural editor, 1964—. *Member:* Actors Equity Association, American Federation of Television and Radio Artists, Modern Language Association of America, Phi Beta Kappa. *Awards, honors:* Fulbright Fellow, 1953-55; Guggenheim Fellow; Ford Foundation grantee; George Jean Nathan Award for best drama criticism, 1962; LL.D., Lawrence University, 1968.

WRITINGS: The Theatre of Revolt (essays and criticism), Atlantic-Little, Brown, 1964; (editor) *The Plays and Prose of August Strindberg,* Holt, 1964; *Seasons of Discontent,* Simon & Schuster, 1966; *The Third Theatre,* Knopf, 1969; *Revolution as Theatre,* Liveright, 1971. Contributor to *Harper's, Observer, Partisan Review, Encounter, Commentary, New York Times,* and other periodicals and newspapers.

SIDELIGHTS: Brustein is one of the most controversial men in theater today. As a critic he is both loved and hated, and at the same time respected. The same can be said of him as an educator. Since the beginning of his role as dean of the Yale Drama School, when he painted the interior of the theater a "cheery theatrical red," he has been in the center of a "vivid furor in on-campus and off-campus New Haven, in university theater circles across the country and (in Brustein's words) 'wherever there were alumni,'" according to Alan Levy. Helen Dawson calls Brustein a "watchdog on the prowl for a theatrical renaissance."

Brustein finds much wrong with both Broadway and the resident theaters as they are operating in America today. In his reviews and essays he is constantly trying to change people's thinking, to get them to demand something other than what is available to them in theatre today. For a time he had faith in what he called the "third theatre," and his collection of essays and reviews titled *The Third Theatre* illustrates what he means by the term: "[An] underground expression now being developed in the cabarets, workshops, and studios—where all assumptions are questioned, all shibboleths rejected, all dogma destroyed. A theatre, in short, where reality and joy are once more being combined and drama is once again becoming superb, gay, and wild." Miss Dawson calls Brustein "a man quietly but passionately in love with his country, worried by its morality, disturbed by unfulfilled promises, who is brave enough to conclude that Americans ought to stop all this pretence about loving culture.'"

Gary Houston writes of Brustein and *The Third Theatre:* "Mr. Brustein is trying to steer a course between the shallow, insipid standards and formulas to which the American films, television, and now television-influenced theater is prone, on the one hand, and, on the other, the puerile, destructive and neurotic traits of the Third Theater. Both have bourgeois roots. For both exhibit a mentality which, to him, is simply unwilling or perhaps unable to grow up." Julius Novick writes: "Brustein has wit, but I wonder about his sense of humor; he never seems to unbend. 'How can one love the theatre,' he asks, 'unless it functions as the instrument of some higher purpose?' Millions can and do, but Brustein does not want to; he prefers to regard them as his enemies. He is the Savonarola of drama criticism. Fortunately, he writes cogently even about what he doesn't like. And being Savonarola has some positive aspects. Mr. Brustein never loses sight of the theater's 'higher purpose'; he writes out of what George Bernard Shaw called 'moral passion.' But this quality in Brustein has such a keen cutting edge that it never loses itself in mere pieties, and he manages . . . to keep himself this side of annoying self-righteousness." Novick quotes Brustein as saying of *America Hurrah* that "the truest poetic function of the theater is 'to invent metaphors which can poignantly suggest a nation's nightmares and afflictions.' "

"Bob's character has been completely misrepresented by the conflict he's been thrust into," Philip Roth told Levy. "He's combative as an intellectual, but as a person he's quite gentle. He's not liked for the things he takes for granted, so he's usually surprised by the conflict he arouses. Basically, he thinks of himself as lovable." Brustein told Levy that he's "not a fanatic, . . . I'm flexible. But the ideals I've set down in my writing and for the school are impossible ideals. Ideals *have* to be impossible, but they're not to be followed puristically. What I'm discovering here [at Yale] is the collision between theory and doing. Maybe where I'm fanatical is that I don't believe in gradualism." Novick says that Brustein "has been discovering . . . that democratic and humanistic values can be threatened by the Left as well as the Right, the young as well as the old. But though events have revealed the radical Brustein to be something of a conservative, his position has remained essentially constant: he is merely now applying to the *avant-garde* the same vigorous standards he has always applied to other segments of the theatre. The vigor and lucidity of his mind and style remain undiminished, and the value of his criticism is, if anything, increased."

"On the basis of the record he keeps of our theater," Roth wrote, "[Brustein] would certainly qualify as one of our most valuable cultural historians. What makes him to my mind the most important drama critic in America as well, is that to his melancholy task of distinguishing . . . between the genuine and the fake, the inspired and the commonplace, he brings an erudition and intelligence of the highest order. His analyses and judgments reflect the critical clarity of a first-rate mind, and rise out of a deep knowledge of dramatic literature, and the taste of a cultivated man. His language, though on occasion a little swollen with metaphor, is generally clear, rich and witty. But his distinction as a critic is not that he possesses all the equipment; rather, that it is employed in the service of a strong moral concern for the quality of the lives we live."

*   *   *

BRUSTLEIN, Janice Tworkov (Janice)

PERSONAL: Married Daniel Brustlein (an artist), 1941. *Home:* 8 rue du General Bertrand, Paris 7, France.

CAREER: Writer of books for children.

WRITINGS—All juveniles under name Janice: *It's Spring! It's Spring!* Lothrop, 1956; *The Lonely Little Lady and Her Garden,* Lothrop, 1958; *Little Bear's Sunday Breakfast,* Lothrop, 1958; *Minette,* Whittlesey House, 1959; *Little Bear's Pancake Party,* Lothrop, 1960; *Angelique,* Whittlesey House, 1960; *Little Bear's Christmas,* Lothrop, 1964; *Little Bear's Thanksgiving,* Lothrop, 1967; *Little Bear Marches in the St. Patrick's Day Parade,* Lothrop, 1967; *Little Bear Learns to Read the Cookbook,* Lothrop, 1969.

*   *   *

BRUTON, J(ack) G(ordon) 1914-

PERSONAL: Surname is pronounced *Bru*-ton; born July 4, 1914, in London, England; son of John Albert and Dulcie (Hale) Bruton; married Josephine Stewart, August 4, 1948; children: Clive, Anthony. *Education:* King's College, London, B.A. (honors in Spanish), 1935. *Office:* c/o British Council, 65 Davies St., London W.1, England.

CAREER: Central Institute of English, Hyderabad, India, director of studies, 1958-61; British Institute, Madrid, Spain, director of studies, 1961-65; British Council representative, Madrid, 1965-69, Teheran, Iran, 1969-70. *Awards, honors:* Order of the British Empire.

WRITINGS: The English Verb in Context, Cambridge University Press, 1964; *Exercises on the English Verb for Intermediate Students,* Cambridge University Press, 1965; *The Story of Western Science,* Cambridge University Press, 1966; *Ejercicios de espanol,* Pergamon, 1968; *The Bruton English Course for Adults,* nine books and teacher's book, Thomas Nelson, 1969; *Exercises on English Prepositions and Adverbs,* Thomas Nelson, 1969; *Our New English Book,* four textbooks, three teacher's books, and three exercise books, Editorial Mangold, 1969.

WORK IN PROGRESS: Workbooks for *The Bruton English Course for Adults.*

*   *   *

BRYANT, Edward (Albert) 1928-

PERSONAL: Born July 23, 1928, in Lenoir, N.C.; son of Edmond Henry and Shelton Emmaline (Robbins) Bryant; married Tamara Thompson, May 28, 1965; children: Adam Edmond. *Education:* University of North Carolina, B.A., 1950, M.A., 1954; University of Pisa, Fulbright scholar, 1954-55; graduate study, University of Ravenna, 1955, North Carolina State College, 1956, and Columbia University, 1958. *Home:* Versailles Pike, Lexington, Ky. 40504. *Office:* University of Kentucky Art Gallery, Lexington, Ky. 40506.

CAREER: Brooklyn Museum, Brooklyn, N.Y., museum training fellow, 1957-58, travel grant to Italy, 1958-59; Wadsworth Atheneum (art museum), Hartford, Conn., general curator, 1959-61; Whitney Museum of Modern Art, New York, N.Y., associate curator; University of Kentucky Art Gallery, Lexington, director. Painter.

WRITINGS: (With Frieda Tenenbaum) *African Sculpture,* Brooklyn Museum, 1958; (with Lloyd Goodrich) *Forty Artists Under Forty, From the Collection of the Whitney Museum of American Art,* Praeger, 1962; (with Marcello Venturoli) *Sarai Sherman,* Edizioni Penelope, 1963; *Jack Tworkov,* Praeger, 1964; (author of introduction) *Robert Broderson: 32 Drawings,* Duke University Press, 1964. Author of exhibition catalogues and articles on artists and on aspects of twentieth-century art.

WORK IN PROGRESS: A book on abstract expressionism; a book on pop art.

*   *   *

BRYER, Jackson R(obert) 1937-

PERSONAL: Born September 11, 1937, in New York, N.Y.; son of Joseph Jerome (a lawyer) and Muriel (Jackson) Bryer; married Deborah Churchill Chase, August 27, 1960 (divorced April, 1972); children: Kathryn Chase, Jeffrey Russell, Elizabeth Jackson. *Education:* Friends Seminary, New York, N.Y., diploma, 1955; Amherst College, B.A., 1959; Columbia University, M.A., 1960; University of Wisconsin, Ph.D., 1965. *Religion:* Congregational. *Home:* 1429 Kanawha St., Hyattsville, Md. 20783. *Office:* Department of English, University of Maryland, University College, College Park, Md. 20742.

CAREER: University of Maryland, College Park, instructor in English department, 1964—. *Member:* Modern Language Association of America.

WRITINGS: (With Samuel French Morse and Joseph N. Riddel) *Wallace Stevens Checklist and Bibliography of*

Stevens Criticism, Alan Swallow, 1963; (with Robert A. Rees) A Checklist of Emerson Criticism, 1951-1961, Transcendental, 1964; The Critical Reputation of F. Scott Fitzgerald: A Bibliographical Study, Shoe String, 1967; (contributor) Irving Malin, editor, Critical Views of Isaac Bashevis Singer, New York University Press, 1969; Fifteen Modern American Authors: A Survey of Research and Criticism, Duke University Press, 1969, revised edition published as Sixteen Modern American Authors: A Survey of Research and Criticism, Norton, 1973; (editor with Matthew J. Bruccoli) F. Scott Fitzgerald in His Own Time: A Miscellany, Kent State University Press, 1971; (editor with John Kuehl) Dear Scott— Dear Max: The Fitzgerald-Perkins Correspondence, Scribner, 1971. Contributor to Texas Studies, Modern Drama, Modern Fiction Studies, Books Abroad, Bulletin of Bibliography, New Mexico Quarterly, and other periodicals.

WORK IN PROGRESS: A History of The Little Review.

AVOCATIONAL INTERESTS: Collecting

* * *

BUCHANAN, George (Henry Perrott) 1904-

PERSONAL: Born January 9, 1904, in Larne, Northern Ireland; son of Henry and Florence (Moore) Buchanan; married Janet Margesson, August 22, 1952 (died, 1968); children: Florence Leggett, Emily Margesson. Education: Studied at Campbell College and University of Belfast. Home: 27 Ashley Gardens, Westminster, London, England.

CAREER: Times, London, England, sub-editor, 1930-35; News Chronicle, London, England, columnist and drama critic, 1935-38; author and poet. Northern Ireland Town and Country Development Committee, chairman, 1949-53. Military service: Royal Air Force, Coastal Command, 1940-45; served as operations officer. Member: European Society of Culture (executive council, 1954—), International P.E.N. (executive committee, London, 1960-64); Athenaeum and Savile Clubs (both London).

WRITINGS: Passage Through the Present (journal), Constable, 1932, Dutton, 1933; Dance Night (three-act comedy; first produced in London at Embassy Theatre, 1934), Samuel French, 1935; A London Story, Constable, 1935, Dutton, 1936; Words for Tonight (journal), Constable, 1936; Rose Forbes: The Biography of an Unknown Woman (novel), Constable, 1937, augmented edition, Faber, 1950; Entanglement, Constable, 1938, Appleton, 1939; Serious Pleasures: The Intelligent Person's Guide to London, London Transport, 1938, 2nd edition, 1939; The Soldier and the Girl, Heinemann, 1940; A Place to Live (novel), Faber, 1952; Bodily Responses (poems), Gaberbocchus, 1958; Green Seacoast (autobiographical account of childhood in Ireland), Gaberbocchus, 1959, Red Dust, 1968; Conversation with Strangers (poems), Gaberbocchus, 1961; Morning Papers (autobiography from the ages 18 to 28), Gaberbocchus, 1965; Annotations (poetry), Carcanet Press, 1970; Naked Reason (novel), Holt, 1971; Minute-Book of a City (poems), Carcanet Press, 1972.

Unpublished plays: "A Trip to the Castle," first produced in London at Arts Theatre, 1960; "Tresper Revolution," first produced in London at Arts Theatre, 1961; "War Song," first produced in London at Hampstead Theatre Club, 1965. Book reviewer for Times Literary Supplement, 1928-40.

WORK IN PROGRESS: The Umbra, an autobiography from the ages 29 to 39; a novel.

BUCHANAN, Pegasus 1920-

PERSONAL: Born December 29, 1920, in Pomona, Calif.; daughter of Milton Hazard (a manufacturer) and Gladys (Bradshaw) Perry; married Barney Barnum (owner-manager of a golf course), December 28, 1949; children: Daniel Buchanan, Samuel Perry. Education: Attended Michigan State University, 1939-41, and Lansing Business University, 1941. Politics: Republican. Religion: Science of Mind. Home: 740 Washington Ave., Pomona, Calif. 91767.

CAREER: Professional model for art classes at Michigan State University during student days (to help pay tuition), and later a photographer's model for commercial advertising; author and poet. Regular guest on Pamela Mason's television and radio shows, 1961—. Member: California Writers' Guild, California Federation of Chaparral Poets, Pomona Writers' Workshop, Pomona Valley Writers' Club (honorary), Pomona Friends of the Library Association (vice-president, 1958-62). Awards, honors: Sweepstakes Trophy from California Federation of Chaparral Poets, 1961, for poem, "Night Song"; Pomona Valley Literary award, 1964, for Kingsley Alley.

WRITINGS: Wilderness Trail, Story Book Press, 1948; Chestnut Street, Humphries, 1956; Kingsley Alley, Humphries, 1963. Contributor of poems to Saturday Evening Post, Ladies' Home Journal, Good Housekeeping, McCall's, Saturday Review, New York Herald Tribune, New York Times, and to other periodicals and newspapers.

WORK IN PROGRESS: River Path, a book of gypsy poems; another "Street" book similar to Chestnut Street and Kingsley Alley; a novel, Make Bright the Wagons.

* * *

BUCHER, Charles A (ugustus) 1912-

PERSONAL: Born October 2, 1912, in Conesus, N.Y.; son of Grover C. and Elizabeth (Barr) Bucher; married Jacqueline Dubois, August 24, 1941; children: Diana, Richard, Nancy, Gerald. Education: Ohio Wesleyan University, A.B., 1937; Columbia University, M.A., 1941; New York University, Ph.D., 1948; Yale University, postdoctoral study. Home: 3 The Knoll, Whippoorwill, Armonk, N.Y. 10504.

CAREER: Elementary and high school teacher and vice-principal, East Pembroke, and Pleasantville, N.Y., 1937-41; taught at New Haven State Teachers College, 1946-50; New York University, New York, N.Y., 1950—, now professor of education. Appleton-Century-Crofts, Inc., consulting editor. Military service: U.S. Air Force, 1941-46; became captain. Member: National Education Association, American Association for Health, Physical Education and Recreation (fellow), American College of Sports Medicine (fellow), National College Physical Education Association, American School Health Association (fellow), Philippine Association for Health, Physical Education and Recreation (life member). Awards, honors: School Bell Award from National Education Association, 1960.

WRITINGS: Foundations of Physical Education, Mosby, 1952, 6th edition, 1972; Methods and Materials for Physical Education and Recreation: School and Community Activities, Mosby, 1954; Administration of School Health and Physical Education Programs, Mosby, 1955, 4th edition published as Administration of School and College Health and Physical Education Programs, 1967, 5th edition, 1971; (with Evelyn Reade) Physical Education in the Modern Elementary School, Macmillan, 1958, 2nd edition published as Physical Education and Health in the Elementary School, 1964, 3rd edition, 1971; (with Eugene Smith Wilson) College Ahead!: A Guide for High School Students and Their Parents, Harcourt, 1958, revised edition published as *College Ahead!: A Guide for High School Students*, 1961; (with Constance Koenig and Milton Barnhard) *Methods and Materials for Secondary School Physical Education*, Mosby, 1961, 3rd edition, 1970; *Interscholastic Athletics at the Junior High School Level*, State Education Department, University of the State of New York, 1965; (with Ralph K. Dupee, Jr.) *Athletics in Schools and Colleges*, Center for Applied Research in Education, 1965; (with Einar A. Olsen and Carl E. Willgoose) *The Foundations of Health*, Appleton, 1967; (with Helmuth W. Joel and Gertrude A. Joel) *Guiding Your Child Toward College*, Abingdon, 1967; *Physical Education for Life*, McGraw, 1969; (editor with Myra Goldman) *Dimensions of Physical Education*, Mosby, 1969; *Administrative Dimensions of Health and Physical Education Programs, Including Athletic*, Mosby, 1971. Contributor of articles to newspapers and magazines, including *Manila Times* and other foreign publications.

BIOGRAPHICAL/CRITICAL SOURCES: Saturday Review, February 15, 1969.

*   *   *

BULL, Geoffrey Taylor   1921-

PERSONAL: Born June 24, 1921, in London, England; son of William John (a company director) and Ethel Edith (Taylor) Bull; married Agnes Johnstone Templeton, June 11, 1955; children: Ross Templeton, Geoffrey Peter, Alister William. *Education:* Attended Christ's College, Finchley, England. *Religion:* Christian. *Home:* 16, Southview Rd., Blanefield by Glasgow, Scotland. *Agent:* Curtis Brown Ltd., 60 East 56th St., New York, N.Y. 10022.

CAREER: Worked in banking, 1937-42, for British national service, 1942-46; missionary evangelical and bible teacher in Great Britain and abroad, 1947—.

WRITINGS: When Iron Gates Yield (first in a trilogy), Moody, 1955; *God Holds the Key* (2nd in the trilogy), Moody, 1959; *Coral in the Sand*, Hodder & Stoughton), 1962, Moody, 1963; *The Sky is Red* (last in the trilogy), Hodder & Stoughton, 1965, Moody, 1966; *Tibetan Tales*, Hodder & Stoughton, 1966, published in America as *Forbidden Land: A Saga of Tibet*, Moody, 1967; *A New Pilgrim's Progress: John Bunyan's Classic Imagined in a Contemporary Setting*, Hodder & Stoughton, 1969; *The City and the Sign: An Interpretation of the Book of Jonah*, Hodder & Stoughton, 1970, Baker Book, 1972.

Booklets: *Out of the Low Dungeon* (six broadcast talks), Pickering & Inglis, 1964; *Out of the Mouth of the Lion*, Pickering & Inglis, 1967. Author of radio and television scripts for British Broadcasting Corp.

WORK IN PROGRESS: A book, tentatively titled *Love-Song in Harvest*, completed and awaiting publication; devotional Christian literature; a series of six children's books, to be published together by Pickering & Inglis.

SIDELIGHTS: When Iron Gates Yield is a first-hand account of the Communist takeover of eastern Tibet, and of three years' brainwashing experienced by the author in Chinese prisons; the book has been translated into German, Danish, Swedish, Finnish, Norwegian, and Chinese. *Tibetan Tales* has also been translated into German.

*   *   *

BULL, Storm   1913-

PERSONAL: Born October 13, 1913, son of Eyvind Hagerup (a graduate engineer and composer) and Agnes Bull; married Ellen Cross (a writer), October 6, 1939; children: Kristine, Thomas, Edward. *Education:* Studied at American Conservatory of Music, Chicago, Ill., 1919-31, Ecole Normale de Musique, and Sorbonne, University of Paris, 1931-32, under Bela Bartok at Liszt Academy of Music, Budapest, Hungary, 1932-35, University of Budapest, 1933-35. *Residence:* Sunshine Canyon, Boulder, Colo. *Office:* College of Music, University of Colorado, Boulder, Colo. 80302.

CAREER: Made debut as pianist with Oslo Philharmonic Orchestra at age of fifteen; private teacher of piano in Chicago, Ill., 1935-39, and concert pianist and soloist with orchestras in United States, Canada, and Europe, 1935-42; Chicago Conservatory of Music, Chicago, Ill., member of piano faculty, 1939-42; Baylor University, Waco, Tex., assistant professor of piano, 1945-47; University of Colorado, Boulder, professor of music and head of division of piano, 1947—. Fulbright visiting professor of musicology, University of Oslo, 1956-57. Boulder United Fund, member of board of directors, 1959-62; Boy Scouts of America, vice-president of Longs Peak Council. *Military service:* U.S. Naval Reserve, 1942-45; became chief specialist in athletics. *Member:* American Musicological Society, American Music Teachers Association (chairman, senior piano committee, 1952-56; board of directors, 1953-56), College Music Society, American College of Musicians (honorary), Music Educators National Conference (member, 1967 National Committee on Piano Instruction; chairman, Southwest Reg. Com. on Piano Instruction), American Association of University Professors, Colorado Music Teachers Association (former president), Rotary International. *Awards, honors:* Silver Beaver Award of Boy Scouts of America, 1958; Distinguished Achievement Award "for extraordinary contributions to the community, to education, and to the cultural life of the U.S. and Norway," Scandinavian American Foundation/University of Denver, 1969.

WRITINGS: Selected List of Contemporary Composers, University of Colorado, 1958; *Index to Biographies of Contemporary Composers*, Scarecrow, 1964. Author of articles on contemporary music and related subjects. North American editor, *Musikkens Verden*, 1951, revised and enlarged edition, 1963.

WORK IN PROGRESS: A study of the development of skills in the reading of music; research on immigration and emigration habits of twentieth-century composers; a revised and enlarged edition of *Index to Biographies of Contemporary Composers*, for Scarecrow.

AVOCATIONAL INTERESTS: Golf, skiing, and walking in the mountains.

*   *   *

BULLOUGH, Vern (LeRoy)   1928-

PERSONAL: Born July 24, 1928, in Salt Lake City, Utah; son of David Vernon (a tool and die maker) and Augusta (Rueckert) Bullough; married Bonnie Uckerman (a nurse-teacher), August 2, 1947; children: David, James, Steven, Susan, Robert. *Education:* University of Utah, B.A., 1951; University of Chicago, M.A., 1951, Ph.D., 1954. *Home:* 7849 White Oak Ave., Reseda, Calif. 91335.

CAREER: Youngstown University, Youngstown, Ohio, assistant professor, department of history, 1954-59; San Fernando Valley State College (now California State University), Northridge, Calif., 1959—, began as associate professor, became professor of history. Lecturer, California College of Medicine, Los Angeles; visiting lecturer, School of Public Health, University of California, Los Angeles, and in history department, University of Southern California. American Civil Liberties Union, member of southern California board. *Military service:* U.S. Army, Army Security Agency, 1946-48. *Member:* American Historical Association, American Association for Advancement of Science, Mediaeval Academy, Renaissance Society, American Association for History of Medicine, History of Technology Society, American Association of University Professors. *Awards, honors:* Newberry fellowship; Huntington Library fellowship; American Philosophical Society grant; grants from National Science Foundation, U.S. Department of Education, and Erickson Educational Foundation.

WRITINGS: The History of Prostitution, University Books, 1964; *The Development of Medicine as a Profession: The Contribution of the Medieval University to Modern Medicine,* S. Karger, 1966; *Man in Western Civilization,* Holt, 1970; *The Scientific Revolution,* Holt, 1970; (with Raoul Naroll and Frada Naroll) *Military Deterrence in History: A Statistical Survey,* State University of New York Press, 1971.

With wife, Bonnie Bullough: *The Emergence of Modern Nursing,* Macmillan, 1964, 2nd edition, 1969; (editor) *Issues in Nursing,* Springer Publishing, 1966; (editor) *New Directions for Nurses,* Springer Publishing, 1971.

Contributor to *Nation, Saturday Review, Progressive, New Leader, Isis, Speculum, Humanist, Journal of History of Medicine, Bulletin of History of Medicine,* and other professional journals.

WORK IN PROGRESS: A history of sexual attitudes; research on poverty, minority status, ethnic identity, and health cure.

* * *

BULPIN, T(homas) V(ictor) 1918-

PERSONAL: Born March 31, 1918, in Umkomaas, Natal, South Africa; son of Thomas Richard (a journalist) and Constance (MacNab) Bulpin; married Marie Michele Dumont, November 5, 1955; children: Mark Robert, John Anthony. *Education:* Attended St. John's College, Johannesburg, South Africa. *Home:* 60 Exeter Rd., Plumstead, Cape Town, South Africa. *Office:* Books of Africa (Pty.) Ltd., 1005 Cape of Good Hope Savings Bank Building, St. Georges St., Cape Town, South Africa.

CAREER: Pathe Pictures, London, England, producer and script writer in Africa, 1946-50; *Unie Volkspers,* Cape Town, South Africa, roving correspondent in Africa, 1950-55; Howard Timmins, Cape Town, South Africa, publisher's representative, 1955-61; Thomas Nelson & Sons Ltd. (publishers), London, England, editor in South Africa, 1961-66. Books of Africa (Pty.) Ltd. (publishing house), editorial director. *Military service:* South African Air Force, aerial photographer, 1940-46.

WRITINGS: Lost Trails of the Low Veld, Howard Timmins, 1950, 3rd edition, 1953; *Shaka's Country,* Howard Timmins, 1952, 2nd edition published as *Shaka's Country: All About Zululand,* Natal, Howard Timmins, 1954, 3rd edition published as *Shaka's Country: A Book of Zululand,* Bailey Bros. & Swinfen, 1956; *To the Shores of Natal,* Howard Timmins, 1953, Bailey Bros. & Swinfen, 1955; (self-illustrated) *The Golden Republic: The Story of the South African Republic from Its Foundation Until 1883,* Howard Timmins, 1953, Bailey Bros. & Swinfen, 1955; *South Africa's Animal Kingdom,* South African Tourist Corp., c.1954; (editor and author of preface) *Wild Company,* Bodley Head, 1954; (with Cecil Barnard) *The Ivory Trail,* Howard Timmins, 1954, 2nd edition, 1955, Tri-Ocean, 1968; *Storm Over the Transvaal,* Howard Timmins, 1955, 2nd edition, Bailey Bros. & Swinfen, 1955; *Lost Trails of the Transvaal,* Howard Timmins, 1956, Bailey Bros. & Swinfen, 1957; (compiler) *East Africa and the Islands,* Bailey Bros. & Swinfen, 1956; (author of foreword) *South Africa: A Pictorial Tour Through the Union of South Africa,* Bailey Bros. & Swinfen, 1956; *Way of the Wild,* Howard Timmins, 1957; *Islands in a Forgotten Sea* (originally announced as "Jewels in the Ocean"), Howard Timmins, 1958, 2nd edition, Tri-Ocean, 1970; *Trail of the Copper King,* Bailey

Bros. & Swinfen, 1959; (author of introduction) *Rhodesia: A Pictorial Tour of a Beautiful Country,* Bailey Bros. & Swinfen, 1959; *The Cape Province: Its Scenery and People,* Bailey Bros. & Swinfen, 1960; *Rhodesia and Nyasaland,* Howard Timmins, 1960; *The White Whirlwind* (fictionalized biography of Johan Colenbrander, South African frontiersman), Thomas Nelson (Johannesburg), 1961; *The Hunter is Death,* Thomas Nelson, 1962, 2nd edition, Books of Africa, 1968; *Southern Africa: Its Life and Scenery,* includes photographs by Bulpin, Thomas Nelson, 1964; *To the Banks of the Zambezi,* Thomas Nelson, 1965, 2nd edition, Books of Africa, 1968; *South Africa: A Preview,* South African Tourist Corp., c.1965; *Lost Trails of the Transvaal* (includes *Lost Trails of the Low Veld, The Golden Republic, Storm Over the Transvaal,* and *Lost Trails of the Transvaal,* 1956 edition), Thomas Nelson, 1965; *Natal and the Zulu Country,* Books of Africa, 1966; *Low Veld Trails,* Books of Africa, 1968; *Discovering Southern Africa,* Books of Africa, 1970; *The Great Trek,* Tri-Ocean, 1970. Contributor of more than five hundred feature stories to periodicals throughout the world.

WORK IN PROGRESS: Continuing research into the history of South Africa.

SIDELIGHTS: Bulpin is competent in Afrikaans, Zulu, and knows some Sotho and Shona; he has traveled extensively in Africa and continues to cover the continent six months each year. *Avocational interests:* Mountaineering, symphonic music.

* * *

BUNGE, Mario A(ugusto) 1919-

PERSONAL: Born September 21, 1919, in Buenos Aires, Argentina; son of Augusto and Marie (Muser) Bunge; married second wife, Marta Cavallo, 1959; children: Carlos Federico, Mario Augusto Julio. *Education:* National University of La Plata, Dr. Physics, 1952. *Home:* Canning 2824, Buenos Aires, Argentina. *Office:* University of Buenos Aires, Florida 656, Buenos Aires, Argentina.

CAREER: Research work in theoretical atomic and nuclear physics, 1943-56; University of La Plata, La Plata, Argentina, professor of theoretical physics, 1956-58; University of Buenos Aires, Buenos Aires, Argentina, professor of theoretical physics, 1956-58, professor of philosophy, 1957-63. Visiting professor, University of Pennsylvania, 1960-61, University of Texas, 1963, and University of Delaware, 1964-65. Attended Interamerican Congress of Philosophy, Santiago, Chile, 1956, and Buenos Aires, 1959, International Congress of Philosophy, Venice, Italy, 1958, International Congress for Logic, Stanford, California, 1960, and Jerusalem, Israel, 1964. *Member:* Association Fisica Argentina (secretary of publications, 1956-63), Agrupacion Rioplatense de Logica y Filosofia Cientifica (board member, 1956-60; president, 1960-63), Club de Regatas "America" (rowing club).

WRITINGS: Temas de educaction popular, El Ateneo (Buenos Aires), 1943; *Le Edad de universo,* Edit. U.M.S.A., 1955; *Que significa la "ley cientifica?,"* Universidad Nacional de Mexico, 1958; *Causality: The Place of the Causal Principle in Modern Science,* Harvard University Press, 1959; *Metascientific Queries,* C.C. Thomas, 1959; *Cinematica del electron relavista,* Facultad de Ciencias Exactas y Tecnologia, Universidad Nacional de Tucuman, 1960; (editor) *Antologia semantica,* Nuevo Vision (Buenos Aires), 1960; *Etica y ciencia,* Siglo Viente (Buenos Aires), 1960; *Intuition and Science,* Prentice-Hall, 1962; *The Myth of Simplicity: Problems of Scientific Philosophy,* Prentice-Hall 1963; (editor) *The Critical Approach to Science and Philosophy,* Free Press, 1964; *Foundations of Physics,* Springer-Verlag, 1967; *Scientific Research,* Springer-Verlag, 1967; *(editor)* Delaware *Seminar in the Foundations of Physics*, Springer-Verlag, 1967; (editor) *Quantam Theory and Reality*, Springer-Verlag, 1967; *Problems in the Foundations of Physics*, Springer-Verlag, 1971. Contributor to physics and philosophy journals. Editor, *Minerva*, 1944-45.

AVOCATIONAL INTERESTS: Literature, music, rowing, and swimming.†

* * *

BUNKE, H(arvey) Charles 1922-

PERSONAL: Born November 7, 1922, in Oshkosh, Wis.; son of Harvey W. (a salesman and Charlotte (Zahn) Bunke; married Margaret A. Carlsten, May 29, 1947; children: Charles Martin, Richard Carlsten, Christine Anna. *Education:* University of Illinois, B.S., 1947, M.S., 1949, Ph.D., 1951. *Home:* 411 High St., Bellingham, Wash. 98225. *Office:* Western Washington State College, Bellingham, Wash. 98223.

CAREER: U.S. Office of Price Stabilization, Seattle, Wash., senior price economist, 1951-52; University of Tennessee, Knoxville, associate professor, 1952-53; State University of Iowa, Iowa City, assistant professor, 1953-57, professor of public policy, 1957-63, chairman of department of economics, 1963-65; Western Washington State College, Bellingham, president, 1965—. *Military service:* U.S. Army Air Forces, 1941-44; became staff sergeant. *Member:* American Economic Association.

WRITINGS: Linear Programming: A Primer, Bureau of Business and Economic Research, College of Business Administration, State University of Iowa, 1960; *The Liberal Dilemma*, Prentice-Hall, 1964; *A Primer on American Economic History*, Random House, 1969. Contributor to scholarly and trade journals.

WORK IN PROGRESS: A book on the appeal of the various intellectual systems to be underdeveloped people of the world.

AVOCATIONAL INTERESTS: Sailing and trout fishing.†

* * *

BURACK, Abraham Saul 1908-

PERSONAL: Born January 31, 1908, in New York, N.Y.; son of Jacob Harry (a merchant) and Elizabeth (Effross) Burack; married Sylvia Ethel Kamerman, November 28, 1940; children: Janet Elizabeth, Susan Helen, Ellen Judith. *Education:* Boston University, special student, 1925-30. *Office:* Writer, Inc., 8 Arlington St., Boston, Mass. 02116.

CAREER: Writer, Inc., Boston, Mass., editor and publisher of *Writer* and *Plays* (magazines), and of books, 1935—. Radcliffe College, annual lecturer, 1946—; Boston University, instructor, 1950-55; staff member and instructor at writers' conferences at University of New Hampshire, Tufts University, Boston College, University of Colorado, and Northeastern University.

WRITINGS: (With R.J. Monteith) *Methods and Procedures in Federal Purchasing*, Bruce, Humphries, 1931.

Editor: *The Craft of Novel Writing*, Writer, 1942; *Writing Detective and Mystery Fiction*, Writer, 1945, revised edition, 1967; *One Hundred Plays for Children: An Anthology of Non-Royalty, One-Act Plays* (selected from *Plays: The Drama Magazine for Young People*), Plays, 1949, revised edition, 1970; *Christmas Plays for Young Actors* (selected from *Plays* Magazine), Plays, 1950, revised edition, 1969; *Four-Star Plays for Boys: A Collection of Fifteen Royalty-Free, One-Act Plays for All-Boy Casts*, Plays, 1957; *Television Plays for Writers: Eight Television Plays with Comment and Analysis by the Authors*, Writer, 1957; *Four-Star Radio Plays for Teen-Agers: A Collection of Royalty-Free Radio Dramas Adapted from Great Literature*, Plays, 1959; *Writing and Selling Fillers and Short Humor*, Writer, 1959, 3rd edition, 1970; *The Writers Handbook*, Writer, 1961, revised and enlarged edition, 1971; *Prize Contest Plays for Young People: A Collection of Royalty-Free, One-Act Plays for Drama Contests and Festivals*, Plays, 1962, revised edition, 1969; *A Treasury of Holiday Plays for Teen-Agers: A Collection of Royalty-Free, One-Act Plays*, Plays, 1963; *Skits, Comedies, and Farces for Teen-Agers*, Plays, 1970; *Techniques of Novel Writing*, Writer, 1973. Author of plays and articles.

* * *

BURANELLI, Vincent 1919-

PERSONAL: Born January 16, 1919, in New York, N.Y.; son of Prosper and Mina (Ackerman) Buranelli; married Nan Gillespie (a writer and translator), October 31, 1951. *Education:* St. John's College, Annapolis, Md., student, 1945-46; National University of Ireland, B.A., 1947, M.A., 1948; Cambridge University, Ph.D., 1951. *Home:* 282 Mount Lucas Rd., Princeton, N.J. 08540.

CAREER: United Press, reporter in Los Angeles, Calif., 1941; *Business Week*, New York, N.Y., editorial writer, 1952; Lowell Thomas Newscasting, New York, N.Y., writer, 1952-65; employed with American Heritage Publishing Co., New York, N.Y., 1966-67, and Silver Burdett Publishing Co., 1967-68; free-lance writer and editor, 1968—. *Military service:* U.S. Army, 1941-45; received Purple Heart. *Member:* American Historical Association, American Studies Association, Authors Guild, Royal Dublin Society, Friends of the Princeton Library, Cambridge Union, Nassau Club. *Awards, honors:* Kaltenborn fellow in journalism, 1952-53; New Jersey Teachers award for best biography of year by a N.J. author, 1964, for *Josiah Royce*.

WRITINGS: (Editor and author of introduction) *The Trial of Peter Zenger*, New York University Press, 1957; *Edgar Allan Poe*, Twayne, 1961; *The King and the Quaker: A Study of William Penn and James II*, University of Pennsylvania Press, 1962; *Josiah Royce*, Twayne, 1964; *Louis XIV*, Twayne, 1966. Contributor of about twenty articles to *New Scholasticism, Social Education, Ethics*, and other scholarly journals, book reviewer for *American Quarterly, William and Mary Quarterly*, and *New York Historical Society Quarterly*.

WORK IN PROGRESS: Swords at Saratoga, to be published by Grosset.

AVOCATIONAL INTERESTS: Watching professional football.

* * *

BURDEN, Jean 1914-
(Felicia Ames)

PERSONAL: Born September 1, 1914, in Waukegan, Ill.; daughter of Harry Frederick (in real estate) and Miriam (Biddlecom) Prussing; divorced. *Education:* University of Chicago, B.A., 1936. *Politics:* Democrat. *Residence:* Altadena, Calif. *Office:* 1129 Beverly Way, Altadena, Calif. 91001.

CAREER: At one time did secretarial work, worked in advertising and in insurance, and edited a house organ, all in Chicago; was West Coast editor of *Faith Today*, and later West Coast editor of *Yankee* magazine; taught a poetry workshop at Pasadena City College, and privately, 1959-61; *Yankee* magazine, poetry editor, 1955—; Meals for Millions Foundation, Los Angeles, Calif., administrative officer, 1956-65; employed with Stanford Research Institute, 1965-66; self-employed in public relations, 1966—. *Awards, honors:* First prize of $300 for "Poem Before Departure," appearing in *Best Poems of*

1962; Silver Anvil award, Public Relations Society of America, 1969, for best product publicity program of year.

WRITINGS: Naked as the Glass (poetry), October House, 1963, 2nd edition, 1964; *Journey Toward Poetry* (essays), October House, 1966.

Pet care books, under pseudonym Felicia Ames—all published by New American Library: *The Dog You Care For,* 1968, *The Cat You Care For,* 1968, *The Bird You Care For,* 1970, *The Fish You Care For,* 1971.

Represented in "Best Poems" anthologies. Contributor to *Poetry, Atlantic, American Scholar, Trace, Saturday Review, Virginia Quarterly Review, Better Homes and Gardens, Mademoiselle, Prairie Schooner, Southern Review,* and other publications.

WORK IN PROGRESS: "More poems, of course, and am also working, somewhat sporadically, on some memoirs."

SIDELIGHTS: Frances Minturn Howard writes that Mrs. Burden "lives with two cats, but has a passion for birds. ... Loves Big Sur, all rocky wild places, and Mozart. Has at times an unexpectedly acid sense of humor."

Her first book of poems was well received by poets Hayden Carruth, Eric Barker, and by James Dickey, who saw her poems as expressions of "the gentle, reasonable urgency of a passionate woman." She is, he writes, "very reticent; one feels that her words are almost *forced* from her, but when they come the clutter of literature's damning artifice is swept away, and we are freed into poetry as it rarely but marvelously exists." Another poet, Howard Nemerov, wrote: "This is an immense, a rare, possibly unique, gift. . . . These poems really do move. With deceptively simple means, they make big effects." May Sarton calls Mrs. Burden's images "concrete, rock-like, . . . like a piece of sculpture. . . . At best she cuts down to the marrow and one gasps!"

Mrs. Burden has recorded some of her poems for the Library of Congress.

BIOGRAPHICAL/CRITICAL SOURCES: Yankee, December, 1963.

*   *   *

BURGER, Chester   1921-

PERSONAL: Born January 10, 1921, in Brooklyn, N.Y.; son of Benjamin W. (an attorney) and Terese (Felleman) Burger; married second wife, Ninki Hart, January 9, 1959 (died, 1969); children: (first marriage) Jeffrey, Todd, Amy. *Education:* Brooklyn College (now Brooklyn College of the City University of New York), B.A., 1946. *Politics:* Republican. *Home:* 279 East 44th St., New York, N.Y. 10017. *Office:* Chester Burger & Co., Inc., 275 Madison Ave., New York, N.Y. 10016.

CAREER: Columbia Broadcasting System, Inc., New York, N.Y., national manager of television news, 1941-54; Ruder & Finn, Inc. (public relations), New York, N.Y., vice-president, 1955-60; Communications Counselors, Inc., New York, N.Y., president, 1960-62; Echelons Office Temporaries, Inc., New York, N.Y., president, 1963-64; Chester Burger & Co., Inc. (management consultants), New York, N.Y., president, 1964—. Consultant to Coca-Cola Export Corp., American Telephone & Telegraph Co., other firms. New York Diabetes Association, director; National Urban League, trustee. *Military service:* U.S. Army, special assignments, 1942-46. *Member:* Public Relations Society of America (director, 1962-63; vice-president of New York chapter, 1962-63), Radio-Newsreel-Television Working Press Association (president, 1954-55), Young Presidents Organization (national public relations committee chairman, 1963).

WRITINGS: (Editor) *Mike and Screen Press Directory,* Radio-Newsreel-Television Working Press Association of New York, 1954-55; *Survival in the Executive Jungle,* Macmillan, 1964; *Executives Under Fire: Personal Case Histories from the Executive Jungle,* Macmillan, 1966; *Executive Etiquette,* Collier, 1969; (author of foreword) Joaquin De Alba, *Violence in America: De Tocqueville's America Revisited,* Acropolis, 1969; *Walking the Executive Plank, Van* Nostrand, 1972. Writer of television documentaries for "Omnibus," 1954-55. Contributing editor, *Public Relations Quarterly* 1959—; contributing editor, *Popular Photography,* 1967-68; general editor, "The New Executive" series, Collier, 1969—; contributor to American Management Association's *Management Handbook,* 1970. Contributor of articles on three-dimensional photography to photographic magazines.

*   *   *

BURGESS, Christopher Victor   1921-

PERSONAL: Born October 17, 1921, in Dublin, Ireland; son of William Henry (an office manager) and Sarah (Ritchie) Burgess; married July 30, 1947, wife's name, Helen; children: Trevor Howard, Melvin Stuart, Owen William, Gillian Shellagh. *Education:* Alsager Teachers Training College, teaching certificate, 1947. *Politics:* Independent. *Home and office:* 92 Pitts Lane, Woodley, Reading, Berkshire, England.

CAREER: Cooper and Kenny (accountants), Dublin, Ireland, junior clerk, 1937-41; teacher in Middlesex and Sussex, England, 1948-62; now full-time writer, teaching at times to maintain contact with practical aspects of education. Lecturer on classroom method. *Military service:* Royal Air Force, 1941-47. *Member:* Poetry Society, National Book League.

WRITINGS: Short Plays for Large Classes, University of London Press, 1953; "Read, Write and Act" series, three books, Pitman, 1954-55; *More Plays for Large Classes,* University of London Press, 1955; *The Burgess Books,* four readers, University of London Press, 1955; *Teacher's Book for The Burgess Books,* University of London Press, 1955; *Talking of the Taylors,* University of London Press, 1956; *By Sword and Spell,* Edward Arnold, 1956; *Careers Plays for Boys,* University of London Press, Book 1, 1957, Book 2, 1958; *Adventure Playground,* University of London Press, 1958; *Verse in Action,* four books and teacher's book, University of London Press, 1958; *Classroom Theatre,* two books, Hulton Educational Publications, 1959.

Sally at the Mop, University of London Press, 1960; *Discovering the Theatre,* University of London Press, 1960; *The Burgess Plays,* four books, University of London Press, 1960; *Mystery on the Move,* University of London Press, 1960; *Teach Yourself Speech Training,* English Universities Press, 1960; (British editor) Clifton Fadiman, *The Lifetime Reading Plan,* English Universities Press, 1963; (compiler) *Junior Verse in Action,* four books and teacher's book, University of London Press, 1964-65; *It's Your Money,* University of London Press, 1967; *A Book of Verse for Girls,* University of London Press, 1967.

WORK IN PROGRESS: Twelve additional "Burgess Books," for University of London Press.

SIDELIGHTS: Burgess believes less attention should be given to systems of education and more to actual classroom methods. He writes: "My main vocational interest is books that afford maximum help to overburdened teachers. My main sympathies are with the less able child. . . . Because my own education was full of gaps, I write books about the subjects I became interested in rather than from a background of solid learning. Thus I am able to appreciate the child's difficulties as my own. For a year I did nothing but write, but I found that one cannot write books for the classroom unless one (also) teaches." *Avocational interests:* Reading science fiction.

* * *

BURGESS, Jackson (Visscher)   1927-

PERSONAL: Born February 21, 1927, in Atlanta, Ga.; son of Dana Mills-Walcott and Elisabeth (Visscher) Burgess; married second wife, Elena Servi, April 7, 1963; children: (first marriage) Dana L., Ann; (second marriage) Antonio C., Thomas Andrew. *Education:* University of Chicago, B.A., 1951; University of North Carolina, M.F.A., 1955. *Home:* 2441 Woolsey St., Berkeley, Calif. 94705. *Agent:* Robert Lescher, 141 East 55th St., New York, N.Y. 10022. *Office:* English Department, University of California, Berkeley, Calif. 94720.

CAREER: Copyreader for *Chicago Daily News,* Chicago, Ill. 1947-49, for *Greensboro Daily News,* Greensboro, N.C., 1953-56; Guilford College, Guilford College, N.C., assistant professor of English, 1956-57; University of California, Berkeley, 1958—, began as assistant professor, became professor of English, 1972. Smith-Mundt Professor of American Literature, University of Capetown, South Africa, 1960; Fulbright lecturer, University of Catania, 1968-69. Director, Centro Studi, Universita di California, Padova, Italy, 1972-74. *Military service:* U.S. Army, 1945-47. *Awards, honors:* Fellow of University Institute for Creative Arts, University of California, Berkeley, 1963-64.

WRITINGS: Pillar of Cloud, Putnam, 1957; *The Atrocity,* Putnam, 1961. Writer of plays and short stories. Editor, *Chicago Review,* 1951; film critic, *Film Quarterly.*

WORK IN PROGRESS: A novel; articles on Italian life.

AVOCATIONAL INTERESTS: Trout fishing, hiking, and camping.

* * *

BURGESS, Robert H(errmann)   1913-

PERSONAL: Born May 27, 1913, in Baltimore, Md.; son of Kirk William (a marine engineer) and Louann (Dixon) Burgess; married M. Adele Plitt (a school teacher), February 4, 1938; children: Robert Bruce, Janet Leigh. *Education:* Studied at Baltimore City College for four years. *Politics:* Republican. *Religion:* Methodist. *Home:* 1504 Gatewood Rd., Newport News, Va. 23601. *Office:* Mariners Museum, Newport News, Va.

CAREER: Mariners Museum, Newport News, Va., 1941—, curator of exhibits, 1955—. *Military service:* U.S. Navy, 1943-45. *Member:* Steamship Historical Society of America, Virginia Skin Diving Association (member of advisory board), Hampton Historical Society (honorary), Richmond Ship Model Society (honorary), Hampton Roads Ship Model Society (honorary).

WRITINGS: This Was Chesapeake Bay, Cornell Maritime, 1963; *Chesapeake Circle,* Cornell Maritime, 1965; (editor) Leonard S. Tawes, *Coasting Captain: Journals of Captain Leonard S. Tawes Relating His Career in Atlantic Coastwise Sailing Craft from 1868 to 1922,* Mariners Museum, 1967; (with H. Graham Wood) *Steamboats Out of Baltimore,* Tidewater, 1968; *Seas, Sails and Shipwreck: Career of the Four-Masted Schooner Purnell T. White,* Tidewater, 1970. Contributor of maritime articles to encyclopedias, magazines, and newspapers. Member of advisory board, *American Neptune.*

WORK IN PROGRESS: Chesapeake Sail, a book covering all kinds of Chesapeake Sailing Craft, illustrated by 250 photographs taken between 1928-1973.

SIDELIGHTS: In 1936 Burgess sailed as a seaman on the "Doris Hamlin," one of the last of the large American sailing ships; he has collected Chesapeake Bay relics, and photographed the bay vessels and people for forty-five years.

BIOGRAPHICAL/CRITICAL SOURCES: Baltimore Magazine, April, 1954; *Newport News Daily Press,* September 1, 1963; *Baltimore Sun,* October 15, 1965; *Norfolk Virginia Pilot,* March 3, 1966; *Port of Baltimore Bulletin,* July, 1966.

* * *

BURKE, Edmund M.   1928-

PERSONAL: Born September 30, 1928, in Boston, Mass.; son of John A. (a truck driver) and Edith (McAuley) Burke; married Leocadia Bajek (a psychologist), February 23, 1957; children: Brian P., Christopher J., Thomas M., Edmund C. *Education:* Champlain College, B.A., 1953; Boston College, M.S.W., 1956; University of Pittsburgh, Ph.D., 1965. *Politics:* Democrat. *Religion:* Catholic. *Office:* Department of Social Work, Boston College, University Heights, Chestnut Hill, Mass. 02167.

CAREER: United Community Service, Marion, Ohio, executive director of social planning, 1959-62; University of Pittsburgh, Pittsburgh, Pa., assistant professor of social work, 1964-65; Boston College Graduate School of Social Work, Chestnut Hill, Mass., associate professor of social work, 1965-70, dean, 1970—. *Military service:* U.S. Navy, 1946-48. *Member:* National Association of Social Workers.

WRITINGS: How to Work with Parish Groups, Bruce, 1964. Contributor of articles to *Marriage, Priest, Ladies' Home Companion, Social Service Review, Journal of the American Institute of Planners, Community Mental Health,* and *Housing Journal.*

WORK IN PROGRESS: A textbook entitled *Theory, Principles and Techniques of Urban Planning.*

* * *

BURKHART, James A(ustin)   1914-

PERSONAL: Born July 7, 1914, in Renovo, Pa.; son of J. Austin and Gertrude (Loeffler) Burkhart; married June Wells, January 25, 1941; children: Deirdre, James Austin III. *Education:* University of Texas, B.A., 1938, M.A., 1943. *Home:* 2019 Hazelwood Dr., Columbia, Mo. 65201. *Agent:* Mandy Welch, 1601 Sixteenth St. N.W., Washington, D.C. 20009; (lectures) W. Colston Leigh Agency, New York, N.Y. *Office:* Department of Social Studies, Stephens College, Columbia, Mo. 65201.

CAREER: Stephens College, Columbia, Mo., professor of political science, 1945—. Public lecturer. *Member:* American Political Science Association, American Association of University Professors.

WRITINGS: (Contributor) *Battle for Free Schools,* Beacon Press, 1950; (contributor) John Berry Biesancz and M.H. Biesancz, *Modern Society: An Introduction to Social Science,* Prentice-Hall, 1954; (editor with Raymond L. Lee and Van Shaw) *Contemporary Social Issues,* Crowell, 1955; (editor with others) *American Government: The Clash of Issues,* Prentice-Hall, 1960, 4th edition, 1972; *An Experiment to Determine the Values of Using Amplified Classroom Telephone Interviews with Significant Individuals to Enrich Certain College Courses,* Stephens College, c.1961; (with Lee) *Guide to American Government,* Prentice-Hall, 1963, 3rd edition, 1969; (with F.J. Kendrick) *The New Politics: Mood or Movement?,* Prentice-Hall, 1971; (with Lee) *Guide to Burns & Peltason's Government by the People,* Prentice-Hall, 1972; (with others) *Strategies for Political Participation,* Winthrop, 1972. Contributor of articles to *Nation, Frontier,*

Progressive, Antioch Review, Science Digest, and *Farm Quarterly.*

WORK IN PROGRESS: A book on American folklore.

AVOCATIONAL INTERESTS: Collecting folk art and folk music.

BIOGRAPHICAL/CRITICAL SOURCES: Christian Science Monitor, December 10, 1960; *Detroit Free Press,* February 27, 1961; *Newsweek,* February 23, 1962; *Oregonian,* December 3, 1962.

* * *

BURNETT, Collins W. 1914-

PERSONAL: Born March 28, 1914, in Anderson, Ind.; son of Charles and Bertha (Liget) Burnett; married B. Kathryn Kaufman; children: Arlita Jean, Michael Collins. *Education:* Ball State Teachers College, A.B., 1935; Ohio State University, M.A., 1940, Ph.D., 1948. *Politics:* Conservative Democrat. *Religion:* Protestant. *Home:* 1735 Doone Rd., Columbus 21, Ohio. *Office:* Department of Higher Education, University of Kentucky, Lexington, Ky. 40506.

CAREER: Ohio State University, Columbus, assistant dean of student personnel, 1950-63, then professor; presently teaching at University of Kentucky, Lexington, in Department of Higher Education. Associate and consultant, Educational Testing Consultants, Columbus, Ohio. Consultant to College of Guam, 1958, and University of the Americas, Mexico City, Mexico, 1963. *Military service:* U.S. Naval Reserve, 1942—; now commander. *Member:* American Psychological Association (fellow), American Personnel and Guidance Association, Student Personnel Association for Teacher Education (president, 1957; member of professional standards and training committee, 1964-67), American Association of University Professors, National Education Association, Reserve Officers Association.

WRITINGS: (With Alice Z. Seeman) *Planning for Education,* College of Education, Ohio State University, 1952; (with H.J. Peters and Farwell Peters) *Introduction to Teaching,* Macmillan, 1963; (editor) *The Community Junior College: An Annotated Bibliography with Introductions for School Counselors,* College of Education, Ohio State University, 1968.

WORK IN PROGRESS: Editing *Student Personnel Work in Higher Education.*

* * *

BURNETT, David 1931-1971
(Terrave Bernarn, Peter Pace)

PERSONAL: Born November 5, 1931, in Vienna, Austria; son of Whit (an editor) and Martha (an editor; maiden name Foley) Burnett. *Education:* Attended Happy Valley School (experimental; Ojai, Calif.), Columbia University, and the Sorbonne, University of Paris. *Politics:* Dissatisfied independent. *Home and office:* 12 East 30th St., New York, N.Y. 10016.

CAREER: Writer. Spent four years in Paris during late 40's and early 50's; did set designing for A.C.T. Theatre, Paris, and worked on the dubbing of French films into English; edited *New Story Magazine,* 1950-52. Conscientious Objector, from personal rather than religious motivations.

WRITINGS: (Editor with Martha Foley) *The Best American Short Stories,* Houghton, annually, 1958-71; (editor) *Beyond the Breaking Point,* Laurel Books, in press. Author, with Terry Southern, of a mystery story, "'His Second Most Interesting Case," published in *London Mystery Magazine.*

WORK IN PROGRESS: A book dealing with capital punishment; an anthology of psychological horror stories, *The Noonday Ghost;* an anthology on new writing, 1955-65; adapting an undisclosed work for the cinema; hoping to bring out a new literary magazine "which will have no pet axe (aside from quality) to grind."

SIDELIGHTS: New Story Magazine, which survived 13 issues, was the first to publish (for distribution in the United States) Jean Genet, Terry Southern, and James Baldwin, among others. Burnett said of himself: "[I] have long been interested in films. [I] made two short 16mm. films in Paris and one in New York with Terry Southern called 'Candy Kisses.' [I made] only films of the funeral of Charlie 'Bird' Parker. [I] have had paintings shown in California, and illustrations in *Stateside, Mademoiselle, Paris Review,* etc."

Concerning literature, he wrote: "There is now a school of writing that manages to treat such subjects as The Bomb ('Strangelove'), Integration (Dick Gregory), Sex ('Lolita') in such a way as to successfully twist a black humor from it. The Beats and the once exotic subject of narcotics have out-lived their short but highly-promoted lives, leaving in their ebbing wake two good writers, Allen Ginsberg and Ken Kesey. To my mind there are three books from this period that will outlive 99% of what is on the market at the moment. They are [William] Gaddis' *The Recognitions,* [John] Barth's *The Sot-Weed Factor* and [Elias] Canetti's *Auto-da-Fe.*

"At this moment one finds that reportage and films have become the *new* medium of many writers—Southern, Baldwin, Mailer, Gelber, etc. But I feel that this may well be a temporary condition."

BIOGRAPHICAL/CRITICAL SOURCES: New York Times, November 22, 1971; *Publishers Weekly,* December 6, 1971.

(Died November 21, 1971)

* * *

BURNS, Alan 1929-

PERSONAL: Born December 29, 1929, in London, England; son of Harold (a company director) and Anne Marks) Burns; married Carol Lynn (a painter), January 5, 1954; children: Daniel Paul. *Education:* Merchant Taylors' School, higher certificate, 1948; Inns of Court, London, England, barrister-at-law, 1954. *Politics:* Socialist. *Home:* Swains Lane Cottage, Whitchurch Canonicorum, near Bridport, Dorset, England,

CAREER: Barrister in London, England, 1954-58; London School of Economics and Political Science, London, England, research assistant, 1959; *Daily Express,* London, England libel lawyer, 1959-62

WRITINGS: Buster (short novel), published in *New Writers One,* J. Calder, 1961; *Europe After the Rain* (novel), Fernhill, 1965; *Celebrations* (novel), Calder & Boyars, 1967, Fernhill, 1968; *Babel* (novel), Calder & Boyars, 1969, John Day, 1970; (with others) *Red Dust Two: New Writing,* Red Dust, 1972. Also author of a play, "Palach," first produced in London at Open Space Theatre, November 11, 1970.

WORK IN PROGRESS: A novel; a screen play based on *Buster.*

SIDELIGHTS: Burns' "experimental" and "surrealistic" style has provoked a variety of critical comment. Writing for *Library Journal,* Elena Sansalone says of *Babel:* "In representing chaos, [Burns] has lost all sense of order. The only unity present is the constant sense of disunity, but Burns fails to come to terms with the disoriented universe he depicts. . . . He says, 'The old narrative form is dead, boring, irrelevant.' His new narrative form, however, does nothing to improve upon the old." A reviewer of the protest play, "Palach," writes that it is "neither theatre nor is it persuasion or argument. . . . [It] is a garble of words, tricks, exercises—and none of them are startling, effective, or original—which leaves only a blank in the mind of the beholder. It doesn't say a thing."

In *Celebrations* Burns fragments time, juxtaposing scenes and events with often startling effect. Stephen Wall believes that his "control of his medium is not really secure enough for this kind of risk." According to B.S. Johnson, however, "the result is that the book is independent of time in something like the same way that Kafka's work is: it will read very much the same in ten, thirty, or a hundred years' time. . . . The techniques necessary to achieve this are staggering. . . . But it seems to be not just an attempt to describe the more-than-real: Burns is trying rather to illuminate more clearly what he believes with impressive conviction to be really there. Alan Burns has remarkable talent of the most important kind, and he is a very serious writer indeed: he deserves to be read widely with at least equal seriousness."

BIOGRAPHICAL/CRITICAL SOURCES: New Statesman, November 17, 1967; *Observer Review,* December 10, 1967; *Library Journal,* July, 1970, November 1, 1970; *Stage,* November 19, 1970.

*   *   *

BURNSHAW, Stanley 1906-

PERSONAL: Born June 20, 1906, in New York, N.Y.; son of Ludwig and Sophy (Kivman) Burnshaw; married Lydia Powsner (a social worker), September 2, 1943; children: Valerie Burnshaw Razavi; stepchildren: Amy Blumberg, David Chaitkin. *Education:* Columbia University, student, 1924; University of Pittsburg, B.A., 1925; graduate study at University of Poitiers, 1927, University of Paris, 1927-28; Cornell University, M.A., 1933. *Home:* Lamberts Cove, Martha's Vineyard, Mass. 02568.

CAREER: Blaw-Knox Steel Corp., Blawnox, Pa., advertising copywriter, 1925-27; Hecht Co., New York, N.Y., advertising manager, 1928-32; *New Masses* (weekly magazine), New York, N.Y., drama critic and associate editor, 1933-36; Cordon Co., Inc. (publishers), New York, N.Y., vice-president, 1937-39; Dryden Press, Inc. (publishers), New York, N.Y., president and editor-in-chief, 1939-58; Holt, Rinehart & Winston, Inc. (publishers), New York, N.Y., vice-president, 1958-68. Judge, National Book Awards, 1966 and 1972; member of Awards Advisory Board, National Book Committee, 1967-70. New York University, lecturer, 1958-62. *Member:* American Institute of Graphic Arts (board of directors, 1960-62), P.E.N. *Awards, honors:* Award for literature, National Institute of Arts and Letters, 1971.

WRITINGS: Poems, Folio Press, 1927; *The Wheel Age,* privately printed, 1928; *Andre Spire and His Poetry* (two essays and 40 translations), Centaur Press, 1933; (editor) Alfred Kreymborg, *Two New Yorkers,* Humphries, 1934; *The Iron Land* (poem), Centaur Press, 1936; *The Bridge,* Dryden Press, 1945; *The Revolt of the Cats in Paradise* (children's book for adults), Crow Hill Press, 1945; *The Sunless Sea* (novel), Peter Davies, 1948, Dial, 1949; *Early and Late Testament* (poems and translations), Dial, 1952; (editor and author of introduction) *The Poem Itself: Forty-Five Modern Poets in a New Presentation,* Holt, 1960; (editor) *Varieties of Literary Experience: Eighteen Essays in World Literature,* New York University Press, 1962; *Caged in an Animal's Mind,* Holt, 1963; (editor with T. Carmi and Ezra Spicehandler) *The Modern Hebrew Poem Itself: Twenty-Four Modern Hebrew Poets in a New Presentation,* bilingual edition, Holt, 1965; *The Seamless Web: Language-Thinking, Creature-Knowledge, Art-Experience,* Braziller, 1970; *In the Terrified Radiance*

(poems) Braziller, 1972. Contributor to *Columbia University Dictionary of Modern European Literature, Dictionary of World Literature,* and to reviews and literary magazines in the United States and abroad.

WORK IN PROGRESS: A new volume of poems; a biography in prose.

SIDELIGHTS: The Modern Hebrew Poem Itself was the first anthology of modern Hebrew poetry to appear in English; each poem is presented in Hebrew with an English phonetic transcription, literal translation, and analysis. This method closely followed that employed in *The Poem Itself,* in which Burnshaw translated and analyzed 150 European poems. Philip Toynbee wrote that "the whole enterprise was heroic, not only in its courage and considerable achievement but also in a certain dogged, even naive, refusal to admit defeat."

With *The Seamless Web,* Toynbee continues, "he has made a more ferocious and sustained effort to define the nature of criticism than almost any of his confreres in the Great Game." The exhaustiveness of Burnshaw's analysis "makes for certain longueurs; but it also makes for what may well turn out to be a major work of theoretical criticism. It is not only that Mr. Burnshaw's persistence is rewarded by a great many flashes of incidental illumination: what is more important is that a major argument emerges which has never quite emerged in any previous work or body of work." D.J. Enright found Burnshaw's "physiological, biological, cerebral, and zoological excursuses less illuminating than they were meant to be." The studied consideration he gives the various facets of a necessarily complex subject, the nature of art, does not, in Enright's opinion, "save the protracted urbanity of attitude, the scrupulously maintained judiciousness, from proving slightly tedious in the long run." Hilton Kramer believes the importance of *The Seamless Web* "lies precisely in its attempt to establish what the author, himself a poet and anthologist of some distinction, calls a 'creature definition' of poetry and its function—in effect, to answer Valery's appeal by writing a natural history of the poetic process. . . . He has written a book of far-reaching importance—a defense of poetry that removes it from the realm of man's spiritual luxuries and places it pre-eminently among his instruments of survival."

BIOGRAPHICAL/CRITICAL SOURCES: New York Times Book Review, December 22, 1963, February 22, 1970; *Poetry,* January, 1968; *New York Times,* February 18, 1970; *Observer Review,* June 28, 1970; *Times Literary Supplement,* August 28, 1970; *New York Review of Books,* September 3, 1970.

*   *   *

BURROUGHS, William (Seward) 1914-
(William Lee, Willy Lee)

PERSONAL: Born February 5, 1914, in St. Louis, Mo.; son of Perry Mortimer (a businessman) and Laura (Lee) Burroughs; married second wife, Joan Vollmer, January 17, 1945 (deceased); children: (second marriage) William Seward. *Education:* Harvard University, A.B., 1936, and, later, graduate study in ethnology and archaelogy; University of Vienna, medical studies. *Home:* 8 Duke Street, St. James, London S.W.1, England.

CAREER: Once held a variety of jobs, including advertising copywriter, newspaper reporter, office employee, private detective, factory worker, exterminator, and bartender; now full-time writer. *Military service:* U.S. Army, June, 1942-September, 1942.

WRITINGS: (Under pseudonym William Lee) *Junkie: Confessions of an Unredeemed Drug Addict* (first printing entitled *Junk*), A.A. Wyn, 1953, published under own name, Ace Books, 1964; *The Naked Lunch* (first in trilogy; extracts published in *Big Table* and *Evergreen*

Review), Olympia Press (Paris), 1959, published in America as *Naked Lunch*, Grove, 1962; (with Brion Gysin) *The Exterminator* (including poems and calligraphs by Gysin), Auerhaun Press (San Francisco), 1960; (with Sinclair Beiles, Gregory Corso, and Gysin) *Minutes to Go* ("cut-up" poems), Two Cities Editions (Paris), 1960; (contributor) Thomas Parkinson, editor, *A Casebook on the Beat*, Crowell, 1961; *The Soft Machine* (second in the trilogy), Olympia Press, 1961, Grove, 1966; *The Ticket That Exploded* (last in the trilogy; originally announced as "Novia Express" and one chapter published under that title in *Evergreen Review*, July-August, 1962; two sections—"In a Strange Bed" and "The Black Fruit"—written in collaboration with Michael Portman), Olympia Press, 1962, revised and expanded edition, Grove, 1967; *Dead Fingers Talk* (contains excerpts from *Naked Lunch*, *The Soft Machine* and *The Ticket That Exploded*), jointly published by J. Calder (London) and Olympia Press, 1963; (with Allen Ginsberg) *The Yage Letters*, City Lights Books (San Francisco), 1963; *Takis* (catalog of an exhibition at Alexander Iolas Gallery, New York), [New York], 1963; *Nova Express*, Grove, 1964; (under pseudonym Willy Lee) *Roosevelt after Inauguration* ("printed, published, and zapped at a secret location in the lower east side"), mimeographed, [New York], 1964; *Health Bulletin: APO-33: A Report on the Synthesis of the Apomorphine Formula*, F.Y. Press, c.1965; (with Lee Harwood) *Darazt*, Lovebooks, 1965; *Time* (with four drawings by Gysin), "C" Press, (New York), 1965; *Valentine's Day Reading* (script presented at the American Theatre for Poets), mimeographed, [New York], 1965; (contributor) Mary Beach and Claude Pelieu, compilers, *APO-33, a Metabolic Regulator: A Report on the Synthesis of the Apomorphine Formula*, Beach Books Texts & Documents (San Francisco), c.1966; (with Nicholas Galas, Corso, and Ginsberg) *Takis: Magnetic Sculpture* (catalog of an exhibition at Howard Wise Gallery, New York), [New York], 1967; (with Pelieu and Carl Weissner) *So Who Owns Death TV?*, Beach Books Texts & Documents, 1967; (author of preface) Jeff Nuttall, *Pig*, Fulcrum Press, 1969; *The Dead Star*, Nova Broadcast, 1969; *Entretiens avec William Burroughs* (interviews with Burroughs by Daniel Odier), P. Belfond (Paris), 1969, revised and enlarged edition published in America as *The Job: Interviews with William S. Burroughs*, Grove, 1970, revised and enlarged edition, 1971; (with Gysin) *Third Mind*, Grove, 1970; (author of preface) Carl Weissner, *The Braille Film: With a Counterscript*, Nova Broadcast, 1970; *The Last Words of Dutch Schultz* (excerpt originally published as transcript of Burroughs' Valentine's Day reading at East End Theatre, February 14, 1965), Cape Goliard, 1970; *The Wild Boys: A Book of the Dead*, Grove, 1971. Excerpts from writings included in *Etats-Unis: William Burroughs, Claude Pelieu, Bob Kaufman*, translated into French by Pelieu and Mary Beach, Editions de l'Herne (Paris), 1967. Contributor to *Big Table*, *Evergreen Review*, *Paris Review*, *Harper's*, *Village Voice*, *Esquire*, and other periodicals. Editor of *Moving Times* (Tangier), 1964.

WORK IN PROGRESS: A Novel, *Exterminator*, completed and awaiting publication by Seaver Books.

SIDELIGHTS: A grandson of the inventor of the Burroughs adding machine, Burroughs has lived in London, Paris, Tangier, Mexico, and traveled in Central America, the Amazon region of South America, and North Africa. He has been linked with Jack Kerouac and Allen Ginsberg as a kind of chronicler of the beat generation which flourished in Greenwich Village and elsewhere in the mid-1950's, and has himself appeared as a major character in at least three of Kerouac's novels. Burroughs has also lived in homes for narcotic addicts. Of this period of his life he has written: "I have learned a great deal from using junk; I have seen life measured out in eyedroppers of morphine solution ..." After many years of addiction (1944-57), after "a month in a tiny room in the Casbah [Tangier, 1957] staring at the toe of my foot," after "the room had filled up with empty Eukodol cartons ... I suddenly realized I was not doing *anything*. I was dying." After that, he flew off to London and was cured by the apomorphine treatment developed by a British doctor, John Yerby Dent.

Since his cure, Burroughs has become almost evangelistic in his recommendation of apomorphine, a metabolic regulator obtained by boiling morphine in hydrochloric acid, as the most effective approach to drug addiction. In a *Life* article on "The Other Culture," Barry Farrell quoted Jeff Nuttall, who has been instrumental in publishing Burroughs' letters, memoranda, and experimental "cut-ups": "[Burroughs] wants as a man what so many of us want—to drift into some area of hallucinatory delirium where there are some optimistic possibilities. [He] attempted to acheve this delirium through various experiments with drugs, experiments with the manipulation of his life and instincts. Finally he discovered himself hung up and his whole fundamental intention made impossible by heroin—and I've never heard a man speak so savagely against heroin, nor so searchingly and accurately as well." Contrary to traditional medical opinion, Burroughs believes that addiction is a purely physiological problem, and should be treated as such. As he mentioned in an article for *Harper's* in 1967, he is particularly opposed to law enforcement officials' treatment of drug users as criminals, and to the "quasi-religious approach" to metabolic illness which has been so prevalent in the past. "Remember that if [heroin] can be readily obtained," he told an interviewer for *Paris Review*, "you will have any number of addicts. The idea that addiction is somehow a psychological illness is, I think, totally ridiculous. It's as psychological as malaria. It's a matter of exposure." Burroughs was on junk for almost fifteen years, and in that time took ten cures, all of which led to relapses. He was never physiologically cured until 1957, when the apomorphine treatment evicted the "addict personality" he called "Opium Jones" ("standing there in his shabby black suit and gray felt hat with his stale rooming-house flesh and cold undersea eyes") from his existence. When asked by the interviewer if he was interested in "turning the body into an environment" from a creative point of view, a popular concept among drug users, Burroughs replied: "No, junk narrows consciousness. The only benefit to me as a writer (aside from putting me into contact with the whole carny world) came to me after I went off it. What I want to do is to learn to see more of what's out there, to look outside, to achieve as far as possible a complete awareness of surroundings."

Burroughs has said that Dr. Benway, one of his famous character creations of *Naked Lunch*, "dates back to a story I wrote in 1938, ... about the only piece of writing I did prior to *Junkie*." According to William James Smith, *Junk* [as the first printing was entitled] "is a more or less journalistic account of the experiences of a drug addict. It rises, however, considerably above the general literary level of sensational *expose*. It is an authentically macabre version of Hell and the flat literalism of the writing makes it more appalling in some ways than Burroughs' later accounts of the same material." The apocalyptic version of *Naked Lunch* is something else again. A tale John Ciardi has called "a surrealistic montage of dramatic scene and dramatic hallucination," it has aroused intense controversy. "It is not surprising," observes Ihab Hassan, "that [Burroughs'] testimony is subject to extravagant praise and hysterical denunciation. In the view of some, Burroughs is the underground king of the Beat Movement for which sweet Jack Kerouac is merely a publicist; in that view *Naked Lunch* is the secret masterpiece through which the movement is vindicated."

An unfavorable review of four of his books appeared under the headline "Ugh ..." late in 1963 in the *Times Literary Supplement.* There followed an extensive correspondence ("we have never had a keener correspondence," the editors wrote) wherein Burroughs was denounced by Dame Edith Sitwell, publisher Victor Gollancz ("Who," queried Burroughs, "is Mr. Gollancz?"), and numerous lesser personalities. When it was over Burroughs had been called a "dirty-minded neurotic" and a writer with a "third-rate sensibility"; his books had been described as nauseating, boring, repetitious, "bogus-highbrow filth," and as extending the boundaries of the novel "towards the public lavatory." To Burroughs' defense came his British publisher, John Calder (three letters in nine weeks), who considers Burroughs "one of the few really important and seminal novelists of today.... To say that he is boring is not to read him properly, to say that he is immoral is to misjudge the intention of the work, and to throw words like 'filthy' at him is to completely sidestep any pretence at an objective or critical approach." Anthony Burgess, a personal friend, wrote: "Dame Edith will have to accept, whether she likes it or not, that Mr. Burroughs is a serious artist trying to extend the boundaries of the novel-form and that his devotion to the craft of writing is not inferior to her own . . . I do not like what Mr. Burroughs writes about; [but] Life is, unfortunately, life.... Mr. Burroughs recognized that Jane Austen (whom he greatly admires) is not to be disparaged for the limitations of her subject-matter." Burroughs himself contributed a letter. Of the reviewer who wrote that he "presents these episodes [in *Dead Fingers Talk*] without a flicker of disapproval," Burroughs demanded: "Precisely how is a writer expected to 'flicker' disapproval? He must announce to the audience whenever a dubious character appears on stage 'you understand I don't approve of this man. Just part of the show you know?' This is absurd."

In 1962, when Burroughs was relatively unknown, two American literary radicals—Norman Mailer and Mary McCarthy—declared that here was the contemporary writer who had most affected the literary cognoscenti. Mailer has gone so far as to call Burroughs "the only American novelist living today who may conceivably be possessed by genius." A *New Statesman* reviewer has said that "*Naked Lunch* ... deserves to be protected as a potpourri of morbidities which belongs jointly to high literature and to psychopathology." Robert Lowell considers it "a completely powerful and serious book," the product, says Jack Kerouac, "of the greatest satirical writer since Jonathan Swift." E.S. Seldon adds: "This is one contemporary writer who can drop dead tomorrow, confident not in promise, but in fulfillment."

Burroughs has repeatedly assured his readers that a good deal of his writing is direct dictation from Hasan-i-Sabbah, the founder of the eleventh-century Ismaili cult, the Assassins. This dictation if supplemented by Burroughs' own "cut-up" and "fold-in" techniques, whereby pages are selected at random, either cut up and juxtaposed, or folded in half vertically and laid alongside a similarly folded page to form new lines of type. The lines are then edited, rearranged, and "let out" ("words know where they belong better than you do") until a satisfactory juxtaposition is achieved. Such a technique, Burroughs believes, facilitates the formation of "association blocks" and striking "wordless" images. "The aim," as stated by Hassan "is to cut oneself out of language, cut oneself *from* language. The aim is to escape a world made by words and perhaps to discover another.... The death machine, Burroughs implies, can only be destroyed by destroying its logic, its logos." In his destruction of "logos," however, Burroughs sometimes loses and often alienates his readers. Smith is "tempted to say that *Nova Express* is pure junk. It has moved into the limbo of incoherent mutterings ... a sort of in-group madness. It is not a message to mankind, but a message to Tompkins Square." Many critics consider Burroughs more of a social phenomenon than an author. Emile Capouya writes: "Those who are clearly of the present do not, as a rule, write novels that seem likely to last, e.g., William Burroughs, who is most important as a symptom but who seems to have no relation to literature ..." Joan Didion, in contrast, is of the opinion that the search for conventional meaning in Burroughs' work is irrelevant. She believes that "the insistent amorphousness of his books encourages the reader to take from them pretty much exactly what he brought to them. Burroughs has been read as a pamphleteer for narcotics reform. He has been read as a parabolist of the highest order. He has been read as a pornographer and he has been read as a prophet of the apocalypse.... Burroughs is read for 'meaning,' for we tend to be uneasy in this country until we can draw from an imaginative work some immediate social application. . . . In this stampede to first discern the 'message' and then take a stand on it, Burroughs' limited but very real virtues tend to be overlooked. In a quite literal sense with Burroughs, the medium *is* the message: The point is not what the voice says but the voice itself, a voice so direct and original and versatile as to disarm close scrutiny of what it is saying. Burroughs is less a writer than a 'sound,' and to listen to the lyric may be to miss the beat."

Burroughs has been compared to such diverse thinkers as Eliot, Joyce, and Lenny Bruce in style, mood, and subject matter. He admits in the *Paris Review* interview that he freely borrows raw material for cut-ups from various sources, including Joyce, Shakespeare, Rimbaud, Jack Stern, Kerouac, Genet, Joseph Conrad, Richard Hughes, Graham Greene, Tom Lea, Eric Frank Russell, and a host of other writers. Several critics have analyzed his work as examples of black humor, "filled with clever puns, sharp satirical asides, and brilliant impressionistic writing," in the words of Douglas Davis. Hassan says that Burroughs, like the later Swift, Breughel and Hieronymous Bosch, "pushes satire toward the threshold of pathology, claiming from self-hate the hate humanity harbors. Personal outrage may be made into an indictment of history." Hassan feels his apocalyptic scenes resemble those of Rimbaud and Orwell, "but the quality of Burroughs which sets him apart ... is his grotesque humor. Above all, *Naked Lunch* is a parody of evil; it crackles with gargoyle laughter." To Marvin Mudrick it is apparent that Burroughs "would rather be a thinker than a comedian.... The reader will not be permitted merely to laugh, since Burroughs insists—all joking aside—that he's as unfunny as any other over-applauded coterie writer: 'There is only one thing a writer can write about: *what is in front of his senses at the moment of writing. . . . I am a recording instrument....* I do not presume to impose "story" "plot" "continuity".... I am not an entertainer . .'" Terry Southern has called Burroughs' work "an absolutely devastating ridicule of all that is false, primitive, and vicious in American life; the abuses of power, hero worship, aimless violence, materialistic obsession, intolerance, and every form of hypocrisy. No one, for example, has written with such eloquent disgust about capital punishment; ... but one must never mistake this author's work for political comment, which, as in all genuine art, is more instinctive than deliberate—for Burroughs is first and foremost a poet. His attunement to contemporary language is probably unequalled in American writing."

Burroughs told *CA* he is interested in ethnology, archaeology, medicine, and pharmacology. "I feel," he writes, "that writers should be more scientific and scientists more creative."

Burroughs appeared in Conrad Rooks's autobiographical film "Chappaqua," which took second prize for the United States in the Silver Lion competition at the Venice Film Festival in 1967. He also acted, with Brion Gysin, in Anthony Balch's "The Cut Ups" in 1968, and played the President of the United States in "Flash Gordon and the Angels," a play by David Mairowitz, first produced off the West End at Open Space Theatre, February 16, 1971. Some of Burroughs' work was recorded for John Giorno's "Dial-a-Poem" program sponsored by the Architectural League of New York.

BIOGRAPHICAL/CRITICAL SOURCES: Saturday Review, June 27, 1959; *Life,* November 30, 1959, February 15, 1967; *Spectator,* July 29, 1960; *Naked Lunch* (reviews by Terry Southern and others, including excerpts from the book), Grove, 1962; "Introduction to *Naked Lunch, The Soft Machine* and 'Novi Express,'" by Burroughs, in *Evergreen Review,* January-February, 1962; *New York Times Book Review,* September 16, 1962; *Kulchur 7,* autumn, 1962; *Time,* November 30, 1962; *New Republic,* December 1, 1962, December 15, 1962, December 29, 1962, January 12, 1963, August 5, 1967; Terry Southern, Richard Seaver, and Alexander Trocchi, editors, *Writers in Revolt,* Berkeley, 1963; *Critique,* spring, 1963; *Times Literary Supplement,* weekly from November 14, 1963 to January 30, 1964, August 6, 1964; *Book Week,* November 8, 1964, September 26, 1965, March 27, 1966; *Minnesota Review,* index issue, 1965; *Langues Modernes,* January-February, 1965; *Commonweal,* January 8, 1965; *Paris Review,* fall, 1965, summer, 1968; *National Observer,* June, 1967; *Harper's,* July, 1967; *Village Voice,* July 6, 1967; *Hudson Review,* autumn, 1967; *Books and Bookmen,* October, 1968; *Guardian,* July 5, 1969; *Library Journal,* March 15, 1970; *Esquire,* October, 1970, September, 1971; Tony Tanner, *City of Words: American Fiction, 1950-1970,* Harper, 1971; E. Mottram, *William Burroughs: The Algebra of Need,* Intrepid Press, 1971.

* * *

BURSTYN, Harold L(ewis) 1930-

PERSONAL: Born February 26, 1930, in Boston, Mass.; son of Julius (a business executive) and Zena (Pezrow) Burstyn; married Joan N. Jacobs (educator), August 19, 1958; children: Judith N., Gail C., Daniel F. *Education:* Harvard University, A.B. (magna cum laude), 1951, Ph.D., 1964; University of Amsterdam, Fulbright scholar, 1951-52; University of California, M.S. in Oceanography, 1957; University College, University of London, postgraduate study, 1957-58, U.S. National Science Foundation postdoctoral fellow at Imperial College, 1965-66. *Religion:* Jewish. *Home:* 1863 Shaw Ave., Pittsburgh, Pa. 15217; and 5 High St., Woods Hole, Mass. 02543. *Office:* Department of History, Carnegie-Mellon University, Pittsburgh, Pa. 15213; and Woods Hole Oceanographic Institution, Woods Hole, Mass. 02543.

CAREER: Brandeis University, Waltham, Mass., instructor in history of science, 1962-65; Woods Hole Oceanographic Institution, Woods Hole, Mass., visiting investigator, 1962-70; Carnegie-Mellon University, Pittsburgh, Pa., assistant professor, 1966-69, associate professor of history of science, 1969—. *Military service:* U.S. Navy, 1952-55; commissioned officer. *Member:* American Historical Association, History of Science Society, Society for Nautical Research, Past and Present Society, Phi Beta Kappa (chapter secretary, 1963-64). *Awards, honors:* Henry Schuman Prize of History of Science Society, 1960, for "Galileo's Attempt to Prove that the Earth Moves," published in *Isis,* 1962.

WRITINGS: At the Sign of the Quadrant: An Account of the Contributions to American Hydrography Made by Edmund March Blunt and His Sons, Marine Historical Association, 1957. Contributor of articles and reviews to scholarly journals, 1958—.

WORK IN PROGRESS: A history of the Challenger Expedition (1872-76) and its Report (1881-95).

* * *

BURT, Jesse Clifton 1921-

PERSONAL: Born August 29, 1921, in Nashville, Tenn.; son of Jesse Clifton and Agnes (Seals) Burt; married Eleanor Bales Jones (a librarian), September 27, 1947. *Education:* George Peabody College for Teachers, B.S., 1942, M.A., 1943; Vanderbilt University, Ph.D., 1950; Harvard University, Ed.M., 1961. *Religion:* Methodist. *Home and office:* B-8 Skyline Apartments, Acklen Park, Nashville, Tenn. 37205.

CAREER: Presbyterian College, Clinton, S.C., instructor in history, 1943; Florence State College, Florence, Ala., assistant professor of history, 1945-47; Vanderbilt University, Nashville, Tenn., teaching fellow, 1947-50; Lambuth College, Jackson, Tenn., dean, 1950-53; University of Tennessee, Nashville Center, extension division instructor in history, 1956—. Radio broadcaster in own series, Nashville, Tenn., 1963. *Awards, honors:* Danforth Award, 1954, for youth writings.

WRITINGS: Your Vocational Adventure, Abingdon, 1959; *Nashville: Its Life and Times,* Tennessee Book Co., 1959; (with Bob Ferguson) *So You Want To Be in Music,* Abingdon, 1970; (with Ferguson) *Indians of the Southeast—Then and Now,* Abingdon, 1973. Contributor to "The Illustrated Library of the Natural Sciences," American Museum of Natural History. Contributor of more than a score of articles to historical and educational journals, articles to fifteen Catholic and Protestant journals of religious thought, and some five hundred book reviews to various publications.

WORK IN PROGRESS: Science and Man's Hope; also research on the achievements of William Tecumseh Sherman.

AVOCATIONAL INTERESTS: Folk music, physical fitness, foreign films, and radio.

* * *

BURTON, Hester (Wood-Hill) 1913-

PERSONAL: Born December 6, 1913, in Beccles, Suffolk, England; daughter of Henry G. (a surgeon) and Amy (Crowfoot) Wood-Hill; married R.W.B. Burton (a tutor-lecturer in classics at Oxford University), August 7, 1937; children: Catharine, Elizabeth, Janet. *Education:* Oxford University, honors degree in English literature, 1936. *Politics:* Liberal Party. *Home:* Mill House, Kidlington, Oxford, England.

CAREER: Part-time grammar school teacher; examiner in public examination. *Awards, honors:* Carnegie Medal, 1963, for *Time of Trial.*

WRITINGS: Barbara Bodichon, 1827-1891, J. Murray, 1949; (compiler and author of commentary) *Coleridge and the Wordsworths,* Oxford University Press (London), 1953; (compiler and author of commentary) *Tennyson,* Oxford University Press, 1954; (editor) *Her First Ball* (short story collection), Oxford University Press, 1959; (editor) *A Book of Modern Stories,* Oxford University Press, 1959; *The Great Gale* (juvenile), Oxford University Press, 1960; *Castors Away!* (juvenile), Oxford University Press, 1962; *Time of Trial* (juvenile), Oxford University Press, 1963, World Publishing, 1964; *A*

Seaman at the Time of Trafalgar, Oxford University Press, 1963; *No Beat of Drum* (youth novel), Oxford University Press, 1966, World Publishing, 1967; *In Spite of All Terror* (youth novel), Oxford University Press, 1968, World Publishing, 1969; *The Flood at Reedsmere* (juvenile), World Publishing, 1968; *Otmoor for Ever!,* Hamish Hamilton, 1968; *Thomas* (youth novel), Oxford University Press, 1969; *Through the Fire* (juvenile), Hamish Hamilton, 1969; *The Henchmans at Home* (juvenile), Oxford University Press, 1970; *Beyond the Weir Bridge,* Crowell, 1970; *The Rebel,* Crowell, 1972. Assistant editor, *Oxford Junior Encyclopaedia,* 1956-61.

SIDELIGHTS: Mrs. Burton's juvenile and youth books are historical fiction, based on actual incidents in British history. According to Robin McKown of *New York Times Book Review,* "Mrs. Burton, not softening reality because her audience is young, has produced a splendid novel of outstanding power and beauty" in *No Beat of Drum,* which focuses on England's underprivileged in the 1830's. Marie Peel said of *In Spite of All Terror,* the story of a working class orphan in World War II Britain: "[Mrs. Burton's] presentation of these people rings true and is without patronage. . . . There is no preconceived attitude in the author, but unusual openness and depth of understanding."

BIOGRAPHICAL/CRITICAL SOURCES: Times Literary Supplement, June 1, 1962, June 26, 1969; *Book World,* December 31, 1967; *New York Times Book Review,* February 4, 1968; *Library Journal,* September, 1968, July, 1969; *Books and Bookmen,* November, 1968.

*　　　*　　　*

BURTSCHI, Mary 1911-

PERSONAL: Born February 22, 1911, in Vandalia, Ill.; daughter of Joseph Charles (a financier) and Olivia (Yoos) Burtschi. *Education:* St. Mary-of-the-Woods College, Terre Haute, Ind., student, 1929-30; Webster College, B.A., 1933; University of Illinois, M.A., 1954. *Home:* 307 North Sixth St., Vandalia, Ill. 62471.

CAREER: Effingham High School, Effingham, Ill., English instructor, 1939-70. Writer and lecturer. Director, James Hall Library, Little Brick House, Vandalia, Ill. Appointed by Governor of Illinois to Historians of Illinois Sesquicentennial Commission. *Member:* Illinois State Historical Society (director, 1965-68; a vice-president, 1968—), University of Illinois College of Education Alumni Association (research historian; field representative, 1969—; director, 1970-72), Vandalia Historical Society (president, 1962-65).

WRITINGS: Biographical Sketch of Joseph Charles Burtschi (monograph), Vandalia Historical Society, 1962; *Vandalia: Wilderness Capital of Lincoln's Land,* Huston-Patterson, 1963; *A Part Folio for James Hall* (monograph), Vandalia Historical Society, 1968. Author of plays, "Three Scenes in George Washington's Life," "Heaven is Thine," and "Mr. Jack." Poem anthologized in *National Poetry Anthology,* 1956. Contributor of an article on James Hall to *Documentary History of Vandalia, Illinois,* 1954; writer of other articles on Illinois history.

WORK IN PROGRESS: A book, *James Hall: Frontier Storyteller of Lincoln's Vandalia;* an article, "Illinois Artist James William Berry," for *Journal* of the Illinois State Historical Society; "An Unlisted Abraham Lincoln Letter" for *Lincoln Herald;* a monograph on Vandalia's Little Brick House.

AVOCATIONAL INTERESTS: Touring visitors through the Little Brick House, an example of a pioneer home when Vandalia was the capital of Illinois (1820-39), supervising the garden of native trees and wildflowers on the acreage; traveling.

*　　　*　　　*

BURTT, Everett Johnson, Jr. 1914-

PERSONAL: Born August 6, 1914, in Jackson, Mich.; son of Everett Johnson and Eve Mildred (Meisenhelter) Burtt; married Cynthia Webb, June 15, 1940; children: Michael Coburn, Judith. *Education:* Berea College, A.B., 1935; Duke University, M.A., 1937, Ph.D., 1950. *Religion:* Unitarian. *Home:* 399 Clapboardtree, Westwood, Mass. 02090. *Office:* Department of Economics, Boston University, 226 Bay State Rd., Boston, Mass. 02215.

CAREER: Instructor in economics at University of Maine, Orono, 1939-41, and at University of Denver, Denver, Colo., 1941-42; analyst for War Manpower Commission, Washington, D.C., 1942-43, and for U.S. Department of Labor, Boston, Mass., 1946-47; Boston University, Boston, Mass., assistant professor, 1947-52, associate professor, 1952-57, professor of economics, 1957—, chairman of economics department, 1952-68. Economic consultant to business, non-profit organizations, and government agencies. *Military service:* U.S. Army, 1943-46. *Member:* American Economic Association, Industrial Relations Research Association, American Association of University Professors.

WRITINGS: Labor Markets, Unions, and Government Policies, St. Martin's, 1963; *Plant Relocation and the Core City Worker: Commuting and Housing Decisions of Relocated Workers—The Boston Experience,* U.S. Government Printing Office, 1967; (with Blanche E. Fitzpatrick and Warren R. Healey) *Regional New England Manpower Shortage Survey in Selected Areas and Industries,* New England Council, 1968; *Social Perspectives in the History of Economic Theory,* St. Martin's, 1972. Author of research reports on the Boston labor force, and of articles in professional journals.

*　　　*　　　*

BUTLER, Francelia McWilliams 1913-

PERSONAL: Born April 25, 1913, in Cleveland, Ohio; daughter of Robert William (an educator) and Grace Lucille (Williams) McWilliams; married Jerome Ambrose Butler (a journalist), July 4, 1939 (deceased); children: Susan Ellen Butler Wandell. *Education:* Oberlin College, A.B., 1934; Georgetown University, M.A., 1959; University of Virginia, Ph.D., 1963. *Politics:* Democrat. *Religion:* Congregational. *Home:* Mansfield Hollow Rd., Mansfield Center, Conn. 06250. *Agent:* Blanche C. Gregory, 2 Tudor Pla., New York, N.Y. 10017. *Office:* Department of English, University of Connecticut, Storrs, Conn. 06268.

CAREER: Paris Herald, Paris, France, drama critic, 1938; University of Tennessee, Knoxville, assistant professor of English, 1963-65; University of Connecticut, Storrs, associate professor of English, 1965—. Northern Virginia Mental Health Association, volunteer secretary, 1957. *Member:* Modern Language Association of America, American Studies Association, American Association of University Professors, Bibliographical Society of Virginia, Tennessee Philological Association. *Awards, honors:* Laurance Rockefeller grant for research and writing on the history of cancer, 1952; University of Tennessee grant for research on Ruskin Commonwealth, 1964; Ford Foundation fellow, Institute of Medieval and Renaissance Studies, University of North Carolina, 1965; Fulbright lecturer, Jagellonian University, Krakow, Poland, 1967-68; University of Connecticut grant for research in England, 1970.

WRITINGS: James Marion Sims, Pioneer American Cancer Protagonist, Hoeber, 1950; *The Sun Dial,* [Arlington], 1952; *Cancer Through the Ages: The Evolution of Hope,* Virginia Press, 1955; (with Gail E. Haley) *The Skip-Rope Book,* introduction by Phyllis McGinley, Dial, 1963; *The Strange Critical Fortunes of Shakespeare's Timon of Athens,* Iowa State University Press, 1966; (editor) Herbert Silvette, *The Doctor on the Stage: Medicine and Medical Men in 17th Century England,* University of Tennessee Press, 1967. Contributor to *Studies in Philology, Tennessee Historical Quarterly, Tennessee Studies in Literature, Shakespeare Quarterly, Extrapolation, Polish Review, Milton Newsletter.* Editor, *Children's Literature* (scholarly journal).

WORK IN PROGRESS: The Ruskin Commonwealth: An American Experiment in Marxian Socialism, 1939-1902; The Sandpile, a novel; "Left About Face," a play.

AVOCATIONAL INTERESTS: Collecting cookbooks.

BIOGRAPHICAL/CRITICAL SOURCES: Washington Post, September 22, 1963; *Knoxville News Sentinel,* December 29, 1963; *Hartford Times,* January 6, 1971.

* * *

BUTLER, Gwendoline Williams   1922-

PERSONAL: Born August 19, 1922, London, England; daughter of Alfred Edward and Alice (Lee) Williams; married Lionel Butler (a professor of medieval history at University of St. Andrews), October 16, 1949; cⱼildren: Lucilla. *Education:* Haberdashers' Aske's Hatcham Girls School, student, 1934-42; Lady Margaret Hall, Oxford, M.A., 1948. *Home:* 54 South St., St. Andrews, Fife, Scotland. *Agent:* John Farquharson Ltd., 15 Red Lion Sq., London W.C.1, England.

CAREER: Writer.

WRITINGS: Receipt for Murder, Bles, 1956; *Dead in a Row,* Bles, 1957; *The Dull Dead,* Bles, 1958, Walker & Co., 1962; *The Murdering Kind,* Bles, 1958, Roy, 1964; *The Interloper,* Bles, 1959; *Dine and Be Dead,* Macmillan, 1960 (published in England as *Death Lives Next Door,* Bles, 1960); *Make Me a Murderer,* Bles, 1961; *Coffin in Oxford,* Bles, 1962; *Coffin for Baby,* Walker & Co., 1962; *Coffin Waiting,* Bles, 1964, Walker & Co., 1965; *Coffin in Malta,* Bles, 1964, Walker & Co., 1965; *A Nameless Coffin,* Walker & Co., 1966; *Coffin Following,* Bles, 1968; *Coffin's Dark Number,* Bles, 1969; *A Coffin From the Past,* Bles, 1970.†

* * *

BUTLER, Jean Campbell (MacLaurin)   1918-

PERSONAL: Born January 10, 1918, in Victoria, British Columbia; daughter of Donald Leslie (an educational administrator) and Nellie Evelyn (Marchant) MacLaurin; married W. Royce Butler (a university librarian), September 6, 1941. *Education:* Victoria College, student, 1934-36; University of British Columbia, B.A. (first class honors in English and history), 1938, graduate study, 1938-39; University of Toronto, M.A., 1940, postgraduate study, 1940-41. *Religion:* Anglican. *Home:* 34 Dalmeny Rd., Willowdale, Ontario, Canada.

CAREER: University of British Columbia, Vancouver, 1941-47, began as assistant, became lecturer in department of English; Marine Lumber Co. Ltd., Vancouver, British Columbia, bookkeeping and other work, 1947-55; Claremont Colleges, Claremont, Calif., concert manager, 1959-61; D.C. Heath and Co. (educational publishers), Boston, Mass., copywriter, 1961-62; McClelland & Stewart (publishers), Toronto, Ontario, free-lance editor, 1965—; York University, Toronto, Ontario, free-lance researcher and editor, 1965—. *Member:* University Women's Club of North York.

WRITINGS: Danger—Shark!, Little, Brown, 1964. Writer of European travel scripts for Canadian Broadcasting Corp., 1956-57.

* * *

BUTOR, Michel (Marie Francois)   1926-

PERSONAL: Born September 14, 1926, in Mons-en-Barouel, France; son of Emile (a railways inspector) and Anne (Brajeux) Butor; married Marie-Josephe Mas, August 22, 1958; children: Cecile, Agnes, Irene. *Education:* Attended Lycee Louis-le-Grand; Sorbonne, University of Paris, License en philosophie, 1946, Diploma d'etudes superieures de philosophie, 1947. *Home:* 104 rue St. Charles, Paris XV, France. *Agent:* Georges Brochardt, 145 E. 52 St., New York, N.Y. 10022.

CAREER: Teacher of philosophy, Sens, France, 1950; teacher of French in Minieh, Upper Egypt, 1950-51, Manchester, England, 1951-53, Salonica, Greece, 1954-55, Geneva, Switzerland, 1956-57; advisory editor, Editions Gallimard, 1958—. Visiting professor of French, Bryn Mawr College, Bryn Mawr, Pa., 1960, and State University of New York, Buffalo, 1962. *Awards, honors:* Prix Fenelon, 1957, for *L'Emploi du temps;* Prix Theophraste Renaudot, 1957, for *La Modification;* Grand Prix de la Critique Litteraire, 1960, for *Repertoire;* Ford Foundation grant, 1964; Chevalier de L'Ordre National du Merite; Chevalier des Arts et des Lettres.

WRITINGS—Novels: Passage de Milan, Editions de Minuit, 1954; *L'Emploi du temps,* Editions de Minuit, 1956, translation by Jean Stewart published as *Passing Time,* Simon & Schuster, 1960; *La Modification,* Editions de Minuit, 1957, translation by Stewart published in England as *Second Thoughts,* Faber, 1968, published in America as *Change of Heart,* Simon & Schuster, 1959, subsequent French edition published as *La Modification* [suivi de] *Le Realisme mythologique de Michel Butor,* the latter by Michel Leiris, Union Generale d'Editions, 1963, French language edition edited by J. Guicharnod published in America by Ginn, 1970; *Degres,* Gallimard, 1960, translation by Richard Howard published as *Degrees,* Simon & Schuster, 1961; *6810000 litres d'eau par seconde: Etude stereophonique,* Gallimard, 1965, translation by Elinor S. Miller published as *Niagara,* Regnery, 1969; *Portrait de l'artiste en jeune singe, capriccio,* Gallimard, 1967; *Passing Time* [and] *A Change of Heart: Two Novels,* translated by Stewart, Simon & Schuster, 1969.

Poems: *Cycle sur neuf gouaches d'Alexandre Calder* (edition consists of 500 copies signed by the artist and the author), La Hune (Paris), 1962; *Illustrations,* Gallimard, 1964; *Litanie d'eau* (contains 10 original engravings by Gregory Masurovsky; edition consists of 105 copies), La Hune, 1964; (author of poems) Ruth Francken, *In den Flammen* (watercolors) epigram by Herbert Read, Belser (Stuttgart), 1965; *Comme Shirley* (contains drawings by Masurovsky), La Hune, 1966; *Tourmente* (contains drawings by P. Alechinsky, Bernard Dufour, and J. Herold; edition of 130 copies), Fata Morgana (Montpellier), 1968; *Illustrations II,* Gallimard, 1969.

Radio scripts: *Reseau aerien* (commissioned by French Broadcasting System; first performed June 16, 1962), Gallimard, 1962.

Nonfiction: (Translator) Aron Gurwitsch, *Theorie du champ de la conscience (The Field of Conscience),* Desclee de Brouwer, 1957; *Zanartu* (brochure on Enrique Zanartu), Galerie Editions, 1958; *Le Genie de lieu* (essays), Volume I: same title, Volume II: *Ou,* Grasset, 1958; *Herold* (catalogue for exhibition, May 26-June 16, 1959), Galerie La Cour d'Ingres (Paris), 1959; *Repertoire: Etudes et conferences, 1948-59* (essays), Editions de Minuit, 1960; *Une histoire extraordinaire: Essai sur un reve de Baudelaire*, Gallimard, 1961, translation by Howard published as *Histoire extraordinaire: Essay on a Dream of Baudelaire's*, J. Cape, 1969; *Mobile: Etude pour un representation des Etats-Unis*, Gallimard, 1962, translation by Howard published as *Mobile: Study for a Representation of the United States*, Simon & Schuster, 1963; *Description de San Marco*, Gallimard, 1963; *Repertoire II: Etudes et conferences*, 1959-63 (essays, addresses, lectures), Editions de Minuit, 1964; (contributor) *Open to the World* (essays), Times Literary Supplement, 1964; (editor) Michael Eyquem de Montaigne, *Essays*, Union Generale d'Editions, 1964; *Les Oeuvres d'art imaginaires chez Proust* (Casal Bequest lecture) Athlone Press (London), 1964; *Bernard Saby* (conversation between Butor and Saby; published in conjunction with exhibition at L'Oeil, Galerie d'Art, Paris), Imprimerie Reunies (Lausanne), 1964; *Herold* (conversation with Herold; not the same as earlier book), Musee de Poche, 1964; *Essais sur les modernes, Gallimard*, 1964; (author of text) Bernard Larsson, *Die ganze Stadt Berlin* (photographs), Butor's French translated by Helmut Scheffel, Nannen (Hamburg), 1964; (author of text with Harold Rosenberg) Saul Steinberg, *Le Masque* (cartoons; photos by Inge Morath), Maeght, 1966; (author of text) *Dialogue des regnes [Cuivres originaux de] Jacques Herold* (original engravings by Herold; edition of 75 copies signed by author and artist), Fequet et Baudier (Paris), 1967; *Paysage de repons, [suivi de] Dialogues des regnes*, Albeuve (Castella), 1968; *La Banlieue de l'aube a l'aurore: Mouvement brownien* (contains illustrations by Dufour), Fata Morgana, 1968; *Repertoire III* (essays), Editions de Minuit, 1968; *Essais sur "Les Essais"* (essays on the essays of Montaigne; contains extracts from *Essays*), Gallimard, 1968; (with Henri Pousseur) *Votre Faust, fantaisie variable, genre opera* (contains a lecture given by Pousseur and an interview with Pousseur and Butor), Centre d'etudes et de recherches marxistes (Paris), 1968; *Inventory: Essays*, edited with an introduction by Richard Howard, Simon & Schuster, 1969; *Essais sur le roman*, Gallimard, 1969; *Les Mots dans la peinture*, Albert Skira (Geneva), 1969; *La Rose des vents: 32 rhumbs pour Charles Fourier*, Gallimard, 1970; *Entretiens avec Georges Charbonnier*, Gallimard, 1970; *Dialogue avec 33 variations de Ludwig van Beethoven sur une valse de Diabelli*, Gallimard, 1971.

Author of introduction: James Joyce, *Finnegans Wake*, Gallimard, 1962; William Styron, *La Proie des flammes (Set This House on Fire)*, Gallimard, 1962; Fyodor Dostoievski, *Le Joueuer (The Gambler)*, Le Livre de Poche, 1963. Translator into French of Shakespeare's *All's Well That Ends Well*. Contributor to numerous publications in France and elsewhere.

SIDELIGHTS: Along with Samuel Beckett, Nathalie Sarraute, and Alain Robbe-Grillet, Butor is at the vanguard of French literature today, engaged in writing what is sometimes referred to by Jean-Paul Sartre's phrase, the "anti-novel," or, more recently, the "new novel." The exponents of the new novel, according to Sartre, "make use of the novel in order to challenge the novel, to destroy it before our very eyes while seeming to construct it, to write the novel of a novel unwritten and unwritable...." The new novel adds an objective exposition of setting and character, and concentrates on "existence as it is being formed rather than analyzing it after it has happened," Patricia J. Jaeger writes.

For Butor, the novel is an instrument of knowledge, a searching depth-study of personality. He avoids chronological time in favor of "human time" measured in the interior of each character's mind. Miss Jaeger comments: "Butor seems to base most of his books ... on an examination of the effect of the past, present and future on each other. He is especially aware of the propensity of the human mind to shift its perception of the past in light of new information available only in the present." In addition to juxtaposing several levels of time, he offers no solutions, preferring to focus on the transition of action not on its outcome.

Butor himself sees the novel form as the perfect instrument for combining the two principal interests of his youth, philosophy and poetry. Of Butor's stylistic qualities Laurent Le Sage writes: "Butor's books are like those European museums and galleries he is fond of visiting with his readers, full to the rafters of the most painstaking and minute word-painting, as if there were nothing he could leave out. His descriptions often have a lyrical, even rhapsodical quality...." The formation of this style can perhaps be traced to Butor's first encounter with Shelley's poetry at the age of fourteen, when he discovered, he writes, "a lyricism of which the French classics gave me no idea, above all a new sonority, a new way of making words take fire from the rhythm."

Butor has been greatly influenced by Proust. He said once that he had read all of *Remembrance of Things Past* ten times. Henri Peyre writes: "Butor's is the finest mind among those who have undertaken to renovate the novel since 1950—the only one who at times recalls the density and the complex orchestration of the Proustian saga fiction or whose universal intellectual and artistic curiosity grants him a place in the literature of the last third of our century comparable to that of Sartre at mid-century. He received Sartre's blessing and he himself has been generous as well as clear-sighted in praising the avatars of Sartrian thought since 1960." Peyre maintains that until the publication of *Degres* Butor was the "favorite of critics and of philosophers."

Butor has also been influenced by Joyce, whom he greatly admired. The structure of *Passage de Milan* —the entire novel covers twelve hours of time and takes place within an apartment house in Paris, where the residents' lives are regulated by a series of rituals which tend to isolate them from each other rather than bring them closer together—is reminiscent of Joyce's structure in *Ulysses*. A similar structure is used in *L'Emploi du temps*. The novel is in five parts, corresponding to the five months during which the main character keeps a diary. The parts of the novel are each divided into five chapters, for each of the weeks, or portions of weeks in a month. Since Revel does not work on weekends each week has five days. Butor has thus created a schedule for the framework of the book, although he can with his title also be referring to the uses of passing of time. The structure can also be seen in Bleston, the city which Butor creates, and all the details which he carefully sets down. Leon Roudiez states that "Butor is concerned with Bleston not as a city contrasted to the country or the sea, but as a city among cities, as a microcosm of civilization, like Paris in *Passage de Milan*." The great scope of these first two novels, although they are contained in the framework Butor has provided for them, includes myriad details about the lives of the many people encountered in both books.

La Modification is unlike the first two novels since it "[focuses] on the single action of one individual," as Roudiez says, "clearly circumscribed in time and space, actually and symbolically." Butor uses the second person narrative here very successfully. Roudiez states that the second person "allows for an ambiguous author-reader-character relationship, with the reader oscillating between identification with the prosecuting author, or with the guilty character." The reader is then able to choose, "he is free to act either in good faith or in bad faith." Peyre comments that *La Modification* is "a paradox sustained through two hundred and thirty pages without artificiality or weariness. The stark simplicity of the theme and the unities of time and place, the stillness in the midst of motion, are arresting." Peyre recounts Butor's statement to a *Figaro Litteraire* interviewer: "The narrative absolutely had to be told from the point of view of a character ... I needed an interior monologue beneath the level of the character himself, with a form between the first and third person. The *vous* allows me to describe the situation of the character and the manner in which language emerges in him."

Degres has elicited both favorable and unfavorable criticism. Peyre considers the novel a failure, "even as an exercise in the technique of fiction." Harry T. Moore describes the novel as "a microscopic investigation of the life processes themselves, more detailed even than the explorations of Sarraute and Robbe-Grillet, with fewer clues as to what is happening. It is therefore somewhat more difficult to read, but the book remains a fascinating experiment; it deals more thoroughly with space-time concepts than other novels of its school." Roudiez states that *Degres* "is a masterpiece. The initial impetus to the narrative lies in an attempt to recapture the meaning and consciousness of a given hour in the life of a contemporary French lycee, its teachers, and its students, at the beginning of the school year." Roudiez finds that the "architecture" of the novel "is one aspect ... of which most readers are not aware, and this in itself is an indication of how successfully it has been integrated into the work as a whole." It is divided into three parts, and these are further divided. There are many triangular relationships among characters as well.

Since *Degres* Butor has used his methods of structure and categorization in even more unusual ways. *Mobile* is considered by some to be a novel, but most people would agree that it is not really a novel. Butor's subtitle, "study," in the sense of the French *etude*, is probably the best way to categorize the work. He has used the experience of a trip across the United States for the material of this work, although it is not an actual trip, and many of the facts are not completely accurate. Miller describes the book as "a tiresome montage of disconnected images relieved by catalogues of names, advertising slogans, the prose of road signs." He says that *Mobile* is "a poor imitation of the expressionist techniques." Roudiez would disagree. He says that Butor's "is the phenomenological approach, whereby the book is examined in its attributes as a material object." He finds "a certain amount of virtuosity" in the book. Again, the architecture is not obvious, and Butor has been criticized for this, but a very definite structure is present. Most important for the reader, Roudiez states, "is the manner in which the components have been assembled in order to produce the picture, or 'representation.' Discontinuous accounts of the 1692 Salem trials and of writings by Franklin and Jefferson, newspaper extracts, advertisements, signs, brief statements, names of people, cities, counties, and states form a strange mosaic or, as the text suggests at one point, a patchwork quilt. Naturally, the juxtaposition is not haphazard; as with the states themselves, the basic order is alphabetical (almond through vanilla for ice cream, B.P. through Texaco for gasoline, among others), and a number of complicated modifications are subsequently introduced in order to achieve maximum effect from various confrontations: the procedure is ... not unrelated to the surrealist image.... *Mobile* is a stunning display of colors. A profusion of contrasting tints is found in the flora, the fauna, the human artifacts, and the people themselves." A resemblance can be seen between *Mobile* and *Description de San Marco*, although the latter is concerned strictly with San Marco, and does not go off in the directions that *Mobile* does. Both of these works have unusual typographical arrangements which help to clarify that which is taking place. Margins

of different sizes are used to differentiate between different elements in the narratives, and in *Mobile* and use of italic as well as Roman type is significant. Both books led the way to *Reseau aerien*, which uses the same devices. The book departs from the printed page in the sense that it was written for radio broadcast, and involves not only dialogue but sound as well, which can only be described, and not actually heard, in print. Roudiez writes that "the total impression is one of a choral song of mankind in which unidentified individuals blend their common preoccupations about different things and countries into elemental melodies of love and hate. Trivial concerns, expressed in prosaic fashion, dominate in the early dialogues. Later, as distance, imagination, and dreams affect each traveler, the themes become more basically human; the language waxes lyrical, discursive logic makes way for instinctive association, and ordinary talk is metamorphosed into poetry."

6810000 litres d'eau par seconde is described by Miller as "a story in which Niagara Falls are thunderously dominant. The action, chiefly concerned with newly married couples and older ones nostalgically returning, covers a year, presenting events somewhat in the manner of *Mobile*, with different kinds of type and with speechs intended to be read at different pitches." Butor visited Niagara Falls at different seasons so that he would have more than one set of impressions to write about. He has even written himself in to the book as Quentin, a visiting professor of French. John Sturrock writes: "In its devious and sybilline way, [the book] embodies everything that Butor believes about the function and lofty moral virtues of literature. Making a book for him is an exemplary effort at anamnensis, the model of how we ought all of us to set about salvaging our own past."

Butor as an essayist should not be overlooked. Audrey Foote comments on the essays included in *Inventory*: "Both [Butor's] choice of subjects and his treatment of them reflect a mind of muscular intellectuality, a Huguenot or puritan taste for austerity and economy, and above all an intense need to impose discipline, almost geometric order and unity." Moore comments: "Butor is a critic of pronounced originality, discernment, versatility, wit, and force."

La Modification was filmed by Rene Thevenet-Fono Roma, 1970.

BIOGRAPHICAL/CRITICAL SOURCES: Les Temps Modernes, April, 1957; *Critique* (Paris), February, 1958; *Yale Review*, June, 1959; *Yale French Studies*, summer, 1959; *French Review*, December, 1961, October, 1962; Laurent Le Sage, *The French New Novel*, Pennsylvania State University Press, 1962; *Livres de France*, June-July, 1963; *New York Times Book Review*, July 7, 1963, December 28, 1969; *New York Herald Tribune Book Review*, August 4, 1963; *Critique: Studies in Modern Fiction*, winter, 1963-64; R.M. Albers, *Michel Butor*, Editions Universitaire, 1964; Leon S. Roudiez, *Michel Butor*, Columbia University Press, 1965; *Saturday Review*, December 18, 1965, May 3, 1969; Harry T. Moore, *French Literature Since World War II*, Southern Illinois University Press, 1966; Henri Peyre, *French Novelists of Today*, Oxford University Press, 1967; *New Statesman*, April 7, 1967; *Times Literary Supplement*, June 22, 1967; *TriQuarterly Review*, winter, 1967; *Books Abroad*, spring, 1968, spring, 1969, spring, 1970, winter, 1971, spring, 1971; *Book World*, February 8, 1969; *New York Review of Books*, April 23, 1970.

* * *

BUTTON, Dick 1929-

PERSONAL: Born July 18, 1929, in Englewood, N.J.; son of George (a businessman) and Evelyn (Totten)

Button. *Education:* Harvard University, B.A., 1952, LL.D., 1955. *Office:* Candid Productions, Inc., 119 West 57th St., New York, N.Y. 10019.

CAREER: Professional ice skater and Olympic champion; Candid Productions, Inc. (television, theatre, and films), New York, N.Y., vice-president, 1959—. Dick Button's Ice-Travaganza at New York World's Fair, co-producer with Paul Feigay, 1964-65. Richmondtown Restoration, Staten Island, N.Y., president of board of trustees. *Member:* U.S. Olympians (vice-president), American Federation of Television and Radio Artists, Actors Equity Association, New York Athletic Club, New York Skating Club. *Awards, honors:* James E. Sullivan Award for Best U.S. Amateur Athlete, 1950.

WRITINGS: Dick Button on Skates, Prentice-Hall, 1955; *Instant Skating,* Grosset, 1964. Contributor to *American Heritage, Skating, Book of Knowledge.*

*   *   *

BUTTS, David P.   1932

PERSONAL: Born May 9, 1932, in Rochester, N.Y.; son of George A. and Susie (Hicks) Butts; married Velma M. Walton, August 2, 1958; children: Carol Sue, Douglas Paul. *Education:* Frankfort Pilgrim College, student, 1949-50; Butler University, B.S., 1954; University of Illinois, M.S., 1960, Ph.D., 1962. *Home:* 1569 Flintridge Rd., Austin, Tex. 78746. *Office:* Science Education Center, University of Texas, Austin, Tex. 78712.

CAREER: Olivet Nazarene College, Kankakee, Ill., assistant professor of science education, 1961-62; University of Texas, Austin, assistant professor, 1962-65, associate professor, 1965-70, professor of science education, 1970—. Station KLRN-TV, Austin, Tex., curriculum consultant, 1962—. Austin Natural Science Center, vice-president, 1963-65. *Military service:* U.S. Air Force, 1954-57; became captain. *Member:* National Science Teachers Association, National Association for Research in Science Teaching, Council of Elementary Science, International, Association for the Education of Teachers in Science, American Association for the Advancement of Science, American Educational Research Association, Texas Academy of Science, Phi Delta Kappa, Kappa Delta Pi.

WRITINGS: (With Addison E. Lee) *Vanilla,* Steck, 1964; *Development of Instructional Materials for a Process-Oriented Curriculum in Science for Grades K-6,* Science Education Center, University of Texas, 1964; *An Inventory of Science Methods,* Science Education Center, University of Texas, 1966; (with Lee) *The Story of Chocolate,* Steck, 1967; (with Lee) *Watermelon,* Steck, 1968; (editor) *Designs for Progress in Science Education,* National Science Teachers Association, 1969; *Teaching Science in the Elementary School,* Free Press, 1971; (with Gene Hall) *Systematic Science Instruction,* Prentice-Hall, 1971; (editor) *Curriculum Implementation in Elementary School Science,* Science Education Center, University of Texas, 1971; (with Hall) *Children and Science: The Process of Teaching and Learning,* Prentice-Hall, 1973. Writer of some twenty television scripts on education science topics. Contributor to *Science: A Process Approach,* Parts 1, 2, 3, 4, 5, 6, and 7, a project of the American Association for the Advancement of Science.

*   *   *

BUXTON, (Edward) John (Mawby)   1912-

PERSONAL: Born December 16, 1912, in Bramhall, Cheshire, England; son of Alfred Mellor and Ethel Marion (Mawby) Buxton; married Marjorie Lockley, April 12, 1939. *Education:* Attended Malvern College, 1926-31; New College, Oxford, B.A., 1935, M.A., 1938. *Politics:* Conservative. *Religion:* Church of England. *Home:* Cole Park, Malmesbury, Wiltshire, England.

CAREER: New College, Oxford University, Oxford, England, lecturer in English literature, 1946-48, fellow, 1949—, university lecturer, 1967-72, reader in English literature, 1972—. Warton Lecturer, British Academy, 1970. *Military service:* British Army, 1939-46, became lieutenant; prisoner of war, 1940-45. *Member:* Society of Antiquaries (fellow), Keats-Shelley Memorial Association (member of committee), Malone Society (member of council). *Awards, honors:* Atlantic award in English literature, Rockefeller Foundation, 1946; Leverhulme grant, 1951.

WRITINGS: Westward, J. Cape, 1942; *Such Liberty* (poems), Macmillan, 1944; *Atropos and Other Poems,* Macmillan, 1946; *A Marriage Song for the Princess Elizabeth,* Macmillan, 1947; *The Redstart,* Collins, 1950, De Graff, 1953; (editor with R.M. Lockley) *Island of Skomer: A Preliminary Survey of the Natural History of Skomar Island, Pembrokeshire,* Staples, 1950; (editor and author of introduction) Michael Drayton, *Poems,* two volumes, Harvard University Press, 1953; *Sir Philip Sidney and the English Renaissance,* St. Martin's, 1954, 2nd edition, 1964; (editor and author of introduction) Charles Cotton, *Poems,* Harvard University Press, 1958; *Elizabethan Taste,* Macmillan, 1963, St. Martin's, 1964; *A Tradition of Poetry,* St. Martin's, 1967; *Byron and Shelley: The History of a Friendship,* Harcourt, 1968. General editor, "Oxford Paperback English Texts." Contributor to *Cambridge Bibliography of English . Literature, Encyclopaedia Britannica, Collier's Encyclopedia,* and to *Modern Language Review, Review of English Studies, Times Literary Supplement, English Literary Renaissance, Apollo, Keats-Shelley Memorial Association Bulletin,* and other journals and newspapers.

WORK IN PROGRESS: An edition of poems of Samuel Daniel; *English Verse Epitaphs to 1700; The Pastoral Mode;* editing an anthology of English poetry, 1500-1660, with G.K. Hunter and B. Morris.

SIDELIGHTS: Buxton spent the years 1935-36 in Palestine, on archaeological work. He has also traveled in the United States, West Indies, and most countries of western Europe. *Avocational interests:* Ornithology and gardening.

BIOGRAPHICAL/CRITICAL SOURCES: Listener, December 21, 1967; *Punch,* May 15, 1968; *New Statesman,* June 28, 1968; *Christian Science Monitor,* December 12, 1968; *London Magazine,* January, 1969.

*   *   *

BYERS, (Amy) Irene   1906-

PERSONAL: Born December 30, 1906, in London, England; married Cyril Martin Byers (retired Bank of England official); children: Christopher Martin, Jennifer Ann. *Education:* Educated in private school and at business college. *Politics:* Conservative. *Home:* 69 Baldry Gardens, London S.W. 16, England. *Agent:* Winant Towers Ltd., 1 Furnival St., London E.C.4, England.

CAREER: Began as free-lance journalist in Fleet Street, London, England; author specializing in books for boys and girls. *Member:* Croydon Writers' Circle (secretary), Society of Authors.

WRITINGS: The Circus, and Other Verses for Children, Muller, 1946; *Mystery at Barber's Reach,* Muller, 1950; *Our Outdoor Friends* (24 leaflets), Meiklejohn & Son, 1949, published in two volumes, 1952-53; *The Adventure of the Floating Flat,* Thomas Nelson, 1952; *The Young Brevingtons,* Parrish, 1953; *Tim of Tamberly Forest,* Parrish, 1954; *Out and About Tales,* Grant Educational, 1954; *The Mystery of Midway Mill,* Hutchinson, 1955; *Adventures at Fairborough's Farm,* Epworth, 1955; *Catherine of Corners,* Parrish, 1955; *Adventure at Dillingdon Dene,* Epworth, 1956; *The Strange Story of Pippin Wood,* Parrish, 1956; *Jewel of the Jungle,* Hutchinson, 1957; *The Missing Masterpiece,* Parrish, 1957; *Adventure at the Blue Cockatoo,* Epworth, 1958; *Flowers for Melissa,* Hutchinson, 1958; *Kennel Maid Sally,* Hutchinson, 1960; *Sea Sprite Adventure,* Hulton Educational, 1961; *The Twins' Good Turn,* Hulton Educational, 1961; *Farm on the Fjord,* Hutchinson, 1961; *Tim Returns to Tamberly,* Parrish, 1962; *Silka, the Seal,* Brockhampton Press, 1962; *Two on the Trail,* J. Cape, 1963; *Foresters of Fourways,* Brockhampton Press, 1963; *Mystery at Mappins,* Scribner, 1964 (published in England as *The Merediths of Mappins,* Oliver & Boyd, 1964); *Trouble at Tamberly,* Parrish, 1964; *Joanna Joins the Zoo,* Brockhampton Press, 1964; *Magic in Her Fingers,* Brockhampton Press, 1965; *Half Day Thursday,* J. Cape, 1966; *Foresters Afield,* Brockhampton Press, 1966; *Danny Finds a Family,* Wheaton, 1966; *The House of the Speckled Browns,* Oliver & Boyd, 1967; *The Stage Under the Cedars,* Chatto & Windus, 1969; *Cameras on Carolyn,* Chatto & Windus, 1971. Occasional contributor to (London) *Times* and *Books and Bookmen.*

SIDELIGHTS: Mrs. Byers' books have been translated into Swedish, Dutch, and Italian; several of them were serialized on British Broadcasting Corp. "Children's Hour." *Avocational interests:* Interior decoration, unusual cookery, and oil painting.

* * *

BYRNE, Donn (Erwin) 1931-

PERSONAL: Born December 19, 1931, in Austin, Tex.; son of Bernard Devine and Rebecca (Singleton) Byrne; married Lois Ann Pugsley, 1953; children: Keven Singleton, Robin Lynn. *Education:* Attended Stanford University, 1949-51; Fresno State College, B.A., 1953, M.A., 1956; Stanford University, Ph.D., 1958. *Politics:* Democrat. *Home:* 515 Hillcrest Rd., West Lafayette, Ind. 47906. *Office:* Purdue University, West Lafayette, Ind. 47907.

CAREER: While attending graduate schools at Fresno State College and Stanford University, worked at various times as teaching assistant, research assistant, intern psychologist, and United States Public Health Service trainee, 1953-57; San Francisco State College, San Francisco, Calif., instructor in psychology, 1957-59; Veterans' Administration Mental Hygiene Clinic, San Francisco, Calif., postdoctoral intern, 1958; University of Texas, Austin, assistant professor, 1959-62, associate professor, 1962-66, professor of psychology, 1966-69, chairman of clinical training committee, 1961-69; Purdue University, West Lafayette, Ind., professor of psychology, 1969—. Visiting professor, Stanford University, 1966-67, University of Hawaii, 1968. *Member:* American Psychological Association, Psychonomic Society, Society of Experimental Social Psychology, American Association for the Advancement of Science, American Association of University Professors.

WRITINGS: (With Henry Clay Lindgren) *Psychology: An Introduction to the Study of Human Behavior* (includes workbook), Wiley, 1961, 2nd edition, with Lindgren and Lewis Petrinovich, published as *Psychology: An Introduction to a Behavioral Science,* 1966, 3rd edition, with Lindgren, 1971; (editor and contributor with Philip Worchel) *Personality Change,* Wiley, 1964; (contributor) Brendan Maher, editor, *Progress in Experimental Personality Research,* Academic Press, 1964; *An Introduction to Personality: A Research Approach,* Prentice-Hall, 1966; (editor with Marshall L. Hamilton) *Personality Research: A Book of Readings,* Prentice-Hall, 1966; (contributor) Gardner Lindzey and Elliott Aronson, editors, *Handbook of Social Psychology,* Addison-Wesley, 1968; (contributor) Leonard Berkowitz, editor, *Advances in Experimental Social Psychology,* Academic

Press, 1969. Contributor to a dozen psychology journals. Consulting editor, *Journal of Experimental Research in Personality, Personality: An International Journal,* and *Journal of Applied Social Psychology.*

WORK IN PROGRESS: The Attraction Paradigm, to be published by Academic Press; a revision of *An Introduction to Personality: A Research Approach,* for Prentice-Hall.

AVOCATIONAL INTERESTS: Reading, music, world peace.

* * *

CALDWELL, Irene Catherine (Smith) 1908-

PERSONAL: Born August 29, 1908, in Santa Fe, Kan.; daughter of Oliver H. (a farmer) and Eva (Henage) Smith; married Mack M. Caldwell (a college professor), December 16, 1944. *Education:* Northwestern State College, Alva, Okla., B.A., 1930; Oklahoma University, M.A., 1936; Anderson College, Anderson, Ind., B.Th., 1939; Oberlin College, M.A., 1944; University of Southern California, Ph.D., 1959. *Office:* Department of Christian Education, Anderson College School of Theology, Anderson, Ind. 46011.

CAREER: Ordained minister, Church of God. Church of God, Anderson, Ind., executive secretary of National Board of Christian Education, 1940-45, now member of national board; Warner Pacific College, Portland, Ore., head of department of Christian education, 1945-66; Anderson College School of Theology, Anderson, Ind., Chairman of Department of Christian Education, 1966—. Consultant on religious education, in Japan, 1961; other mission trips in Europe and Lebanon, 1959, in Latin America, 1962, 1963, 1964; visiting professor, University of West Indies, Kingston, Jamaica, 1968. Member of Portland Council of Churches. *Member:* Christian Education Association, Religious Education Association.

WRITINGS—All published by Warner Press, except as otherwise noted: *Solving Church School Problems,* 1944, *Our Concern Is Children,* 1948, *Teaching That Makes a Difference,* 1950, 2nd edition, 1962, *Adults Learn and Like It: How to Teach Adults in the Church,* 1955, *Responsible Adults in the Church School Program,* published for the Co-operative Publication Association by Warner Press, 1961, (with others) *Basics for Communication in the Church,* 1971; *The Teacher as Evangelist,* Board of Christian Education, Church of God, 1972.

* * *

CALLAGHAN, Morley Edward 1903-

PERSONAL: Born September 22, 1903, in Toronto, Ontario; son of Thomas and Mary (Dewan) Callaghan; married Loretto Florence Dee, April 16, 1927; children: Michael, Barry. *Education:* St. Michael's College, University of Toronto, B.A., 1925; Osgoode Hall Law School, LL.B., 1928. *Home:* 20 Dale Ave., Toronto, Ontario, Canada.

CAREER: Novelist and short story writer, 1926—. Worked as reporter on *Toronto Daily Star* while in college; stories written during this time found their way, via Ernest Hemingway, into the Paris little literary magazines of that day, including Ezra Pound's *Exile,* and he gave up the idea of practicing law to become a professional writer. Spent a year in Paris, 1928-29, other periods in New York and Pennsylvania, before returning to Toronto, Ontario, to live. During World War II worked with the Royal Canadian Navy on assignment for the National Film Board, and traveled across Canada as chairman of the radio program "Citizen's Forum." *Awards, honors:* Governor General's Literary Award for fiction (Canada), 1952, for *The Loved and the Lost;* gold medal of Royal Society of Canada, 1958; Lorne Pierce Medal for achievement of special significance in imaginative literature, 1960; medal of merit, City of Toronto, 1962; LL.D., University of Western Ontario, 1965; Canada Council Molson prize ($15,000), 1970; Royal Bank of Canada award ($50,000) for distinguished work, 1970.

WRITINGS—Novels: *Strange Fugitive*, Scribner, 1928, Hurtig, 1970; *It's Never Over*, Scribner, 1930; *A Broken Journey*, Scribner, 1932; *Such Is My Beloved*, Scribner, 1934, reissued with an introduction by Malcolm Ross, McClelland & Stewart, 1957; *They Shall Inherit the Earth*, Random House, 1935, reissued with an introduction by F.W. Watt, McClelland & Stewart, 1962; *More Joy in Heaven*, Random House, 1937, reissued with an introduction by Hugo McPherson, McClelland & Stewart, 1960; *The Varsity Story*, Macmillan, 1948; *Luke Baldwin's Vow* (juvenile), Winston, 1948; *The Loved and the Lost*, Macmillan, 1951; *The Many Colored Coat*, Coward, 1960; *A Passion in Rome*, Coward, 1961.

Other books: *A Native Argosy* (short stories), Scribner, 1929, Books for Libraries, 1970; *Now That April's Here, and Other Stories*, Random House, 1937; *Morley Callaghan's Stories* (collection of best short stories), Macmillan, 1959; *That Summer in Paris: Memories of Tangled Friendships with Hemingway, Fitzgerald, and Some Others*, Coward, 1963. Also author of novella, *No Man's Meat*, privately printed in Paris, 1931, and of two plays, "Turn Again Home," and "Just Ask for George," both 1940, produced in Toronto by the New Play Society in 1950 and 1949, respectively, under the titles "Going Home" and "To Tell the Truth." Contributor of short stories to *Scribner's, New Yorker, Harper's Bazaar, Esquire, Cosmopolitan, Saturday Evening Post, Yale Review*, and numerous other magazines.

SIDELIGHTS: Edmund Wilson wrote in *O Canada:* "The Canadian Morley Callaghan, at one time well known in the United States, is today perhaps the most unjustly neglected novelist in the English-speaking world." Wilson noted that "when I talked about Callaghan [in the late 1950's], such people as remembered his existence were likely to think he was dead." Wilson offers several explanations for the fact that Callaghan is virtually unknown outside his native country, the most "striking" reason being "the partial isolation of that country [Canada] from the rest of the cultural world.... My further reading of Callaghan's novels has suggested another reason ... for their relative unpopularity. Almost all of them end in annihilating violence or, more often, in blank unfulfilment.... All these endings have their moral point: recognition of personal guilt, loyalty in personal relationships, the nobility of some reckless devotion to a Christian ideal of love which is bound to come to grief in the world. But they are probably too bleak for the ordinary reader.... Only a very sober, self-disciplined and 'self-directed' writer could have persisted, from decade to decade, in submitting these parables to the public. They are almost invariably tragic, but their tragedy avoids convulsions and it allows itself no outbreak in tirades."

In *That Summer in Paris* Callaghan documents his experiences as a *Toronto Daily Star* cub reporter, and his 1929 trip to Paris, where he became acquainted with and formed opinions on various literary figures, most notably Ernest Hemingway and F. Scott Fitzgerald. William Saroyan said in a review: "Each of the three writers was waging a fight of some kind that the others did not know about, could scarcely guess about, and could not help with. Callaghan's fight seems to have been the easiest—simply to write well and to go on writing well, which he managed to do, which he is still doing, which he does in this book, slight and anecdotal as it is."

Wilson mentioned the universal appeal of Callaghan's work, a quality cited frequently in critical reviews: "The

novels of Morley Callaghan do not deal . . . with his native Canada in any editorial or informative way, nor are they aimed at any popular taste, Canadian, 'American' or British. They center on situations of primarily psychological interest that are treated from a moral point of view yet without making moral judgments of any conventional kind." A *Canadian Forum* columnist called *Morley Callaghan's Stories* "one of the few major achievements of Canadian prose, more powerful than any single Callaghan novel and more worthy of enduring than any single work of his better publicized peers: Anderson, Hemingway and Fitzgerald. Mr. Callaghan does have his limits: he plays no games with time and infinity. Literary innovations leave him cold, the corporational vulture which feeds us all never enters into his fiction. . . . There is one major unreality to which he returns time and time again: emotion.... But for his era, when the media, the false prophets, the corporations, did not place so much underbrush between the human being and life (underbrush which the modern writer *must* deal with), Callaghan created a method that worked extraordinarily well. Never has the urban low bourgeois been dealt with quite so humanely, quite so creatively."

In 1958 Klenman-Davidson Productions filmed *Now That April's Here.*

AVOCATIONAL INTERESTS: Spectator sports.

BIOGRAPHICAL/CRITICAL SOURCES: *Queen's Quarterly*, autumn, 1957; *Dalhousie Review*, autumn, 1959; *Canadian Forum*, March, 1960, February, 1968; *New Yorker*, November 26, 1960; *Tamarack Review*, winter, 1962; *New Republic*, February 9, 1963; *Canadian Literature*, summer, 1964; Edmund Wilson, *O Canada*, Farrar, Straus, 1965; Brandon Conron, *Morley Callaghan*, Twayne, 1966; Victor Hoar, *Morley Callaghan*, Copp, 1969.

*   *   *

CALLARD, Thomas Henry   1912-
   (Sutherland Ross)

PERSONAL: Born March 12, 1912, in Plymouth, Devonshire, England; son of Herbert Robert (Royal Navy) and Emily (Putt) Callard; married Stella U. Clark, October 26, 1935; children: Anthony (deceased). *Education:* Peterborough Training College, teaching certificate, 1947. *Religion:* Episcopalian. *Home:* 18 Glenhouse Rd., London S.E. 9, England. *Agent:* Peter Lewin, E.P.S. Lewin & Partners, 7 Chelsea Embankment, London S.W. 3, England. *Office:* St. Margaret's School, Plumstead, London S.E. 18, England.

CAREER: Various clerical posts during depression years, 1929-33; Prudential Assurance Co., London, England, agent, 1933-39; St. Margaret's School, London, England, 1947—, began as teacher, now headmaster. *Military service:* British Army, Royal Artillery, 1939-45; became warrant officer. *Member:* Society of Authors, P.E.N.

WRITINGS—All published under pseudonym Sutherland Ross: *Three Steps to Tyburn*, Hodder & Stoughton, 1954; *The Masque of Traitors*, Hodder & Stoughton, 1954; *Freedom Is the Prize*, Hodder & Stoughton, 1955, Walker & Co., 1964; *The Lazy Salmon Mystery*, Brockhampton Press, 1955; *Twopenny Diamond Mystery*, Brockhampton Press, 1956; *The Vagabond Treasure*, Hodder & Stoughton, 1956; *The Sword Is King*, Hodder & Stoughton, 1958; *The Sailor's Knot*, Brockhampton Press, 1958; *The Queer Fish*, Brockhampton Press, 1959; *Drum and Trumpet Sound*, Hodder & Stoughton, 1960; *Cross-Channel Adventure*, Brockhampton Press, 1961; *The English Civil War*, Faber, 1961, Putnam, 1966; *Plague and Fire of London*, Faber, 1966.

WORK IN PROGRESS: Historical research.
AVOCATIONAL INTERESTS: Camping.

CALLUM, Myles 1934-

PERSONAL: Born April 4, 1934, in Lynn, Mass.; son of A. Edward (a purchasing agent) and Anne (Caswell) Callum. Education: Studied at University of Connecticut, 1951-53, New York University, 1958-61. Residence: Des Moines, Iowa. Office: Better Homes and Gardens, 1716 Locust St., Des Moines, Iowa 50303.

CAREER: Leisure, New York, N.Y., associate editor, 1961; Good Housekeeping, New York, N.Y., assistant editor, 1961-64, associate editor, 1964-68, director of special publications, 1968-70; Better Homes and Gardens, Des Moines, Iowa, managing editor, 1971—. Military service: U.S. Army, Counter–Intelligence Corps, 1954-57. Member: National Association of Science Writers.

WRITINGS: Body-Building and Self-Defense, Sterling, 1962; (editor) Your Personal Health, Hearst Corp., 1968; Body Talk, Bantam, 1971; Teaching Your Child to Read, Bantam, 1971. Contributor to Boys' Life, Pageant, Dude.

WORK IN PROGRESS: A reference book, for Sterling.

AVOCATIONAL INTERESTS: Herpetology, chess, amateur radio, pocket billiards.

*   *   *

CAMERON, Kenneth Neill 1908-
(Warren Madden)

PERSONAL: Born September 15, 1908, in Barrow in Furness, England; son of Henry Murray (a shipbuilder) and Kathleen Anne (McIntyre) Cameron; married Mary Bess Owen (an associate professor at Hunter College), April 26, 1946; children: Kathleen Anne. Education: McGill University, B.A., 1931; Oxford University, B.A., B.Litt., and M.A., 1931-34; University of Wisconsin, Ph.D., 1939. Home: 160 Riverside Dr., New York, N.Y. 10024. Agent: Helga Greene, 61 Eaton Mews West, London S.W.1, England. Office: Carl H. Pforzheimer Library, 41 East 42nd St., New York, N.Y. 10017.

CAREER: Indiana University, Bloomington, instructor, 1939-43, assistant professor, 1943-47, professor of English, 1947-52; Carl H. Pforzheimer Library, New York, N.Y., editor, 1952—; New York University, New York, N.Y., professor of English, 1963—. Member: Modern Language Association of America (chairman, Wordsworth and His Contemporaries section, 1959), P.E.N. Awards, honors: Modern Language Association—Macmillan Award, 1950, for The Young Shelley.

WRITINGS: The Young Shelley: Genesis of a Radical, Macmillan, 1950; (editor and author of introduction and notes) Percy Bysshe Shelley, Selected Poetry and Prose, Holt, 1951; (under pseudonym Warren Madden) The Enormous Turtle, Bobbs-Merrill, 1954; (editor) Shelley and His Circle, 1773-1822, Volumes 1 and 2, Harvard University Press, 1961, Volumes 3 and 4, Oxford University Press, 1970; (editor) Percy Bysshe Shelley, The Esdaile Notebook: A Volume of Early Poems, Knopf, 1964; Humanity and Society: A World History, Indiana University Press, 1973. Also author of a play, "Papp," first produced Off-Broadway at American Place Theatre, May, 1969; author of sixteen scholarly articles, mostly on Shelley.

WORK IN PROGRESS: Two plays, one on Shelley; a critical study of Shelley's later works and life; a book of poems.

BIOGRAPHICAL/CRITICAL SOURCES: New Yorker, May 10, 1969; Cue, May 17, 1969.

*   *   *

CAMMACK, Floyd M(cKee) 1933-

PERSONAL: Born February 20, 1933, in Frankfort, Kentucky; the son of L.D. (an architect) and Helen (Cox) Cammack. Education: University of Kentucky, B.A., 1954; Oxford University, B.A., 1956, M.A., 1960; Columbia University, M.S. in L.S., 1957; Cornell University, Ph.D., 1962; additional study at University of Grenoble, 1955. Office: Department of Linguistics, Oakland University, Rochester, Mich. 48063.

CAREER: Association of College and Research Libraries, Chicago, Ill., publications officer, 1957-58; University of Hawaii, Honolulu, assistant librarian and assistant professor of anthropology, 1962-64, language co-ordinator of the University's Peace Corps training program, 1962-63; Oakland University, Rochester, Mich., librarian, 1964—. Anthropological field worker in Fiji, 1961-62. Hawaii Governor's Committee on State Library Resources, chairman, 1963-64. Member: American Library Association, Linguistic Society of America, American Anthropological Association, Association for Machine Translation and Computational Linguistics, American Association of Rhodes Scholars, Phi Beta Kappa, Phi Sigma Iota, Beta Phi Mu. Awards, honors: Rhodes Scholar, 1954; grants from American Council of Learned Societies, 1959, National Science Foundation, 1960-62.

WRITINGS: (With Shiro Saito) Pacific Island Bibliography, Scarecrow, 1963. Contributor to Collier's Encyclopedia Yearbook, 1958, Americana Annual, 1958, New International Yearbook, 1958, World Book Encyclopedia Annual, 1959. Contributor of book reviews to Richmond News-Leader, 1957-59, short story to Stylus, and articles to professional journals.

WORK IN PROGRESS: A descriptive grammar of Fijian language; Fijian-English teaching text; editing Polynesian Reminiscences, by W.T. Pritchard.

*   *   *

CAMMANN, Schuyler (van Rensselaer) 1912-

PERSONAL: Born February 2, 1912, in New York, N.Y.; son of Herbert Schuyler and Katharine van Rensselaer (Fairfax) Cammann; married Marcia de Forest Post, February 6, 1943 (now separated); children: Frances Worthington, Stephen van Rensselaer, Hamilton Fairfax, Betsy Schuyler, William Bayard. Education: Attended Kent School, Kent, Conn., 1929-31; Yale University, A.B., 1935; Harvard University, M.A., 1941; Johns Hopkins University, Ph.D., 1949; special language study at University of Tours, University of Munich, Peking Language School. Religion: Episcopalian. Office: Department of Oriental Studies, University of Pennsylvania, Philadelphia, Pa.

CAREER: Yale-in-China, Changsha, Hunan, China, instructor in English and history, 1935-37; University of Pennsylvania, Philadelphia, lecturer, 1948, assistant professor, 1949-50, associate professor of Chinese, 1950-65, professor of East Asian studies, 1966—, assistant curator of University Museum, 1948-50, associate curator, 1950-55. Worked for Grenfell Mission in Labrador, 1929; research and travel in west China, Burma, north India, and borders of Tibet, 1937-38; archaeological reconnaissance in Southeast Asia, 1951; member of University Museum's archaelogical expeditions to Turkey and Afghanistan, 1953; taught in International School of America, around the world, 1962-63; N.A.T.O. Professor at University of Copenhagen, 1969. Regular panel member on television program "What in the World," Columbia Broadcasting System, 1950-55. Military service: U.S. Naval Reserve, 1941-46; became lieutenant.

MEMBER: American Association for the Advancement of Science (fellow), American Historical Association, American Oriental Society (vice-president, 1956-57), Council for Old World Archaeology (director), Association for Asian Studies (former director), Philadelphia Anthropological Society (former president), Descendants of the Signers of the Declaration of Independence, Sigma Xi.

WRITINGS: The Land of the Camel, Ronald, 1951; Trade Through the Himalayas: Early British Attempts to Open Tibet, Princeton University Press, 1951; China's Dragon Robes, Ronald, 1952; Toggles and Toggle-Wearing, University of New Mexico, 1960; Substance and Symbol in Chinese Toggles: Chinese Belt Toggles From the C.F. Bilber Collection, University of Pennsylvania Press, 1962. Contributor to Encyclopaedia Britannica and to magazines and professional journals in various countries. Associate editor, Journal of the American Oriental Society, 1948-51.

WORK IN PROGRESS: A catalogue of the Mongol and Tibetan images and paintings in the National Museum of Denmark; a book on magic squares; a book on Chinese symbols and symbolism.

SIDELIGHTS: Cammann has traveled around the world four times and made fourteen visits to Europe. He enjoys language learning as a practical hobby. He has been able to speak at least a dozen European and Asian languages (but some have been forgotten through lack of practice), including French, German, Italian, Spanish, Chinese, Japanese, Turkish, and Persian.

*   *   *

CAMPBELL, Hannah
(Elizabeth Franklin)

PERSONAL: Born in Winston-Salem, N.C.; daughter of Thomas Franklin (a sales manager) and Elizabeth (Longworth) Campbell. Education: Attended High Point College. Religion: Agnostic. Home: 218 East 79th St., New York, N.Y. 10021. Office: Field and Stream, Holt, Rinehart & Winston, Inc., 385 Madison Ave., New York, N.Y. 10017.

CAREER: Cosmopolitan, New York, N.Y., assistant editor, 1957-60; Field and Stream, New York, N.Y., assistant editor, 1962—; also free-lance writer and editor, currently and at other periods.

WRITINGS: Why Did They Name It?, Fleet, 1964. Writer of column, "Why Did They Name It?," for Cosmopolitan, and fabric column for Furniture and Woodworking. Contributor of articles to trade publications.

WORK IN PROGRESS: A sequel to Why Did They Name It?

AVOCATIONAL INTERESTS: The South and its publicity and promotion.

BIOGRAPHICAL/CRITICAL SOURCES: New York Times, February 28, 1964.

*   *   *

CAMPBELL, J(ohn) Ramsey   1946-

PERSONAL: Born January 4, 1946, in Liverpool, England; son of Alexander Ramsey and Nora Bernadette (Walker) Campbell; married in 1971, wife's name, Jenny. Education: St. Edward's College, Liverpool, England, student, 1957-62. Politics: International Socialist. Religion: "Romantic Humanist." Home: Flat 6-25 Princess Ave., Liverpool L8 2UP, England. Office: Edge Hill Public Library, Liverpool, England.

CAREER: Inland revenue tax officer in Liverpool, England, 1962-66; Liverpool Public Libraries, Liverpool, England, librarian, 1966—. Film critic for British Broadcasting Corp.

WRITINGS: The Inhabitant of the Lake and Less Welcome Tenants (short stories), Arkham, 1964; Demons by Daylight (short stories), Arkham, 1971. Represented in several anthologies, including Dark Mind Dark Heart, ed-

ited by August Derleth, Arkham, 1962, Tandem Horror 3, edited by Richard Davis, Tandem Books, 1969, and New Writings in Horror and the Supernatural, edited by David Sutton, Sphere Books, 1971.

WORK IN PROGRESS: Shifts (tentative title), a third collection of short stories, for Arkham; The Other Liverpool, horror tales set in Liverpool, for local publication; and The Dark Muse, a study of horror in the arts.

SIDELIGHTS: Campbell wrote CA: "Interests: As a BBC film critic I have come to view the cinema as the most dynamic of the contemporary arts. Otherwise, music (I would rather listen to a Mahler symphony than do almost anything else) and literature, especially fantasy and science fiction. I began writing horror stories because I liked the field; I continue (although I prefer to call my work 'tales of unease') because I feel that the horror story is one of the few popular forms that hasn't been cheapened, the only one which has retained the force of a cumulative tradition. I hope to see the emergence of a generation of contemporary horror writers, though at the moment it's depressingly unlikely."

BIOGRAPHICAL/CRITICAL SOURCES: Liverpool Daily Post, March 31, 1964.

*   *   *

CAMPBELL, Robert Dale   1914-

PERSONAL: Born December 2, 1914, in Omaha, Neb.; son of Robert Ward (a businessman) and Emma (Klempnauer) Campbell; married Marian McAnelly, December 20, 1962; children: Duncan, Diane, Ken, Margaret. Education: University of Colorado, B.A., 1938, M.A., 1941; Clark University, Ph.D., 1949. Home: 8219 Lilly Stone Dr., Bethesda, Md. 20034.

CAREER: Office of Strategic Services, Washington, D.C., cartographer, 1942-43; U.S. Department of Army, Office of Quartermaster General, Washington, D.C., geographer, 1946-47; George Washington University, Washington, D.C., 1947-64, became professor of geography and chairman of department of geography and regional science; Ford Foundation, Calcutta, India, advisory planning group consultant, 1964-66; Matrix Corp., Alexandria, Va., vice-president, 1966—. Fulbright lecturer, University of Alexandria, 1952-53, University of Peshawar, 1957-58; lecturer, Oxford University, 1955. Principal investigator, Outdoor Recreation Resources Commission, 1960-61, Maryland-National Capital Parks and Planning Commission, 1961—, and National Capital Planning Commission, 1963-64. Associate director, technical assistance project, Southwest Pennsylvania, and director of Planning Study at Pine Ridge, S.D., 1962-63. Consultant to U.S. Department of Army, 1947-49, U.S. Office of Naval Research, 1949-57, U.S. Corps of Engineers, 1953-57, American University, 1959-61, Arctic Institute of North America, 1960—, and National Park Service, 1961—. Member: Association of American Geographers, American Association of University Professors, Regional Science Association, Phi Beta Kappa, Sigma Xi, University Club (Washington, D.C.); Saturday Club and Tollygunge Club (both Calcutta).

WRITINGS: (With Hugh L. LeBlanc) An Information System for Urban Planning, George Washington University, 1962; Pakistan: Emerging Democracy, Van Nostrand, 1963; An Inventory of Public Open Space in the National Capital Region, Department of Geography and Regional Science, George Washington University, 1964; (w th Robert G. Dixon) Some Administrative Aspects of Open Space Planning and Preservation in the National Capital Region, George Washington University, 1964; (with Eric Fischer) A Question of Place, R.W. Beatty, 1967, 2nd edition, 1969.

CANSDALE, George (Soper)   1909-

PERSONAL: Born November 29, 1909, in Brentwood, Essex, England; son of George William (an accountant) and Alice (Soper) Cansdale; married Margaret Sheila Williamson, September 7, 1940; children: David Martin, Richard Hugh. Education: St. Edmund Hall, Oxford University, B.A., 1932, B.Sc., 1934. Religion: Church of England. Home: Dove Cottage, Great Chesterford, Essex, England.

CAREER: Colonial Forest Service, Ghana, 1934-48; Zoological Society of London, London, England, zoo superintendent, 1948-53; United Nations Food and Agriculture Organization, expert in Ghana, 1963. Has made more than three hundred television appearances, mostly with own programs concerning animals, 1948—. Lecturer. Director of Chessington Zoo Ltd. Governor of Stowe School. Member: Linnean Society (fellow). Awards, honors: Television Society Silver medal, 1952, for programs, "Looking at Animals" and "All About Animals."

WRITINGS: (With members of staff of Imperial Forestry Institute) The Black Poplars, Oxford University Press, 1938; Animals of West Africa, Longmans, Green, 1946; Animals and Man, Hutchinson, 1952; Zoo Book, Phoenix House, 1953; Reptiles of West Africa, Penguin, 1955; Pets Book, Phoenix House, 1959; Bush Baby Book, Phoenix House, 1960; West African Snakes, Longmans, Green, 1961, International Publications Service, 1968; Behind the Scenes at a Zoo, Phoenix House, 1965; All the Animals of the Bible Lands, Zondervan, 1970 (published in England as Animals of Bible Lands, Paternoster Press, 1970).

SIDELIGHTS: Cansdale traveled in Palestine, 1960, Uganda, 1961, Israel, 1962, Ghana, Uganda, and Kenya, 1963, collecting lecture and television material.

*   *   *

CANTELON, John E(dward)   1924-

PERSONAL: Born June 20, 1924, in Warroad, Minn.; son of Arthur Edward (a railroad executive) and Georgia (Turnbull) Cantelon; married Joy Elizabeth Norton, August 15, 1953; children: Barbara Jean, Charles Norton. Education: Neepawa Collegiate Institute, student, 1937-41; Reed College, B.A., 1948; Oxford University, D.Phil., 1951. Politics: Democrat. Religion: Presbyterian. Home: 32653 Seagate Dr., Palos Verdes, Calif. 90274.

CAREER: Presbyterian minister. University of Pennsylvania, Philadelphia, staff member of Christian Association, 1953-57; United Presbyterian Church, Board of Christian Education, Philadelphia, Pa., staff member, 1957-60; University of Southern California, Graduate School of Religion, Los Angeles, chaplain and associate professor of contemporary theology, 1960-67, director of school of religion, 1967-69, vice-provost, 1969—. Military service: U.S. Army, 1943-46; U.S. Army Reserve, 1951-57; chaplain corps; became first lieutenant. Member: American Academy of Religion, American Association of University Professors, Academy of Political and Social Science, Phi Beta Kappa.

WRITINGS: (Editor) A Basis for Study, Presbyterian Board of Christian Education, 1959; A Protestant Approach to the Campus Ministry, Westminster, 1964; College Education and the Campus Revolution, Westminster, 1969. Contributor of articles to Exceptional Children, Theology Today, and Christian Century.

*   *   *

CAPE, William H(enry)   1920-

PERSONAL: Born April 6, 1920, in Murdock, Kan.; son of Amos H. and Laura (Trostle) Cape; married Merceda L. Patton, February 1, 1945; children: Charles W., Eve-lyn L. Education: Fort Hays Kansas State College, A.B., 1947, M.S., 1948; University of Kansas, Ph.D., 1952. Religion: Methodist. Home: 1940 Emerald Dr., Lawrence, Kan. 66044. Office: Department of Political Science, Blake Hall, University of Kansas, Lawrence, Kan. 66044.

CAREER: Instructor in political science at University of Wyoming, Laramie, 1948-49, University of Kansas, 1949-52; University of South Dakota, Vermillion, assistant professor, 1962-64, professor of political science, 1964—, as-political science, 1955-61, assistant director of Governmental Research Bureau, 1952-61; University of Kansas, Lawrence, visiting professor, 1957-58, 1961, associate professor, 1962-64, professor of political science, 1964—, associate director of Government Research Center, 1962—. Military service: U.S. Army Air Forces, 1942-45. Member: American Political Association, American Society for Public Administration, Pi Gamma Mu, Pi Sigma Alpha, Phi Kappa Phi, Phi Alpha Theta.

WRITINGS: Handbook for South Dakota Municipal Officials, League of South Dakota Municipalities, 1954, revised edition, 1960; (with Edwin O. Stene) State Civil Service in Kansas, Governmental Research Center, University of Kansas, 1954; (with Franklin O. Felt) Handbook for South Dakota Country Officials, Governmental Research Bureau, University of South Dakota, 1954, revised edition, South Dakota Association of County Commissioners, 1961; Hospital and Medical Care for the Needy, Governmental Research Bureau, University of South Dakota, 1955; Public Employee Retirement Plans in South Dakota, Governmental Research Bureau, University of South Dakota, 1956; Constitutional Revision in South Dakota, Governmental Research Bureau, University of South Dakota, 1957; Constitutional Revision in Kansas, Governmental Research Center, University of Kansas, 1958.

(Contributor) Kansas Resume, Kansas State Federation of Labor, 1961; (with William O. Farber and Thomas C. Geary) Government of South Dakota, Midwest-Beach Co., 1962, revised edition, 1969; (contributor) Changing Dimensions in Public Administration, University of Michigan Press, 1962; (with John Paul Bay) City Clerks School: A Report, Governmental Research Center, University of Kansas, 1962; (editor with Bay) Seminar for Directors of Mental Health: A Report, Governmental Research Center, University of Kansas, 1962; (with Bay) An Analysis of the Kansas Legislative Council and Its Research Department, Governmental Research Center, University of Kansas, 1963; Kansas Voters Guide (pamphlet), Governmental Research Center, University of Kansas, 1964, 2nd revised edition, 1968; (editor) Kansas Peace Officers Regional Schools, Dodge City and Colby, 1963, University of Kansas, 1964; A Guidebook for Governing Boards of Community Mental Health Centers, Governmental Research Center, University of Kansas, 1964; A Guide to Federal Grants and Other Types of Assistance, Governmental Research Center, University of Kansas, 1965; The Emerging Patterns of County Executives, Governmental Research Center, University of Kansas, 1967; (with Leon B. Graves and Burton M. Michaels) Government by Special Districts, Governmental Research Center, University of Kansas, 1969; Scientific and Technological Advice for Kansas Governments and Industry, Governmental Research Center, University of Kansas, 1969; (editor) Hiring the Handicapped, Institute of Government, University of North Carolina at Chapel Hill, 1970.

Author of two booklets on state government topics and of brochures on Indian affairs and state government. Contributor to published symposia reports, and to journals, including Your Government, Public Personnel Review, Personnel Administration, Public Affairs, and

Midwest Journal of Political Science. Editor of research monographs.

* * *

CAPPER, Douglas Parode

PERSONAL: Born in Sydney, Australia; son of Henry Douglas (a naval officer) and Louisa Elizabeth Sarah Mary (Parode) Capper; and married Yolande Marjory Elwell-Smith (an artist), May 16, 1963; children: (previous marriage) Jane Parode Edwards. *Education:* Attended Scottish and English schools and had private tutor. *Home:* 50, Dawlish Dr., Pinner, Middlesex, England.

CAREER: Royal Navy and Royal Air Force; combat service at sea in World War II, then staff officer of British War Cabinet, 1943-45, and British Naval Representative in Japan as commander, 1945-48.

WRITINGS: On the Pilgrims Way, Methuen, 1934; *The Vikings of Britain,* Allen & Unwin, 1937; *Famous Sailing Ships of the World,* Muller, 1957; *Famous Battleships of the World,* Muller, 1959; *Moat Defensive: A History of the Waters of the Nore Command 55 B.C. to 1961,* Arthur Barker, 1963. Other books published under pseudonyms. Contributor to various journals, mainly on maritime subjects.

WORK IN PROGRESS: Autobiographical material; an article on sails and sailing vessels for *Encyclopaedia Britannica.*

* * *

CARAMAN, Philip 1911-

PERSONAL: Born August 11, 1911, in London, England; son of R.A. Caraman. *Education:* Stonyhurst College, student, 1923-30; Campion Hall, Oxford University, M.A. *Address:* c/o Longmans, Green & Co. Ltd., 48 Grosvenor St., London W.1, England.

CAREER: Roman Catholic priest, member of Society of Jesus (Jesuit). *Month,* editor, 1948-63. *Member:* Royal Society of Literature (fellow).

WRITINGS: (Translator) John Gerard, *Autobiography of an Elizabethan,* Longmans, Green, 1951; (editor) J. Keating, *Retreat Notes,* Gill & Sons, 1952; (translator) John Gerard, *Autobiography of a Hunted Priest,* Pellegrini & Cudahy, 1952; (editor) *Saints and Ourselves,* Kenedy, Volume I, 1953, Volume II, 1955, Volume III, 1958; (editor and author of introduction) F.C. Devas, *What Law and Letter Kill,* Burns, 1953; (editor and author of introduction) F.C. Devas, *Law of Love,* Kenedy, 1954; (translator) William Weston, *Autobiography from the Jesuit Underground,* Farrar, Straus, 1955 (published in Canada as *Autobiography of an Elizabethan,* Longmans, Green, 1955); (editor and author of foreword) R.H. Benson, *Come Rack! Come Rope!,* Kenedy, 1957; *Henry Morse, Priest of the Plague,* Farrar, Straus, 1957; (editor with J.J. Dougherty) *Holy Bible for the Family,* Longmans, Green, 1958.

The Other Face: Catholic Life Under Queen Elizabeth I, Longmans, Green, 1960, Sheed, 1961; (editor and author of introduction) Ronald Knox, *Pastoral Occasional Sermons,* Burns, 1960; (editor and author of introduction) Ronald Knox, *Pastoral Sermons,* Sheed, 1960; (editor with James Walsh) *The Fulton J. Sheen Sunday Missal,* Hawthorn, 1961; *Saint Angela: The Life of Angela Merici, Foundress of the Ursulines (1474-1540),* Longmans, Green, 1963, Farrar, Straus, 1964; (editor and author of introduction) Ronald Knox, *University and Anglican Sermons: Together with Sermons Preached on Various Occasions,* Burns & Oates, 1963, published in America as *University Sermons: Together with Sermons Preached on Various Occasions,* Sheed, 1964; *Henry Garnet (1555-*

1606) and the Gunpowder Plot, Farrar, Straus, 1964; (editor) *The Years of Siege: Catholic Life from James I to Cromwell,* Longmans, Green, 1966; *C.C. Martindale: A Biography,* Longmans, Green, 1967; *Norway,* Longmans, Green, 1969, Eriksen, 1970.

(Contributor) Marina Chavchavadze, editor, *Man's Concern with Holiness,* Houghton & Stoughton, 1970. Contributor to *Tablet, Downside Review, Times Literary Supplement,* and to other periodicals.

* * *

CARBONELL, Reyes 1917-

PERSONAL: Born April 8, 1917, in Valencia, Spain; son of Vincente Marshall and Maria (de Picazo) Carbonell; married Regina Gorriz Bastias, 1941. *Education:* University of Valencia, B.A., 1931, M.A., 1940; University of Madrid, Ph.D., 1948. *Office:* Department of Spanish, Duquesne University, Pittsburgh, Pa. 15219.

CAREER: University of Valencia, Valencia, Spain, professor, 1946-48; Duquesne University, Pittsburgh, Pa., professor of Spanish, 1948—. University of Pittsburgh, visiting professor, 1962. *Member:* Modern Language Association of America, American Association of Teachers of Spanish and Portuguese, International Institute of Iberoamerican Literature, American Association of University Professors.

WRITINGS: Poesias en aire y tierra, Ediciones Laurel, 1951; *Espiritu de llama: Estudios sobre poesia hispanica contemporanea,* Duquesne University Press, 1962; *El Hombre sobre al armario* (stories; includes "El Hombre sobre el armario," "El Professor," "El Reloj," "Ay . . . , literatural," "El Loro," "Una Cena," "Desencanto," and "El Robo"), Ediciones Dos Continentes, 1964, reissued as a Spanish reader, under title *El Hombre sobre el armario, y otros cuentos,* edited by Leonardo C. de Morelos and Adela Lafora, Harper, 1967; (editor) *The Fables of Luqman* (elementary Arabic reader), Duquesne University Press, 1965. Contributor to professional journals. Editor, *Estudios,* 1950-56; editor, *Duquesne Hispanic Review.*

WORK IN PROGRESS: Dictionary of Spanish Idioms.

BIOGRAPHICAL/CRITICAL SOURCES: Mensaje (Madrid, Spain), August, 1952.

* * *

CARDONA-HINE, Alvaro 1926-

PERSONAL: Born October 12, 1926, in San Jose, Costa Rica; son of Jorge Cardona Jimenez and Alice Hine; married Orpha Willis, September 4, 1950 (divorced, 1967); children: Alvaro, Aglaia, Elena, Miguel. *Education:* Attended Los Angeles City College, 1945-48. *Residence:* California.

CAREER: Writer; does part-time editorial work for a publishing firm.

WRITINGS: Romance de Agapito Cascante (book-length narrative poem), Repetorio Americano (Costa Rica), 1955; *The Gathering Wave* (48 haiku with drawings, Alan Swallow, 1961; *The Flesh of Utopia* (poems), Alan Swallow, 1966; *Menastash* (poems in English and Spanish), Little Square Review, 1969; *Agapito* (prose elegy), Scribner, 1969.

SIDELIGHTS: Cardona-Hine's main interest is "to create a credible and joyous vision of life."

BIOGRAPHICAL/CRITICAL SOURCES: American Dialog, spring, 1968; *Library Journal,* June 1, 1969, July, 1969; *Best Sellers,* August 1, 1969; *Nation,* October 13, 1969.

CARES, Paul B(enjamin)   1911-

PERSONAL: Born June 1, 1911, in Meadville, Pa.; son of Charles Calvin (an engineer) and Ellen (Oster) Cares; married Alberta McCotter, June 26, 1940; children: Benjamin C. Education: Allegheny College, A.B., 1932; University of Michigan, M.A., 1935, Ph.D., 1941. Politics: Republican. Religion: Episcopal. Home: 483 Sunset Dr., Meadville, Pa. 16335. Office: Allegheny College, Meadville, Pa. 16335.

CAREER: Allegheny College, Meadville, Pa., instructor, 1932-42, assistant professor, 1942-46, associate professor, 1946-51, professor of history, 1951—, chairman of department, 1953—. Trustee, Meadville Public Library; trustee, Crawford County Mental Health Board; member of Meadville Zoning Board of Appeal. Member: American Historical Association, Phi Beta Kappa, Phi Kappa Phi, Delta Sigma Rho, Omicron Delta Kappa, Alpha Chi Rho, Meadville Country Club.

WRITINGS: The Dawn of Modern Civilization, edited by Kenneth A. Strand, Ann Arbor Publishers, 1962; (contributor) Joseph Dunner, editor, Handbook of World History, Philosophical Library, 1967. Contributor of book reviews to journals.

*   *   *

CARLSON, Dale Bick   1935-

PERSONAL: Born May 24, 1935, in New York, N.Y.; daughter of Edgar M. (an orthopedic surgeon) and Estelle (Cohen) Bick; married Albert W.D. Carlson (an artist-illustrator), November 24, 1962; children: Daniel Bick, Hannah Bick. Education: Wellesley College, B.A., 1957. Religion: Jewish. Home and office: 116 East 63rd St., New York, N.Y. 10021. Agent: Toni Mendez, Inc., 140 East 56th St., New York, N.Y. 10022.

CAREER: Started as bookseller in Doubleday & Co. store, New York, N.Y., 1958; Mel Evans & Co. (editors), New York, N.Y., assistant, 1958-59; Thomas Yoseloff, Inc. (publishers), New York, N.Y., assistant editor, 1959-60; Parents League of New York, New York, N.Y., vice-president and editor-in-chief of Parents League Bulletin, 1968-69; free-lance editor for other New York publishing houses.

WRITINGS: Perkins the Brain, Doubleday, 1964; The House of Perkins, Doubleday, 1965; Miss Maloo, Doubleday, 1966; (editor) The Brainstormers: Humorous Tales of Ingenious American Boys, Doubleday, 1966; Frankenstein (adaptation of Mary Shelley's book for children), Golden Press, 1968; The Electronic Teabowl, Golden Press, 1969; Dracula (adaptation of Bram Stoker's book for children), Dell, 1970; Warlord of the Genji, Atheneum, 1970; The Beggar King of China, Atheneum, 1971; (with husband, Al Carlson) Awful Marshall, World Publishing, 1971; Good Morning, Hannah, Atheneum, 1972; Good Morning Danny, Atheneum, 1972; The Mountain of Truth, Atheneum, 1972.

SIDELIGHTS: Mrs. Carlson told CA that she was prompted to write children's books "because of all the pleasure my books gave me as a child. I continue to write books for children because of the pleasure my own children take in reading good books.... Much of my material comes from my husband's childhood, some from my own, most from watching and living with Danny and Hannah."

*   *   *

CAROSSO, Vincent Phillip   1922-

PERSONAL: Born March 20, 1922, in San Francisco, Calif.; son of Vincent G. (a businessman) and Lucia M. (Barale) Carosso; married Rose Celeste Berti, August 23, 1952; children: Steven Berti. Education: University of California, Berkeley, A.B., 1943, M.A., 1944, Ph.D., 1948. Home: 375 Riverside Dr., New York, N.Y. 10025.

CAREER: Harvard University, Cambridge, Mass., post-doctoral fellow in American economic and business history, 1948-49; San Jose State College, San Jose, Calif., instructor in history, 1949-50; Carnegie Institute of Technology (now Carnegie Mellon University), Pittsburgh, Pa., assistant professor of history, 1950-53; New York University, New York, N.Y., assistant professor, 1953-56, associate professor, 1956-61, professor of history, 1962—. Harvard University, visiting associate research professor, 1961-62, visiting research lecturer, 1964-65. Member: American Historical Association (and Pacific Coast branch), Economic History Association, American Studies Association, Organization of American Historians.

WRITINGS: California Wine Industry, University of California Press, 1951; (with George Soule) American Economic History, Holt, 1957; (with H.B. Parkes) Recent America: A History, two volumes, Crowell, 1963; Investment Banking in America: A History, Harvard University Press, 1970. Contributor of articles and book reviews to professional journals. Associate editor, Journal of Economic History, 1955-60; member of editorial board, Business History Review, 1957-58, and Journal of American History, 1968—.

WORK IN PROGRESS: A History of the United States, with Richard Bardolph and Vincent DeSantis, for Dorsey; The House of Morgan: A Biography, publication by Putnam expected in 1974.

AVOCATIONAL INTERESTS: Music.

*   *   *

CARPENTER, (John) Allan   1917-

PERSONAL: Born May 11, 1917, in Waterloo, Iowa; son of John Alex and Theodosia (Smith) Carpenter. Education: State College of Iowa, B.A. Politics: Republican. Religion: Presbyterian. Home: Suite 4602, John Hancock Bldg., 175 East Delaware Pl., Chicago, Ill. 60611.

CAREER: Des Moines (Iowa) public schools, teacher, 1938-40; Teacher's Digest, founder, 1938, and editor and publisher for eight years; Popular Mechanics Co., director of public relations for nineteen years; Carpenter Publishing House, Chicago, Il., president and founder, 1962—. Music Council of Metropolitan Chicago, founder and president, 1954; Chicago Business Men's Orchestra, chairman of the board, 1957, and principal bassist. Member: American Symphony Orchestra League, American Association for State and Local History, Fine Arts Club of Chicago.

WRITINGS: Between Two Rivers, Klipto, 1940; Hi, Neighbor!, King, 1945; (editor) Primer for Home Builders, Windsor Press, 1946; (editor) Your Guide to Successful Singing, Windsor Press, 1950; The Twelve, Farcroft, 1955; (compiler and editor) Home Handyman Encyclopedia and Guide, sixteen volumes, Little & Ives, 1961, supplement, 1963; (compiler and editor) Shop Projects, Popular Mechanics, 1962; "Enchantment of America" series, fifty-two volumes, Childrens Press, 1963-68; "Enchantment of South America" series, thirteen volumes, Childrens Press, 1968-71; "Enchantment of Central America" series, seven volumes, Childrens Press, 1971; "Enchantment of Africa" series, five volumes, Childrens Press, 1972-73.

Contributor to Reader's Digest, Popular Mechanics, and other periodicals.

WORK IN PROGRESS: Editing Complete Illustrated Homeowner's Encyclopedia, for J.G. Ferguson.

BIOGRAPHICAL/CRITICAL SOURCES: Library Journal, July, 1970.

CARPENTER, John A(lcott) 1921-

PERSONAL: Born August 1, 1921, in Boonton, N.J.; son of Charles Francis (a manufacturer) and Marion (Jewett) Carpenter; married Frances H. Thomas, September 22, 1951; children: Thomas Jewett, John Frederic, James Hargnett. Education: Harvard University, A.B., 1942; Columbia University, M.A., 1947, Ph.D., 1954. Politics: Democrat. Religion: Episcopal. Home: 20 Ferncliff Rd., Scarsdale, N.Y.

CAREER: Mount Vernon Junior College, Washington, D.C., professor of history, 1948-57; Washington and Jefferson College, Washington, Pa., associate professor of history, 1957-65; Fordham University, Bronx, N.Y., associate professor of history, 1965—. Military service: U.S. Navy, 1944-46. Member: Organization of American Historians, American Historical Association, American Association of University Professors, Pennsylvania Historical Association.

WRITINGS: (With others) Civil War Studies, Washington and Jefferson College, 1961; Sword and Olive Branch: Oliver Otis Howard, University of Pittsburgh Press, 1964; Ulysses S. Grant, Twayne, 1970. Contributor of articles to Civil War History, Journal of Negro History, Lincoln Herald, Pacific Northwest Quarterly, and Military Affairs.

*   *   *

CARR, Dorothy Stevenson Laird 1912-
(Dorothy Laird)

PERSONAL: Born June 25, 1912; daughter of James William (an architect) and Elizabeth (an artist; maiden name, Stevenson) Laird; married John Griffith Carr (an underwriter), August 21, 1947; children: James Laird, Margaret Laird. Education: Attended schools in England and on Continent. Religion: Church of Scotland. Home: 10 Ferncroft Ave., London N.W.3, England. Agent: David Higham Associates Ltd., 58 Lower John St., Golden Square, London W.1, England.

CAREER: Dock reporter for Glasgow Herald, Bulletin, and Evening Times, Glasgow, Scotland, 1945-47; freelance writer, 1947—. Holds coastal yacht master's certificate, British Ministry of Shipping. During World War II served with Ministry of War Transport and the Admiralty, attached to British Embassy in Stockholm, Sweden, 1942-45, and to Royal Naval Headquarters, Oslo, Norway, 1945. Member: P.E.N., Press Club (London), Association Amicale Internationale des Capitaines au Long Cours Gap-Horniers, Glasgow Cape Horners Association.

WRITINGS: Double Cherry (novel), Mills & Boon, 1934; Opening Meet (novel), Mills & Boon, 1934; Charles Darwin, Naturalist, Blackie & Son, 1955; Our Bonny Royal Children, Pitkin, 1953; How the Queen Reigns, World Publishing, 1959, revised edition, Pan Books, 1961; Paddy Henderson, Outram, 1961; (with others) The Queen's Visit: Elizabeth II in India and Pakistan, Asia Publishing House, 1961. Under pseudonyms, author of several Golden Gift Books on members of the British Royal family. London correspondent of Scottish Field, 1951—; contributor to Homes and Gardens, Sunday Times, other newspapers.

WORK IN PROGRESS: An authorized history of Royal Ascot.

AVOCATIONAL INTERESTS: Shipping, especially sailing ships and mercantile marine matters; horse racing.

*   *   *

CARRIER, Warren (Pendleton) 1918-

PERSONAL: Born July 3, 1918, in Cheviot, Ohio; son of Burley Warren and Prudence (Alfrey) Carrier; married Marjorie Regan, April 3, 1947; children: Gregory Paul. Education: Attended Wabash College, 1938-40; Miami University, Oxford, Ohio, A.B., 1942; University of North Carolina, graduate study, 1942-44; Harvard University, M.A., 1948; Occidental College, Ph.D., 1962. Office: College of Arts and Letters, San Diego State College, San Diego, Calif. 92104.

CAREER: University of North Carolina, Chapel Hill, instructor in Romance languages, 1942-44; Boston University, Boston, Mass., instructor, 1945-49; University of Iowa, Iowa City, assistant professor of English, 1949-52; Bard College, Annandale, N.Y., 1953-57, began as assistant professor, became associate professor of literature; Bennington College, Bennington, Vt., member of literature faculty, 1955-58; Deep Springs College, Deep Springs, Calif., professor of language, literature, and philosophy, 1960-62; Portland State College, Portland, Ore., professor of English, 1962-64; Montana State University, Missoula, professor of English and chairman of department, 1964-68; Rutgers University, New Brunswick, N.J., associate dean of Livingstone College, 1968-69; San Diego State College, San Diego, Calif., dean of College of Arts and Letters, 1969—. Visiting professor, Sweet Briar College, 1958-60. Wartime service: American Field Service, attached to British Army, 1944-45; served in India-Burma. Member: Modern Language Association of America, American Association of University Professors, Phi Beta Kappa. Awards, honors: $500 award, National Endowment for the Arts, 1970, for "The Image Waits."

WRITINGS: (Translator) The City Stopped in Time, New Directions, 1949; The Hunt (novel), New Directions, 1952; (editor with Paul Engle) Reading Modern Poetry, Scott, Foresman, 1955, revised edition, 1968; Bay of the Damned, John Day, 1957; Toward Montebello, Harper, 1966. Contributor to Accent, Colorado Quarterly, Contact, Drama Survey, Los Angeles Times, New Mexico Quarterly, Perspective, Poetry, Renascence, Prairie Schooner, Tiger's Eye, Quarterly Review of Literature, Virginia Quarterly, and other publications. Quarterly Review of Literature, founder, 1943, editor, 1943-44; associate editor, Western Review, 1949-50.

WORK IN PROGRESS: Letting Go, poems.

BIOGRAPHICAL/CRITICAL SOURCES: Poetry, November, 1966.

*   *   *

CARRINGTON, Richard (Temple Murray) 1921-

PERSONAL: Born June 10, 1921, in London, England; son of Murray and Ethel (McDowall) Carrington. Education: Privately educated. Address: c/o Zoological Society of London, Regent's Park, London N.W.1, England.

CAREER: Biologist and writer. British Council, London, England, editor, 1945-46; British Broadcasting Corp., London, scriptwriter, 1946-50. Scientific adviser to New American Library of World Literature, Inc., New York, N.Y., and George Weidenfeld & Nicolson Ltd., London, England, 1959—. Founder and director, International Communications Centre, Nice, France. Military service: Royal Air Force, 1940-45; served in air-sea rescue units. Member: Zoological Society of London (scientific fellow), Royal Anthropological Institute (fellow), Royal Geographical Society (fellow), Institute of Archaeology, International Oceanographic Foundation, Egypt Exploration Society, Fauna Preservation Society.

WRITINGS: The Picture Dictionary of Flowers, Thames Publishing, 1956; The Story of Our Earth, Harper, 1956 (published in England as A Guide to Earth History, Chatto & Windus, 1956); Mermaids and Mastodons: A Book of Natural and Unnatural History, Rinehart, 1957; East From Tunis: A Record of Travels on the Northern Coast of Africa, Chatto & Windus, 1957; Elephants: A

Short Account of Their Natural History, Evolution, and Influence on Mankind, Chatto & Windus, 1958, Basic Books, 1959; *The Tears of Isis: The Story of a New Journey from the Mouth to the Source of the River Nile*, Chatto & Windus, 1959; *A Biography of the Sea: The Story of the World Ocean, Its Animal and Plant Populations, and Its Influence on Human History*, Chatto & Windus, 1960, Basic Books, 1961; (with Mary Eden) *The Philosophy of the Bed*, Putnam, 1961; *A Million Years of Man: The Story of Human Development as a Part of Nature*, World Publishing, 1963; (with the editors of *Life*) *The Mammals*, Time-Life, 1963; (editor with others) Eldred John Henry Corner, *The Life of Plants*, World Publishing, 1964; (editor with others) Vincent Brian Wigglesworth, *The Life of Insects*, World Publishing, 1964; (with Angus Bellairs) *The World of Reptiles*, American Elsevier, 1966; *Great National Parks of the World*, Random House, 1967 (published in England as *Great National Parks*, Weidenfeld & Nicolson, 1967); *The Mediterranean: Cradle of Western Culture*, Viking, 1971.

"Dawn of History" series, published by Chatto & Windus: *Ancient Egypt*, 1959, *Ancient Sumer*, 1959, *Ancient Greece*, 1961, *Ancient Rome*, 1961, *How Life Began*, 1962. General editor, Weidenfeld & Nicolson "Natural History," "Advancement of Science," and "World Naturalist" series; advisory editor, *The Living World of Animals*.

WORK IN PROGRESS: Books on animals in art and animal life of the past; research in zoology, paleontology, and prehistory.

SIDELIGHTS: Carrington compiled a zoological and botanical dictionary at age of twelve, and was elected a fellow of Zoological Society of London at fourteen; he has traveled widely in every continent except Australia and South America.

BIOGRAPHICAL/CRITICAL SOURCES: Christian Science Monitor, November 30, 1967.

*   *   *

CARROLL, Paul Vincent   1900-1968

PERSONAL: Born July 10, 1900, in Dundalk, Ireland; son of Michael (a schoolmaster) and Kitty (a dressmaker; maiden name Sandys) Carroll; married first wife, 1923 (deceased); married Helena O'Reilly, 1944 (died, 1957); children: Kathleen, Helena, Theresa Carroll Perez, Brian. *Education:* Educated by father until age of 13; attended St. Mary's College, Dundalk, Ireland, 1913-16, St. Patrick's Training College, Dublin, 1916-20, teacher's training schools in Dublin and Glasgow, Scotland. *Religion:* Roman Catholic. *Home:* 22 Park Rd., Bromley, Kent, England. *Agent:* Madden Play Co., 52 Vanderbilt Ave., New York, N.Y. 10017.

CAREER: Teacher of mathematics and English in schools in Scotland, 1921-37; playwright, 1937-68. Founder with James. Bridie of Glasgow Citizens' Theatre, 1943, director and productions adviser, 1943-50, honorary director, 1950-68. *Awards, honors:* Abbey Theatre prize, Dublin, Ireland, 1931, for *Things That Are Caesar's;* New York Drama Critics' Circle Award, 1938, for *Shadow and Substance*, and 1939 (for best foreign play), for *The White Steed;* Casement Award of Irish Academy of Letters, 1939, for *Shadow and Substance.*

WRITINGS—Adult plays: "The Watched Pot" (two-act), first produced in Dublin, Ireland at Abbey Theatre, 1928; *Things That Are Caesar's* (three-act tragedy; first produced in Dublin at Abbey Theatre, 1931; produced on Broadway at Martin Beck Theatre, October 17, 1932), Rich & Cowan, 1934 (also published in *Three Plays*—see below); *Shadow and Substance* (four-act; first produced in Dublin at Abbey Theatre, 1936; produced Off-Broad-

way at John Golden Theatre, January, 1938), Random House, 1937, acting edition, Samuel French (London), 1944 (also published in *Two Plays*—see below); *The White Steed [and] The Coggerers* (the former a three-act drama, first produced on Broadway at Cort Theatre, January 10, 1939; the latter first produced Off-Broadway at Hudson Theatre, January 20, 1939), Random House, 1939, *The White Steed* also published separately in acting edition, Samuel French, 1943, and in *Three Plays* (see below); "Kindred," first produced in New York at Maxine Elliott's Theatre, December 26, 1939; *The Old Foolishness* (three-act; first produced in New York at Windsor Theatre, December 20, 1940), Samuel French, 1944; *Three Plays: The White Steed, Things That Are Caesar's, [and] The Strings, My Lord, Are False* (*Strings* first produced in Dublin at Olympia Theatre, 1942; produced on Broadway at Royale Theatre, May 19, 1942), Macmillan, 1944; *Green Cars Go East* (two-act; first produced in Glasgow at Glasgow Citizens' Theatre, 1940), Samuel French, 1947; *The Conspirators* (one-act), Samuel French, 1947; *Interlude* (one-act), Samuel French, 1947; *The Wise Have Not Spoken* (three-act drama; first produced in London at King's Theatre, Hammersmith, March 19, 1946), Samuel French, 1947, Dramatists Play Service, 1954 (also published in *Two Plays*—see below); *Two Plays: The Wise Have Not Spoken [and] Shadow and Substance*, Macmillan, 1948; "The Chuckeyhead Story," first produced in East Hampton, N.Y. at John Drew Memorial Theatre, summer, 1951, retitled "The Devil Came from Dublin," and produced in Dallas, Tex. at Margo Jones Theatre, October 29, 1958; *The Wayward Saint* (satirical comedy; first produced on Broadway at Cort Theatre, February 17, 1955). Dramatists Play Service, 1955; *Farewell to Greatness!: A Three-Act Drama Based on the Life and Loves of Dean Jonathan Swift*, Proscenium, 1966.

Juvenile plays: *Plays for My Children* (includes *The King Who Could Not Laugh, His Excellency, the Governor, St. Francis and the Wolf, Beauty is Fled, Death Closes All*, and *Maker of Roads*), Messner, 1939, each play also published separately in acting edition by Samuel French, 1947.

Also author of *Irish Stories and Plays*, Devin, 1958. Author of screenplay for film, "Saints and Sinners," based on play *The Wayward Saint*, produced by Lopert in 1949. Writer of several short films for Douglas Fairbanks, Jr., for television showing in America.

BIOGRAPHICAL/CRITICAL SOURCES: Paul A. Doyle, *Paul Vincent Carroll*, Bucknell University Press, 1970.

(Died October 20, 1968)

*   *   *

CARROLL, Thomas Theodore, Jr.   1925-
(Ted Carroll)

PERSONAL: Born November 5, 1925, in St. Petersburg, Fla.; son of Thomas Theodore (a town clerk) and Marion (Guerrant) Carroll; married Dorothy Lee Sale, June 22, 1951; children: Patricia Lee, John DeLorme II. *Education:* Attended University of South Carolina before World War II; afterwards attended The Citadel, University of North Carolina, and George Washington University. *Politics:* Independent. *Religion:* Episcopalian. *Home:* 1104 Parkside Dr., Wilmington, Del. 19803. *Agent:* Marie Rodell, 141 East 55th St., New York, N.Y. 10022. *Office: Daily Times*, Chester, Pa.

CAREER: Roanoke World-News, Roanoke, Va., reporter, 1952-55; MacDonald-Cook Co. (advertising agency), South Bend, Ind., public relations account executive, 1955-57; Griffith Advertising Agency, St. Petersburg, Fla., director of public relations division, 1957-59; *Bradenton*

Herald, Bradenton, Fla., editor, 1959-61; *Daily Times*, Chester, Pa., editor of editorial page, 1962—. *Military service:* U.S. Navy, World War II; seaman. *Awards, honors:* Pennsylvania Press Association best editorial award, 1964, for editorial on Folcroft race riots.

WRITINGS: White Pills (novel), Crown, 1964. Contributor to *Christian Science Monitor, Reader's Digest,* and other periodicals.

WORK IN PROGRESS: A novel, *Happy Valley,* a projection of the Welfare State one and two generations into the future.

SIDELIGHTS: Carroll grew up in Eau Claire, S.C.; he likes being outdoors as much as possible. His avocational ambition is to own a tree farm.

*　　　*　　　*

CARRUTH, Estelle　1910-

PERSONAL: Surname is accented on second syllable; born April 14, 1910, in Desdemona, Tex.; daughter of Robin Pierce and Lizzy Jo (Henry) Carruth; divorced. *Education:* Texas Technological College (now Texas Tech University), B.A., 1936; Pennsylvania State University, M.Ed., 1949; Columbia University, postgraduate study. *Politics:* Independent. *Religion:* Protestant. *Home:* 2009 33rd St., Lubbock, Tex. 79411. *Office:* County Superintendent of Schools, Lubbock, Tex.

CAREER: Teacher in public schools in Texas and New Mexico, 1930-43, in Elizabethtown, Pa., 1946-47; Slippery Rock State College (now part of Pennsylvania State University), Slippery Rock, Pa., associate professor and critic teacher, Laboratory School, 1949-57; Brownfield (Tex.) public schools, teacher, 1957-62; Lubbock County (Tex.) schools, county supervisor, 1962—. Organized first School of Little 400 (English-language school for pre-school Mexican children), Brownfield, Tex., 1960. Member of Texas Supervision and Curriculum Development Committee. *Military service:* Women's Army Corps, 1942-45; served in Europe. *Member:* National Education Association, Texas State Teachers Association, Texas Women's Press Club. *Awards, honors:* First prize for travel story, 1953, for "Instructor."

WRITINGS: Three Sides to the River; Naylor, 1963.

WORK IN PROGRESS: A Negro-white story; other fiction.

*　　　*　　　*

CARRUTH, Hayden　1921-

PERSONAL: Surname accented on final syllable; born August 3, 1921, in Waterbury, Conn.; son of Gorton Veeder (an editor) and Margery (Barrow) Carruth; married (third wife) Rose Marie Dorn, October 28, 1961; children: (first marriage) Martha Hamilton; (third marriage) David Barrow. *Education:* University of North Carolina, A.B., 1943; University of Chicago, M.A., 1948. *Politics:* Abolitionist. *Home:* Johnson, Vt.

CAREER: Poet; free-lance writer. Editor of *Poetry* magazine, 1950-51; editor, University of Chicago Press, 1951-52; editor, Intercultural Publications, Inc., 1952-53. Owner and operator of Crows Mark Press, Johnson, Vt. *Military service:* U.S. Army Air Forces, World War II; became staff sergeant; spent two years in Italy. *Member:* Johnson Chamber of Commerce. *Awards, honors:* Bess Hokin prize (*Poetry* magazine), 1954; Vachel Lindsay prize (*Poetry* magazine), 1956; Levinson prize (*Poetry* magazine), 1958; Harriet Monroe poetry award, 1960-61; $1500 grant-in-aid for poetry, Brandeis University, 1960; Bollingen Foundation fellowship in criticism, 1962; Helen Hanson award, University of Washington, 1962; Carl Sandburg award, *Chicago Daily News,* 1963; Emily

Clark prize, *Virginia Quarterly Review,* 1964; Guggenheim Foundation fellowship, 1965; National Endowment fellowship, 1967; Morton Dauwen Zabel prize (*Poetry* magazine), 1967.

WRITINGS: The Crow and the Heart (poems), Macmillan, 1959; *Journey to a Known Place* (long poem), New Directions, 1961; *The Norfolk Poems of Hayden Carruth,* Prairie Press, 1962; *Appendix A* (novel), Macmillan, 1963; *After the Stranger: Imaginary Dialogues with Camus,* Macmillan, 1964; *North Winter* (poems), Prairie Press, 1964; (editor with J. Laughlin) *A New Directions Reader,* New Directions, 1964; *Nothing for Tigers: Poems, 1959-1964,* Macmillan, 1965; *Contra Mortem* (poem; originally published in *Poetry* magazine, April-May, 1965), Crows Mark Press, 1967; (contributor) *Where Is Vietnam?: American Poets Respond,* Anchor, 1967; *For You: Poems,* New Directions, 1970; (editor) *The Clay Hill Anthology,* Prairie Press, 1970; *The Voice That Is Great Within Us: American Poetry of the Twentieth Century,* Bantam, 1970; (editor) *The Bird/Poem Book: Poems on the Wild Birds of North America,* McCall, 1970; *From Snow and Rock, from Chaos* (poems), New Directions, 1973; *Twenty-three Poems,* Kayak, 1973.

WORK IN PROGRESS: "Collected criticism and a new novel; poems as they come."

SIDELIGHTS: For *CA* Carruth wrote simply: "My lights are too dim to show from the side; you got to face me square on. See the books." He has said that Yeats's "work was the first and strongest influence on me when I began to write. There were others too, of course; but Yeats was the one who hit the hardest. The power of his work upon me had little to do with the particulars of what he was saying, or for that matter with most of the generality; I can scarcely imagine a poet in the modern world with a mind and experience farther away from my own. It was a sensuous thing almost completely, Yeats's rhymes and lines and stanzas getting somehow into my actual nerve endings, retuning them, controlling their own impulses and responses." Richard Howard has seen, in Carruth's earlier poems, the influence of Ransom and Tate, as well as Yeats. Robert Regan writes about *North Winter:* "In these rigorously objective, graceful, masculine poems, Carruth achieves a style which sounds occasionally like an echo of Wallace Stevens—an echo one longs to hear more often in American poetry. Yet Carruth's style is distinctively his own." In reviewing the same book Jim Harrison says that Carruth "is able to progressively regenerate himself from a writer of what might aptly be called 'magazine verse,' the rather usual production of the quarterlies, he has become a substantial poet, one of the finest we have." W.T. Scott has noticed Carruth's admiration of Yeats, especially in "Pseudo Prayer," included in *Nothing for Tigers.* Scott finds, though, that "on the whole [the book] is strikingly [Carruth's] own. I suppose a fellow practitioner is first of all impressed by the variety of verse form and the dazzling deftness of Carruth's technique.... His danger is facility, running into wordiness at times. But mostly he is a rewarding poet."

Appendix A, Carruth's novel, has been both praised and criticized. Most critics felt that the book had many good sections, but that it was uneven. G.P. Elliott writes: "Those who require that a novel give formal satisfaction ... had better not undertake to read *Appendix A.* But those who can put up with the imperfections in a novel for the sake of the good parts, in this case some first rate comedy, should find it rewarding." A *Newsweek* reviewer comments that Carruth's "sense of character is deep and steady when he means it to be—altough he is not above filling in the margins with cartoons—and his prose has a nervous, intense precision that owes its discipline, if not its form, to poetry."

Richard Howard calls *After the Stranger: Imaginary Dialogues with Camus* a "work of fiction and criticism which 'of these was neither and was both at once.' " J.S. Rubenstein considers the book to be a satire, although he says Carruth is so deadpan "that only towards the very end of the book did it strike me." Florence Casey finds that the book "is an effective camouflage for Carruth's didactic impulse and appears to have permitted him to make constructive use of some of his own reveries."

Speaking of Carruth's work, Howard concludes: "Hayden Carruth persists . . . and his entire enterprise is evidently a continuing one, insisting one man, the poet's self, as the *mesocosm,* at the boundary of all things, and himself their boundary."

BIOGRAPHICAL/CRITICAL SOURCES: New York Times Book Review, May 12, 1963, April 18, 1965; *Virginia Quarterly Review,* summer, 1963; *Newsweek,* November 18, 1963; *New Republic,* February 15, 1964; *Nation,* February 15, 1965; *Christian Science Monitor,* February 25, 1965; *Commonweal,* March 19, 1965; *Saturday Review,* October 9, 1965, February 12, 1966; *Poetry,* January, 1966.

* * *

CARSON, John F(ranklin) 1920-

PERSONAL: Born August 2, 1920, in Indianapolis, Ind.; son of Fredric P. and Mary (McKenzie) Carson; married Beverly V. Carlisle, February 1, 1942; children: Jacqueline Ann (Mrs. William Phillips, Jr.), John, Bruce. *Education:* Butler University, B.S. in Ed., 1948; Indiana University, M.S. in Ed., 1955. *Politics:* Republican. *Religion:* Presbyterian. *Agent:* Dorothy Markinko, McIntosh & Otis, Inc., 18 East 41st St., New York, N.Y. 10017.

CAREER: Grassyfork Fisheries, Martinsville, Ind., biologist, 1948-49; Indianapolis Children's Museum, Indianapolis, Ind., lecturer-naturalist, 1949-50; Martinsville High School, Martinsville, Ind., teacher of English and biology, 1950-56; Indiana Lumber and Builders Supply Association, Indianapolis, educational coordinator, magazine editor, field representative, 1956-57; principal of schools in Gosport, Ind., 1957-58, North Judson, Ind., 1958-61; Taipei American High School, Taipei, Taiwan, principal, 1961-64. UNESCO-Chinese Ministry of Education, Taipei, guest participant in experimental teaching workshop, 1961, member of advisory group to study prevocational training, 1964. *Military service:* U.S. Coast Guard Reserve, 1943-45. *Member:* Phi Delta Kappa, American University Club (Taipei).

WRITINGS: Floorburns, Farrar, Straus, 1957; *The 23rd Street Crusaders,* Farrar, Straus, 1958; *The Boys Who Vanished* (Junior Literary Guild selection), Duell, Sloan & Pearce, 1959; *The Coach Nobody Liked* (Junior Literary Guild selection), Farrar, Straus, 1960; *Hotshot,* Farrar, Straus, 1961; *The Mystery of the Missing Monkey,* Farrar, Straus, 1963; *Court Clown,* Farrar, Straus, 1963; *The Mystery of the Tarnished Trophy,* Farrar, Straus, 1964.

WORK IN PROGRESS: A play, "Brief Candle"; two juvenile books, *Basketball Bum,* and *Alley Tom.*

AVOCATIONAL INTERESTS: Basketball, fishing, reading, natural history, camping (hopes to build cabin on Beaver Island, Mich.)

* * *

CARSWELL, John (Patrick) 1918-

PERSONAL: Born May 30, 1918; son of Donald (a barrister and author) and Catherine (Macfarlane) Carswell; married Ianthe Elstob, September 5, 1944; children: Catherine Deborah, Harriet Ursula. *Education:* Attended Ecole Montcel, Versailles, France, and Merchant Taylors' School, London, England; St. John's College, Oxford University, B.A., 1940. *Home:* 32 Park Village East, London N.W.1, England.

CAREER: British Civil Service, 1946—, served as assistant secretary, Ministry of Pensions and National Insurance, 1946-60, assistant secretary, Her Majesty's Treasury, 1961-64, assistant undersecretary of State, Department of Education and Science, 1964—. Robbins Committee on Higher Education, treasury assessor, 1962-63. *Military service:* British Army, 1940-46; became major. *Member:* Society of Authors, Garrick Club.

WRITINGS: (Editor) *Travels of Baron Munchausen,* Cresset, 1948, Dutton, 1950; *Romantic Rogue: Being the Singular Life and Adventures of Rudolph Erich Raspe, Creator of Baron Munchausen,* Dutton, 1950 (published in England as *The Prospector: Being the Life and Times of Rudolph Erich Raspe, 1737-1794,* Cresset, 1950); (editor) *Lying Awake,* Secker & Warburg, 1950; (editor) Alexander Somerville, *Autobiography of a Working Man,* Turnstile Press, 1951, new edition, MacGibbon & Kee, 1967; *The Old Cause: Three Biographical Studies in Whiggism,* Cresset, 1954; *The South Sea Bubble,* Cresset, 1960; (with L.A. Dralle) *The Diary and Political Papers of George Bubb Dodington,* Oxford University Press, 1965; *The Civil Servant and His World,* Gollancz, 1966; *The Descent on England: A Study of the English Revolution of 1688 and Its European Background,* John Day, 1969. Contributor to *New Statesman, Times Literary Supplement, Guardian.*

BIOGRAPHICAL/CRITICAL SOURCES: Spectator, October 11, 1969; *Observer Review,* October 26, 1969; *Books and Bookmen,* December, 1969; *Best Sellers,* December 5, 1969.

* * *

CARTER, Charles H(oward) 1927-

PERSONAL: Born April 3, 1927, in Baker, Ore.; son of Ernest H. and Anne E. (Moura) Carter; married Genevieve A.E.E. Torchin (a psychiatric social worker and instructor in social work at Tulane University), July 30, 1960. *Education:* Attended Willamette University and University of Chicago; Columbia University, B.S., 1957, M.A., 1958, Ph.D., 1962. *Office:* Department of History, Tulane University, New Orleans, La. 70118.

CAREER: University of Oregon, Eugene, instructor in history, 1961-63; Tulane University, New Orleans, La., associate professor, 1963-66, professor of history, 1966—. *Member:* American Historical Association, Renaissance Society of America, Historical Association (England). *Awards, honors:* Fulbright travel grants; Tulane University Council on Research grant.

WRITINGS: The Secret Diplomacy of the Habsburgs, 1598-1625, Columbia University Press, 1964; (editor of abridgement and author of introduction) C.J. Burckhardt, *Richelieu: His Rise to Power,* Random House, 1964; (editor, author of introduction, and contributor) *From the Renaissance to the Counter Reformation: Essays in Honor of Garrett Mattingly,* Random House, 1965; *The Western European Powers, 1500-1700,* Cornell University Press, 1971. Contributor of articles to historical journals.

WORK IN PROGRESS: Career biographies of Count Gondomar and Ambrogio Spinola; several articles, mainly on early seventeenth-century Europe.

SIDELIGHTS: Uses French, Spanish, and Italian in his work, and to a lesser degree, German, Latin, Dutch, and Portuguese. Current research is done in own collection of nearly 150,000 folios of microfilmed select original documents.

CARTER, Mary (Arkley) 1923-

PERSONAL: Born November 19, 1923, in Reedsport, Ore.; daughter of Robert P. and Elizabeth M. (Holzlin) Arkley; married Jack H. Carter, August 26, 1950 (divorced); children: William, Robert. *Education:* Attended University of Oregon and Pitzer College. *Politics:* Independent. *Residence:* Iowa City, Iowa. *Agent:* Brandt & Brandt, 101 Park Ave., New York, N.Y. 10017.

CAREER: Free-lance writer, 1958—. Lecturer, graduate program in creative writing, University of Iowa, 1968—.

WRITINGS: A Fortune in Dimes (novel), Little, Brown, 1963; *The Minutes of the Night* (novel), Little, Brown, 1965; *A Tiger Every Morning,* Little, Brown, 1971. Anthologized in *Best Short Stories of 1961,* edited by Martha Foley and David Burnett, Houghton, 1961. Contributor of short stories to *Kenyon Review, Contact, Argosy, Seventeen, Holiday, Redbook, Good Housekeeping,* and other periodicals.

WORK IN PROGRESS: A quartet of novellas.

*   *   *

CARTLAND, Barbara (Hamilton) (Barbara McCorquodale)

PERSONAL: Daughter of Bertram and Polly (Scobell) Cartland; married Alexander George McCorquodale, 1927 (marriage dissolved, 1933); married ˙Hugh McCorquodale, December 28, 1936 (died December 29, 1963); children: Raine (Countess of Dartmouth), Ian, Glen. *Education:* Attended Malvern Girls' College and Abbey House, Netley Abbey, Hampshire, England. *Politics:* Conservative. *Religion:* Church of England. *Home:* Camfield Pl., Hatfield, Hertfordshire, England. *Agent:* Rupert Crew Ltd., King's Mews, Gray's Inn Rd., London W.C. 2, England.

CAREER: Author. Lecturer, historian, political speaker for the Conservative office, and television personality. Was county councillor for Hertfordshire for nine years. Services welfare officer for Bedfordshire, 1941-45; now chairman of the St. John Council and vice-president of St. John Ambulance Brigade (nursing divisions), Hertfordshire, and president of Hertfordshire branch of Royal College of Midwives. *Member:* Romantic Novelists Association (vice-president), Oxfam (vice-president), National Association of Health (president). *Awards, honors:* Dame of Grace, St. John of Jerusalem, Certificate of Merit, Eastern Command, 1946.

WRITINGS—Novels: *Jigsaw,* Duckworth, 1925; *Sawdust,* Duckworth, 1926; *If a Tree Is Saved,* Duckworth, 1929.

For What?, Hutchinson, 1930; *Sweet Punishment,* Hutchinson, 1931, Hurst & Blackett, 1971; *A Virgin in Mayfair,* Hutchinson, 1932; *Just off Piccadilly,* Hutchinson, 1933; *Not Love Alone,* Hutchinson, 1933; *A Beggar Wished. . . ,* Hutchinson, 1934; *Passionate Attainment,* Hutchinson, 1935; *First Class, Lady?,* Hutchinson, 1935; *Dangerous Experiment,* Hutchinson, 1936, published in America as *Search for Love,* Greenberg, 1937; *Desperate Defiance,* Hutchinson, 1936; *The Forgotten City,* Hutchinson, 1936; *Saga at Forty,* Hutchinson, 1937; *But Never Free,* Hutchinson, 1937; *Broken Barriers,* Hutchinson, 1938; *Bitter Winds,* Hutchinson, 1938; *The Gods Forget,* Hutchinson, 1939; *The Black Panther,* Rich & Cowan, 1939.

Stolen Halo, Rich & Cowan, 1940; *Now Rough—Now Smooth,* Hutchinson, 1941; *Open Wings, a Twenty-third Novel,* Hutchinson, 1942; *The Leaping Flame,* R. Hale, 1942; *The Dark Stream,* Hutchinson, 1944; *After the Night,* Hutchinson, 1944; *Yet She Follows,* R. Hale, 1945; *Escape from Passion,* R. Hale, 1945; *Armour Against Love,* Hutchinson, 1945; *Out of Reach,* Hutchinson, 1945;

The Hidden Heart, Hutchinson, 1946, Pyramid Publications, 1970; *Against the Stream,* Hutchinson, 1946; *The Dream Within,* Hutchinson, 1947; *If We Will,* Hutchinson, 1947; *Again This Rapture,* Hutchinson, 1947; *No Heart Is Free,* Rich & Cowan, 1948; *A Hazard of Hearts,* Rich & Cowan, 1949, Pyramid Publications, 1969; *The Enchanted Moment,* Rich & Cowan, 1949; *A Duel of Hearts,* Rich & Cowan, 1949, Pyramid Publications, 1970.

The Knave of Hearts, Rich & Cowan, 1950, Pyramid Publications, 1971; *The Little Pretender,* Rich & Cowan, 1950, Pyramid Publications, 1971; *Love Is an Eagle,* Rich & Cowan, 1951; *A Ghost in Monte Carlo,* Rich & Cowan, 1951; *Love Is the Enemy,* Rich & Cowan, 1952, Pyramid Publications, 1970; *Cupid Rides Pillion,* Hutchinson, 1952; *Elizabethan Lover,* Hutchinson, 1953, Pyramid Publications, 1971; *Love Me for Ever,* Hutchinson, 1954, published in America as *Love Me Forever,* Pyramid Publications, 1970; *Desire of the Heart,* Hutchinson, 1954, Pyramid Publications, 1969; *The Enchanted Waltz,* Hutchinson, 1955, Pyramid Publications, 1971; *The Kiss of the Devil,* Hutchinson, 1955; *The Captive Heart,* Hutchinson, 1956, Pyramid Publications, 1970; *The Coin of Love,* Hutchinson, 1956, Pyramid Publications, 1969; *Sweet Adventure,* Hutchinson, 1957, Pyramid Publications, 1970; *Stars in My Heart,* Hutchinson, 1957, Pyramid Publications, 1971; *The Golden Gondola,* Hutchinson, 1958, Pyramid Publications, 1971; *Love in Hiding,* Hutchinson, 1959, Pyramid Publications, 1969; *The Smuggled Heart,* Hutchinson, 1959.

Love Under Fire, Hutchinson, 1960; *Messenger of Love,* Hutchinson, 1961, Pyramid Publications, 1971; *The Wings of Love,* Hutchinson, 1962, Pyramid Publications, 1971; *The Hidden Evil,* Hutchinson, 1963, Pyramid Publications, 1971; *The Fire of Love,* Hutchinson, 1964, Avon, 1970; *The Unpredictable Bride,* Hutchinson, 1964, Pyramid Publications, 1969; *Love Holds the Cards,* Hutchinson, 1965, Pyramid Publications, 1970; *A Virgin in Paris,* Hutchinson, 1966, Pyramid Publications, 1971; *Theft of a Heart,* Ward, Lock, 1966; *Love to the Rescue,* Hutchinson, 1967, Pyramid Publications, 1970; *Love Is Contraband,* Hutchinson, 1968, Pyramid Publications, 1970; *The Enchanting Evil,* Hutchinson, 1968, Pyramid Publications, 1969; *The Unknown Heart,* Hutchinson, 1969, Pyramid Publications, 1971.

Debt of Honor, Pyramid Publications, 1970; *Innocent Heiress,* Pyramid Publications, 1970; *Lost Love,* Pyramid Publications, 1970; *The Reluctant Bride,* Hutchinson, 1970; *The Royal Pledge,* Pyramid Publications, 1970; *The Secret Fear,* Hutchinson, 1970, Pyramid Publications, 1971; *The Secret Heart,* Pyramid Publications, 1970; *The Pretty Horse Breakers,* Hutchinson, 1971; *The Queen's Messenger,* Pyramid Publications, 1971; *Stars in Her Eyes,* Pyramid Publications, 1971; *Innocent in Paris,* Pyramid Publications, 1971; *The Audacious Adventuress,* Hutchinson, 1971, Pyramid Publications, 1972; *Lost Enchantment,* Hutchinson, 1972; *A Halo for the Dead,* Hutchinson, 1972; *The Irrisible Buck,* Hutchinson, 1972; *Love is Mine,* Pyramid Publications, 1972.

Under name Barbara McCorquodale: *Sleeping Swords* (political novel), R. Hale, 1942; *Love Is Mine,* Rich & Cowan, 1952, Pyramid Publications, 1972; *The Passionate Pilgrim,* Rich & Cowan, 1952; *Blue Heather,* Rich & Cowan, 1953; *Wings on My Heart,* Rich & Cowan, 1954; *The Kiss of Paris,* Rich & Cowan, 1956; *The Thief of Love,* Jenkins, 1957; *Love Forbidden,* Rich & Cowan, 1957; *Lights of Love,* Jenkins, 1958; *The Sweet Enchantress,* Jenkins, 1958; *A Kiss of Silk,* Jenkins, 1959; *The Price Is Love,* Jenkins, 1960; *The Runaway Heart,* Jenkins, 1961; *A Light to the Heart,* Ward, Lock, 1962; *Love Is Dangerous,* Ward, Lock, 1963; *Danger by the Nile,* Ward, Lock, 1964; *Love on the Run,* Ward, Lock, 1965.

History: *Bewitching Women,* Muller, 1955; *The Outrageous Queen: A Biography of Christina of Sweden,* Muller, 1956; *The Scandalous Life of King Carol,* Muller, 1957; *The Private Life of Charles II: The Women He Loved,* Muller, 1958; *The Private Life of Elizabeth, Empress of Austria,* Muller, 1959; *Josephine, Empress of France,* Hutchinson, 1961; *Diane de Poitiers,* Hutchinson, 1962; *Metternich: The Passionate Diplomat,* Hutchinson, 1964.

Biography: *Ronald Cartland,* preface by Winston Churchill, Collins, 1942; *The Isthmus Years: Reminiscences of the Years 1919-1939* (autobiography), Hutchinson, 1943; *The Years of Opportunity 1929-45* (autobiography), Hutchinson, 1948; *Polly, My Wonderful Mother,* Jenkins, 1956; *I Search for Rainbows 1946-66* (autobiography), Hutchinson, 1967; *We Danced All Night 1919-1929* (autobiography), Hutchinson, 1971.

Other nonfiction: *Touch the Stars: A Clue to Happiness,* Rider & Co., 1935; *You—in the Home,* Standard Art Book Co., 1946; *The Fascinating Forties: A Book for the Over-forties,* Jenkins, 1954; *Marriage for Moderns,* Jenkins, 1955; *Be Vivid, Be Vital,* Jenkins, 1956; *Love, Life and Sex,* Jenkins, 1957; *Look Lovely, Be Lovely,* Jenkins, 1958; *Vitamins for Vitality,* W. & G. Foyle, 1959; *Husbands and Wives,* Arthur Barker, 1961, reissued as *Love and Marriage,* Thorson's, 1971; *Etiquette Handbook,* Paul Hamlyn, 1962; *The Many Facets of Love,* W.H. Allen, 1963; *Sex and the Teenager,* Muller, 1964; *Living Together,* Muller, 1965; *The Pan Book of Charm,* Pan Books, 1965; *Woman, the Enigma,* Frewin, 1965; *The Youth Secret,* Corgi, 1968; *The Magic of Honey,* Corgi, 1970; *Health Food Cookery Book,* Hodder & Stoughton, 1972; *Health and Beauty Book,* Hodder & Stoughton, 1972; *Lines on Life and Love,* Hutchinson, 1972.

Editor, Ronald Cartland, *The Common Problem,* Hutchinson, 1943. Other writings: "Blood Money" (play); (with Bruce Woodhouse) "French Dressing" (play); (librettist) "The Rose and the Violet" (radio operetta with music by Mark Lubbock), 1943; "The Caged Bird" (radio play), 1957. Has done writing for television. Contributor of articles to newspapers, and stories to magazines. Author of columns, "Here's Health" and "Instant Cookery."

BIOGRAPHICAL/CRITICAL SOURCES: Books, February 21, 1937; Kenneth Ullyett, *My Key to Life,* Skeffington, 1958; *New Statesman,* August 4, 1967; *Punch,* August 9, 1967, February 3, 1971; *Times Literary Supplement,* November 2, 1967; *Books and Bookmen,* June, 1968, August, 1968, November, 1968, August, 1969, April, 1971.

* * *

CARTWRIGHT, William H(olman) 1915-

PERSONAL: Born September 12, 1915, in Pine Island, Minn.; son of William H. (a school administrator) and Ada (Frisbie) Cartwright; married Elaine M. McGladrey, September 3, 1934; children: John M., Mary Elaine (Mrs. David Wilson), Margaret Ann (Mrs. Edward Bauer). *Education:* University of Minnesota, B.S., 1937, M.A., 1942, Ph.D., 1950. *Politics:* Democrat. *Religion:* Unitarian. *Home:* 3610 Britt St., Durham, N.C. 27705. *Office:* Duke University, Durham, N.C. 27708.

CAREER: Elementary and high school teacher in Minnesota, 1937-45; University of Minnesota, Minneapolis, instructor, 1943-45; Boston University, Boston, Mass., assistant professor, 1946-50, associate professor of education, 1950-51; Duke University, Durham, N.C., professor of education, 1951—, chairman of department, 1951-70. Visiting summer professor at University of California, 1950, University of Colorado, 1957; Fulbright-Hays lecturer on American history, in India, 1963. Curriculum

consultant. *Military service:* U.S. Army, 1945-46; received Commendation Ribbon for historical writing.

MEMBER: American Historical Association, National Council for Social Studies (president, 1957), American Educational Research Association, National Education Association, American Association of University Professors, Association for Higher Education, Association for Supervision and Curriculum Development, New England History Teachers Association (president, 1950), Southern Council on Teacher Education (president, 1959), North Carolina Council for the Social Studies, North Carolina Association of Educators. Phi Delta Kappa, Phi Alpha Theta, Pi Gamma Mu, Kappa Delta Pi. *Awards, honors:* Outstanding Achievement award, University of Minnesota, 1959.

WRITINGS: A History of Newburg Township and the Village of Mabel, Mabel Record, 1943; *The Military District of Washington During the War Years,* Military District of Washington, 1946; (with Arthur C. Bining) *The Teaching of History in the United States,* Comision de Historia de Institute Panamericano de Geografia y Historia (Mexico), 1950; *The Graduate Education of Teachers: Proposals for the Future,* [Washington] 1959; *Current Trends in Teacher Education,* [Menasha, Wis.], 1960; *How to Use a Textbook,* National Council for the Social Studies, 1961; (with Miriam E. Mason) *Trail Blazers of American History,* Ginn, 1961, revised edition, 1966; (with Oscar O. Winther) *The Story of Our Heritage,* Ginn, 1962, 2nd revised edition published as *Our Country's Heritage, 1865-Today,* 1971; *Clio: A Muse Bemused,* [Bloomington], 1963; (with Edgar Bruce Wesley) *Teaching Social Studies in Elementary Schools,* Heath, 1964, 3rd edition, 1968; (with Frederica B. Coons, Milton C. Lee, and John Prater) *Many Peoples, One Country,* Ginn, 1971.

Editor: (With William B. Hamilton) *Historical Papers of the Trinity College Historical Society,* Duke University Press, 1953; (with Richard Watson, Jr.) *Interpreting and Teaching American History,* National Council for the Social Studies, 1961; (with Hamilton) *Duke University Centennial Conference on Teacher Training,* AMS Press, 1967. Contributor of articles on history and education to journals. *Social Education,* member of advisory board, 1947-48, member of executive board, 1950, 1963—.

WORK IN PROGRESS: Books on teaching social studies and the history of American education; editing a volume of interpretations of American history.

* * *

CARY, John H. 1926-

PERSONAL: Born May 4, 1926, in Eau Claire, Wis.; son of John Bernard and Mary (Beschta) Cary; married Kathryn Marie Ditter, June 9, 1956; children: Sean Bernard, Paul Alexander, Kenneth George, Carolyn Ann. *Education:* University of Wisconsin, B.S., 1950; Pennsylvania State University, M.A., 1951; University of Illinois, Ph.D., 1959. *Office:* Cleveland State University, Cleveland, Ohio 44115.

CAREER: De Paul University, Chicago, Ill., instructor in history, 1955-57; Michigan State University, East Lansing, assistant professor, 1958-63; Lehigh University, Bethlehem, Pa., associate professor and head of department of history, 1963-67; Cleveland State University, Cleveland, Ohio, professor of history and chairman of the department, 1967—. *Military service:* U.S. Army Air Forces, 1944-46; became sergeant. *Member:* American Historical Association, Mississippi Valley Historical Association, Conference on British Studies, Conference on Early American History, Ohio Academy of History.

WRITINGS: Joseph Warren: Physician, Politician, Patriot, University of Illinois Press, 1961; *History Study of* the Proposed Tocks Island National Recreation Area, U.S. Department of Interior, c.1964. Contributor of articles to historical journals.

WORK IN PROGRESS: Massachusetts in the American Revolution, 1763-1783, for McGraw.

* * *

CASSELS, Louis 1922-1974

PERSONAL: Born January 14, 1922, in Ellenton, S.C.; son of Horace M. (a banker) and Mollie (Welborn) Cassels; married Charlotte Norling, July 10, 1943; children: Horace M. IV. *Education:* Duke University, A.B., 1942. *Religion:* Episcopalian. *Address:* Box 1117, Aiken, S.C. 29801. *Office:* National Press Building, Washington, D.C. 10004.

CAREER: United Press International, Washington, D.C., correspondent, 1947-67, feature writer, and columnist, "Religion in America," 1955-74, senior editor, 1967-74. *Military service:* U.S. Army Air Forces, communications officer, 1943-46; became first lieutenant. *Member:* Religious Newswriters Association, National Press Club, Sigma Delta Chi. *Awards, honors:* Christopher Award; Faith and Freedom Award of Religious Heritage of America for religious journalism: Front Page award, Newspaper Guild, for best national reporting of race relations.

WRITINGS: Christian Primer, Doubleday, 1964; *What's the Difference?: A Comparison of the Faiths Men Live By,* Doubleday, 1965; *Your Bible,* Doubleday, 1967; *The Real Jesus: How He Lived and What He Taught,* Doubleday, 1968; *The Reality of God,* Doubleday, 1971; *Haircuts and Holiness: Discussion Starters for Religious Encounter Groups,* Abingdon, 1971; *A Feast for a Time of Fasting: Meditations for Lent,* Abingdon, 1973; *This Follows Jesus,* Warner Press, 1973.

BIOGRAPHICAL/CRITICAL SOURCES: New York Times Book Review, March 19, 1967; *Christian Century,* November 8, 1967.

(Died January 23, 1974)

* * *

CASSERLEY, Julian Victor Langmead 1909-

PERSONAL: Born November 28, 1909, in London, England; son of Arthur Langmead (a civil servant) and Ada (Clerke) Casserley; married Edna Mildred Green; children: Richard Francis Langmead, Lawrence Matthew Langmead, Helen Mary Langmead. *Education:* King's College, University of London, B.A., 1931, M.A., 1945, D.Litt., 1949, fellow, 1951. *Home:* 2126 Orrington Ave., Evanston, Ill. 60201. *Office:* Seabury Western Theological Seminary, Evanston, Ill. 62201.

CAREER: Anglican clergyman. Rector of parishes in England, 1934-52; University of Exeter, Exeter, England, lecturer in sociology, 1948-52; General Theological Seminary, New York, N.Y., former professor of dogmatic theology; Seabury Western Theological Seminary, Evanston, Ill., currently professor of philosophical theology.

WRITINGS: Kingdom Come, Church Literature Association (London), 1943; *No Faith of My Own,* Longmans, Green, 1950; *The Christian in Philosophy,* Faber, 1949, Scribner, 1951; *Morals and Man in the Social Sciences,* Longmans, Green, 1951; *The Retreat from Christianity in the Modern World,* Longmans, Green, 1952; *Graceful Reason: The Contribution of Reason to Theology,* Seabury, 1954; *The Bent World,* Oxford University Press, 1955; *Christian Community,* Longmans, Green, 1960; *Apologetics and Evangelism,* Westminster, 1962; *The Church To-day and To-morrow: The Prospect for Post-Christianity,* S.P.C.K., 1965; *Toward a Theology of History,* Holt, 1965; *The Death of Man: A Critique of Christian Atheism,* Morehouse, 1967; *In the Service of*

Man: Technology and the Future of Human Values, Regnery, 1967; (with Robert Speaight and Robert V. Wilshire) *Teilhard de Chardin: Re-mythologization* (three papers originally presented at symposium at Seabury Western Theological Seminary, Evanston, Ill., September, 1968), World Books, 1970.

BIOGRAPHICAL/CRITICAL SOURCES: Christian Century, August 30, 1967; *America,* February 17, 1968.

* * *

CASSILL, R(onald) V(erlin) 1919- (Owen Aherne)

PERSONAL: Born May 17, 1919, in Cedar Falls, Iowa; son of Howard Earl and Mary (Glosser) Cassill; married Karilyn Kay Adams, November 12, 1956; children: Orin, Erica, Jesse. *Education:* State University of Iowa, B.A., 1939, M.A., 1947. *Home:* R.R. 4, Iowa City, Iowa 52240. *Agent:* Lantz & Donadio, 111 West 57th St., New York, N.Y. 10019. *Office:* Department of English, Brown University, Providence, R.I. 02912.

CAREER: State University of Iowa, Iowa City, teacher in writing workshop, 1948-52, 1960-66; Brown University, Providence, R.I., assistant professor, 1966—. Free-lance writer. *Military service:* U.S. Army, 1942-46; became first lieutenant. *Member:* Phi Beta Kappa. *Awards, honors:* Regional prizes for watercolor paintings, 1939-40; *Atlantic* "Firsts" Award for short story, "The Conditions of Justice"; O. Henry Awards, third prize for "The Prize"; Guggenheim fellowship, 1968-69.

WRITINGS: The Eagle on the Coin, Random House, 1950; *Dormitory Women,* Lion Books, 1954; (with Eric Protter) *Left Bank of Desire,* Ace Books, 1955; *The Wound of Love,* Avon, 1956; *A Taste of Sin* (novel), Ace Books, 1956; *The Hungering Shame* (novel), Avon, 1956; *Naked Morning* (novel), Avon, 1957; (with Herbert Gold and James B. Hall) *Fifteen by Three: R.V. Cassill, Herbert Gold, and James B. Hall* (short stories), New Directions, 1957; *Lustful Summer* (novel), Avon, 1958; *Nurses Quarters* (novel), Gold Medal, 1958; *The Wife Next Door* (novel), Gold Medal, 1959; *Tempest* (novel based on film script of same title), Gold Medal, 1959; *The Buccaneers* (novel based on film script), Gold Medal, 1960; *My Sister's Keeper* (novel), Gold Medal, 1961; *Night School* (novel), New American Library, 1961; *Clem Anderson* (novel), Simon & Schuster, 1961; *Writing Fiction* (textbook), Permabooks, 1962; *Pretty Leslie* (novel), Simon & Schuster, 1963, also published with *The Hour of Maximum Danger,* by James Barlow, Doubleday, 1963; *The President* (novel), Simon & Schuster, 1964; *The Father, and Other Stories,* Simon & Schuster, 1965; *The Happy Marriage, and Other Stories,* Purdue University Studies, 1966; *La Vie Passionnee of Rodney Buckthorne: A Tale of the Great American's Last Rally and Curious Death* (novel), Geis, 1968; *In an Iron Time: Statements and Reiterations* (collection of essays and criticisms), Purdue University Studies, 1969; *Doctor Cobb's Game* (novel), Geis, 1970.

Under pseudonym Owen Aherne: *Man on Fire,* Avon, 1957; *An Affair to Remember* (based on film of same title), Avon, 1957.

Editor: *Intro #1* (short stories), Bantam, 1968; (and author of introduction) *Intro #2* (short stories and poems), Bantam, 1969; *Intro #3,* McCall Publishing, 1970; (with Walton Beacham) *Intro #4,* University Press of Virginia, 1972. Contributor of articles, fifty stories, and over 100 book reviews to periodicals.

WORK IN PROGRESS: A novel, as yet untitled, completed and awaiting publication by Doubleday.

SIDELIGHTS: "R.V. Cassill can be thought of as the successor to Sherwood Anderson," Thomas Rogers has said. "Cassill's attitude towards the lives he writes about has the same honest, helpless respect that one finds in Anderson. And there is this further similarity: just as Anderson has been overshadowed by the more willful writers of the Twenties—Hemingway and Fitzgerald—so Cassill has been overshadowed by the corresponding writers of our period." Rogers goes on to say in his review that *La Vie Passionnee of Rodney Buckthorne* is "a mistake," uncharacteristic of Cassill's other fiction. "One either is or is not the kind of writer whose private experience naturally takes the form of those large-scale, mythologically resounding dramas that attract great public attention. R.V. Cassill is not such a writer."

David Roberts considers Cassill "one of the most significant writers of the present generation.... In less than twenty years [he] has published 14 novels and almost 50 short stories; except for the passing portent of reviewers' comments and the slim recognition of having had a number of stories included in yearly anthologies which rather whimsically select the 'best' of that genre, he has received no formal attention at all." Roberts believes Cassill's best work appears in his short fiction: "Perhaps for the good reason that his themes have . . . been involved with the fragmentation of values in the chaotic present, Cassill's most insightful and esthetically complete accomplishments to date have been in his short stories; his novels, despite their considerable merit and consistently similar thematic concerns, do not manage to present that essence of embodied vision necessary to the finest artistic performance."

In his review of *Doctor Cobb's Game*, John Leonard states that "R.V. Cassill's fiction has always been unclassifiable, as omnivorous and idiosyncratic as Mailer's, examining the relations between public life and private obsession, between the institution and the individual, between—in this instance—power and sex." Reminiscent of Britain's Profumo scandal of the early 1960's, Leonard finds the novel "neither a roman a clef nor a salacity sandwich served up for starving libidos. It is a staggeringly complex meditation on irrationality, the forms it assumes, its energy for good and evil, its sources in biology and myth.... [It] is his best book, better than *Clem Anderson* and *The President;* but it is more—it is a text on the inadequacy of life to live up to the expectations of imagination."

In 1967 Cassill offered his own thoughts on the future of the novel in a *New York Times Book Review* column, entitled "Speaking of Books: Whose Novel is Dead?" He wrote: "A lot of mileage is being got from the declaration that 'the realistic novel is dead, dying, doomed or obsolete'.... The decline and demise of one ritual observance [of reality]—the novel, say—would not by any means prove that reality had shrunk or died, only that faith in it had lost one of its noblest props.... Of all the arts, fiction is the one which most broadly connects the homely, private, errant, ridiculous and immature phases of our lives with the ripened abstractions of philosophy. The type of consciousness invested in and replenished by fiction is simply the realistic orientation of the race to being and nothingness.... So perhaps whatever optimism one feels about the novel can only be expressed in the conditional: Only fiction could describe what has coerced mankind into letting it die."

Options for *La Vie Passionnee of Rodney Buckthorne* have been sold to Bri-Wen and Capri Productions for filming.

BIOGRAPHICAL/CRITICAL SOURCES: New York Times Book Review, January 1, 1967, May 19, 1968; *Critique*, Volume IX, number 1; *New York Times*, May 18, 1968, November 3, 1970; *Book World*, June 2, 1968; *Library Journal*, May 15, 1969; *Antioch Review*, fall/winter, 1970-71; *Time*, November 16, 1970; *Newsweek*, November 30, 1970.

* * *

CASSON, Lionel 1914-

PERSONAL: Born July 22, 1914, in New York, N.Y. *Education:* New York University, A.B., 1934, M.A., 1935, Ph.D., 1939. *Office:* Department of Classics, New York University, New York, N.Y. 10003.

CAREER: New York University, New York, N.Y., instructor, 1936-45, assistant professor, 1945-52, associate professor, 1952-59, professor of classics, 1959—. Director of summer session in classics, American Academy in Rome, 1963—. *Military service:* U.S. Naval Reserve, 1942-46; became lieutenant. *Member:* American Philological Association, American Archaeological Association, Association Internationale des Papyrologues, Society for Nautical Research. *Awards, honors:* Guggenheim fellow, 1952-53, 1959-60; fellowship, National Endowment for the Humanities, 1967-68.

WRITINGS: (With E.E. Burriss), *Latin and Greek in Current Use*, Prentice-Hall, 1939, revised edition, 1948; (with E.L. Hettich) *Excavations at Nessana*, Volume II, Princeton University Press, 1950; *The Ancient Mariners: Seafarers and Sea Fighters of the Mediterranean in Ancient Times*, Macmillan, 1959; *Masters of Ancient Comedy*, Macmillan, 1960; (editor) *Selected Satires of Lucien*, Doubleday, 1962; (editor and translator) *Six Plays of Plautus*, Doubleday, 1963; *Illustrated History of Ships and Boats*, Doubleday, 1964; (with the editors of Time-Life books) *Ancient Egypt*, Time, 1965; (editor) *Masterpieces of World Literature: Classical Age*, Dell, 1965; *Ships and Seamanship in the Ancient World*, Princeton University Press, 1971; (editor and translator) *The Plays of Menander*, New York University Press, 1971; (editor and translator) Plautus, *Amphitryon and Two Other Plays*, Norton, 1971; (editor and translator) Plautus, *The Menaechmus Twins, and Two Other Plays*, Norton, 1971. Member of advisory editorial board, *American Neptune* and *Archaeology*.

WORK IN PROGRESS: Travel and Touring in Ancient Times.

* * *

CASTELLANOS, Jane Mollie Robinson 1913-

PERSONAL: Born August 6, 1913, in Lansing, Mich.; daughter of Charles Summers (a biochemist) and Florence (Sherwood) Robinson; married Jose C. Castellanos, November 14, 1942; children: Esther, Elizabeth, Alice Marie. *Education:* Studied at University of Strasbourg, 1930, University of Munich, 1930-31; University of Michigan, B.A., 1934; Stanford University, M.A., 1935, Ph.D., 1938; postdoctoral study at Mills College, 1941, and University of California. *Home:* 742 Brookdale Court, Concord,, Calif. 94518.

CAREER: San Francisco College for Women, San Francisco, Calif., instructor in languages, 1938-40; Mills College, Oakland, Calif., instructor in child development, 1942-50; Contra Costa Junior College District, Martinez, Calif., instructor in family life education and psychology, and counselor, 1950—, chiefly at Diablo Valley College, Concord, Calif. *Member:* Phi Beta Kappa.

WRITINGS: (With Louisa Wagoner) *The Observation of Young Children*, revised edition, privately printed, 1951; *A Shell for Sam*, Golden Gate, 1963; *Something New for Taco*, Golden Gate, 1965; *Tomasito and the Golden Llamas*, Golden Gate, 1968.

BIOGRAPHICAL/CRITICAL SOURCES: New York Times Book Review, May 9, 1965.

CATON, Charles E(dwin)   1928-

PERSONAL: Surname is pronounced *Cay*-ton; born March 21, 1928, in Evanston, Ill.; son of Harold D. and Irma (Fruit) Caton; married Robin McReynolds, 1955; children: Marcia, Dewey, John, George. *Education:* Oberlin College, B.A., 1950; University of Michigan, M.A., 1951, Ph.D., 1956. *Office:* Department of Philosophy, Gregory Hall, University of Illinois, Urbana, Ill. 61801.

CAREER: University of Michigan, Ann Arbor, instructor in philosophy, 1957-58; University of Illinois, Urbana, instructor, 1958-61, assistant professor, 1961-66, associate professor, 1966-68, professor of philosophy, 1968—. Visiting associate professor, Purdue University, 1968. *Member:* American Philosophical Association, Linguistic Society of America. *Awards, honors:* Fulbright scholar, Oxford University, 1956-57.

WRITINGS: (Editor) *Philosophy and Ordinary Language,* University of Illinois Press, 1963. Contributor to *Analysis, Mind, Philosophical Quarterly,* and other philosophy journals.

*   *   *

CAUSLEY, Charles (Stanley)   1917-

PERSONAL: Born August 24, 1917, in Launceston, Cornwall, England; son of Charles Samuel and Laura Jane (Bartlett) Causley. *Education:* Attended Launceston College, and Peterborough Training College. *Home:* 2, Cyprus Well, Launceston, Cornwall, England. *Agent:* David Higham Associates Ltd., 5-8, Lower John St., Golden Square, London WIR 4HA, England.

CAREER: Writer, teacher. Member of Poetry Panel of the Arts Council of Great Britain, 1962-65. *Military service:* Royal Navy, 1940-46. *Member:* Society of Authors, Royal Society of Literature (fellow, 1958—). *Awards, honors:* Traveling scholarships, Society of Authors, 1954 and 1966; Queen's Gold Medal for Poetry, 1967; Cholmondeley Award for poetry, 1971.

WRITINGS—Poetry: *Farewell, Aggie Weston,* Hand & Flower Press, 1951; *Survivor's Leave,* Hand & Flower Press, 1953; *Union Street,* Hart-Davis, 1957, Houghton, 1958; *The Ballad of Charlotte Dymond* (originally published in *Bryanston Miscellany*), privately printed, 1958; *Johnny Alleluia,* Hart-Davis, 1961, Dufour, 1962; (with George Barker and Martin Bell) *Penguin Modern Poets 3,* Penguin, 1962; *Underneath the Water,* Macmillan, 1968; *Figure of 8: Narrative Poems,* Macmillan, 1969; *Figgie Hobbin: Poems for Children,* Macmillan, 1971, published in America as *Figgie Hobbin,* Walker & Co., 1973; *Timothy Winters* (poem set to music), music by Wallace Southam, Turret Books, 1970; (with Laurie Lee) *Pergamon Poets X,* compiled by Evan Owen, Pergamon, 1970; *The Tail of the Trinosaur,* Brockhampton Press, 1973. Also author of a book of short stories, *Hands to Dance,* Carroll & Nicholson, 1951.

Editor: *Peninsula: An Anthology of Verse from the West Country,* Macdonald, 1957; (and author of introduction) *Dawn and Dusk: Poems of Our Time* (juvenile), Brockhampton, 1962, F. Watts, 1963, 2nd edition, Brockhampton; 1972; (and author of introduction) *Rising Early: Story Poems and Ballads of the 20th Century,* Brockhampton, 1964, published in America as *Modern Ballads and Story Poems,* F. Watts, 1965; (and author of introduction) *Modern Folk Ballads,* Studio Vista, 1966; *In the Music I Hear* (poems by children), Arc Press, 1970; (and author of introduction) *Oats and Beans and Barley* (poems by children), Arc Press, 1971.

Contributor to *New Statesman, Spectator, Listener, Encounter, Harper's Bazaar, Ladies' Home Journal, Observer, Sunday Times* (London), *Times Literary Supplement, London Magazine, Twentieth Century, Outposts, Transatlantic Review,* and other periodicals, and to anthologies of verse.

WORK IN PROGRESS: A collection of poems to be published together with a series of drawings by Barbara Hepworth.

SIDELIGHTS: Causley writes: "*Figure of 8,* a collection of narrative poems, was published as a children's book. I'd hope, though, that the book wouldn't be read by children only—in writing such a book I think one should simply aim at widening the age-range of one's audience, and in the process try and avoid producing poetry and water. . . . In the event, one doesn't think about a possible audience at all when writing: only about the problem of getting the poem on the paper as close as possible to what's in one's head in a vague form. After the poem's written is the time to decide (if ever) what kind of audience it might reach."

Causley has traveled widely from Scapa Flow, off the northern coast of Scotland, to Sydney, Australia, and from Freetown, West Africa, to Rabaul, New Britain; he has visited many countries, including Italy, France, Spain, Poland, and the U.S.S.R. He once said that one of the principal delights of travel was the intense pleasure he experienced on returning to his native Cornwall.

He can be heard reading his poetry on the following recordings: "Authopoetry," Poets Lot Ltd.; "Here Today," "The Jupiter Anthology of 20th Century English Poetry: Part III" (which he also edited), and "The Jupiter Book of Contemporary Ballads," all Jupiter Recordings Ltd.; "The Poet Speaks, Record 8," Argo Record Co. Ltd. Poems and interviews have been recorded on tape for the British Council. A number of his poems appear in the series "Poetry and Song," Argo, and in settings by folk-singers on a number of long-playing albums.

BIOGRAPHICAL/CRITICAL SOURCES: R.N. Currey, *Poets of the 1939-1945 War,* published for the British Council and National Book League by Longmans, Green, 1960; Elizabeth Jennings, *Poetry Today,* published for British Council and National Book League by Longmans, Green, 1961; John Pett, *The Guardian,* January 15, *1965; New Statesman,* March 22, 1968; *Punch,* March 27, 1968; *London Magazine,* November, 1968; *Times Literary Supplement,* October 16, 1969; *Books,* January, 1970; *Books and Bookmen,* April, 1971; Norman Hidden, *Times Educational Supplement,* November 17, 1972.

*   *   *

CAVANNA, Betty   1909-
    (Betsy Allen, Elizabeth Headley)

PERSONAL: Given name, Elizabeth Allen; born June 24, 1909, in Camden, N.J.; daughter of Walter and Emily (Allen) Cavanna; married Edward Headley, August 5, 1940 (died, 1952); married George Russell Harrison (a dean of science emeritus, Massachusetts Institute of Technology), March 9, 1957; children: (first marriage) Stephen. *Education:* Douglass College, A.B., 1929. *Religion:* Protestant. *Home:* 170 Barnes Hill Rd., Concord, Mass. 01742.

CAREER: *Bayonne Times,* Bayonne, N.J., reporter, 1929-31; Westminster Press, Philadelphia, Pa., advertising manager, then art director, 1931-41; full-time writer, 1941—. *Member:* Writers Guild, Boston Museum of Fine Arts, Philadelphia Art Alliance, Technology Matrons (program chairman, 1961-62), Phi Beta Kappa, Women's Travel Club of Boston (2nd vice-president, 1972-73), Cosmopolitan Club (New York).

WRITINGS—All juvenile or young adult books: *Puppy Stakes,* Westminster, 1943; *The Black Spaniel Mystery,*

Westminster, 1945; *Secret Passage*, John C. Winston, 1946; *Going on Sixteen*, Westminster, 1946; *Spurs for Suzanna*, Westminster, 1947; *A Girl Can Dream*, Westminster, 1948; *Paintbox Summer*, Westminster, 1949; *Spring Comes Riding*, Westminster, 1950; *Two's Company*, Westminster, 1951; (compiler) *Pick of the Litter* (short stories), Westminster, 1952; *Lasso Your Heart*, Westminster, 1952; *Love, Laurie*, Westminster, 1953; *Six on Easy Street*, Westminster, 1954; *The First Book of Seashells*, F. Watts, 1955; *Passport to Romance*, Morrow, 1955; *The Boy Next Door*, Morrow, 1956; *Angel on Skis*, Morrow, 1957; *Stars in Her Eyes*, Morrow, 1958; *The Scarlet Sail*, Morrow, 1959; *Accent on April*, Morrow, 1960; *A Touch of Magic*, Westminster, 1961; *Fancy Free*, Morrow, 1961; *The First Book of Wildflowers*, F. Watts, 1961; *A Time for Tenderness*, Morrow, 1962; *Almost Like Sisters*, Morrow, 1963; *Jenny Kimura*, Morrow, 1964; *Mystery at Love's Creek*, Morrow, 1965; *A Breath of Fresh Air*, Morrow, 1966; (with husband, George Russell Harrison) *The First Book of Wool*, F. Watts, 1966; *The Country Cousin*, Morrow, 1967; *Mystery in Marrakech*, Morrow, 1968; *Spice Island Mystery*, Morrow, 1969; *The First Book of Fiji*, F. Watts, 1969; *The First Book of Morocco*, F. Watts, 1970; *Mystery on Safari*, Morrow, 1970; *The Ghost of Ballyhooly*, Morrow, 1971; *Mystery in the Museum*, Morrow, 1972.

"Around the World Today" series, published by F. Watts: *Arne of Norway*, 1960, *Lucho of Peru*, 1961, *Paulo of Brazil*, 1962, *Pepe of Argentina*, 1962, *Lo Chau of Hong Kong*, 1963, *Chico of Guatemala*, 1963, *Noko of Japan*, 1964, *Carlos of Mexico*, 1964, *Tavi of the South Seas*, 1965, *Doug of Australia*, 1965, *Ali of Egypt*, 1966, *Demetrios of Greece*, 1966.

Under name Betsy Allen—"Connie Blair Mystery" series, published by Grosset: *Puzzle in Purple*, 1948, *The Secret of Black Cat Gulch*, 1948, *The Riddle in Red*, 1948, *The Clue in Blue*, 1948, *The Green Island Mystery*, 1949, *The Ghost Wore White*, 1950, *The Yellow Warning*, 1951, *The Gray Menace*, 1953, *The Brown Satchel Mystery*, 1954, *Peril in Pink*, 1955, *The Silver Secret*, 1956.

Under name Elizabeth Headley—All published by Macrae Smith: *A Date for Diane*, 1946, *Diane's New Love*, 1955, *Toujours Diane*, 1957, preceding three books published in one volume as *The Diane Stories: All About America's Favorite Girl Next Door*, 1964, *Take a Call, Topsy!*, 1947, *She's My Girl!*, 1949, *Catchpenny Street*, 1951.

Contributor of serials to *American Girl* and other teen-age magazines.

WORK IN PROGRESS: Petey, for Westminster; a novel about a pupil at the United Nations School in New York City, to be published by Morrow.

SIDELIGHTS: Miss Cavanna has been a writer of youth books for almost thirty years, most of them aimed at the limited audience of junior high school girls. She explains this as the result of "an almost total emotional recall for this particular period of my own life, which made it possible for me to identify with a teenage heroine. Fashions in clothes and speech change, but the hopes, dreams, and fears of the young remain fairly constant, and over the years I have explored all sorts of youthful problems—among them loneliness, shyness, jealousy, social maladjustment, and the destructiveness of alcoholism, divorce, race prejudice, and mother-daughter rivalry within family situations."

Miss Cavanna began to travel in search of book material in the early 1950's, lived in a Swiss ski resort (1955-56), and has picked up other background material in the Caribbean, Mexico, Europe, South America, Australia, Japan, Egypt, the South Seas, Morocco, East Africa, Iran, Afghanistan, Nepal, and India. Her present home in

Concord is on a hill just above the historic river. Miss Cavanna's husband, George Russell Harrison, has provided the photographs for her entire "Around the World Today" series.

AVOCATIONAL INTERESTS: Art, gardening, and antiques.

* * *

CAVENDISH, Richard   1930-
(Martin Cornwall)

PERSONAL: Born August 12, 1930, in Henley, England; son of Richard Philip (a clergyman, Church of England) and Mary (Williams) Cavendish; married Mavis Hay (an editor), August 13, 1955. *Education:* Christ's Hospital, Horsham, England, student, 1940-48; Oxford University, B.A., 1953, graduate student, 1954; Chartered Insurance Institute, London, England, associateship, 1956. *Residence:* London, England. *Agent:* Willis Kingsley Wing, 24 East 38th St., New York, N.Y. 10016.

CAREER: British & Overseas Insurance Co., London, England, overseas manager, 1954-58; B. & R. Excess Corp., New York, N.Y., claims manager, 1958-62; free-lance writer, 1962—. *Military service:* British Army, 1948-50; became sergeant.

WRITINGS: Nymph and Shepherds (novel), Doubleday, 1959; *The Balancing Act* (novel), Cassell, 1960; *On the Rocks* (novel), Heinemann, 1963; (under pseudonym Martin Cornwall) *Buying Insurance*, Collier, 1963; *The Black Arts* (nonfiction), Putnam, 1967; (editor) *Man, Myth and Magic*, Purnell & Sons, in press.

WORK IN PROGRESS: Lords of the Treehold, for Putnam.

BIOGRAPHICAL/CRITICAL SOURCES: Book Week, April 9, 1967; *New Yorker*, June 24, 1967.

* * *

CAVNES, Max P(arvin)   1922-

PERSONAL: Born November 15, 1922, in Midway, Ind.; son of Alfred Andrew (a farmer) and Maude (Haynes) Cavnes; married Doris Elaine Williams (a teacher), August 24, 1953. *Education:* Indiana Central College, student, 1940-43; Indiana University, A.B., 1947, M.A., 1950, Ph.D., 1955; Yale University, B.D., 1950. *Home and office:* Centre College, Danville, Ky.

CAREER: Western State College of Colorado, Gunnison, assistant professor of history, 1955-58; Centre College, Danville, Ky., assistant professor, 1958-63, dean of men, 1960—, associate professor of history, 1963—. *Military service:* U.S. Army, 1942-45. *Member:* American Historical Association, Mississippi Valley Historical Association.

WRITINGS: The Hoosier Community at War, Indiana University Press, 1961.

* * *

CAZEL, Fred A(ugustus), Jr.   1921-

PERSONAL: Born February 25, 1921, in Asheville, N.C.; son of Fred A. (a businessman) and Agnes (Petrie) Cazel; married Annarie Peters (a part-time college teacher), January 2, 1946. *Education:* University of North Carolina, B.A., 1941; Johns Hopkins University, M.A., 1943, Ph.D., 1948. *Politics:* Democrat. *Religion:* Protestant. *Home address:* R.F.D. 3, Gurleyville, Storrs, Conn. 06268. *Office:* Department of History, University of Connecticut, Storrs, Conn. 06268.

CAREER: Johns Hopkins University, Baltimore, Md., instructor in history, 1947-48; University of Connecticut, Storrs, assistant professor, 1948-54, associate professor, 1954-62, professor of history, 1962—. Visiting summer assistant professor of history, University of Minnesota, 1950; visiting professor, University of California, Berkeley, 1965-66. Justice of Peace, 1958-60, 1962—. *Military service:* U.S. Army, 1943-45.

MEMBER: American Historical Association, Mediaeval Academy of America, American Association of University Professors (state conference president, 1962-63), American Civil Liberties Union, Conference on British Studies, New England Association of History Teachers, Connecticut Academy of Arts and Sciences, Connecticut Historical Society, Antiquarian and Landmarks Society of Connecticut, Connecticut Horticultural Society, Pipe Roll Society, Mansfield Historical Society (president, 1957-59), county and local Democratic organizations, Phi Beta Kappa, Phi Kappa Phi, Phi Alpha Theta, Johns Hopkins Club. *Awards, honors:* Gustav Bissing fellowship, 1951-52; Fulbright research fellowship, King's College, University of London, 1955-56.

WRITINGS: (Editor) *Feudalism and Liberty: Articles and Addresses of Sidney Painter,* Johns Hopkins Press, 1961. Contributor of articles to historical publications.

WORK IN PROGRESS: A book on Hubert de Burgh with tentative title, *The Great Justiciar;* research on England and France in twelfth and thirteenth centuries, on the crusades, and on mediaeval taxation and finance; editing *Rotulus de diversis compotis,* for the Pipe Roll Society.

*   *   *

CHAGALL, David 1930-

PERSONAL: Surname originally Siegel; born November 22, 1930, in Philadelphia, Pa.; son of Harry Chagall and Ida (Coopersmith) Siegel; married Juneau Joan Alsin (an artist), November 15, 1956. *Education:* Swarthmore Center College, student, 1948-49; Pennsylvania State University, B.A., 1952; Sorbonne, University of Paris, graduate study, 1953-54. *Home:* 28232 W. Foothill Dr., Agoura, Calif. 91301.

CAREER: Social case worker for the State of Pennsylvania; teacher in the public schools of Philadelphia, Pa.; staff editor for British science journal in London, England; member of public relations staff of A.E.I.-Hotpoint Ltd. in London; market research analyst for Chilton Company, Philadelphia; research project director for Haug Associates, Los Angeles; currently marketing and social research consultant; syndicated columnist; lecturer. *Awards, honors:* Poetry prize of University of Wisconsin, 1971; nominee for National Book Award in fiction, 1972, for *Diary of a Deaf Mute;* nominee for Pulitzer Prize in Letters, 1973, for *The Spieler for the Holy Spirit.*

WRITINGS—All novels: *Diary of a Deaf Mute,* Raben & Sjogren, 1960; *Millenium House,* 1971; *The Century God Slept,* Sidgwick & Jackson, 1962; Yoseloff, 1963; *The Spieler for the Holy Spirit,* Ashley Books, 1972. Contributor of short fiction, poetry, articles, and reviews to American and British magazines, journals and newspapers.

WORK IN PROGRESS: Acapulco Smoke Dreams, a novel about the expatriate scene in Mexico; *The Probability Factor,* a novel about religious cults in southern California.

*   *   *

CHAI, Ch'u 1906-

PERSONAL: Born December 26, 1906, in Anhwei, China; son of Y.Y. and Chao Chai; married May Ann Tsao, 1930; children: Winberg, Henry, Al. *Education:* Tsing Hau College, diploma, 1927; Stanford University,

B.A., 1929; Northwestern University, J.D., 1932. *Home:* 220 West 71st St., New York, N.Y. 10023. *Office:* New School for Social Research, 66 West 12th St., New York, N.Y. 10011.

CAREER: Professor at Chinese national universities, 1939-49; National Taiwan University, Taipei, Formosa, professor of law and philosophy, 1952-55; New School for Social Research, New York, N.Y., associate professor, 1955-57, professor of Chinese culture and philosophy, 1957—. Hunter College, visiting lecturer, 1962—. Legislative Yuan, Nanking, China, senior expert, 1932-37; Judicial Yuan, Nanking, China, counselor, 1947-49; Ministry of Education, Taipei, Formosa, senior editor, 1949-52; Ministry of Justice, Taipei, Formosa, adviser and member of minister's commission, 1952-54. *Military service:* Chinese Army, 1937-39. *Member:* American Oriental Society, American Association of Teachers of Chinese Culture and Language, Association for Asian Studies. *Award, honors:* Research grant from Nationalist Chinese Government, 1949-52; leader grant from U.S. Department of State, 1951.

WRITINGS: The Story of Chinese Philosophy, Washington Square, 1961; (with son, Winberg Chai) *The Changing Society in China,* New American Library, 1962, revised edition, 1969; (editor) *I-Ching: Book of Changes,* University Books, 1964; (editor and translator with Winberg Chai, and author of introduction) *The Sacred Books of Confucius, and other Confucian Classics,* University Books, 1965; (with Winberg Chai) *The Humanist Way in Ancient China,* Bantam, 1965; (editor and translator with Winberg Chai) *A Treasury of Chinese Literature: A New Prose Anthology,* Appleton, 1965; (editor) *Li Chi: Book of Rites,* two volumes, University Books, 1967; *Confucianism,* Barron's Educational Services, 1971.

In English and Chinese: (Co-editor) *Essential Idioms in English,* two volumes, Renaissance Book Co., 1954, 2nd edition, 1958; (co-editor) *English Reader,* six volumes, Cheng Chung Book Co., 1955; (co-editor) *The New English Course for Senior High Schools,* six volumes, Renaissance Book Co., 1955, revised edition, 1959.

In Chinese: *Comparative Commentaries on Private International Law,* Cheng Chung Book Co., 1945, revised edition, 1959; *Politics and Diplomacy of Modern Europe,* Commercial Press (Shanghai), 1946, 2nd edition, 1948; (translator) Huntington Cairns, *The Theory of Legal Science,* Taiwan University Law College, 1953.

Contributor of articles on Chinese art, culture, and philosophy, and of legal and political studies to *Free China Review, Social Research,* and other periodicals in United States, China, Taiwan, and Hong Kong.

WORK IN PROGRESS: History of Chinese Art and Culture, in English and Chinese; with Winberg Chai, *Chinese Political Thought* and *Documentary History of the Modern Far East.*

AVOCATIONAL INTERESTS: Collecting Oriental art.

*   *   *

CHAMBERS, M(erritt) M(adison) 1899-

PERSONAL: Born January 26, 1899, in Mount Vernon, Ohio; son of Rufus Ward and Etta Amelia (Miller) Chambers. *Education:* Studied at University of Florida and Harvard University, 1920; Ohio Wesleyan University, B.A., 1922; Ohio State University, M.A., 1927, Ph.D., 1931; University of Washington, Seattle, post-graduate student, 1928. *Office:* Department of Educational Administration, Illinois State University, Normal, Ill. 61761.

CAREER: Teacher of political science at University of North Dakota, Grand Forks, 1926-27, Oregon State University, Corvallis, 1927-30, of social sciences at Teachers

College of Kansas City, Kansas City, Mo., 1931-32; Carnegie Foundation in cooperation with Purdue University, writer on higher education, 1932-34; Brookings Institution, Washington, D.C., researcher on higher education, 1934-35; American Council on Education, Washington, D.C., writer on higher education, 1935-51; Lafayette Farms, Mount Vernon, Ohio, owner-operator, 1951-58; University of Michigan, Ann Arbor, professor of higher education, 1958-63; Indiana University, Bloomington, professor of higher education, 1963-69; Illinois State University, Normal, professor of higher education, 1969—. Michigan Council of State College Presidents, executive director, 1961-62. Consultant on higher education to five states, 1949-50, U.S. Office of Education, 1952-53, Milton Eisenhower's Committee on Government and Higher Education, 1957, New York City, 1961, Kentucky, 1962, 1965-66, Maryland, 1963, Michigan, Iowa, and Southern Illinois University, 1966. Ohio Farm Bureau Federation, president of Knox County Farm Bureau, Inc., 1957-58. *Military service:* U.S. Army Air Forces, 1942-46; became major; received Army Commendation Ribbon.

MEMBER: American Association for the Advancement of Science (fellow), National Education Association (life), American Association of School Administrators, National Organization for Legal Problems of Education, American Educational Research Association, Association for Higher Education, American Association of University Professors, American Society for Public Administration. *Awards, honors:* Fellow in educational administration, Ohio State University, 1930-32; Doctor of Letters, Eastern Kentucky University, 1969; annual honor award, National Organization for Legal Problems of Education, 1970.

WRITINGS: "Every Man a Brick!": The Status of Military Training in American Universities, Public School Publishing Co., 1927; (editor) *The Yearbook of School Law: A Narrative Topical Summary of Decisions of the Higher Courts in All States of the United States,* ten volumes, American Council on Education, 1933-42; (editor with Edward Charles Elliott) *Charters and Basic Laws of Selected American Universities and Colleges,* Carnegie Foundation for Advancement of Teaching, 1934; (with Elliott and W.A. Ashbrook) *Government of Higher Education: Designed for the Use of University and College Trustees,* American Book Co., 1935; (with Ervin Eugene Lewis) *New Frontiers of Democracy: The Story of America in Transition,* American Education Press, 1935; *Some Features of State Educational-Administrative Organization,* American Council on Education, 1936; (with Elliott) *The Colleges and the Courts: Judicial Decisions Regarding Institutions of Higher Education in the United States,* Carnegie Foundation for Advancement of Teaching, 1936, sole author of five supplementary volumes, Carnegie Foundation for Advancement of Teaching, 1941, 1946, Columbia University Press, 1952, Interstate, 1964, 1967; *Youth-Serving Organizations: National Nongovernmental Associations,* American Council on Education, 1937, 3rd edition, 1948; (with H.P. Rainey and others) *How Fare American Youth,* American Council on Education, 1938; (with Louise Arnold Menefee) *American Youth: An Annotated Bibliography,* American Council on Education, 1938; (with Howard M. Bell) *How to Make a Community Youth Survey,* American Council on Education, c.1938.

The Community and Its Young People, American Council on Education, 1940; *Looking Ahead with Youth: A Study Guide for Use with the General Report of the American Youth Commission,* American Council on Education, 1942; *Opinions on Gains for American Education from Wartime Armed Services Training,* American Council on Education, 1946; *Charters of Philanthropies: A Study of Selected Trust Instruments, Charters, By-laws,*

and Court Decisions, Carnegie Foundation for the Advancement of Teaching, 1948; (with Elaine Exton) *Youth, Key to America's Future: An Annotated Bibliography,* American Council on Education, 1949; (editor) *Universities of the World Outside U.S.A.,* American Council on Education, 1950.

The Campus and the People: Organization, Support, and Control of Higher Education in the United States in the Nineteen Sixties, Interstate, 1960; *Voluntary Statewide Coordination in Public Higher Education,* University of Michigan, 1961; *Chance and Choice in Higher Education,* Interstate, 1962; *Appropriation of State Tax Funds for Operating Expenses of Higher Education, 1961-62,* Joint Office of Institutional Research (Washington), 1962; *Appropriation of State Tax Funds for Operating Expenses of Higher Education, 1962-63,* Joint Office of Institutional Research, c.1962; (with Thomas G. Pullen, Jr. and Broadus E. Sawyer) *The Future of Kentucky State College: A Report,* Kentucky Council on Public Higher Education, 1962; *Financing Higher Education,* Center for Applied Research in Education (Washington), 1963; *State Appropriations of State Tax Funds for Operating Expenses for Publicly-Supported Institutions of Higher Learning,* Virginia State Council of Higher Education, 1964; *Freedom and Repression in Higher Education,* Bloomcraft, 1965; *Appropriations of State Tax Funds for Operating Expenses of Higher Education, 1964-65,* National Association of State Universities and Land Grant Colleges, c.1965; *A Brief Bibliography of Higher Education in the Middle Nineteen Sixties,* Bureau of Educational Studies and Testing, Indiana University, 1966; (with Harry Kenneth Newburn) *Higher Education in Arizona,* Arizona State University, 1967; *Nine Years of Grapevine: State Tax Support of Higher Education in the Fifty States, 1959-1968,* Student Association for Higher Education of Indiana University, 1968; *Higher Education: Who Pays?, Who Gains?: Financing Education Beyond High School,* Interstate, 1968; *A Record of Progress: Ten Years of State Tax Support of Higher Education 1959-60 through 1968-69,* Interstate, 1969; *Higher Education in the Fifty States,* Interstate, 1970; (with Frank Robert Paulsen and others) *Higher Education: Dimensions and Directions,* University of Arizona Press, 1970; *Above High School,* Interstate, 1970; *Record of Progress: Three Years of State Tax Support of Higher Education 1969-70 through 1971-72,* Interstate, 1972.

Contributor to *Social Work Yearbook,* 1939, 1941, *Encyclopedia of Educational Research,* 1950, and *Macmillan Encyclopedia of Education,* 1970; contributor of some three hundred articles to forty educational journals.

WORK IN PROGRESS: The Developing Law of the Student and His College, for Interstate; continuing research and writing on administration and financing of higher education.

BIOGRAPHICAL/CRITICAL SOURCES: Saturday Review, April 17, 1971.

* * *

CHAMBERS, Margaret Ada Eastwood 1911-
(Peggy Chambers)

PERSONAL: Born August 13, 1911, in Long Eaton, Derbyshire, England; daughter of Henry (a schoolmaster) and Mary Ellen (Eastwood) Chambers. *Education:* Attended high school in Nottingham, England. *Home:* 316 Derby Rd., Nottingham, England. *Agent:* David Higham Associates Ltd., 5-8 Lower John St., Golden Square, London WIR 3PE, England.

MEMBER: Society of Women Writers and Journalists, Nottingham Writers' Club.

*WRITINGS—*All under name Peggy Chambers: *Women and the World Today* (short biographies), Forbes Robertson, 1954; *Great Company* (short biographies), Bodley Head, 1954; *They Fought for Children* (short biographies), Bodley Head, 1956; *A Doctor Alone* (biography), Bodley Head, 1956, Abelard, 1958; *Six Great Christians* (short biographies), Hamish Hamilton, 1958; *The Governess* (novel), Bodley Head, 1960. Contributor to *Nottingham Journal, Woman's Magazine, Children's Book of Great Lives, Young Opinion,* and to *Collier's Encyclopedia.*

WORK IN PROGRESS: A novel on Lady Jane Grey (1537-1554).

*   *   *

CHAMBERS, Mortimer Hardin, Jr. 1927-

PERSONAL: Born January 9, 1927, in Saginaw, Mich.; son of Mortimer Hardin (a businessman) and Nell (Bishop) Chambers; married Gail Hamilton, June 11, 1949; children: Pamela, Julia, Blake. *Education:* Harvard University, A.B., 1949, Ph.D., 1954; Wadham College, Oxford, M.A., 1955. *Home:* 2122 Selby Ave., Los Angeles, Calif. 90025. *Office:* Department of History, University of California, Los Angeles, Calif. 90024.

CAREER: Harvard University, Cambridge, Mass., instructor in classics, 1954-55; University of Chicago, Chicego, Ill., assistant professor of ancient history, 1955-58; University of California, Los Angeles, 1958—, began as assistant professor, now professor of ancient history. *Military service:* U.S. Army, 1945-46; became sergeant. *Member:* American Historical Association, American Philological Association.

WRITINGS: (With James Day) *Aristotle's History of Athenian Democracy,* University of California Press, 1962; (editor) *The Fall of Rome: Can It Be Explained?,* Holt, 1963, 2nd edition, 1970; (translator) Polybius, *The Histories,* edited by E. Badian, Washington Square Press, 1966, revised edition, Twayne, 1967. Contributor of articles to journals.

*   *   *

CHANDLER, Alfred D(upont), Jr. 1918-

PERSONAL: Born September 15, 1918, in Guyencourt, Del.; son of Alfred DuPont and Carol (Ramsáy) Chandler; married Fay Martin, January 8, 1944; children: Alpine Douglas, Mary Morris, Alfred D. III, Howard Martin. *Education:* Harvard University, A.B., 1940, M.A., 1947, Ph.D., 1952; University of North Carolina, M.A., 1951. *Home:* 1010 Memorial Dr., Cambridge, Mass. 02138. *Office:* 207 Morgan Hall, Graduate School of Business Administration, Harvard University, Boston, Mass. 02163.

CAREER: Massachusetts Institute of Technology, Cambridge, research associate, 1950-51, instructor, 1951-53, assistant professor, 1953-58, associate professor, 1958-62, professor of history, 1962-63; Harvard University, Cambridge, Mass., research fellow, 1953; Johns Hopkins University, Baltimore, Md., professor of history, 1963-71, chairman of the department, 1966-70; Graduate School of Business Administration, Harvard University, Straus Professor of Business History, 1971—. Ford Distinguished Visiting Professor, Harvard University, 1970-71. Chairman, Advisory Historical Committee, U.S. Atomic Energy Commission, 1969—; member, National Advisory Council on Education Professions Development, 1970—. Consultant, U.S. Naval War College, 1954. Park School, Brookline, Mass., trustee, 1957-63, 1965-69, chairman, 1961-63; Brookline Public Library, trustee, 1959-63 trustee, Johns Hopkins University, 1966-70. *Military service:* U.S. Navy, 1941-45; became lieutenant commander; awarded Commendation Ribbon. *Member:* American Historical Association, Organization of American Historians (member of executive board, 1969-72), Economic History Association (trustee, 1966-70, president-elect, 1970, presi-

dent, 1971-72), American Academy of Arts and Sciences, Association for Higher Education (executive committee, 1962-63), Guana Island Club (Virgin Islands), Harvard Club (New York), Nantucket Yacht Club (governor, 1963-66), St. Botolphs Club. *Awards, honors:* Guggenheim fellow, 1958-59; Thomas Newcomen Award, 1964, for *Strategy and Structure.*

WRITINGS: (Assistant editor) *Letters of Theodore Roosevelt,* four volumes, Harvard University, 1952-54; *Henry Varnum Poor: Business Editor, Analyst and Reformer,* Harvard University Press, 1956; *Strategy and Structure: Chapters in the History of the Industrial Enterprise,* M.I.T. Press, 1963; (editor) *Giant Enterprise: Ford, General Motors, and the Automobile Industry,* Harcourt, 1964; (editor) *The Railroads: The Nation's First Big Business: Sources and Readings,* Harcourt, 1965; (editor with Stuart Bruchey and Louis Galambos) *The Changing Economic Order: Readings in American Business and Economic History,* Harcourt, 1968; (editor) *The Papers of Dwight David Eisenhower: The War Years,* five volumes, Johns Hopkins Press, 1970; (with Stephen Salsbury) *Pierre S. Du Pont and the Making of the Modern Corporation,* Harper, 1971; *The New American State Papers,* nine volumes, Scholarly Research, 1972. General editor, "Forces in Economic Growth" series, Harcourt, 1963—. Member of editorial board, *Business History Review,* 1954-60, *Explorations in Entreprenurial History,* 1963-70.

WORK IN PROGRESS: A history of American business enterprise.

*   *   *

CHANDLER, George 1915-

PERSONAL: Born July 2, 1915, in Birmingham, England; married Dorothy Lowe; children: Malcolm George. *Education:* University of London, F.L.A., 1935, B.A., 1939, M.A., 1946, Ph.D., 1951. *Home:* 23 Dowesfield Lane, Liverpool 18, England. *Office:* Central Libraries, William Brown St., Liverpool 3, England.

CAREER: Public Library, Dudley, England, borough librarian, 1947-49; Public Library, Liverpool, England, deputy city librarian, 1950-52, city librarian, 1952—. Member, Library Advisory Council, 1966—. Extra-mural lecturer for Universities of Birmingham, Leeds, and Liverpool, and for the Foreign Office. Director, Technical Information Center, Liverpool. Honorary secretary, Liverpool and District Scientific Industrial and Research Library Advisory Council. *Member:* International Association of Metropolitan City Libraries (president, 1968-71), Library Association (chairman of executive committee, 1966-70, president, 1971), Royal Historical Society (fellow), Society of Municipal and County Chief Librarians (former secretary; president), Historic Society of Lancashire and Cheshire (honorary librarian), Athenaeum Club (Liverpool). *Awards, honors:* Cross of Cavaliere dell' Ordine "Al Meitor Della Republica Italiana."

WRITINGS: *Dudley,* Batsford, 1949; *William Roscoe,* Batsford, 1956; *Liverpool, 1207-1957,* Batsford, 1957; *Liverpool Shipping: A Short History,* Phoenix House, 1960; *Liverpool Under James I,* Brown, Picton, & Hornby, 1960; *How to Find Out: A Guide to Sources of Information for All,* Macmillan, 1963, 3rd edition, Pergamon, 1968; *Four Centuries of Banking,* Batsford, Volume I, 1964, Volume II, 1968; *Libraries in the Modern World,* Pergamon, 1965; *Liverpool Under Charles I,* Picton & Hornby Libraries, 1965; *How to Find Out About Literature,* Pergamon, 1968; *Libraries in the East: An International and Comparative Study,* Seminar Press, 1971. Contributor of articles on literary and historical topics to *Times Literary Supplement, Listener,* and to library journals; writer of catalogues and articles on International

Library. General editor, "International Series of Monographs on Libraries and Information Science" and series on the "Library and Information Division of the Commonwealth and International Library," published by Pergamon.

* * *

CHANG-RODRIGUEZ, Eugenio 1924-

PERSONAL: Born November 15, 1924, in Trujillo, Peru; son of Enrique and Peregrina (Rodriguez) Chang. Education: University of San Marcos, Ph.B., 1946; William Penn College, B.A., 1949; University of Arizona, M.S., 1950; University of Washington, Seattle, M.A., 1952, Ph.D., 1956. Home: 116 Pinehurst Ave., New York, N.Y. 10033. Office: Department of Romance Languages, Queens College, City University of New York, Flushing, N.Y. 11367.

CAREER: La Tribuna, Lima, Peru, foreign correspondent, 1946-48; University of Washington, Seattle, instructor in Spanish and assistant to dean of College of Arts and Sciences, 1950-56; University of Pennsylvania, Philadelphia, assistant professor of Romance languages and literatures, 1956-61; Queens College of the City University of New York, Flushing, N.Y., assistant professor, 1961-64, associate professor of Romance languages and literature, 1964—. University of Southern California, visiting summer professor, 1950, 1961, 1962; lecturer at Columbia University, Barnard College, other universities. Member: International League for the Rights of Man (council president, 1970—), International Linguistic Association (president, 1969—), Modern Language Association of America, United Nations Correspondents Association, American Association of Teachers of Spanish and Portuguese (chapter president, 1954-56), Hispanic Institute, Instituto Internacional de Literatura Iberoamericana, Academy of Political Science, Linguistic Circle of New York, Foreign Correspondents Association, American Association of University Professors, Overseas Press Club, Phi Sigma Iota, Sigma Delta Pi.

WRITINGS: Literatura Politica de Gonzalez Prada, Mariategui y Haya, Studium, 1957; (editor with H. Kantor) La America Latina de Hoy (anthology), Ronald, 1961; (with Alphonse G. Juilland) Frequency Dictionary of Spanish Words, Humanities, 1965; (with L. Poston and others) Continuing Spanish, five volumes, American Book Co., 1969; The Lingering Crisis: A Case Study of the Dominican Republic, Las Americas, 1969. Associate editor, Hispania.

WORK IN PROGRESS: Fundamental Dictionary of Spanish; The Structure of the Spanish Grammar (Lexical, Sintactical, and Phonological), three volumes; Indoamerica: Its Civilization and Culture.

AVOCATIONAL · INTERESTS: Fencing, swimming, skiing, horseback riding.

BIOGRAPHICAL/CRITICAL SOURCES: Seattle Times, June 12, 1952, October 7, 1952; Seattle Post-Intelligencer, August 19, 1953; La Prensa, September 11, 1956; Peruvian Times, September 28, 1956; Denver Post, August 24, 1961.

* * *

CHAPMAN, Brian 1923-

PERSONAL: Born April 6, 1923, in London, England; son of Berthold Parry (a postmaster) and Mable Alice (Lewis) Chapman; children: Alexander Brian, Paul Martin. Education: Magdalen College, Oxford, B.A., M.A., 1947; Nuffield College, Oxford, D. Phil., 1950. Home and office: University of Manchester, Manchester, England.

CAREER: Research associate, lecturer, and professor of political science, 1949-60; University of Manchester, Manchester, England, professor of government, 1961—.

Military service: Royal Navy, 1941-45; became lieutenant.

WRITINGS: French Local Government, Allen & Unwin, 1952; Prefects of Provincial France, Allen & Unwin, 1954; (contributor) Great Cities of the World, Allen & Unwin, 1955; (with wife, J.M. Chapman) The Life and Times of Baron Haussmann, Weidenfeld & Nicolson, 1956; The Profession of Government: The Public Service in Europe, Allen & Unwin, 1959, Humanities, 1970; British Government Observed: Some European Reflections, Allen & Unwin, 1963; Future of Government (pamphlet), Conservative Political Centre, 1968; The Police State, Praeger, 1970. Editor, Allen & Unwin's "Minerva Series." Contributor to Guardian, Sunday Times, and political science journals.

WORK IN PROGRESS: The Auchinlock Papers.

SIDELIGHTS: Chapman's books have been translated into French and Spanish.

* * *

CHAPMAN, Hester W (olferstan) 1899-

PERSONAL: Born November 26, 1899, in London, England; daughter of T. and E. (Thomas) Pellatt; married N.K. Chapman, 1926 (deceased); married R.L. Griffin, 1938 (deceased). Education: Privately educated. Home: 13 Conway St., London W.1, England. Agent: Hughes Massie, 18 Southampton Pl., London W.C., England.

CAREER: Writer. Mannequin in Paris, France, in early years, then, intermittently, telephone operator, secretary, governess, and schoolmistress, in London, England. During World War II worked for Fighting French and American Red Cross.

WRITINGS: She Saw Them Go By (novel), Houghton, 1933; To Be a King: A Tale of Adventure, Gollancz, 1934; Long Division (novel), Secker & Warburg, 1943; I Will Be Good (novel), Secker & Warburg, 1945, Houghton, 1946; (editor with Princess Romanovsky-Pavlovsky) Diversion, introduction by Rebecca West, Collins, 1946; Worlds Apart (novel), Secker & Warburg, 1947; Great Villiers: A Study of George Villiers, Second Duke of Buckingham, 1628-1687, Secker & Warburg, 1949; Ivor Novello's King's Rhapsody (novel based on the musical romance by Novello), Harrap, 1950, published in America as King's Rhapsody, Houghton, 1951; Ever Thine (novel), J. Cape, 1951; Mary II, Queen of England (biography), J. Cape, 1953; Falling Stream (novel), J. Cape, 1954; Queen Anne's Son: A Memoir of William Henry, Duke of Gloucester, 1689-1700, Deutsch, 1954; The Stone Lily (novel), J. Cape, 1957; The Last Tudor King: A Study of Edward VI, October 12th, 1537-July 6th, 1553, J. Cape, 1958, Macmillan, 1959; Two Tudor Portraits: Henry Howard, Earl of Surrey, and Lady Katherine Grey, J. Cape, 1960, Little, Brown, 1963; Eugenie (novel), Little, Brown, 1961; Lady Jane Grey, October, 1537-February, 1554, J. Cape, 1962, Little, Brown, 1963; The Tragedy of Charles II in the Years 1630-1660, Little, Brown, 1964; Lucy, J. Cape, 1965; Privileged Persons: Four Seventeenth-Century Studies (includes biographies of Louis XIII, Electress Sophia, Hortense Mancini, Duchess Mazarin, and Thomas Bruce, Earl of Ailesbury), Reynal, 1966; Fear No More (historical novel), Reynal, 1968; The Sisters of Henry VIII: Margaret Tudor, Queen of Scotland (November, 1489-October, 1541), Mary Tudor, Queen of France and Duchess of Suffolk (March, 1496-June, 1533), J. Cape, 1968, published in America as The Thistle and the Rose, Coward, 1971; Caroline Matilda, Queen of Denmark, 1751-1775, J. Cape, 1971, Coward, 1972; Limmerston Hall, Coward, 1972.

AVOCATIONAL INTERESTS: Theatre, interior decorating, travel.

BIOGRAPHICAL/CRITICAL SOURCES: New Statesman, May 5, 1967; National Review, May 30, 1967;
Punch, September 25, 1968; Books and Bookmen, August,
1969; Preston Slosson, Detroit News, May 28, 1972.

* * *

CHARLES, Don C(laude)   1918-

PERSONAL: Born April 22, 1918; son of Claude C. and
Helen D. (Miller) Charles; married Anne Palmer Mal-
lonee, August 12, 1947; children: Linda, Christopher,
Laura, Andrew. Education: State College of Iowa, B.A.,
1941; University of Nebraska, M.A., 1947, Ph.D., 1951.
Politics: Democrat. Religion: Lutheran. Home: Wood-
view, Route 3, Ames, Iowa 50010. Office: Old Botany
Hall, Iowa State University, Ames, Iowa 50010.

CAREER: University of Nebraska, Lincoln, guidance
consultant and counselor, 1948-51; Iowa State University
of Science and Technology, Ames, assistant professor,
1951-55, associate professor, 1955-59, professor of psychology, 1959—, acting head of honors program, 1970—.
Military service: U.S. Army, 1942-46; became first lieutenant; received Bronze Star Medal. Member: American
Psychological Association (fellow), Gerontological Society (fellow), Midwestern Psychological Association, Iowa
Psychological Association.

WRITINGS: Getting Along with Others, Keystone Education Press, 1957; (with Warren R. Baller) The Psychology of Human Growth and Development, Holt, 1962, 2nd
edition, 1968; Psychology of the Child in the Classroom,
Macmillan, 1964; (contributor) L.R. Goulet and Paul B.
Baltes, editors, Life Span Developmental Psychology: Research and Theory, Academic Press, 1970.

* * *

CHARLES, Searle F(ranklin)   1923-

PERSONAL: Born May 6, 1923, in Lyons, Ohio; son of
Thurman P. (a teacher) and Roxie Ellen (Allman)
Charles; married Barbara A. Yount, June 3, 1944; children: Donald, Lyn Ellen, Judith, Janne. Education: Butler University, B.S., 1946; University of Wisconsin, M.S.,
1947; University of Illinois, Ph.D., 1953. Religion: Protestant. Home address: R.F.D. 2, Willimantic, Conn.
06226. Office: 1 Niles St., Hartford, Conn. 06105.

CAREER: Butler University, Indianapolis, Ind., instructor in history, 1947-49; New York (N.Y.) public schools,
teacher, 1951-53; Fairmont State College, Fairmont, W.
Va., assistant professor of history, 1953-54; Flint Junior
College, Flint, Mich., instructor in history, 1954-56, assistant dean, 1957-62; Willimantic State College, Willimantic, Conn., dean of the college, 1962-66; Eastern Connecticut State College, Willimantic, president of the college,
1966-69; Regional Community College of Connecticut,
Hartford, executive secretary, 1970—. United Churchmen
Council, Flint, Mich., member, 1959-61. Military service:
U.S. Army, 1943-44. Member: National Education Association, American Association of University Professors,
Phi Beta Kappa, Kappa Delta Pi.

WRITINGS: Minister of Relief: Harry Hopkins and the
Depression, Syracuse University Press, 1963.

WORK IN PROGRESS: Biography of Harry L.
Hopkins; a history of the New Deal.

AVOCATIONAL INTERESTS: Travel, sports, reading
in the recent American historical period.

* * *

CHARLESWORTH, James Clyde   1900-1974

PERSONAL: Born May 21, 1900, in Westmoreland
County, Pa.; son of James and Priscilla (Hawkins)
Charlesworth; married Dorothy Louise Coy, August 14,

1928 (died 1945); married Berenice Lucille Steward,
July 6, 1946; children:˜ (first marriage) Audrey Elaine
Charlesworth Kingsley, Sylvia Jean Charlesworth Schafer;
(second marriage) Pamela Steward, Rodney J. Educa-
tion: Carnegie Institute of Technology, student, 1919-23,
University of Pittsburgh, A.B., 1926, A.M., 1927, Ph.D.,
1932; Harvard University, postgraduate study, 1938. Pol-
itics: Non-partisan. Religion: Episcopalian. Home: 7125
Penarth Ave., Upper Darby, Pa. 19082. Office: American
Academy of Political and Social Science, 3937 Chestnut
St., Philadelphia, Pa. 19104.

CAREER: Miller Machinery Co., Pittsburgh, Pa., assistant chief engineer, 1922-24; University of Pittsburgh,
Pittsburgh, Pa., instructor, 1927-33, assistant professor,
1933-35, associate professor of political science, 1935-39;
University of Pennsylvania, Philadelphia, associate professor, 1939-45, professor of political science, 1945-70, director of graduate division of Wharton School, 1942-43. Institute of Local and State Government, supervisor of educational program, 1939-55; Commonwealth of Pennsylvania, Harrisburg, secretary of administration, 1955-56;
Pennsylvania Reorganization Commission, executive director, 1956. Trustee, National Parks Association; member
of national council, United World Federalists. Military
service: U.S. Army, 1943-46; chief of management planning branch, Adjutant General's Office, 1944-46; became
lieutenant colonel; awarded Legion of Merit and Army
Commendation Ribbon. Member: American Academy of
Political and Social Science (president, 1953-70), American
Political Science Association, American Society for Public
Administration (president of Philadelphia region, 1947-
49), Southern Political Science Association, Western Political Science Association, Phi Beta Kappa, Pi Sigma Alpha, Pi Gamma Mu, Franklin Inn Club.

WRITINGS: Governmental Administration, Harper,
1951; Governmental Reorganization, State of Pennyslva-
nia, 1956; (editor and contributor) Contemporary Political Analysis, Free Press, 1967.

Editor—All published by American Academy of Political
and Social Science: (With others) Ethical Standards in
American Political Life, 1952, Meaning of the 1952 Presidential Election, 1952, America and a New Asia, 1954,
Bureaucracy and Democratic Government, 1954, The Future of the Western Alliance, 1957, Asia and Future
World Leadership, 1958, American Civilization and Its
Leadership Needs, 1960-1990, 1959, Resolving the Rus-
sian-American Deadlock, 1959, Whither American For-
eign Policy?, 1960, Is International Communism Win-
ning?, 1961, American Foreign Policy Challenged, 1962,
The Limits of Behavioralism in Political Science, 1962,
(with Stephen B. Sweeney) Achieving Excellence in Pub-
lic Service, 1963, Mathematics and the Social Sciences:
The Utility and Inutility of Mathematics in the Study of
Economics, Political Science, and Sociology, 1963, The
New Europe: Implications for the United States, 1963,
Leisure in America: Blessing or Curse?, 1964, Africa in
Motion, 1964, Latin America Tomorrow, 1965, Ethics in
America: Norms and Deviations, 1966, American Civili-
zation: Its Influence on Our Foreign Policy, 1966, A Design for Political Science: Scope, Objectives, and Methods, 1966, Governing Urban Society, 1967, Realignments
in the Communist and Western Worlds, 1967, The Changing American People: Are We Deteriorating or Improving?, 1968, Theory and Practice of Public Administration: Scope, Objectives, and Methods, 1968, America's
Changing Role as a World Leader, 1969, New American
Posture Toward Asia, 1970; (with Alfred J. Eggers, Jr.)
Harmonizing Technological Developments and Social Policy in America, 1970, Integration of the Social Sciences
through Policy Analysis, 1972.

Associate editor, Annals of the American Academy of
Political and Social Science, 1949-53, acting editor, 1950-

51. Contributor of articles on public administration, state and local government, and political theory to professional journals.

(Died January 23, 1974)

* * *

CHARNEY, Maurice (Myron) 1929-

PERSONAL: Born January 18, 1929, in New York, N.Y.; son of A. Benjamin (a business executive) and Sadie A. (Stang) Charney; married Hanna Kurz (a professor of French), June 20, 1954; children: Leopold Joseph, Paul Robert. *Education:* Harvard University, A.B. (magna cum laude), 1949; Princeton University, M.A., 1951, Ph.D., 1952. *Home:* 168 West 86th St., New York, N.Y. 10024. *Office:* English Department, Rutgers University, New Brunswick, N.J. 08903.

CAREER: Hunter College (now Hunter College of the City University of New York), New York, N.Y., instructor in English, 1953-54; Rutgers University, New Brunswick, N.J., instructor, 1956-59, assistant professor, 1959-62, associate professor, 1962-67, professor of English, 1967—. Fulbright exchange professor at University of Bordeaux and University of Nancy, 1960-61; visiting summer professor at Hunter College, 1963, Harvard University, 1965, Shakespeare Institute of Canada, 1969, Shakespeare Institute of America, 1970. *Military service:* U.S. Army, 1954-56. *Member:* Modern Language Association of America, Shakespeare Association of America, Malone Society, Renaissance Society of America, American Association of University Professors, Phi Beta Kappa.

WRITINGS: Shakespeare's Roman Plays, Harvard University Press, 1961; (editor and author of introduction) *Discussions of Shakespeare's Roman Plays,* Heath, 1964; (editor) Shakespeare, *Timon of Athens,* Signet, 1965; (editor) *The Tragedy of "Julius Caesar,"* Bobbs-Merrill, 1969; *Style in "Hamlet,"* Princeton University Press, 1969; *How to Read Shakespeare,* McGraw, 1971. Contributor of articles and reviews on literary subjects to fifteen journals.

WORK IN PROGRESS: Elizabethan Dramatic Form, for Northwestern University Press; *Shakespeare and His Contemporaries,* for Hutchinson University Library.

* * *

CHARTERS, Samuel (Barclay) 1929-

PERSONAL: Born August 1, 1929, in Pittsburgh, Pa.; son of Samuel and Lillian (Kelley) Charters; married Ann Danberg, March 12, 1959. *Education:* Sacramento City College, A.A., 1949; attended Tulane University, 1954; University of California, Berkeley, A.B., 1956.

CAREER: Folkways Records, New York, N.Y., recording director, 1956-63; Prestige Records, Bergenfield, N.J., recording director, 1963—. *Military service:* U.S. Army, 1951-53.

WRITINGS: Jazz: New Orleans, 1885-1957, W.C. Allen, 1958, revised edition, Oak, 1963; *The Country Blues,* Rinehart, 1959; *8 Poems in the Imagist Manner,* Tunnel Town Press, 1960; (with Leonard Kunstadt) *Jazz: A History of the New York Scene,* Doubleday, 1962; *The Poetry of the Blues,* Oak, 1963; *Heroes of the Prize Ring* (poems), Portents, c.1964; *Looking for Michael McClure at the Corner of Haight and Ashbury,* privately printed, c.1967; *Days; or, Days as Thoughts in a Season's Uncertainties* (poems), Oyez, 1967; *The Bluesmen: The Story and the Music of the Men Who Made the Blues,* Oak, 1967; *Some Poems Against the War,* Portents, c.1968; *Some Poems and Some Poets,* Oyez, 1971; (author of introduction) *Country Joe and the Fish: The Life, The Times, and the Songs,* Quick Fox, 1971.

WORK IN PROGRESS: The Jug Band Book, for Holzman; *The Music of the Bahamas,* for Oak.

SIDELIGHTS: Jack Hirschman describes Charters' poetry as "evoked through a density of notations involving person, place, thing: language fricatives, textures struggling with and against one another like branches of New England trees in the beginning of winter. Basically a nature poet, and romantical, Charters desires to memorialize his moments, has more a sense of the poem as heraldic or remembered image, is closer to the history of the earth's turnings. At the same time, his notation strikes toward a mingle of England and Japan, haiku dropping out of his interestingly predestined and suddenly taut stanzas."

Charters has done much of his research for his books on music in field, with documentary recording in the American South, British Isles, Mexico, and the Bahamas.

BIOGRAPHICAL/CRITICAL SOURCES: Poetry, July, 1968.

* * *

CHASE, Harold W (illiam) 1922-

PERSONAL: Born February 6, 1922, in Worcester, Mass.; son of Louis and Bessie (Lubin) Chase; married Bernice M. Fadden, July 3, 1944; children: Bryce S., Eric L. *Education:* Phillips Academy at Andover, student, 1937-39; Princeton University, A.B., 1943, M.A., 1948, Ph.D., 1956. *Home:* 124 Bedford St., Minneapolis, Minn. 55414.

CAREER: University of Delaware, Newark, assistant professor of political science, 1948-50; Princeton University, Princeton, N.J., assistant professor of political science, 1952-57; University of Minnesota, Minneapolis, associate professor, 1957-60, professor of political science, 1960—. Visiting professor, Columbia University, 1963-64, National War College, 1965-66, University of Chicago, 1966-67. Charles Scribner's Sons, advisory editor in political science. *Military service:* U.S. Marine Corps Reserve, active duty, 1943-46, 1950-52, 1968-69; became colonel; wounded on Iwo Jima; received Purple Heart and Legion of Merit. *Member:* American Political Science Association, Midwest Political Science Association. *Awards, honors:* Distinguished teaching award, University of Minnesota, 1961.

WRITINGS: Security and Liberty, Doubleday, 1955; (with Paul Dolan) *The Case for Democratic Capitalism,* Crowell, 1964; (editor with G.T. Mitau) *Proximate Solutions: Case Problems in State and Local Government,* Scribner, 1964; (editor with Mitau) *Insoluble Problems,* Scribner, 1964; *Federal Judges: The Appointing Process,* Brookings Institution, c.1964; text edition, University of Minnesota Press, 1972; (editor with Allen H. Lerman) *John F. Kennedy and the Press,* introduction by Pierre Salinger, Crowell, 1965. Contributor to law journals.

* * *

CHAYEFSKY, Paddy 1923-

PERSONAL: Born Sidney Chayefsky, January 29, 1923, in New York, N.Y.; son of Harry (a milk company executive) and Gussie (Stuchevsky) Chayefsky; married Susan Sackler, February 24, 1949; children: Dan. *Education:* College of the City of New York (now City College of the City University of New York), B.S.S., 1943; attended Fordham University. *Politics:* Uncommitted. *Religion:* Jewish. *Agent:* Maurice Spanbock, Esq., 10 East 40th St., New York, N.Y. 10016. *Office:* 850 Seventh Ave., New York, N.Y. 10019.

CAREER: Worked in print shop upon return from military service; writer of television dramas and plays, 1952—; Sudan Corp., New York, N.Y., president, 1956—; Carnegie Productions, Inc., New York, N.Y., president, 1957—; S.P.D. Productions, New York, N.Y., president, 1959—; Paddy Chayefsky Foundation, New

York, N.Y., president, 1960—. *Military service:* U.S. Army, 1943-45; received Purple Heart. *Member:* P.E.N., Writers Guild, Screen Writers Guild, Screen Actors Guild, American Guild of Variety Artists, American Guild of Authors and Composers, Songwriters Protective Association, Dramatists Guild (member of council, 1962—), New Dramatists Committee (director). *Awards, honors:* Academy Award, 1955, Cannes Film Festival golden palm, 1955, Catholic award, 1955, New York Film Critics award, 1956, all for "Marty"; Critics' Prize at the Brussels Film Festival, 1958, for "The Goddess"; Academy Award, 1972, for "The Hospital"; awards from film festivals in Edinburgh and elsewhere.

WRITINGS—Television plays: "Holiday Song," produced on NBC network for Philco Television Playhouse, September 14, 1952; *Printer's Measure,* produced on NBC network for Goodyear Playhouse, April 26, 1953; *Marty* (produced on NBC network for Goodyear Playhouse, May 24, 1953), published in *The Lively Arts* (anthology), edited by R.E. Sheratsky and J.L. Reilly, Globe Book Co., 1964; "The Big Deal," produced on NBC network for Goodyear Playhouse, July 19, 1953; "The Bachelor Party," produced on NBC network for Goodyear Playhouse, October 11, 1953; "The Sixth Year," produced on NBC network for Philco Television Playhouse, November 20, 1953; "Catch My Boy on Sunday," produced on NBC network for Philco Television Playhouse, 1953; "The Mother," produced on NBC network for Philco Television Playhouse, April 4, 1954; "Middle of the Night," produced on NBC network for Philco Television Playhouse, September 19, 1954; "The Catered Affair," produced on NBC network for Goodyear Playhouse, May 22, 1955; *Television Plays* (six scripts), Simon & Schuster, 1955; "The Great American Hoax," produced on CBS network for 20th Century-Fox Hour, May 15, 1957; *Marty [and] Printer's Measure,* adapted by Warren Halliburton, McGraw, 1968. Has also written for the CBS series, "Suspense," 1952, and for "Manhunt," 1952.

Plays: *Middle of the Night* (three-act, originally written for television; first produced on Broadway at ANTA Theatre, February 8, 1956), Random House, 1957; *The Tenth Man* (three-act; first produced on Broadway at Booth Theatre, November 5, 1959), Random House, 1960; *Gideon* (two-act; first produced on Broadway at Plymouth Theatre, November 9, 1961), Samuel French (acting edition), 1961, Random House, 1962; *The Passion of Josef D.* (first produced on Broadway, under Chayefsky's direction, at Ethel Barrymore Theatre, February 11, 1964), Random House, 1964; *The Latent Heterosexual* (originally announced as "The Accountant's Tale; or The Case of the Latent Heterosexual"; first produced in Dallas at Dallas Theatre Centre, March 12, 1968; produced on the West End at Aldwych Theatre, September, 1968), originally published in *Esquire,* August, 1967, Random House, 1967. Also author of the book and lyrics for a G.I. musical comedy, "No T.O. for Love," 1943, and of a play, "Fifth from Garibaldi," neither published nor produced. Plays anthologized in *Four Contemporary American Plays,* edited by Bennett Cerf, Vintage, 1961, *Six American Plays for Today,* edited by Cerf, Modern Library, 1961, *Best American Plays: Fifth Series, 1957-1963,* edited by John Gassner, Crown, 1963, *Best Television Plays,* edited by Gore Vidal, Ballantine, 1965, *The Discovery of Drama,* edited by Thomas Sanders, Scott, Foresman, 1968, and other collections.

Screenplays: (Author of screen story) "As Young As You Feel," Fox, 1951; (and associate producer) "Marty" (based on his teleplay), United Artists, 1955; (and associate producer) *The Bachelor Party* (based on his teleplay), United Artists, 1957, screen version published by New American Library, 1957; *The Goddess,* Columbia, 1958, Simon & Schuster, 1958; "Middle of the Night" (based on his teleplay), Columbia, 1959; "The Americanization of Emily" (based on the novel by William Bradford Huie), M-G-M, 1964; (adaptor) "Paint Your Wagon" (based on the musical by Lerner and Loewe), Paramount, 1969; "The Hospital" (originally announced as "The Latent Humanitarian"), United Artists, 1971; "The Habakkuk Conspiracy," 1973. Contributor, during World War II, to an Army film, "The True Glory."

Adaptations for radio: "The Meanest Man in the World," "Tommy," "Over 21," all broadcast by Theatre Guild of the Air, 1951-52.

SIDELIGHTS: Critic Harriet Van Horne wrote in 1955 that "Chayefsky, in his own special way, is as important to television drama in the 1950's as Ibsen was to the stage in 1890's." Chayefsky began writing for radio; he then turned to television mystery shows and to such programs as "Goodyear TV Playhouse" and "Philco TV Playhouse."

As a result of his Broadway productions he has been widely hailed as one of America's best playwrights. Through realistic dialogue he explores urban middle-class life with humor and pathos. Of *Gideon,* Marya Mannes wrote: ". . . the best thing about *Gideon* as a whole is the evidence it supplies of the continuing growth of Chayefsky as a playwright. He has found fresh ways of saying things, and he is achieving a subtlety and lightness of touch that show an expanding sensibility and sophistication; he is moving ahead."

More recently, however, Chayefsky has become increasingly pessimistic about the future of the theatre in America. "At this point in our dehumanization," he wrote in 1969, "I don't think the destiny of Broadway really matters. The issue is not whether the legitimate theater can be maintained in midtown Manhattan but whether it can be maintained anywhere at all. . . . The purpose of any art form is to reveal to its audience some truth about their own lives, and very few people go to the theater for that any more. . . . I think Broadway as a legitimate theater is moribund because drama itself is fast becoming unnecessary. . . . Needless to say, this isn't going to stop playwrights from writing plays because that is our witness, our substance and satisfaction and because the last human identity still remains the artist's suspicion of beauty somewhere imminent in his own solitude."

Author of three Broadway smash hits, Chayefsky refused to put his latest play, "The Latent Heterosexual," on Broadway. He has commented on the "unreality" of the present situation in America. He told *Book World* that "credibility is one of the basic criteria of narrative. The function of the artist is to provide some insight into *why* things happen, *how* it came to be that way. It is precisely because the times are so absurd that literature can't afford to be." Chayefsky believes "that the time may be coming when the most significant drama. . .will come from television." After an absence of fifteen years, he tried to return to television with a series of one-hour dramas for CBS, which "never came to fruition." He told *CA* recently he is now "entirely concerned with the making of my own films"; "The Hospital" and "The Habakkuk Conspiracy" were the first two of these films.

A 90-minute television adaptation of *Gideon* by Robert Hartung was broadcast on the "Hallmark Hall of Fame" by the NBC network, March 26, 1971.

AVOCATIONAL INTERESTS: Chayefsky is "reasonably competent in German, fair in French," and enjoys travel, historical research, and antiquity.

BIOGRAPHICAL/CRITICAL SOURCES: Time, November 17, 1961, February 21, 1964; *Newsweek,*

November 20, 1961, February 24, 1964; *Reporter*, December 7, 1961; *Life*, December 15, 1961; *Theatre Arts*, January, 1962; *Saturday Review*, February 29, 1964; *Esquire*, August, 1967; *New York Times*, December 8, 1967, November 28, 1969; *Book World*, January 12, 1969; *Variety*, March 31, 1971, December 8, 1971.

*   *   *

CHEN, Philip S(tanley) 1903-

PERSONAL: Born August 17, 1903, in Shanghai, China; son of Kung Yung (a merchant) and Siu Ying (Chang) Chen; married Helen Feng; children: Philip, Jr., Helen Chung, John Edward, George D., Ruth Seet, Samuel M. *Education:* Emmanuel Missionary College, B.S., 1929; Michigan State University, M.S., 1931, Ph.D., 1933. *Religion:* Seventh-day Adventist. *Home:* 529 Mission Dr., Camarillo, Calif. 93010.

CAREER: Madison College, Madison, Tenn., professor of chemistry, 1933-38; Atlantic Union College, South Lancaster, Mass., professor of chemistry, 1938-70. *Member:* American Chemical Society, American Soybean Association, Sigma Xi.

WRITINGS: Syntans and Newer Methods of Tanning, Chemical Elements Publishing, 1950; *500 Syntan Patent Abstracts: 1911-1950*, Chemical Elements Publishing, 1950; *Soybeans for Health, Longevity, and Economy*, Chemical Elements Publishing, 1956; *Heart Disease—Cause, Prevention, and Recovery*, Chemical Elements Publishing, 1958; *A New Look at God*, Chemical Elements Publishing, 1962; *Chemistry: Inorganic, Organic, and Biological*, Barnes & Noble, 1968; *Mineral Balance in Eating for Health*, Rodale Books, 1969; *Handbook of Chemistry for High School Students*, Chemical Elements Publishing, 1972. Contributor of articles to chemical and religious journals.

WORK IN PROGRESS: A book on vegetarianism; a book dealing with science and religion.

SIDELIGHTS: Languages (in order of competence) are English, Chinese, Spanish, German, French, and Russian. *Avocational interests:* Photography and travel.

*   *   *

CHENEVIX TRENCH, Charles Pocklington 1914-

PERSONAL: Born June 29, 1914, in Simla, India; son of Richard Henry (in Indian political service) and May (Pocklington) Chenevix Trench; married Mary Elizabeth Kirkbride, October 4, 1954; children: Lucy, Georgia. *Education:* Attended Winchester College; Oxford University, B.A. *Politics:* Independent. *Religion:* Church of Ireland. *Home:* Lisnamoe House, Ballymackey, Nenagh, Tipperary, Ireland. *Agent:* Maurice Michael, 3-4 Fox Ct., London E.C. 1, England.

CAREER: Indian Army, Hodson's Horse, 1935-46; served with 8th Army in North Africa and Italy; became major; received Military Cross on battlefield, 1944. Indian Political Service, assistant political agent, 1946-47; Colonial Administrative Service, district commissioner in Kenya, 1948-64; schoolmaster, 1964-71. *Member:* Cavalry Club (London).

WRITINGS: My Mother Told Me, James Blackwood, 1958, Norton, 1966; *Portrait of a Patriot: A Biography of John Wilkes*, James Blackwood, 1962; *The Royal Malady*, Longmans, Green 1964, Harcourt, 1965; *The Desert's Dusty Face*, James Blackwood, 1964, Morrow, 1966; *The Poacher and the Squire: A History of Poaching and Game Preservation in England*, Longmans, Green, 1967; *The Shooter and His Gun*, Farm Journal Ltd., 1969; *The Flyfisher and His Rod*, Farm Journal Ltd., 1969; *The Western Rising: An Account of the Re-

bellion of James Scott, Duke of Monmouth*, Longmans, Green, 1969; *A History of Horsemanship*, Doubleday, 1970.

WORK IN PROGRESS: A history of marksmanship; a biography of George II.

AVOCATIONAL INTERESTS: Horses, hunting, fishing, polo, and travel.

*   *   *

CHENG, J(ames) Chester 1926-

PERSONAL: Born April 4, 1926, in Hankow, China; married in 1957; children: two. *Education:* St. John's University, Shanghai, China, B.A., 1945; Fletcher School of Law and Diplomacy, Medford, Mass., M.A., 1947; Pembroke College, Cambridge, Ph.D., 1950. *Office:* Department of History, San Francisco State College, San Francisco, Calif. 94132.

CAREER: University of Oregon, Eugene, visiting associate professor of history and political science, 1959-60; San Francisco State College, San Francisco, Calif., associate professor, 1960-65, professor of history, 1965—; Stanford University, Hoover Institution on War, Revolution, and Peace, research associate, 1963—. Fulbright research professor, Japan and Korea, 1966-67. Consultant, U.S. Office of Education, 1959—. *Member:* Association for Asian Studies, American Historical Association.

WRITINGS: Basic Principles Underlying the Chinese Communist Approach to Education, U.S. Office of Education, 1961; *Chinese Sources for the Taiping Rebellion 1850-1864*, Oxford University Press, 1963; (editor) *The Politics of the Chinese Red Army*, Hoover Institution, 1966.

WORK IN PROGRESS: Commander and Commissar: The Dynamics of the Chinese Red Army, 1927-1966.

*   *   *

CHESSER, Eustace 1902-1973

PERSONAL: Born March 22, 1902, in Edinburgh, Scotland; son of Arthur and Rebecca Chesser; married Sheila Blayney-Jones, February 23, 1915; children: Shirley, Edward. *Education:* Attended George Watson's College; Royal Colleges, Edinburgh, Scotland, L.R.C.P., L.R.C.S., L.R.E.P.S., 1926; Tavistock Clinic, training analysis, 1939. *Religion:* Humanist. *Home and office:* 17 Wimpole St., London W.1, England. *Agent:* Curtis Brown Ltd., 13 King St., London W.C.2, England.

CAREER: Consulting psychologist and lecturer, London, England. Research Council in Marriage and Human Relationship, research director. *Member:* Society for Sex Education and Guidance, Royal Institution, Medico-Legal Council, Abortion Law Reform Association, Medico-Legal Society, Royal Medico-Psychological Society, Association for the Advancement of Psycho-Therapy, International Union of Family Organization (British executive committee), British Social Biology Council, Society for Study of Addiction, International Committee for Sexual Equality (Amsterdam).

WRITINGS: Slimming for the Million: The New Treatment for Obesity, Rich & Cowan, 1939; *Love without Fear: A Plain Guide to Sex Technique for Every Married Adult*, Rich & Cowan, 1940, 4th edition, Arrow Books, 1966 (also published with *Marriage and Freedom*—see below); *Marriage and Freedom*, Progress Books, 1945, 3rd edition published as *Love and Marriage*, Pan Books, 1957, first edition published in America with *Love without Fear* as *Love without Fear: How to Achieve Sex Happiness in Marriage*, Roy, 1947; (with Zoe Dawe) *The Practice of Sex Education: A Plain Guide for Parents and Teachers*, Roy, 1946; *Unwanted Child*, Rich & Cowan, 1947; *Children by Choice: An In-

timate Guide to Married Life, Torchstream Book, 1947, reissued as *A Practical Guide to Birth Control,* 1950; *Grow Up—and Live,* Penguin, 1949; *Sexual Behavior, Norman and Abnormal,* Roy, 1949, revised edition published as *Sexual Behavior,* Transworld Publishers, 1964; *Cruelty to Children,* Gollancz, 1951, Philosophical Library, 1952; (with Olive Hawks) *Life Lies Ahead: A Practical Guide to Home-making and the Development of Personality,* Harrap, 1951; *Successful Living,* Penguin, 1952; *Unquiet Minds: Leaves from a Psychologist's Casebook,* Rich & Cowan, 1952; *How to Make a Success of Your Marriage,* Bodley Head, 1952, Roy, 1953; *Humanly Speaking* (essays on sex problems), Hutchinson, 1953, Roy, 1954; (with others) *The Sexual, Marital, and Family Relationships of the English Woman,* Hutchinson, 1956, Roy, 1957, reissued as *Women: A Popular Edition of the Chesser Report,* Jarrolds, 1958, revised and enlarged edition published as *Twentieth Century Woman,* Arrow Books, 1969; *Live and Let Live: The Moral of the Wolfenden Report,* foreword by John Wolfenden, Philosophical Library, 1958; *The Psychology of Everyday Living: How to Live with Yourself—A Simple Guide to Self-Understanding,* British Medical Association, 1958; *An Outline of Human Relationships,* Heinemann, 1959, Hawthorn, 1960; *Odd Man Out: Homosexuality in Men and Women,* Gollancz, 1959; *Is Chastity Outmoded?,* Heinemann, 1960; (with others) *Teenage Morals* (articles originally published in *Education,* March 3-April 14, 1961), Councils and Education Press (London), 1961; *Woman and Love,* Jarrolds, 1962, Citadel, 1963; *Life is for Living, So Relax and Enjoy It,* Harrap, 1962; *When and How to Stop Smoking,* Jarrolds, 1963, published in America as *When and How to Quit Smoking,* Emerson, 1964; *The Cost of Loving,* Methuen, 1964, Citadel, 1965; *Challenge of the Middle Years,* K. Mason, 1964; *Shelley and Zastrozzi: Self-Revelation of a Neurotic,* Archive Press, 1965; *Unmarried Love,* McKay, 1965; *Living with Suicide,* Hutchinson, 1967, reissued as *Why Suicide?,* Arrow Books, 1968; *Sex and the Married Woman,* W.H. Allen, 1968, published in America as *Love and the Married Woman,* Putnam, 1969; *Who Do You Think You Are?,* W.H. Allen, 1970, International Publications Service, 1970; *Strange Loves: The Human Aspects of Sexual Deviation,* Morrow, 1971 (published in England as *The Human Aspects of Sexual Deviation,* Jarrolds, 1971); *Beginner's Guide to Sex,* Pelham Books, 1971, published in America as *Young Adult's Guide to Sex,* Drake Publishers, 1972. Contributor to medical journals and the press. With Alexander Fullerton, under pseudonym Alex Hilton: *The Consultant,* Corgi, 1968; *Waiting for the Night,* Corgi, 1969; *The Heart People,* Corgi, 1969.

AVOCATIONAL INTERESTS: Ideas, people, places and things.

BIOGRAPHICAL/CRITICAL SOURCES: Library Journal, March 1, 1969; *Books,* April, 1970.

(Died December 5, 1973)

* * *

CHILD, Heather 1912-

PERSONAL: Born November 3, 1912, in Winchester, Hampshire, England. *Education:* Studied at St. Swithun's School, Winchester, England, and Chelsea School of Art, London, England.

MEMBER: Society of Scribes and Illuminators (chairman, 1964), Society of Designer Craftsmen, Society for Italic Handwriting, Crafts Centre of Great Britain (council), Heraldry Society.

WRITINGS: Decorative Maps, Studio Publications, 1956; (contributor) *Calligraphers Handbook,* Faber, 1956; *Calligraphy Today: A Survey of Tradition and Trends,* Studio Vista, 1962; *Heraldic Design: A Handbook for Students,* Watson, 1964; (editor) Edward Johnston, *Formal*

Penmanship and Other Papers, Hastings House, 1971; (with Dorothy Colles) *Christian Symbols: Ancient and Modern,* Scribner, 1972.

* * *

CHILDS, Marilyn Grace Carlson 1923-

PERSONAL: Born August 26, 1923, in Springfield, Mass.; daughter of Carl Oscar (a photoengraver) and Dorothy M. (Davis) Carlson; married Harold Lofton Childs (a farm owner and horse trainer), February 2, 1952; children: David Loring, Robert Stuart, Carl Albert. *Education:* Vermont Junior College, A.A., 1942; American International College, B.A., 1945. *Politics:* Independent. *Religion:* Protestant. *Home:* Harolyn Hill, R.F.D., Tunbridge, Vt. 05077.

CAREER: Springfield Union, Springfield, Mass., reporter, 1942-45; *American Horseman-Sportologue,* Lexington, Ky., associate editor, 1945-47; *Popular Horsemen,* Harrisburg, Pa., managing editor, 1948-52; *Lexington Herald-Leader,* Lexington, Ky., feature writer, 1954-63; *Saddle and Bridle,* eastern representative, 1954-67. American Horse Shows Association, judge and steward, 1950—, committeewoman, 1961—; Morgan Horse Club, Inc., director, 1953-63; Mid-Atlantic Morgan Horse Club, president, 1954-60; New England Horsemen's Council delegate, 1965—; New England Morgan Horse Association, vice-president, 1970—.

WRITINGS: Riding Show Horses, edited by Eugene V. Connett, Van Nostrand, 1963; *Mandate for a Morgan Horse: Autobiography of a Real Horse,* Carlton, 1967; *Training Your Colt to Ride and Drive,* Van Nostrand, 1969. Contributor of articles to newspapers and magazines.

* * *

CHILDS, Maryanna 1910-
(C. Sand Childs)

PERSONAL: Born January 16, 1910, in New York, N.Y.; daughter of James Michael (a builder) and Clara (Sand) Childs. *Education:* Ohio Dominican College (formerly College of St. Mary of the Springs), B.A., 1942; Catholic University of America, M.A., 1947; other study at Columbia University, Notre Dame University, Marquette University, and University of Washington, Seattle. *Politics:* "Ticket-splitting Democrat." *Home and office:* Ohio Dominican College, Columbus, Ohio 43219.

CAREER: Roman Catholic religious, member of Order of Dominican Sisters, name in religion, Sister Maryanna; Ohio Dominican College, Columbus, chairman of department of English, 1947-67. Teacher of summer courses in creative writing at Loretto Heights College, 1960, Dominican College, Dublin, Ireland, 1961, Georgetown University, 1962, College of the Holy Names, 1964, Aquinas College, 1966, Capital University, 1968, Wright State University, 1970. Religious consultant, Stanley Greetings, 1950-61. *Member:* Modern Language Association of America, Catholic Poetry Society, Catholic Press Association. *Awards, honors:* Journalism adviser's medal, Catholic School Press Association, 1960; Knights of Columbus grant to Ireland, summer, 1961; author's grant, American Irish Foundation, 1965.

WRITINGS: The Littlest Angel and Other Legends, O'Toole, 1942; *My Little Book of Thanks,* Bruce, 1957; *My Marybook,* Bruce, 1959; *With Love and Laughter,* Doubleday, 1960; *My Little Book of Manners,* Bruce, 1963; *With Joy and Gladness,* Doubleday, 1964; *The Sounds of Ireland,* Our Sunday Press, 1969. Contributor of about two hundred poems, forty articles, and fifty stories to religious and secular publications, 1931—.

WORK IN PROGRESS: Poems and children's stories.

AVOCATIONAL INTERESTS: Detective stories.

CHINITZ, Benjamin 1924-

PERSONAL: Born April 24, 1924, in New York, N.Y.; son of Abraham and Mollie Chinitz; married, wife's name, Ethel; children: Adam, Michael. Education: Yeshiva University, A.B., 1945; Brown University, A.M., 1951; Harvard University, Ph.D., 1956. Home: 5719 Solway St., Pittsburgh, Pa. 15217. Office: Department of Economics, Brown University, Providence, R.I. 02912.

CAREER: Dartmouth College, Hanover, N.H., instructor, 1954-55; Brown University, Providence, R.I., instructor, 1955-56; New York Metropolitan Region Study, senior staff member, 1956-59; Pittsburgh Regional Economic Study, associate director, 1959-62; University of Pittsburgh, Pittsburgh, Pa., professor and chairman of department of economics, associate director of Center for Regional Economic Studies, 1962-65; U.S. Department of Commerce, Washington D.C., deputy assistant secretary of commerce for economic development, 1965-66; Brown University, professor of economics, 1966—, chairman of department, 1967—. Fulbright scholar, University of Glasgow, 1965; visiting professor, Massachusetts Institute of Technology, 1967. Consultant to President's Appalachian Regional Commission, RAND Corp., Connecticut State Development Commission. Transportation Research Foundation, member of board of trustees and research committee; Committee for Economic Development, member of advisory board of area development committee. Member: American Economic Association, Regional Science Association.

WRITINGS: Freight and the Metropolis, Harvard University Press, 1960; (with Barbara Berman and Edgar M. Hoover) Projection of a Metropolis, Harvard University Press, 1961; Differential Regional Economic Growth and Changing Industrial Structure, National Academy of Sciences, 1961; (with Hoover) The Role of Accounts in the Economic Study of the Pittsburgh Metropolitan Region, Johns Hopkins Press, 1961; (co-author) Region in Transition, University of Pittsburgh Press, 1964; (editor with Hoover and I.S. Lowry) Economic Study of the Pittsburgh Region, three volumes, University of Pittsburgh Press, 1964; (editor) City and Suburb: The Economics of Metropolitan Growth, Prentice-Hall, 1965. Contributor to professional journals.

* * *

CHIPPERFIELD, Joseph Eugene 1912-
(John Eland Craig)

PERSONAL: Born April 20, 1912, in St. Austell, Cornwall, England; son of Edward and Lavinia (White) Chipperfield; married Mary Anne Tully, April 26, 1936. Education: Educated privately. Politics: Conservative. Home and office: Innisfree, Raheen Park, Bray Head, County Wicklow, Ireland.

CAREER: Author's Literary Service, Cheapside, England, editor, 1930-34; editor and writer of scripts for documentary films, 1934-40; free-lance writer, 1940—. Member: Auto Club (Great Britain), German Shepherd Dog Club (Ireland).

WRITINGS: Two Dartmoor Interludes, Boswell Press, 1935; An Irish Mountain Tragedy, Boswell, Press, 1936; Three Stories (includes An Irish Mountain Tragedy and Two Dartmoor Interludes), Boswell Press, 1936; This Earth My Home: A Tale of Irish Troubles, Padraic O'Follain, 1937; Storm of Dancerwood, Hutchinson, 1948, Longmans, Green (New York), 1949, revised edition, Hutchinson, 1967; Greatheart, the Salvation Hunter: The Epic of a Shepherd Dog, Hutchinson, 1950, Roy, 1953; Beyond the Timberland Trail, Hutchinson, 1951, Longmans, Green (New York), 1953; Windruff of Links Tor, Longmans, Green (New York), 1951; Grey Chieftain, Hutchinson, 1952, Roy, 1954; (under pseudonym John Eland Craig) The Dog from Castle Crag, Thomas Nelson, 1952; Greeka, Eagle of the Hebrides, Hutchinson, 1953, Longmans, Green (New York), 1954, revised edition, Hutchinson, 1962; Silver Star, Stallion of the Echoing Mountain, Hutchinson, 1953, Longmans, Green (New York), 1955; Rooloo, Stag of Dark Water, Hutchinson, 1955, Roy, 1962, revised edition, Hutchinson, 1962, Roy, 1963; Dark Fury, Stallion of Lost River Valley, Hutchinson, 1956, Roy, 1958; The Story of a Great Ship: The Birth and Death of the Steamship Titanic, Hutchinson, 1957, Roy, 1959; Wolf of Badenoch: Dog of the Grampian Hills, Hutchinson, 1958, Longmans, Green (New York), 1959; Ghost Horse: Stallion of the Oregon Trail, Hutchinson, 1959, Roy, 1962; Grasson, Golden Eagle of the North, Hutchinson, 1960; Petrus, Dog of the Hill Country, Heinemann, 1960; Seokoo of the Black Wind, Hutchinson, 1961, McKay, 1962; The Grey Dog from Galtymore, Heinemann, 1961, McKay, 1962; Sabre of Storm Valley, Hutchinson, 1962, Roy, 1965; A Dog Against Darkness, Heinemann, 1963, published in America as A Dog to Trust: The Saga of a Seeing-eye Dog, McKay, 1964; Checoba, Stallion of the Comanche, Hutchinson, 1964, Roy, 1966; Boru, Dog of the O'Malley, Hutchinson, 1965, McKay, 1966; The Two Fugitives, Heinemann, 1966; Lone Stands the Glen, Hutchinson, 1966; The Watcher on the Hills, Heinemann, 1968; Rex of Larkbarrow, Hutchinson, 1969; Storm Island, Hutchinson, 1970; Banner, the Pacing White Stallion, Hutchinson, 1971. Also author of two short story collections. Author of film scripts, short stories, serials, and articles.

WORK IN PROGRESS: My Pal Wolf; Glen; Rafferty's Mare; a novel about the troubles in Ireland, tentatively titled, No More the Green Isle.

BIOGRAPHICAL/CRITICAL SOURCES: Kathleen Lines, Four to Fourteen, National Book League, 1946; Young Readers' Review, December, 1966; Books and Bookmen, November, 1970.

* * *

CHISOLM, Lawrence W (ashington) 1929-

PERSONAL: Born February 7, 1929, in New York, N.Y.; son of William Garnett and Ruth (Anderton) Chisolm; married Elizabeth Richards, June 14, 1950; children: Anne, Ruth, Elizabeth, Susan, Sarah. Education: Princeton University, A.B., 1950; Yale University, Ph.D., 1957. Home: 49 Autumn St., New Haven, Conn. 06511.

CAREER: Yale University, New Haven, Conn., instructor, 1956-61, assistant professor of history and American studies, 1961—. Military service: U.S. Navy, 1950-53; became lieutenant j.g.

WRITINGS: (Editor) Life and Letters of J. Alden Weir, Yale University Press, 1960; Fenollosa: The Far East and American Culture, Yale University Press, 1963.

* * *

CHITWOOD, Marie Downs 1918-

PERSONAL: Born June 20, 1918, in Boaz, Ala.; daughter of Robert Edward and Minnie (Wills) Downs; married James William Chitwood, August 20, 1937 (deceased); children: Joyce (Mrs. Robert Corey), James William II, Jan. Education: Educated in Alabama public schools. Religion: Baptist. Home: 1210 Goodyear Ave., Gadsden, Ala. 35903.

CAREER: Active in Baptist church work for twenty-five years, serving as superintendent of intermediate department of First Baptist Church, Gadsden, Ala; presently employed as a school librarian.

WRITINGS: This Passing Night, Zondervan, 1955; Laughter in the House, Zondervan, 1961; After the

Storm, Zondervan, 1964. Contributor of articles to *Home Life.*

WORK IN PROGRESS: A novel.

AVOCATIONAL INTERESTS: Sewing, designing clothes, gardening, and entertaining.

* * *

CHRISTENSEN, Gardell Dano 1907-

PERSONAL: Born August 31, 1907, in Shelley, Idaho; son of Anton Erastus (a mining engineer) and Anna Christina (Jensen) Christensen; married Eugenia Burney (now a writer), June 3, 1953; children: Barbara (Mrs. Glenn Collins), Gardell Dano, Jr., Peter Burch, Yahna (Mrs. George Borden). *Education:* Attended public schools in Shelley, Idaho. *Politics:* Republican. *Religion:* Mormon. *Home:* 320 Knoll Dr., San Pedro, Calif. 90731. *Office:* Cabrillo Beach Marine Museum, San Pedro, Calif.

CAREER: American Museum of Natural History, New York, N.Y., exhibits designer, 1928-41; McArthur 3 Dimensional Advertising Corp., New York, N.Y., assistant production manager, 1947-49; National Park Museum Laboratories, Washington, D.C., sculptor, 1950-51; Montana Historical Society, Helena, Mont., exhibits designer, 1951-53; Hagley Museum, Wilmington, Del., exhibits designer, 1956-59; Schenectady Museum, Schenectady, N.Y., curator of exhibits, 1959-62; State University of New York, Department of History and Archives, Albany, exhibits designer for historic sites, 1962-68; Cabrillo Beach Marine Museum, San Pedro, Calif., exhibits designer, 1969—. Wild animal collector on year-long expedition in Africa, on other expeditions in Alaska, Canada, and western United States. Creator of dioramas and sculpture for Colonial Museum, Nairobi, British East Africa, and for other museums, monuments, and battlefields in United States. *Member:* Association of American Museums, Historical Society of Southern California, Torch Club, Society of Animal Artists.

WRITINGS—All self-illustrated: *The Fearless Family,* Holt, 1955; *Mr. Hare,* Holt, 1956; *Chuck Woodchuck's Secret,* Holt, 1957; *Mrs. Mouse Needs a House,* Holt, 1958; *Buffalo Kill,* Thomas Nelson, 1959; *The Buffalo Robe,* Thomas Nelson, 1960; *Buffalo Horse,* Thomas Nelson, 1961; *Colonial New York,* Thomas Nelson, 1969. Also author of *Animal Art,* International Correspondence Schools, 1960. Contributor of articles to natural history magazines.

WORK IN PROGRESS: The Battle of Oriskany, a children's book on Revolutionary War battle.

SIDELIGHTS: Christensen's writing career began out of another interest. He writes: "As a young sculptor and artist at the American Museum of Natural History in New York City, I began to illustrate some of the articles in the magazine published by the museum, *Natural History....* I decided that not enough books about animals were being written for me to illustrate, so I would write one myself.... When one works in the museum field as I have most of my life, he learns to take a subject and research it in depth, no matter how small the subject may be, before he begins to build and exhibit, a diorama or a life-sized group. One museum wanted a diorama of the buffalo kill, the way in which the Indians of Montana killed the buffalo by luring them over a cliff in order to obtain their winter supply of food and clothing. I spent six months doing the research at libraries, the University of Montana, and from aerial photographs of the very cliffs, seeing the big circle where the Indians had danced. Another six months was spent in designing and creating the diorama. A year later *Buffalo Kill* came

from the press. It has remained one of my best sellers to this day."

* * *

CHRISTY, George

PERSONAL: Surname originally Stupakis; born in Monessen, Pa.; son of Stephanos and Calliope (Christy) Stupakis. *Education:* Carnegie Institute of Technology (now Carnegie-Mellon University), B.F.A. *Religion:* Greek Orthodox. *Home:* 11 East 68th St., New York, N.Y. 10021.

CAREER: For over one year, conducted daily radio interview program for American Broadcasting Co. *Military service:* U.S. Army; became sergeant.

WRITINGS: All I Could See From Where I Stood (novel), Bobbs-Merrill, 1963; *The Los Angeles Underground Gourmet,* Simon & Schuster, 1970. Contributor to *Good Housekeeping, McCall's, Reader's Digest,* and other periodicals.

WORK IN PROGRESS: A novel, *Someone, Somewhere.*

* * *

CHU, Valentin (Yuan-ling) 1919-

PERSONAL: Born February 14, 1919, in Shanghai, China; became U.S. citizen; son of Thomas V. D. (a publisher) and Rowena (Zee) Tsu; married Victoria Tsao, September, 1954; children: Douglas Y.C. *Education:* St. John's University, Shanghai, China, B.A. in Journalism, 1940. *Religion:* Protestant. *Home:* 101 Laurel Hill Rd., Croton-on-Hudson, N.Y. 10520. *Office:* Time, Inc., Time & Life Building, Rockefeller Center, New York, N.Y. 10020.

CAREER: Shanghai Municipal Council, International Settlement, Shanghai, China, assistant, 1940-42; Thomas Chu & Sons (publishers and printers), Shanghai, China, assistant manager, 1942-45; *China Press* (English-language daily), Shanghai, China, reporter and correspondent, 1945-49; Central Air Transport Corp., Shanghai, China, and Hong Kong, public relations officer, 1949; Time, Inc., Hong Kong correspondent, 1949-56, member of New York editorial staff, 1956-68, writer and editor of Time-Life Books, 1968—. *Member:* Authors Guild. *Awards, honors:* China winner, United Nations International Essay Contest, 1948, for "The Role of the Individual in the United Nations."

WRITINGS: Ta Ta, Tan Tan: The Inside Story of Communist China (title means "Fight Fight, Talk Talk", Norton, 1963; *Thailand Today: A Visit to Modern Siam,* Crowell, 1968; (co-author) *The U.S.A.: A Visitor's Handbook,* Time-Life, 1969. Contributor of articles and short stories to *Time, Life, New Leader, U.S. News and World Report,* and other publications in United States, France, Italy, Great Britain, China, Japan, and Hong Kong.

WORK IN PROGRESS: Another book on China.

SIDELIGHTS: Ta Ta, Tan Tan has been published in German, Spanish, and Hindi editions. *Avocational interests:* Photography, travel.

* * *

CHURCHILL, R(eginald) C(harles) 1916-

PERSONAL: Born February 9, 1916, in Bromley, Kent, England; son of Edward Wallis (an accountant) and Ellen Amelia (Culverwell) Churchill; married Jeanne Marie Marie, February 19, 1955. *Education:* Downing College, Cambridge, B.A., 1938, M.A., 1943. *Home:* 95 Collinswood Dr., St. Leonards, Sussex, England.

CAREER: Temporary teaching posts in Devonshire, Essex, and Berkshire, England, 1940-42; professional writer and book reviewer, 1942—; Oxford and Cambridge Joint Board, examiner, general certificate of education, 1943-63.

WRITINGS: English Literature and the Agnostic, C.A. Watts, 1944; *Art and Christianity,* C.A. Watts, 1945; *He Served Human Liberty,* Allen & Unwin, 1946; *Disagreements,* Secker & Warburg, 1950; (editor) *Pope's Epistle to Arbuthnot,* University Tutorial Press, 1950; *English Literature of the 19th Century,* University Tutorial Press, 1951; *English Literature of the 18th Century,* University Tutorial Press, 1953; *The English Sunday,* C.A. Watts, 1954; *A Short History of the Future,* Laurie, 1955; *Sixty Seasons of League Football,* Penguin, 1958; (with Maurice Hussey as collaborator in research) *Shakespeare and His Betters,* Reinhardt, 1958, Indiana University Press, 1959; *English League Football,* Kaye, 1961; (contributor) George Sampson, *Concise Cambridge History of English Literature,* 2nd edition, Cambridge University Press, 1961, 3rd edition, 1970; *The Powys Brothers,* British Book Centre, 1962; (editor) H. Radcliffe Wilson, *Official Rules of Sports and Games, 1964-65,* Sportshelf, 1964; *The Frontiers of Fiction,* K.A. Ward, 1970.

Contributor: *Little Reviews Anthology, 1947-48,* Eyre & Spottiswoode, 1948; *Pelican Guide to English Literature,* Penguin, Volume VI, 1958, Volume VII, 1961. Contributor of more than a thousand articles and reviews to forty journals and newspapers, including *Criterion, Scrutiny, Humanist, Spectator, Adelphi, Contemporary Review, Twentieth Century, John o'London's, Everyman, Modern Churchman, Dublin Review, Shakespeare Jahrbuch,* and London and Birmingham newspapers.

WORK IN PROGRESS: Poetry and Politics.

AVOCATIONAL INTERESTS: Sports, gardening.

* * *

CHUTE, William J (oseph) 1914-

PERSONAL: Born June 23, 1914, in New Haven, Conn.; son of William Joseph and Madeline (Beurer) Chute; married Virginia Remington, June 23, 1949; children: Elizabeth Emery, Susan Anne, Robert Courtney. *Education:* Hobart College, student, 1934-36; New York University, B.A., 1945; Cornell University, graduate study, 1946-47; Columbia University, Ph.D., 1951. *Religion:* Protestant. *Office:* Queens College of the City University of New York, Flushing, N.Y. 11367.

CAREER: Walter Hervey Junior College, New York, N.Y., instructor in American history and government, 1947-50; Rutgers University, New Brunswick, N.J., lecturer in history, 1951-54; Queens College of the City University of New York, Flushing, N.Y., instructor, 1954-57, assistant professor, 1958-65, associate professor of history, 1965—. *Military service:* U.S. Army, 1942-43. *Member:* American Historical Association, American Studies Association, Organization of American Historians.

WRITINGS: (Editor) *The American Social Scene, 1600-1860: Contemporary Views of Life and Society,* two volumes, Bantam, 1964. Contributor of articles to professional journals.

WORK IN PROGRESS: Biography of Frederick A.P. Barnard, American scientist and educator; *The Rise and Fall of the "Anglo-Saxon" as an American Proto-type in History.*

* * *

CLARK (of Herriotshall), Arthur Melville 1895-

PERSONAL: Born August 20, 1895, in Edinburgh, Scotland; son of James and Margaret Moyes (McLachlan) Clark. *Education:* University of Edinburgh, M.A. (with first class honors), 1919; Oriel College, Oxford, scholar, D. Phil., 1929. *Politics:* Conservative. *Religion:* Anglican. *Home:* 3 Woodburn Ter., Edinburgh 10, Scotland.

CAREER: University College, Reading, Berkshire, England, lecturer in English language and literature, 1920-21; Oxford University Home Students Society, Oxford, England, tutor in English language, 1921-22; University of Edinburgh, Edinburgh, Scotland, assistant in English literature, 1924-28, lecturer, 1928-46, director of studies, 1932-47, reader, 1946-60. External examiner in English language and literature for University of St. Andrews, 1939-43, University of Aberdeen, 1944-47. Staff officer of Scottish Regional Commission for Civil Defense, 1939-45. Member of Committee of the Baronage of Scotland and of Scottish Landowners' Federation. Chairman of Esdaile Trust. Proprietor of estate in Berwickshire.

MEMBER: Royal Society of Edinburgh (life fellow), Royal Society of Arts (life fellow), Oxford Union Society (secretary, 1923), Oxford Bibliographical Society, Scottish Genealogy Society, Speculative Society of Edinburgh (president, 1926-29), Scottish Arts Club (president, 1948-50), New Club (Edinburgh), Edinburgh Sir Walter Scott Club (president, 1957-58), Royal Society Club, Scottish Artists Benevolent Association, Scottish Students Song Book Committee Ltd. (chairman). *Awards, honors:* Knight of the Military and Hospitaller Order of St. Lazarus of Jerusalem; Knight of Polonia Restitute (for war service); D. Litt., University of Edinburgh, 1947.

WRITINGS: The Realistic Revolt in Modern Poetry, Basil Blackwell, 1922, Haskell House, 1966; *A Bibliography of Thomas Heywood,* Oxford University Press, 1925; *Thomas Heywood: Playwright and Miscellanist,* Basil Blackwell, 1931; *Autobiography: Its Genesis and Phases,* Oliver & Boyd, 1935; (editor with John Purves) *Seventeenth-Century Studies Presented to Sir Herbert Grierson,* Clarendon Press, 1938; (editor with Augustus Muir and John W. Oliver) *George Saintsbury: The Memorial Volume,* Methuen, 1945, published in America as *A Saintsbury Miscellany,* Oxford University Press, 1947; *Studies in Literary Modes,* Folcroft, 1946, 2nd edition, Oliver & Boyd, 1958; (with R.K. Underka) *Spoken English: An Idiomatic Grammar for Foreign Students,* Oliver & Boyd, 1946, 4th edition, 1958; (with Muir and Oliver) *Last Vintage: Essays and Papers by George Saintsbury,* Methuen, 1950; (editor) *Two Pageants by Thomas Heywood,* Basil Blackwell, 1953; *The Background History of the Speculative Society,* Constable, 1968; *Sir Walter Scott: The Formative Years,* Blackwood, 1969, Barnes & Noble, 1970; *Sonnets from the French and Other Verses,* Oliver & Boyd, 1969.

Contributor of articles to *Encyclopaedia Britannica, Collier's Encyclopedia, Philosophical Library's Dictionary of Poetry and Poetics, Cambridge Bibliography of English Literature,* and to a dozen literary and professional journals. Editor, *Edinburgh University Calendar,* 1932-46.

WORK IN PROGRESS: Research in Shakespeare, especially tragedies; King James VI and the drama; rhyme; genealogy; heraldry.

AVOCATIONAL INTERESTS: Pastel-sketching (has exhibited at Royal Scottish Academy, Society of Scottish Artists, and other exhibitions), shooting, illumination, verse-translation, and billiards.

* * *

CLARK, Eleanor 1913-

PERSONAL: Born July 6, 1913, in Los Angeles, Calif.; left at age of four weeks, considers self a native of Roxbury, Conn.; daughter of Frederick Huntington (an engineer) and Eleanor (Phelps) Clark; married Robert Penn Warren (Pulitzer Prize-winning author and poet), 1952; children: Rosanna, Gabriel Penn. *Education:* Vassar College, B.A. *Home:* 2495 Redding Rd., Fairfield, Conn.

CAREER: Writer. U.S. Office of Strategic Services, Washington, D.C., 1943-45; also worked in publishing and editing posts prior to 1952. *Member:* National Institute of Arts and Letters. *Awards, honors:* National Institute of Arts and Letters grant in literature, 1947; Guggenheim fellowships in fiction, 1947, 1960; National Book Award, 1965, for *The Oysters of Locmariaquer.*

WRITINGS: (Translator) Roman Sender, *Dark Wedding* (novel), Doubleday, 1942; *The Bitter Box* (novel), Doubleday, 1946; *Rome and a Villa*, Doubleday, 1952; *Song of Roland*, Random House, 1960; *The Oysters of Locmariaquer*, Pantheon, 1964; *Baldur's Gate* (novel; Book-of-the-Month Club selection), Pantheon, 1970. Contributor to anthologies and periodicals.

SIDELIGHTS: Known until then for her short fiction published in periodicals, Miss Clark was described as a "skillful and ironic writer" for her first novel. She did not write another for 25 years, until *Baldur's Gate*, in which the locale was her own New England countryside.

Eleanor Clark has lived a good deal in foreign parts, and in one of them, the village of Locmariaquer on the Brittany coast of France, she found the subject of one of her books, the Locmariaquer oyster.

She speaks French and Italian, loves to ski (especially in Vermont), and says that her main occupation for quite a few years has been her children, and she "has no time for Women's Lib."

BIOGRAPHICAL/CRITICAL SOURCES: New Yorker, April 27, 1946, May 17, 1952; *Nation,* April 27, 1946, July 6, 1970; *Christian Science Monitor,* July 21, 1964, July 16, 1970; *New York Review of Books,* July 30, 1964; *New Leader,* June 22, 1970; *New York Times Book Review,* June 28, 1970; *Best Sellers,* July 1, 1970; *Saturday Review,* July 4, 1970; *Virginia Quarterly Review,* Autumn, 1970.

*   *   *

CLARK, (Charles) Manning (Hope) 1915-

PERSONAL: Born March 3, 1915, in Sydney, Australia; son of Charles Henry (a clergyman) and Catherine (Hope) Clark; married Dymphna Lodewyckx, January 31, 1939; children: Sebastian, Katerina, Axel, Andrew, Rowland, Benedict. *Education:* University of Melbourne, B.A. (with honors), 1938, M.A., 1944; Balliol College, Oxford, graduate student, 1938-39. *Agent:* Richmond Towers & Benson, 14 Essex St., London W.C.2, England. *Office:* History Department, Australian National University, Canberra, Australia.

CAREER: University of Melbourne, Melbourne, Australia, lecturer, 1944-49; Canberra University College, Canberra, Australia, professor of history and political science, 1949-59; Australian National University, Canberra, professor of history, 1960—. *Member:* Melbourne University Union.

WRITINGS: (Editor) *Select Documents in Australian History,* Angus & Robertson, Volume I (with L.J. Pryor): *1788-1850,* 1950, Volume II: *1851-1900,* 1955, both volumes reissued by International Publications Service, 1970; (author of foreword) Alexander Harris, *Settlers and Convicts; or, Recollections of Sixteen Years' Labour in the Australian Backwoods, by an Emigrant Mechanic,* 2nd edition, Melbourne University Press, 1954, reissued with a new foreword by Clark, 1964; (editor) *Sources of Australian History,* Oxford University Press, 1957; (contributor) Robert Noel Ebbels, compiler, *The Australian Labor Movement, 1850-1907,* Noel Ebbels Memorial Committee and Australasian Book Society, 1960, F.W. Cheshire, 1965; *Meeting Soviet Man,* Angus & Robertson, 1960; *A History of Australia,* Volume 1:

From the Earliest Times to the Age of Macquarie, Cambridge University Press, 1962, Volume 2: *New South Wales and Van Diemen's Land, 1822-1838,* Cambridge University Press, 1968, Volume 3: *Beginning of Australian Civilization, 1824-1854,* Melbourne University Press, in press; (contributor) *The Australian Idiom,* F.W. Cheshire, 1963; *A Short History of Australia,* New American Library, 1963, new edition, Heinemann, 1969; (with others) *Ned Kelly: Man and Myth,* Cassell, 1969, Tri-Ocean, 1971; *Disquiet, and Other Stories,* Angus & Robertson, 1969. Contributor of short stories to *Sydney Bulletin,* and *Quadrant.*

AVOCATIONAL INTERESTS: Music, fishing.

*   *   *

CLARK, Walter Van Tilburg 1909-1971

PERSONAL: Born August 3, 1909, in East Oreland, Me.; son of Walter Ernest (a teacher, economist, president of University of Nevada) and Euphemia Murray (Abrams) Clark; married Barbara Frances Morse, October 14, 1933 (deceased); children: Barbara Anne Clark Salmon, Robert Morse. *Education:* University of Nevada, B.A., 1932, M.A., 1932; University of Vermont, M.A., 1934. *Politics:* Democrat. *Home address:* P.O. Box 5546, Reno, Nev. 89503. *Agent:* International Famous Agency, 1301 Avenue of the Americas, New York, N.Y. 10019. *Office:* University of Nevada Press, Reno, Nev.

CAREER: Cazenovia Central School, Cazenovia, N.Y., teacher of English, drama, sports, 1936-45; head of an English department, and tennis coach, Rye, N.Y., 1945; University of Montana, Missoula, assistant professor of English, 1953-56; San Francisco State College (now California State University), San Francisco, Calif., professor of English, director of creative writing, 1956-62; University of Nevada, Reno, writer-in-residence, 1962-71. Visiting lecturer in creative writing, University of Iowa writers' workshop, and Stanford University writers' workshop. Visiting lecturer or professor at other universities, including University of Utah, University of Wyoming, University of California, University of Illinois, University of Missouri, and University of Arkansas. Fellow in writing at Center for Advanced Studies, Wesleyan University, 1960-61, Rockefeller Foundation lecturer in writing, Reed College, University of Washington, and University of Oregon. *Member:* American Association of University Professors, Authors Guild, American Civil Liberties Union, Sierra Club, Western Historical Association, Western Literary Association, Phi Kappa Phi. *Awards, honors:* O. Henry Memorial Award, 1945, for "The Wind and the Snow of Winter"; Litt.D., Colgate University, 1957.

WRITINGS—All published by Random House (except as indicated): *The Ox-Bow Incident* (novel), 1940, published with an introduction by Clifton Fadiman, Heritage, 1942, published with an afterword by W.P. Webb, New American Library, 1960; *The City of Trembling Leaves* (novel), 1945 (published in England as *Tim Hazard,* Kimber, 1951); *The Track of the Cat* (novel), 1949; *The Watchful Gods, and Other Stories* (contains "Hook," "The Wind and the Snow of Winter," "The Rapids," "The Anonymous," "The Buck in the Hills," "Why Don't You Look Where You're Going?," "The Indian Well," "The Fish Who Could Close His Eyes," "The Portable Phonograph," "The Watchful Gods"), Random House, 1950; (author of foreword) *Robert Cole Caples: A Retrospective Exhibition, 1927-63* (catalog), [Reno], 1964. Contributor to *Saturday Review, Holiday, Western Review, Pacific Spectator, Chrysalis, New York Times, New Yorker, Nation,* and *New York Herald Tribune.*

WORK IN PROGRESS: A biography of Alfred Doten, tentatively titled *The Delegation from Pluckville,* for University of Nevada-University of California Presses; an edition of Doten's journals (1849-1903), for University of Nevada-University of California Presses.

SIDELIGHTS: Clark told *CA:* "Hate cities: too many people ... with nothing else alive except in a zoo or on a leash, which is not really being alive.... Loved the Maine country and sea-shore and the farm. Lots of space and sky and weather, all sorts of things growing, wild and in gardens (had one of my own to ruin from the time I was five).... The deep interest in all kinds of life which I developed then has never left me. On the farm, too, by way of my mother's piano, my father's fine story-telling and reading aloud to us, King Arthur, Robin Hood, Indian and frontier tales, Greek, Roman and Nordic gods and heroes, the Bible, much else, and the kind interest of a neighbor who was a painter, I developed the love of reading and writing, music and art which have also continued. My first painting I can remember, a very wet and mingled water-color of the first football game I ever saw.... My first poem I cannot remember, but have been told it was a quatrain about a pair of rubbers. Unfortunately for posterity, both masterpieces have been lost. Also wrote many very adventurous and very short short-stories, even serials of a distinctly cliff-hanging variety, all of which were 'published' in a very local weekly paper, *The Clark News,* to which I also contributed poems and illustrations."

"*The Ox-Bow Incident* is an adventure story without a hero, a genuine psychological study in a horse-opera setting, with significant overtones drawn from the complex ethics of human justice," L.B. Salomon wrote of Clark's first novel. Robert D. McFadden stated: "In Mr. Clark's account of the Ox-Bow lynching, there were no villains nor special heroes and the book was one of the first in Western fiction that did not glamorize the West of the cowboy and rancher." McFadden quotes Frank T. Marsh as saying that the book "was 'a novelist's study of simple universals with respect to men of very different kinds, both individually and under mass pressure, during a crisis.'" G.G. Stevens wrote that the book "stands by itself for its high grade of psychological insight and expert craftsmanship." Salomon believes that "the book is noteworthy for its restraint, its deliberately subdued sense of drama." "The tenseness that builds and eddies and comes back stronger," Max Gissen states, "is beautifully geared to the temper of each central character and the shifting of the mob, as doubt, anger, stubbornness, physical cold, pity and revulsion hold them in turn."

The Track of the Cat, James Hilton wrote, "constitutes a true exploit of the mind, probing deeply, if perhaps too dourly, beneath the surface of its own excitements." Edmund Fuller maintained that "the actions have implications that go far beyond their limited context. It is masterful, consistently sustained story telling, and it purges with pity and terror." Others, including J.H. Jackson, agreed that the book was something more than a suspense or adventure story. He stated that Clark "says something of universal significance. The black panther is there ... it has always been there ... it will always be there.... Each man ... must hunt his black panther in his own way. It is because Mr. Clark knows this and has made the universal problem the core of his novel that the book is the fine thing it is." Mark Schorer found the "real beauty of Walter Clark's masterful prose [to be] its wonderful capacity to evoke from the homeliest circumstances the quality of grief and loneliness that exists deep in or under every human effort. The sharp visual clarity and the consequent fullness of evocation in scene after scene—many of them sustained in the most lavish detail for page after page—are a constant delight."

Clark was interested in teaching, writing, sports, art and music (though mostly just as looker and listener), hiking and camping, outdoor life in general, and socializing. He wrote: "My favorite diversion, by long odds, is socializing, just sitting around with a beer or more in all kinds of places, talking to all kinds of people about all kinds of things." Other interests: Chess, history (particularly western history as told by those who were personally involved in it, by way of journals, memoirs, letters, etc.), Indian lore, geology, mining and ranching methods (as necessary knowledge for stories). He believed that "the most important concerns of the human race now, all of it everywhere, must be birth control and natural conservation, the preservation and even, where possible, the restoration, of other forms of life and of all natural resources."

The Ox-Bow Incident was filmed by 20th Century Fox, 1943; *The Track of the Cat* was filmed by Warner Brothers, 1954. Clark's works have been translated into twenty languages, including Arabic, Urdu, Korean, and Japanese.

BIOGRAPHICAL/CRITICAL SOURCES: Books, October 12, 1940, October 7, 1950; *New Yorker,* October 12, 1940; *New York Times,* October 13, 1940, May 27, 1945, June 5, 1949, September 24, 1950, November 12, 1971; *Saturday Review of Literature,* October 26, 1940, June 2, 1945, June 4, 1949, September 30, 1950; *Atlantic,* October, 1940; *New Republic,* December 2, 1940; *New York Herald Tribune Weekly Book Review,* June 5, 1949; *San Francisco Chronicle,* June 5, 1949; *Christian Science Monitor,* June 11, 1949; *Catholic World,* July, 1949; *Arizona Quarterly,* 1951; *College English,* February, 1952; *Western Review,* winter, 1956; *Bulletin of Bibliography,* September-December, 1956; *Critique,* winter, 1959; *Washington Post,* November 12, 1971; *Variety,* November 17, 1971; *Newsweek,* November 22, 1971; *Time,* November 22, 1971; *Publishers Weekly,* November 29, 1971.

(Died November 11, 1971)

*   *   *

CLARKE, D(avid) Waldo   1907-
  (Dave Waldo)

PERSONAL: Born August 13, 1907, in Swansea, Wales; son of David Henry (a lawyer) and Alice Mayfield (Turner) Clarke; married Gwen Williams (a headmistress), September 9, 1931; children: Alisoun Jennifer, Joanna Mayfield. *Education:* Swansea University College, B.A. (first class honors), 1929; Jesus College, Oxford, B.A., 1931, M.A., 1938. *Home:* 29 Broom Water, Teddington, Middlesex, England.

CAREER: Egyptian Education Service, Cairo, Egypt, English master, 1931-38; Derby School, Derby, England, senior English master, 1939-43; The Polytechnic, London, England, senior lecturer, 1948-60; West London College, London, England, head of English department, 1960—. Macmillan Company Ltd., literary adviser.

WRITINGS: Modern English Writers, Longmans, Green, 1947; *William Shakespeare,* Longmans, Green, 1950, AMS Press, 1970; *Writers of Today,* Longmans, Green, 1956; (with M.D. Mackenzie) *Modern English Practice,* Longmans, Green, 1957; (with Mackenzie) *The Groundwork of English Sentence Structure,* Macmillan, 1963; (with Ronald Ridout) *A Reference Book of English: A General Guide for Foreign Students of English,* Macmillan, 1970.

Novels under name Dave Waldo: *The Man from Thunder River,* T.V. Boardman, 1951; *Warbonnet,* T.V. Boardman, 1952; *Ride On, Stranger,* T.V. Boardman, 1953; *The Long Riders,* Mills & Boon, 1957; *Lariat,* Mills & Boon, 1958; *Ride the High Hills,* Ward Lock, 1961; *Beat the Drum Slowly,* Ward Lock, 1962; *No Man Rides Alone,* Ward Lock, 1965. General editor, "Pattern Readers," ten volumes, Macmillan (London), 1964.

WORK IN PROGRESS: An anthology of poetry.

AVOCATIONAL INTERESTS: Reading about the 1860-90 period in western frontier history in America; music, mainly eighteenth century; oil painting.

*   *   *

CLARKE, Joan Dorn   1924-

PERSONAL: Born February 4, 1924, in New York, N.Y.; daughter of Hal James (an advertising executive and writer) and Evelyn (an actress under professional name Evelyn Dorn; maiden name, Dornbach) Clarke. *Education:* Elmhurst Academy of the Sacred Heart, Providence, R.I., student, 1936-41; Emmanuel College, Boston, Mass., A.B. (cum laude), 1945; Simmons College, M.S., 1957. *Politics:* Independent. *Religion:* Roman Catholic. *Home:* 37 Concord Ave., Cambridge, Mass. 02138.

CAREER: Advertising fashion copywriter in Boston, Mass., for Sears, Roebuck & Co., 1945-46, and Gilchrist Co., 1946-47; T.W. Rogers Co., Lynn, Mass., advertising manager, 1947-48; Harvard University Library, Cambridge, Mass., librarian, 1948-55; King Philip Regional High School, Wrentham, Mass., librarian, 1957-60; Girls' Latin School, Boston, Mass., librarian, 1960-70; Brighton High School, Brighton, Mass., librarian, 1970—. Library consultant for schools and for technical and medical libraries, 1957—. American Theater Wing, member, 1942-45. *Member:* American Library Association, Women's National Book Association, Authors League of America, New England Library Association, Massachusetts Library Association, Massachusetts School Library Association (member of executive board, 1960—; chairman of Boston area branch), Kappa Gamma Pi.

WRITINGS: Your Future As a Librarian, Rosen Press, 1963. Writer and producer of film, "The King Philip Library Story," used nationally as an educational film on libraries. Contributor of reviews to *Library Journal.*

WORK IN PROGRESS: A book with tentative title *St. Margaret, Queen of Scotland,* for Farrar, Straus; two television scripts; a career novel about the college library field, for young people.

SIDELIGHTS: Speaks and reads French, some Spanish; reads Anglo-Saxon, Latin, and German. *Avocational interests:* Readings, tennis, swimming, idle musing and thinking.

BIOGRAPHICAL/CRITICAL SOURCES: Boston Traveler, April 17, 1963; *Portland Press Herald,* (Portland, Me.), August 16, 1963.

*   *   *

CLAYTON, James E(dwin)   1929-

PERSONAL: Born November 14, 1929, in Johnston City, Ill.; son of John H. and Vinnie (Black) Clayton; married Elise B. Heinz (a lawyer), 1961. *Education:* University of Illinois, B.S., 1951; Princeton University, M.P.A., 1956. *Home:* 2847 Lorcom Lane, Arlington, Va. 22207. *Office: Washington Post,* 1515 L St. N.W., Washington, D.C. 20005.

CAREER: Southern Illinoisan, Carbondale, Ill., reporter, 1951-52; *Washington Post,* Washington, D.C., reporter, 1956-64, assistant managing editor, 1964-67, editorial writer, 1967—. Lecturer, Northwestern University, 1966-67, Johns Hopkins University, 1969. *Military service:* U.S. Army, 1952-53; became first lieutenant. *Member:* Princeton Club, Cosmos Club, (Washington, D.C.). *Awards, honors:* Washington Newspaper Guild awards, 1960, 1963, 1964; Sigma Delta Chi award, 1961; American Bar Association Silver Gavel, 1962, 1963; George Polk Memorial Award, 1971, for editorials on the nomination of Harrold Carswell to the Supreme Court.

WRITINGS: The Making of Justice: The Supreme Court in Action, Dutton, 1964. Contributor to *Reporter, Progressive, American Judicature Journal.*

WORK IN PROGRESS: The Supreme Court and the Criminal Law.

BIOGRAPHICAL/CRITICAL SOURCES: Washington Post, February 17, 1971.

*   *   *

CLEM, Alan L(eland)   1929-

PERSONAL: Born March 4, 1929, in Lincoln, Neb.; son of Remey Leland (a clergyman and school administrator) and Bernice (Thompson) Clem; married Mary Louise Burke, October 24, 1953; children: Andrew, Christopher, Constance, John, Daniel. *Education:* University of Nebraska, B.A., 1950; American University, M.A., 1957, Ph.D., 1960. *Politics:* Republican. *Religion:* Episcopalian. *Home:* 902 Valley View Dr., Vermillion, S.D. 57069. *Office:* Governmental Research Bureau, University of South Dakota, Vermillion, S.D. 57069.

CAREER: Ayres Advertising Agency, Lincoln, Neb., copywriter, then research director, 1950-52; press secretary in Washington, D.C., for U.S. Representative Carl Curtis, 1953-54, and Representative R.D. Harrison, 1955-58; U.S. Department of Agriculture, Foreign Agricultural Service, Washington, D.C., information specialist, 1959-60; University of South Dakota, Vermillion, associate professor, and assistant director of Governmental Research Bureau, 1960-64, professor of government and associate director of the Bureau, 1964—. Partner, Opinion Survey Associates, 1964-66. Television election analyst, KELO-TV. *Member:* American Political Science Association, Midwest Political Science Association, Alpha Tau Omega, Sigma Delta Chi, Phi Alpha Theta, Pi Sigma Alpha, Vermillion Chamber of Commerce, Rotary (member of National Council).

WRITINGS: The U.S. Agricultural Attache: His History and His Work, Foreign Agricultural Service, U.S. Department of Agriculture, 1960; *Spirit Mound Township in the 1960 Election: A Study of Rural Attitudes Toward Issues, Candidates, and Campaign Appeals,* Governmental Research Bureau, University of South Dakota, 1961; *South Dakota Political Almanac: A Presentation and Analysis of Election Statistics, 1889-1960,* Governmental Research Bureau, University of South Dakota, 1962, 2nd edition, Dakota Press, 1970; *The Nomination of Joe Bottum: Analysis of a Committee Decision to Nominate a United States Senator,* Governmental Research Bureau, University of South Dakota, 1963; *Precinct Voting: The Vote in Eastern South Dakota, 1940-1960,* Governmental Research Bureau, University of South Dakota, 1963; (editor) *Proceedings of the Fifth Annual Conference for South Dakota Assessing Officers,* Governmental Research Bureau, University of South Dakota, 1963; *Political Attitudes of South Dakota High School Students,* Governmental Research Bureau, University of South Dakota, 1963; *West River Voting Patterns: The Vote in Western South Dakota, 1940-1960,* Governmental Research Bureau, University of South Dakota, 1965; (compiler with George M. Platt) *A Bibliography of South Dakota Government and Politics,* Governmental Research Bureau, University of South Dakota, 1965; *Popular Representation and Senate Vacancies,* Governmental Research Bureau, University of South Dakota, 1966; *Roll Call Voting Behavior in the South Dakota Legislature,* Governmental Research Bureau, University of South Dakota, 1966; *Prairie State Politics: Popular Democracy in South Dakota,* Public Affairs Press, 1967. Contributor to historical, legal, and political periodicals.

WORK IN PROGRESS: Collaborating on *Comparative State Elections Project,* for University of North Carolina; articles on politics and government.

AVOCATIONAL INTERESTS: Bridge, golf, heraldry, old road maps, church history, game theory, and Edmund Burke.

* * *

CLEVELAND, Philip Jerome 1903-
(A. Don Adams, Rupert Chute, A. Frend, Lettie Lewes, Jerome C. Phillips)

PERSONAL: Born June 1, 1903, in Beverly, Mass.; son of Victor E. and Elizabeth M. (Chute) Cleveland; married Pearle B. Sullivan, 1926; children: Rupert, Priscilla, Wendell, Bruce. *Education:* Studied at Museum of Fine Arts, Boston, Berkshire Christian College, New England School of Theology. *Home:* 20 Tisbury St., New Bedford, Mass. 02745. *Office:* First Congregational Church, Blandford, Mass. 01008.

CAREER: Congregational minister who was chaplain at Babson Institute, Wellesley Hills, Mass., while still a college student. Pastor in Bear River, Nova Soctia, for two years, in Canterbury, Conn., for sixteen years, and in other Connecticut and Pennsylvania towns before becoming pastor of the First Congregational Church, New Bedford, Mass., in 1961. Former county jail chaplain and newspaper editor; commentator and pianist over radio station WBSM, New Bedford, Mass., for one year. Member of executive committee, Congregational-Christian Fellowship of Massachusetts; trustee, Camp Wachogue, Stafford, Conn. *Member:* American Committee for Free Latvia.

WRITINGS: Her Master: A Religious Romance, Plainville Press, 1928; *Beauty's Pilgrim, a Portrait of Jesus,* Ingland, 1937; *End of Dreams* (novel), Ingland, 1943; *Three Churches and a Model T,* Revell, 1960; *It's Bright in My Valley,* Revell, 1962; *Have a Wonderful Time!,* Revell, 1966.

Poems anthologized in *Masterpieces of Religious Verse,* edited by James D. Morrison, Harper, 1948, *A Treasury of Religious Verse,* edited by Donald T. Kauffman, Revell, 1962, *American Lyric Poems,* edited by Elder Olson, Appleton, 1964, *Our American Heritage,* edited by Charles L. Wallis, Harper, 1970, *The Marriage Affair,* compiled by J. Allan Petersen, Tyndale, 1971, and other collections. Contributor of articles and verse, under various pseudonyms, to periodicals, including *Reader's Digest, Saturday Evening Post, Good Housekeeping,* and *Ladies' Home Journal;* author of May-June, 1967 issue of *Manual of Prayer,* published by United Prayer Tower (Minneapolis).

SIDELIGHTS: An oil painter and composer-pianist, Cleveland's versatility also led him to serve for nine years as Santa Claus at a Sears, Roebuck & Co. store in Norwich, Conn. Complete collections of his books and poems are on file at Essex Institute, Salem, Mass., and the University of Mississippi, Hattiesburg.

BIOGRAPHICAL/CRITICAL SOURCES: Standard-Times, New Bedford, Mass., October 7, 1961.

* * *

CLEVELAND, Sidney E(arl) 1919-

PERSONAL: Born January 22, 1919, in Boston, Mass.; son of Herbert Carlos (a pharmacist) and Edith (Willey) Cleveland; married Marjorie L. Spacht, November 27, 1942; children: John A., Carol T., Mark E., Sarah D. *Education:* Brown University, A.B., 1941; University of Nebraska, M.A., 1942; University of Michigan, Ph.D., 1950. *Home:* 12021 Tall Oaks, Houston, Tex. 77024. *Office:* Veterans Administration Hospital, Houston, Tex. 77031.

CAREER: Veterans Administration Hospital, Houston, Tex., chief of psychology service, 1950—; Baylor College

of Medicine, Houston, Tex., 1957—, began as associate professor, became professor of psychology, 1957—. University of Houston, Houston, Tex., lecturer, 1950—; Rice University, Houston, Tex., lecturer, 1962—. Private practice of clinical psychology. City-County Hospital, Houston, Tex., consultant. *Military service:* U.S. Navy, 1942-46; became lieutenant commander. *Member:* American Psychological Association, Southwest Psychological Association, Law Science Academy of America.

WRITINGS: (With Seymour Fisher) *Body Image and Personality,* Van Nostrand, 1958, 2nd revised edition, Dickenson, 1968; (contributor) S.S. Beck and H.B. Molish, editors, *Reflexes to Intelligence,* Free Press, 1959; (contributor) H.E. Adams and W.K. Boardman, editors, *Advances in Experimental Clinical Psychology,* Pergamon, 1971; (contributor) H.C. Lindgren, D. Byrnne, and Fredrica Lindgren, editors, *Current Research in Psychology,* Wiley, 1971. Contributor of about 70 articles to professional journals.

WORK IN PROGRESS: Studies on clinical aspects of various psychosomatic syndromes, on psychological effects of sensory deprivation, on body image and personality, and on organ donor attitudes.

* * *

CLIFFORD, H(enry) Dalton 1911-

PERSONAL: Born August 20, 1911; son of Alex (an engineer) and Marian (Gibson) Clifford; married Mary Buntin, September 3, 1938. *Education:* Attended Tonbridge School. *Politics:* Conservative. *Home:* The Abbey, Penzance, Cornwall, England. *Office:* St. Ann's Gate, Salisbury, England.

CAREER: Articled to Denman & Son, Architects, Brighton, England, 1928-34; assistant in architectural firms of Joseph Emberton and of Sir John Burnet, Tait & Lorne, London, England, 1934-39; British Air Ministry, London, England, camouflage officer, 1940-44; started hotel in Penzance, England, 1947, and a fabric-printing business, 1949; *Home and Gardens,* London, England, furnishings editor, 1952-55; started another hotel, The Abbey, in Penzance, England, 1956, and still operates it and antique and book shops. Registered architect, 1944—, architect in private practice in Salisbury, England, 1962—. Designer of fabrics and Christmas cards. *Member:* Royal Institute of British Architects, Institute of Registered Architects.

WRITINGS: Cyprus for Beginners, Cyprus Mail, 1949; (with R.E. Enthoven) *New Homes from Old Buildings,* Country Life, 1954; *Home Decoration,* Country Life, 1955; *New Houses for Moderate Means,* Country Life, 1957; *The Country Life Book of Houses for Today,* Country Life, 1963. Contributor of articles and cartoon drawings to magazines and newspapers in England and Australia; designer of "Herb and Spice Charts," Bart Prints.

WORK IN PROGRESS: A book on English garden herbs.

* * *

CLIFT, Virgil Alfred 1912-

PERSONAL: Born May 1, 1912, in Princeton, Ind.; son of Joseph Leslie (a farmer) and Arra Bane (Hardiman) Clift. *Education:* Indiana University, B.A., 1934; Indiana State College, M.A., 1939; Ohio State University, Ph.D., 1944. *Home:* 3 Washington Square Village, Apt. 11-5, New York, N.Y. 10012. *Office:* School of Education, New York University, Washington Sq., New York, N.Y. 10003.

CAREER: Rust College, Holly Springs, Miss., professor of education, 1938-39; Agriculture and Technical College of North Carolina, Greensboro, professor of education, 1939-48; Morgan State College, Baltimore, Md., professor of education, 1948-63; New York University, New York, N.Y., professor of education, 1963—. Fulbright lecturer in Pakistan, 1954-55; director of teacher education for Kingdom of Libya, 1956-58. *Member:* National Society for the Study of Education, Society for the Advancement of Education, John Dewey Society (chairman of yearbook commission, 1960-63; member of nominating committee, 1960-63; member of executive board, 1964-66).

WRITINGS: (Editor with Archibald W. Anderson and H. Gordon Hullfish) *Negro Education in America: Its Adequacy, Problems and Needs,* Harper, 1962. Contributor: E. Franklin Frazier, editor, *Integration of Negroes into Public Elementary Schools in the United States,* Howard University Press; William W. Brickman and Stanley Lehrer, editors, *Countdown on Segregated Education,* Society for the Advancement of Education, 1960; *Compensation on the Campus,* Association of Higher Education and National Education Association, 1961; (editor and contributor with W.A. Low) *Encyclopedia of Black America,* McGraw, in press. Contributor of articles and reviews to educational and sociological journals.

WORK IN PROGRESS: Cultural Deprivation of Youth in Urban Areas; Influence of Social Class Factors on High Level Academic Achievement; Social and Cultural Deprivation Among Negro Youth.

*   *   *

COBB, Faye Davis 1932-

PERSONAL: Born June 3, 1932, in Baltimore, Md.; daughter of Paul and Mary Louise (Kain) Davis; married Virgil Wayne Cobb (a Civil Service Commission employee) August 4, 1956; children: Jeffrey W., Gregory B. *Education:* State Teachers College at Towson, Towson, Md., B.S. in Ed., 1954. *Home:* 6215 85th Pl., Hyattsville, Md. 20784.

CAREER: Teacher in Baltimore, Md., 1954-56, in Prince Georges County, Md., 1961—. *Member:* National Education Association, Maryland State Teachers Association.

WRITINGS: A Parent's Guide to Better Babysitting (with babysitter's manual), Pocket Books, 1963. Contributor to community paper.

*   *   *

COBLE, John (Lawrence) 1924-

PERSONAL: Born December 27, 1924, in Springfield, Mo.; son of Le Roy (an executive secretary of Young Men's Christian Association) and Pauline (Woodard) Coble; married Lorraine Virginia Hunt, July 16, 1955. *Education:* University of Redlands, B.A., 1949; University of Denver, M.A., 1950, Ph.D., 1958; University of California, Los Angeles, postgraduate study, 1951-52. *Home:* 844 North Verde, Rialto, Calif. 92376. *Agent:* Elizabeth McKee, MacIntosh, McKee & Dodds, Inc., 22 East 40th St., New York, N.Y. 10016. *Office:* Department of English, San Bernardino Valley College, San Bernardino, Calif. 92403.

CAREER: San Bernardino Valley College, San Bernardino, Calif., 1954—, began as instructor, became assistant professor of English. *Military service:* U.S. Army Air Corps, 1943-45; became staff sergeant; received Air Medal and two Oak Leaf Clusters. *Awards, honors:* Huntington Hartford scholarship for writing.

WRITINGS: Two Eagles (stories), A. Swallow, 1963. Contributor of short story to *PS,* A. Swallow, 1953. Contributor to *Tomorrow.*

WORK IN PROGRESS: A novel about World War II, *To Slay the Tiger.*

COCHRANE, Louise Morley 1918-

PERSONAL: Born December 22, 1918, in New York, N.Y.; daughter of Christopher and Helen (Fairchild) Morley; married James Aikman Cochrane (director of a British printing firm); children: Alison Morley, Janet Fairchild. *Education:* Graduate Institute of International Studies, Geneva, Switzerland,· student, 1938-39; Bryn Mawr College, B.A., 1940. *Religion:* Episcopal. *Home:* Malthouse, Corsley, Westminister, England. *Agent:* Curtis Brown Ltd., 13 King St., London W.C. 2, England.

CAREER: International Student Service, New York, N.Y., conference secretary, 1940-42; U.S. Office of War Information, London, England, education specialist, 1943-46; British Broadcasting Corp., London, England, radio program director in schools department, 1947-50; free-lance broadcaster and writer, mainly for children, 1951—. Fulbright Commission, member, 1952-66. *Member:* English-Speaking Union (life), Bryn Mawr Club of United Kingdom (former chairman).

WRITINGS: (With Sam Williams) *Rag, Tag and Bobtail,* Publicity Products, 1953; (with Williams) *Rag, Tag and Bobtail and the Mushrooms,* Publicity Products, 1954; (with Peter Cochrane) *Digest of British History,* Newman Neame, 1954; *Social Work for Jill,* Chatto & Windus, 1954; *Marion Turns Teacher,* Chatto & Windus, 1955; *Sheila Goes Gardening,* Chatto & Windus, 1957; *Jalopy the Taxicab Cat,* F. Watts, 1957; *Holiday Book of Play Ideas and Things-To-Do,* Chatto & Windus, 1959.

Anne in Electronics, Chatto & Windus, 1960; *Jalopy at the Rally,* Chatto & Windus, 1960; *Puppet Book of Play Ideas and Things-To-Do,* Chatto & Windus, 1962; *Highland Summer,* Chatto & Windus, 1963; (with Duncan Taylor) *The World of Nations,* Whitman Publishing, 1963; *The U.S.A. and Her People,* Lutterworth, 1964; *Shadow Puppets in Color,* Plays, 1972.

Contributor of short stories to anthologies; has done editorial work on translating French texts for English children; author of British Broadcasting Corp. television series, "Rag, Tag and Bobtail," 1953—, and of other television and radio scripts.

WORK IN PROGRESS: Research on historical background for a children's novel; another novel.

*   *   *

COCKBURN, Thomas Aiden 1912-

PERSONAL: Surname is pronounced *Co*-burn; born May 30, 1912, in North Shields, England; son of George Thomas (a sailor) and Margaret J. (Howey) Cockburn; married Eve Gillian Fairhurst; children: Gillian, Erika, Vivian, Alistair, Alison. *Education:* University of Durham, M.B. and B.S., 1935, M.D., 1937; Royal Institute of Hygiene and Public Health, D.P.H., 1940. *Office:* Mayor's Committee for Human Resources Development, 903 West Grand Blvd., Detroit, Mich. 48208.

CAREER: British Army, specialist in hygiene in England, 1941-42, in West Africa, 1942-44, in Middle East, 1944-46; London Zoo, London, England, assistant superintendent, 1946-47; U.S. Public Health Service, Washington, D.C., chief of encephalitis investigations, 1948-54; World Health Organization, adviser on epidemiology to government of Ceylon, 1955-57; International Cooperative Administration, adviser to government of East Pakistan, 1958-60; Health Department, Cincinnati, Ohio, assistant commissioner, 1961-66; Mayor's Committee for Human Resources Development, Detroit, Mich., medical-dental director, 1966—. Visiting fellow at Johns Hopkins University, 1960-61. *Member:* Cincinnati Gilbert and Sullivan Society (president).

WRITINGS: The Evolution and Eradication of Infectious Diseases, Johns Hopkins Press, 1963; Infectious Diseases: Their Evolution and Eradication, C.C Thomas, 1967.

WORK IN PROGRESS: A dozen research projects in infections; Infectious Diseases in Ancient Populations.

* * *

COCKETT, Mary

PERSONAL: Born in Yorkshire, England; married Reginald Cockett; children: Judith, Roger. Education: Studied at Bedford College, and London Institute of Education, University of London. Home: 24, Benville Ave., Bristol BS9 2RX, England.

CAREER: Editorial work for National Institute of Industrial Psychology, 1943-48, and International Congress on Mental Health, 1948-49; free-lance writer of juveniles.

WRITINGS: Jonathan on the Farm, Harrap, 1954; Jonathan and Felicity, Harrap, 1955; Fourteen Stories about Jonathan, Harrap, 1956; More about Jonathan, Harrap, 1957; Jan, the Market Boy, Brockhampton Press, 1957; Bouncing Ball, Hamish Hamilton, 1958; Jasper Club, Heinemann, 1959; When Felicity Was Small, Harrap, 1959.

Rolling On, Methuen, 1960; Seven Days with Jan, Brockhampton Press, 1960; Mary Ann Goes to Hospital, Methuen, 1961; Out with Felicity and Jonathan, Harrap, 1962; Cottage by the Loch, Methuen, 1962; Roads and Travelling, Basil Blackwell, 1964, Soccer Associates, 1966; Benny's Bazaar, Oliver & Boyd, 1964; Acrobat Hamster, Hamish Hamilton, 1965; The Birthday Ride, Oliver & Boyd, 1965; Bridges (nonfiction), Oliver & Boyd, 1965; Sunflower Giant, Hamish Hamilton, 1966; There for the Picking, Oliver & Boyd, 1966; Ash Dry, Ash Green, Oliver & Boyd, 1966, Criterion, 1969; Strange Valley, Oliver & Boyd, 1967; Twelve Gold Chairs, Oliver & Boyd, 1967; Something Big, Oliver & Boyd, 1968; The Wild Place, Oliver & Boyd, 1968; Rosanna the Goat, Chatto, Boyd & Oliver, 1969, Bobbs-Merrill, 1970; Pelican Park, Warne, 1969; Tufty, Macmillan, 1969; Frankie's Country Day, Macmillan, 1969; The Lost Money, Macmillan, 1969; Another Home, Another Country, Oliver & Boyd, 1970; Farthing Bundles, Chatto, Boyd & Oliver, 1970; The Wedding Tea, Macmillan, 1970; Towns (nonfiction) Basil Blackwell, 1971; The Joppy Books, three volumes, Chatto & Windus, 1971; Boat Girl, Chatto & Windus, 1972; The Marvellous Stick, Macmillan, 1972.

Contributor to Young Elizabethan, Guardian, Times (London), Growing Point, Books for Your Children, Nursery World, and other periodicals. Author of radio scripts, mostly for schools programs, for about 150 broadcasts in several countries. Lecturer to schools and libraries on writing.

WORK IN PROGRESS: Two books; several school scripts for British Broadcasting Corp. (radio and television).

BIOGRAPHICAL/CRITICAL SOURCES: Times Literary Supplement, May 25, 1967, June 26, 1969; Books and Bookmen, February, 1968.

* * *

COFFIN, Berton   1910-

PERSONAL: Born April 11, 1910, in Fairmount, Ind.; son of Charles Levi (a professor) and Hazel (Painter) Coffin; married Mildred Wantland (manager of Artist Series, University of Colorado), August 26, 1936; children: Martha Ann. Education: Earlham College, B.A., 1932; Chicago Musical College, B.M., 1934; Eastman School of Music, M.M., 1938; Juilliard School of Music, advanced study, 1945-46, and three summers;

Columbia University, M.A., 1946, Ed.D. 1950. Home: 1240 Holly Pl., Boulder, Colo. 80303.

CAREER: Tarleton State College, Stephenville, Tex., 1936-45, became professor of voice and head of division of fine arts; University of Colorado, College of Music, Boulder, professor of voice, 1946—, head of division of voice, 1959—. Consolidated Vultee Aircraft, Fort Worth, Tex., mathematician and weights analyst, 1944-45. Member: American Academy of Teachers of Singing, National Association of Teachers of Singing (former president of Colorado chapter; member of board of directors, 1956—, president, 1968-69), Pi Kappa Lambda, Phi Mu Alpha, Rotary Club (Boulder).

WRITINGS: The Singer's Repertoire, Volumes I-IV, Scarecrow, 1960, Volume V: (with Werner Singer) Program Notes, Scarecrow, 1962, Volume VI: (with Singer, Pierre Delattre, and Ralph Errolle) Phonetic Readings of Songs and Arias from "The Singer's Repertoire," Pruett Press, 1964, Volume VII: (with Singer and Delattre) Word-by-Word Translations of Songs and Arias from "The Singer's Repertoire," Scarecrow, 1967; Bel Canto: The Nature of Vowels, Milton Press, 1971.

WORK IN PROGRESS: Microfilm research in song literature in connection with The Singer's Repertoire; compilation of music and data for use by graduate students at University of Colorado under grants from the university's Research Council.

* * *

COFFIN, Frank M(orey)   1919-

PERSONAL: Born July 11, 1919, in Lewiston, Me.; son of Herbert Rice and Ruth (Morey) Coffin; married Ruth Ulrich, December 19, 1942; children: Nancy, Douglas, Meredith, Susan. Education: Bates College, A.B., 1940; Harvard Business School, student in industrial administration, 1943; Harvard Law School, LL.B., 1947. Politics: Democrat. Religion: Baptist. Home: 1 Ocean Rd., South Portland, Me. 04106. Office: 156 Federal St., Portland, Me. 04112.

CAREER: Attorney, Lewiston, Me., 1945-57, and partner of Verrill, Dana, Walker, Philbrick and Whitehouse, Portland, Me., 1953-57; U.S. Congressman for Maine, 1957-60, serving on House Foreign Affairs Committee and Joint Economic Committee; U.S. Development Loan Fund, Washington, D.C., managing director, 1961; U.S. Agency for International Development, Washington, D.C., deputy administrator, 1961-64; Development Assistance Committee, Paris, France, U.S. permanent representative, 1964-65; U.S. Court of Appeals for the First Circuit, Portland, Me., judge, 1965—. Military service: U.S. Naval Reserve, 1943-46; served in Pacific theater; became lieutenant.

WRITINGS: Economic Development Assistance and World Stability, Industrial College of the Armed Forces, 1962; Witness for AID, Houghton, 1964.

* * *

COHANE, Tim(othy)   1912-

PERSONAL: Born February 7, 1912, in New Haven, Conn.; son of Sylvester T. and Margaret (Hogan) Cohane; married Margaret U. Hill, December 29, 1936; children: Margaret Mary, Lorraine Elizabeth, Timothy, Jr., Peter, Rosemary, Ellen, Mary Therese. Education: Fordham University, B.A., 1935. Home: 12 Carman Rd., Scarsdale, N.Y. 10583. Office: School of Public Communication, Boston University, 640 Commonwealth Ave., Boston, Mass. 02215.

CAREER: Fordham University, Bronx, N.Y., director of athletic publicity, 1935-40; New York World-Telegram, New York, N.Y., sports writer and columnist, 1940-44; Look, New York, N.Y., sports editor, 1944-65; Sunrise (magazine), editor, 1965-67; Boston University, Boston, Mass., professor of writing, School of Public Communication, 1968—.

WRITINGS: Gridiron Grenadiers: The Story of West Point Football, Putnam, 1948; *The Yale Football Story,* Putnam, 1951; (with Earl H. Blaik) *You Have to Pay the Price* (autobiography of Blaik), Holt, 1960; *Bypaths of Glory: A Sportswriter Looks Back,* Harper, 1963. Also author of *Great College Football Coaches of the Twenties and Thirties,* Arlington House.

* * *

COHEN, B(enjamin) Bernard 1922-

PERSONAL: Born May 30, 1922, in Baltimore, Md.; son of Louis and Lillie (Laken) Cohen; married Lucian Dumas Anderson, July 29, 1952. *Education:* University of Maryland, A.B., 1943, M.A., 1944; Indiana University, Ph.D., 1950. *Politics:* Democrat. *Home:* 7433 Overbrook Dr., St. Louis, Mo. 63121.

CAREER: Wayne University (now Wayne State University), Detroit, Mich., instructor in English, 1948-52; Georgia Institute of Technology, Atlanta, assistant professor of English, 1953-55; Indiana State College, Terre Haute, assistant professor of English, 1955-57; Jacksonville State College, Jacksonville, Ala., associate professor of English, 1957-59; Wichita State University, Wichita, Kan., associate professor, 1960-65, professor of English, 1965-68; University of Missouri, St. Louis, professor of English, 1968—. *Member:* Modern Language Association of America, National Council of Teachers of English, Conference on College Composition and Communication, Midwest Modern Language Association. *Awards, honors:* American Council of Learned Societies research grant, 1952-53; Excellence in Teaching Award, Wichita State University, 1968.

WRITINGS: Writing About Literature, Scott, Foresman, 1963; (editor) *Literature for Understanding,* Scott, Foresman, 1966; *Working for Literary Understanding: A Guide to Critical Reading,* Scott, Foresman, 1966; (editor) *The Recognition of Nathaniel Hawthorne,* University of Michigan Press, 1969; *Guide to Nathaniel Hawthorne: An Essay,* C.E. Merrill, 1970. Contributor of some forty articles to professional journals.

WORK IN PROGRESS: A second edition of *Writing About Literature; Thomas Wentworth Higginson,* a critical study for Twayne's "U.S. Authors" series; *Nathaniel Hawthorne's Library.*

* * *

COHEN, Jerome B(ernard) 1915-

PERSONAL: Born January 18, 1915, in New York, N.Y.; son of Charles Kenneth and Estelle (Bauland) Cohen; married Mina Salmon, June 18, 1941; children: Carla Lee. *Education:* College of the City of New York (now City College of the City University of New York), B.S.S. in Economics (cum laude), 1934; Columbia University, M.A., 1935, Ph.D., 1947. *Home:* 135 East 74th St., New York, N.Y. 10021. *Office:* Bernard M. Baruch School of Business and Public Administration, City University of New York, 17 Lexington Ave., New York, N.Y. 10010.

CAREER: City University of New York (formerly City College of New York), New York, N.Y., 1934—, became professor of economics and assistant dean in charge of graduate studies at Bernard M. Baruch School of Business and Public Administration, 1956—, associate dean of graduate studies, 1963-68, dean of School of Business, 1969-70, acting president of Baruch School of Business, 1970—. On leave from college, serving in U.S. government posts as economist, Coordinator of Inter-American Affairs, 1941-42, assistant regional administrator for territories and possessions, Office of Price Administration, 1942-43, staff of Strategic Bombing Survey, 1945-46, member of tax mission to Japan, 1949, chief of South Asian Branch, Office of Intelligence Research, Department of State, 1950-51. Visiting professor at Columbia University, 1962 and 1963; lecturer at Stonier Graduate School of Banking, 1960-61, New School for Social Research, 1961. Consultant in various anti-trust cases, 1956-64. *Military service:* U.S. Navy, Intelligence, 1943-46; served as Japanese language officer.

MEMBER: American Economic Association, National Association of Business Economists, American Finance Association, American Association of University Professors, National Tax Association, Royal Economic Society (fellow), Metropolitan Economic Association (president, 1954-55), Council on Foreign Relations, Phi Beta Kappa (president of Gamma chapter, 1970-71), Beta Gamma Sigma. *Awards, honors:* Rockefeller Foundation grant, 1956; Social Science Research Council grant, 1963-64.

WRITINGS: Decade of Decision, Institute of Life Insurance, 1948; *Japan's Economy in War and Reconstruction,* University of Minnesota Press, 1949; (contributor) Hugh Borton, editor, *Japan,* Cornell University Press, 1951; *Economic Problems of Free Japan,* Princeton University Press, 1952; (with Arthur Hanson) *Personal Finance: Principles and Case Problems,* Irwin, 1954, 4th edition, 1972; (contributor) Phillip Moseley, editor, *Japan Between East and West,* Harper for Council on Foreign Relations, 1957; *Japan's Postwar Economy,* Indiana University Press, 1958; *Personal Money Management* (monograph), American Bankers Association, 1962; (with Sidney R. Robbins) *The Financial Manager: Basic Aspects of Financial Management,* Harper, 1966; (with Edward D. Zinberg) *Investment Analysis and Portfolio Management,* Irwin, 1967; (editor) *Pacific Partnership: U.S. Japan Trade,* Lexington, 1973.

Contributor of more than sixty articles and reviews to magazines and professional journals, including *New Republic, Fortune, Reader's Digest, Saturday Review, Current History, Journal of Finance, Bankers Magazine, Barron's Financial Weekly.*

* * *

COHN, Robert Greer 1921-

PERSONAL: Born September 5, 1921, in Richmond, Va.; son of Charles A. (a merchant) and Susan (Spilberg) Cohn; children: Stephen A., Richard L. *Education:* University of Virginia, B.A., 1943; Yale University, M.A., 1947, Ph.D., 1949. *Home:* 6 Maywood Lane, Menlo Park, Calif. 94025. *Office:* Department of French and Italian, Stanford University, Stanford, Calif. 94305.

CAREER: Yale University, New Haven, Conn., instructor in French, 1949-50; Swarthmore College, Swarthmore, Pa., assistant professor of French, 1952-54; Vassar College, Poughkeepsie, N.Y., assistant professor of French, 1954-59; Stanford University, Stanford, Calif., associate professor of French, 1959-64, professor of French, 1964—. *Military service:* U.S. Army, 1943-46; became technician fifth class; received Croix de Guerre, Distinguished Unit medal. *Awards, honors:* Guggenheim fellow; Fulbright fellow, 1950-51; fellow, American Council of Learned Societies; fellow, National Endowment for the Humanities, 1969-70.

WRITINGS: Mallarme's "Un Coup de Des": An Exegesis, Yale University Press, 1949; *L'Oeuvre de Mallarme,* Les Lettres, 1951; *The Writers Way in France,* University of Pennsylvania Press, 1960; *Toward the Poems of Mallarme,* University of California Press,

1965; *Mallarme's Masterwork: New Findings,* Mouton & Co., 1966, Humanities, 1967; (contributor) Warren Ramsey, editor, *Jules Laforgue: Essays on a Poet's Life and Work,* Southern Illinois University Press, 1969; (contributor) Walter Langlois, editor, *The Persistent Voice: Hellenism in French Literature Since the Eighteenth Century,* New York University Press, 1971; *The Poetry of Rimbaud,* Princeton University Press, 1973. Founding editor, *Yale French Studies.*

BIOGRAPHICAL/CRITICAL SOURCES: Sewanee Review, spring, 1970.

* * *

COKER, Jerry 1932-

PERSONAL: Born November 28, 1932, in South Bend, Ind.; son of Curtis (a musician) and Mildred Ruth (Collier) Coker; married Patricia Fitz-Patrick (a journalist and jazz singer), September 23, 1955; children: David Curtis. *Education:* Attended Indiana University, 1950-53, Yale University, 1957-58; Sam Houston State Teachers College, B.M.E., 1959, M.A., 1960. *Office:* Department of Music Theory, University of Miami, Coral Gables, Fla. 33124.

CAREER: Jazz composer-arranger and tenor sax soloist with Woody Herman, Stan Kenton, Claude Thornhill, Les Elgart, Ralph Marterie, and Clare Fischer orchestras, on tour and for recordings, 1953-57; Sam Houston State Teachers College (now Sam Houston State University), Huntsville, Tex., instructor in music, 1958-62; Monterey Peninsula College, Monterey, Calif., instructor in music, 1962—. Clinician, lecturer, jazz festival coordinator. Monterey Symphony Orchestra, clarinettist, 1963-64. *Member:* American Federation of Musicians, California Teachers Association.

WRITINGS: Improvising Jazz, forewords by Stan Kenton and Gunther Schuller, Prentice-Hall, 1964.

WORK IN PROGRESS: A saxophone method book; a collection of original jazz instructive etudes.

* * *

COLBY, Vineta (Blumoff) 1922-

PERSONAL: Born May 12, 1922, in New York, N.Y.; daughter of Walter and Vineta (Rolls) Blumoff; married Robert Alan Colby (a professor of library science), May 8, 1947. *Education:* New York University, B.A., 1942, M.A., 1943; Yale University, Ph.D., 1946. *Home:* 33-24 86th St., Jackson Heights, N.Y. 11372. *Office:* Department of English, Queens College, City University of New York, Flushing, N.Y. 11367.

CAREER: Roosevelt University, Chicago, Ill., 1947-49, began as instructor, became assistant professor of English; Queens College, Flushing, N.Y., instructor, 1961-65, assistant professor, 1966-69, associate professor of English, 1970—. *Park East* (weekly newspaper), drama critic, 1964—. *Member:* American Association of University Professors, Modern Language Association of America, Phi Beta Kappa.

WRITINGS: (Assistant editor to Stanley Kunitz) *Twentieth Century Authors: First Supplement,* H.W. Wilson, 1955; (editor) *American Culture in the Sixties,* H.W. Wilson, 1964; (with husband, Robert A. Colby) *The Equivocal Virtue: Mrs. Oliphant and the Victorian Literary Market Place,* Archon, 1966; (editor with Kunitz) *European Authors, 1000-1900,* H.W. Wilson, 1967; *The Singular Anomaly: Women Novelists of the Nineteenth Century,* New York University Press, 1970.

BIOGRAPHICAL/CRITICAL SOURCES: Times Literary Supplement, March 16, 1967.

COLE, Margaret Alice
(Rosemary Manning, Julia Renton, Ione Saunders)

PERSONAL: Born in Meerut, India; daughter of Edward (a regular officer, British Army) and Frances (Hampton) Cole. *Education:* Attended schools on Guernsey, Channel Islands, and Residential Training College and Hartley University, both Southampton, England. *Politics:* Conservative. *Religion:* Roman Catholic. *Home:* 27 Langham Court, London S.W. 20, England. *Agent:* Robert Sommerville Ltd., Mowbray House, Norfolk St., London W.C.2, England.

CAREER: Teacher in Government Educational Service, London, England, prior to 1957, and teacher of English and music for London County Council Evening Institute; full-time writer, 1957—. Pianist. *Member:* Royal Society of Arts (fellow), Royal Overseas League (fellow), Royal Commonwealth Society, Romantic Novelists Association (founder member; literary reader), Society of Women Journalists, London Writers Circle, John O'London Literary Circle.

WRITINGS—Under name Margaret Alice Cole: *Romance at Butlin's,* R. Hale, 1958; *Passport to Paradise,* R. Hale, 1959; *Holiday Camp Mystery* (juvenile), R. Hale, 1959; *Love for a Doctor,* R. Hale, 1960; *Across the World to Love,* Gresham, 1961; *Jill and Joe on Holiday* (juvenile), 1961; *The Doctor Takes a Wife,* R. Hale, 1961; *Give Me Back Yesterday,* Gresham, 1961; *Jill and Joe's Return Holiday* (juvenile), 1962; *Love in Venice,* Gresham, 1962; *Love on the Long Walk,* R. Hale, 1962; *Thrilling Holiday* (juvenile), R. Hale, 1962; *Rainbow Beyond,* Gresham, 1963; *Romance in the Tyrol,* Gresham, 1964; *Doctor Verner's Romance,* R. Hale, 1964; *Another Thrilling Holiday* (juvenile), R. Hale, 1964; *Romance in Capri,* R. Hale, 1965; *Two Hearts Bid,* R. Hale, 1965; *The Doctor Decides,* Gresham 1966; *The Doctor's Fiancee,* Gresham, 1966; *Scottish Rhapsody,* R. Hale, 1966; *Another Holiday Camp Mystery,* R. Hale, 1967; *Flying to Happiness,* Gresham, 1967.

Under pseudonym Rosemary Manning: *Shadowed Starlight,* Gresham, 1961.

Under pseudonym Julia Renton: *Romance in Chelsea,* Gresham, 1961; *Connemara Colleen,* Gresham, 1962; *Starlight for Sheila,* Gresham, 1962; *Life's a Mirror,* Gresham, 1963.

Under pseudonym Ione Saunders: *Rhapsody in Paris,* Gresham, 1963.

Contributor of stories to magazines and newspapers.

* * *

COLE, William (Rossa) 1919-

PERSONAL: Born November 20, 1919, in Staten Island, N.Y.; son of William Harrison (a businessman) and Margaret (O'Donovan-Rossa) Cole; married Peggy Bennett (a writer), May, 1947 (divorced); married Galen Williams (a cultural administrator), July 10, 1967; children: (first marriage) Cambria Bennett, Jeremy Rossa (both daughters); (second marriage) Williams, Rossa (sons) *Education:* High school graduate. *Politics:* Socialist. *Religion:* None. *Home and office:* 201 West 54th St., New York, N.Y. 10019.

CAREER: Alfred A. Knopf, Inc., New York, N.Y., publicity director, 1946-58; Simon and Schuster, Inc., New York, N.Y., publicity director, editor, 1958-61. Co-publisher, with Viking Press, William Cole Books. *Military service:* U.S. Army, Infantry, 1940-45; served in European theater; became sergeant; received Purple Heart. *Member:* International P.E.N. (vice-president, American Center, 1955-56; executive board member, 1956—), Authors Guild.

WRITINGS: *A Cat-Hater's Handbook; or, the Ailuro-phobe's Delight*, Dial, 1963; *Frances Face-Maker: A Going-to-Bed Book*, World Publishing, 1963; *What's Good for a Six-Year-Old?*, Holt, 1965; *Uncoupled Couplets: A Game of Rhymes*, Taplinger, 1966; *What's Good for a Four-Year-Old?*, Holt, 1967; *What's Good for a Five-Year-Old?*, Holt, 1968; *That Pest, Jonathan*, Harper, 1970; *Aunt Bella's Umbrella*, Doubleday, 1970.

Anthologies edited: (With Marvin Rosenberg) *The Best Cartoons from Punch*, Simon & Schuster, 1952; *The Best Humor from Punch*, World Publishing, 1953; (with Florett Robinson) *Women Are Wonderful: A History in Cartoons of a Hundred Years with America's Most Controversial Figure*, Houghton, 1954; (with Douglas McKee) *French Cartoons*, Dell, 1954; (with McKee) *More French Cartoons*, Dell, 1955; *Humorous Poetry for Children*, World Publishing, 1955; *Story Poems, Old and New*, World Publishing, 1957; *I Went to the Animal Fair: A Book of Animal Poems*, World Publishing, 1958; *The Fireside Book of Humorous Poetry*, Simon & Schuster, 1959; *Poems of Magic and Spells*, World Publishing, 1960; (with Julia Colmore *The Poetry-Drawing Book*, Simon & Schuster, 1960; *Poems for Seasons and Celebrations*, World Publishing, 1961; *Folk Songs of England, Ireland, Scotland and Wales*, Doubleday, 1961; (with Colmore) *New York in Photographs*, Simon & Schuster, 1961; (with McKee) *Touche: French Cartoons*, Dell, 1961; (with Colmore) *The Second Poetry-Drawing Book*, Simon & Schuster, 1962; (with McKee) *You Damn Men Are All Alike: French Cartoons*, Gold Medal, 1962; *Erotic Poetry*, Random House, 1963; *The Most of A.J. Liebling*, Simon & Schuster, 1963; *The Birds and the Beasts Were There: Animal Poems*, World Publishing, 1963; *Beastly Boys and Ghastly Girls*, World Publishing, 1964; *A Big Bowl of Punch*, Simon & Schuster, 1964; *A Book of Love Poems*, Viking, 1965; (with Mike Thaler) *The Classic Cartoons*, World Publishing, 1966; *Oh, What Nonsense!*, Viking, 1966; *The Sea, Ships, and Sailors: Poems, Songs and Shanties*, Viking, 1967; *D.H. Lawrence: Poems Selected for Young People*, Viking, 1967; *Poems of W.S. Gilbert*, Crowell, 1967; *Eight Lines and Under: An Anthology of Short, Short Poems*, Macmillan, 1967; *A Case of the Giggles*, two volumes, World Publishing, 1967; *Man's Funniest Friend: The Dog in Stories, Reminiscences, Poems and Cartoons*, World Publishing, 1967; *Poems of Thomas Hood*, Crowell, 1968; *A Book of Nature Poems*, Viking, 1969; *Rough Men, Tough Men: Poems of Action and Adventure*, Viking, 1969; *The Punch Line: Twenty-five Portfolios of Contemporary English Comic Artists*, Simon & Schuster, 1969; *Pith and Vinegar: An Anthology of Short Humorous Poetry*, Simon & Schuster, 1969; *Oh, How Silly!*, Viking, 1970; *The Poet's Tales: A New Book of Story Poems*, World Publishing, 1971; *Poems from Ireland*, Crowell, 1971; *Poetry Brief*, Macmillan, 1971; *Oh, That's Ridiculous!*, Viking, 1972; *Pick Me Up: A Book of Short, Short Poems*, Macmillan, 1972; *. . . And Be Merry!: A Feast of Light Verse and a Soupcon of Prose About the Joy of Eating*, Grossman, 1972.

WORK IN PROGRESS: A second book of folksongs of the British Isles; an anthology of short poems for young people; poems from Ireland; a book of light verse; two children's books; contemplating an immense anthology of British and American humor from all periods.

SIDELIGHTS: As his bibliography and report on work in progress indicate, Cole is a writer of books on his own, but, primarily, he belongs to that distinctive breed of bibliogoners known as *anthologists,* having gotten started some twenty collections or so ago when he was an editor in search of an anthologist and suddenly realized that not only could he do the book he had in mind but that he'd *like* doing it.

"The first requisite for an anthologist," said Cole in a lively and informative article in *Junior Libraries* (May, 1960), "should be a crusading enthusiasm for his subject. He should be a practitioner of literary buttonholing—continually exclaiming, through the medium of his compilations, 'Hey! Take a look at *this* one!' An anthology done without enthusiasm is like a TV dinner: frozen, tasteless, and quickly forgotten."

The anthologist also needs, says Cole, some of the instincts of the pack rat, and since boyhood he has been accumulating files of anything which appealed to him, although in the beginning he had no particular reason for doing so except that "I felt somebody should do it the honor."

When, as Cole puts it, he "feels an anthology coming on," he mouses through his accumulated hoards, lives in libraries, and scouts used book shops carefully. In a month or so of intensive searching he generally uncovers everything he needs for a book—and much more. Then begin the winnowing, the arranging, the re-arranging, the seeking of permissions and the negotiating of reprint fees.

Finally, the finished book arrives—"the biggest thrill of the year." There is excitement in examining the new volume and satisfaction in seeing that the desired mood is created by the selections. But there is a peculiar pleasure, Cole finds, in being able to say concerning little gems rescued from newspapers and magazines that, "Now, they've got a home."

AVOCATIONAL INTERESTS: "Reading poetry, listening to folk songs, admiring pretty girls, eating exotically when possible, playing tennis and ping pong, making puns, and going to good movies."

BIOGRAPHICAL/CRITICAL SOURCES: *Commonweal*, May 26, 1967; *New York Times Book Review*, November 5, 1967, November 9, 1969; *Christian Science Monitor*, November 30, 1967; *Best Sellers*, December 1, 1967, December 15, 1969, January 1, 1970; *New Yorker*, March 30, 1968; *Poetry*, May, 1968; Lee Bennett Hopkins, *Books Are By People*, Citation, 1969; *Writers Digest*, March, 1969; *Saturday Review*, May 10, 1969; *Library Journal*, September, 1970; *Book World*, January 11, 1970; *Horn Book*, January 11, 1970.

*   *   *

COLEMAN, Robert William Alfred   1916-
(James Insight)

PERSONAL: Born July 30, 1916, in Cairo, Egypt; son of Robert (a doctor) and Evans Coleman; married Lucette Bartholomew, July 6, 1945; children: Michael, Sylvia. *Education:* Attended Westminster School, London, England, 1930-35; Christ's College, Cambridge, M.A., 1939. *Home:* Villa Florence, West Dr., Middleton-on-Sea, Sussex, England. *Agent:* John Johnson, 10 Suffield House, 79 Davies St., London, England.

CAREER: Clergyman, Church of England. Curate in Worthing, Sussex, England, 1941-43; vicar in Tiberton, Devonshire, 1946-50, in West Ealing, 1950-59; chaplain to Springfield Hospital, 1959-60, to Seaford College, 1960—. *Military service:* Royal Army Chaplain's Department, chaplain to the forces, 1943-46.

WRITINGS—All under pseudonym James Insight: *I Am the Vicar*, Jenkins, 1956; *Country Parson*, Jenkins, 1961, Fell, 1964; *I Turned My Collar Round*, Fell, 1963; *I Am a Guinea Pig*, P. Davies, 1964. Contributor to various journals.

WORK IN PROGRESS: A book on the theme that Insight (the author) takes a party to the Lord.

COLES, Harry L(ewis) 1920-

PERSONAL: Born April 30, 1920, in Nashville, Tenn.; son of Harry Lewis (a retail merchant) and Zay (Freeman) Coles; married Patricia Lockwood Sinnott, December 26, 1959; children: Christopher Desmond, Carl Edward. Education: Vanderbilt University, A.B., 1939, Ph.D., 1942. Home: 2605 Wellesley Dr., Columbus, Ohio 43221. Office: Department of History, Ohio State University, Columbus, Ohio 43210.

CAREER: Ohio State University, Columbus, instructor, 1949-52, assistant professor, 1952-56, associate professor, 1956-61, professor of history, 1961—, chairman of the department, 1967—.

WRITINGS: (Contributor) The Army Air Forces in World War II, Volume IV, University of Chicago Press, 1950; Ohio Forms an Army, Ohio State University Press, 1962; (editor) Total War and Cold War: Problems in Civilian Control of the Military, Ohio State University Press, 1963; (with Albert Weinberg) Civil Affairs: Soldiers Become Governors, Office of the Chief of Military History, Department of the Army, 1964; The War of 1812, University of Chicago Press, 1965.

* * *

COLLIER, James L(incoln) 1928-
(Charles Williams)

PERSONAL: Born June 27, 1928, in New York, N.Y.; son of Edmund and Katherine (Brown) Collier; married Carol Burrows, September 2, 1952; children: Geoffrey Lincoln, Andrew Kemp. Education: Hamilton College, A.B., 1950. Home: R.D.1, Box 2, Croton-on-Hudson, N.Y. 10520. Agent: Sterling Lord Agency, 660 Madison Ave., New York, N.Y. 10021.

CAREER: Free-lance writer.

WRITINGS: (Under pseudonym Charles Williams) Fires of Youth, Magnet Books, 19(?); Cheers, Avon, 1961; Somebody Up There Hates Me, Macfadden, 1962; The Hypocritical American: An Essay on Sex Attitudes in America, Bobbs-Merrill, 1964; Battleground: The United States Army in World War II, Norton, 1965; (contributor) Walter Brown Gibson, editor, The Fine Art of Swindling, Grosset, 1966; A Visit to the Firehouse, Norton, 1967; The Teddy Bear Habit; or, How I Became a Winner, Norton, 1967; (with others) Sex Education U.S.A.: A Community Approach, Sex Information and Education Council of the United States, 1968; Which Musical Instrument Shall I Play?, Norton, 1969; Rock Star, Four Winds, 1970; Danny Goes to the Hospital, Norton, 1970; Practical Music Theory: How Music Is Put Together from Bach to Rock, Norton, 1970; Why Does Everybody Think I'm Nutty?, Grosset, 1971; The Hard Life of the Teenager, Four Winds, 1972. Contributor of 400 articles to magazines.

* * *

COLLIN, Marion (Cripps) 1928-

PERSONAL: Born May 12, 1928, in Aylesbury, Buckinghamshire, England; daughter of Archibald George (a painter) and Hilda Maud (Packard) Cripps; married John W.H. Collin (a sales engineer); children: Lisa. Education: Educated by state scholarships. Religion: Church of England. Home: 41 Clifton Rd., Heaton Moor, Stockport, Cheshire, England. Agent: Elaine Greene Ltd., 2 Caxton St., London S.W.1, England.

CAREER: Student nurse, Isle of Wight, England, 1945-48; medical secretary in London, England, 1948-52; Tenth International Congress of Dermatologists, London, England, secretary, 1952; Woman's Own, London, don, England, fiction editor, 1952-56. Member: Romantic Novelists Association.

WRITINGS—All published by Mills & Boon, except as otherwise noted: (With Anne Britton) Romantic Fiction, T.V. Boardman, 1960, Nurse Maria, 1963, Nurse at the Top, 1964, Doctors Three, 1964, Nurse in the Dark, 1965, The Doctor's Delusion, 1967, The Shadow of the Court, 1967, The Man on the Island, 1968, Sun on the Mountain, 1969, Nurse on an Island, 1970, House of Dreams, 1971. Contributor of short stories to women's magazines.

WORK IN PROGRESS: Another romantic novel with a medical background, for Mills & Boon.

AVOCATIONAL INTERESTS: Acting for local amateur dramatic societies, gardening.

* * *

COLLINS, Robert O(akley) 1933-

PERSONAL: Born April 1, 1933, in Waukegan, Ill.; son of William G. (a chemist) and Louise (Jack) Collins; married Diana R. Ware, June 22, 1955; children: Catharine L., Randolph W., Robert W. Education: Dartmouth College, A.B. (summa cum laude), 1954; Balliol College, Oxford, B.A., 1956, M.A., 1960; Yale University, M.A., 1958, Ph.D., 1959. Religion: Episcopalian. Home: 425 West Padre St., Santa Barbara, Calif. 93105. Office: Graduate Division, University of California, Santa Barbara, Calif. 93105.

CAREER: Williams College, Williamstown, Mass., instructor in history, 1959-61; Columbia University, New York, N.Y., assistant professor of history, 1961-62; Williams College, assistant professor of history, 1962-65; University of California, Santa Barbara, associate professor, 1965-69, director of Center for Developing Nations, 1968, professor of history, 1969—, associate dean of graduate division, 1969, acting vice-chancellor for research and academic affairs, 1970, dean of graduate division, 1971—. Member: American Historical Association, African Studies Association, Phi Beta Kappa. Awards, honors: Ford Foundation fellowship, 1956-57; N.D.E.A. Language fellowship, 1961; Social Science Research Council fellowship, 1962-63, 1968.

WRITINGS: The Southern Sudan, 1883-1898: A Struggle for Control, Yale University Press, 1962; (with Peter Duignan) Americans in Africa: A Preliminary Guide to Protestant Missionary Archives and Library Manuscript Collection on Africa (monograph), Hoover Institution, 1963; (with Duignan and Clarence Clendenen) Americans in Africa 1865-1900 (monograph), Hoover Institution, 1966; (with R.L. Tignor) Egypt and the Sudan, Prentice-Hall, 1967; (author of introduction) Sir Richard Burton, The Nile Basin, DaCapo Press, 1967; (editor and author of introduction) Problems in African History, Prentice-Hall, 1968; King Leopold, England and the Upper Nile, 1899-1909, Yale University Press, 1968; (editor and author of introduction) Sir Gilbert Clayton, An Arabian Diary, University of California Press, 1969; (editor and author of introduction) The Partition of Africa: Illusion or Necessity?, Wiley, 1969; (editor) Readings in African History, Random House, 1970; Land Beyond the Rivers: The Southern Sudan, 1898-1918, Yale University Press, 1970; (editor and author of introduction) Documents in African History, Random House, 1970; European Imperialism in Africa, Knopf, 1970; (editor and author of introduction) Problems in the History of Colonial Africa, Prentice-Hall, 1970.

Contributor: Stanley Diamond and Fred G. Burke, editors, The Transformation of East Africa: Studies in Political Anthropology, Basic Books, 1966; Robin Winks, editor, The British Empire-Commonwealth: Historiographical Reassessments, Duke University Press, 1966; Prosser Gifford and Roger Louis, editors, British and German Colonialism in Africa, Yale University Press, 1967;

Arnold Rivkin, editor, *Nations by Design: Institution Building in Africa,* Doubleday, 1968; Robert Rotberg, editor, *Africa and Its Explorers,* Harvard University Press, 1969. Contributor of articles and reviews to *Journal of African History, Sudan Notes and Records, Zaire, Uganda Journal, Tarikh, Victorian Studies,* and *American Historical Review.*

WORK IN PROGRESS: Historical writing on the southern Sudan.

*   *   *

COLLINS, Rowland Lee   1934-

PERSONAL: Born September 17, 1934, in Bristow, Okla.; son of John Leland (a businessman) and Velma (Jones) Collins. *Education:* Princeton University, A.B., 1956; Stanford University, M.A., 1959, Ph.D., 1961. *Office:* University of Rochester, River Campus, Rochester, N.Y. 14627.

CAREER: Indiana University, Bloomington, lecturer, 1959-61, instructor, 1961-62, assistant professor, 1962-65, associate professor of English, 1965-67; University of Rochester, Rochester, N.Y., professor of English, 1967—, acting chairman of department, 1970-71, Chairman, 1972—. Montfort and Allie B. Jones Foundation, academic adviser, 1959—; Woodrow Wilson National Fellowship Foundation, Indiana University representative, 1963-67. *Member:* Modern Language Association (chairman, Old English literature group, 1964), Tennyson Society (American representative, 1967—), Medieval Academy of America, Early English Text Society, Cambridge Bibliographical Society, Bibliographical Society (London), Friends of the University of Rochester Libraries (councillor, 1972—), Grolier Club. *Awards, honors:* Woodrow Wilson fellow, 1956, 1959; Guggenheim fellow, 1965-66; fellow, Council of the Humanities, Princeton University, 1965-66.

WRITINGS: (With Charles Tennyson) *The Somersby Tennysons* (includes *The Somersby Tennysons* by C. Tennyson, and *The Frederick Tennyson Collection* by Collins), Victorian Studies, Indiana University, 1963; (author of preface) Alfred, Lord Tennyson, *The Devil and the Lady [and] Unpublished Early Poems,* edited by Charles Tennyson, Indiana University Press, 1964; *Fourteen British and American Poets,* Macmillan, 1964; (editor and author of introduction and notes) *Beowulf,* translated by Lucien Dean Pearson, Indiana University Press, 1965; (contributor) *New Cambridge Bibliography of English Literature,* Cambridge University Press, 1970. Contributor to *Times Literary Supplement, Book Collector, Shakespeare Quarterly, Annuale Mediaevale, Notes and Queries, Anglia, Victorian Poetry, Journal of English and Germanic Philology,* and other journals. Editorial consultant, *Victorian Studies,* 1963-66; founding editor, *Year's Work in Old English Studies,* 1968—.

WORK IN PROGRESS: The Present Past, a study of the origin and exposition of theme in the prose fiction of George Eliot; a critical edition of *The Blickling Homilies.*

AVOCATIONAL INTERESTS: Antiques and historic preservation.

*   *   *

COMAN, Edwin Truman, Jr.   1903-

PERSONAL: Born May 18, 1903, in Colfax, Wash.; son of Edwin Truman (a banker) and Ruth (Martin) Coman; married Evelyn B. Brownell, February 23, 1928. *Education:* Thacher School, graduate, 1922; Yale University, A.B., 1926; University of California, librarian's certificate, 1933; Claremont Graduate School, M.A., 1934. *Religion:* Protestant. *Home:* 5784 Bellevue Ave., LaJolla, Calif. 92037.

CAREER: Business solicitor and bond salesman, San Francisco, Calif., 1926-32; Claremont College, Claremont, Calif., library research assistant, 1933-36, director of library, 1936-42; Stanford University, Graduate School of Business, Stanford, Calif., assistant professor of business history, 1945-50; University of California, Riverside, librarian, 1951-65. American Library Association, consultant on college library buildings; Special Libraries Association, consultant. Trustee, LaJolla Library Association. Senior warden, St. Michael's Episcopal Church, 1962-65. *Military service:* U.S. Army Air Forces, 1942-45; became captain. *Member:* American Library Association (council, 1949-52), Special Libraries Association (president, San Francisco Bay region chapter, 1940), American Association of University Professors, Western Economic Association, California Library Association (president, 1949), San Diego Historical Society (first vice-president), Zamorano Club. *Awards, honors:* National Special Libraries Award for outstanding contribution to special librarianship, 1949, for *Sources of Business Information.*

WRITINGS: Sources of Business Information, Prentice-Hall, 1949, 2nd edition, University of California Press, 1964; (with H.M. Gibbs) *Time, Tide, and Timber,* Stanford University Press, 1949; (contributor) Robert B. Downs and Francis B. Jenkins, editors, *Bibliography, Current State and Future Trends,* University of Illinois Press, 1967; (contributor) Allen Kent and Harold Lancour, editors, *Encyclopedia of Library and Information Science,* Dekker, 1970. Contributor of articles and book reviews to professional journals.

AVOCATIONAL INTERESTS: History of business firms in California and early landholdings.

*   *   *

COMBER, Lillian   1916-
(Lillian Beckwith)

PERSONAL: Born April 25, 1916, in Wirral, Cheshire, England; daughter of Robert and Lillian (Beckwith) Lloyd; married Edward Comber (an artist); children: Geoffrey, Elizabeth Ann. *Residence:* Ballyre House, Kirk Michael, Isle of Man. *Address:* c/o Hutchinson & Co. (Publishers) Ltd., 178-202 Great Portland St., London W.1, England. *Agent:* Curtis Brown Ltd., 60 East 56th St., New York, N.Y. 10022.

CAREER: School teacher, 1936-38; crofter (operator of a small farm), 1943-60. *Member:* Society of Authors, P.E.N.

WRITINGS—All under pseudonym Lillian Beckwith: *The Hills Is Lonely,* Hutchinson, 1959, Dutton, 1963; *The Sea for Breakfast,* Hutchinson, 1961, Dutton, 1962; *The Loud Halo,* Hutchinson, 1964, Dutton, 1965; *Green Hand,* Hutchinson, 1967; *A Rope—In Case,* Hutchinson, 1968, Dutton, 1969; *About My Father's Business,* Hutchinson, 1971. Writer of short stories for magazines.

WORK IN PROGRESS: The Way of the Wind.

AVOCATIONAL INTERESTS: Amateur theatricals, giving children's parties, walking, and beachcombing.

*   *   *

COMFORT, Mildred Houghton   1886-

PERSONAL: Born December 11, 1886, in Winona, Minn.; daughter of Louis (a merchant) and Zerelda (Dustin) Bergemann; married Hollis Murdock Comfort (a lawyer), September 30, 1914 (deceased); children: James D., Nancy H. (Mrs. Maurice D. MacRoberts). *Education:* Carleton College, B.S., 1908. *Politics:* Republican. *Religion:* Episcopal. *Home:* 54 South Cretin Ave., Apartment 202, St. Paul, Minn. 55105. *Agent:* Larry Sternig, 2407 North 44th St., Milwaukee, Wis. 53210.

CAREER: Teacher and head of department of English in high schools in Caledonia, Minn., 1908-10, Stillwater, Minn., 1910-13, Rapid City, S.D., 1913-14; writer of books for children. Member: League of American Pen Women, Christian Writers' Guild. Awards, honors: Boys' Clubs of America award, 1947, for Winter on the Johnny Smoker.

WRITINGS: Peter and Nancy in Europe, Beckley-Cardy, 1932, revised edition, 1935; Happy Health Stories, Beckley-Cardy, 1934; Peter and Nancy in South America, Beckley-Cardy, 1935; Peter and Nancy in Africa, Beckley-Cardy, 1935; Peter and Nancy in Asia, Beckley-Cardy, 1937; Peter and Nancy in Australia and Islands of the Pacific, Beckley-Cardy, 1937; Peter and Nancy in Mexico, Central America, West Indies, and Canada, Beckley-Cardy, 1938.

Peter and Nancy in the United States and Alaska, Beckley-Cardy, 1940; Winter on the Johnny Smoker, Morrow, 1943; Search Through Pirate's Alley, Morrow, 1945; Meet Tom Cooney, Lund Press, 1945; Children of the Mayflower, Beckley-Cardy, 1947; Treasure on the Wheels, Beckley-Cardy, 1948; Children of the Colonies, Beckley-Cardy, 1948; Prairie Schooners West, Beckley-Cardy, 1949.

Temple Town to Tokyo, Beckley-Cardy, 1952; Alpine Paths, Beckley-Cardy, 1953; Kish of India, Beckley-Cardy, 1953; Sergeant Preston and Yukon King, Rand McNally, 1955; Little Lost Kitten, Rand McNally, 1956; Beans from Brazil, Beckley-Cardy, 1956; Moving Day, Rand McNally, 1958; J. Edgar Hoover, Modern Knight Errant, Denison, 1959.

Herbert Hoover, Humanitarian, Denison, 1960; John Foster Dulles, Peacemaker, Denison, 1960; William L. McKnight, Industrialist, Denison, 1962; Conrad N. Hilton, Hotelier, Denison, 1964; Lowell Thomas, Adventurer, Denison, 1965; Herbert Hoover, Boy Engineer, Bobbs-Merrill, 1965; Give and Take, Unity Books, 1966; James J. Hill, Young Empire Builder, Bobbs-Merrill, 1968; Walt Disney, Master of Fantasy, Denison, 1968; Princess Isabel of Brazil and the Glittering Pen, Kenedy, 1969; Danger on the Trail, Scholastic Book Services, 1969.

James Jerome Hill, Railroad Pioneer, Denison, 1971.

WORK IN PROGRESS: Herbert Hoover, Quaker Boy, for Bobbs-Merrill.

SIDELIGHTS: Winter on the Johnny Smoker was published in Canada, England, and Italy.

BIOGRAPHICAL/CRITICAL SOURCES: Carmen Nelson Richards, Minnesota Writers, Denison, 1961.

*   *   *

COMPTON, Henry (Pasfield) 1909-

PERSONAL: Born July 6, 1909, in Coventry, England; son of Frank William (an engineer) and Eleanor (Pasfield) Compton; married Joyce Pawley, July 24, 1937; children: John Pawley, Rosemary Pasfield. Education: Attended Bablake School in England; University of Geneva, student; University of London, B.A., 1935. Home: Oriel Cottage, Aynho, Banbury, Oxford, England.

CAREER: Newspaper reporter, 1929-33; Bournville Works Magazine, editor, 1952-53; College of Advanced Technology, Birmingham, England, senior lecturer in communication, 1953-63. Lecturer and consultant in industrial communication. Military service: British Army, Intelligence Corps, 1940-45; became sergeant.

WRITINGS: Kindred Points (poems), Allen & Unwin, 1951; Chocolate and Cocoa, Educational Supply, 1952; Newspapers, Educational Supply, 1954; Conveying Ideas: Fundamentals of Written Communication, Cleaver-Hume,

1962; Effective Speech, Institute of Supervisory Management, 1964; (with Eric Harlow) Practical Communication, Longmans, Green, 1967; (with William Bennett), Communication in Supervisory Management, Thomas Nelson, 1967; The Trial of a Foreman (management training play), Institute of Supervisory Management, 1969; (contributor) D.E.H. White and R. Martin, editors, Sociology, Theology and Conflict, Basil Blackwell, 1969; A Supervisor to the Rescue (management training play), Institute of Supervisory Management, 1970; How to Study and Pass Examinations, Institute of Supervisory Management, 1971.

*   *   *

CONE, Carl B. 1916-

PERSONAL: Born February 22, 1916; son of Carl S. (a utilities manager) and Lena (Peterson) Cone; married Mary Louise Regan (a librarian); children: Timothy. Education: University of Iowa, B.A., 1936, M.A., 1937, Ph.D., 1940. Politics: Republican. Religion: Roman Catholic. Home: 474 West Third, Lexington, Ky. 40508. Office: History Department, University of Kentucky, Lexington, Ky. 40506.

CAREER: Allegheny College, Meadville, Pa., instructor in history, 1940-41; Louisiana State University, Baton Rouge, assistant professor of history, 1942-47; University of Kentucky, Lexington, 1947—, professor of British history, 1955—, Hallam Professor, 1956-58, chairman of the history department, 1965-70. Member, Lexington Civil Service Commission. Member: American Historical Association, Catholic Historical Association (president, 1967), Southern Historical Association, Phi Beta Kappa. Awards, honors: University of Kentucky Alumni Research award; Ford Foundation faculty fellowship; Guggenheim fellow; book prize, Phi Alpha Theta, for Volume II of Burke and the Nature of Politics; Sory award, 1968, for outstanding contribution to graduate education; grant-in-aid, American Council of Learned Societies, 1971.

WRITINGS: Torchbearer of Freedom, University of Kentucky Press, 1952; Burke and the Nature of Politics, University of Kentucky Press, Volume I, 1957, Volume II, 1964; The English Jacobins: Reformers in Late 18th Century England, Scribner, 1968. Contributor of more than thirty articles to scholarly journals.

WORK IN PROGRESS: A biography of George III.

SIDELIGHTS: Cone spent a total of three years in England on research projects.

BIOGRAPHICAL/CRITICAL SOURCES: Christian Science Monitor, August 31, 1968; New York Review of Books, June 19, 1969.

*   *   *

CONRAD, Barnaby 1922-

PERSONAL: Born March 27, 1922, in San Francisco, Calif.; son of Barnaby and Helen (Hunt) Conrad; married Dale Cowgill, March 19, 1941; married Mary Slater, May 18, 1962; children: (first marriage) Barnaby III, Tani, Winston; (second marriage) Kendall (daughter). Education: Attended Taft School; Yale University, B.A., 1944. Politics: Republican. Religion: Protestant. Home: 2520 Octavia St., San Francisco, Calif. 94123. Office: 22 Darrell Place, San Francisco, Calif. 94133.

CAREER: American vice consul to Vigo, Malaga, Seville, and Barcelona, Spain, 1943-46; student bullfighter with Juan Belmonte, and bullfighter in Spain, Mexico, and Peru, 1943-46; portrait painter and night club pianist in Lima, Peru, 1946; secretary to Sinclair Lewis, 1949. Writer and illustrator. Former collector of exotic birds, fish, and monkeys; co-owner of Enrico's Coffee House, San Francisco, Calif.

WRITINGS: The Innocent Villa (novel), Random House, 1948; (self-illustrated) Matador, Houghton, 1952; La Fiesta Brava: The Art of the Bull Ring, Houghton, 1953; (with Carlos Arruza) My Life as a Matador (autobiography), Houghton, 1954; Gates of Fear, Crowell, 1957; The Death of Manolete, Houghton, 1958; San Francisco: A Profile with Pictures, Studio Books, 1959; (editor and translator) Torcuato Luca de Tena, Second Life of Captain Contreras, Houghton, 1960; Dangerfield, Harper, 1961; Encyclopedia of Bullfighting, Houghton, 1961; (compiler) Famous Last Words, foreword by Clifton Fadiman, Doubleday, 1961; Tahiti, Studio Books, 1962; How to Fight a Bull, Doubleday, 1968; (self-illustrated) Fun While It Lasted (autobiography), Random House, 1969; Zorro: A Fox in the City, Doubleday, 1971. Short story, "Cayetano the Perfect," anthologized in O. Henry Collection of Prize Stories, 1949.

SIDELIGHTS: On publication of Conrad's autobiography at the age of 46, a writer for National Observer noted the appropriateness of the "epitaph he has suggested for himself, 'Gored but never bored.'" Because of two fight injuries to the same knee, Conrad decided in his mid-twenties not to become a professional bullfighter, although, according to Roger Jellinek, "he has probably written more about bullfighting than anybody." Jellinek writes in a review of Fun While It Lasted: "Mr. Conrad started lucky and stayed lucky. Born in 1922 to a wealthy San Francisco investment-banking family, he grew up hardly aware of the Depression. His ancestry was one of his many passports: one grandfather was the first Governor of Puerto Rico, as well as the friend of most of the Presidents from Lincoln to Truman. A great-great-great grandmother was Martha Washington. Conrad himself was proudest of a pirate forebear named Philander Beadle.... As a playboy with an expensive schooling on the Coast and back East (he was the third Conrad generation at Yale), he might easily have slipped into a stereotype. In 1941 he was a student in Mexico City when on a dare he leaped into the bullring, flapping his raincoat (Brooks Brothers) at the charging bull. Miraculously he survived three passes and fled, deserting what was left of his raincoat, and his stereotype, on the horns of the bull. As he was being hustled off to jail, Felix Guzman, another torero that day, appealed to the president of the bullfight for Mr. Conrad's release. He went free, and Guzman volunteered to teach him the art. Mr. Conrad was injured and nearly killed by his first practice bull. This was the beginning of Mr. Conrad's remarkable career as a bullfighter and aficionado."

Fun While It Lasted reminds David Dempsey that Conrad "is one of those modern Renaissance men whose multiple talents are peculiarly attuned to the 20th century and its diversions, without reflecting its real concerns. A romantic at heart, he searched for a personal mystique at a time when his contemporaries were looking for an ideology. As a result, [this autobiography] has a pleasantly anachronistic air about it, as though the author had been set apart, or set back, in an era when it was possible to live a legendary life without being a legend." Jellinek believes the book "is strictly an entertainment: in spite of the astonishing variety in Mr. Conrad's life, one doesn't get to know him. There's no time."

BIOGRAPHICAL/CRITICAL SOURCES: New York Times Book Review, May 26, 1968, August 24, 1969; New York Times, August 9, 1969; National Observer, August 25, 1969; The Writer, April, 1972.

*   *   *

CONRAD, Jack (Randolph)   1923-

PERSONAL: Born July 25, 1923, in Atlanta, Ga.; son of Jesse Bowden (a businessman) and Gertrude (Bowden)

Ragsdale; married Madelyn Compton, September 4, 1948; children: Jane Nicole, Roger Scott, Annabel Susan. Education: Emory University, A.B., 1949, M.A., 1951; Duke University, Ph.D., 1954—. Agent: Ann Elmo Agency, Inc., 52 Vanderbilt Ave., New York, N.Y. 10017.

CAREER: Department of Public Health, Atlanta, Ga., survey consultant, 1954-55, Southwestern College, Memphis, Tenn., assistant professor 1955-58, associate professor, 1958-62, professor of anthropology, 1962-63; University of California, Berkeley, research fellow, Institute of Personality Assessment and Research, 1963-64; Yale University, New Haven, Conn., research fellow in psychology, 1965-66; Southwestern College, professor of anthropology, 1966—. Military service: U.S. Air Force, 1943-46; received Air Medal; U.S. Air Force Reserve, 1946—, now lieutenant colonel. Member: American Anthropological Association (fellow), Royal Anthropological Institute (fellow), American Association for the Advancement of Science (fellow). Awards, honors: National Science Foundation research award; National Institute of Mental Health special fellowship award.

WRITINGS: The Horn and The Sword: The History of the Bull as Symbol of Power and Fertility, Dutton, 1957; Museum of Man, University of Wisconsin Press, 1961; The Many Worlds of Man, Crowell, 1964; Man, Myth, and Magic, BPC Publishing, 1969.

WORK IN PROGRESS: Profile of the Playgoer, for Yale University Press; Anthropology and Art.

SIDELIGHTS: Conrad's first book was published in England and France.

*   *   *

CONRADS, Ulrich   1923-

PERSONAL: Born October 27, 1923, in Bielefeld, Germany; son of Theo and Erika (Boerner) Conrads; married Renate Schuppel, 1954. Education: Philipps-Universitaet (Marburg an der Lahn, Germany), Dr. phil., 1951. Home: Hirzbacher Weg 3, West Berlin 46, Germany. Office: Ullstein Verlag, Tempelhofer Damm 1/3, West Berlin 42, Germany.

CAREER: Das Kunstwerk, Baden-Baden, Germany, editor, 1950-52; Baukunst und Werkform, Nuremberg, Germany, editor, 1952-57; Ullstein, Verlag (publishers), West Berlin, Germany, editor-in-chief, Bauwelt (weekly architectural magazine), 1957—, editor, "Bauwelt Fundamente" (monograph series), 1963—. Architecture critic for RIAS (Radio in American Sector of Berlin). Member: International Association of Art Critics (secretary, German section, 1957-62).

WRITINGS: (With Hans G. Sperlich) Phantastiche Architektur, Hatje, 1960, translation by Christiane Crasemann Collins and George R. Collins published, in edited and expanded form, as The Architecture of Fantasy: Utopian Building and Planning in Modern Times, Praeger, 1962 (published in England as Fantastic Architecture, Architectural Press, 1963); (author of introduction) Modern Architecture in Germany, bilingual edition, captions by Werner Marschall, translated by James Palmes, Architectural Press, 1962; Neue deutsche Architektur II, Hatje, 1962; (editor) Bruno Taut, 1920-1922, Ullstein, 1963; (editor) Programme und Manifeste zur Architektur des 20. Jahrhunderts, Ullstein, 1964, translation by Michael Bullock published as Programs and Manifestoes on 20th-Century Architecture, M.I.T. Press, 1970; (editor) Lazar' Markovich Lisitskii, Russland: Architektur fuer eine Weltrevolution, Ullstein, 1965.

*   *   *

COOK, Fred J(ames)   1911-

PERSONAL: Born March 8, 1911, in Point Pleasant, N.J.; son of Frederick P. (a hardware store employee and tax collector) and Huldah (Compton) Cook; married Julia Barbara Simpson, June 5, 1936; children: Frederick P. II, Barbara Jane. *Education:* Rutgers University, B.Litt., 1932. *Politics:* "Mugwump, New Dealish." *Home:* 722 Fernmere Ave., Interlaken, N.J. *Agent:* Barthold Fles Literary Agency, 507 Fifth Ave., New York, N.Y. 10017.

CAREER: Asbury Park Press, Asbury Park, N.J., reporter, 1933-36; *New Jersey Courier,* Toms River, editor, 1936-37, assistant editor, then city editor, 1938-44; *New York World Telegram and Sun,* New York, N.Y., rewriteman, 1944-59; free-lance writer, 1959—. *Awards, honors:* New York Newspaper Guild Page One Awards for best city reporting, 1958, best magazine feature, for "The FBI," 1959, best magazine reporting, for "The Shame of New York," 1960; Sidney Hillman Award, 1960, for magazine article in *Nation,* "Gambling, Inc."

WRITINGS: The Girl in the Death Cell (on the Snyder Gray case), Gold Medal Books, 1953; *The Girl on the Lonely Beach* (on the Starr Faithful case), Fawcett, 1954; (with Robert Hendrickson) *Youth in Danger,* Harcourt, 1956; *The Unfinished Story of Alger Hiss,* Morrow, 1958; *What Manner of Men: Forgotten Heroes of the Revolution,* Morrow, 1959; (editor) Bruce Lancaster, *The Golden Book of the American Revolution* (teen-age book), introduction by Bruce Catton, Golden Press, 1959; (editor) Winston Churchill and editors of *Life* magazine, *The Second World War* (edition for young readers), Golden Press, 1960; *Rallying a Free People: Theodore Roosevelt,* Kingston House, 1961; *A Two-Dollar Bet Means Murder,* Dial, 1961; *John Marshall, Fighting for Justice,* Kingston House, 1961; *Entertaining the World: P.T. Barnum,* Encyclopaedia Britannica, 1962; *The Warfare State,* foreword by Bertrand Russell, Macmillan, 1962; *Building the House of Labor: Walter Reuther,* Encyclopaedia Britannica, 1963; *The FBI Nobody Knows,* Macmillan, 1964; *Barry Goldwater: Extremist of the Right,* Grove, 1964; *The Corrupted Land: The Social Morality of Modern Americans,* Macmillan, 1966; *The Secret Rulers: Criminal Syndicates and How They Control the U.S. Underworld,* Duell, Sloan & Pearce, 1966; *The Plot Against the Patient,* Prentice-Hall, 1967; *What So Proudly We Hailed,* Prentice-Hall, 1968; *Franklin D. Roosevelt, Valiant Leader* (juvenile), Putnam, 1968; *The New Jersey Colony* (juvenile), Collier, 1969; *The Nightmare Decade: The Life and Times of Senator Joe McCarthy,* Random House, 1971; *The Army-McCarthy Hearings, April-June, 1954: A Senator Creates a Sensation Hunting Communists,* F. Watts, 1971; *The Rise of American Political Parties,* F. Watts, 1971; *The Cuban Missile Crisis, October, 1962: The U.S. and Russia Face a Nuclear Showdown,* F. Watts, 1972; *The Demagogues* (juvenile), Macmillan, 1972; *The Muckrakers: Crusading Journalists Who Changed America,* Doubleday, 1972; *Mafia,* Fawcett, 1973.

Contributor to *Reader's Digest, American Heritage, Saturday Review, New York Times, True Detective,* and other publications.

WORK IN PROGRESS: A number of fact-juvenile books, two for Watts, one for Crowell-Collier; articles for magazines.

SIDELIGHTS: Sean Cronin called *What So Proudly We Hailed* "a lively, provocative but, above all, a relevant book. [Mr. Cook's] insight is sharp, his comment always to the point. He is a great one to prick bubble reputations and to explode myths."

"I am essentially a questioner, a critic of our times," Cook has written. "A major concern is the increasing tendency of our mass society to build massive power structures in which the individual becomes increasingly lost and helpless."

AVOCATIONAL INTERESTS: Reading, fishing, swimming, big league baseball, and the fortunes of the Rutgers football team.

BIOGRAPHICAL/CRITICAL SOURCES: Time, December 7, 1959; *Christian Science Monitor,* July 3, 1968; *Nation,* September 2, 1968, April 26, 1971.

*   *

COOK, J(ames) Gordon   1916-

PERSONAL: Born February 19, 1916, in Newcastle, England; son of Russell (a draper) and Sarah Ellen (Laverick) Cook; married Mary Elliott, March 23, 1940; children: Judith Anne (Mrs. Ian Holt), Angela Mary. *Education:* Attended Bootham School; King's College, University of Durham, B.Sc. (first class honors), 1939; Queen's College, Oxford, Ph.D., 1940. *Home and office:* 276 Hempstead Rd., Watford, Hertfordshire, England. *Agent:* Curtis Brown Ltd., 13 King St., Covent Garden, London W.C.2, England.

CAREER: Imperial Chemical Industries Ltd., London, England, research chemist, 1939-54; George Newnes Ltd. (publishers), London, England, managing editor of technical books department, 1956-61; Merrow Publishing Co. Ltd., Watford, Hertfordshire, England, director and managing editor. *Member:* Royal Institute of Chemistry, Textile Institute.

WRITINGS: Last Enemy?: The Story of the Virus, Merrow, 1952; *Sheer Magic: The Story of Textile Fibres,* Merrow, 1953; *Our Astonishing Atmosphere,* Harrap, 1955, Dial, 1957; *The Fight for Food,* Harrap, 1955, Dial, 1957; *The World of Water,* Harrap, 1956, Dial, 1957; *Virus in the Cell,* Harrap, 1956, Dial, 1957; *We Live by the Sun,* Dial, 1957; *Electrons Go to Work,* Dial, 1957; *Handbook of Textile Fibres,* two volumes, Merrow, 1959, Textile Book Service, 1960, 4th edition, Merrow, 1968, Textile Book Service, 1970; *Our Living Soil,* Dial, 1960; *Science for Everyman Encyclopaedia,* Merrow, 1962, 2nd edition, 1964; *Michael Faraday,* A. & C. Black, 1963; *Rubber,* Muller, 1963; *Look at Glass,* Hamish Hamilton, 1963; *Exploring Under the Sea,* Abelard, 1964; *The Miracle of Plastics,* Dial, 1964 (published in England as *Your Guide to Plastics,* Merrow, 1964); *Your Guide to the Soil,* Merrow, 1965; *Your Guide to Plant Growth,* Merrow, 1967; *Your Guide to the Plant Kingdom,* Merrow, 1967; *Handbook of Polyolefin Fibres,* Merrow, 1967, Textile Book Service, 1970; *ABC of Plant Terms,* Merrow, 1968. Author of articles and scripts on popular science.

WORK IN PROGRESS: Your Guide to Textiles.

AVOCATIONAL INTERESTS: Travel, sailing, fishing, walking.

*   *   *

COOK, Roderick   1932-

PERSONAL: Born February 9, 1932, in London, England. *Education:* Queens' College, Cambridge University, B.A., 1953. *Home address:* c/o Lionel Larner Ltd., 850 Seventh Ave., New York, N.Y. 10019.

CAREER: Actor in theater, television, films, and radio, London, England, 1953-61, and in United States and Canada, 1961—. Also director, producer, and writer; president, Wroderick Productions, Inc.

WRITINGS: (With W. N. Jayme) *Know Your Toes,* Clarkson & Potter, 1963. Contributor of poetry to *Harper's,* and of literary criticism to other publications. Also author of sketches and lyrics for various revues in Canada, an adaptation of *Lady in the Dark* for a concert performance, and an adaptation of a work by Noel Coward.

WORK IN PROGRESS: "The Twenty Million Dollar Musical," an Off-Broadway play; "Over the Falls," a musical comedy.

*   *   *

COOLEY, Lee Morrison 1919-

PERSONAL: Born October 3, 1919, in New York, N.Y.; daughter of Harry (a machinist) and Ann (Rosan) Morrison; married Leland Frederick Cooley (a writer), August 6, 1956. Education: Attended Straubenmuller Textile School, New York, N.Y., 1938, and New York School of Applied Design for Women, 1939. Address: 541 Alta Vista Way, Laguna Beach, Calif. 92651.

CAREER: Former dancer, appearing with Metropolitan Opera Co. and in Broadway shows and films; Columbia Broadcasting System, New York, N.Y., choreographer for "Perry Como Show," "Vic Damone Show," and "Peggy Lee Show," 1950-57. Member: Screen Actors Guild, Actors Equity.

WRITINGS—All with husband, Leland F. Cooley: The Simple Truth about Western Land Investment, Doubleday, 1964, revised edition, 1968; The Retirement Trap, Doubleday, 1965; How to Avoid the Retirement Trap, Nash Publishing, 1972.

WORK IN PROGRESS: With husband, a book on housing developments.

*   *   *

COOPER, Barbara (Ann) 1929-

PERSONAL: Born October 10, 1929, in Denbigh, North Wales; daughter of Robert and Ruth (Root) Cooper. Education: Attended school in St. Asaph, North Wales. Politics: Independent Conservative. Religion: Church of England. Home: Lingwood, Grayswood, Haslemere, Surrey, England.

CAREER: Adprint Ltd. (publishers), London, England, editorial assistant, 1950-51; Max Parrish & Co. Ltd. (publishers), London, England, editorial assistant, 1951-54; Woman (magazine), London, England, staff writer, 1954-56; free-lance writer, 1956—. Member: National Trust, Museums Association, National Book League, British Horse Society.

WRITINGS: BOAC Book of Flight, Parrish, 1959; (author with Ches Gudiman and editor) Travellers Digest, two volumes, British Overseas Air Corp., 1961, 7th edition, 1971; (editor) The Speedbird Book, Paul Hamlyn, 1962; Badminton: The Three-day Event, 1949-1969, Pleasure Books, 1969; (with M.J. Ross-Macdonald and others) Explorer Guides, two volumes, British Overseas Air Corp., 1969-70, Tri-Ocean, 1970. Contributor of articles to illustrated magazines. Former member of editorial staff, Associated Rediffusion (television).

WORK IN PROGRESS: A new series of world guides to wildlife areas and public art collections.

SIDELIGHTS: Miss Cooper has traveled in Africa, Asia, West Indies, United States, Canada, Near East, Australia, New Zealand, and Europe. Avocational interests: English history, English and French poetry, wildlife, art and architecture, sports.

*   *   *

COOPER, Jamie Lee

PERSONAL: Born in Richmond, Ind.; daughter of Ralph F. and Esther (Armacost) Kellner. Education: Studied at Fairfax Hall and Cincinnati Art Academy. Politics: Republican, but votes for the man. Religion: Episcopal. Home: 100 South Ninth, Richmond, Ind. 47374.

CAREER: Former commercial writer for radio, staff artist for Children's Playmate, and free-lance illustrator and writer.

WRITINGS: The Horn and the Forest, Bobbs-Merrill, 1963; Shadow of a Star, Bobbs-Merrill, 1965; Rapaho, Bobbs-Merrill, 1967; The Castaways, Bobbs-Merrill, 1970; The Great Dandelion, Bobbs-Merrill, 1972.

WORK IN PROGRESS: A book about French fur traders in the 1680's.

AVOCATIONAL INTERESTS: American Indians and the early history of America.

BIOGRAPHICAL/CRITICAL SOURCES: New York Times Book Review, January 14, 1967, June 28, 1970; Library Journal, June 15, 1970.

*   *   *

COOPER, Kenneth Schaaf 1918-

PERSONAL: Born September 17, 1918, in Doniphán, Kan.; son of William M. and Josephine (Schaaf) Cooper; married Ruthe Meeker, August 15, 1942; children: Barbara Ruth, Kent Meeker. Education: College of Emporia, B.A., 1940; University of Nebraska, M.A., 1941; University of Missouri, Ph.D., 1947. Politics: Independent. Religion: Presbyterian. Home: 2407 Barton Ave., Nashville, Tenn. 37212. Office: Peabody College, Nashville, Tenn. 37203.

CAREER: Kemper Military School, Boonville, Mo., history teacher, 1942-45; University of Missouri, Columbia, instructor in history, 1945-47; George Peabody College for Teachers, Nashville, Tenn., professor of history, 1947—. Member: American Historical Association, National Council for Social Studies, Pi Gamma Mu.

WRITINGS: (With Lewis Paul Todd) Old Ways and New Ways, Silver Burdett, 1954; (with Todd) New Ways in the New World, Silver Burdett, 1954; (with Todd) World Ways, Silver Burdett, 1954; (with Todd) World Ways, Silver Burdett, 1954; (with Todd and C.W. Sorensen) Learning to Look at Our World, Silver Burdett, 1961; (with Todd and Sorensen) The Changing New World, Silver Burdett, Volume I: North and South America, 1963, Volume II: United States and Canada, 1964; (with Todd and Sorensen) The Changing Old World, Silver Burdett, 1964; (with Carl L. Becker) Modern History: Europe Since 1600, Silver Burdett, 1964; Man and Change, Silver Burdett, 1971. Contributor of articles to Book of Knowledge, Social Education, National Elementary Principal, Social Science, Peabody Journal of Education, and Educational Forum.

WORK IN PROGRESS: A book on Western intellectual history.

*   *   *

COOPER, Lettice (Ulpha) 1897-

PERSONAL: Born September 3, 1897, daughter of Leonard (an engineer) and Agnes Helena (Fraser) Cooper. Education: Attended Lady Margaret Hall, Oxford. Politics: Democrat. Home and office: 95 Canfield Gardens, London N.W. 6, England. Agent: A.P. Watt, 26-29 Bedford Row, London W.C.1, England.

CAREER: Writer. Ministry of Food, public relations division, 1940-45. Member: P.E.N., Authors' Society, Children's Book Writers Association, Robert Louis Stevenson Club (president). Awards, honors: Arts Council bursary, 1968.

WRITINGS: The Lighted Room, Hodder & Stoughton, 1925; The Old Fox, Hodder & Stoughton, 1927; Good Venture, Hodder & Stoughton, 1928; Likewise the Lyon, Hodder & Stoughton, 1929; The Ship of Truth, Little, Brown, 1930; Private Enterprise, Hodder & Stoughton, 1931; Hark to Rover!, Hodder & Stoughton, 1933; We Have Come to a Country, Gollancz, 1935; The New House, Macmillan, 1937; National Provincial, Macmillan, 1938.

Black Bethlehem, Macmillan, 1947; *Robert Louis Stevenson,* Home & Van Thal, 1947, A. Swallow, 1948, 2nd edition, Arthur Barker, 1967; *Yorkshire West Riding,* R. Hale, 1950, Macmillan, 1951; *George Eliot,* Longmans, Green, 1951, new edition, .1960; *Fenny* (Book Society selection), Gollancz, 1953; *Great Men of Yorkshire—West Riding,* Bodley Head, 1955; *Three Lives,* Gollancz, 1957; (author of introduction) Edward George Lytton, *The Last Days of Pompeii,* Norton, 1959.

The Young Florence Nightingale, Parrish, 1960, Roy, 1961; *A Certain Compass,* Gollancz, 1960; *The Young Victoria,* Parrish, 1961, Roy, 1962; *Blackberry's Kitten,* Brockhampton Press, 1961, Vanguard, 1963; *The Double Heart,* Gollancz, 1962; *The Bear Who Was Too Big,* Parrish, 1963, Follett, 1966; *Bob-a-Job,* Brockhampton Press, 1963; *James Watt,* A. & C. Black, 1963; *Contadino,* J. Cape, 1964; *Garibaldi,* Methuen, 1964, Roy, 1966; *The Young Edgar Allan Poe,* Parrish, 1964, Roy, 1965; *The Twig of Cypress,* Deutsch, 1965, Washburn, 1966; *The Fugitive King,* Parrish, 1965; *We Shall Have Snow,* Brockhampton Press, 1966; *A Hand Upon the Time: A Life of Charles Dickens,* Pantheon, 1968; *Gunpowder, Treason and Plot,* Abelard, 1970; *Late in the Afternoon,* Gollancz, 1971.

Contributor to *Times Literary Supplement, Observer, Spectator,* and other journals and newspapers in England. Associate editor, *Time and Tide,* 1939-40.

WORK IN PROGRESS: An adult novel.

BIOGRAPHICAL/CRITICAL SOURCES: Best Sellers, June 15, 1971; *Observer Review,* June 20, 1971.

*   *   *

COOTNER, Paul H(arold)   1930-

PERSONAL: Born May 25, 1930, in Logansport, Ind.; son of William David and Rose (Singer) Cootner; married Cathryn Mae Marcho, December 2, 1962. *Education:* University of Florida, B.S., 1949, M.A., 1950; Massachusetts Institute of Technology, Ph.D., 1953. *Religion:* Jewish. *Home:* 676 Mayfield Ave., Stanford, Calif. 94305. *Office:* Graduate School of Business, Stanford University, Stanford, Calif.

CAREER: Brown University, Providence, R.I., Ford Foundation teaching intern, 1955-56; Resources for the Future, Inc., Washington, D.C., researcher, 1956-58; Massachusetts Institute of Technology, Cambridge, assistant professor of finance, 1959-62, associate professor, 1962-66, professor, 1966-70; Stanford University, C.O.G. Miller Professor of Finance, 1970—. Northwestern University, visiting summer professor, 1956; taught at All-India Management Conference, Srinigar, Kashmir, summer, 1964; visiting professor, Harvard University, 1969-70. B.C. Morton Mutual Funds, member of advisory board; consultant to U.S. Federal Trade Commission, U.S. Treasury, private industry. *Military service:* U.S. Army, Quartermaster Corps, 1953-55. *Member:* American Economic Association, Econometric Society, Phi Beta Kappa, Phi Kappa Phi, Phi Eta Sigma.

WRITINGS: (Contributor) *The Takeoff into Sustained Economic Growth,* Macmillan (London), 1960; (contributor) William Fellner and others, *Fiscal and Debt Management Policies,* published for Commission on Money and Credit by Prentice-Hall, 1963; (contributor) George Fisk, editor, *Frontiers of Management Psychology,* Harper, 1963; (editor) *The Random Character of Stock Market Prices,* M.I.T. Press, 1964; (contributor) Paul M. Horvitz and others, *Private Financial Institutions,* published for Commission on Money and Credit by Prentice-Hall, 1964; (with George Loef) *Water Demand for Steam Electric Generation: An Economic Projection*

Model, published for Resources for the Future by Johns Hopkins Press, 1966.

Contributor of more than fifteen articles to *Business Scope, Journal of Political Economy, Industrial Management Review,* other journals in field.

WORK IN PROGRESS: Research on risk and risk premiums of businessmen as reflected in future markets, supported by Sloan Foundation.

*   *   *

COPE, Robert Knox   1913-
(Jack Cope)

PERSONAL: Born June 3, 1913, in Mooi River, Natal, South Africa; son of Charles Frederick (a farmer) and May Knox) Cope; married Lesley de Villiers (a painter), June 4, 1942 (divorced May, 1958); children: Raymond, Michael. *Education:* Attended schools in South Africa. *Home:* Sea Girt, Second Beach, Clifton, Cape Town, South Africa. *Agent:* Cyrilly Abels, 119 West 57th St., New York, N.Y. 10019.

CAREER: Natal Mercury, Durban, Natal, South Africa, reporter, 1930-35; South African Morning Newspapers, correspondent in London, England, 1936-40; farming in Natal, South Africa, 1941-42; shark-fishing enterprise in Cape Town, South Africa, 1943-45; South African Association of Arts, Cape Town, director, 1946-48; free-lance writing, farming, fishing, and occasional newspaper work, 1949-59; full-time writer, 1959—. *Member:* P.E.N. *Awards, honors:* British Council scholarship, 1961; South African Literary Prose Prize for manuscript of volume of short stories, 1963; Carnegie traveling scholarship, 1966; Veld Trust award, 1971, for *The Rain-Maker.*

WRITINGS: Comrade Bill (biography), Stewart, 1944; *Lyrics and Diatribes* (poems), privately printed, 1948; *Marie* (verse satire), Stewart, 1948; *The Fair House* (novel), MacGibbon & Kee, 1955; *The Golden Oriole* (novel), Heinemann, 1958; *The Road to Ysterberg* (novel), Heinemann, 1959; *The Tame Ox* (short stories), Heinemann, 1960; *Albino* (novel), Heinemann, 1964; *The Man Who Doubted, and Other Stories,* Heinemann, 1967; (compiler and author of introduction with Uys Krige) *The Penguin Book of South African Verse,* Penguin, 1968; (translator with William Plomer) Ingrid Tunker, *Selected Poems,* J. Cape, 1968; *The Dawn Comes Twice,* Heinemann, 1969; (editor) *Seismograph,* Reijger, 1970; *The Rain-Maker* (novel), Heinemann, 1971.

Contributor of short stories, literary and critical articles, and poetry to anthologies. Short stories also have been published in magazines in United States, twelve countries of Europe, Australia, India, and South Africa, including *Harper's, Harper's Bazaar, Gentlemen's Quarterly, New Yorker, Mademoiselle.* Founder, 1960, and editor of South African literary magazine, *Contrast.*

WORK IN PROGRESS: The Student of Zend, a novel.

SIDELIGHTS: Cope told *CA:* "Writing in South Africa is not easy. There's a high voltage of tension; there's censorship—one's books get banned. I don't write dirt for its own sake or for sale. There's a lot of dirt in life and if it gets into a book, it must be there of necessity. I remain an African and Africa has a certain innocence, a certain freshness and strength. It's not a political slogan, or a garbage dump. To fight against isolation I've always tried to draw together our younger writers, to raise critical standards, demand sound craftsmanship, and for ten years, *Contrast* has been a workshop and a mouthpiece for new South African writing."

BIOGRAPHICAL/CRITICAL SOURCES: Miller and Sergeant, *Survey of South African Poetry,* Balkema, 1957; Roy Macnab and Maskew Miller, *Poets in South*

Africa, [Cape Town], 1958; *Times Literary Supplement,* July 20, 1967; *Listener,* July 27, 1967; *Books and Bookmen,* September, 1967, October, 1969.

*   *   *

COPELAND, E(dwin) Luther 1916-

PERSONAL: Born January 24, 1916, in Drennen, W. Va.; son of Luther Lowell (a lumberman) and Nannie (Hurt) Copeland; married Louise E. Tadlock, June 5, 1946; children: Judith Carol, Joy Marie, Sarah Elizabeth, Rebecca Louise, John Luther. *Education:* Mars Hill College, A.A., 1942; Furman University, B.A., 1944; Southern Baptist Theological Seminary, Th.M., 1946; Yale University, Ph.D., 1949. *Home:* 3701 Pembroke Pl., Raleigh, N.C. 27609. *Office:* Southeastern Baptist Theological Seminary, Wake Forest, N.C. 27587.

CAREER: Baptist minister. Southern Baptist Convention, Foreign Mission Board, missionary to Japan, 1948-56; Seiman Gakuin University, Fukuoka, Japan, professor of Christian history, 1949-56, president, 1952-55; Southeastern Baptist Theological Seminary, Wake Forest, N.C., professor of missions, 1956—. Visiting professor of missions at Southern Baptist Theological Seminary, Louisville, Ky., 1953-54; visiting research professor of comparative religion, Banaras Hindu University, Varanasi, India, 1963-64. *Member:* International Congress of Orientalists, American Society of Church History, Association of Missions Professors. *Awards, honors:* Fulbright research scholarship in comparative religion, India, 1963-64; American Association of Theological Schools faculty fellowship, 1969-70.

WRITINGS: *The Japanese Govern....nt and Protestant Christianity, 1889-1900* (pamphlet), Foreign Affairs Association of Japan, 1954; *Christianity and World Religions,* Convention Press, 1963; (contributor) G. Allen West, editor, *Christ for the World,* Broadman, 1963; *Frontiers of Advance,* Convention Press, 1964. Contributor of articles to mission and religious periodicals.

WORK IN PROGRESS: *World Religions: An Introduction;* and *The Christian Mission in Biblical Context.*

AVOCATIONAL INTERESTS: Beekeeping and hiking.

*   *   *

COPPERUD, Roy H. 1915-

PERSONAL: Born June 28, 1915, in Crystal Falls, Mich.; son of Sigurd and Hilma (Hendrickson) Copperud; married Mary E. Lavely, June 22, 1946; children: Wendy Leigh, Jill Ellen, Barry Roy. *Education:* University of Minnesota, B.A. (magna cum laude), 1942. *Politics:* Democrat. *Home:* 2782 McNally Ave., Altadena, Calif. 91001. *Agent:* Harold Matson Co., Inc., 30 Rockefeller Plaza, New York, N.Y. 10020. *Office:* University of Southern California, University Park, Los Angeles, Calif. 90007.

CAREER: Member of editorial staff of newspapers in Baltimore, Md., and Milwaukee, Wis., 1946-48, and in Sacramento, Calif., 1951-52; North American Aviation, Inc., staff assistant for special writing projects, 1952-53; with *Stockton Record,* Stockton, Calif., 1953-59; *Pasadena Independent and Star-News,* Pasadena, Calif., editor of editorial pages, chief editorial writer, and music critic, 1959-64; University of Southern California, School of Journalism, Los Angeles, assistant professor, 1964-66, associate professor, 1966-70, professor of journalism, 1970—. Director of summer training program in writing and editing, *Washington Post,* 1964, 1965. Consultant on writing and editing for various publishers. *Military service:* U.S. Naval Reserve, 1942-46; served in Pacific; became lieutenant. *Member:* American Association of University Professors, Phi Beta Kappa.

WRITINGS: *Words on Paper,* Hawthorn, 1960; *A Dictionary of Usage and Style: The Reference Guide for Professional Writers, Reporters, Editors, Teachers, and Students,* Hawthorn, 1964; *Handbook for Journalists,* School of Journalism, University of Southern California, 1965; *American Usage: The Consensus,* Van Nostrand, 1970. Conductor of column, "Editorial Workshop," in *Editor and Publisher,* 1954—; member of usage panel, *American Heritage Dictionary;* reviewer for newspapers and magazines.

WORK IN PROGRESS: Handbook for use in news editing instruction.

BIOGRAPHICAL/CRITICAL SOURCES: *Atlantic,* September, 1970.

*   *   *

CORBIN, Arnold 1911-

PERSONAL: Born February 16, 1911, in Brooklyn, N.Y.; married Claire Rothenberg (a college professor), August 22, 1937; children: Lee Harrison, Karen Sue. *Education:* Harvard University, B.S. (summa cum laude), 1931, M.B.A. (with distinction), 1934; New York University, Ph.D., 1954. *Home:* 330 Harvard Ave., Rockville Centre, N.Y. 11570. *Office:* Graduate School of Business Administration, New York University, 100 Trinity Pl., New York, N.Y. 10006.

CAREER: Department store research specialist and buyer, New York, N.Y., and Newark, N.J., 1934-40; Corbin Foods Co., New York, N.Y., president, 1946-47; U.S. Army, Quartermaster Corps, Inspection Service, New York, N.Y., chief technologist, 1947-49; College of City of New York, Baruch School of Business (now Baruch College of City University of New York) New York, N.Y., lecturer, then assistant professor, 1947-54; New York University, Graduate School of Business Administration, New York, N.Y., associate professor, then professor of marketing, 1954—. Consultant to private firms, trade associations, and government agencies, 1955—, including General Electric Co., Schenley Industries, Doubleday & Co., Inc., Coca Cola Export Corp., and American Can Co. Member of National Marketing Advisory Committee, U.S. Department of Commerce; member of advertising committee of U.S. Council, International Chamber of Commerce. *Military service:* U.S. Army, Quartermaster Corps, 1940-46; became lieutenant colonel.

MEMBER: American Marketing Association (national board of directors, 1963-65, vice-president, 1967-68), Sales Promotion Executives Association (honorary), Association of Industrial Advertisers, American Arbitration Association (national panel of arbitrators), New York University Graduate School of Business Administration Alumni Association (board of directors), Phi Beta Kappa (first marshal, 1931), Beta Gamma Sigma, Eta Mu Pi, Mu Kappa Tau, Long Island Harvard Club (scholarship committee). *Awards, honors:* Ford Foundation fellow at Graduate School of Business Administration, University of California, Berkeley, 1960.

WRITINGS: (With John Wingate) *Changing Patterns in Retailing,* Irwin, 1956; *Bibliography of Graduate Theses in the Field of Marketing Written at U.S. Colleges and Universities, 1950-1957,* Graduate School of Business Administration, New York University, 1957; (with Hector Lazo) *Management in Marketing,* McGraw, 1961; (with Kelley, Lazo, and Kahn) *Marketing Management: Bibliography,* American Marketing Association, 1963; (with G. Blagowidow and wife, Claire Corbin) *Decision Exercises in Marketing: Using the Principles of SysteMetrics,* McGraw, 1964; (with Claire Corbin) *New Trends in American Marketing,* British Institute of Management, 1965; *Implementing the Marketing Concept,* British Institute of Management, 1966; (contributor) H.B. Maynard, editor, *Handbook of Business Administration*, McGraw, 1968; (contributor) Victor Buell, editor, *Handbook of Modern Marketing*, McGraw, 1970. Contributor to *Collier's Encyclopedia Yearbook*, 1958; contributor to professional and trade periodicals.

WORK IN PROGRESS: Working on several books dealing with financial analysis; a revision of *Implementing the Marketing Concept*.

* * *

CORLEY, Robert N(eil) 1930-

PERSONAL: Born March 21, 1930, in Oak Park, Ill.; son of Paul R. (a railway mail clerk) and Vera M. (Hoobler) Corley; married Elinor A. McAloon, October 5, 1952. *Education:* University of Illinois, B.S., 1952, J.D., 1956. *Politics:* Republican. *Religion:* Methodist. *Home:* 1429 Mayfair Rd., Champaign, Ill.

CAREER: Practicing attorney in Illinois; University of Illinois, Urbana, 1957—, began as associate professor, now professor of business law and administration. *Military service:* U.S. Army Reserve, Finance Corps, 1952-59; became first lieutenant.

WRITINGS: (With R.L. Black) *The Legal Environment of Business*, McGraw, 1963, 3rd edition, 1973; (with O.E. Adams and Black) *Outlines of Commercial Law*, Stipes, 1963; (editor with others) Essel Ray Dillavou and C.G. Howard, *Principles of Business Law*, Prentice-Hall, 1964, 9th edition (with William J. Robert), published as *Dillavou and Howard's Principles of Business*, 1971; *Materials and Cases for Use in Estate Planning*, Stipes, 1964. Contributor to *Illinois Bar Journal*. Editor of case comments in *American Business Law Journal*.

* * *

CORNELL, George W. 1920-

PERSONAL: Born July 21, 1920, in Weatherford, Okla.; son of Charles H. (a rancher) and Gladys (Cameron) Cornell; married Jo Ann Reeves, April 1, 1944; children: Marion Emma, Harrison Reeves. *Education:* University of Oklahoma, A.B., 1943. *Politics:* Democrat. *Religion:* Episcopalian. *Home:* 400 East 20th St., New York, N.Y. 10019.

CAREER: Associated Press, New York, N.Y., news writer, 1947—, reporter covering religious affairs and writer of weekly column, "Religion Today," 1951—. *Military service:* U.S. Army, Infantry, 1943-47; became second lieutenant. *Awards, honors:* Faith and Freedom award of Religious Heritage of America, 1960; Supple Memorial award of Religious Newswriters, 1961; LL.D. from Defiance College, 1962.

WRITINGS: They Knew Jesus, Morrow, 1957; *The Way and Its Ways*, Association Press, 1963; *Voyage of Faith: The Catholic Church in Transition*, Odyssey, 1966; (with Douglas W. Johnson) *Punctured Preconceptions: What North American Christians Think About the Church*, Friendship, 1972.

* * *

CORNWALL, I(an) W(olfran) 1909-

PERSONAL: Born November 28, 1909, in Coonoor, Nilgiri Hills, South India; son of John Wolfran (a lieutenant colonel, Indian Medical Service) and Effie Esme (Sinclair) Cornwall; married Anna Margareta Callear, May 15, 1937 (deceased 1967); children: Geoffrey St. Clair, William John Fenger. *Education:* Wellington College, Berkshire, England, student, 1922-27; St. John's College, Cambridge, B.A., 1931; University of London, Diploma in Prehistoric Archaeology, and Ph.D., 1952. *Politics:* Conservative. *Home:* Flat 8, 11 Netherhall Gardens, Lon-

don N.W.3, England. *Agent:* Winant, Towers Ltd., 14, Clifford's Inn, London E.C.4, England. *Office:* University of London Institute of Archaeology, 31-4 Gordon Sq., London W.C.1, England.

CAREER: Variously employed as salesman, schoolmaster, clerk-accountant, and works chemist in London, England, 1931-39, civil service postal censor, travelers' censor, and press censor in Glasgow, Scotland, 1939-45; Institute of Archaeology, University of London, London, England, lecturer in environmental archaeology, 1951—, reader in human environment, 1964—. *Member:* Geologists' Association, Prehistoric Society, Zoological Society (London; scientific fellow), Royal Anthropological Institute (fellow). *Awards, honors:* Carnegie Medal of Library Association, 1960, for *The Making of Man;* Henry Stopes Memorial Medal, Geologists Association, 1969.

WRITINGS: Bones for the Archaeologist, Macmillan, 1956; *Soils for the Archaeologist*, Macmillan, 1958; (with M.M. Howard) *The Making of Man* (juvenile), Phoenix House, 1960, Dutton, 1961; (contributor) D.R. Brothwell and Eric Higgs, editors, *Science in Archaeology*, Basic Books, 1963; *The World of Ancient Man*, Edward Pyddoke, editor, Day, 1964; (contributor) *The Scientist and Archaeology*, Roy, 1964; *Hunter's Half-Moon* (fiction), John Baker, 1967, Coward, 1969; *Prehistoric Animals and Their Hunters*, Praeger, 1968; *Ice Ages: Their Nature and Effects*, Humanities, 1970. Contributor to *Chambers's Encyclopaedia*, *Bulletin* of the Institute of Archaeology, *Proceedings* of Prehistoric Society, and to professional journals.

SIDELIGHTS: Cornwall told *CA* he is "chiefly interested in things, not people—man not *men!* . . . Favorite leisure pursuits: gardening, fishing. Have natural history convictions and am essentially solitary." He speaks German, Spanish, French; reads Dutch, Danish, Italian.

* * *

CORRIGAN, Robert A(nthony) 1935-

PERSONAL: Born April 21, 1935, in New London, Conn.; son of Anthony John and Rose Mary (Jengo) Corrigan; married Geraldine Marie Brisson, November 24, 1956; children: Kathleen Marie, Anthony John, Robert Anthony. *Education:* Brown University, A.B., 1957; University of Pennsylvania, M.A., 1959, Ph.D., 1967. *Politics:* Democrat. *Home:* 1040 East Court St., Iowa City, Iowa 52240. *Office:* 305 English Philosophy Bldg., State University of Iowa, Iowa City, Iowa 55240.

CAREER: Philadelphia Historical Commission, Philadelphia, Pa., research historian, 1957-59; University of Gothenburg, Gothenburg, Sweden, Smith-Mundt Visiting Professor in American civilization, 1959-60, lecturer in American civilization, 1960-62; Bryn Mawr College, Bryn Mawr, Pa., lecturer in English, 1962-63; University of Pennsylvania, Philadelphia, instructor in American civilization, 1963-64; University of Iowa, Iowa City, instructor in English, 1964-66, assistant professor of American civilization and executive secretary of American civilization program, 1966-69, associate professor of English and acting chairman of American civilization, 1969—. Visiting lecturer at Philadelphia Museum College of Art, 1963-64; director of summer institutes for Afro-American Culture, 1968—; visiting professor of American studies, Grinnell College, 1970-71. Member of Democratic Central Committee, Johnson County, Iowa, 1964-70; Iowa City Human Relations Commission, member, 1970-72, vice-chairman, 1971. *Military service:* U.S. Naval Reserve Officers Training Corps, 1953-54.

MEMBER: American Studies Association, Modern Language Association of America, American Association of

University Professors (Iowa state conference president, 1968-69), National Council of Teachers of English, American Historical Association, Organization of American Historians, National Association for Study of Negro Life and History, National American Studies Faculty (charter member), Popular Culture Association, European Association for American Studies, Nordic Association for American Studies, Midcontinent American Studies Association (executive secretary, 1971—), Midwest Modern Language Association. *Awards, honors:* Clarkson Able Collins Maritime History Prize, 1956; Pennsylvania Colonial Society Award, 1958, 1959; Fulbright lectureship, 1960-61, 1961-62; Standard Oil Foundation award, 1968, for excellence in undergraduate teaching; N.E.H. grants, summers, 1969, 1970, 1971-72; Rockefeller Foundation grant, 1972-75.

WRITINGS: (Editor with Robert E. Fisher, John Hancock, and Norman Schwenk) *American Fiction and Verse: An Anthology,* Gleerups, 1962, 2nd edition, revised, 1970; (editor and author of introduction) Harriet Beecher Stowe, *Uncle Tom's Cabin,* Airmont, 1967; (contributor) Warren French, editor, *The Forties: Fiction, Poetry, Drama,* Edwards, Everett, 1969; (editor) *Ezra Pound Criticism, 1904-1970: An Annotated Checklist,* University of Iowa Press, in press; (editor) *The Diary of Samuel Sewall,* College & University Press, in press. Contributor to *World Book Encyclopedia;* contributor of translations (from Swedish to English) to *Moderna Sprak,* 1959-63, and of articles to several publications, including *American Quarterly, Midcontinent Studies Journal,* and *American Studies.* Member of editorial board, *Studies in Black Literature;* editorial consultant, *American Studies;* member of national advisory board, Afro-Am Press.

WORK IN PROGRESS: Editing, with O.M. Brack, Jr., *The Poetry of Michael Wigglesworth: A Textually Definitive Edition,* for the Center for Editions of American Authors; *What Thou Lovest Well Remains: Ezra Pound and America, 1940-1958,* completed and awaiting publication; editing, with Richard E. Fisher, *Afro-American Fiction and Verse: An Anthology,* for Gleerups; with Charles T. Davis, a series of thirteen original essays from the 1971 Afro-American Culture Summer Institute, *Richard Wright: His Work, His World, and His Influence;* editing, with Donald B. Gibson, a collection of previously published essays, *Richard Wright's Fiction: The Critical Response, 1940-1971; Afro-American Fiction, 1853-1973,* for Gale, expected completion in 1974.

*   *   *

CORT, David   1904-

PERSONAL: Born in 1904, son of Ambrose and Lydia R. (Painter) Cort; married Catharine Whitcomb, 1937 (divorced); children: John Cyrus. *Education:* Columbia University, B.A., 1924. *Address:* The Nation, 333 Sixth Ave., New York, N.Y. 10003.

CAREER: Conde Nast, Inc., New York, N.Y., associate editor of *Vanity Fair,* 1927-30; employed by Time-Life, Inc., New York, N.Y., 1932-47, and *United Nations World,* New York, N.Y., 1950-51. Free-lance writer.

WRITINGS: Once More Ye Laurels, John Day, 1928; *Give Us Heroes,* Liveright, 1932, reissued as *A Constellation of Heroes,* Grosset, 1971; *The Great Union,* Federal Union, 1944; *The Big Picture,* Bobbs-Merrill, 1953; *The Calm Men,* Dell, 1954; *Is There An American in the House?,* Macmillan, 1960; *The Minstrel Boy,* Macmillan, 1961; *Social Astonishments,* Macmillan, 1963; *The Glossy Rats,* Grosset, 1967; *Revolution by Cliche,* Funk, 1970.

BIOGRAPHICAL/CRITICAL SOURCES: Commonweal, October 6, 1967.

COSGROVE, Margaret (Leota)   1926-

PERSONAL: Born June 3, 1926, in Sylvania, Ohio; daughter of Maynard Giles (an engineer) and Leota (Holt) Cosgrove. *Education:* Studied at Chicago Art Institute and American Academy of Art. *Religion:* Protestant. *Home:* 175 East 93rd St., New York, N.Y. 10028.

CAREER: Cornell University Medical College, New York, N.Y., medical artist, 1950; Roosevelt Hospital, New York, N.Y., medical artist, 1953-56; free-lance book and medical illustrator. Good Neighbor Community Center, New York, N.Y., former afternoon program director.

WRITINGS—All self-illustrated; all published by Dodd: *Wonders of the Tree World,* 1953, revised edition, 1970, *The Wonders Inside You,* 1955, *Wonders of your Senses,* 1958, *Wonders Under a Microscope,* 1959, *Wonders at Your Feet: A New World for Explorers,* 1960, *The Strange World of Animal Senses,* 1961, revised edition, edited by J.C.W. Houghton, Phoenix House, 1963, *Your Hospital, a Modern Miracle,* 1962, *Strange Worlds Under a Microscope,* 1962, *A is for Anatomy,* 1965, *Eggs, and What Happens Inside Them,* 1966, *Plants in Time: Their History and Mystery,* 1967, *Bone for Bone,* 1968, *Seeds, Embryos, and Sex,* 1970.

WORK IN PROGRESS: Illustrating medical publications, including a book on chest injuries and thoracic surgery; adult fiction.

BIOGRAPHICAL/CRITICAL SOURCES: Christian Science Monitor, May 4, 1967; *Books and Bookmen,* June, 1967, July, 1968; *Young Readers' Review,* October, 1968.

*   *   *

COULDERY, Fred(erick) A(lan) J(ames)   1928-

PERSONAL: Born June 20, 1928, in Brighton, England; son of Herbert William and Eva Louisa (Cox) Couldery; married Marion Shirley Priddle, June 21, 1948; children: Peter Alan James, Angela Margaret. *Education:* Attended Whitgift School, 1940-45. *Home:* 11 Queen Victoria Ave., Hove 4, Sussex, England. *Office:* Couldery & Co., 173 Dyke Rd., Hove 2, Sussex, England.

CAREER: Couldery & Co. (chartered accountants), Brighton, Sussex, England, partner. Director of Industrial Design Associates Ltd., Alan James Ltd., Editype Ltd., and other firms. *Member:* Institute of Chartered Accountants in England and Wales (fellow), Association of Certified and Corporate Accountants (fellow), Corporation of Secretaries (fellow). *Awards, honors:* Plender Prize of Institute of Chartered Accountants; Kennedy Medal of Corporation of Secretaries.

WRITINGS: (With Allen J.G. Sheppard) *Your Business Matters,* J. Murray, 1958; (editor) A. Stephen Noel, *Manual of Business Training: A Complete Guide to Office Routine and Modern Methods of Business,* 14th edition, Pitman, 1958, 15th edition, 1967; *An Accountant's Working Papers,* Gee & Co., 1960; *Critical Path Analysis,* Editype Ltd., 1967. Editor of *Auditor,* 1956-61.

*   *   *

COULSON, Felicity Carter   1906-
(Emery Bonett)

PERSONAL: Born December 2, 1906, in Sheffield, Yorkshire, England; daughter of John Louis and Winifred (Naylor) Carter; married John Coulson (now a writer), February, 1939; children: Nicholas. *Education:* Educated in English schools. *Home:* Tamariu, Palafrugell, Gerona, Spain. *Agent:* Curtis Brown Ltd., 13 King St., London W.C. 2, England.

CAREER: Author. *Member:* Arts Theatre Club (London).

WRITINGS—All under pseudonym Emery Bonett: *A Girl Must Live,* Arthur Barker, 1937; *Never Go Dark,* Heinemann, 1940; *Make Do with Spring,* Heinemann, 1942; *Old Mrs. Camelot,* Blakiston Co., 1944 (published in England as *High Pavement,* Heinemann, 1944).

With husband, John Coulson, under pseudonyms Emery and John Bonett: *Dead Lion,* Doubleday, 1949; *Not in the Script,* Doubleday, 1951 (published in England as *A Banner for Pegasus,* M. Joseph, 1951); *No Grave for a Lady,* Doubleday, 1959; *Better Off Dead,* Doubleday, 1964 (published in England as *Better Dead,* M. Joseph, 1964); *The Private Face of Murder,* Doubleday, 1966; *This Side Murder?,* M. Joseph, 1967, published in America as *Murder on the Costa Brava,* Walker & Co., 1968; *The Sound of Murder,* Harrap, 1970, Walker & Co., 1971; *No Time to Kill,* Walker & Co., 1972.

Film scripts: "The Glass Mountain"; (with John Coulson) "Children Galore." Radio and television plays: "One Fine Day"; "Mr. Beverly Plays God"; "Blue Murder"; "Face to Face"; other plays. Contributor of short stories to magazines.

WORK IN PROGRESS: A detective novel.

SIDELIGHTS: The Coulsons have been doing their joint writing since 1949. In 1964 they built a home (named La Golondrina) in the village of Tamariu, a Costa Brava resort with a winter population of eighty; the population swells in the summer to several thousand. Two of Mrs. Coulson's solo books, *Old Mrs. Camelot* and *A Girl Must Live,* were made into motion pictures.

* * *

COULSON, John H(ubert) A(rthur)   1906-
(John Bonett)

PERSONAL: Born August 10, 1906, in Benton, Northumberland, England; son of Hubert and Constance (Tayler) Coulson; married Felicity Carter, February, 1939; children: Nicholas. *Education:* Attended Durham School in England. *Home:* Tamariu, Palafrugell, Gerona, Spain. *Agent:* Curtis Brown Ltd., 13 King St., London W.C. 2, England.

CAREER: In banking, 1924-37; company secretary, 1937-39; Admiralty officer, 1940-45; sales promotion executive, 1945-63. *Member:* National Book League, Instituto Britanico (Barcelona), Garrick Club (London).

WRITINGS—With wife, Felicity Coulson, under pseudonyms Emery and John Bonett: *Dead Lion,* Doubleday, 1949; *Not in the Script,* Doubleday, 1951 (published in England as *A Banner for Pegasus,* M. Joseph, 1951); *No Grave for a Lady,* Doubleday, 1959; *Better Off Dead,* Doubleday, 1964 (published in England as *Better Dead,* M. Joseph, 1964); *The Private Face of Murder,* Doubleday, 1966; *This Side Murder?,* M. Joseph, 1967, published in America as *Murder on the Costa Brava,* Walker & Co., 1968; *The Sound of Murder,* Harrap, 1970, Walker & Co., 1971; *No Time to Kill,* Walker & Co., 1972. Author of story, and co-author with Felicity Coulson of film script, "Children Galore." Contributor of short stories to *Maclean's Magazine, Argosy,* and other magazines.

WORK IN PROGRESS: A detective novel.

SIDELIGHTS: Coulson writes he is listed in *Burke's Peerage* under Lord Byron, and that his descent can be traced and confirmed via a subsequently legitimised bastard (John Beaufort, Earl of Somerset, who was the son of John of Gaunt by his third wife, Catherine), from William the Conqueror.

In regard to writing with his wife, Coulson dislikes being asked, "Now, how do you and your wife collaborate?"

* * *

COULTER, E(llis) Merton   1890-

PERSONAL: Surname is pronounced *Coal*-ter; born July 20, 1890, in Catawba County, N.C.; son of John Ellis (a farmer, lumberman, and stockman) and Lucy Ann (Propst) Coulter. *Education:* University of North Carolina, A.B., 1913; University of Wisconsin, M.A., 1915, Ph.D., 1917. *Politics:* Independent Democrat. *Religion:* Lutheran. *Home:* 110 Fortson Dr., Athens, Ga. 30601.

CAREER: Marietta College, Marietta, Ohio, member of history faculty, 1917-19; University of Georgia, Athens, associate professor, 1919-23, professor of history, 1923-58, Regents' Professor Emeritus of History, 1958—. Visiting professor at University of Texas, 1929-30, 1942-45, Louisiana State University, 1934-35, Hebrew University of Jerusalem, 1952; visiting summer professor at Harvard University, Ohio State University, University of Chicago, Duke University, National University of Mexico, six other U.S. universities. *Member:* American Historical Association, Organization of American Historians, Southern Historical Association (former president), Georgia Historical Society. *Awards, honors:* Litt.D., Marietta College, 1948; LL.D., University of North Carolina, 1952.

WRITINGS: (With W.E. Connelley) *History of Kentucky,* two volumes, American Historical Society, 1922; *The Civil War and Readjustment in Kentucky,* University of North Carolina Press, 1926; *College Life in the Old South,* Macmillan, 1928.

Short History of Georgia, University of North Carolina Press, 1933, reissued as *Georgia: A Short History,* 1947; (editor) *Georgia's Disputed Ruins,* University of North Carolina Press, 1937; *William G. Brownlow: Fighting Parson of the Southern Highlands,* University of North Carolina Press, 1937; (editor) *The Other Half of Old New Orleans,* Louisiana State University Press, 1939; (editor) *The Course of the South to Secession: An Interpretation by Ulrich Bonnell Phillips,* Appleton, 1939.

Thomas Spalding of Sapelo, Louisiana State University Press, 1940; *John Jacobus Flournoy, Champion of the Common Man in the Antebellum South,* Georgia Historical Society, 1942; *The South During Reconstruction, 1865-1877,* Louisiana State University Press, 1947; *Travels in the Confederate States: A Bibliography,* University of Oklahoma Press, 1948; (editor with A.B. Saye) *A List of the Early Settlers of Georgia,* University of Georgia Press, 1949, 2nd edition, 1967.

The Confederate States of America, 1861-65, Louisiana State University Press, 1950; *Wormsloe: Two Centuries of a Georgia Family,* University of Georgia Press, 1955; *Lost Generation: The Life and Death of James Barrow, C.S.A.,* Confederate, 1956; *Auraria: The Story of a Georgia Gold-Mining Town,* University of Georgia Press, 1956; *The Myth of Dade County's Seceding from Georgia in 1860,* Georgia Historical Society, 1957; (editor) *The Journal of William Stephens,* University of Georgia Press, Volume I: *1741-43,* 1958, Volume II: *1743-45,* 1959.

(Editor) *Confederate Receipt Book,* University of Georgia Press, 1960; *James Monroe Smith, Georgia Planter, Before Death and After,* University of Georgia Press, 1961; *John Ellis Coulter, Small-Town Businessman of Tarheelia,* privately printed, 1962; (editor) *The Journal of Peter Gordon, 1732-35,* University of Georgia Press, 1963; *Joseph Vallence Bevan, Georgia's First Official Historian,* University of Georgia Press, 1964; *Old Petersburg and the Broad River Valley of Georgia: Their Rise and Decline,* University of Georgia Press, 1965; *Georgia Waters: Tallulah Falls, Madison Springs, Scull Shoals,* and the Okefenokee Swamp, Georgia Historical Quarterly, 1965; The Toombs Oak, the Tree That Owned Itself, and Other Chapters of Georgia, University of Georgia Press, 1966; (editor) Warren Grice, Georgia Through Two Centuries, Lewis Historical Publishing, 1966; William Montague Brown, Versatile Anglo-Irish American, University of Georgia Press, 1967; Negro Legislators in Georgia During the Reconstruction Period, Georgia Historical Quarterly, 1968.

Daniel Lee, Agriculturist: His Life North and South, University of Georgia Press, 1971; The Last Visit of Jefferson Davis to Georgia and Other Topics in the History of the State, Georgia Historical Quarterly, 1971. Editor, Georgia Historical Quarterly, 1924—.

SIDELIGHTS: "My writings are more descriptive than critical or interpretative, . . . directed to illuminating the dark historical corners—mainly local and regional."

Coulter has pursued his hobbies—walking, color photography, and mountain climbing—in travel on four continents. Other interest: Music.

*   *   *

COURLANDER, Harold   1908-

PERSONAL: Born September 18, 1908, in Indianapolis, Ind.; son of David (a primitive painter) and Tillie (Oppenheim) Courlander; married Emma Meltzer, June 18, 1949; children: Erika Courlander Wolfson, Michael, Susan. Education: University of Michigan, B.A., 1931. Home: 5512 Brite Dr., Bethesda, Md. 20034. Office: Voice of America, U.S. Information Agency, Washington, D.C. 20025.

CAREER: Farmer in Romeo, Mich., 1933-38; Douglas Aircraft Co., Eritrea (now Ethiopia), historian, 1942-43; U.S. Office of War Information, New York, N.Y., and Bombay, India, editor, 1943-45; U.S. Information Agency, Voice of America, New York, N.Y., editor, 1945-54; Washington, D.C., senior political analyst, 1960—; U.S. Mission to United Nations, New York, N.Y., press officer, 1954; United Nations, New York, N.Y., writer and editor on United Nations Review, 1956-59. Awards, honors: Avery Hopwood Award, 1931, 1932; Franz Boas Fund research grant for folklore study in Dominican Republic, 1939; American Council of Learned Societies grants for research in Haiti, 1939, 1940; American Philosophical Society grants for studies in New World Negro cultures, 1946, 1954, 1955; Wenner-Gren Foundation grants for work in United States and West Indian Negro folk music, 1946, 1954, 1955, 1956, 1962; Guggenheim fellowships for studies in African and Afro-American cultures, 1948, 1955.

WRITINGS: Swamp Mud, Blue Ox Press, 1936; Home to Langford County, Blue Ox Press, 1938; Haiti Singing, University of North Carolina Press, 1939, Cooper Square, 1973; The Caballero, Farrar & Rinehart, 1940; The Drum and the Hoe: Life and Lore of the Haitian People, University of California Press, 1960; Shaping Our Times: What the United Nations Is and Does, Oceana, 1960, revised edition, 1962; On Recognizing the Human Species, Anti-Defamation League of B'nai B'rith, 1960; Negro Songs From Alabama, Oak, 1960; The Big Old World of Richard Creeks, Chilton, 1962; Negro Folk Music U.S.A., Columbia University Press, 1963; (with Remy Bastien) Religion and Politics in Haiti, Institute for Cross-Cultural Research, 1966; Vodounin Haitian Culture, Institute for Cross-Cultural Research, 1966; The African, Crown, 1967; The Fourth World of the Hopis, Crown, 1971.

Folk tale collections: Uncle Bouqui of Haiti, Morrow, 1942; (with George Herzog) The Cow-Tail Switch, and Other West African Stories, Holt, 1947; (with Robert Kane) Kantchil's Lime Pit, and Other Stories from Indonesia, Harcourt, 1950; (with Wolf Leslau) The Fire on the Mountain, and Other Ethiopian Stories, Holt, 1950; Ride With the Sun, Whittlesey House, 1955; Terrapin's Pot of Sense, Holt, 1957; (with Albert K. Prempeh) The Hat Shaking Dance, and Other Tales from the Gold Coast, Harcourt, 1957; The Tiger's Whisker, and Other Tales and Legends from Asia and the Pacific, Harcourt, 1959; The King's Drum, and Other African Folk Tales, Harcourt, 1962; The Piece of Fire, and Other Haitian Tales, Harcourt, 1964; (with Ezekiel A. Eshugbayi) Olode the Hunter, and Other Tales from Nigeria, Harcourt, 1968 (published in England as Ijapa the Tortoise, and Other Nigerian Tales, Bodley Head, 1969); People of the Short Corn: Tales and Legends of the Hopi Indians, Harcourt, 1970; Tales of Yoruba Gods and Heroes, Crown, 1972.

Albums, compiled and edited from own field recordings: "Cult Music of Cuba," Ethnic Folkways Library, 1949; "Meringues," Folkways Records, 1950; "Drums of Haiti," Ethnic Folkways Library, 1950; "Folk Music of Haiti,' Ethnic Folkways Library, 1950; "Folk Music of Ethiopia," Ethnic Folkways Library, 1951; "Songs and Dances of Haiti," Ethnic Folkways Library, 1952; "Haitian Piano," Folkways Records, 1952. Compiler and editor of other collections for Ethnic Folkways Library, including "Caribbean Folk Music," "Folk Music, U.S.A.," "African and Afro-American Drums," "Afro-American Folk Music."

Contributor, Miscelanea de estudios dedicados a Fernando Ortiz, published in Havana, 1955. Contributor of articles to Saturday Review, Musical Quarterly, New Republic, Journal of Negro History, Opportunity, and other periodicals.

WORK IN PROGRESS: A treasury of African and Afro-American folklore.

BIOGRAPHICAL/CRITICAL SOURCES: New York Times Book Review, April 28, 1968; Book World, May 5, 1968; National Observer, September 22, 1968. Times Literary Supplement, October 16, 1969.

*   *   *

COURSE, Alfred George   1895-

PERSONAL: Born February 20, 1895, in London, England; son of William (a station master) and Mary (Scudder) Course; married Alice Sims, November 17, 1921; children: Edwin Alfred, Pamela Mary. Education: Attended school in Chelsea, London, England. Home: 26 Weldon Ave., Bear Cross, Bournemouth, England.

CAREER: Began working at fifteen as apprentice in sailing ships on world voyages; served in North Atlantic Fleet Auxiliary in World War I, then in passenger and cargo vessels in the Far East, commanding a mail, passenger, and cargo vessel; returned to London to join service of Port of London Authority; served as dockmaster at London Docks during World War II; retired in 1956 to devote full time to writing. Member: Authors' Society, Institute of Transport (associate), Honourable Company of Master Mariners, International Association of Master Mariners (chairman, British section). Awards, honors: Dock and Harbour Authorities awards, for papers on dock subjects, 1934, 1946; Institute of Shipping award, 1945, for papers on shipping and related subjects.

WRITINGS: The Wheel's Kick and the Wind's Song: The Story of the John Stewart Line of Sailing Ships, Percival Marshall, 1950, 3rd revised edition, Augustus M. Kelley, 1968; Ships of the P & O, Adlard Coles, 1954; The Merchant Navy To-Day, Oxford University Press, 1956; The Deep Sea Tramp, Hollis & Carter, 1960, Barre, 1963; Painted Ports: The Story of the Ships of Devitt and Moore, Hollis & Carter, 1961; (with R.B. Oram)

Glossary of Cargo Handling Terms, Brown, Son & Ferguson, 1961; *A Dictionary of Nautical Terms,* Arco Publications, 1962, Philosophical Library, 1963; *The Merchant Navy: A Social History,* Muller, 1963, Sportshelf, 1964; *The Dock and Harbours of Britain,* Ian Allen, 1964; *A Seventeenth-Century Mariner,* Muller, 1965, Sportshelf, 1966; *Pirates of the Eastern Seas,* Muller, 1966, Transatlantic, 1970; *Windjammers of the Horn: The Story of the Last British Fleet of Square-Rigged Sailing Ships,* Fernhill, 1969; *Pirates of the Western Seas,* Muller, 1969, Transatlantic, 1971.

Contributor of articles and short stories to monthly journals.

WORK IN PROGRESS: The Golden Years of Sail.

* * *

COURTENAY, William J(ames) 1935-

PERSONAL: Born November 5, 1935, in Neenah, Wis.; son of Walter Rowe (a minister) and Emily (Simpson) Courtenay. *Education:* Vanderbilt University, A.B., 1957; Harvard University Divinity School, S.T.B., 1960, Ph.D., 1967. *Home:* 3420 Blackhawk Dr., Shorewood Hills, Madison, Wis. 53705.

CAREER: Institute for European History, Mainz, Germany, fellow, 1964-65; Stanford University, Stanford, Calif., instructor in history, 1965-66; University of Wisconsin, Madison, assistant professor, 1966-69, associate professor, 1969-71, professor of history, 1971—. *Member:* Mediaeval Academy of America, American Society of Church History, American Society for Reformation Research, Phi Delta Theta. *Awards, honors:* Younger Scholar award, National Endowment for the Humanities, 1968-69; grant-in-aid, American Council of Learned Societies, 1968-69.

WRITINGS: (Editor with H.A. Oberman) *Gabrielis Biel Canonis Misse Expositio,* four volumes, Franz Steiner Verlag, 1963-67; (editor) *The Judeo-Christian Heritage,* Holt, 1970. Contributor to *Harvard Theological Review, Speculum,* and *Research Studies of Washington State University.*

WORK IN PROGRESS: A study of Nominalist Eucharistic thought, for Franz Steiner Verlag; articles for journals.

SIDELIGHTS: Courtenay knows Latin, Greek, French, German, Spanish, and Italian. *Avocational interests:* Tennis, sailing, skiing.

* * *

COWASJEE, Saros 1931-

PERSONAL: Born July 12, 1931, in Secundrabad, Deccan, India; son of Dara and Meher (Bharucha) Cowasjee. *Education:* St. John's College, Agra, India, B.A., 1951; Agra University, M.A., 1955; University of Leeds, Ph.D., 1960. *Religion:* Zoroastrian. *Office:* Department of English, University of Saskatchewan, Regina, Saskatchewan, Canada.

CAREER: Times of India Press, Bombay, India, assistant editor, 1961-63; University of Saskatchewan, Regina, instructor, 1963-64, assistant professor, 1964-66, associate professor of English, 1966—. *Member:* Humanities Club, I.S.A.I.L. *Awards, honors:* Canada Council leave fellowship, 1968-69; Canada Council grant, 1970-71.

WRITINGS: Sean O'Casey: The Man Behind the Plays, Oliver & Boyd, 1963, St. Martin's, 1964, revised edition, Oliver & Boyd, 1965; *O'Casey,* Oliver & Boyd, 1966, Barnes & Noble, 1967; *His Father's Medals and Other Stories and Sketches,* Writers Workshop (Calcutta), 1970; (editor and author of introduction) Mulk Raj Anand, *Private Life of an Indian Prince,* Copp, 1970; (editor

and author of introduction) Mulk Raj Anand, *Untouchable,* Copp, 1970; (editor and author of introduction) Mulk Raj Anand, *Seven Summers,* Cedric Chivers, 1970; (editor and author of introduction) Mulk Raj Anand, *Coolie,* Copp, 1971.

Contributor of articles and short stories to *Guardian, Review of English Literature, Journal of Commonwealth Literature, Dublin, Drama Survey, Literary Criterion, Literary Half-Yearly, Wascana Review, Illustrated Weekly of India, Thought, Irish Times, Times of India, Indian Literature,* and to several other publications in India and the United Kingdom.

WORK IN PROGRESS: The Novels of Mulk Raj Anand, for Copp; a screenplay; abridging novels for Macmillan (Bombay).

* * *

COWLES, Fleur

PERSONAL: Born in New York, N.Y.; daughter of Matthew M. and Eleanor (Pearl) Fenton; married Atherton Pettingell (an advertising executive), February 13, 1938; married second husband, Gardner Cowles (a publisher), December 27, 1946 (divorced, 1955); married Tom Montague Meyer (owner of a timber company), November 18, 1955. *Education:* Studied at Pratt Institute. *Home and office:* A5 Albany, Piccadilly, London W.1, England. *Agent:* Monica McCall, Ashley Famous Agency, Inc., 1501 Avenue of the Americas, New York, N.Y. 10019.

CAREER: New York World Telegram, New York, N.Y., columnist, 1935-38; executive vice-president of an advertising agency, New York, N.Y., 1938-46; *Look,* New York, N.Y., assistant editor, 1946-55, foreign agency correspondent, 1955-58; *Flair,* New York, N.Y., founder and editor, 1950-53; *Quick,* New York, N.Y., assistant editor, 1951-53. Special consultant to Famine Emergency Commission, 1946; personal representative of President Eisenhower, with rank of ambassador, at coronation of Queen Elizabeth II, 1952; member of advisory committee on women's participation, Civil Defense Administration, 1953-55. Trustee of Social Rehabilitation of the Facially Disfigured, and of Elmira College; member of council, American Museum, Bath, England.

MEMBER: Ordre les Compagnons de Rabelais, Women's National Press Club, Overseas Press Club, Theta Sigma Phi. *Awards, honors:* Chevalier of the Legion of Honor (France), 1951; Queen's Medal (England), 1952; Order of the Southern Cross, Cavalier Class (Brazil), 1953; Order of Bienfascene (Greece), 1955; LL.D., Elmira College, 1955.

WRITINGS: Bloody Precedent, Random House, 1951; *Flair Book,* Random House, 1963; *The Case of Salvador Dali,* Little, Brown, 1960; *The Hidden World of the Hadramoutt,* Stevens, 1962; *Tiger Flower: Paintings,* text by Robert Vavra, introduction by Yehudi Menuhin, Collins, 1968, Reynal, 1969. Contributor to *Atlantic Monthly, Daily Telegraph* (London), *Vogue* (London), *Queen* (London), and other newspapers and magazines.

WORK IN PROGRESS: A book of personal anecdotes.

* * *

COX, Bill 1910-

PERSONAL: Born March 18, 1910, in Wimbledon, London, England; married Enid Vera Cocking, September 3, 1937; children: Peter Coulston, Graham Charles. *Politics:* Conservative. *Religion:* Church of England. *Home:* 23 Montana Rd., Wimbledon, London S.W.20, England.

CAREER: Fulwell Golf Club, Hampton Hill, Middlesex, England, currently golf professional. Represented Great Britain in Ryder Cup golf matches, 1935, 1937; official golf coach to Royal and Ancient Golf Club of St. Andrews, 1956-59. British Broadcasting Corp., golf commentator. Adviser to Castle Equipment Co. Ltd. and Slazengers. *Military service:* British Army, 1941-46; became captain. *Member:* Conservative Club, 19th Hole Club.

WRITINGS: *Golf with Bill Cox,* Niblick, 1937; *Play Better Golf,* Muller, 1951; *Can I Help You?,* Benn, 1954; *Improve Your Golf,* Penguin, 1963; (with Nicholas Tremayne) *Bill Cox's Golf Companion,* Dent, 1969. Contributor to *Golf Illustrated, Italian Golf, Evening News* (London).

*   *   *

COX, LaWanda Fenlason 1909-

PERSONAL: Born September 24, 1909, in Aberdeen, Wash.; daughter of O.C. and Jennie (Boomsliter) Fenlason; married John H. Cox (a professor of history). *Education:* University of Oregon, A.B., 1930; Smith College, M.A., 1932; University of California, Berkeley, Ph.D., 1941. *Home:* 372 Central Park West, New York, N.Y. 10025.

CAREER: Northeast Missouri State Teachers College, Kirksville, instructor in history, 1940-41; Goucher College, Baltimore, Md., assistant professor of history, 1944-46; Hunter College of the City University of New York; New York, N.Y., 1942-44, 1946—, began as instructor, became professor of history. Member of doctoral faculty, City University of New York. *Member:* American Historical Association, American Association of University Professors, Southern Historical Association, Phi Beta Kappa. *Awards, honors:* Research grants from Social Science Research Council and American Philosophical Society; John H. Dunning Prize, American Historical Association; book award, Phi Alpha Theta, for *Politics, Principle, and Prejudice.*

WRITINGS: (With husband, John H. Cox) *Politics, Principle, and Prejudice, 1865-1866: Dilemma of Reconstruction America,* Free Press, 1963; (editor with J. H. Cox) *Reconstruction, the New South, and the Negro,* University of South Carolina Press, 1973. Contributor to historical journals.

*   *   *

COX, Miriam Stewart

PERSONAL: Born in Logan, Utah; daughter of James Zebulon and Johanna (Kotter) Stewart; married Dee Cox (a teacher), July 12, 1938; children: Janet Elaine. *Education:* Utah State University, B.S., 1934; University of Idaho, M.S., 1942; also studied summers at University of California, Los Angeles. *Office:* Fullerton Junior College, Fullerton, Calif. 93734; Department of English, California State College at Fullerton, 800 North State College, Fullerton, Calif. 92631.

CAREER: Has held a variety of teaching positions, including nursery school and kindergarten teacher, and secondary school teacher in Utah, California, and Idaho; Fullerton Junior College, Fullerton, Calif., English instructor, 1957—. Part-time English instructor at California State College at Fullerton, 1961—. Has also taught at University of Idaho and University of Redlands. *Member:* National Council of Teachers of English, College English Association, California Council of Teachers of English, California Federation of Chaparral Poets (president, Compton chapter, 1953-58; state secretary, 1955-57), Phi Kappa Phi.

WRITINGS: *The Magic and the Sword* (Greek myths retold), Row, Peterson, 1956; *The Three Treasures: Myths of Old Japan,* Harper, 1964. Contributor of articles to professional journals.

WORK IN PROGRESS: Research on Persian epic and mythology and on Goethe's *Faust.*

AVOCATIONAL INTERESTS: Social dancing; music, particularly opera; and writing poetry.

*   *   *

COX, William R(obert) 1901-
(Joel Reeve)

PERSONAL: Born 1901, in Peapack, N.J.; son of William and Marion Grace (Wenz) Cox; married Lee Frederic. *Home:* 4438 Bellingham Ave., Studio City, Calif. 91604. *Agent:* Lenninger Literary Agency, Inc., 11 West 42nd St., New York, N.Y. 10036.

CAREER: Professional writer. *Member:* Writers Guild of America, West; Western Writers of America; Academy of Magical Arts; Kansas State Historical Society.

WRITINGS: *Make My Coffin Strong,* Fawcett, 1954; *The Lusty Men,* Pyramid Books, 1957; *The Tycoon and the Tigress,* Fawcett, 1957; *Hell to Pay,* New American Library, 1958; *Comanche Moon: A Novel of the West,* McGraw, 1959; *Death Comes Early,* Dell, 1959; *The Duke,* New American Library, 1959; *Murder in Vegas,* New American Library, 1960; *Luke Short and His Era,* Doubleday, 1961 (published in England as *Luke Short, Famous Gambler of the Old West,* Fireside Press, 1962); *The Outlawed,* New American Library, 1961; *Death on Location,* New American Library, 1962; *Bigger than Texas,* Fawcett, 1962; *The Mets Will Win the Pennant* (nonfiction), Putnam, 1964; (editor) *Rivers to Cross* (collection of stories by members of Western Writers of America), Dodd, 1966; *Chicano Cruz,* Bantam, 1972; *The Sixth Horseman,* Ballantine, 1972.

Young adult books: *Five Were Chosen: A Basket Ball Story,* Dodd, 1956; *Gridiron Duel,* Dodd, 1959; *The Wild Pitch,* Dodd, 1963; *Tall on the Court,* Dodd, 1964; *Third and Eight to Go,* Dodd, 1964; *Big League Rookie,* Dodd, 1965; *Trouble at Second Base,* Dodd, 1966; *The Valley Eleven,* Dodd, 1967; (under pseudonym Joel Reeve) *Goal Ahead,* S.G. Phillips, 1967; *Jump Shot Joe,* Dodd, 1968; *Rookie in the Backcourt,* Dodd, 1970; *Big League Sandlotters,* Dodd, 1971; *Third and Goal,* Dodd, 1971; *Playoff,* Bantam, 1972; *Gunner on the Court,* Dodd, 1972.

Contributor of more than one thousand stories to magazines including *Saturday Evening Post, Collier's, This Week, Argosy, American, Pic, Blue Book, Cosmopolitan,* Popular Publication magazines, Fiction House magazines, Street & Smith magazines.

Writer of several motion pictures and of more than one hundred television shows for "Fireside Theater," "Broken Arrow," "Bonanza," "Zane Grey Theater," "The Virginian," "The Grey Ghost," "Alcoa Theater," "Wells Fargo," "Route 66," other network programs.

WORK IN PROGRESS: One novel; several untitled juveniles; screen and television scripts.

*   *   *

COX, William Trevor 1928-
(William Trevor)

PERSONAL: Born May 24, 1928, in Mitchelstown, County Cork, Ireland; son of James William (a banker) and Gertrude (Davison) Cox; married Jane Ryan, August 26, 1952; children: Patrick, Dominic. *Education:* St. Columba's College, Dublin, Ireland, student, 1942-46; Trinity College, University of Dublin, B.A., 1950. *Politics:* A liberal. *Home:* Stentwood House, Dunkeswell, Honiton, Devonshire, England. *Agent:* Sterling Lord Agency, 75 East 55th St., New York, N.Y. 10022; and John Johnson, 3 Albemarle St., London W.1, England.

CAREER: History teacher in Armagh, Northern Ireland, 1950-52; art teacher in Rugby, England, 1952-56, in Taunton, England, 1956-60; advertising copywriter in London, England, 1960-65. Member: Irish Academy of Letters. Awards, honors: Winner of Irish section, "Unknown Political Prisoner" sculpture competition, 1953; second prize, Transatlantic Review short story competition, 1964; Hawthornden prize, 1965; Society of Authors' traveling scholarship, 1972.

WRITINGS—Under name William Trevor: A Standard of Behavior, Hutchinson, 1958; The Old Boys, Viking, 1964; The Boarding-House, Viking, 1965; The Love Department, Bodley Head, 1966, Viking, 1967; The Day We Got Drunk on Cake, and Other Stories, Bodley Head, 1967, Viking, 1968; Mrs. Eckdorf in O'Neill's Hotel, Bodley Head, 1969, Viking, 1970; The Old Boys (play; adapted from his novel; first produced in the West End at Mermaid Theatre, July 29, 1971), Davis-Poynter, 1971; Miss Gomez and the Brethren, Bodley Head, 1971; The Ballroom of Romance, and Other Stories, Viking, 1972; "Lonely People" (one-act play), first produced in London at King's Head Islington, February 29, 1972.

Stories anthologized in Voices 2, edited by Michael Ratcliffe, M. Joseph, 1964, Winter's Tales 14, edited by Kevin Crossley-Holland, Macmillan, 1968, Splinters: A New Anthology of Modern Macabre Fiction, edited by Alex Hamilton, Hutchinson, 1968, Walker & Co., 1969, The Bedside Guardian, edited by W.L. Webb, Collins, 1969, The Seventh Ghost Book, edited by Rosemary Timperley, Barrie & Jenkins, 1972, Modern Irish Short Stories, edited by David Marcus, Sphere, 1972, The Eighth Ghost Book, edited by Rosemary Timperley, Barrie & Jenkins, 1973, Winter's Tales from Ireland, 2, edited by Kevin Casey, Macmillan, 1973, and in other collections. Contributor of short stories to Transatlantic Review, London Magazine, Town, Queen, Nova, Encounter, Times (London) Irish Press, Penguin Modern Stories, Listener, Argosy, Redbook, Antioch Review, and other periodicals. Author of television and radio plays for British Broadcasting Corp. and ITV, including "The Old Boys," "O Fat White Woman," and "The Grass Widows."

WORK IN PROGRESS: A novel; a new stage play.

SIDELIGHTS: In a review of Mrs. Eckdorf in O'Neill's Hotel, Berry Cole states that "Trevor has created a dotty, twilight, ultimately inconsequential world which is enhanced by a quiet but persistently nudging tone: he uses the right language for what he wants to say." Peter Buitenhuis, however, finds Trevor's world depressing and seemingly aimless. "These clever, meticulously—written, brittle tales almost all lead the reader into a blind alley, where it seems that the best, if not the only thing to do, is accept the limitations life has inexorably imposed. In William Trevor's world, when illusion and liquor do not free him, man's lot is isolation, just as Eliot described it in 'The Waste Land.' From this constriction, as the good American phrase goes, I want out."

In an article in London Magazine, Trevor stated that he does not write with a particular social or political cause in mind. "In my case I can only work on my own terms: I possess neither the instinct nor the kind of equipment that's necessary if public opinion is to be influenced in a specific manner or for a specific cause. I am all for protest and misbehaviour in a smug society and my own writing appears to me to be based on an objection to the intolerances and conventions that just such a society has generated. Yet I am very far from being, in the ordinary and contemporary sense, a writer of protest. And while I am in no way whatsoever against the idea of the novelist as a polemicist, for me to perform as such would not, I'm certain, be a happy experience for anyone, including myself."

AVOCATIONAL INTERESTS: Eating, drinking, friends, traveling; prefers listening to talking.

BIOGRAPHICAL/CRITICAL SOURCES: Books and Bookmen, July, 1967; Vogue, February 1, 1968; New York Times Book Review, February 11, 1968; London Magazine, August, 1968; Spectator, October 11, 1969; Time, January 26, 1970; Christian Science Monitor, February 26, 1970; Plays and Players, September, 1971; Stage, March 9, 1972; New York Times, September 31, 1972.

*   *   *

COZZENS, James Gould   1903-

PERSONAL: Born August 19, 1903, in Chicago, Ill.; son of Henry William and Bertha (Wood) Cozzens; married Bernice Baumgarten, December 31, 1927. Education: Graduate of Kent (Conn.) School, 1922; attended Harvard University, 1922-24. Home: Shadowbrook, Williamstown, Mass. Agent: Brandt and Brandt, 101 Park Ave., New York, N.Y. 10017.

CAREER: Taught children of American engineers in Santa Clara, Cuba, 1925; spent one year in Europe, 1926-27; associate editor of Fortune magazine, 1938; farmer; writer. Military service: U.S. Army Air Forces, 1942-45; became major. Member: National Institute of Arts and Letters. Awards, honors: O. Henry Award, 1936; Pulitzer Prize, 1949, for Guard of Honor; Litt.D., Harvard University, 1952; William Dean Howells Medal, American Academy of Arts and Letters, 1960, for By Love Possessed.

WRITINGS: Confusion, B.J. Brimmer, 1924; Michael Scarlett, A & C Boni, 1925; Cockpit, Morrow, 1928; The Son of Perdition, Morrow, 1929; S.S. San Pedro, Harcourt, 1931; The Last Adam, Harcourt, 1933 (published in England as A Cure of Flesh, Longmans, Green, 1934, new edition, Longmans, Green, 1958); Castaway, Random House, 1934; Men and Brethren, Harcourt, 1936; Ask Me Tomorrow, Harcourt, 1940 (reissued as Ask Me Tomorrow; or, the Pleasant Comedy of Young Fortunas, Harcourt, 1969); The Just and the Unjust, Harcourt, 1942, new edition, Longmans, Green, 1958; Guard of Honor, Harcourt, 1948; S.S. San Pedro [and] Castaway, Modern Library, 1956; By Love Possessed, Harcourt, 1957; Children and Others (stories), Harcourt, 1964; Morning Noon and Night, Harcourt, 1968.

WORK IN PROGRESS: A novel.

SIDELIGHTS: In 1957 John Fischer wrote: "The essential difference between Cozzens and his contemporaries lies in the character of his work. Here he is the complete nonconformist: a classic man, operating in a romantic period. This, I suspect, is the basic reason why he has missed both popular and critical appreciation."

With the publication of By Love Possessed, Cozzens could no longer be considered as one ignored—either popularly or critically. Orville Prescott has called him "One of the most distinguished living American writers." Granville Hicks wrote of him in 1959: "He should not be ignored because he is unfashionable nor should be be disparaged because John Fischer nominated him for the Nobel Prize. He has been writing for a long time now, and he has shown a greater capacity for growth than the majority of his contemporaries. He clings tenaciously to his own point of view, and it yields him a vision of human experience that the reader has to respect even when he doesn't like it."

Cozzens' point of view is that of the white American Republican Protestant. Writes Chester E. Eisinger: "Cozzens not only defends the status quo against attack, but he is eager to assert his approval of its essential character."

Cozzens countered to *CA:* "This is just plain crap. I don't defend anything; I don't eagerly assert anything."

Eisinger goes on to maintain that "All these strains are to be detected in Cozzens—Christian orthodoxy, classical conservatism, ancient Stoicism, and modern pragmatism. His is an eclectic conservatism."

Cozzens himself once wrote: "I am more or less illiberal, and strongly antipathetic to all political and artistic movements. I was brought up an Episcopalian, and where I live the landed gentry are Republican. I do not understand music, I am little interested in art, and the theatre seems tiresome to me. My literary preferences are for writers who take the trouble to write well. This necessarily excludes most of my contemporaries. . . I like Shakespeare and Swift and Steele and Gibbon and Jane Austen and Hazlitt." Cozzens indeed seems to have little respect for his literary contemporaries. He has called Hemingway "a great bleeding heart. . . ," described Sinclair Lewis as "a crypto-sentimentalist and a slovenly writer. . . ," and stated that he "can't read ten pages of Steinbeck without throwing up."

Although most critics concentrate upon the content and meaning in Cozzens' novels, a few are particularly impressed with his style. "I know of no modern novelist who commands such a range of idiom, allusion, cadence, rhetorical radiation and vocabulary," Louis O. Coxe maintains. "It is a muscular, virile style with certain strong affinities to seventeenth-century prose. . . ." In his narratives, writes Prescott, Cozzens is "a master of dialogue, of interior monologues, of flashbacks, of narrative pace and selective form. His style is precise and smooth, graceful and unobtrusive, always so subordinated to the matter of his novels that it is hardly noticeable at all."

Frederick C. Crews notes that Cozzens' strength "lies in the patient, cumulative rendering of institutions.... In other words, he is a traditional novelist, yet without the great traditional novelist's psychological penetration." Cozzens eschews emotional involvement and sentimentality. Richard Ellmann has said that Cozzens "walks away from us cool, disenchanted, a little superior, pleased to have kept his distance." Cozzens said in 1939: "I simply put down, then I write, what the things I have seen and known look like to me."

Walter Allen describes Cozzens as "the novelist of man in society, of man as a member of an organization.... He is not only anti-sentimental, he is anti-romantic. His characteristic spokesmen are middle-aged men who have. . . learnt from experience that . . . man cannot do what he wants but only what circumstances—the nature of society, the constitution of human institutions and the clash of interests all about him—allow him to do. . . ."

Eisinger believes that Cozzens' literary realism constitutes a deficiency in imagination and emotion. "He is a writer who says all he knows, and who expects that to be enough.... No ultimate mystery, never to be plumbed, throws its shadow upon his word. The great writer says more than he knows." Another view is set forth by Howard Nemerov, who writes: "I respect and admire the somber intelligence in Mr. Cozzens' sermons on reason, futility, and the will. I also am impressed, and a little amazed, at the obedience of a large reading public which, having heard for years from its popular critics that the Great American Novel would be optimistic, sane, cheerful, and full of positive values, now accepts from the same critics, as the same Great American Novel, this work of a mind whose cold temper and grim austerity and firm conviction of despair makes existentialists look somewhat cozy and Rotarian, if not evangelical."

BIOGRAPHICAL/CRITICAL SOURCES—Books: Harold C. Gardiner, *Fifty Years of the American Novel:* *1900-1950,* Scribner's, 1951; Maxwell Geismar, *American Moderns from Rebellion to Conformity,* Hill & Wang, 1958; F.G. Bracher, *The Novels of James Gould Cozzens,* Harcourt, 1959; Chester E. Eisinger, *Fiction of the Forties,* University of Chicago Press, 1963; H.J. Mooney, *James Gould Cozzens,* University of Pittsburgh Press, 1963; Howard Nemerov, *Poetry and Fiction: Essays,* Rutgers University Press, 1963; Orville Prescott, *In My Opinion,* Bobbs-Merrill, 1963; D.E.S. Maxwell, *Cozzens,* Oliver & Boyd, 1964; Walter Allen, *Then Modern Novel,* Dutton, 1965; Thomas B. Whitbread, editor, *Seven Contemporary Authors,* University of Texas Press 1966; Arthur Mizener, *Twelve Great American Novels,* New American Library, 1967; Daniel Madden, editor, *Proletarian Writers of the Thirties,* Southern Illinois University Press, 1968.

Articles: *New York Herald Tribune,* January 8, 1933, August 25, 1957; *Harper's,* February, 1949, September, 1957, October, 1968; *New Mexico Quarterly,* winter, 1949; *English Journal,* January, 1950; *Perspectives USA,* winter, 1954; *American Literature,* May, 1955; *New Republic,* January 20, 1957, September 16, 1957, June 9, 1958; *New Yorker,* August 24, 1957, February 8, 1958, November 2, 1968; *Saturday Review,* August 24, 1957, August 8, 1959; *New York Times Book Review,* August 25, 1957, August 9, 1959, August 2, 1964, August 25, 1968; *New York Times,* August 25, 1957, August 9, 1959, August 20, 1968; *House and Garden,* September, 1957; *Time,* September 2, 1957, August 8, 1968; *Reporter,* October 3, 1957, September 10, 1964; *America,* October 5, 1957; *Catholic World,* November, 1957; *Nation,* November 2, 1957, September 9, 1968; *Vogue,* November 15, 1957; *American Scholar,* winter, 1957; *Commentary,* January, 1958, September, 1968; *Commonweal,* April 4, 1958; *Newsweek,* April 28, 1958, August 26, 1968; *Atlantic,* August, 1964, September, 1968; *Book Week,* August 2, 1964, *Kenyon Review,* November, 1966; *Life,* August 30, 1968; *Book World,* September 8, 1968; *Christian Science Monitor,* September 19, 1968; *National Review,* November 11, 1968; *Observer Review,* January 29, 1969; *Spectator,* February 21, 1969; *Best Sellers,* April 1, 1969, September 1, 1969; *Virginia Quarterly Review,* winter, 1969.

*   *   *

CRAFT, Robert   1923-

PERSONAL: Born October 20, 1923, in Kingston, N.Y.; son of Raymond and Arpha (Lawson) Craft. *Education:* Juilliard School of Music, B.A., 1946. *Home:* 1218 North Wetherly Dr., Hollywood, Calif. 90069. *Agent:* Virginia Rice, 301 East 66th St., New York, N.Y. 10021.

CAREER: Conductor of orchestras in Europe, Japan, and the United States, 1952—. Lecturer at Dartington School, England, 1957, at Princeton Seminar for Contemporary Music, 1959. Conducted 25 record albums for Columbia Records. *Military service:* U.S. Army, 1943-44.

WRITINGS—With Igor Stravinsky: *Conversations with Igor Stravinsky,* 4 volumes, Doubleday, 1959; *Memories and Commentaries,* Doubleday, 1960; *Expositions and Developments,* Doubleday, 1962; *Dialogues and a Diary,* Doubleday, 1963; *Themes and Episodes,* Knopf, 1966; *Retrospectives and Conclusions,* Knopf, 1969; *Themes and Conclusions* (comprises most of material in *Themes and Episodes* and *Retrospectives and Conclusions*), Faber, 1972.

Other books: (With Alessandro Piovesan and Ramon Vlad) *Le Musiche religiose di Igor Stravinsky con il catalogo analitico completo di tutte le sue opere di Craft, Piovesan, Vlad,* Lombroso (Venice), 1957; *Table Talk,* Doubleday, 1965; (with Arnold Newman) *Bravo Stravin-*

sky (includes photographs by Newman, text by Craft), World Publishing, 1967; *Stravinsky: The Chronicle of a Friendship, 1948-1971,* Knopf, 1972. Columnist, *World* magazine.

SIDELIGHTS: For two decades Craft enjoyed a rather unique position as resident house guest of Igor Stravinsky, recording his impressions of life with the composer and his wife in a journal which resulted in the publication of several books, beginning with *Conversations with Stravinsky.* In the words of a writer for *Time,* "together, these collections of interviews, essays on music and reviews make up an extraordinary loose-leaf monument to the 20th century's leading composer. Professionally speaking, Stravinsky has always been brilliant but baffling. A fierce and uncompromising pioneer who quite literally revolutionized the music of his century, he was also as modishly conscious of musical fashions as Picasso was addicted to changing taste in art and sculpture. Craft has made Stravinsky's one of the best-documented lives since Beethoven's, and his book [*Retrospectives and Conclusions*], music aside, presents some of the most lively and intelligent casual reading available."

In his review of the book, Robert Evett speculates on "how large an influence Craft has had on Stravinsky. In the fifties, Stravinsky made a radical break with his own tradition; he not only gave aid and comfort to the enemy, he became one of them, leaving his own forces in the 20th century musical wars of religion hopelessly confused. His defection, his heresy, was so astonishing that it is almost impossible to believe that he did it all by himself.... Since Robert Craft was making a name for himself as an interpreter of the Viennese moderns, it would appear that, in the marriage of Stravinsky and Dodecaphony, it was Craft who instructed the postulant in the articles of faith, received him into the church, and officiated at the wedding."

Anatole Broyard writes: "There are so many brilliant and moving things in Robert Craft's *Stravinsky* that one hardly knows where to begin in praising the book. In the last two decades of Stravinsky's life, Mr. Craft functioned as friend, sounding board, musical catalyst and stand-in conductor under Stravinsky's supervision. Having collaborated on six books with Stravinsky, Mr. Craft is a practiced writer: he is also an extremely good one." Broyard is especially appreciative of Craft's "description of remote places" while on concert tours, and considers the book "a treasury of cameos" in its vignettes of celebrities—W.H. Auden, Albert Camus, Aldous Huxley, Edith Sitwell, T.S. Eliot. Broyard points out that "Mr. Craft's objectivity in writing about Stravinsky has recently been a subject of controversy. In the absence, at this point, of concrete evidence to the contrary, his book impresses one as too deeply felt, too eloquently consistent, to be doubted."

BIOGRAPHICAL/CRITICAL SOURCES: Book World, December 31, 1967; *Time,* December 19, 1969; *New Republic,* January 10, 1970; *Nation,* June 15, 1970; *New York Times,* June 15, 1972.

*   *   *

CRAFTS, Glenn Alty   1918-

PERSONAL: Born November 29, 1918, in Allen's Hill, N.Y.; son of Thomas S. Alty (a minister) and Mina Crafts; married Betty M. Jacox, August 16, 1941; children: Stephen A., Gordon A., Phillip A., Rebecca J., Jeffrey A. *Education:* Alfred University, B.A., 1940; Colgate Rochester Divinity School, B. D., 1943. *Politics:* Liberal. *Home:* 219 Terre Vista, Terre Haute, Ind. 47803.

CAREER: Ordained to Methodist ministry, 1943. Christ Methodist Church, Snyder, N.Y., minister, 1949-67; Centenary United Methodist Church, Terre Haute, Ind., min-

ister, 1967—. Member, Southern Indiana Conference of United Methodist Church; president, United Methodist Union of Terre Haute. Active in Vigo County Mental Health Association and Wabash Valley Audubon Society. *Military service:* U.S. Navy, chaplain, World War II; became lieutenant junior grade.

WRITINGS: Life is Forever, Abingdon, 1963. Occasional contributor to religious journals.

*   *   *

CRAIG, Elizabeth (Josephine)

PERSONAL: Born in Addiewell, West Lothian, Scotland; daughter of John Adam (a clergyman) and Katherine (Nicholl) Craig; married Arthur E. Mann (a war correspondent, now retired), December 29, 1919. *Education:* Attended George Watson's Ladies' College and Forfar Academy. *Home:* "St. Catherine's," Botesdale, Near Diss, Norfolk, England. *Agent:* E.P. Lewin, E.P.S. Lewin and Partners, 7 Chelsea Embankment, London S.W.3, England; and Innes Rose, John Farquharson Ltd., 15 Red Lion Sq., Holborn, London W.C.1, England.

CAREER: Woman's page editor and reporter in Scotland, 1912-15, in London, England, 1915-18; editor of *Woman's Life,* 1915-18; cookery editor of *Woman's Journal,* 1927-59; also free-lance columnist, interviewer, and feature writer. Lecturer, British Ministry of Agriculture and Ministry of Food, throughout World War II. Consultant on food products. *Member:* Royal Society of Arts (fellow), Food and Cookery Association (fellow), Institute of Hygiene, Dame de la Chaine des Rotisseurs, Chevaliere de l'Ordre des Coteaux (de Champagne), Women's Press Club, Circle of Wine Writers, P.E.N., Wine and Food Society, Royal Horticultural Society.

WRITINGS: The State Favourites Cook Book, Hutchinson, 1924; *Cooking with Elizabeth Craig,* Collins, 1932, new edition, 1961; (editor) *New Standard Cookery Illustrated,* Oldhams Press, 1932; *Entertaining with Elizabeth Craig,* Collins, 1933; (with Andre Simon) *Madeira: Wine, Cakes and Sauce,* Constable, 1933; *Elizabeth Craig's Economical Cookery,* Collins, 1934, revised edition, 1940; *Elizabeth Craig's Standard Recipes,* Collins, 1934; *Wine in the Kitchen,* Transatlantic, 1934; *Elizabeth Craig's Everyday Cookery,* Collins, 1935; *Elizabeth Craig's Family Cookery,* Collins, 1935; *Cookery Illustrated and Household Management,* Oldhams Press, 1936; *Bubble and Squeak,* Chapman & Hall, 1936; *The Housewives Monthly Calender,* Chapman & Hall, 1936; *Keeping House with Elizabeth Craig: A New Guide to Planning and Running Your Home,* Collins, 1936; (editor) *278 Tested Recipes,* Clerke & Cockeran, 1936; *Woman, Wine and a Saucepan,* Chapman & Hall, 1936; *The Way to a Good Table: Electric Cookery,* British Electrical Development Association, 1937; *Gardening,* Collins, 1937; *Housekeeping,* Collins, 1937; *Needlecraft,* Collins, 1937; *1500 Everyday Menus,* Collins, 1937; *1000 Household Hints,* Collins, 1937; *Cookery,* Collins, 1937; *Enquire Within: The Happy Housewife,* Collins, 1938; *Simple Gardening,* Collins, 1938; *Simple Housekeeping,* Collins, 1938.

Cooking in War-Time, Collins, 1940; *Gardening with Elizabeth Craig: A Complete Guide to all Aspects of Gardening in War-Time,* Collins, 1940; *Elizabeth Craig's Household Library,* six volumes (includes *Gardening, Housekeeping, Needlecraft, 1000 Household Hints, Cookery, 1500 Everyday Menus*), Collins, 1940; *Cooking for Today,* Woman's Journal, 1948; *Court Favourites: Recipes from Royal Kitchens,* British Book Centre, 1953; *Waterless Cooking,* Milbro Products, 1953; *Beer and Vittels,* Museum Press, 1955; *The Scottish Cookery Book,* Deutsch, 1956; *Instructions to Young Cooks,* Museum Press, 1957, Sportshelf, 1958, 2nd edition, Museum Press, 1960; *Collins Family Cookery,* Collins, 1957; *The Eliza-*

beth Craig Complete Family Cookery, Educational Book Co., 1957; *Scandinavian Cooking*, Deutsch, 1958; *A Cook's Guide to Wine*, Constable, 1959.

Cottage Cheese and Yogurt, Jenkins, 1960; (editor) Thora H. Campbell, *The Potluck Cookery Book*, revised edition, Oliver & Boyd, 1962; *Banana Dishes*, Wehman, 1962; (editor) Victor Bennett and Cecil Kalıman, *Around the World in a Salad Bowl*, revised edition, Oliver & Boyd, 1963; *Cook Continentale*, Oliver & Boyd, 1965, International Publications Service, 1966; *What's Cooking in Scotland*, Rand McNally, 1965; *The Art of Irish Cooking*, Ward, Lock, 1969; *The Business Woman's Cook Book*, Pelham Book, 1970; (editor) *The Penguin Salad Book*, Penguin, 1972.

Contributor to *Scottish Annual, Jewish Chronicle Supplement, Doctor on Holiday, House and Garden, Wine Magazine, Scottish Field, People's Friend*, and other periodicals, and to most national newspapers in Great Britain and some in United States. Former cookery editor, *Woman's Journal, Woman's Pictorial*, and *Mother and Home.*

WORK IN PROGRESS: Traditional English Cookery, for Ward, Lock.

SIDELIGHTS: Miss Craig has traveled all over Europe, the United States, Canada, and North Africa, gathering material for articles on food, wine, and travel.

*   *   *

CRAIG, Gerald M(arquis)   1916-

PERSONAL: Born October 2, 1916, in Brighton, Ontario, Canada; son of Clarence Marquis (a civil servant) and Florence (Cryderman) Craig; married Janet Stier (an editor), March 9, 1943; children: Alan, Constance. *Education:* University of Toronto, B.A., 1939; Brown University, graduate study, 1939-40; University of Minnesota, Ph.D., 1947. *Home:* 137 Roxborough St. E., Toronto 5, Ontario, Canada. *Office:* Department of History, University of Toronto, Toronto 5, Ontario, Canada.

CAREER: University of Toronto, Toronto, Ontario, professor of history, 1947—. *Military service:* Royal Canadian Air Force, 1942-46. *Member:* American Historical Association, Organization of American Historians, Canadian Historical Association, Ontario Historical Association. *Awards, honors:* Two Canada Council senior fellowships.

WRITINGS: (Editor and author of introduction) *Early Travellers in the Canadas, 1791-1867*, Macmillan, 1955; (editor) *Lord Durham's Report*, McClelland & Stewart, 1963; *Upper Canada: The Formative Years, 1784-1841*, Oxford University Press, 1963; *The United States and Canada*, Harvard University Press, 1968.

Booklets: *American Government in the World Crisis*, Canadian Association for Adult Education, 1952; *Canada's Foreign Policy: A Look at the Record*, Canadian Institute of International Affairs and Canadian Association for Adult Education, 1953; *Electing an American Government*, Canadian Institute of International Affairs, 1956. Former member of editorial board, *Canadian Historical Review;* member of editorial board, Yale and McGill Canadian-American Project.

WORK IN PROGRESS: Historical Documents of Canada, Vol. III (1815-1867), with J.M.S. Careless, for Macmillan [Canada]; *Discontent in Upper Canada*, for Copp Clark; *The Rebellion of 1837*, for Prentice-Hall.

*   *   *

CRANE, Caroline   1930-

PERSONAL: Born October 30, 1930, in Chicago, Ill.; daughter of Roger Alan (a foundation executive) and

Jessie Louise (a social worker; maiden name, Taft) Crane; married Yoshio Kiyabu (now a travel agent), July 11, 1959; children: Crane Ryo, Laurel Rei. *Education:* Bennington College, A.B., 1952; Columbia University, graduate study at Russian Institute, 1952-53. *Politics:* Democrat. *Home:* 317 West 93rd St., New York, N.Y. 10025. *Agent:* Muriel Fuller, P.O. Box 193, Grand Central Station, New York, N.Y. 10017.

CAREER: U.S. Committee for United Nations Children's Fund, New York, N.Y., writer, 1957-60; author of books for young people. *Member:* Authors Guild of Authors League of America.

WRITINGS: Pink Sky at Night, Doubleday, 1963; *Lights Down the River*, Doubleday, 1964; *A Girl Like Tracy*, McKay, 1966; *Wedding Song*, McKay, 1967; *Don't Look at Me That Way*, Random House, 1970; *Stranger on the Road*, Random House, 1971.

WORK IN PROGRESS: Two adult novels, *The Finger of Jupiter* and *Orchids in the Bathtub;* an adult mystery, *Flowers for Her Grave;* and two adult biographical novels.

AVOCATIONAL INTERESTS: The ancient history and archaeology of Asia and Africa; dogs, animal welfare.

BIOGRAPHICAL/CRITICAL SOURCES: Young Readers' Review, May, 1966; *Best Sellers*, October 1, 1967; *Christian Science Monitor*, November 2, 1967; *Library Journal*, May 15, 1970.

*   *   *

CRANE, Philip Miller   1930-

PERSONAL: Born November 3, 1930, in Chicago, Ill.; son of George Washington and Cora (Miller) Crane; married Arlene Catherine Johnson, February 14, 1959; children: Catherine Anne, Susanna Marie, Jennifer Elizabeth, Rebekah Caroline, George Washington, Rachel Ellen, Sarah Emma. *Education:* DePauw University, student, 1948-50; Hillsdale College, A.B., 1952; graduate study at University of Michigan, 1952, 1953-56, and at University of Vienna, 1953, 1956; Indiana University, A.M., 1961, Ph.D., 1963. *Politics:* Republican. *Religion:* Methodist. *Office:* House Office Building, Washington, D.C. 20515.

CAREER: Worked in advertising and selling, on newspapers, 1956-58; Bradley University, Peoria, Ill., assistant professor of history, 1963-67; Westminster Academy, Northbrook, Ill., director of schools, 1967-69; U.S. Congress, Washington, D.C., representative from 13th district in Illinois, 1969—. Hopkins Syndicate, Inc., member of board of directors, 1960—. Member of board of trustees, Hillsdale College, Hillsdale, Mich. Republican Party, public relations consultant, 1962; Goldwater for President Committee, research chairman, 1964. *Military service:* U.S. Army, 1954-56. *Member:* American Historical Association, American Society of Composers, Authors, and Publishers, Intercollegiate Studies Institute (member of board of directors), Young Americans for Freedom (member of national advisory board), Young Republicans, Organization of American Historians, Indiana Historical Society.

WRITINGS: The Democrat's Dilemma, Regnery, 1964. Contributor of reviews to historical periodicals.

SIDELIGHTS: Crane wrote the lyrics to "Little Sandy Sleighfoot," recorded by Jimmy Dean for Columbia Records.

*   *   *

CRAWFORD, Joanna   1941-

PERSONAL: Born January 14, 1941, in Pennsylvania; daughter of William W. and Miriam Elizabeth (Whorle)

Crawford. *Religion:* Presbyterian. *Agent:* Annie Laurie Williams, Inc., 18 East 41st St., New York, N.Y. 10017; (acting) William Morris Agency, Beverly Hills, Calif.

CAREER: Traveled about the country, mostly on foot or by bicycle, before settling in Hollywood, Calif., to study acting, 1962-64; appeared in a Martin Manulis film, did some television work, and wrote her first novel; worked on second novel at her home in Pennsylvania for eight months, then returned to Hollywood to write the screen play of *Birch Interval* for a United Artists production. *Member:* Screen Actors Guild, Writers Guild of America.

WRITINGS: Birch Interval, Houghton, 1964.

WORK IN PROGRESS: A novel, *James Hefflebower Quigley;* a short story, "Great Responsibilities from Small Jellyfish Grow."

AVOCATIONAL INTERESTS: Folklore, antiques, seventeenth-century music, people, sailing, bicycling.

*   *   *

CREAGH-OSBORNE, Richard   1928-

PERSONAL: Surname is pronounced Cray-osborne; born April 5, 1928, in England; son of Frank (a captain; Royal Navy) and Mabel (Poulton) Creagh-Osborne; married Augusta Heymoz, October 8, 1949; children: Edward Frank, Charles Pearson. *Education:* Attended Royal Naval College at Dartmouth and Royal Naval Engineering College at Keyham. *Home and office:* 7 Station St., Lymington, Hampshire, England.

CAREER: Adlard Coles Ltd. (publishers), London, England, director, 1962-69. Director of two commercial farming firms. Partner, Nautical Publishing Co. Yachtsman, competing as member of British Olympic team, 1956, 1960, 1964. *Military service:* Royal Navy, 1942-47; became midshipman; invalided out.

WRITINGS: Dinghy Management, Adlard Coles, 1962; *Dinghy Building,* Adlard Coles, 1963, DeGraff, 1964; (editor and translator) Paul Elvstrom, *Expert Dinghy Racing,* privately printed, 1964, revised edition published as *Expert Dinghy and Keelboat Racing,* Nautical Publishing Co., 1967; (editor and author of introduction) *Paul Elvstrom Explains the Yacht Racing Rules,* Nautical Publishing Co., 1965, revised edition, DeGraff, 1969; (editor and author of introduction) *Paul Elvstrom Speaks on Yacht Racing,* Quadrangle, 1970; (editor and author of introduction) *Paul Elvstrom Speaks to His Sailing Friends on His Life and Racing Career,* Nautical Publishing Co., 1970. Editor of Adlard Coles' *Dinghy Year Book,* 1962-65. Contributor to yachting periodicals.

*   *   *

CREESE, Bethea

PERSONAL: Born in England. *Education:* Attended Alice Ottley School, Worcester, England. *Religion:* Anglican. *Home:* Flat 14, 65 Courtfield Gardens, London S.W.5, England. *Agent:* Curtis Brown Ltd., 13 King St., Covent Garden, London W.C.2, England.

CAREER: Fleetway Publications Ltd., London, England, member of editorial staff of *Woman and Home* and *My Home* for twenty-one years, careers expert for *My Home* for fourteen years; now retired. *Member:* Society of Women Writers and Journalists, Romantic Novelists Association.

WRITINGS—All published by Mills & Boon, except as indicated: *The Family Face,* 1950, Pocket Books, 1970; *The Winter Bud,* 1951; *The Checquered Flat,* 1952; *White Laurel,* 1953; *Flower-Piece,* 1954; *Evergreen Oak,* 1955; *The Locket,* 1956; *The Young Rose,* 1957; *Glorious Haven,* 1958; *Fortune Thy Foe,* 1959; *Beauty Queen,* 1960; *Little Angel,* 1962; *My Heart Is Fast,* 1963; *Irish Rose,* 1964, *Count Roger,* 1965; *Careers in Catering and Domestic Science,* Bodley Head, 1965, revised edition, Evans Brothers, 1967; *New Girl,* 1967; *King of Hearts,* 1967; *Sea Rapture,* 1968; *Fire Down Below,* 1969; *A Rose in Wales,* 1969; *Damsel of Cyprus,* 1970; *Love for Love,* in press.

WORK IN PROGRESS: A new novel.

*   *   *

CRISP, Frank R(obson)   1915-

PERSONAL: Born November 30, 1915, in Durham, England; son of Frank Robson and Sarah (Sinton) Crisp; married Margaret Diston, December 6, 1941; children: Judith, Sally Ann, Kathleen. *Home:* 57 Castleton Ave., Wembley, Middlesex, England.

CAREER: Served in British Merchant Navy; spent several years as bosun aboard inter-island steamer in Indonesia; pearled in Western Australia; settled in London, England after World War II and became a writer; made two whaling trips to the Antarctic; became a businessman in London; currently director of a catering service and part-time writer.

WRITINGS: Within This House, Stanley Paul, 1947; *The Voice from Yesterday,* Stanley Paul, 1948; *The Sea Robbers,* Bodley Head, 1949, Coward, 1953; *The Nail of Suspicion,* John Long, 1949; *The Haunted Reef,* Bodley Head, 1950, Coward, 1952; *By Whose Hand,* Stanley Paul, 1951; *The Golden Quest: A Seventeenth Century Tale of Adventure for Older Boys and Girls,* Bodley Head, 1952, Coward, 1953; *The Weird Archer,* Bodley Head, 1953, abridged edition published as *The Rogues of Alwyn,* Collins, 1964; *The Adventure of Whaling,* St. Martin's, 1954; *The Devil Driver,* Coward, 1954; *The Chandu Men,* Stanley Paul, 1955; *Ships,* St. Martin's, 1955; *Fazackerley's Millions,* Stanley Paul, 1955; *The Treasure of Barby Swin,* Coward, 1955; *The Java Wreckmen: A Dirk Rogers Adventure,* Hodder & Stoughton, 1955, Coward, 1956; *Maori Jack's Monster,* Hodder & Stoughton, 1956; *The Manila Menfish,* Hodder & Stoughton, 1956, Coward, 1957; *The Manila Stranger,* John Long, 1957; *The Sea Ape,* Hodder & Stoughton, 1958, Coward, 1959; *The Demon Wreck,* Hodder & Stoughton, 1958; *The Giant of Jembu Gulf,* Hodder & Stoughton, 1959; *The Ape of London,* Hodder & Stoughton, 1959; *The Night Callers,* John Long, 1960; *The Ice Divers,* Hodder & Stoughton, 1960; *The Coral Wreck: A Dirk Rogers Adventure,* J. Cape, 1964; *The Sanguman: A Dirk Rogers Adventure,* J. Cape, 1965, McCutcheon, 1966.

SIDELIGHTS: Crisp's books are based on seafaring and travels abroad; they have been adapted and serialized on television and radio in England, and translated into several languages. In 1967 World Entertainment produced a film of *The Night Callers,* entitled "Blood Beast from Outer Space." *Avocational interests:* Sailing in his own boat.†

*   *   *

CROFT-COOKE, Rupert   1903-
(Leo Bruce)

PERSONAL: Born June 20, 1903, in Edenbridge, Kent, England; son of Hubert Bruce and Lucy (Taylor) Cooke. *Education:* Attended Tonbridge School and Wellington College (now Wrekin College) in England. *Agent:* A.M. Heath & Co., Ltd., 35 Dover St., London WIX 4EB, England and Curtis Brown Ltd., 575 Madison Ave., New York, N.Y. 10022.

CAREER: Founded and edited a weekly, *La Estrella,* in Argentina, 1923-24; antiquarian bookseller, 1929-31; lecturer, English Institute Montana, Zugerberg, Switzerland,

1931; book critic, *Sketch*, 1947-53; free-lance writer. *Military service:* British Army Intelligence Corps, 1940; served in Madagascar campaign, 1942 (awarded the British Empire Medal); commander 3rd (Queen Alexandra's Own) Gurkha Rifles, 1943; captain (field security officer) Poona district, 1944; instructor, intelligence school, Karachi, West Pakistan, 1945; field security officer, Delhi district, 1945-46.

WRITINGS: Songs of a Sussex Tramp (poems), Vine Press, 1922; *Tonbridge School* (poem), Free Press, 1923; *Songs South of the Line*, Lincoln Torrey, 1925; *The Viking* (poem), privately printed, 1926; *How Psychology Can Help*, C.W. Daniel, 1927; (author of introduction) G.A. Dominguez Becquer, *Twenty Poems from the Spanish of Becquer*, Basil Blackwell, 1927; *Some Poems*, Galleon Press, 1929.

Banquo's Chair (play), H.W.F. Deane, 1930; *Troubadour*, Chapman & Hall, 1930; *Give Him the Earth*, Chapman & Hall, 1930, Knopf, 1931; *Cosmopolis*, Dial, 1932; *Night Out*, Dial, 1932; *Release the Lions*, Jarrolds, 1933, Dodd, 1934; *Her Mexican Lover*, Mellifoul Press, 1934; *Picaro*, Dodd, 1934; *Tap Three Times* (play), Samuel French, 1934; *Darts*, Bles, 1936; *God in Ruins*, Fortune Press, 1936; *Kingdom Come*, Jarrolds, 1936; *Shoulder the Sky*, Jarrolds, 1936; *Pharaoh with His Wagons and Other Stories*, Jarrolds, 1937; *The World Is Young*, Hodder & Stoughton, 1937; *Escape to the Andes*, Messner, 1938; *How to Get More Out of Life*, Bles, 1938; *The Man in Europe Street*, Putnam, 1938; *Rule, Britannia*, Jarrolds, 1938; (translator and author of introduction) S. Casado, *The Last Days of Madrid*, P. Davies, 1939; (editor) *Major Road Ahead*, Methuen, 1939; *Same Way Home*, Jarrolds, 1939, Macmillan (New York), 1940.

The Circus Has No Home, Methuen, 1940, revised edition, with drawings by Laurence Scarfe, Falcon Press, 1950; *Glorious*, Jarrolds, 1940; *Ladies Gay*, MacDonald & Co., 1946; *Octopus*, Jarrolds, 1946, published in America as *Miss Allick*, Holt, 1947; (editor) *The Circus Book*, Low, 1948; *How to Enjoy Travel Abroad*, Rockliff, 1948; *The Moon in My Pocket: Life with the Romanies*, Low, 1948; *Rudyard Kipling*, A. Swallow, 1948; *Wilkie*, MacDonald & Co., 1948, published in America as *Another Sun, Another Home*, Holt, 1949.

Brass Farthing, Laurie, 1950; *A Football for the Brigadier*, Laurie, 1950; (with Gladys B. Stern) *Gala Night at 'The Willows'* (play), H.W.F. Deane, 1950; (with Noel Barber) *Cities*, Wingate, 1951; *Three Names for Nicholas*, Macmillan (London), 1951; (with W.S. Meadmore) *The Sawdust Ring*, Odhams, 1951; (with Meadmore) *Buffalo Bill*, Sidgwick & Jackson, 1952; *The Life for Me*, Macmillan (London), 1952, St. Martin's, 1953; *Nine Days with Edward*, Macmillan (London), 1952; *The Blood-Red Island*, Staples, 1953; *Harvest Moon*, St. Martin's, 1953; *Fall of Man*, Macmillan (London), 1955; *A Few Gypsies*, illustrated by Peter Emmerich, Putnam, 1955; *Seven Thunders*, St. Martin's, 1955; *Sherry*, Putnam, 1955, Knopf, 1956; *The Verdict of You All*, Secker & Warburg, 1955; *The Tangerine House*, St. Martin's, 1956; *Port*, Putnam, 1957; *Barbary Night*, Eyre & Spottiswoode, 1958; *The Gardens of Camelot*, Putnam, 1958; *The Quest for Quixote*, Secker & Warburg, 1959, published in America as *Through Spain with Don Quixote*, Knopf, 1960; *Smiling Damned Villain: The True Story of Paul Axel Lund*, Secker & Warburg, 1959.

The Altar in the Loft, Putnam, 1960; *English Cooking: A New Approach*, W.H. Allen, 1960; *Thief*, Eyre & Spottiswoode, 1960, Doubleday, 1961; *The Drums of Morning*, Putnam, 1961; *Madeira*, Putnam, 1961; *Clash by Night*, Eyre & Spottiswoode, 1962; *The Glittering Pastures*, Putnam, 1962; *Wine and Other Drinks*, Collins, 1962; *Bosie: Lord Alfred Douglas, His Friends and Enemies*, W.H. Allen, 1963, Bobbs-Merrill, 1964; *Cooking for Pleasure*, Collins, 1963; *The Numbers Came*, Putnam, 1963; *Tales of a Wicked Uncle* (poems), drawings by Quentin Blake, J. Cape, 1963; *The Last of Spring*, Putnam, 1964; *The Wintry Sea*, W.H. Allen, 1964; *The Gorgeous East: One Man's India*, W.H. Allen, 1965; *Paper Albatross*, Eyre & Spottiswoode, 1965, Abelard-Schuman, 1968; *The Purple Streak*, W.H. Allen, 1966; *St. George for England*, P. Dulwich, 1966; *The Wild Hills*, W.H. Allen, 1966; *Feasting with Panthers: A New Consideration of Some Victorian Writers*, W.H. Allen, 1967, Holt, 1968; *The Happy Highways*, W.H. Allen, 1967; *The Ghost of June: A Return to England and the West*, W.H. Allen, 1968; *Three in a Cell*, Eyre & Spottiswoode, 1968; *Exotic Food: Three Hundred of the Most Unusual Dishes in Western Cookery*, illustrated by John Stoddart, Allen & Unwin, 1969, Herder & Herder, 1971; *The Sound of Revelry*, W.H. Allen, 1969; *Wolf from the Door*, W.H. Allen, 1969.

Exiles, W.H. Allen, 1970; *The Licentious Soldiery*, W.H. Allen, 1971; *Under the Rose Garden*, W.H. Allen, 1970; *While the Iron's Hot*, W.H. Allen, 1971; *The Unrecorded Life of Oscar Wilde*, McKay, 1972.

(Under pseudonym Leo Bruce): *Case for Three Detectives*, Bles, 1936, Frederick A. Stokes, 1937; *Case Without a Corpse*, Frederick A. Stokes, 1937; *Case with Four Clowns*, Frederick A. Stokes, 1939; *Case with No Conclusion*, Bles, 1939; *Case with Ropes and Rings*, Nicholson & Watson, 1940; *Case for Sergeant Beef*, Nicholson & Watson, 1947; *Neck and Neck*, Gollancz, 1951; *Cold Blood*, Gollancz, 1952; *At Death's Door*, Hamish Hamilton, 1955; *Dead for a Ducat*, P. Davies, 1956; *Death of Cold*, P. Davies, 1956; *Dead Man's Shoes*, P. Davies, 1958; *A Louse for the Hangman*, P. Davies, 1958; *Our Jubilee Is Death*, P. Davies, 1959; *Furious Old Woman*, P. Davies, 1960; *Jack in the Gallows Tree*, P. Davies, 1960; *Die All, Die Merrily*, P. Davies, 1961; *Nothing Like Blood*, P. Davies, 1962; *A Bone and a Hank of Hair*, P. Davies, 1962; *The Crack of Doom*, P. Davies, 1963; *Such Is Death*, London House, 1963; *Death in Albert Park*, W.H. Allen, 1964; *Death at Hollows End*, W.H. Allen, 1965; *Death on the Black Sands*, W.H. Allen, 1966; *Death of a Commuter*, W.H. Allen, 1967; *Death on Romney Marsh*, W.H. Allen, 1968; *Death with Blue Ribbon*, W.H. Allen, 1969; *Death on Allhallowe'en*, W.H. Allen, 1970.

Author of play "Deliberate Accident," 1934. Contributor to *Poetry* (Chicago) and many British literary journals.

SIDELIGHTS: With reference to *Exiles*, Reginald Moore has written: "There are few novelists with as much style and grace in their writing as Rupert Croft-Cooke. And now that we have had to endure a decade of graffiti rubbish masquerading as fiction, Mr. Croft-Cooke's skill in the mere shaping of a sentence is even more welcome." *Seven Thunders* was made into a motion picture in 1957.

BIOGRAPHICAL/CRITICAL SOURCES: Atlantic, April, 1968; *New York Times Book Review*, April 14, 1968; *Spectator*, August 23, 1969; *Books and Bookmen*, August, 1970, March, 1971.

*   *   *

*   *   *

CROMIE, Alice Hamilton 1914-
(Alice Hamilton, Vivian Mort)

PERSONAL: Born May 29, 1914, in Chariton, Iowa; daughter of James Albert and Margaret (Bertrand) Hamilton; married Robert Allen Cromie (now *Chicago Tribune* book editor), May 22, 1937; children: Michael Allen, Richard Allen, Barbara Allen, James Allen. *Educa-*

tion: Attended Kansas City Junior College, 1932-33, and University of Missouri, 1934; University of Texas, A.B., 1937. *Politics:* Independent. *Religion:* Protestant. *Home address:* Route 1, Box 42, Grayslake, Ill. 60030. *Agent:* Henry Volkening, Russell & Volkening, Inc., 551 Fifth Ave., New York, N.Y. 10017.

CAREER: Free-lance writer and lecturer; work has included promotional advertising and greeting card verses. *Member:* Mystery Writers of America, Critics Circle, Confederate Memorial Literary Society, Midland Authors, Illinois Historical Society, Theta Sigma Phi.

WRITINGS: (Editor) *A Tour Guide to the Civil War,* Quadrangle, 1965; (author of preface) *The Charlotte Armstrong Reader,* Coward, 1970. Anthologized in *Post Scripts,* McGraw, 1943. Under pseudonym Vivian Mort, author of "Crime on My Hands," a mystery review column for *Chicago Tribune,* 1963-66, weekly book reviewer for *Chicago Tribune* under own name, 1966—. Contributor of fiction, light verse, and humorous verse to *Saturday Evening Post, Reader's Digest, Ladies' Home Journal, Collier's, Look, American.*

WORK IN PROGRESS: A novel, *To See the Elephant,* for St. Martin's; a juvenile book, for Doubleday; *A Tour Guide to the Old West,* for Quadrangle.

* * *

CRONE, Ruth 1919-

PERSONAL: Born June 24, 1919, in Lincoln, Neb.; daughter of Burley R. and Willie Ethel (Jones) Crone. *Education:* Nebraska State College, A.B., 1942; George Washington University, M.A., 1945; New York University, Ph.D., 1960. *Politics:* Independent. *Religion:* Christian. *Home:* 1723 East Lincoln Blvd., Beatrice, Neb. 68310.

CAREER: U.S. Department of Commerce, Washington, D.C., writer, 1940-44; Port of New York (N.Y.) Authority, reports editor, 1945-49; U.S. Department of State, Economic Cooperation Administration, information specialist in Shanghai, China, and Seoul, Korea, 1949-50; staffer, *New York Times,* New York, N.Y., 1952-54; *Beatrice Daily Sun,* Beatrice, Neb., 1954-58; Gustavus Adolphus College, St. Peter, Minn., assistant professor of English and journalism, 1958-59; Nebraska State Teachers College, Peru, assistant professor of literature, 1959-60; General Beadle State College, Madison, S.D., assistant professor of English and journalism, 1960-62; Omaha (Neb.) public schools, teacher, 1962-63; Wisconsin State College, Superior, assistant professor of English and journalism, 1963—.

MEMBER: National Federation of Presswomen, National Council of Teachers of English, American Association of University Women, Association of Wisconsin State College Faculties, Nebraska Presswomen, Wisconsin Council of Teachers of English, Nebraska Writers Guild, Sigma Tau Delta, Kappa Delta Pi. *Awards, honors:* Adult fiction award, National Federation of Presswomen; twelve first-place awards, Nebraska Presswomen.

WRITINGS: (With Marion Marsh Brown) *The Silent Storm* (Junior Literary Guild selection), Abingdon, 1963, (with Brown) *Willa Cather: The Woman and Her Works,* Scribner, 1970. Contributor of articles, features, and reviews to magazines.

WORK IN PROGRESS: Three books, one under a research grant from the State of Wisconsin.

BIOGRAPHICAL/CRITICAL SOURCES: Omaha World-Herald, July 8, 1963.

CRONIN, Vincent 1924-

PERSONAL: Born May 24, 1924, in Tredegar, Wales; son of Archibald Joseph (an author) and Agnes (Gibson) Cronin; married Chantal De Rolland, August 25, 1949; children: Sylvelie, James, Luan, Dauphine. *Education:* Attended Ampleforth College, 1937-39; Harvard University, student, 1941-43; Trinity College, Oxford, B.A. (with honors), 1947. *Religion:* Roman Catholic. *Home:* 44 Hyde Park Sq., London W.2, England.

CAREER: Author. William Collins Ltd., London, England, editor of "Companion Travel Guides," 1959—. *Military service:* British Army, Rifle Brigade, 1943-46; became lieutenant. *Member:* Royal Society of Literature (fellow). *Awards, honors:* Heinemann Award, 1955; Rockefeller Foundation Award, 1958.

WRITINGS: The Golden Honeycomb (study of Sicily), Dutton, 1954; *The Wise Man from the West* (on Father Matteo Ricci), Dutton, 1955; *The Last Migration* (on the Falqani tribe in Southern Persia), Dutton, 1957; *A Pearl to India: The Life of Roberto de Nobili,* Dutton, 1959; *The Letter after Z,* Collins, 1960; (translator) *L'Amour profane,* Pantheon, 1961 (published in England as *Profane Love,* Collins, 1961); *The Companion Guide to Paris,* Harper, 1963; (compiler) *A Calendar of Saints,* Newman, 1963; *Louis XIV,* Collins, 1964, Houghton, 1965; (translator) Jean Danielou and Henri Marrou, *The Christian Centuries: A New History of the Catholic Church,* Volume I: *The First Six Hundred Years,* McGraw, 1964; *Four Women in Pursuit of an Ideal,* Collins, 1965, published in America as *The Romantic Way,* Houghton, 1966; (editor with Elizabeth Nicholas and Leonard Russell) *The Sunday Times Travel and Holiday Guide,* revised edition, Thomas Nelson, 1966, International Publications Service, 1966; *The Florentine Renaissance,* Dutton, 1967; *Mary Portrayed,* Darton, Longman & Todd, 1968, Borden, 1970; *The Flowering of the Renaissance,* Dutton, 1969; (editor) Errol Brathwaite, *The Companion Guide to the North Island of New Zealand,* Collins, 1970, Tri-Ocean, 1971; *Napoleon,* Collins, 1971, published in America as *Napoleon Bonaparte: An Intimate Biography,* Morrow, 1972.

AVOCATIONAL INTERESTS: France, particularly French literature and arts; the psychological novel and psychological biography.

BIOGRAPHICAL/CRITICAL SOURCES: Books and Bookmen, November, 1967; *New York Times Book Review,* November 2, 1969; *Washington Post,* November 15, 1969; *Books,* January, 1970.

* * *

CROSBIE, (Hugh) Provan 1912- (John Carrick)

PERSONAL: Born June 28, 1912, in Girvan, Scotland; son of James Jackson and Marion (Provan) Crosbie; married Patricia Mary Allan, June 27, 1953. *Education:* Attended secondary school in Girvan, Scotland.

CAREER: National Commercial Bank of Scotland Ltd., London, England, 1929—c.70, manager at time of retirement. *Military service:* Royal Artillery, 1939-45; became captain; seconded to U.S. Army Air Forces, 57th Pursuit Group, 1943; received Military Cross (Tobruk, 1941), mentioned in dispatches (Italy, 1944).

WRITINGS: They Shall Not Die, R. Schindler, 1943; *Fairways and Foul,* R. Hale, 1964.

Under pseudonym John Carrick—All published by R. Hale, unless otherwise noted: *Richer the Dust,* Kimber & Co., 1962, *The Vulture,* 1964, *Mario,* 1965, *Bond of Hate,* 1966, *Beware the Shadows,* 1967, *The Killer Conference,* 1968, *The Young and Deadly,* 1969.

SIDELIGHTS: Crosby told CA, "Since retirement from business, writing and painting are full-time activities."

* * *

CROSS, Colin (John) 1928-
(John Weir)

PERSONAL: Born January 12, 1928, in Cardiff, Wales; son of William (an insurance manager) and Winifred (Francis) Cross; married Jean Caldwell, July 16, 1954 (divorced, 1967); married Josefina Aguero, March 16, 1970; children: (first marriage) Michael William, Harriet Jane, Stephen Alexander. *Education:* Attended Portsmouth Grammar School, 1936-46; Queens' College, Cambridge, B.A., 1950. *Home:* 50 Rodenhurst Rd., London S.W.4, England. *Office:* The Observer, 160 Queen Victoria St., London E.C.4, England.

CAREER: Evening Standard, London, England, reporter, 1950-51; *Southern Times,* Weymouth, Dorsetshire, England, chief reporter, 1951-53; *Express and Star,* Wolverhampton, Staffordshire, England, features editor, 1953-56; Portsmouth and Sunderland Newspapers Ltd., London editor, 1956-61; *Sunday Express,* London, England, feature writer on political and foreign affairs, 1961-65; *Observer,* London, England, writer on political and foreign affairs, 1965—. *Member:* Travellers' Club.

WRITINGS: The Fascists in Britain, Barrie & Rockcliff, 1961, St. Martin's, 1963; *The Liberals in Power 1905-1914,* Barrie & Rockcliff and Pall Mall, 1963, Dufour, 1964; *Philip Snowden,* Barrie & Rockcliff, 1966; *The Fall of the British Empire, 1918-1968,* Hodder & Stoughton, 1968, Coward, 1969; *Who Was Jesus?* Atheneum, 1970.

WORK IN PROGRESS: A biography of Adolph Hitler for McKay.

SIDELIGHTS: Cross has traveled on assignments in Europe, United States, Africa, India, and the Middle East.

BIOGRAPHICAL/CRITICAL SOURCES: Times Literary Supplement, January 5, 1967, September 25, 1970; *Observer Review,* September 8, 1968; *Punch,* September 18, 1968; *New Yorker,* February 1, 1969; *Esquire,* May, 1969; *New York Review of Books,* December 16, 1969.

* * *

CROTEAU, John T(ougas) 1910-

PERSONAL: Born March 10, 1910, in Holbrook, Mass.; son of Narcisse L. and Mary M. (Tougas) Croteau; married Gertrude D. Gallant, June 2, 1936 (deceased); married Jeanne R. Miller, August 20, 1969. *Education:* Holy Cross College, A.B., 1931; Clark University, M.A., 1932, Ph.D., 1935. *Religion:* Roman Catholic. *Home:* 124 North Eddy St., South Bend, Ind. 46617.

CAREER: Prince of Wales College and St. Dunstan's College, Charlottetown, Prince Edward Island, Carnegie Chair of Economics and Sociology, 1933-45; Xavier University, Cincinnati, Ohio, associate professor of economics, 1946-47; Catholic University of America, Washington, D.C., associate professor of economics, 1947-53; University of Notre Dame, Notre Dame, Ind., associate professor, 1953-56, professor of economics, 1956—. Prince Edward Island Credit Union League, managing director, 1933-45; Rochdale Cooperatives, Washington, D.C., director and vice-president, 1947-53; University of Notre Dame Federal Credit Union, current president. Consultant to Credit Union National Association.

MEMBER: American Economic Association, American Finance Association, Agricultural History Society, American Association of University Professors, Royal Economic Society (fellow), Canadian Political Science Association (director, 1946-47). *Awards, honors:* LL.D., St. Joseph's University, New Brunswick, 1956.

WRITINGS: A Regional Library and Its Readers, American Association for Adult Education, 1940; *Cradled in the Waves: The Story of a People's Cooperative Achievement in Economic Betterment on Prince Edward Island, Canada,* Ryerson, 1951; *The Federal Credit Union: Policy and Practice,* Harper, 1956; *The Economics of the Credit Union,* Wayne State University Press, 1963.

Contributor: *The Economic Aspects of Social Life,* University of Notre Dame Press, 1955; *Money and Banking,* Pitman, 1957; *Compendium of Papers on Broadening the Tax Base Submitted to the Committee on Ways and Means,* U.S. Government Printing Office, 1959.

Monographs: *Co-operatives: A Guide to Reading,* Canadian Legion Educational Services, 1944; *A National Central Credit Society and the Liquidity Problem of the Credit Union Movement,* Credit Union National Association, 1960; *Credit Union Members by Income Groups,* Credit Union National Association, 1963. Contributor to economics and other professional journals, including *Journal of Finance, Agricultural History, Journal of Business.*

WORK IN PROGRESS: Research in credit union growth and management efficiency.

* * *

CROUCH, Marcus 1913-

PERSONAL: Born February 12, 1913, in Tottenham, Middlesex, England. *Education:* University of London, B.A., 1934. *Home:* 34 Glebe Lane, Maidstone, Kent, England. *Office:* Springfield, Maidstone, Kent, England.

CAREER: Kent County Library, Maidstone, England, deputy county librarian, 1948—. *Member:* Library Association (fellow), Society of Authors.

WRITINGS: (Editor) *Chosen for Children: An Account of the Books Which Have Been Awarded the Library Association's Carnegie Medal, 1936-1957,* Library Association, 1957; *Beatrix Potter,* Bodley Head, 1960, Walck, 1961; *Treasure Seekers and Borrowers: Children's Books in Britain 1900-1960,* Library Association, 1962; *Britain in Trust: England and Wales,* International Publications Service, 1963; (editor) *Books about Children's Literature,* Library Association, 1963, revised edition, 1966; *Rivers of England and Wales,* Verry, 1965; *Kent,* Hastings House, 1966, 2nd edition, Batsford, 1967; *Fingerprints of History,* Longmans, Green, 1968; *Heritage of Sussex,* Macdonald & Evans, 1969; *Essex,* Hastings House, 1969; *Canterbury,* Longmans, Green, 1970; *The Nesbit Tradition: Children's Novels 1945-1970,* Rowman and Littlefield, 1973.

BIOGRAPHICAL/CRITICAL SOURCES: Times Literary Supplement, October 16, 1969, October 30, 1970; *Observer Review,* November 29, 1970.

* * *

CROUZET, Francois Marie-Joseph 1922-

PERSONAL: Born October 20, 1922, in Monts-sur-Guesnes, France; son of Maurice (a historian) and Henriette (Pactat) Crouzet; married Francoise Dabert, March 27, 1947; children: Marie-Anne, Denis, Joel. *Education:* Attended Lycee Hoche (Versailles), 1932-39, Lycee de Poitiers, Lycee Louis-le-Grand (Paris), 1940-41; Ecole Normale Superieure and the Sorbonne, Universite de Paris, 1941, licence es-lettres, 1943, diplome d'etudes superieures, 1944, agregation d'histoire, 1945, doctorat es-lettres, 1956; attended London School of Economics and Political Science, 1946-49. *Religion:* Roman Catholic. *Home:* 6, rue Benjamin-Goddard, Paris, France. *Office:* Universite de Paris-Sorbonne, 7 rue Victor-Cousin, 75005 Paris, France.

CAREER: Instructor at Lycee de Beauvais, France, 1945, Lycee Janson-de-Sailly, France, 1953-56; research fellow in Great Britain, 1945-46; Centre National de la Recherche Scientifique, France, research associate, 1947-49; Universite de Paris, faculte des lettres, Paris, France, assistant lecturer, 1949-53; Universite de Bordeaux, Bordeaux, France, associate professor of history, 1956-58; Universite de Lille, Lille, France, professor of contemporary history, 1958-64; Universite de Paris, Nanterre, France, professor of economic and social history, 1964-69; Universite de Paris-Sorbonne, Paris, France, professor of northern European history, 1969—; Visiting professor, Columbia University, spring, 1961, and University of California, Berkeley, summer, 1964. Member: Societe d'histoire moderne, Association Marc Bloch, Economic History Society, Commission for Research in Economic History of the French Revolution, Association francaise des historiens economistes (vice-president). Awards, honors: Centre National de la Recherche scientifique, bronze medal, 1957; Academie des science morales et politiques, Prix G. Mauguin, 1959.

WRITINGS: L'Economie du Commonwealth, Presses Universitaires de France, 1950; L'Economie britannique et le blocus continental, 1806-1813, Presses Universitaires de France, 1958; (editor with Guy S. Metraux) The Nineteenth-Century World: Readings from the History of Mankind, New American Library, 1963; (editor with Metraux) The Evolution of Science: Readings from the History of Mankind, New American Library, 1963; (editor with Metraux) The New Asia, New American Library, 1965; (editor with Metraux) Religions and the Promise of the Twentieth Century, New American Library, 1965; (editor with Metraux) Studies in the Cultural History of India, Verry, 1965; (editor with W.H. Chaloner and W.M. Stern) Essays in European Economic History, 1789-1914, published for Economic History Society by Edward Arnold, 1969, St. Martin's, 1970; (editor and author of introduction) Capital Formation in the Industrial Revolution, Barnes & Noble, 1972. Assistant editor, Journal of World History, 1952-68. Contributor of articles and book reviews to journals in field of economic history.

WORK IN PROGRESS: Books on the Cyprus conflict, and on the origins of industrial arbitration; research project on French industrial production in the nineteenth century.

SIDELIGHTS: Crouzet's main field of interest and research is the economic history of Britain and France in the late eighteenth and early nineteenth centuries, with secondary interest in recent British history.

*   *   *

CROWE, Bettina Lum   1911-
(Peter Lum)

PERSONAL: Born April 27, 1911, in Minneapolis, Minn.; daughter of Burt Francis (a lawyer) and Bertha (an artist; maiden name, Bull) Lum; married Colin Crowe (British Ambassador to the U.N.), May 21, 1938. Education: Educated privately. Religion: Episcopalian. Agent: Curtis Brown Ltd., 13 King St., London W.C.2, England.

CAREER: Writer, whose early life was spent in the United States and Peking, China; now resident of New York, N.Y. Member: Society of Women Geographers, Royal Central Asian Society.

WRITINGS: Fairy Tales of China, Dutton, 1959; The Holiday Moon, Abelard, 1963; Fairy Tales from the Barbary Coast, Muller, 1967; The Growth of Civilization in East Asia: China, Japan and Korea to the 14th Century, S.G. Phillips, 1969.

Under pseudonym Peter Lum: Stars in Our Heaven, Pantheon, 1948; Fabulous Beasts, Pantheon, 1951; Peking 1950-1953, R. Hale, 1958; The Purple Barrier: The Great Wall of China, R. Hale, 1960; Italian Fairy Tales, Muller, 1953.

AVOCATIONAL INTERESTS: Far and Middle East, myths and legends, the stars.

*   *   *

CROWELL, Norton B.   1914-

PERSONAL: Born January 10, 1914, in Sioux City, Iowa; son of Norman H. (a writer) and Grace (Noll) Crowell; married Ruth Mary Needham (a violinist), September 11, 1954; children: Lawrence, Dring, Steven, Donald. Education: Southern Methodist University, B.S. in Commerce, 1935, M.A., 1937; Harvard University, M.A., 1939, Ph.D., 1946; Sorbonne, University of Paris, postdoctoral study, 1953-54. Home: 1119 Broadway, Normal, Ill. 61761. Office: Illinois State University, Normal, Ill. 61761.

CAREER: Carnegie Institute of Technology, Pittsburgh, Pa., instructor, 1940-46, assistant professor of English, 1946-47; University of New Mexico, Albuquerque, started as assistant professor, 1947, became professor of English; now professor of English at Illinois State University, Normal. Military service: U.S. Naval Reserve, 1943. Member: Modern Language Association of America, Phi Beta Kappa. Awards, honors: Ford Foundation fellow, 1953-54.

WRITINGS: Alfred Austin: Victorian, University of New Mexico Press, 1953; The Triple Soul: Browning's Theory of Knowledge, University of New Mexico Press, 1963; The Convex Glass: The Mind of Robert Browning, University of New Mexico Press, 1968; A Browning Guide, University of New Mexico Press, 1973.

*   *   *

CROZIER, Brian   1918-

PERSONAL: Born August 4, 1918, in Kuridala, Queensland, Australia; son of Robert Henry (a mining engineer) and Elsa (McGillivray) Crozier; married Lila Samuel, September 7, 1940; children: Kathryn (Mrs. Charles L. Choguill), Isobel, Michael, Caroline. Education: Trinity College of Music, London, England, student, 1935-36. Home: 112 Bridge Lane, Temple Fortune, London N.W.11, England.

CAREER: Sub-editor for Reuters, then for News Chronicle, London, England, 1943-48; Sydney Morning Herald, Sydney, Australia, feature writer, 1948-51; Reuter-Australian Associated Press, correspondent in Melbourne, Australia, in Saigon, Viet Nam, and in other locations, 1951-52; Straits Times, Singapore, features editor, 1952-53; Foreign Report (a confidential bulletin published by The Economist), London, England, editor, 1954-64; British Broadcasting Corp., London, England, political commentator, 1954-65; Forum World Features, London, England, president, 1965—. Director, Institute for the Study of Conflict, 1970—. Member: Royal Institute of International Affairs, Institute for Strategic Studies, Travellers' Club and Royal Automobile Club (both London).

WRITINGS: I Was Wrong About Free China (pamphlet), Friends of Free China Association, 1957; The Rebels: A Study of Post-War Insurrections, Beacon Press, 1960; The Morning After: A Study of Independence, Oxford University Press (New York), 1963; The Pursuit of Plenty: The Sino-Indian Economic Race, Peal, Ashdown & Hart, 1963; Neo Colonialism: A Background Book, Dufour, 1964; South-East Asia in Turmoil, Penguin, 1965, revised edition, 1968; The Struggle for the Third World, Dufour, 1966; Franco: A Biographical History, Eyre & Spottiswoode, 1967, published in America as

Franco, Little, Brown, 1968; *The Masters of Power,* Little, Brown, 1969; (editor) Max Beloff, *The Future of British Foreign Policy,* Taplinger, 1969; (editor) Hubert Gladwyn, *Europe After De Gaulle,* Taplinger, 1969; *Since Stalin: An Assessment of Communist Power,* Coward, 1970; *The Future of Communist Power,* Eyre & Spottiswoode, 1970; *De Gaulle,* Scribner, 1973.

Contributor to *Daily Telegraph, Le Monde Diplomatique, Encounter,* and other periodicals.

WORK IN PROGRESS: De Gaulle in History, for Scribner.

BIOGRAPHICAL/CRITICAL SOURCES: Observer Review, October 29, 1967; *Spectator,* November 24, 1967, October 18, 1969; *Listener,* December 21, 1967; *New York Times,* April 1, 1968; *Book World,* April 21, 1968; *Best Sellers,* May 1, 1968; *New Republic,* May 4, 1968; *National Observer,* May 20, 1968; *New York Times Book Review,* June 28, 1968; *L'Express,* November 10-16, 1969; *New Yorker,* February 7, 1970.

* * *

CRUMP, Fred H., Jr. 1931-

PERSONAL: Born June 7, 1931, in Houston, Tex.; son of Fred H. and Carol Crump. *Education:* Sam Houston State Teachers College, B.S., 1953, M.S., 1961. *Home:* 38-206 Paradise Way, Cathedral City, Calif. 92234.

CAREER: Formerly junior high school art teacher in Orange, Tex., in Palm Springs, Calif., 1960—. Illustrator of children's books.

WRITINGS—Self-illustrated: *Marigold and the Dragon,* Steck, 1964; *The Teeny Weeny Genie,* Steck, 1966.

Illustrator of books by Garry and Vesta Smith, published by Steck: *Creepy Caterpillar,* 1961, *Flagon the Dragon,* 1962, *Mitzi,* 1963; *Jumping Julius,* 1964, *Leander Lion,* 1966, *Florabelle,* 1968, *Crickety Cricket,* 1969.

WORK IN PROGRESS: Illustrations for a book by the Smiths with a Mexican locale.

SIDELIGHTS: Crump told *CA:* "I wrote *Marigold and the Dragon* because it was the type of thing I had in mind when I submitted *Flagon the Dragon* illustrations to the Smiths. Their direction took a turn toward a modern setting so I was still left with a dragon. . . . Have several ideas for future work, none too ambitious. I am an incurable idler."

* * *

CUBER, John F(rank) 1911-

PERSONAL: Surname is pronounced Soo-bur; born August 31, 1911, in Chicago, Ill.; son of John Charles (a cabinet maker) and Lillian (Vomacka) Cuber; married Armine Gulesserian (a teacher), December 10, 1949 (divorced, 1964); married Peggy Buckwalter Harroff, December 15, 1964; children: (first marriage) Armine Anne. *Education:* Western Michigan University, A.B., 1932; University of Michigan, fellow in sociology, 1932-35, Ph.D., 1937. *Home address:* R.F.D. 1, Mt. Gilead, Ohio 43338. *Office:* Ohio State University, 1775 South College Rd., Columbus, Ohio 43210.

CAREER: Sioux Falls College, Sioux Falls, S.D., chairman of economics and sociology departments, 1935-36; Marietta College, Marietta, Ohio, assistant professor of sociology, 1936-37; Kent State University, Kent, Ohio, assistant professor, 1937-39, associate professor, 1939-41, professor of sociology, 1941-44; Ohio State University, Columbus, associate professor, 1944-46, professor of sociology, 1946—. National Council on Family Relations, member of board of directors, 1948-53. Visiting scientist, National Science Foundation and American Sociological

Association. *Member:* American Sociological Association, Society for the Study of Social Problems, American Association of Marriage Counsellors, Ohio Valley Sociological Association, Phi Beta Kappa.

WRITINGS: Sociology: A Synopsis of Principles, Appleton, 1947, 6th edition, 1968; (with Robert A. Harper) *Problems of American Society,* Holt, 1948, 4th edition (with Harper and William F. Kenkel), 1964; *Marriage Counseling Practice,* Appleton, 1948; (with Kenkel) *Social Stratification in the United States,* Appleton, 1954; (with Peggy B. Harroff) *Readings in Sociology: Sources and Comment,* Appleton, 1962; (with Harroff) *The Significant Americans: A Study of Sexual Behavior Among the Affluent,* Appleton, 1965, also published as *Sex and the Significant Americans: A Study of Sexual Behavior Among the Affluent,* Penguin, 1965. Editor, *Ohio Valley Sociologist,* 1946-48, Appleton "Sociology Series," 1949—. Contributor of about fifty articles to professional journals.

* * *

CULBERTSON, Don S(tuart) 1927-

PERSONAL: Born January 12, 1927, in Detroit, Mich.; son of William Homer and Etta (Grubaugh) Culbertson; married Lillian Dallas Williams, November 17, 1956. *Education:* Albion College, A.B., 1950; University of Denver, M.A., 1958. *Home:* 836 West Prospect, Fort Collins, Colo. 80521. *Office:* Colorado State University Library, Fort Collins, Colo. 80521.

CAREER: Instructor in English at public schools in Reese, Mich., 1950-52, and Milford, Mich., 1952-57; University of Wichita, Wichita, Kan., circulation librarian, 1958-60; University of Illinois, Undergraduate Division, Chicago, chief of data processing, 1960-64; Colorado State University Library, Fort Collins, librarian for research and development, 1964—. *Military service:* U.S. Army, 1945-47. *Member:* American Library Association, American Documentation Institute, Colorado Library Association.

WRITINGS: (With Louis A. Schultheiss and Edward M. Heiliger) *Advanced Data Processing in the University Library,* Scarecrow, 1962. Contributor of articles to *Library Journal, American Behavioral Scientist,* other journals in library field.

AVOCATIONAL INTERESTS: Sports cars.

* * *

CULBERTSON, J(ohn) M(athew) 1921-

PERSONAL: Born August 25, 1921, in Detroit, Mich.; son of Glen A. and Lydia (Hawley) Culbertson; married Frances Mitchell (a psychologist), August 27, 1947; children: John, Joanne, Lyndall, Amy. *Education:* University of Michigan, B.A., 1946, M.A., 1947, Ph.D., 1956. *Home:* 5305 Burnett Dr., Madison, Wis. 53705. *Office:* Department of Economics, University of Wisconsin, Madison, Wis. 53706.

CAREER: Federal Reserve System, Board of Governors, Washington, D.C., economist, 1950-57; University of Wisconsin, Madison, assistant professor, 1957-59, associate professor, 1960-62, professor of economics and commerce, 1962—, director of Financial and Fiscal Research Center, Social Systems Research Institute, 1963-65. Consultant to Federal Reserve Bank of St. Louis, 1959-60, to U.S. House of Representatives Banking and Currency Committee, 1963. *Military service:* U.S. Air Force, 1943-46; became first lieutenant; received Air Medal. *Member:* American Economic Association, American Finance Association, Econometric Society, Western Economic Association.

WRITINGS: Full Employment or Stagnation?, McGraw, 1964; Macroeconomic Theory and Stabilization Policy, McGraw, 1968; Economic Development: An Ecological Approach, Knopf, 1971; Money and Banking, McGraw, 1972. Contributor of articles on economics to academic journals. Associate editor, Journal of Finance, 1963-66.

WORK IN PROGRESS: An introductory textbook, Economics; articles developing a dynamic and evolutionary approach to economics.

* * *

CULKIN, Ann Marie 1918-

PERSONAL: Born October 6, 1918, in Scranton, Pa.; daughter of John Joseph (an engineer) and Margaret (Loftus) Culkin. Education: Marywood College, B.A., 1940. Politics: Democrat. Religion: Catholic. Home: 1081 West Market St., Scranton, Pa. 18508. Office: 612 Connell Building, Scranton, Pa. 19603.

CAREER: Originator of Anne Culkin Course of Personality Development. Writer of newspaper column, "Talk It Over." Member: Catholic Press Association.

WRITINGS: Charm for Young Women, Paulist/Newman, 1963.

* * *

CULVER, Dwight W(endell) 1921-

PERSONAL: Born February 15, 1921, in New Haven, Conn.; son of Mearl P. (a minister) and Louisa (Collier) Culver; married Margaret L. Augustine, June 7, 1943; children: Enid Louise, Timothy Dwight, Jane Christine, Laura Bernice. Education: Carleton College, B.A., 1941; Yale Divinity School, B.D., 1944; Yale University, Ph.D., 1948. Religion: Methodist. Home: 1831 Bayard Ave., St. Paul, Minn. 55116. Office: College of St. Catherine, St. Paul, Minn. 55105.

CAREER: Purdue University, Lafayette, Ind., assistant professor, 1947-52; associate professor of sociology, 1952-63, on leave as executive director of National Council for the Panel of Americans, New York, N.Y., 1956-58, as associate director of Lilly Endowment Study of Pre-Seminary Education, Minneapolis, Minn., 1961-63; St. Olaf College, Northfield, Minn., professor of sociology and chairman of department, 1963-68; College of St. Catherine, St. Paul, Minn., academic dean, 1968-71, professor of sociology, 1971—. Methodist minister, member of Minnesota Conference of United Methodist Church. Musician (French horn) in community orchestras.

MEMBER: American Sociological Association (fellow), Religious Research Association, Society for the Scientific Study of Religion, Religious Education Association, American Association of University Professors, Phi Beta Kappa.

WRITINGS: Negro Segregation in the Methodist Church, Yale University Press, 1953; "We Can and We Will. . . ," Methodist Church, 1961; (editor with Keith R. Bridston) The Making of Ministers: Essays on Clergy Training Today, Augsburg, 1964; (with Bridston) Pre-Seminary Education: Report of the Lilly Study, Augsburg, 1965. Contributor to Ashmore Project, a study of school desegregation. Contributor of articles and reviews to religious and professional journals.

* * *

CUNNINGHAM, Julia W(oolfolk) 1916-

PERSONAL: Born October 4, 1916, in Spokane, Wash.; daughter of John G.L. and Sue (Larabie) Cunningham. Education: Attended art school in Charlottesville, Va., one year. Home: 1812 Anacapa St., Santa Barbara, Calif. 93101.

CAREER: G. Schirmer, Inc. (publishers), New York, N.Y., editorial coordinator, four years; Metropolitan Museum of Art, saleswoman in book and art shop, three years; Dell Publishing Co., New York, N.Y., associate editor of Screen Stories, three years; Tecolote Book Shop, Santa Barbara, Calif., assistant to owner, 1959—. Former bank and machine company employee and recordings saleswoman. Member: Authors Guild, International P.E.N. Awards, honors: First prize, New York Herald Tribune, for Dorp Dead.

WRITINGS: The Vision of Francois, the Fox, Houghton, 1960; Dear Rat, Houghton, 1961; Macaroon, Pantheon, 1962; Candle Tales, Pantheon, 1964; Dorp Dead, Pantheon, 1965; Violett, Pantheon, 1966; Onion Journey, Pantheon, 1967; Burnish Me Bright, Pantheon, 1970; Wings of the Morning, Golden Gate, 1971; Far in the Day, Pantheon, 1972.

WORK IN PROGRESS: A children's book, as yet untitled.

SIDELIGHTS: Miss Cunningham told CA: "Like Beatrix Potter, I do not consciously write for children, but rather just to tell a story. And my characters are some of the best friends I have, as real as any other. I was not aware of being a writer until age twelve when I received my first rejection letter. It's a good road to follow, full of darkness and joy, and, if one is very lucky indeed, one meets and is championed by one of the greatest gifts of all, a good editor."

Miss Cunningham has lived in France and Mexico.

AVOCATIONAL INTERESTS: Music.

BIOGRAPHICAL/CRITICAL SOURCES: Library Journal, July, 1970; New Statesman, June 4, 1971; Antiquarian Bookman, January 18, 1971.

* * *

CUNNINGHAM, Rosemary 1916-

PERSONAL: Born October 6, 1916, in Chicago, Ill.; married Angus Cunningham (a missionary); children: John, Carol, Mark, Donald, Laurie, Mary-Ellen. Education: Attended St. Paul Bible College and Nyack Missionary Training College. Address: c/o Unevangelized Fields Mission, Bala Cynwyd, Pa.

CAREER: Unevangelized Fields Mission, Bala Cynwyd, Pa., missionary among an Indian tribe and in lower Amazon region, Brazil, 1939-64. Lecturer.

WRITINGS: Under a Thatched Roof, Evangelical Publishers, 1946; Harvest Moon on the Amazon, Zondervan, 1956; When the Arrow Flies, Prairie Bible Institute, 1966.

WORK IN PROGRESS: Lord, My Face Is to the Wind.

* * *

CURLEY, Daniel 1918-

PERSONAL: Born October 4, 1918, in East Bridgewater, Mass. Agent: John Schaffner, 425 East 51st St., New York, N.Y. 10022.

CAREER: Writer. Associate, University of Illinois Center for Advanced Study, 1968. Awards, honors: Guggenheim fellowship in fiction, 1958; National Council on the Arts award, for In the Hands of Our Enemies.

WRITINGS: That Marriage Bed of Procrustes (stories), Beacon Press, 1957; How Many Angels? (novel), Beacon Press, 1958; A Stone Man, Yes (novel), Viking, 1964; In the Hands of Our Enemies (stories), University of Illinois Press, 1970. Also author of several plays produced on college campuses. Contributor of short stories, poetry, and criticism to Kenyon Review, Epoch, Modern Fiction Studies, other literary periodicals. Member of editorial board, Accent, 1955-60.

CURTIS, Charlotte

PERSONAL: Born in Chicago, Illinois; daughter of George Morris and Lucile (Atcherson) Curtis. *Education:* Vassar College, B.A. *Agent:* Littauer & Wilkinson, 500 Fifth Ave., New York, N.Y. 10036. *Office: New York Times,* 229 West 43rd St., New York, N.Y. 10036.

CAREER: New York Times, New York, N.Y., news reporter, 1961-65, women's news editor, 1965—. *Member:* Junior League.

WRITINGS: First Lady, Pyramid Books, 1963; (contributor) Harrison E. Salisbury, editor, *The Soviet Union: The Fifty Years,* Harcourt, 1967. Contributor to *Sports Illustrated, Town & Country, New York Times Magazine, Ladies' Home Journal, Gentlemen's Quarterly,* and other periodicals.

*   *   *

CURTIS, Rosemary Ann (Stevens) 1935-

PERSONAL: Born December 29, 1935, in Greenwich, London, England; daughter of John Felgate (in naval service) and Mary (Gilkes) Stevens; married T.J. O'Connor Curtis (a sales manager), September 5, 1959; children: Lucinda Mary, Mathew Timothy, Catherine Love. *Education:* National Cathedral School, Washington, D.C., graduate, 1952. *Politics:* Liberal. *Religion:* Episcopalian. *Home:* 101 Oakwood Ct., London W.14, England.

WRITINGS: Jenny, the Young Lady Churchill, Chilton, 1963. Contributor to *Ladies' Home Journal, Woman's Own, Woman, Grit,* and *New York Daily Mirror.*

WORK IN PROGRESS: A book on the clipper ship era; *Moonmen,* a children's historical book.

*   *   *

CUSACK, (Ellen) Dymphna

PERSONAL: Born in Wyalong, New South Wales, Australia; daughter of James (a sheep farmer) and Beatrice (Crowley) Cusack; married Norman Randolph Freehill (a journalist and writer). *Education:* University of Sydney, B.A., 1925, diploma of education, 1925. *Politics:* Progressive. *Home:* 1 Bungan Head Rd., Newport, Sydney, Australia. *Agent:* Madame Odette Arnaud, 11 rue de Teheran, Paris, France. *Office address:* c/o Commonwealth Bank, Australia House, London W.C.2, England.

CAREER: Department of Education, New South Wales, Australia, high school teacher, 1926-43. Lecturer in extra-mural university studies, 1942-43. Lecturer, broadcaster, and writer. *Member:* Society of Authors (England). Fellowship of Australian Writers (vice-president, 1949-61), P.E.N. *Awards, honors:* West Australian drama prizes, 1942, for "Morning Sacrifice," and 1943, for "Comets Soon Pass"; Playwrights' Advisory Board drama prizes, 1945, for "Shoulder the Sky," and 1946, for "Stand Still Time"; British Arts Council Award, for "The Golden Girls"; *Sydney Daily Telegraph* novel award, 1948, for *Come in Spinner!;* Commonwealth literary fellowship for *Southern Steel;* Coronation Medal for services to Australian literature, 1953.

WRITINGS: Jungfrau (novel), Bulletin Publishing (Sydney), 1936; (with Miles Franklin) *Pioneers on Parade,* Angus & Robertson, 1939; (with Florence James) *Come in Spinner!,* Morrow, 1951; *Say No to Death,* Heinemann, 1951, published in America as *The Sun in My Hands,* Morrow, 1952; *Southern Steel,* Constable, 1953; *The Sun in Exile,* Constable, 1955; *Chinese Women Speak* (travel), Angus & Robertson, 1958; *Heatwave in Berlin,* Heinemann, 1961; *Picnic Races,* Heinemann, 1962; *Holidays Among the Russians* (travel), Heinemann, 1964; *Black Lightning* (novel), Heinemann, 1964; (with Flor-

ence James) *Four Winds and a Family,* new edition, Lansdowne, 1965, Angus & Robertson, 1966; *Ilyria Reborn* (travel in Albania), Heinemann, 1966; *The Sun Is Not Enough,* Heinemann, 1967; *The Half-Burnt Tree,* Heinemann, 1969.

Plays: *Red Sky at Morning* (three-act), Melbourne University Press and Oxford University Press, 1942; *Three Australian Three-Act Plays* (includes "Comets Soon Pass," "Shoulder the Sky," and "Morning Sacrifice"), Australasian Publishing Co., 1950; *The Golden Girls* (three-act), Baker, 1955. Also author of British and Australian sound or television productions, "Stand Still Time," "Exit," and "Pacific Paradise."

SIDELIGHTS: Miss Cusack's novels and plays have been translated for publication or production in thirty-one countries; *Heatwave in Berlin* was adapted for a British Broadcasting Corp. series, "The Sun in Exile," adapted for Australian Broadcasting Commission presentation. She speaks French, Italian, German, Chinese, and some Russian, and has traveled throughout Australia, in China, Southeast Asia, Europe, Panama, the Caribbean, and Egypt.

*   *   *

CUTFORTH, John Ashlin 1911-
(John Ashlin)

PERSONAL: Born May 8, 1911, in Woodville, Burton-on-Trent, England; son of Edwin Henry and Cecilia (King) Cutforth; married Isabel Eacott. *Education:* University College, University of London, B.A., 1933. *Religion:* Church of England. *Home:* Masons House, Marsh Gibbon, Bicester, Oxfordshire, England.

CAREER: Schoolmaster at English School, Chateau d'Oex, Switzerland, 1934-35, at St. Cyprians, Eastbourne, England, 1935-39, at Worksop College, Nottinghamshire, England, 1948-49; H.M. inspector of schools, 1949-51; Basil Blackwell & Mott Ltd. (publishers), Oxford, England, staff member, 1951—, board of directors, 1954—. *Military service:* British Army, 1939-48; became staff captain. *Member:* Savage Club (London).

WRITINGS: English in the Primary School, Basil Blackwell, 1952, 2nd edition, 1959; (compiler) *Mystery, Magic and Adventure* (anthology), Basil Blackwell, 1956; (with S.H. Battersby) *Children and Books,* Fernhill, 1962, revised edition, Basil Blackwell, 1963; *Light and Shadow,* Basil Blackwell, 1969. Editor with J.C. Gagg of Blackwell's "Learning Library." Contributor to *School Librarian,* educational journals, and to *New English Encyclopedia.*

AVOCATIONAL INTERESTS: Music, choir training, film-making and photography.

*   *   *

CUTSHALL, Alden 1911-

PERSONAL: Born April 12, 1911, in Olney, Ill. *Education:* Eastern Illinois University, B.Ed., 1932; University of Illinois, M.A., 1935; Ohio State University, Ph.D., 1940. *Religion:* Methodist. *Home:* 667 North Elizabeth, Lombard, Ill. 60148. *Office:* University of Illinois at Chicago Circle, Chicago, Ill. 60680.

CAREER: Public school teacher in Illinois, 1932-34, 1937-39; University of Illinois, Urbana and Chicago, started as instructor, 1940, professor of geography, 1955—, head of department of geography, Chicago campus, 1964—, associate member of Center for Advanced Study, 1962-63. Principal research analyst, U.S. Office of Strategic Services and Department of State, 1944-46. Fulbright lecturer in Philippines, 1957-58. *Member:* American Association for the Advancement of Science, Association of American Geographers, National Council for Geographic

Education, Illinois Geographic Society (president, 1963-64), Illinois State Academy of Science, Philippine Geographic Society, Chicago Geographic Society. *Awards, honors:* Fulbright research grant, Philippines, 1950-51.

WRITINGS: (Associate author) *World Political Geography,* Crowell, 1948, revised edition, 1957; *The Philippines: Nation of Islands,* Van Nostrand, 1964. Contributor to *Encyclopaedia Britannica, Encyclopedia Americana,* other encyclopedias, and of some seventy-five articles to scientific journals. Associate editor, *Philippine Geographic Journal.*

WORK IN PROGRESS: Continuing research into economic and political geography of Southeast Asia, especially the Philippines.

* * *

CYKLER, Edmund A(lbert) 1903-

PERSONAL: Born September 2, 1903; son of Emanuel Emil (a brewer) and Theresa (Pircher) Cykler; married Marian M. Rhodes, August 6, 1926; children: Carol A. Cykler Bratton, Noel B. *Education:* University of California, Berkeley, A.B., 1926; Charles University, Prague, Czechoslovakia, Ph.D., 1928. *Politics:* Democrat. *Religion:* Unitarian. *Home:* 1055 West 17th Ave., Eugene, Ore. 97402. *Office:* School of Music, University of Oregon, Eugene, Ore. 97403.

CAREER: Sacramento Junior College, Sacramento, Calif., instructor in music, 1928-29; Los Angeles City College, Los Angeles, Calif., head of music department, 1929-44; Occidental College, Los Angeles, Calif., associate professor of music, 1944-47; University of Oregon, Eugene, professor of music, 1947—, director of university's German Center for International Music Education, 1963-64 and 1966-67. Conducted music educators on tours of Europe, summers of 1958, 1961. *Member:* Music Educators National Conference (research council), American Society for Aesthetics, American Musicological Society, College Music Society, International Society for Music Education, American Association of University Professors (national council), American Civil Liberties Union. *Awards, honors:* Exchange fellowship from Czechoslovakian Government, 1926-28; Fulbright research grant for University of Innsbruck, 1955-56.

WRITINGS: (With Milo A. Wold) *An Introduction to Music and Art in the Western World,* W.C. Brown, 1955, 4th edition, 1972; workbook, 1959; (with Wold) *An Outline History of Music,* W.C. Brown, 1963, 2nd edition, 1973; (with Egon Kraus) *121 Canons.* Contributor to music educators' journals in America, Germany, Czechoslovakia, and Yugoslavia.

WORK IN PROGRESS: Research in comparative music education.

AVOCATIONAL INTEREST: Farming.

* * *

DABNEY, William M(inor) 1919-

PERSONAL: Born January 6, 1919, in Norfolk, Va.; son of James Cabell (a lawyer) and Mary Beverley (Whittle) Dabney; married Jeanne Lavender Paterson (a teacher), August 27, 1946; children: Virginia Page, Mary Beverley, Daniel Patterson, Elizabeth Sinclair. *Education:* College of William and Mary, student, 1935-37; University of Virginia, A.B., 1939, M.A., 1941, Ph.D., 1951. *Politics:* Democrat. *Religion:* Episcopalian. *Home:* 3041 Mackland Ave. N.E., Albuquerque, N.M. 87106. *Office:* Department of History, 1154 Mesa Vista Hall, University of New Mexico, Albuquerque, N.M. 87106.

CAREER: Armstrong College, Savannah, Ga., instructor in social sciences, 1941-42, 1946-50; University of New

Mexico, Albuquerque, assistant professor, 1951-56, associate professor, 1956-63, professor of history, 1963—, acting chairman of the department, 1955-57, 1963-64, assistant dean of Graduate School, 1961-63. Fulbright lecturer in American history, University of Edinburgh, 1958-59. President, 1965, Albuquerque Tutoring Council. *Military service:* U.S. Naval Reserve, 1942-46; became lieutenant. *Member:* American Historical Association, Organization of American Historians, Phi Kappa Phi, Phi Alpha Theta (national councillor), Blue Key.

WRITINGS: (Editor and contributor with Josiah C. Russell) *Dargan Historical Essays: Historical Studies Presented to Marion Dargan by His Colleagues and Former Students,* University of New Mexico Press, 1952; *After Saratoga: The Story of the Convention Army,* University of New Mexico Press, 1954; (with Marion Dargan) *William Henry Drayton and the American Revolution,* University of New Mexico Press, 1962. Contributor of articles and reviews to historical journals. Board of editors, *New Mexico Historical Review,* 1970—.

WORK IN PROGRESS: Editing the letters of James Steuart Denham; research on Charles Cochrane's career in the American Revolution.

* * *

DAHLBERG, Edward 1900-

PERSONAL: Born July 22, 1900, in Boston, Mass.; son of Elizabeth Dahlberg. *Education:* University of California, Berkeley, student, 1921-23; Columbia University, B.S., 1925. *Residence:* New York, N.Y.

CAREER: Writer. New York University, New York, N.Y., visiting lecturer in Graduate School, 1950, 1961, lecturer in School of General Education, 1961-62. University of Missouri at Kansas City, Carolyn Benton Cockefair Professor, 1964-65, professor of language and literature, 1966—. *Awards, honors:* Attended McDowell Colony, 1930; grants from National Institute of Arts and Letters, 1961, and from Longview Foundation to complete autobiography, *Because I Was Flesh;* Rockefeller Foundation grant, 1965; elected to membership to National Institute of Arts and Letters, 1968.

WRITINGS: Bottom Dogs (novel), introduction by D.H. Lawrence, Putnam, 1929, Simon & Schuster, 1930; *From Flushing to Calvary* (novel), Harcourt, 1932; *Kentucky Blue Grass Henry Smith* (prose-poem), White Horse Press, 1932; *Those Who Perish* (novel), John Day, 1934; *Do These Bones Live* (criticism), Harcourt, 1941, revised edition published in England as *Sing O Barren,* Routledge, 1947, 2nd revised edition published as *Can These Bones Live,* New Directions, 1960; *The Flea of Sodom* (essays), New Directions, 1950; *The Sorrows of Priapus* (philosophy), New Directions, 1957; *Moby Dick: An Hamitic Dream,* Fairleigh Dickinson University, 1960; (with Herbert Read) *Truth Is More Sacred* (critical exchange on modern literature), Horizon, 1961; *Alms for Oblivion* (essays on American literature), University of Minnesota Press, 1964; *Because I Was Flesh* (autobiography), New Directions, 1964; *Reasons of the Heart,* Horizon, 1965; *Cipango's Hinder Door,* University of Texas Press, 1966; *The Leafless American,* edited by Harold Billings, Roger Beacham, 1967; *The Edward Dahlberg Reader,* edited by Paul Carroll, New Directions, 1967; *Epitaphs for Our Times: The Letters of Edward Dahlberg,* edited by Edwin Seaver, Braziller, 1967; *The Carnal Myth: A Search into Classical Sensuality,* Weybright, 1968; *Edward Dahlberg: American Ishmall of Letters,* edited by Harold Billings, Roger Beacham, 1970; *The Confessions of Edward Dahlberg,* Braziller, 1971; (compiler and author of essay) *The Gold of Ophiv: Travels, Myths and Legends in the New World,* Dutton, 1972.

Contributor: Martha Foley and David Burnett, editors, *Best American Short Stories 1961-1962,* Houghton, 1962; Stanley Burnshaw, editor, *Varieties of Literary Experience,* New York University Press, 1962; Louis Filler, editor, *The Anxious Years,* Putnam, 1963; James Laughlin, editor, *New Directions in Prose and Poetry,* New Directions, 1937—. Contributor of poetry, articles, and short stories to *Poetry, Sewanee Review, Fortnightly Review, Nation, Prairie Schooner, First Person, Big Table, Texas Quarterly, Massachusetts Review, New Directions, New Republic,* and other periodicals.

WORK IN PROGRESS: A volume of stories, *The Tailor's Daughter,* for Roger Beacham; and an untitled volume of literary portraits for Weybright.

SIDELIGHTS: "I feel," said Dahlberg several years ago, "I have been writing posthumously for a generation." The public had never heard of him and, throughout his long and, until recently, obscure literary career, Dahlberg has presented critics with something of a dilemma. Some, such as Josephine Herbst, who praise his work, often find it impossible to define: "It is easy," she writes, "to describe second rate talents.... But first rate powers defy comparison and can be defined only by themselves." Most critics, however, seek to explain and define. Raymond Rosenthal writes: "That Edward Dahlberg is one of contemporary America's most important writers is becoming clearer with every book he publishes. . . .Allen Tate, Herbert Read, and Alfred Kazin rub elbows with a number of younger men who have espoused Dahlberg's cause. But," he asks, "what is his cause? It is interesting to note that the critics although almost uniformly laudatory, are not quite sure of its limits and lineaments. Allen Tate, for example locates Dahlberg's mystique in his opposition to the state, and connects him with that line of American loners that runs from Thoreau to Randolph Bourne; he is 'the poet as the perpetual dissenter and outcast'. . . .On the other hand, Herbert Read hails him as our twentieth century Thoreau, seeking an understanding of the past which will be the understanding of our land and ourselves. . . .His career demonstrates that there is no tradition for American writers: 'We are the eternal infant aboriginals,' as he has said, and each artist must take the journey into the backwoods alone if he is to reach the plateau of achievement where Edward Dahlberg stands." Rosenthal himself believes that Dahlberg's "importance lies in his ingrained suspicion of the rationalistic, scientific heritage which has imprisoned intellect in our time. He knows, instinctively—and this is the virtue and defect of his autodidactic limitations—that above reason and the soul or spirit stands what Dante called 'il bene dell' intelletto,' that is, the good of the intellect, the light of wisdom which is a perpetual source of interpretation and transformation. Dahlberg intuitively knows that the method of this form of intellect is the explanation of myth, the presentation of symbols, the search for ancient wisdom." Edmund White, avowing that "the problems Dahlberg raises for the critic are certainly not intellectual," believes that he is simply reiterating easily understood opinions, i.e., "that sexuality is permanently at war with man's higher aspirations and must be disciplined; that human companionship is a great good, but difficult to find or keep; that instinct is often more trustworthy than reason; that accumulating reason, however, is an honorable, if vain practice; that each person's character is so inflexible it cannot be significantly improved; that the machine age is an abomination; and that life is tragic."

Such critical analyses are not incorrect but incomplete. Dahlberg is *sui generis,* "a man of letters in the European sense," according to X.J. Kennedy, and therefore he cannot be easily categorized. He has been a prophet with few disciples, at times intransigent, "his hortatory complexities," according to Arno Karlen, often recalling John Donne's, "the poet-preacher whose bitterness and warmth were also those of essential man alive to regret, whose life's lessons were also burned to his bones, making him somber and sardonic, witty and kind with sensual pessimism." According to Rosenthal, Dahlberg is also "a religious writer without a religion, or rather in search of one." "He utilizes myth, which, in his best work," writes Robert M. Adams, "functions as a way of giving depth, perspective, and perhaps order to the chaos of raw experience." He is at the same time modern and traditional. But, says Rosenthal, "he cannot settle down comfortably in an uncomfortable epoch." Myth and tradition are not "lifeless institutions for him but rather the reminders of tragedy that goad him to feats of incomparable juxtaposition and analogy. . . .Dahlberg is important because he points a new way," especially for the American continent. Dahlberg writes: "Until he is connected with the fens, the ravines, the stars, [man] is more solitary than any beast. Man is a god, and kin to men, when he is a river, a mountain, a horse, a moon. . . . The American legend is the mesa and the bison; it is the myth of a tragic terrain stalked by banished men." Dahlberg is nortorious for his rejection of contemporary life, but it must be noted that his attitude is similar to Thoreau's.

As Frank MacShane notes, "he is a nay-sayer only because he loves his country." Dahlberg once said: "Do you take a weak affirmation when there is a strong negation that is better? . . . I am by nature an iconoclast, but one who is always in search of images, fables and proverbs—the wine for an aching heart." Dahlberg is always in search of positive values, "the old values of family, the land, ancient wisdom, animals and good prose, whose qualities he celebrates in order to cure the ills of the nation and avert its destruction," writes Frank MacShane. Even Melvin Maddocks, who cannot be considered a Dahlberg admirer, admits that, "just as behind his cosmic disgust there is a hard-bitten affection, so also behind the theatrical arrogance lies a genuine humility: 'I do what I can, and later pray that it is not horrible.' "

He is a "lord of the language," according to Herbert Read. Victor Lipton calls him "one of the finest prose stylists of our age, [one who combines] the moral strictures of Leviticus with the sensuousness of The Song of Solomon." His letters are "as passionate as Keat's letters [and] have the massive variety and control of Flaubert's," writes MacShane, who considers Dahlberg "easily the most remarkable writer in America today." His prose, which is often aphoristic, is "avidly quotable; he is perhaps our most consummate rhetorician, but he also has a great deal to say," Rosenthal adds. "His books are worth the trouble of meditation, of rereading, of pondering over again and again. I myself wonder whether he *knows* fully and intimately the profundity of his own wisdom. He is indeed like a seer whose vision sometimes escapes himself; the delight of the imaginative transport blurs the clarity of perception. . . .The truth is in his rhythms, his eloquence, not in his explanation." Dahlberg believes that "character is fate and that's what writes the books, not grammar, not being clever, or imagining that one is the lion or the fox. . . .When the body is false unto itself, the intellect is a liar. . . . A writer should employ a language that can pierce the heart or awaken the mind. Style ought to have some kinship with mountains, seas, glens, orchards, furrows, if it is to have a symbolic and human value. . . .There has to be love in a book if it is to be useful to society.... And there also has to be people or a strong and pungent sense of them in words which we employ to persuade others. I find, however, the academic vocabulary is as peopleless as our commonwealth." MacShane relates how Dahlberg "rejoices that he never lost connection with the European mind. 'Of course, everything American is in my marrow, a tree, a ravine, a sumac, the Rockies, but unless I know the experiences of Attica and Rome, what else can I be except a provincial scribbler?' "

In the thirties he was something of a "provincial scribbler." He now says that "the defect of [*Bottom Dogs*] lies in its jargon, . . . the rude American vernacular." MacShane notes that Dahlberg's early work was naturalistic literary journalism. (Recently Dahlberg said, "I detest my three novels.") Then suddenly he virtually stopped writing and remained in a kind of limbo for nearly twenty years, reading his mentors, says Kerrigan, "an improbable list" which includes Macrobius, Pausanias, Herodian, Suetonius, Clement of Alexandria, Josephus, Plutarch, the Elizabethans, the Comedy of the Restoration, Livy, Thucydides, Coleridge, Ruskin, Herzen, [and] Saint-Simon." Since then, says Lipton, "he has startled the literary world by both the quantity and quality of his production."

His poetry is also highly regarded, even though Allen Tate points out that "Dahlberg runs the risk of not knowing where to stop. He is, though, one of the inspired *namers* of American poetry, who (like Wallace Stevens) loves to rotate an exotic name upon his tongue. He would have been happy, one suspects, in the role of Adam in Eden, given the task of finding names for all of the animals." Kennedy calls him "a remarkable poet," and Donald W. Baker adds: "Edward Dahlberg's imagination is rich in history and myths; his style is fresh in allusion and muscular with verbs. The best of his work, alive with incantatory rhythms and a prophetic tone, generates the power of psalm or prayer. . . .Although Mr. Dahlberg's shorter poems are not wholly successful, . . . [he does] achieve that Shakespearean quickening of speech that distinguishes poetry from artifice, that living language that Mr. Dahlberg himself prays for. . . ." "If he falls at times below the mark," writes Karlan, "he also rises above it—past wit, past insight, past shrewdness, to a vatic poetry that is the final reach of art."

In his autobiography, *Because I Was Flesh*, he tells, says Kennedy, "how, born out of wedlock, he was brought up by his mother, a lady barber in Kansas City. This background, and his years in a Jewish orphanage, may help us understand the central importance to him of a search for parents, a family and an identity. There is an engaging humor in a poem rejecting all of Manhattan above 13th St. . . . Most of the time, however, to read Dahlberg is to feel transfixed by the eye of some Ancient Mariner who grips one's lapels with a terrible urgency. The nightmare he has to tell is hard to ignore." He has been a lonely man. Kerrigan adds that Dahlberg is idiosyncratic. "He is, that is to say, a private person, one not susceptible to 'education' by mass-teachers, and when he says . . . 'I make my own,' that is literally what he does in making judgments. He is also a fool, a divine fool, of the breed of Unamuno . . . and St. Theresa. . . . He learned nothing from any textbook, his texts being his 'life-experience' . . . with certain men of the past, masters, wise men—most of whom were literary and social miscreants, from Socrates to Baudelaire to Ford Maddox Ford. . . . He has no truck with savants and scholars, and none with the Angry, Young or Old. He himself is far more furious than any of the latter. . . . His most characteristic quotation is from the sage Roman who pontificated 'O my friends, there are no friends!' He has been true, in all his books and all his life, to his natural state. . . . 'I have always been loyal to my beginnings, by which I mean I have always been an orphan!' "

August Derleth succinctly expresses Dahlberg's position in the literary world today. "Nobody speaks so well for Edward Dahlberg as Edward Dahlberg himself. His kind of honesty is unhappily far too rare in any time, but most especially in our own. He has never hidden behind any mask, he has always been completely himself, and in prose that is richer than almost any other to be found— in America or elsewhere. He is as much a genius as anyone of whom I can think, past or present, and he is consistently in the core tradition of American literature. . . . The world is seldom ready to extend genius a helping hand, but only to salute genius when he who possessed it is safely underground."

BIOGRAPHICAL/CRITICAL SOURCES: D.H. Lawrence, *Selected Literary Criticism*, edited by Anthony Beale, Viking, 1956; *New York Times Book Review*, December 19, 1965, June 19, 1966, January 15, 1967, March 5, 1967, August 18, 1968; *Newsweek*, January 23, 1967; *Poetry*, March, 1967; *Christian Science Monitor*, April 13, 1967; *New York Review of Books*, August 24, 1967, January 2, 1969; *National Review*, September 19, 1967; *Book World*, June 2, 1968; July 21, 1968, February 16, 1969; *Best Sellers*, June 15, 1968, February 1, 1971; *New Republic*, August 3, 1968, February 6, 1971; *Nation*, November 11, 1968; *TriQuarterly*, fall, 1970; *Atlantic*, March, 1971; *Saturday Review*, March 6, 1971.

*   *   *

DAIN, Norman 1925-

PERSONAL: Born October 5, 1925, in New York, N.Y.; son of Joseph and Bessie (Gordon) Dain; married Phyllis Segal (a librarian), March 10, 1950. *Education:* Brooklyn College (now Brooklyn College of the City University of New York), B.A. (cum laude), 1953; Columbia University, M.A., 1957, Ph.D., 1961. *Home:* 110 Crescent Ave., Leonia, N.J. 07605. *Office:* Department of History, Rutgers University, Newark, N.J. 07102.

CAREER: Polytechnic Institute of Brooklyn, Brooklyn, N.Y., instructor in history and economics, 1958; Cornell University, Medical College, New York, N.Y., research assistant, 1958-61; Rutgers University, Newark, N.J., instructor, 1961-62, assistant professor, 1962-64, associate professor, 1964-68, professor of history, 1968—. *Military service:* U.S. Navy, 1943-46. *Member:* American Historical Association, American Association for Medical History, American Association of University Professors, Organization of American Historians. *Awards, honors:* Social Science Research Council grants-in-aid, 1963-65; U.S. Public Health Service research grants, 1966-67, 1968-69.

WRITINGS: Concepts of Insanity in the United States, 1789-1865, Rutgers University Press, 1964; *Disordered Minds: The First Century of Eastern State Hospital in Williamsburg, Virginia, 1766-1866*, Colonial Williamsburg, 1970. Contributor of articles to professional periodicals. Member of editorial board of *History of Behavioral Sciences Newsletter*, 1960-64, and *Journal of the History of the Behavioral Sciences*, 1965—.

WORK IN PROGRESS: A biography of Clifford W. Bears; concepts of mental disorder in the United States, 1865 to present; research in American intellectual, social, and medical history.

*   *   *

DAINTON, (William) Courtney 1920-

PERSONAL: Born December 13, 1920, in Turleigh, Bradford-on-Avon, Wiltshire, England; son of George Edward and Annie Dorothy (Mew) Dainton. *Education:* University of London, diploma in public administration. *Home:* 34 Bourne Rd., Farncombe, Goldalming, Surrey, England.

CAREER: Wiltshire County Council, Trowbridge, England, clerical officer, 1936-40, 1946-48; South West Metropolitan Regional Hospital Board, Winchester, England, administrative officer, 1948-50; Godalming, Milford, and Liphook Group Hospital Management Committee, Godalming, England, administrative officer, 1950-61; Guildford and Godalming Hospital Management Committee, Guildford, England, senior administrative officer, 1961-66; Cyclists Touring Club, clerk, 1966—. *Military service:* British Army, 1940-46; became sergeant.

WRITINGS: Clock Jacks and Bee Boles, Phoenix House, 1957; *The Story of England's Hospitals,* Museum Press, 1961, C.C Thomas, 1962.

AVOCATIONAL INTERESTS: Walking, photography, stamp-collecting, travel.

*   *   *

DAIUTE, Robert J(ames)   1926-

PERSONAL: Surname is pronounced Die-you-tee; born December 27, 1926, in Braintree, Mass.; son of Carroll F. (an attorney and tax adviser) and Dorothy (Park) Daiute; married Eleanor Mae Stevens, June 6, 1953; children: Robert James, Jr., Eleanor Maria. *Education:* Princeton University, A.B., 1951; University of Pennsylvania, M.B.A., 1954. *Office:* Rider College, Trenton, N.J. 08602.

CAREER: Norwich University, Northfield, Vt., instructor in business administration, 1955-57; Alfred University, Alfred, N.Y., assistant professor of business, 1957-60; Rider College, Trenton, N.J., assistant professor of business administration, 1960—. Co-director, research project in library leadership, 1969-70. *Military service:* U.S. Navy, 1944-46. *Member:* Academy of Management, American Economic Association, Alpha Kappa Psi.

WRITINGS: Scientific Management and Human Relations, Holt, 1964; *Land-Use Data Sources for an Interstate Region,* Department of Commerce (Harrisburg), 1966; (editor) *Management Education,* Eastern Academy of Management, 1969; *Economic Highway Planning,* Chandler-Davis, 1970. Contributor to *Better Roads, Public Works, Advanced Management,* other journals.

WORK IN PROGRESS: Research in history of management thought, economic impact of highways, and land use information.

*   *   *

DALY, Emily Joseph   1913-

PERSONAL: Born August 2, 1913, in Utica, N.Y.; daughter of George Aloysius (a pharmacist) and Maria (Hurley) Daly. *Education:* D'Youville College, A.B., 1933; Catholic University of America, A.M., 1941; Fordham University, Ph.D., 1946. *Home:* 979 Madison Ave., Albany, N.Y. 12203. *Office:* Department of Classics, College of Saint Rose, 432 Western Ave., Albany, N.Y. 12203.

CAREER: Roman Catholic nun, member of Sisters of St. Joseph, name in religion, Sister Emily Joseph; College of Saint Rose, Albany, N.Y., professor of classics, 1940—. Member, Mohawk-Hudson Council on Educational Television; member of regional interviewing committee, Fulbright Grants under Teacher Exchange Program. *Member:* American Classical League, American Association of University Professors, American School of Classics Studies (Rome), Classical Association of Middle Atlantic States, Virgil Society of London, Delta Epsilon Sigma. *Awards, honors:* Fulbright grant to Italy, 1955.

WRITINGS: (Editor) *The Spiritual Legacy of John Peter Medaille, S.J.,* St. Anthony Guild Press, 1959; (editor) *Joseph, Son of David* (anthology), St. Anthony Guild Press, 1961; (editor) *Paul, Trumpet of the Spirit: An Anthology,* St. Anthony Guild Press, 1963. Translator of Tertullian's writings, appearing in Volume X and Volume

XL of *The Fathers of the Church.* Contributor to religious, classical, and literary journals.

WORK IN PROGRESS: Deux Hommes Revoltes, a comparison of Lucretius and Camus; history of Congregation of Sisters of St. Joseph of Carondelet; further translations from Tertullian.

SIDELIGHTS: Sister Emily Joseph has a reading knowledge of Latin, Greek, French, Italian, and German.

*   *   *

DALY, Robert Welter   1916-

PERSONAL: Born March 13, 1916, in Chicago, Ill.; son of Charles Lawrence (a lawyer) and Elizabeth (Welter) Daly; married Mary Lauretta Kennedy (a teacher), September 18, 1943; children: Deborah, Brian, John, William (deceased). *Education:* Loyola University, Chicago, Ill., Ph.B., 1939, M.A., 1940, Ph.D., 1949. *Religion:* Roman Catholic. *Home address:* P.O. Box 31, Arnold, Md. 21012. *Agent:* Brandt & Brandt, 101 Park Ave., New York, N.Y. 10017. *Office:* Department of History, U.S. Naval Academy, Annapolis, Md. 21402.

CAREER: U.S. Coast Guard Academy, New London, Conn., instructor in general studies, 1941-43; U.S. Naval Academy, Annapolis, Md., 1946—, professor of history, 1961—. *Military service:* U.S. Coast Guard Reserves, 1941—; now captain. *Member:* American Society for Russian Naval History.

*WRITINGS—*Fiction: *Broadsides,* Macmillan, 1940 (published in England as *Heart of Oak,* P. Davies, 1941); *Soldier of the Sea,* Morrow, 1942; *Cleared for Action,* Adventure Magazine, 1946; *To the Vigilant,* Blue Book Magazine, 1947; *Guns of Yorktown,* Dodd, 1953; *Guns of Roman Nose,* Dodd, 1957.

Nonfiction: *The Seven Years War* (pamphlet), U.S. Naval Institute, 1952; *How to Write a Research Paper* (pamphlet), U.S. Naval Institute, 1953; (contributor) Potte and Fredland, editors, *The U.S. and World Sea Power,* Prentice-Hall, 1955; (contributor) Malcolm George Saunders, editor, *The Soviet Navy,* Praeger, 1958; *How the Merrimac Won: The Strategic Story of the C.S.S. Virginia,* Crowell, 1957; (editor) William Frederick Keeler, *Aboard the U.S.S. Monitor, 1862, Letters to His Wife, Anne,* U.S. Naval Institute, 1964; (with J.E. Cooke and A.F. Davis) *Age of Responsibility,* Scribner, 1965; *Raphael Semmes, Confederate Admiral,* Kenedy, 1965; (editor) *Aboard the U.S.S. Florida: The Letters of Paymaster William Frederick Keeler, U.S. Navy, to His Wife, Anne,* U.S. Naval Institute, 1968. Military editor, *Dictionary of American History,* 2nd editor, Scribner, in press. Contributor of stories to *Saturday Evening Post, Esquire, Argosy,* and other magazines, and of articles to U.S. military periodicals.

WORK IN PROGRESS: An outline of Russian Wars; A Short History of the Russian Navy, for Little, Brown.

*   *   *

DANAGHER, Edward F.   1919-

PERSONAL: Born July 11, 1919, in Chicago, Ill.; son of John Joseph (a salesman) and Eleanor (Tonry) Danagher. *Education:* St. Mary's Seminary, Perryville, Mo., B.A., 1942, advanced study, 1942-46; St. Louis University, summer study, 1946-49. *Home:* 621 West Adams Blvd., Los Angeles, Calif. 90007.

CAREER: Roman Catholic priest.

WRITINGS: Son, Give Me Your Heart, Bruce, 1964.

WORK IN PROGRESS: A humorous novel on suburban parochial life.

DANGERFIELD, George Bubb 1904-

PERSONAL: Born October 28, 1904, in Newbury, Berkshire, England; became American citizen, 1943; son of George (a clergyman) and Ethel (Tyrer) Dangerfield; married Helen Mary Deey Spedding, 1928; married second wife, Mary Louise Schott, June 29, 1941; children: (second marriage) Mary Jo, Hilary, Anthony. *Education:* Hertford College, Oxford, B.A., 1926, M.A., 1968. *Politics:* "Peace and Freedom." *Religion:* Church of England. *Home:* 883 Toro Canyon Rd., Santa Barbara, Calif. 93103.

CAREER: Brewer, Warren & Putnam (publishers), New York, N.Y., assistant editor, 1930-32; *Vanity Fair*, New York, N.Y., literary editor, 1933-35; University of California, Santa Barbara, lecturer in Anglo-American history, 1968—. *Military service:* U.S. Army, Infantry, 1942-45. *Member:* American Historical Association, Americans for Democratic Action, American Civil Liberties Union, National Association for the Advancement of Colored People, Friends of Santa Barbara Public Library. *Awards, honors:* Pulitzer Prize in history and Bancroft Prize of Columbia University, 1953, for *The Era of Good Feelings;* Benjamin D. Shreve Fellow, Princeton University, 1957-58; California Literature Silver Medal award and Marquis Biographical Award, 1961, for *Chancellor Robert R. Livingston of New York;* Guggenheim fellow, 1970-71.

WRITINGS: *Bengal Mutiny,* Harcourt, 1932; *The Strange Death of Liberal England,* Smith & Haas, 1935; *Victoria's Heir,* Harcourt, 1942; *The Era of Good Feelings,* Harcourt, 1952; *Chancellor Robert R. Livingston of New York,* Harcourt, 1960; (editor and author of introduction with O.M. Scruggs) Henry Adams, *The History of the United States During the Administrations of Jefferson and Madison,* two volumes, Prentice-Hall, 1963; *The Awakening of American Nationalism 1815-1828,* Harper, 1965; *Defiance to the Old World,* Putnam, 1970.

WORK IN PROGRESS: A study of the Irish Easter uprising of 1916.

* * *

DANIERE, Andre L(ucien) 1926-

PERSONAL: Surname is pronounced *Dan*-nee-air; born December 29, 1926, in Roanne, France; son of Pierre Emile and Simone (Duverne) Daniere; married Nirmal Chawla (a radio announcer), August 1, 1958; children: Amrita, Jyoti. *Education:* Institut National Agronomique, Diplome d'Ingenieur Agronome, 1948; Amherst College, graduate student, 1949-51; University of Massachusetts, M.A., 1950; Harvard University, Ph.D., 1956. *Home:* 28 Adams St., Brookline, Mass. 02160. *Office:* Department of Economics, Boston College, University Heights, Chestnut Hill, Mass. 02167.

CAREER: Harvard University, Cambridge, Mass., assistant professor of economics, 1959-64, lecturer in economics, Graduate School of Education, 1964-68; Boston College, Chestnut Hill, Mass., associate professor of economics, 1968—. *Military service:* French Army, 1952-53. *Member:* Econometric Society.

WRITINGS: *Higher Education in the American Economy,* Random House, 1964; *Financing of Education in India,* Education Commission (New Delhi), 1965; *Some Economics of Quality in School Education,* Seminar on Quality in Education, American University, 1966; *Statistical Investigation of Financial Aid to Students in Higher Education and Related Activities,* U.S. Department of Health, Education, and Welfare, 1966; *Program Report on Indian Education,* Agency for International Development, 1967; *Inequalities of Educational Opportunities in Massachusetts,* Massachusetts Advisory Council on Education and New England School Development Council, 1967; (with Jerry Mechling) *Direct Marginal Productivity of College Education in Relation to College Aptitude of Students and Production Costs of Institutions,* Institute of Economic Research, Harvard University, 1968; *Cost-Benefit Analysis of General Purpose State School-Aid Formulas in Massachusetts* (monograph), Massachusetts Advisory Council on Education, 1969; (with George F. Madaus) *The Measurement of Alternative Costs of Educating Catholic School Children in Public Schools* (monograph), Massachusetts Advisory Council on Education, 1969; *Impact of Alternative Patterns of Parochial School Closings on Public Budgets in the State of New York,* New York State Commission on the Quality, Cost and Financing of Elementary and Secondary Education, 1971.

Contributor: *Needs in Massachusetts Higher Education,* Massachusetts Special Commission on Audit of State Needs, 1958; Seymour Harris, editor, *Challenge and Change in American Education,* McCutchan, 1965; *Economic Effect of Vietnam Spending,* U.S. Government Printing Office, 1967; Stanley Elam and Gordon I. Swanson, editors, *Educational Planning in the United States,* F.E. Peacock, 1969; *The Economics and Financing of Higher Education in the United States,* Joint Economic Committee, United States Congress, 1969; *The Social Sciences and the Education of Administrators,* University Council for Educational Administration, in press. Contributor to *Economia Internationale, Journal of Economic History, Public Policy, Journal of Human Resources,* and *NCEA Bulletin.*

WORK IN PROGRESS: *Student Loan Systems: A Comparative Analysis.*

* * *

DANOWSKI, T(haddeus) S(tanley) 1914-

PERSONAL: Born September 6, 1914, in Wallington, N.J.; son of Anton and Theresa (Kosciuh) Danowski; married Phyllis Little, June 22, 1949: children: Stanley T. *Education:* Yale University, B.A., 1936, M.D. (magna cum laude), 1940. *Home:* 5415 Howe St., Pittsburgh, Pa. 15232.

CAREER: Diplomate, National Board of Medical Examiners, 1941, American Board of Internal Medicine, 1947. New Haven Hospital, New Haven, Conn., intern, 1940-41, assistant resident, 1941-43, associate physician, instructor in medicine, 1943-46, assistant professor, 1946-47; University of Pittsburgh, Pittsburgh, Pa., Renziehausen Professor of Research Medicine, 1947-56, professor of medicine, 1956—, chief of section of endocrinology and metabolism, 1956—. Senior staff physician at Presbyterian Hospital, Woman's Hospital, and Children's Hospital, all Pittsburgh, Pa., 1947—, at Elizabeth Steel Magee Hospital, Pittsburgh, 1949—, at Shadyside Hospital, Pittsburgh, 1958—; chief of department of medicine, Magee Womens Hospital.

MEMBER: American Medical Association, American Association for the Advancement of Science (fellow), American College of Physicians (fellow), American Diabetes Association (fellow; council, 1957—; vice-president, 1963-64; president, 1965-66), American Geriatrics Society (council, 1961), American Physiological Society, American Society for Clinical Investigation, American Thyroid Association, Association of American Physicians, Endocrine Society, Society for Experimental Biology and Medicine, American Cancer Society (president, Pennsylvania division, 1961-62; Allegheny County and Pennsylvania State board, 1951—), Pittsburgh Academy of Medicine, New York Academy of Sciences (fellow), Indian Society of Endocrinology (honorary), Phi Beta Kappa, Sigma Xi, Alpha Omega Alpha, Phi Beta Pi (honorary).

Awards, honors: Guggenheim fellowship, 1953-54; distinguished achievement award, Polish Medical Alliance, 1964; Banting Memorial Award, 1964; Sword of Hope, Pennsylvania Division of the American Cancer Society, 1966; national bronze medal, American Cancer Society, 1968; Alfred Jurzykowski Award, 1969.

WRITINGS: (Contributor) Victor A. Drill, editor, *Pharmacology in Medicine,* McGraw, 1954, 2nd edition, 1958; (contributor) S.C. Werner, editor, *The Thyroid,* Hoeber Medical Division, 1955, 2nd edition, 1962; (with J.R. Elkinton) *The Body Fluids: Basic Physiology and Practical Therapeutics,* Williams & Wilkins, 1955; (contributor) W.B. Kiesewetter, editor, *Pre- and Post-operative Care in the Pediatric Surgical Patient,* Year Book Medical Publishers, 1956; *Diabetes Mellitus with Emphasis on Children and Young Adults,* Williams & Wilkins, 1957; *Diabetes as a Way of Life,* Coward, 1957, 3rd edition, 1970; *Clinical Endocrinology,* four volumes, Williams & Wilkins, 1962; (editor with Harvey C. Knowles and Arthur Krosnick) *Juvenile Diabetes: Adjustments and Emotional Problems,* privately printed, 1963; (editor) *Diabetes Mellitus: Diagnosis and Treatment,* American Diabetes Association, Volume I, 1964, Volume II (with G.J. Hamwi), 1967; *Outline of Endocrine Gland Syndromes,* Williams & Wilkins, 1965, 2nd edition, 1968; *Sustained Weight Control: The Individual Approach,* F.A. Davies, 1969.

Contributor of more than four hundred articles to medical journals in United States and abroad, 1941—. Member of editorial board, *Circulation,* 1952, 1953-56, of *Diabetes,* 1957—, of *Metabolism,* 1959—, of *Clinical Pharmacology and Therapeutics,* 1966.

WORK IN PROGRESS: Third edition of *Outline of Endocrine Gland Syndromes.*

* * *

DANTON, J(oseph) Periam 1908-

PERSONAL: Born July 5, 1908, in Palo Alto, Calif.; son of George Henry (a professor) and Annina (Periam) Danton; married Lois King, December 25, 1948; children: Jennifer, Joseph Periam, Jr. *Education:* University of Leipzig, student, 1925-26; Oberlin College, B.A. (magna cum laude), 1928; Columbia University, B.S., 1929; Williams College, M.A., 1930; University of Chicago, Ph.D., 1935. *Politics:* Democrat. *Home:* 700 Grizzly Peak Blvd., Berkeley, Calif. 94708. *Office:* School of Librarianship, University of California, Berkeley, Calif. 94720.

CAREER: With New York (N.Y.) Public Library, 1928-29, American Library Association, Chicago, Ill., 1930-33; Colby College, Waterville, Me., librarian and associate professor of bibliography, 1935-36; Temple University, Philadelphia, Pa., librarian and associate professor of bibliography, 1936-42; University of California, Berkeley, associate professor, 1946-47, professor, 1947—, dean of School of Librarianship, 1946-61. Lecturer at The Hague, 1961, University of Toronto, 1963, Hebrew University and Universities of Belgrade, Ljubljana, and Zagreb, 1965, McGill University, 1969, University of Puerto Rico, 1970; visiting professor, University of Chicago, summer, 1942, Columbia University, spring, 1946. Director, U.S. Department of State—American Library Association multi-area group librarian program, 1963-64. Library consultant, U.S. Department of State, in Ethiopia, 1961, to U.S. Veterans Administration 1961-65, and to academic and private libraries; Ford Foundation library consultant, Southeast Asia, 1963; UNESCO library consultant, 1968. *Military service:* U.S. Naval Reserve, Intelligence Corps, 1942-45; became lieutenant commander; served in South Pacific in the island campaigns, 1943-44; received Presidential Unit Citation with two stars, Pacific theater ribbon with seven battle stars.

MEMBER: American Library Association, Association of College and Research Libraries (treasurer, 1938-40), Association of American Library Schools (vice-president, 1948-49; president, 1949-50), Bibliographical Society of America, California Library Association, Sigma Alpha Epsilon. *Awards, honors:* Fulbright research grants, 1960-61, 1964-65; Association of College and Research Libraries grant, 1960-61, 1963-64; Council on Library Resources grant, 1967-69; Guggenheim fellowship, 1971-72.

WRITINGS: (Translator of sections on German libraries) *Popular Libraries of the World,* American Library Association, 1933; (compiler with others) *Library Literature, 1921-32,* American Library Association, 1934; (compiler with M.F. Tauber) *Graduate Theses and Dissertations, 1894-1940,* Temple University Press, 1940; *Education for Librarianship,* UNESCO, 1949; (contributor) Bernard Berelson, editor, *Education for Librarianship,* American Library Association, 1949.

(Editor) *A Symposium in Public Librarianship,* University of California School of Librarianship, 1952; *United States Influence on Norwegian Librarianship, 1890-1940,* University of California Press, 1957; (editor) *The Climate of Book Selection: Social Influences on School and Public Libraries* (symposium), University of California School of Librarianship, 1959; (with L.C. Merritt) *The Vallejo, California, Public Library: A Survey,* [Berkeley], 1959; (editor) *New and Continuing Problems in an Expanding University,* University of California Press, 1962; *Book Selection and Collections: A Comparison of German and American University Libraries,* Columbia University Press, 1963; (editor) *Index to Festschriften in Librarianship,* Bowker, 1970; *Between M.L.S. and Ph.D.: A Study of Sixth-Year Specialist Programs in Accredited Library Schools,* American Library Association, 1970.

Co-compiler of *Union List of Microfilms,* 1942-46. Contributor of forty-odd articles and more than thirty reviews to *Books Abroad, Library Journal, School and Society, College and Research Libraries, Booklist, Wilson Library Bulletin,* and other library periodicals. Member of editorial boards, Association of College and Research Libraries *Monographs,* 1966-69, *Library Quarterly,* 1968—; and *International Library Review,* 1968—.

WORK IN PROGRESS: The Dimensions of Comparative Librarianship.

SIDELIGHTS: Danton has lived and traveled in China and Japan, 1916-24, in Europe, 1925-26, 1960-61, 1964-65. *Avocational interests:* Sailing, reading, skiing, gardening, classical music.

* * *

D'ARCY, G(eorge) Minot 1930-

PERSONAL: Born July 31, 1930, in Bristol, N.H.; son of G. Austin and Harriet (Cavis) D'Arcy; married Ann Giles, June 12, 1955. *Education:* Tufts College (now Tufts University), B.A., 1952. *Home:* 7 Hawks Hill Rd., New Canaan, Conn. 06840. *Office:* D'Arcy, McCarter & Chew, Inc., 22 East 40th St., New York, N.Y. 10016.

CAREER: With Merrill Lynch, Pierce, Fenner & Beane, 1953-56; Saddler, Stevens & Clark, investment counsel, 1956-59; D'Arcy, McCarter & Chew, Inc., New York, N.Y., president, 1959—. Lecturer, University of Connecticut, 1962-64.

WRITINGS: Investment Counsel: Profit and Peace of Mind for the Investor, Obolensky, 1963.

* * *

DARLINGTON, Cyril Dean 1903-

PERSONAL: Born December 19, 1903, in Chorley, England; son of William Henry Robertson (a schoolmaster) and Ellen (Frankland) Darlington; married Margaret Upcott; married second wife, Gwendolen Adshead, June 2, 1950; children: Oliver, Andrew (deceased), Clare, Deborah, Rachel. *Education:* Foundation scholar, St. Paul's School, London, England; Wye College, University of London, D.Sc., 1930. *Home:* Woodside, Frilford Heath, near Abingdon, Berkshire, England. *Office:* Botany School, Oxford University, Oxford, England.

CAREER: Rockefeller Foundation traveling fellow, 1932-33; John Innes Institute, Hertford, Hertfordshire, England, director, 1939-53; Oxford University, Oxford, England, professor of botany, fellow of Magdalen College, and keeper of Oxford Botanic Garden, 1953-71. President, Oxford Chromosome Conferences, 1964, 1967, 1970. *Member:* Genetical Society (president, 1943-46), Royal Society (fellow), Eugenics Society (fellow), American Botanical Society (honorary), Accademia dei Lincei (foreign member), Royal Danish Academy (foreign member). *Awards, honors:* Royal Medal of Royal Society, 1946.

WRITINGS: Recent Advances in Cytology, J. & A. Churchill, 1932, 2nd edition, 1936, Blakiston, 1937, reissued as *Cytology,* Little, Brown, 1965; *Chromosomes and Plant-Breeding,* Macmillan (London), 1932; *The Evolution of Genetic Systems,* Macmillan (New York), 1939, 2nd edition, Basic Books, 1958; (with L.F. LaCour) *The Handling of Chromosomes,* Allen & Unwin, 1942, 5th edition, Hafner, 1970; (with Janaki Ammal) *Chromosome Atlas of Cultivated Plants,* Macmillan (New York), 1946, 2nd edition (with A.P. Wylie) published as *Chromosome Atlas of Flowering Plants,* Macmillan, 1956; (editor) *The Fruit and the Soil,* Oliver & Boyd, 1948, 2nd edition published as *The Fruit, the Seed, and the Soil,* 1949; *The Conflict of Science and Society,* C.A. Watts, 1948; (with Kenneth Mather) *The Elements of Genetics,* Allen & Unwin, 1949, revised edition, Schocken, 1969; (with Mather) *Genes, Plants and People: Essays on Genetics,* Blakiston, 1950; *The Facts of Life,* Allen & Unwin, 1953, Macmillan (New York), 1955, revised edition published as *Genetics and Man,* Macmillan, 1964, new edition, Penguin, 1966, Schocken, 1969; *The Place of Botany in the Life of a University,* Clarendon Press, 1954; *Chromosome Botany,* Allen & Unwin, 1956, 2nd edition published as *Chromosome Botany and the Origins of Cultivated Plants,* Hafner, 1963; *Oxford Botanic Garden Guide,* Basil Blackwell, 1957; *Darwin's Place in History,* Basil Blackwell, 1959, Macmillan (New York), 1961; (author of introduction) Sir Francis Galton, *Hereditary Genius,* Collins, 1962; (editor with A.D. Bradshaw) *Teaching Genetics in School and University,* Oliver & Boyd, 1963, Philosophical Library, 1965, revised edition, Oliver & Boyd, 1966; (editor with K.R. Lewis) *Chromosomes Today,* Plenum, Volume I, 1966, Volume II, 1969, Volume III, 1972; *The Evolution of Man and Society,* Simon & Schuster, 1970.

Co-founder and editor, *Heredity,* 1947-57.

SIDELIGHTS: The Facts of Life has been translated into French, German, Italian, and Japanese; *The Evolution of Man* has also been published in Spanish, Dutch, and Finnish editions. Scientific travels have taken Darlington to South and East Africa, Australia, New Guinea, New Zealand, Russia, United States, Persia, Japan, and India.

BIOGRAPHICAL/CRITICAL SOURCES: Observer Review, September 7, 1969; *New York Times,* June 26, 1970; *New York Times Book Review,* August 2, 1970.

*   *   *

DAVELUY, Paule Cloutier 1919-

PERSONAL: Born April 6, 1919, in Ville-Marke, Temiscamingue, Quebec; daughter of Philippe and Gabrielle (Guay) Cloutier; married Andre Daveluy (a writer), June 26, 1944; children: Danielle, Sylviane, Pierre, Brigitte, Marie-Claude, Andre, Jr. *Education:* Studied at Pensionnat Mont-Royal, Bon Conseil Institute, and University of Montreal. *Politics:* "French-Canadian, so: a touch of nationalism." *Religion:* Roman Catholic. *Home:* 12062 Saint-Germain Blvd., Montreal 9, Quebec, Canada.

CAREER: Secretary to Andre Daveluy before marriage, and still his secretary at home. Member of board of directors, Editions Jeunesse (publishers). *Member:* La Societe des Ecrivains Canadiens, Communications-jeunesse (president), Federation des Unions de Familles. *Awards, honors: L'Ete Enchante* received Prix du Roman of the Canadian Association of Educators in the French Language, bronze medal of Canadian Library Association as best children's book of the year, and the English translation, *Summer in Ville-Marie* was included on the *New York Times* list of the hundred best books for children, 1962; *Drole d'Automne* received the Prix du Salon du Livre and bronze medal of Canadian Library Association, 1962; *Cet hiver-la,* received the Quebec literary award, 1968.

WRITINGS: Les Guinois, L'Atelier, 1957; *Cherie Martin* (novel), L' Atelier, 1957; *L'Ete enchante* (novel for teenagers), L'Atelier, 1958, translation by Monroe Stearns published in America as *Summer in Ville-Marie,* Holt, 1962; *Drole d'Automne* (novel for teenagers), Le Pelican, 1962; *Sylvette et les adultes* (novel for teenagers), Editions Jeunesse, 1962; *Sylvette sous la tente bleue,* Editions Jeunesse, 1964; *Cinq Filles Compliques,* Editions Jeunesse, 1965; *Cet hiver-la,* Editions *Jeunesse,* 1967; *Cher printemps,* Editions Jeunesse, 1971; (translator into French) Elizabeth Yates, *Pipe, Paddle and Song,* Editions Jeunesse, 1971. Contributor to French-Canadian newspapers, magazines, radio, and television.

SIDELIGHTS: Mrs. Daveluy is one of the few authors writing for French-Canadian teen-agers. The lack of books for this category of youth, she feels, "makes patriotism a difficult affair for young people quartered between two countries."

BIOGRAPHICAL/CRITICAL SOURCES: Montreal Gazette, November 22, 1962; *La Presse* (Montreal), November 22, 1962.

*   *   *

DAVENPORT, Gwen 1910-

PERSONAL: Born October 3, 1910, in Colon, Canal Zone, Panama; daughter of James Farquharson (a vice-admiral, U.S. Navy) and Gwen (Wigley) Leys; married John Davenport (a stockbroker), February 5, 1937; children: Christopher W., John F., Juliet R. *Education:* Vassar College, A.B., 1931. *Politics:* Democrat. *Religion:* Episcopalian. *Home:* 6 Rio Vista Dr., Louisville, Ky. 40207. *Agent:* Curtis Brown Ltd., 60 East 56th St., New York, N.Y. 10022.

CAREER: Author.

WRITINGS: A Stranger and Afraid, Bobbs-Merrill, 1943; *Return Engagement,* Bobbs-Merrill, 1945; *Belvedere,* Bobbs-Merrill, 1947; *Family Fortunes,* Doubleday, 1949; *Candy for Breakfast,* Doubleday, 1950; *The Bachelor's Baby,* Doubleday, 1957; *The Wax Foundation,* Doubleday, 1961; *Great Loves in Legend and Life,* F. Watts, 1964. Author of play, "Belvedere." Contributor of short stories to *McCall's, Good Housekeeping,* and other magazines.

SIDELIGHTS: Belvedere was made into the film "Sitting Pretty," which starred Clifton Webb.

DAVENPORT, Marcia 1903-

PERSONAL: Born June 9, 1903, in New York, N.Y.; daughter of Alma Gluck (opera singer); stepdaughter of Efrem Zimbalist (concert violinist); married Russell Wheeler Davenport, 1929 (died, 1954). *Education:* Attended Shipley School, Wellesley College, University of Grenoble. *Agent:* Brandt & Brandt, 101 Park Ave., New York, N.Y. 10017.

CAREER: New Yorker, New York, N.Y., member of editorial staff, 1928-31; free-lance author, music critic, lecturer, 1931—. Music critic of *Stage,* 1934-39; commentator for Metropolitan Opera broadcasts, 1936-37; other radio broadcasts on musical subjects.

WRITINGS: Mozart (biography), Scribner, 1932, revised edition, 1956; *Of Lena Geyer* (novel), Scribner, 1936; *The Valley of Decision* (novel), Scribner, 1942; *East Side, West Side* (novel), Scribner, 1947; *My Brother's Keeper* (novel), Scribner, 1954; *Garibaldi: Father of Modern Italy,* (juvenile biography), Random House, 1956; *The Constant Image* (novel), Scribner, 1960; *Too Strong for Fantasy* (autobiography), Scribner, 1967. Contributor to *Fortune, McCall's, Saturday Evening Post, Reader's Digest,* other national magazines.

SIDELIGHTS: Ellen Moers writes that although Mrs. Davenport's autobiography "is too long, too gushing, sometimes to improbable; it is nevertheless a thoroughly readable, even a compelling production."

BIOGRAPHICAL/CRITICAL SOURCES: New York Times Book Review, October 22, 1967; *Harper's,* November, 1967; *Book World,* November 12, 1967; *Best Sellers,* December 1, 1967; *Time,* December 8, 1967; *New Statesman,* February 12, 1968; *Punch,* April 10, 1968; *Washington Post,* September 2, 1968.

*   *   *

DAVES, Michael 1938-

PERSONAL: Surname is pronounced Dave's; born March 4, 1938, in Wichita Falls, Tex.; son of Floyd Lee and Johnnie (Dunn) Daves; married Patricia McLean, August 29, 1958; children: Paul Lee, Donna Michelle. *Education:* Midwestern University, B.A., 1959; Southern Methodist University, Th.M., 1963; D.D., 1969. *Politics:* Democrat. *Home:* 1021 Northeast 20th, Grand Prairie, Tex. 75050.

CAREER: Minister, North Texas Conference, United Methodist Church, serving churches in Wichita Falls, Tex., 1957-59, Addison, Tex., 1959-62, Plano, Tex., 1962-63, Holliday, Tex., 1963-66; Prairie Heights United Methodist Church, Grand Prairie, Tex., 1966—. Vice-chairman, North Texas Conference, Commission on Worship, 1963-70. *Member:* Dallas County Mental Health Association, Grand Prairie Symphony Orchestra Association, Grand Prairie Ministerial Association, Grand Prairie Chamber of Commerce (member of executive division). *Awards, honors:* Best children's book award, Texas Institute of Letters, 1967, for *Young Reader's Book of Christian Symbolism.*

WRITINGS: Devotional Talks for Children, Baker Book, 1961, 2nd edition, 1967; *Sermon Outlines on Romans,* Revell, 1962; *Famous Hymns and Their Writers,* Revell, 1962; *George Matheson: The Free Captive* (booklet), Upper Room, 1962; *Meditations on Early Christian Symbols,* Abingdon, 1964; *Come with Faith,* Abingdon, 1965; *A Young Reader's Book of Christian Symbolism,* Abingdon, 1967; *The Service of Marriage* (booklet), T-M Press, 1968; *Advent: A Calender of Devotion,* Abingdon, 1971.

Regular contributor of columns in *Texas Methodist* and *Grand Prairie Daily News.* Contributor of articles and sermons to religious magazines and journals, including *Pulpit, Pulpit Preaching, Pulpit Digest, Together, Christian Century, Motive, Upper Room, Christian Advocate, Church School, Music Ministry,* and *Methodist Story.*

AVOCATIONAL INTERESTS: Reading novels and plays, swimming, tennis, hiking.

*   *   *

DAVIDSON, Mickie (Compere) 1936-
(Mickie Compere, Margaret Davidson)

PERSONAL: Born May 14, 1936, in New York, N.Y.; daughter of Thomas Stephen (an editor) and Ruth (Davis) Compere; married Carson Davidson (a film producer), April 27, 1964. *Education:* Baylor University, B.A., 1958. *Politics:* Democrat. *Home and office:* 86 Bedford St., New York, N.Y. 10014.

CAREER: Ellington Advertising Agency, New York, N.Y., employee, 1958-60; Military Publishing Institute, New York, N.Y., writer, 1960-63; elementary school teacher, New York, N.Y., 1963; juvenile author, 1963—.

WRITINGS—Under name Mickie Compere: *The Story of Thomas A. Edison, Inventor: The Wizard of Menlo Park,* Four Winds, 1966; *Dolphins!,* Four Winds, 1966.

Under name Mickie Davidson: *The Pirate Book,* Random House, 1965; *The Adventures of George Washington,* Four Winds, 1965; *Helen Keller's Teacher,* Four Winds, 1965.

Under pseudonym Margaret Davidson: *Frederick Douglass Fights for Freedom,* Four Winds, 1968; *The Story of Eleanor Roosevelt,* Four Winds, 1969; *Helen Keller,* Hastings House, 1971; *Louis Braille, the Boy Who Invented Books for the Blind,* Hastings House, 1972.

WORK IN PROGRESS: Priscilla, the story of a dolphin, and *Herman,* the story of a pilot whale, both for ages five-eight; *A Gold Doubloon for You, A Gold Doubloon for Me,* an adventure story for ages seven-nine.

SIDELIGHTS: Mickie Davidson, whose mail sometimes comes addressed to Mr. Davidson ("I'm a girl"), writes books for children because "they come naturally to me."

"I like the drama," she adds, "the immediate quality inherent in children's stories . . . . I don't wish to bring a message to *any* book I write, and if I have an urge to educate, I'll write a textbook. Too many writers try to impose their own brand of adult and intangible morality on children. Or they try to keep anything real and perhaps a bit ugly away from children. This to me is insulting—a child is tougher and smarter than this. It is also futile, for children pay little attention to written propaganda.

"Above all, I write children's books because I have a fantastic amount of fun doing it. This to me seems the only valid reason for writing anything."

AVOCATIONAL INTERESTS: Art, especially design elements; collecting recipes, and reading "almost everything."

BIOGRAPHICAL/CRITICAL SOURCES: Young Readers' Review, October, 1966.

*   *   *

DAVIES, David W(illiam) 1908-

PERSONAL: Born May 23, 1908, in Winnipeg, Manitoba, Canada; son of Owen H. and Catherine (McCaffery) Davies; married Thelma E. Stengel (a cataloguer, Francis Bacon Library), November 11, 1936. *Education:* University of California, Los Angeles, B.A., 1932; University of California, Berkeley, B.L.S., 1934, M.A., 1940; University of Chicago, Ph.D., 1947. *Politics:* Democrat. *Home:* 524 West 10th St., Claremont, Calif. 91711. *Office:* Department of Library Science, California State University, Fullerton, Calif. 92631.

CAREER: Huntington Library, San Marino, Calif., staff member, 1936-38; University of California, Bancroft Library, Berkeley, in charge of rare books and manuscripts, 1938-41; Utah State University, Logan, librarian, 1941-43; University of Vermont, Burlington, director of libraries, 1946-47; Claremont Colleges, Claremont, Calif., librarian, 1947-67; Immaculate Heart College, Los Angeles, Calif., professor of library science, 1965-70; California State University, Fullerton, lecturer in library science, 1970—. Senior visiting lecturer, College of Librarianship, Wales, 1967-68; professor of library science, University of Southern California, summers, 1970, 1972. *Military service:* U.S. Army, 1943-45; became first sergeant. *Member:* Renaissance Society of America, Society for British Studies, California Library Association, Zamorano Club (president, 1963—), Grolier Club. *Awards, honors:* Guggenheim fellow, 1963-64.

WRITINGS: A Primer of Dutch 17th Century Overseas Trade, Nijhoff, 1941; *The World of the Elseviers, 1580-1712,* Greenwood Press, 1954; *Dutch Influences on English Culture, 1558-1625,* Cornell University Press, 1964; (editor) Sir Roger Williams, *The Action of the Low Countries,* Cornell University Press, 1964; *Elizabethans Errant: The Strange Fortunes of Sir Thomas Sherley and His Three Sons,* Cornell University Press, 1967; *An Enquiry into the Reading of the Lower Classes,* Castle, 1970; *The Evergreen Tree,* Castle, 1971; (editor with Elizabeth S. Wrigley) *Concordance to the Essays of Francis Bacon,* Holt, 1972. Also author of "Death at La Coruna: The Last Campaign of Sir John Moore," as yet unpublished. Contributor to magazines and journals.

WORK IN PROGRESS: A book on the unbookish activities of librarians.

BIOGRAPHICAL/CRITICAL SOURCES: New York Times Book Review, October 29, 1967.

* * *

DAVIES, John Paton, Jr. 1908-

PERSONAL: Born April 6, 1908, in Kiating, China; son of John Paton and Helen (MacNeil) Davies; married Patricia Grady, August 24, 1942; children: Alexandra, Patricia, John, Susan, Jennifer, Deborah, Megan. *Education:* Attended University of Wisconsin, 1928 and 1929, Yenching University, 1930; Columbia University, B.S., 1931. *Home:* 3646 Cumberland St. N.W., Washington, D.C. 20008.

CAREER: U.S. Department of State, Foreign Service officer, 1932-54, serving in Canada, China, Burma, India, U.S.S.R., Germany, and Peru; Estilo S.A. (furniture manufacturers), Lima, Peru, president 1956-64. *Awards, honors:* Two awards from American Institute of Interior Designers for furniture design.

WRITINGS: Foreign and Other Affairs, Norton, 1964, new edition, with an introduction by Hans J. Morgenthau, 1966; *Dragon by the Tail: American, British, Japanese, and Russian Encounters with China and One Another,* Norton, 1972. Contributor of articles to *New York Times Magazine, Reporter,* and *Harper's.*

* * *

DAVIES, Mansel Morris 1913-

PERSONAL: Born March 24, 1913, in Aberdare, Wales; son of Thomas Morris (a schoolmaster) and Caroline (Thomas) Davies; married Rhiannon Williams, June 25, 1942; children: Huw, Rhodri (sons). *Education:* University College of Wales, University of Wales, B.Sc. (honors), 1933, M.Sc., 1935; Cambridge University, Ph.D.,

1938, Sc.D., 1958. *Home:* Talfan, Buarth Rd., Aberystwyth, Wales.

CAREER: Cambridge University, Cambridge, England, research fellow, 1938-40; teacher of chemistry and physics in Caernarvonshire, Wales, 1940-42; University of Leeds, Leeds, England, research associate, department of biomolecular structure, 1942-47; University College of Wales, University of Wales, Aberystwyth, lecturer, 1947-54, senior lecturer, 1954-61, reader, 1961-68, professor of chemistry, 1968—.

WRITINGS: An Outline of the Development of Science, C.A. Watts, 1948; (with wife, Rhiannon Davies) *Hanes Datblygiad Gwyddoniaeth,* University of Wales Press, 1948; *The Physical Principles of Gas Liquefaction and Low-Temperature Rectification,* Longmans, Green, 1949; (editor and contributor) *Infra-Red Spectroscopy and Molecular Structure: An Outline of the Principles,* Elsevier, 1963; *Some Electrical and Optical Aspects of Molecular Behaviour,* Pergamon, 1965; (editor and contributor) *Dielectric Properties and Molecular Behaviour,* Van Nostrand, 1969; (contributor) *Dielectric and Related Molecular Processes,* Volume I, London Chemistry Society, 1972. Contributor of research articles to professional journals.

* * *

DAVIES, Margaret C(onstance Brown) 1923-

PERSONAL: Born May 4, 1923, in Manchester, England; married Robert Davies (a company director), August 9, 1944; children: Martin, Philippa. *Education:* Attended Queen Mary School, Lytham, England; Somerville College, Oxford, B.A., 1944, M.A., 1949; La Sorbonne, Doctorat de L'Universite de Paris, 1948. *Home:* 10 River Close, Loddon Dr., Wargrave, Berkshire, England. *Office:* Department of French Studies, University of Reading, Reading, England.

CAREER: Harrow County School for Girls, London, England, French mistress, 1951-53; University of Reading, Reading, England, French tutor, 1961-63; Westfield College, University of London, London, England, lecturer in French 1963. University of Reading, lecturer, 1964, reader in French studies, 1969—. Governor of St. Paul's Girls Preparatory School, London. *Member:* P.E.N., Oxford Club.

WRITINGS: Two Gold Rings (novel), Hart-Davis, 1958; *Colette,* Grove, 1961; *Apollinaire,* Oliver & Boyd, 1964, St. Martin's, 1965. Contributor to *French Studies, Times Literary Supplement, French Review, Time and Tide, Listener, La Revue des Lettres Modernes,* and *Review of English Literature.*

WORK IN PROGRESS: A critical biography of Balzac; a full-length study of Rimbaud; articles on Apollinaire and Rimbaud.

AVOCATIONAL INTERESTS: Painting, music, antiques, and travel.

* * *

DAVIES, R(eginald T(horne) 1923-

PERSONAL: Born November 5, 1923, in Weston-super-Mare, England; son of Daniel and Beatrice (Thorne) Davies. *Education:* Alderman Newton's School, Leicester, England, student, 1934-41; Magdalen College, Oxford, M.A., 1948. *Religion:* Church of England. *Office:* University of Liverpool, Liverpool, England.

CAREER: University of Liverpool, Liverpool, England, lecturer, 1948-64, senior lecturer, 1964-67, reader in department of English literature, 1967—, warden of residence hall, and for three years sub-dean of Faculty of Arts. *Military service:* British Army, Royal Artillery, 1942-45; became lieutenant.

WRITINGS: Chaucer's Prologue to the Canterbury Tales, Harrap, 1953; (contributor) K. Muir, editor, *John Keats: A Reassessment,* Liverpool University Press, 1958; (editor) *Medieval English Lyrics: A Critical Anthology,* Faber, 1963, Northwestern University Press, 1964; (contributor) J.A.W. Bennett, editor, *Essays on Malory,* Oxford University Press, 1963; (editor) *Samuel Johnson: Selected Writings,* Northwestern University Press, 1965; (editor) Sir Thomas Malory, *King Arthur and His Nights,* Barnes & Noble, 1967; (translator) *Documents Illustrating the History of Medieval England 1066-1500,* Barnes & Noble, 1969; (editor) *The Corpus Christi Story of the English Middle Ages,* Rowman & Littlefield, 1972. Contributor to professional journals.

WORK IN PROGRESS: "Songs and Lyrics" in revised Cambridge bibliography; *Sir Thomas Malory,* Hutchinson.

AVOCATIONAL INTERESTS: Walking in the country, exploring interesting buildings and places, writing, reading, music, dancing, making and running things.

* * *

DAVIES, Rhys 1903-

PERSONAL: Born November 9, 1903, in Rhondda Valley, Wales; son of Thomas Rhys (a shopkeeper) and Sarah (Lewis) Davies. *Agent:* Curtis Brown Ltd., 13 King St., London W.C.2, England.

CAREER: Writer. Served in War Office, London, England, 1939-45. *Member:* Society of Authors, P.E.N. *Awards, honors:* Edgar Allan Poe Award, Mystery Writers of America, for short story "The Chosen One."

WRITINGS: The Withered Root, Holden, 1927; *A Pig in a Poke,* Joiner & Steele, 1931; *Count Your Blessings,* Putnam, 1932; *The Red Hills,* Putnam, 1932; *Love Provoked,* Putnam, 1933; *Honey and Bread,* Putnam, 1935; *The Things Men Do,* Heinemann, 1936; *A Time to Laugh,* Heinemann, 1937; *My Wales,* Jarrolds, 1937; *Jubilee Blues,* Heinemann, 1938.

Under the Rose, Heinemann, 1940; *Tomorrow to Fresh Woods,* Heinemann, 1941; *A Finger in Every Pie,* Heinemann, 1942; *The Story of Wales,* Collins, 1943; *The Black Venus,* Heinemann, 1944; *The Trip to London,* Heinemann, 1946; *The Dark Daughters,* Heinemann, 1947; *Boy with a Trumpet,* Heinemann, 1949; *Marianne,* Heinemann, 1951; *The Painted King,* Heinemann, 1954; *Collected Stories,* Heinemann, 1955; (with Archibald Batty) *No Escape* (three-act play; adapted from Davies' novel *Under the Race),* Evans Brothers, 1955; *The Perishable Quality,* Heinemann, 1957; *The Darling of Her Heart,* Heinemann, 1958; *Girl Waiting in the Shade,* Heinemann, 1960; *The Chosen One and Other Stories,* Dodd, 1967; *Print of a Hare's Foot: An Autobiographical Beginning,* Dodd, 1969; *Nobody Answered the Bell,* Dodd, 1971. Adapter of several of own novels and short stories for radio and television. Contributor to *New Yorker, House and Garden, Esquire,* and anthologies.

BIOGRAPHICAL/CRITICAL SOURCES: R.L. Megroz, *Rhys Davies,* W. & G. Foyle, 1932; G.F. Adam, *Three Contemporary Anglo-Welsh Novelists,* A. Francke, 1948; *John O' London's,* October 24, 1952; *New Statesman,* April 7, 1967; *Times Literary Supplement,* July 20, 1967; *New York Times Book Review,* August 13, 1967; *Observer Review,* June 22, 1969; *New Yorker,* November 8, 1969.

* * *

DAVIN, D(aniel) M(arcus) 1913-

PERSONAL: Born September 1, 1913, in Invercargill, New Zealand; son of Patrick (a railway worker) and Mary (Sullivan) Davin; married Winifred Gonley (an editor), July 22, 1939; children: Anna Hodgkin, Delia Jenner, Brigid Sanford-Smith. *Education:* Attended

Sacred Heart College, Auckland, New Zealand; Otago University, M.A., Dip. M.A., 1936; Balliol College, Oxford, M.A. *Home:* 103 Southmoor Rd., Oxford, England. *Agent:* David Higham Associates Ltd., 5-8 Lower John St., London W1R 4HA, England. *Office:* Clarendon Press, Walton St., Oxford, England.

CAREER: With Clarendon Press, Oxford, England, 1945—; Oxford University Press, Oxford, England, assistant secretary to the delegates, 1948-70, deputy secretary to the delegates, 1970—. *Military service:* British Army, 1939-40, New Zealand Division, 1940-45; became major; mentioned in dispatches; received the Order of the British Empire. *Member:* P.E.N., Authors Society, Royal Society of Arts (fellow).

WRITINGS: Cliffs of Fall (novel), Nicholson & Watson, 1945; *For the Rest of Our Lives* (novel), Nicholson & Watson, 1947; *The Gorse Blooms Pale* (short stories), M. Joseph, 1947; *Crete,* New Zealand Government War History Department, 1953; *The Sullen Bell* (novel), M. Joseph, 1956; *No Remittance* (novel), M. Joseph, 1947; *Not Here, Not Now* (novel), R. Hale, 1970; *Brides of Price* (novel), Coward, 1973.

Editor: (With John Mulgan) *Introduction to English Literature,* Clarendon Press, 1947; *World Classics: New Zealand Short Stories,* Oxford University Press, 1953; (and author of introduction) *World Classics: Katherine Mansfield's Short Stories,* Oxford University Press, 1953; *English Short Stories of Today,* Oxford University Press and English Association, 1958.

* * *

DAVIS, Christopher 1928-

PERSONAL: Born October 23, 1928, in Philadelphia, Pa.; son of Edward (a lawyer) and Josephine (Blitzstein) Davis; married Sonia Fogg, June 6, 1953; children: Kirby Gray, Katherine Hart, Emily Fogg, Sarah Baldwin. *Education:* University of Pennsylvania, A.B., 1955. *Home:* 6436 Overbrook Ave., Philadelphia, Pa. 19151. *Agent:* William Morris Agency, 1350 Avenue of the Americas, New York, N.Y. 10019.

CAREER: Free-lance writer. Lecturer in creative writing, University of Pennsylvania, 1958-69. *Member:* Authors Guild, P.E.N., Phi Beta Kappa. *Awards, honors:* National Arts Council fellowship; Guggenheim fellowship, 1972-73.

WRITINGS: Lost Summer, Harcourt, 1958; *First Family,* Coward, 1961; *A Kind of Darkness,* Hart-Davis, 1962; *Belmarch: A Legend of the First Crusade,* Viking, 1964; *Sad Adam, Glad Adam,* Crowell-Collier, 1966; *The Shamir of Dachau,* New American Library, 1966: *Ishmael: A Self Portrait,* Cassell, 1967, Harper, 1969; *A Peep into the Twentieth Century,* Harper, 1971; *The Producer,* Harper, 1972. Contributor of stories and essays to *Philadelphia Bulletin, Saturday Evening Post, Esquire, Los Angeles Times,* and *Holiday.*

WORK IN PROGRESS: A Chronicle, a novel, publication by Harper expected in 1974.

SIDELIGHTS: Characterized by a *Time* reviewer as "a painstaking craftsman," Davis is also lauded by Robert Steiner of *Nation* as having the "ability to write boldly of moral matters without ever losing sight of fiction as art." Edmund Fuller describes *Ishmael: A Self Portrait* as "a book of beauty and fascination that does not yield its meanings or intentions easily, or at one reading."

Davis' novel, *A Peep into the Twentieth Century,* has also been well received by critics. D.K. Mano calls it a "brawny, hard, enlightening book—truthful and sad," and D.W. McCullough believes that it is "a novel that demands serious attention. It never entertains, but it is as sparse; as unblinking, even as cruel as an unfaded daguerrotype."

BIOGRAPHICAL/CRITICAL SOURCES: Best Sellers, September 15, 1966; Saturday Review, September 24, 1966, September 4, 1971; New York Times Book Review, October 2, 1966, December 21, 1969, May 30, 1970; Book Week, November 13, 1966; Times Literary Supplement, May 4, 1967; Book World, November 23, 1969; Atlantic, January, 1970; Nation, June 21, 1970; Time, July 19, 1971; New York Times, February 7, 1972.

* * *

DAVIS, Curtis Carrol 1916-

PERSONAL: Born February 18, 1916, in Baltimore, Md.; son of Hoagland Cook (a medical doctor) and Katharine (Carroll) Davis. Education: Yale University, A.B., 1938; Columbia University, M.A., 1939; Duke University, Ph.D., 1947. Politics: Independent. Religion: Roman Catholic. Home and office: A-2, Homewood Apartments, Charles at 31st St., Baltimore, Md. 21218.

CAREER: U.S. Central Intelligence Agency, Washington, D.C., desk chief, 1947-49. Free-lance writer. Star-Spangled Banner Flag House Association, Baltimore, Md., member of directorate. Military service: U.S. Army Air Corps, 1942-46; became captain; received Bronze Star and Presidential Unit Citation. U.S. Army Reserve, Intelligence, 1946-68; now lieutenant colonel (retired). Member: American Studies Association (president, Chesapeake chapter, 1954-55), Society of American Historians, American Historical Association, Maryland Historical Society (library committee, 1964), Virginia Historical Society, North Carolina Literary and Historical Association, Society for the Preservation of Maryland Antiquities.

WRITINGS: Early Historical Novelist Goes to the Library: William A. Chandler and His Readings, 1823-29 New York Public Library, 1948; Chronicler of the Cavaliers: A Life of the Virginia Novelist, Dr. William A. Caruthers, Dietz, 1953; The King's Chevalier: A Biography of Lewis Littlepage, Bobbs-Merrill, 1961; (editor) John S. Wise, The End of an Era, revised edition, A.S. Barnes, 1965; (editor) Belle Boyd in Camp and Prison, revised edition, A.S. Barnes, 1968; (contributor) Louis D. Rubin, Jr., editor, A Bibliographic Guide to the Study of Southern Literature, Louisiana State University Press, 1969; (editor) William A. Caruthers, The Knights of the Golden Horse-Shoe, revised edition, University of North Carolina Press, 1970; That Ambitious Mr. Legare of South Carolina, Including a Collected Edition of His Verse, University of South Carolina Press, 1970.

Contributor to World Book Encyclopedia and Concise Dictionary of American Biography. Contributor of more than forty articles on historical topics to American Heritage, Virginia Cavalcade, Baltimore Sun, Southern Humanities Review, other newspapers and history journals. Editor, annual brochure, Society of the War of 1812 in the State of Maryland.

AVOCATIONAL INTERESTS: Collecting fine, old beer mugs.

BIOGRAPHICAL/CRITICAL SOURCES: Time, August 9, 1968.

* * *

DAVIS, Moshe 1916-

PERSONAL: Born June 12, 1916, in Brooklyn, N.Y.; son of William and Ida (Schenker) Davis; married Lottie Keiser, June 11, 1939; children: Zev (son), Tamar (daughter). Education: Columbia University, B.A., 1937; Jewish Theological Seminary of America, Bachelor of Jewish Pedagogy, 1937, Rabbi and M.H.L., 1942; Hebrew University of Jerusalem, Ph.D., 1946. Address in Israel: Institute of Contemporary Jewry, Hebrew University of Jerusalem, Jerusalem, Israel. Address in U.S.A.: American Jewish History Center, Jewish Theological Seminary of America, 3080 Broadway, New York, N.Y. 10027.

CAREER: Jewish Theological Seminary of America, New York, N.Y., registrar, 1942-46, dean of Teachers Institute, 1946-51, seminary provost, 1950-63, co-director of American Jewish History Center, 1953—, associate professor of American Jewish history, 1956-63, Research Professor, 1963—. Hebrew University of Jerusalem, Jerusalem, Israel, visiting professor, 1959-63, head of Institute of Contemporary Jewry, 1959—, associate professor of American Jewish history, 1963-70, Stephen S. Wise Professor in American Jewish History and Institutions, 1970—. Organizer of conferences for Institute of Contemporary Jewry in Argentina, England, Europe, and Israel, to measure impact of environing culture on Jews and Judaism. Chairman, Committee on Education and Youth, Government Aliyah Absorption Advisory Council, 1969—. Hebrew Arts Foundation, founder and first president. Member: American Jewish Historical Society (vice-president), Histadruth Ivrith of America (former vice-president). Awards, honors: Louis La Med Award in Hebrew Literature, 1953; Guggenheim fellowships, 1956 and 1959.

WRITINGS: (Contributor) L. Finkelstein, editor, The Jews, Harper, 1949, 3rd edition, 1960; Yahadut Amerikah be-hitpathutah (title means "The Shaping of American Judaism"), Jewish Publication Society, 1950; (editor and contributor) Mordecai M. Kaplan Jubilee Volume, two volumes, Jewish Theological Seminary, 1953; Darkhe ha-Yahadut be Amerikah (title means "Jewish Religious Life and Institutions in America"), [Tel Aviv], 1953; (editor) Israel: Its Role in Civilization, Jewish Theological Seminary, 1956; The Synagogue in American Judaism, Monde Publishers, 1957; (editor with Isidore Meyer) The Writing of American Jewish History, American Jewish Historical Society, 1957; The Human Record: Cyrus Adler at the Peace Conference, 1919, privately printed c.1958; (with Victor Ratner) The Birthday of the World, Farrar, Straus, 1959; (contributor) B. Mandelbaum, editor, Assignment in Israel, Harper, 1960; The Emergence of Conservative Judaism: The Historical School in 19th Century America, Jewish Publication Society, 1963; (contributor) Daniel J. Silver, editor, In the Time of Harvest, Macmillan, 1963; (editor with Salo W. Baron and Allan Nevins) Regional History Series of American Jewish History Center, Volume I, 1963, Volumes II-III, 1970; (editor with B. Mazar and H.H Ben Sasson) Illustrated History of the Jews, Harper, 1964; (editor) Publications of the Study Circle on Diaspora Jewry, Series I-IV, 1967-71; (with Isaac Levy) Journeys of the Children of Israel: A Guide to the Study of the Bible, Vallentine Mitchell, 1966, 2nd edition, 1967; (editor) Contemporary Jewish Civilization, three volumes, Random House, 1970; (editor with A. Karp) Text and Studies in American Jewish History, Magnes Press, Volume I, 1970, Volumes II-III, 1971; (contributor) Jewish Existence in an Open Society, Ritchie, 1970; (in Hebrew) From Dependence to Mutuality: The American Jewish Community and World Jewry, Magnes Press, 1970.

Monographs: (With wife, Lottie K. Davis) Land of Our Fathers: Biblical Names in America, Associated American Artists, 1954; Mixed Marriage in Western Jewry: Historical Background to the Jewish Response, 1969. Contributor of monographs to assembly proceedings, articles to historical and social science journals, Encyclopaedia Britannica and Encyclopedia Judaica. Editor of "Eternal Light" program, National Broadcasting Co., radio, 1942-52, and "Frontiers of Faith," National Broadcasting Co., television, 1951-53.

WORK IN PROGRESS: Metamorphosis of the Jewish People; American Settlement in the Holy Land; research in aspects of contemporary world Jewry.

SIDELIGHTS: Davis has traveled to major areas of Jewish residence in England, France, South America and throughout United States and Canada.

* * *

DAVIS, Paxton   1925-

PERSONAL: Born May 7, 1925, in Winston-Salem, N.C.; son of James Paxton (a tobacco executive) and Emily (McDowell) Davis; married Wylma Elizabeth Pooser, June 6, 1951; children: Elizabeth Keith, Anne Beckley, James Paxton III. *Education:* Virginia Military Institute, cadet, 1942-43; Johns Hopkins University, B.A., 1949. *Politics:* Democrat. *Religion:* Presbyterian. *Home:* 703 McMath St., Lexington, Va. *Agent:* Curtis Brown Ltd., 60 East 56th St., New York, N.Y. 10022. *Office:* Department of Journalism, Washington and Lee University, Lexington, Va. 24450.

CAREER: Reporter for *Winston-Salem Journal,* Winston-Salem, N.C., 1949-51, *Richmond Times Dispatch,* Richmond, Va., 1951-52, *Twin City Sentinel,* Winston-Salem, N.C., 1952-53; Washington and Lee University, Lexington, Va., assistant professor, 1953-58, associate professor, 1958-63, professor of journalism, 1963—, head of the department, 1968—. *Military service:* U.S. Army, 1943-46, served two years in China-Burma-India Theater; became sergeant; received two battle stars for Burma campaigns of 1944-45. *Awards, honors:* First place in interpretive reporting, Virginia Press Association, 1951; fellow, Bread Loaf Writers' Conference, 1956; Shenandoah Award for distinguished writing, 1956.

WRITINGS: Two Soldiers: Two Short Novels, Simon & Schuster, 1956; *The Battle of New Market: A Story of VMI,* Little, Brown, 1963; *One of the Dark Places,* Morrow, 1965; *The Seasons of Heroes,* Morrow, 1967. Contributor of short stories to *Playboy, Hopkins Review, Bluebook,* and *Shenandoah,* poems to *Shenandoah* and *Lyric.* Book editor, *Roanoke Times* (Roanoke, Va.), 1961—.

WORK IN PROGRESS: Two novels.

BIOGRAPHICAL/CRITICAL SOURCES: Best Sellers, September 15, 1967; *New York Times Book Review,* September 17, 1967.

* * *

DAVIS, Rex D.   1924-

PERSONAL: Born June 11, 1924, in Skiatook, Okla.; son of Ivan Francis and Ruth (Nabors) Davis; married Patricia M. Humphreys, August 31, 1946; children: Deborah Ruth, Kathleen Marie. *Education:* University of Oklahoma, student, 1942-43, 1946-49, LL.B., 1949. *Home:* 826 Carini Lane, Cincinnati, Ohio 45218. *Office:* Internal Revenue Service, 550 Main St., Cincinnati, Ohio 45202.

CAREER: U.S. Treasury Department, criminal investigator (agent), in McAlester, Okla., 1949-55, part-time law instructor and assistant director at Treasury Law Enforcement School, Washington, D.C., 1953-61, special investigator in Richmond, Va., 1955-58, enforcement examiner on national office staff, Washington, D.C., 1958-62, executive assistant to assistant regional commissioner, Alcohol and Tobacco Tax Division, Internal Revenue Service, Cincinnati, Ohio, 1962-66, assistant regional commissioner, 1966—. *Military service:* U.S. Army Air Forces, 1942-45; flew thirty-three missions with Eighth Air Force, England; became first lieutenant; received Air Medal and Purple Heart. *Member:* International Platform Association, Federal Bar Association, Federal Business Association, Pi Kappa Alpha, Greenhills (Ohio) Golf and Coun-

try Club. *Awards, honors:* William A. Jump Memorial Foundation Meritorious Award for contributions to operating procedures in administering the Alcohol and Tax Division of the Internal Revenue Service.

WRITINGS: Federal Searches and Seizures, C.C Thomas, 1964. Contributor to *Police.*

WORK IN PROGRESS: Research for *The Critical Balance Between Individual Liberties and Effective Law Enforcement;* keeping material current for revision of *Federal Searches and Seizures.*

* * *

DAVIS, Roy Eugene   1931-

PERSONAL: Born March 9, 1931, in Levittsburg, Ohio; son of DeWitt Talmage (a farmer and trucker) and Eva Lee (Carter) Davis; married Patricia A. Neeley, November 15, 1959; married second wife, Carolyn Crosby, June, 1965; children: (first marriage) Jeannette Frances, Clark Edward. *Education:* Attended schools in Ohio. *Politics:* Republican. *Religion:* New Thought. *Residence:* St. Petersburg, Fla.

CAREER: Minister of Self-Realization Fellowship Church, Phoenix, Ariz., 1952-53; ordained minister of Divine Science Church, 1960; now guest lecturer and teacher for Unity, Science of Mind, and other groups in the United States, Japan, and Canada. *Military service:* U.S. Army, 1953-55.

WRITINGS: Time, Space, and Circumstance, privately printed, 1960; *How You Can Use the Technique of Creative Imagination,* privately printed, 1961; *Secrets of Inner Power,* Fell, 1964; *This Is Reality,* CSA Press, 1967, 2nd edition, 1970; *Studies in Truth,* CSA Press, 1969; *God's Revealing Word,* CSA Press, 1969; *The Way of the Initiate,* CSA Press, 1970; *Miracle Man of Japan: The Life and Work of Masaharu Taniguchi,* CSA Press, 1970; *Hidden Teachings of Jesus Revealed,* CSA Press, 1971; *Finding Your Place in Life,* CSA Press, 1971; *How to Have a Personal Experience with God,* CSA Press, 1971; *Reincarnation and Your Life,* CSA Press, 1971; *Sex and the Spiritual Life,* CSA Press, 1971; *Third Eye,* CSA Press, 1971; *Darshan: The Vision of Light,* CSA Press, 1971; *Success Through Superconscious Power,* two books, CSA Press, 1971; *The Bhagavad-Gita,* CSA Press, 1972; *Reincarnation and Your Destiny,* CSA Press, 1972. Contributor of articles to religious and metaphysical journals.

* * *

DAVISON, Kenneth E(dwin)   1924-

PERSONAL: Born May 4, 1924, in East Cleveland, Ohio; son of Gordon Edwin and Mildred (Smith) Davison; married Virginia Nell Rentz, June 14, 1959; children: Robert Edwin, Richard Allen. *Education:* Heidelberg College, A.B., 1946; Western Reserve University, (now Case Western Reserve University), A.M., 1951, Ph.D., 1953. *Politics:* Independent. *Religion:* Presbyterian. *Home:* 125 Hampden Park, Tiffin, Ohio 44883. *Office:* Heidelberg College, Tiffin, Ohio 44883.

CAREER: Heidelberg College, Tiffin, Ohio, assistant professor, 1952-56, associate professor, 1956-59, professor of history, 1959-67, professor of American studies and chairman of the department, 1967—. Bowling Green State University, Bowling Green, Ohio, lecturer, 1960; historian-in-residence, Rutherford B. Hayes Library, 1968-69. *Member:* American Historical Association, Society of American Archivists, American Association of University Professors, Manuscript Society, Society for Historical Archaeology, Society of Architectural Historians, Organization of American Historians, American Studies Association (member of national executive council, 1968—), Canadian Association for American Studies, American

Association for State and Local History, American Association of Museums, Southern Historical Association, Ohio-Indiana American Studies Association (secretary-treasurer, 1957-63; vice-president, 1963-64; president, 1965-66), Ohio Academy of History. *Awards, honors:* Faculty research fellowship, Heidelberg College, 1963-64; American Philosophical Society research grant, 1963-64, 1964-65.

WRITINGS: Cleveland and the Civil War, Ohio State University Press, 1962; *Presidential Papers and Their Use,* [Tiffin, Ohio], 1963; (contributing editor on presidents) *Dictionary of Political Science,* Philosophical Library, 1964; *The Presidency of Rutherford B. Hayes,* Greenwood Press, 1972. Contributor to *Collier's Encyclopedia, American Educator's Encyclopedia, American Quarterly, Ohio History,* and *American Archivist.*

*   *   *

DAVISON, Peter   1928-

PERSONAL: Born June 27, 1928, in New York, N.Y.; son of Edward (a poet) and Natalie (Weiner) Davison; married Jane Auchincloss Truslow, March 7, 1959; children: Edward Angus, Lesley Truslow. *Education:* Harvard University, A.B. (magna cum laude), 1949; Fulbright Scholar, St. John's College, Cambridge University, 1949-50. *Home:* 11 Mellen St., Cambridge, Mass. 02138. *Agent:* Henry Volkening, Russell & Volkening, Inc., 551 Fifth Ave., New York, N.Y. *Office:* Atlantic Monthly Co., 8 Arlington St., Boston, Mass. 02116.

CAREER: U.S. Senate, Washington, D.C., page, 1944; Harcourt, Brace & Co., New York, N.Y., editorial assistant, 1950-51, assistant editor, 1953-55; Harvard University Press, Cambridge, Mass., assistant to director, 1955-56; Atlantic Monthly Press, Boston, Mass., associate editor, 1956-59, executive editor, 1959-64, director, 1964—. Poetry critic, *Atlantic.* Lecturer. *Military service:* U.S. Army, 1951-53. *Member:* Phi Beta Kappa, Harvard Club, Century Association (both New York); Examiner Club, St. Botolph Club, Signet Society (all Boston). *Award, honors:* Yale Series of Younger Poets prize, 1963.

WRITINGS: The Breaking of the Day, and Other Poems, Yale University Press, 1964; *The City and the Island,* Atheneum, 1966; *Pretending to Be Asleep,* Atheneum, 1970. Anthologized in *A Controversy of Poets,* edited by Paris Leary and Robert Kelly, Doubleday-Anchor, 1965, and in several volumes of *Borestone Mountain Poetry Awards.* Contributor of poems and critical essays to *Encounter, Kenyon Review, Partisan Review, Atlantic, New Yorker, Hudson Review, Harper's, Poetry,* and other publications.

WORK IN PROGRESS: Poems.

SIDELIGHTS: In a review of *Pretending to Be Asleep,* Victor Howes states that Davison succeeds in his work "because he is a poet with something to say. Unlike the parrot, or the parodist, who deals only in echoes of things overheard, Peter Davison reads like a man talking to men. He writes about life-and-death concerns, about being aware (awake), and about being unaware (asleep), and about pretending to be asleep when you are really awake. . . .[His] third book of poems is the virtuoso performance of a man trying on a variety of poetic hats in an effort to find one that fits. Fits, that is, for everyday and for all days in all kinds of weathers." Phoebe Adams also praises Davison's work, adding: "[His] poems are the loot of a borderer's raids into the territory between wish and truth, imagination and reality, dream and waking, and they display what is normally half-understood or willfully forgotten. . . .There is edge and bite in all these poems."

BIOGRAPHICAL/CRITICAL SOURCES: New York Times Book Review, December 11, 1966; *Contemporary Literature,* winter, 1968; *Atlantic,* May, 1970; *Christian Science Monitor,* June 4, 1970.

*   *   *

DAWE, Roger David   1934-

PERSONAL: Born September 15, 1934, in Bristol, England; son of Charles Vivian and Louisa (Butler) Dawe; married Kerstin Wallner, November 12, 1961. *Education:* Attended Clifton College; Gonville and Caius College, Cambridge, B.A., 1957, M.A., 1961, Ph.D., 1962. *Office:* Trinity College, Cambridge, England.

CAREER: Cambridge University, Cambridge, England, research fellow in classics at Gonville and Caius College, 1957-63, fellow in classics at Trinity College, 1964—. *Member:* Cambridge Philological Society.

WRITINGS: Investigation and Collation of Manuscripts of Aeschylus, Cambridge University Press, 1964; *Repertory of Conjectures on Aeschylus,* Humanities, 1965. Contributor of articles to scholarly publications.

WORK IN PROGRESS: Literary and textual work on Greek dramatists.

*   *   *

DAY, Beth (Feagles)   1924-
(Elizabeth Feagles)

PERSONAL: Born May 25, 1924, in Fort Wayne, Ind.; daughter of Ralph L. (an engineer) and Mary A. (West) Feagles; married Donald Day, 1945 (divorced, 1960); married Harry Padva, June 15, 1962 (deceased). *Education:* University of Oklahoma, B.A., 1945. *Politics:* Democrat. *Religion:* Presbyterian. *Home:* 35 East 38th St., New York, N.Y. 10016. *Agent:* Paul R. Reynolds & Son, 599 Fifth Ave., New York, N.Y. 10017.

CAREER: Free-lance writer. Teacher of writing in adult education courses. *Member:* Society of Magazine Writers, Authors League of America, Society of Women Geographers.

WRITINGS: (With Donald Day) *Will Rogers, the Boy Roper* (juvenile), Houghton, 1950; *Joshua Slocum, Sailor* (juvenile), Houghton, 1953; *Gene Rhodes, Cowboy* (juvenile), Messner, 1954; *America's First Cowgirl* (juvenile), Messner, 1955; *Little Professor of Piney Woods,* Messner, 1955; (under name Elizabeth Feagles) *Talk Like a Cowboy* (dictionary of Western lingo), Naylor, 1955; *Grizzlies in Their Back Yard* (juvenile), Messner, 1956, reissued as *The World of the Grizzlies,* Doubleday, 1969; *Glacier Pilot,* Holt, 1957; *No Hiding Place,* Holt, 1957; *A Shirttail to Hang to,* Holt, 1959; *This Was Hollywood: An Affectionate History of Filmland's Golden Years,* Doubleday, 1960; *Passage Perilous,* Putnam, 1962; (with Helen Klaben) *Hey, I'm Alive,* McGraw, 1964; (with Tom Pyle) *Pocantico: Fifty Years on the Rockefeller Domain,* Duell, Sloan & Pearce, 1964; (with Frank Wilson) *Special Agent,* Holt, 1965; (with Margaret Liley) *Modern Motherhood,* Random House, 1967, revised edition, 1969; (with Liley) *The Secret World of the Baby,* (juvenile), Random House, 1968; (with Louanne Ferris) *I'm Done Crying,* M. Evans, 1969; (with Jacqui Schiff) *All My Children,* M. Evans, 1971; *Life on a Lost Continent: A Natural History of New Zealand,* Doubleday, 1971; *Sexual Life Between Blacks and Whites: The Roots of Racism,* introduction by Margaret Mead, World Publishing, 1972.

Also author of a television play, "The Man Nobody Wanted" networked on "Four Star Playhouse." Contributor to *Ladies' Home Journal, McCall's, Reader's Digest, Cosmopolitan, Good Housekeeping, Catholic Digest, Parents, Woman's Day, Redbook, New York Times Magazine.*

WORK IN PROGRESS: A book on the influence of slavery on modern society, for World Publishing.

SIDELIGHTS: Mrs. Day's books reflect her special interests—fetology, biography, personalities, travel (in Europe, Caribbean, Mexico, Canada, Alaska, New Zealand, Thailand, Malta, and Japan).

BIOGRAPHICAL/CRITICAL SOURCES: New York Times Book Review, April 21, 1968, November 3, 1968; Saturday Review, February 22, 1969; Best Sellers, February 15, 1971; Writer's Digest, March, 1971.

* * *

DAY, Douglas (Turner III)   1932-

PERSONAL: Born May 1, 1932, in Colon, Republic of Panama; son of Douglas Turner, Jr. (an officer, U.S. Navy) and Bess (Turner) Day; married Mary Hill Noble, July 3, 1954; children: Douglas T. IV, Ian Christopher, Emily Forsyth. Education: University of Virginia, B.A., 1954, M.A., 1959, Ph.D., 1962. Politics: Democrat. Religion: Episcopal. Home: 1616 King Mountain Rd., Charlottesville, Va. 22901. Agent: Peter Matson, Harold Matson Co., Inc., Rockefeller Plaza, New York, N.Y. 10020. Office: Department of English, 530 Cabell Hall, University of Virginia, Charlottesville, Va. 22903.

CAREER: Washington and Lee University, Lexington, Va., instructor in English, 1960-62; University of Virginia, Charlottesville, assistant professor, 1962-64; associate professor of English, 1964—. Military service: U.S. Marine Corps, naval aviator, 1954-57; became first lieutenant. Member: Modern Language Association of America, Phi Beta Kappa. Awards, honors: Fellowships or grants from Folger Shakespeare Library, American Philosophical Society, and American Council of Learned Societies.

WRITINGS: Swifter Than Reason: The Poetry and Criticism of Robert Graves, University of North Carolina Press, 1963; The Stranger: A Critical Commentary, American Research Development Corp., c.1965; (editor with Margaret Lowry) Dark as the Grave Wherein My Friend Is Laid, New American Library, 1968. Contributor of articles to scholarly journals. Former editor of Shenandoah.

WORK IN PROGRESS: The Literary Career of Malcolm Lowry; editing unpublished novel of William Faulkner, Flags in the Dust, for Random House.

BIOGRAPHICAL/CRITICAL SOURCES: Book World, June 30, 1968; Spectator, August 9, 1969.

* * *

DAY, Kenneth   1912-

PERSONAL: Born January 4, 1912, in London, England; married Grace Wagstaff. Education: Attended Stationers' Company School and London School of Printing. Home: The Elephant, Newport, Essex, England. Office: Ernest Benn Ltd., 154 Fleet St., London E.C. 4, England.

CAREER: Ernest Benn Ltd. (publishers), London, England, a director. Chairman, Publishers Association Production Committee, 1969—. Member: National Book League (chairman of printing group, 1956-62), Book Production Managers Group (chairman, 1962-64), Wynkyn de Worde Society (chairman, 1962-63; chairman of publication committee, 1963—), Galley Club (chairman, 1959-60), Paternosters (chairman, 1965), Freeman and Liveryman of the Stationers and Newspaper Makers Co. Awards, honors: Order of the British Empire, 1971.

WRITINGS: The Typography of Press Advertisement, De Graff, 1956; (with Stanley Morison) The Typographic Book 1450-1935, Benn, 1963, University of Chicago Press, 1964; (editor and author of introduction) Book Typography 1815-1965 in Europe and the U.S.A., University of Chicago Press, 1966. Contributor of articles to printing trade journals and graphics periodicals. Editor of Book Design and Production (quarterly), 1961-63.

WORK IN PROGRESS: Copy Preparation.

AVOCATIONAL INTERESTS: Architecture and the arts, book collecting, antiques, country living.

* * *

DEAN, Beryl   1911-

PERSONAL: Born August 2, 1911, in Bromley, Kent, England; daughter of Herbert C. and Marion (Petter) Dean. Education: Royal School of Needlework, teachers diploma, 1932; Bromley College of Art, diploma, 1935; Royal College of Art, associate, 1938. Home: 27 Canonbury Grove, London N.1, England.

CAREER: Teacher of embroidery, dress, and millinery at schools and colleges of art, 1938—. Designer and embroiderer of ecclesiastical vestments and furnishings for Chelmsford, Guildford, and Gloucester Cathedrals, and other churches throughout England. Designer and maker of decor and costumes for several ballet companies in England, 1940-45. Embroideries shown in exhibitions in England, other countries. Lecturer on aspects of embroidery in England, and on U.S. tour, 1962. Member: World Craft Council (British council), Craft Center of Great Britain, Embroiderers' Guild (council).

WRITINGS: Ecclesiastical Embroidery, Branford, 1958; (contributor) Handbook of Crafts, Edward Hulton, 1960; Church Needlework, Batsford, 1961, Branford, 1962; Ideas for Church Embroidery, Batsford, 1968; Creative Applique, Watson, 1970. Contributor of articles on church embroidery to Embroidery, Church Maintenance and Equipment News, and other publications.

WORK IN PROGRESS: Research into the history of church embroidery; collecting information on examples of contemporary embroidery in relation to contemporary churches.

AVOCATIONAL INTERESTS: Interior decorating, gardening.

* * *

de BEDTS, Ralph F(ortes)   1914-

PERSONAL: Born March 4, 1914, in Kearny, N.J.; son of Charles (an accountant) and Bertha (Fortes) de Bedts; married Elizabeth M. Seelinger (a librarian), May 23, 1963. Education: University of Miami, Coral Gables, Fla., B.B.A., 1950, M.A., 1957; University of Florida, Ph.D., 1960. Home: 1123 Manchester Ave., Norfolk, Va. 23508. Office: Department of History, Old Dominion University, Norfolk, Va. 23508.

CAREER: Dade County Board of Commissioners, Miami, Fla., chief accountant, 1947-57; University of Florida, Gainesville, assistant instructor, 1958-60; Old Dominion University (formerly Old Dominion College), Norfolk, Va., assistant professor, 1960-63, associate professor, 1963-65, professor of history and chairman of the department, 1966—, director of graduate studies, 1966-67. Fulbright Lecturer in American History, University of Hong Kong, 1964. Military service: U.S. Army, 1941-42. Member: American Historical Association, American Studies Association, Organizaton of American Historians, American Association of University Professors (chapter president, 1963), Society of Historians of American Foreign Policy, Southern Historical Association, Phi Beta Kappa. Awards, honors: American Philosophical Society grants, 1966, 1967.

WRITINGS: The New Deal's SEC: The Formative Years, Columbia University Press, 1964; The United

States Since 1933, Dorsey, 1973. Contributor to *American Journal of Economics and Sociology.*

WORK IN PROGRESS: A figure study of General Hugh S. Johnson and the New Deal, tentatively titled *Old Ironpants.*

* * *

DECHANT, Emerald V (ictor) 1926-

PERSONAL: Born April 26, 1926, in Antonino, Kan.; son of Cornelius J. (a businessman) and Ursula (Legleiter) Dechant; married Deloris Milke, 1952; children: Randy, Lorianne, Pamela. *Education:* Pontifical College Josephinum, A.B., 1948; Fort Hays Kansas State College, M.S., 1955; University of Kansas, Ph.D., 1958. *Home:* 613 Briarcliff, Salina, Kan. 67401.

CAREER: High school teacher, 1954-56; University of Wichita, Wichita, Kan., director of language arts, 1958-59; Fort Hays Kansas State College, Hays, assistant professor, 1959-62, associate professor and director of guidance and counseling, 1962-64, professor of education and director of counseling center, 1964-70; Marymount College, Salina, Kan., president, 1970—. *Military service:* U.S. Army, 1952-54; psychiatric social worker. *Member:* International Platform Association, National Education Association, American Personnel and Guidance Association (former president of Kansas branch), International Reading Association, Kansas State Teachers Association, Phi Delta Kappa, Knights of Columbus (Hays; former grand knight), Lions International.

WRITINGS: (With Henry P. Smith) *Psychology in Teaching Reading,* Prentice-Hall, 1961, 2nd edition, 1970; *Improving the Teaching of Reading,* Prentice-Hall, 1964, 2nd edition, 1970; *Diagnosis and Remediation of Reading Disability,* Parker Publishing, 1968; *Linguistics, Phonics and the Teaching of Reading,* C.C Thomas, 1969; (editor) *Detection and Correction of Reading Difficulties,* Appleton, 1971; *How to Be Happily Married,* Alba, 1972; *Reading Improvement in the Secondary School,* Prentice-Hall, 1973. Also co-author of "Listen and Read," a series of tapes and accompanying workbook for high schools and colleges, prepared for Educational Development Laboratories, 1961.

SIDELIGHTS: Reads six foreign languages, speaks two.

* * *

DECKER, Leslie E (dward) 1930-

PERSONAL: Born June 14, 1930, in Wellington, Me.; son of Laurence Franklin (an engineer) and Velma (Pushor) Decker; married Eva Lois Wildes, September 11, 1948; children: Margurite Velma, Laurence John. *Education:* University of Maine, B.A., 1951; Oklahoma State University of Agriculture and Applied Science, M.A., 1952; Cornell University, 1952-55, Ph.D., 1961. *Agent:* The Sterling Lord Agency, 660 Madison Ave., New York, N.Y. 10021. *Office:* History Department, University of Oregon, Eugene, Ore. 97403.

CAREER: Cornell University, Ithaca, N.Y., research fellow, Social Science Research Center, 1955-56; *Wisconsin Magazine of History,* Madison, editor, 1956-57; free-lance editor, Salem, Me., 1957-58; State University College at Potsdam, Potsdam, New York, assistant professor of history, 1958-61; University of Maine, Orono, assistant professor, 1961-66, associate professor, 1967-69; University of Oregon, Eugene, professor of history, 1969—. Consultant, and editor of books on American history for academic and commercial publication, 1957—. *Member:* Organization of American Historians, American Historical Association, Economic History Association, Agricultural History Society, Business History Association.

WRITINGS: *Railroads, Lands, and Politics: The Taxation of the Railroad Land Grants, 1864-1897,* Brown University Press, 1964; (with Forrest McDonald) *The Torch Is Passed: A History of the United States in the Twentieth Century,* Addison-Wesley, 1968; (with McDonald and Thomas P. Govan) *The Last Best Hope: A History of the United States,* two volumes, Addison-Wesley, 1972; (with Robert Seager II) *America's Major Wars: Crusaders, Critics, and Scholars,* two volumes, Addison-Wesley, 1973. Contributor of articles to historical journals and festschriften.

WORK IN PROGRESS: A book of essays on the peopling and politics of the mid-continent country, tentatively titled *Pioneers, Promoters, and Politicians,* for completion in 1974; research in the history of rural abandonment in New England, leading to one or more books and several articles.

SIDELIGHTS: Decker told *CA:* "My writing and editing, like my teaching, is an exercise in translation. Learning and understanding I do for my own satisfaction. Communicating what I have learned I do in an attempt to pay the debt I owe to the society I live in, a society that not only permits me but actually pays me to follow my curiosity wherever it leads." *Avocational interests:* Hunting, fishing, sailing, carpentry and cabinetry, smoking a pipe; enjoying good music, drama, food and drink; and reading everything—good, bad, and indifferent—within reach.

* * *

DeCRISTOFORO, R (omeo) J (ohn) 1917- (R.J. Cristy, Cris Williams)

PERSONAL: Born April 28, 1917, in New York, N.Y.; married Mary A. Ferrari (a writer and artist), June 7, 1942; children: Daniel Taft, David, Ronald John. *Education:* Special courses in universities. *Home:* 27861 Natoma Rd., Los Altos Hills, Calif. 94022.

CAREER: Sometime inspector of experimental aircraft, director of education materials for Magna Engineering Corp., and teacher of arts and crafts; combined two hobbies (writing and manual arts) to become free-lance writer on manual arts, 1946—. *Awards, honors:* Short story award, *Writer's Digest* contest.

WRITINGS: *Power Tool Woodworking for Everyone,* McGraw, 1953, reissued as *Modern Power Tool Woodworking,* Magna Publications, 1967; *The New Handy Man's Carpentry Guide,* Fawcett, 1959; *Handy Man's Concrete and Masonry Handbook,* Arco, 1960; *Home Carpentry Handbook,* Fawcett, 1960; *How to Choose and Use Power Tools,* Arco, 1960 (also published under title *Mechanix Illustrated: How to Choose and Use Power Tools,* Fawcett, 1960); *Fun with a Saw,* McGraw, 1961; *Concrete and Masonry Ideas for the Homeowner,* Fawcett, 1962; *Mechanix Illustrated: The How-to Book of Carpentry,* Fawcett, 1963, reissued as *The How-to Book of Carpentry,* Arco, 1966; *How-to Book of Concrete and Masonry,* Fawcett, 1964; *How to Build Your Own Furniture,* Harper, 1965; *The Practical Book of Carpentry,* Arco, 1969; *De Cristoforo's Complete Book of Power Tools,* Popular Science, 1972. Contributor of poetry and fiction, and of more than a thousand how-to articles to magazines, including *Popular Science, Popular Mechanics, Better Homes and Gardens.*

AVOCATIONAL INTERESTS: Photography; art, including charcoal nudes and portraits.

* * *

DEDMON, Emmett 1918-

PERSONAL: Born April 16, 1918, in Auburn, Neb.; son of Roy Emmett and Cora (Frank) Deadman; married

Claire Lyons, June 19, 1945; children: Jonathan. *Education:* University of Chicago, A.B., 1939. *Religion:* Lutheran. *Office: Chicago Sun-Times* and *Chicago Daily News,* 401 North Wabash Ave., Chicago, Ill. 60611.

CAREER: Chicago Times, Chicago, Ill., assistant foreign editor, 1940-41; *Chicago Sun,* Chicago, Ill., columnist, critic, and editor of literary supplement, *Book Week,* 1946-47; *Chicago Sun-Times,* Chicago, Ill., literary editor, 1947-50, drama critic, 1950-53, assistant Sunday editor, 1953-55, assistant managing editor, 1955-58, managing editor, 1958-62, executive editor, 1962-65, editor, 1965-68; *Chicago Sun Times* and *Chicago Daily News,* Chicago, Ill., vice-president and editorial director, 1968—. Young Men's Christian Association of Metropolitan Chicago, former president and member of board of managers; trustee, Chicago Historical Society, University of Chicago, and George M. Pullman Educational Fund. Director of Welfare Council of Metropolitan Chicago, National Academic Council of Valparaiso University, Northwestern University Associates, and of Chicago Chapter of American National Red Cross. *Military service:* U.S. Army Air Forces, 1940-45; became captain; received Air Medal, European Ribbon with two Bronze Stars, American Theater Ribbon with Bronze Star. *Member:* American Society of Newspaper Editors, Society of American Historians, Society of Midland Authors, Chicago Press Club, Air Force Association, Sigma Delta Chi, Phi Kappa Psi, Chicago Club, Tavern Club, Economic Club, Arts Club.

WRITINGS: Duty to Live, Houghton, 1946; *Fabulous Chicago,* Random House, 1953; *Great Enterprises,* Rand McNally, 1957; *A History of the Chicago Club,* Chicago Club, 1960.

*   *   *

DeFERRARI, Sister Teresa Mary   1930-

PERSONAL: Born February 21, 1930, in Washington, D.C., daughter of Roy Joseph (an educator) and Evelyn M. (Biggi) DeFerrari. *Education:* Dunbarton College, A.B., 1951; St. Mary's School of Theology, Notre Dame, Ind., M.A., 1958; Catholic University of America, Ph.D., 1962. *Politics:* Democrat. *Office:* Department of Theology, St. John's University, Jamaica, N.Y. 11432.

CAREER: Roman Catholic nun of Holy Cross order, name in religion, Sister Teresa Mary; Dunbarton College, Washington, D.C., member of faculty; St. John's University, Jamaica, N.Y., member of faculty of theology department. *Member:* Catholic Biblical Association of America (associate member), Society of Catholic College Teachers of Sacred Doctrine.

WRITINGS: The Problem of Charity for Self: A Study of Thomistic and Modern Theological Discussion, Daughters of St. Paul, 1960, also published as *The Problem of Charity for Self: A Study of the Doctrine and Its Presentation to College Students,* St. Paul Editions, 1962. Contributor to religious and education journals.

WORK IN PROGRESS: Writing for *New Catholic Encyclopedia.*

SIDELIGHTS: Sister Teresa Mary is competent in Latin, Greek, French, German and Italian.

*   *   *

DeFREES, Sister Madeline   1919-
(Sister Mary Gilbert)

PERSONAL: Born November 18, 1919, in Ontario, Ore.; daughter of Clarence C. and Mary T. (McCoy) DeFrees. *Education:* Maryhurst College, B.A., 1948; University of Oregon, M.A., 1951. *Politics:* Democrat. *Home:* 1310 Gerald # 5, Missoula, Mont. 59801. *Office:* Department of English, University of Montana, Missoula, Mont. 59801.

CAREER: Entered Roman Catholic order of Sisters of the Holy Names of Jesus and Mary, 1936; elementary school teacher in Bend, Coos Bay, and Portland, Ore., 1938-42; high school teacher in Medford and The Dalles, Ore., 1943-49; Fort Wright College, Spokane, Wash., began as instructor, 1950, associate professor of English and journalism, 1963-67; University of Montana, Missoula, visiting associate professor, 1967-69, associate professor of English, 1969—. *Member:* American Association of University Women, Theta Sigma Phi. *Awards, honors:* Litt.D., Gonzaga University, 1959.

WRITINGS: The Springs of Silence, Prentice-Hall, 1953; *Later Thoughts from the Springs of Silence,* Bobbs-Merrill, 1962; *From the Darkroom* (poetry), Bobbs-Merrill, 1964. Works anthologized in *Best Poems of 1960* and *Best Poems of 1965* (Borestone Mountain Poetry Awards), Pacific Books, 1962, 1966, and *Best American Short Stories, 1962,* edited by Martha Foley and David Burnett, Houghton, 1962. Contributor to journals and magazines, including *America, New American Review, Poetry Northwest, Sewanee Review, Northwest Review, New Republic, Nation.*

WORK IN PROGRESS: A second volume of poems.

*   *   *

de GRUNWALD, Constantine

PERSONAL: Born in St. Petersburg, Russia; children: Anatole, Dmitri (both motion picture producers). *Education:* Attended University of St. Petersburg. *Religion:* Orthodox. *Home:* 23, rue Fortuny, Paris XVII, France. *Agent:* Odette Arnaud, 12, rue de Teheran, Paris VIII, France.

CAREER: Writer. Has lectured at Oxford University, University of London and University of Nottingham. *Military service:* Imperial Russian Army; received St. George Medal. *Awards, honors:* Laureat de l'Academie Francaise; laureat de l'Institut de France.

WRITINGS: Stein, L'ennemi de Napoleon, Grasset, 1936, translation by Charles Francis Atkinson published as *Napoleon's Nemesis: The Life of Baron Stein,* Scribner, *1936* (published in England as *Baron Stein, Enemy of Napoleon,* J. Cape, 1936); *La Vie de Metternich,* Calmann-Levy, 1938, translation by Dorothy Todd published as *Metternich,* Falcon Press, 1953; *Portrait de la Hongrie,* Plon, 1939.

Trois siecles de diplomatie russe, Calmann-Levy, 1945; *La Vie de Nicolas Ier,* Calmann-Levy, 1946 translation by Brigit Patmore published as *Tsar Nicholas I,* MacGibbon & Kee, 1954, Macmillan, 1955; *Bismarck,* Albin-Michel, 1949.

Le Duc de Gramont, gentilhomme et diplomate, Hachette, 1950; *La Russie de Pierre le Grand,* Hachette, 1953, translation by Viola Garvin published as *Peter the Great,* Macmillan, 1956; *Alexandre Ier, le tsar mystique,* Amiot-Dumont, 1955; *Quand la Russie avait des saints,* Fayard, 1958, translation by Roger Capel published as *Saints of Russia,* Macmillan, 1960.

L'Assassinat de Paul Ier, tsar de Russie, Hachette, 1960; *La Vie Religieuse en U.R.S.S.,* Plon, 1961, translation by G.J. Robinson-Pashevsky published as *God and the Soviets,* Hutchinson, 1961, published in America as *The Churches and the Soviet Union,* Macmillan, 1962; *La Vraie histoire de Boris Godounov,* Fayard, 1961; *Le Tsar Alexandre II et son temps,* Berger-Levrault, 1963; *Histoire de Moscou et des Moscovites,* Pont-Royal, 1963; *La Campagne de Russie,* Julliard, 1964; *Les Alliances Franco-Russe: Neuf siecles de malentendus,* Plon, 1965; *Le Tsar Nicholas II,* Berger-Levrault, 1965; *Louis II, le roi romantique,* P. Waleffe, 1967; (author of essay) *Friedrich der Grosse,* Marion von Schroeder, c.1967; *His-*

toire du peuple russe, P. Waleffe, 1968; *Les Nuits blanches de Saint-Petersbourg,* Berger-Levrault, 1968. Contributor to *Revue des Deux Mondes, Miroir de l'Histoire, Horizon,* and other periodicals.

* * *

DEIGHTON, Len 1929-

PERSONAL: Born February 18, 1929, in Marylebone, London, England; married Shirley Thompson (an illustrator), 1960. *Education:* Attended Marylebone Grammar School; studied at St. Martin's School of Art, London, three years; Graduate of the Royal College of Art. *Residence:* London, England.

CAREER: Has worked as a railway lengthman, as an assistant pastry cook at the Royal Festival Hall, 1951 (which led him to the writing of a syndicated cooking column), a manager of a gown factory in Aldgate, a waiter in Piccadilly, an advertising man in London and New York, a teacher in Brittany, a co-proprietor of a glossy magazine, and as a magazine artist and news photographer; worked as a B.O.A.C. steward, 1956-57; founded Continuum 1, a literary agency, in London; producer of motion pictures, including "Only When I Larf," based on his own novel, 1968, was originally a producer of "Oh What a Lovely War," but withdrew.

WRITINGS: The Ipcress File (novel), Fawcett, 1962; *Horse Under Water* (novel), J. Cape, 1963, (Literary Guild selection), Putnam, 1967; (editor) *Drinks-man-ship: Town's Album of Fine Wines and High Spirits,* Haymarket Press (London), 1964; *Funeral in Berlin* (novel), J. Cape, 1964, Putnam, 1965; *Ou est le garlic; or, Len Deighton's French Cookbook* (includes 50 cookstrips), Penguin, 1965; *Action Cookbook: Len Deighton's Guide to Eating,* J. Cape, 1965; *Len Deighton's Cookstrip Cookbook,* Bernard Geis Associates, 1966; *The Billion Dollar Brain* (novel), Putnam, 1966; *An Expensive Place to Die,* (novel), Putnam, 1967; (compiler and designer with Michael Rand and Howard Loxton) *The Assassination of President Kennedy,* J. Cape, 1967; (compiler and contributor) *Len Deighton's London Dossier,* J. Cape, 1967; *Only When I Larf* (novel; originally a screenplay, produced by Paramount, 1968), Sphere Books, 1968; *Len Deighton's Continental Dossier: A Collection of Cultural, Culinary, Historical, Spooky, Grim and Preposterous Fact,* compiled by Victor and Margaret Pettitt, M. Joseph, 1968; *Bomber: Events Relating to the Last Flight of an R.A.F. Bomber over Germany on the Night of Je. 31, 1943* (novel), Harper, 1970; *Declarations of War,* J. Cape, 1971; *Close-Up,* Atheneum, 1972.

Writer of weekly comic strip on cooking for Sunday *Observer,* 1962—. Also wrote one of the original filmscripts for "From Russia with Love"; wrote screenplay for "Oh! What a Lovely War," produced by Paramount, 1969 (as a result of difference of opinion with director, Deighton had his name removed from credits).

SIDELIGHTS: Deighton told a *Tatler* interviewer: "Basically I am not a writer, but I am interested in narration and in the pattern of events. The pleasure of a book is, I feel, more important than the syntax. The thriller gives one a good, bold pattern, a geometric shape."

Each of his books is done in six or eight drafts and takes a year of continuous work. "I type masterpieces," he says, "and the machines turn out crap: I am not interested in producing the greatest best-sellers or acquiring a large number of readers. I am happy to acquire a strong rapport from a smaller number."

Deighton's books, however, have been extremely successful, and many have been on the best-seller lists in England and America. He chose a spy format, he said, because of the political possibilities he could incorporate. For each book he does "a lot of painstaking personal investigation and research," writes Hugh Moffett. "He finds his most valuable details still come from travel and from association with people who know what they are talking about. His travels in Communist countries have exposed him to the thongs of Communist bureaucracy. Once he was hauled into police barracks in Czechoslovakia when he neglected to renew his visa. In Riga, Latvia, he could obtain no map of the city—and his style demands accurate geography—so he drew one. (I was a little neurotic about having that document on me,' he says.)" Moffett writes that Deighton keeps notebooks, and in one of them he wrote: " 'Few writers are ever completely happy with a manuscript, but finally they abandon it to a publisher and it appears in print. Several years of syntax polishing might produce a hymn to literacy, but all too often the initial dynamic vulgarity is lost. Knowing the time to abandon the tickling up process is an important part of a writer's skill.' "

All of his books, from *The Ipcress File* to his most recent, have involved suspense in some way. He began with a spy story. R.D. Spector writes of *The Ipcress File:* "Len Deighton has combined picaresque satire, parody and suspense and produced a hybrid more humorous than thrilling. Inevitably, his comedic attack on modern espionage agencies and his burlesque of the fictional techniques of Ambler, Fleming, and Greene reduce the intensity and intrigue of his narrative. . . . Where Deighton allows his humor to dominate, he is bitingly and savagely funny. He recognizes that the spy—whose survival depends on his guile, cunning, and adaptability— is today's picaro." *Funeral in Berlin* continues in this tradition, as Sergeant Cuff says, a "sure-footed, and thoroughly adult espionage number." The *New York Times* called it "a ferociously cool fable of the current struggle between East and West. . . ."

J.V. D'Anna praises *The Billion Dollar Brain:* "Len Deighton's writing manifests that the art of constructing a lucid, logical plot still has some future in English fiction. . . . It is a very good show: Deighton's dialogue suits his characters who become flesh as they speak, and his descriptions of various locales are original." The same nameless spy who is the main character in his previous books also appears in *An Expensive Place to Die.* Anthony Boucher writes: "Len Deighton is always a pleasure to read. He offers crisp prose, fast action, vivid scenes and an anonymous agent-narrator whose attitude is cynical, professional and completely of the 1960's. . . . [This book] has a good unified workable plot . . . [and] is easily Deighton's second-best novel; and second place after 'Funeral' is no real disgrace." This book was thought by many to be more tightly constructed than his others.

Only When I Larf is a suspense story which involves confidence tricksters rather than spies. It is a slight departure for Deighton. Still suspenseful, but in a different way, is *Bomber.* William McPherson says that this "is Deighton's 'big' book. It is not really a suspense novel in the usual sense, but there is a definite tension experienced. As Robert Maurer comments: "As the sickening tension mounts, a reader cares not about who will be the vanquished, who the victor, but about when, if ever, all such journeys of destruction will cease." McPherson says that the novel is "not so much a novel about people as it is about machines and the ineluctable force of technology." He finds that it is "overlong, overpopulated and underedited." But, he continues, "persevere, and don't worry about keeping the characters straight and the facts sorted, for despite its gross faults the final impact of *Bomber* stuns. I have never been in a war but having just read *Bomber* I feel shell shocked and battle-fatigued, and I was moved beyond tears."

Close-Up is a departure for Deighton. It is not a suspense novel, but takes place in Hollywood. A *Times Literary Supplement* reviewer comments: "The film industry is in many ways the ideal subject for Mr. Deighton's talents. In a business so obsessed with surface he can exploit his eye for what one might (reluctantly) call the 'furniture' of the world.... Mr. Deighton seems to have ... settled down to what he does best: reporting, lucidly, and readably, on what his imagination sees."

Deighton's books are well-supplied with footnotes and appendices which explain secret channels and undercover organizations. His knowledge of military history and weapons is encyclopedic. He is an expert rifle and pistol shot, as well as an experienced frogman. He travels widely and is reputed to have a special knowledge of and contacts in Havana, Darwin, Macao, Casablanca, Tokyo, and Anchorage.

The Ipcress File was filmed by Universal, 1965; *Funeral in Berlin* was produced by Paramount, 1966; *Billion Dollar Brain* was produced by United Artists, 1967; *Only When I Larf* was released by Paramount, 1968; *An Expensive Place to Die* has been purchased for filming.

BIOGRAPHICAL/CRITICAL SOURCES: *Book Week*, November 17, 1963, May 1, 1966, May 7, 1967; *Wine and Food*, autumn, 1964; *Tatler*, November 4, 1964; *Saturday Review*, January 30, 1965; *Newsweek*, January 31, 1966, June 26, 1972; *Life*, March 25, 1966; *Playboy*, May, 1966; *Observer Review*, March 26, 1967, May 14, 1967; *National Observer*, April 24, 1967, February 12, 1968; *New Statesman*, May 12, 1967; *New York Times Book Review*, May 21, 1967, January 14, 1968, October 4, 1970; *Times Literary Supplement*, June 1, 1967, June 22, 1967, September 25, 1970, June 16, 1972; *Books & Bookmen*, September, 1967; *New Yorker*, February 3, 1968; *Book World*, February 4, 1968, September 22, 1970, June 25, 1972; *Listener*, April 11, 1968; *Bookseller*, September 19, 1970; *Washington Post*, October 9, 1970; *New York Times*, October 17, 1970; *Books*, November, 1970; *Atlantic*, December, 1970; *Variety*, June 21, 1972.

*   *   *

DEINDORFER, Robert Greene   1922-
(Jay Bender, Jay Dender, Robert Greene)

PERSONAL: Born July 3, 1922, in Galena, Ill.; son of Charles Robert and Marion (Greene) Deindorfer; married Joan Brown (in public relations work), May 4, 1963. *Education:* University of Missouri, student, 1940-43. *Politics:* Democrat. *Religion:* Episcopalian. *Home:* 114 East 71st St., New York, N.Y. 10021. *Agent:* Sterling Lord Agency, 660 Madison Ave., New York, N.Y. 10021. *Office:* Booke & Co., 919 Third Ave., New York, N.Y. 10022.

CAREER: Free-lance magazine writer, 1949—; New York Stock Exchange, New York, N.Y., magazine manager, 1955-70; Booke & Co., New York, N.Y., magazine director, 1970—. New York University, New York, N.Y., teacher of course in magazine writing, 1960-61. Peace Corps, consultant, 1961-65; City of New York, public relations adviser. *Wartime service:* U.S. Marine Corps, 1942-43. U.S. Merchant Marine, 1944. *Member:* Society of Magazine Writers, National Press Club, New York University Faculty Club.

WRITINGS: *The Great Gridiron Plot*, Whitman, 1946; *True Spy Stories*, Crest Books, 1961; (with George Ratterman) *Confessions of a Gypsy Quarterback*, Coward, 1962; (with Robert Rowan) *Secret Service: 33 Centuries of Espionage*, revised edition, Hawthorn, 1967; (editor) *The Spies*, Fawcett, 1969. Contributor to *Redbook*, *Ladies' Home Journal*, *Life*, *Look*, *Reader's Digest*, *Good Housekeeping*, *This Week*, *Cosmopolitan*, *Nation's Busi-

ness, Pageant, Saturday Review, Parade, Saturday Evening Post, True, Argosy.*

WORK IN PROGRESS: Two books on espionage; magazine articles.

SIDELIGHTS: Research for articles has taken Deindorfer to Europe a number of times, to the Middle East, and to Africa (once for an eighteen-month period).

*   *   *

DeKRUIF, Paul (Henry)   1890-1971

PERSONAL: Surname pronounced da Krife; born March 2, 1890, in Zeeland, Mich.; son of Hendrik (a farm implement dealer) and Hendrika J. (Kremer) deKruif; first marriage ended in divorce; married Rhea Elizabeth Barbarin, December 11, 1922 (died, 1957); married Eleanor Lappage, September 1, 1959; children: (first marriage) Hendrik, David. *Education:* University of Michigan, B.S., 1912, Ph.D., 1916. *Home:* Wake Robin, Holland, Mich.

CAREER: University of Michigan, Ann Arbor, assistant professor of bacteriology, 1916-17; Pasteur Institute, Paris, researcher, 1918; Rockefeller Institute for Medical Research, New York, N.Y., associate in pathology, 1920-22; free-lance writer and popularizer of medical science, 1922-71. Former consultant to Chicago Board of Health, Michigan State Health Department. National Foundation for Infantile Paralysis, secretary of general scientific committee, 1940; President's Birthday Ball Commission for Infantile Paralysis Research, co-founder, 1934, and longtime secretary. *Military service:* U.S. Army, Sanitary Corps, 1917-18; served in France; became captain.

WRITINGS: (Contributor), *Civilization in the United States: An Inquiry by Thirty Americans*, Harold Stearns, editor, Harcourt, 1922; *Our Medicine Men* (collection of articles from *Century* magazine), Century, 1922; (collaborator on medical background) Sinclair Lewis, *Arrowsmith*, Harcourt, 1925; *Microbe Hunters*, Harcourt, 1926 published as *Dr. Ehrlich's Magic Bullet and the Discoveries of Eleven Other Microbe Hunters*, Pocket Books, 1940; *Hunger Fighters*, Harcourt, 1928; *Seven Iron Men*, Harcourt, 1929; *Men Against Death*, Harcourt, 1932; (with Sidney Howard) *Yellow Jack* (play, produced in New York, 1934), Harcourt, 1933; (with wife, Rhea deKruif) *Why Keep Them Alive?*, Harcourt, 1936; *The Fight for Life*, Harcourt, 1938; *Toward a Healthy America*, Public Affairs Committee, 1939; *Activities of the National Foundation for Infantile Paralysis in the Field of Virus Research*, National Foundation for Infantile Paralysis, 1939; *Health Is Wealth*, Harcourt, 1940; *Kaiser Wakes the Doctors*, Harcourt, 1943; *The Male Hormone*, Harcourt, 1945; (with R. deKruif) *Life among the Doctors*, Harcourt, 1949; *A Man against Insanity*, Harcourt, 1957; *The Sweeping Wind, a Memoir*, Harcourt, 1962.

Regular contributor to Curtis Publishing Co. magazines, including *Country Gentlemen*, *Ladies' Home Journal*, 1925-1971; *Reader's Digest*, contributing editor, 1940-71. Contributor to other magazines.

SIDELIGHTS: *The Microbe Hunters* and *The Hunger Fighters* both were best sellers, with the former selling more than a million copies in a total of eighteen languages. *Yellow Jack* was made into a motion picture by Metro-Goldwyn-Mayer, 1938 and produced on radio by The Theatre Guild, 1946; a Pare Lorentz film of *Fight for Life* was made by Columbia, 1940; "Dr. Ehrlich's Magic Bullet," based on *The Microbe Hunters*, was filmed by Warner Bros., 1940.

BIOGRAPHICAL SOURCES: *Newsweek*, August 26, 1940; *Reader's Digest*, December, 1946, January, 1947;

Paul Henry deKruif, *Sweeping Winds, a Memoir,* Harcourt, 1962 Detroit Free Press, March 2, 1971; New York Times, March 2, 1971; Washington Post, March 3, 1971.

(Died February 28, 1971)

* * *

de LAUNAY, Jacques F(orment) 1924-

PERSONAL: Born January 28, 1924, in Roubaix, France; son of Jean (an industrialist) and Maria (Herman) de Launay; married December 21, 1950, wife's maiden name, Delcroix; children: Marie-Christine. *Education:* University of Lille, Licence en Droit; University of Paris, advanced study in political science. *Religon:* Roman Catholic. *Home:* Faisanderie 68, Brussels, Belgium. *Agent:* Gheysens, Pecheries, 78, Brussels, Belguim. *Office:* Helene Boucher, 2, Marcq-en-Baroeul, Nord, France.

CAREER: French Government, Paris, France, attached to Office of Minister of Public Health, 1946-47; European Movement, Brussels, Belgium, deputy secretary, 1948-51; European Bureau for Youth and Childhood, Brussels, general manager, 1950-63; Transassim-France, Marcq-en-Baroeul, France, general manager, 1960—. *Military service:* French Army, volunteer, 1944-45. *Awards, honors:* Medaille de la Resistance.

WRITINGS: Le Monde en guerre, 1939-1945, J.B. Janin, 1945; (with Claude Murat) *Jeunesse d'Europe,* introduction by Andre Gide, France-Empire, 1948; *Fascisme rouge: Contribution a la defense de l'Europe,* Editions Montana, 1954; *The Vocational Training of Young Agricultural Workers in the Member Countries of the E.O.E.C.,* European Bureau for Youth and Childhood, c.1954; *European Resistance Movements,* two volumes, Pergamon, 1960; *L'Education professionelle en Europe meridionale,* H. & M. Schaumans, 1960; *La Formation des formateurs,* Societe d'Etudes et d'Expansion, 1961; (editor) Louis Loucheur, *Carnets secrets, 1908-1932,* Brepols, 1962; *Secrets diplomatiques, 1914-1918,* Brepols, 1963; *Secrets diplomatiques, 1939-1945,* Brepols, 1963, translation by Edouard Nadier published as *Secret Diplomacy of World War II,* Simmons-Boardman, 1963; (with Henri Bernard, George-Andre Chevallaz, and Roger Gheysens) *Les Dossiers de la seconde guerre mondaile,* Marabout Universite, 1964; *Les Grandes controverses de l'histoire contemporaine, 1914-1945,* Editions Rencontre, 1964, translation by J.J. Buckingham published as *Major Controversies of Contemporary History,* Pergamon, 1965; *Le Congres de Vienne et l'Europe,* Brepols, 1964, translation by J. Granger published as *The Congress of Vienna and Europe,* Pergamon, 1964; *Histoire contemporaine de la diplomatie secrete, 1914-1945,* Editions Rencontre, 1965, reissued as *Histoire de la diplomatie secrete, de 1914 a 1945,* L'Inter, 1966; *Emile Mayrich et la politique du patronat european 1926-1933,* P. de Meyere, 1965; *Napoleon III and Europe,* Pergamon, 1965; *Les Deux guerres mondials,* Brepols, 1965 translation by J. Granger published as *Two World Wars,* Pergamon, 1965; *Histoire de la diplomatie secrete, 1789-1914,* Editions Rencontre, 1966; *Le Dossier de Vichy,* Julliard, 1967; *Les Grandes controverses du temps present, 1945-1965,* Editions Rencontre, 1967; *Les Derniers jours du fascisme,* Dargaud, 1968; *Napoleon: Un Portrait psychopolitique,* P. de Meyer, 1968; *De Gaulle et sa France,* Dargaud, 1968, translation by Dorothy Albertyn published as *De Gaulle and His France: A Political and Historical Portrait,* Julian Press, 1968; *Les Derniers jours de nazisme,* Dargaud, 1969; (with Gheysens) *Histoire de la guerre psychologique et secrete, 1939-1963,* Editions Rencontre, 1970; *Les Morts mysterieuses de l'histoire contemporaine,* Dargaud, 1970; (with Gheysens) *Les Grands espions de notre temps,* Hatchette, 1971.

SIDELIGHTS: Secret Diplomacy in World War II has been translated into eight languages; two other books have also appeared in foreign-language editions.

* * *

DELGADO, Alan (George) 1909-

PERSONAL: Born October 11, 1909, in London, England; son of Gershom (a greetings card publisher) and Sophia (Cohen) Delgado; married Mary Elise Politzer, October 20, 1944; children: Jane, Martin Gershom, Susan. *Education:* Attended Stowe School, Buckinghamshire, England, 1923-27. *Religion:* Jewish. *Home:* 29 Parkhill Rd., London NW3 27H, England.

CAREER: Former employee of publishing firms, Putnam & Co. Ltd. and William Collins Sons & Co. Ltd.; since 1955, with firm of Brown, Knight & Truscott Group. *Military service:* British Army, Royal Artillery, 1939-45; served with British Eighth Army in Africa. *Member:* Savile Club (London).

WRITINGS: Introducing Ponies, Spring Books, 1960; *The Very Hot Water-Bottle,* Brockhampton Press, 1962, Follett, 1964, reissued as *The Hot Water Bottle Mystery,* Scholastic Book Services, 1967; *Hide the Slipper,* Brockhampton Press, 1963; *Winner on Points,* Parrish, 1964; *Return Ticket,* Brockhampton Press, 1965; *Nothing Up My Sleeve,* Harrap, 1966; *Mile-a-Minute Ernie,* Constable, 1967; *Edwardian England,* Longmans, Green, 1967; *Printing,* Wheaton, 1969; *A Hundred Years of Medical Care,* Longmans, Green, 1969; *As They Saw Her: Florence Nightengale,* Harrap, 1970; *Victorian Entertainment,* American Heritage Press, 1971. Contributor to newspapers and journals. Editor of *Pony Club Annual,* Numbers 1-6, and *Pony Club Book,* Numbers 7-14, for British Horse Society, 1950-63.

* * *

de LONGCHAMPS, Joanne (Cutten) 1923-

PERSONAL: Born January 7, 1923, in Los Angeles, Calif.; daughter of Alfred Beverly (a building contractor) and Ruth (Avery) Cutten; married Galen Edward de Longchamps (a teacher), January 21, 1941; children: Galen Dare. *Education:* Graduate of Mar-Ken Professional School, 1939; attended Los Angeles City College, 1939-40, University of Nevada, 1941-47, as auditor, 1956-62. *Politics:* Democrat. *Home:* 895 North Center St., Reno, Nev. 89501. *Office address:* P.O. Box 2526, Reno, Nev. 89505.

CAREER: Poet. Has taught classes in poetry, and lectured at the University of Nevada, 1962, 1971; has exhibited paintings and collages in local and regional shows, 1941—. *Member:* Poetry Society of America. *Awards, honors:* Reynolds Lyric Award, Poetry Society of America, 1954; *Carolina Quarterly* annual award, University of North Carolina, 1959.

WRITINGS—All poetry: And Ever Venus, Wagon & Star, 1944; *Eden Under Glass* (Book Club for Poetry selection), Golden Quill, 1957; *The Hungry Lions,* Indiana University Press, 1963; *The Wishing Animal,* Vanderbilt University Press, 1970. Poetry represented in several anthologies, including *Borestone Mountain Poetry Awards,* 1953, 1955, 1960, 1966, *Southern Poetry Review: A Decade of Poems,* edited by Guy Owen, Southern Poetry Review Press, 1969, and *The New York Times Book of Verse,* edited by Thomas Lask, Macmillan, 1970. Contributor of poems to *Accent, American Scholar, Antioch Review, Contact, Poetry, Prairie Schooner, San Francisco Review, Sparrow, Trace, Voices,* and other publications. Associate editor, *Destinies,* 1944.

WORK IN PROGRESS: New book of poems.

DeMARCO, Angelus A. 1916-

PERSONAL: Born March 11, 1916, in Philadelphia, Pa.; son of Joseph (an employee of U.S. Mint) and Carmela (Littieri) DeMarco. *Education:* St. Bonaventure University, St. Bonaventure, N.Y., B.A., 1938; Pontifical Institute of Sacred Music, Rome, Italy, B. Mus., 1953; University of Notre Dame, M.A., 1956; Catholic University of America, S.T.D., 1960. *Home:* Holy Name College, 14th & Shepherd Sts. N., Washington, D.C. 20017.

CAREER: Roman Catholic priest, member of Order of Friars Minor (Franciscans); pastor in Youngsville, N.Y., 1942-52; Franciscan House of Theology, Holy Name College, Washington, D.C., professor of patrology, sacred liturgy, and Christian archeology, 1953—; Catholic University of America, Washington, D.C., professor of dogmatic theology, 1960—. *Member:* Franciscan Educational Conference, Catholic Theological Society of America, National Catholic Liturgical Conference.

WRITINGS: *Rome and the Vernacular,* Newman, 1961; *A Key to the New Liturgical Constitution: An Alphabetical Analysis,* Desclee, 1964; *The Tomb of St. Peter: A Representative and Annotated Bibliography of the Excavations,* E.J. Brill, 1964, Humanities, 1965. Contributor to *New Catholic Encyclopedia,* and to *American Ecclesiastical Review, Friar, Interest,* and other journals.

WORK IN PROGRESS: Articles for *New Catholic Encyclopedia.*

*   *   *

de MARE, Eric S(amuel) 1910-

PERSONAL: Born September 10, 1910, in Enfield, Middlesex, England; son of Bror (a timber broker) and Ingrid (Tellander) de Mare; married Marjorie Vanessa Vallance, December 12, 1936 (died, 1972). *Education:* St. Paul's School, London, England, graduate, 1927; Architectural Association School of Architecture, A.A. diploma, 1934, A.R.I.B.A., 1935. *Politics:* Social Crediter. *Home and office:* 27 Grenville Ct., Dulwich Wood Park, London S.E.19, England.

CAREER: Architectural Press, London, England, editor, 1944-48; free-lance writer and photographer on architectural, topographical, and related subjects, 1948—. *Military service:* British Army, Home Guard, 1940-45. *Member:* Architectural Association, Special Committee on Industrial Archaeology.

WRITINGS: (Translator with I.R. de Mare) Brynjolf Bjoerset, *Distribute or Destroy!: A Survey of the World's Glut of Goods with a Description of Various Proposals and Practical Experiments for Its Distribution,* Stanley Nott, 1936; *Britain Rebuilt,* Sidgwick & Jackson, 1942; (editor) *New Ways of Building,* Praeger, 1948, 3rd edition, Architectural Press, 1958.

The Canals of England, Architectural Press, 1950, British Book Centre, 1951, revised edition, Architectural Press, 1961; *Time on the Thames,* Architectural Press, 1952, British Book Centre, 1953; *Scandinavia: Sweden, Denmark and Norway,* Hastings House, 1952; (editor) *New Ways of Servicing Buildings,* Architectural Press, 1954; *The Bridges of Britain,* Batsford, 1954; *Gunnar Asplund, a Great Modern Architect,* Art & Technics, 1955; *Photography,* Penguin, 1957, 5th edition, 1970; (illustrator with photographs) J.M. Richards, *The Functional Tradition in Early Industrial Buildings,* Architectural Press, 1958; *London's Riverside: Past, Present and Future* (Book Society choice), Dufour, 1958.

Photography and Architecture, Praeger, 1961; (illustrator with photographs) William Gaunt, *London,* Batsford, 1961; (illustrator with photographs) Michael de la Bedoyere, *Francis of Assisi,* Collins, 1962; *Your Book of*

Bridges, Faber, 1963; *Swedish Cross Cut: A Book on the Goeta Canal,* Allhems, 1964; *London's River: The Story of a City,* Bodley Head, 1964, McGraw, 1965, new edition, Bodley Head, 1972; (illustrator with photographs) F.A. Reeve, *Cambridge,* Batsford, 1964; (illustrator with photographs) William Gaunt, *Oxford,* Batsford, 1965; *Your Book of Waterways,* Faber, 1965; *Colour Photography,* Penguin, 1968, new edition, 1973; *The City of Westminster: Heart of London,* Batsford, 1968, Hastings House, 1969; (with wife, Vanessa de Mare) *Your Book of Paper Folding,* Faber, 1968; *London 1851: The Year of the Great Exhibition,* Folio Society, 1972; *The London Dore Saw: A Victorian Evocation,* Allen Lare, 1972.

Contributor to journals and newspapers in England and United States, including *Times Literary Supplement, House and Garden, Guardian, New York Times, Observer, Daily Telegraph* (London), and architectural periodicals. Editor, *Architects' Journal,* 1944-48; founder and editor, *The Sun: The Social Credit World Review,* 1950-57.

SIDELIGHTS: de Mare writes of his "inherited fanaticism," (from Huguenot ancestors) which he now applies to "a private war against the tyranny of banksterdom." He believes in the need to establish a leisure age culture through mechanization. He also believes that solutions to architectural and town-planning problems are primarily philosophical and then financial.

*   *   *

DEMING, Richard 1915-
(Max Franklin)

PERSONAL: Born April 25, 1915, in Des Moines, Iowa; son of Fred Kemp (a history teacher) and Erva Pearl (Smyers) Deming; married Ruth Lorraine DuBois; children: Tracey Lou, Barbara, Patricia. *Education:* Attended Central Methodist College, Fayette, Mo., two years; Washington University, St. Louis, Mo., A.B., 1937; University of Iowa, M.A., 1939. *Religion:* Unitarian. *Agent:* Scott Meredith Literary Agency, 580 Fifth Ave., New York, N.Y. 10026.

CAREER: Social worker in St. Louis, Mo., 1939-41; American National Red Cross, Dunkirk, N.Y., chapter manager, 1945-50; free-lance writer, 1946—, now in Ventura, Calif. *Military service:* U.S. Army, 1941-45; served in European theater; became captain. *Member:* Mystery Writers of America, American Legion, Masons, Elks. *Awards, honors:* Distinguished alumni citation from Central Methodist College, 1958.

WRITINGS: *The Gallows in My Garden,* Rinehart, 1952; *Tweak the Devil's Nose,* Rinehart, 1953; *Whistle Past the Graveyard,* Rinehart, 1954.

Under pseudonym Max Franklin: *Justice Has No Sword,* Rinehart, 1953; *Hell Street,* Rinehart, 1954; *Dragnet* (juvenile), Whitman Publishing, 1957; *The Case of the Courteous Killer,* Pocket Books, 1958; *The Case of the Crime King,* Pocket Books, 1959; *Fall Girl,* Zenith, 1959; *Hit and Run,* Pocket Books, 1960; *Kiss and Kill,* Zenith, 1960; *American Spies* (juvenile), Whitman Publishing, 1960; *Edge of the Law,* Berkley Publishing, 1960; *This Is My Night,* Monarch Books, 1961; *Vice Cop,* Belmont Books, 1961; *Body For Sale,* Pocket Books, 1962; *Anything But Saintly,* Pocket Books, 1963; *She'll Hate Me Tomorrow,* Monarch Books, 1963; *Famous Investigators* (juvenile), Whitman Publishing, 1963; *Death of a Pusher,* Pocket Books, 1964; *This Game of Murder,* Monarch Books, 1964; *The Police Lab at Work,* Bobbs-Merrill, 1967; *The Mod Squad: The Greek God Affair,* Pyramid Publications, 1968; *The Mod Squad: A Groovy Way to Die,* Pyramid Publications, 1968; *The Mod Squad: The Sock-It-to-Em Murders,* Pyramid Publications, 1969; *The*

Mod Squad: Spy-In, Pyramid Publications, 1969; The Mod Squad: Assignment, the Arranger (juvenile), Whitman Publishing, 1969; Heroes of the International Red Cross, Meredith, 1969; The Mod Squad: The Hit, Pyramid Publications, 1970; The Mod Squad: Assignment, the Hideout (juvenile), Whitman Publishing, 1970; Man and Society: Criminal Law at Work, Hawthorn, 1970; What's the Matter with Helen?, Beagle Books, 1971; Man Against Man: Civil Law at Work, Hawthorn, 1972; Sleep: Our Unknown Life, Thomas Nelson, 1972; Vice Cop, Belmont Books, 1972.

Short stories in seven editions of Dutton's Best Detective Stories of the Year, and in other mystery, crime, western, and science fiction anthologies. Also contributor of about six hundred short stories and novelettes to sixty magazines, and to television and films.

WORK IN PROGRESS: Man and the World: International Law at Work, for Hawthorn.

AVOCATIONAL INTERESTS: Swimming, fishing, bowling, and travel.

* * *

DENHOLM, Therese Mary Zita White 1933-
(Zita White)

PERSONAL: Born May 29, 1933, in Brisbane, Queensland, Australia; daughter of Luton John Isidore and Enid (King) White; married David Desmond Denholm (an author and student), September 29, 1962. Education: Attended All Hallows' College; University of Queensland, B.A., 1961. Religion: Roman Catholic. Home: Apfel Baum, 23 Edson St., Kenmore, Brisbane, Queensland, Australia. Office: University of Queensland, St. Lucia, Brisbane, Queensland, Australia.

CAREER: Associated with 4BH (broadcasters), Brisbane, Queensland, Australia, 1951-52; Queensland Department of Education, English and history teacher in various secondary schools, 1954-57, 1958-59; Jacaranda Press, Ltd., Brisbane, Queensland, editor, 1960-62; University of Queensland, Brisbane, tutor in history, 1963-69. Member: Pony Club Association of Queensland (founder; publicity officer, 1956—; treasurer, 1956-62).

WRITINGS: The One Day Ponies, Lutterworth, 1958; Ride Across the Ocean, Lutterworth, 1959; (editor) A Race of Horsemen, Jacaranda Press, 1963. Regular columnist in Queensland Country Life, 1959—, Hoofs and Horns, 1960—. Author of radio and television scripts.

WORK IN PROGRESS: Research for Suburbia in Arcadia, an objective survey of the Australian urban character; James Tyson, a biography.

* * *

DeNOVO, John A(ugust) 1916-

PERSONAL: Born November 5, 1916, in Galva, Ill.; son of August (a grocer) and Paula (LaMantia) DeNovo; married Jeanne Humphreys, December 22, 1948; children: Anne, Jay. Education: Knox College, B.A., 1938; University of Minnesota, M.A., 1940; Yale University, Ph.D., 1948; postdoctoral study at Harvard University, 1956-57, Johns Hopkins University, summer, 1957. Office: Department of History, Humanities Building, University of Wisconsin, Madison, Wis. 53706.

CAREER: Yale University, New Haven, Conn., assistant in instruction, 1947; Pennsylvania State University, University Park, 1948-64, started as instructor, became professor of American history; University of Wisconsin, Madison, professor of history, 1964—. Visiting professor at Cornell University, 1963-64; summer lecturer or professor at George Washington University, 1949, University

of Wisconsin, 1961. Military service: U.S. Naval Reserve, 1941-45; became lieutenant. Member: American Historical Association, Mississippi Valley Historical Association, American Association of University Professors, Society of Historians of American Foreign Relations (member of board of managers, 1969—), Middle East Studies Association. Awards, honors: Phi Alpha Theta book award for American Interests and Policies in the Middle East.

WRITINGS: (Contributor) George L. Anderson, editor, Issues and Conflicts: Studies in Twentieth-Century American Diplomacy, University of Kansas Press, 1959; American Interests and Policies in the Middle East, 1900-1939, University of Minnesota Press, 1963; (editor with others, and contributor) Selected Readings in American History, two volumes, Scribner, 1969. Contributor of articles and book reviews to historical journals.

WORK IN PROGRESS: The United States and the Middle East, 1939-1950.

* * *

DENT, Alan (Holmes) 1905-

PERSONAL: Born January 7, 1905, in Ayrshire, Scotland; son of John and Margaret (Holmes) Dent. Education: University of Glasgow, medical and arts student, 1921-26. Home: 85 Aylesbury End, Beaconsfield, Buckinghamshire, England. Agent: Miss Stephens, A.D. Peters, 10 Buckingham St., London W.C.2, England.

CAREER: Started as secretary to James Agate, London drama critic, 1926-41; critic in own right, 1935—, serving as drama and film critic of Manchester Guardian (now Guardian), 1935-43, drama critic of Punch, 1943, 1963, film critic of Sunday Telegraph, 1960-62, film critic of Illustrated London News, 1947-68; British Broadcasting Corp., London, England, critic, 1942—. Military service: Royal Navy, 1943-45.

WRITINGS: Preludes and Studies (criticism), Macmillan, 1942, Kennikat, 1970; Nocturnes and Rhapsodies (criticism), Hamish Hamilton, 1950; (editor) Bernard Shaw and Mrs. Patrick Campbell: A Correspondence, Gollancz, 1952; My Dear America (travel), Arthur Barker, 1954; Mrs. Patrick Campbell (biography), Museum Press, 1961; How Well Do You Know Your Shakespeare?, Macdonald & Co., 1964; Robert Burns in His Time, Thomas Nelson, 1966; Vivien Leigh: A Bouquet, Hamish Hamilton, 1969, International Publications Service, 1971; The World of Shakespeare, foreword by Sir Ralph Richardson, Osprey Publications, 1971. Film scripts for Sir Laurence Olivier's "Henry V," "Hamlet," "Richard II."

WORK IN PROGRESS: Plants for Osprey Publications; Laurence Olivier: A Garland, for Hamish Hamilton.

AVOCATIONAL INTERESTS: Shakespeare, poetry, painting, wine, Victoriana, Beerbohmiana, Burnsiana, Boswelliana.

* * *

DERING, Joan (Rosalind Cordelia) 1917-

PERSONAL: Born April 29, 1917, in Nottingham, England; daughter of Anthony Lionel Yea (a club secretary) and Gertrude Frances Cordelia (Boyd) Dering. Religion: Church of England. Home: 2 Thellvsson Lodge, Aldeburgh, Suffolk, England.

WRITINGS: Louise, Hodder & Stoughton, 1956, Washburn, 1957; Mrs. Winterton's Rebellion, Hodder & Stoughton, 1958; The Caravanners, Hodder & Stoughton, 1959; Marianne, Hodder & Stoughton, 1960; The Silent Witness, Hodder & Stoughton, 1962; Number Two, North Steps, Hodder & Stoughton, 1965; Not Proven, Hodder & Stoughton, 1966.

De ROOS, Robert (William) 1912-

PERSONAL: Surname rhymes with "de dose"; born June 18, 1912, in San Jose, Costa Rica; son of Alfred Benjamin and Mary (Boyle) de Roos; married Betty Jane Hedden, April 11, 1936; children: Barbara (Mrs. Michael Mitchell III), Betsy (Mrs. Thomas Dority). *Education:* Stanford University, A.B., 1933; Harvard University, Nieman Fellow, 1948-49. *Politics:* Democrat. *Home and office:* 145 Pinehill Rd., Hillsborough, Calif. 94010.

CAREER: Time, Inc., San Francisco, Calif., bureau chief, 1942-45; *San Francisco Chronicle*, San Francisco, Calif., feature writer, 1945-51, columnist, "Now Hear This," 1950-51, weekly column, 1966—; Crowell-Collier Publishing Co., San Francisco, Calif., senior editor, 1954-56; free-lance writer, 1956—. *Member:* Society of Magazine Writers, Society of Nieman Fellows, Sigma Delta Chi. *Awards, honors:* National Headliners Club award for reporting, 1947, for article on first postwar year in the Pacific coast economy.

WRITINGS: The Thirsty Land: The Story of Central Valley Project, Stanford University Press, 1948; (with Stanton Delaplane) *Delaplane in Mexico*, Coward, 1958; (ghost writer) Gladys Workman, *Only When I Laugh*, Prentice-Hall, 1959; (ghost writer) *The Check List for a Perfect Wedding*, Doubleday, 1960; *Monument Valley: An Exploration of Red-rock Land Where the Desert Becomes Magic and Wonder*, Northland Press, 1965. Writer of articles on Los Angeles, Disneyland, Arizona, Philippines, Costa Rica, and other locations for *National Geographic* and other major periodicals.

WORK IN PROGRESS: A novel with tentative title, *Faith of Our Fathers;* a personal narrative of travels.

AVOCATIONAL INTERESTS: Fishing, travel in Mexico and Central America.

*   *   *

DeSANTIS, Mary Allen (Carpe) 1930-

PERSONAL: Born November 5, 1930, in New York, N.Y.; daughter of Allen and Kathleen (MacBain) Carpe; married Anthony DeSantis (an architect), March 22, 1956; children: Claudia Allen. *Education:* Cambridge School of Weston, Weston, Mass., graduate, 1947; Bennington College, B.A., 1951. *Office: Ingenue*, 750 Third Ave., New York, N.Y. 10017.

CAREER: Ingenue, New York, N.Y., beauty editor, 1960—. Free-lance writer and editor for Dell Books.

WRITINGS: Bubble Baths and Hair Bows: A Little Girl's Guide to Grooming, Doubleday, 1963.

*   *   *

DeSANTIS, Vincent P. 1916-

PERSONAL: Born December 25, 1916, in Birdsboro, Pa.; son of Antonio and Martha (Templin) De Santis; married Helene O'Brien (a teacher), June 24, 1946 (divorced, 1971); children: Vincent, Jr., Edmund, Philip, John. *Education:* West Chester State College, B.S., 1941; Johns Hopkins University, Ph.D., 1952. *Home:* 1236 East Madison St., South Bend, Ind. 46617. *Office address:* Box 562, Notre Dame, Ind. 46556.

CAREER: University of Notre Dame, Notre Dame, Ind., 1949—, now professor of history and chairman of department of history. Member, Catholic Commission on Intellectual and Cultural Affairs. Fulbright professor, 1967-68. *Military service:* U.S. Army, 1941-45; became captain. *Member:* American Historical Association, American Studies Association, American Association of University Professors, American Catholic Historical Association (president, 1964), Society of American Historians, Organization of American Historians, National Geograph-

ic Society, Southern Historical Association. *Awards, honors:* American Philosophical Society awards, 1955, 1962, 1963; R.D.W. Connor Award of North Carolina Historical and Literary Society, 1960; Guggenheim fellowship, 1960-61; distinguished alumni award, West Chester State College, 1970.

WRITINGS: Republicans Face the Southern Question: The New Departure Years, 1877-1897, Johns Hopkins Press, 1959; (with Dwight Follett and others) *Our Country*, Follett, 1960; (with T.T. McAvoy and others) *Roman Catholicism and the American Way of Life*, University of Notre Dame Press, 1960; (with Morton Borden and others) *America's Ten Greatest Presidents*, Rand McNally, 1961, revised edition, published as *America's Eleven Greatest Presidents*, 1971; (with H. Wayne Morgan and others) *The Gilded Age*, Syracuse University Press, 1961; (with Louis B. Wright and others) *The Democratic Experience*, Scott, Foresman, 1963, 3rd edition, 1973; (with Joseph J. Huthmacher and Benjamin W. Labaree) *America Past and Present: An Interpretation with Readings*, two volumes, Allyn & Bacon, 1968; *The Shaping of Modern America*, Allyn & Bacon, 1973. Contributor of articles to historical journals.

WORK IN PROGRESS: American Politics, 1877-1897; A History of the United States; The United States in the Twentieth Century; The United States, 1877-1897; The United States, 1897-1917; The Gilded Age: A Bibliography; The Presidential Life of the Gilded Age.

*   *   *

DESMOND, (Clarice) J(oanne) Patrick (Scholes) 1910-

PERSONAL: Born March 28, 1910, in Batesville, Ark.; daughter of Joseph Samuel (a medical doctor) and Mary Etta (Reed) Scholes; married Michael Laurence Desmond, January 1, 1930 (died, 1932); children: Joanne Kathleen (Mrs. Douglas S. MacLennan). *Education:* Mountain Home Baptist College and Conservatory of Music, A.A.; also studied at business colleges in Chillicothe and Kansas City, Mo. *Religion:* Roman Catholic (convert). *Office:* 603 New High St., Los Angeles, Calif. 90012.

CAREER: Onetime Western Union telegraph operator, teletypist, and office manager; Los Angeles County, Los Angeles, Calif., civil service typist-clerk for accountant, 1949—. *Member:* National Writers Club.

WRITINGS: (With Ace Corson) *Ace Corson, Railroader 1878-1960*, Fell, 1964.

WORK IN PROGRESS: Through a Strange World on a Mule, based upon factual experiences among San Blas Indians of Central America; *Ace Corson, the Boy*, based on his life among Osage Indians.

AVOCATIONAL INTERESTS: Flowers, good music, books, paintings, all nature, and photography.

*   *   *

DEWART, Leslie 1922-
   (Philomythes, William Ross)

PERSONAL: Original name, Gonzalo Gonzalez; name legally changed in 1945; born December 12, 1922, in Madrid, Spain; son of Gerardo (a surveyor) and Adamina (Duarte) Gonzalez; married Joanne McWilliam (a theology professor), August 19, 1954 (legally separated August 2, 1972); children: Leslie, Elizabeth, Sean, Colin. *Education:* University of Toronto, B.A., 1951, M.A., 1952, Ph.D., 1954. *Politics:* "Nil." *Religion:* Roman Catholic. *Home:* St. Michael's College, University of Toronto, Toronto M5S 104, Ontario, Canada. *Office:* Institute of Christian Thought, St. Michael's College, University of Toronto, Toronto M5S 1J4, Ontario, Canada.

CAREER: University of Detroit, Detroit, Mich., instructor in philosophy, 1954-56; St. Michael's College, University of Toronto, Toronto, Ontario, assistant professor, 1956-61, associate professor, 1961-68, professor of religious studies, 1968—. Military service: Royal Canadian Air Force, pilot, 1942-47; became flying officer. Member: Canadian Theological Society, Societe Europeenne de Culture. Awards, honors: Catholic Book award, Catholic Press Association, for The Future of Belief.

WRITINGS: Christianity and Revolution: The Lesson of Cuba, Herder & Herder, 1963 (published in England as Cuba, Church and Crisis: Christianity and Politics in the Cuban Revolution, Sheed, 1964); The Future of Belief: Theism in a World Come of Age, Herder & Herder, 1966; The Foundations of Belief, Herder & Herder, 1969; Religion, Language and Truth, Herder & Herder, 1970.

Contributor: Thomas Roberts, editor, Contraception and Holiness: The Catholic Predicament, Herder & Herder, 1964; Abraham Rotstein, editor, The Prospect of Change: Proposals for Canada, McGraw (Toronto), 1965; Paul T. Harris, editor, Brief to the Bishops: Canadian Catholic Laymen Speak Their Minds, Longmans (Don Mills, Ont.), 1965; Paul Goodman, editor, Seeds of Liberation, Braziller, 1965; Walter Stein, editor, Peace on Earth: The Way Ahead, Sheed, 1966; William B. Dunphy, editor, The New Morality: Continuity and Discountinuity, Herder & Herder, 1967; Gregory Baum, editor, The Future of Belief Debate, Herder & Herder, 1967; Martin Emil Marty and Dean G. Peerman, editors, New Theology: No. 5, Macmillan, 1968; Christopher F. Mooney, editor, The Presence and Absence of God, Fordham University Press, 1969; Robert Campbell, editor, The Spectrum of Catholic Attitudes, Bruce, 1969; Daniel John Callahan, editor, God, Jesus and Spirit, Herder & Herder, 1969; Robert Alexander Divine, editor, The Cuban Missile Crisis, Quadrangle, 1971. Contributor of about one hundred and fifty articles to magazines and journals, including Thomist, Canadian Forum, Commonweal, Continuum, Critic, Cross Currents, and Nation. Associate editor, Concurrence, 1968-70, Continuum, 1964-70, Internationale Dialog Zeitschrift, 1967—, Convergence, and Ecumenist; member of editorial board, SR: Studies in Religion—Sciences Religieuses, 1970; contributing editor, The Ecumenist, 1968.

SIDELIGHTS: Late in 1969 an investigation by the Vatican Congregation for the Doctrine of Faith was convened to examine the theological implications of Dewart's writings. The investigation was generated by the publication of The Future of Belief, and, although no condemnation was issued, it was reported that the Congregation asked Dewart not to authorize further editions of the book, a request which the author refused. Dewart also declined to defend his book or his orthodoxy, stating that "to have struck any such defensive posture would have implicitly granted the legitimacy ... of the Congregation as a tribunal at whose bar transgressions of the bounds of legitimate speculation may be tried."

Dewart has continued to write about his own interpretation of Christianity in the contemporary world and to delineate what he believes are needed reforms in the Catholic Church. C. Pearson, Jr. describes Christianity and Revolution: The Lesson of Cuba as a clarification of America's "role in the creation and maintenance of the cold war. Observing a fundamental American ambivalence toward the world represented by incompatible ideals of total victory and co-existence, Dewart considers the former to rest on a misunderstanding of the present historical situation as a contest between superhuman forces of good and evil rather than as one between very human societies. He sees in the latter ideal the sole hope for mankind."

Pearson adds: "The discussion of Christian conscience and war constitutes a significant addition to current literature on this topic. Dewart argues the irrelevance of concepts of a just war in the context of total war where even survival is contingent upon total destruction of the enemy and thus itself aggressive. He insists that the Judeo-Christian tradition excludes survival at all costs no less than peace at all costs and that the only defensive war permissible to the Christian today is on war itself."

Walter Arnold describes The Foundations of Belief as "the most considerable contribution so far by a contemporary Catholic thinker to the reconstruction of the basic concepts of faith vis-a-vis the traditional ones. In particular Mr. Dewart's writings represent the most thoroughgoing alternative within the tradition to the concepts formulated by St. Thomas Aquinas and his revisionists down to the present."

BIOGRAPHICAL/CRITICAL SOURCES: Times Literary Supplement, September 14, 1967; Gregory Baum, editor, The Future of Belief Debate, Herder & Herder, 1968; Library Journal, May 15, 1969; New York Times Book Review, July 20, 1969; Encounter, summer, 1969; Washington Post, November 22, 1969; Christian Century, December 24, 1969.

* * *

DEWEY, Robert D(yckman) 1923-

PERSONAL: Born March 14, 1923, in Maumee, Ohio; son of Henry Evert (a teacher) and Elizabeth (Blanchard) Dewey; married Eleanor Bowen Hootman, December 8, 1951; children: Janet, Martha, Paula, Eric. Education: Kalamazoo College, B.A., 1947; Yale University, B.D., 1951; graduate study at State University of Iowa, 1964, and at University of Utah, 1968. Politics: Democrat. Home: 1316 West Lovell, Kalamazoo, Mich. 49007. Office: Kalamazoo College, Kalamazoo, Mich. 49001.

CAREER: Worked in England under Congregational Service Committee, 1948-49; Ohio Congregational Christian Conference, minister to youth, 1951-53; Congregational Church, Birmingham, Mich., minister, 1953-58; Garden City Community Church, Long Island, N.Y., minister, 1958-61; First Congregational Church, Grinnell, Iowa, minister 1961-65; Kodaikanal School, Madras State, South India, chaplain, 1965-67; Kalamazoo College, Kalamazoo, Mich., dean of the chapel and assistant professor of religion, 1967—. United Church of Christ, Iowa Conference, chairman of ministry on youth. Member of youth commission, Iowa Council of Churches, of the Iowa Governor's Commission on Children and Youth, and Iowa Board of International Education. Poweshiek County Mental Health Association, president; Grinnell United Fund, board member. Military service: U.S. Army, 1943-46; received Bronze Star.

WRITINGS: Youth Ministry Manual: A Manual for Adults Who Work with Youth in the Local Church, United Church Press, 1963; The Language of Faith, United Church Press, 1963; A Manual for Confirmation Education, United Church Press, 1968; (with Charles Murphy) My Commitment, Herder & Herder, 1968. Contributor to religious journals.

* * *

DEXTER, Lewis Anthony 1915-

PERSONAL: Born November 13, 1915; son of Robert Cloutman (a sociologist) and Elizabeth (Antho) Dexter. Education: University of Chicago, A.B., 1935; Harvard University, A.M., 1938; Columbia University, Ph.D., 1960. Politics: Democrat. Home: 536 Pleasant St., Belmont, Mass. 02178. Office: University of Massachusetts, 250 Stuart St., Boston, Mass. 02116.

CAREER: Teacher of political science and related courses at Park College, Parkville, Mo., at Bryn Mawr College, Bryn Mawr, Pa., prior to 1950, and at University of Puerto Rico, Rio Piedras, 1961, 1963, 1968-70; free-lance consultant on social science research projects, on mental retardation, and in political campaign field, working for one hundred employers on several hundred projects, 1950—; University of South Florida, teaching political science and sociology, 1963-65; University of Massachusetts, Boston, professor of politics and sociology, 1969—. Part-time teacher at St. Anselm's College, Manchester, N.H., and Lowell Technological Institute, Lowell, Mass., 1957-58, at Howard University, 1959; visiting professor at Michigan State University, Ohio State University, Dalhousie University, State University of New York at Albany, and University of California at Berkeley, 1965-69; summer instructor at other schools. Elections analyst, Democratic National Committee, 1956; research director for Democratic gubernatorial campaign in Massachusetts, 1956, for Republican gubernatorial campaign in Massachusetts, 1960. Sometime consultant to National Research Council advisory committee on civil defense, to Puerto Rico Department of Education, to U.S.-Japan Trade Council, other groups and firms. Member: American Sociological Society (fellow), Society for Applied Anthropology (fellow), American Association on Mental Deficiency (fellow), American Political Science Association (honorary life member), National Association of Social Workers. Awards, honors: Woodrow Wilson Award, 1963, for American Business and Public Policy; Social Science Research Council grant, 1966-69.

WRITINGS: How Candidates Lend Strength to Tickets, privately printed, 1956; (contributor) R. Peabody and N. Polsby, editors, New Perspectives on Congress, Rand McNally, 1963; (with Raymond Bauer and Ithiel Pool) American Business and Public Policy, Atherton, 1963; (editor with David M. White) People, Society, and Mass Communications, Free Press, 1964; The Tyranny of Schooling: An Inquiry into the Problem of Stupidity, Basic Books, 1964; How Organizations Are Represented in Washington, Bobbs-Merrill, 1969; Elite and Specialized Interviewing: Handbooks for Research in Political Behavior, Northwestern University Press, 1970; The Ideology and Politics of Congress, Rand McNally, 1970. Articles on political and sociological subjects published in academic journals and in magazines.

AVOCATIONAL INTERESTS: Tennis, reading detective stories, badminton, hiking.

*   *   *

DIAMOND, Robert Mach 1930-

PERSONAL: Born March 5, 1930, in Schenectady, N.Y.; son of Henry Gordon and Ruth (Mach) Diamond; married Dolores Jacobs, April 14, 1957; children: Harli Fait, H. Gordon. Education: Union College, Schenectady, N.Y., A.B., 1951; New York University, M.A., 1953, Ph.D., 1962. Religion: Jewish. Home: 7405 South West 140th Ter., Miami, Fla.

CAREER: Schenectady Public Schools, Schenectady, N.Y., teacher of mathematics, 1956-58; Plainedge Public Schools, North Massapequa, N.Y., television coordinator, 1958-59; California State University (formerly San Jose State College), San Jose, Calif., associate professor of education, 1959—; University of Miami, University College, Coral Gables, Fla., visiting professor, and director of instructional resources, 1953—. Owner and chief artist, Diamond Card Co. Consultant on instructional resources and instructional television. Former swimming competitor and holder of state and district records. Military service: U.S. Army, 1952-54. Member: Department of Audio-Visual Instruction, National Association of Educational Broadcasters, Kappa Delta Pi.

WRITINGS: (Editor) A Guide to Instructional Television, McGraw, 1964; (with Bertha Grattan Lee) A Storage and Retrieval System for Documents in Instructional Resources, Office for the Study of Instruction, University College, University of Miami, 1965; (with John C. Woodward) The Amateur Psychologists' Dictionary, Arco, 1966; (with Anthony Barresi) A Modular Approach to Music Appreciation with Emphasis on Independent Study, Instructional Resources Center, State University of New York at Fredonia, 1970. Contributor of articles to educational publications.

WORK IN PROGRESS: Research projects in the area of instructional resources and instructional improvement.

*   *   *

DICKEN, E(ric) W(illiam) Trueman 1919-

PERSONAL: Born January 18, 1919, in Uttoxeter, Staffordshire, England; son of Walter Trueman (a cinematograph exhibitor) and Mary Gertrude (Wilkinson) Dicken; married Helene Sylvia Margaret Humphries, September 5, 1940; children: Anne Felicity Trueman, Mark Nicholas Trueman, Ruth Magdalen Trueman. Education: University of Besancon, student, 1936-37; Exeter College, Oxford, B.A. (honors), 1939, M.A. (first class honors), 1946; additional study at Cuddesdon College, 1949; Oxford University, B.D. and D.D., 1964. Home: The Warden's House, Lenton Hall, University of Nottingham, Nottinghamshire, England.

CAREER: Ordained deacon, Church of England, 1949, priest, 1950; vicar of Caunton and Maplebeck, Nottinghamshire, 1954-65; University of Nottingham, Nottinghamshire, England, warden of Lenton Hall and senior lecturer in Christian theology, 1965—. Military service: British Army, Somerset Light Infantry, 1939; intelligence staff officer, 1942-45; senior British displaced persons officer, Vienna, Austria, 1946; mentioned in dispatches; became major. Member: Society for Old Testament Study, Association for Promoting Retreats.

WRITINGS: Living With God, Mowbray, 1957; The Crucible of Love: A Study of the Mysticism of St. Teresa of Jesus and St. John of the Cross, Shccd, 1963; (translator) G. von Rad, Collected Studies in the Old Testament, Oliver & Boyd, 1966; Not This Way, Faith Press, 1968; Loving on Principal, Darton, Longman & Todd, 1969.

WORK IN PROGRESS: A textbook of biblical ethics and spirituality.

SIDELIGHTS: Competent in French, German, Spanish, Italian, Latin, Greek, and Hebrew.

*   *   *

DICKEY, James (Lafayette) 1923-

PERSONAL: Born February 2, 1923, in Atlanta, Ga.; son of Eugene and Maibelle (Swift) Dickey; married Maxine Syerson, November 4, 1948; children: Christopher Swift, Kevin Webster. Education: Attended Clemson College, 1942; Vanderbilt University, B.A. (magna cum laude), 1949, M.A., 1950. Office: Department of English, University of South Carolina, Columbia, S.C. 29208. Permanent address: 166 Wesley Dr. N.W., Atlanta, Ga. 30305.

CAREER: Instructor in English, Rice Institute (now Rice University), Houston, Tex., 1950, 1952-54, University of Florida, Gainesville, 1955-56; worked for next five years, as copywriter for McCann-Erickson, New York, N.Y., then as official for Liller, Neal, Battle & Lindsey and Burke Dowling Adams, both in Atlanta, Ga.; poet-in-residence, Reed College, Portland, Ore., 1963-64, San Fernando Valley State College, Los Angeles, Calif., 1964-65, and University of Wisconsin,

Madison, 1966, Milwaukee, 1967; Library of Congress, Washington, D.C., consultant in poetry, two terms, 1966-68, honorary consultant in American Letters, 1968-71; University of South Carolina, Columbia, professor of English and poet-in-residence, 1968—. *Military service:* U.S. Army Air Forces, World War II, flew 100 combat missions in 418th Night Fighter Squadron; served in Korean War; awarded Air Medal. *Member:* Phi Beta Kappa. *Awards, honors: Sewanee Review* poetry fellowship, 1954; Union League Civic and Arts Foundation Prize (*Poetry* magazine), 1958; Longview Foundation award, 1959; Vachel Lindsay Prize (*Poetry* magazine), 1959; Guggenheim fellowship, 1961; National Book Award for poetry, and Melville Cane Award of Poetry Society of America, 1966, both for *Buckdancer's Choice;* National Institue of Arts and Letters grant, 1966; Medicis prize for best foreign book of year (Paris), 1971, for *Deliverance.*

WRITINGS—Poetry: *Into the Stone, and Other Poems,* Scribner, 1960; *Drowning with Others,* Wesleyan University Press, 1962; *Helmets,* Wesleyan University Press, 1964; *Two Poems of the Air,* Centicore Press (Portland), 1964; *Buckdancer's Choice,* Wesleyan University Press, 1965; *Poems, 1957-1967* (selections issued as miniature edition prior to publication), Wesleyan University Press, 1967; *Poems,* Sun Books (Melbourne), 1968; *The Eye-Beaters, Blood, Victory, Madness, Buckhead and Mercy,* Doubleday, 1970; (adaptor of English versions, with others) Evgenii Evtushenko, *Stolen Apples: Poetry,* Doubleday, 1971.

Prose: *The Suspect in Poetry* (literary criticism), Sixties Press, 1964; *A Private Brinksmanship* (address given at Pitzer College, June 6, 1965), Castle Press (Pasadena), 1965; (contributor) Howard Nemerov, editor, *Poets on Poetry,* Basic Books, 1966; *Spinning the Crystal Ball: Some Guesses at the Future of American Poetry,* Library of Congress, 1967; *Metaphor as Pure Adventure* (lecture given at Library of Congress, December 4, 1967), Library of Congress, 1968; *Babel to Byzantium: Poets and Poetry Now* (literary criticism), Farrar, Straus, 1968; *Deliverance* (novel; Literary Guild selection; excerpt entitled "Two Days in September" published in *Atlantic,* February, 1970), Houghton, 1970; *Self-Interviews* (informal monologues; excerpt entitled "The Poet Tries to Make a Kind of Order" published in *Mademoiselle,* September, 1970), recorded and edited by Barbara Reiss and James Reiss, Doubleday, 1970; *Sorties: Journals and New Essays,* Doubleday, 1971. Also author of screenplay for film, "Deliverance," produced by Warner Bros. in 1972.

Contributor: Louis D. Rubin, Jr. and Robert D. Jacobs, editors, *Modern Southern Literature in Its Cultural Setting,* Doubleday, 1961; Morton Dauwen Zabel, editor, *Selected Poems of Edwin Arlington Robinson,* Macmillan, 1965; Howard Nemerov, editor, *Poets on Poetry,* Basic Books, 1966; Oscar Williams, editor, *Master Poems of the English Language,* Trident Press, 1966; *Teaching in America,* Fifth Annual Conference of the National Committee for Support of the Public Schools, 1967; (author of introduction) Paul Carroll, editor, *New American Poets,* Follett, 1968; Robert M. Hutchins and Mortimer J. Adler, editors-in-chief, *The Great Ideas of Today, 1968,* Encyclopedia Britannica, 1968. Contributor of poems, essays, articles, and reviews to over thirty periodicals, including *Atlantic, Harper's, Hudson Review, Nation, New Yorker, Paris Review, Poetry, Sewanee Review, Times Literary Supplement,* and *Virginia Quarterly Review.* Poems included in over twenty anthologies, including *Contemporary American Poetry,* edited by Donald Hall, Penguin, 1962, *American Poetry Since 1945,* edited by Stephen Stepanchev, Harper, 1965, *Poems on Poetry,* edited by Robert Wallace and James G. Taaffe, Dutton, 1965, *The New Modern Poets,* edited by M.L. Rosenthal,

Macmillan, 1967, *Southern Writing in the Sixties,* edited by John William Corrington and Miller Williams, Louisiana State University Press, 1967, *Where is Viet Nam?: American Poets Respond,* edited by Walter Lowenfels, Doubleday, 1967, and *Poems of Our Moment: Contemporary Poets of the English Language,* edited by John Hollander, Pegasus, 1968.

WORK IN PROGRESS: A second novel, *Death's Baby Machine.*

SIDELIGHTS: "All poetry, I suspect," Dickey has written, "is nothing more or less than an attempt to discover or invent conditions under which one can live with oneself. I have been called a mystic, a vitalist, a pantheist, an anti-rationalist, and a good many other things. I have not been conscious of the applicability of any of these labels, although they very well may all apply. At any rate, what I have always striven for is to find some way to incarnate my best moments—those which in memory are most persistent and obsessive." Geoffrey Wolff of *Time* magazine writes: "It has become almost obligatory when writing about James Dickey to name his biographical paradoxes, to say that this wonderfully gifted poet was an advertising executive, that he cherishes powerful machinery as well as wilderness quiet, that he was a fighter pilot, that he plays the guitar, that he was an athlete, that he hunts. . . . It is the special signature of Dickey's verse that it both contains and resolves opposites." Dickey believes "that the isolated episodes and incidents of a human life make up, in the end, a kind of sum, a continuous story with different episodes, and that these moments of natural responsiveness show what [the poet] is and in a sense explain him; in the case of a poet they are not so much what he writes but what he *is.*" The critics, too, have noted the feeling of totality in Dickey's work, disparate elements and separate poems fusing into a cohesive whole. "In a sense," John William Corrington observes, "hardly any single poem of Dickey's stands alone. Each seems to lead backward to something else, forward to something more. . . . In surface and in depth, each operates in almost kaleidoscopic fashion, revealing with each reading new facets, new angles of entry previously unseen." As Peter Davison writes, "his poetry is, in the words of his poem 'Buckdancer's Choice,' 'the thousand variations of one song.' "

Paul O'Neil of *Life* has called Dickey "the unlikeliest poet"; a *Time* reviewer hails him as "everyone's notion of a poet." Paradoxically, both labels ring true. A star back in high school and college, even now, O'Neil notes, Dickey "looks, acts and often talks exactly like a professional football coach." He began writing poetry at the age of 24, and his first real poem, Dickey affirms, was a description of football players dressing in a locker room. Davison observes that, at that time, "his technique was still at some distance behind his aspirations. He was handicapped as a poet by coming to his craft late, already knowing what to say, but not how to say it." Dickey writes, in an essay in *Poets on Poetry:* "I came to poetry with no particular qualifications. I had begun to suspect, however, that there is a poet—or a kind of poet—buried in every human being like Ariel in his tree, and that the people whom we are pleased to call poets are only those who have felt the need and contrived the means to release this spirit from its prison." Seeking this means, his ventures into technique centered at first on rhythms, on anapests and iambs, and later on the split line and free-flowing form of his prize-winning collection, *Buckdancer's Choice.* "Although I didn't care for rhyme and the 'packaged' quality which it gives even the best poems," Dickey says, "I did care very much for meter, or at least rhythm. . . . I was then, without knowing it, involved in the question of style and with that I wrestled for a long time—am still wrestling." (A writer for *Antioch Review* recently noted that, "for a man whose poems give the id free reign, Dickey is obsessed with technique and form: at one time he made a list of all the poems he could think of to write.") Dickey employs both lyric and narrative styles in the service of a free verse which many have called "unmannered and businesslike." The content of his work, the various facets of living with which it treats, often, to quote O'Neil, "strikes the spark of recognition" in his readers. In a review of *Poems, 1957-1967,* Donald Baker remarks that "Mr. Dickey continues to shape a suburban mythology of poems nostalgic for youth, for home, for the 'heroic' pathos of love, adultery, flying, and sport, for mystic virility, for rebirth into non-human nature, even for death—in short, for salvation in a 'purely private/Embrace of impossibility'.... His energies burst so blindingly into words, he chants in so confident and successful a voice, and his illusions so closely resemble our own that a reader goes drunk on his work as he might on a strong, familiar music. As a bourgeois American scop Mr. Dickey deserves his rings."

One of the "bourgeois American" traits which receives frequent attention in reviews of his work is his fascination with violence and the manipulation of power. Robert Bly writes that his concern with the imposition of will becomes almost obsessive in the three long poems of *Buckdancer's Choice,* "Slave Quarters," "The Fiend," and "The Firebombing," the last recounting of the night fighter's bombing of Japan seen from the distance of suburban life twenty years later. Ralph J. Mills, Jr. believes that in this poem "Dickey's imaginative gift collapses at the moral level.... [He] would appear to be reliving this segment of his past more for aesthetic than for any other reasons, for the pain and terror of his victims are dwelt on and vividly presented (though without sympathy).... Any real concern for the terrible fate imposed upon others seems secondary." Many of Dickey's fellow poets, including Bly, have taken him to task for feeling "so little anguish" in this regard. Bly was especially repulsed by "The Firebombing" because, "in its easy acceptance of brutality, the poem is deeply middleclass. . . . Dickey balances on his shoulders an absolutely middle class head. He embraces the psychoses of the country, and asks us to wait until he dresses them up a bit with breathless words: then all the liberals will see those psychoses are really 'life-giving'.... As someone said recently, more and more Mr. Dickey takes his life and laminates poetry onto it." Along these same lines, Norman Friedman writes that Dickey "is sweet, he is winning, he is high-minded even while writing of bestiality and violence and lust, and he writes damnably well. . . . He seems so real, and yet at the same time he is so very safe. In the midst of all the apparent daring of his concern with strangeness, with hunting, with war, with death, and so on, nowhere is there the slightest hint that he is anything but the gentlest of domestic men and the most naive of model citizens. He deals with turbulent subjects, but he has no turbulent feelings; he walks through a chamber of horrors clucking with compassion, but almost never is dumb with terror, sick with despair, or wild with desperation. He gives us the illusion of confronting reality but without the danger of being touched by it, and he allows us to preserve our complacency even while we are congratulating ourselves on our temerity."

Dickey's first novel ("and very likely the only one I will write, since my main concern is poetry," Dickey told *Library Journal), Deliverance,* centers on the theme of the suburban dweller fulfilling his potential for brutality. The book was published in the spring of 1970, pre-sold to Warner Bros. for filming, with Dickey writing the script. In progress for eight years before publication, the novel has proved to be an astonishing popular success. "Mr. Dickey is to be praised," wrote L.E. Sissman of the *New Yorker,* "for resisting the temptation of the poet to write 'poetical' prose, to lose his story in lyrical metaphor. He writes in a neat, terse, matter-of-fact prose, level in pitch and perfectly suited to carry the burden of the action." The plot concerns four Southern suburban businessmen who set out on a weekend canoe trip in the wilds of Georgia; but what begins as a stimulating encounter with nature quickly becomes a savage battle for survival. In Dickey's words: "I wished to write a novel having to do with the violence that is at the periphery of all modern experience.... We all fear being set upon by malicious strangers. In fact that feeling is so strong among us that it might well be identified as the characteristic *Angst* of twentieth century man, particularly the American variety. It has come to be as strong, almost, as the fear of death, and in a great many cases it turns out to have been synonymous with it.... *Deliverance* is a novel about how decent men kill.... [It] is also about the bringing forth of qualities in a man that usually lie buried for his whole lifetime. Norman Mailer has always been preoccupied with such themes, and I think rightly: there is something of ourselves being left out of us." However, several reviewers, including Lucy Rosenthal of *Book World,* have observed that with this novel Dickey again seems to be raising moral questions without supplying any answers. Christopher Ricks believes there is, in the book, "a moral insensitivity comparable to the stylistic, for all the studied fineness. [It] is too patently a concoction of a situation in which it will be morally permissible—nay, essential—to kill men with a bow and arrow. Such is clearly what the book wants to do from the outset, and the contrivance of such circumstances has its cold prurience." Commenting on the conspicuously masculine imagery of the novel, Calvin Bedient of the University of California, borrowing a distinction from philosopher Karl Jaspers, writes that *"Deliverance* is a novel of consciousness, not of spirit.... While it merely opens the flesh of the mind to the fiercely specific arrowhead of an adventure that ends without resonance or healing. Dickey's poems open the ego to the restoring draughts of the universal that pour from spiritually apprehended particulars."

Dickey, of course, is the first to agree that he is primarily a poet, and a poet of the spirit at that, although he has the ability to give his poems a strong physical presence. His images are intense, primitive, and animistic. The hunting of animals with bow and arrow is a frequent motif in his work. (Although he is concerned about animal extinction, Dickey views archery hunting "as part of the ecology.") Mills comments on "the notion of exchange" in his poems on hunting, "where the poet ... divides his intuitive powers so as to depict his own inner state in the role of human perceiver or hunter and the sensations of the animal who knows he is pursued." Mills goes on to say that this "notion of exchange ... encompasses the imaginative devices of bodily and spiritual extension, metamorphosis, and metempsychosis.... All of these characteristics, and in addition a preoccupation (strong in his first three books and still present in more recent work) with ritual and archetypal modes of experience, confirm Dickey as a poet who possesses an imagination of a primitive, magical type." In a *New Leader* review of *Poems, 1957-1967,* Jean Garrigue calls his poems "a series of flights," pointing to his *Two Poems of the Air* and his experience as a pilot in the Pacific Theatre as supportive of the fact that "he is a heady poet ... wrapped up in his own imaginative coil, airborne and fighting the earthbound. . . . In short, he treads air as much as he can; he is trying to say the impossible and, if we are to believe him, to do the impossible. Identities change hands, so do parts of the world, things flow into one another; the too too solid world melts, thaws, objects become transparent, metamorphosis occurs or would always be occurring."

In contrast to Miss Garrigue's conception of the "airborne" in Dickey's poetry, Richard Howard notes that "images of the earth" were prevalent in *Helmets,* published in 1964. Howard said that this volume "confirmed him as the telluric maker Wallace Stevens had called for in prophesying that the great poems of heaven and hell have been written and the great poem of the earth remains to be written. Here, more loosely cast in the emblems of battle and quest, are the same gerundive preoccupations with process, though they are now content with the poem as its own reward, rather than a magical charm or source of control over nature. The poet is no longer a necromancer, a magus, but a man speaking to himself.... That impulse—to disarm and confront one's naked humanity—is what governs this entire book, its celebrations of life on earth and its imagined figures." Several critics and fellow poets have expressed the opinion that *Helmets* represents the best of Dickey's achievement, that later efforts show a tendency toward overwriting and "fuzzy Dickeyese," in Friedman's words. Although Corrington believes that *Poems, 1957-1967* is a lucid and exciting demonstration of "the growth of a poet's mind," Harry Morris remarks that he can see "little or no growth in this collection of the work of ten years; the only change is in the direction of greater dispersal, to be found both in the author's self-permissiveness in greater rambling and in his adoption of the long line." A *Times Literary Supplement* reviewer of the book made the following observation: "Mr. Dickey's effect is usually less powerful than it aims to be because, in spite of the concreteness of his detail, his syntax is so loose and cloudy that lines spill over with participles, prepositions, conjunctions and subordinate clauses, smothering whatever main verb is meant to be carrying the central sense." Friedman writes that "Dickey would do well to climb up out of his lush and woolly style, cast it off like excess clothing, and cut into his fuzzy dream-like vision with the pressure of actual confrontations with reality.... He is developing, changing slowly, and taking more risks: he may stand naked, tough, and eloquent yet." However, as John Alfred Avant has suggested, perfection of style may sometimes lead to irrelevance of content. Avant finds Dickey's most recent collection, *The Eye-Beaters, Blood, Victory, Madness, Buckhead, and Mercy,* "very exciting, despite certain alarming elements. Dickey is now an Important Poet ... so he is writing about Big Subjects. As his poetry becomes depersonalized, the poetic effects are blurred, although his images remain vivid in themselves. Thus much of this work is beautiful but rather remote."

Dickey himself is probably aware of this tendency. Saul Maloff has said that he cares desperately about poetry, both his own and that of his contemporaries, believing that "the issues at stake are those of the life and death of the mind and spirit." Nowhere is this more evident than in his literary criticism. He admires what is simplistic, elemental, and genuine in the work of his peers, deplores purely intellectual maneuvers and "overrefined, university-pale subtleties." Howard Kaye says that *Babel to Byzantium,* Dickey's collected criticism of the previous twelve years, reveals him as "a democratic liberal of the poetry shelf ... impatient with the pretensions of the radicals to his left—the Charles Olsons, the Duncans, the Ginsbergs, the coffee-house warblers of woodnotes wild.... To Dickey's right are the traditional poets, characterized by strict adherence to metrical forms, rhymes, and abstractions; he is unsympathetic to them too. Much of the center, as well, comes under attack, particularly the 'school of charm' (James Merrill, Richard Wilbur, Anthony Hecht), which tries 'to raise banalities, through verbal manipulation alone, to what passes for consequence.'" Dickey admires the work of Robert Lowell, John Berryman, Rolfe Humphries, Robert Penn Warren, Howard Nemerov, William Jay Smith, May Sarton, Richard Eberhart, and Margaret Tongue, stating that Theodore Roethke "is the greatest poet we have ever had in

this country." "When I began writing," Dickey has said, "I thought Keats and Wordsworth were great—and so they are, of course. Milton bored me [Dickey has classified Milton among "the great stuffed goats of English literature"], and I mistrusted modern guys like Hopkins. As I worked with words, I especially came to admire the things that Sydney, Shakespeare, Spenser and all those cats could do with the language way back in their time."

Possibly "the most serious defect of Dickey's critical sensibility," according to Kaye, "is in the area of traditional poetry. As he says, 'I have always had trouble distinguishing between artificiality and the traditional modes and methods of verse.'" He publishes criticism prolifically and admits that he gets poison-pen letters about articles he does not recall having written.

A *Virginia Quarterly* reviewer of *Babel to Byzantium* writes: "When Mr. Dickey was asked at a reading his opinion of the usefulness of criticism *to poets,* he said *he* never learned anything from it. This reaction is typical of the man, whose approach is always personal, filtering the 'universal' tenets of criticism through his own taste." Victor Howes is decisive in his acclaim of Dickey's critical aplomb in *The Suspect in Poetry:* "Here is no ponderous tome of literary officialdom uttering canons and commandments, no high court distributing poetic justice right and left. Here, rather, is an exercise in taste by a man who believes each of us is potentially 'master of a superior secret.' In seeking to clear away the deadwood of the suspect, Mr. Dickey reveals a passionate desire to hear truths of the human heart."

Dickey's "sprawling energies . . . a gladdening unwillingness to lie flat on the page," to quote John Simon, is perhaps the single most striking quality in his work. In an *Atlantic* article entitled "The Difficulties of Being Major," Davison lists W.H. Auden's five suggested rules for the major poet, and asserts that there are really only two American poets the age of fifty or younger who qualify: Robert Lowell and James Dickey. "If American poetry needs a champion for the new generation," writes Davison, "Dickey's power and ambition may supply the need.

"His archetypal concerns are universal to all languages and will no doubt carry over into translation; his sense of urgency is overwhelming; his volume, his range, his style, his technique, his process of maturing—all might supply W.H. Auden's five categories (and so might the number of bad poems he has written!)." Morris' denial of Dickey's growth notwithstanding, many have commented on Dickey's emergence as a major poet in just over a decade. Louis Untermeyer believes that Dickey's "development has been so recent and his fecundity so rapid that the appraisers and compilers have not caught up with him. Practically everything he has written has been accomplished in a ten-year span."

To Lawrence Lieberman, "the subject of Dickey's new poetry is being in extremity, being stretched to the outer —or inner—limits of joy and terror. Dickey at his best is now able to give us the radically new experience in poetry that D.H. Lawrence superbly demonstrated to be America's most singular contribution to world literature. He is an expansional poet. Those voices he is able to release through self-expansion in the poem are themselves the substance and make-up of his total personality. The poems he writes enlarge his personality, in fact, to the degree that he enlarges his experience of humanity—or ultrahumanity—in the writing of them. The expansional poet has learned to harness his personality, to make it run at full gallop in the poetry, to open it up and let it flow outward into the world, constrained neither by experience it has already mastered in life, nor by traditional forms and meters. For the expansional poet, form is developmental, self-discovering." What new impact or insight will emerge from Dickey's "mystique of self" in the future is a subject for fervent discussion. The following statement from the *Literary Times*, May-June, 1967, may be indicative of the way in which the entire field of American poetry is evolving: "James Dickey is emerging, not with inchworm progress, but with explosive acceptance and fanatical followers as the new Robert Lowell. . . . He has the drift of things and the drift takes him away from the merely self analytical and into the social history of self, the importance of living and *acting* upon the world and not warming beneath the forlorn [billets-doux] of E.S.V. Millay. Aside from stringent political entanglements, Dickey's voice will cry the loudest and perhaps the longest in the next decade."

Dickey has recorded his poetry for the Library of Congress, and Spoken Arts released a recording (SA 984), in 1968, of the poet reading thirteen of his poems.

In 1970 Stanley Croner produced and directed a 37-minute, 16mm sound film about Dickey and his poetry. The film, entitled "Lord, Let Me Die But Not Die Out," is distributed by Encyclopaedia Britannica Educational Corp.

Warner Bros. released a motion picture of *Deliverance* in 1972, in which Dickey plays a small part as a rural sheriff.

BIOGRAPHICAL/CRITICAL SOURCES: Chad Walsh, *Today's Poets*, Scribner, 1964; *Times Literary Supplement*, October 29, 1964, May 18, 1967; *Christian Science Monitor*, December 3, 1964; *Sixties*, winter, 1964, spring, 1967; *New York Times Book Review*, January 3, 1965, February 6, 1966, March 22, 1970; *Chicago Review*, Number 1, 1966; *Milwaukee Journal*, March 20, 1966; *Partisan Review*, summer, 1966; *Sewanee Review*, summer, 1966, spring, 1969; *Life*, July 22, 1966; *Nation*, April 24, 1967, April 6, 1970, March 23, 1970; *Saturday Review*, May 6, 1967; *New Leader*, May 22, 1967, May 20, 1968; *Literary News*, May-June, 1967; *Hudson Review*, autumn, 1967, autumn, 1968; *Atlantic*, October, 1967; *Commonweal*, December 1, 1967; Paul Carroll, *The Poem in its Skin*, Follett, 1968; Laurence Lieberman, editor, *The Achievement of James Dickey*, Scott, Foresman, 1968; *Georgia Review*, spring, 1968, summer, 1969; *Poetry*, March, 1968; *New Republic*, June 29, 1968, April 18, 1970; *Book World*, June 30, 1968, March 15, 1970; *Triquarterly*, winter, 1968; *Yale Review*, winter, 1968; *Newsweek*, March 30, 1970; *Best Sellers*, April 1, 1970; *Time*, April 20, 1970, August 7, 1972; *New York Review of Books*, April 23, 1970; *New Yorker*, May 2, 1970; *Antioch Review*, fall/winter, 1970-71; *Esquire*, December, 1970; Eileen Glancy, *James Dickey: The Critic as Poet* (annotated bibliography with introductory essay), Whitston Publishing Co., 1971; *Playboy*, May, 1971.†

*   *   *

DICKEY, William 1928-

PERSONAL: Born December 15, 1928, in Bellingham, Wash.; son of Paul C. (a contracting officer) and Anne (Hobart) Dickey; married Shirley Anne Marn (a psychiatric nurse), January 7, 1959. *Education:* Reed College, B.A. 1951; Harvard University, M.A., 1955; State University of Iowa, M.F.A., 1956. *Politics:* Democrat. *Religion:* None. *Home:* 478 Chenery St., San Francisco, Calif. 94131. *Office:* Department of English, San Francisco State College, San Francisco, Calif. 94132.

CAREER: Cornell University, Ithaca, N.Y., instructor in English, 1956-59; Denison University, Granville, Ohio, assistant professor of English, 1960-62; San Francisco State College, San Francisco, Calif., assistant professor, 1962-65, associate professor, 1965-70, professor of English and

creative writing, 1970—. *Member:* Modern Language Association of America, American Federation of Teachers, Society for Italic Handwriting (England), Phi Beta Kappa. *Awards, honors:* Woodrow Wilson fellowship, 1951-52; Yale Series of Younger Poets prize, 1959, for *Of the Festivity;* Fulbright award, Jesus College, Oxford, 1959-60; Union League Foundation prize, *Poetry* magazine, 1962.

WRITINGS: Of the Festivity (poems), foreword by W.H. Auden, Yale University Press, 1959; *Interpreter's House* (poems), Ohio State University Press, 1963; *Rivers of the Pacific Northwest* (long poem), Twowindows, 1969; *More Under Saturn* (poems), Wesleyan University Press, 1971. Anthologized in *Poet's Choice*, edited by Paul Engle and Joseph Langland, Dial, 1962, *Erotic Poetry*, edited by William Cole, Random House, 1963, and *The Contemporary Poet as Artist and Critic: Eight Symposia*, edited by Anthony Ostroff, Little, Brown, 1964. Contributor of about one hundred poems to *New Yorker, Harper's, Saturday Review, Atlantic,* and other periodicals. Regular reviewer of poetry for *Hudson Review.* Former managing editor of *Western Review*, and editorial assistant for *Civil War History.*

WORK IN PROGRESS: A study of the poetry of Jonathan Swift.

SIDELIGHTS: Critics have said that Auden is the prime influence in Dickey's early poetry. Thom Gunn believes that Dickey is attempting to loosen this tie, striving to achieve his individual style. This process may, Gunn says, be a difficult task for Dickey. "There are . . . some . . . self-consciously serious poems, . . . some of which are a trifle awkward, but others of which really say something in an interesting way. . . . Most . . . [are] the enjoyable and competent work of an apprentice who has good chances of becoming a master." Dudley Fitts is more unqualified in his praise. "Mr. Dickey is skilful and engaging . . . . He is also witty, in a donnish sort of way, and very successful in establishing an air of casual inconsequence that turns out, upon reflection, to be anything but inconsequential."

BIOGRAPHICAL/CRITICAL SOURCES: Saturday Review, July 25, 1959; *New York Times Book Review*, September 6, 1959, July 5, 1964; *Yale Review*, December, 1959; *Poetry*, January, 1960, May, 1964; *Antioch Review*, spring, 1963; *Times Literary Supplement*, May 7, 1964.

*   *   *

DICKINSON, Patric Thomas 1914-

PERSONAL: Born December 26, 1914, in Nasirabad, India; son of Arthur Thomas (an army officer) and Eileen (Kirwan) Dickinson; married Sheila Shannon (an editor and anthologist), December 19, 1947; children: David Dunbar, Virginia Kirwan. *Education:* St. Catharine's College, Cambridge, B.A. (with honors), 1936. *Home:* 38 Church Square, Rye, Sussex, England. *Agent:* Curtis Brown Ltd., 13 King St., London W.C.2, England.

CAREER: British Broadcasting Corp., producer, transcription service, 1942-45, poetry editor, Home Service and Third Programme, 1945-48; free-lance broadcaster and critic, 1948—. Lecturer and reader. Director, Poetry Festival, Royal Court Theater, 1963. *Member:* International P.E.N., Saville Club, Rye Golf Club. *Awards, honors:* Atlantic award in literature, 1948.

WRITINGS: The Seven Days of Jericho (poetry), Andrew Dakers, 1944; (compiler) *Soldiers' Verse* (anthology), Muller, 1945; *Theseus and the Minotaur, and Poems*, J. Cape, 1946; *Stone in the Midst, and Poems*, Methuen, 1948; (editor and author of introduction) Byron, *Poems*, Grey Walls Press, 1949; (editor with wife Sheila Shannon) *Personal Portraits*, Parrish, 1950; *A*

Round of Golf Courses: A Selection of the Best Eighteen, Evans Brothers, 1951; *The Sailing Race, and Other Poems,* Chatto & Windus, 1952; *The Scale of Things* (poems), Chatto & Windus, 1955; (editor with others) *New Poems, 1955,* M. Joseph, 1955; (translator) *Aristophanes Against War: The Acharnians, The Peace, Lysistrata,* Oxford University Press, 1957; (compiler with Shannon) *Poems to Remember: A Book for Children* (anthology), Harvill, 1958.

The World I See (poems), Chatto & Windus and Hogarth, 1960, Dufour, 1962; (translator) Vergil, *The Aeneid,* New American Library, 1962; *This Cold Universe* (poems), Chatto & Windus and Hogarth, 1964; *The Good Minute: An Autobiographical Study,* Gollancz, 1965; (compiler with Shannon) *Poets' Choice: An Anthology of English Poetry from Spenser to the Present Day,* Evans Brothers, 1967; (editor and author of introduction and notes) C. Day Lewis, *Selections from His Poetry,* Chatto & Windus, 1967; *Selected Poems,* Chatto & Windus, 1968; *More Than Time* (poetry), Chatto & Windus and Hogarth, 1970, Wesleyan University Press, 1971; (translator into English verse) Aristophanes, *Plays,* Oxford University Press, 1970; (translator into English verse) Aristophanes, *Plays II,* Oxford University Press, 1970.

Plays: *Stone in the Midst* (first produced in London at Mercury Theatre, 1951), published in *Stone in the Midst, and Poems,* Methuen, 1948; "The Golden Touch," first produced in Wolverhampton, 1956; *A Durable Fire* (first produced at Canterbury Festival, 1962), Chatto & Windus, 1962. Contributor of numerous scripts to British Broadcasting Corp. Third Programme.

SIDELIGHTS: Literary critics are mixed in their reactions to Dickinson's poetry. They approve of its technique and craftsmanship; yet they also find fault with its often quiet and settled tone. Robin Skelton writes of *Selected Poems:* "The poems are all well-made. The observations are acute and sometimes original. The lyrics flow easily without slackness. The ironic passages are effective. The moral fables are pointed. There is nothing wrong. And yet over and over again I find myself unimpressed. It is partly, I think, that there is a surfeit of generalized expressions of emotion such as the words 'beautiful,' 'wonderful,' 'miraculous' and that the poems too often hinge upon such words at a crucial point in their structures. It is partly, perhaps, that the easiness of tone too often results in predictability, and in the presentation of what oft was thought and oft as well expressed." Douglas Dunn believes that Dickinson's poetry "seldom disturbs, probes, excites, exasperates, hurts, in any forceful way. This subdued tone usually is right, for him, though sometimes the poems need a bit more propulsion than he seems able to give.... But Dickinson is a fair minor poet, who, particularly in the later work, appears less appreciated than he deserves."

Alan Brownjohn is less qualified in his praise. "The Georgian quietness of Dickinson's early verse was always a little deceptive. Even where the plots were conventional and the diction plain and limited ... he was always a skillful craftsman with an excellent ear, and [had] a way of giving a poem a disconcerting edge which held the attention.... In the poems of his last two books ... there is a readiness to come out from behind the mask of the gentle, elegiac poet concerned with time, history and inadequate mankind, and to write in a more strongly personal way. The patient craftsmanship and the quiet, unembroidered manner are still there, but used with much more conciseness and point. ... This kind of scrupulous directness in a deceptively simple mode ... suggests more interesting developments to come yet from a poet strengthening and maturing his talent in a way worth watching."

AVOCATIONAL INTERESTS: Collecting Sunderland lustre poetry and playing golf.

BIOGRAPHICAL/CRITICAL SOURCES: Times Literary Supplement, August 24, 1967; *New Statesman,* February 28, 1969, September 25, 1970; *Poetry,* September, 1969; *London Magazine,* October, 1969.

* * *

DICKLER, Gerald 1912-

PERSONAL: Born August 20, 1912, in New York, N.Y.; son of Michael and Lillian (Fischoff) Dickler; married Ruth A. Crohn, June 1, 1933; children: Abby, Jane, Susan. *Education:* Columbia University, A.B., 1931, LL.B., 1933. *Office:* 460 Park Ave., New York, N.Y. 10022.

CAREER: Admitted to New York Bar; attorney in private practice; Hall, Casey, Dickler & Howley (attorneys), New York, N.Y., partner, 1959—. Director and secretary, Capital Cities Broadcasting Corp. and Odyssey Productions, Inc.; director of Hall Syndicate, Inc. Trustee of Walden School, 1947-51. *Military service:* U.S. Naval Reserve, 1943-45. *Member:* Federal Bar Association of New York, New Jersey, and Connecticut, Bar Association of the City of New York.

WRITINGS: Man on Trial: History-Making Trials from Socrates to Oppenheimer, Doubleday, 1962.

* * *

DICKSON, Gordon R(upert) 1923-

PERSONAL: Born November 1, 1923, in Edmonton, Alberta; son of Gordon Fraser (a mining engineer) and Maude Leola (a teacher; maiden name, Ford) Dickson. *Education:* University of Minnesota, B.A., 1948, graduate study, 1948-50. *Home:* 7400 10th Ave. S., Minneapolis, Minn. 55423. *Agent:* Robert Mills, McIntosh, McKee & Dodds, 30 East 60th St. New York, N.Y. 10022.

CAREER: Writer, 1950—. *Military service:* U.S. Army, 1943-46. *Member:* Authors League of America, Mystery Writers of America, Minnesota Historical Society, Minneapolis Institute of Arts, Milford Science-Fiction Writers Conference. *Awards, honors:* Hugo award, 1965, for *Soldier, Ask Not;* Nebula award, Science-Fiction Writers of America, 1966, for *Call Him Lord.*

WRITINGS—Adult science fiction novels, except as indicated: (With Nick Boddie Williams) *Alien from Arcturus [and] The Atom Curtain* (the former by Dickson, the latter by Williams), Ace Book, 1956; (with Andre Norton) *The Crossroads of Time [and] Mankind on the Run* (the former by Norton, the latter by Dickson), Ace Books, 1956; (with Poul Anderson) *Earthmen's Burden,* Gnome Press, 1957; *Time to Teleport [and] The Genetic General,* two volumes in one, Ace Books, 1960 (*The Genetic General* published in England in a separate volume, Brown, Watson, 1961); *Naked to the Stars,* Pyramid Books, 1961; *Delusion World [and] Spatial Delivery,* two volumes in one, Ace Books, 1961; *Necromancer,* Doubleday, 1962, reissued as *No Room for Man,* Macfadden, 1963; *The Alien Way,* Bantam, 1965; *Mission to Universe,* Berkley Publishing, 1966; (with Keith Laumer) *Planet Run,* Doubleday, 1967; *The Space Swimmers,* Berkley Publishing, 1967; *Soldier, Ask Not,* Dell, 1967; *Wolfling,* Dell, 1969; *Spacepaw,* Putnam, 1969; *None But Man,* Doubleday, 1969; *Hour of the Horde,* Putnam, 1970; *Danger—Human* (short stories), Doubleday, 1970; *Mutants,* Macmillan, 1970; *Sleepwalker's World,* Lippincott, 1971; (with others) *Five Fates,* Doubleday, 1971; *The Tactics of Mistake,* Doubleday, 1971; *The Outposter,* Lippincott, 1972; (with Anderson and Robert Silverberg) *The Day the Sun Stood Still: Three Original Novellas of Science Fiction* (contains *A Chapter of Revelation* by

Anderson, *Thomas the Proclaimer* by Silverberg, and *Things Which Are Caesar's* by Dickson), T. Nelson (Nashville), 1972; *The Pritcher Mass*, Doubleday, 1972.

Juveniles: *Secret Under the Sea*, Holt, 1960; *Secret Under Antarctica*, Holt, 1963; *Secret Under the Caribbean*, Holt, 1964; *Space Winners*, Holt, 1965. Author of more than 150 short stories and novelettes, some of them anthologized. Also author of radio plays.

WORK IN PROGRESS: *Alien Art*, for Dell; *Pilgrim and Professional*, for Putnam; *Stoneman's Walk*, a contemporary novel; two historical novels, *Swords to Poitiers* and *Hawkhood*.

BIOGRAPHICAL/CRITICAL SOURCES: *Times Literary Supplement*, May 25, 1967.

*　　*　　*

DILLARD, Polly Hargis 1916-

PERSONAL: Born April 22, 1916, in Somerset, Ky.; daughter of Charles Parker (a religious educator) and Sarah (Boyd) Hargis; married Badgett Dillard (an educational administrator), June 2, 1957; children: Stephen, Ann. *Education:* University of Kentucky, B.A.; George Peabody College for Teachers, M.A. *Religion:* Baptist. *Home:* 610 Upland Rd., Louisville, Ky. 40206.

CAREER: Southern Baptist Theological Seminary, Louisville, Ky., assistant professor of children's work, 1953-58; Head Start, Louisville, Ky., supervisor, 1968—.

WRITINGS—All published by Broadman, except as indicated: *Teaching the Beginner Child*, 1948; *Sunday with Stevie*, 1956; *Peter and the Rain*, 1957; *The Church Kindergarten*, 1958; *Improving Nursery Departments*, 1960; *Bible Stories for Me*, 1961; *Good Food to Eat: A Unit for Nursery Children in the Church Study* Course, Convention Press, 1961; *My Thank-You Book*, 1964; *My Book about Jesus*, 1968; *Tony's Triumph*, Home Mission Board, Southern Baptist Convention, 1970.

*　　*　　*

DILLON, Eilis 1920-

PERSONAL: Given name is pronounced El-*eesh*; born March 7, 1920, in Galway, Ireland; daughter of Thomas (a university professor) and Geraldine (Plunkett) Dillon; married Cormac O'Cuilleanain (a university professor), March 28, 1940 (died, 1970); children: Eilean, Maire, Cormac. *Education:* Ursaline Convent, Sligo, Ireland, student, 1931-38. *Politics:* Irish Nationalist. *Religion:* Roman Catholic. *Home:* 7 Templemore Ave., Dublin, Ireland. *Agent:* Harold Ober Associates, Inc., 40 East 49th St., New York, N.Y. 10017; and Bolb & Watson, 8 Storey's Gate, London S.W.1, England.

CAREER: Originally a professional cellist, but turned to writing. Lecturer on creative writing, Trinity College, Dublin, 1971-72; lecturer at American universities and colleges on three tours, speaking on Anglo-Irish literature, especially poetry. *Member:* Societa Dante Alighieri (Cork; vice-president). *Awards, honors: A Herd of Deer* was listed as a 1970 American Library Association "notable book."

WRITINGS: *An Choill bheo* (in Gaelic), Oifig an tSolathair, 1948; *Midsummer Magic*, Macmillan, 1949; *Oscar agus an Coiste se nEasog* (in Gaelic), Oifig an tSolathair, 1952; *The Lost Island*, Faber, 1952, Funk, 1954; *Death at Crane's Court*, Faber, 1953, Walker & Co., 1963; *The San Sebastian*, Faber, 1953, Funk, 1954; *Sent to His Account*, Faber, 1954, Walker & Co., 1969; *Ceol na Coille* (in Gaelic), Oifig an tSolathair, 1955; *The House on the Shore*, Faber, 1955, Funk, 1956; *The Wild Little House*, Faber, 1955; *The Island of Horses*, Faber, 1956, Funk, 1957; *Death in the Quadrangle*, Faber, 1956,

Walker & Co., 1968; *Plover Hill*, Hamish Hamilton, 1957; *The Bitter Glass*, Faber, 1958, Appleton, 1959; *Aunt Bedelia's Cats*, Hamish Hamilton, 1958.

The Head of the Family, Faber, 1960; *The Fort of Gold*, Faber, 1961, Funk, 1962; *King Big-Ears*, Faber, 1961, Norton, 1963; *A Pony and A Trap*, Hamish Hamilton, 1962; *The Cat's Opera*, Faber, 1962, Bobbs-Merrill, 1963; *The Coriander*, Faber, 1963, Funk, 1964; *A Family of Foxes*, Faber, 1964, Funk, 1965; *Bold John Henebry*, Faber, 1965; *The Sea Wall*, Farrar, Straus, 1965; *The Lion Cub*, Hamish Hamilton, 1966, Duell, Sloan & Pearce, 1967; *The Road to Dunmore*, Faber, 1966; *The Cruise of the Santa Maria*, Funk, 1967; *Two Stories: The Road to Dunmore* [and] *The Key*, Meredith, 1967; *The Key*, Faber, 1967; *The Seals*, Faber, 1968, Funk, 1969; *Under the Orange Grove*, Faber, 1968, Meredith, 1969; *A Herd of Deer*, Faber, 1969, Funk, 1970; *The Wise Man on the Mountain*, Hamish Hamilton, 1969, Atheneum, 1970; *The Voyage of Mael Duin*, Faber, 1969; *The King's Room*, Hamish Hamilton, 1970; *The Five Hundred*, Hamish Hamilton, 1972; *Across the Bitter Sea*, Simon & Schuster, 1973; *The Hamish Hamilton Book of Wise Animals*, Hamish Hamilton, 1973; *Life in Ancient Rome* (tentative title), Faber, in press. Also author of "A Page of History" (stage play), "Manna" (radio play), and other radio scripts.

SIDELIGHTS: "My father was [a] professor of chemistry at a university. We lived in a village on the sea coast, a few miles west of Galway, where the common language of the people was Irish. From visiting our neighbors, from going to the village school, and mainly from my early knowledge of the Irish language and of old Irish songs, I came gradually to know the mind of these people. Later I spent summers in the Aran Islands, and also in the remote parts of Connemara where we used to camp in tents which as I remember occasionally blew away in the middle of the night. My school was the Ursuline Convent in Sligo, where William Butler Yeats lived as a boy. It is a beautiful country, dominated by two mountains, Benbulben and Knocknarea, whose names are associated with the oldest of the Irish folk tales.

"I never remember a time when I did not want to write. I composed my first story at the age of seven, about a mouse called Harry who got into bad company, committed murder and was hanged. I would not choose such a subject for a children's book now."

Miss Dillon has lectured and broadcast frequently in Ireland. Many of her books have been translated into French, German, Dutch, Swedish, Czech, Polish, and Norwegian.

AVOCATIONAL INTERESTS: Music, travel, and the theatre.

BIOGRAPHICAL/CRITICAL SOURCES: *Creation*, August, 1962; *Books for Children, 1960-1965*, American Library Association, 1966; *Times Literary Supplement*, May 25, 1967; *Best Sellers*, October 1, 1967; *Listener*, November 16, 1967; *Books and Bookmen*, December, 1967, August, 1968, March, 1970, May, 1970; *Book World*, December 31, 1967; *New Statesman*, November, 1968; Nancy Larrick, *A Parent's Guide to Children's Reading*, 3rd edition, Doubleday, 1969; *New York Times Book Review*, April 27, 1969; *Punch*, December 19, 1969; *Horn Book*, June, 1970.

*　　*　　*

DINES, (Harry) Glen 1925-

PERSONAL: Born November 19, 1925, in Casper, Wyo.; son of Harry G. and Caroline (Maltby) Dines; married Ruth Goldberg, February, 1954; children: Debby Lisa, Woody. *Education:* Attended University of Washington,

Seattle, and Art Center School, Los Angeles, Calif.; Sacramento State College, B.A. and M.A., 1957. *Home:* Fairfax, Calif.

CAREER: Before becoming full-time writer and illustrator worked at variety of jobs, including apple picker, handicraft instructor in Young Men's Christian Association camp on Santa Catalina Island, high school teacher, and department store layout artist. *Military service:* U.S. Army, Eighth Army Special Services, Tokyo, Japan, staff artist on Pacific edition *Stars and Stripes,* World War II; became sergeant.

WRITINGS: (With Raymond Price) *Dog Soldiers: The Famous Warrior Society of the Cheyenne Indians,* Macmillan, 1962; *End 'o Steel: Man and Rails Across a Wilderness,* Macmillan, 1963.

Author and illustrator: *The Useful Dragon of Sam Ling Toy,* Macmillan, 1956; *The Mysterious Machine,* Macmillan, 1957; *A Tiger in the Cherry Tree,* Macmillan, 1958; *Pitidoe, the Color Maker,* Macmillan, 1959; *The Fabulous Flying Bicycle,* Macmillan, 1960; *Overland Stage: The Story of the Famous Overland Stagecoaches of the 1860's,* Macmillan, 1962; *Long Knife: The Story of the Fighting U.S. Cavalry of the 1860 Frontier,* Macmillan, 1962; *Bull Wagon: Strong Wheels for Rugged Men—The Frontier Freighters,* Macmillan, 1963; *Indian Pony: The Tough, Hardy Little Horse of the Far-Roving Red Man,* Macmillan, 1963; *Crazy Horse,* Putnam, 1966; *Gilly and the Whicharoo,* Lothrop, 1968; *Golden Cities, Golden Ships,* McGraw, 1968; *Kit Carson's Black Deed and Other True Stories from Marin's Lively Past,* Academy Press, 1968; *Sir Cecil and the Bad Blue Beast,* S.G. Phillips, 1970; *Sun, Sand, and Steel: Costumes and Equipment of the Spanish-Mexican Southwest,* Putnam, 1972; *John Muir* (biography), Putnam, 1973.

Illustrator: Richard Watkins, *Milliken's Ark,* Thomas Nelson, 1956; Patricia Miles Martin, *The Bony Pony,* Putnam, 1965; Don Berry, *Mountain Men: The Trappers of the Great Fur-Trading Sea,* Macmillan, 1966.

AVOCATIONAL INTERESTS: Camping and hiking, especially in wilderness areas, skin diving, tennis, good books, and people.

*   *   *

DIVERRES, Armel Hugh   1914-

PERSONAL: Born September 4, 1914, in Liverpool, England; son of Paul (a university teacher) and Elizabeth (Jones) Diverres; married Ann Williams, November 25, 1945; children: Branwen, Catrin, Paul. *Education:* University College of Swansea, B.A. (with honors), 1936, M.A., 1938; University of Rennes, L. es L., 1938; University of Paris, Docteur de l'Universite, 1950. *Religion:* Presbyterian. *Home:* 202 Queen's Rd., Aberdeen, Scotland.

CAREER: University of Manchester, Manchester, England, assistant lecturer, 1946-49, lecturer in French, 1949-54; University of Aberdeen, Aberdeen, Scotland, senior lecturer, 1954-57, professor of French, 1958—. *Military service:* British Army, 1940-46; became captain.

WRITINGS: (Editor) Froissart, *Voyage en Bearn,* Manchester University Press, 1953; (editor) *La Chronique metrique attribuee a Geffroy de Paris,* Belles-Lettres, 1956; (editor with Frederick Whitehead) *Medieval Miscellany,* Barnes & Noble, 1965; (editor and author of introduction) Alfred Vigny, *Chatterton,* University of London Press, 1967. Contributor of articles and reviews to learned journals.

WORK IN PROGRESS: Editing Joinville's *Vie de Saint Louis,* publication expected in 1974.

AVOCATIONAL INTERESTS: Hill-walking, travelling in western Europe.

*   *   *

DIXON, John W(esley), Jr.   1919-

PERSONAL: Born August 18, 1919, in Richmond, Va.; son of John Wesley (a minister) and Margaret Collins (Denny) Dixon; married Vivian Slagle, January 9, 1943; children: Susan, Judith, Miriam. *Education:* University of Bristol, student, 1938-39; Emory and Henry College, B.A., 1941; University of Chicago, Ph.D., 1953. *Politics:* Democrat. *Religion:* Episcopal. *Home:* 216 Glenhill Lane, Chapel Hill, N.C. 27514. *Office:* Department of Religion, University of North Carolina, Chapel Hill, N.C. 27514.

CAREER: Michigan State University, East Lansing, instructor in literature and fine arts, 1950-52; Emory University, Atlanta, Ga., assistant professor of humanities and art history, 1952-57; Dickinson College, Carlisle, Pa., associate professor of art history, 1957-60; Florida Presbyterian College, St. Petersburg, associate professor of humanities and art history, 1960-63; University of North Carolina, Chapel Hill, associate professor, 1963-67, professor of religion and art, 1967—. *Military service:* U.S. Army, 1941-46; became first lieutenant. *Member:* College Art Association.

WRITINGS: Form and Reality: Art As Communication, Methodist Student, 1951; *Nature and Grace in Art,* University of North Carolina Press, 1964; *Aesthetics and Art Criticism,* Faculty Christian Fellowship, 1964; *Criticism,* Faculty Christian Fellowship, 1964. Contributor of articles to religious publications.

WORK IN PROGRESS: Continued studies on the relation of religion and art.

*   *   *

DOBB, Maurice (Herbert)   1900-

PERSONAL: Born July 24, 1900, in London, England; son of Walter Herbert and Elsie Annie (Moir) Dobb; married Barbara Marian Nixon, November 6, 1931. *Education:* Attended Charterhouse School; Pembroke College, Cambridge, first class in economics tripos, 1922; London School of Economics and Political Science, London, research student, 1922-24; Cambridge University, M.A.; University of London, Ph.D. *Home:* College Farmhouse, Fulbourn, Cambridgeshire, England.

CAREER: Cambridge University, Cambridge, England, university lecturer, 1925-60, reader in economics, 1960-67, reader emeritus, 1967—, fellow and lecturer of Trinity College, 1948—. Visiting professor of economics at University of Delhi, India, 1951. *Member:* Royal Economic Society, Association of University Teachers.

WRITINGS: The Development of Capitalism: An Outline Course for Classes and Study Circles, Labour Research Department, 1922, 2nd edition, 1925; *Money and Prices: An Outline Course for Students,* Labour Research Department, 1924; *An Outline of European History from the Decay of Feudalism to the Present Day,* Plebs League, 1925; *Capitalist Enterprise and Social Progress,* Routledge & Sons, 1925; *Modern Capitalism: Its Origin and Growth,* Labour Research Department, 1928; (with H.C. Stevens) *Russian Economic Development Since the Revolution,* Dutton, 1928, 2nd edition, Routledge & Sons, 1929; *Wages,* introduction by John Maynard Keynes, Harcourt, 1928, 4th revised edition, Nisbet and Cambridge University Press, 1956.

Russia To-day and To-morrow (pamphlet), Leonard & Virginia Woolf, 1930; *On Marxism Today* (pamphlet), Leonard & Virginia Woolf, 1932; *An Introduction to Economics,* Gollancz, 1932; *Soviet Russia and the World* (pamphlet), Sidgwick & Jackson, 1932; *Social Credit Discredited,* Martin Lawrence, 1936; *Planning and Capitalism,* W.E.T.U.C., 1937; *Political Economy and Capitalism,* International Publishers, 1937 (published in England as *Political Economy and Capitalism: Some Essays in the Economic Tradition,* Routledge & Sons, 1937).

Trade Union Experience and Policy, 1914-18: An Outline, Lawrence & Wishart, 1940; *Soviet Economy and the War,* Routledge & Sons, 1941, International Publishers, 1943; *Production Front,* Labour Monthly, 1941; *How Soviet Trade Unions Work,* Labour Research Department, 1941; *Soviet Planning and Labour in Peace and War: Four Studies,* Routledge & Sons, 1942, International Publishers, 1944; *U.S.S.R.: Her Life and Her People,* University of London Press, 1943; *Economics of Capitalism: An Introductory Outline,* Lawrence & Wishart, 1943; *Marx as an Economist,* Lawrence & Wishart, 1943, International Publishers, 1945; *Economics of Private Enterprise: An Introductory Outline,* Current Book, 1944; *Studies in the Development of Capitalism,* Routledge & Sons, 1946, International Publishers, 1947, revised edition, Routledge & Sons, 1963, International Publishers, 1964; *Soviet Economic Development Since 1917,* Routledge & Kegan Paul, 1948, International Publishers, 1949, 6th edition, Routledge & Kegan Paul, 1966, International Publishers, 1967.

(Editor with P. Sraffa) *Works and Correspondence of David Ricardo,* ten volumes, Cambridge University Press, 1950-54; *Some Aspects of Economic Development: Three Lectures,* Ranjit (Delhi), 1951; *On Economic Theory and Socialism: Collected Papers,* International Publishers, 1955, revised edition, Routledge & Kegan Paul, 1965; (with others) V.B. Singh, editor, *Keynesian Economics: A Symposium,* Peoples Publishing House, 1956; *Capitalism, Yesterday and Today,* Lawrence & Wishart, 1958, Monthly Review Press, 1962.

An Essay on Economic Growth and Planning, Monthly Review Press, 1960, 2nd edition, 1969; *Economic Growth and Underdeveloped Countries,* International Publishers, 1963; *Transition from Feudalism to Capitalism* (pamphlet), University of Bologna, 1963; *Argument on Socialism,* Lawrence & Wishart, 1966; *Papers on Capitalism, Development and Planning,* International Publishers, 1967; *Socialism, Capitalism and Economic Growth,* edited by C.H. Feinstein, Cambridge University Press, 1967; *Welfare Economics and the Economics of Socialism,* Cambridge University Press, 1969; (editor) Karl Marx, *Contribution to the Critique of Political Economy,* International Publishers, 1971; *Theories of Value and Distribution Since Adam Smith: Ideology and Economic Theory,* Cambridge University Press, 1973.

Contributor to *Encyclopaedia Britannica, Encyclopaedia of Social Sciences,* and to professional journals.

BIOGRAPHICAL/CRITICAL SOURCES: Times Literary Supplement, January 26, 1967, February 29, 1968.

*   *   *

DOBBIN, John E.   1914-

PERSONAL: Born July 8, 1914, in Eau Claire, Wis.; son of Ernest L. and Ida (Nordlie) Dobbin; married Elizabeth W.I. Esser, October 29, 1938. *Education:* University of Minnesota, B.S., 1942, M.A., 1949. *Home:* 16111 Redington Dr., Redington Beach, Fla. 33708. *Office:* Educational Testing Service, Princeton, N.J. 08540.

CAREER: Hoisting and stationary engineer and heavy machinery operator, 1933-42; high school teacher of English in Wisconsin, 1942-43; Educational Test Bureau, Minneapolis, Minn., editor, 1943-48; University of Minnesota, Minneapolis, resident fellow in Bureau of Educational Research, 1948-50; Educational Testing Service,

Princeton, N.J., project director of college board program, 1950-51, director of cooperative test division, 1951-60, project director, 1961—. Atomic Energy Commission, member of advisory committee on technical information, 1961—. Princeton Township Board of education, member, 1957-60. *Member:* Florida Educational Research Association, Florida Association of Deans and Counselors.

WRITINGS: (Contributing editor) *Higher Education in Minnesota,* University of Minnesota Press, 1951; (editor) *Elementary School Objectives,* Russell Sage, 1953; (editor) *Goals of General Education in High School,* Russell Sage, 1956; (contributor) *Encyclopedia of Educational Research,* Macmillan, 1960; (with Henry Chauncey) *Testing: Its Place in Education Today,* Harper, 1964. Contributor of articles to educational journals.

WORK IN PROGRESS: Research and development in the area of impact of racial and cultural integration on interpretation of school test performance; with David Leeb, *Learning System in Communication,* publication by Glencoe Press expected in 1974.

AVOCATIONAL INTERESTS: Sailing and flying.

*   *   *

DOBER, Richard P.

PERSONAL: Born in Philadelphia, Pa.; son of L.J. and V.R. (Brake) Dober; married E. Lee Lyman; children: Patrick Lee, Claire Brake. *Education:* LaSalle College, Philadelphia, Pa., student; Brooklyn College (now Brooklyn College of City University of New York), B.A. (honors); Harvard University, M.C.P., graduate study, 1959. *Home:* 10 Buena Vista Park, Cambridge, Mass. 02140. *Office:* 12 Arrow St., Cambridge, Mass. 02138.

CAREER: Various junior architecture and planning positions, 1948-53; James L. Harris (architect and planner), Cambridge, Mass., planner, 1955-56; Cambridge (Mass.) Planning Board, assistant to the director, 1957-58; Sasaki, Walker and Associates, Inc., Watertown, Mass., executive director, 1958-62; private practice as planning consultant, Cambridge, Mass., 1963—. Massachusetts Institute of Technology, member of research staff for Form of the City Project (Rockefeller Foundation), 1956; Harvard University, Graduate School of Design, visiting lecturer, 1959-62, visiting critic in planning, 1963-65; lecturer at University of Chicago, Radcliffe College, University of Alabama, and other universities. Vice-president, Boston Architecture Center; director, Cambridge Community Center. Member of board of overseers, Shady Hill School. *Military service:* U.S. Army, 1953-55. *Member:* American Institute of Planners, American Society of Planning Officials, Urban Land Institute, Renaissance Society of America, Society for College and University Planning (director).

WRITINGS: Campus Planning, Reinhold, 1964; *The New Campus in Great Britain: Ideas of Consequence for the United States,* Educational Facilities Laboratories, Inc., 1965; *Environmental Design,* Van Nostrand, 1969. Contributor of more than forty articles to *Progressive Architecture, Landscape, Architecture, Design* (Bombay, India), and other publications. Special issue editor, *Landscape Architecture,* January, 1962.

*   *   *

DODD, A(rthur) E(dward)   1913-

PERSONAL: Born May 29, 1913, in Stoke-on-Trent, England; son of William Henry and Alice (Cotton) Dodd; married Evelyn Mary Williams, June 9, 1936. *Education:* University of London, B.Sc., 1934, M.Sc., 1936, Ph.D., 1950. *Home:* Hall Lodge, Ellastone, Ashbourne, England.

CAREER: British Refractories Research Association, Stoke-on-Trent, England, research assistant, 1930-34; Guest, Keen, Baldwins Iron & Steel Co., Port Talbot, Wales, refractories technologist, 1934-38; British Refractories Research Association, information officer, 1938-48; British Ceramic Research Association, Stoke-on-Trent, England, information officer, 1948-70; now full-time writer. Member: Royal Institute of Chemistry (fellow), Institute of Ceramics (fellow).

WRITINGS: Poems from Belmont, Fortune Press, 1955; Three Journeys (verse), Fortune Press, 1958; The Flower-Spun Web (play), Fortune Press, 1960; Words and Music (verse), Fortune Press, 1963; Dictionary of Ceramics, Philosophical Library, 1964 2nd edition, George Newnes, 1967; To Build a Bridge (play), Fortune Press, 1966; Weaver Hills and Other Poems, Fortune Press, 1967; The Fifth Season (poems), Mitre Press, 1971. Contributor to Chambers's Encyclopaedia, Thorpe's Dictionary of Applied Chemistry, Britannica Book of the Year.

WORK IN PROGRESS: Verse.

* * *

DODSON, Daniel B. 1918-

PERSONAL: Born March 21, 1918, in Portland, Ore.; son of William Daniel Boone (a businessman) and Besse E. (Krum) Dodson; married Judith Ware, August, 1943; children: Dorian, Elizabeth. Education: University of Vienna, student, 1937-38; Reed College, B.A., 1941; Columbia University, M.A., 1947, Ph.D., 1954. Politics: Democrat. Home: 1 Sparkill Ave., Sparkill, N.Y. 10976. Agent: Mavis McIntosh, McIntosh, McKee & Dodds, 30 East 60th St., New York, N.Y. 10022. Office: English Department, Columbia University, New York, N.Y. 10027.

CAREER: Columbia University, New York, N.Y., instructor, 1948-54, assistant professor, 1954-59, associate professor, 1959-70, professor of English, 1970—. Military service: U.S. Army Air Forces, 1942-46; became first lieutenant; received Distinguished Flying Cross, Air Medal with oak-leaf cluster. Member: Modern Language Association of America.

WRITINGS: The Man Who Ran Away, Dutton, 1961; (editor) Eight Russian Short Stories, Fawcett, 1962; (editor and author of introductions) Twelve Modern Plays, Wadsworth, 1970; Malcolm Lowry, Columbia University Press, 1970; (with M.S. Barranger) Generations: An Introduction to Drama, Harcourt, 1971. Contributor of short fiction to Esquire and Story, and of articles to scholarly journals.

WORK IN PROGRESS: A manuscript of Joseph Conrad; a novel; a study of the modern theatre.

* * *

DOHERTY, Charles Hugh 1913-

PERSONAL: Born March 31, 1913, in London, England; son of Edward Henry and Florence (Whittingham) Doherty; married Ruby May Singleton, June 29, 1939. Educated: Attended Polytechnic School, London, England, 1924-29. Home: 2 Leconfield Ave., London S.W. 13, England. Agent: Robert Sommerville Ltd., Mowbray House, Norfolk St., London W.C. 2, England.

CAREER: Air Ministry, London, England, draftsman, 1934-36; London County Council, London, England, technical assistant, 1936-40; Ministry of Public Building and Works, London, England, senior engineer, 1940-65, superintending engineer, 1965—. Member: Institution of Civil Engineers (associate), Institution of Mechanical Engineers (associate), Institution of Heating and Ventilating Engineers.

WRITINGS—All juveniles: Brian Decides on Building, Chatto & Windus, 1960; Science on the Building Site, Brockhampton Press, 1962, 2nd edition, 1969; Science Inside the Building, Brockhampton Press, 1963; Science Builds the Bridges, Brockhampton Press, 1964; Science and the Tunneller, Brockhampton Press, 1967; Tunnels: The Construction, Types and History of Subterranean Transit, Meredith, 1968; Bridges, Hawthorn, 1969; New Gas for Old: The Story of Natural Gas, Clifton Books, 1970. Short stories in various publications in Britain and Australia under a pseudonym.

WORK IN PROGRESS: A book on the subject of roads, for Thomas Nelson.

AVOCATIONAL INTERESTS: Caravanning, the gramophone.

BIOGRAPHICAL/CRITICAL SOURCES: Best Sellers, March 1, 1970; Times Literary Supplement, April 16, 1970.

* * *

DOHERTY, Ivy R. Duffy 1922-
(Sylvia Hardwick)

PERSONAL: Born June 22, 1922, in Sydney, New South Wales, Australia; came to United States in 1948, naturalized in 1957; daughter of Oliver Andrew (a highway maintenance employee) and Lily Emily (Gogerly) Duffy; married Walter Doherty (a public school vice principal), November 5, 1942; children: Walter John, Charmaine Louise, Grahame Vivian. Education: Attended Avondale College, Cooranbong, New South Wales, Australia, 1939-41. Politics: Republican. Home: 646 Upper River Rd., Gold Hill, Ore. 97525.

CAREER: Teacher in private school, one year; Hanby School, Gold Hill, Ore., secretary to principal, 1959-64; teacher's aide, 1966-67. Church organist and teacher.

WRITINGS: Susan Haskell, Missionary, Review & Herald, 1958; The Extra Mile, Southern Publishing, 1962; No Need for a Magic Carpet, Review & Herald, 1962; My Magic Carpet Never Wears Out, Review & Herald, 1963; (under pseudonym Sylvia Hardwick) Singing Tree and Laughing Water, Pacific Press Publishing Association, 1970. Contributor of articles to Youths' Instructor, 1952—, and to magazines for children in U.S., England, South Africa, and South America. Contributor of adult articles to Oregon Journal and Oregon Farmer.

WORK IN PROGRESS: The Kind Shepherd, stories for children; Forever the Blue Tattoo, a biography of Olive Ann Oatman.

* * *

DOLAN, John Richard 1893-

PERSONAL: Born January 20, 1893, in Warren, Ohio; son of James A. and Helen (Murphy) Dolan; married Betty Dyer; children: Richard Dyer, Margaret (Mrs. E.L. Andrews). Education: Catholic University of America, A.B., 1917, A.M. 1918. Politics: Independent. Religion: Roman Catholic. Home: 535 Tarragona Way, Daytona Beach, Fla. 32014.

CAREER: Advertising and promotion writer, now retired. Military service: U.S. Navy, World War I. Member: Halifax River Yacht Club (Daytona Beach, Fla.)

WRITINGS: Yankee Peddler in Early America, C.N. Potter, 1964; English Ancestral Names: The Evolution of the Surname from Medieval Occupations, C.N. Potter, 1971. Contributor of historical articles to periodicals.

SIDELIGHTS: Dolan told CA: "My book on the Yankee peddler was an effort to write the kind of history not taught in schools. I selected the peddler because he knew far more about the way people lived than the generals or politicians."

DOLAN, Paul   1910-

PERSONAL: Born May 13, 1910, in Philadelphia, Pa.; son of Peter Patrick (an upholsterer) and Julia Marie (Fei) Dolan; married Mildred Anna Horner, June 14, 1938; children: Peter Anton, Louise Ann. Education: University of Pennsylvania, B.S., 1933, M.A., 1936; Johns Hopkins University, Ph.D., 1949. Home: 115 Townsend Rd., Newark, Del. 19711. Office: University of Delaware, Newark, Del. 19711.

CAREER: University of Delaware, Newark, instructor, 1940-48, assistant professor, 1948-49, associate professor, 1950-61, professor of political science, 1961—. Member of Delaware Council on Administration of Justice, of Delaware Youth Services Commission, and of Newark Planning Commission. Military service: U.S. Navy, 1943-45; served in Pacific theater. Member: American Political Science Association, American Association of University Professors, Kappa Phi Kappa, Phi Kappa Phi. Awards, honors: Fulbright fellow in Europe, 1957; Governmental Affairs fellowships; National Health Institute grant.

WRITINGS: Organization of State Administration, Johns Hopkins Press, 1951; Government and Administration of Delaware, Crowell, 1956; (with Harold William Chase) The Case for Democratic Capitalism, Crowell, 1964; Penjerdel Studies (on local government in eleven countries of Penjerdel region), Pennsylvania Economy League, 1964. Contributor to Britannica Yearbook, 1961-1962, and Collier's Yearbook. Contributor of articles to law and political science journals.

WORK IN PROGRESS: The Ombudsman in the U.S.

*   *   *

DOMINY, Eric (Norman)   1918-

PERSONAL: Born August 4, 1918, in Leeds, England; son of Gerald (a bank manager) and May (Prile) Dominy; married Sylvia Margaret Hackett, June 26, 1947; children: John Andrew, Robert Gerald. Education: Attended Christ's College, Finchley, London, England. Religion: Church of England. Home: 18 Hamilton Way, Finchley, London N.3, England. Office: Inland Revenue, H.M. Inspector of Taxes, 120 Finchley Rd., Hampstead, London, N.W. 3, England.

CAREER: H.M. Inspector of Taxes, Inland Revenue, London, England, 1946—, now executive officer. Teacher of judo. Military service: British Army, 1939-46; became sergeant major; wounded and taken prisoner in France, escaped, 1945; mentioned in dispatches. Member: British Judo Association (senior examiner; member of executive committee; coaching and courses secretary; team manager; third Dan, British International), British Judo League (secretary), Institute of Advance Motorists, Civil Service Judo Association (chairman).

WRITINGS: The Art of Judo, London Judo Society, 1952; Teach Yourself Judo, English Universities Press, 1954, Emerson, 1963; Teach Yourself Self Defence, English Universities Press, 1955, Emerson, 1964; Judo: Beginner to Black Belt, Foulsham, 1956, Sterling, 1958; Judo: Throws and Counters, Sterling, 1956; Judo: Basic Principles, Jenkins, 1958, Sterling, 1964; Camping: Home and Abroad, Foulsham, 1965; Judo: Contest Techniques and Tactics, Jenkins, 1966; Teach Yourself Karate, English Universities Press, 1967, Emerson, 1968.

WORK IN PROGRESS: Books with tentative titles, Teach Yourself Camping and The Science of Judo.

SIDELIGHTS: Dominy's books have also been published in Holland, Spain, and South America. Avocational interests: Driving cars, athletics, camping.

DOMJAN, Joseph   1907-

PERSONAL: Born March 15, 1907, in Budapest, Hungary; now an American citizen; married Evelyn (a graphic artist), March 13, 1944; children: Alma, Michael Paul, Daniel George. Education: Attended Royal Academy of Fine Arts, Budapest, Hungary, 1935-42. Home: Tuxedo Park, N.Y. 10987.

CAREER: Hungarian Royal Academy of Fine Arts, Budapest, Hungary, assistant professor of fine arts, 1941-42; self-employed woodcut artist in Budapest, Hungary, 1942-56, in Switzerland, 1956-57, in United States, 1957—. Work exhibited at one-man shows in Scandinavia, 1948, fifteen one-man shows in China, 1955, in Geneva, Switzerland, 1956, and in America at one-man shows at museums, libraries, and universities, including Cincinnati Art Museum, Georgia Museum of Art. Works, mostly color woodcuts, in permanent collections of more than a hundred museums on three continents, among them Victoria and Albert Museum, Metropolitan Museum of Art, Bibliotheque National, Smithsonian Institution, Library of Congress. Lecturer and author.

MEMBER: Metropolitan Museum of Art (life fellow), Print Council of America, American Color Print Society, Silvermine Guild of Artists, Goetheanum (Switzerland), Society of Illustrators, Society of American Graphic Artists, Societe d'Encouragement au Progres (Paris), National Academy of Design, National Register of Prominent Americans. Awards, honors: National Salon prize, 1936; Fine Arts Hall prize, 1941; Nemes Marcell prize, 1942; purchase award, Johansen Abstract Collection, 1948; purchase award, International Color Woodcut Exhibition, Victoria and Albert Museum, 1950; purchase award, International Exhibition of Graphic Arts, and Mihaly Zichy Prize for Graphic Arts, 1952; Munkacsy Prize of Fine Arts and "Master of the Color Woodcut" (China), 1955; Kossuth Prize of Fine Arts, 1956; Rockefeller Foundation grant, 1957; Printmaker of 1961, Print Club of Albany, 1961; book awards from National Educational Society and American Institute of Graphic Arts, 1964; award of faithfulness, Washington-Kossuth Historical Society, 1966; Sonia Watter Award, American Color Print Society, and award of merit, Society of Illustrators, 1967; award of excellence, Society of Illustrators, 1968; silver medal and diploma, Societe d'Encouragement au Progres, 1969; medal of honor, Hungarian Helicon Society, George Washington award, American Hungarian Studies Foundation, and silver medal and diploma, International Academy of Literature, Arts and Science, 1970.

WRITINGS—Self-illustrated and designed: Wildflowers, Medimpex (Budapest), 1954; (fine arts editor) Hunyadi (album), [Budapest], 1956; 32 Color Woodcuts, Corvina (Budapest), 1956; Ungarische Legende, Atlantis Verlag (Zurich), 1957; Henry Hudson of the River, Art Edge, 1959; Janos Hunyadi: 10 Woodcuts, Art Edge, 1960; Hungarian Heroes and Legends, Van Nostrand, 1963; Peacock Festival, Art Edge, 1964; The Proud Peacock, Holt, 1965; The Little Princess Goodnight, Holt, 1966; Domjan the Woodcutter (monograph), Art Edge, 1966; The Fifteen Decisive Battles of the World, Limited Editions Club, 1969; The Little Cock, Lippincott, 1969; Hungarian Song, American Hungarian Literary Guild, 1969; Domjan Portfolio, Art Edge, 1970; I Went to the Market, Holt, 1970; The Joy of Living, Holt, 1971.

SIDELIGHTS: Domjan was in Switzerland opening an exhibition at the Musee d'Art et d'Histoire when the Hungarian revolution broke out in 1956; he remained there until his family could join him.

BIOGRAPHICAL/CRITICAL SOURCES: Hans Vollmer, Algemeines Lexicon den Bildenden Kunstler, Volume I, 1953; John R. Biggs, Woodcuts, Bradford Press, 1958; Library Journal, March 15, 1970.

DOMMEN, Arthur J(ohn) 1934-

PERSONAL: Born June 24, 1934, in Mexico City, Mexico; came to United States in 1940, naturalized in 1958; son of John Henry and Sarah Doris (Hall) Dommen. Education: Institut Le Rosey, Rolle, Switzerland, student, 1947-51; Cornell University, B.Sc., 1955. Home: 12 Rajdoot Marg, Diplomatic Enclave, New Delhi, India. Agent: Bill Berger Associates, Inc., 535 East 72nd St., New York, N.Y. 10021.

CAREER: United Press International, reporter in New York, N.Y., 1957-59, bureau manager in Saigon, Vietnam, 1959-61, in Hong Kong, 1961-63; Los Angeles Times, Los Angeles, Calif., staff member, 1965—, bureau chief, New Delhi, India, 1966—. Member: Sigma Delta Chi. Awards, honors: New York Council on Foreign Relations fellow, 1963-64.

WRITINGS: Conflict in Laos: The Politics of Neutralization, Praeger, 1964, revised edition, 1971.

*   *   *

DONALD, David (Herbert) 1920-

PERSONAL: Born October 1, 1920, in Goodman, Miss.; son of Ira Unger and Sue Ella (Belford) Donald; married Aida Di Pace, 1955; children: Bruce Randall. Education: Holmes Junior College, student, 1937-39; Millsaps College, A.B., 1941; University of Illinois, A.M., 1942, Ph.D., 1946. Religion: Episcopal. Office: Johns Hopkins University, Baltimore, Md. 21218.

CAREER: University of North Carolina, Chapel Hill, teaching fellow, 1942; University of Illinois, Urbana, research associate, 1946-47; Columbia University, New York, N.Y., instructor in history, 1947-49, assistant professor, 1951-52, associate professor, 1952-57, professor of history, 1957-59; Smith College, Northampton, Mass., associate professor of history, 1949-51; Princeton University, Princeton, N.J., professor of history, 1959-62; Johns Hopkins University, professor of history, 1962—, Harry C. Black Professor of American History, 1963—, director, Institute of Southern History, 1966—. Amherst College, visiting associate professor of history, 1950; University College of North Wales, Fulbright lecturer in American history, 1953-54; Institute for Advanced Study, Princeton, N.J., member, 1957-58; Oxford University, Harmsworth Professor of American History, 1959-60; Center for Advanced Study in the Behavioral Sciences, visiting professor, 1969-70. Member: American Historical Association, Society of American Historians, Organization of American Historians, Southern Historical Association (president, 1969-70), Phi Beta Kappa, Phi Kappa Phi, Pi Kappa Delta, Pi Kappa Alpha, Omicron Delta Kappa. Awards, honors: Social Science Research Council fellowship, 1945-46; George A. and Eliza G. Howard fellowship, 1957-58; Pulitzer Prize in biography for Charles Sumner and the Coming of the Civil War, 1961; Guggenheim fellowship, 1964-65; American Council of Learned Societies fellowship, 1969-70.

WRITINGS: Lincoln's Herndon, introduction by Carl Sandburg, Knopf, 1948; (editor) Divided We Fought: A Pictorial History of the War, 1861-1865, Macmillan, 1952; (editor) Inside Lincoln's Cabinet: The Civil War Diaries of Salmon P. Chase, Longmans, Green, 1954; Lincoln Reconsidered: Essays on the Civil War, Knopf, 1956, 2nd enlarged edition, Random House, 1961; (author of introduction) George Cary Eggleston, A Rebel's Recollections, Indiana University Press, 1959; (editor) Why the North Won the Civil War, Louisiana State University Press, 1960; An Excess of Democracy: The American Civil War and the Social Process, Clarendon Press, 1960; Charles Sumner and the Coming of the Civil War, Knopf, 1960; (with James G. Randall) The Divided Union, Little, Brown, 1961; (with Randall) The Civil War and Reconstruction, 2nd edition, Heath, 1961, revised and enlarged edition, 1969; (editor with wife Aida Donald) Diary of Charles Francis Adams, two volumes, Harvard University Press, 1964; (with others) Grant, Lee, Lincoln and the Radicals, Northwestern University Press, 1964; The Politics of Reconstruction, 1863-1867, Louisiana State University Press, 1965; The Nation in Crisis, 1861-1877, Appleton, 1969; Charles Sumner and the Rights of Man, Knopf, 1970. Contributor to historical journals. General editor, "The Making of America" series and "Documentary History of American Life" series.

BIOGRAPHICAL/CRITICAL SOURCES: New York Times Book Review, March 12, 1961; Library Journal, October 7, 1970; New Republic, January 9, 1971; New York Times, January 30, 1971; Saturday Review, February 20, 1971.

*   *   *

DONLEAVY, J(ames) P(atrick) 1926-

PERSONAL: Born April 23, 1926, in Brooklyn, N.Y.; married, wife's name Mary; children: Philip, Karen. Education: Attended Trinity College, Dublin. Office: Levington Park, Mullinger, Westmeath, Ireland.

CAREER: Writer. Military service: U.S. Navy; served in World War II. Awards, honors: Brandeis University Creative Arts award, 1961-62, for two plays, The Ginger Man and Fairy Tales of New York; Evening Standard Drama Critic's Award for Fairy Tales of New York.

WRITINGS: The Ginger Man (novel), Olympia Press (Paris), 1955, published with an introduction by Arland Ussher, Spearman (London), 1956, Obolensky, 1958, complete and unexpurgated edition, Delacorte, 1965; The Ginger Man (play, produced on Broadway at Orpheum Theatre, November 21, 1963; contains introduction, "What They Did in Dublin"), Random House, 1961 (published in England as What They Did in Dublin, with The Ginger Man, McGibbon, 1961); Fairy Tales of New York (play), Random House, 1961; A Singular Man (novel), Atlantic-Little, Brown, 1963; A Singular Man (play; produced in Dublin at the Eblana Theatre, November 20, 1971), Bodley Head, 1964; Meet My Maker the Mad Molecule (stories and sketches), Atlantic-Little, Brown, 1964; The Saddest Summer of Samuel S (novel), Dial, 1966; The Beastly Beatitudes of Balthazar B (novel), Dial, 1968; The Onion Eaters (novel), Delacorte, 1971; The Plays of J.P. Donleavy; with a Preface by the Author, Delacorte, 1972; A Fairy Tale of New York, Delacorte, 1973.

WORK IN PROGRESS: A novel entitled Gratz.

SIDELIGHTS: Donleavy's first novel, The Ginger Man, although well-received, caused some controversy. It was not until 1965 that an unexpurgated version was published in the United States. He has been considered one of the "Angry Young Men," while also being called a link between the "angries" and the "beats." Philip Toynbee wrote of The Ginger Man in 1968: "It was, indeed, an exceedingly funny book, written with splendid panache and inventiveness. This New Yorker-turned-Dubliner showed very clearly that he had the gift of the gab, and that more and better things were to be expected of him" Donleavy has produced four novels since The Ginger Man, and although all have done well, none has had quite the impact of the first.

Dangerfield is perhaps Donleavy's most memorable character, not only because he was considered one of the first of his kind, the coarse, comic, desperate anti-hero, but because despite all his faults, and he has many, he is also "a man in love with life, ready and able to take the good with the bad," as William David Sherman wrote. "Such a man is indeed worthy of our admiration." Donleavy has used variations of this same character in other novels. George Smith in *A Singular Man* is Sebastian grown rich and turned inward, absorbed with defending himself against life rather than going out to live it. Samuel S in *The Saddest Summer of Samuel S* has been seen by Dean Cohen as the final evolution of Sebastian. Beefy in *The Beastly Beatitudes of Balthazar B* is much like Sebastian, and much of the novel takes place in Dublin, where the Ginger Man roared through much of his life.

Critical opinions of Donleavy's work are divided. The *Times Literary Supplement* considered *The Ginger Man* to be fresh, original, and humorous. Vivian Mercier comments: "Portions of this book are obscene and/or blasphemous; other portions may give offense to those who are Irish by birth or sentiment. She concludes, however, that "Donleavy has written an Irish comic masterpiece in the tradition of the twelfth-century Vision of the MacGonglinne." Richard Sullivan expressed "disgust, indignation, and boredom," as the result of reading the book. Many stated that the novel had a Joycean quality, and others that it reminded them of Henry Miller. Gene Baro found it "A fascinating portrait, harrowingly real, of a man of promise gone somehow awry and astray, a sensitive man out of control. What Mr. Donleavy is able so notably to convey might be called the sheer ache of being."

A *Newsweek* reviewer found *A Singular Man* to be "a darker novel than its predecessor, in tone and in lucidity, and it has less of the mad buoyancy that sent Sebastian Dangerfield winging among the chandeliers. If the earlier book was a manic hymn of freedom, this one is a threnody of indefinable sorrows and terrors." He found some similarities to *The Ginger Man,* but concluded: "Nevertheless, *A Singular Man* is almost always a singular and original novel, and the echo from the earlier novel should not be permitted to drown out the fresh chords being struck here." Granville Hicks was disappointed by the novel, but on another occasion wrote that Donleavy's writing is "distinguished by humor, often inelegant, even coarse, but explosive and irresistable. Humor and poetry are his weapons."

Donleavy consistently employs both humor and poetry in his books, and a rather specialized style, using both first and third person for his protagonists' voices. It is his use of language, perhaps, which made *The Ginger Man* so outstanding, but in subsequent books it has been said that his style has become mannered, and that the seemingly easy language of *The Ginger Man* has now become forced.

The Saddest Summer of Samuel S brings something new, a character who, William David Sherman says, makes "a tenuous accommodation to the social community." Samuel is "under psychiatric treatment in Vienna after a life of womanizing and wandering in Europe." What he really wants, he says, is to have a wife and kids. Sherman says that this is "Donleavy's saddest book. There is no evasive irony, no reciting of an odd little poem [the usual ending for a Donleavy chapter] and then skipping off merrily to another picaresque adventure." Sherman says further that in this novel "Donleavy reexamines, through the major character, the anarchic life he has chosen for his past heroes. He finds that the decision to live life passionately and to affirm isolation as a life style, is the only possible choice a man can make if he is to remain totally free from manipulation. But Donleavy also finds that to live this kind of life leads a man to the brink of unbearable loneliness and despair. Samuel is the most 'human' of all Donleavy's heroes."

Balthazar, Donleavy's hero in *The Beastly Beatitudes of Balthazar B,* is passive, and through the course of the narrative seems to learn nothing. He is the same at the beginning and end. He is wealthy, but his wealth brings him neither happiness nor comfort. He is not an instigator, and the action in the book is provided by his school chum Beefy, a Sebastian-like rogue who goes on at length about his adventures. Toynbee believes that one of the problems with this novel is that it is too long, that "Mr. Donleavy simply lacks the staying power to write a novel of this length. Becoming unsure of his own purposes, he seems to become equally unsure of his words and tone.... But in the course of [the book] Mr. Donleavy has shown again that he is a splendid writer, even if he has not yet managed to make himself into a great novelist."

BIOGRAPHICAL/CRITICAL SOURCES: Saturday Review, May 10, 1958, November 23, 1963, November 23, 1968; *New York Herald Tribune Book Review,* May 11, 1958; *New York Times,* May 11, 1958, November 18, 1968; *Nation,* May 24, 1958, December 14, 1963, January 20, 1969; *Chicago Sunday Tribune,* May 25, 1958; Kenneth Alsop, *The Angry Decade,* Peter Owen, 1958; *Times Literary Supplement,* July 26, 1963, May 11, 1967, March 20, 1969, July 23, 1971; *Newsweek,* November 11, 1963, November 18, 1968; *Book Week,* November 17, 1963, October 4, 1964, March 13, 1966; *New Statesman,* April 17, 1964, May 12, 1967; *Books and Bookmen,* May, 1964, September, 1967; *New York Times Book Review,* September 27, 1964, December 29, 1968, September 5, 1971; Harry T. Moore, *Contemporary American Novelists,* Southern Illinois University Press, 1964; *Wilson Library Bulletin,* May, 1965; Pierre Dommergues, *Les Ecrivains americains d'aujourd'hui,* Presses Universitaires de France, 1965; *Best Sellers,* April 1, 1966, December 15, 1968, August 1, 1971; *Commonweal,* December 2, 1966, March 7, 1969; *Observer Review,* May 14, 1967, February 9, 1969; *Punch,* May 24, 1967, February 4, 1969; *Twentieth Century Literature,* January, 1968; *Life,* November 22, 1968; *National Observer,* December 2, 1968; *Time,* December 6, 1968; *Washington Post,* December 6, 1968; *Book World,* December 15, 1968, August 22, 1971; *Village Voice,* December 26, 1968; *New York Review of Books,* January 2, 1969; *New Republic,* May 1, 1969; *Critique,* Vol. XII, No. 3, 1971; *Vogue,* November 1, 1971; *Variety,* December 15, 1971.

* * *

DONNA, Natalie 1934-

PERSONAL: Born December 25, 1934; daughter of Patrick B. and Maryanne (Tritto) Donna. *Education:* New York University, B.A. *Home:* 1729 East 31st St., Brooklyn, N.Y. 10034.

CAREER: Advertising agency copywriter, working in all media, in New York, N.Y., and Boston, Mass. Package and product design consultant and copywriter; designer of three historically-based games for children; creator of history, science, math, literature, and geography quizzes for children; currently free-lance writer.

WRITINGS: Boy of the Masai, Dodd, 1964; *Bead Craft,* Lothrop, 1972.

WORK IN PROGRESS: Two adult plays; a fact-fiction book on pygmies of the Congo, and the Masai of East Africa; a musical.

* * *

DONOVAN, James Britt 1916-

PERSONAL: Born February 29, 1916, in New York, N.Y.; son of John J. (a physician and surgeon) and Harriet F. (a recital pianist and teacher; maiden name, O'Connor) Donovan; married Mary E. McKenna, June 30, 1941; children: Jane Ann, John, Mary Ellen, Clare. *Education:* Attended All Hallows Institute; Fordham University, A.B., 1937; Harvard University, LL.B., 1940. *Politics:* Independent Democrat. *Religion:* Roman Catholic. *Home:* 35 Prospect Park W., Brooklyn, N.Y. 11215. *Office:* 161 William St., New York, N.Y. 10038.

CAREER: Admitted to the Bar of New York State, 1941, the Bar of U.S. Supreme Court, 1944, and the Bar of the District of Columbia, 1951; attorney in private practice, New York, N.Y., 1940-42, 1946-49, and as partner of Watters & Donovan, New York, N.Y., and Washington, D.C., 1950—, serving as chief counsel in cases in more than thirty states, 1946—. Associate general counsel, U.S. Office of Scientific Research and Development, Washington, D.C., 1942-43; associate prosecutor at major Nuremburg Trial, 1946; government-appointed attorney in trial and appeals of Rudolf Ivanovich Abel, convicted as Soviet master spy, 1958; negotiated release of U-2 pilot Francis Gary Powers by Soviet Russia, and release of U.S. student Frederick Pryor by East German government, in exchange for Abel, 1962; negotiated with Castro government for release of Bay of Pigs prisoners, their relatives, and other political prisoners in Cuba, 1962-63. Lecturer on legal subjects at Cornell University, Villanova University, University of Chicago, and other universities. Democratic candidate for U.S. Senate, 1962. Director, Forest Press, 1960—. Secretary, New York City Art Commission, 1951-61; president, New York City Board of Education, 1963-65. Chairman-emeritus, Council of Regents of St. Francis College, Brooklyn, N.Y.; member of governing committee, Brooklyn Museum; trustee, Brooklyn Institute of Arts and Sciences; trustee of other school and institutions. *Military service:* U.S. Naval Reserve, 1943-45, serving as general counsel, Office of Strategic Services, 1943-45; became commander; received Legion of Merit, Commendation Ribbon with clusters.

MEMBER: International Academy of Trial Lawyers (fellow), American Law Institute, American Bar Association (chairman of insurance negligence, and compensation law section, 1961-62), American College of Trial Lawyers (fellow), American Society of International Law (fellow), American Judicature Society, New York State Bar Association (chairman of committee on insurance section, 1951; chairman of administrative law, 1959-61), Association of the Bar of the City of New York, National Lawyers Club (Washington, D.C.), Fordham College Alumni Association (former vice-president), Harvard Law School Association of New York (trustee), American Legion, Knights of Malta, Phi Delta Phi (honorary), Harvard Club, Metropolitan Club, Lake Placid Club, Grolier Club, Drug and Chemical Club, Montauk Club, Bath and Tennis Club (Spring Lake, N.J.), Rembrandt Club (Brooklyn), Friendly Sons of St. Patrick.

AWARDS, HONORS: Tyne Award, Federation Insurance Council, 1952; Gold Medal award, Greater New York Insurance Brokers Association, 1958; Distinguished Intelligence medal, U.S. Central Intelligence Agency, at direction of President Kennedy, 1962, for negotiating Soviet-American prisoner exchange; American Red Cross Decoration, 1963, for release of Cuban prisoners; Distinguished Service medallion of City of New York, 1963; Humanities award, College Insurance Association, 1966; LL.D., Fordham University, 1962, Albany Law School, Union University, and Gannon College, 1965; Litt.D., St. Francis College, 1963; L.H.D., Villanova University and Bryant College, 1963; other achievement awards from universities and schools.

WRITNGS: Strangers on a Bridge: The Case of Colonel Abel, Atheneum, 1964; *Challenges: Reflections of a Lawyer-at-Large,* Atheneum, 1967. Contributor of articles on intelligence, foreign languages, and law to periodicals.

AVOCATIONAL INTERESTS: Collecting rare books and illuminated manuscripts and playing golf.

BIOGRAPHICAL/CRITICAL SOURCES: Coronet, October, 1960; *Life,* February 23, 1962, January 4, 1963; *True,* September, 1962; *Saturday Evening Post,* February 2, 1963; *Nation,* April 13, 1963.

*   *   *

DORCY, Sister Mary Jean   1914-
(Jean Frances Bennett)

PERSONAL: Born March 10, 1914, in Anacortes, Wash.; daughter of William Jeremiah (a farmer) and Emma (Knapp) Dorcy. *Education:* Gonzaga University, B.A., 1941; California College of Arts and Crafts, M.F.A., 1944. *Politics:* Democrat. *Home:* St. Helen Hospital, Chehalis, Wash. 98532.

CAREER: Roman Catholic nun, member of Order of Preachers (Dominican), 1934—, name in religion, Sister Mary Jean; teacher of junior high school English, 1932-42; Mexican missionary, 1964-71. Free-lance writer, and illustrator of books for children. *Member:* Gallery of Living Catholic Authors, Delta Phi Delta.

WRITINGS: Mary My Mother, Sheed, 1944; (under pseudonym Jean Frances Bennett) *A Shady Hobby,* Bruce, 1944; *Silhouette Cutting,* Bruce, 1944; *Shepherd's Tartan* (essays), Sheed, 1953; *Our Lady of Springtime,* St. Anthony, 1953; *Our Lady's Feasts,* Sheed, 1954; *Fount of our Joy* (poetry), Newman, 1955; *Shrines of our Lady,* Sheed, 1956; *The Carrying of the Cross,* St. Anthony, 1957; *Mary,* Sheed, 1958; *Never the Golden City* (fiction), Sheed, 1962.

Biography: *Hunters of Souls,* Bruce, 1946; *A Crown for Joanna,* Sheed, 1946; *Truth Was Their Star,* Bruce, 1947; *Army in Battle Array,* Bruce, 1948; *Master Albert,* Sheed, 1955; *St. Dominic,* Herder, 1959; *St. Dominic's Family: Lives and Legends,* Priory, 1964. Contributor of short stories, essays, poems, and silhouettes to periodicals.

WORK IN PROGRESS: A book of historical fiction about the Spanish and Indian civilization in the Rio Grande Valley.

SIDELIGHTS: Sister Mary Jean illustrates her children's books and those of others with cut-out silhouette designs, an art form practiced in Germany, Austria, and China, but rare in the United States. Now confined to a hospital because of severe arthritis, she is no longer able to do art work but continues to write.

*   *   *

DORE, Claire (Morin)   1934-
(Claire Morin; pseudonym, Claire France)

PERSONAL: Born December 24, 1934, in Roberval, Quebec, Canada; daughter of Rodolphe and Maria (Tremblay) Morin; married Marc Dore (a comedian-author-producer), October 9, 1961. *Education:* Cours Hattemer-Prignet (Paris), B.A.; Sorbonne, University of Paris, diploma in literature; studied classical dancing for thirteen years and dramatic art for six years in Quebec and at Cours Dullin and Ecole Lecoq in Paris. *Religion:* Catholic. *Home:* 48, Ave. Ste-Genevieve, Quebec, Canada.

CAREER: Ecole Secondaire Thevenet, Sillery, Quebec, teacher of French diction, 1963—. Teaches classical dancing to children. *Member:* Composers, Authors and Publishers Association of Canada. *Awards, honors:* Grand Prix du Maine, 1962, for *Autour de toi Tristan.*

WRITINGS—All under pseudonym Claire France: *Les Enfants qui s'aiment,* Beauchemin (Montreal), 1956, translation by Antonia White published as *Children in Love,* Ryerson, 1959; *Et le septieme jour. . . ,* Beauchemin, 1958; *Autour de toi Tristan,* Flammarion (Paris), 1962. Also author of poetry, radio scripts, and plays. Contributor of articles to French and Canadian journals.

WORK IN PROGRESS: A fourth novel and a play.

SIDELIGHTS: Mrs. Dore has a great interest in dramatic art. In connection with her study and teaching of classical dancing, she states, "I find rhythm very important in writing." She has traveled through Europe and Africa.

*   *   *

DOSS, Helen (Grigsby) 1918-

PERSONAL: Born August 9, 1918, in Sanderstead, Surrey, England; daughter of Owen Eugene and Maude (Menely) Grigsby; married Carl M. Doss (a Methodist minister), June 20, 1937; children: Donald, Richard, Dorothy (Mrs. Roy Abey), Elaine (Mrs. David Minyard), Ted, Laura, Susan, Rita, Diane, Tim, Alex, Gregory. *Education:* Eureka College, student, 1934-35; Santa Ana Junior College, A.A., 1936; University of Redlands, B.A., 1954. *Religion:* Protestant. *Home:* 365 Rosalinde, Azusa, Calif. 91702.

CAREER: Free-lance writer. *Member:* California Writers' Guild.

WRITINGS: The Family Nobody Wanted, Little, Brown, 1954; *A Brother the Size of Me,* Little, Brown, 1957; (with husband, Carl Doss) *If You Adopt a Child,* Holt, 1957; *All the Children of the World,* Abingdon, 1958; *The Really Real Family,* Little, Brown, 1959; *Friends Around the World,* Abingdon, 1959; *Jonah,* Abingdon, 1964; *King David,* Abingdon, 1967; *Where Can I Find God?,* Abingdon, 1968; *Young Readers Book of Bible Stories,* Abingdon, 1970. Contributor of articles to juvenile magazines, including *American Girl.*

WORK IN PROGRESS: An adult novel on King David, *David, My Love, My King.*

SIDELIGHTS: The Dosses are the parents of twelve adopted children—six boys and six girls—of minority and mixed racial backgrounds. The ancestries of the children include strains of Japanese, Chinese, Filipino, Hawaiian, Mexican, American Indian, East Indian, and various European nationalities. The story of this unusual family is told in *The Family Nobody Wanted, A Brother the Size of Me,* and *The Really Real Family.* The children are now grown and scattered, with homes of their own. So far, Mrs. Doss has sixteen grandchildren.

*   *   *

DOUGLAS, William O(rville) 1898-

PERSONAL: Born October 16, 1898, in Maine, Minn.; son of William (a Presbyterian home missionary) and Julia Bickford (Fiske) Douglas; married Mildred Riddle, 1923 (divorced, 1953); married Mercedes Hester Davidson, 1954 (divorced, 1963); married Joan Carol Martin, August 5, 1963 (divorced, 1966); married Cathleen C. Heffernan, July 5, 1966; children: (first marriage) Mildred (Mrs. Frank Wells II), William O., Jr. *Education:* Whitman College, A.B., 1920; Columbia University, LL.B., 1925. *Politics:* Democrat. *Religion:* Presbyterian. *Home:* 4852 Hutchins Pl. N.W., Washington, D.C. 20007. *Office:* United States Supreme Court, Washington, D.C. 20543.

CAREER: High school teacher in Yakima, Wash., 1920-22; Columbia University, Law School, New York, N.Y., lecturer in law, 1924-28; admitted to New York Bar, 1926; Cravath, de Gersdorff, Swaine, and Wood (law firm), member, 1925-27; Yale University Law School, New Haven, Conn., professor of law, 1928-32, Sterling Professor of Law, 1932-39; U.S. Securities and Exchange Commission, Washington, D.C., director of protective committee study, 1934-36, commissioner, 1936-39, chairman, 1937-39; United States Supreme Court, Washington, D. C., associate justice, 1939—. Conducted studies on bankruptcy for U.S. Department of Commerce and Yale

Institute of Human Relations, 1929-32; National Commission on Law Observance and Enforcement, secretary of committee on business of federal courts, 1930-32; Temporary National Economic Committee, member, 1938-39; Center for the Study of Democratic Institutions, board chairman. *Military service:* U.S. Army, 1918.

MEMBER: Royal Geographical Society (London), Overseas Press Club, P.E.N., Explorers Club and Yale Club (both New York), Himalayan Club (New Delhi), University Club (Washington, D.C.), Phi Beta Kappa, Phi Alpha Delta, Delta Sigma Rho, Beta Theta Pi. *Awards, honors:* Geographical Society of Chicago Publication Award for *Beyond the High Himalayas,* 1952; Horace Marden Albright Medal, 1961; M.A., Yale University, 1932; LL.D., Whitman College, 1938, Wesleyan University, 1940, Washington and Jefferson College, 1942, William and Mary College, 1943, Rollins College, 1947, National University, 1949, New School for Social Research, 1952, University of Toledo, 1956, Bucknell University, 1958, Dalhousie University, 1958, Colby College, 1961; L.H.D., Wayne State University, 1964.

WRITINGS: (with Carroll M. Shanks) *Cases and Materials on the Law of Corporate Reorganization,* West Publishing, 1931; (with Shanks) *Cases and Materials on the Law of Financing of Business Units,* Callaghan, 1931; (with Shanks) *Cases and Materials on the Law of Management of Business Units,* Callaghan, 1931; (with Shanks) *Cases and Materials on Business Units, Losses, Liabilities, and Assets,* Callaghan, 1932; (with Charles Edward Clark) *Cases on the Law of Partnership, Joint Stock Associations, Business Trusts, and Other Non-corporate Business Organization,* West Publishing, 1932.

Democracy and Finance: The Addresses and Public Statements of William O. Douglas as Member and Chairman of the Securities and Exchange Commission, edited by James Allen, Yale University Press, 1940; *Being an American* (selected speeches and articles), John Day, 1948; *Stare Decisis,* Association of the Bar of the City of New York, 1949; *Lectures, February 18-19, 1949,* Occidental College, 1949.

Of Men and Mountains (partial autobiography), Harper, 1950; *Strange Lands and Friendly People,* Harper, 1951 (published in England as *Strange Lands and Friendly People: An Account of the Author's Travels in Persia, India, and the Middle East,* Gollancz, 1952); *Beyond the High Himalayas,* Doubleday, 1952 (published in England as *Beyond the High Himalayas: An Account of a Journey to Afghanistan and Ladakh,* Gollancz, 1953); *North from Malaya: Adventure on Five Fronts,* Doubleday, 1953; *Washington and Manifest Destiny* (speech), Library of Congress, 1953; *Democratic Fronts Against Communism: The Middle East and South Asia* (lecture), Walter J. Shepard Foundation, Ohio State University, 1954; *An Almanac of Liberty,* Doubleday, 1954; *The French Are Facing Disaster Again in Morocco* (pamphlet), 1954; *We the Judges: Studies in American and Constitution Law from Marshall to Mukherjea,* Doubleday, 1956 (published in India as *From Marshall to Mukherjea: Studies in American and Indian Constitutional Law,* Eastern Law House, [Calcutta], 1956); *America and Russia,* 1956 (pamphlet), Roosevelt University, 1956; *Russian Journey* (travel book), Doubleday, 1956; *Law and Psychiatry* (pamphlet), William Alanson White Institute of Psychiatry, Psychoanalysis, and Psychology, 1956; *Exploring the Himalaya,* Random House, 1958; *The Bill of Rights and America—at Home and Abroad,* University of Wichita, 1958; *The Right of the People* (essays), Doubleday, 1958, reissued with new introduction, Pyramid Books, 1962; *West of the Indus,* Doubleday, 1958; (editor) *The Mind and Faith of A. Powell Davies,* Doubleday, 1959; *Douglas of the Supreme Court: A Selection of His Opinions,* edited by Vern Countryman,

Doubleday, 1959; *Democracy vs. Communism in Asia* (pamphlet), Los Angeles City College, 1959.

The Rule of Law in World Affairs, [New York], 1960; *My Wilderness: The Pacific West,* Doubleday, 1960; *Vagrancy and Arrest on Suspicion,* University of New Mexico School of Law, 1960; *America Challenged* (essays), Princeton University Press, 1960; *Judges, Juries, and Bureaucrats* (pamphlet), University of New Hampshire, 1960; *A Living Bill of Rights,* Doubleday, 1961; *The Rule of Law in World Affairs: A Contribution to the Discussion of Free Society* (not the same as the 1960 publication), Center for the Study of Democratic Institutions, 1961; *Muir of the Mountains* (biography), Houghton, 1961; *My Wilderness: East to Katahdin,* Doubleday, 1961; *Counter Plan,* 1961; *Mr. Justice Douglas Dissents!: A Statement by the Virginia Commission on Constitutional Government,* [Richmond], 1961; *Democracy's Manifesto,* Doubleday, 1962; *Freedom of the Mind,* American Library Association, 1962, hardcover edition, Doubleday, 1964; *Speech to the Minnesota Historical Society,* 1962; *The Anatomy of Liberty: The Rights of Man without Force,* Trident, 1963; *Mr. Lincoln and the Negroes: The Long Road to Equality,* Atheneum, 1963; (contributor) Thomas C. Wheeler, editor, *A Vanishing America,* Holt, 1964; *A Wilderness Bill of Rights,* Little, Brown, 1965; *Changing Role of Government* (lectures), West Georgia College, 1965; *The Bible and the Schools,* Little, Brown, 1966; *Farewell to Texas: A Vanishing Wilderness,* McGraw, 1967; *Towards a Global Federalism* (essays), New York University Press, 1968; *ABM: Yes or No?,* Center for the Study of Democratic Institutions, 1969; (author of preface) *The Sacco-Vanzetti Case: A Transcript,* Appel, 1969.

International Dissent, Random House, 1970; *Points of Rebellion* (politics), Random House, 1970; (author of introduction) *This Beautiful Land: America in Pictures,* Scribner, 1971; *Holocaust or Hemispheric Co-Op,* Random House, 1971; *The Three Hundred Year War: A Chronicle of Ecological Disease,* Random House, 1972.

Anthologized in *Voices in Dissent,* edited by Arthur A. Ekirch, Citadel, 1964. Contributor to law journals and to *New Republic, Holiday, Audubon, Bulletin of the Atomic Scientists, Saturday Review, Field and Stream, Saturday Evening Post, National Geographic, Look,* and other periodicals.

SIDELIGHTS: A figure of national controversy since his appointment to the Supreme Court, Douglas has encouraged both admiration and disapproval with his legal and political views on the weaknesses and needs of modern society. While critics are divided about the method and style Douglas employs, they generally acknowledge his books as representative of the mood of a dissenting segment in America. Milton Viorst believes that *Points of Rebellion,* "while not particularly good, was particularly provocative and it came out during a crisis in public order in the nation. It predictably gave offense to many...." Others assert that Douglas oversimplifies issues. "He reduces the most complex political and legal difficulties to a few abstract moral principles, and the sharpest antagonisms to a flabby and homogeneous togetherness," states Yosal Rogat. "Douglas' homogenizing tendencies carry him beyond facile optimism and inconsistency to outright inaccuracy." Roger Baldwin is more sympathetic to Douglas' aims and method. "Justice Douglas' treatment of American and international law cases and principles. . .meets very practically the need for faith in law as the alternative to nuclear holocaust. . . .For a champion of liberty in high office who has often voiced his distress over the state of American freedoms, this testament of faith in the achievement of universal agreement on law is indeed heartening."

In addition to his political and social works, Douglas also writes extensively on travel and conservation. His absorbing interest in out-of-the-way places and peoples has taken him to the northern provinces of India, Malaya, Vietnam, Indo-China, Thailand, Burma, Soviet Union, Afghanistan, Cyprus, Iran, and many other countries. He has produced several volumes which describe the people and the lands he visits. Critics like Hasan Ozbekkan find that these books are "hard to match when it comes to directness of perception, accuracy and warmth. There has always been another dimension to Justice Douglas' writings. One is tempted to call it the dimension of concern. . . .This quality makes the books something to be enjoyed at several levels [and] above all, as the report of an educated and open-minded American on certain forces emerging in the world today." While he dislikes what he feels are Douglas' use of generalization and occasional inaccuracies, Harrison Salisbury thinks that *Russian Journey* "has all the merits which keen eyes and an open and reflective mind can give it. . . ."

Douglas' legal opinions and dissensions as a Supreme Court Justice are, however, the writings which most clearly reveal his philosophy and which make him an object of both hatred and adulation. He represents, as Viorst states, "the liberalism inherent in the domestic programs of Democratic Administrations since the New Deal and, perhaps more important, in almost two decades of bold judicial opinions by the Earl Warren Court." Haynes Johnson regards Douglas' decisions as placing him "on the side of enforcement of antitrust laws, against discrimination whether of race or religion or sex or the background of poverty. He has been a vigorous advocate for a strict construction of the First Amendment, insisting that government can never abridge a man's right to speak his mind or worship his God—or not to—in his own way, and without interference by the government." Such stances have brought Douglas outraged criticism. Representative Gerald Ford of Michigan has attacked Douglas as being involved with "pornographic publications and espousal of hippie-yippie style revolution." Representative G.V. Montgomery of Mississippi stated: "In a time when we have law-abiding citizens clamoring for law and order in America, it is totally wrong in my opinion to have an associate justice of the Supreme Court encouraging just the opposite. I just cannot condone Mr. Douglas openly taking the side of violent protestors, protestors whose fate he will be asked to rule on in future decisions."

Louis Nizer, however, finds an appropriate mixture of the administration of justice and a compassion for the individual in Douglas' opinions. "Justice Douglas serves the concept that the law is a silent magistrate, but the magistrate is a speaking law. Sympathy without judgment is like wine without water, apt to be intoxicating. But judgment without sympathy is like water without heat, destined to be ice. Justice Douglas combines sympathy with judgment in nice balance."

BIOGRAPHICAL/CRITICAL SOURCES: Columbia Law Review, February, 1932; *Harvard Law Review,* April, 1932; *Yale Review,* winter, 1941, June, 1958; Wesley McCune, *Nine Young Men,* Harper, 1947; Louis Nizer, *Between You and Me,* Yoseloff, 1948, revised edition, 1963; *US News and World Report,* January 30, 1948, September 14, 1951, February 11, 1955, December 24, 1962, August 1, 1966, April 27, 1970; *New Republic,* June 14, 1948, June 15, 1953, September 14, 1959, January 9, 1971; *Nation,* July 10, 1948, December 1, 1951, April 26, 1952, February 18, 1956; *Christian Science Monitor,* August 14, 1948, April 15, 1950, November 1, 1951, May 29, 1953, June 7, 1956, November 26, 1958, July 7, 1960, November 17, 1960, March 26, 1966, July 27, 1967; *New York Herald Tribune Book Review,* August

15, 1948, April 9, 1950, November 4, 1951, September 21, 1952, May 31, 1953, November 14, 1954, June 24, 1956, January 26, 1958, June 14, 1959, June 12, 1960, November 6, 1960, August 27, 1961; *Commonweal,* August 20, 1948, November 7, 1952, July 25, 1969; *Life,* August 15, 1949; Tom Walter Campbell, *Four Score Forgotten Men,* Pioneer Publishing, 1950; *New York Times,* April 9, 1950, September 21, 1952, November 14, 1954, June 10, 1956, January 19, 1958, November 9, 1958, August 9, 1959, April 17, 1970; *Saturday Review,* April 15, 1950, September 20, 1952, November 6, 1954, February 4, 1956, June 9, 1956, January 18, 1958, November 22, 1958, July 2, 1960, June 24, 1961, January 4, 1964; *Library Journal,* May 1, 1950, November 15, 1954, January 1, 1956, April 15, 1956, February 1, 1958, January 1, 1959, June 1, 1959, June 15, 1961, October 15, 1961, April 1, 1962, May 1, 1967, November 1, 1968; *New Yorker,* September 20, 1952, June 6, 1953, November 6, 1954; *Time,* November 8, 1954, June 11, 1956, August 16, 1963, June 9, 1967, June 6, 1969, April 27, 1970, May 11, 1970; *Atlantic,* December, 1954; *Christian Century,* August 17, 1960, January 26, 1966, December 16, 1970; *New York Times Book Review,* November 20, 1960, November 5, 1961, September 29, 1963; *Field and Stream,* May, 1961; *Best Sellers,* September 15, 1963; *Book Week,* September 22, 1963, September 19, 1965, July 16, 1967; *America,* October 19, 1963; John Frank, *Warren Court,* Macmillan, 1964; *New York Review of Books,* October 22, 1964; *Newsweek,* August 1, 1966, June 2, 1969, June 9, 1969, February 16, 1970, April 27, 1970, July 13, 1970, August 17, 1970, December 28, 1970, January 14, 1971; *Choice,* April, 1969; *Washington Post,* May 19, 1969, February 20, 1970, April 12, 1970, April 17, 1970, April 26, 1970, December 4, 1970, December 18, 1970; *National Review,* February 24, 1970, December 29, 1970, March 23, 1971; *Book World,* March 29, 1970; *New York Times Magazine,* June 14, 1970.

*   *   *

DOUGLAS-SCOTT-MONTAGU, Edward John Barrington 1926-
(Montagu of Beaulieu)

PERSONAL: Born October 20, 1926 (heir to title of 3rd Baron Montagu of Beaulieu), in London, England; son of Lord Montagu of Beaulieu (2nd Baron) and Pearl Crake; married Elizabeth Crossley, April 11, 1959; children: Mary, Ralph. *Education:* Attended Ridley College at St. Catharines, Ontario, Canada, 1940-42, Eton College, 1942-44, New College, Oxford, 1948-49. *Politics:* Independent Conservative. *Religion:* Church of England. *Home:* Palace House, Beaulieu, Hampshire, England. *Agent:* Curtis Brown Ltd., 13 King St., Covent Garden, London W.C.2, England. *Office:* Veteran and Vintage Magazine, 3 Wyndham Pl., London W.1, England.

CAREER: Voice and Vision Ltd. (public relations), London, England, director, 1950-53; *Veteran and Vintage Magazine,* London, England, editor, 1956—; Pioneer Publications Ltd., London, England, chairman, 1956—. Montagu Motor Museum, Beaulieu, Hampshire, England, founder, 1952, and director, 1952—. Lecturer on tours in United States, South Africa, Australia, and New Zealand. *Military service:* British Army, Grenadier Guards, 1945-48; became lieutenant. *Member:* Historic Commercial Vehicle Club (president).

WRITINGS: The Motoring Montagus: The Story of the Montagu Motoring Museum, Cassell, 1959; *Lost Causes of Motoring,* Cassell, 1960, 2nd edition, 1966, Sportshelf, 1967; *Jaguar: A Biography,* Cassell, 1961, Norton, 1962, 3rd edition, Cassell, 1967, A.S. Barnes, 1969; *The Gordon Bennett Races,* Cassell, 1963; *Rolls of Rolls Royce: A Biography of Hon. C.S. Rolls,* Cassell, 1966, A.S. Barnes, 1967; *Gilt and the Gingerbread; or, How to Live in a*

Stately Home and Make Money, M. Joseph, 1967; *Lost Causes of Motoring: Europe,* two volumes, A.S. Barnes, 1969; *More Equal Than Others: The Changing Fortunes of British and European Aristocracies,* M. Joseph, 1970.

AVOCATIONAL INTERESTS: Shooting, fishing, water skiing, and photography.

*   *   *

DOWDELL, Dorothy (Florence) Karns 1910-

PERSONAL: Surname is accented on first syllable; born May 5, 1910, in Reno, Nev.; daughter of Albert Berdell (a federal employee) and Florence (Lusk) Karns; married Joseph A. Dowdell (a retired college botany instructor), June 21, 1931; children: Joan Eva (Mrs. William R. Moore), John Lawrence. *Education:* Sacramento City College, student, 1927-29; University of California, Berkeley, A.B., 1931; additional study at Sacramento State College, 1948-50. *Politics:* Republican. *Religion:* Episcopalian. *Home:* 21549 Old Mine Rd., Los Gatos, Calif. 95030. *Agent:* Edith Margolis, Lenniger Literary Agency, 437 Fifth Ave., New York, N.Y. 10016.

CAREER: Sacramento City Unified School District, Sacramento, Calif., elementary school teacher, 1948-61; full-time writer, 1961—. *Member:* American Association of University Women (member of Sacramento branch board, 1964-65), Authors Guild of Authors League of America, California Writers Club (Sacramento branch president, 1953-54, 1963-64), California Congress P.T.A. (honorary life), P.E.O. Sisterhood (chapter president, 1944-46).

WRITINGS: Karen Anderson, Illustrator (for young adults), Bouregy, 1960; *Strange Rapture* (for young adults), Bouregy, 1961; *Border Nurse* (for young adults), Bouregy, 1963; *Roses for Gail* (for young adults), Bouregy, 1964; *How to Help Your Child in School,* Macfadden, 1964; *Secrets of the ABC's* (juvenile), Oddo, 1965; *Arctic Nurse* (for young adults), Bouregy, 1966; *The Allerton Rose* (for young adults), Dell, 1972.

With husband, Joseph Dowdell: *Tree Farms: Harvest for the Future,* Bobbs-Merrill, 1965; *Your Career in Teaching,* Messner, 1967; *Sierra Nevada: The Golden Barrier,* Bobbs-Merrill, 1968; *Careers in Horticultural Sciences,* Messner, 1969; *The Japanese Helped Build America,* Messner, 1970; *Your Career in the World of Travel,* Messner, 1971; *The Chinese Helped Build America,* Messner, 1972.

WORK IN PROGRESS: Hawk Over Hollyhedge Manor, a romantic suspense story, for Avon.

SIDELIGHTS: Mrs. Dowdell lived in Europe for one year, and has traveled to Alaska, Hawaii, Canada, and throughout the United States studying plant life with her botanist-husband.

BIOGRAPHICAL/CRITICAL SOURCES: Best Sellers, May 1, 1967, September 1, 1968, April 1, 1969; *Library Journal,* September, 1968, July, 1969, October 15, 1970.

*   *   *

DOWDEN, Anne Ophelia 1907-
(Anne Ophelia Todd)

PERSONAL: Born September 17, 1907, in Denver, Colo.; daughter of James Campbell (head of department of clinical pathology at University of Colorado) and Edith (Brownfield) Todd; married Raymond Baxter Dowden (head of art department at Cooper Union School of Art and Architecture), April 1, 1934. *Education:* University of Colorado, student, 1925-26; Carnegie Institute of Technology (now Carnegie-Mellon University), B.A., 1930; additional study at Art Students League of New York and Beaux Arts Institute of Design, New York,

N.Y. *Religion:* Protestant. *Home:* 205 West 15th St., New York, N.Y. 10011.

CAREER: Pratt Institute, Brooklyn, N.Y., instructor in drawing, 1930-33; Manhattanville College, Purchase, N.Y., head of art department, 1932-53; free-lance textile designer, 1935-55; botanical illustrator, 1950—. Paintings, textiles, and botanical water colors have been exhibited at Carnegie Institute, Whitney Museum, Metropolitan Museum of Art, Newark Museum, Silvermine Artists Guild, Cooper Union Museum, Brooklyn Botanic Garden, and Hunt Botanical Library. *Awards, honors:* Fellow of Tiffany Foundation, 1929, 1930, 1932.

WRITINGS—Self-illustrated: (Under name Anne Ophelia Todd) *CUAS 8*, Cooper Union Art School, 1961; *The Little Hill: A Chronicle of Flora on a Half Acre at the Green Camp, Ringwood, New Jersey*, Cooper Union Art School, 1961; *Look at a Flower*, Crowell, 1963; *The Secret Life of the Flowers*, Odyssey, 1964; (with Richard Thomson) *Roses*, Odyssey, 1965; *Wild Green Things in the City: A Book of Weeds*, Crowell, 1972.

Illustrator: Jessica Kerr, *Shakespeare's Flowers*, Crowell, 1969; Hal Borland, *Plants of Christmas*, Golden Press, 1969; Louis Untermeyer, editor, *Roses*, Golden Press, 1970; Louis Untermeyer, *Plants of the Bible*, Golden Press, 1970. Botanical illustrations published in four issues of *Life*, 1952-57, in *House Beautiful, Natural History*, and *Audubon*.

*   *   *

DOWDEY, Clifford (Shirley, Jr.)   1904-

PERSONAL: Born January 23, 1904, in Richmond, Va.; son of Clifford Shirley (a Western Union employee) and Bessie (Bowis) Dowdey; married Frances Gordon Wilson (a clinical psychologist), July 13, 1944 (died July, 1970); married Carolyn DeCamps (a librarian), September 9, 1971; children: Frances, Sarah Bowis. *Education:* Attended Columbia University, 1921-22, 1923-25. *Politics:* "Virginia Democrat." *Religion:* Episcopalian. *Home and office:* 2504 Kensington Ave., Richmond, Va. 23220. *Agent:* Harold Ober Associates, Inc., 40 East 49th St., New York, N.Y. 10017.

CAREER: Professional writer, 1929—. Started career as a reporter and book reviewer for *Richmond News Leader*, Richmond, Va., 1925-26; member of editorial staff of *Munsey's Magazine* and *Argosy*, 1926-28; editor of pulp magazines, Dell Publishing Co., New York, N.Y., 1928-29, 1933-35; former associate editor of *Redbook*; part-time lecturer in English, University of Richmond, Richmond, Va., 1958-69. Nominal editor of *Virginia Record*, 1955—. During World War II did propaganda work for U.S. War Department, 1942-43, and served on confidential assignment as special appointee of Secretary Stimson, 1943-44. Virginia Civil War Commission, vice-chairman, 1957-59. Richmond Professional Institute, member of board of visitors, 1962-64. *Member:* Authors Guild, Virginia Historical Society, Virginia Museum of Fine Arts. *Awards, honors:* Guggenheim fellowship for creative writing, 1937; LL.D., Ripon College, 1961; Fletcher Pratt Memorial award, 1965; National Humanities grant, 1967.

WRITINGS—Novels: *Bugles Blow No More*, Little, Brown, 1937; *Gambles Hundred*, Little, Brown, 1939; *Sing for a Penny*, Little, Brown, 1941; *Tidewater*, Little, Brown, 1943; *Where My Love Sleeps*, Little, Brown, 1945; *Weep for My Brother*, Doubleday, 1950; *Jasmine Street*, Doubleday, 1952; *The Proud Retreat*, Doubleday, 1954; *Last Night the Nightingale*, Doubleday, 1962.

Non-fiction: *Experiment in Rebellion*, Doubleday, 1946; *The Land They Fought For: The Story of the South as the Confederacy*, Doubleday, 1955; *The Great Plantation:*

A Profile of Berkeley Hundred and Plantation Virginia from Jamestown to Appomatox, Rinehart, 1956; *Death of a Nation*, Knopf, 1958; *Lee's Last Campaign: The Story of Lee and His Men against Grant—1864*, Little, Brown, 1960; (editor with Louis Manarin, and author of connective narratives) *The Wartime Papers of R.E. Lee*, Little, Brown, 1961; *The Seven Days: The Emergence of Lee*, Little, Brown, 1964; *Lee*, Little, Brown, 1965; *The Virginia Dynasties: The Emergence of "King" Carter and the Golden Age*, Little, Brown, 1969; *The Golden Age: A Climate for Greatness, Virginia, 1732-1775*, Little, Brown, 1970.

Writer for motion pictures. Contributor of short stories, novels, and articles to *Saturday Evening Post, Atlantic, Collier's, McCall's, Ladies' Home Journal, Holiday, American Mercury, Saturday Review, American Heritage, American Home, Journal of Southern History, Virginia Quarterly, New York Times*, and *Richmond Sunday Times Dispatch*.

SIDELIGHTS: After living (and writing) from coast to coast, Dowdey returned to where he began writing in the twenties—using the bedroom-of-his-youth in the family home as a workroom. He said the re-rooting was gradual. "After the war I returned to Richmond as a base for research on my first non-fiction book ... kept postponing leaving until my children were born ... then decided to settle permanently with the ambition of becoming an enlightened provincial. The summarization behind all this is that I believe it to be of extreme importance today for a writer to work with a sense of roots, and for individuals to be a part of the perpetuity of a social pattern."

Between times Dowdey resided in New York in the midtwenties ("magazines were flourishing there"), in Connecticut, Florida, Texas, Arizona, Mexico, California, Vermont, and New York again. Having drawn on the "struggle and tragedy of the Confederacy" during the Civil War for his earliest novels, Dowdey became known as an authority on The Army of Northern Virginia. However, as he told *CA* recently, "the deluge of pop books that flooded the market during the Civil War Centennial sated the public with the subject, and I found myself an authority in a dead field." Since the loss of his subject Dowdey believes he has gone into a decline as a writer. He expresses some bitterness "at the callousness of publishers to a professional writer *the moment* he cases to produce for them," saying that he feels like "an impotent relic of another age." He nevertheless considers his writing career a fulfilling one: "I would not have wanted to do anything else."

Dowdey's avocational (as well as vocational) interests are history and literature—history on a broad range of the cultural history of the Western world from the Greeks on, and reading in philosophy, psychology, biography. Another interest is music, particularly classical works of the eighteenth century, but also show music and Mexican music.

*   *   *

DRACKETT, Phil(ip Arthur)   1922-
(Paul King)

PERSONAL: Born December 25, 1922, in London, England; son of Arthur Ernest (a builder) and Mary Jane (King) Drackett; married Joan Isobel Davies, June 19, 1948. *Education:* University of London, general schools certificate. *Home:* 217 Lauderdale Mansions, London W. 9, England.

MEMBER: National Union of Journalists, Guild of Motoring Writers, Sports Writers Association.

WRITING: Fighting Days, A-American, 1944; *Come Out Fighting*, A-American, 1945; *Speedway*, W. & G. Foyle,

1951; *Motor Racing*, W. & G. Foyle, 1952; *Motoring*, W. & G. Foyle, 1955; (with Leslie Webb) *You and Your Car*, W. & G. Foyle, 1957; (with A. Thompson) *You and Your Motor Cycle*, W. & G. Foyle, 1958; *Great Moments in Motoring*, Roy, 1958; *Automobiles Work Like This*, Phoenix House, 1958, Roy, 1960; *Veteran Cars*, W. & G. Foyle, 1961; *The Young Car Driver's Companion*, Sportshelf, 1961; *Vintage Cars*, W. & G. Foyle, 1962; *Motor Rallying*, W. & G. Foyle, 1963; *Driving Your Car: Passing the Test, and After*, Sportshelf, 1964; *Taking Your Car Abroad*, W. & G. Foyle, 1965; *International Motor Racing Book*, four volumes, Souvenir Press, 1967-70; *Let's Look at Cars*, Muller, 1967; *Slot Car Racing*, Souvenir Press, 1968; *Like Father, Like Son: The Story of Malcolm and Donald Campbell*, Clifton Books, 1969; *Rally of the Forests: The Story of the RAC International Rally of Great Britain*, Pelham Books, 1970. Contributor to programs of British Broadcasting Corp. and Independent Television; contributor of articles to many periodicals and newspapers.

WORK IN PROGRESS: A History of Motor Racing.

* * *

DRAYER, Adam Matthew 1913-

PERSONAL: Born January 12, 1913, in Worcester, Mass.; son of Paul (an organist) and Lottie (Frydrych) Drayer; married Rita Frances Martini, January 11, 1943; children: Michael Edward, Barbara Mary. *Education:* University of Notre Dame, A.B., 1935; Boston College, M.A., 1939; Fordham University, Ph.D., 1953. *Politics:* Republican. *Religion:* Catholic. *Home:* 86 Walnut St., Forty Fort, Pa. 18704. *Office:* King's College, 133 North River St., Wilkes-Barre, Pa. 18702.

CAREER: Harvard University, Cambridge, Mass., vocational counselor, 1945-48; King's College, Wilkes-Barre, Pa., 1948—; began as instructor, now professor of education and chairman of the department. Visiting lecturer at College Misericordia, Dallas, Pa. *Military service:* U.S. Army Air Forces, 1942-45; became staff sergeant. *Member:* American Association of Colleges for Teacher Education, National Education Association, Pennsylvania State Education Association, Association for Student Teaching, Pennsylvania Association of Liberal Arts Colleges for the Advancement of Teaching, Delta Epsilon Sigma.

WRITINGS: Problems and Methods in High School Teaching, Heath, 1963; *The Teacher in a Democratic Society: An Introduction to the Field of Education*, C.E. Merrill, 1970. Contributor of articles to professional journals.

AVOCATIONAL INTERESTS: Fishing and coin collecting.

* * *

DRESCHER, Seymour 1934-

PERSONAL: Born February 20, 1934, in New York, N.Y.; son of Sidney (a hatter) and Eva Rita (Levine) Drescher; married Ruth Lieberman (an artist), June 19, 1955; children: Michael, Jonathan, Karen. *Education:* College of City of New York (now City College of City University of New York), B.A., 1955; University of Wisconsin, M.S., 1956, Ph.D., 1960. *Home:* 5550 Pocusset St., Pittsburgh, Pa. 15217. *Office:* University of Pittsburgh, Pittsburgh, Pa. 15213.

CAREER: Harvard University, Cambridge, Mass., instructor in history, 1960-62; University of Pittsburgh, Pittsburgh, Pa., assistant professor, 1962-65, associate professor, 1965-69, professor of history, 1969—. *Member:* American Historical Association, Society for French Historical Studies, American Association of University Professors.

WRITINGS: Tocqueville and England, Harvard University Press, 1964; (editor, translator, and author of introduction) *Tocqueville and Beaumont on Social Reform*, Harper, 1968; *Dilemmas of Democracy: Tocqueville and Modernization*, University of Pittsburgh Press, 1968. Co-producer and writer of film, "Confrontation: Paris 1968." Contributor to *Journal of the History of Ideas, American Quarterly, Journal of American History, Jewish Social Studies*.

WORK IN PROGRESS: Co-editing *Retrospective Analysis of the French Uprising of 1968; Abolition and Race in Britain and France, 1790-1860.*

* * *

DRESSEL, Paul L(eroy) 1910-

PERSONAL: Born November 29, 1910, in Youngstown, Ohio; son of David Calvin (carpenter) and Aura Olive (Jacobs) Dressel; married Wilma Frances Sackett, September 18, 1933; children: Carol Ann, Linda Kathleen, Jeana Lynn. *Education:* Youngstown College, A.A., 1929; Wittenberg University, A.B., 1931; Michigan State University, M.A., 1934; University of Michigan, Ph.D., 1939. *Religion:* Protestant. *Home:* 235 Maplewood Dr., East Lansing, Mich. 48823. *Office:* Office of Institutional Research, Michigan State University, East Lansing, Mich. 48223.

CAREER: Michigan State University, East Lansing, instructor and assistant professor of mathematics, 1934-40, counseling head of board of examiners, 1940-44, professor of education and head of board of examiners, 1944-54, professor of education and director of evaluation services, 1954-57, now Professor of University Research, director of institutional research, and assistant provost. Director, Cooperative Study of Evaluation in General Education, American Council on Education, 1949-53. *Member:* American Association for the Advancement of Science (fellow), American Psychological Association (fellow), American Educational Research Association, National Education Association, National Council for Measurement in Education, American Association for Higher Education (president, 1970-71), National Society for the Study of Education, Association for Institutional Research, Association for General and Liberal Studies. *Awards, honors:* LL.D., Wittenberg University, 1966.

WRITINGS: (With others) *Comprehensive Examination in a Program of General Education*, Michigan State College Press, 1949; (with John Schmid) *An Evaluation of the Tests of General Educational Development*, American Council on Education, 1951; (with Raymond Hatch) *Guidance Services in the Secondary School*, W.C. Brown, 1953; (with Lewis B. Mayhew) *General Education: Explorations in Evaluation*, American Council on Education, 1954; (with Mayhew) *Handbook for Theme Analysis*, W.C. Brown, 1954; (with Mayhew) *Science Reasoning and Understanding*, W.C. Brown, 1954; (with Mayhew) *Critical Thinking in the Social Sciences*, W.C. Brown, 1954; *Research in General Education Instruction*, Association for Higher Education, Volume I, 1955, Volume II (with Margaret F. Lorimer), 1957; (with Clarence H. Nelson) *Test Item Folios*, Educational Testing Service, 1956; (with Mayhew) *Critical Analysis and Judgement in the Humanities*, W.C. Brown, 1956; (with Mayhew and Earl J. McGrath) *The Liberal Arts as Viewed by Faculty Members in Professional Schools*, Teachers College, Columbia University, Institute of Higher Education, 1959; *A Report of Differential Prediction and Placement in Colleges and Universities*, [East Lansing], c. 1959; (with Irvin J. Lehmann) *Critical Thinking, Attitudes and Values in Higher Education*, Michigan State University, 1959; *Liberal Education and Journalism,* Teachers College, Columbia University, Institute of Higher Education, 1960; (with Lorimer) *The Attitudes of Liberal Arts Faculty Members Toward Liberal and Professional Education,* Teachers College, Columbia University, 1960; (with others) *Evaluation in Higher Education,* Houghton, 1961; *The Undergraduate Curriculum in Higher Education,* Center for Applied Research in Education, 1963; (with Jeannette A. Lee) *Liberal Education and Home Economics,* Teachers College, Columbia University, 1963; *College and University Curriculum,* McCutchan, 1968; (with Frances DeLisle) *Undergraduate Curriculum Trends,* American Council on Education, 1969; (with F. Craig Johnson and Philip Marcus) *The Confidence Crisis,* Jossey-Bass, 1970; *New Colleges,* Jossey-Bass, 1971; (with others) *Institutional Research in the University,* Jossey-Bass, 1971; (with Sally B. Pratt) *The World of Higher Education,* Jossey-Bass, 1971; (with William H. Faricy) *Return to Responsibility: Higher Constraints on Autonomy in Higher Education,* Jossey-Bass, 1972; (with DeLisle) *Blueprint for Change: Doctoral Programs for College Teachers* (monograph), American College Testing Program, 1972.

Contributor: C.E. Erickson, editor, *A Basic Text for Guidance Workers,* Prentice-Hall, 1947; Ralph F. Berdie, editor, *Concepts and Programs of Counseling,* University of Minnesota Press, 1951; William G. Tyrrell, editor, *Social Studies in the College Program for the First Two Years,* National Council for the Social Studies, 1953; Sidney J. French, editor, *Accent on Teaching,* Harper, 1954; Ralph F. Berdie, editor, *Counseling and the College Program,* University of Minnesota Press, 1954; Thomas H. Hamilton, editor, *The Basic College of Michigan State College,* Michigan State College Press, 1955; Melvene Hardee, editor, *Counseling and Guidance in General Education,* World Book, 1955; Lewis B. Mayhew, editor, *General Education: An Account and Appraisal,* Harper, 1960; Earl J. McGrath, editor, *Cooperative Long-Range Planning in Liberal Arts Colleges,* Institute of Higher Education, Teachers College, Columbia University, 1964; Herman A. Estrin and Delmer M. Goode, *College and University Teaching,* W.C. Brown, 1964; Morris Keeton and Conrad Hilberry, *Struggle and Promise: A Future for Colleges,* McGraw, 1969; Asa S. Knowles, editor, *Handbook of College and University Administration,* McGraw, 1970.

Editor: (And contributor) *Evaluation in General Education,* W.C. Brown, 1954; (with Clarence H. Nelson) *Questions and Problems in Science,* Educational Testing Service, 1956; (and contributor) *Evaluation in the Basic College of Michigan State University,* Harper, 1958; (with Horace T. Morse) *General Education for Personal Maturity,* W.C. Brown, 1960; (and contributor) *Evaluation in Higher Education,* Houghton, 1961; *The New Colleges: Toward An Appraisal* (monograph), American College Testing Program and American Association for Higher Education, 1971.

Contributor to encyclopedias, education association yearbooks, and published conference reports; also contributor of almost one hundred mongraphs, articles, and book reviews to educational journals.

WORK IN PROGRESS: Revision of *Evaluation in Higher Education;* a proposed book on higher education as a discipline.

* * *

DREW, Katherine Fischer 1923-

PERSONAL: Born September 24, 1923, in Houston, Tex.; daughter of Herbert H. (a small businessman) and Martha (Holloway) Fischer; married Ronald F. Drew (a professor at University of Houston), 1951. *Education:* Rice Institute (now Rice University), B.A., 1944, M.A.,

1945; Cornell University, Ph.D., 1950. *Home:* 509 Buckingham, Houston, Tex. 77024. *Office:* 408 Fondren Library, Rice University, Houston, Tex. 77001.

CAREER: Rice University, Houston, Tex., assistant professor, 1950-57, associate professor, 1957-64, professor of history, 1964—, acting chairman of department of history. *Member:* American Historical Association, Mediaeval Academy of America, Renaissance Society of America, Phi Beta Kappa. *Awards, honors:* Guggenheim fellow, 1959; Fulbright seminarist, 1965.

WRITINGS: (Editor with F. S. Lear) *Perspectives in Medieval History,* University of Chicago Press, 1963; (editor) *The Barbarian Invasion: Catalyst of a New Order, Holt,* 1970; (translator and author of introduction) *The Lombard Laws,* University of Pennsylvania Press, 1972.

Monographs: (Translator) *The Burgundian Code,* University of Pennsylvania Press, 1949; *Notes on Lombard Institutions; Lombard Laws and Anglo-Saxon Dooms,* Rice University Press, 1956. Contributor to *Speculum, Traditis, Manuscripta,* and other professional journals. Editor, *Rice University Studies.*

* * *

DRINAN, Robert F(rederick) 1920-

PERSONAL: Born November 15, 1920, in Boston, Mass.; son of James J. and Anne (Flanagan) Drinan. *Education:* Boston College, A.B., 1940, M.A., 1947; Weston College, S.T.L., 1954; Georgetown University, LL.B., 1949, LL.M., 1950. *Home:* Boston College, 140 Commonwealth Ave., Chestnut Hill, Mass. 02167. *Office:* 509 Cannon Bldg., Washington, D.C. 20515.

CAREER: Entered Roman Catholic order, Society of Jesus, 1942; ordained priest, 1953. Admitted to District of Columbia Bar, 1950, Bar of U.S. Supreme Court, 1955; Boston College, Law School, Brighton, Mass., assistant dean, 1955-56, dean, 1957-70; U.S. Congress, representative from Massachusetts, 1970—. *Member:* American Bar Association, American Judicature Society (executive committee), Massachusetts Bar Association (vice-president), Boston Bar Association.

WRITINGS: Federal Aid to Education, Clergy Conference, Archdiocese of Chicago, 1962; *Religion, the Courts and Public Policy,* McGraw, 1963; *New Dimensions in the Professional Responsibilities of the Bar,* Maine Bar Association, 1963; (contributor) Dallin H. Oaks, editor, *The Wall Between Church and State,* University of Chicago, 1963; *The Changing Order of the Lawyer in an Era of Non-Violent Action,* Congress of Racial Equality, 1964; *The Constitution, Governmental Aid and Catholic Higher Education,* National Catholic Educational Association, 1968; (editor) *The Right to Be Educated,* foreword by Arthur J. Goldberg, Corpus Publications, 1968; *Democracy, Dissent and Disorder: The Issues and the Law,* Seabury, 1969; *Vietnam and Armageddon: Peace, War and the Christian Conscience,* Sheed, 1970. Corresponding editor, *America.*

WORK IN PROGRESS: A book on legal-moral problems in America, tentatively titled *Law and Morality in America.*

BIOGRAPHICAL/CRITICAL SOURCES: Christian Century, February 4, 1970; *Library Journal,* June 15, 1970.

* * *

DRINKALL, Gordon (Don) 1927-
(Don Demaine)

PERSONAL: Born December 29, 1927, in Ryhope, Durham, England; son of Cyril and Ellen Drinkall. *Edu-*

cation: Attended Imperial College of the University of London, and Enfield Technical College. *Religion:* Church of England. *Home:* 12 Newfield Way, Dedmore Ct., Marlow on Thames, Buckinghamshire, England.

CAREER: Autocar Magazine, London, England, editorial assistant, one and one-half years; *Courier* Magazine, London, feature writer, one year; Rolls House Feature Agency, London, assistant editor, three years; Focal Press, London, executive editor, three years; *Photography* Magazine, London, editor, five years; Astral Marketing (advertising), London, chief copywriter; now free-lance photographer and writer. *Military service:* Royal Air Force, 1945-48.

WRITINGS: All About Pictures at the Seaside with your Camera, Focal Press, 1955. Author of motion picture scripts. Contributor of motoring features and reports and feature photography to *Daily Express, Life, Scotsman, Photorama, Autosport,* and television magazines. Editor, *Clarion;* co-editor, *Photography Annual,* World's Press.

WORK IN PROGRESS: Documentary film scripts; various nonfiction books; travel writing.

AVOCATIONAL INTERESTS: Motor sport (racing and rallying), natural history and wildlife photography, travel, and geographical research.

* * *

DRURY, Clifford Merrill 1897-

PERSONAL: Born November 7, 1897, in Early, Iowa; son of William (a farmer) and Mae Charity (Dell) Drury; married Miriam Leyrer, November 17, 1922; children: Robert Merrill, Patricia, Philip Edward (deceased). *Education:* Buena Vista College, B.A., 1918; San Francisco Theological Seminary, B.D., 1922, S.T.M., 1928; University of Edinburgh, Ph.D., 1932. *Politics:* Republican. *Home:* 2889 San Pasqual St., Pasadena, Calif. 91107.

CAREER: Ordained to Presbyterian ministry, 1922; Community Church (American), Shanghai, China, pastor, 1923-27; First Presbyterian Church, Moscow, Idaho, pastor, 1928-38; San Francisco Theological Seminary, San Anselmo, Calif., professor of church history, 1938-63; now retired. *Military service:* U.S. Army, 1918. U.S. Naval Reserve, 1933-58, serving on active duty, 1941-46; official historian of U.S. Navy Chaplain Corps, 1944-56; became captain; received Secretary of Navy Commendation with medal. *Member:* Church History Society, Phi Beta Kappa. *Awards, honors:* D.D., Buena Vista College, 1941; Litt.D., Whitworth College, 1955; Distinguished Service Award, Presbyterian Historical Society, 1960; D.H.L., Whitman College, 1964; first recipient of Captain Robert Gray Medal, Washington State Historical Society, 1968.

WRITINGS: Nicodemus: A Three-act Religious Drama Based Upon the Three New Testament References to Nicodemus, the Pharisee, privately printed, 1934; *Pioneer of Old Oregon: Henry Harmon Spalding,* Caxton, 1936; *Marcus Whitman, M.D., Pioneer and Martyr,* Caxton, 1937; *Elkanah and Mary Walker: Pioneers Among the Spokanes,* Caxton, 1940; (contributor) Ward Willis Long, editor, *Ninetieth Anniversary, March 17, 1940, First Presbyterian Church, Stockton, California,* Simarel Printing Co., 1940; *United States Navy Chaplains, 1778-1945,* U.S. Government Printing Office, 1945; (compiler) *The History of the Chaplain Corps, United States Navy,* five volumes, U.S. Government Printing Office, 1948-57; *A Tepee in His Front Yard: A Biography of H.T. Cowley, One of the Four Founders of the City of Spokane, Washington,* Binfords, 1949.

Presbyterian Panorama: One Hundred and Fifty Years of National Missions History, Westminster, 1952; (editor)

Diary of Titian Ramsay Peale: Oregon to California, Overland Journey, September and October, 1841, G. Dawson, 1957; (editor and author of introduction) *The Diaries and Letters of Henry H. Spalding and Asa Bowen Smith Relating to the Nez Pearce Mission, 1838-1842,* Arthur Clark, 1958; *The Beginnings of Talmaks "Galloping Over the Butte"* (address), privately printed, 1958; (editor) *First White Women Over the Rockies: Diaries, Letters, and Biographical Sketches of the Six Women of the Oregon Mission Who Made the Overland Journey in 1836 and 1838,* three volumes, Arthur Clark, 1963-66; *San Francisco YMCA: 100 Years by the Golden Gate, 1853-1963,* Arthur Clark, 1963; *William Anderson Scott, "No Ordinary Man,"* Arthur Clark, 1967; *Rudolph James Wig, Engineer, Pomona College Trustee, Presbyterian Layman,* Arthur Clark, 1968.

California Imprints, 1846-1876: Pertaining to Social, Educational, and Religious Subjects, Arthur Clark, 1970. Contributor of forty articles to historical journals. Editor, *Army-Navy Chaplain,* 1945-46.

WORK IN PROGRESS: A two-volume biography of Dr. Marcus and Narcissa Whitman.

* * *

DUBOIS, Elfrieda T(heresia Pichler) 1916-

PERSONAL: Born March 28, 1916, in Vienna, Austria; married Pierre Dubois (a university lecturer), September 11, 1948; children: Dominique J. Michael. *Education:* University of Birmingham, B.A. (first class honors), 1943, M.A., 1945; University of Vienna, Dr. Phil., 1953; University of Paris, Docteur es lettres. *Religion:* Roman Catholic. *Home:* 82 Newlands Rd., Newcastle on Tyne 2, England. *Office:* University of Newcastle, Newcastle on Tyne 1, England.

CAREER: Teacher in Durham and Cambridge, England, 1943-46; University of Sheffield, Sheffield, England, university lecturer, 1947-48; University of Newcastle, Newcastle on Tyne, England, university lecturer, 1948-64, senior lecturer in French, 1964—.

WRITINGS: Leon Bloy, Sheed, 1952; (editor) *Essays Presented to C.M. Girdlestone,* University of Durham Press, 1960; (editor) *Eighteenth-Century French Studies: Literature and the Arts,* Oriel Press, 1969; (editor) R. Rapin, *Reflexions sur la poesie,* Droz (Geneva), 1970; (editor) Mme. de Sevigne, *Lettres,* Folens (Dublin), 1971; (editor) Martene, *Vie de C. Martin,* Gregg Press (London), 1971. Contributor to learned journals.

WORK IN PROGRESS: Literary criticism in seventeenth-century France; modern German novel; editing Rotrov's *Saint-Genest,* for Droz.

SIDELIGHTS: Ms. Dubois speaks French and German, reads Spanish, Italian, and classical languages. *Avocational interests:* Walking, cycling.

* * *

DUCHE, Jean 1915-

PERSONAL: Born March 17, 1915, in Chabanais, Charente, France; son of Joseph and Berthe (Jaulin) Duche; married Natacha Epstein, March 20, 1946; children: Caroline. *Education:* Attended Ecole Montalembert, Limoges, and Lycee Louis le Grand, Paris; Faculte de Droit de Paris, licence en droit, 1936; Faculte des Lettres de Paris (Sorbonne), licence es-lettres, 1940. *Home:* Manoir de Remauville, par Nemours, Seine-et-Marne, France.

CAREER: Free-lance journalist, 1944—. *Elle,* editorial writer, 1951—. *Military service:* Armee francaise, 1936-38, 1939-40. *Awards, honors:* Prix de l'Humour (premium of one franc), 1951, for *Elle et Lui;* Chevalier de la Legion d'honneur.

WRITINGS: Liberte europeenne, Flammarion, 1949; *Elle et lui,* Flammarion, 1951, translation by Virginia Graham published as *I Said to My Wife,* Deutsch, 1953; *Trois san toit,* Flammarion, 1952, translation by Diana Athill published as *Not at Home,* Deutsch, 1955; *L'Histoire de France racontee a Juliette,* Presses de la Cite, 1954, revised edition, 1968, translation by R.H. Stevens published as *The History of France as Told to Juliette,* Burke Publishing, 1958, Roy, 1960; *L'Histoire de France racontee a Francois et Caroline,* Editions G.P., 1955, revised edition, Flammarion, 1970; *Les Grandes heures de Lyon,* Amiot-Dumont, 1956; *On s'aimera toute la vie,* Amiot-Dumont, 1956; *Histoire de monde,* Flammarion, Volume I: *L'Animal vertical,* 1958, Volume II: *Le Feu de Dieu,* 1960, Volume III: *L'Age de raison,* 1963, Volume IV: *Le Grand tournant,* 1966; *Le Coeur a l'ouvrage,* Livre Contemporain, 1960; *Pourquoi Jaccoud a-t-il tue?,* Flammarion, 1960; (with F.A. Roulhec) *Deux siecles d'histoire de France par la caricature, 1760-1960,* Le Pont Royal, 1961; (with wife, Natalie Duche) *Des Jeunes filles parlent,* Flammarion, 1965; *The Great Trade Routes,* McGraw, 1969; *Rever des Iles britanniques,* Editions Vilo, 1969; *Pecus,* Robert Laffont, 1970; (with Anne-Marie Bryan) *Pour parler: Manuel de conversation francaise,* Prentice-Hall, 1970; *La Premier sexe,* Robert Laffont, 1971.

WORK IN PROGRESS: Six more volumes in series *Histoire du monde.*

SIDELIGHTS: Duche told *CA:* "I live as little as possible in Paris and as much as possible in the country. If I don't have books to write, I participate every day in the hunt."

BIOGRAPHICAL/CRITICAL SOURCES: Books and Bookmen, January, 1970; *Library Journal,* June 15, 1970.

* * *

DULLES, Avery (Robert) 1918-

PERSONAL: Born August 24, 1918, in Auburn, N.Y.; son of John Foster (U.S. Secretary of State, 1953-59) and Janet (Avery) Dulles. *Education:* Harvard University, A.B., 1940, law student, 1940-41; Woodstock College, Ph.L., 1950, S.T.L., 1957; Gregorian University, Rome, Italy, S.T.D., 1960. *Office:* Woodstock College, 475 Riverside Dr., New York, N.Y. 10027.

CAREER: Entered Society of Jesus (Jesuits), 1946; ordained a Roman Catholic priest, 1956; Fordham University, New York, N.Y., instructor in philosophy, 1951-53; Woodstock College, Woodstock, Md., 1960—, began as associate professor, now professor of fundamental theology. Member of board of trustees, Fordham University, 1969-72. *Military service:* U.S. Naval Reserve, 1942-46; became lieutenant; received Croix de Guerre. *Member:* Catholic Theological Society of America (member of board of directors, 1970—), U.S. Catholic Conference (member of advisory council, 1969—), Catholic Commission on Intellectual and Cultural Affairs. *Awards, honors:* LL.D., St. Joseph's College, Philadelphia, Pa., 1969; Cardinal Spellman Award for distinguished achievement in theology, 1970; Christopher Award, 1972, for *The Survival of Dogma.*

WRITINGS: Princeps Concordiae, Harvard University Press, 1941; *A Testimonial to Grace,* Sheed, 1946; (with James M. Demske and Robert J. O'Connell) *Introductory Metaphysics,* Sheed, 1955; *Protestant Churches and the Prophetic Office,* Woodstock College Press, 1961; *Apologetics and the Biblical Christ,* Newman, 1963; *The Ignatian Experience as Reflected in the Spiritual Theology of Karl Rahner,* Program to Promote the Spiritual Exercises, 1965; *The Dimensions of the Church,* Newman, 1967; (with others) *Toward a Theology of Christian Faith: Readings in Theology,* Kenedy, 1968; *Revelation and the Quest for Unity,* foreword by Robert McAfee Brown, Corpus, 1968; *Myth, Biblical Revelation and Christ,* Corpus, 1969; *Revelation Theology: A History,* Herder, 1969; (with Wolfgang Pannenberg and Carl E. Braaten) *Spirit, Faith and Church,* Westminster, 1970; *A History of Apologetics,* Corpus, 1971; *The Survival of Dogma,* Doubleday, 1971.

Contributor of articles to English-language theological journals. Associate editor for Ecumenism, *Concilium,* 1963—.

SIDELIGHTS: Dulles has lived in France, Germany, Switzerland, Belgium, and Italy, mostly for study.

BIOGRAPHICAL/CRITICAL SOURCES: Christian Century, January 22, 1969, February 10, 1971; *Commonweal,* December 19, 1969.

* * *

DULLES, Eleanor Lansing 1895-

PERSONAL: Born June 1, 1895, in Watertown, N.Y.; daughter of Allen Macy and Edith (Foster) Dulles; married David Blondheim, December 9, 1932 (died, 1934); children: David Dulles, Ann Dulles (Mrs. David Joor). *Education:* Bryn Mawr College, A.B., 1917, M.A., 1920; postgraduate study at London School of Economics, University of London, 1921-22, at University of Paris, 1924-25; Radcliffe College, M.A., 1924; Harvard University, Ph.D., 1926. *Politics:* Independent. *Religion:* Presbyterian. *Home:* 1114 Spring Hill Rd., McLean, Va. 22101. *Office:* Center for Strategic Studies, Massachusetts Ave. at 17th St., Washington, D.C.

CAREER: Shurtleff Memorial Relief, Paris, France, relief work, 1917; American Friends Service, Paris, France, relief work, 1917-1919; American Tube and Stamping Co., Bridgeport, Conn., assistant personnel manager, 1920-21; Harvard and Radcliffe Bureau of Research, research associate in France, 1925-27, in Switzerland, 1920-32; Simmons College, Boston, Mass., teacher, 1924-25, 1927-28; Bryn Mawr College, Bryn Mawr, Pa., associate professor, 1928-30, lecturer in economics, 1932-36; University of Pennsylvania, Philadelphia, research associate, 1932-36; U.S. Government, Washington, D.C., chief of finance division, Social Security Board, 1936-42, economist, Board of Economic Welfare, 1942; U.S. Department of State, Washington, D.C., economic officer, 1942-45, financial attache in Austria, 1945-48, with Western European Division, 1949-51, on detail to National Production Authority, Department of Commerce, 1951-52, special assistant, Office of German Affairs, holding personal rank of minister, 1952-59, special assistant to director of intelligence, 1959-62; Duke University, Durham, N.C., professor of political science, 1962-63; Georgetown University, Washington, D.C., professor of political science, 1963—. Investigated unemployment insurance, President Hoover's Committee, 1931; economic advisor, Geneva Conference on Investment Social Security Funds, 1938; represented U.S. Government at Bretton Woods Conference on International Monetary Fund, 1944. Visiting professor, Hoover Institution, 1967-68.

MEMBER: American Economic Association, Phi Beta Kappa, Cosmopolitan Club (New York), Tavern Club, International Club (both Washington, D.C.), Henderson Harbor Yacht Club. *Awards, honors:* LL.D., Wilson College, 1950, Western College, 1957, and Mount Holyoke College, 1963; Distinguished Achievement award, Radcliff College, 1955; honorary doctorate, Free University of Berlin, 1957; Carl Schurz Plaque, 1958; Ernst Reuter Plaque from City of West Berlin, 1959; citation for distinguished service, Bryn Mawr College, 1960; Grand

Cross of Merit (Germany), 1962; Litt.D., Duke University, 1965.

WRITINGS: *The French Franc, 1914-1928: The Facts and Their Interpretation,* Macmillan, 1929; *The Bank for International Settlements at Work,* Macmillan, 1932; *The Dollar, the Franc and Inflation,* Macmillan, 1933; (compiler with others) *Catalogue of the Library of David S. Blondheim,* privately printed, 1935; *Depression and Reconstruction: A Study of Causes and Controls,* University of Pennsylvania Press, 1936; *The Evolution of Reparation Ideas* (monograph), Harvard University, 1936; *The Export-Import Bank of Washington: The First Ten Years,* U.S. Government Printing Office, 1944; *John Foster Dulles: The Last Year,* foreword by Dwight D. Eisenhower, Harcourt, 1963; (editor with Robert Dickson Crane and Mary Catherine McCarthy) *Detente: Cold War Strategies in Transition,* Praeger for Center for Strategic Studies, 1965; *Berlin: The Wall Is Not Forever,* forword by Konrad Adenauer, University of North Carolina Press, 1967; *American Foreign Policy in the Making,* Harper, 1968; *One Germany or Two: The Struggle at the Heart of Europe,* Hoover Institution Press, 1970; (with Richard C. Walker) *The Wall: A Tragedy in Three Acts,* University of South Carolina Press, 1972. Contributor of articles on economic subjects to journals.

* * *

DULSEY, Bernard M. 1914-

PERSONAL: Born February 27, 1914, in Chicago, Ill.; son of Louis (a lawyer) and Rose (Gollis) Dulsey; married Elaine S. Cann (a teacher of ballet), June 8, 1940. *Education:* University of Chicago, A.B., 1938, A.M., 1939; University of Illinois, Ph.D., 1950. *Home:* 5927 Cherokee Dr., Shawnee Mission, Kan. 66205. *Office:* University of Missouri at Kansas City, Kansas City, Mo. 64110.

CAREER: De Pauw University, Greencastle, Ind., instructor in Spanish, 1941-42; taught Spanish at Purdue University, Lafayette, 1946-51; University of Missouri, Kansas City, professor of Spanish, 1951—. Visiting summer professor at New Mexico Highlands University, 1952, University of Kansas, 1960. *Military service:* U.S. Army, 1943-46; became second lieutenant. *Member:* American Association of Teachers of Spanish and Portuguese (president, Missouri chapter, 1955), Modern Language Association of America, American Association of University Professors (chapter president, 1959), Central States Modern Language Teachers Association.

WRITINGS: (Translator and author of introduction) Jorge Icaza, *The Villagers* (original title, *Huasipungo*), Southern Illinois University Press, 1964. Associate editor, *University Review* (quarterly literary journal); prose fiction editor for Colombia, Ecuador, and Peru for Library of Congress' *Handbook of Latin-American Studies,* 1961-66. Contributor to *Hispania, American Book Collector,* other language journals.

WORK IN PROGRESS: Studies in contemporary Spanish and Latin American literature.

SIDELIGHTS: In addition to earlier travel in South America, Latin-American countries, and western Europe, Dulsey spent the last half of 1964 in Spain and Portugal becoming acquainted with contemporary writers and their work. He is fluent in Spanish and French, manages in Italian and Portuguese, and knows some German.

* * *

DUNBAR, Dorothy 1923-

PERSONAL: Born October 3, 1923, in Olympia, Wash.; daughter of John H. (an attorney) and Marie (Rowe) Dunbar; divorced (legally regained maiden name). *Edu-*cation: University of Washington, Seattle, student, 1941-42. *Politics:* Independent. *Religion:* Catholic. *Home:* 1203 Howard, San Antonio, Tex. 78212.

CAREER: WLW-Television, Cincinnati, Ohio, assistant to continuity director, 1949-54; Fabian Advertising, Cincinnati, Ohio, copywriter, 1954-59; KUTV, Salt Lake City, Utah, member of program department staff, 1963-64.

WRITINGS: *Blood in the Parlor,* A.S. Barnes, 1964.

WORK IN PROGRESS: *Legends of the Lincoln County War, New Mexico.*

* * *

DUNBAR, Janet 1901-

PERSONAL: Surname is accented on second syllable; born May 15, 1901, in· Glasgow, Scotland; married Clifford Ernest Webb (a scientist, now retired), June 30, 1923; children: Lysbeth (Mrs. Ralph Merrifield), Philip (deceased), Frances (Mrs. Ronald Presley). *Education:* University of London, student, 1920-23. *Religion:* Nondenominational. *Agent:* John Cushman Associates, 24 East 38th St., New York, N.Y. 10016; and Curtis Brown Ltd., 13 King St., Covent Garden, London W.C. 2, England.

CAREER: Free-lance writer, 1920—. Lecturer on travel and literary subjects. British Broadcasting Corp., London, England, broadcaster on Overseas Services, and on other services, 1942—. *Member:* Society of Authors, Guild of Travel Writers.

WRITINGS: *The Early Victorian Woman* (Book Society recommendation), Harrap, 1953; *Golden Interlude: The Edens in India, 1936-42* (Daily Mail Book-of-the-Month choice in England), J. Murray, 1955; *The Radio Talk,* Harrap, 1957; *Five Festival Plays,* Harrap, 1958; *Flora Robson,* Harrap, 1960; *Mrs. G.B.S.: A Portrait,* Harper, 1963 (published in England as *Mrs. G.B.S.: A Biographical Portrait of Charlotte Shaw,* Harrap, 1963); *A Prospect of Richmond,* Houghton, 1966; *Script-Writing for Television,* Sportshelf, 1966; *Peg Woffington and Her World,* Houghton, 1968; *J.M. Barrie: The Man Behind the Image,* Houghton, 1970. Writer of radio scripts and two documentary films. Travel adviser, *Woman's Journal.*

WORK IN PROGRESS: Authorized biographies of Dame Laura Knight and Compton Mackenzie.

AVOCATIONAL INTERESTS: Theatre, music, and travel.

BIOGRAPHICAL/CRITICAL SOURCES: *Punch,* September 11, 1968; *Times Literary Supplement,* September 19, 1968; *Christian Science Monitor,* September 26, 1968; *Drama,* winter, 1968; *New York Times,* August 28, 1970; *Atlantic,* September, 1970; *Library Journal,* September 1, 1970; *Listener,* September 24, 1970; *Books and Bookmen,* October, 1970; *New Statesman,* October 9, 1970; *Esquire,* January, 1971.

* * *

DUNCAN, Kenneth S(andilands) 1912-

PERSONAL: Born April 26, 1912, in Lancashire, England; son of William Arthur (a doctor) and Ethel M. (Edwards) Duncan; married Katharine Darwall, March 14, 1941 (died, 1955); married Dorothy Williamson, August 20, 1957; children: Peter Andrew; (stepchildren) Nicholas, Elizabeth Perera, Jillian. *Education:* New College, Oxford, B.A. (with honors in chemistry), 1934. *Home:* 46 A Elvaston Pl., London S.W.1, England. *Office:* British Olympic Association, 12 Buckingham St., London WC2N GDJ, England.

CAREER: Bradfield College, Berkshire, England, chemistry master, 1935-39; Eton Manor Clubs, London, England, manager, 1945-48; British Olympic Association, London, general secretary, 1948—; British Empire and Commonwealth Games, general secretary, council for England, 1948—; British Empire and Commonwealth Games Federation, honorary secretary, 1948—. Parliamentary Sports Committee, honorary secretary. *Military service:* British Army; became major. *Member:* Achilles Club (honorary secretary). *Awards, honors:* Order of the White Rose and Lion, Finland; Member of Order of the British Empire.

WRITINGS: (With John Barlee) *Athletics—Do It This Way,* J. Murray, 1937; *The Oxford Pocketbook of Athletic Training,* Oxford University Press, 1948, 2nd edition (with Kenneth Bone), 1956.

AVOCATIONAL INTERESTS: Collecting pre-1909 operatic gramophone records, and travel.

* * *

DUNCAN, Robert 1919-

PERSONAL: Born January 7, 1919, in Oakland, Calif.; name at birth, Edward Howard Duncan; son of Edward Howard (a day laborer) and Marguerite (Wesley) Duncan (who died at the time of his birth); adopted, March 10, 1920, by Edwin Joseph (an architect) and Minnehaha (Harris) Symmes; adopted name, Robert Edward Symmes; in 1941 he took the name Robert Duncan. *Education:* Attended University of California, Berkeley, 1936-38, 1948-50, studying in the Civilization of the Middle Ages under Ernst Kantorowicz. *Residence:* San Francisco, Calif. *Address:* c/o New Directions Publishing Corp., 333 6th Ave., New York, N.Y. 10014.

CAREER: Duncan's early work appeared in *Phoenix,* edited by James Peter Cooney and Henry Miller, 1938-40; in 1940-41, he edited *Experimental Review,* with Sanders Russell, publishing works of Henry Miller, Anais Nin, Lawrence Durrell, Kenneth Patchen, William Everson, Aurora Bligh (Mary Fabilli), Thomas Merton, Robert Horan, and Jack Johnson; in 1948-49, edited *Berkeley Miscellany* to publish Jack Spicer and Mary Fabilli; since 1950 his work has been closely associated with that of Charles Olson, Robert Creeley, and Denise Levertov; lived in Banyalbufar, Majorca, 1955-56; taught at Black Mountain College, Black Mountain, N.C., spring and summer, 1956; assistant director of Poetry Center, San Francisco State College, under a Ford grant, 1956-57; associated with the Creative Writing Workshop, University of British Columbia, 1963; lecturer in Advanced Poetry Workshop, San Francisco State College, spring, 1965. *Awards, honors:* Union League Civic and Arts Foundation Prize (*Poetry* magazine), 1957; Harriet Monroe Prize (*Poetry* magazine), 1961; Guggenheim fellowship, 1963-64; Levinson Prize (*Poetry* magazine), 1964; Miles Poetry Prize, 1964; National Endowment for the Arts grant, 1965, 1966-67; Eunice Tietjens Memorial Prize (*Poetry* magazine), 1967.

WRITINGS: Heavenly City, Earthly City (poems, 1945-46), Bern Porter, 1947.

Medieval Scenes (poems, 1947), Centaur Press (San Francisco), 1950; *Poems, 1948-49* (actually, poems written between November, 1947 and October, 1948), Berkeley Miscellany, 1950; *Song of the Border-Guard* (poem), Black Mountain Graphics Workshop, 1951; The Artist's View, [San Francisco], 1952; *Caesar's Gate* (poems, 1949-55), Divers Press (Majorca), 1956, 2nd edition, 1972; *Letters* (poems, 1953-56, with drawings by Duncan), J. Williams (Highlands, N.C.), 1958; *Faust Foutu* (an entertainment in four parts, written 1954, with decorations by Duncan), Part I, White Rabbit Press (San Francisco), 1958, entire play, Enkidu sur Rogate (Stinson Beach, Calif.), 1959; *Selected Poems* (1942-50), City Lights Books, 1959.

The Opening of the Field (poems, 1956-59), Grove, 1960, new edition, New Directions, 1973; (author of preface) Jess, *O!* (poems and collages), Hawk's Well Press (New York), 1960; (author of preface) Jonathan Williams, *Elegies and Celebrations,* Jargon, 1962; *On Poetry* (radio interview, broadcast on WTIC, Hartford, Conn., May 31, 1964), Yale University, 1964; *Roots and Branches* (poems, 1959-63), Scribner, 1964; *Writing Writing: A Composition Book* (poems and essays, 1953), Sumbooks, 1964; *As Testimony: The Poem & the Scene* (essay, 1958), White Rabbit Press, 1964; *Wine,* published by Auerhahn Press for Oyez Broadsheet Series (Berkeley), 1964; *The Sweetness and Greatness of Dante's "Divine Comedy"* (lecture presented at Dominican College of San Rafael, October 27, 1965), Open Space (San Francisco), 1965; *Medea at Kolchis; or, The Maiden Head* (play, first produced at Black Mountain College, 1956), Oyez, 1965; (contributor) Howard Nemerov, editor, *Poets on Poetry,* Basic Books, 1966; *Of the War: Passages 22-27,* Oyez, 1966; *A Book of Resemblances* (poems, 1950-53), Henry Wenning, 1966; *Fragments of a Disordered Devotion* (poems, 1952), Gnomon Press, 1966; *Six Prose Pieces,* Perishable Press (Rochester, Mich.), 1966; *The Years as Catches: First Poems, 1939-46,* Oyez, 1966; *Boob* (poem), privately printed, 1966; *Audit/Robert Duncan* (published as special issue of *Audit/Poetry,* Volume 4, number 3), Audit/Poetry, 1967; *Christmas Present, Christmas Presence!* (poem), [Los Angeles], 1967; *The Cat and the Blackbird* (children's storybook), illustrated by Jess, White Rabbit Press, 1967; *Epilogos,* P. Klein, 1967; *My Mother Would Be a Falconress,* Oyez, 1968; *Names of People* (poems, 1952-53), illustrated by Jess, Black Sparrow Press, 1968; *The Truth and Life of Myth: An Essay in Essential Autobiography,* House of Books (New York), 1968, Sumac, 1972; *Bending the Bow,* New Directions, 1968; *The First Decade: Selected Poems, 1940-50,* Fulcrum Press (London), 1968; *Derivations: Selected Poems, 1950-1956,* Fulcrum Press, 1968; *Achilles' Song,* Phoenix, 1969; *A Selection of Sixty-Five Drawings from One Drawing-Book, 1952-1956,* Black Sparrow Press, 1970; *Tribunals: Passages 31-35,* Black Sparrow Press, 1970; *Poetic Disturbances,* Maya (San Francisco), 1970; (contributor) Edwin Haviland Miller, editor, *The Artistic Legacy of Walt Whitman: A Tribute to Gay Wilson Allen,* New York University Press, 1970; *Poems from the Margins of Thom Gunn's Moly,* privately printed, 1972.

Represented in various anthologies, including *Faber Book of Modern American Verse,* edited by W.H. Auden, Faber, 1956, *The New American Poetry: 1945-1960,* edited by Donald M. Allen, Grove, 1960, *Contemporary American Poetry,* edited by Donald Hall, Penguin, 1962, *The New Modern Poetry,* edited by M.L. Rosenthal, Macmillan, 1967. Contributor to *Atlantic, Poetry, Nation, Quarterly Review of Literature,* and other periodicals.

WORK IN PROGRESS: The H.D. Book, a study of the mythopoeic experience at work; works on Shakespeare's *Romeo and Juliet;* editing *Selected Poems of Henry Vaughan,* for Penguin in England; a Dante notebook for his next collection of poetry, planned for 1983.

SIDELIGHTS: In some pages from a notebook published in *The New American Poetry: 1945–1960,* Duncan makes these comments on poetry: "Every moment of life is an attempt to come to life. Poetry is a 'participation,' a oneness. Can the ambitious artist who seeks success, perfection, mastery, ever get nearer to the universe, can he ever know 'more' or feel 'more' than a child may? To be a child is not an affair of how old one is. 'Child' like 'angel' is a concept, a realm of possible being. Many children have never been allowed to stray into childhood. Sometimes I dream of at last becoming a child. A child can be an artist, he can be a poet. But can a child be a banker? . . . The secret of genius lies in this: that here experience is not made to count.

"I once dreaded happiness, for I thot that ones being, ones art, sprang full grown from suffering. But I found that one suffers happiness in that sense. There is no magic of poetry that will not remain magic because one has sought wisdom. The wisdom of the hearth is, one finds, an other magic. It was the disappearance of dread itself that made suffering unessential—as, indeed, happiness had become unessential. . . . Happiness itself is a forest in which we are bewildered, run wild, or dwell, like Robin Hood, outlawd and at home."

Concerning form and quality in a poem he writes: "A longing grows to return to the open composition in which the accidents and imperfections of speech might awake intimations of human being. . . . There is a natural mystery in poetry. We do not understand all that we render up to understanding. . . . I study what I write as I study out any mystery. A poem, mine or anothers, is an occult document, a body awaiting vivisection, analysis, X-rays." Although frequently obscure in its imagery, Duncan's language is also musical and effusive. He writes: "I work at language as a spring of water works at the rock, to find a course, and so, blindly. In this I am not a maker of things, but, if maker, a maker of a way. For the way is itself. . . . And vast as the language is, it is no end but a resistance thru which a poem might move—as it flows or dances or puddles in time—making it up in its going along and yet going only as it breaks the resistance of the language."

X.J. Kennedy considers some of the early Duncan poems as "tentative jottings from his laboratory," and, because of the experimental nature of much of Duncan's work, has this advice to the reader of *Roots and Branches:* "In approaching Duncan's poems, the reader may find a bit of blind faith useful. With it, he may surmount a few private allusions, mysterious gaps in syntax and quirky spellings (meant to distinguish the sounds of *-ed* endings: *calld, many-brancht*). His pay will be . . . movingly beautiful pieces. . . ." Kennedy adds: "One of that large clan of poets who emerged in the fifties from Black Mountain College and the cafes of San Francisco, Duncan in this book stands as the most serious of them all, the most capable." Jim Harrison calls the structure of his poetry multi-layered and four-dimensional ("moving through time with the poet"), and compares it to "a block of weaving. . . . The poem is not the paradigm but the source, the competitor not the imitator, of nature." Harrison continues: *"Bending the Bow* is for the strenuous, the hyperactive reader of poetry; to read Duncan with any immediate grace would require Norman O. Brown's knowledge of the arcane mixed with Ezra Pound's grasp of poetics. . . . [Duncan] is personal rather than confessional and writes within a continuity of tradition. It simply helps to be familiar with Dante, Blake, mythography, medieval history, H.D., William Carlos Williams, Pound, Stein, Zukofsky, Olson, Creeley and Levertov." Hayden Carruth called the publication of *Bending the Bow* "an event exceeding questions of quality. I cannot imagine my friends, the poets who gather to dismember each other, asking of this book, as they would of the others in this review, those narrower in scope, smaller in style, 'Is it good or is it bad?' The question doesn't arise; not because Duncan is a good poet, though he is superb, but because the comprehensiveness of his imagination is too great for us."

Other critics and fellow poets are of the opinion that Duncan "has desperately needed for many years to retrieve his poetry from the incantatory monologue of private reverie and myth." Laurence Lieberman believed *"The Opening of the Field* had announced the birth of a surpassingly individual talent: a poet of mysticism,

visionary terror, and high romance. . . . But in his recent books he had produced numerous exercises—lacking all vividness—while he waits for the return of his demon." Frederic Will agrees that "as poet he is priest," but that "something is wrong" here. "Duncan's cult is his own, and we have on the whole been left outside it. Have never gotten in. As Duncan obviously—we see—knew, this feeling-of-being-excluded gives some pleasure. . . . We have obeyed signals. It has all made us feel in the control, at least under the influence, of a higher power. More than in the usual poet-reader relationship. And in retrospect, like all who have been hypnotized, we begin to worry."

Indeed, the visionary quality of his imagination is what lends an aura of mysticism to his poetry. Imagination, according to Stephen Stepanchev, is one of Duncan's three major subjects, the other two being his God of light and love, and poetry. "Sometimes the three are bound in so close a relationship that they seem interchangeable: aspects of the same reality," Stepanchev writes. It is Duncan's own reality; "reading his poems is like walking through a brilliant, subjective landscape." Donald W. Baker adds: "He floats in a world of his own making, travelling tirelessly among . . . creatures and faces projected out of his own inner life." The explanation of the poem is the poem itself. "As we start the sentence," Duncan says in *Letters,* "we notice that birds are flying thru it; phrases are disturbd where these wings and calls flock; wings are a wind, featherd, a beating of the air in passage or a word, the word 'word,' hovers, sailing before dropping down the empty shafts of sense toward. . ."

BIOGRAPHICAL/CRITICAL SOURCES: Donald M. Allen, *The New American Poetry: 1945-1960,* Grove, 1960; *New York Times Book Review,* December 20, 1964, September 29, 1968; Stephen Stepanchev, editor, *American Poetry Since 1945,* Harper, 1965; *New York Review of Books,* June 3, 1965, May 7, 1970; *Poetry,* September, 1965, March, 1968, April, 1969, May, 1970; A. Kingsley Weatherhead, *Edge of the Image: Marianne Moore, William Carlos Williams, and Some Other Poets,* University of Washington Press, 1967; *Hudson Review,* summer, 1968; Roy Harvey Pearce, *Historicism Once More: Problems and Occasions for the American Scholar,* Princeton University Press, 1969; Serge Fauchereau, *Lecture de la poesie americaine,* Editions de Minuit, 1969.

*   *   *

DUNLOP, Ian G(eoffrey) D(avid)   1925-

PERSONAL: Born August 19, 1925, in Rajkot, Kathiawar, India; son of Walter N.U. (in Indian civil service) and Irene (Shakerley) Dunlop; married Deirdre Jamieson, November 2, 1957. *Education:* Winchester College, student, 1938-43; New College, Oxford, B.A., 1948, M.A., 1956; Strasbourg University, diplome, 1953; other study at Lincoln Theological College, 1954-56. *Home:* The Vicarage, Bures, Suffolk, England.

CAREER: English teacher at schools in Strasbourg, France, 1952-53, in Versailles, France, 1953-54; Church of England, curate in Hertfordshire, 1956-59, chaplain at Westminster School, London, 1959-62; currently vicar at Bures, Suffolk. Trustee, Historic Churches Preservation Trust, 1970. *Military service:* Irish Guards, 1943-45. *Member:* National Book League, Society of Antiquaries (fellow), Guards Boat Club.

WRITINGS: Versailles, Batsford, 1956, revised edition, Taplinger, 1970; *Palaces and Progresses of Elizabeth I,* J. Cape, 1962, Verry, 1964; *Piet Mondrian,* Purnell, 1967; *Chateux of the Loire,* Taplinger, 1969. Contributor to *Country Life, Connoisseur.*

WORK IN PROGRESS: French Cathedrals Built During the 'Cathedrals' Crusade,' 1150-1250.

AVOCATIONAL INTERESTS: Birdwatching; the countryside, especially the Scottish Highlands.

* * *

DUNN, Edgar S(treeter), Jr. 1921-

PERSONAL: Born August 15, 1921, in Gainesville, Fla.; son of Edgar S. (a salesman) and Francis Martina (Lacey) Dunn; married Lillian Jean Bowness, August 31, 1947; children: Marion Charlotte, James Edgar. Education: University of Florida, B.S.B.A. (with high honors), 1943, M.A., 1947; Harvard University, M.A., 1949, Ph.D., 1951. Politics: Democrat. Religion: Protestant. Home: 7615 Range Rd., Alexandria, Va. 22306. Office: Resources for the Future, Inc., 1755 Massachusetts Ave., Washington, D.C. 20036.

CAREER: University of Florida, Gainesville, assistant professor, 1950-51, associate professor, 1951-56, professor of economics, 1957-58, 1959-62; Resources for the Future, Inc., Washington, D.C., research consultant, 1956-57; Organization for European Economic Cooperation, Paris, France, economic consultant, 1958-59; U.S. Department of Commerce, Washington, D.C., deputy assistant secretary for economic affairs, 1962-64; Resources for the Future, Inc., Washington, D.C., senior research associate, 1964—. Consultant to Tennessee Valley Authority, 1951, and U.S. Bureau of the Budget, 1965-66. Military service: U.S. Army, 1943-46; became master sergeant. Member: American Statistical Association, American Economic Association, Southern Economic Association (vice-president, 1962-63, president, 1967-68), Regional Science Association, Phi Beta Kappa, Phi Kappa Phi, Beta Gamma Sigma.

WRITINGS: The Location of Agricultural Production, University of Florida Press, 1954; (with Perloff, Lamphard, and Muth) Regions, Resources and Economic Growth, Johns Hopkins Press, 1960; Recent Southern Economic Development, University of Florida Press, 1962; Review of Proposal for a National Data Center, Office of Statistical Standards, U.S. Bureau of the Budget, 1965; Economic and Social Development: A Process of Social Learning, Johns Hopkins Press, 1971; Information Resources, Statistical System Reform and Human Freedom, Johns Hopkins Press, in press. Editor, Southern Economic Journal, 1957-60.

WORK IN PROGRESS: The Transformation of Urban Systems, for Johns Hopkins Press.

* * *

DUNN, Harold 1929-

PERSONAL: Born April 18, 1929, in Heavener, Okla.; son of William Levi and Lora (Stuart) Dunn. Education: Southwest Missouri State College, B.S. in Ed., 1950; Baylor University, M.S. in Mus.Ed., 1954; Washington University, St. Louis, Mo., postgraduate study, 1961. Religion: Baptist. Home: 323 Shady Meadow, St. Louis, Mo. 63011.

CAREER: Public school teacher in Seymour, Mo., 1955-56, Gallup, N.M., 1956-58, Jefferson City, Mo., 1958-60, Ballwin, Mo., 1960—. Military service: U.S. Army, Ordnance, served at White Sands Proving Grounds, 1951-53.

WRITINGS: Those Crazy, Mixed-Up Kids, New American Library, 1961; (compiler) How to Run a Country, Etc.: Kids Write Their Congressmen, Horizon, 1963; (editor) A Blizzard Is When It Snows Sideways, Western Publishing, 1970. Contributor of articles to Home and Highway, Empire, Suburbia Today, Christian Science Monitor, Family Weekly, Yankee, TV Guide, This Week,

Science Digest, Maclean's, Discovery, Ford Times, Golfing, Catholic Digest, and other magazines.

WORK IN PROGRESS: A book tentatively titled Stop the Election!, a compilation of youngsters' ideas on the election process.

AVOCATIONAL INTERESTS: Music, playing the violin, travel, hunting and fishing, golfing, tennis, and table tennis.

* * *

DUPRE, Louis Karel 1925-

PERSONAL: Born April 16, 1925, in Veerle, Belgium; son of Clemens Vincent and Francisca (Verlinden) Dupre; married Constance Pierson (an attorney), December 17, 1965; children: Christian. Education: Berchmanianum Nijmegen, Holland, Licence (philosophy), 1950; University of Louvain, Ph.D. (philosophy), 1952; Berchmanscollege Louvain, Belgium, Licence (theology), 1958; graduate study in Denmark, 1957. Religion: Catholic. Home: 2328 37th St. N.W., Washington, D.C. 20007. Office: Georgetown University, Washington, D.C. 20007.

CAREER: Georgetown University, Washington, D.C., 1958—, began as associate professor became professor of philosophy. Taught course in Marxist philosophy at St. Louis University, 1962. Member: Wijsgerig Gezelschap (Belgium). Awards, honors: American Philosophical Association, American Metaphysical Society, American Council of Learned Societies (fellow), American Catholic Philosophical Association (president, 1970-71). Huyghe Prize for best study in field of sociology, jurisprudence, or journalism by an alumnus of University of Louvain, 1954, for Het Vertrekpunt der Marxistische Wijsbegeerte.

WRITINGS: Het Vertrekpunt der Marxistische wijsbegeerte: De kriteek op Hegels staatsrecht (title means "The Starting Point of Marxist Philosophy"), Standaard-Boekhandel, 1954; Kierkegaard's Theologie: De Dialectiek van het Christen-worden, Spectrum, 1958, published in America as Kierkegaard as Theologian: The Dialectic of Christian Existence, Sheed, 1963; Contraception and Catholics: A New Appraisal, Helicon, 1964; The Philosophical Foundations of Marxism, Harcourt, 1966; (editor and author of introduction) Faith and Reflection: A Selection from the Writings of Henry Dumery, Herder, 1969; The Other Dimension: A Search for the Meaning of Religious Attitudes, Doubleday, 1971. Contributor to philosophical and religious periodicals in Europe and America.

WORK IN PROGRESS: Books on the early philosophy of Marx and on the philosophy of religion.

* * *

DUPREE, A(nderson) Hunter 1921-

PERSONAL: Born January 29, 1921, in Hillsboro, Tex.; son of George W. (a lawyer) and Sarah (Hunter) Dupree; married Marguerite L. Arnold, July 18, 1946; children: Marguerite W., Anderson Hunter, Jr. Education: Oberlin College, B.A. (summa cum laude), 1942; Harvard University, M.A., 1947, Ph.D., 1952. Religion: Congregationalist. Home: 114 Morris Ave., Providence, R.I. 02906. Office: Brown University, Department of History, Providence, R.I. 02912.

CAREER: Texas Technological College, Lubbock, assistant professor of history, 1950-52; Harvard University, Gray Herbarium, Cambridge, Mass., research fellow, 1952-54, 1955-56; University of California, Berkeley, visiting assistant professor, 1956-58, associate professor, 1958-61, professor of history, 1961-68; Brown University, Providence, R.I., George L. Littlefield Professor of History, 1968—. Consultant to committee on science and public policy, National Academy of Sciences; consultant, Panel on Science and Technology and Astronautics, U.S. House of Representatives, N.A.S.A. History Advisory Committee, A.E.C. History Advisory Committee. *Military service:* U.S. Naval Reserve, 1942-46; became lieutenant. (Belgium). *Awards, honors:* American Philosophical Associate Member: American Academy of Arts and Sciences, American Association for the Advancement of Science, American Historical Association, American Association of University Professors, American Studies Association, History of Science Society, Society for the History of Technology, Organization of American Historians, Phi Beta Kappa.

WRITINGS: Science in the Federal Government: A History of Policies and Activities to 1940, Belknap Press, 1957; *Asa Gray: 1810-1888,* Belknap Press, 1959; (editor) Asa Gray, *Darwiniana,* Belknap Press, 1963; (editor) *Science and the Emergence of Modern America, 1865-1916,* Rand McNally, 1963. Contributor of articles to professional journals.

WORK IN PROGRESS: A sequel to *Science in the Federal Government* for the period since 1940.

*   *   *

DUPUIS, Adrian M(aurice) 1919-

PERSONAL: Born October 6, 1919, in Menominee, Mich.; son of Edmund B. and Emilie (Archambault) Dupuis; married Mary E. Thompson, May 1, 1948; children: Marie, Therese, Thomas, Laurence. *Education:* Catholic University of America, A.B., 1944, M.A., 1948; University of Edinburgh, graduate study, 1946; University of Minnesota, Ph.D., 1955. *Politics:* Independent. *Religion:* Roman Catholic. *Home:* 5352 North 48th St., Milwaukee, Wis. 53218. *Office:* Marquette University, Milwaukee, Wis. 53233.

CAREER: College of St. Teresa, Winona, Minn., 1948-57, became professor of philosophy and education; Marquette University, Milwaukee, Wis., professor of philosophy of education, 1957—. Summer visiting professor, University of Minnesota, Minneapolis, 1955, 1956, 1968. Youth director, Catholic Order of Foresters, 1950-57. *Military service:* U.S. Army, Infantry and Graves Registration, 1944-46; became sergeant. *Member:* Philosophy of Education Society, National Association for Mental Health, John Dewey Society, Educational Studies Association, Phi Delta Kappa.

WRITINGS: (With R. C. Craig) *American Education: Its Origins and Issues,* Bruce, 1963; (with R. Nordberg) *Philosophy of Education: A Total View,* Bruce, 1964, revised edition, 1968; *Philosophy of Education in Historical Perspective,* Rand McNally, 1966; (editor) *Nature, Aims and Policy,* University of Illinois Press, 1970. Contributor to *New Catholic Encyclopedia.* Contributor of articles to educational and psychological journals.

WORK IN PROGRESS: History of Curriculum Development; Teaching Religion in the Public Schools.

AVOCATIONAL INTERESTS: Outdoor sports and woodworking.

*   *   *

DURANT, Ariel K(aufman) 1898-

PERSONAL: Original given name Ida, legally changed; born May 10, 1898, in Proskurov, Russia; came to United States in 1900; naturalized in 1913; daughter of Joseph Michael and Ethel (Appell) Kaufman: married Will Durant (author and philosopher), October 13, 1913; children: Ethel Benvenuta (Mrs. Stanislas Kwasniewski), Louis R. (adopted). *Education:* Educated privately. *Home:* 5608 Briarcliff Rd., Los Angeles, Calif. 90028.

AWARDS, Honors: (With husband, Will Durant) Huntington Hartford award for literature, 1963, for *The Age of Louis XIV; Los Angeles Times* Woman of the Year in Literature award, 1965; (with Will Durant) Pulitzer Prize, 1968, for *Rousseau and Revolution.*

WRITINGS—With Will Durant: *The Story of Civilization,* Simon & Schuster, Volume VII: *The Age of Reason Begins,* 1961, Volume VIII: *The Age of Louis XIV,* 1963, Volume IX: *The Age of Voltaire,* 1965, Volume X: *Rousseau and Revolution,* 1967; *The Lessions of History,* Simon & Schuster, 1968; *Interpretations of Life,* Simon & Schuster, 1970.

WORK IN PROGRESS: A Dual Autobiography, with Will Durant.

SIDELIGHTS: Mrs. Durant, whose original role in *The Story of Civilization* was that of researcher, became a full fledged co-author with her husband, beginning with the seventh volume.

*   *   *

DURANT, John 1902-

PERSONAL: Born January 10, 1902, in Waterbury, Conn.; son of Harold R. and Mary (Walker) Durant; married Alice Kobbe Rand (an author-photographer), August 6, 1942. *Education:* Yale University, B.A., 1925. *Politics:* Independent Republican. *Home:* 600 Gordon Dr., Naples, Fla. 33940. *Agent:* Brandt & Brandt, 101 Park Ave., New York, N.Y. 10017.

CAREER: New York Times, New York, N.Y., reporter, 1927-28; New York Stock Exchange, member, 1929-44; free-lance writer, 1936—. *Military service:* U.S. Naval Reserve, 1942-44; became lieutenant. *Member:* Society of American Travel Writers, Racquet and Tennis Club (New York), Lac Desert Fish and Game Club (Maniwaki, Quebec).

WRITING: (With Edward Rice) *Come Out Fighting,* Duell, Sloan & Pearce, 1946; *The Story of Baseball in Words and Pictures,* Hastings House, 1947, new and enlarged edition, 1959; *The Dodgers: An Illustrated Story of Those Unpredictable Bums,* Hastings House, 1948; *The Yankees: A Pictorial History of Baseball's Greatest Club,* Hastings House, 1949, revised edition, 1950; *National Baseball Hall of Fame and Museum,* National Baseball Hall of Fame & Museum, 1949, 2nd revised edition, 1960; (with Otto Bettmann) *Pictorial History of American Sports from Colonial Times to the Present,* A.S. Barnes, 1952, revised edition, 1965; (with wife, Alice Rand Durant) *Pictorial History of American Ships on the High Seas and Inland Waters,* A.S. Barnes, 1953; (with Alice Rand Durant) *Pictorial History of American Presidents,* A.S. Barnes, 1955, 5th revised edition, 1969; *Predictions: Pictorial Predictions from the Past,* A.S. Barnes, 1956; (editor) *Yesterday in Sports: Memorable Glimpses of the Past as Selected from the Pages of Sports Illustrated,* A.S. Barnes, 1956; (with Alice Rand Durant) *Pictorial History of the American Circus,* A.S. Barnes, 1957.

The Heavyweight Champions, Hastings House, 1960, 4th edition, revised and enlarged, 1971; *Highlights of the Olympics from Ancient Times to the Present,* Hastings House, 1961, 3rd edition, revised and enlarged, 1969; *Highlights of the World Series,* Hastings House, 1963, 2nd edition, revised and enlarged, 1971; *The Sports of Our Presidents,* Hastings House, 1964; (with L.F. Etter) *Highlights of College Football,* Hastings House, 1970. Contributor of articles to *Saturday Evening Post, Look, Sports Illustrated, True, American Heritage, Outdoor Life,* and other magazines. Free-lance travel correspondent (Florida west coast and the Keys) for *New York Times.*

AVOCATIONAL INTERESTS: Outdoor life, fishing, camping, sports, and history.

DURANT, Will(iam James) 1885-

PERSONAL: Born November 5, 1885, in North Adams, Mass.; son of Joseph (superintendent of a Du Pont branch) and Marie (Allors) Durant; married Ariel Kaufman (now his collaborator), October 31, 1913; children: Ethel Benvenuta (Mrs. Stanislas Kwasniewski), Louis R. (adopted). Education: St. Peter's College, Jersey City, N.J., B.A., 1907; attended Seton Hall, 1907-11; Columbia University, Ph.D., 1917. Religion: Agnostic, formerly Catholic. Home: 5608 Briarcliff Rd., Los Angeles, Calif. 90028.

CAREER: New York Evening Journal, New York, N.Y., reporter, 1908; Seton Hall, South Orange, N.J., instructor in Latin and French, 1907-11; Ferrer Modern School, New York, N.Y., sole teacher, 1911-13; Labor Temple School, New York, N.Y., director, 1914-27; Columbia University, New York, N.Y., instructor in philosophy, 1917; University of California, Los Angeles, professor of philosophy, 1935; full-time writer. Member: National Institute of Arts and Letters. Awards, honors: L.H.D., Syracuse University, 1930; (with wife, Ariel Durant) Huntington Hartford Foundation award for literature, 1963, for The Age of Louis XIV; (with Ariel Durant) Pulitzer Prize, 1968, for Rousseau and Revolution.

WRITINGS—All published by Simon & Schuster, except as indicated: Philosophy and the Social Problem, Macmillan, 1917; The Story of Philosophy, 1926, revised edition, 1933; Transition: A Sentimental Story of One Mind and One Era (autobiographical novel), 1927; (editor) Arthur Schopenhauer, Works, 1928, revised edition, Ungar, 1962; Mansions of Philosophy: A Survey of Human Life and Destiny, 1929, reissued as The Pleasures of Philosophy: A Survey of Human Life and Destiny, 1953; The Case for India, 1930; Adventures in Genius (essays and articles), 1931; A Program for America, 1931; On the Meaning of Life (correspondence), R.R. Smith, 1932; Tragedy of Russia: Impressions from a Brief Visit, 1933; 100 Best Books for an Education (excerpted from Adventures in Genius), 1933; Great Men of Literature (excerpted from Adventures in Genius), 1936; The Story of Civilization, Volume I: Our Oriental Heritage, 1935, introduction published as The Foundations of Civilization, 1936, Volume II: The Life of Greece, 1939, Volume III: Caesar and Christ, 1944, Volume IV: The Age of Faith, 1950, Volume V: The Renaissance, 1953, Volume VI: The Reformation, 1957, (with wife, Ariel Durant) Volume VII: The Age of Reason Begins, 1961, (with A. Durant) Volume VIII: The Age of Louis XIV, 1963, (with A. Durant) Volume IX: The Age of Voltaire, 1965, (with A. Durant) Volume X: Rousseau and Revolution, 1967; (with A. Durant) The Lessons of History, 1968; (with A. Durant) Interpretations of Life, 1970.

SIDELIGHTS: Durant is considered one of the foremost popularizers of history, and has been attacked by scholars for "softmindedness" and inaccuracies, and "of small service to students." He has said himself that "the probability of error increases with the scope of the undertaking," and his scope encompasses 110 centuries. Other critics, however, find his work "brilliant and engrossing," combining a "high regard for scholarship with a sense of drama." Clifton Fadiman said "tribute must be paid. . . to his ease of style . . . and concise epigrammatic statement," and Andre Maurois wrote of The Story of Civilization that it revealed "with laudable objectivity the lights and shadows of a great age in a highly readable book that is crystal-clear without being shallow." Durant is recognized as an able and conscientious writer, of whom Theodore Morrison said: "[he] has given the common reader an interesting and enlivening introduction to a variety of thinkers who have profoundly influenced the modern world." Reviewing The Lessons of History, Herman Ausubel wrote: "[This] is a modest, balanced and helpful statement of the beliefs and values that have resulted from the Durants' immersion in historical investigation these many years. Here are their fair-mindedness, their respect for human dignity, their exaltation of reason, their horror of bigotry and their faith in education as the clue to the betterment of the human condition. To be sure, their book is not without a few weaknesses. . . . [It] contains its share of platitudes, but at least it is reassuring that the Durants make no phony claims to originality. And like every history book that has ever been written, [it] has its share of errors. . . . [However, this] will be a welcome book to the host of readers who have been encouraged to explore the past because of the extraordinary ability of the Durants to inspire them."

The genesis of The Story of Philosophy was a lecture series, begun in New York City in 1914, before audiences of working people "who demanded complete clarity," and was published originally in pamphlet form by E. Haldeman-Julius.

AVOCATIONAL INTERESTS: Walking, music.

*   *   *

DURDEN, Robert Franklin 1925-

PERSONAL: Born May 10, 1925, in Graymont, Ga.; son of Virgil Edward (a planter) and Mildred (Donaldson) Durden; married Anne Oller, September 3, 1952; children: Molly, Frances. Education: Emory University, B.A., 1944, M.A., 1948; University of Havana, graduate study, 1947; Princeton University, Ph.D., 1952. Home: 2532 Wrightwood Ave., Durham, N.C. 27705. Office: History Department, Duke University, Durham, N.C. 27708.

CAREER: Duke University, Durham, N.C., instructor, 1952-56, assistant professor, 1956-60, associate professor, 1961-64, professor of history, 1965—. Fulbright professor of history, Johns Hopkins School for Advanced International Studies, Bologna, Italy, 1965-66; James Pinckney Harrison Professor of History, College of William and Mary, 1970-71. Military service: U.S. Naval Reserve, served in South Pacific and Japan, as Japanese language officer, 1943-46; became lieutenant junior grade. Member: American Historical Association, Organization of American Historians (member of executive board, 1968-70), Southern Historical Association, Historical Society of North Carolina, Phi Beta Kappa. Awards, honors: Jules F. Landry Prize, Louisiana State University Press, 1972.

WRITINGS: James Shepherd Pike: Republicanism and the American Negro, 1850-1882, Duke University Press, 1957; Reconstruction Bonds and Twentieth-Century Politics: South Dakota v. North Carolina (1903), Duke University Press, 1962; The Climax of Populism: The Election of 1896, University of Kentucky Press, 1965; (contributor) Martin Duberman, editor, The Abolitionist Vanguard, Princeton University Press, 1965; (contributor) R.J. Cunningham, The Populists in Historical Perspective, Heath, 1968; (editor and author of introduction) James Shepherd Pike, The Prostrate State: South Carolina Under Negro Government, Harper Torchbooks, 1968; The Gray and the Black: The Confederate Debate on Emancipation, Louisiana State University Press, 1972. Contributor of articles to historical and other journals.

WORK IN PROGRESS: The Dukes of Durham: A Family History.

AVOCATIONAL INTERESTS: Gardening, hiking, and fishing.

*   *   *

DURHAM, Philip 1912-

PERSONAL: Born February 7, 1912, in Portland, Ore.; son of Darr (a printer) and Greta (Phillips) Durham; married Jeanne Grandy, June 15, 1955; children: Christine, Darran. *Education:* Linfield College, B.S., 1935; Claremont Graduate School, M.A., 1946; Northwestern University, Ph.D., 1949. *Politics:* Democrat. *Home:* 920 Bienveneda Ave., Pacific Palisades, Calif. 90272. *Agent:* Collins, Knowlton, Wing, 60 East 56th St., New York, N.Y. 10022.

CAREER: University of California, Los Angeles, instructor, 1953-55, assistant professor, 1955-61, associate professor, 1961-66, professor of English, 1966—. Fulbright professor of American literature, University of Helsinki, 1955-56. *Military service:* U.S. Marine Corps, 1942-46; became major. *Member:* Authors Guild, American Studies Association, Modern Language Association of America, American Literature Group, Western History Association, Western Literature Association. *Awards, honors:* American Council of Learned Societies fellow, 1952-53, research fellowship, 1964; Guggenheim fellow, 1960-61; American Philosophical Society fellow, 1964; Edgar Award of Mystery Writers of America, 1964, for *Down These Mean Streets a Man Must Go: Raymond Chandler's Knight;* National Endowment for the Humanities grant, 1967-69.

WRITINGS: (With Mark Schorer and Everett Jones) *Harbrace College Reader,* Harcourt, 1959, 3rd edition, 1968, (with Jones) *Readings in Science and Engineering,* Holt, 1961; *Down These Mean Streets a Man Must Go: Raymond Chandler's Knight,* University of North Carolina Press, 1963; (author of introduction) Raymond Chandler, *Killer in the Rain,* Houghton, 1964; (with Jones) *The Negro Cowboys,* Dodd, 1965, juvenile edition published as *The Adventures of the Negro Cowboys,* 1966; (editor) Edward Sylvester Ellis, *Seth Jones and Deadwood Dick,* Odyssey, 1966; (with Jones) *The West: From Fact to Myth* (catalogue of an exhibit at U.C.L.A. Library), [Los Angeles], 1967; (editor) Owen Wister, *The Virginian,* Houghton, 1968; (editor with Jones) *The Frontier in American Literature,* Odyssey, 1969. Contributor to journals in United States and Finland.

WORK IN PROGRESS: A Literary Investigation of American Popular Culture; The Cowboy and the Mythmakers.

*   *   *

DUROSELLE, Jean-Baptiste Marie Lucien Charles 1917-

PERSONAL: Born November 17, 1917, in Paris, France; son of Albert and Jeanne (Peronne) Duroselle; married Christiane Viant, October 1, 1940; children: Henri, Genevieve, Dominique, Michel. *Education:* Attended Lycee Louis-le-Grand, 1935-38; Ecole Normale Superieure, Agrege d'histoire et geographie, 1943, Docteur es lettres, 1949. *Religion:* Catholic. *Home:* 15, rue Laurent-Gaudet, Le Chesnay, Yvelines 78, France. *Office:* Sorbonne, 17 rue de la Sorbonne, Paris V, France.

CAREER: Lycee de Chartres, Chartres, France, history teacher, 1943-45; Sorbonne, Universite de Paris, Paris, France, assistant d'histoire contemporaine, 1945-49; Lycee Hoche, Versailles, France, history teacher, 1949-50; Universite de la Sarre, Saarbruecken, Germany, 1950-56, professeur titulaire, 1953—; doyen de la Faculte des lettres, two years; Universite de Lille, Lille, France, professor of contemporary history, 1957-58; Fondation Nationale des Sciences Politiques, Paris, France, professeur, and directeur, Centre d'Etude des Relations Internationales, 1958-64; Sorbonne, Universite de Paris, professor of contemporary history, 1964—. Director, United States Educational Commission for France, 1964-69. Has conducted courses at Bologna, Italy, center of School for Advanced International Studies, Johns Hopkins University, since 1955. Visiting professor at University of Notre Dame, 1951, 1953, Brandeis University, 1958, Harvard

University, 1959, Colegio de Mexico, 1963, University of Seattle, 1970. *Military service:* French Army, artillery reserve officer, 1939-40. *Member:* International Association for the History of Ideas (vice-president), Societe d'Histoire Moderne (honorary president). *Awards, honors:* Chevalier de la Legion d'Honneur. Chevalier des Palmes Academiques.

WRITINGS: Histoire de catholicisme, Presses Universitaires de France, 1949, 3rd edition, 1967; *Les Debuts du catholicisme social en France (1822-1870),* Presses Universitaires de France, 1951; *Histoire diplomatique de 1919 a nos jours,* Dalloz, 1953, 5th edition, 1970; *De l'utilisation des sondages d'opinion en histoire et en science politique,* Institut Universitaire d'Information Sociale et Economique, 1957; *Les Relations internationales, 1871-1918: Les Hommes d'etat,* Centre de Documentation Universitaire, 1958; *De Wilson a Roosevelt: Politique exterieure des Etats-Unis de 1913-1945,* A. Colin, 1960, translation by Nancy Lyman Roelker published as *From Wilson to Roosevelt: Foreign Policy of the United States, 1913-1945,* Harvard University Press, 1963; *Histoire: Le Monde contemporaine,* Fernand Nathan, c.1960; (with Pierre Gerbet) *Histoire, 1848-1914,* Fernand Nathan, 1961; *L'Europe de 1815 a nos jours: Vie politique et relations internationales,* Presses Universitaires de France, 1964, 2nd edition, 1967; (with Pierre Renouvin) *Introduction a l'histoire des relations internationales: Forces profondes et hommes d'etat,* A. Colin, 1964, 2nd edition, 1966, translation by Mary Ilford published as *Introduction to the History of International Relations,* Praeger, 1967; *L'Idee d'Europe dans l'histoire,* preface by Jean Monnet, Denoel, 1965; *La Politique exterieure de la France de 1914 a 1945,* Centre de Documentation Universitaire, 1965; *Le Conflit de Trieste, 1945-1954,* Dotation Carnegie, 1966; *Les Relations franco-allemandes de 1918 a 1950,* Centre de Documentation Universitaire, 1966; *Les Relations internationales de l'Allemagne et de l'Italie de 1919 a 1939,* Centre de Documentation Universitaire, 1967; *Les Relations franco-allemandes de 1914 a 1939,* Centre de Documentation Universitaire, 1967; *Le Drame de l'Europe,* two volumes, Richelieu, 1969; *Le Monde dechire, 1945-1970,* two volumes, Richelieu, 1970.

Editor: *La Politique etrangere et ses fondements,* A. Colin, 1954; *Les Relations germano-sovietiques de 1933 a 1939,* A. Colin, 1954; *Les Frontieres europeennes de l'U.R.S.S., 1917-1941,* A. Colin, 1957; (with Jean Meyriat) *Les Nouveaux Etats dans les relations internationales,* A. Colin, 1962; (with Meyriat) *La Communaute internationale face aux jeunes Etats,* A. Colin, 1964; (with Meyriat) *Politiques nationales envers les jeunes Etats,* A. Colin, 1964.

Contributor to *Encyclopedie francaise,* and of articles to periodicals in France, United States, U.S.S.R., and other countries.

*   *   *

DURRELL, Lawrence (George)   1912-
(Charles Norden, Gaffer Peeslake)

PERSONAL: Surname is accented on first syllable; born February 27, 1912, in Julundur, India, of Irish and English parents; son of Lawrence Samuel (an engineer) and Louise Florence (Dixie) Durrell; married Nancy Myers, 1935 (divorced, 1947); married Yvette Cohen, February 26, 1947 (divorced); married Claude Marie Vineenden (a writer), March 27, 1961 (died, 1967); children (first marriage) Penelope Berengaria, (second marriage) Sappho-Jane. *Education:* Attended College of St. Joseph, Darjiling, India, and St. Edmund's School, Canterbury, England. *Religion:* "Of course I believe in God; but every kind of God. But I rather dread the word religion because I have a notion that the reality of it dissolves the minute it is uttered as a concept." *Residence:* Provence,

France. *Address:* c/o National and Grindlay's Bank, Parliament St., Whitehall, S.W.1, England.

CAREER: Held many odd jobs, including that of jazz pianist at the Blue Peter Night Club, London; also was automobile racer, jazz composer, real estate agent, and ran a photographic studio with his first wife; taught at British Institute in Athens, Greece, 1940; foreign press service officer in British Information Office, Cairo, Egypt, 1941-44; press attache, Alexandria, 1944-45; public relations director, Dodecanese Island, Greece, 1946-47; director of Institute, British Council in Cordoba, Argentina, 1947-48; press attache at British Legation, Belgrade, Yugoslavia, 1949-52; taught school, 1951; teacher of English, then director of public relations for British government in Cyprus during the fifties; special correspondent for the *Economist,* Cyprus, 1953; moved to France and became full-time writer, 1957. *Member:* Royal Society of Literature (fellow, 1954). *Awards, honors:* Duff Cooper Memorial Prize, 1957, for *Bitter Lemons;* Prix du Meilleur Livre Etranger (France), 1959, for *Justine,* and *Balthazar.*

WRITINGS: Ten Poems, Caduceus Press, 1932; *Ballade of Slow Decay,* [London], 1932; (under pseudonym Gaffer Peeslake) *Bromo Bombastes,* Caduceus Press, 1933; *Transition: Poems,* Caduceus Press, 1934; *Pied Piper of Lovers* (novel), Cassell, 1935; (under pseudonym Charles Norden) *Panic Spring,* Covici-Friede, 1937; *The Black Book, An Agon,* Obelisk 1938, 2nd edition, Olympia Press, 1959, Dutton, 1960.

A Private Country (poems), Faber, 1943; *Prospero's Cell: A Guide to the Landscape and Manners of the Island of Corcyra,* Faber, 1945 (published with *Reflections on a Marine Venus,* Dutton, 1960); *Cities, Plains, and People* (poems), Faber, 1946; (translator) *Six Poems from the Greek of Sekilianos and Seferis,* [Rhodes], 1946; *Zero and Asylum in the Snow,* [Rhodes], 1946, published in America as *Two Excursions Into Reality,* Circle Editions, 1947; *Cefalu* (novel), Editions Poetry, 1947, reprinted with minor alterations, as *The Dark Labyrinth,* Ace Books, 1958, Dutton, 1962; *On Seeming to Presume* (poems), Faber, 1948; (translator, with Bernard Spence and Nanos Valaoritis) George Seferis, *The King of Asine, and Other Poems,* Lehmann, 1948; *A Landmark Gone,* [Los Angeles], 1949.

Deus Loci (poem), [Ischia], 1950; *Nemea,* [London], 1950; *Sappho; A Play in Verse* (broadcast on BBC, March 25, 1957; staged in Hamburg on November 21, 1959, in Edinburgh, summer, 1961), Faber, 1950, Dutton, 1958; *Key to Modern Poetry,* Peter Nevill, 1952, published in the United States as *A Key to Modern British Poetry,* University of Oklahoma Press, 1952; *Reflections on a Marine Venus,* Faber, 1953; (translator) Emmanuel Royidis, *Pope Joan; A Romantic Biography,* Verschoyle, 1954, revised edition, Deutsch, 1960, Dutton, 1961, Overlook Press, 1972; *Private Drafts,* Proodos Press, 1955; *The Tree of Idleness, and Other Poems,* Faber, 1955; *Selected Poems,* Grove, 1956; *Bitter Lemons,* Faber, 1957, Dutton, 1958; *Esprit de Corps; Sketches from Diplomatic Life,* Faber, 1957, Dutton, 1958 (also see below); *Justine; A Novel,* Dutton, 1957, 2nd edition, Faber, 1963 (also see below); *White Eagles Over Serbia* (detective stories), Criterion, 1957, abridged edition, edited by G.A. Verdin, Chatto & Windus, 1961; *Balthazar; A Novel,* Dutton, 1958 (also see below); (contributor, in French) *Hommage a Roy Campbell,* [Montpellier], 1958; *Mountolive; A Novel,* Faber, 1958, Dutton, 1959 (also see below); *Stiff Upper Lip; Life among the Diplomats,* Faber, 1958, Dutton, 1959, published with *Esprit de Corps,* Dutton Everyman, 1961; (contributor) *Art and Outrage* (a correspondence about Henry Miller between Alfred Perles and Durrell, including letters by Miller), Putnam, 1959, Dutton, 1961; (editor and author of introduction) *The Henry Miller Reader,* New Directions, 1959, reprinted, Books for Libraries, 1972 (published in England as *The Best of Henry Miller,* Heinemann, 1960).

Clea: A Novel, Dutton, 1960 (also see below); *Collected Poems,* Dutton, 1960, revised edition, Faber, 1968; *The Alexandria Quartet* (contains *Justine, Balthazar, Mountolive,* and *Clea),* Dutton, 1961; (author of introduction) Georg Walther Groddeck, *The Book of the It,* [Wiesbaden], 1961; *Briefwechsel ueber Actes* (correspondence between Durrell and Gustaf Gruendgens concerning *Acte)* Rowohlt Verlag, 1961; *The Poetry of Lawrence Durrell,* Dutton, 1962; (editor) *New Poems, 1963: A.P.E.N. Anthology of Contemporary Poetry,* Hutchinson, 1963, Harcourt, 1964; *Lawrence Durrell and Henry Miller: A Private Correspondence,* edited by George Wickes, Dutton, 1963; *Beccafico* (limited edition), [Montpellier], 1963; *An Irish Faustus: A Morality in Nine Scenes* (produced in Hamburg, 1963), Dutton, 1964; *Selected Poems, 1935-1963,* Faber, 1964; *Drei dramatische Dichtungen,* Rohwohlt Verlag, 1964; *La descente du Styx* (limited edition), [Montpellier], 1964 published in America as *Down the Styx,* Capricorn Press, 1971; *Acte* (verse play; produced in Hamburg, 1962), Dutton, 1965; *The Icons, and Other Poems,* Faber, 1966, Dutton, 1967; *Sauve qui peut* (more sketches from diplomatic life), Faber, 1966, Dutton, 1967; *Nothing is Lost, Sweet Self* (poem, set to music by Wallace Southam), Turret Books, 1967; *Tunc: A Novel,* Dutton, 1968; *In Arcadia* (poem, set to music by Southam), Turret Books, 1968; (author of introductory essay) Gyula Halasz Brassai, *Brassai,* Museum of Modern Art, 1968; *Spirit of Place: Letters and Essays on Travel,* edited by Alan G. Thomas, Dutton, 1969; *Nunquam: A Novel* (Book of the Month Club selection), Dutton, 1970; *Red Limbo Lingo: A Poetry Notebook,* Dutton, 1971.

Contributor to *The Booster, Delta, New English Weekly, Geographical Magazine, Seven, Poetry* (London), *T'ien Hsia Monthly* (Shanghai), *Poetry World, Experimental Review, Furioso, View, Chimera, Counterpoint, Circle, Partisan Review, Neurotica, New Statesman, Time and Tide, Quarterly Review of Literature, Spectator, London Magazine, Encounter, Holiday, Mademoiselle, Esquire, New York Times Book Review, Realities* (Paris), and other publications. Edited, with Robin Fedden, *Personal Landscape,* in Cairo, 1941-44; with Henry Miller and Alfred Perles, edited *The Booster,* later known as *Delta;* edited *Cyprus Review,* 1954-55.

SIDELIGHTS: Durrell's baroque prose is reminiscent of that of Thomas De Quincey, Joseph Conrad, and more recently, Vladimir Nabokov. "The style," writes George Steiner, "is mosaic. Each word is set in its precise and luminous place. Touch by touch, Durrell builds his array of sensuous, rare expressions into patterns of image and idea so subtle and convoluted that the experience of reading becomes one of total sensual apprehension."

Principally he is a poet, or what he calls a "hander on of sound." He told his *Paris Review* interviewer: "Poetry turned out to be an invaluable mistress. Because poetry is form, and the wooing and seduction of form is the whole game...." His style and poetic vision he has termed "heraldic," transcending ordinary syntax and logic, invading "a realm where unreason reigns, and where the relations between ideas are sympathetic and mysterious—affective—rather than casual, objective, substitutional."

His opus magnum, *The Alexandria Quartet,* he calls "a yarn on one plane, and a sort of poetic parable on another.... Every good work should have a good deal of bone meal and manure mixed with it, or the cultural humus you manufacture won't be rich enough to allow for the growth of future flowers...." The *Quartet* is principally an investigation of modern love. In it Durrell applies the principles of Einsteinian time, trying to create the idea of a continuum of words (" ... ideally, all four volumes should be read simultaneously," he once said). To answer the critics of this ambitious scheme he light-heartedly comments: "I'm trying to give you stereoscopic narrative with stereophonic personality, and if that doesn't mean anything to anybody at least it should be of interest to radio engineers."

Each of the novels in the *Quartet* is prefaced by a quotation from the Marquis de Sade who is for Durrell "the most typical figure of our century, with his ignorance and cruelty. I regard him as both a hero and a pygmy.... The very apotheosis of our infantile unconscious." He feels, however, that morality "should not have an explicit place in an art context; to the artist everyone is primally good, however bad or ignorant their actions.... [Art] doesn't read sermons, but teaches by example," urging people "to wake up by giving them the vicarious feel of the poetic illumination." Despite the references to Sade, Durrell's view of life is generally positive, unlike that of many of his contemporaries. Gerald Sykes notes the distinction between him and Samuel Beckett, for example: "Durrell celebrates life 'heraldically' as a blessing; Beckett wishes it had never been inflicted on him."

Durrell's longtime friend, Henry Miller, once observed that Durrell took his work seriously, but not himself. "Me change the world?" says Durrell. "Good Lord, no. Or only perhaps indirectly by persuading itself to see itself and relax; to tap the source of laughter in itself." And, he warns, "it's possible my ideas are altogether too explicit not to be suspect. Beware!"

Upon publication of *The Black Book*, the book and its author were praised by such people as Henry Miller ("You are *the* master of the English language.") and T.S. Eliot ("The first piece of work by a new English writer to give me any hope for the future of prose fiction."). Durrell himself does not regard this book as a good one.... "There are parts of it which I think probably are a bit too obscene."

Though many consider the *Quartet* "the highest performance in the modern novel since Proust or Joyce," George Steiner has noted that other critics call Durrell "a pompous charlatan," "a mere word-spinner," a "gatherer of flamboyant cliches," a "late Victorian decadent," a "minor disciple of Henry Miller." He admits that he always feels he is overwriting, and that he has done a good deal of potboiling in his career. His comment on the latter: "Let them riddle me with arrows so long as I can keep it up and avoid jobs." In defense of Durrell's use of language, poet Hayden Carruth has written: "Durrell is a writer, embodying perhaps as well as any man alive all the refinements and conscientiousness that has been bred into the genus since antiquity, and his protests are well-fashioned, the products of as much intelligence as a very intelligent man can bring to bear; and they are beautiful as well...."

About *Tunc* Sykes writes: "The author may be moving in a new direction.... One gets the impression that ... Durrell has deliberately thrown overboard the charm that won him so many readers in *Justine*.... [Durrell] seems to be trying to come to grips, at least in concept, with 'the real world.'" Cassill reports of *Nunquam*: "One feels that Durrell has been alert to the whole significant culture of his time and grasps it with almost dismaying facility." And, comparing *Nunquam* with the *Quartet*, Durrell himself told an interviewer: "[It] is much more contemporary. It's no longer an historical dream of a city which gave us our sources; it's where we are now."

"A born writer," Henry Miller calls him, though Durrell himself says he was driven to writing "by sheer inepti-

tude," perhaps recalling his futile attempts to get into Cambridge University "about eight times." Except for poetry, he writes on a typewriter, and writes prolifically and often rapidly: *Bitter Lemons* took six weeks; *Justine* about four months; *Balthazar* six weeks; *Mountolive* two months; *Clea* seven weeks.

Durrell's personal and literary sympathies lie with Henry Miller (whom he greatly admired in the thirties, while now it is Miller's turn to affirm Durrell's mastery), Henry de Montherlant, Marcel Proust, Kazantzakis, Borges, and Italo Svevo. He has almost always been an expatriate, though H. T. Moore quotes him as saying, "I'm as English as Shakespeare's birthday." The Irish element "means the fire, the hysteria, the mental sluttishness, the sensuality and' intuition." He told one interviewer: "... with all my love-hate complex for England I keep in touch and try not to become a 'professional foreigner'."

AVOCATIONAL INTERESTS: Painting (he has been called an accomplished watercolorist), and though he refers to himself as a "dauber," he has said he would have preferred to be a painter rather than a writer; at one time listed travel, but he told the *Paris Review:* "You know I'm so travel-stained with fifteen or sixteen years of it—the great anxiety of being shot at in Cyprus, being bombed, being tormented by the Marxists in Yugoslavia—that now for the first time I've a yen for my tiny roof. Staying put is so refreshing that it's almost anguish to go into town for a movie."

Film rights to both *Tunc* and *Nunquam* have been sold to American producer Ronald J. Kahn. An adaptation of *Stiff Upper Lip* was produced on BBC-TV in 1968. Durrell may be heard on several recordings: "Grecian Echoes," selections from *Bitter Lemons, Prospero's Cell* and *Reflections on a Marine Venus,* LVA 1003-4; "An Irish Faust," LVA 201; and "The Love Poems of Lawrence Durrell, Spoken Arts.

BIOGRAPHICAL/CRITICAL SOURCES: Encounter, December, 1959; *Paris Review,* autumn-winter, 1959-60; *Books and Bookmen,* February, 1960; *Manchester Guardian,* May 6, 1961; Alfred Perles, *My Friend, Lawrence Durrell,* Scorpion Press, 1961; Robert A. Potter and Brooke Whiting, *Lawrence Durrell: A Checklist,* University of California Library, 1961; H. T. Moore, editor, *The World of Lawrence Durrell,* Southern Illinois University Press, 1962; John Unterecker, *Lawrence Durrell* (essay with bibliography), Columbia University Press, 1964; *Saturday Review,* March 21, 1964; John A. Weigel, *Lawrence Durrell,* Twayne, 1966; *Virginia Quarterly Review,* Summer, 1967; George Sutherland Fraser, *Lawrence Durrell: A Study* (with complete bibliography by Alan G. Thomas), Dutton, 1968; *New York Times Book Review,* April 14, 1968; *Times Literary Supplement,* May 22, 1969; Allen Warren Friedman, *Lawrence Durrell and the Alexandria Quartet: Art for Love's Sake,* University of Oklahoma Press, 1970; *Shenandoah,* Winter, 1971; *Modern Fiction Studies,* Summer, 1971.†

*   *   *

DUTTON, Joan Parry   1908-

PERSONAL: Born September 4, 1908, in Herefordshire, England; married William S. Dutton (an American). *Home:* St. Helena, Calif.

CAREER: Author and garden enthusiast.

WRITINGS: Enjoying America's Gardens, Reynal, 1958 (published in England as *Exploring America's Gardens,* Secker & Warburg, 1959); *The Good Fare and Cheer of Old England,* Reynal, 1960; *The Flower World of Williamsburg,* Colonial Williamsburg, 1962, revised edition, Holt, 1973; (author of commentary) Letha Booth and others, compilers, *The Williamsburg Cookbook: Traditional and Contemporary Recipes*, Colonial Williamsburg, 1971.

*   *   *

DYNES, Russell R(owe) 1923-

PERSONAL: Born October 2, 1923, in Dundalk, Ontario, Canada; son of Oliver Wesley (a college professor) and Carlotta (Rowe) Dynes; married Susan M. Swan, July 25, 1947; children: Russell, Jr., Patrick, Gregory, Jon. *Education:* University of Tennessee, B.A., 1948, M.A., 1950; Ohio State University, Ph.D., 1954. *Politics:* Independent Democrat. *Religion:* Methodist. *Home:* 1604 Grenoble Rd., Columbus, Ohio. 43221.

CAREER: Ohio State University, Columbus, associate professor, 1951-65; professor of sociology, 1965—. Co-director of Disaster Research Center. *Military service:* U.S. Army Engineers, 1942-46; became sergeant. *Member:* American Sociological Association (fellow), Religious Research Association (fellow), Society for the Scientific Study of Religion, Ohio Valley Sociological Society (editor, 1958-63; vice-president, 1970-71), Ohio Council of Family Relations (editor, 1960-63).

WRITINGS: (With A. Clarke, S. Dinitz, and I. Ishino) *Social Problems: Dissensus and Deviation in an Industrial Society*, Oxford University Press, 1964; (editor with Dinitz and Clarke) *Deviance: Studies in the Process of Stigmatization and Societal Reaction*, Oxford University Press, 1969; *Organized Behavior in a Disaster*, Heath, 1970.

WORK IN PROGRESS: Research on organizational reactions in disasters and in various types of crisis.

*   *   *

EALES, John R(ay) 1910-

PERSONAL: Born November 3, 1910, in Rushville, Ill.; son of Charles Lancaster (a dentist) and Edith (Bogue) Eales; married Edna Elizabeth Neal, December 26, 1938; children: Meredith Ann, April Christine. *Education:* Washington University, St. Louis, Mo., B.A., 1934; Northwestern University, M.A., 1946; University of California, Los Angeles, Ed.D., 1956. *Religion:* United Church of Christ. *Home:* 8012 Maybelline Way, Sacramento, Calif. 95823.

CAREER: J.D. Colt School, Litchfield, Ill., teacher and principal, 1937-39; Missouri Military Academy, Mexico, teacher and coach, 1939-43, 1945-46; Nichols Junior High School, Evanston, Ill., principal, 1946-48; Los Angeles County (Calif.) Schools Office, consultant in secondary education, 1948-56; California State Department of Education, Sacramento, consultant in secondary education, 1956—. *Military service:* U.S. Army Air Corps, 1943-45; served in Africa and Italy, 1944-45. *Member:* National Education Association, American Driver and Traffic Safety Education Association, California Teachers Association, California Association of Secondary School Administrators, California Association of Secondary School Curriculum Coordinators, California Driver Education Association, Phi Delta Kappa, Tau Kappa Epsilon, Masons, Elks, Parkway Swimming Club.

WRITINGS: (With Strasser, Zaun, and Mushlitz) *When You Take the Wheel*, Laidlaw Brothers, 1961; (with Strasser, Aaron, and Bohn) *Fundamentals of Safety Education*, Macmillan, 1964; (with Strasser and Aaron) *Driver Education*, Laidlaw Brothers, 1969.

AVOCATIONAL INTERESTS: Swimming, golf, bowling, and reading.

EARL, Lawrence 1915-

PERSONAL: Born April 29, 1915, in Saint John, New Brunswick, Canada; married Jane Armstrong (a foreign correspondent), June 9, 1943. *Education:* Dalhousie University, student, 1933-34. *Home:* M/45 Eaton Sq., London S.W. 1, England. *Agent:* Collins-Knowlton-Wing, Inc., 60 East 56th St., New York, N.Y. 10022.

CAREER: Montreal Standard, Montreal, Quebec, feature writer, war correspondent, 1941-45; Mirror Features, London, England, writer, 1946-47; John Bull (magazine), London, writer, 1947-50; free-lance writer of books and magazine articles, 1950-58; Star Weekly, Toronto, Ontario, magazine editor, 1958-59. *Member:* Society of Authors, Royal Mid-Surrey Golf Club. *Awards, honors:* Stephen Leacock Award for Humor, for *The Battle of Baltinglass*.

WRITINGS: Yangtse Incident: The Story of H.M.S. Amethyst, April 20, 1949 to July 31, 1949, Harrap, 1950, Knopf, 1951; *The Battle of Baltinglass*, Knopf, 1951; *Crocodile Fever*, Knopf, 1954; *The Frozen Jungle*, Collins, 1955, Knopf, 1956; *She Loved a Wicked City: The Story of Mary Ball, Missionary*, Dutton, 1962 (published in England as *One Foreign Devil*, Hodder & Stoughton, 1962); *The Riddle of the Haunted River* (juvenile), Little, Brown, 1962; *Risk*, Harrap, 1969. Contributor to *Saturday Evening Post, American, National Geographic, Maclean's*, and other magazines.

WORK IN PROGRESS: A novel; a nonfiction book.

AVOCATIONAL INTERESTS: Travel, golf, trout and salmon angling in Scotland and Eastern Canada.

*   *   *

EASTMAN, Max (Forrester) 1883-1969

PERSONAL: Born January 4, 1883, in Canandaigua, N.Y.; son of Samuel Elijah (a minister) and Annis (a minister, maiden name Ford) Eastman; married Ida Rauh, 1911 (divorced, 1922); married Eliena Krylenko, 1924 (died, 1956); married Yvette Szekely (a social worker), March 22, 1958; children: (first marriage) Daniel. *Education:* Williams College, B.A., 1905; attended Columbia University, 1907-11, fulfilled, he said, "all the requirements for a Ph.D., but preferred not to receive it." *Politics:* Independent. *Residence:* Chilmark, Mass.; also maintained an apartment in Greenwich Village and a winter residence in Barbados.

CAREER: Columbia University, New York, N.Y., assistant in philosophy, 1907-10, associate, 1911; editor of *The Masses*, 1913-17, and of *The Liberator*, 1918-22; lectured, translated, taught, and conducted a radio program; roving editor, *Reader's Digest*, 1941-69. Organized first Men's League for Woman Suffrage in U.S., 1910. *Member:* Delta Psi, Phi Beta Kappa.

WRITINGS: Enjoyment of Poetry, Scribner, 1913, revised and enlarged edition published as *Enjoyment of Poetry, and Other Essays in Aesthetics*, Scribner, 1939, also published with *Anthology for the Enjoyment of Poetry* (see below); *Child of the Amazons, and Other Poems*, Kennerley, 1913; *Journalism versus Art* (four essays originally published in *The Masses, Vanity Fair, New Republic*, and *North American Review*), Knopf, 1916; *Understanding Germany: The Only Way to End War, and Other Essays*, Kennerley, 1916; *The Colors of Life* (poems, songs, and sonnets), Knopf, 1918; *The Sense of Humor*, Scribner, 1921, Octagon, 1972; *Since Lenin Died*, Liveright, 1925; *Leon Trotsky: Portrait of a Youth*, Greenberg, 1925, AMS Press, 1970; *Marx, Lenin, and the Science of Revolution*, Allen & Unwin, 1926, Boni Brothers, 1927; *Venture* (novel), Boni Brothers, 1927; *Kinds of Love* (poems), Scribner, 1931; *The Literary Mind: Its Place in an Age of Science* (essays), Scribner, 1931; (editor and author of introduction) Karl Marx, *Capital, The*

Communist Manifesto, and Other Writings, Modern Library, 1932; *Artists in Uniform: A Study of Literature and Bureaucratism,* Knopf, 1934; *Art and the Life of Action, with Other Essays,* Knopf, 1934; *Last Stand of Dialectic Materialism: A Study of Sidney Hook's Marxism* (pamphlet), Polemic, 1934; *Enjoyment of Laughter,* Simon & Schuster, 1936; *The End of Socialism in Russia,* (originally published in *Harper's,* January 20, 1937) Little, Brown, 1937; (compiler) *Anthology for the Enjoyment of Poetry,* Scribner, 1939, also published with *Enjoyment of Poetry* (see below); *Stalin's Russia and the Crisis in Socialism,* Norton, 1940; *Marxism: Is It Science?,* Norton, 1940; *Lot's Wife* (dramatic poem), Harper, 1942; *Heroes I Have Known: Twelve Who Lived Great Lives,* Simon & Schuster, 1942; *Enjoyment of Living* (memoirs), Harper, 1948; *Enjoyment of Poetry* [and] *Anthology for the Enjoyment of Poetry,* single-volume edition, Scribner, 1951; (with Jacob Rosin) *The Road to Abundance,* McGraw, 1953; (author of biographical note) Claude McKay, *Selected Poems,* introduction by John Dewey, Bookman Associates, 1953; *Poems of Five Decades,* Harper, 1954; (contributor) *John Dos Passos: An Appreciation,* Prentice-Hall, 1954; *Reflections on the Failure of Socialism,* Devin-Adair, 1955; *Great Companions: Critical Memoirs of Some Famous Friends,* Farrar, Straus, 1959, reissued as *Einstein, Trotsky, Hemingway, Freud, and Other Great Companions,* Collier, 1962; *Love and Revolution: My Journey Through an Epoch* (sequel to *Enjoyment of Living*), Random House, 1964; *Seven Kinds of Goodness,* Horizon, 1967; (author of afterword) William L. O'Neill, editor, *Echoes of Revolt: "The Masses," 1911-1917,* Quadrangle, 1967.

Translator: Leon Trotsky, *The Real Situation in Russia,* Harcourt, 1928; Alexander Pushkin, *Gabriel,* Covici-Friede, 1929; Leon Trotsky, *The History of the Russian Revolution,* Simon & Schuster, 1932; Leon Trotsky, *The Revolution Betrayed,* Doubleday, 1937; Leon Trotsky, *In Defense of Marxism,* Pioneer Publishers, 1942.

Compiler and narrator of film, "From Czar to Lenin," 1937. Contributor to numerous periodicals, including *National Review, Harper's, Saturday Review, Atlantic, American Scholar, New Republic,* and *American Mercury.*

SIDELIGHTS: An influential literary representative of the radical left in the United States during the first quarter of this century, Eastman was a friend of Sidney Hook and a protege of John Dewey at Columbia. He was cofounder and editor of *The Masses* which, according to Walter Sutton, was "fired by a spirit of social idealism unparalleled in this dark century and lightened with gaiety.... [It] provided a focus for a highly gifted group of artists and political and social crusaders and critics." A vehicle for radical social protest, the magazine's uncompromising opposition to World War I led to its demise in 1917, when the U.S. Government banned it from the mails. After launching his next magazine, *The Liberator,* Eastman and three other staff members were tried twice for sedition, but both trials ended in hung juries.

Eastman's life was never dull. Both his private and public lives became exceedingly complex because of his tendency to move on to new relationships or concepts when be began to feel too comfortable with the old. "The interesting thing," a *Newsweek* reviewer of *Love and Revolution* notes, "is that the opinions themselves do not seem to matter very much. He arrives at them languidly and holds them loosely; yet he has suffered for them as much as any fanatic. It finally seems that hysteria itself, 'true belief,' is his only real enemy—because true belief threatens his selfhood almost as much as monogamy does." William S. Schlamm wrote: "In spite of his considerable sophistication and even refinement, Eastman has gone through his long and stormy life with the untouched in-

nocence of a happy pagan. This unpretentious man has the wholesome self-righteousness of the nineteenth century." Eastman's fascination with the concept of revolution took him to Lenin's Russia in the early twenties, which led to disillusionment with Stalinist Communism and to a series of books attacking Marxism as unscientific. This in turn provoked hostile criticism in the United States, although David Cort was moved to remark, only half in jest, that "a little Eastman then might have spared us a lot of McCarthy later." In an interview with Alden Whitman of the *New York Times,* Eastman commented on the New Left: "They want to make a revolution but they have no ultimate purpose.... We had a program, a purpose, which was to make over capitalism into Socialism ... but when Socialism failed and produced a totalitarian tyranny, it left social ideas without a theoretical basis."

Although probably best known for his political works, Eastman had an equally intense interest in the relation of art to science (which he examined in *The Literary Mind*) and in the psychology of literature. His most popular book is his first; it has never been out of print. He told *CA:* "*Enjoyment of Poetry,* published in 1913, was selling at the rate of more than two a day in 1963-64—its fiftieth anniversary. (My only boast!)" He traveled extensively, visiting western Europe, North Africa, the Near East, Central America, and the Caribbean, as well as Russia. He enjoyed swimming and tennis into his eighties. "At eighty-two," wrote William Barrett in a review of *Love and Revolution,* "he is still as vital as ever, and the story of his life is not only a very lively revelation of his own engaging and complex personality, but a valuable chronicle of three eras in American intellectual life—the progressive period of the teens, the literary bohemia of the twenties, and the Red decade of the thirties." "Long, racy, candid and vain," according to *Time,* "... [his autobiography] has the egalitarian earnestness of a Tom Paine, the lighthearted sexual adventures of a Casanova, the self-preoccupation of a Cellini."

BIOGRAPHICAL/CRITICAL SOURCES: New Republic, February 10, 1941; *Partisan Review,* May-June, 1942; Edmund Wilson, *Classics and Commercials,* Farrar, Straus, 1950; Daniel Aaron, *Writers on the Left,* Harcourt, 1961; *Newsweek,* January 4, 1965; *Time,* January 8, 1965; *National Review,* January 26, 1965; *Commonweal,* February 5, 1965; *Saturday Review,* February 6, 1965, May 17, 1969; *Atlantic,* March, 1965; *Minnesota Review,* Number 1, 1967; *New York Times,* January 9, 1969.

(Died March 25, 1969)

*   *   *

EBELING, Gerhard 1912-

PERSONAL: Born July 6, 1912, in Berlin-Steglitz, Germany; son of Adolf (a teacher) and Elizabeth (Nain) Ebeling; married Kometa Richner, May 23, 1939; children: Charitas. *Education:* Attended Universities of Marburg/Lahn and Berlin; University of Zurich, Dr. Theol., 1938. *Religion:* Evangelical. *Home:* Naegelistrasse 5, Zurich 7/44, Switzerland.

CAREER: Bekennende Kirche, Berlin-Brandenburg, Germany, minister, 1939-45; University of Tuebingen, Tuebingen, Germany, professor of church history, 1946-54, professor of systematic theology, 1954-56; University of Zurich, Zurich, Switzerland, professor of systematic theology, 1956—. *Awards, honors:* D. Theol., University of Bonn.

WRITINGS: Evangelische Evangelienauslegung: Eine Untersuchung zu Luthers Hermeneutik, Christian Kaiser, 1942; *Kirchenzucht,* Kohlhammer, 1947; *Kirchengeschichte als Geschichte der Auslegung der Heiligen*

Schrift, Mohr, 1947; *Die Geschichtlichkeit der Kirche und ihrer Verkuendigung als theologisces Problem,* Mohr, 1954, translation by Grover Foley published as *The Problem of Historicity in the Church and Its Proclamation,* Fortress, 1967; *Was heisst Glauben?,* Mohr, 1958; (editor) *Die Frage nach dem historischen Jesus,* Mohr, 1959; *Das Wesen des Christlichen Glaubens,* Mohr, 1959, 3rd edition, Siebenstern Taschenbuch, 1967, translation by Ronald Gregor Smith published as *The Nature of Faith,* Collins, 1961, Muhlenberg, 1962; *Wort und Glaube,* Mohr, 1960, translation by James W. Leitch published as *Word and Faith,* Fortress, 1963, 3rd edition, 1967; *Theologie und Verkuendingung: Ein Gesprach mit Rudolph Bultmann,* Mohr, 1962, revised edition, 1965, translation by John Riches published as *Theology and Proclamation: Dialogue with Bultmann,* Fortress, 1966 (published in England as *Theology and Proclamation: A Discussion with Rudolph Bultmann,* Collins, 1966); *Vom Gebet: Predigten ueber das Unser-Vater,* Mohr, 1963, translation by James W. Leitch published as *On Prayer: Nine Sermons,* Fortress, 1966 (published in England as *The Lord's Prayer in Today's World,* S.C.M. Press, 1966); *Luther: Einfuehrung in sein Denken,* Mohr, 1964, translation by R.A. Wilson published as *Luther: An Introduction to His Thought,* Fortress, 1970; *Im Dienste der Verstaendigung: Beitraege zur Konfessionskunde,* Vandenhoeck & Ruprecht, 1964; *Wort Gottes und Tradition: Studien zu einer Hermeneutik der Konfession,* Vandenhoeck & Ruprecht, 1964, 2nd edition, 1966, translation by S.H. Hooke published as *The Word of God and Tradition: Historical Studies Interpreting the Divisions of Christianity,* Fortress, 1968; *Gott und Wort,* Mohr, 1966, translation by James W. Leitch published as *God and Word,* Fortress, 1967; *Verstehen und Verstandigung in der Begegnung der Konfessionen,* Vandenhoeck & Ruprecht, 1967; *Frei aus Glauben,* Mohr, 1968; *Psalmenmeditationen,* Mohr, 1968; (contributor) Robert W. Funk, editor, *Schleiermacher as Contemporary,* Herder & Herder, c.1970; (editor with Robert W. Funk) *God and Christ: Existence and Province,* Gannon, 1970; (editor with Funk) *Distinctive Protestant and Catholic Themes Reconsidered,* Gannon, 1970; (editor with Funk) *History and Hermeneutic,* Gannon, 1970; (editor with Funk) *The Bultmann School of Biblical Interpretation,* Gannon, 1970.

BIOGRAPHICAL/CRITICAL SOURCES: Christian Century, July 19, 1967, October 25, 1967, December 3, 1969; *Times Literary Supplement,* July 20, 1967; *Encounter,* winter, 1968; *Observer Review,* May 17, 1970; *Library Journal,* July, 1970.

* * *

EBERMAN, (Gilbert) Willis 1917-

PERSONAL: Born December 30, 1917, in Portland, Ore.; son of Richard Larkin (a policeman) and Violet (Gilbert) Eberman. *Home:* 120 Northwest Macleay Blvd., Portland, Ore. 97210.

CAREER: Poet. *Member:* Order of St. Genesius (charter member).

WRITINGS: Lines to Be Left in the Earth, and Other Poems, Binfords, 1951; *This My Bequest, and Other Poems,* Golden Quill, 1955; *The Pioneers, and Other Poems,* Binfords, 1959; *Dear Editor, and Other Poems,* Binfords, 1962; *Chants for the Shades of Animals, and Other Poems,* Dunham Publishing, c.1967.

WORK IN PROGRESS: Poetry, using as a locale the northwest coast of Oregon.

* * *

ECCLES, W(illiam) J(ohn) 1917-

PERSONAL: Born July 17, 1917, in Yorkshire, England; son of John (a merchant) and Jane Ellen (Thorpe) Ec-

cles; married Margaret Jean Jaffray Low, September 18, 1948; children: Michael John, Robin Christina, Peter Alexander. *Education:* McGill University, B.A., 1949, M.A., 1951, Ph.D., 1955; Sorbonne, University of Paris, postgraduate study, 1951-52. *Home:* 108 Cluny Dr., Toronto 5, Ontario, Canada.

CAREER: University of Manitoba, Winnipeg, lecturer in history, 1953-57; University of Alberta, Edmonton, professor of history, 1957-63; University of Toronto, Toronto, Ontario, professor of history, 1963—. Visiting professor, University of Chile, 1966, McGill University, 1966-67. *Military service:* Royal Canadian Air Force, 1941-45; became flight sergeant. *Member:* International Congress of Americanists, Canadian Historical Association (council, 1961-64), Humanities Research Council of Canada. *Awards, honors:* Pacific Coast Branch of American Historical Association book award, 1959, for *Frontenac the Courtier Governor.*

WRITINGS: Frontenac the Courtier Governor, McClelland & Stewart, 1959, revised edition, 1965; *Canada Under Louis XIV,* Oxford University Press, 1964; *The Government of New France,* Canadian Historical Association, 1965; (with J.W. Chalmers and H. Fullard) *Philip's Historical Atlas of Canada,* Philip & Son, 1966; *The Ordeal of New France,* C.B.C. International Service, 1966; *Canadian Society During the French Regime,* Harvest House, 1968; *The Canadian Frontier 1534-1760,* Holt, 1969; *France in America,* Harper, 1972. Contributor of historical articles to scholarly journals. Series editor, "Canadian Historical Controversies," Prentice-Hall (Canada).

WORK IN PROGRESS: Volume I of *Oxford Social History of Canada;* Volume I of "Historical Documents of Canada" series, for Macmillan (Canada).

BIOGRAPHICAL/CRITICAL SOURCES: La Presse (Montreal), May 4, 1963.

* * *

ECHEVERRIA, Durand 1913-

PERSONAL: Born February 26, 1913, in Short Hills, N.J.; son of Charles Manuel and Marie (Durand) Echeverria; married Patricia R. Smith, February 9, 1945 (divorced, 1966); married Barbara V. Forigberg, June 10, 1967; children: (first marriage) Peter D., Ann Teresa, John D. *Education:* Princeton University, A.B., 1935, M.A., 1937, Ph.D., 1949; Middlebury College, M.A., 1946. *Politics:* Independent. *Religion:* Episcopalian. *Office:* Department of French, Brown University, Providence, R.I. 02912.

CAREER: Brown University, Providence, R.I., instructor, 1949-50, assistant professor, 1951-55, associate professor, 1955-62, professor of French, 1962-67, head of department of French, 1965-68, professor of French and comparative literature, 1967—. *Military service:* U.S. Naval Reserve, 1942—; now commander. *Member:* International Comparative Literature Association, Modern Language Association of America, American Association of Teachers of French, American Comparative Literature Association, Society for French Historical Studies, Societe d'Historie Moderne, Phi Beta Kappa, Narragansett Boat Club (former president). *Awards, honors:* Fulbright grants, 1950-51, 1957-58; Guggenheim fellowship, 1957-58.

WRITINGS: Mirage in the West: A History of the French Image of American Society to 1815, Princeton University Press, 1957; *Materials for the Study of French History in the John Carter Brown Library of Brown University,* privately printed, 1961; (editor, and translator with Mara Soceanu Vamos) J. P. Brissot, *New Travels in the United States of America, 1788,* John Harvard Library and Harvard University Press, 1964.

WORK IN PROGRESS: French Political and Social Thought, 1770-74; a bibliography of French works related to British colonies and the U.S., 1607-1815.

*   *   *

EDELMAN, Paul S.   **1926-**

PERSONAL: Born January 2, 1926, in Brooklyn, N.Y.; son of Joseph S. (an advertising man) and Rose (Kaminsky) Edelman; married Rosemary H. Jacobs, June 15, 1951; children: Peter, Jeffrey. *Education:* Harvard University, A.B., 1947, LL.B., 1950. *Politics:* Democrat. *Religion:* Jewish. *Home:* 57 Buena Vista Dr., Hastings, N.Y. 13076. *Office:* Kreindler & Kreindler, 99 Park Ave., New York, N.Y. 10016.

CAREER: Admitted to Bar of New York State, 1951; Kreindler & Kreindler (law firm), New York, N.Y., partner, specializing in maritime and aviation law, 1953—. Chairman, Planning Board, Hastings, N.Y. Member of New York chapter executive board, American Jewish Committee. *Military service:* U.S. Army, 1944-46. *Member:* National Association of Claimants' Compensation Attorneys, Trial Lawyers Association of New York, New York County Lawyers Association.

WRITINGS: Maritime Injury and Death, Central Book Co., 1960; (contributor) L.R. Frumer and R.L. Benoit, editors, *Personal Injury: 1960 Cumulative Supplement,* Matthew Bender, 1961. Contributor of articles on maritime subjects to legal periodicals. Admirality editor of publication of National Association of Claimants' Compensation Attorneys; associate editor, *Journal of the Insurance Law Section,* New York State Bar Association.

WORK IN PROGRESS: A supplement to *Maritime Injury and Death;* a chapter for *The Noise Handbook.*

*   *   *

EDIE, James M.   **1927-**

PERSONAL: Born November 3, 1927, in Grand Forks, N.D. *Education:* Attended University of Paris; University of Louvain, Ph.D., 1958. *Home:* 3950 North Lake Shore Dr., Chicago, Ill. 60613. *Office:* Northwestern University, Evanston, Ill. 60201.

CAREER: Hobart and William Smith Colleges, Geneva, N.Y., assistant professor of philosophy, 1959-61; Northwestern University, Evanston, Ill., assistant professor, 1961-65, associate professor of philosophy, 1965—. *Member:* American Philosophical Association, American Metaphysical Society, Society for Existential Philosophy and Phenomenology, American Society for Aesthetics, British Society for Phenomenology.

WRITINGS: (Editor and author of introduction, and translator with others) Pierre Thevenaz, *What is Phenomenology, and Other Essays,* Quadrangle, 1962; (editor and translator with John Wild) Maurice Merleau-Ponty, *In Praise of Philosophy,* Northwestern University Press, 1963; (with William Earle and Wild) *Christianity and Existentialism,* Northwestern University Press, 1963; (editor and author of introduction) Merleau-Ponty, *The Primacy of Perception, and Other Essays on Phenomenological Psychology, the Philosophy of Art, History, and Politics,* Northwestern University Press, 1964; (editor with James P. Scanlan and Mary-Barbara Zeldin) *Russian Philosophy: An Historical Anthology,* three volumes, Quadrangle, 1965; (editor and author of introduction) *Invitation to Phenomenology: Studies in the Philosophy of Existence,* Quadrangle, 1965; (editor and author of introduction) *Phenomenology in America: Studies in the Philosophy of Existence,* Quadrangle, 1967; (editor and author of introduction) *New Essays in Phenomenology,* Quadrangle, 1969; (editor) *Patterns of the Life-World: Essays in Honor of John Wild,* Northwestern University

Press, 1970. Editor, "Northwestern University Studies in Phenomenology and Existential Philosophy"; consulting editor, *American Philosophical Quarterly* and *Journal of Value Inquiry.*

BIOGRAPHICAL/CRITICAL SOURCES: New York Review of Books, December 5, 1968.

*   *   *

EDLIN, Rosabelle Alpern   **1914-**

PERSONAL: Born January 23, 1914, in Chicago, Ill.; daughter of Isadore Mayer and Anna (Block) Alpern; married Morris Edlin, September 3, 1944; children: Arlene Esther. *Education:* Received formal education, and tutoring in the arts, literature, and music. *Religion:* Jewish. *Home:* 19710 Northwest Sixth Ct., Miami, Fla. 33169.

CAREER: Wilcox & Follett (now Follett Publishing Co.), Chicago, Ill., formerly administrative department head.

WRITINGS: (With Sushannah Spector) *My Jewish Kitchen: The Momele's Ta'am Cookbook,* edited by Arthur Pell, Liveright, 1964.

WORK IN PROGRESS: Research on the flight of the Yemenites from the period of Nebuchadnezzar to the flight from Yemen into Israel, for a book for Liveright; research on Babylon before and during the reign of Hammurabi; with Daniel Medvin, a book on the distinction between the Hammurabi and Mosaic code of laws.

AVOCATIONAL INTERESTS: Music (plays piano and organ).

*   *   *

EDWARDS, Herbert Charles   **1912-**
  (Bertram Edwards)

PERSONAL: Born July 22, 1912, in London, England; son of John Quilton and Eliza (Conybeare) Edwards; married Lilian Florence Hinton, December 25, 1937; children: John Charles, Michael Vernon, Nigel Philip. *Education:* Attended Newlands Park Training College, Buckinghamshire, England, and Cambridge Institute of Education. *Religion:* Church of England. *Home:* 20 Whitehurst Ave., Hitchin, Hertfordshire, England. *Office:* Longfield School, Stevenage, Hertfordshire, England.

CAREER: Teacher, now at Longfield Special School, Stevenage, Hertfordshire, England. *Military service:* British Army, 1940-45; became staff sergeant. *Member:* National Union of Teachers. *Awards, honors:* Runners-up Junior Book award certificate from Boys' Clubs of America for *The Mystery of Barrowmead Hill.*

WRITINGS—Under pseudonymn Bertram Edwards: *The Restless Valley,* Brockhampton Press, 1956; *Midnight on Barrowmead Hill,* Brockhampton Press, 1957, published in America as *The Mystery of Barrowmead Hill,* McKay, 1959; *Strange Traffic,* Brockhampton Press, 1959, McKay, 1960; *Danger in Densmere,* Thomas Nelson, 1965; *The Rise of the U. S. A.,* Blackie & Son, 1968; "Captain Swing at the Penny Gaff" (play), first produced in London at Unity Theatre, 1971.

*   *   *

EDWARDS, James Don(ald)   **1926-**

PERSONAL: Born November 12, 1926, in Ellisville, Miss.; son of Thomas Terrell and Reitha Mae (Cranford) Edwards; married Clara Florence Maestri, August 16, 1947; children: James Donald, Jr. *Education:* Louisiana State University, B.S., 1949; University of Denver, M.B.A., 1950; University of Texas, Ph.D., 1953. *Religion:* Protestant. *Home:* 1967 Lagoon Dr., Okemos, Mich. 48864. *Office:* Department of Accounting and Financial Adminstration, Michigan State University, East Lansing, Mich. 48823.

CAREER: Certified public accountant; Michigan State University, East Lansing, instructor, 1951-53, assistant professor, 1953-55, associate professor, 1955-57, professor of accounting, 1957—, acting head of the department of accounting and financial administration, 1957-58, head of the department, 1958—, associate dean of Graduate School of Business Administration, 1960. Consultant, Touche, Ross, Bailey & Smart. *Military service:* U.S. Navy, two years; became petty officer third class.

MEMBER: American Accounting Association (vice-president, 1964), National Association of Accountants (national director, 1962-63), American Institute of Certified Public Accountants (chairman of education committee, 1960-61), American Management Association, American Economics Association, American Finance Association, Midwest Economics Association (program chairman, 1959), Michigan Association of Certified Public Accountants, Phi Kappa Phi, Beta Gamma Sigma, Beta Alpha Phi, Delta Sigma Pi, Masons.

WRITINGS: (With A.W. Holmes and others) *Elementary Accounting,* revised edition (Edwards was not associated with earlier editions), Irwin, 1956, 3rd edition, 1962; (with Holmes and others) *Intermediate Accounting,* 3rd edition (Edwards was not associated with earlier editions), Irwin, 1958; *History of Public Accounting in the United States,* Bureau of Business and Economic Research, Graduate School of Business Administration, Michigan State University, 1960; (editor with B.C. Lemke) *Administrative Control and Executive Action,* C.E. Merrill, 1961, 2nd edition, 1972; (with Roland F. Salmonson) *Contributions of Four Accounting Pioneers: Kohler, Littleton, May, Paton—Digests of Periodical Writings,* Bureau of Business and Economic Research, Graduate School of Business Administration, Michigan State University, 1961; (with John W. Ruswinckel) *The Professional C.P.A. Examination,* two volumes, McGraw, 1963; (with Salmonson and Roger H. Hermanson) *Accounting: A Programmed Text,* two volumes, Irwin, 1967, revised edition, 1970. Also author of *Controllo Aziendale, I.P.S.O.A.,* c.1961. Contributing editor, *Journal of Accountancy.*

*   *   *

EDWARDS, Monica le Doux Newton   1912-

PERSONAL: Born November 8, 1912, in Belper, Derbyshire, England; daughter of Harry (a clergyman) and Beryl F. le Doux (Sargeant) Newton; married William Ferdinand Edwards (a farmer), 1931; children: Shelley C. Edwards Paton, Sean R. *Education:* Attended Beecholm College, Thornes House School, and St. Brandon's School for the Daughters of Clergy. *Home:* Punch Bowl Farm, Thursley, Surrey, England. *Agent:* Curtis Brown Ltd., 13 King St., Covent Garden, London W.C. 2, England.

CAREER: Author, mainly of children's books. *Member:* Society of Authors, Royal Horticultural Society, International Camellia Society, Burmese Cat Club, National Farmers' Union. *Awards, honors:* Co-recipient of Foyles' Children's Book Club Author of the Year designation, 1957.

WRITINGS—All published by Collins, except as indicated: *Wish for a Pony,* 1947, *No Mistaking Corker,* 1947, *The Summer of the Great Secret,* 1948, *The Midnight Horse,* 1949, Vanguard, 1950.

The White Riders, 1950, *Black Hunting Whip,* 1950, *Punchbowl Midnight,* 1951, *Cargo of Horses,* 1951, *Spirit of Punchbowl Farm,* 1952, *Hidden in a Dream,* 1952, *The Wanderer,* 1953, *Storm Ahead,* 1953, *No Entry,* 1954, *The Unsought Farm,* M. Joseph, 1954, *Punchbowl Harvest,* 1954, *Joan Goes Farming,* John Lane, 1954, *The Nightbird,* 1955, *Rennie Goes Riding,* Bodley Head, 1956,

Frenchman's Secret, 1956, *Strangers to the Marsh,* 1957, *Operation Seabird,* 1957, *The Cownappers,* 1958, *Killer Dog,* 1959.

No Going Back, 1960, *The Outsider,* 1961, *The Hoodwinkers,* 1962, *Dolphin Summer,* 1963, Hawthorn, 1971, *The Cats of Punchbowl Farm,* Doubleday, 1964, *Fire in the Punchbowl,* 1965, *The Badgers of Punchbowl Farm,* M. Joseph, 1966, *The Wild One,* 1967, *Under the Rose,* 1968, *A Wind Is Blowing,* 1969, *The Valley and the Farm,* M. Joseph, 1971.

Author of film script, "The Dawn Killer," for Children's Film Foundation. Contributor of short stories to English magazines.

SIDELIGHTS: Twelve books have been translated for publication in other European languages, one transcribed into Braille, some serialized and broadcast. *Avocational interests:* Natural history, wildlife conservation, photography, gardening, needlework, riding, music, reading, and cats.

*   *   *

EGGENBERGER, David   1918-

PERSONAL: Born July 25, 1918, in Pontiac, Ill.; son of Florian E. (a farmer) and Rose (Huber) Eggenberger; married Lorraine Angstman, August 27, 1943; children: Lynn, April. *Education:* University of Illinois, B.S. in Journalism, 1941. *Politics:* "F.D.R. Democrat." *Religion:* Roman Catholic. *Home:* 16 Van Breemen Ct., Upper Montclair, N.J. 07043. *Office:* McGraw-Hill Book Co., 330 West 42nd St., New York, N.Y. 10036.

CAREER: Compton's Pictured Encyclopedia, Chicago, Ill., an editor, 1946-57; McGraw-Hill Book Co., New York, N.Y., managing editor and executive editor of encyclopedia division, 1957—. *Military service:* U.S. Army, Infantry, 1942-46; became captain; received Bronze Star.

WRITINGS: Flags of the U.S.A., Crowell, 1959, revised edition, 1964; *A Dictionary of Battles,* Crowell, 1967.

WORK IN PROGRESS: Research on the decisive battles in the history of the world.

*   *   *

EHLE, John (Marsden, Jr.)   1925-

PERSONAL: Surname is pronounced *E*-lee; born December 13, 1925, in Asheville, N.C.; son of John Marsden (an insurance executive) and Gladys (Starnes) Ehle; married Gail Oliver, August 30, 1951 (divorced April 20, 1967); married Rosemary Harris (an actress), October 21, 1967; children: (second marriage) Jennifer Anne. *Education:* University of North Carolina, A.B., 1949, M.A., 1952. *Politics:* Democrat. *Religion:* Protestant. *Home:* 1 Westview Drive N., Winston-Salem, N.C. 27108. *Agent:* Robert Lantz-Candida Donadio Literary Agency, Inc. 111 West 57th St., New York, N.Y. 10019.

CAREER: University of North Carolina, Chapel Hill, 1952-65, began as instructor in Communication Center, became associate professor; Office of the Governor, Raleigh, N.C., special assistant to the governor, Terry Sanford, 1962-64; program officer for Ford Foundation, 1964-65. New York University, New York, N.Y., visiting associate professor, 1957-58. Former board member, National Commission for UNESCO, 1964-66, North Carolina Fund, 1964-69, National Council on the Humanities, 1966-70, North Carolina Governor's School. Board member, Anne C. Stouffer Foundation, North Carolina School of the Arts Foundation, and Outdoor Drama Institute of University of North Carolina. *Military service:* U.S. Army, Infantry, rifleman, 1942-46. *Member:* Authors Guild, Roanoke Historical Society (former board member). *Awards, honors:* Special citation from National Conference of Christians and Jews; two Freedoms

Foundation awards; best novel by a North Carolinian annual award, 1964, 1967; best nonfiction book by a North Carolinian award, 1965.

WRITINGS: Move Over, Mountain (novel), Morrow, 1957; *The Survivor* (biography of a stateless person), Holt, 1958; *Kingstree Island* (novel), Morrow, 1959; *Shephard of the Streets: The Story of Reverend James A. Gusweller and His Crusade on the New York West Side,* Sloane, 1960; *Lion on the Hearth* (novel), Harper, 1961; *The Land Breakers* (novel), Harper, 1964; *The Free Men* (biography of civil rights activists), Harper, 1965; *The Road* (novel), Harper, 1967; *Time of Drums* (novel), Harper, 1970; *Journey of the August King,* Harper, 1971; *The Cheeses and Wines of England and France,* Harper, 1972. Author of twenty-six plays in series, "American Adventure," broadcast on National Broadcasting Co. network, 1952-53, and by Radio Free Europe, Voice of America, Armed Forces Network, Network of the National Association of Educational Broadcasters.

WORK IN PROGRESS: A novel, for Harper.

SIDELIGHTS: Although Ehle describes himself as "designed to be a writer," an article written for *Newsweek* reports: "As a brain-truster for North Carolina's Governor Terry Sanford, the 38-year-old Ehle has functioned as a one-man Rand Corporation, dreaming up ways and means of raising the admittedly low level of education in the Tar Heel state. ... He has provided a creative spark for what will probably be considered one of the most successful administrations in North Carolina history."

Ehle does most of his writing at his mountain house in Penland, N.C. In recent years, he has spent about a third of the time in London and Paris. His most outstanding publishing successes abroad have been in Holland.

BIOGRAPHICAL/CRITICAL SOURCES: Newsweek, June 1, 1964; *Best Sellers,* April 15, 1970; *Library Journal,* June 15, 1970.

*   *   *

EHRE, Edward 1905-

PERSONAL: Born June 4, 1905, in Rochester, N.Y.; son of Abraham and Mollie (Karpf) Ehre; married Gertrude Siltzbach, January 1, 1934; children: Stephen, Paul. *Education:* University of Rochester, A.B., 1932; Columbia University, M.A., 1934. *Home:* 96 Ivy Way, Port Washington, N.Y. 11050.

CAREER: Taught English in Manasquin, N.J., 1935-38; Port Washington (N.Y.) Board of Education, teacher of English and speech, 1938—. *Member:* National Council of Teachers of English, National Education Association, New York Teachers Association.

WRITINGS: (Editor with Irving T. Marsh) *Best Sports Stories,* Dutton, annually, 1944—; *Athletic Astro-Nuts: The Sportsman's Guide to Space Travel,* Chilton, 1960; (editor) *Best of the Best Sports Stories,* Dutton, 1964.

WORK IN PROGRESS: Twenty-seventh volume of *Best Sports Stories.*

*   *   *

EIBL-EIBESFELDT, Irenaus 1928-

PERSONAL: Born June 15, 1928, in Vienna, Austria; son of Anton and Maria (von Hauninger) Eibl-Eibesfeldt; married Eleonore Siegel, February 10, 1950; children: Bernolf, Roswitha. *Education:* University of Vienna, Ph.D. *Home:* Soecking, Fichtenweg, West Germany. *Office:* Max-Planck-Institut, Percha near Starnberg, West Germany.

CAREER: Biological Station Wilhelminenberg, near Vienna, Austria, zoologist, 1946-49; Max-Planck-Institute for Physiology of Behavior, Percha near Starnberg, West Germany, zoologist, 1951-69, head of research group for human ethnology, 1969—; University of Munich, Munich, West Germany, docent, 1963-69, professor of zoology, 1969—. Member of skin-diving expeditions to Galapagos, Caribbean Sea, Indian Ocean, Africa, and South America. *Member:* American Society of Herpetologists and Ichthyologists, Charles Darwin Foundation, Deutsche Gesellschaft fuer Saugetierkunde, Deutsche Ornithologische Gesellschaft, Deutsche Zoologische Gesellschaft, Senckenbergische Naturforschende Gesellschaft.

WRITINGS: Das Verhalten der Nagetiere, W. De-Gruyter, 1958; *Survey on the Galapagos Islands,* UNESCO (Paris), 1960; *Galapagos: Die Arche Noah im Pazifik,* Piper, 1960, translation by Alan Houghton Brodrick published as *Galapagos: The Noah's Ark of the Pacific,* MacGibbon & Kee, 1960, Doubleday, 1961; *Im Reich der tausend Atolle: Als Tierpsychologe in den Korallenriffen der Malediven und Nikobaren,* Piper, 1964, translation by Gwynne Vevers published as *Land of a Thousand Atolls: A Study of Marine Life in the Maldive and Nicobar Islands,* MacGibbon & Kee, 1965, World Publishing, 1967; *Haie: Angriff, Abwehr, Arten,* Kosmos, 1965; *Ethologie: Die Biologie des Verhaltens,* Akademische Verlagsgesellschaft Athenaion, 1966, reissued as *Grundriss der Vergleichenden Verhaltensforschung,* Piper, 1967, translation by Erich Klinghammer published as *Ethology: The Biology of Behavior,* Holt, 1970; *Liebe und Hass,* Piper, 1970, translation by Geoffrey Strachan published as *Love and Hate: The Natural History of Behavior Patterns,* Holt, 1971.

Scriptwriter for scientific and educational films. Contributor of more than one hundred articles to scientific journals and handbooks.

*   *   *

EIGNER, Laurence (Joel) 1927-
   (Larry Eigner)

PERSONAL: Born August 7, 1927, in Swampscott, Mass.; son of Israel and Bessie (Polansky) Eigner. *Education:* Correspondence courses from University of Chicago. *Politics:* "Safety is no more than a by-product of well-being." *Residence:* Swampscott, Mass.

CAREER: Poet.

WRITINGS—Under name Larry Eigner: *From the Sustaining Air* (poems), Divers Press (Mallorca), 1953, Toad Press (Eugene, Ore.), 1967; *Look at the Park* (poems), privately printed, 1958; *On My Eyes* (poems), foreword by Denise Levertov, Jargon, 1960; *Murder Talk. The Reception. Suggestions for a Play. Five Poems. Bed Never Self Made,* [Placitas, N.M.], 1964; *The Music, the Rooms; a Poem,* Desert Review Press, 1965; *Another Time in Fragments* (poems), Fulcrum Press (London), 1967; *Six Poems,* Wine Press, 1967; *Air; the Trees* (poems), Black Sparrow Press, 1967; *The Breath of Once Live Things/In The Field with Poe* (poem), Black Sparrow Press, 1968; *A Line That May Be Cut: Poems from 1965* (edition of 250 numbered copies), Circle Press (London), 1968; *Valleys, Branches* (poems), Big Venus, 1969; *Selected Poems,* Oyez, 1971; *Watery Air/earth/clouds* (poems), The Land Press, 1971; *Looks like nothing/the shadow/through air* (poems), Tetrad Press, 1971. Author of two prose broadsides, *Clouding,* Portents, 1968, and *Farther North* (edition of 200 copies), Portents, 1969.

Anthologized in *A New Folder, Americans,* Folder editions, 1959, *New American Poetry,* Grove, 1960, *Neue Amerikanische Lyrik,* Carl Hanser Verlag (Munich), 1962, *A Controversy of Poets,* Doubleday Anchor, 1965, *Poems Now,* Kulchur Press, 1966; *Panama Gold, San*

Francisco, 1969, edited by T.L. Kryss, Zero Publications (Cleveland), 1969.

Contributor to *Poetry, Ann Arbor Review, Kulchur,* and *Black Mountain Review.*

SIDELIGHTS: Eigner, palsied as a result of injury at birth, has spent much of his life writing. In discussing *Another Time in Fragments* Andrew Hoyem wrote: "Many poets have been fascinated by the apparently disjointed random notations scattered over the page in the poems of Eigner . . . . A service rendered by this book is that Eigner *in toto* is neither invalid nor superior because of his confinement to a wheelchair. . . . He has, as Robert Duncan says, come into the full of his poetic voice. He is truly modern in his conception of reality. What he discovers to us is indigenous to mankind. It is uncommon; it is physical. While I welcome the cogent intervals, wish for personal commerce and less selfishness in the poems, I must insist that we have an important poet in Larry Eigner."

BIOGRAPHICAL/CRITICAL SOURCES: Paris Leary and Robert Kelly, *A Controversy of Poets,* Doubleday Anchor, 1965; *Listener,* February 1, 1968; *Poetry,* March, 1969, July, 1969.

* * *

EINZIG, Paul 1897-

PERSONAL: Born August 25, 1897, in Brasov, Transylvania, Hungary (now Rumania); son of Bernard and Giselle (Weisz) Einzig; married Eileen Ruth Telford Quick, 1931; children: Richard, Penelope Juliet (Mrs. Robert Retallick). *Education:* Oriental Academy, Budapest, Hungary, diploma, 1919; University of Paris, doctor of political and economic sciences, 1923. *Home:* Suffolks, Ashursttwood, East Grinstead, Sussex, England. *Agent:* Curtis Brown Ltd., 13 King St., London W.C.2, England. *Office:* 120 Cliffords Inn, London EC4A 1BX, England.

CAREER: Financial News, London, England, Paris correspondent, 1921-23, foreign editor, 1923-39, political correspondent, 1939-45; *Financial Times,* London, political correspondent, 1945-56; *Commercial and Financial Chronicle,* New York, N.Y., London correspondent, 1945—. *Member:* Association of American Correspondents, Reform Club (both London).

WRITINGS: International Gold Movements, Macmillan, 1929, 2nd edition, 1931; *The Bank for International Settlements,* Macmillan, 1930, 3rd edition, revised and enlarged, 1932; *Behind the Scenes of International Finance,* Macmillan, 1931; *The World Economic Crisis, 1929-31,* Macmillan, 1931, 3rd edition, revised, 1932; *The Fight for Financial Supremacy,* Macmillan, 1931, 3rd edition, 1932; *Finance and Politics,* Macmillan, 1932; *The Tragedy of the Pound,* Routledge, 1932; *Montagu Norman: A Study in Financial Statesmanship,* Routledge, 1932; *The Comedy of the Pound,* Routledge, 1933; *The Sterling-Dollar-Franc Tangle,* Macmillan, 1933; *The Economic Foundations of Fascism,* Macmillan, 1933, 2nd edition, 1934; *Exchange Control,* Macmillan, 1934; *France's Crisis,* Macmillan, 1934; *Germany's Default: The Economics of Hitlerism,* Macmillan, 1934; *The Future of Gold,* Macmillan, 1934; *The Economics of Rearmament,* Routledge, 1934; *The Exchange Clearing System,* Macmillan, 1935; *Bankers, Statesmen and Economists,* Macmillan, 1935, Books for Libraries, 1967; *World Finance, 1914-1935,* Macmillan, 1935 (published in England as *World Finance Since 1914,* Routledge, 1935); *Monetary Reform in Theory and Practice,* Macmillan, 1936; *World Finance, 1935-1937,* Macmillan, 1937; *The Theory of Forward Exchange,* Macmillan, 1937; *Will Gold Depreciate?,* Macmillan, 1937; *Foreign Balances,* Macmillan, 1938; *World Finance, 1937-38 to 1939-40,* three volumes, Macmillan, 1938-40; *Bloodless Invasion: German Economic Penetration into the Danubian States and the Balkans,* Duckworth, 1938, 2nd edition, 1939; *The Economic Problems of the Next War,* Macmillan, 1939, revised edition published as *Economic Warfare,* 1940.

Europe in Chains, Penguin, 1940; *Economic Warfare, 1939-1940,* Macmillan, 1941; *Hitler's "New Order" in Europe,* Macmillan, 1941; *Appeasement Before, During and After the War,* Macmillan, 1941; *Can We Win the Peace?,* Macmillan, 1942; *The Japanese "New Order" in Asia,* Macmillan, 1943; *Currency After the War: The British and American Plans,* Nicholson & Watson, 1944, Transatlantic, 1945; *Freedom From Want,* Nicholson & Watson, 1944; *Primitive Money in Its Ethnological, Historical and Economic Aspects,* Eyre & Spottiswoode, 1949, British Book Centre, 1950, revised and enlarged edition, Pergamon, 1966.

Inflation, Macmillan, 1952; *How Money is Managed: The Ends and Means of Monetary Policy,* Penguin, 1954, reissued as *Monetary Policy: Ends and Means,* 1964; *The Economic Consequences of Automation,* Secker & Warburg, 1956, Norton, 1957; *The Control of the Purse: Progress and Decline of Parliament's Financial Control,* Secker & Warburg, 1959.

In the Centre of Things (autobiography), Hutchinson, 1960; *A Dynamic Theory of Forward Exchange,* St. Martin's, 1961, 2nd edition, 1967; *The History of Foreign Exchange,* St. Martin's, 1962, 2nd edition, 1970; *The Euro-Dollar System: Practice and Theory of International Interest Rates,* St. Martin's, 1964, 4th edition, 1970; *Foreign Dollar Loans in Europe,* St. Martin's, 1965, 2nd edition published as *The Euro-Bond Market,* 1969; *A Textbook of Foreign Exchange,* St. Martin's, 1966, 2nd edition, 1969; *Why London Must Remain the World Banking Centre,* Aims of Industry, 1966; *Leads and Lags: The Main Cause of Devaluation,* St. Martin's, 1968, 2nd edition, 1971; *The Case Against Unearned Wage Increases,* Aims of Industry, 1968; *Foreign Exchange Crises: An Essay in Economic Pathology,* St. Martin's, 1968, 2nd edition, 1970; *Decline and Fall?: Britain's Crisis in the Sixties,* St. Martin's, 1969, 2nd edition, 1970.

The Case Against Floating Exchanges, St. Martin's, 1970; *The Case Against Joining the Common Market,* St. Martin's, 1971; *Parallel Money Markets,* St. Martin's, Volume I, 1971, Volume II, 1972; *The Destiny of Gold,* St. Martin's, 1972; *The Destiny of the Dollar,* St. Martin's, 1972; *A Textbook on Monetary Policy,* St. Martin's, 1973. Contributor to *Economic Journal, Banker, National Banking Review, Journal of Finance,* and other professional periodicals, 1956—.

BIOGRAPHICAL/CRITICAL SOURCES: Punch, January 31, 1968; *Times Literary Supplement,* July 9, 1970.

* * *

EISENSTADT, A(braham) S(eldin) 1920-

PERSONAL: Born June 18, 1920, in Brooklyn, N.Y.; son of Ben-Zion and Sarah (Seldin) Eisenstadt; married Paulette D. Smith, September 4, 1949; children: Elizabeth Anne, Laura Jane, Jonathan. *Education:* Brooklyn College (now Brooklyn College of the City University of New York), A.B., 1940; Columbia University, Ph.D., 1955. *Home:* 567 First St., Brooklyn, N.Y. 11215. *Office:* Department of History, Brooklyn College of the City University of New York, Brooklyn, N.Y. 11210.

CAREER: Brooklyn College, of the City University of New York, Brooklyn, N.Y., instructor, 1956-60, assistant professor, 1961-63, associate professor, 1964-67, professor of history, 1968—. Fulbright lecturer, Johns Hopkins University, School of Advanced International Studies, Bologna, Italy, 1962-63; visiting professor, Council of American Studies, Rome, 1963. *Military service:* U.S. Army, 1942-46; became master sergeant. *Member:* American Historical Association, American Studies Association, Conference on Early American History, Conference on British Studies, Organization of American Historians. *Awards, honors:* American Philosophical Society grant, 1965; City University of New York grant, 1966-67.

WRITINGS: (Contributor) *Some Modern Historians of Britain,* Dryden Press, 1952; *Charles Mclean Andrews: A Study in American Historical Writing,* Columbia University Press, 1956; (editor) *American History: Recent Interpretations,* two volumes, Crowell, 1962, revised edition, 1969; (editor) *The Craft of American History: Selected Essays,* two volumes, Harper, 1966. Contributor to *American Historical Review, Encyclopedia Judaica, Labor History Review, Nation, Southwestern Social Science, American Review, Centennial Review, Journal of Higher Education, Political Science Quarterly,* and other journals. Editor with John Hope Franklin of "Crowell Series in American History"; history and social science editor, Pitman Publishing Co.

* * *

ELDRIDGE, Paul 1888-

PERSONAL: Born May 5, 1888, in Philadelphia, Pa.; son of Leon and Jeanette (Lefleur) Eldridge; married Sylvette De Lamar (a writer). *Education:* Temple University, B.S., 1909; University of Pennsylvania, M.A., 1911; University of Paris, Docteur de l'Universite, 1913. *Home:* 227 Riverside Dr., New York, N.Y. 10025.

CAREER: High school teacher of Romance languages in New York, N.Y., 1914-45; retired, 1945. Lecturer on American literature at the Sorbonne, University of Paris, 1913, at University of Florence, 1923; instructor in English literature at St. John's College, Philadelphia, Pa., 1910-12. *Member:* Authors League and Dramatists League of Authors Guild of America.

WRITINGS: Life Throbs, Poet Lore, 1911; *Vanitas* (verse), Stratford, 1920; *Our Dead Selves, Anthology of the Lowly* (verse), Stratford, 1923; *The Intruder* (play), Sheridan, 1928; *Cobwebs and Cosmos* (verse), Liveright, 1930; *Horns of Glass* (maxims), Yoseloff, 1943; *I Bring a Sword* (verse), Fine Editions, 1945; *Leaves From the Devil's Tree,* 1946; *The Bed Remains* (play), Haldeman-Julius, 1948; *Moon Nets of the Master Spider* (verse), Haldeman-Julius, 1948; *Maxims are Gadflies,* Haldeman-Julius, 1950; *Anatole France, Erasmus, Montaigne, Schopenhauer* (essays), 1950; *The Kingdom Without God* (prose poem), 1954; *Crown of Empire: The Story of New York,* Yoseloff, 1957; *Seven Against the Night* (essays), Yoseloff, 1960; *Maxims for A Modern Man,* Yoseloff, 1965; *Parables of Old Cathay* (verse), A.S. Barnes, 1969; *Francois Rabelais, the Great Storyteller,* A.S. Barnes, 1971.

Novels: (With George Sylvester Viereck) *My First Two Thousand Years,* Sheridan, 1928; (with Viereck) *Salome,* Liveright, 1930; (with Viereck) *The Invincible Adam,* Liveright, 1932; *Prince Pax,* Duckworth, 1933; *If After Every Tempest,* Yoseloff, 1941; *Madonna with the Cat,* Yoseloff, 1942; *Two Lessons in Love* (two short novels; includes "Master of Hearts" and "Mr. Lowell and the Goddess"), Yoseloff, 1946; *And Thou Shalt Teach Them,* Sheridan, 1947; *The Second Life of John Stevens,* Yoseloff, 1960; *The Tree of Ignorance,* Yoseloff, 1962; *The Homecoming: A Chronicle of a Refugee Family,* Yoseloff, 1966.

Short stories: *And the Sphinx Spoke,* Stratford, 1921; *Irony and Pity: A Book of Tales,* Liveright, 1926; *One Man Show,* Liveright, 1933; *Men and Women,* Yoseloff, 1946; *Tales of the Fortunate Isles,* Yoseloff, 1959. Contributor to magazines.

Also author of a number of other books of verse, novels, short stories, and plays, published by Haldeman-Julius.

BIOGRAPHICAL/CRITICAL SOURCES: Books and Bookmen, May, 1970.

* * *

ELIZABETH MARIE, Sister 1914-

PERSONAL: Born September 1, 1914, in El Paso, Tex.; daughter of William Paul (a lawyer and judge) and Mabel Ellen (Rarey) Brady. *Education:* Immaculate Heart College, B.A., 1940, M.A. 1960. *Politics:* Democrat. *Home:* 5515 Franklin Ave., Los Angeles, Calif. 90027. *Office:* Immaculate Heart College Library, 2070 East Live Oak Dr., Los Angeles, Calif. 90028.

CAREER: Roman Catholic nun of Sisters of the Immaculate Heart of Mary; teacher in parochial elementary schools in California and Canada, 1934-54; Immaculate Heart Generalate, Los Angeles, Calif., clerk, 1954-56; Immaculate Heart Library, Los Angeles, Calif., student clerk, 1957-60; Immaculate Heart College Library, Los Angeles, Calif., periodical librarian, 1960-62, reference librarian, 1962—. *Member:* National Catholic Educational Association, American Library Association, Catholic Library Association.

WRITINGS: Eric Gill, Twentieth Century Book Designer, Scarecrow, 1962. Contributor of articles on typography, librarianship, and art to journals.

WORK IN PROGRESS: Idea Merchandising, about book exhibit design; *Maker of Beauty,* a biography of Eric Gill; *Compassionate City,* a novel; *A Bibliography of the History of Libraries.*

* * *

ELKIN, Stanley L(awrence) 1930-

PERSONAL: Born May 11, 1930, in New York, N.Y.; son of Phil (a salesman) and Zelda (Feldman) Elkin; married Joan Marion Jacobson, February 1, 1953; children: Philip Aaron, Bernard Edward, Molly Ann. *Education:* University of Illinois, A.B., 1952, M.A., 1953, Ph.D., 1961. *Religion:* Jewish. *Home:* 225 Westgate, University City, Mo. 63130. *Agent:* Georges Borchardt, Inc., 145 East 52nd St., New York, N.Y. 10022. *Office:* Department of English, Washington University, St. Louis, Mo. 63130.

CAREER: Washington University, St. Louis, Mo., instructor, 1960-62, assistant professor, 1962-66, associate professor, 1966-69, professor of English, 1969—. Visiting professor, Smith College, 1964-65. *Military service:* U.S. Army, 1955-57. *Member:* Modern Language Association of America. *Awards, honors:* Longview Foundation award, 1962; Paris Review humor prize, 1964; Guggenheim fellow, 1966-67; Rockefeller Foundation grant, 1968-69; National Endowment for the Arts and Humanities grant, 1972.

WRITINGS: Boswell (novel), Random House, 1964; *Criers and Kibitzers, Kibitzers and Criers* (stories), Random House, 1966; *A Bad Man* (novel), Random House, 1967; *The Dick Gibson Show* (novel), Random House, 1970; (editor) *Stories from the Sixties,* Doubleday, 1971; *The Making of Ashenden* (novella), Covent Garden Press, 1972; *Searches and Seizures: Three Short Novels,* Random House, 1973. Author of film scenario "The Six-year-old Man" (published in *Esquire,* December, 1968). Contributor to *Epoch, Views, Accent, Perspective, Chicago Review, Journal of English and Germanic Philology, Southwest Review, Esquire, Paris Review, Harper's, Oui,* and *Saturday Evening Post.* Stories appear in *Best American Short Stories,* 1962, 1963, and 1965.

SIDELIGHTS: Although critics have tended to describe Elkin as a "black humorist," he dislikes this classification. "I don't think of myself in categories," Elkin states. He prefers, he says, to emphasize "the flow of feeling and character. I'm interested in the physics of personality, not in schemes."

"Black" or not, Elkin's humor is appreciated by the critics. Josh Greenfeld praises him for his "fanciful diction, boffo wit, prize punning, razzle-dazzle mimicry, picturesque conceits and one-handed insights. For Elkin is at once a bright satirist, a bleak absurdist, and a deadly moralist, with a brisk and busy imagination. . . . I know of no serious funny writer in this country who can match him." Others, though they admit that the novels are funny, believe that Elkin's humor is undisciplined. "Mr. Elkin is . . . better at invention than in following through," Bernard Bergonzi states, "and his narrative has an air of almost desperate improvisation. . . . He has plenty of stamina, but very little of the blend of manic concentration and absolute conviction that one finds in Pynchon or Heller, and his prose has a slightly effortful quality, without any of their dazzle."

Elkin uses his humor to create a world of grotesqueness and despair. Greenfeld describes Elkin's world as "one of expansive, glib, Jewish-American schizophrenia . . . a joyous joylessness in which energy and eccentricity are the disguises of disintegration or deadened inner life." R.Z. Sheppard believes that Elkin's "Jewishness" is central in providing a basis for the themes in his fiction. "Elkin uses the Jew and his dispersion in the world as an analogy for man's striving for absolute freedom: a kind of philosophic Second Law of Thermodynamics, according to which the unchecked will, diffusing like a gas, moves from order to disorder." In a review of A Bad Man, Webster Schott suggests that Elkin's vision necessitates a departure from a conventional style. "Elkin is the artist fully aware. He sees his culture exceeding human limits, moving outside emotion and into a wilderness of sensations. He knows that the convention of straight-line fictional realism cannot contain the new reality of human beings beyond accountability. . . . Like all art, his novel is truth masquerading as deception."

BIOGRAPHICAL/CRITICAL SOURCES: Book Week, June 21, 1964; New York Times Book Review, July 12, 1964, January 23, 1966, October 15, 1967; Saturday Review, August 15, 1964, January 15, 1966, November 18, 1967; Times Literary Supplement, October 22, 1964; Library Journal, January 15, 1966; New York Review of Books, February 3, 1966, January 18, 1967; Christian Science Monitor, May 12, 1966; Choice, October, 1966; Book World, October 22, 1967, October 29, 1967; Life, October 27, 1967; Time, October 27, 1967, March 1, 1971; Nation, November 27, 1967; New Leader, December 4, 1967; Commonweal, December 8, 1967; New Yorker, February 24, 1968; Punch, March 27, 1968, January 1, 1969; Listener, March 28, 1968; Books and Bookmen, May, 1968; Allan Guttman, The Jewish Writer in America, Oxford University Press, 1971; New York Times, February 17, 1971; Raymond M. Olderman, Beyond the Wasteland: A Study of the American Novel in the 1960's, Yale University Press, 1972.

* * *

ELLERY, John Blaise 1920-

PERSONAL: Born February 3, 1920, in New York, N.Y.; son of William Hoyt and Thea (Kavanagh) Ellery; married Ellen Jane Savacool (captain, Army Nurse Corps), September 21, 1946; children: Thea, Martha, Sarah, Jessica, John. Education: Hamilton College, A.B., 1948; University of Colorado, M.A., 1950; University of Wisconsin, Ph.D., 1954. Home: 4217 Janick Circle N., Stevens Point, Wis. 54481.

CAREER: University of Colorado, Boulder, instructor in English, 1948-50; University of Iowa, Iowa City, assistant professor, 1952-56; Alabama College, Montevallo, associate professor, 1956-57; Wayne State University, Detroit, Mich., associate professor, 1957-61, manager of university radio station, 1958-61; East Tennessee State University, Johnson City, professor and chairman of department of English, 1961-66; Njala University College, Freetown, Sierra Leone, head of English department and acting dean, 1966-68; Wisconsin State University, Stevens Point, assistant to president and dean of College of Natural Sciences, 1968—. Qualified parachutist. Licensed radio operator and navigator. U.S. Coast Guard Academy, chairman of cadet procurement committee for Ninth Coast Guard District, 1960-61. Honorary admissions counselor, U.S. Naval Academy, 1969. Military service: U.S. Army Infantry, 1941-45. U.S. Naval Reserve, Maritime Service, 1937-45; Corps of Cadets, 1938-41; received Bronze Star with oak-leaf cluster, Purple Heart with oak-leaf cluster, Conspicuous Service Cross, Medaille Militaire Fourragere.

MEMBER: National Association of Educational Broadcasters (national research committee, 1958—), Military Order of the Purple Heart (national chief of staff, 1956-57), Sons of the American Revolution, Retired Officers Association, U.S. Naval Institute, American Military Institute, American Motorcycle Association, Association of American Motorcycle Road Racers, Alpha Psi Omega, Delta Sigma Rho, Eta Sigma Phi, Pi Kappa Delta, Sigma Tau Delta, Sigma Phi Epsilon. Awards, honors: Saga prize, 1953, for short story, "Local Action"; National Educational Television and Radio Center research grant, 1957; National Association of Educational Broadcasters research fellow, 1958.

WRITINGS: A Pilot Study of the Nature of Aesthetic Experience in Educational Television (monograph), Division of Broadcasting, Wayne State University, 1959; (contributor with Rupert Cortright) Introduction to Graduate Work in Speech and Drama, Michigan State University Press, 1961; John Stuart Mill, Twayne, 1964. Contributor of poetry to National Anthology of Poetry, 1964. Television script writer. Contributor of articles to professional journals and popular publications. Editor, Watauga Review, 1963-66.

WORK IN PROGRESS: African Ambush; the role of the military in West Africa.

AVOCATIONAL INTERESTS: Motorcycle racing, amateur baseball, pistol shooting, sports cars.

* * *

ELLIS, David Maldwyn 1914-

PERSONAL: Born October 14, 1914 in Utica, N.Y.; son of Samuel (a businessman) and Margaret (Jones) Ellis; married Carolyn Crawford, June, 1953. Education: Hamilton College, B.A., 1938; Cornell University, M.A., 1939, Ph.D., 1942. Religion: Presbyterian. Home: 250 College Hill Rd., Clinton, N.Y. 13323. Office: Hamilton College, Clinton, N.Y. 13323.

CAREER: University of Vermont, Burlington, instructor in history, 1942-44; Social Science Research Council fellow, 1944-45; Hamilton College, Clinton, N.Y., assistant professor, 1946-51, associate professor, 1951-57, Rogers Professor of History, 1957—. Member: American Historical Association, American Studies Association of New York (president, 1963-64), Mississippi Valley Historical Association, New York Historical Association, Agricultural History Society, New York State Historical Association (fellow), Phi Beta Kappa. Awards, honors: John Dunning Award of American Historical Association, 1946, for Landlords and Farmers in Hudson-Mohawk Region; Ford fellowship, 1951-52.

WRITINGS: *Landlords and Farmers in Hudson-Mohawk Region, 1790-1850,* Cornell University Press, 1946; (with Harold Syrett, Harry Carman, and James Frost) *A Short History of New York State,* Cornell University Press, 1957, revised edition published as *A History of New York State,* 1967; (with Frost and William Fink) *New York: The Empire State,* Prentice-Hall, 1961, 3rd edition, 1969; (with W.R. Ellis) *Geography Around Us,* University of London Press, 1964; (editor with others) *The Frontier in American Development: Essays in Honor of Paul Wallace Gates,* Cornell University Press, 1969; *The Saratoga Campaign,* McGraw, 1969. Contributor to *Encyclopaedia Britannica* and *Collier's Encyclopedia.* Contributor of articles to historical journals.

*   *   *

ELLIS, Leo R(oy)   1909-

PERSONAL: Born June 3, 1909, in Norton Kan.; son of Lee Roy (a cabinetmaker) and Maude (Sager) Ellis; married Margaret L. Kouns (a recreation and dance supervisor), July 10, 1937. *Home:* 1505 Pilgrim Way, Monrovia, Calif. 91016. *Agent:* Larry Sternig, 2407 North 44th, Milwaukee, Wis. 53210.

CAREER: Walt Disney Studios, Burbank, Calif., writer, 1936-40; free-lance radio writer, Hollywood, Calif., 1940-42; now free-lance writer. *Military service:* U.S. Naval Reserve, served with Office of Strategic Services, 1942-45; became photographers mate, second class. *Member:* Writers Guild of America, Mystery Writers of America, California Writers Guild.

WRITINGS: *Nights of Danger,* Funk, 1964; *King Rooster* (juvenile), Funk, 1965; *The Bronc Tattoo,* Funk, 1966; *To Kill an Octopus,* Western Publishing, 1971. Contributor to *Alfred Hitchcock's Mystery Magazine, Manhunt, Ellery Queen's Mystery Magazine, Men's Digest,* and other men's magazines.

*   *   *

ELLISON, Ralph (Waldo)   1914-

PERSONAL: Born March 1, 1914, in Oklahoma City, Okla.; son of Lewis Alfred (a construction worker and tradesman) and Ida (Millsap) Ellison; married Fanny McConnell, July, 1946. *Education:* Attended Tuskegee Institute, 1933-36. *Home and office:* 730 Riverside Dr., New York, N.Y. 10031, and Plainfield, Mass. *Agent:* William Morris Agency, 1740 Broadway, New York, N.Y. 10019.

CAREER: Began writing seriously in 1939; worked as a researcher on New York Federal Writers' Project, 1938-42; edited *Negro Quarterly,* 1942; lecture tour in Germany, 1954; lecturer at Salzburg Seminar, Austria, fall, 1954; Bard College, Annandale-on-Hudson, N.Y., instructor in Russian and American literature, 1958-61; New York University, New York, N.Y., Albert Schweitzer Professor in Humanities, 1970—. Alexander White Visiting Professor, University of Chicago, 1961; visiting professor of writing, Rutgers University, 1962-64; visiting fellow in American studies, Yale University, 1966. Gertrude Whittall Lecturer, Library of Congress, January, 1964; delivered Ewing Lectures at University of California, Los Angeles, April, 1964. Member of Carnegie Commission on Educational Television, 1966-67; honorary consultant in American Letters, Library of Congress, 1966-72. Trustee, Colonial Williamsburg Foundation, Museum of the City of New York, John F. Kennedy Center for the Performing Arts, New School for Social Research, Bennington College, and Educational Broadcasting Corp. Member of National Council of the Arts, 1965-67, and of National Advisory Council, Hampshire College. *Military service:* U.S. Merchant Marine, World War II.

MEMBER: P.E.N. (vice-president, c.1964), Authors Guild, National Institute of Arts and Letters (vice-president, 1967), American Academy of Arts and Sciences, Institute of Jazz Studies (member of board of advisors), Century Association (resident member). *Awards, honors:* Rosenwald grant, 1945; National Book Award, 1953, and National Newspaper Publishers Russwurm Award, 1953, both for *Invisible Man;* American Academy of Arts and Letters fellowship in Rome, 1955-57; Medal of Freedom, 1969; Chevalier de l'Ordre des Artes et Lettres (France), 1970; Ph.D. in Humane Letters, Tuskegee Institute, 1963; Litt.D., Rutgers University, 1966, University of Michigan, 1967, Williams College, 1970, Long Island University, 1971; L.H.D., Grinnell College, 1967, Adelphi University, 1971, College of William and Mary, 1972.

WRITINGS: *Invisible Man* (novel; vignette published in *American Writing,* edited by Hans Otto Storm and others, J.A. Decker, 1940; "Battle Royal" sequence published in *Horizon,* October, 1947; prologue published in *Partisan Review,* Number 1, 1952), Random House, 1952; (author of introduction) *The Red Badge of Courage and Four Great Stories by Stephen Crane,* Dell, 1960; *Shadow and Act* (essays), Random House, 1964; (with Karl Shapiro) *The Writer's Experience* (lectures given at Library of Congress; includes "Hidden Name and Complex Fate," by Ellison, and "American Poet?," by Shapiro), Gertrude Clarke Whittall Fund, 1964; (with Whitney M. Young and Herbert Gans) *The City in Crisis,* A. Philip Randolph Educational Fund, 1968; (author of introduction) *Paintings and Projects* (of Romare Bearden; catalog of exhibition, November 25-December 22, 1968), State University of New York at Albany, c.1968. Also author of an unpublished novel, as yet untitled, portions of which have been published under various titles in several periodicals, including "And Hickman Arrives," *Nobel Savage,* March, 1960, "The Roof, the Steeple, and the People," *Quarterly Review of Literature,* Number 3, 1960, "It Always Breaks Out," *Partisan Review,* spring, 1963, "Juneteenth," *Quarterly Review of Literature,* Numbers 3-4, 1965, "Night Talk," *Quarterly Review of Literature,* Numbers 3-4, 1969, "Song of Innocence," *Iowa Review,* spring, 1970, and "Cadillac Flambe," *American Review,* February, 1973.

Short stories, articles, essays, and excerpts from novel anthologized in *American Writing,* edited by Hans Otto Storm and others, J.A. Decker, 1940, *The Best Short Stories, 1941,* edited by E.J. O'Brien, Houghton, 1941, *Cross-Section,* edited by Edwin Seaver, Fischer, 1944, *The Antioch Review Anthology,* edited by Paul Bixler, World Publishing, 1953, *New World Writing, 5,* New American Library, 1954, *New World Writing, 9,* New American Library, 1956, *Best Short Stories of World War II,* edited by Charles A. Fenton, Viking, 1957, *The Living Novel,* edited by Granville Hicks, Macmillan, 1957, *A New Southern Harvest,* edited by Robert Penn Warren and Albert Erskine, Bantam, 1957, *The Book of Negro Folklore,* edited by Langston Hughes and Arna Bontemps, Dodd, 1958, *I Have Seen War,* edited by Dorothy Sterling, Hill & Wang, 1960, *Stories of Modern America,* edited by Herbert Gold and D.L. Stevenson, St. Martin's, 1961, *The Angry Black,* edited by John Alfred Williams, Lancer, 1962, *Soon, One Morning* (includes previously unpublished section from original manuscript of *Invisible Man*), edited by Herbert Hill, Knopf, 1963 (published in England as *Black Voices,* Elek Books, 1964), *Writers at Work,* edited by George Plimpton, Viking, 1963, *Who Speaks for the Negro?,* edited by Robert Penn Warren, Random House, 1965, *The Best Short Stories by Negro Writers,* edited by Langston Hughes, Little, Brown, 1967, *To Heal and to Build,* McGraw, 1968. Also contributor of short stories, articles, critical essays, and reviews to *Nation, New Masses, Tomorrow, Noble Savage, Negro World Digest, Common Ground, Saturday Review, Quar-*

terly *Review of Literature, Partisan Review, Phylon, Horizon,* and other periodicals. Member of editorial board of *American Scholar,* 1966-69.

WORK IN PROGRESS: A second novel, as yet untitled, to be published by Random House.

SIDELIGHTS: Invisible Man, hailed by F.W. Dupee as "the 'Moby Dick' of the racial crisis," was cited in a *Book Week* poll of 200 American writers and cirtics as the most significant work of fiction written between 1945 and 1965. Wright Morris said that the book "belongs on the shelf with the classical efforts man has made to chart the river Lethe from its mouth to its source." "*Invisible Man* is not a great Negro novel," wrote Harvey Curtis Webster; "it is a work of art any contemporary writer could point to with pride."

Shadow and Act, a spiritual and intellectual autobiography, has been similarly acclaimed. Comparing it to Ellison's novel, Bell Gale Chevigny wrote: "In *Invisible Man,* freedom is precious because won by the protagonist's leap of courage and insight, his decision 'to run the risk of his own humanity.' In *Shadow and Act* we sense that the author values freedom because he had it all along. . . . The invisible man, whose fate was to undergo 'a kind of jiu-jitsu of the spirit,' learning to live in a doubleness of vision, is replaced here by the Renaissance Man who must simply, patiently cultivate and unfold his best self." *Newsweek* notes: "The theme, which is a great one, is this: what it means to be Ralph Waldo Ellison (in a marvelous essay, 'Hidden Name and Complex Fate,' he meditates upon the meaning fo. him of the name which his father, who hoped his son would become a poet, gave him)—what it means to be *that* man and *that* artist and *that* Negro in America."

"Boy and man," John Corry writes in the *New York Times Magazine,* "Ellison has had a multiplicity of cultural influences." He grew up in Oklahoma City, which was where his mother canvassed for the Socialists and "was thrown into jail with the utmost regularity for violating the segregation orders laid down by Governor 'Alfalfa' Bill Murray." Ellison discovered music early in life, brushing shoulders with young greats like Jimmy Rushing, Hot Lips Paige, Lester Young, and the Blue Devils, who later became Count Basie's band. After three years at Tuskegee Institute studying music and composition, a growing interest in sculpture took him to New York City and a chance meeting with Langston Hughes. By this time he had read T.S. Eliot's *The Wasteland,* which he believes was the most influential thing he had ever read. "It got me interested in literature," Ellison recalled in an interview with Harvey Breit. "I tried to understand it better and that led me to reading criticism. I then started looking for Eliot's kind of sensibility in Negro poetry and I didn't find it until I ran into Richard Wright." Ellison met Wright through Hughes, "when he hadn't yet begun to be famous." He learned much of his craft under Wright, who encouraged him to write and introduced him to the work of Dostoyevsky, Conrad, and Henry James. These masters, in addition to Joyce, Faulkner, Hemingway, Lawrence, and the Greek classics, seem to have been the major influences on Ellison. Ellin Horowitz described *Invisible Man* as "the result of a union between the Negro folk culture (blues, jazz, folk tales, the Bible, etc.) and the modern Western art of such men as Joyce and Eliot." Albert J. Murray believes that "*Invisible Man* is *par excellence* the literary extension of the blues. It was as if Ellison had taken an everyday twelve-bar blues tune (by a man from down South sitting in a manhole up North in New York singing and signifying about how he got there) and scored it for a full orchestra."

Corry theorizes that *Invisible Man,* seven years in the writing, occupies a position, both chronologically and ideologically, between the very different kinds of protest which characterised the Depression years and the beginning civil rights movement of the early fifties. Ellison has been reproached by Irving Howe and by numerous black militants for not writing as a political activist, for lacking social consciousness. At a time when many blacks, especially the young, are denying all influences of American culture, Ellison continues to affirm his identity as a Negro-American, a product of the blending of both cultures. To charges of "Uncle Tomism" he repeatedly asserts his belief in the primacy of the artist's freedom to be an artist. "The problem of becoming an artist is related to that of becoming a man, of becoming visible," he once said. "You need a discipline far more demanding than loyalty to your racial group. . . . The point of our struggle is to be both Negro and American and to bring about that condition in American society in which this would be possible. . . . I've always written out of a sense of the group experience as filtered through my individual experiences, talent, and vision." Chevigny notes that "Ellison's inventiveness appeals to the mind and imagination, not the stomach queasy with guilt. . . . But when, in the first and fullest section [of *Shadow and Act*], Ellison searches the problems of being an artist and of American literature, he tells us the most about being a Negro and about American society." In a recent conversation with James Alan McPherson, Ellison said: "I'm saying that I'm in a better position to see certain things about American literature or American culture precisely because I'm a black man; but I'm not restricted by those frames which have been imposed upon us. I think that one has to keep this constantly in mind; otherwise, somebody else is going to be interpreting your experience for you, and you're going to be repeating it. And they might be in error."

Commenting on the future popularity of black writers, Ellison says: "I'm hesitant to make a prediction because so many of them seem to be still caught up at the point of emphasizing *inwardness* without emphasizing the inward outwardness." He agrees with Wright that the most valuable resource available to the black author is his double vision, his simultaneous position "*inside* and *outside* of our culture. These are positions of observation; positions where values can be studied in action. . . . If our black writers are going to become more influential in the broader community, they will do it in terms of style; by imposing a style upon a sufficient area of American life to give other readers a sense that this is true, that here is a revelation of reality."

A highly disciplined artist ("Craft to me is an aspect of morality") and something of a perfectionist, Ellison has been working on his long-awaited second novel for more than a decade. He revealed to McPherson that he now has enough typed manuscripts to publish three novels, but is concerned how the work will hold up as a total structure. Ellison has been extremely reticent about its expected date of publication. Richard Kostelanetz notes that one old friend said: "Ralph is insanely ambitious. He actually writes quickly, but won't release this book until he is sure that it is the greatest American novel ever written."

BIOGRAPHICAL/CRITICAL SOURCES—Books: Harvey Breit, *The Writer Observed,* World Publishing, 1956; Joseph W. Waldmeir, editor, *Recent American Fiction: Some Critical Views,* Houghton, 1963; Richard Kostelanetz, editor, *On Contemporary Literature,* Avon, 1964; Walter Allen, *The Modern Novel in Britain and the United States,* Dutton, 1965; Jonathan Baumbach, *Studies in the Contemporary American Novel,* New York University Press, 1965; Herbert Hill, editor, *Anger and Beyond: The Negro Writer in the United States,* Harper, 1966; Seymour L. Gross and John Edward Hardy, editors, *Images of the Negro in American Literature,* University of Chicago Press, 1966; Donald B. Gibson, editor,

Five Black Writers, New York University Press, 1970; John M. Reilly, editor, *Twentieth Century Interpretations of "Invisible Man"*, Prentice-Hall, 1970; Ronald Gottesman, compiler, *The Merrill Studies in "Invisible Man"*, Merrill, 1971.

Articles: *Saturday Review*, April 12, 1952, January 1, 1955; *New York Times Book Review*, April 13, 1952; *Nation*, May 10, 1952, November 9, 1964, September 20, 1965; *Atlantic*, July, 1952, December, 1970; *Commentary*, November, 1953; *Paris Review*, spring, 1955, spring-summer, 1957; *Time*, February 1, 1963; *Newsweek*, August 12, 1963, October 26, 1964; *Tamarach Review*, summer, 1964; *Village Voice*, November 19, 1964; *Motive*, April, 1966; *New York Times Magazine*, November 20, 1966; *Chicago Review*, Number 2, 1967; *Harper's*, March, 1967; *Critique*, Number 2, 1968; *Shenandoah*, summer, 1969; *English Journal*, September, 1969; *Modern Fiction Studies*, winter, 1969-70; *Phylon*, spring, 1970.

*   *   *

ELLISTON, Valerie Mae (Watkinson)   1929-
(Valerie Watkinson)

PERSONAL: Born May 16, 1929, in Sydney, New South Wales, Australia; daughter of Raymond Leslie and Sonoma Muriel (McKay) Watkinson; married Kenneth Edward Elliston (a sales manager), January 27, 1951; children: Mark Ashleigh, Brett Edward Raymond. *Education:* Attended University of Sydney and Metropolitan Business College, Sydney, Australia. *Politics:* Liberal. *Religion:* Church of England. *Agent:* Curtis Brown Ltd., 60 East 56th St., New York, N.Y. 10022.

CAREER: Started as copy girl on *Australian Women's Weekly*, Sydney, then worked for *Sydney Sunday Telegraph* and *Sydney Daily Telegraph*; Hansen Rubensohn, Sydney, copywriter, 1951-53. *Member:* Mystery Writers of America.

WRITINGS—Under name Valerie Watkinson: *The Sped Arrow* (novel), Scribner, 1964. Contributor of short stories to magazines in Australia, United States, England, Canada, and Finland.

WORK IN PROGRESS: A novel; short stories.

AVOCATIONAL INTERESTS: Gardening, conversation, the sea, good food, books, Tschaikovsky, and cats.

*   *   *

ELSNER, Gisela   1937-

PERSONAL: Born May 2, 1937, in Nuremberg, Germany; daughter of Richard (an engineer) and Gertrud (Buch) Elsner. *Education:* Attended University of Vienna. *Residence:* London, England.

CAREER: Writer. *Awards, honors:* Julius Campe Stipendium, 1964; Prix Formentor, 1964, for *Die Riesenzwerge*.

WRITINGS: (With Klaus Roehler) *Triball: Lebens laufeines erstaunlichen Mannes*, Walter Olten, c.1956; *Die Riesenzwerge, ein Beitrag*, Rowohlt, 1964, translation by Joel Carmichael published as *The Giant Dwarfs: A Contribution*, Grove, 1965; *Der Nachwuchs*, Rowohlt, 1968. Contributor of short stories to periodicals.

SIDELIGHTS: Miss Elsner, a proponent of the "new novel," has drawn acclaim for her first book (not a novel, she says, but a "contribution"). The *Times Literary Supplement* reviewer believes that she has learned much from a fellow-countryman, Gunter Grass, namely "the use of incomplete or meaningless phrases in dialogue to render the inarticulateness or, more often, the utterly brainless, banal, mechanical conformism of a character, [and] the use of almost unbearably pedantic elaboration in the description of trivial scenes and events." (Miss Elsner herself would rather acknowledge the influence of Franz Kafka.) Though she eliminates the inner life of her characters, this very exclusion, according to the *Times Literary Supplement* writer, "amounts to a *tour de force* carried off with uncommon rigour and skill."

She has traveled to France, Italy, Spain, Portugal, Scandinavia, Switzerland, and Austria.

BIOGRAPHICAL/CRITICAL SOURCES: Le *Figaro Litteraire*, May 7-13, 1964; *L'Express*, May 14, 1964; *Times Literary Supplement*, June 4, 1964; *Books Abroad*, summer, 1969.

*   *   *

ELTING, Mary   1906-
(Benjamin Brewster, Davis Cole, Campbell Tatham, Michael Gorham)

PERSONAL: Born June 21, 1906, in Creede, Colo.; daughter of Charles T. (a merchant) and Clara (Shawhan) Elting; married Franklin Folsom (a writer), September, 1936; children: Michael, Rachel. *Education:* University of Colorado, B.A., 1927; attended University of Strasbourg, Strasbourg, France, 1929-30. *Residence:* Roosevelt, N.J. *Agent:* Evelyn Singer, 41 West 96th St., New York, N.Y. 10025.

CAREER: Member of editorial staff, *Forum* magazine, 1927-29, *Golden Book Magazine*, 1931-35. *Member:* Authors Guild, Phi Beta Kappa, Horticultural Society of New York, Archeological Society of New Jersey.

WRITINGS—Nonfiction: (With Robert T. Weaver) *Soldiers, Sailors, Fliers and Marines* (Junior Literary Guild selection), Doubleday, 1943; (under pseudonym Campbell Tatham) *The First Flying Book*, F. Watts, 1944; (with others) *Battles: How They Are Won* (Junior Literary Guild selection), Doubleday, 1944; (with Margaret Gossett) *We Are the Government*, Doubleday, 1945, revised edition, 1967; (under pseudonym Campbell Tatham) *The First Book of Boats*, F. Watts, 1945; (with Gossett) *The Lollypop Factory—and Lots of Others* (Junior Literary Guild selection), Doubleday, 1946; *Trucks at Work*, Garden City, 1946, revised edition, Harvey House, 1962; *Trains at Work*, Garden City, 1947, revised edition, Harvey House, 1962; (under pseudonym Campbell Tatham) *The First Book of Trains*, F. Watts, 1948; (with Gossett) *Now You're Cookin'*, Westminster, 1948; *Who Lives on the Farm?*, Wonder Books, 1949; (under pseudonym Campbell Tatham) *The First Book of Automobiles*, F. Watts, 1949.

(Under pseudonym Benjamin Brewster) *The First Book of Baseball*, F. Watts, 1950, 4th revised edition published as *Baseball*, 1970; (under pseudonym Benjamin Brewster) *The First Book of Indians*, F. Watts, 1950, revised edition, Mayflower, 1960; (under pseudonym Benjamin Brewster) *The First Book of Cowboys*, F. Watts, 1950; *Wheels and Noises*, Wonder Books, 1950; (under pseudonym Benjamin Brewster) *Columbus*, Whitman, 1951; *The First Book of Nurses*, F. Watts, 1951; (under pseudonym Michael Gorham) *The Real Book About Abraham Lincoln*, Garden City, 1951; (under pseudonym Davis Cole) *The Real Book About Trains*, Garden City, 1951; (under pseudonym Benjamin Brewster) *The First Book of Firemen*, F. Watts, 1951; (under pseudonym Benjamin Brewster) *The Big Book of the Real Circus*, Grosset, 1951; *The Big Book of Real Boats and Ships*, Grosset, 1951; (under pseudonym Campbell Tatham) *The First Book of Trucks*, F. Watts, 1952; (under pseudonym Michael Gorham) *The Real Book of American Tall Tales*, Garden City, 1952; (under pseudonym Michael Gorham) *The Real Book About Cowboys*, Garden City, 1952; (under pseudonym Benjamin Brewster) *The First Book of Eskimos*, F. Watts, 1952; *Machines at Work*, Garden City, 1953, revised edition, Harvey House, 1962; (under pseudonym Michael Gorham) *The Real Book of Great*

American Journeys, Garden City, 1953; (under pseudonym Michael Gorham) *The Real Book About Indians,* Garden City, 1953; *Ships at Work,* Garden City, 1953, revised edition, Harvey House, 1962; (with Felix Sutton) *The Big Book of the Real Circus* (adapted from the 1951 book), Grosset, 1958; *The Answer Book,* Grosset, 1959, abridged edition published as *Arrow Book of Science Facts,* Scholastic Book Services, 1960 (published in England as *Why? What? Where?: Answers to 300 Questions Children Ask,* Odhams, 1962).

(With husband, Franklin Folsom) *The Story of Archeology in the Americas,* Harvey House, 1960; *Flowers and What They Are,* Whitman, 1961; *Answers and More Answers: Answers to Questions That Every Child Asks,* Grosset, 1961, abridged edition published as *Arrow Book of Answers,* Scholastic Book Services, 1962 (published in England as *Every Child's Answer Book,* Odhams, 1963); *Arrow Book of Nurses* (adapted from *The First Book of Nurses),* Scholastic Book Services, 1963; (with son, Michael Folsom) *The Secret Story of Pueblo Bonito,* Harvey House, 1963; *Question and Answer Book,* Grosset, 1963; (with Franklin Folsom) *The Answer Book of Geography,* Grosset, 1964; *Aircraft at Work,* Harvey House, 1964; *How the Animals Get to the Zoo,* Grosset, 1964; *Water Come, Water Go,* Harvey House, 1964; *Spacecraft at Work,* Harvey House, 1965; (with Franklin Folsom) *The Answer Book of History,* Grosset, 1966; (with Franklin Folsom) *Flags of All Nations and the People Who Live Under Them,* Grosset, 1967, revised edition, 1970; (with Michael Folsom) *The Mysterious Grain,* M. Evans, 1967; *What's Going On Here?,* Grosset, 1968; (with Franklin Folsom) *If You Lived in the Days of the Wild Mammoth Hunters,* Four Winds, 1968; *All Aboard!,* Four Winds, 1969, revised edition, 1971; *The Hopi Way,* M. Evans, 1969.

(with Robin A. McKown) *Mongo Homecoming,* M. Evans, 1970; *Still More Answers,* Grosset, 1971; (with Judith Steigler) *Helicopters at Work,* Harvey House, 1972.

Fiction: *Smoky, the Baby Goat,* Whitman, 1947; (with Grossett) *Patch,* Doubleday, 1948; *Speckles and the Triplets,* Whitman, 1949; *Pussycat's Secret,* Whitman, 1949; *Runaway Ginger,* Whitman, 1949; (under pseudonym Benjamin Brewster) *The Baby Elephant,* Wonder Books, 1950; (under pseudonym Benjamin Brewster) *It's a Secret,* Wonder Books, 1950; *The Big Red Pajama Wagon,* Whitman, 1950; *Lady, the Little Blue Mare,* Whitman, 1950; *Wishes and Secrets,* Bobbs-Merrill, 1956; *The Helicopter Mystery,* Harvey House, 1958; *Miss Polly's Animal School,* Grosset, 1961; *The Mysterious Milk Robber, and Other Stories,* Harvey House, 1970.

Translator: *Manon Lascaut,* 1931; (with E.I. Holt) Ferenc Kormendi, *Escape to Life,* Morrow, 1933.

SIDELIGHTS: Mary Elting belongs to a writing family, for her husband, Franklin Folsom, is also a prolific author of books for young people; they have worked on many books together, although authorship is usually "somewhat arbitrarily assigned to one or the other," according to their agent. Even their children, now grown, have participated in many books, according to Mrs. Folsom. She told *CA,* "when the children were young, they too were enthusiastic travellers and campers, and they used to deny indignantly that they were tourists. They were researchers, they said, and the fact is that our books usually do reflect the adventures that we and they have had together."

Mrs. Folsom is always pleased to hear from her readers, and likes to answer their letters, too, but, she wrote *CA,* "I find that I often do not mail an answer as soon as I should because the writer did not enclose a carefully self-addressed envelope. Somehow, the task of deciphering the sometimes obscure address on the letter takes that final minute or two of time I never feel I can really spare." Addressed envelopes would help boys and girls get faster replies to their letters. "No stamps on the envelopes, of course, because I realize that eight cents is a lot for many kids. Just something to expedite the reply."

BIOGRAPHICAL/CRITICAL SOURCES: *Best Sellers,* March 1, 1970; *Library Journal,* March 15, 1970, July, 1970.

* * *

ELTON, Geoffrey R(udolph) 1921-

PERSONAL: Surname originally Ehrenberg; born August 17, 1921, in Tuebingen, Germany; son of Victor L. (a classical scholar) and Eva (Sommer) Ehrenberg; married Sheila Lambert (a historian), August 30, 1952. *Education:* Attended Rydal School, Colwyn Bay, Wales, 1939-40; University of London, B.A., Ph.D.; Cambridge University, M.A., Litt.D. *Office:* Clare College, Cambridge University, Cambridge, England.

CAREER: University of Glasgow, Glasgow, Scotland, assistant in history, 1948-49; Cambridge University, Cambridge, England, assistant lecturer, then lecturer in history, 1949-63, fellow and director of studies in history at Clare College, 1954-67, reader in Tudor studies, 1963-67, professor of English constitutional history, 1967—. Cambridge University Press, syndic. *Military service:* British Army, World War II, Infantry and Intelligence; became sergeant. *Member:* British Academy (fellow), Royal Historical Society (fellow).

WRITINGS: *The Tudor Revolution in Government: Administrative Changes in the Reign of Henry VIII,* Cambridge University Press, 1953; *England under the Tudors,* Putnam, 1955; *Star Chamber Stories,* Methuen, 1958; (editor) *New Cambridge Modern History,* Volume II, Cambridge University Press, 1958; (editor) *The Reformation, 1520-1559,* Cambridge University Press, 1958; (editor) *The Tudor Constitution: Documents and Commentary,* Cambridge University Press, 1960; *Henry VIII: An Essay in Revision,* Routledge & Kegan Paul, 1962; (editor) *Ideas and Institutions: Renaissance and Reformation,* Macmillan, 1963, 2nd edition, 1968; (with George Kitson Clark) *Guide to Research Facilities in History in the Universities of Great Britain and Ireland,* Cambridge University Press, 1963, 2nd edition, 1965; *Reformation Europe, 1517-1559,* Collins, 1963, Meridian Books, 1964; (editor) Albert Frederick Pollard, *Wolsey,* Collins, 1965; *The Practice of History,* Methuen, 1967, Crowell, 1968; *The Future of the Past: An Inaugural Lecture,* Cambridge University Press, 1968; *The Body of the Whole Realm: Parliament and Representation in Medieval and Tudor England,* University Press of Virginia, 1969; *England 1200-1640,* Cornell University Press, 1969; *Political History: Principles and Practice,* Basic Books, 1970; *Modern British Historians on British History, 1485-1945: A Critical Bibliography, 1945-1969,* Methuen, 1970, Cornell University Press, 1971; *Twenty-Five Years of Modern British History: A Bibliograpical Survey 1945-1969,* British Book Centre, 1971; *Policy and Police: The Enforcement of the Reformation in the Age of Cromwell,* Cambridge University Press, 1972. Contributor to historical journals.

WORK IN PROGRESS: Studies on the reign of Henry VIII, especially concerning the enforcement of treason and heresy laws, and on the King's Council between 1485 and 1547.

BIOGRAPHICAL/CRITICAL SOURCES: *Listener,* January 11, 1968; *South Atlantic Quarterly,* summer 1968; *Books and Bookmen,* June, 1969; *Spectator,* S⸱ ⸱⸱er 27, 1969; *Observer Review,* November 16, 196⸱ *Journal,* July, 1970; *New Statesman,* Septembe⸱ *Times Literary Supplement,* October 16, 197⸱

EMMERICH, Andre 1924-

PERSONAL: Surname is pronounced Emmerik; born October 11, 1924; son of Hugo and Lily (Marx) Emmerich; married Constance Marantz, August 25, 1958; children: Adam Oliver, Tobias David Hugo, Noah Nicholas. Education: Oberlin College, B.A., 1944. Home: 1060 Fifth Ave., New York, N.Y. 10028. Office: Andre Emmerich Gallery, Inc., 41 East 57th St., New York, N.Y. 10022.

CAREER: Member of staff of Time International, Life International, New York Herald Tribune, all New York, N.Y., and of Realities, Paris, France, 1948-53; Andre Emmerich Gallery, New York, N.Y., owner, 1954—. Member: Art Dealers Association of America (vice-president, 1970—).

WRITINGS: Art Before Columbus: The Art of Ancient Mexico from the Archaic Villages of the Second Millenium to the Splendor of the Aztecs, Simon & Schuster, 1963; The Sweat of the Sun and the Tears of the Moon: Gold and Silver in Pre-Columbian Art, University of Washington Press, 1964. Contributor of some twenty articles to American Heritage, American Mercury, Art in America, and other periodicals.

AVOCATIONAL INTERESTS: Archaeology, photography.

*   *   *

EMMET, Dorothy Mary 1904-

PERSONAL: Born September 29, 1904, in England; daughter of Cyril William (a clergyman) and Gertrude (Weir) Emmet. Education: Attended St. Mary's Hall, Brighton, England; Lady Margaret Hall, Oxford, B.A., 1927, M.A., 1931; Radcliffe College, A.M., 1930. Religion: Church of England. Home: 21 Yew Tree Lane, Manchester 2, England. Office: The University, Manchester 13, England.

CAREER: University of Manchester, Manchester, England, lecturer, 1932-46, professor of philosophy, 1946—.

WRITINGS: Whitehead's Philosophy of Organism, Macmillan (London), 1932, 2nd edition, St. Martin's, 1966; Philosophy and Faith, S.C.M. Press, 1936; (editor and author of introduction) John Leofric Stocks, Reason and Intuition, and Other Essays, Oxford University Press, 1939; The Nature of Metaphysical Thinking, Macmillan, 1945; The Foundations of a Free University (pamphlet), S.C.M. Press, 1946; Presuppositions and Finite Truths, Geoffrey Cumberlege, 1949; Alfred North Whitehead, 1861-1947, Oxford University Press, 1949; Coleridge on the Growth of the Mind, [Manchester], 1952; Function, Purpose and Powers: Some Concepts in the Study of Individuals and Societies, St. Martin's, 1958, 2nd edition, Temple University Press, 1971; Justice and the Law, Lindsey Press, 1963; Rules, Roles, and Relations, St. Martin's, 1966; (editor and author of introduction with Alasdair MacIntyre) Sociological Theory and Philosophical Analysis, Macmillan, 1970.

WORK IN PROGRESS: Relations between sociology and ethics.

*   *   *

ENDACOTT, M(arie) Violet 1915-

PERSONAL: Born August 4, 1915, in London, England; daughter of William Leonard (a customs and excise man) and Ida Alberta (a teacher; maiden name, Bloor) Endacott. Education: Homerton College, teacher's certificate, 1936; College of Handicraft, Froebel Trainer's Diploma, 1953; University of London, Academic Diploma in Education, 1956. Politics: Socialist. Religion: Church of England.

CAREER: Teacher in infant school, Middlesex, England, 1936-38; head of art and craft department of secondary school, Middlesex, England, 1938-48; lecturer in art and craft at Weymouth Teacher Training College, Weymouth, England, 1948-49, and Newland Park Teacher Training College, Newland Park, England, 1949-53; Eastbourne Training College, Eastbourne, England, now principal lecturer in needlecraft. Member: Crafts Council of Great Britain. Awards, honors: College of Handicraft fellowship, 1954, for research on teaching handwriting.

WRITINGS: Needlecraft in Schools Today, Blackie & Son, 1961; Design in Embroidery, J. Murray, 1963, Macmillan, 1964; Introducing Needlecraft: A Handbook for Teachers in Primary Schools, Parrish, 1966; Instructions in Needlecraft, Museum Press, 1966, SportShelf, 1967. Contributor of articles on teaching of embroidery and needlecraft to journals in England.

AVOCATIONAL INTERESTS: Comparative education (has visited educational institutions in United States, Soviet Union, Norway, Denmark, and Germany), entertaining, reading.

*   *   *

ENGLEMAN, Finis E(wing) 1895-

PERSONAL: Born August 19, 1895, in Dunnegan, Mo.; son of George W. and Malissa (Hopper) Engleman; married Ruby Lane, November 17, 1921; children: Virginia (Mrs. Adolf Dehn), Nancy (Mrs. Frederick Lowe). Education: Southwest Missouri State College, B.S., 1917; University of Missouri, M.A., 1926; Yale University, Ph.D., 1934. Politics: Independent. Religion: Protestant. Home and office: 115 South Fernwood Ave., Pitman, N.J. 08071.

CAREER: Teacher, principal, and superintendent of schools in Missouri, 1919-32; Yale University, New Haven, Conn., 1932-34, began as instructor, became lecturer; New Haven College, West Haven, Conn., associate director, 1933-34; Southern Connecticut State College (formerly New Haven State Teachers College), New Haven, president, 1935-43; State of Connecticut, deputy commissioner of education, 1945-48, commissioner, 1948-56; American Association of School Administrators, Washington, D.C., executive secretary, 1956-63, executive secretary emeritus, 1964—. Head of U.S. delegation, International Conference on Education, Geneva, Switzerland, 1951, 1956, 1957; U.S. delegate, UNESCO, Paris, France, 1958. Military service: U.S. Naval Reserve, naval aviator, 1917-19; became flight ensign; returned to active duty, 1943-45; became commander.

MEMBER: National Education Association, American Association of School Administrators, Phi Delta Kappa, Kappa Delta Pi, Rotary International. Awards, honors: Litt.D., Trenton State College, 1960; LL.D., University of Maine; American Education award, 1964.

WRITINGS: (With Julia Salmon) Airways, Heath, 1931; (with Salmon and Wilma McKemy) Scales and Fins, Heath, 1938; (with J.C. Matthews) Progress Report on Seven Teachers Colleges Participating in the Cooperative Study of Teacher Education, American Association of Teachers Colleges and Commission on Teacher Education of American Council on Education, 1941; Music and Public Education, Music Educators National Conference, c.1961; (with Shirley Cooper and William J. Ellena) Vignettes on Theory and Practice of School Administration, Macmillan, 1963; The Consent of the Governed, Northeast Missouri State Teachers College, 1963; (with others) American Dependents' Schools, Near East and South Asia: A Survey Report, National Education Association, 1964; The Pleasure Was Mine: 70 Years in Education, Interstate, 1971. Author of bulletins, pamphlets, and editorials published by American Association of

School Administrators and State of Connecticut. Contributor of articles to magazines.

WORK IN PROGRESS: A study of roles and responsibilities of school boards; gathering data for speeches on history of school administration.

* * *

ENGLISH, Maurice 1909-

PERSONAL: Born October 21, 1909, in Chicago, Ill.; son of Michael and Agnes (Sexton) English; married Fanita Blumberg (a psychotherapist), April 25, 1945; children: Jonathan Brian, Deirdre Elena. *Education:* Harvard University, A.B. (magna cum laude), 1933. *Home:* 1530 Locust St., Philadelphia, Pa. 19102.

CAREER: Foreign correspondent in France and Spain, 1938-41; editor and publisher of *Chicago Magazine,* 1953-1956; University of Chicago Press, Chicago, Ill., managing editor, 1961-63, senior editor, 1963-69; Temple University Press, Philadelphia, Pa., founder and director, 1969—. *Member:* American Association of University Presses, Phi Beta Kappa, Harvard Club (New York), Franklin Inn Club (Philadelphia). *Awards, honors:* Ferguson Award, Friends of Literature, 1964, for *Midnight in the Century;* Fulbright fellowship in creative writing, 1966-67.

WRITINGS: (Editor) *The Testament of Stone,* Northwestern University Press, 1963; *Midnight in the Century* (poems), Prairie School Press, 1964; (translator with others) *The Selected Poems of Eugenio Montale,* New Directions, 1965. Also author of a play "The Saints in Illinois," as yet neither published nor produced. Poetry is anthologized in *The New Yorker Book of Verse,* Harcourt, 1935, *100 Modern Poets,* edited by Selden Rodman, Pelligrini & Cudahy, 1949, *Where Steel Winds Blow,* edited by Robert Cromie, McKay, 1969.

WORK IN PROGRESS: "The Seven Ages," a play; *The Air Strike and Other Poems.*

SIDELIGHTS: English wrote *CA:* "It's better to just write and publish, and not offer all sorts of explanations, which rarely go beyond the first four lines in *Midnight in the Century:* 'Since no one is someone without a disguise / And the truths of the parlor in the bedroom are lies / And my everyday self is a shoddy disgrace, / I have put on these masks to show you my face.' " *Avocational interests:* Translating from French, Italian, and Spanish.

* * *

EPP, Margaret A(gnes)
(Agnes Goossen)

EDUCATION: Graduate of Bethany Bible Institute, Hepburn, Saskatchewan, Canada; additional study at Prairie Bible Institute, Three Hills, Alberta. *Home:* P.O. Box 178, Waldheim, Saskatchewan, Canada.

CAREER: Writer, mainly of books for juniors and teenagers.

WRITINGS: Peppermint Sue, Moody, 1955; *North to Sakitawa,* Moody, 1955; *Light on Twin Rocks* [and] *Music in the Wapawekkas,* Moody, 1956; *The Long Chase* [and] *Budworms and Tepees,* Moody, 1956; *Vicki Arthur,* Moody, 1956; *The Sign of the Tumbling T,* Moody, 1956; *Come Back, Jonah* [and] *The Secret of Larrabie Lake,* Moody, 1956; *Sap's Running,* Moody, 1956; *Thirty Days Hath September* (story collection), Moody, 1956; *Canadian Holiday,* Moody, 1956; *Shades of Great Aunt Martha,* Moody, 1956; *Anita and the Driftwood House,* Moody, 1957; *All in the April Evening* (story collection), Moody, 1959; *No Hand Sam* (missionary stories), Mennonite Publishing House, 1959; (under pseudonym Agnes Goossen) *Mystery at Pony Ranch,* Moody, 1963; *But God Hath Chosen: The Story of John and Mary Dyck,* Mennonite Publishing House, 1963; *Come to My Party* (nonfiction), Zondervan, 1964; *A Fountain Sealed,* Zondervan, 1965; *The Brannans of Bar Lazy B,* Moody, 1965; *Trouble on the Flying M,* Moody, 1966; *The North Wind and the Caribou,* Moody, 1966; *Search Down the Yukon,* Moody, 1967; *Walk in My Woods* (autobiography), Moody, 1967; *Prairie Princess,* Moody, 1967; *No Help Wanted,* Moody, 1968; *The Princess and the Pelican,* Moody, 1968; *This Mountain Is Mine* (biography), Moody, 1969; *The Princess Rides a Panther,* Moody, 1970; *Call of the Wahoa and Other Adventures,* Moody, 1971; *Great Frederick and Friends,* Moody, 1971; *Runaway at the Running K,* Moody, 1972.

SIDELIGHTS: In 1971 Miss Epp participated in a tour of mission fields in thirty countries. Most of her books have also been serialized.

* * *

EPSTEIN, Samuel 1909-
(Adam Allen and Douglas Coe, joint pseudonyms with Beryl Williams Epstein; Bruce Campbell, Martin Colt, Charles Strong)

PERSONAL: Born November 22, 1909, in Boston, Mass.; son of Joseph David and Sarah (Gershofsky) Epstein; married Beryl M. Williams (an author), April 26, 1938. *Education:* Rutgers University, Litt.B., 1932. *Agent:* McIntosh & Otis, Inc., 18 East 41st St., New York, N.Y. 10017.

CAREER: Author, 1936—. *Military service:* U.S. Army, 1944-46. *Member:* Authors League.

WRITINGS: Peter Platypus, Speller, 1946; (with David W. De Armand) *How to Develop, Print and Enlarge Pictures,* Grosset, 1950, revised edition, 1971.

With wife, Beryl Williams Epstein: *Miracles from Microbes: The Road to Streptomycin,* Rutgers University Press, 1946; *The Great Houdini, Magician Extraordinary,* Messner, 1950; *William Crawford Gorgas: Tropic Fever Fighter,* Messner, 1953; *The Rocket Pioneers: On the Road to Space,* Messner, 1955, reissued with an introduction by Wernher von Braun, 1958 (published in England as *Rocket Pioneers,* Lutterworth, 1957; *Francis Marion, Swamp Fox of the Revolution,* Messner, 1956; *Young Faces in Fashion,* Lippincott, 1956; *The Andrews Raid; or, The Great Locomotive Chase,* Coward, 1956; *Prehistoric Animals,* F. Watts, 1957; *Jacknife for a Penny,* Coward, 1958; *Change for a Penny,* Coward, 1959; *George Washington Carver, Negro Scientist,* Garrard, 1960; *Plant Explorer, David Fairchild,* Messner, 1961; *Grandpa's Wonderful Glass,* Wonder Books, 1962; *Junior Science Book of Seashells,* Garrard, 1963; *Pioneer Oceanographer: Alexander Agassiz,* Messner, 1963; *The Story of the International Red Cross,* Thomas Nelson, 1963; *Spring Holidays: A Holiday Book,* Garrard, 1964; *Hurricane Guest,* Random House, 1964; *Medicine from Microbes: The Story of Antibiotics,* Messner, 1965; *Baseball: Hall of Fame,* Garrard, 1965; *The Game of Baseball,* Garrard, 1965; *Young Paul Revere's Boston,* Garrard, 1966; *The Sacramento: Golden River of California,* Garrard, 1968; *European Folk Festivals: A Holiday Book,* Garrard, 1968; *Harriet Tubman: Guide to Freedom,* Garrard, 1968; *The Picture Life of Franklin Delano Roosevelt,* F. Watts, 1968; *Who Says You Can't?,* Coward, 1969; *Take This Hammer,* Hawthorn, 1969; *Who Needs Holes?,* Hawthorn, 1970; *Enrico Fermi: Father of Atomic Power,* Garrard, 1970; *Scientific Instruments: How To Build and Use Them,* Franklin Publishing, 1970; *Michael Faraday: Apprentice to Science,* Garrard, 1971; *Winston Churchill, Lion of Britain,* Garrard, 1971; *Pick It Up, Friday* House, 1971; *Charles DeGaulle: Defender of* Garrard, 1973.

"Real Book" series, with B.W. Epstein; all published by Garden City Books: *The Real Book About Inventions*, 1951, revised edition, 1961; *... About Benjamin Franklin*, 1952; *... About Pirates*, 1952; *... About Alaska*, 1952, revised edition, 1961; *... About Spies*, 1953 (published in England as *Real Book of Spies*, edited by Helen Hoke and Patrick Pringle, Dobson, 1959); *... About the Sea*, 1954; *... About Submarines*, 1954, revised edition, 1962.

"First Book" series with B.W. Epstein; all published by F. Watts: *First Book of Electricity*, 1953, revised edition, 1966; *... of Words, Their Family Histories*, 1954; *... of Hawaii*, 1954; *... of Printing*, 1955, revised edition, 1972; *... of Glass*, 1955; *... of Mexico*, 1955, revised edition, 1967; *... of Codes and Ciphers*, 1956; *... of Italy*, 1958, revised edition, 1972; *... of Maps and Globes*, 1959; *... of Measurement*, 1960; *... of the Ocean*, 1961; *... of Washington, D.C., The Nation's Capital*, 1961; *... of Teaching Machines*, 1961; *... of Switzerland*, 1964; *... of World Health Organization*, 1964; *... of News*, 1965.

"All About" series, with B.W. Epstein; all published by Random House: *All About the Desert*, 1957; *... Prehistoric Cave Men*, 1959; *... Engines and Power*, 1962.

With B.W. Epstein and John Gunther: *Meet North Africa*, Harper, 1956; *Meet South Africa*, Harper, 1958.

With B.W. Epstein under joint pseudonym Adam Allen: *Tin Lizzie*, Stackpole, 1937; *Printer's Devil*, Macmillan, 1939; *Dynamo Farm*, Lippincott, 1942; *Water to Burn*, Lippincott, 1943; *Dollar a Share*, Random House, 1943; *New Broome Experiment*, Lippincott, 1944.

Under pseudonym Bruce Campbell, "Ken Holt" series; all published by Grosset: *The Secret of Skeleton Island*, 1949; *The Riddle of the Stone Elephant*, 1949; *The Black Thumb Mystery*, 1950; *The Clue of the Marked Claw*, 1950; *The Clue of the Coiled Cobra*, 1951; *The Secret of Hangman's Inn,* 1951; *The Mystery of the Iron Box*, 1952; *The Clue of the Phantom Car*, 1953; *The Mystery of the Galloping Horse*, 1954; *The Mystery of the Green Flame*, 1955; *The Mystery of the Grinning Tiger*, 1956; *The Mystery of the Vanishing Magician*, 1957; *The Mystery of the Shattered Glass*, 1958; *The Mystery of the Invisible Enemy*, 1959; *The Mystery of Gallows Cliff*, 1960; *The Clue of the Silver Scorpion*, 1961; *The Mystery of the Plumed Serpent*, 1962; *The Mystery of the Sultan's Scimitar*, 1963.

With B.W. Epstein under joint pseudonym Douglas Coe: *Marconi, Pioneer of Radio*, Messner, 1943; *Road to Alaska: The Story of the Alaska Highway*, Messner, 1943; *Burma Road*, Messner, 1946.

Under pseudonym Martin Colt: *The Secret of Baldhead Mountain*, Messner, 1946; *The Riddle of the Hidden Pesos*, Messner, 1948.

Under pseudonym Charles Strong: *Stranger at the Inlet*, Messner, 1946 (published in England under pseudonym Martin Colt, Museum Press, 1949).

SIDELIGHTS: Epstein told CA: "My wife and I wrote our first book for young people before we were married. We liked writing it so much that we just went on writing books.

"Most of the books we write, either in collaboration or individually, are nonfiction, probably because we are endlessly curious about people, and things, and events. Sometimes we get a book idea from reading about something or someone in a newspaper. We wrote *Who Says You Can't?* after reading reports of a number of determined individuals who decided that it was possible to fight—and defeat—such overpowering adversaries as the automobile industry, the drug industry, powerful government agencies, and intrenched political machines."

BIOGRAPHICAL/CRITICAL SOURCES: *Best Sellers*, May 1, 1969; *Saturday Review*, May 10, 1969; *Commonweal*, May 23, 1969; *Library Journal*, July, 1969.

* * *

ERB, Paul 1894-

PERSONAL: Born April 26, 1894, in Newton, Kan.; son of Tillman M. (a minister) and Lizzie (Hess) Erb; married Alta Mae Eby (a librarian), May 26, 1917; children: Winifred (Mrs. Milford Paul), John Delbert. *Education:* Hesston College, student, 1915-16; Bethel College, North Newton, Kan., B.A., 1918; State University of Iowa, M.A., 1923; summer study at University of Kansas, University of Chicago. *Politics:* Independent. *Home:* Mennonite Apartments, Scottdale, Pa. 15683. *Office:* Mennonite Publishing House, Scottdale, Pa. 15683.

CAREER: Ordained to ministry of Mennonite Church, 1919; Hesston College, Hesston, Kan., 1917-41, started as instructor, became professor of English, then dean, 1933-41; Goshen College, Goshen, Ind., professor of English, 1941-45; Mennonite Publishing House, Scottdale, Pa., editor of *Gospel Herald*, 1944-62, book editor, 1959-65. Visiting professor of English, Eastern Mennonite College, 1969-71. Mennonite Church, executive secretary of General Conference, 1954-61, president of Board of Education, 1962-65, field representative of Board of Missions 1962-64.

WRITINGS: *The Alpha and the Omega: A Restatement of the Christian Hope in Christ's Coming*, Herald Press, 1955; (with Harold S. Bender) *Later History and Poetry*, revised edition, 1956; *Old Testament Poetry and Prophecy*, 2nd edition, Herald Press, 1956; *Don't Park Here: Discussions on Dynamic Christian Living*, Herald Press, 1962; (with Henry S. Smith) *Mennonites and Their Heritage*, Herald Press, 1964; *Our Neighbors South and North: A Textbook for the Study of Mennonite Missions on the Perimeter of North America*, Herald Press, 1965; (editor) *From the Mennonite Pulpit*, Herald Press, 1965; *We Believe: An Interpretation of the 1963 Mennonite Confession of Faith for the Younger Generation*, Herald Press, 1969; *Orie O. Miller*, Herald Press, 1969. Co-editor, *Family Worship*, 1962-68.

WORK IN PROGRESS: *History of the South Central Mennonite Conference*, for Herald Press.

* * *

ERICKSON, M(elvin) E(ddy) 1918-

PERSONAL: Born April 3, 1918, in Tugaske, Saskatchewan, Canada; son of Otto and Alma (Skrove) Erickson; married Lorna Joy Stickle (a secretary); children: Melvin Lloyd, Clare Lavern. *Education:* Canadian Union College, B.Th., 1947; Syracuse University, M.A., 1961. *Religion:* Seventh-day Adventist. *Home:* 4342 Riverwood Cir., Decatur, Ga. 30032. *Office address:* Southern Union Conference of Seventh-day Adventists, Box 849, Decatur, Ga. 30032.

CAREER: Schoolteacher and principal in Canada, 1938-48; Seventh-day Adventists, educational superintendent in Alberta, Canada, 1952-56, in New York, N.Y., 1956-62, with Georgia-Cumberland Conference, Decatur, Ga., 1962-66, secretary-treasurer of Ontario-Quebec Conference, 1966-67, secretary of education of Canadian Union Conference, 1967-70, associate secretary of education of Southern Union Conference, 1970—. *Member:* National Geographic Society, American Association of School Administrators, American Association of Elementary-Kindergarten-Nursery Educators, National Education Association, Association for Supervision and Curriculum Development.

WRITINGS: *Bible Quizzes,* Review & Herald, 1963; *In Tune with God: A Junior Devotional,* Review & Herald, 1966. Also deviser of a game, "Blackout," issued by Review & Herald, 1962, and contributor to Seventh-day Adventist periodicals.

WORK IN PROGRESS: *Pioneer Days in Saskatchewan, Canada.*

* * *

ERLICH, Victor 1914-

PERSONAL: Born November 22, 1914, in Petrograd, Russia; son of Henryk and Sophie (Dubnov) Erlich; married Iza Sznejerson (a social worker), February 27, 1940; children: Henry Anthony, Mark Leo. *Education:* Free Polish University, M.A., 1937; Columbia University, Ph.D., 1951. *Office:* Yale University, New Haven, Conn. 06520.

CAREER: *New Life,* Warsaw, Poland, assistant literary editor, 1937-39; *Yiddish Encyclopedia,* New York, N.Y., research writer, 1942-43; University of Washington, Seattle, assistant professor, later associate professor, 1948-58, professor of Slavic languages and literature, 1958-62, assistant director of Far Eastern and Russian Institute, 1961-62; Yale University, New Haven, Conn., visiting professor of Slavic literature, 1962-63, Bensinger Professor of Russian Literature, 1963—. *Military service:* U.S. Army, 1943-45; received Purple Heart. *Member:* International Association of Slavonic Languages and Literatures (member of executive council), Modern Language Association of America (executive council), American Association for the Advancement of Slavic Studies (board of directors), American Society for Aesthetics, American Council of Learned Societies. *Awards, honors:* Ford Foundation fellow, 1953-54; Guggenheim fellow, 1957-58, 1964; M.A., Yale University, 1963.

WRITINGS: *Russian Formalism: History, Doctrine,* Mouton & Co., 1955, 2nd edition, Humanities, 1966, 3rd edition, Mouton & Co., 1969; (contributor) *For Roman Jakobson,* Mouton & Co., 1956; (contributor) *Stil- und Formprobleme in der Literatur,* [Heidelberg], 1959; (contributor) *Russia Under Khrushchev,* Praeger, 1962; *The Double Image: Concepts of the Poet in Slavic Literatures,* Johns Hopkins Press, 1964; *Gogol,* Yale University Press, 1969. Contributor to *Comparative Literature, Studies in Romanticism, Slavic Review,* other periodicals.

BIOGRAPHICAL/CRITICAL SOURCES: *Library Journal,* March 15, 1970; *Virginia Quarterly Review,* spring, 1970.

* * *

ERTEL, (Richard) James 1922-

PERSONAL: Born December 6, 1922, in Williamsport, Pa.; son of Herbert H. (a social worker) and Hilda (Yount) Ertel; married Jeanette Rubsam, September 1, 1951; children: Christopher J. *Education:* Roanoke College, A.B., 1947; graduate study at Columbia University and University of Virginia. *Politics:* Democrat. *Home:* 1009 Rush St., Chicago, Ill. 60611. *Agent:* Barthold Fles Literary Agency, 507 Fifth Ave., New York, N.Y. 10017. *Office:* Encyclopaedia Britannica Press, 425 North Michigan Ave., Chicago, Ill. 60611.

CAREER: *Wall Street Journal,* New York, N.Y., rewrite, 1948; *Jersey Journal* (Bergen County edition), Hackensack, N.J., city editor, 1954-57; *Daily Mirror,* New York, N.Y., rewrite, 1957; *Golden Book Encyclopedia,* New York, N.Y., managing editor, 1958-59; Encyclopaedia Britannica Press, Chicago, Ill., managing editor, 1959—. *Military service:* U.S. Navy, 1943-46; became lieutenant junior grade. *Member:* Society of Midland Authors, National Society for Programmed Instruction, Chicago Book Clinic.

WRITINGS: *Toads, Frogs, and Salamanders,* Golden Press, 1959; *Colonial Williamsburg,* Golden Press, 1960; *How to Run for Office,* Sterling, 1960; (adapter) *The Ugly Duckling,* Encyclopaedia Britannica, 1962; *Adventures of a Squirrel,* Encyclopaedia Britannica, 1963.

WORK IN PROGRESS: A complete language arts series for elementary grades.

* * *

ESCHER, Franklin (Jr.) 1915-

PERSONAL: Born September 11, 1915, in New York, N.Y.; son of Franklin (a banker and author) and Mildred (Gleason) Escher; married Julia Ross Neel, May 6, 1949; children: Alfred Franklin. *Education:* Yale University, B.A., 1938; Syracuse University, M.S., 1959. *Religion:* Episcopalian. *Office:* Houghton Mifflin Co., 2 Park St., Boston, Mass. 02107.

CAREER: *Young America* (magazine), New York, N.Y., 1946-52, began as associate, became executive editor; 1946-52; L.W. Singer Co. (publishers), Syracuse, N.Y., social studies editor, 1953-64; Houghton Mifflin Co. (publishers), Boston, Mass., senior associate editor for social studies, 1964—. *Military service:* U.S. Army, Intelligence, 1942-45.

WRITINGS: *A Brief History of the United States,* New American Library, 1954, revised edition, 1962.

WORK IN PROGRESS: Text and materials covering American history from its origins through the Revolutionary War period, in an experiment with new inductive thinking approaches to high school American history curriculum.

SIDELIGHTS: *A Brief History of the United States* was sponsored by the U.S. Information Agency, translated into dozens of languages, and circulated world-wide. The author comments: "Social studies texts and curriculum must be broadened to include objective discussion of such controversial issues as civil rights and federal versus states' rights. Educators should be less concerned with crusading than with examining and experimenting."

* * *

ESKOW, Seymour 1924-

PERSONAL: Born April 19, 1924; son of Joseph (a tailor) and Bluma (Kravitz) Eskow; married Lynette Temple, March 4, 1946; children: John, Gary, Richard. *Education:* University of California, Berkeley, A.B., 1943; Columbia University, M.A., 1945; Syracuse University, postgraduate study, 1957—. *Home:* 7 Kevin Dr., Suffern, N.Y. 10901. *Office:* Rockland Community College, 145 College Rd., Suffern, N.Y. 10901.

CAREER: Instructor in English at Fairleigh Dickinson University, Rutherford, N.J., and at City College (now City College of City University of New York), New York, N.Y., 1945-46; Mohawk Valley Community College, Utica, N.Y., teacher of English and chairman of liberal studies, 1946-56, dean, 1956-63; Rockland Community College, Suffern, N.Y., president, 1963—. Consultant to new community colleges. Member of advisory committee, New York State College Proficiency Examination Program. *Member:* American Association of Junior Colleges, Phi Delta Kappa.

WRITINGS: *Barron's Guide to the Two-Year College,* Barron's, 1960, revised edition published as *Barron's Guide to the Two-Year Colleges: All the Facts About 859 Two-Year Colleges,* 1966.

* * *

ETTELDORF, Raymond P. 1911-

PERSONAL: Born August 12, 1911, in Ossian, Iowa; son of Andrew and Regina (Wagner) Etteldorf. *Educa-*

tion: Loras College, A.B., 1934; Gregorian University, Rome, Italy, theology student, 1934-38; Lateran University, J.C.L., 1957. *Office:* 112 Queen's Dr., Wellington 3, New Zealand.

CAREER: Ordained priest of Roman Catholic church, Rome, Italy, 1937; now an archbishop. Curate in Ryan, Iowa, 1937; *Witness* (Catholic periodical), Dubuque, Iowa, managing editor, 1939-45, assistant editor, 1945-46, editor, 1946-51; Sacred Congregation for the Oriental Church, Rome, Italy, official, 1951-64; Papal Society for the Propagation of the Faith, Rome, Secretary General, 1964-68; Prefecture for Economic Affairs, Vatican City, Italy, secretary, 1968; Apostolic delegate to New Zealand and the Islands of the Pacific, with the rank of Titular Archbishop of Tindari, 1968—.

WRITINGS: The Catholic Church in the Middle East, Macmillan, 1959; *The Soul of Greece,* Newman, 1963; *Christian Greece and Rome,* St. Paul Publications, 1965. Contributor to *America, Ave Maria.*

*   *   *

EULLER, John E(lmer) 1926-

PERSONAL: Born January 7, 1926, in Buffalo, N.Y.; son of Elmer J. (a machine designer) and Flora (Darstein) Euller; married Carol J. Nauth (a librarian), September 13, 1947; children: Roald John. *Education:* Pennsylvania State College (now Pennsylvania State University), student, 1944-45; University of Buffalo, B.A., 1949; graduate study at McGill University, 1957, and Pennsylvania State University, 1960. *Home:* 350 Ellinwood Dr., Rochester, N.Y. 14622. *Agent:* Scott Meredith Literary Agency, Inc., 580 Fifth Ave., New York, N.Y. 10036.

CAREER: Cornell Aeronautical Laboratory, Buffalo, N.Y., flight research, 1947; free-lance writer in Alberta and British Columbia, Canada, 1950-54; teacher of physics, and department and curriculum supervisor in New York State secondary schools, 1959—. Free-lance observer with U.S. Navy forces in Antarctica, 1963. *Military service:* U.S. Army, 1944-46. *Member:* Arctic Institute of North America, New Zealand Antarctic Society, Friends of Scott Polar Research Institute, Rochester Authors' Club.

WRITINGS: Arctic World, Abelard, 1958; *Antarctic World,* Abelard, 1960; *Ice, Ships, and Men,* Abelard, 1964; *Our Navy Explorers,* Abelard, 1966; *Whaling World,* Doubleday, 1970. Contributor to *Hunting and Fishing, Bluebook, Saga, Boys' Life, Ships and the Sea,* and other outdoor magazines, 1952-56.

SIDELIGHTS: Euller traveled by ice-breaker from New Zealand to Antarctica in his most recent writing-research trip. His earlier trips were to Alaska, and the subarctics of Canada and Iceland.

BIOGRAPHICAL/CRITICAL SOURCES: Rochester Times Union, October 22, 1963.

*   *   *

EVANS, Constance May 1890-
(Jane Gray, Mairi O'Nair)

PERSONAL: Born March 15, 1890, in Montreal, Quebec, Canada; daughter of James Grainger and Elizabeth (Tweedale) Evans. *Education:* Educated privately; studied music under Julius Benedict, and art under several London teachers. *Politics:* Conservative. *Religion:* Church of England. *Home and office:* Raventhorpe, Carmel Rd. N., Darlington, Durham, England.

CAREER: Before becoming an author, played the piano at local cinema in England, and illustrated stories and posters. Nurse in convalescent home, Voluntary Aid Detachment, World War I. *Member:* Romantic Novelists Association, Authors' Society.

WRITINGS—All romantic novels; all published by Mills & Boon, except as indicated: *The Pattern of a Star,* 1932, *The Hidden Door,* Warne, 1933, *Fortune's Wing Feather,* 1933, *The Cedar-Wood Box,* Warne, 1934, *The Other Wife,* 1934, *Rosemary Comes Home,* 1934, *Secret Daughter,* 1935, *Sandra Goes Downstairs,* 1935, *Green Satin Girl,* 1935, *The Secret River,* Warne, 1936, *Janna, the Actress,* 1936, *Gay Holiday,* 1936, *Second-Hand Cinderella,* 1937, *Lilac for My Lady,* 1937, *Orchid—Ltd.,* 1937, *The Brown Rose,* Warne, 1937, *Dancing Partner,* 1938, *Road of Dreams,* 1938, *April Roses,* 1938, *Secret of the Brown Shed,* R.T.S., 1939, *Blue Silk Slip,* 1939, *At Heart a Rake,* 1939, *Bargain Price,* 1939, *A Lover from London,* 1940, *Part-Time Mother,* 1940, *Holiday Wife,* 1940, *Temptation in Silver,* 1941, *Sweetheart Time,* 1941, *Good-Time Girl,* 1942, *Bachelor Aunt: An Impossible Comedy,* 1942, *Three for Jane,* 1943, *Life Comes to Mary Willand,* 1943, *Miss Streamline,* 1944, *Enter: A Land Girl,* 1944, *Second Act,* 1945, *My Heart Goes With You,* 1946, *Flat No. 49,* 1946, *A Wish Is Granted,* 1946, *Romance for Four,* 1947, *My Husband's People,* 1948, *Quiet Rhapsody,* 1949; *Glamorous Adventure,* 1950, *Joy Was in the Dawn,* 1950, *Appointment with Love,* 1951, *Assistant Matron,* 1952, *Portrait of Delilah,* 1952, *Generous Heart,* 1953, *Love That Is Nearest* 1954, *Summer Symphony,* 1954, *Stand-In,* 1955, *The Trysting Tree,* 1956, *No. 6 Green Acres,* 1957, *The Wind Through the Pines,* 1957, *Looking for Catalina,* 1958, *The World Is Mine,* 1959; *Ward to Andrew,* 1959; *My Johnny,* 1960, *Diamonds for Chloe,* 1961, *Simon's Wife,* 1962, *Always Another Spring,* 1963, *Ann Logan District Nurse,* 1964, *The Five-Shilling Holiday,* 1964, *Grass Widows,* 1965; *Suddenly Came Summer,* 1966, *The Castle of Dreams,* 1967, *Where Is Elizabeth?,* 1968, *The Uphill Road,* 1969, *Companion Housekeeper,* 1971.

Romantic novels under pseudonym Mairi O'Nair; all published by Mills & Boon: *The House with Orange Curtains,* 1933, *The Inn Without a Name,* 1934, *The Turned-Down Page,* 1934, *Dangerous Lady,* 1934, *Peggy Paradine, House Agent,* 1935, *The Girl with the X-Ray Eyes,* 1935, *Jennifer Disappears,* 1935, *Enchanter of Women,* 1936, *Unexpected Lover,* 1936, *Red Hair Means Trouble,* 1936, *Smith's the Man!,* 1937, *Beautiful Crook,* 1937, *Fay Draper, Widow,* 1937, *Anne Gilling, Receptionist,* 1938 *The Rich Mrs. Van,* 1938, *Trouble-Maker,* 1938, *She Couldn't Say "No!,"* 1939, *False Darkness,* 1940, *Blue Tinsel,* 1940, *Someone Else's Shoes,* 1941, *Some Were Lucky,* 1941, *A Date with Destiny,* 1941, *Husband for Sale,* 1942, *Who Follows Pan?,* 1943, *Storm Over Sandham Park,* 1944, *Judy Ashbane, Police Decoy,* 1944, *Four Steps Upwards,* 1945, *Nerida Speaks Twice,* 1945, *The Girl in Red,* 1946, *The Stars Are Green,* 1946, *Night Club Hostess,* 1947, *Nun of the Market Place,* 1947, *They Chose Felicity,* 1949, *Housekeeper to John,* 1949; *Flower of the Dust,* 1950, *Desirable Widow,* 1951, *I Bequeath My Daughter,* 1952, *Shadows on the Water,* 1953, *The House on the Hill,* 1953, *The Bend of the Road,* 1954, *Patchwork Horizon,* 1955, *The Girl Next Door,* 1955, *Of Interest to Women,* 1956, *The Soft Touch,* 1957, *Pink Lady,* 1958, *Country Club,* 1958, *Second Blossoming,* 1959, *Singing Star,* 1960, *Mystery at Butlin's,* 1960, *Scent of Wood Smoke,* 1961, *A Girl They Called Pam,* 1962, *Cottage Hospital,* 1963, *A Thing of Beauty,* 1964, *Breaking Point,* 1965, *The Daring Adventure,* 1966, *The Bird of Passage,* 1967, *The Torch of Pleasure,* 1970. Also author of short stories, serials, and articles appearing in popular periodicals.

SIDELIGHTS: Miss Evans describes her capsule career ("haven't a minute to spare"): "Started to write, sent a novel to Mills & Boon, a serial to *Thompson's,* and a children's story to *Little Folks.* All accepted so took [to] writing. Engaged three times, one killed, one died from old wounds, one heart failure, so found a family to adopt and have three (foster) daughters.... Am now (alas!) too old for much research in my subject." *Avocational Interests:* Poking about ("a few years ago did a river from source to end"), cinephotography, tape recording, reading, and listening to interesting people.

*   *   *

EVANS, K(athleen) M(arianne)   1911-

PERSONAL: Born February 25, 1911, in Pembrey, Carmarthenshire, South Wales. *Education:* Bedford College, London, B.Sc., 1932; University of London, M.A., 1946, Ph.D., 1952. *Home:* 33 Axminster Rd., Roath, Cardiff CF2 5AR, Wales.

CAREER: Grammar school teacher, 1933-46; training college lecturer, 1946-50; University College of South Wales and Monmouthshire, University of Wales, Cardiff, lecturer and research officer, 1950-72.

WRITINGS: Saint David: Dewi Sant, S.P.C.K., 1957; *In Their Own Tongue,* Church in Wales, 1958; *A Book of Welsh Saints,* Church in Wales, 1959; *Club Members Today,* National Association of Mixed Clubs and Girls' Clubs, 1960; *Birth of a Diocese,* Church in Wales, 1961; *Sociometry and Education,* Humanities, 1962; *Attitudes and Interests in Education,* Routledge & Kegan Paul, 1965; *Planning Small-Scale Research: A Practical Guide for Teachers and Students,* National Foundation for Educational Research in England and Wales, 1968. Contributor to education journals and other periodicals.

*   *   *

EVANS, Richard L(ouis)   1906-

PERSONAL: Born March 23, 1906, in Salt Lake City, Utah; son of John Alldridge and Florence (Neslen) Evans; married Alice Thornley, August 9, 1933; children: Richard Louis, Jr., John Thornley, Stephen Thornley, William Thornley. *Education:* University of Utah, B.A., 1931, M.A., 1932. *Religion:* Church of Jesus Christ of Latter-day Saints (Mormon). *Address:* P.O. Box 30, Salt Lake City, Utah 84110.

CAREER: Church of Jesus Christ of Latter-day Saints, missionary in England, 1926-29; Radio Station KSL, Salt Lake City, Utah, staff announcer, 1929, writer, director, and production manager, 1930-36, most widely known in radio world as writer, producer, and commentator for Salt Lake Tabernacle Choir weekly broadcasts carried by National Broadcasting Co., 1930-32, Columbia Broadcasting System, 1932—; *Improvement Era* (magazine), Salt Lake City, Utah, managing editor, 1936-49, editor, 1950-70; King Features Syndicate, feature writer, 1946-52. Directorships in Salt Lake City include David W. Evans Advertising Agency, 1947—, Temple Square, 1947-66, Salt Lake Union Stockyards, 1958-68, First Security Corp., 1963—. Church of Jesus Christ of Latter-day Saints, member of Council of the Twelve, 1953—. University of Utah, member of board of regents, 1950-69; Brigham Young University, trustee, 1953—; member, Utah Higher Board of Education, 1969—.

MEMBER: Utah Academy of Science, Arts and Letters, Newcomen Society, University of Utah Alumni Association (president, 1950-53), Rotary International (local president, 1949-50; district governor, 1956-57; district counselor, 1957-58; international director, 1959-61; third vice-president, 1960-61; president 1966-67), Bonneville Knife and Fork Club (president, 1953-54; circuit speaker). *Awards, honors:* LL.D., University of Utah, 1956; D.H.L., California College of Medicine, 1957; D. Litt., Eastern Kentucky State College, 1964; achievement awards from College of Business, University of Utah,

1958, from Pi Kappa Alpha, 1961; Freedoms Foundation award, 1962.

WRITINGS: Unto the Hills, Harper, 1940; *This Day ... and Always,* Harper, 1942; *... And the Spoken Word,* Harper, 1945; *At This Same Hour,* Harper, 1949; *Tonic for Our Times,* Harper, 1952; *From the Crossroads,* Harper, 1955; *The Everlasting Things,* Harper, 1957; *From Within These Walls,* Harper, 1959; *May Peace Be with You,* Harper, 1961; *Faith in the Future,* Harper, 1963; *Faith, Peace, and Purpose,* World Publishing, 1966; *Thoughts for One Hundred Days as Heard on Radio,* Publishers Press, Volume I, 1966, Volume II: *An Open Door,* 1967, Volume III: *An Open Road,* 1968, Volume IV, 1970.

Contributor to *Encyclopaedia Britannica.* Also contributor of articles to newspapers and magazines, including *Reader's Digest, Coronet,* and *Look.*

*   *   *

EVERETT, Donald E(dward)   1920-

PERSONAL: Born December 10, 1920, in Auburn, Ala.; son of Edward (a veterinarian) and Mary (Hopkins) Everett; married Mary L. Melancon, September 4, 1949; children: John Lauchlin, Mary Melancon. *Education:* University of Florida, B.A., 1941; Tulane University, M.A., 1950, Ph.D., 1952. *Politics:* Democrat. *Religion:* Presbyterian. *Home:* 142 Laurel Heights Place, San Antonio, Tex. 78212.

CAREER: Tulane University, New Orleans, La., instructor in history and editorial assistant of *Mississippi Valley Historical Review,* 1952-53; Trinity University, San Antonio, Tex., assistant professor, 1953-57, associate professor, 1957-64, professor of history, 1964—, chairman of the department, 1966—. Chairman of board of editors, Trinity University Press; member, Bexar County (Texas) Historical Survey Commission. *Member:* Mississippi Valley Historical Association, Southern Historical Association, Texas State Historical Association, San Antonio Historical Association (president, 1962), Phi Alpha Theta, Pi Sigma Alpha. *Awards, honors:* Ford fellowship, 1951-52; Piper Professor, 1970.

WRITINGS: (Editor) *Chaplain Davis and Hood's Texas Brigade,* Principia Press of Trinity University, 1962; *Trinity University: A Record of One Hundred Years,* Trinity University Press, 1968. Contributor to historical journals.

WORK IN PROGRESS: San Antonio: Its Antiquated Foreignness.

*   *   *

EVERSOLE, Finley T.   1933-

PERSONAL: Born December 24, 1933, in Birmingham, Ala.; son of Finley Pratt and Frieda Mae (Traweek) Eversole; married Mary Ann Knox (a teacher) June 8, 1958. *Education:* Birmingham-Southern College, A.B., 1956; Vanderbilt University, B.D. (honors), 1958; Drew University, graduate study, 1958-59, 1963—; studied at University of Chicago Divinity School, 1959-60. *Politics:* Democrat. *Home:* 52 Symor Dr., Convert Station, N.J. 07961. *Office:* National Council of the Churches of Christ in the U.S.A., 475 Riverside Dr., New York, N.Y. 10027.

CAREER: Methodist clergyman; *Motive Magazine,* Nashville, Tenn., staff associate, 1959-61; National Student Christian Federation, New York, N.Y., director of Interseminary Movement, 1961-63; National Council of Churches, New York, N.Y., director and editor of adult department of Friendship Press, 1963—. Lecturer on Arts to schools and colleges, and on religion to seminaries and universities. *Member:* American Society of Church History, Institute for Religious and Social

Studies. American Society for Aesthetics, Authors Guild, Pi Kappa Alpha, Eta Sigma Phi.

WRITINGS: (Editor) *Christian Faith and the Contemporary Arts,* Abingdon, 1962. Contributor of articles and reviews to religious journals. Founding editor, *Interseminarian,* 1961-63; editor *Communique,* 1961-63.

WORK IN PROGRESS: The Rebirth of Dionysus, attempting a new philosophy of modern art; study of "the dark vision" of Baudelaire and Rimbaud; articles on art and myth and the politics of modern art; editing a book on church architecture; collaborating on a book of literary and art criticism.

AVOCATIONAL INTERESTS: Collecting primitive and oriental sculpture and carving, pole arms, armor, and old shipping and whaling items; woodworking.

*   *   *

*   *   *

EVERSON, William (Oliver) 1912-
(Brother Antoninus)

PERSONAL: Surname rhymes with "weaver's son"; born September 10, 1912, in Sacramento, Calif.; son of Louis Waldemar (a bandmaster, composer, and printer) and Francelia Marie (Herber) Everson; married twice, now divorced. *Education:* Attended Fresno State College (now California State University), 1931, 1934-35. *Religion:* Roman Catholic convert, 1949. *Home:* St. Albert's College, 6172 Chabot Rd., Oakland 18, Calif.

CAREER: Left college in 1935 to write poetry; conscientious objector, 1943-46; after war joined the anarchopacifist group around Kenneth Rexroth in San Francisco; joined Catholic Worker Movement, 1950; entered Dominican Order as a lay brother without vows, 1951; reentered literary scene in 1957 during the San Francisco Renaissance; since then has given poetry readings across the country. *Awards, honors:* Guggenheim fellowship, 1949.

WRITINGS—All poetry except as noted; under name William Everson: *These Are the Ravens,* Greater West, 1935; *San Joaquin,* Ward Ritchie, 1939; *The Masculine Dead: Poems, 1938-1940,* Press of J.A. Decker, 1942; *Ten War Elegies,* 3rd edition, Untide, 1943, new edition published as *War Elegies,* 1944; *The Waldport Poems,* Untide, 1944; *The Residual Years: Poems, 1940-41,* Untide, 1944, published with additional poems, as *The Residual Years,* New Directions, 1948, enlarged edition published as *The Residual Years: Poems, 1934-48. The Pre-Catholic Poetry of Brother Antoninus,* introduction by Kenneth Rexroth, New Directions, 1968; *Poems MCMXLII,* Untide, 1945; *A Privacy of Speech: Ten Poems in Sequence,* Equinox, 1949; *Triptych for the Living,* Seraphim, 1951; *There Will Be Harvest,* [Berkeley], 1960; *The Year's Declension,* [Berkeley], 1961; *Single Source: Early Poems, 1934-1940,* introduction by Robert Duncan, Oyez, 1966; *The Blowing of the Seed,* H.W. Wenning, 1966; *In the Fictive Wish,* Oyez, 1967; (author of introduction) Robinson Jeffers, *Californians,* Cayucos Books, 1971.

Under name Brother Antoninus: (Liturgy and ritual) *Novum Psalterium Pii xii,* an unfinished folio edition, [Los Angeles], 1955; *A Fragment for the Birth of God,* Albertus Magnus, 1958; (biography; with Brother Kurt) *Friar Among Savages: Father Luis Cancer,* Benzinger, 1958; *An Age Insurgent,* Blackfriars, 1959; *The Crooked Lines of God: Poems, 1949-1954,* University of Detroit Press, 1959, 2nd edition, 1960, 3rd edition, 1962; *The Hazards of Holiness: Poems, 1957-1960,* Doubleday, 1962; *The Poet Is Dead: A Memorial for Robinson Jeffers,* Auerhahn, 1964; *The Rose of Solitude,* Oyez, 1964, Doubleday, 1967; *The Achievement of Brother Antoninus,* selection of poems with introduction by William E. Staf-

ford, Scott, Foresman, 1967; *A Canticle to the Waterbirds,* Eizo, 1968; (editor) *Robinson Jeffers: Fragments of an Older Fury,* Oyez, 1968; *The Springing of the Blade,* Black Rock Press, 1968.

Contributor to *Ramparts, Evergreen Review,* and to other periodicals.

WORK IN PROGRESS: New Poems, *The Ecstasy of the Rose;* a prose book on the assassination of President Kennedy, *The Tongs of Jeopardy.*

SIDELIGHTS: "Brother Antoninus is a rough, urgent startlingly honest poet, with a passionate identification with the Californian landscape," writes Kenneth Rexroth. "His verse has the same kind of integrity as that of Whitman, D.H. Lawrence, the early Sandburg.... Brother Antoninus is more or less a disciple of Robinson Jeffers, but I think he has made a harder and more honest instrument of [poetry] than his master, . . . [perhaps because] he has come through a lot of agony to present peace. Honesty, simplicity, modesty, complete commitment to communication—these are the outstanding virtues of good poetry in any case. In the telling of a spiritual odyssey of the sort Brother Antoninus has traveled . . . , they make all the difference. They make, in fact, a collection of poems of stunning impact, utterly unlike anything else being written nowadays.... His poems are the record of grueling struggle to prepare himself for vision."

There was some critical controversy over the merit of *The Rose of Solitude.* William Dickey called the book "pretentious and dishonest, ... 125 pages of overheated verse, and a lengthy prose preface which may represent the fullest statement of a narcissist theology yet made in our time.... The language of the book is, like its substance, overblown. Antoninus makes a simple equation between suffering and unintelligibility: the greater the pain the more tortured the syntax." The *Virginia Quarterly Review* writer, however, considered the book as a continuation of Antoninus' spiritual autobiography, an attempt at "a Christian meditation and confession, a revelation of the mystery of man and nature, of Me and the Not-Me, of man becoming Man through Woman.... The book, has a religious and a human intensity that transcends its occasional failures and its often alien abstraction. It is the poem of a thinking and living man; more important, it is the poem of a praying man, is in fact, a prayer."

BIOGRAPHICAL/CRITICAL   SOURCES: Kenneth Rexroth, *Assays,* New Directions, 1961; *Atlantic,* December, 1963; *National Observer,* July 10, 1967; *Commonweal,* October 19, 1962, December 20, 1968; *New York Times Book Review,* September 9, 1962, October 8, 1967; *Hudson Review,* winter, 1967-68; *Virginia Quarterly Review,* winter, 1968; *Choice,* June, 1969; *Poetry,* autumn, 1968, December, 1969.

*   *   *

EYSENCK, H(ans) J(urgen) 1916-

PERSONAL: Born March 4, 1916, in Berlin, Germany; son of Eduard Anton (an actor) and Ruth (Werner) Eysenck; married Margaret Malcom Davies, 1938; married second wife, Sybil Bianca Giuletta Rostal, 1950; children: (first marriage) Michael; (second marriage) Gary, Connie, Kevin, Darrin. *Education:* University of London, B.S., 1938, Ph.D., 1940, D.Sc., 1962. *Politics:* Liberal. *Religion:* Church of England. *Home:* 10 Dorchester Dr., London S.E.24, England. *Office:* Maudsley Hospital, Denmark Hill, London S.E.5, England.

CAREER: University of London, London, England, reader in psychology, Institute of Psychiatry, 1950-55, professor of psychology, 1955—. Institute of Psychiatry, director of research laboratories; Maudsley and Bethlem

Royal Hospitals, psychologist. *Member:* American Psychological Association (fellow), British Psychological Society, Eugenics Society.

WRITINGS: (With others) *Dimensions of Personality: A Record of Research,* Routledge & Kegan Paul, 1947, Macmillan, 1948; *The Scientific Study of Personality,* Macmillan, 1952; *The Structure of Human Personality,* Wiley, 1953, 3rd edition, Barnes & Noble, 1970; *Uses and Abuses of Psychology,* Penguin, 1953; *The Psychology of Politics,* Routledge & Kegan Paul, 1954, Praeger, 1955; *Psychology and the Foundations of Psychiatry,* H.K. Lewis, 1955; *Sense and Nonsense in Psychology,* Penguin, 1957, revised edition, 1958; *The Dynamics of Anxiety and Hysteria: An Experimental Application of Modern Learning Theory to Psychiatry,* Praeger, 1957; *Manual of the Maudsley Personality Inventory,* University of London Press, 1959; *The Structure of Human Personality,* University of London Press, 1959; (contributor) George Wills Beadle, *The Language of the Game,* University of London Press, 1961; *Know Your Own I.Q.,* Penguin, 1962; (with wife, Sybil Bianca Eysenck) *Manual of the Eysenck Personality Inventory: Personality Questionnaire,* University of London Press, 1964; *Crime and Personality,* Houghton, 1964, revised edition, Pallidan Press, 1970; (with Stanley Rachman) *The Causes and Cures of Neuroses: An Introduction to the Modern Behaviour Therapy Based on Learning Theory and the Principles of Conditioning,* Robert R. Knapp, 1965; *Fact and Fiction in Psychology,* Penguin, 1965; *Smoking, Health and Personality,* Basic Books, 1965; *Check Your Own I.Q.,* Penguin, 1966; *The Effects of Psychotherapy,* International Science Press, 1966; *The Biological Basis of Personality,* C.C Thomas, 1967; *Personality Structure and Measurement,* Robert R. Knapp, 1969; *The I.Q. Argument: Race, Intelligence and Education,* Liberty Press, 1971 (published in England as *Race, Intelligence and Education,* M.T. Smith, 1971; *Psychology Is About People,* Liberty Press, 1972.

Editor: *Handbook of Abnormal Psychology: An Experimental Approach,* Pitman, 1960, Basic Books, 1961; *Experiments in Personality,* two volumes, Routledge & Kegan Paul, 1960, Humanities, 1961; *Behaviour Therapy and the Neuroses: Readings in Modern Methods of Treatment Derived from Learning Theory,* Macmillan, 1960; *Experiments with Drugs: Studies in the Relation between Personality, Learning Theory and Drug Action,* Macmillan, 1963; *Experiments in Motivation,* Macmillan, 1964; *Experiments in Behaviour Therapy: Readings in Modern Methods of Treatment of Mental Disorders Derived from Learning Theory,* Macmillan, 1964; *Readings: Extroversion, Introversion,* three volumes, Staples, 1970, Wiley, 1972.

Editor, *Behaviour Research and Therapy,* and "International series of Monographs on Experimental Psychology," Pergamon, 1964—.

AVOCATIONAL INTERESTS: History of science, tennis, squash, swimming, sailing, table tennis, photography, filming.

BIOGRAPHICAL/CRITICAL SOURCES: New Statesman, July 2, 1971.

* * *

FADNER, Frank (Leslie) 1910-

PERSONAL: Born January 11, 1910, in Neenah, Wis.; son of Frank Leslie and Elizabeth Teresa (Regenfusz) Fadner. *Education:* Georgetown University, C.F.S, 1933, B.S., 1939, M.A., 1940; Woodstock College, Ph.L., 1939, Th.L., 1944; University of London, Ph.D., 1949. *Home and office:* Georgetown University, Washington, D.C. 20007.

CAREER: Ordained a Roman Catholic priest, member of Society of Jesus (Jesuits), 1943. Georgetown University,

Washington, D.C., executive assistant regent, School of Foreign Service, 1949-55, regent, School of Foreign Service, 1955-61, associate professor, 1949-61, professor of Russian history, regent, head of Russian division, Institute of Languages and Linguistics, 1961—. *Member:* American Association for the Advancement of Slavic Studies, American Association of Teachers of Slavic and East European Languages, American Historical Association, American Catholic Historical Association, Gold Key Society, Delta Phi Epsilon, Delta Sigma Pi, Gamma Rho Sigma, Pi Gamma Nu. *Awards, honors:* Fundacion Eloy Alfaro; Encomienda, Orden de Isabel la Catolica; Al Merito por Servicios Distinguidos (Peru).

WRITINGS: The Russian Five Year Plan in Operation: The Cultural Front, Education and Religion, [Washington, D.C.], 1933; *Seventy Years of Pan-Slavism in Russia, Karazin to Danilevskii, 1800-1870,* Georgetown University Press, 1962.

SIDELIGHTS: Student of Spanish, Russian, French, Portuguese, Italian, German, Latin, and Esperanto. *Avocational interests:* Painting in oils and watercolors.

* * *

FAGAN, Edward R(ichard) 1924-

PERSONAL: Born November 14, 1924, in Waterbury, Conn.; son of Paul A. and Agnes (Costello) Fagan; married Rosemarie Niro, September 14, 1946; children: Patricia Ann, Timothy, Paul, Barry, Christopher, Cori. *Education:* University of Connecticut, Waterbury Extension, student, 1946-48; University of Wisconsin, B.S., 1950, M.S., 1953; Columbia University, Ed.D., 1961. *Politics:* Independent. *Religion:* Catholic. *Home:* 672 Wiltshire Rd., State College, Pa. 16801. *Office:* Pennsylvania State University, University Park, Pa. 16802.

CAREER: High school teacher of English in Waukesha and Madison, Wis., and Tarrytown and Albany, N.Y., 1950-58; State University of New York, Albany, associate professor of education, 1953-57; New York State Education Department, Albany, research associate, 1957-58; State University of New York, Albany, director of foreign study project, 1958-61; Pennsylvania State University, University Park, professor of English and education, 1962—. Director, NDEA Title VI Institute for Teachers of Disadvantaged. Consultant on Indonesian teacher education to Ford Foundation, Institute of International Education, and State University of New York. Boy Scouts of America, institutional representative. Little League manager and coach. *Military service:* U.S. Marine Corps, 1942-45; became sergeant; received Guadalcanal, Tulagi, Munda, Pelelieu, and Okinawa battle stars and Presidential Unit Citation.

MEMBER: National Council of Teachers of English (director), American Educational Research Association, Conference on English Education, Pennsylvania Council of Teachers of English (vice-president for professional development, 1970-71), Phi Delta Kappa (president, Pennsylvania State University chapter, 1968). *Awards, honors:* Ford Foundation grant to study Indonesian teacher education, 1960.

WRITINGS: Field: A Process for Teaching Literature, Pennsylvania State University Press, 1964; (editor) *English and the Disadvantaged,* International Textbook Co., 1967; (with Jean Van Dell) *Minorities: Communicating the Dream's Responsibilities,* National Council of Teachers of English, 1969; (with Van Dell) *Humanizing English: Do Not Fold, Spindle or Mutilate,* National Council of Teachers of English, 1970; (with Van Dell) *Teaching English: Through a Glass, Darkly,* National Council of Teachers of English, 1971; *Research and the English Teacher,* National Council of Teachers of English, 1971.

AVOCATIONAL INTERESTS: Motion picture photography, sports.

* * *

FALK, Leslie A. 1915-

PERSONAL: Born April 19, 1915, in St. Louis, Mo.; son of Albert and Eleanor Falk; married Joy Hume, 1942; children: Gail, Ted, Don, Beth. *Education:* University of Illinois, A.B., 1935; Oxford University, Rhodes Scholar, 1937-40, D.Phil., 1940; Johns Hopkins University, M.D., 1942. *Office:* Department of Family and Community Health, Meharry Medical College, Nashville, Tenn. 37208.

CAREER: Licensed to practice medicine in Maryland, New York State, and Pennsylvania; Johns Hopkins Hospital, Baltimore, Md., intern, 1942-43; worked with United Nations Relief and Rehabilitation Association, 1946, U.S. Public Health Service, 1947-48; Welfare and Retirement Fund, United Mine Workers of America, Pittsburgh, Pa., area medical administrator; Meharry Medical College, Nashville, Tenn., now faculty member. Diplomate, American Board of Preventive Medicine and Public Health, 1951. Lecturer, American University, 1948; University of Pittsburgh, lecturer, School of Social Work, and adjunct associate professor of medical and hospital administration, Graduate School of Public Health, 1949—. *Military service:* U.S. Army, Medical Corps, 1943-46.

MEMBER: American Public Health Association (fellow; life), Group Health Association of America, American College of Preventive Medicine (fellow), American Medical Association, American Sociological Association, American Association of the History of Medicine (fellow), Association of Teachers of Preventive Medicine, National Rehabilitation Association, Medical Committee for Human Rights, Pennsylvania Public Health Association, Pennsylvania State Medical Society, Pennsylvania Academy of Preventive Medicine (vice-president-elect), Allegheny County Medical Society.

WRITINGS: (With Grace J. Mushrush and Mariam E. Skrivanek) *Administrative Aspects of Prepaid Group Practice: An Annotated Bibliography, 1950-62,* University of Pittsburgh Press, 1964. Co-author or co-editor of four reports by U.S. Senate Subcommittee on Wartime Health, including *The Experimental Health Programs of the U.S. Department of Agriculture* (monograph), and *International Health.* Contributor of about twenty articles to *Public Affairs* (Canada), *Nation,* and to public health and medical journals in United States and Great Britain.

WORK IN PROGRESS: Articles on black medical history.

* * *

FALLERS, Lloyd A(shton, Jr.) 1925-

PERSONAL: Born August 29, 1925, in Nebraska City, Neb.; son of Lloyd A. (an insurance salesman) and Fannie (Lincoln) Fallers; married Margaret Elinor Chave (a high school teacher), June 18, 1949; children: Winnifred Mary, Beth Laura. *Education:* Attended University of Utah, 1943-44, and Deep Springs College, 1944-45; University of Chicago, Ph.B., 1946, M.A., 1949, Ph.D., 1953; London School of Economics, graduate study, 1949-50. *Politics:* Democrat. *Religion:* Episcopal. *Home:* 1361 East 56th St., Chicago, Ill. 60637. *Office:* Department of Anthropology, University of Chicago, Chicago, Ill. 60637.

CAREER: East African Institute of Social Research, Kampala, Uganda, research fellow, 1950-52, 1954-55, director, 1956-57; Princeton University, Princeton, N.J., lecturer in anthropology, 1953-54; University of California, Berkeley, 1957-60, began as assistant professor, became associate professor of anthropology; University of Chicago, Chicago, Ill., 1960—, began as associate professor, now professor of anthropology. Fellow, Center for Advanced Study of the Behavioral Sciences, 1958-59. *Member:* International African Institute, American Anthropological Association, Association of Social Anthropologists (England), Royal Anthropological Institute, African Studies Association, Middle East Studies Association, American Academy of Arts and Sciences (fellow).

WRITINGS: Bantu Bureaucracy: A Study of Integration and Conflict in the Political Institutions of an East African People, Heffer for East African Institute of Social Research, 1956, published in America as *Bantu Bureaucracy: A Century of Political Evolution Among the Basoga of Uganda,* University of Chicago Press, 1965; *Some Determinants of Marriage Stability in Basoga: A Reformation of Gluckman's Hypothesis,* Oxford University Press, 1957; *Customary Law in the New African States,* Committee for the Comparative Study of New Nations, University of Chicago, c.1962; *An Introductory Syllabus on African Anthropology,* Department of Anthropology, University of Chicago, 1962; (editor) *The King's Men: Leadership and Status in Buganda on the Eve of Independence,* Oxford University Press, 1964; (editor) *Immigrants and Associations,* Mouton & Co., 1967; *Law without Precedent: Legal Ideas in Action in the Courts of Colonial Buganda,* University of Chicago Press, 1969. Associate editor, *International Encyclopedia of Social Sciences,* 1962—.

WORK IN PROGRESS: The Social Anthropology of the Nation-State; Inequality: Social Stratification Reconsidered.

* * *

FARON, Louis C. 1923-

PERSONAL: Born July 16, 1923, in New York, N.Y.; son of Louis C. (a salesman) and Erna (Rost) Faron; married Amy Brewster (divorced); married Barbara Kearnes; children: (first marriage) Amy, Kenneth; (second marriage) John, Alice. *Education:* Columbia University, A.B., 1949, Ph.D., 1954. *Politics:* Democrat. *Home:* Main Street, Stony Brook, Suffolk, N.Y. 11790. *Office:* Department of Anthropology, State University of New York at Stony Brook, Stony Brook, N.Y. 11790.

CAREER: University of Illinois, Urbana, research associate in anthropology, 1955-59; Los Angeles State College (now California State College at Los Angeles), Los Angeles, Calif., assistant professor of anthropology, 1959-62; University of Pittsburgh, Pittsburgh, Pa., associate professor of anthropology, 1962-64; State University of New York at Stony Brook, professor of anthropology, 1964-71. *Military service:* U.S. Army, 1943-46. *Member:* American Anthropological Association, American Association for the Advancement of Science. *Awards, honors:* National Institute of Mental Health fellowship; National Science Foundation fellowships; Doherty fellowship; Guggenheim fellow, 1970-71.

WRITINGS: (With Julian H. Steward) *Native Peoples of South America,* McGraw, 1959; *Mapuche Social Structure: Institutional Reintegration in a Patrilineal Society of Central Chile,* University of Illinois Press, 1961; *Hawks of the Sun: Mapuche Morality and Its Ritual Attributes,* University of Pittsburgh Press, 1964; *The Mapuche Indians of Chile,* Holt, 1968. Contributor of articles to *Encyclopaedia Britannica* and *Grolier Encyclopedia* and to anthropological journals. Associate editor, *Journal of Ethnology* (University of Pittsburgh), 1962-64.

WORK IN PROGRESS: Social Structure of Peru; Mapuche Culture Constancy and Change; Otomi of Mexico.

SIDELIGHTS: Faron speaks Spanish and reads French, Portuguese, Italian, and German.

FARRIS, Paul L(eonard) 1919-

PERSONAL: Born November 10, 1919, in Vincennes, Ind.; son of James David (a farmer) and Fairy (Kahre) Farris; married Rachel Rutherford, August 16, 1953; children: Nancy Ruth, Paul James, John Lewis, Carl Stephen. *Education:* Purdue University, B.S.A., 1949; University of Illinois, M.S., 1950; Harvard University, Ph.D., 1954. *Office:* Department of Agricultural Economics, Purdue University, Lafayette, Ind.

CAREER: Purdue University, Lafayette, Ind., 1952—, started as assistant professor, became professor of agricultural economics, 1959. Project leader, National Commission on Food Marketing, 1965-66. *Military service:* U.S. Air Force, 1941-46; became captain. *Member:* American Economic Association, American Farm Economics Association.

WRITINGS: Dairying in Indiana: Trends and Facts, Purdue University, 1958; (editor) *Market Structure Research: Theory and Practice in Agricultural Economics,* Iowa State University Press, 1964. Contributor to *Journal of Farm Economics* and *Journal of Marketing.*

WORK IN PROGRESS: A study of industrial organization and market performance of agricultural industries.

*   *   *

FEDDEN, Henry (Romilly) 1908-
(Robin Fedden)

PERSONAL: Born November 26, 1908, in Burford, Oxfordshire, England. *Education:* Magdalene College, Cambridge, M.A. (honors). *Home:* 20 Eldon Rd., London W.8, England.

CAREER: Writer. *Member:* St. James Club, Alpine Club, Beefsteak Club.

WRITINGS—All under pseudonym Robin Fedden, except as noted: *As the Unicorn* (novel), Macmillan, 1933; *Suicide: A Social and Historical Study,* P. Davies, 1938; *The Land of Egypt,* Scribner, 1939; *A Study of the Monastery of Saint Anthony in the Eastern Desert,* [Cairo], 1939; (under name H. Romilly Fedden) *The Elizabethan Mind,* Goldberg's Press (Jerusalem), 1943; (compiler) *Personal Landscape: An Anthology of Exile,* Edition Poetry, 1945; (translator) Peter Bruegel, the Elder, *The Dulle Griet,* Lund, Humphries, 1946; *Syria: An Historical Appreciation,* R. Hale, 1946, 3rd edition published as *The Phoenix Land: The Civilization of Syria and Lebanon,* Braziller, 1965 (published in England as *Syria and Lebanon,* J. Murray, 1965); (author of introduction and notes) Alexander William Kinglake, *Eothen,* Methuen, 1948; *Crusader Castles: A Brief Study in the Military Architecture of the Crusades,* Art & Technics, 1950, revised edition (with John Thomson) published as *Crusader Castles,* J. Murray, 1957, Transatlantic, 1958; (with Clement W. Parish) *Bateman's Sussex,* Country Life, 1950; *The Ascott Collection,* Country Life, 1951; *Castlecoole, Enniskillen,* Country Life, 1952; *Oxburgh Hall, Norfolk,* Country Life, 1953; *Penrhyn Castle, Bangor, Caernarvon,* Country Life, 1953; *Powis Castle, Montgomeryshire,* Curween Press, 1953; (under name H.R. Fedden) *Treasurer's House, York,* Country Life, 1954; *Alpine Ski Tour: An Account of the High Level Route,* Putnam, 1956, New Directions, 1957; (under name Henry Romilly Fedden) *Petworth House, Sussex: A Property of the National Trust,* [London], 1957; (with Peter Waddell and C.A. de Linde) *Ski-ing in the Alps,* Hulton, 1958; *English Travellers in the Near East,* Longmans, Green, 1958; *The Enchanted Mountain: A Quest in the Pyrenees,* J. Murray, 1962, Transatlantic, 1963; *Chante mesle* (autobiography), J. Murray, 1964, Braziller, 1966; *The Continuing Purpose: A History of the National Trust, Its Aims and Works,* Longmans, Green, 1968,

International Publications Service, 1968; *The White Country* (verse), J. Murray, 1968; *The Giant's Causeway,* Garnstone Press, 1971.

*   *   *

FEINBERG, Abraham L. 1899-

PERSONAL: Born September 14, 1899, in Bellaire, Ohio; son of Nathan (a rabbi) and Sarah (Abramson) Feinberg; married Ruth E. Katsh, November 4, 1930; children: Jonathan Frome, Sarah Jane Feinberg Growe. *Education:* University of Cincinnati, B.A., 1920; Hebrew Union College—Jewish Institute of Religion, Cincinnati, Ohio, Rabbi, 1924; graduate study at University of Chicago and Columbia University; also studied at American Conservatory, Fontainebleau, France. *Politics:* "Left of center." *Home:* 154 Old Forest Hill Rd., Toronto 10, Ontario, Canada. *Office:* Holy Blossom Synagogue, 1950 Bathurst St., Toronto, Ontario, Canada.

CAREER: Rabbi to congregations in Niagra Falls, N.Y., Wheeling, W. Va., New York, N.Y., and Denver, Colo.; Holy Blossom Synagogue, Toronto, Ontario, became rabbi, 1943, now rabbi emeritus. Professional singer on radio and stage under name Anthony Frome, 1932-34. Journalist, television panelist, and lecturer. Canadian Campaign for Nuclear Disarmament, national vice-chairman; member of peace missions to England, West Germany, and Soviet Union. *Member:* Central Conference of American Rabbis, Phi Beta Kappa. *Awards, honors:* LL.D., University of Toronto; D.D., Hebrew Union College—Jewish Institute of Religion, Cincinnati, Ohio.

WRITINGS: A Rabbi Visits Germany, [Montreal], 1959; *Storm the Gates of Jericho,* McClelland & Stewart, 1964, Marzani & Munsell, 1965; *Hanoi Diary,* Longmans, Green (Toronto), 1968; *Christus-killer,* F.A. Herbig (Munich), 1969. Contributor to *Macleans, Globe, Canadian Weekly, Toronto Star, Globe and Mail,* and other periodicals.

WORK IN PROGRESS: Sex and the Pulpit.

*   *   *

FELLOWS, Malcolm Stuart 1924-

PERSONAL: Born September 11, 1924, in Bilston, Staffordshire, England; son of Edward and Jennie Fellows. *Education:* University College, London, B.A. (with honors). *Home:* Denham, 42 Queen's Walk, London N.W.9, England. *Agent:* Carl Routledge, Charles Lavell Ltd., Mowbray House, Norfolk St., London W.C.2, England.

CAREER: Hendon County School, London, England, assistant master, 1950-54; Owen's School, London, England, head of English department, 1954—. Senior tutor, Television Writing School Ltd.; member of educational advisory council, Thames Television Ltd. Reader for publishers and literary agents. Fellow, Salzburg Seminar in American Studies. Chairman of Governors, St. Nicholas School. *Military service:* British Army, Intelligence Corps, 1943-47; became staff sergeant. *Member:* Writers Guild of Great Britain (member of executive council), Bureau of Free-lance Photographers (fellow), Incorporated Association of Assistant Masters, Screenwriters' Guild, English-Speaking Union, Society of Authors. *Awards, honors:* Television Play of the Year award, 1961, for "The Truth about Helen."

WRITINGS: (Contributor) *Dogs-Dogs-Dogs: The Dog in Literature* (a symposium), Paul Hamlyn, 1962; *Shame in Summer,* Horwood, 1963; (editor) *Eight Plays,* Cassell, 1964; *Projects for Schools,* Museum Press, 1965; *Come Fly With Me* (play), Samuel French, 1966; *Behind the Wheel,* Cassell, 1968. Author of television scripts, including serial, "Plateau of Fear," and play, "The Truth about Helen." Contributor to *Theatre Arts, Times Educa-*

tional Supplement, Courier, Listener, Stage, Television Today, New Bedford Standard Times, and to education journals.

WORK IN PROGRESS: Several plays.

* * *

FELT, Margaret Elley 1917-

PERSONAL: Born December 19, 1917, in Payette, Idaho; daughter of Walter Orie and Lavina (Schwabauer) Elley; married Horace Woodruff Felt (a heavy equipment operator), January 21, 1940; children: Vicki-Anne Felt Davis, Kimberley Jane. Education: Griffin-Murphy Business College, student, 1937; additional study at University of Washington, Seattle. Politics: Democrat. Religion: Protestant. Home address: Route 18, Box 201, Olympia, Wash. 98501.

CAREER: Washington State Department of Natural Resources, Olympia, information officer with division of public affairs, 1961—. Director, Olympia YMCA; director of publicity, Washington State YMCA Youth Legislature. Member, State-Federal Resource Information and Education Officers Council. Occasionally conducts talk shows on local television. Member: Pacific Northwest Industrial Editors Association, Pacific Northwest Writers Conference, Washington Press Women, Washington State Employees Association (member of board), Washington State Information Council. Awards, honors: Several writing awards from Washington Press Women contests and from Washington Information Council contests; Photographer-Journalist award of experience, 1969.

WRITINGS: Gyppo Logger, Caxton, 1963. Contributor of articles on Washington to encyclopedias and historical books; author of various recreation and travel brochures and state agency biennial reports; contributor of articles to Saturday Evening Post, Westways, Traveler, National Wildlife, Washington Farmer, Tacoma News Tribune, Pacific Sea and Boating, Parents, and Seattle Times. Editor, TOTEM, Washington Department of Natural Resources publication.

WORK IN PROGRESS: Grandma Was a Truck Driver, a book on the background and work of a female information officer; The History of Capitol Forest; Blowdown, a novel.

* * *

FELTON, Ronald Oliver 1909-
   (Ronald Welch)

PERSONAL: Born December 14, 1909, in Aberavon, Glamorganshire, Wales; son of Oliver (an accountant) and Alice (Thomas) Felton; married Betty Llewellyn Evans, 1934; children: Mary Felton Simmons. Education: Berkhamsted School, student, 1922-28; Clare College, Cambridge University, M.A. (honors), 1931. Religion: Church of England. Home: Carreg Cennen, Okehampton, Devonshire, England. Office: Okehampton Grammar School, Okehampton, Devonshire, England.

CAREER: Okehampton Grammar School, Okehampton, Devonshire, England, headmaster, 1947—; writer of historical books for children. Military service: Territorial Army, 1933-39. Welch Regiment, World War II; served in Normandy and Germany; became major. Awards, honors: Carnegie Medal of Library Association for outstanding children's book published in 1954, for Knight Crusader.

WRITINGS—Under pseudonym Ronald Welch: The Black Car Mystery, Pitman, 1950; The Clock Stood Still, Pitman, 1951; The Gauntlet, Oxford University Press (New York), 1951; Knight Crusader, Oxford University Press (New York), 1954; Ferdinand Magellan (biography), Oxford University Press, 1955, Criterion, 1956;

Captain of Dragoons, Oxford University Press, 1956; Mohawk Valley, Criterion, 1958; Captain of Foot, Oxford University Press, 1959; Escape from France, Oxford University Press, 1960, Criterion, 1961; For the King, Oxford University Press, 1961, Criterion, 1962; Nicholas Carey, Criterion, 1963; Bowman of Crecy, Oxford University Press, 1966, Criterion, 1967; The Hawk, Oxford University Press, 1967, Criterion, 1969; Sun of York, Oxford University Press, 1970; The Galleon, Oxford University Press, 1971.

As Ronald Oliver Felton: Sker House, Hutchinson, 1954.

WORK IN PROGRESS: Story on the first tanks of World War I; book of short stories of the nineteenth century.

AVOCATIONAL INTERESTS: Military history, collecting model soldiers, motoring on the continent, photography.

BIOGRAPHICAL/CRITICAL SOURCES: Times Literary Supplement, May 25, 1967; Books and Bookmen, June, 1967; Book World, October 8, 1967.

* * *

FENIN, George N(icolaievich) 1916-

PERSONAL: Born September 24, 1916, in Kharkov, Russia; son of Nicholas (an engineer and industrialist) and Lubov (Andreev) Fenin; married February 9, 1946 (wife's maiden name Carducci); children: Nicholas. Education: University of Naples, Law Degree, 1939; Royal African Society of Italy, Diploma in Colonial Sciences, 1939. Politics: Democrat. Religion: Russian Orthodox. Home: 215 West 98th St., New York, N.Y. 10025.

CAREER: Free-lance writer on films and theatre, and later critic for Italian dailies, including Il Mattino, Il Corriere di Napoli, and Il Veneto, 1937-48; civilian posts with U.S. Army, British Army, and as regional officer of Displaced Persons Division of United Nations Relief and Rehabilitation Administration, 1943-47; film correspondent for magazines and newspapers in Italy and other countries, 1948—. Juror at Golden Reel Film Festival, New York, N.Y., 1955, at film festivals in Punta del Este, Uruguay, 1955, Mar del Plata, Argentina, 1960, 1961. Organizer of U.S. Retrospective Films Showing for VII Film Exposition, Trento, Italy, 1958. Member: Foreign Press Association (vice-president, 1957-61; president, 1962).

WRITINGS: Italian Cinema, 1945-51, Bestetti, 1951; Almanacco Cinema Italiano 1952, Bestetti, 1953; (translator) Zavattini, Film—Book I, Grove, 1959; (with W. K. Everson) The Western, from Silents to Cinerama, Orion, 1962. Author of film scripts. Correspondent of Italian dailies, La Nazione, La Notte, La Voce Republicana, and of the magazines, Cinema Nuovo (Milan), Cinema 62 (Paris), Tiempo de Cine (Buenos Aires), Marcha (Montevideo), Films and Filming (London). Contributor of geographical monographs to L'Universo (publication of Italian Geographical Military Institute), articles and book reviews to Saturday Review, movie section to MD Magazine. Editor, Film Culture.

WORK IN PROGRESS: The U.S. Social Cinema, in several volumes; a revised and updated edition of The Western.

BIOGRAPHICAL/CRITICAL SOURCES: Il Western Maggiorenne, Zigiotti, 1953; Mass Culture, Free Press, 1957.

* * *

FENN, Charles (Henry) 1907-

PERSONAL: Born June 19, 1907, in London, England; son of Robert William (a manufacturer's agent) and

Jane Elizabeth (Boxley) Fenn; married Mair Lewis (writer of children's stories and poetry), October 29, 1958; children: (previous marriage) Katherine Alison; (present marriage) Alyn Elizabeth, Robert Kerry. *Home:* Schull, County Cork, Ireland. *Agent:* London Management, 235/241 Regent St., London W.1, England.

CAREER: Cunard Steamship Line "S.S. Aquitania," bell-boy, other posts, 1925-30; Cannon Mills, Inc. (textiles), New York, N.Y., salesman, 1930-39; self-employed color photographer in New York, N.Y., 1939-40; Associated Press, Far Eastern war correspondent, 1941-43; New York Enterprises Corp. (oriental art, educational toys), New York, N.Y., London, England, and Hongkong, president, 1946-48; Lars Schmidt Theatre Group, London, England, and Stockholm, Sweden, London representative, 1950-58; author and playwright. *Military service:* U.S. Marine Corps, 1943-46; became captain; awarded Bronze Star, Order of Cloud and Banner, with ribbon. *Member:* Cosmo Club (Hongkong; founder and life president).

WRITINGS: Love and Politics: Two Plays, Wide World Publishing, 1947; *Vice Amongst the Veterans,* Wide World Publishing, 1948; *Kampffische,* Henschel 1954; *The Golden Rule of General Wong,* Arthur Barker, 1961; *Crimson Joy,* Hart-Davis, 1962; *Tropic Zero-3,* Heinemann, 1964; *Floating Pagoda-Boat,* Heinemann, 1965; *Pyramid of Night,* Elek, 1966; *Journal of a Voyage to Nowhere,* Chatto & Windus, 1971, Norton, 1972.

Plays produced in London: "School for Scoundrels," 1950; "The Sea Breeze," 1951; "The Purple Fire-Eaters," 1953; "The Pleasure Dome," 1954; "The Final Ace," 1955; "Sorcerer's Apprentice," 1955; "A for Angel," 1956; "Skyrocket," 1959.

WORK IN PROGRESS: A war autobiography, *My Two Years with the Slivy Toves;* a novel, *Exit First Soldier.*

SIDELIGHTS: Fenn brackets his interests in progressing five-year cycles: (1) Paris, wine, and horseracing; (2) Shaw, riding horses, and travel; (3) Proust, music, "the intellect"; (4) intensive money-making; (5) writing, which goes on and on. He now lives in Ireland because it seems to have the least money, cars, intellectuals, progress, and theatres, and more leisure, cart-horses, and wonderful bread. Another attraction is "The Standing Stone," described by Fenn as "a seashore haven for artists, writers, craftsmen, etc., offering beauty, quiet, and non-pollution."

* * *

FENTON, Edward 1917-

PERSONAL: Born July 7, 1917, in New York, N.Y.; son of Henry Clemence and Fannie (Golden) Fenton; married Sophia Harvati (a psychologist and educator), March 23, 1963. *Education:* Attended Amherst College. *Home:* 12 Dionysiou Areopagitou, Athens 119, Greece.

CAREER: Metropolitan Museum of Art, New York, N.Y., staff member in department of prints, 1950-55; self-employed writer, formerly in New York State, currently in Athens, Greece. *Awards, honors:* Mystery Writers of America "Edgar" for best juvenile of year in its field, 1961, for *The Phantom of Walkaway Hill.*

WRITINGS: Soldiers and Strangers (poems), Macmillan, 1945; *The Double Darkness* (novel), Doubleday, 1947.

Juveniles—All published by Doubleday, except as indicated: *Us and the Duchess,* 1947; *Aleko's Island,* 1948; *Hidden Trapezes,* 1950; *Nine Lives; or, The Celebrated Cat of Beacon Hill,* Pantheon, 1951; *The Golden Doors,* 1957; *Once Upon a Saturday,* 1958; *Fierce John: A Story,* 1959; *The Nine Questions,* 1959; *The Phantom of Walkaway Hill,* 1961; *An Island for a Pelican,* 1963; *The Riddle of the Red Whale,* 1966; *The Big Yellow Balloon,* 1967; *A Matter of Miracles,* Holt, 1967; *Penny Candy,* Holt, 1970.

WORK IN PROGRESS: An adult novel dealing with the eighteenth century in Venice.

SIDELIGHTS: Fenton writes to *CA:* "For the moment I'm living in Athens, with my Greek wife. I have lived and worked in Italy and Greece chiefly. I have been translated into French, Italian, German, Dutch, Polish, Greek, Spanish. When asked why I write for children, I can only reply that it's because certain books turn out that way."

Fenton has definite ideas as to what children require in a book. "Children hunger for plot. The recognition of this desire for a story is another way of saying that they require form. Subconsciously they recognize that the function of art is to wrest shape out of chaos. They abhor chaos—unless, of course, they are creating it themselves. They are absolutely logical, and impossible to deceive. They know when the Emperor is wearing no more than his underdrawers. Even when engrossed in fantasy, they demand of the story that it be based on almost geometric logic and that it advance with the inevitableness of an equation."

BIOGRAPHICAL/CRITICAL SOURCES: New York Times Book Review, August 6, 1967; *Book World,* September 10, 1967, November 5, 1967; *Young Reader's Review,* October, 1967; *The Writer,* April, 1969; *Saturday Review,* May 10, 1969; *Library Journal,* July, 1970.

* * *

FERGUSSON, Bernard Edward 1911-

PERSONAL: Born May 6, 1911, in London, England; son of Sir Charles (an army general) and Lady Alice (Boyle) Fergusson; married Laura Grenfell, November 22, 1950; children: George Duncan. *Education:* Studied at Eton College and Royal Military College at Sandhurst. *Religion:* Presbyterian. *Home:* Auchairne, Ballantrae, Ayrshire, Scotland. *Agent:* Curtis Brown Ltd., 13 King St., Covent Garden, London W.C.2, England.

CAREER: British Army, began service as second lieutenant in Black Watch, 1931, retired as brigadier, 1958; Governor-General and Commander-in-Chief of New Zealand, 1962-67. Served in Palestine and as instructor at Royal Military College prior to World War II, in Middle East, India, and Burma in World War II, receiving Distinguished Service Order, Order of the British Empire and being twice mentioned in dispatches. Special correspondent traveling abroad for *Sunday Times* and *Daily Telegraph,* both from London, England, 1958-61. *Member:* Royal Geographical Society (fellow), Royal Society of Literature (fellow). *Awards, honors:* Knight Grand Cross of Order of St. Michael and St. George, Knight Grand Cross of Royal Victorian Order, Knight of Order of St. John of Jerusalem; honorary degrees from Universities of Canterbury and Waikato (both New Zealand) and from University of Strathclyde (Scotland); created Life Peer as Lord Ballantrae, 1972.

WRITINGS: Eton Portrait, with one chapter by Philip Brownrigg, John Miles, 1937; *Essential French Military Terms, English-French,* Gale & Polden, 1942; *Beyond the Chindwin: Being an Account of the Adventure of Number Five Column of the Wingate Expedition into Burma, 1943,* Collins, 1945, new edition, 1951; *Lowland Soldier* (poems), Collins, 1945; *The Wild Green Earth,* Collins, 1946, reissued as *The Wild Green Earth: Burma Campaign,* English Book Store, 1967; (author of introduction) Laszlo Moholy-Nagy, *Portrait of Eton,* Muller, 1949; *The Black Watch and the King's Enemies,* Crowell, 1950; *The Wattery Maze: The Story of Combined Operations,* Collins, 1951, Holt, 1961; *Rupert of the Rhine,* Collins, 1952, Macmillan, 1953; *The Rare Adventure,*

Collins, 1954, Rinehart, 1955; (editor and author of preface) Sir John Noble Kennedy, *The Business of War*, Hutchinson, 1957, Morrow, 1958; *Wavell: Portrait of a Soldier*, Collins, 1961; *Look at the Army*, Hamish Hamilton, 1962; *Return to Burma*, Collins, 1962; *Five Addresses on Church Unity*, A.H. & A.W. Reed, 1967; *The Trumpet in the Hall, 1930-1958* (autobiography), Collins, 1970; *Captain John Niven*, 1972. Contributor to *Punch*, 1933—, and to other periodicals.

SIDELIGHTS: In a review of *The Trumpet in the Hall*, Stephen Vaughan says of Fergusson: "He has seen some of the most vicious fighting on record, terrorism, the three-cats-in-a-sack Syrian business. Burma, where the wounded had to be left to fend or die, and his descriptions, humorously and humanely tempered, are the real thing. He has long Scots roots in the soil of his profession, and even those who recoil automatically from the man who directed psychological warfare over Suez may glean something from this book about the heart and head of soldiering."

AVOCATIONAL INTERESTS: Travel, sailing, shooting.

BIOGRAPHICAL/CRITICAL SOURCES: Observer Review, September 27, 1970.

*   *   *

FERGUSSON, Francis   1904-

PERSONAL: Born February 21, 1904, in Albuquerque, N.M.; son of Harvey Butler (a lawyer) and Clara (Huning) Fergusson; married Marion Crowne, January 16, 1931 (died, 1959); married Peggy Watts, July 26, 1962; children: (first marriage) Harvey, Honora. *Education:* Attended Harvard University, 1921-23; Oxford University, Rhodes Scholar, B.A., 1926. *Address:* Box 143, Kingston, N.J. 08528. *Office:* Princeton University, Princeton, N.J. 08540.

CAREER: American Laboratory Theatre, New York, N.Y., associate director, 1926-30; *The Bookman*, New York, N.Y., theater critic, 1930-32; New School for Social Research, New York, N.Y., lecturer and executive secretary, 1932-34; Bennington College, Bennington, Vt., professor of literature and drama, 1934-47; Princeton University, Princeton, N.J., member of Institute for Advanced Study, 1948-49, director of Gauss Seminars, 1949-52; Rutgers University, New Brunswick, N.J., professor of comparative literature, 1952-73; Princeton University, Princeton, N.J., professor, 1973—. Indiana University, fellow, 1950, visiting professor, 1952-53. *Member:* Modern Language Association, National Institute of Arts and Letters, P.E.N. *Awards, honors:* Christian Gauss Award, Phi Beta Kappa, 1953, for *Dante's Drama of the Mind;* National Institute of Arts and Letters Grant in Literature, 1953; D.Litt., University of New Mexico, 1955; *Kenyon Review* Fellow in Criticism, 1957.

WRITINGS: (Adaptor) Sophocles, *Electra: A Version for the Modern Stage*, William R. Scott, 1938; (contributor of essay) James Joyce, *Exiles*, New Directions, 1945; *The Idea of a Theater* (study of ten plays), Princeton University Press, 1949; *The King and the Duke: A Melodramatic Farce from Huckleberry Finn* (play; produced Off-Broadway, June, 1955), published in *From the Modern Repertoire*, Series Two, edited by Eric Bentley, University of Indiana Press, 1952; *Dante's Drama of the Mind: A Modern Reading of the "Purgatorio"*, Princeton University Press, 1953; *The Human Image in Dramatic Literature* (essays), Doubleday-Anchor, 1957; *Poems, 1929-1961*, Rutgers University Press, 1962; *Dante Alighieri: Three Lectures*, Gertrude Clarke Whittall Poetry and Literature Fund, U.S. Library of Congress, 1965; (translator with others) Sophocles, *Oedipus the King, Philoctetes, Electra,* [and] *Antigone*, Dell, 1965; *Dante*, Macmillan, 1966; *Shakespeare: The Pattern in His Carpet*, Dela-

corte, 1970. General editor and contributing editor, "Laurel Shakespeare" series, Dell, 1959—. Member of editorial board, *Comparative Literature.*

SIDELIGHTS: Stanley Edgar Hyman calls Fergusson the only important American critic to be centrally concerned with the theatre. Fergusson's theory of the drama involves the human soul's movement from purpose to passion to perception, a movement analogous to the one found in Dante's *Purgatorio*. A reviewer for the *New York Times Book Review* has called his *Dante* "the most lucid and intelligent general introduction to Dante in English."

Of his *Poems* Paul Engle has written: "Reading the brief play 'Penelope' in Francis Fergusson's volume, one wishes that he had written far more for theatre, and that he had used his poetic gift more eloquently in his prose. . ."

He is the brother of Harvey Fergusson, a novelist, and Erna Fergusson, a regional writer.

BIOGRAPHICAL/CRITICAL   SOURCES: Stanley Edgar Hyman, *The Armed Vision*, Vintage, 1955; *New 20, 1966; Book Week*, July 24, 1966; Alan Cheuse and Richard Koffler, editors, *The Rarer Action: Essays in York Times Book Review*, September 1, 1963, November *Honor of Francis Fergusson*, Rutgers University Press, 1970; *Library Journal*, September 1, 1970; *New York Review of Books*, November 19, 1970.

*   *   *

FERGUSSON HANNAY, Lady
(Doris Leslie)

PERSONAL: Born in London, England; married John Leslie (an actor) while in her teens (he died a short time later); in accordance with her religion, Lady Fergusson Hannay does not acknowledge a subsequent marriage to R. Vincent Cookes (deceased); married, 1936, Walter Fergusson Hannay (a London physician, who was knighted in 1951, and died in 1961). *Education:* Attended private schools in London, England, and Brussels, Belgium; studied art and drama in London and Florence. *Religion:* Roman Catholic convert, 1961. *Home:* Cintra, Budleigh, Salterton, Devonshire, England. *Agent:* A.P. Watt & Son, 26-28 Bedford Row, London W.C.1, England.

CAREER: Actress for a brief period in London, England, before starting to write (more or less without plan). First book, centered in Florence, Italy, led to several additional books (through *Puppet's Parade*) which the author considers "not good enough" to list; then *Full Flavor* became an international best-seller, and other novels and biographical studies have followed, in varying degrees, its success—six of them as National Book Club choices in England. During World War II, Lady Fergusson Hannay served in London's Civil Defence, 1941-45, was wounded on duty. She now lives in retirement in Devonshire. *Member:* Society of Authors, P.E.N., United Hunts Club (London). *Awards, honors: As the Tree Falls* selected as best historical novel of the year by *Books and Bookmen*, 1958; named Woman of the Year for Literature by the Catholic Women's League, 1970.

*WRITINGS—*All under name Doris Leslie: *The Starling*, Century Press, 1927; *Fools in Mortar*, Century Press, 1928; *The Echoing Green*, Hurst & Blackett, 1929; *Terminus*, Hurst & Blackett, 1931; *Puppet's Parade*, John Lane, 1932; *Full Flavor*, Macmillan, 1934; *Fair Company*, Macmillan, 1936; *Concord in Jeopardy*, Macmillan, 1938; *Another Cynthia: The Adventures of Cynthia, Lady Ffulkes (1780-1850) Reconstructed from Her Memoirs*, Macmillan, 1939; *House in the Dust*, Macmillan, 1942; *Folly's End*, Hutchinson, 1944; *The Peverills*, Hutchinson, 1946; *Tales fo Grace and Favour* (contains *Folly's End, The Peverills,* and *Another Cynthia),* Hutchinson, 1956; *As the Tree Falls,* Hodder & Stoughton, 1958.

Biographical studies, all under name Doris Leslie: *Royal William: The Story of a Democrat,* Hutchinson, 1940, Macmillan, 1941; *Polonaise,* Hutchinson, 1943; *Wreath for Arabella,* Hutchinson, 1948, Roy, 1949; *That Enchantress,* Hutchinson, 1950; *The Great Corinthian: A Portrait of the Prince Regent,* Eyre & Spottiswoode, 1952, Oxford University Press, 1953, new edition, Heinemann, 1967; *A Toast to Lady Mary,* Hutchinson, 1954; *Peridot Flight: A Novel Reconstructed from the Memoirs of Peridot, Lady Mulvarnie, 1872-1955,* Hutchinson, 1956; *The Perfect Wife,* Hodder & Stoughton, 1960, published in America as *The Prime Minister's Wife,* Doubleday, 1961; *Vagabond's Way: The Story of Francois Villon,* Doubleday, 1962 (published in England as *I Return: The Story of Francois Villon,* Hodder & Stoughton, 1962); *This for Caroline,* Heinemann, 1964; *Paragon Street,* Heinemann, 1965; *The Sceptre and the Rose,* Heinemann, 1967; *The Marriage of Martha Todd,* Heinemann, 1968; *The Rebel Princess,* Heinemann, 1970.

SIDELIGHTS: In a nationwide poll conducted several years ago Lady Fergusson Hannay was named the second most popular historical novelist of Britain, an honor that also took into account the fictional aspects of her historical biographies. *Full Flavor* was dramatized and translated into five languages; *Peridot Flight* was televised in ten weekly episodes by British Broadcasting Corp. in 1960. *Avocational interests:* Exhibiting prize bulldogs.

* * *

FERM, Vergilius (Ture Anselm) 1896-

PERSONAL: Born January 6, 1896, in Sioux City, Iowa; son of O. W. (a clergyman) and Mathilda (Slattengren) Ferm; married Nellie Nelson, June 25, 1919; children: Vergil H., Deane, Robert. *Education:* Augustana College, B.A. 1916; Augustana Theological Seminary, B.D., 1919; Yale University, M.A., 1923, Ph.D., 1925; also attended Northwestern University and State University of Iowa. *Religion:* United Lutheran Church of America. *Home:* 1586 Beall Ave., Wooster, Ohio 44691; (summer) Mercer, Wis.

CAREER: Ordained Lutheran minister, 1919; pastor in Iowa and Connecticut, 1919-26; Albright College, Reading, Pa., professor of philosophy and chairman of department of social sciences, 1926-27; College of Wooster, Wooster, Ohio, began as assistant professor, 1927, professor of philosophy, 1928-38, Compton Professor of Philosophy, and head of department, 1938-64, dean of summer sessions, 1940-44, now professor emeritus; Ashland College, Ashland, Ohio, professor of philosophy, 1968—. Visiting professor of philosophy, Sweet Briar College, 1964-65, Wake Forest University, 1965-68; Heidelberg College, 1966. Editor for book publishers. *Member:* American Theological Society (past president, Eastern division), American Philosophical Association, Phi Beta Kappa.

WRITINGS: *The Crisis in American Lutheran Theology: A Study of the Issue Between American Lutheranism and Old Lutheranism,* Zondervan, 1927; *First Adventures in Philosophy,* Scribner, 1936; *First Chapters in Religious Philosophy,* Round Table, 1937; *What Can We Believe?* Philosophical Library, 1948; *A Protestant Dictionary,* Philosophical Library, 1951, revised edition published as *A Concise Dictionary of Religion: A Lexicon of Protestant Interpretation,* 1965; *Their Day Was Yesterday* (novel), Library Publishers, 1954; *A Dictionary of Pastoral Psychology,* Philosophical Library, 1955; *In the Last Analysis,* 1956; *Pictorial History of Protestantism: A Panoramic View of Western Europe and the United States,* Philosophical Library, 1957; *A Brief Dictionary*

of American Superstitions, Philosophical Library, 1959; *Inside Ivy Walls: Observations from a College Professor's Notebook,* Citadel, 1964; *Toward an Expansive Christian Theology,* Philosophical Library, 1964; *Basic Philosophy for Beginners,* Christopher, 1969; *Memoirs of a College Professor,* Christopher, 1971; *So . . . You're Going to College,* Christopher, 1972; *Cross-Currents in the Personality of Martin Luther,* Christopher, 1972.

Editor: *What is Lutheranism?: A Symposium in Interpretation,* Macmillan, 1930; *Contemporary American Theology: Theological Autobiographies,* Round Table, Volume I, 1932, Volume II, 1933; Sarvepalli Radhakrishnan and others, *Religion in Transition,* Macmillan, 1937; *An Encyclopedia of Religion,* Philosophical Library, 1945; *Religion in the Twentieth Century,* Philosophical Library, 1948, reissued as *Living Schools of Religion,* Littlefield, 1956; *Forgotten Religions, Including Some Living Primitive Religions,* Philosophical Library, 1950, reissued as *Ancient Religions,* Citadel, 1965; *A History of Philosophical Systems,* Philosophical Library, 1950; (and contributor) *The American Church of the Protestant Heritage,* Philosophical Library, 1953; *Puritan Sage: The Collected Writings of Jonathan Edwards,* Library Publishers, 1953; *The Protestant Credo,* Philosophical Library, 1953; *An Encyclopedia of Morals,* Philosophical Library, 1956; *Classics of Protestantism,* Philosophical Library, 1959.

Ghost writer of one book; contributor of chapters to others. Contributor to encyclopedias, and of articles and reviews to journals.

SIDELIGHTS: *A Histroy of Philosophical Systems* has been translated into Japanese.

* * *

FERRIER, Janet Mackay 1919-
(Janet Love)

PERSONAL: Born June 6, 1919, in Girvan, Ayrshire, Scotland; daughter of Herbert Victor and Janet (Mackay) Ferrier; married William Love (a gynecologist), September 3, 1948; children: Janet Victoria. *Education:* St. Hilda's College, Oxford, B.A., 1940, M.A., 1945; University of Manchester, research student, 1940-41. *Home:* 226 Dialstone Lane, Stockport, Cheshire, England.

CAREER: British Foreign Office, temporary junior administrative officer of special department, 1941-45; Neville's Cross College, Durham, England, lecturer in French, 1945-46; University of Manchester, Manchester, England, assistant lecturer in French, 1946-48. Oral examiner in French, Northern Universities Joint Matriculation Board, 1956—.

WRITINGS: *L'Histoire de Messire Guido de Plaisance et de Fleurie sa Femme, and Its Antecedents: A Study in Fifteenth-Century Narrative Methods,* Manchester University Press, 1949; *Forerunners of the French Novel: An Essay on the Development of the Nouvelle in the Late Middle Ages,* Manchester University Press, 1954; (translator under name Janet Love) Guillaume Mollat, *The Popes at Avignon, 1305-1378,* Thomas Nelson, 1963; *French Prose Writers of the Fourteenth and Fifteenth Centuries,* Pergamon, 1966; (compiler) *100 Modern French Unseens,* Duckworth, 1970. Contributor to *French Studies.*

* * *

FESSLER, Loren W. 1923-

PERSONAL: Born July 17, 1923, in Thompson Falls, Mont.; son of Elmer I. and Kathryn E. (Kramer) Fessler; married Stella Lau, October 7, 1956 (divorced, 1968); children: Freeman D. *Education:* Lingnan University, Canton, China, student, 1948-49; Harvard University, B.A., 1950, M.A., 1968; University of Washington, graduate study, 1950-52. *Politics:* Independent. *Office address:* American Universities Field Staff, P.O. Box 150, Hanover, N.H. 03755.

CAREER: Asia Foundation, Taipei, Taiwan, English teacher, 1955-58; National Broadcasting Co. and Time-Life, Taipei stringer correspondent, 1955-58; Time-Life News Service, Hong Kong, British Crown Colony, correspondent, 1958-66; American Universities Field Staff, Associate, 1969—. *Military service:* U.S. Army, Office of Strategic Services, 1943-46; received Bronze Star. *Member:* Foreign Correspondents' Club (Hong Kong), Overseas Press Club (New York).

WRITINGS: (With the editors of *Life*) *China*, Time, Inc., 1963.

WORK IN PROGRESS: Research on current affairs in Communist and Nationalist China.

* * *

FIELD, Thomas P(arry)   1914-

PERSONAL: Born June 6, 1914, in Waynesburg, Pa.; son of Frank (a college administrator) and Jane Wood (Parry) Field; married Nancie Emerson Davis (a music teacher), July 29, 1944; children: Julia Davis, Gwendolyn Parry. *Education:* East Tennessee State College, B.S., 1935; George Peabody College for Teachers, M.A., 1940; University of North Carolina, Ph.D., 1948. *Politics:* Independent. *Religion:* Presbyterian. *Home:* 1014 Castleton Way S., Lexington, Ky. 40502.

CAREER: Public school teacher in Johnson City, Tenn., 1935-36, Greenville, N.C., 1936-39; East Tennessee State College, Johnson City, teacher in civilian pilot training program, 1940-42; University of Kentucky, Lexington, 1948—, began as instructor, became professor of geography. *Military service:* U.S. Navy, 1942-45. *Member:* Association of American Geographers, American Names Society, American Association of University Professors.

WRITINGS: (With I. T. Sanders and others) *Societies Around the World*, two volumes, Dryden Press, 1953, 2nd edition, 1956; *Swanland, 1829-1956: The Agricultural Districts of Western Australia*, University of Kentucky, 1956; *A Guide to Kentucky Place Names*, College of Arts and Sciences, University of Kentucky, 1961; *Postwar Land Settlement in Western Australia*, University of Kentucky Press, 1963.

WORK IN PROGRESS: An article for *A Pictorial History of Kentucky; An Evaluation of the War Service Land Settlement Scheme in Western Australia;* editing an atlas of Kentucky.

AVOCATIONAL INTERESTS: Photography.

* * *

FIELDING, Daphne Winifred Louise   1904-

PERSONAL: Born July 11, 1904, in London, England; daughter of Lord Vivian and Cecile (Wunenburger); married Marquess of Bath; married second husband, Xan Fielding, July 11, 1953; children: (first marriage) Lady Caroline Somerset, Viscount Weymouth, Lord Christopher Thynne, Lord Valentine Thynne. *Education:* Attended Queen's College, London, England, St. James School, West Malvern, England, and Villa St. James, Neuilly, Paris, France. *Politics:* Conservative. *Religion:* Church of England. *Home:* La Galerie des Patres, Uzes, Gard, France. *Agent:* Curtis Brown Ltd., 13 King St., Covent Garden, London W.C.2, England.

CAREER: Writer. American Red Cross librarian during World War II.

WRITINGS: Longleat: From 1566 to the Present Time, Longleat Estate Co., 1951; *Before the Sunset Fades: Recalled by the Marchioness of Bath,* Longleat Estate Co., 1951; *Cheddar Aves,* Longleat Estate Co., 1952; *Mercury Presides,* Eyre & Spottiswoode, 1954, Harcourt, 1955; *The Adonis Garden,* Eyre & Spottiswoode, 1961; *The Duchess of Jermyn Street: The Life and Good Times of Rosa Lewis of the Cavendish Hotel,* preface by Evelyn Waugh, Little, Brown, 1964; *Those Remarkable Cunards: Emerald and Nancy,* Atheneum, 1968 (published in England as *Emerald and Nancy: Lady Cunard and Her Daughter,* Eyre & Spottiswoode, 1968); *The Nearest Way Home,* Eyre & Spottiswoode, 1970. Contributor of articles to English newspapers.

WORK IN PROGRESS: The Thirties; The Rainbow Picnic.

SIDELIGHTS: In a review of *Those Remarkable Cunards: Emerald and Nancy,* Alice Andrews writes: "Though [Daphne Fielding] tells us that both were her friends, there is singularly little of the personal in the book—especially of either condemnation or defence. She leaves them to speak for themselves, and by so doing has produced a book that will be not only enjoyed by those with a more or less superficial interest in leading personalities of the social world in the first half of this century, but with deeper undertones to fascinate those with some knowledge of psychology, and interested in the underlying thought of one of the most pregnant and shattering 50 years of world history."

AVOCATIONAL INTERESTS: Painting, riding, gastronomy, and playing the recorder.

* * *

FIEDLER, Leslie A(aron)   1917-

PERSONAL: Born March 8, 1917, in Newark, N.J.; son of Jacob J. (a pharmacist) and Lillian (Rosenstrauch) Fiedler; married Margaret Ann Shipley, October 6, 1939; married Sally Andersen, February, 1973; children: (first marriage) Kurt, Eric, Michael, Deborah, Jenny, Miriam; (second marriage; stepchildren) Soren Andersen, Eric Andersen. *Education:* New York University, B.A., 1938; University of Wisconsin, M.A., 1939, Ph.D., 1941; Harvard University, post-doctoral study as Rockefeller fellow, 1946-47. *Religion:* Jewish. *Home:* 154 Morris Ave., Buffalo, N.Y. *Office:* State University of New York at Buffalo, Buffalo, N.Y.

CAREER: Montana State University, Missoula, assistant professor, 1941-48, associate professor, 1948-52, professor of English, 1954-64, department chairman and director of humanities courses, 1954-56; State University of New York at Buffalo, professor of English, 1964—. Fulbright fellow and lecturer, Universities of Rome and Bologna (Italy), 1951-53, University of Athens (Greece), 1961-62; resident fellow in creative writing and Gauss Lecturer, Princeton University, 1956-57; visiting professor, University of Sussex (England), 1967-68, University of Vincennes (France), 1971. Summer professor at New York University, Columbia University, University of Vermont, and Indiana University. Lecturer. *Military Service:* U.S. Naval Reserve, 1942-46; Japanese interpreter; became lieutenant j.g. *Member:* American Association of University Professors, Modern Language Association of America, English Institute, Dante Society of America, P.E.N., Phi Beta Kappa. *Awards, honors:* Rockefeller fellowship, 1946-47; junior fellow, School of Letters, Indiana University, 1953, *Kenyon Review* fellow in Literary Criticism, 1956-57; National Book Awards Judge, 1956, 1972; American Council of Learned Societies grants-in-aid, 1960, 1961; Furioso prize for poetry; National Institute of Arts and Letters prize for excellence in creative writing, 1957; Guggenheim fellowship, 1970-71.

WRITINGS: (Author of introduction) Robert Louis Stevenson, *Master of Ballantrae*, Rinehart, 1954; *An End to Innocence: Essays on Culture and Politics*, Beacon Press, 1955; (contributor) Milton Hindus, editor, *Leaves of Grass One Hundred Years After*, Stanford University Press, 1955; (with others) *Negro and Jew: Encounter in America*, [New York], 1956; (editor) *The Art of the Essay*, Crowell, 1958, 2nd edition, 1969; (author of introduction) *Walt Whitman: Selections from Leaves of Grass*, Dell, 1959; *The Jew in the American Novel*, Herzl Press, 1959, second edition, 1966; *Love and Death in the American Novel* (first in a trilogy), Criterion, 1960, revised edition, Stein & Day, 1966; *No! In Thunder: Essays on Myth and Literature*, Beacon Press, 1960; *Pull Down Vanity, and Other Stories* (contains "The Teeth," "The Fear of Innocence," "An Expense of Spirit," "Nobody Ever Died From It," "Pull Down Vanity," "The Stain," "Nude Croquet," "The Dancing of Reb Hershl with the Withered Hand") Lippincott, 1962; (with others) *The Riddle of Shakespeare's Sonnets* (interpretive essays) Basic Books, 1962; *The Second Stone: A Love Story*, Stein & Day, 1963; *Waiting for the End* (second in the trilogy, Stein & Day, 1964 (published in England as *Waiting for the End: The American Literary Scene from Hemingway to Baldwin*, Cape, 1965); (editor, with Jacob Vinocur) *The Continuing Debate: Essays on Education*, St. Martin's Press, 1964; *Back to China* (novel), Stein & Day, 1965; (contributor) Fred Eychaner, editor, *Reflections on Rebellion: The 1965 Northwestern Student Symposum*, [Evanston], 1965; *The Last Jew in America* (three novelettes: "The Last Jew in America," "The Last WASP in the World," "The First Spade in the West") Stein & Day, 1966; (author of afterword) Samuel Langhorne Clemens, *The Innocents Abroad*, New American Library, 1966; *The Return of the Vanishing American* (third in the trilogy), Stein & Day, 1968; (editor, with Arthur Zeiger) *A Critical Anthology of American Literature*, Dell, Volume I: *O Brave New World: American Literature From 1600 to 1840*, 1968; *Nude Croquet: The Stories of Leslie Fiedler* (contains "Nude Croquet," "The Teeth," "Let Nothing You Dismay," "Dirty Ralphy," "The Fear of Innocence," "An Expense of Spirit," "Nobody Ever Died From It," "Pull Down Vanity," "The Stain," "Bad Scene at Buffalo Jump," [appears in novel, *Back to China*], "The Girl in the Black Raincoat," "The Dancing of Reb Hershl With the Withered Hand"), Stein & Day, 1969; *Being Busted*, Stein & Day, 1969; (editor, with J.W. Field, and author of introduction) *Bernard Malamud and the Critics*, New York University Press, 1970; *Collected Essays* (two volumes), Stein & Day, 1971; (contributor) Arthur A. Cohen, compiler, *Arguments and Doctrines: A Reader of Jewish Thinking in the Aftermath of the Holocaust*, Harper, 1970; *The Stranger in Shakespeare*, Stein and Day, 1972; *Unfinished Business*, Stein and Day, 1972; *To the Gentiles*, Stein and Day, 1972; *Cross the Border, Close the Gap*, Stein and Day, 1972. Contributor to *Kenyon Review*, *Partisan Review*, *Poetry*, *Commentary*, *New Republic*, *Encounter*, and other periodicals in the United States and Europe. Work included in collections. Advisory editor, *Ramparts* and *Studies in Black Literature;* regular columnist for *American Judaism;* advisory editor in English to St. Martin's Press.

WORK IN PROGRESS: Further volumes of *A Critical Anthology of American Literature*; a book of poems.

SIDELIGHTS: Upon publication of *An End to Innocence*, the same critic who called Fiedler "one of the most vigorous social and literary critics to appear recently in this country," also said: "Many ... will be annoyed with him at points, and some will be shocked." This tendency toward a polarization of his readers has remained a characteristic of his work. Robert Adams asks: "Is he really provocative or just provoking"? In much the same way, C.A. Raines describes him as the "exasperating, exhaustive, provocative Professor Fiedler."

Brilliantly intelligent, and acknowledged as an exceptional teacher, Fiedler, in the words of Kingsley Widmer, "as a learned critic, punched away at the bland decorum which dominates humanistic studies." And John Leonard writes that he has been able "to reveal the richness and complexity of our literary legacy.... He permits us to argue with our own writers, not simply worship their semicolons and explicate their disguises."

Fiedler's critical works are sometimes seen as superior to his fiction. Charlotte Croman wrote: "It is a tribute to Fiedler that he can create as well as criticize.... Unfortunately, Fiedler's magnificent, hyperbolic and imaginative use of American English never quite shines the way it does in his non-fictional creations." Guy Daniels wants "to cry out, 'Fiction should be at least as well written as criticism,' " and is convinced *Back to China* is "wilfully bad writing, literary Pop Art." Annette Grant finds that while the hypocrisies and ambivalences of the liberal mind have been brilliantly explored in his essays and criticism, Fiedler's "strength as a social, intellectual and literary historian is his weakness as a writer of fiction." Fiedler told *CA* that "Joyce Carol Oates, on the other hand, finds his fiction superior to his non-fiction."

In 1967 Fiedler was arrested on a charge of "maintaining premises where marijuana was used." Shocked by what he felt was political oppression and the resulting personal persecution and harassment, he was moved to examine his life in the light of his "pattern of dissent." He explores his "ambivalence" as a literary-academic rebel in *Being Busted*, which he himself described to an interviewer as "a kind of cultural-political autobiography—not really a very personal book, but one concerned chiefly with my own life at points where it has touched public issues, usually via the interference of the cops." Widmer says the book reveals "a deep uncertainty about the role of the 'established liberal humanist,' as Fiedler describes himself, playing 'disturber of the peace.' " At his trial, Fiedler was found guilty as charged and sentenced to six months in jail, a sentence later reversed by the Court of Appeals of the State of New York, which found that Fiedler "had never been convicted of a crime, or charged with a crime."

BIOGRAPHICAL/CRITICAL SOURCES: U.S. Quarterly Book Review, September, 1955; *Nation*, August 15, 1959, September 22, 1969; *Saturday Review*, July 2, 1960; *New Republic*, May 22, 1965; *Commonweal*, January 6, 1967; *New York Review of Books*, April 10, 1969; *Book World*, August 17, 1969; *Village Voice*, December 25, 1969.

* * *

FILBY, P(ercy) W(illiam) 1911-

PERSONAL: Born December 10, 1911, in Cambridge, England; came to United States in 1957, naturalized in 1961; son of William Lusher (a builder) and Florence Ada (Stanton) Filby; married Nancie Elizabeth Giddens, Aug. 20, 1936 (divorced, 1957); married Vera Ruth Weakliem (a U.S. government research analyst), May 23, 1957; children: (first marriage) Ann Veronica (Mrs. Ward Chesworth), Jane Vanessa, Roderick, Guy. *Education:* Attended Cambridge University, 1928-29. *Politics:* Democrat. *Religion:* Church of England. *Home:* 307 Madison St., Savage, Md. 20863. *Office:* Maryland Historical Society, 201 W. Monument, Baltimore, Md. 21201.

CAREER: Cambridge University, Cambridge, England, library staff, 1929-37, chief librarian of Science Library, 1937-40; British Foreign Office, London, England, senior researcher, 1946-57; Peabody Institute Library, Baltimore, Md., assistant director, 1957-65; Maryland Historical Society, Baltimore, librarian and assistant director, 1965-72, director, 1972—. Secretary to Sir James G. Frazer, 1935-40. Lecturer to universities on calligraphy, fine printing, genealogy, heraldry, James Frazer. *Military service:* British Army, Intelligence Corps, 1942-46; became captain. *Member:* American Library Association, Grolier Club, Typophiles, Special Libraries Association (president, Baltimore chapter), Bibliographical Society of America, Baltimore Bibliophiles (president), and twenty antiquarian societies in England.

WRITINGS: Cambridge Papers, Cambridge University Library, 1935; *Calligraphy and Handwriting in America, 1710-1962,* Italimuse, 1963; *English, Irish, Scottish, Welsh Genealogy and Heraldry: A List of Basic Books,* Peabody Institute Library, 1964; *2,000 Years of Calligraphy,* American Library Association, 1965; *American and British Genealogy and Heraldry: A Selective List of Books,* American Library Association, 1970; (with Edward G. Howard) *Star Spangled Books: Books, Sheet Music, Newspapers, Manuscripts, and Persons Associated with the Star-Spangled Banner,* Maryland Historical Society, 1972. Regular contributor to *RQ, Baltimore Evening Sun, Baltimore Sunday Sun,* and to *Library Journal.*

WORK IN PROGRESS: Under the Golden Bough: Life With the Frazers; manuscript collections of the Maryland Historical Society; some Shakespearean works.

AVOCATIONAL INTERESTS: Genealogy and heraldry, particularly British sources.

BIOGRAPHICAL/CRITICAL SOURCES: Antiquarian Bookman, yearbook, 1970.

*   *   *

FINK, Merton   1921-
(Matthew Finch, Merton Finch)

PERSONAL: Born November 17, 1921, in Liverpool, England; son of Norman (a secret service agent) and Francoise (le Pretre) Fink; married Ruth E. Tennant (a novelist, March 15, 1953; children: Frances, Peter. *Education:* University of Liverpool, B.S., 1941, Licence in Dental Surgery, 1952. *Home:* 1 Barkhill Rd., Liverpool 17, England. *Agent:* Laurence Pollinger Ltd., 18 Maddox St., Mayfair, London W.1, England.

CAREER: Dental surgeon in private practice, 1952—; administrative grade civil servant. Has own radio show, "Matthew Finch on Paradise Street." *Military service:* British Army, Royal Engineers, staff officer, War Office, 1940-48; became captain. *Member:* British Dental Association, Royal Engineers Association, Civil Service Writers Association, British Society of Aesthetics, P.E.N., Liverpool Rifle Club.

WRITINGS—All under pseudonym Matthew Finch, except as indicated; all published by Dobson, except as indicated: *Dentist in the Chair,* 1955; *Teething Troubles,* 1956; *The Third Set,* 1957; *Hang Your Hat on a Pension,* 1958; *The Empire Builder,* 1959; *Snakes and Ladders,* 1960; *Solo Fiddle,* 1961; *The Beauty Bazaar,* 1962; *The Match Breakers,* 1963; *Five Are the Symbols,* 1964; *Jones in a Rainbow,* 1965; *Chew This Over: The Life of a Dentist,* Education Explorers, 1965; *The Succubus,* 1966; *Eye With Mascara,* 1968; (under pseudonym Merton Finch) *Simon Bar Cochba: Rebellion in Judea,* Dutton, 1969; (under pseudonym Merton Finch) *Josephus Flavius,* Dutton, in press. Writer of film and television scripts. Author of monthly column in *Dental Practice.*

WORK IN PROGRESS: Matilda the Ironside.

SIDELIGHTS: Dentist in the Chair was filmed in 1961; film scripts have been written for *Hang Your Hat on a Pension* and *The Empire Builder.*

FINLAY, Winifred Lindsay Crawford (McKissack)   1910-

PERSONAL: Born April 27, 1910, in Newcastle upon Tyne, Northumberland, England; daughter of James and Susan (Crawford) McKissack; married Evan Finlay (a college lecturer), July, 1935; children: Gillian. *Education:* Kings College, Newcastle upon Tyne, England, M.A., 1933. *Home:* The Old House, Walgrave, Northampton, England.

CAREER: Schoolmistress at Newcastle, England, 1933-35, Stratford on Avon, England, 1941-44, and Leeds, England, 1945-48; writer. Lecturer on books to school children and librarians. *Member:* Society of Authors, National Book League, Northampton Arts Association. *Awards, honors:* Edgar Allan Poe special award, Mystery Writers of America, 1969, for *Danger at Blade Dyke.*

WRITINGS—All published by Harrap, except as indicated: *The Witch of Redesdale,* 1951, *Peril in Lakeland,* 1953, *Peril in the Pennines,* 1953, *Cotswold Holiday,* 1954, *Lost Silver of Langdon,* 1955, *Storm Over Cheviot,* 1955, *Judith in Hannover,* 1955, *Canal Holiday,* 1957, *The Cruise of the Susan,* 1958, *The Lost Emeralds of Black Howes,* 1961, *The Castle and the Cave,* 1961, *Alison in Provence,* 1963, *Mystery in the Middle Marches,* 1965, *Castle for Four,* 1966, *Adventure in Prague,* 1967, *Danger at Black Dyke,* S.G. Phillips, 1968, *Folk Tales from the North,* Kaye & Ward, 1968, F. Watts, 1969, *The Cry of the Peacock,* 1969, *Summer of the Golden Stag,* 1969, *Folk Tales from Moor and Mountain,* Kaye & Ward, 1969, Roy, 1970, *Singing Stones,* 1970.

WORK IN PROGRESS: A junior novel with a fourth century background of struggle for power between Picts and Celts of Iona and Argyll.

SIDELIGHTS: Mrs. Finlay told *CA:* "All my stories for young people are set in real places which I know well; each book has a map to show where the imaginary adventure takes place, and I generally try to work in local history and folklore." She lives in a seventeenth-century house in a small Midland village. *Avocational interests:* Reading, gardening, cooking, archaeology.

BIOGRAPHICAL/CRITICAL SOURCES: Books and Bookmen, December, 1963, September, 1968; *Best Sellers,* December 1, 1968; *Times Literary Supplement,* June 26, 1969; *Book World,* August 17, 1969.

*   *   *

FINNEY, Gretchen Ludke   1901-

PERSONAL: Born December 12, 1901, in Browns Valley, Minn.; daughter of Henry W. (a businessman) and Janet (Florance) Ludke; married Ross Lee Finney (a composer), September 3, 1930; children: Ross Finney III, Henry Christopher. *Education:* Carleton College, A.B., 1923; Radcliffe College, graduate study, 1923-24; University of California, Berkeley, M.A., 1925. *Home:* 2015 Geddes Ave., Ann Arbor, Mich. 48104.

CAREER: Carleton College, Northfield, Minn., instructor in English, 1925-29; Smith College, Northampton, Mass., instructor in English, 1944-48. *Member:* Renaissance Society of America, Phi Beta Kappa.

WRITINGS: Musical Backgrounds for English Literature: 1580-1650, Rutgers University Press, 1962.

WORK IN PROGRESS: A history of the use of music for prevention and cure of disease, with research in medical collections in Paris.

*   *   *

FIRMAGE, George J (ames)   1928-

PERSONAL: Born July 3, 1928, in New York, N.Y. *Education:* Attended Massachusetts Institute of Technology,

1947-48, College of City of New York (now City College of City University of New York), 1949; New York University, B.A., 1952; University of Massachusetts, graduate study, 1952-54. *Home:* 27 Jones St., New York, N.Y. 10014.

CAREER: First National City Bank, New York, N.Y., publications supervisor in advertising and marketing services department, 1954—.

WRITINGS: A Checklist of the Published Writings of Gertrude Stein, University of Massachusetts, 1954; (editor and author of introduction) *E.E. Cummings: A Miscellany,* Argophile Press, 1958, 2nd edition published as *E.E. Cummings: A Miscellany Revised,* Clarke & Way, 1964; *E.E. Cummings: A Bibliography,* Wesleyan University Press, 1960; (editor) *A Garland for Dylan Thomas,* Clarke & Way, 1963; (editor and author of introduction) E.E. Cummings, *Three Plays and a Ballet,* October House, 1967.

WORK IN PROGRESS: Two books on Dylan Thomas' works, *Dylan Thomas: A Bibliography,* and *Dylan Thomas: The Uncollected Poetry and Prose; E.E. Cummings: Collected Works.*

* * *

FISCHER, John 1910-

PERSONAL: Born April 27, 1910, in Texhoma, Okla.; son of John S. and Georgia (Caperton) Fischer; married Elizabeth Wilson, 1936; children: (daughters) Nicolas Fischer Hahn, Sara Fischer Geeson. *Education:* University of Oklahoma, B.A., 1932; Lincoln College, Oxford, Rhodes Scholar, 1933-35. *Religion:* Unitarian. *Home:* Shell Beach Rd., Guilford, Conn. 06437. *Office: Harper's,* 2 Park Ave., New York, N.Y. 10016.

CAREER: Began newspaper work with *Globe News,* Amarillo, Tex., while in high school, and later worked as reporter for *Current-Argus,* Carlsbad, N.M., *Oklahoma Daily,* Norman, and *Daily Oklahoman,* Oklahoma City, 1928-33; United Press, reporter in England and Germany, 1933-35; Associated Press, Washington, D.C., correspondent, 1935-37, head of Senate staff, 1937; U.S. Government, Washington, D.C., with Department of Agriculture in Farm Security Administration and Bureau of Agriculture Economics, 1937-41, with Board of Economic Welfare and Foreign Economic Administration, 1941-44, serving as chief representative in India and Burma, 1943-44, and as economic intelligence officer on General Stilwell's staff; *Harper's Magazine,* New York, N.Y., associate editor, 1944-47; Harper & Brothers (Now Harper & Row, Publishers, Inc.), New York, N.Y., chief editor of general books, 1947-53; *Harper's Magazine,* editor-in-chief, 1953-67, contributing editor, 1967-71, associate editor, 1971—. Member of United Nations Relief and Rehabilitation Administration team in Russia, 1945. Advisor and speech writer on staff of Adlai Stevenson during presidential campaign, 1952-56. Member, Presidential Commission on Rural Poverty, 1966-67. Consultant or member of selection committees of Institute for International Education, John Hay Whitney Foundation, Rhodes Trust, Fund for Adult Education, Markle Foundation, and National Book Committee. Trustee, Brookings Institution. Regent's Professor at University of California and lecturer at other universities in United States and in Europe.

MEMBER: Council on Foreign Relations, American Political Science Association, Phi Beta Kappa, Century Association. *Awards, honors:* LL.D., Bucknell University and Kenyon College, 1954; D.H.L., University of Massachusetts, 1956; Society of Magazine Writer's award for editorial distinction.

WRITINGS: Why They Behave Like Russians (Book-of-the-Month Club selection), Harper, 1947 (published in England as *The Scared Men in the Kremlin,* Hamish Hamilton, 1947); *India's Insoluble Hunger,* Vora (Bombay), 1947; *Master Plan U.S.A.: An Informal Report on America's Foreign Policy and the Men Who Make It,* Harper, 1951 (published in England as *America's Master Plan,* Hamish Hamilton, 1951); (with Hugo Kalnoky and Leslie Le Nard) *Forced Labor and Confinement without Trial in Hungary,* National Committee for a Free Europe, Mid-European Studies Center, 1952; (editor with Robert B. Silvers) *Writing in America,* Rutgers University Press, 1960; (editor with Lucy Donaldson) *Humor From Harper's,* foreword by Ogden Nash, Harper, 1969; *The Stupidity Problem, and Other Harassments* (selections from "The Easy Chair" column), Harper, 1964. Author of monthly column, "The Easy Chair," in *Harper's.* Contributor of articles to *Life, New Yorker, Reader's Digest,* and other national magazines.

* * *

FISHMAN, Jack 1920-

PERSONAL: Born July 14, 1920, in London, England; married Lillian Richman, February 13, 1944; children: Ian, Paul. *Education:* Left school at age of fourteen; later attended night school. *Home:* London, England. *Address:* c/o David McKay Co., Inc., 119 West 40th St., New York, N.Y. 10018.

CAREER: Junior reporter; sub-editor, *Sunday Referee* (later absorbed by Kemsley newspapers); Kemsley Newspaper and Thomson Newspaper organizations, England, news editor and deputy editor for twenty years. *Military service:* Royal Air Force, World War II.

WRITINGS: The Seven Men of Spandau, Rinehart, 1954; (editor) *The Official Radio Luxembourg Book of Record Stars,* introduction by Frank Sinatra, Souvenir Press, 1962, supplement number five, 1966; (with J. Bernard Hutton) *The Private Life of Josef Stalin,* W.H. Allen, 1962; *My Darling Clementine: The Story of Lady Churchill,* introduction by Eleanor Roosevelt, McKay, 1963, revised edition, Pan Books, 1964.

SIDELIGHTS: Fishman had long exposure to Winston Churchill's activities before he wrote the best-selling *My Darling Clementine.* His coverage of events in which Churchill figured dated to pre-war elections, continued through the war years, and later to Parliament. He also obtained exclusive stories from Joseph Stalin and Pope Pius XII. *The Seven Men of Spandau* was one of the authoritative books used by William Shirer in the preparation of *The Rise and Fall of the Third Reich.* Fishman's hobby as composer-lyricist has been converted into a second profession—he has written compositions for some twenty major films.

BIOGRAPHICAL/CRITICAL SOURCES: New York Times, July 21, 1963, September 1, 1963.

* * *

FITZGERALD, Patrick (John) 1928-

PERSONAL: Born September 30, 1928, in Walsall, England; son of Thomas Walter (a medical doctor) and N.J. (Twomey) Fitzgerald; married Brigid Aileen Judge, August 15, 1959; children: Katherine, Liam, Michael. *Education:* Studied at University College, Oxford, 1945-49. *Religion:* Roman Catholic. *Office:* Department of Law, Carleton University, Ottawa, Canada.

CAREER: Lincoln's Inn, London, England, barrister-at-law, 1951-56; Trinity College, Oxford University, Oxford, England, law fellow, 1956-60; University of Leeds, Leeds, England, professor of law, 1960-66; University of Kent, Canterbury, England, professor of law, 1966-71; Carleton University, Ottawa, professor of law, 1971—. Visiting professor of law at the University of Louisville, Louisville, Ky., 1962-63. Research worker on *British Digest of International Law,* 1958-59. *Military service:* Royal Air Force, 1951-53; became pilot officer. *Member:* United Nations Association (secretary of Oxford City branch, 1959-60; chairman of Leeds district council, 1963-66), Lincoln's Inn.

WRITINGS: (Contributor) A.G. Guest, editor, *Oxford Essays in Jurisprudence,* Oxford University Press, 1961; *Criminal Law and Punishment,* Clarendon Press, 1962; *Crime, Sin and Negligence: An Inaugural Lecture,* Leeds University Press, 1962; (editor) *Salmond on Jurisprudence,* 12th edition, Sweet & Maxwell, 1966; (contributor) David Layton, editor, *University Teaching in Transition,* Oliver & Boyd, 1968; (with others) *Road Accident: Prevent or Punish?,* Cassell, 1969. Contributor of articles to legal periodicals.

WORK IN PROGRESS: English Civil Liberties, for Oxford University Press; *Law the Oppressor,* a review of common law, for Oxford University Press.

SIDELIGHTS: Fitzgerald is interested in computer language and its application to law. *Avocational interests:* Music, choral singing, string playing.

*   *   *

FITZMYER, Joseph A(ugustine)   1920-

PERSONAL: Born November 4, 1920, in Philadelphia, Pa.; son of Joseph A. and Anna C. (Alexy) Fitzmyer. *Education:* Loyola University, Chicago, B.A., 1943, M.A., 1945; Facultes St. Albert de Louvain, S.T.L., 1952; Johns Hopkins University, Ph.D., 1956; Pontifico Instituto Biblico, S.S.L., 1957. *Home:* Faber Hall, 4906 South Greenwood Ave., Chicago, Ill. 60615. *Office:* 232 Oriental Institute, University of Chicago, 1155 East 58th St., Chicago, Ill. 60637.

CAREER: Roman Catholic priest, member of Society of Jesus (Jesuits); Gonzaga High School, Washington, D.C., instructor in Latin, Greek, and German, 1945-48; Woodstock College, Woodstock, Md., assistant professor, 1958-59, associate professor, 1959-64, professor of New Testament and Biblical languages, 1964-69; University of Chicago, Chicago, Ill., professor of Aramaic and Hebrew, 1969—. Visiting lecturer, Johns Hopkins University, 1958-61, University of Pennsylvania, 1965-66; visiting professor of New Testament, Yale Divinity School, 1967-68. Member, International Study Commission of the Lutheran World Federation and the Vatican Secretariat for Promoting Christian Unity, 1969-71. *Member:* American Oriental Society, Studiorum Novi Testamenti Societas, Catholic Biblical Association of America, Society of Biblical Literature and Exegesis, Catholic Commission on Intellectual and Cultural Affairs, Phi Beta Kappa. *Awards, honors:* Fellow of American School of Oriental Research, Jerusalem, 1957-58.

WRITINGS: (With George S. Glanzman) *An Introductory Bibliography for the Study of Scripture,* Newman, 1961; *The Historical Truth of the Gospels,* Paulist-Newman, 1964; (editor) Augustin Bea, *The Study of the Synoptic Gospels: New Approaches and Outlooks,* Harper, 1965; *The Genesis Apocryphon of Qumran Cave I: A Commentary,* Pontifical Biblical Institute (Rome), 1966; *Pauline Theology: A Brief Sketch,* Prentice-Hall, 1967; *The Aramaic Inscriptions of Sefire,* Pontifical Biblical Institute (Rome), 1967; (editor with others) *The Jerome Biblical Commentary,* Prentice-Hall, 1968; (author of prolegomenon) S. Schechter, *Documents of Jewish Sectaries,* Library of Biblical Studies, 1970; *Essays on the Semitic Background of the New Testament,* Geoffrey Chapman, 1971.

Contributor of numerous articles to periodicals. Associate editor, *Catholic Biblical Quarterly,* 1963—; chairman of editorial board, *Catholic Biblical Quarterly* monograph series, 1968—; Consulting editor, *Journal of Near Eastern Studies* and *Journal for the Study of Judaism,* 1969—; editor, *Journal of Biblical Literature,* 1971—.

WORK IN PROGRESS: Commentary on Luke's Gospel; Early Extrabiblical Aramaic Documents.

*   *   *

FLESCH, Rudolf (Franz)   1911-

PERSONAL: Born May 8, 1911, in Vienna, Austria; came to United States in 1938, naturalized, 1944; son of Hugo (a lawyer) and Helene (Basch) Flesch; married Elizabeth Terpenning, September 6, 1941; children: Anne (Mrs. Peter Wares), Hugo, Gillian, Katrina, Abigail, Janet. *Education:* University of Vienna, Jur.D., 1933; Columbia University, B.S., 1940, M.A., 1942, Ph.D., 1943. *Home:* 24 Belden Ave., Dobbs Ferry, N.Y. 10522.

CAREER: Free-lance writer. New York University, New York, N.Y., lecturer, 1946—; Famous Writers School, Westport, Conn., member of guiding faculty, 1960—.

WRITINGS—All published by Harper except as indicated: *Marks of Readable Style: A Study in Adult Education,* Teachers College, Columbia University, 1943; *The Art of Plain Talk,* 1946; (with A.H. Lass) *The Way to Write,* 1947, 2nd edition, McGraw, 1955, new edition published as *A New Guide to Better Writing,* Popular Library, 1963; *The Art of Readable Writing,* 1949; *How to Test Readability,* 1951; *The Art of Clear Thinking,* 1951; (editor) *Best Articles: Most Memorable Articles of the Year,* Hermitage House, 1953; *How to Make Sense,* 1954; *Why Johnny Can't Read—And What You Can Do About It,* 1955; *Teaching Johnny to Read,* Grosset, 1956; (with others) *How You Can Be a Better Student,* Sterling, 1957; *The Book of Unusual Quotations,* 1957; *A New Way to Better English,* 1958; *How to Write, Speak and Think More Effectively,* 1960; *How to Be Brief: An Index to Simple Writing,* 1962, published with title *How to Express Yourself Clearly and Briefly,* Citadel, 1968; *The ABC of Style: A Guide to Plain English,* 1964; (editor) *The Book of Surprises,* 1965; *The New Book of Unusual Quotations,* 1966; *Say What You Mean,* Harper, 1972. Also author of two booklets, *Some Writing Hints,* Prentice-Hall, 1948, and *How to Write Better,* Science Research Associates, 1951.

*   *   *

FLETCHER, Charlie May Hogue   1897-
  (Charlie May Simon)

PERSONAL: Born August 17, 1897, in Monticello, Ark.: daughter of Charles Wayman and Mary (Gill) Hogue; married John Gould Fletcher, January 18, 1936 (deceased). *Education:* Attended Memphis State University, Chicago Art Institute, and Le Grande Chaumiere, Paris, France. *Politics:* Independent. *Religion:* Episcopal. *Home:* 10314 Cantrell Rd., Little Rock, Ark. 72207.

CAREER: Author of books for children. *Awards, honors:* Albert Schweitzer Book Prize for *A Seed Shall Serve;* LL.D., University of Arkansas, 1960; Charles and Bertie G. Schwartz Award, Jewish Book Council of America, 1970, for *Martin Buber: Wisdom in Our Time.*

WRITINGS—All under pseudonym Charlie May Simon; all published by Dutton, except as indicated: *Robin on the Mountain,* 1934, *Lost Corner,* 1935, *Tenny Gay,* 1936, *The Sharecropper,* 1937, *Popo's Miracle,* 1938, *Bright Morning,* 1939, *The Faraway Trail,* 1940, *Roundabout,* 1941, *Younger Brother,* 1942, *Lonnie's Landing,* 1942, *Lays of the New Land: Stories of Some American Poets and Their Work,* 1943, *Song of Tomorrow: Stories of American Artists and Their Work,* 1945, *Joe Mason: Apprentice to Audubon,* 1946, *The Royal Road,* 1948, *Satur-*

day's Child, 1950, *The Long Hunt,* 1952, *Johnswood,* 1953, *Secret on the Congo,* Ginn, 1955, *Green Grows the Prairie: Arkansas in the 1890's,* Aladdin Books, 1956, *All Men Are Brothers: A Portrait of Albert Schweitzer,* 1956, *A Seed Shall Serve: The Story of Toyohiko Kagawa, Spiritual Leader of Modern Japan,* 1958, *The Sun and the Birch: The Story of Crown Prince Akihito and Crown Princess Michiko,* 1960, *The Andrew Carnegie Story,* 1965, *Dag Hammarskjold,* 1967, *Martin Buber: Wisdom in Our Times,* 1969. Contributor to *Collier's Encyclopedia;* contributor of short stories and articles to magazines.

WORK IN PROGRESS: A biography of Teilhard de Chardin.

BIOGRAPHICAL/CRITICAL SOURCES: Book Week, May 28, 1967.

* * *

FLETCHER, H(arry) L(utf) V(erne) 1902-
(John Garden, John Hereford)

PERSONAL: Born March 21, 1902, in Christchurch, Hampshire, England; son of Julien James and Alicia Anne (Merry) Fletcher; married Nora Lillian Stidwill, September 26, 1925; children: Barbara Fletcher Attwell, Peter. *Education:* Goldsmiths' College, University of London, teacher's certificate, 1925. *Religion:* Christian. *Home:* The Shieling, Llandrindod Wells, Wales. *Agent:* Laurence Pollinger Ltd., 18 Maddox St., London W.1, England.

CAREER: Former headmaster of a small country school; later deputy head teacher of secondary school in Llandrindod Wells, Wales; now retired from teaching. Author, 1940—, started with short stories, then sold six thrillers for cash to a pulp publisher, and began concentrating on the book field. *Member:* Society of Authors, Royal Horticultural Society.

WRITINGS—Novels; all published by Macdonald & Co., except as indicated: *Miss Agatha,* Wells Gardner, Darton & Co., 1942, *The Woman's House,* 1944, Messner, 1948, *Forest Inn,* 1946, *The Devil Has the Best Tunes,* 1947, *Miss Agatha Doubles for Death,* Messner, 1947, *The Whip and the Tongue,* 1949, *The Rising Sun,* 1951, *The Storm,* 1954, *High Pastures,* 1957, *The Lonely Island,* 1958, *The Reluctant Prodigal,* 1958

Country and garden books: *By Saint Phocas!,* Gifford, 1943; *Purest Pleasure: A Book of Garden Gossip,* Hodder & Stoughton, 1948; *Herefordshire,* R. Hale, 1948; *The Gardener's Pocket Companion,* Hodder & Stoughton, 1949; *The Water Garden,* Lehmann, 1951; *Fletcher's Folly,* Hodder & Stoughton, 1952; *Gardening on a Shoestring: The Pleasures of Plant Propagation,* Phoenix House, 1953; *North Wales,* Hodder & Stoughton, 1955, International Publications Service, 1972; *South Wales,* Hodder & Stoughton, 1956, International Publications Service, 1972; *The Feature Garden,* Phoenix House, 1960, Branfrod, 1961; *The Beginner's Garden: A Short Guide for the Complete Novice in the Garden,* Phoenix House, 1962, Branford, 1969; (compiler) *The Rose Anthology,* George Newnes, 1963; *The Fragrant Garden,* George Newnes, 1965; *The Pleasure Garden,* Hodder & Stoughton, 1967; (compiler) *The Happy Gardener,* Hodder & Stoughton, 1967, Funk, 1969; *Portrait of the Wye Valley,* R. Hale, 1968, International Publications Service, 1968; *The Coasts of Wales,* R. Hale, 1969, International Publications Service, 1970; *Gardening in Window Boxes and Other Containers,* Pelham Books, 1969; *Popular Flowering Plants,* Pelham Books, 1970; *Popular Flowering Shrubs,* Pelham Books, 1971.

Detective novels under pseudonym John Garden: *Six to Ten,* M. Joseph, 1947; *All on a Summer's Day,* M. Joseph, 1949; *Murder Isn't Private,* M. Joseph, 1950, published in America as *Day of Reckoning,* Lippincott, 1951; *A Little Time to Stay,* M. Joseph, 1953; *Death in the Village,* R. Hale, 1967.

Novels under pseudonym John Hereford; all published by Hodder & Stoughton: *Shepherd's Tump,* 1947, *The May Fair,* 1948, *Hay Harvest,* 1949, *A Day to Remember,* 1950, *The Ostriches in the Wilderness,* 1951, *The Well,* 1953, *The Good Summer,* 1956, *The Man Who Was Angry,* 1957.

Author of a film and several radio plays. Short stories have appeared in a number of magazines in Britain. Gardening editor, *Home and Gardens.*

WORK IN PROGRESS: A book about shrubs.

SIDELIGHTS: Fletcher says that his gardening books developed as sort of a side line. "I first wrote them because gardening is my hobby—at present they are crowding out the fiction.... Would like to write a really good novel (whatever that may be) but might settle (with an uneasy conscience) for a real smacking best seller."

Three of his novels have been serialized for radio, and one was used by Alfred Hitchcock for a television play.

* * *

FLETCHER, Helen Jill 1911-
(Carol Lee, Charles Morey)

PERSONAL: Born February 25, 1911; daughter of Charles Morey and Celia (Sperling) Siegel; married Jack Fletcher; children: Carol Joan (Mrs. Jules Viglielmo). *Education:* New York University, teaching certificate; also studied at Columbia University. *Home:* 101 West 57th St., New York, N.Y. 10019.

CAREER: Writer, primarily for children. Substitute teacher, New York Public Schools, New York, N.Y.

WRITINGS: (With Jack Deckter) *The Puppet Book: Everything You Need to Know for Putting on a Puppet Show,* Greenberg, 1947; (with Deckter) *Storyland Cook Book,* Maxton Publishers, 1948; *Let's Make Something,* House of Little Books, 1948; *Let's Cook Something,* House of Little Books, 1948; *The Big Top Circus Books,* S. Gabriel Sons, 1949; *Everything Goes,* S. Gabriel Sons, 1949; *The Art Apprentice's Handbook,* Pitman, 1949; *Christmas at the Zoo,* Doehla, 1952; *Trucks, Trailers and Tractors,* Rand McNally, 1954; (compiler) *The Trumpet Book of Laughs,* S. Gabriel Sons, 1955; *Trains,* S. Gabriel Sons, 1955; *The Secret of Cookies, Candies and Cakes,* Harvey House, 1957; *Trumpet Book of Boats,* S. Gabriel Sons, 1958; *Trumpet Book of Music,* S. Gabriel Sons, 1958; *Horses,* S. Gabriel Sons, 1958; *X-Word Puzzles for Children,* Samuel Lowe, 1958; *Paper Play,* Platt, 1958; *Finger Play Poems and Stories,* Educational Publishing Corp., 1958; *Blue Angel Book of Birds,* S. Gabriel Sons, 1959; *Strange and Unusual Birds,* S. Gabriel Sons, 1959; *Georgie Graymouse Finds a Home,* S. Gabriel Sons, 1959; *Indoor Gardens,* Educational Publishing Corp., 1959; *Travel and Stay-at-Home Fun,* Capitol Publishing, 1959; *Private Eye,* Capitol Publishing, 1959; *Golden Puppet Playhouse,* Golden Press, 1959; *The First Book of Bells,* F. Watts, 1959; *Christmas Book of Arts and Crafts,* Scholastic Book Services, 1960; *Coloring and Counting,* Golden Press, 1960; *Coloring and Writing,* Golden Press, 1960; *Coloring and Reading,* Golden Press, 1960; *The Make and Do Book of Arts and Crafts,* Random House, 1961; *The Airplane Book,* Paxton-Slade, 1961; *The Big Book of Things to Do and Make,* Random House, 1961; *For Junior Doctors Only,* Bobbs-Merrill, 1961; (with Renatus Hartogs) *How to Grow Up Successfully,* Bobbs-Merrill, 1961; *Action Songs,* Teachers Publishing Corp., 1961; *Children's Dances Around the World,* Educational Publishing Corp., c.1961; *Adventures in Archaeology,* Bobbs-Merrill, 1962; *Beginning Reading,* Harvey House, 1962; (editor) *The Children's Book of Games and Puzzles,* Bobbs-Merrill, 1962; *Creative Dramatics for Elementary Grades,* Teachers Publishing Corp., 1962; *The Stay-at-Home Book for 6-, 7-, and 8-Year-Olds,* Random House, 1962; *Finger Play Poems for Children,* Teachers Publishing Corp., 1964; *The Color Wheel Book,* McGraw, c.1965; *Show and Tell,* Platt, 1968; *Put On Your Thinking Cap,* Abelard, 1969; *Would You Believe?,* Platt, 1969; *Puzzles, Puzzles and More Puzzles,* Abelard, 1969; *ABC's of Contract Bridge,* McGraw, 1970; *Puzzles and Quizzes,* Abelard, 1971.

"Child Approved" series, published by Paxton-Slade, 1950-53: *Things to Do; Things to Make; Let's Have a Party: Menus, Decorations, Favors, Hats, Costumes, Games; Let's Play Together; Paper Fun; Paper Pastimes; Cook Book; Arts and Crafts Book; Quick and Easy Arts and Crafts; Quick and Easy Projects;* (self-illustrated) *The Nature Book; The Magic Book; How, When and Why; Games Around the World; Raising and Training Pets; Playbook of Learning; Hobbies; What Makes It Work; Advanced Arts and Crafts.*

"See and Do" series, published by H.S. Stuttman, 1959; *The See and Do Encyclopedia of Arts and Crafts; ...Book of Boxes, Cartons, and Containers; ...Book of Dolls and Doll Houses; ...Book of Crayons, Charcoal and Chalk; ...Cooking—Indoors and Out; ...Modeling and Sculpture.*

Adult books: *Your Face,* Will Roberts, 1952; *Your Hair,* Will Roberts, 1952; *Your Hands and Feet,* Will Roberts, 1952; *Your Body,* Will Roberts, 1952; *Your Clothes,* Will Roberts, 1952; *Your Charm and Personality,* Will Roberts, 1952; *Your Face Can Be Beautiful,* Padell, 1960; *Your Hair Can Be Beautiful,* Padell, 1961; *Arthritis,* Padell, 1961; (with Pauline N. Cagen) *Speech Aids for Elementary Grades,* Teachers Publishing Corp., c.1965.

Also author of "Peter Rabbit's Easter Egg Shop" (motion picture), 1953; "Peter Rabbit's Mother's Day Surprise" (motion picture), 1953; "The Old Woman Who Lived in a Shoe" (for marionettes), 1953; "Margie from Mars" (for marionettes), 1953; "School Days" (for marionettes), 1954. Contributor to newspapers, magazines, radio, and television.

*   *   *

FLETCHER, Jesse C.   1931-

PERSONAL: Born April 9, 1931, in San Antonio, Tex.; son of Jesse N. and Ruby (Arnold) Fletcher; married Dorothy Jordan, 1953; children: Jordan Scott, Melissa Dupree. *Education:* Texas A&M University, B.B.A., 1952; Southwestern Baptist Theological Seminary, B.D., 1955, Th.D., 1958. *Office:* P.O. Box 6597, Richmond, Va. 23230.

CAREER: Baptist clergyman. Baptist Foreign Mission Board, Richmond, Va., associate secretary, department of missionary personnel, 1960-63, secretary of department, 1963-68, director of Mission Support Division, 1968—. *Military service:* U.S. Army Reserve, chaplain, 1952-62; became captain. *Member:* Young Men's Christian Association, Lions Club.

WRITINGS—All published by Broadman: *Bill Wallace of China,* 1963, *The Wimpy Harper Story,* 1966, *Wimpy Harper of Africa,* 1967, *Journeyman Missionary,* 1967, *The Search for Blonnye Foreman: The Absorbing Story of a Missionary Who Found Deeper Meaning,* 1969. Contributor to religious periodicals.

WORK IN PROGRESS: A book on a contemporary philosophy of the missionary task.

SIDELIGHTS: Mr. Fletcher has traveled throughout America, Europe, Middle East, and Asia, visiting missionary stations. *Avocational interests:* Flying (private pilot), golf, hunting, fishing.

*   *   *

FLOOD, Kenneth Urban   1925-

PERSONAL: Born August 26, 1925, in Fond du Lac, Wis.; son of Urban S. (a barber) and Florence (Schorr) Flood; married Anita Freuhbroot, 1947; children: Sandra Kay, Patti Ann, Robert A. *Education:* Marquette University, B.S., 1949; University of California, Berkeley, M.A., 1951; Emory University, J.D., 1959; Harvard University, D.B.A., 1963. *Politics:* Republican. *Religion:* Catholic. *Home:* 1301 Fieldcrest, Columbia, Mo. 65201. *Office:* Department of Agricultural Economics, University of Missouri, Columbia, Mo. 65201.

CAREER: George J. Meyer Co., Cudahy, Wis., traffic manager, 1951-54; Georgia State College, Atlanta, associate professor, 1954-61; University of Illinois, Urbana, associate professor, 1962-64; John Sexton & Co., Chicago, Ill., director of distribution, 1964; University of Missouri, Columbia, distinguished professor of agricultural economics, 1964—. Visiting lecturer, Harvard University, 1961-62. Attorney-at-law. Business consultant to approximately fifty business firms. *Military service:* U.S. Army, 1943-46; became staff sergeant. *Member:* American Society of Traffic and Transportation (vice-president), Association of Interstate Commerce Commission Practitioners, National Council of Physical Distribution Management, Georgia Bar Association.

WRITINGS: Advanced Traffic Management, W.C. Brown, 1959, 2nd edition published as *Traffic Management,* 1963; *Research in Transportation Sources and Procedures,* Association of Interstate Commerce Commission Practitioners, 1960; *Research in Transportation: Legal/Legislative and Economic Sources and Procedure,* Gale, 1970. Contributor of about twenty articles to business law, business, and economics journals.

WORK IN PROGRESS: Research into systems analysis as applied to distribution.

*   *   *

FLORY, Jane Trescott   1917-

PERSONAL: Born June 29, 1917, in Wilkesbarre, Pa.; daughter of Leroy Charles (an engineer) and Hazel (Nixon) Trescott; married Arthur Louis Flory (an artist and college instructor), September 29, 1941; children: Cynthia Jane, Christine Kate, Erika Susan. *Education:* Philadelphia Museum School of Industrial Art (now Philadelphia Museum College of Art), diploma, 1939. *Home:* 1814 Beech Ave., Melrose Park, Philadelphia, Pa. 19126.

CAREER: Free-lance writer and illustrator of children's books, 1939—; Philadelphia Museum College of Art, Philadelphia, Pa., director of evening division, 1958—.

WRITINGS—Juveniles; all self-illustrated, except as indicated: *Snooty, the Pig Who Was Proud,* Whitman Publishing, 1944; *How Many?,* Holt, 1944; *What Am I?,* Domesday, 1945; *The Wide Awake Angel,* Grosset, 1945; (illustrator) Laura Harris, *Away We Go,* Garden City Books, 1945; *The Hide-Away Ducklings,* Grosset, 1946; (with husband, Arthur Flory) *The Cow in the Kitchen,* Lothrop, 1946; *Fanny Forgot,* Whitman Publishing, 1946; *Once Upon a Windy Day,* Whitman Publishing, 1947; *Toys,* Whitman Publishing, 1948; *The Powder Puff Bunny Book,* Capitol Publishing Co., 1948; *The Lazy Lion,* Whitman Publishing, 1949; *Timothy, the Little Brown Bear,* Rand McNally, 1949; *ABC,* Whitman Publishing, 1949; *Farmer John,* Whitman Publishing, 1950; *Mr.*

Snitzel's Cookies, Rand McNally, 1950; *The Too-Little Fire Engine,* Wonder Books, 1950; *The Pop-up Runaway Train,* Avon, 1951; *Count the Animals,* Loew, 1952; *Surprise in the Barn,* Whitman Publishing, 1955; *Jeremy's ABC Book,* Behrman, 1957; *Peddler's Summer,* Houghton, 1960; *A Tune for the Towpath,* Houghton, 1962; *One Hundred and Eight Bells,* Houghton, 1963; *Clancy's Glorious Fourth,* Houghton, 1964; *Mist on the Mountain,* Houghton, 1966; *Faraway Dream,* Houghton, 1968; *Ramshackle Roost,* Houghton, 1972.

WORK IN PROGRESS: A juvenile novel, set in the 1920's; research on a book about Puerto Rico.

BIOGRAPHICAL/CRITICAL SOURCES: Young Readers' Review, May, 1966.

*   *   *

FLOWER, Desmond (John Newman) 1907-

PERSONAL: Born August 25, 1907; son of Sir Newman (a publisher) and Evelyne (Redwin) Flower; married Margaret Cameron Coss, February 3, 1931; married second wife, Anne Elizabeth Smith, May 14, 1952; children: (first marriage) Nicholas; (second marriage) Susan Elizabeth Caysetana, Caroline Louise, David Newman. *Education:* Attended Lancing College; King's College, Cambridge, B.A., 1929, M.A., 1930. *Home:* 187 Clarence Gate Gardens, London N.W.1, England.

CAREER: Cassell & Co. Ltd. (publishers), London, England, 1930-71, director, 1931-38, literary director, 1938-40, 1943-46, 1951-71, deputy chairman, 1951-58, chairman, 1958-71. Former chairman of Cassell Australia Ltd., and Folio Society Ltd. Chairman, Thomas Harrison Memorial Fund (craft book-binding). *Military service:* British Army, 1940-45; received Military Cross, mentioned in dispatches. *Member:* Association Internationale de Bibliophilie (British representative), Alliance Francaise en Grande Bretagne (president), P.E.N., Royal and Ancient St. Andrews Golf Club. *Awards, honors:* Officier de la Legion d'honneur, 1950; D.Litt., University of Caen, 1957.

WRITINGS: A Thousand Years of French Books (catalogue of an exhibition), Macmillan (New York), 1948; *History of the Argyll and Sutherland Highlanders, 5th Battalion, 91st Anti-Tank Regiment, 1939-45,* Thomas Nelson, 1950; *Versailles: The Chateau and Its History in Books and Pictures* (catalogue of an exhibition), National Book League, 1953; *The Paper-back: Its Past, Present and Future,* Arborfield, 1959.

Editor: (And author of introduction) *The Poetical Works of Ernest Christopher Dowson,* Cassell and John Lane, 1934, 3rd edition, Cassell, 1967, published in America as *The Poetry of Ernest Dowson,* Fairleigh Dickinson University Press, 1970; (with Francis Meynell and A.J.A. Symons) *The Nonesuch Century: An Appraisal, a Personal Note and a Bibliography of the First Hundred Books Issued by the Press, 1923-1934,* Nonesuch, 1936; (with A.N.L. Munby) *English Poetical Autographs: A Collection of Facsimiles of Autograph Poems from Sir Thomas Wyat to Rupert Brooke,* Cassell, 1938; (with wife, Margaret Flower) *Cassell's Anthology of English Poetry,* Cassell, 1938, 2nd edition, 1946; *The Pursuit of Poetry: A Book of Letters about Poetry Written by English Poets, 1550-1930,* Cassell, 1939; *Voltaire's England,* Philip C. Duschnes, 1950; *Voltaire's Essay on Milton,* Cambridge University Press, 1954; (with James Reeves) *The Taste of Courage: The War, 1939-1945,* Harper, 1960 (published in England as *The War, 1939-1945,* Cassell, 1960); Sidney Bechet, *Treat It Gentle,* Hill & Wang, 1960; (with Howard Nixon) *Treasures from Private Libraries in England,* West Brothers, 1965; (with Henry Maas) *The Letters of Ernest Dawson,* Cassell, 1967, Fairleigh Dickinson University Press, 1968.

Translator: Paul Morand, *Orient Air Express,* Cassell, 1932; Paul Morand, *Indian Air: Impressions of Travel in South America,* Houghton, 1933; Paul Morand, *A Frenchman's London,* Cassell, 1934; Michael Matveev, *Weep Not for the Dead,* Knopf, 1935 (published in England as *Bitter Draught,* Cassell, 1935); (and editor) *Louis XIV at Versailles: A Selection from the Memoirs of the Duc de Saint-Simon,* Folio Society, 1953, Philip C. Duschnes, 1954; Hughues Panassie and Madeleine Gautier, *Guide to Jazz,* Houghton, 1956 (published in England as *Dictionary of Jazz,* Cassell, 1956); (and editor) *The Memoirs of Louis de Rouvroy Duc de Saint-Simon Covering the Years 1691-1723,* Heritage Press, 1959; Guy de Maupassant, *The Tellier House,* Cassell, 1964. Founder and editor with A.J.A. Symons of *The Book Collector's Quarterly,* Cassell, 1930-34.

WORK IN PROGRESS: Television historical subjects.

SIDELIGHTS: Flower's Voltaire collection (since sold to the University of Texas) was considered one of the two finest in private hands in the world (Theodore Besterman of Geneva, Switzerland, owns the other); Flower's library also extends to first editions of French literature of the seventeenth to twentieth century. His travels have ranged over much of Europe, United States, Australia, and the Far East. *Avocational interests:* Golf.

*   *   *

FLOWERS, Ann Moore 1923-

PERSONAL: Born November 25, 1923, in Bemidji, Minn.; daughter of Daniel Joseph and Elsie (Wolff) Moore; married Colman Horowich, December 23, 1943 (deceased); married M.A.L. Flowers, 1953 (divorced); children: Martha Moore. *Education:* Minnesota State College, B.S.; University of Wisconsin, M.S.; University of Virginia, Ed.D., 1965. *Home:* 300 West Franklin, Richmond, Va. 23220. *Office address:* Box 66, Medical College of Virginia, Richmond, Va. 23298.

CAREER: Speech Clinic, Augusta, Ga., director, 1949-53; Florida Department of Special Education, St. Petersburg, area worker, 1957-60; Danville Speech and Hearing Clinic, Danville, Va., director, 1961-63; Medical College of Virginia, Richmond, director of speech pathology, 1963—. *Member:* American Speech and Hearing Association, Speech and Hearing Association of Virginia.

WRITINGS: The Big Book of Sounds, Interstate, 1963; *Good Morning, Mr. Moon: An Album for the Aphasic Adult,* Interstate, 1966; *The Big Book of Language Through Sounds,* Interstate, 1972. Contributor of articles to speech and hearing journals. Editor, *Fair Force Times.*

WORK IN PROGRESS: Research in Speech and Hearing.

*   *   *

FLUCK, Reginald Alan Paul 1928-

PERSONAL: Born February 3, 1928, in Pontypridd, Glamorganshire, Wales; son of Reginald and Ellen (Fowles) Fluck. *Education:* Attended Cheltenham Grammar School, 1939-46; Royal College of Music, A.R.C.M. 1950, L.R.A.M., 1951. *Home:* Fairholme, Firgrove Hill, Farnham, Surrey, England. *Office:* Farnham Grammar School, Farnham, Surrey, England.

CAREER: Farnham Grammar School, Farnham, Surrey, England, director of music, 1951—. Farnham Festival of New Music for Young People, founder and organizer, 1961—. Lecturer, British Ministry of Education. Sometime educational consultant to Decca Records (London) and Glasgow & Baker Ltd. Member of executive board of Youth and Music Ltd., and of advisory committee of National Operatic Association.

WRITINGS: *The Sour Sweet Music: A Beginners Guide to Contemporary Music*, Putnam, 1957; (author of orchestral transcription) *Berkeley*, Chester, 1967; (author of orchestral transcription) *Weber*, Chester, 1968; *The Confident Young Musician*, Chester, 1968; (author of orchestral transcription) *Kodaly*, Boosey & Hawkes, 1970; "Love on the Dole" (musical), first produced at Nottingham Playhouse, 1970. Co-author of script, "Book into Musical," for Cheltenham Festival, 1963. Contributor to music and music education journals, and to concert program notes.

WORK IN PROGRESS: Two new musical plays; a television version of "Love on the Dole."

      *   *   **

FLYGT, Sten G(unnar) 1911-

PERSONAL: Born April 6, 1911, in New Britain, Conn.; son of Carl Bernhard (a machinist) and Thekla (Almquist) Flygt; married Lavinia Witherspoon, September 18, 1954; children: Carl Hardin, Tertia Lavinia Dale. *Education:* Wesleyan University, Middletown, Conn., B.A., 1932, M.A., 1933; graduate study at Yale University, 1934-36, University of Cologne, 1936-37; Northwestern University, Ph.D., 1938. *Politics:* "Nonpartisan." *Home:* Clovercroft Rd., Franklin, Tenn. 37064. *Office:* Vanderbilt University, Nashville, Tenn. 37203.

CAREER: Wesleyan University, Middletown, Conn., instructor in German, 1933-36; Northwestern University, Evanston, Ill., assistant professor of German, 1938-42; Princeton University, Princeton, N.J., assistant professor of German, 1946-47; Office of Military Government for Bavaria, Erlangen and Wuerzburg, Germany, university specialist, 1947-49; Reed College, Portland, Ore., associate professor of German, 1949-51; Muhlenberg College, Allentown, Pa., visiting lecturer in German, 1952-53; Vanderbilt University, Nashville, Tenn., professor of German, 1953—. *Member:* Modern Language Association of America, Society for the Advancement of Scandinavian Riksforeningen for Svenskhetens Bevarelse i Utlandet, Phi Beta Kappa. *Awards, honors:* Scholar's award of American Council of Learned Societies; Guggenheim fellowship.

WRITINGS: (Editor with T.M. Campbell) *Wilhelm Karl Raab, Die Schwarze Galeere: Geschichtliche erzaehlung*, Crofts, 1935; (with C.R. Goedsche and Meno Spann) *A Modern Course in German*, Houghton, 1947; *Friedrich Hebbel's Conception of Movement in the Absolute and in History*, University of North Carolina Press, 1952; *A Review of German: Grammar Practice Based on Selected Texts*, Norton, 1959; *The Notorious Dr. Bahrdt*, Vanderbilt University Press, 1963; *Friedrich Hebbel*, Twayne, 1968. Contributor to language journals, principally those on German studies.

WORK IN PROGRESS: Studies in the poetry of Annette von Droste-Huelshoff.

AVOCATIONAL INTERESTS: Raising chickens, turkeys, peafowl, and guinea hens (on a small scale).

      *   *   **

FOLEY, (Cedric) John 1917-
(John Sawyer, Ian Sinclair)

PERSONAL: Born March 7, 1917, in Stevenage, Hertfordshire, England; son of John James (an engineer) and Madge (Wilderspin) Foley; married Alice May Dorey, August 8, 1940; children: Christopher John, Wendy Elizabeth. *Education:* Attended Royal Military Academy at Sandhurst, 1941-42. *Home:* 9 Romney Rd., New Malden, Surrey, England. *Agent:* A.M. Heath & Co. Ltd., 35 Dover St., London W.1, England. *Office:* Campbell-Johnson Ltd., 16 Bolton St., London W.1, England.

CAREER: British Army, career service, 1936-54; received Order of the British Empire, 1948; retired as major. Campbell-Johnson Ltd., London, England, public relations consultant, 1954—, now member of board of directors. Granada Television Network Ltd., military adviser. *Member:* Institute of Public Relations, Society of Authors, Royal Aero Club of London.

WRITINGS: *ABC of British Army Vehicles*, Ian Allan 1955; *ABC of the Army*, Ian Allan, 1955; *Mailed Fist*, Hamish Hamilton, 1957; *Bull and Brass*, Cassell, 1958; *Death of a Regiment*, Cassell, 1959; *Man in the Moon*, Four Square Books, 1960; (as John Sawyer) *D-Day*, Four Square Books, 1960; *Double Bunk*, Four Square Books, 1961; *No Need to Go Home*, Cassell, 1961; *Very Important Person*, May Fair Books, 1962; (as Ian Sinclair) *Tenpin Bowling*, Four Square Books, 1962; (as John Sawyer) *A Basic Guide to Tenpin Bowling*, Collins, 1963; *The Boilerplate War*, Muller, 1963, Walker & Co., 1964. Contributor of short stories to radio and magazines; writer of television scripts.

      *   *   *

FOLTZ, William J(ay) 1936-

PERSONAL: Born January 24, 1936, in Mount Vernon, N.Y.; son of William E. and Margaret (Cockerill) Foltz; married Anne-Marie Abrahamsen (a writer), July 12, 1958; children: Peter W., Jeremy D. *Education:* Princeton University, A.B., 1957; Yale University, M.A., 1958, Ph.D., 1963. *Office:* Department of Political Science, Yale University, New Haven, Conn. 06520.

CAREER: Yale University, New Haven, Conn., 1962—, now associate professor of political science. *Member:* American Political Science Association, African Studies Association.

WRITINGS: (Editor with Karl W. Deutsch) *Nation-Building*, Atherton, 1963; *From French West Africa to the Mali Federation*, Yale University Press, 1965; (with Leonard W. Doob and others) *Resolving Conflict in Africa*, Yale University Press, 1970. Contributor of articles on African politics to journals.

      *   *   *

FONER, Philip (Sheldon) 1910-

PERSONAL: Born December 14, 1910, in New York, N.Y.; son of Abraham (a garage owner) and Mary (Smith) Foner; married Roslyn Held (a technical editor), 1939; children: Elizabeth (Mrs. Robert S. Van der Paer), Laura. *Education:* College of City of New York (now City College of City University of New York), B.A., 1932; Columbia University, M.A., 1933, Ph.D., 1940. *Office:* Department of History, Lincoln University, Lincoln University, Pa. 19352.

CAREER: College of the City New York (now City College of the City University of New York), New York, N.Y., instructor in history, 1932-41; International Fur and Leather Workers, New York, N.Y., educational director, 1941-45; Citadel Press, New York, N.Y., member of firm, 1945-67, became publisher; Lincoln University, Lincoln University, Pa., professor of history, 1967—. *Member:* American Historical Association, Organization of American Historians, Association for the Study of Negro Life and History, Phi Beta Kappa.

WRITINGS: *Business and Slavery: The New York Merchants and the Irrepressible Conflict*, University of North Carolina Press, 1941; *Morale Education in the American Army: War for Independence, War of 1812, Civil War*, International Publishers, 1944; *The Jews in American History, 1645-1865*, International Publishers, 1946; *Jack London, American Rebel: A Collection of His Social Writings Together with an Extensive Study of the Man* and His Times, Citadel, 1947, revised edition, 1964; History of the Labor Movement in the United States, International Publishers, Volume I: From Colonial Times to the Founding of the American Federation of Labor, 1947, Volume II: From the Founding of the American Federation of Labor to the Emergence of American Imperialism, 1956, Volume III: The Policies and Practices of the American Federation of Labor, 1900-1909, 1964, Volume IV: The Industrial Workers of the World, 1905-1917, 1966; The Fur and Leather Workers Union: A Story of Dramatic Struggles and Achievements, Nordan Press, 1950; Mark Twain: Social Critic, International Publishers, 1958, 2nd edition, 1966.

A History of Cuba and Its Relations with the United States, International Publishers, Volume I, 1962, Volume II, 1963; Frederick Douglass: A Biography, Citadel, 1964, 2nd edition, 1969; The Case of Joe Hill, International Publishers, 1966; The Bolshevik Revolution: Its Impact on American Radicals, Liberals, and Labor, International Publishers, 1967; American Labor and the Indochina War: The Growth of Union Opposition, International Publishers, 1971; The Spanish-Cuban-American War, and the Birth of American Imperialism, 1895-1902, two volumes, Monthly Review Press, 1972.

Editor: (And author of introduction) Thomas Jefferson: Selections from His Writings, International Publishers, 1943; Basic Writings of Thomas Jefferson, University of North Carolina Press, 1944; (and author of introduction) Abraham Lincoln: Selections from His Writings, International Publishers, 1944; George Washington: Selections from His Writings, International Publishers, 1944; (and author of introduction) Frederick Douglass: Selections from His Writings, International Publishers, 1945; (and author of biographical essay, notes, and introduction) The Complete Writings of Thomas Paine, two volumes, Citadel, 1945, reissued as The Life and Major Writings of Thomas Paine, 1961; Franklin Delano Roosevelt: Selections from His Writings, International Publishers, 1947; The Life and Writings of Frederick Douglass, four volumes, International Publishers, 1950-55; (and author of notes) The Letters of Joe Hill, Oak, 1965; (and author of introduction) Helen Keller: Her Socialist Years, International Publishers, 1967; (and author of introduction) The Autobiographies of the Haymarket Martyrs, Humanities for A.I.M.S., 1969; The Black Panthers Speak, Lippincott, 1970; W.E.B. Du Bois Speaks: Speeches and Addresses, two volumes, Pathfinder, 1970; The Voice of Black America: Major Speeches by Negroes in the U.S., 1797-1971, Simon & Schuster, 1972. Member of board of editors, Journal of Negro History, and Pennsylvania History.

WORK IN PROGRESS: Memorial Tributes to Karl Marx; Organized Labor and the Black Worker: From Slavery to Black Power; American Labor Songs of the Nineteenth Century.

SIDELIGHTS: Foner has traveled in Egypt, U.S.S.R., Japan, Cuba, Hungary, Germany, Scandinavia, the Netherlands, France, Latin America, Mexico, and Israel. Avocational interests: Tennis, sailing, swimming, mountain climbing; opera and music in general.

* * *

FOOT, Hugh Mackintosh 1907-
(Lord Caradon)

PERSONAL: Born October 8, 1907, in Plymouth, England; son of Isaac (one-time Liberal member of British Cabinet) and Eva (Mackintosh) Foot; married Sylvia Tod, 1936; children: Paul, Sarah Foot Burbury, Oliver, Benjamin. Education: Attended Leighton Park School; St. John's College, Cambridge, B.A., 1929. Religion: Methodist. Home: Trematon Castle, Saltash, Cornwall, England.

CAREER: From Cambridge went into British Colonial Service, and served overseas all but one year of the period, 1929-60, retiring from post as Britain's last governor of Cyprus when Cyprus attained independence; United Kingdom Mission to the United Nations, advisor and ambassador, 1960-62; resigned, 1962; consultant to United Nations Special Fund, 1962-64, Minister of State for Foreign Affairs, and permanent representative of United Kingdom to the United Nations, 1964-70. Administrative officer, Palestine, 1929-37; assistant British resident, Trans-Jordan, 1939-42; colonial secretary, Cyprus, 1943-45, and Jamaica, 1945-47; chief secretary, Nigeria, 1947-51 (helped government leaders draw up Nigerian constitution); governor-in-chief and captain-general of Jamaica, 1951-57; governor and commander-in-chief of Cyprus, 1957-60. Member: Travelers' Club, West Indian Club. Awards, honors: Commander, Order of St. Michael and St. George, 1946, Knight Commander, 1951, Knight Grand Cross, 1957; Knight of Order of St. John of Jerusalem, 1952; Knight Commander of Royal Victorian Order; Fellow, St. John's College, Cambridge University, 1960.

WRITINGS: Constitutional Reform: A New System of Government for Jamaica—Three Broadcast Talks, Government Printer (Kingston), 1953; Empire Into Commonwealth (lectures), Liberal Publication Department, 1962; A Start in Freedom, Harper, 1964; (with Charles Coulson and Trevor Huddleston) Three Views on Commitment, Longmans, 1967; Southern Africa in International Relations, Africa Bureau, 1970.

SIDELIGHTS: A Start in Freedom was described in Time as a "sprightly autobiography, which combines exploits worthy of James Bond with a scholar's critical look at current history." But adventure was incidental, as Time emphasizes: "Even among the many superbly qualified colonial administrators that Britain produced, Hugh Foot is a standout."

BIOGRAPHICAL/CRITICAL SOURCES: Time, September 11, 1964.

* * *

FORBES, DeLoris (Florine) Stanton 1923-
(De Forbes, Stanton Forbes; joint pseudonym, Forbes Rydell)

PERSONAL: Born July 10, 1923, in Kansas City, Mo.; daughter of Lawrence and Florence (Ellis) Stanton; married William J. Forbes, Jr., October 29, 1948; children: Daniel William, Anne Stanton, William Andrew. Education: Attended schools in Kansas. Home address: P.O. Box 133, Wellesley, Mass. 02181. Office: Wellesley Townsman, 1 Crest Rd., Wellesley, Mass. 02181.

CAREER: Wellesley Townsman, Wellesley, Mass., assistant editor, 1958—. Writer of mystery novels. Member: Mystery Writers of America, Quota Club. Awards, honors: Mystery Writers of America scroll for Grieve for the Past; nominated for Edgar Allen Poe Award, 1964.

WRITINGS—With Helen B. Rydell under joint pseudonym Forbes Rydell; all published by Doubleday, except as indicated: Annalisa, Dodd, 1955, If She Should Die, 1961, They're Not Home Yet, 1962, No Questions Asked, 1963.

Under name Stanton Forbes; all published by Doubleday, except as indicated: Grieve for the Past, 1963; The Terrors of the Earth, 1964 (published in England as The Long Hate, R. Hale, 1966), reissued as Melody of Terror, Pyramid Publications, 1967; Relative to Death, 1965; A Business of Bodies, 1966; Terror Touches Me, 1966; Encounter Darkness, 1967; Go to Thy Deathbed, 1968; If Two of Them Are Dead, 1968; The Name's Death,

Remember Me?, 1969; *She Was Only the Sheriff's Daughter,* 1970; *If Laurel Shot Hardy the World Would End,* 1970; *The Sad Sudden Death of My Fair Lady,* 1971; *All for One and One for Death,* 1971; *A Deadly Kind of Lonely,* 1971; *But I Wouldn't Want to Die There,* 1972.

Under pseudonym Tobias Wells; all published by Doubleday: *A Matter of Love and Death,* 1966, *What Should You Know of Dying,* 1967, *Dead by the Light of the Moon,* 1967, *Murder Most Fouled Up,* 1968, *The Young Can Die Protesting,* 1969, *Die Quickly, Dear Mother,* 1969, *Dinky Died,* 1970, *What to Do Till the Undertaker Comes,* 1971, *The Foo Dog,* 1971, *How to Kill a Man,* 1972, *A Die in the Country,* 1972.

Contributor to anthologies, *Best Detective Stories,* 1961, 1963, and to magazines and newspapers, as De Forbes.

SIDELIGHTS: Mrs. Forbes writes: "There are writers who opt for exotic locales such as Katmandu and the Ryukyu Islands, but as for me—give me Kansas and Boston and all the places in between. I know how to spell them and I've been there, besides! All of which is apropos of the books I write . . . mystery novels, all of them Crime Club selections. As Tobias Wells I write of the Boston scene . . . Stanton Forbes roams the United States, Stanton Forbes being my alter ego.

I must confess that I do not always stay put in red-white-and-blue locations. After a couple of trips to Ireland, I put *Terror Touches Me* on that lovely isle, and I've dealt with the Caribbean. . . . Which is to say, people are the story and there are fascinating people everywhere . . . at least in the view of a mystery writer, who finds that much that glitters is gold, and excitement lies in the labyrinth passages of the human mind."

All of her books have been published in British editions.

AVOCATIONAL INTERESTS: Travel, crossword puzzles, bridge, antiques, home decorating.

BIOGRAPHICAL/CRITICAL SOURCES: Writer, September, 1969; *Library Journal,* May 15, 1970.

*   *   *

FORBES, Elliot   1917-

PERSONAL: Born August 30, 1917, in Cambridge, Mass.; son of Edward Waldo (a museum director) and Margaret (Laighton) Forbes: married Kathleen Brooks Allen (a teacher), June 7, 1941; children: Diana, Barbara Anne, Susan. *Education:* Attended Milton Academy, 1932-36; Harvard University, B.A., 1941, M.A., 1947. *Home:* 182 Brattle St., Cambridge, Mass. 02138. *Office:* Music Building, Harvard University, Cambridge, Mass. 02138.

CAREER: Teacher at Cate School, Santa Barbara, Calif., 1941-43; Belmont Hill School, Belmont, Mass., 1945-47; Princeton University, Princeton, N.J., assistant professor, 1947-54, bicentennial preceptor, 1951-54, associate professor of music, 1954-58; Harvard University, Cambridge, Mass., professor of music, 1958-61, Fanny Peabody Professor of Music, 1961—. Director of Harvard Glee Club and Radcliffe Choral Society, 1958-70. *Member:* International Musicological Society, American Musicological Society, College Music Society.

WRITINGS: (Editor) Beethoven, *Funeral Cantata,* E.C. Schirmer, 1961; (editor and reviser) Alexander Wheelock Thayer, *Life of Beethoven,* two volumes, Princeton University Press, 1964; (editor) *The Harvard Song Book,* E.C. Schirmer, 1966; *The Choral Music of Beethoven,* American Choral Foundation, 1969; (editor) Beethoven, *Symphony No. 5 in C Minor: An Authoritative Score, the Sketches, Historical Background, Analysis, Views and Comments,* Norton, 1971. Editor, "Harvard-Radcliffe

Choral" series, E.C. Schirmer. Contributor of article on Beethoven to *American People's Encyclopedia.*

*   *   *

FORBES, J(ohn) V(an) G(elder)   1916-

PERSONAL: Born December 27, 1916, in Oak Park, Ill.; son of James Bruff and Stella (Rogers) Forbes; married Lydia Brinton; children: Catharine, Sarah, James, Anna. *Education:* University of Rochester, B.A., 1939, M.A. 1942; University of Pennsylvania, Ph.D., 1951. *Politics:* Democrat. *Religion:* Society of Friends. *Home:* 429 College Ave., Carlinville, Ill. 62626. *Office:* History Department, Blackburn College, Carlinville, Ill. 62626.

CAREER: Blackburn College, Carlinville, Ill., 1949—, now chairman of department of history. Visiting professor of history, Queen's University summer school, 1969, 1970, St. Jerome's College, University of Waterloo, 1970-71. U.S. Congress Joint Economic Committee, staff member, 1956. Accredited correspondent for Democratic and Republican national campaigns, 1952, for national campaigns and conventions, 1956, 1960, 1964. Deputy director of Downstate Citizens for Douglas, 1954; manager of downstate headquarters of Illinois Citizens for Stevenson-Kefauver, 1956; manager of Bob Wilson's campaign for U.S. House of Representatives, 1962; director of national farm desk, Eugene McCarthy campaign, 1968. *Member:* American Historical Association, American Political Science Association, American Association of University Professors.

WRITINGS: The Quaker Star Under Seven Flags, 1917-1927: The Work of the American Friends Service Committee with Seven Governments to Relieve Civilian Victims of World War I, University of Pennsylvania Press, 1962; *The Springfield Mitre: The Politics and Consequence of an Episcopal Election in Illinois, 1962-1967,* Diocese of Springfield, 1971.

*   *   *

FORD, LeRoy   1922-

PERSONAL: Born January 14, 1922, in Sayre, Okla.; son of Walter C. (a farmer) and Lucinda (Lakey) Ford; married Jeanette White, June 3, 1950; children: Judy, Daniel, Cindy. *Education:* Southwestern State College, Weatherford, Okla., B.S., 1943; Southwestern Baptist Theological Seminary, Fort Worth, Tex., M.R.E., 1949, D.R.E., 1958, *Religion:* Baptist. *Home:* 5832 Sycamore Creek Rd., Fort Worth, Texas 76134. *Office:* School of Religious Education, Southwestern Baptist Theological Seminary, 2001 West Seminary Dr., Fort Worth, Texas 76115.

CAREER: U.S. government, Washington, D.C., training specialist, 1943-47; First Baptist Church, Norman, Okla., minister of education, 1947-56; Baptist Sunday School Board, Nashville, Tenn., editor of Training Union adult lesson courses, 1958-66; Southwestern Baptist Theological Seminary, Fort Worth, Texas, professor of principles of education, 1966—.

WRITINGS: Tools for Teaching and Training, Broadman, 1961; *Adults Learning to Witness: A Training Union Resource Unit,* Sunday School Board, Southern Baptist Convention, 1962; *A Primer for Teachers and Leaders,* Broadman, 1963; *Developing Skills for Church Leaders,* Convention Press, 1968; *Using the Lecture in Teaching and Training,* Broadman, 1968; *Using the Case Study in Teaching and Training,* Broadman, 1969; *Using the Panel in Teaching and Training,* Broadman, 1970; *Using Problem Solving in Teaching and Training,* Broadman, 1972. Contributor to *Church Administration, AV Education,* and denominational periodicals.

WORK IN PROGRESS: The Learning Bridge: From Theory to Practice in Teaching.

FORD, Margaret Patricia 1925-

PERSONAL: Born March 17, 1925, in Erie, Pa.; daughter of Ralph Boughton (a salesman) and Margaret (Carnes) Ford. *Education:* Lake Erie College for Women, A.B., (cum laude), 1945; Western Reserve University (now Case Western Reserve University), M.A., 1946, Ph.D., 1957. *Politics:* Republican. *Religion:* Protestant. *Home:* Burton, Ohio 44021. *Office:* Department of English, Hood College, Frederick, Md. 21701.

CAREER: Lake Erie College, Painesville, Ohio, instructor, 1946-48; instructor in English at Valparaiso University, Valparaiso, Ind., 1948-51, and Louisiana State University, Baton Rouge, 1955-57; Grove City College Grove City Pa., 1957-64, began as assistant professor, became professor of English; Hood College, Frederick, Md., associate professor, 1964-68 professor of English, 1968—. *Member:* Modern Language Association of America, College English Association, National Council of Teachers of English, American Association of University Professors, American Association of University Women.

WRITINGS: (With Suzanne Kincaid) *Who's Who in Faulkner,* Louisiana State University Press, 1963, revised edition, 1966; (contributor) James Austin and Donald A. Koch, editors, *Popular Literature in America,* Bowling Green University Press, 1972.

WORK IN PROGRESS: An article on Faulkner and women; editing nineteenth-century set of Ohio personal diaries.

* * *

FORD, Mary Forker 1905-

PERSONAL: Born October 25, 1905, in Noble County, Ind.; daughter of Simon Edward and Mina Mae (Bowen) Forker; married Harland B. Ford (deceased); children: Jane Leigh (Mrs. Ira Carlton Crandall). *Education:* Attended public schools in Fort Wayne, Ind. *Politics:* Democrat. *Religion:* Methodist. *Home:* 2949 Holton Ave., Fort Wayne, Ind. 46806.

CAREER: Employed by Lincoln National Life Insurance Co. before marriage; now free-lance writer. *Member:* Newspaper Institute of America.

WRITINGS—All published by Bouregy, except as noted: *Murder Country Style,* 1964, *The Silent Witness,* 1964, *The Dude Ranch Murders,* 1965, *Shadow of Murder,* 1965, *Long Journey Home,* 1966, *Roswell Heritage,* 1968, *Shadow of Danger,* 1971, *Harvest of Years,* 1972, *Along Came a Stranger,* Lancer, 1973.

* * *

FORD, W(illiam) Herschel 1900-

PERSONAL: Born November 21, 1900, in Monroe, Ga.; son of William Henry (a merchant) and Martha (Cox) Ford; married Maybelle Archibald, October 15, 1919; children: Walter M., Robert A. *Education:* Wake Forest College, B.A. (magna cum laude), 1932; also studied at Southwestern Baptist Theological Seminary. *Politics:* Independent. *Home:* 7061 Old King Rd. S., Jacksonville, Fla. 32217.

CAREER: Pastor of Baptist churches for forty-eight years, now pastor of San Jose Baptist Church, Jacksonville, Fla. Southern Baptist Convention, vice-president, 1961-62; Southern Baptist Pastors Conference, president, 1962-63. *Awards, honors:* D.D., Carson-Newman College, 1938.

WRITINGS: God Bless America, and Other Sermons, Zondervan, 1941, reissued as *Simple Sermons on Simple Themes,* 1957.

"Simple Sermon" series; all published by Zondervan, except as indicated: *Seven Simple Sermons on the Second Coming,* 1945; *Simple Sermons from the Book of Acts,* two volumes, 1950; *. . . on the Great Christian Doctrines,* Broadman, 1951; *. . . on the Saviour's Last Words,* 1953; *. . . for Saints and Sinners,* 1953; *. . . on Salvation and Service,* 1955; *. . . on the Ten Commandments,* 1955; *. . . for Special Days and Occasions,* 1956; *. . .* from the *Gospel of John,* two volumes, 1958; *. . . on the Seven Churches of Revelation,* 1959; *. . . for Today's World,* 1960; *. . . for Christian Workers,* 1961; *. . . about Jesus Christ,* 1961; *. . . on the Christian Life,* 1962; *. . . for Funeral Services,* 1962; *. . . from the Gospel of Matthew,* 1963; *. . . for Time and Eternity,* 1964; *. . . for Times Like These,* 1965; *. . . for Sunday Morning,* 1966; *. . . for Sunday Evening,* 1967; *. . . for Twentieth-Century Christians,* 1968; *. . . on Prophetic Themes,* 1968; *. . . on the Old-Time Religion,* 1968; *. . . on Heaven, Hell, and Judgment,* 1969; *. . . on Prayer,* 1969; *. . . for a Sinful Age, 1970; . . . for the Midweek Service,* 1970; *. . . on Evangelistic Themes,* 1971, *. . . for Modern Man,* 1972.

WORK IN PROGRESS: Other books in "Simple Sermons" series.

* * *

FORDE-JOHNSTON, James (Leo) 1927-

PERSONAL: Born May 7, 1927, in Liverpool, England; son of James and Elsie (Thompson) Forde-Johnston; married Kathleen Mary Healy, September 8, 1962; children: James, Kathleen, Richard, Andrew. *Education:* University of Liverpool, B.A., 1952, M.A., 1954. *Home:* 6 Greystoke Ave., Sale, Cheshire, England.

CAREER: Liverpool Museum, Liverpool, England, assistant keeper of archaeology, 1954-56; Royal Commission on Historical Monuments, England, investigator on archaeological field work, 1956-58; University of Manchester Museum, Manchester, England, keeper of ethnology and general archaeology, 1958-70, keeper of ethnology, 1970—. *Military service:* British Army, 1946-48; became sergeant. *Member:* Society of Antiquaries (fellow), Royal Archaeological Institute, Royal Anthropological Institute, Prehistoric Society, Lancashire and Cheshire Antiquarian Society (council).

WRITINGS: Neolithic Cultures of North Africa: Aspects of One Phase in the Development of African Stone Age Culture, Liverpool University Press, 1959, Humanities, 1960. Contributor of articles to archaeological and antiquarian journals.

WORK IN PROGRESS: The Iron Age Hill Forts of England and Wales, for Liverpool University Press; *An Introduction to Archaeology,* for Pall Mall Press.

* * *

FOREMAN, Lawton Durant 1913-

PERSONAL: Born March 8, 1913, near Lavaca, Sebastian County, Ark.; son of Jessie J. and Willie Ann (Matthews) Foreman; married Mary Opal Henry, June 21, 1936; children: Rebekah Foreman Beam, Lynn, Pricilla, Betty Jane. *Education:* Missionary Baptist Seminary, graduate, 1936, Master of Bible, 1937, Doctor of Bible Languages, 1939. *Home:* 12313 Sardis Rd., Mabelvale, Ark. 72103.

CAREER: Ordained Baptist minister, 1935; Missionary Baptist Seminary, Little Rock, Ark., professor, 1939—, dean, 1945, president, 1946-66. Pastor of Baptist churches in Cave City, Ark., 1939-42, Sheridan, Ark., 1942-47; Antioch Missionary Baptist Church, Little Rock, Ark., pastor, 1947-66; Woodhaven Baptist Church, Mabelvale, Ark., pastor, 1966—. Chaplain, United Commercial Travelers Council, 1967. *Member:* American Baptist Association (publications committee, 1940—; president,

1950-51), State Association of Missionary Baptist Churches of Arkansas (president, 1949-53), Free and Accepted Masons, Hugh de Payens Commandry, Knights Templar (commander, 1956), Grand Council of Royal and Select Masters of Arkansas, Royal Arch Masons, Scottish Rite Bodies—Arkansas Consistory.

WRITINGS—All published by Seminary Press, except as indicated: *The Bible in Eight Ages*, 1942, 3rd edition, 1952, (editor) *Credenda: Being a Treatise of Thirteen Bible Doctrines*, 1950, *Handbook on Ordinations*, 1952, *A Study Course in the Gospel of John*, 1953, *Biblical Proofs for Identifying the True Church*, 1955, *Ordination Handbook*, 1956, *Ministerial Practicalities*, 1961, (with Alta Payne) *The Life and Works of Benjamin Marcus Bogard*, two volumes, privately printed, 1966, *The Golden Key to Bible Analysis*, 1970. Editor, *Baptist World*.

* * *

FORMAN, Brenda 1936-

PERSONAL: Born August 1, 1936, in Hollywood, Calif.; daughter of Harrison (a writer) and Sandra (Carlyle) Forman. *Education:* Barnard College, B.A., 1956; City University of New York, Ph.D., 1969. *Home:* 301 North Beauregard St., Alexandria, Va. 22312. *Office:* Mitre Corp., Westgate Research Park, McLean, Va. 22101.

CAREER: Mitre Corp., McLean, Va., began as analyst, systems analyst, 1969—. *Member:* Phi Beta Kappa.

WRITINGS: (With father, Harrison Forman) *The Land and People of Nigeria*, Lippincott, 1964, revised edition, 1972; *The Story of Thailand*, McCormick-Mathers, 1965; *America's Place in the World Economy*, Harcourt, 1969.

"Famous First Name" series for children, published by Frommer-Pasmantier: *Is Your Name James?*, 1965; . . . *John?*, 1965; . . . *Richard?*, 1965; . . . *Robert?*, 1965; . . . *William?*, 1965; . . . *Michael?*, 1965.

SIDELIGHTS: Miss Forman told *CA:* "My writing aim is to make historical and political subjects interesting and stimulating to young readers, particularly the teen-age groups."

BIOGRAPHICAL/CRITICAL SOURCES: *Saturday Review*, August 16, 1969.

* * *

FORMAN, James Douglas 1932-

PERSONAL: Born November 12, 1932, in Mineola, Long Island, N.Y.; son of Leo Erwin (a lawyer) and Kathryn (Forman) Forman; married Marcia Fore, September 3, 1956; children: Karli. *Education:* Princeton University, A.B., 1954; Columbia University, LL.B., 1957. *Home:* 2 Glen Rd., Sands Point, Port Washington, N.Y. 11501. *Agent:* Theron Raines, 244 Madison Ave., New York, N.Y. 10016. *Office:* 290 Old Country Rd., Mineola, Long Island, N.Y. 11501.

CAREER: Practice of law, 1957—. *Member:* Lightning Fleet 142 (sailboats; past president).

WRITINGS: (With wife, Marcia Forman) *Islands of the Eastern Mediterranean* (booklet), Doubleday, 1959; *The Skies of Crete*, Farrar, Straus, 1963; *Ring the Judas Bell*, Farrar, Straus, 1965; *The Shield of Achilles*, Farrar, Straus, 1966; *Horses of Anger*, Farrar, Straus, 1967; *The Traitors*, Farrar, Straus, 1968; *The Cow Neck Rebels*, Farrar, Straus, 1969; *My Enemy, My Brother*, Meredith, 1969; *Ceremony of Innocence*, Hawthorn, 1970; *So Ends This Day*, Farrar, Straus, 1970; *Song of Jubilee*, Farrar, Straus, 1971; *Law and Disorder*, Thomas Nelson, 1971; *Capitalism: Economic Individualism to Today's Welfare State*, F. Watts, 1972; *Communism: From Marx's Manifesto to 20th Century*, F. Watts, 1972; *Socialism: Its*

Theoretical Roots and Present-Day Development, F. Watts, 1972; *People of the Dream*, Farrar, Straus, 1972.

WORK IN PROGRESS: *Chief Joseph*, a biography of the Nez Perce leader in the last major Indian war.

AVOCATIONAL INTERESTS: Travel, photography (some photographs appear in his works), and antique arms of the eighteenth century.

BIOGRAPHICAL/CRITICAL SOURCES: *Best Sellers*, May 1, 1967, November 1, 1968, November 1, 1969, January 15, 1971, July 15, 1971; *Young Readers' Review*, June, 1967, November, 1968; *Saturday Review*, June 28, 1969; *New York Times Book Review*, November 30, 1969; *Library Journal*, June 15, 1970.

* * *

FORMAN, Robert E(dgar) 1924-

PERSONAL: Born July 17, 1924, in Minneapolis, Minn.; son of Phillip E. (a salesman) and Lotta (Holmgren) Forman; married Ruth Anne Linsley, June 9, 1945; children: Lucy Jeanne, Mark Richard, Dan Robert. *Education:* University of Minnesota, B.A. (cum laude), 1948, M.A., 1949, Ph.D., 1959. *Office:* University of Toledo, Toledo, Ohio 43606.

CAREER: St. Olaf College, Northfield, Minn., assistant professor of sociology, 1951-53; University of Minnesota, Minneapolis, counselor, office of dean of students, 1955-58, assistant foreign student adviser and research fellow, 1958-59; Rockford College, Rockford, Ill., assistant professor of sociology, 1959-61; Wisconsin State University, Oshkosh, associate professor, 1961-66, chairman of department of sociology, 1961-69, professor of sociology, 1966-69; University of Toledo, Toledo, Ohio, professor of sociology, 1969. *Military service:* U.S. Army, 1944-46. *Member:* American Sociological Association, American Association of University Professors, Ohio Valley Sociological Association.

WRITINGS: (With Forrest G. Moore) *The University and Its Foreign Alumni* (monograph), University of Minnesota Press, 1964; *Black Ghettos, White Ghettos, and Slums*, Prentice-Hall, 1971. Contributor of articles to *American Journal of Sociology* and other periodicals.

* * *

FORSYTH, David P(ond) 1930-

PERSONAL: Born October 2, 1930, in Price, Utah; son of Sterling C. (an accountant) and Abbie (Pond) Forsyth; married Carmela Tanner, May 6, 1954; children: Tamara, Todd, Thomas, Terence. *Education:* Brigham Young University, B.S., 1954; Northwestern University, M.S.J., 1959, Ph.D., 1962. *Politics:* Republican. *Religion:* Church of Jesus Christ of Latter-day Saints (Mormon). *Home:* 12 Longview Ave., North Caldwell, N.J. 07006.

CAREER: Chilton Co., Philadelphia, Pa., manager, communications research, 1962-68; Temple University, Philadelphia, Pa., professor of business journalism, 1962-68; Hagen Communications, Inc., Montclair, N.J., vice-president, 1968—. *Consultant* in business communications. *Military service:* U.S. Army, 1954-57. *Member:* Society for the Study of Communication, Sigma Delta Chi, Kappa Tau Alpha. *Awards, honors:* Sigma Delta Chi distinguished service award for research in journalism for *The Business Press in America*.

WRITINGS: *The Business Press in America, 1750-1865*, Chilton, 1964. Contributor to *Journalism Quarterly, Quill*, and other magazines.

WORK IN PROGRESS: Second volume of *The Business Press in America*.

FOSTER, G(eorge) Allen 1907-

PERSONAL: Born March 28, 1907, in Plymouth, N.H.; son of George Rice (a manufacturer) and Christabel (Allen) Foster; married Hazel Gronberg (a pianist), July 15, 1936 (deceased); married Mary Jeter, December 27, 1957; children: George Thaddeus. *Education:* Dartmouth College, student, 1924-27; Eastman School of Music, B.Mus., 1930; additional study at Plymouth State Teachers College. *Politics:* Democrat. *Religion:* Congregational. *Home and office:* 180 North Main St., Plymouth, N.H. 03264.

CAREER: Greenwich House Music School, New York, N.Y., chairman of theory department, 1930-35; Works Progress Administration Federal Music Project, regional director in Boston, Mass., 1935-39; deputy national director, Washington, D.C., 1939-42, national director, 1942-44; New Orleans Symphony Orchestra, New Orleans, La., manager, 1944-53; Plymouth High School, Plymouth, N.H., music instructor, 1954-59; New Hampshire Democratic State Committee, executive secretary, 1959-61; free-lance writer, 1961—. Chairman, Plymouth Red Cross; vice-chairman, Plymouth Zoning Board of Adjustment, 1960—. *Member:* New Hampshire Historical Society, New Hampshire Council on World Affairs, Grafton County Democratic Committee, Dartmouth Alumni Association (area admissions chairman), Plymouth Rotary Club.

WRITINGS: The Eyes and Ears of the Civil War, Criterion, 1963; *Impeached: The President Who Almost Lost His Job,* Criterion, 1964; *Communications: From Primitive Tom-toms to Telstar,* Criterion, 1965; *Votes for Women,* Criterion, 1966; *Advertising: Ancient Market Place to Television,* Criterion, 1967; *Sunday in Centreville: The Battle of Bull Run, 1861,* David White, 1971. Author of New Orleans Symphony Orchestra *Program Notes,* 1944-53. Contributor to *Washington Post* and *Ebony.*

WORK IN PROGRESS: A Presidential Tragedy: The Biography of Franklin Pierce; The Flute at the Crescent Saloon and Other Madrigals, a book of musical anecdotes; *The Road to the White House,* for Criterion.

AVOCATIONAL INTERESTS: Education, foreign affairs, hunting, fishing, and gardening.

BIOGRAPHICAL/CRITICAL SOURCES: Manchester Union-Leader, January 20, 1963; *Young Readers' Review,* January, 1967; *Best Sellers,* January 1, 1968; *Saturday Review,* March 20, 1971.

*   *   *

FOXALL, Raymond (Jehoiada Campbell) 1916-

PERSONAL: Born March 26, 1916, in Irlam, Lancashire, England; son of Robert Christopher and Agnes Currie (Campbell) Foxall; married Audrey Pamela Owen, January, 1940; children: Rosalind Wyndham (Mrs. Wayne Grant), Wendy Campbell (Mrs. Ian G. Whitehall). *Education:* Attended Manchester College of Commerce. *Home:* Cruachan, 12 Woodside, Knutsford, Cheshire, England; and The Old Crossing House, Balgowan, Perthshire, Scotland. *Agent:* David Higham Associates, 5 Howes St., London W.1, England. *Office:* Sunday Express, Manchester, England.

CAREER: Reporter for newspapers and a news agency in Manchester and Warrington, England, then in London for *Daily Mirror,* Press Association, *Sunday Express, Daily Telegraph,* 1936-52; commercial traveler selling ties, 1952-58; *Sunday Express,* Manchester, reporter and feature writer, 1958—. *Military service:* British Army, World War II. *Member:* Society of Authors, National Union of Journalists, Writers' Guild of Great Britain,

Press Club of Britain, Highland Association, Knutsford Society.

WRITINGS—Novels, except as indicated; all published by R. Hale, except as indicated: *Here Lies the Shadow,* 1957, *Song for a Prince,* 1959, *The Devil's Smile,* 1960, *The Wicked Lord,* 1962, *John McCormack* (biography), 1963, *Alba,* 1964, *The Devil's Spawn,* 1965, *Squire Errant,* 1968, *The Little Ferret,* 1968, *Brandy for the Parson,* 1970, *The Dark Forest,* 1971. Contributor of short stories and articles to magazines and newspapers.

WORK IN PROGRESS: The Silver Tassle.

AVOCATIONAL INTERESTS: Golf, walking, gardening, antique-collecting.

*   *   *

FOXE, Arthur N(orman) 1902- (Aun Foda)

PERSONAL: Born June 28, 1902, in New York, N.Y.; son of David (a businessman) and Jennie (Nash) Foxe; married Jane Millicent Langeloh, August 1, 1936; children: Jon Langeloh. *Education:* College of the City of New York (City College of the City University of New York), B.S., 1923; Jefferson Medical College, M.D., 1927. *Politics:* Independent. *Religion:* Episcopalian. *Home and office:* 9 East 67th St., New York, N.Y. 10021.

CAREER: Qualified psychiatrist, New York State, 1937; diplomate of American Board of Psychiatry and Neurology, 1939, American Board of Legal Medicine, 1950. Bellevue Hospital, New York, N.Y., intern and resident, 1928-30, assistant visiting physician, 1930-32; New York University, Medical College, New York, N.Y., instructor in neurology, 1930-32; St. Lawrence State Hospital, Ogdensburg, N.Y., physician, 1933; Great Meadow Prison, Comstock, N.Y., psychiatrist and director of classification, 1933-39; private practice of psychiatry, New York, N.Y., and Glens Falls, N.Y., 1939—. Attending psychiatrist at Gracie Square Hospital, New York, N.Y., 1961—; consulting psychiatrist at other New York institutions, 1947—. Founding fellow, American Board of Legal Medicine, 1952—; Academy of Psychosomatic Medicine, founder, 1953, vice-president, 1962. Member of National Committee on Mental Hygiene, 1941, National Committee on Alcoholic Hygiene, 1945, National Council on Family Relations, 1945—, National Committee on Alcoholism, 1951. Medical Correctional Association, councilor, 1952-56, vice-president, 1970. *Military service:* U.S. Army Reserve, Medical Corps, 1927-33; became first lieutenant.

MEMBER: American Psychiatric Association, American Psychopathological Association (vice-president), New York Academy of Medicine (fellow), American Geriatrics Society (fellow), Authors League of America, American Academy of Forensic Sciences, United States Figure Skating Association, Eastern Psychiatric Research Association, New York Society for Medical History, New York Society for Clinical Psychiatry, New York Neurological Society, New York State Society for Medical Research, state and county medical societies, New Jersey Figure Skating Club, Alpha Omega Alpha.

WRITINGS: Dilettantism, Afe Press, 1930; *Plague: Laennec (1782-1826) Inventor of the Stethoscope and Father of Modern Medicine,* Hobson Book Press, 1930, 2nd edition, 1947; *Auscultation of the Abdomen,* Monograph Editions, 1931; (under pseudonym Aun Foda) *Garbo: A Commentary on the Times,* Afe Press, 1932; *Crime and Sexual Development: Movement and Fixation of the Libido in Crimonotic Individuals,* Monograph Editions, 1936; *The Life and Death Instincts—The Vita and the Fatum,* Monograph Editions, 1939; *Studies in Criminology,* Williams & Wilkins, 1948; (editor with Alfred

Joseph Cantor) *Psychosomatic Aspects of Surgery*, Grune, 1956; *Catherine Eden Moore, 1742-1818, Wife of John Moore, Archbishop of Canterbury, 1783-1805*, Monograph Editions, 1958; *The Common Sense from Heraclitus to Pierce: The Sources, Substance, and Possibilities of Common Sense*, Tunbridge, 1962; *Skating for Everyone*, Deerhill, 1966; *Early Poems*, Tunbridge, 1971.

Contributor of more than three hundred articles and book reviews to handbooks, encyclopedias, and professional journals. Associate managing editor of *Journal of Nervous and Mental Diseases*, 1939-59; associate editor of *Psychoanalytic Review*, 1939-59, *Psychosomatics*, 1960-63, *Corrective Psychiatry*, 1968; collaborating editor, *Journal of Criminal Psychopathology*, 1945-48, *Journal of Clinical Psychopathology*, 1949-50, *Archives of Criminal Psychodynamics*, 1958-63; consulting editor, *Alcoholic Hygiene*, 1948-52.

WORK IN PROGRESS: American Wildflowers, photographs in color; additional studies in criminology; poems of childhood.

AVOCATIONAL INTERESTS: Figure skating; snowshoeing and climbing mountains in New England.

*   *   *

FRAHM, Anne B. Schwerdt   1927-

PERSONAL: Born June 29, 1927, in Esher, Surrey, England; daughter of Edmund Arthur and Helen (Lucas) Schwerdt; married Robert N. Frahm (a consultant bacteriologist), October 20, 1945; children: Robert B., Susan K., Fredericka, C. Joseph, Elizabeth C., John E. *Education:* Attended schools in England, and Katharine Gibbs School, New York, N.Y., 1943-44. *Politics:* Republican. *Religion:* Protestant. *Home:* 535 Cambridge S.E., Grand Rapids, Mich. 49506.

CAREER: Sheffield Farms Milk Co., New York, N.Y., assistant editor of house organ, 1944-45; now assists her husband in his business, writing brochures and other materials.

WRITINGS: True Book of Bacteria, Childrens Press, 1963 (published in England as *The Junior True Book of Bacteria*, Muller, 1966); *Crew's Manual for Small Boat Racing*, De Graff, 1967.

WORK IN PROGRESS: Dr. Goggle, about a small boy's guardian angel; *Mushrooms*, a science book for early grades; *Heraldry*, for early readers; *American Government*, for early readers; science teaching materials and manuals for elementary grades.

AVOCATIONAL INTERESTS: Sailing, and working with children in arts, crafts, and drama.

*   *   *

FRANK, Nathalie D.   1918-

PERSONAL: Born January 28, 1918, in St. Petersburg (now Leningrad), Russia; came to United States in 1923; daughter of Dimitry N. (a mining and electrical engineer) and Claudia (Potapoff) Frank. *Education:* Barnard College, A.B., 1939; Columbia University, B.S. in L.S. (with honors), 1941. *Politics:* Independent. *Religion:* Russian Greek Orthodox. *Home:* 120 Vermilyea Ave., New York, N.Y. 10034. *Office:* Geyer, Morey, Ballard, Inc., 555 Madison Ave., New York, N.Y. 10022.

CAREER: Clarke, Sinsabaugh & Co. (investment counselors), New York, N.Y., assistant librarian, 1941-42; U.S. Office of War Information, New York, N.Y., library assistant, 1942-43; Geyer, Morey, Ballard, Inc. (advertising agency), New York, N.Y., librarian, 1943—. Instructor in elementary cataloging, Ballard School, New York, N.Y., 1954—. Consultant, Special Libraries Association, 1958—. *Member:* Special Libraries Association (chair-

man of Russian Scientific Periodicals Project, 1942-44; secretary of advertising division, 1949-50; chairman of elections committee, 1950-51), American Documentation Institute, American Marketing Association, American Translators Association, American Association of Teachers of Slavonic and East European Languages in America, Council of Advertising Agency Librarians (chairman, 1953-54; member of program committee for American Association of Advertising Agencies Eastern Conference, 1951), Advertising Women of New York, Advertising Club of New York.

WRITINGS: Current Sources of Information for Market Research: A Selected and Annotated Bibliography, American Marketing Association, 1954; *Library File Data: Information File Sources—Their Selection and Scope*, Special Libraries Association, New York Advertising Group, 1958; *Market Analysis: A Handbook of Current Data Sources*, Scarecrow, 1964, 2nd edition published as *Data Sources for Business and Market Analysis*, 1967. Contributor to *Advertising Agency* and *Special Libraries*. Editor, *What's New in Advertising and Marketing*, 1949-50, and American Marketing Association *New York Chapter Newsletter*, 1955-56.

AVOCATIONAL INTERESTS: Travel and color photography.

*   *   *

FRANKENBERG, Celestine Gilligan

PERSONAL: Born in New York, N.Y.; daughter of James Bartholomew and Kathryn (Murphy) Gilligan; married Robert C. Frankenberg (an artist), April 4, 1959. *Education:* Hunter College, B.A., 1946; Pratt Institute, M.L.S., 1948. *Office:* Young & Rubicam, Inc., 285 Madison Ave., New York, NY. 10017.

CAREER: New York Public Library, New York, NY., picture collection librarian, 1946-50; Pan American World Airways, New York, N.Y., photo librarian, 1950-55; Young & Rubicam, Inc., New York, N.Y., photo and art librarian, 1955-68, assistant director of library services, 1968-71, director of library services, 1971—. *Member:* Special Libraries Association (secretary-treasurer, New York picture group, 1955; chairman, New York picture group, 1962-63).

WRITINGS: (Editor) *Picture Sources 2*, Special Libraries Association, 1964. Contributor to *Special Libraries*.

AVOCATIONAL INTERESTS: Travel, natural history, theatre, and preservation of natural resources.

*   *   *

FRANKENSTEIN, Carl   1905-

PERSONAL: Born February 16, 1905, in Berlin, Germany; son of Emil (a merchant) and Rosa (Czempin) Frankenstein; married Rehuma Druckmann (formerly a nurse), April 29, 1949. *Education:* University of Berlin, Ph.D., 1927. *Religion:* Jewish. *Home:* Shmaryahu Levin St., Jerusalem, Israel.

CAREER: Mandatory Government, Jerusalem, Palestine, probation officer, 1937-46; private practice as psychotherapist, 1946-51, and during other periods; Szold Institute for Child Research, Jerusalem, Israel, director, 1948-53; Hebrew University, Jerusalem, Israel, professor of special education, 1951-69. Member of government, municipal, and voluntary agency advisory committees. *Member:* International Child Psychiatry Association, American Group Psychotherapy Association.

WRITINGS: Wayward Youth, Henrietta Szold Institute, 1947; (editor) *Child Care in Israel: A Guide to the Social Services for Children and Youth*, Henrietta Szold Institute, 1950; (editor) *Between Past and Future: Essays and Studies on Aspects of Immigrant Absorption in Israel*, Henrietta Szold Institute, 1953; *Die Aeusserlichkeit des Lebensstils: Ein Beitrag zur Pathologie der Ichentwicklung*, J.M. Meulenhoff (Amsterdam), 1959; *Psychopathy: A Comparative Analysis of Clinical Pictures*, Grune, 1959; *Yaldut ve-ont* (title means "childhood and poverty"), [Jerusalem], 1959; *Die Wege der Verinnerund*, Urban & Schwarzenberg, 1964; *Persoenlichkeitswandel durch Fuersorge, Erziehung und Therapie*, Urban & Schwarzenberg, 1964; *Ha-Adam bi metsukato* (title means "man in distress"), [Jerusalem], 1965; *The Roots of the Ego: A Phenomenology of Dynamics and of Structure*, Williams & Wilkins, 1966; *Psychodynamics of Externalization: Life from Without*, Williams & Wilkins, 1968; *Vareties of Juvenile Delinquency*, Gordon & Breach, 1970; *Impaired Intelligence: Pathology and Rehabilitation*, Gordon & Breach, 1970. Contributor of essays on education, child care, psychopathology, delinquency, and other topics, in English, German, and Hebrew, to journals. Editor of "Studies in Education," Hebrew University, 1963, and of child research quarterly, *Megamoth*.

WORK IN PROGRESS: Intelligence Resurrected.

* * *

FRANKLYN, Charles Aubrey Hamilton 1896-

PERSONAL: Born August 25, 1896, in Brentwood, Essex, England; son of Aubrey Hamilton (a member of London Stock Exchange) and Ethel Mary (Gray) Franklyn. *Education:* Tonbridge School, student, 1910-14; St. Thomas's Hospital Medical School, University of London, M.B. and B.S., 1924; University of Lausanne, M.D., 1925; Exeter College, Oxford, postgraduate study, 1940-41. *Politics.* Conservative. *Religion:* "Officially Church of England, de facto agnostic." *Home:* Wickham Hill House, Hassocks, Sussex, England.

CAREER: Member, Royal College of Surgeons, and licentiate, Royal College of Physicians, 1923; physician in private practice, 1925—. University of London, member of standing committee, 1927-61, senior member, 1954-61, bedell of convocation, 1932—, provincial supervisor in charge of final degree examinations, 1941-56. Designer of official robes and academical dress for University of Malaya, Australian National University, University of Southampton, University of Hull; lecturer on heraldry. *Military service:* British Army, 1915-20; served in France, and Flanders, 1916-19; became lieutenant. *Member:* British Medical Association, Society of Antiquaries of Scotland (fellow), Linnean Society (fellow), Oxford Society (life), Philosophical Society (fellow), American Institute for Philosophical Studies. *Awards, honors:* M.A., University of Malaya, 1951; D.Litt., Geneva Theological College, 1972.

WRITINGS: The Bearing of Coat-Armour by Ladies: A Guide to the Bearing of Arms by Ladies of All Ranks, J. Murray, 1923; *A Short History of the Family of Tiarks of Foxbury*, Adlard, 1929, 2nd edition, privately printed, 1965; *The Genealogy of the Chavasse Family*, privately printed, 1929; *Academic Costume*, Oxonion Press, 1930; *A Short Genealogical and Heraldic History of the Families of Frankelyn of Kent and Franklyn of Antigua and Jamaica, B.W.I.*, Edward O. Beck, 1932; (compiler with Cecil W. Brand) *Pedigree of Hanson Family of Osmandthorpe*, [Hassocks], 1955; *A Genealogical History of the Families of Paulet (or Pawlett), Berewe (or Barrow), Lawrence, and Parker*, Farming Press, 1963; *A Genealogical History of the Families of Montgomerie of Garboldisham, Hunter of Knap, and Montgomerie of Fittleworth*, Ditchling Press, 1967; *Supplement to A Genealogical History of the Familes of Paulet*, Baxter, 1969; *Academical Dress from the Middle Ages to the Present Day, Including Lambeth Degrees*, Baxter, 1970; (with Rogers, Shaw, and Boyd) *Degrees and Hoods of the World's Universities and Colleges*, 5th edition (Franklyn was not associated with earlier editions), Baxter, 1972.

Contributor to *Encyclopaedia Britannica, Grove's Dictionary of Music and Musicians, Chambers' Encyclopaedia, Pears' Cyclopaedia, Illustrated London News, Sphere, Graphic*, and other periodicals. Honorary assistant to editor of *Armorial Families*, 7th edition, two volumes, 1929-30, to editor of *Burke's Landed Gentry*, centenary edition, 1937.

AVOCATIONAL INTERESTS: Music, travel, cats; also a student of the Higher Criticism.

* * *

FREE, Ann Cottrell

PERSONAL: Born in Richmond, Va.; daughter of Emmett Drewry and Emily (Blake) Cottrell; married James Stillman Free (a newspaper correspondent in Washington, D.C.), February 24, 1950; children: Elissa. *Education:* Attended Barnard College; Columbia University, A.B., 1938. *Religion:* Protestant. *Home and office:* 4700 Jamestown Rd., Washington, D.C. 20016.

CAREER: Correspondent in Washington, D.C., for *Richmond Times-Dispatch, Newsweek, Chicago Sun*, and *New York Herald Tribune*, 1938-46; United Nations Relief and Rehabilitation Administration, chief of public information in Shanghai, China, 1936-48; Marshall Plan, special writer in Europe, 1948-49; North American Newspaper Alliance, Washington correspondent, 1950—. Columnist with husband, James Stillman Free, for McClure Syndicate, 1962. *Member:* Women's National Press Club (founder of Eleanor Roosevelt Memorial Commission), American Newspaper Women's Club. *Awards, honors:* Albert Schweitzer Medal of Animal Welfare Institute, and *Boys' Life*—Dodd, Mead writing award, 1963, both for *Forever the Wild Mare;* citation for establishment of Rachel Carson National Wildlife Refuge.

WRITINGS: Forever the Wild Mare, Dodd, 1963. Contributor to magazines.

WORK IN PROGRESS: A second animal book; a novel on China.

BIOGRAPHICAL/CRITICAL SOURCES: Washington Post, October, 13, 1963; *Congressional Record*, October 17, 1963; *Richmond News Leader*, October 28, 1963; *Washington Star*, December 12, 1963, August 5, 1970.

* * *

FREE, William Joseph 1933-

PERSONAL: Born March 18, 1933, in Chattanooga, Tenn.; son of Albert F. and Kate (Bridges) Free; married Ruby Ann Smith, September 1, 1957; married second wife, Mary Gilbert (a teacher), September 17, 1971; children: (first marriage) David William. *Education:* University of Chattanooga, A.B., 1957; University of North Carolina, M.A., 1959, Ph.D., 1962. *Home:* 109 Westchester Circle, Apt. 8, Athens, Ga. 30601. *Office:* Department of English, University of Georgia, Athens, Ga. 30601.

CAREER: Free-lance drama director and radio-television writer, 1954-57; *Times*, Chattanooga, Tenn., movie critic, 1955-57; North Carolina Symphony Orchestra, Chapel Hill, N.C., publicity director, 1957-58; University of North Carolina, Chapel Hill, instructor in English, 1958-62; University of Georgia, Athens, assistant professor, 1962-67, associate professor of English, 1967—. *Member:* Modern Language Association of America, American Society for Aesthetics, South Atlantic Modern Language Association.

WRITINGS: (Editor with Charles B. Lower) *History Into Drama: A Source Book of Symphonic Drama,* Odyssey, 1963; *The Columbian Magazine and American Literary Nationalism,* Mouton & Co., 1968; (contributor) Ellsworth Barnard, editor, *E.A. Robinson Centenary Essays,* University of Georgia Press, 1969. Contributor to professional journals.

WORK IN PROGRESS: Creative writing in drama; a book on drama and film.

*   *   *

FREEDMAN, Ronald   1917-

PERSONAL: Born August 8, 1917, in Winnipeg, Manitoba, Canada; son of Issador (a merchant) and Ada (Greenstone) Freedman; married Deborah G. Selin (an economist), December 4, 1941; children: Joseph Selin, Jane Ilene. *Education:* University of Michigan, B.A., 1939, M.A., 1940; University of Chicago, Ph.D., 1947. *Religion:* Jewish. *Home:* 1404 Beechwood Rd., Ann Arbor, Mich. 48103. *Office:* Sociology Department, University of Michigan, Ann Arbor, Mich. 48104.

CAREER: University of Michigan, Ann Arbor, 1946—, started as instructor, now professor of sociology, director of Population Studies Center, and research associate of Survey Research Center. *Military service:* U.S. Army Air Forces, 1942-45; became warrant officer junior grade. *Member:* Population Association of America (president, 1964-65), American Sociological Association, American Statistical Association, Phi Beta Kappa. *Awards, honors:* Award for Excellence in Teaching, University of Michigan, 1952; Guggenheim fellow and Fulbright fellow, 1957; Distinguished Faculty Service award, 1970.

WRITINGS: *Recent Migration to Chicago,* University of Chicago Press, 1950; (with others) *Principles of Sociology: A Text with Readings,* Holt, 1952, revised edition, 1956; *Future School and College Enrollments in Michigan: 1955 to 1970,* J.W. Edwards, 1955; (with Samuel J. Eldersvald) *Political Affiliation in Metropolitan Detroit,* Michigan Governmental Studies, 1957; (with Pascal K. Whelpton and Arthur A. Campbell) *Family Planning, Sterility, and Population Growth,* McGraw, 1959; *The Sociology of Human Fertility,* Basil Blackwell, 1963; (editor) *Population: The Vital Revolution,* Doubleday, 1964; (with Lolagene C. Coombs) *Use of Telephone Interviews in a Longitudinal Fertility Study,* University of Michigan Population Studies Center, 1964; *The Accelerating Fertility Decline in Taiwan,* University of Michigan Population Studies Center, 1965; (with David Goldberg and Doris Slesinger) *Current Fertility Expectations of Married Couples in the United States,* University of Michigan Population Studies Center, 1965, revised edition (with Goldberg and Larry Bumpass), 1965; (editor) *Fertility and Family Planning: A World View,* University of Michigan Press, 1969; (with John Y. Takeshita and others) *Family Planning in Taiwan: An Experiment in Social Change,* Princeton University Press, 1969.

Contributor of about fifty articles to professional journals.

*   *   *

FREEMAN, Margaret N(adgwick)   1915-

PERSONAL: Born April 7, 1915, in Essex, Iowa; daughter of Joseph A. (a farmer) and Vilma (Hart) Nadgwick; married Stanley O. Freeman (a paint store manager), May 29, 1941; children: Dennis Stanley, Douglas Joseph. *Education:* Educated in Iowa schools. *Politics:* Republican. *Religion:* Protestant. *Home:* 1203 South Maple St., Shenandoah, Iowa 51601.

MEMBER: Covenant Women (national education committee).

WRITINGS: *Twelve Devotional Programs for Women's Meetings,* Moody, 1963; *Thank You God,* Standard Publishing, in press. Contributor to more than fifty periodicals, mainly religious.

WORK IN PROGRESS: Research for a juvenile biography; a youth program book.

*   *   *

FRENCH, Dorothy Kayser   1926-

PERSONAL: Born February 11, 1926, in Milwaukee, Wis.; daughter of Paul (in public relations) and Gertrude (Ament) Kayser; married Louis N. French (a patent attorney for Phillips Petroleum Co.), July 2, 1948; children: Nancy, Laura. *Education:* University of Wisconsin, B.A., 1948. *Home:* 2136 Starlight Ct., Bartlesville, Okla. 74003.

CAREER: *Shorewood Herald,* Shorewood, Wis., society editor, 1947; *Wisconsin State Journal,* Madison, women's editor, 1948-50; *Bartlesville Record,* Bartlesville, Okla., society editor, 1951; free-lance writer, 1951—. *Member:* American Association of University Women (branch secretary, 1950-52), Theta Sigma Phi, Mortar Board, Kappa Delta.

WRITINGS: *Mystery of the Old Oil Well, F.* Watts, 1963; *Swim to Victory,* Lippincott, 1969; *A Try at Tumbling,* Lippincott, 1970. Contributor of short stories and articles to magazines.

WORK IN PROGRESS: Sports, mystery, and nonfiction books for juveniles.

*   *   *

FRIEDMAN, Bruce Jay   1930-

PERSONAL: Born April 26, 1930, in New York, N.Y.; son of Irving (a manufacturer) and Molly (Liebowitz) Friedman; married Ginger Howard (an actress and model), June 13, 1954; children: Josh Alan, Drew Samuel, Kipp Adam. *Education:* University of Missouri, B.J., 1951. *Home:* 11 Gateway Dr., Great Neck, N.Y. 11021. *Agent:* Candida Donadio, Lantz-Donadio, 111 West 57th St., New York, N.Y.

CAREER: Magazine Management Co., New York, N.Y., editorial director, 1954-66. *Military service:* U.S. Air Force, 1951-53. *Member:* P.E.N., Sigma Delta Chi.

WRITINGS: *Stern* (novel), Simon & Schuster, 1962; *Far From the City of Class, and Other Stories,* Frommer-Pasmantier, 1963; *A Mother's Kisses* (novel), Simon & Schuster, 1964; (editor and author of introduction) *Black Humor* (anthology), Bantam, 1965; *Stern* [and] *A Mother's Kisses,* Simon & Schuster, 1966; *Black Angels* (stories), Simon & Schuster, 1966; "23 Pat O'Brien Movies" (one-act play), produced Off-Broadway on triple bill with "The Floor" by May Swenson, and "Miss Pete" by Andrew Glaze as "Double Opposites," at American Place Theatre, May 11, 1966; *Scuba Duba: A Tense Comedy* (play; first produced Off-Broadway at New Theatre, October 10, 1967), Simon & Schuster, 1968; "A Mother's Kisses" (musical based on his novel), first produced in New Haven, Conn., September 21, 1968 (closed prior to Broadway); (contributor with Gregory Corso and others) *Pardon Me, Sir, But Is My Eye Hurting Your Elbow?,* Geis, 1968; *The Dick* (novel), Knopf, 1970; *Steambath: A Play* (produced Off-Broadway at Truck and Warehouse Theatre, June, 1970), Knopf, 1971; "The Owl and the Pussycat" (screenplay; based on the play by William Manhof), produced by Columbia, 1971.

WORK IN PROGRESS: A third collection of stories.

SIDELIGHTS: Nelson Algren writes in the *Nation* that "Friedman's craft is in provoking laughter at the same time that the air grows murderous." In this preoccupation with black humor he is similar to Samuel Beckett. "The difference between Friedman and Beckett," says Algren, "is that while Beckett assigns a separate ash can to each of his characters, Friedman uses no props: his people simply live ash-can lives."

Comparing Friedman to other contemporaries, Algren writes: "Friedman has nothing of the cleverness of Roth; he lacks Bellow's intellectualism altogether. Unlike Malamud, his people don't even have connections to a life of the past." But, at a time when these writers are virtually unchallenged as perhaps the most important in America today, Algren can also add; "What makes Friedman more interesting than most of Malamud, Roth and Bellow is the sense he affords of possibilities larger than the doings and undoings of the Jewish urban bourgeois.... What makes him more important is that he writes out of the viscera instead of the cerebrum. What makes him more dangerous is that while they distribute prose designed by careful planning for careful living, Friedman really doesn't know what he's doing. 'I can remember being inside Mommy,' Stern's infant son tells him, 'I knew about the Three Stooges in there.' "

Friedman wrote in *Harper's:* "I write to find out how I really feel about things. If I knew in advance, there really would not be any point to writing.... I find out how I feel about things as I go along and there is no one more curious than I am to find out what I am up to." He usually seems to be up to some funny business.

Alfred Chester describes *Stern,* Friedman's first novel, as a "delightful, moving, and sometimes quite beautiful novel.... More extraordinary even than the creation of a real comic character and a real man is the way that Friedman has, . . . and with barely any of that tiresome sociology which makes books about minorities so unrewarding, somehow rendered transparent the eclectic nature of the American Jew. . . . This mild, comical, slob who lives mainly in fantasy is actually a tour de force, but he lacks one quality—and this is the major weakness in the book—the quality of introspection." Eugene Goodheart states: "The novel is an odd, whimsical descant, complicated by pathos, on the old theme of anti-Semitism. There is certainly enough wit and charm to make us attend to the story, but it leaves us smiling uncertainly at the joke." A *Time* reviewer describes *Stern* as "a strange and touching little first novel . . . about being Jewish in a lawn-proud suburb of mid-century, middle-class America. But Stern is no sociological novel. Blurring fact and fantasy, it is funny and sad at the same time in the tradition of the Jewish *schlemiel* story and the Charlie Chaplin movie." As Stanley Trachtenberg writes, "abrasive rather than comic, Stern reverses the standard pattern of the anti-hero, whose roguery and guile protest the social norm. Rather he is the self-generated victim, the outcast who does not resist society but, accepting its authority as his own, wants only to submerge himself in it."

"*A Mother's Kisses* is one of the funniest and most imaginative novels in many moons," R.J. Cunningham states. "It is a brief, yet arresting story of a few hectic weeks in the life of Meg, a New York Jewish woman ... a fabulous combination of all the women of legend, including Jocasta, Medea, the Wife of Bath and Molly Bloom." "Friedman merges a wild comedy of language and situation with the stark terror of character and theme so that they imperceptibly become one another—riotous comedy suddenly becoming frightening revelation, awful insight [careening] toward zany comedy," a *Newsweek* critic writes. "Friedman explores the real meaning of the national cult of Mother Love; takes the most mawkish of sentimentalities—a mother's love, a mother's kisses—and with furious singlemindedness sets

out to discover its hidden recesses. There is not a trace of psychoanalytic cliche—only an implacably honest writer uncovering his unexpected truths." Daniel Stern states that Friedman's "real victory is one of style. The style *is* the subject, because the characters' lives and their language are identical. Friedman is a wild poet of the secret life, one of the funniest of writers, but with a dark echo to the laughter that gets painfully close to the bone."

When *Scuba Duba* opened Walter Kerr wrote that Friedman, "by all the rules ... shouldn't be able to write a first play as stageworthy and as side-splitting as *Scuba Duba.* . . . It is a genuine original, a zany charade with a mindlessness of its own." A *Life* writer states that the play "has a social conscience but not a messianic complex. It is not concerned with defending the Negro or upholding his civil rights—and does not purport to unify the human race. It is concerned with a wholly different but major aspect of the race problem: the white man's lurid notions and misconceptions of what a Negro is." Harold Clurman believes that the play "is not satire, it is naturalism! It is also 'nihilism.' What Friedman, willynilly, is telling us from the frazzled deeps of his being is that he, they, *we* are all living in a loony bin in which anything goes, and that there's no use feeling anything about it since nothing is what it seems or is given out to be. We are puppets playing unbalanced games on a freak stage."

Marilyn Stasio discusses Friedman's wit in her review of *Steambath:* "It spears the idiosyncratic behavior of the play's characters without losing touch with the poignancy of their existential condition. Although it is set in the afterlife, *Steambath* is actually about the life of reality. Friedman is registering cynicism, pity, horror, and frustrated anger about the fact that we live inconsequential existences in a shoddy limbo that we have the temerity to call life.... While the surface humor of Friedman's situation-comedy form is riotously funny, the underlying philosophical premise is as profoundly tragic as the similar theme of his first play."

Friedman is known for his stories as well as his novels and plays. Webster Schott writes of *Black Angels:* "[Friedman] is trying to make our new intrinsic fiction. To disarm death, erotic disloyalty, matrimonial doom, to laugh at them. To discover the truth of our situation and expand it billboard-size. Friedman succeeds. He's a very funny guy. Like poetry, his black humor leads us to infer personal truths from his ambiguous stories." Martin Tucker finds all the stories "equally coated with bitterness and brilliance, and a kick that surprises even when it is expected. His fourth book ... is less dependent on the surface for its Jewish milieu; its characters rarely mention their nominal religion, but the feeling of an alien stance in a boxed-in world remains."

Scuba Duba, originally scheduled for filming by Warner Brothers, is being produced by Filmways; screen rights for *Stern* and *The Dick* have been sold.

BIOGRAPHICAL/CRITICAL SOURCES: New York Herald Tribune Books, September 23, 1962; *New York Times Book Review,* September 23, 1962, October 2, 1966, August 16, 1970; *Saturday Review,* October 13, 1962, August 15, 1964; *Time,* December 21, 1962, July 13, 1970, September 7, 1970; *Newsweek,* August 17, 1964, August 17, 1970; *Best Sellers,* October 15, 1964, September 15, 1970; *Critique,* spring-summer, 1965; *Harper's,* November, 1965; *Commonweal,* December 9, 1966; *Life,* October 13, 1967; *New York Times,* October 22, 1967, January 21, 1968, July 1, 1970, August 17, 1970; *National Observer,* October 23, 1967; *Nation,* October 30, 1967, November 23, 1970; *Playbill,* October, 1968; *Cue,*

July 11, 1970, July 18, 1970; *New Yorker,* July 11, 1970; *National Review,* October 20, 1970; *New York Review of Books,* November 5, 1970.

*   *   *

FRISCH, O(tto) R(obert)   1904-

PERSONAL: Born October 1, 1904, in Vienna, Austria; son of Justinian (a printer) and Gusti (a pianist; maiden name, Meitner) Frisch; married Ursula Blau (an illustrator), March 14, 1951; children: Monica, Tony. *Education:* University of Vienna, Dr. Phil., 1926. *Home:* Trinity College, Cambridge, England.

CAREER: Researcher in physics in Berlin and Hamburg, Germany, in London, Birmingham, Liverpool, and Harwell, England, in Copenhagen, Denmark, and in Los Alamos, N.M.; Cambridge University, Cambridge, England, professor of physics, 1947—, fellow of Trinity College. *Member:* Royal Society (fellow), Physical Society (fellow), American Physical Society (fellow). *Awards, honors:* Order of British Empire; D.Sc., University of Birmingham; Bronze Medal of Freedom, United States.

WRITINGS: On the Selective Capture of Slow Neutrons, Munksgaard, 1937; (with Hans von Halban and Joergen Koch) *On the Slowing Down and Capture of Neutrons in Hydrogenous Substances,* Munksgaard, 1938; (with Lise Meitner) *On the Products of the Fission or Uranium and Thorium under Neutron Bombardment,* Munksgaard, 1940; *Meet the Atoms: A Popular Guide to Modern Physics,* Wyn, 1947; (editor) *Progress in Nuclear Physics,* Volumes 1-8, Pergamon, 1950-60, Volume 9, Macmillan, 1964; (editor) *The Nuclear Handbook,* Van Nostrand, 1958; (editor) *Beitraege zur Physik und Chemie des 20 Jahrhunderts,* F. Vieweg, 1959; (editor with others) *Trends in Atomic Physics,* Interscience, 1959; *Atomic Physics Today,* Basic Books, 1961; (with Wilhelm Fuchs) *Die Elementarteilchen der Physik* [and] *Mathematische Analyse von Formalstrukturen von Werken der Musik* (the former by Frisch, the latter by Fuchs), Westdeutscher, 1963; *Working with Atoms,* Brockhampton Press, 1965, Basic Books, 1966; *The Nature of Matter,* Dutton, 1973.

Contributor of science articles (popular presentations) to magazines.

WORK IN PROGRESS: Research on the physics of the smallest particles.

AVOCATIONAL INTERESTS: Piano music.

*   *   *

FROMM, Erika   1910-

PERSONAL: Born December 23, 1910, in Frankfurt, Germany; daughter of Siegfried (a physician) and Clementine (Stern) Oppenheimer; married Paul Fromm (a business executive), July 20, 1938; children: Joan (Mrs. J. David Greenstone). *Education:* University of Frankfurt, Ph.D., 1933. *Politics:* Democrat. *Religion:* Jewish. *Home:* 5715 South Kenwood Ave., Chicago, Ill. 60637. *Office:* Department of Psychology, University of Chicago, Chicago, Ill. 60637.

CAREER: Department of Psychiatry, Amsterdam, Netherlands, research associate, 1934-35; State Hospital, Apeldoon, Netherlands, director of psychology laboratory, 1935-38; Francis W. Parker School, Chicago, Ill., chief psychologist, 1944-51; Institute for Juvenile Research, Chicago, Ill., supervising psychologist, 1951-53; Northwestern University Medical School, Chicago, Ill., associate professor, 1954-61; University of Chicago, Chicago, Ill., professor of psychology, 1961—. Fromm Music Foundation, trustee. *Member:* American Psychological Association (fellow), American Association for the Advancement of Science (fellow), American Orthopsychia-

tric Association (fellow; director, 1961-63), Society for Clinical and Experimental Hypnosis (fellow), Society for Projective Techniques (fellow), Sigma Xi. *Awards, honors:* Award of Society of Clinical and Experimental Hypnosis 1965, for best research paper published in 1965; Morton Prince Award, 1970.

WRITINGS: (With Lenore D. Hartman) *Intelligence—A Dynamic Approach,* Doubleday, 1955; (contributor) Albert I. Rabin and M.R. Haworth, editors, *Projective Techniques with Children,* Grune, 1960; (with Thomas M. French) *Dream Interpretation: A New Approach,* Basic Books, 1964; (with Ronald E. Shor) *Hypnosis: Research Developments and Perspectives,* Aldine, 1972. Contributor to scientific journals. Clinical editor, *Journal of Clinical and Experimental Hypnosis.*

AVOCATIONAL INTERESTS: Indoor gardening, knitting, and travel.

*   *   *

FROST, Ernest   1918-

PERSONAL: Born December 19, 1918, in Isleworth, Middlesex, England; son of Ernest (a gown manufacturer) and Mabel (Stanford) Frost; married Phyllis Gadsden, July 2, 1946; children: Nicholas. *Education:* Attended private and state schools in England until sixteen; Gaddesden Training College, student, 1948. *Home:* 2 Main St., Long Whatton, near Loughborough, Leicestershire, England. *Agent:* David Higham Associates Ltd., 5-8 Lower John St., Golden Square, London W.1, England. *Office:* Department of English, Loughborough College of Education, Leicestershire, England.

CAREER: Saturday Review, London, England, editorial assistant, 1934; Krisson Printing Ltd., London, England, reader, 1935-38; schoolmaster in and near London, England, 1949-59; Loughborough College of Education, Leicestershire, England, senior lecturer in English language and literature, 1959—. Guest poet for 1960 at University of Durham and College of Venerable Bede. *Military service:* British Army, 1940-46. *Member:* Association of Teachers in Colleges and Departments of Education, P.E.N.

WRITINGS: (Contributor) *Four in Hand* (poems), Three Arts Club (Naples), 1944; *The Dark Peninsula* (novel), Macdonald & Co., 1949; *The Lighted Cities* (novel), Lehmann, 1950, Harcourt, 1952; *A Short Lease,* Lehmann, 1953; *The Visitants* (novel), Deutsch, 1955; *Down to Hope* (novel), Hodder & Stoughton, 1963; *It's Late By My Watch* (novel), Hodder & Stoughton, 1966.

Anthologized in *Poets of the Forties* and in *New Poems 1965 and 1971,* edited by C.V. Wedgwood, Hutchinson, 1966, and in press. Contributor of poetry to *Yale Review, World Review, New Statesman, Poetry Quarterly, Poetry Folios, Observer, Horizon, Arena, London Magazine,* and other periodicals; author of short stories for British Broadcasting Corp. programs.

WORK IN PROGRESS: In the Hanging Gardens, a novel; a children's entertainment titled *The Cats of Montparnasse.*

AVOCATIONAL INTERESTS: Bicycling in Europe, typography, painting.

BIOGRAPHICAL/CRITICAL SOURCES: Go, December, 1950; *Times Literary Supplement,* August 24, 1951; John Lehmann, editor, *The Craft of Letters,* [London], 1954; *London Magazine,* November, 1958.

*   *   *

FROSTICK, Michael   1917-

PERSONAL: Born October 26, 1917, in Hove, Sussex, England; son of Walter George Frostick; married

Suzanne Harlock, November 3, 1962; children: (previous marriage) Xenia, Robin. *Education:* Attended Brighton College, 1931-34. *Politics:* "Pale" Tory. *Religion:* Anglican. *Home:* 42 Clare Ct., Judd St., London W.C.1, England.

CAREER: Hurok Attractions, Inc., New York, N.Y., European representative, 1952-58; TWW Ltd. (independent television company), London, England, deputy program controller, 1959-61; Old Vic, London, England, general manager, 1961-63; Choiceview (pay television company), London, England, chief executive, 1963—. *Military service:* British Army, Royal Dragoons, 1941-46; became captain. *Member:* Guild of Motoring Writers, Vintage Sports Car Club of Great Britain, British International Rally Drivers' Club.

WRITINGS: (With Richard Hough) *Motor Racing: A Guide for the Younger Enthusiast,* Bodley Head, 1955; *Drivers in Action,* Bodley Head, 1955; *Racing Sports Cars,* Hamish Hamilton, 1956; *British Racing Green, 1946-1956,* Bodley Head, 1957; (with Louis Klemantski) *The Vanwall Story,* Macmillan, 1958; (with Klemantski) *Motor Racing Circuits of Europe,* Macmillan, 1958; (with Klemantski) *For Practice Only,* Bodley Head, 1959; (with Klemantski) *Le Mans: A Picture History,* Hamish Hamilton, 1960; (editor with Anthony Harding) *The Motorist's Weekend Book,* Batsford, 1960, Bentley, 1961; *A History of the Monte Carlo Rally,* Hamish Hamilton, 1963, Sportshelf, 1966; (with Hough) *A History of the World's Classic Cars,* Harper, 1963; *Works Team: The Rootes Competition Department,* Cassell, 1964; (with Hough) *A History of the World's Racing Cars,* Harper, 1965; (with Hough) *Rover Memories,* Sportshelf, 1966; (with Hough) *A History of the World's High-Performance Cars,* Harper, 1967; *The Cars That Got Away: Ideas, Experiments and Prototypes,* Cassell, 1968; *Return to Power: The Grand Prix of 1966 and 1967,* Allen & Unwin, 1968; *Grand Prix,* Hamlyn, 1969; *Advertising and the Motor-car,* Lund, Humphries, 1970; *Mighty Mercedes,* Classic Motorbooks, 1971.

* * *

FRUMKIN, Gene 1928-

PERSONAL: Born January 29, 1928, in New York, N.Y.; son of Samuel (a tailor) and Sarah (Blackman) Frumkin; married Lydia Samuels (a painter), July 3, 1955 (divorced November, 1971); children: Celena, Paul. *Education:* University of California, Los Angeles, B.A., 1950. *Home:* 1332 Princeton Dr. N.E., Albuquerque, N.M. 87106. *Office:* Department of English, University of New Mexico, Albuquerque, N.M. 87106.

CAREER: California Apparel News (weekly trade paper), Los Angeles, managing editor, 1952-66; University of New Mexico, Albuquerque, writer-in-residence, 1966-67, assistant professor, 1967-71, associate professor of English, 1971—.

WRITINGS: The Hawk and the Lizard (poems), Alan Swallow, 1963; *The Orange Tree* (long poem), Cyfoeth Publications, 1964; *The Rainbow Walker,* Grasshopper Press, 1971; *Dostoevsky and other Nature Poems,* Solo Press, 1972; *Locust Cry,* San Marcus Press, 1973; *Clouds and Red Earth,* Alan Swallow, 1973. Anthologized in *Forty Poems Touching on Recent American History,* edited by Robert Bly, Beacon Press, 1971, and *Contemporary American Poetry,* edited by Miller Williams, Random House, 1973. Co-founder of *Coastlines* (literary magazine), 1955, served as poetry editor, 1955-58, editor, 1958-62. Contributor to *Saturday Review, Poetry, Evergreen Review, Choice, San Francisco Review, Prairie Schooner, Talisman, Carolina Quarterly, Folio, California Quarterly, Western Review, Chelsea, Statement, Mainstream, Beloit Poetry Journal, Odyssey, Chicago Review, Nation, Minnesota Review, Cafe Solo, New Mexico Quarterly, Kayak, Vigil, Whetstone, Coastlines,* and other journals.

WORK IN PROGRESS: A Novel, *The Frog Novel,* two books of poems.

SIDELIGHTS: Frumkin's primary concern is poetry and fiction. "Above all," he writes, "my intention is to write seriously, for love. Any money that results is a by-product. There is too little time for anything less."

BIOGRAPHICAL/CRITICAL SOURCES: Poetry, February, 1964, January, 1971.

* * *

FRY, Edward Bernard 1925-

PERSONAL: Born April 4, 1925, in Los Angeles, Calif.; son of Eugene Bert and Frances (Dreier) Fry; married Carol Addison (a school librarian), 1950; children: Shanti, Christopher Mohammed. *Education:* Occidental College, B.A., 1949; University of Southern California, M.S., 1954, Ph.D., 1960. *Home:* 233 Harrison, Highland Park, N.J. 08904. *Office:* Graduate School of Education, Rutgers State University, New Brunswick, N.J.

CAREER: Loyola University, Los Angeles, Calif., associate professor of education, 1954-63; Rutgers University, New Brunswick, N.J., professor of education and director of reading center, 1963—. Fulbright lecturer at University of East Africa, Uganda, 1961-62. Member of board of directors, National Reading Conference. *Wartime service:* U.S. Merchant Marine, 1943-45; became deck officer. *Member:* American Psychological Association, International Reading Association, American Educational Research Association.

WRITINGS: (With Glenn L. Bryan and Joseph Rigney) *Teaching Machines: An Annotated Bibliography,* Psychological Sciences Division, Office of Naval Research, 1960; (contributor) A.A. Lumsdaine and R. Glaser, editors, *Teaching Machines and Programmed Learning,* National Education Association, 1960; *A Survey and Analysis of Current Teaching-Machines Programs and Programming,* Department of Psychology, University of Southern California (Los Angeles), 1961; (with Rigney) *Current Teaching-Machine Programs and Programming Techniques,* Department of Audiovisual Instruction, 1961; (contributor) W.J. Smith and W. Moore, editors, *Programmed Learning,* Van Nostrand, 1962; *Teaching Machines and Programmed Instruction,* McGraw, 1963; *Teaching Faster Reading: A Manual,* Cambridge University Press, 1963; *Reading Faster: A Drill Book,* Cambridge University Press, 1963; (contributor) Albert Harris, editor, *Readings on Reading Instruction,* McKay, 1963; *First Grade Reading Instruction Using a Diacritical Marking System, the Initial Teaching Alphabet and a Basic Reading System,* Rutgers State University, 1965; *Comparison of the Three Methods of Reading Instruction: Final Report,* Rutgers State University, 1967; *The Emergency Reading Teachers Manual,* Dreier Educational Systems, 1969; *Typing Course for Children,* Dreier Educational Systems, 1969; *Ninety-Nine Phonics Charts,* Dreier Educational Systems, 1971; *Sailboat in the Wind,* Dreier Educational Systems, 1971; *Reading Instruction for Classroom and Clinic,* McGraw, 1972.

Co-author of two monographs published by National Education Association. Writer of filmstrips, "Instant Words" and "Instant Word Phrases"; deviser of vocabulary game, "Instant World Pairs"; consultant, "Lessons for Self-Instruction" series, California Test Bureau, 1963-65. Contributor of articles and reviews to professional journals.

FRY, Rosalie Kingsmill 1911-

PERSONAL: Born April 22, 1911, on Vancouver Island, British Columbia; daughter of Lindsay Bowring (an engineer) and Edith Alice (Finch) Fry. *Education:* Attended school in Swansea, Wales, and then Central School of Arts and Crafts, London, England, 1929-34. *Politics:* Conservative (Tory). *Religion:* Anglican. *Home:* 1 Mountain Cottage, Llandybie, Ammanford, Wales.

CAREER: Writer and illustrator. Designer of Christmas cards. *Military service:* Women's Royal Naval Service, 1939-45. *Member:* Society of Authors.

WRITINGS—Self-illustrated, except as indicated: *Bumblebuzz*, Dutton, 1938; *Ladybug Ladybug!*, Dutton, 1940; *Bandy Boy's Treasure Island*, Dutton, 1941; *Baby's Progress Book*, W.H. Smith, 1944; *Adventure Downstream*, Hutchinson, 1946; *In a Rock Pool*, Hutchinson, 1947.

Cherrywinkle, Hutchinson, 1951; *The Little Gipsy*, Hutchinson, 1951; *Pipkin Sees the World*, Dutton, 1951 (published in England as *Pipkin the Woodmouse*, Dent, 1953); *Two Little Pigs* (readers), three books, Hutchinson, 1953; *Cinderella's Mouse and Other Fairy Tales*, Dutton, 1953; *Deep in the Forest*, Hutchinson, 1955, Dodd, 1956; *The Wind Call*, Dutton, 1955; *Lucinda and the Painted Bell*, Dent, 1956, published in America as *A Bell for Ringleblume*, Dutton, 1957; *Child of the Western Isles*, Dent, 1957, published in America as *Secret of the Ron Mor Skerry* (Junior Literary Guild selection), Dutton, 1959; *Secret of the Forest*, Hutchinson, 1958; *Matelot, Little Sailor of Britanny*, Dutton, 1958 (published in England as *Lucinda and the Sailor Kitten*, Dent, 1959).

Fly Home, Colombina, Dutton, 1960; *The Mountain Door*, Dent, 1960, Dutton, 1961; *Princess in the Forest*, Hutchinson, 1961; *The Echo Song* (Junior Literary Guild selection), Dutton, 1962; *The Riddle of the Figurehead*, Dutton, 1963; *September Island*, illustrated by Margery Gill, Dutton, 1965; *The Castle Family*, illustrated by Margery Gill, Dent, 1965, Dutton, 1966; *Promise of the Rainbow*, illustrated by Robin Jacques, Farrar, Straus, 1965; *Whistler in the Mist*, illustrated by Robin Jacques, Farrar, Straus, 1968; *Gypsy Princess*, illustrated by Philip Gough, Dutton, 1969; *Snowed Up*, illustrated by Robin Jacques, Farrar, Straus, 1970; *Mungo*, Farrar, Straus, 1971.

Illustrator of *The Water Babies* in Dutton's "Children's Illustrated Classics," and of other books published by Dent, Dutton, and Hutchinson. Stories included in several anthologies. Contributor of articles and illustrations to *Lady, Parents', Collins' Children Annual, Countryman,* and *Country Life,* of stories to British Broadcasting Corp. and Radio Eireann programs.

WORK IN PROGRESS: Books for publication by Dutton, Dent, and Farrar, Straus.

SIDELIGHTS: When Miss Fry is writing about a particular place, especially abroad, she usually spends several weeks in the area, sometimes doing the first draft on the spot.

BIOGRAPHICAL/CRITICAL SOURCES: Times Literary Supplement, June 26, 1969.

*   *   *

FRYE, Roland Mushat 1921-

PERSONAL: Born July 3, 1921, in Birmingham, Ala.; son of John H. (a banker) and Helen (Mushat) Frye; married Jean Elbert Steiner, January 11, 1947; children: Roland M., Jr. *Education:* Princeton University, A.B., 1943, M.A., 1950, Ph.D., 1952; additional study at Princeton Theological Seminary, 1950-51. *Politics:* Republican.

Religion: Presbyterian. *Home:* 226 West Valley Rd., Wayne, Pa. 19087; (summer) Glen Eyrie, Montreat, N.C. *Office:* Department of English, University of Pennsylvania, Philadelphia, Pa. 19104.

CAREER: Tennessee Coal, Iron & Railroad Co., Birmingham, Ala., public relations representative, 1946-47; Howard College, Birmingham, Ala., instructor in English, 1947-48; Emory University, Atlanta, Ga., 1952-61, began as assistant professor, became professor of English; Folger Shakespeare Library, Washington, D.C., research professor, 1961-65; University of Pennsylvania, Philadelphia, professor of English literature, 1965—. Stone Lecturer, Princeton Theological Seminary, 1959. *Military service:* U.S. Army, Field Artillery, 1943-46; became major; awarded Bronze Star. *Member:* Modern Language Association of America, Modern Humanities Research Association, Shakespeare Association of America, Milton Society, Renaissance Society of America, Society for Religion in Higher Education, Princeton Club (New York), Cosmos Club (Washington, D.C.), Franklin Inn (Philadelphia). *Awards, honors:* Guggenheim fellowship, 1956-57; American Council of Learned Societies grants, 1966, 1971; American Philosophical Society grants, 1968, 1971.

WRITINGS: God, Man, and Satan: Patterns of Christian Thought and Life in "Paradise Lost," "Pilgrim's Progress," and the Great Theologians, Princeton University Press, 1960; *Perspective on Man: Literature and the Christian Tradition,* Westminster, 1961; *Shakespeare and Christian Doctrine,* Princeton University Press, 1963; (editor) *The Bible: Selections from the King James Version for Study as Literature,* Houghton, 1965; *Shakespeare's Life and Times: A Pictorial Record,* Princeton University Press, 1967; *Shakespeare: The Art of the Dramatist,* Houghton, 1970. Contributor of more than fifty articles and reviews to professional and learned journals.

WORK IN PROGRESS: John Milton and the Visual Arts; literature and art.

AVOCATIONAL INTERESTS: Theatre, art, music, and fishing.

*   *   *

FUHRO, Wilbur J. 1914-

PERSONAL: Born April 17, 1914, in Union City, N.J.; son of Charles and Anna (Antony) Fuhro; married Marie Roberta Holscher; children: Lawrence Peter, Stephen Allan. *Education:* Newark College of Engineering, B.S.M.E., 1946. *Home:* 19 Chester Lang Pl., Cranford, N.J. 07016.

CAREER: Keuffel & Esser Co. (engineering supplies), Hoboken, N.J., plant methods engineer, 1939-50; Barbizon Corp. (lingerie), Paterson, N.J., chief industrial engineer, 1950-53; U.S. Metals Refining Co., Carteret, N.J., supervisor of methods and standards, 1953-58; Raritan Arsenal (U.S. Ordnance Corps), Metuchen, N.J., chief of manpower and standards, 1958-61; U.S. Naval Ammunition Depot, Colt's Neck, N.J., industrial manager, 1961—. Teacher of industrial engineering, Fairleigh Dickinson University, Rutherford, N.J., 1947—. Consultant in systems integration, Department of the Navy, Bureau of Ships, Washington, D.C. Consultant for two labor unions. *Member:* Society for Advancement of Management (former president, Northern New Jersey chapter). *Awards, honors:* Department of the Army awards for sustained superior performance and for installation of FAST system.

WRITINGS: How to Practice Motion and Timestudy, Fairleigh Dickinson University Press, 1950; *Work Measurement and Production Control with the FAST System,* Prentice-Hall, 1963. Author of industrial and government brochures.

WORK IN PROGRESS: Research into the nature, characteristics, and attributes of sampling to develop a new approach called "simultaneous repetitive sampling," a book on results to follow.

* * *

FULBRIGHT, J(ames) William 1905-

PERSONAL: Born April 9, 1905, in Sumner, Mo.; son of Jay (a farmer) and Roberta (a newspaperwoman; maiden name Waugh) Fulbright; married Elizabeth Kremer Williams, June 15, 1932; children: Elizabeth (Mrs. John Winnacker), Roberta (Mrs. E. Thaddeus Foote II). *Education:* University of Arkansas, B.A., 1925; Pembroke College, Oxford, Rhodes Scholar, A.B., 1928, M.A., 1931; George Washington University, L.L.B., 1934. *Politics:* Democrat. *Religion:* Disciples of Christ. *Home:* 1000 Shrewsbury St., Fayetteville, Ark. 72701; and 2527 Belmont Rd. N.W., Washington, D.C. 20008. *Office:* U.S. Senate Office Building, Washington, D.C. 20025.

CAREER: Admitted to District of Columbia Bar, 1934; U.S. Department of Justice, Anti-Trust Division, special attorney, 1934-35; George Washington University, Washington, D.C., instructor in law, 1935-36; University of Arkansas, Fayetteville, lecturer in law, 1936-39, president of the University, 1939-41; member of 78th Congress from Arkansas Third District, 1943-45; U.S. Senator from Arkansas, 1945—, chairman, Senate Banking and Currency Committee, 1955-59, chairman, Senate Committee on Foreign Relations, 1959—, also member of Senate Finance Committee, and of Joint Economic Committee. Delegate to 9th General Assembly of United Nations, 1954. Fellow, American Academy of Arts and Sciences. *Member:* Order of the Coif, Phi Beta Kappa, Sigma Chi, Rotary (Fayetteville). *Awards, honors:* Honorary fellow, Pembroke College, Oxford, 1949; D.C.L., Oxford University, 1953; National Institute of Arts and Letters Award, 1954; Longfellow-Glocke Award (Germany), 1958, for "original contribution to the mutual understanding between peoples."

WRITINGS: (Contributor) Robert B. Heywood, editor, *Works of the Mind,* University of Chicago Press, 1947; *Towards a More Creative Foreign Policy* (originally published in *Progressive,* November, 1959), Overbrooke Press, 1959; *What Makes U.S. Foreign Policy?,* [Columbus], 1959; (with others) *The Elite and the Electorate: Is Government by the People Possible?,* Center for the Study of Democratic Institutions, 1963; *Fulbright of Arkansas: The Public Positions of a Private Thinker,* edited by Karl E. Meyer, preface by Walter Lippmann, Luce, 1963; *Prospects for the West,* Harvard University Press, 1963; *The American Character* (pamphlet), Industrial Union Department, AFL-CIO, 1964; *Old Myths and New Realities, and Other Commentaries,* Random House, 1964; *Bridges East and West,* edited by John M. Claunch, Southern Methodist University, 1965; *Yugoslavia 1964,* U.S. Government Printing Office, 1965; *The Two Americas,* University of Connecticut, 1966; (author of introduction) *The Vietnam Hearings: Voices from the Grass Roots,* Doubleday, 1966; *The Arrogance of Power,* Random House, 1967; (contributor) David Lloyd Larson, editor *The Puritan Ethic in United States Foreign Policy,* Van Nostrand, 1967; (with Martin Jeckel) *Laudito zur Verleihung der Wuerde des Ehrendoktors der Rechtswissenschaft an James William Fulbright am 7. Mai 1965* [and] *Education in International Relations* (the former by Heckel, the latter by Fulbright), Mohr (Tuebingen), 1967; *The Pentagon Propaganda Machine,* Liveright, 1970; (author of foreword) John M. Wells and Maria Wilhelm, editors, *The People vs. Presidential War,* Dunellen Co., 1970; (author of introduction) Charles Morrow Wilson, *Black Africa in Microcosm,* Harper, 1971; *The Price of Empire,* Random House, 1972; (with John C. Stennis) *The Role of Congress in Foreign Policy,* American Enterprise Institute for Public Research, 1972.

Anthologized in *Representative American Speeches, 1957-58, 1958-59, 1963-64,* and *1964-65,* and *Challenges to Democracy: The Next Ten Years,* edited by Edward Reed, Praeger, 1963. Contributor to *Christian Century, New York Times Magazine, Saturday Review, Saturday Evening Post,* and other periodicals.

SIDELIGHTS: Recognized as a knowledgable and astute authority on foreign affairs, Fulbright defies easy analysis or classificа.ion. Former senator Paul Douglas describes him as "a child of the eighteenth-century, a throwback to that age of enlightenment, trust in reason, temperate argument, and slightly aristocratic tendencies. That, I think explains why he seems a little aloof, a little different from the rest." Despite his nearly thirty years in politics, Fulbright appears to lack the personal ambition and party regularity which characterize many of his colleagues.

His stands on various political issues present him as something of a paradox. As a freshman representative in 1943, he defied tradition by personally writing and sponsoring a resolution leading to the U.S. commitment to the United Nations. He caused political uproar by suggesting in 1946 that President Truman defer to a strong Republican congress and resign. He opposed Senator Joseph McCarthy almost from the beginning, casting the lone vote against supplying the investigator with funds for his committee; eventually Fulbright led the successful battle to censure McCarthy.

Fulbright can claim practically sole responsibility for the Fulbright-Hays Act of 1946, which has sent more than 12,000 American scholars abroad and brought more than 15,000 foreign students to America. He has supported the southern attitude towards civil rights and was a signer of the Southern Manifesto, a document which attempted to unify the South against Supreme Court decisions on segregation. Though he originally floor-managed the Gulf of Tonkin resolution, which provided funding for the escalation of the Vietnam war, he has since repudiated that stand and is currently one of the outstanding critics of U.S. policy in Southeast Asia.

As an outgrowth of his opposition of Vietnam policy, Fulbright has recently expanded his endeavors to include the effect of that policy on domestic American life. In an article for *New York Times Magazine,* he described what he believes is the damage that the Southeast Asian involvement has wrought upon the U.S. "More and more, we have been treating political philosophy—more exactly, the defense of our own political philosophy and hostility to Communism—as an end in itself, to which, with increasing frequency, it is deemed necessary to subordinate the freedom and the dignity of individual men. More and more, in fear of having an ideology in which power is wielded arbitrarily imposed upon us, we have been imposing a degree of arbitrary power upon ourselves, passively if uneasily accepting half-true explanations of necessity, emergency and defense, while the wielders of power reassure us with a perversion of Lord Acton's maxim, something to the effect of: 'Power, it is true, corrupts, but I am incorruptible and can be trusted to wield power with voluntary benevolence and restraint.' "

Fulbright's words and action have not been allowed to pass without criticism. Edgar Ansel Mowrer believes that Fulbright is "urging his countrymen to take what might be a fatal risk on the basis of a misjudgment of international Communism and of its preponderant role in stimulating and capturing those manifold revolutions which he so welcomes. His is a conspicuous case of the *power of arrogance*, something to which certain U.S. senators seem particularly prone...." "He possesses a generous sympathy for the peoples of the non-Western world," states Wilson Carey McWilliams. "Yet it is the sympathy of the social worker combined with the understanding of an ideologue.... So long as the world conforms to his wish, the liberal ideologue is generous and benign; let it violate his design and he is likely to insist ... that it be 'made to work' according to the plans of his tenderest desiring." His opponents in the political world have attacked Fulbright in less intellectual terms. James D. Johnson, Fulbright's opponent for the Senate in 1968, described him as a "proven socialist," "the most powerful and sinister of our one-worlder senators," and "Ho Chi Minh's pin-up boy...."

Such attacks do not appear unsettling to Fulbright's career or to the man himself. Accused of bring an isolationist, Fulbright meets these charges directly in reasserting his position on foreign affairs, a stand which forms the crux of his philosophy. "It has become almost impossible, therefore, to introduce certain salient points into current discussion, such as that American isolationism was a very wise policy in its time, that it has now become impractical but not necessarily undesirable and, most important of all, that being largely obsolete does not mean that it is entirely obsolete. Indeed, the term 'isolationism,' insofar as it connotes minding one's own business, still makes a good deal of sense in a good many places. Or, to make the point still another way, the fact that we cannot help being involved in some people's affairs does not mean that we ought to be involved in everybody's affairs."

BIOGRAPHICAL/CRITICAL SOURCES: U.S. News and World Report, March 2, 1951, July 23, 1954, March 4, 1955, March 14, 1966, August 1, 1966; *Nation,* February 20, 1954, October 14, 1961; *Harper's,* June, 1956; *Saturday Evening Post,* May 2, 1959; *New York Times Magazine,* May 10, 1959, January 3, 1960, October 1, 1961, April 23, 1967; *Newsweek,* October 16, 1961, August 24, 1964, February 21, 1966, March 25, 1968, August 12, 1968, January 26, 1970, August 17, 1970, August 31, 1970, September 7, 1970; *Time,* November 3, 1961. January 22, 1965, February 10, 1967, July 26, 1968, August 9, 1968; *New Republic,* May 14, 1962, August 22, 1964, October 2, 1965, February 25, 1967, December 12, 1970, January 23, 1971; *Library Journal,* March 1, 1963; *New York Times Book Review,* April 21, 1963, October 20, 1963, August 16, 1964, January 22, 1967, September 22, 1968; *America,* November 23, 1963, August 22, 1964; *Saturday Review,* January 4, 1964, August 15, 1964, February 11, 1967; *Book Week,* January 12, 1964, August 2, 1964, February 19, 1967; *Times Literary Supplement,* January 16, 1964, October 5, 1967; *New Statesman,* April 3, 1964; *Business Week,* April 4, 1964; *Christian Science Monitor,* August 6, 1964, January 26, 1967, August 2, 1969; *Virginia Quarterly Review,* autumn, 1964, autumn, 1967; *Commonweal,* March 17, 1965, March 17, 1967; Tristam Coffin, *Senator Fulbright: Portrait of a Public Philosopher,* Dutton, 1966; *Life,* May 11, 1966; *Village Voice,* February 9, 1967; *Best Sellers,* February 15, 1967; *Atlantic,* March, 1967; *New Yorker,* March 11, 1967; *National Review,* April 4, 1967; *New York Review of Books,* April 6, 1967; *Choice,* September, 1967; Haynes Bonner Johnson and Bernard M. Gwertzman, *Fulbright: The Dissenter,* Doubleday, 1968; *Listener,* January 18, 1968; *Washington Post,* May 19, 1969, February 26, 1971; *Variety,* November 18, 1970; *New York Times,* December 29, 1970; *Observer Review,* June 20, 1971.

FULLER, Blair 1927-

PERSONAL: Born January 18, 1927, in New York, N.Y.; son of Charles F. (an architect) and Jane (White) Canfield; married Diana Burgess; children: Maria, Anthony, Whitney. *Education:* Harvard University, B.A., 1951. *Home:* 844 Bay St., San Francisco, Calif. 94133. *Agent:* Russell & Volkening, Inc., 551 Fifth Ave., New York, N.Y. 10017. *Office:* 111 Kearny St., San Francisco, Calif. 94103.

CAREER: Texaco sales department, New York, N.Y., and West Africa, 1952-55; Barnard College, New York, N.Y., instructor in English, 1956; Stanford University, Stanford, Calif., lecturer in creative writing, 1961-66; California State College, Hayward, professor of English, 1967-69; Universite d'Oran, Algeria, Fulbright professor of American literature, 1969-70; Squaw Valley Community of Writers, Squaw Valley, Calif., director, 1970—. *Military service:* U.S. Navy, 1944-46.

WRITINGS: A Far Place, Harper, 1957; (with Douglas Fairbairn and George Mandel) *Three,* Random House, 1961. Contributor to periodicals. Editor, *Paris Review,* 1955—; book critic, *San Francisco,* 1968-69.

WORK IN PROGRESS: A book.

SIDELIGHTS: His short film, "Dionysus and the Maenads," was presented at the San Francisco Film Festival in 1970.

*   *   *

FULLER, R(ichard) Buckminster 1895-

PERSONAL: Born July 12, 1895, in Milton, Mass.; son of Richard Buckminster and Caroline Wolcott (Andrews) Fuller; married Anne Hewlett, July 12, 1917; children: Alexandra Willets (deceased), Allegra (Mrs. Robert Snyder). *Education:* Attended Milton Academy, 1904-13, Harvard University, 1913-15, and U.S. Naval Academy, 1917. *Home:* 200 Locust, Philadelphia, Pa. 19106. *Office address:* P.O. Box 696, Edwardsville, Ill. 62025.

CAREER: Richards, Atkinson & Kaserick, Boston, Mass., apprentice machine fitter, 1914; Armour & Co., New York, N.Y., apprentice, 1915-17, assistant export manager, 1919-21; Kelly Springfield Truck Co., national account sales manager, 1922; Stockade Building System, president, 1922-27; 4-D Co., Chicago, Ill., founder, 1927, president, 1927-32; Pierce Foundation-American Radiator-Standard Sanitary Manufacturing Co., assistant director of research, 1930; Dymaxion Corp., Bridgeport, Conn., founder, 1932, director and chief engineer, 1932-36, vice-president and chief engineer, 1941-42; Phelps Dodge Corp., assistant to director of research and development, 1936-38; *Fortune Magazine,* technical consultant, 1938-40; Board of Economic Warfare, chief of mechanical engineering section, 1942-44; Foreign Economic Administration, special assistant to director, 1944; Dymaxion Dwelling Machines, chairman of board and administrative engineer, 1944-46; Fuller Research Foundation, Wichita, Kan., chairman of board of trustees, 1946-54; Synergetics, Inc., Raleigh, N.C., president, 1954-59; Southern Illinois University, Carbondale, research professor, 1956—; Plydomes, Inc., Des Moines, Iowa, president, 1957—; Tetrahelix Corp., Hamilton, Ohio, chairman of board, 1959—. Geodesics, Inc., president, 1954-56; Buckminster Fuller Institute, chairman of board, 1959—; Research and Design Institute, trustee, 1966; Temcor Corporation, director, 1967; University of Detroit, Detroit, Mich., R. Buckminster Fuller professor of architecture, 1970—. Trowbridge lecturer, Yale University, 1955; Hill Foundation Lecturer, St. Olaf's College, 1957; Lorado Taft Lecturer, University of Illinois, 1960; Harvard University, Charles Eliot Norton Professor of Poetry, 1961-62; Ullman Lecturer, Brandeis University, 1962; visiting professor of engineering, San Jose State College, 1966; visiting professor, Iowa State University, 1966; visiting professor or lecturer at many universities around the world. U.S. representative to American-Russian Protocol Exchange, U.S.S.R., 1959. Consultant to Time, Inc., 1938-40, Ford Foundation and Calcutta (India) Planning Organization, 1961—, governor of North Carolina, 1962—, Space Science Laboratory of General Electric, 1963, U.S. Steel Space Team, 1964, John Deere and Co., 1964, American Association of University Women, 1965, NASA and ASTRA, 1965—, U.S. Institute of Behavioral Research, 1965—. Director of Oceanographic Study, New York, N.Y.; New York Cancer Research Institute, member of board of trustees, 1964—; International Corporation, member of board of trustees, 1964—; Brandeis University, member of board of trustees of overseers in art, 1965—; architect/trustee for "Denationalized World Man Territory," Cyprus, 1966—; Harmony Hill Music Foundation, president of board of directors, 1966—; Internal Advisory Council of the National Pollution Control Foundation, member of council, 1966. *Military service:* U.S. Navy, 1917-19; became lieutenant.

MEMBER: World Academy of Art and Science (fellow), World Society for Ekistics (vice-president), International Society for Stereology, Royal Society of Arts (Benjamin Franklin life fellow), Society of Venezuelan architects, Mexican College and Institute of Architects, Institute of General Semantics (fellow and honorary trustee), Institute of Human Ecology, American Association for the Advancement of Science (life fellow), American Institute of Architects (honorary life member), National Institute of Arts and Letters (life member), American Society of Professional Geographers, American Association of University Professors, American Society for Metals, Society of Architectural Historians, Harvard Engineering Society, Architectural League of New York, Phi Beta Kappa, Sigma Xi, Alpha Rho Chi, Tau Sigma Delta, Century Club (New York), New York Yacht Club, Northeast Harbor Fleet, Camden Yacht Club.

AWARDS, HONORS: Award of merit from New York chapter of American Institute of Architects, 1952; Award of merit from U.S. Marine Corps, 1954; Gran Premio, Trienniale de Milano, 1954, 1957; Centennial Award, Michigan State University, 1955; gold medal scarab, National Architectural Society, 1958, gold medal, Philadelphia chapter of American Institute of Architects, 1960; Frank P. Brown medal, Franklin Institute, 1960; Allied Professions gold medal, American Institute of Architects, 1963; Plomade de Oro Award, Society of Mexican Architects, 1963; Brandeis University Special Notable Creative Achievement Award of the Year, 1964; Delta Phi Delta Gold Key Laureate, 1964; Industrial Designers Society of America Award of Excellence, 1966; Graham Foundation Fellow, 1966-67; Lincoln Academy of Illinois fellow and Order of Lincoln medal, 1967; gold medal, National Institute of Arts and Letters, 1968. Degrees: Dr. Design, University of North Carolina, 1954; Dr. Arts, University of Michigan, 1955; D.Sc., Washington University, 1957, University of Colorado, 1964; Doctor of Fine Arts, Southern Illinois University, 1959, University of New Mexico, 1964; H.H.D., Rollins College, 1960; Doctor of Letters, Clemson University, 1964; Doctor of Humane Letters, Mommouth College, 1965, Long Island University, 1966; Doctor of Engineering, Clarkson College, 1967.

WRITINGS: 4D Time-Lock, privately printed, 1927; *Nine Chains to the Moon,* Lippincott, 1938; (with others) *New Worlds in Engineering,* Chrysler Co., 1940; *Industrialization of Brazil,* Board of Economic Warfare, 1943; *Survey of the Industrialization of Housing,* U.S. Foreign Economics Administration, 1944; *Geoscope—1960,* edited by James Robert Hillier, Princeton University, 1960; *New Approaches to Structure,* [Washington, D.C.], 1961; *Unti-*tled *Epic Poem of the History of Industrialization,* Jonathon Williams, 1962; *No More Second Hand God, and Other Writings,* Southern Illinois University Press, 1963; *Ideas and Integrities: A Spontaneous Autobiographical Disclosure,* edited by Robert W. Marks, Prentice-Hall 1963; *Education Automation: Freeing the Scholar to Return to His Studies,* Southern Illinois University Press, 1963; *Charles Eliot Norton 1961-62 Lectures at Harvard University,* Harvard University Press, 1963; *Governor's Conference with Buckminster Fuller,* Governor's Office (Raleigh), 1963; (with John McHale) *World Design Science Decade, 1965-1975: Inventory of World Resources, Human Trends and Needs—Phase 1 of 5 Two-year Increments of World Retooling Design Decade Proposed to the International Union of Architects,* Southern Illinois University, 1963; *World Design Science Decade, 1965-1975: The Design Initiative* (includes phase 1, [1964], document 2; also brief outlines of phases 2, 3, 4, and 5), Southern Illinois University, 1964; *What I Am Trying to Do,* Cape Goliard, 1968; (author of foreword) Isamu Noguchi, *A Sculptor's World,* Harper, 1968; (contributor) Richard Kostelanetz, editor, *Beyond Left and Right: Radical Thought for Our Times,* Morrow, 1968; *Operating Manual for Spaceship Earth,* Southern Illinois University Press, 1969; (with others) *The Arts and Man,* Prentice-Hall, 1969; *Utopia or Oblivion: The Prospects for Humanity,* Bantam, 1969; (with others) *Approaching the Benign Environment: The Franklin Lectures in the Sciences and Humanities,* University of Alabama Press, 1970; *I Seem to Be a Verb,* Bantam, 1970; (author of introduction) Samuel Rosenberg, *The Come As You Are Masquerade Party,* Prentice-Hall, 1970; *The Buckminster Fuller Reader,* edited by James Miller, J. Cape, 1970; *Selected Articles,* Bern Porter, 1970; (editor with Henry Dreyfuss) *Symbol Sourcebook: An Authoritative Guide to International Graphic Symbols,* McGraw, 1972; *Intuition,* Doubleday, 1972; *Earth Inc.,* Doubleday-Anchor, 1973. Editor, *Convoy* magazine, 1918-19; publisher, *Shelter* magazine, 1931-32; editor and author, "Notes on the Future" column in *Saturday Review,* 1964—.

WORK IN PROGRESS: Synergetics, a study of the comprehensive mathematical system apparently employed by nature; *Naga to Eden,* a new theoretical maritime reconstruction of prehistory; *Transformation Trends,* a preview of probable world transforming.

SIDELIGHTS: Regarded as eccentric for most of his life, Fuller was largely ignored by industry and government until the early nineteen-fifties. A change in public attitude came in 1952, when the Ford Foundation requested a dome for the exhibition rotunda in Dearborn, Mich. Since that time there has been a growing recognition of Fuller's work. Among his many inventions are the Dymaxion automobile, the Dymaxion World Map, Geodesic Dome, Plydome, Aspension Building, and energetic—synergetic geometry. His numerous structures include the Kaiser aluminum domes, the Golden Dome for the U.S. exhibit in Moscow in 1959, the New York World's Fair of 1964 Pavilion dome, and the United States pavilion at Expo, 1967.

Fuller's inventions and designs are proving to be not only innovative, but extremely useful. His work is so original that he has created the word "dymaxion," a combination of "dynamic" and "maximum efficiency," to describe them. The geodesic dome, his best known creation, combines the sphere, the most efficient container of volume per square foot, and the tetrahedron, the triangle-sided pyramid shape which provides the greatest strength for the least volume of weight. The geodesic dome has been used for factories, restaurants, homes, cotton mills, concert halls, and roundhouses. Its design gives it strength to withstand winds of 210 miles per hour, yet it can be easily moved anywhere in the world.

Despite the recent success of his dome, Fuller's earlier discoveries are still largely ignored. His Dymaxion Car is a three-wheeled vehicle which can obtain speeds of 120 miles per hour and turn full-circle within its own length. The automotive companies avoided the car because of an accident involving Fuller's vehicle and a four-wheeled automobile. Despite the fact that the Dymaxion Car was not at fault, it has been relegated to the status of a museum oddity. The Dymaxion House, an "automated, inexpensive, circular structure," was both prefabricated and collapsible; Fuller offered the patent to the American Institute of Architects and as David Jacobs relates, "not only was the gift rejected, but the entire concept of prefabrication was condemned by the organization in a public position paper."

Despite these and many other setbacks, Fuller has remained firm in his convictions about his work. Foremost in his philosophy is the belief that man must adapt his technology to work with his physical universe. As David Cort states, Fuller "accepts industrialization not only technically, using all its advantages, but also morally and philosophically. In Fuller's opinion it should be written 'universalization.' Modern industry uses some of the techniques of the universe in mass production, but it often resents and perverts them. Fuller preaches an almost religious adherence to the laws of the universe. His domes, for example, are faithful to the true tensions on the surface of a sphere. They do not rest on the ground like a rock; they exist in space in tension like a tree."

Morley Markson directed and produced a film featuring Fuller, along with Allan Gunsberg, Jerry Rubin, Abbie Hoffman, and Fred Hampton. The film, entitled "Breathing Together: Revolution of the Electric Family," premiered at Cannes in May, 1971.

BIOGRAPHICAL/CRITICAL SOURCES: Business Week, May 10, 1958; Time, October 20, 1958, January 10, 1964, March 10, 1967, March 1, 1968, May 11, 1970; David Cort, Social Astonishments, Macmillan, 1959; Newsweek, July 13, 1959, August 5, 1963; New York Times Magazine, August 23, 1959, April 23, 1967; New Yorker, October 10, 1959; Robert W. Marks, The Dymaxion World of Buckminster Fuller, Reinhold, 1960; Nation, January 2, 1960, September 1, 1969, June 15, 1970; John R. McHale, Buckminster Fuller, Braziller, 1962; Vogue, March, 1962; Christian Century, May 8, 1963; Library Journal, June 1, 1963, June 15, 1963, July, 1969; New York Times Book Review, July 28, 1963, May 5, 1968, April 20, 1969; Architectural Forum, October, 1963; Book Week, January 26, 1964; Times Literary Supplement, September 6, 1963, August 6, 1964, September 11, 1969; Science Digest, October, 1964; Books, May, 1967, September, 1967, June, 1968; Horizon, summer, 1968; Sidney Rosen, Wizard of the Dome: R. Buckminster Fuller, Designer for the Future, Little, Brown, 1969; Book World, April 27, 1969; Books and Bookmen, December, 1969; Washington Post, June 10, 1970; Nation, June 15, 1970; Life, February 26, 1971.

*   *   *

GAER, Joseph   1897-
   (Yossef Gaer)

PERSONAL: Original name, Joseph Fishman; born March 16, 1897, in Russia; came to United States in 1917, naturalized in 1926; son of Solomon and Naomi (Shkolnik) Fishman; married Fay Ratner, March 14, 1923; children: Elsa Gay (Mrs. Duncan R. Luce), Paul Joseph. Education: Attended colleges in the United States and Canada. Politics: Democrat. Religion: Jewish. Home: 201 San Vincente Blvd., Santa Monica, Calif. 90402. Agent: Brandt & Brandt, 101 Park Ave., New York, N.Y 10017; and Henry Lewis, 9172 Sunset Blvd.,

Hollywood, Calif. 90028. Office: Jewish Heritage Foundation, 409 North Camden Dr., Beverly Hills, Calif. 90210.

CAREER: University of California, Berkeley, teacher, 1930-35; U.S. Government, Washington, D.C., chief field supervisor and editor-in-chief of Federal Writers Project, 1935-39, consultant to administrator of Farm Security Administration, 1939-41, special assistant to Secretary of Treasury, 1941-43; Congress of Industrial Organizations, publicity director of Political Action Committee, 1943-45; Pamphlet Press (division of Reynal & Hitchcock), founder and director, 1945-46; Boni & Gaer (later Gaer Associates Publishing Co.), New York, N.Y., president, 1946-49; Jewish Heritage Foundation, Beverly Hills, Calif., founder and director, 1958—. Member of American Jewish Committee, Commission of Jewish Affairs. Consultant to film producers. Member: International Institute of Arts and Letters (fellow), Screenwriters Guild, National Jewish Music Council (board member), Foundation for Arts, Religion and Culture. Awards, honors: Distinguished merit citation, National Conference of Christians and Jews, 1964; American Honorarium citation, 1966.

WRITINGS: The Magic Flight: Jewish Tales and Legends, Frank-Maurice, 1926; The Legend Called Meryom (novel), Morrow, 1928; (adapter) The Burning Bush: Adapted Folklore Legends, Sinai Press for Union of American Hebrew Congregations, 1929; How the Great Religions Began (Book Find Club selection), R.M. McBride, 1929, new and revised edition, Dodd, 1935, school edition, Dodd, 1963; (adapter) The Unconquered: Adapted Folklore Legends, Sinai Press for Union of American Hebrew Congregations, 1932; Washington: City and Capital, U.S. Government Printing Office, 1937; Men and Trees: The Problem of Forest Conservation and the Story of the United States Forest Service, Harcourt, 1939; Fair and Warmer: The Problem of Weather Forecasting and the Work of the United States Weather Bureau, Harcourt, 1939; Consumers All: The Problem of Consumer Protection, Harcourt, 1940; Toward Farm Security: The Problem of Rural Poverty and the Work of the Farm Security Administration, U.S. Government Printing Office, 1941; (with J.L. Kaukonen and Elliott H. Moyer) What Uncle Sam Owes You, Funk, 1943; The First Round: The Story of the CIO Political Action Committee, Duell, Sloan & Pearce, 1944; Everybody's Weather (juvenile), Lippincott, 1944, revised edition, 1957; Angels Could Do It Better: The Story of Dunbarton Oaks (pamphlet), American Labor Party, 1945.

Heart Upon the Rock (novel; Jewish Book Guild selection), Dodd, 1950; The Lore of the Old Testament (Book Find Club and Jewish Book Build selection), Little, Brown, 1951; The Lore of the New Testament (Book Find Club and Pulpit Book Club selection), Little, Brown, 1952; Young Heroes of the Living Religions, Little, Brown, 1953; Holidays Around the World, Little, Brown, 1953; The Adventures of Rama: The Story of the Great Hindu Epic Ramayana (youth book), Little, Brown, 1954; The Fables of India, Little, Brown, 1955; The Wisdom of the Living Religions, Dodd, 1956; (with Alfred Wolf) Our Jewish Heritage, Holt, 1957, new edition, Wilshire, 1967; The Legend of the Wandering Jew, New American Library, 1961; What The Great Religions Believe, Dodd, 1963; (with Ben Siegel) The Puritan Heritage: America's Roots in the Bible, New American Library, 1964.

Editor: Our Federal Government and How It Functions, Hastings House, 1939; Our Washington: A Comprehensive Album of the Nation's Capital in Words and Pictures, A.C. McClurg, 1939; Our Lives: American Labor Stories, Boni & Gaer, 1948; (and author of introduction and notes with Chester C. McCown) The Bible for Family Reading, Little, Brown, 1956; (and author of introduction and notes) The Jewish Bible for Family Reading, Yoseloff, 1957; *The Best of Recall,* Yoseloff, 1962; *The Best of Recall #2,* Yoseloff, 1967; *Ambrose Swinett Bierce: Bibliography and Biographical Data* (originally published in mimeographed form, 1935), B. Franklin, 1968; *Bret Harte: Bibliography and Biographical Data* (originally published in mimeographed form, 1935), B. Franklin, 1968; *Frank Norris (Benjamin Franklin Norris): Bibliography and Biographical Data* (originally published in mimeographed form, 1934), Folcroft, 1969; *Bibliography of California Literature: Fiction of the Gold-Rush Period, Drama of the Gold-Rush Period, Poetry of the Gold-Rush Period* (originally published in mimeographed form, 1935), B. Franklin, 1970; *Jack London: Bibliography and Biographical Data* (originally published in mimeographed form, 1934), B. Franklin, 1970; *The Theatre of the Gold Rush Decade in San Francisco* (originally published in mimeographed form, 1935), B. Franklin, 1970; *Bibliography of California Literature: Pre-Gold Rush Period* (originally published in mimeographed form, 1935), B. Franklin, 1970; *Upton Sinclair: Bibliography and Biographical Data* (originally published in mimeographed form, 1935), B. Franklin, 1971; *California in Juvenile Literature* (originally published in mimeographed form, 1935), B. Franklin, 1972.

Editor; all mimeographed pamphlets published under auspices of California Literary Research Project: *Mary Austin: Bibliography and Biographical Data,* 1934; *John M. Letts, An Alphabetical Index to California Illustrated,* 1935; *Index: California and Its Gold Regions by Fayette Robinson,* 1935; *Index: California and Oregon; or, Sights in the Gold Region and Scenes by the Way, by Theodore Taylor Johnson,* 1935; *Index: California Life Illustrated, by William Taylor,* 1935; *Index: Diary of a Physician in California: Being the Result of an Actual Experience, by James L. Tyson,* 1935; *Index: Eldorado; or, Adventures in the Path of Empire: Comprising a Voyage to California, via Panama, by Bayard Taylor,* 1935; *Index: Eldorado; or, California as Seen by a Pioneer, 1850-1900, by D.A. Shaw,* 1935; *Index: Hunting for Gold: Reminiscences of Personal Experience and Research in the Early Days of the Pacific Coast from Alaska to Panama, by William Downie,* 1935; *Index: Life in California During a Residence of Several Years in That Territory: Comprising a Description of the Country and the Missionary Establishments, by Alfred Robinson,* 1935; *Index: Mountains and Molehills; or, Recollections of a Burnt Journal, by Frank Marryat,* 1935; *Index: Personal Adventures in Upper and Lower California in 1848-1849: With the Author's Experience at the Mines, by William Redmond Ryan,* 1935; *Index: Recollections and Opinions of an Old Pioneer, by Peter H. Burnett,* 1935; *Index: Sixteen Months at the Gold Diggings, by Daniel B. Woods,* 1935; *Index: The Annals of San Francisco: Containing a Summary of the History of the First Discovery, Settlement, Progress and Present Condition of California and With a Complete History of All the Important Events Connected with Its Great City, by Frank Soule, John H. Gihon, and James Nisbet,* 1935; *Index: The Gold Regions of California: Being a Succinct Description of the Geography, History, Topography, and General Features of California: Including a Carefully Prepared Account of the Gold Regions of That Fortunate Country, Edited by George G. Foster,* 1935; *Index: The Story of the Mine: As Illustrated by the Great Comstock Lode of Nevada, by Charles Howard Shaw,* 1935; *Index: Three Years in California, by J.D. Borthwick,* 1935; *Index: Three Years in California, by Walter Colton,* 1935; *Index: What I Saw in California: Being the Journal of a Tour by the Emigrant Route and South Pass of the Rocky Mountains, Across the Continent of North America, the Great Desert Basin, and Through California in the Years 1846, 1847, by Edwin Bryant,* 1935.

Contributor to *Universal Jewish Encyclopedia, Encyclopedia of Religion and Ethics, Children's Encyclopedia,* and *Book of Knowledge;* contributor to periodicals, including *Bookman, Dial, Saturday Review,* and *New Republic,* Editor, *Recall* (publication of the Jewish Heritage Foundation).

BIOGRAPHICAL/CRITICAL SOURCES: Muriel Fuller, *More Junior Authors,* H.W. Wilson, 1963.

* * *

GAINES, Ernest J.   1933-

PERSONAL: Born January 15, 1933, in Oscar, La.; son of Manuel (a laborer) and Adrienne J. (Colar) Gaines. *Education:* San Francisco State College, B.A., 1957; Stanford University, graduate study, 1958-59. *Home:* 998 Divisadero St., San Francisco, Calif. 94115. *Agent:* Dorothea Oppenheimer, 866 United Nations Plaza, Room 4029, New York, N.Y. 10017.

CAREER: "Writing, five hours a day, five days a week." *Awards, honors:* Joseph Henry Jackson Award, 1959, for "Comeback" (short story).

WRITINGS: Catherine Carmier (novel), Atheneum, 1964; *Of Love and Dust* (novel), Dial, 1967; *Bloodline* (short stories; includes "A Long Day in November," "The Sky is Gray," "Bloodline," "Three Men," and "Just Like a Tree"), Dial, 1968, *A Long Day in November* published separately by Dial, 1971; *The Autobiography of Miss Jane Pittman* (novel), Dial, 1971.

WORK IN PROGRESS: A novel, *The Last Christian.*

SIDELIGHTS: Gaines told *CA* that his ambition is "to learn as well as I can the art of writing (which I'm sure will take the rest of my life)." In view of the enthusiastic response his books have drawn from critics and fellow writers, he seems to be learning rapidly. Melvin Maddocks recently wrote in a *Time* review that "Ernest J. Gaines has not received anything like the attention he deserves, for he may just be the best black writer in America. He is so good, in fact, that he makes the category seem meaningless, though one of his principal subjects has been slavery—past and present. Born on a Louisiana plantation 38 years ago, Gaines is first and last a country-boy writer. He sets down a story as if he were planting, spreading the roots deep, wide and firm. His stories grow organically, at their own rhythm. When they ripen at last, they do so inevitably, arriving at a climax with the absolute rightness of a folk tale." *A Negro Digest* writer has said that "The Sky is Gray," published in *Bloodline,* "is destined to be one of the most anthologized short stories of the century."

Of Love and Dust, narrative of a young, rebellious Negro serving time on a Louisiana plantation, elicited admiration from a number of reviewers. Joy Melville of *Punch* called it "spellbinding. . . . The atmosphere is timeless; gradually one realises that the date is postwar and a point has been unobtrusively made. . . . Beautifully organised, the novel has the virtues of traditional fiction. Its impact, apart from the skill of the narration, is due to the deadly quietness of tone." Sara Blackburn reviewed the book for *Nation,* calling Gaines "a writer of terrific energy. . . . It takes a lot of nerve to write a novel like this today, and a lot of skill to bring it off. Mr. Gaines has plenty of both." Robert Granat said "Gaines paints some vivid scenes and fine portraits," but that this, his second novel, is "still an 'undergraduate' work, in which the author trusts craft formula too much, himself too little."

When asked by an interviewer if black writers should direct their work toward black audiences, Gaines replied: "No more than French writers should. The artist is the only free man left. He owes nobody nothing—not even himself. He should write what he wants, when he wants, and to whomever he wants. If he is true, he will use that material which is closest to him." Gaines's most recent novel, *The Autobiography of Miss Jane Pittman,* could be called the embodiment of the black experience in America. Jerry Bryant has written a critique of the American Black novel in which he contrasts the form of Gaines's expression with that of Ellison, Baldwin, and John A. Williams, among others. "No American novelist, either white or black," according to Bryant, "has been able to harmonize these discordant notes [of black political and artistic expression]. No novelist, that is, before Gaines. The secret of his success in *The Autobiography of Miss Jane Pittman* is the character of Miss Jane." As Josh Greenfield notes in a *Life* review: "Never mind that Miss Jane Pittman is fictitious, that her 'autobiography,' offered up in the form of taped reminiscences, is artifice. The effect is stunning. I know of no black novel about the South that exudes quite the same refreshing mix of wit and wrath, imagination and indignation, misery and poetry. And I can recall no more memorable female character in Southern fiction since Lena of Faulkner's *Light in August* than Miss Jane Pittman herself."

Of Love and Dust has been optioned by film director Ulu Grosbard, with Gaines to write the screenplay.

BIOGRAPHICAL/CRITICAL SOURCES: Times Literary Supplement, February 10, 1966; *Negro Digest,* November, 1967, January, 1968, January, 1969; *New York Times Book Review,* November 19, 1967; *Nation,* February 5, 1968, April 5, 1971; *Punch,* June 12, 1968; *Best Sellers,* August 15, 1968; *Newsweek,* June 16, 1969; *Life,* April 30, 1971; *Time,* May 10, 1971, December 27, 1971.

* * *

GAITHER, Gant 1917-

PERSONAL: Born August 1, 1917, in Hopkinsville, Ky.; son of Joseph Gant (a surgeon) and Jane Eskridge (Lum) Gaither. *Education:* University of Mexico, student, 1934-35; University of the South, A.B., 1938; Yale University, School of Fine Arts, graduate study, 1938-39. *Religion:* Episcopalian. *Home:* 1527 Sunset Plaza Dr., Los Angeles, Calif. 90069. *Agent:* Ruhl Sampler, Curtis Brown, Inc., 7250 Franklyn Ave., Hollywood, Calif.

CAREER: Broadway writer, producer, and director, 1947-56; executive producer for Paramount Pictures, 1960-63; currently under contract to Qualis Productions, Burbank, Calif. *Military service:* U.S. Air Force, Special Services, World War II; awarded Bronze Star.

WRITINGS: (With Gordon Gaines) *Princess of Monaco: The Story of Grace Kelly,* Holt, 1957; *Sally Seal: The Unexpurgated Love Life of Her Imperial Highness the Grand Duchess of Cod-Sardinska,* Astor-Honor, 1964; *The Sleep-Ins and Outs,* Obolensky, 1964. Author of play, "The Long Street," and "Mother, May I Go Out to Swim?," and a television series for Qualis Productions, "Simon Says."

WORK IN PROGRESS: A Broadway musical, "Vicki."

SIDELIGHTS: Gaither has exhibited his art work at galleries in New York, Palm Beach, Mexico City, and Paris.

* * *

GALE, Robert L(ee) 1919-

PERSONAL: Born December 27, 1919, in Des Moines, Iowa; son of Erie Lee (a sales manager) and Miriam (Fisher) Gale; married Maureen Dowd, November 18, 1944; children: John, James, Christine. *Education:* Dartmouth College, B.A., 1942; Columbia University, M.A., 1947, Ph.D., 1952. *Home:* 131 Techview Ter., Pittsburgh,

Pa. 15213. *Office:* University of Pittsburgh, Pittsburgh, Pa. 15213.

CAREER: University of Delaware, Newark, instructor, 1949-52; University of Mississippi, University, assistant professor, 1952-56, associate professor, 1956-59; University of Pittsburgh, Pittsburgh, Pa., assistant professor of English, 1959-60, associate professor, 1960-65, professor of American literature, 1965—. Fulbright professor at Oriental Institute, Naples, Italy, 1956-58. *Military service:* U.S. Army, Counter Intelligence Corps, 1942-45; became second lieutenant. *Member:* Modern Language Association of America, Phi Beta Kappa.

WRITINGS: The Caught Image: Figurative Language in the Fiction of Henry James, University of North Carolina Press, 1964; *Thomas Crawford, American Sculptor,* University of Pittsburgh Press, 1964; *Barron's Simplified Approach to Thoreau's Walden,* Barron's, 1965; *Plots and Characters in the Fiction of Henry James,* Archon, 1965; *Barron's Simplified Approach to Ralph Waldo Emerson and Transcendentalism,* Barron's, 1966; *Barron's Simplified Approach to Crane's The Red Badge of Courage,* Barron's, 1966; *Barron's Simplified Approach to The Grapes of Wrath by John Steinbeck,* Barron's, 1966; *A Critical Study Guide to James' The American,* Littlefield, 1966; *A Critical Study Guide to James' The Ambassadors,* Littlefield, 1967, also published as *Pennant Key-Indexed Study Guide to Henry James' The Ambassadors,* Educational Research Associates and Bantam, 1967; *A Critical Study Guide to James' The Turn of the Screw,* Littlefield, 1968; *A Critical Study Guide to Dreiser's Sister Carrie,* Littlefield, 1968; *Plots and Characters in the Fiction and Sketches of Nathaniel Hawthorne,* Archon, 1968; *Barron's Simplified Approach to Edgar Allen Poe,* Barron's, 1969; *Plots and Characters in the Fiction and Narrative Poetry of Herman Melville,* Archon, 1969; *Richard Henry Dana, Jr.,* Twayne, 1969; *A Critical Study Guide to Twain's Tom Sawyer,* Littlefield, 1969; *Barron's Simplified Approach to Edith Wharton's Ethan Frome,* Barron's, 1969; *Plots and Characters in the Writings of Edgar Allen Poe,* Archon, 1970; (contributor) Floyd Stovall, editor, *Eight American Authors,* Norton, 1971.

WORK IN PROGRESS: Francis Parkman, for Twayne; *Guide to Salinger's Catcher in the Rye; Plots and Characters in Mark Twain;* "Henry James," for *American Literary Scholarship: An Annual/1970,* to be published by Duke University Press; and *William Bartram.*

* * *

GALOUYE, Daniel Francis 1920-

PERSONAL: Born February 11, 1920, in New Orleans, La.; son of John Baptiste (a businessman) and Hilda (Mouney) Galouye; married Carmel Barbara Jordan, December 26, 1945; children: Denise Marie, Jeanne Arlene Galouye Ingraham. *Education:* Louisiana State University, B.A. in Journalism, 1941. *Politics:* Democrat. *Religion:* Catholic. *Home:* 5669 Catina St., New Orleans, La. 70124. *Agent:* Lurton Blassingame, 60 East 42nd St., New York, N.Y. 10017.

CAREER: New Orleans *States-Item,* New Orleans, La., reporter, later assistant news editor, 1946-55, chief editorial writer, 1955-62, associate editor, 1962-66; retired, 1966. *Military service:* U.S. Navy, Naval Aviation, 1941-46; served as pilot in Pacific theater; became lieutenant, U.S. Naval Reserve, executive officer of public relations company, 8th Naval District.

WRITINGS: Dark Universe, Gollancz, 1962; *Lords of the Psychon,* Bantam, 1963; *Counterfeit World,* Gollancz, 1964; *The Last Leap, and Other Stories of the Super Mind,* Transworld, 1964; *Simulacron-3,* Bantam, 1964; *The Lost Perception,* Gollancz, 1966; *Project Barrier* (collection of five novelettes), Gollancz, 1968; *A Scourge of Screamers,* Bantam, 1968; *The Infinite Man,* Bantam, 1971. Contributor of numerous short stories and novelettes to periodicals.

WORK IN PROGRESS: A novel examining the psycho-sociological foundations of religious expression, for Bantam.

* * *

GANNON, Robert Haines 1931-

PERSONAL: Born March 5, 1931, in White Plains, N.Y.; son of John A. (a business executive) and Dorothy B. Gannon; married June Ormay, June 20, 1963. *Education:* Miami University, Oxford, Ohio, student, 1949-53. *Politics:* Liberal. *Religion:* Non-denominational. *Home:* 5C Tillson Rd., Tillson, N.Y. 12486. *Agent:* Theron Raines, 244 Madison Ave., New York, N.Y. 10016. *Office:* 647 Hudson St., New York, N.Y. 10014.

CAREER: Leo Burnett Co., Inc., New York, N.Y., publicist, 1955-57; WQXR, New York, N.Y., continuity writer, 1955; Daniel J. Edelman & Assoc., New York, N.Y., public relations account executive, 1957-59; freelance writer, 1959—. President, High Falls Civic Association, High Falls, N.Y.; trustee, D & H Canal Historical Society, High Falls, N.Y. *Military service:* U.S. Army, 1953-55; became corporal. *Member:* Society of Magazine Writers, National Association of Science Writers, American Association for the Advancement of Science.

WRITINGS: How to Raise and Train a Scottish Terrier, T.F.H. Publications, 1960; *How to Raise and Train an English Springer Spaniel,* T.F.H. Publications, 1961; *How to Raise and Train an Irish Setter,* T.F.H. Publications, 1961; *How to Raise and Train an English Cocker Spaniel,* T.F.H. Publications, 1962; *Starting Right with Goldfish,* T.F.H. Publications, 1964; *Starting Right with Tropical Fish,* T.F.H. Publications, 1964; *The Complete Book of Archery,* Coward, 1964; (with John Walsh) *Time is Short and the Water Rises: Operation Gwamba—The Story of the Rescue of 10,000 Animals from Certain Death in a South American Rain Forest,* Dutton, 1967; *What's Under a Rock?,* Dutton, 1971.

* * *

GANTT, Fred, Jr. 1922-

PERSONAL: Born November 12, 1922, in Foreman, Ark.; son of Fred (a banker-accountant) and Margaret Elizabeth (Taaffe) Gantt. *Education:* Southern Methodist University, B.A. 1943, M.A., 1948; University of Texas, Ph.D., 1962. *Politics:* Democrat. *Religion:* Methodist. *Office:* Department of Political Science, North Texas State University, Denton, Tex. 76203.

CAREER: Southern Methodist University, Dallas, Tex., instructor in government, 1947-52; Lone Star Ordnance Plant, Texarkana, Tex., assistant to personnel director, 1952-55; Texarkana College, Texarkana, Tex., instructor in social science and dean of adult education, 1955-58; University of Texas, Austin, research associate of Institute of Public Affairs, 1960; Texas Agricultural and Mechanical University, College Station, instructor in government, 1961-62; North Texas State University, Denton, assistant professor, 1962-64, associate professor, 1964-66, professor of government, 1966-69, chairman of department of political science, 1969—. Consultant, Texas Constitutional Revision Commission, 1968, National Governors' Conference Study Committee on Constitutional Revision and General Government Organization, 1968. *Military service:* U.S. Army, 1944-46; became sergeant. *Member:* American Political Science Association, American Association of University Professors, Southern Political Science Association, Southwestern Social Science Association, Southwestern Political Science Association (president, 1970—), Texas Association of College Teachers,

Academy of Political Science of Columbia University, Pi Sigma Alpha, Psi Chi, Phi Theta Kappa.

WRITINGS: The Texas Constitutional Amendments of 1960, Institute of Public Affairs, University of Texas, 1960; *The Chief Executive in Texas: A Study in Gubernatorial Leadership,* University of Texas Press, 1964; (editor with others) *Governing Texas: Documents and Readings,* Crowell, 1966, 2nd edition, 1970; *The Governor's Veto in Texas: An Absolute Negative?,* Institute of Public Affairs, University of Texas, 1969; *Special Legislative Sessions in Texas: The Governor's Bane or Blessing,* Institute of Public Affairs, University of Texas, 1970.

WORK IN PROGRESS: A monograph, *Legislative Perceptions of the Executive's Role in Lawmaking Process,* for Institute of Public Affairs, University of Texas.

* * *

GARDNER, Lloyd C(alvin) 1934-

PERSONAL: Born November 9, 1934, in Delaware, Ohio; son of Lloyd Calvin (a government employee) and Hazel (Grove) Gardner; married Nancy Wintermute, June 3, 1956; children: Rebecca, Julia. *Education:* Ohio Wesleyan University, A.B., 1956; University of Wisconsin, M.S., 1957, Ph.D., 1960. *Home:* 15 Redcoat Dr., East Brunswick, N.J. 08816. *Office:* Rutgers University, New Brunswick, N.J. 08903.

CAREER: Lake Forest College, Lake Forest, Ill., instructor in history, 1959-60; Rutgers University, New Brunswick, N.J., assistant professor, 1963-64, associate professor, 1964-67, professor of history, 1967—, chairman of history department, 1970—. *Military service:* U.S. Air Force, 1960-63; now captain, U.S. Air Force Reserve.

WRITINGS: Economic Aspects of New Deal Diplomacy, University of Wisconsin Press, 1964; (editor and author of introduction) *A Different Frontier: Selected Readings in the Foundations of American Economic Expansion,* Quadrangle, 1966; *Architects of Illusion: Men and Ideas in American Foreign Policy, 1941-1949,* Quadrangle, 1970; (with others) *Origins of the Cold War,* Blaisdell, 1970; (editor and author of introduction) *The Korean War,* Quadrangle, 1972.

WORK IN PROGRESS: Economic Aspects of Progressive Diplomacy; A Diplomatic History of the U.S.; and *American Crisis Diplomacy, 1950-1970.*

BIOGRAPHICAL/CRITICAL SOURCES: Library Journal, March 1, 1970; *Virginia Quarterly Review,* summer, 1970.

* * *

GARFORTH, Francis William 1917-

PERSONAL: Born July 3, 1917, in Jaffna, Ceylon; son of James Wales (a Methodist minister) and Elizabeth Amy (Corby) Garforth; married Francesca Mary Leeke (a teacher), July 1, 1946; children: Anne Margaret, Christopher James, Michael Francis, Bernard Mark. *Education:* Attended Kingswood School, Bath, England; Queens' College, Cambridge, B.A., M.A., *Politics:* "Uncommitted." *Religion:* Methodist. *Home:* 151 Newland Park, Hull, Yorkshire, England. *Office:* Department of Education, University of Hull, Hull, Yorkshire, England.

CAREER: Teacher at St. George's School, Harpenden, Hertfordshire, England, 1939-45; Bristol Grammar School, Bristol, England, 1945-49; University of Hull, Hull, England, teacher of classics, religious education, and philosophy in department of education, 1949—. Methodist lay preacher. *Member:* Association of University Teachers.

WRITINGS: Education and Social Purpose, Oldbourne, 1962; (editor and author of introduction and commentary) *John Locke: Some Thoughts Concerning Education* abridged edition, Barron's, 1964, revised edition, Heinemann, 1969; (editor) John Dewey, *Selected Educational Writings,* Heinemann, 1966; (editor) John Locke, *Of the Conduct of the Understanding,* Teachers College Press, 1966; (editor) *Bede's Historia Ecclesiastica: A Selection,* Bell, 1967; (editor) *Aspects of Education: Education for the Seventies,* Institute of Education, University of Hull, 1969; *The Scope of Philosophy: An Introductory Study-Book,* Humanities, 1971; (editor) *John Stuart Mill on Education,* Teachers College Press, 1971. Contributor of articles to professional journals.

AVOCATIONAL INTERESTS: Gardening and mountain walking.

BIOGRAPHICAL/CRITICAL SOURCES: Times Literary Supplement, February 16, 1967.

* * *

GARLINGTON, Warren K(ing)   1923-

PERSONAL: Born September 9, 1923, in Missoula, Mont.; son of King and Alice (Shephard) Garlington; married June Edna Warren, December 28, 1946; children: Janet Marie, Patricia Ann. *Education:* Montana State University, B.A., 1948; Indiana University, Ph.D., 1953. *Politics:* Democrat. *Home:* 108 City View, Pullman, Wash. 99163.

CAREER: U.S. Veterans Administration Hospital, Sheridan, Wyo., staff psychologist, 1952-54; Montana State University, Missoula, assistant professor, 1954-55; U.S. Veterans Administration Hospital, American Lake, Tacoma, Wash., staff psychologist, 1955-60; Mental Health Research Institute, Fort Steilacoom, Wash., chief psychologist, 1961-63; Long Beach State College, Long Beach, Calif., associate professor of psychology, 1963-64; Washington State University, Pullman, associate professor, 1964-68, professor of psychology, 1968—. *Military service:* U.S. Marine Corps, 1942-45. *Member:* American Psychological Association, Association for Advancement of Behavior Therapy, Western Psychological Association, Washington State Psychological Association (president, 1962-63).

WRITINGS: (With Helen E. Shimota) *Statistically Speaking* (revised version of series originally published in *Northwest Medicine,* 1962), C.C Thomas, 1964. Contributor of papers to medical and psychology journals.

WORK IN PROGRESS: Research on behavior modification in schools and hospitals, and on the treatment of alcoholism.

* * *

GARNER, Claud Wilton   1891-

PERSONAL: Born August 29, 1891, in Hope, Ark.; son of Thomas Jefferson (a physician) and Ida Hope (Hayner) Garner; married Ruth Stewart, April 10, 1935. *Education:* Attended Ouachita Baptist University. *Politics:* Independent. *Religion:* Episcopalian. *Home and office address:* P.O. Box 440, Weatherford, Tex. 76086. *Agent:* Maurice Crain, Inc., 18 East 41st St., New York, N.Y. 10017.

CAREER: Commercial producer of fruits and vegetables all of adult life prior to 1945, also produce distributor for some years; sold business in 1945 and started writing as a hobby. *Member:* Texas Institute of Letters, Sons of the American Revolution, Shrine, Masons, Rotary International. *Awards, honors:* Texas Institute of Letters annual award for book honoring Texas, 1947, for *Wetback.*

WRITINGS: Wetback, Coward, 1947; *Cornbread Aristocrat,* Farrar, Straus, 1950; *The Young Texans,* New American Library, 1960; (with Ruth Admas McKnight)

Word of Honor: A Story about Thoroughbreds, Farrar, Straus, 1964; *Sam Houston: Texas Giant,* Naylor, 1969. Contributor to Texas and Arkansas newspapers.

WORK IN PROGRESS: Yardstick for Living, a story of life in the Deep South from 1900 to 1950.

* * *

GARRETT, Wendell D(ouglas)   1929-

PERSONAL: Born October 9, 1929, in Los Angeles, Calif.; son of Windell Ennis and Lucille (Walker) Garrett; married Martha Jane Nuckols (a librarian and book review editor), June 22, 1957. *Education:* University of California, Los Angeles, B.A., 1954; University of Delaware, M.A., 1957; Harvard University, M.A., 1960. *Politics:* Democrat. *Religion:* Presbyterian. *Home:* 21 Linnaean St., Cambridge, Mass. 02138. *Office:* 1154 Boylston St., Boston, Mass. 02115.

CAREER: Massachusetts Historical Society, Boston, associate editor of Adams Papers, 1959—; Cambridge Historical Society, Cambridge, Mass., editor, 1963—; Society for the Preservation of New England Antiquities, Boston, Mass., librarian, 1964—. Owner and operator of private press, Gallows Hill Press, 1962—. Co-chairman of advisory committee on history and historical sources, Cambridge Historical Commission. *Member:* American Historical Association, Mississippi Valley Historical Association, Massachusetts Historical Society, Colonial Society of Massachusetts (member of council, 1964), Club of Odd Volumes.

WRITINGS: Apthorp House, 1760-1960, Adams House, Harvard University, 1960; (author of bibliography with wife, Jane N. Garrett) Walter Muir Whitehill, *American History: Needs and Opportunities for Study,* University of North Carolina Press, 1965; (editor) Elias Brewster Hillard, *The Last Men of the Revolution,* Barre, 1968; (with Paul F. Norton, Alan Gowans, and Joseph T. Butler) *The Arts in America: The Nineteenth Century,* Scribner, 1969; (author of text) *Thomas Jefferson Redivivus,* photographs by Joseph C. Farber, Barre, 1971. Assistant editor, *Diary and Autobiography of John Adams,* edited by L.H. Butterfield, four volumes, Harvard University Press, 1961; associate editor, Volumes I and II, *Adams Family Correspondence,* edited by Butterfield, Harvard University Press, 1963. Editor, *Cambridge Historical Proceedings,* 1961-63.

WORK IN PROGRESS: Compiling catalogue of early American furniture collection in Rhode Island Historical Society.

* * *

GARTENBERG, Leo   1906-

PERSONAL: Born December 13, 1906, in Hungary; son of Morris (a merchant) and Mali (Lebowitz) Gartenberg; married Gertie Ringler; children: Jacob, Eva Gartenberg Heftler. *Education:* Educated in Jewish and public schools in Europe; also attended night school (high school) in United States. *Religion:* Jewish. *Home:* Pioneer Country Club, Greenfield Park, N.Y. 12435.

CAREER: Operator of resort hotels in New York, New Jersey, and Florida, 1936—, now a partner in Pioneer Country Club, Greenfield Park, N.Y. General insurance broker, 1930—. Children's Salvation, vice-president; Ohel Children's Home, vice-president; Pioneer Milk Fund, Inc., organizer and secretary. *Member:* Agudath Israel of America, Mizrachi Organization of America (life member).

WRITINGS: (With S.Z. Kahana) *Legends of Israel,* Volume 1, 1964; (compiler) *Torah Thoughts,* Jonathan David, Volume 1, 1964, Volume 2, 1965, Volume 3, 1966, Volume 4, 1967, Volume 5, 1969, Volume 6, 1972; *Israel*

Through Eight Eyes, Jonathan David, 1968; *Israel: The Story of a Miracle,* Jonathan David, 1969; (with Morris Mandel) *Sidra by Sidra,* Jonathan David, 1970. Contributor to religious periodicals.

WORK IN PROGRESS: Volume 7 of *Torah Thoughts;* Volume 2 of *Legends of Israel.*

*   *   *

GATELL, Frank Otto   1931-

PERSONAL: Born July 28, 1931, in New York, N.Y.; son of Frank M. and Anna (Gutierrez) Gatell; married Kay Tapper, February 10, 1956; children: Susan Valerie. *Education:* College of City of New York (now City College of City University of New York), B.A., 1956; Harvard University, A.M., 1958, Ph.D., 1960. *Office:* Department of History, University of California, Los Angeles, Calif. 90024.

CAREER: University of Maryland, College Park, assistant professor of history; University of California, Los Angeles, member of history faculty. Visiting lecturer, University of Puerto Rico, 1959; visiting assistant professor of history, Stanford University, 1964-65. *Military service:* U.S. Army, 1952-53. *Member:* American Historical Association, Mississippi Valley Historical Association, Southern Historical Association.

WRITINGS: John Gorham Palfrey and the New England Conscience, Harvard University Press, 1963; (with Paul Goodman) *The American Colonial Experience: An Essay in National Origins,* Holt, 1970; (with Goodman) *Democracy and Union: The United States, 1815-1877,* Holt, 1972; (with Goodman) *America in the Twenties: The Beginnings of Contemporary America,* Holt, 1972; (with Goodman) *USA: An American Record,* Holt, 1972.

Editor: *The Jacksonians and the Money Power, 1829-1840,* Rand McNally, 1967; (with Allen Weinstein) *American Themes: Essays in Historiography,* Oxford University Press, 1968; (with Weinstein) *American Negro Slavery: A Modern Reader,* Oxford University Press, 1968; (and contributor) *Essays in Jacksonian America,* Holt, 1970; (with John M. McFaul) *Jacksonian America, 1815-1840: New Society, Changing Politics,* Prentice-Hall, 1970; (with Weinstein) *The Segregation Era, 1863-1954: A Modern Reader,* Oxford University Press, 1970; (with Weinstein and Goodman) *Readings in American Political History: A Modern Reader,* Oxford University Press, 1972; (with Goodman and Weinstein) *The Growth of American Politics: A Modern Reader,* two volumes, Oxford University Press, 1972. Contributor of articles on United States and Latin American history to historical journals.

*   *   *

GATNER, Elliott S(herman) M(ozian)   1914-

PERSONAL: Born October 24, 1914, in New York, N.Y.; son of Abraham Elliott (a newspaper reporter) and Tillie (Sherman) Gatner; married Shirley V. Golden (a schoolteacher), July 13, 1941; children: Alice Roberta, Deborah Ann. *Education:* Long Island University, B.A., 1936; College of City of New York (now City College of the City University of New York), M.S., 1939; Columbia University, B.S. in L.S., 1947. *Home:* 81-07 248th St., Bellerose, N.Y. 10026.

CAREER: Long Island University, Brooklyn, N.Y., instructor in English, 1938-47, instructor in history, 1948-52, assistant professor, 1953-56, associate professor, 1956-63, professor of history and government, 1963—, assistant director of libraries, 1961—. Library consultant; research consultant to industry; lecturer. *Military service:* U.S. Army, 1941-46, 1950-52; became major (U.S. Army

Reserve); received Bronze Star, Combat Infantryman Badge. *Member:* College English Association, National Council of Teachers of English, American Historical Association, American Association of University Professors, American Library Association, Modern Language Association of America.

WRITINGS: Analytical Survey of Cooperative Agreements Among Institutions of Higher Education in the Metropolitan Area of New York City, Long Island University Alumni Association, 1940; (with Francesco Cordasco and N. Resnick) *Study Guide to English Literature,* two volumes, Lamb, 1947-48; *University Handbook for Research and Report Writing,* Lamb's Book Exchange, 1946, 3rd edition published as *Handbook for Research and Report Writing,* Barnes & Noble, 1948, 4th edition published as *Research and Report Writing,* 1955, 9th edition, 1969. Editor of Long Island University official publications and for Long Island University Press; book reviewer for *Brooklyn Daily Eagle.*

WORK IN PROGRESS: A history of Long Island University, for Long Island University Press; a census of eighteenth-century American libraries; literary antecedents of the American constitution.

AVOCATIONAL INTERESTS: Mass communications, philately, photography, and painting.

*   *   *

GAUNT, William   1900-

PERSONAL: Born July 5, 1900, in Hull, Yorkshire, England; son of William (a designer and lithographer) and Harriet (Spence) Gaunt; married Mary Catherine Connolly, 1935. *Education:* Worcester College, Oxford, B.A. (honors), 1922, M.A., 1926. *Home:* 35B Lansdowne Rd., London W. 11, England. *Agent:* A.P. Watt & Son, 26-28 Bedford Row, London WCIR 4HL, England.

CAREER: Art historian and painter. Studio Publications, London, England, editorial director, 1926-39; Odhams Press Ltd., London, editor of documentary war-time publications, 1939-45; *Evening Standard,* London, art critic, 1945-47; museums correspondent for *Times,* London, 1963-71. *Military service:* British Army, Durham Light Infantry, 1918. *Member:* International Association of Art Critics.

WRITINGS: English Rural Life in the Eighteenth Century, Connoisseur, 1925; (editor) *The Etchings of Frank Brangwyn* (catalog), Studio, 1926; *Rome, Past and Present,* edited by C. Geoffrey Holme, Studio, 1926; (author of introduction) *Etchings of Today,* edited by C. Geoffrey Holme, Studio, 1929; (self-illustrated) *London Promenade,* Harcourt, 1930; *Touring the Ancient World with a Camera,* photographs by C. Geoffrey Holme, W.E. Rudge, 1932; *Bandits in a Landscape: A Study of Romantic Painting from Caravaggio to Delacroix,* Studio Publications, 1937; (editor with Frank A. Mercer) *Poster Progress,* Studio Publications, 1939.

The Pre-Raphaelite Tragedy, Harcourt, 1942, reissued as *The Pre-Raphaelite Dream,* Schocken, 1966; (with Frederic Gordon Roe) *Etty and the Nude: The Art and Life of William Etty,* F. Lewis, 1943; *The Aesthetic Adventure,* Harcourt, 1945; *British Painting from Hogarth's Day to Ours,* Avalon and Central Institute of Art and Design, 1945, revised edition, 1946; (author of introduction and notes) *Hogarth, 1697-1764,* Faber, 1947; (editor and author of introduction) *Selected Writings of William Morris,* Falcon Press, 1948; *The March of the Moderns,* J. Cape, 1949; *Victorian Olympus* (a study of the works of Lord Leighton and other artists of late Victorian times), Oxford University Press, 1952; (author of introduction) *Renoir,* Phaidon, 1952, 2nd edition, Praeger, 1971; *Chelsea,* Batsford, 1954; (editor) Henri Schmidt-

Degener, *The Teach Yourself History of Painting*, English Universities Press, 1954; (author of introduction and notes on illustrations) *London in Colour: A Collection of Colour Photographs by James Riddell*, Batsford, 1955, Studio Publications, 1956; *Arrows of Desire: A Study of William Blake and His Romantic World*, Fernhill, 1956; (editor) *Henri Schmidt-Degener, The Dutch School*, Roy, 1956; (editor) *Henri Schmidt-Degener, The Flemish School*, Roy, 1956; *The Lady in the Castle*, W.H. Allen, 1956; *Teach Yourself to Study Sculpture*, English Universities Press, 1957; (contributor) *Eugene Boudin, 1824-1898* (catalog of exhibition held in London, November-December, 1958), Marlborough Fine Art Ltd., 1958; *Kensington*, Batsford, 1958; *The Observer's Book of Painting and Graphic Art*, Warne, 1958; (author of introduction and notes on illustrations) *Old Inns of England in Colour: A Collection of Colour Photographs*, Batsford, 1958.

(Author of introduction) Benvenuto Cellini, *The Life of Benvenuto Cellini*, translated by Anne Macdonell, Dent, 1960; *London*, Viking, 1961; (compiler) *Everyman's Dictionary of Pictorial Art*, two volumes, Dutton, 1962; (editor and author of introduction) Giorgio Vasari, *The Lives of the Painters, Sculptors and Architects* (revision of translation by A.B. Hinds), four volumes, Dutton, 1963; *A Concise History of English Painting*, Praeger, 1964; *The Observer's Book of Modern Art, from Impressionism to the Present Day*, Warne, 1964; Oxford, Batsford, 1965, Hastings House, 1966; *The Observer's Book of Sculpture*, Warne, 1966; *A Companion to Painting*, Thames & Hudson, 1967; *Dante Gabriel Rossetti*, Purnell, 1967; *A Guide to the Understanding of Painting*, Abrams, 1968; *Flemish Cities—Bruges, Ghent, Antwerp, Brussels: Their History and Art*, Putnam, 1969; *Impressionism: A Visual History*, Praeger, 1970; *The Impressionists*, Thames & Hudson, 1970; *Great Century of British Painting: From Hogarth to Turner*, Praeger, 1971; *Turner*, Praeger, 1971; *William De Morgan*, New York Graphic Society, 1971; *The Restless Century: Painting in Britain, 1800-1900*, Phaidon, 1972; *The Surrealists*, Putnam, 1972. Contributor to *Times Literary Supplement* and to art magazines.

SIDELIGHTS: Gaunt told *CA* that he "has a general appetite for books in English and French. My writing about art is more concerned with making its history intelligible to the wider public than with specialization." His travels include countries of Europe and the Mediterranean, and longer journeys ranging from Lapland to Yucatan. He has always been an "assiduous explorer of the vast chaos of London, especially along the river."

BIOGRAPHICAL/CRITICAL SOURCES: *Times Literary Supplement*, April 23, 1970; *Best Sellers*, November 1, 1970; *Time*, December 14, 1970.

*   *   *

GEDULD, Harry M(aurice) 1931-

PERSONAL: Surname is accented on first syllable; born March 3, 1931, in London, England; son of Sol E. and Anne (Berliner) Geduld; married Carolyn Taft, December 24, 1963. Education: University of Sheffield, B.A. (honors), 1953, M.A., 1954; University of London, Ph.D., 1961. Office: Screen Arts Department, University of Maryland, Baltimore County, 5401 Wilkens Ave., Baltimore, Md. 21228.

CAREER: High school teacher in London, England, 1955-62; Indiana University, Boomington, instructor, 1962-64, assistant professor, 1964-66, associate professor of English, 1966-70, professor of English and comparative literature, 1970-72; University of Maryland, Baltimore, professor of screen arts and English, 1972—. Member: Modern Language Association of America, National Council of Teachers of English, Society for Cinema Studies, Shaw Society of England (general secretary, 1959-61). Awards, honors: Fulbright scholar, 1959-60; Indiana University faculty fellowship, 1963.

WRITINGS: (Editor and author of introduction and notes) George Bernard Shaw, *The Rationalization of Russia*, Indiana University Press, 1964; (compiler and author of introduction) *Film Makers on Film Making: Statements on Their Art by Thirty Directors*, Indiana University Press, 1967; *Prince of Publishers: A Study of the Life and Work of Jacob Tonson*, Indiana University Press, 1969; (editor and contributor with Ronald Gottesman) *Sergei Eisenstein and Upton Sinclair: The Making and Unmaking of 'Que Viva Mexico!'*, Indiana University Press, 1970 (published in England as *The Making and Unmaking of 'Que Viva Mexico!' by Sergei Eisenstein and Upton Sinclair*, Thames & Hudson, 1970; *Sir James Barrie: A Study*, Twayne, 1971; (editor) *Focus on D.W. Griffith*, Prentice-Hall, 1971; (editor with Gottesman) *A Guide Book to Film: An Eleven-in-One Reference*, Holt, 1972; (editor) *Authors on Film*, Indiana University Press, 1972. Contributor of reviews to *Louisville Courier-Journal*, *A-V Communication Review*, *Quarterly Journal of Speech*, *Victorian Studies*, and *Humanist*, of articles to *California Shavian*, *Modern Drama*, *Radio Times*, *Jewish Chronicle*, *Shavian* (London), *Shaw Review*. Contributing editor, *Film Journal*, 1971—.

WORK IN PROGRESS: *The Coming of Sound;* a film guide to Olivier's *Henry V*; with Ronald Gottesman, *Illustrated Glossary of Film Terms*; *The King Kong Book;* *The Busby Berkeley Book;* with wife, Carolyn Geduld, *301 Films*.

BIOGRAPHICAL/CRITICAL SOURCES: *New York Times Book Review*, December 17, 1967; *Hudson Review*, summer, 1968; *Newsweek*, August 10, 1970.

*   *   *

GEE, H(erbert) L(eslie) 1901-

PERSONAL: Born June 16, 1901, in Bridlington, Yorkshire, England; son of Percy and Ellen (Gray) Gee; married Mary Peel, September 23, 1939; children: David Howard, Judith Pamela, Jonathan Peter. Education: Attended City of Leeds Training College. Religion: Methodist. Home: 5 The Courtyard, Bishopthorpe, York, England.

CAREER: Teacher in Bridlington, Yorkshire, England, 1923-31; free-lance journalist, 1920—, and author. Special newspaper correspondent, World War II.

WRITINGS: *Stories of Ahbou, the Owl* (juvenile), Edward Arnold, 1925; *The Romance of the Yorkshire Coast*, Methuen, 1928.

Cheerful Day (apologues and reflections for every day in the year), Methuen, 1934; *The Shining Highway: An Account of a Plain Man's Pilgrimage*, Epworth, 1935; *Another Cheerful Day*, Methuen, 1936; *Caravan Joe: The Story of a Conjuror Who Became Prime Minister* (juvenile), Epworth, 1937; (editor) *Three Hundred Thrilling Tales*, Methuen, 1937; *Winter Journey: Some Account of a Friendly Man's Adventures*, Epworth, 1938; *The Wonders of Your House*, Methuen, 1938; *Every Boy's Book: An Epitome of Information Covering All the Interests and Activities of the Modern Boy* (juvenile), University of London Press, 1938; *The Friendly House, and the Thrilling Adventures of the Little Man Who Built It* (juvenile), University of London Press, 1939, 3rd edition, Epworth, 1954; *Pilgrim Books*, Epworth, 1939—; *Pleasant People*, Epworth, 1939.

Don't Lose Heart: A Book of Comfort and Good Cheer, Methuen, 1940; *Nodding Wold: A Friendly Man's Account of What He Found There and the People He Met*,

Epworth, 1940; *The Friendly Year*, Epworth, 1940; *Funnily Enough: A Pocketful of Humour, Comprising Hundreds of Twice-Told Tales Worth Telling Again*, Methuen, 1941; *Mrs. Bowser Starts Again*, Epworth, 1941; *The Spare Minute [and] Teacher's Book of Answers*, University of London Press, 1942; *Friendly Folk*, Epworth, 1942; *Tales of Today: Contemporary Stories of Breathless Adventure, Brave Deeds, and Humble Service*, Methuen, 1942; *Neighbours: A Discursive Chronicle*, Methuen, 1942; *The Sunny Room: How Penelope Came Into It, What She Did There and the Manner of Her Leaving It*, Epworth, 1942; *American England: An Epitome of a Common Heritage*, Methuen, 1943; *Wartime Pilgrimage: Some Account of a Hopeful Journey*, Epworth, 1943; *Immortal Few: The Story of the Battle of Britain in Verse*, Epworth, 1943; *The Daily Round*, Epworth, 1944; *Easter at Epworth: The Story of a Pilgrimage*, Epworth, 1944; *The Adventures of Billy Bounser and Tommy Terror* (juvenile), Epworth, 1944; (compiler) *Good in Everything: A Treasury of Inspiration, Joy, and Comfort*, Methuen, 1945; *Up Hill and Down: A Springtime Pilgrimage in Sunshine and Shower*, Epworth, 1946; *Gay Adventure: Some Account of What Befell Two Rogues on a Walking Tour*, Epworth, 1948; *The Twins at Peep-o'-Day Farm* (juvenile), Brockhampton Press, 1948; *The Timely Series of Books (Thoughts for Every Day)*, Walter, Book 1, *Some Softening Gleam*, 1949, Book 2, *New Thoughts of God*, 1949, Book 3, *Of Countless Price*, 1949, Book 4, *This and Every Day*, 1949; *Talking Out of Doors*, Ronald, 1948; *Bright Interlude*, Epworth, 1949; *The Twins on Holiday* (juvenile), Brockhampton Press, 1949; *Share My Harvest: An Anthology of Good Things Gathered Through the Years*, Methuen, 1949; *Talking in the Garden: Fact and Fancy, Fun and Fable in the Veriest School of Peace*, Ronald, 1949; (compiler) *The Spirit of Romany*, Hodder & Stoughton, 1949; *The Friendly Series*, Epworth, Book 1, *Country Ways*, 1949, Book 2, *People I Meet*, 1949, Book 3, *Neighbours and Friends*, 1949, Book 4, *This Kind World*, 1949, Book 5, *Busy Streets*, 1950, Book 9, *One Fine Day*, 1956, Book 10, *On My Way*, 1956.

(Editor) *Facts and Figures About London*, Ronald, 1950; (editor) *Facts and Figures About Scotland*, Ronald, 1950; *Talking by the Fire: Discursive Reflections and Some Personal Reminiscences*, Epworth, 1950; *The Twins in London* (juvenile), Brockhampton Press, 1950; (compiler and editor) *Nelson's Encyclopaedia*, Thomas Nelson, 1951; *Always It Is Spring: Some Account of a Plain Man's Pilgrimage in a Brave New World*, Epworth, 1951; *Happy Folk*, Walter, 1952; *The Everyday Books*, four parts, Walter, 1952; *Folk Tales of Yorkshire*, Thomas Nelson, 1952; *Cloud and Sunshine: Some Account of a Plain Man's Journey by Car from Yorkshire to the Cotswolds and Back*, Epworth, 1953; *Through the Year with H.L. Gee*, Walter, 1953; *Brother Lawrence*, Walter, 1953; *Johnny Brown* (juvenile), Brockhampton Press, 1953; *And Pastures New: Relating How a Traveller Who Intended Doing One Thing Did Another*, Epworth, 1954; *Hymns That Came to Life*, Epworth, 1954; *Tales They Tell in Yorkshire*, Methuen, 1954; (compiler) *Five Hundred Tales to Tell Again*, Epworth, 1955, Roy, 1964, selected stories published as *English Stories for Translation and Comprehension/Histoires en anglais pour l'etude et le traduction*, Epworth, 1956; *H.L. Gee's Pleasure Book* (juvenile), Epworth, 1956; *There and Back: Adventures of a Traveller Who Returned Home the Long Way Round*, Epworth, 1956; *H.L. Gee's Second Pleasure Book* (juvenile), Epworth, 1956; *H.L. Gee's Story Book* (juvenile), Roy, 1958; *Little Old Lady* (on Ada Taylor of Holby, a Leicestershire Village), Epworth, 1958.

Do You Agree?, Epworth, 1960; *Dusty Finds the Money* (juvenile), National Savings Committee, 1961; *It Seems to Me*, Epworth, 1962; *Yorkshire Wit and Humour*, Epworth, 1962; *Telling Tales*, Epworth, 1962; *Candle Books*, Epworth, 1963—; *Wings On My Shoes: Some Account of a Plain Man's Midsummer Journey in a Friendly World*, Epworth, 1963; *Briefly: An Anthology of Wit and Wisdom*, Epworth, 1964.

Day is Done, Bagster, 1970. Assistant to the late Arthur Mee in compiling "The King's England," a series of topographical books published by Hodder & Stoughton. Writer of newspaper features and an annual publication under an unrevealed pseudonym.

SIDELIGHTS: Gee summarizes his interests as "everything and everybody. As author and journalist have always felt that cleverer pens can portray the doubtful side of life, and have tried consistently to draw attention to what is good."

*   *   *

GEIS, Gilbert   1925-

PERSONAL: Born January 10, 1925, in Brooklyn, N.Y.; son of Joseph (a salesman) and Ida (List) Geis; married Ruth Steinberg (a teacher), April 4, 1948; married second wife, Robley Huston, December 17, 1966; children: (first marriage) Ellen, Jean. *Education:* Colgate University, A.B., 1947; Brigham Young University, M.S., 1949; University of Wisconsin, Ph.D., 1953. *Politics:* Democrat. *Home:* 1020 Skyline Dr., Laguna Beach, Calif. 92651. *Agent:* Paul R. Reynolds & Son, 599 Fifth Ave., New York, N.Y. 10017. *Office:* Department of Sociology, University of California, Irvine, Calif. 92664.

CAREER: University of Oklahoma, Norman, assistant professor of sociology, 1952-57; California State College at Los Angeles, professor of sociology, 1957-71; University of California, Irvine, professor of social ecology, 1971—. *Military service:* U.S. Navy, 1943-46. *Awards, honors:* Fulbright fellow; Oslo, Norway, 1951-52; fellow in law and sociology, Harvard Law School, 1964-65.

WRITINGS: (With Herbert A. Bloch) *Man, Crime, and Society: The Forms of Criminal Behavior*, Random House, 1962, 2nd edition, revised, 1970; (with William E. Bittle) *The Longest Way Home: Chief Alfred C. Sam's Back-to-Africa Movement*, Wayne State University Press, 1964; (with others) *The Role of the Institutional Teacher: A Report of a Pilot Training Program*, Youth Studies Center, University of Southern California, 1964; (editor and author of introduction and notes) *White-Collar Criminal: The Offender in Business and the Professions*, Atherton, 1968; (with Bruce Bullington and John G. Munns) *Ex-Addicts as Streetworkers: The Boyle Heights Narcotics Prevention Project*, Economic and Youth Opportunities Agency (Los Angeles), c.1968; (with others) *Addicts in the Classroom: The Impact of an Experimental Narcotics Education Program on Junior High School Pupils*, Economic and Youth Opportunities Agency, 1969; (with Eugene Doleschal) *Graduated Release*, National Institute of Mental Health, 1971; *Not the Law's Business?: An Examination of Homosexuality, Prostitution, Abortion, Gambling and Narcotics*, U.S. Government Printing Office, 1973.

*   *   *

GELB, Ignace J(ay)   1907-

PERSONAL: Born October 14, 1907, in Tarnow, Poland; came to U.S. in 1929, naturalized in 1930; son of Salo (a professional soldier) and Regina (Issler) Gelb; married Hester Mokstad (on staff of a children's encyclopedia), May 13, 1938; children: Walter A., John V. *Education:* University of Florence, student, 1925-26; University of of Rome, Ph.D., 1929. *Home:* 5454 Woodlawn Ave., Chicago, Ill. 60615. *Office:* Oriental Institute, University of Chicago, Chicago, Ill. 60615.

CAREER: University of Chicago, Chicago, Ill., traveling fellow and instructor, 1929-41, assistant professor, 1941-43, associate professor, 1943-47, professor of Assyriology, 1947-65, Frank P. Hixon Distinguished Service Professor, 1965—. Visiting professor at University of Michigan, 1956, 1967. Member of archaeological expeditions to Near East in 1932, 1935, 1947, 1963, 1966. *Military service:* U.S. Army, 1943-45. *Member:* American Academy of Arts and Sciences (fellow), American Oriental Society, Archaeological Institute of America, American Schools of Oriental Research, Linguistic Society of America, American Name Society (president, 1963), Societe Hittite (Paris), Accademia Nazionale dei Lincei (foreign member); honorary member of oriental societies of France, Finland, and India; Linguistic Circle of New York, Philological Club, Quadrangle Club, Near East Club (president, 1942-43).

WRITINGS: (Contributor) Edward Chiera, editor, *Joint Expedition of the American School of Oriental Research in Bagdad, with the Iraq Museum at Nuzi,* P. Geuthner (Paris), 1927-39; *Hittite Hieroglyphs I-III,* University of Chicago Press, 1931-32; *Inscriptions from Alishar and Vicinity,* University of Chicago Press, 1935; *Hittite Hieroglyphic Monuments,* University of Chicago Press, 1939; (with Pierre M. Purves and Allan A. MacRae) *Nuzi Personal Names,* University of Chicago Press, 1943; *Hurrians and Subarians,* University of Chicago Press, 1944, *A Study of Writing: The Foundations of Grammatology,* 1952, 2nd edition, 1963; *Sargonic Texts from the Diyala Region,* University of Chicago Press, 1952; *Old Akkadian Writing and Grammar,* University of Chicago Press, 1952, 3rd edition, 1969; *Old Akkadian Inscriptions in Chicago Natural History Museum* (legal and business texts), Chicago Natural History Museum, 1955; *Glossary of Old Akkadian,* University of Chicago Press, 1957, revised edition, 1963; *Sargonic Texts in the Louvre Museum,* University of Chicago Press, 1968; *Sargonic Texts in the Ashmolean Museum,* Oxford University Press, 1968; *Sequential Reconstruction of Proto-Akkadian,* University of Chicago Press, 1968; *Sargonic Texts from the Kish Area,* University of Chicago Press, 1970. Editor, *Assyrian Dictionary,* 1947—.

WORK IN PROGRESS: Structure of the Ancient Mesopotamian Society; The Language of the Amorites; Old Akkadian Inscriptions.

SIDELIGHTS: Gelb has studied some ninety languages, speaks Polish, German, Italian, French, and Turkish, and knows professionally Assyrian, Sumerian, Hebrew, Arabic, and others. *Avocational interests:* Tennis and hiking.

*   *   *

GENDELL, Murray   1924-

PERSONAL: Born February 2, 1924, in New York, N.Y.; married Barbro Winberg, September 7, 1958; children: Ingrid Erika, Martin Aaron. *Education:* New York University, B.A., 1950; Columbia University, Ph.D., 1963. *Office:* Center for Population Research, Georgetown University, Washington, D.C. 20007.

CAREER: Department of Correction, New York, N.Y., senior statistician, 1957-58; Columbia University, New York, N.Y., lecturer in sociology, 1959-60; College of City of New York (now City College of the City University of New York), New York, N.Y., lecturer in sociology, 1960-62; International Labour Organization, Geneva, Switzerland, manpower research, 1963-64; International Population and Urban Research, University of California, Berkeley, population research, 1964-66; Center for Population Research and Department of Sociology, Georgetown University, Washington, D.C., associate professor of sociology and director of demography program, 1966—. *Military service:* U.S. Army Air Forces, 1943-47;

became sergeant. *Member:* International Union for the Scientific Study of Population, Latin American Studies Association, American Association of University Professors, American Association for the Advancement of Science, American Sociological Association, Population Association of America. *Awards, honors:* Research grant from government of Sweden and National Science Foundation.

WRITINGS: (Editor with Hans L. Zetterberg) *A Sociological Almanac for the United States,* Bedminster, 1961, 2nd edition, 1963; *Swedish Working Wives: A Study of Determinants and Consequences,* Bedminster, 1963; (contributor) Steven Polger, editor, *Culture and Population,* Schenkman and Carolina Population Center, University of North Carolina, 1971. Contributor to *Proceedings* of World Population Conference, 1965, of International Population Union, 1969, and of Latin American Regional Population Conference, 1970.

WORK IN PROGRESS: With T.K. Burch, *Family Structure and Fertility in Guatemala and the U.S.*

AVOCATIONAL INTERESTS: Opera.

*   *   *

GENTRY, Curt   1931-

PERSONAL: Born June 13, 1931, in Lamar, Colo.; son of Curtis Herman (a city clerk) and Coral (McMillin) Gentry; married Laura Wilson Spence (a professional librarian), October 30, 1954. *Education:* University of Colorado, student, 1949-50; San Francisco State College, B.A., 1957. *Politics:* Democrat. *Agent:* Paul R. Reynolds, Inc., 599 Fifth Ave., New York, N.Y. 10017.

CAREER: Part-time reporter for Colorado newspapers while student, 1947-50; Paul Elder Books, San Francisco, Calif., head of mail order department, 1954-57; Tro Harper Books, San Francisco, Calif., manager, 1957-61; full-time writer, 1961—. *Military service:* U.S. Air Force, 1950-54; spent one year in Korea editing an Air Force newspaper; became sergeant. *Member:* Authors Guild, California Historical Society. *Awards, honors:* Command prizes in Air Force short story contest, 1953, 1954; honorable mention for novel in progress, first annual Joseph Henry Jackson Competition, 1957; Edgar Allan Poe Special Award, Mystery Writers of America, 1967, for *Frame-Up: The Incredible Case of Tom Mooney and Warren Billings.*

WRITINGS: The Dolphin Guide to San Francisco and the Bay Area—Present and Past, Doubleday, 1962, revised edition, 1969; *The Madams of San Francisco: An Irreverent History of the City by the Golden Gate,* Doubleday, 1964; (with John Browning) *John M. Browning: American Gunmaker,* Doubleday, 1964; *The Vulnerable Americans,* Doubleday, 1966; *Frame-Up: The Incredible Case of Tom Mooney and Warren Billings,* Norton, 1967; *The Killer Mountains: A Search for the Legendary Lost Dutchman Mine,* New American Library, 1968; *The Last Days of the Late, Great State of California* (originally announced as "Goodbye, California"), Putnam, 1968; (with Francis Gary Powers) *Operation Overflight,* Holt, 1970; (editor) Toni L. Scott, *King of Loving,* World Publishing, 1970; (contributor) Eugene C. Lee and Willis D. Hawley, *The Challenge of California, with a Concise Introduction to California Government,* Little, Brown, 1970; (with Edward R. Murphy, Jr). *Second in Command,* Holt, 1971. Contributor of short stories to *Preview* (Tokyo), and *Points* (Paris), articles to *New York Times Magazine, Newsday, Denver Post, San Francisco Chronicle, Fodor Shell Travel Guide to the Pacific, Humble Vacation Guide, Cry California.*

WORK IN PROGRESS: A nonfiction book on a contemporary history subject; a novel trilogy.

BIOGRAPHICAL/CRITICAL SOURCES: *Book World,* May 14, 1967; *New York Times Book Review,* June 18, 1967, July 26, 1970; *Best Sellers,* October 15, 1968, December 1, 1968; *Nation,* December 9, 1968; *New Yorker,* July 18, 1970.

* * *

GEORGE, Charles H(illes) 1922-

PERSONAL: Born May 22, 1922, in Kansas City, Mo.; son of Hilles McIntyre (an industrial manager) and Pearl (Renne) George; married Margaret Young (a college professor), February 20, 1960; children: David, Claudia. *Education:* Gettysburg College, A.B., 1946; Princeton University, Ph.D., 1951. *Home:* 621 Annie Glidden Rd., DeKalb, Ill. 60115. *Office:* Department of History, Northern Illinois University, DeKalb, Ill. 60115.

CAREER: Stanford University, Stanford, Calif., instructor in history, 1951-52; assistant professor of history at Pomona College, Claremont, Calif., 1952-53, Colorado College, Colorado Springs, 1953-54, University of Rochester, Rochester, N.Y., 1954-55, University of Washington, Seattle, 1956-57; University of Pittsburgh, Pittsburgh, Pa., assistant professor, 1958-59, associate professor of history, 1959-61; Northern Illinois University, DeKalb, professor of history, 1961—. *Military service:* U.S. Army, 1942-45; served in European theater; became sergeant; received Bronze Star. *Member:* Conference on British Studies, American Society for Reformation Research, American Historical Association, American Historical Society, American Institute for Marxist Studies, Phi Beta Kappa. *Awards, honors:* Social Science Research Council fellow.

WRITINGS: (With Katharine George) *The Protestant Mind of the English Reformation,* Princeton University Press, 1961; (editor) *Revolution: Five Centuries of Europe in Conflict,* Dell, 1962, reissued as *Revolution: European Radicals from Hus to Lenin,* Scott, Foresman, 1970. Contributor of articles to *Journal of Modern History, Journal of History of Ideas, Journal of Religion, Church History, Past and Present.*

WORK IN PROGRESS: A book on secularism and the English Revolution for Princeton University Press; a monograph, "The Making of the English Bourgeoisie, 1500-1700," for *Past and Present.*

* * *

GERLACH, Don R(alph) 1932-

PERSONAL: Born June 9, 1932, in Harvard, Neb.; son of Ralph R. (a farmer) and Evelyn I. (Bishoff) Gerlach. *Education:* University of Nebraska, B.Sc.Ed., 1954, M.A., 1956, Ph.D., 1961; University of London, postgraduate study, 1956-57. *Politics:* Republican. *Religion:* Anglican. *Home:* 1115 Copley Rd., Akron, Ohio 45420. *Office:* Department of History, University of Akron, Akron, Ohio 45404.

CAREER: University of Maryland, Far East Division, Korea, instructor, 1958-59; University of Nebraska, Lincoln, instructor, 1961-62; University of Akron, Akron, Ohio, assistant professor, 1962-65, associate professor of history, 1965—. Episcopal Diocese of Ohio, licensed lay reader; church school teacher and vestryman. *Military service:* U.S. Army, 1958-60. *Member:* American Historical Association, Royal Historical Society (fellow), American Association of University Professors, Organization of American Historians, Phi Alpha Theta, Pi Sigma Alpha. *Awards, honors:* American Association for State and Local History grant, 1964; American Philosophical Society grants, 1969, 1970.

WRITINGS: *Philip Schuyler and the American Revolution in New York, 1733-1777,* University of Nebraska Press, 1964.

WORK IN PROGRESS: *Philip Schuyler and the Politics of New York in the Confederation and the Federalist Era;* with George E. DeMille, *Samuel Johnson of Stratford in New England, 1696-1772.*

* * *

GERTLER, Menard M. 1919-

PERSONAL: Born May 21, 1919, in Saskatoon, Saskatchewan; son of Franklin and Clare (Delman) Gertler; married Anna Paull, September 4, 1943; children: Barbara Lynn Victor, Stephanie, Jonathan. *Education:* University of Saskatchewan, B.A., 1940; McGill University, M.D.C.M., 1943, M.Sc., 1946; Harvard University, fellow, 1947-50; New York University, D.Sc., 1958. *Home:* 1000 Park Ave., New York, N.Y. 10028. *Office:* Institute of Physical Medicine & Rehabilitation, New York University Medical Center, 400 East 34th St., New York, N.Y. 10016.

CAREER: Licensed to practice medicine in New York State and Massachusetts; McGill University, Montreal, Quebec, demonstrator in physiology, 1945-47; Massachusetts General Hospital, Boston, resident cardiologist and executive director of coronary research project, 1947-50; College of Physicians and Surgeons, Columbia University, New York, N.Y., instructor in medicine, 1950-54; New York University Medical Center, New York, N.Y., associate professor and director of research, 1958—. Assistant, Presbyterian Hospital, 1950-54; assistant attending physician and physician-in-charge of cardiovascular diseases, Francis Delafield Division, Columbia-Presbyterian Medical Center, 1951-54; consultant and lecturer, U.S. Naval Hospital, St. Albans, N.Y., 1959—; chief medical consultant, Sinclair Oil Corp., New York, N.Y. 1958-70. *Military service:* Canadian Armed Services, 1942-44.

MEMBER: American Medical Association, American Heart Association, American College of Physicians (fellow), American Chemical Society, American Federation for Clinical Research, American Physiology Society, American Association for the Advancement of Science, Harvey Society, Society for Experimental Biology and Medicine, New York Academy of the Sciences, New York Academy of Medicine (fellow), New York Heart Association, Sigma Xi, Enzyme Club of New York. *Awards, honors:* Founder's Day award, New York University, 1958.

WRITINGS: (With Paul D. White) *Coronary Heart Disease in Young Adults: A Multidisciplinary Study,* Harvard University Press for Commonwealth Fund, 1954; *You Can Predict Your Heart Attack and Prevent It,* Random House, 1963; (contributor) Howard A. Rusk, *Rehabilitation Medicine,* revised edition, Mosby, 1964. Author or co-author of some 125 articles in medical and scientific journals.

* * *

GETLEIN, Dorothy Woolen 1921-

PERSONAL: Surname is pronounced *Get*-line; born January 20, 1921, in Meriden, Conn.; daughter of Ernest (a printer) and Esther (Gallivan) Woollen; married Frank Getlein (a writer), May 26, 1943; children: Christine, Steve, Mary, Bill, Karl. *Education:* Albertus Magnus College. *Politics:* Independent. *Religion:* Catholic. *Home and office:* 2007 Citadel Pl., Vienna, Va. 22180.

WRITINGS—With husband, Frank Getlein: *Christianity in Art,* Bruce, 1959; *Christianity in Modern Art,* Bruce, 1961; (and Anne Peck) *Wings of an Eagle: The Story of Michelangelo,* Hawthorn, 1963; *The Bite of the Print: Satire and Irony in Woodcuts, Engravings, Etchings, Lithographs and Serigraphs,* C.N. Potter, 1964; *Georges Rouault's Miserere,* Bruce, 1964.

WORK IN PROGRESS: In collaboration with Frank Getlein, *Art and Government,* for Pantheon.

GETLEIN, Frank 1921-

PERSONAL: Surname is pronounced Get-line; born March 6, 1921, in Ansonia, Conn,; son of Frank (an economic supervisor) and Katherine (Sheehan) Getlein; married Dorothy Woollen (a writer), May 26, 1943; children: Christine, Steve, Mary, Bill, Karl. Education: College of the Holy Cross, B.S., 1942; Catholic University of America, M.A., 1947. Politics: Independent. Religion: Catholic. Home: 2007 Citadel Pl., Vienna, Va. 22180. Office: Washington Evening Star, 225 Virginia Ave. S.E., Washington, D.C. 20003.

CAREER: English insrtuctor at St. Ambrose College, Davenport, Iowa and lecturer at Fairfield University, Fairfield, Conn., 1947-51; Otto and Eloise Spaeth Foundation, Milwaukee, Wis., executive secretary, 1951-53; Barkin & Herman (public relations firm), Milwaukee, Wis., 1953-56; Milwaukee Journal, Milwaukee, Wis., art critic, 1956-59; New Republic, Washington, D.C., art critic, 1957—; Washington Evening Star, Washington, D.C., art critic, 1961—, editorial writer, 1963—. Member Fulbright Committee, 1961-64; chairman, Advisory Committee of Department of Agricultural Graduate School Lectures on Design, 1964-65. Lecturer at Marquette University, 1964-65, and at other colleges, universities, and art groups. Military service: U.S. Army, 1942-45; served in Italy. Member: National Press Club.

WRITINGS: (with wife, Dorothy Getlein) Christianity in Art, Bruce, 1959; (author of commentaries) H.W. Janson and Dora Jane Janson, Standard Treasury of World's Great Paintings, Abrams, 1960; Abraham Rattner, American Federation of Arts, Ford Foundation, 1960; (with Dorothy Getlein) Christianity in Modern Art, Bruce, 1961; A Modern Demonology: Being Social Criticism in the Form of a Scholarly Dissertation, Complete with Sociological Findings Collected by the Latest Approved Methods, on the Need for a Rehabilitation of the Ancient Science of Demonology, the Discovery and Destruction of Demons Inhabiting Various Individuals and Groups in the Social Order, the Body Politic and the Economic Milieu, C.N. Potter, 1961; (with Harold C. Gardiner) Movies, Morals and Art, Sheed, 1961; (with Dorothy Getlein and Anne Peck) Wings of an Eagle: The Story of Michelangelo, Hawthorn, 1963; (with Dorothy Getlein) The Bite of the Print: Satire and Irony in Woodcuts, Engravings, Etchings, Lithographs and Serigraphs, C.N. Potter, 1964; (with Dorothy Getlein) Georges Rouall's Miserere, Bruce, 1964; The Trouble with Catholics, Helicon, 1964; (author of text) Jack Levine, Abrams, 1966; (author of introductory text) Walter Kuhn, 1877-1949 (catalogue of an exhibition), Kennedy Galleries, 1967; (compiler and author of commentaries) Ten French Impressionists: A Portfolio of Color Prints, Abrams, 1967; (author of introduction) Herman Maril: A Monograph, Baltimore Museum of Art, 1967; Art Treasures of the World: 100 Most Precious Masterpieces of All Time in Full Color, C.N. Potter, 1968; (author of introductory text) The Silver Sculpture of Earl Krentzen (catalogue of an exhibition), Kennedy Galleries, 1968; (author of introductory text) Peter Blume (catalogue of an exhibition), Kennedy Galleries, 1968; (author of introductory text) Ben Shahn (catalogue of an exhibition), Kennedy Galleries, c.1968; The Politics of Paranoia, Funk, 1969; Harry Jackson: Monograph—Catalogue, Kennedy Galleries, 1969; (author of introductory text) Colleen Browning (catalogue of an exhibition), Kennedy Galleries, 1969; (author of introductory text) Abraham Rattner (catalogue of an exhibition), Kennedy Galleries, 1969; (author of introduction) Bruce Harris and Seena Harris, editors, The Complete Etchings of Rembrandt, Bounty Books, 1970; Milton Hebald, Viking, 1971; Playing Soldier: A Diatribe, Holt, 1971. Contributor to Country Beautiful, Horizon, Commonweal, Jubilee, Sign, American Scholar, Time, and other publications. Washington correspondent for Art in America and Burlington Magazine.

WORK IN PROGRESS: Collaborating with Dorothy Getlein on Art and Government, for Pantheon.

BIOGRAPHICAL/CRITICAL SOURCES: Best Sellers, August 15, 1971.

*   *   *

GEYER, Alan (Francis) 1931-

PERSONAL: Born August 3, 1931, in Dover, N.J.; son of Curtis Bayley (a clergyman) and Ada (Wehrly) Geyer; married Joanne Shirley Goodnow, March 28, 1953; children: Nancy Kathryn, Peter Lincoln, David Curtis. Education: Attended University of California, 1951; Ohio Wesleyan University, B.A., 1952; Boston University, S.T.B., 1955, Ph.D., 1961. Politics: Democrat. Home: 938 Donaghe St., Staunton, Va. 24401. Office: Department of Political Science, Mary Baldwin College, Staunton, Va. 24401.

CAREER: Ordained to Methodist ministry; juvenile probation officer, Delaware County, Ohio, 1952; adviser to Methodist Student Movement at Harvard University, Cambridge, Mass., and Boston University, Boston, Mass., 1953-55, concurrently pastor of church in Cambridge, 1954-55; Lycoming College, Williamsport, Pa., assistant professor of political science and sociology, 1957-58; pastor in Newark, N.J., 1958-60; Mary Baldwin College, Staunton, Va., chairman of George Hammond Sullivan Department of Political Science, 1960—. American Political Science Association, member of World Travel-Seminar, meeting with leaders in fourteen countries, 1963. Tenor soloist, Staunton Choral Society. Director, Lycoming County Council of Community Services, 1957-58.

MEMBER: American Political Science Association, American Sociological Association (fellow), Society for Religion in Higher Education (fellow), Council on Religion and International Affairs, Southern Political Science Association, Phi Beta Kappa, Omicron Delta Kappa, Alpha Kappa Delta, Delta Sigma Rho.

WRITINGS: Piety and Politics: American Protestantism in the World Arena, John Knox, 1963; (editor) The Maze of Peace: Conflict and Reconciliation Among Nations, Friendship, 1969; (editor with Dean Peerman) Robert McAfee Brown and others, Theological Crossings, Eerdmans, 1971. Contributor of articles to Worldview.

WORK IN PROGRESS: Study in two fields, ethics and decision-making in foreign policy, and politics and the arts.

*   *   *

GIBBS, Paul T(homas) 1897-

PERSONAL: Born February 16, 1897, in Moline, Kan.; son of John M. (a teacher and farmer) and Jennie Gibbs; married Gladys Ruth Clark; children: Marilyn (Mrs. Perry Beach). Education: Union College, Lincoln, Neb., B.A., 1919; University of Nebraska, M.A., 1926; University of Washington, Seattle, Ph.D., 1937. Politics: Republican. Religion: Seventh-day Adventist. Home: 200 Grove Ave., Berrien Springs, Mich. 49103.

CAREER: Enterprise Academy, Enterprise, Kan., instructor in English, 1922-25; Broadview College, Lagrange, Ill., instructor in English, 1926-28; Walla Walla College, Walla Walla, Wash., professor of English, 1928-37; Washington Missionary College (now Columbia Union College), Takoma Park, Md., professor of English, 1937-46; Emmanuel Missionary College, Berrien Springs, Mich., professor of English, 1946-65, department chairman, 1946-62; Andrews University, Berrien Springs,

Mich., professor of English, 1959-65, department chairman, 1959-62, professor emeritus of English, 1966—. *Awards, honors:* Citation for Distinguished Service, Emmanuel Missionary College, 1961.

WRITINGS: Men Such as We, Review & Herald, 1963; *Job and the Mysteries of Wisdom,* Southern Publishing, 1967; *Men Come Alive,* Review & Herald, 1968; *Crossroads of the Cross,* Review & Herald, 1969; *David and His Mighty Men,* Review & Herald, 1970; *Paul the Conqueror,* Review & Herald, 1972. Writer of more than fifty magazine articles, mainly in *Youth's Instructor.*

WORK IN PROGRESS: A book on Moses.

AVOCATIONAL INTERESTS: Photography, gardening, walking.

* * *

GIBBS-SMITH, Charles Harvard   1909-
(Charles Harvard)

PERSONAL: Born March 22, 1909, in London, England; son of Edward Gibbs (a physician) and Ethel (Watts) Gibbs-Smith. *Education:* Attended King's College Choir School, Cambridge, England, and Westminster School, London, England; Harvard University, A.M., 1932. *Politics:* "Conservative/liberal." *Agent:* A.M. Heath & Co. Ltd., 35 Dover St., London W.1, England. *Office:* Victoria and Albert Museum, London S.W.7, England.

CAREER: Victoria and Albert Museum, London, England, assistant keeper, 1932-39, keeper of public relations department (formerly department of extension services), 1947-71, keeper emeritus, 1971—. British Ministry of Information, London, 1939-45, rose to director of photograph division. Adviser on early aeronautical history to *Encyclopaedia Britannica, Chambers's Encyclopaedia,* and *World Book Encyclopedia.* Organizer of *Radio-Times* Hulton Picture Library (formerly Hulton Library). Has participated in more than one hundred radio programs, and appeared on television. *Member:* Royal Society of Arts (fellow; Cantor Lecturer), Royal Aeronautical Society of Great Britain (honorary companion), Museums Association (fellow), English-Speaking Union (London; member of board of governors, 1956-59), Institute of Journalists, Royal Aero Club, Danish Club (London). *Awards, honors:* Medal of Aero-Club de France for *The Aeroplane: An Historical Survey;* Chevalier, Royal Danish Order of the Dannebrog.

WRITINGS: Costume: An Index to the More Important Material in the Library, revised edition, Victoria and Albert Museum, 1936; *Basic Aircraft Recognition,* Country Life, 1942, reissued as the *Aircraft Recognition Manual,* George Newnes, 1949; (editor and contributor) *The New Book of Flight,* Oxford University Press, 1948; (compiler) *The Great Exhibition of 1851; A Commemorative Album,* H.M.S.O., 1950, revised edition, 1964; *The Air League Aircraft Recognition Manual,* Putnam, 1952, new edition published as *The Aircraft Recognition Manual,* De Graff, 1954; *Operation Caroline* (novel), Heinemann, 1953, published in America as *The Caroline Affair,* Viking, 1954; *A History of Flying,* Batsford, 1953, Praeger, 1954; (editor with Geoffrey Grigson) *People, Places and Things,* Volume I: *People: A Volume of the Good, Bad, Great and Eccentric Who Illuminate the Admirable Diversity of Man,* Hawthorn, 1954, 2nd edition, 1957, Volume II: *Places: A Volume of Travel in Space and Time,* Grosvenor Press, 1954, Hawthorn, 1955, 2nd edition, Hawthorn, 1957, Volume III: *Things: A Volume of Objects Devised by Man's Genius Which Are the Measure of His Civilization,* Grosvenor Press, 1954, 2nd edition, Hawthorn, 1957, Volume IV: *Ideas: A Volume of Ideas, Notions, and Emotions, Clear or Confused, Which Have Moved the Minds of Men,* Grosvenor Press, 1954, 2nd edition, Hawthorn, 1957; *Yankee Poodle: A Roman-tic Mystery,* Heinemann, 1955; (with L.E. Bradford) *World Aircraft Recognition Manual,* De Graff, 1956; *Escape and Be Secret* (novel), Heinemann, 1957; *The Aeroplane: An Historical Survey of Its Origins and Development,* H.M.S.O. for Science Museum, 1960, 2nd edition published as *Aviation: An Historical Survey from Its Origins to the End of World War II,* 1970; *The Fashionable Lady in the 19th Century,* Victoria & Albert Museum, 1960; *Sir George Cayley's Aeronautics,* Science Museum, 1962; *A Dictionary and Nomenclature of the First Aeroplanes, 1809 to 1909,* H.M.S.O., 1966; *The Invention of the Aeroplane (1700-1909),* Taplinger, 1966; *Clement Alder: His Flight-Claims and His Place in History,* H.M.S.O., 1968.

Shorter works: (compiler) *Winston Churchill,* Hodder & Stoughton, 1941; (compiler) *Roosevelt* (photographs and speeches), Hodder & Stoughton, 1942; *An Introduction to Aircraft Recognition: German Aircraft and How to Know Them,* George Newnes for British Aviation Publications, 1943; *Man Takes Wings,* H.M.S.O. for Air Ministry, 1948; *Ballooning,* Penguin, 1948; *How to Remember Sea Signal Flags and the Morse Code,* Gale & Polden, 1951; (with H.V.T. Percival) *The Wellington Museum, Apsley House: A Guide,* H.M.S.O., 1952, 4th edition, 1964; (with Percival) *The Wellington Museum, Apsley House: The Paintings,* H.M.S.O., 1952; (editor and author of introduction and notes) *Balloons,* Ariel Press, 1956; *Women Who Defied Prejudice,* National Union of Townswomen's Guilds, 1956; *The History of Flying* (bibliography), Cambridge University Press for National Book League, 1957; *The Wright Brothers: A Brief Account of Their Work, 1899-1911,* H.M.S.O., 1963; *The World's First Aeroplane Flights, 1903-1908, and Earlier Attempts to Fly,* H.M.S.O., 1965; (author of introduction with Oliver Warner) *Balloons and Ships,* Van Nostrand, 1965; *Aeronautics: Early Flying Up to the Reims Meetings,* H.M.S.O., 1966; *A Brief History of Flying, from Myth to Space Travel,* H.M.S.O., 1967; *Leonardo Da Vinci's Aeronautics,* H.M.S.O., 1967; *Sir George Cayley (1773-1857),* H.M.S.O., 1968; *Copyright Law Concerning Works of Art, Photographs and the Written Word,* Museums Association, 1970; *The Uses of Deep Breathing in Health and Disease,* privately printed, 1970; *The Art of Observation: A Booklet for Museum Warders,* Victoria and Albert Museum, 1971; *The Arrangement and Organization of Lectures,* Museums Association, 1971; *The Art of Observation: A Manual for Police Officers,* Sussex Constabulary, 1972; *The Bayeux Tapestry,* Phaidon, 1973; *How to Learn the Sea Signal Flags and the Morse Code,* privately printed, 1973. Contributor to Royal Society of Arts *Notes and Records,* and to *Punch, Spectator, Flight, New Scientist, Country Life, Lilliput, Saturday Book, Sphere, Times* (London), *Daily Telegraph,* and *Argosy* (London).

WORK IN PROGRESS: Re-Birth of European Aviation 1902-1908: A Study of the Wright Brothers' Influence, for Science Museum (London).

* * *

GIBSON, William   1914-
(William Mass)

PERSONAL: Born November 13, 1914, in New York, N.Y.; son of George Irving (a bank clerk) and Florence (Dore) Gibson; married Margaret Brenman (a psychoanalyst), September 6, 1940; children: Thomas and Daniel. *Education:* Attended College of City of New York (now City College of the City University of New York), 1930-32. *Politics:* Democrat. *Religion:* None. *Residence:* Stockbridge, Mass. *Agent:* Leah Salisbury, 790 Madison Ave., New York, N.Y. 10021.

CAREER: Author and playwright. Piano teacher at intervals in early writing days to supplement income. President and co-founder of Berkshire Theatre Festival, Stockbridge, Mass., 1966—. *Member:* Dramatists Guild, P.E.N. *Awards, honors:* Harriet Monroe Memorial Prize for group of poems published in *Poetry,* 1945; Topeka Civic Theatre award for "A Cry of Players," 1947; Sylvania Award for his first ("and last," he says) television play, "The Miracle Worker," 1957.

WRITINGS—Plays: *I Lay in Zion* (one-act; first produced in Topeka, Kan., at Topeka Civic Theatre, Easter, 1943), Samuel French (acting edition), 1947; (under pseudonym William Mass) *The Ruby* (one-act lyrical drama), with libretto (based on Lord Dunsany's *A Night at an Inn*) by Norman Dello Joio, Ricordi, 1955; *The Miracle Worker* (three-act; originally written as a television drama; produced by CBS for "Playhouse 90" in 1957; rewritten for stage, and first produced on Broadway at Playhouse Theatre, October 19, 1959), Knopf, 1957; *Dinny and the Witches* [and] *The Miracle Worker* (the former first produced Off-Broadway at Cherry Lane Theatre, December 9, 1959; also see below), Atheneum, 1960; *Two for the Seesaw* (three-act comedy; copyrighted in 1956 as "After the Verb to Love"; first produced on Broadway at Booth Theatre, January 16, 1958), Samuel French, 1960; *Dinny and the Witches: A Frolic on Grave Matters,* Dramatists Play Service, 1961; (with Clifford Odets) *Golden Boy* (musical adaptation of Odet's original drama, with lyrics by Lee Adams, and music by Charles Strouse; first produced on Broadway at Majestic Theatre, October 20, 1964), Atheneum, 1965; *A Cry of Players* (three-act; first produced at Topeka Civic Theatre, Topeka, Kansas, February, 1948, produced on Broadway at the Vivian Beaumont Theatre, November 14, 1968), Atheneum, 1969; "John and Abigail" (three-act drama; first produced in Stockbridge, Mass., at Berkshire Theatre Festival, summer, 1969, produced in Washington, D.C., at Ford's Theatre, January 9, 1970), published as *American Primitive: The Words of John and Abigail Adams Put into a Sequence for the Theater, with Addenda in Rhyme,* Atheneum, 1972. Author of screenplays for "The Miracle Worker," produced by United Artists in 1962, and "A Cry of Players," filmed by Columbia in 1969.

Other publications: *Winter Crook* (poems), Oxford University Press, 1948; (under pseudonym William Mass) *The Cobweb* (novel), Knopf, 1954; *The Seesaw Log* (a chronicle of the stage production, including the text of *Two for the Seesaw,* Knopf, 1959; *A Mass for the Dead* (chronicle and poems), Atheneum, 1968; *Grove of Doom,* Grosset-Tempo, 1969.

SIDELIGHTS: A Mass for the Dead is a memorial to the author's parents and to the continuity of the generations. Granville Hicks has called it "a strong book, written out of compunction, love, and hope." In a recent interview with Jerrold Phillips, Gibson said that "the prime responsibility of a writer is to master certain conflicts in himself. If he masters them in himself and puts them on the stage in a controlled form, the audience sits there, and the audience which lacks the artistic or creative faculties for self-mastery in this gets it vicariously." He comments on the present generation of American playwrights: "The writing is very small, it's very transient. There're hardly any of the younger writers that know how to write a three-act play. They write one-act plays. They haven't had the training in the theatre or they don't have the structural, technical abilities to handle their audience, to handle a piece of material over two hours."

A Cry of Players won the Topeka Civic Theatre award in 1947, and was snapped up for Broadway by Margaret Webster and Carly Wharton, but somehow got lost in the shuffle. It only recently came to public attention with its production at Lincoln Center in 1968. It is a drama

about the young Shakespeare (although he is never really named in the play) and his rebellion against a premature marriage, fatherhood, and the pettiness of his Elizabethan workaday world. Harold Clurman writes that Gibson "must have a special attachment to [this play] . . . because it is the work of his youth with clearly autobiographical overtones. He also esteems it because it is written in a cherished mode from which his later plays—*Two for the Seesaw* and *The Miracle Worker*—have departed." In a review of the Lincoln Center production, Henry Zeiger judges *A Cry of Players* "more relevant to the early 20th Century than to the English Renaissance. Dressing the actors up in costumes (which comes off rather well) does not disguise the fact that this is the same old turkey about the sensitive lad who leaves home to create Art in the big city because he is discouraged by the drab life of the surrounding rubes. The pattern, while it fits Sherwood Anderson or Thomas Wolfe (and possibly Gibson), is simply not appropriate to Shakespeare."

The film rights to *A Cry of Players* have been purchased by Columbia. *The Cobweb,* a best seller, was filmed by M-G-M in 1957. In 1973, "Seesaw", a musical version of *Two for the Seesaw,* opened on Broadway.

BIOGRAPHICAL/CRITICAL SOURCES: Cosmopolitan, August, 1958; *Newsweek,* March 16, 1959, July 27, 1970; *Tulane Drama Review,* May, 1960; *Saturday Review,* March 23, 1968; *New York Times Book Review,* April 14, 1968; *New Yorker,* November 23, 1968; *Nation,* December 2, 1968; *New Leader,* December 16, 1968; *New England Theatre* (interview), spring, 1970; *Variety,* February 21, 1971.

*   *   *

GIELGUD, Val (Henry) 1900-

PERSONAL: Born April 28, 1900, in London, England; son of Frank and Kate Terry (Lewis) Gielgud; married 1921 (marriage dissolved); succeeding marriages to Barbara Druce, 1928, Rita Vale, 1946, Monica Grey, 1955, also dissolved; married fifth wife, June Vivienne Bailey, 1960; children: (second marriage) one son. *Education:* Attended Rugby School and Trinity College, Oxford. *Home:* Wychwood, Barcombe, near Lewes, Sussex, England. *Agent:* David Higham Associates Ltd., 5-8 Lower John St., London W1R 4HA, England.

CAREER: Joined *Radio Times* in 1928 after periods as secretary to member of British Parliament, actor, sub-editor of comic paper; British Broadcasting Corp., London, England, head of drama department, 1929-63. *Military service:* Grenadier Guards, World War I. *Member:* Crime Writers (chairman, 1961), Savile Club (London). *Awards, honors:* Order of the British Empire, 1942, Commander, 1958.

WRITINGS: Black Gallantry (novel), Constable, 1928; *Old Swords,* Houghton, 1928; *White Eagles: A Story of 1812,* Houghton, 1929 (published in England as *Gathering of Eagles: A Story of 1812,* Constable, 1929); *Imperial Treasure* (novel), Houghton, 1931; *How to Write Broadcast Plays* (includes three examples, "Friday Morning," "Red Tabs," and "Exiles"), Hurst & Blackett, 1932; *The Broken Men* (novel), Constable, 1932, Houghton, 1933; *Gravelhanger: The Story of an Adventure,* Cassell, 1934; *The Ruse of the Vanished Women,* Doubleday, 1934; *Outrage in Manchukuo: The Story of an Adventure,* Cassell, 1937; *The Red Account: The Story of an Adventure,* Rich & Cowan, 1938; (with Eric Maschwitz) *The First Television Murder,* Hutchinson, 1940; *Beyond Dover, Announcer's Holiday, [and] Africa Flight,* Hutchinson, 1940; *Confident Morning,* Collins, 1943; (editor and author of foreword) *Radio Theatre* (plays written for broadcasting), Macdonald & Co., 1946; *Years of the Locust* (autobiography), Nicholson & Watson, 1947; *The Right Way to Radio Playwriting,* Andrew George Eliot,

1948; *Fall of a Sparrow: The Story of an Adventure,* Collins, 1949, published in America as *Stalking-Horse,* Morrow, 1950; *One Year of Grace* (autobiography), Longmans, Green, 1950; *Special Delivery: The Story of an Adventure,* Collins, 1950; *Ride for a Fall* (novel), Morrow, 1953; *The High Jump* (novel), Collins, 1953; *Cat* (novel), Collins, 1956, Random House, 1957; *British Radio Drama, 1922-1956: A Survey,* Harrap, 1957; *Gallows' Foot,* Collins, 1958; *To Bed at Noon,* Collins, 1959; *And Died So?,* Collins, 1961; *Through a Glass Darkly,* Scribner, 1963 (published in England as *The Goggle-Box Affair,* Collins, 1963); *Prinvest-London,* Collins, 1965; *Years in a Mirror* (autobiography), Bodley Head, 1965; *Cats: A Personal Anthology,* Newnes, 1966; *Conduct of a Member,* Collins, 1967; *A Necessary End,* Collins, 1969; *The Candle-Holders,* Macmillan, 1970; *The Black Sambo Affair,* Macmillan, 1972.

With Holt Marvell: *Under London,* Rich & Cowan, 1933; *London Calling,* Doubleday, 1934 (published in England as *Death at Broadcasting House,* Rich & Cowan, 1934); *Death as an Extra,* Rich & Cowan, 1935; *Death in Budapest,* Rich & Cowan, 1937.

Plays: *Chinese White* (three-act), Rich & Cowan, 1933; (compiler) "Gallipoli" (libretto of a broadcast program), 1936; *Away from It All* (two-act), Sampson Low, 1948; *Party Manners* (three-act comedy), Muller, 1950. Other plays produced: "Iron Curtain," "The Bombshell," "Mediterranean Blue," "Not Enough Tragedy." Adaptor of C.S. Forester's "Hornblower and the Crisis," for radio.

WORK IN PROGRESS: The Sky Suspended, a novel.

AVOCATIONAL INTERESTS: Military history, cats, watching polo, the Dreyfus Case.

* * *

GILBERT, Allan H. 1888-

PERSONAL: Born March 18, 1888, in Rushford, N.Y.; son of Eddy Clifton (a druggist) and Helen Josephine (White) Gilbert; married Katharine Everett, 1913 (died, 1952); married Mary Moss Wellborn, 1953 (died, 1968); children: (first marriage) Everett Eddy, Creighton Eddy. *Education:* Cornell University, B.A., 1909, Ph.D., 1912; Yale University, A.M., 1910. *Home:* 503 Compton Pl., Durham, N.C. 27707; 69 West Ninth St., New York, N.Y. 10011. *Office:* Library, Drew University, Madison, N.J. 07940.

CAREER: Instructor in English at Cornell University, Ithaca, N.Y., 1912-19, Rice University, Houston, Tex., 1919-20; University of Tennessee, Knoxville, professor of English, 1920-21; Duke University, Durham, N.C., started as professor of English, 1921, professor emeritus, 1957—. Visiting professor or lecturer at University of Florence, 1948, Wayne State University, 1957, 1960, University of Southern California, 1958, University of Oregon, 1958-59, University of Pennsylvania, 1959-60, New York University, 1961, Rutgers University, 1961-62, Columbia University, 1962-63, City College of the City University of New York, 1962-63, Drew University, 1963—.

MEMBER: Modern Language Association of America (vice-president, 1955-56; founder of group for literature and arts), American Society of Teachers of Italian (vice-president, 1957-58), American Dante Society, South Atlantic Modern Language Association (president, 1946-47), Southeastern Renaissance Conference (founder; president, 1956), Southern Humanities Association (chairman, 1957), Phi Beta Kappa, Erasmus Club (founder and chairman). *Awards, honors:* Fulbright research grant to Italy, 1955-56; Cavaliere nel Ordine al Merito della Repubblica Italiana, 1967.

WRITINGS: A Geographical Dictionary of Milton, Cornell University Press, 1919; *Dante's Conception of Jus-*

tice, Duke University Press, 1925; *Milton's Art of Logic,* Columbia University Press, 1935; *Machiavelli's Prince and Its Forerunners: The Prince as a Typical Book de Regimine Principum,* Duke University Press, 1938; (editor) *Literary Criticism: Plato to Dryden,* Wayne State University Press, 1940; *On the Composition of Paradise Lost: A Study of the Ordering and Insertion of Material,* University of North Carolina Press, 1947; *The Symbolic Persons in the Masques of Ben Jonson,* Duke University Press, 1948; (editor) *Renaissance Papers* (selection of papers presented at Renaissance Meeting in Southeastern States, Duke University, April 23-24, 1954), University of South Carolina, 1954; *The Principles and Practice of Criticism: Othello, The Merry Wives, Hamlet,* Wayne State University Press, 1959; *Dante and His Comedy,* New York University Press, 1963.

Translator: (And author of introduction and notes) *Machiavelli: The Prince, and Other Works,* Packard & Co., 1941; (and author of introduction and notes) Lodovico Ariosto, *Orlando Furioso,* two volumes, S.F. Vanni, 1954; *Translator or Betrayer?: Some Translations of Dante* (originally published in *Proceedings* of the ICLA Congress in Chapel Hill, N.C.), edited by W.P. Friederich, University of North Carolina Press, 1959; (and editor and author of introduction) *The Letters of Machiavelli: A Selection,* Putnam, 1961; Niccolo Machiavelli, *The Chief Works, and Others,* three volumes, Duke University Press, 1965; (and author of notes) Dante Alighieri, *Inferno* (includes Italian text), Duke University Press, 1969. Contributor of more than one hundred articles on Italian and English Renaissance literature to periodicals.

WORK IN PROGRESS: Aristotle's Poetics Reinterpreted; Plato, Artist in Dialog; and *Plato's Laws,* a new translation with introduction.

* * *

GILBERT, Martin 1936-

PERSONAL: Born October 25, 1936, in London, England; son of Peter (a manufacturing jeweler) and Miriam (Green) Gilbert; married Helen Robinson (a potter), July 29, 1963; children: Natalie. *Education:* Magdalen College, Oxford, B.A. (first class honors), 1960; St. Antony's College, Oxford, graduate research, 1960; Merton College, Oxford, M.A., 1964. *Politics:* Sceptic. *Home:* Merton College, Oxford, England.

CAREER: Merton College, Oxford, England, fellow, and member of governing body, 1962—, official biographer of Sir Winston Churchill, 1968—. University of South Carolina, Columbia, visiting professor, 1965. Research assistant to Randolph S. Churchill on offiicial life of Winston Churchill, 1962-67; consultant on modern history to *Sunday Telegraph,* 1963-64, and to *Sunday Times,* 1967-68. Lecturer on historical topics to schools and universities, 1960—. *Military service:* British Army, student at Joint Service School for Linguists, 1955-57.

WRITINGS: (With Richard Gott) *Anthropologist at Work,* Houghton, 1963; (with Gott) *The Appeasers,* Houghton, 1963, 2nd edition, Weidenfeld & Nicolson, 1967; (editor) *Britain and Germany Between the Wars,* Longmans, Green, 1964, Barnes & Noble, 1966; *The European Powers, 1900-1945,* Weidenfeld & Nicolson, 1965, New American Library, 1966; (editor) *Plough My Own Furrow: The Life of Lord Allen of Hurtwood,* Longmans, Green, 1965; *Recent History Atlas: 1870 to the Present Day,* Weidenfeld & Nicolson, 1966, 2nd edition, 1967, Macmillan, 1968; *The Roots of Appeasement,* Weidenfeld & Nicolson, 1966, New American Library, 1967; (editor) Sir James Robert Dunlop Smith, *Servant of India: A Study of Imperial Rule from 1905 to 1910* (as told through Smith's correspondence and diaries), Longmans, Green, 1966; (editor) *A Century of Conflict, 1850-1950* (essays for A.J.P. Taylor), Hamish Hamilton,

1966, Atheneum, 1967; *Winston Churchill* (Clarendon biography, for grades 6-9), Oxford University Press (London), 1966, Dial, 1967, 2nd edition, Oxford University Press, 1970; (editor) *Churchill* ("Great Lives Observed" series), Prentice-Hall, 1967; (editor) *Lloyd George*, Prentice-Hall, 1968; *British History Atlas*, Weidenfeld & Nicolson, 1968, Macmillan, 1969; *American History Atlas*, Weidenfeld & Nicolson, 1968, Macmillan, 1969; *Jewish History Atlas*, Macmillan, 1969; (editor) *Winston Churchill, 1874-1965*, Grossman, 1969 (published in England as *Winston Churchill: A Collection of Contemporary Documents*, J. Cape, 1969); (editor with Randolph S. Churchill) *Winston S. Churchill: Companion Volume 2* (companion volume to Randolph Churchill's *Winston S. Churchill: Young Statesman, 1901-1914*, Houghton, 1968), Part 1: *1901-1907*, Part 2: *1907-1911*, Part 3: *1911-1914*, Houghton, 1969; *Atlas of World War I*, Macmillan, 1970, reissued as *First World War History Atlas*, 1971; *The Second World War*, Chatto & Windus, 1970; *Winston S. Churchill: Volume 3, 1914-1916*, Houghton, 1971; *Russian History Atlas*, Macmillan, 1972. Contributor of reviews to *History*, *Sunday Telegraph*, *Evening Standard*, and articles to *Sunday Times* (London), *Spiegel* (Hamburg), and *Tworczosz* (Warsaw).

WORK IN PROGRESS: Life of Sir Horace Rumbold.

SIDELIGHTS: Gilbert makes a special effort to travel each year. Between 1957 and 1971, he visited Persia, Afghanistan, Pakistan, India, Egypt, Poland, Bulgaria, Hungary, Rumania, Turkey, and the United States. His second book, *The Appeasers,* was published in four languages. *Avocational interests:* Meeting people.

BIOGRAPHICAL/CRITICAL SOURCES: New York Times Book Review, June 11, 1967; Detroit News, November 28, 1971; Best Sellers, December 15, 1971.

*   *   *

GILBERT, Ruth Gallard Ainsworth 1908-
   (Ruth Ainsworth)

PERSONAL: Born October 16, 1908, in Manchester, England; daughter of Percy Clough (a Methodist minister) and Gertrude (Fisk) Ainsworth; married Frank Lathe Gilbert (managing director of chemical works), March 29, 1935; children: Oliver Lathe, Christopher Gallard, Richard Frank. *Education:* Attended Ipswich High School and Froebel Training Centre, Leicester, England. *Politics:* Labour. *Home:* West Cheynes, Corbridge, Northumberland, England.

CAREER: Writer.

WRITINGS—All juveniles, under name Ruth Ainsworth: *Tales About Tony*, Epworth, 1936; *Mr. Popcorn's Friends*, Epworth, 1938; *The Gingerbread House*, Epworth, 1938; *The Ragamuffins*, Epworth, 1939; *Richard's First Term: A School Story*, Epworth, 1940; *All Different* (poems), Heinemann, 1947; *Five and a Dog*, Epworth, 1949; *Listen with Mother Tales*, Heinemann, 1951; *Rufty Tufty the Golliwog*, Heinemann, 1952; *The Evening Listens* (poems), Heinemann, 1953; *The Ruth Ainsworth Readers*, Books 1-12, Heinemann, 1953-55; *Rufty Tufty at the Seaside*, Heinemann, 1954; *Charles Stories, and Others* (selected from BBC radio program, "Listen with Mother"), Heinemann, 1954; *More About Charles, and Other Stories* (selected from "Listen with Mother" program), Heinemann, 1954; *Three Little Mushrooms* (four puppet plays), Heinemann, 1955; *More Little Mushrooms* (four puppet plays), Heinemann, 1955; *The Snow Bear*, Heinemann, 1956; *Rufty Tufty Goes Camping*, Heinemann, 1956; *Rufty Tufty Runs Away*, Heinemann, 1957; *Five Listen with Mother Tales About Charles*, Adprint, 1957; *Nine Drummers Drumming* (stories), Heinemann,

1958; *Rufty Tufty Flies High*, Heinemann, 1959; *Cherry Stones* (fairy stories), Heinemann, 1960 *Rufty Tufty's Island*, Heinemann, 1960; *Lucky Dip*, Penguin, 1961; *Rufty Tufty and Hattie*, Heinemann, 1962; *Far-Away Children*, Heinemann, 1963, Roy, 1968; *The Ten Tales of Shellover*, Deutsch, 1963, Roy, 1968; *The Wolf Who Was Sorry*, Heinemann, 1964, Roy, 1968; *Rufty Tufty Makes a House*, Heinemann, 1965; *Daisy the Cow*, Hamish Hamilton, 1966; *Horse on Wheels*, Hamish Hamilton, 1966; *Jack Frost*, Heinemann, 1966; *The Look About You Books*, Heinemann, Book 1: *In Woods and Fields*, 1967, Book 2: *Down the Lane*, 1967, Book 3: *Beside the Sea*, 1967, Book 4: *By Pond and Stream*, 1969, Book 5: *In Your Garden*, 1969, Book 6: *In the Park*, 1969; *Roly the Railway Mouse*, Heinemann, 1967, published in America as *Roly the Railroad Mouse*, F. Watts, 1969; *The Aeroplane Who Wanted to See the Sea*, Bancroft & Co., 1968; *Boris the Teddy Bear*, Bancroft & Co., 1968; *Dougal the Donkey*, Bancroft & Co., 1968; *More Tales of Shellover*, Deutsch, 1968, Roy, 1969; *Mungo the Monkey*, Bancroft & Co., 1968; *The Old Fashioned Car*, Bancroft & Co., 1968; *The Rabbit and His Shadow*, Bancroft & Co., 1968; *The Noah's Ark*, Lutterworth, 1969; *The Bicycle Wheel*, Hamish Hamilton, 1969; *Look, Do and Listen* (anthology), F. Watts, 1969; (editor) *Book of Colours and Sounds*, Purnell Juvenile, 1969; *The Ruth Ainsworth Book* (stories), F. Watts, 1970.

Educational books, under name Ruth Ainsworth, with Ronald Ridout: *Look Ahead Readers*, Books 1-8 (includes supplementary readers for each book), Heinemann, 1956-58; *Books for Me to Read*, six volumes, Bancroft & Co., 1964; *Bancroft Red Books* (includes *Jill and Peter, House of Hay, Come and Play, Name of My Own, Duck That Ran Away*, and *Tim's Hoop*), Bancroft & Co., 1965; *Bancroft Blue Books* (includes *At the Zoo, What Are They?, Colors, Silly Billy, Jane and John*, and *Pony, Pony*), Bancroft & Co., 1965; *Bancroft Green Books* (includes *Susan's House, What Can You Hear?, Tim's Kite, Flippy the Frog, Huff the Hedgehog*, and *A House for a Mouse*), Bancroft & Co., 1965, each book also published separately by Initial Teaching Publishing Co., 1968; *Dandy the Donkey*, Bancroft & Co., 1971; *The Wild Wood*, Bancroft & Co., 1971. Writer of puppet plays and stories for television. Contributor of stories to British Broadcasting Corp., programs (also broadcast in Australia and New Zealand), "Listen with Mother" and "English for Schools."

*   *   *

GILBERTSON, Merrill Thomas 1911-

PERSONAL: Born June 28, 1911, in Avoca, Wis.; son of Thomas (a farmer) and Maria (Husam) Gilbertson; married Olga Coltvet, June 26, 1942; children: Mary, Ruth, Lois. *Education:* University of Wisconsin, B.A., 1938; Luther Theological Seminary, C.T., 1942; Biblical Seminary in New York and Union Theological Seminary, M.R.E., 1951. *Home:* 4020 Quincy N.E., Minneapolis, Minn. 55421. *Office:* First Lutheran Church, 4000 Quincy N.E., Minneapolis, Minn. 55421.

CAREER: Lutheran minister; pastor of Lutheran churches in Joplin, Mont., 1942-47, and Butte, Mont., 1947-49; Waldorf College, Forest City, Iowa, professor of religion, 1949-57; Grace Lutheran Church, Albert Lea, Minn., pastor, 1957-66; First Lutheran Church, Minneapolis, Minn., pastor, 1966—. Rocky Mountain District Luther League, president, 1947-49.

WRITINGS: The Way It Was in Bible Times, Augsburg, 1959; *Where It Happened in Bible Times* (sequel to *The Way It Was in Bible Times*), edited by Harriet L. Oberholt, Augsburg, 1963; *Uncovering Bible Times: A Study in Biblical Archaeology*, Augsburg, 1968.

GILBRETH, Frank B., Jr. 1911-

PERSONAL: Born March 17, 1911; son of Frank Bunker (a scientific management engineer) and Lillian Evelyn (an engineer, professor, and author; maiden name, Moller) Gilbreth; married Elizabeth Cauthen September 9, 1934 (died, 1954); married Mary Manigault, June 4, 1955; children: (first marriage) Betsy; (second marriage) Edward M., Rebecca. Education: Attended St. Johns College, 1928-29; University of Michigan, B.A., 1933. Home: 430 Maybank Hwy. Charleston, S.C. 29412. Office: Post-Courier, 134 Columbus St., Charleston, S.C. 29402. Agent: Paul R. Reynolds, 599 Fifth Ave., New York, N.Y. 10017; McIntosh & Otis, 18 East 41st St., New York, N.Y. 10017.

CAREER: Worker as reporter for New York Herald Tribune, New York, N.Y., Associated Press, and Buenos Aires Herald before joining staffs of The News and Courier, and The Evening Post, Charleston, S.C., in 1947, where is is now vice-president and assistant publisher. Military service: U.S. Navy, 1942-45; aerial photographer, and onetime aide to admiral in South Pacific; became lieutenant commander; received Bronze Star and Air Medal.

WRITINGS: (With sister, Ernestine Carey) Cheaper by the Dozen, Crowell, 1948, expanded edition, 1963; (with Ernestine Carey) Belles on Their Toes, Crowell, 1950; I'm a Lucky Guy, Crowell, 1951; (with John Held, Jr.) Held's Angels, Crowell, 1952; Innside Nantucket, Crowell, 1954; Of Whales and Women: One Man's View of Nantucket History, Crowell, 1956; How to Be a Father, Crowell, 1958; Loblolly, Crowell, 1960; He's My Boy (biography of son, Teddy), Dodd, 1962; Time Out for Happiness (biography of parents), Crowell, 1971.

SIDELIGHTS: Frank Gilbreth, Jr., and his sister wrote a best seller about their own family—the already widely known senior Gilbreths, and their six sons and six daughters—in Cheaper by the Dozen; a dramatized version by Christopher Sergei was issued by Dramatic Publishing in 1950. Belles on Their Toes also describes his family life. Both books were filmed by 20th Century-Fox.

BIOGRAPHICAL/CRITICAL SOURCES: Writings of the Gilbreths, Irwin, 1953; New York Times, February 4, 1962; Best Sellers, February 15, 1971.

* * *

GILDEN, Katya
(K.B. Gilden, joint pseudonym with Bert Gilden)

PERSONAL: Born in Bangor, Me.; married Bert Gilden (publicist and writer, with whom she collaborated), 1947 (died, 1971); children: David Ethan, Jairus Matthew, Daniel Mordecai. Education: Radcliffe College, A.B., 1936. Home: 250 Algonquin Rd., Fairfield, Conn. 06604. Agent: Peter Matson, 22 East 40th St., New York, N.Y.

CAREER: Formerly a fashion copywriter, and information and research director for the overseas relief division of the Unitarian Service Committee. Lived in Harlem with six different Negro families on a writing-research project, 1940-43; also worked with the U.S.O., developing an interracial program for G.I.'s. Co-founder of Van Wyck Brooks Memorial Awards. Member: Authors' Guild, Connecticut Civil Liberties Union, Fairfield County Board.

WRITINGS—With Bert Gilden, under pseudonym K.B. Gilden: Hurry Sundown (novel; Literary Guild selection), Doubleday, 1965; Between the Hills and the Sea (novel; Literary Guild alternate selection), Doubleday, 1971. Collaborator with Ber. Gilden on many short stories, an original screenplay, and four television scripts.

WORK IN PROGRESS: A Naked Man at the Door, a novel; a volume of short stories.

SIDELIGHTS: Mrs. Gilden's books have been published in several other countries. Hurry Sundown was filmed by Paramount, 1967. Avocational interests: Political and scientific developments; camping in United States and Canada.

* * *

GILL, Evan Robertson 1892-

PERSONAL: Born April 24, 1892, in Brighton, Sussex, England; son of Arthur Tidman (a clergyman) and Cicely Rose (King) Gill; married Mabel Rimmer, September 20, 1921; children: Francis Peter, John Michael, Susan Mary Gill Stiff. Education: Educated in private schools in Bognor Regis, Sussex, England. Politics: Conservative. Religion: Church of England. Home: 67 A Hanger Lane Ealing, London W.5, England.

CAREER: Associated with Law, Guarantee, Trust & Accident Society Ltd., London, England, 1907-11, Imperial Bank of Canada, Fernie, British Columbia, and Regina, Saskatchewan, 1911-14; Spillers Ltd. (flour millers), Liverpool, England, head of costings and statistical department, 1920-55. School manager, Liverpool Education Committee. Military service: Canadian Field Artillery Reserve, 1912-20, active service in France and Belgium, 1915-18; twice wounded; became lieutenant. Member: Royal Philatelic Society (fellow), Liverpool Philatelic Society (former president, vice-president, and secretary; librarian, 1921—). Awards, honors: Medals for international and national philatelic exhibitions for exhibit of Papua, at London, 1950, New York, 1956, Sydney, 1959, London, 1960, and Melbourne, 1963.

WRITINGS: Bibliography of Eric Gill, Cassell, 1953; New Guinea: Catalogue of Books Relating to New Guinea (But with Special Reference to Papua) in the Library of Evan R. Gill, privately printed, 1957; The Inscriptional Work of Eric Gill: An Inventory, Cassell, 1964, Dufour, 1965. Contributor to philatelic journals on the stamps and postal history of Papua.

* * *

GILL, Joseph 1901-

PERSONAL: Born November 8, 1901, in Killamarsh, England; son of Daniel (a coal mining official) and Charlotte (Roddis) Gill. Education: Studied in England at St. Michael's College, St. Mary's Hall, Heythrop College; University College, London, B.A., 1924, B.A. (honors in Greek and Latin), 1938, Ph.D. 1949; Gregorian University Ph.D., 1926. S.T.L., 1933. Home: Campion Hall, Oxford OX1 1QS, England.

CAREER: Entered Society of Jesus (Jesuits), 1918, ordained Roman Catholic priest; Pontifical Oriental Institute, Rome, Italy, professor of Byzantine history and Byzantine Greek, 1938-39, 1946-66, rector, 1962-67; Gregorian University, Rome, Italy, professor of Anglican theology, 1948-66; Heythrop College, Chipping Norton, England, professor, 1968—. Military service: Royal Air Force, chaplain, 1940-46; mentioned in dispatches.

WRITINGS: La Chiesa Anglicana, Instituto Editoriale Galileo, 1948; (editor) Quae supersunt Actorum graecorum Concilii Florentini, Pontificium Institutum Orientalium Studiorum, 1953; The Council of Florence, Cambridge University Press, 1959, 2nd edition, 1961; Eugenius IV, Pope of Christian Union, Newman, 1961; (with Edmund Flood) The Orthodox: Their Relations with Rome, Paulist Press, 1964; Personalities of the Council of Florence, and Other Essays, Basil Blackwell, 1964, Barnes & Noble, 1965; Orationes Georgii Scholarii in Concilio Florentino habitae, Pontificium Institutum

Orientalium Studiorum, 1964; *Constance et Bale-Florence* (history of the 9th Ecumenical Council), l'Orante, 1965.

Contributor: A. Piolanti, *Il Protestantesimo ieri e oggi*, F. Ferrari, 1958; C. Boyer, *Il Problema ecumenico oggi*, Editrice Queriniana, 1960; *Le Concile et les conciles*, Editions du Cerf, 1960; *L'Unita della Chiesa*, Vita e Pensiero, 1962; Wilhelm de Vries, *Rom und die Patriarchate des Ostens*, Karl Alber, 1963; Ivanka, Tyciak and Wiertz, editors, *Handbuch der Ostkirchenkunde*, Patmos-Verlag, 1970. Contributor of articles to encyclopedias and historical journals.

WORK IN PROGRESS: Byzantium and Rome, 1200-1400: A Study in Church Relations.

*   *   *

GILSTRAP, Robert L(awrence)   1933-

PERSONAL: Born August 10, 1933, in Marshall, Tex.; son of J.D. (in advertising) and Elizabeth (Cabbiness) Gilstrap; married Dorothy Ann Barclay, November 28, 1964; children: Greg, Guy. *Education:* Kilgore College, A.A., 1953; North Texas State University, B.S., 1954, M.Ed., 1960; George Peabody College for Teachers, Ed.D., 1963. *Religion:* Catholic. *Home:* 505 Holland St., Marshall, Tex. 75670.

CAREER: North Texas State University, Laboratory School, Denton, instructor in elementary education, 1958-60; San Leandro (Calif.) Public Schools, instructor, 1960-61; University of Florida, Gainesville, assistant professor of elementary education, 1963-66; National Education Association, American Association of Elementary-Kindergarten-Nursery Educators, Washington, D.C., executive secretary and director of publications, 1966-71; University of Virginia, George Mason College, Fairfax, associate professor of elementary education, 1971—. *Military service:* U.S. Air Force, Information Services, 1954-58. *Member:* National Education Association, National Council of Teachers of English, American Association of Elementary-Kindergarten-Nursery Educators, Association of Teacher Educators.

WRITINGS: (With Irene Estabrook) *The Sultan's Fool, and Other North African Tales*, Holt, 1958; *Ten Texas Tales*, Steck, 1963; (with Rembert W. Patrick) *New Land, New Lives: The Story of Our Country's Beginning*, Steck, 1967. Author of "Guiding the Student Teaching Process," an educational television series for teachers in the University of Florida student teaching program, 1966. Contributor of reviews and articles to professional journals, and short stories to church publications.

WORK IN PROGRESS: The Tricky Turtle and Other American Animal Tales; A Day in the Life of Greg and Guy, a guide for parents of pre-school children.

SIDELIGHTS: The Sultan's Fool, and Other North African Tales has been published in Arabic.

*   *   *

GILZEAN, Elizabeth Houghton Blanchet   1913-
(Elizabeth Houghton, Mary Hunton)

PERSONAL: Born March 1, 1913, in Lachine, Montreal, Quebec, Canada; daughter of Geoffrey Orme (a banker) and Muriel Wylie (Liffiton) Blanchet; married Stanley John Gilzean, February 15, 1940 (deceased); children: Brian John, Sandra Elizabeth. *Education:* Attended Convent of Sacred Heart, Vancouver, British Columbia, and Ottawa Model School. *Politics:* Conservative. *Religion:* Church of England. *Home:* Lletty's Hwsmon, Llanfachreth, Dolgellau, Merioneth, Wales. *Agent:* Gerald Pollinger, 18 Maddox St., London WIR OEU, England.

CAREER: Nurse in Canada and England, 1930-56; writer, 1956—. Also building restorer and interior decora-

tor in Dolgellou, Wales. *Member:* 'Rendy-Vous' Postal-Women Writers' Group.

WRITINGS—All published by Mills & Boon, except as indicated: *Next Patient, Doctor Anne*, 1958; *On Call, Sister!*, 1959; *Love From a Surgeon*, 1959; *Staff Nurse at St. Laura's*, 1959; *Sister Maclean Goes West*, 1959; *The Healing Word*, 1960; *Another Child for Sister Lorraine*, 1960; *A Yankee Surgeon at St. Bride's*, 1961; *Sister Kate of Outpatients*, 1961; *Senior Surgeon at St. David's*, 1962; *Sister Grant's Last Case*, 1962; *A Baby for Doctor Jane*, 1963; *Arctic Nurse*, 1963; *Something to Do at Home: Hobbies, Crafts, and Gainful Occupations*, Soccer, 1964; *No Place for Surgeons*, 1965; *Doctor of Mercy*, 1965; *Sister Mary's Babies*, 1966; *The Rebellion of Nurse Smith*, 1967; *Murder on Sundays*, R. Hale, 1967; *Marriage Problems*, Corgi, 1967, published in America as *Why Marriages Fail*, Bantam, 1968; *Hobbies for Women*, Corgi, 1967; *Coins: A Collector's Guide*, Corgi, 1970; *Doctors Don't Cry*, 1971.

Under pseudonym Elizabeth Houghton; all published by Mills & Boon, except as indicated: *A Sister in the Backwoods*, 1959, *Staff Nurse in the Tyrol*, 1960, *Dr. Sara Comes Home*, 1961, *Love for the Matron*, 1961, *Surgeon for Tonight*, 1962, *Part-Time Angel*, 1964, *Simon Dane, Doctor of Research*, 1965, *Return of Sister Barnett*, 1966, Pocket Books, 1971, *New Surgeon at St. Lucien's*, 1966, *The Stubborn Doctor Stephens*, 1967.

Under pseudonym Mary Hunton; all published by Mills & Boon: *Nurse Blade's First Week*, 1961, *Surgeons at Arms*, 1962, *House Surgeon at St. Anne's*, 1963, *Maple Leaves are Lucky*, 1965, *Sister for Tomorrow*, 1966.

Contributor to *Good Housekeeping Encyclopaedia of Family Health*, National Magazine Co., 1956, and to newspapers and magazines.

WORK IN PROGRESS: A novel, *For Love of Doctor Jonathan;* nonfiction, *Stories from Gingerbread;* and case studies in self-help among 'group' for one-parent families.

*   *   *

GIOVANNETTI, Alberto   1913-

PERSONAL: Born July 20, 1913, in Rome, Italy; son of Francesco (a farmer) and Vittoria (Aloisi) Giovannetti. *Education:* Attended Gregorian University, 1940-44, and Pontificial Academy for Diplomacy, Rome, Italy, 1943-45. *Home:* 315 East 47th St., New York, N.Y. 10017. *Office:* 323 East 47th St., New York, N.Y. 10017.

CAREER: Roman Catholic priest, now domestic prelate of Pope Paul VI with title of right reverend monsignor. Teacher and managing editor of Catholic periodical, 1935-40; diplomatic post as attache to papal nunciature in Germany, 1945-48; now permanent observer of the Holy See to the United Nations. *Awards, honors:* Commander of Italian Republic.

WRITINGS: The Red Book of the Persecuted Church, Newman, 1957; (editor) *Pio XII parla alla chiesa del silenzio*, Editrice Ancora, 1958; *We Have a Pope: A Portrait of His Holiness John XXIII*, translation by John Chapin, Newman, 1959; *Il Vaticano e la guerra*, Citta del Vaticano, 1960; *Roma, citta aperta*, Editrice Ancora, 1962; *Il Palazzo é di Vetro*, Coines (Rome), 1971. Contributor to *L'Osservatore Romano* and *Citta del Vaticano*.

*   *   *

GIRARD, Rene N(oel)   1923-

PERSONAL: Born December 25, 1923, in Avignon, France; son of Joseph and Therese (Fabre) Girard; married Martha V. McCullough, June 18, 1951; children: Martin J., Daniel C., Mary P. *Education:* Ecole Nationale des Chartes, Sorbonne, University of Paris, Archiviste-paleographe, 1947; Indiana University, Ph.D., 1950. *Home:* 126 Kandahar Dr., East Aurora, N.Y. 14052. *Office:* Department of Art and Letters, State University of New York College at Buffalo, Buffalo, N.Y.

CAREER: Indiana University, Bloomington, instructor in French, 1947-52; Duke University, Durham, N.C., instructor in French, 1952-53; Bryn Mawr College, Bryn Mawr, Pa., assistant professor of French, 1953-57; Johns Hopkins University, Baltimore, Md., associate professor, 1957-61, professor of French, 1961-68; State University of New York College at Buffalo, professor in faculty of arts and letters, 1968—. Institut d'Etudes Francaises d'-Avignon, professor, 1962—. *Member:* Modern Language Association of America (executive council, 1969—).

WRITINGS: Mensonge romantique et verite romanesque, Grasset, 1961, translation by Yvonne Freccero published in America as *Deceit, Desire and the Novel,* Johns Hopkins Press, 1965; *Marion, la mal aimee* (novel), R. Solar, 1962; (editor) *Proust: A Collection of Critical Essays,* Prentice-Hall, 1962; *Dostoievsky: Du double a l'unite,* Plon, 1963; *Lenz, 1751-1792: Genese d'une dramaturgie du tragicomique,* C. Klincksieck, 1968.

BIOGRAPHICAL/CRITICAL SOURCES: Partisan Review, fall, 1968.

*　　*　　*

GIRTIN, Thomas 1913-
(Tom Girtin)

PERSONAL: Born July 25, 1913, in London, England; son of Thomas and Sabina (Cooper) Girtin; married Mary Monica Don, October 14, 1944. *Education:* Attended Shrewsbury School; Pembroke College, Cambridge, B.A., 1935, M.A., 1948. *Politics:* Independent. *Religion:* Catholic. *Home:* 19 Montpelier Sq., London S.W.7, England. *Agent:* Fraser & Dulop Ltd., Regent St., London W.1, England. *Office:* Tom Girtin Publications Ltd., 19 Montpelier Sq., London S.W.7, England.

CAREER: Taylor & Humbert, Solicitors, London, England, articled clerk, 1935-37; Gordon Harbord Literary Agency, London, partner, 1937-39; full-time writer in Sussex, England, 1945-47; White Horse Public House, Longford, Middlesex, England, proprietor, 1947-54; full-time writer in London, England, 1954—. Freeman, City of London; liveryman, Clothworkers' Company. *Military service:* British Army, Royal Artillery, 1939-45; official historian, Anti-Aircraft Command, 1944-45; became captain. *Member:* Royal Historical Society, (fellow), Society of Authors, P.E.N., Garrick Club (London).

WRITINGS: Lord Mayor of London, Oxford University Press, 1948; *Come, Landlord!,* Hutchinson, 1957; *The Golden Ram: A Narrative History of the Clothworkers' Company, 1528-1958,* Hutchinson, 1958; *Not Entirely Serious,* Hutchinson, 1958; *Doctor with Two Aunts. A Biography of Dr. John Wolcot* (Peter Pindar), Hutchinson, 1959; *Nothing but the Best: The Tradition of English Craftsmen from Edwardian to Elizabethan,* Obolensky, 1959, Astor-Honor, 1960; *Unnatural Break: A Commercial Novel,* Hutchinson, 1959; *Makers of Distinction: Suppliers to the Town and Country Gentleman,* Harvill, 1959; *In Love and Unity: A Book About Brushmaking,* Hutchinson, 1961; *The Abominable Clubman,* Hutchinson, 1964; *The Triple Crowns: A Narrative History of the Drapers' Company, 1364-1964,* Hutchinson, 1964. Ghost writer of two autobiographies; contributor to *Punch* and other periodicals, and to British Broadcasting Corp. programs.

WORK IN PROGRESS: Death in the Loving Cup.

SIDELIGHTS: Originally a humorous writer, Girtin is now more involved in histories. He researches in London, and does a large part of his writing in a medieval house in a tiny village in Provence, insulated from most modern distractions. *Avocational interests:* Early English watercolors, auction sales, singing polyphony in a small choir.

*　　*　　*

GLASSER, Allen 1918-

PERSONAL: Born September 4, 1918, in New York, N.Y.; son of Abraham Barnett and Julia (Joseph) Glasser; married Selma Goldstein, November 18, 1948; children: Gary Thomas, Gloria Iris. *Education:* Educated in New York public schools. *Home:* 241 Dahill Rd., Brooklyn, N.Y. 1128. *Office:* O'Brien Communications Ltd., 155 East 44th St., New York, N.Y. 10017.

CAREER: American Management Association (business publications), New York, N.Y., editorial assistant, 1946-54; Cantor Publications, Inc. (trade magazine publishing), New York, N.Y., production manager, 1954-67; *1001 Decorating Ideas* (consumer magazine), New York, N.Y., production editor, 1967-69; *Inside News* (weekly newspaper), New York, N.Y., staff writer, 1969-70; O'Brien Communications Ltd. (trade magazine publisher), New York, N.Y., managing editor, 1970—. *Member:* Association of Publication Production Managers, National Contesters Association (convention chairman, 1960), The Productioneers, Brooklyn Contest Club (president, 1958, 1962). *Awards, honors:* First prize, Mars advertising contest, 1954; first prize, *New York Daily News* caption contest, 1958; second prize, National Safety Council contest, 1963; poetry medal, Freedoms Foundation, 1964.

WRITINGS: Fell's Official Guide to Prize Contests and How to Win Them, Fell, 1963; *Analogy Anthology,* A.D. Freese & Sons, 1964. Columnist, *Men's Digest, National Insider, Rogue Magazine.* Contributor to *Saturday Review, Science Digest, True, Playboy, Harvest Years, Sexology, Coronet, National Enquirer.*

WORK IN PROGRESS: A collection in book form of syndicated astrology feature, "Star Stanzas," a series of rhymed horoscopes.

*　　*　　*

GLAZIER, Kenneth MacLean 1912-

PERSONAL: Born September 21, 1912, in Carnduff, Saskatchewan, Canada; son of Harry MacLean (a merchant) and Martha (Heslip) Glazier; married Teresa Ferster (a teacher), August 2, 1940; children: Gretchen, Christopher, Kenneth. *Education:* University of Toronto, B.A., 1936; Union Theological Seminary, New York, N.Y., B.D., 1939; Yale University, M.A., 1942, Ph.D., 1944; University of California, Berkeley, M.L.S., 1962. *Home:* 763 Esplanada Way, Stanford, Calif. 94305. *Office:* Hoover Institution, Stanford University, Stanford, Calif. 94305.

CAREER: Presbyterian minister; Glenview Presbyterian Church, Toronto, Ontario, minister, 1946-59; Canadian Missions Schools, Georgetown, British Guiana, manager, 1960-61; Stanford University, Hoover Institution, Stanford, Calif., deputy curator of Africa collection, 1962-65, librarian, 1965—. *Member:* American Library Association, Society of American Archivists, Canadian American Association.

WRITINGS: (With Peter Duignan) *A Checklist of Serials for African Studies,* Hoover Institution, Stanford University, 1963; *Africa South of the Sahara: A Select and Annotated Bibliography,* Hoover Institution, Stanford University, Book 1: *1958-63,* 1964, Book 2: *1964-68,* 1969; (with James R. Hobson) *International and English-*

Language Collections: A Survey of Holdings at the Hoover Institution on War, Revolution and Peace, Hoover Institution Press, 1971. Writer of regular column, "Recent Reference Works on Africa," in *Africana Newsletter.*

WORK IN PROGRESS: *Canadians in the United States,* a study of the influence of the Canadians on the American scene.

* * *

GLEADOW, Rupert Seeley   1909-
   (Justin Case)

PERSONAL: Born January 22, 1909, in Leicester, England; son of Frank and Mary Phyllis (Seeley) Gleadow; married Marguerite Rendu; married second wife, Helen Cooke (a painter and theatrical designer), June 21, 1940; children: (first marriage) Sylvie. *Education:* Trinity College, Oxford, M.A., 1933. *Religion:* Polytheist. *Home:* 18 Lawrence St., London S.W.3, England.

WRITINGS: *Astrology in Everyday Life,* Faber, 1940, McKay, 1941; *Magic and Divination,* Faber, 1941; *The Gorilla and the Angel* (poems), Fortune Press, 1948; (editor) Cyril Fagan, *Ephemeris,* new edition, Robert Anscombe & Co., 1949; *The Unclouded Eye: An Exploration Among the Roots of Religion,* Skeffington & Son, 1953; *Your Character in the Zodiac,* Phoenix House, 1968, Funk, 1970; *The Origin of the Zodiac,* J. Cape, 1968, Atheneum, 1969. Translator from the German and French for encyclopedias. Contributor to *American Astrology, Spica, Aquarian Agent, Poetry London,* and *Jubilee.*

WORK IN PROGRESS: *Meaning Is the Only Reality.*

SIDELIGHTS: Gleadow is an authority on magic and the Kabalah; he has a continuing interest in the evidence for reincarnation.

BIOGRAPHICAL/CRITICAL SOURCES: *Library Journal,* July, 1969, May 15, 1970; *Virginia Quarterly Review,* autumn, 1969.

* * *

GLEAVES, Suzanne   1904-

PERSONAL: Born October 13, 1904, in New York, N.Y.; daughter of Edward (an opera manager) and Suzanne (Van Valkenburg) Ziegler; married Charles Lucian Gleaves (present of American Land Co.), December 6, 1933; children: Susan (Mrs. Timothy Simon). *Education:* Primary and grammar school. *Politics:* Republican. *Religion:* Episcopalian. *Home and office:* 220 East 61st St., New York, N.Y. 10021. *Agent:* Paul R. Reynolds, Inc., 599 Fifth Ave., New York, N.Y. 10017.

CAREER: Started doing editorial work on magazines in 1926 and became copy editor, editor, or managing editor of various periodicals, including *House and Garden, Vanity Fair, House and Home, House Beautiful, Interiors, Cue, Popular Gardening, Harper's Bazaar,* 1926-58; free-lance writer, 1958—. *Member:* Cosmopolitan Club.

WRITINGS—All with Lael Wertenbaker: *Tip and Dip,* Lippincott, 1960; *You and the Armed Services: An Up-to-Date Guide to Selective Service, the Draft, and Enlistment,* Simon & Schuster, 1961; *Mercy Percy,* Lippincott, 1961; *Rhyming Word Games,* Simon & Schuster, 1964; (editor with Wertenbaker) William Bertalen, *A Ship Called Hope,* Dutton, 1964; (with Lane Lee) *I Gathered the Bright Days: A Courageous Woman's Story of Her Family, Struggles, and Triumphs,* Dial, 1973. Editor and reviser of other books.

* * *

GLEESON, Ruth (Ryall)   1925-

PERSONAL: Born October 11, 1925, in Sparta, Wis.; daughter of Ernest V. (a county agricultural agent) and

Henrietta (Achtenberg) Ryall; married Frederick W. Gleeson, August 6, 1953 (deceased). *Education:* University of Wisconsin, B.A., 1948. *Politics:* Democrat. *Religion:* Unitarian. *Home:* 11483 Hessler Rd., Cleveland, Ohio 44106.

CAREER: Continuity writer at radio station in Janesville, Wis., 1948; *Kenosha News,* Kenosha, Wis., reporter, 1949-52; free-lance research writer in partnership with husband, 1958-62; Case Western Reserve University, Cleveland, Ohio, research assistant, 1962—. *Member:* American Sociological Association, Society for the Study of Social Problems, Ohio Valley Sociological Society.

WRITINGS: (With James Colvin) *Words Most Often Misspelled and Mispronounced,* Pocket Books, 1963.

WORK IN PROGRESS: *Predictors and Non-Predictors of Upward Mobility,* report on high school talent study.

* * *

GLENN, Jacob B.   1905-

PERSONAL: Born May 2, 1905; son of Moses J. (a rabbi) and Treine (Tcherback) Glenn; married Elizabeth Hampel; children: Melvyn H., Gabriel R., David J. *Education:* University of Pittsburgh, B.S., 1929; Columbia University, M.A., 1931; postgraduate study at University of Vienna and University of Zurich, 1933-40. *Religion:* Hebrew. *Office:* 201 Brighton I Rd., Brooklyn, N.Y. 11235.

CAREER: Formerly with New York City (N.Y.) Department of Hospitals as assistant hospital administrator. Physician in private practice. Lecturer. *Member:* Kings County Medical Society, Manhattan Beach Jewish Center. *Awards, honors:* Maimonides Award, Chicago, 1968.

WRITINGS: *Asphyxia Sub Partu,* Verlag Karger, 1941; *The Bible and Modern Medicine* (originally published in *Jewish Forum,* 1958), Jewish Forum, 1959, reissued as *The Bible and Modern Medicine: An Interpretation of the Basic Principles of the Bible in the Light of Present Day Medical Thought,* Bloch, 1963; *Zu Gesunt und zu Leben,* Shulsinger, c.1970. Contributing editor, *Das Israel-itische Wochenblatt* (Zurich), 1938-44, *Syn Light,* 1955—; staff medical writer, *Forward* (Jewish daily); staff writer, *Jewish Press.*

* * *

GLOVER, Leland E (llis)   1917-

PERSONAL: Born November 13, 1917, in Satanta, Kan.; son of Ed Hanley (a rancher) and Mary Elizabeth (Burton) Glover; married Jeanne Dunford, August 3, 1951; children: Mary Beth, Robert Edward, Julie Ann. *Education:* Stanford University, A.B., 1939, M.A., 1940; University of Southern California, Ph.D., 1950. *Religion:* Presbyterian. *Home:* 8544 East Fairview Ave., San Gabriel, Calif. 91775. *Agent:* August Lenniger, Literary Agency, 11 West 42nd St., New York, N.Y. 10036. *Office:* Los Angeles County Schools Office, 155 West Washington, Los Angeles, Calif. 90015.

CAREER: Teacher and counselor in public schools in Redwood City, Oakdale, and Long Beach, Calif., 1940-43; U.S. Veterans Administration, Los Angeles, Calif., counselor, 1946-48; Office of Los Angeles County Superintendent of Schools, Los Angeles, Calif., research and guidance consultant, 1950—. Lecturer at University of Southern California, Occidental College, Claremont Graduate School, California State College at Los Angeles, and University of California, Los Angeles. Host and participant on "Paging Parents," syndicated public service television series. *Military service:* U.S. Army Air Forces, 1943-46. *Member:* American Association of Marriage Counselors, American Psychological Association, National Council on Family Relations, National Congress of

Parents and Teachers, National Education Association, California Congress of Parents and Teachers (life), California Teachers Association, Los Angeles County Psychological Association.

WRITINGS: Sex Life of the Modern Adult, Belmont Books, 1961; *Sex Life of the Modern Teen-Ager: A New Report,* Belmont Books, 1961; *How to Give Your Child a Good Start in Life,* Collier, 1962; *How to Help Your Teen-Ager Grow Up,* Collier, 1962; *The Impotent Male,* Monarch Books, 1963; *How to Marry Someone You Can Live With All Your Life,* Prentice-Hall, 1964; *How Do You Feel About Sex?,* Gold Medal Books, 1964; *How to Guide Your School-age Child,* Collier, 1965. Writer of about one hundred public service television programs, including "Paging Parents."

WORK IN PROGRESS: A book on remarriage, for Odyssey; a book on early marital adjustment.

*   *   *

GLUBB, John Bagot   1897-

PERSONAL: Born April 16, 1897, in Preston, England; son of Frederick Manley (a general, British Army) and Frances Letitia (Bagot) Glubb; married Rosemary Forbes, August 20, 1938; children: Godfrey, Naomi, Mary, John. *Education:* Attended Cheltenham College and Royal Military Academy at Woolwich. *Religion:* Church of England. *Home:* Westwood, Mayfield, Sussex, England.

CAREER: British Army, Royal Engineers, regular officer, 1915-26, serving on Western Front in France and Belgium, 1915-18 (wounded three times), in Iraq, 1920-26; became captain; resigned, 1926. Iraq Government, administrative inspector, 1926-30. Transjordan (now Jordan) Army, officer commanding desert area, 1930-38, chief of staff (in effect, commanding general since king was titular commander) of Arab Legion, 1938-56; became lieutenant general. *Awards, honors:* Military Cross, World War I; Knight Commander of the Bath; Commander of the Order of St. Michael and St. George; Distinguished Service Order; Order of the British Empire, Rafidain (Iraq); Jordan orders of Istiqlal and Nahdha, first class; Knight of the Order of St. John of Jerusalem.

WRITINGS: (With Henry Field) *The Yezidis, Sulubba, and Other Tribes of Iraq and Adjacent Regions,* G. Banta, 1943; *The Story of the Arab Legion,* Hodder & Stoughton, 1948; (author of foreword) Godfrey Lias, *Glubb's Legion,* Evans Brothers, 1956; *A Soldier with the Arabs,* Harper, 1957; *The British and the Arabs: A Study of Fifty Years, 1908 to 1958,* Hodder & Stoughton, 1959; *War in the Desert: An R.A.F. Frontier Campaign,* Hodder & Stoughton, 1960, Norton, 1961; *The Great Arab Conquests,* Hodder & Stoughton, 1963, Prentice-Hall, 1964; *The Empire of the Arabs,* Hodder & Stoughton, 1963, Prentice-Hall, 1965; *The Course of Empire: The Arabs and Their Successors,* Hodder & Stoughton, 1965, Prentice-Hall, 1966; *The Lost Centuries: From the Muslim Empires to the Renaissance of Europe, 1145-1453,* Prentice-Hall, 1967; *Syria, Lebanon and Jordan,* Walker & Co., 1967; *The Mixture of Races in the Eastern Arab Countries* (lecture given at New College, Oxford, April 25, 1967), Blackwell Bookshop, 1967; *The Middle East Crisis: A Personal Interpretation,* Hodder & Stoughton, 1967; *A Short History of the Arab Peoples,* Stein & Day, 1969; *The Life and Times of Muhammad,* Stein & Day, 1970; *Peace in the Holy Land: An Historical Analysis of the Palestine Problem,* Hodder & Stoughton, 1971.

WORK IN PROGRESS: Continuation of series on Arab history.

SIDELIGHTS: Glubb's thirteenth study on the military and political history of the Islamic empires, *The Life and Times of Muhammad* "reveals the simple and open reflections of the soldier-author," as Reverend James M. Murphy wrote in a review for *Best Sellers.* "This is not the work of a professional historian. Had it been so it would have been a worthless book. By Glubb's own confession, it is a popular work." C.M. Woodhouse calls the book "more than a mere biography. . . . Fourteen years ago Sir John Glubb was dismissed from his post as Commander of the Arab Legion with peremptory and brutal discourtesy. . . . Such treatment as Glubb Pasha received in the country of his adoption would have led to a blood-feud lasting many generations if he had been himself a Jordanian. This is just one symptom of the gulf which separates even so sympathetic an observer as Sir John from the people he knows so well. He writes from the point of view of an outsider who can profoundly understand and brilliantly interpret their philosophy of life, but does not share it."

BIOGRAPHICAL/CRITICAL SOURCES: New Yorker, March 30, 1968; *Library Journal,* June 1, 1969, March 15, 1970; *Spectator,* March 28, 1970; *Best Sellers,* June 1, 1970.

*   *   *

GLUCKMAN, Max   1911-

PERSONAL: Born January 26, 1911, in Johannesburg, South Africa; son of Emmanuel and Kate (Cohen) Gluckman; married Mary Brignoli (a research assistant), June 23, 1939; children: John, Peter, Timothy. *Education:* University of the Witwatersrand, B.A., 1930, B.A. (honors), 1934; Exeter College, Oxford, D.Phil., 1936, postdoctoral study, 1938-39. *Politics:* Labour. *Religion:* Jewish. *Home:* Sheen, Ladybrook Rd., Bramhall, Cheshire, England. *Agent:* Curtis Brown Ltd., 13 King St., London W.C.2, England. *Office:* University of Manchester, Manchester 13, England.

CAREER: Field work in anthropology in Zululand, South Africa, 1936-39; Rhodes-Livingstone Institute, Rhodesia, research officer, 1939-41, director 1941-47; Oxford University, Oxford, England, lecturer in social anthropology, 1947-49; University of Manchester, Manchester, England, professor of social anthropology, 1949—. Visiting professor at University of Delhi and M.S. University of Baroda, 1960; Frazer Lecturer at University of Glasgow, 1952; Mason Lecturer at University of Birmingham, 1955; Munro Lecturer at University of Edinburgh, 1958, 1960; Storrs Lecturer, Yale University Law School, 1963; Marett Lecturer, Exeter College, Oxford; fellow, Center for Advanced Study in the Behavioral Sciences, Stanford, Calif., 1967—; lecturer at other universities in Netherlands, France, Israel. Member of UNESCO Tensions Project, 1948, of inter-professional advisory committee of World Federation of Mental Health, 1951-55, of Department of Scientific and Industrial Research Human Sciences Committee, 1958-63; co-chairman of social anthropology section, Third International Congress of Sociology, 1959. Fieldwork, in addition to Zululand, in Barotseland, Tonga, Lamba.

MEMBER: International African Institute (executive council, 1956—), Association of Social Anthropologists of the British Commonwealth (honorary secretary, 1951-57; chairman, 1962—), Royal Anthropological Institute (formerly on council), British Association for the Advancement of Science (section president, 1961), Royal Commonwealth Society, Lancashire County Cricket Club. *Awards, honors:* Rhodes Scholar, 1934-36, 1938-39; Wellcome Medal of Royal Anthropological Institute, 1945; Rivers Memorial Medal, 1954.

WRITINGS: Economy of the Central Barotse Plain, Rhodes-Livingstone, 1941; *Essays on Lozi Land and Royal Property,* Rhodes-Livingstone, 1943; *Administrative Organization of the Barotse Native Authorities,* two volumes, Rhodes-Livingstone, 1943; *An Analysis of the Sociological Theories of Bronislaw Malinowski* (essays), Oxford University Press, 1949; *Rituals of Rebellion in South-east Africa: The Frazer Lecture, 1952,* Manchester University Press, 1954; *The Judicial Process Among the Barotse of Northern Rhodesia,* Free Press, 1955, 2nd edition, revised and enlarged, Manchester University Press, 1967; *Custom and Conflict in Africa* (originally a series of lectures broadcast by British Broadcasting Corp., 1955), Free Press, 1956; *Analysis of a Social Situation in Modern Zululand,* Manchester University Press, 1958; *Order and Rebellion in Tribal Africa: Collected Essays with an Autobiographical Introduction,* Free Press, 1963; *Politics, Law and Ritual in Tribal Society,* Aldine, 1965; *The Ideas in Barotse Jurisprudence* (Storrs Lectures), Yale University Press, 1965.

Contributor: Meyer Fortes and E.E. Evans-Pritchard, editors, *African Political Systems,* Oxford University Press for International African Institute, 1940; *Land Holding and Land Usage Among the Platean Tonga of Northern Rhodesia,* Oxford University Press for Rhodes-Livingstone Institute, 1948; Meyer Fortes, editor, *Social Structure: Essays Presented to A.R. Radcliffe-Brown,* Oxford University Press, 1949; (and editor with Elizabeth Colson) *Seven Tribes of British Central Africa,* Oxford University Press for Rhodes-Livingstone Institute, 1951; E.E. Evans-Pritchard, editor, *The Institutions of Primitive Society* (originally a radio program), Free Press, 1954; Edward Adamson Hoebel and Jesse D. Jennings, compilers, *Readings in Anthropology,* McGraw, 1955, 2nd edition, 1966; Lewis A. Coser and Bernard Rosenberg, editors, *Sociological Theory: A Book of Readings,* Macmillan, 1957; Morton Herbert Fried, *Readings in Anthropology,* Crowell, 1959; Aiden William Southall, editor, *Social Change in Africa: Studies Presented and Discussed,* Oxford University Press for International African Institute, 1961; Harold Dwight Lasswell and Harlan Cleveland, editors, *The Ethic of Power: The Interplay of Religion, Philosophy and Politics,* Jacob Ziskind Memorial Publication, 1962; (and editor) *Essays on the Ritual of Social Relations,* Humanities, 1963; Paul Bohannan, editor, *Law and Warfare: Studies in the Anthropology of Conflict,* Natural History Press for American Museum of Natural History, 1967.

Editor: (With J.M. Winterbottom and Colson) *Human Problems in British Central Africa,* Volumes 1-5 (with Winterbottom), Rhodes-Livingstone, 1944-48, Volumes 6-7 (with Colson), Oxford University Press, 1948-50; Ian George Cunnison, *History on the Luapula: An Essay on the Historical Notions of a Central African Tribe,* Oxford University Press for Rhodes-Livingstone Institute, 1951; James Arundel Barnes, *Marriage in a Changing Society,* Oxford University Press, 1952; Arnold Leonard Epstein, *Juridical Techniques and the Judicial Process,* Manchester University Press, 1954; James Arundel Barnes, *Politics in a Changing Society,* Oxford University Press for Rhodes-Livingstone Institute, 1954; James Clyde Mitchell, *The Yao Village: A Study in the Social Structure of a Nyasaland Tribe,* Manchester University Press for Rhodes-Livingstone Institute, 1956; Toslim Olawale Elias, *The Nature of African Customary Law,* Manchester University Press, 1956; F.G. Bailey, *Caste and the Economic Frontier,* Manchester University Press, 1957; Peter M. Worsley, *The Trumpet Shall Sound: A Study of Cargo Cults in Melanesia,* MacGibbon & Kee, 1957; (and author of introduction) Ronald J. Frankenberg, *Village on the Border: A Social Study of Religion, Politics and Football in a North Wales Community,* Cohen & West, 1957; Emil Solomon Sachs, *Rebels Daughter,* MacGibbon & Kee, 1957; (and author of introduction) Victor Witter Turner, *Schism and Continuity in an African Society: A Study of Ndema Village,* Manchester University Press, 1957, Humanities, 1958; (and

author of introduction) W. Watson, *Tribal Cohesion in a Money Economy,* Manchester University Press for Rhodes-Livingstone Institute, 1958; Arnold Leonard Epstein, *Politics in an Urban African Community,* Humanities, 1958; (and author of introduction) L.H. Gunn, *The Birth of a Plural Society,* Manchester University Press, 1958; E.J. Hobsbawm, *Primitive Rebels,* Manchester University Press, 1959, published in America as *Social Bandits and Primitive Rebels,* Free Press, 1960; F.G. Bailey, *Tribe, Caste and Nation,* Manchester University Press, 1960; Ian George Cunnison, *The Lunda Peoples of the Luapula: Customs and History in Tribal Politics,* Humanities, 1960; Victor Witter Turner, *Ndemu Divination: Its Symbolism and Techniques,* Manchester University Press, 1961; (and author of foreword) Elizabeth Colson, *The Plateau Tonga of Northern Rhodesia: Social and Religious Studies,* Humanities, 1962; Trude Scarlett Epstein, *Economic Development and Social Change in India,* Humanities, 1962; Tom Lupton, *On the Shop Floor,* Pergamon, 1962; *Closed Systems and Open Minds: The Limits of Naivety in Social Anthropology,* Oliver & Boyd, 1964, Aldine, 1965; J. van Velsen, *The Politics of Kinship: A Study in Social Manipulation Among the Lakeside Tonga of Nyasaland,* Humanities, 1964; (and author of foreword) William Allan, *The African Husbandman,* Barnes & Noble, 1965; (and author of foreword) Mervyn John Meggitt, *The Lineage System of the Mae Enga of the New Guinea Highlands,* Barnes & Noble, 1965; Sheila Cunnison, *Wages and Work Allocation: A Study of Social Relations in a Garment Workshop,* Tavistock Publications, 1966; *Ideas and Procedures in African Customary Law: Studies presented and Discussed at the Seminar,* [Addis Ababa], 1966, Oxford University Press for the International African Institute, 1969; (and contributor) *Allocation of Responsibility,* Humanities, 1972.

Member of editorial board of *African Studies,* 1942-47; *Rhodes-Livingstone Papers,* editor, 1942-47, member of editorial board, 1947-63; founder and editor of *Rhodes-Livingstone Communications,* 1943-47; *Rhodes-Livingstone Journal: Human Problems in British Central Africa,* founder and chief editor, 1944-47, member of editorial board, 1947-63. Contributor of more than seventy articles to anthropology journals and African journals, and to *Listener.*

SIDELIGHTS: Gluckman's studies of African society and culture have been praised by many critics for their appropriate blending of scholarship and accurate personal observation. S.E. Stumpf describes Gluckman's work as dealing "with a solid, wide, and rich variety of fact, not with generalizations. [His] analysis is . . . exciting . . . since his data is firsthand and recent and not derived from ancient literature." Characterizing one of Gluckman's works as "a major contribution to anthropology, and . . . of prime importance to African Studies," C.M. Turnbull believes that Gluckman's writings "afford an exciting glimpse of an exact, forthright academic mind at work. . . ."

BIOGRAPHICAL/CRITICAL SOURCES: *Manchester Guardian,* June 28, 1955, March 6, 1956; *Harvard Law Review,* February, 1956; *American Sociological Review,* April, 1956; *Times Literary Supplement,* April 27, 1956, May 24, 1963; *Annals of American Academy of Political and Social Science,* November, 1956, July, 1964; *New Statesman,* February 1, 1963; *Natural History,* May, 1964.

*   *   *

GLYN, Caroline 1947-

PERSONAL: Born August 27, 1947; daughter of Anthony (a writer) and Susan (Rhys-Williams) Glyn. *Education:* Attended primary and grammar schools; studied graphic art in Paris. *Religion:* Christian (Anglican). *Ad-*

dress: c/o Victor Gollancz Ltd., 14 Henrietta St., London W.C.2, England.

CAREER: Linguist-telephonist; journalist. *The Observer,* London, England, teenage correspondent for color supplement, 1965-66. Has exhibited paintings in one-man shows in England and France. *Awards, honors: Good Housekeeping* prize, 1956, for a design; poem-titling first prize, Poetry Society, 1959; second prize, "Jeune Espoir," France, 1964, for a painting; La Libre Belgique award for best foreign novel, 1964, for *Don't Knock the Corners Off;* runner-up for Society of Authors award to young writers, 1966, for *Love and Joy in the Mabillon.*

WRITINGS—(All novels, unless otherwise noted): *Dream Saga* (poems), Outposts, 1962; *Don't Knock the Corners Off,* Gollancz, 1963, Coward, 1964; *Love and Joy in the Mabillon,* Gollancz, 1965, Coward, 1966; *The Unicorn Girl* (first in a trilogy), Gollancz, 1966, Coward, 1967; *Heights and Depths* (2nd in the trilogy), Gollancz, 1968; *The Tree* (last in the trilogy), Gollancz, 1969; *The Tower and the Rising Tide,* Gollancz, 1971. Her poems have appeared in numerous journals, including *Cornhill;* contributor of articles to periodicals, including *Punch.*

WORK IN PROGRESS: A novel.

SIDELIGHTS: Miss Glyn, the great-granddaughter of author Elinor Glyn, was writing short stories and poetry at the age of six; with her first novel, *Don't Knock the Corners Off,* she became a celebrity at 15. She writes with a professional skill belied by her years, and with a "flying imagination" which seems to be her personal trademark. Her books are liberally sprinkled with mythological references and allusions to her own private world of fantasy, but her sense of detail is extremely realistic. Reviewing *Heights and Depths,* Mary Sullivan remarked that "period detail seems to come to Caroline Glyn on the wind, and is imparted as lightly . . . a gift that can't be willed or worked at." In a review of *Love and Joy in the Mabillon,* G.M. Casey said that she looks at "this dreary world . . . with the uncritical clarity of innocence. Only the young can afford the despair which underscores [her first two] novels. Usually only the experienced can achieve such technical ease and grace. Should Miss Glyn grow up and learn to love, her work could be very interesting indeed." Miss Glyn told *CA,* however: "I would deny that I had ever felt despair of anything but the British school system, and even that seems to have ameliorated with the introduction of large-scale streaming! The title of *Love and Joy* . . . was not sarcastic; I meant love and joy to be represented and vindicated in the young hero."

Miss Glyn speaks fluent if colloquial French and Spanish, and has traveled widely in most European countries, America, and Mexico. She has exhibited her paintings several times, and has two permanently installed in churches. She told *CA:* "My painting and my writing complement each other and I could not live without either. I paint trees, stars, and religious abstracts, and my books come into being while I am about it. . . . Because of such an intense imaginative life, I need lots of ordinary hard work to balance it—farming, housework, and helping run a printing press."

BIOGRAPHICAL/CRITICAL SOURCES: New York Times Book Review, January 5, 1964; *Seventeen,* July, 1964; *Best Sellers,* April 15, 1966; *Life,* May 13, 1966; *Listener,* February 1, 1968; *Times Literary Supplement,* February 8, 1968.

*   *   *

GOLD, Herbert 1924-

PERSONAL: Born March 9, 1924, in Cleveland, Ohio; son of Samuel S. and Frieda (Frankel) Gold; married Edith Zubrin, April, 1948 (divorced, 1956); married Melissa Dilworth, January, 1968; children: (first marriage) Ann, Judith; (second marriage) Nina, Ari, Ethan. *Education:* Columbia University, B.A., 1946, M.A., 1947; Sorbonne, University of Paris, license-es-lettres, 1951. *Home:* 1051-A Broadway, San Francisco, Calif. 94133. *Agent:* James Brown Associates, Inc., 22 East 60th St., New York, N.Y. J0022.

CAREER: Hotel manager; employee of Cleveland, Ohio. Regional Planning Commission; lived in Haiti, one year; Western Reserve University (now Case Wes'ern Reserve), Cleveland, Ohio, lecturer in philosophy and literature, 1951-53; Wayne State University, Detroit, Mich., member of English department, 1954-56; University of California. Davis, regents professor, 1973. Visiting professor, Cornell University, 1958, University of California, Berkeley, 1963. 1968, Harvard University, summer, 1964, Stanford University, 1967; McGuffey lecturer in English, Ohio University, 1971. *Military service:* U.S. Army Intelligence. 1943-46. *Awards, honors:* Fulbright fellow to Sorbonne, University of Paris, 1950—; Inter-American Cultural Relations grant to Haiti, 1954; Hudson Review fellow, 1956; Guggenheim fellow, 1957; Ohioana Book award. 1957, for *The Man Who Was Not With It;* National Institute of Arts and Letters grant in literature, 1958; Longview award, 1959; Ford Foundation fellow, 1960.

WRITINGS: Birth of a Hero (novel), Viking, 1951; *The Prospect Before Us,* World Publishing, 1954, published as *Room Clerk,* New American Library, 1956; *The Man Who Was Not With It,* Little, Brown, 1956, published as *The Wild Life,* Permabooks, 1957; (contributor) Granville Hicks, editor, *The Living Novel,* Macmillan, 1957; (with R. V. Cassill and James B. Hall) *Fifteen (Short Stories) By Three,* New Directions, 1957; (edi'or) *Fiction of the Fifties: A Decade of American Writing,* Doubleday, 1959; *The Optimist* (novel), Little, Brown, 1959; *Love and Like* (short stories), Dial, 1960; *Therefore Be Bold* (novel), Dial, 1960; (editor, with David L. Stevenson) *Stories of Modern America,* St. Martin's, 1961; *The Age of Happy Problems* (essays), Dial, 1962; (editor) *First Person Singular: Essays for the Sixties,* Dial, 1963; *Salt* (novel), Dial, 1963; *Fathers: A Novel in the Form of a Memoir* (key sections originally published as short stories, including "The Heart of the Artichoke," first published in the *Hudson Review;* several sections, in slightly different form, also included in *Love and Like),* Random House, 1967; (contributor) Bob Booker and George Foster, editors, *Pardon Me Sir, But is My Eye Hurting Your Elbow?* (screenplays), Geis, 1968; *The Great American Jackpot,* Random House, 1969; *Biafra Goodbye,* Twowindows Press, 1970; *The Magic Will: Stories and Essays of a Decade,* Random House, 1971; *My Last Two Thousand Years,* Random House, 1972; *The Young Prince and the Magic Cone* (juvenile), Doubleday, 1973.

Contributor of essays and stories to *Botteghe Oscure, New Yorker, Yale Review, Hudson Review, Transatlantic Review, Playboy, New York Times Book Review, Atlantic, Harper's, Esquire, Discovery, Partisan Review, Furioso,* and *Antioch Review.*

WORK IN PROGRESS: A novel, *Swiftie the Magician.*

SIDELIGHTS: Gold's style is unique in American fiction, blending the colloquial and the baroque, "a cerebral performance," writes James Kelly, "with a tangle of long, long thoughts, most of them entertainingly presen!ed in colorful, runaway language." The *New York Herald Tribune Book Review* called the handling of filial love in the stories in *Love and Like* "reminiscent of Chekhov ir its seeming artlessness." Harvey Swados writes: "Gold writes with charm and talent. He understands the phenomena at which he is smiling, and he communicates adroitly his delighted recognition of the significance of such neglected rituals as the office party and the commuter's daily journey."

"The Heart of the Artichoke," his most celebrated short story, Gold calls "my most personally crucial story because, by writing it, I learned to be a writer. I had a sense of mastering my experience. Not just examining, not just using, but *riding* my world, with full use of my faculties in the open air. . . . I was ready to throw a rock at the Henry James hive, a rock even at the great juicy Dostoyevsky swarm, and secrete my own gathered sweets into my own homemade jug." At another time he said: "[I write] *to master my experience.* But I write also to entertain myself and to make things I know mysterious again and to make the mysterious things manageable again. I used to write very much out of dream and nightmare; the dreams because I enjoyed them and the nightmares in order to control them. There is still an element of that. It is the way I know the world."

As Granville Hicks has observed, Gold's novels involve an open world where possibility remains. In *The Living Novel,* Gold writes: "The novelist must reach for the grownup, risking, athletic personality, surely must in some way be this person, in order to find a hero who gives the sense of men at their best on earth; and catch him finally where his great gifts do not suffice: this is tragedy." Gold dares, says Hicks, "to look for heroes, and he finds them in unlikely places."

Describing *Fathers,* the story of the Jewish immigrant seeking fortune and dynasty in America, Leonard Kriegel wrote: "In his previous novels, Gold's language, always rich and sensuous, stood in the way of what he was trying to do. He was that peculiar creature, a 'natural' novelist who had not written the novel one felt he was capable of writing. It is probably this that accounts for the smugness with which Gold has been dismissed by a number of critics and fellow novelists, most of whom should have known better. Gold was generally accused of not being tough enough, of not being contemporary, of lacking what Hemingway called *cojones* (a much traveled novelistic commodity), of being too sentimental. Some of this was true. Perhaps it still is. But Gold at his best, and he is at his best in *Fathers,* is a warm, lyrical, zestful writer. . . . Gold has taken the myth of the Jew as wanderer and molded it to his own purposes. While some of us search for superman, he has been content to write a novel which is decidedly uncontemporary and remarkably good."

Two of Gold's short stories have been made into films, and a play, based on the book *Love and Like,* was produced in Los Angeles.

BIOGRAPHICAL/CRITICAL SOURCES: The Creative Present, edited by Nona Balakian and Charles Simmons, Doubleday, 1963; *Poetry and Fiction: Essays by Howard Nemerov,* Rutgers University Press, 1963; *Contemporary American Novelists,* edited by Harry T. Moore, Southern Illinois University Press, 1964; *The Modern Novel in Britain and the United States,* edited by Walter Allen, Dutton, 1965.

Nation, October 6, 1951, July 3, 1967; *New York Times Book Review,* February 14, 1954, September 4, 1966, March 19, 1967, October 19, 1969, January 25, 1970; *New York Herald Tribune Book Review,* March 27, 1960; *Saturday Review,* April 2, 1960, April 20, 1963, March 25, 1967; *Christian Science Monitor,* March 23, 1967; *Time,* March 31, 1967; *National Observer,* March 27, 1967, March 2, 1970; *Newsweek,* March 27, 1967, January 26, 1970; *Vogue,* April 1, 1967; *Life,* April 7, 1967; *Book Week,* April 9, 1967; *New Leader,* May 22, 1967; *New York Review of Books,* June 1, 1967, May 21, 1970; *New Republic,* June 17, 1967; *Hudson Review,* summer, 1967; *Yale Review,* autumn, 1967; *Books and Bookmen,* February, 1968; *Harper's* February, 1970; *Writer's Digest,* September, 1972; *New York Times,* October 20, 1972.

*   *   *

GOLDBERG, Herman Raphael 1915-

PERSONAL: Born November 20, 1915, in Brooklyn, N.Y.; son of Isidore Baruch (a businessman) and Rose (a teacher; maiden name, Saltser) Goldberg; married Harriette Balacaier, January 23, 1943; children: Robert Ira, Arnold. *Education:* Brooklyn College (now Brooklyn College of the City University of New York), B.S., 1935; Columbia University, M.A., 1944; New York University, graduate study. *Home:* 105 Beckwith Ter., Rochester, N.Y. 14610. *Office:* Board of Education, 13 South Fitzhugh St., Rochester, N.Y. 14614.

CAREER: Professional baseball player, 1937-38; New York (N.Y.) Public Schools, teacher, 1939-48; Rochester (N.Y.) Board of Education, director of special education, 1948-58, coordinator of instruction, 1958-63, superintendent of schools, 1963-71; U.S. Office of Education, Washington, D.C., Associate Commissioner for Elementary and Secondary Education, 1971—. University of Bologna, Bologna, Italy, Fulbright professor, 1960-61; lecturer in education at New York University and University of Rochester, and demonstration teacher at Columbia University; Distinguished Visiting Professor, Oregon State University, 1970. Consultant to ministries of education of Italy and Israel, 1960-61, and to New York State Department of Education. Chairman, President's National Advisory Council on Education of the Disadvantaged, 1970. Member of state or local boards of United Cerebral Palsy Association, American National Red Cross, Visiting Nurses Association. Inventor of teaching machine, manufactured under the name of Chromovox. Member of U.S. Olympic baseball team, 1936.

MEMBER: National Education Association, American Association of School Administrators, Council of School Superintendents, New York State Teachers Association, Rochester Teachers Association, Chamber of Commerce, Rotary International, Phi Delta Kappa. *Awards, honors:* John Hay fellowship to Bennington College, 1964; LL.D., University of Rochester, 1965.

WRITINGS: (Contributor) M.E. Frampton and E.D. Gall, editors, *Special Education for the Exceptional,* Sargent, 1955; (editor with W.T. Brumber) *Gas Stations,* Science Research Associates, c.1959; *Otolaryngology,* William Prior Corp., 1960; (editor with Brumber) *The Job Ahead,* Science Research Associates, 1963; (contributor) Walter M. Lifton, editor, *Educating for Tomorrow: The Role of Media, Career Development, and Society,* Wiley, 1970; (with Gilbert B. Schiffman) *Dyslexia: Problems of Reading Disabilities,* Grune, 1972. Senior editor of "Rochester Occupational Reading Series," Syracuse University Press, 1954—.

*   *   *

GOLDBERGER, Arthur Stanley 1930-

PERSONAL: Born November 20, 1930, in New York, N.Y.; son of David M. (a dress cutter) and Martha (Greenwald) Goldberger; married Iefke Engelsman (a teacher and poet), August 19, 1957; children: Nina, Nicholas. *Education:* New York University, B.S., 1951; University of Michigan, M.A., 1952, Ph.D., 1958. *Office:* Department of Economics, University of Wisconsin, Madison, Wis. 53706.

CAREER: Fulbright research fellow in Netherlands, 1955-56, 1959-60; Stanford University, Stanford, Calif., acting assistant professor of economics, 1956-59; University of Wisconsin, Madison, associate professor, 1960-63, professor of economics, 1963—. Visiting professor

University of California, Berkeley (Athens Project), 1964-65, University of Essex, England, 1968-69, University of Hawaii, 1969. *Member:* American Economic Association, American Statistical Association (fellow, 1968—), Econometric Society (fellow, 1964—). *Awards, honors:* Ford Foundation faculty fellowship, 1963-64.

WRITINGS: (With Lawrence Robert Klein) *An Econometric Model of the United States, 1929-52,* Humanities, 1955; *Impact Multipliers and Dynamic Properties of the Klein-Goldberger Model,* Humanities, 1959, 2nd edition, North-Holland Publishing, 1970; *Econometric Theory,* Wiley, 1964; (contributor) Pan A. Yotopoulos, editor, *Economic Analysis and Economic Policy,* Center of Planning and Economic Research (Athens), 1966; *Topics in Regression Analysis,* Macmillan, 1968. Contributor of articles to professional journals. Member of board of editors, *American Economic Review,* 1964-66.

WORK IN PROGRESS: Research on statistical methodology in the social sciences.

*   *   *

GOLDMAN, Marshall I (rwin)   1930-

PERSONAL: Born July 26, 1930, in Elgin, Ill.; son of Sam and Bella (Silvian) Goldman; married Merle Rosenblatt, June 14, 1953; children: Ethan, Avra Lea, Karla Ann, Seth. *Education:* University of Pennsylvania, B.S., 1952; Harvard University, M.A., 1956, Ph.D., 1961. *Religion:* Jewish. *Home:* 17 Midland Rd., Wellesley, Mass. 02181.

CAREER: Harvard University, Russian Research Center, Cambridge, Mass., researcher, 1957—; Wellesley College, Wellesley, Mass., began as assistant professor, became professor of economics, 1958—, chairman of department, 1971—. Brandeis University, Waltham, Mass., visiting professor of economics, 1961. Member of State Department delegation studying marketing in Soviet Union, 1960. Consultant to International Marketing Institute, 1960—, to Raytheon Corp., 1962, Arthur D. Little, 1967, Cambridge Economic Research Group, 1968—, Charles Rives Associates, 1969. Director, Century Bank & Trust, Somerville, Mass. *Military service:* U.S. Army, 1953-55. *Member:* American Economic Association, American Marketing Association, American Association of University Professors (secretary, vice president, Wellesley chapter), Wellesley Clean Air Committee, Town Meeting (Wellesley). *Awards, honors:* Brookings Institution research professorship to study Soviet foreign aid, 1964.

WRITINGS: Soviet Marketing: Distribution in a Controlled Economy, Macmillan, 1963; (editor) *Comparative Economic Systems: A Reader,* Random House, 1964, 2nd edition, 1971; *Soviet Foreign Aid,* Praeger, 1967; (editor) *Controlling Pollution: The Economics of a Cleaner America,* Prentice-Hall, 1967, revised and enlarged edition published as *Ecology and Economics: Controlling Pollution in the 1970's,* 1972; *The Soviet Economy: Myth and Reality,* Prentice-Hall, 1968; *Critical Issues in Controlling Pollution,* Prentice-Hall, 1972; *The Spoils of Progress: Environmental Pollution in the Soviet Union,* MIT Press, 1972. Contributor of articles to *Foreign Affairs, Journal of Political Economy,* other professional journals in America, Italy, Germany, England, France, Japan.

SIDELIGHTS: Study on Soviet foreign aid has taken Goldman to Africa, Europe, Asia, and the Soviet Union. On his fifth trip to the U.S.S.R. in 1970, he participated in an American Friends Service Conference.

BIOGRAPHICAL/CRITICAL SOURCES: New York Times Book Review, May 28, 1967.

GOLDMAN, Richard Franko   1910-

PERSONAL: Born December 7, 1910, in New York, N.Y.; son of Edwin Franko and Adelaide (Maibrunn) Goldman; married Alexandra Rienzi (an artist), June 8, 1934; children: Daniel Franko. *Education:* Columbia University, A.B. (with honors), 1930, advanced study in fine arts and archaeology, 1930-31. *Office:* Peabody Institute, Baltimore, Md. 21202.

CAREER: Goldman Band, New York, N.Y., associate conductor, 1937-56, conductor, 1956—. Director, Peabody Conservatory of Music, Baltimore, Md., 1968—; president, Peabody Institute of City of Baltimore, 1969—; member of board of directors, Baltimore Symphony Orchestra, 1969—; chairman, Council of Independent Professional Schools of Music, 1970—. Juilliard School of Music, New York, N.Y., faculty member and chairman of literature and materials of music department, 1947-60. Visiting associate professor of music at Columbia University, 1961; visiting lecturer at Princeton University, 1952-56, New York University, 1963. Composer of works for orchestra and band, and of chamber music, piano music, songs. *Military service:* U.S. Army, Office of Strategic Services, 1942-45. *Member:* American Bandmasters Association, American Society of Composers, Authors and Publishers, Music Library Association, National Association of American Composers and Conductors, Phi Mu Alpha (honorary member), Phi Beta Kappa. *Awards, honors:* Alice M. Ditson Conductor's Award, 1961; Guggenheim fellowship, 1962; L.H.D., Lehigh University, 1964.

WRITINGS: The Band's Music, Pitman, 1938; *The Concert Band,* Rinehart, 1946; *The Wind Band: Its Literature and Technique,* Allyn & Bacon, 1962; (contributor) Paul Henry Lang, editor, *100 Years of Music in America,* G. Schirmer, 1961; (contributor) Arthur Jacobs, editor, *Choral Music: A Symposium,* Penguin, 1963; *Harmony in Western Music,* Norton, 1965; (translator from the Portuguese) Jose Maria de Eca de Queiroz, *The Mandarin and Other Stories,* Ohio University Press, 1965; (contributor) *Challenges of College Teaching,* Basic Books, 1971.

Editor or arranger: (And compiler) *Five Pre-Classical Pieces for Three Trumpets (Cornets) and Drums (Ad Lib),* Music Press, 1942; *Sonatina,* Mercury Music Corp., 1943; (and compiler, with Roger Smith) *Landmarks of Early American Music, 1760-1800* (32 compositions for orchestra or band; includes historical and biographical notes, suggestions for performance), G. Schirmer, 1943; *Grand Symphony for Band, Funeral and Triumphal, Op. 15* (Berlioz' "Symphonie funebre et triomphale"), Mercury Music Corp., 1947; *Eight Russian Folk Songs, Op. 58* (Liadov's "Chants populaires russes," transcribed for band), Mills Music, 1948; *Athletic Festival March, Op. 69, No. 1* (Prokofev's work arranged and edited for American band), American-Russian edition, Leeds Music Corp., 1948; *Two Airs for Trumpet* (Purcell's "Bonduca," selections, figured bass realized for piano by Goldmen), Mercury Music Corp., 1949; *Aubades: Piano Solo,* Mercury Music Corp., 1949; *Le Bobino: Burlesque in Three Scenes, for Two Pianos, Four Hands,* Southern Music Publishing Co., 1950.

Opera libretti: *The Mandarin,* music by Jonathan Elkus, Carl Fischer, 1969; *Athaliah,* music by Hugo Weisgall, Presser, 1971. Contributor to *New Oxford History, Grolier Encyclopedia, Book of Knowledge,* and to other encyclopedias, anthologies, and periodicals. Editor, *Juilliard Review,* 1953-58

WORK IN PROGRESS: History, Information and Art.

GOLDMAN, William W.   1931-
(Harry Longbaugh)

PERSONAL: Born August 12, 1931, in Chicago, Ill.; son of Maurice Clarence and Marion (Weil) Goldman; married Ilene Jones, April 15, 1961; children: Jenny Rebecca, Susanna. Education: Oberlin College, B.A., 1952; Columbia University, M.A., 1956. Home: 740 Park Ave., New York, N.Y. 10021. Agent: Monica McCall, International Famous Agency, 1301 Avenue of the Americas, New York, N.Y.

CAREER: "I've only been a writer. My first novel was taken the summer I finished graduate school, so I've never known anything else." Military service: U.S. Army, 1952-54. Awards, honors: Academy of Motion Picture Arts and Sciences Award (Oscar), 1970, for Best Original Screenplay, for "Butch Cassidy and the Sundance Kid."

WRITINGS—Novels: The Temple of Gold, Knopf, 1957; Your Turn to Curtsy, My Turn to Bow, Doubleday, 1958; Soldier in the Rain, Atheneum, 1960; Boys and Girls Together, Atheneum, 1964; (under pseudonym Harry Longbaugh) No Way to Treat a Lady, Gold Medal, 1964, published under own name, Harcourt, 1968; The Thing of It Is . . . , Harcourt, 1967; Butch Cassidy and the Sundance Kid (screenplay), Bantam, 1969; Father's Day, Harcourt, 1971; The Princess Bride, Harcourt, in press.

Nonfiction: The Season: A Candid Look at Broadway (an excerpt originally published in Esquire, January, 1969), Harcourt, 1969.

Plays: (With brother James Goldman) "Blood, Sweat and Stanley Poole," produced on Broadway at Morosco Theatre, October 5, 1961; (with James Goldman and John Kander) "A Family Affair" (musical), produced on Broadway at Billy Rose Theatre, January 27, 1962.

Screenplays: "Harper," produced by Warner Brothers, 1966; "Butch Cassidy and the Sundance Kid," produced by 20th Century Fox, 1969; "The Hot Rock," produced in 1972.

SIDELIGHTS: Goldman has attracted attention not only with his novels, plays, and films, but with his nonfiction book, The Season, which was cause of controversy on and off Broadway, as well. Goldman chose an entire Broadway season, 1967-68, and decided to "take it apart, and write a book explaining how [the season] works." Christopher Lehmann-Haupt states that "the book that Mr. Goldman has written is very nearly perfect. It is a loose-limbed, gossipy, insidey, savvy, nuts-and-bolts report on the annual search for the winning numbers that is now big-time American commercial theater." John Simon states that he does not think that Goldman has gone far enough, that he fell "prey to middlebrow prejudices and resentments, or bogged down in careless inconsistency. He is not unaware of the problems, and sometimes willing to expose them, but he does not name enough names, rake enough muck, or think things through rigorously enough." Simon also believes that the breezy style of the book detracts rather than adds to the material. Harold Clurman states that the book was written in Broadway's terms, and as such is not as uncompromising as it might have been had Goldman been impartially on the outside. Roderick Nordell comments: "As he pursues his anatomy of hits and misses, Mr. Goldman brings some fresh analysis to familiar materials."

Goldman's novels have been quite successful. Dan Wickenden writes of The Temple of Gold: "[It] is a considerable achievement. Mr. Goldman has worked out his own adroit way of conveying a novel across a considerable span of time; he has devised for his narrator a fresh and vigorous idiom; and he has fulfilled the novelist's basic function of bringing his characters wholly alive and engrossing to us in their actions." Richard Schickel comments on Boys and Girls Together: [Goldman] has a solid gift for gag lines, plenty of hairpin curves in his story line and a flair for good old-fashioned melodrama. . . . One must fault Goldman for his unwillingness to firmly place his characters against backgrounds of felt reality; they relate only to one another, never to the world at large." "Mr. Goldman has a fine ear for dialogue," Anthony Boucher stated in reviewing No Way to Treat a Lady, "his style is unbelievably economic, rich in adroitly-used narrative and typographical devices. In all, pretty dazzling."

Martin Levin writes of Father's Day: "Weaving together flashbacks and current happenings, the author composes his hero's personality with offhand expertise. It is a virtuoso performance in which the lightning tempo counteracts a tendency to cloy."

"Butch Cassidy and the Sundance Kid," in addition to being a critical success, has been extremely popular with filmgoers.

Goldman told CA: "I'm not all that crazy about the act of writing, which is probably why I write quickly. The sooner I'm done, the sooner I can go to the movies. Besides movies I like tennis, swimming, mysteries, the New York Knicks, and working out baseball statistics."

Soldier in the Rain was filmed by Allied Artists, 1963; No Way to Treat a Lady was produced by Paramount, 1968.

BIOGRAPHICAL/CRITICAL SOURCES: Chicago Sunday Tribune, October 13, 1957; Saturday Review, October 19, 1957, July 25, 1964; New York Herald Tribune Book Review, November 3, 1957; New York Times, November 17, 1957, August 31, 1969, September 19, 1969; Commonweal, November 29, 1957; Christian Science Monitor, April 27, 1967, October 9, 1969; Best Sellers, May 1, 1967, September 15, 1969, March 15, 1971; New York Times Book Review, April 14, 1968, September 28, 1969, January 31, 1971; New Yorker, May 20, 1967; Books and Bookmen, January, 1968; Variety, August 13, 1969; New Leader, September 15, 1969; Life, October 31, 1969; Book World, April 18, 1971.

*   *   *

GOLDSCHMIDT, Walter Rochs   1913-

PERSONAL: Born February 24, 1913, in San Antonio, Tex.; son of Hermann and Gretchen (Rochs) Goldschmidt; married Beatrice Gale (a psychiatric social worker); children: Karl G., Mark S. Education: University of Texas, B.A. (cum laude), 1933, M.A., 1935; University of California, Berkeley, Ph.D., 1942. Home: 978 Norman Pl., Los Angeles, Calif. 90049. Office: Department of Anthropology, University of California, Los Angeles, Calif. 90024.

CAREER: U.S. Bureau of Agricultural Economics, Washington, D.C., social science analyst, 1940-46; University of California, Los Angeles, assistant professor, 1946-50, associate professor, 1950-56, professor of anthropology, 1956—, chairman of department, 1964-69. Summer lecturer or visiting assistant professor at Stanford University, 1945, University of California, Berkeley, 1949, Harvard University, 1950. Director of Ways of Mankind Radio Project, National Association of Educational Broadcasters, 1951-53, and director of Culture and Ecology in East Africa Project, 1960-69.

MEMBER: African Studies Association (founder; board of directors, 1957-60), American Anthropological Association (fellow), American Association for the Advancement of Science, American Association of University Professors, Society for Applied Anthropology, American Ethnological Society (president, 1969-70), Southwestern Anthropological Society (president, 1950-51), International African Institute, Phi Beta Kappa (president of California chapter, 1970-71), Sigma Xi. *Awards, honors:* Fulbright research grant, 1953; Social Science Research Council grant-in-aid, 1953; Wenner Gren Foundation postdoctoral fellowship, 1953, and grant for travel, 1958; fellow of Center for Advanced Study in the Behavioral Sciences, 1964; National Science Foundation postdoctoral fellow, 1964; Phi Beta Kappa visiting scholar, 1969-70; senior scientist award, National Institute of Mental Health, 1970-75.

WRITINGS: (With Harold E. Driver) *The Hupa White Deerskin Dance,* University of California, 1940; *Small Business and the Community: A Study in Central Valley of California on Effects of Scale of Farm Operations,* U.S. Senate, Small Business Committee, 1946; *As You Sow,* Harcourt, 1947; *Nomlaki Ethnography,* University of California Press, 1951; (editor and author of commentary) Lister Sinclair and others, *Ways of Mankind: Thirteen Dramas of Peoples of the World and How They Live,* Beacon Press, 1954; (contributor) Lister Sinclair, *Ways to Justice: An Adult Discussion Program* (background essays by Goldschmidt), Fund for Adult Education, 1955; (editor) *Readings in the Ways of Mankind,* two volumes, Beacon Press, 1957, 2nd edition published as *Exploring the Ways of Mankind,* Holt, 1960, 3rd edition, 1971; (editor) *The United States and Africa,* American Assembly, Columbia University, 1958, 3rd edition, Books for Libraries, 1970; (editor) *The Anthropology of Frank Boas: Essays on the Centennial of His Birth,* Chandler Publishing, 1959; *Man's Way: A Preface to the Understanding of Human Society,* Holt, 1959 (published in England as *Understanding Human Society,* Routledge & Kegan Paul, 1959); (editor) *Discussion Leader's Guide for Use with "Exploring the Ways of Mankind",* Holt, 1961; *Comparative Functionalism: An Essay in Anthropological Theory,* University of California Press, 1966; *Sebei Law,* University of California Press, 1967; *Cultural Anthropology,* American Library Association, 1967; *Kambuya's Cattle: The Legacy of an African Herdsman,* University of California Press, 1969; *On Becoming an Anthropologist* (career pamphlet), American Anthropological Association, 1970. Editor, *American Anthropologist,* 1956-59.

WORK IN PROGRESS: Research on culture and ecology in East Africa; ethnographic study of the Sebei of Uganda.

* * *

GOLDSTEIN, E. Ernest 1918-

PERSONAL: Born October 9, 1918, in Pittsburgh, Pa.; son of Nathan E. and Annie (Ginsberg) Goldstein; married Peggy Rosenfeld (a sculptor), June 22, 1941; children: Susan Martha, Daniel Frank. *Education:* Amherst College, A.B. (cum laude), 1939; Georgetown University, LL.B., 1947; University of Wisconsin, S.J.D., 1956. *Office:* 52 Champs Elysees, 75 Paris VIII, France.

CAREER: Began private practice of law, Washington, D.C., 1947; U.S. Government, assistant counsel of Special Crime Committee, U.S. Senate, 1951, general counsel of Antitrust Subcommittee, U.S. House of Representatives, 1951-52, restrictive trade practices specialist, Foreign Operations Administration, Paris, France, 1952-53; University of Texas School of Law, Austin, associate professor, 1955-57, professor, 1957-65; Coudert Freres, Paris, France, counsel, 1966-67; special assistant to the President of the United States, 1967-69; Coudert Freres, Paris, partner, 1969—. Visiting professor at University of

Puerto Rico Law School, summer, 1962, at Salzburg Seminar in American Studies, summer, 1963; lecturer, National University of Mexico, summer, 1964. Anti-Defamation League of B'nai B'rith, member of Southwest regional advisory board, chairman, 1957-58; member, Austin Commission on Human Relations. *Military service:* U.S. Army, Army Security Agency, 1941-46; became master sergeant; received Legion of Merit.

MEMBER: American Bar Association, International Law Association, American Society of International Law. *Awards, honors:* Ford Foundation international legal studies fellowship.

WRITINGS: (Editor) *Cases and Other Materials on the Fundamentals of Patent, Trade-Mark, and Copyright Law,* two volumes, University of Texas Law School Foundation, 1957, reissued in a single volume as *Cases and Materials on Patent, Trademark and Copyright Law,* Foundation, 1959; *American Enterprise and Scandinavian Antitrust Law,* University of Texas Press, 1963; (contributor) *The Craft and Context of Translation,* Doubleday, 1964. Contributor to legal journals, and to *Harper's, Les Echos* (Paris), other journals in France and Netherlands.

WORK IN PROGRESS: A paper on licensing to be published by Europa Institut, University of Amsterdam.

AVOCATIONAL INTERESTS: Horticulture, philately, sailing.

* * *

GOLDSTEIN, Edward 1923-

PERSONAL: Born December 18, 1923, in New York, N.Y.; son of Henry and Sarah (Gordon) Goldstein; married Ann Silverman, March 19, 1958; children: Jill Susan. *Education:* Long Island University, B.S., 1950; Columbia University, M.A., 1953. *Home:* 173-17 89th Ave., Jamaica, N.Y. 11432.

CAREER: Bethpage Schools, Bethpage, N.Y., special education teacher, 1956-60; Prince George County (Md.) Association for Retarded Children, director, 1960-62; George Washington University, Washington, D.C., lecturer, 1961-62; Union Free School District #5, Copiague, N.Y., teacher of special education classes, 1962-65; City of New York (N.Y.) Board of Education, guidance counselor in College Bound Program, Morris High School, Bronx, N.Y., 1965—. Brooklyn Home for Children, Forest Hills, N.Y., consultant in reading. *Military service:* U.S. Army Air Forces, World War II. *Member:* New York State Personnel and Guidance Association.

WRITINGS: Selective Audio-Visual Instruction for Mentally Retarded Pupils, C.C Thomas, 1964. Contributor to *Pointer* and other periodicals.

AVOCATIONAL INTERESTS: Drama and literature.

* * *

GOLDSTEIN, Roberta Butterfield 1917-

PERSONAL: Born December 25, 1917, in North Troy, Vt.; daughter of Alfred Mitchell and Anne (Huckins) Butterfield; married Harold Levin, 1939 (died, 1947); married Frank Goldstein (an actor and restaurateur), November 13, 1949; children: (first marriage) Michael, Mark; (second marriage) Jan Mordecai, Ethel Faith. *Education:* University of Vermont, Ph.B. (cum laude), 1939, M.S., 1969. *Politics:* Independent. *Religion:* Hebrew. *Home:* 30 Adsit Ct., Burlington, Vt. 05401.

CAREER: Co-owner and advertising manager of Henry's Diner, 1954—, and A & W Island of Refreshment, 1959—, both Burlington, Vt.; Burlington (Vt.) School System, speech therapist, 1966—; Enosburg Falls, Vt., director of summer speech therapy program, 1970. Burlington Community Chest, chairman of Women's Division, 1955. Ohavi Zedek Hebrew School, secretary of education board, 1959-67. Narrator of FM radio program, "Your Literary Heritage," 1961-62. Advisor, Marquis Biographical Society.

MEMBER: International Platform Association, World Poetry Society Intercontinental, Poetry Society of America, National League of American Pen Women, National Council of Jewish Women (state legislative chairman, 1949-51), Jewish Publications Society, Jewish Infomation Society, Poetry Society of Vermont (executive committee, 1963—; publicity director, 1964-67; vice president, 1968-70; president, 1970—), Vermont Historical Society, Hadassah (president of Burlington Chapter, 1969-70), Centro Studi e Scambi Internazionali, Accademia Leonardo da Vinci of Rome (fellow, 1964-67), Avalon World Arts Academy, United Poets Laureate, Phi Beta Kappa, Alpha Xi Delta. *Awards, honors:* Certificate of Merit, *Dictionary of International Biography,* 1969; Magna cum Laude Citation for Poetry, World Poetry Society Intercontinental, 1970; poet laureate, United Amateur Press Association, 1970-71.

WRITINGS—All poetry: *The Searching Season: Poems of Faith, Hope and Love, by a Modern Mother,* Queen City Press, 1961; *Fling Jeweled Pebbles,* Golden Quill, 1963; *Un Cahier de poesie* (selections from *The Searching Season),* Centro Studi e Scambi Internazionali, 1964; *The Wood Burns Red,* Golden Quill, 1966. Contributor of poetry to *Jewish Spectator,* drama reviews and interviews to *Burlington Free Press* and *Writers Voice,* and poetry, essays, and short stories to other periodicals.

WORK IN PROGRESS: A children's book, *The First Spring of Jennifer;* a book of poetry, *Cry Before Dawn,* for Mitre Press; and a documentary for ETV, "The Snowflake Man—Wilson Alwyn Bentley."

SIDELIGHTS: Scotti D'Arcy produced a recording of Mrs. Goldstein reading her poetry, "The Wood Burns Red, and Other Poems," released by Aseb Record Co., 1970.

BIOGRAPHICAL/CRITICAL SOURCES: Vermont Sunday News, December 22, 1963, October, 1968; *Vermont Catholic Tribune,* February 28, 1964; *Burlington Free Press,* November 19, 1964; *Rural Vermonter,* Number 3, 1964.

*   *   *

GOODFIELD, (Gwyneth) June   1927-

PERSONAL: Born June 1, 1927, in Stratford-on-Avon, England; daughter of Richard Morgan and Eleanor Francis (Ashton) Goodfield; married Stephen Toulmin (director of Nuffield Foundation Unit for History of Ideas), July 25, 1961. *Education:* University of London, B.Sc., 1949; University of Leeds, Ph.D., 1950. *Home:* Tile Barn, Alfriston, Polegate, Sussex, England. *Office:* Nuffield Foundation Unit for History of Ideas, 6-10 Gordon St., London W.C.1, England.

CAREER: Medical Research Council, Oxford, England, research assistant in zoology, 1949-50; Cheltenham Ladies' College, Cheltenham, England, senior biology mistress, 1950-54; Benenden School, Kent, England, physics mistress, 1954-56; University of Leeds, Leeds, England, Leverhulme Research Fellow and lecturer in history of science, 1956-60; Nuffield Foundation Unit for History of Ideas, London, England, assistant director, 1960—, mainly writing books and directing documentary films, including direction of "The God Within" (greek science), selected for showing at Edinburgh, San Francisco, Warsaw, and Toronto film festivals. *Member:* Royal Society of Medicine (fellow), Zoological Society of London (fellow).

WRITINGS: The Growth of Scientific Physiology: Physiological Method and the Mechanist-Vitalist Controversy, Illustrated by the Problems of Respiration and Animal Heat, Hutchinson, 1960; (with husband, Stephen Toulmin) *The Ancestry of Science,* Volume I: *The Fabric of the Heavens,* Hutchinson, 1961, published in America as *The Fabric of the Heavens: The Development of Astronomy and Dynamics,* Harper, 1962, Volume II: *The Architecture of Matter,* Hutchinson, 1962, Harper, 1963, Volume III: *The Discovery of Time,* Harper, 1965; *Courier to Peking,* Dutton, 1972. Contributor to *Isis, Observer,* and *Times* (London).

WORK IN PROGRESS: Teaching Guide to the History of Science; Science in Its Environment, Volume IV of *Ancestry of Science* written with Stephen Toulmin.

AVOCATIONAL INTERESTS: Music, gardening, and travel.

*   *   *

GOODMAN, Walter   1927-

PERSONAL: Born August 22, 1927, in New York, N.Y.; married Elaine Egan (an artist), February 10, 1951; children: Hal, Bennett. *Education:* Syracuse University, B.A. (magna cum laude), 1949; University of Reading, England, M.A., 1953. *Home:* 4 Crest Dr., White Plains, N.Y. 10607.

CAREER: New Republic, Washington, D.C., staff writer, 1954-55; *Playboy,* Chicago, Ill., contributing editor, 1960-61; *Redbook,* New York, N.Y., senior editor, 1957—. *Awards, honors:* Christopher Award for nonfiction for children, 1972, for *The Rights of the People: The Major Decisions of the Warren Court.*

WRITINGS: The Clowns of Commerce, Sagamore, 1957; *All Honorable Men: Corruption and Compromise in American Life,* Little, Brown, 1963; *Smoking and the Public Interest* (Part IV), Consumer's Union, 1963; *The Committee: The Extraordinary Career of the House Committee on Un-American Activities,* Farrar, Straus, 1968; *Black Bondage: The Life of Slaves in the South* (youth book), Farrar, Straus, 1969; *A Percentage of the Take,* Farrar, Straus, 1971; (with wife, Elaine Goodman) *The Rights of the People: The Major Decisions of the Warren Court,* Farrar, Straus, 1972. Writer of magazine articles and book reviews.

SIDELIGHTS: In the opinion of Saul Maloff, *The Committee* is a "lively, sobering, definitive, hilarious and depressing study of America's peculiar institution, the House Un-American Activities Committee—from its start in 1938 under the ineffable Martin Dies to the three-ring circus conducted by the inimitable Joe Pool." Irony is the tool Goodman uses to relate the tragicomic, three-decade history of HUAC, which "gives him three important advantages," according to Mitchel Levitas. "As a writer, [the use of irony] enables him to be funny—no small edge, considering the solemn idiocy of many Committee proceedings. As a historian, irony gives him distance; he can step back a few paces from events. And as a political analyst who makes no secret of his anti-Communist liberalism, it leaves him free to take aim at both prosecutors and witnesses without feeling guilty." Arthur Schlesinger, Jr. notes that Goodman "regards the Committee as a disaster; but he does not make his book a crusade. One is particularly impressed by his understanding of the symbiotic relationship between the Committee and its witnesses. The fact that the Committee consisted in the main of a collection of clowns does not in Goodman's view sanctify its victims. . . . In its own terms, *The Committee* is a first-rate historical study—exhaustive in research, cool in judgment, brilliantly perceptive and eminently readable. It is also a glorious piece of Americana." James W. Carey agrees that the HUAC experience has been peculiarly American: "Witch-hunting happens to be a perennial part of American politics, a fact liberals sometimes conceal by fastening anti-democratic labels on nativist groups. Goodman understands this, and *The Committee* is as much a history of the American left since 1930 as of the right; of stupidity, duplicity and intolerance on both sides; and of a moralizing tendency to make partisan heroes, from Alger Hiss to Martin Dies, out of dubious political actors."

As Levitas has said, however, "there are readers who will regret Goodman's lack of outrage." Reviewing the book for *Ramparts,* L.M. Bensky wrote: "Walter Goodman is a prudent man. He has managed an extraordinary feat: he has produced a 564-page book on the House Un-American Activities Committee without once describing the structure of the Committee's staff; without ever analyzing its expenditures; without giving the reader a glimpse into its famous files; without more than summarily describing the lives and careers of its members and counsels; without seemingly having interviewed anyone but the drawer of old newspaper clippings he has rewritten; having devoted less than a half-dozen pages to the Committee's relations with the FBI; with only one mention of the CIA.... After a while the stream of self-consciousness which is Walter Goodman at work becomes an impossible barrier to learning anything." Eliot Fremont-Smith believes Goodman "writes fairly, or at least openly, and with suave good humor; but he fails to recapture either the drive of the investigators (the smell of blood) or the desperation of many of its victims. He makes it seem all quite hilarious, which it was, but only in part and not at the time."

Goodman's most recent book, *A Percentage of the Take,* is another example of lucid muckraking, this time focusing on the Marcus-Itkin-De Sapio case of 1967. Roger Starr calls the book "a succinct and entertaining morality play." In a review for *New Leader* Richard Reeves complains that "there are no characterizations in this book; the principals do not even make it as cardboard figures," despite the fact that *"A Percentage of the Take*—actually the story of a most unclassical case of American municipal corruption—fits the definition of the good magazine article. It is a fine piece of work, beautifully and professionally organized, with no holes in the telling." "Although this is journalism," writes Russell J. Williams of the State University of New York, "there are structural, thematic, and stylistic similarities between this work and the tragedies of Shakespeare, the moods of Herman Melville. But the sense of tragedy and pathos is perverted to satire. . . . Mr. Goodman is able. Well tried in no less than five fine documentaries, now his mockery intrudes and begins to weigh against him. He would be careful to measure it, advantage for disadvantage, science for art. A turn of fiction might serve him well: allow expression to his sense of farce, or force him to rein in on it, on deep-six tedious or impotent caustics. I hope he would try, rein, and still let the genius of intermittent raving flavor his work. He could write no innocuous love story. And kinds and quality are needed."

BIOGRAPHICAL/CRITICAL SOURCES: New York Times, March 22, 1968; *Book World,* March 24, 1968; *Newsweek,* March 25, 1968; *New Republic,* April 13, 1968; *Commonweal,* May 17, 1968, May 23, 1969; *New Leader,* May 20, 1968, March 22, 1971; *Ramparts,* June 15, 1968; *Commentary,* July, 1968, May, 1971; *National Review,* August 27, 1968; *New York Review of Books,* December 5, 1968; *New York Time Book Review,* May 4, 1969; *Harper's,* February, 1971; *Best Sellers,* February 15, 1971.

GORE, William Jay 1924-

PERSONAL: Born February 23, 1924; son of Jay I. and Gertrude (Moore) Gore; married Dorothy Elaine Mathison; children: Edmond, Kathleen, Brian. *Education:* University of Washington, Seattle, B.A., 1948; University of Southern California, M.P.A., 1950, D.P.A., 1951. *Religion:* Methodist. *Home:* 4310 43rd Ave. N.E., Seattle, Wash. 98105. *Office:* Department of Political Science, University of Washington, Seattle, Wash.

CAREER: University of Washington, Seattle, instructor in political science, 1951-56; University of Kansas, Lawrence, assistant professor of political science, 1957-58, 1960-62; Cornell University, Ithaca, N.Y., assistant professor of public administration, 1958-59; Indiana University, Bloomington, associate professor of government, 1962-66; University of Washington, Seattle, professor of political science, 1966—. *Military service:* U.S. Army, 1943-46. *Member:* American Political Science Association, American Society for Public Administration.

WRITINGS: (With Robert L. Peabody) *The Functions of the Political Campaign: A Case Study* (originally published in *Western Political Quarterly,* March, 1958), [Salt Lake City], 1958; (with Evelyn Shipman) *Commuters vs. the Black Ball Line: Washington Purchases the Puget Sound Ferries,* published for Inter University Case Program by University of Alabama Press, c.1959; (with Fred S. Silander) *A Bibliographical Essay on Decision Making* (originally published in *Administrative Science Quarterly,* June, 1959), Graduate School of Business and Public Administration, Cornell University, 1961; *Administrative Decision-Making: A Heuristic Model,* Wiley, 1964; (editor with James W. Dyson) *The Making of Decisions: A Reader in Administrative Behavior,* Free Press, 1964; (with William Bicker, David Brown, and Herbert Malakoff) *Comparative Urban Development: An Annotated Bibliography,* Comparative Administration Group, American Society for Public Administration, 1965; (editor with Leroy C. Hodapp) *Change in the Small Community: An Interdisciplinary Survey,* Friendship, 1967. Associate editor, *Administrative Science Quarterly;* contributing editor, *Public Administration Review.*

WORK IN PROGRESS: Analysis of processes of change in two community health service systems, to be published as research reports.

*   *   *

GORHAM, Maurice Anthony Coneys 1902- (Walter Rault)

PERSONAL: Born August 19, 1902, in London, England; son of James John (a medical doctor) and Mary (Smith) Gorham. *Education:* Attended Stonyhurst College; Balliol College, Oxford, B.A. (honors). *Religion:* Catholic. *Home:* 33 Sydney Parade Ave., Dublin 4, Ireland.

CAREER: Weekly Westminster, London, England, assistant editor, 1923-26; *Radio Times,* London, assistant editor and art editor, 1926-33; editor, 1933-41; British Broadcasting Corp., London, director of North American Service, 1941-44, began and directed Allied Expeditionary Forces Programme, 1944, and Light Programme, 1945, head of Television Service, 1945-47; Radio Eireann, Ireland, director of broadcasting, 1953-60. Consultant to Irish Tourist Board, 1960-63. *Member:* Society of Authors (London), Irish Georgian Society, Irish United Nations Association (president, 1967—), Tailors Hall Fund, Dublin Regional Tourism Association.

WRITINGS: (Editor) Kenneth Norman Bell, *The Way of History,* four volumes, Collins' Clear-Type Press, 1924; *The Local,* Cassell, 1939; *Sound and Fury: 21 Years in the BBC,* Percival Marshall, 1948; *Back to the Local,*

Percival Marshall, 1949; *Training for Radio*, UNESCO, 1949; (with Harding MacGregor Dunnett) *Inside the Pub*, Architectural Press, 1950; *Showmen and Suckers: An Excursion on the Crazy Fringe of the Entertainment World*, Percival Marshall, 1951; *Londoners*, Percival Marshall, 1951; *Broadcasting and Television Since 1900*, Dakers, 1952; *Forty Years of Irish Broadcasting*, published for Radio Telefis Eireann by Talbot Press, 1967; *Ireland Yesterday*, Viking, 1971 (published in England as *Ireland from Old Photographs*, Batsford, 1971).

AVOCATIONAL INTERESTS: Architecture, painting, sculpture, social history, caricature, drinks and drinking places, films, theater and music hall, typography, boxing, and preservation of amenities.

BIOGRAPHICAL/CRITICAL SOURCES: Times Literary Supplement, June 13, 1967.

* * *

GOSLIN, David A. 1936-

PERSONAL: Born October 27, 1936, in New York, N.Y.; son of Omar Pancoast (a minister) and Ryllis (Alexander) Goslin; married Ann Davis Compter (a teacher), September 6, 1958; children: Jean Davis. *Education:* Swarthmore College, B.A., 1958; Yale University, M.A., 1959, Ph.D., 1962. *Home:* 325 East 79th St., New York, N.Y. 10021. *Office:* Department of Education, Teachers College, Columbia University, New York, N.Y. 10027.

CAREER: Russell Sage Foundation, New York, N.Y., associate sociologist, 1961—; Columbia University, New York, N.Y., associate in sociology, 1961—. *Member:* American Sociological Association, Eastern Sociological Society, Yale Club (New York).

WRITINGS: The Search for Ability: Standardized Testing in Social Perspective, Russell Sage, 1963; *The School in Contemporary Society*, Scott, Foresman, 1965; (with Robert R. Epstein and Barbara A. Hallock) *The Use of Standardized Tests in Elementary Schools*, Russell Sage, 1965; *Teachers and Testing*, Russell Sage, 1967; (editor) *Handbook of Socialization Theory and Research*, Rand McNally, 1969. Contributor of articles to educational and sociological journals.

* * *

GOULD, Joseph E(dmund) 1912-

PERSONAL: Born November 30, 1912, in New York, N.Y.; son of Joseph E. and Alice (McDonough) Gould; married Phyllis Goranson, April 29, 1944. *Education:* University of Rochester, A.B., 1941; Syracuse University, Ph.D., 1951. *Office:* St. Andrew's School, Boca Raton, Fla. 33432.

CAREER: Fulbright lecturer, Pakistan, 1952-53; State University of New York College of Education at Fredonia, dean, 1952-62; St. Andrew's School, Boca Raton, Fla., head of history department, 1962—. *Member:* Phi Beta Kappa.

WRITINGS: The Chatauqua Movement: An Episode in the Continuing American Revolution, State University of New York Press, 1961; *Challenge and Change*, Harcourt, 1969.

WORK IN PROGRESS: Development of American education and its relation to political trends in the nineteenth century.

* * *

GOVER, (John) Robert 1929-

PERSONAL: Born November 2, 1929, in Philadelphia, Pa.; son of Bryant Addison and Anna (Wall) Gover; married Mildred Vitkovich (a nurse-anesthetist), March 15, 1955 (divorced, 1966); married Jeanne-Nell Gement, December 23, 1968; children: (second marriage) Bryant. *Education:* University of Pittsburgh, B.A., 1953. *Politics:* Anarchist. *Home:* 540 Picacho Lane, Montecito, California 93103. *Agent:* Scott Meredith Literary Agency, Inc., 580 Fifth Ave., New York, N.Y. 10036.

CAREER: Reporter for various small dailies in Pennsylvania and Maryland, 1954-60; also employed as a construction worker and bookstore salesman, and operator of a beach shop near Convention Hall, Atlantic City, N.J., 1960; full-time writer, 1961—. *Member:* Authors Guild, P.E.N.

WRITINGS—All novels: *One Hundred Dollar Misunderstanding* (first in a trilogy), Ballantine, 1961; *The Maniac Responsible*, Grove, 1963; *Here Goes Kitten* (second in the trilogy), Grove, 1964; *Poorboy at the Party*, Trident, 1966; *J.C. Saves* (last in the trilogy), Trident, 1968; *Going for Mr. Big*, Bantam, 1973.

Editor: *The Portable Walter* (anthology of prose and poetry of Walter Lowenfels), International Publishers, 1968. Also author of short stories and non-fiction; contributor to periodicals.

WORK IN PROGRESS: Two novels; the launching of a film company; various poems, essays, and journals.

SIDELIGHTS: Gover told *CA:* "I have tended to avoid public exposure or publicity about myself; I'd prefer to have my work succeed or fail on its own, keeping myself free to think and do the unexpected without the need to explain. If, later in life, my work has counted for something, I'd very much enjoy being honored ... [My] major vocational interest is human nature and the suicidal course our species is on, how we got on it and how we might get off it. Avocations: Digging people, the various styles they live in and the range of 'realities' they believe in."

BIOGRAPHICAL/CRITICAL SOURCES: L'Express, August 30, 1962; *Contemporary American Novelists*, edited by Harry T. Moore, Southern Illinois University Press, 1964; *New York Times Book Review*, August 25, 1968.

* * *

GOWING, Lawrence (Burnett) 1918-

PERSONAL: Born April 21, 1918, in London, England; son of Horace and Louise (Lawrence) Gowing; married Julia Frances Strachey, 1952. *Education:* Attended Leighton Park School; studied art under William Coldstream. *Home:* 17 Percy St., London W.1, England.

CAREER: University of Durham, Durham, England, professor of fine arts, 1948-58; King Edward VII School of Art, Newcastle upon Tyne, England, principal, 1948-58; Chelsea School of Art, London, England, principal, 1958—. Painter and art critic; work exhibited at one-man shows in 1942, 1946, 1948, 1955, and included in permanent collections of Tate Gallery, National Gallery of Canada, British Council, Arts Council, other collections. Trustee of Tate Gallery, 1953-60, 1961-64, of National Portrait Gallery, 1961—. Member of art panel of Arts Council of Great Britain, 1952—. *Awards, honors:* Commander, Order of the British Empire.

WRITINGS: (Author of introduction) *Paintings* (by Pierre Auguste Renoir), Lindsay Drummond, 1947; *Vermeer*, Faber, 1952, Beechhurst Press, 1953, 2nd edition, Faber, 1970; *Cezanne* (exhibition catalogue), Arts Council of Great Britain, 1953; (author of text) *Constable, 1776-1837*, Abrams, 1960; *Jan Vermeer*, Blandford Press, 1961, Barnes & Noble, 1962; *Francisco Goya*, Purnell, 1965; *Turner: Imagination and Reality*, Museum of Modern Art, 1966; (author of introduction) *Matisse, 1869-*

1954: A Retrospective Exhibition at the Hayward Gallery (catalogue), Arts Council of Great Britain, 1968. Contributor of articles and reviews to periodicals.

BIOGRAPHICAL/CRITICAL SOURCES: Criticism, spring, 1967.

*   *   *

GRAF, Rudolf F.   1926-

PERSONAL: Born August 17, 1926, in Vienna, Austria; came to United States in 1941; son of Oskar (an importer and manufacturer) and Berta (Witler) Graf; married Bettina Knisbacher (an interior decorator), April 20, 1952; children: Jeffrey Howard, Debra Helene. Education: RCA Institutes, Inc., New York, N.Y., degree in general technology, 1947; Polytechnic Institute of Brooklyn, B.E.E., 1951; New York University, M.B.A., 1954; Sussex College of Technology, Ph.D. (with honors), 1971. Home: 111 Van Etten Blvd., New Rochelle, N.Y. 10804.

CAREER: Hudson American Corp., Brooklyn, N.Y., test engineer, 1943-45; Radio City Products Co., Inc., New York, N.Y., design and development engineer, 1945-48; French-van Breems, Inc. (export agent for various electronic equipment firms), New York, N.Y., assistant to vice-president, 1948-49; Gotham Radio Institute, Bronx, N.Y., chief instructor, 1949-52; Camburn, Inc., Woodside, N.Y. director of engineering and sales, 1952-54; Sprague Electric Co., New York, N.Y., sales engineer, 1954—. Consultant on electronic projects. Holder of first class radio telephone operator's license. Military service: U.S. Navy, 1944-45. Member: Institute of Electrical and Electronics Engineers.

WRITINGS: Using and Understanding Probes, Sams, 1960; Modern Dictionary of Electronics, Sams, 1962, 4th edition, 1972; The Safe and Simple Book of Electricity: 101 Exciting Experiments Using Common Household Articles, Rider, 1964, reissued as Practical Electricity and Magnetism: 101 Exciting Electricity Experiments Using Common Household Articles, Lutterworth, 1967; The ABC's of Electronic Test Probes, 2nd edition, Sams, 1966, reissued with additional chapter by W. Oliver, Foulsham, 1967; (with George Whalen) Twenty-Five Solid State Projects, Hayden, 1970; Electronic Design Data Book, Van Nostrand, 1971; (with Whalen) Automotive Electronics, Sams, 1971 (published in England as The Manual of Car Electronics: With a Specially Written Chapter for the Guidance of the English Reader, Foulsham, 1972). Contributor of about fifty articles and charts to a dozen periodicals. Eastern editor of Radio-TV Maintenance, 1949-52.

WORK IN PROGRESS: Updating Modern Dictionary of Electronics; a book, How Everyday Gadgets Work.

SIDELIGHTS: Graf traveled extensively throughout Europe before coming to the United States, and achieved proficiency in several languages.

*   *   *

GRAHAM, Frank, Jr.   1925-

PERSONAL: Born March 31, 1925, in New York, N.Y.; son of Frank (a newspaperman) and Lillian (Whipp) Graham; married Ada Cogan, October 31, 1953. Education: Columbia University, A.B., 1950. Home: Milbridge, Me. 04658.

CAREER: New York Sun, New York, N.Y., copy boy, summers, 1947-49; Brooklyn Dodgers Baseball Club, Brooklyn, N.Y., publicity director, 1951-55; Sport (magazine), New York, N.Y., assistant managing editor, 1956-58; free-lance writer, 1958-69; Audubon Magazine, field editor, 1969—. Military service: U.S. Navy, 1943-46; served as torpedoman's mate aboard escort carrier "Marcus Island," and saw action at Palau, Philippines, and

Okinawa. Member: Authors Guild of the Authors League of America, National Audubon Society, Sierra Club, American Association for the Advancement of Science.

WRITINGS: Casey Stengel—His Half Century in Baseball, John Day, 1958; (with Mel Allen) It Takes Heart, Harper, 1959; Margaret Chase Smith, Woman of Courage (young people's book), John Day, 1964; Austria (juvenile), Macmillan, 1964; (with Jo Wasson Hoyt) For the Love of Mike, Random House, 1966; Disaster by Default: Politics and Water Pollution, M. Evans, 1966; Great Pennant Races of the Major Leagues (juvenile), Random House, 1967; (with Stanley Woodward) Sportswriter, Doubleday, 1967; Great No-Hit Games of the Major Leagues (juvenile), Random House, 1968; Great Hitters of the Major Leagues (juvenile), Random House, 1969; (with wife, Ada Graham) The Great American Shopping Cart: How America Gets Its Food Today (juvenile; originally announced as "Food from Farm to Table"), Simon & Schuster, 1969; Since Silent Spring, Houghton, 1970; (with Ada Graham) Wildlife Rescue (juvenile), Cowles, 1970; Man's Dominion: The Story of Conservation in America, M. Evans, 1971; (with Ada Graham) Puffin Island (juvenile), Cowles, 1971; (with Ada Graham) The Mystery of the Everglades, Random House, 1972. Contributor to American Heritage, Atlantic, Sports Illustrated, Audubon, and other periodicals and newspapers.

WORK IN PROGRESS: Books and magazine articles on conservation and the environment.

SIDELIGHTS: Published in 1964, Rachel Carson's Silent Spring was instrumental in awakening the public conscience to the dangers of pesticides. Since Silent Spring, "an ecological treatise in its own right," according to Tommy W. Rogers of Christian Century, continues that tradition with biographical information on Miss Carson and a hard-line case against the use of DDT and organic phosphate insecticides. Regrettably, as Deborah Kaetz of Harper's suggests, "in 1962 it was the giant chemical companies and their government lobbyists who were the loudest and strongest critics of Rachel Carson, and who will probably not listen to this second installment. . . . As factually up-to-date as [Graham's] book might be in its description of the problem, its message seems doomed not to reach the people that count."

BIOGRAPHICAL/CRITICAL SOURCES: New York Times Book Review, August 6, 1967, March 14, 1971; Washington Post, February 18, 1970; Harper's, March, 1970; Christian Century, October 7, 1970; Newsday, March 6, 1971; Saturday Review, April 24, 1971.

*   *   *

GRAHAM, Lorenz (Bell)   1902-

PERSONAL: Born January 27, 1902, in New Orleans, La.; son of David Andrew (a minister) and Etta (Bell) Graham; married Ruth Morris, August 20, 1929; children: Lorenz, Jr., Jean (deceased), Joyce (Mrs. Campbell C. Johnson), Ruth (Mrs. Herbert R. May), Charles. Education: Attended University of Washington, Seattle, 1921, University of California, Los Angeles, 1923-24; Virginia Union University, A.B., 1936; also studied at New York School of Social Work for two years, and at Columbia University and New York University. Politics: "Liberal, Democratic, sometimes called Left." Religion: Disciples of Christ. Home: 1400 Niagara Ave., Claremont, Calif. 91711

CAREER: Monrovia College, Liberia, West Africa, teacher and missionary, 1924-28; lecturer and fund raiser in United States for Foreign Mission Board, National Baptist Convention, 1929-32; teacher in Richmond, Va., 1933-35; U.S. Civilian Conservation Corps, camp educational adviser in Virginia and Pennsylvania, 1936-42;

manager of public housing, Newport News, Va., 1943-45; free-lance writer, real estate salesman, and building contractor, Long Island, N.Y., 1946-49; Queens Federation of Churches, New York, N.Y., social worker, 1950-57; Los Angeles County (Calif.) probation officer, 1958-66. Lecturer, California State Polytechnic College, 1970-71.

MEMBER: P.E.N. International, Authors League of America, National Association for the Advancement of Colored People, California Writers Guild. *Awards, honors:* Thomas Alva Edison Foundation special citation for *Ten Commandments;* Follett $3,000 Award, 1958, and Child Study Association of America award, 1959, both for *South Town;* Association for Study of Negro Life and History award, 1959; Los Angeles (Calif.) City Council award, 1966; Southern California Council on Literature for Children and Young People award, 1968; first prize, *Book World,* 1969, for *Whose Town?.*

WRITINGS—All juveniles: *How God Fix Jonah* (collection of Biblical tales told in Liberian dialect), Reynal & Hitchcock, 1946; *Tales of Momolu,* Reynal & Hitchcock, 1946; (adapter) *The Story of Jesus,* Gilberton, 1955; *The Ten Commandments,* Gilberton, 1956; *South Town,* Follett, 1958; *North Town,* Crowell, 1965; *I, Momolu,* Crowell, 1966; *Whose Town?,* Crowell, 1969; *Every Man Heart Lay Down* (originally published in *How God Fix Jonah*—see above), Crowell, 1970; *A Road Down in the Sea,* Crowell, 1970; *God Wash the World and Start Again,* Crowell, 1971; *John Brown,* Scholastic Magazines, 1971; *David He No Fear,* Crowell, 1971; *Hongry Catch the Foolish Boy,* Crowell, 1973. Author of plays for amateur groups, schools, and colleges. Contributor of articles to agency and department publications.

SIDELIGHTS: Graham told *CA:* "As a Negro I grew up with fears and hatreds for white people and came to understanding of these destructive emotions only after being outside the United States and separated from the 'race problem.' I concluded that people, all people, should be brought to better understanding of other people.

"For this I work and write. . . . My personal problem with publishers has been the difference between my images and theirs. Publishers have told me that my characters, African and American black people, are 'too much like white people.' And I say, 'If you look closely you will see that people are people.' "

BIOGRAPHICAL/CRITICAL SOURCES: Charlotte S. Huck and D.A. Young, *Children's Literature in the Elementary School,* Holt, 1961; *The Children's Bookshelf,* Child Study Association of America, Bantam, 1965; *Books for Children, 1960-1965,* American Library Association, 1966; Nancy Larrick, *A Parent's Guide to Children's Reading,* 3rd edition, Doubleday, 1969; *Young Readers' Review,* May, 1969; *Saturday Review,* May 10, 1969, March 20, 1971; *Horn Book,* August, 1969, December, 1970, April, 1971; *Commonweal,* May 21, 1971.

*   *   *

GRAHAM, Margaret Althea 1924-

PERSONAL: Born April 1, 1924, in Greenwood, S.C.; daughter of Frank Kirkland and Alice Elizabeth (McKnight) Graham. *Education:* National Bible Institute (now Shelton College), Bachelor of Religious Education, 1948; special courses at Northwestern University, other colleges. *Politics:* Republican. *Religion:* Presbyterian. *Office address:* Box 1162, Laurinburgh, N.C. 28352.

CAREER: Scripture Press, Wheaton, Ill., editor and writer, 1950-52; free-lance writer for religious press, 1952-54; Laurinburg (N.C.) Public Schools, teacher of Bible, 1954—. *Member:* National Education Association, North Carolina Education Association.

WRITINGS: (With Nels Andersen) *Vacation Bible School,* Evangelical Teacher Training Association; *Careers for Christian Young People,* VanKampen, 1954; (compiler and contributor with Nancy Bates) *How to Win a Sunday School Contest,* Scripture Press, 1958; *Marilyn's Adventures* (teen-age fiction), Zondervan, 1963; *How to Teach the Bible to Children in the Home,* National Press, c.1966; *Teen-age Devotionals,* Moody, 1971. Contributor of articles to *Christianity Today, Christian Life,* and other religious publications.

WORK IN PROGRESS: A historical novel of late eighteenth and early nineteenth-centuries.

AVOCATIONAL INTERESTS: Painting.

*   *   *

GRAHAM, William Franklin 1918- (Billy Graham)

PERSONAL: Born November 7, 1918, in Charlotte, N.C.; son of William Franklin (a dairy farmer) and Morrow (Coffey) Graham; married Ruth McCue Bell, August 13, 1943; children: Virginia Leftwich (Mrs. Stephan Tchividjian), Ann Morrow (Mrs. Daniel Lotz), Ruth Bell (Mrs. Ted Dienert), William Franklin, Jr., Nelson Edman. *Education:* Florida Bible Institute, Th.B., 1940; Wheaton College, Wheaton, Ill., B.A., 1943. *Home:* Montreat, N.C. *Agent:* Bennett Advertising Agency, 20 North Wacker Dr., Chicago, Ill. 60606. *Office:* 1300 Harmon Pl., Minneapolis, Minn. 55403.

CAREER: Ordained to Baptist ministry, 1940; pastor in Western Springs, Ill., and radio personality, "Songs in the Night," on WCFL, Chicago, Ill., 1943-45; began Crusades for Christ, 1946; Northwestern Schools (now Northwestern College), Minneapolis, Minn., president, 1947-52; Billy Graham Evangelistic Association, Minneapolis, Minn., founder and president, 1950—. Youth for Christ International, first vice-president, 1946—. Leader of weekly "Hour of Decision," television and radio program on American and Canadian broadcasting networks, and on worldwide short-wave hookups. Head of Billy Graham Evangelistic Films, Inc., producers of religious films; president of Blue Ridge Broadcasting Corp. (operator of non-commercial radio station WFGW), Black Mountain, N.C.

MEMBER: Royal Geographic Society (fellow), Royal Literary Society, Suburban Professional Men's Club (founder), 1943—. *Awards, honors:* Bernard Baruch Award, 1955; Freedoms Foundation Awards, 1955, 1969; Clergyman-Churchman of the Year, National Pilgrim Society, 1956; Gold Medal, National Institute of Social Science, 1957; Humane Order of African Redemption, 1960; Gutenberg Award, Chicago Bible Society, 1962; Gold Medal, George Washington Carver Memorial Institute, 1963; speaker of the Year Award, 1964; Horatio Alger Award, 1965; Gold Plate Award, American Academy of Achievement, 1965; National Citizenship Award, Military Chaplains Association of the United States, 1965; Big Brother of the Year Award at the White House, Washington, D.C., 1966; Silver Medallion, 1967, International Brotherhood Award, 1971, from the National Conference of Christians and Jews; Torch of Liberty Plaque, Anti-Defamation League of B'nai B'rith, 1969; Distinguished Service Award from the National Association of Broadcasters, 1972; Franciscan International Award, 1972; International Youth's Distinguished Service Citizen; Distinguished Service Medal, Salvation Army; LL.D. from Houghton College, 1950, The Citadel, Baylor University; D.D. from King's College, 1948, Wheaton College, Wheaton, Ill., and William Jewell College; D.Hum. from Bob Jones University, 1948.

WRITINGS: *Calling Youth to Christ,* Zondervan, 1947; (with others) *Revival in Our Time,* Van Kampen, 1950; (contributor) *America's Hour of Decision* (radio sermons), Van Kampen, 1951; (author of introduction) James Edwin Orr, *Full Surrender,* Christian Li erature Crusade, 1951; *The Chance of a Lifetime: Helps for Servicemen,* Zondervan, 1952; *The Work of an Evangelist: An Address,* World's Evangelical Alliance (London), 1953; *Peace with God,* Doubleday, 1953; *I Saw Your Sons at War: The Korean Diary of Billy Graham,* Billy Graham Evangelistic Association (Minneapolis), 1953; (author of speeches) Charles Thomas Cook, *The Billy Graham Story,* Van Kampen, 1954; *The Secret of Happiness: Jesus' Teaching on Happiness as Expressed in the Beatitudes,* Doubleday, 1955 (published in England as *The Secret of Happiness: The Teaching of Jesus as Expressed in the Beatitudes,* World's Work, 1956); *The Seven Deadly Sins,* Zondervan, 1956; George Burnham, *To the Far Corners with Billy Graham in Asia* (includes excerpts from Graham's diary), Revell, 1956 (published in England as *With Billy Graham in Asia,* with an introduction by Graham, Marshall, Morgan & Scott, 1956); (author of foreword and message) Robert O. Ferm, editor, *They Met God at the New York Crusade,* Billy Graham Evangelistic Association, 1957; *Billy Graham Talks to Teenagers,* Miracle Books, 1958; (author of message) Robert O. Ferm, *Persuaded to Live: Conversion Stories from the Billy Graham Crusades,* Revell, 1958; (with Hubert Eaton) *Mass Public Education: The Tool of the Dictator* [and] *Hope for Tommorrow* (the former by Eaton, the latter by Graham), Forest Lawn Memorial Park Association, 1958; (author of foreword and keynote sermon) Sherwood Eliot Wirt, *Crusade at the Golden Gate,* Harper, 1959; (author of foreword) Warner Hutchinson and Cliff Wilson, *Let the People Rejoice,* Crusader Bookroom Society, Ltd. (Wellington, N.Z.) 1959.

My Answer, Doubleday, 1960; *World Aflame,* Doubleday, 1965; *The New Birth* (excerpts from *World Aflame*), [Washington, D.C.], 1965; *The Quotable Billy Graham,* compiled and edited by Cort R. Flint and the staff of *Quote,* Droke, 1966; (author of preface) Curtis Mitchell, *Those Who Came Forward: Men and Women Who Responded to the Ministry of Billy Graham,* Chilton, 1966 (published in England as *Those Who Came Forward: An Account of Those Whose Lives Were Changed by the Ministry of Billy Graham,* World's Work, 1966); (author of introduction) Lewis F. Brabham, *A New Song in the South: The Story of the Billy Graham Greenville, S.C. Crusade,* Zondervan, 1966; (contributor) Bill Adler, compiler, *My Favorite Funny Story,* Four Winds, 1967; *The Wit and Wisdom of Billy Graham,* edited and compiled by Bill Adler, Random House, 1967; (contributor) Cliff Barrows, editor, *Crusade Hymn Stories,* Hope Publishing, 1967; *The Faith of Billy Graham,* compiled and edited by T.S. Settel, Droke, 1968; *The Challenge: Sermons from Madison Square Garden,* Doubleday, 1969; *The Jesus Generation,* Zondervan, 1971.

Represented in several anthologies, including *Best Sermons: 1955,* edited by George Paul Butler, Crowell, 1955; *American Principles and Issues: The National Purpose,* edited by Oscar Handlin, Holt, 1961, and *White on Black: The Views of Twenty-two White Americans on the Negro,* edited by Era Bell Thompson and Herbert Nipson, Johnson Publishing Co. (Chicago), 1963.

Author of syndicated daily newspaper column, "My Answer." Editor-in-chief, *Decision* Magazine.

Contributor to *Church Today, Good Housekeeping, McCall's, Reader's Digest, Redbook, Saturday Evening Post, Christian Century, Cosmopolitan, American Mercury,* and other periodicals.

SIDELIGHTS: "The meaning of the word 'evangelist' is 'proclaimer,' a proclaimer of good news.... My job is not to defend the Gospel; my job is simply to proclaim the Gospel, and to let the Spirit of God apply in the individual hearts." Thus, Billy Graham succinctly describes what he and his followers believe to be their mission in the world. Emphasizing that he is no theological scholar ("My only specialty is soul-winning. I'm not a great philosopher, not a theologian, not an intellectual...."), Graham modestly describes himself as "just a small item on the back page of heaven's newspapers...." Despite this personal humility, he has sought to reach souls on six continents and has received over one million "Decisions for Christ." He uses extensively radio, television, and motion pictures; and has appeared in or promoted numerous films which usually deal with the process of conversion in his various crusades.

Because he is the most famous and successful evangelist in recent times, Graham is also the subject of much discussion. Many of his more orthodox contemporaries regard him as too liberal. John Pollock, Graham's authorized biographer, describes the evangelist's initial dismay when he was first attacked by some fundamentalists. "Certain conservatives such as Dr. John R. Rice and Dr. Carl McIntire pronounced him guilty of association with men of false beliefs on the Bible, the atonement and other 'fundamentals' of the faith; he should separate himself from all who were unsound...." A 1956 editorial in *Christian Century* expresses the view of more liberal Christians toward Graham. "Our concern is ... with the attenuation of the Christian gospel which comes about because of too close a linkage of evangelism with the promotional methods which are routine in the advertising profession. For example, few insiders believe Billy Graham writes the syndicated newspaper columns which appear over his name in papers from coast to coast. Isn't simple, ordinary honesty a requirement in mass evangelism? ... Can a man who is surrounded by the entourage which has snowballed up around Billy Graham be sensitive to the promptings of the Holy Spirit in our time? It is a well-known fact that it is about as difficult to penetrate this dedicated corps of Graham assistants to reach the man himself, either personally or by letter, as it is to reach President Eisenhower.... There are dangers in such insulation, and Billy Graham's Master recognized them and refused to submit when solicitous disciples sought to wall him off."

Other critics find fault with Graham's theological techniques. Reinhold Niebuhr believes that Graham oversimplifies moral issues to the detriment of his goal. "Thus Graham declares: 'Every human problem can be solved and every hunger satisfied and every potential can be fulfilled when a man encounters Jesus Christ and comes in vital relation to God in him.' Perhaps these solutions are rather too simple in any age, but particularly so in a nuclear one with its great moral perplexities, such a message is not convincing to anyone—Christian or not—who is aware of the continual possibilities of good and evil in every advance of civilization, every discipline of culture, and every religious convention. Graham offers Christian evangelism less complicated answers than it has ever before provided.... [He] promises a new life, not through painful religious experience but merely by signing a decision card. Thus, a miracle of regeneration is promised at a painless price by an obviously sincere evangelist. It is a bargain."

Many clergy and layman, however, feel that Graham is performing a valuable service. Dr. John Sutherland Bonnell, a Presbyterian pastor in New York City, believes that Graham's crusades will have a continuing impact on the modern world. "For years to come these churches will be vitalized by the influence of the crusade, as the churches of Britain for decades felt the impact of the revival they made under Dwight L. Moody's leadership. . . . [Another] readily discernable contribution is the creation of spiritual climate favorable to religious decision." In a public statement Richard Cardinal Cushing said: "I have never known of a religious crusade that was more effective.... Dr. Graham's crusade has something tremendously needed in our day and age. I only wish we had half a dozen men of his caliber to go forth and do likewise—that is, to preach Christ and Him crucified to the modern world."

Graham accepts criticism and praise with equal composure, although he believes the majority of Christians support his cause. "Some of the extreme fundamentalists are among my most vocal critics," says Graham, "and extreme liberals think I'm too fundamentalist. But I think the vast majority of church people support me." In any case there is little indication that either liberal or conservative critics have changed the message he has been preaching for over twenty years, a belief that the process of conversion is available to anyone who will sincerely embrace it. "In conversion, as you stand at the foot of the cross, the Holy Spirit makes you realize that you are a sinner," Graham preaches. "He directs your faith to the Christ who died in your place. You must open your heart and let Him come in. At that precise moment the Holy Spirit performs the miracle of the new birth. You actually become a new moral creature.... Conversion is so simple that the smallest child can be converted.... God has made the way of salvation so plain that 'the wayfaring men, though fools, shall not err therein.' [No one is] barred from the Kingdom of God because he did not have the capacity to understand. The rich and the poor, the sophisticated and the simple—all can be converted."

BIOGRAPHICAL/CRITICAL SOURCES—Books: *America's Hour of Decision*, Van Kampen, 1951; Arthur R. Chapple, *Billy Graham*, Marshall, Morgan & Scott, 1954; Charles Thomas Cook, *The Billy Graham Story*, Van Kampen, 1954; Lewis W. Gillenson, *Billy Graham: The Man and His Message*, Fawcett, 1954; Charles Thomas Cook, *London Hears Billy Graham*, Grason Co., 1954; Tom Allan, editor, *Crusade in Scotland*, Pickering & Inglis, 1955; George Burnham, *Billy Graham: A Mission Accomplished*, Revell, 1955; Frank Colquhoun, *Harringay Story*, Hodder & Stoughton, 1955; Stanley High, *Billy Graham: The Personal Story of the Man, His Message and His Mission*, McGraw, 1956; George Burnham, *To the Far Corners with Billy Graham in Asia*, Revell, 1956; Edward Oliver England, *Afterwards: A Journalist Sets Out to Discover What Happened to Some of Those Who Made a Decision for Christ During the Billy Graham Crusades in Britain in 1954 and 1955*, Elim, 1957; George Burnham and Lee Fisher, *Billy Graham and the New York Crusade*, Zondervan, 1957; Curtis Mitchell, *God in the Garden: The Story of the Billy Graham New York Crusade*, Doubleday, 1957; J.B. Priestley, *Thoughts in the Wilderness*, Harper, 1957; Robert O. Ferm, *Cooperative Evangelism: Is Billy Graham Right or Wrong?*, Zondervan, 1958; Robert O. Ferm, *Persuaded to Live: Conversion Stories from the Billy Graham Crusades*, Revell, 1958; Reinhold Niebuhr, *Essays in Applied Christianity*, selected and edited by D.B. Robertson, Meridian Books, 1959; Warner Hutchinson and Cliff Wilson, *Let the People Rejoice*, Crusader Bookroom Society, 1959; Sherwood Eliot Wirt, *Crusade at the Golden Gate*, Harper, 1959; William Gerald McLoughlin, *Billy Graham: Revivalist in a Secular Age*, Ronald, 1960; Stuart Barton Babbage and Ian Siggins, *Light Beneath the Cross*, Doubleday, 1960; Maurice R. Stein, Arthur J. Vidich, and David Manning White, editors, *Identity and Anxiety: Survival of the Person in Mass Society*, Free Press, 1960; Harold E. Fey and Margaret Frakes, editors, *The Chris-*

tian Century Reader: Representative Articles, Editorials, and Poems Selected from More than Fifty Years of the Christian Century, Association Press, 1962; *Meet Billy Graham: A Pictorial Record of the Evangelist, His Family and His Team*, Pitkin, 1966; Lewis F. Brabham, *A New Song in the South: The Story of the Billy Graham Greenville, S.C. Crusade*, Zondervan, 1966; Curtis Mitchell, *Billy Graham: The Making of a Crusader*, Chilton, 1966; John C. Pollock, *Billy Graham: The Authorized Biography*, McGraw, 1966; James E. Kilgore, *Billy Graham the Preacher*, Exposition, 1968; Alan Levy, *God Bless You Real Good: My Crusade with Billy Graham*, Essandess, 1969.

Articles: *Life*, November 21, 1949, May 27, 1957, July 1, 1957, March 21, 1960, June 30, 1961, August 30, 1963; *Time*, March 20, 1950, July 15, 1966, July 21, 1967, February 7, 1969, June 27, 1969; *Newsweek*, May 1, 1950, February 25, 1957, May 20, 1957, July 22, 1957, February 3, 1958, June 23, 1958, October 6, 1958, February 16, 1959, March 9, 1959, March 28, 1960, February 26, 1962, September 2, 1963, July 24, 1967; *Library Journal*, November 15, 1953, November 15, 1955, November 1, 1960, January 15, 1970; *New York Times*, December 6, 1953, December 11, 1955, May 5, 1969; *Chicago Sunday Tribune*, December 13, 1953, December 18, 1955; *New Republic*, August 22, 1955; *Nation*, April 7, 1956, May 11, 1957, February 8, 1958; *Christian Century*, November 21, 1956; *New York Times Magazine*, April 21, 1957; *Atlantic*, June, 1957; *New Yorker*, June 8, 1957; *Commonweal*, June 21, 1957, July 25, 1969; *Holiday*, March, 1958; *Observer*, June 25, 1967; *Harper's*, February, 1969; *Village Voice*, July 19, 1969; *Choice*, May, 1970.

*   *   *

GRANGER, Clive W(illiam) J(ohn) 1934-

PERSONAL: Born September 4, 1934, in Swansea, Glamorganshire, Wales; son of Edward John (a divisional sales manager) and Evelyn (Hessey) Granger; married Patricia Anne Loveland, May 14, 1960; children: Mark William John, Claire. *Education:* University of Nottingham, B.A. (first class honors), 1955, Ph.D., 1959. *Home:* Croft House, Hall Croft, Beeston, Nottingham, England. *Office:* Mathematics Department, University of Nottingham, Nottingham, England.

CAREER: University of Nottingham, Nottingham, England, reader in economics, 1956—. Research associate, Econometric Research Program, Princeton University, 1960—; visiting assistant professor of statistics, Stanford University, 1963; visiting professor of economics, University of California, San Diego, 1969. Consultant, Pricing Research Ltd., 1971. *Member:* Royal Statistical Society (fellow), Institute of Mathematical Statistics. *Awards, honors:* Harkness fellow, Commonwealth Fund, 1960.

WRITINGS: (With Michio Hatanaka) *Spectral Analysis of Economic Time Series*, Princeton University Press, 1964; *Investigating the Future: Statistical Forecasting Problems* (lecture), University of Nottingham, 1967; (with Morgenstern) *Predictability of Stock Market Prices*, Heath Lexington, 1970; (with Walter C. Labys) *Speculation Hedging, and Commodity Price Forecasts*, Heath Lexington, 1970. Author of approximately fifty research papers. Contributor to academic journals in Europe and America, including *Information and Control, Kyklos*, and *L'Industria*.

WORK IN PROGRESS: Research on econometrics, time series analysis, and forecasting and marketing.

SIDELIGHTS: Granger told *CA*: "I have the usual Englishman's interest in travel combined with incompetence in other people's languages." Granger camped his way around the United States in 1960.

GRAY, John 1913-

PERSONAL: Born June 9, 1913, in Kelso, Roxburgh-shire, Scotland; son of James Telfer and Mary Ann (Patterson) Gray; married Janet J. Gibson, July 22, 1942; children: James, Ian, Walter, Alastair, Jean. Education: University of Edinburgh, M.A. (honors), 1935, B.D. (with distinction in Oriental languages), 1939, Ph.D., 1939. Home: Inverawe, Persley, Aberdeen, Scotland.

CAREER: Ordained to ministry, Church of Scotland, 1939; colonial chaplain in Palestine, 1939-41; minister, Isle of Arran, Scotland, 1942-47; University of Manchester, Manchester, England, lecturer in Semitic languages and literatures, 1947-53; University of Aberdeen, Aberdeen, Scotland, lecturer, 1953-62, professor of Hebrew and Semitic languages at King's College, 1962—. Member: Society for Old Testament Study.

WRITINGS: The KRT Text in the Literature of Ras Shamra: A Social Myth of Ancient Canaan, E.J. Brill (Leiden), 1955, 2nd edition, 1964; (contributor) Alan Rowe, editor, Cyrenacian Expedition of the University of Manchester, 1952, Victoria University, 1956; The Legacy of Canaan: The Ras Shamra Texts and Their Relevance to the Old Testament, E.J. Brill, 1957, 2nd revised edition, 1965; Archaeology and the Old Testament World, Thomas Nelson, 1962; I and II Kings: A Commentary, Westminster, 1963, 2nd revised edition, S.C.M. Press, 1970, Westminster, 1971; The Canaanites, Praeger, 1964; (editor) Joshua, Judges and Ruth, Thomas Nelson, 1967; A History of Jerusalem, Praeger, 1969; Near Eastern Mythology, Hamlyn, 1969; What About the Children?, S.C.M. Press, 1970. Contributor to Bible dictionaries and commentaries; contributor of articles to academic journals.

WORK IN PROGRESS: Bible commentaries for Abingdon and Century Press.

SIDELIGHTS: Gray is competent in French, German, Norwegian, Arabic, and Greek. Avocational interests: Fishing, beekeeping, and gardening.

*   *   *

GRAYLAND, Valerie Merle (Spanner) (Lee Belvedere, V. Merle Grayland)

PERSONAL: Born in Thames, New Zealand; daughter of Jens Koeford (a farmer) and Eva (Howe) Spanner; married Eugene Charles Grayland (a journalist), November 13, 1948. Education: Attended Seddon Memorial Technical College, Auckland, New Zealand. Religion: Anglican. Home: 55 Athens Rd., One Tree Hill, Auckland, New Zealand.

CAREER: Office worker until 1948; free-lance writer of mystery novels and books for children, 1948—. Member: P.E.N., Mystery Writers of America.

WRITINGS—Mystery novels under name V. Merle Grayland: The Dead Men of Eden, R. Hale, 1962; Night of the Reaper, R. Hale, 1963; The Grave-Digger's Apprentice, R. Hale, 1964; Jest of Darkness, R. Hale, 1965.

Novels under pseudonym Lee Belvedere: Farewell to a Valley, Bouregy, 1971.

Children's books under name Valerie Grayland: The First Strawberry, Colenso Press, 1954; John and Hoani, Blackie & Son, 1962; Early One Morning, Rand McNally, 1963; Baby Sister, Rand McNally, 1964. Children's stories anthologized in White Robin Story-Book, Longacre Press, 1960, and Lucky Dip, edited by Barbara Ker Wilson, Angus & Robertson, 1970.

Nonfiction, with husband, Eugene C. Grayland: Coromandel Coast, A.H. & A.W. Reed, 1965, revised edition, 1968; Historic Coromandel, A.H. & A.W. Reed, 1969; Tarawera, Hodder & Stoughton, 1971. Contributor of articles and short stories to magazines in Australia and New Zealand. Joint editor, Hearing News.

WORK IN PROGRESS: A novel under pseudonym Lee Belvedere, Meet a Dark Stranger; a Gothic mystery, The Heights of Havenrest.

SIDELIGHTS: Mrs. Grayland created a Maori detective, Hoani Mata, for her mystery novels. She has given her children's book manuscripts to the Southern Mississippi University Library for a special collection, and, as a hobby, runs a private press with her husband.

*   *   *

GREEN, Constance McLaughlin 1897-

PERSONAL: Born August 21, 1897, in Ann Arbor, Mich.; daughter of Andrew Cunningham (a historian) and Lois Thompson (Angell) McLaughlin; married Donald Ross Green, February 14, 1921 (died, 1946); children: Lois Angell (Mrs. Jack Ladd Carr), Donald Ross, Elizabeth L. (deceased). Education: University of Chicago, student, 1914-16; Smith College, A.B., 1919; Mount Holyoke College, M.A., 1925; Yale University, Ph.D., 1937. Politics: Democrat. Religion: Congregational. Home and office: 19 Second St. N.E., Washington, D.C. 20002. Agent: Margot Johnson Agency, 405 East 54th St., New York, N.Y. 10022.

CAREER: University of Chicago, Chicago, Ill., instructor in English, 1919-20; Mount Holyoke College, South Hadley, Mass., instructor in history, 1925-32; Smith College, Northampton, Mass., instructor in history, 1938-39, director of research, Council of Industrial Studies, 1939-46; U.S. Army Ordnance Department, Springfield, Mass., historian, 1942-45; American National Red Cross, Washington, D.C., historian, 1947-48; U.S. Army Ordnance Corps, Washington, D.C., chief historian, 1948-51; Office of Secretary of Defense, Research and Development Board, historian, 1951-54; Washington History Project administered by American University, Washington, D.C., director, 1954-60. University College, University of London, Commonwealth Fund lecturer in American history, 1951; visiting professor of history, Dartmouth College, 1971. National Capital Planning Commission, member of landmarks committee.

MEMBER: American Historical Association, Economic History Association, Americans for Democratic Action, Organization of American Historians, Committee on the History of Social Welfare, U.S. Capitol Historical Society, Capitol Hill Restoration Society, Washington Literary Society (corresponding secretary, 1961-63). Awards, honors: Eggleston Prize in history, Yane University, for Holyoke, Massachusetts: A Case History of the Industrial Revolution in America; Pulitzer Prize in history, 1963, for Washington, Village and Capital, 1800-1878; Litt.D. from Smith College, 1963, and Pace College.

WRITINGS: Holyoke, Massachusetts: A Case History of the Industrial Revolution in America, Yale University Press, 1939; The Role of Women as Production Workers in War Plants of the Connecticut Valley, Smith College, 1946; History of Naugatuck, Connecticut, Yale University Press, 1949; Eli Whitney and the Birth of American Technology, Little, Brown, 1956; American Cities in the Growth of the Nation, De Graff, 1957; Washington, Village and Capital, 1800-1878, Princeton University Press, 1962; Washington, Capital City, 1879-1950, Princeton University Press, 1963; The Rise of Urban America, Harper, 1965; The Secret City: A History of Race Relations in the Nation's Capital, Princeton University Press, 1967; The Church on Lafayette Square: A History of St. John's Church, Washington, D.C., 1815-1970, Potomac, 1970; (with Milton Lomask) Vanguard: A History, Smithsonian Institution Press, 1971.

Contributor: A.B. Hart, editor, *Commonwealth History of Massachusetts*, Volume I, States History Co., 1929; Caroline Ware, editor, *The Cultural Approach to History*, Columbia University Press, 1939; E.A.J. Johnston and Harold Williamson, editors, *Growth of the American Economy*, Prentice-Hall, 1943; *The Ordnance Department*, Office of Chief of Military History, Department of the Army, 1955-68. Contributor of articles to *Encyclopaedia Britannica, Encyclopedia Americana*, book reviews to historical journals.

WORK IN PROGRESS: Urban Life in American History, for Dial.

AVOCATIONAL INTERESTS: Reading thrillers, travel, gardening.

BIOGRAPHICAL/CRITICAL SOURCES: American, November, 1950; *New York Times Book Review*, May 14, 1967; *South Atlantic Quarterly*, autumn, 1967.

*   *   *

GREEN, Otis H(oward)   1898-

PERSONAL: Born December 11, 1898, in Monroe, Mich.; son of John Howard (a clergyman) and Cora (Dike) Green; married Mabel Barnett, June 11, 1924; children: Eleanor Irving (Mrs. John Laing Wise, Jr.), Paul Barnett. *Education:* Colgate University, A.B., 1920; Pennsylvania State College, M.A., 1923; University of Pennsylvania, Ph.D., 1927. *Politics:* Republican. *Religion:* Protestant. *Home:* 60 East Levering Mill Rd., Bala-Cynwyd, Pa. 19004. *Office:* Logan Hall, University of Pennsylvania, Philadelphia, Pa. 19104.

CAREER: Peddie School, Hightstown, N.J., teacher of French and Spanish, 1920-21; Pennsylvania State College, University Park, instructor in French and Spanish, 1921-23; University of Pennsylvania, Philadelphia, instructor, 1923-28, assistant professor, 1928-36, associate professor, 1936-39, chairman of department of romance languages, 1938-45, professor of Spanish, 1939—. University of Colorado, visiting professor, five summers, 1934-57. *Member:* Modern Language Association of America (president, 1968), American Association of Teachers of Spanish, Modern Humanities Research Association, Mediaeval Academy of America, Renaissance Society of America. *Awards, honors:* Guggenheim fellow, 1964-65.

WRITINGS: Life and Works of Lupercio Leonardo de Argensola, University of Pennsylvania Press, 1927; (editor) Lucio Victorio Mansilla, *Una Excursion a los Indios Ranqueles*, Holt, 1944; *Courtly Love in Quevedo*, University of Colorado Press, 1952; *Spain and the Western Tradition: The Castilian Mind in Literature from El Cid to Calderon*, four volumes, University of Wisconsin Press, 1963-66; *The Literary Mind of Medieval and Renaissance Spain* (essays), University Press of Kentucky, 1970. Contributor of articles to philological journals in Europe and North and South America. *Hispanic Review*, co-editor, 1939-69, honorary editor, 1969—.

AVOCATIONAL INTERESTS: Camping, mountaineering, wilderness travel.

BIOGRAPHICAL/CRITICAL SOURCES: Books Abroad, autumn, 1967, winter, 1967.

*   *   *

GREEN, Vivian Hubert Howard   1915-

PERSONAL: Born November 18, 1915, in Wembley, Middlesex, England; son of Hubert J. and Edith (Howard) Green. *Education:* Attended Bradfield College, 1929-34; Trinity Hall, Cambridge, B.A., 1937, M.A., 1941; Cambridge University, B.D., 1945; D.D., 1957; Oxford University, B.D., 1951, D.D., 1957. *Home:* Lincoln College, Oxford and Calendars, Sheep St., Burford, Oxford, England.

CAREER: Clergyman, Church of England; St. Augustine's College, Canterbury, England, fellow and lecturer, 1938-40; St. Luke's College, Exeter, England, chaplain and lecturer, 1940-42; Sherborne School, Dorsetshire, England, chaplain and master, 1942-51; Lincoln College, Oxford University, Oxford, England, fellow and lecturer, 1951—, senior tutor, 1953-61, chaplain, 1957-69, subrector, 1970—.

WRITINGS: Bishop Reginald Pecock: A Study in Ecclesiastical History and Thought, Cambridge University Press, 1945; *From St. Augustine to William Temple: Eight Studies in Christian Leadership*, Latimer House, 1948; *The Hanoverians, 1714-1815*, Edward Arnold, 1948; *Renaissance and Reformation: A Survey of European History Between 1450 and 1660*, Edward Arnold, 1952, 2nd edition, St. Martin's, 1964; *The Later Plantagenets: A Survey of English History Between 1307 and 1485*, Edward Arnold, 1955; *Oxford Common Room: A Study of Lincoln and Mark Pattison*, Edward Arnold, 1957; *The Young Mr. Wesley: A Study of John Wesley and Oxford*, St. Martin's, 1961; *The Swiss Alps*, Batsford, 1961; *Luther and the Reformation*, Putnam, 1964 (published in England as *Martin Luther and the German Reformation*, Batsford, 1964); *John Wesley*, Thomas Nelson, 1964; *Religion at Oxford and Cambridge*, S.C.M. Press, 1964; *The Universities*, Penguin, 1969; *Medieval Civilization*, St. Martin's, 1971 (published in England as *Medieval Civilization in Western Europe*, Edward Arnold, 1971).

*   *   *

GREENBERG, Sidney   1917-

PERSONAL: Born September 27, 1917, in Brooklyn, N.Y.; son of Morris (a presser) and Sadie (Armel) Greenberg; married Hilda Weiss, October 31, 1942; children: Shira Beth, Reena Keren, Adena Joy. *Education:* Yeshiva University, A.B., 1938; Jewish Theological Seminary, Rabbi, 1942, Doctor of Hebrew Literature, 1947. *Home:* 300 Old Farm Rd., Wyncote, Pa. 19095.

CAREER: Temple Sinai, Philadelphia, Pa., rabbi, 1942—. *Military service:* U.S. Army, chaplain, 1944-46; became captain. *Member:* Zionist Organization of America, Jewish Chaplains Association, Rabbinical Assembly of America (president, Philadelphia branch, 1954-56), B'nai B'rith.

WRITINGS: (Editor) *A Treasury of Comfort*, Crown, 1954, 1967 edition, Wilshire, 1967; (editor with Abraham Rothberg) *The Bar Mitzvah Companion*, Behrman, 1959; *Adding Life to Our Years*, J. David, 1959; (editor) *A Modern Treasury of Jewish Thoughts*, Yoseloff, 1960; (compiler and editor with Morris Silverman) *Our Prayer Book: A New and Original Siddur Text for Religious Schools*, Prayer Book Press, 1961; *A Jew for All Seasons* (cantata), [Philadelphia], 1963; *A Treasury of the Art of Living*, Hartmore House, 1963; *Finding Ourselves: Sermons on the Art of Living*, J. David, 1964; *High Holiday Services for Children*, Prayer Book Press, 1968; (with S. Allan Sugarman) *Sabbath and Festival Services for Children*, Prayer Book Press, 1970; (with Sugarman) *A Contemporary High Holiday Service for Teenagers and. . . .*, Prayer Book Press, 1970. Member of editorial board, *Reconstructionist*.

*   *   *

GREENE, Jack P(hillip)   1931-

PERSONAL: Born August 12, 1931, in Lafayette, Ind.; son of Ralph B. (an agricultural engineer) and Nellie (Miller) Greene; married Sue Neuenswander, June 27, 1953; children: Megan, Granville. *Education:* University of North Carolina, A.B., 1951; Indiana University, M.A., 1952; graduate study at University of Nebraska, 1952-55, University of Bristol, 1953-54; Duke University, Ph.D., 1956. *Politics:* Democratic. *Religion:* Protestant. *Residence:* Baltimore, Md. *Office:* History Department, Johns Hopkins University, Baltimore, Md. 21218.

CAREER: Michigan State University, East Lansing, instructor in history, 1956-59; Western Reserve University, (now Case Western Reserve University), Cleveland, Ohio, associate professor of history, 1959-65; University of Michigan, Ann Arbor, associate professor of history, 1965-66; Johns Hopkins University, Baltimore, Md., professor of history, 1966—, chairman of history department, 1970—. Visiting associate professor at Johns Hopkins University, 1964-65. *Military service:* U.S. Army Reserve, Military Intelligence, 1956-63. *Member:* American Historical Association, Organization of American Historians, Conference on British Studies.

WRITINGS: The Quest for Power: The Lower Houses of Assembly in the Southern Royal Colonies, 1689-1776, published for Institute of Early American History and Culture by University of North Carolina Press, 1963; (editor and author of introduction) *The Diary of Colonel Landon Carter of Sabine Hall, 1752-1778*, two volumes, published for Virginia Historical Society by University Press of Virginia, 1965, revised introduction published separately as *Landon Carter: An Inquiry into the Personal Values and Social Imperatives of the 18th-Century Virginia Gentry*, University Press of Virginia, 1967; (editor) *Settlements to Society, 1584-1763*, McGraw, 1966; (editor) *Colonies to Nation, 1763-1789*, McGraw, 1967; *The Reappraisal of the American Revolution in Recent Historical Literature*, Service Center for Teachers of History, 1967; (editor) *The Ambiguity of the American Revolution*, Harper, 1968; (editor and author of introduction) *The Reinterpretation of the American Revolution, 1763-1789*, Harper, 1968; (compiler with Edward C. Papenfuse, Jr.) *The American Colonies in the Eighteenth Century, 1689-1763*, Appleton, 1969; (editor) *Great Britain and the American Colonies, 1606-1763*, Harper, 1970; *The Nature of Colony Constitutions*, University of South Carolina Press, 1970; (editor and author of introduction with Robert Forster) *Preconditions of Revolution in Early Modern Europe*, Johns Hopkins Press, 1970; (editor with Robert Forster) *Preconditions of Revolution in Early Modern Europe*, Johns Hopkins Press, 1971, 2nd edition, 1972; (editor with David W. Cohen) *Neither Slave Nor Free: The Freedmen of African Descent in the Slave Societies of the New World*, Johns Hopkins Press, 1972. Contributor to *Huntington Library Quarterly*. Visiting editor, *William and Mary Quarterly*, 1961-62.

WORK IN PROGRESS: With Keith B. Berwick, a study of politics in revolutionary Virginia, 1763-1789; *The English Colonies in the Eighteenth Century, 1713-1763*, for Harper's "New American Nation" series.

*　*　*

GREENE, Thomas M(cLernon) 1926-

PERSONAL: Born May 17, 1926, in Philadelphia, Pa.; son of George Durgin (an executive) and Elizabeth (McLernon) Greene; married Liliane Massarano (a teacher), May 20, 1950; children: Philip James, Christopher George, Francis Richard. *Education:* Principia College, student, 1943-45; Yale University, B.A., 1949, Ph.D., 1955; Sorbonne, University of Paris, graduate study, 1949-51. *Home:* 125 Livingston St., New Haven, Conn. 06511.

CAREER: Yale University, New Haven, Conn., 1954—, began as associate professor, became professor of English and comparative literature. *Military service:* U.S. Army, Counter Intelligence Corps, 1945-47; special investigator

in Korea. *Member:* Modern Language Association of America, Renaissance Society of America, Elizabethan Club (Yale University). *Awards, honors:* Morse grant for research, 1958-59; American Council of Learned Societies fellowship for research, 1963-64; Harbison Prize for Distinguished Teaching, 1968.

WRITINGS: The Descent from Heaven: A Study in Epic Continuity, Yale University Press, 1963; (editor with Peter Demetz and Lowry Nelson, Jr.) *The Disciplines of Criticism: Essays in Literary Theory, Interpretation, and History*, Yale University Press, 1968; *Rabelais: A Study in Comic Courage*, Prentice-Hall, 1970. Contributor of articles to learned journals.

WORK IN PROGRESS: Studies in the imagery of Renaissance poetry.

*　*　*

GREENFIELD, Stanley B(rian) 1922-

PERSONAL: Born March 19, 1922, in New York, N.Y.; son of Solomon C. (a teacher and administrator) and Olga (Benov) Greenfield; married Thelma C. Nelson (a college professor), January 22, 1951; children: Tamma Lucille, Sayre Nelson. *Education:* Cornell University, B.A., 1942; University of California, Berkeley, M.A., 1947, Ph.D., 1950. *Home:* 2056 Orchard St., Eugene, Ore. 97403. *Office:* Department of English, University of Oregon, Eugene, Ore. 97403.

CAREER: University of Wisconsin, Madison, instructor in English, 1950-54; Queens College (now Queens College of the City University of New York), Flushing, N.Y., instructor in English, 1954-59; University of Oregon, Eugene, assistant professor, 1959-61, associate professor, 1961-64, professor of English, 1964—, teacher at John Hay Summer Institute. Portland (Ore.) High School Curriculum Project, consultant and writer, 1960-61. *Military service:* U.S. Army, Signal Corps, 1943-45. *Member:* Modern Language Association of America (chairman of research and bibliography committee, Old English group), Mediaeval Academy of America, Modern Humanities Research Association, American Association of University Professors, Phi Beta Kappa, Phi Kappa Phi. *Awards, honors:* Ersted Award for Distinguished Teaching, University of Oregon, 1963; Guggenheim fellow, 1965-66; National Endowment for the Humanities senior fellow, 1970-71.

WRITINGS: (Compiler of bibliographies) David M. Zesmer, *Guide to English Literature from Beowulf Through Chaucer and Medieval Drama*, Barnes & Noble, 1961; (editor and contributor) *Studies in Old English Literature in Honor of Arthur G. Brodeur*, University of Oregon Books, 1963; *A Critical History of Old English Literature*, New York University Press, 1965; (contributor) E.G. Stanley, editor, *Continuations and Beginnings: Studies in Old English Literature*, Thomas Nelson, 1966; (editor with A. Kingsley Weatherhead) *The Poem: An Anthology*, Appleton, 1968; 2nd edition, 1972; *The Interpretation of Old English Poetry*, Routledge & Kegan Paul, 1972. Contributor of articles to learned journals.

WORK IN PROGRESS: Old English poetry section for *New Cambridge Bibliography of English Literature;* editing three Old English poems, for Methuen.

*　*　*

GREENLEAF, William 1917-

PERSONAL: Born July 1, 1917, in Brooklyn, N.Y.; son of Harry and Anna (Goldstein) Greenleaf; married Ellen Nora Chanin (a medical doctor), January 18, 1952 (died, 1965); children: Peter, David, Eric, Allan. *Education:* College of City of New York (now City College of the City University of New York), B.S.S. (magna cum laude), 1942; Columbia University, M.A., 1948, Ph.D., 1955. *Politics:* Democrat. *Home:* 70 Mill Rd., Durham, N.H. 03824. *Office:* Department of History, Social Science Center, University of New Hampshire, Durham, N.H. 03824.

CAREER: Columbia University, New York, N.Y., research associate full-time, 1952-55, part-time, 1955-63, visiting professor of economic history, 1966-67; Colorado State University, Fort Collins, assistant professor of history, 1956-58; University of New Hampshire, Durham, professor of American history, 1958—. Ford Foundation, consultant, 1955-56, 1957-58, 1960-61. *Military service:* U.S. Army, 1943-46; served in Europe. *Member:* American Historical Association, Organization of American Historians. *Awards, honors:* Guggenheim fellow, 1964-65; American Council of Learned Societies grant-in-aid, 1970-71.

WRITINGS: *John D. Rockefeller* (abridgement of Allan Nevins' two-volume *Study in Power*), Scribner, 1959; *Monopoly on Wheels: Henry Ford and the Selden Automobile Patent*, Wayne State University Press, 1961; *From These Beginnings: The Early Philanthropies of Henry and Edsel Ford, 1911-1936*, Wayne State University Press, 1964; (editor) *American Economic Development Since 1860*, University of South Carolina Press, 1968; (author of introduction) Keith Sward, *The Legend of Henry Ford*, Russell, 1968; *The Rise of Industrial America, 1840-1900*, Macmillan, 1969; (with Richard B. Morris) *U.S.A.: The History of a Nation*, two volumes, Rand McNally, 1969; (with Morris and Robert H. Ferrell) *America: A History of the People*, Rand McNally, 1971. Research associate for *Ford*, by Allan Nevins and Frank Ernest Hill, three volumes, Scribner, 1954, 1957, 1963. Contributor to *Encyclopedia Americana* and *Dictionary of American Biography;* member of editorial staff, *Encyclopedia of American History*, Harper, and *New Century Cyclopedia of Names*, Appleton.

WORK IN PROGRESS: Research for a book on the impact of the American Civil War on business organization and leadership, for Knopf's "Civil War Impact" series; a book on the Motion Picture Patents Company and its effect on the formative era of the film industry in the United States.

*   *   *

GREENSTOCK, David Lionel 1912-

PERSONAL: Born April 2, 1912, in Dublin, Ireland; son of David and Mary (Barton) Greenstock. *Education:* Attended Xaverian College and St. Joseph's College in England; St. Alban's College, Valladolid, Spain; Pontifical University of Salamanca, Th.D. (summa cum laude), 1947. *Home:* English College, Valladolid, Spain.

CAREER: Roman Catholic priest; began as curate in working-class parish in London, England; English College, Valladolid, Spain, professor of dogmatic theology, experimental psychology, and preaching, 1947—, vice-rector, 1947-63, rector, 1963—. Vice-chairman, Henry Doubleday Research Assoc., 1970. *Military service:* British Army, officiating chaplain, World War II. *Member:* Centro Studi e Scambi Internazionali (executive committee, 1963), International Institute of Arts and Letters (fellow, 1963).

WRITINGS: *Christopher's Talks to Catholic Children*, Burns & Oates, 1946; *Christopher's Talks to the Little Ones*, Burns & Oates, 1948; *Christopher's Talks to Catholic Parents*, Burns & Oates, 1951; *Be Ye Perfect*, Herder, 1952; *Christopher's Talks to Catholic Teachers*, Burns & Oates, 1953; *Death: The Glorious Adventure*, Burns & Oates, 1956; (with Jordan Aumann) *The Meaning of Christian Perfection*, Herder, 1956; *With Christ to Calvary: Lenten Meditations*, Burns & Oates, 1957; *Lenten*

Meditations, Bruce, 1960; *La Armadura de Dios*, FAX, 1960; *El Sacramento de la Misericordia*, FAX, 1960; (editor and translator) Angel Herrera Oria, *The Preacher's Encyclopedia*, four volumes, Newman, 1964; *Controlling the Colorado Beetle*, H.D.R.A., 1970; *Garlic as a Pesticide*, H.D.R.A., 1970. Contributor to theological journals.

WORK IN PROGRESS: A definitive report on a new organic pesticide, to be published by H.D.R.A.

*   *   *

GREENWAY, John 1919-

PERSONAL: Original surname, Groeneweg, legally translated to Greenway; born December 15, 1919, in Liverpool, England; immigrated to the United States, 1922; became U.S. citizen by derivation; son of Cornelis Paul and Mary (Rafferty) Groeneweg; married 2nd wife, Joan Disher (an anthropologist), October 27, 1966; children: (first marriage) John Leonard. *Education:* University of Pennsylvania, A.B. (honors), 1947, M.A. (English), 1948, Ph.D., 1951; University of Colorado, M.A. (anthropology), 1958. *Politics:* "Aggressively illiberal Independent." *Home:* 100 Inca Parkway, Boulder, Colo. 80303. *Office.* University of Colorado, Boulder, Colo. 80302.

CAREER: Carpenter, later building contractor, 1938-45; Rutgers University, New Brunswick, N.J., instructor in English, 1951-53; University of Denver, Denver, Colo assistant professor of English, 1953-56; University of Sydney, Sydney, Australia, Fulbright research scholar, 1956-57; University of Colorado, Boulder, instructor, 1957-58, assistant professor, 1958-63, associate professor, 1964-65, professor of anthropology, 1965—. Visiting assistant professor at University of California, Los Angeles, 1960-61; visiting fellow, Davenport College, Yale University, 1961. Folk singer, appearing on radio and television and in public performances, and folk-song recording artist; master of ceremonies at Newport Folk Festival, 1960, Colorado Folk Festival, 1961. John Edwards Memorial Foundation, member of advisory board, 1963. *Military service:* U.S. Army, 1943-44.

MEMBER: American Anthropological Association (fellow), American Folklore Society (fellow), Society for Ethnomusicology, National Folk Festival Association (advisory council), Colorado Archaeological Society, California Folklore Society, Folklore Society of the Northeast, Phi Beta Kappa, Pi Gamma Nu. *Awards, honors:* Nuffield Foundation award (one thousand pounds) to complete an anthropological bibliography of Australian aborigines; winner of Ohio State University's Fine Arts and Humanities Radio Program award for lecture in radio series, "Primitive Music," 1963; National Institute of Mental Health grant for field work in Australia, 1965-66; Carpenter Center for the Visual Arts grant, Harvard University, 1968.

WRITINGS: *American Folksongs of Protest*, University of Pennsylvania Press, 1953; *Anthropology in Australia*, University of Colorado, 1958; (contributor) Horace Beck, editor, *Folklore in Action: Essays in Honor of MacEdward Leach*, American Folklore Society, 1962; *Bibliography of the Australian Aborigines and the Native Peoples of Torres Strait to 1959*, Angus & Robertson, 1963; *Literature Among the Primitives*, Folklore Associates, 1964; *The Inevitable Americans*, Knopf, 1964; (contributor) Arnold Pilling, editor, *Change Among the Australian Aborigines*, Wayne State University Press, c.1965; (editor) *The Primitive Reader: An Anthology of Myths, Tales, Songs, Riddles, and Proverbs of Aboriginal Peoples Around the World* (supplement to *Literature Among the Primitives*), Folklore Associates, 1965; (editor with Melville Jacobs) *The Anthropologist Looks at Myth*, University of Texas Press, 1966; *Gormless Tom, and Other Tales from the British Isles* (folktales for children), Silver Burdett, 1968; *Don't Talk to My Horse: Tall Tales from the U.S.A.*, Silver Burdett, 1968; (compiler and author of commentary) *Folklore of the Great West: Selections from 83 Years of the Journal of American Folklore* (originally announced as "Treasury of Western Folklore"), American West, 1969; *The Last Frontier*, Dodd, 1972; *Down Among the Wild Men: The Narrative Journal of Fifteen Years Spent Pursuing the Old Stone Age Aborigines of Australia's Western Desert*, Atlantic-Little, Brown, 1972.

Booklets: *A Guide Through James Joyce's "Ulysses"; Folklore Research Around the World*, Indiana University Press, 1961. Also writer of University of Colorado Extension syllabus, *Social Science 101-102: Foundations of the Social Order* (with others) 1961, and textbooks, *Primitive Music*, 1962, *Peoples and Cultures of Australia*, 1963, *Peoples and Cultures of the Pacific*, 1963. Contributor of approximately 300 articles and reviews to scholarly and popular periodicals, including *National Review, Nation, Saturday Review, New York Times Book Review, New York Times Magazine, American Anthropologist, Current Anthropology, Book Week, American Speech, Book World, Delphian Quarterly, Australian Literary Studies, Quadrant* (Australia), *Sydney* (Australia) *Bulletin, American West, Reader's Digest*, and *Atlantic*. Writer of notes and background material for nine albums of own recordings and for a dozen folklore albums recorded by others.

Editor of *Southwestern Lore* (journal of Colorado Archaeological Society), 1959-63, *Journal of American Folklore*, 1964-68; *Western Folklore*, acting editor, 1960-61, record review editor, 1960-62; member of editorial council, American Anthropological Association, 1964-68.

AVOCATIONAL INTERESTS: Chess (ranked fifth in Colorado State Chess Championship, 1962).

BIOGRAPHICAL/CRITICAL SOURCES: Donald Knight Wilgus, *Anglo-American Folksong Scholarship Since 1898*, Rutgers University Press, 1959; Ray McKinley Lawless, *Folksingers and Folksongs in America*, Duell, Sloan & Pearce, 1960; *A Guide to the Study of the United States of America*, Library of Congress, 1960; *Caravan, the Folk Music Magazine*, March-April, 1960; *Library Journal*, January 1, 1970.

* * *

GREENWOOD, Marianne (Hederstrom) 1926-

PERSONAL: Born April 5, 1926, in Lapland, Sweden; daughter of Sune (president of state forests) and Elin (Pettersson) Hederstrom; children: Christer K. Hederstrom, Allan Greenwood. *Education:* Studied at art academy in Stockholm, Sweden, for three years; also studied in Switzerland, one year. *Agent:* Bertha Klausner, International Literary Agency, Inc., 71 Park Ave., New York, N.Y. 10016.

CAREER: Photographer and self-described "bird and gypsy," who adds that "being on a perpetual journey I sometimes find the time to write about what I feel and see, but I think that living in itself is a profession, taking up all time."

WRITINGS: Det tatuerade hjaertat (autobiography; includes photographs by Greenwood), Raben & Sjoegren, 1964, translation by Greenwood published in America as *The Tattooed Heart of Livingston*, Stein & Day, 1965.

Photographs for: *Vignette pour les vignerons*, text by Jacques Prevert, Falaize, 1950; Andre Verdet, *Picasso in Musee d'Antibes*, Falaize, 1951; *Svarta Tjurar*, text by Evert Taube, Raben & Sjoegren, 1958; *Aterkomst*, text by E. Taube, Raben & Sjoegren, 1958; Dor de la Souchere, *Picasso in Antibes*, Pantheon, 1961; *Land of the Mayas:*

Yesterday and Today, text by Carleton Beals, Abelard, 1967. Also author of *Land of the Incas*, text by Carleton Beals, published by Abelard. Also illustrator of small art books published in France. Contributor of photographs to accompany various articles in *Mankind;* contributor of articles to *VI* (weekly magazine, Stockholm), and of eight short stories to *Cad, Adam*, and *Knight* (magazines).

WORK IN PROGRESS: A picture book about the Navajo Indians, to be published by Mankind; second part of autobiography.

* * *

GRENVILLE, John A(shley) S(oames) 1928-

PERSONAL: Surname originally Guhrauer; born January 11, 1928, in Berlin, Germany; son of Adolf (a judge) and Charlotte (Sandberg) Guhrauer; married Betty Anne Rosenberg, March 24, 1960; children: Murray Charles, Edward Samson, George Daniel. *Education:* London School of Economics and Political Science, University of London, B.A., 1951, Ph.D., 1954; Yale University, postdoctoral student, 1959-60. *Politics:* "Conservative tendencies but no active affiliations." *Home:* 42 Selly Wick Rd., Birmingham B29 7JA, England. *Office:* University of Birmingham, Birmingham, England.

CAREER: University of Nottingham, Nottingham, England, assistant lecturer, 1953-55, lecturer, 1955-64, reader in history, 1964-65; University of Leeds, Leeds, England, professor of international history, 1965-68; University of Birmingham, Birmingham, England, professor of modern history, 1968—. Yale University, postdoctoral fellow, 1961-63; University of Ghana, external examiner. *Member:* Royal Historical Society (fellow), Commonwealth Fund (fellow), Yale Alumni Association of England.

WRITINGS: (With G. Joan Fuller) *The Coming of the Europeans: A History of European Discovery and Settlement, 1415-1775*, Longmans, Green, 1962; *Lord Salisbury and Foreign Policy: The Close of the Nineteenth Century*, Oxford University Press, 1964; (with George Berkley Young) *Politics, Strategy and American Diplomacy: Studies in Foreign Policy, 1873-1917*, Yale University Press, 1966; *National Prejudice and International History* (inaugural lecture given at University of Leeds, October 23, 1967), Leeds University Press, 1968. Writer of documentary films, "The Munich Crisis, 1938," 1968, and "The End of Illusions, from Munich to Dunkirk," 1970, for Inter-University History Film Consortium. Contributor to historical journals in England and America, and to *Transactions of the Royal Historical Society*. Editor, *War and Society*, Collins, 1970—; area editor, *Historical Abstracts*.

WORK IN PROGRESS: International Treaties, 1815-1870, for Methuen; *The World Powers, 1871-1945*, for Oxford University Press; *The Fontana History of Europe, 1848-1878*, for Collins; and *The Spanish-American War*, for Macmillan.

AVOCATIONAL INTERESTS: Gardening, travel.

* * *

GRICE, Frederick 1910-

PERSONAL: Born June 21, 1910, in Durham, England; son of Charles Oliver (a miner) and Mary Jane (Hewitt) Grice; married Gwendoline Simpson, April 8, 1939; children: Gillian (Mrs. C.G. Clarke), Erica. *Education:* King's College, London, B.A. (honors); Hatfield College, Durham, D.Th.P.T. *Religion:* Anglican. *Home:* 91 Hallow Rd., Worcester, England.

CAREER: City of Worcester Training College, Worcester, England, head of English department, 1946—. *Mili-*

tary service: Royal Air Force, 1941-46; became flight lieutenant.

WRITINGS: Folk Tales of the North Country, Drawn from Northumberland and Durham, Thomas Nelson, 1944; *Folk Tales of the West Midlands,* Thomas Nelson, 1952; *Folk Tales of Lancashire,* Thomas Nelson, 1953; *Night Poem, and Other Pieces,* Peter Russell, 1955; *Aidan and the Strolling Players,* Duell, Sloan & Pearce, 1960 (published in England as *Aidan and the Strollers,* J. Cape, 1960); *The Bonny Pit Laddie,* Oxford University Press (London), 1960, published in America as *Out of the Mines: The Story of a Pit Boy,* F. Watts, 1961; *The Moving Finger,* Oxford University Press (Toronto), 1962, published in America as *The Secret of the Libyan Caves,* F. Watts, 1963; *Rebels and Fugitives,* Batsford, 1963, Norton, 1964; *A Northumberland Missionary,* Oxford University Press, 1963; *Jimmy Lane and His Boat,* F. Watts, 1963; *The Rescue* [and] *The Poisoned Dog* (two tales), F. Watts, 1963; *Bill Thompson's Pigeon,* Oxford University Press (London), 1963, F. Watts, 1968; *A Severnside Story,* Oxford University Press, 1964; (with Dora Saint) *The Lifeboat Haul* [and] *Elizabeth Woodcock* (the former by Grice, the latter by Saint), Oxford University Press, 1965; *The Luckless Apple,* Oxford University Press, 1966; *The Oak and the Ash,* Oxford University Press, 1968; *Dildrum, King of the Cats, and Other English Folk Stories* (includes "Dildrum, King of the Cats," "Black Vaughan," "The Magic Ointment," "The Iron Gates," "The Boy and the Fairies," "The Three Rivers," "The Pedlar of Swaffham," and "The Well at the World's End"), F. Watts, 1968; *The Courage of Andy Robson,* Oxford University Press, 1969; *The Black Hand Gang,* Oxford University Press, 1971. Author of textbooks for slow readers. Contributor to periodicals and to British Broadcasting Corp. feature and poetry programs.

SIDELIGHTS: Grice writes to *CA:* "I am deeply interested in France. Passionately fond of Provence. Would like to be an artist as well as a writer—or a collector."

BIOGRAPHICAL/CRITICAL SOURCES: Books and Bookmen, July, 1968, June, 1969.

*   *   *

GRIEVE, Andrew W.   1925-

PERSONAL: Born June 19, 1925, in Yonkers, N.Y.; son of Andrew (a machinist) and Janet (Wilson) Grieve; married Eva Ann D'Eufemia, November 25, 1947; children: Douglas, Kevin. *Education:* Attended Colgate University and Villanova College (now Villanova University); New York University, B.S., 1948; Ithaca College, M.S., 1952; additional postgraduate courses. *Religion:* Protestant. *Home:* 2 South St., Sherburne, N.Y. 13460.

CAREER: High School science and physical education teacher, Wellsburg, N.Y., 1948-49; athletic director and coach at central schools in Van Etten, N.Y., 1949-56, Wyalusing, Pa., 1956-57, and Sherburne, N.Y., 1957—. Secretary-treasurer, Center State Conference, 1964-65. *Military service:* U.S. Naval Air Corps, 1942-45. *Member:* American Association for Health, Physical Education and Recreation, American Football Coaches Association, New York State Association for Health, Physical Education and Recreation (Central Eastern Zone secretary, 1962, and president, 1964-65), New York State Athletic Directors Association, New York State Coaches Association, Masons.

WRITINGS: Directing High School Athletics, Prentice-Hall, 1963; *The Legal Aspects of Athletics,* A.S. Barnes, 1969. Contributor of more than fifty articles, dealing mainly with athletics and physical education activities, to *Parents' Magazine, Athletic Journal, Scholastic Coach,* and other periodicals.

GRIFFITH, A(rthur) Leonard   1920-

PERSONAL: Original name, Arthur Leonard Griffiths; born March 19, 1920, in Lancashire, England; son of Thomas (an opera singer) and Sarah Jane (Taylor) Griffiths; married Anne Merelie Cayford (a teacher), June 17, 1947; children: Anne (Mrs. Douglas Rutherford), Mary. *Education:* McGill University, B.A., 1942; United Theological College, Montreal, Quebec, student, 1942-45; Queens University Kingston, Ontario, B.D., 1958; additional study at Mansfield College, Oxford, 1957-58. *Home:* 73 Eastbourne Ave., Toronto 195, Canada. *Office:* Deer Park United Church, 129 St. Clair Ave. W., Toronto 195, Canada.

CAREER: Ordained to ministry of United Church of Canada, 1945; pastor of churches in Arden, Ontario, 1945-47, Grimsby, Ontario, 1947-50, and Ottawa, Ontario, 1950-60; City Temple, London, England, minister, 1960-66; Deer Park United Church, Toronto, Ontario, minister, 1966—. *Member:* Rotary Club of Canada. *Awards, honors:* D.D., United Theological College, 1962.

WRITINGS: The Roman Letter Today, Abingdon, 1959; *God and His People: The Renewal of the Church,* Lutterworth, 1960, Abingdon, 1961; *Beneath the Cross of Jesus,* Abingdon, 1961; *What Is a Christian?: Sermons on the Christian Life,* Abingdon, 1962; *Barriers to Christian Belief,* Hodder & Stoughton, 1962, Harper, 1963, revised edition, Forward Movement Miniature Books, 1969; *A Pilgrimage to the Holy Land,* Epworth, 1962; *The Eternal Legacy: From an Upper Room,* Hodder & Stoughton, 1963, Harper, 1964; *Pathways to Happiness: A Devotional Study of the Beatitudes,* Abingdon, 1964; *God's Time and Ours: Sermons for the Christian Year,* Abingdon, 1964; *The Crucial Encounter: The Personal Ministry of Jesus,* Hodder & Stoughton, 1965, published in America as *Encounters with Christ: The Personal Ministry of Jesus,* Harper, 1966; *This Is Living: Paul's Letter to the Philippians,* Lutterworth, 1966, Abingdon, 1967; *God in Man's Experience: The Activity of God in the Psalms,* Word Books, 1968; *Illusions of Our Culture,* Hodder & Stoughton, 1969, Word Books, 1970, revised edition, Forward Movement Miniature Books, 1972; *The Need to Preach,* Hodder & Stoughton, 1971; *Hang On to the Lord's Prayer,* Upper Room, 1973; *We Have This Ministry,* Word Books, 1973.

WORK IN PROGRESS: A Time for Affirmations; We Have This Ministry.

AVOCATIONAL INTERESTS: Music, drama, and golf.

*   *   *

GRIFFITH, Winthrop   1931-

PERSONAL: Born June 17, 1931, in Los Angeles, Calif.; son of Evan Cadwalader and Florence (Gold) Griffith; married Patricia King, October 4, 1958; children: Kevin Winthrop, Christina. *Education:* Stanford University, A.B., 1955. *Politics:* Democrat. *Religion:* Episcopal. *Residence:* Carmel Valley, Calif. *Agent:* Curtis Brown Ltd., 60 East 56th St., New York, N.Y. 10022.

CAREER: San Francisco Examiner, San Francisco, Calif., reporter, 1955-59; news secretary to Senator Hubert H. Humphrey, Washington, D.C., 1960-64; chief deputy state controller, Sacramento, Calif., 1965-67; President's Council on Youth Opportunity, Washington, D.C., director of public affairs, 1968; free-lance writer and political consultant, 1969—.

WRITINGS: Humphrey: A Candid Biography, Morrow, 1965. Contributor of numerous articles to *New York Times Magazine,* 1969-71.

WORK IN PROGRESS: A book on Great Falls, Mont., to be published by Dial.

GRINSELL, Leslie Valentine 1907-

PERSONAL: Born February 14, 1907, in London, England; son of Arthur John and Janet (Tabor) Grinsell. *Education:* Attended Highgate School, London, England. *Religion:* Anglican. *Home:* 32 Queen's Ct., Bristol 8, England. *Office address:* City Museum, Bristol 8, England.

CAREER: Barclays Bank Ltd., officer, 1925-41, 1945-49; Victoria County History of Wiltshire, member of staff, 1949-52; Bristol City Museum, Bristol, England, curator of archaeology, 1952-72. *Military service:* Royal Air Force, 1941-45; served in Egypt; became flight lieutenant. *Member:* Society of Antiquaries (fellow), Prehistoric Society (treasurer, 1947-70), British Association (recorder, anthropology and archaeology section, 1955-58). *Awards, honors:* M.A., Bristol University, 1971.

WRITINGS: The Ancient Burial-Mounds of England, Methuen, 1936, 2nd edition, 1953; *White Horse Hill and the Surrounding Country,* St. Catherine Press, 1939; *Egyptian Pyramids,* John Bellows, 1947; (contributor) *Studies in the History of Swindon,* Swindon (England) Borough Council, 1950; (contributor) *Victoria History of Wiltshire,* published for University of London Institute of Historical Research by Oxford University Press, 1957; *The Archaeology of Wessex: An Account of Wessex Antiquities from the Earliest Times to the End of the Pagan Saxon Period, with Special Reference to Existing Field Monuments,* Methuen, 1958; *Dorset Barrows,* Dorset Natural History and Archaeological Society, 1959; *A Brief Numismatic History of Bristol: Being a Guide to Bristol Coins, Tokens, and Medals in the City Museum, Bristol and in Other Collections,* Bristol City Museum 1962; (editor) *A Survey and Policy Concerning the Archaeology of the Bristol Region,* two volumes, Bristol Archaeological Research Group, 1964-66; *Prehistoric Sites in the Mendip, South Cotswold and Bristol Region,* Bristol Archaeological Research Group, 1966; (with Philip Rahtz and Alan Warhurst) *The Preparation of Archaeological Reports,* 2nd edition, Bristol Archaeological Research Group, 1962, 3rd edition, Humanities, 1966; *Guide Catalogue to the South Western British Prehistoric Collections,* Bristol City Museum, 1968; (with Max Hebditch) *Roman Sites in the Mendip, Cotswold, Wye Valley and Bristol Region,* Bristol Archaeological Research Group, 1968; *Archaeology of Exmoor: Bideford Bay to Bridgwater,* Augustus M. Kelley, 1970; *Regional Archaeology: South-Western England,* International Publications Service, 1970.

WORK IN PROGRESS: Biographical Dictionary of English Field Archaeologists; research on prehistoric sepulchral monuments, and on the later history of prehistoric sites, including their folklore.

* * *

GRIVAS, Theodore 1922-

PERSONAL: Born July 11, 1922; son of John Theodore and Angy (Jahalidis) Grıvas; married Jacqueline Kay Smith, June 17, 1955; children: Deborah Leigh, Melanie Cynthia, Theodore Gregory. *Education:* University of Southern California, A.B., 1952, A.M., 1953, Ph.D., 1957. *Politics:* Democrat. *Religion:* Protestant. *Home:* 1127 Winding Ridge Rd., Santa Rosa, Calif. 95404.

CAREER: University of Southern California, Los Angeles, instructor, 1956-57; Fresno State College (now California State University-Fresno), Fresno, Calif., assistant professor of history, 1957-62; Sonoma State College, Rohnert Park, Calif., associate professor, 1962-65, professor of history, 1965—, chairman of Social Science Division, 1965-66, chairman of history department, 1966—. Director of history institutes for NDEA, 1965, 1967, and EPDA, Stuttgart, Germany, 1969. *Military service:* U.S. Navy, 1942-45; became coxswain. *Member:* American Historical Association, Organization of American Historians, California Historical Society, Phi Beta Kappa, Phi Kappa Phi, Phi Alpha Theta, Pi Gamma Mu.

WRITINGS: History of the Los Angeles YMCA, Los Angeles Young Men's Christian Association, 1957; (with Robert G. Comegys) *Outline of Western Civilization, History I,* Barbor Associates, 1959, revised edition, 1961; *Military Governments in California, 1846-1850,* Arthur H. Clark, 1963. Contributor to *Encyclopedia Britannica Yearbook of 1963.* Contributor of articles and reviews to historical journals.

WORK IN PROGRESS: A biography, *General Richard Barnes Mason;* a monographic study, *The Impact of the U.S. Military on Frontier Civilian Communities.*

AVOCATIONAL INTERESTS: Bookbinding, electronics, photography.

* * *

GROCH, Judith (Goldstein) 1929-

PERSONAL: Surname is pronounced Grosh; born May 14, 1929, in New York, N.Y.; daughter of Eli (a physician) and Caroline (Kleppner) Goldstein; married Sigmund N. Groch (a physician), 1953 (died, 1961); married Wilbert Minowitz (a physicist), October 6, 1962; children: Deborah Susan, Emily Louise; Peter (stepson). *Education:* Vassar College, student, 1946-48; Columbia University, B.S., 1952. *Home:* 168 West 86th St., New York, N.Y. 10024. *Agent:* Marie Rodell, 141 East 55th St., New York, N.Y. 10022

CAREER: Mayo Clinic, Department of Biophysics, Rochester, Minn., research technician, 1953-56; free-lance writer. *Member:* Phi Beta Kappa, Authors Guild, Authors League of America. *Awards, honors:* Winner of National Mass Media award, Thomas Alva Edison Foundation, 1963, for *You and Your Brain.*

WRITINGS: You and Your Brain (juvenile), Harper, 1963; *The Right to Create,* Little, Brown, 1970. Contributor of articles and short stories to magazines, including *McCall's, Seventeen, American Girl,* articles to medical journals.

WORK IN PROGRESS: A children's book, *Play the Bach, Dear.*

AVOCATIONAL INTERESTS: Painting, playing piano, figure skating.

BIOGRAPHICAL/CRITICAL SOURCES: Saturday Review, February 21, 1970; *Library Journal,* November 1, 1970.

* * *

GROSS, Gerald 1932-

PERSONAL: Born September 29, 1932, in New York, N.Y.; son of Nathan (an electrician) and Helen Stieglitz) Gross; married Arlene B. Cohen, June 2, 1957; children: Alison Moira-Claire. *Education:* City College of City University of New York, B.A. (cum laude), 1963. *Politics:* Democrat. *Religion:* Jewish. *Home:* 136 Joralemon St., Brooklyn, N.Y. 11201. *Office:* Paperback Library, Inc., 260 Park Ave. S., New York, N.Y. 10010.

CAREER: With Paperback Library, Inc., New York, N.Y. *Member:* National Association of Book Editors.

WRITINGS: (Editor and author of introduction and commentary) *Publishers on Publishing,* Grosset, 1961; (editor and author of introduction and commentary) *Editors on Editing,* Grosset, 1962; (editor and author of essay) *Masterpieces of Murder: An Edmund Pearson True Crime Reader,* Little, Brown, 1963; *The Responsibility of the Press,* Fleet Press, 1966.

GROSS, Helen Shimota 1931-

PERSONAL: Born May 14, 1931, in St. Paul, Minn.; daughter of Emanuel E. (an accountant) and Emma (Novak) Shimota; married Nathan Gross. *Education:* College of St. Catherine, A.B., 1952; University of Minnesota, Ph.D., 1956. *Religion:* Catholic. *Home:* 24009 248th Ave. S.E., Maple Valley, Wash. 98038. *Office:* Rainier School, Box 600, Buckley, Wash. 98321.

CAREER: U.S. Veterans Administration Hospital, St. Cloud, Minn., staff psychologist, 1956-57; Seattle University, Seattle, Wash., assistant professor of psychology, 1957-59; Mental Health Research Institute, Fort Steilacoom, Wash., research psychologist, 1959-63; University of Southern California, Los Angeles, research psychologist in Youth Studies Center, 1963-65; Rainier School, Buckley, Wash., coordinator of community services, 1965-66, chief psychologist, 1966—. *Member:* American Psychological Association, American Academy of Arts and Sciences, Western Psychological Association, Washington State Psychological Association.

WRITINGS—Under name Helen E. Shimota: (With Warren K. Garlington) *Statistically Speaking,* C.C Thomas, 1964; *Delinquent Acts as Perceived by Gang and Non-Gang Adolescents,* Youth Studies Center, University of Southern California, 1964. Contributor of articles to professional journals.

WORK IN PROGRESS: Research on education of children with learning handicaps.

*   *   *

GROSS, Martin L. 1925-

PERSONAL: Born August 15, 1925, in New York, N.Y. *Education:* College of City of New York (now City College of City University of New York), B.S.S., 1947; Columbia University, graduate study, 1950-52. *Agent:* Sterling Lord Agency, 660 Madison Ave., New York, N.Y. 10021.

CAREER: Free-lance writer. Teacher of modern social criticism, New School for Social Research, New York, N.Y. Moderator, "Protest," WNBC Radio, New York, N.Y. *Military service:* U.S. Army Air Corps, 1943-46. *Member:* Authors Guild, Society of Magazine Writers.

WRITINGS: The Brain Watchers, Random House, 1962; *The Doctors,* Random House, 1966. Contributor of about 160 articles to magazines, including *Life, Saturday Evening Post, Reader's Digest, Good Housekeeping,* and *New Republic.*

WORK IN PROGRESS: A book for Random House.

BIOGRAPHICAL/CRITICAL SOURCES: Carlton Miscellany, spring, 1967

*   *   *

GROSSACK, Martin Myer 1928-

PERSONAL: Born June 11, 1928, in Boston, Mass.; son of Albert L. (a salesman) and Rose Grossack; married Judith Tractenberg, June 29, 1952; children: David, Richard. *Education:* Northeastern University, B.A., 1948; Boston University, M.A., 1949, Ph.D., 1952. *Religion:* Jewish. *Home and office:* 99 Revere St., Hull, Mass. 02045.

CAREER: Clinical and social psychologist, in private practice; Grossack Research Co., Hull, Mass., president 1957—. *Military service:* U.S. Air Force, 1952-55; became captain. *Member:* American Psychological Association.

WRITINGS: (Editor) *Mental Health and Segregation: A Selection of Papers and Some Book Chapters,* Springer Publishing, 1963; (editor) *Understanding Consumer Behavior,* Christopher, 1964, 2nd edition, 1966; *You Are*

Not Alone: A Guide for Mental Health in Our Times, Christopher, 1965; (with Howard Gardner) *Man and Men: Social Psychology as a Social Science,* International Textbook Co., 1970; *Consumer Psychology: Theory and Practice,* Branden Press, 1971.

*   *   *

GRUBEL, Herbert G(unter) 1934-

PERSONAL: Born February 26, 1934, in Frankfurt am Main, Germany; son of Ernst (a businessman) and Elisabeth (Hessler) Grubel; married Joan Arlene Longbreak, July 20, 1958; children: Eric, Heidi. *Education:* Realgymnasium Koenigstein, Abitur, 1954; Rutgers University, B.A., 1958; Yale University, Ph.D., 1963. *Home:* 1501 Surrey Lane, Philadelphia, Pa. 19151. *Office:* Department of Finance, University of Pennsylvania, Philadelphia, Pa. 19104.

CAREER: Stanford University, Stanford, Calif., assistant professor of economics, 1962-63; University of Chicago, Chicago, Ill., assistant professor of economics, 1963-66; University of Pennsylvania, Philadelphia, associate professor of finance, 1966—. *Member:* American Economic Association, Royal Economic Society.

WRITINGS: (Editor) *World Monetary Reform: Plans and Issues,* Stanford University Press, 1963; *Forward Exchange, Speculation, and the International Flow of Capital,* Stanford University Press, 1966; *The International Monetary System: Efficiency and Practical Alternatives,* Penguin, 1969; (editor with Harry G. Johnson) *Effective Tariff Protection,* Unipub, 1971. Contributor to economic and finance journals.

*   *   *

GRUENBAUM, Adolf 1923-

PERSONAL: Born May 15, 1923, in Cologne, Germany; became U.S. citizen; son of Benjamin (a businessman) and Hannah (Freiwillig) Gruenbaum; married Thelma Braverman, June 26, 1949; children: Barbara Susan. *Education:* Wesleyan University, Middletown, Conn., B.A., 1943; Yale University, M.S. (physics), 1948, Ph.D. (philosophy), 1951. *Home:* 2270 McCrea Rd., Pittsburgh, Pa. 15235. *Office:* University of Pittsburgh, Pittsburgh, Pa. 15213.

CAREER: Columbia University, New York, N.Y., consulting physicist in government-aided research work, 1946-48; Lehigh University, Bethlehem, Pa., instructor, 1950-51, assistant professor, 1951-53, associate professor, 1953-55, professor of philosophy, 1955-56, Selfridge Professor, 1956-60; University of Pittsburgh, Pittsburgh, Pa., Andrew Mellon Professor of Philosophy and director of Center for Philosophy of Science, 1960—. Visiting research professor, University of Minnesota Center for Philosophy of Science, 1956, 1959, visiting fellow, Center for Advanced Study in the Behavioral Sciences, Stanford University, summer, 1967. Member, International Congress for Logic and the Philosophy of Science, 1964, 1971. *Military service:* U.S. Army, Military Intelligence, 1944-46. *Member:* International Union for the History and Philosophy of Science, Institute for the Unity of Science (member of governing board), American Philosophical Association (executive committee), Philosophy of Science Association (president, two terms, 1965-70), American Association for the Advancement of Science (fellow; vice-president, 1963), Sigma Xi. *Awards, honors:* Alfred Noble Robinson Award for Teaching, Lehigh University, 1953; J. Walker Tomb Prize from Princeton University for publications on the time problem, 1958; National Science Foundation research grants.

WRITINGS: Philosophical Problems of Space and Time, Knopf, 1964; (author of prologue and epilogue) Percy

Williams Bridgman, *A Sophisticate's Primer of Relativity,* Routledge & Kegan Paul, 1967; *Modern Science and Zeno's Paradoxes,* Wesleyan University Press, 1967, revised edition, Allen & Unwin, 1968; *Geometry and Chronometry in Philosophical Perspective,* University of Minnesota Press, 1968. Essays anthologized in over 35 collections, including *The Validation of Scientific Theories,* edited by P. Frank, Beacon Press, 1957, *Studies in Logic and the Foundations of Mathematics,* North Holland Publishing, 1959, *The Nature of Physical Knowledge,* edited by L.W. Friedrich, Indiana University Press, 1960, *Current Issues in the Philosophy of Science,* edited by H. Feigl and G. Maxwell, Holt, 1961, *Frontiers of Science and Philosophy,* edited by R. Colodny, University of Pittsburgh Press, 1962, *Boston Studies in the Philosophy of Science,* edited by R.S. Cohen and M. Wartofsky, Reidel, 1963, *The Philosophy of Rudolf Carnap,* edited by Paul A. Schilpp, Open Court Publishing, 1964, *Problems of Space and Time,* edited by J.J.C. Smart, Macmillan, 1964, *Relativity Theory: Its Origins and Impact on Modern Thought,* edited by L. Pearce Williams, Wiley, 1968, *Zeno's Paradoxes,* edited by W.C. Salmon, Bobbs-Merrill, 1970, and *The Philosophy of Karl Popper,* edited by Paul A. Schilpp, Open Court Publishing, 1970. Contributor of essays, articles, reviews, and letters to *Scientific Monthly, Philosophy of Science, American Scientist,* and numerous other journals, and to encyclopedias. Member of editorial board, *Philosophy of Science, Encyclopedia of Philosophy, Philosopher's Index, American Philosophical Quarterly, Studies in History and Philosophy of Science.*

WORK IN PROGRESS: Philosophical Aspects of Cosmology and Cosmogony; books on the special theory of relativity and on philosophical problems of physical cosmology and cosmogony.

* * *

GUEDE, Norina (Maria Esterina) Lami 1913-

PERSONAL: Born October 12, 1913, in Modena, Italy; daughter of Carlo Giovanni (a machinist) and Maria Pia (Linari) Lami; married Auguste Georges Guede, October 31, 1940. *Education:* Ospedale Maggiore, Milan, Italy, diploma d'Infermiera, 1933; British Military Field Hospital, Ben Aknoun, Algeria, anesthetist's certificate, 1944. *Religion:* Roman Catholic. *Home:* 136 Avenue Olivier Heuze, La Mans, Sarthe, France; (temporary) c/o Lloyd Cabot Briggs, Hancock, N.H. *Office:* Peabody Museum, Harvard University, Cambridge, Mass. 02138.

CAREER: Laboratory assistant and clinic surgical nurse in Algeria, 1935-43, 1944-47; independent anesthetist, Algiers, Algeria, 1947-62; independent anthropological research in collaboration with Peabody Museum of Harvard University, Cambridge, Mass., and Centre de Transfusion Sanguine, Toulouse, France, 1962—. Field work in anthropology in the Sahara, 1961-62. Served with anti-Fascist underground, Associazione Matteoti, in Italy, 1924-35, with French Resistance in Algiers, 1940-43, with Allied Intelligence, 1943-45.

WRITINGS: (With Lloyd Cabot Briggs) *No More for Ever: A Saharan Jewish Town,* Peabody Museum, Harvard University, 1964. Contributor, in collaboration with Briggs, of articles to *Bulletin de la Societe d'Anthropologie de Paris.*

WORK IN PROGRESS: Comparative studies of social structures in mountains of northern Italy as they were forty years ago and as they are today; general anthropology of peoples of the Sahara and adjoining regions.

SIDELIGHTS: Mrs. Guede speaks Italian and French well, English and Arabic less fluently.†

GUNN, James E(dwin) 1923-
(Edwin James)

PERSONAL: Born July 12, 1923, in Kansas City, Mo.; son of J. Wayne (a printer) and Elsie (Hutchinson) Gunn; married Jane Anderson, February 6, 1947; children: Christopher, Kevin. *Education:* University of Kansas, B.S. in Journalism, 1947, M.A., 1951. *Home:* 2149 Quail Creek Dr., Lawrence, Kan. 66044. *Agent:* Robert P. Mills, 156 East 52nd St., New York, N.Y. 10022. *Office:* University of Kansas, 222 Carruth-O'Leary Hall, Lawrence, Kan. 66044.

CAREER: Western Printing and Lithographing Co., Racine, Wis., editor, 1951-52; University of Kansas Alumni Association, Lawrence, editor of alumni magazine, 1955-58; University of Kansas, Lawrence, administrative assistant to the chancellor for university relations, and instructor in English, 1958-70, lecturer in English and journalism, 1970—. Civil Defense, assistant director, Kansas City, Mo., 1952; Douglas County (Kan.) Centennial Committee, vice-chairman, 1960-61; Kansas State Chamber of Commerce, member of Education Council, 1961-67; chairman, Mid-America District, American College Public Relations Association, 1969-70; member of Information Committee, National Association of State Universities and Land-Grant Colleges, 1966-70. *Military service:* U.S. Naval Reserve, active duty, 1943-46; became lieutenant j.g. *Member:* Science Fiction Writers of America (member, Public Relations Committee, Nebula Rules Committee; president, 1971-72).

WRITINGS: (With Jack Williamson) *Star Bridge,* Gnome Press, 1955; *This Fortress World,* Gnome Press, 1955; *Station in Space* (collection), Bantam, 1958; *The Joy Makers,* Bantam, 1961; *The Immortals,* Bantam, 1962; *Future Imperfect* (collection), Bantam, 1964; (editor) *Man and the Future* (papers presented at Inter-Century Seminar, University of Kansas, 1966), University Press of Kansas, 1968; *The Witching Hour,* Dell, 1970; *The Immortal* (novelization of screenplay for ABC-TV "Movie of the Week" of the same title, 1969), Bantam, 1970; *The Burning,* Dell, 1971; *Breaking Point* (collection of short stories and novelettes), Walker & Co., 1972; *The Listeners,* Scribner, 1972; *Alternate Worlds* (illustrated history of science fiction), Prentice-Hall, in press.

Contributor: Frederick R. Pohl, editor, *Shadow of Tomorrow,* Permabooks, 1953; H.L. Gold, editor, *Second Galaxy Reader of Science Fiction,* Crown, 1954; *The Golfer's Own Book,* Lantern Press, 1956; Judith Merril, editor, *The Year's Greatest Short Science Fiction and Fantasy,* Gnome Press, 1956; H.L. Gold, editor, *Five Galaxy Short Novels,* Doubleday, 1958; Edmund Crispin, editor, *Best Tales of Terror,* Faber, 1962; Poul Anderson, editor, *Nebula Award Stories Four,* Doubleday, 1969; Robert Hoskins, editor, *The Stars Around Us,* New American Library, 1970; Robert Hoskins, editor, *Infinity Two,* Lancer, 1971; Harry Harrison, editor, *Nova Two,* Walker & Co., 1972.

Author of more than sixty short stories in magazines, mainly science fiction periodials like *Beyond Fantasy Fiction, Astounding Science Fiction, Planet Stories,* and *Galaxy Science Fiction;* from 1949-52 these stories appeared under the pseudonym Edwin James. Also author of some plays, radio scripts, articles, poetry, and criticism.

SIDELIGHTS: Gunn teaches university courses in fiction writing and in the literature of science fiction, believing that "science fiction speaks most clearly to modern man about the matters which most concern him today and will be even more pressing tomorrow."

He sold nine of the first ten science fiction stories he wrote. Four of his stories have been dramatized on National Broadcasting Co. radio; another story, "The Cave of Night," was adapted for Columbia network television presentation on "Desilu Playhouse," anthologized, and reprinted in two magazines; in all, the stories have been reprinted in Australia, South America, England, France, Spain, Germany, Italy, Portugal, Scandinavia, Russia, and Japan.

One of his books, *The Immortals*, was the inspiration for an ABC-TV "Movie of the Week" (called "The Immortal") in 1969 and an hour-long weekly series with Christopher George in 1970.

* * *

GUNTHER, John   1901-1970

PERSONAL: Born August 30, 1901, in Chicago, Ill.; son of Eugene McClellan and Lisette (Schoeninger) Gunther; married Frances Fineman, 1927 (divorced, 1944); married Jane Perry Vandercook, 1948; children: (first marriage) John (deceased), (second marriage) Nicholas. *Education:* University of Chicago, Ph.B., 1922. *Home:* 1 East End Ave., New York, N.Y. *Agent:* Harold Ober Associates, Inc., 40 East 49th St., New York 17, N.Y.

CAREER: Chicago Daily News, Chicago, Ill., reporter, 1922, correspondent in London, 1924-26, in other capitals of Europe and Near East, 1926-29, in Vienna, 1930-35, in London, 1935-36; North American Newspaper Alliance, special correspondent in Persia, India, China, and Japan, 1937-39; National Broadcasting Co., roving correspondent in Europe, 1939, later that year covering outbreak of war in London; war correspondent in London, 1941, at invasion of Sicily, 1943; traveled throughout Latin American countries, 1940-41, United States, 1944-45, in Europe as correspondent for *Look* and special writer for *New York Herald Tribune*, 1948, around the world, 1950; covered Summit Conference, Paris, 1960; author, network radio commentator, and lecturer. *Member:* New York Council on Foreign Relations, Association of Radio News Analysts, Century Club (New York), Bucks Club (London). *Awards, honors:* D.Litt., Gettysburg College, 1955.

WRITINGS: The Red Pavilion, Harper, 1926; *Peter Lancelot: An Amusement*, M. Secker, 1927; *Eden for One: An Amusement*, Harper, 1927; *The Bright Nemesis*, Bobbs, 1932; *Inside Europe*, Harper, 1936, 5th edition, 1942; *The High Cost of Hitler*, Hamish Hamilton, 1939; *Inside Asia*, Harper, 1939, school edition, 1942; *Inside Latin America*, Harper, 1941; *D Day*, Harper, 1944; *The Troubled Midnight*, Harper, 1945; *Inside U.S.A.*, Harper, 1947, 2nd revised edition, 1956; *Behind the Curtain*, Harper, 1949 (published in England as *Behind Europe's Curtain*, Hamish Hamilton, 1949); *Death Be Not Proud: A Memoir*, Harper, 1949, new edition, 1970, memorial edition, 1971.

Roosevelt in Retrospect: A Profile in History, Harper, 1950; *The Riddle of MacArthur: Japan, Korea, and the Far East*, Harper, 1951; *Eisenhower, the Man and the Symbol*, Harper, 1952; *The Story of TVA* (reprinted from *Inside U.S.A.*, with updating), Harper, 1953; *Inside Africa*, Harper, 1955; (with Bernard Quint) *Days to Remember: America, 1945-1955*, Harper, 1956; *Inside Russia Today*, Harper, 1958, revised edition, 1962, 2nd revised edition, Penguin, 1964; *Taken at the Flood: The Story of Albert D. Lasker*, Harper, 1960; *Inside Europe Today*, Harper, 1961, revised edition, 1962; *A Fragment of Autobiography: The Fun of Writing the Inside Books*, Harper, 1962 (published in England as *The Story of the Inside Books: A Fragment of Autobiography*, Hamish Hamilton, 1962); *The Lost City* (novel; Literary Guild selection), Harper, 1964; *Procession* (biography), Harper, 1965; *Inside South America*, Harper, 1967; *Twelve Cities* (travel), Harper, 1969; *The Indian Sign* (novel), Harper, 1970 (published in England as *Quatrain*, Hamish Ham-

ilton, 1970); *Inside Australia*, completed and edited by William H. Forbis, Harper, 1972.

Juvenile books: *The Golden Fleece* (novel), Harper, 1929; *Alexander the Great*, Random House, 1953; "Meet the World Series," Harper: (with Beryl and Sam Epstein) *Meet North Africa*, 1957, (with Beryl and Sam Epstein) *Meet South Africa*, 1958 (published in England as *Meet Southern Africa*, Hamish Hamilton, 1959), *Meet the Congo and Its Neighbors*, 1959 (published in England as *Meet Central Africa*, Hamish Hamilton, 1959), *Meet Soviet Russia*, two volumes, 1962; *Julius Caesar*, Random House, 1959 (published in England as *All About Julius Caesar*, W.H. Allen, 1967). Contributor to more than thirty magazines, including *Harper's, Reader's Digest*, and *Look*. Editor, "Mainstream of Modern World History Series," for Doubleday.

SIDELIGHTS: In his "Inside" books Gunther combined the basic skills of a gifted, hard-working reporter with what John Chamberlain called "the charm, humor, balance, factual richness and ultimate theoretical weakness that are inseparable from Mr. Gunther's character as a person." Although not considered profound or scholarly, Gunther's work was said by W.E. Garrison to "unite the best qualities of the newspaperman and the historian," and Joseph Barnes wrote of *Inside Latin America* that "his sampling of a continent will make up in timeliness and usefulness what it may lack in erudition." While the tone and atmosphere of his novels is accurate and true, critics called his stories "trite" and "mediocre." Ten of his books have been Book of the Month Club selections. At his death Mr. Gunther had completed three chapters of a new book, *Inside Australia*.

BIOGRAPHICAL/CRITICAL SOURCES: New Republic, February 12, 1936, June, 28, 1939; *New Yorker*, November 1, 1941, February 10, 1945, September 26, 1964; *Books*, November 2, 1941; *Christian Century*, November 26, 1941; *Kirkus*, December 1, 1944; *Saturday Review*, April 12, 1958, July 10, 1965, September 13, 1969; John Gunther, *A Fragment of Autobiography*, Harper, 1962; *Commonweal*, November 16, 1962; *New York Times Book Review*, May 12, 1963; *Book World*, June 21, 1970.

(Died May 29, 1970)

* * *

GUNTHER, Peter F.   1920-

PERSONAL: Born March 20, 1920, in Bakersfield, Calif.; son of John Peters (a farmer) and Lena (Johnson) Gunther; married Phyllis J. Merkes (a piano instructor), June 15, 1944; children: Marilyn, Alan, Evan. *Education:* Bible Institute of Los Angeles, student, 1938-42; Wheaton College, Wheaton, Ill., student, 1942-46, M.A., 1950. *Religion:* Mennonite background. *Home:* O-N 468 Ellis, Wheaton, Ill. 60187. *Office:* Moody Bible Institute, 820 North LaSalle St., Chicago, Ill. 60610.

CAREER: Indiana Rural Bible Crusade, onetime director with headquarters in Wheaton, Ill.; Moody Literature Mission, Chicago, Ill., director, 1950—. Board member, Literatura Evangelica para America Latina, 1955—, and Evangelical Literature Overseas, 1958—; council member, National Home Missions Fellowship, 1960—.

WRITINGS: (Editor) *Great Sermons by Great Preachers*, Moody, 1960; (editor) *The Fields at Home: Studies in Home Missions*, Moody, 1963. Contributor of articles to religious periodicals.

WORK IN PROGRESS: A Christian career book.

SIDELIGHTS: Gunther has traveled to home mission fields in Latin America and Europe, touring Central

America, 1964, and Africa, 1965. He traveled around the world in 1967, 1969, and 1971, and plans to visit Mexico, Africa, and Europe in 1973.

* * *

GUSTAFSON, Donald F. 1934-

PERSONAL: Born October 17, 1934, in Austin, Tex.; son of Carl Algot Franklin (a businessman) and Esther (Swenson) Gustafson; married Mary Fleming, August 31, 1956; children: Joseph, Benjamin, Samuel. Education: University of Texas, B.A., 1957, M.A., 1959, Ph.D., 1961. Politics: Independent. Residence: Boulder, Colo.

CAREER: University of Colorado, Boulder, 1961—, began as assistant professor, became professor of philosophy. Member: American Philosophical Association, Mind Association, American Civil Liberties Union, American Federation of Teachers.

WRITINGS: (Editor) Essays in Philosophical Psychology, Doubleday-Anchor, 1964. Contributor of articles and reviews to Mind, Analysis, Theoria, Journal of Philosophy, Personalist, Philosophy and Phenomenological Research, other philosophical journals.

* * *

GUTTERSON, Herbert (Lindsley, Jr.) 1915-

PERSONAL: Born May 19, 1915, in New Rochelle, N.Y.; son of Herbert Lindsley and Janet (Miller) Gutterson; married Dorrit Becker, April 10, 1948; children: Eric Norman, Dorrit Constable. Education: Choate School, graduate; Williams College, B.A., 1937. Religion: Episcopalian. Home and office: Choate School, Wallingford, Conn. 06492. Agent: Curtis Brown Ltd., 60 East 56th St., New York, N.Y. 10022.

CAREER: Northwood School, Lake Placid, N.Y., teacher of English, one year; Choate School, Wallingford, Conn., teacher of English, 1949—. Sometime editorial employee at Time, Inc. and William Morrow & Co. (publishers). Military service: U.S. Naval Reserve, 1940-45; became lieutenant commander; received Secretary of Navy Commendation. Member: New Haven Lawn Club.

WRITINGS: The Last Autumn (novel), Morrow, 1958. Contributor of short stories to Woman's Home Companion, American, Collier's, Cosmopolitan, Vogue, Woman's Day, Farm Journal, and other periodicals.

WORK IN PROGRESS: A contemporary novel; freelance short stories and articles.

SIDELIGHTS: A television adaptation by Arthur Heinemann of The Last Autumn was produced by the Theatre Guild for "United States Steel Hour," November 18, 1959. Avocational interests: Golf, tennis, and watching other sports, especially football.

* * *

GUTTSMAN, Wilhelm Leo 1920-

PERSONAL: Born August 23, 1920 in Germany; son of Walter Johann and Helen (Kamerase) Guttsman; married Valerie Lichtig, July 11, 1942; children: Janet Helen. Education: Attended school in Berlin, Germany, 1930-37; London School of Economics, University of London, student, 1943-50. Politics: Socialist. Home: 20 Mill Hill Rd., Norwich, England. Office: University of East Anglia, Wilberforce Rd., Norwich, England.

CAREER: London School of Economics, University of London, London, England, sub-librarian, 1948-62; University of East Anglia, Norwich, England, librarian, 1963—. Member: British Sociological Association, Society for Study of Labour History.

WRITINGS: (Contributor) Dwaine Marvick, editor, Political Decision Makers, Free Press, 1962; The British Po-

litical Elite, MacGibbon & Kee, 1963, Basic Books, 1964; (editor) A Plea for Democracy: An Edited Selection from the 1867 "Essays on Reform" and "Questions for a Reformed Parliament," with an Introduction and Bibliographical Index, MacGibbon & Kee, 1967; (editor and author of introduction) The English Ruling Class, Weidenfeld & Nicolson, 1969. Contributor to British Journal of Sociology, International Review of Social History.

WORK IN PROGRESS: A comparative study of the basis of social democracy in England and a number of European countries, for the period 1870-1914; further work on the British ruling class.

BIOGRAPHICAL/CRITICAL SOURCES: Times Literary Supplement, January 1, 1970.

* * *

HAAS, Ben(jamin) L(eopold) 1926-
(Richard Meade)

PERSONAL: Born July 21, 1926, in Charlotte, N.C.; son of Otto and Lorena (Michael) Haas; married Douglas Thornton Taylor, 1950; children: Joseph Elliott, Benjamin Michael, John Douglas. Education: Attended schools in Charlotte, N.C. Home: 2818 Bedford Ave., Raleigh, N.C. 27607. Agent: Paul R. Reynolds, Inc., 599 Fifth Ave., New York, N.Y. 10017; and H.N. Swanson, Inc., 8523 Sunset Blvd., Los Angeles, Calif. 90069. Office: Box 5332, Raleigh, N.C. 27607.

CAREER: Charlotte News, Charlotte, N.C., proofreader, 1947; American Oil Co., Charlotte, N.C., clerk, 1947-52; Southern Engineering Co., Charlotte, N.C., steel estimator, 1953-56; B.L. Montague Co., Inc., Sumter, S.C., chief estimator and assistant sales manager, 1956-59; Raleigh Metal Products, Inc., Raleigh, N.C., manager, 1959-61; full-time writer, 1961—. Military service: U.S. Army, two years; became sergeant. Member: Authors League of America, North Carolina Writer's Conference.

WRITINGS: The Foragers, Simon & Schuster, 1962; KKK, Regency, 1963; Look Away, Look Away (Literary Guild selection), Simon & Schuster, 1964; The Last Valley, Simon & Schuster, 1966; The Troubled Summer, Bobbs-Merrill, 1966; (under pseudonym Richard Meade) Beyond the Danube, P. Davies, 1967, published in America as The Danube Runs Red, Random House, 1968 (reissued in England as The Gun Runner, New English Library, 1969); (under pseudonym Richard Meade) Big Bend, Doubleday, 1968; (under pseudonym Richard Meade) The Lost Fraulein, Random House, 1969 (published in England as A Score of Arms, P. Davies, 1969); The Chandler Heritage, Simon & Schuster, 1971. Also author of forty paperback novels, mostly under pseudonyms.

WORK IN PROGRESS: The Blue Windows.

SIDELIGHTS: Haas sold his first story in 1944, then none until 1961, when he broke into the paperback field, and had a novel accepted for hardback publication. Avocational interests: Outdoor activities.

BIOGRAPHICAL/CRITICAL SOURCES: Commonweal, May 26, 1967.

* * *

HAAS, Mary R(osamond) 1910-

PERSONAL: Born January 23, 1910, in Richmond, Ind.; daughter of Robert Jeremiah (a dairy inspector) and Leona (Crowe) Haas. Education: Earlham College, A.B., 1930; University of Chicago, graduate study, 1930-31; Yale University, Ph.D., 1935. Office: Department of Linguistics, University of California, Berkeley, Calif. 94720.

CAREER: University of California, Berkeley, assistant professor of Siamese and linguistics, 1947-52, associate professor, 1952-57, professor of linguistics, 1957—, chairman of department, 1958-63. Walker-Ames Visiting Professor of Linguistics, University of Washington, 1961; Linguistic Society of America Professor, Ohio State University, summer, 1970; Virginia Gildersleeve Visiting Professor of Linguistics, Barnard College and Columbia University, 1971. Member: Linguistic Society of America (vice-president, 1956; president, 1963); American Anthropological Association, American Folklore Society, American Oriental Society, Ethnohistory Conference, Linguistic Circle of New York, Sigma Xi. Awards, honors: Guggenheim fellowship for studies on American Indian languages, 1964-65; fellow of National Foundation for the Humanities, and Center for Advanced Study in the Behavioral Sciences, 1967-68.

WRITINGS: Tunica Grammar, J.J. Augustin, 1941; Beginning Thai: Introductory Lessons in the Pronunciation and Grammar of the Thai Language, American Council of Learned Societies, 1942; The Thai System of Writing, American Council of Learned Societies, 1942, revised edition, 1956; (with Heng R. Subhanka) First Thai Reader, [Berkeley], 1945; Manual of Thai Conversation, [Berkeley], 1945; Special Dictionary of the Thai Language, University of California (Berkeley), 1945; Thai Phrases, [Berkeley], 1945; (with Subhanka) Spoken Thai: Basic Course, two volumes, American Council of Learned Societies, 1945; Phonetic Dictionary of the Thai Language, two volumes, University of California Press (Berkeley), 1947; (editor) Tunica Texts, University of California Press, 1950; Tunica Dictionary, University of California Press, 1953; Thai Reader, American Council of Learned Societies, 1954; Thai Vocabulary, American Council of Learned Societies, 1955; (editor) Edward Sapir and Morris Swadish, Yana Dictionary, University of California Press, 1960; (with others) Thai-English Student's Dictionary, Stanford University Press, 1964; The Prehistory of Languages, Mouton & Co., 1969, Humanities, 1970.

WORK IN PROGRESS: Editing Readings in North American Indian Linguistics; compiling Natchez-English and English Natchez Dictionary; a study of genetic relationships among American Indian languages.

*   *   *

HABER, Samuel   1928-

PERSONAL: Born May 5, 1928, in New York, N.Y.; son of Max (a tailor) and Celia (Mondschein) Haber; married Janice Grodman, December 3, 1949; children: Sarah, Kate, Ruth. Education: University of California, Berkeley, B.A., 1952, M.A., 1957, Ph.D., 1961. Religion: Jewish. Office: Department of History, University of California, Berkeley, Calif. 94720.

CAREER: University of Delaware, Newark, assistant professor of history, 1961-65; University of California, Berkeley, assistant professor, 1965-68, associate professor of history, 1968—.

WRITINGS: Efficiency and Uplift: Scientific Management in the Progressive Era, 1890-1920, University of Chicago Press, 1964.

WORK IN PROGRESS: A History of the Professions in America, completion expected in 1974.

*   *   *

HAKES, Joseph Edward   1916-

PERSONAL: Born October 22, 1916, in New York, N.Y.; son of Joseph William (a clergyman) and Emily (Faron) Hakes; married Lois Ruth Wyngarden, September 5, 1941; children: Jay, James, Joseph. Education: Wheaton College, Wheaton, Ill., B.A., 1937; Columbia University, law student, 1937-38; Eastern Baptist Theological Seminary, B.D., 1941; University of Pittsburgh, Ed.D., 1967. Politics: Democrat. Home: 180 Valdon Rd., Mundelein, Ill. 60060. Office: Trinity College, Deerfield, Ill. 60015.

CAREER: Ordained to Baptist ministry, 1941; pastor in Beacon, N.Y., 1940-42, in Gallipolis, Ohio, 1942-48, in Kalamazoo, Mich., 1948-53; Grand Rapids Baptist Seminary, Grand Rapids, Mich., president, 1953-58; Wheaton College, Wheaton, Ill., assistant professor of Bible, 1958-66, department chairman, 1964-66; Trinity Evangelical Divinity School, Deerfield, Ill., professor of Christian education and department chairman, 1966-69; Trinity College, Deerfield, Ill., vice-president for undergraduate studies and dean of the college, 1969—.

WRITINGS: (Editor) An Introduction to Evangelical Christian Education, Moody, 1964; (contributor) M.J. Taylor, editor, An Introduction to Christian Education, Abingdon, 1966.

*   *   *

HALL, A(lfred) Rupert   1920-

PERSONAL: Born July 26, 1920, in Stoke on Trent, England; son of Alfred Dawson and Margaret (Ritchie) Hall; married Marie Boas (a reader), June 10, 1959; children: Two daughters. Education: Alderman Newton's School, student, 1931-38; Christ's College, Cambridge, B.A., 1941, M.A., 1944, Ph.D., 1950. Home: 23 Chiswick Staithe, London W.4, England. Agent: Curtis Brown Ltd., 13 King St., London W.C.2, England. Office: Imperial College of Science and Technology, London S.W.7, England.

CAREER: Cambridge University, Cambridge, England, fellow and steward of Christ's College, 1949-59, university lecturer in history of science, 1950-59; University of California, Los Angeles, associate research medical historian, 1959-60, professor of philosophy, 1960-61; Indiana University, Bloomington, professor of history and philosophy of science, 1961-63; Imperial College of Science and Technology, University of London, London, England, professor of history of science and technology, 1963—. Military service: British Army, Royal Corps of Signals, 1940-45; became lieutenant. Member: International Academy of History of Science, Royal Society of Arts (fellow), Royal Historical Society (fellow).

WRITINGS: Ballistics in the Seventeenth Century: A Study in the Relations of Science and War with Reference Principally to England, Cambridge University Press, 1952; (editor with Charles Joseph Singer and others) A History of Technology, Oxford University Press, 1954-58; The Scientific Revolution, 1500-1800: The Formation of the Modern Scientific Attitude, Longmans, Green, 1954, Beacon Press, 1956, 2nd edition, Longmans, Green, 1962, Beacon Press, 1966; (with wife, Marie Boas Hall) Newton's Chemical Experiments, [Paris], 1958; Cambridge and the Royal Society, Cambridge University Press, 1960; (editor and author of foreword) The Making of Modern Science, Leicester University Press, 1960; (with C. Donald O'Malley) Scientific Literature in Sixteenth and Seventeenth Century England, University of California (Los Angeles), 1961; (editor and translator with Marie Boas Hall) Unpublished Scientific Papers of Isaac Newton, Cambridge University Press, 1962; From Galileo to Newton, 1630-1720, Harper, 1963; (with Marie Boas Hall) A Brief History of Science, New American Library, 1964; (editor and translator with Marie Boas Hall) The Correspondence of Henry Oldenburg, eight volumes, University of Wisconsin Press, 1965-71; The Abbey Scientists, R. & R. Nicholson, 1966; Hooke's "Micrographia," 1665-1965, Athlone Press, 1966; The Cambridge Philosophical Society: A History, Heffer, 1969.

Contributor to *Isis* and other journals. General editor, "The Rise of Modern Science" series, Harper, 1962—.

WORK IN PROGRESS: Volumes nine through twelve of *The Correspondence of Henry Oldenburg.*

AVOCATIONAL INTERESTS: Antiquities, especially those connected with science; collecting scientific books.

BIOGRAPHICAL/CRITICAL SOURCES: Times Literary Supplement, January 19, 1967.

* * *

HALL, John O.P.   1911-

PERSONAL: Born June 7, 1911, in Lynn, Mass.; son of John (a mariner) and Carrie (Farrell) Hall; married Mary G. Phillips, September, 1950; children: Tabitha, Jonathan. *Education:* Harvard University, student, 1929-32; University of New Hampshire, B.S. (with honors), 1939; Columbia University, Ph.D., 1953. *Politics:* Democrat. *Religion:* Unitarian. *Home:* 336 Delta Lane, Charlotte, N.C. 28215. *Office:* Department of History, University of North Carolina, Charlotte, N.C. 28205.

CAREER: Teacher of American history, 1939-61; American Federation of Labor and Congress of Industrial Organizations, Industrial Union Department, Washington, D.C., research historian, 1961-63; Charlotte College, Charlotte, N.C., professor of history, 1963-64; University of North Carolina, Charlotte, professor of history, 1964—. Consultant to the U.S. Department of Labor; lecturer for Bureau of International Labor Affairs. *Member:* American Historical Association, Economic History Association, Labor Historians (president, 1963-65), American Association of University Professors, Organization of American Historians, Southern Historical Association.

WRITINGS: History of the University of New Hampshire, University of New Hampshire Press, 1941; (with John Brophy) *A Miner's Life: An Autobiography,* University of Wisconsin Press, 1964. Contributor of historical articles and of reviews to a dozen journals. Associate editor, *Labor History,* 1959-63.

WORK IN PROGRESS: The Gentle Craft; The Henderson Strike.

AVOCATIONAL INTERESTS: Music, walking, and comparative religion.

* * *

HALL, Marie Boas   1919-

PERSONAL: Born October 18, 1919, in Springfield, Mass.; daughter of Ralph Philip (a professor) and Louise (Schutz) Boas; married A. Rupert Hall (a professor), June 10, 1959; children: Two daughters. *Education:* Radcliffe College, A.B., 1940, M.A., 1942; Cornell University, Ph.D., 1949. *Home:* 23 Chiswick Staithe, Hartington Rd., London W.4, England.

CAREER: University of Massachusetts, Amherst, assistant professor of history, 1949-52; Brandeis University, Waltham, Mass., assistant professor of history of science, 1952-58; University of California, Los Angeles, associate professor of history of science, 1958-61; Indiana University, Bloomington, professor of history and logic of science, 1961-63; Imperial College of Science and Technology, University of London, London, England, senior lecturer in history of science and technology, 1963-64, reader in history of science and technology, 1964—. *Member:* History of Science Society (secretary, 1952-58), Academie Internationale d'Histoire des Sciences, British Society for History of Science, Royal Society of Arts (fellow), Newcomen Society. *Awards, honors:* Guggenheim fellowship, 1955-56; Pfizer Award of History of Science Society, 1959, for best book in its field by an American author, for *Robert Boyle and Seventeenth Century Chemistry.*

WRITINGS: (With husband, A.R. Hall) *Newton's Chemical Experiments,* [Paris], 1958; *History of Science,* Service Center for Teachers of History (Washington), 1958, 2nd edition, 1964; *Robert Boyle and Seventeenth Century Chemistry,* Cambridge University Press, 1958; *The Scientific Revolution, 1450-1630,* Harper, 1962; (editor and translator with A.R. Hall) *Unpublished Scientific Papers of Isaac Newton,* Cambridge University Press, 1962; (editor) *Robert Boyle's Experiments and Considerations Touching Colours,* Johnson Publications, 1964; (with A.R. Hall) *A Brief History of Science,* New American Library, 1964; *Robert Boyle on Natural Philosophy: An Essay with Selections from His Writings,* Indiana University Press, 1965; (editor and translator with A.R. Hall) *The Correspondence of Henry Oldenburg,* eight volumes, University of Wisconsin Press, 1965-71; (editor) Henry Power, *Experimental Philosophy,* Johnson Reprint, 1966; (editor) *Nature and Nature's Laws: Documents of the Scientific Revolution,* Harper, 1969; (editor) *The Pneumatics of Hero of Alexandria,* Macdonald & Co., 1970. Contributor to scientific and historical journals in England and France.

WORK IN PROGRESS: Volumes nine through twelve of *The Correspondence of Henry Oldenburg.*

AVOCATIONAL INTERESTS: Old scientific instruments, old silver, books.

* * *

HALL, Oakley (Maxwell)   1920-
(O. M. Hall, Jason Manor)

PERSONAL: Born July 1, 1920, in San Diego, Calif.; son of Oakley M. and Jessie (Sands) Hall; married Barbara Edinger, June 28, 1945; children: Oakley III, Mary Barbara Sands, Tracy Elizabeth, Sara Brett. *Education:* University of California, Berkeley, B.A., 1943; State University of Iowa, M.F.A., 1950. *Home address:* P.O. Box 2101, Olympic Valley, Calif. 95730. *Agent:* Harold Matson & Co., 22 East 40th St., New York, N.Y. 10016.

CAREER: State University of Iowa Writer's Workshop, staff member, 1950-52; University of California, Irvine, professor of English and director of graduate program in writing, 1968—. *Military service:* U.S. Marine Corps, 1939-45.

WRITINGS: (Under name O.M. Hall) *Murder City,* Farrar, Straus, 1949; *So Many Doors,* Random House, 1950; *Corpus of Joe Bailey,* Viking, 1953; *Mardios Beach,* Viking, 1955; *Warlock,* Viking, 1958; *The Downhill Racers,* Viking, 1963; *The Pleasure Garden,* Viking, 1966; *A Game for Eagles,* Morrow, 1970; *Report from Beau Harbor,* Morrow, 1971.

Under pseudonym Jason Manor: *Too Dead to Run,* Viking, 1953; *The Red Jaguar,* Viking, 1954; *The Pawns of Fear,* Viking, 1955; *The Tramplers,* Viking, 1956.

Contributor of short stories to *Western Review, Epoch,* and other little magazines.

SIDELIGHTS: In a review of *The Pleasure Garden,* Wirt Williams writes: "[Oakley Hall] . . . has always had an X-ray penetration of social orders, big and little, and the keenest sensitivity to their nuances and subtleties. And he has always had a skill with plot that was absolutely dangerous.

"His great and manifest growth here is in the range and intensity of language and imagery. The dimension that the edited image creates was in the past his most serious lack: the absence of poetry was almost all that kept his *Warlock* from being the culminating, *fin de series* work in a century of fiction about the American West. Now he has that dimension." *Warlock,* nominated for the Pulitzer Prize in 1958, was filmed by Twentieth Century-Fox in 1959, *The Downhill Racers* by Paramount in 1969 as "Downhill Racer."

BIOGRAPHICAL/CRITICAL SOURCES: Hudson Review, spring, 1967; *Kenyon Review,* Volume 30, number 1, 1968; *Variety,* December 24, 1969; *Best Sellers,* December 1, 1970.

*   *   *

HALL, Rosalys Haskell 1914-

PERSONAL: Born March 27, 1914, in New York, N.Y.; daughter of Henry Marion (an author) and Alice Louise (Haskell) Hall. *Education:* Studied at Ecole Sevigne, Paris, France, at New Jersey College for Women (now Douglass College of Rutgers University) and Ethical Culture Norman Training School; special courses at Columbia University and New York University. *Politics:* Republican. *Religion:* Dutch Reformed. *Home:* 56 Barrow St., New York, N.Y. 10014.

CAREER: Sutton Beekman School, New York, N.Y., former kindergarten and French teacher; Doubleday Bookshop, New York, N.Y., seller of children's books, 1938-44; Longmans, Green & Co. (now merged with David McKay Co., Inc., under McKay name), New York, N.Y., editor in children's book department, 1944—. Freelance editor for other publishers. *Member:* Roger Williams Family Association, Audubon Society of Rhode Island, Junior Writers Forum (New York), Newport Historical Society, Redwood Library (Newport, R.I.).

WRITINGS: Animals to Africa, Holiday House, 1939; *Out of Provincetown,* Farrar & Rinehart, 1941; *The Merry Miller,* Oxford University Press, 1952; *No Ducks for Dinner,* Oxford University Press, 1953; *Baker's Man,* Lippincott, 1954; *The Tailor's Trick,* Lippincott, 1955; *Bertie and Eddie,* Oxford University Press, 1956; *Green as Spring,* Longmans, Green, 1957; *Seven for Saint Nicholas,* Lippincott, 1958; (with sister, Julia Hall) *Animal Hide and Seek,* Lothrop, 1958; *Young Fancy,* Longmans, Green, 1960; *The Dog's Boy,* Lothrop, 1962; *Miranda's Dragon,* McGraw, 1968; *The Bright and Shining Breadboard,* Lothrop, 1969.

WORK IN PROGRESS: A biography of Roger Williams; a sequel to *Seven for Saint Nicholas.*

AVOCATIONAL INTERESTS: Tennis, swimming, gardening, cats, and nature walks.

BIOGRAPHICAL/CRITICAL SOURCES: Young Readers' Review, December, 1968; *Library Journal,* March 15, 1970.

*   *   *

HALLER, Mark H(ughlin) 1928-

PERSONAL: Born December 22, 1928, in Washington, D.C.; son of Mark H. (a scientist) and Sarah (Gillogley) Haller. *Education:* Wesleyan University, Middletown, Conn., B.A., 1951; Johns Hopkins University, graduate study, 1951-52; University of Maryland, M.A., 1954; University of Wisconsin, Ph.D., 1959. *Office:* Department of History, Temple University, Philadelphia, Pa. 19122.

CAREER: University of Chicago, Chicago, Ill., instructor, 1959-61, assistant professor of history, 1961-68; Temple University, Philadelphia, Pa., associate professor of history, 1968—. *Military service:* U.S. Army, Counter Intelligence Corps., 1953-55. *Member:* American Historical Association, Organization of American Historians, American Association of University Professors, American Civil Liberties Union. *Awards, honors:* Herfurth Award for *Eugenics: Hereditarian Attitudes in American Thought.*

WRITINGS: Eugenics: Hereditarian Attitudes in American Thought, Rutgers University Press, 1963; (with Allen F. Davis) *The Peoples of Philadelphia,* Temple University Press, 1973. Contributor to historical journals.

WORK IN PROGRESS: A history of crime and criminal justice in Chicago, 1890-1935.

*   *   *

HALLINAN, Nancy 1921-

PERSONAL: Born February 5, 1921, in London, England; daughter of Charles T. Hallinan (a journalist) and Hazel (Hunkins) Hallinan; divorced; children: Rosalind Addison Goethals. *Education:* Vassar College, B.A., 1942; graduate study at Columbia University, 1946-47, and New School for Social Research, 1947-48. *Politics:* Registered Democrat. *Religion:* Episcopal. *Home and office:* 276 Riverside Dr., New York, N.Y. 10025. *Agent:* Mavis McIntosh, McIntosh, McKee & Dodds, 22 East 40th St., New York, N.Y. 10016.

CAREER: Reporter for newspapers in Newburgh, N.Y., and Binghamton, N.Y., 1942-44; Office of War Information, New York, N.Y., editorial assistant, 1944-45; freelance writer. *Awards, honors:* Writing fellowships at Yaddo, Saratoga Springs, N.Y., and Edward MacDowell Artists' Colony, Peterborough, N.H.

WRITINGS: Rough Winds of May, Harper, 1955; *A Voice from the Wings,* Knopf, 1965. Contributor of short stories to *Cornhill, New Voices, American Writing Today, Touchstone, American Vanguard.*

WORK IN PROGRESS: A novel, *Wild Men Who Court.*

SIDELIGHTS: Rough Winds of May has been issued in six foreign editions. *Avocational interests:* Theatre, ballet and modern dance, good movies, painting, sculpture, travel.

*   *   *

HALPERIN, Morton H. 1938-

PERSONAL: Born June 13, 1938, in Brooklyn, N.Y.; son of Harry (a lawyer) and Lillian (Neubart) Halperin; married Ina Weinstein, June 19, 1960; children: David Elliott. *Education:* Columbia University, A.B., 1958; Yale University, M.A., 1959, Ph.D., 1961. *Religion:* Jewish. *Office:* Brookings Institution, 1775 Massachusetts Ave., Washington, D.C. 20034.

CAREER: Harvard University, Cambridge, Mass., research associate, Center for International Affairs, 1960-66, instructor, 1961-63, assistant professor of government, 1964-66; Office of the Assistant Secretary of Defense, Washington, D.C., special assistant, 1966-67, deputy assistant secretary of defense, 1967-69; Brookings Institution, Washington, D.C., senior fellow, 1969—. Member of senior staff, National Security Council, 1969. Consultant to RAND Corp. *Member:* American Political Science Association, American Civil Liberties Union, Council on Foreign Relations, Institute for Strategic Studies. *Awards, honors:* Rockefeller Foundation grant for research on China's military and foreign policy.

WRITINGS: (With Sheldon Raab) *The Columbia College Student, 1956-57: A Study of the Whole Man,* Columbia College, 1957; *Nuclear Weapons and Limited War,* Harvard University, Center for International Affairs, 1960; (with Thomas C. Schelling) *Strategy and Arms Control,* Twentieth Century Fund, 1961; *Limited War: An Essay on the Development of the Theory and an Annotated Bibliography,* Harvard University, Center for International Affairs, 1961; *A Proposal for a Ban on the Use of Nuclear Weapons,* Institute for Defense Analysis, 1961; *Arms Control and Inadvertent General War,* Institute for Defense Analysis, 1962; *The Limiting Process in the Korean War,* Harvard University, Center for

International Affairs, 1962; *Limited War in the Nuclear Age*, Wiley, 1963; *China and the Bomb*, Praeger, 1965; (with Dwight Perkins) *Communist China and Arms Control*, Praeger, 1965; *Chinese Nuclear Strategy: The Early Post Detonation Period*, Institute for Strategic Studies, 1965; *Is China Turning In?*, Harvard University, Center for International Affairs, 1965; *China and Nuclear Proliferation*, University of Chicago Center for Policy Study, 1966; *Contemporary Military Strategy*, Little, Brown, 1967, revised edition published as *Defense Strategy for the Seventies*, 1971; (editor) *Sino-Soviet Relations and Arms Control*, M.I.T. Press, 1967.

Contributor to professional journals. Member of editorial board, *American Political Science Review* and *Foreign Policy*.

WORK IN PROGRESS: Bureaucratic Politics and Foreign Policy.

* * *

HALPERN, Manfred 1924-

PERSONAL: Born February 1, 1924, in Mittweida, Germany; came to United States in 1937, naturalized in 1944; son of Jacob (a hat-maker) and Edith (Aron) Halpern; married Betsy Steele (a clinical psychologist), November 5, 1948; children: Jeffrey Kim, Tamara Steele, Katrina Ann, David Nicholas. *Education:* University of California, Los Angeles, B.A. (summa cum laude), 1947; Johns Hopkins School of Advanced International Studies, M.A., 1948, Ph.D., 1960. *Home:* 27 MacLean Cir., Princeton, N.J. 08540. *Office:* Department of Politics, Princeton University, Princeton, N.J. 08540.

CAREER: U.S. Department of State, Washington, D.C., research analyst to chief of Division of Research for Europe, 1948-50, research analyst, 1950-53, special assistant to chief of Division of Research for Near East, South Asia and Africa, 1953-58; Princeton University, Princeton, N.J., 1958—, now professor of politics and faculty associate of Center of International Studies. Faculty member, George Washington University, 1951-53, and Johns Hopkins University, 1956; lecturer, National War College, Foreign Service Institute, and Strategic Intelligence School. Consultant to RAND Corp., 1958-66, and to U.S. Department of State, 1963-70. *Military service:* U.S. Army, served in European Theater, 1944-46; became technical sergeant; received Combat Infantry Badge and three battle stars.

MEMBER: American Political Science Association, African Studies Association (fellow; program chairman), Royal Central Asian Society, Middle East Studies Association (program chairman), Adlai Stevenson Institute for International Affairs, American Society for Social Psychiatry (council member), Middle East Institute (fellow), Phi Beta Kappa. *Awards, honors:* Meritorious service award, U.S. Department of State, 1952.

WRITINGS: (Contributor) John J. Johnson, editors, *The Role of the Military in Underdeveloped Countries*, Princeton University Press, 1962; *The Politics of Social Change in the Middle East and North Africa*, Princeton University Press, 1963; *The Morality and Politics of Intervention*, Council on Religion and International Affairs, 1963; (contributor) Cyril Edwin Black and T.P. Thornton, editors, *Communism and Revolution: The Strategic Uses of Political Violence*, Princeton University Press, 1964; (contributor) James N. Rosenau, editor, *International Aspects of Civil Strife*, Princeton University Press, 1964; *Applying a New Theory of Human Relations to the Comparative Study of Racism* (monograph), Center on International Race Relations, University of Denver, c.1970. Contributor to *World Politics, Middle East Journal, Africa Report,* and *Worldview*.

WORK IN PROGRESS: The Political Process in a Traditional Society: Islam; The Revolution of Modernization in National and International Society.

* * *

HAMMER, Jeanne-Ruth 1912-

PERSONAL: Born January 10, 1912, in Odessa, Russia; daughter of Max (a dressgoods salesman) and Frieda (Kravitz) Lipsky; married Manuel Hammer (an assistant plant manager), August 17, 1929; children: Alvan Dale, Lianne Hammer Juster, Carl Helman. *Education:* Attended classes at New York University, Columbia University, and New School for Social Research. *Politics:* Progressive. *Religion:* Jewish. *Home and office:* 1117 Mahantongo St., Pottsville, Pa. 17901. *Agent:* Jeanne Hale, 31 West Tenth St., New York, N.Y. 10011.

CAREER: Worked in the export-import business, 1950-52, then ran own export business; worked in the Columbia University Library, 1955-56; wrote feature articles for the *Brooklyn Daily* for about four years, and a column, "Window on the World," for the weekly *Brooklyn Graphic*. *Member:* American Translators Association.

WRITINGS: Little Thorn (juvenile), Reilly & Lee, 1964. Contributor of own work, and of translations of such authors as Germain Nouveau and Sabine Sicaud to *Neon, American Weave, The Sixties, Transatlantic Review, Migrant,* and other publications.

WORK IN PROGRESS: Collaborating with Robert Kishko on a novel, a trilogy of novelettes, several juveniles, and short stories.

SIDELIGHTS: Mrs. Hammer writes: "[I] have traveled in France, Italy, Mexico (I spent a year in Mexico, living with a Mexican family, writing poetry). [I] have long been interested in poetry—Mr. Ezra Pound gave me generously of his time, working with me on my poetry. [I] can translate from French, Yiddish, German, Spanish, Italian."

* * *

HAMMOND, Thomas T(aylor) 1920-

PERSONAL: Born September 15, 1920, in Atlanta, Ga.; son of Percy Waters (a journalist) and Elizabeth (Denman) Hammond; married Alena Vithova; children: Thomas Kent. *Education:* University of Mississippi, B.A., 1941; University of North Carolina, M.A., 1943; Columbia University, M.A., 1948, Ph.D., 1954. *Office:* Randall Hall, University of Virginia, Charlottesville, Va. 22901.

CAREER: Emory University, Atlanta, Ga., instructor in history, 1946; Louisiana State University, Baton Rouge, assistant professor of history, 1948; Columbia University, New York, N.Y., lecturer in history, 1948-49; University of Virginia, Charlottesville, assistant professor, 1949-56, associate professor, 1956-63, professor of history, 1963—. Visiting associate professor of history, University of Wisconsin, 1959-60. Southern Conference on Slavic Studies, vice-president, 1963-64, president, 1964-65; associate of Russian Research Center, Harvard University, 1967. *Military service:* U.S. Naval Reserve, active duty, 1942-46. *Member:* American Historical Association, American Association for the Advancement of Slavic Studies. *Awards, honors:* Ford Foundation faculty fellow, 1951-52; Fulbright fellow, 1956-57, 1968-69; American Council of Learned Societies fellow, 1961, 1962; exchange scholar at Moscow University, 1964.

WRITINGS: Yugoslavia Between East and West, Foreign Policy Association, 1954; *Lenin on Trade Unions and Revolution*, Columbia University Press, 1957; (editor) *Soviet Foreign Relations and World Communism: A Selected, Annotated Bibliography of 7,000 Books in 30 Languages*, Princeton University Press, 1965; *Proposal for*

Bibliographic Documentation and Information Center, Conference of Bibliographic and Research Aids in Soviet Studies, 1966.

Contributor: E.J. Simmons, editor, *Continuity and Change in Russian and Soviet Thought,* Harvard University Press, 1955; Robert F. Byrnes, editor, *Yugoslavia,* Praeger, 1957; John Curtiss, editor, *Essays in Russian and Soviet History,* Columbia University Press, 1963. Contributor to *National Geographic, Slavic Review, Foreign Affairs, Political Science Quarterly, Journal of International Affairs, Virginia Quarterly Review, New Leader,* and *American Historical Review.*

WORK IN PROGRESS: *The Anatomy of Communist Takeovers.*

*   *   *

HAMORI, Laszlo Dezso   1911-

PERSONAL: Born May 10, 1911, in Budapest, Hungary; son of Ignac and Sidonia (Neumann) Salamon; married Magda Foldes, September 18, 1938; children: Susan, Katrine. *Education:* University of Budapest, Dr. Juris, 1934. *Politics:* Independent liberal. *Religion:* Jewish. *Home:* Canadastigen 17, Lidingo, Stockholm, Sweden. *Agent:* Gunther Stuhlmann, 65 Irving Pl., New York, N.Y. 10003.

CAREER: Law clerk in Budapest, Hungary, 1934-42; interned in Nazi forced labor camp in Ukraine, 1942-44; *Nepszava* (daily newspaper), Budapest, Hungary, political editor, 1945-48; political refugee in Zurich, Switzerland, and Stockholm, Sweden, 1948-49; free-lance journalist and author, Stockholm, Sweden, 1949—; International Feature Service, New York, N.Y., foreign correspondent, 1960—. *Military service:* Hungarian Army, officer candidate, 1933-34. *Member:* Free Hungarians Federation in Sweden, Minerva Authors Federation, Publicist Club (Stockholm). *Awards, honors:* Swedish Authors' Foundation prize, 1962.

WRITINGS: *Amiroel Beszelnek: A 20. szazad politikai es gazdaszgi problemainak roevid attekintese,* Forras, 1946; (editor with others) *Hundra miljoner faangar: Oesteuropa under kommunistisk regim,* Natur och Kultur, 1953; *Jugoslavien,* Natur och Kultur, 1955; *Schweden,* Verlat Volk und Land, 1957; *Ungern efter andra vaerldskriget,* Kooperativa foer Bundets Bokfoerlag, 1957; *Oesteuropa efter ungerskrisen,* Raben & Sjoegren, 1959; *Det Fjarde riket: En Bok on Tysklandsfraagan,* Horsta Foerlag, 1959; *Farlig resa,* Svensk Laeraetidnings Foerlag, 1959, translation by Annabelle Macmillan published as *Dangerous Journey,* Harcourt, 1962; *Schalom kommer till Israel,* Saga, 1961, translation by Annabelle Macmillan published as *Flight to the Promised Land,* Harcourt, 1963; *Israel—loefte sem infrias,* Horsta Foerlag, 1961; *Samurajer och neonljus: Japan utan romantik,* Wahlstrom och Wistrand, 1962; *Israel: En Turisthandbok,* Wahlstrom och Wistrand, 1965; *Adventure in Bangkok* (originally published in Swedish), translation by Annabelle Macmillan, Harcourt, 1966; (with Erik Gate) *Varldspolitisk upplagsbok,* Natur. och Kultur, 1969.

WORK IN PROGRESS: A book about the foreign workers in Western Europe.

SIDELIGHTS: Hamori's books have been translated into Norwegian, Dutch, Danish, German, and Hebrew.

*   *   *

HANCE, William A(dams)   1916-

PERSONAL: Born December 29, 1916, in New York, N.Y.; son of George C. and Grace (Adams) Hance; married Margaret Dorst (an assistant in English at Barnard College), March 23, 1940; children: Jean (Mrs. Andrew L. Zagayko), Bronwen. *Education:* Columbia

University, A.B., 1938, Ph.D., 1949. *Politics:* Independent. *Religion:* Episcopalian. *Home:* 106 Morningside Dr., New York, N.Y. 10027.

CAREER: Columbia University, New York, N.Y., head of graduate placement, 1941-43, assistant to the dean, Columbia College, 1943-44, 1946-48, assistant dean, 1948-49, associate professor, 1949-59, professor of economic geography, 1959—, department chairman, 1964—. Young Men's Christian Association, member of board of managers of Uptown Branch, 1950-60. *Military service:* U.S. Naval Reserve, 1944-46; became lieutenant commander. *Member:* American Geographic Society, Association of American Geographers, Royal Geographic Society, Council on Foreign Relations, Royal African Society, African Studies Association (board of directors, 1958-60; executive secretary, 1959; chairman of archives and libraries committee, 1963-64; chairman of policies and plans committee, 1963—), Men's Faculty Club (Columbia; member of board of directors, 1959-62), Phi Beta Kappa.

WRITINGS: *The Outer Hebrides in Relation to Highland Depopulation,* E. Edwards, 1949; (with Irene S. Van Dongen) *The Port of Lobito and the Benguela Railway,* American Geographical Society, 1956; *Madagascar: Ports, Roads, Railroads, Air Transport,* Columbia University, Division of Economic Geography, 1958; *African Economic Development,* Harper, 1958, 2nd edition, Praeger, 1967; (with Van Dongen) *Matadi: Focus of Belgian African Transport,* [Washington], 1959; *Export Production in Tropical Africa by Commodity or Group and by Percent of Total Value in 1957,* privately printed, 1960; *The Geography of Modern Africa,* Columbia University Press, 1964; (editor) *Southern Africa and the United States,* Columbia University Press, 1968; *Population, Migration and Urbanization in Africa,* Columbia University Press, 1970. Contributor to geographic periodicals.

WORK IN PROGRESS: *Regional Development in Western Europe; Demographic Problems in Africa.*

AVOCATIONAL INTERESTS: British scenery and architecture.

BIOGRAPHICAL/CRITICAL SOURCES: *New Republic,* June 29, 1968.

*   *   *

HANDOVER, P(hyllis) M(argaret)

EDUCATION: St. Anne's College, Oxford, M.A. *Home:* Lyon House, Aldersey Rd., Guildford, Surrey, England. *Office:* The Times Publishing Co., Printing House Sq., London E.C.4, England.

CAREER: The Times Publishing Co., London, England, publicity and feature writer, and correspondent. *Member:* Royal Historical Society (fellow).

WRITINGS: *The Site of the Office of The Times,* Times Publishing, 1955; *Arbella Stuart: Royal Lady of Hardwick and Cousin to King James,* Eyre & Spottiswoode, 1957; *The Second Cecil: The Rise to Power, 1563-1604, of Sir Robert Cecil, Later First Earl of Salisbury,* Eyre & Spottiswoode, 1959, Dufour, 1963; *Stanley Morison: A Second Handlist, 1950-59,* Sheval Press, c.1959; *Printing in London: From 1476 to Modern Times,* Harvard University Press, 1960; (editor) Stanley Morison, *Of Type Designs,* Benn, 1962. Contributor to *Motif,* and other journals.

*   *   *

HANDY, Rollo   1927-

PERSONAL: Born February 20, 1927, in Kenyon, Minn.; son of John Robert (a mechanic) and Alice (Kispert) Handy; married Toni E. Scheiner, September 17, 1950; children: Jonathan David, Ellen Joan, Benjamin

Paul. *Education:* Carleton College, B.A., 1950; Sarah Lawrence College, M.A., 1951; University of Minnesota, postgraduate study, 1951-52; University of Buffalo, Ph.D., 1954. *Home:* 185 Oakgrove Dr., Williamsville, N.Y. 14221. *Office:* Foster Hall, State University of New York at Buffalo, Buffalo, N.Y. 14214.

CAREER: University of South Dakota, Vermillion, 1954-60, started as assistant professor, became professor and head of department of philosophy; Union College, Schenectady, N.Y., associate professor of philosophy, 1960-61; State University of New York at Buffalo, associate professor and acting chairman of department of philosophy, later professor and chairman of department, 1961-67, provost of Faculty of Educational Studies, 1967—. *Military service:* U.S. Naval Reserve, 1945-46. *Member:* American Philosophical Association, Philosophy of Science Association, International Phenomenological Society, American Association of University Professors (chapter president, 1964-66), American Anthropological Association, Mind Association, American Civil Liberties Union, Phi Beta Kappa, Creighton Club.

WRITINGS: (With Paul Kurtz) *A Current Appraisal of the Behavioral Sciences,* Behavioral Research Council, 1964, revised edition, in press; *Methodology of the Behavioral Sciences,* C.C Thomas, 1964; (editor with E.H. Madden and M. Farber) *Philosophical Perspectives on Punishment,* C.C Thomas, 1968; (editor with Madden and Farber) *The Idea of God,* C.C Thomas, 1968; (editor with A. DeGrazia, E.C. Harwood, and Kurtz, and contributor) *The Behavioral Sciences: Essays in Honor of George A. Lundberg,* Behavioral Research Council, 1968; (contributor) Jerry Gill, editor, *Philosophy Today,* Macmillan, 1968; Paul Kurtz, editor, *Modern Problems in Contemporary Society,* Prentice-Hall, 1969; *Value Theory and the Behavioral Sciences,* C.C Thomas, 1969; *The Measurement of Values,* Warren H. Green, 1970; (contributor) Geoffrey A. Petersen, editor, *Philosophic Essays in Honor of Martin Eshleman,* Carleton College, 1971; (contributor) David H. DeGrood, John Somerville, and Dale Riepe, editors, *Radical Currents in Contemporary Philosophy,* Warren H. Green, 1971; (contributor) Dale Reipe, editor, *Naturalism and Phenomenology: Essays in Honor of Marvin Farber,* State University of New York Press, in press; (editor) *Education and the Behavioral Sciences,* Warren H. Green, in press; (with Harwood) *Useful Procedures of Inquiry,* Behavioral Research Council, in press. Contributor of articles to academic journals.

*   *   *

HANGEN, (Putnam) Welles   1930-

PERSONAL: Born March 22, 1930, in New York, N.Y.; son of Herman Cecil and Helen (Brunig) Hangen; married Patricia Dana (a part-time writer), April 1, 1958. *Education:* University of Virginia, student, 1945-46; Brown University, A.B. (cum laude), 1949; Columbia University, graduate work, 1950. *Politics:* Independent. *Religion:* Protestant Episcopal. *Home:* Robert Kochstrasse 54, Bad Godesberg, West Germany. *Agent:* Willis Kingsley Wing, 24 East 38th St., New York, N.Y. 10016. *Office:* National Broadcasting Company, Dahlmannstrasse 32, Bonn, West Germany.

CAREER: New York Herald Tribune, New York, N.Y., reporter for European edition, Paris, France, 1948-49; *New York Times,* New York, N.Y., correspondent in Moscow, Paris, Ankara, and Middle East, 1949-56; National Broadcasting Co., New York, N.Y., chief of news bureaus in Cairo, New Delhi, and now Bonn, 1956—. North American Newspaper Alliance, correspondent in Middle East, 1957-59. *Military service:* U.S. Army, 1951-53; became first lieutenant. *Member:* Overseas Press Club, National Press Club, Foreign Press Association of

Bonn, Phi Beta Kappa. *Awards, honors:* Overseas Press Club citation for excellence, 1957, for news broadcasts from Middle East; Overseas Press Club of New York award for best book on foreign affairs, 1967, for *The Muted Revolution.*

WRITINGS: (Contributor) *Memo to JFK,* Putnam, 1961; (with others) *The Best of Emphasis,* Newman, 1962; *After Nehru, Who?* Harcourt, 1963; *The Muted Revolution: East Germany's Challenge to Russia and the West,* Knopf, 1966. Contributor of articles to *Journal of International Affairs, New Yorker, New Republic,* and *New York Times Sunday Magazine.*

BIOGRAPHICAL/CRITICAL SOURCES: New York Review of Books, March 9, 1967; *Virginia Quarterly Review,* spring, 1967; *Times Literary Supplement,* August 24, 1967.

*   *   *

HANLEY, Boniface Francis   1924-

PERSONAL: Born September 27, 1924, in Brooklyn, N.Y.; son of James Joseph and Mary (Riordan) Hanley. *Education:* St. Bonaventure University, B.A., 1947; Holy Name College, theology studies, 1947-51. *Politics:* Democrat. *Office:* Department of Religious Studies, Siena College, Loudonville, N.Y. 12211.

CAREER: Entered Franciscan Order, 1945; ordained Roman Catholic priest, 1956; Bishop Timon High School, Buffalo, N.Y., teacher, 1951-53; Franciscan Provincial Headquarters, New York, N.Y., secretary, 1953-55; Franciscan Mission, LaPaz, Bolivia, pastor, 1956-58; St. Francis College, Rye Beach, N.H., master of students, 1958-67; Siena College, Loudonville, N.Y., superior of Franciscan Community, 1967—.

WRITINGS: (With Salvator Fink) *The Franciscans: Love at Work,* St. Anthony Guild Press, 1962.

WORK IN PROGRESS: Research on early Franciscan history; gathering material on present missionary activities of Americans in Latin America.

*   *   *

HANLEY, Clifford   1922-
(Henry Calvin)

PERSONAL: Born October 28, 1922, in Glasgow, Scotland; son of Henry and Martha (Griffiths) Hanley; married Anna Easton Clark, January 10, 1948; children: Clifford, Jane, Joanna. *Education:* Attended schools in Glasgow, Scotland. *Home:* 36 Munro Rd., Glasgow, Scotland. *Agent:* Curtis Brown Ltd., 13 King St., London W.C.2, England.

CAREER: Scottish Newspaper Services (news agency), Glasgow, Scotland reporter, 1941-46; *Daily Record,* Glasgow, Scotland, columnist, 1946-57; *TV Guide,* Glasgow, Scotland, columnist, 1957-58; *Evening Citizen,* Glasgow, Scotland, columnist, 1958-60; *Spectator,* London, England, television critic, 1963. Glasgow Films Ltd., director, 1957-63. Appears regularly on television in Scotland "as subversive social commentator." Lecturer. *Member:* National Union of Journalists, P.E.N. (Glasgow council, 1962—), Glasgow Literary and Philological Society (president, 1962-63), Screenwriters Guild, Scottish Arts Council, Inland Waterways Advisory Council.

WRITINGS: Dancing in the Streets (autobiography), Hutchinson, 1958; *Love from Everybody,* Hutchinson, 1959, reissued as *Don't Bother to Knock,* Brown, Watson, 1961; *The Taste of Too Much,* Hutchinson, 1960, revised edition, edited by Vincent Whitcombe, Blackie & Son, 1967; *Second Time Around,* Houghton, 1964 (published in England as *Nothing But the Best,* Hutchinson, 1964); *A Skinful of Scotch,* Houghton, 1965; *The Hot Month,* Houghton, 1967; *The Redhaired Bitch,* Houghton, 1969.

Under pseudonym Henry Calvin: *The System,* Hutchinson, 1962; *It's Different Abroad,* Harper, 1963; *The Italian Gadget,* Hutchinson, 1966; *The DNA Business,* Hutchinson, 1967; *A Nice Friendly Town,* Hutchinson, 1967; *Miranda Must Die,* Hutchinson, 1968; *Boka Lives!,* Harper, 1969; *The Chosen Instrument,* Hutchinson, 1969; *The Poison Chasers,* Hutchinson, 1971.

Plays: "The Durable Element," produced in Dundee, 1961; "Saturmacnalia" (musical), produced at Glasgow Citizens Theatre, 1962; "Dear Boss" (television play), produced in England, 1962; "Oh for an Island" (musical), produced at Glasgow Citizens Theatre, 1963; "Dick McWhitty" (musical), produced in 1964; "Oh Glorious Jubilee" (musical), produced at Leeds Playhouse Theatre, December 10, 1970; "Down Memory Lane," networked by STV, 1971. Song lyrics include unofficial national anthem, "Scotland the Brave." Contributor of several hundred articles to newspapers in Great Britain.

AVOCATIONAL INTERESTS: Music and talk, brewing own beer, sailing in self-built boat.

BIOGRAPHICAL/CRITICAL SOURCES: Times Literary Supplement, March 9, 1967, June 29, 1967, September 21, 1967; *Books and Bookmen,* May, 1967, September, 1968, June, 1969; *Punch,* March 15, 1969, April 23, 1969, September 3, 1969; *Book World,* May 18, 1969; *Library Journal,* July, 1969; *New York Times Book Review,* July 20, 1969.

*   *   *

HANLEY, Hope Anthony 1926-

PERSONAL: Born January 13, 1926, in Washington, D.C.; daughter of Alfred (an engineer and author) and Margaret (McWade) Anthony; married Walter A. Hanley (a research administrator), March 14, 1953; children: Lee (daughter), Walter A. III. *Education:* Tufts University, B.A., 1949.

CAREER: Medford (Mass.) Public Schools, elementary teacher, 1949-51; U.S. Government, Washington, D.C., and foreign posts, 1951-54. *Member:* Kenwood Golf and Country Club (Chevy Chase, Md.).

WRITINGS: Needlepoint, Scribner, 1964; *New Methods in Needlepoint,* Scribner, 1966; *Needlepoint in America, 1600-1900,* Scribner, 1969; *Needlepoint Rugs,* Scribner, 1971; *Fun with Needlepoint,* Scribner, 1972.

AVOCATIONAL INTERESTS: Animals, especially dogs; gardening, modern art, antiques.

*   *   *

HANNAN, Joseph F(rancis) 1923-

PERSONAL: Born February 26, 1923, in Paterson, N.J.; son of Frank and Alice (O'Neill) Hannan; married Margaret M. Condon, April 13, 1944; children: Joseph, Kathleen, Frank, Matthew, Eileen. *Education:* Rutgers State University, A.B., 1955; Seton Hall University, M.A., 1960. *Religion:* Catholic. *Home:* Pompton Lakes, N.J. 07742.

CAREER: Semi-skilled worker before entering teaching profession, 1955; elementary and secondary school teacher of social studies and English, 1955-60; Anthony Wayne Junior High School, Wayne, N.J., guidance counselor, 1960-63; Wayne Valley High School, Wayne Valley, N.J., 1963-69; Fair Lawn High School, Fair Lawn, N.J., guidance counselor, 1969—. *Military service:* U.S. Coast Guard, 1941-45. *Member:* National Education Association, American Personnel and Guidance Association, New Jersey Guidance Association, New Jersey Education Association, Wayne Education Association, Authors Guild.

WRITINGS: Never Tease a Dinosaur: Tales of a Man in a Woman's World, Holt, 1962; *Killing Time,* Holt, 1964. Contributor of humorous articles to magazines.

WORK IN PROGRESS: A novel.

AVOCATIONAL INTERESTS: Bowling, golf, and fishing.

*   *   *

HANO, Arnold 1922-

PERSONAL: Surname is pronounced *Hay*-no; born March 2, 1922, in New York, N.Y.; son of Alfred Barnard (a salesman) and Clara (Millhauser) Hano; married Marjorie Mosheim, October 4, 1942; married second wife, Bonnie Abraham, June 30, 1951; children: (first marriage) Stephen, Susan; (second marriage) Laurel. *Education:* Long Island University, A.B., 1941. *Politics:* Democrat. *Religion:* Jewish. *Home:* 1565 Bluebird Canyon Dr., Laguna Beach, Calif. 92651.

CAREER: New York Daily News, New York, N.Y., copy boy and junior reporter, 1941-42; New York State Department of Labor, New York, N.Y., editor of news bulletin, 1946-47; Robert Louis Stevenson School, New York, N.Y., teacher, 1947-48; Bantam Books, New York, N.Y., editor, 1948-50; Magazine Management Co., New York, N.Y., editor, 1950-54; free-lance writer, 1954—; University of California, Irvine, instructor in writing, 1966—. Founder, Laguna Beach Interracial Citizens Committee, 1963-64; member of local executive board, National Association for the Advancement of Colored People, 1962; member, Laguna Beach Greenbelt Committee, 1969—, Laguna Beach Chamber of Commerce, 1970—, Laguna Beach Board of Adjustment and Design Review, 1971—. *Military service:* U.S. Army, 1942-46; became second lieutenant; awarded combat ribbons for Pacific Theater, Bronze Arrowhead for Kwajalein. *Member:* Society of Magazine Writers. *Awards, honors:* Sidney Hillman Foundation Prize Award, 1963, for an article on California farm labor; selected magazine sportswriter of the year, National Sportscasters and Sportswriters Association, 1963; Boys' Clubs of America junior book award, 1967.

WRITINGS: (Editor) *Western Roundup,* Bantam, 1948; *The Big Out* (novel), A.S. Barnes, 1951; *A Day in the Bleachers,* Crowell, 1955; *Willie Mays: The Say-Hey Kid,* Bartholomew House, 1961, reissued as *Willie Mays,* Grosset, 1966; *The Executive* (novel), New American Library, 1964; *Sandy Koufax, Strikeout King,* Putnam, 1964, revised edition, 1967; *Marriage, Italian Style,* Popular Library, 1965, *Bandolero,* Popular Library, 1968; *Greatest Giants of Them All,* Putnam, 1968; *Roberto Clemente, Batting King,* Putnam, 1968; (with William Gargan) *Why Me?,* Doubleday, 1969. Represented in *Best Sports Stories of the Year, 1963, 1965, 1967,* edited by Irving T. Marsh and Edward Ehre, Dutton, 1963, 1965, 1967, and in other anthologies. Book reviewer, *New York Times;* contributor of short stories and articles to magazines.

SIDELIGHTS: Hano told *CA:* "I feel I am cheating if I do not write something every day."

*   *   *

HANSEN, Bertrand Lyle 1922-

PERSONAL: Born March 20, 1922, in North Royalton, Ohio; son of George Gabriel and Myrtle (Green) Hansen; married Ann Moroney, October 3, 1952; children: Stephanie Ann, George Geoffrey. *Education:* Ohio State University, B.A., 1947, graduate study, 1951; Baldwin Wallace College, graduate study, 1950-51. *Home:* 2190 Obeck Crescent, Mississanga, Ontario, Canada.

CAREER: U.S. Army, Cleveland Ordnance District, Cleveland, Ohio, chief of quality control, 1950-55; Ordnance Management Engineering Training Agency, Rock Island Arsenal, Rock Island, Ill., training officer in industrial management, 1955-57; National Institute of Management, Cleveland, Ohio, director of research, 1957-59; American Management Institute, Inc., Cleveland, Ohio, founder and president, 1959—; Ohio State University, College of Commerce and Administration, Columbus, research associate, 1961-66; University of Toronto, Toronto, Ontario, director of institutional research, 1966-69; University of Ontario, director of research and lecturer in higher education, 1969—. Consultant in industrial management. *Member:* American Institute of Industrial Engineers, American Society for Quality Control, American Economic Association, American Association for the Advancement of Science, American Association for Higher Education, American Association of Institutional Research, Canadian Society for the Study of Higher Education.

WRITINGS: Sampling Aids for Management Control, American Management Institute, 1959; *Work Sampling for Modern Management,* Prentice-Hall, 1960; *Quality Control: Theory and Applications,* Prentice-Hall, 1963; (co-author) *Toward Two Thousand,* McCelland & Stewart, 1971. Contributor to professional journals.

WORK IN PROGRESS: Writings in management, institutional research, and higher education.

* * *

HANSEN, Gary B(arker) 1935-

PERSONAL: Born October 4, 1935, in Ogden, Utah; son of Clarence James (a teacher) and Lena (Barker) Hansen; married Helen Ure, September 7, 1962; children: Mark Gary, Ann Marie, Janet Kay. *Education:* Utah State University, B.S., 1957, M.S., 1963; Cornell University, Ph.D., 1971. *Home:* 1950 North 1050 East, Logan, Utah 84321. *Office:* Department of Economics, Utah State University, Logan, Utah 84321.

CAREER: London School of Economics, London, England, Fulbright scholar, 1965-66; Utah State University, Logan, assistant professor of economics, 1967—. *Military service:* U.S. Army, 1957-59; became first lieutenant. *Member:* Industrial Relations Research Association, British Association for Commercial and Industrial Education.

WRITINGS: (With Leonard J. Arrington) *The Richest Hole on Earth: The History of the Bingham Copper Mine,* Utah State University Press, 1963; *Britain's Industrial Training Act: Its History, Development and Implications for America,* National Manpower Policy Task Force, 1967. Contributor to *Labor Law Journal, Personnel Management* (Great Britain), *Training and Development Journal,* Industrial Relations Research Association *Proceedings, Comparative Education Review,* and *Utah Historical Quarterly.*

WORK IN PROGRESS: Britain's Industrial Training Act: A Case Study in the Development of Public Manpower Policy; studies of manpower training in industry in Utah and collective bargaining in public employment.

AVOCATIONAL INTERESTS: Travel, camping, music, reading.

* * *

HANSON, Robert P(aul) 1918-

PERSONAL: Born May 14, 1918, in Sarona, Wis.; son of Fred E. (a farmer) and Marian (Bergquist) Hanson; married Martha M. Goodlet, January 7, 1946; children: Allan N., Diane G. *Education:* Northland College, B.A., 1940; University of Wisconsin, M.S., 1947, Ph.D., 1949. *Religion:* Methodist *Home:* 5730 Dogwood Pl., Madison, Wis. 53705. *Office.* Department of Veterinary Science, University of Wisconsin, Madison, Wis. 53706.

CAREER: University of Wisconsin, Madison, assistant professor, 1949-52, associate professor, 1952-57, professor of veterinary science and bacteriology, 1957—. Member of International Commission on Foot and Mouth Disease; consultant to U.S. Department of Agriculture and U.S. Public Health Service. *Military service:* U.S. Army, assigned to a war research project, 1942-45. *Member:* American Society of Tropical Medicine, American Society for Microbiology, Wildlife Disease Association, American Association of Avian Pathology, Conference of Research Workers in Animal Diseases, Animal Health Association, National Academy of Sciences-National Research Council (member of animal health committee), American Association for the Advancement of Science, American Veterinary Medicine Association, Wisconsin Academy of Science, Arts and Letters.

WRITINGS: (Editor with Duard Lee Walker and A.S. Evans) *Symposium on Latency and Masking in Virus and Rickettsial Infections,* Burgess, 1958; *Manual for Evaluation of Poultry Biologics,* National Academy of Sciences, 1963; (editor) *Newcastle Disease Virus: An Evolving Pathogen,* University of Wisconsin Press, 1964. Author of more than 100 published papers on virology and epidemiology.

* * *

HARBRON, John D(avison) 1924-

PERSONAL: Born September 15, 1924, in Toronto, Ontario, Canada; son of Tom and Sara Lillian (Peace) Harbron; married Sheila Elizabeth Lester, September 20, 1950; children: Patrick, Christopher, Ann. *Education:* Attended Lawrence Park College Institute; University of Toronto, B.A., 1946, M.A., 1948; graduate study at University of Havana and Hispanic Foundation, Library of Congress, 1947-48. *Home:* 4 Elstree Rd., Islington, Ontario, Canada. *Agent:* Sterling Lord Agency, 15 East 48th St., New York, N.Y. 10017. *Office:* 440 Front St. W., Toronto 135, Ontario, Canada.

CAREER: Canadian Services College, Royal Roads, Victoria, British Columbia, chairman of department of history and economics, 1948-51; *Business Week,* New York, N.Y., Canadian editor, 1956-60; *Executive Magazine,* Toronto, Ontario, editor 1961-66; *The Telegram,* Toronto, associate editor, 1966—. Vice-chairman, Center for Adult Education, Y.M.C.A., Toronto, 1958-60; member of board of governors, St. George's College, Toronto. *Military service:* Royal Canadian Navy, 1944-45, 1948-53. Royal Canadian Navy Reserve; became lieutenant commander; now retired. *Member:* U.S. Naval Institute, Royal Canadian Military Institute, Barrie Yacht Club. *Awards, honors:* Decorated commander, Order of Isabella The Catholic (Spain), 1969; Maria Moors Cabot Prize, Columbia University, 1970.

WRITINGS: Crisis and Change in Latin America, Canadian Institute of International Affairs, 1960; *Communist Ships and Shipping,* Adlard Coles, 1963, Praeger, 1963; *The Conservative Party and National Unity,* [Kingston, Ont.], 1962; *Canada and the Organization of American States,* Canadian-American Committee, 1963; *The Mexican Model,* Baxter Publishing, 1966; *This Is Trudeau,* Longmans Canada (Don Mills), 1968. Editor, "Century" Southam Press Centennial Supplement, 1964-67. Contributor to journals, magazines, newspapers, radio, and television.

AVOCATIONAL INTERESTS: Fencing, sailing, philately.

* * *

HARGREAVES, John D(esmond) 1924-

PERSONAL: Born January 25, 1924, in Colne, Lancashire, England; son of Arthur S. and M. Hilda (Duckworth) Hargreaves; married Sheila E. Wilks, September 30, 1950; children: Alastair Michael, Sara Margaret Ayodele, Catherine Juliet. *Education:* University of Manchester, B.A., 1943, M.A., 1948. *Politics:* Fabian Socialist. *Religion:* Anglican. *Home:* 146 Hamilton Pl., Aberdeen, Scotland.

CAREER: British Civil Service, 1948; University of Manchester, Manchester, England, assistant lecturer, then lecturer in history, 1948-52; Fourah Bay College, Sierra Leone, senior lecturer in history, 1952-54; University of Aberdeen, Aberdeen, Scotland, lecturer, 1954-62, professor of history and head of department, 1962—. Visiting professor at Union College, Schenectady, N.Y., 1960-61, and at University of Ibadan, 1970-71. *Military service:* British Army, Infantry, 1943-46; served in Germany and Malaya.

WRITINGS: Problems of Constitutional Development in West Africa: An Outline for Group Discussion, Fourah Bay College, 1953; *A Life of Sir Samuel Lewis,* Oxford University Press, 1958; *Prelude to the Partition of West Africa,* St. Martin's, 1963; *West Africa: The Former French States,* Prentice-Hall, 1967; (editor and author of introduction) *The Expansion of Europe: A Selection of Articles from History Today,* Oliver & Boyd, 1968; (editor) *France and West Africa: An Anthology of Historical Documents,* Macmillan (London), 1969; (co-editor) *Nations and Empire,* Macmillan (London), 1969. Contributor of articles on modern European and African history to periodicals.

WORK IN PROGRESS: West Africa Partitioned.

AVOCATIONAL INTERESTS: Walking, reading.

* * *

HARGREAVES-MAWDSLEY, W(illiam) Norman 1921-
(Norman Mawdsley)

PERSONAL: Born November 13, 1921, in Clifton, Bristol, Gloucestershire, England; son of Reginald (an antiquary and author) and Olga (Edelston) Hargreaves-Mawdsley; married Josefa-Deo Laguens, March 23, 1960. *Education:* Attended Clifton College; Oriel College, B.A. and M.A., 1948, D.Phil., 1958. *Politics:* Liberal. *Home:* 7 Lathbury Rd., Oxford, England. *Office:* Department of History, Brandon University, Brandon, Manitoba, Canada.

CAREER: Literary work and private tutoring, Oxford, England, 1948-52; full-time research and writing, Oxford, England, 1952-59; Exeter College, Oxford University, Oxford, England, tutor in Latin, 1959-61; University of Edinburgh, Edinburgh, Scotland, senior research fellow, 1961-64; St. Andrews University, St. Andrews, Fife, Scotland, lecturer in history, 1964-70; Brandon University, Brandon, Manitoba, professor of history and head of the department, 1970—. Visiting professor of history, University of South Carolina, 1970. Examiner in history, Oxford and Cambridge Universities Examination Board for English Schools, 1959-64. *Member:* Royal Historical Society (fellow), Society of Antiquaries of London (fellow), Society of Antiquaries of Scotland (fellow), Oxford University Union Society, Cambridge University Union Society, Old Cliftonian Society.

WRITINGS: A History of Academical Dress in Europe until the End of the Eighteenth Century, Clarendon Press, 1963; *A History of Legal Dress in Europe, until the End of the Eighteenth Century,* Clarendon Press, 1963; *The English Della Cruscans and Their Time, 1783-1828,* Nijhoff, 1967; (editor) *Everyman's Dictionary of European Writers,* Dutton, 1968, revised edition, in press; *Woodforde at Oxford, 1759-76,* Clarendon Press, 1969; *Oxford in the Age of John Locke,* University of Oklahoma Press, 1972.

Under name Norman Mawdsley: *Night Pieces,* Fortune Press, 1948; *Poetry from Oxford,* Fortune Press, 1949; *Robert Nichols,* Poetry Review Publishing, 1952. Contributor to *Poetry Review, Oxford Magazine* and other journals. Literary editor, *Isis,* 1947-48.

WORK IN PROGRESS: A Documentary History of Spain under the Bourbons, for Macmillan.

SIDELIGHTS: Hargreaves-Mawdsley studied Greek and Latin from the age of nine or ten onwards; he is competent in French, Spanish, German, Italian.

* * *

HARGROVE, Merwin Matthew 1910-

PERSONAL: Born January 22, 1910, in Enid, Okla.; son of Frank Kirk (a minister) and Effie (Matthews) Hargrove; married Jane Marshall, September 2, 1933; children: Linda Jean, Charles Marshall. *Education:* Municipal University of Omaha, B.A., 1932; University of Iowa, M.A., 1934. *Religion:* Christian. *Office:* College of Business Administration, University of Tulsa, Tulsa, Okla. 74104.

CAREER: Municipal University of Omaha, Omaha, Neb., instructor in business administration, 1934; Lincoln College, registrar, 1935-37; University of Tulsa, Tulsa, Okla., 1937—, began as instructor, now dean of College of Business Administration, head of 75th College Training Detachment at university during World War II. *Member:* American Economics Association, American Association of Collegiate Schools of Business (member dean), American Management Association, National Association of Accountants, Financial Executives Institute, Southwest Social Science Association, Southern Economic Association, Southern Case Writers Association (president), Oklahoma Council for Economic Education, Oklahoma Society of Certified Public Accounts, Tulsa Society of Certified Public Accountants. *Awards, honors:* LL.D., Phillips University, 1951.

WRITINGS: (Editor with Eugene L. Swearingen and Ike Harrison) *Business Policy Cases With Behavior Science Implications,* Irwin, 1963, 3rd edition, 1969.

WORK IN PROGRESS: Administrative Policies and Contemporary Problems.

* * *

HARKNESS, David J(ames) 1913-

PERSONAL: Born April 19, 1913, in Jellico, Tenn.; son of David Alexander and Jessie (Jones) Harkness. *Education:* University of Tennessee, B.A., 1934; Columbia University, M.A., 1939, postgraduate summer study, 1946, 1951. *Politics:* Republican. *Religion:* Presbyterian. *Home:* 1411 Kenesaw Ave., Knoxville, Tenn. 37919. *Office:* University of Tennessee Extension Division, Knoxville, Tenn. 37916.

CAREER: Parkdale High School, Parkdale, Ore., English teacher, 1934-35; English teacher and principal in Jellico (Tenn.) schools, 1935-40, 1943-46; Lincoln Memorial University, Harrogate, Tenn., English instructor, 1940-43; East Tennessee State College, Johnson City, director of training school, 1946-47; University of Tennessee, Extension Division, Knoxville, director of program planning and library services, 1947—. *Member:* Adult Education Association of U.S.A., American Library Association, American Studies Association, National University Extension Association, Speech Association of Tennessee (president, 1953-55), Tennessee Education Association, Tennessee Library Associa'ion, East Tennessee Historical Society, Phi Kappa Phi, Phi Delta Kappa, Pi Kappa Alpha, Masons.

WRITINGS: (With R. Gerald McMurtry) *Lincoln's Favorite Poets,* University of Tennessee Press, 1959.

Brochures; all published by Division of University Extension, University of Tennessee: *Tennessee in Literature,* 1949; *Tennessee in Recent Books, Music and Drama,* 1950; *The Biographical Novel: A Bibliography with Notes,* 1950; *Famous Women of Tennessee and Literary Landmarks of the Volunteer State,* 1951; *Music and Legends for American Holidays: A Manual for Program Planners,* 1951; *Some First Facts about Tennessee: A Manual for School and Club Programs,* 1952; *Literary Profiles of the Southern States: A Manual for Schools and Clubs,* 1953; *The American Heritage in Historical Fiction,* 1953; *The Southwest and West Coast in Literature: A Manual for Schools and Clubs,* 1954; *Literary Trails of the Western States,* 1955; *Literary New England: A Manual for Schools and Clubs,* 1956; *The Bible in Fiction and Drama: A Bibliography with Notes,* 1956; *Literary Mideast U.S.A.,* 1957; *Legends of the Holidays: A Manual for Program Planners,* 1957; *The Literary Midwest: A Manual for Schools and Clubs,* 1958; *Arts and Letters in Fiction and Drama: A Bibliography with Notes,* 1958; *The Great Lakes States and Alaska and Hawaii in Literature: A Manual for Schools and Clubs,* 1959; *Abraham Lincoln and Cumberland Gap,* 1959; *Heroines of the Blue and Gray: A Civil War Centennial Program Manual,* 1960; *Heroines of the American Revolution,* 1961; (compiler) *Legends and Lore: Southern Indians, Flowers, Holidays,* 1961; *Southern Heroes, Heroines and Legends,* 1962; *Lincoln and the Land-Grant Idea,* 1962; *Southern Heroines of Colonial Days,* 1963; (compiler) *The Dogwood in Legend and Literature,* 1964; *Tennessee—The Most Interesting State,* 1965, revised edition, 1968; *Kentucky and Tennessee,* 1966; (compiler) *Tennessee and Mississippi: Where the Old South Meets the New,* 1967; *Forgotten Heroes of the American Revolution,* 1968; *Tennessee and Arkansas,* 1968; *Tennessee and North Carolina,* 1969; *Tennessee and Virginia,* 1970.

* * *

HARMAN, Richard Alexander 1917-
(Alec Harman)

PERSONAL: Born November 19, 1917, in Gooty, Madras State, India; son of Richard Ashbee (a teacher) and Ida (Stockwell) Harman; married Gillian Margaret Luce (a lecturer), August 5, 1948; children: Anna Jane, Stephen Richard, Julia Margaret. *Education:* Royal College of Music, London, A.R.C.M. and G.R.S.M., 1943; University of Durham, M.Bus., 1949. *Religion:* Society of Friends. *Home:* 17 Church St., Durham City, England. *Office:* Music Department, University of Durham, Palace Green, Durham, England.

CAREER: Durham School, Durham, England, music director, 1943-49; University of Durham, Durham, lecturer, 1949-64, senior lecturer on Renaissance and Baroque music, 1964—. Music advisor, Philharmonic Records Ltd. *Member:* American Musicological Society, Galpin Society.

WRITINGS: (Editor and author of commentary) Thomas Morley, *A Plain and Easy Introduction to Practical Music,* Norton, 1952, 2nd edition, 1963; *Man and His Music: The Story of Musical Experience in the West,* Volume I: *Mediaeval and Early Renaissance Music (up to c.1525),* Barrie & Rockliff, 1957, Essential Books, 1958, (with Anthony Milner) Volume II: *Late Renaissance and Baroque Music (c.1525-c.1750),* Essential Books, 1959, reissued in one volume with two sections by Wilfred Mellers, Oxford University Press, 1962; (editor of Marenzio's madrigals) *Music Transalpina,* Stainer & Bell, 1958; (contributor) Alec Robertson and D.W. Stevens, editors, *The Pelican History of Music,* Volume II: *Renaissance and Baroque,* Pelican, 1963; (editor and translator) Palestrina, *Ten Four-Part Motets for the*

Church's Year, Oxford University Press, 1964; *A Catalogue of the Printed Music and Books on Music in Durham Cathedral Library,* Oxford University Press, 1968. Contributor of articles to *Die Musik in Geschichte und Gegenwart,* 1955—; regular reviewer of gramophone records of music up to 1750 in *Audio and Record Review.*

WORK IN PROGRESS: Scoring Vaugham William's "Household Music" for orchestra, for Oxford University Press; a book on the operas of Alessandro Scarlatti.

AVOCATIONAL INTERESTS: Model railways; sports, including cricket, tennis, and soccer.

BIOGRAPHICAL/CRITICAL SOURCES: Friedrich Blume, editor, *Die Musik in Geschichte und Gegenwart,* Volume IV, Barnereiter, 1949.

* * *

HARMER, Mabel 1894-

PERSONAL: Born September 28, 1894, in Logan, Utah; daughter of John Jacob (a merchant) and Bertine (Berg) Spande; married Earl W. Harmer, September 14, 1922; children: Marian Harmer Nelson, Earl W., Jr., Patricia Harmer Spencer, John Loren, Alan Spande. *Education:* Utah State University, B.S., 1923. *Politics:* Republican. *Religion:* Church of Jesus Christ of Latter-day Saints. *Home:* 1177 Yale Ave., Salt Lake City, Utah 84105.

CAREER: Teacher in Logan, Utah, 1916-22; now teacher of creative writing at Brigham Young University Adult Education Center, Salt Lake City, Utah. *Member:* National Federation of Press Women, National League of American Pen Women (president, Salt Lake branch, 1958-60), Utah League of Writers (president, Salt Lake chapter, 1950-52; state president, 1956-58), Daughters of the Utah Pioneers. *Awards, honors:* Second prize, Utah Fine Arts Contest; first award for published story, National League of American Pen Women.

WRITINGS: (With Clarissa Y. Spencer) *Brigham Young at Home,* Caxton, 1940; (with Spencer) *One Who Was Valiant,* Caxton, 1940; *The Story of the Mormon Pioneers,* Deseret, 1943; *Famous Mascots and K-9's,* Deseret, 1945; *The Youngest Soldier,* Deseret, 1953; *The True Book of the Circus,* Childrens Press, 1955; *The True Book of Pioneers* (Junior Literary Guild selection), Childrens Press, 1957, reissued as *My Easy-to-Read True Book of Pioneers,* Grosset, 1957; *About Dams,* Melmont, 1963; *About Penguins, and Other Antarctic Animals,* Melmont, 1964; *Our Utah Pioneers,* Deseret, 1966; *The Boy Who Became a Prophet,* Bookcraft, 1969; *Lizzie: The Lost Toys Witch,* Macrae, 1970. Contributor of daily juvenile story to *Deseret News,* 1947-57.

WORK IN PROGRESS: Boy on a Trapeze, teen-age fiction for Golden Gate Junior Books; *Hours of Glory,* nonfiction.

AVOCATIONAL INTERESTS: Knitting, gardening, travel, classical music.

* * *

HARMER, Ruth Mulvey 1919-
(Ruth Watt Mulvey)

PERSONAL: Born June 18, 1919, in New York, N.Y.; daughter of Charles Watt (a postal inspector) and Mary E. (Gierloff) Mulvey; married Lowell Harmer (a teacher and writer), October 31, 1950; children: Felicia. *Education:* Boston University, student, 1938-40; Barnard College, A.B., 1941; Columbia University, M.A., 1942; University of Southern California, Ph.D., 1972. *Politics:* Democrat. *Home:* 437 Crane Blvd., Los Angeles, Calif. 90065. *Agent:* Blanche C. Gregory, 2 Tudor City Pl., New York, N.Y. 10017. *Office:* Department of English,

California State Polytechnic College, Pomona, Calif. 91766.

CAREER: Reporter for *Hartford Courant*, Hartford, Conn., and *Washington Times-Herald*, Washington, D.C., 1942-46; reporter and editor in Mexico for *Mexico City Herald* and *Mexico City News*, and correspondent for U.S. publications, 1947-51; *Modern Mexico* (magazine), California editor, 1948-51; University of Southern California, Los Angeles, instructor in English, 1950-60; California State Polytechnic College, Pomona, 1960—, began as assistant professor, now professor of English. Instructor in extension division, University of California, Los Angeles, 1952-59; visiting summer lecturer, Mexico City College, 1960-62. Member of National Advisory Veterinary Medicine Committee, U.S. Food and Drug Administration; member, Los Angeles County Committee on Affairs of the Aging; president, Continental Association of Funeral and Memorial Societies. *Member:* American Association of University Professors (chapter secretary, 1962-64), P.E.N., Cooperative League of the U.S.A., Women's National Press Club, United Professors of California, Washington Press Club.

WRITINGS: (Under name Ruth Watt Mulvey; with L.M. Alvarez) *Good Food from Mexico*, Barrows, 1950; *The High Cost of Dying*, Crowell-Collier, 1963; *Unfit for Human Consumption*, Prentice-Hall, 1970. Author of "Know Your Government" series of network radio programs, 1944. Contributor of more than two hundred articles to various publications.

WORK IN PROGRESS: A book on medical care; a book on modern fiction writers in Mexico.

AVOCATIONAL INTERESTS: Anthropology, archaeology, Spanish language, and Latin American studies.

BIOGRAPHICAL/CRITICAL SOURCES: *Barnard Alumnae Quarterly*, winter, 1963.

*   *   *

HARRELL, John G(rinnell) 1922-

PERSONAL: Born May 24, 1922, in Los Angeles, Calif.; son of Orville Jones (a real estate developer) and Charlotte (Grinnell) Harrell; married Mary Jane Pyburn, June 6, 1959. *Education:* Occidental College, A.B., 1944; Virginia Theological Seminary, student, 1944-45; Church Divinity School of the Pacific, B.D., 1947. *Home and office:* 148 York Ave., Berkeley, Calif. 94708.

CAREER: Ordained Episcopal priest, 1947. National Council of Episcopal Church, Greenwich, Conn., executive secretary for audio-visual education, 1957-62; St. Margaret's House (Episcopal graduate school for women), Berkeley, Calif., lecturer in communications, 1962-66; independent producer of multimedia materials, 1966—.

WRITINGS: (Editor and translator) *Selected Writings of Richard Rolle*, S.P.C.K., 1963; *Teaching is Communicating: An Audio-Visual Handbook for Church Use*, Seabury, 1965; *Hello in Exile* (poem), privately printed, 1965. Contributor to *Christian Century, Theology Today, Motive, Liturgy, Religion Teachers Journal*, and other religious journals.

Television and films: "Let Us Pray," an experimental jazz liturgy presented by Columbia Broadcasting System; "Jazz Evensong," also presented by Columbia Broadcasting System and first performed by Modern Jazz Quartet at International Jazz Festival, Washington, D.C. Also author of educational films, including "Here and Now," and filmstrips including "Teaching Tools." With wife, Mary Harrell, creator and producer of multimedia productions, including "The Fire and the Mind," "Lord, Come!," "Communicating the Gospel Today," and "Time Being."

HARRELSON, Walter (Joseph) 1919-

PERSONAL: Born November 28, 1919, in Winnabow, N.C.; son of Isham Danvis and Mae (Rich) Harrelson; married Idella Aydlett, September 20, 1942; children: Marianne, David A., Robert J. *Education:* Mars Hill College, student, 1940-41; University of North Carolina, A.B., 1947; Union Theological Seminary, New York, N.Y., B.D., 1949, Th.D., 1953; postgraduate study at University of Basel, 1950-51, at Harvard University, part-time, 1951-53. *Politics:* Democrat. *Home:* 305 Bowling Ave., Nashville, Tenn. 37205. *Office:* Vanderbilt University, Nashville, Tenn. 37203.

CAREER: Ordained to ministry of Baptist Church, 1949. Andover Newton Theological School, Newton Center, Mass., professor of Old Testament, 1951-55; University of Chicago Divinity School, Chicago, Ill., dean and associate professor of Old Testament, 1955-60; Vanderbilt University, Nashville, Tenn., professor of Old Testament, 1960—, chairman of graduate department of religion, 1961-62, 1964-67, dean of divinity school, 1967—. Oberlin College Graduate School of Theology, Haskell Lecturer, 1965. World Council of Churches, member of study commissions. Nashville Christian Leadership Council, member of board, 1963—. *Military service:* U.S. Naval Reserve, 1941-45; became chief storekeeper.

MEMBER: Society of Biblical Literature and Exegesis, American Schools of Oriental Research, Society for Religion in Higher Education, American Society for the Study of Religion, Chicago Society for Biblical Research, Phi Beta Kappa. *Awards, honors:* American Council of Learned Societies research award, 1950-51; Fulbright research award for Rome, 1962-63.

WRITINGS: *Jeremiah, Prophet to the Nations*, Judson, 1959; (editor with Bernhard W. Anderson, and contributor) *Israel's Prophetic Heritage: Essays in Honor of James Muilenburg*, Harper, 1962; (contributor) M.E. Marty, editor, *The Place of Bonhoeffer*, Association Press, 1963; *Interpreting the Old Testament*, Holt, 1964; *From Fertility Cult to Worship*, Doubleday, 1969. Contributor to *Encyclopaedia Britannica, Encyclopedia Americana, Interpreter's Dictionary of the Bible, Hastings' Dictionary of the Bible*, and to professional journals.

BIOGRAPHICAL/CRITICAL SOURCES: *Christian Century*, January 21, 1970.

*   *   *

HARRINGTON, William 1931-

PERSONAL: Born November 21, 1931, in Marietta, Ohio; son of William K. (an oil producer) and Virginia (Pickens) Harrington; married Margaret Phillips, August 29, 1953. *Education:* Marietta College, A.B., 1953; Duke University, M.A., 1955; Ohio State University, LL.B., 1958. *Home:* 2578 Berwyn Rd., Upper Arlington, Columbus, Ohio 43221.

CAREER: Lawyer in private practice, Marietta, Ohio, 1958-62; Office of Ohio Secretary of State, Columbus, elections counsel, 1962-65; Ohio State Bar Association, Columbus, counsel, 1965—. *Member:* American Bar Association, Ohio Bar Association, Phi Beta Kappa, Masons.

WRITINGS: *Which the Justice, Which the Thief*, Bobbs-Merrill, 1963; *The Power*, Bobbs-Merrill, 1964; *Yoshar the Soldier*, Dial, 1966, reissued as *One Over One*, McKay, 1970; *The Gospel of Death*, M. Joseph, 1966; *The Search for Elisabeth Brandt*, McKay, 1969; *Trial*, McKay, 1970; *The Jupiter Crisis*, McKay, 1971.

WORK IN PROGRESS: An untitled novel, for McKay.

SIDELIGHTS: The motion picture rights to *Trial* have been acquired by MGM.

BIOGRAPHICAL/CRITICAL SOURCES: Observer Review, August 6, 1967; New York Times Book Review, February 26, 1969, April 12, 1970; Best Sellers, March 15, 1969, February 15, 1970, October 15, 1970; Variety, December 17, 1969; Library Journal, January 1, 1970.

* * *

HARRIS, Leon A., Jr. 1926-

PERSONAL: Born June 20, 1926, in New York, N.Y.; son of Leon A. (a merchant) and Lucile (Herzfeld) Harris; married Marina Svetlova (a ballerina), September 10, 1963. Education: Phillips Academy at Andover, student, 1941-43; Harvard University, B.A., 1947. Home: 4512 Fairfax, Dallas, Tex. 75205. Agent: Sterling Lord Agency, 660 Madison Ave., New York, N.Y. 10021. Office: 1505 Elm St., Dallas, Tex. 75201.

CAREER: A. Harris & Co. (department store), Dallas, Tex., executive vice-president, 1947-60; Empire State Bank, Dallas, Tex., director, 1962—; Trammell Crow Realty Trust, Dallas, Tex., chairman, 1963—. Trustee of Dallas Museum of Fine Arts, Dallas Public Library, Dallas Historical Society, and of St. Mark's School; member of board of directors of Dallas Community Chest, Dallas Symphony, Friends of the Dallas Public Library, Friends of the Texas Libraries, and Dallas Association for the United Nations. Military service: U.S. Naval Reserve, 1944-46. Member: City Club (Dallas), Harvard Club (New York). Awards, honors: Italian Order of the Star of Solidarity.

WRITINGS: The Night Before Christmas in Texas, Lothrop, 1952; The Great Picture Robbery, Atheneum, 1963; Young France: Children of France at Work and at Play, Dodd, 1964; The Fine Art of Political Wit: Being a Lively Guide to the Artistic Invective, Elegant Epithet, and Polished Impromptus as Well as the Gallant and Graceful Worldly Wit of Various British and American Politicians from the 18th Century Through Our Own Days of Grace, Dutton, 1964; Only to God: The Extraordinary Life of Godfrey Lowell Cabot, Atheneum, 1967; Maurice Goes to Sea, Norton, 1968; Young Peru: Children of Peru at Work and at Play, Dodd, 1969; The Moscow Circus School, Atheneum, 1970; Yvette, McGraw, 1970; The Russian Ballet School, Atheneum, 1970; Behind the Scenes in a Car Factory, photographs by Harris, Lippincott, 1972; Behind the Scenes in a Department Store, photographs by Harris, Lippincott, 1972; Behind the Scenes of Television Programs, photographs by Harris, Lippincott, 1972. Contributor to Esquire, Playboy, and Boy's Life.

BIOGRAPHICAL/CRITICAL SOURCES: Times Literary Supplement, May 25, 1967; New York Times Book Review, November 15, 1967, May 12, 1968, March 29, 1970; New Yorker, December 2, 1967; Young Readers' Review, October, 1968; Library Journal, May 15, 1970, September, 1970.

* * *

HARRISON, K(enneth) C(ecil) 1915-

PERSONAL: Born April 29, 1915, in Hyde, Cheshire, England; son of Thomas and Anne (Wood) Harrison; married Doris Taylor, August 26, 1941; children: David John, Timothy Michael. Education: Attended schools in Hyde, Cheshire, England. Home: 50 West Hill Way, Totteridge, London N20 8QS, England. Office: Marylebone Library, Marylebone Rd., London NW1 5PS, England.

CAREER: Assistant librarian in Hyde, Cheshire, England, 1931-36; branch librarian in Coulsdon, England, and in Purley, England, 1936-39; borough librarian in Hyde, Cheshire, England, 1939-47, in Hove, Sussex, England, 1947-50, in Eastbourne, Sussex, England, 1950-58,

and in Hendon, London, England, 1958-61; city librarian of Westminster, London, England, 1961—. Chairman of joint organizing committee, National Library Week, 1964-69. Governor, Westminster Technical College. Lecturer on librarianship, travel and literary subjects. Military service: British Army, Infantry, 1940-46; served in North Africa, Sicily, France, Belgium, Holland, took part in D-Day landing; became major; awarded Order of British Empire.

MEMBER: International Association of Metropolitan Libraries (secretary), Commonwealth Library Association (president, 1972-75), National Central Library (chairman of executive committee), Central Music Library Council, National Book League (council member), Library Association (council member; president, 1973), Westminster Arts Council (honorary secretary), Eastbourne Rotary Club (president, 1956-57), Marylebone Cricket Club, Surrey County Cricket Club.

WRITINGS: First Steps in Librarianship: A Student's Guide, Grafton & Co., 1950, 4th revised edition, Deutsch, 1973; Sixty Years of Service: The Diamond Jubilee of the Eastbourne Public Libraries, 1896-1956, Eastbourne Public Libraries, 1956; Libraries in Scandinavia, Grafton & Co., 1961, International Publications, 1962, 2nd edition, revised, Deutsch, 1969; The Library and the Community, Deutsch, 1963, 2nd revised edition, 1966; Public Libraries Today, Philosophical Library, 1963; Facts at Your Fingertips: Everyman's Guide to Reference Books, Mason Publications, 1964, 2nd edition, 1967; (with S.G. Berriman) British Public Library Buildings, Deutsch, 1966; Libraries in Britain, Longmans for British Council, 1968; Libraries and the Three Cultures, George Peabody College for Teachers, 1969. Contributor to Times (London), Listener, UNESCO Bulletin for Libraries, and to library journals in United States, Europe, and India. Editor, Library World, 1961-71.

AVOCATIONAL INTERESTS: Reading, travel, motoring, holidays in the sun, and watching cricket and football.

* * *

HARROD, Roy Forbes 1900-

PERSONAL: Born February 13, 1900, in London, England; son of Henry Dawes (a member of copper exchange) and Frances (a novelist; maiden name, Forbes Robertson) Harrod; married Wilhelmine Cresswell, January 8, 1938; children: Henry Mark, Dominick Roy. Education: Attended Westminster School, London, England, 1913-18; New College, Oxford, M.A., 1922; other study at King's College, Cambridge, 1922, Handelshochscule, Berlin, Germany, 1923. Politics: Formerly Liberal, now Conservative. Home: Old Rectory, Holt, Norfolk, England; 51 Campden Hill Square, London W.8, England.

CAREER: Christ Church, Oxford University, Oxford, England, lecturer, 1922-24, member of governing body, 1924—, curator of pictures, 1956-64. British Admiralty, member of Winston Churchill's private statistical branch, 1940-45, later member of Prime Minister's Office; International Monetary Fund, Washington, D.C., member of research staff, 1952-53. Visiting lecturer at University of Pennsylvania, 1964, 1967, 1969, 1970. Military service: British Army, Royal Garrison Artillery, 1919; became second lieutenant. Member: Royal Economic Society (president; member of council, 1933—), British Association for the Advancement of Science (president, economic section, 1938), Athenacum Club and Beefsteak Club (both London), Norfolk Club (Norwich). Awards, honors: Knighted, 1959; fellow of British Academy, doctorates from University of Poitiers, University of Aberdeen, University of Glasgow, University of Warwick, University of Pennsylvania.

WRITINGS: International Economics, introduction by John Maynard Keynes, Harcourt, 1933, revised edition, Cambridge University Press, 1957, University of Chicago Press, 1958; *The Trade Cycle: An Essay,* Oxford University Press, 1936, Augustus M. Kelley, 1961; *Meeting a Trade Recession: Case for Monetary Reflation,* Times Publishing, 1938; *Britain's Future Population,* Oxford University Press, 1943; *A Page of British Folly,* Macmillan (London), 1946; *Are These Hardships Necessary?,* Hart-Davis, 1947; *Towards a Dynamic Economics: Some Recent Developments of Economic Theory and Their Application to Policy,* Macmillan (London), 1948, St. Martin's, 1956.

(Reviser) John A. Hobson, *The Science of Wealth,* Oxford University Press, 1950; *The Life of John Maynard Keynes,* Harcourt, 1951; *And So It Goes On: Further Thoughts on Present Mismanagement,* Hart-Davis, 1951; *The Pound Sterling, 1951-1958,* Department of Economics and Social Institutions, Princeton University, 1952; *Economic Essays,* Macmillan (London), 1952, Harcourt, 1953, 2nd edition, St. Martin's, 1972; *The Dollar,* Macmillan (London), 1953, Harcourt, 1954, 2nd edition, Norton, 1963; *Foundations of Inductive Logic,* St. Martin's, 1956; *British Experience of Disflationary Policy in 1955-1956,* [Stockholm], 1957; *Policy Against Inflation,* St. Martin's, 1958; *The Prof: A Personal Memoir of Lord Cherwell,* Macmillan (London), 1959; *The Trade Cycle: An Essay,* Cass, 1961, Augustus M. Kelley, 1965; *Topical Comment: Essays in Dynamic Economics Applied,* St. Martin's, 1961; (editor with Douglas Hague) *International Trade Theory in a Developing World,* Macmillan (London), 1963, St. Martin's, 1964; *The British Economy,* McGraw, 1963; *Reforming the World's Money,* St. Martin's, 1965; *The International Monetary Fund, Yesterday, Today and Tomorrow,* University of Kiel, 1966; *Dollar-Sterling Collaboration: Basis for Initiative,* Atlantic Trade Study, 1967; *Towards a New Economic Policy,* Augustus M. Kelley, 1967; *Money,* St. Martin's, 1969; *Sociology, Morals and Mystery,* St. Martin's, 1971; *Economic Dynamics,* St. Martin's, 1973.

Regular contributor to *Financial Times* (London), 1948-63; contributor to more than one hundred other journals. Editor, *Economic Journal,* 1945-61.

BIOGRAPHICAL/CRITICAL SOURCES: Times Literary Supplement, October 26, 1967, July 24, 1969.

*   *   *

HART, A(rthur) Tindal   1908-

PERSONAL: Born December 18, 1908, in Sawbridgeworth, England; son of Robert Ernest Sperling and Amy Frances (Rackham) Hart; married Vera Constance Pitt, September 15, 1935. *Education:* Attended Felsted School; Emmanuel College, Cambridge, B.A., 1931, M.A., 1936; Ripon Hall, B.D., 1944, D.D., 1952. *Politics:* Conservative. *Home:* Selmeston Vicarage, Near Polegate, Sussex, England.

CAREER: Clergyman, Church of England; assistant curate in Kent, England, 1932-37; vicar in Birmingham, England, 1937-46; rector of Blatherwycke and Kingscliffe, England, 1946-55, of Blatherwycke and Laxton, England, 1955-59, of Appleton, Berkshire, England, 1959-66; Selmeston-with-Aliston, Sussex, England, vicar, 1966—. Rural dean of Kingscliffe Deanery, 1947-59. *Member:* English Church Historical Society, English Ecclesiastical History Society.

WRITINGS: The Life and Times of John Sharp, Archbishop of York, Macmillan (New York), 1949; *William Lloyd, 1627-1717: Bishop, Politician, Author, and Prophet,* S.P.C.K. for Church Historical Society, 1952; (with Edward Frederick Carpenter) *The Nineteenth Century Country Parson (Circa 1832-1900),* Wilding & Son, 1954; *The Eighteenth Century Country Parson (Circa 1689-1830),* Wilding & Son, 1955; (with others) *History of St. Paul's Cathedral,* Phoenix House, 1957; *The Country Clergy in Elizabethan and Stuart Times, 1558-1660,* Phoenix House, 1958; *The Country Priest in English History,* Phoenix House, 1959, Transatlantic, 1960; *Country Counting House: The Story of Two Eighteenth-Century Clerical Account Books,* Phoenix House, 1962, Transatlantic, 1963; *The Man in the Pew, 1588-1660,* Humanities, 1966; (with others) *History of Westminster Abbey: A House of Kings,* Baker Publishers, 1966; *Clergy and Society, 1600-1800,* S.P.C.K. for Church Historical Society, 1968; *The Curate's Lot: The Story of the Unbeneficed English Clergy,* Baker Publishers, 1970. Regular contributor and reviewer, *Modern Churchman.* Editor, *Church and Countryside,* 1952-61.

WORK IN PROGRESS: Some Clerical Oddities in the Church of England from Medieval to Modern Times.

*   *   *

HART, Donald J(ohn)   1917-

PERSONAL: Born August 9, 1917, in Milwaukee, Wis.; son of Edward William and Minnie (Keller) Hart; married Margaret E. Thorpe, June 22, 1940; children: Roger L., Susan E., Charles W., Mary M. *Education:* Lake Forest College, B.A., 1938; University of Wisconsin, M.A., 1941, Ph.D., 1951. *Religion:* Presbyterian. *Home:* 612 South Main St., Laurinburg, N.C. 28352. *Office:* St. Andrews Presbyterian College, Laurinburg, N.C. 28352.

CAREER: Lake Forest College, Lake Forest, Ill., director of publicity, 1938-40; Allis-Chalmers Manufacturing Co., Milwaukee, Wis., chief priorities clerk, 1941-42; Iowa State University of Science and Technology, Ames, assistant business manager, 1942-43; Carroll College, Waukesha, Wis., associate professor of economics, 1947-50; University of Idaho, Moscow, dean of College of Business Administration, 1950-56; University of Florida, Gainesville, dean of College of Business Administration, 1956-68; Virginia Polytechnic Institute, Blacksburg, 1968-69; St. Andrews Presbyterian College, Laurinburg, N.C., president, 1969—. Member of board of directors of Research Corporation of America, 1959-66, and Research Capital Corp., 1960-64. Member of Regional Expansion Council, U.S. Department of Commerce, 1962-66; chairman and public member of advisory council, Idaho Employment Security Agency, 1951-56. Vice-president and trustee, Idaho Institute of Christian Education, 1951-56. Advisory member, Florida Atlantic University Planning Commission, 1959-60; trustee, Florida Presbyterian College, 1960-65. *Military service:* U.S. Naval Reserve, 1943-46; served in European theater; became lieutenant.

MEMBER: American Economic Association, American Association of Collegiate Schools of Business (member of executive committee, 1962-68; president, 1967-68), Southern Economic Association, Beta Gamma Sigma (executive committee, 1963-68), Phi Chi Theta, Pi Sigma Epsilon, Delta Sigma Pi.

WRITINGS: Business in a Dynamic Society, Macmillan, 1963, 2nd edition published as *Introduction to Business in a Dynamic Society,* 1970. Annual contributor to *Encyclopaedia Britannica Book of the Year,* 1949-64; author of articles and book reviews in professional journals.

AVOCATIONAL INTERESTS: Music, spectator sports, reading, and travel.

HART, Herbert Michael 1928-

PERSONAL: Born October 19, 1928, in St. Louis, Mo.; son of Herbert Malcolm (a career naval officer and lawyer) and Helen (Quigley) Hart; married Teresa V. Keating (a nurse anesthetist), October 13, 1958; children: Bridget Erin, Bret, Tracy, Megan, Michael, Patrick. Education: Northwestern University, B.S. in Journalism. Religion: Roman Catholic. Home address: P.O. Box 194, Quantico, Va. 22134. Agent: Albert P. Salisburg, Box 1710, Seattle, Wash. 98111. Office: Marine Corps Education and Development Command, Quantico, Va. 22134.

CAREER: U.S. Marine Corps, 1946—; commissioned, 1951, now lieutenant colonel; served in Korea, 1952-53, and aboard "U.S.S. Randolph," 1953-54; graduate of Amphibious Warfare Course, Quantico, Va., 1962-63; operational intelligence officer, Amphibious Group Two, 1963-65; battalion executive officer and regimental operations officer, 2nd Marine Division, Europe and Caribbean, 1965-67; plans and policies officer, Arab, Israeli, Persian states, J-5 Plans Directorate, U.S. Strike Command, 1967-69; infantry battalion commander, Southeast Asia, and operations officer, 1st Marine Division, Vietnam, 1969-70; now on staff of Marine Corps Education and Development Command, Quantico, Va.; holds Legion of Merit (with combat "V"), Meritorious Service Medal, Navy Commendation Medal (with combat "V"), Army Commendation Medal, five Air Medals, two Purple Hearts.

MEMBER: Association of the United States Army, Marine Corps League, Westerners, Western History Association, Council on Abandoned Military Posts (past president and director), U.S. Cavalry Memorial Association (director), National Parks Association, National Trust for Historic Preservation, South Dakota Historical Society (life), North Dakota Historical Society, Montana Historical Society, Colorado State Historical Society, Oregon Historical Society, Washington State Historical Society, Arizona Pioneers Historical Society, New Mexico Museum Society, New Mexico Historical Society, Florida Historical Society, Historical Society of Southern California, West Texas Historical Society, El Paso Historical Society, Sigma Delta Chi, Delta Phi Epsilon, Theta Xi, Knights of Columbus. Awards, honors: Army Commendation Medals, for Old Forts of the Northwest and Old Forts of the Southwest.

WRITINGS: Old Forts of the Northwest, Superior, 1963; Old Forts of the Southwest, Superior, 1964; Old Forts of the Far West, Superior, 1965; Pioneer Forts of the West, Superior, 1967; The Guide to Western Forts, Superior, 1971.

WORK IN PROGRESS: Frontier Forts of the West; The Forts of Florida; supervisory editor of nine-volume Guardians of the Old West, for Arthur Clark.

SIDELIGHTS: Hart has traveled 100,000 miles in the United States to photograph sites of about 800 old Army forts of the nineteenth century to illustrate his books.

* * *

HARTER, Lafayette George, Jr. 1918-

PERSONAL: Born May 28, 1918, in Des Moines, Iowa; son of Lafayette George (a food broker) and Helen E. (Ives) Harter; married Charlotte Mary Toshach (an economics professor), August 23, 1950; children: Lafayette G. III, James, Charlotte. Education: Antioch College, B.A., 1941; Stanford University, M.A., 1948, Ph.D., 1960. Politics: Democrat. Religion: United Church of Christ. Home: 3755 Van Buren, Corvallis, Ore. 97331. Office: Department of Economics, Oregon State University, Corvallis, Ore. 97331.

CAREER: Menlo College, Menlo Park, Calif., instructor in economics and accounting, 1948-50; College of Marin, Kentfield, Calif., instructor in economics and accounting, 1950-60; Oregon State University, Corvallis, associate professor, 1960-65, professor of economics, 1965—, chairman of the department, 1967—. Member of arbitration panels, Federal Mediation and Conciliation Service, and Oregon Conciliation Service; Vice-Chairman, Oregon Advisory Council on Unemployment Compensation; member of board, Oregon Council on Economic Education. Military service: U.S. Naval Reserve, active duty, 1941-46; became lieutenant commander. Member: American Economic Association, Western Economic Association, Industrial Relations Research Association, American Association of University Professors, Evolutionary Economic Association, American Arbitration Association (member of national labor panel).

WRITINGS: John R. Commons: His Assault on Laissez-faire, foreword by Wayne Morse, Oregon State University Press, 1962; (editor with John Keltner) Labor in America: The Union and Employer Responses to the Challenge of Our Changing Society, Oregon State University Press, 1967; Economic Responses to a Changing World, Scott, Foresman, 1971. Contributor of articles and reviews to economic and sociology journals.

WORK IN PROGRESS: A case study of San Francisco hotel and restaurant workers.

* * *

HARTLEY, Marie 1905-

PERSONAL: Born September 25, 1905, in Morley, Yorkshire, England; daughter of Harry (a cloth manufacturer) and Gertrude (Hinchliffe) Hartley. Education: Studied at Leeds College of Art and Slade School of Art, London, England. Home: Coleshouse, Askrigg, Leyburn, Yorkshire, England.

CAREER: Author, illustrator, and lecturer. Yorkshire Dales National Park Committee, member, 1956-62. Member: Society of Authors, National Book League, Yorkshire Archaeological Society, York Georgian Society.

WRITINGS—Self-illustrated: Ella Pontefract, Swaledale, Dent, 1934; Ella Pontefract, The Charm of Yorkshire Churches, Yorkshire Weekly Post, 1935; (with Pontefract) Wensleydale, Dent, 1936; (with Pontefract) Wharfedale, Dent, 1938; (with Pontefract) Yorkshire Tour, Dent, 1939; (with Pontefract) Yorkshire Cottage, Dent, 1942; Yorkshire Heritage: A Memoir to Ella Pontefract, Dent, 1950; (with Joan Ingilby) The Old Handknitters of the Dales, Dalesman Publishing, 1951; (with Ingilby) Yorkshire Village, Dent, 1953; (with Ingilby) The Yorkshire Dales, Dent, 1956; (with Ingilby) The Wonders of Yorkshire, Dent, 1959; (with Ingilby) Yorkshire Portraits, Dent, 1961; (with Ingilby) Getting to Know Yorkshire, Dent, 1964; (with Ingilby) Life and Tradition in the Yorkshire Dales, Dent, 1968, published in America as Vanishing Folkways: Life and Tradition in the Yorkshire Dales, A.S. Barnes, 1971. Contributor to Yorkshire Post, Country Life, and Dalesman.

AVOCATIONAL INTERESTS: Visiting European art galleries, taking color slides.

BIOGRAPHICAL/CRITICAL SOURCES: Yorkshire Evening Post, March 12, 1956; Yorkshire Evening News, August 24, 1962.

* * *

HARTSHORNE, Charles 1897-

PERSONAL: Surname is pronounced Harts-horn; born June 5, 1897, in Kittanning, Pa.; son of Francis Cope (an Episcopal clergyman) and Marguerite (Haughton) Hartshorne; married Dorothy Eleanore Cooper, December 22, 1928; children: Emily Lawrence (Mrs. Nicolas D. Goodman). *Education:* Haverford College, student 1915-17; Harvard University, A.B., 1921, A.M., 1922, Ph.D., 1923. *Politics:* Independent. *Home:* 724 Sparks Ave., Austin, Tex. 78705. *Office:* University of Texas, 313 Waggener Hall, Austin, Tex. 78712.

CAREER: Harvard University, Cambridge, Mass., Sheldon traveling fellow, 1923-25, instructor in philosophy, then research fellow, 1925-28; University of Chicago, Chicago, Ill., 1928-55, began as instructor, became professor of philosophy, 1945-55; Emory University, Atlanta, Ga., professor of philosophy, 1955-62; University of Texas, Austin, Ashbel Smith Professor, 1962—. Visiting professor at Stanford University, 1937, New School for Social Research, 1941-42, Goethe University, 1948-49, University of Washington, Seattle, 1958. Fulbright professor, Melbourne, Australia, 1952, Kyoto, Japan, 1958, 1966; Terry Lecturer, Yale University, 1947; Matchette Lecturer, Wesleyan University, 1964; Dudleian Lecturer, Harvard University, 1964; Morse Lecturer, Union Theological Seminary, 1964; visiting professor, Banaras Hindu University, 1966.

MEMBER: American Philosophical Association (president, Western division, 1949), C.S. Peirce Society (president, 1951), Metaphysical Society of America (president, 1955), Southern Society for Philosophy of Religion (president, 1963), Southern Society for Philosophy and Psychology (president, 1965), Phi Beta Kappa, Phi Kappa Phi. *Awards, honors:* Pierre Lecomte du Nouey Award, medal and $1,000, for *The Logic of Perfection,* 1963; L.H.D., Haverford College, 1967; Litt.D., Emory University, 1969.

WRITINGS: (Editor with Paul Weiss) *Collected Papers of Charles Sanders Peirce,* six volumes, Harvard University Press, 1931-35; *The Philosophy and Psychology of Sensation,* University of Chicago Press, 1934; *Beyond Humanism: Essays in the New Philosophy of Nature,* Willett, Clark & Co., 1937; *Man's Vision of God and the Logic of Theism,* Willett, Clark & Co., 1941, Harper, 1948; *The Divine Relativity: A Social Conception of God* (Terry Lectures), Yale University Press, 1948; (with Victor Lowe and A.H. Johnson) *Whitehead and the Modern World,* Beacon Press, 1950; *Reality as Social Process: Studies in Metaphysics and Religion,* Free Press, 1953; (editor with William L. Reese) *Philosophers Speak of God,* University of Chicago Press, 1953; *The Logic of Perfection, and Other Essays in Neoclassical Metaphysics,* Open Court, 1962; *Anselm's Rediscovery: A Re-examination of the Ontological Proof for God's Existence,* Open Court, 1965; *A Natural Theology for Our Time,* Open Court, 1967; *Creative Synthesis and Philosophic Method,* Open Court, 1970; *Whitehead's Philosophy: Selected Essays, 1935-1970* University of Nebraska Press, 1972; *Born to Sing: An Interpretation and World Survey of Bird Song,* Indiana University Press, 1973.

Contributor: *Philosophical Essays for Alfred North Whitehead,* Longmans, Green, 1936; Marvin Farber, editor, *Philosophical Essays in Memory of Edmund Usserl,* Harvard University Press, 1940; P.A. Schlipp, editor, *The Philosophy of George Santayana,* Northwestern University Press, 1940; P.A. Schlipp, editor, *The Philosophy of Alfred North Whitehead,* Northwestern University Press, 1941; Vergilius Ferm, editor, *An Encyclopedia of Religion,* Philosophical Library, 1945.

Vergilius Ferm, editor, *A History of Philosophical Systems,* Philosophical Library, 1950; *The Encyclopedia Hebraica,* Volume III, Encyclopedia Publishing Co. (Jerusalem), 1951; *Structure, Method and Meaning: Essays in Honor of Henry M. Sheffer,* Liberal Arts Press, 1951; Philip P. Wiener and Frederick H. Young, editors, *Studies in the Philosophy of Charles Sanders Peirce,* Har-

vard University Press, 1952; P.A. Schlipp, editor, *The Philosophy of Sarvepalli Radhakrishnan,* Tudor, 1952; Charles W. Kegsley and Robert W. Bretall, editors, *The Theology of Paul Tillich,* Macmillan, 1952; Sidney Hook, editor, *American Philosophers at Work,* Criterion, 1956; Walter Leibrecht, editor, *Religion and Culture: Essays in Honor of Paul Tillich,* Harper, 1959.

Ivor Leclerc, editor, *The Relevance of Whitehead,* Allen & Unwin, 1961; Sidney Hook, editor, *Religious Experience and Truth: A Symposium,* New York University Press, 1961; Irwin C. Lieb, editor, *Experience, Existence, and the Good: Essays in Honor of Paul Weiss,* Southern Illinois University Press, 1961; (author of introduction) *Saint Anselm: Basic Writings,* translated by S.W. Deane, 2nd edition, Open Court, 1962; Jordan M. Scher, editor, *Theories of the Mind,* Free Press, 1962; P.A. Schlipp and Maurice S. Friedman, editors, *Martin Buber,* Kohlhammer Verlag, 1963; George L. Kline, editor, *Alfred North Whitehead: Essays on His Philosophy,* Prentice-Hall, 1963; Sydney Rome and Beatrice Rome, editors, *Philosophical Interrogations,* Holt, 1964; John Hick, editor, *Faith and the Philosophers,* St. Martin's, 1964; Edward G. Moore and Richard S. Robin, editors, *Studies in the Philosophy of Charles Sanders Peirce,* University of Massachusetts Press, 1964; Alvin Plantinga, editor, *The Ontological Argument,* Doubleday, 1965; Gordon Mills, editor, *Innocence and Power,* University of Texas Press, 1965; Douglas Browning, editor, *Philosophers of Process,* Random House, 1965; Charles H. Monson, Jr., editor, *Great Issues Concerning Theism,* University of Utah Press, 1965; Konstantin Kolenda, editor, *Insight and Vision: Essays in Philosophy in Honor of Radoslav Andrea Tsanoff,* Rice University Studies, 1965; Frederick C. Dommeyer, editor, *Current Philosophical Issues: Essays in Honor of Curt John Ducasse,* C.C Thomas, 1966; Leroy S. Rouner, editor, *Philosophy, Religion and the Coming World Civilization,* Nijhoff, 1966; J. Clayton Feaver and William Horosz, editors, *Religion in Philosophical and Cultural Perspective,* Van Nostrand, 1967; P.A. Schlipp, editor, *The Philosophy of Martin Buber,* Open Court, 1967; John Lachs, editor, *Animal Faith and Spiritual Life,* Appleton, 1967; Perry Le Fevre, editor, *Philosophical Resources for Christian Thought,* Abingdon, 1968; John Hick and Arthur McGill, editors, *The Many-Faced Argument,* Macmillan, 1968; George L. Abernathy and Thomas A. Langford, editors, *Philosophy of Religion,* 2nd edition, Macmillan, 1968; Paul G. Kuntz, editor, *The Concept of Order,* University of Washington Press, 1968; Jerry H. Gill, editor, *Philosophy and Religion: Some Contemporary Perspectives,* Burgess, 1968; P.A. Schlipp, editor, *The Philosophy of C.I. Lewis,* Open Court, 1968; Herbert W. Richardson and Donald R. Cutler, editors, *Transcendence,* Beacon Press, 1969.

Dwight Van de Vate, Jr., editor, *Persons, Privacy and Feeling: Essays in the Philosophy of Mind,* Memphis State University Press, 1970; (author of preface) David Bonner Richardson, *Berdyaev's Philosophy of History,* Nijhoff, 1970.

Contributor of more than 150 articles and about 100 book reviews to philosophy and religion journals; contributor of articles on ornithology to *Victorian Naturalist* (Australia), *Elepaio* (Hawaii), *Emu* (Australia), *Ibis* (Great Britain), *Oriole, Wilson Library Bulletin,* and *Auk.*

WORK IN PROGRESS: A book on Alfred North Whitehead; a book on idealism; articles for symposia.

SIDELIGHTS: Hartshorne has pursued his hobby of bird-song study on five trips to Europe, in Australasia, Hawaii, Philippines, Taiwan, Japan, Central America, South America, Africa, India, Nepal, Malaya, Thailand, Hong Kong, Mexico, Fiji, and Jamaica.

HARVEY, C(harles) J(ohn) D(errick) 1922-

PERSONAL: Born July 2, 1922, in Pretoria, South Africa; son of Herbert (a bookseller) and Mildred (Robinson) Harvey; married Patricia O'Connor, December 6, 1947. Education: University of Natal, B.A., 1942, M.A., 1946. Home: 10 Binnekringweg, Stellenbosch, South Africa. Office: University of Stellenbosch, Stellenbosch, Cape Province, South Africa.

CAREER: Lecturer in English literature and language at University of the Witwatersrand, Johannesburg, South Africa, 1947, at University of Stellenbosch, Stellenbosch, South Africa, 1948-54; University of Natal, lecturer in English literature and language at Pietermaritzburg, South Africa, 1955, senior lecturer at Durban, 1956-60; University of South Africa, Pretoria, professor of English, 1961; University of Stellenbosch, professor of English and head of department, 1962—. Director, Standpunte (periodical), Cape Town. Military service: South African Air Force, air navigator, 1942-45; became lieutenant. Member: English Academy of Southern Africa.

WRITINGS: (Editor with A.G. Hooper) Poems for Discussion, with Commentaries and Questions, Oxford University Press, 1955; (editor with Hooper) Talking of Poetry (annotated anthology), Oxford University Press, 1961; Language, Literature and Criticism, University of South Africa, 1961; (editor with A.P. Grove) Afrikaans Poems with English Translations, Oxford University Press, 1962. English editor, Standpunte.

* * *

HASKELL, Francis (James Herbert) 1928-

PERSONAL: Born April 7, 1928, in London, England; son of Arnold (a writer) and Vera (Saitroff) Haskell; married Larissa Salmina, August 10, 1965. Education: Attended Eton College, 1941-46; King's College, Cambridge, M.A. (first class honors), 1951. Residence: Oxford, England. Office: Trinity College, Oxford, England.

CAREER: House of Commons, London, England, junior library clerk, 1953-54; Cambridge University, Cambridge, England, fellow, 1954-67, librarian of Faculty of Fine Arts, 1961-67; Trinity College, Oxford University, Oxford, England, professor of art history, 1967—. Lecturer at universities and art galleries in Europe and United States.

WRITINGS: (Translator) Franco Venturi, Roots of Revolution: A History of the Populist and Socialist Movements in Nineteenth Century Russia, Knopf, 1960; Patrons and Painters: A Study of the Relations Between Italian Art and Society in the Age of the Baroque, Knopf, 1963; Gericault, Purnell & Sons, 1966; (with Anthony Burgess) The Age of the Grand Tour: Containing Sketches of the Manners, Society, Customs of France, Flanders, the United Provinces, Germany, Switzerland and Italy in the Letters, Journals and Writings of the Most Celebrated Voyages Between the Years 1720-1820, Crown, 1967. Contributor of articles and reviews to Burlington Magazine, Art Bulletin, New Statesman, Nation, and other periodicals.

WORK IN PROGRESS: Research into the reception of modern art in England and France during the nineteenth century.

BIOGRAPHICAL/CRITICAL SOURCES: New York Times Book Review, December 3, 1967; Time, December 15, 1967.

* * *

HASSLER, Warren W., Jr. 1926-

PERSONAL: Born January 13, 1926; son of Warren W. (a movement director, Pennsylvania Railroad) and

Naomi (Jacobs) Hassler; married Elizabeth S. Vaughn, June 9, 1961; children: Christopher C., Suzanne Ellen, Carol W. Education: Johns Hopkins University, B.A., 1950, Ph.D., 1954; University of Pennsylvania, M.A., 1951. Religion: Protestant. Office: History Department, Pennsylvania State University, University Park, Pa. 16802.

CAREER: Pennsylvania State University, University Park, instructor, 1955-57, assistant professor, 1957-59, associate professor, 1959-64, professor of history, 1964—. Military service: U.S. Army Air Forces, 1944-46. Member: American Military Institute, Organization of American Historians, American Historical Association. Awards, honors: Southern Book of the Year award, 1957, for General George B. McClellan: Shield of the Union.

WRITINGS: General George B. McClellan: Shield of the Union, Louisiana State University Press, 1957; Commanders of the Army of the Potomac, Louisiana State University Press, 1962; Crisis at the Crossroads: The First Day at Gettysburg, University of Alabama Press, 1970. Contributor of articles to Encyclopaedia Britannica, and of articles and reviews to Civil War History, Virginia Librarian, Military Affairs, American Historical Review, and other journals.

WORK IN PROGRESS: American Military Affairs from Colonial Times to the Present.

AVOCATIONAL INTERESTS: Golf, bowling, hiking, traveling, and stamp collecting.

* * *

HASTINGS, Phyllis Dora Hodge
(John Bedford, E. Chatterton Hodge, Rosina Land, Julia Mayfield)

PERSONAL: Born in Bristol, England; daughter of William and Dora Rosina (Miles) Hodge; married Philip Norman Hastings, August 20, 1938; children: Kerry. Education: Attended Edgebaston Church of England College for Girls. Politics: Tory. Home: Mayfield, Sussex, England. Agent: Scott Meredith Literary Agency, 44 Great Russell St., London W.6, England.

CAREER: Ballet dancer as a child; started writing short stories and poetry at sixteen; owned and operated a dairy farm in 1953; began an antique business in 1960.

WRITINGS: As Long as You Live, Jenkins, 1951; Far from Jupiter, Jenkins, 1952; Crowning Glory, Jenkins, 1952; Rapture in My Rags, Dutton, 1954, reissued as Scarecrow Lover, Pan Books, 1960; Dust Is My Pillow, Dutton, 1955; The Field of Roses, Dent, 1955, published in America as Her French Husband, Dutton, 1956; The Black Virgin of the Gold Mountain, Dent, 1956; The Signpost Has Four Arms, Dent, 1957; (under pseudonym Julia Mayfield) The Forest of Stone, R. Hale, 1957; The Happy Man, Hutchinson, 1958; Golden Apollo, Hutchinson, 1958; The Fountain of Youth, Hutchinson, 1959; Sandals for My Feet, Hutchinson, 1960; Long Barnaby, Hodder & Stoughton, 1961, reissued as Hot Day in High Summer, May Fair Books, 1962; The Night the Roof Blew Off, Hodder & Stoughton, 1962; Their Flowers Were Black, R. Hale, 1967; The Swan River Story, R. Hale, 1968; An Act of Darkness, R. Hale, 1969, published in America as The House on Malador Street, Putnam, 1970; All Earth to Love (part one of "The Sussex Saga"), Howard Barker, 1969; The Stars Are My Children, R. Hale, 1970; The Temporary Boy, R. Hale, 1971; Day of the Dancing Sun (part two of "The Sussex Saga"), Corgi Books, 1971; When the Gallows Is High, R. Hale, in press.

Author of about 450 short stories published in magazines in many countries, of poems, and of stories and plays for radio.

WORK IN PROGRESS: A third part of "The Sussex Saga"; *The End of a String.*

SIDELIGHTS: Mrs. Hastings told *CA:* "My chief interest is country life, pure air, and escaping from crowds. I dabble in painting and musical composition, and study seriously the history of agriculture. In collecting, I am the complete magpie. I collect dogs, old and rare books, pictures, and every bit of Victorian curiosa on which I can lay my hands.

"In the garden I grow flowers, trees, and vegetables, and try to raise from seed everything from a violet to a cedar. I have now embarked upon the adventure of providing a home for lonely old ladies."

BIOGRAPHICAL/CRITICAL SOURCES: Best Sellers, February 1, 1970.

* * *

HATCH, John (Charles) 1917-

PERSONAL: Born November 1, 1917, in Manchester, England. *Education:* Sidney Sussex Colllege, Cambridge, B.A., 1940. *Politics:* Socialist. *Home:* 67 Parliament Hill Mansions, Lissenden Gardens, London N.W. 5, England. *Agent:* Innes Rose, John Farquharson Ltd., 15 Red Lion Sq., London W.C. 1, England; and Oliver Swan, Paul Reynolds & Son, 599 Fifth Ave., New York, N.Y. 10017.

CAREER: University of Glasgow, Glasgow, Scotland, lecturer in international relations, 1948-53; British Labour Party, London, England, head of Commonwealth Department, 1954-61; University College of Sierra Leone, Freetown, director of extramural studies, 1961-62. Director, Houston Inter-University African Studies Program, 1965—. Commonwealth correspondent for *New Statesman;* contributor to *L'Express, Progressive, Frankfurter Rundschau.*

WRITINGS: Coal for the People: The Mines for the Miners, Independent Labour Party, 1946; *The Dilemma of South Africa,* Dobson, 1952; *New from Africa,* Dobson, 1956; *Everyman's Africa,* Dobson, 1959, revised edition published as *Africa Today—and Tomorrow: An Outline of Basic Facts and Major Problems,* Praeger, 1960, 2nd revised edition, 1965; *A History of Post-War Africa,* Praeger, 1965; *Africa—the Rebirth of Self-Rule,* Oxford University Press, 1967; *The History of Britain in Africa from the Fifteenth Century to the Present,* Praeger, 1969; *Nigeria: The Seeds of Disaster,* Regnery, 1970; *Tanzania: A Profile,* Praeger, 1972.

SIDELIGHTS: Hatch was banned from South Africa after taking part in a number of history-making events in Africa—the movement against Central African Federation, helping train African politicians like Kaunda and Nyerere. He is a personal friend of many African leaders, and has traveled all over that continent since 1950.

BIOGRAPHICAL/CRITICAL SOURCES: New Statesman, December 5, 1969.

* * *

HATHAWAY, Dale E(rnest) 1925

PERSONAL: Born June 28, 1925, in Decatur, Mich.; son of Roy C. (a farmer) and Ruth Marie Hathaway; married Helen Pollock, July 16, 1947; children: four. *Education:* Michigan State University, B.A., 1947, M.A., 1948; Harvard University, D.P.A., 1952. *Home:* 1155 Daisy Lane, East Lansing, Mich. 48823. *Office:* Michigan State University, East Lansing, Mich. 48823.

CAREER: Michigan State University, East Lansing, 1948—, now professor of agricultural economics and head of the department. Consultant to Committee for Economic Development, 1960-62, U.S. Department of Agriculture, 1961, U.S. Department of Labor, 1961, Council

of Economic Advisers, 1961-62. *Military service:* U.S. Naval Reserve, 1944-54; active duty, 1944-46; became ensign. *Member:* American Farm Economic Association (vice-president, 1962-63), Phi Kappa Phi. *Awards, honors:* Carnegie fellow, 1950-52; awards for best published research in field of agricultural economics in 1952, 1953, 1955, and 1957; Distinguished Faculty Award, Michigan State University, 1964.

WRITINGS: The Impact of Price Support Programs upon the Available Supplies of Farm Products, 1948-56, Department of Agricultural Economics, Michigan State University, 1960; *Government and Agriculture: Public Policy in a Democratic Society,* Macmillan, 1963; *The Problems of Progress in the Agricultural Economy,* Scott, Foresman, 1964; (with Arley D. Waldo) *Multiple Jobholding by Farm Operators: An Interregional Publication for the State Agricultural Experiment Stations,* Department of Agricultural Economics, Michigan State University, 1964; *The Search for New International Arrangements to Deal with the Agricultural Problems of Industrialized Countries,* Department of Agricultural Economics, Michigan State University, 1965; *Michigan Farmers in the Mid-Sixties: A Survey of Their Views of Marketing Problems and Organizations,* Agricultural Experiment Station, Michigan State University, 1966; (with Allan Beegle and W. Keith Bryant) *People of Rural America* (monograph), U.S. Department of Commerce, Bureau of the Census, 1968.

* * *

HAWKEN, William R. 1917-

PERSONAL: Born February 25, 1917, in San Francisco, Calif.; son of Samuel Leslie (an engineer) and Barbara (George) Hawken; divorced; children: Roderick Leslie, Paul Gary, Pamela Rose. *Education:* Attended public schools and junior college.

CAREER: Eastman Kodak Co., San Francisco, Calif.; V-mail microfilm project, 1942-44; itinerant microphotographer, 1944-46; University of California, Berkeley, head of Library Photographic Service, 1947-59; self-employed consultant in field of document reproduction, 1960—, currently working on American Library Association Library Technology Project under grants from Council on Library Resources, Inc. *Member:* American Library Association, National Microfilm Association, Microfiche Foundation (Delft, The Netherlands; member of board).

WRITINGS: Full-Size Photocopying, Rutgers State University, 1960; *Photocopying from Bound Volumes: A Study of Machines, Methods, and Materials,* American Library Association, 1962; *Enlarged Prints from Library Microfilms: A Study of Processes, Equipment, and Materials,* American Library Association, 1963; *Copying Methods Manual,* American Library Association, 1966. Contributor of occasional articles to library periodicals.

WORK IN PROGRESS: A manual on methods of reproducing research materials.

AVOCATIONAL INTERESTS: Photography of works of art, and black and white abstracts; an occasional poem, spoonerisms; jazz, baroque, and flamenco music.

* * *

HAY, Eloise K(napp) 1926-

PERSONAL: Born November 19, 1926, in Chicago, Ill.; daughter of George Griff Prather and Lucy (Norvell) Knapp; married Stephen N. Hay (an educator), June 11, 1954; children: Catherine, Edward. *Education:* Elmira College, B.A., 1948; Radcliffe College, M.A., 1951, Ph.D., 1961. *Politics:* Independent. *Religion:* Roman Catholic. *Home:* 3310 Los Pinos Dr., Santa Barbara, Calif. 93105.

CAREER: University of Illinois, Chicago Division, assistant professor of English, 1961-64; Radcliffe Institute for Independent Study, Cambridge, Mass., associate scholar, 1964-66; University of California, Santa Barbara, lecturer in English, 1967-70; Delhi University, Delhi, India, visiting professor of American literature, 1970-71. *Member:* Phi Beta Kappa.

WRITINGS: The Political Novels of Joseph Conrad: A Critical Study, University of Chicago Press, 1963. Contributor to *Comparative Literature, Contemporary Literature, Conradiana,* and various essay collections.

WORK IN PROGRESS: A study of prescience and hindsight in the English novel of politics.

*　　　*　　　*

HAYES, Robert M(ayo) 1926-

PERSONAL: Born December 3, 1926, in New York, N.Y.; son of Dudley Lyman and Myra Wilhelmina (Lane) Hayes; married Alice Peters, September 2, 1952; children: Robert Dendrou. *Education:* University of California, Los Angeles, B.A., 1947, M.A., 1949, Ph.D., 1952. *Home:* 3943 Woodfield Dr., Sherman Oaks, Calif. 91403. *Office:* School of Library Service, University of California, Los Angeles, Calif. 90024.

CAREER: National Bureau of Standards, Washington, D.C., and Los Angeles, Calif., mathematician, 1949-52; Hughes Aircraft Co., Los Angeles, Calif., research mathematician 1952-53; National Cash Register Co., Los Angeles, Calif., application specialist, 1953-55; Magnavox Co., research laboratory, Los Angeles, Calif., head of business systems department, 1955-59; Electrada Corp., Los Angeles, Calif., vice-president and scientific director, 1959-63; Advanced Information Systems, Los Angeles, president, 1960-64; University of California, Los Angeles, visiting lecturer, 1952-64, professor in School of Library Service, 1964—. Teacher of special courses in information science at various universities. Holder of several patents on equipment developments in field of information storage. *Member:* American Library Association (former president of Information and Automation Division), American Mathematical Society, American Documentation Institute (former president), Association for Computing Machinery, Special Libraries Association, Phi Beta Kappa, Sigma Xi.

WRITINGS: (With Joseph Becker) *Information Storage and Retrieval: Tools, Elements, Theories,* Wiley, 1963; (with Gordon Martin and Irving Lieberman) *Recruitment and Training of Staff and Support of Staff Dissemination Activities at the American Library Association, Library 21 Exhibit,* School of Librarianship, Washington State University, 1963; (with R.M. Shoffner) *The Economics of Book Catalogue Production: A Study,* Stanford University Libraries, 1964; *Simulation and Modeling in the Information Sciences,* Institute of Government and Public Affairs, University of California (Los Angeles), 1964; (with Becker) *Data Processing for Library Operations,* Washington State Library, 1965; *Urban and Regional Information Systems,* University of California Extension, 1966; (with Becker) *A Proposed Library Network for Washington State,* Washington State Library, 1967; (with Becker) *Handbook of Data Processing for Libraries,* Wiley, 1970. Author of articles on the information sciences. Former associate editor, journal of Association for Computing Machinery.

*　　　*　　　*

HAYWARD, Charles H(arold) 1898-

PERSONAL: Born April 26, 1898, in London, England; son of Albert Charles (a woodworker) and Elizabeth (Richards) Hayward; married Ivy Edith Peronne, April, 1939; children: C.G. Alan, Sylvia R., Lorna H.J. *Education:* Attended Westminster City School, London, England. *Home:* 187 Marshalswick Lane, St. Albans, Hertfordshire, England. *Office:* Montague House, Russell Sq., London W.C.1, England.

CAREER: Self-employed cabinetmaker in London, England, 1913-25; *Handicrafts,* London, England, editor, 1925-35; *Woodworker,* London, England, editor, 1935-68. Shoreditch Training College, lecturer, 1938-39. *Military service:* Royal Field Artillery, 1916-18. *Member:* Authors Club, Arts Theatre Club.

WRITINGS: English Furniture at a Glance: A Simple Review in Pictures of the Origin and Evolution of Furniture from the Sixteenth to the Eighteenth Centuries, Architectural Press, 1924, Putnam, 1925; *English Rooms and Their Decoration at a Glance: A Simple Review in Pictures of English Rooms and Their Decorations from the Eleventh to the Eighteenth Centuries,* Architectural Press, 1925, Putnam, 1926; (contributor) Richard Greenhalgh, editor, *Joinery and Carpentry,* six volumes, Pitman, 1928, 2nd edition, 1939.

English Period Furniture: An Account of the Evolution of Furniture from 1500 to 1800, Evans Brothers, 1936, new edition, Lippincott, 1949, 11th edition, Scribner, 1971; *Practical Veneering: The Theory and Practice of Veneering in Cabinet Work,* Evans Brothers, 1937, Lippincott, 1938, new edition published as *Practical Veneering: Hammer and Caul Methods, Presses, Built-up Patterns, Marquetry, Inlays,* Evans Brothers, 1949, Lippincott, 1950, 2nd revised edition, Evans Brothers, 1961; *The Carpentry Book,* Van Nostrand, 1938, new edition published as *Teach Yourself Carpentry,* English Universities Press, 1938, 2nd edition, 1941, revised and enlarged edition published under 1938 title, English Universities Press, 1946, Van Nostrand, 1955.

Hammer and Nails Carpentry, Evans Brothers, 1942; *How to Make Strong Wooden Toys,* Evans Brothers, 1942; *Home Hobbies in Wood: Useful Things That You Will Enjoy Making,* Evans Brothers, 1943; *New Woodwork from Old: What to Make with Old Wood,* Evans Brothers, 1943; *The ABC of Woodwork,* Evans Brothers, 1945; (editor) *Staining and Polishing,* Evans Brothers, 1945, revised edition published as *Polishing Your Furniture: Staining, French Polishing, Ebonising, Limed Oak Effect, Jacobean Rubbed Finish, Ivory Bleached Treatment, Wax Polishing, Repolishing,* 1953, new edition published as *Staining and Polishing: How to Finish Woodwork,* Lippincott, 1959, revised edition, Evans Brothers, 1960; *Tools for Woodwork: The Sharpening, Care and Use of Hand Tools,* Evans Brothers, 1946, Lippincott, 1949, new edition, Evans Brothers, 1960; *Wood Carving for Beginners,* Evans Brothers, 1946; *How to Make Woodwork Tools,* Evans Brothers, 1946; *Cabinet Making for Beginners,* Evans Brothers, 1947, Lippincott, 1948, revised edition, Evans Brothers, 1960, Drake Publishers, 1971; (editor) *The Woodworker's Pocket Book: Recipes, Materials, Fittings, Tools, Geometry, Woodworking Data,* Evans Brothers, 1949, revised edition, 1959.

Woodwork Joints: Kinds of Joints, How They Are Cut and Where Used, Evans Brothers, 1950, Lippincott, 1951, revised edition, Evans Brothers, 1960, Drake Publishers, 1971; (editor) *Carpentry for Beginners: How to Use Tools, Basic Joints, Workshop Practice, Designs for Things to Make,* Evans Brothers, 1950, Lippincott, 1951, revised edition, Evans Brothers, 1965, Emerson, 1969; (editor) *Furniture Designs for Dining Room, Sitting Room, Bedroom, Kitchen and Hall,* Evans Brothers, 1950; *The Junior Woodworker,* Evans Brothers, 1951, Lippincott, 1952, revised edition, Evans Brothers, 1963; *Light Machines for Woodwork: Saws, Planers, Spindles,*

Sanders, Powered Hand Tools, Evans Brothers, 1952, revised edition, 1960; (editor) *The Handyman's Pocket Book: Materials, Processes, Repairs, and Data for the Householder,* Evans Brothers, 1952, 2nd edition, 1960; (editor) *The Second Book of Furniture Designs,* Evans Brothers, 1953; *Polishing Your Woodwork,* Evans Brothers, 1953; *The Complete Book of Woodwork,* Lippincott, 1955; *Period Furniture Designs,* Evans Brothers, 1956, revised edition, 1968, published in America as *English Period Furniture Designs,* Arco, 1969.

(Editor) *The Complete Handyman,* Lippincott, 1960; (editor) *Garden Woodwork: Greenhouse Sheds, Seats, Beach Chalet, Swings, Gates, Frames, Cycle Sheds, Garage, Poultry House, Pigeon Cote,* Lippincott, 1961; *Modern Power Woodwork,* English Universities Press, 1962; (with William Wheeler) *Practical Wood Carving and Gilding,* Evans Brothers, 1963, reissued as *Wood Carving,* Drake Publishers, 1972; (editor) *Making Toys in Wood,* Evans Brothers, 1963, Drake Publishers, 1971; *Practical Woodwork,* Evans Brothers, 1965, Emerson, 1967; *Making Furniture,* Evans Brothers, 1966; *Furniture Repairs,* Van Nostrand, 1967; (editor) *Woodworkers Question Box,* Evans Brothers, 1968, Drake Publishers, 1971; *Antique or Fake?: The Making of Old Furniture,* Evans Brothers 1970, St. Martin's, 1972.

Editor, *Woodworkers Annual,* Evans Brothers, 1949-50, 1956-59.

* * *

HAYWARD, John F(orrest)   1916-

PERSONAL: Born February 10, 1916, in Hounslow, England; son of Walter Henry (a professor of music) and Anne (Forrest) Hayward; married Helena Martyn (a writer), April 1, 1939; children: Anthony Richard, Monica Verena. *Education:* Magdalen College, Oxford, B.A., 1937. *Politics:* Conservative. *Home:* 28 Chepstow Villas, London W.11, England.

CAREER: Victoria and Albert Museum, London, England, deputy keeper, department of woodwork, 1946-65; Suthebys-Parke-Bernet, London, England, associate director, 1965—. *Military service:* British Army, World War II; became major; decorated Officer of the Order of Leopold II of Belgium. *Member*—Honorary: American Society of Arms Collectors, Accademia di S. Marciano (Turin, Italy), Polish Society of Arms Collectors.

WRITINGS: Swords and Daggers (booklet), H.M.S.O., 1951, 2nd edition, 1963; *European Armour* (booklet), H.M.S.O., 1951; *Silver Bindings from the J.R. Abbey Collections,* H.M.S.O., 1952; *Viennese Porcelain of the Du Paquier Period,* Rockliff, 1952; *European Firearms* (booklet), Philosophical Library, 1955, revised edition, H.M.S.O. 1958; *English Cutlery, Sixteenth to Eighteenth Century,* H.M.S.O., 1956; *English Watches,* H.M.S.O, 1956, 2nd edition, 1969; *Huguenot Silver in England 1688-1727* (monograph), Faber, 1959, Macmillan (New York), 1961; *Chests of Drawers and Commodes in the Victoria and Albert Museum* (booklet), H.M.S.O., 1960; *Tables in the Victoria and Albert Museum* (booklet), H.M.S.O., 1961; *The Art of the Gunmaker,* St. Martin's, Volume I, 1962, Volume II, 1964, 2nd edition, Barrie & Rockliff, 1965; *English Cabinets in the Victoria and Albert Museum* (booklet), H.M.S.O., 1964; (editor) Torsten Link, *The Flintlock: Its Origin and Development,* Holland Press, 1965; *English Desks and Bureaux* (booklet), H.M.S.O., 1968.

WORK IN PROGRESS: Renaissance Goldsmith's Work.

SIDELIGHTS: Hayward is competent in German, French, Italian, Spanish, and Dutch.

HAZZARD, Shirley   1931-

PERSONAL: Born January 30, 1931, in Sydney, Australia; daughter of Reginald (a government official) and Catherine (Stein) Hazzard; married Francis Steegmuller (a novelist and biographer), December 22, 1963. *Education:* Educated at Queenwood College, Sydney, Australia. *Home:* 200 East 66th St., New York, N.Y. 10021. *Agent:* McIntosh & Otis, Inc., 18 East 41st St., New York, N.Y. 10017.

CAREER: Worked for British Intelligence, Hong Kong, 1947-48, and for British High Commissioner's Office, Wellington, New Zealand, 1940-50. United Nations, New York, N.Y., general service category assistant, Technical Assistance to underdeveloped countries, 1952-62, serving in Italy, 1957. *Awards, honors:* U.S. National Institute of Arts and Letters award in literature, 1966; National Book Award nominee, 1971.

WRITINGS: Cliffs of Fall, and Other Stories, Knopf, 1963; *The Evening of the Holiday* (novel), Knopf, 1966; *People in Glass Houses: Portraits from Organization Life,* Knopf, 1967; *The Bay of Noon* (novel), Atlantic-Little, Brown, 1970; *Defeat of an Ideal: A Study of the Self-Destruction of the United Nations,* Atlantic-Little, Brown, 1973. Regular contributor of fiction to *New Yorker.*

WORK IN PROGRESS: A novel.

SIDELIGHTS: Shirley Hazzard's work has met with unusual critical approval. Economy and subtlety of language, underlying intense but controlled emotion, and a witty and sophisticated approach to her subjects are characteristics which reviewers find abundant in her writing. A *Time* reviewer describes her prose as "so understated that it forces the reader to become uncommonly attentive. But mostly it is because she chooses her words with such delicacy and precision that even ordinary situations acquire poetic shadings." Robie Macauley called *The Bay of Noon* "one of those rare novels that tries to address itself to the reader's intelligence rather than his nightmares. Its assumptions are firm and modest: that the reader will enjoy a sense of place if that place is drawn for him so perfectly that it seems to breathe, that the reader will understand a story based on the interactions of personality rather than mere violence, that the reader will take pleasure in a style that is consciously elegant and literary."

For L.E. Sissman Miss Hazzard's work is "an art of beauty, precision, and perception, which is in the long view fashionable, as all excellence should be fashionable." Charles Poore emphasizes the humor in her work. "Do not fail to savor the felicity in Miss Hazzard's style. Her joyful lampooning of pomposities, her solemn owls who shuffle multilingual papers, her vivid foreign scenes, her tenderness toward the few who are truly dedicated and ask no fanfare for devotion, places her on a high ground between Katherine Mansfield and Evelyn Waugh."

She has lived in Australia, New Zealand, the Far East, the U.S., and in Italy, which she has visited annually since 1957.

BIOGRAPHICAL/CRITICAL SOURCES: New York Times Book Review, January 9, 1966, November 12, 1967, April 5, 1970; *Time,* January 14, 1966, November 24, 1967; *New York Review of Books,* March 17, 1966; *Atlantic,* April, 1966; *Times Literary Supplement,* July 7, 1966, October 19, 1967, May 7, 1970; *Times* (London), October 14, 1967, October 21, 1967; *Observer Review,* October 15, 1967; *Listener,* October 19, 1967; *Spectator,* October 20, 1967, May 16, 1970; *Christian Science Monitor,* October 19, 1967, April 30, 1970; *New Statesman,* October 20, 1967; *Book World,* November 5, 1967; *Na-*

tional Observer, November 6, 1967; *Best Sellers,* November 15, 1967, May 1, 1970; *Commonweal,* December 1, 1967; *New York Times,* December 13, 1967, March 25, 1970; *Nation,* January 8, 1968; *National Review,* February 27, 1968; *Reporter,* May 16, 1968; *Life,* April 3, 1970; *New Yorker,* April 13, 1970.

*   *   *

HEANEY, John J.   **1925-**

PERSONAL: Born December 7, 1925, in County Wicklow, Ireland; son of William and Caroline (Keogh) Heaney. *Education:* Boston College, B.A., 1949, M.A., 1950; Woodstock College, S.T.L., 1957; Institut Catholique, Paris, France, S,T.D., 1963. *Home:* 278 Bedford Park Blvd., Bronx, N.Y. 10458. *Office:* Fordham University, Bronx, N.Y. 10458.

CAREER: Roman Catholic priest, member of Society of Jesus. Fordham University, New York, N.Y., instructor, 1958-61, assistant professor, 1964-68, associate professor of theology, 1968—.

WRITINGS: (Editor) *Faith, Reason and the Gospels: A Selection of Modern Thought of Faith and the Gospels,* Newman, 1961; *The Modernist Crisis: Von Huegel,* Corpus Publications, 1968. Contributor to *New Catholic Encyclopedia, Heythrop Journal,* and *Continuum.*

*   *   *

HEARD, J(oseph) Norman   **1922-**
   (Joe Norman)

PERSONAL: Born October 29, 1922, in Austin, Tex.; son of Henry B. and Winifred (Benson) Heard; married Joyce Boudreaux, July 7, 1945; children: Steven Paul, Diane Rachelle, William St. John. *Education:* Texas College of Arts and Industries, student, 1939-41; University of Texas, B.J., 1947, M.J., 1949, M.L.S., 1951. *Politics:* Democrat. *Religion:* Roman Catholic. *Home:* 140 Oakridge St., Lafayette, La. 70501. *Office:* University of Southwestern Louisiana Library, Lafayette, La. 70501.

CAREER: Texas Technological College, Lubbock, order librarian, 1951-53; Texas College of Arts and Industries, Kingsville, assistant librarian, 1953-55; Pan American College, Edinburg, Tex., director of libraries, 1955-62; Northwestern State College of Louisiana, Natchitoches, order librarian, 1962-63; Louisiana State University, Baton Rouge, chief acquisitions librarian, 1963-64; Southeastern Louisiana College, Hammond, librarian, 1964-69; University of Southwestern Louisiana, Lafayette, acquisitions librarian, 1969—. Founding president, Valley Botanical Garden Association, 1959-62; member of board of directors, Louisiana Association for Retarded Children, 1964. *Military service:* U.S. Navy, 1942-45. *Member:* American Library Association, Louisiana Library Association, Phi Kappa Phi, Civitan. *Awards, honors:* First prize in Foundation for Voluntary Welfare national essay contest on child welfare, 1957.

WRITINGS: (Contributor) *Handbook of Texas,* Texas State Historical Association, 1952; *Bookman's Guide to Americana,* Scarecrow, Volume I, 1953, Volume II, 1956, 6th edition (with J.H. Hoover), 1971; (contributor) *Grassroots Private Welfare,* New York University Press, 1957; (editor) *A Place of Their Own,* Times Publishing, 1958; *Hope Through Doing: The Rewards of Working for Your Retarded Child and Others,* John Day, 1968; *The Black Frontiersmen: Adventures of Negroes Among American Indians 1528-1918,* John Day, 1969. Contributor of articles on historical topics to regional magazines.

WORK IN PROGRESS: A bibliography of American Indians; a dictionary of American frontiersmen; and a study of assimilation of white children captured by Indians.

SIDELIGHTS: Heard told *CA:* "Because all three of my children are brain damaged, my major interest is in work for the mentally retarded." This, combined with an interest in tropical plants, led Heard to found the Valley Botanical Garden at McAllen, Tex., as a place for handicapped persons to work.

*   *   *

HEATH, Roy   **1917-**

PERSONAL: Born May 31, 1917, in Trenton, N.J.; son of S. Roy (a lumberman) and Janet (Curtis) Heath; married Dorothy Thayer Heck, May 2, 1946 (divorced, 1956); children: Douglass, Peter. *Education:* Princeton University, A.B., 1939; University of Pennsylvania, M.A., 1947, Ph.D., 1952. *Politics:* Democrat. *Religion:* Episcopalian. *Home:* 1187 Southeast St., Amherst, Mass. 01002. *Office:* Department of Psychology, Amherst College, Amherst, Mass. 01002.

CAREER: Princeton University, Princeton, N.J., instructor in psychology, 1950-54; Knox College, Galesburg, Ill., associate professor of psychology, 1954-56; University of Pittsburgh, Pittsburgh, Pa., director of counseling, 1956-63; Amherst College, Amherst, Mass., visiting professor, 1963-64; professor of psychology, 1970—; Trinity College, Hartford, Conn., dean of students, 1964-70. National representative, Woodrow Wilson Foundation, 1958-63. *Military service:* U.S. Army, World War II; became major; received Army Commendation Ribbon. *Member:* American Psychological Association. *Awards, honors:* American Personnel and Guidance Association research award, 1960.

WRITINGS: The Reasonable Adventurer: A Study of the Development of Thirty-six Undergraduates at Princeton, University of Pittsburgh Press, 1964.

*   *   *

HEATH, Royton E(dward)   **1907-**

PERSONAL: Born August 7, 1907, in Dulwich, London, England; married Mary Thoburn, August 12, 1933; children: Jennifer. *Education:* Attended Westminster Technical College, London, England. *Home:* 78 Kingsway, Petts Wood, Orpington, Kent, England.

CAREER: Savoy Hotel Ltd., London, England, head floors superintendent for twenty-eight years. *Member:* Society of Authors, Linnean Society (fellow), Royal New Zealand Institute of Horticulture (fellow). *Awards, honors:* Gold, silver, and bronze medals for Alpine plants.

WRITINGS: Alpines Under Glass, Gifford, 1951; *Shrubs for the Rock Garden and Alpine House,* Collingridge, 1954, Transatlantic, 1955; *Miniature Rock Gardening in Troughs and Pans,* Collingridge, 1957, Transatlantic, 1958, revised edition published as *Rock Plants for Small Gardens,* Collingridge, 1969, Transatlantic, 1970; *Collectors' Alpines: Their Cultivation in Frames and Alpine Houses,* Taplinger, 1964; *Encyclopedia of Gardening,* Collingridge, 1970; *Encyclopedia of Rock Plants,* Collingridge, 1971.

AVOCATIONAL INTERESTS: Philately, especially New Zealand issues.

*   *   *

HEBARD, Edna L(aura Henriksen)   **1913-**

PERSONAL: Born August 22, 1913, in Missoula, Mont.; daughter of Edward and Laura (Hutchinson) Henriksen; married William Bartlett Hebard (associate professor of biology, New York University), July 1, 1933. *Education:* Attended Montana State University, 1931-33; New York University, B.S., 1953, M.B.A., 1954, Ph.D., 1957. *Home:* 269 River Vale Rd., River Vale, N.J. 07675.

Office: Department of Real Estate, School of Commerce, New York University, New York, N.Y. 10003.

CAREER: Certified abstractor of titles for abstract companies in Missoula, Mont., 1936-41; Puget Sound Title Insurance Co., Seattle, Wash., title searcher, 1942-45, 1947-49; Title Guaranty Co., Missoula, Mont., manager, 1946-47; New York University, New York, N.Y., 1956—, began as instructor, became associate professor, chairman of department of real estate, 1963—. Consultant in real estate economics and market studies. *Member:* Real Estate Board of New York (associate), Metropolitan Economic Association (New York), Phi Chi Theta (honorary), Rho Epsilon (district director).

WRITINGS: (With John R. White) *Manhattan Housing Market,* privately printed, 1959; (with Gerald S. Meisel) *Principles of Real Estate Law,* Simmons-Boardman, 1964, revised edition, Schenkman, 1967; (with David Clurman) *Condominiums and Cooperatives,* Interscience, 1970.

BIOGRAPHICAL/CRITICAL SOURCES: Iris, May, 1961; *Binder,* October, 1963.

* * *

HECHT, Anthony (Evan) 1923-

PERSONAL: Born January 16, 1923, in New York, N.Y.; son of Melvyn Hahlo (a businessman) and Dorothea (Holzman) Hecht; married Patricia Harris (divorced); married Helen D'Alessandro, June 12, 1971; children: (first marriage) Jason, Adam; (second marriage) Evan Alexander. *Education:* Bard College, B.A., 1944; Columbia University, M.A., 1950. *Home:* 19 East Boulevard, Rochester, N.Y. 14610. *Office:* Department of English, University of Rochester, Rochester, N.Y. 14627.

CAREER: Has taught at Kenyon College, State University of Iowa, New York University, and Smith College; Bard College, Annandale-on-Hudson, N.Y., associate professor of English, 1962-67; University of Rochester, Rochester, N.Y., John H. Deane Professor of Poetry and Rhetoric, 1967—. *Military service:* U.S. Army, three years; served in Europe and Japan; temporary duty with Counter-Intelligence Corps. *Member:* National Institute of Arts and Letters. *Awards, honors:* Prix de Rome fellowship, 1951; Guggenheim fellowships, 1954, 1959; *Hudson Review* fellowship, 1958; Ford Foundation fellowships, 1960, 1968; Brandeis University Creative Arts Award in Poetry, 1965; Russell Loines Award, 1968; Miles Poetry Prize, 1968; Pulitzer Prize in poetry, 1968, for *The Hard Hours;* Academy of American Poets fellowship, 1969; chancellor, Academy of American Poets.

WRITINGS—All poetry: *A Summoning of Stones,* Macmillan, 1954; *The Seven Deadly Sins* (pamphlet; includes wood engravings by Leonard Baskin), Gehenna Press, 1958; *Struwwelpeter, a Poem,* Gehenna Press, 1958; (editor with John Hollander) *Jiggery-Pokery: A Compendium of Double Dactyls,* Atheneum, 1967; *The Hard Hours,* Atheneum, 1967; *Aesopic* (couplets; includes wood engravings by Thomas Bewick), Gehenna Press, 1968. Translator, with Helen Bacon, of Aeschylus' *Seven Against Thebes,* Oxford University Press, in press. Poems included in *New Pocket Anthology of American Verse,* edited by Oscar Williams, World Publishing, 1955, *Contemporary American Poetry,* edited by Donald Hall, Penguin, 1962, *Poet's Choice,* edited by Paul Engle and Joseph Langland, Dial, 1962, *A Controversy of Poets,* edited by Paris Leary and Robert Kelly, Doubleday-Anchor, 1965, *Poems of Our Moment,* edited by John Hollander, Pegasus, 1968, and in other anthologies. Has done translations from French and German. Contributor to *Hudson Review, New York Review of Books, Quarterly Review of Literature, Transatlantic Review,* and *Voices.*

WORK IN PROGRESS: A translation, with George Dimock, of Sophocles' *Oedipus at Colossus.*

SIDELIGHTS: Labeled a "good instance of donnish humor" by the *New Yorker, Jiggery-Pokery* is an exercise in a new light-verse form invented by poet-professors Hecht and John Hollander. The book is a collection of "Clerihewesque" limericks composed entirely of double dactyls. As a testimonial to the universality of the book's wit and appeal, a rash of double dactyls broke out on college campuses and in literary circles across the country after its publication in 1967.

However, as Martin Dodsworth has observed, "Mr. Hecht is primarily a poet, secondarily a wit." Always an accomplished practitioner of metrical verse, he was frequently criticised a decade ago for sacrificing content to form, for being a technician rather than an artist. According to several critics and fellow poets, including Booth, John Thompson, and Louis Simpson, his most recent, Pulitzer Prize-winning collection, *The Hard Hours,* shows a marked difference in style; he has begun to write with a new, pared-down directness and emotional sensitivity not evident in his earlier work. Since *The Hard Hours* contains most of the poems from his original collection, *A Summoning of Stones,* the new volume invites comparison. In the opinion of Lisel Mueller, Hecht "has discarded the baroque, decorative elements of his earlier verse; he no longer writes the poem which is essentially one long, dazzling conceit; he has a new simplicity and strength. But he is still brilliant; he still employs literary sources; his poems are still tightly woven, excellently constructed forms." In a review of *The Hard Hours,* Hayden Carruth writes: "Some of his poems, especially the sequence called 'Rites and Ceremonies,' are so well controlled yet so fierce that in them the irony fades out, the rhetoric, left free, clings to the experience, and the formal fury binds us so tightly that our only hope of escape is to realize the poem in ourselves—and thus to submit to it." Hecht has been noted for the versatility and abundance of his language, and for the wide range of forms and subjects he has at his command. He is as expressive with domestic themes as he is with the religious, sharing personal insights, "the painfully earned joy of tragic self-knowledge," to quote Philip Booth, with his readers. Laurence Lieberman calls his new poetry "a powerful synthesizing art. . . . In 'More Light! More Light!' and 'Rites and Ceremonies,' the interlocking of dramas mercilessly batters the reader's sensibility with excoriating facts, and judges his conscience. The scissoring movement between story and story provides the reader's nervous system with a series of shocks, a jackknifing of emotions, comparable to that produced by the interplay of plot and subplot in *King Lear,* and in some story sequences of the Old Testament. I don't know any other poetry in English, outside poetic drama, that creates anything like this effect."

Although considered a modern poet, Hecht's technique is traditional; he leans to realism rather than symbolism, relying, as Lieberman has said, "on the power of quiet overtones to transmit the intense emotional experience hidden below the casual surface." "His real concern is human suffering and cruelty," Dodsworth remarks. "He is Jewish, and writes about the concentration camps with decency, without posturing. 'More Light! More Light!' is the best poem on the subject known to me, because it does not make poetry seem irrelevant in the context of that suffering."

BIOGRAPHICAL/CRITICAL SOURCES: Perspective, spring, 1962; Atlantic, February, 1967; New Yorker, February 25, 1967; Listener, October 19, 1967; Observer, November 12, 1967; Times Literary Supplement, November 23, 1967; New York Times Book Review, December 17, 1967; Christian Science Monitor, February 1, 1968; Reporter, February 22, 1968; London Magazine, Volume 7, number 12, 1968; Shenandoah, spring, 1968; Carleton Miscellany, Volume IX, number 3, 1968; New York Review of Books, August 1, 1968; Harper's, August, 1968; Poetry, September, 1968; Yale Review, spring, 1969; Contemporary Literature, spring, 1969.

*   *   *

HECKEL, Robert V. 1925-

PERSONAL: Born June 12, 1925, in Columbia, S.C.; son of Verne Kennedy (an engineer) and Martha (Vero) Heckel; married Belle Mead Martin, 1957; children: Robert, Verne Kennedy, Belle Mead. Education: Pennsylvania State University, B.S., 1948, M.S., 1949, Ph.D., 1955. Politics: "Northern Republican, Southern Democrat." Religion: Episcopalian. Office: University of South Carolina, Columbia, S.C. 29208.

CAREER: Greenville Mental Health Clinic, Greenville, S.C., chief psychologist, 1951-57; psychiatrist in private practice, Greenville, S.C., 1954-58; Medical College of Georgia, Augusta, assistant professor of psychiatry, 1958; U.S. Veterans Administration Hospital, Augusta, Ga., coordinator of psychology research and training, 1961-64; University of South Carolina, Columbia, professor of psychology, 1964—, director, Social Problems Research Institute, 1968—. Director, Psychological Supply Co., 1953-60. Military service: U.S. Navy, 1943-45. Member: American Psychological Association, Southeastern Psychological Association, Psi Chi.

WRITINGS: (With Rose Jordan) Psychology: The Nurse and the Patient, Mosby, 1963, 3rd edition, in press; (with Grider and Cinotti) Applied Psychology in Dentistry, Mosby, 1964, 2nd edition, 1971; (with Lelon Peacock) Textbook of General Psychology, Mosby, 1966, 2nd edition, in press; (with Helen C. Latham) Pediatric Nursing, Mosby, 1967, 2nd edition, 1971; (with Peacock) Instructor's Guide for Use with Textbook of General Psychology, Mosby, 1967; (with Colgan, Borasio, and Walsh) Study Guide for Textbook of General Psychology, Mosby, 1967; (with Charles Perry, Arliss J. Epps, and P.G. Reeves) The Return Home: A Study of the Effects of Chemo-Therapy on Released Psychiatric Patients, State Printing Co., 1967; (with Weatherbee and Rempel) Contemporary University: An Evaluation of an Educational Experiment, University of Southern California, 1970; (with Elizabeth Mandell) Crime and Delinquency, Social Problems Research Institute, University of Southern California, 1970; Generation in Revolt, Mosby, 1971; Group Psychotherapy, Mosby, 1971; (with Perry) The Discharged Mental Patient: A Five-Year Statistical Survey, University of South Carolina Press, 1973.

Wrote, produced, and acted in educational film, "Mary Stewart," and three other educational films. Contributor of more than one hundred articles to professional periodicals.

WORK IN PROGRESS: The Renaissance Man in the Modern World; with William Wilson, Approaches to Community Mental Health: The Development of Humor; and The Psychology of Popularity.

*   *   *

HEDGE, Leslie (Joseph) 1922-

PERSONAL: Born February 21, 1922, in Old Windsor, England; son of George Charles (a clerk) and Edith (Cannon) Hedge; married Joan Olga Stutt (a schoolteacher), April 20, 1946; children: Barbara, Philip, Penelope. Education: Attended House of the Sacred Mission, Kelham, England, 1938-40, and King Alfred's College, Winchester, England, 1940-42; University of London, LL.B., 1955. Home: 5 Evendons Lane, Wokingham, Berkshire, England. Agent: Curtis Brown Ltd., 60 East 56th St., New York, N.Y. 10022. Office: Patent Office, 25 Southampton Buildings, London W.C.2, England.

CAREER: Former teacher in English schools; barrister of Gray's Inn, London, England; British Patent Office, London, examiner, 1957—. Part-time lecturer, City Literary Institute, London. Military service: Royal Navy, 1942-47, became lieutenant. British Army, 1954-56, became captain. Member: Society of Authors.

WRITINGS: After the Flesh (novel), Hamish Hamilton, 1963, Coward, 1964.

WORK IN PROGRESS: A novel tentatively titled Gooseberry Fool.

SIDELIGHTS: "I have two main literary preoccupations. The first is solving the purely technical problems of novel-writing. I have even started teaching a night school class in 'the craft of fiction' on the principle that (pace GBS) the surest way to learn anything is to teach it to others. The second is working out a valid and consistent moral attitude to the world; this sounds stuffy, but I think it is essential, for me anyway, as a novelist."

*   *   *

HEDGES, Sid(ney) G(eorge) 1897-

PERSONAL: Born March 25, 1897, in Bicester, Oxfordshire, England; son of G.W. and Mary Hedges; married Mary Dixon; children: Anthony John. Religion: Christian. Home: Ginkgo House, Bicester, Oxfordshire, England.

CAREER: Went to work as a carpenter at age fourteen, then a clothing salesman, soldier, music teacher, violinist, lecturer, journalist, and free-lance writer. Onetime European adjudicator of Federation Internationale de l'Harmonica, member of board of National Sunday School Union, and president of British Temperance Youth. Member: Society of Authors, Royal Commonwealth Society.

WRITINGS: The Pillars of Piloh, Warwick Brothers, 1922; Self-Help for the Violinist, Scribner, 1925; The Boy's Book of Swimming, J. Brown & Son, 1926; Holding the Senior Boys, National Sunday School Union, 1926; The Book of Swimming and Diving, Hutchinson, 1927; The Girl's Book of Swimming, Brown, Son & Ferguson, 1927; Ice and Roller Skating, Warne, 1928; (with Theodore Ruete) The African Heir, Warne, 1928; Swimming in Twelve Lessons, Athletic Publications, 1928, 5th edition, 1951; Swimming, Diving, and Life-Saving, Warne, 1928, 4th edition published as Swimming and Diving, Athletic Publications, 1949; Games for Socials, National Sunday School Union, 1929, enlarged edition, 1941; Modern Swimming and Diving, Athletic Publications, 1929, 3rd edition published as Swimming and Diving, 1945; Holding the Senior Boys, National Sunday School Union, 1929; Tales of Pendlecliffe School, Sheldon Press, 1929.

Musical Games for Socials, National Sunday School Union, 1930; Swimming, Pearson, 1930; Class Party Games for Juniors, Intermediates, and Seniors, Cook, 1930; The Weir Boyd Mystery, Jenkins, 1930; Book of Swimming and Diving, Hutchinson, 1931; More Games for Socials, National Sunday School Union, 1931; The Pendlecliffe Swimmers, Sheldon Press, 1931; Our Senior Class, Independent Press, 1931; The Channel Tunnel Mystery, Jenkins, 1932; The Malta Mystery, Jenkins, 1932; Swimming: How to Succeed, Evans Brothers, 1932, revised edition, 1938; Seeing Europe Cheaply, Methuen, 1932; How *to Swim Crawl,* Methuen, 1932, 5th edition, 1950; *Ice Rink Skating,* Pearson, 1932; *Indoor and Community Games,* Methuen, 1932, Lippincott, 1933, 5th edition, Methuen, 1943; *Venetian Swimmer Mystery,* Jenkins, 1933; *Swimming and Watermanship,* Hutchinson, 1933; *Do You Know This Game?,* National Sunday School Union, 1933; *Games for Small Lawns,* Lippincott, 1933; (with Nellie Ferrers-Nicholson) *Art of Badminton,* Methuen, 1934; *The Swim Book,* Methuen, 1934, 2nd edition, 1951; *Indoor Games and Fun,* Lippincott, 1934, 2nd edition, 1939; *The Boys of Pendlecliffe School,* Hutchinson, 1934; *Plague Panic,* Jenkins, 1934; *Outdoor Games,* National Sunday School Union, 1935; *Outdoor and Community Games,* Lippincott, 1935; *Games to Play,* Cassell, 1935; *Indoor and Party Games,* Evans Brothers, 1935; *Modern Swimming,* Cassell, 1935; *Diamond Duel,* Jenkins, 1935; *How to Teach Swimming,* Methuen, 1935; (editor) *The Universal Book of Hobbies and Handicrafts,* Odhams, 1936; *Open-air Games for Every Occasion,* Warne, 1936; *Indoor Games for All,* National Sunday School Union, 1936; *One Hundred Garden Games,* Country Life, 1936; *How Well Do You Swim?,* Methuen, 1936; *Swim!,* National Sunday School Union, 1937; *More Indoor and Community Games,* Methuen, 1937, Chemical Publishing Co., 1940; *Outdoor and Holiday Games,* Evans Brothers, 1937; *The Boys' and Girls' Swim Book,* Methuen, 1937, 3rd edition, 1951; *Hohner Harmonica Band Book,* Pilgrim Press, 1938; *Swimming Complete,* Methuen, 1939, 2nd edition published as *The Complete Swimmer,* British Book Centre, 1950; (editor) *The Home Entertainer,* Odhams, 1939.

Knowledge for the Growing Boy, Pilgrim Press, 1940; *Mediterannean Mystery,* Mellifont Press, 1940; *Club Games and Activities,* National Sunday School Union,; 1940; *Musical Games for Socials,* Pilgrim Press, 1942; *Youth Club Games and Contests,* Methuen, 1942; *Christian Youth, the Alternative to Hitler Youth,* National Sunday School Union, 1942; *Youth Club Work,* Pilgrim Press, 1943, revised edition, 1960; *Educational Activities for Youth Clubs,* Pilgrim Press, 1943, revised edition published as *Educational Fun for Youth Groups,* 1954; *War Ends at Malta,* Mellifont Press, 1943; (editor) *The Christian Youth Handbook,* National Sunday School Union, 1944; *Youth Club Epilogues,* Methuen, 1944, revised edition published as *Youth Worshipping,* Pilgrim Press, 1958; *Club Games for Outdoors,* National Sunday School Union, 1945; *Junior Club Work,* National Sunday School Union, 1945; *Youth Club Activities,* Methuen, 1945; (editor) *Youth Club Songs,* National Sunday School Union, 1946; (editor) *Be Your Own Boss: Twenty-one Suggestions for Making an Independent Living,* Allenson & Co., 1946; *A Youth Club Band: The Romance of Red Rhythmics,* National Sunday School Union, 1946; *I Write for a Living,* Allenson & Co., 1946; *The Book of Stunts and Tricks,* Allenson & Co., 1947; *Youth Club Technique,* Methuen, 1947; *The Sunday School Ideas Book,* National Sunday School Union, 1948; *Youth Club Quizzes,* Methuen, 1948; *Games for Your Home,* Allenson & Co., 1949.

(Editor) *The School Entertainment Book,* Pilgrim Press, 1950; *Modern Party Games,* Mellifont Press, 1950; *Youth Club Entertainment Stunts,* Methuen, 1951; *The Bible Quiz Book,* Pilgrim Press, 1951; *Toi, the Swimmer,* Epworth, 1952; (compiler) *Youth Sing Book with Music,* National Sunday School Union, 1953; *The Home Entertainer,* Odhams, 1953; *Crawl and Butterfly Swimming,* Methuen, 1954; (editor) *Second School Entertainment Book,* Pilgrim Press, 1954; *Sunday School Ideas Book,* revised edition, National Sunday School Union, 1955; *Children's Party Games,* Pilgrim Press, 1955; (compiler) *Everybody's Book of Hobbies,* Odhams Press, 1955; *Social Fun and Games,* Pilgrim Press, 1955; *Tom Thumb Tales, with Morals if You Want Them,* Pilgrim Press, 1955;

Games for the Not-So-Young, Methuen, 1956, Philosophical Library, 1957; *Youth Club Contest Quizzes,* Methuen, 1957; *Team Quizzes for the Under Fourteen's,* Pilgrim Press, 1957; *Fun for the Not-So-Young,* Philosophical Library, 1958; *Pilgrim by Plane to the Holy Land,* Pilgrim Press, 1959; *Sunday Celebrations and Special Features,* Pilgrim Press, 1959; *Bible Contest Quizzes,* Pilgrim Press, 1959.

Step Out to Music: Group Dances and Games, Pilgrim Press, 1960; *Youth Club Programmes,* Methuen, 1961; (compiler) *Prayers for Youth Clubs,* Methuen, 1962; *Outdoor Games for Youth Club and Home,* Methuen, 1963; *What to Do for Under 15's: Club and Group Programmes,* Pilgrim Press, 1963; (compiler) *Down to Earth and Up to Heaven: Prayers for the Youthful,* Pilgrim Press, 1964; *The Youth Club Ideas Book,* Methuen, 1964; *Responsive Prayers for Youth,* National Christian Education Council, 1964; *Youth Club Skits and Stunts,* Methuen, 1966; *Swimming for Everyone,* Methuen, 1967; *Bicester Wuz a Little Town,* Bicester Advertiser, 1968; *With One Voice: Prayers and Thoughts from World Religions,* Religious Education Press, 1969.

Group Activities and Fun for Groups of All Ages, Methuen, 1970; National Sunday School Union, 1970; *Is There Anybody There?,* Mowbray, 1971; *Prayers and Thoughts from World Religions,* John Knox, 1972.

Author of booklets on swimming, games, youth activities. Editor of "Things to Do" series, Allenson & Co. Contributor to American juvenile periodicals, and to magazines and newspapers throughout the world.

WORK IN PROGRESS: Compilations of prayers and quotations from all faiths, showing their relevance and interest to Christians.

SIDELIGHTS: Hedges' books have been translated into Norwegian, Dutch, French, and Hindustani.

*   *   *

HEFFLEY, Wayne 1927-

PERSONAL: Born July 15, 1927, in Bakersfield, Calif.; son of Arnold and Ann Lee (Woods) Heffley; married fourth wife, Ilene Nemerski, December 14, 1962; children: (previous marriages) Michael Wayne, Patricia Louise, Devon Jeanne, Kendis Ann. *Education:* Studied at dramatic schools. *Politics:* Liberal. *Agent:* Kurt Frings Agency, 9025 Wilshire Blvd., Beverly Hills, Calif. 90211; and Ruth Cantor, 156 Fifth Ave., New York, N.Y. 10011.

CAREER: Originally went to Hollywood to write for films, wound up as actor appearing in more than 150 television films, and in stage plays and motion pictures, 1953—. *Military service:* U.S. Marines, Infantry, World War II and Korean War; became sergeant. *Member:* Screen Actors Guild, Actors' Equity Association, American Federation of Television and Radio Artists, Academy of Motion Picture Arts and Sciences, Academy of Television Arts and Sciences.

WRITINGS: Television as a Career, Macfadden, 1964. Author and producer of play "Through a Dirty Window"; also author of "Pygmy" (screenplay) and "Tulip Growing" (novel). Writer of several television shows.

WORK IN PROGRESS: A novel about divorce, *No One There to Greet Me;* a book of essays, *Portfolio of Minor Angers.*

AVOCATIONAL INTERESTS: Chess, classical music (has collection of more than two thousand operas and classical works), politics.

HEITMAN, Sidney 1924-

PERSONAL: Born April 24, 1924, in Elizabeth, N.J.; son of Joseph and Pauline (Bacher) Heitman; married Frances R. Korchok, November 23, 1950; children: Jody Ellen, David Kermit. Education: University of Missouri, A.B., 1949, M.A., 1950; Columbia University, Certificate of Russian Institute, 1952, Ph.D., 1963. Home: 1900 Sheely Dr., Fort Collins, Colo. 80521. Office: Department of History, Colorado State University, Fort Collins, Colo. 80521.

CAREER: University of Missouri, Columbia, instructor, 1949-50; Colorado State University, Fort Collins, assistant professor, 1955-62, associate professor, 1962-64, professor of history, 1964—. Military service: U.S. Army Air Corps, 1942-46; became first lieutenant. Member: American Historical Association, American Association for the Advancement of Slavic Studies, American Association of University Professors, Western Slavic Association, American Association of University Professors, American Civil Liberties Union, Rocky Mountain Social Science Association, Rocky Mountain Association for Slavic Studies, Southwestern Association for the Advancement of Slavic Studies. Awards, honors: Social Science Research Council fellowship; Ford Foundation fellowship; Rockefeller Foundation research award; Ecole Pratique des Hautes Etudes, research associate; Hoover Institution research grant; American Council of Learned Societies research grant; Colorado State University research grants; Distinguished Service Award, Colorado State University, 1968.

WRITINGS: An Annotated Bibliography of Nikolai Bukharin's Published Works, privately printed, 1958; (co-author) Revisionism: Essays on the History of Marxist Ideas, edited by Leopold Labedz, Praeger, 1962; (author of introduction) N. Bukharin and E. Preobrazhensky, The ABC of Communism, University of Michigan Press, 1966; (contributor) Sowjetsystem und demokratische Gesellschaft, Volume I, Verlag Herder, 1966; (editor and author of introduction) The Path to Socialism in Russia: Selected Works of N.I. Bukharin, Omicron Books, 1967; Nikolai I. Bukharin: A Bibliography with Annotations, Including the Locations of His Works in Major American and European Libraries, Hoover Institution, 1969; (contributor) Francis B. Randall, editor, Problems in Russian History, Pitman, 1970; Bukharin on Revolution: The Making of Communist Doctrine, 1912-1929, Stanford University Press, in press. Contributing editor of three hundred historical biographies to New Wonder World Encyclopedia, Parents' Magazine Press, 1959. Contributor to journals, including Historian, Saturday Review, Political Science Quarterly, American Historical Review, Slavic Review, Rocky Mountain Social Science Journal, Problems of Communism. Managing editor, Rocky Mountain Social Science Journal, 1965—.

*   *   *

HELFERT, Erich A(nton) 1931-

PERSONAL: Born May 29, 1931, in Aussig/Elbe, Sudetenland (now part of Czechoslovakia); came to United States in 1950; son of Julius (an executive director) and Anna Maria (Wilde) Helfert. Education: Oberrealschule Neuburg, Abitur (with honors), 1950; University of Nevada, B.S., in B.A., 1945; Harvard University, M.B.A. (with high distinction), 1956, D.B.A., 1958. Religion: Roman Catholic. Home: 580 Arastradero Rd., Apt. 501, Palo Alto, Calif. 94306. Office: Crown Zellerbach, 1 Bush St., San Francisco, Calif. 94119.

CAREER: Expelled to West Germany from homeland with other Sudeten Germans in 1946; Neuburger Zeitung, Neuburg, West Germany, newspaper reporter and correspondent, 1948-51; Semenza & Kottinger (certified public accountants), Reno, Nev., accountant, 1952-55; Harvard University, Cambridge, Mass., research assistant, 1956-57, assistant professor of business policy, 1959-65; San Francisco State College, San Francisco, Calif., assistant professor of business policy, 1958-59; Crown Zellerbach, San Francisco, Calif., internal consultant, 1965-67, assistant to executive vice-president, 1967-69, assistant to president and director of corporate planning, 1969—. Consultant to American Telephone and Telegraph, Caltex, Coca Cola, General Electric Co., United Nations, and various banks, 1959-65. Member: American Accounting Association, American Finance Association, American Economic Association, Corporate Planners Association, Commonwealth Club of California, Harvard Business School Club of Northern California (treasurer), Sierra Club, Phi Kappa Phi.

WRITINGS: (With others) Case Problems in Finance, 4th edition, Irwin, 1962; Techniques of Financial Analysis, Irwin, 1963, revised edition, 1967, 3rd edition, 1972; (with Malcolm P. McNair and Eleanor G. May) Controllership in Department Stores, Division of Research, Harvard University, Graduate School of Business Administration, 1965; Wirklichkeitsnahe Ausbildung des Management-Nachwuchses in den USA, Kohlhammer, 1965; Valuation: Concepts and Practice, Wadsworth, 1966; (with others) Financial Executive's Handbook, Irwin, 1970. Contributor of articles to California Management Review, Revue Economique et Sociale (Switzerland), Business Scope, and Zeitschrift fuer Betriebswirtschaft (West Germany).

*   *   *

HELLER, Deane 1924-

PERSONAL: Born January 14, 1924, in Milwaukee, Wis.; daughter of Edmund J. and Delphine Ann Fons; married David Heller (an author), September 1, 1943 (died May, 1968); children: David, Douglas. Education: Attended University of Chicago, 1943-44, correspondence courses, 1945; attended University of Maryland, 1948-49. Home and office: 612 Ellsworth Dr., Silver Spring, Md. 20910; and 1501 Vernon Ave., Key West, Fla. 33040. Agent: Scott Meredith Literary Agency, 580 Fifth Ave., New York, N.Y. 10036.

CAREER: Reporter for Chicago Sun, Chicago, Ill., 1943-44; free-lance writer in collaboration with husband, 1948-68, by herself, 1968—. Photographer, illustrating many of joint articles, 1955—.

WRITINGS—All with husband, David Heller, except as indicated: John Foster Dulles: Soldier for Peace, Holt, 1960; Jacqueline Kennedy: The Complete Story of America's Glamorous First Lady, Monarch, 1961, new edition published as Jacqueline Kennedy: The Warmly Human Life Story of the Woman All Americans Have Taken to Their Hearts, 1963; The Kennedy Cabinet: America's Men of Destiny, Monarch, 1961; The Berlin Crisis: Prelude to World War III?, foreword by Konrad Adenauer, Monarch, 1961; The Cold War, Monarch, 1962; The Berlin Wall, Walker & Co., 1962; Events 1941, Monarch, 1964; Paths of Diplomacy: America's Secretaries of State, Lippincott, 1967; (sole author) Hero of Modern Turkey: Ataturk, Messner, 1972.

WORK IN PROGRESS: The Florida Keys; an adventure novel with a Rio and Acapulco background.

*   *   *

HELLYER, A(rthur) G(eorge) L(ee) 1902-

PERSONAL: Born December 16, 1902, in Bristol, England; son of Arthur Lee and Maggie (Parlett) Hellyer; married Grace Charlotte Bolt, January 18, 1933; children: Edward, Peter, Penelope Susan. Education: Attended Dulwich College. *Politics:* Liberal. *Home and office:* Orchards, Rowfant, near Crawley, Sussex, England.

CAREER: Employed in nursery gardens, Bristol, England, 1921-29; assistant editor of *Amateur Gardening,* London, England, 1929-46; editor of *Gardening Illustrated,* London, England, 1947-56, of *Amateur Gardening,* 1947-67. W. H. & L. Collingridge Ltd., director, 1958-67. *Member:* Royal Horticultural Society (associate of honor), Linnean Society (fellow). *Awards, honors:* Member of the British Empire, Victoria Medal of Honour.

WRITINGS: Simple Rose Growing, edited by Albert James Macself, Collingridge, 1930, 3rd revised edition, Transatlantic, 1955, 5th revised edition, Collingridge, 1961; *Fifty-two Week-end Jobs in My Garden,* Collingridge, 1932; *Practical Gardening for Amateurs,* Collingridge, 1935, 3rd edition, Transatlantic, 1951, 5th edition, Collingridge, 1967; *Your New Garden,* Collingridge, 1937, 3rd revised edition, Transatlantic, 1957; *Your Garden Week by Week,* Collingridge, 1938, 3rd revised edition, Transatlantic, 1950; *War-Time Gardening for Home Needs,* Collingridge, 1939, revised edition published as *Utility Gardening for Home Needs,* Transatlantic, 1950; *Amateur Gardening Pocket Guide,* Collingridge, 1941, new edition, Transatlantic, 1957; *Garden Pest Control,* Collingridge, 1944; *The Amateur Gardener,* Collingridge, 1948, 2nd revised edition, Transatlantic, 1964.

(Reviser) Ernest Markham, *The Large and Small Flowered Clematis,* 3rd edition, Scribner, 1951; (reviser) *Sander's Encyclopaedia of Gardening with Supplement,* 22nd edition, Collingridge, 1952, Translatlantic, 1972; (editor) *The Horticultural Exhibitor's Manual,* Collingridge, 1952, Transatlantic, 1953; *The Encyclopaedia of Plant Portraits,* Transatlantic, 1953; (editor, and author, except as indicated) *The Amateur Gardening Picture Books,* Collingridge, Volume I: *Chrysnthemums,* 1954, Volume II: *Roses,* 1954, revised edition, 1966, Volume III: *Tomatoes,* 1954, Volume IV: *Plant Propagation,* 1955, Volume V: *Herbaceous Borders,* 1955, Volume VI: *Garden Making* (by G.B. Walkden), 1956, Volume VII: *Dahlias,* 1956, Volume VIII: *Indoor Plants* (by A.J. Huxley), 1957, Volume IX: *Pruning* (by J.P. Wood), 1957, Volume X: *Greenhouse Management* (by Wood), 1959; *The Encyclopaedia of Garden Work and Terms,* Transatlantic, 1954; *Flowers in Colour: An Amateur Gardening Encyclopaedia,* British Book Centre, 1955, revised edition, 1959; (editor) *The Gardener's Golden Treasury,* Collingridge, 1956, Transatlantic, 1957; *Amateur Gardening Picture Book of Gardens,* Collingridge, 1956, Transatlantic, 1957; *Garden Pests and Diseases: A Guide to Recognition and Control,* Collingridge, 1956; *English Gardens Open to the Public,* Country Life, 1956, Transatlantic, 1957; (editor) *Garden Work for the Week,* Collingridge, 1956, Transatlantic, 1957; (compiler) *Diary and Horticultural Directory,* Collingridge, 1957; *Popular Encyclopaedia of Flowering Plants: Description and Cultivation of the Best Plants for Garden and Greenhouse,* Collingridge, 1957, Transatlantic, 1958; (editor) *Amateur Gardening Spring Guide,* Collingridge, 1957; *Garden Plants in Colour: An Amateur Gardening Encyclopaedia,* Collingridge, 1958, British Book Centre, 1959; (reviser) Albert James Macself, *The Amateur's Greenhouse,* Transatlantic, 1960; *The Treasury of Flowers and Plants in Colour* (contains *Flowers in Colour* and *Garden Plants in Colour*), Collingridge, 1961, Transatlantic, 1962; (editor) *An Amateur Gardening Book of Garden Plans and Designs,* Collingridge, 1961, Transatlantic, 1962; (compiler) *Photo Album of Garden Plants,* Collingridge, 1961, Transatlantic, 1962; *Shrubs in Colour,* Collingridge, 1965, published in America as *Shrubs in Color: An Amateur Gardening Encyclopedia,* Doubleday, 1967; *Starting with Roses,* Collingridge, 1966; (editor)

Amateur Gardening Planter's Guide, Collingridge, 1966; *Find Out About Gardening,* Collingridge, 1967.

Gardens to Visit in Britain, Paul Hamlyn, 1970, International Publications Service, 1970; *Your Lawn,* Paul Hamlyn, 1970, Transatlantic, 1972; *Arthur Hellyer's Gardening Cards,* Paul Hamlyn, 1970; *Carter's Book for Gardeners,* Heinemann, 1970.

Gardening correspondent, *Country Life, Financial Times;* editor, *Amateur Gardening Annual,* Collingridge, 1948-49, 1958-64.

WORK IN PROGRESS: The ABC of Gardening.

AVOCATIONAL INTERESTS: Motoring, travel.

*   *   *

HELM, P(eter) J(ames) 1916-

PERSONAL: Born June 16, 1916, in Waterfoot, Lancashire, England; son of James Edgar (a doctor) and Marjorie (Ashworth) Helm; married October 7, 1942 (wife's name, Joan Ellen); children: Ann. *Education:* Attended St. Bees School; Magdalene College, Cambridge, B.A., 1938, M.A., 1946. *Home:* The Croft, Bradford-on-Tone, Taunton, Somerset, England. *Agent:* John Johnson, 10 Suffield House, 79 Davies St., London, England. *Office:* Queen's College, Taunton, Somerset, England.

CAREER: Queen's College, Taunton, Somerset, England, senior history master, 1946—, second master, 1952—.

WRITINGS: Dead Men's Fingers, John Long, 1960, published in America as *A Walk into Murder,* Scribner, 1961; *History of Europe, 1450-1660,* G. Bell, 1961, Ungar, 1964; *Death Has a Thousand Entrances* (Mystery Book Guild selection), John Long, 1962; *Alfred the Great,* R. Hale, 1963, Crowell, 1965; *Modern British History, 1815-1964,* G. Bell, 1965; *The Man with No Bones,* John Long, 1966; *Jeffreys,* R. Hale, 1966, published in America as *Jeffreys: A New Portrait of England's Hanging Judge,* Crowell, 1967; *England Under the Yorkists and Tudors 1471-1603,* G. Bell, 1968, Humanities, 1969; *Discovering Prehistoric England,* R. Hale, 1971. Contributor to *Time and Tide, Outposts, Archaeological Journal,* and other periodicals.

WORK IN PROGRESS: John Dee: His Life and Times.

AVOCATIONAL INTERESTS: Travel, painting, poetry.

BIOGRAPHICAL/CRITICAL SOURCES: Times Literary Supplement, January 26, 1967; *Virginia Quarterly Review,* autumn, 1967.

*   *   *

HELMERICKS, Constance Chittenden 1918-

PERSONAL: Born January 4, 1918, in Binghamton, N.Y.; daughter of Arthur Smith (a physician and surgeon) and Winifred (Browning) Chittenden; married Harmon Helmericks, April 27, 1941 (divorced, 1956); married Gilbert Doyle Bertie Kitchner Barrett, July 2, 1969 (divorced, February 17, 1970); children: (first marriage) Constance Jean, Carol Ann. *Education:* University of Arizona, B.A., 1954. *Politics:* Republican. *Religion:* Protestant. *Home:* 2648 East 6th St., Tucson, Ariz. 85716.

CAREER: Writer and lecturer, mainly on Alaska, Canada, and Mexico. Made seven U.S. lecture tours; also appeared on series of three network television shows with own Alaskan films. University of Arizona, Bureau of Business and Public Research, field researcher, 1962. *Member:* Arctic Institute of North America (charter), Associated Press Clubs of America.

WRITINGS: We Live in Alaska, Little, Brown, 1944; *Hunting in North America,* Stackpole, 1957; *Down the*

Wild River North, Little, Brown, 1968; *Australian Adventure,* Prentice-Hall, 1971.

With Harmon (Bud) Helmericks; all published by Little, Brown: *We Live in the Arctic,* 1947, *Our Summer with the Eskimos,* 1948, *Our Alaskan Winter,* 1949, *The Flight of the Arctic Tern,* 1952.

Anthologized in *Better Reading,* Book two, Science Research Associates, 1962, *Literature of Adventure* and *Literature of Achievement,* Ginn. Also contributor to *New American Oxford Encyclopedia* and *New Horizons,* Book two, 1958.

WORK IN PROGRESS: Films based on travels.

SIDELIGHTS: Books have been published in ten foreign countries.

BIOGRAPHICAL/CRITICAL SOURCES: Life, March 24, 1947, August 31, 1953; *Detroit News,* April 2, 1972.

* * *

HENDERSON, Dion (Winslow) 1921-

PERSONAL: Born December 14, 1921, in Dassel, Minn.; son of Charles and Myrtle (Butler) Henderson; married Beth von Kleist, April 5, 1941; children: Amy, Jane, Bruce, Charles. *Home:* Madera Circle, Elm Grove, Wis. *Agent:* Harold Matson, Inc., 22 East 40th St., New York, N.Y. 10016. *Office:* Associated Press, 922 North Fourth St., Journal Sq., Milwaukee, Wis. 53208.

CAREER: Daily News, Fort Atkinson, Wis., city editor, 1941-42; Associated Press, writer and news supervisor, 1942-68, bureau chief in Milwaukee, 1968—.

WRITINGS: Algonquin: The Story of a Great Dog (novel), Holt, 1953; *The Last One* (novel), Holt, 1956; *Here Is Your Hobby: Hunting,* Putnam, 1963; *On the Mountain* (novel), McKay, 1969; *The Wolf of Thunder Mountain and Other Stories,* Western Publishing, 1970. Contributor of more than one hundred short stories to *Saturday Evening Post, Collier's, Argosy, Boys' Life, Playboy,* and other magazines; stories reprinted in anthologies and textbooks.

WORK IN PROGRESS: A novel based on Coupe de Foudre stories that appeared in national magazines in last decade.

SIDELIGHTS: Henderson's writings have been translated into eight foreign languages. *Avocational interests:* Ecology, sporting dogs, arts of the chase.

* * *

HENKEL, Barbara Osborn 1921-
(Barbara M. Osborn)

PERSONAL: Born March 14, 1921, in Oakland, Calif.; daughter of Russell Jerome (a deputy coroner) and Ruth (Watson) Monroe; married Robert W. Osborn, 1941 (divorced); married William H. Henkel, September 14, 1968; children: (first marriage) Robert S., Patricia J. Osborn McClean. *Education:* University of California at Los Angeles, B.S. in Nursing, 1943, Ed.D., 1960; California State College at Los Angeles, M.A., 1956. *Politics:* Republican. *Religion:* Protestant. *Home:* 236 North Windsor Blvd., Los Angeles, Calif. 90004. *Office:* California State College at Los Angeles, 5151 State College Dr., Los Angeles, Calif. 90032.

CAREER: Head nurse and assistant director of nursing at hospitals in San Francisco, Calif., 1943-47; National Foundation, foster home work in San Francisco, Calif., 1948-50; California Physician's Service, Los Angeles, Calif., supervisor, 1950-52; American National Red Cross, director of chapter nursing services, Pasadena, Calif., 1952-55; East Los Angeles College, Los Angeles, Calif., instructor in nursing, 1955-56; California State

College at Los Angeles (formerly Los Angeles State College), 1956—, began as associate professor, became professor of health education. *Member:* American Public Health Association, American School Health Association (fellow), California Association for Health, Physical Education and Recreation, Southern California Public Health Association.

WRITINGS: (Under name Barbara M. Osborn) *Introduction to Community Health,* Allyn & Bacon, 1964, 2nd edition (under name Barbara Osborn Henkel) published as *Community Health,* 1970; (under name Barbara M. Osborn, with Richard K. Means, Jack Smolensky, and James Sawrey) *Foundations of Health Science,* Allyn & Bacon, 1968, 2nd edition (under name Barbara Osborn Henkel), 1971. Writer of health education pamphlets.

WORK IN PROGRESS: Determination of Incidence of Pulmonary Dysfunction Among College Students: A Research Study.

* * *

HENNESSY, Jossleyn (Michael Stephen Philip) 1903-

PERSONAL: Born 1903, in London, England; son of Philip Mather (a banker) and Ida (Countess Seilern) Hennessy; married October 26, 1932 (wife's maiden name Noel-Paton); children: Flavian (deceased), Armyn, Aminta. *Education:* Attended Charterhouse School; New College, Oxford, B.A. (honors), 1924, diploma in economics (with distinction), 1925, M.A., 1935. *Home:* 95 Linden Gardens, London W2 4EX, England.

CAREER: International Chamber of Commerce, Paris, France, founding editor of journal, 1928-31; successively Paris correspondent of Reuters News Agency and chief Paris correspondent of *News Chronicle,* London, England, 1931-37; Government of India, director of public relations, 1937-45, inaugurating India Information Services in U.S. and Canada, 1942-45; *Sunday Times,* London, England, chief correspondent in India and Pakistan, 1946-48; *Eastern Economist,* New Delhi, India, columnist, 1948-64, editor-in-chief for Europe, 1953—. Broadcaster in India, United States, France, and England. *Member:* British Institute of Journalists (fellow), Bengal Club (Calcutta); Turf Club, Beefsteak Club, and Coningsby Club (all London). *Awards, honors:* Chevalier of French Legion of Honor for services to Franco-British friendship, 1935.

WRITINGS: India and Pakistan in World Politics, King-Hall, 1950; *India, Democracy and Education,* Luzac, 1955; *Socialism Tomorrow,* Eastern Economist Press, 1956; *Britain in Europe: Viewpoint for Industry,* Federal Research Trust, 1958; *The European Free Trade Area,* Westminster Chamber of Commerce, 1959; *The European Common Market: What Will It Mean to You?,* Westminster Chamber of Commerce, 1959; *The Outer Seven: What Will It Mean to You?,* Westminster Chamber of Commerce, 1959; (with Vera Lutz and Giuseppe Scimone) *Economic "Miracles": Studies in the Resurgence of the French, German, and Italian Economies Since the Second World War,* Deutsch, 1964, Transatlantic, 1965; (author of bibliography) David Graham Hutton, *Sourcebook on Restrictive Practices in Britain,* Institute of Economic Affairs, 1966; (with Frank Knox) *Restrictive Practices in the Building Industry,* Institute of Economic Affairs, 1966; (with Frank Paish) *Policy for Incomes?* Economic Affairs, Part I: *The Limits of Income Policies* (by Paish), 1964, Part II: *Income Policies in Europe* (by Hennessy), 1964, 4th edition, 1968; (contributor) Rupert Wilkinson, editor, *Governing Elites: Studies in Training and Selection,* Oxford University Press, 1969.

Contributor to *Encyclopaedia Britannica, Encyclopedia Americana;* contributor to periodicals, including *Encoun-*

ter, Observer, Economist, Spectator, Statist, New Society, International Affairs, Times (London).

WORK IN PROGRESS: Autobiography in three parts, entitled *The Amazing Ancestors, The Amazing Marriage,* and *The Amazing Ego.*

SIDELIGHTS: Hennessy covered the Spanish Civil War for *News Chronicle.* Franco disapproved of Hennessy's dispatches and had his picture posted with a reward offered for his capture. As *Sunday Times* correspondent in India, he was twice ambushed by tribesmen while accompanying Nehru on the northwest frontier.

*   *   *

HENRY, Bessie Walker   1921-
(Bessie Walker)

PERSONAL: Born June 17, 1921, in Leeds, England; daughter of Rowland and Martha Ann (Naylor) Walker; married Denis Valentine Henry (a schoolmaster), February 11, 1956; children: Patrick Denis, Jessica Ellen, Martha Olive. *Education:* University of Manchester, B.A. (first class honors), 1942, M.A., 1947. *Home:* 9 White Rd., Blackburn, Lancashire, England.

CAREER: University of Manchester, Manchester, England, lecturer in classics, 1945-47; University of Sheffield, Sheffield, England, lecturer in education, 1954-57.

WRITINGS: (Under name Bessie Walker) *The Annals of Tacitus: A Study in the Writing of History,* Barnes & Noble, 1952, 2nd edition, Manchester University Press, 1960. Regular reviewer for *Times Educational Supplement* and *Classical Philology;* contributor to *Greece and Rome.*

WORK IN PROGRESS: Collaborating with husband, Denis Henry, on studies of the dramas of Seneca.

*   *   *

HENSHALL, A(udrey) S(hore)   1927-

PERSONAL: Born April 11, 1927, in Oldham, Lancashire, England; daughter of Edward and Marjory A. Shore. *Education:* Attended Hulme Grammar School for Girls, Oldham, Lancashire, England, 1937-38, and Howell's School, Denbigh, North Wales, 1938-45; University of Edinburgh, student, 1945-50, M.A. (honors in history), 1949. *Religion:* Anglican. *Office:* National Museum of Antiquities, Queen St., Edinburgh, Scotland.

CAREER: National Museum of Antiquities, Edinburgh, Scotland, research assistant, 1951-56, assistant keeper, 1956-70; Society of Antiquaries of Scotland, Edinburgh, assistant secretary, 1970—. *Member:* Society of Antiquaries of London, Society of Antiquaries of Scotland, Prehistoric Society.

WRITINGS: (With others) *The Dungiven Costume,* Ulster Journal of Archaeology, 1961; *Chambered Tombs of Scotland,* Volume I, Edinburgh University Press, 1963, volume 2, Aldine, 1972. Contributor of papers to *Proceedings* of the Society of Antiquaries of Scotland; occasional contributor to other archaeological journals.

WORK IN PROGRESS: Volume II of *Chambered Tombs of Scotland.*

AVOCATIONAL INTERESTS: Prehistoric and early European textiles, history of architecture (especially medieval churches), gardening, color photography, embroidery.

*   *   *

HERBERT, Robert L(ouis)   1929-

PERSONAL: Born April 21, 1929, in Worcester, Mass.; son of John Newman (a drawbridge operator) and Rosalia (Harr) Herbert; married Eugenia Warren (an au-

thor), June 6, 1953; children: Timothy, Rosemary, Catherine. *Education:* Wesleyan University, Middleton, Conn., B.A., 1951; University of Paris, graduate study, 1951-52; Yale University, M.A., 1954, Ph.D., 1957. *Politics:* Socialist. *Home:* Beacon Rd., Bethany, Conn. 06525. *Office:* Department of History of Art, Yale University, 56 High St., New Haven, Conn. 06520.

CAREER: Yale University, New Haven, Conn., instructor, 1956-60, assistant professor, 1960-63, associate professor, 1963-67, professor of history of art, 1967—, chairman of the department, 1965-68. Organizer of art exhibitions for museums and other public institutions. *Awards, honors:* American Council of Learned Societies grant-in-aid, 1961.

WRITINGS: Essay on Drawing in Yale University School of Fine Arts, Yale University, c.1960; *Barbizon Revisited: Essay and Catalogue,* Clarke & Way, 1962; *Seurat's Drawings,* Shorewood, 1963; (editor and author of introduction) *The Art Criticism of John Ruskin,* Doubleday-Anchor, 1964; (editor) *Modern Artists on Art: Ten Unabridged Essays,* Prentice-Hall, 1965; (editor with W.E. Mitchell) *Neo-Impressionists and Nabis in the Collection of Arthur G. Altschul,* Yale University Art Gallery, 1965; *Neo-Impressionism,* Solomon R. Guggenheim Museum, 1968; (contributor) Jean Sutter, editor, *The Neo-Impressionists,* New York Graphic Society, 1970; *David's Brutus,* Penguin, 1972. Contributor of about thirty articles to scholarly journals.

WORK IN PROGRESS: Jean-Francois Millet, a monograph.

*   *   *

HERNDON, Booton   1915-

PERSONAL: Born December 9, 1915, in Charlottesville, Va.; son of Booton and Bertie Shirley (Wood) Herndon; married Bernadette Ann Dorrity, August 5, 1949; children: Booton III, John, Sue. *Education:* Attended Woodberry Forest School, University of Missouri, and University of Virginia. *Politics:* Democrat. *Home:* 2422 Jefferson Park Ave., Charlottesville, Va. 22903. *Agent:* Sterling Lord, 660 Madison Ave., New York, N.Y. 10021.

CAREER: Reporter and editor for newspapers in New Orleans, La., 1938-42; free-lance writer, 1945—. Public relations consultant, U.S. Interstate Commerce Commission, 1961. *Military service:* U.S. Army, World War II; received five battle stars, invasion arrowhead. *Member:* Society of Magazine Writers, Kappa Sigma, Farmington Country Club.

WRITINGS: Praised and Damned: The Story of Fulton Lewis, Jr., edited by Gordon Carroll, Duell, Sloan & Pearce, 1951, reissued as *Stormy Petrel: The Story of Fulton Lewis, Jr.,* Human Events, 1958; *Bergdorf's on the Plaza: The Story of Bergdorf Goodman and a Half-Century of American Fashion,* Knopf, 1956; *Young Men Can Change the World,* McGraw, 1960, revised edition, 1965; *The Seventh Day: The Story of the Seventh-Day Adventists,* McGraw, 1960; (with Violeta C. Kokenes) *On Wings of Faith,* Random House, 1960; *Football's Greatest Quarterbacks,* Bartholomew House, 1961; (with William H. Tunner) *Over the Hump,* Meredith, 1964; *The Sweetest Music This Side of Heaven: The Guy Lombardo Story,* McGraw, 1964; (with Victor F. Obeck) *How to Exercise Without Moving a Muscle,* Geis, 1964; (editor) *The Humor of J.F.K.,* Gold Medal Books, 1965; *The Unlikeliest Hero: The Story of Desmond T. Doss, Conscientious Objector, Who Won His Nation's Highest Military Honor,* Pacific Press Publishing Association, 1967; (editor) *Rickenbacker,* Prentice-Hall, 1967; *Ford: An Unconventional Biography of the Two Henry Fords and Their Times,* Weybright, 1969; *The Great Land,* Weybright, 1971. Ghost writer of other books. Contributor of several hundred articles and short stories to national magazines.

BIOGRAPHICAL/CRITICAL SOURCES: *Newsday,* October 11, 1969; *New York Times Book Review,* November 16, 1969; *Times Literary Supplement,* April 23, 1970; *Best Sellers,* June 15, 1971.

* * *

HERNTON, Calvin C(oolidge) 1932-

PERSONAL: Born April 28, 1932, in Chattanooga, Tenn.; son of Magnolia Jackson; married Mildred Webster, May 28, 1958; children: Antone. *Education:* Talladega College, B.A., 1954; Fisk University, M.A., 1956; attended Columbia University, 1961. *Office:* Department of Afro-American Studies, Oberlin College, Oberlin, Ohio 44074.

CAREER: Writer. Benedick College, Columbia, S.C., instructor in history and sociology, 1957-58; Edward Waters College, Jacksonville, Fla., instructor in sociology, 1958-59; Alabama A. & M. College, Normal, instructor in social sciences, 1959-60; Southern University, Baton Rouge, La., instructor in sociology, 1960-61; New York State Department of Welfare, New York, social worker, 1961-62; now faculty member at Oberlin College, Oberlin, Ohio.

WRITINGS: *The Coming of Chronos to the House of Nightsong: An Epical Narrative of the South* (poetry), Interim Books, 1963; *Sex and Racism in America,* Doubleday, 1965, new edition published in England as *Sex and Racism,* Deutsch, 1969; *White Papers for White Americans,* Doubleday, 1966; *Coming Together: Black Power, White Hatred, and Sexual Hangups,* Random House, 1971. Anthologized in *Beyond the Blues,* edited by Rosey E. Pool, Hand & Flower Press, 1962, and in other publications. Author of plays. Contributor to *Negro Digest, Freedomways,* and other periodicals.

SIDELIGHTS: In a review of *White Papers for White Americans,* Brooks Johnson writes: "It is virtually impossible to bring something new to the area of race, but, infrequently, the very gifted see and are able to express the centuried problems with something that approaches creativity because of the sensitivity and forcefulness with which they relate the old truths. Calvin C. Hernton's work is an example of such a process. He has the ability to tell, narrate, and explain, which he does at varying tempos and moods—in the manner of a good, highly polished jazz group. I don't mean to imply that his technique is slick—it isn't. Mr. Hernton is smooth because he is a man who knows his subject matter and has mastered the delicate balance between what observation and honesty dictate and what natural talent makes possible. The product in this case is a book that knows no time."

BIOGRAPHICAL/CRITICAL SOURCES: *Saturday Review,* February 12, 1966; *Negro Digest,* May, 1967.

* * *

HERRMANNS, Ralph 1933-

PERSONAL: Born January 31, 1933, in Berlin, Germany; now Swedish citizen; son of Otto (a chief justice) and Edith (Jacoby) Herrmanns. *Education:* University of Uppsala, B.A., 1953. *Religion:* Jewish. *Home:* Herkulesgatan 4, Stockholm C, Sweden. *Office:* Ahlen & Akerlunds Foerlag (The Bonnier Magazine Group), Sveavaegen 53, Stockholm Va., Sweden.

CAREER: Journalist for Swedish newspapers, and foreign correspondent, 1953-1962; Ediciones Albon Medellin, Colombia (affiliate of The Bonnier Group, Stockholm), editor-in-chief and publisher, 1962-64; Ahlen & Akerlunds Foerlag (The Bonnier Magazine Group), Stockholm, Sweden, editor-in-chief, 1964—. *Military service:* Royal

Swedish Horse Guards Reserve. *Member:* Publicistklubben, Svenska Journalistfoerbundet (both Stockholm).

WRITINGS: *Lee Han, Hing och draken,* Bonniers, 1961, translation by Annabelle Macmillan published as *Lee Lan Flies the Dragon Kite,* Harcourt, 1963; *Barnen vid Nordpolen,* Bonniers, 1963, translation by Annabelle Macmillan published as *Children of the North Pole,* Harcourt, 1964; *Bilen Julia,* Bonniers, 1963, translation by Annabelle Macmillan published as *Our Car Julia,* Harcourt, 1964; *Pojken och folden,* Bonniers, 1964, translation by Joan Tate published as *River Boy: Adventure on the Amazon,* Harcourt, 1965; *Flickan som hade braatom,* Bonniers, 1967. Contributor to journals in Sweden.

WORK IN PROGRESS: *May It Rain When She Swims,* a book on Central America; a novel involving conflicts of a Swedish community in Latin America.

SIDELIGHTS: *Lee Lan Flies the Dragon Kite* has been published in nine languages and was filmed by Stephen Bosutow Productions. *Avocational interests:* Modern paintings, antique Chinese bronzes, dogs and horses.

* * *

HERSEY, Jean 1902-

PERSONAL: Born September 29, 1902; daughter of John Jay and Mary (Mattocks) McKelvey; married Robert Wilson Hersey, December 5, 1924; children: Joan Carr, Robert Huntington, Timothy Wilson. *Education:* Attended Brearley School. *Religion:* New Thought. *Home address:* Box 1452, Tryon, N.C. 28782. *Agent:* McIntosh & Otis, 18 East 41st St., New York, N.Y. 10017.

MEMBER: Tryon Garden Club. *Awards, honors:* Asta award for best garden writing of the year, 1962.

WRITINGS: *I Like Gardening,* Hale, Cushman & Flint, 1941; *Halfway to Heaven: Guatemala Holiday,* Prentice-Hall, 1947; *Garden in Your Window,* Prentice-Hall, 1949; *Carefree Gardening: New and Easier Ways to Have an Abundance of Flowers and Vegetables,* Van Nostrand, 1961; *Wild Flowers to Know and Grow,* Van Nostrand, 1964; *A Sense of Seasons,* Dodd, 1964; *A Woman's Day Book of House Plants,* Simon & Schuster, 1965; *The Shape of a Year,* Scribner, 1967; (with husband, Robert Hersey) *These Rich Years: A Journal of Retirement,* Scribner, 1969; (with R. Hersey) *Cooking with Herbs,* Scribner, 1972; (with R. Hersey) *Growing Herbs Indoors,* Scribner, 1972; (with R. Hersey) *Change in the Wind,* Scribner, 1972.

Writing for *Woman's Day* includes series of booklet-inserts on wild flowers, houseplants, flowering shrubs, and trees, and other subjects, each with two hundred color paintings, introductory article, and indentifications. Contributor of several hundred other articles to *House and Garden, Flower Grower, House Beautiful,* and other magazines.

WORK IN PROGRESS: *Change in the Wind.*

AVOCATIONAL INTERESTS: Traveling in Europe, particularly Switzerland; camping in a tent trailer in the North Carolina mountains and on the southern beaches; water color painting.

* * *

HERTSENS, Marcel 1918-

PERSONAL: Born March 29, 1918, in East Finchley, England; son of Georges and Ghislaine (Jordens) Hertsens. *Education:* Two years of study in philosophy, four in theology. *Home:* 167, rue Leon Theodor, Brussels, Belgium.

CAREER: Ordained Roman Catholic priest, July 27, 1942; Institut Saint-Pierre, Brussels, Belgium, professor, 22 years.

WRITINGS: Seigneur, ton serviteur ecoute (book of meditations), Oeuvre des Tracts (Brussels), 1961 published in America as *Lord, Your Servant Listens,* Newman, 1964; *Tresors mystiques de l'Inde: Les Grandes Textes de l'hindouisme et du bouddhisme,* Editions du Centurion (Paris), 1968; (with Marie Ina Bergeron) *Sagesse eternelle de la Chine: Pensees et Preceptes,* Editions du Centurion, 1970. Contributor to *Lumen Vitae* and *Educatrices Paroisiales.*

WORK IN PROGRESS: Preparing a book "to teach young people that they are able to live in the Lord's presence, to listen to His Word, to know His still young and actual message and to follow it with generosity."

SIDELIGHTS: Seigneur, ton serviteur ecoute has been translated into over fifteen languages, including Portuguese, Japanese, Sinhalese, Hindi, and Tamil.

*   *   *

HERTZMAN, Lewis   1927-

PERSONAL: Born July 7, 1927, in Toronto, Ontario, Canada; son of Harry and Pauline (Munis) Hertzman. *Education:* University of Toronto, B.A. (first class honors), 1949; Harvard University, A.M., 1950, Ph.D., 1955. *Office:* Department of History, York University, Downsview 463, Ontario, Canada.

CAREER: Princeton University, Princeton, N.J., instructor in history, 1956-59; University of Alberta, Edmonton, Canada, assistant professor, 1959-63, associate professor of history, 1963-65; York University, Toronto, Ontario, associate professor, 1965-68, professor of history, 1968—, chairman of the department, 1967-70. *Member:* Canadian Historical Association, American Historical Association, Historical Association (Great Britain), Societe d'Histoire Moderne, Comite International des Sciences Historiques, Racing Club of France, Harvard Club (New York).

WRITINGS: DNVP: Right-Wing Opposition in the Weimar Republic, 1918-1924, University of Nebraska Press, 1963; (with others) *Alliances and Illusions: Canada and the NATO-NORAD Question,* M.G. Hurtig, 1969. Contributor of articles to *Queen's Quarterly, Dalhousie Review, International Review of Social History, Journal of Modern History,* and other journals; contributor to newspapers, radio, and television.

SIDELIGHTS: Hertzman is fluent in German and French and does research in French and German libraries and archives; he has a working knowledge of Italian, Spanish, Russian, and other languages.

BIOGRAPHICAL/CRITICAL   SOURCES: Canadian Forum, December, 1969.

*   *   *

HERVEY, Michael   1920-

PERSONAL: Born October 11, 1920, in London, England; settled in Australia, 1951; married Lilyan Stella (a secretary), October 27, 1951; children: Gordon Selwyn. *Education:* Attended Coopers Foundation College, London, England. *Home:* 5 Dick St., Henley, New South Wales, Ausralia.

CAREER: Abandoned commercial art career at age of nineteen and went to sea as ship's interpreter; Everybody's Publications Ltd., London, England, editor, four years; *Observer,* London, England, drama critic, three years; British War Office, London, England, editorial assistant, secret publications department, two years; author of "Smoke Rings," syndicated column, 1953—. Hampton Press, Henley, New South Wales, Australia, managing director, twenty years. Justice of the peace, nineteen years. *Member:* Australian Journalist Association (acting president, authors and artists section), Institute of Journalists

(London), Writers Guild of England (vice-president), Centro Studi e Scambi Internationali. *Awards, honors:* Awarded B.E.M. by Queen Elizabeth II for services to literature.

WRITINGS: Save Your Pity, Mitre Press, 1943; (with Preston Yorke) *The Astounding Crime,* Everybody's Books, 1943; *Travel the Hard Way: Michael Hervey's Rough and Tough Autobiographical Story of the Sea,* Mitre Press, 1944; *Dames Spell Trouble,* Bear Hudson, 1944; *Death Tolls the Bell,* Mitre Press, 1944; *Imperfect Alibi,* Mitre Press, 1944; *Murder at the Movies,* Mitre Press, 1944; *Murder by Installments,* War Facts Press, 1944; *Murder Thy Neighbor,* Mitre Press, 1944; *No Crime Like the Present,* Mitre Press, 1944; *The Queer Looking Box,* Everybody's Books, 1944; (with Sidney Denham and Harold Kelly) *She Loves Me,* Fudge & Co., 1944; *The Silver Death,* Mitre Press, 1944; *Thrilling Tales,* Gulliver Books, 1944; *Laughter in the Ranks,* Alliance Press, 1945; (editor) *The Book of Master Crimes: Amazing True Stories of the World's Most Notorious Crimes,* Mitre Press, 1945; *Accent on Romance,* Pictorial Art, 1945; *The Book of Master Crimes,* Mitre Press, 1945; *Death at My Heels, and Other Short Stories,* Mitre Press, 1945; *The Devil and Miss Thrace, and Other Stories,* Pan Books, 1945; *Exploits That Amazed the World,* Gulliver Books, 1945; *Gold-Digger, and Fourteen Other Short Stories,* Alliance Press, 1945; *Horror Medley,* Hampton Press, 1945; *Murder Medley,* Peal, Ashdown & Hart, 1945; *No More Love,* Hampton Press, 1945; *Wide Boy!,* Hampton Press, 1945; *Wide Girl,* Hampton Press, 1945; *Twisted Tales,* Alliance Press, c.1945; *Toughs Afloat: Sequel to "Travel the Hard Way,"* Alliance Press, 1946; *Corpse Parade,* Hampton Press, 1946; *Creeps Medley,* Hampton Press, 1946; *Dumb Witness [and] The Other Side of the Curtain,* M.B. Books, 1946; *G Is for Ghoul!,* Hampton Press, 1946; *Ghost Voice,* Hampton Press, 1946; *Stranger Than Fiction,* Gulliver Books, 1946; *Suspicion,* Hampton Press, 1946; *Toughs Ashore: A Sequel to "Travel the Hard Way,"* Alliance Press, 1947; *The Case of the Missing Hand [and] Initiation to Murder,* Hampton Press, 1947; *Brooklyn Angel,* Hamilton & Co., 1947; *The Body in the Drum Mystery,* Modern Publishing Co., 1951; *No Time for Tears,* Elek, 1963; *Strange Happenings,* Ace Books, 1969; *They Walk by Night,* Ace Books, 1969; *Fraternity of the Weird,* Ace Books, 1969; *UFOs over the Southern Hemisphere,* Horwitz, 1969; *Book of Amazing Records and Achievements,* Ace Books, 1970.

Plays: *No Peace for the Living* (three-act; produced in London), Hampton Press, 1947; *Ours Is a Nice House* (one-act), Hampton Press, 1947; *Pro Bono Publico* (one-act), Hampton Press, 1947; *Room Without a View* (one-act), Hampton Press, 1947; *Shipwreck* (one-act), Hampton Press, 1947; *Trapped* (one-act), Hampton Press, 1947; *Walls Have Mouths* (one-act), Hampton Press, 1947; *The Original Mr. Fix-it?* (one-act), Hampton Press, 1949; *Running Commentary* (one-act), Hampton Press, 1949; *A Voice in the Wilderness* (one-act), Hampton Press, 1949; *Wanted—Dead or Alive* (comedy), Hampton Press, 1949; *Let's Be Civilised* (one-act), Leonard's Plays, 1952. Also author of "The Crime of Your Life," produced in London.

Film scripts include "Operation Countdown." Television plays include "Happy Birthday," "Contract," "Errant Husband," and others. Short stories have been broadcast in England, Australia, New Zealand, Holland, Germany, Malta, and Scandinavia. Editor, *Examinor* (Sydney); film critic, *The Australian* (daily). Contributor to more than 300 publications.

SIDELIGHTS: Hervey is listed in the *Guinness Book of Records* as the world's most prolific writer of short stories (3,500).

HESELTINE, Nigel 1916-

PERSONAL: Born July 3, 1916, in London, England; son of Philip Arnold and Maria Lucia (Shannon) Heseltine. Education: Attended Shrewsbury School and Royal Military College, Sandhurst; University of London, L.S.E., B.Sc. (honors); University of Dublin, M.A. Religion: Catholic. Address: B.P. 3658, Tananarive, Madagascar.

CAREER: Farmer in Ireland and Tanganyika, 1937-49; United Nations Food and Agriculture Organization, 1950-65, agricultural adviser in Congo, Nigeria, Cameroun, and Ivory Coast, later agricultural adviser to Office of the President of Republic of Madagascar, 1961-65; rural development adviser to President of Madagascar, 1965-68; Office of National Development and Planning, Zambia, under-secretary, 1968-72. Lecturer in United States, 1960, under auspices of (then) Senator John F. Kennedy and African American Institute; lecturer in Italy, Israel, Madagascar, and a number of countries in Africa. Member: International African Institute, International Institute of Agricultural Economics, Royal Geographical Society (fellow).

WRITINGS: Scarred Background: A Journey Through Albania, Dickson, 1938; Violent Rain: A Poem, Latin Press, 1938; The Four-Walled Dream (poems), Fortune Press, 1941; (translator) Dafydd, ap Gwilym, Selected Poems, Cuala Press (Dublin), 1944, reissued as Twenty-five Poems, Piers Press, 1968; Tales of the Squirearchy: Short Stories, Druid Press, 1946; The Mysterious Pregnancy, Gollancz, 1953, published in American as Inconstant Lady, Lippincott, 1954; From Lybian Sands to Chad, Museum Press, 1959; Remaking Africa, Museum Press, 1961; Madagascar, Praeger, 1971. Contributor to New Writing, Irish Times, Studii Catholici, World Crops, and other periodicals.

*   *   *

HEUSCHER, Julius E(rnst) 1918-

PERSONAL: Born March 19, 1918, in Zurich, Switzerland; son of John and Anna (Cramer) Heuscher; married Ruth B. Isler (a physician), May 4, 1946; children: Enno Francis, Dominic Julius. Education: Attended University of Lausanne, 1937-38, 1945-46, and Zurich University, 1938-40; University of California, M.D., 1944; Basel University, F.M.H. in Psychiatry, 1949. Home: 18500 Hillview Dr., Monte Sereno, Calif. 95030. Office: 491 North Santa Cruz Ave., Los Gatos, Calif. 95030.

CAREER: Psychiatrist in private practice, 1950—. University of California, Berkeley, clinical instructor in psychiatry; assistant clinical professor, Stanford University Medical School. Member: American Medical Association, American Psychiatric Association (fellow), American Ontoanalytic Association, Society for Phenomenology and Existential Psychotherapy (chairman, 1964).

WRITINGS: A Psychiatric Study of Fairy Tales: Their Origin, Meaning, and Usefulness, C.C Thomas, 1963. Contributor of more than fifty articles and papers to professional journals in United States and Europe.

WORK IN PROGRESS: A Contribution to the Phenomenology of Thinking; various articles on existential psychiatry, and on the meaning and usefulness of fairy tales and myths.

*   *   *

HEWLETT, Richard Greening 1923-

PERSONAL: Born February 12, 1923, in Toledo, Ohio; son of Timothy Y. (an architect) and Gertrude (Greening) Hewlett; married Marilyn E. Nesper, September 6, 1946. Education: Attended Dartmouth College, 1941-43, Bowdoin College, 1943-44; University of Chicago, M.A., 1948, Ph.D., 1952. Religion: Episcopalian. Home: 7909 Deepwell Dr., Bethesda, Md. 20034. Office: U.S. Atomic Energy Commission, Washington, D.C. 20545.

CAREER: U.S. Air Force, Washington, D.C., intelligence specialist, 1951-52; U.S. Atomic Energy Commission, Washington, D.C., reports analyst, 1952-57, chief historian, 1957—. Member of U.S. delegation, United Nations International Conference on Peaceful Uses of Atomic Energy, Geneva, Switzerland, 1958. Military service: U.S. Army Air Forces, 1943-46. Member: American Historical Association, Organization of American Historians, American Nuclear Society (Washington, D.C. section), Society for the History of Technology.

WRITINGS: (With Oscar E. Anderson, Jr.) A History of the U.S. Atomic Energy Commission, Pennsylvania State University Press, Volume I: The New World, 1939-1946, 1962, Volume II: Atomic Shield, 1947-1952, 1969; (contributor) M. Kranzberg and Carroll W. Pursell, Jr., editors, Technology in Western Civilization, Volume II, Oxford University Press, 1967.

WORK IN PROGRESS: A History of Nuclear Power in the U.S. Navy.

*   *   *

HEYM, Stefan 1913-

PERSONAL: Born April 10, 1913, in Chemnitz, Germany; son of Daniel and Else (Primo) Flieg; married Gertrude Peltyn, March 4, 1944 (died January, 1969); married Inge Hohn (a dramaturgist for DEFA Films), 1971. Education: Attended University of Berlin; University of Chicago, M.A., 1935. Home: Rabin-dranath-Tagore-St. 9, Berlin-Gruenau, German Democratic Republic. Agent: Laurence Pollinger Ltd., 18 Maddox St., Mayfair, London W.1, England.

CAREER: Writer. Deutsches Volksecho (anti-Nazi, German-language weekly), New York, N.Y., editor, 1937-39. Military service: U.S. Army, World War II; received Bronze Star. Member: P.E.N. Awards, honors: National prize of German Democratic Republic.

WRITINGS: Hostages (novel), Putnam, 1942, reissued as The Glasenapp Case, Seven Seas Publishers, 1962; Of Smiling Peace, Little, Brown, 1944; The Crusaders, Little, Brown, 1948; The Eyes of Reason (novel), Little, Brown, 1951; Goldsborough (novel), P. List (Leipzig), 1953, Blue Heron Press, 1954; Im Kopf-Sauber: Schriften zum Tage, P. List, 1954; Keine Angst von Russlands Baeren: Neugierige Fragen und Fragen und offene Antworteh ueber die Sowjetunion (originally written in English, but published in German), Bruecken-Verlag (Dusseldorf), 1955; Offen Gesagt: Neue Schriften zum Tage, Verlag Volk und Welt (Berlin), 1957; The Cannibals and Other Stories, Seven Seas Publishers, 1958; A Visit to Soviet Science, Marzani & Munsell, c.1959 (published in India as The Cosmic Age: A Report, People's Publishing House [New Delhi], 1959); Schatten und Licht: Geschichten aus einem geteilten Lande (originally written in English, but published first in German), P. List, 1960, translation published as Shadows and Lights, Cassell, 1963; The Lenz Papers, Cassell, 1964; Casimir und Cymbelinchen: Zwei Maerchen, Kinderbuchverlag (Berlin), 1966; The Uncertain Friend (novel), Cassell, 1969; Die Schmaehschrift; oder, Koenigin gegen Defoe (title means "Queen Against DeFoe"; originally written in English, but published in German). Diogenes Verlag, 1970; The King David Report (novel), Kindler's (Munich), 1972, Putnam, 1973.

BIOGRAPHICAL/CRITICAL SOURCES: Washington Post, April 25, 1968.

HICK, John (Harwood) 1922-

PERSONAL: Born January 20, 1922, in Scarborough, England; son of Mark D. (a lawyer) and Aileen (Hirst) Hick; married Hazel Bowers, August 30, 1953; children: Eleanor, Mark, Peter, Michael. Education: University of Edinburgh, M.A. (first class honors), 1948; Oxford University, D.Phil., 1950; Westminster Theological College, Cambridge, theological study, 1950-53. Home: 277 Hawthorne Ave., Princeton, N.J. 08540. Office: Princeton Theological Seminary, Princeton, N.J. 08540.

CAREER: Presbyterian minister in Northumberland, England, 1953-56; Cornell University, Ithaca, N.Y., assistant professor of philosophy, 1956-59; Princeton Theological Seminary, Princeton, N.J., Stuart Professor of Christian Philosophy, 1959—. Wartime service: Served with Friends' Ambulance Unit, 1942-45. Member: Royal Institute of Philosophy, American Philosophical Association, American Theological Society, Society of Psychical Research, Mind Association. Awards, honors: Guggenheim fellowship, 1963-64.

WRITINGS: Faith and Knowledge: A Modern Introduction to the Problem of Religious Knowledge, Cornell University Press, 1957, 2nd edition, 1966; Philosophy of Religion, Prentice-Hall, 1963 2nd edition, 1973; (editor) Classical and Contemporary Readings in the Philosophy of Religion, Prentice-Hall, 1964, 2nd edition, 1970; (editor) Faith and the Philosophers, St. Martin's, 1964; (editor and author of introduction) The Existence of God, Macmillan, 1964; Evil and the Love of God, Harper, 1966; (compiler with Arthur C. McGill) The Many-Faced Argument: Recent Studies on the Ontological Argument for the Existence of God, Macmillan, 1967; Christianity at the Centre, Macmillan (London), 1968, Herder & Herder, 1970; Arguments for the Existence of God, Macmillan (London), Herder & Herder, 1971; Biology and the Soul, Cambridge University Press, 1972; (editor) M.J. Charlesworth, Philosophy of Religion: The Historic Approaches, Herder & Herder, 1972; (editor) William A. Christian, Oppositions of Religious Doctrine, Herder & Herder, 1972; (editor) Kai Neilsen, Contemporary Critiques of Religion, Herder & Herder, 1972. Member of editorial board, Enclyclopedia of Philosophy; member of editorial council, Theology Today.

SIDELIGHTS: In a review of Christianity at the Centre, Frederick Sontag states: "Hick makes Christianity as doctrine seem easy and obvious and natural, and he ends his examination of God with a reaffirmation of resurrection belief. His mode of argument is essentially to show that things we accept in everyday life make belief reasonable. . . ."

BIOGRAPHICAL/CRITICAL SOURCES: Christian Century, March 22, 1967, November 18, 1970; Encounter, autumn, 1967.

*   *   *

HICKS, David E. 1931-

PERSONAL: Born January 1, 1931, in Indianapolis, Ind.; son of John Arthur (a land developer) and Marguerite (Barnes) Hicks; married Shirlene L. Barlow, January 22, 1958; children: Sharon Lynn, Brenda Kay. Education: Graduate of National Radio Institute, 1953, Florida Police Academy, 1958; special courses at Purdue University, 1959. Politics: Independent. Religion: Protestant. Home: 6105 Northwest 110th St., Miami, Fla. 33167.

CAREER: Radio, television, and industrial equipment technician in Indianapolis, Ind., and Pensacola, Fla., 1950-58, also working for two years in same period as private detective in Pensacola, three years as member of Pensacola City Police; Howard W. Sams & Co., Inc., Indianapolis, Ind., technical editor, book department, 1958-

64; self-employed writer and technical consultant, Miami, Fla., 1964—. Licensed amateur radio operator; private pilot; trumpet player in Indianapolis Philharmonic Orchestra, 1947-49. Military service: U.S. Navy, 1948. Member: American Radio Relay League.

WRITINGS: Citizens Band Radio Handbook, Sams & Co., 1961, 4th edition, 1971; CB Radio Antenna Guidebook, Sams & Co., 1961, 2nd edition published as CB Radio Antennas, 1967; Handbook of Ham Radio Circuits, Sams & Co., 1963; Understanding and Using Citizens Band Radio, Allied Radio Corp., 1963; (reviser) Edwin P. Anderson, Audels Radioman's Guide, 2nd edition, Audel, 1964; Amateur Radio-VHF and Above, Sams & Co., 1964; Audels Practical Guide to Citizens Band Radio, Audel, 1965. Contributor of articles to electronics magazines.

AVOCATIONAL INTERESTS: Photography and golf.

*   *   *

HICKS, Granville 1901-

PERSONAL: Born September 9, 1901, in Exeter, N.H.; son of Frank Stevens and Carrie Weston (Horne) Hicks; married Dorothy Dyer, June 27, 1925; children: Stephanie. Education: Harvard University, A.B., 1923, A.M., 1929; also studied at Harvard Theological School. Home: Grafton, N.Y.

CAREER: Smith College, Northampton, Mass., instructor in biblical literature, 1925-28; Rensselaer Polytechnic Institute, Troy, N.Y., assistant professor of English, 1929-35; Harvard University, Cambridge, Mass., counselor in American civilization, 1938-39; New School for Social Research, New York, N.Y., instructor in novel writing, 1955-58. New Masses, member of editorial staff, 1934-39. Macmillan Co., manuscript reader, 1930-65. Chairman of radio program, "Speaking of Books," 1941-43. New Leader, literary consultant, 1951-58. Director, Corporation of Yaddo, 1942—. Visiting professor, New York University, 1959; Syracuse University, 1960; McGuffey visiting professor, Ohio University, 1967-68. Awards, honors: Guggenheim fellow in literature, 1936-37; D.H.L., Skidmore College, 1968, Ohio University, 1969.

WRITINGS: Eight Ways of Looking at Christianity, Macmillan, 1926; The Great Tradition: An Interpretation of American Literature Since the Civil War, Macmillan, 1933, revised edition 1935, 2nd revised edition, Biblo, 1967, with a new foreword and afterword, Quadrangle, 1969; (with Lynd Ward) One of Us, The Story of John Reed, Equinox, 1935; (editor with others) Proletarian Literature in the United States, International Publishers, 1935; (with John Stuart) John Reed: The Making of a Revolutionary, Macmillan, 1936; (editor with Ella Winter) The Letters of Lincoln Steffens, two volumes, Harcourt, 1938; I Like America, Modern Age Books, 1938; Figures of Transition: A Study of British Literature at the End of the Nineteenth Century, Macmillan, 1939; (with Richard M. Bennett) The First to Awaken, Modern Age Books, 1940; Only One Storm (novel), Macmillan, 1942; Behold Trouble (novel), Macmillan, 1944; Small Town, Macmillan, 1946; There Was a Man In Our Town (novel), Viking, 1952; Where We Came Out, Viking, 1954; (editor) The Living Novel: A Symposium, Macmillan, 1957; (author of introduction) Banned, Berkley, 1961; (author of afterword) Banned #2, Berkley, 1962; Part of the Truth (autobiography), Harcourt, 1965; James Gould Cozzens, University of Minnesota Press, 1966; (author of introduction) Wright Morris: A Reader, Harper, 1970; Literary Horizons: A Quarter Century of American Fiction, New York University Press, 1970.

Poem, "New Light," set to music by Stuart B. Hoppin and published by Birchard. Contributor to *Mercury, Forum, Nation,* and other magazines. Contributing editor, *Saturday Review,* 1958-1969.

SIDELIGHTS: A onetime storm figure in academic circles, Hicks resigned from the Communist Party in 1939, and testified as a "cooperative" witness before the House Committee on Un-American Activities in 1953. His autobiography might have been expected to be an important addition to the history of the early days of American Marxism, but *Newsweek's* critic stated: "For a man who wrote books of Marxist criticism, defended the Bolsheviks on public platforms, and wrote a biography of the American radical, John Reed, Hicks offers a simple-minded and unconvincing explanation of Marxism's appeal for himself and other intellectuals. . . .He skimps on Thornton Wilder, but chats for pages about the Grafton Free Library and Grafton politics. . . .He registers little of the American earthquake of the '30s, focusing instead on a placid backwater—a very small part of the truth." Conversely, Ambrose Agius mentions admiringly the book's small-town atmosphere, its attractive presentation of famous literary figures, and says that "the chief interest of the book is and will remain the Communist commitment." Malcolm Cowley, too, applauds, writing that "[the autobiography] has told more than it seems to be telling. *Part of the Truth* casts new light not only on a man one respects, but on a whole misunderstood period in American history."

BIOGRAPHICAL/CRITICAL SOURCES: Granville Hicks, *Small Town,* Macmillan, 1946; *Newsweek,* December 2, 1946; August 2, 1965; Vernon Louis Parrington, *American Dreams,* Brown University Press, 1947; Julien Steinberg, editor, *Verdict of Three Decades,* Duell, Sloan & Pearce, 1950; Daniel Aaron, *Writers on the Left,* Harcourt, 1961; Granville Hicks, *Part of the Truth,* Harcourt, 1965; *Saturday Review,* July 31, 1965; *New York Times Book Review,* August 1, 1965; *Best Sellers,* August 2, 1965.

*   *   *

HIGDON, Hal 1931-

PERSONAL: Born June 17, 1931, in Chicago, Ill.; son of H.J. (an editor) and Mae (O'Leary) Higdon; married Rose Musacchio, April 12, 1958; children: Kevin, David, Laura. *Education:* Carleton College, B.A., 1953. *Politics:* "Revolutionary." *Home:* 2815 Lake Shore Dr., Michigan City, Ind. 46360. *Agent:* Max Siegel, 154 East Erie, Chicago, Ill. 60611.

CAREER: Kiwanis Magazine, Chicago, Ill., assistant editor, 1957-59; free-lance magazine writer, 1959—. *Military service:* U.S. Army, 1954-56. *Member:* Society of Magazine Writers, National Road Runners Club.

WRITINGS: The Union Versus Dr. Mudd, Follett, 1964; *Heroes of the Olympics,* Prentice-Hall, 1965; (editor) *Pro Football, U.S.A.,* Putnam, 1968, abridged edition published as *Inside Pro Football,* Grosset, 1970; *The Horse That Played Center Field,* Holt, 1969; *The Business Healers,* Random House, 1970; *On the Run from Dogs and People,* Regnery, 1971; *Thirty Days in May: The Indy 500,* Putnam, 1971; *Champions of the Tennis Court,* Prentice-Hall, 1971; *The Electronic Olympics,* Holt, 1971; *Finding the Groove,* Putnam, 1973.

WORK IN PROGRESS: The Corporate Guerillas.

SIDELIGHTS: Higdon competes as a long distance runner and was the first American to finish in the 1964 Boston Marathon.

HIGGINS, Aidan 1927-

PERSONAL: Born March 3, 1972, in County Kildare, Ireland; son of Bartholomew Joseph and Lillian Ann (Boyd) Higgins; married Jill Damaris Anders, November 25, 1955; children: Carl, Julien, Elwin. *Education:* Attended Clongowes Wood College. *Residence:* Muswell Hill, London, England.

CAREER: Laborer in light industry in and around London for about two years; brief career in advertising; lived for two years in Johannesburg, South Africa, after extensive tour of Europe and Africa with John Wright's Marionette Co.; full-time writer, 1958—. *Awards, honors:* Somin Trust Award, 1963, for *Felo de Se;* James Tait Black Memorial Prize, 1967, for *Langrishe, Go Down;* Irish Academy Award.

WRITINGS: Killachter Meadow (stories), Grove, 1960 (published in England as *Felo de Se,* Calder, 1960); *Langrishe, Go Down* (novel), Grove, 1966; *Images of Africa: Diary (1956-60),* Calder, 1971; *Balcony of Europe,* Delacorte, 1973. Contributor to *X* Magazine, *Art & Literature, Evergreen Review, Les Lettres nouvelles, Transatlantic Review, Malahat Review,* and *Tri-Quarterly.*

SIDELIGHTS: Higgins is "one of the best known of the younger Irish prose writers," John Montague states. "His collection of stories, *Killachter Meadow,* showed an arrogant, though slightly unfocused, feeling for language, and a relish for exotic settings from Berlin to Johannesburg." Higgins submitted the book to his English publisher at the suggestion of novelist-playwright Samuel Beckett, who later recommended it to his French publisher. Julian Moynihan wrote that the book "recalled Joyce in its harsh distinction of style and was very up to date in its tendency to sacrifice character to the demands of various coldly calculated technical procedures, but its closest affinities were with Beckett."

Such a family is the subject of *Langrische, Go Down,* about the women of the Langrische family, and what Moynihan has termed "entropy, the slow running down of sequestered lives." A *Times Literary Supplement* reviewer wrote: "Mr. Higgins clearly feels his responsibilities towards prose rather acutely, but his style is sustained not so much by ambition as by an unremitting attention, and although his particularities can verge on the gratuitous, they do make you see. The relation of the bits of the novel to the whole piece is not always convincing . . . but [the book] certainly reveals a promising talent." Moynihan states that Higgins "shows us, . . . entirely in terms of the phenomenal, that failing and decaying—the dissipation of physical, moral and psychic energy—entail the same, and the same amounts of, energy conversion as succeeding and flowering. As it is surveyed and occupied in this book the ground of the phenomenal is anything but barren, and life seen at dead level is anything but dead." He concludes: "It is too early to put Higgins in the company of Joyce and Beckett [which many have done] as a major innovator in modern fiction. Yet *Langrische, Go Down* is without question the most interesting work of fiction to come out of the British-Irish Isles in any number of years and should be read attentively by all who seriously care whether the novel as a genre still exists and has a future."

Killachter Meadow has been published in France, Germany, Italy, Holland, Portugal, and Denmark. *Langrishe, Go Down* is to be filmed by Harold Pinter.

BIOGRAPHICAL/CRITICAL SOURCES: Times Literary Supplement, March 3, 1966; *Saturday Review,* March 4, 1967; *Christian Century,* April 1, 1967; *New York Times Book Review,* April 16, 1967, January 28, 1973; *New Leader,* September 25, 1967.

HIGGINS, Rosalyn (Cohen) 1937-
(Rosalyn Cohen)

PERSONAL: Born June 2, 1937, in London, England; daughter of Lewis (a company director) and Fay (Inberg) Cohen; married Terence Langley Higgins (an economist). *Education:* Attended Burlington Grammar School, London, England, 1942-55; Girton College, Cambridge, B.A. (first class honors), 1958, LL.B., (first class honors), 1959; Yale University, J.S.D., 1962. *Religion:* Jewish. *Home:* 18 Hallgate, Blackheath Park, London S.E.3, England. *Office:* Royal Institute of International Affairs, 10 St. James's Sq., London S.W.1, England.

CAREER: United Kingdom intern at United Nations, 1958; London School of Economics and Political Science, University of London, London, England, junior fellow in international studies, 1961-63; Royal Institute of International Affairs, London, England, international lawyer, 1963—. Visiting fellow, Brookings Institution, 1960. Occasional lecturer. *Member:* International Law Association, American Society of International Law (vice-president), Oxford and Cambridge Club. *Awards, honors:* Commonwealth Fund fellowship to Yale, 1959-61; Rockefeller Foundation award for research on United Nations, 1961-63; annual award, American Society of International Law, 1971.

WRITINGS: The Development of International Law Through the Political Organs of the United Nations, Oxford University Press, 1963; (contributor) Ronald Segal, editor, *Sanctions Against South Africa,* Penguin, 1964; (with others) *United Nations Forces: A Legal Study,* Stevens & Sons, 1964, Praeger, 1966; *Conflict of Interests: International Law in a Divided World,* Dufour, 1965; *The Administration of United Kingdom Foreign Policy Through the United Nations,* edited by Gerard J. Mangone, Maxwell School of Citizenship and Public Affairs, Syracuse University, 1966; *South West Africa: The Court's Judgment,* International Commission of Jurists, 1967; (compiler) *United Nations Peacekeeping, 1946-1967: Documents and Commentary,* Oxford University Press, Volume I: *The Middle East,* 1969, Volume II: *Asia,* 1970. Contributor of articles to *World Today, International Affairs,* and of articles and reviews to yearbooks and journals of law and politics, some under name Rosalyn Cohen.

WORK IN PROGRESS: United Nations Peacekeeping, 1946-1967: Documents and Commentary, Volume III: *Africa and Europe.*

*   *   *

HIGGS, E(ric) S(idney) 1908-

PERSONAL: Born November 26, 1908, in Bridgnorth, Shropshire, England; son of Sidney (an artist) and Florence (Pryce) Higgs; children: Sonia (Mrs. Richard Wright). *Education:* London School of Economics, University of London, Bachelor of Commerce, 1932; Magdalene College, Cambridge, Diploma in Archaeology, 1956, M.A., 1957. *Home:* 35 Panton St., Cambridge, England; and Tuffley House, Clee St., Margaret Craven Arms, England.

CAREER: Cambridge University, Cambridge, England, director of research, department of archaeology. Participant in three expeditions to the Libyan desert, and two to Greece and numerous other countries. *Member:* Zoological Society of London (scientific fellow).

WRITINGS: (Editor with D.R. Brothwell) *Science in Archaeology: A Comprehensive Survey of Progress and Research,* Basic Books, 1963, 2nd edition, Thames & Hudson, 1969, Praeger, 1970; (with J.M. Coles) *The Archaeology of Early Man,* Praeger, 1969; *The History of*

Domestication, Methuen, 1971; (editor) *Papers in Economic Prehistory,* Cambridge University Press, 1972.

WORK IN PROGRESS: Greece: A Study in Palaeolthology, for Faber.

*   *   *

HILL, (John Edward) Christopher 1912-
(K.E. Holme)

PERSONAL: Born February 6, 1912, in York, England; son of Edward Harold (a solicitor) and Janet (Dickenson) Hill; married Inez Bartlett, January, 1944, married second wife, Bridget Irene Sutton, January 2, 1956; children: Frances Catherine (Mrs. John Stein), Andrew Oliver, Dinah Jane. *Education:* Attended St. Peter's School, York, England, 1921-31; Balliol College, Oxford, B.A., 1934, M.A., 1938. *Politics:* Socialist. *Religion:* None. *Home:* 21 Northmoor Rd., Oxford, England. *Office:* Balliol College, Oxford University, Oxford, England.

CAREER: University College, Cardiff, Wales, assistant lecturer in history, 1936-38; Balliol College, Oxford University, Oxford, England, fellow and tutor in modern history, 1938-65, master, 1965—. Oxford University, special lecturer in history, 1959-65, Ford Lecturer, 1961-62. *Military service:* British Army, 1940-45; became major. *Member:* Royal Historical Society (fellow), Association of University Teachers, British Academy (fellow). *Awards, honors:* D.Litt., Oxford University, 1965.

WRITINGS: (Editor and contributor) *The English Revolution: Three Essays,* Lawrence & Wishart, 1940; (under pseudonym K.E. Holme) *Two Commonwealths,* Harrap, 1945, Transatlantic, 1946; *Lenin and the Russian Revolution,* Hodder & Stoughton, 1947, Macmillan, 1950; (editor with Edmund Dell) *The Good Old Cause: The English Revolution of 1640-60,* Lawrence & Wishart, 1949, 2nd edition, Cass, 1969, Augustus M. Kelley, 1970; *Economic Problems of the Church, from Archbishop Whitgift to the Long Parliament,* Clarendon Press, 1956; *Puritanism and Revolution: Studies in Interpretation of the English Revolution of the 17th Century,* Humanities, 1958; *Oliver Cromwell, 1658-1958* (pamphlet), Routledge & Kegan Paul, 1958; *The Century of Revolution, 1603-1714,* Thomas Nelson, 1961, Norton, 1966, new edition, Sphere Books, 1969; (editor) Henry Noel Brailsford, *The Levellers and the English Revolution,* Stanford University Press, 1961; *Society and Puritanism in Pre-Revolutionary England,* Schocken, 1964, 2nd edition, 1967; *Intellectual Origins of the English Revolution,* Clarendon Press, 1965; *Reformation to Industrial Revolution: A Social and Economic History of Britain, 1530-1780,* Volume II, Weidenfeld & Nicolson, 1967, published in America as *Reformation to Industrial Revolution: The Making of Modern English Society, 1530-1780,* Volume II, Pantheon, 1968; *God's Englishman: Oliver Cromwell and the English Revolution,* Dial, 1970; *Antichrist in 17th Century England,* Oxford University Press, 1971; *The World Turned Upside Down,* Viking, 1972.

Contributor to *English Historical Review, Spectator, New Statesman,* and other periodicals. Member of editorial board, *Complete Prose Works of John Milton,* Yale University Press, 1953—; member of editorial board, *Past and Present,* 1952-68.

WORK IN PROGRESS: 17th century English history.

SIDELIGHTS: Peter Dickinson describes Hill's method as "a patterned accumulation of facts and quotations, to suggest the richness and complexity of the historical process. He distrusts the broad generalisation and the single theme, preferring (surely rightly) to see the past as an almost infinite collection of interlocking variables, many of them in conflict with each other, and all affecting each other so that a historian who tries to emphasize one strand can do so only by cheating about the rest. In lesser hands the method would produce a baffling mess, but here all is clear and ordered into a pattern as rich as life."

BIOGRAPHICAL/CRITICAL SOURCES: Punch, September 13, 1967; Spectator, September 20, 1967; New Statesman, September 22, 1967, July 31, 1970; Observer Review, October 8, 1967, August 20, 1970; Books and Bookmen, March, 1968, January, 1969, April, 1970; New York Times Book Review, November 3, 1968; New York Review of Books, February 13, 1969; Washington Post, October 3, 1970; National Review, November 17, 1970.

* * *

HILL, Evan 1919-

PERSONAL: Born January 20, 1919, in Philadelphia, Pa.; son of Louis and Marie Eugenia (Schmeltz) Hill; married Priscilla Anne Fiske, September 21, 1946; children: Lucinda, Peter. Education: Stanford University, B.A., 1948; Boston University, M.S., 1950. Home and office address: Box 566, Newport, N.H. 03773.

CAREER: Daily Alaska Empire, Juneau, Alaska, general reporter, 1940-41; U.S. Army, Infantry, serving in Alaska, United States, and Europe, 1941-48, discharged as captain; Argus-Champion, Newport, N.H., editor, 1948-49; Boston University, Boston, Mass., 1949-56, started as teaching fellow, became associate professor of journalism; Ohio State University, Columbus, associate professor of journalism, 1956-57; full-time free-lance writer, 1957-64; University of Connecticut, Storrs, professor of journalism and chairman of the department, 1964—. Trustee, Richards Free Library, Newport, N.H., 1953-64; member, Newport Planning Board, 1961—. Member: Society for the Protection of New Hampshire Forests. Awards, honors: Winner of American Newspaper Publishers Association Essay Contest, 1950; Freedoms Foundation Medal, 1950.

WRITINGS: (With George Gallup) The Secrets of Long Life, Geis, 1960; (ghost writer) A Life After Death, Simon & Schuster, 1963; Beanstalk: The History of Miniature Precision Bearings, [Keene, N.H.], 1966, The Connecticut River, Wesleyan University Press, 1972. Contributor of articles to Reader's Digest, True, Saturday Evening Post, New York Times Magazine, Saturday Review, Redbook, Coronet, and other magazines.

WORK IN PROGRESS: A book on the Connecticut River, for Wesleyan University Press; a book on the state of New Hampshire, for New York Times Co.

AVOCATIONAL INTERESTS: Forestry, conservation, and the American North.

* * *

HILL, Hamlin (Lewis) 1931-

PERSONAL: Born November 7, 1931, in Houston, Tex.; son of Hamlin Lewis and Marguerite (Courtin) Hill; married Arlette Crawford, December 29, 1952; children: Cynthia, Scott, Sondra, William. Education: University of Texas, student, 1949-51, M.A., 1954; University of Houston, B.A., 1953; University of Chicago, Ph.D., 1959. Office: Department of English, University of Chicago, Chicago, Ill. 60637.

CAREER: University of New Mexico, Albuquerque, instructor in English, 1959-61; University of Wyoming, Laramie, assistant professor of English, 1961-63; University of New Mexico, assistant professor, 1963-65, associate professor of English, 1965-68; University of Chicago, Chicago, Ill., professor of English, 1968—. Summer lecturer at University of Nebraska, 1960; visiting lecturer at University of California, Berkeley, spring, 1965; Fulbright lecturer, University of Copenhagen, 1966-67; lecturer at

University of Wyoming, summer, 1968. Military service: U.S. Army, 1954-56. Member: Modern Language Association of America, American Studies Association, National Council of Teachers of English, American Association of University Professors. Awards, honors: Grant-in-aid, American Council of Learned Societies, 1963, 1965, 1967.

WRITINGS: Mark Twain's Book Sales, privately printed, c.1961; (editor with Walter Blair) The Art of Huckleberry Finn, Chandler Publishing, 1962, revised edition, 1969; (editor) Mark Twain, The Adventures of Huckleberry Finn: A Facsimile of the First Edition, Chandler Publishing, 1962; (editor) Mark Twain, A Connecticut Yankee in King Arthur's Court: A Facsimile of the First Edition, Chandler Publishing, 1963; Mark Twain and Elisha Bliss, University of Missouri Press, 1964; (editor) Mark Twain's Letters to His Publishers, 1867-1894, University of California Press, 1967. Contributor of articles to professional periodicals.

WORK IN PROGRESS: Editing The Gilded Age for the Iowa-California edition of The Works of Mark Twain; Modern American Humor, for Twayne.

BIOGRAPHICAL/CRITICAL SOURCES: Book Week, March 5, 1967; New Statesman, June 23, 1967; New York Times Book Review, July 30, 1967; Times Literary Supplement, August 24, 1967; South Atlantic Quarterly, summer, 1968.

* * *

HILL, Kathleen Louise 1917-
(Kay Hill)

PERSONAL: Born April 7, 1917, in Halifax, Nova Scotia; daughter of Henry and Margaret Elizabeth (Ross) Hill. Education: Attended schools in Halifax, Nova Scotia. Religion: Protestant. Residence: Ketch Harbour, Nova Scotia, Canada. Agent: Collins-Knowlton-Wing, 60 East 56th St., New York, N.Y. 10022.

CAREER: Secretary and court reporter before becoming full-time free-lance writer, 1957—. Member: Association of Canadian Television and Radio Artists. Awards, honors: "Best Juvenile Book in Canada" award, Canadian Library Association, 1969, for And Tomorrow the Stars.

WRITINGS—Under name Kay Hill: Glooscap and His Magic: Legends of the Wabanaki Indians, Dodd, 1963; Three to Get Married (three-act comedy), Samuel French, 1964: Badger, the Mischief Maker, Dodd, 1965; Cobbler, Stick to Thy Last (one-act play; produced in Ottawa at National Arts Centre, July 5, 1969), Dramatic Publishing, 1967; And Tomorrow the Stars: The Story of John Cabot, Dodd, 1968; More Glooscap Stories: Legends of the Wabanaki Indians, Dodd, 1970; Anthologized in Beyond the Footlights, edited by Hugh Duncan McKellar, Macmillan, 1963; children's stories and plays appear in other anthologies. Writer of radio and television plays, short stories, articles, serials, and documentaries.

WORK IN PROGRESS: A children's book on the modern Indian, for Dodd.

AVOCATIONAL INTERESTS: Oil painting, Scottish country dancing.

* * *

HILL, Richard Johnson 1925-

PERSONAL: Born September 9, 1925, in New York, N.Y.; son of Archie S. and Esther (Johnson) Hill; married Barbara J. Beall, June 28, 1947; children: Suzan E., Laura K. Education: Rutgers University, student, 1946-48; Stanford University, B.A., 1950, M.A., 1951; University of Washington, Seattle, Ph.D., 1955. Office: Department of Sociology, University of Oregon, Eugene, Ore. 97403.

CAREER: University of Washington, Seattle, acting instructor, 1953-55, research assistant professor and director of Basic Nursing Research Project, School of Nursing, 1955-56; Bell Telephone Laboratories, New York, N.Y., staff member, 1956-57; University of California, Los Angeles, assistant professor of sociology, 1957-60; University of Texas, Austin, 1960-65, began as associate professor, became professor of sociology and director of Statistical Laboratory; Purdue University, Lafayette, Ind., professor of sociology, 1965-71; University of Oregon, Eugene, professor of sociology and head of department, 1971—. Visiting summer professor, University of Alberta, 1961, and University of Washington, 1962. Consultant to William J. Millard and Associates, 1960-65, and Texas League for Nursing, 1961-65. Visiting scientist, National Science Foundation and American Sociological Association, 1963-65. Member, Governor's Committee for Comprehensive Mental Health, Texas, 1963-65; member, Long Range Planning Committee, Community Council of Austin and Travis County, 1964-65. Military service: U.S. Marine Corps., 1942-46; became staff sergeant. Member: American Sociological Association (fellow; chairman, section on methodology, 1966-67), American Association for Advancement of Science, American Academy of Political and Social Science, Psychometric Society, Phi Beta Kappa.

WRITINGS: A Comparative Study of Lecture and Discussion Methods, Fund for Adult Education, 1960; (with Wendell Bell and Charles R. Wright) Public Leadership, Chandler Publishing, 1961; (with S. Dale McLemore) Management Training Effectiveness: A Study of Nurse Managers, Bureau of Business Research, University of Texas, 1965; (with McLemore and Charles M. Bonjean) Sociological Measurement: An Inventory of Scales and Indices, Chandler Publishing, 1967. Contributor to professional journals. Sociometry, editorial consultant, 1961-62, associate editor, 1962-65, editor, 1973—.

WORK IN PROGRESS: Studies on leadership structure in metropolitan growth areas, conformity to social pressure, and effectiveness of graduate research training.

* * *

HILL, Robert W(hite) 1919-

PERSONAL: Born September 12, 1919, in Richmond, Va.; son of Dudley J. and Mary (Banks) Hill; married Barbara Whitall, October 20, 1956; children: Matthew Banfield, Elizabeth Brinton, Anthony Whitall. Education: Haverford College, B.A., 1944, M.A., 1947. Home: 156 De Forest Rd., Wilton, Conn. 06897. Office: Association Press, 291 Broadway, New York, N.Y. 10007.

CAREER: Harcourt, Brace & Co. (publishers), New York, N.Y., sales representative and editorial reader, 1948-53; free-lance editor and Book-of-the-Month Club reader, 1953-54; John Day Co., Inc. (publishers), New York, N.Y., associate editor, 1955-58, secretary of corporation and member of board of directors, 1958, managing editor, 1959, vice-president, 1960-66; J.B. Lippincott Co. (publishers), New York, N.Y., editor-in-chief, 1966-68; Association Press, New York, N.Y., director and editor-in-chief, 1969—. Member of book selection committee, Wilton Public Library. Military service: U.S. Navy, 1943-46; became lieutenant j.g. Member: P.E.N., Beta Rho Sigma, Publishers' Lunch Club, Wilton Riding Club, Saunderstown Yacht Club.

WRITINGS: What Colonel Glenn Did All Day, John Day, 1962; What the Moon Astronauts Will Do All Day: The Official Plan of Project Apollo, John Day, 1963, 2nd revised edition published as What the Moon Astronauts Do, 1971; The Chesapeake Bay Bridge-Tunnel, John Day, 1972.

BIOGRAPHICAL/CRITICAL SOURCES: Library Journal, May 15, 1969.

HILL, Samuel S(mythe), Jr. 1927-

PERSONAL: Born October 25, 1927, in Richmond, Va.; son of Samuel Smythe (a minister) and Mary L. (Brown) Hill; married Claire Cohen, August 22, 1958; children: Sarah, Charles. Education: Georgetown College, Georgetown, Ky., A.B., 1949; Vanderbilt University, M.A., 1952; Southern Baptist Theological Seminary, B.D., 1953; Cambridge University, postgraduate study, 1955-56; Duke University, Ph.D., 1960. Politics: Democrat. Home: 237 Knollwood Dr., Chapel Hill, N.C. 27514.

CAREER: Pastor in Burlington, Ky., 1953-55; Stetson University, De Land, Fla., assistant professor of religion, 1959-60; University of North Carolina, Chapel Hill, assistant professor, 1960-64, chairman of department of religion, 1961-70, associate professor, 1964-67, professor of religion, 1967—. Member: American Academy of Religion, Society for the Scientific Study of Religion. Awards, honors: Tanner Award for undergraduate teaching, University of North Carolina, 1964; Society for Religion in Higher Education postdoctoral fellowship, 1964-65, spent in research at Harvard University on American intellectual history.

WRITINGS: (With Robert G. Torbet) Baptists North and South, Judson, 1964; (contributor) Kyle Haselden and Martin E. Marty, editors, What's Ahead for the Churches? (symposium), Sheed, 1964; Southern Churches in Crisis, Holt, 1967; Religion and the Solid South, Abingdon, in press. Contributor of numerous articles and reviews to periodicals.

WORK IN PROGRESS: A textbook, Major Forms and Forces of American Religion, for Harper; a monograph on indigenous American Christian traditions.

BIOGRAPHICAL/CRITICAL SOURCES: Christian Century, May 31, 1967; Encounter, summer, 1967; South Atlantic Quarterly, winter, 1968.

* * *

HILLIARD, Noel (Harvey) 1929-

PERSONAL: Born February 6, 1929, in Napier, Hawke's Bay, New Zealand; son of Jack Lockhart (a public servant) and Laura (Glink) Hilliard; married Kiriwai Mete, September 8, 1954; children: Reremoana Eleanor, Harvey Matthew, Hinemoa May, Howard Muriwai. Education: Studied at Victoria University of Wellington, 1946-50, Wellington Teachers' College, 1954-55. Home: 21 Moana Crescent, Mangakino, North Island, New Zealand. Agent: David Higham Associates Ltd., 5-8 Lower John St., London W1R 4HA, England.

CAREER: Southern Cross, Wellington, New Zealand, journalist, 1945-50; teacher in Wellington, New Zealand, 1955-56; high school teacher in Mangakino, New Zealand, 1956-62; primary school teacher, 1964—. Mangakino-Pouakani Maori Executive Committee, chairman; Waiariki District Council of Maori Executive Committees, delegate. Member: P.E.N. (New Zealand center), New Zealand Educational Institute. Awards, honors: Hubert Church Memorial Award for Maori Girl, 1961; New Zealand State Literary Fund scholarship in letters, 1962.

WRITINGS: Maori Girl, Heinemann, 1960; A Piece of Land, R. Hale, 1963; Power of Joy, M. Joseph, 1965, Regnery, 1966; A Night at Green River, R. Hale, 1969. Contributor to New Zealand Listener, Mate, Fernfire, Overland, and other periodicals.

* * *

HILSDALE, (Eric) Paul 1922-

PERSONAL: Born November 28, 1922, in Eureka, Utah; son of Paul (a mining engineer) and Maud (Fitch) Hilsdale. Education: Early education in France and England; Gonzaga University, M.A., 1949; Alma College, S.T.L., 1956; St. Louis University, M.A., 1959. *Politics:* Democrat. *Home:* Loyola University, 7101 West 80th St., Los Angeles, Calif. 90045.

CAREER: Roman Catholic priest of Jesuit order; Institute of Social Order, St. Louis, Mo., research assistant, 1959-60; Ryan Preparatory College, Fresno, Calif., seminary teacher, 1960-63; Loyola University of Los Angeles, Los Angeles, Calif., instructor in theology, 1963—. *Member:* American Sociological Association, American Association of University Professors.

WRITINGS: (Editor) *Prayers from Saint Paul*, Sheed, 1964. Author of several pamphlets on religious topics; contributor to *America, Columbia, Marriage and Family Living*, and other journals. Former editor, *Western Jesuit*.

* * *

HINDS, (Evelyn) Margery
(E.M. Hinds)

PERSONAL: Born in Kent, England; became Canadian citizen, 1955. *Education:* Studied at University College, University of London, and at University of Grenoble. *Home address:* Box 552, Postal Station B, Ottawa 4, Ontario, Canada.

CAREER: Lecturer in England for H.M. Forces, 1940-45, for Central Office of Information, 1945-48; Canadian government, Arctic Service, 1948-62, working among Eskimos as educator and administrator; lecturer in England for Commonwealth Institute, 1962—, for City Literary Institute, London, 1963—. *Member:* Royal Geographical Society (fellow), Society of Authors, Society of Women Writers and Journalists, Photographic Society of America.

WRITINGS: (Under name E.M. Hinds) *Nothing Venture*, Gifford, 1941; (under name E.M. Hinds) *Victorious Venture*, Gifford, 1946; *School House in the Arctic*, Bles, 1958; *Kanayu, the Young Hunter*, Basil Blackwell, 1965; *High Arctic Adventure*, Ryerson, 1968; *Makpa: The Story of an Eskimo-Canadian Boy*, Ryerson, 1971. Anthologized in *Writing for Young Canada*, Gage, 1963, 1964. Contributor to periodicals and newspapers, including *Lady, Cornhill Magazine, Field, Beaver*, and *Toronto Star*.

WORK IN PROGRESS: A personal story of life on Baffin Island, for adults; a school book about peoples of the far north, in an effort to correct some misconceptions about these regions.

SIDELIGHTS: Miss Hinds is competent in French, Swedish, Italian, and Eskimo. She has visited Lapland many times, and has lived among the Lapps. She has also traveled to Australia, New Zealand, Africa, Central America, and Europe.

BIOGRAPHICAL/CRITICAL SOURCES: Nunny Bag 2, Gage, 1963; *Nunny Bag 3*, Gage, 1964.

* * *

HINES, Robert Stephan 1926-

PERSONAL: Born September 30, 1926, in Kingston, N.Y.; son of Harry Jacob (a businessman) and Gertrude (Payne) Hines; married Germaine Marie Lahiff, December 9, 1950. *Education:* Juilliard School of Music, B.S., 1952; University of Michigan, M. Mus., 1956. *Religion:* Lutheran. *Home:* 6020 East Murdock, Wichita, Kan. 67208. *Office:* School of Music, Wichita State University, Wichita, Kan. 67208.

CAREER: Choral director for General Motors Corp., and director of music, Our Saviour Lutheran Church, Detroit, Mich., 1952-57; Southern Illinois University, Carbondale, assistant professor of music, 1957-61; Wichita State University, Wichita, Kan., 1961—, began as associate professor, now professor of music and chairman of choral-voice department. Visiting professor, University of Michigan, summer, 1960; visiting lecturer, Northwestern University, summer, 1960; lecturer, University of Texas, summer, 1968. *Military service:* U.S. Navy, Construction Battalion, 1944-46. *Member:* American Choral Directors Association, Music Teachers National Association, Music Educators National Conference, Phi Kappa Lambda.

WRITINGS: (Editor) *The Composer's Point of View: Essays on Twentieth-Century Choral Music by Those Who Wrote It*, University of Oklahoma Press, 1963; (co-editor) *Selected Lists of Choral Music*, Music Educators National Conference, 1968; (editor) *The Orchestral Composer's Point of View: Essays on Twentieth-Century Music by Those Who Wrote It*, University of Oklahoma Press, 1970. Editor or arranger of choral works for Belwin-Mills, Concordia, Elkan-Vogel, Lawson-Gould, Marks, G. Schirmer, and Schmitt, Hall & McCreary. Contributor to *Choral Journal*.

WORK IN PROGRESS: "Robert Hines Choral" series, for Belwin-Mills.

AVOCATIONAL INTERESTS: Collecting religious art works, fishing.

BIOGRAPHICAL/CRITICAL SOURCES: Antiquarian Bookman, yearbook, 1970.

* * *

HIRST, Rodney Julian 1920-

PERSONAL: Born July 28, 1920, in Sheffield, England; son of William (a minister) and Elsie (Billington) Hirst; married Jessica Podmore, 1942; children: Jennifer Margaret, Susan Irene. *Education:* Magdalen College, Oxford, B.A. (honors) and M.A., 1948. *Home:* 109 Maxwell Dr., Glasgow S. 1, Scotland. *Office:* University of Glasgow, Glasgow W. 2, Scotland.

CAREER: University of St. Andrews, St. Andrews, Scotland, lecturer in logic and metaphysics, 1948-49; University of Glasgow, Glasgow, Scotland, lecturer, 1949-61, professor of logic and head of department, 1961—, dean of arts, 1971—. *Military service:* British Army, 1940-45. *Member:* Mind Association, Aristotelian Society, Scots Philosophical Club.

WRITINGS: The Problems of Perception, Macmillan (New York), 1959; (with G.M. Wyburn and R.W. Pickford) *Human Senses and Perception*, Oliver & Boyd, 1964; (editor and author of introduction) *Perception and the External World* (readings), Macmillan, 1965; (editor and contributor) *Philosophy: An Outline for the Intending Student*, Humanities, 1968. Contributor to *Encyclopedia of Philosophy* and to professional journals.

* * *

HIRT, Michael L(eonard) 1934-

PERSONAL: Born February 19, 1934, in Poland; son of Arthur (a lawyer) and Amalia (Reiss) Hirt; married Myrna York, November 20, 1956; children: Arthur Michael. *Education:* Drake University, B.A., 1954; Iowa State University, M.S., 1955; University of Nebraska, Ph.D., 1958. *Office:* Department of Psychology, Kent State University, Kent, Ohio 44242.

CAREER: U.S. Army, civilian clinical psychologist, 1956-62; U.S. Disciplinary Barracks, Fort Leavenworth, Kan., chief of psychology service, 1960-61; National Jewish Hospital, Denver, Colo., chief of rehabilitation research, 1962-63, chief of psychological services, 1963-64; Marquette University Medical School, Milwaukee, Wis., assistant professor, 1964-65; Veterans Administration Center, Wood, Wis., chief of gerontology research section, 1964-65; University of Cincinnati, Cincinnati, Ohio, associate professor of psychology, 1965-67; Kent State University, Kent, Ohio, professor of psychology, 1967—. *Member:* American Psychological Association.

WRITINGS: A Career as a Psychologist, Bellman Publishing, 1962; (editor) *Rorschach Science: Readings in Theory and Method,* Free Press, 1962; (editor) *Psychological and Allergic Aspects of Asthma,* C.C Thomas, 1965. Contributor of articles to *Journal of Clinical Psychology, Journal of Applied Psychology,* and other professional publications.

*   *   *

HOARE, Robert J(ohn) 1921-

PERSONAL: Born November 5, 1921, in Manchester, England; son of John William (a journalist) and Margaret (Giles) Hoare; married Eileen Mary Hodgkinson, July, 1952; children: Clare Susan, Zoe Therese. *Education:* Alsager Training College, Cheshire, England, Ministry of Education teaching certificate; Reading University, diploma in advanced study of education. *Politics:* "Undecided." *Religion:* Catholic. *Home:* "Karina," Wells Lane, Ascot, Berkshire, England.

CAREER: Allied Newspapers (later Kemsley Newspapers), Manchester, England, sub-editor, 1937-41, 1946-48; St. Cuthbert's Senior Mixed School, Manchester, England, assistant master, 1949-56; St. Peter's Primary School, Marlow, Buckinghamshire, England, assistant master, 1956-59; St. Mary's College, Twickenham, Middlesex, England, tutor and librarian, 1959—. Author of juveniles and texts. *Military service:* Royal Air Force, 1941-46; became leading aircraftsman. *Member:* Association of Training Colleges and Departments of Education, Society of Authors, Simmarian Athletic Club.

WRITINGS—Juveniles: *Wings Over the Atlantic,* Phoenix House, 1956, Branford, 1957; *The Sinister Hoard,* Parrish, 1958; *The First Book of Aviation,* Cassell, 1958; *The Second Book of Aviation,* Cassell, 1958; *Desperate Venture,* Parrish, 1958; *The Story of Aircraft and Travel by Air,* A. & C. Black, 1958, 4th edition, 1968; (with Jim Peters) *Spiked Shoes,* Cassell, 1959; *Rangi to the Rescue,* Hamish Hamilton, 1960; *Secret in the Sahara,* Parrish, 1960; *Temba Becomes a Tiger,* Hamish Hamilton, 1960; (compiler) *True Stories of Capture and Rescue* (anthology), Hamish Hamilton, 1960, new edition, 1961; *Travel by Sea,* A. & C. Black, 1961, Dufour, 1965, 2nd edition, A. & C. Black, 1967; (editor) Margaret Hyde, *Flight Today and Tomorrow,* Brockhampton Press, 1961; *First Person: An Anthology of Achievement,* Odhams, 1963; *Christianity Comes to Britain,* Geoffrey Chapman, 1968; *The Old West,* Muller, 1969; *Messages,* Muller, 1969.

"Champion Library" series, published by Macmillan: *Four-Minute Miler and the Boy from Bowral,* 1962, *The Fighting Marine and the Boy Who Loved Horses,* 1962, *Queen of Tennis and She Jumped to Fame,* 1962.

Textbooks: "Planned Composition," series, published by Odhams: *Planned Composition,* 1957, *Easier Planned Composition,* 1959, *More Planned Composition,* 1959, *Towards Planned Composition,* 1960, *Advanced Planned Composition,* 1961; "Understanding Through Interest" series, four books, Longmans, Green, 1961; "Modern Age Readers," Books 1-4, Odhams, 1962, Books 5-8, Ginn, 1966; (with Sister John) "Catholic Workbooks," four books, Macmillan, 1963-64; "The Mitre Histories," published by Macmillan: *From the Earliest Times to the Assyrian Empire,* 1963, *From the New Babylon to the Time of Christ,* 1964, (with Sean D. Healy) *From the Roman Empire to the Crowning of Harold,* 1964, (with A.M. Dyer) *From the Norman Conquest to the Flight of James II,* 1964, (with F.C. Price) *From William and Mary to the Mechanical Age,* 1965; "Planned English" series, four books, Ginn, 1966; (with Adolf Heuser)

Christ Through the Ages: A Church History for Secondary Schools, Geoffrey Chapman, Volume I: *From the Beginning to the Fifteenth Century,* 1966, Volume II: *From the Reformation to Second Vatican Council,* 1966; "Our Saints" series, eight books, Longmans, Green, 1967; "Write Away" series, four books, Longmans, Green, 1969; "Words in Action" series, four books, Philograph Publications, 1970; *Topic Work with Books,* Geoffrey Chapman, 1971.

Contributor to *Times Educational Supplement, Teachers World, Teacher, School Librarian, Books for Your Children, Bookseller.*

WORK IN PROGRESS: Information books for the youngest readers; *Men of the Old West,* for Chatto & Windus; *Saints,* for Chatto & Windus; "Junior Science Topic" series, eight books, for Philograph Publications.

SIDELIGHTS: The Sinister Hoard was broadcast in installments on British Broadcasting Corp. "Children's Hour," 1960. *Avocational interests:* Running, swimming.

BIOGRAPHICAL/CRITICAL SOURCES: Books and Bookmen, October, 1959, December, 1968.

*   *   *

HOBSBAUM, Philip (Dennis) 1932-

PERSONAL: Born June 29, 1932, in London, England; son of Joseph (an engineer) and Rachel (Sapera) Hobsbaum; married Hannah Kelly, August 7, 1957 (marriage dissolved, 1968). *Education:* Downing College, Cambridge, B.A., 1955, M.A., 1960; Royal Academy of Music, licentiate, 1956; Guildhall School of Music, licentiate, 1957; research at University of Sheffield, 1959, Ph.D., 1968. *Home:* 6 Princes Ter., Glasgow W.2, Scotland. *Office:* Department of English, University of Glasgow, Glasgow W.2, Scotland.

CAREER: Writer, 1955—; part-time lecturer and teacher, 1955-59; Queen's University, Belfast, Northern Ireland, lecturer in English, 1962-66; University of Glasgow, Glasgow, Scotland, lecturer in English, 1966—. Member of Northern Ireland Civic Theatre Committee, 1963-64. *Member:* Association of University Teachers, BBC Club (Glasgow).

WRITINGS: (Editor with Edward Lucie-Smith) *A Group Anthology,* Oxford University Press, 1963; *The Place's Fault, and Other Poems,* St. Martin's, 1964; *Snapshots,* Festival Publications, 1965; *In Retreat, and Other Poems,* Macmillan, 1966, Dufour, 1968; *Coming Out Fighting* (poems), Dufour, 1969; *Ten Elizabethan Poets,* Longmans, Green, 1969; *A Theory of Communication,* Macmillan, 1969, published in America as *A Theory of Criticism,* Indiana University Press, 1970; *A Readers' Guide to Charles Dickens,* Thames & Hudson, 1971; *Women and Animals,* Macmillan, 1972.

Represented in several anthologies, including *Happenings,* edited by Maurice Wollman and David Grugeon, Harrap, 1964, *Young Commonwealth Poets,* edited by Peter L. Brent, Heinemann, 1965, and *The Pattern of Poetry,* edited by William K. Seymour and John Smith, F. Watts, 1967. Contributor to *Listener, Spectator, Encounter, Scottish International, Transatlantic Review, Encore, The Review, Times Literary Supplement, Twentieth Century, Outposts, Poetry Review, New York Times, London Magazine, Ambit, Priapus,* and *Texas Quarterly.* Editor, *Delta,* 1954-55; co-editor, *Poetry from Sheffield,* 1959-61; member of editorial board, *Northern Review,* 1964-66.

WORK IN PROGRESS: Tradition and Experiment.

SIDELIGHTS: Describing *Women and Animals,* Derek Stanford wrote: "Self-pity is not the rarest motive impulse in poetry, but Philip Hobsbaum goes one better in discovering the motor-power inherent in self-hatred and disgust. . . . It is a great pity Dr. Hobsbaum cannot succeed in liking himself (in due moderation) just a little more, since he is a worthy person, both as man and academic. . . . Meanwhile, he entertains us with the *saeva indignatio* of his impressions which—being the bone and sinew of his passion—fascinate us a good deal more than another's flat philanthropy."

Hobsbaum founded "The Group," a creative writing seminar, 1955, which has since become a movement in contemporary poetry. He appears regularly on British Broadcasting Corp. "Third Programme."

AVOCATIONAL INTERESTS: Walking, music, theatre, arguing, and cooking.

BIOGRAPHICAL/CRITICAL SOURCES: Twentieth Century, June, 1960; G.S. Fraser, *The Writer and the Modern World,* Penguin, 1964; *Kenyon Review,* Volume 30, number 5, 1968; *Poetry,* July, 1969; *Times Literary Supplement,* July 24, 1969; *Library Journal,* June 15, 1970; *New Statesman,* September 18, 1970; *Hudson Review,* summer, 1972; *Times Literary Supplement,* October 20, 1972; *Books and Bookmen,* December, 1972; *Review of English Studies,* February, 1973.

* * *

HODGES, Elizabeth Jamison

PERSONAL: Born in Atlanta, Ga.; daughter of William Lemmon (an electrical engineer) and Elizabeth Jamison (Hodges) Hodges. *Education:* Radcliffe College, A.B., 1931; Simmons College, B.S. in L.S., 1937. *Home:* 19 Lowell St., Cambridge, Mass. 02138. *Agent:* McIntosh & Otis, Inc., 18 East 41st St., New York, N.Y. 10017. *Office:* Robbins Library, 700 Massachusetts Ave., Arlington, Mass. 02174.

CAREER: Worked in public libraries in Boston, Mass., and Detroit, Mich., 1937-43; Westover Army Air Base, Westover, Mass., post librarian, 1943-45; Overseas Army Library Service, corps librarian, Third Army, command librarian, First Military District, Europe, 1945-47; librarian in Watertown, Mass., 1947-49, Leominster, Mass., 1949-58, Belmont, Mass., 1958-61; Robbins Library, Arlington, Mass., assistant librarian and supervisor of adult services, 1961—. Part-time lecturer, Northeastern University, 1966—. Member of chapter board, American Red Cross and Detroit, Mich., 1937-43; Westover Army Air Base, Cross, Leominster, Mass., 1951-52. *Member:* English-Speaking Union, American Library Association, Women's National Book Association, New England Library Association, New England Poetry Club, Poetry Society of New Hampshire, Massachusetts Library Association, Charles River Library Club (vice-president, 1958-60; president, 1960-61). *Awards, honors:* Three-time winner in juvenile short story contest, University of New Hampshire Writers' Conference.

WRITINGS: The Three Princes of Serendip, Atheneum, 1964, revised edition, Constable, 1965; *Serendipity Tales* (adaptation of Christoforo Armeno's *Peregrinaggio di tre giovani*), Atheneum, 1966; *Free as a Frog,* Addison-Wesley, 1969; *A Song for Gilgamesh,* Atheneum, 1971. Author of booklet on Leominster Public Library; contributor to *Library Journal, Wilson Library Bulletin, Best Articles and Stories, American Weave,* and other periodicals and newspapers.

WORK IN PROGRESS: A modern fiction book; a juvenile with an ancient oriental background.

SIDELIGHTS: Miss Hodges writes: "In general, for writers, I believe in what might be called deep immersion in their special seas and related streams. I read about writing and authors, and I have spent part of my time teaching children's literature and the writing of it. I sometimes tell stories to children, and I keep writing. All of such activities, I believe, make for the kind of life in which serendipity can keep on happening."

AVOCATIONAL INTERESTS: People, poetry, painting, politics, international peace.

BIOGRAPHICAL/CRITICAL SOURCES: Horn Book, June, 1967, April, 1971; *Library Journal,* March 15, 1970.

* * *

HODGSON, Peter E(dward) 1928-

PERSONAL: Born November 27, 1928, in London, England. *Education:* Imperial College of Science and Technology, University of London, B. Sc. and A.R.C.S., 1948, Ph.D., and D.I.C., 1951, D. Sc., 1964; Oxford University, M.A., 1961. *Office:* Nuclear Physics Laboratory, Oxford, England.

CAREER: University of Reading, Reading, England, lecturer in physics, 1957-58; Oxford University, Oxford, England, 1958—, lecturer in theoretical physics at Pembroke College, 1960-62, senior research fellow at Corpus Christi College, 1962—, university lecturer in nuclear physics, 1967—, senior research officer, university department of nuclear physics. Consultant to United Kingdom Atomic Energy Authority. *Member:* Atomic Scientists Association (council, 1952-59), Institute of Physics (fellow), American Physical Society, Newman Association (member of council, 1959-61).

WRITINGS: This Atomic Age, Catholic Truth Society, 1953; *The Catholic Church and Science,* Catholic Truth Society, 1954; *Science and Human Society,* Catholic Truth Society, 1957; (with Margaret M. Feeny) *Just War?: Papal Teaching on Nuclear Warfare, with a Scientific Commentary* (pamphlet), Sword of the Spirit, 1959; *Nuclear Physics in Peace and War,* Hawthorn, 1961; (with L.L. McReavy) *Nuclear Warfare: An Account of the Basic Physics of Nuclear Weapons, the Teaching of the Church on the Morality of Nuclear Warfare and the Possibility of International Control,* Catholic Truth Society, 1962; *The Optical Model of Elastic Scattering,* Oxford University Press, 1963; *Nuclear Reactions and Nuclear Structure,* Oxford University Press, 1971. Author of about a hundred published research papers in experimental and theoretical nuclear physics. General editor, "Newman Philosophy of Science" series, Sheed, 1958—. Editor, *Atomic Scientists' Journal,* 1953-55.

WORK IN PROGRESS: Research in theoretical nuclear physics, with special reference to the optical model analysis of elastic scattering processes and the distorted wave analysis of direct nuclear reactions.

* * *

HOEKEMA, Anthony A(ndrew) 1913-

PERSONAL: Surname is pronounced *Hook*-uh-ma; born July 26, 1913, in Drachten, Friesland, Netherlands; son of Peter (a tailor) and Jessie (Weeber) Hoekema; married Ruth A. Brink (a teacher), August 4, 1942; children: Dorothy Ruth, James Anthony, David Andrew, Helen Jean. *Education:* Calvin College, A.B., 1936; University of Michigan, A.M., 1937; Calvin Theological Seminary, Th.B., 1942; Princeton Theological Seminary, Th.D., 1953. *Home:* 1887 Woodcliff S.E., Grand Rapids, Mich. 49506. *Office:* Calvin Theological Seminary, 3233 Burton St. S.E., Grand Rapids, Mich. 49506.

CAREER: Minister of Christian Reformed Church. Pastor in Grand Rapids, Mich., 1944-50, 1954-56, in Paterson, N.J., 1950-54; Calvin College, Grand Rapids, Mich., professor of Bible, 1956-58; Calvin Theological Seminary, Grand Rapids, Mich., associate professor, 1958-64, professor of systematic theology, 1964—. *Member:* Evangelical Theological Society, Christian Association for Psychological Studies.

WRITINGS: The Four Major Cults: Christian Science, Jehovah's Witnesses, Mormonism, Seventh-Day Adventism, Eerdmans, 1963; *What About Tongue-Speaking?,* Eerdmans, 1966; *Holy Spirit Baptism,* Eerdmans, 1972. Contributor to religious periodicals, both national and denominational.

SIDELIGHTS: Hoekema knows German, Dutch, Latin, Greek, and Hebrew. *Avocational interests:* Classical music, camping, swimming.

*   *   *

HOFFMAN, Betty Hannah   1918-

PERSONAL: Born January 22, 1918, in Glen Ridge, N.J.; daughter of William and Ann (Leslie) Hannah; married C. Robert Hoffman (a lawyer), June 6, 1942; children: Clement, Bruce, Nell. *Education:* Smith College, B.A. (cum laude), 1939. *Politics:* Democrat. *Religion:* Quaker. *Home and office:* Buck and Stonyford Rds., Newton, Pa. 18940.

CAREER: Mademoiselle, New York, N.Y., guest managing editor, summer, 1939; *Ladies' Home Journal,* Philadelphia, Pa., an assistant editor, 1939-45, associate and contributing editor in Philadelphia and New York, N.Y., 1962-63; free-lance writer, 1946-61, 1963—. *Member:* League of Women Voters (Newton; publicity and voters' service chairman, 1952-56), Overseas Press Club of America, Society of Magazine Writers, Phi Beta Kappa. *Awards, honors:* University of Illinois Benjamin Franklin Award for "How America Lives" series in *Ladies' Home Journal,* 1956.

WRITINGS: (With staff of Netherlands News Agency) *Born to Be a Queen,* Public Relations Department, Lago Oil & Transport Co., 1955; (with Cornelius Vanderbilt) *Queen of the Golden Age,* McGraw, 1956; (with Kathryn Murray) *My Husband, Arthur Murray,* Simon & Schuster, 1960. Contributor of approximately one hundred articles and series of articles to *Ladies' Home Journal, Saturday Evening Post, Readers' Digest, Cosmopolitan,* and *Smith Alumnae Quarterly.*

WORK IN PROGRESS: Research on social problems affecting American families.

SIDELIGHTS: Mrs. Hoffman spent two months in Holland writing personal story of Dutch royal family, serialized in *Ladies' Home Journal* as "Born to be Queen." Another series, "How America Lives," ran in the same magazine, 1945-63; subjects for feature pieces have included Prince Philip, Joan Kennedy, Teddy Nadler, Paul Popenoe, Ruth Lyons. *Avocational interests:* Painting in water color, gardening (flowers), politics.

BIOGRAPHICAL/CRITICAL SOURCES: Saturday Evening Post, February 14, 1959.

*   *   *

HOGAN, (Robert) Ray   1908-
(Clay Ringold)

PERSONAL: Born December 15, 1908, in Willow Springs, Mo.; son of Thomas Newton and Sarah (Gooch) Hogan; married Lois Easterday Clayton, August 13, 1927; children: Betty Gwynn Hogan Grady, R.R. Hogan, Jr. *Education:* Attended schools in Albuquerque, N.M.; studied two years at Hoosier Institute of Journalism. *Religion:* Presbyterian. *Home:* 700 Stagecoach Rd. S.E., Albuquerque, N.M. 87123.

CAREER: Various work in Arizona, Texas, Colorado, and New Mexico, but mainly free-lance writer, 1928—. Active in conservation. *Member:* Writers Guild of America, West, Western Writers of America, Shrine, Scottish Rite, Mason.

WRITINGS: Ex-Marshall, Ace Books, 1956; *The Friendless,* Ace Books, 1956; *Walk a Lonely Trail,* Ace Books, 1957; *Land of Strangers,* Ace Books, 1957; *Longhorn Law,* Ace Books, 1957; *Marked Man,* Ace Books, 1958; *Outlaw Marshall,* Muller, 1959; *Hangman's Valley,* Ace Books, 1959; *Wanted Alive,* Ace Books, 1959; *Marshal Without a Badge,* Gold Medal Books, 1959.

Guns Against the Sun, Avon, 1960; *Lead Reckoning,* Avon, 1960; *The Ghost Raider,* Pyramid Publications, 1960; *The Shotgunner,* Avon, 1960; *Hasty Hangman,* Ace Books, 1960; *Raider's Revenge,* Pyramid Publications, 1960; *Rebel Raid,* Berkeley, 1961; *The Life and Death of Clay Allison,* Signet, 1961; *The Ridge-Runner,* Ace Books, 1961; *Ride to the Gun,* Avon, 1961; *Ambush at Riflestock,* Ace Books, 1961; *Track the Man Down,* Ace Books, 1961; *Marshal for Lawless,* Ace Books, 1961; *The Jim Hendren Story,* Pyramid Publications, 1962; *Rebel in Yankee Blue,* Avon, 1962; *Hell to Hallelujah,* Macfadden, 1962; *Shot Gunner,* Ace Books, 1962; *New Gun for Kingdom City,* Ace Books, 1962; *Strangers in Apache Basin,* Avon, 1963; *Outside Gun,* Ace Books, 1963; *The Life and Death of Johnny Ringo,* Signet, 1963 (published in England as *Johnny Ringo: Gentleman Outlaw,* John Long, 1964); *Trail of the Fresno Kid,* Ace Books, 1963; *Last Gun at Cabresto,* Ace Books, 1963; *Hoodoo Guns,* Ace Books, 1964; *Man from Barranca Negra,* Ace Books, 1964; *Trackers,* New American Library, 1964; *Rebel Ghost,* Macfadden, 1964; *Night Raider,* Avon, 1964; *Mosby's Last Raid,* Macfadden, 1966; *Panhandle Pistolero,* Ace Books, 1966; *Killer's Gun,* Ace Books, 1966; *Dead Man on a Black Horse,* New American Library, 1966; *Hellsfire Lawman,* Ace Books, 1966; *Outlaw Mountain,* Ballantine, 1967; *Legacy of Slash M,* Ace Books, 1967; *Border Bandit,* Lancer Books, 1967; *The Wolver,* Ace Books, 1967; (with Brian Wynne) *Badge for a Badman* [and] *Devil's Butte* (the former by Wynne, the latter by Hogan), Ace Books, 1967; *Texas Lawman,* Lancer Books, 1967; *The Moonlighters,* Avon, 1968; *Trouble at Tenkiller,* Ace Books, 1968; (under pseudonym Clay Ringold) *Return to Rio Fuego,* Ace Books, 1968; *The Gunmaster,* New American Library, 1968; *The Hell Road,* New American Library, 1968; *Killer on Warbucket,* Ace Books, 1968; *Man Who Killed the Marshal,* New American Library, 1969; (under pseudonym Clay Ringold) *Reckoning in Fire Valley,* Ace Books, 1969; *Trail to Tucson,* New American Library, 1969; *Bloodrock Valley War,* Ace Books, 1969; *Texas Guns,* Lancer Books, 1969; (under pseudonym Clay Ringold) *The Hooded Gun,* Ace Books, 1969.

The Rimrocker, New American Library, 1970; *The Searching Guns,* New American Library, 1970; *Guns Along the Jicarilla,* Ace Books, 1970; *Jackman's Wolf,* Doubleday, 1970; *The Outlawed,* New American Library, 1970; *Three Cross,* New American Library, 1970; *Deputy of Violence,* New American Library, 1971; *Duel Lagrima Valley,* Ace Books, 1971; *Bullet for Mr. Texas,* New American Library, 1971; *Marshall of Babylon,* New American Library, 1971; *Brandon's Posse,* New American Library, 1971; (with Clemence Hardin) *A Man Called Ryker* [and] *Stage Line to Rincon* (the former by Hogan, the latter by Hardin), Ace Books, 1971; *The Devil's Gunhand,* New American Library, 1972; *New Gun for Kingdom City,* Ace Books, 1972; *Passage to Dodge City,* New American Library, 1972; (with Barry Cord) *Hell in Paradise Valley* [and] *The Night Hell's Corner Died* (the former by Cord, the latter by Hogan), Ace Books, 1972; *The Hangmen of San Sabal,* New American Library, 1972; *The Hell Merchant,* New American Library, 1972; *Lawman for Slaughter Valley,* New American Library, 1972; *Passage to Dodge City,* New

American Library, 1972; *Showdown at Texas Flat,* Ace Books, 1972; *Conger's Woman,* Doubleday, 1973; *The Guns of Stingaree,* New American Library, 1973.

Also writer of several hundred stories and articles in magazines, one motion picture, television scripts. Editor, *New Mexico Sportsman,* 1956-57; weekly sports columnist, *Albuquerque Tribune,* for four years.

SIDELIGHTS: Hogan's books have been reprinted in Great Britain, Canada, and Australia, and have been translated for readers in five countries in continental Europe.

* * *

HOGBIN, H(erbert) Ian 1904-

PERSONAL: Surname is pronounced *Ho*-bin; born December 17, 1904, in Bawtry, Yorkshire, England; son of Herbert and Edith (Smart) Hogbin. *Education:* University of Sydney, B.A., 1926, M.A., 1929; University of London, Ph.D., 1931. *Office:* Department of Anthropology, Macquarie University, North Ryde, New South Wales, Australia.

CAREER: University of Sydney, Sydney, Australia, senior lecturer, 1931-32, 1936-48, reader in social anthropology, 1948-69; Australian School of Pacific Administration, instructor, 1946-48; Australian National University, Canberra, fellow, 1948-49; Macquarie University, North Ryde, New South Wales, Australia, 1970—. Munro Lecturer, University of Edinburgh, 1949; Josiah Mason Lecturer, University of Birmingham, 1953; Marett Lecturer, Oxford University, 1961. Adviser to British Solomon Islands Government, 1943. Member of anthropological expedition to Ontong-Java, 1928-39, Solomon Islands, 1933, New Guinea, 1934-35, 1946-50. *Military service:* British Solomon Islands Defence Force, 1943; became captain. Australian Army, 1944-46; became lieutenant colonel. *Awards, honors:* Wellcome Medal, 1944, and Rivers Medal, 1946, both from Royal Anthropological Institute of London; Harbison-Higinbotham Prize from University of Melbourne, 1951, 1958.

WRITINGS: Law and Order in Polynesia: A Study of Primitive Legal Institutions, Harcourt, 1934; *Experiments in Civilization: The Effects of European Culture on a Native Community of the Solomon Islands,* Routledge & Kegan Paul, 1939, Transatlantic, 1944; (with Camilla Wedgwood) *Development and Welfare in the Western Pacific,* Australian Institute of International Affairs, 1943; *Peoples of the Southwest Pacific,* John Day, 1946; *Transformation Scene: The Changing Culture of a New Guinea Village,* Humanities, 1951; *Social Change,* C.A. Watts, 1958; *Kinship and Marriage in a New Guinea Village,* Athlone Press, 1963; *A Guadalcanal Society: The Kaoka Speakers,* Holt, 1964; (compiler with L.R. Hiatt) *Readings in Australian and Pacific Anthropology,* Cambridge University Press, 1966; (with Peter Lawrence) *Studies in New Guinea Land Tenure,* Pennsylvania University Press, 1967; *The Island of Menstruating Men,* Intext, 1970. Contributor of articles to *Royal Anthropological Institute Journal, American Anthropologist, Oceania, Pacific Affairs, Asia,* and other journals.

WORK IN PROGRESS: New Guinea Politics.

* * *

HOGGART, Richard 1918-

PERSONAL: Born September 24, 1918, in Leeds, England; son of Tom Longfellow and Adeline Emma (Long) Hoggart; married Mary Holt France, July 18, 1942; children: Simon, Nicola, Paul. *Education:* University of Leeds, B.A. (first class honors in English), 1939, M.A., 1940. *Address:* UNESCO, Place de Fontenoy, Paris 7e, France.

CAREER: University of Hull, Hull, Yorkshire, England, extra-mural staff tutor in English literature, 1946-56, senior staff tutor, 1957-59; University of Leicester, Leicester, England, senior lecturer in English, 1959-62; University of Birmingham, Birmingham, England, professor of English, 1962—. Visiting professor of English, University of Rochester, 1956-57. Governor, Royal Shakespeare Theatre; Birmingham Repertory Theatre Fellow of the Royal Society of Literature, 1957-63. Director, Centre for Contemporary Cultural Studies, 1964—; assistant director-general, UNESCO, Paris. Member, Albemarle Committee on Youth Service, 1958-60; member, Pilkington Committee on Broadcasting, 1960-62; British Broadcasting Corp., member of general advisory council, 1964-70, Reith Lecturer, 1971. *Military service* British Army, Royal Artillery, 1940-46; became captain.

WRITINGS: (Editor with John Hewett) *Four In Hand: An Excursion* (poetry anthology), Three Arts Club, 1945; *Auden: An Introductory Essay,* Yale University Press, 1951; *The Uses of Literacy: Changing Patterns in English Mass Culture,* Essential Books, 1957 (published in England as *The Uses of Literacy: Aspects of Working Class Life,* Chatto & Windus, 1957); *Prefabricated Thinking,* Newman Neame, 1958; (editor *W.H. Auden—A Selection,* Hutchinson, 1961; *Teaching Literature,* National Institute of Adult Education, University of Hull, 1963; *Schools of English and Contemporary Society* (lecture), University of Birmingham, 1963; *Higher Education and Cultural Change* (lecture), University of Newcastle upon Tyne, 1965; (with M.C. Bradbrook) *W.H. Auden [and] T.S. Eliot* (the former by Hoggart, the latter by Bradbrook), University of Nebraska Press, 1965; (author of introduction) George Orwell, *The Road to Wigan Pier,* Heinemann, 1965; (editor) Samuel Butler, *The Way of All Flesh,* Penguin, 1966; (editor) *Your Sunday Newspaper,* University of London Press, 1967; *Speaking to Each Other,* Oxford University Press, Volume I: *About Society,* 1970, Volume II: *About Literature,* 1970; *On Culture and Communication* (originally announced as *Only Connect),* Oxford University Press, 1972.

Contributor: *W.H. Auden,* Longmans, Green, 1957, new edition, 1961; Norman Mackenzie, editor, *Conviction,* MacGibbon & Kee, 1958; Boris Ford, editor, *The Modern Age,* Penguin, 1961; John Butt, editor, *Of Books and Mankind: Essays and Poems Presented to Bonamy Dobree,* Routledge & Kegan Paul, 1964. Author of monographs and introductions. Contributor of reviews to periodicals. Member of editorial advisory board, *Twentieth Century* (critical quarterly).

SIDELIGHTS: In a review of *Speaking to Each Other,* Julian Mitchell describes Hoggart as "a socio-literary-cultural critic, trying to keep a proper distance from material which must sometimes cry out for a direct response; he is a working-class boy grown into an international professor, striving to be honest in a language which keeps trying to be someone else's. His tone, when he's at his best, is that of a man under very great tensions, forcing himself to stay calm and clear. Often this tone is more interesting than what he actually has to say—which may sound absurd to Americans, but as Hoggart himself observes, Americans simply don't have the stylistic problems the English have.

"The essays give the impression of a marvelous teacher: he is tough as well as scrupulous, patient, concerned and, above all, reasonable. He seems an extraordinarily *English* Englishman, somehow combining the best qualities of the two classes he does and doesn't belong to—middle-class responsibility and sense of service, working-class honesty and warmth."

BIOGRAPHICAL/CRITICAL SOURCES: Times Literary Supplement, March 5, 1970; *New Statesman,* March

13, 1970; *Economist,* April 18, 1970; *Books and Book-men,* May, 1970; *New York Times Book Review,* May 17, 1970; *London Magazine,* June, 1970; *Encounter,* June, 1970; *Commonweal,* June 12, 1970; *New Yorker,* June 27, 1970.

* * *

HOLLOWAY, Harry (Albert) 1925-

PERSONAL: Born August 28, 1925, in Seattle, Wash.; son of Albert Cecil (a newsman) and Maude (Hall) Holloway; married Jean Gretchen Connorton, June 7, 1951 (divorced, 1972); chidren: Linda Jean, Diana Lee, Scott Douglas. *Education:* University of Washington, Seattle, B.A., 1950; University of London, M. Sc. in Economics, 1954; Cornell University, Ph.D., 1957. *Politics:* Usually Democrat. *Religion:* None. *Home:* 333 East Brooks #9, Norman, Okla. 73069. *Office:* Department of Political Science, University of Oklahoma, Norman, Okla. 73069.

CAREER: University of Texas, Austin, instructor, 1957-61, assistant professor of political science, 1961-62; University of Oklahoma, Norman, associate professor, 1962-66, professor of political science, 1967—. *Military service:* U.S. Marine Corps Reserve, 1943-46. *Member:* American Association of University Professors, American Civil Liberties Union, National Association for the Advancement of Colored People, Southern Political Science Association, Southwest Social Science Association. *Awards, honors:* Rockefeller Foundation grant, 1964-65.

WRITINGS: (With James R. Soukup and H.C. McCleskey) *Party and Factional Division in Texas,* University of Texas Press, 1964; *The Politics of the Southern Negro: From Exclusion to Big City Organization,* Random House, 1969; (contributor) Norval D. Glenn and Charles M. Bonjean, editors, *Blacks in the United States,* Chandler Publishing, 1969. Contributor to scholarly journals.

WORK IN PROGRESS: A textbook on public opinion; an essay on violence in America; writing on black-white differences, giving evidence from the surveys.

* * *

HOLLOWAY, Maurice 1920-

PERSONAL: Born February 13, 1920, in St. Louis, Mo.; son of John Joseph and Maude (Kopp) Holloway; married Betty O'Daniel, July 21, 1966; children: Mary Patricia, Thomas Aquinas. *Education:* St. Louis University, A.B., 1944, M.A., 1945; Gregorian University, Ph.D., 1954. *Home:* RD1, Florek Rd., Edinboro, Pa. 16412. *Office:* 133 Faculty Annex, Edinboro State College, Edinboro, Pa. 16412.

CAREER: Entered Order of Society of Jesus (Jesuits), 1937, ordained Roman Catholic Priest, 1950; St. Louis University High School, St. Louis, Mo., instructor in Latin and English, 1945-47; Bellarmine House of Studies, St. Louis, Mo., extraordinary professor in the text of St. Thomas and in medieval philosophy, 1954-57, ordinary professor in natural theology, 1957-64; St. Louis University, St. Louis, Mo., instructor, 1954-57, assistant professor, 1957-62, associate professor of philosophy, 1962-64; Rockhurst College, Kansas City, Mo., associate professor of philosophy and religion and chairman of philosophy department, 1964-67, head of division of philosophy and religion, 1965-67; Edinboro State College, Edinboro, Pa., professor of philosophy and chairman of the department, 1967—. *Member:* American Catholic Philosophical Association, Jesuit Philosophical Association, Missouri Philosophical Association.

WRITINGS: An Introduction to Natural Theology, Appleton, 1959; (with G.P. Klubertanz) *Being and God: An Introduction to the Philosophy of Being and to Natural Theology,* Appleton, 1963; (editor with Vincent F. Daues and Leo Sweeney) *Wisdom in Depth: Essays in Honor of Henry Renard, S.J.,* Bruce, 1966. Contributor to *Catholic Youth Encyclopedia* and *New Catholic Encyclopedia,* and to *Thought* and *Social Justice.* Editor, *Modern Schoolman,* 1959-64.

WORK IN PROGRESS: A textbook in ethics, *Fundamental Principles of Morality;* a college text, *Introduction to Existentialism; The Finite God,* for Appleton.

SIDELIGHTS: Holloway is competent in Latin, and has a reading knowledge of French, German, Italian, and Spanish.

* * *

HOLLOWOOD, Albert Bernard 1910-

PERSONAL: Born June 3, 1910, in Burslem, Staffordshire, England; son of Albert and Sarah Elizabeth Hollowood; married Marjorie Duncan Lawrie, 1938; children: Jane (Mrs. M. Jeremy Barlow), Susan, Duncan. *Education:* Attended St. Paul's College, Cheltenham, England, and University of London. *Home:* Blackmoor Paddock, Haldish Lane, Shamley Green, Surrey, England. *Office: Punch,* 10 Bouverie St., London E.C.4, England.

CAREER: Stoke and Loughborough College, London, England, lecturer in economics, 1932-43; *Economist,* London, staff member, 1944-45; *Pottery and Glass,* London, editor, 1944-50; *Punch,* London, editor, 1958-68. Cartoonist for *Times* (London), *Telegraph,* and other newspapers. Broadcaster, 1939—. Visiting professor at universities in the United States. Research officer, Council of Industrial Design, 1946. Governor, London School of Economics, University of London. *Member:* Marylebone Cricket Club. *Awards, honors:* M.A., University of Keele, 1968.

WRITINGS: (Self-illustrated) *Direct Economics,* Thomas Nelson, 1943; (self-illustrated) *Money Is No Expense,* Sidgwick & Jackson, 1946; *An Innocent at Large,* Sidgwick & Jackson, 1947; *Pottery and Glass,* Penguin, 1947; *Britain Inside-Out,* Sidgwick & Jackson, 1948; *Scowle and Other Papers,* Penguin, 1948; (self-illustrated) *Poor Little Rich World,* Thomas Nelson, 1948; *The Hawksmoor Scandals,* Harrap, 1949; *The Cornish Engineers,* Samson Clark, 1951; *The Story of Morro Velho,* Samson Clark, 1954; (with Wren) *These Fuelish Things,* Esso Petroleum Co., c.1955; *Money,* Newman Neame, 1957; *Tory Story: Incorporating Living with Labour and Liberal Outlook,* Hammond, 1964; *Pont: An Account of the Life and Work of Graham Laidler (1908-1940), the Great Punch Artist,* Collins, 1969; *Cricket on the Brain,* Eyre & Spottiswoode, 1970; *Tales of Tammy Barr,* Chatto & Windus, 1970.

Editor: *The Pick of Punch,* Arthur Barker, 1960-62, Hutchinson, 1963-68. Contributor to *Sunday Times* (London), *Sunday Telegraph, New York Times,* and to various periodicals.

WORK IN PROGRESS: A book on specialist economic planning.

BIOGRAPHICAL/CRITICAL SOURCES: Punch, November 12, 1969.

* * *

HOLMAN, Dennis (Idris) 1915-

PERSONAL: Born January 14, 1915, in Lahore, India (now Pakistan); son of Edward Allan and Rose (Harrington) Holman; married Elizabeth Keily, June 15, 1948; children: Neil, Pamela, Denise, Judith, Miranda. *Education:* Attended St. George's College, Mussoorie, India; Punjab University, B.A., 1936. *Religion:* Roman

Catholic. *Home:* 48 Christchurch Rd., Sidcup, Kent, England. *Agent:* Julian S. Bach Jr., 249 East 48th St., New York, N.Y. 10017.

CAREER: Free-lance journalist. *Military service:* British Army, 1939-45; became major. *Member:* Society of Authors, League of Dramatists, Screenwriters Guild, National Union of Journalists.

WRITINGS: Lady Louis: Life of the Countess Montbatten of Burma, Odhams, 1952; (with W. Ellery Anderson) *Expedition South,* Evans Brothers, 1957; *Noone of the Ulu,* Heinemann, 1958; *The Man They Couldn't Kill,* Heinemann, 1960; *Sikander Sahib: The Life of Colonel James Skinner, 1778-1841,* Heinemann, 1961; *The Green Torture: The Ordeal of Robert Chrystal,* R. Hale, 1962; (with G.T. Cooper) *Ordeal in the Sun,* R. Hale, 1963; *Bwana Drum,* W.H. Allen, 1964, Norton, 1965; (editor) *Earlier Nineteenth Century, 1783-1867,* Hutchinson, 1965, Fernhill, 1968; (with C.J.P. Ionides) *A Hunter's Story,* W.H. Allen, 1965, published in America as *Mambas and Man-Eaters,* Holt, 1966; *Massacre of the Elephants,* Holt, 1967 (published in England as *The Elephant People,* J. Murray, 1967); *Inside Safari Hunting with Eric Rundgren,* W.H. Allen, 1969, Putnam, 1970. Author of filmscript, "Adventure On," and of several radio and television scripts. Regular contributor to British newspapers and magazines, 1945—, including more than sixty short stories.

WORK IN PROGRESS: Rape of the Dream People; and The Hills of Atrocity.

SIDELIGHTS: Holman told *CA:* "I travel the world as a roving free lance looking for feature material, in particular stories which will serialize in magazines and newspapers. . . . My main interest is the theatre. I have two hobbies: In England it is growing rare rock plants; abroad it is goggling with a spear gun in tropical coral gardens. I can also cook a fairly good curry."

*   *   *

HOLMES, David Charles 1919-
(David Charlson)

PERSONAL: Born August 18, 1919, in Spokane, Wash.; son of David Charlson and Maude (Bunce) Holmes; married Virginia Romar, July 15, 1944; children: Dian Carolyn, David C., Jr. *Education:* Gonzaga University, student, 1938-39; U.S. Naval Academy, B.S., 1942. *Home:* Lysehagen 4, Oslo, Norway. *Agent:* Donald Mac-Campbell, Inc., 12 East 41st St., New York, N.Y. 10017. *Office:* Allied Forces Northern Europe (NATO), Kolsas, Norway.

CAREER: U.S. Navy, 1942—; served aboard ships and in squadrons; designated naval aviator in 1947; member of Advanced Research Projects Agency and manager of Defense Department's space-tracking network, 1959-62; currently captain, serving with North Atlantic Treaty Organization forces in Oslo, Norway. *Member:* American Institute of Aeronautics and Astronautics.

WRITINGS: Young People's Book of Radar, McBride Co., 1951, 3rd edition, 1955; (under pseudonym David Charlson) *Frenchie,* Zenith Books, 1955; (with Marvin Pitkin) *On the Wings of the Wind,* McBride Co., 1955; (with Pitkin) *Young People's Book of Weather,* McBride Co., 1955; *The Velvet Ape,* Mystery House, 1957; *What's Going on in Space?: A Chronicle of Man's Exploration into Space Beyond This Earth,* Funk, 1958; *The Story of Weather,* Pyramid Publications, 1963, revised edition published as *Weather Made Clear,* Sterling, 1965 (revised edition published in England as *Understanding the Weather,* Oak Tree Press, 1966); *The Search for Life on Other Worlds,* Sterling, 1967. Contributor of articles to magazines and journals.

BIOGRAPHICAL/CRITICAL SOURCES: Best Sellers, May 1, 1967.

*   *   *

HOLMES, John Clellon 1926-

PERSONAL: Born March 12, 1926, in Holyoke, Mass.; son of John McClellan (a sales representative) and Elizabeth (Emmons) Holmes; married Marian Miliambro, August, 1944; married second wife, Shirley Allen, September 9, 1953. *Education:* Studied at Columbia University, 1943, 1945-46, New School for Social Research, 1949-50. *Politics:* Independent. *Home:* Box 75, Old Saybrook, Conn. 06475. *Agent:* Sterling Lord Agency, 660 Madison Ave., New York, N.Y. 10021.

CAREER: Writer. State University of Iowa, visiting lecturer, 1963-64; University of Arkansas, writer-in-residence, 1966. Visiting professor, Bowling Green State University, 1968, Brown University, 1971-72. *Military service:* U.S. Navy, Hospital Corps, 1944-45. *Member:* P.E.N. *Awards, honors: Playboy* awards, 1964, 1971, runner up, 1970, 1972.

WRITINGS: Go (novel), Scribner, 1952 (published in England as *The Beat Boys,* Harborough Publishing Co., 1959); *The Horn* (novel), Random House, 1958; *Get Home Free* (novel), Dutton, 1964; *Nothing More to Declare* (essays; excerpts originally published in *Books,* December, 1966), Dutton, 1967.

Represented in many anthologies. Contributor of poetry, articles, and stories to *Holiday, Esquire, New York Times Magazine, Harper's, Partisan Review, Glamour, Poetry, Audience, Writer,* and other literary magazines and periodicals.

WORK IN PROGRESS: Autobiographical travel book, *Walking Away from the War;* a novel, tentatively titled *The Taboo Hunters.*

SIDELIGHTS: As a representative of the "Beat Generation" of artists and writers, Holmes has never achieved the fame of such contemporaries as Allen Ginsberg or Jack Kerouac. Holmes has not, however, been disregarded by critics, who consider *Nothing More to Declare* a succinct and accurate chronicle of the people and aspirations that comprised that post-war movement. Daniel Aaron believes that Holmes's book "is an absolutely honest testament in addition to being a kind of mosaic of a generation. . . . Throughout this far-ranging commentary, . . . Holmes is invariably pertinent r.ad unfailingly alive. Perhaps he overstates the cultural importance of his Beat heroes and the profundity of their psychic and social disclosures, but exaggeration is usually undercut by wit and candor."

An important distinction Holmes makes is that between the "beats" of his generation and the activists of the present. "Non-violence, pacifism and reverence for life are mostly means of action to young people today," Holmes states, "whereas, to us, they were ends in themselves: you were nonviolent not because it was one way of changing institutions, but because it was the only way of remaining a human being."

A John Clellon Holmes collection was established at Boston University in 1966.

AVOCATIONAL INTERESTS: Music, especially Baroque and guitar; renovating old houses (specifically the Connecticut Victorian house in which he lives, and a clammer's shack in Maine); travel, history, films, cooking, wine.

BIOGRAPHICAL/CRITICAL SOURCES: Saturday Review, October 11, 1952, August 2, 1958, June 6, 1964; *New York Herald Tribune Book Review,* October 12, 1952, July 20, 1958; *Library Journal,* October 15, 1952,

June 1, 1964, February 15, 1967; *New York Times,* November 9, 1952, August 10, 1958; *Chicago Sunday Tribune,* July 27, 1958; *San Francisco Chronicle,* July 27, 1958; *New Yorker,* September 6, 1958; *Nation,* November 15, 1958; *New York Times Book Review,* May 3, 1964, April 9, 1967; *Atlantic,* June, 1964; *Book Week,* June 7, 1964, *Books,* December, 1966; *Newsweek,* March 13, 1967; *Christian Science Monitor,* March 16, 1967; *Commonweal,* May 5, 1967; *Choice,* September, 1967; *Listener,* June 27, 1968; *London Magazine,* July, 1968; *Times Literary Supplement,* June 12, 1969.

* * *

HOOK, Sidney 1902-

PERSONAL: Born December 20, 1902, in New York, N.Y.; son of Isaac and Jennie (Halpern) Hook; married Carrie Katz, March 31, 1924; married second wife, Ann E. Zinken, May 25, 1935; children: (first marriage) John Bertrand; (second marriage) Ernest Benjamin, Susan Ann. *Education:* College of the City of New York (now City College of the City University of New York), B.S., 1923; Columbia University, M.A., 1926, Ph.D., 1927. *Residence:* South Wardsboro, Vt. 05355.

CAREER: Public school teacher in New York City, 1923-28; New York University, Washington Square College, New York, N.Y., instructor, 1927-32, assistant professor, 1932-34, associate professor and chairman of department, 1934-39, professor of philosophy, 1939-72, head of department of philosophy of graduate school, 1948-67, chairman of division of philosophy and psychology of the graduate school, 1949-55, head of all-university department, 1957-72. Lecturer at New School for Social Research, New York, N.Y., 1931—. One of organizers of Americans for Intellectual Freedom, American Committee of Cultural Freedom, Conference on Methods in Science and Philosophy, New York University Institute of Philosophy, Conference on Scientific Spirit and Democratic Faith, University Centers for Rational Alternatives, and Committee Against Academic Discrimination and for Academic Integrity.

MEMBER: International Committee for Academic Freedom, International Committee for the Rights of Man, American Philosophical Association (Eastern Division, vice-president, 1958, president, 1959-60), American Association of University Professors (former council member), John Dewey Society, New York Philosophy Club. *Awards, honors:* Guggenheim fellowships, 1928-29, 1953; Nicholas Murray Butler Silver Medal of Columbia University, 1945, for *The Hero in History;* Ford Foundation traveling fellowship, 1958; D.H.L., University of Maine, 1960, University of Utah, 1970; fellow, Center for Advanced Study in the Behavioral Sciences, Stanford, Calif., 1961-62; fellow, American Academy of Arts and Sciences, 1965; fellow, National Academy of Education, 1966; LL.D., University of California, 1966, Rockford College, 1971, University of Florida, 1971.

WRITINGS: The Metaphysics of Pragmatism, introduction by John Dewey, Open Court, 1927; (translator with David Kvitko) *Collected Works of Vladimir Ilich Lenin,* Volume XIII, International Publications, 1927; *Towards the Understanding of Karl Marx: A Revolutionary Interpretation,* John Day, 1933; *The Democratic and Dictatorial Aspects of Communism* (Part II of a work of which Part I was *The Political and Social Doctrine of Communism,* by Joseph Stalin), Carnegie Endowment for International Peace, 1934; (with Francis Henson and Henry P. Van Deusen) *Christianity and Marxism,* Polemic, 1935; *From Hegel to Marx: Studies in the Intellectual Development of Karl Marx,* Reynal & Hitchcock, 1936, reissued with a new introduction by Hook, University of Michigan Press, 1950; *John Dewey: An Intellectual Portrait,* John Day, 1939; *Reason, Social Myths, and Democracy,*

John Day, 1940, reissued with a new introduction, Harper, 1965; *The Hero in History: A Study in Limitation and Possibility,* John Day, 1943; *What is the Future of Socialism?,* [London], 1945; *Education for Modern Man,* Dial, 1946, revised and enlarged edition published as *Education for Modern Man: A New Perspective,* Knopf, 1963; *Democracy and Desegregation,* Tamiment Institute, 1952; *Heresy, Yes—Conspiracy, No!,* John Day, 1953; *Modern Education and Its Critics,* American Association of Colleges for Teacher Education, 1954; *Dialectical Materialism and Scientific Method,* Manchester University Press, 1955; *Marx and the Marxists: The Ambiguous Legacy,* Van Nostrand, 1955; *Common Sense and the Fifth Amendment,* Criterion, 1957; *Democracy and Desegregation* (pamphlet), Tamiment Institute, 1958; *John Dewey: His Philosophy of Education and Its Critics* (pamphlet), Tamiment Institute, 1959; *Political Power and Personal Freedom: Critical Studies in Democracy, Communism, and Civil Rights,* Criterion, 1959; *The Quest for Being, and Other Studies in Naturalism and Humanism,* St. Martin's, 1961; *The Paradoxes of Freedom* (Thomas Jefferson Memorial lecture series), University of California Press, 1962; *The Fail-Safe Fallacy,* Stein & Day, 1963; *Religion in a Free Society* (Montgomery Lectures given at University of Nebraska, March 23 and 25, 1964), University of Nebraska Press, 1967; *Contemporary Philosophy,* American Library Association, 1968; (with Tom Wicker and C. Vann Woodward) *Social Justice and the Problems of the Twentieth Century* (William D. Carmichael, Jr. Lecture series, 1968; includes "Human Rights and Social Justice" by Hook, "Black and White Democracy" by Wicker, and "Ironies of Peace and War" by Woodward), North Carolina State University, 1968; *Academic Freedom and Academic Anarchy* (expanded version to book length of an address originally delivered on June 20, 1968, and published by Institute for the Comparative Study of Political Systems, University of Colorado, 1968; excerpt entitled "What Student Rights in Education?" published in *Current,* April, 1970), Cowles, 1970; *Education and the Taming of Power,* Open Court, 1973.

Editor: (And contributor) *The Meaning of Marx* (symposium; originally published in *Modern Monthly,* April, 1934), Farrar & Rinehart, 1934; (with Horace M. Kallen) *American Philosophy Today and Tomorrow,* Furman, 1935; (with Milton R. Konvitz) *Freedom and Experience: Essays Presented to Horace M. Kallen,* Cornell University Press, 1947; *John Dewey, Philosopher of Science and Freedom: A Symposium,* Dial, 1950; *American Philosophers at Work: The Philosophic Scene in the United States,* Criterion, 1956; (and author of introduction) *World Communism: Key Documentary Material,* Van Nostrand, 1962; (with E. Chalfant) *In Defense of Academic Freedom,* Pegasus, 1971. Editor of annual proceedings of the New York University Institute of Philosophy, published by New York University Press, including *Determinism and Freedom in the Age of Modern Science,* 1958, *Psychoanalysis, Scientific Method and Philosophy,* 1959, *Dimensions of Mind,* 1960, *Religious Experience and Truth,* 1961, *Philosophy and History,* 1963, *Law and Philosophy,* 1964, *Art and Philosophy,* 1966, *Human Values and Economic Policy,* 1967, *Language and Philosophy,* 1969.

Contributor: *Essays in Honor of John Dewey,* Holt, 1929; Max Eastman, *Art and the Life of Action,* Knopf, 1934; *Studies in the History of Ideas,* Columbia University Press, 1935; Findlay MacKenzie, editor, *Planned Society: Yesterday, Today, and Tomorrow,* Prentice-Hall, 1937; Y.A. Krikorian, editor, *Naturalism and the Human Spirit,* Columbia University Press, 1944; (author of introduction) Karl Kautskey, *Social Democracy verses Socialism,* edited by David Shub, translated by Joseph Shaplen, Rand School Press, 1946; Jerome Nathanson, editor, *Pa-*

pers: *Science for Democracy*, King's Crown Press, 1946; *Theory and Practice in Historical Study: A Report of the Committee on Historiography*, Social Science Research Council, 1946; *American Thought, 1947*, introduction by Philip Wylie, Gresham Press, 1947; J.R. Chamberlain, W.B. Pressey, and R.E. Watters, editors, *Living, Reading, and Thinking*, Scribner, 1948; Julien Steinberg, *Verdict of Three Decades*, Duell, Sloan & Pearce, 1950; Marvin Farber, editor, *Philosophic Thought in France and the United States*, University of Buffalo Press, 1950; Paul A. Schilpp, editor, *Philosophy of Bertrand Russell*, Tudor, 1951; Salo Baron, Ernest Nagel, and K.S. Pinson, editors, *Freedom and Reason*, Free Press, 1951; Horace T. Morse, editor, *General Education in Transition*, University of Minnesota Press, 1951; H.M. Gloster, W.E. Farrison, and N. Tillman, editors, *My Life, My Country, My World*, Prentice-Hall, 1952; Sidney Ratner, editor, *Vision and Action: Essays in Honor of Horace Kallen on His 70th Birthday*, Rutgers University Press, 1953; *The Contemporary Scene* (symposium held at Metropolitan Museum of Art, March 28-30, 1952), New York Metropolitan Museum of Art, 1954; *Science and Freedom* (proceedings of Congress for Cultural Freedom, Hamburg, 1953), Beacon Press, 1955; Adrienne Koch, *Philosophy for a Time of Crisis*, Dutton, 1959; Brand Blanshard, editor, *Education in the Age of Science*, Basic Books, 1959; *Science and Philosophy of Reading*, University of Delaware Press, 1959; Milton R. Konvitz and Gail Kennedy, editors, *The American Pragmatist*, Meridian Books, 1960; George B. Huszar, editor, *The Intellectuals*, Free Press, 1960; C.A. Moore, editor, *Philosophy and Culture—East and West*, University of Hawaii Press, 1962; Don C. Travis, editor, *A Hegel Symposium*, University of Texas, 1962; Abraham Brumberg, editor, *Problems of Communism: Russia Under Khrushchev*, Praeger, 1962; (author of introduction) R.R. Abrahamovich, *The Soviet Revolution*, International Universities Press, 1962; *The Role of the Humanities in Ordering a Peaceful World*, Central Connecticut State College, 1962; *In Quest of Value* (readings selected by San Jose State College Associates in Philosophy), Chandler Publishing, 1963; (author of introduction) Eric Hoffer, *The True Believer*, Time-Life, 1963; *Health-Care Issues of 1960* (symposium), Group Health Insurance, 1963; Mahir Nasim, editor, *World Politics* (originally presented as English language radio program, 1956), Dar Al-kurrnek (Cairo), 1964; H.A. Bedau, editor, *The Death Penalty in America*, Aldine, 1964; Jozef Stankiewicz, editor, *Political Thought Since World War II: Critical and Interpretive Essays*, Free Press, 1964; Earl Rabb, *Religious Conflict in America*, Doubleday, 1964; (author of introduction) Walter Lippmann, *Preface to Morals*, new edition, Time-Life, 1964; Seymour Martin Lipset, *The Berkeley Student Revolt*, Doubleday-Anchor, 1965; Michael V. Miller and Susan Gilmore, editors, *Revolution at Berkeley*, Dial, 1965; James E. Dougherty and John F. Lehman, Jr., editors, *The Prospects for Arms Control*, Macfadden, 1965; (author of introduction) Rebecca West, *The New Meaning of Treason*, new edition, Time-Life, 1966; Milorad M. Drachkovitz, editor, *Marxist Ideology in the Contemporary World—Its Appeal and Paradoxes*, Stanford University Press and Praeger for the Hoover Institute on War, Revolution and Peace, 1966; Paul Kurtz, editor, *American Philosophy in the Twentieth Century*, Macmillan, 1966; Lionel Abel, editor, *Moderns on Tragedy*, Fawcett, 1966; E.J. Faulkner, editor, *Man's Quest for Security: A Symposium*, University of Nebraska Press, 1966; Milorad M. Drachkovitz, editor, *Marxism in the Western World* (contains chapter by Hook originally published in *Encounter*, 1965), Stanford University Press, 1968; (author of introduction) Thomas Paine, *The Essential Thomas Paine*, New American Library, 1969. Contributor to encyclopedias, to the Proceedings of various conferences and symposia, to *New Leader, Saturday Review, Partisan Review, Commentary, New Republic, Nation, Open Court*, and to numerous philosophical journals.

WORK IN PROGRESS: An autobiography.

SIDELIGHTS: Lecturing his last New York University philosophy class before retiring in December of 1972, Hook said that as a student, "and at great distance a colleague of John Dewey," he has always believed that intelligence is "the chief moral virtue," and that it includes "being able to judge the limitations of knowledge." He added: "But in the last few years I've come to the conclusion that though there is no substitute for intelligence it is not enough. I've discovered that people may be intelligent but lack the moral courage to act."

Hook studied under Morris Cohen at City College in the early 1920's, and with Frederick J.E. Woodbridge and Dewey at Columbia. Considered by many America's leading pragmatist and philosopher of democracy, his works touch on all the major social issues of our time. Paul Kurtz wrote in his preface to *Sidney Hook and the Contemporary World*: ". . . Hook occupies a special place in American philosophy and life. He is, without peer, the leading philosopher deeply involved in social affairs: He is *engage* at a time when others are non-*engages*. One may not always agree with the positions Sidney Hook has taken on moral and social issues; one may not deny that he has expressed stands on virtually all the major public issues of our time, and that his counsel and judgment have been heard in the highest chambers of decision-making, not only in America, but throughout the world. Like Jean-Paul Sartre in France and Bertrand Russell in Britain, as heir to John Dewey's mantle in the United States, Hook speaks to the actual conditions of contemporary life; and he has persistently attempted to apply pragmatic intelligence to concrete issues of practical concern . . . Like Socrates, Hook has been a controversial figure because he has frequently taken unpopular positions, and he has attacked many of the sacred cows of contemporary life. Moreover, his brilliant pragmatic intelligence has often devastated the views of some of the leading intellectual figures of our time. . . . Hook has few rivals in his ability to engage in continuing dialogue." This ability was once demonstrated in a series of fiery debates with Max Eastman concerning differing concepts of Marxism. Their bitter personal exchange finally yielded to mutual respect and "cooperation in activities opposed to Stalinism and other varieties of totalitarianism," according to Hook. Brand Blanshard has described Hook as "that inexhaustible geyser of books, lectures, and essays, a philosopher who scents the smell of battle from afar and is soon in the midst of it, giving as well as he gets, and usually somewhat better." Adrienne Koch explains that Hook has "made enemies, scores of them," because his devastating assessments of people and situations are so often "revelations of reality." Koch writes: "Nature, to be sure, creates no saints, and Hook himself would find a halo an impediment. So lively a man, and one possessed of such copious courage, can be scrappy as a gamecock. He has little reverence for merely conventional politeness and never bothers to hide a yawn. As for those who vend empty ideals or proffer ersatz ideas as the real thing, Hook can be merciless. His criticism is always enlightening but sometimes unrelieved by the hint of a contrived exit for the offender. His reputation as a controversialist is formidable, justifiably so. When others merely *lamented* the stupidities or the malignant distortions of the liberal faith, Hook was prepared and able to do battle for it. He knew how to provide effective leadership for democracy and wisely understood that it required a militant and vigilant advance guard."

Hook considers *Education for Modern Man*, which Dewey called a "wisely sane" appraisal of current controversies, philosophies, and movements in the field of education, his major educational work. Eric Bentley stated that "those who enjoy the human individual will like [this book] all the more for its crotchets and aggressions, its petulance and its boyish earnestness. And even severe impersonalists will have to admit that Mr. Hook has the qualities of his defects." Irwin Edman especially recommended Hook's "excellent chapter on The Good Teacher, where he permits himself a little less dialectic and controversy, a little more enkindling eloquence, than generally marks the book. Himself a notably good teacher, his account of such a rarity is both exciting and true talk." In her essay on Hook's theory of education, Bella K. Milmed seems to agree: "Sidney Hook's recent rebuke to American intellectuals for failure to concern themselves with the problems of education comes from one of the few in a position to administer such a rebuke without self-incrimination. A possible reply may be that few people have either the intellectual versatility or the inexhaustible energy that have enabled Professor Hook to bring philosophical resources to bear on so many of the urgent problems of our perplexing and distressing world."

While studying in Germany and the Soviet Union in 1928-29, Hook resided briefly at the Marx-Engels Institute in Moscow. As Andrew Reck affirms in *The New American Philosophers*, "Hook's concern with Marxism covers half a century. So numerous are his writings on Marxism that they vie with pragmatism for central position in the structure and genesis of his thought. No doubt his study of Marxism was in the first instance triggered by his adherence to democratic socialism which, in the days before communism had taken a Stalinist form, he sometimes referred to as communism. . . . In truth, the temper of Sidney Hook's thinking owes more to John Dewey than to Karl Marx. But this must not obscure the overriding significance of Hook's philosophy for contemporary thought—a significance which resides neither in his Marxism nor in his pragmatism alone, but in that crucial and insufficiently noted juncture in the intellectual history of the present epoch—the confrontation of pragmatism and Marxism, an Americanized version of democratic socialism." In his review of *The Fail-Safe Fallacy* (a refutation of the 1962 best-selling novel, *Fail-Safe*, by Eugene Burdick and Harvey Wheeler), J.G. Campaigne calls the book "a multi-megaton bomb. Sidney Hook has mounted a tight, five-pronged offensive which wholly obliterates the jungle of confusion and hysteria now suffocating the whole range of anti-Communist thought and action. The book is . . . a devastating appraisal of the intellectual sclerosis and moral ambiguity of the American Establishment, . . . [and] the most concise short course in Communist political warfare, motivation, philosophy, psychology and history ever penned."

One of the chief targets of philosophical and political attack in the press of Communist countries, Hook has consistently maintained a democratic socialist position which takes on added dimensions in opposition to the New Left. His most recent book, *Academic Freedom and Academic Anarchy*, has aroused intense controversy among those concerned with the future of American universities. A critique of student rebels and their faculty sympathizers, the book is, in the opinion of H.D. Aiken (whom Hook considers a partisan of the radical students), "a call to arms against every form of resistance to legitimated power." Hook bases his position on the tenet that "the university is not a political community. Its business [should be] not government but primarily the discovery, publication, and teaching of the truth." How one defines "truth" without taking into account the "enormous overlap of university and governmental concerns and personnel" is what baffles many, among them Edgar Friedenberg, who himself has been the target of Hook's criticisms. He believes that Hook's assessment is so divorced from a realistic appraisal of the modern univer-

sity's role in relation to student needs that "it leaves the reader who does not share his assumptions with the sinking feeling of trying to confront an enclosed system of delusions." On the other hand, L.B. Mayhew believes the book is "a needed corrective for the flood of apologist-for-youth literature that characterized the first five post-Berkeley years."

Hook said recently that he is working on an autobiography, which he will call *Out of Step*. "I've always been out of step," he told his philosophy class. "A premature Marxist. A premature anti-Fascist. A premature anti-Communist."

BIOGRAPHICAL/CRITICAL SOURCES: Max Eastman, *Last Stand of Dialectic Materialism: A Study of Sidney Hook's Marxism*, Polemic, 1934; *Nation*, April 20, 1946; *Saturday Review of Literature*, April 20, 1946, January 24, 1970; Julien Steinberg, editor, *Verdict of Three Decades*, Duell, Sloan & Pearce, 1950; Brand Blanshard, editor, *Education in the Age of Science*, Basic Books, 1959; *Commentary*, March, 1963; *National Review*, November 19, 1963, January 27, 1970; *Christian Century*, August 30, 1967; Paul Kurtz, editor, *Sidney Hook and the Contemporary World*, John Day, 1968; Andrew J. Reck, *The New American Philosophers*, Louisiana State University Press, 1968; *New York Review of Books*, February 12, 1970; *New York Times Book Review*, March 8, 1970; *New York Times*, December 21, 1972.

*   *   *

HOOKHAM, Hilda Henriette (Kuttner)   1915-

PERSONAL: Born May 22, 1915, in London, England; daughter of Arthur and Emily (Allen) Kuttner; married Maurice Hookham (a university lecturer), February 16, 1934; children: Jeremy Marlowe. *Education:* London School of Economics, University of London, B.Sc. (first class honors), 1936. *Home:* The Lawns, 486 Groby Rd., Leicester, England.

CAREER: Ashby de la Zouch, Leicestershire, England, senior history mistress, 1953-63. Lecturer, Goldsmiths College, University of London, 1963. *Member:* Royal Asiatic Society.

WRITINGS: Tamburlaine the Conqueror, Hodder & Stoughton, 1962, Verry, 1964; *A Short History of China*, Longmans, 1969, St. Martin's, 1970. Contributor to *Times* (London), and to history journals in England and America. Author of film strip, "History of China," Hulton Educational Press.

WORK IN PROGRESS: History of the Trans-Siberian Railway; Jane Austen and the Gentry.

*   *   *

HOPE, Ronald (Sidney)   1921-

PERSONAL: Born April 4, 1921, in London, England; son of George William (a laborer) and Martha (Turrell) Hope; married Marion Whittaker, December 20, 1947; children: Marion Elizabeth, Ronald Anthony. *Education:* New College, Oxford, B.A., 1941, M.A., 1946, D. Phil., 1949. *Home and office:* 207 Balham High Rd., London S.W. 17, England.

CAREER: Brasenose College, Oxford University, Oxford, England, fellow and lecturer in economics, 1946-47; Seafarers' Education Service and College of the Sea, London, England, director, 1947—. Justice of the peace, 1963-70; former chairman of Social Workers Pension Fund and of Social Service Supplies. *Military service:* Royal Naval Volunteer Reserve, 1941-45; became lieutenant. *Member:* Marine Society (chairman). *Awards, honors:* Officer, Order of the British Empire.

WRITINGS: Spare Time at Sea, Maritime Press, 1954; *Economic Geography*, Philip & Son, 1956, 5th edition, 1969; *Dick Small in the Half-Deck*, Chatto & Windus, 1958; *Ships*, Macmillan, 1958; (editor) *The Harrap Book of Sea Verse*, Harrap, 1960, Books for Libraries, 1969; (editor) *The Shoregoer's Guide to World Ports*, Maritime Press, 1963; *Introduction to the Merchant Navy*, Seafarers' Education Service, 1965, 3rd edition, 1967; (editor) *Seamen and the Sea: A Collection of New Sea Stories by Merchant Seamen*, Harrap, 1965; *In Cabined Ships at Sea: Fifty Years of the Seafarer's Education Service*, Harrap, 1969. Regular contributor to *Fairplay* and *Seafarer*.

WORK IN PROGRESS: Beginnings of the British Merchant Navy, 1600 B.C.-1600 A.D.

BIOGRAPHICAL/CRITICAL SOURCES: Seafarer, spring, 1964.

*   *   *

HOPKINS, Bill 1928-

PERSONAL: Born May 15, 1928, in Cardiff, South Wales; son of Ted (an actor and dramatist) and Violet (an actress; maiden name, Brodrick) Hopkins. *Education:* Privately educated. *Home and office:* 36 Kirkstall Rd., Streatham Hill, London S.W.2, England. *Agent:* David Higham Associates Ltd., 76 Dean St., London W.1, England.

CAREER: British United Press, night editor, 1946; Royal Air Force, Air Ministry news correspondent with occupational forces, Europe, 1946-49; *The Diplomatist* (journal of the Corps Diplomatique), editor, 1949; *Across Frontiers* (journal of the Crusade for World Government), associate editor, 1950-55; *New York Times*, London, England, night editor, 1954-57. Writer.

WRITINGS: (Contributor) Tom Maschler, editor, *Declaration*, MacGibbon & Kee, 1957, Dutton, 1958; *The Divine and the Decay* (novel), McGibbon & Kee, 1957; (translator) Roger Bragard and F.J. de Hen, *Musical Instruments in Art and History*, Studio Books, 1968; (editor, translator, and author of introduction) Karl Heinrich Woerner, *Stockhausen: Life and Work*, University of California Press, 1973. One of the dramatists committed to providing plays for the Royal Court Theatre, London. Author of television play, "The Burying Party," and stage play, "Someone for the Night." Editorial director of *Penthouse*, an English version of *Playboy*, 1965—. Contributor to *News Chronicle, Daily Express, New York Times, Lilliput, Time and Tide, Spectator, Town Today*, and other publications.

WORK IN PROGRESS: Time of Totality, and *The Parcels*, two novels for McGibbon & Kee; another novel, *The Unwanted*; "The Titans," the first in a cycle of plays; other projected titles of cycle: "Genius," "The Orator," and "The Dukedoms of Demonia."

SIDELIGHTS: Hopkins told *CA:* "[I] am interested in evolving new types of heroic characters and a new type of novel of which *The Divine and The Decay* is a first prototype. [I] am interested in paleontology, archaeology, anthropology, zoology, biology, mysticism, human pathology (crime especially), philosophy, theology, politics, and too many other subjects to be listed. [I am] specifically interested in early Chinese culture and its evolution; in fact, I have an interesting collection of Ancient Ritual Bronzes of the Shang-Yin, Chou, Han Dynasties, and various early examples of Jade, Ivory, Pottery and Ceramics. [I] have travelled throughout Europe."

Because he is an experimentalist, Hopkins says he rarely gets an impartial review. "In fact," he writes, "the reason I've remembered the few I've quoted is purely because they've either been venomous attacks, such as in Sartre's rag *Les Temps Modernes*, or eulogistic defences by other writers. . . . As one of the most attacked authors in Britain, advocating some of the most radical and unorthodox arguments against our social structure in the West, I have deliberately not published any major work for several years."

BIOGRAPHICAL/CRITICAL SOURCES: Kenneth Allsop, *The Angry Decade*, P. Owen, 1958; *Les Temps Modernes*, spring, 1958; Stuart Holroyd, *Flight and Pursuit*, Gollancz, 1959; *Hamburger Abendblatt*, December, 1961; James Gindin, *Postwar British Fiction: New Accents and Attitudes*, University of California Press, 1962; Bernard Kops, *The World Is a Wedding*, Coward, 1963.

*   *   *

HOPKINS, Terence K(ilbourne) 1928-

PERSONAL: Born November 20, 1928, in New Rochelle, N.Y.; son of Frank Warren (an artist) and Eleanor (Matthews) Hopkins; married Elizabeth Erickson (an anthropologist), April 29, 1961. *Education:* Oberlin College, student, 1947-49; New York University, A.B. (cum laude), 1952; Columbia University, Ph.D., 1959. *Office:* Department of Sociology, State University of New York at Binghamton, Binghamton, N.Y., 13901.

CAREER: Columbia University, New York, N.Y., research associate, Bureau of Applied Social Research, 1952-58, instructor, 1958-59, assistant professor, 1959-64, became associate professor of sociology, 1964; State University of New York at Binghamton, presently member of sociology department. Associate, East African Institute of Social Research, Makerere University College, Kampala, Uganda, 1961-62. *Member:* American Sociological Association, Economic History Association, Academy of Political Science, African Studies Association, Social Science Research Council (fellow), American Federation of Scientists, American Association of University Professors, Phi Beta Kappa, Alpha Kappa Delta. *Awards, honors:* Social Science Research Council and American Council of Learned Societies award; Fulbright award; Columbia Council for Research in the Social Sciences award.

WRITINGS: (With Herbert H. Hyman and Charles R. Wright) *Applications of Methods of Evaluation: Four Studies of the Encampment for Citizenship*, University of California Press, 1962; *The Exercise of Influence in Small Groups*, Bedminster, 1964; *On Economic Planning in Tropical Africa*, Institute of African Studies, Columbia University, 1964; (with Perezi Kamunarive) *A Study Guide for Uganda*, Development Program, African Studies Center, Boston University, 1969.

WORK IN PROGRESS: Group Structure and Opinion Change: An Analysis of an Effective Training Program; The Feasibility of Staggered Working Hours: A Sociological Analysis; The Colonial Transformation: The Kingdom of Ankole, 1890-1960; An Introduction to Sociological Analysis; and *Patterns of Consumer Credit;* co-authoring a comparative study of national societies.

*   *   *

HOPPE, Emil Otto 1878-

PERSONAL: Born April 14, 1878, in Munich, Bavaria, Germany; children: Frank, Muriel. *Education:* Educated in Vienna, Austria, and Paris, France. *Home:* Wildhern, near Andover, Hampshire, England. *Agent:* Laurence Pollinger Ltd., 18 Maddox St., London W.C.1, England.

CAREER: Trained for a banking career, but turned professional photographer without any formal training; now represented in collections of Smithsonian Institution, other national and municipal art galleries and museums, with a permanent collection of four hundred prints in Japan. International Photographic Exhibition, Dresden,

Germany, commissioner for Great Britain. *Member:* Royal Photographic Society (fellow), Royal Geographical Society, Authors Club, Savage Club. *Awards, honors:* Gold medals for photography at international exhibitions.

WRITINGS: Studies from the Russian Ballet, Fine Arts Society, 1913; (with J.D. Beresford) *Taken from Life,* Collins, 1922; (with Richard King) *The Book of Fair Women,* Knopf, 1922; *In Gipsy Camp and Royal Palace: Wanderings in Rumania,* Scribner, 1924; *Picturesque Great Britain,* Brentano's, 1926, reissued as *Great Britain: The Architecture and the Landscape,* Benn, 1930; *Romantic America, Picturesque United States,* B. Westermann, 1927 (published in England as *The United States of America,* Studio Ltd., 1929); *Loveable London,* Methuen, 1928; *Romantik der kleinstadt: Eine Entdeckungsfahrt durch das alte Deutschland,* F. Bruckmann, 1929; *Deutsche arbeit, bilder vom wiederaufstieg Deutschlands,* Ullstein, 1930; *Achievement,* Ullstein, 1930; *Cities Time Has Passed By,* F. Bruckmann, 1931; *The Fifth Continent,* Simpkin Marshall, 1931; *London,* Medici Society, 1932, Hale, Cushman & Flint, 1933; *Bali,* Schlutz, 1933; *Round the World with a Camera,* Hutchinson, 1934; *The Image of London,* Chatto & Windus, 1935; *A Camera on Unknown London,* Dent, 1936; *The London of George VI,* Chatto & Windus, 1937; *Hundred Thousand Exposures: The Success of a Photographer,* with an introduction by Cecil Beaton, Focal Press, 1945, Transatlantic, 1946; *Rural London in Pictures,* Odhams, 1951; *Jamaica, Land of Rivers,* Safari Ltd., 1959; *Pirates, Buccaneers and Gentlemen Adventurers,* A.S. Barnes, 1972.

Also author of *Gods of Modern Grub Street* (with A. St. John Adcock), *More Gods* (with Adcock), and *London Types* (with Pett Ridge). Writer of articles on art and travel, published in British Commonwealth, United States, Canadian, and European periodicals. Editor, *Colour.*

SIDELIGHTS: As a photographer traveler Hoppe has covered much of New Zealand, West Indies, North America (camping in the Southwest United States and visiting Indian reservations), Australia, and countries of the Far East. *Avocational interests:* Fly-fishing, motoring.

*   *   *

HORAK, M. Stephan   1920-

PERSONAL: Born October 23, 1920, in Horodok, Ukraine; came to United States in 1956, naturalized in 1963; son of Mykhailo and Anna (Halushka) Horak; married Mary L. Breiner, September 9, 1954; children: Christine Anne, Julia Marie, Arkady Michael. *Education:* Gymnasium, Lviv, Ukraine, graduate diploma, 1941; University of Erlangen, Ph.D., 1949; University of Bonn, postdoctoral study, 1952; University of Michigan, M.A. in L.S., 1960. *Home:* 1508 Fourth, Charleston, Ill. 61920. *Office:* Department of History, Eastern Illinois University, Charleston, Ill. 61920.

CAREER: Gymnasium, Regensburg, Germany, teacher, 1949-51; University of Tuebingen, Tuebingen, Germany, research assistant at East European Institute, 1953-56; Indiana University Library, Bloomington, Slavic librarian, 1960-64; Eastern Illinois University, Charleston, currently member of faculty. Visiting assistant professor, University of Kentucky, 1964-65. *Military service:* Ukranian National Army, 1943-45; became first lieutenant. *Member:* American Historical Association, American Association for the Advancement of Slavic Studies. *Awards, honors:* Indiana University, faculty grants-in-aid, 1961, 1962, 1963.

WRITINGS: Ukraine in der internationalen Politik (title means "Ukraine in World Affairs"), Verlag Ukraine (Munich), 1957; *Istorychnyi shliakh rosli do bolshevyzmu* (title means "Russia's Historical Way to Bolshevism"), [London], 1958; (with others) *Handbuch Po-*len, Boehlau, 1959; *Poland and Her National Minorities, 1919-1939: A Case Study,* Vantage, 1961; *The First Phase of Soviet International Relations, 1917-1923,* Institute for the Study of the USSR (Munich), 1961; *Poland's International Affairs: A Calendar of Treaties, Agreements, Conventions, and Other International Acts,* Indiana University, 1964; *Ukranian Historiography, 1953-1963,* American Association for the Advancement of Slavic Studies, 1965; (compiler) *Junior Slavica: A Selected Bibliography of Books in English on Russia and Eastern Europe,* Libraries Unlimited, 1968; *The Kiev Academy: A Bridge to Europe in the 17th Century,* University of Colorado, 1968. Contributor of articles to periodicals in Germany, Great Britain, and United States.

WORK IN PROGRESS: Lenin on the United States.

SIDELIGHTS: Horak speaks Russian, German, Polish, and Ukrainian, with a good working knowledge of all other Slavic languages, and of French and Latin.

*   *   *

HORNBY, John (Wilkinson)   1913-
(Joseph Grace, Gordon Summers)

PERSONAL: Born April 5, 1913; son of Joseph (a gamekeeper) and Grace (Wilkinson) Hornby. *Education:* Attended schools in Northumberland, England. *Politics:* Conservative. *Religion:* Church of England. *Home and office:* 48 Jackson Ave., Northumberland, England.

CAREER: Free-lance writer; historian.

WRITINGS: Missing Cargo, Thomas Nelson, 1947; "Crusader" series, twelve readers, Blackie & Son, 1947-49; *The Red Scarf,* Thomas Nelson, 1950; *The Young Traders,* Blackie & Son, 1951; *The Iron Hills,* Blackie & Son, 1952; (under pseudonym Joseph Grace) *A Bone for Biff,* Blackie & Son, 1952; *The Winbeck Whistle,* Blackie & Son, 1952; *The Puppet Theatre [and] No Show without Toby,* Blackie & Son, 1952; *Alpine Crack-up,* Hamish Hamilton, 1952; "Pegasus" series, eight school readers, George Newnes, 1952; *Priory Island,* Thomas Nelson, 1953; "Far and Wide" series, four school readers, Macmillan (London), 1953-55; (under pseudonym Joseph Grace) *The Secret of the Sails,* Blackie & Son, 1954; *Jacko Comes Home,* Blackie & Son, 1954; *The United Nations,* Macmillan (London), 1954, 2nd edition, 1959; *The Sailor in the Merchant Service and in the Royal Navy,* Macmillan, 1955; *Forestry in Britain,* Macmillan (London), 1957; *Undersea World,* St. Martins, 1960; "Turret Readers," three books, Macmillan (London), 1962; *Clowns Through the Ages,* Oliver & Boyd, 1962, Walck, 1965; *Swords for the King,* St. Martin's, 1964; *Gypsies,* Oliver & Boyd, 1965, Walck, 1967; *Travel by Water,* Oliver & Boyd, 1968, published in America as *The True Book of Travel by Water,* Childrens Press, 1969; *Toys Through the Ages,* Chatto & Windus, 1971; *Goliaths to Conquer,* War on Want, in press.

Writer of more than twenty stories for radio programs in Dublin, Ireland, and of forty historical articles for Tyne Tees Television, England. Contributor of articles and stories to British Broadcasting Corp. programs, and to more than a dozen religious and general periodicals in England, Ireland, Australia, New Zealand, United States, Canada, and India.

WORK IN PROGRESS: A book on archaeology, for Macmillan (London), a book on Christian missions; a three-volume series on the specialized agencies of the United Nations, for Macmillan.

SIDELIGHTS: A descendent of seventeenth-century English gamekeepers and foresters, Hornby never has lost his interest in the lore of the countryside although he has been a shut-in for most of his life, the result of an illness at sixteen. Three of his "Far and Wide" readers and *The United Nations* have been translated into Dutch. *Avocational interests:* Helping teenagers with school work and personal problems; helping aspiring young writers.

* * *

HORNE, Geoffrey 1916-
(Gil North)

PERSONAL: Born July 12, 1916, in Skipton, Yorkshire, England; son of Joshua P. (a town clerk) and Louise (Binns) Horne; married Betty Duthie, February 3, 1949; children: Joshua R.P., Sarah R. *Education:* Christ's College, Cambridge, B.A., 1938, M.A., 1942, diploma in social anthropology, 1952. *Religion:* Church of England. *Home and office:* North Bank, 1 Raikes Ave., Skipton, Yorkshire, England.

CAREER: British Colonial Administrative Service, 1938-55, district officer in West Africa; writer, 1955—. *Member:* Crime Writers Association, Mystery Writers of America, Society of Authors.

WRITINGS: Beware of the Dog, Morrow, 1939; *Winter,* Hutchinson, 1957; *Land of No Escape,* Hutchinson, 1958; *Quest for Gold,* Hutchinson, 1959; *The Man Who Was Chief,* Chapman & Hall, 1960; *The Portuguese Diamonds,* Chapman & Hall, 1961.

Under pseudonym Gil North: *Sergeant Cluff Stands Firm,* Chapman & Hall, 1960; *The Methods of Sergeant Cluff,* Chapman & Hall, 1961; *Sergeant Cluff Goes Fishing,* Chapman & Hall, 1962; *More Deaths for Sergeant Cluff,* Chapman & Hall, 1963; *Sergeant Cluff and the Madmen,* Chapman & Hall, 1964; *Sergeant Cluff and the Price of Pity,* Chapman & Hall, 1965; *The Confounding of Sergeant Cluff,* Chapman & Hall, 1966; *Sergeant Cluff and the Day of Reckoning,* Chapman & Hall, 1967; *The Procrastination of Sergeant Cluff,* Eyre & Spottiswoode, 1969; *No Choice for Sergeant Cluff,* Eyre & Spottiswoode, 1971. Author of twenty "Sergeant Cluff" television scripts for British Broadcasting Corp.

WORK IN PROGRESS: A new series of novels; another "Sergeant Cluff" book; television scripts.

AVOCATIONAL INTERESTS: Social questions and contemporary society; the country.

* * *

HOROWITZ, Robert S. 1924-

PERSONAL: Born September 25, 1924, in Baltimore, Md.; son of Charles (a toy wholesaler) and Rose (Blumenthal) Horowitz; married Sandra Bergstein; children: Ellen, Carol, Charles. *Education:* Attended Washington College, Chestertown, Md., 1941-42, and George Washington University, 1946-47. *Office:* Army Times, 475 School St. S.W., Washington, D.C. 20024.

CAREER: Worked for *Portsmouth Star* (daily newspaper), Portsmouth, Va., 1947, Transradio Press (radio wire service), New York, N.Y., 1947-51; *Army Times,* Washington, D.C., associate editor, 1951—. Congressional editor and political columnist, Army Times Publishing Co. *Military service:* U.S. Army, rifleman, World War II; served in Europe; received Bronze Star and three battle stars.

WRITINGS: (With editors of *Army Times*) *Military Leaders of World War II,* Putnam, 1962; (with editors of *Army Times*) *Famous Fighters of World War I,* Dodd, 1963; (with editors of *Army Times*) *The Tangled Web,* Robert B. Luce, 1963; (with Forrest Kleinman) *The Modern United States Army,* Van Nostrand, 1964; (with Gene Famiglietta and John J. Ford) *Ramparts We Watch,* Monarch Books, 1964.

HORTON, John (William) 1905-

PERSONAL: Born October 22, 1905, in Nottingham, England; son of John Henry (a factory manager) and Sarah (Nixon) Horton; married Olwen Morfydd Griffiths, August 16, 1937; children: John Nicholas, Sarah Catherine, Jane Elizabeth. *Education:* Attended Nottingham High School for Boys; University of London, B.A., 1931; University of Durham, B. Mus., 1935; F.R.C.O., A.R.C.M *Home:* The Cottage, Burland Rd, Brentwood, Essex, England.

CAREER: Teacher of music and other subjects, 1925-37; British Broadcasting Corp., Schools Department, program assistant, 1937-47; Ministry of Education, H.M. inspector of schools, 1947-59, staff inspector, 1959-67; part-time college lecturer, free-lance examiner, author, broadcaster, 1967—.

WRITINGS: Three Nursery Songs, Novello, 1942; *Stories of Great Music,* Thomas Nelson (New York), 1943; *The Chamber Music of Mendelssohn,* Oxford University Press, 1946; *Legends in Music,* Thomas Nelson (New York), 1948; *Cesar Franck,* Oxford University Press, 1948; (contributor) G.E.H. Abraham, editor, *Grieg: A Symposium,* Lindsay Drummond, 1948; *Approach to Music,* Allen & Unwin, 1950; *Grieg: A Biography,* Dufour, 1950; *Some Nineteenth Century Composers,* Oxford University Press, 1950; *Scandinavian Music: A Short History,* Norton, 1963; *Brahms Orchestral Music: A Short History,* BBC Publications, 1968, University of Washington Press, 1969; *Mendelssohn Chamber Music,* University of Washington Press, 1972; *Music,* Scholastic Book Services, 1972.

* * *

HORWITZ, Julius 1920-

PERSONAL: Born August 18, 1920, in Cleveland, Ohio; son of Samuel (a merchant) and Jennie (Chazen) Horwitz; married Lois Sandler, June 1, 1947; children: Jonathan, David. *Education:* Attended Ohio State University, 1940-42, 1946, and Columbia University, 1947-50; New School for Social Research, B.A., 1953. *Religion:* Hebrew. *Home:* 10 Stuyvesant Ave., Larchmont, N.Y. 10538. *Agent:* Lois Wallace, William Morris Agency, 1350 Avenue of the Americas, New York, N.Y. 10019.

CAREER: New York City (N.Y.) Department of Welfare, social investigator, 1956-62; New York State Senate, Albany, consultant on public welfare to majority leader, 1963-65; New York State Joint Legislative Committee on Public Health, Albany, consultant, 1965-67; City of New York, director of Medicaid Information Office, 1967-70; Health Insurance Plant of New York, New York, N.Y., director of public relations, 1970—. Faculty member, The New School, Center for New York City Affairs. *Military service:* U.S. Air Force, 1942-45; received Europe-Africa-Middle Eastern theater ribbon with six Bronze Stars, and Distinguished Unit Citation. *Member:* Authors League of America, P.E.N., New School Alumni Association (president). *Awards, honors:* Guggenheim fellowship for writing, 1954, 1963; Silver Gavel award, American Bar Association, 1967.

WRITINGS: The City, World Publishing, 1953; *The Inhabitants,* World Publishing, 1960; *Can I Get There by Candlelight,* Atheneum, 1964; *The W.A.S.P.,* Atheneum, 1967; *The Diary of A.N.: The Story of the House on West 104th Street,* Coward, 1970; *The Married Lovers,* Dial, 1973. Contributor of articles to *Look, Commentary, Midstream, Contact, New York Times Sunday Magazine, Reader's Digest.*

WORK IN PROGRESS: A novel, for Dial.

SIDELIGHTS: Critics have found *The Diary of A.N.* impressive in its portrayal of the deadening influence of welfare on the lives of its recipients. Alfred Sundel describes Horwitz's ghetto as a "painful human enclave at the gates of affluent America, [where] drugs, promiscuity, and crime are outgrowths of lethally deprived needs, with the primary need being to lean on something or someone other than yourself in order to stand, because, man, you are beat, from cradle to hopscotch to rape on the roof. This is the nature of their crippledness, that they are terribly dependent, and Horwitz has caught this. . . ." Gerald Walker believes that the "narrative is so powerful one wonders why the publisher felt compelled to issue the book as nonfiction. Surely, everything in it is factual in the sense that it can happen and has happened, even down to the death-by-overdose of A.N.'s 12-year-old brother . . . but the book is clearly a novel, and a fine, compassionate one at that."

Charles Gordone is adapting *The W.A.S.P.* for production as a film.

BIOGRAPHICAL/CRITICAL SOURCES: Books and Bookmen, September, 1967; *Time*, September 8, 1967; *Christian Science Monitor*, August 31, 1967, February 26, 1970; *New York Times Book Review*, September 10, 1967, March 22, 1970; *Atlantic*, October, 1967; *Book World*, November 26, 1967; *Nation*, February 5, 1968; *Observer Review*, July, 1968; *Listener*, August 15, 1968; *Saturday Review*, February 21, 1970; *Newsweek*, March 9, 1970; *Library Journal*, March 15, 1970; *Village Voice*, March 12, 1970; *New York Times*, May 17, 1970.

*   *   *

HOUGH, (Helen) Charlotte 1924-

PERSONAL: Surname is pronounced *How;* born May 24, 1924, in Brockenhurst, England; daughter of Henry Constantine (a doctor) and Helen (Littler) Woodyatt; married Richard Hough (an author), July 17, 1943; children: Sarah Hough Garland, Alexandra, Deborah, Bryony. *Education:* Attended Fresham Heights School, 1935-40. *Religion:* Church of England. *Home:* 25 St. Ann's Ter., London N.W.8, England. *Agent:* Curtis Brown Ltd., 13 King St., Covent Garden, London W.C.2, England.

CAREER: Writer and illustrator of children's books. *Military service:* Women's Royal Naval Service, 1942-43.

WRITINGS—Juveniles; all self-illustrated: *Jim Tiger,* Faber, 1956, Bobbs-Merrill, 1958; *Morton's Pony,* Faber, 1957, Transatlantic, 1958; *The Home-Makers,* Hamish Hamilton, 1957; *The Story of Mr. Pinks,* Faber, 1958; *The Hampshire Pig,* Hamish Hamilton, 1958; *The Animal Game,* Faber, 1959; *The Trackers,* Hamish Hamilton, 1960; *Algernon,* Faber, 1961, A.S. Barnes, 1962; *Anna and Minnie,* Faber, 1962; *Three Little Funny Ones,* Hamish Hamilton, 1962, Penguin (Baltimore), 1966; *The Owl in the Barn,* Faber, 1964; *More Funny Ones,* Hamish Hamilton, 1965; *Red Biddy, and Other Stories,* Faber, 1966; *Educating Flora, and Other Stories,* Faber, 1968; *Sir Frog, and Other Stories,* Faber, 1968; *My Aunt's Alphabet, with Billy and Me,* Hamish Hamilton, 1969; *Abdul the Awful, and Other Stories,* McCall Publishing, 1970; *Bad Child's Book of Moral Verse,* Faber, 1970, Walck, 1971; *Queer Customer,* Heinemann, 1972.

Illustrator: A. Stephen Tring, *Barry's Big Day,* Oxford University Press, 1954; Anita Hewett, *Elephant Big and Elephant Little, and Other Stories,* John Lane, 1955; Barbara Euphan Todd, *Boy with the Green Thumb,* Hamish Hamilton, 1956. Illustrator of many other juveniles.

WORK IN PROGRESS: Three picture books, for Heinemann and Penguin.

BIOGRAPHICAL/CRITICAL SOURCES: Books and Bookmen, November, 1968.

HOUSTON, John Porter 1933-

PERSONAL: Born April 21, 1933, in Wilmar, Calif.; son of William Bascom (a manufacturer) and Sappho (Davis) Houston; married Mona Tobin (a professor), July 6, 1959; children: Natalie Melissa. *Education:* University of California, Berkeley, B.A., 1954; University of Aix-Marseilles, graduate study, 1954-55; Yale University, Ph.D., 1959. *Office:* French Department, Indiana University, Bloomington, Ind. 47401.

CAREER: Yale University, New Haven, Conn., instructor in French, 1958-62; Indiana University, Bloomington, assistant professor, 1962-65, associate professor, 1965-70, professor of French, 1970—. *Member:* Modern Language Association of America. *Awards, honors:* Morse fellowship, Yale University, 1961-62.

WRITINGS: The Design of Rimbaud's Poetry, Yale University Press, 1963; (editor with wife, Mona Tobin Houston) Francois Mauriac, *Genitrix,* Prentice-Hall, 1966; *The Demonic Imagination: Style and Theme in French Romantic Poetry,* Louisiana State University Press, 1969.

*   *   *

HOVDA, Robert W(alker) 1920-

PERSONAL: Surname is pronounced *Hahv*-da; born April 10, 1920, in Clear Lake, Wis.; son of Leslie Raymond and Helma Regina (Lohn) Hovda. *Education:* Hamline University, student, 1938-41; St. John's University, Collegeville, Minn., B.A., 1945; St. John's Seminary, seminarian, 1945-49; Catholic University of America, S.T.L., 1960. *Politics:* "Democrat (left wing)." *Home:* 1141 North University Dr., Fargo, N.D. 58102.

CAREER: Ordained Roman Catholic priest, 1949; Diocese of Fargo, Fargo, N.D., parish priest, 1949-59; Catholic University of America, Washington, D.C., instructor in theology, 1959-62; North Dakota State University, Fargo, chaplain of St. Paul's Student Center, 1963—. Member of board of directors, National Catholic Liturgical Conference, 1963—. *Wartime service:* Conscientious objector serving in Civilian Public Service Camp. *Member:* American Civil Liberties Union, National Association for the Advancement of Colored People, Congress of Racial Equality.

WRITINGS: (Editor, author of introduction, and contributor) *Sunday Morning Crisis: Renewal in Catholic Worship,* Helicon, 1963; (editor) *Church Architecture: The Shape of Reform,* Liturgical Conference, Inc., 1965; (editor) *Jesus Christ Reforms His Church,* Liturgical Conference, Inc., 1966; *Manual of Celebration,* Liturgical Conference, Inc., 1970; (with Gabe Huck) *There's No Place Like People: Planning Small Group Liturgies,* 2nd edition, Argus, 1971.

Contributor: *Problems Before Unity,* Helicon, 1962; *The Layman in the Church, and Other Essays,* Alba, 1963; F.R. McManus, editor, *The Revival of the Liturgy,* Herder & Herder, 1963. Contributor of essays and book reviews to religious and educational periodicals. Editor, *Liturgy* (quarterly bulletin of National Catholic Liturgical Conference), 1963—.

WORK IN PROGRESS: Research in ecclesiology, with special reference to the layman, and in liturgy, ecumenism, and Christian social thought.

*   *   *

HOWARD, Kenneth Samuel 1882-

PERSONAL: Born April 12, 1882, in Le Roy, N.Y.; son of Samuel Talcott and Marietta Annette (Ballintine) Howard; married Lucille Gilson, July 2, 1919; children: Rebekah Gilson (Mrs. Andrew J. Martin). *Education:*

University of Rochester, B.S., 1904. *Home:* 1 West McFarlan St., Dover, N.J. 07801.

CAREER: Engaged during most of career in advertising, sales, sales promotional activities, and editorial work.

WRITINGS: How to Write Advertisements, McGraw, 1937; *Methods of Sales Promotion,* McGraw, 1940; *The Enjoyment of Chess Problems,* McKay, 1943, 4th edition, Dover, 1967; *How to Solve Chess Problems,* McKay, 1945, 2nd edition, Dover, 1961; *One Hundred Years of the American Two-Move Chess Problem: A Collection of 212 Compositions by United States Problemists,* Dover, 1962, 2nd edition, 1965; (editor) *Spectacular Chess Problems: 200 Gems by American Composers,* Dover, 1965, 2nd edition, 1967; *Classic Chess Problems by Pioneer Composers,* Dover, 1970; *Chess Problem Gems by Eight Eminent American Composers,* Dover, 1973.

* * *

HOWE, Irving 1920-

PERSONAL: Born June 11, 1920, in New York, N.Y.; son of David and Nettie (Goldman) Howe; married Arien Hausknecht; children: Nina, Nicholas. *Education:* City College of New York (now City College of the City University of New York), B.Sc., 1940; Brooklyn College (now Brooklyn College of the City University of New York), graduate study, one-half year. *Politics:* Socialist. *Home:* 90 Riverside Dr., New York, N.Y. 10024. *Office:* Department of English, Hunter College of the City University of New York, New York, N.Y. 10021.

CAREER: Brandeis University, Waltham, Mass., 1953-61, began as associate professor, became professor of English; Stanford University, Stanford, Calif., professor of English, 1961-63; Hunter College of the City University of New York, New York, N.Y., professor of English, 1963-70, distinguished professor, 1970—. Visiting professor, University of Vermont and University of Washington. Christian Gauss Seminar Chair Professor, Princeton University, 1953. National Book Awards judge, 1969. *Military service:* U.S. Army, 1942-45. *Member:* Modern Language Association of America. *Awards, honors:* Indiana University, School of Letters, fellow; *Kenyon Review* fellow, 1953; Longview Foundation prize for literary criticism; Bollingen award, 1959-60; National Institute of Arts and Letters award, 1960; Guggenheim fellow, 1964-65, 1971.

WRITINGS: A rendition of Leo Baeck's *Essence of Judaism,* Schocken, 1948; (with B.J. Widick) *The U.A.W. and Walter Reuther,* Random House, 1949; *Sherwood Anderson,* Sloane, 1951; *William Faulkner: A Critical Study,* Random House, 1952, 2nd edition, Vintage, 1962; (editor with Eliezer Greenberg) *A Treasury of Yiddish Stories,* Viking, 1954; *Politics and the Novel,* Horizon, 1957; (editor) *Modern Literary Criticism: An Anthology, 1919-1957,* Beacon, 1958; (with Lewis Coser) *The American Communist Party: A Critical History,* Beacon, 1958.

(Editor) George Gissing, *New Grub Street,* Houghton, 1962; (editor) *Edith Wharton: A Collection of Critical Essays,* Prentice-Hall, 1962; (editor and author of introduction) Leon Trotsky, *Basic Writings,* Random House, 1963; *A World More Attractive: A View of Modern Literature and Politics,* Horizon, 1963; (editor) George Orwell, *Nineteen Eighty-Four* (source book), Harcourt, 1963; (editor and author of introduction) *Selected Short Stories of Isaac Bashevis Singer,* Modern Library, 1966; *Steady Work: Essays in the Politics of Democratic Radicalism, 1953-1966,* Harcourt, 1966; (editor and author of introduction) *The Radical Papers,* Doubleday, 1966; (compiler) *Student Activism,* Bobbs-Merrill, 1967; (editor) *The Radical Imagination: An Anthology from Dissent Magazine,* New American Library, 1967; (author of introduction) William O'Neill, editor, *Echoes of Revolt: The Masses, 1911-1917,* Quadrangle, 1967; *Thomas Hardy: A Critical Study,* Macmillan, 1967; (compiler) *Literary Modernism,* Fawcett, 1967; (editor and author of introduction) *The Idea of the Modern in Literature and the Arts,* Horizon, 1968; (editor with Jeremy Larner) *Poverty: Views from the Left,* Morrow, 1968; (author of introduction) Henry James, *The American Scene,* Horizon, 1968; (editor) *A Dissenter's Guide to Foreign Policy,* Praeger, 1968; (compiler) *Classics of Modern Fiction: Eight Short Novels,* Harcourt, 1968; (editor with Greenberg) *A Treasury of Yiddish Poetry,* Holt, 1969; (editor and author of introduction) *Beyond the New Left: A Confrontation and Critique,* McCall, 1970; *Decline of the New* (literary essays), Harcourt, 1970; (compiler with Mark Schorer and Larzer Ziff) *The Literature of America: Nineteenth Century,* McGraw, 1970; (editor) *Essential Works of Socialism,* Holt, 1970 (published in England as *A Handbook of Socialist Thought,* Gollancz, 1972); (compiler and editor with Greenberg) *Voices from the Yiddish: Essays, Memoirs, Diaries,* University of Michigan Press, 1972.

Contributor to *Partisan Review, Commentary, New Republic, New York Review of Books, Harper's, New York Times Book Review,* and other journals and periodicals. Editor of *Dissent,* 1953—; alternate book critic, *Harper's,* 1968-71.

WORK IN PROGRESS: A study of the Jewish social-cultural immigrant milieu in the United States, 1880-1950.

SIDELIGHTS: Typical comments when Howe began his career were those of Arthur Schlesinger—"A brilliant young critic," and of F.R. Dulles, who praised him for writing "with knowledgeable understanding, critical acumen and forthright candor." Newton Arvin called *Sherwood Anderson* "a literary event [which] indicates the definite arrival upon the scene of a considerable critical talent." His work was described by Melvin Maddocks as "a full-blooded and three-dimensional approach to literature."

The criticism Howe published in *Dissent,* and which was reflected in several of his books, has been called "some of the most worthwhile social criticism published in America today," and his magazine was hailed as "notable for radical criticism that is consistently intelligent, literate, and non-authoritarian."

More recently, Howe has been criticized for, in the words of Raymond Williams, "the rancor of his response to the present." Jack Newfield says: "A believer in empirical logic, [he] cannot comprehend the irrationality of the new generation, spawned by Watts, Dallas and LSD." Newfield mentions "how much Howe and I share—the same radical democratic values, as well as a curiosity concerning the linkage between culture and politics . . . still, I feel deeply alienated from Howe at other times in this book." Newfield does add: "Howe is brilliant, honest with himself, and has much to teach my generation of dissenters. Just as Howe would stretch his soul by listening to Dylan, everyone in the Movement could stretch his mind by reading this book." George Stade offers a somewhat similar attitude, saying: "Howe . . . stands 'for the values of liberalism, for the politics of democratic radicalism, for the norms of rationality and intelligence, for the standards of seriousness, for the life of the mind as a human dedication. He also says: "At this moment in American history, the praise of moderation, even of 'liberal humaneness and rational discourse,' is just a bit priggish and is a form of aggression against the young. . . . However, Irving Howe is a man we should more honor than reject. He is aware that in his struggle for 'the preservation of the residual decencies' he may have to 'face intellectual isolation and perhaps dismissal.' Dismissal would be a mistake; we should come to regret it; Howe tells us too many things that nobody else seems to want to know anymore." Howe's integrity and intellect have never been in question. As stated by Arnold Beichman: "Older radicals and liberals, even conservatives, might well profit from reading Mr. Howe's important collection of essays. . . . It is not that I am inclined to agree with Mr. Howe's social prescriptions let alone his analysis of the American condition. . . . But the quality of his thought and the power of his moral commitment is such that we must deal with his political ideas which he has been re-thinking in the era of what he calls the garrison-welfare state . . . Of all our radicals, Mr. Howe makes some sense because he will not compromise his radicalism with that of the New Left to whom politics is a psychedelic experience."

BIOGRAPHICAL/CRITICAL SOURCES: Nation, September 24, 1949; *New York Times,* September 28, 1949, April 8, 1951, March 18, 1970; *Christian Science Monitor,* April 25, 1957, October 27, 1966, July 22, 1967; *Village Voice,* January 12, 1967; *Commentary,* February, 1969; *New York Times Book Review,* April 12, 1970.

*   *   *

HOWES, Barbara   1914-

PERSONAL: Born May 1, 1914, in New York, N.Y.; daughter of Osborne (a stock broker) and Mildred (Cox) Howes; married William Jay Smith (a teacher and writer), October 1, 1947 (divorced, 1964); children: David E., Gregory Jay. *Education:* Attended Beaver Country Day School, Chestnut Hill, Mass.; Bennington College, B.A., 1937. *Politics:* Kennedy Democrat. *Religion:* Episcopalian. *Home:* Brook House, North Pownal, Vt. *Agent:* John Schaffner, 425 East 51st St., New York, N.Y. 10022.

CAREER: Writer. *Awards, honors:* Bess Hokin Prize, 1949, from *Poetry* magazine; Guggenheim fellowship, 1955; Brandeis University poetry grant, 1958; Eunice Tietjens Memorial Prize, 1959; award in literature from the National Institute of Arts and Letters, 1971.

WRITINGS: The Undersea Farmer (poems), Banyan Press, 1948; *In the Cold Country* (poems), Bonacio & Saul, with Grove Press, 1954; *Light and Dark* (poems), Wesleyan University Press, 1959; (editor) *23 Modern Stories,* Vintage, 1963; *Looking Up at Leaves* (poetry), Knopf, 1966; (editor) *From the Green Antilles: Writings of the Caribbean,* Macmillan, 1966; (contributor) Howard Nemerov, editor, *Poets on Poetry,* Basic Books, 1966; (editor with Gregory Jay Smith) *The Sea-Green Horse* (short stories), Macmillan, 1970; *The Blue Garden* (poems), Wesleyan University Press, 1972; (editor) *The Eye of the Heart: Short Stories from Latin America,* Bobbs-Merrill, 1973.

Anthologized in *New Poems by American Poets,* Ballantine, 1957, *Modern Verse in English,* Macmillan, 1958, *Modern American Poetry,* Harcourt, 1962, *Poet's Choice,* Dial, 1962, *Modern Poets,* McGraw, 1963; *Of Poetry and Power,* Basic Books, 1964; *The Girl in the Black Raincoat,* edited by George Garrett, Duell, Sloane & Pierce, 1966; *The Marvelous Light,* edited by Helen Plotz, Crowell, 1970; *Inside Outer Space,* edited by Robert Vas Dias, Anchor Books, 1970.

Contributor to *New Yorker, Saturday Review, Atlantic, Poetry, Virginia Quarterly Review, Southern Review, New Republic, American Scholar, University of Kansas Review, New Directions, Chicago Review, New York Times Book Review, Yale Review.*

Editor of literary magazine, *Chimera,* 1943-47.

WORK IN PROGRESS: New book of poems; an anthology of short stories from Latin America.

SIDELIGHTS: Dudley Fitts wrote of *The Undersea Farmer:* "It is refreshing to turn to Miss Howes's exquisitely printed book. . . . At least four times in [it] we find finished poems of considerable merit . . . and many others have passages of memorable force. The technique is aware and skilled; the structure . . . is subtly designed and harmoniously realized; the poems—the best ones are passionate *saying.*" Louise Bogan commented on *In the Cold Country:* "Miss Howes is daring with language, but she is also accurate. Her originality stands in constant close reference to the material in hand, and although much of that material is fantastic or exotic, it is never so simply for its own sake. Her diction becomes more exact the more it is applied to certain dissolving effects in nature that attract her, and her poems are full of movement."

Miss Howes lists her main interests as "literary and familial; also concerned about fauna and flora, to say nothing about the state of the world." She has lived in Italy, France, and also in Haiti.

BIOGRAPHICAL/CRITICAL SOURCES: Nation, January 15, 1949; *Saturday Review,* March 19, 1949, October 9, 1954, December 31, 1956; *Poetry,* June, 1949, January, 1967; *New York Times,* April 4, 1954; *New Yorker,* June 5, 1954; Louis Untermeyer, editor, *Modern American Poetry,* Harcourt, 1962; *New York Times Book Review,* February 20, 1966, April 1, 1967; *Kenyon Review,* June, 1966; *Virginia Quarterly Review,* autumn, 1966; Howard Nemerov, editor, *Poets on Poetry,* Basic Books, 1966; *Times Literary Supplement,* June 29, 1967.

*   *   *

HOYEM, Andrew   1935-

PERSONAL: Born December 1, 1935, in Sioux Falls, S.D.; son of Albert G. (a doctor) and Ellen (Lewison) Hoyem; married Sally Cameron Heimann, June 24, 1961 (divorced, 1965); married Judith Bordin Laws, December 31, 1970. *Education:* Pomona College, B.A., 1957. *Home:* 2319 California St., Berkeley, Calif. 94703. *Office:* 566 Commercial St., San Francisco, Calif. 94111.

CAREER: Auerhahn Press, San Francisco, Calif., partner, 1961-65; Grabhorn-Hoyem, San Francisco, Calif., partner, 1966—. *Military service:* U.S. Navy, 1957-60; became lieutenant junior grade.

WRITINGS: The Wake (poems), Auerhahn Press, 1963; *The Music Room* (poems), Dave Haselwood Books, 1965; *Chimeras,* Dave Haselwood Books, 1966; (translator with John F. Crawford) *The Pearl,* Grabhorn-Hoyem, 1967; *Articles: Poems 1960-67,* Grossman, 1969. Contributor to *Poetry.*

WORK IN PROGRESS: Poems.

BIOGRAPHICAL/CRITICAL SOURCES: Books and Bookmen, November, 1969.

*   *   *

HOYT, Murray   1904-

PERSONAL: Born December 8, 1904, in Worcester, Mass.; son of Prentiss Cheney (a college professor) and Hortense (Drake) Hoyt; married Margaret O'Hare (a dietician), July 16, 1932; children: Margaret Marion (Mrs. Malcolm R. Randall). *Education:* Middlebury College, A.B., 1926; Columbia University, summer graduate student, 1928. *Politics:* Republican. *Religion:* Congregational. *Home and office:* 8 Green Mountain Pl., Middlebury, Vt. 05753. *Agent:* Collins-Knowlton-Wing, 60 East 56th St., New York, N.Y. 10022.

CAREER: Waterville High School, Waterville, N.Y., teacher, 1926-31; free-lance writer, 1931—. Co-owner of Owl's Head Harbor (Lake Champlain resort), 1933—. Green Mountain Council Boy Scouts, member of executive board. *Member:* Vermont Hotel Association (former secretary), Associated Alumni of Middlebury College (former national president), Sigma Phi Epsilon, Hawthorne Club.

WRITINGS: Does It Always Rain Here, Mr. Hoyt?, Rinehart, 1950; (co-editor) Green Mountain Treasury, Harper, 1960; The Fish in My Life, Crown, 1964; The World of Bees, Coward, 1965; Jewels from the Ocean Deep: The Complete Guide to Shell Collecting, Putnam, 1967; (with Ralph N. Hill and Walter R. Hard) Vermont: A Special World, Houghton, 1969; The Young Investor's Guide to the Stock Market, Lippincott, 1972. Contributor to anthologies; contributor of over 400 short stories and articles to Saturday Evening Post, Ladies' Home Journal, Collier's, American, Good Housekeeping, Reader's Digest, Woman's Day, Family Circle, Woman's Home Companion, Writer, Writer's Digest, and other periodicals in America, Canada, England, Australia, Italy. Senior editor, Vermont Life, 1954—.

WORK IN PROGRESS: A book on the stock market, Don't Feed the Bears, for Lippincott.

SIDELIGHTS: Hoyt started writing for pulps, worked up through Canadian slick paper magazines to popular magazines in United States; originally a fiction writer, he is now doing more articles. One Collier's story, "No Sum too Small," is included in three anthologies and was used on the radio; a Vermont Life and Reader's Digest article, "The Strange Wedding of the Widow Ward," has also been anthologized.

Hoyt played semi-pro baseball until the age of forty; he now fishes in his spare time, in Florida in the winter, in Vermont in the summer.

* * *

HUANG, David S(hih-Li) 1930-

PERSONAL: Born September 15, 1930, in Taipei, Taiwan, China; son of Chih Lai and Yueh Nu (Lin) Huang; married Ruth Woan-Rong Lin, January 7, 1961; children: Milton Peechuan, Lena Lin. Education: University of Washington, Seattle, B.A., 1953, M.A., 1954, Ph.D., 1961. Office: Department of Economics, Southern Methodist University, Dallas, Tex. 75222.

CAREER: University of Texas, Austin, assistant professor of economics, 1961-65; Southern Methodist University, Dallas, Tex., associate professor, 1965-66; professor of economics, 1966—. Research associate, University of Wisconsin, Social Systems Research Institute, 1961-66; visiting professor, University of Chicago, 1967-68. Member: American Economic Association, American Statistical Association, Econometric Society.

WRITINGS: Introduction to the Use of Mathematics in Economic Analysis, Wiley, 1964; A Microanalytic Model of Automobile Purchase (monograph), Bureau of Business Research, University of Texas, 1964; A Multi-Cross-Section Investigation of Demand for Automobiles (monograph), Bureau of Business Research, University of Texas, 1966; Regression and Econometric Methods, Wiley, 1970. Contributor to economic and statistical journals.

WORK IN PROGRESS: Conducting research on mortgage credit and housing market.

BIOGRAPHICAL/CRITICAL SOURCES: Journal of American Statistical Association, September, 1963.

* * *

HUDSON, Derek (Rommel) 1911-

PERSONAL: Born July 20, 1911, in London, England; son of Ernest Walter (a solicitor) and Emily Louise (Rommel) Hudson; married Yvonne Patricia O'Neill, September 2, 1939; children: Katherine Frances. Educa-

tion: Shrewsbury School, student, 1925-30; Merton College, Oxford, B.A., 1933, M.A. Home: 33 Beacon Hill Ct., Hindhead, Surrey, England.

CAREER: Birmingham Post, Birmingham, England, member of editorial staff, 1937; Times, London, England, member of editorial staff, 1939-49; Spectator, London, England, literary editor, 1949-53; Oxford University Press, London, England, publisher's editor, 1955-65, part-time adviser, 1965—. Member: Royal Society of Literature (fellow), Garrick Club.

WRITINGS: (Editor with A.M.E. Goldschmidt and George Playfair) The Cherwell Wine Book, Cherwell Press, 1932; (author of introduction) L.A. Willoughby, editor, Letters of Justinus Kerner to Graf Alexander von Wuerttemberg, English Goethe Society, 1938; A Poet in Parliament: The Life of Winthrop Mackworth Praed, 1802-1839, J. Murray, 1939; An Oxford Dialogue, and Other Papers, Shakespeare Head Press, 1940; Thomas Barnes of the Times, Cambridge University Press, 1943, Macmillan, 1944; British Journalists and Newspapers, Hastings House, 1945; Norman O'Neill: A Life of Music, Slant (three-act play), Quality Press, 1946; Charles Keene, Pleiades Books, 1947; Martin Tupper: His Rise and Fall, Constable, 1949, published in America as Unrepentant Victorian: His Rise and Fall, Macmillan, 1950; James Pryde, 1866-1941, Constable, 1949, Macmillan, 1950.

Lewis Carroll, Macmillan, 1954; (with Kenneth W. Luckhurst) The Royal Society of Arts, 1754-1954, Transatlantic, 1954; (author of introduction) Lewis Carroll, Useful and Instructive Poetry, Macmillan, 1954; (editor and author of introduction) Modern English Short Stories: Second Series, Oxford University Press, 1956; Sir Joshua Reynolds: A Personal Study, Bles, 1958, Essential Books, 1959; (editor and author of introduction) English Critical Essays: Twentieth Century, Second Series, Oxford University Press, 1958; Lewis Carroll (not the same as 1954 title), Longmans, Green for British Council, 1958; Arthur Rackham: His Life and Work, Scribner, 1960; The Forgotten King, and Other Essays, Constable, 1960; (editor) Essays and Studies, 1961-1962, two volumes, Humanities, 1961-62; (author of introduction) Lord Alfred Douglas, Oscar Wilde: A Summing Up, Icon Books, 1962; (author of notes) Sir William Schwenck Gilbert, The Savoy Operas, two volumes, Oxford University Press, 1962-63; The Boys' Book of the Press, Burke Publishing, 1964; Writing between the Lines: An Autobiography, High Hill Books, 1965; Oxford University Press in Scotland, Oxford University Press, 1966; (editor and author of introduction) The Diary of Henry Crabb Robinson: An Abridgement, Oxford University Press, 1967; Holland House in Kensington, P. Davies, 1967; Kensington Palace, P. Davies, 1968, Fernhill, 1969; Quality Press, 1945; (with Anthony Goldsmith) On the Talks with Fuddy and Other Papers, Centaur Press, 1968; Munby, Man of Two Worlds, Gambit, 1972.

Contributor to Spectator, Cornhill, National Review, Time and Tide, Dictionary of National Biography supplement, Encyclopaedia Britannica, and other publications.

WORK IN PROGRESS: Munby: Man of Two Worlds, for J. Murray.

SIDELIGHTS: In a review of Kensington Palace, John Hayes states: "[Hudson] is exceedingly good at interesting us in the frailties and foibles of his royal subject and their debts; he has a nice sense of wit; and an unerring instinct for a good story. . . ."

BIOGRAPHICAL/CRITICAL SOURCES: Times Literary Supplement, October 12, 1967; Books and Bookmen, December, 1967; Punch, December 4, 1968; Yale Review, winter, 1968.

HUGGETT, Frank E(dward) 1924-

PERSONAL: Born March 25, 1924, in London, England; son of Hubert George and Caroline (Cant) Huggett; married Renee Bell (a writer), May 25, 1924; children: Diana Tarrant. Education: Attended Emanuel School; Wadham College, Oxford, B.A., 1948. Home: Bridgefoot Cottage, Stedham, Midhurst, Sussex, England.

CAREER: Westminster Press Provincial Newspapers, reporter, 1949-52; Daily Telegraph, London, England, subeditor, 1952-55; Look and Listen, London, England, editor, 1956-57; Regent Street Polytechnic, London, England, lecturer in journalism, 1958-65; Ministry of Defence, London, England, lecturer, 1966-68. Lecturer in Britain and Europe.

WRITINGS: The Coal Miner, Ward, Lock, 1955; The True Book About Newspapers, Muller, 1955; South of Lisbon: Water Travels in Southern Portugal, Gollancz, 1960; Farming, Dufour, 1963; The Newspapers, Heinemann, 1968; Modern Belgium, Praeger, 1969; A Short History of Farming, Macmillan, 1970; What They've Said about Nineteenth Century Reformers, Oxford University Press, 1971; The Modern Netherlands, Praeger, 1971; How It Happened, Basil Blackwell, 1971, Barnes & Noble, 1972; Travel and Communications, Harrap, 1971. Contributor to various journals.

WORK IN PROGRESS: Various historical works.

SIDELIGHTS: Huggett resided in Portugal, 1957-58.

*   *   *

HUGHES, Anthony John 1933-

PERSONAL: Born July 15, 1933, in Hemel Hempstead, Hertfordshire, England; son of George Arthur and Doris (Sommerville) Hughes. Education: Attended Berkhamsted School, 1947-52, and Wadham College, Oxford, 1954-56. Politics: Socialist. Religion: Agnostic. Home: P.O. Box 12786, Nairobi, Kenya, East Africa. Office: P.O. Box 30050, Nairobi, Kenya, East Africa.

CAREER: Went to East Africa as a political reporter with interest in African affairs from a radical viewpoint, 1959; became press liaison and public relations officer of Kenya National Union, 1963; senior press officer, Kenya Ministry of Information, Broadcasting and Tourism, Nairobi, 1964—. Military service: British Army, 1952-54; became lieutenant. Member: Kenya Union of Journalists.

WRITINGS: (Contributor) Colin Legum, editor, Africa: A Handbook to the Continent, Praeger, 1962; East Africa: The Search for Unity, Penguin, 1963, revised edition published as East Africa: Kenya, Tanzania, Uganda, 1969. Contributor of articles on African affairs to British publications.

WORK IN PROGRESS: Political History of Tanganyika, for Praeger; editing Writings and Speeches of Jomo Kenyatta, for Presence Africaine and Kenya government.

AVOCATIONAL INTERESTS: Reading, parties and dancing, good eating, organized sport and impromptu games, the cinema (but not television), and going on safari.

*   *   *

HUGHES, Gervase (Alfred Booth) 1905-

PERSONAL: Born September 1, 1905, in Birmingham, England; son of Alfred (a university professor) and Hester (Booth) Hughes; married Gwyneth Edwards (formerly an operatic soprano), April 24, 1934; children: Ann (Mrs. Derck Glynne-Percy), Mary Caroline. Education: Attended Malvern College; Corpus Christi College, Oxford, B.A. and B.Mus., 1927, M.A., 1949. Home: 83 Winchester Ct., London W.8, England.

CAREER: British National Opera Company, London, England, member of musical staff and occasional conductor, 1926-29; associated with Sir Frank Benson and Oscar Asche in Shakespeare productions, 1926-33; London Opera Festival, London, England, conductor, 1929-30; London, Midland & Scottish Railway, executive positions, 1934-46; manager of travel agency specializing in European tours by Rolls-Royce, 1947-59. Composer and author. Member: Savage Club (life), Warwickshire Cricket Club.

WRITINGS: Castle Creevy (operetta), Novello, 1928; The Music of Arthur Sullivan, St. Martin's, 1960; Composers of Operetta, St. Martin's, 1962; The Pan Book of Great Composers, Pan Books, 1964, reissued as The Handbook of Great Composers, Arthur Barker, 1965, published in America as Great Composers of the World, Crowell, 1966; Dvorak: His Life and Music, Dodd, 1967; Sidelights on a Century of Music: 1825-1924, MacDonald & Co., 1969, St. Martin's, 1970. Contributor to international edition of World Book Encyclopedia, 1965—and to Encyclopedia Americana, 1969. Contributor to Opera, Monthly Musical Record, Railway Magazine and other periodicals.

WORK IN PROGRESS: Fifty Famous Composers, for Pan Books.

AVOCATIONAL INTERESTS: Mountain walks, wine, watching cricket, world geography, railways.

BIOGRAPHICAL/CRITICAL SOURCES: Daily Telegraph (London), March 19, 1960; Times Literary Supplement, May 6, 1960, June 15, 1962; Listener, June 9, 1960; Observer, April 1, 1962; Christian Science Monitor, July 30, 1962; Library Journal, November 1, 1962, April 15, 1966, November 1, 1967; Choice, September, 1966, May, 1968; Punch, May 10, 1967.

*   *   *

HUGHES, Harold K(enneth) 1911-

PERSONAL: Born December 31, 1911, in New York, N.Y.; son of John Watt and Rachel (Mulgrew) Hughes; married Mildred M. Wells, July 22, 1936; children: Phyllis L. Hughes Rojakovick, Marilyn P. Hughes Patrik. Education: Columbia University, A.B., 1934, M.A., 1943, Ph.D., 1948. Religion: Unitarian-Universalist. Home: 12236 Hannawa Rd., Potsdam, N.Y. 13676. Office: Vicepresident for Academic Affairs, State University College at Potsdam, Potsdam, N.Y. 13676.

CAREER: Columbia University, New York, N.Y., instructor in physics, 1935-40; University of Newark, Newark, N.J., assistant professor and head of physics department, 1940-45; Columbia Radiation Laboratory, scientist, 1944-45; Socony Mobil Oil Co., Inc., assistant supervisor of special analytical section, 1945-52; Celanese Corp. of America, 1952-58, superintendent of technical extrusion department, 1955-57, director of manufacturing development extrusion, 1957-58; Markite Corp., assistant technical director, 1958-59; Continental Can Co., Inc., director of physics research, 1959-62; Indiana State University, Terre Haute, professor of physics, department head, 1962-69; State University College at Potsdam, Potsdam, N.Y., vice-president for academic affairs, 1969—. Developer of seventeen patented industrial processes.

MEMBER: Society for Applied Spectroscopy (president, 1950-51), American Physical Society (fellow), American Chemical Society, Institute of Electronic and Electrical Engineers, American Association of Physics Teachers, Scientific Research Society of America, American Society for Cybernetics (director, 1969—), Society for General Systems Research, World Future Society, American Association for the Advancement of Science, Phi Beta Kappa, Epsilon Chi, Sigma Xi. Awards, honors: Citation by executive council of American Association of Physics

Teachers for work as chairman of committee on letter symbols.

WRITINGS: Short Radio Dictionary, Fieldston School, 1935; (co-author) American Standard Letter Symbols for Physics, American Standards Association, 1948; (contributor) Methods for Emission Spectro-Chemical Analysis, American Society for Testing Materials, 1953; (editor with M.A. Coler) Essays on Creativity in the Sciences, New York University Press, 1963; (contributor) Edmund Dewan, editor, Cybernetics and the Management of Large Systems, Spartan, 1969; (contributor) E.O. Attinger, editor, Global Systems Dynamics, Albert J. Phiebig, 1970. Also author of The Boundaries of Modern Science, Indiana State University. Included in later editions of Handbook of Chemistry and Physics and Lange's Handbook of Chemistry. Contributor of about sixty articles and reports on scientific subjects to journals. Associate editor, Applied Spectroscopy, 1950-55.

* * *

HUGHES, Paul L(ester) 1915-

PERSONAL: Born November 25, 1915, in Cedar Rapids, Iowa; married Virginia Alice Schnare. Education: Coe College, B.A., 1941; State University of Iowa, M.A., 1947, Ph.D., 1950. Home: 240 Woodland Dr., Whitewater, Wis. 53190. Office: Department of History, Wisconsin State University, Whitewater, Wis. 53190.

CAREER: State University of Iowa, Iowa City, instructor in history, 1948-51; DePaul University, Chicago, Ill., 1951-66, became professor of history; Wisconsin State University, Whitewater, professor of history, 1966—. Military service: U.S. Army Air Forces, 1942-45. Member: American Historical Association, American Association of University Professors, Midwest Archeological Association, Organization of American Historians, Chicago University Renaissance Seminar.

WRITINGS: (Editor with Robert F. Fries) Readings in Western Civilization, Littlefield, 1956, revised edition published as European Civilization: Basic Historical Documents, 1965; Crown and Parliament in Tudor-Stuart England, 1485-1714, Putnam, 1959; (editor with James F. Larkin) Tudor Royal Proclamations, three volumes, Yale University Press, 1964-69; Stuart Royal Proclamations: The Proclamations of King James I, Clarendon, in press.

WORK IN PROGRESS: Stuart Royal Proclamations: The Proclamations of King Charles I, for Oxford University Press.

* * *

HUGHES, Philip Edgcumbe 1915-

PERSONAL: Born April 30, 1915, in Sydney, New South Wales, Australia; son of Randolph William (an author) and Muriel (Stanley-Hall) Hughes; married Margaret Byers, April 22, 1945; children: Marion. Education: University of Cape Town, B.A., 1937, M.A., 1939, D.Litt., 1955; University of London, B.D., 1946. Home: 1565 Cherry Lane, Rydal, Pa. 19046.

CAREER: Clergyman, Church of England; Tyndale Hall, Bristol, England, lecturer, 1947-52, vice-principal, 1951-52; University of Bristol, Bristol, lecturer in theology, 1948-52; Churchman (quarterly of Anglican theology), London, England, editor, 1959-68; Conwell School of Theology, Philadelphia, Pa., professor of historical theology, 1968-70. Guest professor of New Testament exegesis at Columbia Theological Seminary, Decatur, Ga., 1964; visiting professor of New Testament, Westminster Theological Seminary, Philadelphia, Pa., 1970—. Lecturer and preacher in Europe, United States, and Canada. Member: Studiorum Novi Testamenti Societas, Renaissance Society of America, American Society for Reformation Research.

WRITINGS: Revive Us Again, Marshall, Morgan & Scott, 1947; The Divine Plan for Jew and Gentile, Tyndale Press, 1949; (translator) Pierre Marcel, The Biblical Doctrine of Infant Baptism: Sacrament of the Covenant of Grace, James Clarke, 1953; (editor) Canon Law and the Church of England: An Examination of the Present Revision, Church Book Room Press for the Church Society, 1955; Scripture and Myth: An Examination of Rudolf Bultmann's Plea for Demythologization, Tyndale Press, 1956; The Position of the Celebrant at the Service of Holy Communion, Church Book Room Press, 1957; The Revision of Canon Law: Where Is It Leading Us?, Church Book Room Press, 1957; (translator with P.J. Allcock and others) J.J. von Allmen, editor, Companion to the Bible, Oxford University Press, 1958 (published in England as Vocabulary of the Bible, Lutterworth, 1958); The Public Baptism of Infants, Church Book Room Press, 1959.

(Editor) Edward Arthur Litton, Introduction to Dogmatic Theology, new edition, James Clarke, 1960; Paul's Second Epistle to the Corinthians, Eerdmans, 1962; Christianity and the Problem of Origins, Presbyterian & Reformed, 1964; But for the Grace of God: Divine Initiative and Human Need, Hodder & Stoughton, 1964, Westminster, 1965; (with James Atkinson) Anglicanism and the Roman Church, Church Book Room Press, 1964; Theology of the English Reformers, Hodder & Stoughton, 1965, Eerdmans, 1966; (editor and translator) The Register of the Company of Pastors of Geneva in the Time of Calvin, Eerdmans, 1966; (editor and contributor) Creative Minds in Contemporary Theology: A Guidebook to the Principal Teachings of Karl Barth, G.C. Berkouwer, Dietrich Bonhoeffer, Emil Brunner, Rudolf Bultmann, Oscar Cullman, James Denney, C.H. Dodd, Herman Dooyeweerd, P.T. Forsyth, Charles Gore, Reinhold Niebuhr, Pierre Teilhard de Chardin, and Paul Tillich, Eerdmans, 1966, 2nd edition, revised, 1969; (editor and author of foreword) Churchmen Speak: Thirteen Essays, Marcham Manor Press, 1966; The Control of Human Life, Presbyterian & Reformed, 1971. Contributor to other theological works and symposia. Contributor of articles to philosophical and theological journals in England, United States, France and The Netherlands. Editor, Christian Foundations, Hodder & Stoughton, 1964—.

* * *

HUIE, William Bradford 1910-

PERSONAL: Born November 13, 1910, in Hartselle, Ala.; son of John Bradford and Margaret Lois (Brindley) Huie; married Ruth Puckett, October 27, 1934. Education: University of Alabama, A.B., 1930. Residence: Hartselle, Ala. 35640.

CAREER: Birmingham Post, Birmingham, Ala., reporter, 1932-36; American Mercury, associate editor, 1941-43, editor and publisher until 1952; lecturer and free-lance writer, 1941—. Military service: U.S. Navy, 1943-45; became lieutenant. Member: Phi Beta Kappa.

WRITINGS: Mud on the Stars (novel), L.B. Fischer, 1942; The Fight for Air Power, L.B. Fischer, 1942; Seabee Roads to Victory, Dutton, 1944; Can Do!: The Story of the Seabees, Dutton, 1944; From Omaha to Okinawa: The Story of the Seabees, Dutton, 1945; The Case Against the Admirals: Why We Must Have a Unified Command, Dutton, 1946; The Revolt of Mamie Stover, Duell, Sloan & Pearce, 1951; The Execution of Private Slovik, Duell, Sloan & Pearce, 1954; Ruby McCollum, Woman in the Suwannee Jail, Dutton, 1956 (published in England as The Crime of Ruby McCollum, Jarrolds, 1957); Wolf Whistle, and Other Stories, New American Library, 1959; The Americanization of Emily (novel), Dutton, 1959; The Hero of Iwo Jima, and Other Stories, New American Library, 1962; Hotel Mamie Stover, Allen, 1962, C.N. Potter, 1963; *The Hiroshima Pilot: The Case of Major Claude Eatherly*, Putnam, 1964; *Three Lives for Mississippi*, Whitney Communications Corp., 1965; *The Klansman* (novel), Delacorte, 1967; *He Slew the Dreamer: My Search with James Earl Ray for the Truth About the Murder of Martin Luther King*, Delacorte, 1970. Contributor to *New Republic, Look*, and other publications.

WORK IN PROGRESS: A novel, *In the Hours of the Night*, for Delacorte.

SIDELIGHTS: Huie has been a dabbler in controversial themes since the publication of *The Fight for Air Power* in 1942, the book in which he charged that U.S. air power was crippled by Army and Navy ground hogs during the war. In October of 1954, while collecting material for *Ruby McCollum* (a Negro woman accused of murdering a white doctor in Florida), Huie was convicted of contempt of court allegedly for attempting to influence a psychiatrist who was a witness in the case. An outspoken opponent of white supremacy in his native Alabama, Huie again stirred widespread controversy with *The Klansman.* A fictionalized account of the evolution of power of the Ku Klux Klan in the South, the book aroused the ire of local Klansmen to the point where the lives of the author's family were endangered. After a cross was burned on his lawn in July of 1968, Huie asked Alabama Governor Albert Brewer for the same police protection as that given former Governor George Wallace during the presidential campaign. It is no coincidence that the title of Huie's novel parallels that of Thomas Dixon's *The Clansman,* a 1905 eulogy of the Klan which inspired the classic D.W. Griffith film, "The Birth of a Nation." Huie states that 16 mm. versions of the film are still shown regularly in backwoods areas to recruit Klan members, and that the Klan has been able to murder with impunity because of the passive acquiescence of the white power structure in much of the deep South.

Late in 1968 Huie paid approximately $35,000 to James Earl Ray, convicted assassin of Martin Luther King, Jr., for a handwritten manuscript detailing Ray's travels and activities prior to his arrest. Huie used the manuscript as the basis for a three-article *Look* magazine series on Ray, published in 1970 in book form as *He Slew the Dreamer.* In February of 1969 Huie was again arrested on a contempt of court citation, based on a strict order issued by Judge W. Preston Battle against pre-trial publicity. Bond was posted and Huie was freed following his arrest.

Fourteen of Huie's books have been best sellers; *The Revolt of Mamie Stover* sold over five million copies. Several of his books have been made into motion pictures, including *The Revolt of Mamie Stover,* produced by 20th Century-Fox in 1956, *Mud on the Stars,* filmed by 20th Century-Fox in 1960 as "Wild River," *The Hero of Iwo Jima,* produced by Universal in 1961 with the title "The Outsider," and *The Americanization of Emily,* produced by M-G-M in 1964. A musical production of the last also ran on Broadway in 1969. Robert J. Leder produced a motion picture version of *The Klansman* in 1968, and Jalem Productions has begun a film version of *Three Lives for Mississippi,* a dramatization of the 1964 murder of three civil rights workers in the South, to be entitled "Three Lives."

BIOGRAPHICAL/CRITICAL SOURCES: Time, May 30, 1949, December 8, 1952, September 13, 1968; *Publishers' Weekly,* June 19, 1967; *National Observer,* December 11, 1967; *Books and Bookmen,* June, 1968; *Commentary,* August, 1968; *New York Times,* February 8, 1969.†

* * *

HULL, Eleanor (Means)   1913-

PERSONAL: Born August 19, 1913, in Denver, Colo.; daughter of Carleton Bell and Florence (an author; maiden name, Crannell) Means; married Angus Clifton Hull (a clergyman), January 9, 1938; children: Mary Margaret (Mrs. Joseph Philip Hammer), Angus Crannell, Stephen Carleton, Peter Henrich, Jeremy Robert. *Education:* Colorado Woman's College, A.A., 1930; University of Redlands, B.A., 1932; University of Denver, B.F.A., 1934. *Politics:* Democrat. *Religion:* Baptist. *Home:* 41 Healy Ave., Hartsdale, N.Y. 10530.

CAREER: Department of Welfare, New York, N.Y., social caseworker, 1964-69. *Awards, honors:* Degree from Wilberforce College, Yellow Springs, Ohio.

WRITINGS: Tumbleweed Boy, Friendship, 1949; *The Third Wish,* Friendship, 1950; *Papi,* Friendship, 1953; *The Turquoise Horse,* Friendship, 1955; *Suddenly the Sun: A Biography of Shizuko Takahashi,* Friendship, 1957; *In the Time of the Condor,* Friendship, 1961; *Through the Secret Door,* Pilgrim Press, 1963; *The Sling and the Swallow,* United Church Press, 1963; *Moncho and the Dukes,* Friendship, 1964; *Everybody's Somebody,* Pilgrim Press, 1964; (with Elinor G. Galusha and Sarah D. Schear) *Let Us Worship God,* United Church Press, 1964; *The Church Not Made with Hands,* Judson, 1965; *A Trainful of Strangers,* Atheneum, 1968.

WORK IN PROGRESS: A teen-age novel on Mexico, *The Second Heart,* for Atheneum; a book about welfare clients.

* * *

HULSE, James Warren   1930-

PERSONAL: Born June 4, 1930, in Pioche, Nev.; son of James Gordon (a miner) and Berene (Cutler) Hulse; married Betty Kay Wynkoop (a teacher), June 20, 1962; children: Jane, James Charlton. *Education:* University of Nevada, B.A., 1952, M.A., 1958; Stanford University, Ph.D., 1961. *Politics:* Democrat. *Religion:* Unitarian. *Home:* 940 Grandview Ave., Reno, Nev. 89503. *Office:* Department of History, University of Nevada, Reno, Nev. 89507.

CAREER: Nevada State Journal, Reno, Nev., reporter, 1954-58; Central Washington State College, Ellensburg, instructor, 1961-62; University of Nevada, Reno, assistant professor, 1962-66, associate professor, 1966-70, professor of history, 1970—. Member of Nevada Commission on Equal Rights of Citizens, 1963-65. *Military service:* U.S. Army, 1952-54. *Member:* American Historical Association, American Association for the Advancement of Slavic Studies, American Civil Liberties Union.

WRITINGS: The Forming of the Communist International, Stanford University Press, 1964; *The Nevada Adventure: A History,* University of Nevada Press, 1965, 3rd edition, 1972; *Revolutionists in London: A Study of Five Unorthodox Socialists,* Oxford University Press, 1970; *Lincoln County, Nevada, 1864-1909: History of a Mining Region,* University of Nevada Press, 1971.

WORK IN PROGRESS: A history of the University of Nevada, publication expected in 1974; a study of Christian Socialism, 1974.

BIOGRAPHICAL/CRITICAL SOURCES: New Statesman, March 13, 1970; *London Magazine,* May, 1970.

* * *

HUMPHREVILLE, Frances Tibbetts   1909-

PERSONAL: Born February 12, 1909, in Pittsfield, Me.; daughter of Leonard (a businessman) and Frances (Gordon) Tibbetts; married Byron Humphreville (president of Niantic Co.), April 25, 1942. *Education:* Columbia University, Ph.D., 1952. *Politics:* Independent. *Religion:* Methodist. *Home:* 536 Huntington St., Shelton, Conn. 06484. *Agent:* Mrs. Betty J. Russell, Russylvania, Summan Rd., R.R. 1, Box 118, Valparaiso, Ind. 46383; and A.L. Fierst, 545 Fifth Ave., New York, N.Y. 10017.

CAREER: Chance Vought Aircraft Co., Westport, Conn., head of personnel department, 1943-45; New Haven Reading Center, New Haven, Conn., director, 1950-55; Danbury State College, Danbury, Conn., associate professor, 1947-61; general supervisor of schools, Bridgeport, Conn., 1959—. Treasurer, Niantic Co., Inc. Conducts radio program, "Going Places in Connecticut." *Member:* International Reading Association, National Association of Supervision, National Book Women, National Education Association, Connecticut Education Association, Connecticut Reading Research. *Awards, honors:* National Aeronautics and Space Administration science scholarship, 1963-64.

WRITINGS: The Story of Sam Coho, House of Field-Doubleday, 1947; (editor) *The Years Between: 12 Stories,* Scott, Foresman, 1953; (editor) *In Other Days: 15 Stories,* Scott, Foresman, 1956; (editor with Frances S. Fitzgerald) *Top Flight: Reading for Pleasure,* Scott, Foresman, 1961; (editor with Fitzgerald) *On Target,* Scott, Foresman, 1963; (with Albert E. Van Dusen) *This Is Connecticut,* Singer, 1963; (editor with Charlotte B. Diamant) *On the Threshold: Twelve Stories,* Scott, Foresman, 1964; (with others) *Resource Units in Planetarium-Oriented Space Science Teaching,* National Aeronautics and Space Administration, 1964; *Harriet Tubman: Flame of Freedom,* Houghton, 1967; *For All People: The Story of Frederick Douglass,* Houghton, 1969. Also writer and photographer of five sets of filmstrips for Eye Gate, Inc., and of thirteen scripts of the history of Connecticut for radio programs and recordings. Contributor of short stories, two of them later anthologized, to magazines, and of some twenty articles on English, citizenship, and journalism to professional journals.

WORK IN PROGRESS: A study of reading methods and techniques to help reluctant readers in early grades; a novel; a children's book; another reading book.

AVOCATIONAL INTERESTS: Photography, swimming, reading, and travel.

* * *

HUNT, Raymond G(eorge)   1928-

PERSONAL: Born July 1, 1928, in Buffalo, N.Y.; son of William R. (in automotive services) and Florence (Elkington) Hunt; married Viola C. Wannenwetsch, June 3, 1949; children: Gregory W., Karen S. *Education:* State University of New York at Buffalo, B.A., 1952, Ph.D., 1958. *Politics:* Democrat. *Home:* 616 Cottonwood Dr., Williamsville, N.Y. 14221. *Office:* Psychology Department, State University of New York, Buffalo, N.Y. 14226.

CAREER: Washington University, St. Louis, Mo., assistant professor of psychology, 1958-61; State University of New York at Buffalo, 1961—, began as assistant professor, now professor of psychology. Consultant in social psychology, U.S. Veterans Administration. *Military service:* U.S. Army, 1945-48. *Member:* American Psychological Association, American Sociological Association, Academy of Management, American Association of University Professors, Phi Beta Kappa. *Awards, honors:* Co-recipient of Helen M. DeRoy Award Society for Study of Social Problems, 1960, for research and writing in the field of social problems.

WRITINGS: (Editor with E.P. Hollander) *Current Perspectives in Social Psychology,* Oxford University Press, 1963, 3rd edition, 1971; (with others) *Nurses, Patients and Social Systems,* University of Missouri Press, 1967; (editor with Hollander) *Classic Perspectives in Social Psychology,* Oxford University Press, in press; *Counsel-*

ing: The Interpersonal Dimension of Management, Wadsworth, in press. Regular contributor to psychological, sociological, and management journals.

WORK IN PROGRESS: Research in organizational behavior and management, and in social psychiatry.

* * *

HUNT, Richard N(orman)   1931-

PERSONAL: Born February 23, 1931, in Syracuse, N.Y.; son of Herbert James (a chemist) and Verda (Engst) Hunt; married Margery A. Kohl, May 9, 1953; children: Christopher Paul, Jennifer Leigh. *Education:* Rutgers University, B.A., 1952; Yale University, M.A., 1953, Ph.D., 1958; University of Bonn, postgraduate study, 1953-54. *Office:* History Department, University of Pittsburgh, Pittsburgh, Pa., 15213.

CAREER: Connecticut College, New London, instructor in history, 1958-59; State University of Iowa, Iowa City, assistant professor of history, 1959-61; University of Pittsburgh, Pittsburgh, Pa., assistant professor of history, 1961—. *Member:* American Historical Association, American Association of University Professors. *Awards, honors:* Fulbright fellow, 1953-54.

WRITINGS: German Social Democracy, 1918-1933, Yale University Press, 1964; (editor and author of introduction) *The Creation of the Weimar Republic: Stillborn Democracy?,* Heath, 1969.

WORK IN PROGRESS: A book on Marx's and Engel's attitude toward political democracy.

* * *

HUNTER, A(rchibald M(acbride)   1906-

PERSONAL: Born January 16, 1906, in Kilwinning, Ayrshire, Scotland; son of Archibald (a minister) and Crissie (MacNeish) Hunter; married Margaret Wylie Swanson, March 14, 1934; children: Archibald Stewart, Fiona Mary (Mrs. John L. Harper). *Education:* University of Glasgow, M.A. (first class honors), B.D. (with distinction), Ph.D.; University of Marburg, advanced study; Oxford University, D.Phil. *Home:* 12 Westfield Ter., Aberdeen, Scotland. *Agent:* S.C.M. Press, London, England.

CAREER: Clergyman, Church of Scotland, Minister at Comrie, Perthshire, Scotland, 1934-37; Mansfield College, Oxford University, Oxford, England, professor of New Testament, 1937-42; minister at Kinnoull, Perthshire, Scotland, 1942-45; University of Aberdeen, Aberdeen, Scotland, professor of New Testament, 1945—, master of Christ's College, 1957—. Sprunt Lecturer at Richmond, Va., 1954; Sir D. Owen Evans Lecturer, 1962. *Awards, honors:* D.D., University of Glasgow, 1950.

WRITINGS: Paul and His Predecessors, Nicholson & Watson, 1940, revised edition, Westminster, 1961; *The Unity of the New Testament,* S.C.M. Press, 1943, published in America as *The Message of the New Testament,* Westminster, 1944; *Introducing the New Testament,* S.C.M. Press, 1945, Westminster, 1946, 2nd edition, 1957; *The Gospel According to St. Mark,* S.C.M. Press, 1948, Macmillan, 1949; *The Work and the Words of Jesus,* S.C.M. Press, 1950, Westminster, 1951; *Interpreting the New Testament, 1900-1950,* S.C.M. Press, 1951, Westminster, 1952; *A Pattern for Life: An Exposition of the Sermon on the Mount,* Westminster, 1953, revised edition, 1965 (published in England as *Design for Life: An Exposition of the Sermon on the Mount,* S.C.M. Press, 1953, revised edition, 1965); *Interpreting Paul's Gospel,* S.C.M. Press, 1954, Westminster, 1955, revised edition published as *The Gospel According to St. Paul,* S.C.M. Press, 1966, Westminster, 1967; *The Epistle to the Romans,* Macmillan, 1955, reissued as *The Epistle to the*

Romans: The Law of Love, 1968; Introducing New Testament Theology, S.C.M. Press, 1957, Westminster, 1958; The First Epistle of Peter, Abingdon, 1959; The Letter of Paul to the Galatians. The Letter of Paul to the Ephesians. . . . Philippians [and]. . . . Colossians, John Knox, 1959 (published in England as Galatians, Ephesians, Philippians, Colossians, S.C.M. Press, 1960).

Interpreting the Parables, S.C.M. Press, 1960, Westminster, 1961, 2nd edition, S.C.M. Press, 1964; Teaching and Preaching the New Testament, Westminster, 1963; Commentary on St. John's Gospel, Cambridge University Press, 1964; The Gospel According to John, Cambridge University Press, 1965, published in America as According to John: A New Look at the Fourth Gospel, Westminster, 1968; (editor) Thomas Murray Taylor, Speaking to Graduates, Oliver & Boyd, 1965; Bible and Gospel, Westminster, 1969; The Parables Then and Now, S.C.M. Press, 1971, Westminster, 1972; Exploring the New Testament, Saint Andrew Press, 1971, published in America as Probing the New Testament, John Knox, 1972.

*   *   *

HUNTER, Alan (James Herbert)   1922-

PERSONAL: Born June 25, 1922, in Hoveton St. John, Norwich, England; son of Herbert Ernest (a poultry farmer) and Isabella (Andrew) Hunter; married Adelaide Cubitt (an antique dealer), March 6, 1944; children: Helen. Religion: Zen Buddhist. Home: Rigby House, 4 Bathurst Rd., Norwich, England.

CAREER: Poultry farmer, Hoveton St. John, Norwich, England, 1936-40; bookseller, Norwich, England, 1946-57; full-time writer, 1957—. Military service: Royal Air Force, 1940-46; became leading aircraftsman. Member: Society of Authors, Crime Writers Association, Norwich Writer Circle (vice-president, 1955—), Yare Valley Sailing Club (rear commodore, 1961-62; vice commodore, 1962-63; commodore, 1963—).

WRITINGS: The Norwich Poems, 1943-44, Soman Wherry Press, 1945; Gently Does, It, Rinehart, 1955; Gently by the Shore, Rinehart, 1956; Gently Down the Stream, Cassell, 1957, Roy, 1960; Landed Gently, Cassell, 1957, Roy, 1960; Gently Through the Mill, Cassell, 1958; Gently in the Sun, Cassell, 1959; Gently with the Painters, Cassell, 1960; Gently to the Summit, Cassell, 1961; Gently Go Man, Cassell, 1961; Gently Where the Roads Go, Cassell, 1962; Gently Floating, Cassell, 1963; Gently Sahib, Cassell, 1964; Gently with the Ladies, Cassell, 1965; Gently in an Omnibus: Three Complete Novels (contains Gently Does It, Gently Through the Mill, Gently in the Sun), Cassell, 1966, St. Martin's, 1972; Gently North-West, Cassell, 1967; Gently Continental, Cassell, 1967; Gently Coloured, Cassell, 1969; Gently in Another Omnibus (contains Gently Go Man, Gently Where the Roads Go, Gently Floating), Cassell, 1969, St. Martin's, 1972; Gently with the Innocents, Cassell, 1970; Gently at a Gallop, Cassell, 1971.

Contributor of reviews of crime books to Eastern Daily Press, 1955—; author of humorous short stories for British Broadcasting Corp., and of several plays.

SIDELIGHTS: Hunter told CA: "My principal writing has been in the form of crime novels, which for a number of years I held to be the major literary form of the period. After much practise and experiment with the genre, and a critic's watching brief of fifteen years, I think I was wrong; perhaps being misled by the accomplishments of such writers as Chandler and Simenon. The form has severe limitations imposed upon it by dramatic necessity, and so tends towards mediocrity and resistance to development. If it is to survive as a literary vehicle I believe it must seek a new technique, in which connection it may be worth noticing the impressionism of Alain Robbe-Grillet's The House of Assignation.

"My long love affair with sail-cruising on the river-lake system known as The Norfolk Broads has cooled recently, owing to their over-popularity. In consequence I am much more aligned towards travel, with a particular interest in mountain and lake scenery. For me, this is quite a profound change of attitude and I feel it reflecting in my work."

Gently Does It has been dramatized as "That Man Gently," by Mrs. August Belmont, and produced at Harlow England, November, 1961. Hunter's books have been issued in translation in Germany, Sweden, Norway, France, Italy, Spain, and Yugoslavia.

BIOGRAPHICAL/CRITICAL SOURCES: Books and Bookmen, April, 1970, March, 1971; Punch, June 14, 1967, April 16, 1969.

*   *   *

HUNTER, Jim   1939-

PERSONAL: Born June 24, 1939, in Stafford, England; son of David (a teacher) and Gwendolyn (Castell-Evans) Hunter. Education: Gonville and Caius College, Cambridge University, M.A. (first class honors), 1960; Indiana University, postgraduate student, 1960-61; University of Bristol, Certificate of Education (with distinction), 1962. Agent: Harold Matson Co., Inc., 30 Rockefeller Plaza, New York, N.Y. 10022.

CAREER: Bradford Grammar School, Bradford, England, English master, 1962-66; Bristol Grammar School, Bristol, England, 1966—. Awards, honors: Authors Club (London) award for best first novel of 1961 for The Sun in the Morning.

WRITINGS: The Sun in the Morning, Faber, 1961; Sally Cray, Faber, 1963; Earth and Stone, Faber, 1963, published in America as A Place of Stone, Pantheon, 1964; (editor and author of introduction) Modern Short Stories (school anthology), Faber, 1964, Transatlantic, 1967; The Metaphysical Poets, Evans Brothers, 1965; The Flame, Pantheon, 1966; Gerard Manley Hopkins, Evans Brothers, 1966; (editor) The Modern Novel in English Studied in Extracts, Faber, 1966; (editor) Modern Poets, four volumes, Faber, 1968; (editor) Shakespeare, Henry IV, Part I, Evans Brothers, 1969. Contributor to Evening News, Spectator, Time and Tide, and College English.

*   *   *

HUNTER, Maud L(ily)   1910-
(Christine Hunter, John Hunter)

PERSONAL: Born June 29, 1910, in Longtown, Cumberland, England; daughter of John (a grocer) and Charlotte (Steer) Wheeler; married John Edward Hunter (a conference speaker), July 14, 1934; children: Kathleen Patricia (Mrs. Leonard Ward), Malcolm Ian, Michael Stuart, Colin Alistair. Education: Edge Hill Training College, Certificate of Teaching. Politics: Conservative. Religion: Evangelical. Home: 98 Helmside Rd., Oxenholme, Kendal, Westmorland, England.

CAREER: Teacher in elementary council schools in Liverpool and Wiltshire, England, for sixteen years. Assistant in youth conference work for sixteen years.

WRITINGS: Cousin John, Waters, 1961; Bunty and Peter, Pickering & Inglis, 1969; Tangled Threads, Zondervan, 1971.

Under pseudonym Christine Hunter: Against Great Odds, Christian Literature Crusade, 1950; All the Way, Christian Literature Crusade, 1950; Mysterious Neighbours, Christian Literature Crusade, 1953; Escape to Adventure, Christian Literature Crusade, 1953; A Mender of Broken

Hearts, Stirling Tract Enterprise, 1956; *Laughing Waters,* Pickering & Inglis, 1956; *The Coutier Treasure,* Pickering & Inglis, 1956; *Come On, Spencer's!,* Victory Press, 1957; *Tentenbury Manor,* Victory Press, 1957; *The Boy from Down Under,* Pickering & Inglis, 1964; *The Years of Our Days,* Zondervan, 1967; *To Life Anew,* Zondervan, 1968; *Deep Waters,* Zondervan, 1969; (with Gladys Aylward) *The Small Woman of the Inn,* Moody, 1970.

Under pseudonym John Hunter: *Michael Graham, Police Cadet,* Elim, 1959; *Michael Graham, Police Constable,* Victory Press, 1963.

Contributor of serials and short stories to *Sunday Companion, Scottish Journal, Crusade,* and other periodicals.

WORK IN PROGRESS: A series of three books, each entitled *One Thousand Bible Quiz Questions,* for C.R. Gibson; *Book of Party Games,* for Gibson; a novel, *Life at Innercairn,* for Zondervan; four books, *Annalisa, Living Stones, Mystery Next Door, Gold Tried in the Fire,* for Moody; *Linda Rowlands,* for Christian Literature Crusade.

AVOCATIONAL INTERESTS: Travel and speaking.

* * *

HUNTINGTON, (E.) Gale   1902-

PERSONAL: Born June 4, 1902; son of Elon Obed (in U.S. Navy) and Hannah (Blackwell) Huntington; married Mildred Tilton (a bank clerk), October 14, 1931; children: Emily Huntington Rose. *Education:* Stetson University, A.B., 1925; Boston University, M.A., 1947. *Politics:* Republican. *Religion:* Congregationalist. *Home:* Hine's Point, Vineyard Haven, Mass. 02568. *Agent:* Curtis Brown Ltd., 60 East 56th St., New York, N.Y. 10022. *Office:* Dukes County Historical Society, Cooke St., Edgartown, Mass. 02539.

CAREER: Self-employed commercial fisherman and farmer, 1926-44; high school teacher of history, 1944-55, of Latin, 1955-61; free-lance short story writer, 1961—. *Member:* Northeast Folklore Society, Massachusetts Archaeological Society, Martha's Vineyard Conservation Society, Dukes County Historical Society (vice-president).

WRITINGS: Songs the Whaleman Sang, Barre, 1964, 2nd edition, Dover, 1970; *Folksongs From Martha's Vineyard,* Northeast Folklore Society, 1967; *An Introduction to Martha's Vineyard,* Martha's Vineyard Printing Co., 1969. Editor of Dukes County Historical Society Bulletin.

WORK IN PROGRESS: A book on the Indians of Martha's Vineyard; editing *Sam Henry's Songs of the People,* a collection of folksongs from Northern Ireland.

* * *

HURE, Anne   1918-

PERSONAL: Born October 25, 1918, in Paris, France; daughter of Pierre Adolphe Auguste and Andree Eugenie (Gellee) Hure. *Education:* Etudes superieures, Paris, France, Licence Philosophie; studied at Louvain, Belgium, received Doctorate de Theologie. *Politics:* Rightist-monarchist. *Religion:* Catholic. *Home:* 8, rue Henri Duchene, Paris XV, France.

*WRITINGS—*Novels: *Les Deux moniales,* R. Julliard, 1962, translation by Emma Craufurd published as *The Two Nuns,* Sheed, 1964; *Entretiens avec Monsieur Renan,* R. Julliard, 1962; *En Prison,* R. Julliard, 1963, translation by Emma Craufurd published as *In Prison,* Macdonald & Co., 1965; *Le Peche sans merci,* Plon, 1964, translation by Emma Craufurd published as *The Word Made Flesh,* Macdonald & Co., 1967; *Discente en enfer,* Plon, 1966; *Le Haut chemin,* La Table Ronde, 1966; *Les Vendanges,* La Table Ronde, 1968; *Tendresses d'ete,* Plon, 1970. Contributor to *Nation Francaise, Monde et la Vie,* and other publications.

WORK IN PROGRESS: A novel; essays on Luther and Lamennais.

SIDELIGHTS: Miss Hure is interested in the history of the Catholic Church. She enjoys travel, especially to Greece and Italy. *Avocational interests:* Classical music (especially Bach), Rembrandt, cats, 50-year-old men, and old wines.

BIOGRAPHICAL/CRITICAL SOURCES: Realities, August, 1963; *Ecrits de Paris,* October-November, 1963; *Punch,* November 29, 1967.

* * *

HURLEY, William James, Jr.   1924-

PERSONAL: Born December 31, 1924, in Chicago, Ill.; son of William James and Marian (Clark) Hurley; married Jane Ellen Hezel (an elementary teacher), 1954; children: Ellen Maureen, Jane Ann, William III, Michael Sean, Patrick Vincent, Matthew John. *Education:* DePaul University, B.A., 1950, M.A., 1952; Rutgers State University, postgraduate student, 1960; Loyola University, Chicago, Ill., graduate study. *Religion:* Roman Catholic. *Home:* 7346 Pottawatomi Dr., Palos Heights, Ill. 60463. *Office:* Chicago State College, 6800 South Stewart Ave., Chicago, Ill. 60621.

CAREER: Chicago (Ill.) Public Schools, elementary teacher, 1950-54, high school teacher, 1954-61; Chicago State College, Chicago, Ill., assistant professor of English, 1961—. Loyola University, Chicago, Ill., part-time lecturer, 1960—. *Military service:* U.S. Air Force, 1943; served in European theater; awarded six battle stars; currently major, Illinois Air National Guard. *Member:* Illinois Education Association, International Reading Association (Chicago region secretary, 1956-57; treasurer, 1957-58), American Association of University Professors, Alpha Delta Gamma, Pi Gamma Mu, O'Hara Air Force Base Officer's Club. *Awards, honors:* Ford fellowship, 1960.

*WRITINGS—*All published by Benefic: *Dan Frontier,* 1959, *Dan Frontier Goes Hunting,* 1959, *Dan Frontier and the Wagon Train,* 1959, *Dan Frontier with the Indians,* 1959, *Dan Frontier, Sheriff,* 1960, *Dan Frontier and the New House,* 1961, *Dan Frontier and the Big Cat,* 1961, *Dan Frontier, Trapper,* 1962, *Dan Frontier Scouts with the Army,* 1962, *Dan Frontier Goes Exploring,* 1963, *Dan Frontier Goes to Congress,* 1964.

WORK IN PROGRESS: A travelogue and geography book, tentatively titled *Operation Creek Party.*

SIDELIGHTS: All the "Dan Frontier" books have been recorded on L.P. records. *Avocational interests:* Pilot of light aircraft, amateur herpetologist, numismatics.

* * *

HUSSEY, Maurice Percival   1925-

PERSONAL: Born June 7, 1925, son of Percival John and Ella (Burrough) Hussey. *Education:* Downing College, Cambridge University, B.A., 1947, education diploma, 1948, M.A., 1951. *Politics:* Labour. *Religion:* Roman Catholic. *Home:* 15 Highsett, Hills Rd., Cambridge, England.

CAREER: Cambridge College of Arts and Technology, Cambridge, England, lecturer in English literature, 1948—; supervisorship in English literature at other colleges, 1948—. Salzburg Seminar in American Studies, fellow, 1963. *Member:* Royal Commonwealth Society (fellow).

WRITINGS: (Contributor) *Pelican Guide to English Literature III,* Pelican, 1956; (adapter into modern English)

The Chester Mystery Plays: Sixteen Pageant Plays from the Chester Craft Cycle, Heinemann, 1957; (with R.C. Churchill) Shakespeare and His Betters: A History and a Criticism of the Attempts Which Have Been Made to Prove that Shakespeare's Works Were Written by Others, University of Illinois Press, 1958; Scrutiny, Volume XX—Indexes, Cambridge University Press, 1963; (editor and author of introduction) Jonson and the Cavaliers, Heinemann, 1964, Barnes & Noble, 1966; (editor) Ben Jonson, Bartholomew Fair, Benn, 1964; (editor and author of introduction) Chaucer, The Canon's Yeoman Tale, Cambridge University Press, 1965; (editor and author of introduction) Chaucer, The Nun's Priest's Tale, Cambridge University Press, 1965; (with others) An Introduction to Chaucer, Cambridge University Press, 1965; (editor and author of introduction) Chaucer, The Merchant's Tale, Cambridge University Press, 1966; (compiler) Chaucer's World: A Pictorial Companion, Cambridge University Press, 1967; (editor) Poetry of the First World War, Longmans, Green, 1967; (editor) Ben Jonson, Devil Is an Ass, University Tutorial Press, 1967; (adapter with Surenda Agarwala) John Heywood, Play of the Weather, and Other Tudor Comedies, Theatre Arts, 1967; (editor) Criticism in Action: A Critical Symposium on Modern Poems, Longmans, Green, 1969; (editor and author of foreword) John Purkis, Preface to Wordsworth, British Book Centre, 1971, Scribner, 1972; (editor and author of foreword) James Winney, Preface to Donne, Scribner, 1972; The World of Shakespeare and His Contemporaries, Viking, 1972. General editor, Longman's English series, Preface Books.

Contributor of scripts on literary and other subjects to British Broadcasting Corp. programs.

WORK IN PROGRESS: A book on Shakespeare's iconography, for Heinemann.

AVOCATIONAL INTERESTS: Music, opera, theatrical history.

*   *   *

HUTCHINGS, Margaret (Joscelyne)   1918-

PERSONAL: Born December 18, 1918, in Brentwood, Essex, England; daughter of William Jabez (a draper) and Marjorie Winifred (Golding) Howard; married Sidney Alfred Hutchings (a consulting optician), June 1, 1939; children: Richard John, Christopher William, David George. Education: Attended Endsleigh House School, Colchester, England, 1931-35. Religion: Church of England. Home: Mimosa House, South Weald, Brentwood, Essex, England.

CAREER: Toymaker; free-lance writer; designer. Chairman, Bon Marche Ltd. Demonstrator of toymaking on British Broadcasting Corp. television. Past president, Ongar Women's Institute. Member: British Toy Makers' Guild. Awards, honors: International Handicrafts Exhibition (Olympia, London, England) awards for Father Christmas and sledge, 1956, for giant monkey, 1957, for toy village, 1958.

WRITINGS: Glove Toys, Studio Books, 1958; Modern Soft Toy Making, Mills & Boon, 1959, Branford, 1960; (self-illustrated) Toying with Trifles, Mills & Boon, 1960; (contributor) The Marchioness of Anglesey, editor, The Country Woman's Year, M. Joseph, 1960; Hints on Soft Toys, Mills & Boon, 1961; (self-illustrated) Patchwork Playthings, Branford, 1961; Dolls and How to Make Them, Branford, 1963; What Shall I Do with This?, Mills & Boon, 1963, Taplinger, 1965; The Book of the Teddy Bear, Mills & Boon, 1964, Branford, 1965; What Shall I Do Today?, Mills & Boon, 1965, Taplinger, 1966; What Shall I Do This Month?, Mills & Boon, 1965, Taplinger, 1966; What Shall I Do: From Scandinavia, Mills & Boon, 1966, Taplinger, 1967; Making New Testament Toys, Taplinger, 1972; Making Old Testament Toys, Taplinger 1972. Contributor of articles to newspapers and magazines, including Home and Country, Housewife, Sunday Times, She, and Good Housekeeping.

WORK IN PROGRESS: Plans and research for more books for children and adults; Making Things from the Bible and Making Finger Puppets, both for Mills & Boon.

SIDELIGHTS: Mrs. Hutchings hates insincerity, indecision, two-faced people, procrastination, cold weather, eggs, and cocktail parties. She loves babies, old people, small animals (except mice), sunshine, the music of a round-a-bout, deserted seashores, fruit, and spaghetti.

*   *   *

HUTCHINGS, Monica Mary   1917-

PERSONAL: Born July 3, 1917, in Cardiff, Glamorganshire, Wales; daughter of John Lawler Scott and Elizabeth Mills; married Lewis George Baber (a farmer and yachtsman), April 10, 1951. Politics: Liberal. Religion: Agnostic; vegetarian. Home: Broad Mead, Church Knowle, Wareham, Dorset, England.

CAREER: Author. Active in campaigns of Royal Society for Prevention of Cruelty to Animals and Captive and Performing Animals Defence League; operator of free ballet and music studio for children in her own home for two decades; lecturer at American Institute for Foreign Study and at other institutions. Member: Romantic Novelists' Association, South Western Museums Group, South Western Arts Association, Farmwomen's Club, Parkstone Yacht Club.

WRITINGS: The Chronicles of Church Farm, Hodder & Stoughton, 1945; Romany Cottage, Silverlake: The True Story of an "Ordinary" Adventure, Hodder & Stoughton, 1946; Rural Reflections, Hodder & Stoughton, 1947; Hundredfold, Hodder & Stoughton, 1948; Green Willow, Longmans, Green, 1950; The Walnut Tree: An Autobiography of Kindness, Hodder & Stoughton, 1951; The Special Smile, Hodder & Stoughton, 1951; The Isle of Wight, R. Hale, 1953; Dorset River, Macdonald & Co., 1956; The Blue Island, Ward, Lock, 1959; The Heart Mender, Ward, Lock, 1960; Blow the Wind Southerly, Ward, Lock, 1960; Tamarisk Summer, Ward, Lock, 1961; Two for Joy, Ward, Lock, 1961; The Man for Gill, Ward, Lock, 1962; Highway to Dreams, Ward, Lock, 1962; The Visitors' Brief Guide to the Hardy Country of Dorset, Raleigh Press, 1962; The Visitors' Brief Guide to Somerset, Mendip, and Avalon, edited by E.R. Delderfield, Raleigh Press, 1963; A Thing Apart, Ward, Lock, 1963; Inside Somerset, Abbey Press, 1963; A Farmer's Wife Looks at Hunting (pamphlet), National Society for the Abolition of Cruel Sports, 1965; Things to See and Do in Dorset, Mendip, and Avalon, David & Charles, 1966; The Isle of Purbeck, Abbey Press, 1967; Things to See and Do in Somerset, David & Charles, 1967; Hardy's River, Abbey Press, 1967; The Fight for Tyneham, Dorset Publishing Co., 1968; (with Mavis Caver) Man's Dominion: Our Violation of the Animal World, Hart-Davis, 1970.

Also author of script for documentary, "New Face of Britain." Contributor to Western Gazette and to specialized magazines.

AVOCATIONAL INTERESTS: Nature, archaeology, animal welfare.

*   *   *

HUTCHINS, Ross Elliott   1906-

PERSONAL: Born April 30, 1906, in Ruby, Mont.; son of Elliott J. (a rancher) and Hellen M. Hutchins; married Annie L. McClanahan, June 5, 1931. Education: Montana State College, B.S., 1929, Mississippi State University, M.S., 1932; Iowa State College, Ph.D., 1935. *Address:* Drawer EH, State College, Miss. 39762.

CAREER: Mississippi State College, State College, 1929—, became professor of entomology and entomologist, now professor emeritus. Executive officer of Mississippi Plant Board, 1951-1968. *Military service:* U.S. Navy, epidemic disease control officer, 1942-45; became lieutenant commander. *Member:* American Entomological Society, Mississippi Entomological Society, Authors Guild, Sigma Xi, Phi Kappa Phi.

WRITINGS: Insects: Hunters and Trappers, Rand McNally, 1957; *Strange Plants and Their Ways,* Rand McNally, 1958; *Insect Builders and Craftsmen,* Rand McNally, 1959 (published in England as *Insects: Builders and Craftsmen,* Burke Publishing, 1960); *Strange Ways of the Plant and Insect World* (contains *Strange Plants and Their Ways* and *Insects: Builders and Craftsmen,* Burke Publishing, 1960; *Wild Ways: A Book of Animal Habits,* Rand McNally, 1961 (published in England as *Wild Ways of the Animal World,* Burke Publishing, 1962); *Lives of an Oak Tree,* Rand McNally, 1962; *This Is a Leaf,* Dodd, 1962; *This Is a Flower,* Dodd, 1963; *This Is a Tree,* Dodd, 1964; *The Amazing Seeds,* Dodd, 1965; *Plants without Leaves: Lichens, Fungi, Mosses, Liverworts, Slime-Molds, Algae, Horsetails,* Dodd, 1966; *The Travels of Monarch X,* Rand McNally, 1966; *Insects,* Prentice-Hall, 1966; *Caddis Insects: Nature's Carpenters and Stone-masons,* Dodd, 1966; *The Ant Realm,* Dodd, 1967; *The Last Trumpeters,* Rand McNally, 1967; *Galls and Gall Insects,* Dodd, 1969; *The World of Dragonflies and Damselflies,* Dodd, 1969; *Adelbert the Penguin,* Rand McNally, 1969; *Little Chief of the Mountains,* Rand McNally, 1970; *The Mayfly,* Addison-Wesley, 1970; *Hop, Skim and Fly: An Insect Book,* Parents' Magazine Press, 1970; *Scaly Wings: A Book About Moths and their Caterpillars,* Parents' Magazine Press, 1971; *Saga of Pelorus Jack,* Rand McNally, 1971; *Hidden Valley of the Smokies: With a Naturalist in the Great Smoky Mountains,* Dodd, 1971; *Cicada,* Addison-Wesley, 1971; *Insects in Armor: The Beetle Book,* Parents' Magazine Press, 1972; *The Carpenter Bee,* Addison-Wesley, 1972; *Grasshoppers and their Kin,* Dodd, 1972; *The Bug Clan,* Dodd, 1973; *Paper Hornets,* Addison-Wesley, 1973. Contributor to *National Geographic.*

BIOGRAPHICAL/CRITICAL SOURCES: Christian Science Monitor, November 2, 1967, December 21, 1967; *New York Times Book Review,* November 5, 1967, November 3, 1968; *Book World,* January 7, 1968; *Commonweal,* May 23, 1969; *Library Journal,* October 15, 1970.

* * *

HUXLEY, Anthony J(ulian) 1920-

PERSONAL: Born December 2, 1920, in Oxford, England; son of Julian (a biologist and writer) and Marie-Juliette (Baillot) Huxley. *Education:* Dauntsey's School, student, 1934-39; Trinity College, Cambridge, B.A., 1941, M.A., 1954. *Home and office:* 32 Becklay House, Eagle St., London W.C.1, England.

CAREER: Royal Air Force, civilian scientific officer in operational research, 1941-47; British Overseas Airways Corp., economic research, 1947-49; *Amateur Gardening,* London, England, assistant editor, 1949-67, editor, 1967-71; free-lance writer, photographer, and tour leader, 1971—. *Member:* Royal Horticultural Society, Royal Geographical Society, Horticultural Club (London; secretary, 1951—).

WRITINGS: Cacti and Succulents, Collingridge, 1953; *House Plants,* Collingridge, 1954, revised edition, 1961; (translator and editor) Marcel Belvianes, *Exotic Plants of the World,* Doubleday, 1957; *Indoor Plants,* edited by

A.G.L. Hellyer, Collingridge, 1957; *Treasures of the Garden,* Doubleday, 1959 (published in England as *Beauty in the Garden,* Rathbone Books, 1960); (translator and editor) Aloys Duperrex, *Orchids of Europe,* Blandford, 1961; *Wild Flowers of the Countryside,* Blandford, 1962; *Garden Terms Simplified,* Collingridge, 1962; (editor and contributor) *Standard Encyclopedia of the World's Mountains,* Putnam, 1962; (editor and contributor) *Standard Encyclopedia of the World's Oceans and Islands,* Putnam, 1962; *Flowers in Greece: An Outline of the Flora,* Royal Horticultural Society, 1963; (with Oleg Polunin) *Flowers of the Mediterranean,* Chatto & Windus, 1965, Houghton, 1966; (editor with R. Kay Gresswell, and contributor) *Standard Encyclopedia of the World's Rivers and Lakes,* Putnam, 1966; *Mountain Flowers in Color,* Blandford, 1967, Macmillan, 1968; (editor) *Garden Perennials in Color,* Macmillan, 1971; (editor) *Garden Annuals and Bulbs in Color,* Macmillan, 1971. Regular contributor to *Country Life.*

WORK IN PROGRESS: A Plant's World, for Viking; *A History of Gardening Methods.*

AVOCATIONAL INTERESTS: Photography, gardening, looking for wild flowers, conducting botanical tours.

* * *

HUXLEY, Julian (Sorell) 1887- (Balbus)

PERSONAL: Born June 22, 1887, in London, England; son of Leonard (an essayist, master of Charterhouse) and Julia (Arnold) Huxley; married Marie Juliette Baillot, 1919; children: Anthony Julian, Francis John Heathorn. *Education:* Eton College, King's Scholar; Balliol College, Oxford, Brakenbury Scholar, degree in natural science (with first class honours), 1909; Naples Zoological Station Scholar, 1909-10. *Religion:* Humanist. *Home:* 31 Pond St., Hampstead N.W. 3, England. *Agent:* A.D. Peters, 10 Buckingham St., London W.C.2, England.

CAREER: Balliol College, Oxford University, Oxford, England, lecturer in zoology, 1910-12; Rice Institute, Houston, Tex., research associate, 1912-13, assistant professor, 1913-16; New College, Oxford University, Oxford, fellow and senior demonstrator in zoology, 1919-25; King's College, University of London, London, England, professor of zoology, 1925-27, honorary lecturer, 1927-35; Royal Institution, London, Fullerian Professor of Physiology, 1926-29; general supervisor of biological films, G. B. Instructional Ltd., 1933-36, Zoological Film Productions Ltd., 1937; director general, UNESCO, 1946-48. Galton Lecturer, 1937, 1962; Romanes Lecturer, Oxford University, 1943; William Alanson White Lecturer, Washington, D.C., 1951; first Alfred P. Sloan Lecturer, Sloan-Kettering Institute for Cancer Research, 1955; Beatty Lecturer, McGill University, 1956; visiting professor, University of Chicago, 1959. Participated in Oxford University's expedition to Spitsbergen, Norway, 1921; participated in Jordan Expedition, 1963; visited East Africa to advise on native education, 1929; member of General Committee for Lord Hailey's African Survey, 1933-38; member of Commission on Higher Education in West Africa, 1944; secretary, Zoological Society of London, 1935-42; member, Committee on National Parks, 1946; visited East Africa, 1960, and Ethiopia, 1963, to report to UNESCO on wildlife conservation there; vice-president of UNESCO Commission for Scientific and Cultural History of Mankind. *Military service:* British Army, General Headquarters in Italy, staff lieutenant, World War I.

MEMBER: Institute of Animal Behaviour (former president), Eugenics Society (president), Association for the Study of Systematics (former chairman), Academie des Sciences (Paris; corresponding member), Hungarian

Academy of Science (foreign member), Saville Club, Atheneum Club. *Awards, honors:* Academy of Motion Picture Arts and Sciences "Oscar," 1934, for "The Private Life of the Gannets"; Anisfield award, 1935, for *We Europeans;* made a Fellow of the Royal Society, 1938; honorary member of faculty of biology and medicine, University of Santiago de Chile, 1947; honorary member of Society of Biology, University of Montevideo, 1947; Kalinga Prizeman, 1953; Darwin medal, Royal Society, 1957; Darwin-Wallace commemorative medal, Linnean Society, 1958; knighted, 1958; honorary degrees from University of Caracas, 1947, University of San Carlos de Guatemala, 1947, University of Athens, 1949, Columbia University, 1954, University of Birmingham, 1959.

WRITINGS: Holyrood (poems), Blackwell, 1908; *The Individual in the Animal Kingdom,* Putnam, 1912; *Essays of a Biologist,* Knopf, 1923, 3rd edition, 1926, reprinted, Books for Libraries, 1970; *The Outlook in Biology* (pamphlet), Rice Institute (Houston), 1924; (editor) *Text-Books of Animal Biology,* Sidgwick & Jackson, 1926; *Essays in Popular Science,* Chatto & Windus, 1926, Knopf, 1927; *The Stream of Life,* Watts & Co., 1926, Harper, 1927; (with J.B.S. Haldane) *Animal Biology,* Oxford University Press, 1927; *Religion Without Revelation,* Harper, 1927, revised edition, Harper, 1957; *Towards the Open,* Chatto & Windus, 1927; *Biology and Society,* British Social Hygiene Council, 1928; (with H.G. Wells and G.P. Wells) *The Science of Life,* Amalgamated Press, 1929, revised edition, 1938; *What Darwin Really Said,* Routledge, 1929.

Bird-watching and Bird Behavior, Chatto & Windus, 1930, 2nd edition, Dobson, 1950; *Science, Religion, and Human Nature* (Conway Memorial Lecture), Watts & Co., 1930; *Ants,* J. Cape and H. Smith, 1930, reprinted, AMS Press, 1969; *Africa View,* Harper, 1931; *What Dare I Think?,* Harper, 1931; *Problems of Relative Growth,* Dial, 1932; *A Scientist Among the Soviets,* Harper, 1932; *A Captive Shrew and Other Poems of a Biologist,* Blackwell, 1932, Harper, 1933; *Evolution, Fact and Theory,* Doubleday, 1932; (with Andrade) *Introduction to Science,* Blackwell, 1932, reissued as *Simple Science,* Blackwell, 1934, published in America as *Simple Science,* Harper, 1935; *If I Were a Dictator,* Harper, 1934; (with G.R. De Beer) *The Elements of Experimental Embryology,* Cambridge University Press, 1934, Hafner, 1963; (with H.G. Wells and G.P. Wells) *Living Body,* Cassell, 1934; *Scientific Research and Social Needs,* Watts & Co., 1934, published in America as *Science and Social Needs,* Harper, 1935; (with R.M. Lockley) "Private Life of the Gannets," (film script), produced, 1934; (with Andrade) *More Simple Science,* Blackwell, 1935, Harper, 1936; *Problems in Experimental Embryology* (Robert Boyle Lecture), Oxford University Press, 1935; (editor) T.H. Huxley, *Diary of the Voyage of the H.M.S. Rattlesnake,* Chatto & Windus, 1935, reprinted, Kraus, 1972; (with A.C. Haddon) *We Europeans: A Survey of 'Racial' Problems,* J. Cape, 1935, Harper, 1936; *At the Zoo,* Allen & Unwin, 1936; (author of introduction) Adolf Portmann, *The Beauty of Butterflies,* Batsford, 1936, Oxford University Press (New York), 1945; (with H.G. Wells and G.P. Wells) *Biology of the Human Race,* Cassell, 1937; (with H.G. Wells) *How Animals Behave,* Cassell, 1937; (with H.G. Wells and G.P. Wells) *Man's Mind and Behavior,* Cassell, 1937; *Beginnings of Life,* Tuck, 1938; *Animal Language,* Country Life Ltd., 1938, new edition, Grosset, 1964; (contributor) Sandor Forbat, *Love and Marriage,* Liveright, 1938; *'Race' in Europe,* Farrar & Rinehart, 1939; (editor) *The Living Thoughts of Darwin,* Longmans, Green, 1939, new edition, Fawcett, 1959.

(Editor) *The New Systematics,* Clarendon Press, 1940; *Argument of Blood: The Advancement of Science,* Macmillan, 1941; (under pseudonym Balbus) *Arm Now*

Against Famine and Pestilence, Universal Distributors, 1941; *Democracy Marches,* Harper, 1941; *Man Stands Alone,* Harper, 1941 (published in England as *The Uniqueness of Man,* Chatto & Windus, 1941); (under pseudonym Balbus) *Reconstruction and Peace: Needs and Opportunities,* K. Paul, Trench, Trubner & Co., 1941, New Republic, 1942; (contributor) H. Thomas, editor, *The Brains Trust Book,* Hutchinson, 1942; (contributor) A. Low, editor, *Science Looks Ahead,* Oxford University Press, 1942; *Evolution, the Modern Synthesis,* Allen & Unwin, 1942, Harper, 1943, 2nd edition, Allen & Unwin, 1963, Wiley, 1964; *Evolutionary Ethics* (Romanes Lecture), Oxford University Press, 1943; *TVA, Adventures in Planning,* Architectural Press, 1943; (with Phyllis Deane) *The Future of the Colonies,* Pilot Press, 1944; (with others) *Humanism,* Watts & Co., 1944; *On Living in a Revolution,* Harper, 1944; (with others) *Reshaping Man's Heritage,* Allen & Unwin, 1944; *Julian Huxley on T.H. Huxley: A New Judgment,* Watts & Co., 1945; (with others) *Science at Your Service,* Allen & Unwin, 1945; *Religion as an Objective Problem,* Watts & Co., 1946; *UNESCO, Its Purpose and Philosophy,* Preparatory Commission of UNESCO, 1946, Public Affairs Press, 1947; *Man in the Modern World,* Chatto & Windus, 1947, New American Library, 1948; (with T.H. Huxley) *Touchstone for Ethics, 1893-1943,* Harper, 1947 (published in England as *Evolution and Ethics, 1893-1943,* Pilot Press, 1947), reprinted, Kraus, 1969; *The Vindication of Darwinism,* Pilot Press, 1947; (with Jaime Torres Bodet) *This Is Our Power,* UNESCO Publications, 1948; *Heredity, East and West: Lysenko and World Science,* H. Schuman, 1949, reprinted, Kraus, 1969 (published in England as *Soviet Genetics and World Science,* Chatto & Windus, 1949).

Natural History in Ireland, Smithsonian Institution, 1951; *Evolution in Action,* Harper, 1953; *New Bottles for New Wine: Ideology and Scientific Knowledge* [Singapore], 1953, published as *New Bottles for New Wine: Essays,* Harper, 1957, and as *Knowledge, Morality, and Destiny: Essays,* New American Library, 1960; *Evolution as a Process,* Allen & Unwin, 1954, 2nd edition, 1958, Collier, 1963; *From an Antique Land: Ancient and Modern in the Middle East,* Crown, 1954, 2nd edition, Parrish, 1961, Harper, 1966; *Kingdom of the Beasts,* Vanguard, 1956; *Biological Aspects of Cancer,* Harcourt, 1958; (with others) *A Book That Shook the World,* University of Pittsburgh Press, 1958; *The Story of Evolution: The Wonderful World of Life,* Rathbone Books, 1958, published in America as *The Wonderful World of Life: The Story of Evolution,* Doubleday, 1958, 2nd edition, published as *The Wonderful World of Evolution,* Macdonald, 1969; (with others) *The Destiny of Man,* Hodder & Stoughton, 1959.

(Contributor) Corliss Lamont, editor, *A Humanist Symposium on Metaphysics,* American Humanist Association, 1960; *Man's New Vision of Himself,* edited by Peter Hey, University of Natal, 1960; *On Population, Three Essays,* (includes work by Huxley, Thomas Malthus, and Frederick Osborn), New American Library, 1960; *The Conservation of Wild Life and Natural Habitats in Central and East Africa,* UNESCO, 1961; (editor with James Fisher) *The Doubleday Pictorial Library of Nature: Earth, Plants, Animals,* Doubleday, 1961; (editor and contributor) *The Humanist Frame,* Allen & Unwin, 1961, Harper, 1962; *Education and the Humanist Revolution,* Fawley Foundation, University of Southampton, 1962; *The Human Crisis,* University of Washington Press, 1963; (author of introduction and postscript) Marie Juliette Huxley, *Wild Lives of Africa,* Collins, 1963; *Essays of a Humanist,* Harper, 1964; (author of foreword) Henry Eliot Howard, *Territory in Bird Life,* Collins, 1964; (editor) *Aldous Huxley, 1894-1963: A Memorial Volume,* Harper, 1965; (with H.B. Kettlewell) *Charles Darwin and His World,* Viking, 1965; (editor) *The Doubleday Pictorial Library of Growth of Ideas,* Doubleday, 1966; *The Future of Man: Evolutionary Aspects,* Ethical Culture Publications, 1966; (author of foreword) George Brown Barbour, *Unterwegs mit Teilhard de Chardin: Auf den Spuren des Lebens in drei Kontinenten,* Walter-Verlag, 1967; *The Courtship Habits of the Great Crested Grebe,* J. Cape, 1968; *Memories,* volume I, Allen & Unwin, 1970, Harper, 1971.

Contributor to *Animals* magazine. Biological editor of *Encyclopaedia Britannica,* 14th edition; advisory editor, *Animal and Zoo Magazine,* 1935-42; member editorial board, *New Naturalist,* 1944—.

SIDELIGHTS: Sir Julian has developed and put forward an integrated system of ideas which he calls evolutionary humanism. It bases itself on the fact that evolution is at work everywhere, and on earth has passed through three phases, the inorganic, the biological (operated by natural selection), and the human or psychosocial (operated largely by psychological factors). It also stresses the fact that evolutionary processes are directional; that improvement has occurred both in the biological and psychosocial phases, and that further psychosocial improvement is possible in the human phase. Its main conclusion is that man is now the agent for the whole future evolution of our planet. Sir Julian believes that man has initiated a new psychosocial stage of evolution, and his humanism is based on the understanding of man, his past, and his possible future, and man's relations with his environment. It avoids all metaphysical or theological absolute, and asserts the unity of the human species.

Sir Julian told *CA* that among the major challenges to man's progress he lists the threat of nuclear war, the threat of over-population, the rise of communist and fascist ideologies, and the widening gap between the rich and poor nations.

He is a member of an illustrious family whose notable members include his biologist grandfather T(homas) H(enry) Huxley, great-uncle Matthew Arnold, and brother Aldous Huxley.

AVOCATIONAL INTERESTS: Travel and bird watching.

BIOGRAPHICAL/CRITICAL SOURCES: R.W. Clark, *Sir Julian Huxley,* Phoenix House, 1960; *New York Times Book Review,* May 24, 1964, April 3, 1966; *Scientific American,* October, 1964; *Times Literary Supplement,* November 4, 1965, June 28, 1970; R.W. Clark, *The Huxleys,* McGraw, 1968; *Books and Bookmen,* June, 1968, August, 1970; *New York Times,* October 12, 1969; *Saturday Review,* April 24, 1971; *Atlantic,* June, 1971.†

*   *   *

HYATT, J(ames) Philip 1909-

PERSONAL: Born February 16, 1909, in Monticello, Ark.; son of Robert Lee (a banker) and Mamie (Stanley) Hyatt; married Elizabeth Bard, September 12, 1932; children: James Lee (deceased), Charles Sidney, David Philip. *Education:* Baylor University, A.B., 1929; Brown University, M.A., 1930; postgraduate study at American School of Oriental Research, Jerusalem, 1931-32, and University of Marburg, summer, 1932; Yale University, B.D., 1933, Ph.D., 1938; Hebrew Union College, postdoctoral study, 1952. *Politics:* Democrat. *Home:* 3614 Saratoga Dr., Nashville, Tenn. 37205. *Office:* Vanderbilt Divinity School, Nashville, Tenn. 37240.

CAREER: Ordained minister of Disciples of Christ. Wellesley College, Wellesley, Mass., instructor, 1935-38, assistant professor of Biblical history, 1938-41; Vanderbilt University, Nashville, Tenn., associate professor, 1941-44, professor of Old Testament, 1944—, director of graduate

studies in religion, 1944-64. *Member:* Society of Biblical Literature and Exegesis (president of Southern section, 1949-50; national president, 1956), Archaeological Institute of America, American Oriental Society (vice-president, Middle West section, 1943-44), American Academy of Religion, Society for Religion in Higher Education (fellow). *Awards, honors:* Ford faculty fellow, 1952; D.D., Christian Theological Seminary, 1967; LL.D., Baylor University, 1969; L.H.D., Texas Christian University, 1969; Harvie Branscomb Distinguished Professor Award, Vanderbilt University, 1969-70.

WRITINGS: The Treatment of Final Vowels in Early Neo-Babylonian, Yale University Press, 1941; *Prophetic Religion,* Abingdon, 1947; *Jeremiah: Prophet of Courage and Hope,* Abingdon, 1958; *Meeting God Through Isaiah,* Upper Room, 1958; *The Prophetic Criticism of Israelite Worship,* Hebrew Union College Press, 1963; *The Heritage of Biblical Faith: An Aid to Reading the Bible,* Bethany Press, 1964; (editor) *The Bible in Modern Scholarship,* Abingdon, 1966; *Commentary on Exodus* (New Century Bible), Oliphants, 1971. Contributor to *Encyclopaedia Britannica, Encyclopedia Americana,* and *Hastings Dictionary of the Bible.* Editor, *Journal of Biblical Literature,* 1948-49.

WORK IN PROGRESS: Commentary on Exodus, for Oliphants.

SIDELIGHTS: Hyatt has reading knowledge of German, French, Hebrew, Greek, and several Semitic languages.

*   *   *

HYLAND, (Henry) Stanley 1914-

PERSONAL: Born January 26, 1914, in Shipley, Yorkshire, England; son of Harry Hugh and Annie (Rhodes) Hyland; married Nora Hopkinson, April 20, 1940; children: Jeremy, Henry. *Education:* Attended Bradford Grammar School; Birkbeck College, London, B.A., 1946. *Religion:* Church of England. *Home:* 37 South Croxted Rd., Dulwich, London, England. *Agent:* David Higham Associates Ltd., 76 Dean St., London W.1, England. *Office:* British Broadcasting Corp. Television, London, England.

CAREER: House of Commons, London, England, research librarian; British Broadcasting Corp., London, television producer. *Military service:* Royal Naval Volunteer Reserve, World War II; became lieutenant.

WRITINGS: (Editor) *King and Parliament: A Selected List of Books,* Cambridge University Press, 1951; *Curiosities from Parliament,* Wingate, 1955, De Graff, 1956; *Who Goes Hang?* (novel), Gollancz, 1958, Dodd, 1959; *Green Grow the Tresses-O,* Gollancz, 1963, Bobbs-Merrill, 1967; *Top Bloody Secret* (novel), Bobbs-Merrill, 1969. Author of plays and features for the British Broadcasting Corp.

AVOCATIONAL INTERESTS: Bookmanship, politics, history, sport, and travel.

BIOGRAPHICAL/CRITICAL SOURCES: Spectator, June 7, 1969.†

*   *   *

IAMS, Thomas M., Jr. 1928-

PERSONAL: Surname is pronounced *Eye-*amz; born February 13, 1928; son of Thomas M. (a librarian) and Dorothy (Finer) Iiams; married Nicole Harle, September 3, 1964. *Education:* Colgate University, B.A., 1950; Fletcher School of Law and Diplomacy, M.A., 1951; Institut d'Etudes Politiques, Paris, France, student, 1956-57; Columbia University, Ph.D., 1959. *Home:* 17 University Ave., Hamilton, N.Y. 13346. *Office:* Pennsylvania Military College, Chester, Pa. 19013.

CAREER: Queens College (now Queens College of the City University of New York), Flushing, Long Island, N.Y., lecturer in history, 1957-60; Pennsylvania Military College, Chester, associate professor of history, 1963—. Visiting assistant professor of history, Northwestern University, 1960-61. Staff aide to U.S. Mission, United Nations General Assembly, Paris, 1951-52. Commentator, Radio Station WEEZ, Chester, Pa. *Member:* American Historical Association, American Association of University Professors, Societe d'Histoire Moderne, French Historical Society. *Awards, honors:* Research grant, French Ministry of Foreign Affairs, 1956-57.

WRITINGS: The Administration of the Pan-American Union, Columbus Library (Washington, D.C.), 1951; *Dreyfus, Diplomatists and the Dual Alliance: Gabriel Hanotaux at the Quai d'Orsay (1894-1898),* E. Droz, (Geneva), 1962; (with Edwin P. Dunbaugh) *Teach Yourself World History,* Crowell-Collier, 1963.

WORK IN PROGRESS: The Meaning of the Last Hundred Years, a guide to contemporary world history.

SIDELIGHTS: Iiams is a specialist in French diplomatic history, particularly the period of the Third Republic. He lived abroad 1951-52, 1956-57, and 1961-62.

*   *   *

IDYLL, C(larence) P(urvis) 1916-

PERSONAL: Born February 10, 1916, in Edmonton, Alberta, Canada; son of A. Charles (a salesman) and Annabelle (Purvis) Idyll; married Marion Janet Daniels (a music teacher), June 28, 1941; children: Marilyn Judith (Mrs. Richard Dana Hamly), Janice Leah (Mrs. John Francis Barr III), Jacqueline. *Education:* University of British Columbia, B.A. (first class honors), 1938, M.A., 1940; University of Washington, Seattle, Ph.D., 1951. *Religion:* Protestant. *Home:* Viale Pasteur 33, Int. 9, Rome, Italy. *Office:* Food and Agriculture of the UN, Via della Terme di Carocalla, Rome, Italy.

CAREER: Pacific Salmon Fisheries, biologist, 1941-48; University of Miami, Coral Gables, Fla., assistant professor of zoology, 1948-50, associate professor, 1950-54, professor of marine science 1948-72, chairman of division of fisheries, Institute of Marine Science, 1956-72; Food and Agriculture of the UN, Rome, Italy, fishery research advisor, 1972—. Friends of Chamber Music of Miami, vice-president, 1965-72; Friends of the University Library, member of editorial board. Chairman, Gulf Caribbean Fisheries Institute, 1950-72. *Member:* American Institute of Biological Science Marine Technology Society American Institute of Fishery Research Biologists, American Institute of Ichthyologists and Herpetologists, American Fisheries Society, American Association for Advancement of Science, Florida Academy of Science, Sigma Xi, Phi Sigma.

WRITINGS: The Commercial Shrimp Industry of Florida, Marine Laboratory, University of Miami, 1950; (with Charles E. Dawson) *Investigations on the Florida Spiny Lobster, Panulirus argus,* (Florida) State Board of Conservation, 1951; (with William Saenz) *Preliminary Report on the Marine Fisheries of Honduras,* Marine Laboratory, University of Miami, 1957; (with Edwin S. Iversen) *The Tortugas Shrimp Fishery: The Fishing Fleet and Its Method of Operation,* State Board of Conservation, 1959; *Commercial Fishery of St. John, Virgin Islands,* Marine Laboratory, University of Miami, 1959; (with John E. Randall) *Addendum to Sport and Commercial Fisheries Potential of St. John, Virgin Islands,* Marine Laboratory, University of Miami, 1960; *Abyss: The Deep Sea and the Creatures That Live In It,* Crowell, 1964, revised edition, 1971; (editor and contributor) *Exploring the Ocean World: A History of Oceanography,* Crowell, 1970, revised edition, 1972; *The Sea Against*

Hunger: Harvesting the Oceans to Feed a Hungry World, Crowell, 1970. Contributor to Smithsonian Institution *Annual Report,* 1959, and *Transactions* of American Fisheries Society, 1957, 1960; contributor to encyclopedias, magazines, and professional journals.

WORK IN PROGRESS: A book on migrations of marine animals; scientific and popular articles on marine science.

*   *   *

IGGULDEN, John Manners 1917-

PERSONAL: Born February 12, 1917, in Brighton, Victoria, Australia; married; children: two daughters. *Home:* 50 Wells Rd., Beaumaris, Victoria, Australia. *Agent:* A.D. Peters, 10 Buckingham St., Adelphi, London W.C.2, England: Harold Matson Co., Inc., 22 East 40th St., New York, N.Y. 10016.

CAREER: Partner in family-owned engineering and business concerns in Australia, and active in production and general management capacities in those firms prior to 1959; primarily a writer, 1959—. Glider pilot, 1932—; Australian national gliding champion, 1959-60; represented Australia in Ninth World Gliding Championships in Argentina, 1963; director of Australian National Gliding School, 1960-64. *Member:* Port Philip Conservation Council (president), Gliding Federation of Australia (life governor).

WRITINGS: Breakthrough, Chapman & Hall, 1960; *The Storms of Summer,* Chapman & Hall, 1960; *The Clouded Sky,* Macmillan, 1964; *Dark Stranger,* McGraw, 1965; (editor with Kylie Tennant) *Summer's Tales 3* (three-volume short story collection; Volumes 1 and 2 edited by Tennant, Volume 3 by Iggulden), St. Martin's, 1966.

WORK IN PROGRESS: Sounds Before an Echo; The Modification of Freedom.

SIDELIGHTS: "Questionnaires bug me," Iggulden wrote *CA.* "I hope you will regard it as no more than an amiable eccentricity that I supply some of the information you require in my own way. . . . My name can be pronounced any way anyone likes. . . . With my wife and children I share an interest in farming, which we propose to develop further on a 300-acre mountain property we have bought near Melbourne. I like fishing, landscape gardening, squash, and reading. These are things I do whenever I can. I smoke heavily, drink moderately, and talk a good deal."

*   *   *

IGNATOW, David 1914-

PERSONAL: Surname is accented on second syllable; born February 7, 1914, in Brooklyn, N.Y.; son of Max (a businessman) and Henrietta (Reinbach) Ignatow; married Rose Graubart (an artist and writer), July, 1939; children: David, Jr., Yaedi. *Education:* High school graduate. *Home:* 17th and Gardiner Ave., East Hampton, N.Y. 11967. *Office:* School of the Arts, Columbia University, New York, N.Y. 10027; and York College of the City University of New York, Jamaica, N.Y. 11432.

CAREER: Free-lance writer and editor. New School for Social Research, New York, N.Y., instructor, 1964-65; University of Kentucky, Lexington, visiting lecturer, 1965-66; University of Kansas, Lawrence, lecturer, 1966-67; Vassar College, Poughkeepsie, N.Y., instructor, 1967-68; York College of the City University of New York, Jamaica, N.Y., poet-in-residence, 1969—; Columbia University, New York, N.Y., adjunct professor, 1969—. Member of field faculty, Goddard College. *Member:* Modern Language Association of America, American Association of University Professors, P.E.N. *Awards, honors:* National Institute of Arts and Letters award, 1964, "for a lifetime of creative effort"; Guggenheim fellowship, 1965, and Shelley Memorial Prize, Poetry Society of America, 1966; Rockefeller Foundation grant, 1968-69; National Endowment for the Arts grant, 1970, for "Against the Evidence."

WRITINGS—All poetry: *Poems,* Decker Press, 1948; *The Gentle Weight Lifter,* Morris Gallery Press, 1955; *Say Pardon,* Wesleyan University Press, 1961; *Figures of the Human,* Wesleyan University Press, 1964; *Rescue the Dead,* Wesleyan University Press, 1968; *Earth Hard,* Rapp & Whiting, 1968; *Poems, 1934-1969,* Wesleyan University Press, 1970.

Editor: *Political Poetry* (anthology), Chelsea, 1960; *Walt Whitman: A Centennial Celebration,* Beloit College, 1963; *William Carlos Williams: A Memorial Chapbook,* Beloit College, 1963.

Poems included in *A Treasury of Jewish Poetry,* edited by Nathan and Marynn Older Ausubel, Crown, 1957, *Erotic Poetry,* edited by William Cole, Random House, 1963, *America Forever New,* edited by John Edmund and Sara Westbrook Brewton, Crowell, 1968, *Contemporary American Poetry,* edited by Donald Hall, Penguin, 1970, and other anthologies. Contributor of poems to *Quarterly Review of Literature, Sixties, Goddard Journal, Poetry, Kayak, Choice, Commentary, New Yorker, Saturday Review,* and other periodicals. An editor of *Beloit Poetry Journal,* 1949-59, guest editor, 1963; poetry editor of *Nation,* 1962-63; co-editor of *Chelsea,* 1967—; associate editor, *American Poetry Review,* 1972—.

WORK IN PROGRESS: Two books, tentatively titled *Notebooks: 1934-1971,* and *Facing the Tree: 1970 to Date,* publication by Swallow Press expected in 1973; another collection, tentatively titled *Selected Poems: 1934-1972,* for possible publication in 1974.

SIDELIGHTS: Ignatow told *CA:* "My avocation is to stay alive; my vocation is to write about it; my motivation embraces both intentions and my viewpoint is gained from a study and activity in both ambitions. The book important to my career is the next one or two or three on the fire.... The modern poet most influential in my work was William Carlos Williams. Earlier influences were the Bible, Walt Whitman, Baudelaire, Rimbaud, Hart Crane. Prose writers Theodore Dreiser, Ernest Hemingway, Chekov, Dostoyevsky, Flaubert, and Tolstoy also played influential roles in my thinking and writing."

Norman Friedman, commenting on Ignatow's first collection, calls his style somewhat "flaccid and prosy." He remarks however, that *"The Gentle Weight Lifter* is, for the reader of the Wesleyan Series, an agreeable surprise. It is full of exciting things, and seems, for its chronological position, to be a happy spurt in the curve of Ignatow's career. There is more variety and grace and penetration here than in any of his other groups, and yet it comes somewhere in the middle. There was, apparently, a tremendous growth between 1948 and 1955, and then a leveling off in 1961 and 1964." After his second book, Ignatow turned to surrealism and the "anguished existence" of the urban dweller, according to Ralph J. Mills, Jr. Many critics have noted that with *Rescue the Dead,* published in 1968, Ignatow began to move away from the surreal urban landscape of his earlier work into himself, into fantasy and self-analysis. Mills has pointed out that his prose poems of this period combine dreamlike or nightmare effects with social and moral concerns, and that themes of the poet's life dominate his later poetry: "his desires and failures, the difficulties, pains and resolutions of marriage, the arrival of middle-age, and the promise of death which generates a sense of bleakness and futility." Hayden Carruth writes: "As Ignatow has moved away from the flat bitterness of his earlier poems,

those terrible vignettes of urban degradation, his attitudes have become, without doubt, not only more complex and philosophical, but more deeply humane and personal as well; and this, though much of his work continues to fall into poems of only a dozen lines or so." [It is this emotional purity, his "intense vision" of inner existence, which links him to the collective human experience.] Mills writes: "Authenticity speaks to us from every line of Ignatow's poetry, reaching into our lives with the force and deliberation of the seemingly unassuming art which he has subtly and skillfully shaped." Mills goes on to say that, following the example of Whitman and Williams, Ignatow "has placed himself in the tradition of those genuine poets who have, in independent ways, struggled to create a living American poetry from the immediacies of existence in this country, from the tragedies and potentialities of its legacy, and from the abundant music and vitality of its language."

Robert Bly has observed that Ignatow, belonging to the generation of Roethke, Berryman, Lowell, Shapiro, and Ciardi, "is the only member of this generation to whom the young have rallied." He believes this is because "Ignatow notices that human emotions are not becoming less insistent, but more insistent, and they have a greater influence upon events. As Western man sinks nearer to the instincts, his emotions become more demanding."

BIOGRAPHICAL/CRITICAL SOURCES: New Mexico Quarterly, spring, 1961; *Chelsea,* 12, September, 1962; James Dickey, *The Suspect in Poetry,* Sixties Press, 1964; *Chicago Review,* number 2, 1967; *University Review,* spring, 1968; *New Leader,* May 20, 1968; *Hudson Review,* summer, 1968; *Sixties,* summer, 1968; *Yale Review,* summer, 1970; *Tennessee Poetry Journal,* winter, 1970; *Nation,* April 20, 1970; *New York Times Book Review,* August 2, 1970; *American Libraries,* November, 1971; *Crazy Horse 9,* December, 1971; *Kayak #27,* 1971; *New York Review of Books,* December 30, 1971; Ralph J. Mills, Jr., *Cry of the Human,* Swallow Press, 1973; *North Stone Review,* winter, 1973.

*   *   *

ILLINGWORTH, Ronald Stanley 1909-

PERSONAL: Born October 7, 1909, in Harrogate, England; son of Herbert Edward (an architect) and Ellen (Brayshaw) Illingworth; married Cynthia-Mary Redhead (a pediatrician); children: Andrea, Robin, Corinne. *Education:* University of Leeds, M.B., Ch.B., 1934, M.D., 1936, Diploma in Public Health (with distinction), 1938; Diploma in Child Health, 1938. *Politics:* Conservative. *Religion:* Baptist. *Home:* 8 Harley Rd., Sheffield, England. *Office:* Children's Hospital, Sheffield, England.

CAREER: University of Sheffield, Sheffield, England, professor of child health, 1947—. Pediatrician at Children's Hospital and United Sheffield Hospitals. *Military service:* Royal Army, Medical Corps, served in Middle East, 1941-45; became lieutenant colonel. *Member:* Royal Photographic Society (fellow), Royal College of Physicians (fellow).

WRITINGS: Some Aspects of Child Health, University of Sheffield, 1949; *The Normal Child: Some Problems of the First Three Years and Their Treatment,* Little, Brown, 1953, 2nd edition published as *The Normal Child: Some Problems of the First Five Years and Their Treatment,* 1957, 4th edition, 1968; (with wife, Cynthia-Mary Illingworth) *Babies and Young Children: Feedings, Management and Care,* Churchill, 1954, 5th edition, Churchill Livingstone, 1972; *Children and Sleep,* Family Health Publications, 1956; (editor) *Recent Advances in Cerebral Palsy,* Little, Brown, 1958; *Common Ailments in Babies,* British Medical Association, 1959, reissued as

Common Ailments in Toddlers, 1960: *The Development of the Infant and Young Child, Normal and Abnormal,* Livingstone, 1960, 2nd edition, Williams & Wilkins, 1963, 4th edition, 1970; *Your Child from Five to Twelve,* British Medical Association, 1962; *An Introduction to Developmental Assessment in the First Year,* National Spastics Society, Education and Information Unit, 1962; *The Normal School Child: His Problems, Physical and Emotional,* Heineman, 1964; (with C.M. Illingworth) *Lessons from Childhood: Some Aspects of the Early Life of Unusual Men and Women,* Williams & Wilkins, 1966; *All About Feeding Your Baby,* British Medical Association, 1966; *Common Symptoms of Disease in Children,* F.A. Davis, 1967, 3rd edition, Blackwell Scientific Publications, 1971; (with D. Egan and R.C. MacKeith) *Developmental Screening, 0-5 Years,* Heinemann, 1969; *Treatment of the Child at Home,* F.A. Davis, 1971. Contributor of articles to medical and photographic journals.

*   *   *

ILSLEY, Velma (Elizabeth)   1918-

PERSONAL: Born August 6, 1918, in Edmonton, Alberta, Canada; daughter of Rowland Sutherland and Lily E. (Thomas) Ilsley; married James W. Ledwith (a physician), May 1, 1962. *Education:* Studied at Douglass College, 1936-38, Moore Institute of Art, 1938-40. *Politics:* Independent. *Home:* 320 East 42nd St., New York, N.Y. 10017. *Studio:* 45 Tudor City Pl., New York, N.Y. 10017.

CAREER: Illustrator of children's books, and painter, primarily of children. Began career as a fashion illustrator. *Member:* Society of Illustrators, Authors League of America.

WRITINGS—All self-illustrated: *The Pink Hat,* Lippincott, 1956; *A Busy Day for Chris,* Lippincott, 1957; *The Long Stocking,* Lippincott, 1959; *Once Upon a Time* (baby record book in verse), C.R. Gibson, 1960; *M Is for Moving,* Walck, 1966. Also author of *Boxes and Boxes of Hats,* published by Vanguard.

Illustrator: Gladys Adshead, *Brownies, It's Christmas,* Oxford University Press, 1955; Mabel Leigh Hunt, *Miss Jellytot's Visit,* Lippincott, 1955; Mabel Leigh Hunt, *Stars for Cristy,* Lippincott, 1956; Mabel Leigh Hunt, *Cristy at Skippinghills,* Lippincott, 1958; Norma Simon, *My Beach House,* Lippincott, 1958; Gladys Adshead, *The Smallest Brownie's Fearful Adventure,* Walck, 1961; Beman Lord, *Our New Baby's ABC,* Walck, 1964; Rosalie K. Fry, *Mungo,* Farrar, Straus, 1972.

AVOCATIONAL INTERESTS: Ship travel and ballet.

*   *   *

INGE, William Motter   1913-1973

PERSONAL: Surname rhymes with "hinge"; born May 3, 1913, in Independence, Mo.; son of Luther Clayton (a merchant) and Maude Sarah (Gibson) Inge. *Education:* University of Kansas, A.B., 1935; George Peabody College for Teachers, A.M., 1938.

CAREER: Playwright, whose almost life-long interest in the stage was sidetracked at various times for periods of more lucrative teaching and journalism. Started as a child monologist, acted in high school and college plays, in a tent show, and in summer stock; lacking money to further his acting career on Broadway, turned to teaching as high school instructor in Columbus, Kan., 1937-38, instructor at Stephens College, Columbia, Mo., 1938-43, working last three years under Maude Adams in drama department; left to become drama, music, and movie critic for *St. Louis Star-Times,* St. Louis, Mo., 1943-46; returned to teaching at Washington University, St. Louis,

Mo., 1946-49. Taught at University of North Carolina, 1969, and at University of California, Irvine, 1970. *Awards, honors:* George Jean Nathan Award and Theatre Time Award, 1950, for *Come Back, Little Sheba;* Pulitzer Prize in Drama, Outer Circle Award, New York Drama Critics Circle Award, and Donaldson Award, 1953, for *Picnic;* "Oscar" from Academy of Motion Picture Arts and Sciences, 1961, for *Splendor in the Grass.*

WRITINGS—Plays: *Come Back, Little Sheba* (first produced by Theatre Guild in Westport, Conn., September 12, 1949, produced on Broadway at Booth Theatre, February 15, 1950), Random House, 1950, acting edition published as *Come Back, Little Sheba; a Drama in Two Acts,* S. French, 1951; *Picnic* (based on Inge's short play "Front Porch"; one version titled *Summer Brave* produced at Hyde Park, N.Y., August, 1952 [see below], subsequently revised and retitled version produced on Broadway at Music Box Theatre, February 19, 1953), Random House, 1953, acting edition, Dramatists Play Service, 1955; *Bus Stop* (reworking and expansion of his one-act "People in the Wind"; first produced on Broadway at Music Box Theatre, March 2, 1955), Random House, 1955, acting edition published as *Bus Stop; a Three-act Romance,* Dramatists Play Service, 1956 (also collaborated on musical adaptation, originally titled "Beau," then changed to "Cherry," cancelled prior to Broadway); *The Dark at the Top of the Stairs* (typescript; originally a short play titled "Farther Off From Heaven," first produced by Margo Jones's Little Theatre Group in Dallas, Tex., 1947, expanded retitled version first produced on Broadway at Music Box Theatre, December 5, 1957), A. Meyerson (New York), 1957, published with an introduction by Tennessee Williams, Random House, 1958, acting edition, Dramatists Play Service, 1960; *Four Plays: Come Back, Little Sheba, Picnic, Bus Stop, The Dark at the Top of the Stairs,* Random House, 1958; *The Mall* (originally appeared in *Esquire,* January, 1969), [Chicago], 1959; *A Loss of Roses* (first produced on Broadway at Eugene O'Neill Theatre, November 28, 1959), Random House, 1960, acting edition, Dramatists Play Service, 1963; *Summer Brave, and Eleven Short Plays,* (contains *Summer Brave,* "To Bobolink for Her Spirit," "People in the Wind," "A Social Event," "The Boy in the Basement," "The Tiny Closet," "Memory of Summer," "Bus Riley's Back in Town," "The Rainy Afternoon," *The Mall,* "An Incident at the Standish Arms," "The Strains of Triumph"), Random House, 1962; *Natural Affection* (produced on Broadway at Booth Theatre, January 31, 1963), Random House, 1963; *Where's Daddy?* (first produced as "Family Things" in Westport, Conn., 1965, revised version, retitled, produced on Broadway, February 28, 1966), Random House, 1966, acting edition published as *Where's Daddy?: A Two-act Comedy,* Dramatists Play Service, 1966; *Two Short Plays: The Call* [and] *A Murder,* Dramatists Play Service, 1968; "The Last Pad" (originally titled "Don't Go Gentle"), produced Off-Broadway at 13th Street Theatre, December, 1970; "Overnight," scheduled for production in spring, 1970, as yet not produced.

Screenplays: *Splendor in the Grass* (produced by Warner Brothers, 1961), Bantam, 1961; "All Fall Down" (from novel by James Leo Herlihy), produced by Metro-Goldwyn-Mayer, 1962; "Bus Riley's Back in Town" (from his own short play; he had his name removed from the credits prior to release and the name Walter Gage appears instead), produced by Universal, 1964.

Television plays: "Out on the Outskirts of Town," produced on Bob Hope Chrysler Theatre," November 6, 1964.

Novels: *Good Luck, Miss Wyckoff,* Atlantic-Little, Brown, 1970; *My Son Is a Splendid Driver,* Atlantic-Little, Brown, 1971.

Contributor to *Esquire.*

WORK IN PROGRESS: Two filmscripts, "Off the Main Road," and "Almost a Love Song."

SIDELIGHTS: William Inge has been called the playwright of the Mid-west, since he was the first, and really only person to write exclusively about the people who have lived their ordinary lives away from the mainstream of America. He is perhaps best known for his psychological portraits of these people, whose lives to him are so important. He said in an interview in 1967: "It seems to me that I'm usually concerned with Man's realization of himself, with his place in the universe." Inge's place was established in the theater with the production of *Come Back, Little Sheba,* which was well-received, although it did not actually have as long a run on Broadway as might be thought. Inge told Digby Diehl: "It was successful, but moderately so. It was a hit as a movie but the play only got about half the New York critics. Happily, Brooks Atkinson liked it. . . . On the road we had great success. The audiences were much more responsive and alive." R. Baird Shuman states that *Come Back, Little Sheba* "is generally considered Inge's best play. In it Inge's primary concern is to present human motivations and behavior; however, the play, based on one of Inge's early short stories, has greater structural unity and a stronger story line than any of his other plays with the possible exception of his scenario, *Splendor in the Grass.*"

Picnic, Inge's second play to bow in New York, solidified his standing in New York theater. Shuman wrote: "If Inge's first play had established his reputation in the theater, *Picnic* assured the skeptics that *Come Back, Little Sheba* had not been just a unique stroke of good fortune. The widespread recognition which *Picnic* received . . . caused Inge to be favorably compared to Williams and Miller." *Picnic* was based on a short sketchy play which Inge had called "Front Porch." He developed and expanded it for Broadway. Another version of the play, *Summer Brave,* is considered by Inge to be the final version, although it was produced before *Picnic* went to Broadway. Jean Gould wrote of *Picnic:* "It has been called by [John] Gassner a 'pathetic pastoral,' but it also possesses the richness, the earthiness of an al fresco bacchanale, in terms of American folkways in the Middle West."

Inge expanded his one-act "People in the Wind" into *Bus Stop,* which he considers a romantic comedy. Miss Gould says that *Bus Stop* "has serious overtones and moments of sadness, and in its way is a commentary on the haphazard lives of those who try to live by their talents, beauty, or wits, without a penny in the world, homeless and rootless." Shuman says that Inge changed the focus from loneliness, in the short play, to the different aspects of love in the longer work. Inge told Digby Diehl that the play is "the closest thing to fantasy that I ever wrote. It's pretty close to being a fairy tale. The town in Kansas was kind of an archetype." Shuman points out that in *Bus Stop* the emotions "are, in the final analysis, stark and undramatized. Herein is the greatest strength of Inge's extreme realism. His clinical objectivity increased steadily from *Come Back, Little Sheba* to *The Dark at the Top of the Stairs,* and it was increasingly reinforced by his unadorned use of language and by the classic starkness of his settings."

In *The Dark at the Top of the Stairs* Inge adds to the theses that Shuman believes is evident in his work, "that love is to be discovered through sex and that problems are more often to be solved in bed than in the parlor. Inge is aware most fully of what Brooks Atkinson calls 'the illusiveness of experience.' His characters often seek to overcome this illusiveness and to escape from their loneliness through sex." The end of the play finds Rubin urging Cora to come upstairs, where they will reconcile their differences in bed.

Inge told an interviewer that although *The Dark at the Top of the Stairs* is not an autobiographical play, "I did kind of base a piece of fiction around the members of my family. But they are only a vague resemblance to my family."

Harold Clurman wrote that Inge "writes sparsely, almost laconically, but his choice of words and of situations is so shrewd that he makes them go a long way in creating a stage of life far more potent than the written page may indicate."

Farther Off from Heaven, which he expanded to *The Dark at the Top of the Stairs,* was the first play Inge wrote. He had the opportunity to interview Tennessee Williams in 1945, and as a result of that interview confided his interest in writing to Williams. Inge showed him the play, and Williams made it possible for Margo Jones to produce the play in Dallas in 1947. Although they see each other infrequently, Inge and Williams have remained friends.

The plays which followed *The Dark at the Top of the Stairs, A Loss of Roses, Natural Affection,* and *Where's Daddy?* have not had the success that the earlier plays had. Difficulties with script changes and a substitution of the leading actress caused *A Loss of Roses* to be a virtual disaster when it opened. Inge had been practically the only backer for the production and the financial and personal losses were great. Neither *Natural Affection* nor *Where's Daddy?* proved to be very successful, although both were thought to have many good sections. In both *Natural Affection* and *A Loss of Roses* Inge was concerned with the mother-son relationship, as he was in *The Dark at the Top of the Stairs,* and had difficulty in focusing on one aspect of the relationships rather than going off in many directions. Many believe that as Inge moved further away from the more familiar territory of the earlier plays he moved away from some of the elements which were the best in his work. Most agree that he is best at writing about ordinary Midwestern townspeople. His naturalistic style, his psychological perceptions all contributed to the success of his plays. His understanding of children and young people, seen especially in the characters in *The Dark at the Top of the Stairs* and in *Splendor in the Grass* has been praised by many.

Splendor in the Grass, for which Inge won an Oscar, was very successful, especially in the presentation of the adolescent characters. Shuman states that "Inge's understanding and recording of adolescent behavior is nothing short of amazing. The small touches which were almost entirely lacking in *A Loss of Roses* are present with vigor in *Splendor in the Grass.*" Shuman also points out that the dialogue was much more spare than in *A Loss of Roses* and *Natural Affection,* and he thinks that this might have something to do with the success or failure of his plays.

Inge has thusfar produced two novels, both about small people in the Midwest, both strong on character, and more in line with the material of his earlier plays. *Good Luck, Miss Wyckoff,* Haskel Frankel thought, does not contain anything that Inge has not already covered in his plays, and that the latter form suited him better. He says that Miss Wyckoff is "either a new girl in town, or an old hat. Or, for those of us who remember four very happy evenings in the theater, a sentimental journey." Eugene J. Linehan wrote: "The language is strong; the sexuality often gross; but the sense of reality is profound." D. Keith Mano discusses *My Son Is a Splendid Driver* and states: "William Inge writes in the form of a memoir, which, by his own admission, approximates autobiography. . . . This is a sad, clinical tale, written with dignity and imagination and restraint, yet I doubt if many readers would care to have Mr. Inge's depressing, bitter memories of another era imposed on them with such remitting emphasis."

Inge grew up in small-town Kansas, and did not reach New York for the first time until he was twenty seven. But, he says, he did not consider himself a Kansan until he was away from home. He told Digby Diehl: "I'm one of those people who grew up in Kansas feeling very superior to it. I felt out of place in that forlorn mid-western agricultural state. I had nothing in common with it at all. It was boring as hell and I wanted out. It wasn't until I got to New York that I became Kansan. Everyone there kept reminding me that they were Jewish or Irish, or whatever, so I kept reminding them that I was midwestern. . . . I discovered I had something a bit unique, but it was the nature of New York that forced me to claim my past." His strong sense of his rural past infuses all his work. Inge originally wanted to be an actor, and Jean Gould says that "he had the kind of countenance that could have made a 'matinee idol': his deep-set eyes, classic nose and full, curving lips combines in round contour to form, according to Tennessee Williams' description, 'the very handsome and outwardly serene face of William Inge.' He was tall and well-proportioned, and moved with the easy gait of an actor." Fortunately he did discover his true role in the theater.

Inge said in an interview that he believes foreign actors to be better trained than Americans, and that this is one problem to contend with in doing plays. Digby Diehl asked Inge for a solution to the "Broadway dilemma." Inge responded: "I read somewhere, in Robert Graves, I think, about a tribe which created gods in order to destroy them. I think that the instant a person becomes famous in America a machine is set in motion to destroy him. If you look at the personal lives of people in theater in this country most of them are despairingly unhappy people. Some of our most talented actors are miserable. We have no future or security to offer them. We still think of our artists in the *La Boheme* portrait. America can't believe in the artist as a working man. He becomes famous, but he's not respected. I think it's time now that we get respected and quit being famous."

Come Back, Little Sheba, adapted by Ketti Frings, was produced by Paramount, 1952; *Picnic* was produced by Warner Brothers, 1955; *Bus Stop*, adapted by William Axelrod, was produced by Twentieth Century Fox, 1960; *The Dark at the Top of the Stairs* was produced by Warner Brothers, 1960; *A Loss of Roses* was produced as "The Stripper" by Twentieth Century Fox, 1963. Film rights for *Where's Daddy?* and *Good Luck, Miss Wyckoff* have been sold.

Picnic was adapted as a musical titled "Hot September," first produced in Boston at Shubert Theatre, September 4, 1965, closed prior to Broadway opening; *Come Back, Little Sheba* has been adapted as a musical titled "The Word Is Love," scheduled for Broadway production.

A television series based on *Bus Stop,* was broadcast during the 1961-62 season.

BIOGRAPHICAL/CRITICAL SOURCES: Theater Arts, May, 1950; *American Annals,* 1954; *Vogue,* May 1, 1954; *Nation,* December 2, 1957; *Time,* December 16, 1957; *Life,* January 6, 1958; John Gassner, *Theatre at the Crossroads,* Holt, 1960; George Oppenheimer, *Passionate Playgoer,* Viking, 1958; *Newsweek,* May 14, 1962; R. Baird Shuman, *William Inge,* Twayne, 1965; Allan Lewis, *American Plays and Playwrights of the Contemporary Theatre,* Crown, 1965; Horst Frenz, editor, *American Book Collector,* October, 1965; Jean Gould, *Modern Playwrights on Drama,* Hill & Wang, 1965; *American Playwrights,* Dodd, 1966; *Choice,* July, 1967; Walter Wager editor, *The Playwrights Speak,* Delacorte, 1967; Robert Brustein, *Seasons of Discontent,* Simon & Schuster, 1967; Frederick Lumley, *New Trends in 20th Century Drama,* Oxford University Press, 1967; *Transatlantic Review,* autumn, 1967; *Best Sellers,* June 1, 1970, June 15, 1971; *Book World,* June 14, 1970; *New York Times Book Review,* June 14, 1970; *Show Business,* December 12, 1970; *National Review,* June 29, 1971.

(Died June 10, 1973)

*   *   *

INGILBY, Joan Alicia   1911-

PERSONAL: Born December 11, 1911, in North Stainley, Yorkshire, England; daughter of John Uchtred McDowall (an army officer) and Marjorie Cecily (Phelips) Ingilby. *Education:* Attended Runton Hill School, and French Academy, Edinburgh, Scotland. *Home:* Coleshouse Askrigg, Leyburn, Yorkshire, England.

MEMBER: Yorkshire Archaeological Society, Yorkshire Naturalists' Union, Bronte Society, Poetry Society, National Book League.

WRITINGS—All with Marie Hartley: *The Old Hand-Knitters of the Dales,* Dalesman Publishing Co., 1951; *Yorkshire Village,* Dent, 1953; *The Yorkshire Dales,* Dent, 1956; *The Wonders of Yorkshire,* Dent, 1959; *Yorkshire Portraits,* Dent, 1961; *Getting to Know Yorkshire* (juvenile), Dent, 1964; *Life and Tradition in the Yorkshire Dales,* Dent, 1968, published in America as *Vanishing Folkways: Life and Tradition in the Yorkshire Dales,* A.S. Barnes, 1972. Occasional contributor to *Country Life, Dalesman, Yorkshire Post.*

AVOCATIONAL INTERESTS: Contemporary poetry and art; reading, especially poetry and history; gardening, walking, the theatre; sightseeing abroad, especially art galleries and churches.

*   *   *

INGRAM, Derek (Thynne)   1925-

PERSONAL: Born June 20, 1925, in Westcliff-on-Sea, Essex, England; son of Stanley Arthur (a businessman) and Amy Clara (Wettlauffer) Ingram. *Education:* Attended Highgate School, London, England, 1939-42. *Religion:* Church of England. *Home:* 5 Wyndham Mews, London W.1, England. *Office:* Gemini News Service, John Carpenter House, John Carpenter St., London E.C. 4, England.

CAREER: Kemsley Newspapers, London, England, editorial assistant on *Daily Sketch,* 1942-43, 1946-47; *Daily Express,* Manchester, England, sub-editor, 1947-49; *Daily Mail,* London, 1949-66, began as sub-editor, became deputy editor; Gemini News Service, London, managing editor, 1966—. *Military service:* Royal Navy, 1943-46. *Member:* National Union of Journalists, Royal Commonwealth Society, National Book League, London Press Club, Royal Society of Arts.

WRITINGS: Partners in Adventure: A New Look at the Commonwealth Today, Pan Books, 1960, expanded edition published as *The Commonwealth Challenge,* Allen & Unwin, 1962; (contributor) Colin Legum, editor, *Africa: A Handbook to the Continent,* Praeger, 1962; *Commonwealth for a Color-Blind World,* Humanities, 1965; *The Commonwealth at Work,* Pergamon, 1969.

SIDELIGHTS: Ingram has traveled extensively in Africa and Asia, studying, in particular, the development of Zambia and Rhodesia. *Avocational interests:* Opera and theatre.

BIOGRAPHICAL/CRITICAL SOURCES: Evening News of India, November 22, 1963.

IONESCO, Eugene 1912-

PERSONAL: Born November 26, 1912, in Slatina, Romania; now a French citizen; son of Eugene (a lawyer) and Marie-Therese (Icard) Ionesco; married Rodika Burileano, July 12, 1936; children: Marie-France. *Education:* Attended University of Bucharest, Romania; University of Paris, Sorbonne, licencie es lettres, agrege des lettres. *Home:* 14 rue de Rivoli, Paris 4, France.

CAREER: Professor of French in Romania, 1936-39; worked for publisher in France; now full-time writer. *Member:* Academie Francaise. *Awards, honors:* Prix de la Critique, Tours Festival, 1959, for film "Monsieur Tete"; Chevalier des Arts et Lettres, 1961; Grand Prix Italia, 1963, for ballet version of "La Lecon" as shown on Eurovision; Grand Prix du Theatre de la Societe des Auteurs, 1966, for total body of work; Le Prix National du Theatre, 1969; Prix Litteraire de Monaco, 1969; Austrian Prize for European Literature, 1971; Jerusalem Prize (Israel), 1973, for total body of work, with special mention of "Rhinoceros" as being "one of the great demonstrations against totalitarianism."

WRITINGS—Plays—Omnibus volumes: *Theatre* (includes "La Cantatrice chauve" [one-act; first produced in Paris at Theatre des Noctambules, May 11, 1950; produced under title "The Bald Soprano" Off-Broadway at Sullivan Street Playhouse, June 3, 1958], "La Lecon" [one-act; first produced in Paris at Theatre de Poche-Montparnasse, February 20, 1951; produced under title "The Lesson" Off-Broadway at Phoenix Theatre, January 9, 1958], "Jacques, ou la soumission" [one-act; first produced in Paris at Theatre de la Huchette, October, 1955; produced under title "Jack" at Sullivan Street Playhouse, June 3, 1958], and "Le Salon de l'automobile" [first produced at Theatre de la Huchette, September 1, 1953]), Arcanes, 1953; *Theatre*, four volumes, Gallimard, Volume I, 1954, new edition, 1970, Volume II, 1958, new edition, 1970, Volume III, 1963, Volume IV, 1966, Volume I: Includes "La Cantatrice chauve," "La Lecon," "Jacques, ou la soumission," "Les Chaises" (first produced in Paris at Theatre Nouveau-Lancry, April 22, 1952; produced under title "The Chairs" Off-Broadway at Phoenix Theatre, January 9, 1958), "Victimes du devoir" (one-act; first produced in Paris at Theatre du Quartier Latin, February, 1953; produced under title "Victims of Duty" Off-Broadway at Theatre de Lys, January 19, 1960), and "Amedee, ou Comment s'en debarasser" (three-act; first produced in Paris at Theatre de Babylone, April 14, 1954; produced under title "Amedee, or How to Disentangle Yourself" in New York at Tempo Playhouse, October 31, 1955, ["La Cantatrice chauve" "La Lecon," and "Les Chaises" published as *Three Plays*, edited by H.F. Brookes and C.E. Fraenkel, Heinemann, 1965], Volume II: Includes "L'Impromptu de l'Alma, ou Le Cameleon du berger" (first produced in Paris at Studio des Champs-Elysses, February, 1956; produced under title "Improvisation, or The Shepherd's Chameleon" Off-Broadway at Theatre de Lys, November 29, 1960), "Tuer sans gages" (three-act; first produced in Paris at Theatre Recamier, February 27, 1959; produced under title "The Killer" in New York at Seven Arts Theatre, March 22, 1960), "Le Nouveau Locataire" (one-act; first produced in Helsinki, 1955; produced in Paris at Theatre d'Aujourd'hui, 1957; produced under title "The New Tenant" in New York at Royale Playhouse, March 9, 1960), "L'Avenir est dans les oeufs" (first produced in 1957), "Le Maitre" (first produced at Theatre de la Huchette, September 1, 1953; produced in London at The Theatre Upstairs [Royal Court Theatre], August 31, 1970), and "La Jeune Fille a marier" (first produced at Theatre de la Huchette, September 1, 1953; produced Off-Broadway at Barbizon-Plaza Theatre, May, 1970; produced at The Theatre Upstairs, August 31, 1970), Volume III: Includes "Rhinoceros" (three-act; first

produced in Dusseldorf, 1959; produced in Paris at Theatre l'Odeon, January 25, 1960; produced in London at Royal Court Theatre, April 28, 1960; produced on Broadway at Longacre Theatre, January 9, 1961), "Le Pieton de l'air" (ballet-pantomime; first produced at Theatre l'Odeon, February 8, 1963; produced on Broadway at New York City Center Theatre, February, 1964), "Delire a deux" (one-act; first produced at Studio des Champs-Elyssees, 1962), "Le Tableau" (first produced at Theatre de la Huchette, October, 1955; produced under title "The Painting" Off-Off-Broadway at Cafe Deja-vu, September, 1969), "Scene a quatre" (first produced in Italy for the Spoleto Festival, 1959; produced at The Theatre Upstairs, August 31, 1970), "Les Salutations" (first produced at The Theatre Upstairs, August 31, 1970), and "La Cholere," Volume IV: Includes "Le Roi se meurt" (one-act; first produced in Paris, December 15, 1962; produced under title "Exit the King" at Royal Court Theatre, September 12, 1963; produced by APA-Phoenix in Ann Arbor, Mich. at Lydia Mendelsshon Theater, October 10, 1967), "La Soif et la faim" (three-act; first produced in Paris at Comedie-Francaise, February 28, 1966; produced under title "Hunger and Thirst" in Stockbridge, Mass. at Berkshire Theatre Festival, July, 1969), "La Lacune" (produced at Theatre l'Odeon; produced at Barbizon-Plaza Theatre, May, 1970; produced at The Theatre Upstairs, August 31, 1970), "Le Salon de l'automobile," "L'Oeuf dur, pour preparer un oeuf dur" (first produced at The Theatre Upstairs, August 31, 1970), "Le Jeune Homme a marier" (often cited as the ballet version of "Jacques, ou la soumission"), and "Apprendre a marcher" (scenario for the ballet by Deryk Mendal; first performed in Paris at Theatre de l'Etoile, April, 1960).

Plays—Omnibus volumes in translation: *Plays*, seven volumes, translated by Donald Watson, J. Calder, Volume I: Includes "The Chairs," "The Bald Prima Donna," "The Lesson," and "Jack, or Obedience" ("Jacques, ou la soumission"), 1958, translation by Donald M. Allen published in America as *Four Plays: The Bald Soprano* [and] *The Lesson* [and] *Jack, or the Submission* [and] *The Chairs*, Grove, 1958, Volume II: Includes "Amedee, or How to Get Rid of It" ("Amedee, ou Comment s'en debarasser"), "The New Tenant," and "Victims of Duty," 1961, translation by Allen published in America as *Amedee* [and] *The New Tenant* [and] *Victims of Duty*, Grove, 1958, Volume III: Includes "The Killer," "Improvisation, or The Shepherd's Chameleon," and "Maid to Marry" ("La Jeune Fille a marier"), 1962, published in America as *The Killer, and Other Plays*, Grove, 1960, Volume IV: Includes "Rhinoceros," "The Leader" ("Le Maitre"), and "The Future is in Eggs, or It Takes All Sorts to Make a World," ("L'Avenir est dans les oeufs"), 1963, translation by Derek Prouse published in America as *Rhinoceros and Other Plays*, Grove, 1960, Volume V: Includes "Exit the King," "The Motor Show," ("Le Salon de l'automobile"), and "Foursome" ("Scene a quatre"), 1963, Volume VI: *A Stroll in the Air* [and] *Frenzy for Two* ("Le Pieton de l'air" and "Delire a deux"), 1965, published in America as *A Stroll in the Air* [and] *Frenzy for Two or More*, Grove, 1968, Volume VII: Includes "Hunger and Thirst," "The Picture" ("Le Tableau"), "Anger" ("La Cholere"), and "Salutations" ("Les Salutations"), 1968, published in America as *Hunger and Thirst, and Other Plays*, Grove, 1969.

Plays—Published singly: *The Chairs* (acting edition), translated by Donald Watson, Samuel French, 1958; *The Lesson* (acting edition), translated by Watson, Samuel French, 1958, French version published as "La Lecon" in Samuel Beckett, *Fin de Partie*, [Paris], 1957; *Le Rhinoceros*, Galliamrd, 1959, edited by Reuben Y. Elliseon and Stowell C. Gooding, Holt, 1961, translation by Derek Prouse published as *Rhinoceros: A Play in Three Acts*, acting edition, Samuel French, 1960; *La Cantatrice, chauve* Gallimard, 1962, enlarged edition, 1964, published with "La Lecon," 1970, translation by Watson published as *The Bald Prima Donna: A Pseudo-play* (acting edition), Samuel French, 1961, published as *The Bald Soprano: Anti-play*, Grove, 1965 (published in England as *The Bald Prima Donna: Anti-Play*, J. Calder, 1966); *Le Roi se meurt*, Gallimard, 1963, translation by Watson published as *Exit the King*, Grove, 1963, French edition, with notes in English, edited by Robert J. North, Harrap, 1966; *La Soif et la faim*, [Paris], 1966; *Delire a deux*, Gallimard, 1966; *Jeux de massacre* (one-set; first produced in Dusseldorf, 1970; produced in Paris at Theatre Montparnasse, October 17, 1970; produced under title "Wipe-out Games" in Washington, D.C. at Kreeger Theater, April, 1971), Gallimard, 1970; *"The Niece-wife"* ("La Niece-Epouse"; first produced at Theatre de la Huchette, September 1, 1953; produced in London, March, 1971), in Richard N. Coe, *Ionesco: A Study of His Plays*, Methuen, 1971; *Victimes du devoir and Une Victime du devoir* (play and short story; illustrated by Ionesco), edited by Vera Lee, Houghton, 1972; *Macbett* (version of Shakespeare's *Macbeth*), Gallimard, 1972.

Unpublished plays: "Les Grandes Chaleurs," "Le Connaissez-vous?," and "Le Rhume Onirique" (all first produced in 1953); "Impromptu pour la Duchesse de Windsor," privately performed for the Duke and Duchess of Windsor, May, 1957; "Ches [sic] le docteur," "Le Cocotier en flammes," "D'Isidione," "Histoire des bandits," "Il y eut d'abord," and "Lecons de francais pour Americains" (all produced at The Theatre Upstairs, August 31, 1970); "Melees et demelees."

Other: (Translator with G. Gabrin) Pavel Dan *Le Vieil Urcan*, Editions Jean Vigneau, 1945; *Ionesco: Les Rhinoceros au theatre* (includes a short story and selections from his journal), R. Julliard, 1960; *La Photo du Colonel* (narratives later adapted as plays [except last two]; includes "Oriflamme" [basis for "Amedee"], "La Photo du Colonel" [basis for "Tuer sans gages"], "Le Pieton de l'air," "Une Victime du devoir," "Rhinoceros," "La Vase," and "Printemps, 1939"), Gallimard, 1962, new edition, 1970, translation by Jean Stewart (except "A Stroll in the Air," translated by John Russell) published as *The Colonel's Photograph*, Faber, 1967, Grove, 1969; *Notes et contre-notes* (essays, addresses, lectures on drama), Gallimard, 1962, new edition, 1970, translation by Donald Watson published as *Notes and Counter-notes*, Grove, 1964; (author of notes) Joan Miro, *Quelques fleurs pour des amis*, Societe Internationale d'Art, 1964; *Journal en miettes* (autobiography), Mercure de France, 1967, translation by Stewart published as *Fragments of a Journal*, Grove, 1968; *Story Number 1: For Children under Three Years of Age* (illustrated by Etienne Delessert), translated by Calvin K. Towle, Harlin Quist, 1968; *Present passe, passe present* (autobiography), Mercure de France, 1968, translation by Helen R. Lane published as *Present Past, Past Present*, Grove, 1971; *Decouvertes* (essay on literature; illustrated by Ionesco), Skira (Geneva), 1969; (with Michael Benamou) *Mise en train: Premiere Annee de francais* (textbook for grades 11-12), Macmillan, 1969; (author of text) *Monsieur Tete* (animated film by Jan Lenica), Bruckmann (Munich), 1970; *Story Number 2: For Children under Three Years of Age* (illustrated by Delessert), Harlin Quist, 1970; (author of text) Gerard Schneider, *Catalogo* (art exhibit), [Torino], 1970; *Story Number 3: For Children over Three Years of Age* (illustrated by Philippe Corentin), translated by Ciba Vaughan, Harlin Quist, 1971; (with Jean Delay) *Discours de reception d'Eugene Ionesco a l'Academie francaise et reponse de Jean Delay*, Gallimard, 1971.

Co-author of the filmscript for "Seven Capital Sins," produced by Embassy in 1962.

Work is represented in many anthologies and critical studies, including *Absurd Drama*, edited by Martin Esslin, and *New Directions*, edited by Alan Durrand.

Contributor to *Les Lettres nouvelles, Les Lettres francaises, Encore, Evergreen Review, Mademoiselle, L'Express, Tulane Drama Review, Theatre Arts, Commentary, London Magazine*, and other publications.

SIDELIGHTS: Ionesco's early failure to appeal to his audiences has been replaced by such resounding success that now he is, along with Brecht, one of the two most widely-performed contemporary playwrights in the world. Unquestionably an original talent, he has discarded plot in order to "rediscover the rhythms of drama in their purest state and to reproduce them in the form of pure scenic movement." Committed to a belief in an absurd universe where everything is contradiction, where "only myth is true," where communication is probably impossible, he must conclude, "what else can one do but laugh at it?"

And laugh he does. Richard Coe has written: "To a greater or less degree, all Ionesco's drama is a satire upon the bourgeoisie, its speech, its manners, and its morals. . . ." "Humor," writes Ionesco, "is my outlet, my release and my salvation." Yet his humor holds no optimism but rather what Coe has called a "profound and ineradicable pessimism" inculcated by a world where the senselessness of death is the ultimate absurdity.

Critic Susan Sontag, who considers Ionesco "a minor writer even at his best," does grant him these triumphs: "What Ionesco did—no mean feat—was to appropriate for the theater one of the great technical discoveries of modern poetry: that all language can be considered from the outside, as by a stranger. . . . His next discovery, also long familiar in modern poetry, was that he could treat language as a palpable thing. (Thus, the teacher kills the student in *The Lesson* with the word 'knife.')"

Ionesco's favorite dramatic device is the platitude. By its use he demonstrates the absurdity of language and the futility of communication. "But in my view," he writes *(Cahiers des Quatres Saisons*, No. 1, 1955), "the unusual can spring only from the dullest and most ordinary routine and from our everyday prose, when pursued beyond their limits; . . . nothing surprises me more than banality; the 'surreal' is there, within our reach, in our daily conversation." A master at creating illusion, he begins with an unrealistic situation, develops it to its limits, engaging himself in "an adventure, a hunt, the discovery of a universe that reveals itself to me, at the presence of which I am the first to be astounded."

Criticized by Kenneth Tynan and Orson Welles for his allegedly apolitical position, Ionesco continues to affirm that the source of his plays is "a mood and not an ideology, an impulse not a program. . . ." Coe, however, asserts Ionesco's commitment to the cause of man, though his concern is with ultimates and absolutes, not with ephemeral political situations. Even Utopia cannot eliminate absurdity, death, and loneliness. Moreover, true revolutions are not political, Ionesco maintains. "Science and art have done far more to change thinking than politics have. The real revolution is taking place in the scientists' laboratories and in the artists' studios. . . . Penicillin and the fight against dipsomania are worth more than politics and a change of government."

Though he continues to believe that "the work of art is untranslatable," his work has appeared in 27 languages.

Several of Ionesco's plays have been adapted as operas and ballets. "The Great Man," an opera based on "Le Maitre," was performed in New York in 1963. With Flemming Flindt, Ionesco adapted three of his plays as ballets: "La Lecon" was first performed on European television in 1963 (for which it won the 1963 Grand Prix Italia), and later at L'Opera Comique in 1964; "Le Jeune Homme a marier," based on "Jacques, ou la soumission" and produced in 1965, and "The Triumph of Death," based on "Jeux de Massacre" and produced in 1971, were both performed first on Danish television and later taken into the repertoire of the Royal Danish Ballet.

Ionesco directed a Zurich production of "Victims of Duty" at Theatre am Neumacht, November, 1968. He has acted in various productions, including a 1951 adaptation of Dostoevsky's *The Possessed*, and as the teacher in his play "Lecons de francais pour Americains" at the Theatre de Poche-Montparnasse, February, 1965.

"Rhinoceros" was first produced in English on the BBC, August 20, 1959, and "Le Tableau" was first presented in English as "The Picture," BBC, March 11, 1957. Several other plays, including "Exit the King," "The Lesson," and "The Picture," have been shown on American television. The film rights to "Rhinoceros" were sold to Woodfall Films in 1971.

BIOGRAPHICAL/CRITICAL SOURCES: Laurence Kitchin, *Mid-Century Drama,*. Faber, 1960; Toby Coll, editor, *Playwrights on Playwriting*, Hill & Wang, 1961; Richard N. Coe, *Ionesco*, Grove, 1961, revised and enlarged edition, Methuen, 1971; David I. Grossvogel, *Four Playwrights and a Postscript: Brecht, Ionesco, Beckett, Genet*, Cornell University Press, 1962; Leonard C. Pronko, *Avant-Garde: The Experimental Theatre in France*, University of California Press, 1962; Terry Southern, Richard Seaver, Alexander Trocchi, editors, *Writers in Revolt*, Fell, 1963; George Wellworth, *Theatre of Protest and Paradox*, New York University Press, 1964; David I. Grossvogel, *The Blasphemers*, Cornell University Press, 1965; Leonard C. Pronko, *Eugene Ionesco*, Columbia University Press, 1965; Harry T. Moore, *French Literature Since World War II*, Southern Illinois University Press, 1966; Walter Wager, editor, *The Playwrights Speak*, Delacorte, 1967; Martin Esslin, *The Theatre of the Absurd*, Doubleday, 1968; J. Jacobson and W. R. Mueller, *Ionesco and Genet*, Hill & Wang, 1968; Claude Bonnefoy, *Conversations with Eugene Ionesco*, Holt, 1971; J.H. Wulbern, *Brecht and Ionesco: Commitment in Context*, University of Illinois Press, 1971; C. Duckworth, *Angels of Darkness*, Barnes & Noble, 1972; R. Hayman, *Eugene Ionesco*, Heinemann, 1972.†

* * *

IRELAND, Norma Olin 1907-

PERSONAL: Born March 27, 1907, in Wadsworth, Ohio; daughter of Carl Leroy (a farmer) and Jessie (a musician; maiden name, Latimer) Olin; married David E. Ireland (an industrial engineer), August 15, 1931. *Education:* University of Akron, B.A., 1928; Western Reserve University (now Case Western Reserve University), B.S. in L.S., 1929. *Politics:* Republican. *Religion:* Congregationalist. *Home:* 2237 Brooke Rd., Fallbrook, Calif. 92028.

CAREER: University of Akron, Akron, Ohio, reference and reserve room librarian in Bierce Library, 1929-36; night school instructor, 1936; Pomona College Library, Claremont, Calif., acting head of loan department, 1936-37; Glendale Public Library, Glendale, Calif., acting head of reference department, assistant to librarian, 1937-38; University of Southern California, Los Angeles, associate professor in Library School, 1938, acting head of education library, 1938; Ireland Book and Library Service, Altadena, Calif., co-owner, 1938—; Ireland Indexing Service, Altadena, and Spring Valley, Calif., director, 1938—; free-lance technical indexer and researcher, 1956—; certified genealogy records searcher, 1969—. *Member:* Society of Mayflower Descendants, Daughters

of the American Revolution, National Contesters Association (president, 1953-54), American Library Association national chairman, 1938-39), American Society of Indexers, Phi Mu, Chi Delta Phi, Alpha Phi Gamma, Pi Gamma Mu.

WRITINGS: Historical Biographies for Junior and Senior High Schools, Universities, and Colleges: A Bibliography, McKinley Publishing, 1933; *The Picture File in School, College, and Public Libraries*, Faxon, 1935, revised edition, 1952; *The Pamphlet File in School, College, and Public Libraries*, Faxon, 1937, revised edition, 1954; (with husband, David E. Ireland) *An Index to Monologs and Dialogs*, Faxon, 1939, revised edition, 1949, supplement, 1959; *An Index to Indexes: A Subject Bibliography of Published Indexes*, Faxon, 1942; (editor) *Local Indexes in American Libraries*, Faxon, 1947; (editor) *N.C.A. Handbook*, A.D. Freese, 1954; (with John Mead Atwater) *Long Word Books*, Book 1, A.D. Freese, 1956; *An Index to Skits and Stunts*, Faxon, 1958; *Index to Scientists of the World, from Ancient to Modern Times: Biographies and Portraits*, Faxon, 1962; *Index to Full-Length Plays, 1944-64*, Faxon, 1965; *Index to Women, from Ancient to Modern Times: Biographies and Portraits*, Faxon, 1970. Editor, junior librarians' section, *Wilson Library Bulletin*, 1936-37; editor, *NCA Bulletin*, 1953-54; editor, "Practical Contester" section, *Contest Magazine*, 1954-59. Contributor to *Encyclopedia of Education*, and to magazines.

WORK IN PROGRESS: Index to Fairy Tales, 1949-1971, to be published by Faxon.

AVOCATIONAL INTERESTS: Genealogy, philately, contesting, book collecting, travel, music (plays organ and piano), tape recording, oil painting, copper work, jewelry making and repair, pets, needlepoint, sewing, reading.

BIOGRAPHICAL/CRITICAL SOURCES: Library Journal, March 1, 1934; *Contest Magazine*, October, 1953; *American Magazine*, June, 1954.

* * *

IREMONGER, Lucille (d'Oyen)

PERSONAL: Married T.L. Iremonger (a member of Parliament, and Lloyd's underwriter); children: Pennant (daughter). *Education:* St. Hugh's College, Oxford, M.A. *Politics:* Conservative. *Religion:* Church of England. *Home:* 34 Cheyne Row, Chelsea, London S.W.3, England.

CAREER: Author and political journalist. Participant in British Broadcasting Corp. programs, 1948—. London County Council, member. Ilford Conservative Association, vice-president; Norwood Conservative Association, patron; King George's Hospital Patients League, president. *Member:* Authors Society, Forum Club. *Awards, honors:* Society of Women Journalists' Lady Brittain trophy for best book of the year, 1948, for *It's A Bigger Life*, and Lady Violet Astor trophy for best article of the year, 1948; Silver Musgrave Medal (Jamaica) for contributions to literature in connection with the West Indies, 1962.

WRITINGS: It's a Bigger Life, Hutchinson, 1948; *Creole* (novel), Hutchinson, 1950; *The Cannibals* (novel), Hammond, Hammond & Co., 1952; *The Young Traveller in the South Seas*, Phoenix House, 1952; *The Young Traveller in the West Indies*, Phoenix House, 1952, Dutton, 1955; *West Indian Folk Tales: Anansi Stories* (retold for English children), Harrap, 1956; *The Ghosts of Versailles: Miss Moberly and Miss Jourdain and Their Adventure—A Critical Study*, Faber, 1957; *Love and the Princess* (on Princess Sophia, daughter of George III), Crowell, 1958, reissued as *Love and the Princesses*, 1960; *And His Charming Lady*, Secker & Warburg, 1961; *Yes, My*

Darling Daughter (autobiographical), Secker & Warburg, 1964; *The Fiery Chariot: A Study of British Prime Ministers and the Search for Love,* Secker & Warburg, 1970.

Contributor: *Adventure and Discovery* (anthology), J. Cape, 1949—; *On the Air: An Anthology of the Spoken Word,* Oxford University Press, 1951; *Caribbean Anthology of Short Stories,* Pioneer Press (Jamaica), 1953; *Independence Anthology,* Pioneer Press, 1962. Contributor to *The Radio Listener's Week End Book,* published by Odhams, and to *Magazine Digest,* 1950; contributor to *Times* (London), *Sunday Times* (London), *Daily Telegraph, Observer, Evening Standard,* and other newspapers and journals.

WORK IN PROGRESS: A biography of the fourth Earl of Aberdeen, Prime Minister of Britain, 1852-1855.

SIDELIGHTS: The Young Traveller in the West Indies and *The Young Traveller in the South Seas* have been translated for a number of foreign-language editions.

BIOGRAPHICAL/CRITICAL SOURCES: Punch, December 2, 1970; *New Statesman,* December 4, 1970; *Books and Bookmen,* April, 1971.

*   *   *

IRISH, Marian D (oris)   1909-

PERSONAL: Born May 29, 1909, in Scranton, Pa.; daughter of William Stitt (an illustrator) and Martha (Williams) Irish. *Education:* Barnard College, B.A., 1930; Bryn Mawr College, M.A., 1932; Yale University, Ph.D., 1939. *Politics:* Democrat. *Religion:* Episcopalian. *Home:* 5903 Calla Dr., McLean, Va. 22101. *Office:* Department of International Relations, American University, Washington, D.C. 20016.

CAREER: Lafayette College, Easton, Pa., research librarian in government and law, 1930-31; Florida State University (formerly Florida State College for Women), Tallahassee, associate professor, 1933-40, professor of political science, 1940-63, professor of government, 1963-66, head of department of political science, 1940-63, head of department of government, 1959-63; American University, Washington, D.C., Lerche Professor of International Relations, 1966—. Guest scholar, Brookings Institution, 1963-64. Consultant, Florida Legislative Committee on Economy and Efficiency, 1945, Florida Citizens Committee on Taxation, 1947, and State Merit Council of Florida, 1948.

MEMBER: American Political Science Association (secretary; vice-president; council member), American Association of University Women, National Civil Service League (member of executive council), Southern Political Science Association (former president), Phi Beta Kappa. *Awards, honors:* Harvard Littauer fellow and Ford Foundation fellow, 1952-53; distinguished professor award, Florida State University; senior research award in American government, Social Science Research Council.

WRITINGS: (With Laurence G. Paquin) *The People Govern,* Scribner, 1954, revised edition, 1958, supplement, 1961; (with James Prothro) *The Politics of American Democracy,* Prentice-Hall, 1959, 5th edition, 1971; (with Prothro) *State and Local Supplement to The Politics of American Democracy,* Prentice-Hall, 1959, 2nd edition, 1962; (editor) *Continuing Crisis in American Politics,* Prentice-Hall, 1963; (editor) *World Pressures on American Foreign Policy,* Prentice-Hall, 1964; (editor) *Political Science: Advance of the Discipline,* Prentice-Hall, 1968; (editor with Prothro and Robert L. Lineberry) *Readings on the Politics of American Democracy,* Prentice-Hall, 1969; (with Elke Frank) *An Introduction to Comparative Politics: Twelve Nation States,* Appleton, 1972. Contributor of articles and book reviews to political and educational journals. Editor, *Journal of Politics,* 1965-69.

WORK IN PROGRESS: Presidential Transition and American Foreign Policy.

BIOGRAPHICAL/CRITICAL SOURCES: University Bookman, winter, 1968.

*   *   *

ISAACS, Alan   1925-

PERSONAL: Born January 14, 1925, in London, England; son of Stanley (a company director) and Regina (Hiller) Isaacs; married Fleur Richmond, May 21, 1955 (died, 1964); married Jacqueline Boulting, 1966; children: (first marriage) Amanda Valentine, Penelope Ann; (second marriage) Lucy, Joanna, Emma. *Education:* St. Paul's School, London, England, student, 1938-42; Imperial College of Science and Technology, University of London, B.Sc., Ph.D. *Politics:* Liberal. *Religion:* Agnostic. *Home:* Heathbourne Lodge, Bushey Heath, Hertfordshire, England.

CAREER: Imperial College of Science and Technology, University of London, London, England, research assistant in physical chemistry, 1946-50; Polish University College, London, part-time lecturer, 1947-49; Alfred Isaacs & Sons (raw material suppliers), London, director, 1951-55; free-lance writer, lexicographer, publisher, 1970—. City and Guilds of London Institute, associate. Technical adviser to Constable & Co. (publishers).

WRITINGS: Introducing Science, Penguin, 1961, Basic Books, 1962, revised edition, 1971; (with E.B. Uvarov and D.R. Chapman) *Penguin Dictionary of Science,* Penguin, 1964; *Survival of God in the Scientific Age,* Penguin, 1966. Author of television scripts. Contributor to journals. Scientific editor of *Hamlyn World Dictionary,* 1971.

SIDELIGHTS: Introducing Science has been translated into Dutch, Spanish, German, Portuguese, and Japanese. *Avocational interests:* Music, painting.

*   *   *

IVES, Sumner   1911-

PERSONAL: Born December 11, 1911, in Arkadelphia, Ark.; son of Sumner Albert and Gladys (Sharp) Ives; married Ruth Fleming, 1945 (died, 1964); married Josephine Piekarz, 1965; children: (first marriage) Sumner William. *Education:* Furman University, B.A., 1932, M.A., 1938; University of Texas, Ph.D., 1950. *Home:* 2 Washington Square Village, New York, N.Y. 10012. *Office:* 19 University Pl., New York University, Washington Square, New York, N.Y. 10003.

CAREER: Tulane University, New Orleans, La., assistant professor, 1950-54, associate professor, 1954-59; North Texas State University, Denton, professor, 1959-61; Syracuse University, Syracuse, N.Y., professor of English, 1961-66; New York University, New York, N.Y., professor of English education, 1966-68; Hunter College of the City University of New York, N.Y., professor of English, 1968-69; New York University, professor of English, 1969—. Lecturer at summer workshops on application of linguistics to English teaching; television lecturer, New Orleans, 1958-59. *Military service:* U.S. Army, Counter Intelligence Corps, 1942-45; became staff sergeant. *Member:* Modern Language Association of America (section chairman, 1957), National Council of Teachers of English, Conference on College Composition and Communications, Linguistic Society of America. *Awards, honors:* Ford Foundation fellowship, 1953-54.

WRITINGS: The Phonology of the Uncle Remus Stories, American Dialect Society, 1954; *A New Handbook for Writers,* Knopf, 1960; (editor with Stephen O. Mitchell) *Language, Style, Ideas: The Writer's Challenge,* Harcourt, 1964; (with Harry W. Sartrain) *English is Our Lan-*

guage: *Language Arts for Beginners—A Portfolio of Charts,* Heath, grades k-1, 1967, grades 2-6, 1968; (contributor with wife, Josephine P. Ives) Albert H. Marckwardt, editor, *Linguistics in School Programs,* National Society for the Study of Education, 1970; (contributor with J.P. Ives) Thomas A. Sebeok, editor, *Linguistics in North America* (Volume 10 of *Current Trends in Linguistics),* Humanities, 1971.

WORK IN PROGRESS: A report on pedagogical grammars of English, for Center for Applied Linguistics.

* * *

IVIE, Robert M. 1930-

PERSONAL: Born August 30, 1930, in Brooklyn, N.Y.; son of Morris W. and Madelyn (Engelhardt) Ivie; married Carol Ann Nystuen, January 23, 1954; children: Deborah Anne, Daniel Eric. *Education:* Washington and Jefferson College, B.A., 1952; Stanford University, M.B.A., 1957. *Home:* 715 Monte Rosa, Menlo Park, Calif. 94025.

CAREER: United Vintners, Inc., San Francisco, Calif., vice-president in charge of distribution, 1958—. *Military service:* U.S. Army, 1953-55. *Member:* Phi Gamma Delta, Pi Sigma Alpha, Alpha Kappa Alpha, Pi Delta Epsilon, San Francisco Olympic Club.

WRITINGS: Information Systems for Logistics Management, American Transportation Research Forum, 1962; (with J.L. Heskett and N.A. Glaskowsky) *Business Logistics,* Ronald, 1964.

WORK IN PROGRESS: Research in inventory management.

* * *

JACKSON, Herbert C(ross) 1917-

PERSONAL: Born May 13, 1917, in War, McDowell County, W. Va.; son of John Henry (a railroad station agent) and Sara Martha (Cross) Jackson; married Mary London, August 30, 1941; children: Charlotte Grey, Carolyn Elizabeth, Bruce Carver, Stephen Allen. *Education:* University of Nebraska, student, 1935-37; William Jewell College, B.A., 1939; Southern Baptist Theological Seminary, Th.M., 1942; Yale University, M.A., 1944, Ph.D., 1954. *Home:* 1927 Tomahawk Rd., Okemos, Mich. 48864. *Office:* 244 Akers Hall, Michigan State University, East Lansing, Mich. 48823.

CAREER: Minister, American Baptist Convention, serving as pastor in Cheshire, Conn., then as missionary in South India for six years; Central Baptist Theological Seminary, Kansas City, Kan., assistant professor of missions, 1950-51; Eastern Baptist Theological Seminary, Philadelphia, Pa., professor of missions, 1951-54; Southern Baptist Theological Seminary, Louisville, Ky., associate professor, 1954-59, professor of comparative religion and missions, 1959-61; Missionary Research Library, New York, N.Y., director, 1961-66; Union Theological Seminary, New York, N.Y., adjunct professor of missions and history of religions, 1961-66; Michigan State University, East Lansing, professor of Asian religions, 1966—. National Council of the Churches of Christ in the United States, member of executive staff, 1961-66; Columbia University, seminars associate, 1963—.

MEMBER: National Association of Professors of Missions (secretary-treasurer 1962-66), National Association of Professors of Ecumenics, American Association of University Professors, American Academy of Religion, Deutsche Gesellschaft fer Missionswissenschaft, International Association for the History of Religions, American Oriental Society, Association for Asian Studies, All-India Oriental Congress, Michigan Academy of Science, Arts, and Letters, Phi Beta Kappa, Phi Epsilon. *Awards, hon-*

ors: Citation for Achievement, William Jewell College, 1956; Sealantic Fund fellowship for nine months at University of Ceylon and three months travel in Asia, American Association of Theological Schools, 1958-59.

WRITINGS: Man Reaches Out to God: Living Religions and the Christian Missionary Obligation, Judson, 1963; (author of introduction) *Missionary Biography: An Initial Bibliography,* Missionary Research Library, 1965; (with Helen Bailey) *A Study of Missionary Motivation, Training, and Withdrawal, 1953-1962,* Missionary Research Library, 1965; (editor) *Judaism, Jewish-Christian Relations and the Christian Mission to the Jew: A Selected Bibliography,* Missionary Research Library, 1966. Contributor of articles to publications in the United States and India. Member of editorial board of "World Christian Books," published by World Council of Churches.

WORK IN PROGRESS: A book on studies in comparative religion.

* * *

JACKSON, Robert 1911-

PERSONAL: Born February 25, 1911, in Leeds, England. *Home:* 49 Cumberland Mansions, Bryanston Sq., London W. 1, England.

CAREER: Journalist in England, war and foreign correspondent for London and provincial newspapers and magazines, and author, 1929—. *Military service:* British Army, served in India, Burma, and Malaya, 1941-45; became captain. *Member:* Savage Club, Press Club (both London).

WRITINGS: Gardening on Chalk and Lime Soil, Williams & Norgate, 1940; *Gordon Richards—First Day,* Mason & Ford, 1952; (editor) *Beautiful Gardens of the World,* Evans Brothers, 1953; (with Willi Frischauer) *The Altmark Affair,* Macmillan, 1955 (published in England as *The Navy's Here: The Altmark Affair,* Gollancz, 1955); (with Asja Mercer) *One Woman's War,* Wingate, 1958; *The Chief: The Biography of Gordon Hewart, Lord Chief Justice of England, 1922-40,* Harrap, 1959; *Thirty Seconds at Quetta: The Story of an Earthquake,* Evans Brothers, 1960; (with Robert G. Thelwell) *I Captained the Big Ships,* Arthur Barker, 1961; *Case for the Prosecution: The Biography of Sir Archibald Bodkin, Director of Public Prosecutions, 1920-1930,* Arthur Barker, 1962; *Coroner: The Biography of Sir Bentley Purchase,* Harrap, 1963; *A Taste of Freedom: Stories of the German and Italian Prisoners Who Escaped from Camps in Britain During World War II,* Arthur Barker, 1964; *The Nuffield Story,* Muller, 1964; *The Crime Doctors,* Muller, 1966. Editor, *Gardening Illustrated.* Contributor of numerous articles to newspapers and magazines.

* * *

JACOBI, Jolande (Szekacs) 1890-

PERSONAL: Born March 25, 1890, in Budapest, Hungary; daughter of Anton Szekacs (an industrialist, senator, and privy councillor to Austro-Hungarian court); married Andreas Jacobi (an attorney), 1909 (died, 1944); children: Andrew, Ernest. *Education:* University of Vienna, Ph.D.; also studied under Carl Gustav Jung in Switzerland. *Home and office:* Wilfriedstrasse, 8, Zurich, Switzerland.

CAREER: Psychotherapist, teacher, and scientific writer, Zurich, Switzerland, 1938—. Institute for Applied Psychology, Zurich, instructor in Jungian psychology, 1944—; C.G. Jung Institute, Zurich, founder, member of board of directors, and instructor, 1948—. Also lecturer at Public University of Zurich and instructor at Summer School of European Studies, Zurich. Lecturer at major universities in United States, 1953-54, in France, Holland, Germany, England. Managing vice-president of Austrian Cultural Association, 1928-38. *Awards, honors:* Decorated by president of Austria for cultural activities, 1935.

WRITINGS: Die Psychologie von C.G. Jung, foreword by Jung, Rascher (Zurich), 1940, translation by K.W. Bash published in England as *The Psychology of C.G. Jung,* Kegan Paul & Co., 1942, published in America as *The Psychology of Jung,* Yale University Press, 1943, 6th edition (translated by Ralph Manheim), 1962, 7th edition, Routledge & Kegan Paul, 1968; (editor) *Paracelsus, Selected Writings,* Pantheon, 1951, 2nd edition, 1958; (editor) Carl Gustav Jung, *Psychological Reflections: An Anthology,* Pantheon, 1953; *Komplex, Archetypus, Symbol in der Psychologie C.G. Jung,* foreword by Jung, Rascher, 1957, translation by Ralph Manheim published in America as *Complex, Archetype, Symbol in the Psychology of C.G. Jung,* Pantheon, 1959; (contributor) *Case Studies in Counselling and Psychotherapy,* Prentice-Hall, 1959; (editor and contributor with others, including Jung) *Man and His Symbols,* Doubleday, 1964; *Der Weg zur Individuation,* Rascher, 1965, translation by R.F.C. Hull published in America as *The Way of Individuation,* Harcourt, 1967; (editor) Carl Gustav Jung, *L'Ame et la vie,* translated from the German by Roland Cohen and Yves Le Lay, Buchet/Chastel, 1965; *Frauenprobleme—Eheprobleme,* Rascher, 1968; *Vom Bilderreich der Seele,* Walter, Olten, 1969; (editor and compiler with R.F.C. Hull) Carl Gustav Jung, *Psychological Reflections: A New Anthology of His Writings, 1905-1961,* Princeton University Press, 1970.

Contributor of about one hundred articles on psychology, problems of modern women, religion, art therapy, and education to journals in Switzerland, France, England, United States.

SIDELIGHTS: Mrs. Jacobi's family left Budapest in 1919 to establish residence in Vienna. Both her father and husband were killed by National Socialists.

* * *

JACOBS, Hayes B(enjamin)　1919-

PERSONAL: Born December 8, 1919, in Toppenish, Wash.; son of Hayes Benjamin (a merchant) and Maude Joanna (Tucker) Jacobs; married Gretchen Hall, July 25, 1942. *Education:* Whitman College, student, 1937-38; Harvard University, A.B., 1947. *Politics:* Independent. *Religion:* Episcopalian. *Home address:* R.F.D. 3, Box 366, Saugerties, N.Y. 12477. *Office:* 54 West 12th St., New York, N.Y. 10011. *Agent:* Candida Donadio, 111 West 57th St., New York, N.Y. 10019.

CAREER: Yakima Daily Republic, Yakima, Wash., reporter, feature writer, 1940-41; Associated Press, Tacoma, Wash., editor, 1941-42; Bell Telephone Laboratories, New York, N.Y., press information supervisor, 1948-58; Remington Rand Corp., New York, N.Y., press information manager, 1958-59; Columbia Broadcasting System television network, New York, N.Y., publications manager, 1959; free-lance writer and editor, New York, N.Y., 1959—. New School for Social Research, instructor, 1963-65, director of writing workshops, 1963—. Lecturer at numerous writers' conferences. *Military service:* U.S. Army, 1942-45. *Member:* Authors Guild.

WRITINGS: (Editor and author of preface) *New Voices, '64* (anthology of short stories and poetry), Macmillan, 1964; *A Complete Guide to Writing and Selling Non-Fiction,* Writer's Digest, 1967. Contributor of short stories, articles, and reviews to anthologies and to *New Yorker, Harper's, Esquire, Saturday Review, Saturday Evening Post, Reporter, Coronet, New York Times Magazine, Catholic Digest, Writer's Yearbook,* and other periodicals. Contributing editor and columnist, *New York Market Letter* and *Writer's Digest*

WORK IN PROGRESS: Writing and Selling Fiction.

* * *

JACOBS, Helen Hull　1908-
　　(H. Braxton Hull)

PERSONAL: Born August 6, 1908, in Globe, Ariz.; daughter of Roland Herbert and Eula (Hull) Jacobs. *Education:* Attended Anna Head School for Girls and University of California, Berkeley, 1926-29, College of William and Mary, 1942. *Religion:* Episcopalian. *Home:* Ocean Ave., East Hampton, N.Y. 11937.

CAREER: Former national and international tennis star, and senior editor, Grolier Council for Educational Research, New York, N.Y. U.S. tennis titles include junior champion, 1924-25, women's singles champion, 1932-35, women's doubles champion (with Sarah Palfrey), 1932, 1934, 1935, mixed doubles champion (with George Lott), 1934; in international tennis was finalist at Wimbledon, England, six times, Wimbledon singles champion, 1936, member of Wightman Cup team for thirteen consecutive years, 1927-39, and winner of titles in Egypt, Austria, Switzerland, and Greece. Designer of women's sports clothes. *Military service:* U.S. Naval reserve, on active duty, mainly as commandant of seamen and public relations officer at WAVES Training School, New York; public information officer and administrative assistant, Naval Gun Factory, Washington, D.C., 1943-45, Naval Proving Ground, Dahlgren, Va., 1949-54; retired as commander, 1968.

MEMBER: National Geographic Society (honorary), Mark Twain Society (honorary), English Speaking Union (honorary), Eugene Field Society (honorary), California Writers' Club, Kappa Alpha Theta, Oakland Junior League (charter), All England Lawn Tennis and Cricket Club (honorary), Nice Tennis Club (France; honorary), Women's Athletic Club (Oakland), San Francisco Press Club (honorary), Berkeley Tennis Club (California; honorary). *Awards, honors:* Inducted into Lawn Tennis Hall of Fame, Newport, R.I., 1962; Tennis Immortal award, Tennis Writers Association of America, 1968.

WRITINGS: Modern Tennis, Bobbs-Merrill, 1933; *Improve Your Tennis,* Methuen, 1936; *Beyond the Game: An Autobiography,* Lippincott, 1936; (under pseudonym H. Braxton Hull) *Barry Cort,* Faber, 1938; *Tennis,* A.S. Barnes, 1941; *"By Your Leave, Sir": The Story of a WAVE,* Dodd, 1943; *Storm Against the Wind,* Dodd, 1944; *Laurel for Judy,* Dodd, 1945; *Adventure in Bluejeans,* Dodd, 1947; *Gallery of Champions,* A.S. Barnes, 1949; *Center Court,* A.S. Barnes, 1950; *Judy, Tennis Ace,* Dodd, 1951; *Proudly She Serves: The Realistic Story of a Tennis Champion Who Becomes a WAVE,* Dodd, 1953; *Golf, Swimming and Tennis,* Creative Educational Society, 1961; *The Young Sportsman's Guide to Tennis,* Thomas Nelson, 1961; *Famous American Women Athletes,* Dodd, 1964; *Better Physical Fitness for Girls,* Dodd, 1964; *Courage to Conquer,* Dodd, 1967; *The Tennis Machine,* Scribner, 1972. Contributor of articles to major American magazines, to *Sketch, Country Life,* and *Britannia* in England, and to newspapers in United States, England, and Egypt.

BIOGRAPHICAL/CRITICAL SOURCES: John Durant and Otto Bettman, *Pictorial History of American Sports: From Colonial Times to the Present,* A.S. Barnes, 1952; John Durant, editor, *Yesterday in Sports: Memorable Glimpses of the Past as Selected from the Pages of Sports Illustrated,* A.S. Barnes, 1956; Parke Cummings, *American Tennis: The Story of a Game and Its People,* Little, Brown, 1957; *Best Sellers,* January 1, 1968; *National Observer,* January 15, 1968.

JACOBSON, Edmund 1888-

PERSONAL: Born April 22, 1888, in Chicago, Ill.; son of Morris and Fannie (Blum) Jacobson; married Elizabeth Ruth Silberman, December 16, 1926; children: Ruth Frances Jacobson Grommers, Edmund, Jr., Nancy Elizabeth Jacobson Engelsberg. *Education:* Northwestern University, B.A., 1907; Harvard University, A.M., 1909, Ph.D., 1910; Cornell University, fellow, 1911; University of Chicago, M.D., 1915. *Home:* 5532 South Shore Dr., Chicago, Ill. 60637. *Office:* Laboratory for Clinical Physiology, 55 East Washington St., Chicago, Ill. 60602; Hotel Commodore, 42nd and Lexington, New York, N.Y. 10017.

CAREER: Private practice of internal medicine and psychiatry, Chicago, Ill., 1917—, in New York, N.Y., 1932—; Laboratory for Clinical Physiology, Chicago, Ill., director, 1936—. University of Chicago, Chicago, Ill., research associate, 1926-30, assistant professor of physiology, 1930-36. Foundation for Scientific Relaxation (non-profit), director. Developer of instruments for measuring nervous and muscular states, and the direct measurement of mental activities.

MEMBER: International Society of Internal Medicine (fellow), American College of Physicians (fellow), American Association for the Advancement of Science (fellow), American Medical Association, Academy of Psychosomatic Medicine (fellow), American College of Sports Medicine (fellow), International Society for Research on the Coagulation of Blood, Capillary Function and Practical Myology, International College of Angiology, American Physicians Society for Physiological Tension Control (president, 1962-63), American Physiological Society, American Psychosomatic Society, American Geriatrics Society (fellow), American Academy of Physical Education (associate fellow), Academy of Political Science, U.S. Naval Institute, Illinois State Medical Society, Chicago Medical Society, St. Louis Medical Society (honorary life member), Midwestern Psychological Society, University of Stuttgart (honorary member), Phi Beta Kappa, Sigma Xi. *Awards, honors:* LL.D., George Williams College.

WRITINGS: Progressive Relaxation: A Physiological and Clinical Investigation of Muscular States and Their Significance in Psychological and Medical Practice, University of Chicago Press, 1929, 3rd edition, 1965; *You Must Relax: A Practical Method of Reducing the Strains of Modern Living,* McGraw, 1934, 4th edition, 1962; (contributor) *Nerve and Muscle in the Problem of Mental Disorder,* McGraw, 1934; *You Can Sleep Well: The ABC's of Restful Sleep for the Average Person,* McGraw, 1938; (contributor) *The Principles and Practice of Physical Therapy,* Volume I, revised edition, W.F. Prior, 1940; *The Peace We Americans Need: A Plea for Clearer Thinking About Our Allies, Our Foes, Ourselves and Our Future,* Kroch, 1944; *How to Relax and Have Your Baby,* McGraw, 1959; *Tension Control for Businessmen,* McGraw, 1963; *Anxiety and Tension Control: A Physiologic Approach,* Lippincott, 1964; *Biology of Emotions: New Understanding Derived from Biological Multidisciplinary Investigation—First Electrophysiological Measurements,* C.C Thomas, 1967; (compiler and editor) *Tension in Medicine,* C.C Thomas, 1967; *Modern Treatment of Tense Patients, Including the Neurotic and Depressed with Case Illustrations, Follow-Ups and EMG Measurements,* C.C Thomas, 1969.

Contributor of more than eighty articles to medical, physiology, psychology, and philosophy journals, principally on the topics of nervous states, high blood pressure, coronary heart disease, salt-free diets, electrical measurements, mental activities, and muscular contractions.

WORK IN PROGRESS: Physiological Psychiatry, completed and awaiting publication; a book on effective teaching, classroom methods, following ten NBC broadcasts to improve learning, attention, memory; laboratory work: further direct electrical measurements of tension in health and disorder, using digital computer; research in new medical methods of tension control for heart maladies, high blood pressure, and digestive disorders.

* * *

JACOBSON, Harold Karan 1929-

PERSONAL: Born June 28, 1929, in Detroit, Mich.; son of Harold Kenneth (a businessman) and Maxine A. (Miller) Jacobson; married Merelyn Jean Lindbloom, August 25, 1951; children: Harold Knute, Eric Alfred, Kristoffer Olaf, Nils Karl. *Education:* University of Michigan, A.B., 1950; Yale University, M.A., 1952, Ph.D., 1955. *Politics:* Democrat. *Religion:* Episcopal. *Home:* 2174 Delaware Dr., Ann Arbor, Mich. 48103. *Office:* Department of Political Science, University of Michigan, Ann Arbor, Mich. 48104.

CAREER: University of Houston, Houston, Tex., assistant professor of political science, 1955-57; University of Michigan, Ann Arbor, assistant professor, 1957-61, associate professor, 1961-65, professor of political science, 1965—. Visiting professor, University of Geneva, 1965-66, 1970-71. *Military service:* U.S. Army Reserve, 1951-62; became lieutenant. *Member:* International Political Science Association, International Studies Association (president, midwest division, 1969-70), American Political Science Association, Society for Religion in Higher Education, Midwestern Conference of Political Scientists, Phi Beta Kappa, Phi Eta Sigma, Phi Kappa Phi. *Awards, honors:* Fellow, World Affairs Center, 1959-60.

WRITINGS: (Editor) *America's Foreign Policy,* Random House, 1960, 2nd edition, 1965; *The USSR and the UN's Economic and Social Activities,* University of Notre Dame Press, 1963; (with Eric Stein) *Diplomats, Scientists and Politicians: The United States and the Nuclear Test Ban Negotiations,* University of Michigan Press, 1966; (editor with William Zimmerman) *The Shaping of Foreign Policy,* Atherton, 1969. Contributor of articles to *Foreign Affairs* and other professional journals. Member, board of editors, *International Organization;* member of editorial board, *Journal of Conflict Resolution.*

* * *

JACOT de BOINOD, Bernard Louis 1898-
(B.L. Jacot)

PERSONAL: Born February 25, 1898, in Birmingham, England; son of Louis and Isabella Millner (Wilkinson) Jacot de Boinod; married Claribel Mandy, 1937; children: P.L.B., D.C.P., C.W.B., and D.B.V. (sons), Bernadine. *Education:* Attended King Edward's School, Birmingham, England, 1908-15; St. John's College, Oxford, M.A. (honors), 1923; Inner Temple, London, England, Barrister-at-Law, 1922. *Religion:* Church of England. *Home:* Beech Hill, Buckland-St.-Mary, Somerset, England.

CAREER: Barrister-at-law and author; has been member of editorial staff of *Times* (London), deputy editor for *News-Chronicle* (London), and a Foreign correspondent for *New York Herald-Tribune. Military service:* British Army, Royal Flying Corps, pilot, 1916; served on staff of General Eisenhower during World War II; became colonel. *Member:* Vincent's Club (Oxford).

*WRITINGS—*All under pseudonym B.L. Jacot: *The Longer Shadow* (stories), Noel Douglas, 1926; *Trust Wesley!,* Little, Brown, 1929; *Frogs Don't Grow Feathers, and Other Outstanding Epics Laid to the Charge of the Hon.*

Winslow Moult, Hutchinson, 1930; *Winslow Moult* (short stories), Rich & Cowan, 1944; (with D.M.B. Collier) *Marconi: Master of Space,* Hutchinson, 1935; *The House of Madame Jacqueminet, with Other Stories,* Muller, 1944; *The Hands of Wan Lu, with Other Stories,* Muller, 1946; *Villa Mar,* Macdonald & Co., 1948; (with Helen Astrup) *Night Has a Thousand Eyes,* Macdonald & Co., 1953, published in America as *Oslo Intrigue: A Woman's Memoir of the Norwegian Resistance,* McGraw, 1954; *The Summer of Uncle Jean-Marie,* Knopf, 1964 (published in England as *A Kingdom for My Horse,* M. Joseph, 1964); *The Tulip Tree,* Dent, 1967; *Crying for the Moon,* Dent, 1969. Author of television plays for British Broadcasting Corp. and Columbia Broadcasting System. Contributor of short stories to *Collier's, Liberty, New Yorker,* and *Good Housekeeping.*

BIOGRAPHICAL/CRITICAL SOURCES: Books and Bookmen, November, 1967.

* * *

JAFFE, Frederick S. 1925-

PERSONAL: Born November 27, 1925, in New York, N.Y.; son of Samuel and Clara (Cherno) Jaffe; married Phyllis Shelley (an attorney), August 8, 1947; children: Paul, David, Richard. *Education:* Queens College (now Queens College of the City University of New York), B.A., 1947. *Home:* 2 Knollwood Dr., Ossining, N.Y. 10562. *Office:* Planned Parenthood Federation, 515 Madison Ave., New York, N.Y. 10022.

CAREER: Daily Compass, New York, N.Y., legislative correspondent and reporter, 1949-52; United Packinghouse Workers, Chicago, Ill., editor and public relations director, 1953; Planned Parenthood Federation, New York, N.Y., associate director of information, 1954-64, vice-president, 1964—, director, Center for Family Planning Program Development, 1968—. *Military service:* U.S. Army Air Corps, 1944-46; became staff sergeant. *Member:* American Public Health Association, Population Association of America, Society for Study of Social Problems, National Association of Science Writers.

WRITINGS: (Editor with Winfield Best) *Simple Methods of Contraception,* Planned Parenthood, 1958; (with Alan F. Guttmacher and Best) *The Complete Book of Birth Control,* Ballantine, 1961, revised and enlarged edition published as *Planning Your Family: The Complete Guide to Birth Control, Overcoming Infertility, Sterilization, with a Special Section on Abortion,* Macmillan, 1964, 3rd edition published as *Birth Control and Love,* 1969.

Contributor: Louis Ferman, editor, *Poverty in America,* University of Michigan Press, 1965; Talcott Parsons and Kenneth B. Clark, editors, *The Negro American,* foreword by Lyndon B. Johnson, Houghton, 1966; Hanna H. Meissner, editor, *Poverty in the Affluent Society,* Harper, 1966. Contributor to *Parents' Magazine, McCall's, Reader's Digest, Good Housekeeping, Journal of Social Issues, American Journal of Public Health, Science, Journal of Marriage and the Family,* and *Public Health Reports.*

* * *

JAHER, Frederic Cople 1934-

PERSONAL: Born March 17, 1934, in Beverly, Mass.; son of Sidney Mortrey and Henrietta (Fox) Jaher; married Susan Lichtenstein. *Education:* College of City of New York (now City College of the City University of New York), B.A. (magna cum laude), 1955; Harvard University, A.M., 1957, Ph.D., 1961. *Home:* 406 West Iowa St., Urbana, Ill. 61801. *Office:* History Department, University of Illinois, Urbana, Ill. 61801.

CAREER: City College of the City University of New York, New York, N.Y., instructor in history, 1961-64; Long Island University, New York, N.Y., assistant professor of history, 1964-65; University of Chicago, Chicago, Ill., assistant professor of history and social sciences, 1965-68, University of Illinois, Urbana, associate professor of history, 1968—. *Member:* American Historical Association, American Studies Association, Congress on Racial Equality, American Civil Liberties Union, Society Against Nuclear Explosion, Mississippi Valley Historical Association, Phi Alpha Theta, Phi Beta Kappa.

WRITINGS: Doubters and Dissenters: Cataclysmic Thought in America, 1880-1918, Free Press, 1964; *Oscar Handlin's The Uprooted: A Critical Commentary,* American R.D.M., 1966; (editor) *The Age of Industrialism in America: Essays in Social Structure and Cultural Values,* Free Press, 1968; (editor with Leonard Dinnerstein) *The Aliens: A History of Ethnic Minorities in America,* Appleton, 1970.

WORK IN PROGRESS: A study of the rise and decline of urban elites in America.

* * *

JAHN, Melvin E(dward) 1938-

PERSONAL: Born October 4, 1938, in Galveston, Tex.; son of Edward A. (an attorney) and Carmen Estelle (Wood) Jahn. *Education:* University of California, Berkeley, B.A., 1961, M.A., 1963; University of California, San Francisco, Ph.D. candidate, 1969—. *Home:* 2509 Haste St., Berkeley, Calif. 94704. *Office:* Department of History of Health Sciences, University of California, San Francisco Medical Center, San Francisco, Calif. 94122.

CAREER: University of California, Berkeley, research paleontologist working under National Science Foundation grant, 1963-66. Macy Fellow, University of California, San Francisco, 1967-69. *Member:* Society for the Bibliography of Natural History, History of Science Society, Ray Society (fellow), Zoological Society of London, Palaeontological Association of London.

WRITINGS: (Translator and annotator with Daniel J. Woolf) *The Lying Stones of Dr. Johann Bartholomew Adam Beringer: Being His Lithographie Wirceburgensis,* University of California Press, 1963.

WORK IN PROGRESS: With D.J. Woolf, *The Wreck of a World: Dr. Scheuchzer, Dr. Woodward and the Deluge,* materials toward a history of the Noachian Flood concept in paleontology, for University of California Press; a critical edition of Edward Topsell's *Historie of Foure-Footed Beastes; Paleontology in the Philosophical Transactions: 1665-1800,* a source book in the early history of paleontology.

* * *

JAIN, Girilal 1922-

PERSONAL: Born July 10, 1922, in Piplikhera, Punjab, India; son of Shahzadrai (a businessman) and Bhagwani (Devi) Jain; married Sudarshan Kumari, December 10, 1951; children: Meenakshi, Meera, Sandhya, Sunil. *Education:* Delhi University, B.A. (honors), 1943. *Religion:* Jainist. *Home:* 300 Dollis Hill Lane, London N.W.2, England. *Office: Times of India,* 3 Albermarle St., London, W.1, England.

CAREER: Indian News Chronicle (English daily), Delhi, India, sub-editor, 1948-50; *Times of India* (English-language daily), Delhi and Bombay, India, sub-editor, 1950-51, reporter, 1951-58, chief reporter, 1958-60, foreign correspondent in Karachi, Pakistan, 1961, London editor, and columnist, 1962—. *Member:* Commonwealth Correspondents Association, Indian Journalists Association.

WRITINGS: Chinese "Panchsheela" in Burma, Democratic Research Service (Bombay), 1956; What Mao Really Means, Siddhartha Publications, 1957; India Meets China in Nepal, Asia Publishing House, 1959; Panchsheela and After: A Re-appraisal of Sino-Indian Relations in the Context of the Tibetan Insurrection, Asia Publishing House, 1960.

WORK IN PROGRESS: A study of possible consequences for India of growth of Chinese power.

SIDELIGHTS: Although no longer active in politics, Jain courted imprisonment in Gandhi's "Quit India" anti-British campaign in 1942.

* * *

JANIFER, Laurence M(ark) 1933-
(Alfred Blake, Andrew Blake, Larry M. Harris, Barbara Wilson; Mark Phillips, joint pseudonym)

PERSONAL: Born March 17, 1933, in Brooklyn, N.Y.; son of Bernard N. and Hilda (Warshauer) Harris; married Sylvia Siegel, 1955 (divorced, 1958); married Sue Blugerman, 1960 (divorced, 1962); married Rae Montor, 1966 (divorced, 1966); married Beverly Goldberg, October 8, 1969; children: (fourth marriage) Mary Elizabeth. Education: Attended City College of the City University of New York, one year. Politics: Independent Conservative. Religion: Roman Catholic. Agent: Seligmann & Collier, 280 Madison Ave., New York, N.Y. 10016.

CAREER: Pianist, arranger, accompanist, bandsman, New York, N.Y., 1950-59; Scott Meredith Literary Agency, New York, N.Y., editor, 1952-57; editor, managing editor, or art director for various detective and science fiction magazines, New York, N.Y., 1953-57; comedian, appearing in floor shows and plays, and on radio and television, New York, N.Y., 1957—.

WRITINGS: Slave Planet, Pyramid Publications, 1963; The Wonder War, Pyramid Publications, 1963; You Sane Men, Lancer Books, 1964, reissued as Bloodworld, 1969; The Woman Without a Name, Signet, 1966; (editor) Masters' Choice: The Best Science-Fiction Stories of All Time Chosen by the Masters of Science-Fiction, Simon & Schuster, 1966; The Final Fear, Belmont Books, 1967; A Piece of Martin Cann, Belmont Books, 1968; Impossible?, Belmont Books, 1968; (with S.J. Treibich) Target: Terra, Ace Books, 1968; (with Treibich) The High Hex, Ace Books, 1969; (with Treibich) The Wagered World, Ace Books, 1969, also published as Tonight We Steal the Stars [and] The Wagered World (the former by John Jakes), Ace Books, 1969; You Can't Escape, Lancer Books, 1969.

Under pseudonym Alfred Blake: The Bed and I!, Intimate Books, 1962; Faithful for 8 Hours, Beacon Press, 1963.

Under pseudonym Andrew Blake: I Deal in Desire, Boudoir, 1962; Sex Swinger, Beacon Press, 1963; Love Hostess, Beacon Press, 1963.

Under pseudonym Larry M. Harris: The Pickled Poodles, Random House, 1959; (with Randall Garrett) Pagan Passions, Beacon-Galaxy, 1960; The Protector, Random House, 1960.

Under pseudonym Barbara Wilson: The Pleasures we Know, Lancer Books, 1964; The Velvet Embrace, Lancer Books, 1965.

With Randall Garrett under joint pseudonym Mark Phillips: Brain Twister, Pyramid Publications, 1962; The Impossibles, Pyramid Publications, 1963, 2nd edition. 1966; Supermind, Pyramid Publications, 1963.

Ghost writer: Ken Murray's Giant Joke Book, Ace Books, 1957; The Henry Morgan Joke Book, Avon, 1958; Jeff Harris, The Foot in my Mouth, Caravan Book, 1958; Ed Goldfader, Tracer!, Nash Publishing, 1970. Ghost editor, Thomas Sutton, Yes, I'm Here with Someone, Caravan Book, 1958.

Writer under various pseudonyms of more than 400 stories and articles appearing in detective and science fiction magazines, including Ellery Queen's Mystery Magazine, Alfred Hitchcock's Mystery Magazine, Michael Shayne, Analog, Dapper, Galaxy, Fantasy and Science-Fiction, Fantastic Universe, Manhunt, If, Amazing; occasional columnist, Realist; film reviewer for Escapade and Triumph; other articles in Variety, Esquire, and Reader's Digest. Writer of comedy routines, some music.

WORK IN PROGRESS: Several novels and plays; one music comedy with Frederick Bassoff, as well as occasional liturgical and secular music; short stories and novels set in a future society, 1993-2500 A.D.

SIDELIGHTS: Janifer told CA: "I was born 'Harris,' changed my name in 1962 when the original name was rediscovered for me. . . . an Immigration officer had saddled Harris on my father's father, and I'd rather be named for where I come from than for an Immigration officer's odd whim. Have never made the change legal— why bother? . . . . I write every day, or nearly. My interests are writing, music, history of various sorts, cartooning, and a few more, I imagine." (Janifer later added math and mathematical physics, various sorts of law and forensic medicine, theology, the history of the detective story, and the history of humor.)

"I don't travel. . . . I want to persuade people that the arts are fun, and meant to be fun. If I know of a talented writer anywhere in the world I will blow my last cent and my last bit of energy (as I have done) on getting him or her to work and into some form of knowledge and capability." Janifer has used about thirty-two pseudonyms in his magazine work. He makes the point that he is "not a member of the Science-Fiction Writers of America, and would not be for large amounts of money."

* * *

JARRETT, H(arold) Reginald 1916-

PERSONAL: Born May 6, 1916, in Salford Priors, Evesham, Warwickshire, England; son of Thomas Reginald (a gardener) and Amy (Whyborn) Jarrett; married Edna Smith, February 5, 1944; children: Diana Reed Ayodele, Valerie Reed. Education: University of Birmingham, B.A. (with honors), 1938, diploma in education, 1939; University of London, B. Sc. (with honors), 1945, M.Sc., 1946, Ph.D., 1951. Home: 42 Roslin Rd. S., Talbot Woods, Bournemouth BH3 7EG, England.

CAREER: Methodist missionary, Bathurst, Gambia, 1941-45; Fourah Bay University College, Freetown, Sierra Leone, senior lecturer in geography, 1950-56; University College, Ibadan, Nigeria, senior lecturer in geography, 1957-58; Newcastle University College, New South Wales, Australia, senior lecturer in geography, 1963-67. Member: Royal Geographical Society (fellow), Geographical Association, Institute of British Geographers.

WRITINGS: A Geography of Sierra Leone and Gambia, Longmans, Green, 1954, 2nd edition, 1964; A Geography of West Africa, Dent, 1956, 2nd edition published as A Geography of West Africa, Including the French Territories, Portuguese Guinea, and Liberia, 1957, 3rd edition, 1971; Physical Geography for West Africa, Longmans, Green, 1958, 2nd edition, 1968; A General World Geography for African Schools, Methuen, 1958; An Outline Geography of Africa, Methuen, 1962, 3rd edition, 1971; Africa, Macdonald & Evans, 1962, 3rd edition, 1970; Land and Landscape, University of London Press, 1965;

Landscape and Livelihood, University of London Press, 1967; *A Geography of Manufacturing,* Macdonald & Evans, 1969; (with J.J. Branigan) *The Mediterranean Lands,* Macdonald & Evans, 1969, International Publications Service, 1970. Contributor to *Encyclopaedia Britannica, Book of Knowledge, American Peoples Encyclopedia.* Contributor of other articles to geographical journals.

WORK IN PROGRESS: Further work on west Africa, central Africa, and tropical geography.

* * *

JAURAND, Yvonne 1912-
(Yves Duplessis)

PERSONAL: Born January 26, 1912, in Paris, France; married December 22, 1936; married, husband's surname, Tuchmann (a professor, La Faculte de Medecine); children: Evelyne, Alain. *Education:* Institut Catholique, Paris, Diplome d'Etudes Superieures de Philosophie, 1934; Faculte des Lettres de Paris, Certificate d'Ethnologie, 1935; Faculte des Lettres de Montpellier, Doctorat d'Universite, 1945. *Religion:* Catholic. *Home:* 67 Avenue Raymond-Poincare, Paris XVI, France.

CAREER: Centre National de Tele-Enseignement, Vanves, Seine, France, professeur de philosophie (by correspondence), 1960—. *Member:* Societe des Amis de l'Institut Metapsychique International, Centre Vedantique Ramakrichna.

WRITINGS: (Under pseudonym Yves Duplessis) *Le Surrealisme,* Presses Universitaires de France, 1950, 7th edition, revised, 1967, translation by Paul Capon published as *Surrealism,* Walker & Co., 1963. Contributor to *Prabuddha Bharata* (India), *Connaitre,* and *Concours medical.*

WORK IN PROGRESS: Study of mystic philosophies, especially the relationship between Western mystics and the Vedanta.

SIDELIGHTS: She has given many lectures on Hindu spirituality, which have been illustrated by her films, chiefly of temples, taken during travels to India, Nepal, and Ceylon in 1962. She wrote to *CA:* "My knowledge of English has permitted me to read translations of the great sages of India whose conceptions can enlarge and enrich occidental thinking about existence."

BIOGRAPHICAL/CRITICAL SOURCES: Prabuddha Bharata, January 1948; *Bulletin Officiel de l'Education Nationale,* February, 1951.

* * *

JAYME, William North 1925-

PERSONAL: Surname rhymes with *Pay-me;* born in 1925, in Pittsburgh, Pa.; *Education:* Princeton University, student, 1943-44 1947-49. *Home:* 1853 Jones St., San Francisco, Calif. 94109.

CAREER: Time, Inc., New York, N.Y., assistant circulation promotion manager of *Fortune,* then *Life,* 1950-53; Columbia Broadcasting System, New York, N.Y., copy director, sales and advertising promotion for CBS radio, 1953-55; McCann-Erickson, Inc., New York, N.Y., senior copy writer, 1955-58; advertising creative consultant, 1958—. Municipal Art Society of New York, director, 1953-62; Museum of Modern Art, member of junior council, 1954-58. *Member:* Century Association (New York). *Military service:* U.S. Army, 2nd Armored Division, 1944-46; became sergeant.

WRITINGS: (With Roderick Cook) *Know Your Toes (And Other Things to Know),* C.N. Potter, 1963; (with Helen McCully and Jacques Pepin) *The Other Half of the Egg,* Barrows, 1967. Stories anthologized in *Best De-*

tective Stories, Dutton, 1964, and *Boucher's Choicest,* Dutton, 1969. Writer-producer of U.S. Army radio program, "Music Motorized," 1945-46, and of Time Inc., television program, "Background for Judgment," and "Citizen's View of '52," both 1952. Author of free-lance dramatic scripts for "Studio One," and other television programs, and of libretto for "Carry Nation" (opera; first produced by Unviersity of Kansas, 1966; produced by San Francisco Opera, 1966), with music by Douglas Moore, Galaxy Music Corp., 1968. Contributor of articles and short humor items to *Harper's, Show, Today's Living, Esquire, Ellery Queen's Mystery Magazine,* and *Queen.*

SIDELIGHTS: "Carry Nation" was recorded by Desto Records in 1968.

* * *

JENKINS, Harold 1909-

PERSONAL: Born July 19, 1909, in Shenley, Buckinghamshire, England; son of Henry and Mildred (Carter) Jenkins; married Gladys Puddifoot, January 23, 1939. *Education:* Attended Wolverton Grammar School, 1920-27; University College, London, B.A. (first class honors), 1930, M.A. (distinction), 1933. *Home:* 24 Brantwood Rd., London SE 24 ODJ, England.

CAREER: University of Liverpool, Liverpool, England, William Noble Fellow, 1935-36; University of the Witwatersrand, Johannesburg, South Africa, 1936-45, began as lecturer, became senior lecturer in English; University of London, London, England, lecturer at University College, 1945-46, reader in English at University College, 1946-54, professor of English at Westfield College, 1954-67; University of Edinburgh, Edinburgh, Scotland, Regius Professor of Rhetoric and English Literature, 1967-71. Visiting professor, Duke University, 1957-58.

WRITINGS: The Life and Work of Henry Chettle, Sidgwick & Jackson, 1934; (editor) Henry Chettle, *The Tragedy of Hoffman, 1631,* Malone Society, 1951; *Edward Benlowes, 1602-1676: Biography of a Minor Poet,* Harvard University Press, 1952; *The Structural Problem in Shakespeare's Henry the Fourth* (lecture), Methuen, 1956; (editor with S. Brigid Younghughes) *The Fatal Marriage,* Oxford University Press, 1959; *Hamlet and Ophelia* (lecture), Oxford University Press, 1963; *The Catastrophe in Shakespearean Tragedy* (lecture), University of Edinburgh Press, 1969. General editor with H.F. Brooks, "Arden Shakespeare" series, 1958—. Contributor of articles on Elizabethan literature and seventeenth century to *Modern Language Review, Review of English Studies,* and other journals. Member of advisory board, *Shakespeare Survey* and *Studies in English Literature.*

WORK IN PROGRESS: An edition of *Hamlet.*

* * *

JENKINS, Roy Harris 1920-

PERSONAL: Born November 11, 1920, in Abersychan, Monmouthshire, Wales; son of Arthur (a member of Parliament) and Hattie (Harris) Jenkins; married Jennifer Morris, January 20, 1945; children: Charles, Cynthia, Edward. *Education:* Balliol College, Oxford, B.A. (first class honors). *Politics:* Labour. *Home:* 33 Ladbroke Sq., London W.11, England. *Office:* House of Commons, London S.W.1, England.

CAREER: Journalist and author; member of Parliament, 1948—; Minister of Aviation, 1964-65; Home Secretary, 1965-67; Chancellor of the Exchequer, 1967-70; Deputy Leader of the Labour Party, 1970. John Lewis Partnership Ltd., director, 1963—. *Military service:* British Army, Royal Artillery, 1944-46; became captain. *Member:* Fabian Society (executive committee, 1949-61; chairman, 1957-58), Society of Authors (management committee, 1956-60).

WRITINGS: (Editor) Clement Richard Attlee, *Purpose and Policy: Selected Speeches*, Hutchinson, 1947; *Mr. Attlee: An Interim Biography*, Heinemann, 1948; (with others) *Post-War Italy: A Report on Economic Conditions*, Fabian Books, 1950; *Fair Shares for the Rich*, Tribune Publications, 1951; (contributor) *New Fabian Essays*, Fabian Books, 1952; *Pursuit of Progress: A Critical Analysis of the Achievement and Prospect of the Labour Party*, Heinemann, 1953; *Mr. Balfour's Poodle: An Account of the Struggle Between the House of Lords and the Government of Mr. Asquith*, Heinemann, 1954, new edition published in America as *Mr. Balfour's Poodle: Peers vs. People*, Chilmark, 1968; *Sir Charles Dilke: A Victorian Tragedy*, Collins, 1958, revised edition published as *Victorian Scandal: A Biography of the Right Honourable Gentleman Sir Charles Dilke*, Chilmark, 1965; *The Labour Case*, Penguin (Harmondsworth), 1959; (with Douglas Jay) *The Common Market Debate*, Fabian International Bureau, 1962; (contributor W.T. Rodgers, editor, *Hugh Gaitskell*, Thames & Hudson, 1964; *Asquith: Portrait of a Man and an Era*, Chilmark, 1964 (published in England as *Asquith*, Collins, 1964); *Essays and Speeches*, edited by Anthony Lester, Collins, 1967, Chilmark, 1968; *Afternoon on the Potomac: A British View of America's Changing Position in the World*, Yale University Press, 1972.

SIDELIGHTS: Film rights to *Victorian Scandal* have been sold to Sam Spiegel, with John and Penelope Mortimer writing the screenplay.

* * *

JENKINS, Will(iam) F(itzgerald) 1896- (Murray Leinster)

PERSONAL: Born June 16, 1896, in Norfolk, .Va.; son of George Briggs and Mary Louise (Murry) Jenkins; married Mary Mandola, August 9, 1921; children: Mary (Mrs. Vahan Daniels), Elizabeth (Mrs. William De Hardit), Wenllian (Mrs. Peyton Stallings), Joan P. *Education:* Educated in public and private schools in Norfolk, Va. *Religion:* Catholic. *Home and office:* Arduwy, Gloucester, Va. 23061. *Agent:* Littauer & Wilkinson, 500 Fifth Ave., New York, N.Y. 10036.

CAREER: Self-employed fiction writer, 1918—. Guest lecturer, City College of the City University of New York, and College of William and Mary. Served with Committee of Public Information, World War I, in Office of War Information, World War II. Holder of two patents. *Military service:* U.S. Army, Infantry, 1917-18. *Awards, honors:* Liberty Short-Short Story Award of $1,000 for "A Very Nice Family," 1937.

WRITINGS: *Murder Will Out*, John Hamilton, 1932; *The Gamblin' Kid*, A.H. King, 1933; *Mexican Trail*, A.H. King, 1933; *Sword of Kings*, John Long, 1933; *Fighting Horse Valley*, A.H. King, 1934; *Outlaw Sheriff*, A.H. King, 1934 (published in England as *Rustlin' Sheriff*, Eldon, 1934); *Kid Deputy*, A.H. King, 1935; *Murder in the Family*, John Hamilton, 1935, Gateway Books, 1944; *No Clues*, Wright & Brown, 1935; *Black Sheep*, Messner, 1936; *Guns for Achin*, Wright & Brown, 1936; *The Man Who Feared*, Gateway Books, 1942; *The Murder of the U.S.A.*, Crown, 1946; *Dallas: From the Warner Bros. Motion Picture Written by John Twist*, Fawcett, 1950; *Son of the Flying Y*, Fawcett, 1951.

Under pseudonym Murray Leinster: *Scalps: A Murder Mystery*, Harcourt, 1930; *Murder Mystery*, Harcourt, 1930; *Murder Madness*, Harcourt, 1931; *Wings of Chance*, John Hamilton, 1938; *The Last Space Ship*, Fell, 1949; *Sidewise in Time, and Other Scientific Adventures*, Shasta, 1950; *Wanted Dead or Alive*, Wright & Brown,

1951; (editor) *Great Stories of Science Fiction*, introduction by Clifton Fadiman, Random House, 1951; *Space Ferry*, Shasta, 1952; *Space Platform*, Shasta, 1953, revised edition, Belmont Books, 1966; *Space Tug*, Shasta, 1953, 2nd edition, Belmont, 1969; *The Brain-Stealers*, Ace Books, 1954; *The Forgotten Planet*, Gnome Press, 1954; *Gateway to Elsewhere*, Ace Books, 1954; *Operation: Outer Space*, Fantasy Publishing, 1954; *The Other Side of Here*, Ace Books, 1955; *City on the Moon*, Avalon, 1957; *Colonial Survey*, Gnome Press, 1957; *Out of This World*, Avalon, 1958; *The War with the Gizmos*, Fawcett, 1958; *The Monster from Earth's End*, Fawcett, 1959; *Four from Planet 5*, Fawcett, 1959; *Pirates of Zan*, Ace Books, 1959; *Monsters and Such*, Avon, 1959; *The Aliens*, Berkley, 1960; *Wailing Asteroid*, Avon, 1960; *Twists in Time*, Avon, 1960; *Men Into Space*, Berkley, 1960; *Talents, Inc.*, Avon, 1961; *This World is Taboo*, Ace Books, 1961; *Creatures of the Abyss*, Berkley, 1961 (published in England as *The Listeners*, Sidgwick & Jackson, 1969); *Operation Terror*, Berkley, 1962; *The Greks Bring Gifts*, Macfadden, 1964; *The Duplicators*, Ace Books, 1964; *Time Tunnel*, Pyramid Books, 1964; *The Other Side of Nowhere*, Berkley, 1964; *Doctor to the Stars*, Pyramid Books, 1965; *Space Captain*, Ace Books, 1965; *Checkpoint Lambda*, Berkley, 1965; *Get Off My World!*, Belmont Books, 1965; *Miners in the Sky*, Avon, 1966; *S.O.S. from Three Worlds*, Ace Books, 1966; *Space Gypsies*, Avon, 1966; *Timeslip*, Pyramid Publications, 1966; (with Jack Williamson and John Wyndham) *Three Stories* (includes "The Mole Pirate," by Leinster, "The Moon Era," by Williamson, and "Exiles on Asperus," by Wyndham), edited and introduced by Sam Moskowitz, Doubleday, 1967 (published in England as *A Sense of Wonder: Three Science-Fiction Stories*, Sidgwick & Jackson, 1967); *Land of the Giants*, Pyramid Publications, 1967; *Land of the Giants No. 2: The Hot Spot*, Pyramid Publications, 1968; *A Murray Leinster Omnibus* (includes *Operation Terror*, *Invaders of Space*, and *Checkpoint Lambda*), Sidgwick & Jackson, 1968; *Land of the Giants No. 3: The Unknown Danger*, Pyramid Publications, 1969; *Mutant Weapon* [and] *The Pirates of Zan*, Ace Books, 1972.

Writer of television scripts, radio plays, and fourteen motion pictures, more than a thousand short stories in *Saturday Evening Post* and other national magazines, many of the stories included in anthologies.

SIDELIGHTS: Jenkins' books have been published in eighteen languages—including Japanese, Hebrew, Arabic, Afrikaans—on every continent but Antarctica, and transcribed into Braille. In 1967 Embassy produced a motion picture of *The Wailing Asteroid*, entitled "The Terrornauts." *Avocational interests:* Science, history, Thomistic philosophy.

BIOGRAPHICAL/CRITICAL SOURCES: *Saturday Evening Post*, May 12, 1962, May 19, 1962; Samuel Moskowitz, *Seekers of Tomorrow: Masters of Modern Science Fiction*, World Publishing, 1966.

* * *

JENKS, C(larence) Wilfred 1909-

PERSONAL: Born March 7, 1909, in Bootle, Lancashire, England; son of Richard (a marine engineer) and Alice Sophia (Craig) Jenks; married Jane Louise Broverman, October 19, 1949; children: Craig Broverman, Bruce Frederick Edward. *Education:* Attended Liverpool Collegiate School; Gonville and Caius College, Cambridge, B.A., 1931, M.A., 1936, LL.D., 1953; Gray's Inn, Barrister-at-Law, 1936; additional study at Geneva School of International Studies. *Home:* 3 rue de Contamines, Geneva, Switzerland. *Office:* International Labour Office, Geneva, Switzerland.

CAREER: Called to the Bar, London, England, 1936; International Labour Office, Geneva, Switzerland, member of legal section. 1931-40, legal adviser, 1940-48, assistant director-general, 1948-64, deputy director-general, 1964-67, principal deputy director-general, 1967-70, director-general, 1970—. Assistant secretary general of Labour Conferences of American States in South American countries and Cuba, at regional conferences in India and Turkey, 1947, in India, 1950; member of International Labour Office delegation at United Nations Monetary and Financial Conference at Bretton Woods, 1944, at the Conference on International Organization, San Francisco, 1945, at International Copyright Conference, 1952, at International Conference on Peaceful Uses of Atomic Energy, 1955, 1958, at United Nations Conference on Law of the Sea, 1958, 1960, at United Nations Conference on Diplomatic Intercourse and Immunities, 1961, at United Nations Conference on Law of Treaties, 1968, and at other international conferences. Professor, Hague Academy of International Law, 1950, 1955, 1966. Honorary fellow of Gonville College and Caius College, University of Cambridge; honorary professor of Universidad Nacional Mayor de San Marcos de Lima and University of Lima. Chairman of Board, International Institute of Labour Studies, Geneva, and International Centre for Advanced Technical and Vocational Training, Turin.

MEMBER: Institute of International Law, International Society for Labour Law and Social Legislation, International Academy of Comparative Law, International Academy of Astronautics (corresponding), Athenaeum Club, Reform Club, Cosmos Club (Washington, D.C.) Awards, honors: Cecil Peace Prize, 1928; annual award, American Society of International Law, 1959; LL.D., University of Edinburgh, 1967, University of Delhi, 1971, Seoul National University, 1971, University of La Plata, 1972, and University of Costa Rica, 1972.

WRITINGS: (Editor) The International Labour Code, 1939: A Systematic Arrangement of the Conventions and Recommendations Adopted by the International Labour Conference, 1919-1939, International Labour Office, 1941, revised edition published as The International Labour Code, 1951: A Systematic Arrangement of the Conventions and Recommendations Adopted by the International Labour Conference, 1919-1951, 1952; (edior) Constitutional Provisions Concerning Social and Economic Policy: An International Collection of Texts Covering 450 Countries and Other Governments, International Labour Office, 1944; The Headquarters of International Institutions: A Study of Their Location and Status, Royal Institute of International Affairs, 1945; The International Protection of Trade Union Freedom, Praeger, 1957; The Common Law of Mankind, Praeger, 1958.

Human Rights and International Labour Standards, Praeger, 1960; International Immunities, Oceana, 1961; The Proper Law of International Organizations, Oceana, 1962; La Organizacion Internacional del trabajo y la protecion de los derechos humanos de America, Instituto de Derecho Social Facultad de Derecho y Ciencias Sociales, Universidad Nacional de Buenos Aires, 1962; Law, Freedom and Welfare, Oceana, 1963; (with others) International Law in a Changing World, Oceana, 1963; The Prospects of International Ajudication, Oceana, 1964; Space Law, Praeger, 1965; (with Arthur Larson and others) Sovereignity within the Law, Oceana, 1965; Law in the World Community, McKay, 1967; The World Beyond the Charter in Historical Perspective: A Tentative Synthesis of Four Stages of World Organization, Allen & Unwin, 1969; Britain and the I.L.O., David Davies Memorial Institute of International Studies, 1969; A New World of Law?: A Study of the Creative Imagination in International Law, Longmans, 1969; Social Justice in the Law of Nations: The I.L.O. Impact After Fifty Years,

Oxford University Press, 1970. Contributor to British Year Book of International Law and to legal journals.

AVOCATIONAL INTERESTS: Rowing, swimming, mountain walking, skiing, and skating.

*   *   *

JENKS, Randolph   1912-

PERSONAL: Born March 17, 1912, in Morristown, N.J.; son of William Pearson and Bertha (Cooke) Jenks; married Julia Post Swan, September 2, 1936; children: Julia Josephine (Mrs. John Trant III), Randolph, Marie Hamilton, Bertha Cooke. Education: Princeton University, B.A., 1936; University of Arizona, postgraduate study. Politics: Republican. Religion: Society of Friends. Home: 2146 East Fourth St., Tucson, Ariz. 72114.

CAREER: Museum of Northern Arizona, Flagstaff, curator of ornithology, 1932-36; teacher at Arizona Desert School and Greenfield's Preparatory School, 1937-40; Unit Laundry & Dry Cleaners, Tucson, Ariz., president, 1945-50; U. Diamond Cattle Ranch, Tucson, Ariz., owner and operator, 1956—. Member: American Ornithologists' Union, Nature Conservancy, Cooper Ornithology Society, Arizona Academy of Science, Arizona Pioneers Historical Society, Arizona State Park Association, Tucson Audubon Society (vice-president, 1954-58), Phi Beta Kappa, Sigma XI, Theta Chi; Elks Club, Princeton Club (both Tucson).

WRITINGS: (With Lou Blachly) Naming the Birds at a Glance, Knopf, 1963.

SIDELIGHTS: Jenks has worked among the Papago, Pima, and Seri Indian tribes, and done missionary work (as a Quaker) in the Sierra Madre Mountains of Sonora and Chihuahua, Mexico.

*   *   *

JENNINGS, Paul Francis   1918-

PERSONAL: Born June 20, 1918, in Leamington Spa, England; son of William Benedict and Mary Gertrude (Hewitt) Jennings; married Celia Blom, February 9, 1952; children: Susanna, Matthew, Theodora, Hilary, Quentin, Christiana. Education: Attended King Henry VIII and Douai Schools. Religion: Roman Catholic. Home: Hill House, Rectory Hill, East Bergholt, Suffolk, England. Office: Hill House, East Bergholt, Sussex, England.

CAREER: British Government, Central Office of Information, London, England, film strip writer, 1946-47; Colman Prentis & Varley (advertising firm), London, copywriter, 1947-49; Observer, London, columnist, 1949-66. Writer. Singer in Oriana Madrigal Society for fifteen years; now in Philharmonia Chorus, London; organizer of own madrigal group. Military service: British Army, Royal Corps of Signals; became lieutenant.

WRITINGS—All collections of Observer columns: Oddly Enough, Reinhardt, 1951; Even Oddlier, Reinhardt, 1952; Oddly Bodlikins, Reinhardt, 1953; Next to Oddliness, Reinhardt, 1955; Model Oddlies, Reinhardt, 1956; Gladly Oddly, Reinhardt, 1958; Idly Oddly, Reinhardt, 1959; I Said Oddly, Diddle I?, Reinhardt, 1961; Oodles of Oddlies, Reinhardt, 1963, Dufour, 1964; The Jenguin Pennings, Penguin, 1964; Oddly Ad Lib, Reinhardt, 1965; I Was Joking, Of Course, Reinhardt, 1968; It's an Odd Thing But, Reinhardt, 1971.

Other books: Fun, Newman Neame, 1957; Dunlopera: The Works and Workings of the Dunlop Rubber Company, Dunlop Rubber Co., 1961; The Hopping Basket (juvenile), Macdonald & Co., 1965; The Great Jelly of London (juvenile), Faber, 1967; The Living Village: A Report on Rural Life in England and Wales, Hodder

& Stoughton, 1968; *Just a Few Lines: Guinness Trains of Thought,* Guinness Superlatives, 1969.

WORK IN PROGRESS: Lyrics for a musical, "Vile Bodies"; libretto for chamber opera commissioned by Gulbenkian Foundation; a revue.

BIOGRAPHICAL/CRITICAL SOURCES: Punch, November 29, 1967, October 30, 1968; *Spectator,* October 25, 1968; *Books and Bookmen,* December, 1968; *Listener,* December 19, 1968; *New Statesman,* December 27, 1968.

* * *

JENNISON, Peter S(axe) 1922-

PERSONAL: Born July 2, 1922, in Swanton, Vt.; son of Clark Saxe and Louise (Warren) Jennison; married Jane Dryden Lowe, May 11, 1946; children: Andrew Clark. *Education:* Attended Phillips Academy, Andover, Mass., 1940; Middlebury College, B.A., 1947. *Politics:* Democrat. *Religion:* Episcopalian. *Home:* 99 Sturges Highway, Westport, Conn. 06880. *Agent:* Paul R. Reynolds, 599 Fifth Ave., New York, N.Y. 10017. *Office:* National Book Committee, One Park Ave., New York, N.Y. 10016.

CAREER: Publishers' Weekly, New York, N.Y., assistant editor, 1947-52; Economic Cooperation Administration, Stockholm, Sweden, information officer, 1948-49; American Book Publishers Council, New York, N.Y., assistant managing director, 1952-57; New York University, Graduate Institute of Book Publishing, New York, N.Y., assistant director, 1959-62; American Book Publishers Council, New York, N.Y., assistant managing director, 1962-64; National Book Committee, New York, N.Y., executive director, 1964—. Lecturer, School of Library Service, Columbia University. Consultant, Bureau of Educational and Cultural Affairs, Department of State, 1961; consultant, Franklin Book Programs, 1962-64. Chairman, Weston (Conn.) Democratic Town Committee, 1960-62; chairman, Friends of Weston Public Library, 1961-63. *Military service:* U.S. Army, Office of Strategic Services, 1943-46; became technical sergeant. *Member:* P.E.N., Authors League of America, American Library Association, The Players, The Coffee House.

WRITINGS: American Books in the Near East, Central Africa and Asia (report of 2nd conference on American books abroad, Harriman, N.Y., 1957), Bowker, 1957; *The Mimosa Smokers,* Crowell, 1959; (with William Kurth) *Books in the Americas: A Study of the Principal Barriers to the Booktrade in the Americas,* published for American Book Publishers Council by Pan American Union, 1960, summary published separately as *Report on Book Distribution,* 1960; *Freedom to Read* (pamphlet), Public Affairs Committee, 1963; *The Governor,* Morrow, 1963; (editor with Robert N. Sheridan) *The Future of General Adult Books and Reading in America,* American Library Assoiation, 1971.

WORK IN PROGRESS: A novel, tentatively titled *Visas.*

SIDELIGHTS: Jennison has done research in West Africa, the Middle East, Europe, and Asia.

* * *

JENSEN, De Lamar 1925-

PERSONAL: Born April 22, 1925, in Roseworth, Idaho; son of Jacob A. and Johanna (Petersen) Jensen; married Mary White, May 18, 1951; children: Jonna Lu, Marde, Bradford, Emily, Christine. *Education:* Brigham Young University, B.A., 1952; Columbia University, M.A., 1953, Ph.D., 1957. *Politics:* Independent. *Religion:* Latter-Day Saints. *Home:* 1079 Briar Ave., Provo, Utah 84601.

CAREER: High school teacher in Idaho, 1947-48; New York University, New York, N.Y., instructor in history, 1954-57; Brigham Young University, Provo, Utah, in-structor, 1957-58, assistant professor, 1958-61, associate professor, 1961-66, professor of history, 1966—, chairman of history department, 1967—. *Military service:* U.S. Army Air Forces, 1943-46; served as second lieutenant. *Member:* American Historical Association, Renaissance Society of America, Historical Association (England), Verein fer Reformations-Geschichte. *Awards, honors:* Rockefeller Foundation research fellowship, 1964; research grant from the National Foundation for the Humanities, 1970.

WRITINGS: (Editor and author of introduction) *Machiavelli: Cynic, Patriot, or Political Scientist?,* Heath, 1960; *Diplomacy and Dogmatism: Bernardino de Mendoza and the French Catholic League,* Harvard University Press, 1964; (compiler) *The Expansion of Europe: Motives, Methods, and Meanings,* Heath, 1967. Contributor to *Wye, Western Humanities Review, Brigham Young University Studies, History and Theory,* and other history journals.

WORK IN PROGRESS: Research on international relations theory in early modern Europe.

* * *

JEROME, Judson (Blair) 1927-

PERSONAL: Born February 8, 1927, in Tulsa, Okla.; son of Ralph (an oil royalty broker) and Gwen (Stewart) Jerome; married Martha-Jane Pierce, June 20, 1948; children: Michelle, Elizabeth, Polly, Jennifer, Christopher. *Education:* University of Oklahoma, student, 1943-45; University of Chicago, M.A., 1950; Ohio State University, Ph.D., 1953. *Agent:* Ann Elmo Agency, Inc., 545 Fifth Ave., New York, N.Y. 10017. *Office:* Downhill Farm, Hancock, Md. 21750.

CAREER: Antioch College, Yellow Springs, Ohio, chairman of literature department, 1953-63; College of the Virgin Islands, St. Thomas, chairman of the humanities division, 1963-65; Antioch College, professor of literature and director of Inner College, 1965-69, professor of literature at Washington-Baltimore campus, 1969-71; Twentieth Century Fund, New York, N.Y., research director of Contemporary Commune Study, 1971-72; free-lance writer and lecturer, 1972—. *Military service:* U.S. Air Force, 1945-47; became sergeant. *Awards, honors:* Huntington Hartford fellow, 1959; Amy Lowell traveling scholarship, 1960-61.

WRITINGS: "Winter in Eden" (verse drama), produced in Yellow Springs, Ohio, at Antioch College, 1955; (editor with Nolan Miller) *New Campus Writing: Number Three,* Grove, 1959; *Light in the West* (poetry), Golden Quill, 1962; (editor with Miller) *New Campus Writing: Number Four,* Grove, 1962; *Poet and the Poem* (essays), Writer's Digest, 1963, revised edition, 1973; "The Wandering Jew" (verse drama), produced in Yellow Springs at Antioch College, 1963; "Candle in the Straw" (verse drama), produced in St. Paul, Minn., at Hamline University, 1963 (later published in *Religious Theatre,* fall, 1964); *The Ocean's Warning to the Skin Diver and Other Love Poems,* Crown Point Press, 1964; "The Glass Mountain" (verse drama), produced in St. Thomas, at College of the Virgin Islands, 1964; *The Fell of the Dark* (novel), Houghton, 1966; *Serenade* (poetry), Crown Point Press, 1968; *Poetry: Premeditated Art* (textbook), Houghton, 1968; *Culture Out of Anarchy: The Reconstruction of American Highter Learning,* Herder & Herder, 1970; *Plays for an Imaginary Theater* (poetry), University of Illinois Press, 1970.

Anthologized in *Contemporary Ohio Poetry: An Anthology of Mid-Century Ohio Poetry,* edited by George Abbe, Poets of America Publishing Co., 1959, *Borestone Mountain Poetry Awards, 1962-64: A Compilation of Original Poetry Published in Magazines of the English-Speaking*

World in 1961-1963, edited by Lionel Stevenson and others, three volumes, Pacific Books, 1962-64, *Reflections on a Gift of Watermelon Pickle . . . and Other Modern Verse*, edited by Stephen Dunning and others, Scott, Foresman, 1966, *Borestone Mountain Poetry Awards, 1966*, Pacific Books, 1966, *Honey and the Gall*, edited by Chad Walsh, Macmillan, 1967, and *The Creative Writer*, edited by Aron M. Mathieu, revised edition, Writer's Digest, 1968. Author of column "Poetry: How and Why," *Writer's Digest*, 1961—. Contributor of poetry, fiction, drama, criticism, and social commentary to some sixty periodicals, including *Antioch Review, Poetry, Nation, Saturday Review, Prairie Schooner*, and *Colorado Quarterly*.

WORK IN PROGRESS: *Nude*, a novel; *The Compleat Poet*, on the profession of poetry; *Crimes of Innocence*, short stories; *Rumors of Change*, poems; and *Communal Living*, a study of contemporary commune movements.

SIDELIGHTS: Critical reaction to Jerome's poetry has been mixed. Of *Light in the West*, John Engels states that Jerome "often fails through a formal baffling of his vision; his tone is 'structural,' deriving from an exaggeratedly sedate, obvious, and conventional form. But he's a good poet, and there's no temptation to dismiss the book.... [He] accomplishes [his] themes with a real vitality of metaphor, his forms remaining unobtrusive and functional, the conceptions and executions subtle, the images sharply visible, the themes true and noble."

Jerome's novel has had a rather positive critical reaction. Kenneth Lamott praises Jerome's ability to involve the reader in the action of the story. "[He] has a quite unusual ability to breathe life into even the most unlikely clay. He forces us both to care about his people and to care for them, to feel the gray horror of guilt, the despair of alcoholic escape, the salvation that can come with lovemaking, the terror of facing a dreaded and desired solution. In the end we find ourselves observing not merely characters in a novel but a coherent world of people who have been made to matter."

On the subject of art in literature, Jerome has said: ". . .I believe good art is popular art (though the terms aren't reversible). As did Einstein (whom I do not otherwise resemble), I believe that important truths are ultimately simple; the job of the artist (like the job of the scientist) is to find in the jumble and complexity of experience its underlying structure and pattern and to make that evident. . . .The model I try to work on is that of drama rather than fiction: I would like to develop (who wouldn't) Shakespeare's faculty for combining rich suggestiveness with compelling characterization and story."

Jerome adds: "I'm rather old-fashioned in my literary taste. Recent fiction (of which I read less than I ought) depresses me with its self-conscious artiness and preoccupation with the exotic, the *avant*, with meaningless formal liberty. Though one hesitates to mention it in literary circles, I admire *The Grapes of Wrath* and *For Whom the Bell Tolls*. . . . I like Henry James, too. And Twain and Melville and Flaubert and Dostoevsky and Jane Austen—though I can't put them all together in any tradition which would lead to my book. I like each word, each detail, especially each scene to matter, to advance, for the prose to be lean and necessary and transparent (in the sense that the reader is never distracted by the writing for its own sake). I aim for economy, force and the beauty of simple language long deliberated."

BIOGRAPHICAL/CRITICAL SOURCES: *Poetry*, September, 1963; *Saturday Review*, October 26, 1963, May 21, 1966; *Virginia Quarterly Review*, autumn, 1963; *Library Journal*, February 1, 1966, March 15, 1966; *New York Times Book Review*, April 10, 1966; *Book Week*, June 5, 1966.

* * *

JESSOP, Thomas Edmund   1896-

PERSONAL: Born September 10, 1896, in Huddersfield, England; son of Newton and Georgiana (Swift) Jessop; married Dora Anne Nugent Stewart, July 7, 1930. *Education:* University of Leeds, B.A., 1921, M.A., 1922; Oriel College, Oxford, B.Litt., 1924. *Religion:* Methodist. *Home:* 73 Park Ave., Hull, England.

CAREER: University of Glasgow, Glasgow, Scotland, lecturer in logic and metaphysics, 1925-28; University of Hull, Hull, England, professor of philosophy, 1928-61, professor emeritus, 1961—. Visiting lecturer at Universities of Paris, Brussels, Athens, Bombay, Calcutta, and others, and at California State University at Los Angeles and San Francisco State College; educational work with H.M. Forces, 1940—. British Council of Churches,, chairman of adult religious education committee, 1948-62; World Methodist Council, member of executive board, 1956—. *Military service:* British Army, 1916-18; became lieutenant; received Military Cross. *Member:* Institut International de Philosophie (assessor, 1960-62), Archives Inernationales d'Histoire d'Idees (editorial committee), Royal Institute of Philosophy (council, 1950—), Mind Association, Aristotelian Society, British Psychological Society (fellow). *Awards, honors:* Order of British Empire for educational work with British forces; Litt.D. from University of Dublin and University of Hull; Medaille d'Honneur from University of Brussels.

WRITINGS: *Montreux and Lake of Geneva* (guide book), Hazel, Watson & Viney, 1926; *Locarno and Its Valleys*, Orell Fuessli, 1928; *A Bibliography of George Berkeley* (includes inventory of Berkeley's manuscript remains by A.A. Luce), Oxford University Press, 1934, B. Franklin, 1968; (editor) *Berkeley's Principles of Human Knowledge*, A. Brown, 1937; *Science and Religion*, Industrial Christian Fellowship, 1938; *Nature, History and God* (address given at annual conference of Fellowship of the Kingdom), Epworth, 1938; *A Bibliography of David Hume and of Scottish Philosophy from Francis Hutcheson to Lord Balfour*, A. Brown, Russell, 1966; (translator with J.W. Harvey) R. Metz, *A Hundred Years of British Philosophy*, Allen & Unwin, 1938; *Has the Christian Way Failed?*, Epworth, 1940; *Law and Love: A Study of the Christian Ethic*, S.C.M. Press, 1940, revised edition, Epworth, 1948; *The Treaty of Versailles: Was It Just?*, Thomas Nelson, 1942; *Science and the Spiritual: The Threshold of Theology*, Macmillan, 1942; *Basic Religion* (seven broadcast talks), Epworth, 1944; *Effective Religion*, Epworth, 1944; *The Christian Faith*, Churches' Committee (for Supplementing Religious Education Among Men in H.M. Forces), 1944; *The Christian Way*, Churches' Committee, 1944; *Reason and Religion: A Plea for a Rational Faith*, Union of Modern Free Churchmen, 1945; *The Christian Institutions*, Churches' Committee, 1945; *The Padre's Hour: Technique of Adult Religious Education*, Churches' Committee, 1945; *Man, God and Society: An Outline of Christian Truth*, Churches' Committee, briefing notes published as *Life in the Christian Society*, 1947; *Evangelism and Education: The Presentation of Religion to Adults*, S.C.M. Press, 1947; *The Freedom of the Individual in Society* (lectures given at Queens University, Toronto, January, 1948), Ryerson, 1948; *Reasonable Living*, S.C.M. Press, 1948; (editor with A.A. Luce) *The Works of George Berkeley*, nine volumes, Thomas Nelson, 1948-57; *Why Religion?*, Bureau of Current Affairs, 1949; *Christianity for Adults*, Epworth, 1950; *Ideals and Realities*, Epworth, 1950; (editor) *Berkeley's Philosophical Writings*, Thomas Nelson, 1952; *Social Ethics, Christian and Natural: A Problem for the Teaching Church*, Epworth, 1952; *On Reading the English Bible*, Allenson, 1958; *George Berkeley*, published for British Council by Longmans, Green, 1959, London House, 1961; *An Introduction to Christian*

Doctrine, Thomas Nelson, 1960; *The Christian Morality* (six lectures given at Cambridge, 1958), Epworth, 1960, Verry, 1964; *Thomas Hobbes,* published for British Council by Longmans, Green, 1960, London House, 1962; *The Enduring Passion,* Allenson, 1961; (editor and translator) *Spinoza on Freedom of Thought: Selections from Tractatus Theologico-Politicus and Tractutus Politicus,* Casalini, 1962; *Church and Society: Social Service and Social Challenge* (inaugural lecture, City Temple, London, November 18, 1963), Independent Press, 1963; *Not This Way: A Methodist Examination of the Final 1968 Anglican-Methodist Union Scheme, with Special Reference to the Service of Reconciliation and the Theology Which Lies Behind It, and a Plea for Theological Integrity,* Marcham Manor Press, 1969. Contributor to *Proceedings* of British Academy, 1964.

WORK IN PROGRESS: Revised editions of *A Bibliography of George Berkeley* and *A Bibliography of David Hume and of Scottish Philosophy from Francis Hutcheson to Lord Balfour.*

AVOCATIONAL INTERESTS: Gardening and travel.

* * *

JOHNS, John E(dwin) 1921-

PERSONAL: Born November 15, 1921, in Ozark, Ala.; son of Thomas Maxwell (a citrus grower) and Susan (Spires) Johns; married Martha Mauney, August 23, 1947; children: John Edwin, Jr., Steven Maxwell, Marcus Mauney. *Education:* Furman University, A.B., 1947; University of North Carolina, M.A., 1948, Ph.D., 1959. *Politics:* Democrat. *Religion:* Baptist. *Home:* 418 North Blvd., De Land, Fla. 32720. *Office:* Stetson University, De Land, Fla. 32720.

CAREER: Stetson University, DeLand, Fla., 1948—, former professor of history and political science, business manager, now president. Johns Enterprises, Lakeland, Fla., vice-president, 1958—; DeLand Federal Savings & Loan Association, director; West Volusia Industrial Board, chairman. DeLand Chamber of Commerce, vice-president. *Military service:* U.S. Army Air Forces, 1942-45; became first lieutenant; received Distinguished Flying Cross, Air Medal with four oak leaf clusters, Purple Heart, three battle stars. *Member:* Southern Historical Association, Southern Association of College Business Officers, Florida Historical Society, Rotary Club (president, 1959-60; district governor, 1962-63).

WRITINGS: Florida During the Civil War, University of Florida Press, 1963.

* * *

JOHNSON, Albert (Franklin) 1904-

PERSONAL: Born August 14, 1904, in Arkansas; son of George Webster and Lena (Keep) Johnson; married Bertha French (a teacher and drama director), January 30, 1932; children: Christina. *Education:* University of Redlands, A.B., 1930; graduate study at Yale University, 1930-32, State University of Iowa, 1937-38. *Politics:* Democrat. *Religion:* Baptist. *Home:* 2010 South Lane, Redlands, Calif. 92373. *Office:* Department of Drama, University of Redlands, Redlands, Calif. 92373.

CAREER: Cornell College, Mount Vernon, Iowa, director of department of drama, 1932-47, and founder of first summer theatre west of the Mississippi; La Jolla Players, La Jolla, Calif., director, 1948-50; University of Redlands, Redlands, Calif., director of department of drama, 1951—. Co-director with wife of more than four hundred plays produced for stage and air, of Redlands Bowl summer productions, 1952-58, of residence company at National Christian Writers Center, Green Lake, Wis., 1959-62, and of Drama Trio on cross-country tours. Adapter of "Hamlet" and "Romeo and Juliet" for National

Broadcasting Co. television spectaculars, 1961, 1962. Member of theatre for victory committee, National Theatre Conference, 1942-45; national president, American Communal Theatre, 1943-45; National Council of Churches, member of religious drama committee, 1957—, of broadcasting and film commission, 1962—.

MEMBER: International Christian Writers Conference, American Educational Theatre Association, National Writers Conference, American Association of University Professors. *Awards, honors:* Freedoms Foundation award, 1957; citation, National Christian Writers Conference, 1961.

WRITINGS: Drama Technique and Philosophy, Judson, 1963; *Psalms for the New Millenium* (verse), Wake-Brock, 1964; *Church Plays and How to Stage Them,* United Church Press, 1966; *Best Church Plays: A Bibliography of Religious Drama,* Pilgrim Press, 1968; (with wife, Bertha Johnson) *Drama for Classroom and Stage,* A.S. Barnes, 1969; (with Bertha Johnson) *Directing Methods,* A.S. Barnes, 1970; *Shakespeare Vignettes: Adaptations for Acting,* A.S. Barnes, 1970; (with Bertha Johnson) *Drama for Junior High with Selected Scenes,* A.S. Barnes, 1971; (with Bertha Johnson) *Oral Reading: Creative and Interpretive,* A.S. Barnes, 1971; (with Bertha Johnson) *To See a Play: A Primer for Playgoers,* A.S. Barnes, 1972; (with Bertha Johnson) *Shakespeare at My Shoulder,* A.S. Barnes, 1972.

Plays: *Leave to Marry* (three-act comedy), Row, Peterson, 1943; *Days without Daddy* (three-act comedy), Row, Peterson, 1944; *Go Ye to Bethlehem* (spoken cantata), Row, Peterson, 1944; *Parents Are Like That* (three-act comedy), Iowa Art Craft Play Co., 1948; *Westward from Eden: A Choric Drama for Churches* Row, Peterson, 1944; *Love Your Neighbor* (three-act comedy), Row, Peterson, 1945; *So Help Me!* (three-act comedy), Heuer 1946; *Maybe It's Love* (three-act comedy-drama), Heuer, 1947; *If This Be Bliss* (three-act comedy), Heuer, 1947; *Boys About Babbette* (three-act comedy-drama), Heuer, 1947; *People Are Talking* (three-act comedy), Heuer, 1948; *Glory to Goldy* (three-act comedy), Heuer, 1948; *We're in the Money* (three-act comedy), Baker's Plays, 1949; *Dear Dexter* (three-act comedy), Heuer, c.1950; *Head Over Heels* (three-act comedy), Heuer, c.1950; *Out on a Limb* (three-act comedy), Art Craft, c.1950; *Sweet Sue* (three-act comedy), Heuer, c.1950; *Roger Williams and Mary: A Drama for Three Players,* Friendship, 1957; *Conquest in Burma,* Friendship, 1962; *The People Versus Christ: A Drama Trio Play,* Baker's Plays, 1962; *Even the Hater: A Drama Trio Play,* Baker's Plays, 1967.

WORK IN PROGRESS: "Lower Than Angels," commissioned by National Council of Churches of Christ, and "Except for John Leland"; a television adaptation of "This Union Under God," a play about Abraham and Mary Lincoln.

SIDELIGHTS: Johnson's method of teaching is unconventional. He tries to "draw out rather than cram full." He and his wife talk theory and technique only after their students have discovered their need for such things—then theory and technique are related to what they are trying to do in performance. "I probably do my best teaching in rehearsals," he says.

* * *

JOHNSON, Annabell Jones 1921-
(A. Johnson; A.E. Johnson, joint pseudonym)

PERSONAL: Born June 18, 1921, in Kansas City, Mo.; daughter of Burnam R. and Mary Estelle (Ball) Jones; married Edgar Raymond Johnson (a ceramic artist, now a writer), September 14, 1949. *Education:* College of William and Mary, student, 1939-40. *Home:* 2925 South Teller St., Denver, Colo. 80227.

CAREER: Worked in publishing houses, as a librarian, legal secretary, in other secretarial posts prior to 1957; author, mainly in collaboration with husband. 1957—. *Awards, honors:* Friends of American Writers award, 1960, for *The Secret Gift;* Western Writers of America Golden Spur award, 1966, for *The Burning Glass;* William Allen White Children's Book Award, 1967, for *The Grizzly.*

WRITINGS—With husband, Edgar Johnson: *The Big Rock Candy,* Crowell, 1957; *The Black Symbol,* Harper, 1959; *Torrie,* Harper, 1960; *The Bearcat,* Harper, 1960; *The Rescued Heart,* Harper, 1961; *Pickpocket Run,* Harper, 1961; *Wilderness Bride,* Harper, 1962; *A Golden Touch,* Harper, 1963; *The Grizzly,* Harper, 1964; *A Peculiar Magic,* Houghton, 1965; *The Burning Glass,* Harper, 1966; *Count Me Gone,* Simon & Schuster, 1968; *The Last Knife* (five short stories), Simon & Schuster, 1971.

With husband, under joint pseudonym A.E. Johnson: *The Secret Gift,* Doubleday, 1961; *A Blues I Can Whistle,* Four Winds, 1969.

Under name A. Johnson: *As a Speckled Bird,* Crowell, 1956.

AVOCATIONAL INTERESTS: Ceramics and gardening.

BIOGRAPHICAL/CRITICAL SOURCES: The Children's Bookshelf, Child Study Association of America, Bantam, 1965; *Books for Children, 1960-1965,* American Library Assocation, 1966; G. Robert Carlsen, *Books and the Teen-Age Reader,* Harper, 1967; *Young Readers' Review,* June, 1968; *Book World,* October 13, 1968; Nancy Larrick, *A Parent's Guide to Children's Reading,* 3rd edition, Doubleday, 1969; *New York Times Book Review,* November 9, 1969, May 2, 1971.

*   *   *

JOHNSON, B(ryan) S(tanley William)   1933-

PERSONAL: Born February 5, 1933, in London, England; children: two. *Education:* King's College, London, B.A. (honours in English), 1959. *Home:* 9 Dagmar Terrace, London N1, England. *Agent:* Michael Bakewell Assoc., 118 Tottenham Court Road, London W1, England.

CAREER: Writer; film and television director/producer. *Awards, honors:* Gregory awards for *Travelling People,* and for *Poems;* Somerset Maugham award, 1967, for *Trawl;* Grand Prix, Tours International Short Film Festival, and Melbourne International Short Film Festival, both 1968, for *You're Human Like the Rest of Them;* First Gregynog Arts fellow, University of Wales, 1970.

WRITINGS: Travelling People (novel), Constable, 1963, *Poems,* Constable, 1964, Chilmark, 1964; *Albert Angelo* (novel), Constable, 1964; (with Zulfikar Ghose) *Statement Against Corpses* (short stories), Constable, 1964; (author of text for photographs by Julia Trevelyan Oman) *Street Children,* Hodder & Stoughton, 1964; *Trawl* (novel), Secker & Warburg, 1966; (editor) *The Evacuees* (personal narratives), Gollancz, 1968; *The Unfortunates* (novel), Panther House, 1969; *House Mother Normal: A Geriatric Comedy,* limited edition, Trigram Press, 1971, Collins, 1971. *Poems Two,* Trigram Press, 1972; *Christie Malry's Own Double-Entry* (novel), Collins, 1973, Richard Seaver, in press; *All Bull: The National Servicemen,* (edited personal accounts), Alison & Busby, in press; *Aren't You Rather Young to be Writing Your Memoirs?* (selected short prose), Hutchinson, in press.

Plays: "One Sodding Thing After Another" (commissioned by Royal Court Theatre, 1967); "Whose Dog Are You?," first produced in London at Quipu Basement Theatre, January, 1971 (also see below); "B.S. Johnson versus God" (includes "Whose Dog Are You" and *You're Human Like the Rest of Them*), first produced in London at Basement Theatre, January 18, 1971.

Radio play: "Entry," produced on BBC Third Programme, 1965.

Films: *You're Human Like the Rest of Them* (produced by British Film Institute, 1967; also see above), published in *New English Dramatists 14,* Penguin, 1970; "Up Yours Too, Guillaume Apollinaire!," produced by British Film Institute, 1968; "Paradigm," produced by Elisabeth Films, 1969.

Television Films: "The Evacuees," documentary based on his own book, first produced on BBC 2, October, 1968; "The Unfortunates," documentary based on his own book, produced on BBC 2, February, 1969; "Charlie Whildon Talking, Singing, and Playing," documentary produced on BBC 2, March, 1969; "Bath," documentary on architecture of city, produced on BBC 2, June, 1969; "The Smithsons on Housing," architectural documentary, produced on BBC 2, July, 1970; "On Reflection: Sam Johnson," documentary produced by London Weekend Television, January, 1971; "On Reflection: Alexander Herzen," produced by London Weekend Television, April, 1971; "Not Counting the Savages," produced on BBC-TV, January, 1972; "Hafod a Henref," produced by Harlech Television, April, 1972.

Represented in anthologies. Contributor to *London Times, Observer, New Statesman, Spectator, Times Literary Supplement, Encounter, Ambit, Listener,* and other periodicals. Poetry editor, *Transatlantic Review,* 1965—.

WORK IN PROGRESS: The Matrix Trilogy, novels, publication of first of three by Hutchinson, expected in 1974.

*   *   *

JOHNSON, Carol Virginia   1928-

PERSONAL: Born September 7, 1928, in Rockford, Ill.; daughter of Harry Ernest (a pharmacist) and Pearl (Ryburn) Johnson. *Education:* College of St. Catherine, B.A., 1950; Marquette University, M.A., 1958; Indiana University, postgraduate study, 1958; State University of Iowa, M.F.A., 1959; University of Bristol, postgraduate study, 1961-63. *Politics:* Liberal. *Religion:* Roman Catholic. *Office:* English Department, University of North Carolina, Greensboro, N.C. 27412.

CAREER: University of North Carolina, Greensboro, university lecturer in English, 1959-60, 1963—. *Member:* Modern Language Association of America. *Awards, honors:* Academy of American Poets prize for "Threnode," 1959.

WRITINGS: Figure for Scamander: Poems and Translations, Martinsville High School, 1960, reissued as *Figures for Scamander and Others* (poems, 1950-1963), Swallow Press, 1964. Contributor of poetry, articles, essays, criticism, and reviews to periodicals, including *Sewanee Review, Shenandoah, Commonweal, Poetry, Spectator.*

WORK IN PROGRESS: Strategies of Reason, a study of the uses of reason in poetry; poetry and translations.

SIDELIGHTS: Lived and traveled independently in Europe, 1960-61, then spent two years in England. *Avocational interests:* Theater, painting, music.

BIOGRAPHICAL/CRITICAL SOURCES: The Seminars at Martinsville, T.H. Carter, 1960.

*   *   *

JOHNSON, David G(eorge)   1906-

PERSONAL: Born August 5, 1906, in London, England; married; wife's maiden surname, Thornes; children: Michael, Colin. *Education:* Attended school in England.

Home: 172 Purley Downs Rd., Sanderstead, Surrey, England. *Office:* Link House Publications Ltd., Link House, Dingwall Ave., Croydon, Surrey, England.

CAREER: Link House Publications, Croyden, Surrey, England, 1923—, worked in advertising and editorial sections of specialist publications, now editor-in-chief of do-it-yourself books. *Member:* Royal Horticultural Society, Royal Automobile Club.

WRITINGS: (With Oscar Heidenstam) *Modern Body Building: A Complete Guide to the Promotion of Fitness, Strength, and Physique,* Faber, 1955, Emerson, 1958, 3rd edition, Faber, 1969; *Man About the House: A Do it Yourself Guide,* Faber, 1963, Transatlantic, 1964; *Home Improvements: A Do-it-Yourself Guide,* Stanley Paul, 1973. Managing editor, *Do it Yourself, Do it Yourself Annual, Do it Yourself Gardening Annual,* and *Do it Yourself Retailing.*

* * *

JOHNSON, Edgar 1901-

PERSONAL: Born December 1, 1901, in Brooklyn, N.Y.; son of Walter Conover (a sales manager) and Emily (Haas) Johnson; married Eleanor Kraus (an editor, teacher, and literary researcher), June 21, 1933; children: Judith Evelyn (Mrs. James T. Sherwin), Laurence Michael. *Education:* Columbia University, A.B. (honors), 1922, graduate student, 1922-24, 1926-27.

CAREER: Instructor or lecturer in English at Columbia University, New York, N.Y., 1922-24, Washington University, St. Louis, Mo., 1924-26, Hunter College (now Hunter College of the City University of New York), New York, N.Y., 1926-27; City College of the City University of New York, New York, N.Y., 1927-71, began as tutor, became professor and chairman of English department, 1949-64, and Distinguished Professor of English. Visiting professor at Vassar College, 1943, University of Hawaii, 1955, University of Chicago, 1956, Princeton University, 1967; Kenan Distinguished Visiting Professor, Vanderbilt University, 1969-70. *Member:* Modern Language Association of America, Council for Basic Education, American Association of University Professors, P.E.N. (vice-president, 1959-61, 1963—; president, 1961-63), Dickens Fellowship (London; vice-president, 1963), Phi Beta Kappa, Century Association, Lotos Club. *Awards, honors:* Fulbright senior scholar, University of Edinburgh, and Guggenheim fellow in England and Scotland, 1956-57, 1966-67; Officier de l'Ordre des Palines Academiques (France), 1966; fellow, Royal Society of Arts (England), 1968; American Heritage biography prize, 1969, for *Sir Walter Scott: The Great Unknown.*

WRITINGS: Unweave a Rainbow: A Sentimental Fantasy, Doubleday, 1931; *One Mighty Torrent: The Drama of Biography,* Stackpole, 1937; *The Praying Mantis,* Stackpole, 1937; (editor) *A Treasury of Biography,* Howell, Soskin, 1941; (editor and author of introduction) *A Treasury of Satire,* Simon & Schuster, 1945; (editor) *The Heart of Charles Dickens, as Revealed in His Letters to Angela Burdett-Coutts,* Duell, Sloan & Pearce, 1952 (published in England as *Letters from Charles Dickens to Angela Burdett-Coutts, 1841-1865,* J. Cape, 1953); *Charles Dickens: His Tragedy and Triumph* (biography; Book-of-the-Month Club selection), Simon & Schuster, 1952; (editor with wife, Eleanor Johnson) *The Dickens Theatrical Reader,* Little, Brown, 1964; *Sir Walter Scott: The Great Unknown,* Macmillan, 1970. Contributor to scholarly publications. Editor-in-chief, Dell's "Great Lives and Thoughts" series. Also editor of Bulwer Lytton, *Last Days of Pompeii,* Limited Editions Club, Dickens, *A Christmas Carol,* Columbia University Press, *Oliver Twist,* Houghton, *A Tale of Two Cities,* Pocket Books, *Dombey and Son, Martin Chuzzlewit, Pickwick Papers,* and *Bleak House,* all Dell, *David Copperfield,* New American Library, Walter Scott, *Rob Roy,* Houghton, and *Waverley,* New American Library.

SIDELIGHTS: Johnson began research on *Sir Walter Scott: The Great Unknown* in 1956, started writing in 1961, and ended up with a manuscript of 500,000 words in 78 chapters, a biography which many critics, including Thomas Lask, have called "the definitive life for this century." "The first response to this magnificent work," said C.P. Snow, "is a mixture of gratitude, admiration and nationalistic envy. Here is an American scholar who, after giving us a biography of Dickens so complete that the task won't be tried again for generations, has done precisely the same for Walter Scott. One would have thought that these books might have been written slightly more easily this side of the Atlantic. The simple fact is, they haven't been. They are supreme examples of American literary scholarship at its best, with its energy, its total conscientiousness, its willingness to devote years of a life-time to a big job."

Winner of the first American Heritage biography prize in 1969 (at $20,000 believed to be the largest literary award in the U.S.), Johnson obviously loves his subject. According to Harry Gilroy of the *New York Times,* Johnson's "ultimate judgment about Scott ... was this: 'He was one of the great voices of sanity in the 19th century. People read him for the adventure and the melodrama, but I imagine that the sanity would seep and percolate into their minds, and that contributed to his lasting popularity.'" Noting the unreality and flatness of most of Scott's characters, however, Geoffrey Wolff writes that "the life rather than the work, and Johnson's story of the life rather than his almost wholesale endorsement of the work, is a thing of grace and genius."

AVOCATIONAL INTERESTS: Drama, music, art, architecture, swimming, contract bridge, conversation.

BIOGRAPHICAL/CRITICAL SOURCES: Library Journal, September 15, 1952, June 15, 1970; *New York Times,* January 11, 1953, November 5, 1968, September 18, 1970; *Commonweal,* January 16, 1953; *New Republic,* January 26, 1953; *Atlantic,* February, 1953; *Virginia Quarterly Review,* autumn, 1970; *Newsweek,* September 7, 1970; *Nation,* October 26, 1970; *Washington Post,* December 25, 1970.

* * *

JOHNSON, Edgar Raymond 1912-
(A. E. Johnson, joint pseudonym)

PERSONAL: Born October 24, 1912, in Washoe, Mont.; son of Oscar and Martha Johnson; married Annabell Jones (a writer), September 14, 1949. *Education:* Studied at Billings Polytechnic Institute, Kansas City Art Institute, New York State College of Ceramics at Alfred University. *Home:* 2925 South Teller, Denver, Colo. 80227.

CAREER: Ceramic artist, heading department of ceramics at Kansas City (Mo.), Art Institute, 1948-49; also model maker, jeweler, and wood carver, with work exhibited in one-man show in New York, N.Y., and included in Museum of Modern Art exhibition of best in American handcraft; now a free-lance writer, mainly in collaboration with wife. Sometime restorer of antique musical instruments for Smithsonian Institution, Washington, D.C. *Awards, honors:* Friends of American Writers award, 1960, for *The Secret Gift;* Western Writers of America Golden Spur award, 1966, for *The Burning Glass;* William Allen White Children's Book Award, 1967, for *The Grizzly.*

WRITINGS With wife, Annabel Johnson: The Big Rock Candy, Crowell, 1957; *The Black Symbol,* Harper, 1959; *Torrie,* Harper, 1960; *The Bearcat,* Harper, 1960; *The Rescued Heart,* Harper, 1961; *Pickpocket Run,* Harper,

1961; *Wilderness Bride*, Harper, 1962; *A Golden Touch*, Harper, 1963; *The Grizzly*, Harper, 1964; *A Peculiar Magic*, Houghton, 1965; *The Burning Glass*, Harper, 1966; *Count Me Gone*, Simon & Schuster, 1968; *The Last Knife* (five short stories), Simon & Schuster, 1971. With wife, under joint pseudonym A.E. Johnson: *The Secret Gift*, Doubleday, 1961; *A Blues I Can Whistle*, Four Winds, 1969.

AVOCATIONAL INTERESTS: Seventeenth-century music, fishing.

BIOGRAPHICAL/CRITICAL SOURCES: The Children's Bookshelf, Child Study Association of America, Bantam, 1965; *Books for Children, 1960-1965*, American Library Association, 1966; G. Robert Carlsen, *Books and the Teen-Age Reader*, Harper, 1967; *Young Readers' Review*, June, 1968; *Book World*, October 13, 1968; Nancy Larrick, *A Parent's Guide to Children's Reading*, 3rd edition, Doubleday, 1969; *New York Times Book Review*, November 9, 1969, May 2, 1971.

*   *   *

JOHNSON, Elmer Douglas   1915-

PERSONAL: Born August 2, 1915, in Durham, N.C.; son of Ulysses S. (a farmer and merchant) and Nancy M. (Smith) Johnson; married Rosa Shepherd, November 7, 1936; children: Eric Shepherd, Lynn Douglas, Elaine Carol, Giles Kerry. *Education:* University of North Carolina, B.A., 1936, M.A., 1942, Ph.D., 1951. *Religion:* Presbyterian. *Home:* 1200 Milton Lane, Radford, Va. 24141. *Office:* Library, Radford College, Radford, Va. 24141.

CAREER: Tennessee Valley Authority, Guntersville, Ala., camp librarian, 1936-40; U.S. War Department, Arlington, Va., research analyst, 1942-44; Limestone College, Gaffney, S.C., librarian and professor of history, 1944-53; University of Southwestern Louisiana, Lafayette, director of libraries, 1954-63; Radford College, Radford, Va., librarian and professor of history, 1963—. *Member:* American Library Association, Bibliographical Society of America, American Historical Association, Organization of American Historians, Virginia Social Science Association, Phi Beta Kappa, Phi Alpha Theta.

WRITINGS: Communication: A Concise Introduction to the History of the Alphabet, Writing, Printing, Books, and Libraries, Scarecrow, 1955, 3rd edition, 1966; *Of Time and Thomas Wolfe: A Bibliography, with a Character Index of His Works*, Scarecrow, 1959; *History of Libraries in the Western World*, Scarecrow, 1965, 2nd edition, 1970; *Thomas Wolfe: A Checklist*, Kent State University Press, 1970; (with Katherine Sloan) *South Carolina: A Documentary Profile of the Palmetto State*, University of South Carolina Press, 1971. Contributor of articles and reviews to history and library journals. Editor, *Southwestern Louisiana Journal*, 1957-60, *Louisiana Library Association Bulletin*, 1956, 1958; editor of index, *Louisiana Schools, 1924-63.*

WORK IN PROGRESS: The Prestons of Virginia: An All American Family.

AVOCATIONAL INTERESTS: Collecting works by and about Thomas Wolfe, gardening, flower photography.

*   *   *

JOHNSON, Harry Morton   1917-

PERSONAL: Born October 25, 1917, in Cambridge, Mass.; son of Harry Morton (a printer) and Helen Frances (Roche) Johnson; married Ilene Louise Edelstein, 1955 (divorced, 1957); married Danielle Cousin, 1969. *Education:* Harvard University, A.B., 1939, A.M., 1942, Ph.D., 1949. *Home:* 804 West Indiana Ave., Urbana, Ill. 61801.

CAREER: Simmons College, Boston, Mass., 1942-64, started as instructor, became professor of sociology; Massachusetts School (now College) of Art, Boston, associate professor of sociology, 1945-55; University of Illinois, Urbana, visiting professor, 1963-64, associate professor, 1964-66, professor of sociology, 1966—. *Member:* American Sociological Association.

WRITINGS: Sociology: A Systematic Introduction, Harcourt, 1960.

WORK IN PROGRESS: A book on race relations in the United States, for Harcourt.

*   *   *

JOHNSON, Hildegard Binder   1908-

PERSONAL: Born August 20, 1908, in Berlin, Germany; daughter of Albert Wilhelm and Emma (Gartenschlaeger) Binder; married Palmer Oliver Johnson (a professor; died January 24, 1960); children: Gisela Charlotte, Karin Luise. *Education:* Attended University of Rostock, University of Marburg, University of Innsbruck, 1928-30; University of Berlin, M.A., 1933, Ph.D., 1934. *Home:* 3312 Edmund Blvd., Minneapolis, Minn. 55406. *Office:* Department of Geography, Macalester College, St. Paul, Minn. 55101.

CAREER: Assistant at high school in England, 1934-35; Mills College, Oakland, Calif., assistant instructor, 1935-36; Macalester College, St. Paul, Minn., 1947—, began as assistant professor in department of geography, now professor and chairman of department. Visiting professor at University of Minnesota, University of Georgia, and University of California, Berkeley. *Member:* Association of American Geographers, American Geographical Society, National Council for the Social Studies, National Council for Geographic Education (fellow), Society of Women Geographers, Izaac Walton League of America (Minnesota division), Minnesota Historical Society, Minnesota Council for the Social Studies (president, 1957-59). *Awards, honors:* Social Science Research Council grants, 1940, 1946; Izaac Walton League award, 1950, for conservation education; Association of American Geographers award, 1958, for meritorious contribution to geography.

WRITINGS: (Contributor) Adolf Eduard Zucker, editor, *The Forty-Eighters: Political Refugees of the German Revolution of 1848*, Columbia University Press, 1950; (contributor) *Forschungen zu Staat und Verfassung*, Duncker & Humblot (Berlin), 1958; *A Comparative Study of an Introductory Geography Course on ETV and in the Classroom*, Department of Geography, Macalester College, 1960; *Carta Marina: World Geography in Strassburg, 1525*, University of Minnesota Press, 1963; *An Introduction to the Geography of the Twin Cities*, Department of Geography, Macalester College, 1970. Contributor of approximately fifty articles to professional journals in United States, Canada, and Germany. Editor, *Minnesota Geographer*, 1950-62.

WORK IN PROGRESS: Settlement and Land Usage in American Middle West.

*   *   *

JOHNSON, James Rosser   1916-

PERSONAL: Born September 2, 1916, in Scranton, Pa.; son of John Solomon (a construction engineer) and Rose (Rosser) Johnson; married Ida M. McCabe, November 19, 1949; children: David, Eric, Ethan. *Education:* Harvard University, A.B., 1941; Sorbonne, University of Paris, graduate student, 1947; Columbia University, Ph.D., 1960. *Home:* 98 Mather Lane, Cleveland, Ohio 44108.

CAREER: Columbia University, New York, N.Y., instructor in art history, 1952-54; Western Reserve University (now Case Western Reserve University), Cleveland, Ohio, assistant professor of art, 1954-159; Cleveland Museum of Art, Cleveland, Ohio, curator, art history and education, 1959—. *Military service:* U.S. Army, 1942-45; became lieutenant. *Member:* American Council of Learned Societies, American Society for Aesthetics (secretary-treasurer), Mediaeval Academy of America, College Art Association of America.

WRITINGS: *Modern and Mediaeval Stained Glass: A Microscopic Comparison of Two Fragments* (originally published in *Bulletin* of College Art Association of America, Vol. 38, no. 3), [New York], 1956; *The Tree of Jesse Window of Chartres: Laudes regiae* (originally published in *Speculum,* January, 1961), [Cambridge], 1961; *The Radiance of Chartres: Studies in the Early Stained Glass of the Cathedral,* Phaidon Press, 1964, Random House, 1965. Contributor to art journals. Assistant editor, *Journal of Aesthetics and Art Criticism.*

WORK IN PROGRESS: Research on color perception, stained glass, medieval heraldry.

AVOCATIONAL INTERESTS: Photography, music.

* * *

JOHNSON, John J. 1912-

PERSONAL: Born March 26, 1912, in White Swan, Wash.; son of George E. (a farmer) and Mary (Whitford) Johnson; married Maurine Amstutz (a librarian); children: George Michael. *Education:* Central Washington College, B.A., 1940; University of California, Berkeley, M.A., 1943, Ph.D., 1947; additional study at University of Chicago, 1943-44, University of Chile, 1946. *Home:* 774 Esplanada, Stanford, Calif. 94305. *Office:* Department of History, Stanford University, Stanford, Calif. 94305.

CAREER: Stanford University, Stanford, Calif., assistant professor, 1946-50, associate professor, 1950-58, professor of history, 1958—. U.S. Department of State, Washington, D.C., acting chief of South America Branch, Division of Research, American Republics, 1952-53. Public lecturer. RAND Corp., consultant; *Encyclopaedia Britannica,* adviser. *Member:* American Historical Association, Conference on Latin American History (chairman, 1961), Latin American Studies Association (vice-president, 1969; president, 1970). *Awards, honors:* American Council of Learned Societies fellow, 1942; William Harrison Mills traveling fellow, 1943-44, 1945-46; Bolton Prize, 1959; Social Science Research Council fellow, 1962-63.

WRITINGS: *Pioneer Telegraphy in Chile, 1852-1876,* Stanford University Press, 1948; *Political Change in Latin America: The Emergence of the Middle Sectors,* Stanford University Press, 1958; (editor and contributor) *The Role of the Military in Underdeveloped Countries,* Princeton University Press, 1962; *The Military and Society in Latin America,* Stanford University Press, 1964; (editor and contributor) *Continuity and Change in Latin America,* Stanford University Press, 1964; (with Doris M. Ladd) *Simon Bolivar and Spanish American Independence, 1783-1830,* Stanford University Press, 1968; *The Mexican American: A Selected and Annotated Bibliography,* Center for Latin American Studies, Stanford University, 1969.

WORK IN PROGRESS: *Nationalism and Neutralism in Latin America.*

BIOGRAPHICAL/CRITICAL SOURCES: *Times Literary Supplement,* September 19, 1968.

* * *

JOHNSON, Marion Georgina Wikeley 1912-
(Georgina Masson)

PERSONAL: Born March 23, 1912, in Rawal Pindi, Pakistan, daughter of James and Christine (Duns) Masson Wikeley. *Education:* Royal School for Officers of the Army, Bath, England, student, 1922-24. *Religion:* Church of England. *Home:* Villa Pamphilj, 12 via S. Pancrazio, Rome, Italy. *Agent:* Curtis Brown Ltd., 13 King St., Covent Garden, London W.C.2, England.

CAREER: British government, London, England, served with Ministry of Information, 1941-43, Foreign Office, 1943-47; Italian correspondent for *Times Educational Supplement* and *Architectural Review,* both London, 1947—. *Member:* Society of Authors (London).

WRITINGS—All under name Georgina Masson: *Frederick II of Hohenstaufen: A Life,* Secker & Warburg, 1957, Dufour, 1958; *Italian Villas and Palaces,* Abrams, 1959, new edition, 1966; *Italian Gardens,* Abrams, 1961, new edition, Thames & Hudson, 1966; *The Companion Guide to Rome,* Harper, 1965, revised edition published as *Fodor's Rome: A Companion Guide,* edited by Eugene Fodor, McKay, 1971; *Queen Christina,* Secker & Warburg, 1968; *Italian Flower Conoisseurs,* Apollo, 1968, Farrar, Straus, 1969; *Dumbarton Oaks: A Guide to the Gardens,* [Washington, D.C.], 1968. Contributor to *Conoisseur, Country Life, Geographical, Daily Telegraph, Vogue, Studio,* and other periodicals and newspapers.

BIOGRAPHICAL/CRITICAL SOURCES: *Punch,* September 25, 1968; *Observer Review,* October 13, 1968; *Book World,* January 12, 1969; *Newsweek,* January 13, 1969; *New York Times Book Review,* January 19, 1969; *Best Sellers,* February 15, 1969; *New York Times,* February 22, 1969; *Virginia Quarterly Review,* spring, 1969.

* * *

JOHNSON, Patrick Spencer 1938-

PERSONAL: Born November 24, 1938, in Watertown, S.D.; son of Jerauld O. (an investment broker) and Madeline (Sankey) Johnson. *Education:* University of Southern California, A.B., 1963; medical student at Royal College of Surgeons, Dublin, Ireland. *Home:* 15515 Del Gado Dr., Sherman Oaks, Calif. 91403.

MEMBER: Sigma Alpha Epsilon, Psi Chi, Phi Sigma Tau.

WRITINGS: *Fraternity Row,* foreword by Dick Powell, Brewster Publications, 1963.

WORK IN PROGRESS: *Happiness Is White.*

AVOCATIONAL INTERESTS: Rugby, swimming, and golf.

* * *

JOHNSON, Quentin G. 1930-

PERSONAL: Born January 4, 1930, in New Rockford, N.D.; son of Quentin M. (an electrical contractor) and Marie (Trudeau) Johnson; married Margaret S. Brennan (a teacher), July 20, 1957; children: Quentin M., Thomas M., David G. *Education:* Gonzaga University, A.B., 1951; University of Oregon, M.A., 1956, Ph.D., 1967. *Home:* 608 Hodge, Ames, Iowa 50010.

CAREER: University of Oregon, Eugene, instructor in English, 1958-61; Iowa State University of Science and Technology, Ames, assistant professor, 1961-68, associate professor of English, 1968—, consultant in business communications and technical writing to Engineering Extension Service. Bi-monthly speaker on language and communication, Station WOI, Ames, Iowa.

WRITINGS: (Editor with W. Paul Jones) *Essays on Thinking and Writing in Science, Engineering, and Business,* 3rd edition (Johnson was not associated with earlier editions), W.C. Brown, 1963; (with Jones) *Writing Scientific Papers and Reports,* 5th edition, W.C. Brown, 1965.

JOHNSON, Ronald 1935-

PERSONAL: Born November 25, 1935, in Ashland, Kan.; son of A.T. and Helen (Mayse) Johnson. *Education:* Columbia University, B.A., 1960. *Home:* 4566 Eighteenth St., San Francisco, Calif. 94119.

CAREER: Employed at various occupations during the past ten years. Presently writer-in-residence at University of Kentucky, Lexington. *Awards, honors:* Inez Boulton Award, *Poetry* Magazine, 1965; National Endowment for the Arts Award, 1970.

WRITINGS—All poems: *A Line of Poetry, A Row of Trees*, Jargon Press, 1964; *Sports and Divertissements* (contains poems written by Johnson from Eric Satie's notes, in French, to the piano pieces "Sports" and "Divertissements"), Wild Hawthorn Press, 1965; *Assorted Jungles: Rousseau*, Auerhahn Press, 1966; *GORSE/ GOOSE/ROSE, and Other Poems*, Indiana University Fine Arts Department, 1966; *The Book of the Green Man*, Norton, 1967; *Valley of the Many-Colored Grasses*, Norton, 1969; *The Aficianado's Southwestern Cooking* University of New Mexico Press, 1969; *Balloons for Moonless Nights, Arrows Like S's, Gs Ae Rc Fr Ee NtS: Three Concrete Poems* (edition of twenty copies), Finial Press, 1969; *The Spirit Walks, The Rocks Will Talk*, Jargon Press, 1969; *Songs of the Earth*, Grabhorn-Hoyem Press, 1970.

Anthologized in *An Anthology of Concrete Poetry*, Something Else Press, 1967; *Young American Poets*, Follett, 1968; *Holding Your Eight Hands*, Doubleday, 1969.

WORK IN PROGRESS: Head Poems, for Norton.

SIDELIGHTS: Johnson told *CA:* "After quite a few years of travel I have finally settled in the only civilized city in America—San Francisco. From there I am available for readings, Poetry Workshops and teaching in Universities, etc., but I consider the Bay Area my home."

Martin Dodsworth considers *The Book of the Green Man* to be "charming—an American idealisation of England, seen through the eyes of Samuel Palmer, Francis Kilvert and other authors.... The result is slight, literary, precious, and pleasurable." Charles Philbrick finds the book a "most unusual volume ... which is both original and profoundly traditional. The reader becomes absorbed in the young Kansan as he tramps through the English countryside, discovering it with eyes that record the sights of a year's visit and that have also drawn into his brain the recorded lore of centuries.... Mr. Johnson has worked into his poem the writings of a multitude who knew 'the green man'—from Giraldus Cambrensis to Tolkien, and including Vaughan, Smart, Blake, and the Wordsworths. This book may be called literary mistletoe, since it is both symbiotic and magical." A *Beloit Poetry Journal* writer states that the book is "tightly written and beautifully planned—a tribute to Johnson's imagination and scholarship."

Valley of the Many Colored Grasses was very well-received. According to Dan Jaffe the poems "are frankly romantic ... they are verbal equivalents of the Rousseau paintings that Johnson celebrates, calculated expressions of the energy of the universe. These are symbolist poems in intention, but they are informed by the facts of art and flora. Writing in an often extremely elevated diction, hardly fashionable today, Johnson utilizes words most contemporary poets shun, words like ultimate, exquisite, chaos, fronds, gorgeous, and celestial. But Johnson is no purveyor of poesy. He counterpoints carefully."

BIOGRAPHICAL/CRITICAL SOURCES: Saturday Review, June 3, 1967, September 9, 1969; *Beloit Poetry Journal*, summer, 1967; *Listener*, October 19, 1967; *Poetry*, February, 1968.

JOHNSON, Shirley K(ing) 1927-

PERSONAL: Born March 18, 1927, in Adair County, Iowa; daughter of Roland E. (a farmer) and Gladys (Evans) King; married Thomas G. Johnson, June 2, 1946; children: Elaine, Evan; Barry and Bryan (twins). *Education:* Graduated from high school in Cumberland, Iowa. *Home:* 4118 Randolph St., Lincoln, Neb. 68510.

WRITINGS: A Dog Named Chip, Zondervan, 1963.

WORK IN PROGRESS: A biography for teens, *William Jennings Bryan.*

SIDELIGHTS: Mrs. Johnson enlivened a farm childhood by writing adventure stories, and has been turning out fiction, on and off, since then. *A Dog Named Chip* is her first published book. *Avocational interests:* Collecting poetry, flower gardening.

*   *   *

JOHNSON, Thomas Frank 1920-

PERSONAL: Born September 27, 1920, in Lynchburg, Va.; son of Thomas Frank (in real estate and construction) and Inez (McDaniel) Johnson; married Margaret Ann Emhardt, December 29, 1951; children: Thomas Emhardt, Sarah Lee, William Harrison. *Education:* Lynchburg College, student, 1939-41; University of Virginia, B.A., 1943, M.A., 1947, Ph.D., 1949. *Religion:* Episcopal. *Home:* 1113 North Gaillard Pl., Alexandria, Va. 22304. *Office:* 1012 14th St. N.W., Washington, D.C. 20005.

CAREER: U.S. Department of Agriculture, Washington, D.C., economist, 1949-50; U.S. Chamber of Commerce, Washington, D.C., research economist, 1951-54; Federal Housing Administration, Washington, D.C., assistant commissioner, 1955-58; American Enterprises Institute for Public Policy Research, Washington, D.C., 1958—, director of research, 1959—; Institute for Social Science Research, Washington, D.C., secretary and trustee, 1959—. *Military service:* U.S. Naval Reserve, lieutenant commander, 1943-46. *Member:* American Economic Association, American Finance Association, Royal Economic Society, Southern Economic Association.

WRITINGS: (Contributor) *The American Competitive Enterprise Economy*, U.S. Chamber of Commerce, 1953; (with James R. Morris and Joseph G. Butts) *Renewing America's Cities*, Institute for Social Science Research, 1962. Author of other Chamber of Commerce publications, *Small Business, Its Prospects and Its Problems* and *The Price of Price Controls*. Contributor to professional journals.

*   *   *

JOHNSTON, Angus James II 1916-

PERSONAL: Born May 5, 1916, in Chicago, Ill.; son of Angus James and Abbie (Cooper) Johnston; married Ruth E. Coad, 1941; children: Heather E., Angus James III. *Education:* University of Wisconsin, B.A.; Northwestern University, M.A., 1950, Ph.D., 1959. *Religion:* Episcopalian. *Home:* 1935 Highland Ave., Wilmette, Ill. 60091. *Office:* New Trier High School, Winnetka, Ill. 60093.

CAREER: Taught at Indiana State Teachers College, Terre Haute, 1943-44; Diversey Corp., Chicago, Ill., market analyst, 1945-48; New Trier High School, Winnetka, Ill., teacher, 1954—. Visiting instructor at Macalester College, St. Paul, Minn., 1967, and Northwestern University, Evanston, Ill., summer, 1968. *Member:* American Historical Association, Organization of American Historians, Southern Historical Association, State Historical Society of Wisconsin, Historical Association (England), Sigma Phi, Phi Delta Kappa, Illinois St. Andrew Society.

WRITINGS: Virginia Railroads in the Civil War, published for Virginia Historical Society by University Press of Virginia, 1961; (with Ray Allen Billington and others) *The Historian's Contribution to Anglo-American Misunderstanding*, Routledge & Kegan Paul, 1966. Contributor to history journals.

*   *   *

JOHNSTON, John H(ubert) 1921-

PERSONAL: Born January 18, 1921, in Norfolk, Va.; son of John Hubert and Alice (Greeley) Johnston; married Agnes Haney, July 24, 1948; children: Brian, Kieran, Christopher, Patrick, Ann Elizabeth, Timothy, Carol. *Education:* University of Notre Dame, B.A., 1947; University of Chicago, M.A., 1950; University of Wisconsin, Ph.D., 1960. *Religion:* Roman Catholic. *Home:* 232 Grand St., Morgantown, W. Va. 26505. *Office:* 306 Armstrong Hall, West Virginia University, Morgantown, W. Va. 26505.

CAREER: West Virginia University, Morgantown, instructor, 1954-56, 1957-60, assistant professor, 1960-64, associate professor of English, 1964—. *Military service:* U.S. Army, Parachute Infantry, 1943-45. *Member:* National Council of Teachers of English, Modern Language Association of America. *Awards, honors:* Claude Worthington Benedum Foundation award, 1963.

WRITINGS: English Poetry of the First World War: A Study in the Evolution of Lyric and Narrative Form, Princeton University Press, 1964. Contributor to *Encyclopedia of World Literature in the Twentieth Century*, and to *Review of Politics.*

WORK IN PROGRESS: A study of the relationships between poetry and the effects of modern technology, with the aim of evaluating some of the modes whereby contemporary poets have sought to interpret the phenomena of twentieth-century civilization.

SIDELIGHTS: As a teacher who happens to be a critic, Johnston takes this view: "We need the artist today much more than we need the critic, but criticism can help a little."

*   *   *

JOHNSTONE, Kathleen Yerger 1906-

PERSONAL: Born August 19, 1906, in Mobile, Ala.; daughter of Arthur Warren and Kathleen Hughes (Williamson) Yerger; married Harry Inge Johnstone (an architect), June 24, 1930; children: Montgomery Inge, Yerger, Douglas Inge. *Education:* Mississippi State College for Women, B.A.; summer study at Columbia University, Denishawn School of Dance, and Art Students League, New York, N.Y. *Politics:* Independent. *Religion:* Episcopalian. *Home:* 2209 River Forest Rd., Mobile, Ala. 36605.

CAREER: Dancing teacher at Lausanne School, Memphis, Tenn., 1928-29, Arlington Hall, Arlington, Va., 1929-30. Organizer in Mobile, Ala., of Women's Committee for Home Defense, Civilian Defense, Volunteer Bureau; chairman of Home Arts School (domestic servant training); also served as member of board of Mobile Public Library, Council of Social Agencies, Community Chest. *Member:* American Malacological Union, Audubon Society, Alabama Ornithological Society, Historic Mobile Preservation Society, Friends of the Mobile Public Library, Junior League of Mobile (city editor; volunteer placement chairman for two years; president, 1941-43), Colonial Dames of America.

WRITINGS: Sea Treasure: A Guide to Shell Collecting, Houghton, 1957; *Collecting Seashells*, Grosset, 1970. Contributor to *Junior League Magazine, Antiques* and *Holidays.*

WORK IN PROGRESS: A manuscript for Grosset.

AVOCATIONAL INTERESTS: Malacology, ornithology, archaeology, local history.

BIOGRAPHICAL/CRITICAL SOURCES: Mobile Register, February 22, 1957, April 11, 1957, July 6, 1958; *Birmingham News*, March 6, 1960.

*   *   *

JONAS, Carl 1913-

PERSONAL: Born May 22, 1913, in Omaha, Neb.; son of August F. (a surgeon) and Jessica (Stebbins) Jonas; married Edith Larsen. *Education:* Attended Phillips Exeter Academy and Governor Dummer Academy; Williams College, B.A., 1936. *Address:* Box 101, Florence Station, Omaha, Neb. 68501. *Agent:* James Brown, 22 East 60th St., New York, N.Y. 10022.

CAREER: Author. Municipal University of Omaha, Omaha, Neb., lecturer in English department at various periods, 1957—. *Military service:* U.S. Coast Guard Reserve, 1942-45.

WRITINGS: Beachhead on the Wind, Little, Brown, 1945; *Snowslide*, Little, Brown, 1950; *Jefferson Selleck*, Little, Brown, 1952; *Riley McCullough*, Little, Brown, 1954; *Our Revels Now Are Ended*, Norton, 1957; *Lillian White Deer*, Norton, 1964; *The Observatory*, Norton, 1966; *A Trout in the Milk*, Norton, 1972; *The Sputnik Rapist*, Norton, 1973.

*   *   *

JONES, David 1895-

PERSONAL: Born November 1, 1895, in Brockley, Kent, England; son of James and Alice Ann (Bradshaw) Jones. *Education:* Attended Camberwell School of Art, 1909-14, Westminster Art School, 1919-21. *Religion:* Roman Catholic convert, 1921. *Address:* c/o Monksdene, 2, Northwick Park Rd., Harrow, Middlesex, England.

CAREER: Among other engravings, did a series of wooden ones for the Chester Cycle play "The Deluge," and copper engravings for Coleridge's "The Ancient Mariner," 1924-29; painter, principally in water-color, 1927—, represented at Venice Biennale International Exhibition of the Fine Arts, 1934, National Gallery, 1940-42, and at various exhibitions in England, Wales, and the United States; his works are on permanent exhibition at Tate Gallery, Victoria and Albert Museum, British Museum, Sydney Art Gallery, British Council, National Museum of Wales, and Toronto Art Gallery. *Military service:* Royal Welch Fusiliers, 1915-18; served with 15th Battalion.

MEMBER: Honorable Society of Cymmrodorion, Society for Nautical Research, Royal Society of Painters in Watercolours (honorary), Royal Society of Literature (fellow). *Awards, honors:* Royal Drawing Society Prize, 1904; Hawthornden Prize, 1938, for *In Parenthesis;* Russell Loines Memorial Award (for poetry), 1954, for *The Anathemata;* made Commander of the Order of the British Empire, 1955; Harriet Monroe Memorial Prize, 1956, for poem "The Wall"; D.Litt., University of Wales, 1960; Arts Council (Welsh Committee) prize, 1960, for *Epoch and Artist;* Levinson Prize, 1961; Royal National Eisteddfod of Wales, Gold Medal Award of Visual Arts Section, 1964; Midsummer prize, Corporation of London, 1968.

WRITINGS: In Parenthesis: Seinnyessit e gledyf ym penn mameu, Faber, 1937, Chilmark, 1961, reissued with an introduction by T.S. Eliot, Viking, 1961; *The Anathemata: Fragments of an Attempted Writing*, Faber, 1952, Chilmark, 1963; *Epoch and Artist: Selected Writings*, edited by Harman Grisewood, Chilmark, 1959; *The Fatigue: A.V.C. DCCLXXIV, Tantus labor non sit cassus*, Rampant Lions Press, 1965; *The Tribune's Visitation*, Fulcrum Press, 1969.

Illustrator: Eleanor Farjeon, *The Town Child's Alphabet,* Poetry Bookshop, 1924; H.D.C. Pepler, *Libellus Lapidum,* St. Dominic's Press, 1924; Jonathan Swift, *Travels into Several Remote Nations of the World,* two volumes, Golden Cockerel Press, 1925; *The Book of Jonah,* Golden Cockerel Press, 1926; *Llyfr y pregeth-wr,* Gwasg Gregynog, 1927; J. Isaacs, editor, *The Chester Play of the Deluge,* Golden Cockerel Press, 1927; Samuel Taylor Coleridge, *The Rime of the Ancient Mariner,* Douglas Cleverdon, 1929. Represented in several collections, including *An Anthology of Modern Verse, 1940-1960,* edited by Elizabeth Jennings, Methuen, 1961, and Edith Sitwell's two volume anthology. Contributor to *Poetry, Listener,* and other publications.

WORK IN PROGRESS: Continuing with the writing of interrelated pieces, some fragments of which have appeared in periodicals; watercolors, inscriptions, and drawings.

SIDELIGHTS: Jones has described himself as "a Londoner, of Welsh and English parentage, of Protestant upbringing, of Catholic subscription." Certainly his attraction to painting and possibly his desire to write can be traced to his childhood. "At the time of my birth," he once wrote, "my father was a printer's overseer and that meant that I was brought up in a home that took the printed page and its illustration for granted." He told *CA:* "I began drawing when I was aged five and regarded it as a natural activity which I would pursue as I grew older. I was backward at lessons, could not read till I was about seven or eight, and did not take to writing in the sense of writing books until I was thirty-three years old."

Though he remains primarily a painter, the recent publication of his books in America has resulted in the growth of his literary audience. His best known work, *In Parenthesis,* is described by T.S. Eliot as "a work of genius." Eliot goes on: "The work of David Jones has some affinity with that of James Joyce (both men seem to me to have the Celtic ear for the music of words) and with the later work of Ezra Pound, and with my own. I stress the affinity, as any possible influence seems to me slight and of no importance.... [Of this group] David Jones is the youngest, and the tardiest to publish. The lives of all of us were altered by that War [World War I], but David Jones is the only one to have fought in it."

While the whole content of the book was evoked by his experiences as an infantry soldier, Jones writes in his preface: "I did not intend this as a 'War Book'—it happens to be concerned with war (because, he says, "that was my most vivid experience."). I should prefer it to be about a good kind of peace—but as Mandeville says, 'Of Paradys ne can I not speken propurly I was not there; it is fer beyonde and that for thinketh me. And also I was not worthi.' We find ourselves privates in foot regiments. We search how we may see formal goodness in a life singularly inimical, hateful, to us."

Jones is also a poet, and sees the function of a poet thus: "Rather than being a seer or endowed with the gift of prophecy, he is something of a vicar whose job is legatine—a kind of Servus Servorum to deliver what has been delivered to him, who can neither add to nor take from the deposits. It is not that that we mean by 'originality.' There is only one tale to tell even though the telling is patient of endless development and ingenuity and can take on a million variant forms." His long poem, *The Anathemata,* is roughly described by Babette Deutsch as "a revery on the Mass by a Catholic convert," and is both recondite and witty, a poem "that even an agnostic can enjoy."

A series of exhibitions of Jones' work, entitled "Word and Image," Works by a Man who Practices the Art of Writing as well as of Painting, were shown at the National Book League, London, February, 1972, at the National Museum of Wales, December, 1972, and at other Welsh Centers, culminating at the National Library of Wales, Aberystwyth, May, 1973.

BIOGRAPHICAL/CRITICAL SOURCES: Robin Ironside, *David Jones,* Penguin, 1949; *Blackfriars,* April, 1951; *New Statesman,* November 22, 1952; *Dublin Review,* fourth quarter, 1952; Babette Deutsch, *Poetry in Our Time,* Holt, 1952; *Encounter,* February, 1954; *Times Literary Supplement,* August 6, 1954, July 22, 1965, July 27, 1967; *Selections II,* Sheed, 1954; *Studio,* April, 1955; *Listener,* May 14, 1959; *Twentieth Century,* July, 1960; *Apollo,* February, 1963; Howard Nemerov, *Poetry and Fiction,* Rutgers University Press, 1963; *Lectures on Modern Novelists,* Department of English, Cambridge University, 1963; John H. Johnston, *English Poetry of the First World War,* Princeton University Press, 1964; *New Yorker,* August 22, 1964; Bernard Bergonzi, *Heroes' Twilight,* Constable, 1965; *Agenda,* summer, 1967; *Sewanee Review,* autumn, 1967; D.M. Blamires, *David Jones: Artist and Writer,* Manchester University Press, 1971.

*   *   *

JONES, Dorothy Holder (Duane Jones)

PERSONAL: Born in Houston, Tex.; daughter of B.F. and Jennie (Stokely Holder; married Thomas A. Jones, Jr. (an air transport examiner), September 7, 1943; children: Bryan Kimberly, Vicki Lynn. *Education:* Attended thirteen elementary and high schools in Texas, Kansas, and Georgia; studied commercial art at Georgia Evening College, 1945-46. *Religion:* Christian Scientist. *Home:* 1300 Tracy Pl., Falls Church, Va. 22046. *Agent:* McIntosh & Otis, Inc., 18 East 41st St., New York, N.Y. 10017.

CAREER: Free-lance writer of articles and short stories, 1950-57; writer of books for young people, 1959-69. Taught writing courses at St. Simon's, Ga., for Dixie Council of Authors and Journalists Writing Conferences, 1968 and 1969. Public practitioner of Christian Science. *Awards, honors:* Seventeenth Summer Literary Competition award from Dodd (now "Calling All Girls" Prize Competition), 1959, for *The Wonderful World Outside.*

WRITINGS: The Wonderful World Outside, Dodd, 1959; *The Oldest One,* Funk, 1963; *Those Gresham Girls,* Funk, 1965; *Dress Parade,* Funk, 1966; *An Understanding Heart,* Funk, 1967; (with Ruth Sexton Sargent) *Abbie Burgess, Lighthouse Heroine,* Funk, 1969. Contributor of articles on Christian Science to *Christian Science Monitor* and other publications.

SIDELIGHTS: Several of Mrs. Jones' articles on Christian Science have been reprinted in foreign languages.

*   *   *

JONES, Evan   1915-

PERSONAL: Born May 6, 1915, in Le Sueur, Minn.; son of Lewis R. and Elizabeth (McLeod) Jones; married Judith Bailey (an editor); children: Bronwyn (Mrs. John L. Ernst), Pamela (Mrs. Haig Akmakjian). *Education:* Attended public schools in Minneapolis and Le Sueur, Minn. *Home and office:* 108 East 86th St., New York, N.Y. 10028. *Agent:* Robert Lescher, 159 East 64th St., New York, N.Y. 10021.

CAREER: Free-lance writer. *Weekend Magazine,* Paris, France, editor, 1947-49.

WRITINGS: (With Roland Wells Robbins) *Hidden America,* Knopf, 1959; (editor) *The Father: Letters to Sons and Daughters,* Holt, 1960; *Trappers and Mountain Men,* American Heritage, 1961; *The Minnesota: Forgotten River,* Holt, 1962; (contributor) *American Heritage*

Cook Book and Illustrated History of American Eating and Drinking, American Heritage, 1964; *Citadel in the Wilderness: The Story of Fort Snelling and the Old Northwest Frontier,* Coward, 1966; (with others) *The Plains States: Iowa, Kansas, Minnesota, Missouri, Nebraska, North Dakota, and South Dakota,* Time-Life, 1968; (editor and author of notes) Jane Grigson, *Good Things,* Knopf, 1971; *Food and Cooking: The American Story,* Dutton, 1972.

* * *

JONES, Francis P(rice) 1890-

PERSONAL: Born December 28, 1890, in Dodgerville, Wis.; son of Jonathan Thomas (a farmer) and Eva (Baker) Jones; married Lucile Williams, June 26, 1915; children: Edwin, Dorothy, Philip, Donald. *Education:* Northwestern University, B.A., 1915; Garrett Biblical Institute, B.D., 1915; University of Chicago, M.A., 1915; Union Theological Seminary, New York, S.T.M., 1930, Th.D., 1938. *Home:* 47 Prospect St., Madison, N.J. 07940.

CAREER: Methodist minister; missionary in China, 1915-51; Drew University, Madison, N.J., lecturer on missions, 1951-61. National Council of Churches of Christ, consultant, 1951-62.

WRITINGS: Syllabus for Study of the Life of Jesus, Association Press of Shanghai, 1940; (translator and editor) *The Abingdon Bible Commentary* (in Chinese), Volume I, Christian Literature Society (Shanghai), 1950; (translator and editor) *Doctrines and Discipline of the Methodist Church* (in Chinese), Methodist Church (Nanking), 1950; *The Church in Communist China,* Friendship, 1962; (editor) *Documents of the Three Self Movement,* National Council of Churches, 1963.

General editor, "Christian Classics Library in Chinese," published by Council on Christian Literature for Overseas Chinese (Hong Kong): *John Calvin: Institutes of the Christian Religion,* three volumes, 1955, 1957, 1959; *John Wesley's Journal,* 1956; *The Social Gospel of Rauschenbusch,* 1956; *Selected Works of William Temple,* 1956; *Selected Works of John Henry Newman,* 1957; *Selected Works of Martin Luther,* two volumes, 1957, 1959; *Confessions, Catechisms, and Church Councils,* 1957; *The Latin Church,* 1959; *Reinhold Niebuhr: The Nature and Destiny of Man,* 1959; *Patristic and Mediaeval Sermons,* 1960; *Quaker Classics,* 1960; *The Age of Reason in Religion,* 1960; *Kant's Moral Philosophy,* 1960; *Selected Writings of Jonathan Edwards, Sr.,* 1960; *Ernest Troeltsch: The Social Teaching of the Christian Churches,* 1960; *Modern Idealism,* 1961; *Ante-Nicene Fathers,* 1962; *The Christian School of Alexandria,* 1962; *Selected Works of Aurelius Augustine,* 1962; *Mediaeval Christian Thinkers,* 1962; *British Presbyterianism and Puritanism,* 1962; *Selected Writings of Soeren Kierkegaard,* 1963; *The Eastern Church,* 1964.

Contributor to *Christian Century, Religion in Life,* other religious publications. Editor, *China Bulletin,* 1951-62. Member of editorial board, *Hymns of Universal Praise,* Christian Literature Society (Shanghai), 1936.

WORK IN PROGRESS: Other books in "Christian Classics Library in Chinese," planned to include fifty-four volumes.

* * *

JONES, Glyn 1905-

PERSONAL: Born February 28, 1905, in Merthyr Tydfil, Wales; son of William Henry (a government clerk) and Margaret (Williams) Jones; married Doreen Jones, August, 1935. *Education:* Attended St. Paul's College, Cheltenham, England. *Home:* 158 Manor Way, Whitchurch, Cardiff, Wales. *Agent:* Laurence Pollinger Ltd., 18 Maddox St., London W.1, England.

CAREER: Former schoolmaster and English teacher in Cardiff, Wales. Reviewer, interviewer, and translator (from Welsh) for radio. *Awards, honors:* Welsh Arts Council award, 1968, for *The Dragon Has Two Tongues.*

WRITINGS: The Blue Bed, and Other Stories, J. Cape, 1937, Dutton, 1938; *Poems,* Fortune Press, 1939; *The Water Music, and Other Stories,* Routledge & Kegan Paul, 1944; *The Dream of Jake Hopkins* (poems), Fortune Press, 1945; (translator and adapter with T.J. Morgan) *The Saga of Llywarch the Old,* Golden Cockerel Press, 1955; *The Valley, the City, the Village* (novel), Dent, 1956; *The Learning Lark* (novel), Dent, 1960; *The Island of Apples* (novel), John Day, 1965; *The Dragon Has Two Tongues* (essays on Anglo-Welsh writers and writing), Dent, 1968; *Selected Short Stories,* Dent, 1971.

Short Stories and poems anthologized in *Welsh Short Stories,* Faber, 1937, *Best Short Stories,* 1938 and 1940, *Modern Welsh Poetry,* edited by Keidrych Rhys, Faber, 1944, *New British Poets,* edited by Kenneth Rexroth, New Directions, 1949, *World's Classics,* Oxford University Press, 1956, *Presenting Welsh Poetry,* Faber, 1959, *Welsh Voices,* Dent, 1967, *This World of Wales,* edited by Gerald Morgan, University of Wales Press, 1968, *The Lilting House,* Dent, 1969, *The Shining Pyramid,* 1971, and in *New Poems* (P.E.N. anthologies), 1958, 1961, and others. Reviewer for periodicals in Wales and England, including *Western Mail* (Wales) and *Times* (London).

WORK IN PROGRESS: A book of poems, *Images of Light and Darkness.*

* * *

JONES, Goronwy J(ohn) 1915-

PERSONAL: Born September 23, 1915, in Nantymoel, Glamorganshire, Wales. *Education:* Attended Caerleon Training College for Teachers, Monmouthshire, England. *Home:* The Croft, Litchard Ter., Bridgend, Glamorganshire, Wales.

CAREER: Schoolmaster in British schools 1937—, as lecturer in general studies at Bridgend Technical College, Bridgend, Glamorganshire, 1957—. United Nations Association (Wales), member of executive committee, 1947—; member of United Kingdom delegation to UNESCO Seminar on Education for Living in a World Community, Netherlands, 1952. *Military service:* British Army, 1940-45. *Member:* Society of Authors, Royal Society of Literature, Royal Historical Society (fellow). *Awards, honors:* United Kingdom division awards in United Nations essay competition, 1948, for "The Veto," and 1949, for, "The Implementation of Human Rights."

WRITINGS: The Veto Controversy, Priory Press, 1948; *Security from Aggression,* Priory Press, 1949; *Challenge to the Peacemakers,* Wingate, 1951; (with Evan Thomas Davis) *United Nations for the Classroom,* Routledge & Kegan Paul, 1956, 4th edition, 1962; *From Stalin to Khrushchev,* Linden Press, 1960; *General Studies for Technical Students,* two volumes, English Universities Press, 1965; *Fundamentals of Workshop Technology,* Heinemann, 1965; *Wales and the Quest for Peace,* University of Wales Press, 1969. Contributor to *Western Mail* (Cardiff), *New Commonwealth,* and *United Nations News.*

WORK IN PROGRESS: Gilbert Murray's Philosophy of International Relations.

* * *

JONES, H(enry) John F(ranklin) 1924-

PERSONAL: Born May 6, 1924; son of James Walker and Doris Marjorie (Franklin) Jones; married Jean Verity Robinson, December 10, 1949; children: Janet

Armstrong, Jeremy William. *Education:* Attended Blundell's School and Merton College, Oxford. *Politics:* Liberal. *Region:* Church of Engand. *Home:* Holywell Cottage, Oxford, England.

CAREER: Merton College, Oxford University, Oxford, England, fellow and tutor in law, 1949-55; Oxford University, senior lecturer in English literature, 1956-63; Merton College, Oxford University, fellow and tutor in English, 1963—. *Military service:* Royal Navy Volunteer Reserve, Japanese specialist, 1943-46; became sub-lieutenant.

WRITINGS: *The Egotistical Sublime: A History of Wordsworth's Imagination,* Chatto & Windus, 1954; *On Aristotle and Greek Tragedy,* Oxford University Press, 1962; (contributor) John Jacob Gross and Gabriel Pearson, editors, *Dickens and the Twentieth Century,* Routledge & Kegan Paul, 1962; (editor) Heathcote W. Garrod, *The Study of Good Letters,* Clarendon Press, 1963; *John Keats's Dream of Truth,* Barnes & Noble, 1969; *The Same God: A Novel,* Hodder & Stoughton, 1971. Contributor to *Proceedings* of British Academy, 1962, and to *New Statesman, Observer, Times Literary Supplement, Sunday Telegraph,* and *Review of English Studies.*

*   *   *

JONES, Jenkin Lloyd 1911-

PERSONAL: Born November 1, 1911, in Madison, Wis.; son of Richard Lloyd and Georgia (Hayden) Jones; married Juanita Carlson, November 12, 1935; children: Jenkin, Jr., David, Georgia. *Education:* Attended Culver Military Academy, 1925, Tome School, 1926-29; University of Wisconsin, Ph.B., 1933. *Politics:* Republican. *Religion:* Unitarian. *Home:* 2272 East 38th St., Tulsa, Okla. 74105. *Office:* Tulsa Tribune Co., Tulsa, Okla., 74103.

CAREER: Tulsa Tribune Co., Tulsa, Okla., reporter and columnist, 1933-36, managing editor, 1936-38, associate editor, 1938-41, vice-president of company, 1938—, editor and publisher, 1941—. Director, Newspaper Printing Corp., Tulsa, Okla., Holder of commercial pilot rating (inactive). *Military service:* U.S. Naval Reserve, active duty, 1944-46; now lieutenant commander (retired). *Member:* American Society of Newspaper Editors (president, 1957), National Press Club, United States Chamber of Commerce (president, 1969), Oklahoma Historical Society, Phi Gamma Delta, Sigma Delta Chi, Veterans of Foreign Wars. *Awards, honors:* William Allen White Award, 1958.

WRITINGS: *The Inexact Science of Truth-telling,* William Allen White School of Journalism and Public Information, University of Kansas, 1958; *The Changing World: An Editor's Outlook,* Fleet Press, 1964. Writer of weekly column, "An Editor's Outlook," syndicated by General Features Corp.

SIDELIGHTS: Jones has traveled in seventy-three countries, twice above the Arctic Circle, and to the South Pole.

*   *   *

JONES, Stanley L(lewellyn) 1918-

PERSONAL: Born September 7, 1918, in Shell Lake, Wis.; son of Owen (a farmer) and Esther (Isack) Jones; married Adele Joan Tuman (a teacher), December 18, 1942; children: Glenna, Maia, Lois. *Education:* University of Wisconsin, B.S., 1940, M.A., 1941; University of Illinois, Ph.D., 1947. *Home:* 2204 West Market St., Greensboro, N.C. 27403. *Office:* Vice-chancellor for Academic Affairs, University of North Carolina, Greensboro, N.C. 27412.

CAREER: University of Illinois, Chicago, instructor, 1947-48, assistant professor, 1949-56, associate professor,

1957-63, professor of history, 1963-70, chairman of history department, 1964-68, acting dean of College of Liberal Arts and Sciences, 1965-66; University of North Carolina, Greensboro, professor of history and vice-chancellor for academic affairs, 1971—. *Military service:* U.S. Army, 1942-45. *Member:* American Historical Association, American Association of University Professors, Mississippi Valley Historical Association, Phi Beta Kappa.

WRITINGS: *The Presidential Election of 1896,* University of Wisconsin Press, 1964. Contributor of articles to historical journals.

WORK IN PROGRESS: Research for two book-length studies, political attitudes toward government regulation in nineteenth-century United States and the rise and decline of political bosses in late nineteenth- and early twentieth-century United States.

*   *   *

JORDAN, Philip Dillon 1903-

PERSONAL: Born November 7, 1903, in Burlington, Iowa; son of Edwin C. (president of a paper company) and Ida (Unterkircher) Jordan; married Marion Westervelt Valentine, June 10, 1933; children: Martha Dillon. *Education:* Northwestern University, B.S., 1927, M.A., 1928; University of Iowa, Ph.D., 1935. *Home:* 26 Cascade Ter., Burlington, Iowa 52601. *Agent:* McIntosh & Otis, Inc., 18 East 41st St., New York, N.Y. 10017.

CAREER: Long Island University, Brooklyn, N.Y., assistant professor of history, 1928-33; Miami University, Oxford, Ohio, associate professor of history, 1935-45; University of Minnesota, Minneapolis, associate professor, 1945-46, professor of history, 1946-69. Former consultant to St. Paul Public Library, Oliver Mining Co., U.S. Steel Corp. and Farmers Union Grain Terminal Association. Minneapolis Public School System, member of curriculum coordinating committee, 1954-57; Minnesota Department of Education, member of committee on revision of social studies, 1959-60.

MEMBER: American Historical Association, Mississippi Valley Historical Association, Southern Historical Society, Western Historical Association, Iowa Historical Society, Minnesota Historical Society, Lambda Chi Alpha, Tau Kappa Epsilon (honorary), Sigma Delta Chi, Kappa Phi Kappa, Alpha Kappa Delta, Phi Mu, Delta Phi Lambda, Pi Gamma Mu, Kappa Tau Alpha, Phi Alpha Theta, Press Club of Minnesota. *Awards, honors:* Ohioana Library Award, 1943; Award of Merit of American Association for State and Local History, 1954; LL.D. from Monmouth College, 1959.

WRITINGS: (Compiler) *The Juvenilia of Mary Belson Elliot* (includes additions and revisions by Daniel C. Haskell), New York Public Library, 1936; *William Salter, Western Torchbearer,* Mississippi Valley Press, 1939; (with Lillian Kessler) *Songs of Yesterday: A Song Anthology of American Life,* Doubleday, 1941; *Ohio Comes of Age,* Ohio Historical Society, 1943; *Singin' Yankees,* University of Minnesota Press, 1946; *The National Road,* Bobbs-Merrill, 1948; (with Theodore C. Blegen) *With Various Voices: Recordings of North Star Life,* Itasca Press, 1949; *The People's Health: A History of Public Health in Minnesota to 1948,* Minnesota Historical Society, 1953; *Uncle Sam of America* (juvenile), Webb Publishing Co., 1953; *The Night Before Christmas,* Acres-Blackmar, 1956; *These Are the People* (paper read at annual Illinois Folklore Society meeting, November 16, 1956), Southern Illinois University Press, 1957; *Fiddlefoot Jones of the North Woods* (juvenile), Vanguard, 1957; *Rip Van Winkle,* Acres-Blackmar, 1957; *The Nature and Practice of State and Local History,* Service Center for Teachers of History, 1958; *The Burro Bendicto, and*

Other Folk Tales and Legends of Mexico (juvenile), Coward, 1960; *The World of the Historian* (Burton Lecture, 1962), Historical Society of Michigan, 1963; *Frontier Law and Order* (ten essays), University of Nebraska Press, 1970.

Contributor: John F. McDermott, *Research Opportunities in American Cultural History*, University of Kentucky Press, 1961; Henry S. Commager, *Immigration and American History*, University of Minnesota Press, 1961.

Editor—All published by Mississippi Valley Press, except as indicated: Charles M. Thomas, *Thomas Riley Marshall, Hoosier Statesman*, 1939, William J. McNiff, *Heaven on Earth: A Planned Mormon Society*, 1940, Huntley Dupre, *Lazare Carmot, Republican Patriot*, 1940, Frank H. Heck, *The Civil War Veteran*, 1941, Alta H. Heiser, *Quaker Lady*, 1941, Alta H. Heiser, *Hamilton in the Making*, 1941, Lee F. Crippen, *Simon Cameron: Ante-Bellum Years*, 1942, F. Garvin Davenport, *Ante-Bellum Kentucky*, 1943, Israel G. Blake, *The Holmans of Veraestau*, 1943, Edward Bonney, *Banditti of the Prairies*, University of Oklahoma Press, 1963.

Contributor of more than 500 articles and reviews to professional journals, magazines, and newspapers.

SIDELIGHTS: Jordan traveled on sabbatical leave for research in Mexico, 1958, and for study in Europe and the Middle East, 1963-64. He is full blood brother in Chippewa and Sioux tribes. *Avocational interests:* Hunting, fishing, and sailing.

BIOGRAPHICAL/CRITICAL SOURCES: Carmen Nelson Richards, editor, *Minnesota Writers*, Denison, 1961.

* * *

JOSEPH, David I(glauer) 1941-

PERSONAL: Born April 11, 1941, in Cincinnati, Ohio; son of David J., Jr. (a businessman) and Josephine (Iglauer) Joseph; married Alice Louise Weinstein (a psychology research assistant), June 28, 1964. *Education:* Yale University, B.A., 1963; Case Western Reserve University, School of Medicine, student, 1963-64. *Home:* 3096 Livingston Rd., Cleveland, Ohio 44120.

WRITINGS: The Art of Rearrangement: E.M. Forster's Abinger Harvest, Yale University Press, 1964.

WORK IN PROGRESS: An intensive study of two non-pathogenic organisms, nocardia canicruria and nocardia erythropolis, in hopes of illuminating their biochemical characteristics.

* * *

JOSEPH, M(ichael) K(ennedy) 1914-

PERSONAL: Born July 9, 1914, in Chingford, Essex, England; son of George Frederick (a company director), and Ernestine (Kennedy) Joseph; married August 23, 1947; children: Anthony, Charles, Barbara, Peter, Nicholas. *Education:* Early education in Belgium, France, and New Zealand schools; Auckland University College, B.A., 1933, M.A., 1934; Merton College, Oxford, B.A., 1938, B. Litt., 1939, M.A., 1946. *Politics:* Tory Radical. *Religion:* Catholic. *Home:* 185 Victoria Ave., Remuera, Auckland S.E.2, New Zealand. *Office:* c/o University of Auckland, Auckland, New Zealand.

CAREER: University of Auckland, Auckland, New Zealand, junior lecturer in English, 1935-36, lecturer, 1946-49, senior lecturer, 1950-59, associate professor, 1960-69, professor of English literature, 1970—. *Military service:* British Army, Royal Artillery, 1940-46; became bombardier. *Member:* Oxford Society, British Film Institute. *Awards, honors:* Hubert Church Prose Award, 1958, for *I'll Soldier No More;* Jessie Mackay Poetry Award, 1959, for *The Living Countries.*

WRITINGS: Imaginary Islands (verse), privately printed, 1950; *Charles Aders* (biographical note), Auckland University College, 1953; *The New Zealand Short Story*, R.E. Owen, c.1956; *I'll Soldier No More* (novel), Gollancz, 1958; *The Living Countries* (verse), Paul's Book Arcade, 1959; *A Pound of Saffron* (novel), Gollancz, 1962; *Byron, the Poet* (criticism), Gollancz, 1964, Humanities, 1966; *The Hole in the Zero* (novel), Gollancz, 1967, Dutton, 1968; (editor and author of introduction) Mary W.G. Shelley, *Frankenstein; or, The Modern Prometheus* (text based on 3rd edition of 1831), Oxford University Press, 1969. Contributor of articles to *Landfall, New Zealand Listener, Comment,* and *Studies in Philology.*

WORK IN PROGRESS: Literature and the Visual Arts, 1800-1825.

SIDELIGHTS: Joseph heads for the Mediterranean countries of Europe whenever circumstances permit; says he is not wholly at home either in Europe or New Zealand, but wouldn't want to be without either.

BIOGRAPHICAL/CRITICAL SOURCES: Times Literary Supplement, September 21, 1967; *New York Times Book Review,* February 11, 1968.

* * *

JOSEPH, Stephen 1921-

PERSONAL: Born June 13, 1921, in London, England; son of Michael Joseph and Hermione Gingold (stage, screen, and television actress). *Education:* University of Iowa, M.F.A., 1952; Jesus College, Cambridge, M.A., 1953. *Politics:* "Anarchistic." *Home:* 119 Longwestgate, Scarborough, Yorkshire, England.

CAREER: Teacher and lecturer, 1939—; director of Studio Theatre Ltd., Stoke on Trent, England, 1955—, of Theatre in the Round Ltd., Leicester, England, 1962—, of Scarborough Theatre Trust Ltd., Scarborough, England, 1964—; University of Manchester, Manchester, England, lecturer in drama, 1962—. Theatre consultant, 1960—. *Military service:* Royal Navy, 1941-46; became lieutenant; received Distinguished Service Cross. *Member:* Association of British Theatre Technicians, Society of Theatre Consultants (Scarborough; secretary, 1964—).

WRITINGS: Theatre in the Round (pamphlet), Studio Theatre, 1955; (editor) *Adaptable Theatres*, Association of British Theatre Technicians, 1962; *Planning for New Forms of Theatre*, Strand Electric & Engineering Co., 1962, 3rd edition, revised and enlarged, 1966; (self-illustrated) *The Story of the Playhouse in England*, Barrie & Rockliff, 1963, Dufour, 1966; *Scene Painting and Design*, Pitman, 1964; (editor) Tyrone Guthrie and others, *Actor and Architect*, Manchester University Press, 1964; *Theatre in the Round*, Taplinger, 1967; *New Theatre Forms*, Theatre Arts, 1968. Occasional contributor to *Encore, Stage, Plays and Players, Guardian,* and *New Theatre.*

WORK IN PROGRESS: Research in dramatic theory.

SIDELIGHTS: "[I am] interested particularly in the form of theatre in the round, but also in new plays, new styles of acting and presentation; [I am an] advocate of small theatres with a meaningful place in their own community; [I have a] tendency to iconoclasm." *Avocational interests:* Gardening, motorcycles, and listening to music.

* * *

JOSEPHS, Ray 1912-
(Jay Raphael)

PERSONAL: Born January 1, 1912, in Philadelphia, Pa.; son of Isaac and Eva (Borsky) Josephs; married Juanita Wegner, February 22, 1941. *Education:* Attended University of Pennsylvania. *Home:* 415 East 52nd St., New York, N.Y. 10022. *Agent:* William Morris Agency, 1350

Avenue of the Americas, New York, N.Y. 10019. *Office:* 230 Park Ave., New York, N.Y. 10017.

CAREER: Philadelphia Evening Bulletin, Philadelphia, Pa., staff member, 1929-39; free-lance writer and correspondent in South America, mainly in Argentina, 1939-44, representing at various periods *Time, Christian Science Monitor, Chicago Sun, Variety,* and others; writer, lecturer on South America, in United States, 1944-50; writer, lecturer, and broadcaster, specializing in Latin American subjects, and public relations consultant, 1950—. President and chairman of board of Ray Josephs Public Relations Ltd. and Ray Joseph Associates, Inc., both New York, N.Y.; president of International Public Relations Co. Ltd., New York, N.Y., an affiliate of a Japanese firm. Harvard University, Graduate School of Business Administration, member of founder's committee of Tobe Lecture Series; Brandeis University, member of development committee. *Member:* Overseas Press Club of America, Writers Guild of America, East, Society of Magazine Writers (New York), American Club (Buenos Aires).

WRITINGS: Spies and Saboteurs in Argentina, privately printed, 1943; *Argentina Diary,* Random House, 1944; *Latin America: Continent in Crisis,* Random House, 1948; (with James Bruce) *Those Perplexing Argentines,* Longmans, Green, 1952; *How to Make Money from Your Ideas,* Doubleday, 1954; *How to Gain an Extra Hour Every Day,* Dutton, 1955; (with David Kemp) *Memoirs of a Live Wire,* privately printed, 1956; *Streamlining Your Executive Workload,* Prentice-Hall, 1958; (with Oscar Steiner) *Our Housing Jungle and Your Pocketbook,* University Publishers, 1960; (with Stanley Arnold) *The Magic Power of Putting Yourself Over with People,* Prentice-Hall, 1962. Contributor to books, magazines, and newspapers; writer for radio and television.

WORK IN PROGRESS: Writing on business and cultural activity, Japan and the United States, personnel efficiency and time saving, Latin America.

SIDELIGHTS: Josephs' books have been published in French, Portuguese, Italian, Japanese, Chinese, Spanish, and German editions.

* * *

JOY, Edward T(homas) 1909-

PERSONAL: Born September 27, 1909, in London, England; son of Michael and Annie (Blaikie) Joy; married Elsie Shaw, August 30, 1933; children: Alison Anne (Mrs. Michael Barnes), Ruth Veronica (Mrs. David Richardson). *Education:* University College, London, B.A., 1931; University of London, B.Sc., 1945; Institute of Historical Research, University of London, M.A., 1955. *Home and office:* The Rotunda Ickworth, Bury St., Edmunds, Suffolk, England.

CAREER: History teacher in grammar schools in England, 1932-48; Shoreditch Training College, Egham, Surrey, England, lecturer in history, 1948-69. University of London, extramural lecturer in history, 1945-60, chief examiner in history, General Certificates of Education, 1952-57, 1959-63, instructor, 1968. Lecturer on furniture. Curator, Ickworth National Trust, 1969—. *Wartime service:* British Home Guard, 1940-45; became captain. *Member:* Historical Association (chairman of Windsor and Eton branch), Royal Historical Society, Furniture History Society.

WRITINGS: English Furniture, A.D. 43-1950, Arco, 1962; *Country Life Book of English Furniture,* Country Life, 1964, published in America as *The Book of English Furniture,* A.S. Barnes, 1966, new edition published as *Antique English Furniture,* Drake Publications (San Francisco), 1972; *Woodwork in Winchester Cathedral,*

Friends of Winchester Cathedral, 1964; *Country Life Book of Clocks,* Country Life, 1967; *The Country Life Book of Chairs,* Country Life, 1967; *Chippendale,* Country Life, 1971, Transatlantic, 1972. Contributor to *Concise Encyclopaedia of Antiques,* Connoisseur, 1954, 1957, and to three volumes of "Connoisseur Period Guides," 1956-58. Also contributor to *Country Life, Connoisseur, Apollo, Antiques* (New York), *Burlington Magazine, Antique Collector, Discovering Antiques, Journal* of the Furniture History Society, and *Harper's,* 1951—.

WORK IN PROGRESS: The Firm of Holland & Son, to be published by Cassell; general research on 19th century furniture.

AVOCATIONAL INTERESTS: European craftsmanship, especially furniture, and collecting antique furniture on modest scale.

* * *

JOYCE, James Daniel 1921-

PERSONAL: Born January 12, 1921, in Spencer, Va.; son of James G. (a farmer) and Mary (Taylor) Joyce; married Beatrice Campbell, August 2, 1946; children: Kevin Campbell. *Education:* Johnson Bible College, A.B., 1945; Lynchburg College, A.B., 1946; Christian Theological Seminary, B.D., 1949, M.A., 1950; Yale University, M.A., 1952, Ph.D., 1958. *Home:* 1118 West York, Enid, Okla. 73701. *Office:* Phillips Graduate Seminary, Enid, Okla. 73701.

CAREER: Minister, Christian Church; Christian theological Seminary, Indianapolis, Inc., associate professor of Biblical theology, 1960-62; Phillips Graduate Seminary, Enid, Okla., dean and professor of Biblical theology, 1962—.

WRITINGS: The Living Christ in Our Changing World, Bethany Press, 1962; *The Place of the Sacraments in Worship,* Bethany Press, 1967. Book editor, *Encounter,* 1960-62.

* * *

JUDA, L(yon) 1923-

PERSONAL: Born February 3, 1923, in Istanbul, Turkey; married Flora de Mayo (a bookbinder), June 17, 1950. *Education:* Attended English High School for Boys, Istanbul, Turkey; American Robert College, Istanbul, Turkey, B.A. *Home:* Greystoke, Mayfield Dr., Pinner, Middlesex, England.

CAREER: Williams & Williams Ltd. (manufacturers of metal doors and windows), Chester, England, London export manager. *Member:* Society of Authors.

WRITINGS: The Wise Old Man: Turkish Tales of Nasreddin Hodja, Thomas Nelson, 1963. Contributor of short stories and articles to *Blackwood's Magazine, Evening News,* and other periodicals and newspapers.

WORK IN PROGRESS: A novel with London background.

* * *

JUNKER, Karin Stensland 1916-

PERSONAL: Born October 7, 1916, in Lidingo, Stockholm, Sweden; daughter of Josef Gottfrid (a publisher and translator) and Elisabet M. (Samuelsson) Jonsson; married Bengt Junker, March 2, 1940 (died, 1970); children: Sten, Lena, Boel, Riken, Anders. *Education:* University of Stockholm, student, 1935-37, 1954-58, Phil. Mag., 1958, Ph.D., 1968. *Politics:* Liberal (moderate). *Religion:* Lutheran. *Home:* Asogatan 211, S-11632 Stockholm, Sweden. *Agent:* A. B. Europapress, Drottninggatan 10, Stockholm C., Sweden. *Office:* Blockhusringen 17, S-115 25 Stockholm, Sweden.

CAREER: Writer, 1944—. Swedish State Institute for Building Research, editor, 1947-53. Committee member of Royal Board of Education, 1957-58, of Department of Social Work, 1958-59. Member of board of Swedish Scouts' and Guides' Association foundations for handicapped children, of Swedish National Association for Retarded Children, and of other foundations and boards for handicapped youth. *Wartime service:* Special service in Security Guard, 1941-44.

RITINS: Du kanner mig icke (novel; title means "You Don't Know Me"), Fahlcrantz & Gumaelius, 1944; *Det okuvliga hjaertat* (title means "The Unsubduable Heart"), Fahlcrantz & Gumaelius, 1945; *Building Production Methods of Scandinavia,* State Institute of Building Research, 1950; *Auditory Training of Deaf and Hard of Hearing,* Scout Association Publication, 1952; (with Lennart Holmgren) *Hoerseltraening och fostran av doeva smaabarn,* 2nd edition, Scoutfoerlaget, 1952; *What Shall We Do With Ture?,* Scout Association Publication, 1956; *De ensamma,* Natur & Kultur, 1961, 3rd edition, 1963, translation by Gustaf Lannestock published as *The Child in the Glass Ball,* Abingdon, 1964; *Samhallets samvetsbarn* (title means "Community's Conscience Children"), Natur & Kultur, 1964; (with Bengt Barr) *Children with Speech Disorders,* Kooperativa oerb. (Stockholm, c. 1964; (contributor) *Annorlunda barn* (title means "Otherwise Children"), 1965; *Paralinguistics and Kinesics in Pathological Speech Development,* University of Stockholm, 1965; *On the Behavioral Pattern in Infants at Sound Perception Against the Background of Later Developed Speech and Communicative Behavior,* University of Stockholm, 1968; (contributor) *Foeraeldraboken* (title means "Parents' Book"), Bernce's, 1968; (with Evy Blid) *How a "Lekotek" Was Started, and How It Works,* 1969; (with Barr) *Functional Contact Test for Babies as a Screening Method,* 1970; (with Erik Wedenberg) *Auditory Training of Hearing Impaired Children,* 1971; *Lekoteket paa Blockhusudden* (title means "A Program for Training Through Systematic Play Activity"), 1971; *Selective Attention in Infants and Consecutive Communicative Behavior,* Almqvist & Wiksell, 1972. Also author of *Litta, lyssna, le—tre hoernstenar i barns mentala utveckling* (title means "Look, Listen, Smile—Three Cardinal Steps in Children's Mental Development"), published by Bonniers.

WORK IN PROGRESS: Haer slutar allmaen vaeg (title means "End of the General Highway"), a sequel to *The Child in the Glass Ball; Solo Part for Cello,* a novel, completed and awaiting publication.

SIDELIGHTS: Dr. Junker told *CA:* "As the mother of two children mentally retarded (in different ways), I switched over my interests to the field of child psychology in 1953 . . . and thus left the field of building research. . . . I want to keep the door open to artistic writing, though." During journeys in Europe, India, and United States, Dr. Junker says that she has found the problems of the mentally handicapped much the same: "Too little is done to employ and occupy them; much more could be done to fight prejudice against them." She is now focusing on the early diagnosis of handicaps in children, and has developed a screening test for 7-to-9-month-old infants, which has been applied to all Swedish babies since 1971.

*　　*　　*

JUSTUS, May 1898-

PERSONAL: Born May 12, 1898, in Del Rio, Tenn.; daughter of Stephen (a teacher) and Margaret (Brooks) Justus. *Education:* Studied at University of Tennessee. *Politics:* Democrat. *Home:* Route 1, Tracy City, Tenn. 37387.

CAREER: Writer of children's books, dealing with ways and lore of Smoky Mountain region, 1927—. Teacher of handicapped and retarded children in her home. *Awards, honors:* Julia Ellsworth Ford Prize, 1935, for *Gabby Gaffer's New Shoes,* and 1936, for *Near-Side-and-Far;* Boys' Club Award, 1950, for *Luck for Little Lihu.*

WRITINGS: Peter Pocket: A Little Boy of the Cumberland Mountains, Doubleday, 1927; *Betty Lou of Big Log Mountain,* Doubleday, 1928; *Gabby Gaffer,* Volland, 1929; *At the Foot of Windy Low,* Volland, 1930; *Peter Pocket's Luck,* Doubleday, 1930; *The Other Side of the Mountain,* Doubleday, 1931; *Peter Pocket's Books* (including *Peter Pocket* and *Peter Pocket's Luck*), Doubleday, 1934; *Gabby Gaffer's New Shoes,* Suttonhouse, 1935; *Honey Jane* (Junior Literary Guild selection), Doubleday, 1935; *Near-Side-and-Far,* Suttonhouse, 1936; *The House in No-End-Hollow* (Junior Literary Guild selection), Doubleday, 1938.

Here Comes Mary Ellen, Lippincott, 1940; *Mr. Songcatcher and Company,* Doubleday, 1940; *The Mail Wagon Mystery* (Junior Literary Guild selection), Albert Whitman, 1940; *Cabin on Kettle Creek* (Junior Literary Guild selection), Lippincott, 1941; *Dixie Decides,* Random House, 1942; *Fiddle Away,* Grosset, 1942; *Nancy of Apple Tree Hill,* Albert Whitman, 1942; *Step Along* [and] *Jerry Jake,* Albert Whitman, 1942; *Bluebird, Fly Up!,* Lippincott, 1943; *Jerry Jake Carries On,* Albert Whitman, 1943; *Banjo Billy and Mr. Bones,* Albert Whitman, 1944; *Lizzie,* Albert Whitman, 1944; *Fiddlers' Fair,* Albert Whitman, 1945; *Hurray for Jerry Jake,* Albert Whitman, 1945; *Sammy* (Junior Literary Guild selection), Albert Whitman, 1946; *Mary Ellen,* Broadman, 1947; *Susie,* Albert Whitman, 1948; *Toby Has A Dog,* Albert Whitman, 1949; (with others) *Big Meeting Day, and Other Festival Tales,* Aladdin, 1950; *Luck for Little Lihu,* Aladdin, 1950; *Lucky Penny,* Aladdin, 1951; *Children of the Great Smoky Mountains,* Dutton, 1952; *Whoop-ee Hunkydory!,* Albert Whitman, 1952; *Peter Pocket and His Pickle Pup,* Holt, 1953; *Little Red Rooster Learns to Crow,* Albert Whitman, 1954; *Surprise for Peter Pocket,* Holt, 1955; *Use Your Head, Hildy,* Holt, 1956; *Peddler's Pack,* Holt, 1957, 2nd edition published as *The Complete Peddler's Pack: Games, Songs, Rhymes, and Riddles from Mountain Folklore,* University of Tennessee Press, 1967; *Big Log Mountain,* Holt, 1958; *Jumping Johnny and Skedaddle,* Row, Peterson, 1958, revised edition, Garrard, 1971; *Let's Play and Sing,* Broadman, 1958; *Barney, Bring Your Banjo,* Holt, 1959; *Then Came Mr. Billy Barker,* Hastings House, 1959.

Lester and His Hound Pup, Hastings House, 1960; *The Right House for Rowdy,* Holt, 1960; *Winds A'Blowing* (poems), Abingdon, 1961; *Smoky Mountain Sampler* (stories), Abingdon, 1962; *New Boy in School* (chosen Ambassador Book by English Speaking Union, 1963; chosen Brotherhood Book by National Conference of Christians and Jews, 1963; Catholic Book Club selection, 1963), Hastings House, 1963; *The Tale of a Pig* (adaption of American folk song), Abingdon, 1963; *A New Home for Billy,* Hastings House, 1966; *The Wonderful School of Miss Tillie O'Toole,* Golden Press, 1969; *It Happened in No-End Hollow,* Garrard, 1969; *Eben and the Rattlesnake,* Garrard, 1969; *Tales from Near-Side-and-Far,* Garrard, 1970; *Holidays in No-End Hollow,* Garrard, 1970; *Jumping Johnny Outwits Skedaddle,* Garrard, 1971; *Surprise for Perky Pup,* Garrard, 1971; *You're Sure Silly, Billy,* Garrad, 1972.

WORK IN PROGRESS: Two collections of poems for children published in juvenile magazines from 1925-1970: *All Through the Year,* a book of seasonal poems, and *Some One Is Knocking,* poems about childhood experience.

SIDELIGHTS: Miss Justus told CA: "I was born and reared in Coche County in East Tennessee, in the shadow of the Great Smoky Mountains. My mother had a remarkable memory for the old folk songs and the folk tales of that region. These have all been included in my books about life in the Great Smokies. There are now over fifty of them. ... It makes me happy to know that my writing has helped preserve the ways of my people for children of other areas for generations to come."

Miss Justus still lives in the little mountain home where she has spent the greater part of her life. There is a May Justus Collection at the University of Tennessee containing all her books, many manuscripts, and a vast correspondence.

New Boy in School was on the New York Times Best Book List for 1963, and The Tale of a Pig was used by the Canadian Broadcasting Corp. in their television series, "The Friendly Giant," in 1970.

*   *   *

KAHRL, Stanley J.   1931-

PERSONAL: Born June 30, 1931, in Mount Vernon, Ohio; son of George Morrow (a teacher) and Faith (Jessup) Kahrl; married Julia Gamble, June 20, 1954; children: Jennifer, George, Sarah. Education: Harvard University, A.B., 1953, Ph.D., 1962; St. Catherine's College, Cambridge, B.A., 1958, M.A., 1962. Politics: Republican. Religion: Episcopal. Home: 48 Amazon Pl., Columbus, Ohio 43214. Office: Department of English, Ohio State University, Columbus, Ohio 43214.

CAREER: University of Rochester, Rochester, N.Y., instructor, 1962-65, assistant professor of English, 1965-69; Ohio State University, Columbus, professor of English, 1969—. Member of board of directors, Allendale School, 1968-69. Military service: U.S. Navy, 1953-56; became lieutenant j.g. Member: Modern Language Association of America, Modern Humanities Research Association, Mediaeval Academy of America, Renaissance Society of America, Ars Antiqua Society (member of board of directors).

WRITINGS: (Editor with Curt Buhler) Two Early Chapbooks: The Merry Tales of the Mad-Men of Gotham and The History of Tom Thumb the Little, Northwestern University Press for Renaissance English Text Society, 1964; (with J.B. Bessinger) Essential Articles for the Study of Old English Poetry, Archon Books, 1968. Contributor of articles and reviews to journals. Assistant editor, Journal of British Studies, 1963-66, Research Opportunities in Renaissance Drama, 1967—; editor, Old English Newsletter, 1969—.

WORK IN PROGRESS: Editing The N-Town Cycle; Fifteenth and Sixteenth Century English Drama, for Hutchinson; writing on allegory and on stylistic origins of Renaissance jest-books.

AVOCATIONAL INTERESTS: Choral singing, birdwatching, hunting, skiing, fishing.

*   *   *

KAISER, Robert Blair   1930-

PERSONAL: Surname was originally Piser; born December 3, 1930, in Detroit, Mich.; son of Robert (an engineer) and Olive Blair (Hungate) Piser; married Susan Ann Mulcahey, November 28, 1959; children: Margaret Anne, John Gustave. Education: Santa Clara University, student, 1948-52; Gonzaga University, B.A., 1952, M.A., 1955. Religion: Roman Catholic. Agent: Henry Volkening, Russell, Volkening & Donadio, 551 Fifth Ave., New York, N.Y. 10017. Office: 9570 Wilshire Blvd., Beverly Hills, Calif. 90212.

CAREER: Time-Life News Service, New York, N.Y., foreign correspondent, 1961-64, Los Angeles correspondent, 1964—. Awards, honors: Overseas Press Club Award for best magazine reporting of foreign affairs, 1962.

WRITINGS: Pope, Council and World: The Story of Vatican II, Macmillan (New York), 1963 (published in England as Inside the Council: The Story of Vatican II, Burns & Oates, 1963); "R.F.K. Must Die!": A History of the Robert Kennedy Assassination and Its Aftermath, Dutton, 1970.

SIDELIGHTS: As Lance Morrow wrote in 1971, "just why Sirhan Sirhan killed Robert Kennedy may never be fully explained. But few have tried harder to solve the mystery than Journalist Robert Blair Kaiser." Kaiser was able to gain intimate access to his subject through sheer determination and an offer to pay a portion of Sirhan's defense from the proceeds of his writings. His final analysis of the Robert Kennedy assassination contains so detailed a portrait of Sirhan, in fact, that Sirhan's family tried, unsuccessfully, to halt publication of the book through a court order.

"The result of Kaiser's effort is ...", like the case itself, weirdly incomplete," Morrow opines. D.B. Duval agrees that Kaiser "fails to uncover the ultimate truth, but he does succeed in raising a number of fascinating questions, most of which he thinks he could answer with another year's research. He gathers a large amount of circumstantial evidence, some significant, some not, to show that Sirhan either programmed himself to kill Kennedy or that he was programmed by another, as in The Manchurian Candidate." Several critics, among them Geoffrey Wolff, have noted that the book's "most import contribution to the burgeoning literature of American mayhem is its study of Sirhan." Kaiser was even allowed to sit in on sessions during which Sirhan was hypnotized by the chief defense psychiatrist. After months of investigation and close contact with the journalist, Kaiser said, "Sirhan began to discover he didn't like me very much. The feeling was mutual."

BIOGRAPHICAL/CRITICAL SOURCES: Ladies' Home Journal, May, 1970; Washington Post, October 15, 1970; Newsweek, October 19, 1970; Best Sellers, November 1, 1970; Time, January 4, 1971; National Review, February 23, 1971.†

*   *   *

KALISH, Donald   1919-

PERSONAL: Born December 4, 1919, in Chicago, Ill., son of Lionel (a manufacturer) and Mildred (Pareira) Kalish; divorced. Education: University of California, Berkeley, B.A., 1943, M.A., 1945, Ph.D., 1949. Home: 15142 Mulholland Dr., Los Angeles, Calif. 90024. Office: University of California, Los Angeles, Los Angeles, Calif. 90024.

CAREER: Swarthmore College, Swarthmore, Pa., instructor in philosophy, 1946-47; University of California, Los Angeles, instructor, 1949-51, assistant professor, 1951-56, associate professor, 1957-64, professor of philosophy, 1964—, chairman of the department, 1964-70. Member: Association for Symbolic Logic, Mind Association, American Philosophical Association, American Association of University Professors.

WRITINGS: (With Richard Montague) Logic: Techniques of Formal Reasoning, Harcourt, 1964.

*   *   *

KALLENBACH, W(illiam) Warren   1926-

PERSONAL: Surname is pronounced Col-len-bock; born July 16, 1926, in Eugene, Mo.; son of Frederick Valentine (a farmer, businessman, and politician) and Alma (Thompson) Kallenbach; married Patricia Adams (a teacher), April 6, 1947; children: Ann, Sally, Sue. *Education:* Drury College, A.B. (magna cum laude), 1949; Stanford University, M.A., 1953, Ed.D., 1959. *Politics:* Democrat. *Religion:* Unitarian. *Home:* 1232 Harriet St., Palo Alto, Calif. 94301.

CAREER: San Jose State College, San Jose, Calif., member of department of education, 1957—, director of intern teaching program, 1959-62, now co-director. Research coordinator for IOTA teaching effectiveness study, 1959—; consultant on teacher evaluation, micro-teaching, and individualized instruction, Palo Alto, Calif., 1961—. Project director on various studies. Co-holder of copyright on instrument for observation of teacher activities. Member of Palo Alto Community Players, 1955-58; president, Friends of Palo Alto Childrens Theatre, 1970—. Chairman, Palo Alto Citizens' Committee on School Finance. *Military service:* U.S. Naval Reserve, 1944-46; became noncommissioned officer. *Member:* American Educational Research Association, American Psychological Association, National Council on Measurement in Education, American Association of University Professors, California Educational Research Association, California Teachers Association (president, Los Altos branch, 1955-56), Phi Delta Kappa.

WRITINGS: (Senior editor with Harold M. Hodges, Jr.) *Education and Society,* C.E. Merrill, 1963; (with Lucien Kinney and others) *Measuring Teacher Competence,* California Teachers Association, 1965, 2nd edition, 1967; *The Role of the Teacher in Society: Six Areas of Teacher Competence,* Arizona State University Bookstore, 1970; *Contemporary Approaches to the Social Foundations of Education,* Prentice-Hall, in press. Contributor of articles to education journals.

WORK IN PROGRESS: Handbooks for school district teacher evaluation programs, and for workshops for individualizing instruction and learning.

* * *

KAMM, Josephine (Hart) 1905-

PERSONAL: Born December 31, 1905, in London, England; daughter of Percy M.C. (a lawyer) and Hilda (Marx) Hart; married George Emile Kamm (a publisher; now deceased), April 4, 1929; children: Antony. *Education:* Attended Queen's College School, London, England, and Parents' National Educational School, Burgess Hill, Sussex, England. *Agent:* Winant Towers Ltd., 1 Furnival St., London E.C.4, England.

CAREER: Held secretarial post until marriage; British Ministry of Information, London, England, literary and administrative posts, 1939-45; writer. *Member:* National Book League (member of council). *Awards, honors:* Isaac Siegel Juvenile Award of Jewish Book Council of America, 1962, for *Return to Freedom.*

WRITINGS: All Quiet at Home (novel), Longmans, Green, 1936; *Disorderly Caravan* (novel), Harrap, 1938; *Nettles to My Head* (novel), Duckworth, 1939; *Progress Towards Self-government in the British Colonies,* Fosh & Cross, 1945; *Peace, Perfect Peace* (novel), Duckworth, 1947; *Come, Draw This Curtain* (novel), Duckworth, 1948; *Abraham: A Biography,* Union of Liberal & Progressive Synagogues, 1948; *Gertrude Bell: Daughter of the Desert,* Vanguard, 1956 (published in England as *Daughter of the Desert: The Story of Gertrude Bell,* Bodley Head, 1956); *How Different from Us: A Biography of Miss Buss and Miss Beale,* Bodley Head, 1958; *Hope Deferred: Girls' Education in English History,* Methuen, 1965; *Rapiers and Battleaxes: The Women's Movement and Its Aftermath,* Humanities, 1966.

Juveniles: *African Challenge: The Story of the British in Tropical Africa,* Thomas Nelson, 1946; *He Went with Captain Cook,* Harrap, 1952; *Janet Carr: Journalist,* Bodley Head, 1953; *They Served the People,* Bodley Head, 1954; *Student Almoner,* Bodley Head, 1955; *Men Who Served Africa,* Harrap, 1957; *Leaders of the People,* Abelard, 1959; *The Story of Sir Moses Montefiore,* Valentine, Mitchell, 1960; *The Story of Mrs. Pankhurst,* Methuen, 1961, published in America as *The Story of Emmeline Pankhurst,* Meredith, 1968; *Return to Freedom,* Abelard, 1962; *Out of Step,* Brockhampton Press, 1962; *Malaya and Singapore,* Longmans, Green, 1963; *Malaria Ross,* Methuen, 1963, Criterion, 1964; *A New Look at the Old Testament,* Gollancz, 1965, published in America as *Kings, Prophets and History: A New Look at the Old Testament,* McGraw, 1966; *Young Mother,* Duell, Sloan & Pearce, 1965; *The Story of Fanny Burney,* Methuen, 1966, Meredith, 1967; *The Hebrew People: A History of the Jews from Biblical Times to the Present Day,* Gollancz, 1967, published in America as *The Hebrew People: A History of the Jews,* McGraw, 1968; *Joseph Paxton and the Crystal Palace: A Story Biography,* Methuen, 1967; *No Strangers Here,* Constable, 1968; *First Job,* Brockhampton Press, 1969, 2nd edition, 1971; *Explorers into Africa,* Crowell, 1970; *A Duty to Survive: A Centenary History of the Girls' Public Day School Trust,* Allen & Unwin, 1971.

BIOGRAPHICAL/CRITICAL SOURCES: New Statesman, May 26, 1967; *Book World,* March 17, 1968; *Books and Bookmen,* July, 1968, June, 1970; *Best Sellers,* December 1, 1968; *Times Literary Supplement,* June 26, 1969.

* * *

KANE, Robert S. 1925-

PERSONAL: Born April 19, 1925, in Albany, N.Y.; son of Samuel Charles and Stella (Weiss) Kane. *Education:* Syracuse University, B.S. in Journalism, 1947; University of Southampton, graduate study, 1948. *Home:* 145 East 74th St., New York, N.Y. 10021. *Agent:* Anita Diamant, 51 East 42nd St., New York, N.Y. 10017. *Office:* Cue Magazine, 20 West 43rd St., New York, N.Y. 10036.

CAREER: Started as reporter for *Daily Tribune,* Great Bend, Kan., later worked in New York, N.Y., for *Staten Island Daily Advance* and *New York Herald Tribune,* then for *New York World-Telegram and Sun,* 1954-59; *Playbill,* New York, N.Y., travel editor, 1961-63; *Cue,* New York, N.Y., travel editor, 1963—. Working-party member, President Johnson's Task Force on Travel, 1968. Travel lecturer; photographer. *Military service:* U.S. Navy, World War II; served in Pacific; became petty officer. *Member:* Society of American Travel Writers (regional secretary, 1962-63; national secretary, 1963-64; national president, 1968-69; chairman of board, 1970), Overseas Press Club of America, New York Travel Writers' Association. *Awards, honors:* Austrian Gold Medal of Touristic Merit, 1969.

WRITINGS—All published by Doubleday: (Contributor) Nelson Doubleday and C. Earl Cooley, editors, *Encyclopedia of World Travel,* 1961; *Africa A to Z: A Guide for Travelers—Armchair and Actual,* 1961, 2nd edition, 1972; *South America A to Z,* 1962, revised edition, 1971; *Asia A to Z,* 1963; *Canada A to Z,* 1964; *South Pacific A to Z,* 1966; *Eastern Europe A to Z,* 1968; (contributor) *Around the World with the Experts,* 1969; *The Grand Tour A to Z: The Capitals of Europe,* 1972. Contributor to magazines and newspapers, including *Atlantic, Saturday Review, Harper's Bazaar, Venture, Popular Photography, Life, House and Garden, New York Times,* and *Christian Science Monitor.*

SIDELIGHTS: Kane has visited well over one hundred countries on six continents. Avocational interests: Swimming, reading.

* * *

KAPLAN, Charles 1919-

PERSONAL: Born May 15, 1919, in Chicago, Ill.; son of Bernard R. and Lillian (Muchnick); married Geraldine Weber (a teacher), February 21, 1943; children: Jean Laura, Robert Barry, Judith Claire. Education: University of Chicago, A.B., 1940; Northwestern University, M.A., 1942, Ph.D., 1952. Home: 17136 Lisette St., Granada Hills, Calif. 91344. Office: San Fernando Valley State College, Northridge, Calif. 91324.

CAREER: Roosevelt University, Chicago, Ill., instructor in English, 1946-54; Los Angeles State College (now California State University at Los Angeles), Los Angeles, Calif., assistant professor of English, 1954-56; San Fernando Valley State College, Northridge, Calif., associate professor, 1957-59, professor of English, 1959—. Fulbright lecturer in France, 1963-64. Military service: U.S. Naval Reserve, 1941-46. Member: National Council of Teachers of English, Modern Language Association of America, American Studies Association, American Association of University Professors.

WRITINGS: (With others) The Technique of Composition, Holt, 1960; (editor) Criticism: Twenty Major Statements, Chandler Publishing, 1964; Instructor's Manual for "The Experience of Literature" by Lionel Trilling, Holt, 1967; Guided Composition, Holt, 1968; Approaches to the Short Story, Holt, 1969; (editor) The Overwrought Urn: A Potpourri of Parodies of Critics Who Triumphantly Present the Real Meaning of Authors from Jane Austen to J.D. Salinger, Pegasus, 1969; (editor) Literature in America: The Modern Age, Free Press, 1971.

WORK IN PROGRESS: Study of historiography of American literature.

AVOCATIONAL INTERESTS: Reading, travel, fishing.

BIOGRAPHICAL/CRITICAL SOURCES: Book World, September 28, 1969; Christian Science Monitor, October 9, 1969.

* * *

KAPPEN, Charles Vaughan 1910-

PERSONAL: Born May 25, 1910, in Eureka Springs, Ark.; son of William Gilbert (a retail merchant) and Charlotta Tempest (Vaughan) Kappen; married Nora Elizabeth Wood, January 15, 1931; children: Patricia Ann (Mrs. Edward E. Terrill), Charles Gilbert. Education: University of Arkansas, B.A., 1933; Arkansas State Teachers College, graduate student, 1933; University of Wisconsin, M.A., 1947. Politics: Republican. Religion: Methodist. Home: 2201 Peachtree Lane, San Jose, Calif. 95128. Office: Department of Journalism and Advertising, San Jose State College, San Jose, Calif. 95114.

CAREER: Newspaper reporter, then editor, in Southwest and Middle West, 1927-42; University of Wisconsin, Madison, assistant professor of journalism, 1946-47; University of Tulsa, Tulsa, Okla., assistant professor of journalism, 1947-48; San Jose State College, San Jose, Calif., assistant professor, 1948-51, associate professor, 1951-59, professor of journalism, 1959—. Military service: U.S. Army, 1942-46, 1951-53; became major; received Bronze Star. Member: Association for Education in Journalism, American Association of University Professors, California State Numismatic Association (member of board of directors, 1949-62; vice-president, 1963-65), California Exonumist Society (member of board of directors, 1963-65), San Jose Coin Club (president, 1950-51), Sigma

Delta Chi, Pi Delta Epsilon, Kappa Tau Alpha, Kappa Delta Pi.

WRITINGS: (With Ralph A. Mitchell) Depression Scrip of the United States: Period of the 1930's, Globe Printing Co. (San Jose, Calif.), 1961; (with Harold E. Hibler) So-Called Dollars: An Illustrated Standard Catalogue with Valuations, Coin and Currency Institute (New York), 1963; (contributor) James L. Betton, editor, Money Talks, Hendricks Printing Co., 1970. Editor and author of introduction of Lyman H. Low's Hard Times Tokens, William F. Dunham's Easy Finding List, and Edgar H. Adams' photographic plates, Globe Printing Co., 1955. Contributor to International Communication as a Field of Study, edited by James W. Markham, Economy Advertising Co. Contributor to coin journals, magazines, and newspapers. Member of editorial advisory committee of two reprints of coin books; editor, Calcoin News (magazine), 1949-62.

WORK IN PROGRESS: California Merchant Cards and Tokens, describing more than fifteen thousand pieces.

BIOGRAPHICAL/CRITICAL SOURCES: Calcoin News, November, 1951, spring, 1962.

* * *

KARLIN, Robert 1918-

PERSONAL: Born October 16, 1918, in New York, N.Y.; son of David and Rose Karlin; married Edith Schur, December 25, 1943; children: Andrea, Paul. Education: College of City of New York (now City College of the City University of New York), A.B., 1939; New York University, M.A., 1940, Ph.D., 1955. Home: 6 Laurel Way, Sea Cliff, N.Y. 11579.

CAREER: Hofstra University, Hempstead, N.Y., instructor in reading, 1953-55; New York University, New York, N.Y., assistant professor of educational psychology, 1955-59; Southern Illinois University, Carbondale, professor of education and director, reading center, 1959-65; Queens College of the City University of New York, Queens, N.Y., professor of education and coordinator of graduate reading programs, 1965—. Member, National Conference on Research in English. Member: International Reading Association, National Council of Teachers of English, American Association of University Professors, National Society for the Study of Education.

WRITINGS: Teaching Reading in High School, Bobbs-Merrill, 1964; (editor and contributor with Eugene B. Grant) Developmental Reading, Office of Superintendent of Public Instruction of Illinois, 1964; (editor with others) College-Adult Reading Instruction, International Reading Association, 1964; (editor with others) Secondary School Reading Instruction, International Reading Association, 1964; (editor with others) Children, Books and Reading, International Reading Association, 1964; Teaching Reading in High School: Selected Articles, Bobbs-Merrill, 1969, 2nd edition, 1972; (compiler) Reading for Achievement, Holt, 1969; (with others) "Bookmark Reading Program," thirteen volumes, Harcourt, 1970; Teaching Elementary Reading: Principles and Strategies, Harcourt, 1971. Contributor of more than thirty articles and book reviews to professional journals. Contributing editor, Journal of Reading; member of editorial board, Reading Improvement.

WORK IN PROGRESS: Text revisions.

AVOCATIONAL INTERESTS: Sailing, traveling.

* * *

KATZ, Robert L. 1917-

PERSONAL: Born September 18, 1917, in Fort Dodge, Iowa; son of Raphael M. and Rebecca Katz; married Miriam Katz (a social worker); children: Amy Jean,

Michael, Jonathan. *Education:* Lake Forest College, B.A., 1938; Hebrew Union College, M.H.L., 1943, D.H.L., 1952. *Home:* 4187 Rose Hill, Cincinnati, Ohio. 45229. *Office:* Department of Human Relations, Hebrew Union College, Clifton Ave., Cincinnati, Ohio, 45220.

CAREER: Hebrew Union College, Cincinnati, Ohio, 1947—, now professor of human relations. Former teacher of sociology at University of Cincinnati and Antioch College. *Military service:* U.S. Army, chaplain, World War II; served with Fifth Army in Italy; became captain. *Member:* Central Conference of American Rabbis, American Sociological Association.

WRITINGS: Empathy: Its Nature and Uses, Free Press, 1963. Also author or co-author of experimental texts published by Hebrew Union College-Jewish Institute of Religion; department editor, *Central Conference of American Rabbis Journal.*

* * *

KATZ, Stanley Nider 1934-

PERSONAL: Born April 23, 1934, in Chicago, Ill.; son of William Stephen (a businessman) and Florence (Nider) Katz; married Adria Holmes, January 16, 1960; children: Derek Holmes. *Education:* Harvard University, A.B. (magna cum laude), 1955, A.M., 1959, Ph.D., 1961; King's College, London, Fulbright fellow, 1959-60. *Politics:* Democrat. *Office:* University of Chicago Law School, 1111 East 60th St., Chicago, Ill. 60637.

CAREER: Harvard University, Cambridge, Mass., instructor, 1961-64, Allston Burr Senior Tutor in Leverett House, 1963-65, assistant professor of history, 1964-65; University of Wisconsin, Madison, assistant professor, 1965-68, associate professor of history, 1968-71; University of Chicago Law School, Chicago, Ill., professor of legal history 1971—. *Member:* American Historical Society, Mississippi Valley Historical Society, Phi Beta Kappa. *Awards, honors:* Fellowships from American Bar Foundation, 1966-67, Harvard University, 1966-67, 1969-70, and American Council of Learned Societies, 1969-70.

WRITINGS: (Editor) James Alexander, *A Brief Narrative of the Case and Trial of John Peter Zenger,* Harvard University Press, 1963; *Newcastle's New York: Anglo-American Politics, 1732-1753,* Harvard University Press, 1968; (editor with Stanley I. Kutler) *New Perspectives on the American Past,* two volumes, Little, Brown, 1969, 2nd edition, 1972; (contributor) A.G. Olson and R.M. Brown, editors, *Anglo-American Political Relations, 1675-1775,* Rutgers University Press, 1970; (editor) *Colonial America: Essays in Politics and Social Development,* Little, Brown, 1971. Editor, "Studies in Legal History" series, Harvard University Press. Contributor to New York Historical Society *Quarterly, Chicago Law Review, Perspectives in American History,* and *William and Mary Quarterly.* Associate editor, *Journal of Interdisciplinary History,* 1969—.

BIOGRAPHICAL/CRITICAL SOURCES: Library Journal, June 1, 1968; *Times Literary Supplement,* June 12, 1969.

* * *

KAUFMAN, Rosamond (Arleen) V(an) P(oznak) 1923-

PERSONAL: Born July 23, 1923, in Newark, N.J.; daughter of Ira and Esther (Tepper) Van Poznak; married William I. Kaufman (a writer and editor), December 15, 1946; children: Iva Anne, Lazarus Seley. *Education:* Upsala College, B.A., (magna cum laude), 1945. *Religion:* Hebrew. *Home:* 1361 Madison Ave., New York, N.Y. 10028. *Office:* 208 East 50th St., New York, N.Y. 10022.

CAREER: Singer and actress, appearing in operettas and on network television, under name Rosamund Vance, 1941-53; Hillside (N.J.) public schools, teacher, 1946-47; Jewish Museum, executive secretary of education and acquisition fund, 1961-65; Dell Publishing Co., New York, N.Y., indexer for "The Wonderful World of Cooking," 1964-65; Food Photographers, Inc., New York, N.Y., vice-president, 1967—; interpreter, Simmons Tours, 1967—. *Member:* Volunteers of Shelter, Alliance Francaise, Metropolitan Opera Guild (New York), Lambda Sigma Alpha.

WRITINGS: Checklist for Expectant Mothers, Doubleday, 1964; (adapter with Joan Gilbert Van Poznak) William I. Kaufman, compiler, *UNICEF Book of Children's Legends,* Stackpole, 1970; (adapter with Van Poznak) William I. Kaufman, *UNICEF Book of Children's Prayers,* Stackpole, 1970; (with Sybil Leek) *Astrological Guide to Love and Sex,* Pyramid Publications, 1971. Editor, writer, and/or researcher for several cook books by husband, William I. Kaufman, 1949-67. Writer of television show, "Van and the Genie," 1950.

AVOCATIONAL INTERESTS: Swimming, reading, travel.†

* * *

KAY, Kenneth (Edmond) 1915-

PERSONAL: Born February 12, 1915, in Atlanta, Ga.; son of Kenneth Edmond and Dorothy (Bennett) Kay; married Phyllis Charline Bockhold, March 31, 1953; children: Nancy, Elizabeth, Alice, Ariane, Kenneth. *Education:* Studied at Young Harris Junior College, 1932-34, and Northwestern University, 1938-39; University of Denver, B.A., 1952. *Address:* Armed Forces Staff College, Norfolk, Va. 23511. *Agent:* Curtis Brown Ltd., 60 East 56th St., New York, N.Y. 10022.

CAREER: Great American Insurance Co., 1934-41, 1946-47, started as mail clerk, became special agent in Chicago, Ill., then in Nashville, Tenn. U.S. Army, 1941-45; served in India and China; rose from private to major; received Distinguished Unit Emblem, Commendation Ribbon, Asiatic-Pacific Campaign Medal with two battle stars. U.S. Air Force, career service, 1947—, with major foreign assignments as exchange officer with Royal Air Force in England, and staff officer of U.S. European Command in Paris, France; now lieutenant colonel. *Member:* Toastmasters International (chapter president, 1963), Authors League of America. *Awards, honors:* Winner of annual U.S. Air Force short story contest, 1954, 1956.

WRITINGS: Trouble in the Air (novel), Eyre & Spottiswoode, 1959. Short stories have appeared in *Saturday Evening Post, Country Gentlemen, Argosy,* and in military and foreign magazines; contributor of articles to *Writer* and military periodicals.

WORK IN PROGRESS: A novel set in the late 1930's.

SIDELIGHTS: Kay's novel was published in Spanish and Norwegian; his three stories, "Ballad of Jubal Pickett," "Mechanical Cook," and "Fair Young Ghost," were adapted for television presentation on network programs.

* * *

KEELING, Clinton Harry 1932-

PERSONAL: Born January 3, 1932, in Westcliff on Sea, Essex, England; son of Arthur Clinton (a professional soldier) and Alice Louise (Lent) Keeling; married Jill Annette Shaw (a zoo director and writer), August 24, 1953; children: Anthony, Jeremy, Diana, Phoebe. *Education:* Attended council and grammar schools in England. *Politics:* Ex-Conservative, now non-political. *Religion:* Agnostic. *Home and office:* Zoological Gardens, Ashover, Derbyshire, England.

CAREER: Worked as laborer, shop assistant, gardener, private tutor, and at other jobs, 1945-49, then as a free-lance lecturer on natural history, 1949-55; opened Zoological Gardens at Ashover, Derbyshire, England, 1955, and has operated it since. Zoological consultant; writer and lecturer (at about 200 schools a year) on natural history subjects. Founder, Junior Zoological Society, 1965.

WRITINGS: Unusual Pets, W. & G. Foyle, 1958; Cavies, W. & G. Foyle, 1961; Mice and Rats, W. & G. Foyle, 1962; Meet the Mammals, F. Watts, 1962; (with Louisa Stoeckicht) Baby Animals (text by Keeling, photographs by Stoeckicht), Anthony Blond, 1962; (compiler with wife, J. A. Keeling) Keeling's Ark, Harrap, 1970; Guinea Pigs, Arco, 1972. Meet the Reptiles, F. Watts, 1964. Contributor of articles to magazines.

SIDELIGHTS: Keeling says he decided to become a zoologist at age five and left school at thirteen to get on with earning the necessary capital to launch out on his own. His Zoological Gardens are run on educational concepts, the fulfillment of his childhood ambition. Avocational interests: History, philology, Egyptology, geography, decent music, good food.†

* * *

KEEP, John (Leslie Howard) 1926-

PERSONAL: Born January 21, 1926, in Keston, Kent, England; son of Norman M.H. (a businessman) and Phyllis (Austin) Keep. Education: University of London, B.A., 1950, Ph.D., 1953. Office: Department of History, University of Toronto, Toronto 181, Ontario, Canada.

CAREER: University of London, School of Slavonic and East European Studies, London, England, lecturer and reader in modern Russian history, 1954-70; University of Toronto, Toronto, Ontario, professor of Russian history, 1970—. Military service: British Army, 1943-47; became staff captain.

WRITINGS: The Rise of Social Democracy in Russia, Clarendon Press, 1963; (editor with Liliana Brisby) Contemporary History in the Soviet Mirror, Praeger, 1964. Contributor to New Cambridge Modern History, and to historical and political science journals.

WORK IN PROGRESS: Aspects of the Russian revolution, 1917-1921.

AVOCATIONAL INTERESTS: Travel, mountaineering.

* * *

KEESING, Nancy (Florence) 1923-

PERSONAL: Born September 7, 1923, in Sydney, New South Wales, Australia; daughter of Gordon Samuel (an architect) and Margery I.R. (Hart) Keesing; married A.M. Hertzberg, February 2, 1955; children: Margery, John. Education: University of Sydney, Diploma of Social Studies. Religion: Jewish. Home: 3 Garrick Ave., Hunter's Hill, New South Wales, Australia.

CAREER: Department of Navy, Sydney, Australia, clerk, 1942-45; Royal Alexandra Hospital for Children, Sydney, social worker, 1947-51; free-lance writer, 1951—. Member: English Association Sydney branch; vice-president), Australian Society of Authors (executive member).

WRITINGS: Imminent Summer (poetry), Lyre-Bird Writers, 1951; Three Men and Sydney (poetry), Angus & Robertson, 1955; (editor with Douglas Stewart) Australian Bush Ballads, Angus & Robertson, 1955; (editor with Stewart) Old Bush Songs and Rhymes of Colonial Times, Angus & Robertson, 1957; (editor) Australian Poetry, 1959, Angus & Robertson, 1959; By Gravel and Gum: The Story of a Pioneer Family (juvenile), Macmillan, 1963; Douglas Stewart, Lansdowne Press, 1965, revised edition, Oxford University Press, 1969; (author of commentary) Elsie Carew: Australian Primitive Poet, Wentworth Press, 1965; (editor with Stewart) The Pacific Book of Bush Ballads, Angus & Robertson, 1967; (editor and author of introduction, notes, and commentary) Gold Fever: The Australian Goldfields 1851 to 1890s (anthology), Angus & Robertson, 1967; Showground Sketchbook and Other Poems, Angus & Robertson, 1968; (editor) Transition (anthology), Angus & Robertson, 1971. Contributor to Bulletin, Southerly, Bridge, Overland, and other periodicals, and to Australian Broadcasting Commission programs.

WORK IN PROGRESS: A critical and biographical study of John George Lang; a series of short stories; a collection of poems; editing Australian Short Stories, for Pergamon.

SIDELIGHTS: Miss Keesing told CA: "My main interest is poetry. More or less by accident I seem to find myself writing mostly criticism and 'popular' history."

* * *

KELEN, Emery 1896-

PERSONAL: Born December 22, 1896, in Gyor, Hungary; came to United States in 1938; son of Ignace and Julia (Grunwald) Kelen; married Betty Stones, September 25, 1940; children: Julia. Education: Attended schools in Munich, Germany, in Budapest, Hungary, and Paris, France, 1920-38. Home: Housatomic River Rd., Salisbury, Conn. 06068.

CAREER: Left Hungary in 1919; lived in Munich, 1919-22, in Geneva and Paris, 1922-38. As artist and writer, covered all international conferences, 1922-38, for newspapers and magazines throughout the world; syndicated writer in United States, 1939-42; United Nations, New York, N.Y., television director, 1948-57, radio newscaster, 1957-63. Political caricaturist; art director; television adviser. Military service: Austro-Hungarian Army; became lieutenant; received Military Verdienstkreutz, third class. Member: Foreign Press Association (New York). Awards, honors: Academy of Television Arts and Sciences Emmy award and George Foster Peabody Award for United Nations television.

WRITINGS: Guignol a Lausanne, Near East Peace Conference (Lausanne), 1922; Les Guardiens de la paix, League of Nations, 1923; (with Alois Derso) A L'hotel Astoria: Commission de reparations, [Paris], 1924; La Bourse de Paris, Editions aux Ecoutes, 1925; Debts and Reparations, [Paris], 1926; La Testament de Geneve, Ten Years of International Cooperation, 1931; The Indian Round Table Conference, [London], 1930-31; Disarmament, [Geneva], 1932; (illustrator) George Edward Slocombe, A Mirror to Geneva, J. Cape, 1937; (with Derso) The League at Lunch, Allen & Unwin, 1938; (with Derso) The United Nations Sketch Book: A Cartoon History of the United Nations, Funk, 1950; Platypus at Large, Dutton, 1960; (co-illustrator, and author) Peace in Their Time: Men Who Led Us In and Out of War, 1914-1945, Knopf, 1963; Hammarskjold: The Dangerous Man, Putnam, 1966; The Political Platypus, Living Books, 1966; (editor) Hammarskjold: The Political Man, Funk, 1968.

Juveniles: (Self-illustrated) Yussuf the Ostrich, Hyperion Press, 1943; (illustrator) Aesop, Fables, edited by Elizabeth Stone, Hyperion Press, 1944; (self-illustrated) Calling Dr. Owl, Hyperion Press, 1945; (self-illustrated) The Valley of Trust, Lothrop, 1962; Let's Learn about the United Nations: A Coloring Book for Children, Lothrop, 1963; (self-illustrated) Food for the Valley, Lothrop, 1964; (compiler and illustrator) Proverbs of Many Nations, Lothrop, 1966; Peace Is an Adventure: The

Men and Women of the United Nations in Action Around the World, Meredith, 1967; *Stamps Tell the Story of the United Nations,* Meredith, 1968; *Stamps Tell the Story of John F. Kennedy,* Meredith, 1968; *Stamps Tell the Story of the Vatican,* Meredith, 1969; *Dag Hammarskjold: A Biography,* Meredith, 1969; *Fifty Voices of the Twentieth Century,* Lothrop, 1970; *Fantastic Tales, Strange Animals, Riddles, Jests and Prophecies of Leonardo de Vinci,* Thomas Nelson, 1971; *Stamps Tell the Story of Space Travel,* Thomas Nelson, 1972; (self-illustrated) *The Temple of Dendur: A Visit to Ancient Egypt,* Bobbs-Merrill, 1972; *Mr. Nonsense,* Thomas Nelson, 1973.

Author of limited editions books about diplomats, privately printed, 1922-38. Writer of weekly column, syndicated in the United States and abroad.

WORK IN PROGRESS: The Human Face, for Bobbs-Merrill.

AVOCATIONAL INTERESTS: Constitutional psychology (the physical basis of personality), television, films, cooking, philosophy, and fishing.

BIOGRAPHICAL/CRITICAL SOURCES: Christian Science Monitor, July 18, 1968; *Best Sellers,* May 1, 1970.

* * *

KELLAWAY, Frank (Gerald) 1922-

PERSONAL: Born April 19, 1922, in London, England; son of Charles Halliley (a scientist) and Eileen Ethel (Scantlebury) Kellaway; married Carlotta Jane Ellis, November, 1952; children: Dan, Maria Anna Theresa. *Education:* University of Melbourne, B.A., (honors), 1949. *Home:* 469 Victoria St., West Melbourne, Victoria 3033, Australia. *Agent:* Charles Lavell Ltd., Mowbray House, Norfolk St., London W.C.2, England. *Office:* Preston Institute of Technology, St. George's Rd., Preston, Victoria 3072, Australia.

CAREER: Laborer in orchards, Mangrove Mountain, New South Wales, Australia, 1953; Wangaratta Regional Library Service, Wangaratta, Victoria, Australia, librarian, 1954-59; owner-manager of farm and orchard in Eldorado, Victoria, Australia, 1955-59; city librarian of Warrnambool, Victoria, Australia, 1960; University of Melbourne, Melbourne, Australia, branch librarian, School of Architecture, 1961-64; abalone diver, 1965; Heidelberg Regional Library, Heidelberg, Germany, librarian, 1966-67; Preston Institute of Technology, Preston, Victoria, Australia, lecturer, 1968—. Lecturer, Victoria Council of Adult Education. *Military service:* Royal Australian Naval Volunteer Reserve, 1941-46; served in Mediterranean; became lieutenant.

WRITINGS: A Straight Furrow (novel), Cassell, 1960; *The Quest for Golden Dan* (novel), F.W. Cheshire, 1962; *Early Australians: A Whaler,* Oxford University Press, 1967. Also author of "A Kite's Dinner," "A Wish to Be Riding," and "Middentop," all novels as yet unpublished. Contributor of poems to journals. Co-editor of *Present Opinion,* 1948.

WORK IN PROGRESS: A first person narrative of a woman married to an artist.

AVOCATIONAL INTERESTS: Collecting works of Australian painters, collecting vocal records, spearfishing.

BIOGRAPHICAL/CRITICAL SOURCES: Fiction Chronicles, December, 1961; John K. Ewers *Creative Writing in Australia,* Angus & Robertson, 1963; Geoffrey Dutton, editor, *The Literature of Australia,* Penguin, 1964.

KELLER, Thomas F(ranklin) 1931-

PERSONAL: Born September 22, 1931, in Greenwood, S.C.; son of Alonzo (an entrepreneur) and Helen (Seago) Keller; married Margaret Query, June 15, 1956; children: Thomas Crafton, Neel McKay, John Caldwell. *Education:* Duke University, A.B., 1953; University of Michigan, M.B.A., 1957, Ph.D., 1960. *Home:* 1024 West Markham Ave., Durham, N.C. 27701. *Office:* Graduate School of Business Administration, Duke University, Durham, N.C. 27706.

CAREER: Peat, Marwick, Mitchell & Co., Charlotte, N.C., auditor, 1953; University of Michigan, Ann Arbor, instructor, 1958-59; Duke University, Durham, N.C., 1959—, began as assistant professor, now professor of accounting. Visiting associate professor, University of Washington, 1963-64, Carnegie-Mellon University, 1966-67. *Military service:* U.S. Army, 1953-55. *Member:* American Institute of Certified Public Accountants, American Accounting Association (vice-president, 1968-69), Financial Executives Institute, North Carolina Association of Certified Public Accountants, Beta Alpha Sigma, Phi Kappa Sigma, Alpha Kappa Psi, Beta Gamma Sigma. *Awards, honors:* Ford Foundation summer research fellowship, 1960, 1961.

WRITINGS: Accounting for Corporate Income Taxes, School of Business Administration, University of Michigan, 1961; (with Walter Meigs and Charles Johnson) *Intermediate Accounting,* McGraw, 1963, revised edition, 1968; (editor with Stephen Zeff) *Financial Accounting Theory: Issues and Controversies,* two volumes, McGraw, 1964-69; (contributor) Morton Backer, editor, *Modern Accounting Theory,* Prentice-Hall, 1966; (with Meigs and Johnson) *Advanced Accounting,* McGraw, 1966; (contributor) Sidney Davidson, editor, *Handbook of Modern Accounting,* McGraw, 1970. Contributor to *Journal of Accountancy, Accounting Review, Cooperative Accountant, Management Accounting, Hospital Administration,* and *Law and Contemporary Problems.*

WORK IN PROGRESS: Uniformity, Comparability and Reliability, for Prentice-Hall; a 3rd edition of *Intermediate Accounting,* McGraw; *Foundations of Accounting,* Prentice-Hall, 1975.

* * *

KELLOGG, Gene (Defrees) 1916-
(Sally Jackson, Jean Kellogg)

PERSONAL: Born December 28, 1916, in Chicago, Ill.; daughter of Donald (a lawyer) and Florence (Baker) Defrees; married James H. Kellogg, November 4, 1939 (died February 15, 1967; children: Frances (Mrs. George Smith), James M. *Education:* Smith College, B.A. (highest honors), 1939; University of Chicago, M.A. (honors), 1964, Ph.D., 1968. *Politics:* Independent. *Religion:* Catholic. *Home:* 179 East Lake Shore Dr., Chicago, Ill. 60611. *Office:* Mundelein College, 6363 Sheridan, Chicago, Ill. 60626.

CAREER: Henry Regnery Co., Chicago, Ill., assistant editor, 1950-55, associate editor, 1955-59, editor-in-chief, 1959-64; Mundelein College, Chicago, Ill., assistant professor of English, 1968—. Chairman of the board, Harders Engineering; director, Kelran Corp. *Member:* College Theology Society, Society for Arts, Religion, and Culture, Phi Beta Kappa.

WRITINGS—Under name Jean Kellogg; all published by Reilly & Lee, except as indicated: (Adapter) L. Frank Baum, *The Wizard of Oz* (juvenile), 1961; (adapter) Baum, *The Land of Oz* (juvenile), 1961; (adapter) Baum, *Dorothy and the Wizard in Oz* (juvenile), 1961; (adapter) Baum, *Ozma of Oz* (juvenile), 1962; *Hans and the Winged Horse* (juvenile), 1964; *The Rod and the Rose* (juvenile), 1964; *The Vital Tradition: The Catholic*

Church in a Period of Convergence, Loyola University Press, 1970.

Juveniles under pseudonym Sally Jackson; all published by Reilly & Lee: *The Littlest Star: A Story about Ballet,* 1961; *The Littlest Skater: The Story of Johnny One-Skate,* 1961; *Here We Go,* 1962; *Is This Your Dog?,* 1962.

WORK IN PROGRESS: *The Metaphysical Novel in the Nineteenth Century.*

*   *   *

KELLY, William W (atkins) 1928-

PERSONAL: Born September 21, 1928, in Asheville, N.C.; son of John Jackson, Jr. (an educator) and Trula (Watkins) Kelly; married Jane Kelly, February 14, 1953; children: William W., Jr., Robert Jackson, Blair Massey, Gregory Clark. *Education:* Virginia Military Institute, B.A., 1950; Duke University, A.M., 1955, Ph.D., 1957. *Politics:* Democrat. *Religion:* Episcopalian. *Home:* 46 Ridgeview Rd., Staunton, Va. 24401.

CAREER: Virginia Military Institute, Lexington, instructor, 1952-53, assistant professor of English, 1960-62; Michigan State University, East Lansing, assistant professor, 1962-66, associate professor of American thought and language, 1966-69, associate director of Honors College, 1965-67, director of Honors College, 1967-69; Mary Baldwin College, Staunton, Va., president, 1969—. *Military service:* U.S. Air Force Reserve, 1950—, serving on active duty as assistant professor of English at Air Force Academy, 1957-60; now major. *Member:* Modern Language Association of America, Society for Religion in Higher Education, American Studies Association, American Association of University Professors, Association for Higher Education.

WRITINGS: *Ellen Glasgow: A Bibliography,* University of Virginia Press, 1964. Contributor of reviews to *American Literature.*

WORK IN PROGRESS: A study of the novelist, Mary Johnston, for Twayne's "U.S. Authors" series; a study of Ellen Glasgow for Steck's "Southern Writers" series.

*   *   *

KEMELMAN, Harry 1908-

PERSONAL: Born November 24, 1908, in Boston, Mass.; son of Isaac and Dora (Prizer) Kemelman; married Anne Kessin (a medical secretary-technician), March 29, 1936; children: Ruth (Mrs. George Rooks), Arthur Frederick, Diane (Mrs. Stanley Neustadter). *Education:* Attended Boston Latin School, 1920-26; Boston University, A.B., 1930; Harvard University, M.A., 1931, postgraduate study, 1932-33. *Politics:* Independent. *Religion:* Jewish. *Home:* 47 Humphrey St., Marblehead, Mass. 01947. *Agent:* Scott Meredith Literary Agency, Inc., 580 Fifth Ave., New York, N.Y. 10036.

CAREER: Substitute high school teacher, Boston, Mass., 1935-37, full-time English teacher, 1937-41; Manter Hall School, Cambridge, Mass., part-time teacher, 1936-40; Northeastern University, Boston, Mass., English instructor in evening division, 1938-41; U.S. Army Transportation Corps, Boston Port of Embarkation, Boston, Mass., chief wage administrator (civilian), 1942-46; War Assets Administration, New England Division, chief job analyst and wage administrator, 1948-49; operated own business, and did free-lance writing, 1949-63; Franklin Technical Institute, Boston, Mass., assistant professor of English, 1963-64; Boston State College, Boston, Mass., associate professor of English, 1964-70. *Member:* Authors League of America, Mystery Writers of America. *Awards, honors:* Edgar Award for best first novel, 1965, for *Friday*

the Rabbi Slept Late; Faith and Freedom Communications Award, 1967.

WRITINGS—All novels, except as otherwise indicated: *Friday the Rabbi Slept Late,* Crown, 1964; *Saturday the Rabbi Went Hungry,* Crown, 1966; *The Nine Mile Walk: The Nicky Welt Stories of Harry Kemelman* (includes "The Nine Mile Walk," "The Straw Man," "The Ten O'Clock Scholar," "End Play," "Time and Time Again," "The Whistling Tea Kettle," "The Bread and Butter Case," and "The Man On the Ladder"), Putnam, 1967; *Sunday the Rabbi Stayed Home,* Putnam, 1969; *Common Sense in Education* (nonfiction), Crown, 1970; *Monday the Rabbi Took Off,* Putnam, 1972; *Tuesday the Rabbi Saw Red,* Author Fields' Books, 1973. Author of "Nicky Welt" series in *Ellery Queen's Mystery Magazine;* contributor to *Bookman.*

SIDELIGHTS: Kemelman's popular mystery novels on Rabbi David Small had their beginning in the Nicky Welt stories he has long written for *Ellery Queen's Mystery Magazine.* According to a reviewer for *New York Times Book Review,* Kemelman, who is Jewish, wrote a novel entitled *The Building of the Temple* for a change of pace. An editor with Crown Publishers suggested he combine the two forms. The result was *Friday the Rabbi Slept Late,* the first in a series of best sellers combining suburban American Judaism, social commentary, and amateur sleuthing. Kemelman plans to write seven "rabbi" books—one for each day of the week.

In the opinion of several critics, including Judith Crist, *The Nine Mile Walk* (a collection of Professor Nicky Welt stories) exemplifies some of the best "armchair detection" fiction being written today. She cautions the reader not to read all eight stories at once, as "you might become attuned to the Professor's brand of logic and find yourself out-racing his armchair toward a logical solution. This last is an indirect compliment to Mr. Kemelman, who gives the reader his fair share in facts and clues. For this we honor him—and even more for providing us with the classic cool of a cerebral sleuth."

A motion picture of *Friday the Rabbi Slept Late* is scheduled for production in 1973.

BIOGRAPHICAL/CRITICAL SOURCES: *New Statesman,* March 24, 1967; *Books and Bookmen,* May, 1967; *Book World,* November 12, 1967, May 25, 1969; *Christian Science Monitor,* January 6, 1968; *Show Business,* February 1, 1969; *New York Times,* February 21, 1969; *New York Times Book Review,* March 2, 1969; *Best Sellers,* September 1, 1970.

*   *   *

KEMP, Betty 1916-

PERSONAL: Born November 5, 1916, in Bowdon, England; daughter of William and Gertrude (Hampson) Kemp. *Education:* University of Manchester, B.A., 1940; Oxford University, M.A., 1947. *Office:* St. Hugh's College, Oxford University, Oxford, England.

CAREER: H.M. Treasury, London, England, administrative officer, 1940-45; University of Manchester, Manchester, England, lecturer in modern history, 1945-46; St. Hugh's College, Oxford University, Oxford, England, fellow and tutor in modern history, 1946—. *Member:* Royal Historical Society (fellow), Society of Antiquaries (fellow).

WRITINGS: (Contributor) Richard Pares and A.J.P. Taylor, editors, *Essays Presented to Sir Lewis Namier,* St. Martin's, 1956; *King and Commons, 1660-1832,* St. Martin's, 1957; (contributor) Alex Natan, editor, *Silver Renaissance: Essays in Eighteenth Century English History,* Macmillan, 1961, St. Martin's, 1962; (contributor) Martin Gilbert, editor, *A Century of Conflict: Essays*

Presented to A.J.P. Taylor, Hamish Hamilton, 1966, Atheneum, 1967; Sir Francis Dashwood: An Eighteenth Century Independent, St. Martin's, 1967; Votes and Standing Orders of the House of Commons: The Beginning, H.M.S.O., 1971. Contributor to professional journals.

WORK IN PROGRESS: Parliamentary Diary of Sir Richard Cooks, for Oxford University Press; eighteenth-century parliamentary procedure.

BIOGRAPHICAL/CRITICAL SOURCES: Times Literary Supplement, February 16, 1967.

*   *   *

KEMP, Charles F.   1912-

PERSONAL: Born October 25, 1912, in Des Moines, Iowa; son of Fred H. and Mable (Brown) Kemp; married Jean Serrill, 1937; children: Frederick Douglas, James Charles. Education: Drake University, A.B., and M.A.; Colgate-Rochester Divinity School, B.D.; University of Nebraska, Ph.D. Home: 3619 Shelby Dr., Fort Worth, Tex. 76109. Office: Brite Divinity School, Texas Christian University, Fort Worth, Tex. 76129.

CAREER: Ordained minister in Christian Church; pastor of churches in Wellsville, N.Y., Red Oak, Iowa, and Lincoln Neb.; Texas Christian University, Brite Divinity School, Fort Worth, professor of practical ministries, 1957—. Former member of board of directors, Child Guidance Center, Lincoln, Neb.; member, Fort Worth Community Council. Member: American Psychological Association.

WRITINGS: Physicians of the Soul: A History of Pastoral Counseling, Macmillan, 1947; A Pastoral Triumph: The Story of Richard Baxter and His Ministry at Kidderminster, Macmillan, 1948; (editor) Life-Situation Preaching, Bethany Press, 1956; The Church: The Gifted and the Retarded Child, Bethany Press, 1958; Preparing for the Ministry, Bethany Press, 1959; The Pastor and Community Resources, Bethany Press, 1960; The Pastor and Vocational Counseling, Bethany Press, 1961; (editor) Pastoral Preaching, Bethany Press, 1963; Student's Guidebook: Theological School Study Habits Inventory, Texas Christian University, 1963; Christian Dimensions of Family Living, Bethany Press, 1964; Counseling with College Students, Prentice-Hall, 1964; (with Richard A. Hunt) Theological School Check List of Study Skills and Attitudes, Bethany Press, 1965; The Preaching Pastor, Bethany Press, 1966; Learning About Pastoral Care: A Workbook and Study Guide in Pastoral Counseling and Pastoral Care, Abingdon, 1970; Pastoral Counseling Guidebook, Abingdon, 1971; Pastoral Care with the Poor, Abingdon, 1972. Contributor of regular column to Christian, and of articles to other religious journals.

*   *

KEMP, Roy Z(ell)   1910-
(Zell Kay)

PERSONAL: Born June 14, 1910, in Cornelius, N.C.; son of George W. (a salesman) and Ethel (Nicholson) Kemp. Education: Attended schools in Greensboro, N.C. Religion: Protestant. Home: 15 West Franklin St., Baltimore, Md. 21201. Office: Social Security Administration, Baltimore, Md. 21235.

CAREER: U.S. Social Security Administration, 1939-69, became correspondence examiner, Baltimore, Md. Military service: U.S. Army Air Forces, 1943-46; served in European theater. Member: Maryland Poetry Society.

WRITINGS: Measure of a Heart, and Other Poems, Golden Quill, 1962; Shining Towers of Faith, and Other Poems, Johnson Publishing Co. (Murfreesboro, N.C.), 1966; Measure for Living: Devotions and Poems of Affir-

mation, C.R. Gibson, 1967; Testaments of Faith (poems), C.R. Gibson, 1970; The Shield of Faith, C.R. Gibson, 1973. Represented in several anthologies, including This Singing Earth, edited by Lilith Lorraine, Flame Press, 1961, Rhyme Time for the Very Young, edited by Jeanne Hollyfield, Young Publications, 1964, Gold Star Anthology, edited by Marie H. King, Revell, 1970, and Today, Well Lived, edited by William Arthur Ward, Droke, 1971. Contributor of poems to religious periodicals of various denominations; free-lance feature writer for newspapers in Maryland and North Carolina; reviewer for Greensboro Daily News, Greensboro, N.C.

WORK IN PROGRESS: Two adult poetry collections; three children's poetry collections; two works of religious and inspirational nonfiction.

SIDELIGHTS: Kemp told CA: "Since poetry moves on the higher levels of power and emotion, it must be the product of a maker of ideas. The truly creative artists of the written word are gifted with the ability to take the common facts and experiences of life and invest them with epic and enduring qualities. Also, since the heart and core of inspirational poetry is a spirit of devotion and reverence, being idealistic in nature, spiritual in quality, and moral at its center, its writer must be constantly aware of the eternal secret of friendship with God. He must also be possessed with what has been termed 'religious insight.' He must not let himself be limited to any one nation or people, nor to any one age, for to do so would admit to a partiality. The appeal of inspirational poetry is universal, since universality must be expressed in its writing. Eternal verities will ever remain the same, regardless of the change made in other things. Inspirational poetry is the true language of the heart. It is composed of emotional feeling, deep and sincere."

*   *   *

KENNEDY, Malcolm D(uncan)   1895-

PERSONAL: Born January 5, 1895, in Edinburgh, Scotland; son of James Young (a broker) and Anna (McLeod) Kennedy; married Margaret Coutts, September 15, 1921; children: Mungo Hamilton McLeod (killed on active duty), Jean (Mrs. Lennox Abraham), Aline (Mrs. Laidlaw Buxton). Education: Attended Trinity College, Glenalmond, Scotland, and Royal Military College, Sandhurst, England. Politics: "Mildly conservative." Religion: Episcopal. Home: Inverurr, Kippford, by Dalbeattie, Kirkcudbrightshire, Scotland.

CAREER: Started career as regular officer in The Cameronians (Scottish Rifles), 1914-22, rising to captain and receiving Order of the British Empire; invalided out owing to war wounds, 1922. Rising Sun Petroleum Co., employee in Japan and Korea, 1922-24; Reuters News Agency, London, England, correspondent in Tokyo, Japan, 1925-34; British Foreign Office, researcher on Far East, 1935-55. Member: Royal Institute of International Affairs, Royal Commonwealth Society, Japan Society (London).

WRITINGS: The Military Side of Japanese Life, Constable, 1924, Houghton, 1925; Some Aspects of Japan and Her Defence Forces, Kegan Paul, 1928; The Changing Fabric of Japan, Constable, 1930, R. Smith, 1961; The Problem of Japan, Nisbet, 1935; A History of Communism in East Asia, Praeger, 1957 (published in England as A Short History of Communism in East Asia, Weidenfeld & Nicholson, 1957); A Short History of Japan, Weidenfeld & Nicolson, 1963, New American Library, 1964; The Estrangement of Great Britain and Japan, 1917-35, University of California Press, 1969. Contributor of articles and book reviews to periodicals.

WORK IN PROGRESS: Japan's Road to War.

SIDELIGHTS: Kennedy was one of four brothers serving as officers in World War I. He himself received permanent injuries during the assault on Neuve Chapell, 1915; his eldest brother was among 13,000 British killed in the engagement, another brother died later of injuries received in 1914, another was wounded three times. In the devastating Japanese earthquake of 1923, he, his wife, and infant son were buried under the wreckage of their house, but escaped with minor injuries; the son died in a British submarine operation against the Japanese off Penang in 1945. Onetime holder of an offical interpretership in Japanese, Kennedy was attached to the Japanese Army, 1917-20, later ranged widely in the Far East, traveling in Manchuria, Inner Mongolia, and Siberia, among other countries.

BIOGRAPHICAL/CRITICAL SOURCES: Library Journal, February 1, 1970; *Times Literary Supplement,* October 16, 1970.

* * *

KENNELLY, Brendan 1936-

PERSONAL: Born April 17, 1936, in Ballylongford, County Kerry, Ireland; son of Timothy (a pub keeper) and Bridget (Ahern) Kennelly. *Education:* Attended St. Ita's College, Tarbert, Ireland, 1948-53; Trinity College, Dublin, D.P.A., B.A.; attended University of Leeds, 1962-63. *Religion:* Catholic. *Home:* Ballylongford, County Kerry, Ireland. *Office:* 39 Trinity College, Dublin, Ireland.

CAREER: Trinity College, Dublin, Ireland, lecturer in English literature, 1963—.

WRITINGS—All poetry, unless otherwise indicated: (With Rudi Holzapfel) *Cast a Cold Eye,* Dolmen Press, 1959; (with Holzapfel) *The Rain, The Moon,* Dolmen Press, 1961; (with Holzapfel) *The Dark About Our Loves,* John Augustine, 1962; (with Holzapfel) *Poems, Green Townlands,* University Bibliographical Press (Leeds), 1963; *Let Fall No Burning Leaf,* New Square Publications, 1963; *The Crooked Cross* (novel), Figgis & Co., 1963, Little, Brown, 1964; *My Dark Fathers,* New Square Publications, 1964; *Up and At It,* New Square Publications, 1965; *Collection One: Getting Up Early,* Figgis & Co., 1966; *Good Souls, to Survive,* Figgis & Co., 1967; *The Florentines* (novel), Figgis & Co., 1967; *Dream of a Black Fox,* Figgis & Co., 1968; *Selected Poems,* Figgis & Co., 1969, Dutton, 1972; (compiler and author of introduction) *The Penguin Book of Irish Verse,* Penguin, 1970; *A Drinking Cup: Poems from the Irish,* Figgis & Co., 1970; *Bread,* Gallery Books, 1971; *Love Cry,* Figgis & Co., 1972; *Salvation, the Stranger,* Gallery Books, 1972.

WORK IN PROGRESS: A novel, *Across the Pond.*

SIDELIGHTS: Kennelly has written poetry in Irish and translated poems from the Irish, including Brendan Behan's, among others.

BIOGRAPHICAL/CRITICAL SOURCES: Times Literary Supplement, November 9, 1967; *Punch,* February 26, 1969.

* * *

KENT, Allen 1921-

PERSONAL: Born October 24, 1921, in New York, N.Y.; son of Samuel and Anne (Begun) Kent; married Rosalind Kossoff, January 24, 1943; children: Merryl Frances, Emily Beth, Jacqueline Diane, Carolyn May. *Education:* College of City of New York, (now City College of the City University of New York), B.S., 1942. *Office:* University of Pittsburgh, Pittsburgh, Pa. 15213.

CAREER: Essex Chemicals, Inc., Chester, Conn., chief chemist, 1946-47; Interscience Publishers, New York, N.Y., associate editor, 1947-51; Massachusetts Institute of Technology, Cambridge, research associate, 1951-53; Battelle Memorial Institute, Columbus, Ohio, principal documentation engineer, 1953-55; Western Reserve University (now Case Western Reserve University), Cleveland, Ohio, associate director, Center for Documentation of Communication Research, and professor of library science, 1955-63; University of Pittsburgh, Pittsburgh, Pa., director of Knowledge Availability Systems Center, and professor of library and information sciences, 1963—, director of communications programs, 1969—. Allen Kent Associates (consultants), Pittsburgh, Pa., president, 1961—. Consultant on information retrieval to Special Assistant to the President, and to several government agencies, 1955—. Lecturer in Europe and South America.

MEMBER: American Institute of Chemists (fellow), American Association for the Advancement of Science (fellow), International Committee on Information Retrieval and Machine Translation (general secretary), American Chemical Society (chairman, committee on chemical documentation, 1956-57), Special Libraries Association (chairman, advisory council, 1956-57), American Documentation Institute, American Library Association.

WRITINGS: Literature Research as a Tool for Creative Thinking, Western Reserve University, 1956; (editor with Jess H. Shera and James W. Perry) *Documentation in Action,* Reinhold, 1956; (with others) *Machine Literature Searching,* Interscience, 1956; (with Helen Loftus) *Automation in the Library: An Annotated Bibliography,* American Documentation, 1956; *Automation in Literature Research: A Report on the ASM Mechanized Literature Searching Project,* Metals Division, Special Libraries Association, 1956; (with Perry) *The Western Reserve University Searching Selector: Summary of Functions and Capabilities,* [Cleveland], 1956; (with Perry) *New Indexing-Abstracting System for Formal Reports, Development and Proof Services,* privately printed, 1957; (editor with Shera and Perry) *Information Systems in Documentation,* Interscience, 1957; (with Perry) *Documentation and Information Retrieval: An Introduction to Basic Principles and Cost Analysis,* Western Reserve University Press, 1957; (editor with others) *Information Resources,* Western Reserve University Press, 1957; (with Perry and Robert E. Booth) *Machine Searching of Metallurgical Literature,* [Cleveland], 1957; (with T.H. Rees) *The Jargon of Machine Literature Searching,* Center for Documentation and Communication Research, Western Reserve University, 1957; (with Booth) *Trend in Information Services: U.S. versus U.S.S.R. Developments in Scientific and Engineering Fields,* privately printed, 1957; (with T.H. Rees and Perry) *A Demonstration in Automation Correlation for Purposes of Commercial Intelligence,* School of Library Science, Western Reserve University, 1957; (editor with Perry) *Tools for Machine Literature Searching: Semantic Code Dictionary, Equipment, Procedure,* Interscience, 1958; (editor with Perry and Gilbert Peakes) *Progress Report in Chemical Literature Retrieval,* Interscience, 1958; (with Perry) *Centralized Information Services, Opportunities and Problems,* Western Reserve University Press, 1958; (editor with others) *Punched Cards,* Reinhold, 1958; (with Perry and T.H. Rees) *Machine Documentation Equipment,* School of Library Science, Western Reserve University, 1958; *Nonconventional Retrieval Systems in Documentation: Preliminary Comparative Analysis,* School of Library Science, Western Reserve University, 1958; (with Janet Rees) *Mechanized Searching Experiments Using the WRU Searching Selector: Preliminary Report,* Western Reserve University, 1958; *Minimum Criteria for a Coor-*

dinated *Information Service,* U.S. Air Force, 1959; (with Perry) *The Storage and Retrieval of Nonnumerial Data in Large and Complex Documentation Systems,* Western Reserve University, 1959.

Exploitation of Recorded Information, privately printed, 1960; (editor with others) *Information Retrieval and Machine Translation,* Interscience, 1960; (contributor) *Searching and Chemical Literature,* American Chemical Society, 1961; (contributor) *Dissemination and Implementation,* Indiana University Press, 1962; *Textbook on Mechanized Information Retrieval,* Interscience, 1962, 3rd edition, 1971; (editor) Lev I. Gutenmakher, *Electronic Information-Logic Machines,* Wiley, 1963; (editor with Orrin E. Taulbee) *Electronic Information Handling,* Spartan, 1965; (editor) *Library Planning for Automation,* Spartan, 1965; (with John Canter) *Specialized Information Centers,* Spartan, 1965; (editor with others) *Electronic Handling of Information, Testing and Evaluation,* Thompson Book Co., 1967; (editor with Harold Lancour) *Encyclopedia of Library and Information Science,* eight volumes, Dekker, 1968-72; *Information Analysis and Retrieval,* Becker & Hayes, 1971; (editor with Lancour) *Copyright: Current Viewpoints on History, Laws, Legislation,* Bowker, 1972; (with Edward M. Arnett) *Computer Based Chemical Information,* Dekker, 1973.

WORK IN PROGRESS: More volumes of *Encyclopedia of Library and Information Science.*

* * *

KENT, Homer A(ustin), Jr. 1926-

PERSONAL: Born August 13, 1926, in Washington, D.C.; son of Homer Austin (a professor and clergyman) and Alice (Wogaman) Kent; married Beverly Jane Page, August 1, 1953; children: Rebecca Anne, Katherine Ruth, Daniel Arthur. *Education:* American University, student 1945; Bob Jones University, A.B., 1947; Grace Theological Seminary, B.D., 1950, Th.M., 1952, Th.D., 1956. *Home:* 305 Sixth St., Winona Lake, Ind. 46590. *Office:* Grace Theological Seminary, Wooster Rd., Winona Lake, Ind. 46590.

CAREER: Minister, National Fellowship of Brethren Churches; Grace Theological Seminary, Winona Lake, Ind., professor of New Testament, 1951—, dean, 1962—. *Member:* Evangelical Theological Society.

WRITINGS: The Pastoral Epistles: Studies in I and II Timothy and Titus, Moody, 1958; (contributor) *Wycliffe Bible Commentary,* Moody, 1962; *Ephesians: The Glory of the Church,* Moody, 1971; *Jerusalem to Rome: Studies in the Book of Acts,* Baker Book, 1972; *The Epistle to the Hebrews: A Commentary,* Baker Book, 1972. Contributor of articles to *Bibliotheca Sacra* and *Baker's Dictionary of Theology.* Editor, *Grace Journal.*

* * *

KENT, John Henry Somerset 1923-

PERSONAL: Born April 24, 1923, in Coleford, Somerset, England; son of Walter Harold and Dora (Burndred) Kent; married Deborah Joan Trower (a schoolteacher), August 12, 1954; children: Oliver, Catherine. *Education:* Emmanuel College, Cambridge, B.A., 1944; Cambridge University, M.A., 1947, Ph.D., 1951. *Politics:* Socialist. *Home:* 40 Springbridge Rd., Manchester 16, England.

CAREER: Ordained a Methodist minister, 1954. Cambridge University, Emmanuel College, Cambridge, England, lecturer, 1955-59; Hartley Victoria Methodist Theological College, Manchester, England, tutor in church history, 1959-65; University of Bristol, Bristol, England, member of theology faculty, 1965—, reader in theology, 1969—. Associated with Ecumenical Movement, Student

Christian Movement. *Member:* Royal Historical Society (fellow).

WRITINGS: Jabez Bunting, the Last Wesleyan, Epworth, 1955; (contributor) *Anglican-Methodist Relations,* Darton, Longman & Todd, 1961; *Elizabeth Fry,* Batsford, 1962, Arco, 1963; (contributor) *Institutionalism and Church Unity,* Association Press, 1963; *Federation or Union?,* Epworth, 1965; *The Age of Disunity,* Epworth, 1966; *From Darwin to Blatchford: The Role of Darwinism in Christian Apologetic, 1875-1910,* Dr. Williams's Trust, 1966; (with Jean Danielou and A.H. Couratin) *The Pelican Guide to Modern Theology,* Volume 2: *Historical Theology,* Penguin, 1969; (contributor) Joseph Rhymer and Nicholas Lash, editors, *The Christian Priesthood: The Ninth Downside Symposium,* Darton, Longman & Todd, 1970; (editor) *Intercommunion and Church Membership,* Darton, Longman & Todd, 1973; (contributor) *The Victorian City,* Routledge & Kegan Paul, in press. Also contributor to *Encyclopaedia of World Religions,* Hutchinson, 1959; contributor to *London Quarterly.*

WORK IN PROGRESS: Preparing for Edinburgh Croall Lectures, for 1974-75.

* * *

KENYON, J(ohn) P(hilipps) 1927-

PERSONAL: Born June 18, 1927, in Sheffield, England; son of William Houston and Edna Grace (Philipps) Kenyon; married Angela Jane Ewert, September 26, 1962; children: Charlotte Clare, Daniel Louis. *Education:* University of Sheffield, B.A., 1948; Cambridge University, Ph.D., 1954. *Home:* Nicholsen Hall, Cottingham, Yorkshire, England. *Office:* Department of History, University of Hull, Hull, England.

CAREER: Cambridge University, Cambridge, England, fellow of Christ's College, 1954-62, assistant lecturer in history, 1955-60, lecturer, 1960-62; University of Hull, Hull, England, professor of history, 1962—. Visiting associate professor, Columbia University, 1959-60. *Military service:* Royal Air Force, 1948-50; became flying officer. *Member:* Historical Association.

WRITINGS: Robert Spencer, Earl of Sunderland, 1641-1702, Longmans, Green, 1958; *The Stuarts: A Study in English Kinship,* Batsford, 1958, Macmillan, 1959, 2nd edition, Wiley, 1967; *The Nobility in the Revolution of 1688,* University of Hull, 1963; (editor) *Samuel Pepys, Diary,* revised and abridged edition, Macmillan, 1963; (editor) *The Stuart Constitution, 1603-1688: Documents and Commentary,* Cambridge University Press, 1966; (editor and author of introduction) George Savile Halifax, *Complete Works,* Penguin, 1969; *The Popish Plot,* St. Martin's, 1972. Contributor to historical journals, including *English Historical Review.*

WORK IN PROGRESS: Research on early 18th century English politics and political thought.

* * *

KEOGH, Lilian Gilmore 1927-
(Lilian Patrick)

PERSONAL: Born July 15, 1927, in Belfast, Northern Ireland; daughter of Alexander and Mary (Eagleson) Gilmore; married Conal Patrick Keogh (a teacher), July 29, 1950; children: Nigel, Shevaun, Rory. *Education:* Trinity College, Dublin, B.A. (first class honors), 1948, M.A., 1952, B.Litt., 1955. *Home:* Box 401, Kent School, Kent, Conn. 06757.

CAREER: Ashleigh House School, Belfast, Northern Ireland, teacher of English, 1949-50; Uppsala University, Uppsala, Sweden, seminar leader, 1950-54; Balmoral Hall School, Winnipeg, Manitoba, teacher of English and

French, 1956-57; University of Connecticut, Waterbury, lecturer in English, 1961-62; Kent Girl's School, Kent, Conn., teacher of English, 1964—.

WRITINGS—Under pseudonym Lilian Patrick: *Short Engagement* (novel), R. Hale, 1959; *Hold Back the Tide*, R. Hale, 1960.

* * *

KERNER, Fred 1921-
(Frohm Fredericks, E.R. Kern, Frederick Kerr, M.N. Thaler)

PERSONAL: Born February 15, 1921, in Montreal, Quebec, Canada; son of Sam and Vera (Goldman) Kerner; married second wife, Sally Dee Stouten, May 18, 1959; children: (first marriage) Jon; (second marriage) David, Diane. *Education:* Sir George Williams University, B.A., 1942. *Home:* 400 Lansdowne Ave., Westmount, Montreal 217, Quebec, Canada.

CAREER: *Montreal Gazette*, Montreal, Quebec, assistant sports editor, 1942-44; Canadian Press, variously newsman, editor, news executive, in Montreal, Toronto, New York, 1944-50; Associated Press, New York, N.Y., assistant night city editor, 1950-56; Hawthorn Books, Inc., New York, N.Y., editor, 1957-58, president and editor-in-chief, 1965-67; Fawcett Publications, Inc., New York, N.Y., editor-in-chief, Crest and Premier Books, 1958-64; Hall House, Inc., Greenwich, Conn., editor, 1963-64; Centaur House Publishers, Inc. New York, N.Y., president and editor-in-chief, 1964—; Fred Kerner Publishing Projects, New York, N.Y., managing director, 1968—. Publishing director, Book and Educational Division, Reader's Digest Association (Canada), 1969—. Director, Publitex International Corp., Peter Kent, Inc., Pennorama Crafts, Inc., Diaque Design, Inc., National Mint, Inc., Personalized Services, Inc. Lecturer, Long Island University, 1968. Chairman, International Affairs Conference for College Editors, 1965. Committee panelist at various conferences. Member of local school boards.

MEMBER: International Platform Association, Canadian Authors Association, Mystery Writers of America, Authors' Club (London, England), Overseas Press Club (chairman of election committee, 1960-64; chairman of library and book-night committee, 1961), Canadian Society of Professional Journalists, Authors' Guild, Authors League of America, American Academy of Political and Social Science, American Management Association, Edward R. Murrow Fund (chairman of publisher's committee), Advertising Club of New York, Association of Alumni of Sir George Williams University (member of executive committee), Toronto Men's Press Club, Canadian Society (New York), Dutch Treat Club (New York), Deadline Club (New York), Sigma Delta Chi.

WRITINGS: (With Leonid Kotkin) *Eat, Think, and Be Slender*, Hawthorn, 1954, new edition, Wilshire, 1960; (with Walter Germain) *The Magic Power of Your Mind*, Hawthorn, 1956; (with Joyce Brothers) *Ten Days to a Successful Memory*, Prentice-Hall, 1957; (editor) *Love Is a Man's Affair*, Fell, 1958; (contributor) Larston Farrar, editor, *Successful Writers and How They Work*, Hawthorn, 1958; (contributor) Roy Copperud, editor, *Words on Paper*, Hawthorn, 1960; *Stress and Your Heart*, Hawthorn, 1961; (contributor) Sigrid Schultz, editor, *The Overseas Press Club Cookbook*, Doubleday, 1962; (under pseudonym Frederick Kerr) *Watch Your Weight Go Down*, Pyramid Publications, 1963; (editor) *A Treasury of Lincoln Quotations*, Doubleday, 1965; (with Germain) *Secrets of Your Supraconscious*, Hawthorn, 1965; (with David Goodman) *What's Best for Your Child—and You*, Hawthorn, 1966; (with Jesse Reid) *Buy High, Sell Higher!*, Hawthorn, 1966; (under pseudonym M.N. Thaler) *It's Fun to Fondue*, Centaur Press, 1968.

Contributor to *Chambers's Encyclopedia*, and to *Coronet*, *American, American Weekly, Reporter, Today's Health, Science Digest, Sports Digest, Reader's Digest, Liberty, Best Years, Weight Watchers, Byline, Weekend, True*, and other magazines. Writer of television scripts for Joyce Brothers' program for two years; writer of Anita Colby column, and of Enid Haupt column. Editor, *Third Degree*.

WORK IN PROGRESS: *A Dictionary of Canadian Place Names; The Complete Fondue Cookbook*.

* * *

KETCHAM, Ralph (Louis) 1927-

PERSONAL: Born October 28, 1927, in Berea, Ohio; son of Sherman Gordon and Laura (Murphy) Ketcham; married Julia Stillwell, November 30, 1958. *Education:* Allegheny College, A.B., 1949; Colgate University, M.A., 1952; Syracuse University, Ph.D., 1956. *Home:* 1002 Ackerman Ave., Syracuse, N.Y. 13210. *Office:* Maxwell School, Syracuse University, Syracuse, N.Y. 13210.

CAREER: Syracuse University, Syracuse, N.Y., instructor, 1953-56, associate professor of political science, history, and American Studies, 1960-61; University of Chicago, Chicago, Ill., research associate in political science, 1956-60; Yale University, New Haven, Conn., research associate in history, 1961-63; Syracuse University, professor of Political Science, history, and American Studies, 1963—. Visiting lecturer, University of Tokyo, 1965; visiting professor of American civilization, University of Texas, Austin, 1967-68. *Military service:* U.S. Coast Guard, 1945-47. *Member:* American Studies Association, Mississippi Valley Historical Association.

WRITINGS: (With Whitfield Jenks Bell and others) *A Tribute to John Bartram*, [Philadelphia], 1959; (editor with W.T. Hutchinson, W.M.E. Rachal, and others) *The Papers of James Madison*, Volumes I and II, University of Chicago Press, 1962; (with L.W. Labaree and others) *The Papers of Benjamin Franklin*, Volume VI-VII, Yale University Press, 1962-63; (editor with Labaree and others) *The Autobiography of Benjamin Franklin*, Yale University Press, 1964; *Benjamin Franklin* (biography), Washington Square Press, 1965; (editor) *The Political Thought of Benjamin Franklin*, Bobbs-Merrill, 1965; *James Madison: A Biography*, Macmillan, 1971.

WORK IN PROGRESS: *Transitions in American Thought: The Revolutionary Era, 1750-1820*, for Prentice-Hall.

BIOGRAPHICAL/CRITICAL SOURCES: *Best Sellers*, May 15, 1971; *National Review*, June 29, 1971.

* * *

KETCHUM, Creston Donald 1922-

PERSONAL: Born August 20, 1922, in Jaffray, British Columbia, Canada; son of Clarence Wilbur and Laura Belle (Wamacks) Ketchum; married Florence Marion Clark, March 29, 1948; children: Donald Chris, Curtis Clark. *Education:* Mates and Masters School, Vancouver, British Columbia, Canada, Mate's Certificate, 1946. *Home and office:* CPO Box 363, Naha, Okinawa, Ryukyu Islands.

CAREER: Professional seaman, 1940-50; Powell River Foursquare Church, Powell River, British Columbia, pastor, 1950-52; International Church of Foursquare Gospel, boat missionary in Pacific islands, including Marshalls, Carolines, and Ryukyus, 1952—. Church World Service, welfare officer in Ryukyu Islands, 1954-58. *Military service:* Canadian Navy, 1942-43.

WRITINGS: *His Path Is In the Waters*, Prentice-Hall, 1955 (published in England as *The Great Waters: The*

Remarkable Story of a Young Seaman Who Combined His Love of the Sea with His Love for His Fellow Men, Hutchinson, 1956); Bread Upon the Waters, Tuttle, 1964.

AVOCATIONAL INTERESTS: Sailing, working with Boy Scouts, reading World War II memoirs.

* * *

KETTLE, Arnold 1916-

PERSONAL: Born March 17, 1916, in London, England; son of Charles and Ethel (Barry) Kettle; married Marguerite Gale, January 30, 1946; children: Martin James, Nicholas David. Education: Merchant Taylor's School, student, 1928-34; Pembroke College, Cambridge, B.A., Ph.D. Politics: Communist Party of Great Britain. Home: 36 Moor Rd., Leeds 6, England.

CAREER: University of Leeds, Leeds, England, senior lecturer in English literature, 1947—. Military service: British Army, 1942-46; became captain.

WRITINGS: An Introduction to the English Novel, two volumes, Rinehart, Volume I: To George Eliot, 1951, also published as Defoe to George Eliot, Harper, 1960, Volume II: Henry James to the Present Day, 1953, 2nd edition of both volumes, Hutchinson, 1967, Harper, 1968; Karl Marx, Founder of Modern Communism, Weidenfeld & Nicolson, 1963, Roy, 1964, 2nd edition, revised, Weidenfeld & Nicolson, 1968; (editor and contributor) Shakespeare in a Changing World: Essays, International Publishers, 1964; (editor and author of introduction) Thomas Hardy, Tess of the d'Urbervilles: A Pure Woman Faithfully Presented, Harper, 1966; Hardy the Novelist: A Reconsideration (W.D. Thomas memorial lecture, given at University College of Swansea, November 28, 1966), University College of Swansea, 1967; (with V.G. Hanes) Man and the Arts: A Marxist Approach (articles originally published in Horizons [Toronto]; includes "Man and the Arts," by Kettle, and "Frye's Theory of Literature and Marxism," by Hanes), American Institute for Marxist Studies, 1968. Contributor to Encyclopaedia Britannica and to journals, including Review of English Studies and Marxism Today.

WORK IN PROGRESS: Research on the nineteenth and twentieth-century English novel.

* * *

KEVE, Paul W(illard) 1913-

PERSONAL: Born October 5, 1913, in Omaha, Neb.; son of Oliver and Vera (Moore) Keve; married Constance Conway, 1936; children: Anne B., Paula M. Education: George Washington University, B.A., 1943; College of William and Mary, M.S., 1947. Religion: Presbyterian. Residence: McLean, Va. Office: Research Analysis Corp., McLean, Va. 22101.

CAREER: National Training School for Boys, Washington, D.C., shop instructor, 1941-42; Virginia State Probation and Parole System, Arlington, probation and parole officer, 1942-45; Virginia Department of Welfare and Institutions, Richmond, various positions in juvenile corrections, 1945-52; Hennepin County District Court, Minneapolis, Minn., director of court services, 1952-67; State of Minnesota, Minneapolis, commissioner of corrections, 1967-71; Research Analysis Corp., McLean, Va., director of department of public communications and safety, 1971—. Member: National Association of Social Workers, National Council on Social Work Education, National Council on Crime and Delinquency, American Correctional Association (board member).

WRITINGS: Prison, Probation or Parole?: A Parole Officer Reports, University of Minnesota Press, 1954; The Probation Officer Investigates: A Guide to the Presentence Report, University of Minnesota Press, 1960; Imagi-

native Programming in Probation and Parole, University of Minnesota Press, 1967. Contributor of articles to professional journals.

AVOCATIONAL INTERESTS: Woodworking.

* * *

KEWES, Karol 1924-
(K.S. Karol)

PERSONAL: Born August 4, 1924, in Lodz, Poland. Education: Attended University of Rostov (U.S.S.R.), 1944-46, University of Grenoble, 1947-49. Home: 17 bis quai Voltaire, Paris VII, France.

CAREER: L'Express, Paris, France, staff member (from founding), 1953-64; New Statesman, London, England, Paris correspondent, 1954; Le Nouvel Observateur, Paris, France, staff member, 1964—.

WRITINGS—Under pseudonym K.S. Karol: Visa pour la Pologne, Gallimard, 1958, translation by Mervyn Savile published as Visa for Poland, MacGibbon & Kee, 1959; Khrouchtchev et l'Occident, Julliard, 1960; (translator into French and author of preface) Evgenii Aleksandrovich Evtushenko, Autobiographie precoce, Julliard, 1963; La Chine de Mao: L'Autre communisme, R. Laffont, 1966, translation by Tom Baistow published as China: The Other Communism, Hill & Wang, 1967, 2nd edition, 1968; Guerillas in Power: The Course of the Cuban Revolution (originally published in French), translation by Arnold Pomerans, Hill & Wang, 1970. Contributor to Le Monde.

WORK IN PROGRESS: A second book about Mao's China.

SIDELIGHTS: In a review of China: The Other Communism, Harry Schwartz states that Kewes brings to his study "the background of a veteran journalist dealing with Communist affairs as well as the personal experience of having lived as a citizen first of the Soviet Union and then of Communist Poland." John Israel believes that Kewes "went to China looking for Stalinism and found it not in the society or the economy, but in the minds of his hosts. [Kewes] is well-informed and generally skeptical. Pre-arranged interviews with victims of the old order are recognized for what they are, and reports that students volunteer to live in rural villages are discounted...." Jonathan Spence finds Kewes's work "careful and lucid," adding: "It has good summaries of recent Chinese history, of the communes, of the Sino-Soviet dispute, of the background to the Great Proletarian Cultural Revolution . . . and a critical analysis of the United States role in Vietnam."

Kewes's works have been translated into Italian, German, Spanish, Finnish, Portugese, Swedish, Dutch, Norwegian, Cathalan, and Turkish.

BIOGRAPHICAL/CRITICAL SOURCES: Saturday Review, May 6, 1967, March 6, 1971; Newsweek, May 8, 1967, January 25, 1971; New Republic, May 20, 1967; New Leader, May 22, 1967, April 19, 1971; New York Times Book Review, August 6, 1967; New York Review of Books, October 26, 1967; Books and Bookmen, November, 1967; New Statesman, December 1, 1967; Listener, December 28, 1967; Commonweal, December 29, 1967; Times Literary Supplement, February 29, 1968; Book World, March 17, 1968; Nation, May 6, 1968, May 31, 1971; Antioch Review, winter, 1968-69; Best Sellers, February 1, 1971; Observer Review, May 20, 1971.

* * *

KEYS, John D. 1938-

PERSONAL: Born August 9, 1938, in San Francisco, Calif.; son of John Jacques and Dorothy (Lucas) Keys.

Education: University of California, Los Angeles, special courses in music composition and Oriental languages. *Home:* 202 Solano Ave., San Rafael, Calif. 94901. *Office:* Yarnell Co., 1681 Galvez Ave., San Francisco, Calif. 94124.

CAREER: Self-employed caterer, Beverly Hills, Calif., 1961-63; Yarnell Co. (cosmetics manufacturer), San Francisco, Calif., owner, 1963—.

WRITINGS: Food for the Emperor: Recipes of Imperial China with a Dictionary of Chinese Cuisine, Ritchie, 1963, reissued as *Food for the Emperor: Mandarin Chinese Cooking, The San Francisco Chinatown Restaurant Guide,* privately printed, 1964; *Japanese Cuisine: A Culinary Tour,* Tuttle, 1966. Translator and compiler of thirty-odd Chinese cookbooks. Contributor to *Gourmet.*

WORK IN PROGRESS: Rice-wine and Buckwheat Noodles, a culinary tour of Japan, publication by Tuttle expected in 1965; a ballet score.

SIDELIGHTS: Competent in written Chinese and Japanese.

*   *   *

KIDNEY, Dorothy Boone 1919-

PERSONAL: Born February 4, 1919, in Presque Isle, Me.; daughter of Frank R. (a blacksmith) and Bertha (Libby) Boone; married Milford L. Kidney (a calculating machine salesman). *Education:* Gorham State Teachers College (now University of Maine at Gorham), B.S., 1960. *Religion:* Church of the Nazarene. *Home address:* Box 394, Washburn, Me. 04786.

CAREER: Teacher of English in Maine schools, 1960—.

WRITINGS: Come and See, Moody, 1963; *Lively Youth Meetings,* Moody, 1964; *Away from It All,* A.S. Barnes, 1969; *I Like,* Moody, 1971; *That Upside Down Feeling,* Moody, 1971; *Portrait of Debec,* Moody, 1972. Contributor of short stories, articles, and poems to newspapers and magazines, including *Seventeen, Charm,* and religious periodicals (almost exclusively since 1947). Columnist, "Glimpses of the Allagash," in *Moosehead Gazette.*

*   *   *

KIEV, Ari 1933-

PERSONAL: Born December 30, 1933, in New York, N.Y.; son of I. Edward (a librarian) and Mary (a librarian; maiden name, Nover) Kiev; married Phylliseve Kovens (a concert pianist), March 27, 1960; children: Jonathan, Marshall. *Education:* Harvard University, A.B., 1954; Cornell University, M.D., 1958; University of London, postdoctoral study at Institute of Psychiatry, 1961-62. *Office:* Cornell University Medical College, Cornell Program in Social Psychiatry, New York, N.Y. 10021.

CAREER: Diplomate, American Board of Psychiatry; Kings County Hospital Center, Kings Country, N.Y., intern, 1958-59; Johns Hopkins Hospital, Baltimore, Md., resident, 1959-61; Columbia University, College of Physicians and Surgeons, research associate in psychiatry, 1964-67, field station director, Psychiatric Epidemiology Research Unit, 1966-67; New York State Psychiatric Institute, New York, assistant attending psychiatrist, 1964-67; Cornell University Medical College, New York, N.Y., clinical associate professor of psychiatry and head of program in social psychiatry, 1967—; New York Hospital, New York, N.Y., associate attending psychiatrist, 1967—. Visiting professor of anthropology, Brandeis University, 1967-68. *Member:* International Committee Against Mental Illness (medical director), American Psychiatric Association, American Medical Association, Society for Applied Anthropology, Royal Medico-Psychological Association.

WRITINGS: (Editor) *Magic, Faith and Healing: Studies in Primitive Psychiatry Today,* Free Press, 1964; (contributor) Joseph Zubin, editor, *Comprehensive Psychopathology: Animal and Human,* Grune, 1967; (contributor) Joseph Zubin and George A. Jervis, editors, *Psychopathology of Mental Development,* Grune, 1967; (author of introduction) L.M. Epstein, *Sex Laws and Customs in Judaism,* Ktav, 1967; *Curanderismo: Mexican-American Folk Psychiatry,* Free Press, 1968; (editor) *Psychiatry in the Communist World,* Science House, 1968; (editor) *Social Psychiatry,* Volume I, Science House, 1969; (contributor) E. Mansell Pattison, editor, *Clinical Psychiatry,* Volume V, Little, Brown, 1969; (contributor) Jules H. Masserman, editor, *Transcultural Psychiatric Approach,* Grune, 1969; (contributor) Stanley C. Plog and Robert B. Edgerton, editors, *Changing Perspectives in Mental Illness,* Holt, 1969; (contributor) Raymond Prince, editor, *Trance and Possession States,* 1969; (contributor) *Multidisciplinary Conference on Identifying Suicide Potential,* Columbia University Press, 1970; *Transcultural Psychiatry,* Free Press, 1972; (with Mario Argandona) *Mental Health in a Developing World: A Case Study in Latin America,* Free Press, 1972.

Contributor of articles to neurology, psychiatry, and anthropology journals. Member of editorial board, *Transcultural Psychiatric Research Review and Newsletter* and *Journal of Pastoral Counselling;* member of editorial advisory board, *International Journal of Social Psychiatry;* associate editor, *International Journal of Psychiatry,* 1965—; editor, *Attitude.*

*   *   *

KILLIAN, Lewis M(artin) 1919-

PERSONAL: Born February 15, 1919, in Darien, Ga.; son of Lewis Martin (an accountant) and Edith (Robinson) Killian; married Katharine Goold, April 11, 1942; children: Katharine, Lewis, John. *Education:* University of Georgia, A.B., 1940, M.A., 1941; University of Chicago, Ph.D., 1949. *Politics:* Democrat. *Religion:* Episcopal. *Home:* 19 Hickory Lane, Amherst, Mass. 01002. *Office:* Department of Sociology, University of Massachusetts, Amherst, Mass. 01002.

CAREER: University of Oklahoma, Norman, assistant professor of sociology, 1949-52; Florida State University, Tallahassee, professor of sociology, 1952-68; University of Connecticut, Storrs, professor of sociology and chairman of the department, 1968-69; University of Massachusetts, Amherst, professor of sociology, 1969—. Visiting professor, University of California, Los Angeles, 1965-66. Consultant to Operations Research Office, 1951-53, National Research Council, Committee on Disaster Research, 1953-59, Attorney-General of Florida, 1954-55. *Military service:* U.S. Army, 1942-46; U.S. Army Reserve, 1946—; currently colonel, Military Police Corps. *Member:* American Sociological Association, Society for Study of Social Problems, Eastern Sociological Society.

WRITINGS: The Georgia Rural Youth Council, Its Relation to Community Development: Description and Evaluation of the Program for the Period, August, 1940 to September, 1941, University of Georgia, 1942; (with others) *A Study of Response to the Houston, Texas, Fireworks Explosion,* National Academy of Sciences, National Research Council, 1956; *An Introduction to Methodological Problems of Field Studies in Disasters,* Natice-Hall, 1957, 2nd edition, 1972; (with Charles U. Smith) *The Tallahassee Bus Protest,* Anti-Defamation League of B'nai B'rith, 1958; (with Charles M. Grigg) *An Inventory of Community Living Conditions and Attitudes in Daytona Beach, Florida,* Florida State University, 1962; (with Grigg) *Racial Crisis in America: Leadership in Conflict,* Prentice-Hall, 1964; (contributor) R.E.L. Faris, editor, *Handbook of Modern Sociology,* Rand McNally,

1964; *The Impossible Revolution?: Black Power and the American Dream,* Random House, 1968; *White Southerners,* Random House, 1970; (contributor) T. Shibutani, editor, *Human Nature and Collective Behavior,* Prentice-Hall, 1970. Associate editor, *American Sociological Review,* 1961-63.

WORK IN PROGRESS: Studies of the Black power movement in the United States.

BIOGRAPHICAL/CRITICAL SOURCES: New Republic, June 8, 1968; *Georgia Review,* winter, 1968.

* * *

KIMBROUGH, Robert (Alexander III) 1929-

PERSONAL: Born June 26, 1929, in Philadelphia, Pa.; son of Robert Alexander, Jr. (a physician) and Agnes (McComb) Kimbrough; married Gertrude Bolling Alfriend, July 11, 1953; children; Elizabeth, Robert, John. *Education:* Williams College, B.A., 1951; Stanford University, M.A., 1955; Harvard University, Ph.D., 1959. *Home:* 1118 Waban Hill, Madison, Wis. 53711. *Office:* Bascom Hall, University of Wisconsin, Madison, Wis. 53706.

CAREER: University of Wisconsin, Madison, instructor, 1959-60, assistant professor, 1960-64, associate professor, 1964-68, professor of English, 1968—. *Military service:* U.S. Marine Corps, 1951-54; became lieutenant; received Purple Heart and Bronze Star. U.S. Marine Corps Reserve, 1948—; now lieutenant colonel. *Member:* Modern Language Association of America, Shakespeare Association, Wisconsin Academy of Sciences, Arts and Letters, American Association of University Professors, Renaissance Society.

WRITINGS: (Editor) Joseph Conrad, *Heart of Darkness: An Authoritative Text, Backgrounds and Sources, Essays in Criticism,* Norton, 1963, revised edition, 1972; *Shakespeare's Troilus and Cressida and Its Setting,* Harvard University Press, 1964; *Trolius and Cressida: A Scene-by-Scene Analysis with Critical Commentary,* American R.D.M., 1966; (editor) Henry James, *The Turn of the Screw: An Authoritative Text, Backgrounds and Sources, Essays in Criticism,* Norton, 1967; (contributor) Shiv K. Kumar, editor, *Victorian Literature: Recent Reevaluations,* New York University Press, 1969; (editor) Sir Philip Sidney, *Selected Prose and Poetry,* Holt, 1969; *Sir Philip Sidney,* Twayne, 1970. Contributor of articles and reviews to learned journals.

WORK IN PROGRESS: A critical/biographical study of Marlowe, for University of Nebraska Press; a critical study of the love poetry of the 1590's.

* * *

KINCAID, Suzanne (Moss) 1936-

PERSONAL: Born February 25, 1936, in Rushville, Ill.; daughter of Lawrence W. (a cost accountant) and Evelyn (Tucker) Moss; married James R. Kincaid (a university professor), December 28, 1962. *Education:* University of Omaha, B.A., 1958; Northwestern University, M.A., 1959; Case Western Reserve University, Ph.D., 1966. *Home:* 59 West Schreyer Pl., Columbus, Ohio 43214.

CAREER: Grove City College, Grove City, Pa., instructor in English, 1959-61; Western Reserve University (now Case Western Reserve University), Cleveland, Ohio, teaching fellow in English, 1961-64; John Carroll University, Cleveland, Ohio, assistant professor of English, 1964-66; Wittenberg University, Springfield, Ohio, assistant professor of English, 1966—. *Member:* Modern Language Association of America.

WRITINGS: (With Margaret P. Ford) *Who's Who in Faulkner,* Louisiana State University Press, 1963.

WORK IN PROGRESS: A critical book on *The Owl and the Nightingale.*

SIDELIGHTS: Mrs. Kincaid has a reading knowledge of French, German, old and middle English, Gothic, and Latin.

* * *

KING, Betty Patterson 1925-

PERSONAL: Born April 11, 1925, in Winston-Salem, N.C.; daughter of Thomas Pearson (a banker) and Frances (Whitlow) Patterson; married Ware Garbett King (an Episcopal priest), June 14, 1947; children: Sarah, Martha, Ann, David. *Education:* Agnes Scott College, B.A., 1947. *Religion:* Christian. *Home address:* P.O. Box 27, Ethete Rural Station, Lander, Wyo. 82520.

CAREER: Winston-Salem Journal, Winston-Salem, N.C., reporter, 1943-45; Missionary Research Library, New York, N.Y., clerical worker, 1947-49; Riverton High School, Riverton, Wyo., teacher of Latin and classics, 1959-60. *Member:* American Association of University Women (local vice-president, 1958-60), Phi Beta Kappa, Mortar Board.

WRITINGS: (with Lorraine Juliana) *The Wall Between Us: A Protestant-Catholic Dialogue,* Bruce, 1964. Co-editor with husband, Ware G. King, of *Wyoming Churchman,* 1959-61, regular columnist of same magazine, 1956—.

SIDELIGHTS: Mrs. King lives on an Indian reservation and enjoys "moving back and forth between cultures." Besides the American Indian, she is interested in natural childbirth, the ecumenical movement, and the theology of romantic love.

* * *

KING, Glen D. 1925-

PERSONAL: Born April 29, 1925, in Van Zandt County, Tex.; son of William Henry and Jennie (Taylor) King; married Dorothy Gray, 1949; children: Kathy, Marc, Kenneth, Corey. *Education:* Lon Morris Junior College, A.A.; Southern Methodist University, B.S.; Sam Houston State University, M.A. *Home:* 1606 Ebbots Pl., Crofton, Md. 21113. *Office:* 1319 18th St. N.W., Washington, D.C. 20036.

CAREER: Dallas Morning News, Dallas, Tex., reporter, 1946-48; Dallas Police Department, Dallas, Tex., 1948-70, became a captain; International Association of Chiefs of Police, Washington, D.C., director of information services, 1970—. Chairman of traffic safety, Dallas Junior Chamber of Commerce, 1960. *Military service:* U.S. Navy, 1943-46. *Member:* Dallas Police Athletic League (vice-president, 1961-62).

WRITINGS: (Editor) *First Line Supervisor's Manual,* C.C Thomas, 1961; (with Jesse E. Curry) *Race Tensions and the Police,* C.C Thomas, 1961. Editor, *Texas Police Journal,* 1946-47.

* * *

KING, James W. 1920-

PERSONAL: Born April 1, 1920, in Oregon City, Ore.; son of Luther Andrew and Audra Anne (Rinehart) King. *Education:* Sherwood Music School, diploma in voice; Gonzaga University, M.A., 1951; Alma College, S.T.B., 1957; Institute Gregorien de Paris, diploma; also studied at Institut Superieur de Liturgie, Paris, France, Catholic University of America, St. John's Abbey. *Home and office:* Seattle University, Seattle, Wash. 98122.

CAREER: Roman Catholic priest, member of Society of Jesus; Seattle University, Seattle, Wash., 1961—, began as assistant professor, now associate professor of theology.

Military service: U.S. Army, 1942-45. *Member:* Liturgical Conference, National Catholic Association of College Theology Professors.

WRITINGS: The Liturgy and the Laity, Newman, 1963. Writer of narration, with Webster T. Patterson, for "Holy Land Then and Now in University Slide Sets," twelve sets of slides on historical subjects of Old and New Testaments. Contributor to several periodicals on subjects of liturgy and sacred music.

WORK IN PROGRESS: Doctoral dissertation, *U.S. Bishops; Implementation of the Constitution on the Sacred Liturgy and Vatican II Liturgical Reforms.*

*   *   *

KINGERY, Robert E(rnest) 1913-

PERSONAL: Born August 5, 1913, in Dayton, Ohio; son of Ernest and Lavina Marie (Needham) Kingery. *Education:* Wittenberg University, B.S., 1937; Columbia University, B.S. in L.S., 1939, graduate study, 1945-46.

CAREER: Dayton (Ohio) Public Library, assistant, 1931-37; New York (N.Y.) Public Library, reference assistant, 1937-46, readers' adviser, 1947-48, personnel representative, 1948-49, chief of Preparation Division. 1950-63, special assisant to the director, 1964—. Pratt Institute, Brooklyn, N.Y., instructor in library service, 1956—. Consultant to libraries and library systems in other states. International Standards Organization Technical Committee 46, chief of U.S. delegation at meetings in Paris, 1962, Budapest, 1964. *Military service:* U.S. Army Air Forces, 1941-45; became master sergeant. *Member:* Council of National Library Associations (chairman, 1962-63), American Library Association, Special Libraries Association, American Standards Association (chairman, committee 239 on library work and documentation, 1958—), American Documentation Institute, New York Library Association.

WRITINGS: Opportunities in Library Careers, Vocational Guidance Manuals, 1952; *How-To-Do-It Books: A Selected Guide,* Bowker, 1950, 3rd edition, revised, 1963, (editor with Maurice F. Tauber) *Book Catalogs,* Scarecrow, 1963. Also author with Tauber, or Adelaide Smith, of various library and cataloging studies; chief bibliographer of *Collier's Encyclopedia,* 1950.

*   *   *

KINNELL, Galway 1927-

PERSONAL: Born February 1, 1927, in Providence, R.I.; son of James Scott and Elizabeth (Mills) Kinnell; children: Maud Natasha, Fergus. *Education:* Princeton University, A.B., 1948; University of Rochester, M.A., 1949. *Home address:* Sheffield, Vt. 05866. *Agent:* Diarmuid Russell, Russell & Volkening, Inc., 551 Fifth Ave., New York, N.Y. 10017.

CAREER: University of Chicago, Chicago, Ill., supervisor of liberal arts program at downtown campus, 1951-54; lived in France, 1955-57, and taught at the University of Grenoble; Fulbright professor at University of Iran, 1959-60. Poet-in-residence, Juniata College. Writer-in-residence, Colorado State University, Fort Collins. Poet. Field worker for Congress of Racial Equality (CORE), 1963. *Military service:* U.S. Navy, 1945-46. *Awards, honors:* National Institute of Arts and Letters grant, 1962; Longview Foundation award, 1962; Guggenheim fellowship, 1963-64; Bess Hokin prize of *Poetry* Magazine, 1965; Eunice Tietjens prize of *Poetry* Magazine, 1966; Rockefeller Foundation grant, 1968; Cecil Hemley Poetry Prize of Ohio University Press, 1968, for translation of Yves Bonnefoy work; Amy Lowell traveling scholarship, 1969; Brandeis University creative arts award, 1969; special mention by judges of National Book Awards for Poetry, 1969, for *Body Rags.*

WRITINGS—Poetry: *What a Kingdom It Was,* Houghton, 1960; *Flower Herding on Mount Monadnock,* Houghton, 1964; *Body Rags,* Houghton, 1968; *Poems of Night,* Rapp & Carroll (London), 1968; *First Poems: 1946-1954,* Perishable Press, 1970; *The Hen Flower,* Sceptre Press, 1969; *The Shoes of Wandering,* Perishable Press, 1971; *The Book of Nightmares,* Houghton, 1971.

Prose: *Black Light,* Houghton, 1966.

Translator: Rene Hardy, *Bitter Victory (Amere Victoire),* Doubleday, 1956; Henri Lehmann, *Pre-Columbian Ceramics (Les Ceramiques precolumbienne),* Studio, 1962; *The Poems of Francois Villon,* New American Library, 1965; Yves Bonnefoy, *On the Motion and Immobility of Douve (Du mouvement et de l'immobilite de douve),* Ohio University Press, 1968; Iwan Goll, *Lackawanna Elegy,* Sumac Press, 1970.

Other: (With Anthony Ostroff and Winfield Townley Scott) *3 Self Evaluations,* Beloit Poetry Journal Chapbook 2, 1953; *The Poetics of the Physical World* (annual writer-in-residence lecture) Colorado State University, 1969. Represented in anthologies, including *Contemporary American Poetry,* edited by Donald Hall, Penguin, 1962; *Where is Vietnam?: American Poets Respond,* edited by Walter Lowenfels, Doubleday, 1967; and *Pocket Book of Modern Verse.* Contributor of poetry to *Harpers, Hudson Review, Nation, Choice, New Yorker, New World Writing, Poetry,* and other literary journals and periodicals.

SIDELIGHTS: Of Kinnell's first book of poems John Logan wrote: ". . . . One of the finest books of the past decade .. It is a full book and it gets better and better—thirty three poems, many of them sizable, plus a remarkable, 450-line final poem hard to match in American literature...." Although James Dickey found the book "not as deep and abiding as we might like," he also said: "Mr. Kinnell has made an authentic beginning ... [his] development will depend on the actual events of his life. And it is a life that I think we should watch. It is warm, generous, reflective, and friendly." Later on, John Malcolm Brinnin described him as "deft, meditative, scrutinizing correspondences, hearkening to intimations.... he is conscious of the penumbra of a 'second' reality ... all impenetrable otherness." He has also been acclaimed as poet-novelist. Mona Van Duyn wrote: "It is in its images that this novel is really; *they* are its compelling action. A strange, haunting book." A reviewer for the *Times Literary Supplement* said: "*Black Light* is a rewarding novel but not by any means a full achieved one," but referred to it as "poetic in its pared-down language and precise sensuous imagery."

Eight years after the first book appeared, Michael Goldman said of *Body Rags:* "Galway Kinnell's third volume adds to his growing reputation as a superior lyric poet.... the most impressive thing about [the poems] is the distance they travel inward from beginning to end.... the poems move deeper line by line, without any heavy breathing on the poet's part. We are kept in an easy commerce with the outer world—until we discover that the inner world has spoken." A writer for the *Beloit Poetry Journal* agreed on his growth, saying: "Kinnell has developed steadily ... In the long poem, 'The Last River,' he has his finest work to date.... It is good to see a poet fulfill his early promise." Of that same long poem Hayden Carruth wrote: "As far as I know, it is the strongest single piece of writing the Movement has produced so far." Thomas Lask feels Kinnell "has been preparing us for some time for *The Book of Nightmares.* [It] is his most integrated book, a work of one mood, one subject really, a tormented cry of what the poet is and feels at this moment. The nightmares of [the] title are not nocturnal happenings or hallucinatory experiences of the mind but those constrictions of the heart that are a function of living. The book is all of a piece, no more to be broken off than a piece of one's heart. After reading it, one turns without plan or forethought to the beginning and starts anew."

BIOGRAPHICAL/CRITICAL SOURCES: *Commonweal*, November 4, 1960; *Poetry*, February, 1961, February, 1967; Glauco Cambon, *Recent American Poetry*, University of Minnesota, 1962; *Princeton University Library Chronicle*, 1964; *New York Times Book Review* July 5, 1964, February 18, 1968; *Partisan Review*, Winter, 1967; *Beloit Poetry Journal*, Spring, 1968; *Hudson Review*, Summer, 1968; *Times Literary Supplement*, September 21, 1969; *New York Times*, September 1, 1971.

*　　*　　*

KINNEY, C. Cle (land)   1915-

PERSONAL: Born December 15, 1915, in Victoria, British Columbia, Canada; son of C. Robert (an engineer) and Jane (Cleland) Kinney; married Jean Stout Brown (an advertising consultant and author), June 10, 1960; children: Gwen Kinney Bates, Peter, Thomas, Charles; (stepchildren) Susan (Mrs. Thomas Fisher), Dina (Mrs. Ernest Anastasio). *Education:* Massachusetts School of Art, student, 1931-35. *Politics:* Democrat. *Religion:* Methodist. *Home and studio:* Squash Hollow Rd., New Milford, Conn. 06776.

CAREER: Artist, writer, and operator of real estate firm, Possibilities Unlimited, New Milford, Conn. Watercolors exhibited at one-man show in New York, N.Y., photographs in other shows. *Member:* Art Directors Club (New York).

WRITINGS—All with wife, Jean Kinney, except as indicated: *How to Tell a Living Story with Home Slides*, Rosen Press, 1963; *Who Does the Baby Look Like?*, Rosen Press, 1963; *97 Special Effects for Your Home Slide Show*, Rosen Press, 1964; *The Neurotic Inanimates*, Rosen Press, 1964; *How to Get 20 to 90% Off on Everything You Buy*, Parker Publishing, 1966; *21 Sure-Fire Ways to as Much as Double Your Income in One Year*, Parker Publishing, 1970; (with others) *The Doctor's Quick Guide to Home Treatments for Over 200 Common Ailments*, Prentice-Hall, 1972; *How to Beat the High Cost of Medical Care by Treating Yourself at Home as Doctors Recommend*, Parker Publishing, 1972; *Fifty-seven Tests That Reveal Your Hidden Talents*, Hawthorn, 1972; *21 Kinds of American Folk Art and How to Make Each One*, Atheneum, 1972.

Illustrator of juveniles by Jean Kinney: *What Does the Tide Do?*, Young Scott Books, 1966; *What Does the Sun Do?*, Young Scott Books, 1967; *What Does the Cloud Do?*, Young Scott Books, 1967.

*　　*　　*

KINNEY, Jean Stout   1912-

PERSONAL: Born March 17, 1912, in Waukon, Iowa; daughter of C.A. (a dentist) and Bernadette (Mooney) Stout; married William H. Brown, 1937; married second husband, C. Cleland Kinney (an artist, author, and operator of real estate firm), June 10, 1960; children: (previous marriage) Susan (Mrs. Thomas Fisher), Dina (Mrs. Ernest Anastasio); (stepchildren) Gwen Kinney Bates, Peter, Thomas, Charles. *Education:* University of Iowa, B.A. in Journalism, 1934. *Politics:* Independent. *Religion:* Episcopalian. *Home and Office:* Squash Hollow Rd., New Milford, Conn. 06776.

CAREER: Biow Agency (advertising firm), copy writer, 1948-53; Grey Agency (advertising firm), copy supervisor, 1953-55; Benton & Bowles Advertising Agency, New York, N.Y., vice-president, 1956-61; Knox Reeves Advertising Corp., Minneapolis, Minn., vice-president, 1964-67; now advertising consultant and writer. Consultant, Dorland Agency, Paris France, 1964. *Member:* International Platform Association, Advertising Women of New York (first vice-president, 1964), Fashion Group of New York, Theta Sigma Phi. *Awards, honors:* Cited by *Printers' Ink* as one of eighteen top advertising women of all time; Jane Arden Award, State of Iowa, 1968.

WRITINGS: *What Does the Tide Do?*, illustrated by husband, Cle Kinney, Young Scott Books, 1966; *What Does the Sun Do?*, illustrated by Cle Kinney, Young Scott Books, 1967; *What Does the Cloud Do?*, illustrated by Cle Kinney, Young Scott Books, 1967; *Start with an Empty Nest*, Harcourt, 1968; *Living with Zest in an Empty Nest*, Hawthorn, 1970.

With Cle Kinney: *How to Tell a Living Story with Home Slides*, Rosen Press, 1963; *Who Does the Baby Look Like?*, Rosen Press, 1963; *97 Special Effects for Your Home Slide Shows*, Rosen Press, 1964; *The Neurotic Inanimates*, Rosen Press, 1964; *How to Get 20 to 90% Off on Everything You Buy*, Parker Publishing, 1966; *21 Sure-Fire Ways to Double Your Income in One Year*, Parker Publishing, 1970; *How to Beat the High Cost of Medical Care by Treating Yourself at Home as Doctors Recommend*, Parker Publishing, 1972; *21 Kinds of American Folk Art and How to Make Each One*, Atheneum, 1972; *Fifty-Seven Tests That Reveal Your Hidden Talents*, Hawthorn, 1972. Contributor to popular magazines.

WORK IN PROGRESS: *Cook Book for Empty Nesters*, for Hawthorn.

*　　*　　*

KINROSS, Patrick   1904-
(Patrick Balfour)

PERSONAL: Born June 25, 1904 (inheriting title of 3rd Baron of Glasclune), in Edinburgh, Scotland; son of Lord Patrick and Lady Caroline Kinross. *Education:* Attended Winchester College; Balliol College, Oxford, B.A., 1925. *Home:* 4 Warwick Ave., London W.2, England. *Agent:* Harold Matson Co., Inc., 22 East 40th St., New York, N.Y. 10016.

CAREER: Worked for various newspapers in England, 1926-40; free-lance journalist, writer, and broadcaster, 1947—. *Military service:* Royal Air Force, 1940-47; became squadron leader; detailed to duty in H.M. Diplomatic Service, 1944-47.

WRITINGS: (Under pseudonym Patrick Balfour) *Society Racket: A Critical Survey of Modern Social Life*, John Long, 1933; (under pseudonym Patrick Balfour) *Grand Tour: Diary of an Eastward Journey*, John Long, 1934, Harcourt, 1935; (contributor under pseudonym Patrick Balfour) Ladislas Farago, editor, *Abyssinian Stop Press*, R. Hale, 1936; (under pseudonym Patrick Balfour) *Lords of the Equator: An African Journey*, Hutchinson, 1937; *The Ruthless Innocent* (novel), Hamish Hamilton, 1949; *The Orphaned Realm: Journeys in Cyprus*, Percival Marshall, 1951; *The Century of the Common Peer* (essays), Putnam, 1954; *Within the Taurus: A Journey in Asiatic Turkey*, J. Murray, 1954, Morrow, 1955; *Europa Minor: Journeys in Coastal Turkey*, Morrow, 1956; *Portrait of Greece*, Parrish, 1956, Dufour, 1959; *The Candid Eye*, foreword by Malcolm Muggeridge, Richards Press, 1958; *The Innocents at Home*, J. Murray, 1959, Morrow, 1960; *The Kindred Spirit: A History of Gin and the House of Booth*, Newman Neame, 1959; *Ataturk: The Rebirth of a Nation*, Weidenfeld & Nicolson, 1964, published in America as *Ataturk: A Biography of*

Mustafa Kemel, Father of Modern Turkey, Morrow, 1965; *Portrait of Egypt,* Morrow, 1966; *The Windsor Years: The Life of Edward, as Prince of Wales, King, and Duke of Windsor,* Viking, 1967; *Between Two Seas: The Creation of the Suez Canal,* J. Murray, 1968, Morrow, 1969; (with Dorothy H. Gary) *Morocco,* Viking, 1971; *Hagia Sophia,* Newsweek, 1972.

WORK IN PROGRESS: A History of the Ottoman Empire.

BIOGRAPHICAL/CRITICAL SOURCES: Times Literary Supplement, January 5, 1967; *Harper's,* November, 1967; *Christian Science Monitor,* November 30, 1967; *New York Times Book Review,* December 3, 1967, March 2, 1969; *Best Sellers,* April 15, 1969.

*   *   *

KIRK, Robert Warner

PERSONAL: Born in Amory, Miss.; son of William H. (a physician) and Nell (Thomas) Kirk; married Rose Marie Collette, September 13, 1942; children: Robert D. *Education:* University of California, Los Angeles, B.A., 1942; University of Southern California, M.A., 1947, Ph.D., 1959. *Home:* 2451 Silverstrand, Hermosa Beach, Calif. 90254. *Office:* Department of English, El Camino College, Torrance, Calif. 90506.

CAREER: Professional musician (trombonist) in California and Arizona prior to 1942; high school teacher, 1940-42, 1946-47; El Camino College, Torrance, Calif., 1947—, became professor of English, 1968. *Military service:* U.S. Navy, 1942-46; became lieutenant. *Member:* College English Association, American Association of University Professors.

WRITINGS: (With Marvin Klotz) *Faulkner's People: A Complete Guide and Index to Characters in the Fiction of William Faulkner,* University of California Press, 1963. Writer of play, "The Specialist," produced at El Camino College. Contributor of essays to *Georgia Review.*

WORK IN PROGRESS: These Eighteen, a collection of short stories.

*   *   *

KITCHEN, Helen (Angell) 1920-

PERSONAL: Born June 28, 1920, in Fossil, Ore.; daughter of Lloyd Steiwer and Hilda (Miller) Angell; married Jeffrey C. Kitchen (a corporation vice-president), August 12, 1944; children: Jeffrey Coleman, Jr., Erik, Lynn. *Education:* University of Oregon, B.A. (honors), 1942. *Home:* 10401 Riverwood Dr., Potomac, Md. 20854; and P.O. Box 3380, Teheran, Iran.

CAREER: Reader's Digest, Pleasantville, N.Y., member of editorial staff, 1942-44; political researcher in Cairo, Egypt, 1944-47; *Middle East Journal,* Washington, D.C., assistant editor, 1948; U.S. Department of State, Washington, D.C., special assistant to director of research for Africa, Middle East, and South Asia, 1951-58; *Africa Report,* Washington, D.C., editor-in-chief, 1960-68. Member of board of public advisers, U.S. Department of State, African Bureau, 1963-70. Consultant, RAND Corp., 1962-68. Trustee, Georgetown Day School, 1957-63. *Member:* African Studies Association of United States (trustee, 1964-67), Phi Beta Kappa. *Awards, honors:* Outstanding service award, U.S. Secretary of State, 1957.

WRITINGS—Editor and contributor: *Americans and the Middle East,* Middle East Institute, 1950; *The Press in Africa,* Ruth Sloan Associates, 1956; *Africa: Images and Realities,* UNESCO, 1962; *The Educated Africa: A Country-by-Country Survey of Educational Development in Africa,* Praeger, 1962; *A Handbook of African Affairs,*

Praeger, 1964; *Footnotes to the Congo Story: An Africa Report Anthology,* Walker & Co., 1967. Contributor to magazines.

WORK IN PROGRESS: A book on the Sudan, for Stanford University Press.

BIOGRAPHICAL/CRITICAL SOURCES: New York Times Book Review, November 19, 1967.

*   *   *

KLAPERMAN, Libby Mindlin 1921-

PERSONAL: Born December 28, 1921, in Petrikow, Russia; daughter of Charles and Sarah Golda (Saltzman) Mindlin; married Gilbert Klaperman (a rabbi), August 23, 1942; children: Judith, Joel, Frieda, Carol. *Education:* Brooklyn College, B.A., 1942, M.A., 1962. *Religion:* Jewish. *Home:* 64 Muriel Ave., Lawrence, N.Y. 11559.

CAREER: Union Orthodox Congregations, Women's Branch, New York, N.Y., education director, 1950—; *Jewish Life* (magazine), New York, N.Y., editor, 1952—; Far Rockaway High School, New York, N.Y., teacher, 1956—; Stern College for Women, New York, N.Y., instructor, 1960—. *Member:* Authors Guild.

WRITINGS: The Dreidel Who Wouldn't Spin, Behrman, 1950; *Adam and the First Sabbath,* Behrman, 1953; (adapter) *Stories of the Bible,* selected and arranged by Jorn Sann and Ralph Schonberg, Sann's Publishing Co., 1954, reissued as *Stories from the Bible: The Old Testament,* Grosset, 1956, reissued as *Bible Stories from the Old Testament,* Grosset, 1963; *Jeremy and the Torah,* Behrman, 1956; *Jeremy's ABC Book,* Behrman, 1956; (with husband, Gilbert Klaperman) *The Story of the Jewish People,* four volumes, Behrman, Volume I: *From Creation to the Building of the Second Temple,* 1956, Volume II: *From the Second Temple Through the Age of Rabbis,* 1957, Volume III: *From the Golden Age in Spain Through European Emancipation,* 1958, Volume IV: *From the Settlement of America Through Israel Today,* 1959; *Jeremy Learns About God,* Behrman, 1957; *The Scholar-Fighter: The Story of Saadia Gaon,* Farrar, Straus, 1961; *Sisterhood Prayers for All Occasions,* Women's Branch, Union of Orthodox Jewish Congregations of America Press, 1964; *A Different Girl,* Lion Press, 1969; *The Five Brothers Maccabee: A Novel for Young Readers Based on the Story of Chanukah,* Funk, 1969.

SIDELIGHTS: The Dreidel Who Wouldn't Spin has been translated into French, *The Story of the Jewish People* into Danish and Persian.

*   *   *

KLAPP, Orrin E(dgar) 1915-

PERSONAL: Born October 26, 1915, in Chicago, Ill.; son of Orrin Edgar (a salesman) and Mary (Bierbower) Klapp; married Evelyn Gilbert, January 24, 1942; children: Merrie, Curtis. *Education:* University of Chicago, B.A., 1939, M.A., 1940, Ph.D., 1948. *Office:* Department of Sociology, University of Western Ontario, London, Ontario, Canada.

CAREER: San Diego State College. San Diego, Calif., 1948-72, became professor of sociology, 1958; University of Western Ontario, London, professor of sociology, 1972—. Cultural attache, U.S. Embassy, Greece, 1968-69. *Military service:* U.S. Navy, 1942-46; became lieutenant. *Member:* American Sociological Association, Pacific Sociological Association.

WRITINGS: Ritual and Cult: A Sociological Interpretation, Public Affairs Press, 1956; *Heroes, Villains, and Fools: The Changing American Character,* Prentice-Hall, 1962; *Symbolic Leaders: Public Dramas and Public Men,* Aldine, 1964; *Collective Search for Identity,* Holt, 1969;

Currents of Unrest: An Introduction to Collective Behavior, Holt, 1972. Associate editor of *Pacific Sociological Review,* 1959-62.

WORK IN PROGRESS: A book, *Entropy in Social Systems.*

* * *

KLEIN, Marcus 1928-

PERSONAL: Born April 19, 1928, in Cleveland, Ohio; married Marian Weitzman, November 19, 1960; children: Jennifer, Eric. *Education:* Western Reserve University (now Case Western Reserve University), B.A., 1950; Columbia University, M.A., 1952, Ph.D., 1962; University of Munich, postgraduate study, 1956-57. *Home:* 130 Jewett Pkwy., Buffalo, N.Y. 14214.

CAREER: Barnard College, New York, N.Y., assistant professor, 1952-65, associate professor, 1965-68, professor of English, 1968—; State University of New York at Buffalo, chairman of department of English, 1968—. *Military service:* U.S. Army, 1946-47; became staff sergeant. *Member:* Modern Language Association of America, Phi Beta Kappa. *Awards, honors:* Fulbright fellow, 1956-57, 1966-67.

WRITINGS: After Alienation: American Novels in Mid-Century, World Publishing, 1964; (editor with Robert Pack) *Literature for Composition on the Theme of Innocence and Experience,* Little, Brown, 1966; (editor with Pack) *Short Stories: Classic, Modern, Contemporary,* Little, Brown, 1967; (editor) *The American Novel Since World War II,* Fawcett, 1969. Contributor to *Nation, New Leader, New York Post Magazine, Reporter, Kenyon Review, Hudson Review,* and other literary reviews.

WORK IN PROGRESS: American Literature, 1933-1960, for Free Press.

BIOGRAPHICAL/CRITICAL SOURCES: American Literature, January, 1965.

* * *

KLEMENT, Frank L(udwig) 1908-

PERSONAL: Born August 19, 1908, in Leopolis, Wis.; son of Jacob and Barbara (Kutil) Klement; married Laurel Marie Fosnot, 1938; children: Paul Francis, Richard Eugene, Kenneth Raymond. *Education:* Central State College (now Wisconsin State College at Stevens Point), B.E., 1935; University of Wisconsin, Ph.M., 1938, Ph.D., 1946. *Home:* 6627 West Moltke Ave., Milwaukee, Wis. 53210. *Office:* Marquette University, 1309 West Wisconsin Ave., Milwaukee, Wis. 53233.

CAREER: High school teacher in Beloit, Wis., 1938-41; Lake Forest College, Lake Forest, Ill., instructor, 1943-45; Wisconsin State College, Eau Claire, assistant professor of history, 1945-48; Marquette University, Milwaukee, Wis., professor of history, 1948—. Member of advisory council, National Civil War Centennial Commission; chairman of education committee, Wisconsin Civil War Centennial Commission. *Member:* American Historical Society, Mississippi Valley Historical Association, American Catholic Historical Association (executive council, 1957-1960), Wisconsin Historical Society, Civil War Round Table of Milwaukee, Phi Alpha Theta (national councilor, 1963—). *Awards, honors:* Ford Foundation fellowship, 1952-53.

WRITINGS: Lincoln's Critics in Wisconsin (lecture), Lincoln Fellowship of Wisconsin, 1956; *The Copperheads in the Middle West,* University of Chicago Press, 1960; *Wisconsin and the Civil War,* State Historical Society of Wisconsin, 1963; *The Limits of Dissent: Clement L. Vallandigham and the Civil War,* University Press of Kentucky, 1970. Contributor to a score of professional journals, mainly on historical subjects. Editorial board member, *Proceedings* of Wisconsin Academy of Science, Arts and Letters.

WORK IN PROGRESS: A study of subversive secret societies of the Civil War Years.

AVOCATIONAL INTERESTS: Camping, fishing.

* * *

KLINCK, George Alfred 1903-

PERSONAL: Born July 23, 1903, in Elmira, Ontario Canada; son of George (a jeweler, publisher, and grain dealer) and Mary Elizabeth (Devitt) Klinck; married Gladys Jean Smith, June 29, 1929. *Education:* University of Toronto, B.A., 1927, M.A., 1935, B. Paed., 1945; Laval University, Ph.D., 1952. *Politics:* Conservative. *Religion:* Lutheran. *Home:* 194 Dawlish Ave., Toronto 12, Ontario, Canada.

CAREER: Public school teacher in Hamilton, Ontario, 1922-29; North Bay Collegiate Institute, North Bay, Ontario, teacher of art and languages, 1929-31; North Toronto Collegiate Institute, Toronto, Ontario, teacher of modern languages, 1931-69. Supervisor of business English, University of Toronto, Extension Department, Toronto, Ontario, 1946—. *Member:* Ontario Secondary School Teachers Federation, Ontario Modern Language Teachers Association (president, 1948-49), Upper Canada Bible Society (president, 1956-58), Bibliographical Society of Canada, Canadian Colportage Society. *Awards, honors:* Ontario Educational Association Centennial award for service to education, 1960; life membership, Ontario Education Association, 1969.

WRITINGS: (Editor and reviser) *Muenchausens Grossartige Reisen und Abenteuer,* Pitman, 1939; *La Randonnee de L'Oiseau-Mouche,* Librarie Generale Canadienne 1951; (with W.F.H. Whitmarsh) *Parlons Francais!,* Books I-III, Longmans, Green, 1953-57; *Bibliographie: Louis Frechette, Prosateur,* privately printed, 1953; *Louis Frechette, Prosateur: Une Reestimation de son oeuvre,* La Quotidien Ltee, 1955; *Le Retour de L'Oiseau-Mouche,* Librarie Generale Canadienne, 1959; (editor) *Louis Frechette, Memoires Intimes,* Fides, 1961; (editor and author of introduction) Lucien Noel, *La Pere tranquille,* Methuen, 1961, Heath, 1964; (with wife, Gladys Jean Klinck) *Ecouter et chanter,* Holt, 1964; (editor) *Max,* Copp Clark, 1966; *Down to the Sea,* Simon & Schuster (Canada), 1968; (editor) *Max au rallye,* Bellhaven House, 1970.

Compiler of anthologies: *Allons Gai!: A Topical Anthology of French Canadian Prose and Verse,* Ryerson, 1945; *En Avant,* Ryerson, 1947; *Entre Nous,* Ryerson, 1951; *Adventures,* Ryerson, 1954; *Auteurs Francais,* Ryerson, 1954; *Auteurs de nos jours,* Ryerson, 1957. Contributor of articles in English and French to educational and language journals. Editor, Canadian *Modern Language Review.*

WORK IN PROGRESS: L'Oiseau-Mouche aux Indes; Recits pour la jeunesse; Canadian Stories; Legendes de Louis Frechette; The Quest of the Phantom Buffalo.

AVOCATIONAL INTERESTS: Hunting, fishing, traveling.

* * *

KLINEFELTER, Walter 1899-

PERSONAL: Born November 3, 1899, near Glen Rock, Pa.; son of Edwin F. (a farmer) and Sophia (Bricker) Klinefelter; married Mildred Rosenkrans, 1926 (deceased); married Edna McCullough, 1939; children: Mildred Klinefelter Druck, Nancy. *Education:* Gettysburg

College, A.B., 1920. *Home address:* R.D. 1, Dallastown, Pa. 17313.

CAREER: Commonwealth of Pennsylvania, thirty years service as teacher, store manager, other posts; now retired. *Member:* Arthur Machen Society, Baker Street Irregulars, Cartophilatelists.

WRITINGS: Maps in Miniature: Notes Critical and Historical on Their Use on Postage Stamps, Hawthorn, 1936; *Christmas Books* (essay), Southworth-Anthoesen Press, 1936; (editor and author of introduction) *A Bibliographical Checklist of Christmas Books,* Southworth-Anthoesen Press, 1937; *Books about Poictesme: An Essay in Imaginative Bibliography,* Black Cat Press, 1937; (editor) *More Christmas Books,* Southworth-Anthoesen Press, 1938; *Ex Libris A. Conan Doyle: Sherlock Holmes,* Black Cat Press, 1938; *Illustrations in Miniature: Postal Designs from Books and Manuscripts,* Black Cat Press, 1939; *The Fortsas Bibliohoax,* Carteret Book Club, 1941; (translator and author of commentary) Rabelais, *Catalogue of the Choice Books Found by Pantagruel in the Abbey of Saint Victor,* William P. Wreden, 1952; *The World Minutely Mapped,* privately printed, 1953; *A Small Display of Old Maps and Plans,* Prairie Press, 1962; *Sherlock Holmes in Portrait and Profile,* Syracuse University Press, 1963; *A Packet of Sherlockian Bookplates,* privately printed, 1964; *25 Years of Service,* York Junior College, 1968; *The Case of the Conan Doyle Crime Library,* Sumac Press, 1968; *A Further Display of Old Maps and Plans,* Sumac Press, 1969; (contributor) Richard K. Doud, editor, *Portfolio 6,* Winterthur Museum, 1970; *Lewis Evans and His Maps,* American Philosophical Society, 1971.

WORK IN PROGRESS: A Catalog of Catalogs, a translation with commentary, of Johan Fischart's *Catalogus Catalogorum; The ABC Books of the Pennsylvania Germans.*

* * *

KLUGER, Richard   1934-

PERSONAL: Born September 18, 1934, in Paterson, N.J.; son of David (a business executive) and Ida (Abramson) Kluger; married Phyllis Schlain, March 23, 1957; children: Matthew, Theodore. *Education:* Princeton University, B.A. (cum laude), 1956. *Home:* 17 Main St., Ridgefield, Conn. 06870. *Agent:* Sterling Lord Agency, 660 Madison Ave., New York, N.Y. 10022.

CAREER: Wall Street Journal, New York, N.Y., city editor, 1956-57; *Country Citizen,* New City, N.Y., editor and publisher, 1958-60; *New York Post,* New York, N.Y., staff writer, 1960-61; *Forbes* Magazine, New York, N.Y., associate editor, 1962; *New York Herald Tribune,* New York, N.Y., general books editor, 1962-63, book editor, 1963-66; *Book Week,* New York, N.Y., editor, 1963-66; Simon & Schuster, New York, N.Y., managing editor, 1966-68, executive editor, 1968-70; Atheneum Publishers, New York, N.Y., editor-in-chief, 1970-71; Charterhouse Books, New York, N.Y., president and publisher, 1972—. *Member:* Princeton Club of New York.

WRITINGS: When the Bough Breaks (novel), Doubleday, 1964; *National Anthem* (novel), Harper, 1969. Contributor to *Partisan Review, New Republic, Harper's.* 1969. Contributor to *Partisan Review, New Republic, Harper's.*

WORK IN PROGRESS: My Lord, What a Morning, a nonfiction account of 1954 school desegregation cases, for Knopf.

SIDELIGHTS: Kenneth Lamott called *National Anthem* a "funny, sardonic book, pertinent to a world in which the creation of outrageous comedy is one of the few responses left to a sane man. By this test, Richard Kluger

is clearly sane. He also has at his command an admirable gift for comic invention.... Like all truly comic writers, Kluger is involved in a serious business. The outrageousness of his invention allows us to laugh at the madness of our world." A reviewer for *Virginia Quarterly Review* described Kluger as "a fresh, new, and talented writer endowed with high comic gifts and an irrepressible sense of the absurd."

BIOGRAPHICAL/CRITICAL SOURCES: New York Times Book Review, July 12, 1964, June 29, 1969; *Newsweek,* July 13, 1964; *Book World,* December 24, 1967, May 18, 1969; *Best Sellers,* May 1, 1969; *Nation,* June 2, 1969; *Saturday Review,* June 7, 1969; *New Yorker,* June 7, 1969; *Observer Review,* October 26, 1969; *Virginia Quarterly Review,* autumn, 1969.

* * *

KNOX, Vera Huntingdon

PERSONAL: Born in Nova Scotia, Canada; daughter of Elkanah S. and Bridget (Hirtle) Knox. *Education:* Dalhousie University, B.A., 1926. *Religion:* Presbyterian. *Home:* 181 Waverly Pl., New York, N.Y. 10014.

CAREER: Standard & Poor's Corp., New York, N.Y., library assistant, 1927-39; Tax Foundation, Inc., New York, N.Y., librarian, 1939—. *Member:* Special Libraries Association (first vice-president, 1945-46).

WRITINGS: Public Finance: Information Sources, Gale, 1964.

* * *

KOCH, Claude (F.)   1918-

PERSONAL: Surname is pronounced Cook; born November 28, 1918, in Philadelphia, Pa.; son of Claude Quilmer and Madeline (Sauer) Koch; married Mary Kane, September 7, 1941; children: Michael, Christopher, Stephen, Gerard, Mark, Mary Jo. *Education:* LaSalle College, B.S., 1940; graduate study at Niagara University and University of Pennsylvania; University of Florida, M.A., 1957. *Home:* 128 West Highland Ave., Philadelphia, Pa. 19118. *Agent:* Diarmuid Russell, Russell & Volkening, Inc., 551 Fifth Ave., New York, N.Y. 10017.

CAREER: LaSalle College, Philadelphia, Pa., 1946—, became professor of English. *Military service:* U.S. Marine Corps, 1941-46; became major; received Presidential Unit Citation. *Member:* American Association of University Professors. *Awards, honors:* Dodd, Mead Intercollegiate Literary fellowship, 1949; *Sewanee Review* fellowship in fiction, 1957; Rockefeller Foundation fellowship in fiction, 1966.

WRITINGS—All novels: Island Interlude, Dodd, 1951; *Light in Silence,* Dodd, 1958; *The Kite in the Sea,* Chilton, 1964; *A Casual Company,* Chilton, 1965. Contributor of verse and fiction to *Sewanee Review, Antioch Review, Northwest Review, Ave Maria, Four Quarters,* and *Spirit.*

WORK IN PROGRESS: The Thefters, a novel.

* * *

KOCH, Robert   1918-

PERSONAL: Born April 7, 1918, in New York, N.Y.; son of Millard F. and Ella (Heidelberg) Koch; married Gladys L. Rooff (an antiques dealer), August 5, 1942; children: Elaine, Mitchell. *Education:* Harvard University, A.B., 1939; New York University, M.A., 1953; Yale University, Ph.D., 1957. *Politics:* Democrat. *Religion:* Reform Jewish. *Home:* 9 Outer Rd., South Norwalk, Conn. 06854. *Office:* Southern Connecticut State College, Crescent St., New Haven, Conn. 06515.

CAREER: Southern Connecticut State College, New Haven, 1956—, began as associate professor, now professor of art. Board member, Silvermine College of Art. Military service: U.S. Army Air Forces, 1942-45; became first lieutenant. Member: College Art Association, Society of Architectural Historians, National Trust for Historic Preservation.

WRITINGS: Louis Comfort Tiffany, 1848-1933 (catalogue of an exhibition), Museum of Contemporary Crafts, 1958; (author of introduction) Jane Hayward, editor, Art Nouveau, Lyman Allyn Museum, 1963; Louis C. Tiffany, Rebel in Glass, Crown, 1964, 2nd edition, 1967; (author of introduction) Samuel Bing, Artistic America: Tiffany Glass and Art Nouveau, M.I.T. Press, 1970; Louis C. Tiffany, Glass, Bronzes and Lamps: A Complete Collector's Guide, Crown, 1971. Contributor of articles to Art in America, Journal of the Society of Architectural Historians, Gazette des Beaux-Arts, and Art Quarterly.

WORK IN PROGRESS: Art Nouveau, U.S.A.

AVOCATIONAL INTERESTS: Collecting and photographing art nouveau objects.

*　*　*

KOEHLER, W(illiam) R. 1914-

PERSONAL: Surname is pronounced "keeler"; born July 8, 1914, in Freeport, Ill.; son of Clarence E. (a glass maker) and Rena (Johnson) Koehler; married Lillian E. Ward, September 4, 1937; children: Richard D., Elizabeth Ann, Raymond E. Education: University of Wisconsin, extension courses. Politics: Republican. Religion: Protestant. Home: 5059 State St., Ontario, Calif. 91761.

CAREER: Self-employed as dog trainer, with much of present training for Walt Disney Productions, Burbank, Calif. Director of training, Orange Empire Dog Club.

WRITINGS: The Koehler Method of Dog Training, Howell Book, 1961, reissued as The Koehler Method of Guard Dog Training: An Effective and Authoritative Guide for Selecting, Training, and Maintaining Dogs in Home Protection and Police, Security, Sentry, and Military Use, photographs by Koehler and others, 1967; The Koehler Method of Open Obedience for Ring, Home and Field, Howell Book, 1970. Contributor of articles to dog publications and outdoor magazines.

WORK IN PROGRESS: A novel about a dog in Newfoundland.

SIDELIGHTS: Movie dogs trained by Koehler include Asta, Big Red, Shaggy Dog, Bullet, Turk and Duke, Bodger and Luath, and Wildfire; four of them won the American Humane Association's Patsy Award as best animal actor of the year.

*　*　*

KOERNER, James D. 1923-

PERSONAL: Born February 3, 1923, in Cedar Rapids, Iowa. Education: Washington University, St. Louis, Mo., Ph.D., 1952. Home: 60 South Maple Ave., Westport, Conn. 06880. Office: Alfred P. Sloan Foundation, 630 Fifth Ave., New York, N.Y. 10020.

CAREER: Kansas State University, Manhattan, faculty member, 1952-54; Massachusetts Institute of Technology, Cambridge, faculty member, 1955-57; Council for Basic Education, Washington, D.C., executive director, 1957-60; Education Development Center, Boston, Mass., senior research fellow, 1967-68, editor-in-chief, 1968-70; Alfred P. Sloan Foundation, New York, N.Y., program officer, 1970—. Military service: U.S. Army Air Forces, 1942-45. Awards, honors: Ford Foundation fellow, 1954-55.

WRITINGS: The Last of the Muckrake Men, Department of Humanities, Massachusetts Institute of Technology, 1956; (editor) The Case for Basic Education: A Program for Public Schools, Atlantic-Little, Brown, 1959; (editor with Derek K. Colville) The Craft of Writing, Harper, 1961; (with Harold L. Clapp) Teacher Education: Who Holds the Power?, Council for Basic Education, 1963; The Miseducation of American Teachers, Houghton, 1963; Reform in Education: England and the United States, Delacorte, 1968; Who Controls American Education?: A Guide for Laymen, Beacon Press, 1968; The Parsons College Bubble: A Tale of Higher Education in America, Basic Books, 1970. Contributor of articles to Atlantic, Harper's, Saturday Review, Saturday Evening Post, and other journals and newspapers.

WORK IN PROGRESS: A book on Eric Hoffer.

SIDELIGHTS: Maurice R. Berube describes Who Controls American Education? as "a necessary primer on the who's and what's of public education. Uncommonly lucid and direct, this book offers insight into the contending forces for power. Most educational writing lacks either clarity or depth. The reader will learn more of the scope and significance of creative federalism, teacher militancy, local control and state power in this thin book than in a shelfful of thick specialized studies."

BIOGRAPHICAL/CRITICAL SOURCES: Times Literary Supplement, May 9, 1968; Commonweal, April 11, 1969; New Republic, July 11, 1970.

*　*　*

KOGAN, Bernard Robert 1920-

PERSONAL: Born May 16, 1920, in Chicago, Ill.; son of Isaac (a newspaper distributor) and Ida (Perlman) Kogan; married Irene Wishnewsky, August 19, 1962; children: (by wife's previous marriage; adopted) Henry, Sophia; (present marriage) Naomi and Sara (twins). Education: University of Chicago, B.A., 1941, M.A., 1946, Ph.D., 1953. Politics: Democrat. Religion: Jewish. Home: 9034 North Bennett, Skokie, Ill. 60076. Office: University of Illinois at Chicago Circle, Box 4348, Chicago, Ill. 60680.

CAREER: Indiana University, instructor in English at Bloomington, 1946-48, at Gary and Calumet Extension Centers, 1948-53; University of Chicago, Chicago, Ill., instructor in humanities, 1949-51; University of Illinois, Chicago Division, 1952—, began as assistant professor, now professor of English. Military service: U.S. Naval Reserve, 1941-45; served in Pacific theater. Member: Conference on College Composition and Communication (member of executive committee, 1962-65), Modern Language Association of America, National Council of Teachers of English, College English Association, American Association of University Professors, Dickens Fellowship, Phi Beta Kappa.

WRITINGS: (Editor and contributor) The Chicago Haymarket Riot: Anarchy on Trial, Heath, 1959; (editor and contributor) Darwin and His Critics: The Darwinian Revolution, Wadsworth, 1960. Contributor of articles to College Composition and Communicaion, and of reviews to various other publications.

WORK IN PROGRESS: Biographical and bibliographical Problems in Dickens.

AVOCATIONAL INTERESTS: Amateur printing, handball, tennis, and music.

*　*　*

KOGAN, Herman 1914-

PERSONAL: Born November 6, 1914, in Chicago, Ill.; son of Isaac (a newspaper distributor) and Ida (Perilman) Kogan; married Alice Marie Schutt, 1940 (divorced,

1946); married Marilew Cavanagh (a public relations executive), October 1, 1950; children: Rick, Mark. *Education:* University of Chicago, B.A., 1936; also studied music privately, 1919-34. *Home:* 1715 North Park Ave., Chicago, Ill. 60614. *Office: Chicago Sun-Times,* 401 North Wabash Ave., Chicago, Ill. 60614.

CAREER: City News Bureau, Chicago, Ill., reporter, 1935-37; *Chicago Tribune,* Chicago, Ill., reporter, re-write man, 1937-42; *Chicago Sun* and *Chicago Sun-Times,* Chicago, Ill., successively reporter, re-write man, editorial writer, book editor, and drama critic, 1942-58; *Encyclopaedia Britannica,* Inc., Chicago, Ill., director of company relations, 1958-62; *Chicago Daily News,* Chicago, Ill., assistant to executive editor, editor of *Panorama* magazine, 1962-65; Field Communications Corp., Chicago, Ill., assistant general manager, 1965-68; *Chicago Sun-Times,* Chicago, Ill., editor of *Book Week,* 1968-70, editor of *Showcase* Magazine, 1970—. Instructor at Medill School of Journalism, Northwestern University, Evanston, Ill., 1946-48. Director, University of Chicago Alumni Fund, 1960—. Director, Great Books Foundation, 1961-64. *Military service:* U.S. Marine Corps, 1943-46; became technical sergeant; received Presidential Unit Citation.

MEMBER: Authors Guild, Society of Midland Authors, Mental Health Society of Chicago (director, 1960-64), Phi Beta Kappa, Sigma Delta Chi; Arts Club, Press Club (president, 1965), and Tavern Club (all Chicago). *Awards, honors:* Friends of Literature award, 1956, for contribution to letters; American Geography Society award, 1960, for *Chicago: A Pictorial History;* Adult Education of Chicago award, 1963, for magazine, *Panorama;* American Newspaper Guild award, 1964, 1970, for contributions to journalism.

WRITINGS: (With Lloyd Wendt) *Lords of the Levee: The Story of Bathhouse John and Hinky Dink,* Bobbs-Merrill, 1943, reissued as *Bosses in Lusty Chicago: The Story of Bathhouse John and Hinky Dink,* Indiana University Press, 1967; (with others) *Uncommon Valor: Marine Divisions in Action,* Infantry Journal Press, 1946; (with others) *Semper Fidelis,* Sloane, 1947; (with Wendt) *Bet a Million!: The Story of John W. Gates,* Bobbs-Merrill, 1948; (with Wendt) *Give the Lady What She Wants: The Story of Marshall Field & Co.,* Rand McNally, 1952; (with Wendt) *Big Bill of Chicago,* Bobbs-Merrill, 1953; (with Wendt) *Chicago: A Pictorial History,* Dutton, 1958; *The Great EB: The Story of the Encyclopaedia Britannica,* University of Chicago Press, 1958; *The Long White Line: The Story of Abbot Laboratories,* Random House, 1963; *Lending Is Our Business: The Story of Household Finance Corporation,* Donnelley, 1966; (with Robert Cromie) *The Great Fire: Chicago 1871,* Putnam, 1971. Contributor to *Nation, New Republic, Esquire, United Nations World, Saturday Review,* and *American Lawn Tennis.*

WORK IN PROGRESS: Research for biography of Jane Addams; books on Chicago's history.

*   *   *

KOHN, Bernice Herstein   1920-

PERSONAL: Born June 15, 1920, in Philadelphia, Pa.; daughter of Joseph B. and Sarah (Freedman) Herstein; married G. David Weinick (a clinical psychologist); children: Barbara (Mrs. Dan Isaac), Judith (Mrs. Richard Wolman), Eugene. *Education:* Attended University of Wisconsin. *Home:* 490 West End Ave., New York, N.Y. 10024; and 6 Island Rd., East Hampton, N.Y. 11937.

CAREER: Writer.

WRITINGS—Juveniles: *Our Tiny Servants: Molds and Yeasts,* Prentice-Hall, 1962; *Computers at Your Service,* Prentice-Hall, 1962; *The Peaceful Atom,* Prentice-Hall,

1963; *Everything Has a Shape,* Prentice-Hall, 1964; *Everything Has a Size,* Prentice-Hall, 1964; *The Marvelous Mammals: Monotremes and Marsupials,* Prentice-Hall, 1964; *The Scientific Method,* Prentice-Hall, 1964; *Light,* Coward, 1965; *Echoes,* Coward, 1965; *One Day It Rained Cats and Dogs,* Coward, 1965; *Koalas,* Prentice-Hall, 1965; *Light You Cannot See,* Prentice-Hall, 1965; *Fireflies,* Prentice-Hall, 1966; *Telephones,* Coward, 1967; *Levers,* Coward, 1967; *The Bat Book,* Hawthorn, 1967; *Raccoons,* Prentice-Hall, 1968; *Secret Codes and Ciphers,* Prentice-Hall, 1968; *All Kinds of Seals,* Random House, 1968; *The Look-It-Up Book of Transportation,* Random House, 1968; *Ferns: Plants Without Flowers,* Hawthorn, 1968; *Ramps,* Hawthorn, 1969; (with husband, David Weinick) *A First Look at Psychology,* Hawthorn, 1969; *Talking Leaves: The Story of Sequoyah,* Hawthorn, 1969; *The Beachcomber's Book,* Viking, 1970; *Chipmunks,* Prentice-Hall, 1970; *The Armistad Mutiny,* McCall Publishing, 1971; *How High Is Up?,* Putnam, 1971; *Out of the Cauldron: A Short History of Witchcraft,* Holt, 1972; *The Busy Honeybee,* Four Winds, 1972; *One Sad Day,* Third Press, 1972; *The Organic Living Book,* Viking, 1972; *The Gypsies,* Bobbs-Merrill, 1972.

BIOGRAPHICAL/CRITICAL SOURCES: Best Sellers, June 1, 1968; *Library Journal,* May 15, 1970; *New York Times Book Review,* June 7, 1970.

*   *   *

KOLAJA, Jiri Thomas   1919-

PERSONAL: Born October 21, 1919, in Brno, Czechoslovakia. *Education:* Masaryk University, Ph.Dr., 1947; University of Chicago, M.A., 1950; Cornell University, Ph.D., 1959. *Office:* Department of Sociology, West Virginia University, Morgantown, W. Va. 26506.

CAREER: Talladega College, Talladega, Ala., 1954-58, began as assistant professor, became professor of sociology; University of Kentucky, Lexington, 1958-66, began as assistant professor, became associate professor of sociology; McMaster University, Hamilton, Ontario, professor of sociology, 1966-68; State University of New York at Brockport, professor of sociology, 1968-70; West Virginia University, Morgantown, professor of sociology, 1970—. Field work in factories in Poland, 1957, Yugoslavia, 1959. *Member:* American Sociological Association (fellow), International Sociological Institute, Industrial Relations Research Association, Southern Sociological Society. *Awards, honors:* Social Science Research Council grant and training fellowship.

WRITINGS: K Problematice Filmu (title means "Problems of the Motion Picture"), Cs. Filmove Nakladatelstvi, 1948; *A Polish Factory: A Case Study of Worker's Participation in Decision Making,* University Press of Kentucky, 1960; *Workers' Councils: The Yugoslav Experience,* Tavistock, 1965, Praeger, 1966; *Social System and Time and Space: Introduction to the Theory of Recurrent Behavior,* Duquesne University Press, 1969. Contributor to a dozen journals in America and abroad, including *Social Forces, Human Organization, Journal of Central European Affairs, Rural Sociology, Phylon, Industrial and Labor Relations Review, Human Relations,* and *American Journal of Sociology.*

*   *   *

KOLSON, Clifford J(ohn)   1920-

PERSONAL: Born October 20, 1920, in Homestead, Pa.; son of Peter J. (an electrical foreman) and Mary (Hook) Kolson; married L. Evangeline Humm (an educator), June 14, 1959; children: Clifford J. II, Carol Ann, L. Evangeline II. *Education:* University of Pittsburgh, B.S., 1950, M.Ed., 1955, Ed.D., 1959. *Home:* Meadows East, Potsdam, N.Y. 13676. *Office:* Reading

Center, State University of New York College at Potsdam, Pierrepoint Ave., Potsdam, N.Y. 13676.

CAREER: Electrician for U.S. Steel, Homestead, Pa., 1939-41, for Continental Foundries, Coraopolis, Pa., 1946-50; Tarentum (Pa.) public schools, principal, 1950-56; college and university teaching, 1956-62; State University of New York College at Potsdam, professor of education and director of Reading Center, 1962—. Los Angeles School and Vision Forum, member of board of directors, 1962-63. *Military service:* U.S. Army, 1941-45; served in Pacific theater; became sergeant. *Member:* International Reading Association (treasurer, Oregon chapter, 1961), North West Better Vision Institute.

WRITINGS: (With William A. Bennie and others) *Student Teaching,* Miami University Press, 1957; (with Bennie and others) *Guiding Student Teacher Growth,* Miami University Press, 1958; (with George Kaluger) *Clinical Aspects of Remedial Reading,* C.C Thomas, 1963; (with Kaluger) *Reading and Learning Disabilities,* Merrill, 1969. Contributor of eighty-five articles to education journals.

WORK IN PROGRESS: Two series, "Primary Reading Disability Training" and "Patterned Symbol Blending"; *Guiding Growth in the Teaching of Reading; Contralateral Theory of Reading Disability.*

* * *

KONOPKA, Gisela 1910-

PERSONAL: Born February 11, 1910, in Berlin, Germany; came to United States in 1941, naturalized in 1944; daughter of Mendel and Bronia (Buttermann) Peiper; married Erhardt Paul Konopka (a staff engineer), June 23, 1941. *Education:* University of Hamburg, staatsexamen in education, 1933; University of Pittsburg, M.S.S.A., 1943; Columbia University, D.S.W., 1955. *Home:* 3809 Sheridan Ave. S, Minneapolis, Minn. 55410.

CAREER: After leaving Germany in 1937, spent a year in Austria, and three years in France before coming to America in 1941; variously psychiatric group worker for Pittsburgh Child Guidance Clinic, clinical field instructor for School of Social Work, University of Pittsburgh, and lecturer at School of Social Work, Carnegie Institute of Technology (now Carnegie-Mellon University), all Pittsburgh, Pa., 1943-47; University of Minnesota, Minneapolis, professor of social work, 1947—, coordinator, Center for Urban and Regional Affairs, 1968-70, special assistant to vice-president for student affairs, 1969—, director of Center for Youth Development and Research, 1970. Summer teacher at University of California, Berkeley, at Smith College, University of Illinois, University of Utah, Laval University (Quebec, Canada), University of Puerto Rico. Lecturer at various institutions in U.S. and abroad. Consultant and lecturer in Germany under auspices of U.S. Department of State, 1950, 1951, 1956, under auspices of Unitarian Service Committee, 1960; consultant to agencies in Rhode Island, New York, Minnesota. Former member of board of directors, National Conference of Social Welfare; member of advisory committee, Minnesota Department of Corrections; chairman of committee on correctional institutions, Minnesota Governor's Advisory Council on Children and Youth. Participant in conferences, on committees, and on panels.

MEMBER: National Association of Social Workers (former director), American Association of Orthopsychiatry (president, 1963-64), Committee on the History of Social Welfare (former chairman), Minneapolis Urban League (member of executive board). *Awards, honors:* Research grant, University of Minnesota, 1948; Fulbright grant to lecture and research in Holland, 1960-61; named outstanding alumnus of School of Social Work, University of Pittsburgh, 1960; National Institute of Mental Health grant to study the adolescent girl in conflict, 1962-65; award for outstanding service, Association for the Blind, 1966; citation, Department of Health, Education and Welfare, 1966; citation, Volunteers of America, 1968; Distinguished Alumnus award, School of Social Work, University of Pittsburgh, 1968; Outstanding Woman award, National Campfire Girls, 1969.

WRITINGS: Therapeutic Group Work with Children, University of Minnesota Press, 1949; *Report on Public Welfare and Social Work* (pamphlet), U.S. High Commissioner for Germany, 1950; *Group Work in the Institution: A Modern Challenge,* Association Press, 1954, revised edition, 1970; *Eduard C. Lindeman and Social Work Philosophy,* University of Minnesota Press, 1958; *Social Work as a Profession* (pamphlet), National Association of Social Workers, 1959; *Group Work: The Next Ten Years* (pamphlet), National Association of Social Workers, 1959; *Social Group Work and Mental Health* (pamphlet), National Association of Social Workers, 1959; (with Minnie Harlow) *Group Methods in Therapeutic Settings,* University of Pittsburgh, 1960; *Social Group Work: A Helping Process,* Prentice-Hall, 1963, 2nd edition, 1972; (author of introduction) *Group Method and Services in Child Welfare,* Child Welfare League of America, 1964; *Effective Communication with Adolescents in Institutions* (pamphlet), Child Welfare League of America, 1965; (with Vernie-Mae L. Czaky) *An Approach to the Evaluation of Change Through the Group Work Method,* University of Minnesota, 1965; *The Adolescent Girl in Conflict,* Prentice-Hall, 1966; *A Changing Culture Asks for Change Services* (pamphlet), Florence Crittenton Association of America, 1967; *The Teenage Girl* (pamphlet), New York State Division for Youth, 1967; *The Present Crisis in Perspective* (pamphlet), University of North Carolina, 1968.

Contributor: *Proceedings of the National Conference of Social Work, 1946,* Columbia University Press, 1946; Arnold M. Rose, editor, *Race Prejudice and Discrimination,* Knopf, 1948; Charles E. Hendry, editor, *A Decade of Group Work,* Association Press, 1948; *Education for Psychiatric Social Work,* American Association of Psychiatric Social Work, 1950; *Selected Papers in Group and Community Organization,* Health Publications Institute, 1951; *The Handicapped Child in the Mainstream,* Commission for Handicapped Children, State of Illinois, 1953; Mert E. Frampton and Elena D. Gall, editors, *Special Education for the Exception,* Sargent, 1953; *The Social Welfare Forum,* Columbia University Press, 1953; Clyde B. Vedder, editor, *The Juvenile Offender,* Doubleday, 1954; Harleigh B. Trecker, editor, *Group Work: Foundations and Frontiers,* Whiteside, 1955; *Proceedings of the 1955 Social Work Progress Institute,* University of Michigan, 1955; *Out of Their Misfortune,* [Riverside, R.I.], 1956; Alan Keith-Lucas and others, editors, *Readings for House Parents of Children's Institutions,* Workman's Book House, 1956; Walter Friedlander, editor, *Concepts and Methods of Social Work,* Prentice-Hall, 1958; Marjorie Murphy, editor, *The Social Group Work Method in Social Work Education,* Council on Social Work Education, 1959; Henry W. Maier, editor, *Group Work as Part of Residential Treatment,* National Association of Social Workers, 1965; *The Role of Agencies Serving Low-Income Girls,* [Minneapolis], 1966; *Techniques of Probation,* Law-Medicine Institute, Boston University, 1967; Robert J.N. Tod, editor, *Children in Care,* Longmans, Green, 1968; *The Function of Rebellion: Is Youth Creating New Family Values?,* Child Study Association of America, 1968; *Source Book of Teaching Materials on the Welfare of Children,* Council on Social Work Education, 1969; Katherine Kendall, editor, *Teaching of Comparative Social Welfare: A Workshop Report,* Council on Social Work Education, 1969.

Contributor to other published symposia, and of more than one hundred articles and reviews to professional journals. Former member of editorial board, *American Jounal of Orthopsychiatry;* member of editorial board, *Journal of Comparative Studies.*

SIDELIGHTS: Mrs. Konopka's books have been translated into German, Japanese, Italian, Dutch, Arabic, Persian, Turkish, Spanish, and Portuguese.

BIOGRAPHICAL/CRITICAL SOURCES: *American Journal of Orthopsychiatry,* July, 1963.

* * *

KOONCE, Ray F. 1913-

PERSONAL: Born August 15, 1913, in Grenada, Miss.; son of Walter Willis (a merchant) and Lula (Clark) Koonce; married Virginia (a college professor), June 22, 1924; children: Steve, Susan. *Education:* Mississippi College, B.A., 1935; Southwestern Baptist Seminary, M.R.E., 1939; Columbia University, M.A., 1954. *Office:* Department of Psychology, Carson-Newman College, Jefferson City, Tenn. 37760.

CAREER: Carson-Newman College, Jefferson City, Tenn., director of guidance and placement, 1956—. *Military service:* U.S. Army, 1941-45; became staff sergeant. *Member:* East Tennessee Personnel and Guidance Association, Civitan Club (secretary-treasurer, 1963; president, 1964).

WRITINGS: *Growing with Your Children,* Broadman, 1963; *Understanding Your Teenagers,* Broadman, 1965.†

* * *

KOPPMAN, Lionel 1920-

PERSONAL: Born November 24, 1920, in Waco, Tex.; son of Meyer and Ethel (Siegel) Koppman; married Mae Zuckerman (a free-lance proofreader and copy editor), December 5, 1948; children: Stephen, Debra. *Education:* Baylor University, B.A., 1942; Hebrew Union College, New York, N.Y., M.A., 1969. *Religion:* Jewish. *Office:* National Jewish Welfare Board, 15 East 26th St., New York, N.Y. 10010.

CAREER: National Jewish Welfare Board, New York, N.Y., public relations consultant; Temple Isaiah, Forest Hills, N.Y., teacher of Jewish history. *Member:* Health and Welfare Public Relations Association (treasurer), American Jewish Public Relations Society (vice-president). *Awards, honors:* Jewish Book Council award, 1954, for *A Jewish Tourist's Guide to the U.S.*

WRITINGS: (With Bernard Postal) *A Jewish Tourist's Guide to the U.S.,* Jewish Publication Society, 1954; (with Postal) *Jewish Landmarks in New York: An Informal History and Guide,* Hill & Wang, 1964. Writer of one-act play, "Francis Salvador, Patriot." Contributor of more than one hundred articles to magazines and newspapers. Contributing editor, *Jewish Digest.*

WORK IN PROGRESS: A book on American Jewish folklore; a guide for Jewish etiquette; *Judaism for Christians;* a bibliography of multi-media materials on teaching Jewish civics; a textbook on American Jewish history.

* * *

KORBEL, John 1918-

PERSONAL: Born December 13, 1918; son of Mario Joseph and Hilda (Beyer) Korbel; married Jenifer Claridge; married second wife, Isobel Albrecht; children: (first marriage) Wendy, Peter; (step-children) Mark, Peter H. *Education:* Harvard University, S.B., 1939, M.B.A., 1941, Ph.D., 1959. *Home:* Dover Rd., Durham, N.H. 03824. *Office:* University of New Hampshire, Durham, N.H. 03824.

CAREER: University of New Hampshire, Durham, assistant professor of economics, 1950-56; Massachusetts Institute of Technology, Cambridge, research associate, 1957-59; University of Wisconsin, Madison, assistant professor of economics, 1959-65; University of New Hampshire, professor of economics, 1966—. *Military service:* U.S. Navy, 1941-45; became lieutenant.

WRITINGS: (With G.H. Orcutt, Martin Greenberger, and Alice Rivlin) *Microanalysis of Socioeconomic Systems,* Harper, 1961; (contributor) Mark Perlman, editor, *Human Resources in the Urban Economy,* Johns Hopkins Press, 1962. Contributor to *Review of Economics and Statistics* and *Journal of the American Statistical Association.*

* * *

KORBONSKI, Andrzej 1927-

PERSONAL: Born January 2, 1927, in Poznan, Poland; son of S. Korbonski; married Elizabeth Glendinning, June 1, 1955; children: Holly, Ellen. *Education:* University of London, B.Sc., 1950; Columbia University, M.A., 1954, Ph.D., 1962. *Home:* 718 Radcliffe, Pacific Palisades, Calif. 90272. *Office:* Department of Political Science, University of California, Los Angeles, Calif. 90024.

CAREER: Columbia University, New York, N.Y., research associate, research project on national incomes of east-central Europe, 1956-63; University of Calfiornia, Los Angeles, began as assistant professor, 1963, now professor of political science. *Military service:* U.S. Army, 1951-53. *Member:* American Political Science Association, American Economic Association, American Association for the Advancement of Slavic Studies, Polish Institute of Arts and Sciences in America.

WRITINGS: *COMECON,* Carnegie Endowment for International Peace, 1964; *Politics of Socialist Agriculture in Poland, 1945-1960,* Columbia University Press, 1965; (with T.P. Alton) *Polish National Income and Product, in 1954, 1955, and 1956,* Columbia University Press, 1965; *The Warsaw Pact,* Carnegie Endowment for International Peace, 1969. Contributor to *International Organization* and *Comparative Politics.* Also author, with Claus Wittich, of Columbia University indexes (covering 1937 and 1946-65) on Polish transport and communications, construction materials consumption, trade and catering, and housing, service, and government sectors, 1967-68.

WORK IN PROGRESS: Research for a book on economic and political integration in the Communist sphere.

* * *

KOREN, Henry J(oseph) 1912-

PERSONAL: Born December 30, 1912, in Roermond, Netherlands; came to United States in 1948, naturalized in 1954; son of Gerard Hubert (a realtor) and A.M. Catherine (Smolenaers) Koren. *Education:* Seminary Gemert, Netherlands, student, 1931-35; Gregorian University, S.T.L., 1940; Catholic University of America, S.T.D., 1942. *Home address:* Box 328, St. Leo, Fla. 33574. *Office:* Department of Philosophy and Religion, St. Leo College, St. Leo, Fla. 33574.

CAREER: Member of Roman Catholic Order, Congregation of the Holy Ghost (Spiritans), 1933—, ordained priest, 1937; St. Mary's College, Trinidad, West Indies, teacher of Latin and French, 1941-48; Duquesne University, Pittsburgh, Pa., 1948-66, began as instructor, became professor of philosophy, chairman of department of philosophy, 1953-65, chairman of department of theology, 1962-66; St. Leo College, St. Leo, Fla., professor of philosophy, 1967—. *Member:* Metaphysical Society of

America, American Association of University Professors, National Association for the Advancement of Colored People.

WRITINGS: (Translator and editor with Edward A. Bushinski) Gaetano, *The Analogy of Names [and] The Concept of Being*, Duquesne University Press, 1953; *An Introduction to the Science of Metaphysics*, Herder, 1955; *An Introduction to the Philosophy of Animate Nature*, Herder, 1955; *The Spiritans: A History of the Congregation of the Holy Ghost*, Duquesne University Press, 1958; (editor) *Readings in the Philosophy of Nature*, Newman, 1958; (translator and editor) *The Spiritual Writings of Father Claude Francis Poullart des Places*, Duquesne University Press, 1959; *An Introduction to the Philosophy of Nature*, Duquesne University Press, 1960; *Some Contemporary Problems Facing the Church in Africa*, Duquesne University Press, 1960; *Knaves or Knights?: A History of the Spiritan Missionaries in Acadia and North America, 1732-1839*, Duquesne University Press, 1962; *Research in Philosophy: A Bibliographical Introduction to Philosophy and a Few Suggestions for Dissertations*, Duquesne University Press, 1966; (adapter) Bertrand van Bilsen, *The Changing Church*, Duquesne University Press, 1966; *Marx and the Authentic Man: A First Introduction to the Philosophy of Karl Marx*, Duquesne University Press, 1967; (reviser) Gabriel Marcel, *Presence and Immortality*, Duquesne University Press, 1967; (with William A. Luijpen) *A First Introduction to Existential Phenomenology*, Duquesne University Press, 1969; (with Luijpen) *Religion and Atheism*, Duquesne University Press, 1971.

Translator; all published by Duquesne University Press, except as indicated: Andrew G. van Melsen, *From Atomos to Atom: A History of the Atomic Theory*, 1952; P. Henry van Laer, *Philosophico-Scienfic Problems*, 1953; Louis de Raeymaeker and others, *Truth and Freedom*, 1954; van Laer *The Philosophy of Science*, Volume I: *Science in General*, 1956, Volume II: *A Study of the Division and Nature of Various Groups of Sciences*, 1962; Stephan Strasser, *The Soul in Metaphysical and Empirical Psychology*, 1957; William A. Luijpen, *Existential Phenomenology*, 1960, revised edition, 1969; van Melsen, *Science and Technology*, 1961; (with Walter van der Putte) Francis Libermann, *Spiritual Letters to Sisters and Aspirants*, 1962; (with van der Putte) Albert Dondyne, *Faith and the World*, 1963; (with van der Putte) Libermann, *Spiritual Letters to People in the World*, 1963; Remy C. Kwant, *The Phenomenological Philosophy of Merleau-Ponty*, 1963; John A. Peters, *Metaphysics: A Systematic Survey*, 1963; Strasser, *Phenomenology and the Human Sciences: A Contribution to a New Scientific Ideal*, 1963; (with van der Putte) Peter Schoonenberg, *God's World in the Making*, 1964; (with van der Putte) Luijpen, *Phenomenology and Atheism*, 1964; (with van der Putte) Libermann, *Spiritual Letters to Clergy and Religious*, Volume I, 1964, Volume II, 1965, Volume III, 1966; Martin G. Plattel, *Social Philosophy*, 1965; John H. Walgrave, *Person and Society*, 1965; Kwant, *Phenomenology of Social Existence*, 1965; (with Therese Schrynemakers) Joseph P. Kockelman, *Martin Heidegger: A First Introduction to His Philosophy*, 1965; van Melsen, *Evolution and Philosophy*, 1965; (with van der Putte) William H. van der Pol, *Anglicanism in Ecumenical Perspective*, 1965; Kwant, *The Phenomenology of Language*, 1965; Luijpen, *Phenomenology and Metaphysics*, 1965; Joseph J. Kockelmans, *Phenomenology and Physical Science*, 1966; Luijpen, *Phenomenology of Natural Law*, 1967; John A. Heijke, *An Ecumenical Light on the Renewal of Religious Community Life*, 1967; van Melsen, *Physical Science and Ethics*, 1968; (with van der Putte) Higher Institute of Catechetics, *Fundamentals and Programs of a New Catechesis*, 1968; Kwant, *Critique: Its Nature and Function*, 1968; Kwant, *Phenomenology of*

Expression, 1969; (with van der Putte) Herman A. Fiolet, *Ecumenical Breakthrough*, 1969; (with M. Jacobs) J.H. van der Berg, *Things*, 1970; van Melsen, *Science and Responsibility*, 1970; (with van der Putte) Strasser, *The Idea of Dialogal Phenomenology*, 1970; Herman Berger, *Progressive and Conservative Man*, 1971; Guenther Schiwy, *Structuralism and Theology*, 1971; Luijpen, *What Can We Say About God?*, Paulist Press, 1971; Plattel, *Utopian and Critical Thinking*, 1972; van Peursen, *Phenomenology and Reality*, 1972; Luijpen, *Theology as Anthropology*, 1973.

General editor of "Duquesne Studies," 1951-68. Contributor to numerous publications.

WORK IN PROGRESS: Several translations.

SIDELIGHTS: Koren is competent in Dutch, French, German, Portugese, Italian, and Spanish.

*   *   *

KOZLOWSKI, Theodore T(homas)   1917-

PERSONAL: Born May 22, 1917, in Buffalo, N.Y.; son of Theodore (an insurance salesman) and Helen (Zamiara) Kozlowski; married Maude K. Peters, June 29, 1954. Education: Syracuse University, B.S., 1939; Duke University, M.A., 1941, Ph.D., 1947; Massachusetts Institute of Technology, postgraduate study, 1942-43; University of Buffalo, postdoctoral study, summers, 1948, 1949.

CAREER: University of Massachusetts, Amherst, assistant professor, 1947-48, associate professor, 1948-50, head of department of botany, 1950-58; University of Wisconsin, Madison, professor of forestry, 1958-64, chairman of department of forestry, 1961-64. Research collaborator, U.S. Forest Service. Consultant, National Science Foundation and Food and Agriculture Organization of the United Nations. Military service: U.S. Army Air Forces, 1942-46; became captain. Member: Botanical Society of America (chairman, Northeastern section, 1958), American Society of Plant Physiologists (chairman, Northeastern section, 1958), Ecological Society of America, Society of American Foresters (chapter chairman, 1961; chairman of committee on tree physiology, 1963), American Institute of Biological scientists, Sigma Xi, Phi Kappa Phi, Phi Sigma, Phi Sigma Kappa. Awards, honors: Senior Fulbright research scholar, Oxford University, 1964-65.

WRITINGS: *Light and Water in Relation to Growth and Completion of Piedmont Forest Trees* (monograph), privately printed, 1949; *Tree Physiology Bibliography*, U.S. Forest Service, 1956; (with P.J. Kramer) *Physiology of Trees*, McGraw, 1960; (editor) *Tree Growth*, Ronald, 1962; *Water Metabolism in Plants*, Harper, 1964; (editor) *Water Deficits and Plant Growth*, Academic Press, Volume I: *Development, Control and Measurement*, 1968, Volume II: *Plant Water Consumption and Response*, 1968, Volume III, 1972; *Growth and Development of Trees*, Academic Press, Volume I: *Seed Germination, Ontogeny, and Shoot Growth*, 1971, Volume II: *Cambial Growth, Root Growth, and Reproductive Growth*, 1971; (editor) *Seed Biology*, Academic Press, Volume I: *Importance, Development and Germination*, 1972, Volume II: *Germination Control, Metabolism and Pathology*, 1972. Consulting editor, "Physiological Ecology" book series, Academic Press. Contributor of more than two hundred articles on physiology of woody plants to botanical journals. Associate editor, *American Midland Naturalist, Canadian Journal of Forest Research*; member of editorial board, *Forest Science, Ecology*.

*   *   *

KRAEHE, Enno E(dward)   1921-

PERSONAL: Surname is pronounced cray; born December 9, 1921, in St. Louis, Mo.; son of Enno (a realtor) and

Amelia (Henckler) Kraehe; married Mary Alice Eggleston (a librarian), May 25, 1946; children: Laurence Adams, Claudia. *Education:* University of Missouri, A.B., 1943; M.A., 1944; University of Minnesota, Ph.D., 1948. *Religion:* Episcopalian. *Office:* Department of History, University of Virginia, Charlottesville, Va. 22903.

CAREER: University of Delaware, Newark, instructor in history, 1946-48; University of Kentucky, Lexington, assistant professor, 1948-50, associate professor, 1950-63, professor of history, 1963-64; University of North Carolina, Chapel Hill, professor of history, 1964-68; University of Virginia, Charlottesville, professor of history, 1968—. Visiting professor at University of Missouri, University of Texas, University of Virginia, and University of Minnesota, 1946-1963. U.S. Department of State specialist in Germany, 1953. *Member:* American Historical Association, Conference Group for Central European History, Southern Historical Association. *Awards, honors:* Fulbright research scholar in Austria, 1952-53; Guggenheim fellow, 1960-61; fellow, Center for Advanced Study, University of Virginia, 1968-70; fellow, American Council of Learned Societies, 1969.

WRITINGS: (Contributor) I.T. Sanders, editor, *Collectivization of Agriculture in Eastern Europe,* University Press of Kentucky, 1958; *Metternich's German Policy,* Princeton University Press, Volume I: *The Contest with Napoleon, 1799-1814,* 1963, Volume II: *The Contest with Alexander, 1814-1820,* 1971; (editor) *The Metternich Controversy,* Holt, 1971. Contributor of articles and book reviews to *American Historical Review, Journal of Modern History, South Atlantic Quarterly, Revue d'Histoire, Moderne et Contemporaine.* Member of board of editors, *Central European History* and *Austrian History Yearbook.*

* * *

KRAFT, Joseph 1924-

PERSONAL: Born September 4, 1924, in South Orange, N.J.; son of David H. and Sophie (Surasky) Kraft; married Rhoda Winton; children: Mark, David. *Education:* Columbia University, A.B., 1947; Princeton University, graduate study, 1948-49, 1950. *Home and office:* 3021 N St. N.W., Washington, D.C. 20007.

CAREER: Washington Post, Washington, D.C., editorial writer, 1951; *New York Times,* New York, N.Y., writer, 1952-57; *Harper's,* New York, N.Y., Washington correspondent, 1962-65; syndicated columnist for *Washington Post, Chicago Daily News,* and other newspapers, 1965—. *Member:* Council on Foreign Relations, White House Correspondents Association, State Department Correspondents Association, Phi Beta Kappa, Century Club (New York), Federal City Club (Washington, D.C.), Coffee House Club.

WRITINGS: The Struggle for Algeria, Doubleday, 1961; *The Grand Design: From Common Market to Atlantic Partnership,* Harper, 1962; *Profiles in Power: A Washington Insight,* New American Library, 1966; *Chinese Difference* Saturday Review Press, 1973.

* * *

KRAMER, Samuel Noah 1897-

PERSONAL: Born September 28, 1897, in Russia; married Mildred Tokarsky (a university mathematics instructor); children: Daniel C., Judith (Mrs. Robert Greene). *Education:* School of Pedagogy, Philadelphia, Pa., student, 1917; Temple University, B.Sc., 1921; Dropsie College, graduate student, 1926-27; University of Pennsylvania, Ph.D., 1929. *Home:* 5039 Schuyler St., Philadelphia, Pa. 19144. *Office:* University Museum, University of Pennsylvania, 33rd and Spruce Sts., Philadelphia, Pa. 19104.

CAREER: University of Chicago, Oriental Institute, Chicago, Ill., research assistant, 1932-36, research associate, 1936-42; University of Pennsylvania, University Museum, Philadelphia, Pa., research associate, 1942-43, associate curator, 1943-47, curator of tablet collection, 1948—, Clark Research Professor of Assyriology, 1948-68; professor emeritus, 1968—. Fulbright research professor in Turkey, 1951-52. *Member:* American Oriental Society, American Anthropological Association, Archaeological Institute of America, Society of Biblical Literature and Exegesis, American Philosophical Society. *Awards, honors:* Guggenheim fellow, 1937-39; John Frederick Lewis Prize of American Philosophical Society, 1944; D.H.L. from Hebrew Union College, 1956; D.Litt. from Temple University, 1960.

WRITINGS: The Sumerian Prefix Forms Be- and Bi- in the Time of the Earlier Princes of Lagas, University of Chicago Press, c.1936; *Gilgamesh and the Huluppu-Tree: A Reconstructed Sumerian Text,* University of Chicago Press, 1938; *Lamentation Over the Destruction of Ur* (translated from Sumerian tablets), University of Chicago Press, 1940; *Sumerian Mythology: A Study of Spiritual and Literary Achievement in the Third Millennium B.C.,* American Philosophical Society, 1944, revised edition, Harper, 1961; *Enki and Ninhursag: A Sumerian "Paradise" Myth,* American Schools of Oriental Research, 1945; (editor) *Schooldays: A Sumerian Composition Relating to the Education of a Scribe,* University Museum, University of Pennsylvania, c.1950; (editor) *Enmerkar and the Lord of Aratta: A Sumerian Epic Tale of Iraq and Iran,* University Museum, University of Pennsylvania, 1952; *A "Fulbright" In Turkey* (account of researches carried out by Kramer as the first Fulbright research scholar), University Museum, University of Pennsylvania, 1952; *From the Tablets of Sumer: Twenty-five Firsts in Man's Recorded History,* Falcon's Wing Press, 1956, reissued as *History Begins at Sumer,* Thames & Hudson, 1958, Doubleday-Anchor, 1959, 2nd edition, revised and enlarged, Thames & Hudson, 1961; *Two Elegies on a Pushkin Museum Tablet: A New Literary Genre,* bilingual Russian and English edition, Oriental Literature Publishing House (Moscow), 1960; (editor and contributor) *Mythologies of the Ancient World,* Doubleday-Anchor, 1961; (editor and author of introduction and foreword) *Sumerische literarische Texte aus Nippur* (includes text by Professor Hilprecht-Sammlung), Akademie Verlag (Berlin), 1961; *Glory of the Torah: Graded Lessons on Basic Judaism (with Exercises) for Senior Jewish Pupils,* [London], 1962; *The Sumerians: Their History, Culture, and Character,* University of Chicago Press, 1963; (with Cyril J. Gadd) *Literary and Religions Texts* (UR Excavations, Texts 6), Publications of the Joint Expedition of the British Museum and the Museum of the University of Pennsylvania to Mesopotamia, 1963; (with editors of Time-Life Books) *Cradle of Civilization,* Time-Life, 1967; *The Sacred Marriage Rite: Aspects of Faith, Myth, and Ritual in Ancient Sumer* (expanded version of Pattern lectures given at Indiana University in 1968), Indiana University Press, 1969. Contributor to professional journals, including *Harvard Theological Review, Journal of the American Oriental Society,* and *Bulletin* of the American Schools of Oriental Research.

WORK IN PROGRESS: Continuing research in Sumerian language, literature, and culture, using cuneiform tablets as sources.

* * *

KRAVETZ, Nathan 1921-

PERSONAL: Born February 11, 1921, in New York, N.Y.; son of Louis and Anna (Thau) Kravetz; married Evelyn Cottan, December 10, 1944; children: Deborah

Ruth, Daniel. *Education:* University of California, Los Angeles, B.Ed., 1941, M.A., 1949, Ed.D., 1954; Harvard University, fellow in education, 1951-52. *Home:* 95, Rue de la Faisanderie, Paris-16e, France. *Office:* International Institute for Educational Planning, 9, Rue Eugene-Delacroix, Paris-16e, France.

CAREER: Los Angeles (Calif.) City Schools, elementary teacher, principal, 1946-64; Lehman College of the City University of New York, New York, N.Y., professor of education, 1964—. Technical director of education division, U.S. Department of State, U.S. aid program, in Lima, Peru, 1958-60. Summer teacher at University of California, Los Angeles, Los Angeles State College (now California State University at Los Angeles), San Diego State College, Eastern Oregon College. Consultant, System Development Corporation, Santa Monica, Calif.; consultant for educational film, "Allen Is My Brother," Churchill-Wexler Corp. Member of advisory board, Parent-Teachers' Association, Tenth District, Los Angeles. Coordinator of the Peace Corps training program, University of California, Los Angeles, 1963. *Military service:* U.S. Army Air Forces, 1942-46. *Member:* International Education Society, Comparative Education Society, Authors Guild, National Education Association, Association of Elementary School Administrators, Phi Delta Kappa (president, Alpha Chi chapter, Epsilon field chapter), Kappa Delta Phi.

WRITINGS: (With Ted Gordon) *Tips for Teachers,* Fearon, 1962.

Juveniles: *Two for a Walk,* Oxford University Press, 1954; *A Horse of Another Color,* Little, Brown, 1962; *A Monkey's Tale,* Little, Brown, 1964; (with Muriel Farrell) *The Dog on the Ice,* Singer, 1968; *He Lost It! Let's Find It!,* Walck, 1969; (with Farrell) *Is There a Lion in the House?,* Walck, 1970; *The Way of the Condor,* Crown, 1970.

Monographs: *The More Effective Schools Program,* Center for Urban Education, 1966; *The Transitional Schools Program,* Center for Urban Education, 1968, *Academic Excellence in an Inner-City Elementary School,* Center for Urban Education, 1968; *School Boards and School Operations: A Programmed Primer on School Law,* University of the State of New York (Albany), 1968; *Special Primary Programs in Five Schools,* Center for Urban Education, 1969; *The Diagnosis of Educational Systems and Operations as a Prelude to Development Planning,* International Institute for Educational Planning, UNESCO, 1970; *Planning for Change in Educational Structure, Curriculum and Methods,* International Institute for Educational Planning, UNESCO, 1970; (editor) *Management and Decision-Making in Educational Planning,* International Institute for Educational Planning, UNESCO, 1970. Contributor to professional journals and educational yearbooks.

WORK IN PROGRESS: Juvenile book about France; research on educational development.

* * *

KRAWITZ, Ruth (Lifshitz) 1929-

PERSONAL: Surname is pronounced *kraw*-witz; born April 12, 1929, in Bronx, New York, N.Y.; married Irving Krawitz (a druggist) June 19, 1948; children: Stephen, Eileen. *Education:* Hunter College (now Hunter College of the City University of New York), B.A., 1949; Yeshiva University, M.A., 1965. *Religion:* Jewish. *Home:* 22 West Allison Ave., Pearl River, N.Y. 10965.

CAREER: New York (N.Y.) Public Schools, elementary teacher, 1949-59, curriculum assistant, 1959-64, executive assistant to superintendent, 1964—. Owner and director, Blue Rill Day Camp, Monsey, N.Y., 1950—. Educational consultant, Oceana Publications. Adjunct associate profes-

sor, Lehman College of the City University of New York and Columbia University. *Member:* Association for Supervision and Curriculum Development, International Reading Association (Bronx council board of directors, 1962-64), American Camping Association, American Association of University Professors, Phi Beta Kappa.

WRITINGS: (With Lawrence Finkel) *How to Study,* Oceana, 1964; *The Play Is Yours,* Ramapo House, 1970; *You and Drugs,* Ramapo House, 1970; (with Finkel) *Teaching English as a Second Language,* Levels 1-2, Oceana, 1970.

WORK IN PROGRESS: With Finkel, *Teaching English as a Second Language,* Levels 3-4, for Oceana.

AVOCATIONAL INTERESTS: Writing and directing for amateur theatrical group.

* * *

KREININ, Mordechai 1930-

PERSONAL: Born January 20, 1930, in Tel-Aviv, Israel; son of Abraham and Joheved (Naiman) Kreinin; married Marlene L. Miller; children: Tamara, Elana, Miriam. *Education:* University of Tel-Aviv, student, 1947-51; University of Michigan, M.A., 1952, Ph.D., 1955. *Religion:* Jewish. *Home:* 1431 Sherwood, East Lansing, Mich. 48823.

CAREER: University of Michigan, Ann Arbor, study director of Survey Research Center, 1954-57; Michigan State University, East Lansing, assistant professor, 1957-59, associate professor, 1959-61, professor of economics, 1961—. Consultant on international trade problems. *Military service:* Israeli Army. *Member:* American Economic Association, American Association of University Professors. *Awards, honors:* Fellowships from National Science Foundation, Ford Foundation, American Academy of Arts and Sciences, Social Science Research Council.

WRITINGS: Israel and Africa: A Study in Technical Cooperation, Praeger, 1964; (with Bela Balassa and others) *Studies in Trade Liberalization: Problems and Prospects for the Industrial Countries,* Johns Hopkins Press, 1967; *Alternative Commercial Policies: Their Effect on the American Economy,* Institute for International Business and Economic Development, Michigan State University, 1967; *International Economics: A Policy Approach,* Harcourt, 1971. Contributor to Joint Economic Committee study on U.S. balance of payments; contributor to economics journals.

WORK IN PROGRESS: Research in problems of international economics and technical assistance.

* * *

KREVITSKY, Nathan I. 1914-
(Nik Krevitsky)

PERSONAL: Born February 9, 1914, in Chicago, Ill.; son of Joseph and Ida Krevitsky. *Education:* University of Chicago, A.B., 1935; Columbia University, M.A., 1947, Ed.D., 1954; additional study at Bennington College, Mills College, University of Wisconsin, New School for Social Research. *Office:* Tucson Public Schools, Box 4040, Tucson, Ariz. 85717.

CAREER: Chicago (Ill.) Public Schools, high school art teacher, 1936-46; Columbia University, Teachers College, New York, N.Y., instructor, art department, 1946-54; University of California, Los Angeles, assistant professor, art department, 1954-57; San Francisco State College, San Francisco, Calif., assistant professor, art department, 1957-60; Tucson Public Schools, Tucson, Ariz., director of art, 1960—. Work as designer-craftsman in fiber and metal exhibited at Museum of Modern Art, Art Institute of Chicago, Museum of Contemporary Crafts, Smithsonian Institution, and at other museums, galleries, and shows in United States, and at international shows. *Military service:* U.S. Army, Infantry and Signal Corps, 1942-45; became staff sergeant.

MEMBER: National Art Education Association, National Committee on Art Education (member of council), American Craftsmen's Council (research director, study of crafts in American education; vice-president of Southwest regional assembly, 1964-65), International Society for Education through Art, Pacific Arts Association (council, 1962-64), Arizona Art Education Association (president, 1962-64), Arizona Designer-Craftsmen (secretary, 1960-61; president, 1962-63). *Awards, honors:* Awards for enamels and stitchery, Tucson Art Center; merit awards, American Craftsmen's Council.

WRITINGS—Under name Nik Krevitsky: *Knifecraft*, Hunt Pen Co., 1954; *Batik: Art and Craft*, Reinhold, 1964; *Stitchery: Art and Craft*, Reinhold, 1966; (co-author) *Art and the Creative Teacher*, W.S. Benson, 1971. Contributor to art and art education journals. Member of editorial board, *Dance Observer Magazine, Impulse.*

WORK IN PROGRESS: Applique: Art and Craft and *Painting with the Brayer*, both for Reinhold.

BIOGRAPHICAL/CRITICAL SOURCES: Craft Horizons, November-December, 1963; *Creative Crafts*, March-April, 1964.

* * *

KRIEGMAN, Oscar M(arvin) 1930-

PERSONAL: Born December 19, 1930, in Newark, N.J.; son of Morris and Jennie (Lehman) Kriegman; married Ada H. Kesden, August 22, 1959; children: David Jay, Michelle Robin. *Education:* University of Illinois, B.S., 1951, M.S., 1952, Ph.D., 1958. *Office:* New York University, Washington Sq., New York, N.Y. 10003.

CAREER: State of Illinois, certified public accountant, 1954; Miami University, Oxford, Ohio, instructor in accounting, 1953-54; Washington University, St. Louis, Mo., assistant professor of accounting, 1957-58; University of Rochester, Rochester, N.Y., associate professor of accounting, 1958-59; New York University, New York, N.Y., associate professor of accounting, 1959—. Consultant to Bache & Co., Haskins & Sells, Institute of Judicial Administration, National Center for Education in Politics. *Military service:* U.S. Army, 1954-56; became first lieutenant. *Member:* American Institute of Certified Public Accountants, American Accounting Association, New York State Society of Certified Public Accountants.

WRITINGS: (With Arnold W. Johnson) *Intermediate Accounting*, 3rd edition (Kriegman was not associated with earlier editions), Holt, 1964. Contributor to professional journals.

WORK IN PROGRESS: Elementary Accounting.

* * *

KRISLOV, Samuel 1929-

PERSONAL: Born October 5, 1929, in Cleveland, Ohio; son of Isaak and Gertrude (Hutner) Krislov; married Donna Carol Taylor (a pianist), September 15, 1951; children: Sharon Lee, Diana Beth, Daniel Robert, Melanie Bathsheba, Lee Shalom. *Education:* Attended Western Reserve University (now Case Western Reserve University), 1947-48; New York University, B.A., 1951, M.A., 1952; Princeton University, Ph.D., 1955. *Politics:* Democrat. *Religion:* Jewish. *Home:* 1718 Oliver Ave., South Minneapolis, Minn. 55405.

CAREER: University of Vermont, Burlington, instructor in political science, 1955; Hunter College (now Hunter College of the City University of New York), New York, N.Y., instructor in political science, 1955-56; University of Oklahoma, Norman, assistant professor, 1956-60, associate professor of political science, 1960-61; Michigan State University, East Lansing, visiting assistant professor, 1959-61, associate professor of political science and research associate of School of Labor and Industrial Relations, 1961-64; University of Minnesota, Minneapolis, associate professor, 1964-65, professor of political science, 1965—, chairman of department, 1969—. Visiting professor, Columbia University, 1966. Research assistant, New York Joint Legislative Committee on Interstate Cooperation, 1955-56; delegate to Michigan Democratic conventions, 1962-64; member of Ingham County (Mich.) Democratic Committee, 1962-64; member of Minnesota Committee on Judicial Standards, 1971—. *Member:* American Political Science Association, American Association of University Professors, Midwest Conference of American Society for Legal History, Midwest Conference of Political Scientists, Phi Beta Kappa. *Awards, honors:* Social Science Research Council grants, 1958, 1961; Ford Foundation International Relations grant, 1963; National Institute of Mental Health grants, 1963, 1967, 1969, 1971; American Philosophical Society grant, 1964; Russell Sage Fellow, 1966-67; Ford faculty fellowship, 1972-73.

WRITINGS: (With T.S. Sinclair and Lloyd Wells) *The Politics of Judicial Review, 1937-1957* (monograph), Arnold Foundation, 1957; (editor with James A. Burkhart and others) *American Government: The Clash of Issues*, Prentice-Hall, 1960, 4th edition, 1972; (editor with Lloyd D. Musolf) *The Politics of Regulation: A Reader*, Houghton, 1964; (contributor) Gottfried Dietze, editor, *Essays on the American Constitution: A Commemorative Volume in Honor of Alpheus T. Mason*, Prentice-Hall, 1964; (contributor) Donald Cameron Rowat, editor, *The Ombudsman, Citizens Defender*, Allen & Unwin, 1965; *The Supreme Court in the Political Process*, Macmillan, 1965; *The Politics of Legal Advice: Michigan and the ADCU Controversy*, McGraw, 1965; *The Negro in Federal Employment: The Quest for Equal Opportunity*, University of Minnesota Press, 1967; *The Supreme Court and Political Freedom*, Free Press, 1968; *The Judicial Process and Constitutional Law*, Little, Brown, 1972; (editor with others) *Compliance and the Law: A Multi-Disciplinary Approach*, Sage Publications, 1972. Contributor to political science and law periodicals.

WORK IN PROGRESS: Representative Bureaucracy, for Prentice-Hall.

* * *

KRISTELLER, Paul Oskar 1905-

PERSONAL: Born May 22, 1905, in Berlin, Germany; came to United States in 1939, naturalized in 1945; son of Heinrich and Alice (Magnus) Kristeller; married Edith Lewinnek (a physician), 1940. *Education:* University of Heidelberg, Dr. phil. 1928; postdoctoral study at University of Berlin, 1928-31, and University of Freiburg, 1931-33; University of Pisa, Dott. in Filosofia, 1937. *Home:* 423 West 120th St., New York, N.Y. 10027. *Office:* 1161 Amsterdam Ave., New York, N.Y. 10027.

CAREER: Istituto Superiore di Magistero, Florence, Italy, lecturer in German, 1934-35; Scuola Normale Superiore and University of Pisa, Pisa, Italy, lecturer in German, 1935-38; Yale University, New Haven, Conn., lecturer in philosophy, 1939; Columbia University, New York, N.Y., associate, 1939-48, associate professor, 1948-56, professor of philosophy, 1956-68, F.J.E. Woodbridge Professor of Philosophy, 1968—. Visiting professor at Scuola Normale Superiore, 1949 and 1952; lecturer at other institutions in United States and Europe. Member, Institute for Advanced Study, Princeton, N.J., 1954-55, 1961, and 1968-69. Secretary of cooperative research project, Mediaeval and Renaissance Latin Translations and Commentaries, sponsored by learned societies, including Union Academique Internationale.

MEMBER: American Philosophical Association, Mediaeval Academy of America (fellow), American Academy of Arts and Sciences (fellow), American Society of Church History, Italian Teachers Association, Renaissance Society of America (president, 1957-59), Medieval Club of New York (president, 1959-60), Accademia dei Sepolti (Volterra; corresponding fellow), Arcadia (Rome; corresponding fellow), Monumenta Germaniae Historica (Munich; corresponding fellow), Academie des Inscriptions (Paris), Istituto Veneto (Venice), Accademia degli Intronati (Siena), Accademia Toscana La Colombaria (Florence), Accademia Patavina (Padua), Phi Beta Kappa. *Awards, honors:* Research grants from Oberlander Trust, 1939-41, American Philosophical Society, 1949, 1952, 1955, 1958; Fulbright fellowship to Italy, 1952; Guggenheim fellowship, 1958, 1968-69; Serena Medal of British Academy for Italian studies, 1958; Doctor philosophiae from University of Padua, 1962; Premio Internazionale Forte dei Marmi, 1968.

WRITINGS: Der Begriff der Seele in der Ethik des Plotin, Mohr (Tubingen), 1929; *Supplementum Ficinianum: Marsilii Ficini Florentini Opuscula,* two volumes, Olschki, 1937, translation by Virginia Conant published as *The Philosophy of Marsilio Ficino,* Columbia University Press, 1943; (editor with E. Cassirer and J.H. Randall, Jr. and author of introduction with Randall) *The Renaissance Philosophy of Man,* University of Chicago Press, 1948; *Latin Manuscript Books Before 1600: A Bibliography of the Printed Catalogues of Extant Collections,* Cosmopolitan Science & Art Service, 1948, 3rd edition, Fordham University Press, 1965; *Die Italiensichen Universitaten der Renaissance,* Scherpe-Verlag, 1953; *The Classics and Renaissance Thought* (Martin Lectures), Harvard University Press, 1955, revised and enlarged edition published as *Renaissance Thought: The Classic, Scholastic, and Humanist Strains,* Harper, 1961; *Studies in Renaissance Thought and Letters,* Edizioni di Storia e Letteratura, 1956; *Nuove fonti per la medicina salervitana,* [Salerno], 1958; *Humanist Learning in the Italian Renaissance,* privately printed, 1960; *Ludovico Lazzarelli e Giovanni de Corregio,* Agnesotti, 1960; (editor-in-chief) *Catalogus Translationum et Commentariorum, Mediaeval and Renaissance Latin Translations and Commentaries,* Volume I, Catholic University of America Press, 1960; *La Tradizione Aristotelica nel Rinascimento,* Editrice Antenore, 1962; *Iter Italicum: A Finding List of Uncatalogued or Incompletely Catalogued Humantistic Manuscripts of the Renaissance in Italian and Other Libraries,* Brill, Volume I, 1963, Volume II, 1967; *Eight Philosophers of the Italian Renaissance,* Stanford University Press, 1964; *Umanesimo Italiano e Bisanzio,* L.S. Olschki, 1964; *Some Original Letters and Autographed Manuscripts of Marsilio Ficino,* [Verona], 1964; *Renaissance Thought II: Papers on Humanism and the Arts,* Harper, 1965; *Renaissance Philosophy and the Mediaeval Tradition* (Wimmer Lectures), Archabbey Press, 1966; *Le Thomisme et la pensee Italienne de la Renaissance* (Conference Albert-le-Grand), J. Vrin (Paris), 1967; (compiler with Philip P. Werner) *Renaissance Essays,* Harper, 1968; *Der Italienische Humanismus unde seine Bedentung,* Helbing & Lichtenhahn, 1969; *The Renaissance Concept of Man and Other Essays,* Harper, 1973.

Contributor: Vergilius Ferm, editor, *A History of Philosophical Systems,* Philosophical Library, 1950; *Miscellanea Giovanni Galbiati,* [Milan], 1951; *Studi e memorie per la storia dell' universita di Bologna,* University of Bologna, 1956; *Medioevo e rinascimento: Studi in onore di Bruno Nardi,* Volume I, [Florence], 1955; *Studi letterari: Miscellanea in onore di Emilio Santini,* U. Manfredi, 1956; *Artes liberales von der Antiken Bildung zur Wissenschaft des Mittelalters,* Leiden-Koeln, 1959; Karl H. Dannenfeldt, editor, *The Renaissance: Medieval or Modern?,* Heath, 1959; *Facets of the Renaissance* (Arensberg Lectures), University of Southern California Press, 1959; *Medium Aevum Vivum: Festschrift fuer Walther Bulst,* University of Heidelburg, 1960; Tinsley Helton, editor, *The Renaissance: A Reconsideration of the Theories and Interpretations of the Age,* University of Wisconsin Press, 1961; *Chapters in Western Civilization,* Volume I, 3rd edition, Columbia University Press, 1961; S. Prete, editor, *Didascaliae: Studies in Honors of Anselm M. Albareda,* Bernard M. Rosenthal, 1961; *Wort und Text: Festshcrift fuer Fritz Schalk,* Klostermann, 1963; *Melanges Eugene Tisserant,* [Vatican City], 1964; *Classical, Medieval and Renaissance Studies in Honor of Berthold Louis Ullman,* Volume II, Edizioni de Storia e Letteratura, 1964; *Studi di bibliografia e di storia in onore de Tammaro de Marinis,* Mardensteig, 1964; Charles H. Carter, editor, *From the Renaissance to the Counter-Reformation: Essays in Honor of Garrett Mattingly,* Random House, 1965; *Harry Austryn Wolfson Jubilee Volume,* Volume I, [Jerusalem], 1965; Bernard O'Kelly, editor, *The Renaissance Image of Man and the World,* Ohio State University Press, 1966; L. Wallach, editor, *The Classical Tradition: Literary and Historical Studies in Honor of Harry Caplan,* Cornell University Press, 1966; John P. Anton, editor, *Naturalism and Historical Understanding: Essays on the Philosophy of John Herman Randall, Jr.,* State University of New York Press, 1967; John M. Headley, editor, *Medieval and Renaissance Studies: Proceedings of the Southeastern Institute of Medieval and Renaissance Studies,* University of North Carolina Press, 1968.

Contributor of more than one hundred articles on Renaissance and philosophical subjects to professional journals in United States, Italy, and other countries; contributor of book reviews to *American Historical Review, Hispanic Review, Art Bulletin,* and philosophy journals. Member of editorial board, *Journal of the History of Ideas,* 1943—; book editor, *Journal of Philosophy,* 1940-51; editor, *Manuscripta.*

*   *   *

KRONER, Richard 1884-

PERSONAL: Born March 8, 1884, in Breslau, Germany; son of Trangott (a medical doctor) and Margar (Heymann) Kroner; married Alice Kauffman, May 12, 1908; children: Gerda Kroner Seligson. *Education:* Attended Universities of Breslau, Berlin, Heidelberg, Freiburg; Ph.D., 1908. *Religion:* Protestant. *Home:* 4 Framar Rd., Wellesley Hills, Mass. 02181.

CAREER: University of Freiburg, Freiburg, Germany, professor of philosophy, 1918-24; Technical Institute, Dresden, Germany, professor of education and philosophy, 1924-29; University of Kiel, Kiel, Germany, professor of philosophy, 1929-34, now professor emeritus; research professor in philosophy, Berlin, 1934-38; Oxford University, Oxford, England, lecturer in philosophy, 1939; St. Andrews University, St. Andrews, Scotland, Gifford Lecturer, 1939-40; Union Theological Seminary, New York, N.Y., professor of philosophy, 1941-52, now professor emeritus; Temple University, Philadelphia, Pa., adjunct professor of philosophy, 1953-64. *Military service:* German Army Reserve, Light Artillery; became captain. *Member:* International Association for the Study of Hegel (honorary president), American Philosophical Association.

WRITINGS: Ueber Logische und Aethetische Allgemeingueltigkeit, F. Eckardt, 1908; *Das Problem der historischen Biologie,* Gerbruder Borntraeger, 1919; *Von Kant bis Hegel,* J.C.B. Mohr, Volume I, 1921, Volume II, 1924, 2nd edition, 1961; *Die Selbstverwirklichung des Geistes: Prolegomena zur kultur-philosophie,* J.C.B. Mohr, 1928, revised translation published as *Culture and Faith,* University of Chicago Press, 1951; *Idee und Wirklichkeit des Staates,* Lipsius & Tischer, 1930; *Kulturphilosophische*

Grundlegung der Politik, Junker & Dunnhaupt, 1931; *Hegel zum 100. Todestage*, J.C.B. Mohr, 1932; *The Religious Function of Imagination*, Yale University Press for Kenyon College, 1941; *How Do We Know God?: An Introduction to the Philosophy of Religion*, Harper, 1943; *The Primacy of Faith*, Macmillan, 1943; (author of introduction) Hegel, *Early Theological Writings*, University of Chicago Press, 1948; *Kant's Weltanschauung* (originally published in German), translation by John E. Smith, revised edition, University of Chicago Press, 1956; *Speculation and Revelation in the History of Philosophy*, Westminster, Volume I: *Speculation in Pre-Christian Philosophy*, 1956, Volume II: *Speculation and Revelation in the Age of Christian Philosophy*, 1959, Volume III: *Speculation and Revelation in Modern Philosophy*, 1961; *Selbstbesinnung: Drei Lehrstunden*, J.C.B. Mohr, 1958; *The New Dimension of the South: Chapel Addresses*, edited by John E. Skinner, Fortress, 1964; *Between Faith and Thought: Reflections and Suggestions*, Oxford University Press, 1966; *Freiheit und Gnade: Philosophisch-theologischer Traktat*, J.C.B. Mohr, 1969. Co-editor, *Kant—Studien* and *Archiv fuer Philosophie*.

WORK IN PROGRESS: Gedanken betreffend den Sieg des Guten ueber das Boese.

BIOGRAPHICAL/CRITICAL SOURCES: J.E. Skinner, *Self and World*, University of Pennsylvania Press, 1963; *Commonweal*, January 13, 1967.

*   *   *

KRONHAUSEN, Eberhard W(ilhelm) 1915-

PERSONAL: Born September 12, 1915, in Berlin, Germany; married Phyllis Ulrickson (a psychologist), September 12, 1954. *Education:* University of Minnesota, B.S., 1947, M.A., 1951; Columbia University, Ed.D., 1956.

CAREER: Group Community Guidance Center, New York, N.Y., consulting psychologist, 1953-58; National Institute for Mental Health Research Grant, program director, 1956-57; private practice of psychology, 1953—. Painter; has exhibited erotic paintings and drawings throughout Europe. *Member:* American Psychological Association.

WRITINGS—All with wife, Phyllis C. Kronhausen: *Pornography and the Law: The Psychology of Erotic Realism and Pornography*, Ballantine, 1959, 2nd edition, revised and enlarged, 1964; *Sex Histories of American College Men*, Ballantine, 1960; *The Sexually Responsive Woman*, preface by Simone de Beauvoir, Grove, 1964 (published in England as *Sexual Response in Women*, J. Calder, 1965); *Walter, the English Casanova*, Ballantine, 1967 (published in England as *Walter, the English Casanova: A Presentation of His Unique Memoirs, "My Secret Life,"* Polybooks, 1967); *The First International Exhibition of Erotic Art*, privately printed, 1968; (compilers) *Erotic Art: A Survey of Erotic Fact and Fancy in the Fine Arts*, Grove, 1968; (compilers) *Erotic Fantasies: A Study of the Sexual Imagination*, Grove, 1970; *Drs. Eberhard and Phyllis Kronhausen Present the 2nd International Exhibition of Erotic Art* (at Liljevalchs Konsthall, Stockholm, April 2-May 18, 1969), Societe d'Etudes Financieres (Stockholm), 1960; (compilers) *Erotische Exlibris* (erotic book-plates), Gala Verlag (Hamburg), 1970; (compilers) *Erotic Art 2*, Grove, 1970; *Freedom to Love, a Film* (interviews with various persons), Grove, 1971; *More Walter: Being a Further Examination of "My Secret Life,"* Morntide, 1970.

Also author, with P.C. Kronhausen, of script for documentary film, "Freedom to Love," produced by Reginald Puhl in West Germany in 1970. Writer of articles and monographs on psychological topics.

WORK IN PROGRESS: Research in applied psychology, sexology , and cross-cultural studies.

AVOCATIONAL INTERESTS: Experimental films (co-producer with wife, Phyllis C. Kronhausen, of a sound film-short, "Psychomontage No. 1," distributed by Cinema 16).

BIOGRAPHICAL/CRITICAL SOURCES: Washington Post, December 13, 1965; *New Statesman*, December 1, 1967; *Commonweal*, November 7, 1969; *Variety*, February 25, 1970; *Library Journal*, March 15, 1970.

*   *   *

KRONHAUSEN, Phyllis C(armen) 1929-

PERSONAL: Born January 26, 1929, in Minnesota; daughter of Fred J. and Ruby (Hagen) Ulrickson; married Eberhard W. Kronhausen (a psychologist), September 12, 1954. *Education:* University of Minnesota, B.B.A. (summa cum laude), 1951; Columbia University, Ed.D., 1958.

CAREER: University of Minnesota, Minneapolis, administrative assistant, foreign student adviser 1951; U.S. Government, Department of State, assistant vice-counsel, 1951-53; Columbia University, New York, N.Y., lecturer, 1956-58; National Institute for Mental Health Research Grant, program director, 1956-57; now in private practice. *Member:* American Psychological Association.

WRITINGS—All with husband, Eberhard W. Kronhausen: *Pornography and the Law: The Psychology of Erotic Realism and Pornography*, Ballantine, 1959, 2nd edition, revised and enlarged, 1964; *Sex Histories of American College Men*, Ballantine, 1960; *The Sexually Responsive Woman*, preface by Simone de Beauvoir, Grove, 1964 (published in England as *Sexual Response in Women*, J. Calder, 1965); *Walter, the English Casanova*, Ballantine, 1967 (published in England as *Walter, the English Casanova: A Presentation of His Unique Memoirs, "My Secret Life,"* Polybooks, 1967); *The First International Exhibition of Erotic Art*, privately printed, 1968; (compilers) *Erotic Art: A Survey of Erotic Fact and Fancy in the Fine Arts*, Grove, 1968; (compilers) *Erotic Fantasies: A Study of the Sexual Imagination*, Grove, 1970; *Drs. Eberhard and Phyllis Kronhausen Present the 2nd International Exhibition of Erotic Art* (at Liljevalchs Konsthall, Stockholm, April 2-May 18, 1969), Societe d'Etudes Financieres (Stockholm), 1960; (compilers) *Erotische Exlibris* (erotic book-plates), Gala Verlag (Hamburg), 1970; (compilers) *Erotic Art 2*, Grove, 1970; *Freedom to Love, a Film*, (interviews with various persons), Grove, 1971; *More Walter: Being a Further Examination of "My Secret Life,"* Morntide, 1970. Also author, with E.C. Kronhausen, of script for documentary film, "Freedom to Love," produced by Reginald Puhl in West Germany in 1970; producer, with husband, E.C. Kronhausen, of sound film "Psychomontage No. 1." Writer of articles and monographs on psychological topics.

WORK IN PROGRESS: Continuing research in applied psychology, sexology, and cross-cultural studies.

AVOCATONAL INTERESTS: Experimental films.

*   *   *

KRONICK, David A(braham) 1917-

PERSONAL: Born October 5, 1917, in Connelsville, Pa.; son of Barnett L. (a merchant) and Rose (Miller) Kronick; married Marilyn Abramson, October 25, 1959; children: Steven L., Beryl Leah. *Education:* Western Reserve University (now Case Western Reserve University), B.A., 1939, B.L.L.S., 1940; University of Chicago, Ph.D., 1956. *Home:* 10114 Parkwood Dr., Bethesda, Md. 20014.

Office: National Library of Medicine, 8600 Wisconsin Ave., Bethesda, Md. 20014.

CAREER: With Armed Forces Library, 1953-55; Medical Library, University of Michigan, Ann Arbor, chief of divisional library, 1955-59; Cleveland Medical Library, Cleveland, Ohio, director, 1959-64; National Library of Medicine, Bethesda, Md., chief of reference service division, 1964—. *Military service:* U.S. Army, Medical Department, 1941-46; became captain. *Member:* American Library Association, Medical Library Association (member of board of directors, 1963—), American Association for the Advancement of Science (fellow), American Association for History of Medicine.

WRITINGS: The Fielding H. Garrison List of Medical and Scientific Periodicals of the 17th and 18th Centuries, [Baltimore], 1958; *A History of Scientific and Technical Periodicals: The Origins and Development of the Scientific and Technological Press,* Scarecrow, 1962. Contributor to *Bulletin of Medical Library Association.*

*   *   *

KRUMGOLD, Joseph (Quincy)   1908-

PERSONAL: Born April 9, 1908, in Jersey City, N.J.; son of Henry (a film exhibitor) and Lena (Gross) Krumgold; married Helen Litwin, January 10, 1947; children: Adam. *Education:* New York University, A.B., 1928. *Politics:* Democrat. *Religion:* Jewish. *Home:* Shiloh Farm, Hope, N.J. 07844.

CAREER: Writer and producer for film companies, including Metro-Goldwyn-Mayer, Paramount, RKO, Columbia, and Republic, in New York, N.Y., and Hollywood, Calif., 1938-50; Joseph Krumgold Productions (producer of motion pictures and television films), Hope, N.J., proprietor, 1950—. Member, Frelinghuysen Township (N.J.) school board. *Member:* Screen-writers Guild, Authors League of America, Jewish Center (Newton, N.J.), Players (New York), Pi Lambda Phi. *Awards, honors:* John Newbery Medal for most distinguished contribution to literature for American children for *—And Now Miguel* 1954, and for *Onion John,* 1960; first prizes for films at Venice, Edinburgh, and Prague festivals.

WRITINGS: Thanks to Murder, Vanguard, 1935; *Sweeney's Adventure,* Random House, 1942; *—And Now Miguel,* Crowell, 1953; *Onion John,* Crowell, 1959; *Henry 3,* Atheneum, 1967; *The Most Terrible Turk: A Story of Turkey,* Crowell, 1969.

Screenplays: (With Fred Niblo, Jr., Arthur Strawn, and Ben G. Kohn) "Lady from Nowhere," Columbia, 1936; (with Lee Loeb and Harold Buchman) "The Blackmailer," Columbia, 1936; (with Olive Cooper and Karl Brown) "Join the Marines," Republic, 1937; (with Cooper and Octavus Roy Cohn) "Jim Hanvey—Detective," Republic, 1937; (with Cooper) "Lady Behave," Republic, 1938; "Main Street Lawyer" (based on a story by Harry Hamilton), Republic, 1939; "The Phantom Submarine" (from a short story by Augustus Muir), Columbia, 1940; (with Garnett Weston, E.E. Paramore, and Richard Blake) "The Crooked Road," Republic, 1940; "Seven Miles from Alcatraz" (from a novel by John D. Klorer), R.K.O., 1942; (with Robert Riskin) "Magic Town," R.K.O., 1947. Also author of "Dream No More," produced in Israel.

Author of television scripts for Columbia Broadcasting System, National Broadcasting Corp., and National Educational Television.

WORK IN PROGRESS: The Children's Crusade, for Atheneum.

SIDELIGHTS: —And Now Miguel had its beginnings in a film of the same title Krumgold prepared for overseas distribution by the U.S. Department of State; the book has been translated into fifteen languages. *Avocational interests:* Farming in Hope, N.J., fishing, swimming, skating.

BIOGRAPHICAL/CRITICAL SOURCES: Saturday Review, July 19, 1969; *Book World,* September 7, 1969.

*   *   *

KRZYZANIAK, Marian   1911-

PERSONAL: Born February 4, 1911, in Poland. *Education:* University of Poznan, M. Econ. & Pol. Sci., 1932; University of Alberta, M.A., 1954; Massachusetts Institute of Technology, Ph.D., 1959. *Office:* Department of Economics, Rice University, Houston, Tex. 77001.

CAREER: University of Michigan, Ann Arbor, research associate in economics, 1958-59; Montana State University, Missoula, assistant professor of economics, 1959-60; Johns Hopkins University, Baltimore, Md., lecturer and research associate, 1960-61; Wayne State University, Detroit, Mich., assistant professor, 1961-63, associate professor of economics, 1963-64; Rice University, Houston, Tex., associate professor, 1964-67, professor, 1967-69, Henry Fox, Sr. Professor of economics, 1969—. *Military service:* Polish Forces, World War II. *Member:* International Institute of Public Finance, International Platform Association, Polish Institute of Arts and Sciences in America, American Economic Association, Econometric Society, American Statistical Association, Canadian Political Science Association, Royal Economic Society. *Awards, honors:* Research Recognition award, Wayne State Fund, 1963.

WRITINGS: (With Richard A. Musgrave) *The Shifting of the Corporation Income Tax: An Empirical Study of Its Short-run Effect Upon the Rate of Return,* Johns Hopkins Press, 1963; (editor and contributor) *Effects of Corporation Income Tax,* Wayne State University Press, 1966; (contributor) Haller and Tecktenwald, editors, *Finanz und Geld-politik in Umbruch,* Hase & Koehler, 1969; (contributor) R.W. Houghton, editor, *Public Finance,* Penguin, 1970.

WORK IN PROGRESS: A treatise on the incidence of income taxes.

*   *   *

KUBLER, George (Alexander)   1912-

PERSONAL: Born July 26, 1912, in Los Angeles, Calif.; son of Frederick William (a manufacturer) and Ellen (Orloff-Beckmann) Kubler; married Elizabeth Bushnell, February 12, 1937; children: Alexandra, Cornelia, Edward, Elena. *Education:* Studied in France and Switzerland, 1920-24, at Western Reserve Academy, Hudson, Ohio, 1925-29; University of Munich, 1932-33; Yale University, B.A., 1934, M.A., 1936, Ph.D., 1940; other study at University of Berlin, 1931, New York University, 1936-38. *Home:* 406 Humphrey St., New Haven, Conn. 06511. *Office:* Yale University, New Haven, Conn. 06520.

CAREER: Yale University, New Haven, Conn., 1938—, began as instructor in history of art, became professor, 1947-64, Robert Lehman Professor of History of Art, 1964—, chairman of department, 1953-56, director of graduate studies, 1957-63; now director, history of art studies for Tikal Project, University Museum, Philadelphia, Pa. Visiting professor, University of Chicago, 1946, University of San Marcos, Lima, Peru, 1948-49, University of Mexico, 1958, Harvard University, 1966-67. Chief of UNESCO Mission to Cuzco, Peru, 1951. *Member:* American Academy of Arts and Sciences, Spanish Institute (member of board of directors), Hispanic Society (corresponding member), Academy of Franciscan History, Societe des Americanistes de Paris, Real Academia de San Fernando (corresponding member), Connecticut Academy of Arts and Sciences. *Awards, honors:* Grant-in-aid for research in Mexico, American Council of Learned Societies, 1941; Guggenheim fellow in Mexico, 1943-44, in Spain, 1952-53, 1956-57; Alice Davis Hitchcock Prize, 1963, and C.R. Morey Award, 1964, both for *Art and Architecture of Ancient America;* Litt.D., Tulane University, 1972.

WRITINGS: The Religious Architecture of New Mexico in the Colonial Period and Since the American Occupation, Taylor Museum (Colorado Springs), 1940, reissued as *Religious Architecture of New Mexico,* Rio Grande Press, 1962; (translator with Charles Beecher Hogan) Henri Focillon, *The Life of Forms in Art,* Yale University Press, 1942; *Mexican Architecture of the Sixteenth Century,* two volumes, Yale University Press, 1948; *The Tovar Calendar: An Illustrated Mexican Manuscript, ca.1585* (reproduced by Kubler and Charles Gibson), Connecticut Academy of Arts and Sciences, 1951; *Cuzco: Reconstruction of the Town and Restoration of Its Monuments,* UNESCO, 1952; *The Indian Caste of Peru, 1795-1940: A Population Study Based Upon Tax Records and Census Reports,* U.S. Government Printing Office, 1952; *The Arensberg Collection, II,* Philadelphia Art Museum, 1954; *Arquitectura de los siglos XVII and XVIII,* Editorial Plus-Ultra, 1957; (with Martin Soria) *Arquitectura espanola, 1600-1800,* Ars Hispaniae (Madrid), 1957; *The Wurtzburger Collection of Pre-Columbian Art,* Philadelphia Museum of Art, 1958; *The Design of Space in Maya Architecture,* P. Rivet, 1958; *Art and Architecture in Spain and Portugal and Their American Dominions,* Penguin, 1959; *The Art and Architecture of Ancient America: The Mexican, Maya and Andean Peoples,* Penguin, 1962; *The Shape of Time: Remarks on the History of Things,* Yale University Press, 1962; (contributor of essay) *Santos: An Exhibition of the Religious Folk Art of New Mexico,* Amon Carter Museum of Western Art, 1964; (translator with others, and author of introduction and notes) Felix de Costa, *The Antiquity of the Art of Painting,* Yale University Press, 1967; *The Iconography of the Art of Teotihuacan,* Dumbarton Oaks Trustees for Harvard University, 1967; *Studies in Classic Maya Iconography,* Connecticut Academy of Arts and Sciences, 1969; *Portuguese Plain Architecture: Between Spices and Diamonds, 1521-1706,* Wesleyan University Press, 1972.

Contributor to *Handbook of South American Indians,* Smithsonian Institution, 1946; contributor of articles to *New Mexico Historical Review, Gazette des Beaux Arts,* and other art and historical journals. Editor of art section, and contributor, *Handbook of Latin American Studies, 1937-1940,* Harvard University Press, 1938-42; book review editor, *Art Bulletin,* College Art Association of America, 1944; guest editor, *Journal of the Society of Architectural Historians,* 1945; editor, "History of Art" series, Yale University Press, 1953-65.

*   *   *

KUBLIN, Hyman 1919-

PERSONAL: Surname rhymes with "Dublin"; born December 29, 1919, in Boston, Mass.; son of Ralph and Tilly (Goschenberg) Kublin; married Pearl Baru, December 5, 1942; children: Michael B., Barbara J. *Education:* Boston University, A.B., 1941, M.A., 1942; Harvard University, Ph.D., 1947. *Office:* Department of History, Brooklyn College of the City University of New York, Brooklyn, N.Y. 11210.

CAREER: Brooklyn College of the City University of New York, Brooklyn, N.Y., assistant professor, 1947-56, associate professor, 1956-60, professor of history, 1961—; City University of New York, New York, N.Y., associate dean of graduate studies, 1966-69. Fulbright Research Professor in Japan, 1955-56. Visiting

summer professor at University of Delaware, 1948, 1950, 1954, 1955, University of California, 1962, University of Hawaii, 1965, 1967. Consultant to Center for International Programs and Services of New York State Department of Education, and to foundations and cultural organizations. Delegate to XXVth International Congress of Orientalists. *Military service:* U.S. Navy, 1942-46; became lieutenant j.g. *Member:* Association for Asian Studies (member of executive committee, 1954-60), American Historical Association, Japan Society, Asia Society, Society for the History of Discoveries.

WRITINGS: What Shall I Read on Japan?: An Introductory Guide, 3rd edition (Kublin was not associated with earlier editions), Japan Society, 1956, 8th edition, 1965; *The Bonin Islands: An Essay on the Western Language, Literature,* privately printed, 1956; (editor with Leonard S. Kenworthy) *Japan: A Resource Unit for Secondary Schools,* Brooklyn College, 1957; (editor) *Japanese and Chinese Language Sources on Burma: An Annotated Bibliography,* Part I, Human Relations Area File Press, 1957; *An Introductory Reading Guide to Asia,* Asia Society, 1958, 3rd edition, 1962; *Aspects of the Early Labor Movement of Modern Japan* (in Japanese), Yuhikaku, 1959; *Teacher's Manual for Great Civilizations of Asia,* Part I, New York Bureau of Secondary Curriculum Development, 1961; *Useful Japanese: Pronunciation and Basic Words,* Japan Society, 1961; *The Rim of Asia: Japan and Southeast Asia,* Scholastic Book Services, 1963, 3rd edition, 1968; *India and the World Today,* Laidlaw Brothers, 1963; *Asian Revolutionary: The Life of Sen Katayama,* Princeton University Press, 1964; (compiler with Donn V. Hart and Melvin E. Levison) *Education in Asian Countries: An Introductory Reading and Buying Guide for Undergraduate Colleges and Libraries,* Foreign Area Materials Center, State University of New York, 1964; *China,* Houghton, 1968; (editor) *China: Selected Readings,* Houghton, 1968; *India,* Houghton, 1968; (editor) *India: Selected Readings,* Houghton, 1968; (editor) *Japan: Selected Readings,* Houghton, 1968; (editor with Don Peretz) *Middle East: Selected Readings,* Houghton, 1968; *Japan,* Houghton, 1969; (with Peretz) *Middle East,* Houghton, 1969; (editor) *Russia: Selected Readings,* Houghton, 1969; *Russia,* Houghton, 1970; (compiler and author of introduction) *Jews in Old China: Some Western Views,* Paragon, 1971; (compiler and author of preface and introductions) *Studies of the Chinese Jews,* Paragon, 1971. Contributor of about one hundred and fifty articles on history, culture, and education to professional journals.

*   *   *

KUEHNELT-LEDDIHN, Erik Ritter von   1909-
   (Francis Stuart Campbell, Chester F. O'Leary, Tomislav Vitezovic)

PERSONAL: Born July 31, 1909, in Tobelbad, Austria; son of Erik Ritter von Kuehnelt-Leddihn and Isabella (von Leddihn); married Countess Marie-Christiane Goess, July 3, 1937; children: Erik, Isabel, Gottfried. *Education:* Theresianic Academy, Vienna, Austria, B.A., 1927; University of Budapest, M.A., 1934, Dr. Pol. Sc., 1937; University of Vienna, law student, later postdoctoral studies in theology. *Politics:* Liberal Monarchist. *Religion:* Catholic. *Home:* A-6072, Lans, Tyrol, Austria. *Agent:* Mrs. Anthony Gran, 506 La Guardia, New York, N.Y. 10012.

CAREER: Beaumont College, Old Windsor, England, master, 1935-36; Georgetown University, Washington, D.C., assistant professor of political geography, 1937-38; St. Peter's College, Jersey City, N.J., chairman of history department, 1938-43; Fordham University, New York, N.Y., lecturer in Japanese, 1942-43; Chestnut Hill College, Philadelphia, Pa., professor of history and sociology, 1943-47. *Member:* Sovereign Order of Knights of Malta.

Awards, honors: Literary prize, Entr'aide Sociale, Paris, 1936.

WRITINGS: (Under pseudonym Tomislav Vitezovic) *Die Anderen,* Amalthea, 1931; *Jesuiten, Spiesser, Bolschewiken,* Anton Pustet, 1933, translation by I.J. Collins published as *Gates of Hell,* Sheed, 1934; *Ueber dem Osten Nacht,* Anton Pustet, 1935, translation by Edwin Muir and Will Muir published as *Night Over the East,* Sheed, 1936; *Moscow,* Sheed, 1940, revised edition published as *Moscow, 1979,* 1946; (under pseudonym Francis Stuart Campbell) *The Menace of the Herd; or, Procrustes at Large,* Bruce, 1943; (under pseudonym Chester F. O'-Leary) *Mord im Blaulicht,* Amandus, 1948; (under pseudonym Chester F. O'Leary) *Die Urvaeter Amerikas,* Amandus, 1949; *Liberty or Equality?: The Challenge of Our Time,* edited by John P. Hughes, Caxton, 1952; *Black Banners,* Forty-five Press, 1952, Caxton, 1954; *Freiheit oder Gleichheit?: Die Schicksalsfrage des Abendlandes* (incorporating part of *Liberty and Equality),* Otto Mueller, 1952; *El Nuevo conservatismo y el nuevo liberalismi en Europe y Norte-america,* Ateneo, 1955; *Zwischen Ghetto und Katakombe: Von Christlicher Existenz heute,* Otto Mueller, 1960; *Libertad o Igualdad* (containing parts of *Liberty and Equality),* Rialp, 1962; *Die Gottlosen,* Berglandbuch, 1962; *Democracy Revisited,* Intercollegiate Society of Individualists, 1962; *Christliche Sozialromantiker,* Foerderung der schweizerischen Wirtschaft, 1964; *Las Estados Unidos y Europa: El Problema de la comprension, Instituto de Estudios Politicos,* 1965; *Lateinamerika: Geschichte eines Scheiterns?,* Fromm, 1967; *Hirn, Herz und Rueckgrat: Der Zeitlose Christ, Gedanken zu seiner Anatomie,* Fromm, 1968, translation published as *The Timeless Christian,* Herald Press, 1969; *Amerika: Leitbild im Zwielicht,* Johannes Verlag, 1971; *Leftism: From Sade to Marcuse,* Arlington, House, 1972.

Contributor: F.J. Sheed, editor, *Born Catholics,* Sheed, 1954; *Catholicism in America,* Harcourt, 1954; *Handbuch der Weltge-schichte,* Otto Walter, 1956; Dan Herr and Lane Clement, editors, *Realities,* Bruce, 1958; *Gendaiderwege: Festschrift fuer Ida Friederike Goerres,* Thomas Verlag, 1961; *Between Two Cities: God and Man in America,* Loyola University Press (Chicago), 1962; A. Hunold, editor, *Lateinamerika: Land der Sorge, Land der Zukunft,* Eugen Rentsch, 1963; Rafael Lopez Jordan, editor, *Levando el Ancla,* Ediciones Studium, 1964; *Moskau-Peking,* Walter, 1965; *Seeds of Anarchy,* Argus, 1969; *Der Adel in Oesterreich,* Kremayr & Scherian, 1971.

Also contributor to *The Book of Catholic Authors,* 3rd series, 1945, and to *Ordo Jahrbuch,* X and XIII, 1958, 1962. Contributor to periodicals on four continents. European correspondent, *National Review,* 1954—.

WORK IN PROGRESS: Memoirs; *Eros in Theological Perspective; Luftschloesser: Luegen und Legenden,* a critique of our times.

SIDELIGHTS: Kuehnelt-Leddihn travels abroad annually. His books have been translated for publication in five European countries, and in Brazil. *Avocational interests:* Painting, philately, photography.

BIOGRAPHICAL/CRITICAL SOURCES: National Review, August 25, 1970.

*   *   *

KUHN, Alfred 1914-

PERSONAL: Born December 22, 1914, in Reading, Pa.; son of Alvin Boyd (an author) and Mary G. (Leippe) Kuhn; married Nina de Angeli, October 18, 1941; children: David, Jeffrey, Henry. *Education:* Albright College, B.A., 1935; University of Pennsylvania, M.A., 1941,

Ph.D., 1951. *Home:* 574 U.S. 52, New Richmond, Ohio 45157. *Office:* University of Cincinnati, Cincinnati, Ohio 45221.

CAREER: University of Pennsylvania, Philadelphia, instructor in industry, 1946-49; University of Cincinnati, Cincinnati, Ohio, 1949—, began as assistant professor, now David Sinton Professor of Economics. Labor arbitrator. *Member:* American Economic Association, Industrial Relations Research Association, Society for General Systems Research, American Association of University Professors, American Civil Liberties Union, Social Science Education Consortium.

WRITINGS: Study of Racial Discrimination in Cincinnati, Wilder Foundation, 1952; *Arbitration in Transit: An Evaluation of Wage Criteria,* University of Pennsylvania Press, 1952; *Labor: Institutions and Economics,* Rinehart, 1956, revised edition, Harcourt, 1967; *The Study of Society: A Unified Approach,* Irwin, 1963 (published in England as *The Study of Society: A Multidisciplinary Approach,* Tavistock Publications, 1966). Contributor of articles on wage theory, systems theory, and philosophy to professional journals.

WORK IN PROGRESS: An information model of knowledge; *Social System: A Unified, Deductive, System-Based Approach; Social Science,* an introductory textbook; application of systems theory to curriculum in social sciences for grades 4-6.

*   *   *

KUHN, Martin A(rno) 1924-

PERSONAL: Born August 11, 1924, in Mannheim, Germany; son of Sigmund S. and Martha (Ettlinger) Kuhn; married Laura Pape, August 17, 1947; children: Kenneth E., Steven P. *Education:* Queens College of the City University of New York, B.A., 1948; Columbia University, M.S., 1949. *Home:* 36 White Beeches Dr., Dumont, N.J. 07628.

CAREER: U.S. Naval Shipyard, Brooklyn, N.Y., librarian, 1948; College of City of New York (now City College of the City University of New York), New York, N.Y., chief of general reference and life science library, 1949-62; City University of New York, Staten Island Community College, Staten Island, N.Y., 1962—, now chief librarian and professor of political science, associate dean of faculty, 1968—. Library consultant, Dumont (N.J.) Public Schools. *Military service:* U.S. Army, Finance Corps, 1946-47. *Member:* American Library Association, American Association of University Professors, New York Library Association.

WRITINGS: Morris Raphael Cohen: A Bibliography, Journal of the History of Ideas, 1957; (with Joseph R. Dunlap) *Debate Index, Second Supplement,* H.W. Wilson, 1964.

WORK IN PROGRESS: Writing on German librarianship during the Hitler period.

*   *   *

KUHNS, Grant (Wilson) 1929-

PERSONAL: Born April 4, 1929, in Los Angeles, Calif.; son of Grant W. (a building contractor) and Elizabeth (Lary) Kuhns; married Carol Oliver (a secretary). *Education:* University of Southern California, B.S., 1959, M.S., 1960. *Politics:* "Laissez Faire capitalist." *Office:* Consolidated Rock Products Co., 2730 South Alameda, Los Angeles, Calif. 90058.

CAREER: Consolidated Rock Products Co., Los Angeles, Calif., 1957—, began as engineer, now assistant properties manager. *Military service:* U.S. Army, Infantry; served in Korea, 1952. *Awards, honors:* George Washington Honor Medal, Freedoms Foundation, 1967, for essay, "Peace."

WRITINGS: On Surfing, Tuttle, 1963.

* * *

KUMAR, Shiv K(umar) 1921-

PERSONAL: Born August 16, 1921, in Lahore, Punjab, India; son of Bishan Das (a teacher) and Ishwar Kumar; married Anita Chatrath (a teacher), November 21, 1945; children: Neerai K. (son), Ansuya (daughter). *Education:* Forman Christian College, Lashore, India, M.A., 1943; Fitzwilliam House, Cambridge, Ph.D., 1956. *Home:* "Neerajam," 2-2-12/2 Hyderabad, Adikmet, Andhra Pradesh, India. *Office:* Department of English, Osmania University, Hyderabad, Andhra Pradesh, India.

CAREER: Government College, Chandigarh, India, chairman of department of English, 1954-57; Punjab University College, Hoshiarpur, India, reader in English, 1957-59; Osmania University, Hyderabad, India, professor and chairman of department of English, 1959—. Visiting professor at Cambridge University and Yale University. Indian delegate, Harvard International Seminar, 1953. Broadcaster on British Broadcasting Corp. programs, 1951-53, and All India Radio, 1954—. *Member:* Modern Language Association of America, Royal Society of Literature (London), Modern Humanities Research Association (Cambridge), P.E.N. (Indian branch).

WRITINGS: Virginia Woolf and Intuition, Vishveshvaranand Book Agency, 1957; *Virginia Woolf and Bergson's Duree,* Vishveshvaranand Book Agency, 1957; (editor) *Modern Short Stories,* Macmillan (London), 1958; *Bergson and the Stream of Consciousness Novel,* Blackie & Son, 1962, New York University Press, 1963; (editor) Walt Whitman, *Leaves of Grass,* Eurasia Publishing House, 1962; (editor) *Apollo's Lyre,* Macmillan (London), 1962; (with M.M. Maison) *Examine Your English,* Orient Longmans, 1964; (editor) Stephen Crane, *The Red Badge of Courage,* Eurasia Publishing House, 1964; (editor) *British Romantic Poets: Recent Revaluations,* New York University Press, 1966; (compiler with Keith McKean) *Critical Approaches to Fiction,* McGraw, 1968; (editor) *British Victorian Literature: Recent Revaluations,* New York University Press, 1969; (editor and author of introduction) Daniel Defoe, *The Life, Adventures, and Pyracies of the Famous Captain Singleton: Containing an Account of ... His Many Adventures and Pyracies with the Famous Captain Avery and Others,* Oxford University Press, 1969; *Articulate Silences: Poems,* Writers Workshop (Calcutta), 1970. Contributor of articles to literary and philological periodicals in India, Great Britain, Canada, and the United States, and of reviews to newspapers and magazines in India. Member of editorial board of *Indian Journal of English Studies;* editor of *Osmania Journal of English Studies.*

WORK IN PROGRESS: Editing *Representative English Romantic Poets: Contemporary Assessments;* research for *Contemporary Schools of Literary Criticism: A Reassessment.*

SIDELIGHTS: Kumar has traveled extensively in Japan, Europe, Egypt, and the United States, and is competent in French, Urdu, Hindi, and Punjabi. *Avocational interests:* Music, gardening, and walking.†

* * *

KUNSTLER, William M(oses) 1919-

PERSONAL: Born July 7, 1919, in New York, N.Y.; son of Monroe Bradford (a physician) and Frances (Mandelbaum) Kunstler; married Lotte Rosenberger, January 14, 1943; children: Karin K. Goldman, Jane Bradford. *Education:* Yale University, B.A., 1941; Columbia University, LL.B., 1948. *Home:* 210 West St., Mamaroneck, N.Y. 10543. *Agent:* McIntosh & Otis, Inc., 18 East 41st St., New York, N.Y. 10017. *Office:* Kunstler, Kunstler & Kinoy, 511 Fifth Ave., New York, N.Y. 10017; and Center for Constitutional Rights, 588 9th Ave., New York, N.Y. 10036.

CAREER: Admitted to New York Bar in 1948, to District of Columbia Bar in 1958; R.H. Macy & Co., New York, N.Y., executive trainee, 1948-49; Columbia University, New York, N.Y., lecturer in English, 1946-50; Kunstler, Kunstler & Kinoy (attorneys), New York, N.Y., partner, 1948—. Associate professor of law, New York Law School, 1950—, Pace College, 1951—; lecturer at New School for Social Research, 1966—. Volunteer Staff attorney, Center for Constitutional Rights, New York, N.Y. *Military service:* U.S. Army, 1941-46; served in Southwest Pacific Theater; became major; received Bronze Star medal. *Member:* National Association for the Advancement of Colored People, American Civil Liberties Union (director, 1964—; member of national council, 1968—), Association of the Bar of New York City, Authors Guild, Phi Beta Kappa, Phi Delta Phi. *Awards, honors:* Press Award of the New York State Bar Association, 1957; Ohio State University Radio-Television Institute first award, 1960; Civil Rights Scroll, New York State Bar Association, 1963.

WRITINGS: (With William Stone) *Our Pleasant Vices* (poems), privately printed, 1941; *The Law of Accidents,* Oceana, 1954; *First Degree,* Oceana, 1960; *Beyond a Reasonable Doubt?,* Morrow, 1961; *The Case for Courage,* Morrow, 1962; *. . . And Justice for All,* Oceana, 1963; *The Minister and the Choir Singer: The Hall-Mills Murder Case,* Morrow, 1964; *Deep In My Heart,* forewords by James Forman and Martin Luther King, Jr., Morrow, 1966. Author of radio scripts for "Justice" series, WMCA Radio, New York, N.Y. Contributor of book reviews and articles to periodicals.

WORK IN PROGRESS: The Mythology of the Law, a study of the myth and reality of the legal institution.

SIDELIGHTS: "William Kunstler is without doubt the country's most controversial and, perhaps, its best-known lawyer," Victor Navasky wrote in 1970. "The conventional right thinks he should be disbarred, the liberal middle suspects he got what was coming to him when Judge Julius Hoffman sentenced him—without a jury trial—to an unprecedented four years and 13 days for contempt of court [since overturned by a higher court], and the radical left is in the process of looking him over as a potential hero and/or martyr." Navasky quotes Kunstler as saying that "attorneys owe a deeper obligation to humanity than they do to their personal careers," and affirms that Kunstler "no longer takes money for political cases," and seldom even visits his New York law offices (which he shares with his brother Michael). Kenneth Gross says in an article for the *Washington Post* that Kunstler, "the chief attorney for the Chicago Seven and for H. Rap Brown, spends his life fighting off exhaustion, racing between courtrooms, airports and universities, where, like a perennially chilled stranger standing before an open fire, he tries to draw the necessary warmth from his young audiences."

Revered by the young and the radical for his often colorful defense of anti-establishment figures, Kunstler first attracted widespread public attention in the early 1960's with his revival of the Federal provision for "removing" state prosecutions to Federal courts. During the early days of the civil rights movement, Kunstler used this technique as a "countermove" to the Southern practice of harassing civil rights workers. Founder, with other attorneys active in civil rights, of the Law Center in New York (a nonprofit organization which now pays the expenses for his political cases), he also served for a time as special counsel to the late Dr. Martin Luther King, Jr. Navasky writes that "the most striking thing about Kunstler's style is its odd combination of emotional excess (he's a laugher and crier) and ostensible common sense." In addition to Rap Brown (who was married in Kunstler's home) and the Chicago Seven, Navasky lists the following as clients who are strongly attracted to his "loose, honest" style, and commitment to anti-establishment causes: "The Milwaukee 14 (he offered to put up his house and car toward their bail); the Catonsville Nine, the group (including the Berrigans) convicted of napalming draft records to protest the war in Vietnam; Stokely Carmichael; Representative Adam Clayton Powell; Ralph Featherstone, author of S.N.C.C.'s virulent anti-Israel propaganda; the governing boards of Intermediate School 201 and Ocean Hill-Brownsville; and Morton Sobell, convicted of conspiracy to commit espionage with the Rosenbergs and recently released on bail partly as a result of an original Kunstler theory." Kunstler has also represented the Black Panthers, the American Indian Movement (AIM), and Jack Ruby, accused killer of Lee Harvey Oswald, alleged assassin of President John F. Kennedy, and was part of the 12-member defense team recruited by Philip Berrigan and his five co-defendants in the alleged plot to bomb government facilities in Washington and kidnap Presidential aide Henry Kissinger.

Avco Embassy purchased motion picture rights to *The Minister and the Choir Singer.*

BIOGRAPHICAL/CRITICAL SOURCES: Time, December 13, 1968, June 29, 1970; *Esquire,* July, 1969; *Washington Post,* April 12, 1970; *New York Times Magazine,* April 19, 1970; *National Review,* May 5, 1970.

* * *

KURATH, Hans 1891-

PERSONAL: Born December 13, 1891, in Villach, Austria; came to United States in 1907, naturalized in 1912; son of John (a craftsman) and Anna (Raimund) Kurath; married Linda Eidel, 1919 (deceased); married Kathleen Morris, 1926 (deceased); married Gertrude Prokosch (a musicologist and choreographer), 1930; children: (first marriage) Dieter; (third marriage) Ellen, Edward. *Education:* University of Texas, A.B., 1914; University of Chicago, Ph.D., 1920. *Politics:* Democrat (liberal). *Religion:* Christian. *Home:* 1125 Spring St., Ann Arbor, Mich. 48103. *Office:* Angell Hall, University of Michigan, Ann Arbor, Mich. 48104.

CAREER: Northwestern University, Evanston, Ill., instructor, 1920-22, assistant professor of German, 1922-27; Ohio State University, Columbus, professor of Germanics and linguistics, 1927-31; Brown University, Providence, R.I., professor of Germanics and linguistics, 1931-46, chairman of division of modern languages, 1941-46; University of Michigan, Ann Arbor, professor of English, 1946-61, now professor emeritus. *Member:* Modern Language Association of America, Linguistic Society of America (president, 1940), American Dialect Society, American Academy of Arts and Sciences, Austrian Academy. *Awards, honors:* L.H.D., University of Chicago, 1959, University of Wisconsin, 1968.

WRITINGS: The Semantic Sources for the Words for the Emotions in Sanskrit, Greek, Latin, and the Germanic Languages, George Barta Publishing, 1921; *American Pronunciation,* Clarendon Press, 1928; (with others) *Handbook of the Linguistic Geography of New England,* American Council of Learned Societies, 1939; (editor with others) *Linguistic Atlas of New England,* three volumes, American Council of Learned Societies, 1939-43; *A Word Geography of the Eastern United States,* University of Michigan Press, 1949; (with R.I. McDavid) *The Pronunciation of English in the Atlantic States,* University of Michigan Press, 1961; *A Phonology and Prosody of Modern English,* University of Michigan Press, 1964; *Die Lautgestalt einer Kaerntner Mundart und ihre Geschichte,* F. Steiner, 1965; *Studies in Area Linguistics,* Indiana University Press, 1972. Editor, *Linguistic Atlas of the U.S.A.,* 1939-43; editor-in-chief, *Middle English Dictionary,* University of Michigan Press, 1946-72.

* * *

KURLAND, Philip B. 1921-

PERSONAL: Born October 22, 1921, in New York, N.Y.; son of Archibald H. (a lawyer) and Estelle (Polstein) Kurland; married Mary Jane Krensky (a social case worker), May 29, 1954; children: Julie Rebecca, Martha Jennifer, Ellen Sarah. *Education:* University of Pennsylvania, A.B., 1942; Harvard University, LL.B., 1944. *Home:* 4840 Woodlawn Ave., Chicago, Ill. 60615. *Office:* University of Chicago Law School, 1121 East 60th St., Chicago, Ill. 60637.

CAREER: Admitted to New York Bar, 1945, and to U.S. Supreme Court; clerk in office of Judge Jerome Frank, New York, N.Y., 1944-45, in office of U.S. Supreme Court Justice Felix Frankfurter, Washington, D.C., 1945-46; Department of Justice, Washington, D.C., attorney, 1946-47; Kurland & Wolfson (law firm), New York, N.Y., partner, 1947-50; Northwestern University Law School, Chicago, Ill., assistant professor, 1950-53; University of Chicago Law School, Chicago, Ill., associate professor, 1953-56, professor of law, 1956—. Associate general counsel, Economic Stabilization Agency, 1950; chief counsel, subcommittee on separation of powers, U.S. Senate Judiciary Committee, 1967—. *Member:* American Academy of Arts and Sciences (fellow), American Bar Association, American Law Institute, Association of the Bar of the City of New York, Chicago Bar Association; Quadrangle Club and Caxton Club (both Chicago). *Awards, honors:* Guggenheim fellow, 1949-50, 1955-56.

WRITINGS: (With R.F. Wolfson) *Jurisdiction of the Supreme Court,* Matthew Bender, 1951; (editor with Allison Dunham) *Mr. Justice,* University of Chicago Press, 1956, 2nd edition, revised and enlarged, 1964; *Religion and the Law of Church and State and the Supreme Court,* Aldine, 1962; (editor) *The Supreme Court and the Constitution: Essays in Constitutional Law from "The Supreme Court Review",* University of Chicago Press, 1965; (with Harry Kalven, Jr.) *Conscience of a Nation* (series of ten radio discussions, broadcast September 6-17, 1965), Office of Radio and Television, University of Chicago, 1965; (with James William Moore) *Moore's Manual: Federal Practice and Procedure,* Matthew Bender, 1968; *Politics, the Constitution, and the Warren Court,* University of Chicago Press, 1970; (compiler) *Felix Frankfurter on the Supreme Court: Extrajudicial Essays on the Court and the Constitution,* Belknap Press, 1970; (with others) *Constitutionality of Aid to Illinois Non-Public Schools,* Elementary and Secondary Nonpublic Schools Study Commission, 1971; *Mr. Justice Frankfurter and the Constitution,* University of Chicago Press, 1971. Editor, *Harvard Law Review,* 1943-44, *Supreme Court Review* (annual), University of Chicago Press, 1960—; managing editor, *Federal Bar Journal,* 1945-47; contributing editor, *Encyclopaedia Britannica,* 1955—, and various law manuals. Contributor of articles to professional and popular journals.

WORK IN PROGRESS: Biography of Mr. Justice Jackson; Decline and Fall of American Federalism; Business and Jurisdiction of Supreme Court; Primer on Federal Civil Procedure.†

KURSH, Charlotte Olmsted   1912-
(Charlotte Olmsted)

PERSONAL: Born March 2, 1912, in Brookline, Mass.; daughter of Frederick Law (a landscape architect) and Sarah (Sharples) Olmsted; married second husband, Maurice Kursh (an artist), January 7, 1960; children: (first marriage) Sarah Gill, Stephen P. Gill, Jane Gill Beighley, Mary Gill Jordan. *Education:* Sweet Briar College, A.B., 1935; Stanford University, M.A., 1962, Ph.D., 1965. *Politics:* Democrat. *Home:* 80 Valencia Ct., Portola Valley, Calif. 94025. *Office:* Mental Research Institute, 777 Bryant St., Palo Alto, Calif. 94301.

CAREER: Mental Research Institute, Palo Alto, Calif., research associate, 1958—. *Member:* American Philological Association, American Anthropological Association, Southwestern Anthropological Association, League of Women Voters (president, local chapter, 1941-43).

WRITINGS: (Editorial assistant) *Etiology of Schizophrenia,* Basic Books, 1961; *Heads I Win, Tails You Lose,* Macmillan, 1962.

WORK IN PROGRESS: Mermaids and Centaurs, a study of mythological monsters; a community study of Milpitas.

*   *   *

KURSH, Harry   1919-

PERSONAL: Born March 6, 1919, in New York, N.Y.; son of Isadore and Gussie (Feigenbaum) Kurschinsky; married Marilyn Pincus, November 24, 1943; children: Myra, Gail. *Education:* New York University, B.S. in Journalism (cum laude), M.A.; University of Southhampton, postgraduate summer study, 1948. *Politics:* Independent. *Religion:* Jewish. *Home:* Hollowbrook Lake, Peekskill, N.Y. 10566. *Agent:* Evelyn L. Singer Agency, 41 West 96th St., New York, N.Y. 10025.

CAREER: Stringer correspondent for New England newspapers, Eastport, Me., 1939-41; Fairchild Publications, New York, N.Y., reporter, 1950-51; *Sales Management,* New York, N.Y., industrial editor, 1951-52; free-lance writer, 1952—. *Military service:* U.S. Navy, 1941-45. *Member:* Overseas Press Club, Authors Guild, Society of American Travel Writers, Henry Oldtimers (Henry Street Settlement).

WRITINGS: How to Prospect for Uranium, Fawcett, 1954; *How to Get Land from Uncle Sam,* Norton, 1955; (with others) *Inventors Handbook,* Fawcett, 1955; *Apprenticeships in America: A Guide to Golden Opportunities in Industry for Students, Parents, Guidance Counselors, and Leaders in Education, Labor, and Industry,* Norton, 1958, revised edition, 1965; *Inside the U.S. Patent Office: The Story of the Men, the Laws, and the Procedures of the American Patent System,* Norton, 1959; *This is Alaska,* Prentice-Hall, 1961; (with others) *The Man Who Rode the Thunder,* Prentice-Hall, 1961; *The Franchise Boom: How You Can Profit in It,* Prentice-Hall, 1962, revised edition, 1968; *Cobras in His Garden,* Harvey House, 1965; *The United States Office of Education: A Century of Service,* Chilton, 1965. Regular contributor to King Features, North American Newspaper Alliance, and *Christian Science Monitor.*

AVOCATIONAL INTERESTS: Photography, playing the piano (by ear), reading, listening to music.

*   *   *

KURTZ, Stephen G(uild)   1926-

PERSONAL: Born September 9, 1926, in Buffalo, N.Y.; son of George Patterson (a salesman) and Nellie (Crow-

ther) Kurtz; married Katherine Jeanne Godolphin, September 5, 1947; children: Sharon, Thomas, Stephen. *Education:* Princeton University, A.B., 1947; University of Pennsylvania, Ph.D., 1953. *Politics:* Independent. *Religion:* Episcopal. *Home:* 201 South Grant Ave., Crawfordsville, Ind. 47933. *Office:* Wabash College, Crawfordsville, Ind. 47933.

CAREER: University of Pennsylvania, Philadelphia, instructor in history, 1949-51; Kent School, Kent, Conn., history master, 1951-55; Wabash College, Crawfordsville, Ind., assistant professor, 1956-59, associate professor of history and assistant to president, 1959, dean of college, 1964—. Chairman of department of college work, Episcopal Diocese of Indianapolis, 1962-64; chairman, Human Relations Council of Montgomery County, 1963-64. *Military service:* U.S. Naval Reserve, 1944-45. *Member:* American Historical Association. *Awards, honors:* Guggenheim fellow, 1961-62.

WRITINGS: The Presidency of John Adams: The Collapse of Federalism, 1795-1800, University of Pennsylvania Press, 1957; (contributor) Morton Borden, editor, *America's Ten Greatest Presidents,* Rand McNally, 1961; (editor) *Federalists: Creators and Critics of Union,* Wiley, 1971; (editor with James H. Hutson) *Essays on the American Revolution,* University of North Carolina Press, 1973. Reviewer for historical journals.

WORK IN PROGRESS: A biography of John Adams.

*   *   *

KUSAN, Ivan   1933-

PERSONAL: Born August 30, 1933, in Sarajevo, Yugoslavia; son of Jaksa and Marija (Murko) Kusan. *Education:* Studied painting at Academy of Fine Arts, Zagreb, Yugoslavia. *Home:* 24, Banjavcica, Zagreb, Yugoslavia.

CAREER: Former editor at Zagreb-radio, Zagreb, Yugoslavia, and manager of story department at Zagreb Cartoon Motion Picture Studio; now free-lance writer. *Member:* Writers' Union of Yugoslavia. *Awards, honors:* Zagreb Literary Prize, 1961, for juvenile book, *The Homework.*

WRITINGS: Uzbuna na Zelenom vrhu (juvenile), Matica Hrvatska (Zagreb), 1956, translation by Michael B. Petrovich published as *The Mystery of Green Hill,* Harcourt, 1962; *Trenutak unaprijed* (short stories; title means "A Moment in Advance"), Naklada Drustva Knjizevnika Hrvatske (Zagreb), 1957; *Koko i duhovi* (juvenile), Kadok (Belgrade), 1958, translation by Drenka Willen published as *Koko and the Ghosts,* Harcourt, 1966; *Razapet izmedu* (novel; title means "The Crucified"), Nolit (Belgrade), 1958; *Zidom zazidani* (novel; title means "The Walled"), Znanje (Zagreb), 1960; *Domaca zadaca* (juvenile; title means "The Homework"), Matica Hrvatska, 1960; *Tajanstveni djecak* (juvenile; title means "The Mysterious Boy"), Kadok, 1962; *Zagonetni djecak,* Prosveta (Belgrade), 1963; (with Slobodan Novak and Cedo Prica) *Dvadeset godina jugoslavenske proze,* Naprijed (Zagreb), 1966; *Toranj: Ljetopis za razbibrigu,* Kolo Matice Hrvatske (Zagreb), 1970; *Veliki dan: Pripovijetke,* Matica Hrvatska, 1970. Translator of several books from English, French, and Russian into Yugoslav, including Mark Twain's *Tom Sawyer.* Author of radio plays and a television script.

WORK IN PROGRESS: An adult novel; a book of short stories for children; a book of essays; a translation of Mark Twain.

SIDELIGHTS: Kusan's children's books, all self-illustrated in Yugoslav editions, have been translated into five languages. *Avocational interests:* Painting.

KWANT, Remigius C(ornelis) 1918-

PERSONAL: Born January 14, 1918; son of Antonius and Catherina (Stam) Kwant. Education: Institutum Angelicum, Rome, Italy, Phil. Dr., 1945; also studied at Sorbonne, University of Paris, and at Higher Institute of Philosophy, Louvain, Belgium, 1952-54. Home and office: Hezer Enghweg 34, Den Dolder, The Netherlands.

CAREER: Agostinian Seminary, Eindhoven, Netherlands, professor of philosophy, 1945-61; University of Utrecht, Utrecht, Netherlands, professor of philosophy, 1961—. Visiting professor, Duquesne University, Pittsburgh, Pa., 1959, 1965, University of Natal, South Africa, 1965, Manhattanville College, 1968. Member: Association for Thomistic Philosophy, Association for Scientific Philosophy, Dutch Association for Philosophy.

WRITINGS: De Gradibus entis, H.J. Paris, 1946; Idelisme en Christendom, Het Spectrum, 1948; Het Arbeidsbestel: Een Studie over de geest van onze samenleving, Het Spectrum, 1956, 4th edition, 1962; Ontmoeting van wetenschap an arbeid, Het Spectrum, 1958; Wijsbegeerte van de Ontmoeting, Het Spectrum, 1959, translation by Robert C. Adolphs published as Encounter, Duquesne University Press, 1960; De Ontwikkeling van het sociale denken: Tekst van de rede uitgesproken voor het congres ter herdenking van het derde lustrum, Central Staatkundige Vorming, 1960; Philosophy of Labor, Duquesne University Press, 1960; De Wijsbergeerte van Karl Marx, Het Spectrum, 1961, 4th edition, 1966; De Fenomenologie van Merleau-Ponty, Het Spectrum, 1962, revised edition published as Die Wijsbegeerte van Merleau-Ponty, 1968, translation by Henry J. Koren published as The Phenomenological Philosophy of Merleau-Ponty, Duquesne University Press, 1963; Mens en kritiek: Een Analyse van de functie van de kritiek in het menselijke bestaan, Het Spectrum, 1962, translation by Henry J. Koren, published as Critique: Its Nature and Function, Duquesne University Press, 1967; Fenomenologie van de taal, Het Spectrum, 1963, 3rd edition, 1967, translation by Henry J. Koren published as Phenomenology of Language, Duquesne University Press, 1965; Sociale filosofie, Het Spectrum, 1963, 2nd edition, 1967, translation by Henry J. Koren published as Phenomenology of Social Existence, Duquesne University Press, 1965; De Christen en de wereld, Bigot en Van Rossum, 1963; Filosofie van de arbeid, Nederlandsche Boekhandel, 1964; De Stemmen van de stilte: Merleau-Ponty's analyse van de schilderkunst, Paul Brand, 1966; From Phenomenology to Metaphysics: An Inquiry into the Last Period of Merleau-Ponty's Philosophical Life, Duquesne University Press, 1966; Mens en expressie in het licht van de wijsbegeerte van Merleau-Ponty, Het Spectrum, 1968, translation by Henry J. Koren published as Phenomenology of Expression, 1969; Apartheidspolitiek als structureel geweld, Paul Brand, 1969; Een Nieuwe vrijheid, Samson, 1970; Mens en structuur, Samson, 1971. Regular contributor to philosophical journals in the Netherlands.

*   *   *

LA-ANYANE, Seth 1922-

PERSONAL: Born June 12, 1922, in Accra, Ghana; son of Michael Hayfron and Dora (Ofeibea) La; married Muriel Cochrane, March 3, 1955; children: Kojo, Ofeibea, Danso, Nana, Boahema. Education: University of Reading, B.Sc., 1946; London School of Economics, University of London, B.Sc., 1949, M.Sc., 1951; Stanford University, M.A., 1964, Ph.D., 1966. Religion: Christian. Office: University of Ghana, Legon, Ghana.

CAREER: Ghana Department of Agriculture, Accra, agricultural economist, 1952-60; Ghana Ministry of Agriculture, Accra, food commissioner, 1958, chief agricultural economist, 1960-62; University of Ghana, Legon, senior lecturer, 1962-67, associate professor, 1967-70, professor, 1970—, dean, 1966—, pro-vice-chancellor, 1968—. Member: Royal Economic Society (fellow), Ghana Academy of Sciences and Arts (fellow).

WRITINGS: Ghana Agriculture, Oxford University Press, 1963.
Contributor: John Brian Wills, editor, Agriculture and Land Use in Ghana, Oxford University Press, 1962; A.M. Woodruff and others, editors, International Seminar on Land Taxation, Land Tenure, and Land Reform in Developing Countries, John C. Lincoln Institute, University of Hartford, 1966; Background to Agricultural Policy in Ghana, [Legon], 1969; African Encyclopedia, Oxford University Press, 1971. Editor and contributor, Ghanaian Bulletin of Agricultural Economics, 1961-62, Legon Journal of Agriculture, 1967-69.

WORK IN PROGRESS: Study of economic development in tropical Africa.

AVOCATIONAL INTERESTS: Tennis, field hockey, gardening.

*   *   *

LABAREE, Benjamin Woods 1927-

PERSONAL: Born July 21, 1927, in New Haven, Conn.; son of Leonard Woods (a professor) and Elizabeth (Calkins) Labaree; married Linda Carol Prichard, June 27, 1959; children: Benjamin Woods, Jr., Jonathan Martin, Sarah Calkins. Education: Yale University, B.A., 1950; Harvard University, A.M., 1953, Ph.D., 1957. Politics: Democrat. Religion: Congregationalist. Home: Syndicate Rd., Williamstown, Mass. 01267.

CAREER: Phillips Exeter Academy, Exeter, N.H., instructor in history, 1950-52; Connecticut College, New London, instructor in history, 1957-58; Harvard University, Cambridge, Mass., instructor, then assistant professor of history, 1958-63, Allston Burr Senior Tutor, Winthrop House, 1958-62; Williams College, Williamstown, Mass., dean of college, 1963—, associate professor, 1963-67, professor of history, 1968—. Staff member, Munson Institute of Maritime History. Military service: U.S. Navy, 1945-46. Member: American Historical Association, Colonial Society of Massachusetts, Massachusetts Historical Society, American Antiquarian Society.

WRITINGS: (Editor) Samuel McIntire: A Bicentennial Symposium, 1757-1957, Essex Institute, 1957; Patriots and Partisans: The Merchants of Newburyport, 1764-1815, Harvard University Press, 1962; The Road to Independence, 1763-1776, Macmillan, 1963; The Boston Tea Party, Oxford University Press, 1964; (with Vincent P. De Santis) America Past and Present, Allyn & Bacon, 1968; New England and the Sea, Wesleyan University Press, 1971; Colonial America, Allyn & Bacon, 1971; America's Nation-Time 1607-1789, Allyn & Bacon, 1973. American Maritime Library, chairman, board of editors; Essex Institute Historical Collections, member of board of editors, 1956—, editor, 1956-60.

WORK IN PROGRESS: The Decision for Independence, to be published by Oxford University Press.

*   *   *

LA CAPRIA, Raffaele 1922-

PERSONAL: Born October 8, 1922, in Naples, Italy; son of Augusto and Dora (Materasso) La Capria; married Fiore Pucci; married second wife, Ilaria Occhini; children: (first marriage) Roberta, (second marriage) Alessandra. Education: Attended Liceo "Umberto I," Naples, Italy, 1930-40; Naples University, diploma in law, 1947. Politics: Democrat. Religion: Catholic. Home: Piazza Grazioli 5, Rome, Italy. Office: Radio-Television-Italiana, Viale Mazzini 14, Rome, Italy.

CAREER: Radio-Television-Italiana, Rome, Italy, 1950—, started in radio literary section as radio writer, now television script writer. Attended Harvard International Seminar (literature), 1957. Military service: Italian Army, 1943-45, became sergeant. Awards, honors: Premio Strega, 1961, for Ferito a morte; Golden Lion, Venice Film Festival, 1963, for "Le Mani Sulla Citta."

WRITINGS: Un Giorno d'impazienza (novel), Bompiani, 1952, translation by William Fense Weaver published in America as A Day of Impatience, Farrar, Straus, 1954, and as The First Affair, New American Library, 1955; Ferito a morte (novel), Bompiani, 1961, translation by Marguerite Waldman published in America as The Mortal Wound, Farrar, Straus, 1964.

Contributor: Saggi italiani 1959 (title means "Italian Essays, 1959"), Bompiani, 1960; Nuovi racconti italiani (title means "Italian Modern Short Stories"), Nuova Accademia, 1963. Contributor to newspapers and magazines, such as Corriere della Sera, Il Mondo, Tempo Presente. Writes film scripts and translates from English and French.

WORK IN PROGRESS: A new novel.

SIDELIGHTS: La Capria likes the sea, swimming, and the sport of underwater fishing. Many scenes of Ferito a morte take place under water.

* * *

LACEY, Archie L (ouis) 1923-

PERSONAL: Born January 21, 1923, in Boothton, Ala.; son of Joseph Clifton and Mary Belle (Tarrant) Lacey; married Theodora Smiley, April 29, 1956; children: Archie Louis, Jr., Mary Elaine, Clinton Tarrant, Nanette. Education: Alabama State College, B.S., 1947; Howard University, graduate study, 1948-49; Northwestern University, M.A., 1953, Ph.D., 1955. Religion: Unitarian. Home: 168 Stuyvesant Rd., Teaneck, N.J. 07666. Office: Lehman College of the City University of New York, Bronx, N.Y. 10468.

CAREER: High school and junior college science instructor in Alabama, 1947-52; Alabama State College, Montgomery, associate professor of science, 1955-57; Grambling College, Grambling, La., professor of physical science, 1957-60; City University of New York, New York, N.Y., Hunter College, assistant professor, 1960-64, associate professor of education, 1964-68, Herbert H. Lehman College, professor of education, 1968—. Science consultant on special project, Phelps Stokes Foundation, 1955-57. Director of National Science Foundation summer institutes for junior and senior high school teachers, Grambling College, 1960-62. Co-director, National Defense Education Act Institutes in Science, Hunter College, 1966-68. Director, Teacher Education, Federal City College, Washington, D.C., 1969-70. Military service: U.S. Army Engineers. Member: National Science Teachers Association (director, Region IV, 1958-60), National Association for Research in Science Teaching, American Association for Advancement of Science (fellow), National Institute of Science, New York Academy of Sciences, Phi Delta Kappa, Beta Kappa Chi.

WRITING: (With Katherine B. Hoffman) Chemistry of Life, Scholastic Magazines, 1964; (with V.M. Rowley) Guide to Science Teaching in Secondary Schools, Wadsworth, 1966. Contributor of articles to professional journals.

* * *

LADO, Robert 1915-

PERSONAL: Born May 31, 1915, in Tampa, Fla. son of Constantino and Dolores (Canosa) Lado; married Lucia Andrade, September 6, 1950; children: Lucia Dolores, Robert J., Ana Luisa, RoseMary, Margaret, John, Victor, Joseph, Francis Xavier. Education: Rollins College, B.A., 1939; University of Texas, M.S., 1945; University of Michigan, Ph.D., 1950. Religion: Roman Catholic. Home: 5404 Newington Rd., Washington, D.C. 20016. Office: Institute of Languages and Linguistics, Georgetown University, Washington, D.C. 20007.

CAREER: University of Michigan, English Language Institute, Ann Arbor, instructor, 1945-50, assistant professor, 1950-53, associate professor, 1953-58, professor of English, 1958-60, assistant director, 1946-53, associate director, 1953-56, director, 1956-60; Georgetown University, Institute of Languages and Linguistics, Washington, D.C., academic director, 1960-62, dean, 1962—. U.S. Department of State lecturer in South America and Mexico, 1953, Japan, 1958. Member: Fulbright advisory screening committee on linguistics and teaching English, Conference Board of Association of Research Councils, 1955-58; member, National Advisory Committee on Bilingual Education. Organized programs in teaching English in Europe. Member: Modern Language Association of America, Linguistic Society of America, National Association of Foreign Student Advisers (vice-president, 1954-56), Michigan Linguistic Society (president, 1954-56), Washington Linguistics Club (president).

WRITINGS: Oral Pattern Practice, 1949; English Language and Orientation Programs for Foreign Students Offered by Institutions of Higher Learning in the United States, Educational Exchange Section, International Educational Programs Branch, U.S. Office of Education, 1952; Annotated Bibliography for Teachers of English as a Foreign Language, U.S. Government Printing Office, 1955; (with Charles C. Fries) Lessons in Vocabulary, University of Michigan Press, 1956, 3rd revised edition, 1958; Linguistics Across Cultures: Applied Linguistics for Language Teachers, University of Michigan Press, 1957; (with Fries) English Pattern Practices: Establishing the Patterns as Habits, 3rd revised edition, University of Michigan Press, 1958; (with Fries) English Sentence Patterns: Understanding and Producing English Grammatical Structures, University of Michigan Press, 1958, 3rd revised edition, 1962; (with Fries) English Pronunciation: Exercises in Sound Segments, Intonation, and Rhythm, 2nd revised edition, University of Michigan press, 1958, 3rd revised edition, 1965; (editor) An Intensive Course in English, 3rd revised edition, University of Michigan Press, 1958-59.

English Language Test for Foreign Students, Wahr, 1960; Language Testing: The Construction and Use of Foreign Language Tests, Longmans, Green (London), 1961, McGraw, 1964; Language Teaching: A Scientific Approach, McGraw, 1964; (with others) Galeria hispanica, Webster, 1965, 2nd edition, McGraw, 1971; Una Comparacion entre los sistemas fonicos del ingles y del espanol, Department of Linguistics, Faculty of Humanities and Sciences, Universidad de la Republica (Montevideo), 1965; (with Edward Blansitt) Contemporary Spanish, McGraw, 1967; (editor with Norman A. McQuown and Sol Saporta) Current Trends in Linguistics, Volume IV: Ibero-American and Caribbean Linguistics, Mouton & Co., 1968; (with others) Tesoro hispanico, McGraw, 1968; "Lado English" series," Simon & Schuster, 1970—. Author of published tests in English for foreign students.

* * *

LaFEBER, Walter Fredrick 1933-

PERSONAL: Born August 30, 1933, in Walkerton, Ind.; son of Ralph Nichols and Helen (Lidecker) LaFeber; married Sandra Gould, September 11, 1955; children: Scott Nichols, Suzanne Margaret. Education: Hanover College, A.B., 1955; Stanford University, M.A., 1956; University of Wisconsin, Ph.D., 1959. Religion: Presbyterian. Home: 24 Cornell St., Ithaca, N.Y. 14850. Of-

fice: History Department, Cornell University, Ithaca, N.Y. 14850.

CAREER: Cornell University, Ithaca, N.Y., 1959—, now Noll Professor of History. *Member:* American Historical Society, American Association of University Professors, Organization of American Historians. *Awards, honors:* Albert J. Beveridge Prize for *The New Empire* as best manuscript submitted to American Historical Association in 1962.

WRITINGS: The New Empire: An Interpretation of American Expansion, 1860-1898, published for American Historical Association by Cornell University Press, 1963; (editor) *John Quincy Adams and American Continental Empire,* Quadrangle, 1965; *America, Russia and the Cold War, 1945-1966,* Wiley, 1967, 2nd edition, 1972; (compiler) *America and the Cold War: 20 Years of Revolutions and Response, 1947-1967,* Wiley, 1969; *Origins of the Cold War, 1941-1947,* Wiley, 1971. Contributor of articles to professional and popular journals.

WORK IN PROGRESS: United States-Russian Relations, 1780-1917; Biographical Essays on American Foreign Policy.

BIOGRAPHICAL/CRITICAL SOURCES: Nation, April 15, 1968; *New York Times,* May 2, 1968, May 3, 1968.

*   *   *

LAFFERTY, Perry (Francis)   1917-

PERSONAL: Born October 3, 1917, in Davenport, Iowa; son of Herbert Ray and Elizabeth (Perry) Lafferty; married Mary Frances Carden, January 16, 1943; children: Marcy, Steven. *Education:* Yale University, music student for four years. *Home:* 335 South Bristol Ave., Los Angeles, Calif. 90049. *Office:* 7800 Beverly Blvd., Hollywood, Calif. 90036.

CAREER: Columbia Broadcasting System, Hollywood, Calif., vice-president of programs. Conducted seminar on radio and television production, Sarah Lawrence College, 1952. *Military service:* U.S. Army Air Forces, World War II; became captain. *Member:* Directors Guild of America, Screen Producers Guild, Authors League of America.

WRITINGS: Birdies Sing and Everything, Dodd, 1964.

*   *   *

LAIRD, Jean E(louise)   1930-
(Marcia McKeever, Jean L. Wakefield)

PERSONAL: Born January 18, 1930, in Wakefield, Mich.; daughter of Chester A. and Agnes (Petranek) Rydeski; married Jack E. Laird (owner of retail lumberyards), June 9, 1951; children: John E. Jane E., JoanAnn P., Jerilyn S., Jacquelyn T. *Education:* Duluth Business University, graduate, 1948; other courses at University of Minnesota, 1949-50, Michigan State University, 1951. *Religion:* Roman Catholic. *Home:* 10540 South Lockwood Ave., Oak Lawn, Ill. 60453.

CAREER: Former secretary for seven years for firms and schools in Minnesota and Michigan; now free-lance writer, mostly of nonfiction for magazines. Creative writing teacher in adult education courses in Oak Lawn and Concordia, Ill. Lecturer. *Member:* Canterbury Writer's Club (Chicago; president, 1961; member of board, 1962-64).

WRITINGS: Lost in the Department Store (juvenile), Denison, 1964; *Around the House Like Magic,* Harper, 1967; *Around the Kitchen Like Magic,* Harper, 1969; *The Plump Ballerina* (juvenile), Denison, 1970. Travel editor under pseudonym Marcia McKeever, *Oldsmobile's Magazine;* beauty editor under pseudonym Jean L. Wakefield, *Ladycom* (magazine); author of columns in *Mod-*

ern Maturity and *Vacations Unlimited.* Author of 27 National Research booklets, 1969-70. Contributor of over 400 articles to *Parents' Magazine, Suburbia Today, American Home, Popular Medicine, Chatelaine, Victorian, Herald of Health* (India), *Teen, Datebook, Midwest, Catholic Layman, Grit, Chicago Sun-Times,* and other magazines and newspapers.

BIOGRAPHICAL/CRITICAL SOURCES: Life and Health, March, 1964.

*   *   *

LAMANNA, Dolores B.   1930-

PERSONAL: Surname is pronounced La-*man*-na; born July 18, 1930, in Bay Shore, N.Y.; daughter of Anthony S. (a lawyer) and Josephine (Liotta) Lamanna. *Education:* Syracuse University, B.S., 1952. *Home and office:* 1737 York Ave., New York, N.Y. 10028.

CAREER: U.S. Foreign Service, cryptographic clerk in Pretoria, South Africa, 1955-57; Museum of Modern Art, New York, N.Y., coordinator of the Junior Council, 1957-64; free-lance researcher and editor, 1965—. *Member:* American Association of Museums, American Civil Liberties Union, Eta Pi Upsilon.

WRITINGS: (Editor) *Guide to Modern Art in Europe,* Junior Council, Museum of Modern Art, 1963, 2nd edition, 1966.

WORK IN PROGRESS: Compiling and editing an anthology of writings about the Hudson River, tentatively titled *Along the Hudson.*

*   *   *

LAMBERT, William Wilson   1919-

PERSONAL: Born May 10, 1919, in Amherst, Nova Scotia; son of Harry Brown and Alice Grace (Babcock) Lambert; married Elisabeth Carr, June 16, 1950; children: Hilary Ann Barbara, Holly Lee Alison. *Education:* Brown University, A.B., 1942; University of Nebraska, M.A., 1943; Harvard University, Ph.D., 1950. *Politics:* Democrat. *Home Address:* R.D. #2, Hanshaw Rd., Ithaca, N.Y. 14850. *Office:* Department of Psychology, Cornell University, Ithaca, N.Y. 14850.

CAREER: Harvard University, Cambridge, Mass., instructor, 1949-50; Brown University, Providence, R.I., assistant professor of psychology, 1950-51; Cornell University, Ithaca, N.Y., began as assistant professor, 1950, professor of psychology, sociology, and anthropology, 1960—. Fulbright lecturer, University of Oslo, 1958-59. Member of sociology panel, National Science Foundation, 1960-62. *Military service:* U.S. Navy, 1943-46. *Member:* American Psychological Association, American Anthropological Association, American Sociological Association, American Association of University Professors, Phi Beta Kappa, Sigma Xi. *Awards, honors:* Fellow of Center for Advanced Study in the Behavioral Sciences, Palo Alto, Calif., 1956-57.

WRITINGS: (Contributor) Gardner Lindzey, editor, *Handbook of Social Psychology,* two volumes, Addison-Wesley, 1954; (contributor) Paul Henry Mussen, editor, *Handbook of Research Methods in Child Development,* Wiley, 1960; (contributor) Sigmund Koch, editor, *Psychology: A Study of a Science,* Volume VI, McGraw, 1963; (with Wallace E. Lambert) *Social Psychology,* Prentice-Hall, 1964; (with Leigh Minturn) *Mothers of Six Cultures: Antecedents of Child Rearing,* Wiley, 1964; (with others) *Catecholamine Excretion in Young Boys and Their Parents as Related to Behavior: A Preliminary Report,* Psychological Laboratories, University of Stockholm, 1967; (editor with Edgar R. Borgatta) *Handbook of Personality Theory and Research,* Rand McNally, 1968; (with others) *Catecholamine Excretion in Young*

Children and Their Parents as Related to Behavior, Psychological Laboratories, University of Stockholm, 1968; (editor with Rita Weisbrod) *Comparative Perspectives on Social Psychology,* Little, Brown, 1971. Contributor to professional journals.

WORK IN PROGRESS: Cross-cultural studies in personality development and socialization; cross-cultural studies of perception.†

*   *   *

LAMBRICK, Hugh Trevor 1904-

PERSONAL: Born April 20, 1904, in Breaston, Derby, England; son of Charles Menzies (a clergyman) and Jessie (Trevor) Lambrick; married Gabrielle Jennings, October 8, 1948 (died, 1968); children: Charles Trevor, George Henry. *Education:* Attended Rossall School; Oriel College, Oxford University, B.A. (first class honors), 1926, M.A., 1947. *Home:* Picketts Heath, Boars Hill, Oxford, England.

CAREER: Indian Civil Service, posts in Bombay and Sind provinces, 1927-46, serving as assistant commissioner in Sind, 1931, secretary to governor, 1941, civil adviser to commander of Upper Sind Force, 1942-43, special commissioner for Sind, 1943-46; Oxford University, Oxford, England, fellow of Oriel College, 1947-50, 1951—. *Member:* Sind Historical Society (president, 1940-43), Society of Antiquaries (fellow, 1971), East India and Sports Club. *Awards, honors:* Companion, Order of the Indian Empire, 1944; D. Litt., Oxford University, 1971.

WRITINGS: Sir Charles Napier and Sind, Clarendon Press, 1952; *John Jacob of Jacobabad,* Cassell, 1960; *History of Sind,* Volume I: *Sind: A General Introduction,* Sindhi Adabi Board (Pakistan), 1964; (contributor) C.H. Philips and Mary D. Wainwright, editors, *The Partition of India: Policies and Perspectives,` 1935-1947,* Allen & Unwin, 1970. Author of Sind Tables, Volume 12 of Census of India, 1942. Contributor of articles on archeology and history to *Collier's Encyclopedia* and to *Journal of Sind Historical Society,* 1935-46, and *Listener;* book reviews to other journals.

WORK IN PROGRESS: Volume II of *History of Sind; Henry Viscount Hardinge; Franz Schubert's Annus Mirabilis.*

SIDELIGHTS: Lambrick composes music, including symphonic variations and songs. He has written a sonata for violin and piano, cycle of songs without words for oboe and piano, and "Duo Sonatina," "Adagio for Organ," and other piano pieces.

*   *   *

LAMPELL, Millard 1919-

PERSONAL: Born January 10, 1919, in Paterson, N.J.; son of Charles and Bertha Lampell; married Elizabeth Whipple (a researcher), February 29, 1943; children: Peter, Jane. *Education:* West Virginia University, B.S., 1940.

CAREER: During early career worked as silk dryer, process server, coal miner, and fruit picker; formed pioneer folk-singing group, The Almanacs, with Pete Seeger, Woody Guthrie, and Lee Hays, singing throughout America and recording a number of albums; author, and writer of song lyrics. *Military service:* U.S. Army Air Forces, 1943-46; became technical sergeant. *Member:* Dramatists Guild of Authors League of America, Writers Guild of America, Screenwriters Guild. *Awards, honors:* George Foster Peabody Award for "Sometime Before Morning"; Sidney Hillman Award and Anti-Defamation League Award for television play, "No Hiding Place"; eleven major awards for documentary films; Emmy award, 1965, for television production of "Eagle in a Cage."

WRITINGS: The Lonesome Train (cantata), Leeds, 1944; *The Long Way Home* (plays first produced on CBS on official Army Air Force program "First In the Air"), Messner, 1946; *The Hero* (novel), Messner, 1949; (with Sid Grossman, photographer) *Journey to the Cape,* (poems and dialogues), Grove, 1959; (compiler and author of script) Woody Guthrie, *California to the New York Island,* [New York], c.1960; (adapter) *The Wall* (play; produced on Broadway), Knopf, 1961, revised edition, Samuel French, 1964.

Other plays produced: "The Inheritance," 1964; "Jacob and the Angel," 1965; "Hard Travelin' " (one act), 1965. Writer of documentary and feature films, including "A Walk in the Sun," "Chance Meeting," "Eagle in a Cage," and, as adapter, "The Adventures of Augie March." Television plays include "No Hiding Place" for "East Side, West Side" program, a television treatment of "Eagle in a Cage" for "Hallmark Hall of Fame" and of "Hard Travelin' " for New York Television Theatre. Writer of songs, some of them included in published songbooks.

WORK IN PROGRESS: A novel, *The Castle,* for Atheneum.

SIDELIGHTS: The folk cantata *The Lonesome Train,* with music by Earl Robinson, was hailed by the *New York Times* as "an inspired and brilliant evocation of the American spirit." It was premiered over CBS, and performed in the Hollywood Bowl. The recorded version was played hundreds of times across the country as a spontaneous memorial tribute after the death of Franklin D. Roosevelt, and again after the assassination of John F. Kennedy. It has been translated into seven languages. Lampell has lived in England, France, Germany, and Israel, speaks French and German, and has done special work in Biblical archaeology.

*   *   *

LANE, Frank Walter 1908-

PERSONAL: Born August 15, 1908, in London, England; son of John Walter and Agnes Edith (Davis) Lane; married Barbara Katharine Mace, April 25, 1927; children: John Simon Mace, Jean Frances. *Home and office:* Drummoyne, Southill Lane, Pinner, Middlesex, England.

CAREER: British Civil Service, various positions, including work in a technical library, 1922-42; photographic agent specializing in natural history, 1943—; literary agent specializing in natural history, 1949—. Reader in natural history for Jarrolds Publishers Ltd., London, England. Speaker on more than one hundred British Broadcasting Corp. programs. *Member:* American Museum of Natural History, Royal Meteorological Society (fellow), Zoological Society of London (life fellow).

WRITINGS: Nature Parade, Jarrolds, 1939, revised edition, Jarrolds, 1944, Sheridan, 1954, 4th edition, revised, Jarrolds, 1955; *The Elements Rage,* Country Life, 1945, revised and enlarged edition published as *The Elements Rage: The Extremes of Natural Violence,* Chilton, 1965, new edition published in two volumes, Sphere, 1968; *Flight of Birds, Bats and Insects,* Daily Mail School-Aid Department, 1946; *Animal Wonderland: Essays in Natural History,* Country Life, 1948, revised edition, Oliver & Boyd, 1962, published in America as *Animal Wonder World: A Chronicle of the Unusual in Nature,* Sheridan, 1951, revised edition, Dufour, 1964; *Kingdom of the Octopus: The Life History of the Cephalopoda,* Jarrolds, 1957, Sheridan, 1960; (with Eric Hesking) *An Eye for a Bird: The Autobiography of a Bird Photographer,* Hutchinson, 1970. Contributor to journals in Great Britain, continental Europe, and United States.

SIDELIGHTS: Lane, considered a popularizer of science, feels that accuracy should never be sacrificed for sensationalism. "At the same time I strongly deprecate the attitude of some scientists that the world of Nature is the sole preserve of the technician. Everyman, who ultimately pays the scientist's salary, also has a right to be considered. And very few scientists have the necessary skill to translate their technicalities into simple, easily-understood prose." Lane's books have appeared in European translations.

BIOGRAPHICAL/CRITICAL SOURCES: Times Literary Supplement, July 6, 1967.

* * *

LANG, Barbara 1935-

PERSONAL: Born March 31, 1935, in New York, N.Y.; daughter of Bernard D. (a lawyer) and Fannie (Levy) Lang. Education: Cornell University, B.A., 1956. Home: 225 East 46th St., New York, N.Y. 10017. Agent: Robert Lantz Ltd., 111 West 57th St., New York, N.Y. 10019. Office: Rowland Co., 415 Madison Ave., New York, N.Y. 10017.

CAREER: Rowland Co. (public relations and publicity), New York, N.Y., vice-president, 1959—.

WRITINGS: Boys and Other Beasts (humor), Geis, 1964. Contributor of articles to McCall's and New York Times.

WORK IN PROGRESS: Two rhymed children's books; a humorous novel.†

* * *

LANGE, (Hermann Walter) Victor 1908-

PERSONAL: Born July 13, 1908, in Leipzig, Germany; came to United States in 1932; naturalized, 1943; son of Walter (a judge) and Dora (Schellenberg) Lange; married Frances Olrich, February 23, 1945; children: Dora, Thomas. Education: Studied at St. Thomas School, Leipzig, Germany, 1919-28, Oxford University, 1928, Sorbonne, 1929, University of Munich, 1929-30; University of Toronto, M.A., 1933; University of Leipzig, Ph.D., 1934. Politics: Democrat. Religion: Episcopalian. Home: 343 Jefferson Rd., Princeton, N.J. 08540. Office: Department of German Studies, Princeton University, Princeton, N.J. 08540.

CAREER: University of Toronto, Toronto, Ontario, lecturer in German literature, 1932-38; Cornell University, Ithaca, N.Y., assistant professor, 1938-42, associate professor, 1942-45, professor of German literature and chairman of department, 1945-57; Princeton University, Princeton, N.J., professor of German literature and chairman of department of German studies, 1957—, John N. Woodhull Professor of Modern Languages, 1969—. Free University of Berlin, honorary professor of German literature, 1963—. Visiting professor at universities in Europe and United States. Consultant to U.S. Department of State and to Educational Testing Service. Director of Goethe House, New York, N.Y., and Carl-Schurz-National Association. Member: International Association of Germanists (president, 1965-70), Modern Language Association of America (first vice-president, 1956), American Association of Teachers of German, Renaissance Society of America. Awards, honors: Guggenheim fellowship, 1951, 1966; Bundesverdienstkreuz, Germany, 1958.

WRITINGS: Die Lyrik und ihr Publikum im England des 18. jahrhunderts, H. Boehlaus (Weimar), 1935, also issued in part as inaugural dissertation, Die lyrische Anthologie im England des XVIII. jahrhunderts (1670-1780), [Leipzig], 1935; (with Hermann Boeschenstein) Kulturkritik und Literaturbetrachtung in Amerika [and] Irving Babbitt, amerikanischer humanist und kulturkritiker (the former by Lange, the latter by Boeschenstein), Priebatsch (Breslau), 1938; Bibliography, Intended to

Serve as a Select Handlist of Specific Contributions to the Recent Discussion of the Literary Aspects of the Biedermeier Period (reproduced from typewriting), [Ithaca], c.1938; Modern German Literature, 1870-1940, Cornell University Press, 1945; Goethe's Craft of Fiction, English Goethe Society, 1953; Forms of Contemporary German Poetry, 1954; Schlegel's Literary Criticism, Comparative Literature Studies, 1955; Narrative Forms in 18th Century Fiction, Anglia, 1958; Zu Schillers Poetik, Francke (Bern), 1961; Ausklang des 18. jahrhunderts, Francke, 1962; Sifter's Nachsommer, Bagel Verlag (Duesseldorf), 1963; Poets as Critics, Comparative Literature Studies, 1963; Fact in Fiction, Comparative Literature Studies, 1969; Language as the Topic of Fiction, E. Stahl, 1970.

Editor: (And author of introduction and notes) Deutsche briefe, Crofts, 1940; (editor. of German materials) Columbia Dictionary of Modern European Literature, Columbia University Press, 1946; (and translator) Johann Wolfgang von Goethe, The Sorrows of Young Werther, Rinehart, 1949; Goethe, Faust, Modern Library, 1950; (and author of introduction) Great German Short Novels and Stories, revised edition (Lange was not associated with earlier editions), Modern Library, 1952; Goethe, Wilhelm Meister, Collier, 1962; (and author of introduction and prefaces) Classical German Drama (five great plays), translated by Theodore H. Lustig, Bantam, 1963; (with others) Guenter Eich, Die Brandung vor Setubal [und] Das Jahr Lazertis, Harcourt, 1966; Bertolt Brecht, Der kaukasische Kreidekreis, Harcourt, 1966; Modern Literature, Volume II: Italian, Spanish, German, Russian and Oriental Literature, Prentice-Hall, 1968; Bertolt Brecht, Gedichte und Lieder aus Stuecken, Harcourt, 1968; (and author of introduction and prefaces Goethe: A Collection of Critical Essays, Prentice-Hall, 1968.

Author of introduction: Gothold E. Lessing, Hamburg Dramaturgy, Dover, 1962; Johann Wolfgang von Goethe, Elective Affinities, Regnery, 1963; Anthology of Contemporary German Poetry, New Directions, 1964. Contributor of articles on European and American literature to Yale Review, Saturday Review, New Republic, other magazines and journals. Co-editor, Comparative Literature, 1949—, Germanistik.

WORK IN PROGRESS: The Classical Union, to be published by Arnold.

AVOCATIONAL INTERESTS: Printing, wines, chamber music.

* * *

LANGFORD, Thomas Anderson 1929-

PERSONAL: Born February 22, 1929, in Winston-Salem, N.C.; son of Thomas A. Langford (insurance); married Ann Marie Daniel, December 27, 1951; children: Thomas Anderson III, James Howard, Timothy Daniel, Stephen Hughes. Education: Davidson College, A.B., 1951; Duke University, B.D., 1954, Ph.D., 1958. Religion: Methodist. Home: 2002 Dartmouth Dr., Durham, N.C. 27705.

CAREER: Duke University, Durham, NC., 1956—, began as assistant professor, became professor and chairman of department of religion.

WRITINGS: (Editor with George L. Abernethy) Philosophy of Religion, Macmillan, 1962, 2nd edition, 1968; (editor with Abernethy) History of Philosophy, Dickenson, 1965; The Ethical and Religious Thought of Walter Pater, Texas Christian University, 1967; (editor and author of introduction with William H. Poteat) Intellect and Hope: Essays in the Thought of Michael Polanyi, Duke University Press, 1968; In Search of Foundations: English Theology, 1900-1920, Abingdon, 1969; (with Abernethy) Introduction to Western Philosophy, Dickenson, 1970. Contributor of articles to *Christian Scholar, Interpretation, Religion in Life, Motive, Canadian Journal of Theology, Christian Advocate, Christian Century, Journal of Religion, Religious Studies, Scottish Journal of Theology.*

WORK IN PROGRESS: Writing on the nature of authority.

*   *   *

LANHAM, Edwin (Moultrie) 1904-

PERSONAL: Born October 11, 1904, in Weatherford, Tex.; son of Edwin Moultrie (a lawyer) and Elizabeth (Stephens) Lanham; married Joan Boyle, September, 1929 (divorced, 1936); married Irene Stillman, June 3, 1940; children: Evelyn (Mrs. Kazuto Ohira). *Education:* Attended Tome School, Port Deposit, Md., 1915-17, and Polytechnic Preparatory Country Day School, Brooklyn, 1921-22; Williams College, student, 1923-26; studied art in Paris, 1926-30. *Politics:* Democrat. *Home address:* Box 394, Clinton, Conn. 06413. *Agent:* Virginia Rice, 301 East 66th St., New York, N.Y. 10021.

CAREER: *New York Evening Post,* New York, N.Y., reporter, 1930-33; New York City News Association, New York, N.Y., reporter, 1934-39; *New York Herald Tribune,* New York, N.Y., rewrite man, 1939-44; freelance writer, 1944—. Justice of the peace, Clinton, Conn., 1950-60. *Member:* Authors League of America, Mystery Writers of America, Overseas Press Club, Phi Gamma Delta. *Awards, honors:* Guggenheim fellowship, 1940; Texas Institute of Letters award, 1942, for *Thunder in the Earth.*

WRITINGS: *Sailors Don't Care,* Contact Editions (Paris), 1929, Cape & Smith, 1930; *The Wind Blew West,* Longmans, Green, 1935; *Banner at Daybreak,* Longmans, Green, 1937; *Another Ophelia,* Longmans, Green, 1938; *The Stricklands,* Little, Brown, 1939; *Thunder in the Earth,* Harcourt, 1941; *Slug It Slay,* Harcourt, 1946; *It Shouldn't Happen to a Dog,* T.V. Boardman, 1947; *Politics Is Murder,* Harcourt, 1947.

One Murder Too Many, Harcourt, 1952; *Death of a Corinthian,* Harcourt, 1953; *The Iron Maiden,* Harcourt, 1954; *Death in the Wind,* Harcourt, 1956; *Murder on My Street,* Harcourt, 1958; *Double Jeopardy* (originally published as a serial, "I Married Murder," in *Saturday Evening Post,* 1958), Harcourt, 1959; *Six Black Camels,* Harcourt, 1961; *Passage to Danger,* Harcourt, 1962; *No Hiding Place,* Harcourt, 1962; *Monkey on a Chain,* Harcourt, 1963; *Speak Not Evil,* Farrar, Straus, 1964; *The Paste-Pot Man,* Farrar, Straus, 1967.

The Clock at 8:16, Doubleday, 1970. Contributor of short stories to *Saturday Evening Post, Collier's Esquire, Story, Ladies' Home Journal, Good Housekeeping, Redbook, Woman's Home Companion, Harper's Bazaar, Argosy, American,* and *McCall's.*

WORK IN PROGRESS: *Blue Heaven.*

BIOGRAPHICAL/CRITICAL SOURCES: *Book Week,* June 4, 1967; *National Review,* June 27, 1967; *Library Journal,* September 1, 1970.

*   *   *

LANNING, George (William), Jr.   1925-

PERSONAL: Born July 30, 1925, in Lakewood, Ohio; son of George William and Helen (Gravatt) Lanning. *Education:* New School for Social Research, student, 1946; Kenyon College, A.B., 1952. *Politics:* Democrat. *Religion:* Episcopalian. *Home:* 2167 Alger Rd., Lakewood, Ohio 44107. *Agent:* McIntosh & Otis, Inc., 18 East 41st St., New York, N.Y. 10017. *Office:* Educational Research Associates of America, Cleveland, Ohio.

CAREER: *Kenyon Review,* Gambier, Ohio, assistant editor, 1960-67, acting editor, 1964-65, editor, 1967-70. Lecturer in short story and novel at University of New Hampshire Writers' Conference and at Rocky Mountain Writers' Conference, University of Colorado. Visiting writer, Longwood College, 1963. *Member:* Phi Beta Kappa, Phi Kappa Sigma. *Awards, honors: Kenyon Review* fellowship in fiction, 1954-55.

WRITINGS: *This Happy Rural Seat* (novel), World Publishing, 1953; (with Robie Macauley) *Technique in Fiction,* Harper, 1964; *The Pedestal* (novel), Harper, 1966; *Green Corn Moon* (novel), Viking, 1968; (editor with Ellington White) *The Short Story Today: The Kenyon Review Symposium,* Kent State University Press, 1970. Short stories anthologized in *Best American Short Stories, Prize Short Stories: The O. Henry Awards.* Contributor to *Sewanee Review, Prairie Schooner,* other periodicals.

WORK IN PROGRESS: *Two Last Gasps of Alice Grant Rosman,* a novel; *The Coast of Erie,* a collection of short stories; a long historical novel, *Tyrconnell.*

AVOCATIONAL INTERESTS: Reading, dogs, working on his property.

BIOGRAPHICAL/CRITICAL SOURCES: *Times Literary Supplement,* February 2, 1967; *New York Times Book Review,* October 13, 1968; *Book World,* November 24, 1968; *Sewanee Review,* winter, 1969.

*   *   *

LAPPIN, Bernard William   1916-
(Ben Lappin)

PERSONAL: Born May 1, 1916, in Kielce, Poland; son of Louis (a teacher) and Sarah (Burstyn) Lappin; married, wife's name, Adah, June 19, 1949; children: Shalom, David, Naomi, Daniel. *Education:* McMaster University, B.A.; University of Toronto, diploma in social work, 1947; Training Bureau for Jewish Communal Service, New York, N.Y., certificate, 1950. *Religion:* Hebrew. *Office:* School of Social Work, University of Toronto, Toronto 181, Ontario, Canada.

CAREER: Joint Community Relations Committee of Canadian Jewish Congress and B'nai B'rith, Toronto, Ontario, executive secretary, 1942-46; Canadian Jewish Congress, Central Region, Toronto, Ontario, executive director, 1948-58; School of Social Work, University of Toronto, Toronto, Ontario, assistant professor of social work, 1958—. Member of National executive committee, Canadian Jewish Congress. *Member:* Canadian Association of Social Workers, Canadian Welfare Council.

WRITINGS: (Under name Ben Lappin) *The Redeemed Children: The Story of the Rescue of War Orphans by the Jewish Community of Canada,* University of Toronto Press, 1963; (with Murray George Ross) *Community Organization: Theory, Principles, and Practice,* 2nd edition, Harper, 1967; *Community Workers and the Social Role Tradition: Their Quest for a Role Examined in Israel and in Canada,* University of Toronto Press, 1971. Contributor of articles to *Commentary* and *Maclean's.* One of the writers for "Spring Thaw," a satirical review.

*   *   *

LARNER, Jeremy   1937-
(Orson Gouge)

PERSONAL: Born March 20, 1937, in Orlean, N.Y. *Education:* Brandeis University, B.A., 1958; graduate study, University of California, Berkeley, 1958-59. *Agent:* Candida Donadio, Robert Lantz-Candida Donadio Literary Agency, Inc., 111 West 57th St., New York, N.Y. 10019.

CAREER: Writer; principal speechwriter for Eugene McCarthy, presidential candidate, 1968. *Awards, honors:*

Delta Prize, 1964, for *Drive, He Said*; Aga Kahn Prize from *Paris Review* for best short story of 1964; Academy of Motion Picture Arts and Sciences Award (Oscar), 1972, for best original screenplay, "The Candidate."

WRITINGS: Drive, He Said (novel), Delacorte, 1964; (editor and author of introduction, from tape recordings by Ralph Tefferteller) *The Addict in the Street* (interviews with heroin addicts), Grove, 1965; *The Answer* (novel), Macmillan, 1968; (editor with Irving Howe) *Poverty: Views from the Left* (contains articles which first appeared in *Dissent*), Morrow, 1968; *Nobody Knows: Reflections on the McCarthy Campaign of 1968*, Macmillan, 1969; (with Jack Nicholson) "Drive, He Said" (screenplay adapted from his own novel), released by Columbia, 1971; "The Candidate" (screenplay), produced by Warner Brothers, 1972. Contributor to *Partisan Review, Dissent, Atlantic, New Republic, New Leader, Paris Review, Evergreen Review, Nation, Harper's, Life,* and other publications.

WORK IN PROGRESS: A realistic novel.

BIOGRAPHICAL/CRITICAL SOURCES: Saturday Review, October 10, 1964, March 6, 1965, April 6, 1968; *Book Week,* October 18, 1964; *New Republic,* November 14, 1964; *Commonweal,* April 2, 1965, August 28, 1970; *New York Review of Books,* April 11, 1968; *New Yorker,* May 18, 1958; *Book World,* March 1, 1970; *Time,* March 2, 1970, July 17, 1972; *New York Times Book Review,* March 15, 1970; *National Review,* April 28, 1970; *National Observer,* July 8, 1972; *Newsweek,* July 17, 1972.

*   *   *

LARSEN, Egon   1904-

PERSONAL: Surname originally Lehrburger; born July 13, 1904, in Munich, Germany; son of Albert David (a manufacturer) and Beatrice (Koenigsberger) Lehrburger; married second wife, Ursula Lippmann (a translator), July 3, 1940; children: (first marriage) Peter. *Education:* Educated in Munich, Germany. *Home:* 34 Dartmouth Rd., London N.W.2, England. *Agent:* Robert Harben, 3 Church Vale, London N.2, England.

CAREER: Self-employed author and journalist, 1928—. U.S. Office of Strategic Services, civilian staff, London, England, 1944-45; Radio Munich, London correspondent, 1954—; correspondent for *Suddeutsche Zeitung,* Munich, Germany, and for other Central European newspapers. *Member:* P.E.N. (English Centre, London; Centre of German-Speaking Authors Abroad). *Awards, honors:* Diesel Silver Medal, 1963.

WRITINGS: Inventor's Cavalcade (originally written in German but published in English), translation by Ernest W. Dickes, Lindsay Drummond, 1943, Transatlantic, 1946; *Inventor's Scrapbook,* Lindsay Drummond, 1947; *Spotlight on Films: A Primer for Film-Lovers,* Parrish, 1950; *Men Who Changed the World: Stories of Invention and Discovery,* Roy, 1952; *Radar Works Like This,* Roy, 1952, 3rd edition, Phoenix House, 1966; *An American in Europe: The Life of Benjamin Thompson, Count Rumford,* Philosophical Library, 1953; *Men Who Shaped the Future: Stories of Invention and Discovery,* Roy, 1954; *The Young Traveller in Germany,* Phoenix House, 1954, Dutton, 1955, 2nd edition, Soccer, 1961; *The True Book About Inventions,* Muller, 1954, published in America as *The Prentice-Hall Book About Inventions,* Prentice-Hall, 1955, 2nd edition (under original title), Soccer, 1961; *The True Book About Firefighting,* Muller, 1955, 2nd edition, 1962; *Men Under the Sea,* Phoenix House, 1955, Roy, 1956; *You'll See: Report from the Future,* Rider & Co., 1957; *Transistors Work Like This,* Roy, 1957, 2nd edition, Phoenix House, 1963; *Men Who Fought for Freedom,* Roy, 1958; *Atomic Energy: A Layman's Guide to the Nuclear Age,* Hennel Locke, 1958, also published as *Atomic Energy; The First Hundred Years: The Intelligent Layman's Guide to the Nuclear Age,* Pan Books, 1958; (editor) Franklyn M. Branley, *Solar Energy,* English edition, Edmund Ward, 1959; *Transport,* Roy, 1959; *Sir Vivian Fuchs,* Phoenix House, 1959, Roy, 1960; *Power from Atoms,* Muller, 1960, Soccer, 1961; *Ideas and Invention,* Spring Books, 1960; *A History of Invention,* Roy, 1961, revised edition, 1969; *The Atom,* Weidenfeld & Nicolson, 1961; *Film Making,* Muller, 1962; *The Cavendish Laboratory: Nursery of Genius,* F. Watts, 1962; (editor with Eric G. Linfield) *England vorwiegend heiter: Kleine Literaturgeschichte des britischen Humors* (originally written in English but published in German translation by Larsen and wife, Ursula Larsen), Basserman, 1962, reissued as *Laughter in a Damp Climate: 700 Years of British Humour,* Jenkins, 1963, Arc Books, 1965; *Atoms and Atomic Energy* (juvenile), John Day, 1963; (editor) Harry E. Neal, *Communication: From Stone Age to Space Age,* Phoenix House, 1963; (with son, Peter Larsen) *Young Africa,* Roy, 1964; *The Pegasus Book of Inventors,* Dobson, 1965: *Munich,* A.S. Barnes, 1966; (with Maurice F. Allward) *Great Inventions of the World,* Hamlyn, 1966; *The Deceivers: Lives of the Great Imposters,* Roy, 1966; *Great Ideas in Engineering,* edited by Patrick Pringle, Robert C. Maxwell, 1967; (editor with Linfield) *Great Humorous Stories of the World,* Arthur Barker, 1967; *First with the Truth: Newspapermen in Action,* Roy, 1968; *Carlo Pozzo di Borgo: One Man Against Napoleon,* Dobson, 1968; *Lasers Work Like This,* Roy, 1969; *Hovercraft and Hydrofoils Work Like This,* Dent, 1970, Roy, 1971; (editor) Peter Larsen, *The United Nations at Work Throughout the World,* Dent, 1970, Lothrop, 1971; *Great Ideas in Industry,* Robert C. Maxwell, 1971; *Strange Sects and Cults,* Arthur Barker, 1971, Hart Publishing, 1972.

Translator: Erich Weinert, *Stalingrad Diary,* I.N.G. Publications, 1944; *I Escaped from Nazi Germany: A French Deportee's Report,* I.N.G. Publications, 1944; *Free Germans in the French Maquis: The Story of the Committee "Free Germany" in the West,* I.N.G. Publications, 1945; Rene Felix Allendy and Hella Lobstein, *Sex Problems in School,* Staples, 1948; Franz Farga, *Violins and Violinists,* Rockliff, 1950; (with Joseph Avrach) Gustav K.H. Buescher, *The Boys' Book of the Earth,* Burke Publishing, 1960; (with Frank Pickering) Karl Stumpff, *Planet Earth,* University of Michigan Press, 1960. Editor of biographical series, "People from the Past," Dobson, 1963—. Occasional writer for, and director of, documentary films.

SIDELIGHTS: Foreign-language editions of Larsen's books have appeared in eleven European countries, Israel, Japan, Burma, and India (in Hindi, Urdu, Telugu).

BIOGRAPHICAL/CRITICAL SOURCES: Times Literary Supplement, August 17, 1967.

*   *   *

LARSON, Knute (G.)   1919-

PERSONAL: Born April 24, 1919, in Sweden; son of Gunnar A. (a machinist) and Agnes (Berg) Larson; married Ruth Dahlquist, August 21, 1941; children: Kris, Karen, Kristina. *Education:* Clark University, A.B., 1940, Ed.M., 1947; Columbia University, Ed.D., 1951. *Politics:* Democrat. *Religion:* Protestant. *Home:* 254 Wardwell Rd., Mineola, N.Y. 11501. *Office:* Mineola High School, Mineola, N.Y. 11501.

CAREER: Teacher and school administrator, 1945—, serving as high school principal in Cranston, R.I., 1954-63; Mineola High School, Mineola, N.Y., principal, 1963—. *Military service:* U.S. Naval Reserve, on active duty, 1941-45; became commander. *Member:* National

Education Association, National Association of Secondary School Principals, Phi Delta Kappa.

WRITINGS: (With Melvin R. Karpas) *Effective Secondary School Discipline,* Prentice-Hall, 1963; *Guide to Personal Advancement in the Teaching Profession,* Prentice-Hall, 1966; (with J.H. McGoldrick) *Handbook of School Letters,* Parker Publishing, 1970; *School Discipline in an Age of Rebellion,* Parker Publishing, 1972. Occasional contributor to educational journals.

* * *

LASER, Marvin 1914-

PERSONAL: Born November 2, 1914, in Chicago, Ill.; son of Harry and Ida (Preskill) Laser; married Dorothy Kort, February 8, 1948; children: Harvey Richard, Steven Alan. *Education:* Crane Junior College, Chicago, Ill., student, 1931-33; University of Chicago, Ph.B., 1935, M.A., 1937; Northwestern University, Ph.D., 1949. *Politics:* Democrat. *Home:* 3017 Palos Verdes Dr. W., Palos Verdes Estates, Calif. 90274. *Office:* California State College, Dominguez Hills, 1000 East Victoria St., Dominguez Hills, Calif. 90246.

CAREER: High school English teacher, Chicago, Ill., 1937-38; Wilson Junior College, Chicago, Ill., instructor in English, 1938-42, 1946-53; Chicago Teachers College, Chicago, Ill., professor of English, 1953-56; California State College, Los Angeles, professor of English, 1956-65, chairman of division of language arts, 1956-63; California State College, Dominguez Hills, professor of English and dean of School of Humanities and Fine Arts, 1965—. *Military service:* U.S. Army Air Forces, 1942-46; became captain. *Member:* American Studies Association, Modern Language Association of America, College English Association (director, 1959-62), National Council of Teachers of English, California Association of Teachers of English, Phi Beta Kappa. *Awards, honors:* Faculty fellow, Fund for the Advancement of Education, 1953-54; outstanding professor award, California State College, Los Angeles, 1965.

WRITINGS: (Principal author) *Television for the California State Colleges,* California State Printing Office, 1963; (editor with Robert S. Cathcart and Fred H. Marcus) *Ideas and Issues: Readings for Analysis Evaluation,* Ronald, 1963; (editor with Norman Fruman) *Studies in J.D. Salinger: Reviews, Essays, and Critiques of "The Catcher in the Rye" and Other Fiction,* Odyssey, 1963; (editor with John A. Dahl and others) *Student, School and Society: Cross-Currents in Secondary Education,* Chandler Publishing, 1964; (editor with John C. Bushman) *Scope/Reading,* four volumes, Harper, 1965-67; (with Bushman) *Language in Your Life,* four volumes, Harper, 1965-69; (editor with Bushman) *Channel One,* Dickenson, 1970. Contributor to *Junior College Journal, 19th Century Fiction,* and other literary and professional journals.

WORK IN PROGRESS: A study of critical approaches to modern American fiction.

* * *

LASS, Abraham H(arold) 1907-

PERSONAL: Born September 16, 1907, in Brooklyn, N.Y.; son of Samuel and Jennie Lass; married, wife's first name, Betty; children: Janet, Roger. *Education:* College of City of New York (now City College of the City University of New York), B.A., 1929; Columbia University, M.A., 1930. *Home:* 1384 East 10th St., Brooklyn, N.Y. 11230. *Office:* Abraham Lincoln High School, Ocean Parkway and West Ave., Brooklyn, N.Y. 11235.

CAREER: New York City (N.Y.) public schools, teacher of English, 1931-39, chairman of department of English, 1939-50, high school principal, 1950—, at Abra-

ham Lincoln High School, Brooklyn, 1955—. Lecturer in education at College of City of New York, Long Island University; conductor of workshops in teaching of English in other states; consultant to New York State Education Department and College Entrance Examination Board. *Member:* National Educational Association, National Association of Secondary School Principals, National Council of Teachers of English, Metropolitan School Study Council, Metropolitan Association for Study of the Gifted, New York Society for Experimental Study of Education, Civil War Round Table, Grand Street Boys.

WRITINGS: (Editor) Beirne Lay, *I Wanted Wings,* Harper, 1943; (editor) Mary O'Hara, *My Friend Flicka,* Lippincott, 1944; (with Rudolf Franz Flesch) *The Way to Write,* Harper, 1947, 3rd edition, McGraw, 1955; (editor with Earle L. McGill and Donald Axelrod) *Plays from Radio,* Houghton, 1948; (editor with Arnold Horowitz) *Stories for Youth,* Harper, 1950; (contributor) Arno Joseph Jewett and others, compilers, *Literature for Life,* Houghton, 1958; *Business Spelling and Word Power,* Donald, 1961; *How to Prepare for College,* Pocket Books, 1962, David White, 1963; (with Eugene S. Wilson) *The College Students' Handbook,* David White, 1965, revised edition, 1970; (editor) *A Students' Guide to 50 American Novels,* Washington Square Press, 1966; (editor) *A Students' Guide to 50 British Novels,* Washington Square Press, 1966; (editor with Brooks Wright) *A Students' Guide to 50 European Novels,* Washington Square Press, 1967; *Success in High School,* Scholastic Book Services, 1967; (editor with Milton Levin) *A Students' Guide to 50 American Plays,* Washington Square Press, 1969; (editor with Norma L. Tasman) *20 Great Short Stories,* New American Library, 1969; (editor with Tasman) *The Secret Sharer, and Other Great Stories,* New American Library, 1969; (compiler with Richard Henry Goldstone) *The Mentor Book of Short Plays,* New American Library, 1969; (editor) *Plot Guide to 100 American and British Novels: Plot Outlines, Character Analyses, Critical Evaluations; with a Special Introduction on How to Read a Novel,* Writer, Inc., 1971; (editor with Leonard Kriegel) *Masters. of the Short Story,* New American Library, 1971. Contributor of articles to *New York Times Magazine, Coronet,* and to professional journals. Columnist, *World Telegram, New York Post, New York Herald Tribune, Boston Traveler, New York Times.* Contributing and consulting editor, Scholastic Magazines; Member of advisory board, *Journal of Association of College Admissions Officers.*

* * *

LATHAM, Donald Crawford 1932-

PERSONAL: Born December 22, 1932, in Sayre, Pa.; son of Dayton Frederick (in advertising) and Helen (Crawford) Latham; married Mary Elizabeth Livingston, June 5, 1955; children: Sherrie Lizette, Gary Crawford. *Education:* The Citadel, B.S. in E.E., 1955; University of Arizona, M.S. in E.E., 1957; University of Arizona, E.E degree, 1965; Johns Hopkins University, additional postgraduate study. *Politics:* Republican. *Religion:* Methodist. *Home:* 81 Oakleigh Lane, Maitland, Fla. 32751. *Office:* Martin-Marietta Corp., Mail Point 449, P.O. Box 5837, Orlando, Fla. 33105.

CAREER: University of Arizona, Tucson, graduate assistant and instructor in electrical engineering, 1955-57, instructor, 1959-61, research associate, Applied Research Laboratory, 1961-63; Martin-Marietta Corp., Orlando, Fla., manager of Defensive Systems, 1963—. Consultant to National Security Agency and Atomic Energy Commission, Oakridge Physics Division; vice-chairman of Tucson-Pima County Civil Defense Commission, 1962-63. *Military service:* U.S. Air Force, assigned to National Security Agency, 1957-59. U.S. Air Force Reserve, 1959—;

now captain. *Member:* American Institute of Aeronautics and Astronautics, Institute of Electrical and Electronic Engineers, Air Force Association, Sigma Xi, Sigma Pi Sigma.

WRITINGS: (With Thomas L. Martin, Jr.) *Strategy for Survival,* University of Arizona Press, 1963; *Transistors and Integrated Circuits* (textbook), Lippincott, 1966. Contributor to published symposia on war games and electronics; writer of technical reports.

WORK IN PROGRESS: Fundamentals of Strategic Weapon Systems, covering technical aspects of U.S. and enemy strategic offensive and defensive systems, Strategic Arms Control, and U.S. survival.

* * *

LATHAM, Marte Hooper 1924-

PERSONAL: Born March 6, 1924, in Pittsburgh, Pa.; daughter of John Andrew and Blanche (Markle) Hooper; children: William G.H., Jr., Jacquelyn A.H. *Education:* University of Pittsburgh, student, 1942-45, B.A., 1959; University of Southern Illinois, student, 1958. *Religion:* Episcopalian. *Home address:* P.O. Box 22163, Ft. Lauderdale, Fla. 33315.

CAREER: Explorer; collector of rare animals and plants for scientific institutions and associations, including National Institute of Health, Mellon Institute, Smithsonian Institution, University of Michigan, Pfizer, Merck Sharpe & Dhome, Washington Zoo, Baltimore Zoo. Member of expeditions to Panama, Colombia, Ecuador, Peru, and Venezuela; has made two scientific discoveries, the giant earthworm of Colombia and the poison frog. Retired, 1967. Authority on procurement of South American animals, especially monkeys, for research. Professional lecturer. *Member:* National Academy of Sciences, Anteater Association (National Zoo, Washington, D.C.).

WRITINGS: (With John Hunt) *My Animal Queendom,* Chilton, 1962. Contributor to *National Geographic Magazine.*

WORK IN PROGRESS: A cook book, featuring functional recipes using vegetables and herbs for better health and sexual potency, and renewed vigour through aphrodisiac cooking.

* * *

LATTIMORE, Eleanor Frances 1904-

PERSONAL: Born June 30, 1904, in Shanghai, China; daughter of American nationals, David (a professor at Chinese universities, later at Dartmouth college) and Margaret (Barnes) Lattimore; married Robert Armstrong Andrews (a free-lance writer and designer), November 29, 1934 (died, 1963); children: Peter van Etten, Michael Cameron. *Education:* Educated at home by father; studied art at California School of Arts and Crafts, 1920-22, at Art Students League and Grand Central School of Art, New York, N.Y., 1924. *Home:* 324 Duke Rd., Lexington, Ky. 40502.

CAREER: Grew up in China, spent a year in Switzerland as a child, and came to United States with parents in 1920; after art school worked as a free-lance artist until 1930; writer of children's stories, and illustrator, mainly of own books, 1930—. Work exhibited in group shows at galleries in Boston, New York, and Charleston, S.C., and represented in permanent collections of libraries throughout the United States.

WRITINGS— Self-illustrated juveniles, all published by Morrow except as otherwise indicated: *Little Pear: The Story of a Little Chinese Boy,* Harcourt, 1931; *Jerry and the Pusa,* Harcourt, 1932; *The Seven Crowns,* Harcourt, 1933; *Little Pear and His Friends,* Harcourt, 1934; *Tur-*

kestan Reunion, Day, 1934; *The Lost Leopard,* Harcourt, 1935; *The Clever Cat,* Harcourt, 1936; *Junior, a Colored Boy of Charleston,* Harcourt, 1938; *Jonny,* Harcourt, 1939.

The Story of Lee Ling, Harcourt, 1940; *The Questions of Lifu: A Story of China,* Harcourt, 1942; *Storm on the Island,* Harcourt, 1942; *Peachblossom,* Harcourt, 1943; *First Grade,* Harcourt, 1944; *Bayou Boy,* 1946; *Jeremy's Isle,* 1947, *Three Little Chinese Girls,* 1948, *Davy of the Everglades,* 1949, *Deborah's White Winter,* 1949.

Christopher and His Turtle, 1950, *Indigo Hill,* 1950, *Bells for a Chinese Donkey,* 1951, *The Fig Tree,* 1951, *Lively Victoria,* 1952, *Jasper,* 1953, *Wu, the Gatekeeper's Son,* 1953, *Holly in the Snow,* 1954, *Diana in the China Shop,* 1955, *Willow Tree Village,* 1955, *Molly in the Middle,* 1956, *Little Pear and the Rabbits,* 1956, *The Journey of Ching Lai,* 1957, *The Monkey of Crofton,* 1957, *Fair Bay,* 1958, *Happiness for Kimi,* 1958, *The Fisherman's Son,* 1959, *The Youngest Artist,* 1959.

Beachcomber Boy, 1960, *The Chinese Daughter,* 1960, *Cousin Melinda,* 1961, *The Wonderful Glass House,* 1961, *The Bittern's Nest,* 1962, *Laurie and Company,* 1962, *Janetta's Magnet,* 1963, *The Little Tumbler,* 1963, *Felicia,* 1964, *The Mexican Bird,* 1965, *The Bus Trip,* 1965, *The Search for Christina,* 1966, *The Two Helens,* 1967, *Bird Song,* 1968, *The Girl on the Deer,* 1969.

The Three Firecrackers, 1970, *More About Little Pear,* 1971.

Illustrator: Bertha Metzger, *Picture Tales from the Chinese,* Stokes, 1934; E. Freivogel, *All Around the City,* Missionary Education Movement, 1938.

Contributor of short stories to *Jack and Jill, Story Parade, Trailways, American Junior Red Cross Magazine,*

SIDELIGHTS: Miss Lattimore's books have been translated for publication abroad, transcribed into Braille. and *Christian Science Monitor.*

BIOGRAPHICAL/CRITICAL SOURCES: Bertha E. Miller, *Illustrators of Children's Books 1946-56,* Horn Book, 1958.

* * *

LAUBER, Patricia (Grace) 1924-

PERSONAL: Born February 5, 1924, in New York, N.Y.; daughter of Hubert Crow (an engineer) and Florence (Walker) Lauber. *Education:* Wellesley College, B.A., 1945. *Agent:* McIntosh & Otis, Inc., 18 East 41st St., New York, N.Y. 10017.

CAREER: Look, New York, N.Y., writer, 1945-46; Scholastic Magazines, New York, N.Y., writer and editor, 1946-55; Street & Smith, New York, N.Y., editor-in-chief of *Science World,* 1956-59; Grolier, Inc., New York, N.Y., chief editor, science and mathematics, *The New Book of Knowledge,* 1961-66. Writer of children's books, 1954—.

*WRITINGS—*Juvenile nonfiction: *Magic Up Your Sleeve,* Teen-Age Book Club, 1954; *Battle Against the Sea: How the Dutch Made Holland,* Coward, 1956, revised edition, 1971; *Highway to Adventure: The River Rhone of France,* Coward, 1956; *Valiant Scots: People of the Highlands Today,* Coward, 1957; *Penguins on Parade,* Coward, 1958; *Dust Bowl: The Story of Man on the Great Plains,* Coward, 1958; *Rufus, the Red-Necked Hornbill,* Coward, 1958; *The Quest of Galileo,* Doubleday, 1959; *Changing the Face of North America: The Challenge of the St. Lawrence Seaway,* Coward, 1959, revised edition, 1968; *All About the Ice Age,* Random House, 1959; *Our Friend the Forest: A Conservation Story,* Doubleday, 1959; *All About the Planets,* Random House, 1960; *The Quest of Louis Pasteur,* Doubleday,

1960; *Getting to Know Switzerland,* Coward, 1960; *The Story of Numbers,* Random House, 1961; *Junior Science Book of Icebergs and Glaciers,* Garrard, 1961; *The Mississippi, Giant at Work,* Garrard, 1961; *Famous Mysteries of the Sea,* Thomas Nelson, 1962; *All About the Planet Earth,* Random House, 1962; *Your Body and How It Works,* Random House, 1962; *The Friendly Dolphins,* Random House, 1963; *Junior Science Book of Penguins,* Garrard, 1963; *The Congo, River into Central Africa,* Garrard, 1964; *The Surprising Kangaroos and Other Pouched Mammals,* Random House, 1965; *Big Dreams and Small Rockets: A Short History of Space Travel,* Crowell, 1965; *Junior Science Book of Volcanoes,* Garrard, 1965; *The Story of Dogs,* Random House, 1966; *The Look-It-Up Book of Mammals,* Random House, 1967; *The Look-It-Up Book of Stars and Planets,* Random House, 1967; *The Look-It-Up Book of the 50 States,* Random House, 1967; *Bats: Wings in the Night,* Random House, 1968; *The Planets,* Random House, 1968; *This Restless Earth,* Random House, 1970; *Who Discovered America?: Settlers and Explorers of the New World Before the Time of Columbus,* Random House, 1970; *Of Man and Mouse: How House Mice Became Laboratory Mice,* Viking, 1971; *Earthquakes: New Scientific Ideas About Why the Earth Shakes,* Random House, 1972; *Everglades: A Question of Life or Death,* Viking, 1973.

Juvenile fiction: *Clarence, the TV Dog,* Coward, 1955; *Clarence Goes to Town,* Coward, 1957; *Found: One Orange-Brown Horse,* Random House, 1957; *The Runaway Flea Circus,* Random House, 1958; *Clarence Turns Sea Dog,* Coward, 1959; *Adventure at Black Rock Cave,* Random House, 1959; *Champ, Gallant Collie,* Random House, 1960; *Curious Critters,* Garrard, 1969.

Contributor of adult short stories and light essays to magazines. Former editor, Coward's "Challenge Books" series.

WORK IN PROGRESS: Changing America: Cowboys and Cattle, for Crowell.

AVOCATIONAL INTERESTS: The theatre, music, animals, sailing, and travel.

* * *

LAUGHLIN, Florence Young 1910-

PERSONAL: Born June 1, 1910, in Crosby, N.D.; daughter of Richard E. and Ida (Morgan) Young; divorced; children: Andrea Louise, William R. *Education:* San Diego State College, student, 1928-30. *Home:* 2925 East Fifth St., Tucson, Ariz. 58716. *Agent:* Ruth Cantor, 156 Fifth Ave., Room 1005, New York, N.Y. 10010.

CAREER: Writer of books for young people.

WRITINGS: Sally's Lost Shoe, and Other Stories, Rand McNally, 1944; *The Little Leftover Witch,* Macmillan, 1960; *The Mystery of the McGilley Mansion,* Lothrop, 1963; *Mystery Mountain,* Macrae Smith, 1964; *The Seventh Cousin,* Macmillan, 1966; *The Horse from Topolo,* Macrae Smith, 1966; *Four to Get Ready* (picture book), Western Publishing Co., 1968; *Try Again, Sally* (picture book), Whitman Publishing, 1969. Contributor of stories and articles to magazines for adults and children, including *American Home, Jack and Jill.*

WORK IN PROGRESS: A historical novel for juniors.

SIDELIGHTS: Mrs. Laughlin concentrates on humorous mystery stories, believing that "if youngsters find fun in reading, they will make reading a lifelong habit."

* * *

LAUMER, (John) Keith 1925-

PERSONAL: Surname is pronounced *Law-*mer; born June 9, 1925, in Syracuse, N.Y. *Education:* University of

Stockholm, student, 1948; University of Illinois, B.Sc., 1950, B.Sc. in Architecture, 1952. *Residence:* Brooksville, Fla. *Agent:* Robert P. Mills, 156 East 52nd St., New York, N.Y. 10022.

CAREER: U.S. Army, 1943-46; U.S. Air Force, 1953-56; U.S. Foreign Service, vice-consul and third secretary in Rangoon, Burma, 1956-58; U.S. Air Force, 1960-65.

WRITINGS: How to Design and Build Flying Models, Harper, 1960, revised edition, 1970; *Worlds of the Imperium,* Ace Books, 1962, Dobson, 1968; *A Trace of Memory,* Berkley Publishing, 1963; *Envoy to New Worlds,* Ace Books, 1963, Dobson, 1970; *The Great Time Machine Hoax,* Simon & Schuster, 1964; *A Plague of Demons,* Berkley Publishing, 1965; *Galactic Diplomat: Nine Incidents of the Corps Diplomatique Terrestrienne,* Doubleday, 1965; *Embassy,* Pyramid Publications, 1965; *The Other Side of Time,* Berkley Publishing, 1965, Dobson, 1968; *The Time Bender,* Berkley Publishing, 1966; *Enemies from Beyond,* Pyramid Publications, 1966; *Retief's War,* Doubleday, 1966; *Catastrophe Planet,* Berkley Publishing, 1966, Dobson, 1970; (with Rosel George Brown) *Earthblood,* Doubleday, 1966; *The Monitors,* Berkley Publishing, 1966, Dobson, 1968; *Galactic Odyssey,* Berkley Publishing, 1966, Dobson, 1968; *Nine by Laumer,* Doubleday, 1967; (with Gordon R. Dickson) *Planet Run,* Doubleday, 1967; *The Invaders* (based on television series of same title, produced by Quinn Martin for ABC), Pyramid Publications, 1967; *The Avengers, No. 5: The Afrit Affair* (based on television series, "The Avengers," produced for British television by ITV Productions, subsequently networked on ABC), Berkley Publishing, 1968; *The Avengers, No. 6: The Drowned Queen* (based on television series), Berkley Publishing, 1968; *The Avengers, No. 7: The Gold Bomb* (based on television series), Berkley Publishing, 1968; *Retief and the Warlords,* Doubleday, 1968; *Assignment in Nowhere,* Berkley Publishing, 1968, Dobson, 1970; *Greylord,* Berkley Publishing, 1968; *The Day Before Forever* [and] *Thunderhead,* Doubleday, 1968; *The Other Sky,* Dobson, 1968; *Retief, Ambassador to Space: Seven Incidents of the Corps Diplomatique Terrestrienne,* Doubleday, 1969; *The Long Twilight,* Putnam, 1969 (short version published in *Galaxy* as "And Now They Wake," March, April, and May, 1969); *It's a Mad, Mad, Mad Galaxy* (includes "The Body Builders," "The Planet Wreckers," "The Star-Sent Knaves," "The War with the Yukks," and "Goobereality"), Berkley Publishing, 1969; *Time Trap,* Putnam, 1970; *The World Shuffler,* Putnam, 1970; *The House in November,* Putnam, 1970; *Beneath the Planet of the Apes* (based on the film of the same title produced by 20th Century-Fox), Bantam, 1970; *The Glass Tree,* Putnam, 1970; (editor and contributor) *Five Fates,* Doubleday, 1970; *The Star Treasure,* Putnam, 1971; *Retief of the CDT,* Doubleday, 1971; *Dinosaur Beach,* Scribner, 1971; *Once There Was a Giant,* Doubleday, 1971; *Deadfall,* Doubleday, 1971; *Retief's Ransom,* Putnam, 1971; *Timetracks,* Ballantine, 1972; *The Big Show,* Ace Books, 1972; *Night of Delusions,* Putnam, 1972; *The Infinite Cage,* Putnam, 1972; *The Shape Changer,* Putnam, 1972; *The Glory Game,* Doubleday, 1973.

Contributor of over forty short stories to *Galaxy, Fantasy and Science Fiction, If, Analog,* and other science fiction magazines; contributor of about thirty articles to *Young Men, American Modeler, Flying Models, Aeromodeller* (England), and similar periodicals.

WORK IN PROGRESS: Several novels, *The Swedish Adventure, Retief, Emissary to the Stars, Fort Ancient, Judson's Empire,* and *The Universe Maker.*

SIDELIGHTS: In 1969 Commonwealth United and Bell & Howell Productions produced a feature-length film of *The Monitors.*

BIOGRAPHICAL/CRITICAL SOURCES: National Review, January 12, 1971.

*   *   *

LAVIN, Mary   1912-

PERSONAL: Born June 11, 1912, in East Walpole, Mass.; taken to Ireland as a young girl and has lived there since; daughter of Thomas and Nora (Mahon) Lavin; married William Walsh (a Dublin lawyer), September 29, 1942 (died, 1954); married Michael MacDonald Scott, 1969; children: (first marriage) Valentine, Elizabeth, Caroline. Education: Early schooling in East Walpole, Mass., later studied at Loreto Convent, Dublin, Ireland; National University of Ireland, M.A. (first class honors), 1938. Religion: Roman Catholic. Home: Abbey Farm, Bective, County Meath, Eire; Mews 11, Lad Lane, Dublin, Eire.

CAREER: Novelist and short story writer, whose career as an author was set off by publication of a short story in the Dublin Magazine in 1938, and an award-winning collection of stories in 1942. Much of her writing for the past decade has been done at her farm home in Ireland's County Meath (she calls herself a writer and farmer), but she recently bought a disused mews in Dublin and converted it into a town residence while her daughters, one a law student, are being educated. Member: Irish Academy of Letters. Awards, honors: James Tait Black Memorial Prize for best book of fiction published in United Kingdom, 1944, for Tales from Bective Bridge; Guggenheim fellowships for fiction, 1959, 1961, 1962; Katherine Mansfield Prize, 1962, for The Great Wave, and Other Stories; D.Litt., National University of Ireland, 1968; Ella Lyman Cabot fellowship, 1969.

WRITINGS: Tales from Bective Bridge (short stories), Little, Brown, 1942; The Long Ago, and Other Stories, M. Joseph, 1944; The House in Clewe Street (novel), Little, Brown, 1945; The Becker Wives, and Other Stories, M. Joseph, 1946; At Sallygap, and Other Stories, Little, Brown, 1947; Mary O'Grady (novel), Little, Brown, 1950; A Single Lady, and Other Stories, M. Joseph, 1951; The Patriot Son, and Other Stories, M. Joseph, 1956; A Likely Story (juvenile), Macmillan, 1957; Selected Stories, Macmillan, 1959; The Great Wave, and Other Stories, Macmillan, 1961; The Stories of Mary Lavin, Constable, Volume I, 1964, Volume II, 1973; In the Middle of the Fields, and Other Stories, Constable, 1967, Macmillan, 1969; Happiness, and Other Stories, Constable, 1969, Houghton, 1970; Collected Stories, introduction by V.S. Pritchett, Houghton, 1971; A Memory, and Other Stories, 1972; The Second Best Children in the World (juvenile), Houghton, 1972. Short stories anthologized in numerous collections.

WORK IN PROGRESS: A collection of ten short stories.

SIDELIGHTS: Born in America and transplanted to Ireland at an early age, Mary Lavin is "Irish in thought and feeling, and the short story is her most natural form of expression," Edward Weeks writes. He quotes her as saying: " 'It is in the short story that a writer distills the essence of his thought. I believe this because the short story, shape as well as matter, is determined by the writer's own character. Both are one. Short-story writing—for me—is only looking closer than normal into the human heart.' " Jean Stubbs of Books believes "Miss Lavin possesses the strength of gentleness. A serene radiance illuminates all her writing: the radiance of one who observes, accepts and meditates on the human condition. She has, thank God, eschewed mere cleverness in favour of wisdom, so we hear no strident trumpets, no shattering drums. She invites us to contemplate with her the infinite sadness and beauty of the world, the divine inconse-

quence of life. . . . She will not allow us to stand by and marvel, she insists that we become participants."

In a review of In the Middle of the Fields, Roger Baker of Books and Bookmen notes "there is a curiously dated atmosphere about ... [these] stories; it is as though the world came to a halt in 1939. Ironically, this may be some kind of tribute to her ability to isolate characters in their own rigidly bounded worlds. She approaches her people and their emotional conflicts with rich, lyrical poeticism that transcends the business of mere topicality. But this failure to pinpoint a specific space in time is somehow detracting to the total effect." Her Collected Stories have drawn admiration from reviewers and prompted comparisons with "her most noticeable mentors in the genre, Chekhov and Mansfield, and James and Joyce. From them, presumably, she gets the soul, the brittle beauty, the social intricacy, and the technical virtuosity which are the trademarks of her work," according to R.J. Thompson of Canisius College. "In sum," he concludes, "these stories make apparent her position as one of the most artful and perceptive masters of the story form in our day, a fact well recognized by her Irish countrymen who regard her as the only living equivalent of O'Faolain and O'Flaherty."

The House in Clewe Street originally was published in serial form in the Atlantic Monthly under the title of "Gabriel Galloway," and seven of the stories in The Great Wave first appeared in the New Yorker. Another short story was used as the libretto of an opera by South African Eric Chisholm and performed at the South African Festival of Music in London.

BIOGRAPHICAL/CRITICAL SOURCES: Times Literary Supplement, February 16, 1967; Books and Bookmen, May, 1967; Books, January, 1970; New York Times Book Review, March 24, 1970; Library Journal, July, 1970; Atlantic, July, 1970; New York Times, July 2, 1971; Best Sellers, July 15, 1971; Saturday Review, August 7, 1971.

*   *   *

LAVRIN, Janko Matthew   1887-

PERSONAL: Born February 10, 1887, in Krupa, Austria (now Yugoslavia); became British citizen in 1937; son of John and Yera (Golobich) Lavrin; married Nora Fry (an artist), 1928; children: John, David. Education: Early schooling in Austria; university studies in Russia and Paris and at University of Oslo; M.A. Home: 28 Addison Gardens, London W.14, England.

CAREER: Journalist in St. Petersburg (now Leningrad), Russia, writing mainly in Russian and Slovene, 1910-15; war correspondent for a Russian newspaper at Serbian front and in Corfu, 1915-17; when Bolshevist revolution broke out went to London, England, and joined staff of New Age as writer; University of Nottingham, Nottingham, England, university lecturer, 1918-23, professor of Russian language and literature, 1923-52, emeritus professor, 1952—. Broadcaster and supervisor of languages, British Broadcasting Corp., 1939-45. Member: Slovene Academy of Sciences (corresponding), P.E.N., Slovene Authors' Club.

WRITINGS: Dostoevsky and His Creation: A Psycho-Critical Study, Collins, 1920; (author of historical preface) Kossovo: Heroic Songs of the Serbs, translation by Helen Rootham, Basil Blackwell, 1920; Ibsen and His Creation: A Psycho-Critical Study, Collins, 1921; Nietzsche and Modern Consciousness: A Psycho-Critical Study, Collins, 1922; Tolstoy: A Psycho-Critical Study, Collins, 1924; Gogol, Dutton, 1926; Russian Literature, Benn, 1927; Studies in European Literature, Constable, 1929, R.R. Smith, 1930; Aspects of Modernism, from Wilde to Pirandello, Stanley Nott, 1935, Books for Libraries, 1968; (author of preface) Vladimir Segyeevich Solov'ev, *Plato,* translation by Richard Gill, Stanley Nott, 1935.

An Introduction to the Russian Novel, Methuen, 1942, 3rd edition, Methuen, 1945, Whittlesey House, 1947; *Dostoevsky: A Study,* Methuen, 1943, 2nd edition, Methuen, 1943, Macmillan (New York), 1947; *Tolstoy: An Approach,* Methuen, 1944, Macmillan (New York), 1946; (editor) *Russian Poetry,* Reader 1, Basil Blackwell, 1945, International Universities Press, 1946; (author of introduction and notes) *Pushkin's Poems,* translation by Walter Morison, Allen & Unwin for Prague Press, 1945; (author of introductory essay) Nikolai Gogol, *Diary of a Madman, Nevski Prospect,* translation by Beatrice Scott, Lindsay Drummond, 1945; (editor and author of introduction) *A First Series of Representative Russian Stories: Pushkin to Gorky,* Westhouse, 1946; (editor and author of introduction) *A Second Series of Representative Russian Stories: Leskov to Andreyev,* Westhouse, 1946; (editor and author of introduction) *Russian Humorous Stories,* Sylvan Press, 1946; *Pushkin and Russian Literature,* Hodder & Stoughton for English Universities Press, 1947, Macmillan (New York), 1948; *From Pushkin to Mayakovsky: A Study in the Evolution of a Literature,* Sylvan Press, 1948, Greenwood Press, 1971; *Nietzsche: An Approach,* Methuen, 1948; *Ibsen: An Approach,* Methuen, 1950, Russell, 1969; *Nikolai Gogol, 1809-1852: A Centenary Survey,* Sylvan Press, 1951, Macmillan (New York), 1952; *Russian Writers: Their Lives and Literature,* Van Nostrand, 1954; *Goncharov,* Yale University Press, 1954; (author of introduction) William K. Matthews and Anton Slodnjak, editors, *The Parnassus of a Small Nation: An Anthology of Slovene Lyrics,* J. Calder, 1957, 2nd enlarged edition, edited by Lavrin and Slodnjak, Drzavna Zalozba, 1965; *Lermontov,* Hillary, 1959.

(Editor and author of preface) *An Anthology of Modern Yugoslav Poetry in English Translations,* J. Calder, 1962; (translator) France Filipic, *Neka druga dezila: Some Other Land: A Poetic Miscellany* (in Slovenian and English), Zalozba Obzorja, 1964; (author of critical and biographical profile) Fedor Dostoevskii, *Crime and Punishment,* translation by Constance Garnett, F. Watts, 1969; *Russian, Slavdom and the Western World,* Bles, 1969; *Neitzsche: A Biographical Introduction,* Studio Vista, 1971, Scribner, 1972; *A Panorama of Russian Literature,* University of London Press, 1972.

AVOCATIONAL INTERESTS: Travel and mountaineering.

*   *   *

LAWLOR, Monica (Mary)   1926-

PERSONAL: Born May 2, 1926, in London, England; daughter of Geofrey Leo Thomas and Eileen (Bouchier-Hayes) Lawlor. *Education:* Bedford College, London, B.A., 1948, Ph.D., 1959. *Religion:* Roman Catholic. *Office:* Bedford College, Regents Park, London N.W.1, England.

CAREER: Bedford College, University of London, London, England, assistant lecturer in psychology, 1949-53; University of Western Ontario, London, Ontario, research fellow in psychology, 1953-55; Bedford College, University of London, lecturer in psychology, 1955—. *Member:* British Psychological Society, Association for the Study of Animal Behaviour, British Aesthetics Society, Newman Association.

WRITINGS: Personal Responsibility, Hawthorn, 1963 (published in England as *Personal Responsibility: Growth and Limits,* Burns & Oates, 1963); *Out of This World: A Study of Catholic Values,* Sheed, 1965; (with Simon Clements) *The McCabe Affair,* Sheed, 1967. Contributor of articles to *Journal of Abnormal and Social Psychology,*

British Journal of Aesthetics, Advancement of Science, Life of the Spirit, Wiseman Review, and other journals.

WORK IN PROGRESS: A book on personality traits in animals.

AVOCATIONAL INTERESTS: Theology and painting.

BIOGRAPHICAL/CRITICAL SOURCES: Observer Review, November 19, 1967; *Times Literary Supplement,* December 21, 1967.

*   *   *

LAWNER, Lynn   1935-

PERSONAL: Born April 10, 1935, in Dayton, Ohio; daughter of Harry Leon (an attorney) and Irene (Fuchs) Lawner. *Education:* Wellesley College, B.A., 1957; graduate work at Cambridge University, 1957-58, University of Rome, 1958-60; Columbia University, graduate student, 1961-63, Ph.D., 1970. *Religion:* Jewish. *Home:* 531 Belmonte Park N., Dayton, Ohio. *Present address:* Via Adelaide Ristori, 42, Rome, Italy. *Agent:* Georges Borchardt, Inc., 145 East 52nd St., New York, N.Y. 10022.

MEMBER: Phi Beta Kappa. *Awards, honors:* Junior Durant Scholar, Wellesley College; first prize, Borestone Mountain Poetry awards, 1955; Henry fellowship, Newnham College, Cambridge University; Woodrow Wilson fellowship; Fulbright grant in Italy; American Association of University Women fellowship; faculty scholar fellow, Columbia University.

WRITINGS: Wedding Night of a Nun (poems), Little, Brown, 1964; *Triangle Dream, and Other Poems,* Harper, 1969; *Tanit Songs* (poems), Harper, 1971; (translator, compiler, and editor) *Letters from Prison by Antonio Gramsci,* Harper, 1971. Translations of poems by Umberto Saba for *Partisan Review;* translations of young Italian poets for *Chelsea;* translations of poems by Ungaretti for Academy of American Poets, and of other Italian poetry for Bollingen Project. Wrote series of radio programs for Italian Radio's Third Program on American Poetry, doing translations (into Italian) of Robert Lowell, Theodore Roethke, and Richard Wilbur. Contributor to *Botteghe Oscure XXV, Atlantic;* contributor to *New World Writing, No. 10,* New American Library, 1957, and to *Erotic Poetry,* edited by William Cole, Random House, 1963.

WORK IN PROGRESS: A new book of poems; a series of essays.

SIDELIGHTS: Miss Lawner has lived in Italy for several years. She has studied piano and has knowledge of French, Italian, Spanish, Latin, Provencal, and some German.

In 1966 she was commissioned by the Ford Foundation National Translation Center to translate Antonio Gramsci's *Lettere dal carcere* into English.

*   *   *

LAWSON, Ruth C(atherine)   1911-

PERSONAL: Born April 18, 1911, in Batavia, N.Y.; daughter of Frank Edward (a lawyer) and Mary (Burlingham) Lawson. *Education:* Zimmern School, Geneva, Switzerland, student, summer, 1932; Mount Holyoke College, A.B. (magna cum laude), 1933; Bryn Mawr College, M.A., 1934, Ph.D., 1947; additional summer study at University of Michigan, 1938, Academie de Droit International, The Hague, Netherlands, summer, 1939. *Religion:* Episcopalian. *Home:* 2 Jewett Lane, South Hadley, Mass. 01075. *Office:* Mount Holyoke College, South Hadley, Mass. 01075.

CAREER: Tulane University, New Orleans, La., instructor in political science and economics at Newcomb College, 1936-42; Mount Holyoke College, South Hadley, Mass., began as instructor, 1942, professor of political science on Alumnae Foundation, 1960—, chairman of department, 1957-63, 1968. Smith College, Geneva, Switzerland, associate professor of government and director of Smith College junior year of international studies, 1949-50; University of Massachusetts, professor of government in Bologna, Italy, summer, 1966; lecturer in Western Europe under U.S. Specialist grant, 1968; visiting fellow, Center for Contemporary European Studies and Institute for the Study of International Organization, University of Sussex, 1970-71. Director, World Affairs Council of the Connecticut Valley, 1957—, Atlantic Council of the United States, 1964—. *Member:* American Political Science Association (secretary, 1962-63), American Society of International Law (executive council, 1953-56, 1968—), International Studies Association (president, New England section, 1969-70), American Association of University Women, Phi Beta Kappa. *Awards, honors:* Guggenheim fellowship, 1956-57; North Atlantic Treaty Organization fellowship, 1959-60; fellow, American Society of International Law, 1962-63.

WRITINGS: (Editor and author of introductory notes) *International Regional Organizations: Constitutional Foundations,* Praeger, 1962. Contributor: N.J. Padelford, editor, *Contemporary International Relations, 1950-51,* Harvard University Press, 1951; L. Larry Leonard, editor, *Elements of American Foreign Policy,* McGraw, 1953. Contributor of more than fifty articles and book reviews to history, political science, and international law journals, and to *Collier's Year Book.*

WORK IN PROGRESS: NATO and the Problem of European Security.

AVOCATIONAL INTERESTS: Swimming, gardening, photography, travel, and English setters.

*   *   *

LAYMON, Charles Martin   1904-

PERSONAL: Born August 11, 1904, in Dayton, Ohio; son of Charles Burch and Sarah Pearl (Hinkle) Laymon; married Lillian Christina Stenberg, June 18, 1932 (died October, 1964); married Virginia Love Point, May 7, 1967; children: (first marriage) Douglas Burch, John Brooks, Sarah Mildred. *Education:* Ohio Wesleyan University, A.B., 1927; University of Edinburgh, graduate student, 1930-31; Boston University School of Theology, S.T.B., 1931, Th.D., 1941; Harvard University, graduate student, 1940. *Home address:* Box 174, Gatlinburg, Tenn. 37738. *Office:* Department of Religion, Florida Southern College, Lakeland, Fla. 33801.

CAREER: Ordained deacon in Methodist Episcopal Church, 1929, elder, 1931; associate pastor and pastor of congregations in Massachusetts and Ohio, 1924-29; Ohio Wesleyan University, Delaware, instructor in Bible, 1931-34; St. Paul Methodist Church, Delaware, Ohio, pastor, 1933-35; Union College, Barbourville, Ky., professor of Bible and philosophy, 1934-43; Scarritt College for Christian Workers, Nashville, Tenn., professor of literature and Bible history, and dean, 1943-50; Indianola Methodist Church, Columbus, Ohio, pastor, 1950-53; Board of Education, Methodist Church, Nashville, Tenn., editor of adult publications, 1953-60; Florida Southern College, Lakeland, chairman of department of religion, 1960-72, professor emeritus, 1973—. Member of general board of education and chairman of board of ministerial training and qualifications of Ohio Conference, Methodist Church, 1951-53. *Member:* National Education Association, National Association of Biblical Instructors, Franklin County Historical Society, Martha Kinney Cooper Ohioana Library Association, Tau Kappa Epsilon, Theta Alpha Phi, Civitan Club, Torch Club. *Awards, honors:* D.D., Ohio Wesleyan University, 1959; distinguished alumni, Boston University School of Theology, 1964.

WRITINGS: Readings in the Gospel of John, Upper Room, 1946; *The Bible: A Living Book,* Methodist Publishing House, 1947; *Great Prayers of the Bible,* Woman's Division of Christian Service, 1947; *Our Faith in Christ,* Methodist Publishing House, 1949; *A Primer of Prayer,* Tidings, 1949.

New Life in Christ, Tidings, 1950; *Great Moments in the Life of Christ,* Upper Room, 1950; *The Life and Teachings of Jesus,* Abingdon, 1955, revised edition, 1962; *I Follow Christ Above All,* Youth Department, General Board of Education of the Methodist Church, 1956; *Christ in the New Testament,* Abingdon, 1958; *Luke's Portrait of Christ,* Abingdon, 1959.

The Message of the Bible, Abingdon, 1960; *The Book of Revelation: Its Message and Meaning,* Abingdon, 1960; *The Teachings of Jesus for Evangelism,* Methodist Evangelistic Materials, 1961; *The Challenge of the Protestant Faith to Communism,* Methodist Evangelistic Materials, 1962; *The Use of the Bible in Teaching Youth,* Abingdon, 1963; *Thy Kingdom Come: Twenty-five Years of Evangelism,* General Board of Evangelism, Methodist Church, 1964; *Old Testament Survey Guide,* Abingdon, 1964; *New Testament Survey Guide: A Questionnaire,* Abingdon, 1964; *The Lord's Prayer in Its Biblical Setting,* Abingdon, 1968; (editor) *The Interpreter's One Volume Commentary on the Bible,* Abingdon, 1971. Editor, *International Lesson Annual,* Abingdon, 1956—. Contributor to church school publications and religious journals.

*   *   *

LAYTON, Thomas Arthur   1910-

PERSONAL: Born December 31, 1910, in London, England; son of Thomas Bramley (a surgeon) and Edney (Samson) Layton; married Eleanor Marshall; children: T.G., Alice. *Education:* Attended Bradfield College. *Religion:* Anglican. *Home:* Grindfield Farm, Furners Green, near Uckfield, Sussex, England.

CAREER: Wine merchant. Wine and Spirit Association of Great Britain, first public relations officer, 1951. *Miliary service:* British Army, Catering Corps, 1940-43; became second lieutenant.

WRITINGS: Five to a Feast, Duckworth, 1938; *Choose Your Wine,* Duckworth, 1940, 3rd edition, 1959; *Table for Two,* Duckworth, 1942; *Restaurant Roundabout,* Duckworth, 1944; *Dining Round London,* Transatlantic, 1945; *Wine's My Line,* Duckworth, 1955; *Choose Your Cheese,* Duckworth, 1957; *Wines and Castles in Spain,* M. Joseph, 1959; *Wines of Italy,* Harper Trade Journals, 1961; *Choose Your Vegetables,* Duckworth, 1963; *A Year at the Peacock* (autobiographical), Cassell, 1964; *Modern Wines,* Heinemann, 1964; (translator) Louis Jacquelin and Rene Poulain, *The Wines and Vineyards of France,* Putnam, 1962, revised edition, Hamlyn, 1965; *The Wine and Food Society's Guide to Cheese and Cheese Cookery,* Wine and Food Society and World Publishing, 1967; *Wines and Chateaux of the Loire,* Cassell, 1967; *Wines and People of Alsace,* Cassell, 1970. Contributor to some twenty journals. First editor, *Wine Magazine,* 1958; editor, *Anglo-Spanish Society's Quarterly Review,* 1960.

*   *   *

LAZEROWITZ, Morris   1907-

PERSONAL: Surname originally Laizerowitz; born October 22, 1907, in Lodz, Poland; son of Max (a businessman) and Etta (Plochinsky) Laizerowitz; married Alice Ambrose (a professor of philosophy at Smith College), June 15, 1938. *Education:* University of Nebraska, student, 1928-30; University of Michigan, A.B., 1933, Ph.D., 1936; Harvard University, postdoctoral study, 1936-37. *Home:* 31 Langworthy Rd., Northampton, Mass. 01060. *Office:* Department of Philosophy, Smith College, Northampton, Mass. 01060.

CAREER: Smith College, Northampton, Mass. 1938—, now Sophia and Austin Smith Professor of Philosophy. Bedford College, University of London, Fulbright Lecturer, 1951-52. *Member:* American Philosophical Association, Aristotelian Society, Royal Institution of Philosophy, National Council of Foreign Policy Association. *Awards, honors:* Alfred H. Lloyd postdoctoral fellowship from Horace H. Rackham School of Graduate Studies, University of Michigan, 1937-38.

WRITINGS: (With wife, Alice Ambrose) *Fundamentals of Symbolic Logic*, Rinehart, 1948, revised edition, Holt, 1962; *The Structure of Metaphysics*, Routledge & Kegan Paul, 1955, Humanities, 1963; (with Ambrose) *Logic: The Theory of Formal Inference*, 1961; *Studies in Metaphilosophy*, Humanities, 1964; (editor with William E. Kennick) *Metaphysics: Readings and Reappraisals*, Prentice-Hall, 1966; *Philosophy and Illusion*, Humanities, 1968; (editor and contributor with Ambrose) *G.E. Moore: Essays in Retrospect*, Humanities, 1970; (editor and contributor with Charles Hanly) *Psychoanalysis and Philosophy*, International Universities Press, 1971; (editor with Ambrose) *Ludwig Wittgenstein: Philosophy and Language*, Humanities, 1972. Contributor of articles and reviews to philosophical journals.

WORK IN PROGRESS: With wife, Alice Ambrose, *Philosophical Theories*, for Hutchinson.

*   *   *

LEABO, Dick A (lbert)   1921-

PERSONAL: Born October 30, 1921, in Walcott, Iowa; son of A.T. (a railway agent) and Clara (Beinke) Leabo; married Artis Van de Voort, June 11, 1955; children: Thomas William. *Education:* State University of Iowa, B.S., 1949, M.A., 1950, Ph.D., 1953. *Politics:* Democrat. *Religion:* Presbyterian. *Home:* 2424 Londonderry, Ann Arbor, Mich. 48104. *Office:* Graduate School of Business Administration, University of Michigan, Ann Arbor, Mich. 48104.

CAREER: University of Iowa, College of Commerce, Iowa City, assistant professor, and assistant director of Bureau of Business and Economic Research; 1948-56; Michigan State University, College of Business and Public Service, East Lansing, assistant professor, and assistant director of Bureau of Business and Economic Research, 1956-57; University of Michigan, Graduate School of Business Administration, Ann Arbor, associate professor, 1957-62, associate dean, 1962—, professor of statistics, 1963—. *Military service:* U.S. Army Air Forces, 1943-45; became first lieutenant; received Distinguished Flying Cross, Air Medal, Asiatic-Pacific theater ribbon with four battle stars. *Member:* American Statistical Association, American Economic Association, American Association of University Professors, National Association of Business Economists, Midwest Economics Association, Order of Artus (chapter secretary-treasurer, 1953-56), Phi Kappa Phi (University of Michigan chapter, executive committee, 1963-66, president, 1966-67).

WRITINGS: (With C. Frank Smith) *Basic Statistics for Business and Economics*, Irwin, 1960, 3rd edition (with Leabo as sole author) published as *Basic Statistics*, Irwin, 1968, 4th edition (sole author), 1972; (with Louis F. Hampel) *Workbook in Business and Economic Statistics*, 5th edition, Irwin, 1962.

Contributor as writer, consultant, or analyst; all published by Bureau of Business and Economic Research,

State University of Iowa: Robert H. Johnson, *An Analysis of Iowa Income Payments, By Countries*, 1949; Robert H. Johnson and Lewis E. Wagner, *A Comparative Study of the Tax Systems of Iowa and Surrounding States*, 1950; *Retail Trade Area Analysis, 11 Southwest Iowa Towns*, 1950; *Retail Trading Area Analysis, West Branch, Iowa*, 1951.

Monographs: *Retail Trade Area Analysis, Jefferson, Iowa*, Bureau of Business and Economic Research, State University of Iowa, 1951; (with C. Woody Thompson) *An Analysis of Residential Electric Bills in Iowa and Surrounding States*, Bureau of Business and Economic Research, State University of Iowa, 1951; *Selected Trends in Iowa Retail Sales and Use Tax Collections, 1939-52*, Bureau of Business and Economic Research, State University of Iowa, 1954; (with Floyd A. Bond and Alfred W. Swinyard) *Preparation for Business Leadership: Views of Top Executives*, Bureau of Business Research, University of Michigan, 1964.

Contributor to professional journals. Editor, *Iowa Business Digest*, 1948-56.

WORK IN PROGRESS: Stepwise Regression Analysis Applied to Regional Economic Analysis.

*   *   *

LEAR, Martha Weinman   1930-

PERSONAL: Born March 11, 1930, in Malden, Mass.; daughter of Joseph and Kenia (Pugach) Weinman; married Harold Alexander Lear (a physician), May 28, 1961. *Education:* Boston. University, B.S., 1950. *Residence:* West Hartford, Conn. *Agent:* Ashley Famous Agency, Inc., 1301 Avenue of the Americas, New York, N.Y. 10019.

CAREER: Collier's, New York, N.Y., associate editor, 1951-56; *Woman's Home Companion*, New York, N.Y., associate editor, 1956; National Broadcasting Co. Television, New York, N.Y., staff writer, 1957; *New York Sunday Times Magazine*, New York, N.Y., writer and editor, 1957-61. *Member:* Authors League of America, Society of Magazine Writers, American Newspaper Guild.

WRITINGS: The Child Worshippers, Crown, 1963. Contributor to *McCall's, Pageant*, and other publications.

WORK IN PROGRESS: Magazine articles.

*   *   *

LEARD, G (eorge) Earl   1918-

PERSONAL: Born September 5, 1918, on Prince Edward Island, Canada; son of G. Russell (a farmer) and Clara (Lockerby) Leard; married Elinor Harwood (a collegiate teacher), October 20, 1922; children: William Harwood, John Russell, Katherine Alison. *Education:* Prince of Wales College, student, 1935-36, 1938-41; Mount Allison University, B.A., 1944; Union Theological Seminary, New York, N.Y., M.A., 1947; Pine Hill Divinity Hall, B.D., 1950; advanced study at Cheshunt College, Cambridge, England, 1949-50, Columbia University, 1956-57; Syracuse University, Ph.D. candidate, 1970—. *Home:* 249 Poplar Dr., Oakville, Ontario, Canada. *Office:* Berkeley Studio, United Church of Canada, 315 Queen St. E., Toronto 2, Ontario, Canada.

CAREER: United Church of Canada, ordained minister, 1946, secretary for youth work, Board of Christian Education, Toronto, Ontario, 1947-49, director of youth work, Malwa Church Council, Malwa, India, 1950-60, assistant director of instructional communication, Berkeley Studio, Toronto, Ontario, 1961—.

WRITINGS: This Is Southern Asia: India, Pakistan, Ceylon, Nepal, Friendship, 1963. Editor, *Christian Teaching*.

LEARY, John P(atrick) 1919-

PERSONAL: Born October 30, 1919, in Spokane, Wash.; son of Patrick John and Agnes F. (Doyle) Leary. *Education:* Gonzaga University, B.A., 1944, M.A., 1945; Gregorian University, Ph.D., 1955. *Home and office:* New College of California, Sausalito, Calif. 94965.

CAREER: Entered Order of Society of Jesus, 1938, ordained Roman Catholic priest, 1951; Gonzaga University, Spokane, Wash., instructor, 1945-48, assistant professor, 1948-49, associate professor, 1949-55, professor of ethics, 1955-69, dean of education, 1955-58, director of summer sessions, 1956-69, academic vice-president and dean of faculties, 1958-61, president, 1961-69; Utah State University, Logan, professor of philosophy, 1969-70; University of Santa Clara, Santa Clara, Calif., vice-president, 1970-71; New College of California, Sausalito, founder and president, 1971—. Executive board member, United Crusade (Spokane). *Member:* Jesuit Educational Association, Association of American Colleges, Northwest Philology Association, Northwest Education Association (member of higher commission, 1963-69), Washington Education Association, Association of Independent Colleges of Washington (president, 1968-69). *Awards, honors:* Pageant Press award, 1960, for *Introduction to Education.*

WRITINGS: (Editor) *Better a Day,* Macmillan, 1951; (editor) *I Lift My Lamp: Jesuits in America,* Newman, 1955; *Introduction to Education,* Pageant, 1960; *Diamond Jubilee Reflections: Profile of a Pioneer University, 1887-1962,* Gonzaga University, 1961.

*   *   *

LEDERER, Ivo J(ohn) 1929-

PERSONAL: Born December 11, 1929, in Zagreb, Yugoslavia; came to United States in 1944, naturalized in 1952; son of Otto (a businessman) and Ruza (Oppenheim) Lederer; married Johanna Maria Marquardt, September 13, 1952; children: Michael Alexander, Philip Marquardt. *Education:* College of the City of New York (now City College of the City University of New York), student, 1947-49; University of Colorado, B.A., 1951; University of Virginia, graduate study, 1951-52; Princeton University, M.A., 1954, Ph.D., 1957. *Home:* 565 Arastradero, Palo Alto, Calif. 94306. *Office:* Department of History, Stanford University, Stanford, Calif. 94305.

CAREER: Yale University, New Haven, Conn., assistant professor, 1957-63, associate professor, 1963-65; Stanford University, Stanford, Calif., associate professor, 1965-68, professor of history, 1968—. *Member:* American Historical Association, American Association for the Advancement of Slavic Studies. *Awards, honors:* Ford Foundation fellow, 1954-57; Social Science Research Council fellow, 1958; Morse fellow, 1961-62; Rockefeller Foundation fellow, 1961-62; George Louis Beer Prize from American Historical Association, 1964.

WRITINGS: (Editor) *The Versailles Settlement: Was It Foredoomed to Failure?,* Heath, 1960; (editor, contributor, and author of introduction) *Russian Foreign Policy: Essays in Historical Perspective,* Yale University Press, 1962; *Yugoslavia at the Paris Peace Conference: A Study in Frontiermaking,* Yale University Press, 1963; (editor with Peter F. Sugar) *Nationalism in Eastern Europe,* University of Washington Press, 1969. Co-editor of Prentice-Hall's series on Russian civilization.

WORK IN PROGRESS: *Russia's Entry into World War I,* for Oxford University Press; a book of readings on the cold war.

SIDELIGHTS: Lederer is competent in Serbo-Croation, French, German, Italian, and Russian.

BIOGRAPHICAL/CRITICAL SOURCES: *Library Journal,* May 15, 1970.

*   *   *

LEE, Addison E(arl) 1914-

PERSONAL: Born June 18, 1914, in Maydell, Tex.; son of Earl (a teacher) and Alma (Fletcher) Lee; married Neta Warren, August 29, 1937; children: Donald Addison, Neta Susan. *Education:* Stephen F. Austin Teachers (now State) College, B.S., 1934; Texas Agricultural and Mechanical College, M.S., 1937; University of Texas, Ph.D., 1949. *Home:* 4506 Balcones Dr., Austin, Tex. 78731. *Office:* Science Education Center, Ed Annex F-13, University of Texas, Austin, Tex. 78712.

CAREER: Douglas High School, Douglas, Tex., 1934-36, began as biology teacher, became principal; Austin High School, Austin, Tex., 1937-46, began as biology teacher, became head of department; University of Texas, Austin, instructor and associate professor, department of botany, 1946-57, associate professor of botany, 1958-59, professor of science education and biology, director of Science Education Center, 1959—. Principal engineering aide, U.S. Public Health Service, summer, 1944; research associate, Mt. Desert Island Biological Laboratory, Salistury Cove, Me., summer, 1947; consultant, tissue culture laboratory, Harvard University, Cambridge, Mass., summer, 1949; visiting professor, University of Virginia, 1957-58. Austin Natural Science Center, member of board of directors.

MEMBER: American Association for Advancement of Science (fellow), Association for Education of Teachers in Science, American Institute of Biological Sciences, Botanical Society of America, National Association for Research in Science Teaching, National Science Teachers Association (president, 1967), National Education Association, National Association of Biology Teachers, Texas Academy of Science (honorary life fellow; program director of visiting scientist program), Texas State Teachers Association, Science Teachers Association of Texas, Sigma Xi, Phi Sigma, Phi Delta Kappa.

WRITINGS: (With Osmond P. Breland) *Laboratory Studies in Biology* Harper, 1954, 3rd edition, 1971; *Biology, the Science of Life,* Steck, 1958, revised edition, 1964; (with William Lee Evans) *The Fetal Pig: A Photographic Study,* Hemphill's Book Stores, 1954, revised edition, Rinehart, 1958; (with Evans and Earl R. Savage) *Development and Structure of the Frog: A Photographic Study,* Rinehart, 1959; *Laboratory and Field Studies in Biology,* Holt, 1960; (with Charles Heimsch) *Development and Structure of Plants: A Photographic Study,* Holt, 1962; (with others) *The Dogfish Shark: A Photographic Study,* Holt, 1963; *Plant Growth and Development: High School Biology—A Laboratory Block,* Heath, 1963; *Innovations in Techniques and Equipment in the Biology Teaching Laboratory,* Heath, 1963; (with Breland) *Biology in the Laboratory* (alternate edition to *Laboratory Studies in Biology*), Harper, 1965; (editor) *Research and Curriculum Development in Science Education,* Volume I, *The New Programs in High School Biology,* University of Texas Science Education Center, 1968.

Juveniles with David P. Butts: *Vanilla,* Steck, 1964; *The Story of Chocolate,* Steck, 1967; *Watermelon,* Steck, 1968. Contributor to scientific and educational journals.

*   *   *

LEE, C(hin)-Y(ang) 1917-

PERSONAL: Born December 23, 1917, in Hunan, China; came to United States in 1942, naturalized in 1949; son of Sun-an and Huang Li; married Joyce Lackey, April 15, 1963; children: Angela, Jay Ping. *Education:* National South-West Associated University, Kunming,

China, B.A.; Yale University, M.F.A. *Politics:* Democrat. *Religion:* Unitarian. *Home:* 5333 Ellenvale Ave., Woodland Hills, Calif. 91364. *Agent:* Ann Elmo Agency, Inc., 52 Vanderbilt Ave., New York, N.Y. 10017.

CAREER: Secretary to Sawbwa in Mangshih, China, 1941-43; *Chinese World,* San Francisco, Calif., editor, 1949-51; *Young China,* San Francisco, Calif., city editor, 1952-53; Asian Foundation, San Francisco, Calif., writer, 1953-55; U.S. Army Language School, Monterey, Calif., instructor, 1955-57. *Member:* Dramatists Guild, Authors League of America. *Awards, honors:* Commonwealth Club gold medal for fiction for *Flower Drum Song.*

WRITINGS: The Flower Drum Song, Farrar, Straus, 1957; *Lover's Point,* Farrar, Straus, 1958; *The Sawbwa and His Secretary: My Burmese Reminiscences,* Farrar Straus, 1959 (published in England as *Corner of Heaven: My Burmese Reminiscences,* W.H. Allen, 1960); *Madame Goldenflower,* Farrar, Straus, 1960; *Cripple Mah and the New Order,* Farrar, Straus, 1961; *The Virgin Market,* Doubleday, 1964; *The Land of the Golden Mountain,* Meredith, 1967.

WORK IN PROGRESS: "Sing Song Girls and Hatchetmen," for Ballantine.

SIDELIGHTS: Flower Drum Song was made into a Broadway musical in 1958 by Richard Rodgers and Oscar Hammerstein II, and later filmed.

BIOGRAPHICAL/CRITICAL SOURCES: Best Sellers, July 1, 1967.

*   *   *

LEE, Lincoln   1922-
   (Neil Collen)

PERSONAL: Born January 7, 1922, in Stockport, England; son of Harry and Florence (Harrison) Lee; married Helen McCallum, July 6 1945; children: Neil, Nicholas, Dougal. *Education:* Attended Stockport Grammar School. *Home:* The Croft, Ray Park Rd., Maidenhead, Berkshire, England.

CAREER: British South American Airways, captain, 1946-49; British Overseas Airways Corp., 1949—, now senior captain. *Military service:* Royal Air Force, 1939-46; became flight lieutenant. *Member:* Guild of Air Pilots and Navigators (United Kingdom), British Air Line Pilots Association, Institute of Navigation.

WRITINGS: Three-Dimensioned Darkness: The World of the Airline Pilot, Allen & Unwin, 1962, published in America as *Three-Dimensioned Darkness: The World of The Airline Pilot in the Jet Age,* Little, Brown, 1963. Con'ributor of regular column to *World Airports,* and articles to *Times, Observer, New Statesman,* and to aviation publications.

WORK IN PROGRESS: Articles for periodicals.

SIDELIGHTS: Three-Dimensioned Darkness has been translated into French and German.†

*   *   *

LEE, Mark W.   1923-

PERSONAL: Born January 23, 1923, in Akron, Ohio; son of Mark W. and Lura (Oliver) Lee; married Fern Erway, 1943; children: Sharon Anne, Mark, Jr., David, Rachel Jody. *Education:* Nyack College, student, 1940-43; Wheaton College, B.A., 1946, M.A., 1952; University of Minnesota, graduate study, 1950-56; University of Washington, Ph.D., 1966. *Home:* 881 Silver Ave., San Francisco, Calif. 94134. *Office:* Simpson Bible College, 801 Silver Ave., San Francisco, Calif. 94134.

CAREER: Northwestern College, Minneapolis, Minn., associate professor of speech and drama and chairman of the department, 1948-57; Whitworth College, Spokane,

Wash., associate professor, 1957-66, professor of speech and drama, 1967-70, chairman of the department, 1964-70, acting dean of faculty, 1969-70; Simpson Bible College, San Francisco, Calif., president, 1970—. Minister in several churches, 1943—. Public speaker at local, state, and national conventions. Member, Office of Emergency Preparedness. Consultant, Standard Oil of California, credit union leagues, churches, Washington State Board of Health, and Civil Service Commission and Veteran's Administration, 1960—. *Member:* Speech Communication Association of America, American Forensic Association, American Association of Presidents and Universities, Western Speech Association, Pi Kappa Delta (province secretary-treasurer, 1960-62; governor, 1964-66).

WRITINGS: So You Want to Speak: Hints and Helps for Public Speakers, Zondervan, 1951; *The Minister and His Ministry,* Zondervan, 1960; *Our Children Are Our Best Friends: Marriage Is a Family Affair,* Zondervan, 1970. Editor, journal of the Washington State Speech Association, 1965-66.

WORK IN PROGRESS: A book on counseling.

SIDELIGHTS: Lee is interested in library development.

*   *   *

LEE, Peter H(acksoo)   1929-

PERSONAL: Born January 24, 1929, in Seoul, Korea; son of Chong-guk (an educator and publisher) and Insuk (Hwangbo) Lee; married Catherine Y. Lee, August 25, 1962; children: Caroline, Joseph. *Education:* College St. Thomas, St. Paul, Minn., B.A., 1951; Yale University, M.A., 1953; University of Munich, Ph.D., 1958. Further study at University of Fribourg (Switzerland), 1954-55, Universities of Milan, Florence, Perugia, 1955-56, Oxford University, 1959. *Office:* Department of East Asian Literature, University of Hawaii, Honolulu, Hawaii 96822.

CAREER: Columbia University, New York, N.Y., assistant professor of Korean and Japanese, 1960-62; University of Hawaii, Honolulu, associate professor of Korean and comparative literature, 1962—. *Member:* Association for Asian Studies, American Oriental Society, American Comparative Literature Association, Chindan Society (Seoul, Korea). *Awards, honors:* Fellowships from American Council of Learned Societies, Bollingen Foundation, and Alexander von Humboldt-Stiftung.

WRITINGS: Studien zum Saenaennorae: Altkoreanische Dichtung (doctoral dissertation), University of Munich, 1958, enlarged edition published in America as *Studies in the Saenaennorae: Old Korean Poetry,* Paragon, 1959; (compiler and translator) *Kranich am Meer: Koreanische Gedichte,* Carl Hanser, 1959; *Korean Literary History,* American Council of Learned Societies, 1961; *Korean Literary Biographies,* American Council of Learned Societies, 1962; (compiler and translator) *Anthology of Korean Poetry, from the Earliest Era to the Present,* John Day, 1964; *Korean Literature: Topics and Themes,* published for Association for Asian Studies by University of Arizona Press, 1965; (compiler and translator) *Lives of Eminent Korean Monks: The Haedong Kosung Chon,* Harvard University Press, 1969. Contributor to journals, including *Hudson Review, Poetry, T'oung Pao, Oriens Extremus, Monumenta Serica, Journal of the American Oriental Society, Encyclopaedia Britannica.*

WORK IN PROGRESS: A study of heroic poetry in East and West.

SIDELIGHTS: Lee has revealed to *CA* that it was about him that the late poet Wallace Stevens wrote: "Last week I received a letter, greetings on my seventy-fifth birthday, from a young scholar, a Korean. When he was at New Haven, he used to come up to Hartford and the two of us would go out to Elizabeth Park, in Hartford, and sit on a bench by the pond and talk about poetry. He did not wait for the ducks to bring him ideas but always had in mind questions that disclosed his familiarity with the experience of poetry. He spoke in the most natural English. He is now studying in Switzerland at Fribourg, from where his letter came. It was written in what appeared to be the most natural French. Apparently they prize all-round young men in Korea, too."

Lee is deeply interested in the comparative study of Far Eastern and Western poetry and literary criticism. He is fluent in Chinese, Japanese, Korean, English, German, French, and Italian; he can read Spanish and Latin.

BIOGRAPHICAL/CRITICAL SOURCES: Wallace Stevens, *Opus Posthumous,* Knopf, 1957.

* * *

LEE, Robert E.A. 1921-

PERSONAL: Born November 9, 1921, in Spring Grove, Minn.; son of Knute A. (a merchant) and Mathilda (Glasrud) Lee; married Elaine E. Naeseth (a pianist), July 29, 1944; children: Margaret (Mrs. Frank Barth III), Barbara (Mrs. Eric Greenfeldt), Sigrid, Richard, Sylvia, Paul. *Education:* Luther College, Decorah, Iowa, B.A., 1942; additional study at New York University, 1947, and University of Minnesota, 1950. *Religion:* Lutheran. *Home:* 766 Lakeside Dr., Baldwin, N.Y. 11510. *Office:* Lutheran Council, 315 Park Ave. S., New York, N.Y. 10010.

CAREER: Lutheran Film Associates, New York, N.Y., executive secretary, 1954-72, with main assignment as film producer for Lutheran Church in America; Lutheran Council in the U.S.A., New York, N.Y., executive secretary, Division of Public Relations, 1969—. Luther-Film-Gesellshaft, Stuttgart, Germany, chairman of board of directors. National Council of Churches, member of board of managers of Broadcasting and Film Commission. Executive producer of films, "Question 7," 1961, "A Time for Burning," 1967, "Acts," 1970, "Which Way Wisdom?," 1970, and "The World of Martin Luther," "Before the Cock Crows," "Celebration of Learning." *Military service:* U.S. Naval Reserve, naval aviator, 1942-45; became lieutenant; received Distinguished Flying Cross and Air Medal. *Member:* Religious Public Relations Council (former preisdent; now governor), International Radio and Television Society.

WRITINGS: Question 7 (based on motion picture screenplay by Allan Sloane), Eerdmans, 1962; *Behind the Wall,* Eerdmans, 1963; (editor) *Martin Luther: The Reformation Years* (based on the film "Martin Luther"), Augsburg, 1967; (with Roger Kahle) *Popcorn and Parable: A New Look at the Movies,* Augsburg, 1971. Writer of radio, film, and filmstrip scripts.

WORK IN PROGRESS: Bach in Season, completed and awaiting publication.

SIDELIGHTS: Lee was originator of "Children's Chapel," a radio program started in 1949 and now carried by four hundred stations; he was also responsible for worldwide distribution of the motion picture, "Martin Luther."

* * *

LEE, Virginia (Yew) 1927-

PERSONAL: Born May 5, 1927, in San Francisco, Calif.; daughter of She Nam and Shee (Jone) Yew; married Howard F. Lee (an accountant), 1946; children: Dee Dee, Roberta. *Education:* Attended San Francisco State University. *Politics:* Democrat. *Home:* 1232 Fifth Ave., San Francisco, Calif. 90022.

AWARDS, HONORS: Gold medal, Commonwealth Club of California, 1963, for *The House That Tai Ming Built.*

WRITINGS: The House That Tai Ming Built, Macmillan, 1963; *The Magic North,* Seabury, 1972; (with Craig Claiborne) *The Chinese Cookbook,* Lippincott, 1972.

WORK IN PROGRESS: A novel, with background maerial gathered during extended stay in Hong Kong.

* * *

LEE, William R(owland) 1911-

PERSONAL: Born April 3, 1911, in Uxbridge, Middlesex, England; son of William Arthur (a headmaster) and Edith Bridget (Knight) Lee; married Zdena Marie Pausarova, July 9, 1948; children: Miriam Rosalie Zdena, Monica Caroline Janet. *Education:* University of London, Teacher's Diploma, 1934, M.A., 1954; University of Prague, Ph.D., 1950. *Home:* 16 Alexandra Gardens, Hounslow, Middlesex, England.

CAREER: Caroline University, Prague, Czechoslovakia, lecturer in English, 1946-50; Institute of Education, University of London, London, England, research fellow and lecturer, 1952-58, 1959-62. Conductor of teacher-training courses in Ceylon, India, Middle East, other countries, and of an "English by Radio" series for British Broadcasting Corp., 1960. British Council, linguistics adviser, 1958-59, now member of English studies advisory committee. University of London Convocation, member of standing committee, 1959—; Haverstock Comprehensive School, university representative governor, 1961—. *Military service:* British Army, 1940-45. *Member:* Linguistic Society of America, International Phonetic Association, International Society of Phonetic Sciences, International Association of Teachers of English as a Foreign Language (founder and chairman), Linguistic Society of Great Britain, English-Speaking Union, Royal Institute of International Affairs, Overseas Visual Aids Center, Noise Abatement Society, Society of Authors.

WRITINGS: English Intonation: A New Approach (originally published in *Lingua,* Volume V, no. 4), North-Holland Publishing Co., 1958; (with wife, Zdena Lee) *Teach Yourself Czech,* English Universities Press, 1959, 2nd edition, 1964: *Spelling Irregularity and Reading Difficulty in English,* Information Service, National Foundation for Educational Research in England and Wales, 1960, Fernhill, 1970; *An English Intonation Reader,* Macmillan, 1960; (with M. Dodderidge) *Time for a Song,* Longmans, Green, 1963; (with Helen Coppen) *Simple Audio-Visual Aids to Foreign-Language Teaching,* Oxford University Press, 1964, 2nd edition, 1968; *Language-Teaching Games and Contests,* Oxford University Press, 1965; (with Leonides Koullis) *The Argonauts' English Course for Greek-Speaking Children,* Oxford University Press, Book 1, 1965, Book 2, 1966, Book 3, 1968; *English at Home,* Oxford University Press, 1966; (editor) *English Language Teaching Selections 1 & 2: Articles from the Journal "English Language Teaching,"* Oxford University Press, 1967; *The Dolphin English Course,* Oxford University Press, 1969-71. Also author, with Dodderidge, of "Gramophone Records," Longmans, Green; author, with A.W.J. Barron, "Phonetic Wall Charts," Oxford University Press, 1964.

Translator: (With V. Fried) Vaclav Chaloupecky, *The Caroline University of Prague: Its Foundation, Character and Development in the Fourteenth Century,* Caroline University (Prague), 1948; (adapter with Zdena Lee, of additional chapters to 1919 edition) Tomas Garrigue Masaryk, The Spirit of Russia, 2nd edition, Allen & Unwin, 1955. Contributor to *Yearbook of Education, Lingua, Maitre Phonetique,* and other journals. Editor, *English Language Teaching.*

WORK IN PROGRESS: A Study and Practice Book of Contemporary English Usage, for Oxford University Press.

AVOCATIONAL INTERESTS: Playing piano, walking, the fine arts, and scientific developments.

* * *

LEERBURGER, Benedict A., Jr. 1932-

PERSONAL: Born January 2, 1932, in New York, N.Y.; son of Benedict A. (a lawyer) and Kathleen (Goodman) Leerburger; married Julie Loeb (a teacher), June 22, 1958; children: Marian, Ellen. *Education:* Colby College, B.A., 1954. *Home:* 338 Heathcote Rd., Scarsdale, N.Y. 10583. *Agent:* Curtis Brown, Ltd., 60 East 56th St., New York, N.Y. 10022. *Office:* National Micropublishing Corp., 31 Center St., Wilton, Conn. 06897.

CAREER: Associated with Grolier, Inc., 1956-61, and McGraw-Hill Book Co., 1961-63; Cowles Magazines and Broadcasting, Inc., New York, N.Y., managing editor of *Cowles Encyclopedia of Science, Industry, and Technology,* 1963-68; Crowell, Collier and Macmillan Information Corp., New York, N.Y., editor and director, 1968-70; National Micropublishing Corp., Wilton, Conn., vice-president and editorial director, 1970—. Editorial consultant, Chatham Press; book review editor of *Science Digest* and *Popular Science. Military service:* U.S. Navy, 1954-56. *Member:* National Association of Science Writers, History of Science Society, Society for the History of Technology. *Awards, honors:* National Safety Council Award for article in *Product Engineering.*

WRITINGS: Josiah Willard Gibbs, American Theoretical Physicist, F. Watts, 1963. Editor of *Product Engineering,* 1956-61; an editor, *Encyclopedia International,* 1961-62. Contributor to *Factory, Electrical Merchandising Week, Look, Venture, Science Digest, Book of Knowledge, Science News,* other journals.

WORK IN PROGRESS: A book on Antarctica and one on penguins.

* * *

LEES-MILNE, James 1908-

PERSONAL: Born August 6, 1908, in Worcestershire, England; son of George Crompton and Helen (Bailey) Lees-Milne; married Alvilde Bridges, 1951. *Education:* Attended Eton College 1921-26, and Grenoble University, 1927-28; Magdalen College, Oxford, M.A., 1931. *Politics:* Liberal. *Religion:* Roman Catholic. *Home:* Alderley Grange, Wotton-under-Edge, Gloucestershire, England.

CAREER: Private secretary to first Lord Lloyd of Dolobran, high commissioner to Egypt, 1931-34, and to Sir Roderick Jones, chairman of Reuters, 1934-35; National Trust, secretary of Historic Buildings Committee, 1936-51; architectural adviser to National Trust, 1951-66. *Military service:* British Army, Irish Guards, 1940-41; became second lieutenant; invalided. *Member:* Royal Society of Literature (fellow). *Awards, honors:* Heinemann Award, 1956, for *Roman Mornings.*

WRITINGS: (Editor and contributor) *The National Trust: A Record of Fifty Years' Achievement,* Batsford, 1945, 3rd edition, 1948; *The Age of Adam* (on the work and influence of Robert Adam and his brothers), Batsford, 1947; *National Trust Guide: Buildings,* Batsford, 1948; *Tudor Renaissance,* Batsford, 1951; *The Age of Inigo Jones,* Batsford, 1953; *Roman Mornings* (description of eight famous buildings in Rome), Wingate, 1956; *Baroque in Italy,* Batsford, 1959, Macmillan (New York), 1960; *Baroque in Spain and Portugal, and Its Antecedents,* Batsford, 1960; *Earls of Creation, Five Great Patrons of Eighteenth-Century Art,* Hamish Hamilton, 1962, London House, 1963; (author of in-

troduction) Harald Busch and Bernhard Lohse, editors, *Baroque Europe,* translated by Peter Gorge, Batsford, 1962; *Worcestershire: A Shell Guide,* edited by John Betjeman and John Piper, International Publications Service, 1964; *St. Peter's: The Story of St. Peter's Basilica in Rome,* Little, Brown, 1967; *Another Self,* Coward, 1970; *Baroque Country Houses,* Country Life, 1970.

Booklets on National Trust properties, all published for the National Trust by Country Life: *Charlecote Park, Warwickshire,* 2nd edition, 1946, 3rd edition, 1951; *Lyme Park, Cheshire,* 1948; *Blickling Hall, Norfolk,* 1948; *Stourhead, Wiltshire,* 1948, 6th edition, 1961; (with others) *Fenton House, Hampstead,* 1953; *Clivedon, Buckinghamshire,* 1953; *West Wycombe Park, Buckinghamshire,* 1953; *Coughton Court, Warwickshire,* 1954; (under initials J.L.-M.) *Florence Court, Co. Fermanagh,* 1954; (under initials J.L.-M., with J.F.R.) *Packwood House, Warwickshire,* 1954, 2nd edition, 1961; *Berrington Hall, Herefordshire,* 1958; *Mottisfont Abbey, Hampshire,* 1958; *The Vyne, Hampshire,* 1959; *Beningbrough Hall, Yorkshire,* 1961; *Melford Hall, Suffolk,* 1961. Contributor of reviews and articles to *Times Literary Supplement, Connoisseur, Apollo, Country Life,* and other publications.

SIDELIGHTS: Another Self was serialized on the BBC radio program "Woman's Hour" with such success in 1970 that it was repeated in 1971.

BIOGRAPHICAL/CRITICAL SOURCES: Times Literary Supplement, September 28, 1967, April 16, 1970; *Bookseller,* January 2, 1971.

* * *

LEFEVRE, Carl A. 1913-

PERSONAL: Surname is pronounced Lafave, to rhyme with "gave"; born January 14, 1913, in Cedar Rapids, Iowa; son of Charles A. (a teacher) and Kathryn Grace (a teacher; maiden name, Harrington) Lefevre. *Education:* Western Michigan University, B.A., 1934; University of Michigan, M.A., 1937; University of Minnesota, Ph.D., 1943. *Home:* 315 East Wadsworth Ave., Philadelphia, Pa. 19119.

CAREER: University of Minnesota, Minneapolis, instructor in English and speech, 1937-44; propaganda analyst, U.S. Office of War Information, then civilian editor, U.S. Navy, 1944-46; Washington University, St. Louis, Mo., assistant professor of English, 1946-49; Mankato State University, Mankato, Minn., associate professor of English, 1949-51; Pace College, New York, N.Y., professor of English and chairman of communication skills program, 1951-55; Chicago Teachers College, Chicago, Ill., associate professor of English, 1955-60; Northeastern Illinois State College, Chicago, professor of English and chairman, department of communication skills, 1960-66. *Member:* International Reading Association, American Educational Research Association, Linguistic Society of America, National Council of Teachers of English, Modern Language Association of America, Chicago Area Reading Association (president, 1958-60).

WRITINGS: Linguistics and the Teaching of Reading, McGraw, 1964; (with wife, Helen Lefevre) *Writing by Patterns,* Forms A and B, Knopf, 1965-68; (with Helen Lefevre) *English Writing Patterns* (grades 2-12), Random House and Singer, 1968; (with Helen Lefevre) *Oral/Written Practice in Standard English Forms,* Knopf, 1970; *Linguistics, English and the Language Arts,* Allyn & Bacon, 1970. Contributor to reports of International Reading Association, National Reading Conference, Lehigh Reading Conference, Pittsburgh Reading Conference, Temple University Annual Reading Institute; contributor of over fifty articles on language, literature, and reading to professional journals.

WORK IN PROGRESS: Senior author of a language-centered communication and humanities program, grades 3-6; senior author of Reading by Patterns: A Programmed Guide to Reading Sentences and Paragraphs.

* * *

LEFF, Gordon 1926-

PERSONAL: Born May 9, 1926, in London, England; son of Solomon Elvin (a company director) and Eva (Gordon) Leff; married Rosemary Kathleen Fox; children: Gregory Paul. Education: King's College, Cambridge, B.A. (honors) 1951, Ph.D., 1954. Politics: Socialst. Religion: Agnostic. Home: The Sycamores, 12, The Village, Strensall, York, Yorkshire, England. Office: Department of History, University of York, Hestington, Yorkshire, England.

CAREER: University of Manchester, Manchester, England, senior lecturer in history, 1956-65; University of York, York, England, reader, 1965-69, professor of history, 1969—. Fellow, King's College, Cambridge University, 1955-59. Military service: Royal Artillery, 1945-48; served in India.

WRITINGS: Bradwardine and the Pelagians: A Study of His "De Causa Dei" and Its Opponents, Cambridge University Press, 1957; Medieval Thought: St. Augustine to Ockham, Penguin, 1958; Gregory of Rimini: Tradition and Innovation in Fourteenth Century Thought, Barnes & Noble, 1961; The Tyranny of Concepts: A Critique of Marxism, Merlin Press, 1961, Dufour, 1963, 2nd edition, University of Alabama Press, 1969; Richard FitzRalph: Commentator of the Sentences, Barnes & Noble, 1964; John Wyclif: The Path to Dissent, Oxford University Press, 1966; Heresy in the Middle Ages: The Relation of Heterodoxy to Dissent, c.1250-c.1450, two volumes, Barnes & Noble, 1967; Paris and Oxford Universities in the Thirteenth and Fourteenth Centuries: An Institutional and Intellectual History, Wiley, 1968; History and Social Theory, University of Alabama Press, 1969. Contributor of articles to learned journals, and of reviews to Guardian, Spectator, Times Literary Supplement, and New Statesman.

WORK IN PROGRESS: A study of the thought of William of Odham (c.1290-1349).

AVOCATIONAL INTERESTS: Gardening, watching cricket, walking, reading, and listening to music.

BIOGRAPHICAL/CRITICAL SOURCES: Times Literary Supplement, January 25, 1968, August 29, 1969; New York Times Book Review, April 21, 1968; Virginia Quarterly Review, autumn, 1968.

* * *

LEGLER, Philip 1928-

PERSONAL: Born March 7, 1928, in Dayton, Ohio; son of Ellis Peter (a lawyer) and Mary (Ferguson) Legler; married Martha Prater, August 26, 1950; children: David Ferguson, Barbara Finley, Amy. Education: Denison University, B.A., 1951; State University of Iowa, M.F.A., 1953. Politics: Democrat. Religion: Episcopalian. Office: Department of English, Northern Michigan University, Marquette, Mich. 49855.

CAREER: Ohio University, Athens, instructor in English, 1953-56; Central Missouri State College, Warrensburg, assistant professor of literature, 1956-59; New Mexico Highlands University, Las Vegas, assistant professor of literature, 1959-60; Illinois Wesleyan University, Bloomington, assistant professor of literature, 1960-63; Sweet Briar College, Sweet Briar, Va., assistant professor of creative writing, 1963-66; Northern Michigan University, Marquette, associate professor of English, 1966—. Teller

in Building and Loan Association. Military service: U.S. Marine Corps, 1946-47; became sergeant.

WRITINGS: A Change of View (poems), University of Nebraska Press, 1964; The Intruder and Other Poems, University of Georgia Press, 1972. Anthologized in Midland: 25 Years of Fiction and Poetry Selected from the Writing Workshops of the State University of Iowa, edited by Paul Engle and others, Random House, 1961; Borestone Mountain Poetry Awards, 1968: A Compilation of Original Poetry Published in Magazines of the English-Speaking World in 1967, edited by Lionel Stevenson and others, Pacific Books, 1968; New York Times Book of Verse, edited by Thomas Lask, Macmillan, 1970, and Borestone Mountain Poetry Awards, 1970, edited by Lionel Stevenson and others, Pacific Books, 1971. Contributor to Poetry Perspective, Prairie Schooner, Western Review, New Mexico Quarterly, Mss, Motive, Commonweal, Choice, Poetry Northwest, Southwest Review, Epos, Elizabeth, Fiddlehead, Inscape, Sparrow Magazine, Antioch Review, Chelsea, Christian Century, Quarterly Review of Literature, Western Humanities Review, Shenandoah, American Scholar, and New York Times.

WORK IN PROGRESS: A volume of poems, Dale's Flower Shop.

SIDELIGHTS: Legler writes to CA: "I am trying to shape a poetry that is my own, that has its own voice and goes its own way. I have found, in the process of writing, that I have had to unlearn a great deal of what I was taught and of what I taught myself: of course every writer discovers this fact. The most difficult thing in writing, I feel, is to come to terms with yourself, to discover what you really do feel and think. Each poem should be a part of this discovery. Most of what I have written finds itself centered around the family, and the past, and memories. I've become fascinated with how much the past may limit or shape or dominate the present."

BIOGRAPHICAL/CRITICAL SOURCES: Prairie Schooner, summer, 1964; New Mexico Quarterly, summer, 1964; New York Times, September 13, 1964; Poetry, March, 1965; Detroit Free Press, January 28, 1973.

* * *

LEHMAN, Dale 1920-

PERSONAL: Born June 5, 1920, in Nevada, Iowa; son of Ernest L. (a farmer) and Julia (Volkert) Lehman; married Coryn Neff, June 21, 1942; children: Dennis, Linda, Roger. Education: Anderson College and Theological Seminary, B.Th.; Capitol University, A.B. Politics: Republican. Home: 1511 North Tillotson Ave., Muncie, Ind. 47304.

CAREER: Clergyman, Church of God. Minister in New Springfield, Ohio, 1944-47, Barberton, Ohio, 1947-54, and New Boston, Ohio, 1954—. Member: New Boston Ministerial Association (president, 1962-63).

WRITINGS: Living the Christian Life, Warner Press, 1963. Contributor of articles to Vital Christianity.

AVOCATIONAL INTERESTS: Traveling in U.S. West, numismatics, golf, bowling, gardening.

* * *

LEHMAN, F(rederick) K. 1924-

PERSONAL: Born February 5, 1924, in New York, N.Y.; son of D.H. (a lawyer) and Olga (Lurie) Lehman; married Sheila Geyer (an artist), December, 1955; children: Mark A., Charles F.A. Education: New York University, B.A. (cum laude), 1950; University of Pennsylvania, graduate work, 1953-54; Columbia University, Ph.D., 1959. Home: 209 West Henley St., Champaign, Ill. 61820. Office: Department of Anthropology, University of Illinois, Urbana, Ill. 61801.

CAREER: University of Illinois, Urbana, research associate and lecturer in anthropology and linguistics, 1952—. Member: American Anthropological Association, Royal Anthropological Institute, Linguistic Society of America, Association for Asian Studies.

WRITINGS: The Structure of Chin Society: A Tribal People of Burma Adapted to a Non-Western Civilization, University of Illinois Press, 1963; (contributor) J.H. Steward, editor, Asian Rural Societies, University of Illinois Press, 1968. Contributor to anthropological volumes.

WORK IN PROGRESS: Articles on grammar of Burmese and related languages.†

*   *   *

LEHMANN, John (Frederick)   1907-

PERSONAL: Born June 2, 1907, in Bourne End, Buckinghamshire, England; son of Rudolph Chambers (an author and member of Parliament) and Alice Marie (Davis) Lehmann. Education: Attended Eton College; Trinity College, Cambridge, B.A. Home: 85 Cornwall Gardens, London S.W.7, England. Agent: David Higham Associates Ltd., 5-8 Lower John St., London WIR 4HA, England; and A. Watkins, Inc., 77 Park Ave., New York, N.Y. 10016.

CAREER: Poet and journalist in Vienna, Austria, for several years prior to 1936; New Writing and Penguin New Writing, London, England, founder and editor, 1936-50; Hogarth Press, London, partner and general manager, 1938-46; John Lehmann Ltd. (publishers), London, founder and managing director, 1946-52; London Magazine, London, founding editor, 1953-61. Editor, "New Soundings," British Broadcasting Corp. Third Programme, 1952. Visiting professor, University of Texas, 1970-71; California State University, San Diego, 1971-72. Chairman of editorial advisory panel, British Council, 1952-58; president, Alliance Francaise in Great Britain, 1955-64, Royal Literary Fund, 1966—.

MEMBER: Royal Society of Literature (fellow), P.E.N., Bath Club, Garrick Club (all London). Awards, honors: Order of George I of Hellenes, 1954, Commander, 1961; Officer, Legion d'Honneur, 1958; Grand Officier, Etoile Noir, 1960; Prix du Rayonnement Francais, 1961; Commander, Order of the British Empire, 1964; Officier, Ordre des Arts et des Lettres, 1965.

WRITINGS: A Garden Revisited, and Other Poems, L. & V. Woolf, 1931; The Noise of History, Hogarth, 1934; Prometheus and the Bolsheviks, Cresset, 1937, Knopf, 1938; Evil Was Abroad, Cresset, 1938; Down River: A Danubian Study, Cresset, 1939; New Writing in England, Critics Group Press, 1939; New Writing in Europe, Penguin, 1940; Forty Poems, Hogarth, 1942; The Sphere of Glass, and Other Poems, Hogarth, 1944; The Age of the Dragon: Poems, 1930-51, Longmans, Green, 1951, Harcourt, 1953; The Open Night, Harcourt, 1952; Edith Sitwell, Longmans, Green for British Council and National Book League, 1952; The Whispering Gallery: Autobiography I, Longmans, Green, 1955; The Secret Messages, Overbrook Press, 1958; I Am My Brother: Autobiography II, Reynal, 1960; Ancestors and Friends, Eyre & Spottiswoode, 1962; Collected Poems, 1930-1963, Eyre & Spottiswoode, 1965; The Ample Proposition: Autobiography III, Eyre & Spottiswoode, 1966; A Nest of Tigers: The Sitwells in Their Times, Little, Brown, 1968 (published in England as A Nest of Tigers: Edith, Osbert and Sacherwell Sitwell in their Times, Macmillan, 1968); In My Own Time: Memoirs of a Literary Life (revised and condensed version of The Whispering Gallery, I Am My Brother, and The Ample Proposition), Little, Brown, 1969; Holborn: An Historical Portrait of a London Borough, Macmillan (London), 1970.

Editor: (With Denys Roberts and Gerald Gould) The Year's Poetry, three volumes, John Lane, 1934-36; (with T.A. Jackson and C. Day Lewis) Ralph Fox: A Writer in Arms, International Publishing, 1937; (with Stephen Spender) Poems for Spain, Hogarth, 1939; Demetrios Capetanakis: A Greek Poet in England, Lehmann, 1947, published in America as Shores of Darkness: Poems and Essays, Devin, 1949; (and author of introduction) Shelley in Italy: An Anthology, Lehmann, 1947; Orpheus: A Symposium of the Arts, Volume I, New Directions, 1948, Volume II, Lehmann, 1949; (with Day Lewis) The Chatto Book of Modern Poetry, 1915-55, Chatto & Windus, 1956, revised edition, 1959; The Craft of Letters in England: A Symposium, Cresset, 1956, Houghton, 1957; Coming to London, Phoenix House, 1957; (and author of introduction) Italian Stories of Today, Faber, 1959; Edith Sitwell, Selected Poems, Macmillan, 1965; (with Derek Parker) Edith Sitwell, Selected Letters, 1919-1964, Macmillan, 1970, Vanguard, 1971.

Editor, "New Writing" anthologies: New Writing: Spring, 1936, John Lane, 1936; New Writing: Autumn, 1936, John Lane, 1936; New Writing: Spring, 1937, Lawrence & Wishart, 1936, Knopf, 1937; New Writing: Fall, 1937, Knopf, 1937; (with Christopher Isherwood and Stephen Spender) New Writing: Fall, 1938, Knopf, 1938; (with Isherwood and Spender) New Writing: Spring, 1939, Hogarth, 1939; New Writing: Christmas, 1939, Hogarth, 1939; The Penguin New Writing, Penguin, 1940; Folios of New Writing, four volumes, Hogarth, 1940-41; New Writing and Daylight: Summer, 1942, Hogarth, 1942; New Writing and Daylight: Winter, 1942-43, Hogarth, 1943; New Writing and Daylight: Summer, 1943, Hogarth, 1943, Transatlantic, 1944; New Writing and Daylight: Winter, 1943-44, Hogarth, 1944; New Writing and Daylight: Autumn, 1944, Hogarth, 1944, Transatlantic, 1945; New Writing and Daylight: 1945, Hogarth, 1945; New Writing and Daylight: 1946, Lehmann, 1946, New Directions, 1947; Poems from New Writing, 1936-46, Lehmann, 1946; French Stories from New Writing, Lehmann, 1947, published in America as Modern French Stories, New Directions, 1948; Best Stories from New Writing, Harcourt, 1951 (published in England as English Stories from New Writing, Lehmann, 1951); Pleasures of New Writing: An Anthology of Poems, Stories and Other Prose Pieces, Lehmann, 1952. Represented in many anthologies, including Poems of Today, third series, Macmillan, 1938, Penguin Book of Contemporary Verse, Penguin, 1962, Chatto Book of Modern Poetry, edited by Lehmann and C. Day Lewis, Chatto & Windus, 1956, revised edition, 1959, An Anthology of Modern Verse, 1940-1960, edited by Elizabeth Jennings, Methuen, 1961, New Poems, 1963: A P.E.N. Anthology, edited by Patricia Beer and others, Hutchinson, 1963; Poetry of the Thirties, edited by Robin Skelton, Penguin, 1964, and Terrible Rain: The War Poets, 1939-1945, edited by Brian Gardner, Methuen, 1966. Advisory editor, Geographical Magazine, 1940-45; founder and editor, Orpheus, 1948-49.

SIDELIGHTS: Known primarily for his achievements as an editor and publisher, Lehmann was responsible for putting in print some of the first and significant works of such authors as George Orwell, Stephen Spender, Christopher Isherwood, Jean-Paul Sartre, C. Day Lewis, Boris Pasternak, Louis MacNeice, Bertolt Brecht, Paul Bowles, Lawrence Durrell, Edith Sitwell, and Theodore Roethke. Brother of author Rosamond Lehmann and actress Beatrix Lehmann, he has been described by Michael Holroyd, among others, as "one of the most distinguished editors in 20th-century English literature." His poetry has been recorded for the collections of the British Council, Library of Congress, and Harvard University Library.

AVOCATIONAL INTERESTS: Aquatic.

BIOGRAPHICAL/CRITICAL SOURCES: New Statesman, May 31, 1968; Punch, June 5, 1968; New York
Times Book Review, September 22, 1968, October 12,
1969; Book World, September 22, 1968, July 20, 1969;
Prairie Schooner, spring, 1969; New York Times, June 2,
1969; Harper's, July, 1969; Saturday Review, July 12,
1969; New Republic, July 12, 1969; National Observer,
July 21, 1969, Virginia Quarterly Review, autumn, 1969.

*   *   *

LEHMANN-HAUPT, Hellmut (Emile)   1903-

PERSONAL: Born October 4, 1903, in Berlin, Germany;
came to United States, 1929; became U.S. citizen, 1936;
son of Carl F(riedrich) (a historian) and Therese (a playwright; maiden name Haupt) Lehmann-Haupt; married
Letitia Grierson, August 19, 1933 (divorced, 1947); married Rosemarie Mueller, March 11, 1948; children: (first
marriage) Christopher, Carl Andrew, H Alexander; (second marriage) John Peter, Roxana. Education: Schulp-
forta, Thuringia, Germany, graduated, 1922; attended
Universities of Berlin and Vienna; University of Frankfurt, Ph.D., 1927. Religion: Christian. Politics: Democrat. Home: 55 East End Ave., New York, N.Y. 10028,
and New Preston, Conn. Office: H.P. Kraus, Rare Books,
16 East 46th St., New York, N.Y. 10017.

CAREER: Apprentice to a bookseller; Gutenberg Museum, Mainz, Germany, junior curator, 1927-29; Encyclopaedia Britannica, New York, N.Y., indexing editor for
14th edition; Marchbanks Press, New York, N.Y., proofreader; Columbia University, New York, N.Y., curator,
rare book department and instructor, 1930-37, assistant
professor of book arts, 1937-50; New School for Social
Research, New York, N.Y., research principal, 1950-52;
H.P. Kraus, Rare Books, bibliographical consultant,
1952—. Visiting lecturer, Smith College, 1939-41; visiting
professor, University of Illinois, 1940; bibliographical
lecturer, Pratt Institute, 1954-55. Wartime service: Office of War Information, in Europe, 1943-45; U.S. Military Government in Berlin, officer with monuments, fine
arts, and archives branch, 1946-48. Member: Bibliographical Society of America, Gutenberg Gesellschaft,. Grolier
Club. Awards, honors: Rockefeller Foundation grants,
1950-52, 1956.

WRITINGS: Schwaebische Federzeichnungen: Studien
zur Buchillistration Augsburg im 15. Jahrhundert, Walter
de Gruyter (Berlin), 1929, translation by Lehmann-Haupt
published as Book Illustration in Augsburg in the Fifteenth Century (originally published in Metropolitan Museum Studies, volume IV, part I, February, 1932), Metropolitan Museum of Art, 1932.

Five Centuries of Book Design: A Survey of Styles in
the Columbia Library (pamphlet; originally published in
Columbia University Quarterly, June, 1931), Columbia
University School of Library Service, 1931; Lewis Car-
roll, 1832-1932 zum 100. Geburstag, H. Reichner (Vi-
enna), 1932; Russiche Buchholzschnitte, 1840-1850,
Gutenberg-Gesellschaft (Mainz), 1932; Fifty Books
About Bookmaking: Exhibition Prepared by Columbia
University Library for the Twelfth Annual Conference on
Printing Education, June 26, 27, 28, 1933, Columbia Uni-
versity Press, 1933, 2nd edition published as Seventy
Books About Bookmaking: A Guide to the Study and
Appreciation of Printing, 1941, 3rd edition published as
One Hundred Books About Bookmaking: A Guide to the
Study and Appreciation of Printing, 1949; (translator
with wife, Letitia Lehmann-Haupt) Bernhard Ludwig
Diebold, editor, Book of Good Deeds, 1914-1918, Farrar,
Straus, 1933; Ein vollstaendiges Exemplar des xylo-chiro-
graphischen Antichrist, Gutenberg-Gesellschaft, 1934;
Modern Bookbinding (exhibition at Columbia Univer-
sity), Columbia University, 1935; (editor and author of

introduction) A Catalogue of the Epstean Collection on
the History and Science of Photography and Its Applica-
tion to the Graphic Arts, Columbia University Press,
1937; (with Ruth S. Grannis and Lawrence C. Wroth)
Das amerikanische Buchwesen: Buchdruck und Buchhan-
del, Bibliophilie und Bibliothekswesen in den Vereinigten
Staaten von den Anfaengen bis zur Gegenwart, K.W.
Hiesemann (Leipzig), 1937, revised edition, translation by
Lehmann-Haupt published as The Book in America: A
History of the Making, the Selling, and the Collecting of
Books in the United States, Bowker, 1939, 2nd revised
edition (with Wroth and Rollo G. Silver), 1951; The
Heritage of the Manuscript (originally published in Dol-
phin, no. three, 1938), [New York], 1938.

English Illustrators in the Collection of George Arents
(originally published in Colophon, volume I, no. 4,
1940), [New York], 1940; In Search of the Frontispiece
(originally published in Garden Club of America, May,
1940), [New York], 1940; (editor and contributor with
Hannah Dustin French and Joseph W. Rogers) Bookbind-
ing in America: Three Essays, Southworth-Anthoensen
Press, 1941; (with Samuel Ives) An English 13th Century
Bestiary: A New Discovery in the Techniques of Medieval Illumination, H.P. Kraus, 1942; The Terrible Gustave
Dore (originally a lecture given before the Grolier Club,
December 14, 1939), Marchbanks Press, 1943; (editor)
Neue deutsche Gedichte, F. Krause, 1946; (translator)
Carl Linfert, Zeichnungen und Graphik lebender deut-
scher Kuenstler: Ausgewaehlt von einer Gruppe von
Deutschen und Amerikanern in Berlin, Gebr. Mann (Ber-
lin), 1947; (editor) Cultural Looting of the "Ahnnerbe,"
Office of Military Government, Monuments, Fine Arts
and Archives Section (Berlin), 1948; (author of introduc-
tion) Abraham Horodisch, Initials from French Incunab-
ula, Aldus Book Co., 1948.

Peter Schoeffer of Gernheim and Mainz: With a List of
His Surviving Books and Broadsides, Printing House of
Leo Hart, 1950; For Nearly Five Centuries, Oxford University Press, 1953; Art Under a Dictatorship: An Account of Art in Nazi Germany and in Soviet Russia, Oxford University Press, 1954; The Life of a Book: How
the Book Is Written, Published, Printed, Sold, and Read,
Abelard, 1957.

(Editor) Current Trends in Antiquarian Books, University of Illinois Graduate School of Library Science, 1961;
Gutenberg and the Master of the Playing Cards (lecture
originally given at the Rare Book Conference, Coral Gables, June, 1962, and published in Gutenberg Jahrbuch,
1962), Yale University Press, 1966; (editor) Homage to
a Bookman: Essays on Manuscripts, Books and Printing
Written for Hans P. Kraus on His 60th Birthday, October 12, 1967, Gebr. Mann, 1967; On the Rebinding of
Old Books (originally published in Bookbinding in America, Southworth-Anthoensen Press, 1941), Bowker, 1967;
(editor and author of commentary) The Goettingen Model
Book: A Facsimile Edition and Translation of 15th Century Illuminator's Manual, University of Missouri Press,
1972.

Contributor to Gutenberg Jahrbuch, Encyclopedia Americana, Encyclopaedia Britannica, and to professional journals including Publishers Weekly, Print, Columbia University Quarterly, Papers of the Bibliographical Society of
America, College and Research Libraries.

WORK IN PROGRESS: Long range projects concerning
the social history of the graphic arts.

SIDELIGHTS: Highly regarded as an expert in his field,
Lehmann-Haupt has more than two hundred items of
writing to his credit. He told CA: "My dominating interest has been the history of books, writing, and printing,
seen aesthetically as an art, sociologically as a major
form of visual communication, and technologically as

evolution from personal craftsmanship to industrial mass production. [I am] greatly concerned with preservation of personal freedom of expression in these areas [and have] also [a] continuing interest in the relationship between government and art, especially in totalitarian abuse of art and artists." G.W. Gilkey praised *Art Under a Dictatorship* as a "very courageous and scholarly book [which] might well be considered a key to an understanding of the history of the visual arts under the dictatorships of the twentieth century. . . . The peculiarly well-qualified Dr. Lehmann-Haupt views the whole problem with the detachment of a political scientist and the understanding of a creative artist."

AVOCATIONAL INTERESTS: Golf, hunting, and fishing.

BIOGRAPHICAL/CRITICAL SOURCES: Saturday Review, June 24, 1939, July 12, 1941, June 19, 1954; *Publishers Weekly,* July 8, 1939, July 21, 1951, November 5, 1950, December 7, 1959; *New York Times,* August 27, 1939, March 30, 1941, October 12, 1941, June 6, 1954, December 22, 1957; *Times Literary Supplement,* October 21, 1939, January 26, 1951, July 6, 1951, April 13, 1967, January 25, 1968; *Books,* December 31, 1939, July 27, 1941; *Christian Century,* April 23, 1941, October 20, 1954; *Library Journal,* January 1, 1942, January 1, 1952, June 1, 1954, December 15, 1957, January 15, 1967; *New York Herald Tribune Book Review,* August 19, 1951; *Commonweal,* May 28, 1954, November 15, 1957; *New Yorker,* May 29, 1954, February 4, 1967; *Chicago Sunday Tribune,* July 4, 1954; *American Historical Review,* October, 1954; *American Sociological Review,* December, 1954; *New York Times Book Review,* January 22, 1967; *Atlantic,* March, 1967; *Choice,* April, 1967.

*   *   *

LEHNUS, Opal (Hull)   1920-
(Opal Hull)

PERSONAL: Born May 13, 1920, in Summitville, Ind.; daughter of John I. (a farmer) and Ida (Clary) Hull; married Lyle L. Lehnus (a farm store manager), June 20, 1959. *Education:* Anderson College, student, one year; Ball State Teachers College (now Ball State University), B.S., 1951, M.A., 1958. *Religion:* Church of God. *Home:* 76 15th St., Logansport, Ind. 46947.

CAREER: School art supervisor in Rochester, Ind., two years, Elwood, Ind., one year; high school art teacher in Logansport, Ind., nine years. Teacher of handcrafts in youth church camps for ten summers. *Member:* Indiana State Teachers Association, Indiana Art Teachers Association, Delta Phi Delta (life), Delta Kappa Gamma.

*WRITINGS—*As Opal Hull: *More Chalk Talks,* Warner Press, 1952; *Creative Crafts for Churches,* Warner Press, 1958; *Creative Artcrafts for Churches,* Warner Press, 1963; *Something New in Chalk Talks,* Warner Press, 1972. Contributor of short devotional articles to church booklets.

*   *   *

LEIBOWITZ, Irving   1922-

PERSONAL: Born August 5, 1922, in New York, N.Y.; son of Max (a restaurateur) and Frieda (Shiner) Leibowitz; married Frieda Greenwald, December 10, 1950; children: Marilyn; (step-children) Dennis Howard, Alan Leslie. *Education:* Bordertown Military Institute, student, 1937. *Politics:* Independent. *Religion:* Jewish. *Home:* 5537 Beaver Crest Dr., Lorain, Ohio 44053. *Office:* Lorain Journal, 1657 Broadway, Lorain, Ohio 44052.

CAREER: Reporter in Suffolk, Va., 1945-46, sports editor in Portsmouth, Va., 1946-47, and state editor in Mansfield, Ohio, 1947-48; *Indianapolis Times,* Indianapo-

lis, Ind., staff member, 1948-66, columnist, 1951-61, assistant managing editor, 1954-60, managing editor, 1960-66; *Lorain Journal,* Lorain, Ohio, editor, 1966—. Founder and director, Indiana Press Institute, 1958—. Guest lecturer, Indiana University, 1960. Director, 500 Festival. *Military service:* U.S. Army, 1940-45; became sergeant; received Bronze Star; U.S. Marine Corps Reserve, 1958—; now major. *Member:* American Society of Newspaper Editors, Indiana Editors of United Press International (former president), Sigma Delta Chi (former president), Indianapolis Press Club (former president). *Awards, honors:* Indianapolis Junior Chamber of Commerce distinguished service award, 1957.

WRITINGS: My Indiana, Prentice-Hall, 1964. One-time regular contributor to *American Peoples Encyclopedia* and *World Book.†*

*   *   *

LEIGH, James L(eighton)   1930-

PERSONAL: Surname is pronounced *Lee;* born May 24, 1930, in Santa Monica, Calif.; son of Leonard (an actor) and Lily King (Westervelt) Leigh-Valles; married; children: a son. *Education:* San Jose State College, B.A., 1957; graduate study at Stanford University, 1957-58. *Home:* Jose Antonio 25, Fuengirola, Malaga, Spain. *Agent:* Lynn Nesbit, International Famous Agency, 1301 Avenue of the Americas, New York, N.Y. 10019.

CAREER: San Francisco State College, San Francisco, Calif., assistant professor of English, 1954-65. *Awards, honors:* Joseph Henry Jackson Literary Award, 1962, for *What Can You Do?*

WRITINGS: What Can You Do? (novel), Harper, 1965; *Downstairs at Ramsey's* (novel), Harper, 1968; *The Rasmussen Disasters* (novel), Harper, 1969. Contributor of short stories to magazines.

WORK IN PROGRESS: Four novels, tentatively titled *Little Summer, The Pure Products of America, Miss King's People,* and *Green, Green.*

SIDELIGHTS: What Can You Do? was filmed as "Making It," and released by Twentieth Century-Fox, 1970.

BIOGRAPHICAL/CRITICAL SOURCES: New York Times, March 2, 1968, March 22, 1971; *Observer Review,* April 28, 1968; *Spectator,* May 3, 1968; *Commonweal,* May 10, 1968.

*   *   *

LEIGHTON, Margaret (Carver)   1896-

PERSONAL: Born December 20, 1896, in Oberlin, Ohio; daughter of Thomas Nixon (a professor at Oberlin College and Harvard University) and Flora (Kirkendall) Carver; married James Herbert Leighton, May 5, 1921 (died, 1935); children: James Herbert, Jr., Mary (Mrs. Carson Thomson), Thomas Carver, Sylvia (Mrs. Douglas Wikle). *Education:* Studies at schools in Cambridge, Mass., France and Switzerland; Radcliffe College, A.B., 1918. *Politics:* Republican. *Religion:* Protestant. *Home:* 226 Palisades Ave., Santa Monica, Calif. 90402. *Agent:* McIntosh & Otis, Inc., 18 East 41st St., New York, N.Y. 10017.

CAREER: Resident of Westfield, N.J., and Ballston, Va., 1921-35; after husband's death moved to California and started writing books for children. Westfield (N.J.) Board of Education, member, 1930-34. Member of Board of Trustees, Santa Monica (Calif.) Public Library. *Member:* Authors League of America, P.E.N. (president, Los Angeles center, 1957-59). *Awards, honors:* Commonwealth Club of California silver medal, 1945, for *The Singing Cave;* Dorothy Canfield Fisher Memorial Children's Book Award, 1958, for *Comanche of the Seventh;*

Alumnae Achievement Award, Radcliffe College, 1968; Southern California Book Council award, 1971.

WRITINGS—All juvenile or youth books: Junior High School Plays: Ten Short Plays on the American Epic, Samuel French, 1938; The Secret of the Old House, Winston, 1941; Twelve Bright Trumpets, Houghton, 1942 (published in England as The Conqueror, and Other Tales from the Middle Ages, Harrap, 1945); The Secret of the Closed Gate, Winston, 1944; The Singing Cave (Junior Literary Guild selection), Houghton, 1945; Judith of France, Houghton, 1948; The Sword and the Compass: The Far-Flung Adventures of Captain John Smith, Houghton, 1951; The Secret of Bucky Moran, Farrar, Straus, 1952; The Story of Florence Nightingale, Grosset, 1952; The Story of General Custer, Grosset, 1954; Who Rides By?, Farrar, Straus, 1955; Comanche of the Seventh, Farrar, Straus, 1957; The Secret of Smugglers' Cove, Farrar, Straus, 1959; Journey For a Princess, Farrar, Straus, 1960; Bride of Glory: The Story of Elizabeth Bacon Custer (Junior Literary Guild selection), Farrar, Straus, 1962; Voyage to Coromandel, Farrar, Straus, 1965; The Canyon Castaways, Farrar, Straus, 1966; A Hole in the Hedge, Farrar, Straus, 1968; Cleopatra, Sister of the Moon, Farrar, Straus, 1969; The Other Island, Farrar, Straus, 1971.

WORK IN PROGRESS: Another novel for older girls.

SIDELIGHTS: The characters of the four Hill children in the "Secret" books are based on Mrs. Leighton's own four children.

*   *   *

LEISK, David Johnson   1906-
(Crockett Johnson)

PERSONAL: Born October 20, 1906, in New York, N.Y.; son of David and Mary (Burg) Leisk; married Ruth Krauss (a writer and poet), 1940. Education: Studies at Cooper Union, 1924, New York University, 1925. Residence: Rowayton, Conn.

CAREER: Former art editor of several magazines, now geometric painter, book illustrator, and writer. Drew weekly panel, "Little Man with the Eyes," for Collier's, 1938-41, syndicated newspaper comic strip, "Barnaby," 1941-62, syndicated newspaper panel, "Barkis," 1955. Mathematical paintings exhibited in New York, N.Y., 1967. Member: Authors Guild of Authors League of America, Silvermine Guild of Artists.

WRITINGS—All juveniles, under pseudonym Crockett Johnson; mostly self-illustrated: Barnaby, Holt, 1943; Barnaby and Mr. O'Malley, Holt, 1944; Who's Upside Down?, W.R. Scott, 1952; Harold and the Purple Crayon, Harper, 1955; (with wife, Ruth Krauss) Is This You?, W.R. Scott, 1955; Barkis: Some Precise and Some Speculative Interpretations of the Meaning of a Dog's Bark at Certain Times and in Certain (Illustrated) Circumstances, Simon & Schuster, 1956; Harold's Fairy Tale: Further Adventures with the Purple Crayon, Harper, 1956; Harold's Trip to the Sky, Harper, 1957; Terrible, Terrifying Toby, Harper, 1957; Time for Spring, Harper, 1957; The Blue Ribbon Puppies, Harper, 1958; Harold at the North Pole: A Christmas Journey with the Purple Crayon, Harper, 1958; Merry Go Round, Harper, 1958; Ellen's Lion, Harper, 1959; The Frowning Prince, Harper, 1959; Harold's Circus: An Astounding, Colossal Purple Crayon Adventure, Harper, 1959; Will Spring Be Early or Will Spring Be Late?, Crowell, 1960; A Picture for Harold's Room: A Purple Crayon Adventure, Harper, 1960; Harold's ABC, Harper, 1963; The Lion's Own Story: Eight New Stories About Ellen's Lion, Harper, 1963; We Wonder What Will Walter Be When He Grows Up?, Holt, 1964; Castles in the Sand, Holt, 1965; Gordy and the Pirate, and the Circus Ringmaster and the Knight

and the Major League Manager and the Western Marshal and the Astronaut, and a Remarkable Achievement, Putnam, 1965; The Emperor's Gifts, Holt, 1965; Barnaby (selection of best "Barnaby" cartoons), Dover, 1967; Upside Down, Albert Whitman, 1969. Contributor to Harper's, Mathematical Gazette (Cambridge, England), and other magazines.

Illustrator: Ruth Krauss, The Carrot Seed, Harper, 1945; Constance Foster, Story of Money, McBride, 1950; Ruth Krauss, How to Make an Earthquake, Harper, 1954; Margaret Brown, Willie's Adventures, W.R. Scott, 1954; Franklin, Branley, Mickey's Magnet, Crowell, 1956; Bernadine Cook, The Little Fish that Got Away, Saunders, 1957; Ruth Krauss, The Happy Egg, Scholastic Book Services, 1967.

WORK IN PROGRESS: Painting.

SIDELIGHTS: Robert and Lillian Masters wrote a two-act play for children based on the comic strip, Barnaby, published by Samuel French, 1950. Harold and the Purple Crayon, The Frowning Prince, A Picture for Harold's Room, and Barnaby have been made into animated films, the latter winning first place in its category at the 1967 Venice Film Festival.

BIOGRAPHICAL/CRITICAL SOURCES: Bertha Miller, Illustrators of Children's Books, 1946-1956, Horn Book, 1958; Editor and Publisher, July 16, 1960; National Observer, April 22, 1968; Lee Bennett Hopkins, Books Are By People, Citation Press, 1969.

*   *   *

LEISY, James Franklin   1927-
(Frank Lynn)

PERSONAL: First syllable of surname rhymes with "eyes"; born March 21, 1927, in Normal, Ill.; son of Ernest Erwin (an author and professor) and Elva (Krehbiel) Leisy; married Emily Ruth McQueen, June 8, 1949; children: James Franklin, Jr., Scot, Rebecca Ruth. Education: Duke University, student, 1945; Southern Methodist University, B.B.A., 1949. Politics: Republican. Religion: Protestant. Home: 1320 Westridge Dr., Portola Valley, Calif. 94025. Office: Wadsworth Publishing Co., Belmont, Calif. 94002.

CAREER: Prentice-Hall, Inc. (publishers), New York, N.Y., field representative, 1949-52, editor, 1953-54; Allyn & Bacon, Inc. (publishers), Boston, Mass., editor, 1954-56; Wadsworth Publishing Co., Inc., Belmont, Calif., president, 1956—. Member of board of directors, Wadsworth Publishing Co., Inc., Dickenson Publishing Co., Bogden & Quigley, Inc., California Council for Economic Education, Bethel College, Southern Methodist University Alumnae Association. Consultant to Volunteers for International Technical Assistance. Composer. Military service: U.S. Navy, 1945-46. Member: American Folklore Society, Music Industry Council, Music Educators National Conference, Young Presidents' Organization (director), Mystery Writers of America, Alpha Kappa Psi. Awards, honors: Careers Hall of Fame, Southern Methodist University.

WRITINGS: Abingdon Song Kit, Abingdon, 1957; (editor) Let's All Sing, Abingdon, 1959; (under pseudonym Frank Lynn) Songs for Swingin' Housemothers, Chandler Publishing, 1961, revised edition, 1963; (under pseudonym Frank Lynn) Songs for Singin', Chandler Publishing, 1961; (editor) Songs for Pickin' and Singin', Gold Medal Books, 1962, new edition, Fawcett, 1971; (under pseudonym Frank Lynn) The Beer Bust Song Book, Fearon, 1963; Folk Song Fest, S. Fox, 1964; Hootenanny Tonight, Gold Medal Books, 1964; The Folk Song Abecedary, musical autography by Alfredo Seville, Hawthorn, 1966. Writer of classic ballad features in Playboy, 1955, and of articles in various magazines. Composer of more than one hundred published popular songs, choral, and instrumental works.

WORK IN PROGRESS: The Folk Song Omnibus, for S. Fox; a suspense novel; various choral compositions.

* * *

LEKIS, Lisa 1917-

PERSONAL: Born November 19, 1917, in Vicksburg, Miss.; daughter of David A. and Kathryn (Brabston) Crichton; married Walter R. Lekis (a communications media consultant, U.S. Agency for International Development), September 26, 1947; children: Darcy A., Adrianna K. Education: Stanford University, B.A., 1937; University of Chicago, graduate student, 1937-38, 1946; University of Florida, Ph.D., 1956. Home: #1 Las Olas Circle, Ft. Lauderdale, Fla. 33316.

CAREER: Publicity representative in Mexico, 1940-46; American Export Industries, Chicago, Ill., export manager, 1946-48; University of Puerto Rico, San Juan, dance director and director of Caribbean Festivals, 1949-53; Alcoa Steamship Co., New York, N.Y., consultant on Caribbean advertising, 1954-55; U.S. Overseas Mission, Quito, Ecuador, consultant on rural research, Division of Agriculture, 1957-59; Fulbright Commission, Rio de Janeiro, Brazil, executive secretary, 1959-61; University of Bahia, Salvador, Bahia, Brazil, professor of sociology, 1961-63; University of Liberia, Monrovia, professor of sociology, 1963-65. Consultant to AID in Quito, Ecuador, and Washington, D.C., 1966—. Member: Society of Woman Geographers, Eloy Alfaro Foundation, American Folklore Society, Society for Ethnomusicology, People to People Program, California Folk Dance Federation, Phi Beta Kappa, Phi Kappa Phi.

WRITINGS: (Contributor) A. Curtis Wilgus, editor, The Caribbean: Its Culture, University of Florida Press, 1954; Folk Dances of Latin America, Scarecrow, 1958; Province of Loja, Ecuador, U.S. Overseas Mission/Ecuador, 1958; Canton Paltas, U.S. Overseas Mission/Ecuador, 1958; Dancing Gods, Scarecrow, 1960. Contributor to Encyclopedia Americana, Grolier's Encyclopedia, Book of Knowledge, and Richards Illustrated. Author of monographs, and various research studies for AID; contributor to magazines; narrator for recordings.

WORK IN PROGRESS: People of Latin America.

AVOCATIONAL INTERESTS: Little Theater projects; sailing (she has just completed a voyage in a 40-foot sailboat, crossing the North Atlantic to Europe, South Atlantic to Brazil, and sailing north to the Caribbean).

* * *

LENDON, Kenneth Harry 1928-
(Leo Vaughan)

PERSONAL: Born May 16, 1928, in Toronto, Ontario; son of Wilbur Eddy (a teacher) and Claudia (Pollard) Lendon; married Deborah Pierce (a lecturer), September 16, 1950; children: Michael. Education: Queen's University, Kingston, Ontario, B.A. (with honors), 1950; Johns Hopkins University, Ph.D., 1954. Home: Bulak Sumur D/5, Jogjakarta, Indonesia. Agent: Harold Ober Associates, 40 East 49th St., New York, N.Y. 10017.

CAREER: University of California, Santa Barbara, instructor in English, 1954-56; University of Shiraz, Shiraz, Iran, assistant professor, 1958-61. Visiting professor of English, University of Gadiah Mada, Jogjakarta, Indonesia, 1961—.

WRITINGS: (Under pseudonym Leo Vaughan) The Jokeman, Eyre & Spottiswoode, 1962, published in America as A World Full of Nightingales, Morrow, 1963; (under pseudonym Leo Vaughan) It Must Be the Climate, Eyre & Spottiswoode, 1966, Regnery, 1968.

WORK IN PROGRESS: A novel.†

* * *

LENGYEL, Emil 1895-

PERSONAL: Born April 26, 1895, in Budapest, Hungary; came to United States, 1921, naturalized, 1927; son of Joseph (a tradesman) and Johanna (Adam) Lengyel; married Livia Delej, July 17, 1938; children: Peter. Education: Royal Hungarian University, Utriusque Juris Doctor, 1919. Home: 239 East 79th St., New York, N.Y. 10021. Agent: Bertha Klausner International Literary Agency, 71 Park Ave., New York, N.Y. 10022. Office: Fairleigh Dickinson University, Rutherford, N.J. 07070.

CAREER: Journalist in Vienna, Austria, 1920-21; American correspondent for European newspapers, 1922-30; Brooklyn Polytechnic Institute, Brooklyn, N.Y., adjunct professor of history and economics, 1935-42; New York University, New York, N.Y., staff lecturer, 1939-43, assistant professor, 1943-47, associate professor, 1947-51, professor of history, 1951-60, professor emeritus, 1960—; Fairleigh Dickinson University, Rutherford, N.J., professor of history, 1960—, chairman of social science department, 1963-72, adjunct professor of history, 1972—. New School for Social Research, New York, N.Y., lecturer, 1950-55. Lecturer to U.S. Armed Forces in World War II; public lecturer throughout America, 1932—. New York State Department of Education, consultant on Middle Eastern subjects. Military service: Austro-Hungarian Army, World War I; prisoner of war in Sibera almost two years. Member: American Academy of Political and Social Science, American Historical Association, American-European Friendship Association (president, 1956-62, president emeritus, 1962—), American Association for Middle East Studies, American Association of University Professors, P.E.N., Overseas Press Club, Columbia University Seminar on Pre-Industrial Areas, Mongolian Society. Awards, honors: Citation by American-European Friendship Association for distinguished service.

WRITINGS: Cattle Car Express: A Prisoner of War in Siberia, Strassburger Foundation, 1931; Hitler, Dial, 1932; The Cauldron Boils, Dial, 1932; The New Deal in Europe, Funk, 1934; Millions of Dictators: A Study of Public Opinion, Funk, 1936; The Danube, Random House, 1939; Turkey, Random House, 1941; Dakar: Outpost of Two Hemispheres, Random House, 1941; Siberia (Science Book Club selection), Random House, 1943, revised edition published in England as Secret Siberia, R. Hale, 1947; America's Role in World Affairs, Harper, 1946, revised and enlarged editon, 1950; Americans from Hungary, Lippincott, 1948; World Without End: The Middle East, John Day, 1953; Egypt's Role in World Affairs, Public Affairs Press, 1957; 1000 Years of Hungary, John Day, 1958; The Changing Middle East, John Day, 1960; The Subcontinent of India: An Introduction to the History, Geography, Culture, Politics, and Contemporary Life of India, Pakistan, and Ceylon, Scholastic Book Services, 1961; They Called Him Ataturk, John Day, 1962; Krishna Menon, Walker & Co., 1962; From Prison to Power, Follett, 1964; The Land and People of Hungary, Lippincott, 1965, revised edition, 1972; Mahatma Gandhi, the Great Soul, F. Watts, 1966; Jawaharlal Nehru, the Brahman from Kashmir, F. Watts, 1968; Lajos Kossuth, Hungary's Great Patriot, F. Watts, 1969; Asoka the Great, India's Royal Missionary, F. Watts, 1969; Nationalism: The Last Stage of Communism, Funk, 1969; First Book of Turkey, F. Watts, 1970; Ignace Paderewski: Musician and Statesman. F. Watts, 1970; Pakistan: A First Book, F. Watts, 1971, new edition, 1972; Iran: A First Book, F. Watts, 1972; Modern Egypt, F. Watts, 1973.

Foreign Policy Association "Headline Series" publications: (With Joseph C. Harsch) *Eastern Europe Today [and] American Policy in Eastern Europe* (the former by Lengyel, the latter by Harsch), 1949; (with Ernest O. Melby) *Isreal: Problems of Nation-Building [and] Israel: Laboratory of Human Relations* (the former by Lengyel, the latter by Melby), 1951, 2nd edition, 1952; (with Melby) *The Middle East Today*, 1954; (co-author) *Great Decisions*, 1959.

Oxford Book Co. social studies pamphlets: *The Soviet Union: The Land and Its People*, 1951, revised edition, including developments since death of Stalin, 1954, 5th edition, 1962; *The Middle East*, 1951, revised and enlarged edition published as *The Changing Middle East* (not the same as the John Day publication), 1958; *Africa in Ferment*, 1959, revised edition, 1962; *Africa, Past, Present, and Future*, 1966, revised edition, 1967.

Co-author or contributor: *Nazism: An Assault on Civilization*, 1934; *Eye Witness*, Alliance, 1940; *As We See Russia*, published for Overseas Press Club by Dutton, 1948; Arthur Bernard Moehlman and J.S. Roucek, editors, *Comparative Education*, Dryden Press, 1951; Francis James Brown and J.S. Roucek, editors, *One America: The History, Contributions, and Present Problems of Our Racial and National Minorities*, 3rd edition, Prentice-Hall, 1952; (with Thorsten V. Kalijarni and others) *Modern World Politics*, 3rd edition, Crowell, 1953; Charles Angoff, editor, *The Humanities in the Age of Science: In Honor of Peter Sammartino*, Fairleigh Dickinson University Press, 1968. Author of screenplay, "The World in Revolt," produced by 20th Century-Fox in German, and Hungarian, including works of Ferenc Molnar, Erno Szep, Zsigmond Moricz, Sandor Kemeri. Special correspondent and book reviewer for *New York Times*, 1936-46; correspondent of *Toronto Star Weekly*, 1946-56; book reviewer for *Saturday Review;* contributor of articles to *Reporter, Mankind, Asian Student, Annals of the American Academy of Political and Social Science, New York Times Magazine,* and other periodicals.

SIDELIGHTS: Lengyel told *CA:* "[Writing] gives me a feeling of euphoria in the later stages of revision, hunting for *le mot juste.* Also, I hope to reach people to get interested in other people and thereby break down the 'existentialist wall.' I also would like to make my tiny contribution toward a cross-fertilization of civilization. That is why I like to deal with exotic regions." He speaks and writes French, German, Hungarian, reads Italian, some Russian; has traveled in Africa, Asia, Europe, around the world, partly for *New York Times,* and *Toronto Star Weekly,* and partly to collect material for books; five of those books have been translated into a total of six European languages.

BIOGRAPHICAL/CRITICAL SOURCES: New York Times Book Review, March 26, 1967; *Saturday Review,* February 21, 1970; *Library Journal,* July, 1970.

*	*	*

LENTILHON, Robert Ward 1925-

PERSONAL: Born March 8, 1925, in East Orange, N.J.; son of Herbert Danforth and Gertrude (Foss) Lentilhon; 1932. Translator of books and plays from the French, married Marilyn Dutton, September 9, 1950; children: Janet, Thomas, Sally. *Education:* University of Rhode Island, B.S.B.A., 1949; Boston University, M.B.A., 1953. *Politics:* Republican. *Religion:* Congregationalist. *Home:* 77 Rolling Ridge Rd., Amherst, Mass. 01002.

CAREER: Price-Waterhouse & Co., Boston, Mass., junior accountant, 1949-51; Nichols College, Dudley, Mass., instructor in marketing, 1951-52; University of Massachusetts, Amherst, associate professor of accounting, 1952—. *Military service:* U.S. Army, 1943-45; became sergeant;

received Bronze Star. *Member:* American Accounting Association, American Institute of Certified Public Accountants. National Association of Accountants, Massachusetts Society of Certified Public Accountants, Phi Kappa Phi, Beta Gamma Sigma. *Awards, honors:* Gold medal for highest achievement in examination, Massachusetts Society of Certified Public Accountants, 1955.

WRITINGS: (With John W. Anderson) *Principles of Accounting,* Simmons-Boardman, 1965. Contributor of articles to *Accounting Review* (publication of American Accounting Association) and *Massachusetts CPA Review.*

WORK IN PROGRESS: With John W. Anderson, editing *CPA Preparation,* to be published by South-Western.

*	*	*

LEONARD, George B(urr) 1923-

PERSONAL: Born August 9, 1923, in Macon, Ga.; son of George B. (an insurance executive) and Julia (Almand) Leonard; married second wife, Lillie Steele Pitts, October 3, 1959; children: (first marriage) Ellen, Mimi; (second marriage) Lillie, Jr., Emily. *Education:* Georgia Institute of Technology, student, 1941-42; University of North Carolina, A.B., 1948. *Home address:* Box 509, Mill Valley, Calif. 94941.

CAREER: Look, New York, N.Y., senior editor, 1953-56, San Francisco editor and senior editor, San Francisco, Calif., 1956-62, West Coast editorial manager and senior editor, San Francisco, Calif., 1962-70. Esalen Institute, Big Sur, Calif., member of advisory board. *Military service:* U.S. Army Air Forces, 1943-46, combat pilot in Southwest Pacific theater, 1945; received Air Medal, three battle stars. U.S. Air Force, 1950-53; served in Japan and as managing editor of *Air Training;* became captain. *Awards, honors:* Education Writers Association Award for articles in *Look,* for three successive years, 1956-58; School Bell Awards for *Look* articles, 1960, 1962, 1964, 1965, 1966.

WRITINGS: (With William Attwood and J. Robert Moskin) *The Decline of the American Male,* Random House, 1958; *Shoulder the Sky,* McDowell, Obolensky, 1959; *Education and Ecstasy,* Delacorte, 1968; *The Man and Woman Thing, and Other Provocations,* Delacorte, 1970; *The Transformation: A Guide to the Inevitable Changes in Mankind,* Delacorte, 1972.

BIOGRAPHICAL/CRITICAL SOURCES: Christian Science Monitor, October 21, 1968; *Book World,* October 27, 1968; *National Review,* November 19, 1968; *Saturday Review,* December 21, 1968; *New York Times Book Review,* August 24, 1969; *Library Journal,* March 15, 1970.

*	*	*

LEONARD, Joseph T. 1916-

PERSONAL: Born October 8, 1916, in Albany, N.Y.; son of Joseph Henry and Josephine (Sweeney) Leonard. *Education:* Studied at New York University, 1944-47; Epiphany Apostolic College, 1947-49, St. Joseph's Seminary, 1949-55; Catholic University of America, S.T.L., 1957, S.T.D., 1963. *Home:* 1200 Varnum St. N.E., Washington, D.C. 20017.

CAREER: Roman Catholic priest, member of Society of St. Joseph (Josephites); St. Joseph's Seminary, Washington, D.C., professor of moral theology, 1956—.

WRITINGS: Theology and Race Relations, Bruce, 1964. Contributor to *American Ecclesiastical Review.*

*	*	*

LEONHARDT, Rudolf Walter 1921-

PERSONAL: Born February 9, 1921, in Altenburg, Thuringia, Germany; son of Rudolf (a soldier) and

Paula (Zeiger) Leonhardt; married Ulrike Zoerb (a teacher), June 18, 1949; children: (first marriage) Joachim Rudolf; (second marriage) Doerte Susanne, Timm Christopher. *Education:* Attended Universities of Leipzig, Bonn, London; Cambridge University, Dr. Phil., 1951. *Office: Die Zeit*, 1, Speersort, Hamburg 1, Germany.

CAREER: Cambridge University, Cambridge, England, lecturer in modern German literature, 1948-50; British Broadcasting Corporation, foreign correspondent, 1950-53; *Die Zeit*, Hamburg, Germany, 1955—, now cultural editor. German correspondent of *The Guardian*, London.

WRITINGS: 77-mal England: Panorama einen Insel, Piper, 1957; *Der Suendenfall der deutschen Germanistik: Vorschlaege zur Wiederbelebung des literarischen Bewustseins in der Bundesrepublik*, Artemis, 1959; *Leben ohne Literatur?*, Keller, 1961; *X-mall, Deutschland*, Piper, 1961, 5th edition, 1962, abridged student edition, edited by Ottomar Rudolf, 1968, translation by Catherine Hutter published as *This Germany: The Story Since the Third Reich*, New York Graphic Society, 1964; *Zeitnotizen: Kritik, Polemik, Feuilleton*, Piper, 1963; *Junge deutsche Dichter fuer Anfaenger*, Diogenes, 1964; (with Marion Doenhoff and Theo Sommer) *Reise in ein fernes Land*, Wegner, 1964; (editor) Erich Kaestner, *Kaestner fuer Erwachsene*, S. Fischer, 1966; *Sylt fuer Anfaenger*, Diogenes, 1969; *Wer wirft den ersten Stein?*, Piper, 1969; *Haschisch-Report*, Piper, 1970; *Drei Wochen und drei Tage: Ein Europaer in Japan*, Hoffmann & Campe, 1970. Contributor to *Cassell's Encyclopaedia of World Literature*, 1954, and to newspapers, radio, and television in England, Germany, Austria, and Switzerland.

AVOCATIONAL INTERESTS: Sociology of art and literature, people, and "this Germany."

*   *   *

LE ROI, David (de Roche)   1905-
(John Roche)

PERSONAL: Born January 28, 1905, in San Francisco, Calif.; son of John (an officer, Indian Army) and Kathleen (Salazar) Le Roi; married Maude Alice Fox, April 23, 1942; children: Jonathan. *Education:* Attended Herriot-Watt College, Edinburgh, Scotland, Church of England Grammar School, Sydney, Australia, and University of Sydney. *Politics:* Conservative Unionist. *Religion:* Church of England. *Home:* 12 Kirklees Rd., Thornton Heath, Surrey, England. *Agent:* Richmond Towers & Benson Ltd., 14 Essex St., Strand, London W.C.2, England.

CAREER: Daily Guardian, Sydney, New South Wales, Australia, subeditor, 1923-26; *Daily Chronicle*, London, England, reporter, 1927-28; free-lance correspondent for Australian newspapers, 1929-31; free-lance feature writer for English newspapers, 1932-36; Waverley Educational Book Co., London, England, assistant technical editor, 1937-39; Fleetway Publications Ltd., London, technical editor in encyclopedia department, 1945-61, science and technical editor, *Look and Learn*, 1961-64. George Newnes Ltd. (publishers), consultant editor on food technology, processing, and laboratory control, 1954. *Military service:* Royal Air Force, 1939-45. *Member:* International Institute of Arts and Letters (fellow), Institute of Journalists, Society of Authors, National Union of Journalists.

WRITINGS: The Boys' Book of Jets, Thames & Hudson, 1953; *Eagle Book of Modern Wonders*, Hulton Press, 1954; *Invention and Discovery*, Hamish Hamilton, 1955; *Answers to a Thousand Questions*, Hulton Press, 1955; *The Aquarium*, Soccer, 1955; *The Scottie Book of Inventions*, Transworld, 1957; *Hamsters and Guinea Pigs*, Vane, 1955, 2nd edition, 1963; *Pigeons, Doves, and Pigeon-Racing*, Soccer, 1957; *The Boys' Book of Flight*, Il-

iffe, 1957; *Town Dogs*, Soccer, 1957; *Tortoises, Lizards and Other Reptiles*, Soccer, 1958; *Budgerigars, Canaries and Other Cage Birds*, Soccer, 1958; *Aeronautics*, Educational Book Co., 1958; *All About Radar, Radio and Television*, Wheaton & Co., 1959; *All about Nuclear Power*, Wheaton & Co., 1959; *All About Jet-Propulsion and Rocket Power*, Wheaton & Co., 1959; *Things to Make and Do*, Educational Book Co., 1960; *Look at Roads*, Hamish Hamilton, 1960; *Modern Medicine*, Wheaton & Co., 1960; *Modern Agriculture*, Wheaton & Co., 1960; *Man-Made Materials*, Wheaton & Co., 1960; *How We Get and Use Oil*, Routledge & Kegan Paul, 1962; *Land, Sea and Air Weapons*, Educational Book Co., 1962; *Cats*, Vane, 1963; *Aluminum*, Muller, 1964; *Science Today and Tomorrow*, New English Library, 1964; *Towards the Twenty-First Century*, New English Library, 1964; *All about Plastics*, Muller, c.1966; *How Railways Work*, Routledge & Kegan Paul, c.1966; *The Channel Tunnel*, Clifton Books, 1969; *Oceanography*, Machinery Publishing Co., 1971.

Technical editor of *New Universal Encyclopedia, Book of Knowledge, Children's Encyclopedia*, and *Practical Knowledge for All;* executive editor of *The World of Wonder* and *Outline of Nature*. Contributor of articles on popular science, natural history, biography, and history to some fifty magazines and newspapers in Great Britain, many of the articles syndicated by Express Features and P.A.-Reuter Features. Writer of film and television scripts.

*   *   *

LESLIE, Desmond   1921-

PERSONAL: Born June 29, 1921, in London, England; son of Sir Shane (an author and biographer) and American-born Marjorie (Ide) Leslie; married Agnes Bernauer (an actress under name Agnes Bernelle; marriage dissolved); married Helen Jennifer Strong; children: (first marriage) Shaun, Mark, Antonia; (second marriage) Samantha, Camilla. *Education:* Educated in English schools. *Home:* Castle Leslie, Glaslough, Eire. *Agent:* George Greenfield, John Farquharson Ltd., 15 Red Lion Sq., London W.C.2, England.

CAREER: Director of several film companies before establishing Leslie & Leslie Ltd., makers of electronic music for films, plays, radio, television, and commercial records; recordings include twelve Shakespeare plays in stereo, performed by Old Vic players with electronic music as background, a series released in United States under title "The Living Shakespeare." *Military service:* Royal Air Force, World War II; became flight sergeant pilot. *Member:* White Eagle Lodge (London).

WRITINGS: Carless Lives, Macdonald & Co., 1945; *Pardon My Return*, Macdonald & Co., 1946; *Angels Weep*, Laurie, 1946; (with George Adamski) *Flying Saucers Have Landed*, British Book Centre, 1953, revised and enlarged edition, Neville Spearman, 1970; *Hold Back the Night*, P. Owen, 1956; *The Amazing Mr. Lutterworth*, Wingate, 1958. Contributor to *Life, Picture Post, Illustrated, Vogue*, other magazines.

WORK IN PROGRESS: The Jesus File, the case of the rebellious carpenter as seen through the files of the bureaucratic establishment.

SIDELIGHTS: Flying Saucers Have Landed has been translated into sixteen languages.

*   *   *

LESLIE, Warren III   1927-

PERSONAL: Born May 3, 1927, in New York, N.Y.; son of Warren II and Jane (Scales) Leslie; married, wife's name, Bonnie; children: Warren IV, Michael McQueen. *Education:* Educated at Phillips Exeter

Academy and Yale University. *Home:* 11415 Hillcrest, Dallas, Tex. 75230. *Agent:* Harold Matson Co., Inc., 22 East 40th St., New York, N.Y. 10016. *Office:* Neiman-Marcus Co., Main & Ervay, Dallas, Tex. 75201.

CAREER: Started as writer for Jinx Falkenburg-Tex McCrary radio show, New York, N.Y., 1946-47; *Dallas Morning News,* Dallas, Tex., reporter, 1947-51; Neiman-Marcus Co., Dallas, Tex., assistant to president, 1951-53, assistant sales promotion director, 1953-55, director of special events, 1955-58, vice-president in charge of sales promotion, 1958—. Member of board of directors, Dallas Civic Opera; secretary, Dallas Symphony Orchestra. *Military service:* U.S. Marine Corp, 1945-46. *Member:* Texas Institute of Letters; Press Club and University Club (both Dallas).

WRITINGS: The Best Thing That Ever Happened, McGraw, 1952; *Love or Whatever It Is,* McGraw, 1960; *Dallas, Public and Private: Aspects of an American City,* Grossman, 1964; *Under the Skin,* Geis, 1970. Author of radio scripts. Contributor of articles and short stories to magazines.†

*   *   *

LESSING, Doris (May)   1919-

PERSONAL: Born October 22, 1919, in Persia; daughter of Alfred Cook (a farmer) and Emily Maude (McVeagh) Tayler; married Frank Charles Wisdom, 1939 (marriage dissolved, 1943); married Gottfried Anton Lessing, 1945 (marriage dissolved, 1949); children: (first marriage) John, Jean; (second marriage) Peter. *Education:* Attended Roman Catholic Convent, then Girls' High School, both in Salisbury, Southern Rhodesia; left school at the age of 14. *Politics:* Left-wing. *Home:* 60 Charrington St., London N.W.1, England. *Agent:* Greyson & Wigan, 58 Old Compton St., London W.1, England.

CAREER: Held various odd jobs, including work as a nursemaid, a lawyer's secretary, a Hansard typist, and a Parliamentary Commissioner's typist. Lived in Southern Rhodesia, 1924-49. Writer. *Awards, honors:* Somerset Maugham Award of the Society of Authors, 1954, for *Five Short Novels.*

WRITINGS: The Grass Is Singing, Crowell, 1950; *Martha Quest* (also published as Part I, *Children of Violence*), M. Joseph, 1952; *This Was the Old Chief's Country* (stories), M. Joseph, 1952; *A Proper Marriage* (Part II of *Children of Violence*), M. Joseph, 1954; *Five Short Novels,* M. Joseph, 1955; *Retreat. to Innocence,* M. Joseph, 1956; *Going Home,* M. Joseph, 1957; *A Ripple from the Storm* (Part III of *Children of Violence*), M. Joseph, 1958; *Habit of Loving,* Crowell, 1958; "Mr. Dollinger" (play), first produced in Oxford, England, at Oxford Playhouse, 1958; "Each His Own Wilderness" (play; first produced in London at Royal Court, March 23, 1958), published in *New English Dramatists: Three Plays,* edited by E. Martin Browne, Penguin, 1959; *Fourteen Poems,* Scorpion Press (London), 1959; "The Truth About Billy Newton" (play), first produced in Salisbury, England, 1961; *In Pursuit of the English* (nonfiction), Simon & Schuster, 1961; *Play With a Tiger* (play; first produced in London at Comedy Theatre, March 22, 1962; produced in New York at Renata Theatre, December 30, 1964), M. Joseph, 1962; *The Golden Notebook* (novel), Simon & Schuster, 1962; *A Man and Two Women* (stories), Simon & Schuster, 1963; *African Stories,* M. Joseph, 1964, Simon & Schuster, 1965; *Landlocked* (Part IV of *Children of Violence*), Simon & Schuster, 1966; *Particularly Cats,* Simon & Schuster, 1967; *The Four-Gated City* (Part V of *Children of Violence*), Knopf, 1969; *Briefing for a Descent Into Hell,* Knopf, 1971; *The Temptation of Jack Orkney and Other Stories,* Knopf, 1972; *The Summer Before the Dark,* Knopf, 1973.

SIDELIGHTS: Jeremy Brooks considers Doris Lessing to be not only the best woman novelist of our time but one of the finest writers of the post-war generation. Only a woman possessing her special insight and her free intelligence could achieve this kind of success. As Dorothy Brewster notes, "since the conspicuous success in 1950 of her first novel, . . . Doris Lessing . . . has been recognized as one of the most gifted of the younger group of English novelists. . . . Those of Doris Lessing's novels and stories that deal with the people and ways of life of Southern Rhodesia before, during, and after World War II have acquired something of the significance of social and political history. . . . When she came to London, she looked at the English . . . with an alert and fresh vision. . . ." Since the publication of *The Golden Notebook* and "Children of Violence," other contemporary women novelists seem pale by comparison.

In an introductory note to *Declaration* Tom Maschler says of her: "[She was] educated at the Roman Catholic Convent School in Salisbury for five years, and for one year at the girls' High School. Her mother wanted her to be a pianist, and it was a shock when, in Doris Lessing's own words, 'I discovered suddenly that I had no talent whatsoever.' Left school at fourteen. Started writing at eighteen and composed and destroyed six novels. From 1943, . . . was busy politically taking her first lesson from Communists and Socialists in the R.A.F. For the first time in her life she met people who were prepared to do more about the colour bar than deplore it. 1949: came to England. . . . She says, 'England seems to me the ideal country to live in because it is quiet and unstimulating and leaves you in peace.' "

Many of her short stories are actually nouvelles, comprising 25,000 to 45,000 words. Of this form she says: "There is space in them to take one's time, to think aloud, to follow, for a paragraph or two, on a side-trail—none of which is possible in a real short story." Her success in this genre "is primarily a matter of the swift directness and the generalizing intelligence of the voice itself," writes Robert Garis. "Mrs. Lessing's voice has the Laurentian confidence that one can manage the language of fiction by counting the dollars instead of the pennies. This works because she grasps the story as a whole and because it is usually a big story, not [only] in the number of its words but in the number of its events. . . . Almost every paragraph in the story contains [much action] and all of these actions are rendered with the same sufficiency. Sufficiency doesn't sound like much, but it is what makes the minor stories of Lawrence and Chekhov independently valuable, not just failed major works. It is in fact a sign of major talent, for it derives from good judgment in almost the Johnsonian sense. Like Lawrence and Chekhov, Mrs. Lessing has looked at many different kinds of people with unusual curiosity and intelligence and has arrived at sure judgments about them." Despite the success of her novels, Mrs. Lessing will continue to write stories. She says: "Some writers I know have stopped writing short stories because, as they say, 'there is no market for them.' Others like myself, the addicts, go on, and I suspect would go on even if there really wasn't any home for them but a private drawer." Her latest collection, *The Temptation of Jack Orkney and Other Stories,* contains work done over ten years of literary growth, according to Richard Locke, and for which collection he has the highest praise: "I think it's clear that of all the postwar English novelists Doris Lessing is the foremost creative descendant of that 'great tradition' which includes George Eliot, Conrad, and D.H. Lawrence: a literary tradition of intense social concerns and moral realism, a tradition that scrutinizes marriage and sexual life, individual psychology and the role of ideology in contemporary society.... These stories are an excellent place to begin reading or rereading Doris Lessing. It's a voyage very well worth taking, for there are few these days who have the energy and imagination to explore the regions Doris Lessing has now made her own."

J.M. Edelstein believes that, on the basis of *African Stories* alone, "Doris Lessing must be counted as one of the most important fiction writers of our times." As political and social commentaries these stories "confirm in precise and painful detail, like stitches in a wound, the abuse of the native population of Southern Rhodesia by the white settlers of British descent," writes Mary Ellmann. "Doris Lessing's work is an uninterrupted study of loneliness, but here it is particularly the isolation of a few white exiles, claiming vast strange land.... For her first thirty years ... Doris Lessing seems to have listened to Southern Rhodesia as no other writer has been able to do. It remained, even after she had left it, all nature to her. As one associates her English work with flats and offices, one associates the African stories with swollen suns and moons, head-tail grass, and the secret constant stirring of animal life.... Africa is for her not only a society in which the white people use their exile like a weapon against the black; but also a place, supporting both white and black, which endlessly enacts the conflict of forms, the effort of every living thing, at the cost of other living things, to achieve what is right for itself, its sustenance and continuation. Africa, not England, impressed the knowledge of necessary cruelty.... It is disconcerting, in fact, to come so repeatedly upon instances of anarchic hunger, the form of whose seeming formlessness is painful to trace, within stories of straightforward, even old-fashioned, organization. It is this preoccupation with a necessity, which in moral terms can seem a criminal chaos, that disrupts conventional literary form in *The Golden Notebook*." Mrs. Lessing says that she considers Africa to be "the center of a modern battlefield," but, she adds, "there are other things in living besides injustice, even for the victims of it." And, says Edelstein, "It is her knowledge of these larger and 'other things' and her ability to make us see them even while she sustains constantly, like distant drumming, the harsh and bitter realities of life in Africa," which gives these stories their power, accuracy and controlled passion. Africa, concludes Mrs. Lessing, "is not a place to visit unless one chooses to be an exile ever afterwards from an inexplicable majestic silence lying just over the border of memory or of thought. Africa gives you the knowledge that man is a small creature among other creatures, in a large landscape." She told *CA* that she is now "a prohibited immigrant in South Africa and Rhodesia."

Her major and most controversial novel is *The Golden Notebook* wherein she brilliantly explores, as a *New Statesman* reviewer noted, what it is like to be "free and responsible, a woman in relation to men and other women, and to struggle to come to terms with one's self about these things and about writing and politics." Mrs. Lessing considers the book to be "a novel about certain political and sexual attitudes that have force now; it is an attempt to explain them, to objectivize them, to set them in relation with each other. So in a way it is a social novel, written by someone whose training—or at least whose habit of mind—is to see these things socially, not personally." In its structure, the novel is really two novels, divided in four sections, and "the Golden Notebook." Mrs. Lessing split it into four parts, she says, in order to "express a split person. I felt that if the artist's sensibility is to be equated with the sensibility of the educated person, then it is logical to use different styles to express different kinds of people." She feels that the "personality is very

much what is remembered; [the form I used] enabled me to say to the reader: Look, these apparently so different people have got so-and-so in common, or these things have got this in common. If I had used a conventional style, the old-fashioned novel, which I do not think is dead by any means,... I would not have been able to do this kind of playing with time, memory and the balancing of people. ... I like *The Golden Notebook* even though I believe it to be a failure, because it at least hints at complexity." Robert Taubman expresses similar sentiments, although he is a bit confused concerning the book's structure. He calls the book "a very full novel: it not only burst the bounds of the short formal novel, as it set out to do, but overflowed its own bounds as well. It's pretty well inexhaustible on the way women think and behave, notably in the area where their personal feelings and social and political attitudes meet." But, he adds, "its unusual structure is less a matter of subtle organization than of simple, rather haphazard naturalism, ... [or perhaps] an advance in naturalism." Mrs. Lessing is still disturbed by some of the comments on this novel. She told Florence Howe: "When [the book] came out, I was astonished that people got so emotional ... one way or another. They didn't bother to see, even to look at, how it was shaped. I could mention a dozen books by male authors in which the attitudes to women are the obverse, mirror attitudes, of the attitudes to men in *The Golden Notebook*. But no one would say that these men are anti-women.... But I articulated the same things from a female point of view, and this is what was interesting. It was taken as a kind of banner." Mrs. Lessing would not want to be labeled a feminist. She simply states that, "in the last generation women have become what is known as free.... The point is they're still fighting battles to get free—and rightly. And men are still—some men, you know—some men resist it. But what is interesting, ... what interests me in that book, was, in fact, the ideas. ... What I'm trying to say is that it was a detached book. It was a failure, of course, for if it had been a success, then people wouldn't get so damned emotional when I didn't want them to be." This novel, she says, was "extremely carefully constructed.... And the way it's constructed says what the book is about.... What I was doing is this: I was thinking about the kind of ideas we take for granted, ... a complex of ideas which could be described as Left—and which were born with the French Revolution. And they're all to do with freedom. They are revolutionary ideas that are no longer revolutionary and have been absorbed into the fabric of how we live. And they're ideas that fit together in a system, broadly speaking, nonreligious in the old sense, and have to do with the individual in relation to his society and the rights of the individual. Which is a new idea and we don't realize how new it is. We take it absolutely for granted." In one of the sections of this book, says Mrs. Lessing, "I was really trying to express my sense of despair about writing a conventional novel. ... Actually that [part] is an absolutely whole conventional novel, and the rest of the book is the material that went into making it. One of the things I was saying was: Well, look, this is a conventional novel. God knows, I write them myself.... There it is: 120,000 words; it's got a nice shape and the reviewers will say this and that. And the bloody complexity that went into it. And it's always a lie. And the terrible despair. So you've written a good novel or a moderate novel, but what does it actually say about what you've actually experienced? The truth is—absolutely nothing. Because you can't.... I know perfectly well that when I've finished ["Children of Violence"] I shall think, Christ, what a lie. Because you can't get life into it ... no matter how hard you try.... At least I think [*The Golden Notebook* is] more truthful because it's more complex. People are like other people. I mean, I don't think we are as extraordinary as we like to think we are.... The same people occur again and again in our lives. Situations do. And any moment of time is so complicated."

"Children of Violence," the now completed series of self-contained novels which Mrs. Lessing calls "a lie," has been widely acclaimed. Marjorie M. Bitker writes: "There seems no doubt that this work will rank with the foremost fictional commentaries on events of our century up to and perhaps beyond the present." "The series' importance," says Florence Howe, "has to do not only with Mrs. Lessing's reputation as author of *The Golden Notebook;* for she is trying to do something even more ambitious here. She is writing *bildungsroman* and at the same time . . . she is producing good political fiction. Her themes are major: the politics of race and war; . . . the West's changing attitude toward the Soviet Union; the shift from the Second World War to the cold war; worldwide revolutionary struggle against the West and capitalism; the problem of violence." To quote Mrs. Lessing, "Martha did not believe in violence. [Yet] Martha was the essence of violence, she has been conceived, bred, fed, and reared on violence ... because she had been born at the end of one world war, and had spent all her adolescence in the atmosphere of preparations for another which had lasted five years and had inflicted such wounds on the human race that no one had any idea of what the results would be." In "Children of Violence," according to Walter Allen, "Doris Lessing does for a young woman something very similar to what Arnold Bennett in *Clayhanger* and D.H. Lawrence in *Sons and Lovers* did for a young man, but the closer parallel is probably with George Eliot.... Doris Lessing shows her kinship to George Eliot both in her technique here and in her sober, unsentimental scrutiny of behavior, motives and morals." Mrs. Lessing's intent, writes Miss Howe, is "extremely ambitious" and her success, of course, has been debated. "But the canvas large enough to contain world events and small enough to measure the growth of a human being is one that only the very greatest novelists have tried. Martha's half-conscious identification of her own lot with the Africans', as she struggles against the tyranny of paternalistic personal relations, is a motif that lights the novel. Her personal wars are refractions of that other, greater war. And if she is slow to learn how to manage her wars, who is quick?" Miss Bitker concludes that "the bare bones of the plot are the least of the riches of this work; its nuances, complexities and implications for our own time and country are unforgettable. For we, like Martha, are children of violence."

Briefing for a Descent Into Hell, writes Joan Didion, "is entirely a novel of 'ideas,' not a novel about the play of ideas in the lives of certain characters but a novel in which the characters exist only as markers in the presentation of an idea." Pearl K. Bell, too, claims the book "is not a novel but a tract ... [Mrs. Lessing] is making a case for one of the more dubious and treacherous intellectual fads of our time—the apocalyptic view of the British psychiatrist, R.D. Laing, and his follower David Cooper. In this worst of all possible worlds, they contend, schizophrenia is a response to life that is more honest than accepted normality. In all fairness to Mrs. Lessing, it must be said that her commitment to this seductive view of the metaphysics of madness is not the modish tropism it represents in many of Laing's guru-worshipping enthusiasts.... Mrs. Lessing arrived at the moral of her quasi-fable ('inner-space fiction,' she calls it) in her own way, through a deep commitment to and then increasing disenchantment with contemporary life.... In the *Golden Notebook,* she was tentatively suggesting that what the smug world of normality—with its defensive army of psychiatrists, analysts, tranquilizers, and truth serums—calls insanity is actually a higher and purer intuition about the truth of human existence. With The

Four-Gated City ... Mrs. Lessing enlarged these ideas into a substantial thesis that drew her much closer to Laing's position." Exploring further on that theme, Jeffrey Meyers says "Mrs. Lessing 'does not believe that other peoples' crises should be cut short, or blanked out with drugs, or forced sleep, or a pretence that there is no crisis, or that if there is a crisis it should be concealed or masked or made light of.' She feels that certain twilight mental states, what doctors call paranoia, 'have a meaning, are reflections from that other [unconscious] part of ourselves which knows things we don't know.' This complex and compassionate novel, about dead men who awaken with a surge of intuitive insight and are drugged and shocked back to sleep, is a Blakean attack on the limitations of pure Reason . . ." Benjamin De Mott's attitude, in describing *Briefing,* is that "writers who mean to add something to human knowledge in the form of philosophical truth are often more permissive than estheticians about untidy composition, garrulity, repetitiousness, circularity ... they rarely offer readers the pleasures of a perfect design. But the absence of intellectual novelty and of crispness of design doesn't much diminish this writer's significance. Mrs. Lessing in her fifties remains one of the few writers alive in the West whose instinct to feel forward toward a more habitable world is allowed to breathe without shame, hysteria, or ironical defensiveness. If her course as a thinker leads her toward an arraignment of 'sanity' and normality, it does so not in relish of idle tripping, or of supersubtle epistemological argufying about the nature of reality, but rather as a consequence of her moral sense of what men could become and her conviction that self-reduction is a crime against life."

Mrs. Lessing is deeply concerned with what she calls "the individual conscience in its relation with the collective." She believes that "the real gap between people of my age and to choose a point at random, people under thirty [is the rejection of] 'propaganada. . . .' They reject an imaginative understanding of what I am convinced is the basic conflict of our time. The mental climate created by the cold war has produced a generation of young intellectuals who totally reject everything communism stands for; they cut themselves off imaginatively from a third of mankind, and impoverish themselves by doing so." But she also believes that there is a point "where 'committedness' can sell out to expediency. Once you admit that 'art should be willing to stand aside for life,' then the little tracts about progress, the false optimism, the dreadful lifeless products of socialist realism, become inevitable." She feels despair over Vietnam and the possibility of the destruction of the world: "[It is] almost as if there's a permanent boil in the human soul." On the other hand, she is by no means a pessimist: "I believe that the pleasurable luxury of despair, the acceptance of disgust, is as much a betrayal of what a writer should be as the acceptance of the simple economic view of man; both are aspects of cowardice, both fallings-away from a central vision, the two easy escapes of our time into false innocence." Somewhere between isolation and the collective conscience, she believes, is "a resting-point, a place of decision, hard to reach and precariously balanced.... The point of rest should be the writer's recognition of man, the responsible individual, voluntarily submitting his will to the collective, but never finally; and insisting on making his own personal and private judgments before every act of submission."

Many of Mrs. Lessing's stories and novels have been called autobiographical. Miss Brewster writes: "The young woman named Martha Quest in the series 'Children of Violence' grows up, like her creator, Doris Lessing, on a farm in Central Africa, has a father and a mother with some traits resembling those ascribed elsewhere by Doris Lessing to her own father and mother, goes at eighteen or so to earn her living in the capital of the colony, as

Doris Lessing went to Salisbury, and is there shocked and stimulated by new ideas and new relationships in the rapidly changing conditions of the years before and during World War II. We must assume that Mrs. Lessing, in tracing Martha's development, has not forgotten her own." Martha and Anna Wulf, the protagonist in *The Golden Notebook,* are sometimes discussed as similar characters. Miss Brewster relates, however, that "Mrs. Lessing expressed irritation with a review ... which equated Martha Quest with Doris Lessing, and then compared Martha Quest with Anna Wulf, presenting the two women as combinations of the author and her characters."

As Miss Brewster notes, Mrs. Lessing "early in her career chose the straight, broad, direct style of narrative. . . . Her first teachers in fiction were the great nineteenth-century novelists: Tolstoy, Stendhal, Dostoevsky, Balzac, Turgenev, Chekhov—the Realists.... She never felt close to the English novel, 'whereas I feel so close to the Russian novel that it's as if they were all my blood brothers.' ... The artist's sensibility as a mirror for our time has been explored by Proust, Joyce, Lawrence, Mann—the list is Mrs. Lessing's—and she calls this exploration one of the mainstreams of the modern novel. And to her Mann is the greatest.... ['His] whole message was that art is rooted in corruption—in illness, above all,' [says Mrs. Lessing who herself believes] that art is rooted in an overwhelming arrogance and egotism: 'There is a kind of cold detachment at the core of any writer or artist.' "

Mrs. Lessing has very definite opinions on the responsibilities of a writer. She has said: "As a writer I am concerned first of all with novels and stories, though I believe that the arts continuously influence each other, and that what is true of one art in any given epoch is likely to be true of the others. I am concerned that the novel and the story should not decline as art-forms any further than they have from the high peak of literature; that they should possibly regain their greatness, [i.e., through a return to realism].... I define realism as art which springs so vigorously and naturally from a strongly-held, though not necessarily intellectually-defined, view of life that it absorbs symbolism. I hold the view that the realist novel, the realist story, is the highest form of prose writing. . . . The great men of the nineteenth century had neither religion nor politics nor aesthetic principles in common. But what they did have in common was a climate of ethical judgment; they shared certain values; they were humanists." She believes that contemporary literature, on the contrary, is distinguishd by "a confusion of standards and the uncertainty of values." It is now difficult "to make moral judgments, to use words like good and bad," because "we are all of us, directly or indirectly, caught up in a great whirlwind of change; and I believe that if an artist has once felt this in himself, and felt himself as part of it; if he has once made the effort of imagination necessary to comprehend it, it is an end of despair, and the aridity of self-pity. It is the beginning of something else which I think is the minimum act of humility for a writer: to know that one is a writer at all because one represents, makes articulate, is continuously and invisibly fed by, numbers of people . . . to whom one is responsible.... Once a writer has a feeling of responsibility, as a human being, for the other human beings he influences, it seems to me he must become a humanist, and must feel himself as an instrument of change for good or for bad.... The act of getting a story or a novel published is ... an attempt to impose one's personality and beliefs on other people. If a writer accepts this responsibility, he must see himself, to use the socialist phrase, as an architect of the soul.... [Furthermore,] the novelist has one advantage denied to any of the other artists. The novel is the only popular art-form left where the artist speaks directly, in clear words, to the audience.... The

novelist talks, as an individual to individuals, in a small personal voice. In an age of committee art, public art, people may begin to feel again a need for the small personal voice; and this will feed confidence into writers and, with confidence because of the knowledge of being needed, the warmth and humanity and love of people which is essential for a great age of literature."

BIOGRAPHICAL/CRITICAL SOURCES: Tom Maschler, editor, *Declaration,* MacGibbon & Kee, 1959; James Gindin, *Postwar British Fiction,* University of California Press, 1962; *New Statesman,* April 20, 1962, November 8, 1963; Richard Kostelanetz, editor, *On Contemporary Literature,* Avon, 1964; Roy Newquist, editor, *Counterpoint,* Rand McNally, 1964; George Wellwarth, *Theatre of Protest and Paradox,* New York University Press, 1964; Dorothy Brewster, *Doris Lessing,* Twayne, 1965; *Wilson Library Bulletin,* May, 1965; *Nation,* January 17, 1966, June 13, 1966, March 6, 1967; *Commonweal,* January 28, 1966; *Kenyon Review,* March, 1966; *Saturday Review,* April 2, 1966; *Milwaukee Journal,* May 29, 1966; *Partisan Review,* spring, 1966; *Saturday Review,* March 13, 1971; *New York Times Book Review,* March 14, 1971, May 13, 1973; *New Leader,* April 19, 1971; *Commonweal,* May 7, 1971; *New York Times,* October 21, 1972.

*   *   *

LETWIN, William (Louis) 1922-

PERSONAL: Born December 14, 1922, in Milwaukee, Wis.; son of Lazar and Bessie (Rosenthal) Letwin; married Shirley Robin, January 3, 1944; children: Oliver. *Education:* University of Chicago, B.A., 1943, Ph.D., 1951; postgraduate study at London School of Economics and Political Science, London. *Office:* 52-470 Massachusetts Institute of Technology, Cambridge, Mass. 02139; and London School of Economics and Political Science, University of London, London WC2A 2AE, England.

CAREER: University of Chicago Law School, Chicago, Ill., research associate, 1953-55; Massachusetts Institute of Technology, Cambridge, assistant professor, 1955-59, associate professor of economic history, 1959-66; London School of Economics and Political Science, University of London, London, England, reader in political science, 1966—. Consulting editor in economics, Random House, Inc., 1961—, Routledge & Kegan Paul, 1971—. *Military service:* U.S. Army, 1943-46; became second lieutenant; received Bronze Star. *Member:* Phi Beta Kappa.

WRITINGS: Congress and the Sherman Antitrust Law: 1887-1890, Law School, University of Chicago, 1956; *Sir Josiah Child: Merchant, Economist,* Baker Library, Graduate School of Business Administration, Harvard University, 1959; (editor) *A Documentary History of American Economic Policy Since 1789,* Doubleday-Anchor, 1961, hardcover edition, Aldine, 1962, revised and expanded edition, Norton, 1972; *The Origins of Scientific Economics: English Economic Thought, 1660-1776,* Methuen, 1963, Doubleday, 1964; *Law and Economic Policy in America: The Evolution of the Sherman Antitrust Act,* Random House, 1965.

WORK IN PROGRESS: Research (expected to continue for a decade or more) for a four- or five-volume economic history of the United States.

*   *   *

LEVENSON, Dorothy (Perkins) 1927-

PERSONAL: Born September 6, 1927, in Australia; daughter of Aubrey Alan (a butcher) and Lilian (Edwards) Perkins; married Milton Levenson (in public relations), March 18, 1953; children: Michael, Joel, Elizabeth. *Education:* University of Sydney, B.A., 1947. *Home:* 10 Belmont Ave., New Rochelle, N.Y. 10801.

WRITINGS: The Day Joe Went to the Supermarket, Grosset, 1962; Too Many Pockets, Wonder Books, 1963; One Kitten Is Not Too Many, Grosset, 1964; The Magic Carousel, Parents' Magazine Press, 1967; The First Book of the Civil War, F. Watts, 1968; The First Book of the Confederacy, F. Watts, 1968; Reconstruction, F. Watts, 1970; Homesteaders and Indians, F. Watts, 1971. Contributor of short stories to Humpty Dumpty, and articles to Mayfair and other Canadian magazines.

* * *

LEVENSTEIN, Sidney 1917-

PERSONAL: Born March 22, 1917, in Philadelphia, Pa.; son of Harry and Minnie (Sternick) Levenstein; married Phyllis Aronson (a clinical psychologist), November 15, 1946; children: Susan Beth, Daniel Lewis. Education: Columbus University, LL.B., 1941; New York University, A.B., 1949; Columbia University, M.S., 1951, D.S.W., 1963. Home: 3268 Island Rd., Wantagh, N.Y. 11793. Office: Department of Social Work, Adelphi University, Garden City, N.Y. 11530.

CAREER: U.S. Social Security Board, claims reviewer in Washington, D.C., and New York, N.Y., 1938-47; caseworker, supervisor, and assistant director in family agencies, child guidance centers, and psychiatric clinics in New York, N.Y., 1951-62; in private practice of social casework, Wantagh, N.Y., 1955—; Hillside Hospital (psychiatric hospital), Glen Oaks, N.Y., research associate, 1963-67; Graduate School of Social Work, Adelphi University, Garden City, N.Y., professor, 1963—. Member of executive committee, Citizens Committee for Wantagh Public Schools, 1959; member of organizing committee, Wantagh Council on Human Rights. Military service: U.S. Army, 1943-46; served in Europe; became master sergeant. Member: National Association of Social Workers (charter member; member of national committee on private practice, 1961-63), American Orthopsychiatric Association (fellow), Phi Beta Kappa, Alpha Kappa Delta.

WRITINGS: Private Practice in Social Casework: A Profession's Changing Pattern, Columbia University Press, 1964. Contributor to Encyclopedia of Social Work, National Association of Social Workers, 1965. Contributor to numerous professional journals.

WORK IN PROGRESS: Studies involving cognitive and affective development in potentially educationally disadvantaged children.

AVOCATIONAL INTERESTS: Playing piano, golf, table tennis, chess, and bridge.

* * *

LEVIN, Alexandra Lee 1912-

PERSONAL: Surname is pronounced Le-vin; born April 16, 1912, in Washington, D.C.; daughter of Lawrence Rust (an orchardist) and Alexandra (McDannold) Lee; married M. Jastrow Levin (head of a high school science department in Baltimore), August 24, 1934; children: Betsy, Larry, Sally, Lexie. Education: Holton-Arms School, diploma, 1929; Bryn Mawr College, student, 1929-32. Politics: Democrat. Religion: Judaism (convert). Home: 3712 Chesholm Rd., Baltimore, Md. 21216.

CAREER: Baltimore Emergency Relief Commission, Baltimore, Md., nursery school worker, 1933-35. Fairmount Improvement Association, member of board, 1958-59. Member: Maryland Historical Society, Maryland Jewish Historical Society (board, 1964-70), Society of the Lees of Virginia, Bryn Mawr College Club of Baltimore (treasurer, 1953-55). Awards, honors: First prize in Parker Genealogical Contest, Maryland Historical Society, 1959; book award for The Szolds of Lombard Street, Philadelphia Chapter of Hadassah, 1961.

WRITINGS: The Szolds of Lombard Street: A Baltimore Family, 1859-1909 (biography), Jewish Publication Society, 1960; Vision: A Biography of Harry Friedenwald, Jewish Publication Society, 1964. Contributor of articles to Capital Times (Madison, Wis.), Sunday Sun Magazine, Baltimore, Encyclopedia Judaica, London Jewish Chronicle, and to historical journals. Class editor, Bryn Mawr College Alumnae Bulletin, 1960-67.

WORK IN PROGRESS: A biography of Anne Grant, a literary contemporary of Sir Walter Scott, titled The Celebrated Mrs. Grant of Laggan.

AVOCATIONAL INTERESTS: Gardening, tennis, reading, travel.

BIOGRAPHICAL/CRITICAL SOURCES: London Jewish Chronicle, January 15, 1960; Baltimore Sun, November 20, 1960, July 29, 1962, January 15, 1967.

* * *

LEVIN, Beatrice Schwartz

PERSONAL: Born in Providence, R.I.; daughter of Julius and Sarah (Reganthal) Schwartz; married Franklyn K. Levin (a research geophysicist), September 15, 1946; children: Michael, Alan, Philip. Education: Rhode Island College, B.Ed., 1942; University of Wisconsin, M.S., 1947. Politics: Liberal Democrat. Home: 802 West Forest Dr., Houston, Tex. 77024.

CAREER: Encyclopedia Americana, New York, N.Y., research assistant, 1942-43; Edison High School, Tulsa, Okla., English teacher, 1959-60; Benedictine Heights College, Tulsa, Okla., teacher of creative writing, 1960-61; United States Junior Chamber of Commerce, Tulsa, Okla., research consultant, 1963-64; Texas Southern University, Houston, assistant professor of English, 1964-69. Military service: U.S. Women's Army Corps, 1943-45. Member: National Conference of Christians and Jews.

WRITINGS—All fiction: The Lonely Room, Bobbs-Merrill, 1950; Eyewitness to Exodus, Chicago Paperback, 1962; The Singer and the Summer Song, Arcadia House, 1964; Safari Smith, Peace Corps Nurse, Nova, 1966. Regular contributor to St. Louis Post-Dispatch, Oklahoma Orbit, Tulsa World, Universal Science News; travel writer, Chicago News; 55 short stories published in "little magazines."

WORK IN PROGRESS: Voyages of the Vema, a book on oceanography for boys; Best School in Town, a novel about a teacher; Indian Summer, a novel about the Southwest; Nuns and Other People, a collection of thirty previously published short stories; When Thou Art Absent, teen-age fiction; John Hawk, White Man, Black Man, Indian Chief; Creative Games for Teaching English; Walt Whitman, Hippie; The Pomegranate Seed; Vista Volunteer, a teen-age romance; Education of a Sentimentalist, an autobiography.

* * *

LEVIN, Harvey J(oshua) 1924-

PERSONAL: Born July 1, 1924, in New York, N.Y.; son of Leon Levin; married Rhoda Pinsley; children: Adam. Education: Hamilton College, A.B., 1944; Columbia University, A.M., 1948, Ph.D., 1953. Home: 110 Kilburn Rd., Garden City, N.Y. 11530. Office: Department of Economics, Hofstra University, 1000 Fulton Ave., Hempstead, N.Y. 11550.

CAREER: Office of Strategic Services, U.S. War Department, research analyst, 1944-46; Bard College, Annandale-on-Hudson, N.Y., instructor, 1949-50; Pennsylvania State University, University Park, assistant professor, 1950-54; Columbia College, New York, N.Y., instructor, 1954-55; Hofstra University, Hempstead, N.Y., 1955—, professor of economics, 1962—, department chairman,

1961-64, Augustus B. Weller Professor of Economics, 1964—. Senior research associate, Center for Policy Research, 1970—. *Member:* American Economic Associaion, Royal Economic Society, American Association of University Professors, Phi Beta Kappa. *Awards, honors:* Brookings Research grant, 1959-60; Carnegie fellow, Harvard University, 1963-64; research grant from Resources for the Future, 1964-65.

WRITINGS: (Editor) *Business Organization and Public Policy: A Book of Readings,* Rinehart, 1958; *Broadcast Regulation and Joint Ownership of Media,* New York University Press, 1960; *Some Economic and Regulatory Aspects of Liquor Store Licensing in New York State: A Summary of Research,* New York State Moreland Commission on the Alcoholic Beverage Control Law, 1963; *The Invisible Resource: Use and Regulation of the Radio Spectrum,* Johns Hopkins Press for Resources for the Future, 1971. Contributor of articles to professional journals.

*   *   *

LEVIN, Jonathan V (ictor)   1927-

PERSONAL: Born June 11, 1927, in New York, N.Y.; son of Harry and Bertha (Lebendiger) Levin; married Judith Goldstein, 1957. *Education:* Columbia University, B.S. (summa cum laude), 1950; Fletcher School of Law and Diplomacy, M.A., 1951, Ph.D., 1956; University of Strasbourg, diplome, 1952. *Home:* 610 West 173rd St., New York, N.Y. 10032. *Office:* Federal Reserve Bank of New York, 33 Liberty St., New York, N.Y. 10045.

CAREER: The Stars and Stripes (European edition), U.S. zone of Germany, copy editor, writer, 1946-48; International Program in Taxation, Harvard Law School, Cambridge, Mass., research fellow, 1954-56; Federal Reserve Bank of New York, New York, N.Y., economist, research department, 1956—. *Military service:* U.S. Army, 1945-47, became sergeant. *Member:* American Economic Association, American Geographical Society.

WRITINGS: A Theory of Export Economies: Case Studies of Peruvian Guano and Burmese Rice, Fletcher School of Law and Diplomacy, 1956; *The Export Economies: Their Pattern of Development in Historical Perspective,* Harvard University Press, 1960.

*   *   *

LEVIN, Meyer   1905-

PERSONAL: Born October 8, 1905, in Chicago, Ill.; son of Joseph (a tailor) and Goldie (Basiste) Levin; married Mabel Schamp Foy, 1934 (divorced, 1944); married Tereska Szwarc (a French novelist, known under name Tereska Torres), March 25, 1948; children: (first marriage) Eli; (second marriage) Gabriel, Mikael; (stepchildren) Dominique. *Education:* University of Chicago, Ph.B., 1924; attended Academie Moderne art school, Paris, 1925. *Religion:* Reform Judaism. *Home:* Street of the Blue Waves, Herzlia-on-Sea, Israel. *Agent:* Georges Borchardt, 145 East 52nd St., New York, N.Y. 10022.

CAREER: Chicago Daily News, Chicago, Ill., reporter, feature writer, and columnist, 1923-29; one-time member of collective farm community in Palestine (pre-Israel); producer of marionette plays at New School for Social Research, New York, N.Y.; *Esquire,* Chicago, Ill., associate editor, 1933-38, film critic, 1933-39; U.S. Office of War Information, film writer, producer, and director, 1942-43; later war correspondent for Overseas News Agency and Jewish Telegraphic Agency, with special assignment to discover and document the fate of European Jewry; film producer and writer. *Member:* American War Correspondents Association, Authors League, Dramatists Guild. *Awards, honors:* Harry and Ethel Daroff Fiction award, 1966, for *The Stronghold;* Isaac Sie-

gel Memorial Juvenile award of Jewish Book Council of America, 1967, for *The Story of Israel;* special citation by World Federation of Bergen/Belsen Associations, 1969, for "excellence and distinction in literature of the Holocaust and Jewish destiny."

WRITINGS: Reporter (novel), John Day, 1929 (withdrawn shortly after publication); *Frankie and Johnnie: A Love Story,* John Day, 1930, revised edition published as *The Young Lovers,* New American Library, 1952; *Yehuda,* J. Cape & H. Smith, 1931; *The Golden Mountain* (folk tales retold from Hebrew, Yiddish, and German sources), Behrman, 1932, reissued as *Classic Hassidic Tales,* Citadel, 1966; *The New Bridge* (novel), Covici, Friede, 1933; *The Old Bunch* (novel), Viking, 1937; *Citizens* (novel), Viking, 1940; *My Father's House* (novel), Viking, 1947; *If I Forget Thee: A Picture Story of Modern Palestine* (synopsis of the author's film, "My Father's House," with photographs), Viking, 1947; (translator) Sholem Asch, *Tales Of My People,* Putnam, 1948; *In Search* (autobiography), Horizon, 1950; *Compulsion* (novel), Simon & Schuster, 1956; *Eva* (novel); Simon & Schuster, 1959; *The Fanatic* (novel), Simon & Schuster, 1964; *The Stronghold* (novel), Simon & Schuster, 1965; *Gore and Igor: An Extravaganza* (novel), Simon & Schuster, 1968; *The Haggadah Retold* (original paperback), music by Harry Coopersmith, design and illustrations by Miriam Woods, Behrman, 1968, hardcover edition published as *An Israel Haggadah for Passover,* Abrams, 1970; *Beginnings in Jewish Philosophy,* Behrman, 1971; *The Settlers* (novel), Simon & Schuster, 1972.

Juveniles: (With Toby K. Kurzband) *The Story of the Synagogue,* Behrman, 1957; (with Kurzband) *The Story of the Jewish Way of Life,* Behrman, 1959; (with Dorothy K. Kripke) *God and the Story of Judaism,* Behrman, 1962; *The Story of Israel,* includes photographs by Archie Lieberman, sketches by son, Eli Levin, Putnam, 1966.

Editor: (And translator) *Selections from the Kibbutz Buchenwald Diary,* Zionist Organization, 1946; (and author of introduction) David S. Kogan, *Diary,* Beechhurst Press, 1955; Arthur D. Goldhaft, *Golden Egg,* Horizon, 1957; (with Charles Angoff) *The Rise of American Jewish Literature* (anthology of selections from major novels), Simon & Schuster, 1970.

Translator from the French—All written by Levin's wife, under name Tereska Torres: *Not Yet,* Crown, 1957; *Dangerous Games,* Dial, 1957; *The Golden Cage,* Dial, 1959; *Women's Barracks,* Allen, 1960; *The Only Reason,* Allen, 1962.

Plays: "The Good Old Days," first produced in Paris, 1951; *Compulsion* (two-act; revised version first produced on Broadway at Ambassador Theatre, October 24, 1957), original typescript, M. McCall, 1958. Also author of dramatization of *The Diary of Anne Frank,* privately printed "for literary discussion," 1967, produced by The Israel Soldiers Theatre, 1966, and Brandeis University, 1972, although forbidden by the *Diary* owners.

Films: (Writer and co-producer, with Herbert Kline) "My Father's House," feature film produced in Palestine, 1947; "The Illegals," feature-length documentary filmed in eastern Europe, 1948. Also author of two 30-minute documentary films, "The Falashas," and "Bus to Sinai." Author of a report entitled "Another Kind of Blacklist," Congress Bi-Weekly, 1961. Contributor of articles and short stories to *New Yorker,. Reporter, New Republic, Nation, Travel, Saturday Evening Post, Menorah Journal, Commentary, Collier's,* and other periodicals.

WORK IN PROGRESS: The Manipulators, a continuation of the autobiography, *In Search,* publication expected in 1973.

SIDELIGHTS: Levin has said that he began writing in grammar school, setting up his stories in the school print shop. His first novel, Reporter, based on his years as a journalist, was withdrawn shortly after publication in 1929 "due to a threat of suit from a newspaperwoman who thought she had been pictured in the book." The case was subsequently dropped. From 1953 to 1957 Levin was again involved in a lawsuit, this time over the dramatic version of The Diary of Anne Frank. This litigation, Levin told CA, "resulted in a jury decision in the Supreme Court of New York that Meyer Levin had contributed substantially to the Pulitzer Prize play through the use of ideas, conception, and material from an authorized version written by him previous to the Broadway version commissioned from the Hacketts." The Fanatic, a novel about the Communist persecution of an American-Jewish author who has written a dramatization of philosophic fiction by a victim of the Nazis, has been thought to reflect Levin's own difficulties with The Diary of Anne Frank. This book is one of several novels Levin has written (Compulsion, The Stronghold, and Citizens are other examples) which have a basis in fact. Yehuda, which grew out of his experiences on a farm commune in Israel, was the first novel about a modern Palestinian kibbutz to be published in any language.

"In my view," Levin has said, "though always subject to the aesthetic impulse, the function of the writer in modern times is somewhat akin to that of the ancient Hebrew prophet in promulgating his ethical parables, except that the modern writer more consciously is engaged in the interpretation of material that will help humanity toward self-understanding. My own tendency in fiction is to write from the organic point of view: that is, the view embracing society as an organism.... I have consciously sought to define my work as that of an American Jewish writer.... I write largely in the tradition of the realists, having been at the outset impressed by Dreiser and Dos Passos. I hope to develop my work as a novelist performing his share, however small, in the total human search for truth." Levin has always been considered a serious naturalist; Gore and Igor, surprisingly, is a prime example of black humor. A mixture of burlesque and social satire, Time calls the book a "pop war novel" about the Arab-Israeli Seven-Day War of 1967, while Playboy labels it "a fantastic ribald tale of the meeting in Israel of a Dylanesque American folk-rock singer and an Evtushenkoesque Soviet poet amid much travail, many guitars strummed, and myriad ladies mounted."

In 1959, 20th Century-Fox produced a motion picture based on Levin's Compulsion, a dramatization of the Leopold-Loeb case concerning the murder of a boy by two wealthy law students. East Coast Productions has acquired film, television, and non-theatrical rights to "My Father's House," "The Illegals," "The Falashas," and "Bus to Sinai."

AVOCATIONAL INTERESTS: Retouching beach stones into sculptural pieces.

BIOGRAPHICAL/CRITICAL SOURCES: Harry R. Warfel, editor, American Novelists of Today, American Book, 1951; Saturday Review, September 6, November 6, and December 4, 1965, September 24, 1966; Time, February 23, 1968; New York Times Book Review, February 18, 1968; Playboy, March, 1968; Variety, July 7, 1971.

*   *   *

LEVINE, Erwin L(eon)   1926-

PERSONAL: Born June 26, 1926, in Boston, Mass.; son of Henry and Deborah (Baker) Levine; married; children: Dana Lewis. Education: Brown University, A.B., 1948, A.M., 1958, Ph.D., 1961. Home: 80 Court St., Saratoga Springs, N.Y. 12866. Office: Skidmore College, Saratoga Springs, N.Y. 12866.

CAREER: Skidmore College, Saratoga Springs, N.Y., associate professor, 1961-64, professor of government, 1965—. Military service: U.S. Navy, 1944-46. Member: American Political Science Association, American Academy of Political and Social Science. Awards, honors: Howard Foundation fellow, 1967-68.

WRITINGS: Theodore Francis Green: The Rhode Island Years, 1906-1936, Brown University Press, 1963; (with Elmer E. Cornwell, Jr.) An Introduction to American Government, Macmillan, 1968, revised edition, 1972; Theodore Francis Green: The Washington Years, 1937-1960, Brown University Press, 1971. Contributor of articles to Rhode Island History.

*   *   *

LEVINE, Lawrence   1916-

PERSONAL: Born August 1, 1916, in Fargo, N.D.; son of Simon and Fanny (Reichlin) Levine; married Marguerite Lucienne Simonne (a records manager), December 23, 1950. Education: North Dakota State College (now North Dakota State University), student, 1933-35; Alliance Francaise, Paris, France, Diplome Superier, 1952. Home: 110-55 72nd Rd., Forest Hills, N.Y. 11375. Agent: Gunther Stuhlmann, 65 Irving Pl., New York, N.Y. 10003.

CAREER: Motion picture theatre publicity and theatre management, New York, N.Y., 1937-41; U.S. Department of the Army, civilian employee, France, 1946-52; American Society of Mechanical Engineers, New York, N.Y., publications production, 1955-56; free-lance writer, 1956—. Military service: U.S. Army, 1942-46; served in European theater; received two battle stars. Member: Authors Guild of Authors League of America.

WRITINGS: The Great Alphonse, Norton, 1959. Contributor to Kansas Magazine, Pageant, Saturday Review, and Carolina Quarterly.

WORK IN PROGRESS: Two novels, The Little Saga of Dequincey Piip and The Misfortune Cookies.

SIDELIGHTS: "In spite of the absurdity of publication processes and an evident dwindling readership, I believe deeply in the modern novel.... Stylistically and in subject matter, the novel today is at a pinnacle of ingenuity. Never before have so many satisfying novels been written by so many astonishing stylists. I prefer to read and write about the grotesque lives of aliens residing among remarkable strangers. . . ."†

*   *   *

LEVINE, Philip   1928-
  (Edgar Poe)

PERSONAL: Born January 10, 1928, in Detroit, Mich.; son of Harry A. (a buisnessman) and Ester (Priscol) Levine; married Frances Artley (a film actress); children: Mark, John, Theodore Henri. Education: Wayne State University, A.B., 1950, A.M., 1954; State University of Iowa, M.F.A., 1957. Home: 4727 East Dayton, Fresno, Calif. Office: Fresno State College, Fresno, Calif.

CAREER: State University of Iowa, Iowa City, faculty member, 1955-57; Fresno State College, Fresno, Calif., member of English faculty, 1958—. Teacher at Squaw Valley Writers Community. Has read poetry at Poetry Center of San Francisco, Pasadena Art Gallery, Guggenheim Museum, Princeton University, Massachusetts Institute of Technology, University of Michigan, University of California at Los Angeles, Berkeley, Irvine, and Santa Cruz, Stanford University, Wayne State University, State University of Iowa, San Francisco State College, and other schools. Awards, honors: Stanford poetry fellowship, 1958; Joseph Henry Jackson Award, 1961, for "Berenda Slough and Other Poems"; Chaplebrook Foundation Award, 1968; Frank O'Hara Prize of *Poetry* magazine, 1972.

WRITINGS: On the Edge (limited edition), Stonewall Press, 1961; *Silent in America: Vivas for Those Who Failed* (limited edition), Shaw Avenue Press (Iowa City), 1965; (editor with Henri Coulette) *Character and Crisis: A Contemporary Reader,* McGraw, 1966; *Not This Pig* (poems), Wesleyan University Press, 1968; *5 Detroits* (poems), Unicorn Press, 1970; *Thistles* (poems; limited edition), Turret Books (London), 1970; *Pili's Wall* (poems), Unicorn Press, 1971; *Red Dust* (poems), Kayak Books, 1971; *They Feed the Lion* (poems), Atheneum, 1972. Work represented in anthologies, including *Midland,* edited by P. Engle and others, Random House, 1961; *New Poets of England and America,* edited by D. Hall, Meridian, 1962; *Poet's Choice,* edited by P. Engle and J.T. Langland, Dial, 1962; *American Poems,* edited by J.F. Kessler, Southern Illinois University Press, 1964; *Naked Poetry,* edited by S. Berg and R. Mezey, Bobbs-Merrill, 1969. Contributor to *New Yorker, Poetry, Antioch Review, Encounter, New York Review of Books, Kayak, Hudson Review, Paris Review, Harper's.*

SIDELIGHTS: "To distinguish exactly the quality of Philip Levine's poems is not easy," Hayden Carruth writes. "He falls outside our categories. In some respects his horror poems, reciting the barbarities of our time, seem old-fashioned, reverberations from the days of early Jarrell and Shapiro. . . . Levine gives us that inspired loathing, that humane coldbloodedness. But his contempt is even fiercer than his forbears', I should say, and he writes without their neo-metaphysical ornamentation. Face to face with the bomb, what is the use of wit?" Carruth cites Levine's first book, *On the Edge,* "for its individuality, its poems in a classical ascerbic voice," and states that in *Not This Pig* he "writes with an easier, freer, more fluent and versatile command." Ralph J. Mills lists qualities which he sees in *Not This Pig:* "Directness of speech, sudden irruptions of the irrational, use of the ordinary details of contemporary life, and a colloquial intimacy which gives a reader the impression of being spoken to as a person by a person." Mills also finds "two prominent preoccupations which become theme and substance of his art: movement and travel—the poems reflect in oblique fashion the vastness of America, the loneliness of individuals—and finding a tongue for the speechless, for the poor, the outcast, the minorities: the 'submerged population'. . . . Though Levine's presence can be felt everywhere in his poems—and indeed some pieces are about himself or events of a personal nature—he enters the life around him in America, in Spain, suffers it all in himself, and faces his own despair and inner disequilibrium."

Levine has recorded his poems for the Library of Congress. He told *CA* that he has "given up motorcycle racing after creaming self." He "has travelled widely in past four years, lived in Spain for two years and hopes to travel more."

BIOGRAPHICAL/CRITICAL SOURCES: Yale Review, spring, 1964; *Poetry,* February, 1964, January, 1969, July, 1972; *New York Review of Books,* April 25, 1968; *Saturday Review,* June 1, 1968; *Hudson Review,* summer, 1968; *Carleton Miscellany,* fall, 1968.

*   *   *

LEVINE, Sol 1914-

PERSONAL: Born November 16, 1914, in Bentleyville, Pa.; son of Samuel and Bessie (Slesinger) Levine; children: Richard E., James R. *Education:* Waynesburg College, B.S., 1938; New York University, M.S. in Electrical Engineering, 1948. *Home:* 549 Brook Rd., Baltimore, Md. 21204.

CAREER: Edo Corp., College Point, N.Y., chief engineer, 1946-56; Sterling Precision Corp., New York, N.Y., chief engineer, 1956-57; Martin Co., Baltimore, Md., technical director, 1957—. *Member:* Institute of Electrical and Electronic Engineers (senior member), American Institute of Aeronautics and Astronautics (associate fellow).

WRITINGS: Your Future in Electronic Engineering, Rosen Press, 1961; *Appointment in the Sky: The Story of Project Gemini,* Walker & Co., 1964; *Your Future in NASA,* Rosen Press, 1969, revised edition, Arco, 1971; *Mathematics Handbook,* Rosen Press, 1972.

*   *   *

LEVITAN, Sar A. 1914-

PERSONAL: Born September 14, 1914, in Shiauliai, Lithuania; son of Osher N. (a rabbi) and JoAnn (Rapoport) Levitan; married Brita Ann Bouchard, October 16, 1946. *Education:* College of the City of New York (now City College of the City University of New York), B.S.S., 1937; Columbia University, M.A., 1939, Ph.D., 1949. *Home:* 1280 21st St. N.W., Washington, D.C. 20036. *Office:* The Center for Manpower Policy Studies, George Washington University, 1819 H St. N.W., Suite 660, Washington, D.C. 20006.

CAREER: State University of New York College at Plattsburgh, associate professor of economics, 1946-51; various positions in U.S. Government, Washington, D.C., 1951-62; George Washington University, Washington, D.C., research professor of labor economics, 1962-64; Upjohn Institute, Washington, D.C., senior economist, 1964-67; George Washington University, research professor of economics and director of Center for Manpower Policy Studies, 1967—. Vice-chairman, National Manpower Task Force. *Military service:* U.S. Army, 1942-46; became lieutenant colonel. *Member:* American Economic Association, Industrial Relations Research Association (president, Washington chapter, 1958-59), National Association of Business Economists, Economic Round Table of Washington, D.C. *Awards, honors:* Ford Foundation grants, 1962-63, 1967-73.

WRITINGS: Ingrade Wage-Rate Progression in War and Peace: A Problem in Wage Administration Techniques, Clinton Press, 1950; *Federal Assistance to Labor Surplus Areas,* U.S. Government Printing Office, 1957; *Government Regulation of Internal Union Affairs Affecting the Rights of Members,* U.S. Government Printing Office, 1958; (with Harold L. Sheppard) *Impact of Technological Change Upon Communities and Public Policy,* U.S. Department of Commerce, Area Redevelopment Administration, 1960; (with Louise D. Houghteling) *Factors Affecting the Slower Growth of Missouri Population Compared with the U.S.,* revised edition, Legislative Reference Service, U.S. Library of Congress, 1961; *Youth Employment Act,* Upjohn, 1963; *Reducing Worktime as a Means to Combat Unemployment,* Upjohn, 1964; *Federal Manpower Policies and Programs to Combat Unemployment,* Upjohn, 1964; *Federal Aid to Depressed Areas: An Evaluation of the Area Redevelopment Administration,* Johns Hopkins Press, 1964; (with Joseph M. Becker) *Programs to Aid the Unemployed in the 1960's,* Upjohn, 1965; *Programs in Aid of the Poor,* Upjohn, 1965, revised edition published as *Programs in Aid of the Poor for the 1970's,* Johns Hopkins Press, 1969; (editor with Irving H. Siegel) *Dimensions of Manpower Policy: Programs and Research,* Johns Hopkins Press, 1966; *Antipoverty Work and Training Efforts: Goals and Reality,* Institute of Labor and Industrial Relations (University of Michigan/Wayne State University) and National Manpower Policy Task Force, 1967, 2nd edition, 1970; *The Design of Federal Antipoverty Strategy,* Institute of Labor and Industrial Relations, 1967; (with Garth L. Mangum) *Making Sense of Federal Manpower Policy,* Institute of

Labor and Industrial Relations, 1967; (editor with Wilbur J. Cohen and Robert J. Lampman) *Towards Freedom from Want*, Industrial Relations Research Association, 1968; (with Roger H. Davidson) *Antipoverty Housekeeping: The Administration of the Economic Opportunity Act*, Institute of Labor and Industrial Relations, 1968; *The Great Society's Poor Law: A New Approach to Poverty*, Johns Hopkins Press, 1969; (with Mangum) *Federal Training and Work Programs in the Sixties*, Institute of Labor and Industrial Relations, 1969; (with Mangum and Robert Taggart III) *Economic Opportunity in the Ghetto: The Partnership of Government and Business*, Johns Hopkins Press, 1970; (with Taggart) *Social Experimentation and Manpower Policy: The Rhetoric and the Reality*, Johns Hopkins Press, 1971; (editor) *Blue-Collar Workers: A Symposium on Middle America*, McGraw, 1971; (with Barbara Hetrick) *Big Brother's Indian Programs—With Reservations*, McGraw, 1971; (with Taggart) *Job Crisis for Black Youth: A Report for the Twentieth Century Fund*, Praeger, 1971; (with Mangum and Ray Marshall) *Human Resources and Labor Markets: Labor and Manpower in the American Economy*, Harper, 1972; (with Martin Rein and David Marwick) *Work and Welfare Go Together*, Johns Hopkins Press, 1972; *The Federal Dollar in Its Own Backyard*, Bureau of National Affairs, 1973. Contributor to *Encyclopaedia Britannica, Encyclopedia of Education*, and various journals.

WORK IN PROGRESS: Federal Programs for Veterans.

BIOGRAPHICAL/CRITICAL SOURCES: Nation, September 8, 1969; *Commentary*, October, 1969; *Library Journal*, March 15, 1970.

* * *

LEVITAN, Tina (Nellie) 1928-

PERSONAL: Born December 19, 1928, in Boston, Mass.; daughter of Julius and Bella (Rosen) Levitan. *Education:* Hunter College (now Hunter College of the City University of New York), B.A., 1949; Herzliah Hebrew Institute, New York, N.Y., Bachelor of Hebrew Letters, 1950. *Religion:* Jewish. *Home:* 372 Central Park W., Apt. 6H, New York, N.Y. 10025.

CAREER: National Jewish Welfare Board, New York, N.Y., member of Jewish Center Lecture Bureau, 1952—, lecturing on American Jewish history, the Jew in science, Jewish contributions to medicine, Zionism, religon, and public affairs. *Member:* Authors League of America, American Jewish Historical Society, Hunter College Alumni Association. *Awards, honors:* Hunter College award for outstanding achievement, 1959.

WRITINGS: Haolam Hechadash (short stories from American Jewish history, in Hebrew), Charuth, 1949; *The Firsts of American Jewish History, 1492-1951*, Charuth, 2nd edition, 1957; *The Laureates: Jewish Winners of the Nobel Prize*, Twayne, 1960; *Islands of Compassion: A History of the Jewish Hospitals of New York*, Twayne, 1964; *Jews in American Life: From 1492 to the Space Age*, Hebrew Publishing, 1969; *The Scientist and Religion*, Synagogue Light, 1970. Contributor of over one hundred articles on Jewish topics to periodicals in the United States and abroad.

* * *

LEVY, Alan 1932-

PERSONAL: Born February 10, 1932, in New York, N.Y.; son of Meyer and Frances (Shield) Levy; married Valerie Wladaver, August 7, 1956; children: Monica, Erika. *Education:* Brown University, A.B., 1952; Columbia University, M.S. in Journalism, 1953. *Home and office:* Hladkov 4, Praha 6, Czechoslovakia. *Agent:* Theron Raines, 244 Madison Ave., New York, N.Y. 10016.

CAREER: Louisville Courier-Journal, Louisville, Ky., reporter, 1953-60; free-lance writer, New York, N.Y., 1960-67; investigator for President Johnson's Carnegie Commission on Educational Television, 1966-67; free-lance writer and accredited foreign correspondent in Prague, Czechoslovakia, 1967—. *Military service:* U.S. Army, 1953-55. *Member:* Authors Guild of Authors League of America, Overseas Press Club, Society of Magazine Writers. *Awards, honors: New Republic* Younger Writer Award, 1948; Sigma Delta Chi regional award for newspaper coverage of Cuban revolution, 1959; Bernard DeVoto Fellowship in Prose to Bread Loaf Writers' Conference, Middlebury, Vt., 1963.

WRITINGS: (With Bernard Krisher and James Cox) *Draftee's Confidential Guide: How to Get Along in the Army*, Indiana University Press, 1957, revised edition, New American Library, 1966; *Operation Elvis*, Holt, 1960; *The Elizabeth Taylor Story*, Hillman Books, 1961; *Wanted: Nazis Criminals at Large*, Berkley Publishing, 1962; *Interpret Your Dreams*, Pyramid Publications, 1962; (contributor) Leonard Lief and David Hawke, editors, *American Colloquy*, Bobbs-Merrill, 1963; (with Gilbert Stuart) *Kind-Hearted Tiger*, Little, Brown, 1964; (contributor) *Casebook on Godot*, Grove, 1967; (contributor) *College Reading and Writing*, Macmillan, 1968; *The Culture Vultures; or, Whatever Became of the Emperor's New Clothes?*, Putnam, 1968; *God Bless You Real Good: My Crusade with Billy Graham*, Essandess, 1969; (contributor) *Marilyn Monroe: A Composite View*, Chilton, 1969; *Rowboat to Prague*, Grossman, 1972. Contributor to *Life, Harper's, Horizon, Reader's Digest, Saturday Evening Post, Mademoiselle, TV Guide, New York Times Magazine, Reporter, New Republic, Cosmopolitan, Redbook, Theatre Arts, Show, Cavalier, Good Housekeeping*, and other popular magazines. Book reviewer for *New York Post*, 1962-64.

WORK IN PROGRESS: A play.

BIOGRAPHICAL/CRITICAL SOURCES: Redbook, February, 1960; *Life*, January 20, 1967; *Christian Science Monitor*, September 12, 1968; *Harper's*, September, 1969.

* * *

LEVY, William V. 1930-
(Bill Levy)

PERSONAL: Born June 24, 1930, in Cleveland, Ohio; son of Jerome (an accountant) and Bessie (Goldberg) Levy; married Barbara Neuger, June 18, 1955; children: Jody Lynn, Michael Stephen. *Education:* Attended schools in Cleveland, Ohio. *Home:* 14455 Summerfield Rd., Cleveland, Ohio 44118. *Agent:* Donald MacCampbell, Inc., 12 East 41st St., New York, N.Y. 10017.

CAREER: International News Service, Cleveland, Ohio, assistant manager of Cleveland bureau, 1951-58; Cinecraft Productions, Cleveland, Ohio, sales representative, 1959-60; Goodyear Aerospace Corp., Akron, Ohio, manager of public relations, 1960—. *Member:* Public Relations Society of America, Aviation/Space Writers Association.

WRITINGS: How Much Is a College Degree Worth to You?, Macfadden, 1963; *College Scholarships and Loans: Who Gets Them, How and Why?*, Macfadden, 1964; (with Norman A. Palmer) *Five Star Golf*, Duell, Sloan & Pearce, 1964; (under name Bill Levy) *Return to Glory: The Story of the Cleveland Browns*, World Publishing, 1965; (under name Bill Levy) *Three Yards and a Cloud of Dust: The Ohio State Football Story*, World Publishing, 1966; (under name Bill Levy) *The Derby*, World Publishing, 1967. Contributor to *Pageant, TV Guide*, and *Sport*.

WORK IN PROGRESS: 100 Careers for Young Men.†

LEWIS, (Joseph) Anthony   1927-

PERSONAL: Born March 27, 1927, in New York, N.Y.; son of Kassel (a businessman) and Sylvia (Surut) Lewis; married Linda Rannells (a teacher of remedial reading), July 8, 1951; children: Eliza, David Cartmell, Martha. Education: Harvard University, A.B., 1948, Nieman fellow, 1956-57. Religion: Jewish. Home: Canonbury House, London N.1, England; and Deep Bottom Cove, West Tisbury, Mass. 02575. Office: Printing House Sq., London E.C.4, England.

CAREER: New York Times, New York, N.Y., deskman, "Review of the Week," 1948-52; Democratic National Committee, researcher, 1952; Washington Daily News, Washington, D.C., reporter, 1952-55; New York Times, Supreme Court and Department of Justice correspondent in Washington Bureau, 1955-64, chief of London Bureau, 1964-72, columnist, 1972—. Member: Century Association (New York), Garrick Club (London). Awards, honors: Pulitzer Prize for National Reporting, 1955, 1963; Heywood Broun Award, 1955; New York State Bar Association Press award, 1958, 1961; D.Litt., Adelphi University, 1964; award for best fact-crime book, Mystery Writers of America, 1965, for Gideon's Trumpet.

WRITINGS: The Supreme Court: Process and Change, College of Law, State University of Iowa, 1963; Gideon's Trumpet, Random House, 1964; (with others) Portrait of a Decade: The Second American Revolution, Random House, 1964 (published in England as The Second American Revolution: A First-Hand Account of the Struggle for Civil Rights, Faber, 1966); The Supreme Court and How It Works, Random House, 1966. Contributor of articles to law journals and to general periodicals.

*   *   *

LEWIS, Arthur O(reutt), Jr.   1920-

PERSONAL: Born October 8, 1920, in Wellsville, Pa.; son of Arthur O. (a manufacturer) and Janet Morrison (Sanderson) Lewis; married Celeste Cecile Juneau, March 1, 1945; children: Janet Rebecca, Arthur O. III, Mary Jameson. Education: Harvard University, A.B. (cum laude), 1940, A.M., 1942; Pennsylvania State University, Ph.D., 1951. Office: 105 Sparks Building, University Park, Pa. 16802.

CAREER: Rice Institute (now University), Houston, Tex., instructor in English, 1946-48; Pennsylvania State University, University Park, instructor, 1950-52, assistant professor, 1953-56, associate professor of English literature, 1956-60, professor of English, 1960—, associate head of department of English, 1960-65, associate dean, College of Liberal Arts, 1965—, acting dean, 1968-69. Military service: U.S. Army, Signal Corps, 1942-46; became first lieutenant. Member: Modern Language Association of America, American Studies Association, College English Association, Society for the History of Technology, Renaissance Society of America, American Federation of Teachers (president, Pennsylvania State local, 1956-59), Pennsylvania Federation of Teachers (vice-president, 1951-56, 1959-61; president, 1956-59).

WRITINGS—Editor: (With Frederick Landis Gwynn and R.W. Condee) The Case for Poetry, Prentice-Hall, 1954, revised edition, 1965; Emblem Books: An Introduction to the Collection at Penn State, Pennsylvania State College, 1954; (with Philip A. Shelley) Anglo-German and American-German Crosscurrents, University of North Carolina Press, Volume I, 1957, Volume II, 1962, Volume III, 1967, Volume IV, 1972; (with Bernard S. Oldsey) Visions and Revisions in Modern American Literary Criticism, Dutton, 1962; Of Men and Machines, Dutton, 1963; (editor) American Utopias: Selected Short Fiction, Arno, 1971; (editor with Yoshinobui Hakutani) The World of Japanese Fiction, Dutton, 1973. Contributor to

College English, American-German Review, Explicator, Notes and Queries, other professional journals. Editor, "American Utopias" reprint series, Arno (48 volumes).

WORK IN PROGRESS: Utopian and Anti-Utopian Literature; Bibliography of Utopian Works in Pattee Library.

AVOCATIONAL INTERESTS: Reading science fiction.

*   *   *

LEWIS, Claude A.   1934-

PERSONAL: Born December 14, 1934, in New York, N.Y.; son of Robert George and Hazel (Perkinson) Lewis; married Beverly McKelvey, October 18, 1953; children: Pamela, Brian, Craig. Education: Attended City College (now City College of City University of New York). Politics: Democrat. Home: 24 Ivy Hill Dr., Matawan, N.J. 07747. Agent: Donald MacCampbell, Inc., 12 East 41st St., New York, N.Y. 10017. Office: New York Herald Tribune, 230 West 41st St., New York, N.Y.

CAREER: Newsweek, New York, N.Y., began as office boy, 1952, teletype operator, 1957, teletypesetter operator, 1958, editorial assistant, 1959-62, assistant sports editor, 1962-64; New York Herald Tribune, New York, N.Y., on city desk, 1964—. Professional photographer. Consultant, Committee on Civil Rights in Metropolitan New York. Member: National Association for the Advancement of Colored People, Congress on Racial Equality, Matawan Civic Association, Strathmore Democratic Club, Toastmasters.

WRITINGS: Adam Clayton Powell, Fawcett, 1963; Cassius Marcellus Clay, Heavyweight Champion, Macfadden, 1965; Benjamin Banneker: The Man Who Saved Washington, McGraw, 1970. Contributor of poetry, articles, and reviews to periodicals.

AVOCATIONAL INTERESTS: Bicycle riding and collecting books by and about Negroes.

*   *   *

LEWIS, H(ywel) D(avid)   1910-

PERSONAL: Born May 21, 1910, in Llandudno, Caernarvonshire, Wales: son of David John (a minister) and Rebecca (Davies) Lewis; married Megan Elias-Jones, August 17, 1943 (died, 1962); married Megan Pritchard, July 17, 1965. Education: University College of North Wales, B.A. (first class honors in philosophy), 1932, M.A. (with distinction), 1933; Jesus College, Oxford University, B.Litt., 1935. Religion: Presbyterian. Home: 1 Normandy Park, Normandy, near Guilford, Surrey, England. Office: King's College, University of London, Strand, London W.C. 2, England.

CAREER: University College of North Wales, Bangor, lecturer, 1936-46, senior lecturer, 1946-47, professor of philosophy, 1947-55; King's College, University of London, London, England, professor of the history and philosophy of religion, 1955—, fellow, 1963, dean of Faculty of Theology, 1964—, dean of Faculty of Arts, 1967. Visiting professor at Bryn Mawr College, 1958-59, and Yale University, 1964-65. Wilde Lecturer in natural and comparative religion at Oxford University, 1960-63; Edward Cadbury Lecturer at University of Birmingham, 1962-63; visiting lecturer at Center for the Study of Religions, Harvard University, 1963; Owen Evans Lecturer at University College of Wales, 1964-65; Gifford Lecturer at University of Edinburgh, 1966-67, 1967-68; distinguished lecturer at other colleges and universities in England, Scotland, Northern Ireland, and Canada. External examiner at universities in Nigeria and Ghana, 1957; examiner for Universities of Glasgow, Leeds, Wales, Durham, and for Cambridge University. Member of board, Athlone Press; member of Advisory Council on Education, Wales, 1964—.

MEMBER: Royal Institute of Philosophy (chairman of council, 1965—), Society for the Study of Theology (president, 1964-66), Aristotelian Society (president, 1962-63), London Society for the Study of Religion (president, 1970-71), Oxford Society for Historical Theology (president, 1970-71), Mind Association (president, 1948-49), Honourable Society of Cymmrodorion (council). *Awards, honors:* Leverhulme fellow, 1954-55; D.D., University of St. Andrews.

WRITINGS: Morals and the New Theology, Harper, 1947; *Morals and Revelation,* Verry, 1951; (editor and contributor) *Contemporary British Philosophy: Personal Statements,* Series III, Macmillan, 1956; *Our Experience of God,* Macmillan, 1959; *Freedom and History,* Macmillan, 1962; (editor and contributor) *Clarity Is Not Enough: Essays in Criticism of Linguistic Philosophy,* Humanities, 1963; *Philosophy of Religion,* English Universities Press, 1965, Barnes & Noble, 1966; (with Robert Lawson Slater) *World Religions: Meeting Points and Major Issues,* F. Watts, 1966, reissued as *The Study of Religions: Meeting Points and Major Issues,* Penguin, 1969; *Dreaming and Experience* (lecture given at London School of Economics and Political Science, May 11, 1967), Athlone Press, 1968; *The Elusive Mind* (Gifford Lectures given at University of Edinburgh, 1966-68), Humanities, 1969.

Books in Welsh: *Gweriniaeth* (title means "Democracy"), Presbyterian Church of Wales Press, 1940; (with J.A. Thomas) *Y Wladwriaeth a'i Hawdurdod* (title means "The State and Its Authority"), University of Wales Press, 1943; *Ebyrth* (title means "Sacrifices"; poems), Aberystwyth Press, 1943; *Diogelu diwylliant, ac ysgrifian eraill* (title means "In Defense of Culture"), Brython Press, 1945; *Christ a Heddwch,* Gee Press, 1947; *Dilyn Crist* (title means "Christian Discipleship"), Jarvis & Foster, 1951; *Gwybod am Dduw* (title means "Knowledge of God"), University of Wales Press, 1952.

Contributor: Wilfrid Sellars and John Hospers, editors, *Readings in Ethical Theory,* Appleton, 1952, 2nd edition, 1970; Milton K. Munitz, editor, *A Modern Introduction to Ethics,* Free Press, 1958; Victor Gollancz, editor, *The New Year of Grace: An Anthology for Youth and Age,* Doubleday (Toronto), 1961; Ian T. Ramsey, editor, *Prospect for Metaphysics: Essays of Metaphysical Exploration,* Greenwood Press, 1961; Geddes MacGregor and J. Wesley Robb, compilers, *Readings in Religious Philosophy,* Houghton, 1962; Francis George Healey, editor, *Prospect for Theology,* Nisbet, 1966; Rupert Davies, editor, *We Believe in God,* Allen & Unwin, 1968.

Editor: "Muirhead Library of Philosophy," Macmillan, 1948—, including: Radhakrishnan, *The Principal Upanishads;* G.E. Moore, *Some Main Problems of Philosophy;* Moore, *The Common-place Book;* J.N. Findlay, *Values and Intentions;* Brand Blanshard, *Reason and Goodness;* C.A. Campbell, *Selfhood and Godhood.* Also editor of "Religious Studies," Cambridge University Press. Contributor to philosophy and theology journals in England and Wales.

* * *

LEWIS, I(oan) M(yrddin) 1930-

PERSONAL: Born January 30, 1930, in Glasgow, Scotland; son of John Daniel (a journalist) and Mary (Brown) Lewis; married Ann Keir; children: Joanna, David, Sally, Jane. *Education:* University of Glasgow, B.Sc., 1951; Oxford University, Diploma in Social Anthropology, 1952, B.Litt., 1953, D.Phil., 1957. *Home:* 17 Chester Rd., London N. 19, England. *Office:* Department of Anthropology, London School of Economics, London W.C. 2, England.

CAREER: Royal Institute of International Affairs, London, England, research assistant, 1954-55; University College of Rhodesia and Nyasaland, Salisbury, Southern Rhodesia, lecturer in African studies, 1957-60; University of Glasgow, Glasgow, Scotland, lecturer in social anthropology, 1960-63; University College, University of London, London, England, lecturer in anthropology, 1963; now professor of anthropology at London School of Economics, London, England. Africa Research Ltd., London, England, consultant; British Broadcasting Corp., commentator on northeast African affairs; Malinowski Memorial Lecturer, 1966; Social Science Research Council, committee member, 1970—. *Member:* Royal Anthropological Institute (council), Anglo-Somali Society (council), International African Institute, Association of Social Anthropologists of British Commonwealth (secretary, 1964—). *Awards, honors:* Colonial Social Science research fellow in Somaliland Protectorate, 1955-57; Carnegie visiting fellow in Republic of Somalia, East Africa, 1962.

WRITINGS: Peoples of the Horn of Africa: Somali, Afar, and Saho, International African Institute, 1955; *Modern Political Movements in Somaliland* (originally published in *Africa,* July-October, 1958), Oxford University Press, 1958; *A Pastoral Democracy: A Study of Pastoralism and Politics Among the Northern Somali of the Horn of Africa,* published for International African Institute by Oxford University Press, 1961; *Marriage and the Family in Northern Somaliland,* East African Institute of Social Research, 1962; (editor with B.W. Andrzejewski) *Somali Poetry,* Oxford University Press, 1964; *The Modern History of Somaliland, from Nation to State,* Praeger, 1965; (editor and author of introduction) *Islam in Tropical Africa* (studies presented at 5th International African Seminar, Zaria, Nigeria, 1964), Oxford University Press, 1966; (editor) *History and Social Anthropology* (papers presented at annual conference of Association of Social Anthropologists of the Commonwealth, Edinburgh, Scotland, 1966), Barnes & Noble, 1968; *Ecstatic Religion,* Penguin, 1971. Contributor to *Encyclopaedia Britannica, Encyclopaedia of Social Sciences, Collier's Year Book,* and to *Africa, Journal of Modern African Studies,* and other periodicals. Editor, *Man* (journal of Royal Anthropological Institute), 1970—.

WORK IN PROGRESS: Writing on Somali of northeast Africa, and on comparative religion in general.

BIOGRAPHICAL/CRITICAL SOURCES: Times Literary Supplement, December 15, 1966, January 23, 1969; *Choice,* June, 1967; *Social Studies,* March, 1970.

* * *

LEWIS, John P(rior) 1921-

PERSONAL: Born March 18, 1921, in Albany, N.Y.; son of Leon Ray (a lawyer) and Grace (Prior) Lewis; married June Estelle Ryan, July 12, 1946; children: Betsy Prior, Sally Eastman, Amanda Barnum. *Education:* University of St. Andrews, St. Andrews, Scotland, student, 1939-40; Union College, Schenectady, N.Y., A.B., 1941; Harvard University, M.P.A., 1943, Ph.D., 1950. *Politics:* Democrat. *Religion:* Presbyterian. *Home:* 150 Fitzrandolph Rd., Princeton, N.J. 08540. *Office:* Woodrow Wilson School of Public Affairs, Princeton University, Princeton, N.J. 08540.

CAREER: Union College, Schenectady, N.Y., instructor, 1946-48, assistant professor of economics and government, 1948-50; Executive Office of the President, Washington, D.C., staff member of Council of Economic Advisers, 1950-53, 1962-64; Indiana University, Bloomington, associate professor, 1953-56, professor, 1956-64, Distinguished Service Professor of Economics and Public Policy, 1964, chairman of department, 1961-63, director of

International Development Research Center, 1962-64; U.S. AID Mission to India, New Delhi, director, 1964-69; Princeton University, Woodrow Wilson School of Public Affairs, dean, 1969—. Senior staff member in India, Brookings Institution, 1959-60. Economic consultant to United Nations Korean Reconstruction Agency, Pusan, 1953; member of United Nations Committee on Development Planning, 1970—; consultant to Council of Economic Advisers, International Cooperation Administration, and U.S. Department of Labor. Member of board of directors, International Council for Educational Development, Asia Society, and Overseas Development Council. *Military service:* U.S. Navy, 1943-46; served aboard carrier in Pacific; became lieutenant. *Member:* American Economic Association, National Planning Association, American Association of University Professors, Phi Beta Kappa. *Awards, honors:* D.C.L., Union College, 1970.

WRITINGS: (With B.M. Gross) *President's Economic Staff During the Truman Administration,* American Political Science Review, 1954; *Reconstruction and Development in South Korea,* National Planning Association, 1955; *National Income Accounting,* Bureau of Business Research, School of Business, Indiana University, 1956; *Theoretical Tools for Business Conditions Analysis,* Bureau of Business Research, School of Business, Indiana University, 1956; *Business Conditions Analysis,* McGraw, 1959, 2nd edition (with Robert C. Turner), 1966; *Quiet Crisis in India: Economic Development and American Policy,* Brookings Institution, 1962; *Notes on the Nurture of Country Planning,* Bureau of Business Research, Graduate School of Business, Indiana University, 1962; *Wanted in India: A Relevant Radicalism,* Cen'er of International Affairs, Princeton University, 1969.

*   *   *

LEWIS, John W(ilson) 1930-

PERSONAL: Born November 16, 1930, in King County, Wash.; married Hazel Jacquelyn Clark, June 19, 1954; children: Cynthia Jane, Stephen John, Amy Louise. *Education:* University of California, Los Angeles, A.B., 1953, M.A., 1958, Ph.D., 1962. *Home:* 114 Texas Lane, Ithaca, N.Y. 14850. *Office:* Department of Government, Cornell University, Ithaca, N.Y. 14850.

CAREER: Cornell University, Ithaca, N.Y., assistant professor, 1961-64, associate professor of ,government, 1964—. *Military service:* U.S. Navy, 1954-57; became lieutenant. *Member:* American Political Science Association, Association for Asian Studies.

WRITINGS: (Editor) *Chinese Communist Themes in History and Its Study: Selected Readings,* Cornell University, 1961; *Leadership in Communist China,* Cornell University Press, 1963; (editor) *Major Doctrines of Communist China,* Norton, 1964; *Chinese Communist Party Leadership and the Succession to Mao Tse-Tung: An Appraisal of Tensions,* External Research Staff, Bureau of Intelligence and Research, U.S. Department of State, 1964; *Communist China: Crisis and Change,* Foreign Policy Association, 1966; (with George McTurnan Kahn) *The United States in Vietnam,* Dial, 1967, new edition, 1969; (editor) *Party Leadership and Revolutionary Power in China,* Cambridge University Press, 1970; (editor) *The City in Communist China,* Stanford University Press, 1971.

BIOGRAPHICAL/CRITICAL SOURCES: Christian Science Monitor, May 25, 1967; *Commonweal,* August 25, 1967; *Library Journal,* October 7, 1970.

*   *   *

LEWIS, Marianna Olmstead 1923-

PERSONAL: Born July 18, 1923, in New Britain, Conn.; daughter of Bertice Henry (a businessman) and Anna (Bodley) Olmstead; married George Sherman Lewis (an architect), August 8, 1959. *Education:* Stanford University, A.B., 1949. *Politics:* Democrat. *Religion:* Protestant. *Office:* The Foundation Center, 444 Madison Ave., New York, N.Y. 10022.

CAREER: Hamilton College, Clinton, N.Y., secretary to dean of military programs, 1943-44; Hoover Institute and Library, Stanford University, Stanford, Calif., worked with Chinese and Southeast Asian collections, 1948-57; Foundation Center, New York, N.Y., editorial positions, 1957—.

WRITINGS: The Foundation Directory, Russell Sage Foundation, 1st edition (assistant editor), 1960, 2nd edition (editor), 1964, 4th edition, 1971.

*   *   *

LEWIS, Norman 1912-

PERSONAL: Born December 30, 1912, in New York, N.Y. *Education:* College of City of New York (now City College, City University of New York), B.A.; Columbia University, M.A. *Office:* Rio Hondo College, Whittier, Calif. 90608.

CAREER: City College of New York, New York, N.Y., instructor and lecturer, 1942-52; New York University, New York, N.Y., 1957-64, began as instructor, became adjunct associate professor of English, 1963; Rio Hondo College, Whittier, Calif., professor of English and head of Communications Department, 1964—, president of Academic Senate, 1966-68.

WRITINGS: (With others) *Journeys Through Wordland,* four books, Amsco School Publications, 1941; *Lessons in Vocabulary and Spelling,* Amsco School Publications, 1941; *Power with Words,* Crowell, 1943, 3rd edition published as *New Power with Words,* 1964; *How to Read Better and Faster,* Crowell, 1944, 3rd edition, 1958; *The Lewis English Refresher and Vocabulary Builder: A Six-Weeks Course in the Essentials of Effective English,* Wilfred Funk, 1945, revised and updated edition published as *New Guide to Word Power,* Pyramid Publications, 1963; (with Wilfred John Funk) *Thirty Days to a More Powerful Vocabulary,* Wilfred Funk, 1946, revised edition, 1970; *How to Speak Better English,* Crowell, 1948; *Word Power Made Easy: The Complete Three-Week Vocabulary Builder,* Doubleday, 1949.

The Rapid Vocabulary Builder, Grosset, 1951; *How to Get More Out of Your Reading,* Doubleday, 1951, reissued as *How to Become a Better Reader,* Macfadden, 1964; *Twenty Days to Better Spelling,* Harper, 1953; *The Comprehensive Word Guide,* Doubleday, 1958, reissued as *The Modern Thesaurus of Synonyms,* 1965; (editor) *The New Roget's Thesaurus of the English Language in Dictionary Form,* revised and enlarged edition, Putnam, 1961, 2nd edition, 1965, abridged version published as *The New Pocket Roget's Thesaurus in Dictionary Form,* Washington Square Press, 1961; *Dictionary of Correct Spelling,* Harper, 1962; *Correct Spelling Made Easy,* Random House, 1963; *Dictionary of Modern Pronunciation,* Harper, 1963; *30 Days to Better English,* Doubleday, 1965; *R.S.V.P.* (elementary school textbook on word skills), Books 1, 2, 3, Amsco School Publications, 1967.

Contributor of articles to *Harper's, Reader's Digest, Saturday Evening Post, Cosmopolitan, Glamour, Ladies' Home Journal, Scholastic, Vogue, Coronet, Pageant, This Week, Your Life,* and to professional journals. Editor, *Correct English,* 1944-47.

*   *   *

LEWIS, Peter M.H. 1922-

PERSONAL: Born 1922, in London, England; married; children: two daughters. *Education:* Attended Haberdashers' Aske's Hampstead School. *Home:* Delphi, 291 London Rd., Benfleet, Essex SS7 5XP, England.

WRITINGS: Squadron Histories, R.F.C., R.N.A.S., and R.A.F., 1912-59, Putnam (London), 1959, 2nd edition published as *Squadron Histories, R.F.C., R.N.A.S. and R.A.F. Since 1912,* Putnam (New York), 1968; *British Aircraft, 1809-1914,* Putnam (London), 1962, Funk, 1968; *The British Fighter Since 1912: Fifty Years of Design and Development,* Aero, 1965, 2nd edition, Putnam, 1967; *The British Bomber Since 1914: Fifty Years of Design and Development,* Aero, 1967; *British Racing and Record-Breaking Aircraft,* Putnam, 1971.

Contributor: John W.R. Taylor, editor, *Aircraft Annual 1966,* Ian Allen, 1966; John W.R. Taylor, editor, *Aircraft '72,* Ian Allen, 1971. Contributor to *Flight International, Aeroplane, Air Pictorial, American Aviation Historical Society Journal, Aeromodeller, Model Aircraft, R.A.F. Flying Review, Air Cushion Vehicles, Rolls-Royce Owner, Esso Air World,* and other specialty periodicals.

WORK IN PROGRESS: Aircraft of the Royal Flying Corps, 1912-1916, for Putnam.

* * *

LEWIS, Richard 1935-

PERSONAL: Born May 15, 1935, in New York, N.Y.; son of Emanuel Paul and Frances (Weinberg) Lewis; married Nancy Adams (a teacher), August 13, 1965; children: Amanda, Sascha. *Education:* Bard College, B.A., 1957; Mannes College of Music, New York, N.Y., graduate study, 1958-59; student at New York University, 1959-60, New School for Social Research, 1959. *Home and office:* 141 East 88th St., New York, N.Y. 10028. *Agent:* Marilyn Marlow, Curtis Brown Ltd., 60 East 56th St., New York, N.Y. 10022.

CAREER: Teacher of writing and literature to children at Poetry Center of Young Men's Hebrew Association, New York, N.Y., at Art Center of Northern New Jersey, 1961-64, and in private classes at Walden School, New York, N.Y., 1963; New School for Social Research, New York, N.Y., lecturer in education, 1964—; Manhattan Country School, New York, N.Y., drama and writing instructor, 1967—; founder and director, Touchstone Center for Children, 1969—. Assistant to Henry Simon, Simon & Schuster, New York, N.Y., 1962-63; lecturer in children's literature, Wellington Training College, New Zealand, 1965, North Shore Teachers' College, 1965; University of Vermont, 1968. In cooperation with UNESCO, toured English-speaking countries in Asia, Africa, and British Commonwealth, 1964; producer, writer, and narrator of several radio and television programs on children's literature in the United States and abroad. Member of board of advisors, Action for Children's Television. *Military service:* U.S. Army Reserve, 1957-63. *Member:* Authors Guild, P.E.N.

WRITINGS:—Editor or compiler: *In Praise of Music* (anthology), Orion Press, 1963; *The Moment of Wonder: A Collection of Chinese and Japanese Poetry,* Dial, 1964; *In a Spring Garden,* Dial, 1965; *Miracles: Poems by Children of the English-Speaking World,* Simon & Schuster, 1966; *Moon, For What Do You Wait?: Poems by Sir Rabindranath Tagore,* Atheneum, 1967; *The Wind and the Rain* (poems by children), Department of Education (Wellington, New Zealand), 1967, Simon & Schuster, 1968; (and contributor) *The Park,* Simon & Schuster, 1968; *Out of the Earth I Sing: Poetry and Songs of Primitive Peoples of the World,* Norton, 1968; *Journeys: Prose by Children of the English-Speaking World,* Simon & Schuster, 1969; *Muse of the Round Sky: Lyric Poetry of Ancient Greece,* translated by Willis Barnstone and others, Simon & Schuster, 1969; *Of This World: A Poet's Life in Poetry* (biographical sketches and selections of

haiku, in translation, by Japanese poet Issa Kobayashi), Dial, 1969; *Still Waters of the Air: Poems by Three Modern Spanish Poets,* Dial, 1970; (with Haruna Kirmua) *There Are Two Lives: Poems by Children of Japan,* translated by Kirmua, Simon & Schuster, 1970; *The Way of Silence: Prose and Poetry of Basho,* Dial, 1970; *I Breathe a New Song: A Collection of Eskimo Poetry,* Simon & Schuster, 1971.

Theatre productions: (Creator, director, narrator, and writer of music) "I Sing to Myself," first produced at Downstage Theatre, Wellington, New Zealand, 1964; creator and director) "In the Time Before," music by Tony Pagano, first produced at Manhattan Country School, New York, N.Y., 1968; "There Are Two Lives," first produced at Asia Society, New York, N.Y., February, 1971.

Contributor: *The Right to Dissent: Lectures from the University of Curious Cove,* New Zealand University Students Association, 1965; *Explorations in Children's Writing,* National Association of Teachers of English, 1970; Nancy Larrick, editor, *Somebody Turned on a Tap in These Kids,* Dell, 1971. Contributor of articles to *NEA Journal, Young Children, Publishers' Weekly, Instructor, Elementary English,* and other education journals. Editor and music critic, *Musical America,* 1959-61; research editor, *American College Dictionary,* 1961-62; editor, *Touchstone Magazine.*

WORK IN PROGRESS: "The Way of Haiku," a theatre production in which Haiku poetry will be narrated in association with a multi-media presentation based on the photographs of Helen Buttfield (taken from *Of This World* and *The Way of Silence*).

SIDELIGHTS: Lewis created the Touchstone Players in 1964, "a theatrical company whose aim is to create new ways to present children [with] poetic and mythological material through mime, gesture, movement, music, and narrative." The Touchstone Players have presented Lewis's dramatizations of selections from his books, sometimes in collaboration with the National Theatre of the Deaf, to children in the United States, Canada, and New Zealand.

Caedmon Records released two recordings of selections from Lewis's works, entitled "Miracles" and "A Gathering of Great Poetry for Children," in 1967 and 1968. A motion picture, narrated by Lewis and based on *In A Spring Garden,* was produced by Weston Woods Films in 1967.

BIOGRAPHICAL/CRITICAL SOURCES: Hudson Review, spring, 1967; *Poetry,* March, 1968, January, 1969; *Book World,* May 5, 1968; *New York Times Book Review,* December 8, 1968; Lee Bennett Hopkins, *Books Are By People,* Citation Press, 1969; *Library Journal,* March 15, 1970, May 15, 1970.

* * *

LEWY, Guenter 1923-

PERSONAL: Born August 22, 1923, in Breslau, Germany; son of Henry and Rosel (Leipziger) Lewy; married Ilse Nussbaum (a pediatrician), December 29, 1950; children: Barbara Jean, Peter Ralph. *Education:* College of the City of New York (now City College of the City University of New York), B.S.S., 1951; Columbia University, M.A., 1952, Ph.D., 1957. *Home:* 64 Harrison Ave., Northampton, Mass. 01060. *Office:* Department of Government, University of Massachusetts, Amherst, Mass. 01002.

CAREER: Columbia University, New York, N.Y., instructor in government, 1953-56; Smith College, Northampton, Mass., assistant professor of government, 1957-63; University of Massachusetts, Amherst, associate professor, 1964-66, professor of government, 1966—. *Military service:* British Army, 1942-46; became sergeant; received Africa Star and Italy Star. *Member:* American Political Science Association, American Society for Political and Legal Philosophy, American Society of Church History, Phi Beta Kappa. *Awards, honors:* Social Science Research Council fellowship, 1956-57, 1961-62; Rockefeller Foundation fellowship, 1963-64.

WRITINGS: Constitutionalism and Statecraft During the Golden Age of Spain: A Study of the Political Philosophy of Juan de Mariana, S.J., Librairie E. Droz (Geneva), 1960; *The Catholic Church and Nazi Germany,* McGraw, 1964; *The Sinhalese Buddhist Revolution of Ceylon, 1956-1959,* Department of Government, University of Massachusetts, 1967; *The Egyptian Revolution: Nasserism and Islam* [and] *Religion and Revolution: A Study in Comparative Politics and Religion,* University of Massachusetts, 1968.

Contributor: Nils Petter Gleditsch, editor, *Kamp uten Vapen,* Pax Forlag (Oslo), 1965; D.B. and E.R. Schmidt, editors, *The Deputy Reader: Studies in Moral Responsibility,* Scott, Foresman, 1965; David Spitz, editor, *Political Theory and Social Change,* Atherton, 1967; Richard A. Wasserstrom, editor, *War and Morality,* Wadsworth, 1970. Contributor of articles and book reviews to *Political Science Quarterly, Church History, Social Research, Western Political Quarterly, Der Staat, Continuum, Comparative Politics,* and other journals.

WORK IN PROGRESS: Religion and Revolution: A Comparative Study.

BIOGRAPHICAL/CRITICAL SOURCES: New York Post, June 19, 1964; *New York Review of Books,* June 25, 1964; *Saturday Review,* June 27, 1964; *Book Week,* July 5, 1964; *Springfield Union,* July 29, 1964.

*   *   *

LEY, Charles David   1913-

PERSONAL: Born March 11, 1913, in London, England; son of Charles Tulk (member of London Stock Exchange) and Dorothy Mary (Cutcliffe) Ley; married Paz Tarrio, November 17, 1955. *Education:* Magdalene College, Cambridge University, B.A., 1935, M.A., 1939; University of Madrid, Doctor, 1950; King's College, University of London, Ph.D., 1956. *Politics:* Conservative. *Religion:* Catholic. *Home:* 11 Kinnaird Ave., Chiswick, London W.4, England.

CAREER: British Council, lecturer in Lisbon, Portugal, 1939-43, senior lecturer in Madrid, Spain, 1943-48; University of Salamanca, Salamanca, Spain, reader in English language and literature, 1952-58. *Member:* International Association of Hispanists, Royal Commonwealth Society, Cambridge Union.

WRITINGS: A Inglaterra e os escritores portugeses (title means "England and the Portuguese Writers"), Seara Nova (Lisbon), 1939; *Encontro final* (short novel; title means "Final Encounter"), [Lisbon], 1940; *Panorama da literatura inglesa* (title means "Panorama of English Literature"), Seara Nova, 1941; *Escritores e paisagens de Portugal* (title means "Writings and Countrysides of Portugal"), [Lisbon], 1942; *Poems and Poemas,* privately printed, 1942; *Braga* (poems in English and Portuguese), [Lisbon], 1943; *A Vida tragica das Irmas Bronte* (title means "The Tragic Life of the Bronte Sisters"), [Lisbon], 1943; *Semana Santa* (poem; title means "Holy Week"), bilingual edition, Spanish version by Maria Alfaro, Garcilaso, 1945; (editor) Gil Vicente, *Auto da barca do Inferno* (title means "Interlude of the Ship of Hell"), Consejo Superior de Investigaciones Cientificas, 1946; *Shakespeare para espanoles* (title means "Shakespeare for Spaniards"), Revista de Occidente (Madrid), 1951; *La*

Moderna poesia portuguesa (title menas "Modern Portuguese Poetry"), Tito Hombre (Santander), 1951; *Poemas para Espana* (title means "Poems for Spain"), Hordino (Santander), 1952; *El Gracioso en el teatro de le peninsula, siglos XVI-XVII* (title means "The Comic Serving-Man in the Drama of the Peninsula, 16th and 17th Centuries"), Revista de Occidente, 1954; *The Future of the World* (play), Peter Russell, 1955; *2 x 2* (poems), Peter Russell, 1955; editor and author of introduction) *Twentieth Century English Poetry,* Alhambra (Madrid), 1959; *Spanish Poetry Since 1939,* Catholic University of America Press, 1962.

Translator: (From Spanish) Federico Garcia Lorca, "Manana Pineda" (play), first produced in Sheer, England at Barn Theatre, July, 1938; (into Spanish, and author of prologue, with Rafael Morales) Alberto de Serpa, *Poemas de Oporto* (title means "Poems of Oporto"), Adonais, 1947; (and editor) *Portuguese Voyages, 1498-1663* (anthology), Dent, 1947, Dutton, 1948, new edition, Dent, 1953; (with Fernando Trias) *Cinco novelistas inglesas* (translation of *Five English Women Novelists of the Nineteenth Century),* Janes, 1948; (with Jose Garcia Nieto) John Milton, *Sanson Agonistes,* [Madrid], 1949; (with Morales) George B. Shaw, *Pasion, pocima y petrificacion,* c.1950; Jose Ortega y Gasset, *Velazquez,* Random House, 1953; Gregorio Maranon, *Antonio Perez, Spanish Traitor,* Hollis & Carter, 1954, Roy, 1955; Jose Maria Caballero Bonald, *Andalusian Dances,* Noguer, 1957; (from Spanish, with George Ordish) Jose Maria Tey, *Hong Kong to Barcelona in the Junk "Rubia",* Harrap, 1962; (into Spanish, and author of introduction) *Anthology of 20th Century Irish Plays,* Aguilar, 1964; (from Galician) Rosalia de Castro, *Poems,* Ministry of Foreign Affairs (Madrid), 1964; Jose Luis Acquaroni, *Bulls and Bullfighting,* 7th edition, International Publications Service, 1966, 8th edition, Noguer, 1967. Contributor to *Times Literary Supplement, Bulletin of Spanish Studies,* and to Spanish and Portuguese periodicals.

WORK IN PROGRESS: An English-Spanish and Spanish-English dictionary, for Revista de Occidente.

SIDELIGHTS: The Barn Theatre performance of Ley's translation of Lorca's "Manana Pineda," with Peter Ustinov in the cast, was the first performance of a Lorca play in English.

*   *   *

LEY, Willy   1906-1969
(Robert Willey)

PERSONAL: Born October 2, 1906, in Berlin Germany; came to United States, 1935, became U.S. citizen, March, 1944; son of Julius Otto (a wine merchant) and Frida (May) Ley; married Olga Feldman (a fashion consultant), December 24, 1941; children: Sandra, Xenia. *Education:* Studied at University of Berlin and University of Koenigsberg, intermittently, 1922-28. *Religion:* German Lutheran. *Home and office:* 37-26 77th St., Jackson Heights, N.Y. 10072.

CAREER: Free-lance writer in Germany and United States prior to 1940; *PM* (daily newspaper), New York, N.Y., science editor, 1940-44; Washington Institute of Technology, Washington, D.C., research engineer, 1944-47; free-lance writer, and public lecturer on astronautics and space research, 1947-69. Fairleigh Dickinson University, Rutherford, N.J., part-time professor of science, 1959-61. U.S. Department of Commerce, consultant to Office of Technical Services, 1946-47; occasional consultant to industry. Technical adviser for television shows, "Tom Corbett, Space Cadet," and for two Disney programs, "Man in Space," and "Man and the Moon."

MEMBER: American Association for Advancement of Science, American Institute of Aeronautics and Astronautics, Society of American Military Engineers, Deutsche Gesellschaft fuer Raketentechnik und Raumschiffahrt (German Society for Rocket and Space Research; founding member, 1927; vice-president, 1928-33), Institute of Meteoritics (fellow), American Rocket Society, Royal Astronomy Society (Canada), British Interplanetary Society (honorary fellow), Institute of the Aerospace Sciences. *Awards, honors:* Special nonfiction prize in First International Fantasy Fiction Awards for *The Conquest of Space*, 1949, for *Lands Beyond*, 1952; *New York Herald Tribune*, Children's Spring Book Festival Award for *Engineers' Dreams*, 1954; honorary doctorate, Adelphi University, 1960.

WRITINGS: Die Fahrt ins Weltall (title means "Trip into Space"), Hachmeister & Thal (Leipzig), 1926, 2nd edition, 1929; (editor) *Die Moeglichkeit der Weltraumfahrt: Allgemeinverstaendliche Beitraege zum Raumschiffahrtsproblem* (title means "Possibility of Interplanetary Travel"), Hachmeister & Thal, 1928; *Konrad Gesner, Leben und Werk* (title means "Konrad Gesner, Life and Works"), Muenchener Drucke (Munich), 1929; *Grundriss einer Geschichte der Rakete* (title means "An Outline History of the Rocket"), Hachmeister & Thal, 1932.

Bombs and Bombing: What Every Civilian Should Know, Viking, 1941; *The Days of Creation*, Viking, 1941; *The Lungfish and the Unicorn: An Excursion into Romantic Zoology* (Scientific Book Club Selection, May, 1941), Viking, 1941, revised and enlarged edition published as *The Lungfish, The Dodo and the Unicorn: An Excursion into Romantic Zoology*, 1948; *Shells and Shooting*, Viking, 1942; *Rockets: The Future of Travel Beyond the Stratosphere*, Viking, 1944, 2nd revised edition published as *Rockets and Space Travel: The Future of Flight Beyond the Stratosphere*, 1947, 3rd revised edition published as *Rockets, Missiles, and Space Travel*, 1951, 9th revised edition published as *Rockets, Missiles, and Men in Space*, 1968; *Inside the Atom* (originally published in *Natural History Magazine*, October, 1945), American Museum of Natural History, Man and Nature Publications, 1945; *The Conquest of Space*, Viking, 1949.

Dragons in Amber: Further Adventures of a Romantic Naturalist, Viking, 1951; (author of foreword) Jack Coggins and Fletcher Pratt, *Rockets, Jets, Guided Missiles, and Space Ships*, Random House, 1951, revised edition published as *Rockets, Satellites and Space Travel*, edited by Ley, 1958; (contributor) Cornelius Ryan, editor, *Across the Space Frontier*, Viking, 1952; (with Lyon Sprague de Camp) *Lands Beyond*, Rinehart, 1952; (contributor) Jeffrey Logan, editor, *The Complete Book of Outer Space*, Maco Magazine Corp., 1953, 2nd edition published as *The Complete Book of Satellites and Outer Space*, 1957; (with Wernher von Braun and Fred L. Whipple) *Conquest of the Moon*, edited by Cornelius Ryan, Viking, 1953 (published in England as *Man on the Moon*, Sidgwick & Jackson, 1953); (with others) *Mystery of Other Worlds Revealed*, Sterling, 1953; *Engineers' Dreams*, Viking, 1954, revised edition, 1966; *Salamanders and Other Wonders: Still More Adventures of A Romantic Naturalist*, Viking, 1955; (with von Braun) *The Exploration of Mars*, Viking, 1956; (contributor) John Kieran, editor, *Treasury of Great Nature Writing*, Hanover House, 1957; *Satellites, Rockets and Outer Space*, New American Library, 1958, revised edition, 1962; (with von Braun) *Start in dem Weltraum* (title means "Takeoff into Outer Space"), S. Fischer (Frankfurt), 1958; *Exotic Zoology* (compilation of chapters from *The Lungfish, the Dodo and the Unicorn, Dragons in Amber*, and *Salamanders and Other Wonders)*, Viking, 1959; (translator) Herman Oberth, *Moon Car*, Harper, 1959; (editor and author of foreword) Ario Shternfel'd, *Soviet Space Science*, 2nd revised edition, Basic Books, 1959.

Rockets (juvenile), Doubleday, 1960; *Planets*, Doubleday, 1961; (with others) *The Poles*, Time, Inc., 1962; (editor and author of introduction) Jules Verne, *Dr. Ox's Experiment*, translation by George M. Towle, Macmillan, 1963; (with von Braun) *Deutsches Lesebuch: Die Eroberung des Weltraum* (title means "German Reading Book: The Conquest of Outer Space"), edited by Frederick D. Kellerman, Ronald, 1963; (editor and author of introduction and commentary) *Harnessing Space*, Macmillan, 1963; *Watchers of the Skies: An Informal History of Astronomy from Babylon to the Space Age*, Viking, 1963; *Ballistics*, Doubleday, 1964; *Beyond the Solar System*, foreword by von Braun, Viking Press, 1964; *Missiles, Moonprobes, and Megaparsecs*, New American Library, 1964; *Our Work in Space*, Macmillan, 1964; *Ranger to the Moon*, New American Library, 1965; *Fire*, Doubleday, 1966; *Mariner IV to Mars*, New American Library, 1966; (translator and editor) *Otto Hahn: A Scientific Autobiography*, Scribner, 1966 (published in England as *A Scientific Autobiography*, MacGibbon & Kee, 1967); *The Borders of Mathematics*, with illustrations by Ley, Pyramid Publications, 1967; *For Your Information: On Earth and in the Sky*, Doubleday, 1967; *Dawn of Zoology*, Prentice-Hall, 1968; *The Discovery of the Elements*, Delacorte, 1968; *Inside the Orbit of the Earth*, McGraw, 1968; (editor and author of revision, introduction, and appendix) *Kant's Cosmogony: As in His Essay on the Retardation of the Rotation of the Earth and His Natural History and Theory of the Heavens*, translation by W. Hastie, Greenwood Pr 1968; *The Meteorite Craters*, Weybright, 1968; *Another Look at Atlantis, and Fifteen Other Essays*, Doubleday, 1969; *Events in Space*, McKay, 1969; *Visitors from Afar: The Comets*, with drawings by Ley, McGraw, 1969; *The Drifting of the Continents*, Weybright, 1969; *Gas Giants: The Largest Planets*, McGraw, 1970; *Worlds of the Past*, Golden Press, 1971.

"Adventures in Space" series for children, published by Guild Press: *Man-Made Satellites*, 1957, revised edition, 1958; *Space Pilots*, 1958; *Space Stations*, 1958; *Space Travel*, 1958.

Contributor to *Encyclopedia Americana, Compton's Picture Encyclopedia, Britannica Junior Encyclopaedia*, and to popular and scientific periodicals, including *Look, Ordnance, Natural History, Fauna*. Also author of some early science fiction in magazines under the pseudonym Robert Willey.

WORK IN PROGRESS: Historical research on various scientific concepts.

SIDELIGHTS: Herman Oberth's books on space travel influenced Ley to give up plans for a career in geology to look far into space, in advance of his times. In addition to devising some of the basic principles leading to the development of the liquid-fuel rocket, he predicted space travel twenty years before it was actually achieved.

At twenty-one Ley was a founding member in Germany of the Society for Space Travel. He became vice-president in 1928 and held that post until the society was dissolved in 1933. Among those recruited into the society was Werner Von Braun, who became a leader in German military rocket development. Because he read French, Dutch, Latin, and Italian as well as German and English, and some Russian and classical Greek, Ley corresponded with rocket pioneers throughout Europe and America, so that the society eventually served as a world center for information on rockets.

The Nazis became increasingly interested in the experiments of the society and, in 1935, Ley wrote British and Dutch friends that he was in trouble. He had been ordered to cease writing on rocketry for foreign publications and he had done so, but some of his earlier articles began to appear after this command. He left for Britain and then went to America on invitation from the American Rocket Society. He spent the rest of his life writing and lecturing on rocketry; ironically he died three weeks before Apollo 11 lifted into space.

Ley believed it essential that the average layman understand the ideas, achievements, and future of space science. He told *CA* that he wanted "to bring something new, not mentioned by other authors, even into the most routine writing assignment." Most critics feel that he had a particular talent for explaining highly technical scientific data in lucid, comprehensible language. Robert Heinlein stated that Ley "writes with wit and gentle humor, and has a happy ability for stating technical facts so simply that a child may understand, yet an expert will be neither bored nor annoyed. . . ." Others were impressed with his predictions on the future of space travel. A *New Yorker* reviewer believes that Ley presented his material "so matter-of-factly and with such conviction that it would seem only plausible for space conscious members of the younger generation to start drawing up lists of provender and equipment for the hazardous but undoubtedly alluring expeditions awaiting them."

His books have been published from Finland to India, *The Conquest of Outer Space* in eleven languages, *Engineers' Dreams* in ten. *Rockets, Missiles and Space Travel* has run into eighteen printings.

AVOCATIONAL INTERESTS: Classical music, numismatics.

BIOGRAPHICAL/CRITICAL SOURCES: Books, May 25, 1941, December 28, 1941, December 13, 1942; *New York Times,* May 25, 1941, January 18, 1942, May 21, 1944, September 25, 1949, May 30, 1954, August 28, 1955, June 24, 1956, July 22, 1969; *New Republic,* March 16, 1942; *Book Week,* May 14, 1944, July 26, 1964; *New Yorker,* June 10, 1944, August 18, 1951, August 27, 1955; *Library Journal,* April 1, 1947, August, 1948, October 15, 1949, December 1, 1950, July, 1955, July, 1956, May 15, 1958, December 15, 1958, August, 1959, October 15, 1962, December 1, 1963, November 1, 1964; *Nation,* November 13, 1948, October 1, 1949; *Saturday Review,* October 23, 1948, December 24, 1949, June 19, 1954; *New York Herald Tribune Book Review,* November 28, 1948, May 16, 1954, September 11, 1955, July 1, 1956, November 1, 1959, July 28, 1963; *Christian Science Monitor,* July 1, 1954, May 7, 1964; *Christian Century,* July 4, 1956; *New York Times Book Review,* July 15, 1962, December 1, 1963, November 22, 1964; *Atlantic,* December, 1963; *Best Sellers,* July 15, 1964, July 15, 1968, March 1, 1969; *Times Literary Supplement,* August 31, 1967; *Choice,* October, 1968, October, 1969, *Scientific American.* December, 1969.

(Died June 24, 1969)

* * *

LEYDET, Francois G (uillaume) 1927-

PERSONAL: Surname is pronounced *Lay*-day; born August 26, 1927, in Neuilly-sur-Seine, France; son of Bruno (a novelist under pseudonym Bertrand Defos) and Dorothy (Lindsey) Leydet; married Patience Abbe, June 17, 1955; children: Catherine Abbe O'Mahony and Lisa Amanda O'Mahony (stepdaughters). *Education:* University of Paris, Bachelier es-Lettres Philosophie, 1945; Harvard University, A.B., 1947, graduate student, 1950-52; Johns Hopkins University, graduate student, 1952-53. *Politics:* Liberal Republican. *Religion:* Protestant. *Home:* 234 Bella Vista Ave., Belvedere, Calif. 94920. *Office:* Sierra Club, Mills Building, 220 Montgomery, San Francisco, Calif. 94109.

CAREER: San Francisco Chronicle, San Francisco, Calif., staff writer on "This World" (Sunday supplement), 1954-62; *San Francisco Examiner,* San Francisco

Calif., copy editing, layout, make-up, 1962-63. *Military service:* French Army, Tank Corps; became first lieutenant. *Member:* National Parks Association, American Forestry Association, International Hospitality Center, National Wildlife Federation, Save-the-Redwoods League, Wilderness Society, Planned Parenthood Federation (Marin County board member, 1963-65), Sierra Club, California Academy of Sciences, Harvard Club of San Francisco.

WRITINGS: (Editor) *Tomorrow's Wilderness,* Sierra Club, 1963; (with Philip Hyde) *The Last Redwoods,* Sierra Club, 1964; *Time and the River Flowing: Grand Canyon,* edited by David Brower, Sierra Club, 1964, abridged edition, Sierra Club and Ballantine, 1968; *The Last Redwoods, and the Parkland of Redwood Creek,* Sierra Club and Ballantine, 1969.

AVOCATIONAL INTERESTS: Hiking, camping, the outdoors, tennis, sailing, rowing, classical music, playing piano, and gourmet cooking.

* * *

LICHINE, Alexis 1913-

PERSONAL: Born December 3, 1913, in Moscow, Russia; son of Alexander and Alice (Tseits) Lichine; married second wife, Arlene Dahl, December 23, 1965 (divorced, 1968); children: (first marriage) Alexandra, Alexis Jr. *Education:* Attended Ecole Alsacienne and Cours de Droit International, Paris, France; University of Pennsylvania, B.S., 1933. *Home:* 998 Fifth Ave., New York, N.Y. 10028.

CAREER: Director of several wine importing companies, New York, N.Y., prior to 1942; wine importer, New York, N.Y., 1946-68, president of Hedges & Butler Imports Ltd., 1966-68. Founder, 1951, and former director of Alexis Lichine & Co., Margaux, Gironde, France, former proprietor of Chateau Prieure-Lichine and co-proprietor of Chateau Lascombes in Margaux. President or director of development companies in St. Croix, Virgin Islands, and St. Martin, French West Indies. Chairman of board, Synchronex Corp. (sound-on-film). *Military service:* U.S. Army, 1942-46; served as liaison officer, then aide-de-camp to commander of Allied Forces in Morocco, to commanding generals in Corsica, Delta Base Section; served as aide-de-camp to Supreme Allied Commander, Gen. Dwight D. Eisenhower, 1945; became major; received U.S. Bronze Star, other French, Moroccan, and Tunisian decorations, including Chevalier de la Legion d'Honneur, Croix de Guerre (three), Officer, Order of Leopold. *Member:* Academie du Vin de Bordeaux (life), Lucullius Circle, Commanderie de Bordeaux in New York, Commandeur du Bontemps du Medoc, Jurade de St. Emilion.

WRITINGS: (With William E. Massee) *Wines of France,* Knopf, 1951, 7th revised edition, Cassell, 1969; (with others) *Encyclopaedia of Wines and Spirits,* Knopf, 1967, revised edition, 1970. Contributor of articles on wine to *Esquire, Vogue, Harper's Bazaar, New Yorker, Atlantic Monthly, Realites* (France), other magazines.

BIOGRAPHICAL/CRITICAL SOURCES: Book World, November 5, 1967; *Christian Century,* March 6, 1968.

* * *

LIEBERMAN, Herbert Henry 1933-

PERSONAL: Born September 22, 1933, in New Rochelle, N.Y.; son of Arthur Charles (a salesman) and Sylvia (Kissel) Lieberman; married Judith Barsky (an interior decorator), June 9, 1963. *Education:* College of City of New York (now City College of City University of New York), B.A., 1955; Columbia University, M.A., 1956. *Religion:* Jewish. *Home:* 2 Apple Tree Close, Chappaqua,

N.Y. 10514. *Agent:* Georges Borchardt, 145 East 52nd St., New York, N.Y. 10022. *Office:* Reader's Digest Association, Condensed Book Department, Pleasantville, N.Y. 10570.

CAREER: Jamaica High School, New York, N.Y., teacher of English, 1957-59; *New York Times,* New York, N.Y., writer, 1959-60; Macmillan Publishing Co., New York, N.Y., associate editor, 1960-63; McCormick-Mathers Publishing Co., New York, N.Y., senior editor, 1963-67; Reader's Digest Association, Pleasantville, N.Y., associate editor, 1967—. *Military service:* U.S. Army, 1957. *Awards, honors:* First prize, Charles Sergel Drama Award, University of Chicago, 1964, for *Matty and the Moron and Madonna;* Guggenheim fellowship, 1964-65.

WRITINGS: Matty and the Moron and Madonna (play), Hill & Wang, 1964; *The Adventures of Dolphin Green,* Hill & Wang, 1967; *Crawlspace* (novel), McKay, 1971.

Television plays: "Christmas Song," 1960, and "Goodnight Grace Kelly Wherever You Are," 1964, both for Columbia Broadcasting System. Also author of a play, "Tigers in Red Weather," first produced at Tyrone Guthrie Theatre in Minneapolis, Minn., 1966.

WORK IN PROGRESS: A novel, *Lost,* for McKay.

BIOGRAPHICAL/CRITICAL SOURCES: Best Sellers, June 15, 1971; *New York Times,* June 26, 1971.

* * *

LIEBERMAN, Rosalie

PERSONAL: Born in Louisville, Ky.; daughter of Ignace and Dollie (Meyer) Lieberman. *Education:* Columbia University, special work in writing, 1930-35, adult student writers workshop, 1949-53. *Religion:* Roman Catholic.

CAREER: Warner Brothers Pictures, New York, N.Y., script reader, 1932-36; Twentieth Century-Fox Film Corp., New York, N.Y., script reader, 1936-39.

WRITINGS: Heaven Is So High, Bobbs-Merrill, 1950; *The Man Who Sold Christmas,* Longmans, Green, 1951; *The Man Who Captivated New York: The Further Adventures of Brother Angelo,* Doubleday, 1960; *Sister Innocent and the Wayward Miracle,* Newman, 1965. Contributor of short stories to magazines.

SIDELIGHTS: A story from *Heaven Is So High* has been bought by television for a series. *Avocational interests:* Listening to classical music and watching ballet.

* * *

LIMA, Robert 1935-

PERSONAL: Born November 7, 1935, in Havana, Cuba; son of Robert F. (a publisher, editor, and translator) and Joan (Millares) Lima; married Sally Ann Murphy, June 27, 1964. *Education:* Villanova University, B.A., 1957, M.A., 1961; New York University, Ph.D., 1968. *Home:* 485 Orlando Ave., State College, Pa. 16801.

CAREER: Hunter College of the City University of New York, New York, N.Y., lecturer in Romance languages, 1962-65; Pennsylvania State University, University Park, associate professor of Spanish and chairman of comparative literature program, 1965—. Free-lance writer, translator, or editor for T. Y. Crowell Publishing Co., Las Americas Publishing Co., Columbus Publications, New York University Press, Pendulum Productions, Inc., and Voice of America. *Member:* Modern Language Association, Association of Teachers of Spanish and Portuguese, Alpha Psi Omega.

WRITINGS: The Theatre of Garcia Lorca, Las Americas, 1963; (editor and translator) Ana M. Barrenechea, *Borges, the Labyrinth Maker,* New York University,

1965; (editor and translator) Ramon del Valle-Inclan, *Autobiography, Aesthetics, Aphorisms,* privately printed, 1966; *Ramon del Valle-Inclan* (essay), Columbia University Press, 1971.

Contributor: A. Zahareas, editor, *Ramon del Valle-Inclan: An Appraisal of His Life and Works,* Las Americas, 1968; George E. Wellwarth, editor, *The New Wave Spanish Drama: An Anthology,* New York University Press, 1970. Contributor to *McGraw-Hill Encyclopedia of World Drama* and *Reader's Encyclopedia of American Literature;* contributor of articles, poems, and translations of plays and poems to *Athanor, Journal of General Education, Chelsea, Broadside, Gamut, Salted Feathers, Hispania, Modern Drama, Revista de Estudios Hispanicos, Modern International Drama, Drama Critique, Pivot, Theatre Annual, Prairie Schooner, Chicago Review,* and *La Voz.* Founder and former associate editor, *Seventh Street Anthology* and *Judson Review* (both now defunct).

* * *

LIN, Tai-yi 1926-
    (Anor Lin, Wu-shuang Lin)

PERSONAL: Name was originally Anor Lin; born April 1, 1926, in Peking, China; daughter of Yu-t'ang (an author) and Tsuifeng (Liau) Lin; married R. Ming Lai (chief information officer for Hong Kong Government), February 26, 1949; children: Chih-wen (daughter), Chih-yi (son). *Education:* Attended Columbia University, 1946-49. *Office:* Reader's Digest International, Inc., Hang Chong Building, 5 Queen's Rd., Hong Kong.

CAREER: Yale University, New Haven, Conn., instructor in Chinese, 1945-46; Reader's Digest Asia, Ltd., Hong Kong, editor-in-chief of Chinese edition, 1964—. Author and translator.

WRITINGS: War Tide, John Day, 1943; *The Golden Coin,* John Day, 1946; *The Eavesdropper,* Secker & Warburg, 1958, World Publishing, 1959; *The Lilacs Overgrow,* World Publishing, 1960; *Kampoon Street,* World Publishing, 1964; (translator and editor) Ju-chen Li, *Flowers in the Mirror,* University of California Press, 1965.

With sister, Adet Lin: (Under name Anor Lin) *Our Family,* introduction by Pearl S. Buck, John Day, 1939; (translators, under name Adet and Anor Lin) Ping-ying Hsieh, *Girl Rebel* (autobiography, with extracts from her New War Diaries), introduction by Yu-t'ang Lin, John Day, 1940; *Dawn Over Chungking,* John Day, 1941.

Contributor to *Punch* and *United Nations World.* Editor, *Tienfeng Monthly* (New York), 1951-53.

* * *

LIND, Jakov 1927-

PERSONAL: Given name pronounced *Ya*-kov; born February 10, 1927, in Vienna, Austria; son of Simon (a merchant) and Rosa (Birnbaum) Landwirth; married Faith Henry (a literary scout), 1955; children: Simon, Oona. *Education:* Attended Academy of Dramatic Art, Vienna, Austria, two years. *Politics:* "Sharp, anti-rightwing-Barry Goldwater." *Religion:* None. *Home:* 12 A Belsize Park, London N.W.3, England.

CAREER: Writer. Evacuated to Holland for safety in 1938 by a Zionist refugee group; at the German invasion he obtained false papers as a Dutch gentile under the name Jan Overbeek, returning to Germany as a deckhand on a Rhine barge; at the end of World War II he emigrated to Palestine as Jakov Chaklan, but returned to Europe in a few years; has held many jobs, including that of sailor, fisherman, laborer, actor, and editor. Writer-in-residence, Long Island University Brooklyn Center, 1966-67.

WRITINGS: Landscaft in Beton (novel) Luchterhand, 1962, translation by Ralph Manheim published as *Landscape in Concrete*, Grove, 1966; *Eine Seele aus Holz*, Luchterhand, 1963, translation by Manheim published as *Soul of Wood and Other Stories* (contains "Soul of Wood," "Journey Through the Night," "The Pious Brother," "The Judgment," "The Window," "Hurrah for Freedom," and "Resurrection"), J. Cape, 1964, Grove, 1965; *Anna Laub* (play), Luchterhand, 1965; *Das Sterben der Silberfuechse* (play), published with *Die Heiden* by Erich Fried, Luchterhand, 1965; *Eine bessere Welt: In fuenfzehn Kapiteln* (novel), Wagenbach, 1966, translation by Manheim published as *Ergo*, Random House, 1966; *The Silver Foxes Are Dead, and Other Plays* (contains radio plays: "The Silver Foxes Are Dead," "Anna Laub," "Hunger," and "Fear"; also see below), translated by Manheim, Methuen, 1968, Hill & Wang, 1969; *Angst und Hunger* (two radio plays), Wagenbach, 1969; *Counting My Steps: An Autobiography*, Macmillan, 1969; *Numbers: A Further Autobiography*, Harper, 1972; *The Trip to Jerusalem*, Harper, 1973. Also author of "Ergo," a play based on his novel, produced Off-Broadway at Anspacher Theatre, March 3, 1968; television plays, and a film.

SIDELIGHTS: The *Times Literary Supplement* has called the title story of *Soul of Wood* "one man's bizarre vision of mind-defying horror, a vision perfectly valid within its own terms of reference," and described Lind's style as terse and elliptical. Maxwell Geismar considers Lind "the most notable short-story writer to appear in the last two decades." He is a product of that central European Jewish culture which was in effect obliterated by the Nazis, both his parents being victims. And he records this horror, says Geismar, "even more directly and intimately, perhaps more poetically, than [Guenther] Grass or [Rolf] Hochhuth. And with what symbolism, what nightmare visions and surrealistic drama—what art!" "[He] writes the way an existentialist philosophizes," in the view of J.P. Bauke, "with no attention to canons and conventions. In another age, Lind, brilliant and untutored, would have been proclaimed an original genius."

Stuart Hood states: "If a man's experience of life, say the existentialists, has not allowed him to achieve 'primary ontological security,' he is forced to struggle to maintain a sense of his own being. That struggle is the true theme of *Counting My Steps*—a struggle against threats from within and without, a life and death combat in which the hero, to survive, must adopt masks and disguises (thus complicating the question of identity), must live in depth of loneliness and despair, . . . sustained by an unconquerable will to survive. There is no question of conventional nobility of character in such a hero, who must be ruthless, tough, ungrateful, ready to wager his life on the turn of chance or the hazard of fleeting encounter. . . . In these struggles for existence, where the rules and conventions no longer apply, we cannot hope for positive heroes, for paradigms of behaviour or stories with a moral. It is enough if the survivors have the courage, as Jakov Lind has had, to set down honestly what it was like, without sentimentality and without gloss, to write (for example) an uncomfortable, honest book."

BIOGRAPHICAL/CRITICAL SOURCES: Times Literary Supplement, September 17, 1964, September 22, 1966, November 23, 1967, September 19, 1968; *New York Times Book Review*, January 24, 1965, June 26, 1966, October 22, 1967, November 2, 1969, June 11, 1972; *Book Week*, February 21, 1965, October 5, 1969; *Village Voice*, April 7, 1966, March 7, 1968; *Saturday Review*, June 25, 1966; *Books Abroad*, autumn, 1967; *New Statesman*, November 3, 1967; *Listener*, November 23, 1967; *Nation*, November 27, 1967, March 18, 1968; *Commonweal*, January 26, 1968; *Time*, March 18, 1968; *New Leader*, March 25, 1968; *Newsday*, October 11, 1968; *Drama*, winter, 1968; *New Yorker*, October 18, 1969; *Spectator*, April 11, 1970.†

*   *   *

LINDSAY, Jack 1900-
    (Peter Meadows, Richard Preston)

PERSONAL: Born October 20, 1900, in Melbourne, Australia; son of Norman (an artist and writer) and Kathleen (Parkinson) Lindsay; married Meta Waterdrinker (an art potter), June 30, 1958; children: Philip Jan, Helen Marietta. *Education:* University of Queensland, B.A. (first class honors in classics). *Politics:* Communist. *Home:* Castle Hedingham, Queen St., Halstead, Essex, England.

CAREER: Vision (quarterly), Sydney, Australia, co-editor, 1922-23; Fanfrolico Press, London, England, editor and operator, 1927-30, concurrently co-editor of *London Aphrodite* (periodical), 1928-29; *Arena* (periodical), London, England, co-editor, 1949-51; author, poet, editor, and translator. *Military service:* British Army, 1941-45; served in Royal Signal Corps, 1941-43, detailed to War Office as script writer, 1943-45. *Member:* Royal Society of Literature (fellow), Ancient Monuments Society (fellow), Egyptian Exploration Society, Roman and Hellenic Societies, Essex and Suffolk Archaeological Societies. *Awards, honors:* Golden Medal of Australian Literary Society, 1962; Znak Pocheta (a Soviet Order for translating Russian poetry); D.Litt., University of Queensland.

WRITINGS—Nonfiction: (Contributor) William Blake, *Poetical Sketches*, edited by E.H. Partridge, Scholartis Press, 1927; *William Blake: Creative Will and the Poetic Image*, Fanfrolico, 1927, 2nd edition, enlarged, 1929, Haskell House, 1971; *Dionysos: Nietzsche contra Neitzsche* (essay in lyrical philosophy), Fanfrolico, 1928; *A Retrospect of the Fanfrolico Press*, Simpkin Marshall, 1931; *The Romans*, A. & C. Black, 1935; *Marc Antony: His World and His Contemporaries*, Routledge, 1936, Dutton, 1937; *The Anatomy of Spirit: An Inquiry into the Origins of Religious Emotion*, Methuen, 1937; *John Bunyan, Maker of Myths* (biography), Methuen, 1937, Augustus M. Kelley, 1969; *England, My England*, Fore Publications, 1939; *A Short History of Culture*, Gollancz, 1939, published in America as *A Short History of Culture, from Prehistory to the Renaissance*, Citadel, 1962; *Mulk Raj Anand* (critical essay), Hind Kitabs Ltd. (Bombay), 1948, 2nd revised edition published as *The Elephant and the Lotus: A Study of the Novels of Mulk Raj Anand*, Kutub Popular (Bombay), 1965; *Song of a Falling World: Culture During the Break-up of the Roman Empire, A.D. 350-600*, Dakers, 1948; *Marxism and Contemporary Science; or, The Fullness of Life*, Dobson, 1949; *Charles Dickens: A Biographical and Critical Study*, Philosophical Library, 1950; *A World Ahead: Journal of a Soviet Journey*, Fore Publications, 1950; (compiler and author of introduction) Leslie Hurry, *Paintings and Drawings*, Grey Walls Press, 1950; (author of introduction) Dame Edith Sitwell, *Facade, and Other Poems, 1920-1935*, Duckworth, 1950; (reviser and author of introduction) Zaharia Stancu, *Barefoot*, translation by P.M., Fore Publications, 1951; *Byzantium into Europe: The Story of Byzantium as the First Europe, 326-1204 A.D., and its Further Contribution till 1435 A.D.*, John Lane, 1952, Fernhill, 1952; (with Maurice Cornforth) *Rumanian Summer: A View of the Rumanian People's*

Republic, Lawrence & Wishart, 1953; Civil War in England (account of the Civil War of 1642-49), Muller, 1954, Barnes & Noble, 1967; After the Thirties: The Novel in Britain and Its Future, Lawrence & Wishart, 1956; George Meredith: His Life and Work, John Lane, 1956; The Romans Were Here: The Roman Period in Britain and Its Place in Our History, Muller, 1956, Barnes & Noble, 1969; Arthur and His Times: Britain in the Dark Ages, Muller, 1958, Barnes & Noble, 1966; The Discovery of Britain (guide to archaeology), Merlin Press, 1958; Life Rarely Tells (first in an autobiographical trilogy), Bodley Head, 1958; 1764: The Hurlyburly of Daily Life Exemplified in One Year of the 18th Century, Muller, 1959; Death of the Hero (study of French painting from David to Delacroix), Studio, 1960; The Roaring Twenties (2nd in the autobiographical trilogy), Bodley Head, 1960; The Writing on the Wall: An Account of Pompeii in its Last Days, Muller, 1960, Dufour, 1964; Fanfrolico, and After (last in the autobiographical trilogy), Bodley Head, 1962; Our Celtic Heritage (juvenile), Dufour, 1962; Daily Life in Roman Egypt, Muller, 1963; Masks and Faces, Muller, 1963; Nine Days' Hero, Wat Tyler (biography), Dobson, 1964; (contributor) The Paintings of D.H. Lawrence, edited by Mervyn Levy, Viking, 1964; The Clashing Rocks: A Study of Early Greek Religion and Culture and the Origins of Drama, Chapman & Hall, 1965; Leisure and Pleasure in Roman Egypt, Muller, 1965, Barnes & Noble, 1966; Our Anglo-Saxon Heritage (juvenile), Dufour, 1965; J.M.W. Turner: His Life and Work (critical biography), New York Graphic Society, 1966; Our Roman Heritage (juvenile), Dufour, 1967; The Ancient World: Manners and Morals, edited by Richard Friedenthal Putnam, 1968; Meetings with Poets: Memories of Dylan Thomas, Edith Sitwell, Louis Aragon, Paul Eluard, Tristan Tzara, Muller, 1968, Ungar, 1969; Men and Gods on the Roman Nile, Barnes & Noble, 1968; Cezanne: His Life and Art, New York Graphic Society, 1969; The Origin of Alchemy in Graeco-Roman Egypt, Barnes & Noble, 1970; The Origins of Astrology, Barnes & Noble, 1971; Cleopatra, Coward, 1971; Life of Courbet, Adams & Dart, in press; Helen of Troy, Constable, in press; The Normans and Their World, Hart-Davis, in press.

Fiction—(All historical novels, unless otherwise noted): Cressida's First Lover: A Tale of Ancient Greece (fantasy novel), John Lane, 1931, R. Long & R.R. Smith, 1932; Rome for Sale (first in Rome trilogy), foreword by Colin Still, Harper, 1934; Caesar is Dead (2nd in Rome trilogy), Nicholson & Watson, 1934; Despoiling Venus, Nicholson & Watson, 1935; Last Days with Cleopatra (3rd in Rome trilogy), Nicholson & Watson, 1935; Runaway (boys' novel), Oxford University Press, 1935; Storm at Sea (novella), wood engravings by John Farleigh, Golden Cockerel Press, 1935; Adam of a New World (novel about Giordano Bruno), Nicholson & Watson, 1936; Come Home at Last (short stories), Nicholson & Watson, 1936; The Wanderings of Wenamen, 1115-1114, B.C., Nicholson & Watson, 1936; Rebels of the Goldfields (boys' novel), Lawrence & Wishart, 1936; (under pseudonym Richard Preston) Shadow and Flame (contemporary novel), Chapman & Hall, 1936; Sue Verney, Nicholson & Watson, 1937; The Invaders, Oxford University Press, 1938; 1649: A Novel of a Year, Methuen, 1938; To Arms! A Story of Ancient Gaul (boys' novel), Oxford University Press, 1938; (under pseudonym Richard Preston) End of Cornwall (contemporary novel), J. Cape, 1937, Vanguard, 1938; Brief Light: A Novel of Catullus, Methuen, 1939; Lost Birthright, Methuen, 1939; Hannibaal Takes a Hand, Dakers, 1941; Light in Italy, Gollancz, 1941; The Stormy Violence, Dakers, 1941; The Dons Sight Devon (boys' novel), Oxford University Press, 1942; We Shall Return: A Novel of Dunkirk and the French Campaign, Dakers, 1942; Beyond Terror: A Novel of the Battle of Crete, Dakers, 1943; The Barriers Are Down: A Tale of the Collapse of a Civilisation, Gollancz, 1945; Hullo Stranger (contemporary novel), Dakers, 1945; Time to Live (contemporary novel), Dakers, 1946; The Subtle Knot (contemporary novel), Dakers, 1947; Men of Forty-Eight, Methuen, 1948; Fires in Smithfield: A Novel of Mary Tudor's Days, John Lane, 1950; The Passionate Pastoral, John Lane, 1951; Betrayed Spring (contemporary novel), John Lane, 1953; Rising Tide (contemporary novel), John Lane, 1953; The Moment of Choice (contemporary novel), John Lane, 1955; The Great Oak: A Story of 1549, Bodley Head, 1957; A Local Habitation (contemporary novel), John Lane, 1957; The Revolt of the Sons (contemporary novel), Muller, 1960; All on the Never-Never (contemporary novel), Muller, 1961; The Way the Ball Bounces (contemporary novel), Muller, 1962; Choice of Times (contemporary novel), Muller, 1964; Thunder Underground: A Story of Nero's Rome, Muller, 1965.

Poetry: Fauns and Ladies, Kirtley (Sidney), 1923; (contributor) Philip Lindsay, Morgan in Jamaica, includes poem panegyrical by J. Lindsay, Fanfrolico, 1930; The Passionate Neatherd, Fanfrolico, 1930; Into Action: The Battle of Dieppe, Dakers, 1942; Second Front, Dakers, 1944; Clue of Darkness, Dakers, 1949; Peace is Our Answer, linocuts by Noel Counihan, Collets Holdings, 1950; Three Letters to Nikolai Tikhonov, Fore Publications, 1950; Three Elegies, Myriad Press, 1957.

Plays: Helen Comes of Age (three verse plays), Fanfrolico, 1927; Marino Faliero (tragedy in verse), Fanfrolico, 1927; Hereward, Fanfrolico, 1930; "Robin of England," first produced, 1944; "The Whole Armour of God," first produced, 1944; (with B. Coombes) "Face of Coal," first produced at Scala Theatre, London, England, 1946; "Lysistrata," first produced, 1948. Author of other plays, and writer of scripts for documentary and educational films.

Editor: (With K. Slessor) Poetry in Australia, Vision Press (Sydney), 1923; (with Peter Warlock) Sir John Harington, The Metamorphosis of Ajax, Fanfrolico, 1927; Loving Mad Tom (Bedlamite verses of the 16th and 17th centuries), foreword by Robert Graves, musical transcriptions by Peter Warlock, Fanfrolico, 1927, A.M. Kelley, 1970; (under pseudonym Peter Meadows) Robert Herrick, Delighted Earth (selection from "Hesperides"), Fanfrolico, 1927; The Parlement of Pratlers (Elizabethan dialogues and monologues), translated by John Eliot, Fanfrolico, 1928; Inspiration (anthology), Fanfrolico, 1928; Letters of Philip Stanhope, Second Earl of Chesterfield, Fanfrolico, 1930; (with Edgell Rickword) A Handbook of Freedom: A Record of English Democracy Through Twelve Centuries (anthology), International Publishers, 1939, reissued as Spokesmen for Liberty, Lawrence & Wishart, 1941; Giuliano the Magnificent (adaptation of unpublished drama by Dorothy Johnson), Dakers, 1940; (with Maurice Carpenter and Honor Arundel) New Lyrical Ballads, Editions Poetry, 1945; Anvil: Life and the Arts (miscellany), Meridian Books, 1947; Robert Herrick, Selected Poems, includes essay by Lindsay, British Book Centre, 1948; (and author of introduction) Wlliam Morris, Selected Poems, Grey Walls Press, 1948; J.M.W. Turner, The Sunset Ship (collected poems), includes essay by Lindsay, Evelyn, 1966; (and author of introduction) Joseph Priestley, Autobiography: Memoirs written by Himself—An Account of Further Discoveries in the Air, Adams & Dart, 1970, Fairleigh Dickinson University Press, 1971. Also editor of "New Development Series," Bodley Head, 1947-48, and co-editor, with Randall Swingler, of "Key Poet Series," Alan Swallow, 1951.

Translator: Aristophanes, Lysistrata, Fanfrolico, 1926; (and editor) The Complete Works of Petronius Arbiter (comprising The Satyricon and poems), Fanfrolico, 1927, revised edition, including introduction by Lindsay, published as *The Satyricon and Poems*, Elek Books, 1960; *Propertius in Love* (verse), Fanfrolico, 1927; *A Homage to Sappho* (poems, embodying translations of the fragments), Fanfrolico, 1928; *The Complete Poetry of Gaius Catullus,* includes essay by Lindsay, Fanfrolico, 1929, new translation, with introduction and commentary by Lindsay, published as *Catullus: The Complete Poems,* Sylvan Press, 1948; *The Mimiambs of Herondas* (verse), foreword by Brian Penton, Fanfrolico, 1929; Theocritos, *The Complete Poems,* introduction by Edward Hutton, Fanfrolico, 1929; *Women in Parliament* (Aristophanes' *Ecclesiazusae*), foreword by Rickword, Fanfrolico, 1929; D.M. Ausonius, *Patchwork Quilt* (selected poems), Fanfrolico, 1930; *Homer's Hymns to Aphrodite*, Fanfrolico, 1930; *Sulpicia's Garland* (Roman poems), McKee, 1930; Lucius Apuleius, *The Golden Ass,* Limited Editions Club (New York), 1932, revised edition, Indiana University Press, 1962; *I Am a Roman*, Mathews & Marrot, 1934; *Medieval Latin Poets* (verse), Mathews & Marrot, 1934; Longus, *Daphnis and Chloe,* includes critical essay by Lindsay, Daimon Press, 1948; (with Stephen Jolly) Vitezslav Nezval, *Song of Peace,* Fore Publications, 1951; Adam Mickiewicz, *Poems,* Sylvan Press, 1957; (also editor and author of introduction) *Russian Poetry, 1917-1955,* Bodley Head, 1957; Asclepiades, *The Loves of Asklepiades,* Myriad Press, 1959; (and compiler) *Modern Russian Poetry,* Vista Books, 1960; (and editor) *Ribaldry of Greece* (anthology), Bestseller Library, 1961, published in America as *Ribaldry of Ancient Greece: An Intimate Portrait of Greeks in Love,* Ungar, 1965; (and editor) *Ribaldry of Rome* (anthology), Bestseller Library, 1961, published in America as *Ribaldry of Ancient Rome: An Intimate Portrait of Romans in Love,* Ungar, 1965; (and author of introduction) Giordano Bruno, *Cause, Principle and Unity,* Daimon Press, 1962, International Publishers, 1964; Eleonore Bille-de Mot, *The Age of Akhenaton,* Cory, Adams & Mackay, 1967; Euripides, *Iphigeneia in Aulis, Hecuba, Electra, Orestes* (four plays), Mermaid Theatre, 1967; Gotthold Ephraim Lessing, *Nathan the Wise,* Mermaid Theatre, 1967; (and author of introduction) Teukros Anthias, *Greece, I Keep My Vigil for You,* Anthias Publications, 1968.

Booklets: *Perspective for Poetry,* Fore Publications, 1944; *British Achievement in Art and Music,* Pilot Press, 1945; *William Morris, Writer* (lecture given at Caxton Hall, London, November 14, 1958), William Morris Society, 1961. Also author of unpublished book, "The Starfish Road; or, The Poet as Revolutionary," a study of modern poetry in relation to the Industrial Revolution. Contributor to numerous periodicals, including *Life and Letters, Adam, British Ally, New Directions,* and *Horizon.*

WORK IN PROGRESS: Energy Concepts in the Ancient World, for Muller.

SIDELIGHTS: Lindsay is known as an extremely prolific novelist, poet, social and literary critic, verse dramatist, biographer, classical scholar, and translator. He has participated in many of the European literary trends of the past half-century, among them the fine-press movement in London during the late twenties, the French Resistance of the early thirties, mass-declamation poetry in England in the late thirties, and post-war experimental drama techniques, which he used later in documentary films and radio scripts. Since World War II he has turned to the contemporary social scene and a series of analyses of the British way of life, while continuing his work in the area of pure scholarship, linking European with ancient history in critical studies such as his *Byzantium into Europe,* published in 1952. His personal acquaintance with Dylan Thomas and Dame Edith Sitwell is well documented in *Meetings with Poets.* The third section of the book concentrates on the French Resistance poets, Eluard, Aragon,

and Tzara in particular. In his review, Philip Callow writes: "Lindsay certainly succeeds in recapturing the excitement these poets generated for him and his fellow intellectuals at the time. . . . They were going to triumph not only against fascism but the whole world of bourgeois corruption which made it possible. It was the longed-for breakthrough at last, poignantly rising out of the fire and death. Well, it didn't work out that way, but the feeling of a great cultural leap forward out of the ashes is still the dream and inspiration behind this humane and wide-ranging book."

Lindsay, a competent biographer, has recently ventured into the realm of the artist and art critic with his biographies of Turner and Cezanne. Clement Greenberg comments on *J.M.W. Turner: His Life and Work:* "The insights here, such as they are, seem to me to be dulled by a tincture of pedestrian Marxism or, less often, of routine Freudianism. . . . [Mr. Lindsay] fares even worse as an art critic. Turner's pictures are put through the 'parallels-and-diagonals, verticals-and-horizontals' hopper that constituted advanced pictorial analysis 30 years ago. . . . But when he is not an art critic and not an interpreter, [Lindsay] is a scrupulous scholar and sets straight many facts about Turner." Francis Haskell agrees that this "very readable biography does make of [Turner] (for the first time) a credible human being. The task is unusually difficult, for the contradictory elements in his life were more compartmentalized in him than they are in most men." The *Times Literary Supplement* remarks that in *Cezanne: His Life and Art* "we are given a highly romanticized and often contradictory account of the moral, intellectual and professional attitudes which the author thinks can be attributed to the Cezanne of his imagining." However, J.R. Mellow of the *New York Times Book Review* believes that this kind of treatment adds a great deal to biographies of historical figures who, like Cezanne, left few records of a personal nature. "The Cezanne which Jack Lindsay . . . presents is not exactly a new man, but he is a fully realized figure, complex and contradictory. . . . The wealth of personal and literary associations that Lindsay brings to his discussions of the subject-matter of Cezanne's paintings . . . gives his book solidity and weight."

Lindsay lists archaeology as an avocation, an interest which has inspired many of his books. His father, a well-known Australian and British artist, illustrated several of his translations of Latin and Greek authors.

In 1944 Martin Browne and his Pilgrim Players performed a poetic documentary, written by Lindsay, in churches all over England; this concerned the Christian Resistance to Hitler and was entitled "The Whole Armour of God." Over one million copies of Lindsay's novels in translation have been printed in the Soviet Union.

BIOGRAPHICAL/CRITICAL SOURCES: Colin Arthur Roderick, *Twenty Australian Novelists,* Angus & Robertson, 1947; Alick West, *Mountain in the Sunlight: Studies in Conflict and Unity,* Lawrence & Wishart, 1958; *Book Week,* September 11, 1966; *New York Review of Books,* December 1, 1966; *Times Literary Supplement,* August 31, 1967, October 16, 1969, July 16, 1970; *London Magazine,* May, 1968; *Books and Bookmen,* June, 1968, March, 1971; *Economist,* November 9, 1968; *New York Times Book Review,* October 12, 1969.

*   *   *

LINDSAY, (John) Maurice   1918-
(Gavin Brock)

PERSONAL: Born July 21, 1918, in Glasgow, Scotland; son of Matthew (an insurance manager) and Eileen Frances (Brock) Lindsay; married Aileen Joyce Gordon, August 3, 1946; children: Seona Morag, Kirsteen Ann,

Niall Gordon Brock, Morven Morag Joyce. *Education:* Attended Glasgow Academy, 1926-36, Scottish National Academy of Music, 1936-39. *Politics:* Liberal. *Home:* 11, Great Western Terrace, Glasgow W.2, Scotland. *Office:* The Scottish Civic Trust, 24, George Square, Glasgow C. 2, England.

CAREER: *Scottish Daily Mail,* Edinburgh, Scotland, drama critic, 1946-47; *Bulletin,* Glasgow, Scotland, music critic, 1946-60; British Broadcasting Corp., Glasgow, Scotland, free-lance broadcaster, 1946-61; Border Television, Carlisle, Scotland, program controller, 1961-62, production controller, 1962-64, features executive and senior interviewer, 1964-67; Scottish Civic Trust, Glasgow, Scotland, director, 1967—. *Military service:* British Army, World War II; became captain. *Member:* Saltire Society (honorary publications secretary, 1948-52), Royal Scottish Automobile Club. *Awards, honors:* Rockefeller Atlantic Award for *The Enemies of Love,* 1946; holder of Territorial Decoration.

WRITINGS: *The Advancing Day* (poems), privately printed, 1940; *Perhaps To-morrow* (poems), privately printed, 1941; *Predicament* (13 poems), Alden Press, 1942; *No Crown for Laughter* (poems), Fortune Press, 1943; *A Pocket Guide to Scottish Culture,* Maclellan, 1947, Universal Distributors, 1947; *Selected Poems,* Oliver & Boyd, 1947; *Hurlygush: Poems in Scots,* introduction by Hugh MacDiarmid, Serif Books, 1948; *The Scottish Renaissance,* Serif Books, 1948; *At The Wood's Edge* (poems), Serif Books, 1950; *Ode for St. Andrew's Night, and Other Poems,* New Alliance Press, 1951; *The Lowlands of Scotland,* two volumes, R. Hale, Volume I: *Glasgow and the North,* 1953, Volume II: *Edinburgh and the South,* 1956, both volumes, International Publications Service, 1956; *Robert Burns: The Man, His Work, the Legend,* MacGibbon & Kee, 1954, Dufour, 1963, 2nd edition, MacGibbon & Kee, 1968, Hillary, 1969; *Dunoon: The Gem of the Clyde Coast* (guidebook), Town Council of Dunoon, 1954; *The Exiled Heart: Poems, 1941-1956,* edited and introduced by George Bruce, R. Hale, 1957; *Clyde Waters: Variations and Diversions on a Theme of Pleasure,* R. Hale, 1958; *The Burns Encyclopaedia,* Hutchinson, 1959, revised and enlarged edition, 1970; (with David Somervell) *Killochan Castle* (guidebook), Pilgrim Press, 1960; *By Yon Bonnie Banks: A Gallimaufry,* Hutchinson, 1961; *Snow Warning, and Other Poems,* Linden Press, 1962; *The Discovery of Scotland, Based on Accounts of Foreign Travellers from the Thirteenth to the Eighteenth Centuries,* R. Hale, 1964, Roy, 1965; *One Later Day, and Other Poems,* Brookside Press, 1964; *Gottfried Keller: Life and Works,* O. Wolff, 1968; *This Business of Living* (poems), Akros Publications, 1969; *Comings and Goings* (poems), Akros Publications, 1971; *The Eye is Delighted: Some Romantic Travellers in Scotland,* Muller, 1971, Transatlantic, 1972; *Portrait of Glasgow,* R. Hale, 1971.

Editor: *Sailing To-morrow's Seas: An Anthology of New Poems,* introduction by Tambimuttu, Fortune Press, 1944; *Poetry-Scotland,* four volumes, Volume 1, Maclellan, 1944, Volume 2, Maclellan, 1945, Volume 3, Maclellan, 1947, Volume 4 (with Hugh MacDiarmid), Serif Books, 1949; *Modern Scottish Poetry: An Anthology of the Scottish Renaissance, 1920-1945,* Faber, 1946, 2nd edition, 1966; *The Enemies of Love: Poems, 1941-1945,* Maclellan, 1946; (and contributor, with Fred Urquhart) *No Scottish Twilight: New Scottish Short Stories* (includes "Boxing Match," by Lindsay), Maclellan, 1947; *Selected Poems of Alexander Gray,* Maclellan, 1948; *Poems by Sir David Lyndsay of the Mount,* Oliver & Boyd, 1948; (with Helen B. Cruickshank, and author of introduction) *Selected Poems by Marion Angus,* Serif Books, 1950; (and author of introduction) *John Davidson: A Selection of His Poems* (includes essay by Hugh MacDiarmid),

preface by T.S. Eliot, Hutchinson, 1961; (with Edwin Morgan and George Bruce) *Scottish Poetry,* five volumes, Aldine, Numbers 1 and 2, 1966, Number 3, 1968, Number 4, 1969, Number 5, 1970; (and author of introduction) Robert Laird Mackie, compiler, *A Book of Scottish Verse,* 2nd edition, Oxford University Press, 1967; (consultant editor) *Voices of Our Kind: An Anthology of Contemporary Scottish Verse for Schools,* Saltire Society, 1971.

Author of librettos for two operas, "The Abbot of Drimmock," 1957, and "The Decision," music by Thea Musgrave, J. & W. Chester, 1967. Author of commentaries for two films. Contributor to *Grove's Dictionary of Music and Musicians.* Editor, with Douglas Young, of Oliver & Boyd's "Saltire Modern Poets" series, 1947; editor, *Scots Review,* 1949-50.

WORK IN PROGRESS: A book for Faber, *The Pleasures of Scotland;* further poems.

BIOGRAPHICAL/CRITICAL SOURCES: James Kinsley, editor, *Scottish Poetry: A Critical Survey,* Cassell, 1955; *Observer Review,* July, 1968.

* * *

LINDSEY, David 1914-

PERSONAL: Born December 1, 1914, in Waldwick, N.J.; son of Frederick B. (a teacher) and Mary (Krichbaum) Lindsey; children: David Scott. *Education:* Cornell University, B.A., 1936; Pennsylvania State University, M.A., 1938; University of Chicago, Ph.D., 1950. *Office:* 5151 State College Dr., Los Angeles, Calif. 90032.

CAREER: Baldwin-Wallace College, Berea, Ohio, associate professor of history, 1946-55; Oberlin College, Oberlin, Ohio, associate professor of history, 1955-56; California State College, Los Angeles, professor of history, 1956—. Fulbright visiting professor of American history, University of Athens, 1962-63, University of Madrid, 1968-69. *Member:* American Historical Association, Society of American Historians, Organization of American Historians, Southern California Historical Guild (former secretary), Civil War Round Table of Southern California (executive committee).

WRITINGS: *Ohio's Western Reserve: The Story of Its Place Names,* Western Reserve University Press and Western Reserve Historical Society, 1955; *An Outline History of Ohio,* Howard Allen, 1955, 2nd edition (with Esther Davis and Morton Biel), 1960; *"Sunset" Cox, Irrepressible Democrat,* Wayne State University Press, 1959; *A. Lincoln/Jefferson Davis: The House Divided,* Howard Allen, 1960; *H. Clay/Andrew Jackson: Democracy and Enterprise,* Howard Allen, 1963; *Jackson and Calhoun,* edited by Kenneth Colegrove, Barron's, 1971; *The Civil War and Reconstruction,* Houghton, 1973. Contributor of articles to *Washington Post, Columbus Dispatch, Charleston Courier, Los Angeles Examiner,* and to professional journals.

WORK IN PROGRESS: Two books, *The American Civil War and Reconstruction,* and *Los Angeles County: The Story of Its Place Names.*

AVOCATIONAL INTERESTS: Photography.

* * *

LING, Mona

PERSONAL: Born in Lexington, Ky. *Education:* Attended University of Cincinnati and University of Southern California. *Address:* 9735 Wilshire Blvd., Suite 129, Beverly Hills, Calif. 90212.

CAREER: Sales consultant and lecturer, Beverly Hills, Calif., 1956—. *Member:* American Management Association, American Society of Training Directors, International Society of General Semantics, International Platform Association, Soroptimist Club (Beverly Hills).

WRITINGS: How to Increase Sales and Put Yourself Across by Telephone, Prentice-Hall, 1963. Author of booklets on telephone salesmanship. Columnist, Insurance Field and Canadian Insurance; contributor to more than thirty other trade papers, journals, sales services, bulletins, and magazines.

WORK IN PROGRESS: Another book.

AVOCATIONAL INTERESTS: Golf, bowling, dancing and reading.

* * *

LINKLETTER, Art (hur Gordan) 1912-

PERSONAL: Born July 17, 1912, in Moosejaw, Saskatchewan; son of John Fulton and Mary (Metzler) Linkletter; married Lois Foerster, November 28, 1935; children: Jack, Dawn (Mrs. John Zweyer), Robert, Sharon, Diane (deceased). Education: San Diego State University, B.A., 1934. Religion: Protestant. Residence: Bel Air, Calif. Office: 8530 Wiltshire Blvd., Beverly Hills, Calif. 90211.

CAREER: Radio and television personality, 1933—, starting as announcer for Station KGB in San Diego, Calif., 1934; program director of California International Exposition, San Diego, 1935; radio director of Texas Centennial Exposition, Dallas, 1936, of San Francisco World's Fair, 1937-39; writer, producer, and star of West Coast radio shows, 1940-43; partner and co-owner of Guedel-Linkletter Productions (earlier John Guedel Radio Productions), Los Angeles, Calif., 1944—. Star and writer of national network radio and television shows, "People are Funny" and "Art Linkletter's House Party"; star and writer of television films, "Linkletter and the Kids." President of Linkletter Enterprises (oil, real estate, other business holdings), 1954—; partner in Link Research (consumer product development company), 1958—, and Vandebrug-Linkletter Association. Director of Ogden Corp., Inc., Western Airlines, Inc., Neotec, Inc., 15-16 Co., Word, Inc., and National Liberty Insurance Co. Member of board of directors of Flying Tiger Line, and other companies. Member of board of Arthritis and Rheumatism Foundation, Young Men's Christian Association, Linkletter Foundation, and Goodwill Industries. Member: Authors Guild, Chevaliers de Tastevin (gourmet club). Awards, honors: Citations from March of Dimes, Boy Scouts of America, Young Men's Christian Association, Cancer Society, and other national groups for radio and television work on their behalf.

WRITINGS: People Are Funny, Doubleday, 1947; Kids Say the Darndest Things!, illustrated by Charles Schulz, Prentice-Hall, 1957; The Secret World of Kids, Geis, 1959; (with Dean Jennings) Confessions of a Happy Man, Geis, 1960; Kids Still Say the Darndest Things!, illustrated by Charles Schulz, Geis, 1961; (editor) Kids Sure Rite Funny!: A Child's Garden of Misinformation, Geis, 1962; A Child's Garden of Misinformation, Geis, 1965; Oops!; or, Life's Awful Moments, Doubleday, 1967; I Wish I'd Said That!: My Favorite Ad-Libs of All Times, Doubleday, 1968; Linkletter Down Under, Prentice-Hall, 1968. Writer of exposition spectacles, "Cavalcade of the Golden West," 1940, "Cavalcade of America," 1941, and of cartoon panel, "Art Linkletter's Kids," King Feaures Syndicate.

SIDELIGHTS: Linkletter has acted in summer stock company in "Father of the Bride." Avocational interests: Handball, swimming, skiing, travel, and photography.

BIOGRAPHICAL/CRITICAL SOURCES: Best Sellers, September 15, 1967.

LINTON, David (Hector) 1923-

PERSONAL: Born July 20, 1923, in Chicago, Ill.; son of Ralph (an anthropologist) and Margaret (McIntosh) Linton; married Ann Holden Bryant, February 2, 1961; children: Eric, Scott, Bruce. Education: Friends Central School, Overbrook, Pa., student, 1938-42; Swarthmore College, student, 1942-45. Politics: Democrat. Religion: Society of Friends (Quaker). Home: 71 West Sproul Rd., Springfield, Pa. 19064. Office: Natural History Magazine, American Museum of Natural History, 79th and Central Park W., New York, N.Y. 10024.

CAREER: Intercollegiate Broadcasting System, program manager, 1945-47; free-lance magazine photographer, 1948—. Contributing editor, columnist, Natural History Magazine, 1960—. Made six trips to the Arctic and one to the South Pole for polar study; photographic works are included in permanent collection of Museum of Modern Art. Member: American Society of Magazine Photographers (secretary, 1956-57; president, 1957-59; trustee, 1959-60, 1961-62; vice-president, 1960-61, 1962-65; chairman of copyright law committee), American Polar Society. Awards, honors: Gold medal, Parents Institute for Understanding Natural Childbirth.

WRITINGS: (With Herbert J. Thoms and Lawrence G. Roth) Understanding Natural Childbirth: A Book for the Expectant Mother, McGraw, 1950; Photographing Nature, Natural History Press for American Museum of Natural History, 1964; (with Dolores Linton) Practical Guide to Classroom Media, Pflaum and Standard Publishing, 1971. Contributor of articles and pictures to periodicals, textbooks, and encyclopedias.

WORK IN PROGRESS: A book on Norse explorations and settlement in Greenland, and attempted settlement in North America in tenth century, for Natural History Press; Living in the Wilds; with wife, Ann Linton, Cooking in the Wilds.

AVOCATIONAL INTERESTS: Hiking, mountaineering, and camping.

BIOGRAPHICAL/CRITICAL SOURCES: Modern Photography, March, 1953.†

* * *

LIPMAN, Eugene Jay 1919-

PERSONAL: Born October 13, 1919, in Pittsburgh, Pa.; son of Joshua and Bessie (Neaman) Lipman; married Esther Marcuson, 1943; children: Michael, Jonathan, David. Education: University of Pittsburgh, undergraduate student; Hebrew Union College-Jewish Institute of Religion, Cincinnati, Ohio, B.H.L., 1938, M.H.L., 1943, D.D., 1968; University of Cincinnati, A.B., 1941; additional study at University of Washington, Seattle, and Institute for Individual Psychology, New York. Home: 3512 Woodbine St., Chevy Chase, Md. 20015. Office: Temple Sinai, 3100 Military Rd. N.W., Washington, D.C. 20015.

CAREER: Temple Beth El, Fort Worth, Tex., rabbi, 1943-44; Jewish Agency and International Refugee Organization, Germany, work with displaced persons, 1946-48; Hebrew Union College-Jewish Institute of Religion, Cincinnati, Ohio, teaching fellow, 1948-49; University of Washington, Seattle, staff of Hillel Foundation, 1949-50; Union of American Hebrew Congregations, New York, N.Y., staff member, 1951-61; Temple Sinai, Washington, D.C., rabbi, 1961—. Military service: U.S. Army, served in Chaplain Corps, 1944-46, 1950-51; became captain.

WRITINGS: (With Albert Vorspan) Justice and Judaism, Union of American Hebrew Congregations, 1956, revised edition, 1962; (editor with Myron Schoen) The American Synagogue: A Progress Report, Union of American Hebrew Congregations, 1959; (editor with Vorspan) A Tale of Ten Cities: The Triple Ghetto in Ameri-

can Religious Life, Union of American Hebrew Congregations, 1962; (editor and translator) *The Mishnah: Oral Teachings of Judaism,* Norton, 1970.

Contributor: *An American Synagogue for Today and Tomorrow,* Union of American Hebrew Congregations, 1953; Irving I. Katz and M.E. Schoen, *Successful Synagogue Administration,* Union of American Hebrew Congregations, 1963; Angelo A. D'agostino, editor, *Family, Church, and Community,* Kenedy, 1965; Christopher Derrick, editor, *Cosmic Piety: Modern Man and the Meaning of the Universe,* Kenedy, 1965; Bertram Wallace Korn, editor, *Retrospect and Prospect* (essays), Central Conference of American Rabbis, 1965; Daniel J. Silver, editor, *Judaism and Ethics,* Ktav, 1970. Contributor to a dozen journals and magazines.

WORK IN PROGRESS: Compiling a source book in Jewish ethics.

*   *   *

LIPMAN, Vivian David   1921-

PERSONAL: Born February 27, 1921, in London, England; son of Samuel Niman and Cecelia (Moses) Lipman. *Education:* Attended St. Paul's School; Magdalen College and Nuffield College, Oxford University, B.A., 1941, M.A., 1947, D.Phil., 1947. *Religion:* Jewish. *Home:* 21 Cornwall Gardens, London S.W.7, England.

CAREER: British Civil Service, 1947—, with posts including private secretaryship to a minister, and secretaryship of government committees, now assistant secretary, Ministry of Housing and Local Government, London, England. *Military service:* British Army, Royal Signals and Intelligence Corps, 1942-45. *Member:* Royal Historical Society (fellow).

WRITINGS: Local Government Areas, 1834-1945, Basil Blackwell, 1949; *Social History of the Jews in England, 1850-1950,* C.A. Watts, 1954; *A Century of Social Service, 1859-1959: The Jewish Board of Guardians,* Routledge & Kegan Paul, 1959; (editor) *Three Centuries of Anglo-Jewish History* (essays), published for Jewish Historical Society of England by Heffer, 1961, Albert Saifer, 1971; *The Jews of Medieval Norwich* (includes appendix of Latin documents and Hebrew poems of Meir of Norwich), Jewish Historical Society of England, 1967. Honorary editor of publications, Jewish Historical Society of England, 1954-61, chairman of publications committee, 1961—.

WORK IN PROGRESS: A study of the Jews of medieval Norwich, with an appendix of eighty-seven unpublished Latin documents.

*   *   *

LIPPMANN, Walter   1889-

PERSONAL: Born September 23, 1889, in New York, N.Y.; son of Jacob (a clothing manufacturer) and Daisy (Baum) Lippmann; married Faye Albertson, May 24, 1917 (divorced, 1938); married Helen Byrne Armstrong, March 26, 1938. *Education:* Harvard University, A.B. (cum laude), 1909, graduate study, 1909-10. *Politics:* Independent. *Home:* Hotel Lowell, 28 East 63rd St., New York, N.Y. 10021; and Southwest Harbor, Mount Desert, Me.

CAREER: Worked for *Everybody's Magazine* as Lincoln Steffens's secretary, 1910, became associate editor within a year; executive secretary to George R. Lunn, Socialist mayor of Schenectady, N.Y., during four months in 1912; with Herbert Croly, founded the *New Republic,* 1914, served as associate editor until 1917, returned to it in 1919; assistant to Secretary of War Newton D. Baker, 1917; secretary to a governmental organization, 1917, was one of the authors of President Woodrow Wilson's Four-

teen Points: *The Inquiry,* secretary, 1917-18; editorial staff member of *New York World,* 1921-29, editor, 1929-31; columnist ("Today and Tomorrow") for *New York Herald Tribune,* 1931-62, column syndicated by *Washington Post* and *Los Angeles Times* syndicates, 1963-67; also syndicated in over 275 papers around the world; fortnightly columnist, Newsweek, 1962—. Member of board of Overseers, Harvard University, 1933-39; Member of board of directors, Fund for the Advancement of Education, 1951—. *Military service:* U.S. Army Military Intelligence, 1918-19; commissioned a captain; attached to General Pershing's headquarters.

MEMBER: National Institute of Arts and Letters, American Academy of Arts and Letters (fellow), National Press Club, Phi Beta Kappa (senator, 1934-40), Sigma Delta Chi (fellow, 1950); Cosmos Club, Metropolitan Club, Army-Navy Country Club (all Washington, D.C.); Century Club, River Club, Harvard Club, Coffee House Club (all New York); Harvard Club, Tavern Club (both Boston).

AWARDS, HONORS: Commander, Legion of Honor (France), 1946; Commander, Legion of Honor, Officer of Order of Leopold (Belgium), 1947; Knight's Cross of Order of St. Olav (Norway), 1950; Commander, Order of Orange Nassau (Netherlands), 1952; Overseas Press Club Award, 1953, 1955, and 1959; Pulitzer Prizes, 1958 and 1962; George Foster Peabody Award, 1962; Gold Medal, National Academy of Arts and Letters, 1965; LL.D., Wake Forest College, 1926, University of Wisconsin, 1927, University of California and Union College, 1933, Wesleyan University and University of Michigan, 1934, George Washington University and Amherst College, 1935, University of Rochester, 1936, College of William and Mary and Drake University, 1937, University of Chicago, 1955, New School for Social Research, 1959; Litt.D. from Dartmouth College and Columbia University, 1932, Oglethorpe College, 1934, Harvard University, 1944.

WRITINGS: A Preface to Politics, Mitchell Kennerly, 1913; *Drift and Mastery: An Attempt to Diagnose the Current Unrest,* Mitchell Kennerly, 1914, new edition with an introduction and notes by William E. Leuchtenberg, Prentice-Hall, 1961; *The Stakes of Diplomacy,* Holt, 1915, 2nd edition, 1917; *The World Conflict in Its Relation to American Democracy* (originally published in *Annals of the American Academy of Political Science,* July, 1917), Government Printing Office, 1917; *The Political Scene: An Essay on the Victory of 1918,* Holt, 1919; *Liberty and the News* (portions originally published in *Atlantic*), Harcourt, 1920; *France and the European Settlement* (pamphlet), Foreign Policy Association, 1922; *Public Opinion,* Harcourt, 1922; *Mr. Kahn Would Like to Know* (pamphlet; originally published in *New Republic,* July 4, 1923), Foreign Policy Association, 1923; *The Phantom Public,* Harcourt, 1925, reissued as *The Phantom Public: A Sequel to "Public Opinion,"* Macmillan, 1930; *H.L. Mencken* (pamphlet; originally published in *Saturday Review,* December 11, 1926), Knopf, 1926; *Men of Destiny,* drawings by Rollin Kirby, Macmillan, 1927; *American Inquisitors: A Commentary on Dayton and Chicago,* Macmillan, 1928; *A Preface to Morals,* Macmillan, 1929, reissued with the original *New Republic* review by Edmund Wilson, Beacon Press, 1960, reissued with a new introduction by Sidney Hook, Time, Inc., 1964.

Notes on the Crisis (pamphlet; originally published in *New York Herald Tribune,* September, 1931), John Day, 1931; (with W.O. Scroggs and others) *The United States in World Affairs: An Account of American Foreign Relations, 1931,* Harper, Volume I, 1932, Volume II, 1933; *Interpretations, 1931-1932,* edited by Allan Nevins, Macmillan, 1932; *A New Social Order* (pamphlet), John

Day, 1933; *The Method of Freedom*, Macmillan, 1934; (with G.D.H. Cole) *Self-Sufficiency: Some Random Reflections [and] Planning International Trade* (the former by Lippmann; the latter by Cole), Carnegie Endowment for International Peace, 1934; *The New Imperative* (portions originally published in *Yale Review*, June, 1935), Macmillan, 1935; *Interpretations, 1933-1935*, edited by Allan Nevins, Macmillan, 1936; (editor with Nevins) *A Modern Reader: Essays on Present-day Life and Culture*, Heath, 1936, 2nd edition, 1946; *An Inquiry into the Principles of the Good Society*, Little, Brown, 1937, new edition, 1943 (published in England as *The Good Society*, Allen & Unwin, 1938); *The Supreme Court: Independent or Controlled?*, Harper, 1937; *Some Notes on War and Peace*, Macmillan, 1940; *American Trade Policy* (originally published in [London] *Sunday Times*), 1943; *U.S. Foreign Policy: Shield of the Republic*, Little, Brown, 1943 (published in England with an introduction by D.W. Brogan, Hamish Hamilton, 1943); *U.S. War Aims*, Little, Brown, 1944; *In the Service of Freedom* (pamphlet), Freedom House, c.1945; *The Cold War: A Study in U.S. Foreign Policy*, Harper, 1947.

Commentaries on American Far Eastern Policy (pamphlet), American Institute of Pacific Relations, 1950; *Isolation and Alliances: An American Speaks to the British*, Little, Brown, 1952; *Public Opinion and Foreign Policy in the United States* (lectures), Allen & Unwin, 1952; *Essays in the Public Philosophy*, Little, Brown, 1955 (published in England as *The Public Philosophy*, Hamish Hamilton, 1955); *America in the World Today* (lecture), University of Minnesota Press, 1957; *The Communist World and Ours*, Little, Brown, 1959 (British edition edited by Edward Weeks, Hamish Hamilton, 1959); *The Confrontation* (originally published in column "Today and Tomorrow," September 17, 1959), Overbrook Press, 1959; (with Clarence C. Little) *Speeches of Walter Lippmann and Clarence C. Little*, [Cambridge], 1960; *The Coming Tests with Russia*, Little, Brown, 1961; *The Nuclear Era: A Profound Struggle* (pamphlet), University of Chicago Press, 1962; *Western Unity and the Common Market*, Little, Brown, 1962; *The Essential Lippmann; A Political Philosophy for Liberal Democracy*, edited by Clinton Rossiter and James Lare, Random House, 1963; (author of introduction) *Fulbright of Arkansas: The Public Positions of a Private Thinker*, edited by Karl E. Meyer, Luce, 1963; *A Free Press* (pamphlet), Berlingske Bogtrykkeri (Copenhagen), c.1965; *Conversations with Walter Lippmann* (CBS Reports television program), introduction by Edward Weeks, Little, Brown, 1965; (author of introduction) Carl Sandburg, *The Chicago Race Riots, July, 1919*, Harcourt, 1969; *Early Writings*, introduction by Arthur Schlesinger, Jr., Liveright, 1971.

Contributor: Arno Lehman Bader, Theodore Hornberger, Sigmund K. Proctor, and Carlton Wells, editors, *Prose Patterns*, Harcourt, 1933; Edward Simpson Noyes, editor, *Readings in the Modern Essay*, Houghton, 1933; Albert Craig Baird, editor, *Essays and Addresses Toward a Liberal Education*, Ginn, 1934; Joseph Bradley Hubbard and others, editors, *Current Economic Policies: Selected Discussions*, Holt, 1934; Frank Howland McCloskey and Robert B. Dow, editors, *Pageant of Prose*, Harper, 1935; Frank Luther Mott and Ralph D. Casey, editors, *Interpretations of Journalism: A Book of Readings*, F.S. Crofts, 1937; Hillman M. Bishop and Samuel Hendel, editors, *Basic Issues of American Democracy: A Book of Readings*, Appleton, 1948, 6th edition, 1969; William Ebenstein, editor, *Modern Political Thought: The Great Issues*, Rinehart, 1954, 2nd edition, 1960; Robert U. Jamison, editor, *Essays Old and New*, Harcourt, 1955; H.J. Rockel, editor, *Reflective Reader: Essays for Writing*, Holt, 1956; Alan P. Grimes and Robert Horwitz, editors, *Modern Political Ideologues*, Oxford University

Press, 1959; C. Wright Mills, editor, *Images of Man*, Braziller, 1960; Harry K. Girvetz, editor, *Contemporary Moral Issues*, Wadsworth, 1963; Arthur A. Ekirch, editor, *Voices in Dissent: An Anthology of Individualistic Thought in the U.S.*, Citadel, 1964; D.L. Larson, editor, *The Puritan Ethic in United States Foreign Policy*, Van Nostrand, 1966.

Anthologized in numerous volumes, including *Roots of Political Behavior*, edited by Richard Carlton Snyder and H. Herbert Wilson, American Book Co., 1949, *State of the Social Sciences*, edited by L.D. White, University of Chicago Press, 1956, *Conflict and Cooperation Among the Nations*, edited by Ivo D. Duchacek and K.W. Thompson, Holt, 1960, and *Power and Civilization: Political Thought in the Twentieth Century*, edited by David Cooperman and E.V. Walter, Crowell, 1962.

Contributor to many periodicals, including *Atlantic*, *Yale Review*, *New Republic*, *Life*, and *Harper's*.

SIDELIGHTS: "Anything that makes the world more humane and more rational is progress," Lippmann once said, "that's the only measuring stick we can apply to it." This statement exemplifies the attitude that has characterized Lippmann's career for nearly sixty years. And although he is always fully cognizant of the occurrences of the day, he also attempts to place these events in a larger perspective in his effort to make reason out of the chaos of political events. He once stated: "I have led two lives. One of books and one of newspapers. Each helps the other. The philosophy is the context in which I write my columns. The column is the laboratory or clinic in which I test the philosophy and keep it from becoming too abstract."

It is this objective viewing of current events as though they were already part of history that makes Lippmann unique and also brings him criticism as well as praise. Harry S. Ashmore believes that this stance is the most significant aspect of Lippman's work. "[His] aloof and almost bloodless public manner ... is an essential instrument in the execution of the role he has chosen for himself. His style is that of a man who operates at considerable remove from those who occupy the center of the stage of history. Thus, he appears as an informed observer without personal commitment to any individual, or even to any fixed point of view.... The impression, whether it is accurate or not, is that in his long passage through high places he has remained singularly free of the human obligations that accrete to lesser men and sometimes blur their view.... One important result of this calculated disengagement is that Lippmann, although he has expressed firm, forthright, and often unpopular opinions on every important public issue for almost half a century, is not, in the current usage, a controversial figure. He may occasionally stir some passion in upper intellectual reaches, but this is never translated into the kind of public outcry that is likely to send a circulation manager into emergency consultation with his publisher. One reason, doubtless, is that in his careful weighing and balancing of the factors that shape great issues he is rarely entirely satisfactory to the partisans on either side."

Norman Podhoretz also recognizes this quality in Lippmann, although he believes that it has its disadvantages. "His main fault, I think, is a tendency toward pomposity which showed itself even in his most youthful efforts and which, if anything, has been encouraged by the veneration that his advancing years ... have brought upon him. Presidents come and go; Congressmen and Senators come, and even they eventually go; but Walter Lippmann stays on in Washington forever—the last articulate representative of the political ambience of an older America, our last remaining link to the ethos of the Federalist Papers. He is, apparently, heeded and feared in Washington in a way that no other writer is, for his judgment of a government official, or of a policy, or of a bill seems to carry with it all the authority of the basic intentions of the American political system. When he speaks, it is as though the true Constitution were speaking, or as though Jefferson and Madison and Hamilton were communicating a mystical consensus through him— so thoroughly has he steeped himself in their spirit, and with such authenticity is he capable of recapturing the accents of their intellectual style. This, I suspect, is the secret source of his unique power to make the mighty listen: Walter Lippmann's opinion is the closest they can ever come to the judgment of history upon them. Under these circumstances, it is no wonder that Lippmann should occasionally be given to delivering himself of portentous platitudes without being aware that platitudes are what they are. The wonder is that he should be capable of anything else at all."

Podhoretz's comparison of Lippmann to the founding fathers is characteristic of many other analyses of Lippmann's philosophy and writing. Archibald MacLeish describes Lippmann's attitude toward freedom in a democracy as one which closely parallels the idealism of the leaders of the American Revolution. "True freedom, to Mr. Lippmann, is not the freedom of the liberal democracies. True freedom was founded on the postulate that there was a universal order on which all reasonable men were agreed: *within that public agreement* on the fundamentals and on the ultimates, it was sage to permit, and it would be desirable to encourage, dissent and dispute.' True freedom for Mr. Lippmann, in other words, is freedom to think as you please and say as you think provided what you say and think falls within the periphery of what all reasonable men agree to be fundamentally and ultimately true." For Lippmann rationality is not only the highest ideal, but the possible savior of modern society. He once said: "The world will go on somehow, and more crises will follow. It will go on best, however, if among us there are men who have stood apart, who refused to be anxious or too much concerned, who were cool and inquiring, and had their eyes on a longer past and longer future."

It is in the field of foreign affairs that Lippmann reveals the principles central to his view of man and the modern world. In a *New York Times Magazine* interview, Lippmann stated that it is U.S. foreign policy which is most responsible for the current political unrest and social crises. "I ascribe the essence of the failure [of the United States to solve its internal problems] to miscalculation, to misunderstanding our post-World War II position in the world. That has turned our energies away from our real problems. The error is not merely the trouble in Vietnam, but the error lies in the illusion that the position occupied in the world by the United States at the end of the war was a permanent arrangement of power in the world. It wasn't. The United States was victorious; but by then all the imperial structures which set the bounds of American power had been destroyed: the German Reich, the Japanese empire. The result is that we flowed forward beyond our natural limits and the cold war is the result of our meeting the Russians with no buffers between us. That miscalculation, which was made by my generation, has falsified all our other calculations—what our power was, what we could afford to do, what influence we had to exert in the world."

One of Lippmann's chief concerns is that lack of reasonable attitudes toward other nations and domestic dissenters will continue to lead to an illogical disregard for the truly significant issues with which U.S. leaders must deal. "You have only to look at the Senate of the United States," Lippmann wrote in 1912, "to see how that body is capable of turning itself into a court of preliminary hearings for the Last Judgment, wasting its time and our time and absorbing public enthusiasm and newspaper scareheads. For a hundred needs of the nation it has no thought, but about the precise morality of an historical transaction eight years old there is a meticulous interest .. enough to start the Senate on a protracted man-hunt. Now if one half of the people is bent upon proving how wicked a man is and the other half is determined to show how good he is, neither half will think very much about the nation." In recent years he has applied this disparagement of emotional politics to the passionate anti-Communists. "The reactionary radicals, who would like to repeal the twentieth century, are, so they tell us, violently opposed to Communism. But Communism also belongs to the twentieth century and these reactionary radicals do not understand it and do not know how to resist it."

Lippmann believes that it is his ultimate role as a journalist to reveal the absurdity of these emotional diversions. With this goal he hopes to influence the people to accept his creed; he objectifies events so that the populace can comprehend them. "If the country is to be governed with the consent of the governed, then the governed must arrive at opinions about what their governors want them to consent to. How do they do this? They do it by hearing on the radio and reading in the newspapers what the corps of correspondents tells them is going on in Washington and in the country at large and in the world. Here we perform an essential service ... we do what every sovereign citizen is supposed to do, but has not the time or the interest to do for himself. This is our job. It is no mean calling, and we have a right to be proud of it."

BIOGRAPHICAL/CRITICAL SOURCES—Books: David E. Weingast, *Walter Lippmann: A Study in Personal Journalism,* Rutgers University Press, 1949; Max Lerner, *Actions and Passions: Notes on the Multiple Revolution of Our Time,* Simon & Schuster, 1949; Henry Steele Commager, *The American Mind,* Yale University Press, 1950; Kenneth Norman Stewart and John Tibbel, *Makers of Modern Journalism,* Prentice-Hall, 1952; John Mason Brown, *Through These Men: Some Aspects of Our Passing History,* Harper, 1956; Marquis Childs and James Reston, editors, *Walter Lippmann and His Times,* Harcourt, 1959; Felix S. Cohen, *The Legal Conscience,* Yale University Press, 1960; Charles B. Forcey, *The Crossroads of Liberalism: Croly, Weyl, Lippmann, and the Progressive Era 1900-1925,* Oxford University Press, 1961; Hans J. Morgenthau, *The Restoration of American Politics,* University of Chicago Press, 1962; Arthur Schlesinger, Jr., *The Politics of Hope,* Houghton, 1963; Norman Podhoretz, *Doings and Undoings: The Fifties and After in American Writing,* Farrar, Straus, 1964; Anwar H. Syed, *Walter Lippmann's Philosophy of International Politics,* University of Pennsylvania Press, 1964; Aylesa Forsee, *Headliners: Famous American Journalists,* Macrae, 1967; Archibald MacLeish, *A Continuing Journey,* Houghton, 1967; F.C. Cary, *The Influence of Walter Lippmann, 1914-1944,* State Historical Society of Wisconsin, 1967; Edward L. Schapsmeier and Frederick H. Schapsmeier, *Walter Lippmann: Philosopher, Journalist,* Public Affairs Press, 1969; Charles Wellborn, *Twentieth Century Pilgrimage: Walter Lippmann and the Public Philosophy,* Louisiana State University Press. 1969.

*   *   *

LIPSETT, Laurence Cline 1915-

PERSONAL: Born May 8, 1915, in East Aurora, N.Y.; son of William Christopher (a horseshoer) and Flora (Cline) Lipsett; married Agnes Blanche Carter, May 28, 1939; children: Louise Ellen (Mrs. Frank Richens), Judith Ann (Mrs. Everett Eugene Shaver). *Education:* University of Michigan, B.A., 1937; University of Buffalo,

Ed.M., 1948, Ed.D., 1951. *Home:* 207 Curtice Park, Webster, N.Y. 14580. *Office:* Rochester Institute of Technology, 1 Lomb Memorial Dr., Rochester, N.Y. 14623.

CAREER: Erie County Department of Social Welfare, Buffalo, N.Y., senior clerk, 1939-43; U.S. Civil Service Commission, New York, N.Y., personnel investigator, 1943-45; New York State Employment Service, Rochester, interviewer, 1945-46; Rochester Institute of Technology, Rochester, N.Y., counselor, 1946-53, director of Counseling Center, 1953—. Member of board of trustees, Association for the Blind. *Member:* American Psychological Association, American College Personnel Association, National Vocational Guidance Association, New York State Psychological Association, Genesee Valley Psychological Association (president, 1958-59), Genesee Valley Personnel and Guidance Association (president, 1949-50).

WRITINGS: (With Leo F. Smith) *The Technical Institute,* McGraw, 1956; (with Frank P. Rodgers and Harold M. Kentner) *Personnel Selection and Recruitment,* Allyn & Bacon, 1964. Contributor to psychological and educational journals.

WORK IN PROGRESS: A book on psychologial characteristics of salesmen; further work on projective techniques in industrial assessments and in vocational guidance.

* * *

LIPTZIN, Sol(omon) 1901-

PERSONAL: Born July 27, 1901, in Satanov, Russia; son of Benjamin and Fannie (Grossman) Liptzin; married Anna Ohrenstein, 1929; children: Yelva Lynfield, Karen Sitton. *Education:* College of the City of New York (now City College of the City University of New York), B.A., 1921; Univerity of Berlin, graduate student, 1922-23; Columbia University, M.A., 1922, Ph.D., 1924. *Religion:* Jewish. *Home:* 18 Washington St., Jerusalem, Israel.

CAREER: College of the City of New York, New York, N.Y., professor, 1923-64, chairman, department of Germanic and Slavic, 1943-58; American College in Jerusalem, Jerusalem, Israel, professor and chairman, Division of Humanities, 1968—. Visiting professor, Northwestern University, 1931, Univerity of California, 1947, Yeshiva University, 1929-40, Bar-Ilan University, 1955-56, Tel Aviv University, 1963, Haifa Technion, 1963-67. American Jewish Congress, chairman, commission on Jewish affairs, 1960-64; Jewish Book Council of America, president, 1951-53; Yivo Institute of Jewish Research, secretary, academic council, 1933—; Yiddish Dictionary Committee, chairman, administrative board. *Member:* American Association of Teachers of German (secretary, 1927-33), College Yiddish Association (president, 1945-61), Jewish State Zionists (president, 1936).

WRITINGS: Shelley in Germany, Columbia University Press, 1924; *The Weavers in German Literature,* Johns Hopkins Press, 1926; (editor) Heinrich Heine, *Heine,* Johnson Publishing Co. (New York), 1928; *Lyric Pioneers of Modern Germany: Studies in German Social Poetry,* Columbia University Press, 1928; (editor) *From Novalis to Nietzsche: Anthology of Nineteenth Century German Literature,* Prentice-Hall, 1929; *Arthur Schnitzler,* Prentice-Hall, 1932; *Historical Survey of German Literature,* Prentice-Hall, 1936; *Richard Beer-Hofmann,* Bloch Publishing, 1936; *YIVO's Way,* Yiddish Scientific Institute, 1943; *Germany's Stepchildren,* Jewish Publication Society, 1944; *Ben Hecht and Waldo Frank: Flaming Wrath and Olympian Detachment,* Yiddish Scientific Institute, 1945; (editor and translator) Isaac Loeb Peretz, *Peretz* (short stories), bilingual edition, Yiddish Scientific Institute, 1947, reissued as *Stories from Peretz,* Hebrew Publishing, c.1964; *Eliakum Zinser, Poet of His People,* Behrman, 1950; *The English Legend of Heinrich Heine,*

Bloch Publishing, 1954; *Generation of Decision: Jewish Rejuvenation in America,* Bloch Publishing, 1958; *The Flowering of Yiddish Literature,* Yoseloff, 1964; *The Jew in American Literature,* Bloch Publishing, 1966; *The Maturing of Yiddish Literature,* Jonathan David, 1970; *A History of Yiddish Literature,* Jonathan David, 1972. Editor, *Jewish Book Annual,* 1953-55; department editor, *Encyclopedia Hebraica;* divisional editor, *Encyclopedia Judaica.* Contributor to English, Yiddish, and Hebrew journals.

BIOGRAPHICAL/CRITICAL SOURCES: American Literature, January, 1967.

* * *

LISTER, R(ichard) P(ercival) 1914-

PERSONAL: Born November 23, 1914, in Nottingham, England; son of P.T. and Winifred E. (Clapperton) Lister; divorced. *Education:* University of Manchester, B.Sc. (with honors in metallurgy), 1937. *Address:* c/o Lloyds Bank Ltd., 4 Dean Stanley St., London S.W.1, England. *Agent:* International-Famous Agency, Inc., 1301 Avenue of the Americas, New York, N.Y. 10019.

CAREER: United Steel Companies Ltd., Sheffield, England, trainee, 1937-39; Royal Naval Torpedo Factory, Greenock, Scotland, metallurgist, 1940; Royal Aircraft Establishment, Farnborough, England, metallurgist, 1941-43; Ministry of Aircraft Production, London, England, scientific officer, 1943-47; British Non-Ferrous Metals Research Association, London, England, liaison officer, 1947-49; Macdonald & Evans Ltd. (publishers), London, England, general editor, 1954-57; free-lance writer, 1949-54, 1957—.

WRITINGS: The Way Backwards, Collins, 1950; *The Oyster and the Torpedo,* J. Cape, 1951; *Rebecca Redfern,* Deutsch, 1953; *The Idle Demon: A Collection of Verses,* Macmillan, 1958; *The Rhyme and the Reason,* Harcourt, 1963; *The Questing Beast,* Chapman & Hall, 1965; (self-illustrated) *A Journey in Lapland: The Hard Way to Haparanda,* Chapman & Hall, 1965, published in America as *The Hard Way to Haparanda,* Harcourt, 1966; (self-illustrated) *A Muezzin from the Tower of Darkness Cries: Travels in Turkey,* Harcourt, 1967 (published in England as *Turkey Observed,* Eyre & Spottiswoode, 1967); *Genghis Khan,* Stein & Day, 1969 (published in England as *The Secret History of Genghis Khan,* P. Davies, 1969). Contributor of poems, articles and short stories to *Punch, New Yorker, Atlantic Monthly,* and other periodicals.

WORK IN PROGRESS: A historical novel.

AVOCATIONAL INTERESTS: Music, painting, walking, and mountain climbing.

* * *

LITTERER, Joseph A(ugust) 1926-

PERSONAL: Born October 16, 1926, in New York, N.Y.; son of Charles Frank (a printer) and Gladys (Bader) Litterer; married Marie Wilson (a scientific illustrator), October 17, 1953; children: Karin, Susan, David. *Education:* Drexel Institute of Technology, B.S. in E.E., 1950, M.B.A., 1955; University of Illinois, Ph.D., 1959. *Office:* Department of Management, University of Massachusetts, Amherst, Mass. 01002.

CAREER: Radio Corp. of America, Camden, N.J., supervisor of test equipment, 1952-55; University of Illinois, Urbana, instructor, 1957-59, became assistant professor and, associate professor, then professor of business administration; University of Massachusetts, Amherst, presently professor. Consultant to Allis Chalmers, Mobil Oil, Bendix Corp., Corn Products Co., and other business firms. *Military service:* U.S. Army, 1950-52. *Member:* Institute of Management Sciences (chairman of college on organizations, 1963—), American Economic Association, American Sociological Association, Academy of Management, Society for the Advancement of Management.

WRITINGS: (Editor) *Organizations: Structure and Behavior,* Wiley, 1963, 2nd edition in two volumes, 1969; *The Analysis of Organizations,* Wiley, 1965.

WORK IN PROGRESS: A long term research effort on coordinative requirements resulting from different forms of division of work, to be reported in a series of papers and monographs.

AVOCATIONAL INTERESTS: Reading, history, squash, tennis, fishing, sailing, and loafing at the family summer place in Maine.

*   *   *

LIVINGSTON, William S.   1920-

PERSONAL: Born July 1, 1920, in Ironton, Ohio; son of Samuel George (a civil servant) and Bata Aileen (Elkins) Livingston; married Lana Sanor, July 10, 1943; children: Stephen, David. *Education:* Ohio State University, B.A., 1943, M.A., 1943; Yale University, Ph.D., 1950. *Politics:* "Objective neutrality." *Religion:* Episcopal. *Home:* 3203 Greenlee Dr., Austin, Tex. 78703. *Office:* Department of Government, University of Texas, Austin, Tex. 78712.

CAREER: University of Texas, Austin, assistant professor, 1949-54, associate professor, 1954-60, professor of government, 1960—, assistant dean of Graduate School, 1954-58, chairman, Department of Government, 1966-69; University of Texas System, Vice-Chancellor for Academic Programs, 1969—. Visiting lecturer at Yale University, 1955-56; visiting professor at Duke University, 1961. *Military service:* U.S. Army, Field Artillery, 1943-45; served in Europe; became first lieutenant; received Bronze Star and Purple Heart. *Member:* American Political Science Association, Southern Political Science Association (council), Hansard Society (London), Southwestern Social Science Association, Canadian Political Science Association, Phi Beta Kappa, Omicron Delta Kappa, Phi Gamma Delta. *Awards, honors:* Ford Foundation faculty fellow, 1952-53; Guggenheim fellow, 1959-60; Teaching Excellence Award, University of Texas, 1959.

WRITINGS: Federalism and Constitutional Change, Clarendon Press, 1956; (editor and co-author) *Federalism in the Commonwealth: A Bibliographical Commentary,* published for Hansard Society by Cassell, 1963; (contributor) Marian D. Irish, editor, *World Pressures on American Foreign Policy,* Prentice-Hall, 1964; (contributor) Robert H. Connery, editor, *Teaching Political Science,* Duke University Press, 1965; (contributor) Valerie Earle, editor, *Federalism: Infinite Variety in Theory and Practice,* Peacock, 1968. Contributor of about fifteen articles to journals.

WORK IN PROGRESS: A study of the British political system; another general book on federalism.

AVOCATIONAL INTERESTS: Tennis, hunting, philately.

*   *   *

LLEWELLYN, Alun (David William)   1903-

PERSONAL: Born April 17, 1903, in London, England; son of David William and Elizabeth Jane (Lewis) Llewellyn; married Lesley Deane (an actress and producer), January 17, 1953. *Education:* Attended Alleyn's School; St. John's College, Cambridge University, B.A. (honors in history and literature), 1924, LL.B. (honors), 1925, M.A., 1928; Lincolns Inn of Court, called to bar, 1927. *Politics:* Liberal. *Religion:* Christian. *Home:* Garthgwynion, 93 Wood Vale, London S.E.23, England.

CAREER: Liberal Parliamentary candidate from South Croydon, 1931, 1935; League of Nations, Geneva Secretariat, Geneva, Switzerland, engaged in legal translation and treaty revision, 1936-39; also represented Egyptian Government at Montreaux Capitulation Conference, 1937; British Central Valuation Board, secretary, and member of Coal Nationalisation Panel of Arbitrators, 1947-49; counsel to Camberwell Borough, 1951-53. Public speaker for British Ministry of Information, Southern Division, 1940-42, for Commonwealth Industries Association, 1955—. International Commission of Jurists, "Justice." *Military service:* British Army, served in Intelligence Corps, World War II. *Member:* Union Society of London (president, 1935), Hardwicke Society (president, 1953), Bladon Galleries, Confederation of Craft Societies (committee). *Awards, honors:* Chancellor's Gold Medal for English Poetry, St. John's College, Cambridge, 1923; College Literature Prize, St. John's College, 1925; fellow, International Institute of Arts and Letters, 1963-67.

WRITINGS: Ballads and Songs, Stockwell, 1921; *Confound Their Politics,* G. Bell, 1934; *The Deacon* (novel), G. Bell, 1934; *The Strange Invaders,* G. Bell, 1934; (with Kenneth Ingram) *History of the Union Society of London,* Union Society, 1935; *The Soul of Cezar Azan,* Arthur Barker, 1938; *The Emperor of Britain,* Montgomeryshire Society, 1939; *Jubilee John: Being the Record of a Pilgrim's Progress Through an Arabian Night,* Arthur Barker, 1939; *The Tyrant from Below: An Essay in Political Revaluation,* Macdonald & Evans, 1957; *Ways to Love* (one-act comedy), Samuel French, 1958; *The World and the Commonwealth,* British Commonwealth Union, 1968; (with Wynford V. Thomas) *The Shell Guide to Wales,* edited by Jobn Betieman and John Piper, Rainbird, 1969, International Publications Service, 1969.

Contributor: *Public School Verse,* Heinemann, 1921; *Prolusiones Academicae,* Cambridge University Press, 1923; *Icarus, Poetry of Flight,* Macmillan, 1937; *Pick of Punch,* Chatto & Windus, 1953; *Oxford Book of Spoken Verse,* Oxford University Press, 1957; *Modern Lyrical Verse,* Thomas Nelson, 1958; *Penguin Comic Verse III,* Penguin, 1959; *Borestone Mountain Best Poems of Year,* 1961; *Pattern of Poetry,* Burke Publishing Co., 1963.

Author of play, "Shelley Plain," produced by Proscenium Club, 1959. Regular contributor to *Punch,* 1949-53; political commentator, *Truth,* 1958-60; contributor to other periodicals, including *Time and Tide, Country Life, Poetry Review, Chambers Journal, Anglo-Welsh Review, Aryan Path,* and *Contemporary Review.*

WORK IN PROGRESS: A first translation of the ancient Arthurian poems in early medieval Welsh; a study of the idea of "natural justice" from early classic to modern scientific philosophy; plays and novels; a collected edition of poems, lyrics, and stories.

SIDELIGHTS: Llewellyn has spent almost four years in research into the conditions of thought in western Europe in the immediate sub-Roman period as background for translating the early Welsh scripts of Taliesin, Aneirin, and other Arthurian poets. These poems are a series of scientific essays on the formation of the universe in accordance with the stoic philosophy of late classical times. Llewellyn's poems were recorded and distributed by the Library of Congress in 1968.

The Shell Guide to Wales was written for the Installation of the Prince of Wales, a copy being presented for his acceptance. Besides Welsh, Llewellyn speaks French, Spanish, Italian, knows Latin and Greek, and has some knowledge of Portuguese and German.

AVOCATIONAL INTERESTS: Walking (he is chief guide of the Sunday Tramps, an organization for broad philosophical discussion during country walks, founded by Sir Leslie Stephen in 1879), riding, swimming, and archeology.

*   *   *

LOBDELL, Helen   1919-

PERSONAL: Born May 14, 1919, in Royal Oak, Mich.; daughter of Walter Richard (a banker) and Vanessa (Perry) Lobdell. Education: Fenn College, A.B., 1942; Western Michigan University, M.A., 1957. Politics: Independent. Home address: R.R. 2, Box 433, Benton Harbor, Mich. 49022. Agent: Ruth Cantor, 120 West 42nd St., New York, N.Y. 10036.

CAREER: High school history teacher in Mount Eaton, Ohio, 1942-43; Watervliet High School, Watervliet, Mich., art and history teacher, 1943—, on leave as teacher at Belen Junior High School, Belen, N.M., 1964-65. Member: Michigan Education Association. Awards, honors: Outstanding alumni award, Fenn College, 1956; honorable mention award, Friends of American Writers, 1964, for Thread of Victory.

WRITINGS: Golden Conquest, Houghton, 1953; The King's Snare, Houghton, 1955; Captain Bacon's Rebellion, Macrae, 1959; Thread of Victory: A Story of Reform in Britain's Cotton Mills, McKay, 1963; The Fort in the Forest, Houghton, 1963; Terror in the Mountains, Whitman Publishing, 1969; Prisoner of Taos, Abelard, 1970.

WORK IN PROGRESS: A teen-age mystery, set in the early 1900's.

AVOCATIONAL INTERESTS: Gardening, handicrafts, reading, travel.

*   *   *

LOBSENZ, Norman M(itchell)   1919-

PERSONAL: Born May 16, 1919, in New York, N.Y.; son of Philip N. (a painter) and Mabel (Karpe) Lobsenz; married second wife, Dorothea Harding (an actress), May 23, 1969; children: (first marriage) Michael Lewis, James Elliot, George Philip; two stepdaughters. Education: New York University, B.S., 1939; Columbia University, Graduate School of Journalism, M.S., 1940. Religion: Quaker. Home: 300 West End Ave., New York, N.Y. 10023.

CAREER: Newsday (daily newspaper), Nassau County, N.Y., staff member, 1940-43; British Information Services, New York, N.Y., news editor, 1943-44; U.S. Office of War Information, New York, N.Y., news editor, 1944-45; New York Daily Mirror, New York, N.Y., copy editor, 1945-46; Quick, New York, N.Y., managing editor, 1950-53; Hillman Periodicals, New York, N.Y., editorial director, 1955-56; free-lance writer, 1946-50, 1956—. Editorial consultant, Ziff-Davis Publishing Co., and Downe Communications Corp., New York, N.Y. Member: Society of Magazine Writers (former president), Overseas Press Club. Awards, honors: Family Service Association of America national first prize for writings in field of family life, 1959, 1969; American Dental Association Science Writing Award; First Place Magazine Award, Family Service Association, 1969, for article, "The Unexpected Conflict That Upsets New Marriages," published in Redbook, May, 1968.

WRITINGS: The Minister's Complete Guide to Successful Retirement, Channel Press, 1955; (editor) His Bedside Companion, Prentice-Hall, 1957; Emergency!: The Dramatic Story of the Emergency Service Division of the New York City Police Department, McKay, 1958; (with Thelma Keitlen) Farewell to Fear, Geis, 1960; Is Anybody Happy?: A Study of the American Search for Pleasure, Doubleday, 1962; Writing as a Career (youth book), Walck, 1963; The Boots Adams Story, Phillips Petroleum Co., 1965; (with Clark W. Blackburn) How to Stay Married: A Modern Approach to Sex, Money, and Emotions in Marriage, Cowles, 1969.

Juvenile "First Books," all published by F. Watts: The First Book of West Germany, 1959, ... of National Monuments, 1959, revised edition, 1968, ... of National Parks, 1959, revised edition, 1968, ... of Ghana, 1960, revised edition, Edmund Ward, 1966, ... of East Africa: Kenya, Uganda, Tanganika, and Zanzibar, 1964, ... of Peace Corps, 1968, ... of Denmark, 1970. Also author of eight other juvenile non-fiction books, including The Insect World: Ants, Bees, Wasps, Butterflies, and Many Other Insects and Their Relatives, Including Spiders and Centipedes, Golden Press, 1959, revised edition, 1962, and Golden Book Picture Atlas of the World, Volume V: Africa, Golden Press, 1960.

Writer of documentary films and television scripts. Contributor of about 350 articles to Reader's Digest, Redbook, Good Housekeeping, McCall's, Look, Ladies' Home Journal, Woman's Day, and other national magazines.

*   *   *

LOCKERBIE, Jeanette W. Honeyman

PERSONAL: Born in Scotland; daughter of John and Jane (Malcolm) Honeyman; married E.A. Lockerbie, October 5, 1934; children: Donald Bruce, Ernajean. Education: Earlier education in Scotland; also studied at London Bible College, London, Ontario, Canada, and took special courses, chiefly in journalism, at New York University, Los Angeles State College, and University of Washington. Religion: Baptist. Home: 318 West California Blvd., Apt. B, Pasadena, Calif. 91105.

CAREER: Writer. Psychology for Living, Rosemead, Calif., editor, 1969—. Occasional lecturer on writing for publication. Girl Scout captain, 1934-35; town librarian, 1945-46. Member: Pasadena Writers Guild.

WRITINGS: On Your Mark, Zondervan, 1963; Designed for Duty, Moody, 1964; Three 'P's Make Your Program, Regular Baptist Press, 1964; Daily Assignment: Devotional Readings for Teachers, Moody, 1966; Salt in My Kitchen, Moody, 1967; Special Programs for Special Days, Zondervan, 1968; Return of the Rebel, Zondervan, 1968; A Plate of Hot Toast, Moody, 1971; Home Bible Studies for Women, Moody, 1972; The Christ for Everyday, Moody, 1972; Tomorrow's at My Door, Revell, 1973. Contributor of about 250 short stories and articles to religious periodicals; author of Sunday school curricula for publication by D.C. Cook and Lambert-Huffman; author of two movie scripts for Missionary Enterprises.

*   *   *

LOCKLEY, Ronald Mathias   1903-

PERSONAL: Born November 8, 1903, in Cardiff, Wales; son of Harry and Emily (Mathias) Lockley; children: Ann (Mrs. John Mark), Martin, Stephen. Agent: E.P.S. Lewin & Partners, 7 Chelsea Embankment, London S.W.3, England.

CAREER: Author and naturalist, 1921—. Lived on Skokholm, remote Welsh island, 1927-39, establishing first Britsh bird observatory there in 1933; British government, part-time duty with Naval Intelligence, 1940-41, flax field officer with Ministry of Supply, 1941-46, research naturalist with Nature Conservancy, 1955-58. Member of numerous agriculture and naturalist committees, 1938-62. Wes Wales Naturalists' Trust, founder, 1945, former chairman, now honorary chief warden.

WRITINGS: Dream Island: A Record of a Simple Life (autobiography), Witherby, 1930; The Island Dwellers (novel), Putnam, 1932; *Island Days* (autobiographical), Witherby, 1934; *Birds of the Green Belt and the Country Around London*, Witherby, 1936; *The Sea's a Thief* (novel), Longmans, Green, 1936; *I Know an Island*, Harrap, 1938, Appleton, 1939; *Early Morning Island; or, A Dish of Sprats* (juvenile), Harrap, 1939.

A Pot of Smoke: Being the Adventures and Life of D. Owain as Told to R.M. Lockley (novel), Harrap, 1940; *The Way to an Island* (autobiographical), Dent, 1941; *Shearwaters*, William Salloch, 1942; *Dream Island Days. A Record of the Simple Life* (revised version of *Dream Island* and *Island Days*), Witherby, 1943; *Island Farm* (novel), William Salloch, 1943; *Islands Round Britain*, Collins, 1945; *Birds of the Sea*, King Penguin, 1945; *The Island Farmers* (novel), Witherby, 1946; *Letters from Skokholm*, Dent, 1947; *The Golden Year* (novel), Witherby, 1948; *The Cinnamon Bird*, Staples Press, 1948; (author of introduction and notes) Gilbert White, *The Natural History of Selborne*, Dutton, 1949; (compiler with Geoffrey C.S. Ingram and H. Morrey Salmon) *T. Birds of Pembrokeshire*, West Wales Field Society, 1949.

(Editor with John Buxton) *The Island of Skomer: A Preliminary Survey of the Natural History of Skomer Island, Pembrokeshire*, Staples, 1950; *The Charm of the Channel Islands*, Evans Brothers, 1950; (editor) *The Nature-Lovers' Anthology*, Witherby, 1951; *Puffins*, Dent, 1953, Devin, 1954; *Travels with a Tent in Western Europe*, Odhams, 1953; (with Rosemary Russell) *Bird-Ringing: The Art of Bird Study by Individual Marking*, Crosby Lockwood, 1953, De Graff, 1956; *The Seals and the Curragh: Introducing the Natural History of the Grey Seal of the North Atlantic*, Dent, 1954, published in America as *The Saga of the Gray Seal: Introducing the Natural History of the Grey Seal of the North Atlantic*, Devin, 1955; (with James Fisher) *Sea-Birds: An Introduction to the Natural History of the Sea-Birds of the North Atlantic*, Houghton, 1954; *Gilbert White* (biography), Witherby, 1954; (editor) *In Praise of Islands: An Anthology for Friends*, Muller, 1957; *Pembrokeshire*, R. Hale, 1957, 2nd edition, 1969; (editor) *The Bird-Lover's Bedside Book* (anthology), Eyre & Spottiswoode, 1958.

The Pan Book of Cage Birds, Pan Books, 1961; (author of introduction) *Britain in Colour*, Batsford, 1964, Grosset, 1965; *The Private Life of the Rabbit: An Account of the Life History and Social Behaviour of the Wild Rabbit*, Deutsch, 1964, October House, 1966; *Grey Seal, Common Seal: An Account of the Life Histories of British Seals*, October House, 1966; *Wales*, Batsford, 1966, 2nd edition, 1967; *Animal Navigation*, Hart Publishing, 1967; *The Channel Islands*, J. Cape, 1968, revised edition published as *A Traveller's Guide to the Channel Islands*, Corgi, 1971; *The Book of Bird Watching*, Arthur Barker, 1968; *The Island*, Deutsch, 1969, Regnery, 1971.

Man Against Nature, Deutsch, 1970; *The Naturalist in Wales*, David & Charles, 1970. Author with Julian Huxley of film script, "Private Life of the Gannet." Author of scientific papers on sea birds, seals, rabbits, and islands. Editor, "Great Naturalists" series, Witherby, 1954—. Co-editor, *Nature in Wales* (journal of West and North Wales Naturalists' Trusts), 1953—.†

* * *

LOEWENBERG, Bert James 1905-

PERSONAL: Born December 24, 1905, in Boston, Mass.; son of Herman (a lawyer) and Sarah M. (Kelson) Loewenberg; married Anne Cinamon (an assistant medical librarian), October 9, 1931; children: Robert James, Judith Anne, Sarah Miriam. *Education:* Clark University, A.B., 1926, A.M., 1927; Harvard University, A.M., 1930, Ph.D., 1934; postdoctoral study at London School of Economics, University of London, at Cambridge University, Oxford University, and University of Edinburgh, 1934-35. *Politics:* Democrat. *Religion:* Jewish. *Home:* 15 Center Knolls, Bronxville, N.Y. 10708. *Office:* Sarah Lawrence College, Bronxville, N.Y. 10708.

CAREER: University of South Dakota, Vermillion, assistant professor of history, 1937-41; Sarah Lawrence College, Bronxville, N.Y., professor of history, 1941—, currently Esther Rauchenbush Professor of History. Visiting professor of history at University of Missouri, 1938-39, University of Rochester, 1940-41, Mexican universities, 1944, Cornell University, 1946, Northwestern University, 1947, Ruskin College, Oxford, England, 1952, Salzburg Seminar in American Studies, 1953, Hebrew University of Jerusalem, 1953; Fulbright Professor at University of Leeds, 1960, Cambridge University, 1961. *Member:* Royal Historical Society (fellow), Society for American Studies (fellow), American Historical Society, American Studies Association, History of Science Society, Society for the Study of Culture and Technology, American Association of University Professors. *Awards, honors:* Social Science Research Council fellow, 1934-35, 1952, 1962-63; Rockefeller grants, American Council of Learned Societies; fellow, Newberry Library; LL.D., Clark University, 1970.

WRITINGS: (With Ray Allen Billington and Samuel Hugh Brockunier) *United States: American Democracy in World Perspective*, Rinehart, 1947; (editor with Billington and Brockunier) *Making of American Democracy: Readings and Documents*, two volumes, Rinehart, 1950, 2nd edition (with Billington, Brockunier, and D.S. Sparks), Holt, 1960; (editor) *Darwinism: Reaction or Reform?*, Rinehart, 1957; (editor) *Darwin, Wallace, and the Theory of Natural Selection*, G.E. Cinamon, 1957; (editor and author of introduction) Charles Darwin, *Evolution and Natural Selection*, Beacon Press, 1959; (author of introductory essay) Helen Lynd, *Toward Discovery*, Hobbs, Dorman, 1965; *Historical Writing in American Culture*, Editorial Libros (Mexico), 1968; *Darwinism Comes to America, 1859-1900* (originally published in *Mississippi Valley Historical Review*, December, 1941), edited by Richard C. Wolf, Fortress, 1969; *American History in American Thought*, Simon & Schuster, 1972. Member of editorial board, *American Quarterly* and *Sarah Lawrence Journal.*

WORK IN PROGRESS: A multi-volume work, *Darwin: A History of His Life and Thought.*

* * *

LOFTON, John (Marion) 1919-

PERSONAL: Born April 11, 1919, in McClellanville, S.C.; son of John Marion (a farmer) and Harriett (Lucas) Lofton; married Anne Watson, December 27, 1954 (died, 1968); married Priscilla Alvarado, 1969; children: (first marriage) John M., Jr., Charles Lewis; (second marriage) Cathy. *Education:* College of Charleston, B.S., 1940; Duke University, J.D., 1942; University of Pittsburgh, M.A., 1956; Stanford University, postgraduate study, 1960-61. *Politics:* Democrat. *Religion:* Unitarian. *Home:* 6644 Kinsman Rd., Pittsburgh, Pa. 15217. *Office:* Department of Speech, University of Pittsburgh, Pittsburgh, Pa. 15213.

CAREER: Admitted to South Carolina Bar, 1942, but most of career has been spent in newspaper field; member of editorial staff of *Spartanburg Herald*, Spartanburg, S.C., 1945-47, *Seattle Star*, Seattle, Wash., 1947, *Times and Democrat,*, Orangeburg, S.C., 1947-48, *Arkansas Gazette*, Little Rock, Ark., 1948-52; *Pittsburgh Post-Gazette*, Pittsburgh, Pa., associate editor, 1952-66, editor of editorial page, 1966-70; University of Pittsburgh, Pittsburgh, Pa., associate professor of speech, 1970—. Association of Scientists for Atomic Education, conference director, 1947. *Military service:* U.S. Army, 1942-45. *Member:* National Conference of Editorial Writers, American

Bar Association, American Judicature Society, American Civil Liberties Union (board of directors, Pittsburgh branch). *Awards, honors:* American Bar Association Gavel Award for distinguished series of articles and editorials on the roles of judges and lawyers in the American judicial process, 1960; mass media fellowship, Fund for Adult Education, 1960-61.

WRITINGS: (With George Swetnam, William M. Schutte, and Donald M. Goodfellow) *Pittsburgh's First Unitarian Church*, Boxwood Press, 1961; *Insurrection in South Carolina: The Turbulent World of Denmark Vesey*, Antioch Press, 1964; *Justice and the Press*, Beacon Press, 1966. Contributor of articles to *Nature, Progressive, New Republic, Nation, New Leader, Bulletin of the Atomic Scientists, Christian Science Monitor*, and other periodicals and newspapers.

AVOCATIONAL INTERESTS: Civil liberties and rights, conservation, and international relations.

* * *

LOGAN, Gene A (dams) 1922-

PERSONAL: Born June 14, 1922, in Kickapoo, Kan.; son of Frank W. (a farmer) and Myrtle (Hundley) Logan; married Elsie E. Ozal, January 24, 1943; children: Diane, Mark. *Education:* Tulsa University, student, 1941-42; Southwest Missouri State College, B.S. in P.E., 1949; Medical College of Virginia, certificate in physical t erapy, 1951; University of Illinois, M.S. in P.E., 1952; University of Southern California, Ph.D. in P.E., 1960; Kansas University, M.F.A. (sculpture), 1967. *Home:* 473 Guilford Ave., Claremont, Calif. 91711. *Office:* University of Southern California, Los Angeles, Calif. 90007.

CAREER: Athletic trainer at U.S. Military Academy, West Point, N.Y., Tulsa University, Tulsa, Okla., Tulane University, New Orleans, La., and at other schools while studying for degrees, 1940-52; ' University of California, Los Angeles, member of physical education staff, 1952-59; University of Southern California, Los Angeles, visiting assistant professor, later associate professor of physical education, 1959-63, research associate, School of Dentistry, 1961-63; Southwest Missouri State College, Springfield, professor of physical education, 1963-69; University of Southern California, Los Angeles, visiting professor of physical education, 1969—. Practicing sculptor, represented at Ankrum Gallery, Los Angeles, Calif. *Military service:* U.S. Navy, Hospital Corps, 1942-45; served on Okinawa, 1945.

MEMBER: American Academy of Physical Education (fellow), American Association for Health, Physical Education and Recreation (research council), American College of Sports Medicine (fellow), College Physical Education Association for Men, American Registry of Physical Therapists, Laguna Beach Art Association. *Awards, honors:* Creative award, American Academy of Physical Education; first prizes for sculpture at Los Angeles County Fair, 1961, 1962; at Laguna Beach Festival of Arts, All California Exhibit, 1961, 1962; Gold Medal Award, California State Fair, 1962.

WRITINGS: (With Roland F. Logan) *Techniques of Athletic Training*, Franklin-Adams Press, 1952, 3rd edition, 1967; (with James G. Dunkelberg, Gerald W. Gardner, and Glen H. Egstrom) *Student Handbook for Adapted Physical Education*, Adadon Press, 1956, W.C. Brown, 1960; (with Elwood C. Davis) *Biophysical Values of Muscular Activity*, W.C. Brown, 1961, 2nd edition (with Wayne C. McKinney), 1965; (with Earl L. Wallis) *Figure Improvement and Body Conditioning Through Exercise*, Prentice-Hall, 1964; (with Wallis) *Isometric Exercises for Figure Improvement and Body Conditioning* (booklet), Prentice-Hall, 1964; (self-illustrated) *Adaptations of Muscular Activity: A Textbook for Adapted Physical Education*, Wadsworth, 1964; (with Wallis) *Figure Improvement Exercises for Women*, Prentice-Hall, 1965; (with Wallis) *Exercise for Children*, Prentice-Hall, 1966; (with McKinney) *Kinesiology*, W.C. Brown, 1970; (with Harold B. Falls and Wallis) *Foundations of Conditioning*, Academic Press, 1970; *Adapted Physical Education*, W.C. Brown, 1971. Contributor to *Quest* and to professional journals.

* * *

LOGUE, Christopher 1926-
(Count Palmiro Vicarion)

PERSONAL: Born November 23, 1926, in Portsmouth, Hampshire, England. *Home:* 18 Denbigh Close, London W. 11, England. *Agent:* Clive Goodwin, 79, Cromwell Rd., London S.W. 7, England.

CAREER: Poet. *Military service:* British Army, 1944-48.

WRITINGS—All poetry: *Wand and Quadrant*, [Paris], 1953; *Devil, Maggot and Son*, [Amsterdam], 1954, limited edition, P. Russell, 1956; *The Weekdream Sonnets*, Jack Straw (Paris), 1955; *The Song of the Dead Soldier*, Villiers Publications, c.1956; *The Man Who Told His Love: 20 Poems Based on P. Neruda's "Los Cantos d'amores,"* Scorpion Press, 1958, 2nd edition, 1959; *A Song for Kathleen*, Villiers Publications, 1958; *Memoranda for Marchers*, [London], 1959; *Songs*, Hutchinson, 1959, McDowell, Obolensky, 1960; (compiler) *Count Palmiro Vicarion's Book of Limericks*, Olympia Press (Paris), 1959; *Songs from "The Lily-White Boys,"* Scorpion Press, 1960; (translator and adapter) Homer, *Patrocleia: Book 16 of Homer's Illiad Freely Adapted into English*, Scorpion Press, 1962, published in America as *Patrocleia of Homer: A New Version by Christopher Logue*, University of Michigan Press, 1963; *The Arrival of the Poet in the City: A Treatment for a Film*, Mandarin Books, 1964; *I Shall Vote Labour*, Turret Books, 1966; *Christopher Logue's ABC*, Scorpion Press, 1966; *True Stories*, Four Square Books, 1966; *The Establishment Songs*, Poet & Printer, 1966; (translator and adapter) Homer, *Pax, from Book XIX of the Illiad*, Turret Books, 1967, also published as *Pax*, Rapp & Carroll, 1967; (with Wallace Southam and Patrick Gower) *Gone Ladies* (contemporary poetry set to music; words by Logue, music by Southam, and arrangement by Gower), Turret Books, 1968; *The Girls*, Turret Books, 1969; *New Numbers*, J. Cape, 1969, Knopf, 1970.

Plays: "Antigone"; "The Trial of Cob and Leach"; "The Lily-White Boys." Author of screenplay for film, "Savage Messiah," 1972. Also author, under pseudonym Count Palmiro Vicarion, of *Lust*, Ophelia Press, 1969.

SIDELIGHTS: Beginning in 1958 with "To My Fellow Artists," Logue has made many of his poems into posters. When asked by Davina Lloyd if his "prime motive in making posters [is] to get poems out," Logue answered: "One doesn't always know one's own motives. A poster seems two things: both a means to an end and an end in itself. The Iliad would go marvellously on a poster except that it would be a [very] large poster. . . . As for poetry, this fostered, pampered child of the arts, you suddenly realize it's a wide open thing, not a literary thing. . . . I simply feel that I'd like to publish all my poems as posters. For one thing it is easier for people who don't associate themselves with book poems, which is the majority of us. Turner liberated colour from form. At the other end of the scale, the poster can liberate the poem from a book. . . . Now, particularly in America, there is a fantastic upsurge of people doing posters just as creative objects which just are by their very nature multiples. Within this given situation the idea of putting poems with designs or images on them could hardly be more natural. It is an obvious extension of graphic activity."

Recordings of his poems have been issued in London, under the titles "Red Bird," 1961, "Poets Reading," 1961, and "The Death of Patrocleia," 1962.

BIOGRAPHICAL/CRITICAL SOURCES: Books and Bookmen, May, 1967; *London Magazine,* August, 1968, October, 1969.

* * *

LOHF, Kenneth A. 1925-

PERSONAL: Born January 14, 1925, in Milwaukee, Wis.; son of H.A. and Louise (Krause) Lohf. *Education:* Northwestern University, B.A., 1949; Columbia University, M.A., 1950, M.S. in L.S., 1952. *Office:* Special Collections, Columbia University Libraries, New York, N.Y. 10027.

CAREER: Columbia University Libraries, New York, N.Y., assistant librarian, department of special collections (rare book and manuscript library), 1957—. *Military service:* U.S. Army Air Forces, 1943-46; served in India, Germany, France, England; became first lieutenant. *Member:* Bibliographical Society of America, Grolier Club.

WRITINGS: (With Eugene P. Sheehy) *Joseph Conrad at Mid-Century: Editions and Studies, 1895-1955,* University of Minnesota Press, 1957; (with Sheehy) *The Achievement of Marianne Moore: A Bibliography, 1907-1957,* New York Public Library, 1958; (with Sheehy) *Frank Norris: A Bibliography,* Talisman, 1959; (with Sheehy) *Yvor Winters: A Bibliography,* Alan Swallow, 1959; (with Sheehy) *Sherwood Anderson: A Bibliography,* Talisman, 1960; *The Collection of Books, Manuscripts and Autograph Letters in the Library of Jean and Donald Stralem,* privately printed, 1962; (editor and author of preface) Hart Crane, *Seven Lyrics,* Ibex Press, 1966; *XXX for Time* (poems), Humphries, 1966; (compiler) *The Literary Manuscripts of Hart Crane,* Ohio State University Press, 1967; (compiler) *The Engle Collection Presented by Solton and Julia Engel* (catalog), Columbia University Libraries, 1967.

Compiler of *An Index to the Little Review, 1914-1929,* New York Public Library, 1961, and *Index to Little Magazines,* Alan Swallow, 1957, 1958, 1960, 1962, 1964. Contributor to *Twentieth Century Literature, Poetry,* and regional literary reviews.

AVOCATIONAL INTERESTS: American poetry, book collecting.

* * *

LONG, John Frederick Lawrence 1917-
(John Longsword)

PERSONAL: Born July 26, 1917, in London, England; son of Montague Frederick (a surveyor) and Evelyn May (Lawrence) Long; married Patricia Mary Kent, March 13, 1948; children: Nicholas John, Elizabeth Anne. *Education:* Epsom College, student, 1926-36; Queens' College, Cambridge University, B.A. (honors), 1939, M.A., 1943. *Religion:* Agnostic. *Home and office:* Tegelbergstrasse 16, 8 Munich 9, Germany.

CAREER: Rose Hill School, Alderley, Wottan-under-Edge, Gloucestershire, England, head of English department, 1939-41; served in Royal Air Force, 1941-63, except for one-year period, 1946-47, as editor of Soviet and East Europe summary of broadcasts, British Broadcasting Corp. Monitoring Service; Radio Liberty, Munich, Germany, specialist-researcher on Soviet foreign policy and institutions, 1964—. Started Royal Air Force career as navigator/radio, later serving during World War II as specialist intelligence officer in department of Chief of the Air Staff; specialist intelligence officer, then education officer, 1947-63; became wing commander. *Member:* GB-USSR Association, Royal Central Asian Society.

WRITINGS: Modern Russia: An Introduction, Duckworth, 1957, Philosophical Library, 1958. Contributor to *Times Educational Supplement, Financial Times, Royal Air Forces Quarterly, Spectator,* and other periodicals.

WORK IN PROGRESS: Research on the Soviet institutional system.

* * *

LONGMATE, Norman Richard 1925-

PERSONAL: Born December 15, 1925, in Newbury, Berkshire, England; son of Ernest (a photographer) and Margaret (Rowden) Longmate; married Elizabeth Taylor (a teacher), August 8, 1953; children: Jill. *Education:* Attended Christ's Hospital, Horsham, England, 1936-43; Worcester College, Oxford, B.A. (with honors), 1950, M.A., 1954. *Religion:* Anglican. *Home:* 30 Clydesdale Gardens, Richmond, Surrey, England. *Agent:* Bolt & Watson Ltd., Chandos House, Buckingham Gate, London S.W. 1, England. *Office:* British Broadcasting Corp., Broadcasting House, London W. 1, England.

CAREER: Daily Mirror, London, England, feature writer, 1953-57; Electricity Council, London, England, administrator in industrial relations department, 1957-63; British Broadcasting Corp., London, England, radio producer, 1963-65, administrator in secretariat, 1965—. *Military service:* British Army, 1944-47. *Member:* Association of Broadcasting Staff, Oxford Society, Society of Sussex Downsmen.

WRITINGS: (Compiler and author of historical introduction) *A Socialist Anthology and the Men Who Made It,* Phoenix House, 1953; *Oxford Triumphant,* Phoenix House, 1954; *Death Won't Wash,* Cassell, 1957; *A Head for Death,* Cassell, 1958; *Strip Death Naked,* Cassell, 1959; *Vote for Death,* Cassell, 1960; *Death in Office,* R. Hale, 1961; *Keith in Electricity* (career book), Chatto & Windus, 1961; *Electricity Supply,* Sunday Times Publications, 1961; *Electricity as a Career,* Batsford, 1964; *Writing for the BBC,* British Broadcasting Corp., 1966; *King Cholera: The Biography of a Disease,* Hamish Hamilton, 1966; *The Waterdrinkers: A History of Temperance,* Hamish Hamilton, 1968, Fernhill, 1969; *Alive and Well: Medicine and Public Health, 1830 to the Present Day,* Penguin, 1970; *How We Lived Then: Everyday Life in the Second World War,* Hutchinson, 1971. Contributor of articles to *Spectator, Observer, Sunday Mirror, Sunday Express, Daily Telegraph, Teacher, Film User, Industrial Screen,* and *European Broadcasting Union Review,* as well as to British Broadcasting Corp. radio and television.

WORK IN PROGRESS: A book, *The Workhouse: A Social History;* another book for Hutchinson, *The Home Front: An Anthology of Personal Experience.*

AVOCATIONAL INTERESTS: Reading and country walking.

BIOGRAPHICAL/CRITICAL SOURCES: Times (London), November 17, 1966; *Listener,* November 24, 1966; *Observer,* December 10, 1966; *Times Literary Supplement,* December 11, 1966; *British Medical Journal,* January 28, 1967; *Church Times,* February 3, 1967; *Punch,* October 2, 1968; *Guardian,* October 4, 1968; *Observer Review,* October 6, 1968, March 21, 1971.

* * *

LONGRIGG, Jane Chichester 1929-
(Jane Chichester)

PERSONAL: Born August 26, 1929, in London, England; daughter of Marcus Beresford (a company director) and Myra (Jay) Chichester; married Roger Erskine Longrigg (a writer), July 20, 1957; children: Laura Jane, Fanny Angelica, Clare Selma. *Education:* Educated at schools in England and Switzerland; also studied music in

Switzerland. *Politics:* Conservative. *Religion:* Church of England. *Home:* Farley Hill Court, Reading, Berkshire, England. *Agent:* Curtis Brown Ltd., 13 King St., London W.C.2, England.

CAREER: Colman Prentis & Varley (advertising agency), London, England, copywriter, 1954-55; Clifford Bloxham & Partners Ltd. (advertising agency), London, copywriter, 1955-56; Greenlys Advertising, London, television scriptwriter, 1956-57.

WRITINGS: (Under name Jane Chichester) *Take a Deep Breath,* Houghton, 1962; *You're So Lucky, Darling,* M. Joseph, 1968.

WORK IN PROGRESS: A novel.

AVOCATIONAL INTERESTS: Music, horseback riding, fox hunting, gardening, and travel.

BIOGRAPHICAL/CRITICAL SOURCES: Spectator, February 9, 1968; *Books and Bookmen,* May, 1968.

* * *

LONGSTREET, Stephen 1907-
(Thomas Burton, Paul Haggard, David Ormsbee, Henri Weiner)

PERSONAL: Born April 18, 1907, in New York, N.Y.; son of Irwin and Sarah Longstreet; married Ethel Joan Godoff, April 22, 1933; children: Joan, Harry. *Education:* Attended Rutgers University, 1926, and Harvard University, 1927; graduated from New York School of Fine and Applied Art, 1929; studied painting in Paris, Rome, London, and Berlin. *Home:* 1133 Miradero Rd., Beverly Hills, Calif. 90210.

CAREER: Painter, writer, art critic, lecturer on art. Work as an artist has been exhibited in one-man shows and in major museums; cartoons have appeared in *New Yorker, Collier's,* and other national magazines. Radio writer for national networks, doing shows for Deems Taylor, Bob Hope, Rudy Vallee; also writer for "Duffy's Tavern"; also writer of motion pictures and television programs, and associate producer of National Broadcasting Co. series, "The Blue and the Gray." Editor, *Major Bowes Amateur Magazine,* 1936-37; film critic for *Saturday Review of Literature,* 1941; member of editorial staff of *Time,* 1942, *Screenwriters Magazine,* 1947-48, and of *Gourmet;* literary critic for *Readers Syndicate,* 1952-64; literary critic for *Los Angeles Daily News.* Editor, Borden Press. Staff lecturer, Los Angeles Art Association, 1954, University of California, Los Angeles, 1955, 1958-59. Director, Writer's Workshop, University of California at San Diego. Trustee of Los Angeles Art Association and International World Arts. Member of National Civil War Commission. *Wartime service:* Created films for War Department during World War II; awarded Citation of Meritorious Service. *Member:* Dramatists Guild, Writers Guild of America, American Federation of Television and Radio Artists (AFTRA), Screen Writers Film Society, Phi Sigma. *Awards, honors:* Billboard-Donaldson Gold Medal, 1948, for best play of year, *High Button Shoes; Photoplay* Gold Medal Gallup Poll Award, 1948, for most popular film of the year, *The Jolson Story;* California Golden Star, 1949, for *Gauguin; The Greatest Show on Earth* (screenplay), nominated for Academy Award (Oscar) in 1952.

WRITINGS: Decade, 1929-39 (novel; also see below), Random House, 1940; *The Golden Touch,* Random House, 1941; *Great Grab: An American Novel,* Constable, 1941; *Last Man Around the World,* Random House, 1941; *The Gay Sisters,* Random House, 1942; (self-illustrated) *The Last Man Comes Home,* Random House, 1942; *The Land I Live* (novel), Random House, 1943; (with Donald G. Cooley and Tom O'Reilly) *Decade, 1929-1939* (abridged) [and] *Your World Tomorrow* [and] *Purser's Progress,* Literary Classics, Inc.,

1944; (editor with Arch Oboler) *Free World Theatre* (radio plays), Random House, 1944; (self-illustrated) *Nine Lives with Grandfather: The Times and Turmoils of an Early American,* Messner, 1944; *Stallion Road* (novel), Messner, 1945; *The Sisters Liked Them Handsome* (reminiscences), Messner, 1946; *Three Days,* Messner, 1947; *The Crystal Girl,* Messner, 1948; "Gauguin" (play), first produced at Pasadena Playhouse, 1948; *High Button Shoes: A Period Comedy in Two Acts* (adapted from his novel *The Sisters Liked Them Handsome),* Samuel French, 1949.

The Pedlocks, a Family (novel), Simon & Schuster, 1951 (published in England as *The Pedlocks,* W.H. Allen, 1971); *The Beach House* (novel), Henry Holt, 1952; *A Century on Wheels, The Story of Studebaker: A History, 1852-1952,* Henry Holt, 1952; (self-illustrated) *The World Revisited,* (travel), Henry Holt, 1953; (self-illustrated) *The Lion at Morning* (novel), Simon & Schuster, 1954; (self-illustrated) *The Boy in the Model T: A Journey into the Just Gone Past,* Simon & Schuster, 1956; *The Real Jazz, Old and New,* Louisiana State University Press, 1956; *The Promoters* (novel), Simon & Schuster, 1957; (with Alfons M. Dauer) *Knaurs Jazzlexikon,* Droemersche Verlagsanstalt (Munich), 1957; *The Burning Man* (novel), Random House, 1958 (published in England under title *Artist's Quarter,* Hammond, Hammond & Co., 1960); (with wife, Ethel Longstreet) *Man of Montmartre: A Novel Based on the Life of Maurice Utrillo,* Funk, 1958; (with Billy Pearson) *Never Look Back, the Autobiography of a Jockey,* Simon & Schuster, 1958; *Encyclopedie du Jazz,* [Paris], 1958; *The Crime* (novel), Simon & Schuster, 1959; (with Ethel Longstreet) *The Politician* (novel), Funk, 1959.

(With Ethel Longstreet) *Geisha,* Funk, 1960; *Eagles Where I Walk* (novel), Doubleday, 1961; *Gettysburg* (novel), Farrar, Straus, 1961; *A Treasury of the World's Great Prints,* Simon & Schuster, 1961; *The Flesh Peddlers* (novel), Simon & Schuster, 1962; *A Few Painted Feathers,* Doubleday, 1963; *The Figure in Art,* Borden, 1963; *Living High,* Muller, 1963; *The Nylon Island,* Fawcett, 1964; *The Golden Runaways* (novel), Delacorte, 1964; *Sportin' House: A History of the New Orleans Sinners and the Birth of Jazz,* Sherbourne Press, 1965; *War in the Golden Weather* (novel), Doubleday, 1965; (with Hoagy Carmichael) *Sometimes I Wonder: The Story of Hoagy Carmichael,* Farrar, Straus, 1965; *Pedlock & Sons* (novel), Delacorte, 1966; (with J.J. Godoff) *Remember William Kite?* (novel), Simon & Schuster, 1966; *Masts to Spear the Stars,* Doubleday, 1967; *The Young Men of Paris,* Delacorte, 1967; *Senator Silverthorn,* Dell, 1968; (self-illustrated) *The Wilder Shore: A Gala Social History of San Francisco's Sinners and Spenders, 1849-1906,* Doubleday, 1968; (with Ethel Longstreet; self-illustrated) *A Salute to American Cooking,* Hawthorn, 1968; *Pedlock Saint, Pedlock Sinner,* Delacorte, 1969.

She Walks in Beauty (novel), Arbor House, 1970; *War Cries on Horseback: The Stories of the Indian Wars of the Great Plains,* Doubleday, 1970; (with Ethel Longstreet) *Yoshiwara: City of the Senses,* McKay, 1970; *The Canvas Falcons: The Story of the Men and the Planes of World War I,* World, 1970; (editor and author of introduction) Nell Kimball, *Nell Kimball: Her Life as an American Madam,* Macmillan, 1970; *The Pedlock Inheritance,* McKay, 1972; *We All Went to Paris: Americans in the City of Light, 1776-1971,* Macmillan, 1972.

Under pseudonym Thomas Burton: *And So Dedicated,* Harrison-Hilton, 1940; *Bloodbird,* Smith-Durrell, 1941.

Under pseudonym Paul Haggard: *Dead Is the Doornail,* Lippincott, 1937; *Death Talks Shop,* Hillman-Curl, 1938; *Death Walks on Cat Feet,* Hillman-Curl, 1938; *Poison from a Wealthy Widow,* Hillman-Curl, 1938.

Under pseudonym David Ormsbee: *The Sound of an American* (novel), Dutton, 1942; *Chico Goes to the Wars: A Chronicle . . . 1933-43*, Dutton, 1943.

Under pseudonym Henri Weiner: *Crime on the Cuff*, Morrow, 1936; *The Case of the Severed Skull*, Mystery Book of the Month, 1940.

Screenplays: "The Gay Sisters," Warner Brothers, 1942; "The Imposter," Universal, 1944; "Uncle Harry," Universal, 1945; "The Jolson Story," Columbia, 1946; "Stallion Road" (from his own novel), Warner Brothers, 1946; "Duel in the Sun," Selznick, 1946; (with Harriet Frank, Jr.) "Silver River" (from his own novel), Warner Brothers, 1948; "The Greatest Show on Earth," Paramount, 1952; "Stars and Stripes Forever," 20th Century Fox, 1952; "Houdini," Paramount, 1953; (with Devery Freeman) "The First Traveling Saleslady," RKO, 1956; "Untamed Youth," Warner Brothers, 1957; (with others) "The Helen Morgan Story," Warner Brothers, 1957; "Born Reckless," Warner Brothers, 1959; "Wild Harvest," Sutton Pictures Corp., 1961; "Rider on a Dead Horse," Allied Artists, 1963; "Man of Montmartre" (based on his own book), Allied Artists, 1963; "The Secret Door," Allied Artists, 1964.

Author of introduction—All published by Borden: Nicholas Poussin, *Drawings*, 1963; Rembrandt, *Drawings*, 1963; Rubens, *Drawings*, 1964; Adolph von Menzel, *Drawings*, 1964; Paul Cezanne, *Drawings*, 1964; Honore Daumier, *Drawings*, 1964; Edgar Degas, *Drawings*, 1964; Albrecht Durer, *Drawings*, 1964; Paul Gaugin, *Drawings*, 1965; *The Drawings of Rodin*, 1965; Renoir, *Drawings*, 1965; *The Portrait in Art*, 1965; *The Animal in Art*, 1966; *The Horse in Art*, 1966; *The Drawings of LaLyre*, 1966; *The Tree in Art*, 1966; *The Drawings of Watteau*, 1966; *The Child in Art*, 1966; *The Drawings of Augustus John*, 1967; *The Drawings of Kaethe Kollwitz*, 1967; Tintoretto, *The Drawings*, 1967; Daumier, *Lawyers and Law Courts*, 1967; *The Drawings of Fuesli*, 1969; *The Drawings of Hokusai*, 1969.

Writer of television scripts for "Pulitzer Prize Theatre," ABC, "Big Town," CBS, "Playhouse 90," CBS, "Readers' Digest Theatre," "Agent of Scotland Yard," 1959, "Casey Jones," which he also created, 1960, and "The Sea," NBC, 1960, for which he was also master of ceremonies.

SIDELIGHTS: Longstreet had his first exhibition of pencil drawings at the age of four, a water-color show at eight. He spent the latter half of the 1920's in Europe, where he came to know such artists as Utrillo, Suzanne Valadon, Chagall, Matisse, and Picasso, and such notables of the period as Gertrude and Leo Stein, James Joyce, Elliot Paul, and Ernest Hemingway. He is a collector and historian of graphic art and prints.

BIOGRAPHICAL/CRITICAL SOURCES: San Francisco Chronicle, November 29, 1959; *New York Times Book Review*, December 13, 1959, February 13, 1966, March 20, 1966, December 18, 1966, April 23, 1972; *New York Herald Tribune Book Review*, January 10, 1960; *New Yorker*, March 12, 1960, December 3, 1966, April 29, 1972; *New Statesman*, December 3, 1960; *Spectator*, December 16, 1960; July 5, 1968; *Chicago Sunday Tribune*, March 26, 1961; *New York Herald Tribune Lively Arts*, April 16, 1961; *Best Sellers*, November 16, 1963, November 1, 1966, November 1, 1967, September 15, 1970, February 1, 1971; *Saturday Review*, December 7, 1963; *Book Week*, February 6, 1966; *Journal of American History*, June, 1966; *Books & Bookmen*, June, 1969; *Atlantic*, February, 1970; *Choice*, July, 1970; *Economist*, December 26, 1970; *New York Times*, April 12, 1972.

LORD, Priscilla Sawyer 1908-

PERSONAL: Born April 3, 1908, in Woburn, Mass.; daughter of Frank Hayward and Emelyn (Strang) Sawyer; married Philip Hosmer Lord (president of John Carter Co.), February 10, 1938; children: Beverley, Roberta (Mrs. William H. Moore, Jr.). *Education:* Boston University, A.B., 1933. *Religion:* Protestant *Home:* Dennett Rd., Marblehead Neck, Mass. 01945.

CAREER: Public Library, Woburn, Mass., readers' adviser, 1933-38; story teller at other libraries in Massachusetts and Maine. Norway (Me.) Public Library, trustee, 1939-51; Girl Scouts of U.S.A., president of Marblehead (Mass.) Council, 1956-57; currently member of Region I committee. *Member:* Herb Society of America, Inc. (national board, 1963; president, New England Unit, 1970—), Marblehead Garden Club (president, 1962-65), Winter Garden Club (president, 1957-58), Alpha Gamma Delta (director of chapter libraries, 1935-45). *Awards, honors:* Thanks Badge, Massachusetts Girl Scouts.

WRITINGS: (With Daniel J. Foley) *Easter Garland*, Chilton, 1963; (with Foley) *The Folk Arts and Crafts of New England*, Chilton, 1965; (with Foley) *Easter the World Over*, Chilton, 1971; (with Virginia C. Gamage) *Marblehead: The Spirit of '76 Lives Here*, Chilton, 1971. Editor, *Sea Fare* (local cookbook); book reviewer, *Alpha Gamma Delta Quarterly*, 1933-45, *Woburn Daily Times*; contributor to *Potomac Herb Journal* and *Brooklyn Botanic Gardens Handbook*.

WORK IN PROGRESS: A book on eagles.

AVOCATIONAL INTERESTS: Holidays, gardening, sailing.

*   *   *

LOWELL, Robert (Traill Spence, Jr.) 1917-

PERSONAL: Born March 1, 1917, in Boston, Mass.; son of Robert Traill Spence (a naval officer) and Charlotte (Winslow) Lowell; married Jean Stafford (a writer), April 2, 1940 (divorced June, 1948); married Elizabeth Hardwick (a writer), July 28, 1949; children: (second marriage) Harriet Winslow. *Education:* Attended St. Marks School; attended Harvard University, 1935-37; Kenyon College, A.B. (summa cum laude), 1940. *Religion:* Converted to Roman Catholicism, 1940; no longer affiliated with the Church. *Home:* Neilgate Park, Bearsted, Maidstone, Kent, England.

CAREER: Writer, poet. Sheed & Ward, New York, N.Y., editorial assistant, 1941-42; Library of Congress, Washington, D.C., consultant in poetry, 1947-48; at times member of faculty at State University of Iowa, Kenyon School of English, Salzburg Seminar in American Studies (Salzburg, Austria), and Boston University; Harvard University, Cambridge, Mass., lecturer, 1963-64. Yale University, writer-in-residence, 1967. *Wartime activity:* Conscientious objector, World War II; served a prison term as a result, 1943-44. *Member:* American Academy of Arts and Letters, Phi Beta Kappa.

AWARD, HONORS: National Institute Grant in Literature, 1947; Guggenheim fellowship, 1947; Pulitzer Prize, 1947, for *Lord Weary's Castle;* Harriet Monroe Poetry Award, 1952; shared Guiness Poetry Award (Ireland) with W.H. Auden and Edith Sitwell, 1959; National Book Award, 1960, for *Life Studies;* Boston Arts Festival Poet, 1960; Harriet Monroe Memorial Prize, 1961; Bollingen Poetry Translation Prize, 1962, for *Imitations;* Levinson Prize, Poetry Magazine Award, 1963; Golden Rose Trophy, New England Poetry Club, 1964; Obie Award for best new play, 1965, for *The Old Glory;* Sarah Josepha Hale Award, 1966; National Council on the Arts, grant, 1967, to produce *Prometheus Bound;* Litt.D. from

Williams College, 1965, Yale University, 1968; honorary degree from Columbia University, 1969.

WRITINGS: Land of Unlikeness (poems), introduction by Allen Tate, Cummington, 1944; *Lord Weary's Castle* (poems), Harcourt, 1946 (first seventy poems published in England as *Poems, 1938-1949,* Faber, 1950); *The Mills of the Kavanaughs* (poems), Harcourt, 1951; *Life Studies* (poems), Farrar, Straus, 1959, 2nd edition, Faber, 1969; (translator) Eugenio Montale, *Poesie di Montale,* Laterna (Bologna), 1960; (editor and translator) *Imitations* (versions of poems by Homer, Sappho, Rilke, Villon, Mallarme, Baudelaire, and others), Farrar, Straus, 1961; *Lord Weary's Castle [and] The Mills of the Kavanaughs,* two volumes in one, Meridian Books, 1961, hardcover edition, World Publishing, 1964; (translator with Jacques Barzun) Racine and Beaumarchais, *Phaedra [and] Figaro* (the former translated by Lowell, the latter by Barzun), Farrar, Straus, 1961; (translator) Racine, *Phaedra,* Faber, 1963; (author of introduction) Nathaniel Hawthorne, *Pegasus, the Winged Horse,* Macmillan, 1963; *For the Union Dead* (poems), Farrar, Straus, 1964; *Nathaniel Hawthorne, 1804-1864,* Ohio State University Press, 1964; *Selected Poems,* Faber, 1965; *The Old Glory* (three plays: "Endecott and the Red Cross," "My Kinsman, Major Molineaux," based on short stories by Hawthorne, and "Benito Cereno," based on the novella by Melville; first produced Off-Broadway at the American Place Theatre, November 1, 1964), introduction by Robert Brustein, director's note by Jonathan Miller, Farrar, Straus, 1965, revised edition, 1968; (author of appreciation) Randall Jarrell, *The Lost World,* Collier, 1966; (author of introduction) Ford Madox Ford, *Buckshee,* Pyn-Randall Press, 1966; *The Achievement of Robert Lowell: A Comprehensive Selection of His Poems,* critical introduction by William J. Martz, Scott, Foresman, 1966; *Life Studies [and] For the Union Dead,* Noonday, 1967; (editor with Peter Taylor and Robert Penn Warren) *Randall Jarrell: 1914-1965,* Farrar, Straus, 1967; *Near the Ocean* (poems), Farrar, Straus, 1967; *The Voyage and Other Versions of Poems by Baudelaire,* Farrar, Straus, 1968; "Endecott and the Red Cross" (full length play; expanded version of one-act of same title), first produced in New York by the American Place Theatre at St. Clements Episcopal Church, May, 1968; *Prometheus Bound* (derived from the play by Aeschylus; first produced at the Yale School of Drama, May 9, 1967; produced Off-Broadway at Mermaid Theatre, June 24, 1971), Farrar, Straus, 1969; *4,* privately printed, 1969; *Notebook 1967-68,* Farrar, Straus, 1969, revised edition, 1970.

Poems anthologized in over twenty volumes, including *Modern American Poetry,* edited by Louis Untermeyer, Harcourt, 1950, *Criterion Book of Modern American Verse,* edited by W.H. Auden, Criterion, 1956, *The Open Form:- Essays for Our Time,* edited by Alfred Kazin, Harcourt, 1961, *Writers at Work: "Paris Review" Interviews,* edited by George Plimpton, second series, Viking, 1963, and *Where is Vietnam?: American Poets Respond,* edited by Walter Lowenfels and Nan Braymer, Doubleday-Anchor, 1967.

Contributor to periodicals, including *Partisan Review, Kenyon Review, New Republic, New York Review of Books,* and *Observer.*

SIDELIGHTS: "I always liked William Carlos Williams," Lowell told A. Alvarez. "He really is utterly carried away into the object . . . . My things are much more formal, much more connected with older English poetry; there's a sort of formal personality in myself. I think anyone could tell that my free verse was written by someone who'd done a lot of formal verse. I began writing in the thirties. The current I fell into was the southern group of poets—John Crowe Ransom and Allen Tate [Lowell came under the influence of Tate during a two-month period when he literally camped on Tate's lawn]—and that was partly a continuation of Pound and Eliot and partly an attempt to make poetry much more formal than Eliot and Pound did; to write in meters but to make the meters look hard and make them hard to write."

Acknowledged by most critics to be the best American poet of his generation, Lowell is constantly exploring new forms in enlarging the scope of his art. Donald Hall believes that it is this constant change which marks Lowell as an important writer. "While the degree of Robert Lowell's achievement is difficult to assess at this time, he clearly belongs among the changing innovators of modern art. In his twenty-five years of publishing, he has confounded his admirers by renouncing an achieved style and exploring new territory. Because of his dissatisfaction with his achievement and because that achievement has already been considerable, he has the potential to become the major poet in English of the last half of this century, as Yeats—who recurrently judged himself a failure, and set out to improve his art—was the major poet of the first half."

Lowell's search for new poetic forms began with a rather formal, violent approach, colored with what Hall calls a "rigorous Catholicism to which Lowell brought a strong element of New England Calvinism." Lowell then turned to the narrative poem in which he retained some formality but inculcated the character and inclusiveness of the novel, a form which, with the short story, Lowell believes to be "the ideal modern form." He adds: "Maybe Tolstoi would be the perfect example—his work is imagistic, it deals with all experience, and there seems to be no conflict of the form and content. So one thing to get into poetry is that kind of human richness in rather simple descriptive language."

After a lapse of eight years, Lowell published *Life Studies,* a tremendous departure from his former work. Predominantly free verse, *Life Studies* is also autobiographical and, in some editions, contains prose. Hall believes that the change reflected in this book was due to the personal crises Lowell faced in the period prior to its publication. "In the decade of the fifties, Lowell had gone through enormous changes in his personal life; he was divorced, he left the Catholic Church, he experienced the first of the attacks of madness which have committed him to mental hospitals on several occasions, he was remarried and he became a father. His attitude toward his old poetry shifted; in conversation he told friends that his old poetry seemed melodramatic, posturing." In his latest work, Lowell has returned to a somewhat more formal structure, although this work contains an immediacy connected with the events of modern life. Stephen Stepanchev admires this characteristic. "Of the poets who came into public notice in the years immediately after World War II, Robert Lowell has the most inclusive vision, encompassing both the terrors of responsibility and the terrors of alienation, and his career reflects most clearly two major trends in recent American poetry. These are the shift from 'otherness' to the metaphysics and ethics of the individual imagination and the abandonment of the strict measures and dense phrasing of symbolist verse for the looser measures and simpler diction of a poetry responsive to the breath and cadence of contemporary reality."

The critics reveal diversified opinions when they attempt to isolate Lowell's poetic characteristics. Many are particularly impressed with the strong images, dense diction, and intense passions characteristic of much his work. "It is this vividness, the energy and texture of each image, that is Lowell's distinct achievement," Alfred Kazin maintains. "He specializes in place, in eloquent vertigo, in stylizing the communion with self that is the essence of dramatic monologue, and I can't think of any poet of his generation who has polished this dramatic sense, rare enough, to such an acuteness." "Based on a world of opposites and of contrasts, the poems are taut with the strain of linking contraries together," Paul Engle says of Lowell's early work. "There is fury in the lines and that has made the lines furious in sound. There is the feeling that Lowell has not wrestled with an angel but with Christ himself. In the course of that struggle the hand that touched the immaculate body has taken on a radiance which it transfers to the world of poems."

Randall Jarrell emphasizes the influence of history on Lowell's work. He describes the poet as having "a completely unscientific but thoroughly historical mind." Jarrell adds: "It is literary and traditional as well; he can use the past so effectively because he thinks so much as it did. His present contains the past—especially Rome, the late Middle Ages, and a couple of centuries of New England—as an operative skeleton just under the skin. . . . He does not present themes or generalizations but a world; the differences and similarities between it and ours bring home to us themes, generalizations, and the poet himself."

When Lowell was asked whether he revises a great deal he once replied, "Endlessly." More recently he said he "usually" revises extensively. He has said: "I don't believe I've ever written a poem in meter where I've kept a single one of the original lines. Usually when I was writing my old poems I'd write them out in blank verse and then put in the rhymes. And of course I'd change the rhymes a lot. . . . With some of the later poems I've written out prose versions, then cut the prose down and abbreviated it."

The great-grandnephew of James Russell Lowell and distant cousin of Amy Lowell, Robert Lowell has these observations on other poets: "The two I've been closest to are Elizabeth Bishop . . . and [Randall] Jarrell. . . . I like some of [Karl] Shapiro very much, some of [Theodore] Roethke and Stanley Kunitz." He says that Delmore Schwartz was the poet who most "seeped into" him, and considers Hart Crane "the great poet of that generation." He believes Eliot and Frost are "probably equally great poets." The Beats are another story. While he admits that "some of the Beats are quite good," he affirms that "no mass movement like that can be of much artistic importance. . . . You've got to remain complicatedly civilized and organized to keep your humanity under the pressures of our various governments, not go into a bohemian wildness. Quite a few people are genuinely bohemian; the real bohemia is something tremendous, of course. . . ."

Recently his interest in translating poetry has been dominant, and his attempts in this field acclaimed; fellow translator Herma Briffault called his translation of Racine's *Phaedre* "almost miraculous."

BIOGRAPHICAL/CRITICAL SOURCES—Books: Lloyd Frankenburg, *Pleasure Dome: On Reading Modern Poetry*, Houghton, 1949; Babette Deutsch, *Poetry in Our Time*, Holt, 1952, revised edition, Doubleday, 1963; Randall Jarrell, *Poetry and the Age*, Knopf, 1953; Louise Bogan, *Selected Criticism: Prose and Poetry*, Noonday, 1955; Louis Untermeyer, *Lives of the Poets: The Story of 1000 Years of English and American Poetry*, Simon & Schuster, 1959; Jerome Mazzaro, *The Achievement of Robert Lowell*, University of Detroit Press, 1960; M.L. Rosenthal, *The Modern Poets: A Critical Introduction*, Oxford University Press, 1960; Hugh B. Staples, *Robert Lowell: The First Twenty Years*, Farrar, Straus, 1962; Edward Hungerford, editor, *Poets in Progress*, Northwestern University Press, 1962, new edition, 1967; Alfred Kazin, *Contemporaries*, Little, Brown, 1962; Glauco Cambon, *The Inclusive Flame: Studies in Modern American Poetry*, Indiana University Press, 1963; Richard Kostelanetz, editor, *On Contemporary Literature: An Anthol-*ogy of Critical Essays on the Major Movements and Writers of Contemporary Literature, Avon, 1964; Denis Donoghue, *Connoisseurs of Chaos: Ideas of Order in American Poetry*, Macmillan, 1965; Stephen Stepanchev, *American Poetry Since 1945*, Harper, 1965; Harold Clurman, *The Naked Image: Observations on the Modern Theatre*, Macmillan, 1966; Robert Brustein, *Seasons of Discontent: Dramatic Opinions, 1959-1965*, Simon & Schuster, 1967; M.L. Rosenthal, *The New Poets: American and British Poetry Since World War Two*, Oxford University Press, 1967; George Steiner, *Language and Silence: Essays on Language, Literature, and the Inhuman*, Atheneum, 1967; Thomas Francis Parkinson, editor, *Robert Lowell: A Collection of Critical Essays*, Prentice-Hall, 1968; Jay Martin, *Robert Lowell*, University of Minnesota Press, 1970; R.K. Meiners, *Everything to Be Endured*, University of Missouri Press, 1970.

Articles: *New Republic*, October 23, 1944, June 8, 1959, May 31, 1969; *New York Times*, November 3, 1946, April 22, 1951, May 3, 1959, June 3, 1965, October 12, 1965, February 1, 1966, February 6, 1966, May 18, 1967, May 21, 1967, May 7, 1968, October 9, 1948, July 18, 1970; *Saturday Review*, November 16, 1946, July 25, 1959, July 22, 1961, January 6, 1962, September 2, 1967, May 3, 1969, September 6, 1969; *New Yorker*, November 30, 1946, October 24, 1959, January 20, 1962, May 20, 1967, May 11, 1968; *Christian Century*, December 4, 1946; *Commonweal*, December 27, 1946, July 3, 1959, May 12, 1961, May 12, 1967, December 1, 1967, October 17, 1969; *Poetry*, August, 1947, December, 1947, October, 1959, April, 1962, May, 1968; *New York Herald Tribune Book Review*, April 22, 1951, June 7, 1959, February 4, 1962; *Yale Review*, autumn, 1951, December, 1959, March, 1962, summer, 1967; *Spectator*, May 1, 1959, September 1, 1967; *Library Journal*, June 1, 1959, December 1, 1961, March 15, 1966, October 1, 1967, July, 1969; *Atlantic*, July, 1959, August, 1961, December, 1961, October, 1967; *Nation*, September 19, 1959, January 24, 1966, April 24, 1967, June 26, 1967, April 15, 1968, May 27, 1968, December 23, 1968, July 7, 1969, August 25, 1969; *Time*, April 28, 1961, November 3, 1961, October 16, 1964, June 2, 1967, May 10, 1968, March 14, 1969, June 6, 1969; *New York Times Book Review*, May 28, 1961, November 12, 1961, October 4, 1964, January 15, 1967, September 3, 1967, June 15, 1969; *Book Week*, October 11, 1964, February 20, 1966; *Newsweek*, October 12, 1964, May 22, 1967, May 13, 1968; *Encounter*, February, 1965; *New Statesman*, March 26, 1965, July 21, 1967, March 1, 1968; *Hudson Review*, spring, 1965, autumn, 1967, winter, 1967; *American Scholar*, summer, 1965; *Christian Science Monitor*, December 16, 1965, June 5, 1969; *New York Herald Tribune*, February 7, 1966, February 9, 1966; *Tri-Quarterly*, fall, 1966; *American Literature*, January, 1967; *Best Sellers*, February 15, 1967; *Life*, February 17, 1967; *Observer*, March 12, 1967, May 3, 1970; *Punch*, March 15, 1967; *Listener*, March 23, 1967, September 7, 1967, November 26, 1970; *New Leader*, March 27, 1967, June 19, 1967; *National Observer*, May 22, 1967; *Observer Review*, July 2, 1967, January 19, 1969; *New York Review of Books*, July 13, 1967, August 3, 1967, November 23, 1967; *Times Literary Supplement*, August 8, 1967; *Virginia Quarterly Review*, summer, 1967; *Tulane Drama Review*, summer, 1967; *American Quarterly*, fall, 1967; *Books Abroad*, autumn, 1967, summer, 1969, winter, 1969; *Partisan Review*, fall, 1967, summer, 1968; *Prairie Schooner*, winter, 1967-68; *Book World*, March 3, 1968, May 11, 1969; *Washington Post*, May 7, 1969; *Sewanee Review*, spring, 1969; *Contemporary Literature*, spring, 1969; *New York*, July 7, 1969; *Esquire*, September, 1969; *Criticism*, winter, 1969; *Cambridge Review*, May 7, 1971; *Georgia Review*, spring, 1971; *Commentary*, August, 1971.

LOWENSTEIN, Dyno 1914-

PERSONAL: Born November 29, 1914, in Berlin, Germany; son of Kurt and Mara (Kerwel) Lowenstein; married Tilde Hoffman, February 1, 1924; children: Steven, Karin, Tim. Education: Sorbonne, University of Paris, diploma statistician. Home: 63-42 110th St., Forest Hills, N.Y. 11375. Office: 80 West 40th St., New York, N.Y. 10018.

CAREER: Pictograph Corp., New York, N.Y., director, 1950—. Military service: U.S. Army, Office of Strategic Services, 1942-45; became lieutenant.

WRITINGS: Pictographs and Graphs, Harper, 1952; Money: A First Book (for young adults), F. Watts, 1963; (self-illustrated) Graphs: A First Book (juvenile), F. Watts, 1969; (illustrator) Trevor Nevitt Dupuy, The Military History of Revolutionary War Land Battles, F. Watts, 1970.

*   *   *

LOWER, Arthur R(eginald) M(arsden) 1889-

PERSONAL: Born August 12, 1889, in Barrie, Ontario; son of Frederick James and Sarah Anne (Smith) Lower; married Evelyn Marion Smith, October 16, 1920; children: Louise Evelyn (Mrs. William Maxwell Strange). Education: Attended Barrie Collegiate Institute; University of Toronto, B.A., 1914, M.A., 1923; Harvard University, M.A., 1928, Ph.D., 1929. Politics: Liberal ("with small l"). Religion: United Church of Canada. Home: Horizon House, 4205 Bath Rd., Collins Bay, Kingston, Ontario, Canada. Office: Queen's University, Kingston, Ontario, Canada.

CAREER: Canadian Archives, Ottawa, Ontario, assistant to chairman of Board of Historical Publications, 1919-25; Harvard University, Cambridge, Mass., tutor and lecturer in history, 1925-29; United College, University of Manitoba, Winnipeg, head of department of history, 1929-47; Queen's University, Kingston, Ontario, Douglas Professor of Canadian and Commonwealth History, 1947-59; retired, 1959. Military service: Royal Navy, 1916-19; became lieutenant. Member: Royal Society of Canada (president, 1961-62), Canadian Historical Association, American Historical Association, Canadian Political Science Association, Quinte Association (historic sites and parks; president, 1957-65). Awards, honors: Tyrrell Medal in History of Royal Society of Canada, 1947; Governor-General's Literary Award, 1947, for Colony to Nation: A History of Canada, and 1955, for This Most Famous Stream: The Liberal Democratic Way of Life.

WRITINGS: (With C.D. Melvill and N.A. Comeau) Reports on Fisheries Investigations in Hudson and James Bays and Tributary Waters in 1914, Department of the Naval Service, Canada, 1915; (translator) Documents relatifs a la monnaie, au change et aux finances du Canada sous le regime francais, F.A. Acland, 1925; (editor with Harold Adams Innis) Select Documents in Canadian Economic History, 1783-1885, University of Toronto Press, 1933; (with Innis) Settlement and the Forest Frontier in Eastern Canada [and] Settlement and the Mining Frontier (two books in one volume; the former by Lower, the latter by Innis), Macmillan (Toronto), 1936; The North American Assault on the Canadian Forest: A History of the Lumber Trade Between Canada and the U.S., Ryerson, 1938, Greenwood Press, 1969; Canada and the Far East—1940, Institute of Pacific Relations, 1940; (editor with J.F. Parkinson) War and Reconstruction: Some Canadian Issues, Humphries, 1942; The Development of Canadian Economic Ideas (supplement to The Spirit of American Economics by Joao Frederico Normano), Committee on the Study of Economic Thought (New York), 1943; Colony to Nation: A History of Canada, Longmans,

Green, 1946, 4th edition, 1964; (with James Warren Chafe) Canada—A Nation, and How It Came to Be, Longmans, Green (Toronto), 1948, revised edition, 1964; Canada, Nation and Neighbor, Ryerson, 1952; Unconventional Voyages (autobiographical), Ryerson, 1953; This Most Famous Stream: The Liberal Democratic Way of Life, Ryerson, 1954; (with F.R. Scott and others) Evolving Canadian Federalism, Duke University Press, 1958; Canadians in the Making: A Social History of Canada, Longmans, Green (Toronto), 1958; My First Seventy-Five Years, Macmillan (Toronto), 1967; Great Britain's Woodyard: British America and the Timber Trade, McGill-Queen's University Press, 1973.

Essays included in other books. Contributor of articles and essays to most Canadian literary magazines and to American periodicals.

WORK IN PROGRESS: Various articles; a study to be entitled Metropolis and Hinterland; a novel, partially completed.

SIDELIGHTS: Lower looks back: "My whole career has been devoted to clearing up my ideas about Canada, and strengthening the concept contained in the name." He has ranged over much of the English-speaking world in his travels.

*   *   *

LU, David J(ohn) 1928-

PERSONAL: Born September 28, 1928, in Keelung, Formosa; son of Ming (in mining enterprises) and Yeh (Lai) Lu; married I. Annabelle Compton, May 29, 1954; children: David, Jr., Daniel Mark, Cynthia Ellen, Stephen Paul. Education: National Taiwan University, B.A., 1950; Westminster Theological Seminary, student, 1950-52; Columbia University, M.I.A. and certificate of East Asian Institute, 1954, Ph.D., 1960. Politics: Liberal Republican. Religion: Presbyterian. Home: R.D. 1, Lewisburg, Pa. 17837. Office: Bucknell University, Lewisburg, Pa. 17837.

CAREER: Prentice-Hall, Inc., Englewood Cliffs, N.J., editor, Pension and Profit Sharing Service, 1956-60; Rutgers University, New Brunswick, N.J., instructor in history, 1959; Bucknell University, Lewisburg, Pa., began as assistant professor and director, Institute of Asian Studies, became professor of history and director, Center for Japanese Studies, 1960—. Columbia University, associate in University Seminar. Pennsylvania Department of Public Instruction, consultant on world cultures, 1961. Member: Japan Society, Association for Asian Studies, American Historical Association.

WRITINGS: From the Marco Polo Bridge to Pearl Harbor: Japan's Entry into World War II, Public Affairs Press, 1961; Moslems in China Today, International Studies Group (Hongkong), 1964; Sources in Japanese History, McGraw, 1971.

WORK IN PROGRESS: Life and Times of Foreign Minister Yosuke Matsuoka, 1880-1946.

*   *   *

LUBELL, Cecil 1912-

PERSONAL: Born June 6, 1912, in Leeds, England; son of Joseph (a tailor) and Jennie Rachel (Samuel) Lubell; married Winifred A. Milius (an artist-illustrator), September, 1939; children: David, Steven. Education: Harvard University, B.A., 1933, M.A., 1935. Residence: Croton-on-Hudson, N.Y. Office: American Fabrics, 24 East 38th St., New York, N.Y. 10016.

CAREER: Men's Reporter (trade magazine), editor, 1945-50; menswear stylist and design consultant in New York, N.Y., 1950-57; Argosy (magazine), New York, N.Y., menswear columnist, 1955-57; Institute for Motivational Research, Croton-on-Hudson, N.Y., promotional director, 1958-59; *American Fabrics* (quarterly textile journal), New York, N.Y., editor, 1960—; writer of children's books.

WRITINGS—All juveniles, with wife, Winifred Lubell: *The Tall Grass Zoo*, Rand McNally, 1960; *Up a Tree*, Rand McNally, 1961; *Rosalie, the Bird Market Turtle*, Rand McNally, 1962; *Green is for Growing*, Rand McNally, 1964; *In a Running Brook*, Rand McNally, 1968; *A Zoo for You: Some Indoor Pets and How to Keep Them*, Parents' Magazine Press, 1970; *Birds in the Streets: The City Pigeon Book*, Parents' Magazine Press, 1971; *Clothes Tell a Story: From Skin to Space Suits*, Parents' Magazine Press, 1971; *Picture Signs and Symbols*, Parents' Magazine Press, 1972.

BIOGRAPHICAL/CRITICAL SOURCES: Lee Bennett Hopkins, *Books Are by People*, Citation, 1969.

* * *

LUBELL, Harold 1925-

PERSONAL: Born March 29, 1925, in New York, N.Y.; son of Morris and Fannie (Bell) Lubell; married Claudie Marchaut (a physicist), 1962; children: Martin Alexander, Diana Allenc. *Education:* Bard College, B.A., 1944; Harvard University, M.P.A., 1947, M.A., 1948, Ph.D., 1953. *Home:* 14 Chemin de la Tourelle, 1211 Geneva 19, Switzerland. *Office:* International Labour Office, 1211 Geneva 22, Switzerland.

CAREER: Board of Governors of the Federal Reserve System, Washington, D.C., research assistant, 1944-45; United Nations, statistician at Lake Success, N.Y., and Geneva, Switzerland, 1948-49; U.S. Operations Mission to France, Paris, economist, 1949-53; Falk Project for Economic Research, Jerusalem, Israel, senior economist and director, 1954-57; RAND Corp., Santa Monica, Calif., economist, 1957-62; Organization for Economic Cooperation and Development, Paris, France, economist, 1962; Brookings Institution Economic Specialists Group (Ford Foundation), Saigon, Vietnam, economist, 1963-64; Graduate School of Business, Columbia University, New York, N.Y., senior research associate, 1964-65; U.S. Agency for International Development (A.I.D.), economist in Ankara, Turkey, and New Delhi, India, 1965-71; International Labour Office, Geneva, Switzerland, economist, 1971—. *Member:* American Economic Association, American Statistical Association, Econometric Society. *Awards, honors:* Fulbright fellowship, 1951.

WRITINGS: The French Investment Program: A Defense of the Monnet Plan, Mutual Security Agency, 1952; *Provisional Estimates of Israel's National Expenditure, 1952-1953*, Falk Project for Economic Research and Central Bureau of Statistics, 1956; *Israel's National Expenditure: Summary of Results*, RAND Corp., 1957; *Middle East Crises and World Petroleum Movements*, RAND Corp., 1958; (with Hadassah Weisbrod and Rivka Kahana) *Israel's National Expenditure: 1950-1954*, Falk Project for Economic Research and Central Bureau of Statistics, 1958; *World Petroleum Production and Shipping: A Post-Mortem on Suez*, RAND Corp., 1958; *Survey of Energy and Oil Demand Projections for Western Europe*, RAND Corp., 1959.

Security of Supply and Energy Policy in Western Europe, RAND Corp., 1960; *Energy Policy and Security of Energy Supply in Western Europe*, RAND Corp., 1961; *The Public and Private Sector and Investment in Israel*, RAND Corp., 1961; *The Soviet Oil Offensive and Interbloc Economic Cooperation*, RAND Corp., 1961; *A Note on the National Accounts of Algeria, 1950-1959 and 1964*, RAND Corp., 1962; *Middle East Oil Crises and Western Europe's Energy Supplies*, Johns Hopkins Press, 1963.

(Editor with Ronald G. Ridker) *Employment and Unemployment Problems of the Near East and South Asia*, two volumes, Vikas Publications (Delhi), 1971, International Publications Service, 1972; *Urban Development and Employment: The Prospects for Calcutta*, International Labour Office, 1973. Contributor of articles to *New Leader* and to professional journals.

WORK IN PROGRESS: Research on urban employment, and problems in developing countries.

SIDELIGHTS: Lubell is competent in French and Spanish, knows some German, Hebrew, and Turkish. *Avocational interests:* Playing cello in professional-caliber chamber music groups.

* * *

LUDWIG, Charles Shelton 1918-

PERSONAL: Born January 8, 1918, in Macomb, Ill.; son of missionary parents, John Shelton and Twyla Innes (Ogle) Ludwig; married Mary Puchek, 1939; children: Charles II, Brenda M. *Education:* Anderson College, Anderson, Ind., B.S., 1945. *Home:* 7217 East 30th St., Tucson, Ariz. 85710.

CAREER: Church of God, pastor in Palmerton, Pa., 1940-41, Indiana, Pa., 1942, Olympia, Wash., Boise, Idaho, and Tucson, Ariz. *Member:* Associated Church Press, Evangelical Press Association.

WRITINGS: Thirteen Sermons on the Twenty-Third Psalm: Wonderful Jesus, Gospel Trumpet, 1942; *The Adventures of Juma*, Warner Press, 1944; *Witch Doctor's Holiday*, Warner Press, 1945; *Christ at the Door*, Warner Press, 1946; *Leopard Glue*, Warner Press, 1946; *Sankey Still Sings*, Warner Press, 1947; *Cannibal Country*, Warner Press, 1948.

Radio Pals Marooned, Van Kampen, 1952; *Man-Eaters and Masai Spears: A Missionary Adventure Story*, Scripture Press, 1953; *Man-Eaters Don't Knock: A Missionary Adventure Story*, Scripture Press, 1953; *Radio Pals Fight the Flood*, Van Kampen, 1953; *Radio Pals on Bar T Ranch*, Van Kampen, 1953; *Chuma: A Missionary Adventure Story for Girls*, Scripture Press, 1954; *Rogue Elephant: A Missionary Adventure Story for Boys and Girls*, Scripture Press, 1954; *Radio Pals in the Hands of the Mau Mau*, Van Kampen, 1955; *Man-Eaters Don't Laugh: A Missionary Adventure Story*, Scripture Press, 1955; *Radio Pals in the Flaming Forest*, Zondervan, 1955; *Chuma Finds a Baby: A Missionary Adventure Story for Girls*, Scripture Press, 1956; *Man-Eater's Claw: A Missionary Adventure Story*, Scripture Press, 1957.

At the Cross, Warner Press, 1961; *General Without a Gun: The Life of William Booth, Founder of the Salvation Army, for Teens*, Zondervan, 1961; *The Lady General*, Baker Book, 1962; *On Target: Illustrations for Christian Messages*, Warner Press, 1963; *Mama Was a Missionary*, Warner Press, 1963; *Nancy Hanks, Mother of Lincoln*, Baker Book, 1965. Contributor of articles, mostly nonfiction, to magazines.

SIDELIGHTS: Ludwig grew up in Kenya and received his education there, from the age of nine to nineteen.

* * *

LUFF, S(tanley) G(eorge) A(nthony) 1921- (Hugh Farnash)

PERSONAL: Born February 20, 1921, in London, England; son of Edward J. and Elizabeth Eleanor (Woods) Luff. *Education:* St. Joseph's College, Beulah Hill, London, England, student, 1929-36; St. Marys College, Strawberry Hill, Middlesex, England, student, 1951-53; University of London, teacher's qualification; Pontificio Instituto di Archeologia, diploma, 1962-63. *Home:* Pontifical Beda College, Viale San Paolo 18, Rome, Italy.

CAREER: Thomas More School, Frensham, Farnham, Surrey, England, senior master, 1949-51, 1953-54; Burstow School, Horley, Sussex, England, senior master, 1955-58; St. Augustine's Abbey School, Ramsgate, England, senior English master, 1958-61; currently studying for Roman Catholic priesthood. *Military service:* Royal Artillery and Military Government, Germany, 1940-46; became sergeant. *Member:* Collegium Cultorum Martyrum.

WRITINGS: *The First Monks and Hermits,* St. Albert's Press, 1958; *Silent Bedes: Practical Meditations for the Mysteries of the Rosary,* Longmans, Green, 1959; (compiler) *Prayers at Home,* Darton, Longman & Todd, 1962; *Early Christian Writing: An Anthology for Home and School,* S.P.C.K., 1963; *New Library of Catholic Knowledge, Volume I: The Organization of the Church,* Hawthorn, 1963; *Mountains Round Jerusalem* (mediations), Browne & Nolan, 1963, published in America as *The Breezes of the Spirit,* Newman, 1964; *In the Steps of Bernadette* (pamphlet), Carmelite Publications (Dublin), 1964; *The Christian's Guide to Rome,* Fordham University Press, 1967. Contributor of articles on religion, art, history, travel, and poetry to *Tablet, Architectural Review, Art d'Eglise, Life of the Spirit, Lady,* and other periodicals.

WORK IN PROGRESS: A study of Saint Radegund, sixth-century personality; *Anthology of English Literary Epitaphs;* Italian art and architecture.

* * *

LUK, Charles 1898-
(K'uan-yu Lu)

PERSONAL: Born January 17, 1898, in Canton, China; widower; children: one daughter; one son. *Education:* Educated in China. *Religion:* Buddhist. *Home address:* P.O. Box 364, Hongkong.

CAREER: Businessman, now retired; translator of Chinese Buddhist texts.

WRITINGS—All under pseudonym K'uan-yu Lu: (Editor and translator) *Ch'an and Zen Teaching,* 1st series, Rider & Co., 1960, Shambala, 1970, 2nd edition, Rider & Co., 1970, 2nd series, Rider & Co., 1961, Shambala, 1971, 3rd series, Rider & Co., 1962; *The Secrets of Chinese Meditation: Self-Cultivation by Mind Control as Taught in the Ch'an, Mahayana and Taoist Schools in China,* Rider & Co., 1964, new edition, 1969; (translator) *The Surangama Sutra,* Rider & Co., 1966; *Taoist Yoga: Alchemy and Immortality,* Rider & Co., 1970; *Practical Buddhism,* Rider & Co., 1971; (editor and translator) *Vimalakirti Nirdesa Sutra,* Shambala, 1972. Contributor to *World Buddhism* (Ceylon), *Western Buddhist* (London), *Middle Way* (London), *Zen Notes* (New York), and other similar journals.

WORK IN PROGRESS: *The Autobiography of Ch'an Master Han Shan; The Autobiography of Ch'an Master Hsu Yun; The Six Ch'an Patriarchs of China.*

* * *

LURIE, Edward 1927-

PERSONAL: Born April 10, 1927, in New York, N.Y.; son of Alexander and Ella (Lottman) Lurie; marrie: Nancy Oestreich, August 11, 1951 (divorced May, 1963). *Education:* Sarah Lawrence College, B.A., 1949; Northwestern University, M.A., 1951, Ph.D., 1956. *Home:* 630 Merrick, Detroit, Mich. 48202. *Office:* 848 Mackenzie Hall, Wayne State University, Detroit, Mich. 48202.

CAREER: Massachusetts Institute of Technology, Cambridge, instructor in humanities and industrial management, 1953-55; University of Michigan, Ann Arbor, instructor in history, 1955-58; Wayne State University, Detroit, Mich., assistant professor, 1958-61, associate professor, 1961-64, professor of American history, 1964—, chairman of American Studies program, 1959—. Visiting professor, University of Pennsylvania, summer, 1963, Rockefeller Institute, 1963-64, New York University, summer, 1964. Director, International Fulbright-Hays Seminar in American Studies, 1963-64. *Military service:* U.S. Navy, 1944-46. *Member:* Society for the History of Technology (member of executive committee), Committee on Science Manuscripts (member of executive committee), American Studies Association of Michigan (president, 1962-64). *Awards, honors:* Newberry Library fellow, 1960; faculty research fellowship from the Social Science Research Council, 1961-62; Guggenheim fellowship, 1964-65.

WRITINGS: *The Founding of the Museum of Comparative Zoology,* Museum of Comparative Zoology, Harvard University, 1959; *Louis Agassiz: A Life in Science* (selected for inclusion in White House Library), University of Chicago Press, 1960; (editor and author of introduction) Louis Agassiz, *An Assay on Classification,* Belknap Press, 1962. Contributor to *Isis, Victorian Studies,* and *Rockefeller Institute Review.* Member of editorial board of *Technology and Culture.*

WORK IN PROGRESS: *The Transformation of American Culture,* for Oxford University Press.†

* * *

LUZA, Radomir 1922-

PERSONAL: Born October 17, 1922, in Prague, Czechoslovakia; became U.S. citizen in 1959; son of Vojtech (a five-star army general) and Milada (Vecera) Luza; married Libuse Podhrazska, February 5, 1949; children: Radomir. *Education:* Masaryk University, Ju.Dr., 1948; New York University, A.M., 1957, Ph.D., 1959. *Home:* Sonnenweg 113, Vienna 14, Austria. *Office:* Educational Fund, Inc., Sonnenweg 113, Vienna 14, Austria.

CAREER: A member of the Czechoslovakia Resistance, Luza was jailed by the Gestapo in 1941, lived underground during the rest of World War II; became deputy commanding officer of the Partisan Brigade, and later headed the Social Democratic Youth in Czechoslovakia; escaped to France after the Communist take-over in 1948 and remained in Paris until 1953 when he came to the United States. M.L. Annenberg Foundation, Philadelphia, Pa., research associate, 1960-62; Operations and Policy Research, Inc., Washington, D.C., research associate, 1962-63; Educational Fund, Inc., Detroit, Mich., European representative, 1963—. International Union of Socialist Youth, Vienna, member of executive committee; member of Council of Free Czechoslovakia, Washington, D.C. *Member:* American Historical Association.

WRITINGS: *Odsun: Prispevek k historii ceskonemeckych vzatahu v letech 1918-1952,* Nasy Cesty, 1952; *The Transfer of the Sudeten Germans: A Study of Czech-German Relations, 1933-62,* New York University Press, 1964; *History of the International Socialist Youth Movement,* Humanities, 1970; (editor with Victor S. Mamatey) *A History of the Czechoslovak Republic, 1918-1948,* Princeton University Press, 1973. Member of editorial board of *Svedectvi,* an exile Czechoslovak political review, and of *IUSY Bulletin.*

* * *

LYALL, Gavin T(udor) 1932-

PERSONAL: Born May 9, 1932, in Birmingham, England; son of Joseph Tudor (an accountant) and Ann (Hodgkiss) Lyall; married Katharine Whitehorn (a columnist), January 4, 1958; children: two sons. *Education:* Attended King Edward's School, Birmingham, England, 1943-51; Pembroke College, Cambridge, B.A.

(honors). *Religion:* Quaker. *Home:* 14 Provost Rd., London N.W.3, England. *Agent:* A.D. Peters, 10 Buckingham St., London W.C.2, England.

CAREER: Picture Post, London, England, journalist, 1956-57; British Broadcasting Corp., London, television film director, 1958; *Sunday Times,* London, 1959-63, began as journalist, became aviation editor; free-lance writer, 1963—. *Military service:* Royal Air Force, 1951-53; became pilot officer. *Member:* Crime Writers' Association.

WRITINGS: The Wrong Side of the Sky, Scribner, 1961; *The Most Dangerous Game,* Scribner, 1963; *Midnight Plus One,* Scribner, 1965; *Shooting Script,* Scribner, 1966; (editor) *The War in the Air 1939-1945: An Anthology of Personal Experience,* Hutchinson, 1968, published in America as *The War in the Air: The Royal Air Force in World War II,* Morrow, 1969; *Venus with Pistol,* Scribner, 1969; *Blame the Dead,* Viking, 1973.

WORK IN PROGRESS: A crime thriller; research on the history of military aviation.

SIDELIGHTS: Lyall has traveled as a staff journalist in Europe, Libya, India, Pakistan, Persia, Nepal, United States, and Australia. *Avocational interests:* Aviation, firearms, and cats.

BIOGRAPHICAL/CRITICAL SOURCES: Publishers Weekly, April 12, 1965; *New York Times,* September 16, 1969; *Punch,* December 10, 1969.

*　　*　　*

LYLES, Vina Honish 1935-

PERSONAL: Born February 17, 1935, in Victoria, Tex.; daughter of Walter (stepfather) and Doris (Smith) Honish Beran; married Scotty Lyles; children: Peggy Lynn, Thomas Stephen. *Education:* Courses in nursery education. *Religion:* Episcopalian. *Home:* 200 South Norma, La Habra, Calif. 90631.

CAREER: Former nursery school teacher. Office manager for an accounting firm, 1963-70. *Member:* Writers' Club of Whittier (Calif.; treasurer, 1970-71).

WRITINGS: The Terrible Monster on Blackberry Street, Golden Gate Junior Books, 1963; (contributor) *It Happened in the City* (2nd grade reader), Follett, 1968; *Spooky Hand Mystery,* Childrens Press, 1973. Contributor of stories to children's magazines, and of feature articles to *Whittier Review, Southern California Presbyterian,* and *Tempo Magazine.* Contributing special features editor and columnist, *Montebello Journal,* 1970-71.

WORK IN PROGRESS: Free-lance fiction and nonfiction; a nonfiction book on the psychological approach to happiness.

AVOCATIONAL INTERESTS: Travel; reading history, psychology, and philosophy.

BIOGRAPHICAL/CRITICAL SOURCES: East Whittier Review, September 12, 1963.

*　　*　　*

LYNCH, Patrick B(eavis) 1927-

PERSONAL: Born April 4, 1927, in Ilford, Essex, England; son of Alfred (a clergyman) and Annie (Beavis) Lynch; married Anne Maria Kennedy, August 8, 1952; children: Jennifer Alison. *Education:* Attended King Alfred's College, Winchester, England, 1950-52. *Religion:* Anglican. *Home:* 48 Redhill Rd., Rowlands Castle, Hampshire, England.

CAREER: Schoolmaster in Portsmouth, England, 1952-58, Sussex, England, 1958—. Cadet officer, British Red Cross.

WRITINGS: A Million Years of Man, St. Martins, 1959 (published in England as *From the Beginning,* Edward Arnold, 1959); *From the Cave to the City,* St. Martins, 1959; *Man Makes His World,* St. Martins, 1959; (translator) Arno Scholz and Theodor F. Meysels, *Israel, Land of Hope: A Report in Pictures,* William Heinman, 1960; (with Barbara Sewell) *The Story of Ancient Egypt,* Edward Arnold, 1960, St. Martins, 1961; *The Shape of the Earth,* St. Martins, 1962; *Man and Nature,* Edward Arnold, 1963, St. Martins, 1964.

SIDELIGHTS: Lynch's ambition is to earn enough money to take a long caravan tour to Europe.

*　　*　　*

LYON, Peyton V(aughan) 1921-

PERSONAL: Born October 2, 1921, in Winnipeg, Manitoba; son of Hebert Redmond and Frederica (Lee) Lyon; married Frances Hazleton, June 26, 1943; children: Russell Vaughan, Stephen Lee, Barbara Jane. *Education:* University of Manitoba, B.A., 1949; Oxford University, M.A., 1953, D.Phil., 1953. *Home:* 17 Apache Crescent, Ottawa 5, Ontario, Canada. *Office:* Carleton University, Ottawa, Ontario, Canada.

CAREER: Canadian Fire Insurance Co., Winnipeg, Manitoba, Canada, clerk, 1938-40; Canadian Department of External Affairs, Ottawa, Ontario, foreign service officer, 1953-59, serving in Bonn, Germany, four years of that period; University of Western Ontario, London, assistant professor, 1959-61, associate professor, 1961-64, professor of political science, 1964-65; Carleton University, Ottawa, Ontario, professor of political science, 1965—. *Military service:* Royal Canadian Air Force, navigator, 1940-45; served in England and Africa; became flight lieutenant; received King's Commendation. *Member:* Canadian Institute of International Affairs, Canadian Political Science Association.

WRITINGS: The Policy Question: A Critical Appraisal of Canada's Role in World Affairs, McClelland & Stewart, 1963; (contributor) Adam Bromke and Philip E. Uren, editors, *The Communist States and the West,* Praeger, 1967; *Canada in World Affairs, 1961-1963,* Canadian Institute of International Affairs and Oxford University Press, 1968; *NATO as a Diplomatic Instrument,* Atlantic Council of Canada, 1971.

*　　*　　*

LYONS, Eugene 1898-

PERSONAL: Born July 1, 1898, in Uzlian, Russia; came to United States, 1907; naturalized, 1919; son of Nathan and Minnie (Privin) Lyons; married Yetta Siegel, September 6, 1921; children: Eugenie Rose (Mrs. Joseph A. Haimes). *Education:* Attended College of the City of New York (now City College of the City University of New York), 1916-17; Columbia University, 1917. *Religion:* Jewish. *Home:* 220 Madison Ave., New York, N.Y. 10016. *Office: Reader's Digest,* 200 Park Ave., New York, N.Y. 10017.

CAREER: Erie Dispatch, Erie, Pa., reporter, 1919; *Boston Telegram,* Boston, Mass., reporter, 1921; *Soviet Russia Pictorial,* editor, 1922-23; Tass Agency, New York, N.Y., editor, 1924-27; United Press correspondent stationed in Moscow, U.S.S.R., 1928-34; with Ames and Norr (public relations), 1935-39; *American Mercury,* New York, N.Y., editor, 1939-44; *Pageant,* New York, N.Y., editor, 1944-45; *Reader's Digest,* Pleasantville, and New York, N.Y., roving editor, 1946-52, senior editor, 1952—. Onetime writer in Hollywood. First president of the American Committee for the Liberation of the Peoples of Russia (later called Radio Liberty Committee). *Military service:* U.S. Army, 1918. *Member:* Overseas Press Club (president, 1939-40), Dutch Treat Club.

WRITINGS: The Life and Death of Sacco and Vanzetti, International Publishers, 1927; (editor and translator) Six Soviet Plays, Houghton, 1934; Moscow Carrousel, Knopf, 1935 (published in England as Modern Moscow, Hurst & Blackett, 1935); (translator and adapter with Charles Malamuth) Valentin P. Kataev, Squaring the Circle (play; English translation originally published in Six Soviet Plays), Samuel French, 1936; (editor) We Cover the World, by Fifteen Foreign Correspondents, Harcourt, 1937; Assignment in Utopia (autobiography), Harcourt, 1937, abridged edition, Twin Circle, 1967; (with Upton Sinclair) Terror in Russia? Two Views, Richard R. Smith, 1938; Stalin, Czar of All the Russias, Lippincott, 1940; The Red Decade: The Stalinist Penetration of America, Bobbs-Merrill, 1941, reissued as The Red Decade: The Classic Work on Communism in America During the Thirties, Arlington House, 1971; Our Unknown Ex-president: A Portrait of Herbert Hoover, Doubleday, 1948, reissued as The Herbert Hoover Story, Human Events, 1959; Our Secret Allies: The Peoples of Russia, Duell, Sloan, & Pearce, 1953; The Crimes of Khrushchev, U.S. Government Printing Office, 1959; Beware! Tourists Reporting on Russia, U.S. Government Printing Office, 1960; Herbert Hoover: A Biography, Doubleday, 1964; David Sarnoff: A Biography, Harper, 1966; Workers' Paradise Lost: Fifty Years of Soviet Communism—A Balance Sheet, Funk, 1967; Operation Suicide: Those Strange Bridges to Communism, Twin Circle, 1967. Contributor to national magazines.

SIDELIGHTS: In 1966 Harper published Lyons' biography of David Sarnoff, the radio, television, and electronics pioneer and R.C.A. executive. As Clark Kinnaird mentions in a review of the book, Lyons had the edge on other biographers in his relationship to Sarnoff: they shared a grandmother, Rivke (Rebecca) Privin, "the matriarch who came from Uzlian [Russia] to rule over the Sarnoff clan in New York." This made them cousins, and gave Lyons as intimate view into Sarnoff's family background and dramatic rise to fame.

Having spent six years as the United Press correspondent in Moscow, Lyons authored several books on economic and social conditions in the Soviet Union, beginning with Moscow Carrousel in 1935. Assignment in Utopia details his years as a journalist in Moscow and his growing disillusionment with Soviet Russia. In a review of the book for Atlantic, Joseph Barber, Jr. wrote: "Let no one who wishes insight into the baffling complexities of contemporary Russia lay aside this book lightly. It abounds in revealing, often comical, incidents of daily life, interlarded with 'inside' stories on the origin and development of outstanding news stories ... which have been instrumental in shaping world opinion about the U.S.S.R. Not least interesting is the chain of seemingly incredible events which led to the author's expulsion from the country."

While responding favorably to the brilliance of his account, a few critics have faulted Lyons for the "occasional bitterness and abusive exaggeration that creep" into the books on his native country, notably The Red Decade: The Stalinist Penetration of America. Reinhold Niebuhr said: "It cannot be denied that [Lyons'] mastery of his subject gives him a special right to be the historian of the 'red decade' ... this curious undercurrent in American life." As Max Eastman expressed it: "The facts are fabulous, and Lyons relates them with a gusto that rises at times almost to hilarity. He has a gift of slashing satire, and no fear of calling foolish acts and famous people by their exact names. But besides that, and somewhat surprisingly combined with it, he possesses sympathetic understanding."

The most recent of his books on Russia, Workers' Paradise Lost: Fifty Years of Soviety Communism—A Bal-

ance Sheet has sold about 300,000 copies in paperback, and won great admiration from the critics. William J. Parente of the Antioch Review calls it "the most complete treatment of the failures and atrocities of Soviet Communism this writer has seen. Unfortunately, it is at times poorly documented, and one must regret the author's polemical vocabulary and his exaggerations. Nevertheless, almost all of Lyons' conclusions about the regime's past would be accepted by the most fastidious scholar." A writer for the National Review believes the book "should be widely distributed throughout our colleges and high schools. The skill of its presentation makes a forbidding subject come to life and renders it fully comprehensible even to novices in Soviet affairs. ... If the American reader can't learn the salient facts about Communism from Eugene Lyons, he never will be able to protect himself against mental entrapment."

BIOGRAPHICAL/CRITICAL SOURCES: Saturday Review, October 9, 1937, January 22, 1938, March 5, 1966; Atlantic, February, 1938; New York Times, September 7, 1941; Nation, September 20, 1941; Commonweal, September 26, 1941; New York Herald Tribune Book Review, November 22, 1953; Book Week, August 9, 1964, February 27, 1966; National Review, November 14, 1967; New York Times Book Review, November 26, 1967; Antioch Review, winter, 1967-68.

*   *   *

LYONS, Thomas Tolman   1934-

PERSONAL: Born June 21, 1934, in Stoneham, Mass.; son of Louis M. (a journalist) and Margaret (Tolman) Lyons; married Eleanor Coneeney, August 31, 1958; children: John Louis, Kathleen Margaret, David Tolman, Joseph Charles. Education: Brown University, student, 1952-54; Harvard University, B.A., 1957, M.A.T., 1958; postgraduate study at Wesleyan University, Stanford University, and Harvard University. Politics: Democrat. Home and office: Phillips Academy, Andover, Mass. 01810.

CAREER: Mount Hermon School for Boys, Gill, Mass., teacher of history, 1958-63; Phillips Academy, Andover, Mass., teacher of American history and urban studies, 1963—. Visiting fellow, Dartmouth College, 1968-69, Phillips Academy, 1969—. Awards, honors: Distinguished Secondary School Teaching Award, Harvard University, 1966.

WRITINGS: (Editor with Edwin C. Rozwenc) Presidential Power in the New Deal, Heath, 1963; (editor with Rozwenc) Realism and Idealism in Wilson's Peace Program, Heath, 1965; (with Rozwenc) Reconstruction and the Race Problem, Heath, 1968; Black Leadership in American History, Addison-Wesley, 1971.

WORK IN PROGRESS: Research for a book on the Warren Supreme Court.

*   *   *

LYTLE, Andrew (Nelson)   1902-

PERSONAL: Born December 26, 1902, in Murfreesboro, Tenn.; son of Robert Logan (a farmer and lumberman) and Lillie Belle (Nelson) Lytle; married Edna Langdon Barker, June 20, 1938 (deceased); children: Pamela (Mrs. James Law), Katherine Anne (Mrs. Talbot Wilson), Lillie Langdon. Education: Sewanee Military Academy, graduate; Exeter College, Oxford, student, 1920; Vanderbilt University, B.A., 1925; Yale University, School of Drama, student, 1927-29. Home: Log Cabin, Monteagle, Tenn. 37356. Office: Sewanee Review, Sewanee, Tenn. 37375.

CAREER: Southwestern College, Memphis, Tenn., lecturer in American history, 1936; University of the South,

Sewanee, Tenn., lecturer in history and managing editor of *Sewanee Review*, 1942-43, lecturer in creative writing, 1961-68, professor of English, 1968—, editor of *Sewanee Review*, 1961—. University of Iowa, Iowa City, School of Writing, lecturer, 1946, acting head, 1947. Lecturer, University of Florida, 1948-61. Lecturer at writers' workshops and conferences at Universities of North Carolina, Oklahoma, Colorado, Utah, Oregon, Florida, Dallas, and at Eastern Kentucky State College, Morehead College, Converse College, Vanderbilt University, Cumberland College, and Jacksonville University. Chairman of humanities seminar, International Seminar at Harvard University, 1958. *Member:* Association of Literary Magazines of America (chairman of admissions committee), South Atlantic Modern Language Association. *Awards, honors:* Guggenheim fellowships for creative work in fiction, 1940-41, 1941-42, 1960-61; *Kenyon Review* fellowship for fiction, 1956; National Foundation on Arts and Letters grant, 1966-67; Litt.D., Kenyon College, 1965, University of Florida, 1970.

WRITINGS: Bedford Forrest and His Critter Company (biography), Minton, Balch, 1931, revised edition with introduction by Lytle, McDowell, Obolensky, 1960; *The Long Night* (novel), Bobbs-Merrill, 1936; *At the Moon's Inn* (novel), Bobbs-Merrill, 1941; *A Name for Evil* (novel), Bobbs-Merrill, 1947; *The Velvet Horn* (novel), McDowell, Obolensky, 1957; *A Novel, a Novella, and Four Stories*, McDowell, Obolensky, 1958; *The Hero with the Private Parts* (literary criticism), Louisiana State University Press, 1966; *Craft and Vision: The Best Fiction from the "Sewanee Review"*, Delacorte, 1971.

Contributor: *I'll Take My Stand: The South and the Agrarian Tradition* (by twelve Southern writers), Harper, 1930; Herbert Agar and Allen Tate, editors, *Who Owns America?*, Houghton, 1936. Work included in *White Folks Primer, American Harvest, Introduction to Literature*, and other anthologies. Contributor to literary reviews.

WORK IN PROGRESS: A Wake for the Living, a memoir to be published by Seymour Lawrence.

SIDELIGHTS: William Hedges describes Lytle as an "aging and agrarian Southern gentleman"; he is also editor of the literary quarterly, *Sewanee Review*, and a novelist and critic better known to fellow critics than to the public. George Core wrote in the *Georgia Review* that "Lytle has yet to receive his proper share of attention.... As the years pass and the Southern renascence is increasingly viewed within the perspective which only time and dispassionate informed criticism and scholarship can bring, one suspects that Andrew Lytle's reputation will grow more solid and enduring. This is not to say that his work has not always been of high order—quite the contrary.... [His] criticism of Faulkner is some of the best we have: it stands in the same distinguished company as that of Brooks and Warren." Core opines, however, that Lytle "is still the working novelist, not the practicing critic," although "he is indeed a fine critical intelligence at work."

Hedges praises Lytle's essays, collected in *The Hero with the Private Parts*, as "repeated instances of modern academic criticism at its best, patient, respectful, precise, intricate and yet dramatic analyses which show how, through the working of the vital principles of a piece of fiction, usually the controlling image or point of view, 'meaning' radiates through its whole system." Hedges mentions "the palling sameness [which] settles over Lytle's criticism.... One comes to feel that Lytle's anti-liberal, Christian bias controls his sense of what the novel is or should be, that its very form, particularly in its post-Jamesian complexity, is, for him, an almost di-

vinely instituted vehicle for conveying a standardized view of the human condition."

In a detailed review of *The Velvet Horn* for *Critique*, Clinton Trowbridge calls the novel "a deeply Christian book.... It is extraordinary because, with great intensity, with a vivid sense of the concrete and actual, it manages to dramatize its concerns. It is a complex and deeply moving work of the symbolic imagination, a work in which symbolic meaning is never seen as apart from the world of particulars in which it is contained. In a very real sense, Lytle has achieved in his art what he says man must experience in his life. In *The Velvet Horn* the Word, indeed, has become flesh."

BIOGRAPHICAL/CRITICAL SOURCES: San Francisco Chronicle, August 10, 1947; *Saturday Review*, August 17, 1957; *Critique*, Volume X, number 2; *Atlantic*, September, 1958; *New York Times*, August 31, 1958; *Wisconsin Studies in Contemporary Literature*, autumn, 1967; *Georgia Review*, summer, 1968; *Mississippi Quarterly*, fall, 1970.

*   *   *

MacARTHUR, D(avid) Wilson 1903-
(David Wilson)

PERSONAL: Born August 29, 1903, in Glasgow, Scotland; son of Alexander Christie (a doctor) and Margaret (Wilson) MacArthur; married Patricia Maud Knox Saunders, June 2, 1956; children: Iain Charles Wilson, Duncan Edward Wilson. *Education:* University of Glasgow, M.A., 1923, M.A. (with honors), 1925; diploma of Jordanhill Teachers' Training College and parchment of Scottish Education Department, 1926. *Home:* Pumula, Stow Rd., Marandellas District, Rhodesia. *Agent:* Curtis Brown Ltd., 13 King St., London W.C. 2, England; and Ann Watkins, Inc., 77 Park Ave., New York, N.Y. 10016.

CAREER: Free-lance author and journalist. *Military service:* Royal Naval Volunteer Reserve, 1939-45; became lieutenant commander. *Member:* Ancient Monuments Society (fellow), Society of Authors.

WRITINGS: Carlyle in Old Age, 1865-1881 (Volume VI of David Alec Wilson's *Life of Carlyle*), Kegan Paul, 1934; *The Road to the Nile* (travel), Collins, 1940, reissued as *The Broad to Benghazi*, 1941; *The Royal Navy*, Collins, 1940; *The Merchant Service Fights Back*, Collins, 1942; *East India Adventure* (history), Collins, 1945; *The River Windrush* (travel), Cassell, 1946, 2nd edition, 1948; *The Young Chevalier* (history), Collins, 1946; *The River Fowey* (travel), Cassell, 1948; *Auto Nomad in Sweden* (travel), Cassell, 1948; *Auto Nomad in Barbary* (travel), Cassell, 1950; *Traders North* (history), Collins, 1951, Knopf, 1952; *Auto Nomad Through Africa* (travel), Cassell, 1951; *The River Doon* (travel), Cassell, 1952; *The River Conway* (travel), Cassell, 1952; *Auto Nomad in Spain* (travel), Cassell, 1953; *The Desert Watches* (travel), Bobbs-Merrill, 1954; *MacDougall's Land*, College Press, 1971.

Novels: *Yellow Stocking*, Cassell, 1925, film edition, Collins, 1927; *Lola of the Isles*, Cassell, 1926; *The Mystery of the "David M,"* Andrew Melrose, 1932; *Landfall*, Andrew Melrose, 1933; *The Quest of the "Stormalong,"* Andrew Melrose, 1934; *They Sailed for Senegal*, Stokes, 1938; *Convict Captain*, Collins, 1939; *The North Patrol*, Collins, 1941; *Daredevil Dick Takes Wings*, Collins, 1941; *Simba Bwana* (Universal Book Club selection), Hurst & Blackett, 1956; *The Road from Chilanga*, Jarrolds, 1957; *Zambesi Adventure*, Collins, 1960; *Harry Hogbin*, Ward, Lock, 1961; *Death at Slack Water*, Ward, Lock, 1962; (under pseudonym David Wilson) *The Search for Geoffrey Goring*, Jenkins, 1962; *The Valley of Hidden Gold*, Collins, 1962; (under pseudonym David Wilson) *Murder in Mozambique*, Jenkins, 1963; *Guns for the Congo,* Collins, 1963; *A Rhino in the Kitchen,* Ward, Lock, 1964; *The Past Dies Hard,* Ward, Lock, 1965.

Contributor of articles and more than five hundred short stories to newspapers and magazines, 1926-39. Fiction editor, *Daily Mail* (London) and *Evening News* (London), 1935; editor, *Rhodesia and Nyasaland Teachers' Association Journal.*

SIDELIGHTS: MacArthur lived in Spain and Morocco in 1934; he has traveled, mainly by car, through Canada, United States, Europe, Africa (including two trips by motor from London to Spain, then from Algeria to South Africa). He is fluent in French, Spanish, and Kaffir; he also knows Portuguese, Italian, Scottish Gaelic, Danish, Swedish, and Zulu. *Avocational interests:* Tree planting and fruit growing (and the education of Rhodesian Africans in the basic principles of farming and husbandry), archery, yachting, game watching, sheep breeding.

* * *

Mac CAIG, Norman (Alexander) 1910-

PERSONAL: Born November 14, 1910, in Edinburgh, Scotland; son of Robert (a chemist) and Joan (Mac Leod) Mac Caig; married Isabel Munro (a school teacher), April 6, 1940; children: Joan Mac Caig Maclean, Ewen. *Education:* Edinburgh University, M.A. (honors in classics), 1932. *Religion:* None. *Home:* 7 Leamington Ter., Edinburgh, Scotland.

CAREER: Teacher in Edinburgh, Scotland, 1933—; now lecturer in English, University of Stirling. *Member:* Scottish Arts Club (Edinburgh; fellow). *Awards, honors:* Arts Council award, 1955, for *Riding Lights;* Society of Authors award, 1964, for work in general.

WRITINGS—All poetry: *Far Cry,* Routledge, 1943; *The Inward Eye,* Routledge, 1946; *Riding Lights,* Hogarth Press, 1955, Macmillan, 1956; *The Sinai Sort,* Macmillan, 1957; (editor) *Honor'd Shade: An Anthology of New Scottish Poetry to Mark the Bicentenary of Robert Burns,* W. & R. Chambers, 1959; *A Common Grace,* Hogarth Press, 1960, Dufour, 1961; *A Round of Applause,* Hogarth Press, 1962, Dufour, 1963; *Measures,* Hogarth Press, 1965, Dufour, 1966; *Surroundings,* Hogarth Press, 1966; *Rings on a Tree,* Hogarth Press, 1968; *A Man in My Position,* Hogarth Press, 1969, Wesleyan University Press, 1970; (editor with Alexander Scott) *Contemporary Scottish Verse, 1959-1969,* Calder & Boyars, 1970. Contributor of poems and articles to many journals.

WORK IN PROGRESS: *Selected Poems,* for Hogarth.

SIDELIGHTS: Mac Caig told *CA:* "Of the arts other than poetry, I am most interested in music, of all kinds. I get great pleasure from fishing, particularly in the Highlands. I can read French, Italian, Latin, Greek, and Gaelic. I have visited France, Italy, and the U.S.A."

* * *

MacCAMPBELL, James C(urtis) 1916-

PERSONAL: Born October 17, 1916, in Plain City, Ohio; son of Lloyd Z. (a farmer) and Mary (McCullough) MacCampbell; married Barbara Barrett (a librarian), May 9, 1942. *Education:* Ohio Wesleyan University, B.A., 1939; Ohio State University, M.A., 1946, Ph.D., 1957; Simmons College, M.S., 1962. *Home:* 12 Mainewood Ave., Orono, Me. 04473. *Office:* Department of Education, University of Maine, Orono, Me. 04473.

CAREER: Teacher, principal, or elementary supervisor in public schools in Ohio, 1939-48; Kent State University, Kent, Ohio, assistant director of University School and assistant professor of eduation, 1948-50; Ohio State University, Columbus, instructor in education, 1950-52; Cleveland Heights Elementary Schools, Cleveland Heights,

Ohio, director, 1952-57; University of Maine, Orono, began as associate professor of education, 1957, university librarian and professor of education, 1962—. *Member:* National Education Association, National Council of Teachers of English, American Association of University Professors, American Library Association, New England Reading Association, Phi Delta Kappa, Phi Kappa Phi.

WRITINGS: (Editor) *Readings in the Language Arts,* Heath, 1963; (with Eleanor Peck) *Focus on Reading,* New England Reading Association, 1964. Editor, New England Reading Association *Journal,* 1960-68.

* * *

MacCANN, Richard Dyer 1920-

PERSONAL: Born August 20, 1920, in Wichita, Kan.; son of Horace S. (a dry goods salesman) and Marion (Dyer) MacCann; married Donnarae Thompson, October 12, 1957. *Education:* University of Kansas, A.B., 1940; Stanford University, M.A., 1942; Harvard University, Ph.D., 1951. *Politics:* Democrat. *Religion:* Christian Scientist. *Home:* 717 Normandy Dr., Iowa City, Iowa 52240.

CAREER: *Christian Science Monitor,* staff correspondent in Los Angeles, Calif., 1950-56, Hollywood correspondent, 1950-60; University of Southern California, Los Angeles, assistant professor of cinema, 1957-62; U.S. Department of State, Cultural Exchange Program, film writing adviser to Republic of Korea in Seoul, 1963; Subscription Television, Inc., producer, program department, 1964-65; University of Kansas, Lawrence, visiting professor, 1965-66, associate professor, 1966-69, professor of speech and journalism, 1969-70; University of Iowa, Iowa City, professor of film, 1970—. Member of steering committee, Aspen Film Conference, Aspen, Colo., 1963, 1964. *Military service:* U.S. Army, 6th Armored Division, 1942-45; spent two years in England, France, Germany, taught at Shrivenham American University, 1945. *Member:* University Film Association, Society for Cinema Studies, Phi Beta Kappa.

WRITINGS: (With Michael Jorrin) *Good Reading about Motion Pictures: An Annotated List of Books in English,* University of Southern California, 1957, 2nd edition published as *Good Reading about Motion Pictures: The 100 Best Books in English,* 1962; *Hollywood in Transition,* Houghton, 1962; *Film and Society* (textbook), Scribner, 1964; (editor) *Film: A Montage of Theories,* Dutton, 1966. Writer and director of "Degas: Master of Motion," color film produced by University of Southern California, 1960. Contributor of articles to *Encyclopaedia Britannica, Yale Review, Film Quarterly,* and other publications. Editor, *Cinema Journal.*

WORK IN PROGRESS: *Democracy and the Documentary Film,* for Harvard University Press; *The New Film Index,* a bibliography of articles about cinema, for Dutton.

SIDELIGHTS: MacCann abandoned political science in favor of communication after writing his doctoral dissertation on the federal government use of films, 1908-51; he is especially interested in the documentary film and in the relationship between the motion picture and American personality traits and cultural aspirations.

* * *

MacCLOSKEY, Monro 1902-

PERSONAL: Born May 28, 1902, in Fort Worden, Wash.; son of Manus (a brigadier general, U.S. Army) and Sara (Monro) MacCloskey; married Elizabeth Heard, September 8, 1925. *Education:* U.S. Military Academy, B.S., 1924; National War College, Washington,

D.C., graduate, 1948. *Home:* 5064 Lowell St. N.W., Washington, D.C. 20016.

CAREER: Entered real estate business in Chicago, Ill., 1924, while serving as Reserve and National Guard officer. U.S. Army and U.S. Air Force, active duty, 1941-57, becoming brigadier general, 1950; during World War II served successively with headquarters staff of U.S. Army in London, 1942, Northwest African Air Force and Mediterranean Air Command, 1943, 15th Air Force in Italy, 1944; flew fifty combat missions while in command of heavy bomb squadrons and groups engaged in counterinsurgency operations in Europe, 1944-45; post-war assignments included chief of Air Intelligence Policy Division, U.S. Air Force Headquarters, Washington, D.C., 1948-49, U.S. air attache, Paris, France, 1949-52, commanding general of 28th Air Division (Defense), Hamilton Air Force Base, Calif., 1954-57; retired, 1957. Assistant to president of Crosley Division, AVCO Manufacturing Corp., 1958-61.

MEMBER: Army and Navy Club (Washington, D.C.), Corinthian Yacht Club (commodore, 1961-62). *Awards, honors*—Military: Silver Star; Legion of Merit with oak-leaf cluster; Distinguished Flying Cross; Air Medal with seven oak-leaf clusters; Distinguished Unit Citation with oak-leaf cluster; nine Bronze Stars; Bronze Service Arrowhead; Army Commendation Medal with oak-leaf cluster; Order of Partisan Star, Class I; Decoration of Sultan of Morocco; French Legion of Honor (twice); two Croix de Guerre with gold star; two Croix de Guerre with palm.

WRITINGS—All published by Rosen Press, except as indicated: *Your Future in the Air Force,* 1964; *How to Qualify for the Service Academies,* 1964; *Reserve Officers Training Corps: Campus Pathways to Service Commissions,* 1965; *You and the Draft,* 1965; *Secret Air Missions,* 1966; *The American Intelligence Community,* 1967; *The Infamous Wall of Berlin,* 1967; *Pacts for Peace: UN, NATO, SEATO, CENTO, and OAS,* 1967; *The United States Air Force,* Praeger, 1967; *From Gasbags to Spaceships: The Story of the U.S. Air Force,* 1968; *Hallowed Ground: Our National Cemeteries,* 1968; *Our National Attic: The Library of Congress, the Smithsonian Institution, the National Archives,* 1968; *Alert the Fifth Force: Counterinsurgency, Unconventional Warfare, and Psychological Operations of the United States Air Force in Special Air Warfare,* 1969; *Reilly's Battery: A Story of the Boxer Rebellion,* 1969; *Achieving Victory—World War II: A Behind-the-Scenes Account,* 1970; *Planning for Victory—World War II: A Behind-the-Scenes Account,* 1970; *Torch and the Twelfth Air Force,* 1971; *Rearming the French in World War II,* 1972. Contributor to magazines, newspapers, and service journals.

WORK IN PROGRESS: Further writing on military subjects.

AVOCATIONAL INTERESTS: Yachting, model railroading, and amateur radio (call letters: W3MVR).

*   *   *

MacDONALD, Charles B(rown)   1922-

PERSONAL: Born November 23, 1922, in Little Rock, S.C.; son of K.L. and Mary (MacQueen) MacDonald. *Education:* Presbyterian College, A.B., 1942; graduate study at Columbia University, 1946, McGill University, 1947, University of Missouri, 1947, and George Washington University, 1948. *Home:* 1200 North Nash St., Arlington, Va. 22209. *Agent:* Blanche C. Gregory, 2 Tudor City Pl., New York, N.Y. 10017. *Office:* Office of Chief of Military History, Department of the Army, Washington, D.C. 20315.

CAREER: Presbyterian College, Clinton, S.C., instructor in English, 1946-47; Department of the Army, Office of Chief of Military History, Washington, D.C., historian, 1948-52, chief of European section, 1952-56, chief of general history branch, 1956-67, deputy chief historian, 1967—. *Military service:* U.S. Army, 1942-46; became captain; received Purple Heart, Bronze Star, Silver Star. U.S. Army Reserve, 1946—; now colonel. *Awards, honors:* Secretary of the Army research and study fellowship in military history, 1957-58; Litt.D., Presbyterian College, 1967.

WRITINGS: Company Commander, Infantry Journal Press, 1947, revised edition, Ballantine, 1961; (with Sidney T. Mathews) *Three Battles: Arnaville, Altuzzo, and Schmidt,* U.S. Government Printing Office, 1952; (contributor) Kent R. Greenfield, editor, *Command Decisions,* Harcourt, 1961; *The Siegfried Line Campaign,* Office of Chief of Military History, Department of the Army, 1963; *The Battle of the Huertgen Forest,* Lippincott, 1963; *The Mighty Endeavor: American Armed Forces in the European Theater in World War II,* Oxford University Press, 1969; (contributor) Maurice Matloff, editor, *American Military History,* U.S. Government Printing Office, 1969; *Airborne,* Ballantine, 1970 (published in England as *By Air to Battle,* Macdonald & Co., 1970); *The Last Offensive,* U.S. Government Printing Office, in press. Contributor of articles on military subjects to *Encyclopedia Americana, Encyclopaedia Britannica, Grolier Encyclopedia, New York Times Magazine,* and various Army publications.

AVOCATIONAL INTERESTS: Skiing.

BIOGRAPHICAL/CRITICAL SOURCES: Christian Science Monitor, November 29, 1969; *National Review,* December 2, 1969.

*   *   *

MacDONALD, Malcolm John   1901-

PERSONAL: Born August 17, 1901, in Lossiemouth, Morayshire, Scotland; son of James Ramsay and Margaret Ethel (Gladstone) MacDonald; married Audrey Fellowes Rowley, December 6, 1946; children: Fiona. *Education:* Queen's College, Oxford, M.A., 1924. *Religion:* Presbyterian. *Home:* Raspit Hill, Ivy Hatch, Sevenoaks, Kent, England. *Agent:* Peter Jansen Smith, 2 Caxton St., London S.W.1, England.

CAREER: Reader's Library, London, England, editor, 1925-29; London County Council, London, member, 1927-30; member of Parliament, 1929-45; British Government, parliamentary under-secretary in Dominions Office, 1931-35, Secretary of State for Dominion Affairs, 1935-38, 1938-39, Secretary of State for Colonies, 1935, 1938-40, Minister of Health, 1940-41, United Kingdom High Commissioner in Canada, 1941-46, governor-general of Malayan Union and Singapore, 1946, governor-general of Malaya, Singapore, and British Borneo, 1946-48, Commissioner-General of the United Kingdom in Southeast Asia, 1948-55, High Commissioner for the United Kingdom in India, 1955-60, governor of Kenya, 1963, governor-general of Kenya, 1963-64, British High Commissioner in Kenya, 1964-65, British special representative in East and Central Africa, 1963-66, special representative in Africa, 1966-69. Special ambassador at inauguration of Indonesian Republic, 1949; special envoy to Sudan and Somalia, 1967. United Kingdom representative, Southeast Asia Defence Treaty Council, 1955; leader of British delegation and co-chairman, International Conference on Laos, 1961-62. Freeman, City of Singapore, 1955, Burgh of Lossiemouth, 1969. Honorary fellow, Queens College, Oxford University. Rhodes trustee, 1948-57; chancellor, University of Malaya, 1949-61; visitor of Royal College, Nairobi, Kenya, 1963-64. *Member:* Brook's Club, Royal

Island Club (Singapore). *Awards, honors:* Honorary doctorates from University of Hanoi, University of Hong Kong, University of Singapore, and from universities in North America.

WRITINGS: Bird Watching at Lossiemouth, Courant & Courier Office, 1934; *Down North,* Oxford University Press (London), 1943, reissued as *Canadian North,* Oxford University Press, 1945, published in America as *Down North: A View of Northwest Canada,* Farrar & Rinehart, 1944; *The Birds of Brewery Creek,* Oxford University Press, 1947; *Borneo People,* J. Cape, 1956, Knopf, 1958; *Angkor,* J. Cape, 1958, Praeger, 1959; *Birds in My Indian Garden,* J. Cape, 1960, Knopf, 1961; *Birds in the Sun,* Witherby, 1962 (published in India as *Birds in the Sun: Beautiful Birds of India,* D.B. Taraporevala Sons, 1962); *Treasure of Kenya,* Collins, 1965, Putnam, 1966; *People and Places: Random Reminiscences,* Collins, 1969; *Thoughts on the Human Family* (lecture), Longmans for the University of Essex, 1970; *Titans and Others,* Collins, 1972.

AVOCATIONAL INTERESTS: Ornithology, collecting, and skiing.

BIOGRAPHICAL/CRITICAL SOURCES: Punch, May 21, 1969.

* * *

MACDONALD, Robert M(unro) 1923-

PERSONAL: Born July 9, 1923, in Glasgow, Scotland; son of Robert (a carpenter) and Sidney (Wilson) Macdonald; married Mado R. Ambach (an economist), June 22, 1953; children: Laura Anne, Kevin Angus. *Education:* Yale University, B.A. (honors), 1950, M.A., 1951, Ph.D., 1955. *Home:* 19 Rip Rd., Hanover, N.H. 03755. *Office:* Amos Tuck School of Business Administration, Dartmouth College, Hanover, N.H. 03755.

CAREER: University of California, Los Angeles, assistant professor of economics, 1953-56; Yale University, New Haven, Conn., assistant professor of economics, 1956-59; Dartmouth College, Amos Tuck School of Business Administration, Hanover, N.H., associate professor, 1959-65, professor of business economics, 1965—, associate dean, 1970—. *Military service:* British Royal Navy, Fleet Air Arm, 1940-45; became sublieutenant. *Member:* American Economic Association, Industrial Relations Research Association, Phi Beta Kappa.

WRITINGS: (Contributor) Lloyd G. Reynolds and Cynthia H. Taft, *Evolution of Wage Structure,* Yale University Press, 1956; *Unionism and the Wage Structure in the United States Pulp and Paper Industry,* University of California, 1958; *Collective Bargaining in the Automobile Industry: A Study of Wage Structure and Competitive Relations,* Yale University Press, 1963.

WORK IN PROGRESS: Problems in measuring the economic influence of trade unionism; the role of fringe benefits in the compensation system and wage structure; industrial relations systems.

* * *

MacEWEN, Gwendolyn 1941-

PERSONAL: Born September 1, 1941, in Toronto, Ontario, Canada; daughter of Alick James and Elsie (Mitchell) MacEwen.

CAREER: Children's Public Library, Toronto, Ontario, part-time assistant librarian, 1960—. *Awards, honors:* Governor General's award, 1970, for *The Shadow-Maker.*

WRITINGS: Selah (poems), Aleph, 1961; *The Drunken Clock* (poems), Aleph, 1961; *Julian the Magician* (novel), Corinth Books, 1963; *The Rising Fire* (poems), Contact Press, 1963; *A Breakfast for Barbarians* (poems), Ryerson, 1966; *The Shadow-Maker* (poems), Macmillan (Canada), 1970. Contributor of poetry to *Poetry 64* and many literary magazines, and to Canadian Broadcasting Co. poetry broadcasts.

WORK IN PROGRESS: A novel.

AVOCATIONAL INTERESTS: Magic, myth, and ancient history.

* * *

MacINTYRE, Elisabeth 1916-

PERSONAL: Born November 1, 1916, in Sydney, Australia; daughter of Norman John (a grazier) and Laura (Rendall) MacIntyre; married John Eldershaw (an artist), August 21, 1950; children: Jane. *Education:* Attended Sydney Church of England Girls Grammar School; East Sydney Technical College, art student. *Religion:* Christian Science. *Agent:* Monica McCall, Inc., 667 Madison Ave., New York, N.Y. 10021.

CAREER: Lever's Advertising Agency, Lintas, Australia, designer, 1937-42; free-lance artist, 1942—. Writer and illustrator of books for children; cartoonist for magazines and television, including "Ambrose Kangaroo" series carried by Australian Broadcasting Commission and British Broadcasting Corp.; comic-strip artist.

WRITINGS: Self-illustrated, except as indicated: *Ambrose Kangaroo,* Scribner, 1942; *The Handsome Duckling,* Dawfox, 1942; *The Black Lamb,* Dawfox, 1942; *The Forgetful Elephant,* Dawfox, 1942; *The Willing Donkey,* Dawfox, 1942; *Ambrose Kangaroo Has a Busy Day,* Australian Consolidated Press, 1944; *Susan Who Lives in Australia,* Scribner, 1944; *Katherine,* Harrap, 1946; *Willie's Woollies: The Story of Australian Wool,* Georgian House, 1951; *Mr. Koala Bear,* Scribner, 1954, new edition, Angus & Robertson, 1966; *Jane Likes Pictures,* Scribner, 1959; (illustrator) Ruth Fenner, *The Story House,* Angus & Robertson, 1962; *Hugh's Zoo,* Knopf, 1964; *Ambrose Kangaroo Goes to Town,* Angus & Robertson, 1964; *The Affable, Amiable Bulldozer Man,* Knopf, 1965; *Ninji's Magic,* illustrated by Mamoru Funai, Knopf, 1966. Contributor to stories and articles to magazines.

WORK IN PROGRESS: Research on Malaya.

SIDELIGHTS: "Simple and lighthearted as my books may be, they are a sincere attempt to say something quite serious—either a microcosm of another way of life, or an idea which, I like to think, is something worth saying.... I never know whether to describe myself as a writer who draws, or an artist who writes. Most of all I enjoy arranging words and pictures so that each complement the other, working on one dummy book after another, till it all looks so simple, that I wonder however it could have taken so much time!"

BIOGRAPHICAL/CRITICAL SOURCES: Young Reader's Review, March, 1967.

* * *

MACK, Maynard 1909-

PERSONAL: Born October 27, 1909, in Hillsdale, Mich.; son of Jesse Floyd and Pearl (Vore) Mack; married Florence Brocklebank, August 5, 1933; children: Prudence Allen (Mrs. T. Cuyler Young), Sara Bennett (Mrs. George T. Amis), Maynard. *Education:* Taft School, graduate; Yale University, B.A., 1932, Ph.D., 1936. *Religion:* Episcopalian. *Home:* 273 Willow St., New Haven, Conn. 06511. *Office:* 1314 Davenport College, Yale University, New Haven, Conn. 06520.

CAREER: Yale University, New Haven, Conn., instructor, 1936-40, assistant professor, 1940-45, associate professor, 1945-48, professor of English, 1948—. Walker-

Ames Lecturer at University of Washington, Seattle, 1956; Alexander Lecturer at University of Toronto, 1963; Beckman Visiting Professor at University of California, Berkeley, 1964-65; Lord Northcliffe Lecturer at University of London, 1972. New Haven (Conn.) Board of Education, vice-president, 1954-59; consultant in comparative literature to "College English," 1961; member of advisory council, Modern Humanities Research Association, 1971—. Trustee of Hopkins Grammar School, Berkeley Divinity School, Shakespeare Association of America, and American Shakespeare Festival Theatre Association. *Member:* International Association of University Professors of English, American Academy of Arts and Sciences, Modern Language Association of America, Renaissance Society of America, Elizabethan Club, Malone Society, Phi Beta Kappa. *Awards, honors:* Yale University prize for poems, 1932, for *For All Our Fathers, Gentlemen!,* and 1934, for *Mister Scoggins' Saturday Night;* Guggenheim fellow, 1943-43 and 1965; Ford faculty fellow, 1952-53; Fulbright senior research fellow, University of London, 1959-60; senior fellow, National Endowment for the Humanities, 1968-69; fellow, Center for Advanced Study in the Behavioral Sciences, 1971-72; senior research fellow, Clark Library, Los Angeles, 1974.

WRITINGS: For All Our Fathers, Gentlemen! (poem), Profile Press (New Haven), 1932; *Mister Scoggins' Saturday Night* (poem), City Printing Co. (New Haven), 1934; *King Lear in Our Time* (three Beckman lectures given at University of California, 1964-65), University of California Press, Berkeley, 1965; (with Robert Whitney Boynton) *Introduction to the Poem,* Hayden Book Co., 1965, 2nd edition, revised, 1972; (with Boynton) *Introduction to the Short Story,* Hayden Book Co., 1965, 2nd edition, revised, 1972; (with Boynton) *Introduction to the Play,* Hayden Book Co., 1969; *The Garden and the City: Retirement and Politics in the Later Poetry of Pope, 1731-1743,* University of Toronto press, 1969.

Editor: (And author of introduction and notes) Henry Fielding, *The History of the Adventures of Joseph Andrews and His Friend, Mr. Abraham Adams,* Rinehart, 1949, paperback edition published as *Joseph Andrews;* Alexander Pope, *An Essay on Man,* Twickenham edition, Volume 3, pt. 1, Yale University Press, 1951; *Milton* (Volume 4 of *English Masterpieces*), Prentice-Hall, 1957, 2nd edition, 1961; *The Augustans* (Volume 5 of *English Masterpieces*), Prentice-Hall, 1957, 2nd edition, 1961; (with Leonard Dean and William Frost) *Modern Poetry* (Volume 7 of *English Masterpieces*), Prentice-Hall, 1958, 2nd edition, 1961; William Shakespeare, *The Tragedy of Antony and Cleopatra,* Penguin, 1960, revised edition, 1970; *The Morgan and Houghton Library Manuscripts of Alexander Pope's "Essay on Man"* (Roxburghe Club), Yale University Press, 1962; *Essential Articles for the Study of Alexander Pope,* Archon Books, 1964, revised and enlarged edition, 1968; (with Boynton) *Images of Man,* Prentice-Hall, 1964; William Shakespeare, *The History of Henry IV: Part One,* New American Library, 1965; (and author of introduction) *The Poems of Alexander Pope: Translations of Homer,* four volumes, Twickenham edition, Yale University Press, Volumes 7-8: *The Iliad,* 1967, Volumes 9-10: *The Odyssey,* 1967, index, 1969; (with Ian Gregor) *Imagined Worlds: Essays on Some English Novels and Novelists in Honour of John Butt,* Barnes & Noble, 1968.

General editor: *English Masterpieces: An Anthology of Imaginative Literature from Chaucer to T.S. Eliot,* eight volumes, Prentice-Hall, 1950, 2nd edition, 1961; (with others) *World Masterpieces,* two volumes, Norton, 1956, revised editions, 1965, 1973, continental edition (non-English literature), 1962, enlarged continental edition, 1966. Also editor-in-chief of "Twentieth Century Views" essay series, Prentice-Hall, 1962—, and of "Twentieth Century Interpretations" series, Prentice-Hall, 1968—; member of editorial board, *Studies in English Literature,* 1962—.

Contributor: James L. Clifford and Louis A. Landa, editors, *Pope and His Contemporaries,* Clarendon Press, 1949; Cleanth Brooks, editor, *Tragic Themes in Western Literature,* Yale University Press, 1955; John Russell Brown and Bernard Harris, editors, *Jacobean Theatre,* Edward Arnold, 1960, St. Martin's, 1961; Richard Hosley, editor, *Essays on Shakespeare and Elizabethan Drama,* University of Missouri Press, 1962. Also script writer and teacher for four films on *Hamlet,* produced for Council for a Television Course in the Humanities under the auspices of the Ford Foundation.

SIDELIGHTS: In a review of several studies of Shakespeare's *King Lear,* Charles T. Harrison writes that "none is better than Maynard Mack's *King Lear in Our Time.* It is a small volume of condensed but fairly informal talk about *Lear;* in their original cast the essays were lectures. As the title suggests, Professor Mack is centrally concerned with the acute relevance of the play to the twentieth-century world. I think he succeeds in explaining its perpetual relevance: to primitive Britain, to Elizabethan England, to contemporary Europe or America. . . . The second essay, 'Archtype, Parable, and Vision,' must be one of the most humane treatments of literary sources ever composed by a scholar. It makes no effort to pin down detailed indebtednesses. Rather, it informs or reminds the reader of the great range of literary kinds that constitute Elizabethan culture; and it reminds us that Shakespeare's own culture was universal." James Sandoe considers the book "ultimately a private view and a lay sermon, learned, gracefully written," and Terence Hawkes believes it to be "important because its argument that the issues of *King Lear* mirror those of our own day, and in a sense define them, brings the role of drama in our society opportunely into focus."

George Dimock of *Yale Review,* among others, was delighted with the publication in 1967 of *The Poems of Alexander Pope: Translations of Homer.* He mentioned Mack's "heroic task of editorship," and wrote: "Now, after some fifteen years of effort by many hands, the experience of reading Pope's Homer as he meant to have it read is available to all. . . . Maynard Mack's general introduction is excellent. . . . [He] has been able to chase down all but a very few of Pope's vague, not to say lordly, references to other writers in his notes. There are more than four thousand of these and Mack writes that if he had to do it again he is not sure he would make the effort. If he means this, we can only be grateful that he has come through on his first attempt."

Mack's most recent study of Pope, *The Garden and the City,* received similar acclaim from critics. "Most books fit into categories," said a reviewer for *Spectator,* "but this one not readily. At a glance, it is an elegant edition for the coffee-table. . . . Yet one soon realises that this is no coffee-table book for the unlearned. Professor Mack adroitly interweaves much erudition with a little avowed speculation, so as at least to suggest that Pope's loving attention to his villa had its Palladian and indeed perhaps its Platonic overtones. . . . There is a beautiful completeness in the synthesis this book creates: in a certain sense, its varied learning comes out with something that is almost a poetic vision of Pope's last phase. This is indeed far from the coffee-table."

AVOCATIONAL INTERESTS: Gardening, photography.

BIOGRAPHICAL/CRITICAL SOURCES: Yale Alumni Magazine, February, 1959; *New Haven Register,* April 8, 1959; *Yale Review,* winter, 1964, summer, 1967, autumn, 1968; *Times Literary Supplement,* August 25, 1966, December 7, 1967; *Sewanee Review,* autumn, 1967; *Spectator,* February 28, 1970.

MacKAY, Robert A(lexander)   1894-

PERSONAL: Born January 2, 1894, in Victoria County, Ontario, Canada; son of Andrew (a farmer) and Margaret (Jamieson) MacKay; married Mary Kathleen Junkin (deceased); children: Mary Margaret, William Andrew, Janet Kathleen MacKay Brown, Edith Christine MacKay Haliburton. Education: University of Toronto, B.A., 1920; Princeton University, Ph.D., 1924. Office: Carleton University, Ottawa, Ontario, Canada.

CAREER: Cornell University, Ithaca, N.Y., assistant professor of government, 1925-27; Dalhousie University, Halifax, Nova Scotia, professor of political science, 1927-47; Canadian Department of External Affairs, Ottawa, Ontario, head of division, 1947-51, assistant undersecretary, 1951-53, associate undersecretary, 1954-55; Canadian ambassador to United Nations, 1955-58; Canadian ambassador to Norway and Iceland, 1958-61; retired, 1962. Member, Royal Commission on Dominion-Provincial Relations, 1937-40. Visiting professor of political science, Carleton University, 1962—. Military service: Canadian Army, 1915-19; mentioned in dispatches. Member: Royal Society of Canada (fellow), Canadian Political Science Association (president, 1944), Canadian Historical Association, Canadian Institute of International Affairs. Awards, honors: LL.D., Dalhousie University, 1953; Medal of Service, Order of Canada, 1970.

WRITINGS: The Unreformed Senate of Canada, Oxford University Press, 1926, revised edition, McClelland & Stewart, 1963; Changes in the Legal Structure of the British Commonwealth of Nations, Carnegie Endowment for International Peace, 1931; (with S.A. Saunders) The Modern World: Political and Economic, Ryerson, 1935, revised edition published as The Modern World: A Guide to World Conditions and the Political and Economic Problems of the Day, 1937; (with E.B. Rogers) Canada Looks Abroad, Oxford University Press, 1938; (editor) The Paris Peace Conference of 1919, Queen's Printer of Ottawa, 1938; (with others) Treatment of Post-War Germany, edited by Ralph Flenley, Ryerson, 1943; (editor) Newfoundland: Economic, Diplomatic and Strategic Studies, Oxford University Press, 1946; A Review of the Educational Activities of Industries, Association of Technical Institutions, 1951; (editor) Speeches and Documents of Canadian Foreign Policy, 1945-1954, McClelland & Stewart, 1971.

*   *   *

MACKENZIE-GRIEVE, Averil (Salmond)   1903-

PERSONAL: Born April 3, 1903, in Rotherfield, Sussex, England; daughter of Robert and Harriet (Armstrong) Mackenzie-Grieve; married Cyril D. Le Gros Clark (onetime chief secretary of Sarawak; deceased); married second husband, John J. Keevil (surgeon commander, Royal Navy; deceased). Education: Studied with private tutors, in continental convents, and at art schools in England and Italy. Politics: Liberal. Religion: Christian. Home: George Hill House, Robertsbridge, Sussex, England.

CAREER: Author, wood engraver, and sometime freelance broadcaster, journalist, and lecturer. During World War II did censorship work in London, England, and also served four years in Italian Section of British Broadcasting Corp. European Service. Member: Authors Society (London). Awards, honors: Officer of Order of St. John of Jerusalem for published works on the Order's history.

WRITINGS: (Illustrator with woodcuts) Owen Rutter, Fryer of the Bounty, Golden Cockerel, 1939; Sacrifice to Mars (novel), Hutchinson, 1940; (illustrator with woodcuts) Owen Rutter, The Land of Saint Joan, Methuen, 1941; The Last Years of the English Slave Trade, Liverpool, 1750-1807, Putnam, 1941; (translator with Huldine V.

Beamish) Anders Sparrman, A Voyage Round the World with Captain James Cook, Golden Cockerel, 1944; (author of foreword and illustrator) Samuel Johnson, The New London Letter Writer, Golden Cockerel, 1948; The Brood of Time (novel), Hutchinson, 1949; (editor, translator, and annotator) Camillo Spreti, Description of the Island of Malta and a Brief Treatise on Knightly Behavior, Order of St. John of Jerusalem, 1950; The Waterfall (novel), Hutchinson, 1950; The Great Accomplishment, Bles, 1953; Clara Novello, 1818-1908 (biography) Bles, 1955; A Race of Green Ginger (autobiography), Putnam, 1959; Aspects of Elba and Other Islands of the Tuscan Archipelago (history), J. Cape, 1964; Time and Chance (autobiography), Bles, 1970.

Contributor of articles on colonial history to Chambers's Encyclopaedia, Country Life, Crown Colonist, and other periodicals; reviewer for Sunday Times, Times Literary Supplement, and Corona.

WORK IN PROGRESS: Research (reading and travel) into the history of the Mediterranean, particularly Spain and Italy.

SIDELIGHTS: Miss Mackenzie-Grieve researched for four years in Italian and Spanish archives and in private collections in Italy before writing her book on Tuscan Archipelago. She lived in Borneo for twelve years; she speaks Italian, French, German, "rusty Malay and still rustier Chinese."

*   *   *

MACKESY, Piers G(erald)   1924-

PERSONAL: Born September 15, 1924, in Cults, Aberdeenshire, Scotland; son of Pierse Joseph (a major general, British Army) and Leonora (Cook) Mackesy; married Sarah Davies, December 21, 1957; children: William, Catherine, Serena. Education: Wellington College, student, 1938-42; Christ Church, Oxford, B.A., 1950; Oriel College, Oxford, D.Phil., 1953; Harvard University, Commonwealth Fund fellow, 1953-54. Home: Parrotts, Wootton, Woodstock, Oxford, England. Office: Pembroke College, Oxford, England.

CAREER: Pembroke College, Oxford University, Oxford, England, fellow, 1954—. Visiting fellow, Institute for Advanced Study, Princeton, N.J., 1961-62. Military service: British Army, 1943-47.

WRITINGS: The War in the Mediterranean, 1803-1810, Harvard University Press, 1957; (contributor) Michael Howard, editor, Wellingtonian Studies, Wellington College, 1959; The War for America, 1775-83, Harvard University Press, 1964. Contributor to Mariner's Mirror, military history journals.

WORK IN PROGRESS: A study of the Younger Pitt's war ministry, 1798-1802; a study of the Narvik operations in 1940.

AVOCATIONAL INTERESTS: Riding, fox hunting, art.

*   *   *

MACKINNON, Charles Roy   1924-
(Vivian Donald, Rory MacAlpin, Graham Montrose, Hilary Rose, Charles Stuart, Iain Torr)

PERSONAL: Born November 26, 1924, in Scotland; son of Robert Kenneth Leo and Elizabeth (Gauley) Mackinnon; married Evelyn Joan Brown, July 24, 1947; children: Kathryn Deirdre Eve, Fionna Vivienne, Aline Iona. Agent: Charles V. Jackson, Kildare House, 91 Church St., Edmonton, London, England. Office address: C.M.S. (Nigeria) Bookshops, P.O. Box 174, Lagos, Nigeria, West Africa. Address: c/o National Westminster Bank Ltd., 86 High St., Oxford, England.

CAREER: C.M.S. (Nigeria) Bookshops, Lagos, trade manager, 1958—. Military service: Royal Air Force, 1943-48, 1951-58; became flight lieutenant. Member: Royal Society of Arts (fellow), Society of Antiquaries of Scotland (fellow).

WRITINGS: The Clan Mackinnon: A Short History, William Culross & Son, 1958; Tartans and Highland Dress, Collins, 1961; The Highlands in History, Collins, 1961; Scotland's Heraldry, Collins, 1962; The Observer's Book of Heraldry, Warne, 1966.

Under pseudonym Vivian Donald: Better a Neighbour, Ward, Lock, 1962; A Far Cry, Ward, Lock, 1963; Highland Reel, Hurst & Blackett, 1967; Island Paradise, Hurst & Blackett, 1968; Love on Location, Hurst & Blackett, 1968; The Roots of Love, Hurst & Blackett, 1970.

Under pseudonym Iain Torr: Westering Home, Hurst & Blackett, 1963; The Hills of Home, R. Hale, 1964; A Time of Change, Hurst & Blackett, 1965; No Room for Love, R. Hale, 1966; When I Give, Hurst & Blackett, 1966; Sundown, Hurst & Blackett, 1968; The Long Road Home, Hurst & Blackett, 1969; Haven of Peace, Hurst & Blackett, 1970.

Under pseudonym Charles Stuart: Highland Fling, R. Hale, 1964; Diplomatic Baggage, Hurst & Blackett, 1969; Love Royal, Hurst & Blackett, 1970.

Under pseudonym Hilary Rose: Island Rhapsody, R. Hale, 1964; The Rose of Loremia, R. Hale, 1965; Love in Avalon, R. Hale, 1966; Queen's Love, R. Hale, 1966; Cupid's Advocate, R. Hale, 1968; The Golden Island, R. Hale, 1969; A Love Affair, R. Hale, 1969; Runaway Love, R. Hale, 1969.

Also author of "Angel Brown" crime series, under pseudonym Graham Montrose. Contributor of a serial and occasional contributor of short stories to Amber. Book reviewer, Sunday Times of Nigeria. Conducts monthly television programs on books for Nigeria Television Services.

WORK IN PROGRESS: More novels.

* * *

MacLEISH, Archibald 1892-

PERSONAL: Born May 7, 1892, in Glencoe, Ill.; son of Andrew (a partner in Chicago department store of Carson, Pirie, Scott & Co.) and Martha (Hillard) MacLeish; married Ada Hitchcock (a singer), June 21, 1916; children: Kenneth, Brewster Hitchcock (deceased), Mary Hillard, William Hitchcock. Education: Attended Hotchkiss School; Yale University, A.B., 1915; Harvard University, LL.B., 1919. Home: Conway, Mass.

CAREER: Poet, who taught constitutional law at Harvard University, Cambridge, Mass., for one year (1919), then practiced law with firm of Choate, Hall & Stewart, in Boston, Mass., 1920-23. Gave up law to live and write in France, 1923-28; on return to United States settled in Conway, Mass. Spent part of 1929 in Mexico; staff member of Fortune, 1929-38; named first curator of Niemann Collection of Contemporary Journalism at Harvard University, Cambridge, Mass., and adviser to Niemann fellows, 1938. Admitted to U.S. Supreme Court Bar, 1942. In public phase of career served as Librarian of Congress, 1939-44, director of Office of Facts and Figures, 1941-42, assistant director of Office of War Information, 1942-43, Assistant Secretary of State, 1944-45, American delegate to Conference of Allied Ministers of Education in London, 1944. Served as chairman of U.S. delegation to London conference drafting UNESCO constitution, 1945, as first U.S. delegate to General Conference of UNESCO in Paris, 1946, and first U.S. member of Executive Council of UNESCO. In 1949 MacLeish returned

to Harvard University as Boylston Professor of Rhetoric and Oratory, teaching courses in poetry and creative writing until 1962; now Boylston Professor Emeritus. Cambridge University, Rede Lecturer, 1942; U.S. Department of State lecturer in Europe, 1957; Simpson Lecturer, Amherst College, 1964-67. Became trustee of Sarah Lawrence College, Bronxville, N.Y., in 1949, and elected trustee of Museum of Modern Art, New York, N.Y., 1940. Military service: U.S. Army, Field Artillery, 1917-18; served in France, became captain.

MEMBER: American Academy of Arts and Letters (president, 1953-56), National Institute of Arts and Letters, Academy of American Poets (fellow, 1966), League of American Writers (chairman, 1937), National Committee for an Effective Congress Commission on Freedom of the Press, Phi Beta Kappa, Century Club (New York), Tavern Club and Somerset Club (Boston). Awards, honors—Public: Commander, Legion of Honor (France), 1946; Commander, el Sol del Peru, 1947. Literary: John Reed Memorial prize, 1929; Shelley Memorial Award for Poetry, 1932; Pulitzer Prize in poetry for Conquistador, 1933; Golden Rose Trophy of New England Poetry Club, 1934; Levinson Prize for group of poems published in Poetry, 1941; Bollingen Prize in Poetry of Yale University Library, 1952, Pulitzer Prize in poetry, 1953, and National Book Award in poetry, 1953, all for Collected Poems: 1917-1952; Boston Arts Festival poetry award, 1956; Sarah Josepha Hale Award, 1958; Chicago Poetry Day Poet, 1958; Antoinette Perry Award in drama, 1959, and Pulitzer Prize in drama, 1959, for J.B.: A Play in Verse; Academy Award (best screenplay) for Eleanor Roosevelt Story, 1966. Academic: M.A. from Tufts University, 1932; LL.D. from Johns Hopkins University, 1941, University of California, 1943, Queen's University at Kingston, 1948, Carleton College, 1956, and Amherst College, 1963; Litt.D. from Colby College, 1938, Wesleyan University, 1938, Yale University, 1939, University of Pennsylvania, 1941, University of Illinois, 1946, Washington University, 1948, Rockford College, 1953, Columbia University, 1954, Harvard University, 1955, University of Pittsburgh, 1959, Princeton University, 1965, University of Massachusetts, 1969, and Hampshire College, 1970; L.H.D. from Dartmouth University, 1940, and Williams College, 1942; D.C.L. from Union College, 1941, and University of Puerto Rico, 1953.

WRITINGS—Poetry: Songs for a Summer's Day (sonnet cycle), Yale University Press, 1915; Tower of Ivory, Yale University Press, 1917; The Happy Marriage, and Other Poems, Houghton, 1924; The Pot of Earth, Houghton, 1925; Streets in the Moon, Houghton, 1926; The Hamlet of A. MacLeish, Houghton, 1928; Einstein, Black Sun Press, 1929; New Found Land, limited edition, Black Sun Press, 1930, Houghton, 1930; Conquistador (narrative poem), Houghton, 1932; Before March, Knopf, 1932; Poems, 1924-1933, Houghton, 1933; Frescoes for Mr. Rockefeller's City, Day, 1933; Poems, John Lane (London), 1935; Public Speech, Farrar & Rinehart, 1936; Land of the Free, Harcourt, 1938; America Was Promises, Duell, Sloan & Pearce, 1939; Actfive and Other Poems, Random House, 1948; Collected Poems, 1917-52, Houghton, 1952; Songs for Eve, Houghton, 1954; The Collected Poems of Archibald MacLeish, Houghton, 1963; The Wild Old Wicked Man and Other Poems, Houghton, 1968.

Prose: Housing America (articles from Fortune), Harcourt, 1932; Jews in America (first published in Fortune), Random, 1936; Libraries in the Contemporary Crisis, U.S. Government Printing Office, 1939; Deposit of the Magna Carta in the Library of Congress on November 28, 1939, Library of Congress, 1939; The American Experience, U.S. Government Printing Office, 1939; The Irresponsibles, Duell, Sloan & Pearce, 1940; The American Cause, Duell, Sloan & Pearce, 1941; *The Duty of Freedom* (privately printed for the United Typothetae of America, 1941); *The Free Company Presents ... The States Talking* (radio broadcast, April 2, 1941, [New York], 1941; *The Next Harvard*, Harvard University Press, 1941; *Prophets of Doom*, University of Pennsylvania Press, 1941; *A Time to Speak*, Houghton, 1941; *American Opinion and the War* (Rede lecture at Cambridge University, Cambridge, England, 1942), Macmillan, 1942; *A Free Man's Books* (limited edition of 200 copies), Peter Pauper, 1942; *In Honor of a Man and an Ideal ... Three Talks on Freedom, by Archibald MacLeish, William S. Paley, Edward R. Murrow* (radio broadcast, December 2, 1941), [New York], 1942; *Report to the Nation*, U.S. Office of Facts and Figures, 1942; *A Time to Act*, Houghton, 1943; *The American Story: Ten Broadcasts* (presented on NBC Radio, 1944, and for which MacLeish served as commentator), Duell, Sloan & Pearce, 1944, 2nd edition, 1960; *Martha Hillard MacLeish, 1856-1947*, privately printed, 1949; *Poetry and Opinion: The Pisan Cantos of Ezra Pound*, University of Illinois Press, 1950; *Freedom is the Right to Choose: An Inquiry into the Battle for the American Future*, Beacon, 1951; *Poetry and Journalism*, University of Minnesota Press, 1958; *Poetry and Experience*, Riverside Editions, 1960; *The Dialogues of Archibald MacLeish and Mark Van Doren* (televised, 1962), Dutton, 1964; *A Continuing Journey*, Houghton, 1968; *Champion of a Cause: Essays and Addresses on Librarianship*, compiled by Eva M. Goldschmidt, American Library Association, 1971.

Drama: *Nobodaddy* (verse play), Dunster House, 1926; *Panic: A Play in Verse* (produced on Broadway at Imperial Theater, March 14, 1935), Houghton, 1935; *The Fall of the City: A Verse Play for Radio* (presented on CBS Radio, 1937, and on CBS TV, 1962), Farrar & Rinehart, 1937, also see below; *Air Raid: A Verse Play for Radio* (presented on CBS Radio, 1938), Harcourt, 1938, also see below; *The Trojan Horse* (verse play) (presented on BBC Radio, London, c. 1950), Houghton, 1952; *This Music Crept By Me Upon the Waters* (verse play), Harvard University Press, 1953; *J.B.: A Play in Verse* (first produced at Yale School of Drama; produced on Broadway at ANTA Theater, December 11, 1958), Houghton, 1958; *Three Short Plays* (includes *Air Raid, The Fall of the City*, and *the Secret of Freedom*, a television play, produced for Sunday Showcase, 1960), Dramatists Play Service, 1961; *The Eleanor Roosevelt Story* (filmscript, produced by Allied Artists, 1965), Houghton, 1965; *An Evening's Journey to Conway, Massachusetts* (play, produced for NET Playhouse, November 3, 1967), Gehenna Press, 1967; *Herakles* (verse play; produced, 1965), Houghton, 1967; *Scratch* (based on short story by Stephen Vincent Benet, "The Devil and Daniel Webster"; produced on Broadway at St. James Theatre, May 6, 1971), Houghton, 1971.

Other: (Co-author) *Background of War*, by editors of *Fortune*, Knopf, 1937; (author of foreword) William Meredith, *Love Letters from An Impossible Land*, Yale University Press, 1944; (author of introduction) St. John Perse (pseudonym for Alexis Saint-Leger Leger), *Eloges and Other Poems*, Norton, 1944; (editor) Gerald Fitzgerald, *The Wordless Flesh* [Cambridge], 1960; (editor) Edwin Muir, *The Estate of Poetry*, Hogarth, 1962; (editor with E.F. Prichard, Jr., and author of foreword), *Felix Frankfurter, Law and Politics: Occasional Papers, 1913-38*, Peter Smith, 1963; (editor) Leonard Baskin, *Figures of Dead Men*, University of Massachusetts Press, 1968; (contributor) *Let Freedom Ring*, by editors of American Heritage, American Heritage, 1962; (author of introduction) *The Complete Poems of Carl Sandburg*, Harcourt, 1970.

Also author of "The Son of Man," presented on CBS Radio, 1947. Librettist, with Nicolas Nabokoff, for "Union Pacific," a verse ballet, written for Federal Theatre Project (WPA), produced on Broadway at St. James Theatre, April 25, 1934, later performed by Monte Carlo Ballet Russe in Philadelphia, Pa., 1934; librettist for "Magic Prison," 1967.

SIDELIGHTS: "MacLeish represents," writes Signi Falk, "the point of view that grants to poetry the experiences not only of the private but also of the public world; and his poems exemplify his thesis. Although he learned much about metrics and language during his early years in France, he early rejected the mirror-gazing tendency of the 1920's. He believes that poetry has been better served by men of affairs like Chaucer, Dante, Shakespeare, Milton.... He believes that the good poet, as the true revolutionary, crystallizes the essential quality of his time and creates the metaphor by which other men live."

In Paris he came under the influence of Pound, Eliot, Yeats, St.-John Perse, and Laforgue, and, for a time, his work was noticeably influenced by his reading of, and association with, other writers. After his return to America he showed a steady development in his own mode. And, Miss Falk notes, "despite ridicule and parody, he has persisted in expressing in both verse and polemical essay need of Americans to revitalize the principle of individual liberty. Throughout his years of public service and of writing directed to a larger public, he has continued to write the subtly designed personal lyrics that established his position as a major American poet."

Conrad Aiken wrote in 1927 that he felt "from the beginning that [MacLeish] had a very exceptional talent.... On the technical side, there is no living poet to whom he need take off his hat. He has technical genius. He can say things with a cunning, a brilliance, a suppleness, a power, which any living poet might covet." In a review of some of MacLeish's later poems Howard Nemerov writes: "The new poems seem to return to the privacy and seriousness of the earlier ones, but with a more energetic rhythm, a stripped ferocity reminiscent in places of late poems by Yeats." But, as Miss Falk notes, "MacLeish speaks with many voices. There is the delicate insight into human relationship, the robust humor at folly and pretension, the outspoken anger over deceit or treachery or injustice, the compassion for the suffering of others, the forthright candor toward conventional and outmoded beliefs." MacLeish insists that poetry "exists in the context of life; that art is an action on the scene of life; that art is a means of perceiving life; of ordering life; of making life intelligible; and thus also of changing it." He dislikes, writes Malcolm Cowley, "the fashionable school of criticism that confines itself to the study of structure and texture, as if the poem were 'an object in an uninhabited landscape.'" And he addresses himself to "great themes," according to Henry Steele Commager, those "which have engaged the minds and hearts of the greatest writers from Aeschylus to Eliot, above all the theme of the free and confronting world and time and fate."

"MacLeish has certainly made it a central part of his business to 'manipulate a continuous parallel' between the immemorial and the modern," writes John Wain. This is especially evident in his verse plays. MacLeish prefers poetic drama because, he says, "its essence is precision, but precision of the emotion, not the mind. Its quality is to illumine from within, not to describe from without. Its language is not communication, but experience." His best known drama, *J.B.*, is a morality play based on the story of Job. Despite certain reservations, John Gassner considered the play "an exalted work of the dramatic and poetic imagination in a generally commonplace theatre. Though the poetry was rarely MacLeish's best, its quality was still measurably above the level of dialogue in most American prose drama. The work had what an English reviewer called tragic diction. . . ." When *Herakles* was produced, most critics agreed that it surpassed *J.B.* Comparing the two plays, Karl Shapiro wrote that the earlier one "affirmed the pathos of the human condition and the dubious rewards of submission to the blind will of Creation. Herakles, a kind of anti-Job, by virtue of superhuman labors becomes a god in his own right. . . . MacLeish draws from the tangle of the myths and cults of Hercules the parable of the antihumanist modern."

MacLeish said of his latest play, *Scratch,* "I think you can say that my play is about morality and politics. I believe that underneath all political questions there are moral issues." Critics, however, were ambivalent, with Walter Kerr saying: "We do not quite know how to play easy counterpoint to the prosody or to the propositions it is meant to carry forward." At its pre-Broadway tryout in Boston, Kevin Kelly, of the *Globe,* "panned" the play, but an editorial in the same paper refuted its critic's opinion by stating: "When America's greatest living poet—and perhaps her very greatest, living or dead— writes a play about the state of the Union, it is not a matter to be taken lightly with references to 'swirling patriotic rhetoric.' It (the play) is, rather, to be listened to, and read, and learned from." Disagreeing with many of his fellow critics, a reviewer for *Harper's* wrote: "I suspect that the New York critics who slapped it down so casually simply didn't understand what MacLeish was up to. He attempted something utterly unfashionable: to write a serious play, rich in intellectural as well as emotional content, that would deal with a universal moral issue."

When MacLeish turns from the responsibilities of the poet in public life to probe the approach of man to old age, Victor Howes sees his work as breaking new ground, with "the property of greatness . . . richly suggestive, philosophical . . . superbly lyrical." "Like Yeats," writes Chad Walsh, "the older MacLeish is finding new poetic worlds to master."

Miss Falk believes that, because MacLeish "has often written with candor, he has brought himself into sharp conflict with those who are partisan in politics, orthodox in religion, and dogmatic in art. . . . He has developed a theory of poetry that rejects the isolation of an 'ivory tower' and insists that poetry concern itself with all of life. . . . MacLeish has been concerned with the present, with the special and changing quality that seems to predominate in each decade; he has sought to invent the appropriate metaphor for the time and has urged that his fellow poets do the same. In both prose and verse he has written [to oppose] outworn dogmas and conventions that turn man's thought and life back rather than direct them forward. From the time of his Paris sojourn, he has persistently sought a pattern of thought appropriate to the new world."

MacLeish's works have been translated into several languages; *J.B.* has been performed in a number of European countries, in Israel, Egypt, and Mexico. His plays and poetry are included in critical studies, anthologies, and collections. Publications include numerous addresses given before Congress, as lectures at universities, and to mark other important occasions. *America Was Promises* was set to music by Nicolas Nabokoff, and produced on CBS radio, April 5, 1940.

BIOGRAPHICAL/CRITICAL SOURCES: Edmund Wilson, *Classics and Commercials,* Farrar, Straus, 1950; Conrad Aiken, *A Reviewer's ABC,* World, 1958; John Gassner, *Theatre at the Crossroads,* Holt, 1960; Howard Nemerov, *Poetry and Fiction,* Rutgers University Press, 1963; Signi Falk, *Archibald MacLeish,* Twayne, 1965;

New Republic, July 22, 1967; *New York Times Book Review,* August 6, 1967, January 28, 1968; *Book World,* January 21, 1968, November 3, 1968; *Christian Science Monitor,* November 21, 1968; *New York Times,* March 2, 1971, May 16, 1971; *Variety,* April 14, 1971; *Harper's,* December, 1971.

*   *   *

MACLEOD, Jean Sutherland   1908-
(Catherine Airlie)

PERSONAL: Born January 20, 1908, in Glasgow, Scotland; daughter of John (a civil engineer) and Elizabeth (Allen) Macleod; married Lionel Walton (a land surveyor), January 1, 1935; children: David Macleod. *Education:* Educated at schools in Glasgow, Scotland, and Swansea, South Wales. *Politics:* Conservative. *Religion:* Presbyterian. *Home:* "Heather Bloom," Ardmadam, Argyllshire, Scotland.

CAREER: British Ministry of Labor, Newcastle upon Tyne, England, secretary, 1930-35; novelist, 1935—. President of Alne and Tollerton area branch, National Society for Prevention of Cruelty to Children. *Member:* Romantic Novelists' Association, Society of Yorkshire Bookmen, Women of Scotland, Clan Macleod Society (Edinburgh), St. Andrew Society (York). *Awards, honors:* Cartland Historical Novel award, 1962, for *The Dark Fortune.*

WRITINGS—All published by Mills & Boon, except as indicated: *Life for Two,* 1936, *Human Sympathy,* 1937, *Summer Rain,* 1938, *Sequel to Youth,* 1938, *Mist Across the Hills,* 1938, *Dangerous Obsession,* 1939, *Run Away from Love,* 1939, *Return to Spring,* 1939, Pocket Books, 1971, *Rainbow Isle,* 1939.

The Whim of Fate, 1940, *Lonely Furrow,* 1940, *Heatherbloom,* 1940, *Reckless Pilgrim,* 1941, *Shadow of a Vow,* 1941, *One Way Out,* 1941, *Forbidden Rapture,* 1941, *Penalty for Living,* 1942, *Blind Journey,* 1942, *Bleak Heritage,* 1942, Pocket Books, 1971, *Reluctant Folly,* 1942, *Unseen Tomorrow,* 1943, *The Rowan Tree,* 1943, *Flower o' the Broom,* 1943, *Circle of Doubt,* 1943, *Lamont of Ardgoyne,* 1944, *Two Paths,* 1944, *Brief Fulfillment,* 1945, *This Much to Give,* 1945, *One Love,* 1945, Pocket Books, 1971, *Tranquil Haven,* 1946, *Sown in the Wind,* 1946, Pocket Books, 1970, *House of Oliver,* 1947, *And We in Dreams,* 1947, *Chalet in the Sun,* 1948, *Ravenscrag,* 1948, *Above the Lattice,* 1949, *Tomorrow's Bargain,* 1949.

Katherine, 1950, *The Valley of Palms,* 1950, *Roadway to the Past,* 1951, *Once to Every Heart,* 1951, *Cameron of Gare,* 1952, *Music at Midnight,* 1952, *The Silent Valley,* 1953, *The Stranger in Their Midst,* 1953, *Dear Doctor Everett,* 1954, *The Man in Authority,* 1954, *After Long Journeying,* 1955, *Master of Glenkeith,* 1955, Pocket Books, 1971, *Way in the Dark,* 1956, *My Heart's in the Highlands,* 1956, *Journey in the Sun,* 1957, *The Prisoner of Love,* 1958, *Gated Road,* 1959, *Air Ambulance,* 1959.

The Little Doctor, 1960, *The White Cockade,* 1960, *The Silver Dragon,* 1961, *The Country of the Heart,* 1961, *Slave of the Wind,* 1962, Pocket Books, 1971, *The Dark Fortune,* 1962, *Sugar Island,* 1964, *The Black Cameron,* 1965, *Crane Castle,* 1965, *The Wolf of Heimra,* 1965, *The Drummer of Corrae,* 1966, *The Tender Glory,* 1967, *Lament for a Lover,* 1967, *The Master of Keills,* 1967, *The Bridge of Mingulay,* 1967, *The Moonflower,* 1967, *Summer Island,* 1968, Pocket Books, 1971.

The Joshua Tree, 1970, *The Way Through the Valley,* 1970, Pocket Books, 1972, *The Fortress,* 1970, *The Scent of Juniper,* 1971, *Light in the Tower,* Pocket Books, 1971; *Moment of Decision,* Pocket Books, 1972.

Under pseudonym Catherine Airlie: *The Wild Macraes,* 1948, *From Such a Seed,* 1949, *The Restless Years,* 1950,

Fabric of Dreams, 1951, *Strange Recompense*, 1952, *The Green Rushes*, 1953, *Hidden in the Wind*, 1953, *Wind Sighing*, 1954, *Nobody's Child*, 1954, *The Valley of Desire*, 1955, *The Ways of Love*, 1955, *The Mountain of Stars*, 1956, *Unguarded Hour*, 1956, *Land of Heart's Desire*, 1957, *Red Lotus*, 1958, *The Last of the Kintyres*, 1959, *Shadow on the Sun*, 1960, *One Summer's Day*, 1961, *In the Country of the Heart*, 1961, *The Unlived Year*, 1962, *Passing Strangers*, 1963, *The Wheels of Chance*, 1964, *The Sea Change*, 1965.

Contributor to *Woman's Own, People's Journal, Woman's Weekly, People's Friend*, and other magazines.

WORK IN PROGRESS: Research for a novel about South Africa, *The Sugar House*.

AVOCATIONAL INTERESTS: Sailing, gardening, and photography.

*   *   *

MACNICOL, Eona K(athleen) Fraser   1910-

PERSONAL: Born May 12, 1910, in Inverness, Scotland; daughter of John (a draper) and Annie (Fraser) Fraser; married Robert Simson Macnicol (a Presbyterian minister), March 28, 1942; children: Malcolm Fraser, Elizabeth Mary, John Simson. *Education:* University of Edinburgh, M.A. (honors in English), 1932. *Politics:* Liberal. *Religion:* Presbyterian. *Home:* 33 Grange Rd., Edinburgh 9, Scotland.

CAREER: Various teaching posts, with last regular one as English instructor at Women's Christian College, Madras, South India, 1940-42.

WRITINGS: Colum of Derry (novel), Sheed, 1954; *Lamp in the Night Wind: An Account of the Coming of St. Columba to Scotland in 563 A.D.*, W. Maclellan, 1965; *The Hallowe'en Hero, and Other Stories*, W. Blackwood, 1969. Contributor of short stories to *Scots Magazine, Saltire*, and to British Broadcasting Corp. programs.

WORK IN PROGRESS: Another book on Saint Columba.

AVOCATIONAL INTERESTS: Gardening, archeology, knitting.

*   *   *

MACROW, Brenda G(race Joan) Barton   1916-

PERSONAL: Surname is pronounced Mack-*kro;* born June 3, 1916, in London, England; daughter of Joseph William (a company director) and Grace (Tabiner) Barton; married Herbert John Macrow, 1942 (marriage dissolved, 1947); married Dennis Edward Prior, November 5, 1949; children: (second marriage) Lesley Denise. *Education:* Educated in private schools in England and at Wheaton Community High School, Wheaton, Ill. *Politics:* "Liberal by inclination but belong to no party." *Religion:* Anglican. *Home:* Lives on naval pinnace moored near Chicester, Sussex, England.

CAREER: Worked as demonstrator in father's business in London, England, before the war; librarian on American airfield in Essex, England, during World War II; teacher of English literature and composition in private school, 1962-63; free-lance writer, 1934—.

WRITINGS—Scottish books for adults, with photographs by Robert M. Adam: *Unto the Hills*, Oliver & Boyd, 1947; *Kintail Scrapbook*, Oliver & Boyd, 1948; *Hills and Glens*, Oliver & Boyd, 1949; *Torridon Highlands*, R. Hale, 1953, 2nd edition, 1969; *Speyside to Deeside*, Oliver & Boyd, 1956.

Children's books: *Field Folk* (verses), Blackie & Son, 1958; *The Amazing Mr. Whisper*, Blackie & Son, 1958, Dodd, 1963; *The Return of Mr. Whisper*, Blackie & Son,

1959; *Bumbletown Tales* (collection of insect verses), Blackie & Son, 1960; *Babies of the Wild*, Blackie & Son, 1962; *The Little Sleeping Beauty*, Concordia, 1969. Contributor of some sixty articles and poems to *Scottish Field, Scotland's Magazine, Chambers' Journal, Better Homes and Gardens, Scots Magazine, Climber, Braemar Book, Country Life, Good Housekeeping*, and *Weekly Scotsman;* regular contributor of picture-story scripts to children's papers.

SIDELIGHTS: The Amazing Mr. Whisper was transcribed into Braille. *Avocational interests:* Painting, singing, animals, and reading.

BIOGRAPHICAL/CRITICAL SOURCES: Scottish Field, October, 1962; *Climber*, January, 1963.

*   *   *

MacSHANE, Frank   1927-

PERSONAL: Born October 19, 1927, in Pittsburgh, Pa.; son of Frank (a journalist) and A. Elizabeth A. (Morse) MacShane; married Virginia Lynn Fry, July 18, 1959; children: Nicholas Morse. *Education:* Harvard University, A.B., 1949; Yale University, M.A., 1951; Oxford University, D.Phil., 1955. *Office:* Writing Division, School of the Arts, Columbia University, New York, N.Y. 10027.

CAREER: McGill University, Montreal, Quebec, lecturer in English, 1955-57; University of California, Berkeley, assistant professor of English, 1959-64; Williams College, Williamstown, Mass., associate professor of English, 1964-67; Columbia University, New York, N.Y., professor of English and chairman of writing division, 1967—. Fulbright professor at University of Chile, 1957, and at Tribhuvan University, Kathmandu, Nepal; visiting lecturer, Vassar College, 1958-59. *Member:* American Association of University Professors, P.E.N. American Center, Modern Language Association of America, Oxford and Cambridge Club (London).

WRITINGS: (Translator) Miguel Serrano, *The Mysteries*, privately printed, 1960; (translator) Miguel Serrano, *The Visits of the Queen of Sheba*, Asia Publishing House, 1960; *Many Golden Ages: Ruins, Temples and Monuments of the Orient*, Tuttle, 1962; (editor) *Impressions of Latin America: Five Centuries of Travel and Adventure by English and North American Writers*, Morrow, 1963; (translator) Miguel Serrano, *The Serpent of Paradise*, Rider & Co., 1963; (editor) *Critical Writings of Ford Madox Ford*, University of Nebraska Press, 1964; (editor) *The American in Europe: A Collection of Impressions Written by Americans from the Seventeenth Century to the Present*, Dutton, 1965; *The Life and Work of Ford Madox Ford*, Horizon Press, 1965; (translator) Miguel Serrano, *C.G. Jung and Hermann Hesse: A Record of Two Friendships*, Schocken, 1966; (translator) Miguel Serrano, *The Ultimate Flower*, Schocken, 1969; *Ford Madox Ford: The Critical Heritage*, Routledge & Kegan Paul, 1972. Contributor to *New England Quarterly, London Magazine, Prairie Schooner, Centennial Review, New York Times Book Review, Holiday, American Scholar, Chelsea, Shenandoah Columbia Forum*, and other journals.

WORK IN PROGRESS: Ford Madox Ford volume for the "Critical Heritage" series, for Barnes & Noble; *The Dream of Quetzalcoatl*.

*   *   *

MADARIAGA (y Rojo), Salvador de   1886-

PERSONAL: Born July 23, 1886, in La Coruna, Spain; son of Jose (a colonel) and Ascension (Rojo) de Madariaga; married Constance Helen Margaret Archibald, October 10, 1912 (died, 1970); married Emilie Szekely Rauman, November 18, 1970; children: (first marriage)

Nieves and Isabel (daughters). *Education:* Educated in Paris, France, 1900-11, graduating from College Chaptal, 1906, attending Ecole Polytechnique, 1906-08, and graduating from Ecole Nationale Superieure des Mines, 1911. *Politics:* Liberal. *Home:* L'Esplanade, 6600 Locarno, Switzerland.

CAREER: Employed by Railway Company of Northern Spain, Madrid, 1911-16, simultaneously writing political articles for newspapers under a pseudonym; decided to become a writer, and spent 1916-21 in London, doing research and working as a journalist and critic; entered Secretariat of League of Nations, Geneva, Switzerland, 1921, member of press section, 1921-22, head of disarmament section, 1922-27; first occupant of King Alfonso XIII Chair of Spanish Studies at Oxford University, Oxford, England, 1927-30, during which time he also lectured in North America on extended leaves; Spanish Ambassador to United States, 1931, to France, 1932-34, and Spain's permanent delegate to League of Nations Assembly, 1931-36; served briefly as Spain's Minister of Education, 1934, then as Minister of Justice; declining to take sides in Spanish Civil War, returned to Oxford to live, 1936—. Broadcaster to Latin America for British Broadcasting Corp. during war; broadcaster in Spanish, French, and German to European countries. Associated with various international organizations in postwar years, serving as first president of Liberal International (now president of honor) and honorary president of Congress for Cultural Freedom. Honorary co-chairman of Spanish Refugee Aid, Inc. Emory L. Ford Professor of Spanish at Princeton University, 1954; lecturer and speaker in many countries. *Member:* Spanish Academy of Letters and of Moral and Political Sciences, French Academy of Moral and Political Sciences, Academy of History of Caracas, and many other Spanish-American learned societies; Reform Club (London), Ateneo (Madrid).

AWARDS, HONORS: M.A., Oxford University, 1928; gold medalist, Yale University; fellow, Exeter College, University of Pavia; honorary doctor of the Universities of Arequipa, Lima, Poitiers, Liege, and Lille, and of Oxford and Princeton Universities; Ere Nouvelle Prize, for *Englishmen, Frenchmen, Spaniards;* Knight Grand Cross of Order of the Republic (Spain), White Lion (Czechoslovakia), Order of Merit (Chile), Order of Jade in Gold (China), Order of Merit (Hungary), Boyaca (Colombia), Order of the White Rose (Finland), Grand Cross of Legion d'Honneur (France), Aztec Eagle (Mexico), and Order of the Sun (Peru); Europa Prize, Hans Deutsch Foundation, Bern University, 1963; Hanseatic Goethe Prize, 1967.

WRITINGS—Biography and history: *Spain,* Scribner, 1930, 3rd edition, J. Cape, 1942 (see *Spain,* below), Creative Age, 1943, 7th Spanish edition, entitled *Espana,* Editorial Sudamericana (Buenos Aires), 1959; *Christopher Columbus; Being the Life of the Very Magnificent Lord Don Cristobal Colon* (first of the "New World" trilogy), Hodder & Stoughton, 1939, Macmillan, 1940, new edition, Hollis & Carter, 1949, Ungar, 1967; *Hernan Cortes, Conqueror of Mexico* (second in the trilogy), Macmillan, 1941, 2nd edition, Regnery, 1955; *Spain,* two volumes (the first a revision of the 1930 work with the same title), J. Cape, 1942; *Cuadro historico de las Indias,* Editorial Sudamericana, Volume I: *El Auge del imperio espanol en America,* 1945, 2nd edition, 1959, published in America as *The Rise of the Spanish-American Empire,* Macmillan, 1947, Volume II: *El Ocaso del imperio espanol en America,* 1945, English translation by Madariaga entitled *The Fall of the Spanish American Empire,* Hollis & Carter, 1947, Macmillan, 1948, revised edition, Collier, 1963, 2nd Spanish edition, two volumes, 1950; *Bolivar* (third in the trilogy), two volumes, Editorial Hermes (Mexico), 1951, English translation by Madari-

aga, with same title, in abridged edition, Hollis & Carter, 1951, Pellegrini & Cudahy, 1953, 3rd Spanish edition, Editorial Sudamericana, 1959; *De Colon a Bolivar,* E.D.H.A.S.A. (Editorial y Distribuidora Hispano Americana, S.A.; Barcelona) 1956; *ElCiclo hispanico* (omnibus volume), Editorial Sudamericana, Volume I: *Vida del muy magnifico senor Don Cristobal Colon, Hernan Cortes,* [y] *El Auge del imperio espanol en America,* 1958, Volume II: *El Ocaso del imperio espanol en America,* [y] *Bolivar,* 1958; *Spain: A Modern History,* Praeger, 1958.

Political books: *La Guerra desde Londres* (selected articles originally published in *Espana, Imparcial,* and *Publicidad*), Editorila Monclus (Tortosa), 1918; *Disarmament: Obstacles, Results, Prospects,* published by Margaret C. Peabody Fund for League of Nations, 1928, Coward, 1929; *Discursos internacionales,* M. Aguilar (Madrid), 1934; *Anarquia o jerarquia,* M. Aguilar, 1935, English translation by Madariaga published in America as *Anarchy or Hierarchy,* Macmillan, 1937, 3rd Spanish edition, 1970; *Theory and Practice in International Relations* (William J. Cooper Foundation lectures, Swarthmore College, 1937), University of Pennsylvania Press, 1937; *The World's Design,* Allen & Unwin, 1938; (with Edward Hallett Carr) *Future of International Government,* Universal Distributors, 1941; (with others) *The British Commonwealth and the U.S.A. in the Postwar World,* National Peace Council, 1942; *Ojo, Vencedores!,* Editorial Sudamericana, 1945, English translation by Madariaga entitled *Victors, Beware,* J. Cape, 1946; *De l'Angoisse a la liberte,* Calmann-Levy (Paris), 1954, translation by Mrs. M. Marx of second part published in England as *Democracy Versus Liberty?,* Pall Mall Press, 1958; *Rettet die Freiheit!* (selected articles originally published in *Neue Zuercher Zeitung,* 1948-57), Francke (Bern), 1958; *General, marchese usted!* (collection of lectures broadcast for the Spanish Service of the Radiodiffusion Francaise, 1954-57), Ediciones Iberica, 1959; *The Blowing Up of the Parthenon; or, How to Lose the Cold War,* Praeger, 1960, revised edition, 1961; *Latin America Between the Eagle and the Bear,* Praeger, 1962; *Weltpolitisches Kaleidoskop* (second collection of articles originally published in *Neue Zuercher Zeitung*), Fretz & Wasmuth Verlag (Zurich), 1965.

Essays: *Shelley and Calderon, and Other Essays on English and Spanish Poetry,* Constable, 1920; *The Genius of Spain, and Other Essays on Spanish Contemporary Literature,* Clarendon Press, 1923, 2nd edition, 1924; *Semblanzas literarias contemporaneas,* Editorial Cervantes (Barcelona), 1924, revised and enlarged edition published as *De Galdos a Lorca,* Editorial Sudamericana, 1960; *Arceval y los ingleses,* Espasa-Calpe (Madrid), 1925; *Guia del lector del "Quijote",* Espasa-Calpe, 1926, 6th edition, Editorial Sudamericana, 1967, English translation by Madariaga entitled *Don Quixote: An Introductory Essay in Psychology,* Gregynogg Press, 1934, 4th edition, Oxford University Press, 1961; *Englishmen, Frenchmen, Spaniards: An Essay in Comparative Psychology,* Oxford University Press, 1928, 2nd edition, Hill & Wang, 1969; *Americans,* Oxford University Press, 1930; *On Hamlet,* Hollis & Carter, 1948, 2nd edition, F. Cass, 1964, Barnes & Noble, 1964; *Bosquejo de Europa,* Editorial Hermes, 1951, English translation by Madariaga entitled *Portrait of Europe,* Hollis & Carter, 1952, Roy, 1955, revised edition, University of Alabama Press, 1967; *Essays with a Purpose,* Hollis & Carter, 1954; *Presente y porvenir de hispanoamerica, y otros ensayos,* Editorial Sudamericana, 1959; *El Quijote de Cervantes,* Editorial Sudamericana, 1962; *Retrato de un hombre de pie,* E.D.H.A.S.A., 1965, English translation by Madariaga entiled *Portrait of a Man Standing,* University of Alabama Press, 1968; *Memorias de un federalista,* Editorial Sudamericana, 1967; (contributor) Ivar Ivask and Juan Marichal, editors, *Lu-*

...inous Reality: The Poetry of Jorge Guillen, University of Oklahoma Press, 1969; Selecciones de Madariaga (includes selections from Ingleses, franceses, espanoles, Bosqujo de Europa, and El Enemigo de Dios), edited by Frank Sedwick and Elizabeth Van Orman, Prentice-Hall, 1969; Mujeres espanolas, Espasa-Calpe, 1972; Obras selectas: Ensayos, Editorial Sudamericana, 1972.

Novels: The Sacred Giraffe (satire), Hopkinson, 1925; Sir Bob (juvenile), Harcourt, 1930; El Enemigo de Dios, M. Aguilar, 1926; El Corazon de piedra verde (first in a series entitled "Esquiveles y Manriques"), Editorial Sudamericana, 1943, 4th edition, 1967, English translation by Madariaga entitled The Heart of Jade, Creative Age Press, 1944, also published in Spanish in three separate volumes by Editorial Sudamericana, Volume 1: Los Fantasmas, 1952, Volume 2: Los Dioses sanguinarios, 1952, Volume 3: Fe sin blasfemia, 1952; Ramo de errores, Editorial Hermes, 1952, English translation by Madariaga entitled A Bunch of Errors, J. Cape, 1954; La Camarada Ana, Editorial Hermes, 1954, 2nd edition, Editorial Sudamericana, 1956; Guerra en la sangre (2nd novel in the series "Esquiveles y Manriques"), Editorial Sudamericana, 1956, English translation by Madariaga entitled War in the Blood, Collins, 1957; Una Gota de tiempo (3rd novel in the series "Esquiveles y Manriques"), Editorial Sudamericana, 1958, 2nd edition, 1960; El Semental negro (4th novel in the series), Editorial Sudamericana, 1961, French & European Publications, 1969; Sanco Panco, Latino-Americana (Mexico), 1963; Satanael (5th novel in the series), Editorial Sudamericana, 1966.

Poetry: Romances de ciego, Publicaciones Atenea (Madrid), 1922; La Fuente serena: Cantos, romances liricos y sonetos a la espanola, Editorial Cervantes, 1927; Elegia en la muerte de Unamuno, Oxford University Press, 1937; Elegia en la muerte de Federico Garcia Lorca, Oxford University Press, 1938; The Home of Man (18 sonnets), privately printed, 1938; Rosa de cieno y ceniza, Editorial Sudamericana, 1942; Romances a Beatriz: El Sol, la luna y las estrellas, Editorial Juventud (Barcelona), 1954; La que heule a Tomillo y a Romero, Editorial Sudamericana, 1959; Poppy, bilingual Spanish and English edition, Imprenta Bernasconi (Lugano), 1965.

Dramatic works: Elysian Fields, Allen & Unwin, 1937; El Toison de oro, y tres obras mas: La Muerte de Capmen, Don Carlos [y] Mio Cid (the first a lyrical fantasy in three acts; the following three dramatic poems), Editorial Sudamericana, 1940; Don Juan y la Donjuania (one-act verse play), Editorial Sudamericana, 1950; Los Tres estudiantes de Salamanca (includes "Los Tres estudiantes de Salamanca," a three-act tragicomedy; "Viva la muerte," a three-act modern tragedy, produced in the Piccola Scala, Milan, Italy, 1966; and "El Doce de octubre de Cervantes," a one-act historical fantasy), Editorial Sudamericana, 1962; Le Mystere de la Mappemonde et du Pappemonde (three-act French verse play; broadcast by Radiodiffusion Francaise, 1948), O'Hara Gallery (London), 1966; La Cruz y la bandera (romance), Editorial Sudamericana, 1966; Numance: Tragedie lyrique en un acte (opera; first produced in Paris, 1954), libretto by Henri Barraud, Boosey & Hawkes, 1970; Dialogos famosos: Campos eliseos—Adan y Eva, Editorial Sudamericana, 1970.

Radio plays: "Campos eliseos" (Spanish version of Elysian Fields), broadcast by the B.B.C. for Spain, Radio Varsovia, updated version broadcast in German by Radio Berna, 1966; "Cristobal Colon," B.B.C., 1941; "Las Tres carabelas," B.B.C., 1942; "Numancia" (English verse translation of Cervantes' tragedy), B.B.C., 1947; "Christophe Colomb" (dramatization of the discovery of America in French), Radiodiffusion Francaise, 1954.

Other publications: (Author of introduction) Miguel de Unamuno, The Tragic Sense of Life, Macmillan, 1921; (with Henry Noel Brailsford) Can the League Cope with Imperialism? (pamphlet), Foreign Policy Association, 1928; Aims and Methods of a Chair of Spanish Studies, Clarendon Press, 1928; (contributor) A League of Minds (letters), International Institute of Intellectual Cooperation, League of Nations, 1933; The Price of Peace, Cobden-Sanderson, 1935; Spain and the Jews, Jewish Historical Society, 1946; Don Juan as a European Figure, University of Nottingham Press, 1946; (with Robert M. MacIver) First Principles (includes "World Government: Dream or Necessity?", by Madariaga, and "Fundamentals of International Order," by MacIver), published for World Unity Movement by Herbert Joseph, 1946; Europe, a Unit of Human Culture, European Movement (Brussels), 1952; Sobre mi Bolivar, Editorial Sudamericana, c.1953; The Anatomy of the Cold War, M. Boyd (Belfast), 1955; (with others) Franco and the University (pamphlet for Committee on Science and Freedom), [Manchester], 1956; Homenaje a Gabriela Mistral, Hispanic and Luso-Brazilian Councils, 1958; Critique de l'Europe (originally published as preface to European Annual), Council of Europe, 1959; Ueber die Koexistenz in einer freigeteilten Welt (speech delivered in Frankfurt), Rettet die Freiheit, 1960; (author of introduction) Echo de monde, Metz Verlag (Zurich), 1960; (contributor) Dauer im Wandel, Verlag Georg D.W. Callwey (Munich), 1961; (contributor) Die Kraft zu leben, Bertelsmann Verlag (Guetersloh), 1963; Christoph Columbus, translated into German by Emilia Rauman, Amriswiler Buecherei, 1963; Lob Salzburgs (inaugural speech of Festival of Salzburg; includes original French and English, and German translation by Rauman), Festungs Verlag (Salzburg), 1964; Yo-yo y yo-el, Editorial Sudamericana, 1967; On Freedom (lecture given in Bern, Switzerland, 1970), Swiss Eastern Institute Press, 1970; (with others) Ist die Marktwirtschaft noch gesichert? (speech and discussion at 36th Conference of the Aktionsgemeinschaft Soziale Marktwirtschaft, November 25-26, 1970, in Bonn-Bad Godesberg), M. Hoch (Ludwigsburg), 1971; Morgen ohne Mittag (memoirs), Ullstein (Berlin), 1973.

Translator: Manojo de poesias ingleses puestas en verso castellano, William Lewis (Cardiff), 1919; (and compiler) Spanish Folk Songs, Constable, 1922; (and editor) William Shakespeare, Hamlet, bilingual edition, Editorial Sudamericana, 1949. Assisted L. Araquistain in translating Rudyard Kipling's "The Fringes of the Fleet" and "Tales of 'The Trade'" (stories) into Spanish. Contributor to numerous periodicals.

SIDELIGHTS: One of the last great European liberals, a citizen of the world, scholar, and statesman, Madariaga is probably Spain's outstanding intellectual. He writes in English, Spanish, French, and has prepared some of his books in all three languages. He was once described by Aristide Briand as one of the ten best conversationalists in Europe. He assisted in establishing the College of Europe, Bruges, and the European Center of Culture, Geneva.

Many of Madariaga's writings, of both literary and political content, have stimulated heated discussion. The third book in the "New World" trilogy, Bolivar, proved to be "a literary bombshell that caused Spain and Latin America to go to war again, with plenty of ink spilled on both sides," said Marcelle Michelin of Books Abroad. Highly revered in Latin America as a key figure in the struggle for independence, Bolivar, according to Madariaga, was "nothing but a vulgar imitator of Napoleon with dreams of reigning over a South American empire." The Latin American reaction was one of shock and outrage, and the book was banned in Argentina. It was, however, very well received in North America and England. Madariaga's *Sobre mi Bolivar* is, as the subtitle states, a "resena de resenas y critica de criticas."

A severe critic of the Franco regime, Madariaga has lived in England in self-imposed exile since the outbreak of the Spanish Civil War in 1936. Although he bears a passionate love for his homeland, he believes that Spain is caught in the grip of a totally destructive dictatorship. "Fascism hardly counts in Spain," he wrote recently. "It is the Army that keeps its boot on the neck of the Spanish people." In an August, 1969, article in the *New York Times*, he made the statement that Franco, "once an intelligent colonel, ... [has] turned insane by decades of unchecked power. . . . We are told by his friends that he gave Spain thirty years of peace and ten of prosperity. Neither of these assertions is true. Outward quiet is not peace. Before it explodes, a bomb is quiet enough."

BIOGRAPHICAL/CRITICAL SOURCES: New York Herald Tribune Book Review, October 12, 1952; *Books Abroad*, autumn, 1953; *Newsweek*, June 9, 1958; *Saturday Review*, July 2, 1960; *Washington Post*, May 26, 1961; *Times Literary Supplement*, February 22, 1968; *Library Journal*, July, 1969; *New York Times*, August 9, 1969.

* * *

MADDEN, E(dward) S(tanislaus) 1919-

PERSONAL: Born June 19, 1919, in Melbourne, Victoria, Australia; son of Austin Stanislaus (a librarian) and Elsie (Devine) Madden; married Veronica May White, January 28, 1943; children: John Joseph, Gerard Stanislaus, Christopher Campion, Timothy Mark, Mary Louise. *Education:* Studied at Xavier College, St. Joseph's College, and St. Patrick's College, all Melbourne, Australia. *Religion:* Roman Catholic. *Home:* 28 Seventh St., Parkdale, Victoria, Australia. *Office:* 5 Riversdale Rd., Hawthorn, Victoria, Australia.

CAREER: News-Weekly, Melbourne, Victoria, Australia, editor, 1945—. Public relations consultant. Foundation member and national commodore, Australian Coast Guard Auxiliary, 1961—. *Military service:* Australian Imperial Forces, Royal Australian Artillery, 1939-45; became captain. *Member:* Campion Society.

WRITINGS: Craig's Spur, Heinemann, 1961, Vanguard, 1963; *Good Thief*, Heinemann, in press. Author of film and radio scripts. Contributor of short stories to magazines.

WORK IN PROGRESS: The Top of the Mountain, a novel, for Heinemann.

* * *

MADDOX, Gaynor

PERSONAL: Born in San Diego, Calif.; son of William Theobold (a newspaperman) and Clara (Gaynor) Maddox; married Dorothy Manson (an editorial consultant), November 20, 1944; children: Patrick Gaynor. *Education:* University of California, Berkeley, B.A. (with honors), 1918; Harvard University, graduate study, 1920-21. *Politics:* Democrat. *Religion:* Christian. *Home:* 179 East 79th St., New York, N.Y. 10021. *Office:* Newspaper Enterprise Association, 230 Park Ave., New York, N.Y. 10017.

CAREER: U.S. Merchant Marine, purser, 1922-24; Standard Brands, Inc., member of advertising department, 1926-30; Newspaper Enterprise Association, New York, N.Y., 1932—, began as staff correspondent, became food and nutrition editor, working with research scientists at Harvard University, University of California, Berkeley, Columbia University, American Medical Association, American Dietetic Association, Nutrition Foundation, and others; Long Island University, Brooklyn, N.Y., assistant

professor of English, 1934-43. Editor, Domax Service, Inc. (literary service), New York, N.Y. *Member:* National Association of Science Writers, Overseas Press Club, Friends of Old Sturbridge Village (Sturbridge, Mass.).

WRITINGS: Eat Well for Less Money: The American Guide to Modern Nutrition, Dutton, 1942; (editor) *Russian Cook Book for American Homes*, Russian War Relief, 1942, wartime edition, 1943; *The Safe and Sure Way to Reduce*, Random, 1960; *Slim Down, Shape Up Diets for Teenagers*, Avon, 1963; *Cook Out With Gaynor Maddox*, Newspaper Enterprise Association, 1964; *The Good Sense Family Cook Book*, M. Evans, 1966; (reviser and editor) *Cookbook for Diabetics*, Taplinger, 1967; *Food and Arthritis*, Taplinger, 1969. Contributor of articles to *Reader's Digest* and other magazines.

WORK IN PROGRESS: Fitness for Young Adults; Food and Civilization.

SIDELIGHTS: Maddox has made many editorial trips to Europe, and has traveled in Central and South America, China, Japan, Egypt, India, and Hawaii.

* * *

MADISON, Peter 1918-

PERSONAL: Born June 26, 1918; married Karlene Morton, 1944 (divorced October, 1970); children: four. *Education:* University of Oregon, B.S., 1940; Harvard University, M.A., 1947, Ph.D., 1953. *Office:* Psychology Department, University of Arizona, Tucson, Ariz. 85721.

CAREER: Harvard University, Cambridge, Mass., resident psychologist, 1946-49; Swarthmore College, Swarthmore, Pa., instructor, 1949-50, assistant professor, 1950-60, associate professor of psychology, 1960-61; Princeton University, Princeton, N.J., associate professor of psychology and director of counseling service, 1961-63; University of Arizona, Tucson, professor of psychology and consultant on student development, 1963—. Visiting lecturer in psychology at Bryn Mawr College, 1958-59. Part-time research posts at Institute of Pennsylvania Hospital, 1953-54, University of Pennsylvania Medical School, 1957-58. Instructor in Bell Telephone Co. excutives program, 1956-58. Clinical psychologist, Southern Arizona Mental Health Center, 1964—. *Military service:* U.S. Army, clinical psychologist, 1942-46.

WRITINGS: (With Robert Leeper) *Toward Understanding Human Personalities*, Appleton, 1959; *Freud's Concept of Repression and Defense: Its Theoretical and Observational Language*, University of Minnesota Press, 1961; (contributor with R.W. Leeper) D.K. Candland, editor, *Emotion: Bodily Change*, Van Nostrand, 1962; *Personality Development in College*, Addison-Wesley, 1969. Contributor to professional journals.

WORK IN PROGRESS: Working on methods of encouraging optimal personality development during the college years.

* * *

MADOW, Pauline (Reichberg)

PERSONAL: Surname is accented on first syllable, and pronounced with short a; born in Irvington, N.J.; daughter of Jacob (a businessman) and Sonja (Goldin) Reichberg; married Seymour Stephen Madow (an attorney), June 28, 1953; children: Patricia Leslie. *Education:* Rutgers State University, B.A., M.A. *Politics:* Independent. *Home:* 72 Park Terrace W., New York, N.Y. 10034.

CAREER: H.W. Wilson Co., New York, N.Y., *Current Biography* researcher, 1953-59, associate editor, 1959-61; Grolier, Inc., New York, N.Y., chief copy editor, *Encyclopedia International*, 1961-63; Columbia University, w York, N.Y., historian in oral history research office, 969—.

WRITINGS: (Editor and compiler) The Peace Corps, H.W. Wilson, 1964; Recreation in America, H.W. Wilson, 1965. Contributor of articles to Encyclopedia International, Nation, Book Week, and Current Biography.

WORK IN PROGRESS: The Social Thought of H.G. Wells; biographies for Notable American Women, 1607-1950, for Radcliffe College.

BIOGRAPHICAL/CRITICAL SOURCES: Wilson Library Bulletin, June, 1964.

*   *   *

MAGOWAN, Robin 1936-

PERSONAL: Born September 4, 1936, in San Francisco, Calif.; son of Robert A. and Doris (Merrill) Magowan; married second wife, Micaela diLeonardo, April 12, 1969. Education: Harvard University, B.A., 1958; Columbia University, M.A., 1960; Yale University, Ph.D., 1964.

CAREER: University of Washington, Seattle, instructor, 1962-64, assistant professor of American and comparative literature, 1964-65; University of California, Berkeley, assistant professor of English, 1965-70.

WRITINGS: In the Wash, privately printed, 1958; Voyage Noir: Journal of a Trip to Cuba, Haiti, Jamaica, privately printed, 1963; (contributor) Seymour L. Gross, editor, A Benito Cereno Handbook, Wadsworth, 1965; Voyages: Poems, Kayak, c. 1968; (contributor) Eugene Wildman, editor, Experiments in Prose, Swallow Press, 1969; (translator) Henri Michaux, Ecuador, University of Washington Press, 1970; Persian Notes, Frythare Press, 1972; Mary Book, privately printed, 1972; (contributor) Richard Kostelanetz, editor, Breakthrough in Fiction, Something Else Press, 1972. Contributor to College English, New England Quarterly, Voices, Fat Abbot, Jabberwock, Between Worlds, Chicago Review, Poetry, Walt Whitman Review, Comparative Literature, and other periodicals.

WORK IN PROGRESS: Zebeiko; The Founder of Cities and Other Poems; Conventions of Happiness, on pastoral in the work of Sand, Fromentin, Jewett, Alain-Fournier, and Dineson; Iran; a translation of Ungaretti's L'Allegria.

SIDELIGHTS: Magowan's poetic personal comment to CA was these lines: "The pleasure of things innocently grasped/A peacock in the eyes of the rain."

*   *   *

MAILER, Norman 1923-

PERSONAL: Born January 31, 1923, in Long Branch, N.J.; son of Issac Barnett and Fanny (Schneider) Mailer; married Beatrice Silverman, 1944 (divorced, 1952); married Adele Morales, 1954 (divorced, 1962); married Jean Campbell, 1962 (divorced); married Beverly Bentley (an actress), 1963; children: (first marriage) Susan; (second marriage) Danielle, Elizabeth; (third marriage) Kate; (fourth marriage) Michael, Stephen. Education: Harvard University, S.B., 1943. Politics: "Left Conservative." Address: c/o Scott Meredith, Inc., 580 5th Ave., New York, N.Y.

CAREER: Writer. Military service: U.S. Army, infantryman, 1943-46. Awards, honors: National Institute of Arts and Letters grant in literature, 1960; Pulitzer Prize for General Nonfiction, National Book Award, 1969, for The Armies of the Night.

WRITINGS: The Naked and the Dead, Rinehart, 1948, reissued with an introduction by Chester E. Eisinger, Holt, 1968; Barbary Shore, Rinehart, 1951, reissued with an introduction by Norman Podhoretz, Grosset, 1963;

The Deer Park, Putnam, 1955; (contributor) New Short Novels, 2, Ballantine, 1956; Advertisements for Myself, Putnam, 1959; The White Negro, City Lights Books, 1959; Deaths for the Ladies, and Other Disasters (poems), Putnam, 1962; The Presidential Papers, Putnam. 1963; An American Dream (novel; first written in serial form for Esquire), Dial, 1965; Cannibals and Christians, Dial, 1966; (author of text) The Bullfight, Macmillan, 1967; The Deer Park (two-act drama; based on novel; first produced Off-Broadway, at Theatre de Lys, January 31, 1967), Dial, 1967; The Short Fiction of Norman Mailer, Dell, 1967; Why Are We in Vietnam? (novel), Putnam, 1967; The Armies of the Night: History as a Novel, The Novel as History (non-fiction), New American Library, 1968; The Idol and the Octopus (non-fiction), Dell, 1968; Miami and the Siege of Chicago: An Informed History of the Republican and Democratic Conventions of 1968, World, 1968; (contributor) Peter Manso, editor, Running Against the Machine: The Mailer-Breslin Campaign, Doubleday, 1969; Of a Fire on the Moon, Little, Brown, 1970 (published in England as A Fire on the Moon, Weidenfield & Nicholson, 1970); King of the Hill: On the Fight of the Century, New American Library, 1971; Long Patrol: 25 Years of Writing from the Work of Norman Mailer, edited by Robert F. Lucid, World, 1971; Maidstone: A Mystery (transcription of an improvised film dialogue), New American Library, 1971; The Prisoner of Sex, Little, Brown, 1971; Existential Errands: Twenty-Six Pieces Selected by the Author from the Body of His Writings, Little, Brown, 1972; Norman Mailer Convention Book, New American Library, 1972; St. George and the Godfather, New American Library, 1972; Marilyn, Grosset, 1973. Author of screenplay, "The Long Chance," for Cinema Center Films, also author of unpublished play, "D.J." An editor of Dissent, 1953-63; co-founder of Village Voice, 1956, also Esquire columnist. Contributor to New York Post, Partisan Review, New World Writing, Dscovery, Esquire, and numerous other publications.

SIDELIGHTS: Mailer has always been the public personality rather than the secluded artist. His adventures and misadventures are periodically recorded by what he calls that "Godawful Time Magazine world." Admittedly afflicted with self-pity and megalomania, the onetime prophet of Hip has, however, discussed important aspects of contemporary life. In The White Negro, his definitive essay on Hip, he writes of the American existentialist, "the hipster, the man who knows that if our collective condition is to live with instant death by atomic war, relatively quick death by the State as l'univers concentrationnaire, or with a slow death by conformity with every creative and rebellious instinct stifled, . . . the only life-giving answer is to accept the terms of death, to live with death as immediate danger, to divorce oneself with society, to exist without roots, to set out on that uncharted journey into the rebellious imperatives of the self . . ."

Mailer has so set out. Known to be moody and bellicose, he was once convicted of stabbing his wife. He was formerly addicted to Seconal, Benzedrine, and marijuana, and now sees his years as a marijuana smoker as the genesis of his existentialism. He told his Paris Review interviewer: "One's condition on marijuana is always existential. One can feel the importance of each moment and how it is changing one. One feels one's being, one becomes aware of the enormous apparatus of nothingness." In 1969, Mailer ran, unsuccessfully, for mayor of New York.

During a press conference held on March 10, 1965, Mailer said: "Four years ago my life went out of control for a time. Once you become notorious your personality takes on a legendary quality. I am more and more surprised by what I am supposed to have done in the last two years." One of the things he did during that time was hurl obscenities at a lecture audience. "I thought I had God's message at the time," he said, "[but] I regret it."

His literary influences are numerous: First, Jean Malaquais ("He's the only man I know who can combine a powerfully dogmatic mind with the keenest sense of nuance. . . ."), E.M. Forster (from whom he believes he learned the most about technique), James Farrell, John Dos Passos, John Steinbeck, F. Scott Fitzgerald, Thomas Wolfe, and Ernest Hemingway (whom he considers the champion writer of all time).

Concerning style, Mailer quotes Alfred Kazin as saying: "Mailer is fond of his style as an Italian tenor is of his vocal cords." Kazin later wrote: "I believe that *Armies of the Night* is just as brilliant a personal testimony as Whitman's diary of the civil war. . . ." Mailer himself told the *Paris Review:* "A really good style comes only when a man has become as good as he can be. Style is character. A good style cannot come from a bad undisciplined character. Now a man may be evil, but I believe that people can be evil in their essential natures and still have good characters. Good in the sense of being well-tuned. . . . I think good style is a matter of rendering out of oneself all the cupidities, all the cripplings, all the velleities. And then I think one has to develop one's physical grace. Writers who are possessed of some physical grace may tend to write better than writers who are physically clumsy."

An exacting writer, he once said: "I try to go over my work in every conceivable mood. I edit on a spectrum which runs from the high clear manic impressions of a drunk which has made one electrically alert all the way down to the soberest reaches of depression where I can hardly bear my words."

There are critics who say that after his enormously successful *The Naked and the Dead* there is only decline. Mailer is not sure: "The hardest thing for a writer to decide is whether he's burned out or merely lying fallow. I was ready to think I was burned out before I even started *The Naked and the Dead.*" Perhaps critics find some evidence of decline in the clamor that issues from his pages. Gore Vidal once observed: "Mailer is forever shouting at us that he is about to tell us something we must know or has just told us something revelatory and we failed to hear him or that he will, God grant his poor abused brain and body just one more chance, get through to us so that we will know. . . . Each time he speaks he must become more bold, more loud, put on brighter motley and shake more foolish bells. . . . Yet of all my contemporaries I retain the greatest affection for Mailer as a force and as an artist."

Mailer has produced several improvised films, including "Wild 90," "Beyond the Law," and "Maidstone," with a cast of his family and friends. Producer Mitchell Lifton booked *Armies of the Night* for filming in 1970.

AVOCATIONAL INTERESTS: Skiing, boating, and fishing.

BIOGRAPHICAL/CRITICAL SOURCES: Commentary, February, 1960; *American Scholar,* spring, 1961; *Esquire,* May, 1961; Alfred Kazin, *Contemporaries,* Little, Brown, 1962; Myrick Land, *The Fair Art of Literary Mayhem,* Holt, 1962; Richard Kostelanetz, editor, *On Contemporary Literature,* Avon, 1964; *Paris Review,* winter-spring, 1964; *Villiage Voice,* February 18, 1965; *Publisher's Weekly,* March 22, 1965; John W. Aldridge, *Time to Murder and Create: The Contemporary Novel in Crisis,* McKay, 1966; *New York Times Book Review,* September 17, 1967, May 5, 1968; Richard Foster, *Norman Mailer,* University of Minnesota Press, 1968; Robert F. Lucid, *Norman Mailer: The Man & His Work,* Little,

Brown, 1971; *New York Review of Books,* May 6, 1971, June 15, 1972; William R. Poirer, *Norman Mailer,* Viking, 1972; Leo Beal Braudy, editor, *Norman Mailer,* Prentice-Hall, 1972.

* * *

MAIR, Alistair 1924-

PERSONAL: Born June 10, 1924, in Mauchline, Ayrshire, Scotland; son of Alexander (a company director) and Catherine (Robertson) Mair; married Gwenyth E. Minnis, October 22, 1952; children: Alistair Alan, Diana Catriona. *Education:* Attended George Watson's College; University of Glasgow, M.B., Ch.B., 1947. *Home:* Tigh-A-Gharaidh, Port Appin, Argyll, Scotland.

CAREER: Western Infirmary, Glasgow, Scotland, house physician, 1947-48, casualty officer, 1948; Royal Hospital for Sick Children, Glasgow, Scotland, house physician, 1950-51; Royal Infirmary, Stirling, Scotland, house surgeon in maternity department, 1951; general medical practice, Grangemouth, Scotland, 1952-62; now full-time writer. *Military service:* Royal Air Force, pathologist, 1948-50; became flight lieutenant. *Member:* British Medical Association, International P.E.N. (vice-president, Scotland, 1961—). *Awards, honors:* Frederick Niven Award for *The Devil's Minister.*

WRITINGS—All novels: *Rue with a Difference,* R. Hale, 1955; *The Seventeenth Laird,* R. Hale, 1957; *Diana and the Wise Man,* R. Hale, 1957; *The Man Within,* R. Hale, 1959; *The Devil's Minister,* R. Hale, 1961; *The Douglas Affair,* Morrow, 1966; *Yesterday Was Summer,* Heinemann, 1968; *The Ripening Time,* Heinemann, 1970. Contributor to *British Medical Journal.*

WORK IN PROGRESS: Radio and television scripts.

SIDELIGHTS—Principal interest: Observation of the curious behavior of human beings. Ambitions: Few. Hopes: Fewer. Expectations: None. Principal pleasure: Living. *Avocational interests:* Hill walking, shooting, entertaining friends.

BIOGRAPHICAL/CRITICAL SOURCES: Times Literary Supplement, July 7, 1966; *Observer Review,* January 4, 1970.

* * *

MAIZEL, Clarice Matthews 1919-
(C.L. Maizel, Leah Maizel)

PERSONAL: Surname is pronounced My-zel; born December 25, 1919, in Lincolnshire, England; daughter of William Henry (a farmer) and Rose (Markham) Matthews; married Joseph Maizel (a physician), January, 1943; children: Danzil, Judy. *Education:* Trained as nurse, 1939-42. *Home:* Mill Lane, Whitwell, near Worksop, Nottinghamshire, England. *Agent:* Laurence Pollinger Ltd., 18 Maddox St., Mayfair, London W.C.1, England.

CAREER: Did hospital nursing for ten years; justice of the peace, Derbyshire, England, 1960; juvenile court magistrate, 1961—. Lecturer on child care and delinquency and on writing and literature. Adviser, Ministry of National Assistance. Member, Group Hospital Committee; area superintendent, St. John Ambulance Brigade. *Member:* Royal College of Nursing, Magistrates Association.

WRITINGS: Son of Condor, Criterion, 1964. Author of a play, and of scripts for British Broadcasting Corp. and Australia and New Zealand radio. Contributor of short stories and articles to magazines.

SIDELIGHTS: Mrs. Mizel writes to *CA:* "I consider that children's writing is the most important of any. A word can slant their future outlook and attitude. I write to entertain, but also to prise open the oyster of the world, trying to find a pearl." *Avocational interests:* Photography and growing roses.

* * *

MALLORY, Walter Hampton 1892-

PERSONAL: Born July 27, 1892, in Newburgh, N.Y.; son of Edward Wolcott and Mary (Gray) Mallory; married Alice Evans, May 13, 1919; children: Walter Hampton, Jr. (deceased), George Wolcott. *Education:* Columbia University, student, 1913-15. *Politics:* Republican. *Religion:* Episcopalian. *Residence:* Manchester, Vt.; and Hacienda del Sol, Tucson, Ariz. *Office:* 58 East 68th St., New York, N.Y. 10021.

CAREER: Went to Europe as leader of Columbia Relief Expedition to Serbia, 1915, served as executive officer of Near East Relief, 1915-16, as special assistant to U.S. ambassador at Petrograd, Russia, 1916-17; U.S. Shipping Board, foreign representative, 1919; China International Famine Relief Commission, Peking, executive secretary, 1922-26; Council on Foreign Relations, New York, N.Y., executive director, 1927-59, director, 1959—. Member of Allied Mission to Observe the Elections in Greece, with rank of U.S. minister, 1946; U.S. delegate to European-American Assembly, Switzerland, 1962. China Institute in America, president, 1943-47, trustee; member, China Medical Board, 1947-58; director, Asia Foundation. *Military service:* American Expeditionary Forces, Field Artillery, 1917-18.

MEMBER: Asia Society, Council on Foreign Relations, General Society of Mayflower Descendents, National Society of Sons of the Revolution, Century Club, Ekwanok Country Club (Manchester, Vt.). *Awards, honors:* Grand Order of Cristobal Colon (Dominican Republic); Order of Pure Gold (China); Cross of the Order of Mercy (Yugoslavia); Red Cross Decoration (Yugoslavia).

WRITINGS: China: Land of Famine, American Geographical Society, 1926; (editor) *Political Handbook and Atlas of the World,* Harper, annually, 1928—. Contributor of articles on international and Far Eastern affairs to periodicals.

* * *

MALM, William P(aul) 1928-

PERSONAL: Born March 6, 1928, in La Grange, Ill.; son of Royal Dinsmore (an engineer) and Theodora (Drumont) Malm; married Joyce Rutherford, April 24, 1954; children: Elaina Anne, Mia Jeanne, Cecilia Jane. *Education:* Northwestern University, B.M., 1949, M.M., 1950; University of California, Los Angeles, Ph.D., 1959. *Home:* 1419 East Park Pl., Ann Arbor, Mich. 48103. *Office:* School of Music, University of Michigan, Ann Arbor, Mich. 48104.

CAREER: University of Illinois, Urbana, instructor in music, 1950-51; University of California, Los Angeles, lecturer in music, 1957-60; University of Michigan, Ann Arbor, associate professor, 1960-66, professor of music, 1966—. Composer-pianist, New York, N.Y., 1947, 1953. Director of western student performance groups in Japanese music. *Military service:* U.S. Army, 1951-53, instructor at U.S. Naval School of Music; became sergeant. *Member:* Society for Ethnomusicology (board), Society for Asian Music (board), Association for Asian Studies, American Musicology Society, Toyo ongaku gakkai. *Awards, honors:* Monograph prize, American Academy of Arts and Sciences, 1959, for *Nagauta: The Heart of Kabuki Music;* Ford fellowship, 1955-57; American Council of Learned Societies fellowship, 1963-64; Henry Russel Award for Teaching, 1960.

WRITINGS: Japanese Music and Musical Instruments, Tuttle, 1959; *Nagauta: The Heart of Kabuki Music,* Tut-

tle, 1963; *Music Cultures of the Pacific, Near East, and Asia,* Prentice-Hall, 1967. Contributor of chapters to three other books; contributor of articles and reviews to professional journals.

WORK IN PROGRESS: The Acting and Music of Japanese Kabuki.

SIDELIGHTS: Malm can perform on two kinds of Japanese shamisen plucked lutes, in addition to drums and flutes; he sings in two Japanese genre and performs instrumentally in three. His field work includes a video taped expedition in Kelantan, Malaysia.

* * *

MALONE, Wex S(mathers) 1906-

PERSONAL: Born November 17, 1906, in Asheville, N.C.; son of Charles Neilson and Joanna Eleanor (Smathers) Malone; married Helen L. Jeffress, June 14, 1933; children: Helen Malone Monteilh, Charles N. *Education:* University of Chicago, student, 1926-27; University of North Carolina, B.A., 1928, J.D., 1931; Harvard University, LL.M., 1933. *Home:* 1895 East Lakeshore Dr., Baton Rouge, La. 70808. *Office:* Law School, Louisiana State University Baton Rouge, La. 70803.

CAREER: Admitted to New York Bar, 1934. University of Mississippi, University, professor of law, 1931-32, 1935-39; associate in a New York law firm and member of legal department of Irving Trust Co., New York, N.Y., 1933-35; Louisiana State University, Baton Rouge, professor of law, 1939-66, Boyd Professor, 1966—. On leave as senior attorney for Federal Public Housing, 1942-45. Visiting professor at University of Chicago, University of Michigan, other universities and law schools. Adviser, restatement of torts, American Law Institute. *Member:* Association of American Law Schools (national president, 1967), Order of the Coif (national president, 1963-66).

WRITINGS: Louisiana Workmen's Compensation Law and Practice, West Publishing, 1951; (with Green, Pedrick, and Rahl) *Cases on Torts,* West Publishing, 1957; (with Green, Pedrick, and Rahl) *Cases on Injuries to Relations,* West Publishing, 1959; (with Marcus Plant) *Cases on Workmen's Compensation,* West Publishing, 1963; (with Guerry) *Studies in Louisiana Torts Law,* Bobbs-Merrill 1970. Contributor to legal journals.

* * *

MALPASS, E(ric) L(awson) 1910-

PERSONAL: Born November 14, 1910, in Derby, England; son of Tom Riley and Lilias (Lawson) Malpass; married Muriel Gladys Barnett, October 3, 1936; children: Michael Lawson. *Education:* Attended King Henry VIII School, Coventry, England. *Religion:* Anglican. *Home:* 117 Trowell Grove, Long Eaton, Nottingham, England.

CAREER: Barclays Bank Ltd., Long Eaton, Nottingham, England, 1926—, became first cashier, 1947. *Military service:* Royal Air Force, 1941-46; became flight lieutenant. *Member:* Nottingham Writers' Club. *Awards, honors:* Winner of *Observer* short story competition, 1955; Palma D'oro for best humorous novel of year in Italy, for *Beefy Jones.*

WRITINGS—Novels: Beefy Jones, Longmans, Green, 1957; *Operazione Gemelli,* Baldini & Castoldi, 1960; *Morning's at Seven,* Heinemann, 1965, Viking, 1966; *At the Height of the Moon,* Heinemann, 1967; *Oh My Darling Daughter,* Eyre & Spottiswoode, 1970. Regular contributor of short stories to *Argosy* (London) and to British Broadcasting Corp. programs.

WORK IN PROGRESS: A novel.

SIDELIGHTS: *Morning's at Seven* and *At the Height of the Moon* have both been made into motion pictures in Germany. *Avocational interests:* Theatre, countryside, church and charity work, and reading.

BIOGRAPHICAL/CRITICAL SOURCES: *Book Week,* January 30, 1966; *Observer Review,* August 23, 1970; *Times Literary Supplement,* October 2, 1970.

* * *

MAMATEY, Victor S(amuel) 1917-

PERSONAL: Born February 19, 1917, in North Braddock, Pa.; son of Albert P. and Olga (Darmek) Mamatey; married Denise M. Perronne, November 20, 1945; children: Albert R., Peter V. *Education:* Comenius University, Czechoslovakia, diploma, 1938; student at Wittenberg College, 1938-39, University of Chicago, 1939-40; Harvard University, A.M., 1941; University of Paris, Ph.D., 1949. *Politics:* Democrat. *Religion:* Lutheran. *Home:* 142 Spruce Valley Rd., Athens, Ga. 30601. *Office:* Department of History, University of Georgia, Athens, Ga. 30601.

CAREER: Florida State University, Tallahassee, Fla., 1949-67, became professor of history; University of Georgia, Athens, professor of history, 1967—. Visiting professor of history at Russian Institute, Columbia University, 1961, Tulane University, 1963. *Military service:* U.S. Army, 1942-46; served in China-Burma-India, and European theaters; became sergeant. *Member:* American Historical Association, American Association for the Advancement of Slavic Studies. *Awards, honors:* George Louis Beer Prize of American Historical Association, 1958, for *The United States and East Central Europe, 1914-1918;* Guggenheim fellow, 1959.

WRITINGS: *The United States and East Central Europe, 1914-1918: A Study in Wilsonian Diplomacy and Propaganda,* Princeton University Press, 1957; (with Geoffrey Bruun) *The World in the Twentieth Century,* 4th edition (Mamatey was not associated with earlier editions), Heath, 1962, 5th edition, 1967; *Soviet Russian Imperialism,* Van Nostrand, 1964; *Rise of the Habsburg Empire, 1526-1815,* Holt, 1971; (editor with Radomir Luza) *A History of the Czechoslovak Republic, 1918-1948,* Princeton University Press, 1973. Editor, "Florida State University Studies," 1955-58.

WORK IN PROGRESS: A study of East European history.

SIDELIGHTS: Mamatey spent a total of fourteen years as resident, student, and traveler in Europe; he is competent in French, German, and Slavic languages.

* * *

MAMIS, Justin E. 1929-

PERSONAL: Born February 18, 1929, in Providence, R.I.; son of Abraham H. (a salesman) and Anne (Alexander) Mamis; married Nancy Braverman, December 23, 1951; children: Toby, Lisa, Joshua. *Education:* Yale University, B.A., 1950. *Home:* 110 Riverside Dr., New York, N.Y. 10024.

CAREER: Early jobs include bellhop, bus boy, roustabout, horse wrangler, baseball player, and furniture salesman; Zuckerman, Smith & Co., New York, N.Y., stockbroker, 1959-63; Green Mountain Park, Pownal, Vt., mutuel cashier, 1963-64. *Military service:* U.S. Army, 1951-53; became second lieutenant. *Member:* New Dramatists Committee (New York), International Brotherhood of Teamsters.

WRITINGS: *Love* (novel), Stein & Day, 1964.

WORK IN PROGRESS: "A Cup for Elijah," a three-act play; *The Ball Player,* a novel; an untitled three-act play.

MANDEL, William M(arx) 1917-

PERSONAL: Surname is accented on second syllable; born June 4, 1917, in New York, N.Y.; son of Max Gimpel and Dora (Schachter) Mandel; married Tanya Millstein, October 24, 1935; children: Phyllis (Mrs. Keith Glick), Robert, David. *Education:* Attended College of City of New York (now City College of City University of New York); Moscow University, student, 1932; *Home:* 233 Lake Dr., Berkeley, Calif. 94708.

CAREER: American Russian Institute, New York, N.Y., research associate, 1940-44; United Press, New York, N.Y., Russian expert, World War II; Stanford University, Stanford, Calif., postdoctoral fellow in Slavic studies at Hoover Institute, 1947; Stefansson Library, New York, N.Y., research associate, 1948-50; self-employed science translator, from Russian, French, and German, in New York, N.Y., and Berkeley, Calif., 1950-62; International Arts and Sciences Press, New York, N.Y., translator of seven Russian journals in social and behavioral fields, 1962—. Instructor at San Francisco State College, San Jose State College, and University of California, Berkeley. Lecturer and broadcaster on Soviet Union, with radio program originating on KPFA, Berkeley, Calif., and now carried by six stations, 1957—. *Member:* American Association for the Advancement of Slavic Studies, American Translators Association (founding member), Gamma Theta Upsilon (honarary), Alpha Kappa Delta (honorary).

WRITINGS: *The Soviet Far East and Central Asia,* Dial, 1944; *A Guide to the Soviet Union,* Dial, 1946; (compiler) *Soviet Source Materials on USSR Relations with East Asia, 1945-1950* (documents), Institute of Pacific Relations, 1950; *Russia Re-Examined: The Land, the People and How They Live,* Hill & Wang, 1964, revised edition, 1967 (published in England as *A New Look at Russia: The Land, the People and How They Live,* Evans Brothers, 1965); (contributor) Samuel Hendel and R.L. Braham, editors, *The USSR after Fifty Years,* Knopf, 1967; (contributor) Alex Simirenko, editor, *Social Thought in the Soviet Union,* Quadrangle, 1969; (contributor) Arlie Hochschild, editor, *Women,* Trans-Action, 1971; *Soviet Reality,* Free Press, in press. Contributor to *Encyclopedia Arctica, New Republic, Pacific Affairs, Far Eastern Survey, Ski, Current Anthropology, Slavic Review, American Sociological Review, California Social Science Review, Political Affairs,* and other periodicals.

SIDELIGHTS: Mandel lived in Russia, 1931-32, and traveled there in 1959, 1962, 1966, and 1970. Copies of his personal papers are on file in the Contemporary Social Action Collection, State Historical Society of Wisconsin.

* * *

MANDELKORN, Eugenia Miller 1916-
(Eugenia Miller)

PERSONAL: Born May 11, 1916; daughter of Philip (in real estate) and Selda (Vandewarte) Miller; married Robert S. Mandelkorn (a captain, U.S. Navy), June 6, 1937; children: Philip, Richard, Joel. *Education:* Attended Marjorie Webster Junior College. *Politics:* "Democrat from time to time." *Religion:* Jewish. *Home:* I Bis Rue Lavoisier, Le Chesnay, Seine-et-Oise, France. *Office:* c/o Captain R.S. Mandelkorn, Live Oak, SHAPE, APO 55, New York, N.Y.

CAREER: Former newspaper reporter in Annapolis, Md. *Member:* Authors League of America, U.S. Marine and Navy Officers' Wives Club of Paris. *Awards, honors:* First prize for feature article, National League of American Pen Women.

WRITINGS—Under name Eugenia Miller: *Deadline at Spook Cabin,* Holt, 1958; *Rocking Hill Road,* Holt, 1959;

The Golden Spur, Holt, 1964; *The Sign of the Salamander,* Holt, 1967. Contributor to *U.S. Lady, Baltimore Sun,* and *Baltimore American.*

SIDELIGHTS: Mrs. Mandelkorn writes to *CA:* "The *Golden Spur* was my first attempt at historical background and I believe I have found my own special bent at last.... While doing research I find that digging for historical unknown facts is very exciting—and my aim now is to try to transmit that excitement to young readers—to try to let them 'see' back into an earlier time. I am not above sneaking in a bit of history—teaching—but only by means of an authentic background. My main objective is to tell a story.

"As a personal note, I have been living in Paris—or rather, near Paris , . . . and shortly before that lived a year in Italy. I am interested of course in writing about foreign countries for American children. If I ever write a book with a 'message' it will *not* be to stress the sweet thought that 'children everywhere are just alike'—but that people everywhere are quite different, and have different habits—of thinking and otherwise—and that one should accept those differences."

BIOGRAPHICAL/CRITICAL SOURCES: *Best Sellers,* June 1, 1967; *Book World,* October 15, 1967.

*   *   *

MANDELL, Muriel (Hortense Levin)   1921-

PERSONAL: Born August 19, 1921, in New York, N.Y.; daughter of Simon and Gertrude (Maisel) Levin; married Horace Mandell (an auditor), January 23, 1945; children: Mark, Jonathan. *Education:* Brooklyn College, (now Brooklyn College of City University of New York), B.A. (cum laude), 1942; Columbia University, M.S. (journalism), 1943. *Home:* 72 Barrow St., New York, N.Y. 10014.

CAREER: Worked as correspondent for Overseas News Agency in Washington, D.C., police reporter for *Long Branch Daily Record,* Long Branch, N.J., and associate editor of *Tips* (magazine), New York, N.Y.; Radio Station WMGM, New York, N.Y., public relations, 1948-51; New York Board of Education, New York, N.Y., teacher of English, 1951—.

WRITINGS: (With Robert E. Wood) *Make Your Own Musical Instruments,* Sterling, 1957, revised edition, 1959; *101 Best Educational Games,* Sterling, 1958, revised edition published as *Games to Learn By: 100 Best Educational Games,* 1972; *Science for Children,* Sterling, 1959, reissued as *Physics Experiments for Children,* Dover, 1968 (published in England as *Science for Beginners,* Oak Tree Press, 1962); *Jonathan's Sparrow,* Lothrop, 1963; *The 51 Capitals of the U.S.A.,* Sterling, 1965; (with others) *Complete Science Course for Young Experimenters,* Sterling, 1967.

*   *   *

MANFRED, Frederick Feikema   1912-
(Feike Feikema)

PERSONAL: Surname originally Feikema; born January 6, 1912, in Rock Township, Doon, Iowa; son of Feike Feikes (a farmer and carpenter) and Aeltsje (von Engen) Feikema; married Maryanna Shorba (a part-time interviewing supervisor) October 31, 1952; children: Freya, Marya, Frederick F. *Education:* Calvin College, B.A., 1934; other courses at business college, 1937, University of Minnesota (correspondence). *Home:* Blue Mound, Luverne, Minn. 56156. *Agent:* Alan Collins, Curtis Brown Ltd., 60 East 56th St., New York, N.Y. 10022.

CAREER: Novelist whose earlier career included periods as warehouse roustabout, factory hand, filling station at-

tendant, interviewer for an opinion poll, and patient in a tuberculosis sanitarium; *Modern Medicine,* Minneapolis, Minn., an editor, 1942-43; Macalester College, St. Paul, Minn., writer-in-residence, 1949-51; University of South Dakota, Vermillion, writer-in-residence, 1968—. *Member:* Authors League, P.E.N., Society of Midland Writers (vice-president). *Awards, honors:* Grant-in-aid, American Academy of Arts and Letters, 1945; fellowships from Rockefeller Foundation, 1944-46, Field Foundation, 1948-49, Andreas Foundation, 1949, 1952, McKnight Foundation, 1958-59, Huntington Hartford Foundation, 1963.

WRITINGS—Novels, under name Feike Feikema: *The Golden Bowl,* Webb Publishing, 1944; *Boy Almighty,* Webb Publishing, 1945; *This Is the Year,* Doubleday, 1947; *The Chokecherry Tree,* Doubleday, 1948, revised edition, A. Swallow, 1961; *The Primitive* (first in a trilogy entitled "World's Wanderer"), Doubleday, 1949; *The Brother* (second in the trilogy), Doubleday, 1950; *The Giant* (third in the trilogy), Doubleday, 1951; *Wanderlust* (revised edition of *The Primitive, The Brother,* and *The Giant*), A. Swallow, 1962; *Scarlet Plume,* Trident, 1964; *The Man Who Looked Like the Prince of Wales,* Trident, 1965, reissued as *The Secret Place,* Pocket Books, 1967; *King of Spades,* Trident, 1966; *Eden Prairie,* Trident, 1968.

Under own name: *Lord Grizzly,* McGraw, 1954; *Morning Red,* A. Swallow, 1956; *Riders of Judgment,* Random House, 1957; *Conquering Horse,* McDowell-Obolensky, 1959; *Arrow of Love* (story collection), A. Swallow, 1961; *Winter Count: Poems, 1934-1965,* James D. Thueson, 1966; *Apples of Paradise, and Other Stories,* Trident, 1968.

Contributor to *New Republic, Esquire, Minnesota Quarterly, American Scholar, Names, Critique, Roundup, South Dakota Review, Plainsong, Northwest Life, Chicago Sun Times, Saturday Review, Minnesota Review,* and other publications.

WORK IN PROGRESS: A novel about a Minnesota stonecarver-sculptor circa 1918-1968, who becomes a voice for his "place," titled *Milk of Wolves.*

SIDELIGHTS: George Kellogg describes Manfred as "a kind of Thomas Wolfe or Vardis Fisher of the Iowa-Minnesota-South Dakota region which he himself has entitled Siouxland. Like Fisher he has an intimate mastery of authentic rural detail; like Wolfe he has a gigantic lyrical capacity with which to vitalize that detail. Like most Western writers of talent, he failed fully to engage the Eastern critics, at least as far as his treatment of the contemporary scene was concerned."

Manfred told *CA:* "I like long walks alone in the country; I like driving alone in the West; I like getting up alone for breakfast and eating heartily; [I] love to play ball with my boy; [I] can't have enough music around me; [I] enjoy Chaucer to the hilt, all of him; [I] like much of Faulkner; [I] admire the Bible; and, finally, [I] also admire Vardis Fisher, Frank Waters, and Walter Van Tilburg Clark."

He adds: "I have preferred to live in this country I call Siouxland. It is where my roots are; it is where my rich-minded friends live. I have some trouble feeling at home in New York, mostly because I find people there naive and sometimes even sub-human. I also have trouble feeling at home in Hollywood, mostly because I find people there dishonest. Interestingly enough, our best writers have come from the hinterlands, e.g. Faulkner, Steinbeck, Dreiser, Lewis, Fisher, Hemingway, Cather."

BIOGRAPHICAL/CRITICAL SOURCES: *College English,* December, 1957; *Western Review,* spring, 1958; *South Dakota Review,* autumn, 1964, summer, 1966, winter, 1969-70; George Kellogg, *Frederick Manfred: A Bibliography*, Alan Swallow, 1965; Philip Durham and E.L. Jones, *The Frontier in American Literature*, Odyssey, 1969; *Sinclair Lewis Newsletter*, Volume II, number 1, 1970; J. Gorden Taylor, *The Literature of the American West*, Houghton, 1971.

* * *

MANHATTAN, Avro 1914-

PERSONAL: Born April 6, 1914, in Milan, Italy; son of Louis and Marie Antic (Roosevelt) Manhattan. *Education:* Studied for varying periods at Sorbonne, University of Paris, at London School of Economics and Political Science, University of London, and at other universities. *Politics:* "Stubbornly independent." *Religion:* "Genuine believer in God, firm disbeliever in all established churches." *Home:* 24 Ansdell Ter., Kensington, London W.8, England.

CAREER: Onetime director of Radio Freedom, a station in England broadcasting to occupied Europe and partisans; British Foreign Office, staff of political warfare department, 1940-43; British Broadcasting Corp., London, England, writer of political commentaries, 1943-46; free-lance writer. Committee member, Federal Union, London, England; member of executive committee, Stopes Birth Control Clinic, London, England, 1954-59. *Member:* Royal Society of Literature, Society of Authors, Ethical Union, P.E.N., British Interplanetary Society (life).

WRITINGS: The Rumbling of the Apocalypse, Airoldi, 1934; *Towards the New Italy*, preface by H.G. Wells, Lindsay Drummond, 1943; *Latin America and the Vatican*, C.A. Watts, 1946; *The Vatican and the U.S.A.*, C.A. Watts, 1946; *Spain and the Vatican*, C.A. Watts, 1946; *The Catholic Church Against the Twentieth Century*, C.A. Watts, 1947, 2nd edition, 1950; *The Vatican in Asia*, C.A. Watts, 1948; *Religion in Russia*, C.A. Watts, 1948; *The Vatican in World Politics*, Gaer Associates, 1949; *Catholic Imperialism and World Freedom*, C.A. Watts, 1952, 2nd edition, 1959; *Terror over Yugoslavia, the Threat to Europe*, C.A. Watts, 1953; *The Dollar and the Vatican*, Pioneer Press, 1956, 3rd edition, 1957; *Vatican Imperialism in the Twentieth Century*, Zondervan, 1965; *Catholic Power Today*, Lyle Stuart, 1967; *Catholic Terror in Ireland*, Paravision Publications, 1971, 4th edition, Attic Press, 1972; *The Vatican Billions: Two Thousand Years of Wealth Accumulation*, Attic Press, 1972. Stories anthologized in *Fifty Short Science Fiction Tales*, edited by Isaac Asimov and Groff Conklin, and *Untravelled Worlds*, edited by Alan Frank Barter and Raymond Wilson, Macmillan, 1966. Contributor to *Lilliput, Literary Guide, Republic, Everybody's London, Humanist, Fantasy, Rationalist, Churchman, Protestant Telegraph, Freethinker*, and other periodicals.

WORK IN PROGRESS: God and the Universe.

SIDELIGHTS: Manhattan was a friend of George Bernard Shaw, actress Lillah MacCarthy, and H.G. Wells, with whom he cooperated in drafting and distributing a Bill of Human Rights, intended as a basis for a new world community after World War II. *Avocational interests:* Astronomy, ants and termites, painting, sculpture, writing poetry.

* * *

MANN, Dean Edson 1927-

PERSONAL: Born July 22, 1927, in Ogden, Utah; son of Leslie John (an accountant) and Veda (Edson) Mann; married Helen Joyce Krage, February 5, 1951; children: Jeffrey, Karen, Lindsay, Preston, Kimberley, Randall, Tamara. *Education:* Yale University, student, 1945; University of California, Berkeley, A.B., 1951, M.A., 1954, Ph.D., 1958. *Politics:* Democrat. *Religion:*

Latter-Day Saints (Mormon). *Home:* 476 Wakefield Rd., Goleta, Calif. 93017. *Office:* Department of Political Science, University of California, Santa Barbara, Calif. 93106.

CAREER: University of Arizona, Tucson, instructor, 1955-57, assistant professor of government, 1958-60; American Political Science Association, Washington, D.C., congressional fellow, 1957-58; Brookings Institution, Washington, D.C., research associate, senior staff, 1960-63; Ford Foundation, Caracas, Venezuela, program specialist, 1963-65; University of California, Santa Barbara, 1965—, began as associate professor, now professor of political science and chairman of the department. Consultant to Outdoor Recreation Resources Review Commission, 1959, and to General Research Corp. *Military service:* U.S. Navy, 1945-46. *Member:* American Political Science Association, American Society for Public Administration, American Association of University Professors, American Association for the Advancement of Science (secretary of committee on arid lands, 1965—), Western Political Science Association, Phi Beta Kappa.

WRITINGS: (With David A. Bingham) *Government in Arizona's Metropolitan Areas*, Bureau of Business and Public Research, University of Arizona, 1959; *The Politics of Water in Arizona*, University of Arizona Press, 1963; (contributor) Carle Hodge, editor, *Aridity and Man: The Challenge of the Arid Lands in the United States*, American Association for the Advancement of Science, 1963; (with Jameson W. Doig) *The Assistant Secretaries: Problems and Processes of Appointment*, Brookings Institution, 1965; (with Doig) *Federal Political Executives: Selection and Recruitment*, Brookings Institution, 1965; (with William Ebenstein, C. Herman Pritchett, and Henry A. Turner) *American Democracy in World Perspective*, Harper, 1967; (with David Stanley and Doig) *Men Who Govern: A Biographical Profile of Federal Political Executives*, Brookings Institution, 1967; *The Citizen and the Bureaucracy: Complaint-Handling Procedures of Three California Legislators*, Institute of Governmental Studies, University of California (Berkeley), 1968; (contributor) *Human Dimensions of the Atmosphere*, National Science Foundation, 1968; (contributor) Howard Taubenfeld, editor, *Weather Modification and the Law*, Oceana, 1968; (with A.E. Keir Nash and Phil Olson) *Oil Pollution and the Public Interest: A Study of the Santa Barbara Oil Spill*, Institute of Government Studies, University of California (Berkeley), 1972; *Political and Institutional Analysis of the Interbasin Transfers*, National Water Commission, 1972. Contributor of articles to professional journals. Member of board of editors, *Western Political Quarterly*, 1968-70, *Land Economics*, 1969—, *Policy Studies Journal*, 1972—.

WORK IN PROGRESS: Development of a research program in political science at the Escuela de Administracion Publica, Caracas, Venezuela.

* * *

MANNHEIM, Grete (Salomon) 1909-

PERSONAL: Born May 14, 1909, in Celle, West Germany; came to United States in 1949, naturalized in 1955; daughter of Oscar (a businessman) and Nanny Schloss) Salomon; married Ludwig Mannheim, September, 1930 (divorced June, 1949); children: Hanna (Mrs. Joe Baer), Susan (Mrs. Norman Tanen). *Education:* Seminar Frobelhaus, Berlin, Germany, degree in nursery school teaching, 1928; Reiman Art School, Berlin, student, 1930. *Home:* 2609 Ave. L, Brooklyn, N.Y. 11210.

CAREER: Nursery school teacher in Berlin, Germany, 1928-36; operated studio specializing in child photography in Johannesburg, South Africa, 1936-49; free-lance photographer-writer in New York, N.Y., 1949—. Photography teacher, Camp Airy (boys' summer camp), Thurmond,

Md., 1952—. Photographs have appeared in exhibitions, and in magazines and advertising. *Member:* Forum of Writers for Young People, Photographic Historical Society of New York. *Awards, honors:* Awards for photography in national and international competitions.

WRITINGS—All self-illustration with photographs: (Illustrator) Elisabeth S. Helfman, *Patsy Pat: A Duck's Story,* Dutton, 1958; (and author of text with Blossom Budney) *My Pony Joker,* Knopf, 1961; *Farm Animals,* Knopf, 1964; *Touch Me, Touch Me Not,* Knopf, 1965; (compiler) *Feather or Fur: A Collection of Animal Poems,* Knopf, 1967; *The Two Friends,* Knopf, 1968; *The Geese Are Back,* Parents' Magazine Press, 1969; *The Baker's Children: A Visit to a Family Bakery,* Knopf, 1970; *The Veterinarian's Children,* Knopf, 1971. Contributor of articles on photography to *Popular Photography* and *Camera 35,* and of photographs to *Ladies' Home Journal, Parents' Magazine,* and other national magazines.

WORK IN PROGRESS: Two books for children, on zoos, travel, and nature.

*   *   *

MANSCHRECK, Clyde Leonard   1917-

PERSONAL: Surname is accented on both syllables; born January 27, 1917, in Krebs, Okla.; son of Chris G. (a cattleman) and Mary (Schuler) Manschreck; married Ardis Garvene Taylor (a high school teacher), children: Theo Clyde, Lee Allen, Aesta Ann. *Education:* University of Oklahoma, student, 1935-36; George Washington University, B.A., 1941; Garrett Biblical Institute, B.D., 1944; Northwestern University, M.A., 1944; Yale University, Ph.D., 1948. *Politics:* Independent. *Home:* 249 North Sandusky St., Delaware, Ohio 43015. *Office:* Methodist Theological School, Delaware, Ohio 43015.

CAREER: U.S. Department of Commerce, Washington, D.C., printer and editor, 1936-41; ordained to Methodist ministry, 1944, with first pastorate in Yalesville, Conn., 1948-54; Southern Methodist University, Dallas, Tex., assistant professor of religion, 1948-54, and special lecturer at Perkins School of Theology, 1952-53; Duke University, Durham, N.C., associate professor of religion, 1954-61; Methodist Theological School, Delaware, Ohio, professor of church history, 1961—. *Member:* National Association of Biblical Instructors (placement secretary, 1956-60), American Society of Church History, Society for Reformation Research, American Historical Association. *Awards, honors:* Carnegie Research grant, 1949-51; Ford faculty fellow, 1951-52; Guggenheim fellow, 1960-61; Fulbright grant for Melanchthon studies, 1960-61.

WRITINGS: Melanchthon: The Quiet Reformer, Abingdon, 1958; (compiler) *Prayers of the Reformers,* Muhlenberg, 1958; *The Reformation and Protestantism Today,* Association Press, 1960; (editor) *A History of Christianity,* Volume II: *Readings in the History of the Church from the Reformation to the Present,* Prentice-Hall, 1964; (editor and translator) Philipp Melanchthon, *Melanchthon on Christian Doctrine: Loci Communes 1555,* Oxford University Press, 1965; (editor and author of introduction) *An Erosion of Authority,* Abingdon, 1971. Columnist, "Books in Religion," for *All-Church Press.* Contributor to *Encyclopaedia Britannica, Collier's Encyclopedia, Encyclopedia Americana,* and to *Christian Century, Christian Advocate, Pulpit,* and other journals of religion. Editor, *Journal* of Methodist Theological School.

WORK IN PROGRESS: The Council of Trent and Modern Catholicism, for Abingdon; *A Layman's History of the Church.*

AVOCATIONAL INTERESTS: Dabbling in art, golf, and fishing.

BIOGRAPHICAL/CRITICAL SOURCES: Best Sellers, February 15, 1971.

*   *   *

MANSFIELD, Edwin   1930-

PERSONAL: Born June 8, 1930, in Kingston, N.Y.; son of Raymond and Sarah (Haas) Mansfield; married Lucile Howe (a psychologist), 1955; children: Edward, Elizabeth. *Education:* Dartmouth College, A.B., 1951; Duke University, M.A., 1953, Ph.D., 1955; University of London, postgraduate study, 1954-55. *Office:* Department of Economics, University of Pennsylvania, Philadelphia, Pa. 19104.

CAREER: Duke University, Durham, N.C., research associate, 1953-54; Carnegie Institute of Technology (now Carnegie-Mellon University), Pittsburgh, Pa., associate professor of economics, 1955-63; University of Pennsylvania, Wharton School of Finance, Philadelphia, professor of economics, 1963—. Visiting associate professor of economics at Yale University, 1961-62; visiting professor of economics at Harvard University, 1963-64. Consultant to Federal Power Commission, RAND Corp., National Science Foundation, Small Business Administration, U.S. Army, and U.S. Department of Commerce. *Member:* American Economic Association, American Statistical Association, Econometric Society (fellow), Phi Beta Kappa, Delta Upsilon. *Awards, honors:* Fulbright scholar; Ford Foundation faculty research fellow; fellow, Center for Advanced Study in the Behavioral Sciences.

WRITINGS: (Editor and author of introduction) *Monopoly Power and Economic Performance: The Problem of Industrial Concentration,* Norton, 1964, 3rd edition, 1972; (editor) *Managerial Economics and Operations Research: A Non-Mathematical Introduction,* Norton, 1966, revised edition, 1970; *The Economics of Technological Change,* Norton, 1968; *Industrial Research and Technological Innovation: An Econometric Analysis,* Norton, 1968; (compiler) *Defense, Science, and Public Policy,* Norton, 1968; *Macroeconomics: Theory and Application,* Norton, 1970; (compiler) *Elementary Statistics for Economics and Business: Selected Readings,* Norton, 1970; *Research and Innovation in the Modern Corporation,* Norton, 1971; (editor) *Macroeconomics: Selected Readings,* Norton, 1971; *Microeconomic Problems,* Norton, 1971; *Technological Change: An Introduction to a Vital Area of Modern Economics,* Norton, 1971; (compiler) *Microeconomics: Selected Readings,* Norton, 1971. Contributor to half a dozen economics journals. Associate editor, *Journal of ASA.*

WORK IN PROGRESS: Several books for Norton.

*   *   *

MANUEL, Frank Edward   1910-

PERSONAL: Born September 12, 1910, in Boston, Mass.; married October 6, 1936. *Education:* Harvard University, A.B., 1930, M.A., 1931, Ph.D., 1933. *Home:* 29 Washington Square W., New York, N.Y. 10011. *Office:* Department of History, New York University, 19 University Pl., New York, N.Y. 10003.

CAREER: Harvard University, Cambridge, Mass., teacher of history, government, and economics, 1935-37; research and administrative positions with National Defense Commission and Office of Price Administration, 1940-43, 1945-47; Western Reserve University (now Case Western Reserve University), Cleveland, Ohio, professor of history, 1947; Brandeis University, Waltham, Mass., professor of history and moral psychology, 1949-65; New York University, New York, N.Y., 1965—, began as professor, now Kenan Professor of History. *Mili-*

tary service: U.S. Army, 1943-45; served as combat intelligence officer with Twenty-First Corps; received Bronze Star. *Member:* American Historical Association, Authors League, Phi Beta Kappa. *Awards, honors:* Guggenheim fellow, 1957-58; fellow, Center for Advanced Study in the Behavioral Sciences, 1962-63; fellow, American Academy of Arts and Sciences.

WRITINGS: The Politics of Modern Spain, McGraw, 1938; *The Realities of American-Palestine Relations,* Public Affairs Press, 1949; *The Age of Reason,* Cornell University Press, 1951; *The New World of Henri Saint-Simon,* Harvard University Press, 1956; *The Eighteenth Century Confronts the Gods,* Harvard University Press, 1959; *The Prophets of Paris,* Harvard University Press, 1962; *Isaac Newton, Historian,* Harvard *University* Press, 1963; *Shapes of Philosophical History,* Stanford University Press, 1965; *The Enlightenment,* Prentice-Hall, 1965; (editor) *Utopias and Utopian Thought,* Houghton, 1966; (editor, translator, and author of introduction with Fritzie P. Manuel) *French Utopias: An Anthology of Ideal Societies,* Free Press, 1966; *A Portrait of Isaac Newton,* Harvard University Press, 1968; (editor) Johann Gottfried von Herder, *Reflections on the Philosophy of the History of Mankind,* University of Chicago Press, 1968; *Freedom from History, and Other Untimely Essays,* New York University Press, 1971.

BIOGRAPHICAL/CRITICAL SOURCES: Virginia Quarterly Review, spring, 1967, autumn, 1969; *New York Times Book Review,* February 25, 1968; *Saturday Review,* February 1, 1969; *New York Review of Books,* April 10, 1969.

* * *

MARA, Thalia 1911-

PERSONAL: Born June 28, 1911, in Chicago, Ill.; daughter of Louis B. and Lydia (Neminchinska) Symons; married Arthur Mahoney (a ballet teacher), May 23, 1939. *Education:* Attended public schools in Chicago, Ill. *Politics:* Independent. *Religion:* Christian Science. *Home:* 135 Central Park W., New York, N.Y. 10023. *Office:* National Academy of Ballet, 257 West 93rd St., New York, N.Y. 10025.

CAREER: Professional ballet dancer in Europe and United States, 1927-50; School of Dance Arts, New York, N.Y., director and teacher, 1944-47; Jacob's Pillow, Lee, Mass., teacher and director, 1947; Ballet Repertory Co., New York, N.Y., teacher, 1948—, now director and principal choreographer; National Academy of Ballet (nonprofit educational institution chartered as elementary and secondary school), New York, N.Y., founder and president, 1963—.

WRITINGS: (With J.A.L. Hyndman) *First Steps in Ballet,* Doubleday, 1955 (published in England as *Ballet: Home Practice for Beginners,* Constable, 1956); *Do's and Don'ts of Basic Ballet Barre Exercises,* Dance Magazine, 1955; *Second Steps in Ballet: Basic Center Exercises for Home Practice,* Doubleday, 1956; *Do's and Don'ts of Ballet Center Practice,* Dance Magazine, 1957; *Third Steps in Ballet: Basic Allegro Steps for Home Practice,* Doubleday, 1957; *On Your Toes: The Basic Book of Dance on Pointes,* Doubleday, 1959; *So You Want to Be a Ballet Dancer,* Pitman, 1959; *Do's and Don'ts of Basic Allegro Work,* Dance Magazine, 1961; *The Language of Ballet: An Informal Dictionary,* World Publishing, 1966. Contributing editor, *Dance Magazine.*

BIOGRAPHICAL/CRITICAL SOURCES: Dance Magazine, February, 1964; *Backstage,* February 14, 1964; *New York Herald Tribune,* March 8, 1964; *New York Daily News,* April 23, 1968.

MARCHAJ, C(zeslaw) A(ntony) 1918-

PERSONAL: Born July 9, 1918, in Slomniki, Poland; son of Michat and Stanislawa (Mulewicz) Marchaj; married Jana Bartlakowska (a translator), November 7, 1944; children: Martin. *Education:* Aeronautical College, Warsaw, Poland, student, 1936-39; University of Southampton, graduate student, 1960-62. *Home:* Aldony 10, Warsaw 33, Poland; and 4 Shayer Rd., Southampton, England.

CAREER: Regetta competitor and for many years Polish academic champion of regatta sailing in "Finn" class; former glider pilot; University of Southampton, Highfield, Southampton, England, research fellow, 1967—. *Member:* Polish Yachting Association (vice-president), International Yacht Racing Union, Institution of Naval Architects.

WRITINGS: Teoria zeglowania, Ministerstwa Obrony Narodowej, 1957, revised translation by L. Rusiecki published as *Sailing Theory and Practice,* Dodd, 1964; (With A. Chapleo) *Preliminary Note on Results of Rigid Sail Tests in Unheeled Position,* Southampton University Press, 1961; (with Chapleo) *Visual Observation of the Flow Round the Sails of a Model Yacht,* Southampton University Press, 1961; *Wind Tunnel Test of a One-Third Scale Model of an X-One Design Yacht's Sails,* Southampton University Press, 1962; *Wind Tunnel Tests on a One-fourth Scale Dragon Rig,* University of Southampton, 1963; *The Aerodynamic Characteristics of a Two-Fifths Scale Model of the "Finn" Sail and Its Efficiency When Sailing to Windward,* Southampton University Press, 1964; *Skin Friction Drag on Yachts and Its Reduction,* University of Southampton, 1967.

WORK IN PROGRESS: Research on aerodynamics of the sail, and instability of sailing craft.

SIDELIGHTS: Sailing Theory and Practice has been translated into Russian, German, and Polish.

* * *

MARCO, Barbara (Starkey) 1934-

PERSONAL: Born August 19, 1934, in Summit, N.J.; daughter of Rodney Fielding (a partner, Price-Waterhouse & Co.) and Maude (Grebbin) Starkey. *Education:* Studied at Traphagen School of Fashion for three years and Fashion Institute of Technology for two years. *Religion:* Episcopalian *Home:* 229 East 51st St., New York, N.Y. 10022. *Office:* Macfadden-Bartell Corp., 205 East 42nd St., New York, N.Y. 10017.

CAREER: Geyer Advertising, New York, N.Y., secretary to director of media, one year; *Look,* New York, N.Y., assistant food editor, one year; *Vogue,* New York, N.Y., editorial assistant, three years, associate beauty editor, one year; *Vogue Pattern Book,* New York, N.Y., copy editor, three years; Macfadden-Bartell Corp., New York, N.Y., now beauty and fashion editor. Advertising and marketing consultant. *Member:* Fashion Group of New York, Cosmetic Career Women, Pan Pacific and Southeast Asia Woman's Association, Brazilian Culture Society.

WRITINGS: The ABC's of Beauty, Macfaddens, 1963. Author of bi-weekly column for *Vanidades Continental.*

WORK IN PROGRESS: A second beauty book.

AVOCATIONAL INTERESTS: Natural history, lepidoptery, music, horseback riding, haute cuisine, and original fashion design.

BIOGRAPHICAL/CRITICAL SOURCES: Vanidades Continental, January 15, 1964.

MARCUSE, F(rederick) L(awrence) 1916-

PERSONAL: Surname is pronuonced Mar-*kyuse;* born December 5, 1916, in Montreal, Quebec, Canada; son of Feodor (a salesman) and Ethel (Grossman) Marcuse; married Dorothy Powis (an artist), 1939 (died, 1959); married Dvora Wiseman (a musician), October, 1961; children: (first marriage) two; (second marriage) two. *Education:* Queen's University, Kingston, Ontario, Canada, B.A., 1938, M.A., 1940; Cornell University, Ph.D., 1942. *Politics:* Humanist. *Home:* 1614 Fisk, Pullman, Wash. 99163.

CAREER: Cornell University, Ithaca, N.Y., instructor, 1943-46, assistant professor of psychology, 1946-50; Washington State University, Pullman, associate professor, 1950-58, professor of psychology, 1958—. American Board of Examiners in Psychological Hypnosis, member, 1959—, president, 1963. Advisory editor, Julian Press, Inc., 1956; consultant on hypnosis, National Broadcasting Co. Television, 1964. *Member:* American Psychological Association, American Association for the Advancement of Science, Society for Clinical and Experimental Hypnosis (fellow; chairman of committee on legal and professional attitudes, 1955-57; vice-president, 1963), British Society of Medical Hypnotists, American Academy of Psychotherapists, Institute for Research in Hypnosis (member of board of directors, 1959), Washington State Psychological Association (president, 1958), Sigma Xi.

WRITINGS: (Editor) *Areas of Psychology,* Harper, 1954; *Hypnosis—Fact and Fiction,* Penguin, 1959; (editor) *Hypnosis Throughout the World,* C.C Thomas, 1964.

Contributor: *Recent Experiments in Psychology,* 2nd edition, McGraw, 1950; E.L. Hartley and others, editors, *Outside Readings in Psychology,* Crowell, 1950; M.V. Klein, editor, *A Scientific Report on "The Search for Bridey Murphy,"* Julian, 1956. Also contributor of more than one hundred articles and reviews to more than twenty-five journals, including *American Journal of Psychology, Science, British Journal of Medical Hypnotism, Tennessee Law Review, Sexology, Science Activities.* Advisory editor, *Journal of Clinical and Experimental Hypnosis,* 1953—.

WORK IN PROGRESS: Papers on animal hypnosis, children's art, lapsus auditi, and other topics.

*   *   *

MARDUS, Elaine Bassler 1914-

PERSONAL: Born July 13, 1914, in Cincinnati, Ohio; daughter of Harry E. and Ethelle (Falkenstein) Bassler; married Hiram B. Mardus (vice-president of Baker Clothes), September 11, 1941; children: Gail, Craig. *Education:* Wellesley College, B.A., 1936; Columbia University, M.A., 1937. *Home:* 2 Chesterfield Rd., Scarsdale, N.Y. 10583. *Agent:* Toni Strassman, 130 East 18th St., New York, N.Y. 10003.

CAREER: Research Institute of America, New York, N.Y., editorial assistant, 1939; National Broadcasting Co., New York, N.Y., employee-relations writer, 1940; Office of War Information, New York, N.Y., feature writer, 1940-41; Family Service of Westchester, White Plains, N.Y., community relations director, 1962. Teacher of contemporary literature course in adult education program, Mamaroneck, N.Y., 1960-63; substitute teacher in Scarsdale High School, 1962-64; now public school teacher in White Plains, N.Y. and leader of evening seminars at Cooperative College Center, Yonkers. *Member:* National Council of Jewish Women (member of board, 1957), ORT (member of board, 1955-56).

WRITINGS: (With Miriam Lang) *Doctors to the Great,* Dial, 1962; *Man with a Microscope: Elie Metchnikoff,* Messner, 1968. Contributor of articles to *Collier's,*

Coronet, This Week, Pageant, Negro Digest, Leatherneck, and *English Digest.*

WORK IN PROGRESS: The Princess Who Wouldn't.

BIOGRAPHICAL/CRITICAL SOURCES: Best Sellers, December 1, 1968.

*   *   *

MARGULL, Hans J(ochen) 1925-

PERSONAL: Born September 25, 1925, in Danzig (now Poland); son of Walther O. E. H. and Liberta (Doell) Margull; married Maria Angelika Pfaff, 1950; children: Markus A. *Education:* Studied in Germany at University of Greifswald, 1946, University of Halle, 1946-47, University of Mainz, 1948-49; Biblical Seminary in New York, S.T.M., 1950; University of Hamburg, Dr.theol., 1958, Dr. theol. habil., 1960. *Home:* Jenischstrasse 29, 2 Hamburg 52, Germany.

CAREER: Student Christian Movement in Germany, study secretary, 1953-55; University of Hamburg, Hamburg, Germany, assistant professor, 1955-60; World Council of Churches, Geneva, Switzerland, executive secretary of department on studies in evangelism, 1961-65; University of Hamburg, Hamburg, Germany, professor of missiology and ecumenics, 1967—.

WRITINGS: Theologie der missionarischen Verkundigung: Versuch ueber das Problem der Evangelisation in der oekumenischen Diskussion, Ev. Verlagswerk, 1959, revised translation by Eugene Peters published as *Hope in Action: The Church's Task in the World,* Muhlenberg Press, 1962; (editor with Jan Hermelink) *Basileia, Tribute to W. Freytag,* Ev. Missionsverlag, 1959; (editor with Hermelink) W. Freytag, *Reden und Aufsatze,* Chr. Kaiser-Verlag, 1961; (editor) *Die Oekumenischen Konzile der Christenheit,* Ev. Verlagswerk, 1961, translation by Walter F. Bense published as *The Councils of the Church: History and Analysis,* Fortress, 1966; *Aufbruch zur Aukunft: Chiliastisch-messianische Bewegungen in Afrika und Suedostasien,* Gerd Mohn, 1962; (editor) *Zur Sendung der Kirche: Material der oekumenischen Bewund,* Kaiser, 1963; (editor) *Mission als Strukturpinzip,* Oekumenischen Rat der Kirchen, 1965. Contributor to *International Review of Missions, Die Religion in Geschichte und Gegenwart, Ecumenical Review,* and other publications. Editor, *Ansatze,* 1954-56; co-editor, *Evangelische Missions-Zeitschrift,* 1960-68; editor, *Concept,* 1962-65.

*   *   *

MARIAS, Julian 1914-

PERSONAL: Born June 17, 1914, in Valladolid, Spain; son of Julian and Maria (Aguilera) Marias; married Dolores Franco (a professor and author), August 14, 1941; children: Miguel, Fernando, Javier, Alvaro. *Education:* University of Madrid, Lic. Fil., 1936, Ph.D., 1951. *Religion:* Catholic. *Home:* Vallehermoso 34, Madrid 15, Spain.

CAREER: Aula Nueva, Madrid, Spain, professor of philosophy, 1940-48; Instituto de Humanidades, Madrid, co-founder and professor, 1948-50; professor of Spanish at several American colleges in Madrid, Smith College, San Francisco College for Women, Middlebury College, Tulane University, and Mary Baldwin College, 1952-71; University of Puerto Rico, Rio Piedras, visiting professor and research professor, 1956-64; Seminario de Estudios de Humanidades, Madrid, director, 1960—. Visiting professor at Wellesley College, 1951-52, Harvard University, 1952, University of California, Los Angeles, 1955, Yale University, 1956, Mary Baldwin College, 1966, Indiana University, 1967, 1969, 1970, University of Oklahoma, 1968, 1971, Indiana University, 1972, 1973, 1974, 1975, 1976. Lecturer (in Spanish, French, English, German) in most countries of western Europe, United States, Puerto Rico, Mexico, South America, and India. *Military service:* Spanish Republic Army, 1937-39. *Member:* International Institute of Philosophy, International Society for the History of Ideas, Hispanic Society of America, Sociedad Peruana de Filosofia, Sociedad Espanola de Psicologia, Instituto Brasileiro de Filosofia, Real Academia Espanola. *Awards, honors:* Fastenrath Prize of Royal Academy of Spain, 1947, for *Miguel de Unamuno;* Rockefeller Foundation fellowship, 1957-60; Juan Pelonio Prize, 1971, for *Antropologia Metafisica.*

WRITINGS: (With Carlos Alonso del Real and Manuel Granell) *Juventud en el mundo antiguo* (includes "Diario de un estudiante viajero," by Alonso del Real, "Notas de un viaje a Oriente," by Marias, and "Fragmento del diario," by Granell), Espasa-Calpe (Madrid), 1934.

Historia de la filosofia, Revista de Occidente (Madrid), 1941, 25th edition, enlarged, 1972, translation by Stanley Appelbaum and Clarence C. Strowbridge published as *History of Philosophy,* Dover, 1967; *La Filosofia del Padre Gratry,* Ediciones Escorial, 1941, 5th edition, enlarged, Revista de Occidente, 1972, 3rd edition included in *Obras,* Volume 4 (see below); (editor and translator) G.W. Leibnitz, *Discurso de metafisica,* Revista de Occidente, 1942; *Miguel de Unamuno,* Espasa-Calpe, 1943, translation by Frances M. Lopez-Morillas published under same title by Harvard University Press, 1966, 5th edition included in *Obras,* Volume 5 (see below); (editor and translator) Seneca, *Sobre la felicidad,* Revista de Occidente, 1943; *El Tema del hombre,* Revista de Occidente, 1943, 4th edition, Espasa-Calpe, 1968; *San Anselmo y el insensato,* Revista de Occidente, 1944, 3rd edition included in *Obras,* Volume 4 (see below); (editor and translator) Wilhelm Dilthey, *Teoria de las concepciones del mundo,* Revista de Occidente, 1944; (editor and author of prologue) Miguel de Unamuno, *Obras selectas,* Pleyade (Madrid) 1946; *Introduccion a la filosofia,* Revista de Occidente, 1947, 9th edition, 1967, translation by Kenneth S. Reid and Edward Sarmiento published as *Reason and Life: The Introduction to Philosophy,* Yale University Press, 1956; (editor and translator) Plato, *Fedro,* Revista de Occidente, 1948; *Ortega y la idea de la razon vital,* A. Zuniga (Madrid), 1948; *La Filosofia espanola actual,* Espasa-Calpe (Buenos Aires), 1948, 4th edition, 1963; *El Metodo historico de las generaciones,* Revista de Occidente, 1949, translation by Harold C. Raley published as *Generations: A Historical Method,* University of Alabama Press, 1970, 5th edition included in *Obras,* Volume 6 (see below); (editor with German Bleiberg) *Diccionario de literatura espanola,* Revista de Occidente, 1949, 4th edition, revised and enlarged, 1973.

Ortega y tres antipodas, Revista de Occidente (Buenos Aires), 1950; (compiler and author of introduction and notes) *La Filosofia en sus textos* (anthology), Labor (Barcelona), 1950, 2nd edition, 1963; (editor, translator with Maria Araujo, and author of introduction and notes) Aristotle, *Politica,* bilingual edition, Instituto de Estudios Politicos (Madrid), 1951; *El Existencialismo en Espana,* Universidad Nacional de Colombia, 1953, also published with *Filosofia actual* (see below); *La Universidad realidad problematica,* Cruz del Sur (Santiago), 1953; *Idea de la metafisica,* Columba (Buenos Aires), 1954, translation by A.R. Caponigri published in *Contemporary Spanish Philosophy* (anthology), University of Notre Dame Press, 1967, 3rd edition included in *Obras,* Volume 2 (see below); *Biografia de la filosofia,* Emece (Madrid), 1954, 5th edition, Revista de Occidente (Madrid), 1968, translation by Harold C. Raley published as *The Biography of Philosophy,* (includes several additional chapters), University of Alabama Press, 1973; *Ensayos de teoria,* Barna (Barcelona), 1954, 2nd edition included in *Obras,* Volume 4 (see below); *Aqui y ahora,* Espasa-Calpe,

1954, 2nd edition included in *Obras,* Volume 3 (see below); *Universidad y sociedad en los Estados Unidos,* Langa (Madrid), 1954; *Ensayos de convivencia,* Sudamericana (Buenos Aires), 1955, 3rd edition, 1966; *La Estructura social,* Sociedad de Estudios y Publicaciones (Madrid), 1955, 6th edition, 1972, translation by Harold C. Raley published as *The Structure of Society,* University of Alabama Press, in press, 5th edition published in *Obras,* Volume 6 (see below); (translator) Wilhelm Dilthey, *Introduccion a las ciencias del espiritu,* Revista de Occidente, 1956; *Los Estados Unidos en escorzo,* Emece, (Buenos Aires), 1956, 5th edition, 1972, 3rd edition included in *Obras,* Volume 3 (see below); translation by Blanche de Puy and Harold C. Raley published in *America in the Fifties and Sixties: Julian Marias on the United States* (see below); *La Imagen de la vida humana,* Emece, 1956, 2nd edition included in *Obras,* Volume 5 (see below); *El Intelectual y su mundo,* Atlantida (Buenos Aires), 1956, 2nd edition included in *Obras,* Volume 4 (see below); *Don Quixote as Seen by Sancho Panza,* (originally published in Spanish, as "Don Quijote visto desde Sancho Panza" as a prologue to *Biografia de Sancho Panza: Filosofo de la sensatez,* Editorial Aedos, 1952), Indian Institute of Culture, 1956, also included in *El Oficio del pensamiento* (see below); *Ataraxia y alcionismo,* Instituto Ibys (Madrid), 1957; *El Espiritu europeo,* Guadarrama (Madrid), 1957; (editor and author of introduction and notes) Jose Ortega y Gasset, *Meditaciones del Quijote,* Ediciones de la Universidad de Puerto Rico (Rio Piedras), 1957, translation by Evelvn Rugg and Diego Marin published as *Meditations on Quixote,* Norton, 1961; *El Oficio del pensamiento: Ensayos* Biblioteca Nueva (Madrid), 1958, 4th edition published in *Obras,* Volume 6 (see below); *El Lugar del peligro,* Taurus (Madrid), 1958.

(With others) *Experiencia de la vida,* Revista de Occidente, 1960; *Ortega: Circunstancia y vocacion,* Revista de Occidente, 1960, 2nd edition, 1973, translation by Frances M. Lopez-Morillas published as *Jose Ortega y Gasset: Circumstance and Vocation,* University of Oklahoma Press, 1970; (translator with Maria Araujo) Aristotle, *Etica a Nicomaco,* Instituto de Estudios Politicos, 1960; *Imagen de la India,* includes photographs by Marias, Revista de Occidente, 1961, 3rd edition included in *Obras,* Volume 8 (see below); *Ortega ante Goethe,* Taurus, 1961; *Los Espanoles,* Revista de Occidente, 1962, 3rd edition, included in *Obras,* Volume 7 (see below); *La Espana posible en tiempo de Carlos III,* Sociedad de Estudios y Publicaciones, 1963, 2nd edition included in *Obras,* Volume 7 (see below); *El Tiempo que ni vuelve ni tropieza,* Editora y Distribuidora Hispano Americana, S.A. (Barcelona) 1964, 3rd edition included in *Obras,* Volume 7 (see below); (with Pedro Lain Entralgo) *Historia de la filosofia y de la ciencia,* Guadarrama, 1964, 4th edition, 1968; *Modos de vivr: Un Observador espanol en los Estados Unidos* (selections from *Los Estados Unidos en escorzo*), edited by Edward R. Mulvihill and Roberto G. Sanchez, Oxford University Press, 1964; *Nuestra Andalucia,* water colors by Alfredo Ramon, R. Diaz-Casariego, (Madrid), 1966, 2nd edition published in *Obras,* Volume 8 (see below); *Consideracion de Cataluna* (articles originally published in *El Noticiero Universal,* 1965), Ayma (Barcelona), 1966, 2nd edition published in *Obras,* Volume 8 (see below); *El Uso linguistico* (address given at Real Academia Espanola in Madrid, June 20, 1965), Columba, 1966; *Meditaciones sobre la sociedad espanola,* Alianza Editorial, 1966, 3rd edition included in *Obras,* Volume 8 (see below); *Al Margen de estos clasicos: Autores espanoles del siglo XX,* prologue and glossary by Beejee Smith, A. Aguado (Madrid), 1967; *Valle-Inclan en el ruedo iberico,* Columba, 1967; (editor and author of prologue) Gaspar Melchor de Jovellanos, *Diarios,* Alianza Editorial (Madrid), 1967; *Israel: Una Resurrec-*

cion, Columba, 1968, 5th edition included in *Obras,* Volume 8 (see below); *Analisis de los Estados Unidos,* Guadarrama, 1968, 2nd edition included in *Obras,* Volume 8 (see below), translation by B!anche de Puy and Harold C. Raley published in *America in the Fifties and Sixties: Julian Marias on the United States* (see below); *Nuevos ensayos de filosofia,* Revista de Occidente, 1968, 3rd edition published in *Obras,* Volume 8 (see below).

Antropologia metafisica: Le Estructura empirica de la vida humana, Revista de Occidente, 1970, translation by Frances M. Lopez-Morillas published as *Metaphysical Anthropology: The Empirical Structure of Human Life,* Pennsylvania State University Press, 1971; *Esquema de nuestra situacion,* Columba, 1970; *Philosophy as Dramatic Theory,* (collection of 14 essays originally published in Spanish), translated by James Parsons, Pennsylvania State University Press, 1970; *Visto y no visto: Cronicas de cine,* two volumes, Guadarrama, 1970; *America in the Fifties and Sixties: Julian Marias on the United States,* two volumes, edited and introduced by Michael Aaron Rockland, Pennsylvania State University Press, 1972; *Image of Life: Studies in Spanish Literature* (collection of essays originally published in Spanish), University of Georgia Press, in press.

Omnibus volumes: *Filosofia actual [y] Existencialismo en Espana,* Revista de Occidente, 1955, enlarged edition published as *La Escuela de Madrid,* Emece, 1959, 2nd edition included in *Obras,* Volume 5 (see below); *Obras,* Revista de Occidente, Volume 1: *Historia de la filosofia,* 10th edition, 1958, Volume 2: *Introduccion a la filosofia,* 5th edition, *Idea de la metafisica,* 3rd edition, [y] *Biografia de la filosofia,* 3rd edition, 1958, Volume 3: *Aqui y ahora,* 2nd edition, *Ensayos de convivencia,* 2nd edition, [y] *Los Estados Unidos en escorzo,* 3rd edition, 1959, Volume 4: *San Anselmo y el insensato,* 3rd edition, *La Filosofia del Padre Gratry,* 3rd edition, *Ensayos de teoria,* 2nd edition), [y] *El Intelectual y su mundo,* 2nd edition, 1959, Volume 5: *Miguel de Unamuno,* 5th edition, *La Escuela de Madrid,* 2nd edition, [y] *La Imagen de la vida humana,* 2nd edition, 1960, Volume 7: *Los Espanoles,* 3rd edition, *La Espana posible en tiempo de Carlos III,* 2nd edition, *El Tiempo que ni vuelve ni tropieza,* 3rd edition, 1966, Volume 6: *El Metodo historico de las generaciones,* 5th edition, *La Estructura social,* 5th edition, *El Oficio del pensamiento,* 4th edition, 1970, Volume 8: *Analisis de los Estadoa Unidos,* 2nd edition, *Israel: Una Resurreccion,* 5th edition, *Imagen de la India,* 3rd edition, *Meditaciones sobre la sociedad espanola,* 3rd edition, *Consideracion de Cataluna,* 2nd edition, *Nuestra Andalucia,* 2nd edition, *Nuevos ensayos de filosofia,* 3rd edition, 1970; *Coleccion El Alcion de obras completas de Julian Marias* (first volumes include *Acerca de Ortega, La Imagen de la vida humana, Los Espanoles, Nuestra Andalucia [y] Consideracion de Cataluna, Los Estados Unidos en escorze, La Filosofia del Padre Gratry, La Estructura social,* and *Ortega: Circunstancia y vocacion),* Revista de Occidente, in press.

Contributor to *International Encyclopedia of the Social Sciences;* literary adviser and contributor to *Revista de Occidente;* former contributor to *Cruz y Raya, Hora de Espana, Escorial, ABC El Noticiero Universal* (Barcelona), currently contributor to *La Nacion* (Buenos Aires), *Gaceta Ilustrada* (Madrid), *Insula* (Madrid), *La Vanguardia* (Barcelona), *Convivium* (Brazil), and to *Foreign Affairs, Commonweal,* and other journals.

WORK IN PROGRESS: Ortega: Las Trayectorias; editing A. Alcala Baliano's *Historia de Espana, 1700-1843;* research on eighteenth century Spain.

SIDELIGHTS: Marias, well-known Spanish philosopher and essayist, owes a philosophical debt to Kierkegaard, Bergson, Heidegger, and Husserl. He was also greatly influenced by the work of Jose Ortega y Gasset, with whom he was closely associated for twenty-three years, from 1932 to 1955. A reviewer for *Christian Century* calls Marias "the world's foremost authority on Orteguian philosophy." In a review of *Jose Ortega y Gasset: Circumstance and Vocation,* a *Library Journal* writer notes: "Marias' patient, deeply considered study of Ortega contributes significantly to the analysis of this thinker.... Although Ortega as pedagogue and political activist is subordinated here to Ortega as pure philosopher and rhetorician, the entire range of his work is scrutinized with an awareness only possible in a devoted pupil who was later both colleague and friend."

In addition to lecturing in four languages, Marias also translates from the German, Greek, and Latin, and reads Italian and Portuguese. More than a dozen of his books have been translated for foreign publication. Pierre Courtines makes these observations on the recent English translation of *Miguel de Unamuno:* "Marias studies Unamuno from a philosophical point of view and points to him as a forerunner of contemporary existentialism. . . . [He] knew Unamuno personally; has written about him frequently and probes the sum total of his output relentlessly... [This] is not only a work of erudition, but also a popularization of great importance in our age of anxiety, when all our values are being systematically questioned."

Marias says he is independent of official connections in Spain, including state universities. Since 1952 he has lectured and taught at numerous American colleges and universities. His impressions and comments on the American scene are recorded in *America in the Fifties and Sixties: Julian Marias on the United States,* published in translation in this country in 1972. William McCann mentions the meditative quality of the book, observing that Marias "wouldn't be a Spanish philosopher if he were afraid to generalize and to judge. He is sure enough of his insights and intuition to risk being wrong, to make the informed and spirited guess. As a result, we sometimes get interpretations from him as brilliant as Tocqueville's.... Spanish readers can scarcely be expected to realize how grateful they should be for this lucid, profound commentary on a foreign civilization by a man who brings such wide historical and philosophical perspectives to bear on his theme. American readers are bound to recognize the excellence of Marias' achievement, and may be encouraged to read his *History of Philosophy* and his *Philosophy as Dramatic Theory.*"

"Witty, meditative, and cheerful, . . . Marias is a humane philosopher a world apart from the logical positivists," Russell Kirk states in his review. "He does not believe in purely 'national' philosophies, but he thinks that Americans soon will need philosophy so that they may develop into 'the people they *must become.*' His experience at Yale gave him, somewhat to his surprise, new hope for the American future, for the study of philosophy there was broad and earnest." Kirk quotes Marias as stating, "Philosophy, which up to now has figured only as an element in their tradition, will in the near future be a part of their destiny. But the risk is great that on the day when that necessity actually finds full outlet, when man in America truly needs philosophy, there will be no philosophy for him to find. . . . My fear is that he will have had his authentic philosophy falsely supplanted."

Marias observes of Americans that few buy books because of the ubiquitous and well-equipped public library, and feels this may bode ill for the intellectual future of America, since many significant books could go unpublished and unread because the libraries cannot guarantee publishers sufficient sales. In addition, he believes American authors are, in general, too concerned with the material and popular success of their works, to the detriment of ingenuity and "true ambition" in literary endeavor. Kirk considers Marias' book "a success, whether or not it is widely read. As R.B. Cunninghame-Graham wrote, the true Spaniard shrugs at success or failure. 'Your strength lies in the fact that you are not interested in popularity,' a French poet told Marias once. This book of his is successful because he has no eye to popularity."

AVOCATIONAL INTERESTS: Photography.

BIOGRAPHICAL/CRITICAL SOURCES: Juan Lopez-Morillas, editor, *Intelectuales y espirituales: Unamuno, Machado, Ortega, Lorca, Marias,* Revista de Occidente, 1961; *America,* January 14, 1967; *Times Literary Supplement,* June 15, 1967; *Christian Century,* September 9, 1970; *Library Journal,* November 1, 1970; *Books Abroad,* winter, 1970; *University Bookman,* summer, 1972; *Yale Review,* autumn, 1972; Juan Soler Planas, *El Pensamiento filosofico de Julian Marias,* Revista de Occidente, in press.

*　*　*

MARKHAM, Jesse William 1916-

PERSONAL: Born April 21, 1916, in Richmond, Va.; son of John James (a boilermaker) and Edith (Luttrell) Markham; married Penelope Anton, October 15, 1944; children: Elizabeth Markham McLean, John, William. *Education:* University of Richmond, B.A., 1941; Harvard University, M.A., 1947, Ph.D., 1949. *Politics:* Independent. *Religion:* Episcopalian. *Home:* 60 Fresh Pond Pkwy., Cambridge, Mass. 02138. *Office:* Harvard Business School, Anderson 32, Soldiers Field, Boston, Mass. 02163.

CAREER: Vanderbilt University, Nashville, Tenn., associate professor of economics, 1948-53; U.S. Federal Trade Commission, Washington, D.C., chief economist, 1953-55; Princeton University, Princeton, N.J., professor of economics, 1955-68; Harvard University, Cambridge, Mass., professor of business administration, 1968—. Ford Foundation research professor, Geneva, Switzerland, 1958-59; visiting professor at Columbia University, 1957-58, Harvard University, 1961-62. Economic consultant to Tennessee Valley Authority, Federal Communications Commission, Federal Reserve Board, U.S. Department of Commerce, General Electric Co.; economic editorial adviser to Houghton Mifflin Co. U.S. delegate to Organization for European Economic Cooperation, Paris, France, 1956-61. *Military service:* U.S. Naval Reserve, 1942-45; became lieutenant. *Member:* American Economics Association, Econometric Society, American Association for the Advancement of Science, Southern Economic Association, Phi Beta Kappa. *Awards, honors:* Julius Rosenwald fellow, 1942, 1945-46.

WRITINGS: Competition in the Rayon Industry, Harvard University Press, 1952; *Workbook in Modern Economics,* Harcourt, 1953; *The Fertilizer Industry: Study of an Imperfect Market,* Vanderbilt University Press, 1958; (with others) *In the Matter of Study of Radio and Television Network Broadcasting,* U.S. Federal Communications Commission, 1958; (with others) *Prescription Drugs and the Public Health,* [Washington, D.C.], 1962; (editor) R. Joseph Monsen, *Modern American Capitalism: Ideologies and Issues,* Houghton, 1963; (editor and contributor) *The American Economy,* Braziller, 1963; (with Charles Fiero and Howard Piquet) *The Common Market: Friend or Competitor?,* New York University Press, 1964; (editor) Walter Krause, *International Economics,* Houghton, 1965; (editor) Max S. Wortman and Clint W. Randle, *Collective Bargaining,* Houghton, 1966; (with others) *An Economic Media Study of Book Publishers,* American Textbook Publishers Institute, 1966; (editor with Gustav F. Papanek) *Industrial Organization and Economic Develop-*

ment: Essays in Honor of E.S. Mason, Houghton, 1970. Contributor to economic, law, and business journals.

WORK IN PROGRESS: Industrial Pricing: Theory and Practice; Conglomerate Enterprise and Public Policy.

AVOCATIONAL INTERESTS: Tennis, sailing, traveling, horticulture.

*　*　*

MARLYN, John 1912-

PERSONAL: Born April 2, 1912, in Hungary; taken to Canada when six months old; son of Adam (a house painter) and Paula (Kendal) Marlyn; married Ruth Miles (a research assistant), August 16, 1937. *Education:* University of Manitoba, student.

CAREER: Carleton University, Ottawa, Ontario, teacher of creative writing to graduate students. *Military service:* Canadian Army, Signal Corps, 1942-45; became lieutenant. *Awards, honors:* Senior fellowship, Canada Foundation, 1958; Beta Sigma Phi award, 1958, for distinguished first novel.

WRITINGS: Under the Ribs of Death, McClelland & Stewart, 1957. Short stories have appeared in *Queen's Quarterly,* and have been read on Canadian Broadcasting Co. network program, "Anthology," and broadcast on Ottawa program, "Twelve Stories."

WORK IN PROGRESS: A second novel.

*　*　*

MARMUR, Jacland 1901-

PERSONAL: Born February 14, 1901, in Sosnowiec, Poland; became U.S. citizen through father's naturalization, 1908; son of Max and Gertrude (Rechnitz) Marmur; married Vernita Pellow, 1921 (deceased); married Caroline Welter, 1960. *Education:* Attended public schools in Brooklyn, N.Y. *Politics:* Republican. *Agent:* Littauer & Wilkinson, 500 Fifth Ave., New York, N.Y. 10036.

CAREER: Professional seaman, 1920-30; U.S. Navy, observer for research and story material aboard combatant vessels, World War II; free-lance writer. Fellow, International Institute of Arts and Letters. *Member:* U.S. Naval Institute, P.E.N., Masons, San Francisco Press Club.

WRITINGS: Ecola!, Doubleday, Doran, 1928; *Wind Driven,* E. Nash & Grayson, 1930, Dial, 1932; *Three Went Armed,* Dial, 1933; *The Golden Medallion,* Grayson & Grayson, 1934; *The Sea and the Shore,* Holt, 1941; *Sea Duty, and other Stories of Naval Action,* Holt, 1944; *Andromeda,* Holt, 1947; *The Edge of Chaos,* R. Hale, 1969.

Author of original stories for films: "The Ship of State;" "Return from the Sea," Allied Artists, 1954. Fiction anthologized and adapted for television. Contributor of short stories and novelettes to *Collier's, Saturday Evening Post,* and *Scribner's;* occasional contributor of sea fiction to English and Australian magazines.

WORK IN PROGRESS: A sea novel.

SIDELIGHTS: Some of Marmur's books have been translated into Swedish, Danish, and Dutch.

*　*　*

MARROCCO, W(illiam) Thomas 1909-

PERSONAL: Born December 5, 1909, in West New York, N.J.; son of Julius Thomas (a designer) and Elisa (Faccin) Marrocco; married Audrey Jeanette Grein (a piano teacher), September 14, 1937; children: Richard Thomas, Sandra Beth. *Education:* Royal Conservatory of Music, Naples, Italy, Licentiate and Master's Diplomas, 1930; Eastman School of Music, University of Rochester, B.Mus., 1934; University of Rochester, M.A., 1940; University of California, Los Angeles, Ph.D., 1952. *Home:* 1950 Mandeville Canyon Rd., Los Angeles, Calif. 90049. *Office:* Music Department, University of California, Los Angeles, Calif. 90024.

CAREER: Radio Station WHEC, Rochester, N.Y., concertmaster of station orchestra, 1937-42; University of Iowa, Iowa City, lecturer in music, 1945-46; University of Kansas, Lawrence, associate professor of music, 1946-49; University of California, Los Angeles, professor of music, 1950—. Violin member of Roth String Quartet, performing in United States and abroad, and for recordings. *Member:* American Musicological Society, Mediaevel Academy of America, American Philosophical Society (fellow), Phi Kappa Lambda, Phi Beta Lambda. *Awards, honors:* Fulbright research grant to Italy, 1949-50; American Philosophical Society award, 1959, 1972; American Council of Learned Societies fellowship, 1963, 1967, 1969, 1971.

WRITINGS: (Editor and author of introduction) *Fourteenth Century Italian Cacce,* Mediaeval Academy of America, 1942, 2nd edition, revised, 1961; *The Music of Jacopo da Bologna,* University of California Press, 1954; (editor with Harold Gleason) *Music in America: An Anthology from the Landing of the Pilgrims to the Close of the Civil War, 1620-1865,* Norton, 1964; *Secular Music of Trecento Italy,* Volume I, l'Editions de L'Oiseau-Lyre (Monaco), 1964; *The Notation in American Sacred Music,* Baerenreiter (Basel), 1964; (with Arthur C. Edwards) *Music in the United States,* W.C. Brown, 1968. Contributor to *Speculum, Musical Quarterly,* and other music journals.

WORK IN PROGRESS: Volumes II, IV, and V of *Secular Music of Trecento Italy.*

*   *   *

MARSH, Irving T.   1907-

PERSONAL: Surname originally Zablo; born April 15, 1907, in New York, N.Y.; son of David and Bella Zablo; married Eve Kurtz, January 28, 1930; children: Ann (Mrs. Hugh Welborn), Mary Ellen (Mrs. Robert Denny). *Education:* College of the City of New York (now City College of the City University of New York), student, 1924-28. *Politics:* Independent Democrat. *Home:* 235 West 76th St., New York, N.Y. 10023. *Office:* Eastern College Athletic Conference, Royal Manhattan Hotel, New York, N.Y. 10036.

CAREER: Columbia University, New York, N.Y., director of sports information, 1942-53; with *New York Herald Tribune,* New York, N.Y., 1933-67; Eastern College Athletic Conference, director of Service Bureau, 1937—. *Member:* U.S. Basketball Writers Association (vice-president, 1963-64; president, 1964-65), Baseball Writers Association of America, Metropolitan Basketball Writers Association (president, 1950-52), Metropolitan Football Writers Association (president, 1960-62).

WRITINGS: (Editor with Edward Ehre) *Best Sports Stories,* Dutton, annually, 1945—; (editor) *Best of the Best Sports Stories,* Dutton, 1964.

*   *   *

MARSH, (Edith) Ngaio   1899-

PERSONAL: First name is pronounced *Nye-o;* born April 23, 1899, in Christchurch, New Zealand; daughter of Henry Edmund and Rose Elizabeth (Seager) Marsh. *Education:* Attended St. Margaret's College, New Zealand, 1910-14, and Canterbury University College School of Art, 1915-20. *Religion:* Church of England. *Home:* 37 Valley Rd., Christchurch S.2, New Zealand. *Agent:* Harold Ober Associates, Inc., 40 East 49th St., New York, N.Y. 10017.

CAREER: Actress with touring Shakespearean company in Australia and New Zealand, 1920-23; theatrical producer, 1923-27; interior decorator in London, England, 1928-32; returned to New Zealand and has lived there and in London, writing detective novels since 1933; D.D. O'Connor Theatre Management, producer, 1944-52; has directed ten Shakespearean productions and many modern plays; director of first all-New Zealand Shakespearean company, Canterbury University College Student Players, 1946; also directed at Embassy Theatre, London, England, and on a professional tour of Australasia. Honorary lecturer in drama, Canterbury University College, 1948. Head section leader, Red Cross Transport Unit in New Zealand, 1939. *Member:* Royal Society of Arts (fellow), British Authors, Playwrights and Composers Society, P.E.N., Queen's Club (Christchurch). *Awards, honors:* Officer Order of the British Empire, 1948; D.Litt. from University of Canterbury, 1963; Dame Commander, Order of the British Empire, 1966.

WRITINGS—Detective novels: *A Man Lay Dead,* Bles, 1934, Sheridan, 1942; *Enter a Murderer,* Bles, 1935, Sheridan, 1942; (with Dr. Henry Jellett) *The Nursing-Home Murder,* Bles, 1935, Sheridan, 1941; *Death in Ecstasy,* Bles, 1936, Sheridan, 1941; *Vintage Murder,* Bles, 1937, Penguin (New York), 1940; *Artists in Crime,* Furman, 1938; *Death in a White Tie,* Furman, 1938; *Overture to Death,* Furman, 1939; *Death of a Peer,* Little, Brown, 1940 (published in England as *Surfeit of Lampreys,* Collins, 1941); *Death at the Bar,* Little, Brown, 1940; *Death and the Dancing Footman,* Little, Brown, 1941; *Colour Scheme,* Little, Brown, 1943; *Died in the Wool,* Little, Brown, 1945; *Final Curtain* (originally published as serial in *Saturday Evening Post,* March 8-April 12, 1947), Little, Brown, 1947; *A Wreath for Rivera,* Little, Brown, 1949 (published in England as *Swing, Brother, Swing,* Collins, 1949); *Night at the Vulcan,* Little, Brown, 1951 (published in England as *Opening Night,* Collins, 1951); *Spinsters in Jeopardy,* Little, Brown, 1953; *Scales of Justice,* Little, Brown, 1955; *Death of a Fool,* Little, Brown, 1956 (published in England as *Off With His Head,* Collins, 1957); *Singing in the Shrouds,* Little, Brown, 1958, also published with *A Stir of Echoes,* by Richard Matheson, and *The Malignant Heart,* by Celestine Sibley, Walter J. Black for the Detective Book Club, 1958; *False Scent,* Little, Brown, 1959, also published with *The Man Who Followed Women,* by Bert and Dolores Hitchens, and *Tiger on My Back,* by Gordon and Mildred Nixon Gordon, Walter J. Black for the Detective Book Club, 1960; *Hand in Glove,* Little, Brown, 1962; *Dead Water,* Little, Brown, 1963; *Killer Dolphin,* Little, Brown, 1966 (published in England as *Death at the Dolphin,* Collins, 1967); *Clutch of Constables,* Collins, 1968, Little, Brown, 1969; *When in Rome,* Collins, 1970; Little, Brown, 1971; *Tied Up in Tinsel,* Little, Brown, 1972. Author of dramatization, with Eileen MacKay, of *False Scent,* produced in England in 1966; author of dramatization of *Singing in the Shrouds,* entitled "Death Sails at Midnight," produced in England in 1972.

Nonfiction: (With Randal Matthew Burdon) *New Zealand,* Collins, 1942, also included in *The British Commonwealth and Empire,* edited by Walter J. Turner, Collins, 1943; *A Play Toward: A Note on Play Production,* Caxton Press (Christchurch), 1946; *Perspectives: The New Zealander and the Visual Arts,* Auckland Gallery Associates (Auckland), 1960; *Play Production,* R.E. Owen, Government Printer (New Zealand), 1960; *Black Beech and Honeydew* (autobiography), Little, Brown, 1965.

Juveniles: *The Christmas Tree* (play), The Religious Drama Society of Great Britain (London), 1962; *New Zealand* (originally announced as "Islands Down Under"), introduction by Keith Holyoake, Macmillan, 1964.

Omnibus volumes: *Three-Act Special* (includes *A Wreath for Rivera, Spinsters in Jeopardy,* and *Night at the Vulcan*), Little, Brown, 1960; *Another Three-Act Special* (includes *False Scent, Scales of Justice,* and *Singing in the Shrouds*), Little, Brown, 1962. Contributor of short stories, travel articles, and reviews to periodicals; author of an opera libretto.

WORK IN PROGRESS: Another detective novel.

SIDELIGHTS: Dame Ngaio's given name is Maori for "light on the water," and also means "a flowering tree." She has said that her father was descended from an ancient English family, the de Mariscos, Lords of Lundy, rumored to be piratical. Expelled from Lundy for lawlessness, they appeared in Kent, took the name Marsh, and many became Quakers, perhaps as a reaction to their former piracy. Her maternal grandfather was an early colonist of New Zealand.

A well-traveled mystery writer and theatrical producer, Dame Ngaio writes highly literate detective stories which have been classified as among the best of their kind. Her theatrical background and the wide variety of characters and scenery she has met in her travels provide a rich source of material for her novels. In a review of *Killer Dolphin* (the title refers to a crumbling 19th-century London theatre where a murder is committed), Anthony Boucher writes: "Crafty and compelling I certainly agree that this is. Once again Miss Marsh ... writes about the London theatrical scene, delightfully, vividly and inimitably—even bringing off the small miracle of convincing us that her hero, inspired by a genuine Shakespearean relic, has written a good play about Shakespeare.... The mystery, which sets in late, is a good one; the novel of theatre, which dominates throughout, is a joy absolute." *Killer Dolphin* was runner-up for the Edgar Award of the Mystery Writers of America.

Inspector Roderick Alleyn is the detective appearing in most of Dame Ngaio's crime novels. Many of them have been international best-sellers, and fifteen books have borne the Collins Crime Club imprint.

AVOCATIONAL INTERESTS: Art, Shakespeareana.

BIOGRAPHICAL/CRITICAL SOURCES: Wilson Library Bulletin, September, 1940; *Saturday Evening Post,* March 8, 1947; *New York Times Book Review,* June 5, 1960, September 25, 1966, April 7, 1971; *Newsweek,* June 13, 1960; *Christian Science Monitor,* November 2, 1965; *Times Literary Supplement,* June 29, 1967; *Saturday Review,* April 24, 1971; *Detroit News,* June 4, 1972; *National Observer,* July 15, 1972; *New York Times,* July 22, 1972.

* * *

MARSH, Philip M(errill) 1893-

PERSONAL: Born July 29, 1893, in Everett, Mass.; son of James Robert and Effie (Merrill) Marsh. *Education:* University of Maine, student, 1912-14, A.B., 1929, A.M., 1932; Harvard University, A.M., 1932. postgraduate study, 1933-34; University of California, Los Angeles, Ph.D., 1945. *Home address:* Box 794, Chandler, Ariz. 85224. *Agent:* A.L. Fierst, 545 Fifth Ave., New York, N.Y. 10017.

CAREER: Curtis Publishing Co., Philadelphia, Pa., circulation department, 1922-26; Houlton High School, Houlton, Me., chairman of English department, 1934-42; Miami University, Miami, Ohio, 1946-56, began as assistant professor, became associate professor of English; Adrian College, Adrian, Mich., chairman of English department, 1956-57; Texas Lutheran College, Seguin, associate professor of English, 1957-58; Jarvis Christian College, Hawkins, Tex., chairman of English department, 1958-59, 1961-63. Visiting professor at University of Texas, 1948-

49, San Francisco State College (now California State University) 1960-61. *Military service:* U.S. Navy, 1917-19. *Member:* Phi Beta Kappa, Phi Kappa Phi.

WRITINGS: Rebel (novel), Falmouth Book House, 1938; *Poems of a Bachelor,* Aroostook Publications, 1939; *Monroe's Defense of Jefferson and Freneau Against Hamilton,* privately printed, 1948; *American Literature: A Concise History,* Steck, 1950; *Writing Right: A Concise Grammar-Composition,* Steck, 1951; *English Literature: A Concise History,* Steck, 1951; *The Last Bachelor, and Other Poems,* Exposition, 1954; (editor) *The Prose of Philip Freneau,* Scarecrow, 1955; *How to Teach English in High School and College,* Bookman Associates, 1956; *Philip Freneau's Fame,* New Jersey Historical Society, 1962; (editor) *A Freneau Sampler,* Scarecrow, 1963; *Philip Freneau, Poet and Journalist,* Dillon, 1968; *The Works of Philip Freneau: A Critical Study,* Scarecrow, 1968; *The Man Who Stopped World War III* (novel), Vantage, 1968; *Freneau's Published Prose: A Bibliography,* Scarecrow, 1970.

WORK IN PROGRESS: A guide to eighteenth-century American essays; two novels; short stories and essays.

* * *

MARSH, Susan (Raymond) 1914-

PERSONAL: Born January 23, 1914, in Jersey Shore, Pa.; daughter of Allen Arthur (a railroad executive) and Marietta (Persch) Raymond; married Thompson G. Marsh (a professor of law at University of Denver), June 21, 1935; children: Nancy (Mrs. Loy O. Banks), Alice (Mrs. Wilder Kimball Abbott), Lucy (Mrs. Leland Yee), Mary (Mrs. John Zulack). *Education:* Smith College, A.B., 1935. *Home:* 199 Ash St., Denver, Colo. 80220.

CAREER: Professional musician, playing viola with Denver Symphony Orchestra, Denver, Colo., 1949-65; freelance writer. Consultant, Inter-County Regional Planning Commission, 1964—. *Member:* Association of American Geographers, American Federation of Musicians, National Education Association, Rocky Mountain Social Science Association, Colorado Mountain Club (member of board), Colorado Consumer's Council (member of board).

WRITINGS: All About Maps and Mapmaking (youth book), Random House, 1963; *Teaching About Maps, Grade by Grade,* six volumes, Teachers Publishing Corp., 1965. Contributor to *Above and Beyond* (encyclopedia), New Horizons, 1967; contributor of about seventy signed articles on travel, music, and gardens to *New York Times,* and of articles to *Glamour* and other magazines.

WORK IN PROGRESS: The biography of an early nineteenth-century American scientist; another children's book.

AVOCATIONAL INTERESTS: Travel, camping, mountain climbing, ice skating, playing in string quartets, ski touring.

* * *

MARSHALL, John David 1928-

PERSONAL: Born September 7, 1928, in McKenzie, Tenn.; son of Maxwell Cole (a merchant) and Emma (Walpole) Marshall. *Education:* Bethel College, B.A., 1950; Florida State University, M.A., 1951, graduate study, 1951-52. *Politics:* Democrat. *Religion:* Cumberland Presbyterian. *Home:* 802 East Main, Apt. 34, Murfreesboro, Tenn. 37130. *Office:* Andrew L. Todd Library, Middle Tennessee State University, Murfreesboro, Tenn. 37130.

CAREER: Florida State University Library School, Tallahassee, administrative assistant, Office of Library School

Dean, 1951-52; Clemson College Library, Clemson, S.C., reference librarian, 1952-55; Auburn University Library, Auburn, Ala., head of reference department, 1955-57; University of Georgia Libraries, Athens, head of acquisitions division and assistant professor of libraries, 1957-67; Middle Tennessee State University, Murfreesboro, university librarian and associate professor of library science, 1967—. *Member:* American Library Association (life), Association of College and Research Libraries (publications committee member, 1957-62), Bibliographical Society of America, Southeastern Library Association (vice-chairman, College and University Libraries Section, 1970-72, chairman, 1972—), Southeastern Regional Group of Resources and Technical Services Librarians (vice-chairman, 1966-68, chairman, 1968-70), Tennessee Historical Society, Tennessee Library Association (chairman of Intellectual Freedom Committee, 1968-70), English-Speaking Union (Nashville chapter), Phi Kappa Phi, Beta Phi Mu (publications committee member, Gamma Chapter, 1963-64).

WRITINGS: (Editor with Wayne Shirley and Louis Shores) *Books, Libraries, Librarians: Contributions to Library Literature,* Shoe String, 1955; *Books in Your Life,* Bethel College, 1959; (editor) *Of, By, and For Librarians: Contributions to Library Literature,* Shoe String, 1960; (editor) *An American Library History Reader: Contributions to Library Literature,* Shoe String, 1961; (editor) *In Pursuit of Library History,* Florida State University Library School, 1961; *Louis Shores: A Bibliography,* Gamma Chapter, Beta Phi Mu, 1964; (editor) *Louis Shores, Mark Hopkins' Log and Other Essays,* Shoe String, 1965; *A Fable of Tomorrow's Library,* Peacock Press, 1965; (editor) *Approaches to Library History,* Florida State University Library School, 1966; (editor) *The Library in the University,* Shoe String, 1967. General editor, "Contributions to Library Literature" series, Shoe String Press; *Southern Observer,* contributing editor, 1953-66, contributor of column, "Bibliophile's Notebook," 1954-66; book reviewer, *Library Journal,* 1953-64; book review editor, *Journal of Library History,* 1966—.

WORK IN PROGRESS: Revising and bringing up-to-date *Louis Shores: A Bibliography,* for Gamma Chapter of Beta Phi Mu.

SIDELIGHTS: Marshall collects the books of three authors: Louis Shores, dean of Florida State University Library School, Lawrence Clark Powell, dean of School of Library Service at the University of California (Los Angeles), and former Prime Minister Sir Winston S. Churchill. His collection of Churchilliana includes some three hundred items either by or about Churchill (in whom he has been interested since about the seventh grade), including a first edition of *Savrola* (Longmans, Green, 1900), Churchill's only novel. Marshall was privileged to hear the famous "iron curtain" speech which Churchill delivered at Westminster College, Fulton, Mo., on March 5, 1946.

BIOGRAPHICAL/CRITICAL SOURCES: New York Times Book Review, May 6, 1956; *Southern Observer,* April, 1960; *College and Research Libraries,* December, 1967.

*   *   *

MARSON, Philip   1892-

PERSONAL: Surname originally Marzynski; born May 5, 1892, in Boston, Mass.; son of Moritz (a cordage jobber) and Pauline (Levi) Marzynski; married Rose Ulin, January 27, 1918; children: Betty (Mrs. Walter C. Guralnick). *Education:* Tufts University, B.S., 1915; Boston Normal School, diploma, 1916; Teachers College, Boston, Mass., M.Ed., 1928; graduate study at Harvard University and Boston University. *Politics:* Independent. *Religion:* Humanist. *Home:* 86 Boylston St., Chestnut Hill, Mass. 02167.

CAREER: Needham High School, Needham, Mass., head of English department, 1917-18; St. Paul Academy, St. Paul, Minn., master of English and director of athletics, 1918-21, high school English instructor in Newton, Mass., 1921-23; Rivers Country Day School, Brookline, Mass., head of English department and director of student activities, 1923-26; Boston Latin School, Boston, Mass., English teacher, 1926-57; River Dell Regional Schools, River Edge, N.J., consultant in English, 1961-63. Director of summer camps, including Camp Alton, Wolfeboro, N.H., 1937—. *Awards, honors:* Templeton Prize Essay award, Princeton Theological Seminary, 1961, for "A Man's Reach."

WRITINGS: The American Tragedy: Our Schools, Berkshire Publishing, 1958; *A Teacher Speaks,* McKay, 1960; *Breeder of Democracy,* Schenkman, 1963, new edition, c.1970; *Yankee Voices,* Schenkman, 1969.

AVOCATIONAL INTERESTS: Sports, theatre, and contemporary literature.

*   *   *

MARTIN, Anamae   1919-

PERSONAL: Born May 6, 1919, in Lancaster, Ohio; daughter of Lauren E. and Florence (Williamson) Martin. *Education:* Ohio University, B.S., 1943; Ohio State University, M.A., 1952. *Politics:* Republican. *Religion:* Presbyterian. *Home:* 958 Hillsdale Dr., Columbus, Ohio 43224. *Office:* Columbus Board of Education, 270 East State St., Columbus, Ohio 43215.

CAREER: Teacher in Lancaster, Ohio, 1941-45; Columbus Board of Education, Columbus, Ohio, elementary and kindergarten teacher, 1945-51, cadet principal, 1951-52, elementary school principal, 1952-56, supervising principal for elementary grades, 1956-69, principal of Northtower Elementary School, 1969—. *Member:* Social Studies Association, Reading Association, National Education Association, Elementary Principals' Association (local, state, and national levels), Ohio Education Association, Columbus Education Association, Delta Kappa Gamma, English Club, Order of Eastern Star (past chapter matron).

WRITINGS: Columbus, the Buckeye Capital, C.E. Merrill, 1962.

*   *   *

MARTIN, E(rnest) W(alter)   1914-

PERSONAL: Born May 31, 1914, in Devonshire, England; son of Thomas and Elizabeth Martin; married Elisabeth-Editha Mallandaine. *Education:* Educated privately and in English schools. *Politics:* Liberal. *Religion:* Anglican. *Home:* Editha Cottage, Black Torrington, Beaworthy, Devonshire, England.

CAREER: Free-lance writer, 1938—. Began as reviewer for various journals, later turned to social and historical studies, specializing in rural life. Lecturer, Workers' Educational Association. *Member:* Society of Authors.

WRITINGS: Heritage of the West (essays), Heath Cranton, 1938; (editor) *In Search of Faith,* Lindsay Drummond, 1943; (editor) *The New Spirit,* Dobson, 1946; (editor) *The Countryman's Chapbook,* Dobson, 1949; *A Wanderer in the West Country,* Phoenix House, 1951; *The Secret People: English Village Life after 1750,* Phoenix House, 1954, Transatlantic, 1956; (editor and author of introduction and notes) William Cobbett, *Rural Rides,* Macdonald & Co., 1958; *Where London Ends: English Provincial Life after 1750,* Essential Books, 1958; *Dartmoor,* R. Hale, 1958; *The Case against Hunting,* Dobson,

1959; *The Tyranny of the Majority*, Pall Mall, 1961; *The Book of the Village*, Phoenix House, 1962; *The Book of the Country Town*, Phoenix House, 1962; *The Shearers and the Shorn: A Study of Life in a Devon Community*, Humanities, 1965; (editor) *Country Life in England*, Ginn, 1966. Contributor of *Observer, Hibbert Journal, New Society, History Today*, and other periodicals.

WORK IN PROGRESS: History of Social Welfare, for Allen & Unwin.

AVOCATIONAL INTERESTS: Book collecting, walking, gardening, visiting friends.

* * *

MARTIN, George (Whitney) 1926-

PERSONAL: Born January 25, 1926, in New York, N.Y.; son of George Whitney (a lawyer) and Agnes (Hutchinson) Martin. *Education:* Harvard University, B.A., 1948; Trinity College, Cambridge, student, 1949-50; University of Virginia, L.L.B., 1953. *Home and office:* 333 East 68th St., New York, N.Y. 10021.

CAREER: Admitted to bar, 1955; Emmet, Marvin & Martin, Attorneys at Law, New York, N.Y., associate, 1955-58, partner, 1958-59; now full-time writer. Director, Leake & Watts Children's Home, Inc.; director and secretary, Metropolitan Opera Guild. *Military service:* U.S. Navy, 1944-46; U.S. Army, 1953-54.

WRITINGS: The Opera Companion: A Guide for the Casual Opera-Goer, Volume I, Dodd, 1961, Volume II, Apollo, 1972; *The Battle of the Frogs and the Mice: An Homeric Fable* Dodd, 1962; *Verdi: His Music, Life and Times*, Dodd, 1963; *The Red Shirt and the Cross of Savoy: The Story of Italy's Risorgimento 1748-1871)*, Dodd, 1969; *Causes and Conflicts: The Centennial History of the Association of the Bar of the City of New York*, Houghton, 1970. Contributor of articles to *Opera Annual, Yale Review, Opera News*, and *Bulletin of Istituto de Studi Verdiani*, and of book reviews to *Yale Review* and *Book World*.

WORK IN PROGRESS: Biography of Frances Perkins, Secretary of Labor, 1933-1945, publication by Houghton expected in 1974.

SIDELIGHTS: In a review of *Causes and Conflicts: The Centennial History of the Association of the Bar of the City of New York*, a writer for *Virginia Quarterly Review* describes Martin as "a graceful writer and a discriminating historian . . ." and his book as "a near-model institutional history [which] is perceptive, critical, and judicious. It is also appreciative, interesting, and informative."

BIOGRAPHICAL/CRITICAL SOURCES: Book World, May 25, 1969; *Virginia Quarterly Review*, autumn, 1970.

* * *

MARTIN, Harold Clark 1917-

PERSONAL: Born January 12, 1917, in Raymond, Pa.; son of Henry Floyd and Anna (Clark) Martin; married Elma Hicks (a part-time teacher), December 21, 1939; children: Thomas, Joel, Ann, Rebecca. *Education:* University of Wisconsin, certificate of competence in French, 1936; Hartwick College, A.B., 1937; Columbia University, graduate study, 1941; University of Michigan, M.A., 1942; Harvard University, Ph.D., 1954. *Home:* President's House, Union College, Schenectady, N.Y. 12308. *Office:* Union College, Schenectady, N.Y. 12308.

CAREER: Adams High School, Adams, N.Y., teacher of French and English, 1937-39; Goshen High School, Goshen, N.Y., English teacher, 1939-42, principal, 1942-48; Harvard University, Cambridge, Mass., director of General Education A., 1951-65, lecturer in comparative litera-

ture, 1955-65; Union College, Schenectady, N.Y., president, 1965—; Union University, Schenectady, N.Y., chancellor, 1965—. Chairman of Massachusetts State Fulbright Committee, 1957-66; executive secretary, English Institute, 1958-64; chairman of examiners in English, College Entrance Examination Board, 1961-65; member of board of directors, Council on Humanities, 1959—; member of regional committee, Woodrow Wilson Foundation, 1961-63. Consultant, U.S. Bureau of Education, 1963-66. Director, Schenectady Trust Co., 1966—, Volunteers for International Technical Assistance, 1967—. Member of New York State Temporary Commission on Compensation, 1970—. Trustee, Roxbury Latin School, 1964—, and Hartwick College. Director, Schenectady Museum, 1966—.

MEMBER: International Comparative Literature Association (member of advisory board, 1965—), National Council of Teachers of English, Modern Language Association of America. *Awards, honors:* LL.D., Hartwick College, 1965; Litt.D., Elmira College, 1967, Siena College, 1968, Concord College, 1968; D.H.L., Trinity College, 1970.

WRITINGS: (Editor with Richard M. Ohmann) *Inquiry and Expression: A College Reader*, Rinehart, 1958, revised edition, Holt, 1963; *The Logic and Rhetoric of Exposition*, Rinehart, 1958, revised edition (with Ohmann), Holt, 1963, 3rd edition (with Ohmann and James H. Wheatley), Holt, 1969; (editor and contributor) *Style in Prose Fiction*, Columbia University Press, 1959; *The Teaching of Composition and the Study of Style*, College Entrance Examination Board, 1967. Contributor to professional journals.

* * *

MARTIN, James Gilbert 1926-

PERSONAL: Born December 10, 1926, in Paris, Ill.; son of James and Ruth (Gilbert) Martin; married Doris Edmonson, August 23, 1969; children: Bradley. *Education:* Indiana State College, B.A., 1952, M.A., 1953; Indiana University, Ph.D., 1957. *Politics:* Independent. *Home:* 1609 West 5th St. Cedar Falls, Iowa 50613. *Office:* University of Northern Iowa, Cedar Falls, Iowa 50613.

CAREER: Northern Illinois University, DeKalb, 1957-64, became associate professor of sociology; Ohio State University, Columbus, assistant dean of College of Arts and Sciences, 1965-67, associate dean of College of Social and Behavioral Sciences, 1968-70, acting dean of the college, 1970-71; University of Northern Iowa, Cedar Falls, Vice-president, provost, and professor of sociology, 1971—. Consultant, National Association for the Advancement of Colored People. *Military service:* U.S. Army, athletic instructor, 1945-48. *Member:* American Sociological Association, Society for the Study of Social Problems, American Association of University Professors (chapter president, 1960), American Civil Liberties Union (chapter president, 1961). *Awards, honors:* Ellis L. Phillips Foundation intern in academic administration, 1963-64.

WRITINGS: The Tolerant Personality, Wayne State University Press, 1964; *Intergroup Relations*, Merrill, 1973. Contributor of articles to professional journals.

* * *

MARTIN, John Stuart 1900-

PERSONAL: Born November 9, 1900, in Winnetka, Ill.; son of William Hoffman (a grain broker) and Emily (Busch) Martin; third wife, Mary Mitchell Gilbert; children: David B. H., Barry (Mrs. James Stuart), Jill (Mrs. Kenneth Ives, Jr.), Susan (Mrs. B. Danforth Ely). *Education:* Princeton University, A.B., 1923. *Home:* Hope Rd., Great Meadows, N.J. 07838.

CAREER: Time, Inc., New York, N.Y., member of editorial staff, 1922-41; free-lance writer, 1941—. *Member:* Princeton Club of New York. *Awards, honors:* Oscar Award of Academy of Motion Picture Arts and Sciences, 1944, for narration for "The Fighting Lady."

WRITINGS: *General Manpower* (novel), Simon & Schuster, 1938; (editor) *A Picture History of Russia*, Crown, 1945, 3rd edition, 1968; *The Home Owner's Tree Book: A Plain-Spoken Manual for Non-Professional Tree Lovers*, Doubleday, 1962; *Learning to Gun: A Plain-Spoken Manual for the Ardent but Unaccomplished*, Doubleday, 1963; *The Curious History of the Golf Ball: Mankind's Most Fascinating Sphere*, Horizon Press, 1968; (editor with Ellsworth Raymond) *A Picture History of Eastern Europe*, Crown, 1971.

Author of narration for films: (With Eugene Ling) "The Fighting Lady," Fox, 1945; "13 Rue Madeleine," Fox, 1946; "Cinerama Holiday," Stanley Warner, 1955; "Animal Farm," D.C.A., 1955; "Tobaccoland." Also author of narration of several Navy documentaries. Contributor of many articles to *American Heritage, Digest*, and other magazines.

AVOCATIONAL INTERESTS: Gunning, bird dogs, fly-fishing, and golf.

* * *

MARTIN, Ralph C.   1924-

PERSONAL: Born October 11, 1924, in Charleston, S.C.; son of Ralph and Nonia McIntyre (Bartley) Martin; married Sylvia Gerland (a chemistry instructor), March 27, 1948. *Education:* University of Oklahoma, B.S. in Ch.E., 1952; graduate study, Boston University, 1954, Northeastern University, 1954-55, University of Oklahoma, 1959-62. *Home address:* P.O. Box 2188, Norman, Okla. 73069.

CAREER: General Electric Co., New York and Massachusetts, marketing engineer, 1952-55; Arabian American Oil Co., Saudi Arabia, process engineer, 1955-57; University of Oklahoma Research Institute, Norman, technical editor and head of information services, 1960—, conductor of technical writing section of Professional Writing Conference, 1963. Free-lance technical and fiction writer, 1958—. *Member:* American Chemical Society, American Institute of Chemical Engineers, Society of Technical Writers and Publishers, American Association for the Advancement of Science, Alpha Chi Sigma.

WRITINGS: (with Wayne Jett) *Guide to Scientific and Technical Periodicals*, Alan Swallow, 1963; (with Jawaharlal Ramnarace and Bruce Ketcham) *Propellents*, Sams, 1967; (with Ramnarace and Ketcham) *Propulsion*, Sams, 1967. Editor-in-chief, "Rocket and Space Science" series, American Rocket Association and National Aeronautics and Space Administration, 1964. Contributor of fiction to men's magazines. Staff book reviewer, *Daily Oklahoman*, 1960-63.

WORK IN PROGRESS: A novel with a Far East setting; a science book for the general public; a science book for high school readers.

* * *

MARTIN, Thomas Lyle, Jr.   1921-

PERSONAL: Born September 26, 1921, in Memphis, Tenn.; son of Thomas Lyle (an Army officer) and Malvina (Rucks) Martin; married Helene Hartley, June 12, 1943; children: Michele Marie, Thomas Lyle III. *Education:* Rensselaer Polytechnic Institute, B.E.E., 1942, M.E.E., 1948; Stanford University, Ph.D., 1951. *Religion:* Episcopal. *Home:* 7241 Lakehurst Ave., Dallas, Tex. 75230.

CAREER: University of New Mexico, Albuquerque, assistant professor, 1948-50, associate professor of electrical engineering, 1951-53; University of Arizona, Tucson, professor of electrical engineering and head of department, 1953-58, dean of engineering, 1958-63; University of Florida, Gainesville, dean of engineering, 1963-66; Southern Methodist University, Institute of Technology, Dallas, Tex., dean, 1966—. Consultant to industry. *Military service:* U.S. Army, Signal Corps, 1943-46; became captain; received Bronze Star. *Member:* Institute of Electrical and Electronics Engineers, American Society for Engineering Education, Florida Engineering Society. *Awards, honors:* Achievement award, Institute of Radio Engineers (Seventh Region), 1956.

WRITINGS: *Ultrahigh Frequency Engineering*, Prentice-Hall, 1950; *Electronic Circuits*, Prentice-Hall, 1955; *Physical Basis for Electrical Engineering*, Prentice-Hall, 1957; *Radioactive Ionizers* (report), Engineering Experiment Station, University of Arizona, 1958; *The Effects of Nuclear Weapons on Tucson*, University of Arizona Press, 1961; (with Donald C. Latham) *Strategy for Survival*, University of Arizona Press, 1963; (with W.F. Leonard) *Electrons and Crystals*, Brooks-Cole, 1970.

* * *

MARTIN, Walter T(ilford)   1917-

PERSONAL: Born August 26, 1917, in Sherwood, Ore.; son of James Tilford and Clara Irene (Brown) Martin; married Rena Elizabeth Buckley, January 7, 1939; children: Susan E., Kathleen A., Lawrence A., David T. *Education:* University of Washington, Seattle, B.A., 1943, M.A., 1947, Ph.D., 1949. *Home:* 2730 Emerald St., Eugene, Ore. 97403.

CAREER: Washington State Penitentiary, director of classification, 1943-44; Washington State Parole Department, Seattle, parole and probation officer, 1944-45; University of Oregon, Eugene, instructor, 1947-49, assistant professor, 1949-53, associate professor, 1953-59, chairman of department of sociology, 1957-68, professor of sociology, 1959—. Visiting assistant professor at University of Kansas, 1951, Whittier College, 1953; visiting associate professor, University of California, 1956-57, University of Wisconsin, 1958. *Military service:* U.S. Army, 1944. *Member:* Population Association of America (member of board of directors, 1963-66), American Sociological Association (member of executive council, 1960-63), Sociological Research Association, American Association of University Professors, Pacific Sociological Association (vice-president, 1957-58, 1963-64; president, 1964-65). *Awards, honors:* Social Science Research Council fellowship, 1952-53.

WRITINGS: (Editor with Robert W. O'Brien and Clarence Schrag) *Readings in General Sociology*, Houghton, 1951, 4th edition, 1969; *The Rural-Urban Fringe: A Study of Adjustment to Residence Location* (monograph), University of Oregon, 1953; (contributor) William H. Dobriner, *The Suburban Community*, Putnam, 1958; (with John M. Foskett) *Some Factors Related to the Decision of High School Students to Enter the University of Oregon*, University of Oregon, 1959; (contributor) George A. Theodorson, *Studies in Human Ecology*, Row, Peterson, 1961; (contributor) *Problems of Economic Development*, Institute of International Studies and Overseas Administration, 1960; (with Jack P. Gibbs) *Status Integration and Suicide*, University of Oregon Press, 1964; *Social Stress and Chronic Illness*, University of Notre Dame Press, 1970. Contributor of twenty articles to sociological journals.

MARTINEZ, Rafael V. 1923-

PERSONAL: Born December 2, 1923, in Omaja, Ote, Cuba; son of Rafael Martinez; married Wilma Comstock (a teacher), March 16, 1946; children: Alice, Richard, Roland. Education: Havana Provincial Institute, B.S., 1944; Iliff School of Theology, Th.M., 1951; University of Chicago, M.A., 1955; University of Madrid, postgraduate student, 1955-56; Northwestern University, Ph.D., 1964. Home: 2818 Marietta Ave., Lancaster, Pa. 17601. Office: Franklin & Marshall College, Lancaster, Pa. 17604.

CAREER: Presbyterian minister in Roswell, N.M., 1946-47, Fort Morgan, Colo., 1948-50, Chicago, Ill., 1951-53; professor of Spanish language and literature, University of Chicago, 1953-55, Roosevelt University, Chicago, Ill., professor of Spanish, 1956-66; Franklin & Marshall College, Lancaster, Pa., professor of Spanish and Portuguese and chairman of the department, 1966—. Executive director, Chicago Social Service Organization, Chicago, Ill., 1960-63. Director, Pan-American Board of Education, Chicago. Writer-producer of twenty cultural programs for WMBQ Television, 1959. Member: American Association of Teachers of Spanish, American Association of University Professors.

WRITINGS: My House Is Your House, Friendship, 1964; (contributor) L.W. Halvorson, editor, The Church in a Diverse Society, Augsburg, 1964. Author of television scripts.

WORK IN PROGRESS: Our Caribbean Neighbors; a first-year college text on Spanish language; African sociolinguistic influence in the Caribbean.

*　　*　　*

MARTYN, Howe 1906-

PERSONAL: Born August 4, 1906, in Bowmanville, Ontario, Canada; son of H.G. (principal of a teacher's college) and Mabel (Rickard) Martyn; married Marjorie Horwood; children: Nancy Martyn Chadwick, Sylvia Martyn Hubbard, Peter H. Education: University of Toronto, B.A. (first class honors), 1930; Oxford University, M.A. (first class honors), 1932. Residence: Palgrave, Ontario, Canada. Office: American University, Massachusetts and Nebraska Aves. N.W., Washington, D.C. 20016.

CAREER: McKim Advertising Agency, Toronto, Ontario, marketing director, 1940-48; Unilever, London, England, manager of marketing advisory division, 1948-53; Beecham Group (Western Hemisphere), Toronto, Ontario, marketing director, 1954-59; Canadian Food Products, Toronto, Ontario, vice-president of marketing, 1959-60; American University, Washington, D.C., professor of international business, 1961—, and organizer of International Business Research Laboratory. Member, British Dollar Exports Board. Member: University Club (Toronto and New York), Travellers' Club (London, England).

WRITINGS: Foreign Competition and Christian International Relations, Division of Human Relations and Economic Affairs, Methodist General Board of Christian Social Concerns, 1962; International Business: Principles and Problems, Free Press, 1964; Multinational Business Management, Heath, 1970. Contributor to Dalhousie Review, Queen's Quarterly, Maclean's Financial Times, Guardian (England), Canadian Business; also reviewer for other journals and newspapers.

*　　*　　*

MARX, Herbert L(ewis), Jr. 1922-

PERSONAL: Born February 1, 1922, in Albany, N.Y.; son of Herbert Lewis and Ruth (Naumburg) Marx; children: Jonathan B., Timothy S., Alison L. Education: Dartmouth College, A.B., 1943; New York University, M.B.A., 1955. Home: 16 West 16th St., New York, N.Y. 10011. Office: General Cable Corp., 730 Third Ave., New York, N.Y. 10017.

CAREER: Albany Times-Union, Albany, N.Y., reporter, 1941; U.S. Office of Strategic Services, assignments in Washington, D.C., London, England, and Paris, France, 1942-45; Scholastic Magazines, New York, N.Y., associate editor and national affairs editor, 1945-51; General Cable Corp., New York, N.Y., assistant director of personnel relations, 1951—. Member: Industrial Relations Research Association, Phi Beta Kappa, Beta Gamma Delta.

WRITINGS—All published by H.W. Wilson, except as indicated: (Editor) The Welfare State, 1950; (editor) American Labor Unions: Organization, Aims, and Power, 1950; (editor) Universal Conscription for Essential Service, 1951; (editor) Gambling in America, 1952; Facing Military Service (pamphlet), Oxford Book Co., 1953; (editor) Television and Radio in American Life, 1953; (editor) Defense and National Security, 1955; (editor) Community Planning, 1956; (editor) State and Local Government, 1962; (editor) American Labor Today, 1965; (editor) Collective Bargaining for Public Employees, 1969. Contributor of articles to New York Herald Tribune, Mill and Factory, Editor and Publisher, Personnel, Nation, Business Week, and other periodicals.

WORK IN PROGRESS: Editing The American Indians.

*　　*　　*

MARX, Robert F(rank) 1934-

PERSONAL: Born December 8, 1934, in Pittsburgh, Pa.; son of Frank J. and Mary Ann (Salopeck) Marx; married Mary Stanford (an actress and dancer); children: Cheryl. Education: Studied at Los Angeles City College, University of California, Los Angeles, and University of Seville. Politics: Democrat. Religion: Roman Catholic. Home: Generalisimo 28, Madrid, Spain. Agent: Bill Berger Associates, Inc., 535 East 72nd St., New York, N.Y. 10021. Office: Saturday Evening Post, 666 Fifth Ave., New York, N.Y. 10019.

CAREER: Owner of marine salvage company in Yucatan, Mexico, 1956-59; International Mineral and Chemical Corp., Skokie, Ill., oceanographic consultant, 1959-60; Saturday Evening Post, New York, N.Y., adventure editor, 1963—. Leader of underwater and land archaeological expeditions in Mexico, South America, Spain, France, United States, the Caribbean, and Bahamas; in 1955 discovered off Cape Hatteras the USS Monitor of the Civil War; in 1962 was navigator of the Columbus replica, Nina II, following the route of Columbus to America; in 1964 attempted in replica of tenth-century Viking ship to reach America from Yugoslavia, but a gale broke up the ship off Tunisia. Member of board of advisers, American Museum of Underwater Archaeology; member of advisory board, Foul Anchor Archives, Rye, N.Y. Military service: U.S. Marine Corps, 1953-56; ran diving school; became sergeant. Member: Real Academia de la Historia (Spain), Instituto de Estudios Hispano-Americano (Spain), C.E.D.A.M. (marine archaeological group, Mexico), diving clubs. Awards, honors: Knight of Order of Isabel the Catholic (Spain), 1964.

WRITINGS: Historia de Isla de Cozumel, [Merida, Yucatan], 1959; The Voyage of the Nina II, World Publishing, 1963; Following Columbus: The Voyage of the Nina II, World Publishing, 1964; The Battle of the Spanish Armada, 1588, World Publishing, 1965; The Battle of Lepanto, 1571, World Publishing, 1966; They Dared the Deep: A History of Diving, World Publishing, 1967; Always Another Adventure, World Publishing, 1967; Pirate Port: The Story of the Sunken City of Port Royal,

World Publishing, 1967; *The Treasure Fleets of the Spanish Main*, World Publishing, 1968; *Clay Smoking Pipes Recovered from the Sunken City of Port Royal October 1, 1967-March 31, 1968*, Jamaica National Trust Commission, 1968; *Reports on the Sunken City of Port Royal*, Jamaica National Trust Commission, 1968; *Wine Glasses Recovered from the Sunken City of Port Royal: May 1, 1966-March 31, 1968*, Jamaica National Trust Commission, 1968; *Shipwrecks in Florida Waters*, Scott Publishing Co., 1969; (compiler) *Shipwrecks of the Virgin Islands, 1523-1825*, edited by E.L. Towle, Caribbean Research Institute, 1969; *Shipwrecks of the Western Hemisphere, 1492-1825*, World Publishing, 1971; *Sea Fever*, Doubleday, 1972. Contributor to *Saturday Evening Post, Travel, Skin Diver, Cavalier, Paris Match, Stern* (Germany), *Epoca* (Italy), and other periodicals.

SIDELIGHTS: Marx plans to build another Viking ship to sail across the Atlantic; later he plans to duplicate Magellan's around-the-world voyage.

BIOGRAPHICAL/CRITICAL SOURCES: Clay Blair, Jr., *Diving for Pleasure and Treasure*, World Publishing, 1960; *Saturday Evening Post*, December 14, 1964; *New York Times Book Review*, August 6, 1967.

* * *

MASON, Bruce B (onner)   1923-

PERSONAL: Born December 19, 1923, in Cleburne, Tex.; son of Joseph Lee and Daisy (Bonner) Mason; married Jacqueline Tenery (a teacher), January 2, 1928; children: Douglas Lee. *Education:* North Texas State College (now North Texas State University), B.S., 1947; Texas Christian University, M.A., 1949; University of Texas, Ph.D., 1952. *Politics:* Democrat. *Religion:* Unitarian. *Home:* 320 East Fairmont, Tempe, Ariz. 85281. *Office:* Department of Political Science, Arizona State University, Tempe, Ariz. 85281.

CAREER: University of Florida, Gainesville, assistant professor of political science, 1954-58; University of Illinois, Urbana, research assistant professor of political science, 1958-60; Arizona State University, Tempe, professor of public administration, 1960—. Consultant to Central and Southern Florida Flood Control District, 1954-58, Illinois County Problems Commission, 1958-60, governor of Taiwan, 1963-64, and to Arizona Academy, 1964. Member of Arizona Democratic Council, 1964. *Military service:* U.S. Army Air Forces, 1942-45; became sergeant. *Member:* American Political Science Association, American Society for Public Administration (president, Arizona chapter, 1962-63), Western Governmental Research Association, Western Political Science Association.

WRITINGS: Florida Voter's Guide, Public Administrative Clearing Service, University of Florida, 1955; (with Douglas Gatlin) *Reapportionment: Its History in Florida*, Public Administrative Clearing Service, University of Florida, 1956; (editor with Penrose Jackson) *Reports of the Governor's Citizens Committees*, Public Administrative Clearing Service, University of Florida, 1956; *The Public Administration Clearing Service: A Tenth Year Reappraisal*, University of Florida, 1958; (with Heinz R. Hink) *Revision of the Arizona Constitution: A Commentary*, Bureau of Government Research, Arizona State University, 1961; *Arizona General Election Results, 1911-1960*, Bureau of Government Research, Arizona State University, 1961; *Congressional Redistricting in Arizona*, Bureau of Government Research, Arizona State University, 1961; (editor) *The Political-Military Defense of Latin America*, Bureau of Government Research, Arizona State University, 1963; (with Hink) *Constitutional Government in Arizona*, Arizona State University, 1963, 3rd edition, 1968; *Local Government in Taiwan: Some Observations*, Bureau of Government Research, Arizona State University, 1964; *Local Government in Ghana*, Bureau of Government Research, Arizona State University, 1967. Contributor to *Florida Bar Journal, Arizona Frontiers, Western Political Quarterly*, and other journals.

WORK IN PROGRESS: A book on public administration; a monograph on the McCarthy movement in Arizona.

SIDELIGHTS: Mason has traveled to the Far East, 1963-64, spending almost a year in Taiwan, and to Ghana, 1966-67, as a United Nations expert.

* * *

MASON, Haydn T (revor)   1929-

PERSONAL: Born January 12, 1929, in Saundersfoot, Pembrokeshire, Wales; son of Herbert Thomas (a blacksmith) and Margaret (Jones) Mason; married Gretchen Reger, February 5, 1955; children: David, Gwyneth. *Education:* University College of Wales, B.A. (honors), 1949; Middlebury College, Middlebury, Vt., A.M., 1951; Jesus College, Oxford, D.Phil., 1960. *Home:* 14 Claremont Rd., Norwich, England. *Office:* School of European Studies, University of East Anglia, Norwich, England.

CAREER: Princeton University, Princeton, N.J., instructor in French, 1954-57; University of Newcastle upon Tyne, Newcastle upon Tyne, England, lecturer in French, 1960-63; University of Reading, Reading, England, lecturer, 1964-65, reader in French, 1965-67; University of East Anglia, Norwich, England, professor of European literature, 1967—. *Military service:* British Army, 1951-53.

WRITINGS: Pierre Bayle and Voltaire, Oxford University Press, 1963; (editor and author of introduction) Marivaux, *Les Fausses Confidences*, Oxford University Press, 1964, revised edition, 1971; (editor) *The Leibniz-Arnauld Correspondence*, Manchester University Press, 1967; (editor) Voltaire, *Zadig and Other Stories*, Oxford University Press, 1971.

WORK IN PROGRESS: A book on literature and society in France, 1715-1800, tentatively titled *Reason and Sensibility*, for Weidenfeld and Nicolson; a book on Voltaire, for Hutchinson; critical editions of six of Voltaire's philosophical poems, for *Oeuvres completes*, edited by T. Besterman, for University of Toronto Press.

* * *

MASON, Madeline   1913-
(David Bartlett, Tyler Mason)

PERSONAL: Born January 24, 1913, in New York, N.Y.; daughter of Jacob Joshua (a lawyer) and Maud Frederica (Mason) Manheim; married Malcolm Forbes McKesson (an artist), May 6, 1942. *Education:* Educated in private schools in United States and abroad; studied piano under Rudolf Ganz and Alexander Siloti, composition under Ernest Bloch. *Politics:* Democrat. *Religion:* Episcopalian. *Home:* Hotel Seville, 22 East 29th St., New York, N.Y. 10016; and "Casa Benita," Onteora Club, Tannersville, N.Y. 12485.

CAREER: Author and lecturer. Leader of poetry workshops in United States and England, 1950—; founder and director with George Abbe of New England Writers' Conference; poet-in-residence, Shenandoah College, Winchester, Va., 1969—. Read own poetry at Edinburgh Festival, 1953. *Member:* Poetry Society of America (member of executive board, 1971—; vice-president, 1973—), Authors League, Pen and Brush, National League of American Pen Women (national poetry chairman, 1954-56, 1962-64), Composers, Authors, and Artists of America (first vice-president, 1968-70), Women's Press Club, Junior League (New York; chairman of exhibitions committee, 1942-46), P.E.N. (London and New York centers). *Awards, honors:* Diamond Jubilee award of National League of American Pen Women, 1958, for achievement in poetry; Reynolds Lyric Award, 1959; Edna St. Vincent Millay Award for the invention of the Mason Sonnet; Emily Dickinson Award for distinction in poetry; award of distinction, Composers, Authors, and Artists of America, 1970, for superior creative achievements.

WRITINGS: (Translator into French) Kahlil Gibran, *Le Prophete,* Editions du Sagittaire, 1928; (author of foreword) Tolstoy, *Twenty-Three Tales,* Oxford University Press, 1928; *Hill Fragments* (poetry), Coward, 1936; (under pseudonym Tyler Mason, with E.M. House) *Riding for Texas: The True Adventures of Captain Bill Mc-Donald of the Texas Rangers,* John Day, 1936; *The Cage of Years* (poetry), Wheelwright, 1949; *At the Ninth Hour: A Sonnet Sequence in a New Form,* University Press of Washington, D.C., 1958; *Sonnets in a New Form,* Dragon's Teeth Press, 1971. Contributor of poetry, critical articles, and fiction to national magazines. Columnist under pseudonym David Bartlett, "The Political Undercurrent," in *New York Times,* 1933; writer of radio script, "Home on the Range," National Broadcasting Co., 1936.

WORK IN PROGRESS: A book of poetry, *Journey in a Room;* translation of the poems of Verhaeren; *Talks with E.A. Robinson;* memoirs, *As I Knew Them; Only by Love,* poems; *Gerda,* an opera libretto.

SIDELIGHTS: Ms. Mason lists astronomy as a special interest; she is the granddaughter of Oscar Gleason Mason, who made the first photographic studies of the phases of the moon. She also told *CA:* "In my early girlhood, spent in England and France, a visit to Thomas Hardy on his 86th birthday was an outstanding experience."

* * *

MASON, Philip 1906-
(Philip Woodruff)

PERSONAL: Born March 19, 1906, in London, England; son of H.A. and E. Addison (Woodruff) Mason; married Eileen Mary Hayes, 1935; children: two daughters, two sons. *Education:* Sedbergh School, student, 1919-24; Balliol College, Oxford, student, 1924-28. *Home:* Hither Daggons, Cripplestyle, Alderholt, Near Fordingbridge, Hamsphire, England.

CAREER: Indian Civil Service, 1928-47; Institute of Race Relations, London, England, director, 1958-70; writer. Government posts in India included undersecretary, War Department, 1933-36, deputy commissioner, Garhwal, 1936-39, deputy secretary, Defense and War Departments, 1939-42, conference secretary, South-East Asia Command, 1942-44, joint secretary, War Department, 1944-47. *Member:* Travellers Club, Pall Mall Club. *Awards, honors:* Order of British Empire, 1942; Companion of Indian Empire, 1945; fellow, School of Oriental and African Studies, University of London, 1970; D.Sc., University of Bristol, 1971.

WRITINGS: An Essay on Racial Tension, Royal Institute of International Affairs, 1954, Greenwood, 1972; *A New Deal in East Africa,* Royal Institute of International Affairs, 1955; *Christianity and Race,* Lutterworth, 1956, St. Martin's, 1957; *The Birth of a Dilemma: The Conquest and Settlement of Rhodesia,* Oxford University Press for Institute of Race Relations, 1958; (author of introduction and epilogue) *Man, Race and Darwin* (symposium), Oxford University Press, 1960; *Race Relations in Africa Considered Against the Background of History and World Opinion,* S.C.M. Press, 1960; *Year of Decision: Rhodesia and Nyasaland in 1960,* Oxford Uni-

versity Press, 1960; *Common Sense About Race,* Macmillan, 1961; *Prospero's Magic: Some Thoughts on Class and Race,* Oxford University Press, 1962; (editor) *India and Ceylon: Unity and Diversity,* Oxford University Press for Institute of Race Relations, 1967; (editor) *Violence in Southern Africa: A Christian Assessment,* S.C.M. Press, 1970; *Patterns of Dominance,* Oxford University Press for Institute of Race Relations, 1970; *Race Relations,* Oxford University Press, 1970; *How People Differ: An Introduction to Race Relations,* Edward Arnold, 1971.

Under pseudonym Philip Woodruff: *Call the Next Witness,* J. Cape, 1945, Harcourt, 1946; *The Wild Sweet Witch,* Harcourt, 1947; *Whatever Dies,* J. Cape, 1948; *The Sword of Northumbria,* J. Cape, 1948; *The Island of Chamba,* J. Cape, 1950; *Hernshaw Castle,* J. Cape, 1950; *Colonel of Dragoons,* J. Cape, 1951; *The Men Who Ruled India,* Volume I: *The Founders of Modern India,* J. Cape, 1953, St. Martin's, 1954, Volume II: *The Guardians,* St. Martin's, 1954. Contributor to journals and newspapers and to various symposia.

BIOGRAPHICAL/CRITICAL SOURCES: Times Literary Supplement, February 8, 1968; *Library Journal,* July, 1970; *Virginia Quarterly Review,* summer, 1970; *Christian Century,* September 23, 1970.

* * *

MASON, Raymond 1926-

PERSONAL: Legal name, Clarence Ray Mason; born October 8, 1926, in Plattsmouth, Neb.; son of Earl Clarence and Lucille (Bridgewater) Mason; married Marilynn Jane Fike, July 22, 1945; children: Ann. *Education:* Kansas City Junior College, student, 1943, 1948-49; San Francisco State College, A.B., 1952, M.A., 1970. *Politics:* "Belligerent middle of the road." *Home:* 30 Saroni Court, Oakland, Calif. 94611. *Agent:* Joan Foley, Foley Agency, 34 East 38th St., New York, N.Y. 10016.

CAREER: Writer and editor for newspapers; feature writer and advertising copy writer. *Wartime service:* U.S. Merchant Marine, 1944-47; served in Pacific combat zone.

WRITINGS: And Two Shall Meet, Fawcett, 1954; *Forever Is Today,* Fawcett, 1955; *Love After Five,* Fawcett, 1956; (contributor) *The Big Grab,* Pyramid Publications, 1960; *Bedeviled,* Hilton, 1960; *Someone and Felicia Warwick,* Fawcett, 1962. Contributor of stories to *Alfred Hitchcock Magazine* and other publications.

WORK IN PROGRESS: A comic novel.

* * *

MASON, Richard (Lakin) 1919-

PERSONAL: Born May 16, 1919, in England. *Education:* Attended Bryanston School. *Home:* Court St. Lawrence, Llangoven, Monmouthshire, England.

CAREER: Author.

WRITINGS: The Wind Cannot Read, Putnam, 1947; *The Shadow and the Peak,* Hodder & Stoughton, 1949, Macmillan, 1950, reissued as *The Passionate Summer,* Collins, 1958; *The World of Suzie Wong,* World Publishing, 1957; *The Fever Tree,* World Publishing, 1962.

* * *

MASSELMAN, George 1897-

PERSONAL: Born December 9, 1897, in Amsterdam, Netherlands; son of Gerrit Jan and Johanna (Gebuys) Masselman; married Florence Coughlin, January 7, 1941; children: Wilhelmina Masselman Van Hemert, Georgina Masselman Fitchett, Lee Masselman Kallos. *Education:* Navigation Academy, Amsterdam, Netherlands, B.Sc.,

1917. *Politics:* Democrat. *Religion:* Protestant. *Home:* Fox Run, West Redding, Conn. 06896.

CAREER: Java China Trading Co., New York, N.Y., president, 1923-36; Board of Economic Warfare, Washington, D.C., principal economist, 1941-44; U.S. Office of Strategic Services, overseas duty, 1944-45; Industrial College of the Armed Forces, Washington, D.C., geographer, 1945-48; National War College, Washington, D.C., consultant, 1947; New School for Social Research, New York, N.Y., lecturer in social science, 1948-49; Danbury State College, Graduate School, Danbury, Conn., lecturer in social science, 1963-64. Selectman, Town of Redding, Conn., 1956-59. *Member:* Economic History Association, American Historical Association, Nederlands Historisch Genootschap. *Awards, honors:* Research grant, American Philosophical Society, 1964.

WRITINGS: The Cradle of Colonialism (History Book Club selection), Yale University Press, 1963; *The Money Trees: The Spice Trade,* McGraw, 1967; *The Atlantic: Sea of Darkness,* McGraw, 1969. Contributor of articles to professional journals.

WORK IN PROGRESS: Research on a sequel to *The Cardle of Colonialism,* tentatively titled *Empire in Asia.*

* * *

MASTERMAN, John Cecil 1891-

PERSONAL: Born January 12, 1891, in Kingston Hill, Surrey, England; son of John (a captain, Royal Navy) and Edith Margaret (Hughes) Masterman. *Education:* Attended Royal Navy Colleges at Osborne and Dartmouth; Worcester College, Oxford, B.A., 1913, M.A., 1914. *Religion:* Church of England. *Home:* 6 Beaumont St., Oxford, England. *Agent:* Curtis Brown Ltd., 13 King St., Covent Garden, London W.C. 2, England.

CAREER: Oxford University, Oxford, England, lecturer and tutor at Christ Church, 1913-47, provost of Worcester College, 1947-61, vice-chancellor of university, 1957-58. Adviser on personnel matters, Birfield Ltd., London, England, 1961—. Fellow, Eton College; governor, Wellington College. *Awards, honors:* Order of British Empire, 1944, Knight Bachelor, 1959; LL.D., University of Toronto; D.C.L., University of King's College.

WRITINGS: An Oxford Tragedy, Gollancz, 1933; *Fate Cannot Harm Me,* Gollancz, 1935, Penguin (New York), 1940; *Marshall Ney* (five-act play), Cobden-Sanderson, 1937; *To Teach the Senators Wisdom; or, An Oxford Guide Book,* Oxford University Press, 1952; *The Case of the Four Friends: A Diversion in Pre-Detection,* Hodder & Stoughton, 1957, British Book Centre, 1959; *Bits and Pieces,* Hodder & Stoughton, 1961; *The Double-Cross System in the War of 1939-1945,* Yale University Press, 1971.

BIOGRAPHICAL/CRITICAL SOURCES: Publisher's Weekly, February 7, 1972.

* * *

MATCZAK, Sebastian A(lexander) 1914-

PERSONAL: Born January 20, 1914, in Warsaw, Poland; son of Jan (a builder) and Genowefa (Jagodzinska) Matczak. *Education:* Warsaw University, Warsaw, Poland, M.A., 1946; Gregorian University, Rome, Italy, Th.D., 1951; Catholic Institute of Paris, Ph.D., 1956; Sorbonne, University of Paris, Ph.D., 1962. *Religion:* Roman Catholic. *Home:* 83-53 Manton St., Jamaica, N.Y. 11435. *Office:* St. John's University, Jamaica, N.Y. 11432.

CAREER: Warsaw University, Warsaw, Poland, assistant to professor of theology, 1946-48; Manhattan College, New York, N.Y., assistant professor of philosophy, 1956-57; St. John's University, Jamaica, N.Y., associate professor, 1957-65, professor of philosophy, 1965—. *Member:* American Philosophical Association, American Catholic Philosophical Association, History of Science Society, Catholic Theological Society, American Association of University Professors, Polish Institute of Arts and Sciences in America, Fellowship of Religious Humanists.

WRITINGS: St. Hozjusz o sakramentach w ogolnosci, Libella (Paris), 1951; *Karl Barth on God: The Knowledge of the Divine Existence,* St. Paul Publications, 1962; *Research and Composition in Philosophy,* Humanities, 1968; *Philosophy: A Selected, Classified Bibliography of Ethics, Economics, Law, Politics, Sociology,* Nauwelaerts, 1970; (editor) Mary R. Barral, *Progressive Neutralism: A Philosophical Aspect of American Education,* Learned Publications, 1970; *Philosophy: Its Nature, Methods and Basic Sources,* Nauwelaerts, 1972, Humanities, 1972. Editor, "Philosophical Questions" series, St. John's University Press, 1968—. President, Learned Publications, 1968—. Contributor to *Polish Review, Modern Schoolman,* and *Worldmission.*

WORK IN PROGRESS: God in Contemporary Thought, for Nauwelaerts; *Limits of the Universe,* for Nauwelaerts; *Philosophy: Its Histories, Systems and Specific Setting,* to be published by Nauwelaerts in 1974.

SIDELIGHTS: Matczak has traveled extensively through Europe, United States, and Canada. He speaks and writes Polish, German, French, Italian, and English, and has a good knowledge of Latin and Classic Greek.

BIOGRAPHICAL/CRITICAL SOURCES: Review of Metaphysics, September, 1963; *Bibliography of Philosophy* (Paris), Volume X, number 3, 1963; *Theological Studies,* December, 1963; *Polish Review* (New York), winter, 1963.

* * *

MATHEW, (Anthony) Gervase 1905-

PERSONAL: Born March 14, 1905, in London, England; son of Francis James (an author) and Agnes (Woodroffe) Mathew. *Education:* Balliol College, Oxford, M.A., 1928. *Politics:* Liberal. *Religion:* Roman Catholic. *Home:* Blackfriars, St. Giles, Oxford, England.

CAREER: Entered Order of Preachers, 1928, ordained Roman Catholic priest, 1934; Oxford University, Oxford, England, lecturer in Greek patristics and Byzantine art and archaeology, 1937, member of history faculty and lecturer in medieval social theory, 1938—, member of English faculty and lecturer in fourteenth-century English literature, 1945—, member of sub-faculty of anthropology, 1956—. Visiting professor, University of California, 1965. Conductor of archaeological surveys in Tanganyika, 1950, Somaliland Protectorate, 1951, Uganda, 1953, South Arabia, 1962; other archaeological work in Greece and Asia Minor. *Member:* Society of Antiquaries (fellow).

WRITINGS: (With David Mathew) *The Reformation and the Contemplative Life: A Study of the Conflict Between the Carthusians and the State,* Sheed, 1934; (author of introduction and notes) *Byzantine Painting,* Pitman, 1950 (published in England as *Introduction to Byzantine Painting,* Faber, 1950); (with Kenneth Wykeham-George) *Bede Jarret, of the Order of Preachers,* Blackfriars Publications, 1952, Newman, 1953; *Byzantine Aesthetics,* J. Murray, 1963, Viking, 1964; (editor with Roland Oliver) *History of East Africa,* Volume I, Oxford University Press, 1963; (editor with Oliver) *History of East Africa: The Early Period* (reissue of first six chapters of *History of East Africa*), Oxford University Press, 1967; *The Court of Richard II,* J. Murray, 1968, Norton, 1969. Contributor to *Cambridge Mediaeval History, Journal of Roman Studies, Journal of Hellenic Studies, Antiquity,* and *Oriental Art.*

WORK IN PROGRESS: Imperial Rovenna.

BIOGRAPHICAL/CRITICAL SOURCES: Observer Review, May 12, 1968; Best Sellers, June 1, 1969.

* * *

MATHEWS, J(oseph) Howard 1881-

PERSONAL: Born October 15, 1881, in Auroraville, Wis.; son of Joseph and Lydia T. (Cate) Mathews; married Ella Barbara Gilfillan, June 26, 1909; children: Marion Zoe (Mrs. Norman H. Withey), Jean Barbara (Mrs. Charles C. Watson). Education: University of Wisconsin, B.S., 1903, M.A., 1905; Harvard University, M.A., 1906, Ph.D., 1908. Politics: Independent. Religion: Presbyterian. Home: 128 Lathrop, Madison, Wis. 53705. Office: Department of Chemistry, University of Wisconsin, Madison, Wis. 53706.

CAREER: Case Institute of Technology (now Case Western Reserve University), Cleveland, Ohio, instructor in chemistry, 1906-07; University of Wisconsin, Madison, instructor in chemistry, 1908-11, assistant professor, 1911-17, associate professor, 1917-19, professor of chemistry and chairman of department, 1919-52, professor emeritus, 1952—. Former member and president, Madison Police and Fire Commission. Military service: U.S. Army, Ordnance, 1917-18; became major. U.S. Army Reserve, Chemical Warfare, 1918-23; became lieutenant colonel. Member: American Chemical Society, American Association for the Advancement of Science, Alpha Chi Sigma, Sigma Xi.

WRITINGS: (With Farrington Daniels and John Warren Williams) Experimental Physical Chemistry, McGraw, 1929, 4th edition, 1949; Firearms Identification, Volumes I and II, University of Wisconsin Press, 1962, Volume III, C.C Thomas, 1972. Author of sixty scientific papers in the field of chemistry.

WORK IN PROGRESS: Continuing research on identification of firearms.

SIDELIGHTS: Matthews was a pioneer in the field of identification of firearms that have been used in an illegal manner; he built up a laboratory for identification of firearms and for research, and gave a course in scientific methods of criminal investigation at University of Wisconsin for fifteen years.

BIOGRAPHICAL/CRITICAL SOURCES: Guns, March, 1963.

* * *

MATHEWS, Marcia Mayfield

PERSONAL: Born in New Orleans, La.; daughter of Robert Bledsoe (a newspaper editor) and Marie Paige (Allen) Mayfield; married Joseph James Mathews (a professor of history), May 31, 1938; children: Timothy Mayfield. Education: Sophie Newcomb College, B. of Design, 1926; Institute of Art and Archaeology, Paris, France, Brevet, 1934; Wellesley College, B.A., 1935. Politics: Democrat. Religion: Protestant. Home: 924 Clifton Rd. N.E., Atlanta, Ga. 30307. Agent: Scott Meredith Literary Agency, 580 Fifth Ave., New York, N.Y. 10036.

CAREER: Wellesley College, Wellesley, Mass., instructor in fine arts, 1932-35; Duke University, Durham, N.C., instructor in fine arts, 1935-38; Morehouse College, Atlanta, Ga., instructor in humanities, 1958-61. Member: Authors League of America, Authors Guild.

WRITINGS: Richard Allen, Helicon, 1963; Henry Ossawa Tanner, American Artist, University of Chicago Press, 1969; The Freedom Star, Coward, 1971. Contributor to periodicals and newspapers.

WORK IN PROGRESS: A study of the art of Richmond Barthe.

AVOCATIONAL INTERESTS: Art and travel.

BIOGRAPHICAL/CRITICAL SOURCES: Nation, December 21, 1970.

* * *

MATTHEWS, William Henry III 1919-

PERSONAL: Born March 1, 1919, in Henrietta, Okla.; son of William Henry (an engineer) and Douglass (Fain) Matthews; married Jennie Anzalone (a registered nurse), September 7, 1940; children: William Henry IV, James Douglas. Education: Texas Christian University, B.A., 1948, M.A., 1949; graduate study at University of Texas, 1950-51. Religion: Episcopal. Home: 5795 Sul Ross Lane, Beaumont, Tex. 77706. Office: Department of Geology, Lamar State College of Technology, Beaumont, Tex. 77704.

CAREER: Texas Christian University, Fort Worth, assistant professor, 1948-52; Texaco, Inc., subsurface geologist, 1952-55; Lamar State College of Technology, Beaumont, Tex., professor, 1955—. Visiting professor, Sul Ross State College, summers, 1961, 1962. Research scientist, Bureau of Economic Geology, University of Texas, summers, 1958, 1959, 1960. Consulting geologist to Texas Portland Cement Co. and Texas State Highway Department; consultant to various other agencies. Member: American Association for the Advancement of Science, National Association of Geology Teachers (president, Texas Section, 1960-61; national president, 1969-70), Geological Society of America, American Association of Petroleum Geologists, Society of Economic Paleontologists and Mineralogists, Paleontological Society, National Science Teachers Association, Texas Association of College Teachers, Texas Academy of Science, Beaumont Geological Society (former president).

WRITINGS: Marine Ecology as an Aid in Teaching Invertebrate Paleontology, Lamar State College of Technology, c.1957; The Paleontology and Paleoecology of the Biostrome Fauna of the Edwards Formation of Texas, Lamar State College of Technology, 1957; Texas Fossils: An Amateur Collector's Handbook, Bureau of Economic Geology, University of Texas, 1960; Fossils: An Introduction to Prehistoric Life, Barnes & Noble, 1962; Bathymetry of Powell Lake, British Columbia, Institute of Oceanography, University of British Columbia, 1962; The Geologic Story of Longhorn Cavern, Bureau of Economic Geology, University of Texas, 1963; Quaternary Stratigraphy and Geomorphology of the Fort St. John Area, Northeastern British Columbia, British Columbia Department of Mines and Petroleum Resources, 1963; Thirteen Potassium–Argon Dates of Cenozoic Volcanic Rocks from British Columbia, Department of Geology, University of British Columbia, 1963; Geology Made Simple, Doubleday, 1967, revised edition, W.H. Allen, 1970; A Guide to the National Parks: Their Landscape and Geology, Natural History Press for American Museum of Natural History, Volume I: The Western Parks, 1968; Volume II: The Eastern Parks, 1968; The Geologic Story of Palo Duro Canyon, Bureau of Economic Geology, University of Texas, 1969; Science Probes the Earth: New Frontiers of Geology, Sterling, 1969; Invitation to Geology: The Earth Through Time and Space, Natural History Press for American Museum of Natural History, 1971; (compiler) Helping Children Learn Earth-Space Science, National Science Teachers Association, 1971.

Juveniles: Wonders of the Dinosaur World, Dodd, 1963; Exploring the World of Fossils, Childrens Press, 1964 (published in England as The World of Fossils, Odhams, 1966); The Story of the Earth, Harvey House, 1968; Wonders of Fossils, Dodd, 1968; The Story of Volcanoes and Earthquakes, Harvey House, 1969; Soils, F. Watts, 1970; The Earth's Crust, F. Watts, 1971; Introducing the

Earth: Geology, Environment, and Man, Dodd, 1972. General editor, "Earth Science Curriculum Project" series, Prentice-Hall, 1964-65. Contributor to professional and popular publications.

BIOGRAPHICAL/CRITICAL SOURCES: Commonweal, May 24, 1968; *Best Sellers,* March 1, 1970; *Library Journal,* March 15, 1970.

*   *   *

MATHIESON, Theodore   1913-

PERSONAL: I in surname is silent; born March 22, 1913, in San Francisco, Calif.; married Teresa Green (a professional weaver), November 27, 1934; married second wife, Linda L. Bood, April, 1968; children: (first marriage) David, Thalia (Mrs. Richard Rosenfeld), Karen; (second marriage) Colin Jared, Shawn Jeremy. *Education:* University of California, Berkeley, A.B., 1940. *Religion:* "Eclectic." *Agent:* Scott Meredith Literary Agency, Inc., 580 Fifth Ave., New York, N.Y. 10036.

CAREER: High school teacher of English, journalism, and drama in Grass Valley, Calif., and Merced, Calif., 1942-58; Southwestern Oregon Junior College, North Bend, instructor in speech, English, and journalism, 1961-62; free-lance writer, 1958-60, 1962-67. Sometime director of little theatre and summer theatre groups in California, including Sierra Community Playhouse and Thor Theatre. *Member:* Mystery Writers of America.

WRITINGS: The Great Detectives: An Inner Sanctum Mystery, Simon & Schuster, 1960; *The Devil and Ben Franklin,* Simon & Schuster, 1961; *The Door to Nowhere,* Putnam, 1964; *The Sign of the Flame,* Putnam, 1964; *Island in the Sand,* illustrations by son, David Mathieson, Bobbs-Merrill, 1964; *The Nez Perce Indian War: The Compelling True Saga of a Valiant People Who Were Forced to War to Stay Alive,* Monarch Books, 1964; *The Winged Cavalier,* Cowles, 1970. Regular contributor of short stories to *Alfred Hitchcock Mystery Magazine,* and other publications.

WORK IN PROGRESS: Rogue Journey, a novel; short stories.

SIDELIGHTS: Mathieson told *CA:* "I agree with such diverse writers as Thornton Wilder and Tennessee Williams, that renewed contact with *people* is essential in keeping the creative writer fertile. In my case, a year of teaching young men and women on the secondary level, works like magic, and I always return zestfully to the typewriter.

"I speak German fairly well, Spanish a little, and I have been dabbling with the intricacies of Russian, which, next to the violin, is the hardest to play....

"I play piano strictly as an amateur, which means I don't play well when I don't feel like it. I read a lot of biography (a good approach to history, by the way)."

BIOGRAPHICAL/CRITICAL SOURCES: Frederic Dannay (Ellery Queen), introduction to *The Great Detectives,* Simon & Schuster, 1960; *Library Journal,* May 15, 1970.

*   *   *

MATTHEWS, Jack   1917-

PERSONAL: Born June 7, 1917, in Winnipeg, Manitoba, Canada; son of Samuel (a railroader) and Ellen (Walker) Matthews; married Hannah M. Polster (an ecologist and conservation educator), August 16, 1942; children: Rachel Sophia, Rebecca. *Education:* Heidelberg College, Tiffin, Ohio, A.B., 1938; Ohio University, M.A., 1940; Vanderbilt University, postgraduate study, 1942-43; Ohio State University, Ph.D., 1946. *Politics:* Democrat. *Religion:* Jewish. *Home:* 825 Old Mill Rd.,

Pittsburgh, Pa. 15238. *Office:* University of Pittsburgh, Pittsburgh, Pa. 15213.

CAREER: Purdue University, Lafayette, Ind., assistant professor of speech and assistant director of speech and hearing clinic, 1946-48; University of Pittsburgh, Pittsburgh, Pa., assistant professor and director of speech clinic, 1948-56, associate professor of psychology and director of division of psychological services, 1954-56, professor of speech and theater arts, 1956—. Consultant to Veteran's Administration and U.S. Department of Health, Education, and Welfare. *Military service:* U.S. Army Air Forces, 1942-46; became master sergeant.

MEMBER: Speech Association of America (member of executive council, 1962—), American Association for Cleft Palate Rehabilitation (secretary-treasurer, 1952-55; vice-president, 1955-57; president, 1957-59), American Speech and Hearing Association (fellow; vice-president, 1956-57; executive vice-president, 1958-62; president-elect, 1962; president, 1963—), American Association of Advancement of Science (fellow), American Psychological Association (fellow), American Association for Mental Deficiency, Society for Psychological Study of Social Issues, American Association of University Professors, Sigma XI. *Awards, honors:* United Nations Award of Merit.

WRITINGS: The Development of Valid Situational Tests of Leadership, American Institute for Research, 1951; *The Development, Analysis and Validation of Tests to Measure Non-Intellectual Aspects of Officer Aptitude,* American Institute for Research, 1952; (with Jack W. Birch) *Improving Children's Speech,* Public School Publishing, 1958; *Manual for Effective Use of the Best Speech Series with Special Pupils,* Stanwix, 1966; (with Theodore Clevinger) *The Speech Communication Process,* Scott, Foresman, 1971.

"Sound Book" series, with Elizabeth Phillip Wade and Jack W. Birch—All published by Stanwix: *My Sound Book—S,* 1959, *. . . R,* 1959, *. . . L,* 1959, *. . . K,* 1959, *. . . G,* 1959, *. . . Th,* 1960, *. . . Sh,* 1963.

Contributor: *Speech Problems of School Children,* National Society for Crippled Children and Adults, 1953; C.M. Louttit, *Clinical Psychology of Exceptional Children,* 3rd edition (Matthews was not associated with earlier editions), Harper, 1957; Lee E. Travis, editor, *Handbook of Speech Pathology,* Appleton, 1957; S.J. Parnes and H.F. Harding, editors, *A Source Book for Creative Thinking,* Scribner, 1962; T.L. McGarland, editor, *Getting Ready for Functional Basic Reading,* Stanwix, 1963; *Graduate Education in Speech Pathology and Audiology,* American Speech and Hearing Association, 1963; *Operating Procedures in Remedial Speech and Language Training,* Houghton, 1968. Contributor of more than thirty articles to psychology and speech journals, and to *Encyclopedia of the Social Sciences,* 1967. Assistant editor, *Journal of Speech and Hearing Disorders,* 1952-54; member of editorial board, *Speech Monographs,* 1951-53, 1956—, *Journal of Communications,* 1961—.

AVOCATIONAL INTERESTS: Hiking, woodturning, wine making, gardening.

*   *   *

MATTHIESSEN, Peter   1927-

PERSONAL: Surname is pronounced *Math*-e-son; born May 22, 1927, in New York, N.Y.; son of Erard A. and Elizabeth C. Matthiessen; married second wife, Deborah Love, May 16, 1963; children: (first marriage) Lucas, Carey; (second marriage) Rue, Alexander. *Education:* Attended Sorbonne, University of Paris, 1948-49; Yale University, B.A., 1950. *Home:* Bridge Lane, Sagaponack, Long Island, N.Y. 11962. *Agent:* Robert Lantz-Candida

Donadio Literary Agency, Inc., 111 West 57 St., New York, N.Y. 10019.

CAREER: Former commercial fisherman; captain of deep-sea charter fishing boat, Montauk, Long Island, N.Y., 1954-56; member of expeditions to Alaska, Canadian Northwest Territories, and Peru, and of Harvard-Peabody Expedition to New Guinea, 1961; writer. *Awards, honors:* Grant in letters, National Institute/American Academy of Arts and Letters for *The Cloud Forest* and *Under the Mountain Wall,* 1963; *At Play in the Fields of the Lord* nominated for National Book Award, 1966; National Book Awards judge, 1970.

WRITINGS: Race Rock (novel), Harper, 1954; *Partisans* (novel), Viking, 1955; *Wildlife in America,* Viking, 1959; *Raditzer,* Viking, 1961; *The Cloud Forest: A Chronicle of the South American Wilderness,* Viking, 1961; *Under the Mountain Wall: A Chronicle of Two Seasons in the Stone Age,* Viking, 1962; *At Play in the Fields of the Lord* (novel), Random House, 1965; *Oomingmak: The Expedition to the Musk Ox Island in the Bering Sea,* Hastings House, 1967; (with Ralph S. Palmer and artist Robert Verity Clem), *The Shorebirds of North America,* edited by Gardner D. Stout, Viking, 1967; *Profile: Cesar Chavez,* UAW Western Region Six, Los Angeles, Calif., 1969; *Sal si puedes: Cesar Chavez and the New American Revolution,* Random House, 1970; *Blue Meridian: The Search for the Great White Shark,* Random House, 1971; *Everglades: Selections from the Writings of Peter Matthiessen,* edited by Paul Brooks, Sierra Club-Ballantine, 1971; (contributor) Alvin M. Josephy, editor, *The American Heritage Book of Natural Wonders,* American Heritage Press, 1972; *Seal Pool* (juvenile; illustrated by William Pene Du Bois), Doubleday, 1972; (with photographer Eliot Porter) *The Tree Where Man Was Born: The African Experience* (Book of the Month Club special fall selection), Dutton, 1972. Contributor of articles to various popular magazines. Founder and editor, *Paris Review.*

SIDELIGHTS: Peter Farb has characterized Matthiessen as "... one of the three or four most articulate and impassioned nature writers of our time...." Matthiessen, speaks French and some Spanish.†

* * *

MAUGHAM, Robert Cecil Romer 1916-
(Robin Maugham)

PERSONAL: Born May 17, 1916, in London, England; son of Viscount Frederic Herbert (a judge and Lord Chancellor of England) and Helen Mary (Romer) Maugham. *Education:* Educated at Eton and at Trinity Hall, Cambridge. *Religion:* Church of England. *Address:* Casa Cala Pada, Santa Eulalia del Rio, Ibiza, Balcaves, Spain. *Agent:* Julian Bach, Jr., 3 East 48th St., New York, N.Y. 10017; and Eric Glass, 28 Berkeley Sq., London WIX 6HD, England.

CAREER: Barrister, Lincoln's Inn. Wrote first book while hospitalized for almost a year with war injuries, and took up writing as a career, 1945, when health made it impossible for him to resume law practice. Became second Viscount Maugham of Hartfield on father's death, 1958, and took seat in House of Lords, 1960. Lecturer on Middle East to Royal Institute of International Affairs, other groups in England. *Military service:* British Army, 1939-45; served in North Africa with 8th Army, wounded, 1942; later served with Middle East Intelligence Centre; invalided out with honorary rank of captain; mentioned in dispatches. *Member:* Garrick Club.

WRITINGS—Under name Robin Maugham: *The 1946 Ms.,* War Facts Press (London), 1943; (editor) *The Convoy File: Stories, Articles, Poems from the Forces, Factories, Mines and Fields,* Collins, 1945; *Come to Dust*

(an account of the author's experiences in the Libyan Campaign, 1941-42), Chapman & Hall, 1945; *Nomad* (travel book), Chapman & Hall, 1947, Viking, 1948; *Approach to Palestine,* Falcon Press, 1947; *The Servant* (novel), Falcon Press, 1948, Harcourt, 1949; *North African Notebook,* Chapman & Hall, 1948, Harcourt, 1949; *Line on Ginger* (novel), Chapman & Hall, 1949, Harcourt, 1950 (reissued as *The Intruder,* New English Library, 1968); *Journey to Siwa,* photographs by Dimitri Papadimou, Chapman & Hall, 1950, Harcourt, 1951; *The Rough and the Smooth* (novel), Harcourt, 1951; *Behind the Mirror* (novel), Harcourt, 1955; *The Man with Two Shadows* (novel), Harper, 1959; *The Slaves of Timbuktu,* Harper, 1961; *The Joyita Mystery* (nonfiction), Parrish, 1962; *November Reef: A Novel of the South Seas,* Longmans, Green, 1962; *Somerset and All the Maughams,* New American Library, 1966; *The Green Shade,* New American Library, 1966; *The Second Window,* McGraw, 1969; *The Link: A Victorian Mystery,* McGraw, 1969; *The Wrong People,* Heinemann, 1970, McGraw, 1971; *Escape from the Shadows* (autobiography), Hodder & Stoughton, 1972, McGraw, 1973; *The Last Encounter,* W.H. Allen, 1972.

Plays: *Odd Man In* (adaptation of Claude Magnier's "Monsieur Masure"), Samuel French (London), 1958; (with Philip King) *The Lonesome Road* (three-act; first produced in 1957), Samuel French, 1959; *Mister Lear* (three-act comedy; first produced in 1956), English Theatre Guild, 1963 (later retitled "Just in Time"); *The Servant* (adaptation of book of same name; first produced in Worthing, England, 1958), Davis-Poynter, 1972.

Unpublished plays: "The Rising Heifer," first produced in Dallas, Tex., 1952, in England, 1955; "Rise Above it" (television play), produced by British Broadcasting Corp., 1957, also broadcast in Berlin, Germany, 1957; (with Philip King) "The Hermit," first produced in Harrogate, England, 1959; (adapter) "It's in the Bag" (adapted from "Oscar," by Claude Magnier), first produced in Brighton, England, 1959; adapter with Willis Hall) "Azauk," adapted from the play by Alexandre Rivemale), first produced in Newcastle-upon-Tyne, England, 1962; "The Claimant," produced in Worthing, England, 1962; "The Last Hero," produced on radio by the British Broadcasting Corp., 1962, and on television, 1966; "Winter in Ischia," first produced in Worthing, England, 1964; "Enemy" (two-act), first produced in West End at Saville Theatre, December 17, 1969.

Films: (With John Hunter) "The Intruder" (based on *Line On Ginger*), British Lion, 1953; (with Bryan Forbes) "The Black Tent" (adaptation of his serial "Desert Bond," appearing in *Chamber's Journal*), Rank Organization, 1956;

Film scripts: "November Reef"; "How are You Johnnie?" (adaption of Philip King's play); "Willie" (adaptation of his book *Somerset and All the Maughams*); "The Man with Two Shadows" (based on his novel); "The Joyita Mystery" (based on his book); "Curtains"; "Cakes and Ale" (based on the novel by W. Somerset Maugham); "The Barrier" (includes sonnets by John Betjeman).

Also author of plays, "The Leopard" and "The Two Wise Virgins of Hove" as yet neither published nor produced. Editor, "Convoy" (a series of booklets), Collins, 1944—. Contributor to *People, Chamber's Journal, Today, Argosy, Oggi* (Italy).

WORK IN PROGRESS: A screenplay; and a novel about India.

SIDELIGHTS: The work of the nephew of W. Somerset Maugham has generally been well received. The *Times Literary Supplement* reviewer has said that he has a "gift of vivid description [and a] knack of hitting off, if not scoring off, a character in a few lines of dialogue. . . ." Poet John Betjeman states: "Here is a real writer . . . who has something to say and knows how to say it—a rare combination." And the Times (London) reviewer wrote of The Joyita Mystery: "If the benevolent shades of departed artists brood over their disciples, the spirit of Arthur Conan Doyle must have prompted and sustained this persevering investigator. Robin Maugham's deductions are as convincing and as concise as those of Holmes himself."

Critics particularly appreciate the style and construction in Maugham's novels. Kelsey Guifoil praises Line on Ginger as a "story which could be commonplace and unconvincing if it were not for the vitality of Robin Maugham's storytelling. There is no excess baggage, every page of the book is essential to the narrative, and the pace is swift, the interest unflagging. Despite its brevity, it is a most satisfying book to read, and in this brief compass, the author has proved that he is an artist in his own right." In a review of the same book, N.L. Rothman states that "plotting is the thing Mr. Maugham does best. He tells his tale with deceptive ease, he illumines it with meticulously chosen bits of dialogue. Everything contributes, everything builds toward the planned effect. There isn't a wasted word or moment. . . ."

Five of Maugham's books have been translated into French and German, with the translation of The Rough and the Smooth selling over one hundred thousand copies in West Germany alone; some of the books also have appeared in five other languages and the novels in paperback editions in the United States. In addition to the books Maugham himself has adapted for films, other films have been made from The Rough and the Smooth, The Man with Two Shadows, and The Servant.

Maugham's travels in gathering material for his books include trips to the Middle East, 1946-50, India and Kathmandu, 1957, Canary Islands and West Africa, 1958-59, North Africa, 1959, Far East, 1960, Fiji, Samoa, and Tahiti, 1961, and North Africa and Mombasa, 1963.

BIOGRAPHICAL/CRITICAL SOURCES: Manchester Guardian, November 29, 1947, September 24, 1948, October 17, 1950; New Yorker, April 10, 1948, February 10, 1951, September 8, 1951, April 9, 1955, July 18, 1959; Saturday Review, May 1, 1948, March 12, 1949, April 8, 1950, April 16, 1955, September 21, 1968; New York Times, July 11, 1948, February 20, 1949, December 4, 1949, April 2, 1950, September 9, 1951, April 17, 1955, May 31, 1959; Spectator, September 24, 1948, May 26, 1961; Times Literary Supplement, October 2, 1948, March 5, 1949, November 18, 1955, December 5, 1958, June 2, 1961, November 27, 1969; Library Journal, February 1, 1949, April 15, 1955, June 15, 1961, July, 1966, September 1, 1969; Nation, February 12, 1949, November 12, 1955; New York Herald Tribune Book Review, February 13, 1949, March 26, 1950, July 17, 1955; Commonweal, January 6, 1950, September 7, 1951; Christian Science Monitor, February 21, 1951, October 10, 1968; New Statesman, November 12, 1955, November 29, 1958, May 12, 1961, July 29, 1966, October 11, 1968, December 26, 1969; New York Times Book Review, June 19, 1966, November 3, 1968; Best Sellers, October 1, 1968, October 15, 1969; Observer Review, October 6, 1968; Punch, October 9, 1968, November 12, 1969, December 31, 1969; Variety, January 28, 1970; Listener, January 1, 1970, January 22, 1970; Plays and Players, February, 1970.

*   *   *

MAXWELL, (Ian) Robert   1923-

PERSONAL: Surname was originally Hoch; born June 10, 1923, in Selo Slotina, Czechoslovakia; son of Michael and Ann (Slomowitz) Hoch; married Elisabeth Meynard, March 15, 1945; children: Michael, Philip, Anne, Christine, Isabel, Ian, Kevin, Ghislaine. Politics: Labour. Religion: Humanist. Home: Headington Hill Hall, Oxford, England. Office: Robert Maxwell & Co. Ltd., Headington Hill Hall, Oxford, England.

CAREER: Berlin Foreign Office, Berlin, Germany, head of press and publicity division, 1945-47; Pergamon Press, Inc., New York, N.Y., chairman of board and president, 1949—. Former chairman, Pergamon Press Ltd., London, England; chairman, I.R. Maxwell & Co. Ltd., London, England; president, British Book Centre, New York, N.Y.; former director, Gauthier-Villars, Paris, France; former publisher, Commonwealth and International Library of Science, Technology, Engineering and Liberal Studies, Oxford, England. Member of Parliament (Labour Party), 1964-70; chairman, Labour National Fund Raising Foundation, 1960-69; president, Buckingham Constituency Labour Party, 1960-61. Military service: British Army, 1939-45; became captain; received Military Cross. Member: American Nuclear Society, American Vacuum Society, Human Factors Society, Fabian Society.

WRITINGS: (Editor) Information U.S.S.R.: An Authoritative Encyclopaedia About the Union of Soviet Socialist Republics, Pergamon, 1962; Science, Government and Industry: A Report to the Labour Party, British Book Centre, 1963; (author of introduction) Vernon Thornes and Albert Kitts, Steel: The Commanding Height of the Economy, Lincoln-Praeger, 1964; (editor with others) Progress in Nuclear Energy: The Economics of Nuclear Power, Pergamon, 1965; Public Sector Purchasing Report, British Book Centre, 1968; (with Keith Hindell) Man Alive!: A Current Affairs Annual for Schools and Colleges, Pergamon, 1968; (editor with Ferenc Erdie) Information Hungary, Pergamon, 1968.

SIDELIGHTS: Maxwell speaks nine languages, including Czech, Russian, Roumanian, and Serbian; he has traveled throughout the world, covering some two million miles.

BIOGRAPHICAL/CRITICAL SOURCES: Sunday Observer, May 27, 1962; Daily Express, October 25, 1963.

*   *   *

MAY, Edgar   1929-

PERSONAL: Born June 27, 1929, in Zurich, Switzerland; came to United States in 1940, naturalized in 1954; son of Ferdinand (an importer) and Renee (Bloch) May; married Louise T. Breason, September 1, 1965 (deceased). Education: Columbia University, night student, 1948-51; Northwestern University, B.S. in Journalism (with highest distinction), 1957. Home: Muckross, Springfield, Vt. 05156. Agent: Curtis Brown Ltd. 60 East 56th St., New York, N.Y. 10022. Office: 105 East 22nd St., New York, N.Y. 10010.

CAREER: Bellows Falls Times (weekly), Bellows Falls, Vt., 1951-53, began as reporter, became acting editor; Fitchburg Sentinel, Fitchburg, Mass., reporter, 1953; Chicago Tribune, Chicago, Ill., part-time reporter, 1955-57; free-lance writer in United States and Europe, 1957; Buffalo Evening News, Buffalo, N.Y., reporter, 1958-62; State Charities Aid Association, New York, N.Y., director of public welfare projects, 1962-64; U.S. Government, Washington, D.C., member of President's Task Force on War Against Poverty, assistant director of Office of Economic Opportunity (O.E.O.), 1964; special adviser to U.S. ambassador to France, Sargent Shriver, 1968-70; Ford Foundation, New York, N.Y., consultant, 1970—. Lecturer throughout America. Military service: U.S. Army, 1953-55. Member: American Newspaper Guild, Kappa Tau Alpha. Awards, honors: Walter O. Bingham Award for outstanding journalism in western New York, and Page One award, both from Buffalo Newspaper

Guild, 1959; Pulitzer Prize in local reporting, 1961, for public welfare series, "Our Costly Dilemma," in *Buffalo Evening News;* Merit award, Northwestern University Alumni Association, 1962.

WRITINGS: *The Disjointed Trio: Poverty, Politics, and Power,* California State Department of Social Welfare, 1963; *The Wasted Americans: Cost of Our Welfare Dilemmas,* Harper, 1964. Contributor to magazines, including *Harper's* and *Family Weekly.*

WORK IN PROGRESS: Research in social problem field.

SIDELIGHTS: May obtained a job. as a welfare caseworker (while a reporter in Buffalo) and did six months of research for his Pulitzer Prize-winning series.

* * *

MAY, Francis Barns 1915-

PERSONAL: Born December 24, 1915, in Cascilla, Miss.; son of James Marshall (a salesman) and Hallye (Rice) May; married Janice Christensen, June 9, 1956. *Education:* University of Texas, B.B.A. (highest honors), 1941, M.B.A., 1943, Ph.D., 1957. *Home:* 6504 Auburn Hill, Austin, Tex. 78703. *Office:* University of Texas, Austin, Tex. 78712.

CAREER: University of Texas, Austin, instructor, 1941-43, statistician in Office of President, 1946-54, assistant professor, 1947-58, research scientist in Bureau of Business Research, 1954-57, associate professor, 1958-61, statistician in Bureau of Business Research, 1958-64, professor of business statistics, 1961-64, chairman of department of general business, 1964-68, consulting statistician, 1964—. Visiting professor, University of Minnesota, 1960. Dallas Federal Reserve Bank, director, 1966-68, 1969-71, chairman of the board, 1968. Consultant, Southland Corp., 1955, and Humble Oil Refining Co., 1956. *Military service:* U.S. Army Air Forces, Command Statistical Control Office, 1943-46; became captain.

MEMBER: American Association for the Advancement of Science, Institute of Management Sciences, Institute of Mathematical Statistics, American Statistical Association (president of Austin chapter, 1964-66; member of council, 1969-70), Operations Research Society of America, Econometric Society, Southwestern Social Science Association (chairman of business research section, 1956-57; president, 1968-69), Social Science Club (University of Texas chapter; president, 1965-66), Phi Kappa Phi, Beta Alpha Psi, Sigma Iota Epsilon, Beta Gamma Sigma, Phi Eta Sigma.

WRITINGS: *Developments in Mathematics and Statistics Applicable to Business Problems,* Center for Research in Business and Economics, University of Houston, 1960; (with Charles T. Clark, John Lymberopoulds, and Alfred Dale) *Small Business Executive Decision Simulation,* three volumes, Bureau of Business Research, University of Texas, 1963; (with Florence Escott) *Economic Statistics of Texas, 1900-1962,* Bureau of Business Research, University of Texas, 1964; *Introduction to Games of Strategy,* Allyn & Bacon, 1970. Contributor of articles and reviews to business and social science journals. Editor of business research section of *Southwestern Social Science Quarterly;* associate editor, *Texas Business Review,* 1963-64.

* * *

MAY, Henry F(arnham) 1915-

PERSONAL: Born March 27, 1915, in Denver, Colo.; son of Henry F. (a lawyer) and May (Rickard) May; married Jean Louise Terrace, June 18, 1941; children: Hildegarde Clark Dorn, Ann Rickard. *Education:* University of California, Berkeley, B.A., 1937; Harvard University, M.A., 1938, Ph.D., 1947. *Politics:* Democrat. *Religion:* Episcopal. *Home:* 612 Coventry Rd., Berkeley, Calif. 94707. *Office:* History Department, University of California, Berkeley, Calif. 94720.

CAREER: Lawrence College (now Lawrence University), Appleton, Wis., instructor in history, 1941-42; Scripps College, Claremont, Calif., assistant professor, 1947-48, associate professor of history, 1948-49; University of California, Berkeley, associate professor, 1952-56, professor of history, 1956-63, Margaret Byrne Professor of History, 1963—, chairman of department, 1964-66. Visiting associate professor, Bowdoin College, 1950-51; summer teacher at Salzburg Seminar in American Studies and University of Minnesota; Fulbright lecturer at Belgian universities, 1959-60; Pitt Professor of American history and institutions, Cambridge University, 1971—. *Military service:* U.S. Naval Reserve, 1943-45; became lieutenant j.g.; received commendation ribbon. *Member:* American Historical Association, American Academy of Arts and Sciences, Mississippi Valley Historical Association. *Awards, honors:* Social Science Research Council fellowships, 1946-47, 1963-64; American Council of Learned Societies fellowship, 1963-64.

WRITINGS: *Protestant Churches and Industrial America,* Harper, 1949, new edition, 1967; *The End of American Innocence: A Study of the First Years of Our Own Time, 1912-1917,* Knopf, 1959; (with Charles G. Sellers, Jr.) *A Synopsis of American History,* Rand McNally, 1963, 2nd edition, 1969; (editor) *The Discontent of the Intellectuals: A Problem of the Twenties* (pamphlet), Rand McNally, 1963; (editor) Harriet Beecher Stowe, *Oldtown Folks,* Harvard University Press, 1966. Contributor to *Atlantic, Harper's, American Scholar,* historical journals, and other periodicals.

WORK IN PROGRESS: A book on the intellectual history of the United States, 1790-1830, tentatively titled *The American Encounter,* for Oxford University Press.

* * *

MAYBERRY, Florence V(irginia) Wilson

PERSONAL: Born in Sleeper, Mo.; daughter of William Everett and Myrtle (Foose) Wilson; married David Maurice Mayberry (an office manager), August 1, 1936; children: Michael David. *Education:* Ventura Junior College, A.A. *Politics:* Non-partisan. *Religion:* Baha'i World Faith. *Home address:* P.O. Box 369, Santa Paula, Calif. 93060.

CAREER: Chamber of Commerce, Santa Paula, Calif., secretary-manager, two years; now volunteer lecturer for Baha'i Faith, traveling throughout Western hemisphere. Member, Continental Board of Counsellors of North America for the Baha'i Faith. *Member:* Business and Professional Women's Club (Santa Paula, Calif.; president, two years).

WRITINGS: *The Dachshunds of Mama Island,* Doubleday, 1963. Also author of "Pobrecito and the Princesa," as yet unpublished. Contributor of short stories and poetry to national magazines.

WORK IN PROGRESS: Several short stories; *And Now Baha'i,* a nonfiction presentation of the Baha'i faith.

* * *

MAYER, Jane Rothschild 1903-
(Clare Jaynes, joint pseudonym with Clara Spiegel)

PERSONAL: Born December 30, 1903, in Kansas City, Mo.; daughter of Louis P. and Nora (Westheimer) Rothschild; married David Mayer, Jr., December 28, 1927 (deceased); children: David III, Mary Jane Mayer Bezark, Philip. *Education:* Vassar College, A.B., 1925. *Religion:* Jewish. *Home:* 1445 North State Parkway, Chicago, Ill. 60610. *Agent:* Russell & Volkenning, 551 Fifth Ave., New York, N.Y. 10017.

CAREER: Field Enterprises Educational Corp., Chicago, Ill., editorial work, 1961-62. Free-lance writer. Member of Board of Education, Glencoe, Ill. *Member:* Authors League, Society of Midland Authors, Chicago Press Club, Arts Club (Chicago).

WRITINGS: Getting Along in the Family (monograph), Bureau of Publications, Teachers College, Columbia University, 1949; *Betsy Ross and the Flag* (juvenile), Random House, 1952; *Dolly Madison* (juvenile), Random House, 1954; *The Year of the White Trees* (novel), Random House, 1958; *The Listening Heart,* edited by Lucy Freeman, Crown, 1961; *How Do Animals Get to the Zoo* (juvenile), Random House, in press.

With Clara Spiegel under joint pseudonym Clare Jaynes: *Instruct My Sorrows,* Random House, 1942, reissued as *My Reputation,* World Publishing, 1944; *These Are the Times,* Random House, 1944; *This Eager Heart,* Random House, 1947; *The Early Frost,* Random House, 1952. Author of short stories and articles on travel and child development.

*   *   *

MAYER, Tom   1943-

PERSONAL: Born April 7, 1943, in Chicago, Ill.; son of Wally Max and Katherine (Van Stone) Mayer. *Education:* Attended Harvard University, two years; Stanford University, 1964-65. *Politics:* "Generally liberal." *Religion:* None. *Home and office:* 132 East de Vargas, Santa Fe, N.M. 87501.

CAREER: Has worked in the oil fields, for the Santa Fe Opera, and for five years as life guard and swimming coach. *Member:* Fly Club (Harvard).

WRITINGS: Bubble Gum and Kipling (connected short stories), Viking, 1964; *The Weary Falcon* (short stories), Houghton, 1971. Contributor to *New Yorker, Story,* and *Harper's.*

WORK IN PROGRESS: Stories.

SIDELIGHTS: The Weary Falcon, a collection of stories about the Vietnam War, has been described by critics as a fictional representation of the grisly reality of war. William McPherson compares Mayer's style to that of Hemingway: "He has written these stories from the gut. When he's stuck, he spurts blood. Tired blood, perhaps, but still warm and reasonably red, like Hemingway's to whom the author is indebted." Webster Schott acknowledges the Hemingway influence, but states: "Mayer writes like himself, not Hemingway. But he writes under the Hemingway injunction, which may be about the only way to deal imaginatively with the war in Vietnam and have it mean anything real to the rest of us. The war may seem, as one of Mayer's characters says, like a dream out of Franz Kafka. But to envision it symbolically or in fantasy, to see it as a drama of clashing armies or as a conflict of deeply held ideologies, would deny the facts of Vietnam. Young men are being blown apart there, and many don't know or care why. Friends look like enemies, and they die when there is doubt or threat. College boys drop civilization because there is no other way to stay alive."

Peter S. Prescott also notes the reporter's eye Mayer uses to develop his themes. "He keeps his tone cool, his judgments implicit and his focus narrow.... These are conventional stories, with conventional points to make, but they do tell the news, which is one of the things fiction can do well.... Mayer catches the phrasing rhythms and fertile obscenity of soldiers' speech: he knows the cold and the wet; he persuades us that he knows what shells do to flesh and how helicopters fly. More important, he shows us how war makes almost indistinguishable men's good instincts, their brutality and their indifference."

Mayer's favorite writers include F. Scott Fitzgerald, Truman Capote, Ernest Hemingway, and Nelson Algren.

AVOCATIONAL INTERESTS: Baseball, trapezing, and horses.

BIOGRAPHICAL/CRITICAL SOURCES: Esquire, August, 1964; *Book World,* March 14, 1971; *Washington Post,* March 24, 1971; *Life,* March 26, 1971; *Newsweek,* April 19, 1971.

*   *   *

MAYMAN, Martin   1924-

PERSONAL: Born April 2, 1924, in New York, N.Y.; son of Abraham and Anna (Mann) Mayman; married Rosemary Walker, October 3, 1960; children: Sara Alison, Stephen Walker. *Education:* College of City of New York (now City College of the City University of New York), B.S., 1943; New York University, M.A., 1947; University of Kansas, Ph.D., 1953. *Home:* 5006 West 23rd St. Ter., Topeka, Kan. 66614. *Office:* Menninger Foundation, Topeka, Kan. 66601.

CAREER: Menninger Foundation, Topeka, Kan., intern and resident psychologist, 1944-46; Winter Veterans Administration Hospital, Topeka, Kan., psychologist, 1946-51; Menninger Foundation, instructor in School of Psychiatry, 1946—, foundation director of psychological training, 1951—. Fellow, American Board of Examiners in Professional Psychology, 1955—. *Member:* Topeka Psychoanalytic Society (associate).

WRITINGS—With Karl Menninger and Paul Pruyser: *The Vital Balance: The Life Process in Mental Health and Illness,* Viking, 1963; *A Manual for Psychiatric Case Study,* 2nd edition, Grune, 1963. Contributor to *Journal of Abnormal and Social Psychology, Journal of Projective Techniques,* and *Archives of General Psychiatry.*

WORK IN PROGRESS: Research in psychotherapy, in the diagnostic process with attention to the logic of clinical inference, and in the autokinetic phenomenon.

AVOCATIONAL INTERESTS: Bridge, tape recording, and photography.

*   *   *

MAYNARD, Harold Bright   1902-

PERSONAL: Born October 18, 1902, in Northampton, Mass.; son of William Clement (a manufacturer) and Edith (Clark) Maynard; married Hilda Marie Koch, October 29, 1928; children: Barbara Maynard Hattemer, Robert David. *Education:* Cornell University, M.E., 1923. *Politics:* Republican. *Religion:* Presbyterian. *Home:* 2675 Treasure Lane, Naples, Fla. 33940. *Office:* Maynard Research Council, 718 Wallace Ave., Pittsburgh, Pa. 15221.

CAREER: Westinghouse Electric Corp., Pittsburgh, Pa., 1923-29, started as graduate student, became superintendent of Production Steam Division; studied industrial problems in United States and Europe, 1929-34; Methods Engineering Council (management consulting firm), Pittsburgh, Pa., founder and president, 1934-57; H.B. Maynard & Co., Pittsburgh, Pa., president, 1957-60; Maynard Research Council (consulting and special management and training services), Pittsburgh, Pa., president, 1960—. Greater Pittsburgh Capital Corp., chairman, 1962-63, director, 1963-67; president and trustee, Maynard Foundation. Distinguished visiting professor of industrial engineering, Pennsylvania State University, 1963-64. U.S. Government, expert consultant to Secretary of War, 1944, member of advisory groups to Mutual Security Agency, 1952, to Small Business Administration,

1959-61. Director, Council of Churches of Pittsburgh Area, 1962-64.

MEMBER: Society for the Advancement of Management (fellow; executive vice-president, 1944-46; president, 1946-47), American Society of Mechanical Engineers (fellow), Association of Consulting Management Engineers (vice-president, 1951-52; president, 1960-62), National Management Council (president, 1948-49), Comite International de l'Organisation Scientifique (deputy president, 1951-52; president, 1952-54; vice-chancellor of International Academy of Management, 1963-64), Foreign Policy Association, Methods Time Measurement Association for Standards and Research (president, 1951-52; president of international directorate, 1957-67), American Institute of Industrial Engineers (fellow; honorary), American Management Association, American Arbitration Association, Zeta Psi, Rotary, University Club, Duquesne Club, Union League Club (New York); Fort Lauderdale Yacht Club, Venice Yacht Club.

AWARDS, HONORS: Gilbreth Medal, Society for Advancement of Management, 1946; Melville Medal, American Society of Mechanical Engineers, 1949; Wallace Clark Award, Council for International Progress in Management, 1956; LL.D., University of Miami, 1956; Taylor Key, Society for the Advancement of Management, 1964; Gantt Medal, American Management Association and American Society of Mechanical Engineers, 1964; Frank and Lillian Gilbreth Industrial Engineering Award, American Institute of Industrial Engineers, 1968.

WRITINGS: (With S.M. Lowry and G.J. Stegemerten) *Time and Motion Study and Formulas for Wage Incentives,* McGraw, 1927, 3rd edition, 1940; (with others) *Brass and Alloy Founding,* International Textbook Co., 1928; (with Stegemerten) *Operation Analysis,* McGraw, 1939; (editor) *Effective Foremanship,* McGraw, 1941; (with Stegemerten) *Guide to Methods Improvement,* McGraw, 1944; (with Stegemerten and others) *Methods-Time Measurement,* McGraw, 1948; *New Developments in Management,* Australian Institute of Management, 1950; (editor) *Industrial Engineering Handbook,* McGraw, 1956, 3rd edition, 1971; (with William M. Aiken and J.F. Lewis) *Practical Control of Office Costs,* Management Publishing Corp., 1960; (editor) *Top Management Handbook,* McGraw, 1960; (editor) *Handbook of Business Administration,* McGraw, 1967; (editor-in-chief) *Handbook of Modern Manufacturing Management,* McGraw, 1970. Also author of more than two hundred monographs on industrial engineering and general management subjects. Consulting and contributing editor, *McGraw-Hill Encyclopedia of Science and Technology.*

SIDELIGHTS: Maynard coined the term "methods engineering," and conceived the idea of Methods-Time-Measurement (MTM) several decades ago. With his associates, Stegemerten and Schwab, he designed the MTM time standards for basic motions involved in manual work. The 1948 book that the three co-authored on that subject still is considered the classic in its field; it has been translated into six European languages and Japanese. *Avocational interests:* Collecting stamps and coins, fishing, raising tropical fish, gardening, boating.

* * *

MAYNE, William (James Carter) 1928-
(Dynely James, a joint pseudonym)

PERSONAL: Born March 16, 1928, in Kingston upon Hull, Yorkshire, England; son of William and Dorothy (Fea) Mayne. *Home:* New House, Thornton Rust, Leyburn, North Yorkshire, England. *Agent:* David Higham Associates Ltd., 3 Lower John St., London W1R 3PE, England.

CAREER: Writer of children's books. *Awards, honors:* Carnegie Medal of (British) Library Association for best children's book of year, 1957, for *A Grass Rope.*

WRITINGS: Follow the Footprints, Oxford University Press, 1953; *The World Upside Down,* Oxford University Press, 1954; *A Swarm in May,* Oxford University Press, 1955, Bobbs-Merrill, 1957; *The Member for the Marsh,* Oxford University Press, 1956; *Choristers' Cake,* Oxford University Press, 1956, Bobbs-Merrill, 1958; *The Blue Boat,* Oxford University Press, 1957, Dutton, 1960; *A Grass Rope,* Oxford University Press, 1957, Dutton, 1962; *The Long Night,* Basil Blackwell, 1957; *Underground Alley,* Oxford University Press, 1958, Dutton, 1961; (with R.D. Caesar under joint pseudonym Dynely James) *The Gobbling Billy,* Dutton, 1959; *The Thumbstick,* Oxford University Press, 1959; *Thirteen O'Clock,* Basil Blackwell, 1959.

(Contributor) *Over the Horizon; or, Around the World in Fifteen Stories,* Duell, Sloan & Pearce, 1960; *The Rolling Season,* Oxford University Press, 1960; *Cathedral Wednesday,* Oxford University Press, 1960; *The Fishing Party,* Hamish Hamilton, 1960; *Summer Visitors,* Oxford University Press, 1961; *The Changeling,* Oxford University Press, 1961, Dutton, 1963; *The Glass Ball,* Hamish Hamilton, 1961, Dutton, 1962; *The Last Bus,* Hamish Hamilton, 1962; *The Twelve Dancers,* Hamish Hamilton, 1962; *The Man From the North Pole,* Hamish Hamilton, 1963; *On the Stepping Stones,* Hamish Hamilton, 1963; *Words and Music,* Hamish Hamilton, 1963; *Plot Night,* Hamish Hamilton, 1963, Dutton, 1968; *A Parcel of Trees,* Penguin, 1963; *Water Boatman,* Hamish Hamilton, 1964; *Whistling Rufus,* Hamish Hamilton, 1964, Dutton, 1965; (editor with Eleanor Farjeon) *The Hamish Hamilton Book of Kings,* Hamish Hamilton, 1964, published in America as *A Cavalcade of Kings,* Walck, 1965; *Sand,* Hamish Hamilton, 1964; *A Day Without Wind,* Dutton, 1964; *The Big Wheel and the Little Wheel,* Hamish Hamilton, 1965; (editor with Farjeon) *A Cavalcade of Queens,* Walck, 1965 (published in England as *The Hamish Hamilton Book of Queens,* Hamish Hamilton, 1965); *Pig in the Middle,* Hamish Hamilton, 1965, Dutton, 1966; *No More School,* Hamish Hamilton, 1965; *Earthfasts,* Hamish Hamilton, 1966, Dutton, 1967; *Rooftops,* Hamish Hamilton, 1966; *The Old Zion,* Hamish Hamilton, 1966, Dutton, 1967; *The Battlefield,* Dutton, 1967; (compiler) *The Hamish Hamilton Book of Heroes,* Hamish Hamilton, 1967, published in America as *William Mayne's Book of Heroes,* Dutton, 1968; *The Big Egg,* Hamish Hamilton, 1967; *Toffee Join,* Hamish Hamilton, 1968; *Over the Hills and Far Away,* Hamish Hamilton, 1968, published in America as *The Hill Road,* Dutton, 1969; *The Yellow Aeroplane,* Hamish Hamilton, 1968; *The House on Fairmont,* Dutton, 1968; (compiler) *The Hamish Hamilton Book of Giants,* Hamish Hamilton, 1968, published in America as *William Mayne's Book of Giants,* Dutton, 1969. *Ravensgill,* Dutton, 1970; *Royal Harry,* Hamish Hamilton, 1971, Dutton, 1972; *A Game of Dark,* Dutton, 1971; (editor) *Ghosts,* Thomas Nelson, 1971.

SIDELIGHTS: Houston L. Maples described *The Hill Road* as "an engrossing and beautifully polished example of storytelling."

BIOGRAPHICAL/CRITICAL SOURCES: New York Times Book Review, November 3, 1968; *Saturday Review,* May 10, 1969; *Book World,* May 11, 1969; *Commonweal,* May 23, 1969; *Times Literary Supplement,* July 20, 1970; *Observer Review,* August 20, 1970.

* * *

MAZURKIEWICZ, Albert J. 1926-

PERSONAL: Born March 1, 1926, in Shenandoah, Pa.; son of Frank A. (a miner) and Pauline (Polunk)

Mazurkiewicz; married Helen Lipsett, August 29, 1953; children: Katharine. *Education:* Ursinus College, A.B., 1950; University of Pennsylvania, M.A., 1951; Temple University, Ed.D., 1957. *Home address:* R.D. # 1, Coopersburg, Pa. 18036. *Office:* Lehigh University, Bethlehem, Pa. 16601.

CAREER: Philadelphia (Pa.) Public Schools, secondary school teacher, 1950-52, elementary school teacher, 1952-53; Temple University, Philadelphia, Pa., room supervisor in laboratory school of the reading clinic, 1953-55; Lehigh University, Bethlehem, Pa., associate professor of education and director of reading and study clinic, 1955-66; Newark State College, Union, N.J., professor of education, 1966—, chairman of department of education, 1966-69. Consultant to various schools. *Military service:* U.S. Army Medical Corps; received Bronze Star. *Member:* International Reading Association, American Psychological Association, American Educational Research Association, College Reading Association (former president and member of board of directors), National Council of Teachers of English, Phi Delta Kappa. *Awards, honors:* Commonwealth of Pennsylvania leadership in education award.

WRITINGS: (Editor) *Controversial Issues in Reading,* Reading and Study Clinic, Department of Education, Lehigh University, c.1961; (editor) *Explorations in Reading,* Reading and Study Clinic, Department of Education, Lehigh University, 1962; (editor) *Reading, Learning and the Curriculum,* Reading and Study Clinic, Department of Education, Lehigh University, 1963; (with Harold J. Tanyzer) *Early-to-Read I/T/A Program,* seven volumes, Pitman, 1963-65; (with Tanyzer) *The ITA Handbook for Writing and Spelling: Early-to-Read ITA Program,* Initial Teaching Alphabet Publications, 1964; (editor) *New Perspectives in Reading Instruction: A Book of Readings,* Pitman, 1964, 2nd edition, 1969; (editor) *Reading and Child Development,* Reading and Study Clinic, Department of Education, Lehigh University, 1964; *First Grade Reading Using Modified Co-Basal Versus the Initial Teaching Alphabet,* Lehigh University, 1965; (with Tanyzer) *Mie Alfabet Book,* Initial Teaching Alphabet Publications, 1965; (with Tanyzer) *Mie Number Bwk,* Initial Teaching Alphabet Publications, 1965; *The Initial Alphabet and Reading Instruction,* Lehigh University, 1966; (editor) *Wide World of Reading Instruction,* Interstate, 1966; "Training with Language" series, Pitman, 1968. Contributor to *Elementary English, Reading Teacher, Journal of Developmental Reading, Profiles,* and *Educational Leadership.* Editor, *Journal of the Reading Specialist.*

WORK IN PROGRESS: With Tanyzer and A. Decaprio, *The Easy-to-Read i.t.a. Program.*

SIDELIGHTS: Mazurkiewicz has traveled in Portugal, Spain, Switzerland, Italy, Austria, Germany, France, Belgium, Holland, Denmark, and England. *Avocational interests:* Swimming, ice skating, orchid growing, and reading.

* * *

MAZZETTI, Lorenza 1933-

PERSONAL: Born 1933, in Florence, Italy; daughter of Cornado and Olga (Liberati) Mazzetti; married. *Education:* University of Florence, student, 1950. *Home:* Via Vittoria 10, Rome, Italy.

CAREER: Journalist, writer, film director, and television reporter. *Member:* Comunita Europea Scrittori, Associazione Internazionale Documentaristi. *Awards, honors:* Cannes Film Festival Prix de Recherche as director of "Together"; Viareggio Prize, 1963, for *The Sky Falls.*

WRITINGS: Il Cielo cade (part one of trilogy), Garzanti, 1961, translation by Marguerite Waldman published as *The Sky Falls,* Bodley Head, 1962, McKay, 1963; *Con Rabbia* (part two of trilogy), Garzanti, 1963, translation by Isabel Quigly published as *Rage,* McKay, 1965; *Uccidi il padre e la madre* (part three of trilogy), Garzanti, 1969; *Il Lato oscura: L'Opera e stata curata e ordinata da Cosmo Barbato* (on psychoanalysis), Tindalo, 1969. Also author of television documentaries and short stories. Contributor to *Vie Nuove.*

SIDELIGHTS: Mrs. Mazzetti writes: "I believe that to write is to think, and to think is to decide what is good and what is evil, is to choose between indifference and not indifference, it is to decide what is 'good' even if it does not exist, it is to judge, it is executing an act of justice, it is for this reason a social act, a political act." The film "Together" was one of the first efforts of the "Free Cinema Movement" founded by Mrs. Mazzetti, Tony Richardson, Lindsay Anderson, and Karel Reisz.

* * *

McBRIDE, John G. 1919-

PERSONAL: Born April 5, 1919, in Lone Wolf, Okla.; son of William Cleveland and Belle (Taylor) McBride; married Geraldine Gamblin, May 25, 1942; children: John Michael, Don Douglas. *Education:* Texas Technological College, student, 1937-40. *Religion:* Protestant. *Home:* 448 East Norman Ave., Raymondville, Tex. 78580. *Office address:* McBride Gin Co., P.O. Box 807, Raymondville, Tex. 78580.

CAREER: Keisling-McBride (cotton ginning and farming), Lamesa, Tex., bookkeeper, 1940-41; McBride Gin Co., Lamesa and Raymondville, Tex., partner-manager, 1946-60, president, Raymondville, Tex., 1960—. Partner, Chauvin-McBride Vegetable Co., Raymondville, Tex., 1951-53; owner, John McBride Cotton Co., Lamesa, Tex., 1960-62. *Military service:* U.S. Army Air Forces, 1942-46; became major; awarded Legion of Merit, Asiatic-Pacific Theater ribbon with four bronze combat stars, Philippine Liberation ribbon with one star. *Member:* Cotton Producers' Institute, National Cotton Council, Texas Cotton Ginners' Association, Rio Grande Valley Cotton Ginners Association.

WRITINGS: Vanishing Bracero: Valley Revolution, Naylor, 1963.

WORK IN PROGRESS: A novel with the cotton industry as a background.

BIOGRAPHICAL/CRITICAL SOURCES: Lamesa Daily Reporter, November 10, 1963; *Lubbock Avalanche Journal,* November 17, 1963, December 29, 1963.

* * *

McCALL, Storrs 1930-

PERSONAL: Born November 5, 1930. *Education:* McGill University, B.A., 1952; Oxford University, B.Phil., 1955. *Office:* Department of Philosophy, University of Pittsburgh, Pittsburgh, Pa. 15213.

CAREER: McGill University, Montreal, Quebec, 1955-63, began as lecturer, became assistant professor of philosophy; University of Pittsburgh, Pittsburgh, Pa., assistant professor of philosophy, 1963—.

WRITINGS: Aristotle's Modal Syllogisms, North-Holland Publishing, 1963; (editor) *Polish Logic, 1920-1939,* Clarendon Press, 1967.

* * *

McCARTHY, Patrick Joseph 1922-

PERSONAL: Born August 3, 1922, in New York, N.Y.; son of Patrick J. and Anna (Coyle) McCarthy; married

Helen Marcella Lasek (a teacher). *Education:* Fordham University, A.B., 1943; Columbia University, A.M., 1947, Ph.D., 1960. *Politics:* Democrat. *Religion:* Roman Catholic. *Office:* Department of English, University of California, Santa Barbara, Calif. 92706.

CAREER: College of City of New York (now City College of City University of New York), New York, N.Y., lecturer in English, 1947-49; University of Arizona, Tucson, instructor, 1952-60, assistant professor, 1960-64, associate professor of English, 1964-66; University of California, Santa Barbara, associate professor, 1966-70, professor of English and head of the department, 1970—. Visiting summer professor, University of Washington, 1963, Harvard University, 1967. *Military service:* U.S. Army, Infantry, 1943-46; served in Philippines and Japan; became first lieutenant. *Member:* Modern Language Association of America, Modern Humanities Research Association, American Association of University Professors, Philological Association of Pacific Coast, Phi Kappa Phi.

WRITINGS: Matthew Arnold and the Three Classes, Columbia University Press, 1964. Contributor of several articles and reviews to *University of Toronto Quarterly, Victorian Studies, Harvard Library Bulletin,* and other publications.

* * *

McCARTHY, Shaun (Lloyd) 1928-
(Theo Callas, Desmond Cory)

PERSONAL: Born February 16, 1928, in Lancing, Sussex, England; son of William Henry Lloyd and Iris Mary (Chatfield) McCarthy; married Blanca Rosa Poyatos, February 16, 1956; children: John Francis, Alexander Justin Lloyd, Richard Charles, Dewi Anthony. *Education:* St. Peter's College, Oxford, B.A., 1951, M.A., 1960. *Politics:* Liberal. *Religion:* Anglican. *Home:* Eastbrook House, Dinas Powis, Glamorganshire, Wales. *Agent:* Frank C. Betts Ltd., 96 Piccadilly, London, England. *Office:* College of Advanced Technology, Cardiff, Wales.

CAREER: Cenemesa (electrical engineering), Cordoba, Spain, technical translator, 1953; Academia Britanica (language school), Cordoba, Spain, teacher, 1953-60; College of Advanced Technology, Cardiff, Wales, lecturer, department of English studies, 1960—. Part-time journalist. *Military service:* Royal Marines, 45 Commando, 1945-48. *Member:* Institut des Arts et des Lettres (Geneva; fellow), Institute of Linguists (fellow), Society of Authors, Radiowriters' Association, Mystery Writers of America, Press Club (London).

WRITINGS—Under pseudonym Desmond Cory: *Secret Ministry,* Muller, 1951; *Begin, Murderer!,* Muller, 1951; *This Traitor, Death,* Muller, 1952; *This Is Jezebel,* Muller, 1952; *Dead Man Falling,* Muller, 1953; *Lady Lost,* Muller, 1953; *Intrigue,* Muller, 1954; *The Shaken Leaf,* Muller, 1955; *The Height of Day,* Muller, 1955; *The Phoenix Sings,* Muller, 1955; *High Requiem,* Muller, 1956; *Johnny Goes North,* Muller, 1956; *Pilgrim at the Gate,* Muller, 1957, Washburn, 1958; *Johnny Goes East,* Muller, 1958; *Johnny Goes West,* Muller, 1958, Walker & Co., 1967; *Johnny Goes South,* Muller, 1959, Walker & Co., 1964; *Pilgrim on the Island,* Muller, 1959, Walker & Co., 1961; *The Head,* Muller, 1960; *Jones on the Belgrade Express,* Muller, 1960; *Stranglehold,* Muller, 1961; *Undertow,* Muller, 1962, Walker & Co., 1963; *Hammerhead,* Muller, 1963, published in America as *Shockwave,* Walker & Co., 1964; *The Name of the Game,* Muller, 1964; *Deadfall,* Walker & Co., 1965; *Feramontov,* Walker & Co., 1966; *Timelock,* Walker & Co., 1967; *The Night Hawk,* Walker & Co., 1969; *Sunburst,* Walker & Co., 1971; *Take My Drum to England,* Hodder & Stoughton, 1971; *Even If You Run,* Doubleday, 1972.

Under pseudonym Theo Callas: *The City of Kites,* Muller, 1955, Walker & Co., 1964; *Ann and Peter in Southern Spain,* Muller, 1959. Also author of radio play, "Orbit One," British Broadcasting Corp., 1961. Contributor of articles, stories, and translations to periodicals, including *Western Mail, London Magazine, London Mystery Magazine, Observer,* and *Truth.*

WORK IN PROGRESS: An untitled novel; *The Gods of the West,* a survey of expression of philosophical and scientific ideas in contemporary European literature.

SIDELIGHTS: Often asked why he writes thrillers (rather than serious novels or television plays), McCarthy says he believes in applying such talent as one has to the most convenient channel, that "television is a team medium ... which results in a high level of sameness, a lack of individuality."

Thrillers? "It may be because I had in some ways what the British call a Victorian childhood, while at the same time my schooldays coincided exactly with the last war. The war shaped me so much that there's a sense in which I've never got used to peace.... Most of the thriller writers I've met are very mild, unassuming people—Chandler, Fleming and Coles are that way, almost out of touch, you'd say, with the post-war world. The real tough eggs don't have that inner conflict to resolve and don't, as a rule, write thrillers.

"Two things have influenced me particularly, Oxford University and Spain ... semi-private worlds which enable you to sit back and look at what is happening to your own generation from a certain distance. Rather like what Europe was to Malcolm Crowley's exiles.

"My wife is Spanish and my children are bilingual.... I try to be interested in as many things as possible and hence have rather a ragbag of a mind. On the whole I don't feel it matters."

Deadfall was filmed by 20th Century-Fox in 1968.

BIOGRAPHICAL/CRITICAL SOURCES: Times Literary Supplement, June 1, 1967; *New York Times Book Review,* August 6, 1967; *Book World,* August 17, 1969; *Best Sellers,* April 15, 1971.

* * *

McCARTHY, William E(dward) J(ohn) 1925-

PERSONAL: Born July 30, 1925, in London, England; son of Edward (a clerk) and Hyland McCarthy; married Margaret, January 18, 1956. *Education:* Ruskin College, student, 1953-55; Merton College, Oxford, B.A. (first class honors), 1957; Nuffield College, Oxford, Ph.D., 1959. *Politics:* Labour Party. *Religion:* Agnostic. *Home:* 4 William Orchard Close, Old Headington, Oxford, England. *Office:* Nuffield College, Oxford, England.

CAREER: Oxford University, Oxford, England, research fellow of Nuffield College, 1959-63, staff lecturer and tutor in industrial relations, 1964-65; Royal Commission on Trade Unions and Employers' Association, London, England, director of research, 1965-68; Oxford University, Oxford, England, fellow of Nuffield College and Centre for Management Studies, 1968—. University examiner and academic adviser to management schools and technical colleges. *Member:* Consumer's Association, University Industrial Relations Association, Fabian Society.

WRITINGS: The Future of the Unions, Fabian Society, 1962; *The Closed Shop in Britain,* University of California Press, 1964; *The Role of Shop Stewards in British Industrial Relations: A Survey of Existing Information and Research,* H.M.S.O., 1966; (with Arthur Ivor Marsh) *Disputes Procedures in Britain,* H.M.S.O., 1967; (with V.G. Munns) *Employers' Associations: The Results of Two Studies* (contains *The Functions and Organisation* of Employers' Associations in Selected Industries, by Munn, and A Survey of Employers' Association Officials, by McCarthy), H.M.S.O., 1967; The Role of Government in Industrial Relations, Ditchley Foundation, 1968; Shop Stewards and Workshop Relations: The Results of a Study, H.M.S.O., 1968; (editor) Industrial Relations in Britain: Guide for Management and Unions, Lyon, Grant & Green, 1969; The Reform of Collective Bargaining: A Series of Case Studies, H.M.S.O., 1971; Trade Unions, Penguin, 1972.

AVOCATIONAL INTERESTS: The Labour Party and the state of the English theatre.

* * *

McCAULEY, Elfrieda B (abnick) 1915-
(Anne W. House)

PERSONAL: Born August 11, 1915, in Milwaukee, Wis.; daughter of Rudolf (a physical education instructor) and Louise (Hoetzel) Babnick; married Leon McCauley (president of a sales corporation), June 13, 1938; children: Brian, Christopher, Kevin, Matthew. Education: University of Wisconsin, B.S., 1938. Religion: Episcopalian. Home: 32 Longmeadow Rd., Riverside, Conn. 06878.

CAREER: Religious News Service, New York, N.Y., metropolitan reporter, 1943-45; operated publicity service under own name in New York, N.Y., and Brooklyn, N.Y., 1946-51; McCauley Enterprises, Inc., Greenwich, Conn., secretary-treasurer, 1961—.

WRITINGS—Editor: (With husband, Leon McCauley) The Book of Prayers: Compiled for Protestant Worship, Crown, 1954; (with Leon McCauley) A Treasury of Faith: A Personal Guide to Spiritual Peace, Dell, 1957; (under pseudonym Anne W. House) A Girl's Prayer Book: Prayers for Everyday and Special Needs, Seabury, 1957; (with Leon McCauley) A Book of Family Worship, Scribner, 1959; (under pseudonym Anne W. House) The Day Book of the Bible: Devotions for Every Day of the Christian Year, Seabury, 1962; (under pseudonym Anne W. House) The Day Book of Meditations: Meditations for Every Day of the Christian Year, Seabury, 1962. Also author of short stories and articles.

* * *

McCLARY, Ben Harris 1931-

PERSONAL: Born July 8, 1931, in Ocoee, Tenn.; son of Roy Eugene (an engineer) and Arlene (Kimbrough) McClary; married Sandra Carroll Long; children: Katherine Elizabeth, Marcus Harris. Education: University of Tennessee, B.A., M.A., 1955; University of Sussex, Ph.D., 1966. Politics: Democrat, Religion: Episcopal. Home: 548 Wimbish Rd., Macon, Ga. 31204. Office: Department of English, Wesleyan College, Macon, Ga. 31201.

CAREER: Tennessee Wesleyan College, Athens, assistant professor, 1960-64, associate professor of English, 1966-67; Wesleyan College, Macon, Ga., professor of English, 1967-70, chairman of the department, 1967—, Alice Culler Cobb Professor of English Language and Literature, 1970—. Military service: U.S. Army, 1955-56. Member: Modern Language Association of America, East Tennessee Historical Society (life), Phi Kappa Phi. Awards, honors: Fulbright fellowship, 1964-66; American Philosophical Society grants, 1967, 1970; American Council of Learned Societies grant, 1967.

WRITINGS: (Editor with Richard Beale Davis) American Cultural History, 1607-1829, Scholars Facsimiles & Reprints, 1961; (editor) Benjamin Silliman, Letters of Shahcoolen, Scholars Facsimiles & Reprints, 1962; Our Literary Heritage: A Guide for Tennessee in Literature, Tennessee Wesleyan College, 1962; (editor) The Lov-

ingood Papers, University of Tennessee Press, 1962-67; (editor) Washington Irving and the House of Murray: Geoffrey Crayon Charms the British, 1817-1856, University of Tennessee Press, 1969; (editor) Thomas Hughes, Rugby, Tennessee, University of Tennessee Press, 1972; (editor) Complete Writings of Washington Irving, Volume XVII, University of Wisconsin Press, 1972. Contributor of articles on Anglo-American literature and culture to periodicals.

WORK IN PROGRESS: Editing Volume XVIII of Complete Writings of Washington Irving, completion expected in 1975.

BIOGRAPHICAL/CRITICAL SOURCES: Chattanooga Times, January 13, 1963, April 22, 1964; Macon Telegraph and News, October 1, 1967; Macon News, November 30, 1970; Wesleyan Alumnae, May, 1968.

* * *

McCLENDON, James William, Jr. 1924-

PERSONAL: Born March 6, 1924, in Shreveport, La.; son of James William and Mary (Drake) McClendon; married Marie Miles, 1949; children: James William III, Thomas Vernon. Education: University of Texas, B.A. (with high honors), 1947; Southwestern Baptist Theological Seminary, B.D., 1950, Th.D., 1953; Princeton Theological Seminary, Th.M., 1952; postdoctoral study at University of California, 1959-62, research at Oxford University, 1962-63. Home: 50 Marina Vista, Larkspur, Calif. 94939.

CAREER: Minister, Southern Baptist Convention; pastor in Austin, Tex., 1946-47, and Keatchie, La., 1948-50; Princeton University, Princeton, N.J., chaplain to Baptist students, 1950-51; interim pastor in Sydney, Australia, 1952; pastor in Ringgold, La., 1953-54; Golden Gate Baptist Seminary, Mill Valley, Calif., assistant professor, 1954-57, associate professor, 1958-64, professor of theology, 1964-66; University of San Francisco, San Francisco, Calif., associate professor of theology, 1966-69; Church Divinity School, Graduate Theological Union, Berkeley, Calif., professor of theology, 1971—. Visiting professor of religion, Stanford University, 1967, Temple University, 1969; Jeffrey Lecturer in Religion, Goucher College, 1970-71. Member of National Faith and Order Colloquium, National Council of Churches. Trustee, Institute for Ecumenical and Cultural Research, Collegeville, Minn. Military service: U.S. Naval Reserve, 1943-46; became lieutenant junior grade. Member: American Philosophical Association, American Society of Church History, American Academy of Religion, Pacific Coast Theological Group, Stanford-Santa Clara Ecumenical Colloquium, United Nations Association of Marin County (president, 1967-69), Phi Beta Kappa.

WRITINGS: Pacemakers of Christian Thought, Broadman, 1962; (contributor) W. Junker, editor, What Can You Believe, Broadman, 1966; (contributor) Michael Novak, editor, American Philosophy and the Future, Scribner, 1968. Contributor to Baptist Student, Review and Expositor, Theology Today, Concilium, and other publications.

WORK IN PROGRESS: With J.M. Smith, a book analyzing religious convictions.

* * *

McCLOSKEY, Eunice (LonCoske) 1906-

PERSONAL: Born May 25, 1906, in Johnsonburg, Pa.; daughter of Fredrick (a machinist) and Ada (Nelson) LonCoske; married Lewis F. McCloskey (an appliance man), January 9, 1932; children: Eunice Marie McCloskey Minteer. Education: Attended Columbia University, one year. Politics: Republican. Religion: Lutheran. Home: 403 Oak St., Ridgway, Pa. 15853. Agent:

Bertha Klausner, International Literary Agency, Inc., 130 East 40th St., New York, N.Y. 10016.

CAREER: Artist and writer. Paintings have been exhibited in Carnegie Museum, Pittsburgh, Pa., National Museum, Washington, D.C., Galeries Raymond Duncan, Paris, France, and at other galleries in the East; one-man shows include an exhibit at Nelson Art Gallery, Kansas City, Mo. *Member:* International Institute of Arts and Letters (fellow), Professional and Executive Hall of Fame, National League of American Pen Women (former chairman), Associated Artists of Pittsburgh (director), Pennsylvania Federation of Women, Philadelphia Art Alliance, Delta Kappa Gamma. *Awards, honors:* Three national poetry awards, National League of American Pen Women; Associated Artists prizes, 1950, 1953; Henry Posner Prize, 1953; Aime Jackson Short Prize for water color, 1956.

WRITINGS: (Self-illustrated) *Coal Dust and Crystals* (verse), H. Harrison, 1939; *Strange Alchemy* (verse), Driftwind Press, 1940; (self-illustrated) *The Heart Knows This*, Driftwind Press, 1944; (self-illustrated) *This Is the Hour* (verse), Decker Press, 1948; *The Golden Hill*, Humphries, 1952; (self-illustrated) *These Rugged Hills* (poems), privately printed, 1954; *This Is My Art*, four volumes, privately printed, 1956-62; *So Dear to My Heart* (biography), Humphries, 1964; *Potpourri: An Autobiography*, Dorrance, 1966; *Songs and Paintings for the Heart*, privately printed, 1969; *Symbols of My Life*, privately printed, 1970. Contributor of poetry, feature articles, and short stories to magazines and newspapers.

WORK IN PROGRESS: A second biography; *O, Shana, Shana*.

AVOCATIONAL INTERESTS: Travel, preserving Victorian homes, antiques, community projects, and people.

* * *

McCLOSKEY, (John) Robert 1914- (Balfour Dangerfield)

PERSONAL: Born September 15, 1914, in Hamilton, Ohio; son of Howard Hill and Mable (Wismeyer) McCloskey; married Margaret Durand (a librarian), November 23, 1940; children: Sarah, Jane. *Education:* Attended Vesper George Art School, Boston, Mass., 1932-36, National Academy of Design, 1936-38. *Politics:* Democrat. *Home:* Scott Islands, Cape Rosier, Harborside, Me. 04642. *Address:* c/o Viking Press, 625 Madison Ave., New York, N.Y. 10022.

CAREER: Executed bas relief for the municipal building, Hamilton, Ohio, 1935; mural painter for four years; commercial artist; author and illustrator of children's books. Advertising consultant, The Cocked Hat, Paoli, Pa. *Military service:* U.S. Army, 1942-45; became technical sergeant. *Member:* American Academy in Rome (fellow), P.E.N., Authors League. *Awards, honors:* President's award, National Academy of Design, 1936; Tiffany Foundation prize; Prix de Rome, 1939; Caldecott Medal, 1942, for *Make Way for Ducklings*, and 1958, for *Time of Wonder*; Young Readers' Choice award, 1947, for *Homer Price*; Ohioana Book award, 1949, for *Blueberries for Sal*; D.Litt., Miami University, Oxford, Ohio, 1964, Mount Holyoke College, 1967.

WRITINGS—Self-illustrated; all published by Viking: *Lentil*, 1940, *Make Way for Ducklings*, 1941, *Homer Price*, 1943, *Blueberries for Sal*, 1948, *Centerburg Tales*, 1951, *One Morning in Maine*, 1952, *Time of Wonder*, 1957, *Burt Dow, Deep-Water Man*, 1963.

Illustrator: Anne Burnett Malcolmson, *Yankee Doodle's Cousins*, Houghton, 1941; Robert Hobart Davis, *Tree Toad*, Stokes, 1942; Claire Huchet Bishop, *The Man Who Lost His Head*, Viking, 1942; Tom Robinson, *Trigger John's Son*, Viking, 1949; Ruth Sawyer, *Journey Cake, Ho!*, Viking, 1953; Anne H. White, *Junket*, Viking, 1955; Keith Robertson, *Henry Reid, Inc.*, Viking, 1958; Keith Robertson, *Henry Reid's Journey*, Viking, 1963; Keith Robertson, *Henry Reid's Baby-Sitting Service*, Viking, 1966; Keith Robertson, *Henry Reid's Big Show*, Viking, 1970.

SIDELIGHTS: McCloskey told *CA* that he is "primarily an artist, incidentally a writer," who imagines his stories in pictures and then fills in between pictures with the necessary words. He spent two years in Europe, twelve years apart, and two winters in Mexico. He spends May through October in his island home near Cape Rosier, Me. *Avocational interests:* Boats.

BIOGRAPHICAL/CRITICAL SOURCES: Horn Book, July, 1942, July, 1957; Lee Bennett Hopkins, *Books Are By People*, Citation, 1969; Selma Lanes, *Down the Rabbit Hole*, Atheneum, 1971.

* * *

McCONNELL, James Douglas Rutherford 1915- (Douglas Rutherford; Paul Temple, a joint pseudonym)

PERSONAL: Born October 14, 1915, in Kilkenny, Ireland; son of James and Edith (Cooney) McConnell; married Margaret Laura Goodwin (an author's consultant), 1953; children: Mike. *Education:* Educated at Sedbergh School and Clare College, Cambridge. *Home:* Common Lane, Eton, Windsor, England. *Agent:* Curtis Brown Ltd., 13 King St., London W.C.2, England; and 60 East 56th St., New York, N.Y. 10022. *Office:* Cwmgila, Machynlleth, Wales.

CAREER: Eton College, Windsor, England, language teacher and housemaster, 1946—. *Military service:* British Army, Intelligence Corps, 1940-46; served in North Africa and Italy; mentioned in dispatches, 1944. *Member:* Crime Writers Association, Aberdorey Golf Club.

WRITINGS: Learn Italian Quickly, MacGibbon & Kee, 1960; *Learn Spanish Quickly*, MacGibbon & Kee, 1961, Citadel, 1963; *Learn French Quickly*, MacGibbon & Kee, 1966; *Eton: How It Works*, Faber, 1967, Humanities, 1968; *Eton Repointed: The New Structures of an Ancient Foundation*, Faber, 1970.

With Francis Durbridge under joint pseudonym Paul Temple: *The Tyler Mystery*, Hodder & Stoughton, 1957; *East of Algiers*, Hodder & Stoughton, 1959.

Under pseudonym Douglas Rutherford: *Comes the Blind Fury*, Faber, 1950; *Meet a Body*, Faber, 1951; *Flight into Peril*, Dodd, 1952 (published in England as *Telling of Murder*, Faber, 1952); *Grand Prix Murder*, Collins, 1955; *The Perilous Sky*, Collins, 1955; *The Chequered Flag*, Collins, 1956; *The Long Echo*, Collins, 1957, Abelard, 1958; *A Shriek of Tyres*, Collins, 1958, published in America as *On the Track of Death*, Abelard, 1959.

Murder Is Incidental, Collins, 1961; *The Creeping Flesh*, Collins, 1963, Walker & Co., 1965; (editor) *Best Motor Racing Stories*, Faber, 1965; *The Black Leather Murders*, Walker & Co., 1966; *Skin for Skin*, Walker & Co., 1968; (editor and author of introduction) *Best Underworld Stories*, Faber, 1969; *The Gilt-Edged Cockpit*, Collins, 1969, Doubleday, 1971.

Clear the Fast Lane, Collins, 1971, Holt, 1972.

WORK IN PROGRESS: Research on new approaches to language teaching.

SIDELIGHTS: McConnell spends his holidays in a shepherd's cottage in remote Welsh mountains, writing crime novels with a European background. *Avocational interests:* Golf.

BIOGRAPHICAL/CRITICAL SOURCES: New Statesman, March 10, 1967; Times Literary Supplement, April 13, 1967; New York Times Book Review, February 9, 1969; Spectator, November 22, 1969; Best Sellers, April 1, 1971.

*   *   *

McCORD, Howard 1932-

PERSONAL: Born November 3, 1932, in El Paso, Tex.; son of Frank Edward and Sylvia Joy (Coe) McCord; married Dora Garcia Ochoa, April 19, 1953; children: Colman Garcia, Robert Ochoa. Education: Texas Western College, B.A., 1957; University of Utah, M.A., 1960. Politics: None. Religion: Roman Catholic. Home: 1001 Napoleon St., Bowling Green, Ohio 43403. Office: Department of English, Washington State University, Pullman, Wash.

CAREER: Washington State University, Pullman, 1960-71, began as assistant professor, became associate professor of English; Bowling Green University, Bowling Green, Ohio, professor of English and director of M.F.A. program. Secretary and member of executive committee, Coordinating Council of Literary Magazines, 1972—. Military service: U.S. Navy, 1951-53. Member: Federation of Old Cornwall Societies. Awards, honors: National Woodrow Wilson fellowship, 1957-58; Fulbright award, 1965; E.O. Holland fellow, 1967; Borestone Mountain Poetry award, 1969; D.H. Lawrence fellow, University of New Mexico, 1971.

WRITINGS: Precise Fragments (poems), Dolman Press, 1963; Twelve Bones (poems), Goosetree Press, 1964; The Spanish Dark, and Other Poems, Washington State University Press, 1965; (editor) Gordon Curtis, Fire Prayers, Tribal Press, 1966; Fables and Transfigurations (poems), Kayak, 1967; Longjaunes, His Periplus (poems), Kayak, 1968; (with Walter Lowenfels) The Life of Fraenkel's Death, Washington State University Press, 1970; The Fire Visions, Twowindows, 1970; Maps, Kayak, 1971; Gnomonology: A Handbook of Systems, Sand Dollar Press, 1971; Some Notes to Gary Snyder's Myths and Texts, Sand Dollar Press, 1971; The Diary of a Lost Girl, Lillabulero Press, 1972; The Old Beast (poems), Sand Dollar Press, 1973. Contributor to International Poetry Number I, edited by Swadesh Bharati, Prakashan, 1970; contributor to Research Studies, New York Times, Harper's Bazaar, Arena, Partisan Review, Iowa Review, New Mexico Quarterly, Classical Journal, Caterpillar, Tree, and other publications.

WORK IN PROGRESS: New and Selected Poems.

SIDELIGHTS: Edgar Robinson wrote of McCord's Fables and Transfigurations: "McCord is the genuine innocent, the man who can believe in the stars, in St. Paul, in his boots, in his knife. He's very American too, like Gary Snyder or Jack Kerouac in his loneness, in his singleness, in his youth. I don't know where he goes from here, how the grown man will sing or what he will sing about, but these poems of youth's passage are authentic."

McCord told CA: "My work lately focuses on the relationships of the wilderness landscapes of the West and the interior landscapes of dreams and visions."

BIOGRAPHICAL/CRITICAL SOURCES: Chicago Review, Volume 20, number 1, 1968, January-February, 1971; Concerning Poetry, spring, 1969; Lillabulero, winter, 1970.

*   *   *

McCORMICK, (George) Donald (King) 1911-
(Richard Deacon)

PERSONAL: Born December 9, 1911, in Rhyl, Flintshire, Wales; son of Thomas Burnside (a journalist) and Lillie Louise (King) McCormick; married Rosalind Deirdre Buchanan Scott, 1934 (divorced); married Sylvia Doreen Cade, 1947 (deceased); married Eileen Dee Deacon, October 4, 1963; children: (second marriage) Anthony Stuart. Education: Attended Oswestry School, 1925-30. Religion: Church of England. Home: Flat 3, The Old House, 36 Southend Rd., Beckenham, Kent, England.

CAREER: Kemsley Newspapers, foreign correspondent in Northwest Africa 1946-49; Gibraltar Chronicle, Gibraltar, managing editor, 1946—; Sunday Times, London, England, with foreign department, 1949-65, foreign manager, 1965-73. Military service: Royal Navy Volunteer Reserve, 1940-46; served in Combined Operations; became lieutenant commander.

WRITINGS: The Talkative Muse, Lincoln Williams, 1934; Islands for Sale, Garnett, 1949; Mr. France, Jarrolds, 1955; The Wicked City: An Algerian Adventure, Jarrolds, 1956; The Hell-Fire Club: The Story of the Amorous Knights of Wycombe, Jarrolds, 1958; The Mystery of Lord Kitchener's Death, Putnam, 1959; The Identity of Jack the Ripper, Jarrolds, 1959, new and revised edition, Arrow Books, 1970.

The Incredible Mr. Kavanaugh, Putnam, 1960, Devin, 1961; The Wicked Village, Jarrolds, 1960; The Temple of Love, Jarrolds, 1962, Citadel, 1965; Blood on the Sea: The Terrible Story of the Yawl "Migonette," Muller, 1962; The Mask of Merlin: A Critical Study of David Lloyd George, Macdonald & Co., 1963, published in America as The Mask of Merlin: A Critical Biography of David Lloyd George, Holt, 1964; The Unseen Killer: A Study of Suicide, Its History, Causes and Cures, Muller, 1964; Peddler of Death: The Life and Times of Sir Basil Zaharoff, Holt, 1965 (published in England as Pedlar of Death: The Life of Sir Basil Zaharoff, Macdonald & Co., 1965); The Red Barn Mystery: Some New Evidence on an Old Murder, John Long, 1967, A.S. Barnes, 1968; Murder by Witchcraft: A Study of Lower Quinton and Hagley Wood Murders, John Long, 1968; Murder by Perfection: Maundy Gregory, the Man Behind Two Unsolved Murders, John Long, 1970; One Man's Wars: The Story of Charles Sweeney, Soldier of Fortune, Arthur Barker, 1972; How to Buy an Island, David & Charles, 1973.

Under pseudonym Richard Deacon: The Private Life of Mr. Gladstone, Muller, 1966; Madoc and the Discovery of America, Muller, 1967, Braziller, 1968; John Dee, Muller, 1968; A History of the British Secret Service, Muller, 1969, Taplinger, 1970; A History of the Russian Secret Service, Taplinger, 1972.

SIDELIGHTS: McCormick's special interests encompass North Africa, Switzerland, and islands "everywhere in the world," biography, nonfiction requiring the author to be detective as well as writer, and the bibliography of romance and romantic traditions, customs and cults.

BIOGRAPHICAL/CRITICAL SOURCES: Books and Bookmen, July, 1967, October, 1968.

*   *   *

McCORMICK, Jack (Sovern) 1929-

PERSONAL: Born January 19, 1929, in Indianapolis, Ind.; son of James Albert (an attorney) and Betty (Sovern-Smith) McCormick; married Gwendolyn Adele Terry, September 21, 1951 (divorced, 1970); married Janet Berkley Pickens, August 6, 1970; children: (first marriage) James Russell, Wendy Lynn. Education: Butler University, B.S., 1951; Rutgers University, Ph.D., 1955. Office: Waterloo Mills Research Station, 860 Waterloo Rd., Devon, Pa. 19333.

CAREER: American Museum of Natural History, New York, N.Y., in charge of vegetation studies and botany adviser, 1955-61, consultant in ecology at Kalbfleisch Field Research Station, 1961—; Ohio State University, Columbus, assistant professor of botany, and research associate at Institute of Polar Studies, 1961-63; Academy of Natural Sciences of Philadelphia, Philadelphia, Pa., curator and chairman of department of ecology and land management, 1963-70; University of Pennsylvania, Philadelphia, lecturer in biology and landscape architecture, 1963—. Consulting ecologist, 1970—. Member of northeastern forest research advisory council, U.S. Forest Service, 1962-72.

MEMBER: International Society of Bioclimatology and Biometeorology (charter), International Society for Tropical Ecology, International Society for Plant Geography and Ecology, National Geographic Society (life), Ecological Society of America (chairman of committee for study of vegetation, 1960-61), American Association for the Advancement of Science, Nature Conservancy, Pacific Science Association, New Jersey Academy of Science (president, 1970-72), Torrey Botanical Club (member of council, 1957-63), Indiana Academy of Science, Ohio Academy of Science, Sigma Xi, Sigma Nu. *Awards, honors:* Grants from National Science Foundation for study of vegetation of Chiricahua Mountains, 1958-60, for undergraduate research participation program in cooperation with American Museum of Natural History, 1960—; Oak Leaf award, Nature Conservancy, 1961; grants from U.S. Army and Ohio State University Research Foundation for Greenland expedition, 1962, and from U.S. Department of Interior, 1970—.

WRITINGS: Atoms, Energy and Machines (textbook), Creative Educational Society, 1957; (contributor) *The Illustrated Library of the Natural Sciences,* Volume III, Simon & Schuster, 1958; *The Living Forest,* Harper, 1959; (author of foreword) John Muir, *The Mountains of California,* Doubleday-Anchor, 1961; (author of introduction) Peter Farb and the editors of *Life, The Forest,* Time, Inc., 1961; (with John W. Andresen) *Infestation of Pitch and Shortleaf Pines by the Red Pine Sawfly in Southern New Jersey,* American Museum of Natural History, 1961; with George Willard Martin) *Myxomycetes from Shades State Park and Pine Hills Natural Area, Indiana,* [New York], 1962; *Vascular Flora of Shades State Park and Pine Hills Natural Area, Indiana,* American Museum of Natural History, 1962; *The Life of the Forest,* McGraw, 1966; (with August Wilhelm Kuechler) *Bibliography of Vegetation Maps of North America,* privately printed, 1967; *The Pine Barrens: An Ecologi.* ^1 *Inventory,* New Jersey State Museum, 1971.

Contributor to *Encyclopedia Americana* and *McGraw-Hill Encyclopedia of Science and Technology,* Volume XIV. Also contributor of more than one hundred articles to botanical and ecological journals. Natural history editor, *American-Oxford Encyclopedia,* 1957-62.

WORK IN PROGRESS: Trees of Eastern North America, completion expected in 1975; *Natural History of the Seasons,* 1975; *Vegetation of North America,* 1980.

*   *   *

McCORMICK, Richard P (atrick) 1916-

PERSONAL: Born December 24, 1916, in New York, N.Y.; son of Patrick A. (a printer) and Anna (Smith) McCormick; married Katheryne Levis (a college instructor), August 25, 1945; children: Richard Levis, Dorothy Irene. *Education:* Rutgers University, A.B., 1938, M.A., 1940; University of Pennsylvania, Ph.D., 1948. *Politics:* Democrat. *Home:* 938 River Rd., Piscataway, N.J. 08854. *Office:* Department of History, Rutgers University, New Brunswick, N.J. 08903.

CAREER: Philadelphia Quartermaster Depot, Philadelphia, Pa., historian, 1942-44; University of Delaware,

Newark, instructor in history, 1944-45; Rutgers University, New Brunswick, N.J., instructor, 1945-48, assistant professor, 1948-51, associate professor, 1951-56, professor of history and university historian, 1956—. Visiting professor, Cambridge University, 1961-62; Commonwealth Lecturer, University of London, 1971. New Jersey Tercentenary Commission, member, 1959-61, chairman, 1959-60; member, Federal New Jersey Tercentenary Commission, 1960—; New Jersey Historical Commission, member, 1967—, chairman, 1967-70. Research adviser, Colonial Williamsburg, 1952-60. *Member:* American Historical Association, American Association for State and Local History, American Association of University Professors, Organization of American Historians, New Jersey Historical Society (president, 1951-57), New York Historical Society, Phi Beta Kappa. *Awards, honors:* Lindbach Foundation Award; Social Science Research Council fellowship, 1957-58; Fulbright grant, 1961-62; manuscript prize, American Association for State and Local History, 1964.

WRITINGS: Experiment in Independence: New Jersey in the Critical Period, 1781-1789, Rutgers University Press, 1950; *The History of Voting in New Jersey: A Study of the Development of Election Machinery, 1664-1911,* Rutgers University Press, 1954; *Report of Visit to Great Britain for the New Jersey Tercentenary Commission from June to August, 1960,* New Jersey Tercentenary Commission, 1960; (contributor) *Views on the Emancipation Proclamation,* American History Workshop, 1962; *New Jersey from Colony to State, 1609-1789,* Van Nostrand, 1964, 2nd edition, Rutgers University Press, 1970; *New Jersey: A Student's Guide to Localized History,* Bureau of Publications, Teachers College, Columbia University, 1965; *The Second American Party System: ᶠorma-tion in the Jacksonian Era,* University of North Carolina Press, 1966; *Rutgers: A Bicentennial History,* Rutgers University Press, 1966. Contributor of articles to professional journals.

*   *   *

McCOURT, Edward (Alexander) 1907-

PERSONAL: Born October 10, 1907, in Mullingar, Ireland; son of William A. and Elizabeth (Gillespie) McCourt; married Anna Margaret Mackay, September 12, 1938; children: Michael. *Education:* University of Alberta, B.A. (honors), 1932; Oxford University, B.A., 1934, M.A., 1938. *Home:* 1310 Melrose Ave., Saskatoon, Saskatchewan, Canada. *Agent:* Herbert van Thal, 8 Upper Brook St., London W.1, England. *Office:* University of Saskatchewan, Saskatoon, Saskatchewan, Canada.

CAREER: Ridley College, St. Catherines, Ontario, teacher of English, 1935-36; Upper Canada College, Toronto, Ontario, teacher of English, 1936-38; Queen's University, Kingston, Ontario, lecturer in English, 1938-39; University of New Brunswick, Frederiction, professor of English, 1939-44; University of Saskatchewan, Saskatoon, professor of English, 1944—. *Member:* Association of Canadian University Teachers. *Awards, honors:* Rhodes Scholar, 1932.

WRITINGS: The Flaming Hour, Ryerson, 1947; *Music at the Close,* Ryerson, 1947; *The Canadian West in Fiction,* Ryerson, 1949, revised edition, 1970; *Home Is the Stranger* (novel), Macmillan (Canada), 1950; *Buckskin Brigadier: The Story of the Alberta Field Force,* St. Martin's, 1955; *The Wooden Sword,* Arthur Barker, 1956; *Revolt in the West: The Story of the Riel Rebellion,* St. Martin's, 1958; *Walk Through the Valley,* Arthur Barker, 1959; *The Ettinger Affair,* Macdonald & Co., 1963 (published in Canada as *Fasting Friar,* McClelland & Stewart, 1963); *The Road Across Canada,* St. Martin's 1965; *Saskatchewan: The Traveller's Canada,* St. Martin's, 1967; *Remember Butler: The Story of Sir William Butler,*

Routledge & Kegan Paul, 1967; *The Yukon and North-west Territories*, Macmillan (Canada), 1969, St. Martin's, 1970. Author of eight radio plays and of about one hundred short stories.

WORK IN PROGRESS: A biography of Sir William Gregory of Coole.

BIOGRAPHICAL/CRITICAL SOURCES: Guy Sylvester, Brandon Connor, and Carl F. Klinck, editors, *Canadian Writers*, Ryerson, 1964; *Observer Review*, November 12, 1967; *Times Literary Supplement*, January 25, 1968.

* * *

McCRIMMON, James M(cNab)   1908-

PERSONAL: Born June 16, 1908, in Renton, Scotland; came to United States in 1929, naturalized in 1939; son of John and Margaret (Patterson) McCrimmon; married Barbara Smith, June 10, 1939; children: Kevin M., John M. *Education:* Northwestern University, B.A., 1932, M.A., 1933, Ph.D., 1937. *Home:* 1330 West Indian Head Dr., Tallahassee, Fla. 32301.

CAREER: Northwestern University, Evanston, Ill., assistant instructor in English, 1935-36; University of Toledo, Toledo, Ohio, instructor, 1936-38, assistant professor, 1938-43, associate professor of English, 1943-47; University of Illinois, chairman of humanities division at Galesburg Extension, 1947-49, associate professor at Urbana campus, 1949-55, head of division of general studies, 1954-65, professor of humanities, 1955-65, professor emeritus, 1965—; Florida State University, Tallahassee, professor of English, 1965—. *Member:* National Council of Teachers of English, College Conference on Composition and Communication.

WRITINGS: (With George A. Fullette) *Writing Effectively: An Introduction to the Elements of Grammar, Composition, and Usage*, Farrar & Rinehart, 1941; (editor) *Essays for Freshmen*, Harcourt, 1945; (with Ney MacMinn and J.R. Hainds) *Bibliography of the Published Writings of John Stuart Mill*, Northwestern University Press, 1945; (with C.M. Louttit and William Habberton) *Open Door to Education*, University of Illinois Press, 1950; *Writing with a Purpose: A First Course in College Composition*, Houghton, 1950, 5th edition, 1972; (editor with others) *From Source to Statement*, Houghton, 1968; *Writing with a Purpose* [and] *From Source to Statement* (includes 4th edition of former; latter edited by McCrimmon and others), Houghton, 1968.

WORK IN PROGRESS: Developing a sequential curriculum in high school English.

* * *

McCUTCHAN, Philip (Donald)   1920-
(Duncan MacNeil)

PERSONAL: Born October 13, 1920, in Cambridge, England; son of Donald Robert (a master mariner) and Margaret Frances (Gardner) McCutchan; married Elizabeth Ryan, June 30, 1951; children: Donald, Rosemary. *Education:* Attended Royal Military College at Sandhurst, 1939. *Religion:* Church of England. *Home and office:* Myrtle Cottage, 107 Portland Rd., Worthing, Sussex, England.

CAREER: Orient Steam Navigation Company Ltd., London, England, assistant purser on London-Australia run, 1946-49; Anglo-Iranian Oil Company Ltd., London, England, shipping accountant, 1949-51; assistant master in preparatory schools, 1951-53; owner and operator of tea shop, 1953-60; full-time author, 1960—. *Military service:* Royal Naval Volunteer Reserve, 1939-46; became lieutenant. *Member:* Crime Writers Association (chairman, 1965-66).

WRITINGS—Novels: *Whistle and I'll Come*, Harrap, 1957; *The Kid*, Harrap, 1958; *Storm South*, Harrap, 1959; *On Course for Danger* (boys' book), St. Martin's, 1959; *Gilbraltar Road*, Harrap, 1960, Berkley Publishing, 1965; *Hopkinson and the Devil of Hate*, Harrap, 1961; *Redcap*, Harrap, 1961, Berkley Publishing, 1965; *Bluebolt One*, Harrap, 1962, Berkley Publishing, 1965; *Leave the Dead Behind Us*, Harrap, 1962; *The Man from Moscow*, Harrap, 1963, John Day, 1965; *Marley's Empire*, Harrap, 1963; *Warmaster*, Harrap, 1963, John Day, 1964; *Bowering's Breakwater*, Harrap, 1964; *Moscow Coach*, Harrap, 1964, John Day, 1966; *Sladd's Evil*, Harrap, 1965, John Day, 1967; *The Dead Line*, Berkley Publishing, 1966; *A Time for Survival*, Harrap, 1966; *Skyprobe*, Harrap, 1966, John Day, 1967; *Poulter's Passage*, Harrap, 1967; *The Screaming Dead Balloons*, John Day, 1968; *The Day of the Coastwatch*, Harrap, 1968; *The Bright Red Businessmen*, John Day, 1969; *The All-Purpose Bodies*, Harrap, 1969, John Day, 1970; (under pseudonym Duncan MacNeil) *Drums Along the Khyber*, Hodder & Stoughton, 1969; (under pseudonym Duncan MacNeil) *Lieutenant of the Line*, Hodder & Stoughton, 1970; *Man, Let's Go On*, Harrap, 1970; *Hartinger's Mouse*, Harrap, 1970; *Half a Bag of Stringer*, Harrap, 1971; *This Drakotny*, Harrap, 1971; (under pseudonym Duncan MacNeil) *Sadhu on the Mountain Peak*, Hodder & Stoughton, 1971; *The German Helmet*, Harrap, 1972; (under pseudonym Duncan MacNeil) *The Gates of Kunarja*, Hodder & Stoughton, 1972. Author of radio scripts in areas of drama, features, and children's programs for British Broadcasting Corp. and overseas stations. Contributor of articles on seafaring subjects and short stories to magazines; contributor of book reviews to *Books of the Month*.

SIDELIGHTS: Maurice Prior described *Man, Let's Go On* as "a refreshing, purposeful novel written with verve, and encompassing all the tenets of . . . [McCutchan's] craft and his undoubted versatility."

McCutchan draws on countries he visited in ten years at sea as a background for his stories, particularly for books featuring Commander Esmonde Shaw of the Defense Intelligence Staff, an undercover agent appearing in fourteen of his published books.

BIOGRAPHICAL/CRITICAL SOURCES: *News Chronicle* (London), September 26, 1960; *Books and Bookmen*, February, 1968, March, 1968, October, 1968, January, 1969, May, 1970, October, 1970; *Book World*, September 1, 1968.

* * *

McCUTCHEON, Hugh Davie-Martin   1909-

PERSONAL: Born July 24, 1909, in Glasgow, Scotland; son of Alexander (a lawyer) and Anne Campbell (Bain) McCutcheon; married Muriel O'Garr, June 25, 1937. *Education:* University of Glasgow, student, 1928-33; qualified as solicitor, 1933. *Politics:* Independent. *Religion:* Protestant. *Home:* St. Margarets, Woodside Rd., Brookfield, Renfrewshire, Scotland.

CAREER: Hill & Hoggan, Solicitors, Glasgow, Scotland, law apprentice, 1927-32, law clerk, 1933-35; Renfrew County Council, Paisley, Scotland, chief legal assistant, 1935-45; Renfrew Town Council, Renfrew, Scotland, town clerk and legal adviser, 1945—. Former legal associate member and examiner on Scottish town planning law, Town Planning Institute. Justice of the Peace, 1967; honorary sheriff substitute, 1969. *Member:* P.E.N., Society of Authors, Society of Town Clerks of Scotland (former president), Association of Town Clerks of the British Commonwealth (former president), Renfrew Rotary Club (former president), Erskine Golf Club.

WRITINGS: *Alamein to Tunis*, Lutterworth, 1946; *The Angel of Light*, Rich & Cowan, 1951, published in America as *Murder at the Angel*, Dutton, 1952; *None Shall Sleep Tonight*, Dutton, 1953; *Prey for the Nightingale*, Rich & Cowan, 1953; *Cover Her Face*, Rich & Cowan, 1954; *The Long Night Through*, Rich & Cowan, 1956; *Comes the Blind Fury*, John Long, 1959; *To Dusty Death*, John Long, 1960; *Yet She Must Die*, Doubleday, 1962; *The Deadly One*, John Long, 1962; *Suddenly, in Vienna*, John Long, 1963; *Treasure of the Sun*, John Long, 1964; *The Black Attendant*, John Long, 1965; *Killer's Moon*, John Long, 1966, published in America as *And the Moon Was Full*, Doubleday, 1967; *The Scorpion's Nest*, John Long, 1967; *A Hot Wind From Hell*, John Long, 1968; *Brand From the Burning*, John Long, 1969; *Something Wicked*, John Long, 1970. Columnist, "Scottish Notes," in *British Housing and Planning Review*. Contributor of travel articles to *Top Gear* and *Motor World*, of short stories to *Toronto Star Weekly*, *Boys Own Paper*, and to journals, and of serial stories to *Sunday Post*, *Weekly News*, and periodicals in Germany, Denmark, France, and Finland.

SIDELIGHTS: McCutcheon's writings have been published in a total of fifteen countries. One novel, *To Dusty Death*, was made into a film, the film rights to *Suddenly in Vienna* have been sold, and an option taken on *Yet She Must Die*. *Avocational interests:* Motoring, golf, foreign travel.

* * *

McDERMOTT, Thomas J. 1915-

PERSONAL: Born May 12, 1915, in Somerville, Mass.; son of James and Nora (Gallagher) McDermott; married Patsy Ruth Harding, November 21, 1944; children: Christopher H., Susan Fay. *Education:* Boston University, B.B.A., 1939, M.B.A., 1941, Ph.D., 1955. *Politics:* Democrat. *Religion:* Roman Catholic. *Home:* 444 Pacific Ave., Pittsburgh, Pa. 15221. *Office:* Economics Department, Duquesne University, Pittsburgh, Pa. 15219.

CAREER: New Mexico State University, Las Cruces, assistant professor of economics, 1946-48; Holy Cross College, Worcester, Mass., associate professor of economics, 1948-59; Duquesne University, Pittsburgh, Pa., professor of economics and chairman of the department, 1959—. Labor arbitrator, 1954—; permanent arbitrator for Pittsburgh Steel Co. and United Steelworkers of America, 1962-66, and for Glass Container Industry and G.B.B.A., 1970—. Consulting economist to Upper Ohio Valley Association (railroads), 1962-66. Chairman, Massachusetts Personnel Appeals Board, 1958-59. *Military service:* U.S. Army, 1942-46; became captain. *Member:* American Economic Association, Industrial Relations Research Association, Catholic Economic · Association, National Academy of Arbitrators (regional chairman, 1962-65, member of board of governors, 1969-72), American Association of University Professors. *Awards, honors:* Berlin Award, Holy Cross College, 1953, for promotion of sound labor-management relations.

WRITINGS: (Contributor) John J. Foley, editor, *Human History: A Race Between Education and Catastrophe*, Duquesne University Press, 1963; *Economic Growth and Development of Ohio River Counties*, Bureau of Business Research, Duquesne University, 1964. Author of some sixty arbitration decisions published in *Labor Arbitration Reports*, Bureau of National Affairs, *Labor Arbitration Awards*, Commerce Clearing House, and *American Arbitration* Awards, Prentice-Hall. Contributor of editorials to *Worcester Gazette*, 1957-58, of articles to *Labor Law Journal*, *Industrial and Labor Relations Review*, *Arbitration Journal*, and other professional journals.

McDONALD, Forrest 1927-

PERSONAL: Born January 7, 1927, in Orange, Tex.; son of Forrest (a postal clerk) and Myra (McGill) McDonald; married second wife, Ellen Shapiro (a model), August 1, 1963; children: (first marriage) Kathy (Mrs. Brian Rhode), Forrest, Howard, Marcy Ann, Stephen, Kevin. *Education:* University of Texas, B.A., 1949, M.A., 1949, Ph.D., 1955. *Politics:* Republican. *Religion:* Protestant. *Home:* 702 University Pl., Grosse Pointe, Mich. 48236. *Agent:* Sterling Lord Agency, 75 East 55th St., New York, N.Y. 10022. *Office:* Department of History, Wayne State University, Detroit, Mich. 48202.

CAREER: Social Science Research Council, Washington, D.C., research training fellow, 1951-53; Wisconsin Historical Society, Madison, utility research director, 1953-56; American History Research Center, Madison, Wis., executive secretary, 1956-58; Brown University, Providence, R.I., associate professor, 1958-63, professor of history, 1963-67; Wayne State University, Detroit, Mich., professor of history, 1967—. Director of American History Research Center and Lincoln Educational Foundation. State chairman, Goldwater for President Committee of Rhode Island, 1963-64. *Military service:* U.S. Naval Reserve, 1945-46. *Awards, honors:* Volker fellow, 1959; Guggenheim fellow, 1962-63.

WRITINGS: *Let There Be Light: The Electric Utility Industry in Wisconsin, 1881-1955*, American History Research Center, 1957; *We the People: The Economic Origins of the Constitution*, University of Chicago Press, 1958; *Insull*, University of Chicago Press, 1962; (editor) *Empire and Nation*, Prentice-Hall, 1962; *The Anti-Federalists, 1781-1789*, Bobbs-Merrill, 1963; *E Pluribus Unum: The Formation of the American Republic, 1776-1790*, Houghton, 1965, reissued as *The Formation of the American Republic, 1776-1790*, Penguin, 1965; *The Torch Is Passed: The United States in the Twentieth Century*, three volumes, Addison-Wesley, 1968, reissued as *The United States in the Twentieth Century*, 1970; (editor with wife, Ellen S. McDonald) *Confederation and Constitution*, Harper, 1968; *Enough Wise Men: The Story of Our Constitution*, Putnam, 1970; *The Boys Were Men*, Putnam, 1971; (with others) *The Last Best Hope: A History of the United States*, two volumes, Addison-Wesley, 1972. Contributor to historical journals.

WORK IN PROGRESS: A history of the administration of George Washington, for University of Kansas Press.

BIOGRAPHICAL/CRITICAL SOURCES: *Best Sellers*, July 1, 1970.

* * *

McDONALD, Hugh Dermot 1910-

PERSONAL: Born October 29, 1910, in Dublin, Ireland; married Anne Marion Ball; children: Conagh, Beryl, Neil. *Education:* Attended Wilson's College and Irish Baptist College in Ireland; Kings College, London, B.A., B.D., Ph.D. (all with honours). *Home:* Fairhaven, 43, The Rough, Newick, Sussex, England.

CAREER: Baptist minister; minister of churches in England, 1937-48; London Bible College, London, England, professor of the philosophy of religion, 1948—, vice-principal, 1952—. Visiting professor of philosophy and theology at Northern Baptist Theological Seminary, Chicago, Ill., 1960-61, 1968-69, Trinity Evangelical Divinity School, 1972, and Chicago Graduate School of Theology. *Awards, honors:* D.D., University of London.

WRITINGS: *Ideas of Revelation: An Historical Study, A.D. 1700 to A.D. 1860*, St. Martin's, 1959; (contributor) James Dixon Douglas, editor, *The New Bible Dictionary*, Eerdmans, 1962; (contributor) Carl Henry, editor, *Basic Christian Doctrines*, Holt, 1962; *Theories of*

Revelation: An Historical Study, 1860-1960, Allen & Unwin, 1963, Humanities, 1964; *I and He,* Epworth, 1966; *Jesus: Human and Divine,* Zondervan, 1968; *Living Doctrines of the New Testament,* Pickering & Inglis, 1971, Zondervan, 1972; *Freedom in Faith,* Pickering & Inglis, 1973; (contributor) Clark Pinnock and D. Wells, editors, *Towards a Theology of the Future,* Creation Press, in press. Contributor to *Dictionary of the Christian Church* and *Dictionary of Ethics.* Contributor of articles to theological journals.

WORK IN PROGRESS: Books on philosophy and apologetics, Biblical commentary, and Christology.

* * *

McDOWELL, Edwin (Stewart) 1935-

PERSONAL: Born May 13, 1935, in Somers Point, N.J.; son of Samuel Hamilton (a plumber) and Kathryn (Prieser) McDowell; married Carole Ann Foss, July 14, 1956; children: Susan, Amy. *Education:* Temple University, B.A., 1958; New York University, graduate study, 1959. *Agent:* Paul R. Reynolds, 599 Fifth Ave., New York, N.Y. 10017. *Office: Wall Street Journal,* 22 Cortlandt St., New York, N.Y. 10007.

CAREER: Arizona Republic, Phoenix, Ariz., 1960-72, began as columnist and editorial writer, served as foreign correspondent, became editor of editorial pages; *Wall Street Journal,* New York, N.Y., editorial writer, 1972—. Member of Public Relations Advisory Board, Arizona Commission of Indian Affairs. *Military service:* U.S. Marine Corps, 1952-55; became sergeant. *Member:* Sigma Delta Chi.

WRITINGS: Barry Goldwater: Portrait of an Arizonan, Regnery, 1964; *Three Cheers and a Tiger* (novel), Macmillan, 1966. Contributor of articles and reviews to *National Review, New York Times, Modern Age, New Leader, Saturday Review, National Observer,* and *West.*

WORK IN PROGRESS: A novel, *The Sun God.*

SIDELIGHTS: McDowell has traveled in and written articles for various publications from some forty foreign nations in Europe, Asia, Africa, South America, Central America, and the Caribbean.

* * *

McELANEY, (Joseph) Paul 1922-

PERSONAL: Born August 1, 1922, in Providence, R.I.; *Education:* St. Peter's College, Jersey City, N.J., B.A., 1949; graduate study at Seton Hall University, 1957, at Jersey City State College, 1958-59. *Religion:* Roman Catholic. *Home:* 73 Lexington Ave., Jersey City, N.J. 07304.

CAREER: Former reporter for *New York Daily Mirror,* New York, N.Y., and *Jersey Journal,* Jersey City, N.J.; school teacher in New York State, and in New Jersey. *Military service:* U.S. Army, Medical Corps, 1943-45; served in Solomon Islands and Philippines campaigns; received Bronze Star.

WRITINGS—With James O'Donnell and Raymond Taylor: *Help Your Child Succeed in School,* Dell, 1962; *My Catholic Believe-It-or-Not,* Dell, 1963; *Secrets of the Animal World,* Scholastic Book Services, 1964. Author of epigrams appearing in *Look, Reader's Digest, American Mercury, Saturday Evening Post, Catholic Digest, Golf Digest, Coronet, Humorana,* and other periodicals and newspapers.

SIDELIGHTS: McElaney hitchhiked across the country in 1950 as "guest of America" reporter for the *Jersey Journal,* writing a series of articles on the hospitality of Americans.

* * *

McFARLAND, Dorothy Tuck 1938-
(Dorothy Tuck)

PERSONAL: Born June 10, 1938, in Burlingame, Calif.; daughter of Cyrus Edwin and Helen (Davidson) Tuck; married Gerald W. McFarland (a history instructor at University of Massachusetts). *Education:* University of California, Berkeley, B.A., 1960; Columbia University, M.A., 1961. *Residence:* Leverett, Mass.

WRITINGS—Under name Dorothy Tuck: *Crowell's Handbook of Faulkner,* Crowell, 1964 (published in England as *A Handbook of Faulkner,* Chatto & Windus, 1965); (contributor) John Unterecker, editor, *Approaches to the Twentieth Century Novel,* Crowell, 1965; *Willa Cather,* Ungar, 1972.

* * *

McGAW, Naomi Blanche Thoburn 1920-
(Jane Hervey)

PERSONAL: Born September 10, 1920, in Roehampton, London, England; daughter of John Thoburn (a watercolor artist) and Pauline (Tate) McGaw; married third husband, George Nolesworth Salvin Bowlby (a writer); children: (second marriage) Mary Jane Pauline Wilder; (third marriage) Russell Jonathan Dene, Caroline. *Education:* Attended Heron's Ghyll School, 1929-36; studied portrait painting under Frederic Whiting, 1937-39. *Politics:* Conservative. *Religion:* Church of England. *Home:* Hunter's Moon, Cookham Dean, Berkshire, England. *Agent:* Curtis Brown Ltd., 13 King St., Covent Garden, London W.C.2, England.

CAREER: Peak Poultry Ltd., Whaley Bridge, Derbyshire, England, director of packers branch and sales director of services branch, 1952-61.

WRITINGS: (Under pseudonym Jane Hervey) *Vain Shadow,* Gollancz, 1963, Scribner, 1964. Regular contributor to *Sussex County Magazine,* 1941-46; contributor to other local magazines.

WORK IN PROGRESS: A novel; short stories.

SIDELIGHTS: Miss McGaw was a former exhibitor in local art shows, but gave up painting to write for magazines. Her maternal grandfather, Sir Henry Tate, presented Tate Gallery and his collection of oil painting to the British nation, and her father was a well-known watercolor artist. She lived in Paris for two years.

* * *

McGINLEY, Phyllis 1905-

PERSONAL: Born March 21, 1905, in Ontario, Ore.; daughter of Daniel and Julia (Kiesel) McGinley; married Charles L. Hayden (a New York Telephone Co. executive), June 25, 1937; children: Julia Elizabeth, Phyllis Louise. *Education:* Graduate of University of Utah; attended University of California. *Religion:* Roman Catholic. *Home:* 60 Beach Ave., Larchmont, N.Y. 10538.

CAREER: Free-lance writer and poet; taught school in Utah for one year; moved to New York, 1928; before marriage held an assortment of jobs, including English teacher in New Rochelle, copy writer for an advertising agency, and poetry editor for *Town and Country.* Member of advisory board of *American Scholar. Member:* National Institute of Arts and Letters, P.E.N., Poetry Society of America, Catholic Poetry Society, Kappa Kappa Gamma, Cosmopolitan Club of New York City. *Awards, honors:* Catholic Writers Guild award, 1955; Christopher medal, Edna St. Vincent Millay memorial award of Poetry Society of America, both 1955, for *The Love Letters of Phyllis McGinley;* St. Catherine of Siena medal of Theta Phi Alpha, 1956; Catholic Institute of the Press award, 1960; Golden Book award; National Association of Independent Schools award and Pulitzer Prize for poetry, both 1961, for *Times Three*; Spirit gold medal of Catholic Poetry Society of America, 1962; Laetare medal of University of Notre Dame, 1964; Campion award, 1967; D.Litt., Wheaton College (Norton, Mass.), 1956, St. Mary's College (Notre Dame, Ind.), 1958, Marquette University, 1960, Dartmouth College, 1961, Boston College, 1962, Wilson College, 1964, Smith College, 1964, St. John's University, 1964.

WRITINGS—Verse: *On the Contrary*, Doubleday, 1934; *One More Manhattan*, Harcourt, 1937; *A Pocketful of Wry*, Duell, Sloan & Pearce, 1940, revised edition, Grosset, 1959; *Husbands are Difficult; or, The Book of Oliver Ames*, Duell, Sloan & Pearce, 1941; *Stones From a Glass House*, Viking, 1946; *A Short Walk From the Station*, Viking, 1951; *The Love Letters of Phyllis McGinley*, Viking, 1954; *Merry Christmas, Happy New Year*, Viking, 1958; *Times Three: Selected Verse from Three Decades*, foreword by W.H. Auden, Viking, 1960.

Juvenile: *The Horse Who Lived Upstairs*, Lippincott, 1944; *The Plain Princess*, Lippincott, 1945; *All Around the Town*, Lippincott, 1948; *A Name for Kitty*, Simon & Schuster, 1948; *The Most Wonderful Doll in the World*, Lippincott, 1950; *The Horse Who Had His Picture in the Paper*, Lippincott, 1951; *Blunderbus*, Lippincott, 1951; *The Make-Believe Twins*, Lippincott, 1953; *The Year Without a Santa Claus*, Lippincott, 1957; *Lucy McLockett*, Lippincott, 1959; *Sugar and Spice: The ABC of Being a Girl*, F. Watts, 1960; *Mince Pie and Mistletoe*, Lippincott, 1961; *The B Book*, Crowell-Collier, 1962; *Boys Are Awful*, F. Watts, 1962; *How Mrs. Santa Claus Saved Christmas*, Lippincott, 1963; *A Girl and Her Room*, Watts, 1963; *Wonderful Time*, Lippincott, 1966; *A Wreath of Christmas Legends*, Macmillan, 1967; (compiler) *Wonders and Surprises: A Collection of Poems*, Lippincott, 1968.

Essays: *The Province of the Heart*, Viking, 1959; *Sixpence in Her Shoe*, Macmillan, 1964; *Saint-Watching*, Viking, 1969.

Wrote lyrics for "Small Wonder," a Broadway revue, 1948; wrote narration for film, "The Emperor's Nightingale," 1951. Contributor to *New Yorker, America, Horizon, Atlantic, Good Housekeeping, Reader's Digest, Ladies' Home Journal, McCall's, Vogue*, and other publications.

SIDELIGHTS: Miss McGinley is noted for her felicitously-worded verses, technically meticulous, witty, yet often bearing a serious overtone. On occasion she has been compared to Ogden Nash and Dorothy Parker. A writer for the New York *Herald Tribune Book Review* remarked that "even critics who keep telling her that her touch is too light, her heart is too light, her adjustment too good, take her with seriousness." David McCord has praised her "eloquent moments, her compassion, her intuition, her ability to pare the world's wormy apple with a razor blade ... [her] turn of phrase.... This is poetry of delight that she has kept and would keep alive." "The line between light verse and poetry is very thin," Miss McGinley has said. "In fact, the line is practically not there at all. I think, though, I've arrived at a distinction: the appeal of light verse is to the intellect and the appeal of serious verse is to the emotions.... A light-verse writer is a kind of critic. A critic's stock-in-trade is his ability to be angry at injustice, stupidity and pompousness. But today the critic and light-verse writer find it increasingly difficult to express social anger. The whole world is angry. All of us are deflated. In times of ease it is the duty of such a writer to deflate, but in times of unrest and fear it is perhaps his duty to celebrate, to single out some of the values we can cherish, to talk about some of the few warm things we know in a cold world."

Miss McGinley says her formula for juvenile writing is threefold: leanness, rhythm and repetition. "Also, I never attempt to write for a certain age group. I write the story as a story, not for a category on a calendar. I tell the story as I feel it, in the best way that I can and let the public decide what age the book is for. One of my most inflexible standards is that I write my juveniles with as much loving care as I do my poetry. I believe juveniles should be well enough written so adults can read them without pain." Her first two prose collections (for adults) centered on the home and family. A critic for the *New York Times Book Review* noted that *Province. of the Heart* "talks back to those who have patronized, satirized, psychoanalyzed or social science-ized suburban life." Robert F. Capon calls her latest book, *Saint-Watching*, "a brave and welcome achievement.... She takes the very thing we are least prepared to buy [sanctity] and tries to sell it once again," while conveying the "lost human dimension" of the saints.

The mini-musical, "Holiday for Santa," presented at the Colony Square in Atlanta, Georgia, in December, 1970, was based on *The Year Without a Santa Claus*.

AVOCATIONAL INTERESTS: Reading history, cooking, gardening, and "sticking pins into the smugger aspects of the social scene."

BIOGRAPHICAL/CRITICAL SOURCES: Harvey Breit, *The Writer Observed*, World Publishing, 1956; W.H. Auden's introduction to *Times Three*, Viking, 1960; *New York Herald Tribune*, September 25, 1960; *Newsweek*, September 26, 1960; *Commonweal*, December 9, 1960; *Saturday Review*, December 10, 1960; *New York Times Book Review*, September 27, 1964, October 19, 1969; *Harper's*, November 1, 1964; *Time*, June 18, 1965; *Writer's Digest*, February, 1966; Lee Bennett Hopkins, *Books Are By People*, Citation Press, 1969; Nancy Larrick, *A Parent's Guide to Children's Reading*, 3rd edition, Doubleday, 1969; *Best Sellers*, October 15, 1969; *Horn Book*, December, 1969; *Christian Century*, December 17, 1969; Linda Welshimer Wagner, *Phyllis McGinley*, Twayne, 1970; *McCall's*, January, 1970; *Variety*, December 2, 1970.

* * *

McGIVERN, Maureen Daly (Maureen Daly)

PERSONAL: Born in Castle Caufield, County Tyrone, Ireland; daughter of Joseph and Margaret (Kelly) Daly; married William P. McGivern (a writer), December 28, 1948; children: Megan, Patrick. *Education:* Rosary College, River Forest, Ill., B.A. *Politics:* Democrat. *Home:* 10433 Kling St., N. Hollywood, Calif. 91062. *Agent:* Lurton Blassingame, 10 East 43rd St., New York, N.Y. 10017.

CAREER: *Chicago Tribune*, Chicago, Ill., reporter, columnist, 1946-48; *Ladies Home Journal*, Philadelphia, Pa.. associate editor, 1948-54; *Saturday Evening Post*, Philadelphia, Pa., consultant to editors, 1960-69. *Member:* P.E.N. *Awards, honors:* O. Henry Award, 1938; Dodd, Mead Intercollegiate Novel Award for *Seventeenth Summer*, 1942; Freedoms Foundation Award, 1952; Gimbel Fashion Award; Lewis Carroll Shelf award, 1969, for *Seventeenth Summer*.

WRITINGS: *Seventeenth Summer*, Dodd, 1942, illustrated edition, 1948; *Smarter and Smoother; A Handbook on How to Be That Way*, Dodd, 1944; (editor) *My Favorite Stories*, Dodd, 1948; *The Perfect Hostess*, Dodd, 1950; (editor) *Profile of Youth*, Lippincott, 1951; *What's Your P.Q. (Personality Quotient)?* (youth book), Dodd, 1952 revised edition, 1966; *Twelve Around the World*, Dodd, 1957; (under name Maureen Daly McGivern, with husband, William P. McGivern) *Mention*

My Name in Mombasa, Dodd, 1958; *Patrick Visits the Farm* (juvenile), Dodd, 1959; *Patrick Takes a Trip,* Dodd, 1960; *Spanish Roundabout* (travel), Dodd, 1961; *Sixteen, and Other Stories,* Dodd, 1961; *Moroccan Roundabout,* Dodd, 1961; *Patrick Visits the Library* (juvenile), Dodd, 1961; *Patrick Visits the Zoo* (juvenile), Dodd, 1963; *The Ginger Horse,* Dodd, 1964; *The Small War of Sergeant Donkey,* Dodd, 1965; *Spain: Wonderland of Contrasts,* Dodd, 1965; (editor) *My Favorite Mystery Stories,* Dodd, 1966; *Rosie, the Dancing Elephant,* Dodd, 1967; (editor) *My Favorite Suspense Stories,* Dodd, 1968. Author of "High School Career Series," Curtis Publishing Co., 1948—.

SIDELIGHTS: Dramatizations were made of *Seventeenth Summer,* 1949, and of a short story, "You Can't Kiss Caroline." *Seventeenth Summer* was filmed by Warner Bros., *The Ginger Horse,* by Disney Studios.

*   *   *

McGOEY, John Heck 1915-

PERSONAL: Born February 16, 1915, in Toronto, Ontario, Canada; son of Joseph J. and Josephine (Heck) McGoey. *Education:* Studied at St. Michael's College School, Toronto, Ontario, 1926-32, St. Augustine's Seminary, Toronto, 1932-38. *Home:* Blessed Sacrament Church, Harbour Island, Bahamas.

CAREER: Roman Catholic priest, member of Scarboro Foreign Mission Society; missionary to China, 1939-49; Scarboro Foreign Mission Society, Scarboro, Ontario, director of promotion work, 1949-53, superior of Scarboro Missions in Bahamas, 1954-62. Director, Catholic Welfare Committee of China, 1946-49; executive secretary, American Aid to China Committee on Health and Welfare, 1948-49. Handled medical and welfare phases of Marshall Plan for China under auspices of Joint Catholic-Protestant Voluntary Agency Committee. Civilian chaplain, U.S. Navy, Shanghai, 1946-49.

WRITINGS: Fathering Forth, Bruce, 1958 (published in Ireland as *The Priest and the Priesthood,* Clonmore & Reynolds, 1961); *Nor Scrip, Nor Shoes* (autobiography), Little, Brown, 1958; *The Sins of the Just,* Bruce, 1963; *Speak, Lord!* (poems), Bruce, 1966; *The Uncertain Sound,* Bruce, 1967. Contributor of articles to *Homiletic and Pastoral Review* and *Sponsa Regis.* Editor, *Scarboro Missions.*

*   *   *

McGRATH, Thomas 1916-

PERSONAL: Born November 20, 1916, near Sheldon, N.D.; son of James Lang and Catherine (Shea) McGrath; married Eugenia Johnson, February 13, 1960; children: Thomas Samuel Koan. *Education:* University of North Dakota, B.A., 1939; Louisiana State University, M.A., 1940; New College, Oxford, Rhodes Scholar, 1947-48. *Politics:* "Unaffiliated far left." *Address:* Sheldon, N.D. 58068.

CAREER: Poet, along with other writing and periodic teaching at colleges and universities, 1940-41, 1950-54, alternating with intervals of odd jobs and travel. For the past ten years McGrath has mainly written films for a living—primarily documentaries, but some animated films and several low-budget features. *Military service:* U.S. Army Air Forces, 1942-45. *Awards, honors:* Alan Swallow Poetry Book Award, 1954, for *Figures from a Double World;* Amy Lowell travelling poetry scholarship, 1965-66; Guggenheim fellowship, 1968.

WRITINGS: First Manifesto (poetry), Swallow & Critchlow, 1940; (contributor) *Three Young Poets: Thomas McGrath, William Peterson, James Franklin Lewis,* Press of James A. Decker, 1942; *The Dialectics of Love,* Press of James A. Decker, 1944; *To Walk a Crooked Mile* (poems), Alan Swallow, 1947; *Longshot O'Leary's Garland of Practical Poesie,* International Publishers, 1949; *Witness to the Times* (poetry), privately printed, 1954; *Figures from a Double World* (poetry), Alan Swallow, 1955; *The Gates of Ivory, The Gates of Horn* (novel), Mainstream Publishers, 1957; *Clouds* (juvenile), Melmont, 1959; *The Beautiful Things* (juvenile), Vanguard, 1960; *Letter to an Imaginary Friend* (poetry), Volume I, Alan Swallow, 1962, Volume II, Swallow Press, 1970; *New and Selected Poems,* Alan Swallow, 1964; *The Movie at the End of the World: Selected Poems,* Alan Swallow, 1972. Author of about twenty film scripts. Poetry anthologized in *Poetry for Pleasure,* edited by Ian M. Parsons, Doubleday, 1960, *New Poets of England and America,* edited by Donald Hall, Meridian, 1962, *Poets of Today,* edited by Walter Lowenfels, International Publishers, 1964, *Heartland,* edited by Lucien Stryk, Northern Illinois University Press, 1967, and *Where Is Vietnam?,* edited by Lowenfels, Doubleday, 1967. Contributor of poetry, criticism, and short stories to magazines, including *Kayak, Sixties,* and *Poetry.* Editor, *Crazy Horse;* former assistant editor of *California Quarterly* and other literary magazines.

WORK IN PROGRESS: A new, enlarged edition of *New and Selected Poems;* several other books of poems.

SIDELIGHTS: Hugh Gibb said : "The often surrealistic imagery [of the poems] is never allowed to distract the imagination by making it fly off at wild tangents and nearly always succeeds in reinforcing the main meaning of the poem. Moreover, by the subtle use of recurrent symbols which run like threads through all the poems, he contrives to bind them together as a whole."

Many critics believe that McGrath's leftist political views have kept him from the recognition his work warrants. Kenneth Rexroth comments that "It is the other peoples' opinions which have kept him from being as well known as he deserves, for he is a most accomplished and committed poet." Most critics, however, do not believe that McGrath's polemics interfere with his art. Hugh Gibb writes of *To Walk a Crooked Mile:* "In the first place, when contemplating a harsh and chaotic world, he never allows his genuine pity for the oppressed to degenerate into self-pity; and secondly, he is never forced to retreat into a world of private fantasy and introspection. In consequence he has been able not only to sustain the tradition which would otherwise appear to be almost extinct, but has brought to it a new and vigorous honesty."

McGrath has wandered around Europe and Mexico, covered America by car, freight car, and hitchhiking, worked at odd ("some very odd") jobs to finance an interlude of writing poetry. His dream: To find a place where he could teach one semester at a time, and a film producer for whom he could do a few documentaries at intervals—thus clearing the way for working several months at a stretch at poetry.

BIOGRAPHICAL/CRITICAL SOURCES: New York Times, March 7, 1948; *Saturday Review,* April 17, 1948; *New York Times Book Review,* February 21, 1965; *Antioch Review,* fall-winter, 1970-71.

*   *   *

McGUIRE, Joseph William 1925-

PERSONAL: Born March 14, 1925, in Milwaukee, Wis.; son of William B. (a government employee) and Marion (Dunn) McGuire; married Margaret Drewek, August 20, 1946; children: Laurence, Karen, Eileen, Kevin. *Education:* Marquette University, Ph.B., 1948; Columbia University, M.B.A., 1950, Ph.D., 1956. *Home:* 136 Parkside Dr., Berkeley, Calif. 94705. *Office:* Office of the

President, Vice President-Planning, 247 University Hall, University of California, Berkeley, Calif. 94720.

CAREER: University of Washington, Seattle, instructor, 1950-54, assistant professor, 1954-56, associate professor, 1956-61, professor of business economics, 1961-63; University of Kansas, Lawrence, dean of School of Business and professor of business administration, 1963-68; University of Illinois, Urbana, professor of business administration and dean of College of Commerce and Business, 1968-71; University of California, Berkeley, vice-president of planning, 1971—. Visiting professor at Netherlands College of Economics, 1957-58, University of Hawaii, 1962-63; Ford Visiting Research Professor, Carnegie-Mellon University, 1967-68. Consultant to State of Washington, 1954-56, Boeing Co., 1957, 1959-60, Northwest Pulp and Paper Association, 1962, State of Hawaii, 1962-63. *Military service:* U.S. Army Air Forces, 1943-46; became lieutenant. *Member:* American Economic Association, Academy of Management (fellow; member of board of directors, 1969-70, vice president, 1969-72), American Academy of Collegiate Schools of Business (member of board of directors, 1970-71), Association for Social Economics (member of executive council, 1970—, first vice president, 1973—), University of Washington Research Society, Beta Gamma Sigma. *Awards, honors:* Fulbright professor, 1957-58; Ford Research fellow, 1959; Danforth fellow, 1959; Agnes Anderson Award, University of Washington, 1960; Western Management science award, 1961; McKinsey Book Award, Academy of Management, 1963, for *Business and Society;* McKinsey Award, 1965, for best article in *Business Horizons;* LL.D., St. Benedicts College, 1968.

WRITINGS: Allocation of Road and Street Costs: Bases for Weight-Distance Taxation in the State of Washington, University of Washington Press, 1956; (with others) *Forecast of Gross National Product Through 1975 and Projections of Major Expenditure Components,* Boeing Co., 1957; *The American Economy,* U.S. Information Service (The Hague), 1958; *Keynesian and Post-Keynesian Economics,* Nederlandsche Economische Hoogeschool, 1959; *Study of the Market for High Speed Marine Craft,* AeroSpace Division, Boeing Co., 1959; *Study of West Coast Shipbuilding,* AeroSpace Division, Boeing Co., 1960; *Business in Our Contemporary Society* (telecourse book), University of Washington Press, 1961; (editor and contributor) *Interdisciplinary Studies in Business Behavior,* South-Western, 1962; *Economic Indicators for Hawaii,* Economic Research Center, University of Hawaii, 1963; *Factors Affecting the Growth of Manufacturing Firms,* University of Washington Press, 1963; *Business and Society,* McGraw, 1963; *Comparative Prices of Selected Consumer Items: Honolulu, San Francisco, Los Angeles,* Economic Research Center, University of Hawaii, 1963; (with Steve Archer) *Competition and the Growth of Business Enterprise,* University of Washington Press, 1963; (with Warren W. Etcheson) *Methodology for Evaluating Uses of Water in the Pacific Northwest,* [Seattle], 1963; *Theories of Business Behavior,* Prentice-Hall, 1964; (with Joseph A. Pichler) *Inequality: The Poor and the Rich in America,* Wadsworth, 1969; (editor with Clarence C. Walton) Harold Johnson, *Business in Contemporary Society* (not the same as 1961 publication), Wadsworth, 1971.

Contributor: *Nature of Highway Benefits,* Washington State Council for Highway Research, 1954; Fremont Shull, editor, *Selected Readings in Management,* Irwin, 1962; William Greenwood, editor, *Management and Organizational Behavior Theories,* South-Western, 1965; J. Russell Nelson and Aubrey Strickland, editors, *Ethics and Marketing,* Graduate School of Business Administration, University of Minnesota, 1966; Douglas M. Egan and Walter Hill, editors, *Readings in Organizational Theory,* Allyn & Bacon, 1966; Raymond J. Ziegler, editor, *Read-*

ings in Administration, Appleton, 1967; Maneck S. Wadia, editor, *Management and the Behavioral Sciences,* Allyn & Bacon, 1968; T.H. Hailstones, editor, *Readings in Economics,* South-Western, 1968; J.H. Westing and G.S. Albaum, editors, *Modern Marketing Thought,* Macmillan, 1969. Author of other published reports for Economic Research Center, University of Hawaii. Contributor of three dozen articles to professional journals.

WORK IN PROGRESS: Editing and contributing to *Contemporary Management,* for Prentice-Hall; research for articles.

*   *   *

McKAIN, David W.   1937-

PERSONAL: Born December 28, 1937, in Punxsutawney, Pa.; son of Charles VanKirk (a minister) and Ida (an organist and teacher; maiden name Crawford) McKain. *Education:* University of Connecticut, B.A., 1959, M.A., 1960. *Residence:* New York, N.Y. *Office:* McGraw-Hill Book Co., Inc., 330 West 42nd St., New York, N.Y. 10036.

CAREER: Forest ranger's assistant in Big Sur, Calif., 1961; Central Connecticut College, New Britain, instructor in English literature, 1962; McGraw-Hill Book Co., Inc., New York, N.Y., an editor, 1963—.

WRITINGS: (Editor) *Christianity: Some Non-Christian Appraisals,* McGraw, 1964; (editor) *The Whole Earth: Essays in Appreciation, Anger, and Hope,* St. Martin's, 1972.

WORK IN PROGRESS: A novel; a book of poems; the study of poetry.

AVOCATIONAL INTERESTS: Walking, preferably in the country; singing; reading rock-'n-roll lyrics.

*   *   *

McKEE, Alexander (Paul Charrier)   1918-

PERSONAL: Born July 25, 1918, in Ipswich, Suffolk, England; son of Alexander Gray (a surgeon-commander, Royal Navy) and Dorothy (Charrier) McKee; married Ilse Heimerdinger (a writer), February 23, 1952; children: Alexander Michael, Monica Elizabeth, Thomas Paul Gray, Cornelia Barbara, Gabriela Christine. *Education:* Privately educated in England and abroad. *Politics:* "Never voted." *Religion:* Church of Scotland (Presbyterian). *Home and office:* Lorelei, 41 St. Thomas Ave., Hayling Island, Hampshire, England.

CAREER: Soloed at fifteen, received pilot's license two years later, and started selling stories on flying to British aviation magazines at eighteen; served in British Army, 1942-52, becoming a sergeant, and writer, producer, and broadcaster for the Forces Radio Station in Hamburg, Germany, 1948-52; continued writing ("it was hard getting established") in England and eventually divided his time between free-lance features for British Broadcasting Corp. and editing *Conveyor,* the house magazine of a coal and oil company group; now concentrating on books, but occasionally writes television scripts and does broadcasting for Southern Television (south of England) and TWW (West England and Wales). *Member:* British Sub-Aqua Club. *Awards, honors:* Award for best feature script, Writers Guild of Great Britain, 1970, for "The Dark Page."

WRITINGS: The Coal-Scuttle Brigade, Souvenir Press, 1957; *Black Saturday: The Tragedy of the Royal Oak,* Souvenir Press, 1959, published in America as *Black Saturday,* Holt, 1960; *Strike from the Sky: The Story of the Battle of Britain,* Souvenir Press, 1960, Little, Brown, 1961; *The Golden Wreck: The True Story of a Great Maritime Disaster* (Book Society choice), Souvenir Press, 1961, published in America as *The Golden Wreck,* Morrow, 1962; *The Truth About the Mutiny on the Bounty*, Mayflower Books, 1961, published in America as *H.M.S. Bounty*, Morrow, 1962; *The Friendless Sky: The Story of Air Combat in World War I*, Souvenir Press, 1962, Morrow, 1964; *From Merciless Invaders: An Eye-Witness Account of the Spanish Armada*, Souvenir Press, 1963, Norton, 1964; *Caen: Anvil of Victory*, Souvenir Press, 1964, published in America as *Last Round Against Rommel: Battle of the Normandy Bridgehead*, New American Library, 1966; *Gordon of Khartoum*, Mayflower Books, 1965, Lancer Books, 1966; *Vimy Ridge*, Souvenir Press, 1966, published in America as *The Battle of Vimy Ridge*, Stein & Day, 1967; *Farming the Sea: First Steps into Inner Space*, Souvenir Press, 1967, Crowell, 1969; *History Under the Sea*, Hutchinson, 1968, Dutton, 1969; *The Race for the Rhine Bridges: 1940, 1944, 1945*, Stein & Day, 1971. Also author of "The Dark Page" (radio script). Anthologized in *World War II in the Air: Europe*, edited by James F. Sunderman, F. Watts, 1963, and *Combat: The War with Germany*, edited by Don Congdon, Dell, 1963. Contributor to British and Canadian service journals and newspapers in World War II; more recently contributor to *Triton, Diver, New York Times, Radio Times, Yachts and Yachting*, and other publications.

SIDELIGHTS: McKee's forte has been documentary writing in various forms since 1948, something of a discipline for a man who likes to recall that he broadcast a radio commentary while flying a jet fighter near the speed of sound, and who likes to prowl undersea wrecks ("it fascinates me").

Currently he is writing on a number of small projects while waiting for the next big one to be decided. His demands for a story? "One in which ordinary (or for that matter, extraordinary) people are involved in some drama or event in which we really see what they are made of.... A number of my books, such as those on the 'Bounty' or the 'Royal Oak,' involve getting to know a small number of people simultaneously pitchforked into a crisis.

"The other type of book which I write, the campaign history, is a different form. There can obviously be no unity of time and place. The attraction for me lies in finding the reactions of many men (and some women) engaged in these great events...."

One of the campaign histories, *Strike from the Sky*, was published almost simultaneously in four countries, and has since been brought out by two other London publishers. *H.M.S. Bounty* has been published in foreign-language editions and a French edition of *From Merciless Invaders* has been issued.

McKee would like to do more writing on his undersea research, but admits that it has not been remunerative "apart from the sale of the odd article or photograph." For five years he has been handling the explorations of a priory church and village submerged in fourteenth-century floods. Most of his work has been local to the English Channel, but he went on an expedition to the Tyrrhenian Sea in Italy in 1962, and explored six Greek, Roman and Etruscan wrecks plus a Spanish galleon.

The second author in the family is McKee's wife, whose autobiography, *Tomorrow the World*, was published by Dent in 1960.

BIOGRAPHICAL/CRITICAL SOURCES: *Times Literary Supplement*, January 19, 1967; *Books and Bookmen*, April, 1968.

* * *

McKENZIE, John L(awrence) 1910-

PERSONAL: Born October 9, 1910, in Brazil, Ind.; son of Harry James (a salesman) and Myra Belle (Daly) Mc-

Kenzie. *Education:* Xavier University, Litt.B., 1932; St. Louis University, M.A., 1935; Weston College, S.T.D., 1946. *Home:* 1445 North State Pkwy., Chicago, Ill. 60610. *Office:* Department of Theology, DePaul University, Chicago, Ill. 60614.

CAREER: Roman Catholic priest, member of Society of Jesus (Jesuits); West Baden College, West Baden Springs, Ind., professor of Old Testament, 1942-60; Loyola University, Chicago, Ill., professor of Biblical history, 1960-65; University of Notre Dame, Notre Dame, Ind., professor of theology, 1966-70; DePaul University, Chicago, Ill., professor of theology, 1970—. Visiting professor of Old Testament, University of Chicago, 1965-66. *Member:* Society of Biblical Literature (president, 1965-66), American Oriental Society, Catholic Biblical Association (president, 1963-64), Catholic Commission on Intellectual and Cultural Affairs.

WRITINGS: *The Two-Edged Sword: An Interpretation of the Old Testament*, Bruce, 1956; (editor) *The Bible in Current Catholic Thought*, Herder & Herder, 1963; *Myths and Realities: Studies in Biblical Theology*, Bruce, 1963; *A Dictionary of the Bible*, Bruce, 1965; *The Power and the Wisdom: An Interpretation of the New Testament*, Bruce, 1965; *The World of the Judges*, Prentice-Hall, 1966; *Authority in the Church*, Sheed, 1966; *Mastering the Meaning of the Bible*, Dimension Books, 1966; *Vital Concepts of the Bible*, Dimension Books, 1967; (with others) *Reconsiderations: Roman Catholic/Presbyterian and Reformed Theological Conversations, 1966-67*, World Horizons, 1967; (translator and author of introduction and notes) *Second Isaiah*, Doubleday, 1968; *The Roman Catholic Church*, Holt, 1969; (contributor) Clyde Manschreck, *Erosion of Authority*, Abingdon, 1971; *The Power and the Wisdom: An Interpretation of the New Testament*, Doubleday, 1972. Editor, *New Testament for Spiritual Reading*, Herder & Herder, 1969—.

WORK IN PROGRESS: *The Theology of the Old Testament*.

BIOGRAPHICAL/CRITICAL SOURCES: *Time*, December 29, 1967; *Washington Post*, September 15, 1969; *National Observer*, October 13, 1969; *Spectator*, February 14, 1970.

* * *

McKIE, Ronald (Cecil Hamlyn) 1909-

PERSONAL: Surname is pronounced mick-kee; born December 11, 1909, in Toowoomba, Queensland, Australia; son of Allan (a banker) and Nesta (Brown) McKie; married Anne Lindsay, January 5, 1940; children: Iain. *Education:* Attended University of Queensland. *Home:* 147 Sutherland St., Paddington, Sydney, Australia 2021. *Agent:* Sanford Jerome Greenburger, 595 Madison Ave., New York, N.Y. 10022.

CAREER: War correspondent for *Sydney Daily Telegraph* and *London Evening Standard* in Burma, 1943-44, in Europe, 1944-45; reporter and feature writer for newspapers in Australia, Singapore, and China, 1937-60; Eric White Associates, Sydney, Australia, consultant, 1960—. *Military service:* Australian Imperial Forces, 1942-43. *Member:* P.E.N., Australian Society of Authors. *Awards, honors:* Smith-Mundt fellowship to United States, 1952-53.

WRITINGS: *This Was Singapore*, Angus & Robertson, 1942; *The Survivors*, Bobbs-Merrill, 1953 (published in Australia as *Proud Echo*, Angus & Robertson, 1953); (contributor) *With the Australians in Korea*, Australian War Memorial, 1954; (contributor) *Australia at Arms*, Australian War Memorial, 1955; *The Heroes*, Angus & Robertson, 1960, Harcourt, 1961; *The Emergence of Malaysia*, Harcourt, 1963 (published in Australia as *Malaysia in Focus*, Angus & Robertson, 1963); *The Com-*

pany of Animals, Angus & Robertson, 1965, Harcourt, 1966; *Bali,* Angus & Robertson, 1969.

WORK IN PROGRESS: Singapore, for Angus & Robertson.

* * *

McKNIGHT, Thomas Lee 1928-
(Tom Lee McKnight)

PERSONAL: Born October 8, 1928, in Dallas, Tex.; son of Alva Frank (a real estate salesman) and Wacil (Dees) Stagner; married Marian Lee Anderson, September 5, 1953; children: Thomas Clinton, Jill Suzanne. *Education:* Southern Methodist University, B.S., 1949; University of Texas, summer study, 1949; University of Colorado, M.A., 1951; University of Wisconsin, Ph.D., 1955. *Religion:* Methodist. *Home:* 3240 Tilden Ave., Los Angeles, Calif. 90034. *Office:* University of California, Los Angeles, Calif. 90024.

CAREER: Southern Methodist University, Dallas, Tex., instructor in geography, 1953-55; University of Texas, Austin, instructor in geography, 1955-56; University of California, Los Angeles, professor of geography, 1956—. Visiting professor at eight other universities in three countries. *Member:* Association of American Geographers, American Geographical Society, Canadian Association of Geographers, Institute of Australian Geographers, Association of Pacific Coast Geographers, Los Angeles Geographical Society. *Awards, honors:* Fulbright research grant for study in Australia.

WRITINGS: Under name Tom Lee McKnight: *Manufacturing in Dallas: A Study of Effects,* Bureau of Business Research, University of Texas, 1956; *Manufacturing in Arizona,* University of California Press, 1962; (with C. Langdon White and Edwin J. Foscue) *Regional Geography of Anglo-America,* Prentice-Hall, 1964; (with White and Paul Griffin) *World Economic Geography,* Wadsworth, 1964; *Dallas,* Doubleday, 1964; *Feral Livestock in Anglo-America,* University of California Press, 1964; *The Camel in Australia,* Melbourne University Press, 1969; *Australia's Corner of the World: A Geographical Summary,* Prentice-Hall, 1970. Contributor of articles to professional journals. Associate editor, *Annals of the Association of American Geographers,* 1964-69.

WORK IN PROGRESS: A study of feral livestock in Australia; traveling stock routes in Australia.

SIDELIGHTS: McKnight has traveled widely in the United States, Canada, West Indies, Australia, and the Pacific Islands, and has been around the world.

* * *

McLANE, Helen J.

PERSONAL: Born in Indianapolis, Ind.; daughter of Alvin R. and Ethel (Ranck) McLane. *Education:* Northwestern University, B.S. (with distinction), 1951, M.B.A., 1965. *Home:* 1360 Lake Shore Dr., Chicago, Ill. 60610. *Office:* 20 North Wacker Dr., Chicago, Ill. 60606.

CAREER: Management Relations Associates, Chicago, Ill., managing director. *Member:* National Association of Investment Clubs (national trustee; director, Chicago council), Public Relations Society of America.

WRITINGS: (With Patricia Hutar) *The Investment Club Way to Stock Market Success,* Doubleday, 1963; *Profile of a Chief Financial Officer,* Heidrick & Struggles, Inc., 1965.

* * *

McLAUGHLIN, Dean (Jr.) 1931-

PERSONAL: Born July 22, 1931, in Ann Arbor, Mich.; son of Dean Benjamin and Laura (Hill) McLaughlin. *Education:* University of Michigan, A.B., 1953.

CAREER: Slater's, Inc. (book store), Ann Arbor, Mich., buyer. *Member:* Institute for 21st Century Studies.

WRITINGS: Dome World, Pyramid Publications, 1962; *The Fury From Earth,* Pyramid Publications, 1963; *The Man Who Wanted Stars,* Lancer Books, 1965. Contributor of short stories to *Analog, Magazine of Fantasy and Science Fiction,* and other periodicals.

WORK IN PROGRESS: A novel, still untitled; collaborating with Howard DeVore on a history of science fiction conventions, for Advent.

* * *

McLAUGHLIN, Mignon (Bushell)

PERSONAL: Born in Baltimore, Md.; daughter of Max (a businessman) and Joyce Harriet (Kolb) Neuhaus; married Robert McLaughlin (a writer and editor Aug. 30, 1941); children: Thomas Paine, James Joyce. *Education:* Smith College, B.A. *Politics:* Democrat. *Home:* 313 East 51st St., New York, N.Y. 10022. *Office: Glamour,* 420 Lexington Ave., New York, N.Y. 10017.

CAREER: Free-lance writer, 1941—. Reporter for *New York Journal American,* New York, N.Y.; copywriter for *Vogue Magazine,* New York, N.Y., and Arthur Kudner Advertising Agency, New York, N.Y.; play reader and consultant for Herman Shumlin, New York, N.Y.; *Glamour,* New York, N.Y., copy editor, 1960-63, managing editor, 1963—. *Member:* Fashion Group.

WRITINGS: (With husband Robert McLaughlin) *Gayden* (two-act play; first produced on Broadway at Plymouth Theatre, May 10, 1949), Dramatists Play Service, 1950; *The Neurotic's Notebook,* Bobbs-Merrill, 1963; *The Second Neurotic's Notebook,* Bobbs-Merrill, 1966. Contributer of short stories and articles to *Atlantic* and other magazines.

WORK IN PROGRESS: A nonfiction book.

AVOCATIONAL INTERESTS: Philosophy, literature, the theatre, foreign films, politics, and everything French.

* * *

McLEMORE, S(amuel) Dale 1928-

PERSONAL: Born October 12, 1928, in Beaumont, Tex.; son of Samuel Duard (an electrical engineer) and Opal Dane (Gibney) McLemore; married Patsy Marie Reaves, April 15, 1954; children: Jean Marie, Scott David. *Education:* Lamar College, student, 1948-49; University of Texas, B.S., 1952, M.A., 1956; Yale University, Ph.D 1960. *Home:* 5703 Delwood Dr., Austin, Tex. 78723. *Office:* 328 Burdine Hall, University of Texas, Austin, Tex. 78712.

CAREER: Austin (Tex.) public schools, social studies teacher, 1952-55; University of Texas, Galveston, assistant professor of sociology at Medical Branch, 1959-61; University of Texas, Austin, 1961—, began as assistant professor, now professor of sociology. *Military service:* U.S. Marine Corps. *Member:* American Sociological Society, Southwestern Social Science Association, Southwestern Sociological Society. *Awards, honors:* Commonwealth Fund fellowship.

WRITINGS: (With M. Vere De Vault) *Sociology,* Steck, 1962; (with Harley L. Browning) *A Statistical Profile of the Spanish-Surname Population of Texas,* Bureau of Business Research, University of Texas, 1964; (with Richard J. Hill) *Management-Training Effectiveness: A Study of Nurse Managers,* Bureau of Business Research, University of Texas, 1965; (with Hill and Charles M. Bonjean) *Sociological Measurement: An Inventory of Scales and Indices,* Chandler Publishing, 1967.

WORK IN PROGRESS: A continuation of an inventory of sociological scales and indices; the Spanish-surname population.

AVOCATIONAL INTERESTS: Chess, astronomy.

*   *   *

McLENDON, Will L(oving)   1925-

PERSONAL: Born August 26, 1925, in Center, Tex.; son of Will Clifton and Malissa (Loving) McLendon. Education: University of Texas, B.S., 1945; Middlebury College, M.A., 1947; University of Paris, doctorate, 1952. Office: Department of French, University of Houston, Houston, Tex. 77004.

CAREER: Texas Technological College (now Texas Tech University), Lubbock, instructor in French, 1947-48; Southern Methodist University, Dallas, Tex., instructor in French, 1950; University of Houston, Houston, Tex., assistant professor, 1953-63, associate professor, 1963-68, professor of French, 1968—. Television teacher of college French course, KUHT-TV, 1954-55. Military service: U.S. Naval Reserve, 1943-46. Member: American Association of Teachers of French, South-Central Modern Language Association (chairman, modern French literature section, 1955, 1958, 1967; chairman, comparative literature section, 1970), Alliance Francaise de Houston (member of board of directors, 1956-58; president, 1968-69).

WRITINGS: (Translator with Archibald Henderson, Jr.) Charles Mauron, Introduction to the Psychoanalysis of Mallarme, University of California Press, 1963. Contributor to PMLA, French Review, Orbis Litterarum, Comparative Literature, L 'Esprit Createur, Bulletin Marcel Proust, Symposium, Papers of Bibliographical Society of America, and Forum. Co-editor, Le Bayou, 1956-58.

SIDELIGHTS: McLendon lived in France more than three years and has made other trips there and traveled in North Africa, Europe, and Mexico.

BIOGRAPHICAL/CRITICAL SOURCES: Opera (Paris weekly), July 4, 1951.

*   *   *

McLEOD, Alan L(indsey) ' 1928-

PERSONAL: Born March 13, 1928, in Sydney, Australia; son of George B. and Helen (Allen) McLeod; married Marian B., September 11, 1954; children: Ross A. L., Helen E. Education: University of Sydney, B.A., M.A., and diploma in education, 1952; University of Melbourne, B.Ed., 1953; Pennsylvania State University, Ph.D., 1956. Politics: Independent. Religion: Presbyterian. Home: 201 Buckingham Ave., Trenton, N.J. 08618.

CAREER: State University of New York, College at Fredonia, associate professor of English, 1957-62; Lock Haven State College, Lock Haven, Pa., director of division of humanities, and professor of English, 1962-64, dean of liberal arts, 1964-66; Rider College, Trenton, N.J., professor of English and speech and dean of School of Arts and Sciences, 1966—. Member: American Association of University Professors, Modern Language Association of America (bibliographer), Speech Communication Association of America. Awards, honors: State University of New York research fellowship, 1962.

WRITINGS: (Editor with Richard Preston) The Lincoln Anthology, 1951, Futurian Press (Sydney), 1951; Beyond the Cresting Surf (poems), Boxwood Press, 1959; Rex Warner: Writer, Wentworth Press, 1960; (editor) The Commonwealth Pen: An Introduction to the Literature of the British Commonwealth, Cornell University Press, 1961; Chautauqua Canticles and Other Poems, Millbrook Press, 1962: (editor and contributor) The Pattern of Aus-

tralian Culture, Cornell University Press, 1963; (compiler) Walt Whitman in Australia and New Zealand: A Record of His Reception, Wentworth Press, 1964; (editor) The Achievement of Rex Warner, Wentworth Press, c.1965; Malaysian Literature, privately printed, 1966; (compiler with Eleanor Wyland) A Concordance to the Poems of Rex Warner, privately printed, 1967; (editor) The Pattern of New Zealand Culture, Cornell University Press, 1968; Australia Speaks, privately printed, 1969.

WORK IN PROGRESS: A History of Commonwealth Literature.

BIOGRAPHICAL/CRITICAL SOURCES: Books Abroad, summer, 1969.

*   *   *

McLUHAN, (Herbert) Marshall   1911-

PERSONAL: Born July 21, 1911, in Edmonton, Alberta, Canada; son of Herbert Ernest (a real estate and insurance salesman) and Elsie Naomi (Hall) McLuhan; married Corinne Keller Lewis, August 4, 1939; children: Eric, Mary (Mrs. Thomas James Colton), Teresa, Stephanie, Elizabeth, Michael. Education: University of Manitoba, B.A., 1932, M.A., 1934; Cambridge University, B.A., 1936, M.A., 1939, Ph.D., 1942. Religion: Roman Catholic. Home: 3 Wychwood Park, Toronto 4, Ontario, Canada. Office: Centre for Culture and Technology, University of Toronto, Toronto 5, Ontario, Canada.

CAREER: University of Wisconsin, Madison, instructor, 1936-37; St. Louis University, St. Louis, Mo., instructor in English, 1937-44; Assumption University, Windsor, Ontario, Canada, associate professor of English, 1944-46; St. Michael's College, University of Toronto, Toronto, Ontario, Canada, instructor, 1946—, professor of English, 1952—; chairman of Ford Foundation seminar on culture and communications, 1953-55; director of media project for U.S. Office of Education and National Association of Educational Broadcasters, 1959-60; creator (by appointment) and director of Centre for Culture and Technology, 1963—; Fordham University, New York, N.Y., Albert Schweitzer professor of humanities, 1967-68. Consultant to Johnson, McCormick & Johnson, Ltd. (public relations agency), Toronto, 1966—, and to Responsive Environments Corporation, New York, N.Y., 1968—. Appointed by Vatican as consultor of Pontifical Commission for Social Communications, 1973. Frequent lecturer and speaker on television and at universities in U.S. and Canada.

AWARDS, HONORS: Governor General's Literary Award (Canada) for critical prose, 1963, for The Gutenberg Galaxy; fellow, Royal Society of Canada, 1964; Fordham University communications award, 1964; Molson Prize of Canada Council for outstanding achievement in the social sciences, 1967; Niagara University award in culture and communications, 1967; Carl Einstein Preis, West Germany Critics Award, 1967; Companion of the Order of Canada, 1970; Institute of Public Relations President's Award (Great Britain), 1970; Christian Culture Award, Assumption University, 1971; Gold Medal award from President of the Italian Republic, 1971, for original work as philosopher of the mass media; President's Cabinet award, University of Detroit, 1972. D.Litt. from University of Windsor, 1965, Assumption University, 1966, University of Manitoba, 1967, Grinnell College, 1967, Simon Fraser University, 1967, St. John Fisher College, 1969, University of Alberta, 1971, University of Edmonton, and University of Western Ontario, 1972.

WRITINGS: Henry IV: A Mirror for Magistrates (originally published in University of Toronto Quarterly), [Toronto], 1948; The Mechanical Bride: Folklore of In-

dustrial Man, Vanguard, 1951; (editor and author of introduction) Alfred L. Tennyson, *Selected Poetry,* Rinehart, 1956; (editor with Edmund Carpenter) *Explorations in Communication* (anthology), Beacon Press, 1960; *The Gutenberg Galaxy: The Making of Typographic Man,* University of Toronto Press, 1962; *Understanding Media: The Extensions of Man* (originally written as a report to U.S. Office of Education, 1960), McGraw, 1964; (compiler and author of notes and commentary, with Richard J. Schoeck) *Voices of Literature* (anthology), Holt, 1964-65, reissued as *Voices of Literature: Sounds, Masks, Roles,* 1969; (with Quentin Fiore) *The Medium is the Massage: An Inventory to Effects* (advance excerpt published in *Publishers' Weekly,* April 3, 1967), designed by Jerome P. Agel, Bantam, 1967; (with Fiore) *War and Peace in the Global Village* (excerpt entitled "Fashion: A Bore War?" published in *Saturday Evening Post,* July 27, 1968), McGraw, 1968; (with Harley Parker) *Through the Vanishing Point: Space in Poetry and Painting,* Harper, 1968; *The Interior Landscape: The Literary Criticism of Marshall McLuhan, 1943-1962,* edited and compiled by Eugene McNamara & McLuhan, McGraw, 1969; *Counterblast,* designed by Parker, Harcourt, 1969; *Culture is Our Business,* McGraw, 1970; (with Wilfred Watson) *From Cliche to Archetype,* Viking, 1970; (with Barrington Nevitt) *Executives: Die-Hards and Drop-Outs: Management Lore in the Global Village,* Harcourt, 1971; (with Nevitt) *Take Today: The Executive as Dropout,* Harcourt, 1972. Also author of a monthly, multimedia newsletter, *The Marshall McLuhan Dew-Line Newsletter,* published by the Human Development Corporation, 1968—.

Contributor: *The Electronic Revolution* (published as a special issue of *American Scholar,* spring, 1966), United Chapters of Phi Beta Kapppa, 1966; Gerald Emanuel Stearn, editor, *McLuhan: Hot and Cool* (essays), Dial, 1967; Stanley T. Donner, editor, *The Meaning of Commercial Television* (Texas-Stanford seminar held in Asilomar, Calif., 1966), University of Texas Press, 1967; *Verbi-Voco-Visual Explorations* (originally published as Number 8 of *Explorations*), Something Else Press (New York), 1967; Richard Kostelanetz, editor, *Beyond Left and Right: Radical Thoughts for Our Times* (essays), Morrow, 1968; *Exploration of the Ways, Means, and Values of Museum Communication with the Viewing Public* (seminar held at the Museum of the City of New York, October 9-10, 1967), Museum of the City of New York, 1969; Lauro de Oliveira Lima, *Mutacoes em educacao Segundo McLuhan* (includes translation of part of an article by McLuhan), Editora Vozes, 1971. Co-editor of *Explorations,* 1954-59, editor, 1964—; member of editorial board of *Media and Methods,* 1967—. General editor, with Ernest Sirluck and Richard J. Schoeck of "Patterns of Literary Criticism" series, seven volumes, University of Chicago Press and University of Toronto Press, 1965-69. Contributor of articles and essays to numerous periodicals.

SIDELIGHTS: Marshall McLuhan, the Canadian communications specialist, has been described as "pop eschatology," "an intellectual mad-hatter," "the guru of the boob tube," "a communicator who can't communicate," "the Dr. Spock of pop culture," "a master of media mush," "a metaphysical wizard possessed by a spatial sense of madness," and "the high priest of popthink who conducts a Black Mass for dilettantes before the altar of historical determinism." Considered the oracle of the electronic age by advertising, television, and business executives who often admit they can't understand a word he says, he has made now-famous pronouncements on a vast range of contemporary issues, including education, religion, science, environment, politics, minority groups, war, violence, love, sex, hippies, clothing, jobs, music, computers, drugs, automobiles, television, and drop-outs.

His novel insights into the functions of modern mass media, and their implications for the future of our technological culture, have attracted international acclaim and vitriolic criticism. He has been hailed by many as "one of the few really great imaginations in the world today," and Tom Wolfe has suggested that he may be a genius on a level with Newton, Darwin, Freud, Einstein, and Pavlov. Others have denounced him as dangerously wrong-headed, a fakir, charlatan, and (to quote Anthony Quinton) "an academic sheep in Tom Wolfe's clothing." Dudley Young, paraphrasing Hugh Kenner, suggests that there are really three McLuhans, "a pop artist and thinker of considerable genius, a wildly irresponsible funnyman addicted to inaccurate generalization, and an ultimately sinister oracle whose prophecies may hasten the arrival of the millenial nirvana he contemplates." Neil Compton holds the opinion that "McLuhan is in danger of becoming to electronics what Norman Vincent Peale is to capitalism."

Whatever McLuhan may or may not be, one thing he has never been is ignored. In a review of *McLuhan: Hot & Cool,* "an intriguing new olio of things by and about the master," Thomas R. Edwards writes, "we are assured of his importance by ad men, hip Jesuits, Susan Sontag and various Canadians, assured of his folly by Dwight Macdonald, George P. Elliott, Christopher Ricks and other Urizenic tyrants of typographical law, assured of his mixed value by judicious Centrists like Harold Rosenberg, Jonathan Miller and George Steiner. But no one, least of all McLuhan himself, doubts that he has to be dealt with somehow." David Myers notes: "All that McLuhan himself will concede is that 'my work might produce considerable consequences for other people.' Yet it is, of course, these considerable consequences, real or imagined, that animate the controversy." As Elliott has said, "the professor has to be reckoned with.... McLuhan's teaching is radical, new, capable of moving people to social action. If he is wrong, it matters." He is, after all, not only a social analyst, as James P. Carey has observed; "he is also a prophet, a phenomenon, a happening, a social movement. His work has given rise to an ideology . . . and a mass movement producing seminars, clubs, art exhibits, and conferences in his name." According to a writer for *Newsweek,* he has even invaded the language: "The French apply the term *mcluhanisme* to the mixed-media world of pop art; more invidiously, 'McLuhan' has become a synonym for impenetrable prose."

Contrary to his public image, McLuhan is, by training, a man of letters. Richard Kostelanetz writes that his academic field was originally medieval and Renaissance literature; the subject of his Ph.D. thesis at Cambridge was the rhetoric of Thomas Nashe, the Elizabethan writer. Kostelanetz notes: "As a young scholar, he began his writing career, as every professor should, by contributing articles to the professional journals, and to this day, academic circles know him as the editor of a popular paperback textbook of Tennyson's poems. Moreover, his critical essays on writers as various as Gerard Manley Hopkins, John Dos Passos and Samuel Taylor Coleridge are frequently anthologized." At Cambridge "the lectures of I.A. Richards and F.R. Leavis stimulated his initial interest in studying popular culture," an interest which eventually led to his appointment as head of the University of Toronto's newly-founded Center for Culture and Technology, "to study the psychic and social consequences of technology and the media." McLuhan cites the major influences on his thought as Ezra Pound, Lewis Carroll, and James Joyce. When *Understanding Media* appeared in 1964, Kostelanetz writes, "several reviewers noted that [he] must have a book on James Joyce in him," a task he passed on to his son Eric, who has written a comprehensive critical study of the meaning of the ten thunderclaps in *Finnegan's Wake*. John M. Aden, however, in a review of *McLuhan: Pro and Con*, asserts: "Nathan Halper's 'Marshall McLuhan and Joyce' effectively discharges the important mission of disillusioning those, including McLuhan himself, who like to think of Mr. Media as resembling Joyce. 'When it comes to Joyce,' Mr. Halper justly remarks, 'McLuhan is a doodler.' "

In addition to his acknowledged mentors, who also include Harold Adams Innis and T.S. Eliot, McLuhan has been compared to such diverse thinkers as Teilhard de Chardin, Karl Marx (and Groucho Marx), Ralph Waldo Emerson, and Henry Adams, with regard to the various aspects of his view of the history of mass media as central to the history of civilization in general. The core of his argument, in essence, is that all communications media are extensions of [the sensory apparatus of] man which, by their very nature as "determinants of knowledge," dictate, as Carey states, "the character of perception and through perception the structure of mind." All other McLuhanisms (e.g., "linear," print-age man as opposed to "aural-tactile," electronic-age man, "hot" and "cool" media, etc.) are peripheral to his central thesis that "the medium is the message." Upon this basis he predicates seemingly endless hypotheses concerning the past, present, and future of civilization. McLuhan insists that his work is totally experimental and in a state of constant flux, which allows him a great deal of latitude to make the sweeping statements which so infuriate his critics. "Unless a statement is startling," he has said, "no one will pay any attention; they will put it down as a point of view.... I set up possibilities as probes all the time.... I don't necessarily agree with everything I say."

McLuhan is constantly accused of inconsistency, oversimplification, unconcern with truth and deception, indigenous and faulty reasoning, undermining of "the entire humanist heritage of art and science," confusion of origin and import, cause and effect; and myth and reality, and a basic misconception of human nature and behavior and of the methods and means of modern technology. "The force of McLuhan," Aden asserts, "is neither historical nor technological, but purely tendentious, and until we face this fact, and sift accordingly, he will continue to exercise a fatal fascination upon those genuinely desirous of being enlightened about their environment." Theodore Roszak's essay, "Summa Popologica" (included in *McLuhan: Pro and Con*), comes down hard on the pretense of expertise, reminding the reader that McLuhan "is no sort of specialist at all.... [He] doesn't prove his thesis; he browbeats you with it." Tom Nairn of the *New Statesman* seems to agree: "McLuhan is a monomaniac who happens to be hooked on something extremely important. We ought to be grateful. But the colossal evasiveness, the slipshod reasoning and weak-kneed glibness accompanying the mania make him dangerous going.... Capable of the most brilliant and stimulating insight into relationships other historians and social theorists have ignored, he systematically fails to develop this insight critically. Consequently, his view of the connection between media and society is an unbelievable shambles: his dream-logic turns necessary conditions into sufficient conditions, half-truths into sure things, the possible into a *fait accompli*." Kostelanetz finds that "McLuhan embodies that peculiarly North American capacity to push ideas, often derived from others, beyond conventional bounds to the wildest conclusions," which often results in a unique mixture of fact and theory, labeled by Dwight Macdonald as "impure nonsense, nonsense adulterated by sense."

Another characteristic of McLuhan which frequently incurs the wrath of his readers is the intricacy of his style. One critic has said that a decade ago "only McLuhan and God knew what McLuhan was talking about. Today I'm not sure God still knows." Referring to his theories, McLuhan himself admits: "I don't pretend to understand them. After all, my stuff is very difficult." "McLuhanese" has been described by Elliott as "deliberately antilogical, circular, repetitious, unqualified, gnomic, outrageous," and by Christopher Ricks as "a viscous fog through which loom stumbling metaphors." Many believe that he is incapable of making a statement, as D.W. Harding has said, "sufficiently unambiguous, with terms sufficiently defined, to be capable of proof or disproof." Geoffrey Wagner writes: "When the excitable Tom Wolfe yips, 'What if he's right?,' Ricks rightly retorts that he can't be anything but right 'since by now he's committed himself to contradictory opinions on everything.' " Others view this ambivalence as absolute proof of his neutrality in defining the complexities of human interinvolvement. "Such is the Western devotion to facts that the mere stating of any case is considered a hostile act," McLuhan contends. He told a *Playboy* interviewer: "I don't *approve* of the global village. I say we live in it." He claims that he is "merely extrapolating . . . current process[es] to [their] logical conclusion" rather than predicting the future of our technological age, and would in fact prefer the relative simplicity of pre-literate society to the complex pressures of our current electronic culture. John Culkin of Fordham University supports the detachment of McLuhan's viewpoint: "Too many people are eager to write off Marshall McLuhan or to reduce him to the nearest and handiest platitude which explains him to them. He deserves better . . . he didn't invent electricity or put kids in front of TV sets; he is merely trying to describe what's happening out there so that it can be dealt with intelligently. When someone warns you of an oncoming truck, it's frightfully impolite to accuse him of driving the thing." Edward J. Hundert's opinion lends further credence to McLuhan's claim to objectivity: "[He] is a Canadian, thus living in a society exhibiting the marks of cultural imperialism, or what Spengler called 'pseudomorphosis.' The neighboring civilization is so overpowering that it on the one hand absorbs a society as regards the forms of its discourse, yet leaves the consciousness of its population behind. Sociologists have called this cultural lag and McLuhan has made it a central feature of his inquiry. He has often said that the main satisfaction he derived from living in Canada was that it permitted him to lead a 'slower' existence than in the United States, while at the same time be part of a technological revolution. . . . This standing apart from his object has permitted him to see America (for this is his real subject) with the shrewd understanding of Montesquieu's Persians. He writes as a visitor in an alien land, yet the reader is always aware that his amazement at the strange habits of the inhabitants is a device of social commentary. McLuhan sees that we tell each other things in a new way, and because of this, we tell each other new things."

McLuhan the philosopher seems to be a personality apart from McLuhan the conversationalist. Richard Schickel finds that "conversation with McLuhan is by far the most satisfying means of getting to know his mind. There is a charisma about him, a wayward, egocentric, and disarming charm that is absent from his books. . . . He cheerfully admits that the loneliness of the scholar in his library, the writer at his typewriter, is not really for him. 'I have to engage in endless dialogue before I write; I want to *talk* a subject over and over and over.' " Some of his peers see McLuhan as a poet rather than a philosopher or scientist; in this respect they maintain that "you can't argue with him, just as you can't argue with Tennyson or Browning." Rosenberg calls him "a belated Whitman singing the body electric with Thomas Edison as accompanist." Myers considers McLuhan an "elated Teilhard de Chardin . . . a religious ecstatic who attempts . . .

to master the world by rejecting it into the future." "The meaning of McLuhan is not in his message, his sentences," writes Carey in a comparison of McLuhan with Innis, "but is his *persona* as a social actor, in himself as a vessel of social meaning. . . . Unlike the traditional scholar, McLuhan deals with reality not by trying to understand it but by prescribing an attitude to take toward it. McLuhan is a poet of technology. His work represents a secular prayer to technology, a magical incantation of the gods, designed to quell one's fears that, after all, the machines may be taking over. . . . He represents . . . the ultimate triumph of the technical over the moral, for he tells us that concerns for morals and values and meanings in the age of electric circuitry are unnecessary. . . . Ultimately, McLuhan himself is a medium and that is his message."

What McLuhan actually says, to echo his admirers, may not be as important as the way in which he says it. "The first and most vital step of all," McLuhan concludes, "is simply to understand media and its revolutionary effects on all psychic and social values and institutions. . . . If we diagnose what is happening to us, we can reduce the ferocity of the winds of change and bring the best elements of the old visual culture, during this transitional period, into peaceful coexistence with the new retribalized society. If we persist, however, in our conventional rear-view-mirror approach to these cataclysmic developments, all of Western culture will be destroyed and swept into the dustbin of history." In the final analysis, perhaps McLuhan is "profoundly humanistic," as Kostelanetz believes, "precisely because his thought presumes that mankind, by recognizing technology's importance, can overcome its determining power and shape the social environment to his needs."

A happening entitled "McLuhan Megillah," based on *Understanding Media* and *The Gutenberg Galaxy* and combining dance, film, painting, poetry, sculpture, and other art forms, was produced at Al Hansen's Third Rail Time/Space Theatre in Greenwich Village in January of 1966. A McLuhan television special based on *The Medium is the Massage* was produced on NBC-TV, March 19, 1967. In 1967 Columbia Records released a four-track LP (Columbia CL 2701, stereo 9501), based on *The Medium is the Massage* and produced by Jerome P. Agel. The *Marshall McLuhan Dew-Line Newsletter,* billed as "a startling, shocking Early Warning System for our era of instant change," is published in the form of records, courses, sensory retraining kits, and advance chapters from McLuhan's books.

BIOGRAPHICAL/CRITICAL SOURCES: Book Week, June 7, 1964; *Books,* September, 1965, January, 1967; *Harper's,* November, 1965; *Life,* February 25, 1966; *Newsweek,* February 28, 1966, March 6, 1967; *Village Voice,* May 12, 1966, December 26, 1970; *Vogue,* July, 1966; Gerald Emanuel Stearn, editor, *McLuhan: Hot & Cool* (essays), Dial, 1967; *Commonweal,* January 20, 1967; *New York Times Magazine,* January 29, 1967; *Saturday Night,* February, 1967; *Kenyon Review,* March, 1967; *Antioch Review,* spring, 1967; *New Statesman,* September 22, 1967; *Listener,* September 28, 1967, October 19, 1967; *Times Literary Supplement,* September 28, 1967; *American Dialog,* autumn, 1967; *Western Humanities Review,* autumn, 1967; *Book World,* October 29, 1967; *New York Review of Books,* November 23, 1967, January 2, 1969; *Nation,* December 4, 1967; Harry H. Crosby and George R. Bond, compilers, *The McLuhan Explosion* (casebook on McLuhan and *Understanding Media*), American Book Company, 1968; Sidney Walter Finkelstein, *Sense and Nonsense of McLuhan,* International Publishers, 1968; Raymond Rosenthal, editor, *McLuhan: Pro and Con* (essays), Funk, 1968; *Partisan Review,* summer, 1968; *New York Times Book Review,*

September 8, 1968; *National Review,* November 19, 1968; *Canadian Forum,* February, 1969; *Playboy,* March, 1969; *Sewanee Review,* spring, 1969; *New Republic,* February 7, 1970; *Twentieth Century Literature,* July, 1970; *Books and Bookmen,* March, 1971; Jonathan Miller, *Marshall McLuhan,* Viking, 1971; Donald F. Theall, *The Medium is the Rear View Mirror: Understanding McLuhan,* McGill-Queens University Press, 1971; *L'Express,* February 14-20, 1972.†

* * *

McMAHON, Joseph H(enry) 1930-

PERSONAL: Born October 21, 1930, in New York, N.Y.; son of Thomas Anthony (a lawyer) and Catharine (Freeman) McMahon. *Education:* Manhattan College, A.B., 1952; graduate study at University of Paris, 1952-53, and University of Fribourg, 1953-54; Stanford University, A.M., 1959, Ph.D., 1960. *Politics:* Democrat. *Home:* 274 Court St., Middletown, Conn. 06457. *Agent:* Curtis Brown Ltd., 60 East 56th St., New York, N.Y. 10022. *Office:* Department of Romance Languages, Wesleyan University, Middletown, Conn. 06457.

CAREER: Yale University, New Haven, Conn., instructor, 1960-63, assistant professor, 1963-66, associate professor of French, 1967-68, assistant master at Pierson College, 1960-62, dean of Pierson College, 1963-66, fellow of Pierson College, 1968—; Wesleyan University, Middletown, Conn., associate professor of Romance languages, 1968—, dean, 1968-69, chairman of department, 1973—. *Military service:* U.S. Army, 1955-57. *Member:* American Association of University Professors (member of Connecticut State conference, 1964-67), American Association of Teachers of French. *Awards, honors:* Morse fellowship, 1966-67; Guggenheim fellowship, 1972.

WRITINGS: The Imagination of Jean Genet, Yale University Press, 1963; *Humans Being: The World of Jean-Paul Sartre,* University of Chicago Press, 1971. Editor, *Yale French Studies,* 1963-66.

WORK IN PROGRESS: In Reality: A Reading of Jean-Jacques Rousseau's "La Nouvelle Heloise."

BIOGRAPHICAL/CRITICAL SOURCES: New York Times Book Review, March 14, 1971.

* * *

McNEAL, Robert H(atch) 1930-

PERSONAL: Born February 8, 1930, son of Harold George McNeal; married Jacqueline Pickard Frost, October 25, 1952; children: Martha Beatrice, Andrew Frost, Jeffrey Sherman. *Education:* Yale University, B.A., 1952; Columbia University, M.A. and Certificate of Russian Institute, 1954, Ph.D., 1958. *Residence:* Toronto, Ontario, Canada.

CAREER: Princeton University, Princeton, N.J., instructor in history, 1954-58; University of Alberta, Edmonton, 1958-62, began as assistant professor, became associate professor of history; McMaster University, Hamilton, Ontario, associate professor of history, 1962-64; University of Toronto, Toronto, Ontario, associate professor of history, 1964-69; University of Massachusetts, Amherst, professor of history, 1969—. *Military service:* U.S. Army Reserve, 1950-64; became captain. *Member:* American Historical Association, American Association for Advancement of Slavic Studies, Phi Beta Kappa.

WRITINGS: The Russian Revolution: Why Did the Bolsheviks Win?, Rinehart, 1959; (translator with Tova Yedlin) Sergei Germanovich Pushkarev, *The Emergence of Modern Russia, 1801-1919,* Holt, 1963; *The Bolshevik Tradition: Lenin, Stalin, Khrushchev,* Prentice-Hall, 1963; (editor) *Lenin, Stalin, Krushchev: Voices of Bolshevism,* Prentice-Hall, 1963; (compiler) *Stalin's Works: An An-*

notated *Bibliography,* Hoover Institution, 1967; (editor) *International Relations Among Communists,* Prentice-Hall, 1967; (editor) *Russia in Transition 1905-1914: Evolution or Revolution?,* Holt, 1970; *Bride of the Revolution: Krupskaya and Lenin,* University of Michigan Press, 1972; *Guide to the Decisions of the Communist Party of the Soviet Union, 1917-1967,* University of Toronto Press, 1972. Contributor to political science and history journals.

BIOGRAPHICAL/CRITICAL SOURCES: Detroit News, June 18, 1972; *New York Times,* June 19, 1972.

*   *   *

McNEILL, Janet   1907-

PERSONAL: Born September 14, 1907, in Dublin, Ireland; daughter of William (a minister) and Jeannie P. (Hogg) McNeill; married Robert P. Alexander (a civil engineer, now retired), June 24, 1933; children: Robert McNeill, David Bradbury, James Connor, Frances Margaret. *Education:* University of St. Andrews, M.A., 1929. *Home:* 3, Grove Park, Bristol BS 66 PP, England. *Agent:* A.P. Watt & Son, 26/28 Bedford Row, London WC1R 4H1, England.

CAREER: Belfast Telegraph, Belfast, Northern Ireland, staff member, 1929-33; free-lance writer. Northern Ireland British Broadcasting Corp. Advisory Council, member, 1959-63; has appeared on television for British Broadcasting Corp. and for Ulster Television. *Member:* Royal Ulster Academy of Art (patron), Irish P.E.N. Club (chairman, Belfast branch, 1956-57).

WRITINGS—Novels: *A Child in the House,* Hodder & Stoughton, 1955; *Tea at Four O'Clock,* Hodder & Stoughton, 1956; *The Other Side of the Wall,* Hodder & Stoughton, 1957; *A Furnished Room,* Hodder & Stoughton, 1958; *Search Party,* Hodder & Stoughton, 1959; *As Strangers Here,* Hodder & Stoughton, 1960; *The Early Harvest,* Bles, 1962; *The Maiden Dinosaur,* Bles, 1964, published in America as *The Belfast Friends,* Houghton, 1966; *Talk to Me,* Bles, 1965; *The Small Widow,* Bles, 1967, Atheneum, 1968.

Children's books: *My Friend Specs McCann,* Faber, 1955; *A Pinch of Salt,* Faber, 1956; *A Light Dozen* (stories), Faber, 1957; *Specs Fortissimo,* Faber, 1958; *This Happy Morning,* Faber, 1959; *Special Occasions* (stories), Faber, 1960; *Various ,Specs,* Faber, 1961, Thomas Nelson, 1970; *Try These for Size,* Faber, 1963; *The Giant's Birthday,* Walck, 1964; *Tom's Tower,* Faber, 1965, Little, Brown, 1967; *The Mouse and the Mirage,* Walck, 1966; *The Battle of St. George Without,* Little, Brown, 1966; *I Didn't Invite You to My Party,* Hamish Hamilton, 1967; *The Run-Around Robins,* Hamish Hamilton, 1967; *Goodbye, Dove Square* (Junior Literary Guild selection), Little, Brown, 1969; *Dragons, Come Home, and Other Stories,* Hamish Hamilton, 1969; *It's Snowing Outside,* Macmillan, 1969; *Umbrella Thursday,* Hamish Hamilton, 1969; *The Day They Lost Grandad,* Macmillan, 1969; *Best Specs,* Faber, 1970; *The Other People,* Little, Brown, 1970; *The Youngest Kite,* Hamish Hamilton, 1970; *The Prisoner in the Park,* Faber, 1971, Little, Brown, 1972; *Much Too Much Magic,* Hamish Hamilton, 1971; *A Helping Hand,* Hamish Hamilton, 1971; *Wait for It, and Other Stories,* Faber, 1972; *A Snow Clean Pinny,* Hamish Hamilton, 1972; *A Monster Too Many,* Little, Brown, 1972; *A Fairy Called Andy Perks,* Hamish Hamilton, 1972.

Plays: *Gospel Truth,* H.R. Carter Publications, 1951; (librettist) *Finn and the Black Hag* (children's opera), Novello, 1962; (librettist) "Graduation Ode" (opera), first produced in Belfast, 1963; *Switch-On, Switch-Off, and Other Plays,* Faber, 1968. Author of some twenty ra-

dio plays. Contributor of articles and stories to digests, anthologies, newspapers, and magazines.

SIDELIGHTS: Miss McNeill told *CA:* "I have been writing more and more for children as I grow older, which may strike readers as a little contradictory. I think the answer may be that in a rapidly changing world a middle-aged woman tends to feel a little ill-at-ease, perhaps something of an anachronism, and is apt to return to childhood and childhood memories for refreshment and the imaginative exploration a writer seeks for.

"I still find writing laborious, exhausting, sometimes tedious, but am never happy unless I am absorbed in it! I never—except perhaps in an educational book—write consciously with any other child in mind than myself!"

In a review of *The Battle of St. George Without,* Houston L. Maples states: "Miss McNeil renders its [the locale of Dove Square, London] sights and sounds, its congested, noisy vitality with splendid verve, a dry sense of humor and an altogether remarkable ability to reveal with a few beautifully turned phrases the essence of a mood, place or emotional dilemma." Of *The Small Widow,* Martin Levin comments: "The author is very good at shading one emotional state into another: grief, nostalgia, despair. These are universals as old as time, but Miss McNeill is a sensitive observer who sees them afresh."

Search Party and some of her children's stories have been translated into Dutch, a number of stories reproduced in Braille, one included in an Afrikans anthology, and others adapted for television. *Specs McCann* appeared for two years as a cartoon strip in the *Belfast Telegraph; A Child in the House* was filmed and televised, and *The Battle of St. George Without* was televised as a serial by British Broadcasting Corp., December, 1969.

AVOCATIONAL INTERESTS: Gardening, drama, working with the juvenile court and girls' clubs.

BIOGRAPHICAL/CRITICAL SOURCES: Book World, May 5, 1968; *New York Times Book Review,* August 11, 1968; *Times Literary Supplement,* June 29, 1969.

*   *   *

McNEW, Ben(nie) B(anks)   1931-

PERSONAL: Born November 12, 1931, in Greenbrier, Ark.; son of R.H. (a teacher) and Stella (Avery) McNew; married Bonnie Stone, March 31, 1956; children: Bonnie Banks, Mary Kathleen, William Michael. *Education:* Arkansas State Teachers College, B.S., 1953; University of Arkansas, M.B.A., 1954; University of Texas, Ph.D., 1961. *Religion:* Methodist. *Home address:* P.O. Box 122, University, Miss. 38677.

CAREER: U.S. Treasury Department, St. Louis, Mo., assistant national bank examiner, 1954-56; Industrial Research and Extension Center, University of Arkansas, Little Rock, industrial specialist, 1956-59; University of Texas, Austin, lecturer in finance, 1959-61; University of Mississippi, University, professor of economics and banking, 1961-68, dean of School of Business Administration, 1968—. *Military service:* U.S. Army, 1950-51. *Member:* American Finance Association, Southern Economic Association, Southwestern Social Science Association, Beta Gamma Sigma, Phi Kappa Phi, Delta Sigma Pi, Omicron Delta Kappa, Lions International (president, Oxford, Miss. chapter, 1964-65).

WRITINGS: (With John M. Peterson) *Average Hourly Earnings in Arkansas Manufacturing,* Industrial Research and Extension Center, University of Arkansas, 1957; *Financial Resources,* Mississippi Economic Council, State Chamber of Commerce, 1962; (with Charles L. Prather) *Fraud Control for Commercial Banks,* Irwin, 1962; (contributor) L.E. Davids, editor, *Money and Banking Casebook*, Irwin, 1966; (contributor) W.H. Baughn and C.E. Walker, editors, *The Bankers' Handbook*, Dow Jones-Irwin, 1966. Contributor of articles on finance and economics to professional journals.

AVOCATIONAL INTERESTS: Hunting, fishing.

* * *

McNICKLE, (William) D'Arcy 1904-

PERSONAL: Born January 18, 1904, in St. Ignatius, Mont.; son of William (a rancher) and Philomene (Parenteau) McNickle; married Roma Kaufman (an editor), September 13, 1939; children: Antoinette, Kathleen. *Education:* Attended University of Montana, 1921-25, Oxford University, 1925-26, University of Grenoble, 1931. *Politics:* Democrat. *Home:* 205 Devon Pl., Boulder, Colo. 80302.

CAREER: Editorial work in New York, N.Y., 1926-35; Federal Writers Project, Washington, D.C., staff writer, 1935-36; Bureau of Indian Affairs, Washington, D.C., 1936-52, began as assistant to commissioner, became field representative and director of tribal relations; American Indian Development, Inc., Boulder, Colo., director, 1952—. Member of Colorado State Advisory Committee, U.S. Commission on Civil Rights. *Member:* American Anthropological Association (fellow), Society for Applied Anthropology, Current Anthropology (associate). *Awards, honors:* Guggenheim fellowship, 1963-64.

WRITINGS: The Surrounded (fiction), Dodd, 1936; *They Came Here First: The Epic of the American Indian*, Lippincott, 1949; *Runner in the Sun: A Story of Indian Maize* (fiction), Winston, 1954; (with Harold E. Fey) *Indians and Other Americans: Two Ways of Life Meet*, Harper, 1959; *The Indian Tribes of the United States: Ethnic and Cultural Survival*, Oxford University Press, 1962; *Indian Man: A Life of Oliver La Farge*, Indiana University Press, 1971. Contributor to *Encyclopaedia Britannica*.

WORK IN PROGRESS: A novel about contemporary Indian life; book-length report on community development project.

SIDELIGHTS: Member of the Confederated Salish and Kutenai tribes of the Flathead Indian reservation in western Montana.

* * *

McNIERNEY, Mary Alice

PERSONAL: Born in Newark, N.J.; daughter of Edward T. (an engineer) and Regina (Mulcahy) McNierney. *Education:* Trenton State College, B.S. in Education, 1948; Douglass College, B.L.S., 1950; Columbia University, M.L.S., 1960. *Religion:* Roman Catholic. *Home:* 100 West 12th St., New York, N.Y. 10011. *Office:* Bache & Co., 36 Wall St., New York, N.Y. 10005.

CAREER: Cleveland Public Library, Cleveland, Ohio, reference assistant in business information bureau, 1950-52; Special Services Division, U.S. Army, Europe, librarian, 1952-56; Standard & Poor's Corp., New York, N.Y., reference librarian, 1956-60; Bache & Co., New York, N.Y., chief librarian, 1960—. *Member:* Special Libraries Association, Phi Beta Mu. *Awards, honors:* Directory of Business and Financial Services included in Library Journal list of best reference works of 1963.

WRITINGS: (Editor) *Directory of Business and Financial Services*, 6th edition, Special Libraries Association, 1963. Contributor to library journals.

WORK IN PROGRESS: Investment and Investment Analysis Information Sources, for Gale.

McPHAUL, John J. 1904-
(Jack McPhaul)

PERSONAL: Surname is pronounced Mac-*fall;* born June 19, 1904, in Chicago, Ill.; son of Albert A. (a merchant) and Anna (McNamara) McPhaul; married Margaret Collison, January 21, 1929. *Education:* Attended parochial schools in Chicago, Ill. *Politics:* Independent. *Home and office:* 2020 North Howe St., Chicago, Ill. 60614.

CAREER: Chicago Herald-Examiner, Chicago, Ill., 1923-38, began as reporter, became night city editor; *Sun-Times* (formerly *Chicago Times*), Chicago, Ill., 1942-70, news reporter, sports writer, book editor, and feature writer. *Member:* Society of Midland Authors (president, 1965-67), Chicago Newspaper Guild, Chicago Press Veterans Association (director; president, 1966-67), Chicago Press Club. *Awards, honors:* Heywood Broun Medal, American Newspaper Guild, 1946, for best domestic reporting; journalism awards from Sigma Delta Chi, Mystery Writers of America, Headline Club of Atlantic City, and Chicago Newspaper Guild; Friends of Literature award for best nonfiction book of 1962 by a Chicago author, 1963, for *Deadlines and Monkeyshines: The Fabled World of Chicago Journalism;* Chicago Press Veteran of the Year, 1969; Society of Midland Authors award for *Johnny Torrio: First of the Gang Lords.*

WRITINGS: (With John H. Lyle) *The Dry and Lawless Years,* Prentice-Hall, 1960; *Deadlines and Monkeyshines: The Fabled World of Chicago Journalism,* Prentice-Hall, 1962; *Johnny Torrio: First of the Gang Lords,* Arlington House, 1970.

WORK IN PROGRESS: Men and Events of Chicago.

BIOGRAPHICAL/CRITICAL SOURCES: Library Journal, September 1, 1970.

* * *

McPHERSON, James M. 1936-

PERSONAL: Born October 11, 1936, in Valley City, N.D.; son of James Munro (a high school teacher) and Miriam (Osborn) McPherson; married Patricia A. Rasche, December 28, 1957; children: Joanna Erika. *Education:* Gustavus Adolphus College, B.A., 1958; Johns Hopkins University, Ph.D., 1963. *Politics:* Democratic. *Religion:* Presbyterian. *Home:* 15 Randall Rd., Princeton, N.J. 08540. *Office:* Department of History, Princeton University, Princeton, N.J. 08540.

CAREER: Princeton University, Princeton, N.J., instructor, 1962-65, assistant professor, 1965-66, associate professor of history, 1966—. *Member:* American Historical Association, Association for the Study of Negro Life and History, Organization of American Historians, Southern Historical Association, Phi Beta Kappa. *Awards, honors:* Proctor and Gamble faculty fellowship; Anisfield-Wolff Award in Race Relations, 1965, for *The Struggle for Equality: Abolitionists and the Negro in the Civil War and Reconstruction;* Guggenheim fellowship; National Endowment for the Humanities fellowship.

WRITINGS: The Struggle for Equality: Abolitionists and the Negro in the Civil War and Reconstruction, Princeton University Press, 1964; (editor) *The Negro's Civil War: How American Negroes Felt and Acted in the War for the Union,* Pantheon, 1965; (contributor) Martin B. Duberman, editor, *The Anti-Slavery Vanguard: New Essays on Abolitionism,* Princeton University Press, 1965; (editor) *Marching Toward Freedom: The Negro in the Civil War, 1861-1865,* Knopf, 1968; (contributor) Barton J. Bernstein, editor, *Towards a New Past: Dissenting Essays in American History,* Pantheon, 1968; (with others) *Blacks in America: Bibliographical Essays,* Doubleday, 1971. Contributor of articles to *American Histori-*

cal Review, Journal of American History, Journal of Negro History, Caribbean Studies, Phylon, Mid-America, and other publications.

WORK IN PROGRESS: The Antislavery Legacy: From Reconstruction to the NAACP, for Pantheon.

BIOGRAPHICAL/CRITICAL SOURCES: Book World, May 5, 1968; *Commonweal,* May 24, 1968; *National Observer,* November 4, 1968.

*   *   *

McQUAIG, Jack Hunter

PERSONAL: Born in Toronto, Ontario, Canada; married; children: five. *Education:* Queen's University, Kingston, Ontario, B. Com., 1937; University of Toronto, M.A. *Home:* 8 De Vere Gardens, Toronto 12, Ontario, Canada. *Office:* 330 Bay St., Toronto 2, Ontario, Canada.

CAREER: McQuaig Ferguson Ltd. (industrial psychologists), Toronto, Ontario, Canada, 1947—. President, McQuaig Institute of Executive Development, New York, N.Y., 1955.

WRITINGS: How to Pick Men, Fell, 1963; *How to Motivate Men,* Fell, 1967; *Your Business, Your Son and You: A Guide for a Successful Father and Son Business Relationship,* B. Klein, 1971.

*   *   *

McQUOWN, F(rederic) R(ichard) 1907-

PERSONAL: Born January 4, 1907, in London, England; son of Frederic Charles and Dorothy (Billett) McQuown. *Education:* Attended Westminster School; Christ Church, Oxford, B.Æ., 1928, M.A., 1932. *Politics:* Conservative. *Religion:* Anglican. *Home:* 39 Farm Ave., London NW2 2BJ, England.

CAREER: Barrister-at-law in private practice, London, England, 1931—. *Military service:* Royal Air Force, 1940-45; became flight lieutenant. *Member:* British National Carnation Society (president, 1955, 1970), Royal Horticultural Society (chairman, joint border carnation and joint Dianthus committees), Honorable Society of Gray's Inn, Linnean Society (fellow).

WRITINGS: (Editor) *The Pinks Register,* British National Carnation Society, 1952, supplement, 1955; *Pinks: Selection and Cultivation,* MacGibbon & Kee, 1955, Branford, 1956; *Intelligent Gardening: A Practical Guide to Labour-Saving Methods,* Collingridge, 1958; *Plant Breeding for Gardeners: A Guide to Practical Hybridizing,* Collingridge, 1963, revised edition, David & Charles, 1972; *Carnations and Pinks,* Collingridge, 1965, revised edition, David & Charles, 1970, Fernhill, 1971; *Fine-Flowered Cacti: Epiphyllums and Others for Home and Greenhouse,* Collingridge, 1965, revised edition, David & Charles, 1971, A.S. Barnes, 1972. Contributor of articles to *Gardeners Chronicle* and *Amateur Gardening.*

AVOCATIONAL INTERESTS: Gardening, radio, photography.

*   *   *

MEAD, Russell (M., Jr.) 1935-

PERSONAL: Born January 1, 1935, in Pueblo, Colo.; son of Russell M. (a salesman) and Marjorie (Moreno) Mead; married Florence Guyer, September 12, 1956; children: Judith Ann, Roger William, Michael Evin. *Education:* Dartmouth College, A.B., 1956. *Agent:* Brandt & Brandt, 101 Park Ave., New York, N.Y. 10017.

CAREER: Concord Academy, Concord, Mass., teacher of English, 1962-71, headmaster, 1971—. *Member:* Asso-

ciation of American Rhodes Scholars. *Awards, honors:* Rhodes Scholar, 1956; fellow in juvenile literature, Bread Loaf Writers' Conference.

WRITINGS: If a Heart Rings—Answer (teen-age novel), Dutton, 1964; *Tell Me Again About Snow White* (teen-age novel), Dutton, 1965.

WORK IN PROGRESS: The Tales Men Tell, contemporary mythology.

*   *   *

MEAD, (Edward) Shepherd 1914-

PERSONAL: Born April 26, 1914, in St. Louis, Mo.; son of Edward (a salesman) and Sarah (Woodward) Mead; married Annabelle Pettibone, September 18, 1943; children: Sally Ann, Shepherd, Edward. *Education:* Washington University, St. Louis, Mo., B.A., 1936. *Politics:* "Usually votes Democratic." *Home:* La Colombelle, En Marin, 1066 Epalinges, Switzerland. *Agent:* Scott Meredith, 580 Fifth Ave., New York, N.Y. 10036.

CAREER: Benton and Bowles, Inc., New York, N.Y., 1936-56, began as mail room clerk, became vice-president, 1951; S.H. Benson Ltd., London, England, consultant, 1958-62. *Member:* P.E.N., Phi Beta Kappa, Montchoisi Tennis Club.

WRITINGS: The Magnificent MacInnes, Farrar, Straus, 1949; *Tessie, the Hound of Channel One,* Doubleday, 1951; *How to Succeed in Business Without Really Trying: The Dastard's Guide to Fame and Fortune,* Simon & Schuster, 1952; *The Big Ball of Wax: A Story of Tomorrow's Happy World,* Simon & Schuster, 1954; *How to Get Rich in TV Without Really Trying,* Simon & Schuster, 1956; *How to Succeed with Women Without Really Trying: The Dastard's Guide to the Birds and the Bees,* Ballantine, 1957; *The Admen* (Reader's Digest Book Club selection), Simon & Schuster, 1958; *The Four Window Girl; or, How to Make More Money Than Men,* Simon & Schuster, 1959; *"Dudley, There Is No Tomorrow!" "Then How About This Afternoon?,"* Simon & Schuster, 1963; *How to Live Like a Lord Without Really Trying: A Confidential Manual Prepared as Part of a Survival Kit for Americans Living in Britain,* Macdonald & Co., 1964, Simon & Schuster, 1965; *The Carefully Considered Rape of the World,* Simon & Schuster, 1966; *How to Succeed at Business Spying by Trying,* Simon & Schuster, 1968; *Er; or, The Brassbound Beauty, the Bearded Bicyclist, and the Gold-Colored Teen-Age Grandfather,* Simon & Schuster, 1969; *How to Stay Medium-Young Practically Forever Without Really Trying,* Simon & Schuster, 1971; *Free the Male Man!: The Manifesto of the Men's Liberation Movement,* Simon & Schuster, 1972.

SIDELIGHTS: The musical play, based on Mead's book with the same title, "How to Succeed in Business Without Really Trying," was written by Frank Loesser and Abe Burrows, and won the Pulitzer Prize, 1962. It opened on Broadway in October, 1961, ran for more than four years, and was made into a motion picture. The *New Yorker* calls it "the saga of a young egomaniac who skips to the top of the mercantile world by duplicity, chicanery, and just plain gall." On February 10, 1964, the French version opened in Paris, other foreign versions were produced in London, Tokyo, Johannesburg, Copenhagen, Rome, Stockholm and West Berlin.

AVOCATIONAL INTERESTS: Tennis, skiing.

BIOGRAPHICAL/CRITICAL SOURCES: St. Louis Post-Dispatch, December 31, 1961; *New York Times,* May 30, 1968; *Best Sellers,* June 15, 1968, November 1, 1969; *New York Times Book Review,* June 23, 1968, October 26, 1969; *Books and Bookmen,* December, 1969.

MEADE, Dorothy (Joan Sampson) 1923-

PERSONAL: Born in 1923, in Cambridge, England; daughter of Michael Trevisky (a research chemist) and Phyllis (Seward) Sampson; married Peter Meade (a furnishings contracts manager), April 11, 1953; children: Christopher John, Clare Nicola. Education: Attended St. Paul's Girls' School, London, England; Queen Mary College, London, B.A., 1944. Home: 3 Arkwright Rd., Hampstead, London N.W.3, England. Agent: Richmond Towers & Benson Ltd., 14 Essex St., London W.C.2, England.

CAREER: Council of Industrial Design, London, England, exhibitions organizer, 1946-56. Military service: British Women's Reserve Naval Service, 1944-46.

WRITINGS: (With Brenda Rattray) Free for All, English Theatre Guild, 1959; (with Phoebe De Syllas) Design to Fit Family, Penguin, 1965; Bedrooms: Practical Bedrooms for Today, Macdonald & Co. with Council of Industrial Design, 1967, revised edition, 1972. Contributor of fiction and articles on design to periodicals.

AVOCATIONAL INTERESTS: Gardening, entertaining, and going to the theatre.

* * *

MEANS, Marianne Hansen 1934-

PERSONAL: Born June 13, 1934, in Sioux City, Iowa; daughter of Ernest Maynard (president, Ingwersen Bros. Commission Co.) and Else Marie Johanne (Andersen) Hansen. Education: University of Nebraska, B.A., 1956. Home: 1521 31st St. N.W., Washington, D.C. 20037. Office: 1701 Pennsylvania Ave., Washington, D.C. 20006.

CAREER: Dakota County Star, South Sioux City, Neb., reporter, 1954; Lincoln Journal, Lincoln, Neb., copy editor, 1955-57; Northern Virginia Sun, Arlington, Va., woman's editor, 1957-59; Hearst Newspapers, Washington, D.C., Washington bureau correspondent, 1959-61; White House correspondent, 1961-65; King Features Syndicate, Washington, D.C., national affairs columnist, 1965—. Women's Savings Bond Committee, Washington, D.C., member, 1958-63. Member: White House Correspondents Association, Washington Press Club, Phi Beta Kappa, Kappa Tau Alpha, Theta Sigma Phi, Delta Delta Delta. Awards, honors: Front Page Award, New York Newspaperwomen's Club, 1962.

WRITINGS: The Woman in the White House: The Lives, Times, and Influence of Twelve Notable First Ladies, Random House, 1963. Contributor to magazines.

BIOGRAPHICAL/CRITICAL SOURCES: Library Journal, August, 1963, December 15, 1963; Christian Science Monitor, August 22, 1963; New York Herald Tribune Book Review, August 25, 1963; Best Sellers, September 1, 1963.

* * *

MEDLICOTT, William Norton 1900-

PERSONAL: Born May 11, 1900, in Wandsworth, England; son of William Norton (a newspaper editor) and Margaret Louisa (McMillan) Medlicott; married Dorothy Kathleen Coveney (a paleographer), July 18, 1936. Education: University College, University of London, B.A., 1923; Institute of Historical Research, University of London, M.A., 1926, D.Lit., 1952. Religion: Church of England. Home: Cartref, Ellesmere Rd., Weybridge, Surrey, England.

CAREER: University College, Swansea, Wales, lecturer, 1926-45; University of Exeter, Exeter, England, professor of modern history, 1945-53; London School of Economics, University of London, London, England, Stevenson Professor of International History, 1953-67. Visiting professor, University of Texas, 1931-32. Member, Institute for Advanced Study, Princeton University, 1952, 1957. Principal officer, Board of Trade, London, England, 1941; official historian, Ministry of Economic Warfare, London, England, 1942-58. Military service: British Army, 1918-20. Member: British Historical Association (honorary secretary, 1943-46; president, 1952-55), Royal Historical Society, Royal Institute of International Affairs, Athenaeum Club (London). Awards, honors: D.Litt., University College, Swansea, Wales, 1970.

WRITINGS: The Congress of Berlin and After: A Diplomatic History of the Near Eastern Settlement, 1878-1880, Methuen, 1938, 2nd edition, Shoe String, 1963; The Origins of the Second Great War (pamphlet), G. Bell, 1940; British Foreign Policy Since Versailles, 1919-1939, Methuen, 1940, 2nd edition, Barnes & Noble, 1968; The Economic Blockade, H.M.S.O., Volume I, 1952, Volume II, 1959; Bismarck, Gladstone, and the Concert of Europe, Athlone Press, 1956, De Graff, 1957; (compiler) Modern European History, 1789-1945: A Select Bibliography, Routledge & Kegan Paul, 1960; The Coming of War in 1939, Routledge & Kegan Paul, 1963; (editor) From Metternich to Hitler: Aspects of British and Foreign History 1814-1939, Barnes & Noble, 1963, reissued as From Metternich to Hitler: Selected Essays on Diplomacy and Power from 1814-1939, 1966; Bismarck and Modern Germany, Verry, 1965; Contemporary England, 1914-1964, McKay, 1967; Britain and Germany: The Search for Agreement 1930-1937, Oxford University Press (New York), 1969; (editor with wife, Dorothy Coveney) Bismarck and Europe, St. Martin's, 1971; (editor with Dorothy Coveney) The Lion's Tale: An Anthology of Criticism and Abuse, Constable, 1971; general editor, "A History of England," Longmans, Green, 1953—.

WORK IN PROGRESS: Senior editor, Documents on British Foreign Policy 1919-1939, for H.M.S.O.

BIOGRAPHICAL/CRITICAL SOURCES: New Statesman, October 6, 1967; Spectator, February 7, 1969; Times Literary Supplement, June 12, 1969.

* * *

MEEK, Ronald L (indley) 1917-

PERSONAL: Born July 27, 1917, in Wellington, New Zealand; son of Ernest William (a merchant) and Isabel Matilda (Williams) Meek; married Dorothea Luise Schulz, October 20, 1951; children: Roger Duncan, Alison Fiona. Education: Victoria University College, LL.B., 1938, LL.M., 1939, B.A., 1945, M.A., 1946; St. John's College, Cambridge, Ph.D., 1949. Home: 27 The Fairway, Oadby, Leicestershire, England. Office: Department of Economics, University of Leicester, Leicester, England.

CAREER: University of Glasgow, Glasgow, Scotland, lecturer, 1948-61, senior lecturer in political economy, 1961-63; University of Leicester, Leicester, England, professor of economics, 1963—.

WRITINGS: Maori Problems Today: A Short Survey, Progressive Publishing Co., 1943; (editor and translator and author of introduction) Marx and Engels on Malthus, Lawrence & Wishart, 1953, International Publishers, 1954, reissued as Marx and Engels on the Population Bomb, Ramparts Press, 1970; Studies in the Labour Theory of Value, International Publishers, 1956; The Economics of Physiocracy: Essays and Translations, Allen & Unwin, 1962, Harvard University Press, 1963; Hill-Walking in Arran, W. & R. Chambers, 1963; The Rise and Fall of the Concept of the Economic Machine, Humanities, 1965; Economics and Ideology and Other Essays: Studies in the Development of Economic Thought, Barnes & Noble, 1967; (with M. Kuczynski) Quesnay's Tableau Economique, Macmillan, 1971; Figur-

ing Out Society, Fontana, 1971. Contributor to *Science and Society, Soviet Studies*, and other professional journals.

WORK IN PROGRESS: The Economics of Electricity Supply.

BIOGRAPHICAL/CRITICAL SOURCES: Times Literary Supplement, July 17, 1969.

* * *

MEHL, Roger 1912-

PERSONAL: Born May 10, 1912, in Relanges, France; son of Adolphe and Louise (Wasser) Mehl; married Herrade Koehnlein (a professor of religion), July 16, 1938; children: Idelette, Jean-Michel, Claire-Lise. *Education:* Universite de Strasbourg, Licence en Philosophie, 1934, Agregation de Philosophie, 1935, Licence en Theologie, 1945, Doctorat en Theologie, 1956. *Religion:* Reformee. *Home:* Rue Blessig 6, Strasbourg, France.

CAREER: Gymnase Protestant, Strasbourg, France, professeur, 1936-39; Lycee Thiers, Marseille, France, professeur, 1940-44; Eglise Reformee de France, Ales, pasteur, 1944-45; Universite de Strasbourg, Faculte de Theologie Protestante, maitre de conferences, 1945-56, professeur titulaire (ethique), 1956—. Participant at World Council of Churches assemblies, Evanston, Ill., 1954, New Delhi, India, 1961, Upsala, 1968, and at Conference de Foi et Constitution, Montreal, Quebec, 1963. *Member:* Federation Protestante de France, World Council of Churches (member of central committee, Commission on Faith and Order), Commission des Etudes Oecumeniques (president). *Awards, honors:* Commandeur des palmes academiques; chevalier de la Legion d'Honneur; Officier de l'Ordre National du Merite; D.H.L., University of Glasgow.

WRITINGS: La Condition du philosophe chretien, Delachaux & Niestle, 1947, translation by Eva Kushner published as *The Condition of the Christian Philosopher*, James Clarke, 1963, Fortress, 1964; (with Jacques Bois and Jean Boisset) *La Probleme de la morale chretienne*, Delachaux & Niestle, 1948; *Images de l'homme*, Labor & Fides, 1953, translation by James H. Farley published as *Images of Man*, John Knox, 1965; *La Recontre d' Autrui*, Delachaux & Niestle, 1955; *La Vieillisement et la mort*, Presses Universitaires de France, 1956, 2nd edition published as *Notre Vie et Notre Mort*, S.C.E., 1967; *De L'Autorite des valeurs: Essai d'ethique chretienne*, Presses Universitaires de France, 1957; *Du Catholicisme romain: Approche et interpretation*, Delachaux & Niestle, 1957; *Explication de la confession de foi de la Rochelle*, Collection "Les Bergers et Les Mages," 1959; *Societe et amour: Problemes ethiques de la vie familiale*, Labor & Fides, 1961, translation by James H. Farley published as *Society and Love: Ethical Problems of Family Life*, Westminster, 1964; *Decolonisation et missions protestantes*, Societe des Missions Evangeliques de Paris, 1964; *Traite de sociologie de protestantisme*, Delachaux & Niestle, 1965, translation by James H. Farley published as *The Sociology of Protestantism*, Westminster, 1970; *La Theologie protestante*, Presses Universitaires de France, 1966; *Pour une ethique sociale chretienne*, Delachaux & Niestle, 1967; *Ethique Catholique et ethique protestante*, Delachaux & Niestle, 1970, translation by James H. Farley published as *Catholic Ethics and Protestant Ethics*, Westminster, 1971; *Les Attitudes Morales*, Presses Universitaires de France, 1971. Editor-in-chief, *Revue de'Histoire et de Philosophie Religieuses*, 1947-69.

WORK IN PROGRESS: L'Ethique de la politique.

BIBLIOGRAPHICAL/CRITICAL SOURCES: Times Literary Supplement, October 2, 1970.

MEHLINGER, Howard D (ean) 1931-

PERSONAL: Born August 22, 1931, in Marion, Kan.; son of Alex (a businessman) and Alice (Skibbee) Mehlinger; married Carolee Ann Case, December 28, 1952; children: Bradley Case, Barbara Ann, Susan Kay. *Education:* McPherson College, B.A., 1953; University of Kansas, M.S. in Ed., 1959, Ph.D., 1964. *Office:* Social Studies Development Center, Indiana University, 1129 Atwater Ave., Bloomington, Ind. 47401.

CAREER: Lawrence High School, Lawrence, Kan., history teacher, 1953-63, chairman of social studies department, 1961-63; Pittsburgh public schools, Pittsburgh, Pa., co-director of Project Social Studies, 1963-64; North Central Association, Chicago, Ill., assistant director of Foreign Relations Project, 1964-65; Indiana University, Bloomington, 1965—, began as assistant professor, now associate professor of history and education, director of high school curriculum center in government, 1966—, director of Social Studies Development Center, 1968—. *Member:* International Studies Association, American Educational Research Association, American Political Science Association, American Historical Association, American Association for Advancement of Slavic Studies, American Academy of Political and Social Science, National Council for Social Studies, National Education Association, Phi Beta Kappa, Phi Delta Kappa, Phi Alpha Theta, Pi Sigma Alpha.

WRITINGS: (Editor) *Communism in Theory and Practice: A Book of Readings for High School Students*, Chandler Publishing, 1964; (editor) *The Study of Totalitarianism: An Inductive Approach*, National Council for the Social Studies, 1965; *The Study of American Political Behavior*, High School Curriculum Center in Government, Indiana University, 1967; (editor with James M. Becker) *International Dimensions in Social Studies*, National Council for the Social Studies, 1968; (with John M. Thompson) *Count Witte and the Tsarist Government in the 1905 Revolution*, Indiana University Press, 1971; (with John J. Patrick) *American Political Behavior*, Ginn, 1972.

* * *

MEHTA, Rustam Jehangir 1912-
(Roger Hartman, R. Johnson Martin, Plutonius)

PERSONAL: Born June 4, 1912, in Bombay, India; son of Jehangir and Gulestan (Marzban) Mehta. *Education:* Royal Institute of Science, University of Bombay, B.Sc., 1931, M.Sc., 1933; University of Birmingham, Ph.D., 1936. *Religion:* Zoroastrianism. *Home:* Nagin Mahal, Vir Nariman Rd., Bombay 20, India.

CAREER: Writer. *Member:* Photographic Society of India. *Awards, honors:* State award, 1960, for *Handicrafts and Industrial Arts of India.*

WRITINGS—All published by D.B. Taraporevala Sons, except as indicated: *You'll Find It in Bombay*, 1939; *Everyday Letters: 315 Readymade Letters for All Occasions*, 1940; (with Betty Norris) *Good English*, 1941; *Scientific Curiosities of Sex Life*, 1941; (with P.M. Madon) *How to Make Money on the Stock Exchange*, 1942; *Effective Business Letters: Complete Commercial Correspondence*, 1943; (editor) *Secrets of Success and Self-Improvement*, 1946; (under pseudonym R. Johnson Martin) *Expressive English*, 1947; *Scientific Curiosities of Love Life and Marriage: A Survey of Sex Relations, Beliefs and Customs of Mankind in Different Countries and Ages*, 1947; (under pseudonym Roger Hartman) *Thesaurus of English Synonyms and Antonyms*, 1948; *Bombay Today*, 1949.

(Under pseudonym Plutonius) *Oriental Mystic Book of Fortune Telling*, 1952; *Appealing Letters for Securing*

Jobs, Interviews and Favours, 1955; *The Handicrafts and Industrial Arts of India: A Pictorial and Descriptive Survey of Indian Craftsmanship as Seen in Masterpieces*, International Publications, 1960; *1001 Ways of Kissing: The Origin, History, and Technique of Kissing, Based on Indian, Oriental and Western Works on Love, Sex and Romance*, 1962, reissued as *Kama-Chumbana: The Love-Kiss in the East and the West*, 1969; *1001 Useful Phrases and Expressions: Idiomatic, Figurative, and Colloquial*, 1964; *Model Letters for Schools*, 1966; *Masterpieces of Indian Sculpture*, 1968; *Konarak, the Sun-Temple of Love*, 1969; *Masterpieces of Indian Textiles*, Textile Book Service, 1970; (author of introduction) *Masterpieces of Indian Bronzes and Metal Sculpture*, 1971; *Masterpieces of the Female Form in Indian Art*, in press.

AVOCATIONAL INTERESTS: Photography, western music, western and Indian art.

*   *   *

MEIER, August   1923-

PERSONAL: Born April 30, 1923, in New York, N.Y.; son of Frank A. (a chemist) and Clara L. (a teacher and vice-principal; maiden name, Cohen) Meier. *Education:* Oberlin College, A.B., 1945; Columbia University, A.M., 1949, Ph.D., 1957. *Politics:* Democrat. *Religion:* Unitarian. *Home:* 122 North Prospect St., Kent, Ohio 44240. *Office:* Department of History, Kent State University, Kent, Ohio 44242.

CAREER: Tougaloo College, Tougaloo, Miss., assistant professor of history, 1945-49; Fisk University, Nashville, Tenn., assistant professor of history, 1953-56; Morgan State College, Baltimore, Md., 1957-64, began as assistant professor, became associate professor; Roosevelt University, Chicago, Ill., professor of history, 1964-67; Kent State University, Kent, Ohio, professor, 1967-69, university professor of history, 1969—. Adult adviser, Civic Interest Group of Baltimore, 1960-64.

MEMBER: American Historical Association, American Anthropological Association, Association for the Study of Negro Life and History, Organization of American Historians, American Studies Association, American Civil Liberties Union, National Association for the Advancement of Colored People (secretary, Newark branch, 1951-52, 1957), Americans for Democratic Action (chairman, Baltimore chapter, 1960-61; member of national board and executive committee, 1960-61), Congress of Racial Equality, Southern Historical Association. *Awards, honors:* Guggenheim fellowship, 1971-72.

WRITINGS: Negro Thought in America, 1880-1915: Racial Ideologies in the Age of Booker T. Washington, University of Michigan Press, 1963; (with Elliot Rudwick) *From Plantation to Ghetto: An Interpretive History of American Negroes*, Hill & Wang, 1966, revised edition, 1970; (with Milton Meltzer) *Time of Trial, Time of Hope: The Negro in America, 1919-1941*, Doubleday, 1966.

Editor: (With Francis Broderick) *Negro Protest Thought in the Twentieth Century*, Bobbs-Merrill, 1965, 2nd edition, revised (with Broderick and Rudwick) published as *Black Protest Thought in the Twentieth Century*, 1971; (with Rudwick) *The Making of Black America: Essays in Negro Life and History*, Atheneum, 1969; with John H. Bracey and Rudwick) *Black Nationalism in America*, Bobbs-Merrill, 1970; (and author of introduction with Rudwick) *Black Protest in the Sixties*, Quadrangle, 1970; (and author of introduction) *The Transformation of Activism*, Aldine, 1970, 2nd edition published as *Black Experience: The Transformation of Activism*, Transaction Books, 1973; (with Bracey) *American Slavery: The Question of Resistance*, Wadsworth, 1971; (with Bracey) *Black Matriarchy: Myth or Reality?*, Wadsworth, 1971;

(with Bracey) *The Black Sociologist: The First Half Century*, Wadsworth, 1971; (with Bracey) *Black Workers and Organized Labor*, Wadsworth, 1971; (with Bracey) *Blacks in the Abolitionist Movement*, Wadsworth, 1971; (with Bracey) *Conflict and Competition: Studies in the Recent Black Protest Movement*, Wadsworth, 1971; (with Bracey) *Free Blacks in America, 1800-1860*, Wadsworth, 1971; (with Bracey) *The Rise of the Ghetto*, Wadsworth, 1971; (with Bracey) *The Afro-Americans*, Allyn & Bacon, 1972. Contributor to *Journal of Negro History, Crisis, Phylon, Journal of Southern History, New Politics*, and other journals.†

*   *   *

MEIGS, Cornelia Lynde   1884-1973
(Adair Aldon)

PERSONAL: Born December 6, 1884, in Rock Island, Ill.; daughter of Montgomery (a civil engineer) and Grace (Lynde) Meigs. *Education:* Bryn Mawr College, A.B., 1908. *Politics:* Republican. *Religion:* Episcopalian. *Home:* Sion Hill, Havre de Grace, Md. 21078; and (summer) Green Pastures, Brandon, Vt. 05733.

CAREER: St. Katharine's School, Davenport, Iowa, teacher of English, 1912-13; Bryn Mawr College, Bryn Mawr, Pa., 1932-50, began as instructor, became professor of English, then professor emeritus. Civilian employee, U.S. War Department, Washington, D.C., 1942-45. *Member:* American Association of University Women, Pennsylvania Historical Society, Vermont Historical Society, Hartford County (Md.) Historical Society. *Awards, honors:* Drama League prize, 1915, for "The Steadfast Princess"; Newbery Medal, American Library Association, 1934, for *Invincible Louisa*, 1934; Little, Brown & Co. prize for *The Trade Wind*; L.H.D., Plano University, 1967.

WRITINGS: The Kingdom of the Winding Road, Macmillan, 1915; *Master Simon's Garden*, Macmillan, 1916, new edition, 1929; *The Steadfast Princess* (juvenile play), Macmillan, 1916; (under pseudonym Adair Aldon) *The Island of Appledore*, Macmillan, 1917; (under pseudonym Adair Aldon) *The Pirate of Jasper Peak*, Macmillan, 1918; *The Pool of Stars*, Macmillan, 1919, new edition, 1929; (under pseudonym Adair Aldon) *At the Sign of the Heroes*, Century, 1920; *The Windy Hill*, Macmillan, 1921; *Helga and the White Peacock* (juvenile play), Macmillan, 1922; (under pseudonym Adair Aldon) *The Hill of Adventure*, Century, 1922; *The New Moon: The Story of Dick Martin's Courage, His Silver Sixpence and His Friends in the New World*, Macmillan, 1924, new edition, 1929; *Rain on the Roof*, Macmillan, 1925; *As the Crow Flies*, Macmillan, 1927; *The Trade Wind*, Little, Brown, 1927; *Clearing Weather*, Little, Brown, 1928; *The Wonderful Locomotive*, Macmillan, 1928; *The Crooked Apple Tree*, Little, Brown, 1929.

The Willow Whistle, Macmillan, 1931; *Swift Rivers*, Little, Brown, 1932; *The Story of the Author of Little Women: Invincible Louisa*, Little, Brown, 1933, reissued with a new introduction, 1968 (published in England as *The Story of Louisa Alcott*, Harrap, 1935); *Wind in the Chimney*, Macmillan, 1934; *The Covered Bridge*, Macmillan, 1936; *Young Americans: How History Looked to Them While It Was in the Making* (stories), Ginn and Junior Literary Guild, 1936; *Railroad West*, Little, Brown, 1937; *The Scarlet Oak*, Macmillan, 1938.

Call of the Mountain, Little, Brown, 1940; *Mother Makes Christmas*, Grosset, 1940; *Vanished Island*, Macmillan, 1941; *Mounted Messenger*, Macmillan, 1943; *The Two Arrows*, Macmillan, 1949; *The Violent Men: A Study of Human Relations in the First American Congress*, Macmillan, 1949.

The Dutch Colt, Macmillan, 1952; (editor and contributor) *A Critical History of Children's Literature: A Survey of Children's Books in English from Earliest Times to the Present,* Macmillan, 1953, revised edition, 1969; *Fair Wind to Virginia,* Macmillan, 1955; *What Makes a College?: A History of Bryn Mawr,* Macmillan, 1956; *Wild Geese Flying,* Macmillan, 1957; *Saint John's Church, Havre de Grace, Md. 1809-1959,* Democratic Ledger, 1959.

Mystery at the Red House, Macmillan, 1961; *The Great Design: Men and Events in the United Nations from 1945 to 1963,* Little, Brown, 1964; (editor and author of introduction and notes) *Glimpses of Louisa: A Centennial Sampling of the Best Short Stories,* Little, Brown, 1968; *The Dutch Colt,* Macmillan, 1968.

Jane Addams: Pioneer for Social Justice, Little, Brown, 1970; *Louisa M. Alcott and the American Family Story,* Walck, 1971.

BIOGRAPHICAL/CRITICAL SOURCES: *Best Sellers,* October 1, 1968, May 1, 1970; *Book World,* November 3, 1968; *Library Journal,* June 15, 1970.

(Died September 10, 1973)

*   *   *

MEILACH, Dona Zweigoron 1926-

PERSONAL: Surname is pronounced *My*-lack; born August 26, 1926, in Chicago, Ill.; daughter of Julius (an artist and merchant) and Rose (Don) Zweigoron; married Melvin Meyer Meilach (an orthodontist), February 15, 1948; children: Susan Ellen, Allen Edwin. *Education:* University of Chicago, Ph.B., 1946; Art Institute of Chicago, student, 1958-64; Northwestern University, M.A., 1969. *Home:* 13001 Choctaw Rd., Palos Heights, Ill. 60463.

CAREER: Edward Don & Co. (restaurant supply house), Chicago, Ill., advertising manager, 1944-48; Evergreen Park Community High School, Evergreen Park, Ill., teacher of English and art, 1959—. Community resource teacher of creative writing, Fernwood School, 1962; second grade teacher, Beth Torah Religious School, Chicago; instructor at Moraine Valley Junior College, 1970, and at Purdue University, 1970, 1971. Free-lance writer for magazines; exhibiting artist, lecturer. *Member:* College Art Association, National Association of Science Writers, Authors Guild of Authors League of America, National Photographic Society, Art Institute of Chicago, Children's Reading Roundtable, Sigma Delta Chi, B'nai B'rith (president, Freedom chapter, 1946-48), Hadassah, Ridge Camera Club.

WRITINGS: *First Book of Bible Heroes,* five books, Ktav, 1963; (with William G. Birch) *A Doctor Discusses Pregnancy,* Budlong, 1963; (with Elvie Ten Hoor) *Collage and Found Art,* Reinhold, 1964; *Printmaking,* Pitman, 1965; *Papercraft,* Pitman, 1965; (with Don Seiden) *Direct Metal Sculpture: Creative Techniques and Appreciation,* Crown, 1966; *Creating with Plaster,* Reilly & Lee, 1966; (with Elias Mandel) *A Doctor Talks to 5-to-8-Year-Olds,* Budlong, 1966; (contributor) *The Expectant Mother,* Trident, 1967; *Creating Art from Anything: Ideas, Materials, Techniques,* Reilly & Lee, 1968; *Contemporary Art with Wood: Creative Techniques and Appreciation,* Crown, 1968; *Creative Carving: Materials, Techniques, Appreciation,* Reilly & Lee, 1969; *Creative Crafts with Accent,* Illinois Bronze, 1969; (with M. Edward David) *A Doctor Discusses Menopause,* Budlong, 1969.

Making Contemporary Rugs and Wall Hangings, Abelard, 1970; *First Steps in Art Appreciation,* Pitman, 1970; *Contemporary Stone Sculpture: Aesthetics, Methods, Appreciation,* Crown, 1970; (with L. Erlin Snow) *Creative Stitchery,* Reilly & Lee, 1970; *Accent on Crafts,* Illinois Bronze, 1970; *Macrame: Creative Design in Knotting,* Crown, 1971; *Papier-mache Artistry,* Crown, 1971; *Contemporary Leather: Art and Accessories, Tools and Techniques,* Regnery, 1971; *The Artist's Eye,* Regnery, 1972; *Creating Art from Fibers and Fabrics,* Regnery, 1972; *Macrame Accessories: Patterns and Ideas for Knotting,* Crown, 1972; (with Dennis Kowal) *Sculpture Casting: Mold Technique and Materials,* Crown, 1972; *Contemporary Batik and Tie-Dye,* Crown, 1972. Contributor of more than five hundred articles and stories to some forty magazines and newspapers, including *Better Homes and Gardens, Ingenue, Maclean's, Writer, This Week, True Confessions, Redbook, Catholic Digest, Popular Mechanics,* and *Successful Farming.* Correspondent, *Pediatric Herald;* former correspondent and columnist, *Jewish Post and Opinion.*

WORK IN PROGRESS: Several art books and one photography book.

*   *   *

MEISEL, Gerald Stanley 1937-

PERSONAL: Born July 7, 1937, in New York, N.Y.; son of Harry A. (a retailer) and Betty (Greenberg) Meisel. *Education:* New York University, B.S., 1959, LL.B., 1962; City College of City University of New York, graduate student in business administration, 1962—. *Religion:* Jewish. *Home:* 497 Oakdene Ave., Ridgefield, N.J. 07657. *Office:* 4250 Broadway, New York, N.Y. 10033.

CAREER: Admitted to the Bar of New York State, 1962; First-Met Realty (rental management, appraisal), New York, N.Y., vice-president. Adviser and writer for Practicing Law Institute and Condominium Council, both New York, N.Y. *Member:* New York University Law Alumni, Rho Epsilon Alumni (president, New York section, 1963; executive director, New York section, 1963-64), Rho Epsilon, Iota Nu Sigma, Phi Sigma Delta.

WRITINGS: (With Edna L. Hebard) *Principles of Real Estate Law,* Simmons-Boardman, 1964, revised edition, Schenkman, 1967. Contributor of articles to *Real Estate News.*

WORK IN PROGRESS: *Real Estate Construction, Leasing and Financing,* for Practicing Law Institute; a monograph, *Condominium: An Air Rights Concept;* a law textbook, *Principles of Mortgage Law.*

AVOCATIONAL INTERESTS: Oil painting, sports, writing poetry, collecting European hand-carved figurines, and reading history.

*   *   *

MELADY, Thomas Patrick 1927-

PERSONAL: Born March 4, 1927, in Norwich, Conn.; son of Thomas P. and Rose (Belisle) Melady; married Margaret Badum, December 2, 1961; children: Christina, Monica. *Education:* Duquesne University, B.A., 1950; Catholic University of America, M.A., 1952, Ph.D., 1954. *Politics:* Republican. *Religion:* Catholic. *Home:* c/o Seton Hall University, South Orange, N.J. 07079. *Office:* c/o Kampala, U.S. Department of State, Washington, D.C. 20521.

CAREER: U.S. Foreign Operations Administration, Washington, D.C., foreign trade and investment adviser to Ethiopian government, 1954-56; Duquesne University, Pittsburgh, Pa., director of development and founder of Institute of African Affairs, 1956-59; Consultants for Overseas Relations (management consulting firm in international affairs) and Africa Service Institute, New York, N.Y., president, 1959-67; Seton Hall University, South Orange, N.J., professor of Afro-Asian affairs and chairman of department of Asian studies and non-western civilization, 1967-69; ambassador to Burundi, 1969-72; ambassador to Uganda, 1972—. Professor of contemporary

African affairs, St. John's University, Jamaica, N.Y., 1960-66. Adjunct professor of African history, Fordham University, 1966-69. Senior advisor to U.S. delegation to U.N.G.A., 1970. Former adviser to African heads of state. Lecturer on international affairs. *Military service:* U.S. Army, 1945-47.

MEMBER: Academy of Political Science, African Affairs Society, African Studies Association, American Academy of Political and Social Science, American Association for the United Nations, American Economic Association, American Political Science Association, American Society for African Culture, Association for International Development, Association for International Social Justice, Catholic Association for International Peace, Catholic Economic Association, Foundation for Religious Action in the Social and Civil Order, International African Institute, Catholic Interracial Council of New York, Alpha Epsilon, Phi Kappa Theta, Knights of Columbus. *Awards, honors:* Honorary doctorates from seven universities; decorations from four countries; knighted by Pope Paul VI, 1968; Native Son award, Norwalk, Conn.

WRITINGS: Profiles of African Leaders, Macmillan, 1961; (contributor) Mathew H. Ahmann, editor, *The New Negro,* Fides, 1961; *The White Man's Future in Black Africa,* Macfadden, 1962; (contributor) R.S. Payne, editor, *College Readings on Africa,* Catholic Students' Mission Crusade, 1963; *Faces of Africa,* Macmillan, 1964; (editor) *Kenneth Kaunda of Zambia: Selections from His Writings,* Praeger for Africa Service Institute, 1964; *The Revolution of Color,* Hawthorn, 1966; *Western Policy and the Third World,* Hawthorn, 1967; (with wife, Margaret Melady) *House Divided: Poverty, Race, Religion, and the Family of Man,* Sheed, 1969.

Monographs: *Taxation as a Factor in the Development of Underdeveloped Countries,* Catholic University of America Press, 1954; *The Economic Future of Ethiopia,* Institute of African Affairs, Duquesne University, 1959; *An Evaluation of the United States' Position in Guinea, Liberia and Ghana,* Duquesne University Press, 1960; *Race Relations and Harmony Among Men,* Institute of African Affairs, Duquesne University, 1966. Contributor of about fifty articles to *Current History, America, Catholic World, American Mercury, Review of Social Economy,* and other publications.

WORK IN PROGRESS: With R.B. Subartono, *Developing Societies.*

* * *

MELLENCAMP, Virginia Lynn 1917-

PERSONAL: Born May 29, 1917, in Warsaw, Ind.; daughter of Fred A. Mellencamp. *Education:* DePauw University, A.B., 1939; University of New Mexico, graduate study, 1949-50; Stanford University, M.A., 1953; Johns Hopkins University, postgraduate study, 1955-56. *Office:* Crippled Childrens Services, New Mexico State Welfare Department, Santa Fe. 87501.

CAREER: Crippled Children's Services, New Mexico Department of Public Welfare, Santa Fe, audiological consultant, 1956—. Speech and hearing consultant, New Mexico Society for Crippled Children and Adults; member, Council for Exceptional Children. *Military service:* U.S. Navy, 1943-46; became lieutenant junior grade. *Member:* American Speech and Hearing Association, Alexander Graham Bell Association, New Mexico Speech and Hearing Society, New Mexico Hearing Society.

WRITINGS: Play and Say It: A Manual for Helping the Child Learn How to Make and Use Correct Speech Sounds, Expression Co., 1962.

MELTON, John L. 1920-

PERSONAL: Born August 11, 1920, in Walsenburg, Colo.; son of Harry W. (a pharmacist) and Elizabeth (Cahalan) Melton; married Virginia Cadmus, June 1, 1968. *Education:* University of Utah, A.B., 1948, A.M., 1949; Johns Hopkins University, Ph.D., 1955. *Religion:* Roman Catholic. *Home:* 210 Third St. S., St. Cloud, Minn. 56301.

CAREER: Johns Hopkins University, Baltimore, Md., 1950-55, began as junior instructor, became instructor in English; College of Notre Dame of Maryland, Baltimore, lecturer, 1954-55; John Carroll University, University Heights, Ohio, instructor, 1955-57, assistant professor, 1951-61, associate professor, 1961-67, professor of English, 1967-68, director of department of English, 1962-68; St. Cloud State College, St. Cloud, Minn., associate professor, 1968-69, professor of English, 1969—. Consultant, Center for Documentation and Communication Research, Western Reserve University, 1957-63. *Military service:* U.S. Army, Infantry, 1942-46; became major. *Member:* Modern Language Association of America, Modern Humanities Research Association, International Arthurian Society, American Society for Aesthetics, British Society of Aesthetics, National Council of Teachers of English, College English Association, Sierra Club, Phi Beta Kappa, Rowfant Club.

WRITINGS: (Editor) *The Semantic Code Dictionary: A Thesaurus of Scientific and Technical Terms,* Interscience, 1958. Writer of television series, "Literature of the American Frontier." Contributor of articles and reviews to professional journals and popular magazines.

WORK IN PROGRESS: Editing Civil War letters on the Wilderness Campaign; computerized study of the Arthurian cycle; studies in science fiction and Gothic fiction.

AVOCATIONAL INTERESTS: Conservation and the out-of-doors.

* * *

MELTZER, David 1937-

PERSONAL: Born February 17, 1937, in Rochester, N.Y.; son of Louis (a musician and writer) and Rosemunde (Lovelace) Meltzer; married Christina Meyer (a teacher-aide), April 1, 1959; children: Jennifer Love, Margaret Joy, Amanda Rose. *Education:* Attended many high schools, graduated from none; attended Los Angeles City College, and University of California, Los Angeles. *Home address:* P.O. Box 129/Bolinas; Cal. 94924. *Office:* Discovery Book Shop, 241 Columbus Ave., San Francisco, Calif.

CAREER: Discovery Book Shop, San Francisco, Calif., manager, 1959—. Spent some time reading, with jazz, at The Cellar, San Francisco. *Member:* Science Fiction Writers of America.

WRITINGS: (With Donald Schenker) *Poems* (fifteen copies printed comprising Meltzer section only), privately printed, 1957; *Ragas,* Discovery Books (San Francisco), 1959; *The Clown: A Poem,* Semina (Larkspur), 1960; (editor with Lawrence Ferlinghetti and Michael McLure) *Journal for the Protection of All Beings #1: A Visionary and Revolutionary Review,* City Lights (San Francisco), 1960; *We All Have Something to Say to Each Other: Being an Essay Entitled Patchen and Four Poems,* Auerhahn Press (San Francisco), 1962; (author of introduction) *The Outsiders,* [Fort Lauderdale], 1962; *Bazascope Mother,* Drekfesser Press (Los Angeles), 1964; *Station,* [San Francisco], 1964; *The Blackest Rose,* Oyez (Berkeley), 1964; (contributor) *Notes from the Underground Press,* Underground Press, 1964; *In Hope I Offer a Fire-wheel: A Poem,* Oyez, 1965; *The Process,* Oyez,

1965; *The Dark Continent,* Oyez, 1967; *Journal of the Birth* (essay; originally published in *Journal for the Protection of All Beings*), Oyez, 1967; *The Agent,* Essex House, 1968; *How Many Blocks in the Pile?,* Essex House, 1968; *Round the Poem Box: Rustic and Domestic Home Movies for Stan and Jane Brakhage,* Black Sparrow Press (Los Angeles), 1969; *Healer,* Essex House, 1969; *Agency,* Essex House, 1969; *Lovely,* Essex House, 1969; *The Martyr,* Essex House, 1969; *ORF,* Essex House, 1969; *Poem for My Wife,* Maya, 1969; *Yesod,* Trigram Press, 1969; *From Eden Book,* Maya, 1969; *Greenspeech,,* Christopher Books, 1970; *Isle Vista Notes,* Christopher Books, 1970; *Luna,* Black Sparrow Press, 1970; (editor) *The San Francisco Poets,* Ballantine, 1971; *Hero,* Unicorn Press, 1971; *Knots,* Tree Books, 1971; *Hero-Lil,* Black Sparrow Press, 1972. Represented in several anthologies, including: *The New American Poetry: 1945-1960,* edited by Donald M. Allen, Grove, 1960; *Beatitude Anthology,* edited by Lawrence Ferlinghetti, City Lights, 1960; *Junge Amerikanische Lyrik,* edited by Carl Hanser (Munich), 1961; *The Real Bohemia,* edited by Francis J. Regney and L. Douglas Smith, Basic Books, 1961; *On the Mesa: Anthology of Bolinas Writers,* edited by Joel Weishaus, City Lights, 1971; *Mark in Time: Portraits & Poetry—San Francisco,* edited by Nick Harvey, Glide, 1971; *A Caterpillar Anthology: A Selection of Poetry and Prose from Caterpillar Magazine,* edited by Clayton Eshleman, Doubleday, 1971. Author of column, "Green Atom," *Los Angeles Free Press,* 1969. Contributor to *Yale Review, Big Table, Yugen, Lyrik, Renaissance, Beatitude, Floating Bear, Semina, Oyez, Dazzle, White Dove Review,* and other periodicals. Editor of *Tree,* a bi-annual, 1970—, and *The New World,* a bi-annual, 1972—.

WORK IN PROGRESS: A novel, *The Picket; Handbook of the Invisible: A Poetry Primer,* for Ballantine Books; *Birth: A Collection of Texts Through Time Responding to the Event of Birth,* for Mudra Press; a study of the Christian Cabala in America, tentatively titled "QBL/ USA;" a collaboration with John Brandi on geography.

SIDELIGHTS: In 1960 Meltzer described his relationship to his work in the following way: "At 14 left for the West & stayed in L.A. for 6 formative years in which I met Wallace Berman & Robert Alexander, who were instrumental in turning me on to the fantastic possibilities of art & the self. Moved to San Francisco in 1957. . . . Spent many months reading at'The Cellar with Jazz. I no longer believe in the poet as a public target.

"I have decided to work my way thru poetry & find my voice & the stance I must take in order to continue my journey. Poetry is NOT my life. It is an essential PART of my life."

David Kherdian believes that Meltzer has since reevaluated the importance of writing in his life. "Meltzer has taken his religious vows and can not say, as he once did, that writing forms a part of his life, not all of it. What he does say now is that he is not to be judged by his previous work. He has a new responsibility to his writing that is based, one suspects—by viewing the poet as a man—upon the kind of courage that has become a faith." For a time Meltzer concentrated on music rather than writing, but Kherdian asserts that Meltzer has passed into a new phase in which writing is again the most significant aspect of his life. "On the strings of his music he was taking one final exotic flight into fantasy," Kherdian writes, "the voyage was from himself, but inside himself, and now that he has circled the globe of his mind he has come home at last. He made the connective link between hope and actuality, between what a man had hoped for himself and for all humanity, and what indeed was possible. He could only know, he could only

make a beginning by submitting, by assuming a stance that would comprise a life—that of the poet."

BIOGRAPHICAL/CRITICAL SOURCES: David Kherdian, *Six Poets of the San Francisco Renaissance,* Giligia Press, 1965.

* * *

MELVIN, A(rthur) Gordon 1894-

PERSONAL: Born December 19, 1894, in Halifax, Nova Scotia, Canada; came to United States, 1919; son of Arthur Leander and Bessie (Warner) Melvin; married Lorna Reade Strong (an art teacher), August 29, 1931; children: Alice Branch, Mary Lorna. *Education:* Dalhousie University, A.B., 1916; Columbia University, A.M., 1920, Ph.D., 1923. *Religion:* Christian. *Home:* 863 Watertown St., West Newton, Mass. 02165.

CAREER: Central China University, Wuchang, China, professor of education, 1924-27; College of the City of New York (now City College of the City University of New York), New York, N.Y., 1928-54, began as associate professor, became professor of education. Member of national advisory council, Columbia Broadcasting System "School of the Air." 1946-48. Lecturer at universities in England, Egypt, India, China, United States. *Military service:* Canadian Navy, 1917-19; became warrant officer. *Member:* Association for Arts in Childhood (president, 1945-47), Francis W. Parker Society (president, 1941-43), American Association of University Professors, Progressive Education Association, Society of American Travel Writers, Horace Mann League, Boston Malacological Society.

WRITINGS: *The Professional Training of Teachers for the Canadian Public Schools as Typified by Ontario,* Warwick & York, 1923; *Progressive Teaching: An Interpretation for the Guidance of Teaching in the Public Schools,* Appleton, 1929; *The Technique of Progressive Teaching,* John Day, 1932; *Education for a New Era: A Call to Leadership* (pamphlet), John Day, 1933; *Building Personality,* John Day, 1934; *The Activity Program,* Reynal & Hitchcock, 1936; *The New Culture: An Organic Philosophy of Education,* Reynal & Hitchcock, 1937; *Activated Curriculum: A Method and a Model for Class Teachers and Curriculum Committees,* John Day, 1939; *Method for New Schools,* John Day, 1941; *Thinking for Every Man,* John Day, 1942; *People's World,* John Day, 1943; *Teaching: A Basic Text in Education,* John Day, 1944; *Education: A History,* John Day, 1946; *Adventures on Midsummer Evenings,* Exposition, 1951; *General Methods of Teaching,* McGraw, 1952; *Mexican Travel Guide,* Ottenheimer, 1956; *Gems of World Oceans: A Guide to World Sea Shell Collecting,* Naturegraph, 1964; *Sea Shells of the World,* Tuttle, 1966; *Sea Shell Parade,* Tuttle, 1972. Contributor to magazines and professional journals, including *Asia, Design, Dalhousie Review, Educational Forum,* and *Hobbies.*

AVOCATIONAL INTERESTS: Sea shells, Mexico.

* * *

MENDELOWITZ, Daniel M(arcus) 1905-

PERSONAL: Born January 28, 1905, in Linton, N.D.; son of Isaac (a merchant) and Clara (Reichtenstein) Mendelowitz; married Mildred H. Mondschein, September 4, 1935; children: Louis Isaac. *Education:* Stanford University, B.A., in Art, 1926, M.A. in Art, 1927. *Politics:* Democrat. *Religion:* Jewish. *Home:* 800 Lathrop Dr., Stanford, Calif. 94305.

CAREER: Stanford University, Stanford, Calif., 1934—, now professor of art and education. *Member:* National Art Education Association, Pacific Arts Association.

WRITINGS: Children Are Artists: An Introduction to Children's Art for Teachers and Parents, Stanford University Press, 1953, 2nd edition, 1963; A History of American Art, Holt, 1960, revised edition, 1970; Drawing, Holt, 1967.

SIDELIGHTS: Mendelowitz is an exhibiting painter of watercolors, with landscapes of central California and southern France as his favorite subjects.

BIOGRAPHICAL/CRITICAL SOURCES: Time, December 15, 1967.

* * *

MENDELSOHN, Oscar (Adolf) 1896-
(Oscar Milsen)

PERSONAL: Born July 12, 1896, in Nanango, Queensland, Australia; son of Saul and Abigail (Rosensweig) Mendelsohn; married Edna Millward Smale (a sociologist), December 7, 1939; children: Estelle, Frederick, Dorothea. Education: University of Melbourne, B.Sc. (honors). Politics: Labour. Home: 65 Mount St., Heidelberg N22, Melbourne, Victoria, Australia.

CAREER: Private practice as consulting industrial research chemist and examiner of questioned documents, in Australia, 1925—. Member of Australian government industrial mission to Europe and United States, and Australian representative at World Dairy Congress, London, England. Author. Composer, and conductor at various times of Royal Australian Air Force Choir, Melbourne Choral Group, other choirs. Appears on Australian radio and television as member of panels, and on own programs. Military service: Royal Australian Air Force, chemical adviser and head of Scientific Section, 1941-44; became squadron leader. Member: Royal Institute of Chemistry (fellow), Fellowship of Australian Writers (president, 1963), Fellowship of Trenchermen (president, 1945—), Royal Automobile Club, Public Schools Club, Duckboard Club, University Club.

WRITINGS: The Earnest Drinkers' Digest: A Short and Simple Account of Alcoholic Beverages, Consolidated Press (Sydney), 1946, published in America as The Earnest Drinker: A Short and Simple Account of Alcoholic Beverages, Macmillan, 1950; Liars and Letters Anonymous: The Case Book of an Expert Witness, Lansdowne Press, 1961; Drinking with Pepys, Macmillan (London), 1963, St. Martin's, 1964; The Dictionary of Drinks and Drinking, Hawthorn, 1965 (published in England as Glossary of Alcoholic Beverages and Related Terms, Macmillan, c.1965); A Salute to Onions: Some Reflections on Cookery . . . and Cooks, Rigby, 1965, Hawthorn, 1966; A Waltz with Matilda: On the Trail of a Song, Lansdowne Press, 1966; From Cellar and Kitchen, Macmillan (London), 1968; Nicely, Thank You, National Press, 1971.

Composer of serious small musical works published under pseudonym Oscar Milsen by Chester, London, England, and Marks, New York, N.Y. Contributor of articles, short stories, criticism, and poems to journals and magazines in Australia and abroad. Editor of Focus (monthly magazine), 1947-50.

WORK IN PROGRESS: The Lara Papers, a book of essays on country life; an autobiography, tentatively titled One Man's View; Wine Without Tears.

AVOCATIONAL INTERESTS: Gastronomy.

* * *

MENNINGER, Edwin A(rnold) 1896-

PERSONAL: Born March 18, 1896, in Topeka, Kan.; son of Charles Fredrick and Flo Vesta (Knisely) Menninger; married Patsy Underhill, May 19, 1928; children:

Jane Menninger McCrocklin, John U., Edwin, Jr., Barbara. Education: Washburn University, A.B., 1916; Columbia University, graduate study, 1916-18. Religion: Christian Scientist. Home: 201 Martin Rd., Stuart, Fla. 33494. Agent: Carol Woodward, Painter Hill Rd., Roxbury, Conn. 06783. Office: c/o Horticultural Books, Inc., 219 Martin Ave., Stuart, Fla. 33494.

CAREER: New York Tribune, New York, N.Y., telegraph editor, 1917-22; Palm Beach Post, Palm Beach, Fla., city editor, 1922; owner and publisher of newspapers in Stuart, Fla., 1922-58, the South Florida Developer, 1922-27, Stuart Daily News, 1928-31, Stuart News, 1931-58. Member: American Horticultural Society (life), Royal Horticultural Society, Botanical Society of South Africa, Florida Press Association (former president), Fairchild Tropical Garden, Rotary Club (former president, Stuart chapter). Awards, honors: American Horticultural Council Medal; Rio de Janeiro Sesquicentennial Medal; Barbour Medal, Fairchild Tropical Garden; D.Sc., Florida State University, 1964.

WRITINGS: Descriptive Catalog of Flowering Tropical Trees, privately printed, c.1945; (with David Sturrock) Shade and Ornamental Trees for South Florida and Cuba, privately printed, 1946; Flowering Tropical Trees, Doubleday, 1956; What Flowering Tree Is That?: A Handbook for the Tropics, privately printed, 1956, revised edition, 1958; The Cultivated Eugenias in American Gardens, privately printed, 1959; Flowering Trees of the World for Tropics and Warm Climates, Hearthside, 1962; Seaside Plants of the World: A Guide to Planning, Planting, and Maintaining Salt-Resistant Gardens, Hearthside, 1964; Fantastic Trees, Viking, 1967; (with others) Flowering Vines of the World: An Encyclopedia of Climbing Plants, Hearthside, 1970. Occasional contributor of articles to horticultural magazines.

* * *

MERCER, David 1928-

PERSONAL: Born June 27, 1928, in Wakefield, Yorkshire, England; son of Edward and Helen (Steadman) Mercer. Education: University of Durham, B.A. (honors), 1953. Agent: Margaret Ramsay Ltd., 14 Goodwin Court, London W.C.2, England.

CAREER: Technician in pathological laboratory in England, 1943-48; teacher of general subjects, 1956-61; writer of television plays, stage plays, and screenplays, 1961—. Member: Screenwriters' Guild. Awards, honors: Screenwriters' Guild Award for A Suitable Case for Treatment as best television play of 1962; Evening Standard award for most promising playwright, 1965; British Film Academy award for best screenplay, 1966, for "Morgan!"; best British original teleplay award, Writers' Guild, 1967 for In Two Minds; best British original teleplay award, Writers' Guild, 1969, for Let's Murder Vivaldi.

WRITINGS—Television plays, all networked by British Broadcasting Corp., except as indicated: Where the Difference Begins, 1961; A Climate of Fear, 1962; A Suitable Case for Treatment, 1962; "The Buried Man," networked by Associated Television, 1963; "A Way of Living," networked by ABC-TV (England), 1963; The Birth of a Private Man, 1963; For Tea on Sunday, 1963; And Did Those Feet, 1965; In Two Minds, 1967; The Parachute, 1968; Let's Murder Vivaldi, 1968; On the Eve of Publication, 1968; The Cellar and the Almond Tree, 1970; Emma's Time, May 13, 1970; "The Bankrupt," November 27, 1972. Television plays published in: The Generations (contains Where the Difference Begins, A Climate of Fear, and The Birth of a Private Man), J. Calder, 1964; Three TV Comedies (contains A Suitable Case for Treatment, For Tea on Sunday, and And Did

Those Feet), Calder & Boyars, 1966; *The Parachute and Two More TV Plays* (contains *The Parachute, Let's Murder Vivaldi,* and *In Two Minds*), Calder & Boyars, 1967; *On the Eve of Publication and Other Plays* (contains *On the Eve of Publication, Emma's Time,* and *The Cellar and the Almond Tree*), Methuen, 1970.

Plays: *Ride a Cock Horse* (first produced on West End at Piccadilly Theatre, 1965), Hill & Wang, 1966; *The Governor's Lady* (first produced on West End at Aldwych Theatre, 1965), Methuen, 1968; *Belcher's Luck* (first produced on West End at Aldwych Theatre, 1966), Hill & Wang, 1967; (contributor) Kenneth Tynan, *Oh! Calcutta!* (revue; first produced Off-Broadway at Eden Theatre, June 17, 1969; produced in London at Roundhouse Theatre, July 29, 1970), Grove, 1969; *After Haggerty* (two-act; first produced on West End at Aldwych Theatre, February 26, 1970), Methuen, 1970; *Flint* (two-act comedy; first produced on West End at Criterion Theatre, May 5, 1970), Methuen, 1970; "Where the Difference Begins" (based on television play), first produced at Hull Arts Centre, May 19, 1970.

Screenplays: "Morgan!" (based on his television play *A Suitable Case for Treatment*), Cinema V, 1966; "Family Life" (based on his television play, *In Two Minds*), Kestrel Films, 1971, released in America as "Wednesday's Child"; "A Doll's House" (based on the play by Ibsen), Reindeer Productions, 1972.

SIDELIGHTS: John Elsom describes David Mercer as "... one of our best contemporary dramatists, to rank with Bond and Pinter, and as 'representative' ... of the late sixties as Osborne was of the late fifties. He has an excellent eye for a character and a situation: he can relate sensibly the themes of his plays to a wider context—the decline of the Church in *Flint,* of British Imperial Power in *Belcher's Luck,* of changing class attitudes in *After Haggerty.* It has been said that he is far too influenced by Marxism and psychoanalysis. For me, however, these 'philosophies,' if they are such, merely provide a coherent structure through which his various insights emerge, strengthened by the surrounding order." Harold Hobson also believes that Mercer's work has a dimension aside from its political aspects. "What is impressive in Mr. Mercer's writing is the compassion he feels even for people whose actions he cannot help despising. He is aware that human beings fail more often from weakness than from wickedness, and that weakness is frequently deserving of pity."

Mercer has his own very particular thoughts about writing with a social or political framework in his drama. In an interview with Giles Gordon, Mercer remarks: "I think a writer can obviously do something to improve the quality of life in the sense that he can extend people's range of perception. I suppose the basic purpose of works of art is to generalise unique experiences....But politically I wouldn't say at all, except in a most indirect fashion. I think that there are plays which sort of percolate through a society. I think there are detectably different things in this country today simply because *Look Back in Anger* was written. But they are not a consequence of *Look Back in Anger* as a play. *Look Back in Anger* also released quantities of energy and brought in its wake a lot of writers. Which I suppose, insofar as John Osborne is political at all, is related to some kind of anarchic left wing rather muddled view of politics...."

In the same interview Mercer describes his own personal view of the writing process. "... To me the writing of a play is a mystery, the origin of it is a mystery. I don't know where it comes from, or how it comes. I don't even know what it is. I don't mean this in a camp sense, this is a strictly neutral matter of fact for me—I do not

know. I suppose the development, if one had a development in one's work, is a question of everything's being accumulated from previous writing. I wouldn't say that I learn anything in a conscious, rational way but each play that I write, I feel, uses everything that I've discovered in previous pieces of work. But it's in control of me, not the other way round."

BIOGRAPHICAL/CRITICAL SOURCES: Transatlantic Review, summer, 1968; *Listener,* December 19, 1968; *New Statesman,* March 6, 1970; *Variety,* March 11, 1970, February 24, 1971; *New York Times,* May 4, 1970; *Spectator,* May 16, 1970; *Christian Science Monitor,* May 20, 1970, February 26, 1971; *Plays and Players,* June, 1970; *Nation,* July 6, 1970; *London Magazine,* September, 1970.

*   *   *

MEREDITH, George (Marlor)   1923-

PERSONAL: Born April 21, 1923, in Somerville, N.J.; son of Gilbert Judson (a sales executive) and Dorothea (Pope) Meredith; married Elizabeth Jean Moore (an artist), November 15, 1955; children: Gilbert J. III, Scott Arthur. *Education:* Columbia University, student, 1940-42. *Home:* 249 Ridge Rd., Rutherford, N.J. 07070. *Office:* Meredith Associates, Inc., 240 Park Ave., Rutherford, N.J. 07070.

CAREER: Johns-Manville Corp., New York, N.Y., specification writer, 1942-44; U.S. Maritime Service, New York, N.Y., managing editor of *Mast Magazine,* 1944-47; *Outdoor Life,* New York, N.Y., staff editor, 1947; *Premium Practice,* New York, N.Y., managing editor, 1947-51, editor, 1951-54; Frank Associates (business writing service), Chicago, Ill., associate editorial director, 1954-56; Meredith Associates, Inc. (business writing and art service), Rutherford, N.J., president and editorial director, 1956—.

MEMBER: Sales/Marketing Executives International, National Premium Sales Executives, Inc. (executive secretary, 1957-68; executive director, 1968—), National Association of Premium Manufacturers Representatives (executive director, 1963-64), National Association of Food Equipment Manufacturers (executive secretary, 1958-59), American Society of Association Executives, Public Relations Society of America, American Management Association, National Writers Club, New York Society of Association Executives, Advertising Club of New York.

WRITINGS: Effective Merchandising with Premiums, McGraw, 1962. Executive editor, *Marketing Facts,* annual, 1968—. Contributor of articles to business publications. Author of product-application case histories for Surface Combustion, Remington Rand, Eastman Kodak, Standard Register, Eureka Specialty Printing, Mohawk Data Sciences Corp., Charles Beseler Co., American Industries Corp., *Trading Stamp Quarterly,* and *Sales Manager's Notebook.* Also author of a weekly syndicated newspaper column.

*   *   *

MEREDITH, Scott   1923-

PERSONAL: Born November 24, 1923, in New York, N.Y.; son of Henry and Esta Meredith; married Helen Kovet, April 22, 1944; children: Stephen Charles, Randy Beth. *Education:* Studied privately with tutors. *Office:* Scott Meredith Literary Agency, Inc., 580 Fifth Ave., New York, N.Y. 10036; and Scott Meredith Literary Agency, 44 Great Russell St., London W.C. 1, England.

CAREER: Became magazine writer in early teens and an authors agent at the age of seventeen; Scott Meredith Literary Agency, Inc., New York, N.Y., president, 1942—, representing almost five hundred authors. Expert witness in copyright cases. Frequent guest on television panel shows. *Military service:* U.S. Army Air Forces, World War II. *Member:* Rare Book Society, Spectator Club, Three Oaks Tennis Club.

WRITINGS: Writing to Sell, Harper, 1950, revised edition, 1960.

Editor: *The Best of Wodehouse,* Pocket Books, 1949; (with P.G. Wodehouse) *The Best of Modern Humor,* McBride, 1951; *Bar Roundup of Best Western Stories,* Dutton, 1952; (with Wodehouse) *The Week-End Book of Humor,* Washburn, 1952, reissued as *P.G. Wodehouse Selects the Best of Humor,* Grosset, 1965; *Bar Two Roundup of Best Western Stories,* Dutton, 1953; *The Murder of Mr. Malone,* St. John, 1953; *Bar Three Roundup of Best Western Stories,* Dutton, 1954; *Bar Four Roundup of Best Western Stories,* Dutton, 1955; *Bar Five Roundup of Best Western Stories,* Dutton, 1956; (with Ken Murray) *The Ken Murray Book of Humor,* Ace Books, 1957; *Bar Six Roundup of Best Western Stories,* Dutton, 1957; (with Henry Morgan) *The Henry Morgan Book of Humor,* Avon, 1958; (with Sidney Meredith) *The Best from Manhunt,* Pocket Books, 1958; (with Sidney Meredith) *The Bloodhound Anthology,* T.V. Boardman, 1959; *The Fireside Treasury of Modern Humor,* Simon & Schuster, 1963 (published in England as *The Fireside Book of Modern Humour,* Hamish Hamilton, 1964); *Best Western Stories,* Spring Books, 1964; (with Wodehouse) *A Carnival of Modern Humor,* Dial, 1967. Contributor of articles on humor to *Encyclopaedia Britannica,* 1954, 1959, and on fiction writing to *Oxford Encyclopaedia,* 1960. Also contributor of several hundred short stories, articles, novelettes, and serials to magazines.

WORK IN PROGRESS: A biography of George S. Kaufman, for Doubleday.

SIDELIGHTS: Many of Meredith's books have come out in paperback reprints, and in British, Spanish, German, and other foreign-language editions. A number of his stories have been dramatized on television.

* * *

MEREDITH, William (Morris) 1919-

PERSONAL: Born January 9, 1919, in New York, N.Y.; son of William Morris and Nelley Atkin (Keyser) Meredith. *Education:* Princeton University, A.B. (magna cum laude), 1940. *Politics:* Democrat. *Home:* Kitemaug Rd., Uncasville, Conn.

CAREER: New York Times, New York, N.Y., 1940-41, began as copy boy, became reporter; Princeton University, Princeton, N.J., instructor in English and Woodrow Wilson Fellow in writing, 1946-50; University of Hawaii, Honolulu, associate professor of English, 1950-51; Connecticut College, New London, associate professor, 1955-65, professor of English, 1965—. Middlebury College, Middlebury, Vt., instructor at Bread Loaf School of English, 1958-62. Member, Connecticut Commission on the Arts, 1963. *Military service:* U.S. Army Air Forces, 1941-42. U.S. Navy, Naval Aviation, 1942-46; served in Pacific Theater; became lieutenant. U.S. Naval Reserve, active duty in Korean War as naval aviator, 1952-54; became lieutenant commander; received two Air Medals. *Member:* National Institute of Arts and Letters, Academy of American Poets (chancellor), American Choral Society (second vice-president). *Awards, honors:* Yale Series of Younger Poets Award for *Love Letter from an Impossible Land,* 1943; Harriet Monroe Memorial Prize, 1944, and Oscar Blumenthal Prize, 1953, for poems published in *Poetry;* National Institute of Arts and Letters grant in literature, 1958; Loines prize from National Institute of Arts and Letters, 1966; Van Wyck Brooks award, 1971; Ford Foundation Fellow, attached to New York City and Metropolitan Opera companies.

WRITINGS: Love Letter from an Impossible Land (poems), Yale University Press, 1944; *Ships and Other Figures* (poems), Princeton University Press, 1948; *The Open Sea and Other Poems,* Knopf, 1958; (editor and author of introduction) *Shelley: Poems,* Dell, 1962; (translator) Guillaume Apollinaire, *Alcools: Poems 1898-1913,* Doubleday, 1964; *The Wreck of the Thresher and Other Poems.* Knopf, 1964; *Earth Walk: New and Selected Poems,* Knopf, 1970. Librettist for Peter Whiton's opera, "The Bottle Imp," produced at Wilton, Conn., 1958. Contributor to poetry magazines. Opera critic for *Hudson Review,* 1955-56.

* * *

MERRELL, V(ictor) Dallas 1936-

PERSONAL: Born January 25, 1936, in Basalt, Idaho; son of Victor (a rancher and businessman) and Beatrice (Jensen) Merrell; married Karen Dixon, June 8, 1959; children: Ann, Kay, Joan, Paul Dixon. *Education:* Brigham Young University, B.S., 1960, M.S., 1964; University of Southern California, postgraduate study, 1964—. *Home:* 3247 Hollypark Dr. #1, Inglewood, Calif. 90305. *Office:* Brigham Young University, 3141 West Century Blvd., Inglewood, Calif. 90305.

CAREER: Church of Jesus Christ of Latter-day Saints, full-time missionary, 1956-58; Brigham Young University, Provo, Utah, general chairman of Education Week programs throughout United States and Canada, 1962-64, chairman of department of community education, 1963-64, chairman of Brigham Young University's California Center for Continuing Education, 1964—. Member of board of directors, Adult Education Association of Utah, 1963-64; lecturer on leadership and family subjects in western United States and Canada. *Member:* American Sociological Association, Utah Academy of Sciences, Arts and Letters, Alpha Kappa Delta, Blue Key.

WRITINGS: Family Leadership: Inspired Counsel for Parents, Deseret, 1963; *A Genealogical History of William Porter Merrell,* privately printed, 1964; (with wife, Karen Dixon Merrell) *Women in Mormon History,* Deseret, c.1966. Contributor of sociological articles to professional journals, and articles on education to magazines.†

* * *

MERRENS, H(arry) Roy 1931-

PERSONAL: Born July 21, 1931, in Salford, England; came to United States in 1955, naturalized in 1963; resident in Canada since 1968; son of Alec I. (in textiles) and Dora (Nachman) Merrens; married Sheila Van Deventer, June, 1964; children: Mark Clayton Van Deventer (stepson). *Education:* University College, London, B.A. (honors), 1954; University of Maryland, M.A., 1957; University of Wisconsin, Ph.D. 1962. *Politics:* Independent. *Religion:* Agnostic. *Home:* 48 Waverley Rd., Toronto 8, Ontario, Canada. *Office:* Department of Geography, York University, Downsview 463, Ontario, Canada.

CAREER: Rutgers University, New Brunswick, N.J., instructor in geography, 1960-61; University of Wisconsin, Madison, instructor in geography, 1961-62; San Fernando Valley State College, Northridge, Calif., assistant professor, 1962-65, associate professor of geography, 1967-68; York University, Downsview, Ontario, associate professor of geography, 1968—. Visiting professor of geography, University of Wisconsin, 1965-66. *Military service:* British Army, 1949-51; became sergeant. *Member:* Association of American Geographers, American Geographical Society. *Awards, honors:* Fulbright travel grant, 1955-57.

WRITINGS: Colonial North Carolina in the Eighteenth Century: A Study in Historical Geography, University of

North Carolina Press, 1964; *Regions of the United States,* Rand McNally, 1970.

WORK IN PROGRESS: Research on the geography of colonial America, especially the colony of South Carolina.

* * *

MERRILL, James M(ercer)   1920-

PERSONAL: Born April 25, 1920, in Los Angeles, Calif.; son of Clarence Mercer and Helen (Hillman) Merrill; married Ann McIntosh, July 7, 1945; children: Eugenia Louise, James McIntosh. *Education:* Pomona College, B.A., 1947; Claremont Graduate School, M.A., 1949; University of California, Los Angeles, Ph.D., 1954. *Religion:* Episcopalian. *Agent:* Theron Raines, 244 Madison Ave., New York, N.Y. 10016.

CAREER: Whittier College, Whittier, Calif., assistant professor, 1952-58, associate professor of history, 1958-66; University of Delaware, Newark, professor of history, 1966—. *Military service:* U.S. Naval Reserve, 1942-46; became lieutenant j.g.; received Pacific ribbon with three battle stars. *Member:* American Historical Association, Southern Historical Association. *Awards, honors:* Guggenheim research fellowship, 1958-59; Mershon National Security research fellowship, 1961-62.

WRITINGS: Rebel Shore: The Story of Union Sea Power During the Civil War, Little, Brown, 1957; *Quarter-Deck and Fo'c'sle: The Exciting Story of the U.S. Navy,* Rand McNally, 1963; (editor) *Uncommon Valor: The Story of the U.S. Army,* Rand McNally, 1964; *Target Tokyo: The Story of the Halsey-Doolittle Raid,* Rand McNally, 1964; *Spurs to Glory: The Story of the U.S. Cavalry,* Rand McNally, 1966; *Battle Flags South: The Story of the Civil War on Western Waters,* Fairleigh Dickenson University Press, 1970; *William Tecumseh Sherman,* Rand McNally, 1971.

WORK IN PROGRESS: The U.S. Navy in the Pacific during World War II.

BIBLIOGRAPHICAL/CRITICAL SOURCES: *Detroit News,* October 3, 1971.

* * *

MERRILL, Wilfred K.   1903-

PERSONAL: Born November 5, 1903, in Chicago, Ill.; son of Amos Albert (an electrical and mechanical engineer) and Myrtle Alma (Walters) Merrill; married Margaret Rose (an author), October 11, 1930. *Education:* University of California Extension, two years' study in forestry. *Politics:* Republican. *Religion:* Protestant. *Residence:* Sonora, Calif.

CAREER: U.S. Maritime Service, 1919; U.S. Coast and Geodetic Survey, 1919-23; U.S. Forest Service and California Fish & Game Commission, 1922-26, 1927-37, serving as park ranger in Yosemite National Park, 1927-37, acting chief of Lake Mead National Recreational Area, 1938-42, acting chief of General Grant National Park and district ranger of Kings Canyon National Park, 1942-49, various posts at Yosemite National Park and Olympia National Park, 1949-58; retired, 1958. Member of chapter board of directors and adviser to Disaster Service, American National Red Cross. *Military service:* U.S. Navy, 1921-22. *Member:* International Association for Identification, National Rifle Association (life), Toulumne County Peace Officers Association (life.)

WRITINGS: All About Camping, Stackpole, 1962, 2nd edition, 1964; *Getting Out of Outdoor Troubles: The Lifesaving Handbook on Dealing with Emergencies for Careful Families, Outdoorsmen, Boaters, Vacationers,* Stackpole, 1965; *The Hunter's Bible,* Doubleday, 1968; *The Hiker's and Backpacker's Handbook,* Doubleday, 1971; *The Survival Handbook,* Winchester Publishers, 1972. Also author of "The Weekend Boater's Guide for Small Craft Owners," "The Great North American Safari: Vacationing with Saddle and Packhorse Outfit," and "World Wide Survival Manual," as yet unpublished. Contributor to *Camping Illustrated, Western Outdoors,* and *Better Camping.*

WORK IN PROGRESS: Vacationing by Train.

SIDELIGHTS: Merrill traveled more than ten thousand miles in 1963, mostly by train, gathering material for *Getting Out of Outdoor Troubles.* On the trip he ranged as far east as Nova Scotia, and to the Yukon in the north.

* * *

METRAUX, Guy S(erge)   1917-

PERSONAL: Born March 30, 1917, in Montreaux, Vaud, Switzerland; son of Alfred (a physician) and Cecile Metraux; married Ruth Watt (an educational consultant), September 10, 1941; children: Guy P.R., Marc F. *Education:* Primary and secondary schooling in Argentina and Switzerland; University of California, Berkeley, student, 1939-40; University of Michigan, B.A., 1942, M.A., 1942; Yale University, Ph.D., 1949. *Home:* 81, rue de l'Universite, Paris VII, France. *Office:* SCHM - UNESCO, 9, Place de Fontenoy, Paris VII, France.

CAREER: International Committee of the Red Cross, Geneva, Switzerland, delegate to United States, later to British Army of the Rhine, 1944-47; Social Science Research Council, New York, N.Y., consultant, 1950-51; UNESCO, Paris, France, secretary general of International Commission for a History of the Scientific and Cultural Development of Mankind, 1951—. Visiting assistant professor of social sciences, University of Puerto Rico, 1949-50. Member of board of trustees, American College of Paris. *Member:* American Historical Association, Connecticut Academy of Arts and Letters, Yale Club of Paris.

WRITINGS: Exchange of Persons: The Evolution of Cross-Cultural Education (pamphlet), Social Science Research, 1952; (editor with Francois Crouzet) *The Evolution of Science,* New American Library, 1963; (editor with Crouzet) *The Nineteenth Century World,* New American Library, 1963; (editor with Crouzet) *Studies in the Cultural History of India,* Shiva Lal Agarwala, 1965; (editor with Crouzet) *The New Asia,* New American Library, 1965; (editor with Crouzet) *Religions and the Promise of the Twentieth Century,* New American Library, 1965.

WORK IN PROGRESS: Collaborating with Francois Crouzet on *Science in the American Context,* for New American Library; continuing work in supervising and administering the preparation and publication of a six-volume study of the history of mankind, scientific and cultural development, and related topics.

* * *

METZGER, Bruce Manning   1914-

PERSONAL: Born February 9, 1914, in Middletown, Pa.; son of Maurice R. (a lawyer) and Anna Mary (Manning) Metzger; married Isobel Elizabeth Mackay, July 7, 1944; children: John Mackay, James Bruce. *Education:* Lebanon Valley College, A.B., 1935; Princeton Theological Seminary, Th.B., 1938, Th.M., 1939; Princeton University, M.A., 1940, Ph.D., 1942. *Politics:* Republican. *Religion:* Presbyterian. *Home:* 20 Cleveland Lane, Princeton, N.J. 08540. *Office:* Princeton Theological Seminary, Princeton, N.J. 08540.

CAREER: Princeton Theological Seminary, Princeton, N.J., instructor, 1940-44, assistant professor, 1944-48, associate professor, 1948-54, professor of New Testament, 1954—, George L. Collard Professor of New Testament Language and Literature, 1964—. Visiting professor, Presbyterian Seminary, Campinas, Brazil, 1952; scholar-in-residence, Tyndale House, Cambridge, England, 1969; distinguished visiting professor, Fuller Theological Seminary, 1970; Colwell Lecturer, Claremont School of Theology, 1970. Honorary fellow and corresponding member, Higher Institute of Coptic Studies, Cairo, Egypt, 1952—; member, Institute for Advanced Study, Princeton University, 1964-65; member of the Kuratorium, Vetus-Latina-Institut, Beuron, Germany, of advisory committee of Institute for New Testament Text Research, University of Muenster, Germany, and of seminar for New Testament studies, Columbia University. Chairman, American committee of versions, International Greek New Testament Project.

MEMBER: Society of Biblical Literature (delegate to American Council of Learned Societies, 1963-67; president, 1971), National Association of Biblical Instructors, American Philological Association, Studiorum Novi Testamenti Societas (president, 1971), American Society of Church History, American Bible Society (member of board of directors; former chairman of committee on versions). *Awards, honors:* Certificate of distinguished service, National Council of Churches of Christ in the United States, 1957; prizes for books in Christian Research Foundation competitions, 1955, 1962, 1963; D.D., Lebanon Valley College, 1951, and St. Andrews University, 1964; L.H.D., Findlay College, 1962; D.Theol., Muenster University, 1970.

WRITINGS: The Saturday and Sunday Lessons from Luke in the Greek Gospel Lectionary, University of Chicago Press, 1944; *Lexical Aids for Students of New Testament Greek,* privately printed, 1946, 3rd edition, 1969; *A Guide to the Preparation of a Thesis* (pamphlet), Theological Book Agency, 1950, 2nd edition, Princeton Theological Seminary, 1961; *Index of Articles on the New Testament and Early Church Published in Festschriften* (monograph), Society of Biblical Literature, 1951; *Annotated Bibliography of the Textual Criticism of the New Testament, 1914-1939,* Ejnar Munksgaard, 1955; (New Testament editor) *The Twentieth Century Encyclopedia of Religious Knowledge,* two volumes, Baker Book, 1955; (with E.E. Flack) *The Text, Canon and Principal Versions of the Bible,* Baker Book, 1956; *An Introduction to the Apocrypha,* Oxford University Press (New York), 1957; (with others) *Introduction to the Bible,* John Knox, 1959; (contributor) *Bibliographia Patristica,* Volumes I-X, 1959-69.

(Editor) "New Testament Tools and Studies," nine volumes, E.J. Brill, 1960-69; (editor) *Index to Periodical Literature on the Apostle Paul,* Eerdmans, 1960; *Lists of Words Occurring Frequently in the Coptic New Testament,* E.J. Brill, 1961, Eerdmans, 1962; (with Herbert G. May) *The Oxford Annotated Bible,* Oxford University Press (New York), 1962; (compiler with wife, Isobel M. Metzger) *The Oxford Concise Concordance to the Revised Standard Version of the Holy Bible,* Oxford University Press (New York), 1962; *Chapters in the History of New Testament Textual Criticism,* Eerdmans, 1963; *The Text of the New Testament: Its Transmission, Corruption, and Restoration,* Oxford University Press, 1964, 2nd edition, 1968; *The New Testament: Its Background, Growth and Content,* Abingdon, 1965; (editor with May) *The Oxford Annotated Apocrypha,* Oxford University Press (New York), 1965; (editor) *The Apocrypha of the Old Testament,* Oxford University Press (New York), 1965; (editor) *Index to Periodical Literature on Christ and the Gospels,* Eerdmans, 1966; (editor) A.J. Mattill

and M.B. Mattill, *Classified Bibliography of Literature on the Acts of the Apostles,* Eerdmans, 1966; *Historical and Literary Studies, Pagan, Jewish, and Christian,* Eerdmans, 1968; (editor) *The New Testament, Revised Standard Version,* Geoffrey Chapman, 1969; *Text Critical Commentary on the Greek New Testament,* American Bible Society, 1971.

Member of translation committee, *Apocrypha,* Revised Standard Version of the Bible, Thomas Nelson, 1963. Contributor to *Encyclopaedia Britannica, Encyclopedia Americana, World Book, Geschichte und Gegenwart,* to Bible dictionaries published in America and Germany, to Bible commentaries, and to biblical, classical, philological, and theological journals in America and Europe.

WORK IN PROGRESS: Serving on editorial committee of 3rd edition of *The Greek New Testament,* for American Bible Society.

BIOGRAPHICAL/CRITICAL SOURCES: New Testament Abstracts, Volume I, 1957.

* * *

METZGER, Stanley D. 1916-

PERSONAL: Born July 10, 1916, in New York, N.Y.; son of S. David (a businessman) and Malvina (Adler) Metzger; married Mavis Clark, August 23, 1945. *Education:* Cornell University, A.B., 1936, LL.B., 1938. *Home:* 3338 Volta Place N.W., Washington, D.C. 20007. *Office:* Georgetown University Law School, 506 E St., Washington, D.C. 20001.

CAREER: Started legal career with New York Labor Relations Board, 1939; U.S. Government, Washington, D.C., attorney with National Labor Relations Board, Office of Price Administration, Fair Employment Practices Committee, 1939-46, assistant legal adviser in Department of State, 1946-60, member of U.S. Tariff Commission, 1967-69; Georgetown University Law School, Washington, D.C., professor of law, 1960-67, 1969—. *Military service:* U.S. Army Air Corps, 1942-43. *Member:* American Society of International Law (member of executive council), Federal Bar Association, American Law Institute. *Awards, honors:* Medal of Law and Culture from Mexican Academy of International Law.

WRITINGS: International Law, Trade, and Finance: Realities and Prospects, Oceana, 1963; *Trade Agreements and the Kennedy Round: An Analysis of the Economic, Legal, and Political Aspects of the Trade Expansion Act of 1962,* Coiner, 1964; *Documents and Readings in the Law of International Trade,* Lerner Law Book Co., 1965; *Law of International Trade: Documents and Readings* (contains *Documents and Readings in the Law of International Trade*), two volumes, Lerner Law Book Co., 1965-66; *Law and Policy Making for Trade Among "Have" and "Have-Not" Nations,* Oceana, 1968. Member of board of editors, *American Journal of International Law, Journal of World Trade Law.*

* * *

MEYEROWITZ, Eva (Leonie) L(ewin-) R(ichter)

PERSONAL: Born in Germany; daughter of Sigismund (director, German General Electric Co.) and Toni (Richter) Lewin-Richter; married Herbert Vladimir Meyerowitz (founder of West African Institute of Arts, Industries and Social Studies), April 18, 1925 (died June 10, 1945); children: Michael. *Education:* Studied sculpture at Charlottenburger Kunstgewerbe und Handwerkerschule, 1919-23, Hochschule fuer Feine und Angewandte Kunst, 1922-25; University College, University of London, advanced study in anthropology, 1946-48. *Religion:* Jewish. *Address:* 18 Harcourt Ter., London S.W. 10, England.

CAREER: Executed sculptural work on public buildings in Cape Town, Bloemfontein, Pretoria, and Johannesburg, South Africa, and in Dombaschawa, Southern Rhodesia, during period, 1928-35; South African School for Applied Art, Capetown, teacher of sculpture, 1930-33; Achimota College, Gold Coast, art supervisor, 1943-44; writer, 1939—. *Member:* Anti-Slavery Society (member of committee). *Awards, honors:* Grants for anthropological research from Colonial Welfare and Development Fund, 1945-46, Emslie Horniman Anthropological Fund, 1946-48, University College of the Gold Coast, 1949-50, Hugh Le May Fellowship of Rhodes University, 1954-55, Ghana Academy of Sciences, 1964, and Institute of African Studies, Ghana University, 1967.

WRITINGS: The Sacred State of the Akan, Faber, 1951; *Akan Traditions of Origin,* Faber, 1952; *The Akan of Ghana: Their Ancient Beliefs,* Humanities, 1958; *The Divine Kingship in Ghana and Ancient Egypt,* Faber, 1960; *At the Court of an African King,* Faber, 1962, Humanities, 1963; *The Early History of Ghana,* Ghana University, in press. Contributor to *Burlington Magazine, Africa, Man, African Affairs, Contact,* and other periodicals.

SIDELIGHTS: Mrs. Meyerowitz's vocational interests involve ancient history, culture, and art, and modern African politics (she was involved in the foundation of the Brong Federation in Ghana. She writes to *CA:* "The most important of my books is *The Divine Kingship in Ghana and Ancient Egypt,* in which I show that the religion, cult of the king, and matrilineal organisation of the Akan of Ghana is that of ancient Egypt."

She has lived in South Africa, 1925-35, 1940-42, 1954-55, and 1958-60, and in West Africa, 1936-40, 1943-46, 1949-50, 1964, and 1967.

* * *

MICKELSEN, A(nton) Berkeley   1920-

PERSONAL: Born September 20, 1920, in Berwyn, Ill.; son of Anton (a salesman) and Anna Margaret (Hansen) Mickelsen; married Alvera M. Johnson (an editor), August 9, 1952; children: Ruth Ann, Lynnell Margaret. *Education:* Wheaton College, Wheaton, Ill., B.A., 1942, M.A., B.D.; University of Chicago, Ph.D., 1950. *Office:* Department of New Testament, Bethel Seminary, 3949 Bethel Dr., St. Paul, Minn. 55112.

CAREER: Ordained to Baptist ministry, 1951; Wheaton College, Wheaton, Ill., instructor, 1951-52, assistant professor, 1952-56, associate professor, 1956-61, later, professor of Bible and theology; Bethel Seminary, St. Paul, Minn., member of faculty. *Member:* Society of Biblical Literature, Evangelical Theological Society, Chicago Society of Biblical Research. *Awards, honors:* Research grant of Wheaton College Alumni Association for completing *Interpreting the Bible,* 1961-62.

WRITINGS: (Contributor) Carl F.H. Henry, editor, *The Biblical Expositor: The Living Theme of the Great Book,* A.J. Holman, 1960; (contributor) C.F. Pfeiffer, editor, *The Wycliffe Bible Commentary,* Moody, 1962; *Interpreting the Bible,* Eerdmans, 1963; (with others) *Can I Trust My Bible: Important Questions Often Asked About the Bible,* Moody, 1963.†

* * *

MIGDALSKI, Edward C(harles)   1918-

PERSONAL: Born May 3, 1918, in New Haven, Conn.; married Roberta Terrel, 1952; children: Tom, Nancy. *Education:* Attended Yale University, 1940-41, 1952-53; attended Cornell University, 1946-51. *Home:* Main Rd., Hamden, Conn. 06514. *Office:* Outdoor Education and Recreation Department, Yale University, New Haven, Conn. 06520.

CAREER: Yale University, New Haven, Conn., ichthyologist, chief preparator of fishes, fishing coach, and director of outdoor recreation and club sports, 1946—. Participated in twenty-four zoological expeditions to many parts of the world for Yale University's Peabody Museum of Natural History and Bingham Oceanographic Laboratory. Director of water safety, Town of Hamden, Conn. *Military service:* U.S. Air Force, 1942-46; became master sergeant. *Member:* American Association for Health, Physical Education, and Recreation (member of council on Outdoor Education and Camping), American Fisheries Society, American Society of Ichthyologists and Herpetologists, Explorers Club, Anglers Club (New York).

WRITINGS: Angler's Guide to the Salt Water Game Fishes, Atlantic and Pacific, Ronald, 1958; *How to Make Fish Mounts, and Other Fish Trophies,* Ronald, 1960; *Angler's Guide to the Fresh Water Sport Fishes of North America,* Ronald, 1962; *Boy's Book of Fishes,* Ronald, 1964. Contributor of articles on hunting and fishing to scientific publications and magazines.

WORK IN PROGRESS: Teach a Boy to Fish; Expeditions: Field Work and Adventures.

* * *

MIKES, George   1912-

PERSONAL: Born February 15, 1912, in Siklos, Hungary; son of Alfred (a lawyer) and Margit Alice (Gal) Mikes; married Lea Hanak, January 2, 1948; children: Martin Alfred, Judith Pamela. *Education:* University of Budapest, LL.D., 1933. *Religion:* Roman Catholic. *Home:* 24 St. John's Wood Court, London N.W. 8, England. *Agent:* Russell & Volkening, Inc., 551 Fifth Ave., New York, N.Y. 10017.

CAREER: Writer. *Member:* P.E.N. (executive); Garrick Club and Hurlingham Club (both London).

WRITINGS: The Epic of Lofoten, Hutchinson, 1941; *Darlan: A Study,* Constable, 1943; *We Were There to Escape: The True Story of a Jugoslav Officer,* Nicholson & Watson, 1945; *Pont ugye mint az angolok* (songs and verses), Londini Podium, 1945; *How to Be an Alien: A Handbook for Beginners and More Advanced Pupils,* Deutsch, 1946, British Book Centre, 1950; *How to Scrape Skies: The United States Explored, Rediscovered and Explained,* Deutsch, 1948, published in America as *How to Be a Swell Guy: The United States Explored, Rediscovered, and Explained,* Doubleday, 1959.

Wisdom for Others, Deutsch, 1950; *Milk and Honey: Israel Explored,* Deutsch, 1950, Transatlantic, 1965; *Talicska: Humoreszkek, esszek, sohajtasok,* Big Ben Kiadasa, c.1950; *Down With Everybody!: A Cautionary Tale for Children Over Twenty-One, and Other Stories,* Deutsch, 1951, British Book Centre, 1952; *Shakespeare and Myself,* Deutsch, 1952, British Book Centre, 1953; *Uber Alles: Germany Explored,* Deutsch, 1953; *Eight Humorists,* Deutsch, 1954; *Leap Through the Curtain: The Story of Nora Kovach and Istvan Rabovsky,* Weidenfeld & Nicolson, 1955, Dutton, 1956; *Little Cabbages,* Deutsch, 1955; *Italy for Beginners,* Deutsch, 1956, Transatlantic, 1965; *The Hungarian Revolution,* Deutsch, 1957; *East Is East,* Deutsch, 1958; *A Study in Infamy: The Operations of the Hungarian Secret Police,* Deutsch, 1959.

How to Be Inimitable: Coming of Age in England, Deutsch, 1961, Transatlantic, 1966; *Szalka es gerenda, humoreszkek-karcolatak,* Szepirodalmi (Budapest), 1960; *As Others See You,* Newman Neame, 1961; *Tango: A Solo Across South America,* Deutsch, 1961, Transatlantic, 1965; *The Best of Mikes,* Pan Books, 1962; *Switzerland for Beginners,* Deutsch, 1962, Transatlantic, 1965; *Falra hanyt borso: Humoreszk,* Szepirodalmi Koenyvkiado

(Budapest), 1963; *Mortal Passion*, Deutsch, 1963, Transatlantic, 1966; *How to Unite Nations*, Deutsch, 1963, Transatlantic, 1965; (editor) *Prison: A Symposium*, Routledge & Kegan Paul, 1963, Horizon Press, 1964; *How to Be an Alien: In Britain, France, Italy, Germany, Switzerland, Israel, Japan*, Basic Books, 1964; (with John R.R. Bedford) *The Duke of Bedford's Book of Snobs*, P. Owen, 1965, published in America as *The Book of Snobs*, Coward, 1966; *Eureka!: Rummaging in Greece*, Deutsch, 1965; (editor) *Germany Laughs at Herself: German Cartoons Since 1848*, Bassermann (Stuttgart), 1965; *How to Be Affluent*, Deutsch, 1966, James Heineman, 1967; *Not By Sun Alone*, Deutsch, 1967; *Boomerang: Australia Rediscovered*, Deutsch, 1968; *Coat of Many Colors: Israel*, Gambit, 1969 (published in England as *The Prophet Motive: Israel Today and Tomorrow*, Deutsch, 1969; *Laughing Matter*, Library Press, 1971; *Any Souvenirs?*, Gambit, 1972; *How to Run a Stately Home*, Transatlantic, 1972.

Humour in Memoriam, Routledge & Kegan Paul, 1970; *The Land of the Rising Yen: Japan*, Gambit, 1970. Contributor to *Observer, Encounter, Times Literary Supplement*, and other periodicals.

SIDELIGHTS: The *Times Literary Supplement* reviewer states: "Mr. Mikes has made a profession of the paradox, and some twenty books reflect his special gift of observing human behaviour—especially when the humans are English—from the acute angle of the adopted Englishman. Cynical, amused, determined not to be taken in, he is that man with the heavy accent in the corner taking notes: for him face values are no values at all."

Mikes' books have been translated into twenty-one languages. *Avocational interests:* Tennis.

BIOGRAPHICAL/CRITICAL SOURCES: New Statesman, March 17, 1967; Times Literary Supplement, April 27, 1967; Christian Science Monitor, January 18, 1968; Observer Review, October 20, 1968; Books and Bookmen, December, 1968; Punch, March 18, 1970; Listener, December 31, 1970.

* * *

MILBRATH, Lester W(alter) 1925-

PERSONAL: Born October 29, 1925, in Bertha, Minn.; son of Walter R. (a farmer) and Lila (Fischer) Milbrath; married Kirsten M. Oglaend (a native of Norway), February 1, 1952; children: Linda Beate, Erik John. *Education:* University of Minnesota, B.A., 1951, M.A., 1952; University of North Carolina, Ph.D., 1956. *Home:* 9348 Lincolnwood Dr,, Evanston, Ill. 60203. *Office:* Department of Political Science, Northwestern University, Evanston, Ill. 60201.

CAREER: Instructor, and research associate at University of Tennessee, Knoxville, 1952-53, at University of North Carolina, Chapel Hill, 1953-56, at Duke University, Durham, N.C., 1957-58; Brookings Institution, Washington, D.C., postdoctoral research fellow, 1956-57; Northwestern University, Evanston, Ill., 1958—, began as assistant professor, now associate professor of political science. *Military service:* U.S. Navy, 1945-46; became electrician's mate. *Member:* American Political Science Association, American Association of University Professors (secretary, Northwestern chapter), Midwest Political Science Association, Southern Political Science Association, Phi Beta Kappa, Pi Sigma Alpha. *Awards, honors:* Fulbright senior research scholar in Norway, 1961-62.

WRITINGS: *The Washington Lobbyists*, Rand McNally, 1963; *Political Participation: How and Why Do People Get Involved in Politics?*, Rand McNally, 1965. Contributor to *Journal of Politics, American Behavioral Scientist, Public Opinion Quarterly*, and to other periodicals in his field.

WORK IN PROGRESS: Research on political beliefs and political socialization.

AVOCATIONAL INTERESTS: High fidelity stereo reproduction, photography, sailing, fishing, golf, and gardening.

* * *

MILLAR, J(ohn) Halket 1899-

PERSONAL: Born May 2, 1899, in Timaru, New Zealand; son of John Robertson (an electrical engineer) and Ella Isabella (Irwin) Millar; married Una Jane Keay, March 5, 1924; children: John E., Aslin H., Keay (Mrs. K.N. McCormack), Ronella (Mrs. R.H. Cometti), Peter R., Michael J. *Education:* Attended schools in Timaru, New Zealand. *Religion:* Methodist. *Home:* 88A Neale Ave., Stoke, Nelson, New Zealand.

CAREER: Journalist in New Zealand most of adult life, now retired. Also worked for A.H. & A.W. Reed (publishers), Wellington, New Zealand, for two years. Formerly regular broadcaster on historical subjects and book reviewer on national radio service. Actor and producer in repertory; adjudicator for several drama festivals. *Military service:* Territorial Army, instructor, 1918-19; became sergeant. Home Guard, instructor, 1940-42, then in Intelligence. *Member:* Ashburton Club (life).

WRITINGS: *The Bayly Murder Case*, Bullivant, 1934; *A Centennial History*, Trinity Presbyterian Church (Nelson, New Zealand), 1948; *Beyond the Marble Mountain: Tales of the Early Golden Bay, Motueka and Nelson*, R. Lucas, 1948; *High Noon for Coaches*, A.H. & A.W. Reed, 1954, enlarged edition, 1965; *Death Round the Bend*, A.H. & A.W. Reed, 1955; *Gold in New Zealand*, A.H. & A.W. Reed, 1956; *The Merchants Paved the Way: The First Hundred Years of the Wellington Chamber of Commerce*, A.H. & A.W. Reed, 1956; (with Alexander Wyclif Reed) *Roads in New Zealand*, A.H. & A.W. Reed, 1958; *Westland's Golden Sixties*, A.H. & A.W. Reed, 1959; (editor) Frank Alack, *Guide Aspiring*, Oswald-Sealy, 1963; (contributor) Jack Pollard, editor, *One for the Road*, A.H. & A.W. Reed, 1966; *District Directory for the Borough of Richmond, 1968*, R. Lucas, 1968; *To Me, It Wasn't Funny* (autobiography), A.H. & A.W. Reed, 1972. Writer of local histories of textbooks for schools and of three one-act plays. Contributor of historical articles to newspapers and national and overseas magazines.

* * *

MILLAR, Kenneth 1915-
(John Macdonald, John Ross Macdonald, Ross Macdonald)

PERSONAL: Born December 13, 1915, in Los Gatos, Calif.; son of John M. (a newspaper editor) and Anne (Moyer) Millar; married Margaret Sturm (a novelist), June 2, 1938; children: Linda (Mrs. Joseph Pagnusat; deceased). *Education:* University of Western Ontario, B.A., 1938; University of Toronto, graduate study, 1938-39; University of Michigan, M.A., 1943, Ph.D., 1951. *Politics:* Democrat. *Home:* 4420 Via Esperanza, Santa Barbara, Calif. 93110. *Agent:* Harold Ober Associates, 40 East 49th St., New York, N.Y. 10017.

CAREER: Kitchener Collegiate Institute, Kitchener, Ontario, teacher of English and history, 1939-41; free-lance writer. Teacher of writing in adult education program, Santa Barbara, Calif., 1957-59. Trustee, Santa Barbara Natural History Museum, 1970—. *Military service:* U.S. Naval Reserve, 1944-46; became lieutenant j.g. *Member:* Mystery Writers of America (national director, 1960-61, 1964-65; president, 1965), American Civil Liberties Union, Authors League of America, Crime Writers

Association (London), National Audubon Society, Sierra Club, Writers Guild of America West, Santa Barbara Audubon Society (publicity chairman, 1965-66), Coral Casino. *Awards, honors:* Mystery Writers of America scrolls for *The Wycherly Woman,* 1962, and *The Zebra-Striped Hearse,* 1963; Crime Writers Association awards for *The Chill,* 1965, and *The Far Side of the Dollar,* 1966.

WRITINGS: *The Dark Tunnel,* Dodd, 1944, reissued as *I Die Slowly,* Lion Press, 1955; *Trouble Follows Me,* Dodd, 1946, reissued as *Night Train,* Lion Press, 1955; *Blue City,* Knopf, 1947; *The Three Roads,* Knopf, 1948.

Under pseudonym John Macdonald: *The Moving Target,* Knopf, 1949, reissued as *Harper,* Pocket Books, 1966.

Under pseudonym John Ross Macdonald: *The Drowning Pool,* Knopf, 1950; *The Way Some People Die,* Knopf, 1951; *The Ivory Grin,* Knopf, 1952, reissued as *Marked for Murder,* Pocket Books, 1953; *Meet Me at the Morgue* (originally published in *Cosmopolitan* in condensed version as *Experience with Evil,* March, 1953), Knopf, 1953 (published in England as *Experience with Evil,* Cassell, 1954); *Find a Victim,* Knopf, 1954; *The Name Is Archer,* Bantam, 1955.

Under pseudonym Ross Macdonald: *The Barbarous Coast* (originally published in *Cosmopolitan* in condensed version as *The Dying Animal,* March, 1956), Knopf, 1956; *The Doomsters,* Knopf, 1958; *The Galton Case,* Knopf, 1959; *The Ferguson Affair,* Knopf, 1960; *The Wycherly Woman* (originally published in *Cosmopolitan* in condensed version as *Take My Daughter Home,* April, 1961), Knopf, 1961; *The Zebra-Striped Hearse* (originally published in *Cosmopolitan* in condensed version, September, 1962), Knopf, 1962; *The Chill* (originally published in *Cosmopolitan* in condensed version, August, 1963), Knopf, 1964; *The Far Side of the Dollar* (originally published in *Cosmopolitan* in condensed version as *The Far Side,* September, 1964), Knopf, 1956; *Black Money* (originally published in *Cosmopolitan* in condensed version as *The Demon Lover,* December, 1965), Knopf, 1966; *Archer in Hollywood* (contains *The Moving Target, The Way Some People Die,* and *The Barbarous Coast),* Knopf, 1967; *The Instant Enemy,* Knopf, 1968; (editor) William F. Nolan, *Dashiell Hammett: A Casebook,* McNally & Loftin, 1969; *The Goodbye Look,* Knopf, 1969; *Archer at Large* (contains *The Galton Case, The Chill,* and *Black Money),* Knopf, 1970; (with Arthur Kaye) "Ross Macdonald 'In the First Person' " (screenplay), Davidson Films, 1970; *The Underground Man,* Knopf, 1971.

Contributor: Ellery Queen, editor, *Murder by Experts,* Ziff-Davis, 1947; R.W. Lid, editor, *Essays Classic and Contemporary,* Lippincott, 1967; Thomas McCormack, editor, *Afterwords,* Harper, 1969. Represented in several anthologies, including *Maiden Murders,* edited by John Dickson Carr, Harper, 1952, *Ellery Queen's Awards: Ninth Series,* edited by Ellery Queen, Little, Brown, 1954, and *Best Detective Stories of the Year,* edited by Anthony Boucher, Dutton, 1966. Contributor of short stories to *Ellery Queen's Mystery Magazine, American Mercury, Esquire, Argosy, Manhunt,* and other magazines, of articles to *Lyceum, School, Show, Santa Barbara News-Press, Sports Illustrated,* and *New York Times Magazine,* and of reviews to *Santa Barbara News-Press, New York Post, New York Times Book Review, Saturday Night,* and *San Francisco Chronicle.*

WORK IN PROGRESS: *Sleeping Beauty,* an "Archer" detective novel.

SIDELIGHTS: Millar is one of the few novelists writing in the crime genre to receive widespread critical praise

for his abilities. William Goldman calls him "one of the best American novelists now operating." Dick Adler concurs, stating: "Ken Millar . . . is not only the best in his field but an important American novelist on any level. I know of no other writer who catches the spectrum of California life so succinctly, or who can deal with old sadness in such an immediate way."

Millar's ability to recreate the mood and milieu of southern California is one of the qualities which makes him rather unique in critical judgments. Goldman writes: "Like any other first-rate writer, he has created and peopled his own world. Nobody writes southern California like . . . [Millar] writes it. All those new rich people, the perfect front lawns where no one but the gardener ever treads, the dustless houses with their huge picture windows facing other picture windows—there's something unalive about it all. And since . . . [Millar's] characters are all dying anyway, that's what makes him their perfect chronicler."

Although influenced by the works of Dashiell Hammett and Raymond Chandler, Millar's latter works bear his own particular stamp. In acknowledging his debt to Chandler, Millar writes: "Raymond Chandler was and remains a hard man to follow. He wrote like a slumming angel, and invested the sun-blinded streets of Los Angeles with a romantic presence. While trying to preserve the fantastic lights and shadows of the actual Los Angeles, I gradually siphoned off the aura of romance and made room for a completer social realism. My detective Archer is not so much a knight of romance as an observer, a socially mobile man who knows all the levels of Southern California life and takes a peculiar wry pleasure in exploring its secret passages. Archer tends to live through other people, as a novelist lives through his characters."

It is more than setting, however, that gleans critical approval for Millar. Walter Clemons states that Millar "is a deviser of plots of infernal intricacy. What looked like chance proves to be design, random events are gradually drawn tightly together, relationships are revealed that people have spent years building fake fronts and artificial lives to hide. These plots aren't merely ingenious contraptions; they yield illuminations that outlast our engrossed first reading to find out what will happen, and they retain their power on rereading—which isn't a usual experience with detective novels."

Millar, however, seems unimpressed by increasing praise. "One writes on a curve, on the backs of torn-off calendar sheets," he states. "A writer in his fifties will not recapture the blaze of youth, or the steadier passion that comes like a second and saner youth in his forties, if he's lucky. But he can lie in wait in his room . . . and keep open his imagination and the bowels of his compassion against the day when another book will haunt him like a ghost rising out of both the past and the future."

The Moving Target was filmed in 1966 as "Harper."

AVOCATIONAL INTERESTS: Conservation, bird study, and other outdoor activities.

BIOGRAPHICAL/CRITICAL SOURCES: Seattle Times, August 17, 1958; *New York Post,* November 27, 1960, May 9, 1965; *Los Angeles Magazine,* March, 1963; *Book World,* February 25, 1967; *Time,* August 15, 1967; *West Magazine,* December 10, 1967; *New York Times Book Review,* March 3, 1968, June 1, 1969; *New York Times,* July 6, 1968, February 19, 1971; *Books and Bookmen,* October, 1968; *Newsweek,* July 28, 1969; *National Observer,* September 15, 1969, January 5, 1970; Matthew J. Bruccoli, editor, *Kenneth Millar/Ross Macdonald: A Checklist,* Gale, 1971; *Washington Post,* April 21, 1971.

MILLER, Alice McCarthy

PERSONAL: Born in Lynn, Mass.; daughter of William Henry and Julia (McCarthy) McCarthy; married Warren Hudson Miller (an insurance underwriter), April 3, 1942; children: Nancy Lynn, Jacqueline. *Education:* Hunter College (now Hunter College of the City University of New York), B.A.; New School for Social Research, M.S.S.; Columbia University, M.A., 1963. *Home:* 215 Willoughby Ave., Brooklyn, N.Y. 11205.

CAREER: New York City Community College, Brooklyn, N.Y., instructor in English, 1960-61; Pratt Institute, Brooklyn, N.Y., instructor in psychology, 1961-63. Trustee, Levittown (N.Y.) Public Library, 1950-52. *Member:* Women's National Book Association, Authors Guild of Authors League of America, American Psychological Association (associate), Phi Beta Kappa. *Awards, honors:* Indiana University Foundation awards for *The Heart of Camp Whippoorwill* and an unpublished adult nonfiction book.

WRITINGS: The Heart of Camp Whippoorwill, Lippincott, 1960; *Make Way for Peggy O'Brien!,* Lippincott, 1961; *The Little Store on the Corner,* Abelard, 1961; *In Cold Red Ink: How Term Papers Are Graded and Why,* Allwyn Press, 1968; *Kennedy Chronology,* Allwyn Press, 1968; *Who Shares Your Birthday,* Allwyn Press, 1970; (with husband, Warren Hudson Miller) *The 1910-1919 Decade,* Allwyn Press, 1972. Writer for Dave Garroway's "Today" show, National Broadcasting Co. television, 1952-53.

* * *

MILLER, Cecille (Boyd) 1908-

PERSONAL: Born September 21, 1908, in West Frankfurt, Ill.; daughter of Edward and Emma (Bennett) Boyd; married Gordon D. Miller (a sheetmetal worker), July 2, 1938; children: Roger, Mollie, Daniel, John Mark. *Education:* Attended Illinois State Normal University (now Illinois State University), summer sessions, 1929-37. *Home:* 315 North Alexander, Danville, Ill. 61832.

CAREER: Danville public schools, Danville, Ill., English teacher, 1928-38. Sunday school teacher for fifteen years; church deaconess, 1961-64; church librarian, 1966—.

WRITINGS: Missionary Programs for Women's Meetings, Moody, 1963; *Missionary Programs for Church Groups,* Baker Book, 1971. Contributor to *World Vision, Heritage, Lamp, Success,* and other publications.

WORK IN PROGRESS: Missionary Emphasis for Youth, for Baker Book.

* * *

MILLER, Helen Hill 1899-
(Helen Hill)

PERSONAL: Born July 7, 1899, in Highland Park, Ill.; daughter of Russell Day and Lucia Elliott (Green) Hill; married Francis Pickens Miller, August 25, 1927; children: Andrew Pickens, Robert Day. *Education:* Bryn Mawr College, A.B., 1921; Oxford University, diploma in economics and political science, 1922; University of Chicago, Ph.D., 1928; Institute of University of Geneva, certificat, 1928. *Politics:* Democrat. *Home and office:* 2810 P St. N.W., Washington, D.C. 20007; and Tamassee, Kitty Hawk, N.C. 27949.

CAREER: Bryn Mawr College, Bryn Mawr, Pa., tutor, Summer School for Women Workers in Industry, 1921, 1923, 1926; U.S. Department of Agriculture, Washington, D.C., staff writer, 1930-34; National Policy Committee, Washington, D.C., administrative secretary, 1938-41, executive director, 1941-47; *Economist,* London, England, correspondent, 1940, American editorial representative,

1943-50; *Newsweek,* correspondent in Washington Bureau, 1950-52; *New Republic,* contributing editor, 1958-66; free-lance writer, 1930-34, 1953—. Visiting lecturer, St. John's College, Annapolis, Md., 1939-40. Member of board, Bryn Mawr College, 1948-52. *Member:* American Institute of Archaeology, Women's National Press Club (president, 1955-56), Cosmopolitan Club (New York), City Tavern (Washington, D.C.). *Awards, honors:* American Association for Adult Education grant for research work, 1926-27; Bryn Mawr College distinguished alumni honorary citation.

WRITINGS: The Effect of the Bryn Mawr Summer School as Measured in the Activities of Its Students, American Association for Adult Education and Affiliated Summer Schools for Women Workers in Industry, 1929; (with husband, Francis P. Miller) *Giant of the Western World,* Morrow, 1930; *The Spirit of Modern France* (pamphlet), World Peace Foundation, 1934; *Foreign Trade and the Worker's Job* (pamphlet), World Peace Foundation, 1935; *George Mason, Constitutionalist,* Harvard University Press, 1938, condensed version published as *George Mason of Gunston Hall,* Board of Regents of Gunston Hall, 1958; (with Herbert Agar) *Beyond German Victory,* Reynal, 1940; *France, Crossroads of a Continent,* Foreign Policy Association, 1941; *America's Maginot Lines,* Farrar & Rinehart, 1941; *The Kitchen in War Production,* Public Affairs Committee, 1943; *Yours for Tomorrow: A Personal Testament of Freedom,* Farrar & Rinehart, 1943.

(With John Benjamin Hill) *Genetics and Human Heredity,* McGraw, 1955; *You in the U.S.A.,* Carrie Chapman Catt Memorial Fund, 1956; *Carrie Chapman Catt: The Power of an Idea,* Carrie Chapman Catt Memorial Fund, 1958; *Greek Horizons,* Scribner, 1961; (editor) *Health: Are We the People Getting Our Money's Worth?,* [Washington, D.C.], 1963; *Sicily and the Western Colonies of Greece,* Scribner, 1965; *The Case for Liberty,* University of North Carolina Press, 1965; *Greece,* Scribner, 1965; *Bridge to Asia: The Greeks in the Eastern Mediterranean,* Scribner, 1967; *The Realms of Arthur,* Scribner, 1969; *Greece Through the Ages: As Seen by Travelers from Herodotus to Byron,* Funk, 1972. Contributor of articles to *Harper's, Collier's Esquire, National Geographic, Harvard Business Review,* and other periodicals.

BIOGRAPHICAL/CRITICAL SOURCES: Best Sellers, June 1, 1969; *Virginia Quarterly Review,* autumn, 1969.

* * *

MILLER, Henry (Valentine) 1891-

PERSONAL: Born December 26, 1891, in New York, N.Y.; married Beatrice Sylvas Wickens (a pianist), 1917 (divorced, 1924); married June Smith, 1924 (divorced, 1934); married Janina Martha Lepska, December 18, 1944 (divorced 1952); married Eve McClure, December, 1953 (divorced, 1962); married Hoki Tokuda (a jazz pianist and singer), September 10, 1967; children: (first marriage) Barbara; (third marriage) Valentin (daughter), Tony. *Education:* Attended College of the City of New York (now City College of the City University of New York) for two months in 1909. *Religion:* Calls himself religious although he does not espouse any religion: "That means simply having a reverence for life, being on the side of life instead of death." *Residence:* Pacific Palisades, Calif.

CAREER: Worked for Atlas Portland Cement Co., New York, N.Y., 1909-11; traveled through West, working at odd jobs, 1913; worked with father in tailor shop in New York, N.Y. 1914; mail sorter with U.S. Government War Department, 1917; worked for Bureau of Economic Research, 1919; Western Union Telegraph Co., New York, N.Y., 1920-24, began as messenger, became employment manager; sold prose-poems from door to door, 1925; opened speakeasy in Greenwich Village, 1927; toured Europe, 1928; returned to New York, 1929, and then to Europe, 1930, went to London, then to Paris to live until 1939; proofreader for the Paris edition of the *Chicago Tribune*, 1932; with Lawrence Durrell and Alfred Perles, edited *The Booster*, also writing its fashion page; taught English at Lycee Carnot, Dijon, France, 1932; European editor of *Phoenix;* practiced psychoanalysis in New York, N.Y., 1936; was contributing editor, *Volontes*, January, 1938 until February, 1939; lived in Greece, 1939, until ordered by American Consulate to return to U.S. after outbreak of World War II; toured U.S. by auto, 1940-41; painted and exhibited water colors at Santa Barbara Museum of Art, Calif., and in London, 1944; moved to Big Sur, Calif., and made several trips to Europe, 1944-61; painted and exhibited water colors under auspices of Westwood Art Association, Los Angeles, Calif., March, 1966, and at the Daniel Garvis Gallery in the Rue du Bac, Paris, September, 1967; moved to Pacific Palisades, Calif., 1962.

MEMBER: National Institute of Arts and Letters. *Awards, honors:* Special citation from the Formentor Prize Committee, 1961, as "one of the most important literary figures of the twentieth century"; Commander of Order of Arts and Letters of French government, 1972.

WRITINGS: Tropic of Cancer (autobiographical narrative), includes preface by Anais Nin, Obelisk (Paris), 1935, reissued with an introduction by Karl Shapiro, Grove, 1961, also published in *Henry Miller Trilogy* (see below); *Aller Retour New York*, Obelisk, 1935, American edition privately printed, 1945; *What Are You Going To Do About Alf?* (pamphlet), privately printed, 1935, 4th edition, Bern Porter, 1972; *Black Spring*, Obelisk, 1936, Grove, 1963, also published in *Henry Miller Trilogy* (see below); *Scenario* ("a film with sound ... directly inspired by a phantasy called 'The House of Incest' ... by Anais Nin"), Obelisk, 1937; *Un Etre etoilique*, privately printed, 1937; *Money and How It Gets That Way* (broadside), Booster Publications (Paris), 1938, 2nd edition, Bern Porter, 1946; *Max and the White Phagocytes* (contains *The Cosmological Eye*, "Glittering Pie," "Scenario," "The Universe of Death," "Max," "Reflections on 'Extase,'" four letters from "Hamlet," "The Golden Age," "Via Dieppe-Newhaven," "The Eye of Paris," "An Open Letter to Surrealists Everywhere," and *Un Etre etoilique*), Obelisk, 1938, also published with *The World of Sex* (see below); *Tropic of Capricorn* (autobiographical narrative), Obelisk, 1939, Grove, 1962, also published in *Henry Miller Trilogy* (see below); *The Cosmological Eye* (contains selections from *Max and the White Phagocytes*, *Black Spring*, and other, unpublished material), New Directions, 1939; *Hamlet*, Carrefour (Santurce), Volume 1, 1939, 2nd edition, 1943, Volume 2, 1941, two volumes reissued as *The Michael Fraenkel-Henry Miller Correspondence, called Hamlet*, Carrefour (London), 1962.

The World of Sex, privately printed, 1940, revised edition, Olympia (Paris), 1957, Grove, 1965, also published with *Max and the White Phagocytes* (see below); *The Wisdom of the Heart* (short stories and essays), New Directions, 1941; *The Colossus of Maroussi*, Colt Press, 1941; *Sunday after the War* (contains "Reunion in Brooklyn," selections from "Sexus," and other prose pieces from then unpublished writings), New Directions, 1944; *The Plight of the Creative Artist in the United States of America*, includes illustrations by Miller, Bern Porter, 1944, 2nd edition, 1969; *Varda: The Master Builder* (pamphlet), privately printed, 1944, George Leite (Berkeley), 1947, revised edition, Bern Porter, 1972; *Semblance of a Devoted Past* (selected letters from Miller to Emil Schnellock), Bern Porter, 1944, also published with

To Paint is to Love Again (see below); *The Angel is my Watermark!* (essay; originally published in *Black Spring*—see above), Holve-Barrows (Fullerton), 1944; *Murder the Murderer* (an excursus on war from *The Air-Conditioned Nightmare*), Bern Porter, 1944, 2nd edition, 1972; *The Air-Conditioned Nightmare* (stories and essays on Miller's impressions of the United States), New Directions, Volume 1, 1945, Volume 2: *Remember to Remember*, 1947; (with Hilaire Hiler) *Why Abstract?* (discussion on modern painting), includes a letter by Miller and a note by William Saroyan, New Directions, 1945, reissued as *A Letter*, Falcon Press (London), 1948, Wittenborn, 1962; *Henry Miller Miscellanea*, selected and edited by Bernard H. Porter, includes illustrations by Miller, Bern Porter, 1945; *Echolalia* (reproductions of water colors by Miller), Bern Porter, 1945; *Obscenity and the Law of Reflection*, Alicat Book Shop (Yonkers), 1945; *The Amazing and Invariable Beauford Delaney*, (fragment from *The Air-Conditioned Nightmare*, Volume 2), Alicat Book Shop, 1945; *Maurizius Forever* (essay), original drawings and water colors by Miller, Colt Press, 1946, revised edition, Capra Press, 1973; (with Kenneth Patchen) *Patchen: Man of Anger & Light* [and] *A Letter to God* (the former by Miller, the latter by Patchen), Padell, 1946; *Into the Night Life* (includes text originally published in *Black Spring*), illustrated and designed by Bezalel Schatz, privately printed, 1947; (with others) *Of, By and About Henry Miller: A Collection of Pieces by Miller, Herbert Read, and Others*, Alicat Book Shop, 1947; (with Edwin Corle) *The Smile at the Foot of the Ladder* [and] *About Henry Miller* (the former by Miller, the latter by Corle), Duell, Sloan & Pearce, 1948, the former also published separately by New Directions, 1959; *The Rosy Crucifixion* (trilogy of autobiographical narratives), Book 1: *Sexus*, two volumes, Obelisk, 1949, Grove, 1965, Book 2: *Plexus* (written in English but originally published in French), two volumes, translation by Elisabeth Guertic, Obelisk, 1949, English edition, Grove, 1965, Book 3: *Nexus*, Part 1, Olympia, 1957, Grove, 1965.

The Waters Reglitterized ("the subject of water color in some of its more liquid phases"), John Kidis (San Jose), 1950; *Blaise Cendrars*, Denoel (Paris), 1951; *The Books in My Life*, Peter Owen (London), 1952, New Directions, 1957; *Rimbaud* (two essays; written in English but originally published in French), translation by F. Roger-Cornaz, Mermod (Lausanne), 1952, published in America as *The Time of the Assassins: A Study of Rimbaud*, New Directions, 1956; *Nights of Love and Laughter*, (short stories), introduction by Kenneth Rexroth, New American Library, 1955; *Quiet Days in Clichy* (two narratives), includes photographs by Brassai, Olympia, 1956, Grove, 1965; *The Hour of Man* (originally published in *Chicago Review*, fall, 1956), [Chicago], c.1956; *A Devil in Paradise: The Story of Conrad Moricand* (Part 3 of "Big Sur and the Oranges of Hieronymus Bosch"), New American Library, 1956; *Big Sur and the Oranges of Hieronymus Bosch* (reminiscences), New Directions, 1957; (with Bezalel Schatz) *Twelve Illustrations to Henry Miller* (illustrations by Schatz for Hebrew edition of selected writings by Miller, entitled "Half Past Midnight"), [Jerusalem], 1957; *First Letter to Trygve Hirsch* (pamphlet), Henry Miller Literary Society (Minneapolis), 1957; *The Story of George Dibbern's "Quest"* (pamphlet), 1958; (with D.H. Lawrence) *Pornography and Obscenity: Handbook for Censors* (two essays) Fridtjog-Karla Publications, 1958; *The Red Notebook* (autograph notes and sketches; contains Miller's horoscope), Jargon, 1958; *The Last of the Grenadiers; or, Anything You Like* (catalog of an exhibition of Michonze paintings held at Adams Gallery, London, June-July, 1959), Favil Press (London), 1959; (contributor) Lawrence Durrell and Alfred Perles, *Art and Outrage* (correspondence about Miller between Perles and Durrell), includes intermission by Miller, Putnam (London), 1959, Dutton, 1961; *Reunion in Barcelona* (letter to Perles, from *Aller Retour New York*), Scorpion Press, 1959; *The Henry Miller Reader*, edited by Durrell, New Directions, 1959 (published in England as *The Best of Henry Miller*, Heinemann, 1960); *The Intimate Henry Miller* (collection of stories, essays, and autobiographical sketches), includes introduction by Lawrence Clark Powell, New American Library, 1959; *Defence of the Freedom to Read: A Letter to the Supreme Court of Norway, in Connection with the Ban on "Sexus"/Forsvar for lesefrichetera: Brev til Norges Hoeyeste Domstol i anledning av beslagleggelsen av "Sexus"*, bilingual edition, Forlag J.W. Cappelens (Oslo), 1959.

La Table Ronde, [Paris], 1960; *To Paint is to Love Again*, Cambria Books, 1960, revised edition published with the text of *Semblance of a Devoted Past*, Grossman, 1968; *Stand Still Like the Hummingbird* (essays), New Directions, 1962; (with Brassai, Durrell, and Bissiere) *Hans Reichel, 1892-1958*, J. Bucher (Paris), 1962; (with others) *Joseph Delteil: Essays in Tribute*, St. Albert's Press (London), 1962; *Henry Miller: Watercolors, Drawings, and His Essay, "The Angel is My Watermark!"*, Abrams, 1962; *Just Wild About Harry: A Melo-Melo in Seven Scenes* (first produced in Spoleto, 1968), New Directions, 1963; *Henry Miller Trilogy* (consists of *Tropic of Cancer, Tropic of Capricorn*, and *Black Spring*), Grove, 1963; (with Jacques den Haan) *Milleriana* (articles on Miller's work and correspondence between den Haan and Miller), De Beige Bij (Amsterdam), 1963; (with Durrell) *Lawrence Durrell and Henry Miller: A Private Correspondence*, edited by George Wickes, Dutton, 1963; *Books Tangent to Circle: Reviews*, Bern Porter, 1963, 2nd edition, 1971; *Greece*, includes drawings by Anne Poor, Viking, 1964; *Henry Miller on Writing* (selections from published and unpublished works), compiled by Thomas H. Moore, New Directions, 1964; *Letters to Anais Nin*, edited, with an introduction, by Gunther Stuhlmann, Putnam, 1965; *Selected Prose*, two volumes, MacGibbon & Kee, 1965; *Order and Chaos chez Hans Reichel*, includes introduction by Durrell, Loujon Press (Tucson), 1966; (with Helmut Lander) *Torsi* (text by Miller), Verlag der Europaeischen Buecherei Hieronomi (Bonn), 1966; (with Will Slotnikoff) *The First Time I Live: A Romantic Book About the Writing of a Book and the Birth of a Writer* (includes introduction by Miller and an exchange of letters between Slotnikoff and Miller), Manchester Lane Editions (Washington), 1966; *Lawrence Clark Powell: Two Tributes*, Goliard Press, 1966; *Journey to an Antique Land*, Ben Ben Press (Big Sur), c.1967, also published in *On Turning Eighty* (see below); (with William A. Gordon) *Writer and Critic: A Correspondence with Henry Miller*, Louisiana State University Press, 1968; (with J. Rives Childs) *Collector's Quest: The Correspondence of Henry Miller and J. Rives Childs, 1947-1965*, edited and introduced by Richard Clement Wood, published by University Press of Virginia for Randolph-Macon College, 1968.

The World of Sex [and] Max and the White Phagocytes, Calder & Boyars, 1970; *Insomnia; or, The Devil at Large*, Loujon Press, c.1970; (with Georges Belmont) *Entretiens de Paris*, Stock, 1970, translation by Antony Mcnabb and Harry Scott published as *Face to Face with Henry Miller: Conversations with Georges Belmont*, Sidgwick & Jackson, 1971, published in America as *In Conversation*, Quadrangle, 1972; *My Life and Times* (autobiography), edited by Bradley Smith, Playboy Press, 1971; *Reflections on the Death of Mishima*, Capra Press, 1972; *On Turning Eighty* (chapbook; includes text of *Journey to an Antique Land* and preface to *The Angel is My Watermark*), Capra Press, 1972.

Author of preface: Michael Fraenkel, *Bastard Death: The Autobiography of an Idea*, Carrefour, 1936; Alfred Perles, *The Renegade*, George Allen, 1943; James Hanley, *No Directions*, Faber, 1943; Parker Tyler, *Hollywood's Hallucination*, McClelland, 1944; Haniel Long, *The Power Within Us: Cabeza de Vaca's Relation of His Journey from Florida to the Pacific, 1528-1536*, Lindsay Drummond, 1946; Henry David Thoreau, *Life Without Principle* (three essays), Delkin, 1946; Arthur Rimbaud, *Les Illuminations*, Editions des Gaules, 1949; Brassai, *Histoire de Marie*, Editions de Point du Jour, 1949; Lillian Bos Ross, *Big Sur*, Denoel, 1949; Mezz Mezzrow and Bernhard Wolfe, *La Rage de vivre*, Correa, 1950; Claude Houghton, *Je suis Jonathan Scrivener*, Correa, 1954; Harold Maine, *Quand un homme est fou*, Correa, 1954; W.R. Harding, editor, *Thoreau: A Century of Criticism*, Southern Methodist University Press, 1954; Wallace Fowlie, *La Graal du clown*, 1955; Albert Maillet, *Le Christ dans l'oeuvre d'Andre Gide*, Le Cercle du Livre, 1955; Alfred Perles, *My Friend Henry Miller: An Intimate Biography*, Neville Spearman, 1955; T. Lobsang Rampa, *The Third Eye*, privately printed, 1957; Blaise Cendrars, *A l'aventure*, Denoel, 1958; Eric Barker, *In Easy Dark*, privately printed, 1958; Jack Kerouac, *The Subterraneans*, Grove, 1958; Blaise Cendrars, *Edition complete des oeuvres de Blaise Cendrars*, Volume 5: *L'Homme foudroye [et] La Main coupee*, [Paris], 1960; Junichiro Tanizaki, *Deux amours cruelles*, Stock, 1960; Lawrence Durrell, *Justine*, Buchet-Chastel, 1960; Andreas Feininger, *Frauen and Goettinnen von der Steinzeit bis zu Picasso*, M. DuMont Schauberg, 1960; Junichiro Tanizaki, *The Key*, Knopf, 1961; *Bufano: Sculpture, Mosaics, Drawings* (of Beniaminono Bufano), J. Weatherhill, 1968.

Also author of four unpublished novels, still in manuscript form, written in the 1920's: "Clipped Wings," the story of twelve Western Union messengers, "Moloch," "Crazy Cock," and "This Gentile World." Editor of "Villa Seurat" series during the 1930's. Contributor of essays, short stories, and sketches to *Crisis, New York Herald* (Paris), *New English Weekly* (London), *Criterion, The Booster, T'ien Hsia Monthly* (Shanghai), *Cahiers du Sud* (Marseilles), *Volontes* (Paris), *transition, New Republic, Phoenix, Partisan Review, Experimental Review, Story, Horizon* (London), *Nation, Town and Country, Athene, Poetry-London, Interim, Harper's Bazaar, Rocky Mountain Review, London Magazine, Mademoiselle, Evergreen Review*, and other periodicals.

WORK IN PROGRESS: The second part of *Nexus*, which will complete his autobiography. (Miller told *CA:* "Volume 2 will probably never be written. Have about decided to leave *The Rosy Crucifixion* an 'unfinished symphony' "); a book written for George Seferis, the Nobel Prize winning poet, while on the island of Hydra, Greece, in 1939, tentatively titled *First Impressions of Greece*, completed and awaiting publication; seven new lithographs and nine etchings, produced in Japan by S. Kubo; a collection of new short stories; the story of Miller's friendships with thirty or more close friends, beginning at five years of age, tentatively titled *Book of Friends*.

SIDELIGHTS: When Miller got word of the Supreme Court's action in lifting a Florida ban on his novel, *Tropic of Capricorn*, he recalled a British publisher "who as a gag was going to put a slip in the book for the purchaser to sign, saying: 'I am over 21 and am already thoroughly corrupt, and this can do me no harm.' " According to George Wickes, the publication of *Tropic of Cancer* in America "caused a furore, with some sixty lawsuits waged in different states." Perhaps the most censored writer of all time, Miller continues to insist his books are not pornographic (he is against pornography because it is roundabout, but favors the forthrightness of obscenity). He is indignant over the "perverse sadistic writing" of cheap American paperbacks, whereas his writing is, he says, "healthy because it's joyous and natural." The censorship, however, is lifting. Whereas once his books were trafficked under the counter, they now find prominent display in many drug store windows, and Miller has become, along with Jack London, Mark Twain, and Upton Sinclair, one of the most widely read American authors. "If one American can be called a legend in his own time," said a writer for *Variety* in 1971, "Henry Miller is he." But being a bestseller is "unreal" to him: "I'm being accepted for the wrong reasons," he told the *Paris Review.* "It's a sensational affair, it doesn't mean that I am appreciated for my true worth."

Appreciation, however, has also come from such sources as T.S. Eliot, George Orwell, Edmund Wilson, Lawrence Durrell, and Kenneth Rexroth. Wilson claimed for him the discovery of a "new field of picaresque." Durrell sees in the prose of Miller's autobiographical novels an "Elizabethan quality, a rare tonic vitality which comes from the savage health of its creator." George Wickes asserts that like Whitman and Melville, "Miller belongs in the direct line of American genius—a genius which is essentially formless."

It is this comparison with Whitman, favorable and not, that is most often made. Martin Green calls Miller's Whitmanism "perverted"; Anne Fremantle grants him "a faith Walt Whitman would have envied." Miller himself once wrote: "My loyalty and adoration have been constant—for the same men, all throughout my life: Whitman, Emerson, Thoreau, Rabelais, above all. I still think that no one has ever had a larger, freer, healthier view of man and his universe than Walt Whitman." And another time: ". . . perhaps one reason why I have stressed so much the immoral, the wicked, the ugly, the cruel in my work is because I wanted others to know how valuable these are, how equally if not more important than the good things. Always underneath, you see, this idea of 'acceptance'—which is Whitman's great theme, his contribution." Orwell, who called Miller "a sort of Whitman among the corpses," felt Whitman's celebration of life to be poorer than Miller's because Whitman "is one of those writers who tell you what you ought to feel instead of making you feel it." Anthony Burgess, in a review of *My Life and Times,* noted that Orwell once "paid a fine tribute to Miller, asking his readers of the thirties to note in *Tropic of Cancer* what, even at that late date, could still be done with the English language. Orwell saw in Miller what many of us saw then—a liberating force, a cleanser of the dialect of the tribe."

Miller makes no bones about appealing to the heart instead of the intellect. He believes *The Colossus of Maroussi* is his best book because "it expresses joy, it gives joy." His ribaldry, eroticism, and mystical leanings put him in the mainstream of anti-intellectualism; he believes that "it's bad to think. A writer shouldn't think much. . . . I work from some deep down place; and when I write, well, I don't know just exactly what's going to happen." An artist, to him, is "a man who has antennae, who knows how to hook up to the currents which are in the atmosphere, in the cosmos; he has merely the facility for hooking on, as it were." Though Rexroth calls him "a very unliterary writer," who acts "as if he had just invented the alphabet," Miller claims he never turned his back on art: "I may have been defiant, nothing more." It is superficial form, imposed from without, and conscious technique that Miller has shunned. The aesthetic element is certainly present; he was concerned enough for the effect to rewrite *Tropic of Cancer* three times. "What makes Miller distinctive among modern writers," says Herbert Read, "is his ability to combine, without confusion, the aesthetic and prophetic functions."

For Miller, "the highest art is the art of living," and indeed few writers seem so thoroughly alive. He prefers even lonely individualism to "civilization," which is akin to death. Any organization is "a sign of 'impotency,' all imitation is suicide" (Herbert J. Muller). He is completely apolitical because politics "debases everything." The "business of youth—rebellion, longing for freedom—and the business of vision are the two very cardinal points in my orientation," he says. Men of principle bore him. "I am interested—like God—only in the individual." "And I do not want to be a saint! Morality, in fact, drops out of the picture. Maybe the writer will drop out too. Or the man. Never the ego, rest assured. Nor do I give a damn about that." He has no desire to alter the world. "Perhaps I can put it best by saying that I hope to alter my own vision of the world. I want to be more and more myself, ridiculous as that may sound."

Miller has always been attracted to Eastern religious systems. Durrell believes that "only these holy men [of the East] would be able to read his spiritual adventure without prejudice, and would regard his books as a spiritual autobiography." Walker Winslow notes: "I have never known one who was so in love with the miraculous and yet so realistic about his own experience with it" (which bring to mind Wickes' remark about Miller today looking "rather like a Buddhist monk who has swallowed a canary.").

His friend Alfred Perles feels that Miller "is one of those peculiar geniuses who must be approached from the human rather than the literary end; . . . . The failure of literary criticism, at least in England and America, to gauge the portent of his work, to apprehend the fundamental simplicity of his writings, is due to the fact that Henry cannot be shanghaied into any literary category." At the age of 80, Miller said of the critics: "How fatuous it is of them to think that they know why an author did this or that, what influenced him, what he meant to do, and so on. And I end up thinking of how little I myself know about what I do, why I do it, or how. *Then who does?* As any idiot will tell you, the question is irrelevant." Americans today view him with mixed feelings. He says he is seen as "an object of pity, hatred, love, admiration, everything," and that these reactions amuse him. The key to his work, he says, is the utter truth. "And . . . I found it easier to give the truth about the ugly side of my nature than the good." "I wrote all these autobiographical books not because I think myself such an important person but—this will make you laugh—because I thought when I began that I was telling the story of the most tragic suffering any man had endured. As I got on with it I realized that I was only an amateur at suffering."

Miller considers John Cowper Powys "the greatest writer in the English language, the pope of writers," and also admires Robert Musil and Lawrence Durrell (from the latter he learned "to improve my style"). In 1937 he first met Durrell, Eliot, and Dylan Thomas. He still goes on insisting that he is just a Brooklyn boy, though Harold Maine once observed: "I constantly had the feeling that he was on leave of absence from ancient Greece or China, pledged to observe in our day only those things that had eternal currency."

Miller's major avocational interest is painting in watercolor (he is said to be an amateur in the highest sense of the word). According to Peter Bart of the *New York Times,* Miller, having become bored with writing ("I've written everything I want to say"), now turns out about 150 water colors a year, most of them ventures in abstract expressionism. At the opening of an exhibition of some 60 paintings and etchings in Los Angeles in March of 1966, Miller said he considered himself "a beginner." Bart quoted him as saying: " 'That's what fascinates me about it. As a writer I know I can do what I want to do.

As a painter I'm still groping. There's more of a challenge.' "

In 1957 Riverside Records released a recording entitled "Henry Miller Recalls and Reflects." Playboy produced a recording of Henry Miller talking with Bradley Smith in 1973. A motion picture of *Quiet Days in Clichy* was filmed by SBA-ABC Productions (Denmark) in 1969, to be shown in the United States as "Henry Miller's Not So Quiet Days." In 1969 Joseph Strick also produced and directed a feature film of *Tropic of Cancer* for Paramount.

Robert Snyder produced two NET specials on Miller in June of 1970, a half-hour program entitled "Encounter: Buckminster Fuller and Henry Miller," and an hour-long broadcast, "Henry Miller Reads and Muses." Snyder has also produced a feature-length documentary, entitled "The Henry Miller Odyssey." The film was made on the occasion of Miller's 77th birthday, cut to 110 minutes from 15 hours of conversation with Miller and his friends, including Brassai, Durrell, Nin, and Jacob Gimpel. In 1973 Tom Schiller produced a film of Henry Miller in his bathroom, according to Miller "a sort of 'voyage autour de ma chambre,' " as yet untitled.

A Miller archives, founded by Lawrence Clark Powell, is maintained at the University of California, Los Angeles. There is also a Miller collection at the library of Randolph-Macon College in Ashland, Va.

BIOGRAPHICAL/CRITICAL SOURCES — Books: George Orwell, *Inside the Whale, and Other Essays*, Gollancz, 1940; Nicholas Moore, *Henry Miller*, Opus Press, 1943; Michael Fraenkel, *Genesis of the Tropic of Cancer*, Bern Porter, 1944; *The Happy Rock: A Book About Henry Miller* (by various authors), Bern Porter, 1945; *Henry Miller: A Chronology and Bibliography*, Bern Porter, 1945; Claude Mauriac, *The New Literature*, Braziller, 1959; Kenneth Rexroth, *Bird in the Bush: Obvious Essays*, New Directions, 1959; Alfred Perles, *Reunion in Big Sur: A Letter to Henry Miller in Reply to his "Reunion in Barcelona"*, Scorpion Press, 1959; Karl Shapiro, *In Defense of Ignorance*, Random House, 1960; Lawrence Clark Powell, *Books in My Baggage*, World Publishing, 1960; Sydney Omarr, *Henry Miller: His World of Urania*, 9th House, 1960; Thomas H. Moore, editor, *Bibliography of Henry Miller*, Henry Miller Literary Society, 1961; Emil White, editor, *Henry Miller—Between Heaven and Hell: A Symposium*, privately printed, 1961; Annette Kar Baxter, *Henry Miller, Expatriate*, University of Pittsburgh Press, 1961; Wayne C. Booth, *The Rhetoric of Fiction*, University of Chicago Press, 1961; Maxine Renken, *A Bibliography of Henry Miller, 1945-1961*, Alan Swallow, 1962; George Wickes, editor, *Henry Miller and the Critics*, Southern Illinois University Press, 1963; Terry Southern, Richard Seaver, and Alexander Trocchi, editors, *Writers in Revolt*, Berkley, 1963; Madeleine Chapsal, *Quinze Ecrivains*, Julliard, 1963; *Writers at Work: The Paris Review Interviews*, 2nd series, Viking, 1963; Kingsley Widmer, *Henry Miller*, Twayne, 1964; George Wickes, *Henry Miller*, University of Minnesota Press, 1966; Thomas B. Whitbread, *Seven Contemporary Authors*, University of Texas Press, 1966; Julian Symons, *Critical Occasions*, Hamish Hamilton, 1966; Kenneth C. Dick, *Henry Miller: Colossus of One*, E.M. Reynolds, 1967; William A. Gordon, *The Mind and Art of Henry Miller*, J. Cape, 1968; Ihab Habib Hassan, *The Literature of Silence: Henry Miller and Samuel Beckett*, Knopf, 1968; E.R. Hutchison, *Tropic of Cancer on Trial: A Case History of Censorship*, Grove, 1968; Jane A. Nelson, *Form and Image in the Fiction of Henry Miller*, Wayne State University Press, 1970; Charles Rembar, *The End of Obscenity*, Deutsch, 1969, Simon & Schuster, 1970.

Articles: *Prairie Schooner*, summer, 1959; *Life*, July 6, 1959; *Books and Bookmen*, February, 1960, March, 1960; *Newsweek*, February 18, 1963, March 2, 1970; *Time*, March 1, 1963; *Critique*, spring-summer, 1965; *New York Times*, March 23, 1966; *South Atlantic Quarterly*, summer, 1966; *Observer Review*, September 24, 1967; *Virginia Quarterly Review*, spring, 1968; *Washington Post*, February 18, 1970; *Variety*, March 4, 1970, March 10, 1971; *New Republic*, March 7, 1970; *Show*, July 9, 1970; *Punch*, October 7, 1970; *Playboy*, November, 1971; *Saturday Review*, December 11, 1971; *New York Times Book Review*, January 2, 1972.

* * *

MILLER, Merle 1919-

PERSONAL: Born May 17, 1919, in Montour, Iowa; son of Monte Merle (a farmer) and Dora B. (Winders) Miller; married Elinor Green, January, 1948 (divorced). *Education:* State University of Iowa, student, 1935-38, 1939-40; London School of Economics, University of London, student, 1938-39. *Politics:* Radical Socialist. *Religion:* Druid. *Home:* Sherwood Hill, Brewster, N.Y. 10509. *Agent:* Martha Winston, Curtis Brown Ltd., 60 East 56th St., New York, N.Y. 10022.

CAREER: Philadelphia Record, Philadelphia, Pa., Washington correspondent, 1940-41; *Time*, New York, N.Y., associate editor, 1945; *Harper's*, New York, N.Y., editor, 1947-49; free-lance writer, 1949—. *Military service:* U.S. Army, 1941-45; editor of *Yank* in Pacific theater, then in Europe; received Bronze Star with oak-leaf cluster. *Member:* Authors Guild of Authors League of America (president, 1950-54), Writers Guild of America East.

WRITINGS: Island 49 (novel), Crowell, 1945; (with Abe Spitzer) *We Dropped the A-Bomb*, Crowell, 1946; *That Winter* (novel), Sloane, 1948; *The Sure Thing* (novel), Sloane, 1949; *The Judges and the Judged* (nonfiction), Doubleday, 1952; *Reunion* (novel), Viking, 1954; "The Rains of Ranchipur" (screenplay; based on the novel *The Rains Came* by Louis Bromfield), 20th Century-Fox, 1955; *A Secret Understanding* (suspense novel), Viking, 1956; "Kings Go Forth" (screenplay; based on the novel by Joe David Brown), United Artists, 1958; (author of introduction) *Combat European Theatre*, Dell, 1958; *A Gay and Melancholy Sound* (novel), Sloane, 1961; *A Day in Late September* (novel), Sloane, 1963; (with Evan Rhodes) *Only You Dick Darling!; or, How to Write One Television Script, and Make $50,000,000*, Sloane, 1964; *On Being Different: What It Means to Be a Homosexual*, Random House, 1971; *What Happened* (novel), Harper, 1972; *Marshalltown, Iowa* (nonfiction), Holt, in press.

Contributor: *The Best from Yank*, Dutton, 1945; Del Myers and others, editors, *Yank: The G.I. Story of the War*, Duell, Sloan & Pearce, 1947; L.L. Snyder and R.B. Morris, editors, *A Treasury of Great Reporting*, Simon & Schuster, 1949; *Highlights from Yank*, Dell, 1953; Elizabeth Bragdon, editor, *Women Today: Their Conflicts, Their Frustrations and Their Fulfillments*, Bobbs-Merrill, 1953; *Writers Roundtable*, Harper, 1955; John Fischer and R.B. Silvers, editors, *Writing in America*, Rutgers University Press, 1960. Author of television adaptation of *Reunion* and of other television plays for "Playhouse 90" and "Sunday Showcase." Also author of several other film scripts. Contributor to *Show*, *Harper's*, *Esquire*, *Saturday Review*, *Reader's Digest*, *Redbook*, *Collier's*, and *New York Times Magazine*.

WORK IN PROGRESS: A biography of Harry S Truman.

SIDELIGHTS: "In the twenty-two years . . . when I have been as my mother puts it, 'without steady work,' I have become increasingly disciplined, seem to have more to say, seem to say it better, seem to say it to fewer people. My audience is now nearly down to the size of Stendhal—*The Happy Few.*

"I have written some movies that should, I think, be allowed to rest in peace and anonymity. I belong to no organizations—except those required by the complexities of this place and this time. . . . I do not believe in Organizations or Causes. Like E.M. Forster, 'Lord, I disbelieve—help thou my unbelief.' My only real hobby is travel, and I have at the moment a special passion for the people and countries whose temperament or origins are Latin." He adds that he is, however, planning a tour around the world.

BIOGRAPHICAL/CRITICAL SOURCES: Roy Newquist, *Conversations,* Rand McNally, 1967; *New York Times,* March 27, 1968; *Punch,* February 12, 1969; *TV Guide,* November 22, 1969; *Washington Post,* December 8, 1971.

*   *   *

MILLER, Nolan 1912-

PERSONAL: Born May 4, 1912, in Kalida, Ohio; son of John Hiram (a merchant) and Elizabeth (Myers) Miller. *Education:* Wayne State University, A.B 1929, M.A., 1940; University of Wisconsin, graduate study, 1931-32; University of Michigan, postgraduate study, 1943. *Agent:* Russell & Volkening, Inc., 551 Fifth Ave., New York, N.Y. 10017. *Office:* Antioch Review, Yellow Springs, Ohio 45487; and 10A Cleniston Gardens, London W.8, England.

CAREER: Antioch College, Yellow Springs, Ohio, 1946—, began as assistant professor, became professor of literature, now director of Antioch College Center for English Studies. *Military service:* U.S. Army, 1943.

WRITINGS: A Moth of Time (novel), Harper, 1946; *The Merry Innocents* (novel), Harper, 1947; *Why I Am So Beat* (novel), Putnam, 1954.

Compiler: *New Campus Writing #1,* Bantam, 1955; (with Judson Jerome) *New Campus Writing #2,* Putnam, 1957; (with Jerome) *New Campus Writing #3,* Grove, 1959; (with Jerome) *New Campus Writing #4,* Grove, 1962; *New Campus Writing #5,* McGraw, 1966. Contributor of thirty short stories, and of articles and reviews to magazines. Associate editor, *Antioch Review.*

WORK IN PROGRESS: Intelligent Fountains, a novel; *The Fiction of Fiction,* a book on writing.

*   *   *

MILLER, Vassar 1924-

PERSONAL: Born July 19, 1924, in Houston, Tex.; daughter of Jessie Gustavus and Vassar (Morrison) Miller. *Education:* University of Houston, B.S., 1947, M.A., 1952. *Religion:* Episcopalian. *Home:* 1651 Harold St., Houston, Tex. 77006.

CAREER: St. John's School, Houston, Tex., teacher of creative writing, 1964—; poet. *Member:* Writers' Club (University of Houston), Texas Institute of Letters. *Awards, honors:* Texas Institute of Letters awards, 1956, for *Adam's Footprint,* 1961, for *Wage War on Silence,* and 1963, for *My Bones Being Wiser.*

WRITINGS—All poetry: *Adam's Footprint,* New Orleans Poetry Journal, 1956; *Wage War on Silence,* Wesleyan University Press, 1960; *My Bones Being Wiser,* Wesleyan University Press, 1963; *Onions and Roses,* Wesleyan University Press, 1968. Represented in anthologies, including: *New Poets of England and America,* edited by D. Hall, Meridian, 1957, 1962; *Poet's Choice,* edited by P. Engle and J.T. Langland, Dial, 1962; *A Poetry Sampler,* edited by D. Hall, Watts, 1962; *Poems of Doubt and Belief,* edited by T.F. Driver and R. Pack, Macmillan (New York), 1964; *Today's Poets,* edited by C. Walsh, Scribner, 1964; *A Controversy of Poets,* edited by P. Leary and R. Kelly, Doubleday, 1965. Contributor to *New York Times, Paris Review, Transatlantic Review,* and *New Orleans Poetry Journal.* Wrote talk for Voice of America in 1963.

SIDELIGHTS: Miss Miller's poetry is primarily religious. She once said: "Poetry, like all art, has a trinitarian function: creative, redemptive, and sanctifying. It is creative because it takes the raw materials of fact and feeling and makes them into that which is neither fact nor feeling. It is redemptive because it can transform the pain and ugliness of life into joy and beauty. It is sanctifying because it thus gives the transitory at least a relative form and meaning. Hence poetry, whether avowedly so or not, is always religious; it is akin to prayer, an act of love." She later wrote: "I used to say that a poem is an act of love. Now I know that it is an act of hate also. At best, these two emotions are not mutually exclusive."

Denise Levertou wrote: "Miss Miller, with rare exceptions, writes with the clarity and simplicity of someone who is not looking to see if her peers are listening. The result is elegant and strong." Howard Nemerov has written of *Adam's Footprint:* "These pieces ... are at their best brilliant works of language. . . ."

Although afflicted with cerebral palsy since birth, Miss Miller has traveled widely in the United States, and in 1965 she visited Europe.

BIOGRAPHICAL/CRITICAL SOURCES: Howard Nemerov, *Poetry & Fiction: Essays,* Rutgers University Press, 1963; *New York Times Book Review,* June 21, 1964, December 22, 1968; *Times Literary Supplement.*

*   *   *

MILLIGAN, Terence Alan 1918-
(Spike Milligan)

PERSONAL: Born April 16, 1918, in India; son of Leo Alphonso (an Army officer) and Florence Winifred (Kettleband) Milligan; married Margaret Patricia Ridgeway; children: one son, three daughters. *Religion:* Catholic. *Office:* Spike Milligan Productions Ltd., 9 Orme Court, London W.2, England.

CAREER: Free-lance writer, mainly for radio and television. Originator of "Goon Show," which ran for ten years in England; writer for award winning television show, "Fred." Artist. *Awards, honors:* TV Writer of the Year award, 1956.

WRITINGS—All under name Spike Milligan: *Silly Verse for Kids,* Dobson, 1959; (self-illustrated) *A Dustbin of Milligan,* Dobson, 1961; *The Little Pot Boiler: A Book Based Freely on His Seasonal Overdraft,* Dobson, 1963; *Puckoon* (novel), Anthony Blond, 1963; *A Book of Bits; or, A Bit of a Book,* Dobson, 1965; (with Carol Barker) *The Bald Twit Lion,* Dobson, 1968; (self-illustrated) *A Book of Milliganimals,* Dobson, 1968; *The Bedside Milligan; or Read Your Way to Insomnia,* Margaret & Jack Hobbs, 1969; *Values* (poems), Offcut Press, 1969; (with John Antrobus) *The Bedsitting Room* (play; first produced on West End at Mermaid Theatre, January, 1963), Margaret & Jack Hobbs, 1970; *Adolf Hitler: My Part in His Downfall,* M. Joseph, 1971; *Milligan's Ark,* edited by Milligan and Jack Hobbs, Margaret & Jack Hobbs, 1971; *Badjelly the Witch,* M. Joseph, 1971; *The Goon Show Scripts,* St. Martin's, 1973.

SIDELIGHTS: The Bedsitting Room was filmed in 1969; *Adolf Hitler: My Part in His Downfall* was filmed in 1972. *Avocational interests:* Restoration of antiques, oil painting, watercolors, gardening, eating, drinking, talking, wine, and jazz.

BIOGRAPHICAL/CRITICAL SOURCES: Listener, August 8, 1968; Bookseller, May 15, 1971; Observer Review, June 20, 1971.†

*   *   *

MILLS, Betty (Lidstrom) 1926-

PERSONAL: Born July 21, 1926, in Glen Ullin, N.D.; daughter of Leonard C. (a rancher) and Crystal (Sletmoen) Lidstrom; married William R. Mills (an attorney), August 16, 1947; children: Randa, Sherry, William, Nancy Jo. Education: University of Minnesota, student, 1944-47; Mary College, B.A., 1967. Politics: Independent Republican. Religion: Unitarian. Home: 1019 Ave. C W., Bismarck, N.D. 58501.

CAREER: Secretary, North Dakota Broadcasting Council; member, North Dakota Advisory Council on Libraries. Board member, Bismarck Public Library. Member: American Association of University Women, League of Women Voters.

WRITINGS: (With Lucile Hasley) Mind if I Differ?: A Catholic-Unitarian Dialogue, Sheed, 1964. Contributor to Unitarian Christian and Take a Giant Step.

WORK IN PROGRESS: A book on the informal side of the legal profession, as seen by a wife.

*   *   *

MILLS, Ralph J(oseph), Jr. 1931-

PERSONAL: Born December 16, 1931, in Chicago, Ill.; son of Ralph J. (a businessman) and Eileen (McGuire) Mills; married Helen Daggett Harvey, November 25, 1959; children: Natalie, Julian, Brett. Education: Lake Forest College, B.A., 1954; Northwestern University, M.A., 1956, Ph.D., 1963; Oxford University student-at-large, 1956-57. Politics: Democrat. Religion: Roman Catholic. Home: 1451 North Astor St., Chicago, Ill. 60610. Office: Department of English, University of Illinois at Chicago Circle, Chicago, Ill. 60680.

CAREER: University of Chicago, Chicago, Ill., instructor, 1959-61, assistant professor of English, and associate chairman of Committee on Social Thought, 1962-65; University of Illinois at Chicago Circle, associate professor, 1965-67, professor of English, 1967—. Member: Phi Beta Kappa, Phi Kappa Phi, Arts Club (Chicago; member of literary committee, 1962—). Awards, honors: English-Speaking Union fellowship to Oxford, 1956-57.

WRITINGS: Theodore Roethke (pamphlet), University of Minnesota Press, 1963; Eden's Gate: The Later Poetry of Edwin Muir, [Los Angeles], c.1963; The Visionary Poetry of Kathleen Raine, [Milwaukee], c.1963; Contemporary American Poetry, Random House, 1965; (editor) On the Poet and His Craft: Selected Prose of Theodore Roethke, University of Washington Press, 1965; Richard Eberhart (pamphlet), University of Minnesota Press, 1966; Edith Sitwell: A Critical Essay, Eerdmans, 1966; Kathleen Raine: A Critical Essay, Eerdmans, 1967; (editor and author of introduction) Theodore Roethke, Selected Letters, University of Washington Press, 1968; Creation's Very Self: On the Personal Element in Recent American Poetry, Texas Christian University Press, 1969.

Contributor: E.B. Hungerford, editor, Poets in Progress, Northwestern University Press, 1962; Marie Borroff, editor, Wallace Stevens: A Collection of Critical Essays, Prentice-Hall, 1963; Nathan A. Scott, Jr., editor, The Climate of Faith in Modern Literature, Seabury, 1964; Arnold Stein, editor, Theodore Roethke: Essays on the Poetry, University of Washington Press, 1965; Nathan A. Scott, Jr., editor, Four Ways of Modern Poetry, John Knox, 1965; Rosalie Murphy, editor, Contemporary Poets of the English Language, St. James Press, 1970. Contribu-

tor of essays on modern poets to Accent, Poetry, Commentary, Renascence, and other journals.

WORK IN PROGRESS: Cry of the Human: Essays on Contemporary American Poetry, for Swallow Press; editing The Notebooks of David Ignatow, for Swallow Press.

SIDELIGHTS: Mills aims in his critical studies to bring out the chief qualities of the modern poets in sympathetic interpretation. "I have tried to be on the side of the poets first and foremost," he adds, "and so have never supported any particular critical doctrine or aesthetic dogma."

BIOGRAPHICAL/CRITICAL SOURCES: Sewanee Review, summer, 1968; New Republic, September 21, 1968; New York Times Book Review, September 29, 1968; Virginia Quarterly Review, autumn, 1968; New York Times, January 1, 1969; Nation, January 6, 1969; Poetry, February, 1969; London Magazine, September, 1970.

*   *   *

MILNER, Marion (Blackett) 1900-
(Joanna Field)

PERSONAL: Born February 1, 1900, in London, England; daughter of Stuart and Nina (Maynard) Blackett; married Dennis Milner, September 22, 1927; children: John. Education: Attended Godolphin School, Salisbury, England; University College, University of London, B.Sc., 1923. Home: 12 Provost Rd., London N.W. 3, England.

CAREER: National Institute of Industrial Psychology, London, England, investigator, 1924-27; Girls' Public Day School Trust, England, researcher, 1934-39; private practice as psychoanalyst, London, England, 1943—; training analyst for British Psychoanalytic Society, 1947—. Member: British Psychoanalytic Society, British Psychological Society (fellow). Awards, honors: Laura Spelman Rockefeller traveling fellowship in United States, 1927-29.

WRITINGS: (With Frank M. Earle and others) The Use of Performance Tests of Intelligence in Vocational Guidance, Industrial Fatigue Research Board, 1929; (under pseudonym Joanna Field) A Life of One's Own, Chatto & Windus, 1934; (under pseudonym Joanna Field) An Experiment in Leisure, Chatto & Windus, 1937; The Human Problem in Schools: A Psychological Study Carried Out in Behalf of the Girls' Public Day School Trust, Methuen, 1938; (self-illustrated) under pseudonym Joanna Field) On Not Being Able to Paint, Heinemann, 1950, 2nd edition published under own name, with a foreword by Anna Freud, Heinemann, 1957, International Universities Press, 1958; (contributor) J.D. Sutherland, editor, Psychoanalysis and Contemporary Thought, Hogarth, 1958; The Hands of the Living God: An Account of a Psycho-Analytic Treatment, International Universities Press, 1969. Contributor to symposia and to journals, including International Journal of Psychoanalysis and New Era.

WORK IN PROGRESS: A revision of An Experiment in Leisure.

AVOCATIONAL INTERESTS: Painting (Mrs. Milner had her first one-woman show at the Brian Gallery, London, January, 1971.)

*   *   *

MINER, John B(urnham) 1926-

PERSONAL: Born July 20, 1926, in New York, N.Y.; son of John Lynn (a private school headmaster) and Bess (Burnham) Miner; married Sally Tollerton, August 28, 1948 (divorced, 1966); married Mary Green Thompson, January 11, 1967; children: (first marriage) Barbara Ellen, John Tollerton, Cynthia Ann, Frances Mary. Education: Attended Greenwich Country Day School, 1932-40, Deerfield Academy, 1940-44; Princeton University, A.B., 1950, Ph.D., 1955; Clark University, M.A., 1952.

Home: 116 Lillian Lane, Silver Spring, Md. 20904. *Office:* College of Business and Public Administration, University of Maryland, College Park, Md. 20742.

CAREER: Columbia University, New York, N.Y., research associate in psychology, 1956-57; Atlantic Refining Co., Philadelphia, Pa., senior psychologist, 1957-60; University of Oregon, Eugene, associate professor, 1960-62, professor of management, 1962-68; University of Maryland, College Park, professor of business administration, 1968—, chairman of behavioral science division, 1969—. Certified psychologist, New York State. Visiting professor of psychology, University of California, Berkeley, 1966-67. Consultant, McKinsey & Co., 1966-69. *Military service:* U.S. Army, 1944-46; became staff sergeant; received Bronze Star, Combat Infantry Badge. *Member:* American Psychological Association, Industrial Relations Research Association, Academy of Management.

WRITINGS: Intelligence in the United States: A Survey with Conclusions for Manpower Utilization in Education and Employment, Springer Publishing, 1957; (with Silvan Tomkins) *The Tomkins-Horn Picture Arrangement Test,* Springer Publishing, 1957; (with Tomkins) *Picture Arrangement Test Interpretation,* Springer Publishing, 1959; (with others) *Breakdown and Recovery,* Columbia University Press, 1959; *The Management of Ineffective Performance,* McGraw, 1963, abridged edition published as *Introduction to Industrial Clinical Psychology,* 1966; *Scoring Guide for the Miner Sentence Completion Scale,* Springer Publishing, 1964; *Studies in Management Education,* Springer Publishing, 1965; *The School Administrator and Organizational Character,* Center for the Advanced Study of Educational Administration, University of Oregon, 1967; *Personnel and Industrial Relations: A Managerial Approach,* Macmillan, 1969, 2nd edition (with wife, Mary Green Miner), 1973; *Personnel Psychology,* Macmillan, 1969; *Management Theory,* Macmillan, 1971; *The Management Process: Theory, Research and Practice,* Macmillan, 1973. Contributor of more than forty articles to psychology and business journals.

WORK IN PROGRESS: With Allan Nash, editing *Readings in Personnel and Industrial Relations,* for Macmillan; with Stephen Carroll and Frank Paine, editing *Readings in Management* for Macmillan; with wife, Mary Miner, *The Personnel Management Profession* for the Bureau of National Affairs.

*   *   *

MINER, Ward L(ester)   1916-

PERSONAL: Born March 22, 1916, near Wellman, Iowa; son of T. Ralph and Carrie (Talbot) Miner; married Thelma M. Smith (a university professor), October 27, 1950. *Education:* University of Colorado, B.A., 1938; University of Chicago, M.A., 1940; University of Pennsylvania, Ph.D., 1951. *Home address:* RFD 1, North Jackson, Ohio 44451.

CAREER: Instructor in English at South Dakota State College, Brookings, 1940-42, Colorado School of Mines, Golden, 1945-46, Temple University, Philadelphia, Pa., 1946-51; independent research in France, 1951-53; Queens College (now Queens College of the City University of New York), Flushing, N.Y., assistant professor of English, 1953-54; Youngstown State University, Youngstown, Ohio, associate professor, 1957-63, professor of American studies, 1963—, chairman of department of English, 1963-68, head of graduate studies, 1968—. Fulbright professor at Turku, Finland, 1955-56, Elsinore, Denmark, 1960-61, and Reykjavik, Iceland, 1966-67; visiting assistant professor of English, University of Kansas, 1956-57. *Military services:* U.S. Army Air Forces, 1942-45; became first lieutenant; received Distinguished Flying Cross and Air Medal with four oak-leaf clusters. *Member:* American Studies Association (president, Ohio-Indiana

chapter, 1963-64), Modern Language Association of America, American Association of University Professors (chairman of Ohio conference, 1963-64), National Council of Teachers of English, American Civil Liberties Union, Americans for Democratic Action. *Awards, honors:* Fellow, American Council of Learned Societies, 1951-52; American Philosophical Society research award, 1955.

WRITINGS: The World of William Faulkner, Duke University Press, 1952; (with wife, Thelma M. Smith) *Transatlantic Migration: The Contemporary American Novel in France,* Duke University Press, 1955; (contributor) *Ernest Hemingway: Configuration Critique,* Lettres Modernes, 1958; *William Goddard, Newspaperman,* Duke University Press, 1962.

*   *   *

MINOR, Edward Orville   1920-

PERSONAL: Born May 31, 1920, in Gary, Ind.; son of Norton Edward and Margaret (Praul) Minor; married Bertha James (a university instructor), December 24, 1947. *Education:* Indiana University, B.S., 1948, M.S., 1950, Ed.D., 1954. *Politics:* Democrat. *Home:* 3122 Galimore Dr., Tallahassee, Fla. 32304. *Office:* Instructional Media Center, Florida Agricultural and Mechanical University, Tallahassee, Fla. 32307.

CAREER: Indiana University, Bloomington, instructor in School of Education and assistant production supervisor in Audio-Visual Center, 1952-54; Florida Agricultural and Mechanical University, Tallahassee, director of Communications Services, 1956-62; Advanced Teachers College, Yaba, Lagos, Nigeria, 1962-64; University of Hawaii, Honolulu, professor and media specialist, 1971-72; Florida Agricultural and Mechanical University, Tallahassee, director of Instructional Media Center, 1972—. Visiting summer professor, Brigham Young University, 1960; visiting professor of education, University of California, Los Angeles, 1962-64; visiting professor, University of Southern California, 1967. Commercial artist, designing book and magazine covers.

WRITINGS: (Author of film script with Harvey Frye) "Lettering Instructional Materials," Indiana University, 1954; *Simplified Techniques for Preparing Visual Instructional Materials,* McGraw, 1962; (with Frye) *Techniques for Producing Visual Instructional Media,* McGraw, 1970.

BIOGRAPHICAL/CRITICAL SOURCES: Audiovisual Instruction, November, 1962; *McGraw-Hill Technical Education News,* November, 1962.

*   *   *

MINOTT, Rodney G(lisan)   1928-

PERSONAL: Surname is pronounced *My*-not; born June 1, 1928, in Portland, Ore.; son of Joseph Albert and Gainor (Baird) Minott; married Polly Fitzhugh Kennedy, June 28, 1952; children: Katharine, Rodney, Jr., Polly Berry. *Education:* Stanford University, A.B., 1953, M.A., 1956, Ph.D., 1960. *Politics:* Democrat. *Religion:* Episcopal. *Home:* 297 Selby Lane, Atherton, Calif. 94025.

CAREER: Stanford University, Stanford, Calif., instructor, 1960-61, assistant professor of history and director of summer session, 1961-65; California State College at Hayward, associate professor and associate dean of instruction, 1966-67, professor of history, 1967—, head of humanities division, 1967-69. *Military service:* U.S. Army, 1945-47, 1950-52. *Member:* American Historical Association, American Association of University Professors, Association of United States Army, Organization of American Historians, Oregon Historical Society.

WRITINGS: *Peerless Patriots: The Organized Veterans and the Spirit of Americanism, 1898 to the Present*, Public Affairs Press, 1963; *The Fortress that Never Was: The Myth of Hitler's Bavarian Fortress*, Holt, 1964 (published in England as *The Fortress That Never Was: The Myth of Nazi Alpine Redoubt*, Longmans, Green, 1965); *The Sinking of the Lollipop: Shirley Temple vs. Pete McCloskey*, Diablo, 1968.

WORK IN PROGRESS: A social history of the American fighting man during World War II; a book on California politics.

BIOGRAPHICAL/CRITICAL SOURCES: *New York Times Book Review*, November 3, 1968.

* * *

MISHEIKER, Betty Fairly 1919-

PERSONAL: Born June 7, 1919, in Pretoria, Transvaal, South Africa; daughter of Clement and Yetta (Bloch) Fairly; married Aron Misheiker (an educator), October 25, 1942; children: Jonathan, Ilona. *Education:* Educated in South African schools. *Religion:* Hebrew. *Home:* 27 Melrose Gardens, Illoro, Johannesburg, South Africa. *Agent:* A.P. Watt & Son, 26-28 Bedford Row, London WC1R 4HL, England; and Curtis Brown Ltd., 60 East 56th St., New York, N.Y. 10022.

CAREER: Author and composer of songs; television and film advertising script writer; script writer and composer for South African Broadcasting Corp. *Member:* P.E.N., Songwriters Guild of Great Britain, Performing Right Society.

WRITINGS: *Strange Odyssey*, Harrap, 1952, published in America as *Wings on Her Petticoat*, Morrow, 1953; *Handsome Piggywig and Other Stories*, Harrap, 1963; *The Bear Who Wanted the Mostest, and Other Stories*, Harrap, 1963. Composer of "Polly-wiggle," an album of children's songs published by Peter Maurice, and lyrics and music of other records for children. Author of more than 400 children's radio programs, two hour-long radio musicals, as well as stories, articles, and book reviews. Musical play, "Watermelons," was presented by Children's Theatre, Johannesburg.

WORK IN PROGRESS: Collections of her children's stories; a novel.

* * *

MITCHELL, Arthur A(ustin) 1926-

PERSONAL: Born April 9, 1926, in Brooklyn, N.Y.; son of Joseph and Sally (Welling) Mitchell; married Colette Chernoff, May 28, 1949; children: Janet, Brenda, Neil, Anne, David, Lisa. *Education:* Long Island University, B.A., 1952; Columbia University, M.A., 1954. *Home:* Toms River, N.J. 08753.

CAREER: Public school teacher in Cranford, N.J., 1952-54, Malverne, N.Y., 1954-60; principal in Roosevelt, N.J., 1960-64, Toms River, N.J., 1964—. Part-time instructor, Newark State College, 1961—. Captain, Roosevelt (N.J.) First Aid Squad; platoon captain, Roosevelt Fire Company. *Military service:* U.S. Navy, Seabees, 1944-46; became petty officer third class. *Member:* National Education Association (life), New Jersey Education Association, New Jersey Elementary Principals Association.

WRITINGS: *First Aid for Insects, and Much More*, Harvey House, 1964.

WORK IN PROGRESS: *First Aid for Fish*.

MITCHELL, Charles 1912-

PERSONAL: Born January 25, 1912, in London, England; son of Stanley and Mary (Garrard) Mitchell; married Prudence Yalden Thomson, 1935 (died, 1940); married Jean Flower, 1944; children: (first marriage) Simon; (second marriage) John B. *Education:* St. John's College, Oxford, B.A., 1934, B.Litt., 1937, M.A., 1941. *Home:* 139 North Merion Ave., Bryn Mawr, Pa. 19010. *Office:* Department of History, Bryn Mawr College, Bryn Mawr, Pa. 19010.

CAREER: National Maritime Museum, Greenwich, England, assistant, 1935-39; Warburg Institute, University of London, London, England, lecturer, 1945-60; Bryn Mawr College, Bryn Mawr, Pa., Richard M. Bernheimer Professor of History of Art, 1961—. Tallman Visiting Professor, Bowdoin College, 1956-57; lecturer, British Academy, 1961; Whiton Lecturer, Cornell University, 1963; art historian in residence, American Academy in Rome, 1965. *Military service:* Royal Naval War Service, 1939-45; became lieutenant commander, Royal Naval Volunteer Reserve. *Member:* Royal Historical Society (fellow), Walpole Society, Renaissance Society of America, College Art Association of America. *Awards, honors:* American Council of Learned Societies fellowship, 1965-66.

WRITINGS: *Seaman's Portrait*, Collins, 1940, Transatlantic, 1943; (editor) "Peacock Colour Books," six volumes, Collins, 1940-41; *A Book of Ships*, Penguin, 1941; (editor) "Colour Art Books," four volumes, Collins, 1942; (contributor) *England and the Mediterranean Tradition*, Oxford University Press, 1945; (contributor) Bernard Dorival, editor, *Les Peintres celebres*, Lucien Mazenod, 1948; (editor and author of introduction) *Hogarth's Peregrination*, Oxford University Press, 1952; *William Morris at St. James Palace*, William Morris Society, 1960; (contributor) E.F. Jacob, editor, *Italian Renaissance Studies: A Tribute to the Late Cecila M. Ady*, Barnes & Noble, 1960; *A Fifteenth Century Italian Plutarch*, Yoseloff, 1961; (editor with Erna Mandowsky) *Pirro Ligorio's Roman Antiquities*, Warburg Institute, University of London, 1963; (editor and author of introduction) A.P. Oppe, *Raphael*, Praeger, 1970. Contributor of articles to *Thieme-Becker Kuenstlerlexikon* and *Chambers's Encyclopaedia*, to *Listener, Times Literary Supplement, Burlington Magazine, Studi Romagnoli, Italia Medioevale e Umanistica*, and other journals.

WORK IN PROGRESS: Studies on Italian Renaissance art and archaeology and on modern art.

BIOGRAPHICAL/CRITICAL SOURCES: *Listener*, November 26, 1970.†

* * *

MITCHELL, Frank Vincent 1919-

PERSONAL: Born November 11, 1919, in New York, N.Y.; children: two. *Education:* Long Island University, B.S., 1939; New Paltz State Teachers College, (now State University of New York College at New Paltz), M.S., 1953; Hofstra University, M.S., 1954; postgraduate study at New York University, Mexico City College, Indiana University. *Home and office:* 102 Block Blvd., Massapequa, N.Y. 11758.

CAREER: Teacher, 1949-54; high school guidance director in New York State, 1955—. Director, Eastern Correspondence School. Fishing guide licensed by U.S. Coast Guard. *Military service:* U.S. Army Air Forces, 1943-45; received Silver Star, Purple Heart, Air Medal. *Member:* American Society of Psychologists and Guidance Personnel, United States Power Squadrons.

WRITINGS: *How to Buy, Keep and Enjoy Your Car: The Complete Handbook for All Automobile Owners and Drivers*, Arco, 1950; *Handy Guide for Car Owners*,

William H. Wise, 1953; (with Robert W. Mitchell) *The Installation and Servicing of Domestic Oil Burners,* Arco, 1956. Contributor of articles to magazines, including *Better Homes and Gardens, Glamour, Elks, American Legion, Car Life, Auto Age, American Home, Popular Science, Science and Mechanics, Collier's, Motor Boating, Medical Economics,* and *Home Guide.*

WORK IN PROGRESS: A novel, *Land Without a Country;* another novel, *The Chain of Judas.*

SIDELIGHTS: Mitchell has traveled in Europe, Africa, South America, and Cuba. *Avocational interests:* Celestial navigation, safer boating, and boating education.

BIOGRAPHICAL/CRITICAL SOURCES: Motor Boating, July, 1961.

* * *

MITCHELL, Gladys (Maude Winifred) 1901-
(Stephen Hockaby, Malcolm Torrie)

PERSONAL: Born April 19, 1901, in Cowley, Oxford, England; daughter of James and Annie Julia Maude (Simmonds) Mitchell. *Education:* Goldsmith's College, student, 1919-21; University of London, diploma in history, 1926. *Politics:* Conservative. *Religion:* Agnostic. *Home:* 1 Cecil Close, Corfe Mullen, Dorsetshire, England. *Agent:* Curtis Brown Ltd., 1, Craver Hill, London W2 3EW, England.

CAREER: Teacher of English and history, 1921-61. Author of detective stories, 1929—. *Member:* Society of Authors, Crime Writers' Association, Society of Authors, Ancient Monuments Society (fellow), Detection Club.

WRITINGS—All published by M. Joseph, except as indicated: *Speedy Death,* Dial, 1929; *The Mystery of a Butcher's Shop,* Gollancz, 1929, Dial, 1930.

The Longer Bodies, Gollancz, 1930; *The Saltmarsh Murders,* Gollancz, 1932, Macrae Smith, 1933; (with Anthony Berkeley, Milward Kennedy, John Rhode, Dorothy Sayers, and Helen Simpson) *Ask a Policeman,* Arthur Barker, 1933; *Death in the Wet,* Macrae Smith, 1934 (published in England as *Death at the Opera,* Grayson & Grayson, 1934); *The Devil at Saxon Wall,* Grayson & Grayson, 1935; *Dead Men's Morris,* 1936; *Come Away, Death,* 1937; *St. Peter's Finger,* 1938; *Printer's Error,* 1939.

Brazen Tongue, 1940; *Hangman's Curfew,* 1941; *When Last I Died,* 1941, Knopf, 1942; *Laurels Are Poison,* 1942; *The Worsted Viper,* 1943; *Sunset Over Soho,* 1943; *My Father Sleeps,* 1944; *The Rising of the Moon,* 1945; *Here Comes a Chopper,* 1946; *Death and the Maiden,* 1947; *The Dancing Druids,* 1948; *Tom Brown's Body,* 1949.

Groaning Spinney, 1950; *The Devil's Elbow,* 1951; *The Echoing Strangers,* 1952; *Merlin's Furlong,* 1953; *Faintley Speaking,* 1954; *Watson's Choice,* 1955; *Twelve Horses and the Hangman's Noose,* 1956; *The Twenty-Third Man,* 1957; *Spotted Hemlock,* 1958; *The Man Who Grew Tomatoes,* 1959, London House, 1960.

Say It With Flowers, 1960; *The Nodding Canaries,* 1961; *My Bones Will Keep,* 1962; *Adders on the Heath,* London House, 1963; *Death of a Delft Blue,* 1964, London House, 1965; *Pageant of Murder,* London House, 1965; *The Croaking Raven,* 1966; *Skeleton Island,* 1967; *Three Quick and Five Dead,* 1968; *Dance to Your Daddy,* 1969.

Gory Dew, 1970; *Lament for Leto,* 1971; *A Hearse on May-Day,* 1972; *The Murder of Busy Lizzie,* 1973.

Under pseudonym Malcolm Torrie; all published by M. Joseph: *Heavy as Lead,* 1966; *Late and Cold,* 1967; *Your*

Secret Friend, 1968; *Churchyard Salad,* 1969; *Shades of Darkness,* 1970; *Bismarck Herrings,* 1971.

Under pseudonym Stephen Hockaby: *Marsh Hay,* Grayson & Grayson, 1933; *Seven Stars and Orion,* Grayson & Grayson, 1934; *Gabriel's Hold,* Grayson & Grayson, 1935; *Shallow Brown,* M. Joseph, 1936; *Outlaws of the Border,* Pitman, 1936; *Grand Master,* M. Joseph, 1939.

Children's books: *The Three Fingerprints,* Heinemann, 1940; *Holiday River,* Evans Brothers, 1948; *The Seven Stones Mystery,* Evans Brothers, 1949; *The Malory Secret,* Evans Brothers, 1950; *Pam at Storne Castle,* Evans Brothers, 1951; *Caravan Creek,* Blackie & Son, 1954; *On Your Marks,* Heinemann, 1954, new revised edition, Parrish, 1964; *The Light Blue Hills,* Bodley Head, 1959.

WORK IN PROGRESS: A detective story with a college setting.

SIDELIGHTS: "My vocational [writing] interests are governed by British Ordnance Survey maps, as a definite, real setting is usually necessary to the formation of my plots." *Avocational interests:* Athletics, swimming, architecture (from Roman to eighteenth-century English).

BIOGRAPHICAL/CRITICAL SOURCES: Observer Review, September 1, 1968, May 9, 1970; *Punch,* September 11, 1968, May 28, 1969; *Books and Bookmen,* June, 1970.

* * *

MITCHELL, Harold P(aton) 1900-

PERSONAL: Born May 21, 1900, in Carnock, Scotland; son of Alexander Mitchell (a company director) and Meta (Paton) Mitchell; married Mary Pringle, 1947; children: Mary-Jean. *Education:* Attended Eton College and Royal Military College at Sandhurst; Oxford University, B.A., 1921, M.A., 1926; University of Geneva, Docteur es Sciences Politiques, 1963. *Politics:* Conservative. *Religion:* Protestant. *Home address:* P.O. Box 901, Marshall's Island, Bermuda.

CAREER: Conservative Member of Parliament from Brentford and Chiswick, Middlesex, England, 1931-45, and vice-chairman of Conservative Party, 1942-45; business interests include Luscar Group (oil and coal), Alberta, Canada (president), farm lands in Brazil and Central America; Stanford University, Institute of Hispanic American Studies, Stanford, Calif., lecturer, 1959-65; Rollins College, Winter Park, Fla., research professor of Latin American studies, 1965—. *Military service:* British Army, 1940-47; became staff colonel, Anti-Aircraft Command, and Polish liaison officer; decorated Knight of Polonia Restituta, 1944, and received Polish Military Cross, 1945. *Member:* Royal Geographical Society (fellow). *Awards, honors:* Knight of Order of St. John of Jerusalem; created baronet, 1945; LL.D., Rollins College, 1964, University of St. Andrews, 1968, and University of Alberta, 1970.

WRITINGS: Downhill Ski-Racing, Allen & Unwin, 1931, Greenberg, 1936; *Poland in Africa and Asia,* Scottish-Polish Society, 1943; *Into Peace,* Hutchinson, 1945; *In My Stride* (memoirs), W. & R. Chambers, 1951; *Europe in the Caribbean: The Policies of Great Britain, France, and The Netherlands Towards Their West Indian Territories in the Twentieth Century,* Hispanic American Society, Stanford University, 1963; *Cooperation in the Caribbean,* [Edinburgh], 1963; *Caribbean Patterns: A Political and Economic Study of the Contemporary Caribbean,* W. & R. Chambers, 1967, published in America as *Contemporary Politics and Economics in the Caribbean,* Ohio University Press, 1968, 2nd edition, Wiley, 1972; *The Caribbean in Relation to the Integration of Latin America,*

California Institute of International Studies, c.1968. Assistant editor, *Hispanic American Report*, 1959-65.

WORK IN PROGRESS: Research on current Caribbean affairs; the Caribbean section of *L'Histoire du XX siecle.*

* * *

MITCHELL, Jack 1925-

PERSONAL: Born September 13, 1925, in Key West, Fla.; son of Buren R. (an electrician) and Lucile (Dempsey) Mitchell. *Education:* Attended high school in New Smyrna Beach, Fla. *Home:* 435 East 77th St., New York, N.Y. 10021. *Agent:* Carolyn Willyoung Stagg, Lester Lewis Associates, 15 East 48th St., New York, N.Y. 10017.

CAREER: Free-lance photographer doing general magazine work prior to 1957, and specializing in photography of dance and dancers, 1957—. Contributing photographer to *Dance, After Dark,* and *New York Times. Military service:* U.S. Army, 1944-46; did public relations and photography for U.S. Armed Forces Institute at University of Florence; became technician fifth class (sergeant).

WRITINGS: American Dance Portfolio, Dodd, 1964; *Dance Scene U.S.A.: America's Greatest Ballet and Modern Dance Companies,* World Publishing, 1967; *Marisol,* Mobil Oil of Latin America, c.1968.

WORK IN PROGRESS: A book of portraits of leading contemporary painters and sculptors.

AVOCATIONAL INTERESTS: Collecting art.

BIOGRAPHICAL/CRITICAL SOURCES: Dance, June, 1964.

* * *

MITCHELL, John Howard 1921-

PERSONAL: Born February 14, 1921, in West Hartford, Conn.; son of William H., Jr. (a broker) and Grace (French) Mitchell; married Larayne Niers (an artist), September 29, 1945; children: Suzanne, Peter Cole Niers. *Education:* Bowdoin College, B.S., 1943; Harvard University, A.M., 1947. *Home:* 120 Red Gate Lane, Amherst, Mass. 01002. *Office:* Department of English, University of Massachusetts, Amherst, Mass. 01002.

CAREER: Naval Research Laboratory, Washington, D.C., chief writer, 1952-53; Tufts University, Systems Research Laboratory, Medford, Mass., assistant professor of systems analysis, 1953-54; University of Massachusetts, Amherst, associate professor, 1959-67, professor of English, 1967—. Visiting professor of English, University of Hawaii, 1964, Arizona State University, 1968. Writing consultant to Boeing Aircraft, U.S. Navy Mine Defense Laboratory, other companies and organizations. *Military service:* U.S. Navy, naval aviator, 1942-45; became lieutenant. *Member:* American Association for the Advancement of Science, Society of Technical Writers and Publishers, College English Association, American Society for Engineering Education, Presentation of Technical Information (England), Technical Publications Association (England), Institute of Technical Authors and Illustrators of Australia, Technical Communications Association of Australia.

WRITINGS: The Literature of Technical Writing, Boston Chapter, Society of Technical Writers and Editors, 1957; *Handbook of Technical Communication* (textbook), Wadsworth, 1962; *Technical Writing in the United States* (monograph), Presentation of Technical Information, 1962; *A First Course in Technical Writing,* Barnes & Noble, 1967; *Writing for Technical and Professional Journals* (textbook; Reference Book Club selection), Wiley, 1968. Writer of radio script for 260-installment series, "Let's Talk About the Word," produced by Columbia Broadcasting Corp. stations, of television scripts for Johns Hopkins University "Science Review" and for "Discovery." Contributor to technical journals, poetry journals, and to government technical reports.

* * *

MITCHELL, Joseph B(rady) 1915-

PERSONAL: Born September 25, 1915, at Fort Leavenworth, Kan.; son of William Augustus (a brigadier general, U.S. Army) and Margery (Brady) Mitchell; married Vivienne Brown, August 20, 1938; children: Sherwood Mitchell Novick, Joseph Bradford. *Education:* U.S. Military Academy, B.S., 1937. *Politics:* Independent. *Religion:* Episcopalian. *Home:* 606 Beverly Dr., Alexandria, Va. 22305. *Agent:* Brandt & Brandt, 101 Park Ave., New York, N.Y. 10017. *Office:* Fort Ward Museum, 4301 West Braddock Rd., Alexandria, Va. 22304.

CAREER: U.S. Army, career service, 1937-54; commissioned second lieutenant, Field Artillery, 1937; served with Fifth Infantry Division in European theater, World War II, becoming lieutenant colonel; graduate of Command and General Staff College, Fort Leavenworth, Kan., 1945; served as a member of the War Department General Staff, 1945-49, at West Point, 1949-50, as historian, American Battle Monuments Commission, Washington, D.C., 1950-61; Fort Ward Museum, Alexandria, Va., curator, 1963—. *Member:* Society of the Cincinnati, National Temple Hill Association (trustee), Civil War Round Table of Alexandria (former president; now director). *Awards, honors:* American Revolution Round Table prize, 1962, for *Decisive Battles of the American Revolution.*

WRITINGS: Decisive Battles of the Civil War, Putnam, 1955; *Decisive Battles of the American Revolution,* Putnam, 1962; *Twenty Decisive Battles of the World* (revision of Edward Creasy's *Fifteen Decisive Battles of the World*), Macmillan, 1964; *Discipline and Bayonets: The Armies and Leaders in the War of the American Revolution,* Putnam, 1967; *The Badge of Gallantry: Recollections of Civil War Congressional Medal of Honor Winners,* Macmillan, 1968; *Military Leaders of the Civil War,* Putnam, 1972. Contributor to encyclopedias, historical booklets, and magazines.

* * *

MITFORD, Nancy 1904-1973
(Nancy Freeman-Mitford Rodd)

PERSONAL: Born November 28, 1904, in London, England; daughter of David Bertram Ogilvy (second baron of Redesdale) and Sydney (Bowles) Freeman-Mitford; married Peter Rodd, 1933 (marriage dissolved, 1958). *Education:* Educated at home in England, with formal instruction limited to French and riding. *Home:* 4 Rue d'Artois, 78 Versailles, France. *Agent:* A.D. Peters, 10 Buckingham St., Adelphi, London W.C.2, England.

CAREER: Grew up in Cotswold Hills district of England; made debut into society in London, and began writing novels after associating with literary figures there; managed a London bookshop during World War II; resident of France, 1945-73. *Awards, honors:* Chevalier of the Legion d'Honneur; Commander, Order of the British Empire.

WRITINGS: Highland Fling (novel), Butterworth & Co., 1931; *Christmas Pudding* (novel), Butterworth & Co. 1932; *Wigs on the Green* (novel), Butterworth & Co., 1935; (editor) Maria Josepha Stanley and Henrietta Maria Stanley, *The Ladies of Alderley: Their Letters During the Years 1841-1850,* Chapman & Hall, 1938; (editor) Maria Josepha Stanley and Henrietta Maria Stanley, *The Stanleys of Alderley: Their Letters Between the Years 1851-1865,* Chapman & Hall, 1939; *Pigeon Pie: A Warime Receipt* (novel), Hamish Hamilton, 1940, British Book Centre, 1959; *The Pursuit of Love* (novel), Hamish Hamilton, 1945, Random House, 1946; *Love in a Cold Climate* (novel), Random House, 1949; (translator) Madame de La Fayette, *The Princess of Cleves* (novel), Euphorion Books, 1950, New Directions, 1951; *The Blessing*, Random House, 1951; (adapter and translator) Andre Roussin, *The Little Hut* (three-act play; first produced in West End at Lyric Theatre, August 23, 1950, and later in New York), Hamish Hamilton, 1951, British Book Centre, 1952; *Madame de Pompadour* (biography), Random House, 1954, revised edition, Harper, 1968; *The Nancy Mitford Omnibus* (contains *Pursuit of Love, Love in a Cold Climate,* and *The Blessing*), Hamish Hamilton, 1956; (editor) Alan C. Ross and others, *Noblesse Oblige: An Inquiry into the Identifiable Characteristics of the English Aristocracy,* Harper, 1956; *Voltaire in Love: Voltaire and the Marquise du Chatelet* (biography), Harper, 1957; *Don't Tell Alfred* (novel), Harper, 1960; *The Water Beetle* (essays), Hamish Hamilton, 1962, Harper, 1963; *The Sun King: Louis XIV at Versailles* (history), Harper, 1966; *Frederick the Great* (biography), Harper, 1970. Contributor to periodicals, including *Encounter, New Statesman,* and *Sunday Times* (London).

SIDELIGHTS: In 1961 Anne Fremantle wrote of Nancy Mitford: "She is perhaps the nearest our blurred, woolly and sadisto-sentimental age has gotten to the sane simplicity of Jane Austen." Although her work has been praised by many, Miss Mitford's writing has not received the in-depth analysis usually accorded to writers considered "serious." Critics rather emphasize her wit, use of language, sophistication, and portrayal of the upper classes. Elizabeth Janeway once described her writing as "cunningly constructed, artfully written, echoing delightfully in the mind . . . purely frivolous, divinely farcical." V.C. Clinton-Baddeley noted that her "sense of humor is much deeper than her sense of the significant. . . ."

The *Times Literary Supplement* reviewer disagreed with these assessments of Miss Mitford's talents. "Together with her gift for suggesting the lights and shades of high-life, Miss Mitford possesses an easy and unpretentious style which expresses at first hand what she sees and thinks. She writes about things clearly as they appear to her to happen: not about things which might happen if human beings were altogether different; or things described through a fog of verbal obscurity. In doing this she does no small service to the contemporary English novel, sailing its uneasy course between extravaganza and romance. She does not preach or prophesy, she merely watches people behave." Anne Fremantle also believes that "she is . . . a serious writer, an artist who senses and sees the quirks and quiddities of the human condition." Honor Tracy suggests that Miss Mitford is highly successful because she has created her own brand of fiction. "Miss Mitford's difficult art at its best is so fine, so beautifully a-shimmer with wit and nonsense and gaity, that it creates a standard of its own."

The Blessing was filmed by M-G-M in 1959 under the title "Count Your Blessings."

BIOGRAPHICAL/CRITICAL SOURCES: Spectator, January 4, 1946, October 25, 1957; *Times Literary Supplement,* January 29, 1946, October 23, 1970; *New York Times,* June 9, 1946, October 7, 1951; *New Statesman,* July 30, 1949; *Chicago Sunday Tribune,* October 28, 1951, February 23, 1958; *Saturday Review,* August 7, 1954, April 27, 1963; *Atlantic,* April, 1961; *New Republic,* April 10, 1961; *Commonweal,* June 20, 1961; *Washington Post,* October 23, 1970; *National Review,* December 15, 1970; *Daily Telegraph* (London), July 2, 1973; *New York Times,* July 2, 1973; *Washington Post,* July 3, 1973.

(Died, June 30, 1973)

MITGANG, Herbert 1920-

PERSONAL: Born January 20, 1920, in New York, N.Y.; son of Benjamin and Florence (Altman) Mitgang; married Shirley Kravchick, May 13, 1945; children: Esther, Lee, Laura. *Education:* St. John's University, Jamaica, N.Y., LL.B. *Politics:* "New Deal Democrat." *Religion:* Jewish. *Home:* 21 Nirvana Ave., Great Neck, Long Island, N.Y. 11023. *Office: New York Times,* 229 West 43rd St., New York, N.Y. 10036.

CAREER: Admitted to New York State Bar, 1942; *Brooklyn Eagle,* Brooklyn, N.Y., sports stringer, 1938-39; with Universal Pictures in New York, N.Y., and Hollywood, Calif., 1945; *New York Times,* New York, N.Y., writer, critic, editor, 1945-63, member of editorial board, 1963-64; Columbia Broadcasting System, New York, N.Y., executive editor and assistant to president, CBS News, 1964-67; *New York Times,* member of editorial board, 1967—. Evening division instructor in English, College of City of New York (now City College of City University of New York), 1948-49. Co-producer and writer of television documentaries. *Military service:* U.S. Army Air Forces, counterintelligence, 1942-43; army correspondent, then managing editor, *Stars and Stripes,* Oran-Casablanca and Sicily, 1943-45; became staff sergeant; received six battle stars. *Member:* Authors League of America (member of executive council, 1962—), Authors Guild of America (vice-president, 1965-70, president, 1971—), New York Newspaper Guild (member of executive board, 1948-49), Society of American Historians.

WRITINGS: (Editor) *Lincoln as They Saw Him,* Rinehart, 1956, abridged edition, Collier, 1962; *Freedom to See: Television and the First Amendment,* Fund for the Republic, 1958; (editor) Noah Brooks, *Washington in Lincoln's Time,* Rinehart, 1958; (editor) *Civilians Under Arms: The American Soldier, Civil War to Korea,* Pennington Press, 1959; *The Return* (novel), Simon & Schuster, 1959; *The Man Who Rode the Tiger: The Life and Times of Judge Samuel Seabury,* Lippincott, 1963; (editor) *The Letters of Carl Sandburg,* Harcourt, 1968; (editor and author of introduction) *America at Random: From the New York Times' Oldest Editorial Feature, "Topics of the Times": A Century of Comment on America and Americans,* Coward, 1969; *Working for the Reader: A Chronicle of Culture, Literature, War, and Politics in Books from the 1950's to the Present,* introduction by Alfred Kazin, Horizon Press, 1970; (editor) Edward Dicey, *Spectator of America: Edward Dicey's Journal,* Quadrangle, 1971; *Get These Men Out of the Hot Sun* (novel), Arbor House, 1972.

Television documentaries: "Carl Sandburg at Gettysburg," first produced on CBS for "CBS Reports," April 13, 1961; "Carl Sandburg's The Prairie Years," first produced on CBS, February 8, 1962; "D-Day Plus Twenty Years: Eisenhower Returns to Normandy," first produced on CBS for "CBS Reports," June 15, 1964; "Henry Moore: Man of Form," first produced on CBS, October 5, 1965; "Ben Gurion on the Bible," first produced on CBS, April 23, 1967.

BIOGRAPHICAL/CRITICAL SOURCES: Publishers' Weekly, July 24, 1967, February 21, 1972; *New York Times Book Review,* September 29, 1968; *Newsweek,* October 7, 1968; *Virginia Quarterly Review,* autumn, 1968; *Christian Science Monitor,* December 5, 1968; *Saturday Review,* December 7, 1968; *New Republic,* December 7, 1968, December 26, 1970; *Harper's,* August, 1969; *Yale Review,* winter, 1969.

*   *   *

MOEHLMAN, Arthur H(enry) 1907-

PERSONAL: Surname pronounced *Mel*-man; born February 19, 1907, in Rochester, N.Y.; son of Conrad Henry (a professor and church historian) and Bertha (Young) Moehlman; married Marguerite Richebourg (a teacher), December 22, 1933; children: Michael, Stephen, Patricia, Jacqueline. *Education:* University of Rochester, B.A., 1928; University of Basel, international fellow, 1928-29; University of Michigan, M.A., 1930, Ph.D., 1932. *Politics:* Democrat. *Religion:* Episcopalian. *Home:* 4006 Northhills Dr., Austin, Tex. 78712. *Office:* University of Texas, Austin, Tex. 78731.

CAREER: University of Michigan, Ann Arbor, instructor in history and social science, 1930-32; Ohio State University, Columbus, assistant professor, 1932-36, associate professor of history and social science 1937-41; University of Iowa, Iowa City, professor of the history and philosophy of education, 1946-54; University of Texas, Austin, professor of the history and philsophy of education, 1954—, director of Center for History of Education, 1966—. On leave from university posts as research professor at Sorbonne, University of Paris, 1951-52, television writer and professor for Texas Education Agency, 1957-58, Fulbright professor in American studies at Gottingen, Germany, 1961-62, diplomat, and U.S. cultural attache to the Federal Republic, American Embassy, Bonn, Germany, 1962-64. Visiting professor at University of Rochester, University of Maine, and Stanford University. Expert consultant on television in education to Federal Communications Commission, 1951; consultant to Office of Education, U.S. Army. *Military service:* U.S. Army, General Staff officer, Intelligence, 1941-46; served on missions in North Africa, Middle East, and China-Burma-India theater and as member of U.S. Group Control Council in Germany; graduate of Command and General Staff College, 1945; became colonel.

MEMBER: International Academy of Arts and Letters (fellow), American Historical Association, Royal Geographical Society (fellow), Reserve Officers Association, American Studies Association, Deutsche Gesellschaft fuer Amerika Studien, American Geographical Society, Phi Beta Kappa, Kiwanis, Keideans, Quadrangle, Academic Alpine Club.

WRITINGS: (With Harrison M. Sayre) *A History of Our Times,* two volumes, American Education Press, 1936-37; (editor) *Handbook on the German Armed Forces,* Office of the Adjutant General, 1941; (editor with Joseph S. Roucek) *Comparative Education,* Dryden Press, 1952; *Adventures in Education,* Texas Education Agency, 1958; *Comparative Educational Systems,* Center for Applied Research in Education, 1963; (with others) *A Guide to Computer-Assisted Historical Research in American Education,* Center for the History of Education, University of Texas, 1969. Editor, *Our Times,* 1937-39. Writer of television series, "Adventures in Education," carried by nineteen stations in Southwest, 1957-58. Author of monographs in German.

WORK IN PROGRESS: A *Comparative History of Higher Education: Europe and North America* (the Atlantic community); *A Philosophy of Ethical Ecology,* based on Whitehead, Springer, Litt, and Bultmann; *The Impact of the University on American Culture; Foundations of American Education; History of Education in the Americas.*

AVOCATIONAL INTERESTS: Wilderness travel, exploration with gun, rod, and camera, safaris in Africa and India for big game, hunting in Europe and the Americas, and mountain climbing; collecting painting and sculpture.

*   *   *

MOERS, Ellen   1928-

PERSONAL: Born December 9, 1928, in New York, N.Y.; daughter of Robert (a lawyer) and Celia Lewis (a teacher; maiden name, Kauffman) Moers; married Martin Mayer (a writer), June 23, 1949; children: Thomas Moers, James Moers. *Education:* Vassar College, B.A., 1948; Radcliffe College, M.A., 1949; Columbia University, Ph.D., 1954. *Home:* 33 East End Ave., New York, N.Y. 10028. *Agent:* Curtis Brown Ltd., 60 East 56th St., New York, N.Y. 10022.

CAREER: Hunter College (now Hunter College of the City University of New York), New York, N.Y., lecturer in English, 1956-57; Columbia University, New York, N.Y., lecturer in English, 1957-58, senior research associate, 1966-68; Barnard College, New York, N.Y., adjunct associate professor of English, 1968—. *Member:* American Studies Association, Phi Beta Kappa. *Awards, honors:* Guggenheim fellowship for critical study of Theodore Dreiser, 1962-63; National Endowment for the Humanities senior fellowship, 1972-73.

WRITINGS: The Dandy: Brummell to Beerbohm, Viking, 1960; *Two Dreisers,* Viking, 1969. Contributor of critical and scholarly articles to *Commentary, Harper's, Columbia Forum, American Scholar, Victorian Studies, New York Review of Books,* and other publications.

WORK IN PROGRESS: A historical and critical study of major English, French, and American women writers from the eighteenth century to the present.

SIDELIGHTS: In a review of *Two Dreisers,* Herbert Kupferberg writes: "The Dreiser that emerges from Miss Moers' study is indeed an imposing figure, a writer who not only mastered the narrative craft but who drew his people from a real world he knew and understood: a world of the poor, the ambitious, the tormented, the inarticulate. Perhaps she does not present all of the man and his times, to be sure, for her method has its limitations. . . . But there is no doubt that Ellen Moers has made an illuminating voyage of discovery into the life of one of the most important and influential American novelists, and to go along with her is a worth-while literary and human journey."

BIOGRAPHICAL/CRITICAL SOURCES: Book World, July 6, 1969; *National Observer,* August 4, 1969; *New Republic,* July 19, 1969; *New Yorker,* August 30, 1969; *Virginia Quarterly Review,* autumn, 1969; *Commentary,* January, 1970; *Observer Review,* August 20, 1970.

*   *   *

MOFFETT, Samuel Hugh   1916-

PERSONAL: Born April 7, 1916, in Pyengyang, Korea; son of Samuel Austin (a missionary) and Lucia (Fish) Moffett; married Eileen Flower, September 15, 1956. *Education:* Attended Pyengyang Foreign School; Wheaton College, Wheaton, Ill., A.B., 1938; Princeton Theological Seminary, Th.B., 1942; Yale University, Ph.D., 1945; School of Chinese Studies, Peking, China, postdoctoral study, 1947-48. *Home:* 1-1 Yun Chi Dong, Seoul, Korea. *Office:* Program Agency, United Presbyterian Church, 475 Riverside Dr., New York, N.Y. 10027.

CAREER: Presbyterian Board of Foreign Missions, New York, N.Y., director of youth work, 1945-47; Presbyterian missionary in China, 1947-51; member of faculty of Yenching University, Peking, China, 1948-49, Nanking Theological Seminary, Nanking, China, 1949-50; Presbyterian Church, missionary in Korea, 1955—, commission representative in Korea, of United Presbyterian Church, 1960—; Presbyterian Theological Seminary, Seoul, Korea, professor of history and theology, 1960—, dean of graduate school, 1966-71, associate president, 1971—. Visiting lecturer in ecumenics, Princeton Theological Seminary, 1953-55. Member, U.S. Educational Commission in Korea. Director, Yonsei University, Soongjun University, Whitworth College; counselor, Royal Asiatic Society. *Member:* American Missiological Society, Yale Club, Rotary Club (all Seoul, Korea).

WRITINGS: Where'er the Sun, Friendship, 1953; *The Christians of Korea,* Friendship, 1962; (with wife, Eileen Flower Moffett) *Joy for an Anxious Age: A Study Guide on Philippians,* Board of Christian Education, United Presbyterian Church, 1966.

Pamphlets: *The Christian Mission: Its Motive and Its Task,* 1952; *Christ Calls the Church to Mission and to Unity,* 1953; *The Church Today: Obstacles and Opportunities,* 1960. Contributor to *Concise Dictionary of the Christian World Mission,* to *Weltkirchenlexicon,* and to journals in China and Korea. Contributing editor, *Christianity Today;* editorial assistant, *Theology Today,* 1953-55.

WORK IN PROGRESS: Research on the Protestant churches of Asia; *Christianity in Korea: A Bibliographical Guide.*

BIOGRAPHICAL/CRITICAL SOURCES: New York Times, February 27, 1955; *Denver Post,* September 13, 1955; *Time,* April 18, 1960.

* * *

MOK, Paul P.   1934-

PERSONAL: Born September 30, 1934; son of Michel (a writer) and Mary (Watson) Mok; married Violet McMillan Stewart; children: Christopher, Anthony, Steven. *Education:* Attended Cornell University and Harvard University. *Agent:* Oscar Collier, 299 Madison Ave., New York, N.Y. 10017.

CAREER: American Institute for Research, Pittsburgh, Pa., senior research scientist, 1963—. Currently director of U.S. Agency for International Development testing center in Monrovia, Liberia, .West Africa, traveling through the jungle giving aptitude tests to discover potential nursing, engineering, technical, and other talent. *Military service:* U.S. Air Force; became first lieutenant. U.S. Naval Reserve; now lieutenant j.g. *Member:* New York Psychological Association.

WRITINGS: A View from Within: American Education at the Crossroads of Individualism, Carlton, 1962; *Pushbutton Parents and the Schools,* Macrae, 1964; *The Year of the Quicksand* (novel), Trident, 1967; *Recycle Your Lifestyle,* Pinnacle Books, 1972.

WORK IN PROGRESS: A novel dealing with the theme of mercy killing; research scientist on "Project Talent," a twenty-year study of American youth.

BIOGRAPHICAL/CRITICAL SOURCES: Best Sellers, August 15, 1967.

* * *

MOLAN, Dorothy L(ennon)   1911-

PERSONAL: Born July 27, 1911, in Tampa, Fla.; daughter of Luther Brown and Agnes (Hardee) Lennon; married Horace T. Molan (a minister and employee of American Baptist Convention), September 7, 1939; children: Elma (Mrs. John A. Aumick). *Education:* Attended Trinity College, Belair, Fla., three years, and Toccoa Falls Bible College, one year. *Religion:* Baptist. *Home:* 356 Crossfield Rd., King of Prussia, Pa. 19406. *Office:* American Baptist Convention, Valley Forge, Pa. 19481.

CAREER: Toccoa Falls Schools, Toccoa Falls, Ga., teacher, 1937-38, 1940-43, director of personnel, 1940-43; Delaware Township Board of Education, Sergeantsville, N.J., teacher, 1944-45, 1948-51; New Jersey Baptist Convention, East Orange, director of children's work, 1951-54; American Baptist Convention, Valley Forge, Pa., associate director of missionary and stewardship education, 1963—. Vice-president of Christian training and missionary and stewardship education, National Council of American Baptist Women.

WRITINGS: And the Child Grew, Judson, 1961; *Teaching Middlers,* Judson, 1963; *Year 3, Spring,* Unit VIII, Judson, 1964; (with Grace Hatler) *Land of the Lighthouse,* Judson, 1966; *Thank You, God,* Judson, 1969; *With Many Hands—in Many Ways,* Judson, 1969. Also author of several books and picture-story cards for use in church schools. Contributor of Christian education articles and worship materials to *Baptist Leader* and *Bethany Guide,* and author of a number of primary teaching units for Judson. Editor, Adam Morales' *American Baptists with a Spanish Accent* and other missionary education materials.

WORK IN PROGRESS: Editing Elizabeth Anne Hemphill's *A Treasure to Share;* research on ways of observing special days in the church and church school for a book, *Special Ways to Special Days.*

AVOCATIONAL INTERESTS: Creative arts and antiques.

* * *

MOLLO, Victor   1909-

PERSONAL: Born September 17, 1909, in St. Petersburg (now Leningrad), Russia; stepson of Solon and son of Anna Mollo; married Patricia Hyman, 1942 (marriage dissolved, 1948); married Jeanne Forbes, February 22, 1952. *Education:* Received early education from tutors in Paris, later attended preparatory school in Britain, as well as Brighton College, and University of London. *Politics:* Conservative. *Home:* 204 Duncan House, Dolphin Sq., London S.W.1, England. *Office:* British Broadcasting Corp., Bush House, Aldwych, London W.C.2, England.

CAREER: Journalist in various fields, 1928—; British Broadcasting Corp., London, England, news bulletin editor, 1940-70.

WRITINGS: Streamlined Bridge, David Marlowe, 1947, 4th edition, George Newnes, 1960, published in America as *Streamlined Bridge; or, Point-Count Bidding without Tears,* Prentice-Hall, 1956; (with Nico Gardener) *Card-Play Technique; or, the Art of Being Lucky,* George Newnes, 1955; (with Gardener) *Bridge for Beginners,* Duckworth, 1956, A.S. Barnes, 1960; *Bridge Psychology; or, Reading Between the Cards,* Duckworth, 1958; *Will You Be My Partner?,* Duckworth, 1959, published in America as *Bridge with a Master,* A.S. Barnes, 1960; *Bridge: Modern Bidding,* Faber, 1961, 3rd revised edition, 1970; *Success at Bridge,* George Newnes, 1964; *Bridge in the Menagerie: The Winning Ways of the Hideous Hog,* Faber, 1965, Hawthorn, 1967; *Confessions of an Addict,* George Newnes, 1966; *The Bridge Immortals,* Faber, 1967, Harold Hart, 1968; (editor) Edgar Kaplan, *Duplicate Bridge: How to Play, How to Win,* Faber, 1967, Hearthside, 1968; *Victor Mollo's Winning Double: The Shortest Cut to Expert Play,* Faber, 1968, published in America as *How Good Is your Bridge?: The Short Cut to Expert Play,* Harold Hart, 1969; (editor) Oswald Jacoby and James Jacoby, *Win at Bridge with Jacoby and Son,* Faber, 1968; (editor and author of introduction) Samuel M. Stayman, *Do You Play Stayman?,* Faber, 1969; (editor) Ely Culbertson, *Culbertson's Contract Bridge for Everyone,* Faber, 1969, Transatlantic, 1970; *Bridge: Case for the Defence,* Faber, 1970, published in America as *Test Your Defense: Where the Points Are Won,* Prentice-Hall, 1972. Bridge editor, *Evening Standard* (London). Contributor to bridge publications in the U.S., France, Denmark, Sweden, and other countries.

WORK IN PROGRESS: A book on the 1970 world bridge champions, for Aces International.

SIDELIGHTS: Mollo lists his hobbies as "bridge, reading (often about the occult, Buddhism &c.), conversation (often on politics, international affairs), gastronomy and wine. I consider it uncivilised to sit down to dinner ... without wine. I like swimming and I walk on the average 3-4 miles daily. I like the theatre, but not the cinema.

"I dislike mechanical things. I have no car. I use lifts sparingly to go up and never to go down. I detest TV and deplore its effect on society. I hope that some genius will one day disinvent, if not the internal combustion engine, at least some of its soul-destroying manifestations. I deplore alleged Progressives, United Nations enthusiasts, fervent anti-colonialists and people who believe that human nature can be changed by statistics, psychiatry and the expenditure of someone else's money. In short, I am a 'reactionary.' My wife describes my politics as 'right of centre,' but adds that my centre is on the extreme right."

BIOGRAPHICAL/CRITICAL SOURCES: New Statesman, December 2, 1966.

* * *

MOMENT, David 1925-

PERSONAL: Born May 25, in Chicago, Ill.; son of Herman and Corinne (Reisberg) Moment; married Mary-Helen McCain, March 20, 1948 (divorced); children: Rebecca Ann, Peter Jacob. *Education:* Reed College, student, 1946-48; Illinois Institute of Technology, B.S. in Industrial Engineering, 1951; Harvard University, M.B.A., 1957, D.B.A., 1961. *Home:* 664 Worcester St., Wellesley, Mass. 02181.

CAREER: General Etching and Manufacturing Co., Chicago, Ill., assistant production manager and vice-president, 1951-55; Harvard University, Graduate School of Business Administration, Cambridge, Mass., instructor, 1959-61, assistant professor, 1961-64, associate professor of organizational behavior, 1964-68; Boston College, Boston, Mass., associate professor of organizational behavior, 1968—. Associate, National Training Laboratories in Human Relations. *Military service:* U.S. Navy, 1943-46.

WRITINGS—All with Abraham Zaleznik: *Role Development and Interpersonal Competence: An Experimental Study of Role Performances in Problem-Solving Groups,* Division of Research, Graduate School of Business Administration, Harvard University, 1963; *The Dynamics of Interpersonal Behavior,* Wiley, 1964; *Casebook on Interpersonal Behavior in Organizations,* Wiley, 1964; *Role Transition in Career Development,* Center for Research in Careers, Graduate School of Education, Harvard University, 1967.

* * *

MONCURE, Jane Belk 1926-

PERSONAL: Born December 16, 1926, in Orlando, Fla.: daughter of J. Blanton (a Presbyterian minister) and Jennie (Wannamaker) Belk; married James Ashby Moncure (an associate dean at Univeristy College, University of Richmond) June 14, 1952; children: James Ashby, Jr. *Education:* College of William and Mary, B.S., 1952; Columbia University, M.A., 1954. *Religion:* Christian. *Home:* 208 College Rd., Richmond, Va. 23229.

CAREER: First Presbyterian Church Nursery School, New York, N.Y., teacher-director, 1952-54; Richmond Professional Institute, Richmond, Va., instructor in early childhood education, 1955-57; Southside Day Nursery, Richmond, Va., director, 1957-59; Town and Garden School, Richmond, Va., director, 1960-64; Richmond Public Schools, Richmond, Va., junior primary teacher, 1964-66; Virginia Commonwealth University, Richmond, instructor in early childhood education, 1966-70. Part-time consultant on day care for children under six, Department of Welfare and Institutions, Richmond, Va., 1964. Conductor with husband of University of Richmond Summer School Abroad, 1963, 1964; lecturer, summer session, Adelphi College (now Adelphi University), Garden City, N.Y. Member, International Council of Richmond. *Member:* National Association for the Education of Young Children, Virginia Association for Early Childhood Education (first president, 1956), Southern Association for Children Under Six, Delta Kappa Gamma, University of Richmond Faculty Wives Club (president, 1964).

WRITINGS: Pinny's Day at Play School, Lothrop, 1955; *Bunny Finds a Home,* Orion, 1962; *Flip, The True Story of a Dairy Farm Goat,* Farrar, Straus, 1964; *Try on a Shoe,* Child's World, in press.

WORK IN PROGRESS: Four children's books, entitled *The Upside Downside Zoo, The Upside Downside House, What Does a Koala Bear Need?* and *While the Zoo Keeper Slept; Play with the Alphabet Books,* for Child's World.

* * *

MONSEN, R(aymond) Joseph, Jr. 1931-

PERSONAL: Born March 13,^1931, in Payson, Utah; son of Raymond Joseph (a banker) and Lucile (Tilson) Monsen; married Elaine Ranker (an assistant professor at University of Washington), January 21; 1959; children: Maren Ranker. *Education:* University of Utah, B.S., 1953; Stanford University, M.A., 1954; University of California, Berkeley, Ph.D., 1960. *Home:* 2000 East Galer St., Seattle, Wash. 98112. *Office:* MacKenzie Hall, University of Washington, Seattle, Wash. 98105.

CAREER: Brigham Young University, Provo, Utah, assistant professor of economics, 1960-63; University of Washington, Seattle, associate professor, 1963-65, professor of business administration, 1965—, acting chairman of department of business, government, and society, 1967-68. Consultant to Financial Councillors, 1958, Utah Bankers Association, 1962, U.S. Naval Intelligence, 1962-63. Trustee, Contemporary Art Council, Seattle Art Museum, Seattle Opera Association, Salt Lake Art Center. *Member:* American Economic Association, Association for Comparative Economics, Western Economic Association.

WRITINGS: Modern American Capitalism: Ideologies and Issues, Houghton, 1963; (with Mark W. Cannon) *The Makers of Public Policy: American Power Groups and Their Ideologies,* McGraw, 1965; (editor with Boerje O. Saxberg) *The Business World: Introduction to Busienss Readings,* Houghton, 1967, 2nd edition, 1972. Contributor to economic and business journals, and to *Saturday Review* and *Daedalus.*

WORK IN PROGRESS: Two books and five articles on business and society and the modern firm.

AVOCATIONAL INTERESTS: Collector of Oriental and contemporary art, ceramics.

* * *

MONTAGU, Elizabeth 1917-

PERSONAL: Born July 4, 1917; daughter of George (ninth Earl of Sandwich) and Alberta (Sturges) Montagu. *Education:* Attended North Foreland Lodge School; nursing training at St. Thomas's Hospital, London, England, 1940-46. *Politics:* Socialist. *Religion:* "Church of England (but an agnostic)". *Home and office:* Domaine des Colles, Valbonne, Grasse, A.M., France. *Agent:* Curtis Brown Ltd., 13 King St., London WC2E 8HU, England.

CAREER: Royal College of Nursing, lecturer in education department, 1947-50; writer. *Member:* Contemporary Art Society, P.E.N., Arts Theatre Club (London).

WRITINGS: Waiting for Camilla, Heinemann, 1953, Lippincott, 1954; *The Small Corner,* Heinemann, 1955,

Grosset, 1956; *This Side of the Truth,* Heinemann, 1957, Coward, 1958; (translator) Carl Zuckmayer, *The Cold Light: A Drama in Three Acts,* Appleton, 1958; *Change, and Other Stories,* Heinemann, 1966. Contributor to *Botteghe Oscure, Encounter,* and other periodicals.

WORK IN PROGRESS: A novel; a film script.

AVOCATIONAL INTERESTS: Collecting modern pictures, furniture, and works of art.†

* * *

MONTAGUE, John (Patrick) 1929-

PERSONAL: Born February 28, 1929, in New York, N.Y.; son of James Terence and Mary (Carney) Montague; married Madeleine de Brauer, October 18, 1956. *Education:* University College, Dublin, B.A., 1949, M.A., 1953; Yale University, postgraduate studies, 1953-54; State University of Iowa, M.F.A., 1955. *Agent:* A.D. Peters, 10 Buckingham St., Adelphi, London W.C.2, England.

CAREER: Standard (newspaper), Dublin, Ireland, film critic, 1949-52; Bord Failte (Irish tourist board), Dublin, Ireland, executive, 1956-59; *Irish Times,* Paris correspondent, 1961—. Visiting lecturer at University of California, Berkeley, 1964, 1965, University of Dublin, 1966, 1967, and University of Vincennes, 1968. *Awards, honors:* Fulbright fellowship; May Morton Memorial Award for poetry; Arts Council of Northern Ireland grant, 1970.

WRITINGS: Forms of Exile (poetry), Dolmen Press, 1958; *The Old People,* Dolmen Press, 1960; *Poisoned Lands, and Other Poems,* MacGibbon & Kee, 1961, Dufour, 1963; (with Thomas Kinsella and Richard Murphy) *Three Irish Poets* (pamphlet), Dolmen Press, 1961; (editor with Kinsella) *The Dolmen Miscellany of Irish Writing,* Dolmen Press, 1962; *Death of a Chieftain, and Other Stories,* MacGibbon & Kee, 1964, Dufour, 1968; *Old Mythologies: A Poem,* privately printed, c.1965; *All Legendary Obstacles,* Dolmen Press, 1966; *Patriotic Suite,* Dufour, 1966; (editor with Liam Miller) *A Tribute to Austin Clarke on His Seventieth Birthday,* Dufour, 1966; *A Chosen Light* (poetry), MacGibbon & Kee, 1967, Swallow Press, 1969; *Home Again,* Festival Publications, 1967; *Hymn to the New Omagh Road,* privately printed, 1968; *The Bread God* (pamphlet), Dolmen Press, 1968; *Tides* (poetry), Dolmen Press, 1970, Swallow Press, 1971; *The Rough Field* (poetry), Dolmen Press, 1971, Swallow Press, 1972; (editor) *The Faber Book of Irish Verse,* Faber, 1972. Contributor to *Paris Review.*

WORK IN PROGRESS: Translation of an anthology of French poetry.

SIDELIGHTS: M.L. Rosenthal writes: "The Irish poet John Montague is one of the most interesting now writing in English. He tells a story, paints a picture, evokes an atmosphere, suggests the complexities and torments of adult love and marriage—all in the most direct, concrete, involving way. The poems come out of a deeply human speaking personality for whom language and reality are more than just a source of a plastic design of nuances. Montague does have a highly developed sense of the craft; he is a real poet, who works at his desk and drinks of the tradition. But he brings all his engagement with his art directly to bear on the world of our common life, as Frost and Williams so often did, and thus makes immediate contact with his readers. He thinks and talks like a grown-up man, and that fact alone makes him better literary company than most of his poetic contemporaries."

BIOGRAPHICAL/CRITICAL SOURCES: Times Literary Supplement, January 5, 1967, November 9, 1967; *New Statesman,* August 18, 1967; *Punch,* January 3, 1968; *New York Times,* March 23, 1968; *Library Journal,* June 1, 1968; *Nation,* May 17, 1971.

MONTGOMERY, Edward F(inley) 1918-

PERSONAL: Born February 6, 1918, in Greenfield, Mo.; son of Edward Philip (real estate) and Marie (Finley) Montgomery; married Constance Ainley, October 31, 1942; children: John Edward, Karen Sue. *Education:* Studied at Muskogee Junior College; University of Missouri, B.J., 1940. *Politics:* Democrat. *Home:* 1525 Franklin Dr., Norman, Okla. 73069. *Office: Oklahoma City Times,* 500 North Broadway, Oklahoma City, Okla. 73101.

CAREER: Member of editorial staff of *Shelby County Herald,* Shelbyville, Mo., 1940-41, *Bartlesville Evening Enterprise,* Bartlesville, Okla., 1946-48, *Clinton Daily News,* Clinton, Okla., 1948-50, *Norman Transcript,* Norman, Okla., 1950; Oklahoma Publishing Co., Oklahoma City, reporter and book editor, 1950—. *Military service:* U.S. Army and U.S. Army Air Corps, 1941-45; became first lieutenant; received Distinguished Flying Cross and Air Medal. *Member:* Western Writers of America, Oklahoma City Gridiron Club.

WRITINGS: (Contributor) S. Omar Barker, editor, *Spurs West* (anthology), Doubleday, 1960. Contributor of short stories to *Saturday Evening Post, Argosy, Field and Stream,* and other magazines.

WORK IN PROGRESS: A novel based on the life of an Indian athlete.

AVOCATIONAL INTERESTS: Hunting, fishing, and reading.

BIOGRAPHICAL/CRITICAL SOURCES: Saturday Evening Post, June 23, 1956, April 2, 1960.

* * *

MONTGOMERY, Horace 1906-

PERSONAL: Born January 6, 1906, in Derrick City, Pa.; son of Albert (a teacher) and Alice (Gearhart) Montgomery; married Gladys Anderson; children: Thomas Albert. *Education:* Ohio Northern University, A.B., 1927; University of Georgia, M.A., 1930, Ph.D., 1940; additional study at University of Pittsburgh, 1928, 1929, Duke University, 1933. *Politics:* Democrat. *Religion:* Unitarian. *Home:* 160 Rock Glen Rd. Athens, Ga. 30601. *Office:* Department of History, University of Georgia, Athens, Ga. 30601.

CAREER: High school history teacher in Uniontown, Pa., 1927-37; California State College, California, Pa., teacher, social studies, 1937-47; University of Georgia, Athens, 1947—, began as associate professor, now professor of history. Fulbright Visiting Professor at University of Innsbruck, 1959-60; lecturer at London School of Economics, University of London, 1959; visiting professor at universities in United States, 1946-55. Director, University Center in Georgia, 1957-59. *Military service* U.S. Naval Reserve, 1942-45; became lieutenant senior grade. *Member:* American Historical Association, Organization of American Historians, American Association of University Professors (chapter president, 1955-56), Southern Historical Association (chairman of nominating committee, 1963-64), Pennsylvania Historical Association. *Awards, honors:* L.H.D. from Ohio Northern University, 1962.

WRITINGS: Cracker Parties, Louisiana State University Press, 1950; (editor) *Georgians in Profile,* University of Georgia Press, 1958; *Howell Cobb's Confederate Career,* Confederate Publishing Co., 1959; (with Wilbur Devereux Jones) *Civilization through the Centuries,* Ginn, 1960; *Johnny Cobb: Confederate Aristocrat,* University of Georgia Press, 1964; (contributor) Klaus Lanzinger, editor, *Americana Austriaca,* Braumueller, Volume I, 1966, Volume II, 1970. Contributor of articles and reviews to historical journals. Director, "Our World Today," *Atlanta Journal* weekly current events feature, 1952-54. Member of editorial board, Pennsylvania Historical Association.

WORK IN PROGRESS: Koinonia: A Twentieth Century Communitarian Experiment.

AVOCATIONAL INTERESTS: Genealogical studies of Pennsylvania Germans and their movements west and south.

* * *

MONTGOMERY, Rutherford George 1894-
(Al Avery, Everitt Proctor)

PERSONAL: Born April 12, 1894, in North Dakota; son of George Y. and Matilda (Proctor) Montgomery; married Eunice Opal Kirks, February 14, 1930; children: Earl, Polly Montgomery Hecathorn, Marylin Montgomery Fitch. *Education:* Western State College of Colorado, student, three years. *Home:* 33 Walnut Ave., Los Gatos, Calif. 95030.

CAREER: Teacher in Colorado schools, 1921-27; State of Colorado, Gunnison county judge, 1931-36, budget commissioner, 1932-38; free-lance writer, primarily of youth books, 1939—. *Military service:* U.S. Army Air Corps, 1917-19; became sergeant. *Member:* Society of Authors, Western Writers of America, Writers Guild of America West. *Awards, honors:* Commonwealth Club of California juvenile silver medal, 1953, for *Wapiti the Elk; New York Herald Tribune* Children's Spring Book Festival award, 1956, and Boys' Clubs of America junior book award, 1957, both for *Beaver Water.*

WRITINGS: Troopers Three, Doubleday, Doran, 1932; *Call of the West,* Grosset, 1933; *Broken Fang,* M.A. Donohue, 1935, 2nd edition, Caxton, 1939; *Carcajou,* Caxton, 1936; *Yellow Eyes,* Caxton, 1937; *Gray Wolf,* Houghton, 1938; *High Country,* Derrydale Press, 1938; *The Trail of the Buffalo,* Houghton, 1939; *Timberlane Tales,* McKay, 1939.

Midnight, Henry Holt, 1940; *Star Ball of the Rangers,* McKay, 1941; *Iceblink,* Henry Holt, 1941; *Hurricane Yank,* McKay, 1942; *Husky, Co-Pilot of the Pilgrim,* Henry Holt, 1942; *Thumbs Up!* McKay, 1942; *Ghost Town Adventure,* Henry Holt 1942; *Trappers' Trail,* Henry Holt, 1943; *War Wings,* McKay, 1943; *Out of the Sun,* McKay, 1943; *Warhawk Patrol,* McKay, 1944; *Big Brownie,* Henry Holt, 1944; *Thunderboats, Ho!,* McKay, 1945; *Sea Raiders Ho!,* McKay, 1945; *Rough Riders Ho!,* McKay, 1946; *The Mystery of the Turquoise Frog,* Messner, 1946; *Kildee House,* Doubleday, 1949.

The Mystery of the Crystal Canyon, Winston, 1951; *The Capture of the Golden Stallion,* Little, Brown, 1951; *Hill Ranch,* Doubleday, 1951; *Mister Jim,* Faber, 1952, World Publishing, 1957; *Wapiti, the Elk,* Little, Brown, 1952; *White Mountaineer,* Little, Brown, 1953; *Seecatch, a Story of a Fur Seal,* Ginn, 1953; *McGonnigle's Lake,* Doubleday, 1953; *The Golden Stallion's Revenge,* Little, Brown, 1953; *The Golden Stallion to the Rescue,* Little, Brown, 1954; *Amikuk,* World Publishing, 1955; *Black Powder Empire,* Little, Brown, 1955; *The Golden Stallion's Victory,* Little, Brown, 1956; *Beaver Water,* World Publishing, 1956; *Claim Jumpers of Marble Canyon,* Knopf, 1956; *Jets Away!,* Dodd, 1957; *Mountain Man,* World Publishing, 1957; *Tom Pittman, USAF,* Duell, Sloan & Pearce, 1957; *Whitetail: The Story of a Prairie Dog,* World Publishing, 1958; *The Silver Hills,* World Publishing, 1958; *Kent Barstow, Special Agent,* Duell, Sloan & Pearce 1958; *In Happy Hollow,* Doubleday, 1958; *The Golden Stallion and the Wolf Dog,* Little, Brown, 1958; (with Natlee Kenoyer) *A Horse for Claudia and Dennis,* Duell, Sloan & Pearce, 1958; *Tim's Mountain,* World Publishing, 1959; (editor) *A Saddlebag of Tales,* Dodd, 1959; *Missile Away: A Kent Barstow Adventure,*

Duell, Sloan & Pearce, 1959; *The Golden Stallion's Adventure at Redstone,* Little, Brown, 1959; (with Grover Heiman) *Jet Navigator, Strategic Air Command,* Dodd, 1959.

Mission Intruder: A Kent Barstow Adventure, Duell, Sloan & Pearce, 1960; *Walt Disney's Weecha: A Fact-Fiction Nature Story,* Golden Press, 1960; *Walt Disney's The Odyssey of an Otter: A Fact-Fiction Nature Story,* Golden Press, 1960; *Walt Disney's El Blanco: The Legend of the White Stallion,* Golden Press, 1961; *Kent Barstow, Space Man,* Duell, Sloan & Pearce, 1961; *King of the Castle: The Story of a Kangaroo Rat,* World Publishing, 1961; *Klepty,* Duell, Sloan & Pearce, 1961; *Walt Disney's Cougar: A Fact-Fiction Nature Story,* Golden Press, 1961; *Sex Isn't Everything,* Dodd, 1961; *The Golden Stallion,* Grosset, 1962; *The Capture of the West Wind,* Duell, Sloan & Pearce, 1962; *Snowman,* Duell, Sloan & Pearce, 1962; *Monte, the Bear Who Became a Celebrity,* Duell, Sloan & Pearce, 1962; *Crazy Kill Range,* World Publishing, 1963; *The Defiant Heart,* Duell, Sloan & Pearce, 1963; *Kent Barstow and the Commando Flight,* Duell, Sloan & Pearce, 1963; *McNulty's Holiday,* Duell, Sloan & Pearce, 1963; *Kent Barstow on a B-70 Mission,* Duell, Sloan & Pearce, 1964; *Kent Barstow Aboard the Dyna Soar,* Duell, Sloan & Pearce, 1964; *The Living Wilderness,* Dodd, 1964; *Ghost Town Gold,* World Publishing, 1965; *The Stubborn One,* Duell, Sloan & Pearce, 1965; *Into the Groove,* Dodd, 1966; *Thornbush Jungle,* World Publishing, 1966; *The Golden Stallion and the Mysterious Feud,* Little, Brown, 1967; *A Kinkajou on the Town,* World Publishing, 1967; *Smoky Trail,* Ward, Lock, 1967; *Dolphins as They Are,* Duell, Sloan & Pearce, 1969; *Corey's Sea Monster,* World Publishing, 1969; *Pekan the Shadow,* Caxton, 1970; *Big Red, a Wild Stallion,* Caxton, 1971.

"A Yankee Flier" series under pseudonym Al Avery—all published by Grosset: *A Yankee Flier with the R.A.F.,* 1941, *. . . in the Far East,* 1942, *. . . in the South Pacific,* 1943, *. . . in North Africa,* 1943, *. . . Over Berlin,* 1944, *. . . in Italy,* 1944, *. . . on a Rescue Mission,* 1945, *. . . in Normandy,* 1945, *. . . Under Secret Orders,* 1946.

Under pseudonym Everitt Proctor: *The Last Cruise of the Jeannette,* Westminster, 1944; *Thar She Blows,* Westminster, 1945; *Men Against the Ice,* Westminster, 1946.

Also author of screen and television plays. Contributor of more than five hundred short stories to magazines for girls and boys.

AVOCATIONAL INTERESTS: Flying, outdoor life.

BIOGRAPHICAL/CRITICAL SOURCES: Muriel Fuller, *More Junior Authors,* H.W. Wilson, 1963; *New York Times Book Review,* June 25, 1967.

* * *

MOORE, Margaret R(umberger)

PERSONAL: Born in DuBois, Pa.; daughter of George Francis and Euphrasia (Means) Rumberger; married John Travers Moore (a poet and author). *Education:* Syracuse University, B.S. in L.S. *Home:* 1298 Cryer, Cincinnati, Ohio 45208. *Office:* Xavier University Library, Cincinnati, Ohio 45207.

CAREER: Dayton Public Library, Dayton, Ohio, children's librarian; Xavier University, Cincinnati, Ohio, assistant library director, 1947-67, consultant, 1968—.

WRITINGS—All with husband, John Travers Moore: *Sing Along Sary,* Harcourt, 1951; *Little Saints,* Grail Press, 1953; *Big Saints,* Grail Press, 1954; *The Three Tripps (Parents' Magazine* Book Club selection), Bobbs-Merrill, 1959; *On Cherry Tree Hill,* Bobbs-Merrill, 1960; *They Saw Him Fly,* Albert Whitman, 1966; *Here Kitty,* Albert Whitman, 1966; *The Little Band and the Inaug-*

ural Parade (Junior Literary Guild selection), Albert Whitman, 1968; *Pepito's Speech at the United Nations,* Carolrhoda Books, 1971; *Certainly, Carrie, Cut the Cake: Poems A to Z,* Bobbs-Merrill, 1971. Contributor of about eighty poems, stories, and articles to juvenile and other magazines.

WORK IN PROGRESS: An anthology of poetry; juvenile books.

BIOGRAPHICAL/CRITICAL SOURCES: Cincinnati Post and Times Star, September 24, 1958; *Cincinnati Enquirer,* April 19, 1959; *Ohioana Quarterly,* winter, 1970.

*   *   *

MOORE, Russell Franklin 1920-

PERSONAL: Born July 28, 1920, in Woodward, Iowa; son of Lawrence Alva (a businessman) and Sadie (Minger) Moore; married Ruth Emily Moller, May 29, 1946; children: Shelby Lynn. *Education:* State University of Iowa, student, 1937-40; New York Law School, LL.B., 1959. *Office:* Counsel Press, Inc., 55 West 42nd St., New York, N.Y. 10018.

CAREER: Ronald Press Co., New York, N.Y., assistant to the president, 1947-57; Simmons-Boardman Publishing Corp., New York, N.Y., vice-president, 1957-65; private practice of law, 1965-67; American Management Association, New York, N.Y., editor, 1967-70; Counsel Press, New York, N.Y., vice-president, 1970—. *Military service:* U.S. Army, served in European theater, World War II; became captain; received Bronze Star. *Member:* Classical Association (life), American Bar Association, Maison des Ailes (Brussels).

WRITINGS: Mentality and Consciousness, Franklin Publishing, 1937; *Oriental Philosophies,* R.F. Moore Co., 1937, 3rd edition (with William D. Gould and George B. Arbaugh), 1951; (editor) *Ramayana,* R.F. Moore Co., c.1950; (editor) *Readings in Oriental Philosophy,* R.F. Moore Co., 1951; *Bibliography for "Oriental Philosophies,"* R.F. Moore Co., 1951; (editor) *Modern Constitutions: With Brief Commentaries,* Littlefield, 1957; *Stare Decisis: Some Trends in British and American Application of the Doctrine,* Simmons-Boardman, 1958; *Letter from Bern,* Whittier Books, 1960; *Principality of Liechtenstein: A Brief History,* Simmons-Boardman, 1960; *The Family History Book: A Genealogical Record,* Simmons-Boardman, 1961; *Selected Ancestral Lines: Moore-Minger Genealogical Record,* [New York], 1962; (with Max J. Wasserman and Charles W. Hultman) *The Common Market and American Business,* Simmons-Boardman, 1964; (editor) *Compensating Executive Worth,* American Management Association, 1968; (editor) *Law for Executives,* American Management Association, 1968; (editor) *The American Management Association Management Handbook,* American Management Association, 1970. Editor, *Who's Who in Railroading in North America,* Simmons-Boardman, 14th edition, 1959, 15th edition, 1964.

*   *   *

MOORE, Wilfred George 1907-

PERSONAL: Born May 8, 1907, in Burton-on-Trent, England; son of Edward George and Emma (Wainwright) Moore; married Gwenfra Marian Williams, August 10, 1934; children: Nicholas George. *Education:* University of London, B.Sc., 1928. *Home:* Fouroaks, 34 Copsewood Way, Northwood, Middlesex, England.

CAREER: Teacher of geography in schools in London area, England, 1928-39, 1946-67. *Military service:* Royal Air Force, Meteorological Branch, 1939-45; served in Iraq and Persia, organizing Persian meteorological ser-

vice, 1941-44. *Member:* Royal Geographical Society (fellow), Society of Authors.

WRITINGS: The Geography of Capitalism, Gollancz, 1938; *The World's Wealth,* Penguin, 1947; *A Dictionary of Geography: Definitions and Explanations of Terms Used in Physical Geography,* Penguin, 1949, 3rd edition, Praeger, 1967, 4th edition, Penguin, 1968; *The Soil We Live On,* Methuen, 1950; *Work and Rest,* Methuen, 1953; "Essential Geography" series, published by Hulton Educational Publications: *Homes,* 1956, *Food,* 1957, *Clothing,* 1957, *Transport,* 1958; "Adventures in Geography" series, four books, Harrap, 1957-61; "Children Far and Near" series, eight volumes, Hulton Educational Publications, 1958-59; (with Walter Shepherd and Peter Hood) *The World We Live In: The Geography of Our Earth and Its Peoples,* New Educational Press, 1958; *Around the World in Colour,* Paul Hamlyn, 1960; *Find the Answer: Geography,* Hulton Educational Publications, 1961; *A Family in Samoa,* Hulton Educational Publications, 1961; *A Family in Greece,* Hulton Educational Publications, 1962; *A Family in Japan,* Hulton Educational Publications, 1963; (with N.H. Belcher) *A Family in New Zealand,* Hulton Educational Publications, 1964; "More Children Far and Near" series, seven volumes, Hulton Educational Publications, 1965-67; *The Penguin Encyclopedia of Places,* Penguin, 1971.

"New Visual Geography" series, published by Hutchinson: *Ice Cap and Tundra,* 1959, new edition, 1968; *The Northern Forests,* 1959; *The Mining of Coal,* 1960; *Rivers and Their Work,* 1961; *The Production of Oil,* 1961; *The Temperate Grasslands,* 1963; *Deserts of the World,* 1966; *The Sea and the Coast,* 1968; *The Tropical Grasslands,* 1968; *The Weather,* 1968; *The Equatorial Forests,* 1969; *Mountains and Plateaus,* 1971; *Volcanoes,* 1972.

Contributor: *Odhams' Complete Self-Educator,* Odhams, 1939; *Modern Children's Library of Knowledge,* Odhams, 1958; *Geographie Universelle* (English edition), Paul Hamlyn, 1961; G. Manley, editor, *Geography,* Macdonald & Co., 1961.

WORK IN PROGRESS: Further volumes in "New Visual Geography" series.

SIDELIGHTS: Moore has traveled in most countries in Europe and Middle East, and in parts of Africa, West Indies, and in other countries. *Avocational interests:* Reading, conversation, theatre, and films.

*   *   *

MORAN, James Sterling 1909-
(Jim Moran)

PERSONAL: Born November 24, 1909, in Woodstock, Va.; son of J. Sterling and Nellie (Bryant) Moran. *Education:* Educated in public schools. *Agent:* Mrs. Carlton Cole, Waldorf Towers, New York, N.Y. 10022. *Office:* Jim Moran Associates, 300 West End Ave., New York, N.Y. 10023.

CAREER: Varied career as lecturer on sightseeing bus, aviator, teacher of classical guitar, sound engineer, airport engineer, and newspaperman before entering publicity business in 1938; now heads Jim Moran Associates, New York, N.Y. Guest on hundreds of television programs in role of world traveler interested in archaeology, primitive people, unusual inventions, practical jokes, and publicity stunts. Appearances on "Tonight," "Today," "David Frost Show," and "Steve Allen Show."

WRITINGS: Sophocles, the Hyena: A Fable (juvenile), McGraw, 1954; *Miserable: A Story About a Dinosaur* (juvenile), Bobbs-Merrill, 1960; *Why Men Shouldn't Marry,* Lyle Stuart, 1969; *The Frustrations of the Irish,*

Cornerstone Library, 1971; *The Classical Women* (photographs), Playboy Press, 1972.

BIOGRAPHICAL/CRITICAL SOURCES: Saturday Review, April 5, 1969.

*   *   *

MORAN, Patrick Alfred Pierce   1917-

PERSONAL: Surname is accented on first syllable; born July 14, 1917, in Sydney, Australia; son of Herbert Michael (a surgeon) and Eva (Mann) Moran; married Jean Mavis Frame, September 16, 1946; children: Louise, Michael, Hugh. *Education:* University of Sydney, B.Sc., 1937, D.Sc. 1951; Cambridge University, M.A. 1941, Sc.D., 1964. *Religion:* Roman Catholic. *Home:* 17 Tennyson Crescent, Forrest, Canberra, Australia.

CAREER: Australian National University, Canberra, professor of statistics, 1952. *Member:* Australian Academy of Sciences (fellow).

WRITINGS: The Theory of Storage (monograph), Methuen, 1959, Wiley, 1960; *The Statistical Processes of Evolutionary Theory*, Oxford University Press, 1962; (with Maurice George Kendall) *Geometrical Probability*, Hafner, 1963; (with C.A.B. Smith) *Commentary on R.A. Fisher's Paper on the Correlation Between Realtives on the Supposition of Mendelian Inheritance*, Cambridge University Press, 1966; *An Introduction to Probability Theory*, Oxford University Press, 1968. Contributor of papers to scientific journals.

WORK IN PROGRESS: Research on the theory of probability and on genetics.

*   *   *

MOREHOUSE, Clifford P (helps)   1904-

PERSONAL: Born April 18, 1904, in Milwaukee, Wis.; son of Frederic C. (an editor and publisher) and Lilias (Macon) Morehouse; married Ellen L. Smith, March 16, 1927; children: Ellen Louise (Mrs. James L. Henry), Lilias Macon (Mrs. Jackson M. Bruce, Jr.), Frederic Cook. *Education:* Harvard University, A.B., 1925; Marquette University, M.A., 1938. *Religion:* Episcopal. *Home:* 4863 Primrose Path, Sarasota, Fla. 33581.

CAREER: Morehouse-Barlow Co. (formerly Morehouse Publishing Co.), New York, N.Y., secretary, 1925-39, vice-president, 1932-64, president, 1964-68. Delegate to World Conference on Faith and Order in Edinburgh, 1937, Lund, Sweden, 1952, to Assembly of World Council of Churches in Amsterdam, 1948, Evanston, 1954, New Delhi, 1961, Uppsala, 1968; member of executive committee and department of international affairs, National Council of Churches; president, House of Deputies of Episcopal Church, 1961-67; trustee, Cathedral of St. John the Divine, 1948-52. *Military service:* U.S. Marine Corps Reserve, active duty, World War II; assistant editor, *Marine Corps Gazette*, 1943-44, combat historian for Pelieu and Iwo Jima operations; retired as lieutenant colonel. *Member:* American Church Union, Harvard Club (New York). *Awards, honors:* LL.D. from Nashotah House and Brown University; Bishop Chase Medal, Kenyon College; S.T.D., General Seminary; Order of St. John of Jerusalem.

WRITINGS: (Editor) *The Anglican Communion Throughout the World: A Series of Missionary Papers from the Field*, Morehouse, 1927; *Wartime Pilgrimage: An American Churchman's View of Britain in 1942*, Morehouse, 1942; *The Iwo Jima Operation* (monograph), Historical Division, U.S. Marine Corps, 1946; (with Frank E. Wilson) *Life of Christ*, Morehouse, 1947; *A Layman Looks at the Church*, Seabury, 1964; *Mother of*

Churches, Seabury, 1973. Compiler, *Who's Who in the General Convention of the Episcopal Church, 1934*, Morehouse, 1934; editor, *Episcopal Church Annual*, Morehouse, 1962-64, 1967. Editor, *Living Church*, 1932-53.

WORK IN PROGRESS: Volume III of *History of the Parish of Trinity Church in the City of New York.*

*   *   *

MOREHOUSE, Laurence E (nglemohr)   1913-

PERSONAL: Born July 13, 1913, in Danbury, Conn.; son of Howard Lyon and Hazel (Hoyt) Morehouse; married Jane Gotch, September 3, 1939; children: Stephen A., David Bruce. *Education:* Springfield College, B.S., 1936, M.Ed., 1937; State University of Iowa, Ph.D., 1941, *Politics:* Republican. *Religion:* Protestant. *Home:* 10851 Weyburn Ave., Los Angeles, Calif. 90024. *Office:* Department of Kinesiology, University of California, 405 Hilgard Ave., Los Angeles, Calif. 90024.

CAREER: University of Wichita, Wichita, Kan., head of physical education department, 1941-42; University of Kansas, Lawrence, assistant professor of physical education, 1942; Harvard University, Cambridge, Mass., research fellow in fatigue research laboratory, 1945-46; University of Southern California, Los Angeles, associate professor of physical education and research physiologist in aviation medicine, 1946-54; University of California, Los Angeles, professor of kinesiology and director of human performance laboratory, 1954—. U.S. Department of State specialist in sixteen countries, 1960-61; Fulbright Professor, United Arab Republic Ministry of Scientific Research, Cairo, Egypt, 1963. Interim chief of performance physiology, U.S. Air Force School of Aviation Medicine, 1950-52; member of port study project, National Research Council of National Academy of Sciences, San Francisco, Calif., 1958-63; consultant to U.S. Public Health Service, U.S. Military Academy, NASA Manned Spacecraft Center, and other groups, firms, agencies. Member of citizens' advisory committee, President's Council on Fitness; chairman of research committee, California Council on Fitness. *Military service:* U.S. Navy, 1942-45; became lieutenant.

MEMBER: American Physiological Society, Aerospace Medical Association, American Association for Health, Physical Education and Recreation (vice president, health education), Human Factors Society (founding president), Ergonomics Research Society, American Academy of Physical Education, American College of Sports Medicine (fellow; vice president, physiology, 1959), American Association for Advancement of Science (fellow).

WRITINGS: (With Augustus T. Miller, Jr.) *Physiology of Exercise*, Mosby, 1948, 6th edition, 1971; with John M. Cooper) *Kinesiology*, Mosby, 1950; (with David Alvin Armbruster) *Swimming and Diving*, 2nd edition, Mosby, 1950; (with Philip J. Rasch) *Scientific Basis of Athletic Training*, Saunders, 1958; (contributor) *Health and Fitness in the Modern World*, Athletic Institute, 1961; (editor with F.D. Sills and T.L. Delorme) *Weight Training in Sports and Physical Education*, American Association for Health, Physical Education and Recreation, 1962; (with Rasch) *Sports Medicine for Trainers*, 2nd edition, Saunders, 1963; *Laboratory Manual for Physiology of Exercise*, Mosby, 1972. Contributor to professional journals. Associate editor, American Association for Health, Physical Education and Recreation *Research Quarterly*, 1952-60.

WORK IN PROGRESS: Physical Education Tests and Measurement, for Prentice-Hall; *Encyclopedia of Sports Medicine; Anatomy and Physiology.*

MORGAN, Edmund S(ears) 1916-

PERSONAL: Born January 17, 1916, in Minneapolis, Minn.; son of of Edmund Morris (a professor of law) and Elsie (Smith) Morgan; married Helen Mayer (a historian), June 7, 1939; children: Penelope, Pamela. *Education:* Belmont Hill School, graduate, 1933; Harvard University, A.B., 1937, Ph.D., 1942; London School of Economics, University of London, graduate study, 1937-38. *Home:* 244 Livingston St., New Haven, Conn. 06511. *Office:* Department of History, Yale University, New Haven, Conn. 06520.

CAREER: Massachusetts Institute of Technology, Cambridge, instrument maker in Radiation Laboratory, 1942-45; University of Chicago, Chicago, Ill., instructor in social sciences, 1945-46; Brown University, Providence, R.I., assistant professor, 1947-49, associate professor, 1949-51, professor of history, 1951-55; Yale University, New Haven, Conn., professor of history, 1955-65, Sterling Professor of History, 1965—. Member of council, Institute of Early American History and Culture, 1953-56, 1958-60, 1970-72. Johnson Research Professor, University of Wisconsin, 1968-69. *Member:* American Historical Association, American Antiquarian Society, Organization of American Historians (president, 1971-72), American Academy of Arts and Sciences, American Philosophical Society, Massachusetts Historical Society, Colonial Society of Massachusetts. *Awards, honors:* Research fellow, Huntington Library, 1952-53; William Clyde DeVane Medal, 1971; Douglass Adair Memorial Award, 1972.

WRITINGS: The Puritan Family: Essays on Religion and Domestic Relations.in Seventeenth-Century New England, Boston Public Library, 1944, new edition, Harper, 1966; *Virginians at Home: Family Life in the Eighteenth Century,* Colonial Williamsburg, 1952; (with wife, Helen M. Morgan) *The Stamp Act Crisis: Prologue to Revolution,* University of North Carolina Press, 1953, revised edition, Collier, 1963; (editor) *The Stamp Act Crisis: Sources and Documents,* University of North Carolina Press, 1953; *The Birth of the Republic, 1763-89,* University of Chicago Press, 1956; (contributor) *The Mirror of the Indian,* Associates of the John Carter Brown Library, 1958; *The Puritan Dilemma: The Story of John Winthrop,* Little, Brown, 1958; *The American Revolution: A Review of Changing Interpretations,* Service Center for Teachers of History, 1958; *Prologue to the Revolution: Sources and Documents on the Stamp Act Crisis, 1764-1766,* University of North Carolina Press, 1959; (author of introduction) *Paul Revere's Three Accounts of His Famous Ride,* Massachusetts Historical Society, 1961, 2nd edition, 1968; *The Gentle Puritan: A Life of Ezra Stiles, 1727-1795,* Yale University Press, 1962; *Visible Saints: The History of a Puritan Idea,* New York University Press, 1963; (editor) *The Founding of Massachusetts: Historians and the Sources,* Bobbs-Merrill, 1964; (editor) *The American Revolution: Two Centuries of Interpretation,* Prentice-Hall, 1965; (editor) *Puritan Political Ideas, 1558-1794,* Bobbs-Merrill, 1965; (editor) *The Diary of Michael Wigglesworth, 1653-1657: The Conscience of a Puritan,* Harper, 1965; (with others) *The Emergence of the American,* Educational Services, 1965; *Roger Williams: The Church and the State,* Harcourt, 1967; *So What About History?,* Atheneum, 1969. Contributor of articles and reviews to historical journals. Member of editorial board, *New England Quarterly.*

SIDELIGHTS: In a review of *Roger Williams: The Church and the State,* Robert E. Brown writes: "Threading his way skilfully through the intricacies of seventeenth-century language and theology, the author reveals the 'intricate and beautiful' symmetry of Williams's logic which led to his rejection of the Church of England, the Puritan Church, and finally even the Separatist Church. Differing with the late Perry Miller, who held that Williams's mind was theological rather than social, Morgan insists that while Williams's thought took its rise from religion, he was more often concerned with ecclesiastical and political institutions than with theology. The result is a beautifully and lucidly written little book which is must reading for anyone who would understand the controversies that enlivened early New England history."

BIOGRAPHICAL/CRITICAL SOURCES: New York Times, June 28, 1965; *Yale Review,* winter, 1969.

*   *   *

MORGAN, Glenn G(uy) 1926-

PERSONAL: Born April 23, 1926, in Astoria, Ore.; son of Glenn Samuel (a physician and surgeon) and Hope (Worley) Morgan; married Shirley Ann Welt, June 10, 1950 (divorced, February, 1968); children Joanne Hope, Randall David. *Education:* University of Oregon, B.A., 1949, M.A., 1950; additional study at University of Mexico, summer, 1949, Harvard University, 1955-56; University of Virginia, Ph.D., 1961. *Religion:* Protestant. *Home:* 151 Buckingham Dr., Apt. 266, Santa Clara, Calif. 95050. *Office:* San Jose State College, San Jose, Calif. 95114.

CAREER: U.S. Government, Washington, D.C., research analyst, 1952-58; San Jose State College, San Jose, Calif., assistant professor, 1959-63, associate professor, 1963-66, professor of political science, 1966—. Visiting professor at Stanford University, 1962, 1963, University of Oregon, 1963. *Military service:* U.S. Merchant Marine, 1944-45; served in Pacific theater; became warrant officer.

MEMBER: American Political Science Association, American Association for the Advancement of Slavic Studies, Far Western Slavic Association, Phi Beta Kappa (president, faculty club, San Jose State College, 1962-63, 1965-66), Phi Kappa Phi, Sigma Delta Pi, Pi Delta Phi. *Awards, honors:* One of twenty federal employees selected nationally to participate in Third Career Development Program, 1954; Danforth Foundation special grant, 1958-59; research grant from Hoover Institution, Stanford University, 1963-64; Relm Foundation research grants, 1964-65, 1969-70; American Council of Learned Societies research grant, 1966-67; American Philosophical Society research grants for travel in Soviet Union, 1966, 1969; selected Distinguished Scholar of the Year, San Jose State College chapter, Phi Kappa Phi, 1968.

WRITINGS: Soviet Administrative Legality: The Role of the Attorney General's Office, Stanford University Press, 1962; (with Leon Boim and Aleksander W. Rudzinski) *Law in Eastern Europe,* Volume 13: *Legal Controls in the Soviet Union,* Sijthoff (Leiden), 1966; *Soviet Procuracy General Supervision Today,* Sijthoff, 1971. Contributor of articles to journals.

*   *   *

MORGAN, Joe Warner 1912-

PERSONAL: Born July 7, 1919, in Lafayette, Ind.; son of Lee Harry (a businessman) and Rosa (Fluck) Morgan; married Jeanne Murray, June 18, 1938; children: Ann, John, Patrick. *Education:* Knox College, B.A., 1934. *Home:* 66 Cleary Ct., San Francisco, Calif. *Office:* United Press International, Fox Plaza, 1390 Market, San Francisco, Calif. 94102.

CAREER: United Press International, 1934—, with assignments as reporter and writer in Chicago, Ill., Milwaukee, Wis., and Detroit, Mich., 1934-39, bureau manager in Minneapolis, Minn., 1939-43, central division news editor in Chicago, Ill., 1943-48, night news manager in New York, N.Y., 1948-60, foreign editor, 1960-66, Pacific division news editor, 1966—. *Member:* Sigma Delta Chi, Phi Delta Theta.

WRITINGS: Expense Account (novel), Random House, 1958; *Amy Go Home* (novel), McKay, 1964.

* * *

MORGAN, Louise

PERSONAL: Married Gordon Scott Fulcher; married second husband, O.F. Theis (an editor); children: (first marriage) Anne (Mrs. Thomas Hunter), John; (second marriage) Michael. *Education:* Brown University, B.A., M.A.; Byrn Mawr College, Ph.D. *Home:* Dallington, Heathfield, Sussex, England.

CAREER: Onetime college and university instructor in United States, teaching English at University of Wisconsin, Madison, at Miss Madeira's School in Washington, D.C., for two years, at Vassar College, Poughkeepsie, N.Y., for one year; *Everyman,* London, England, literary editor, 1930-33; *News Chronicle,* London, staff reporter, writing mainly on social problems, 1933-53.

WRITINGS: Writers at Work, Chatto & Windus, 1931; (editor and author of introduction) Bala-Sahib Pandita Pratinidhi, *The Ten Point Way to Health,* Dent, 1938; *Inside Yourself: A New Way to Health Based on the Alexander Technique,* foreword by Aldous Huxley, McGraw, 1954; *Inside Your Kitchen: The Source of Good Living,* Hutchinson, 1956; *Home-Made Wines,* Hutchinson, 1958. Contributor to magazines, including a series throughout the war in *Good Housekeeping.*

WORK IN PROGRESS: Personal memoirs in London, in collaboration with husband, O.F. Theis.

SIDELIGHTS: Ten Point Way to Health has been published in Germany and Holland; *Inside Yourself* has been published in Germany.

* * *

MORGAN, (Joseph) Theodore   1910-

PERSONAL: Born May 31, 1910, in Middletown, Ohio; son of Ben and Anna Louella (Knecht) Morgan; married Catharine Moomaw, June 30, 1943; children: Stephanie H., Marian D., Laura S. *Education:* Ohio State University, A.B., B.Sc.Ed., 1930, A.M., 1931; University of Washington, postgraduate study, summer, 1937; Harvard University, M.A., 1940, Ph.D., 1941. *Home:* 3534 Topping Rd., Madison, Wis. 53705. *Office:* Department of Economics, University of Wisconsin, Madison, Wis. 53706.

CAREER: Harvard University, Cambridge, Mass., instructor, 1940-41, 1942-47; Randolph-Macon Woman's College, Lynchburg, Va., assistant professor, 1941-42; University of Wisconsin, Madison, associate professor, 1947-55, professor of economics, 1955—. Consultant to Ford Foundation, 1957, 1963-64; 1967, International Bank for Reconstruction and Development, 1961-62. Advisory, teaching, and research work in Ceylon, Indonesia, Kenya, Singapore, and Thailand. *Member:* American Economic Association (chairman, committee on screening of foreign students), Royal Economic Society, American Association of University Professors, Phi Beta Kappa.

WRITINGS: Income and Employment, Prentice-Hall, 1947, 2nd edition, 1952; *Hawaii: A Century of Economic Change, 1778-1876,* Harvard University Press, 1948; *Introduction to Economics,* Prentice-Hall, 1950, 2nd edition, 1956; (editor with George W. Betz and N.K. Choudhry) *Readings in Economic Development,* Wadsworth, 1963; (editor with Nyle Spoelstra, and contributor) *Economic Interdependence in Southeast Asia,* University of Wisconsin Press, 1969; (editor with Betz, and contributor) *Economic Development: Readings in Theory and Prac-*

tice, Wadsworth, 1970; (editor and contributor) *Report to the Agency for International Development on Economic Cooperation in Southeast Asia,* Agency for International Development, 1970. Contributor of articles to professional journals.

WORK IN PROGRESS: Comparative Theory of Economic Development.

* * *

MORGENSTERN, Oskar   1902-

PERSONAL: Born 1902 in Germany; became American citizen; son of Wilhelm (a businessman) and Margarete (Teichler) Morgenstern; married Dorothy Young (an architectural consultant), June 7, 1948; children: Carl, Karin. *Education:* University of Vienna, Dr. Rer. Pol., 1925. *Politics:* Independent. *Religion:* Lutheran. *Home:* 94 Library Pl., Princeton, N.J. 08540; and Bluff Point Cove, Blue Mountain Lake, N.Y. 12812. *Office:* Tisch Hall, New York University, New York, N.Y. 10003.

CAREER: University of Vienna, Vienna, Austria, lecturer, 1928-35, professor, 1935-38; Princeton University, Princeton, N.J., instructor, 1938-41, associate professor, 1941-44, professor of political economics, 1944-70; New York University, New York, N.Y., professor of economics, 1970—. Consultant to RAND Corp., to U.S. Atomic Energy Commission, 1955-57, White House, 1959-60. Director and chairman of board, Mathematica; director, Midland Capital Corporation; director, Societe Nationale d'Etude et de Construction de Moteurs d'Aviation (SNECMA), Paris; trustee, Institute for Advanced Studies, Vienna. *Member:* International Institute of Statistics, American Economic Association, American Statistical Association, Econometric Society, Academie des Sciences Morales et Politiques (Paris). *Awards, honors:* Rockefeller Foundation fellow at Harvard University, Columbia University, and at Universities of London, Paris, and Rome, 1925-28; Dr. Rer. Pol., University of Mannheim, 1957, University of Basel, 1960; honorary degree, University of Vienna, 1965.

WRITINGS: Wirtschaftsprognose, Springer Verlag, 1928; *Die Grenzen de Wirtschaftspolitik,* Springer Verlag, 1934, translation by Vera Smith published as *The Limits of Economics,* William Hodge & Co., 1937; (with John Von Neumann) *Theory of Games and Economic Behavior,* Princeton University Press, 1944, 3rd edition, 1953; *On the Accuracy of Economic Observations,* Princeton University Press, 1950, 2nd edition, 1963; *Prolegomena to a Theory of Organization,* RAND Corp., 1951; (editor and contributor) *Economic Activity Analysis,* Wiley, 1954; *The Validity of International Gold Movement Statistics,* International Finance Section, Department of Economics and Sociology, Princeton University, 1955; *Der Theoretische unterblau der Wirtschaftspolitik,* Westdeutscher Verlag, c.1957; *International Financial Transactions and Business Cycles,* Princeton University Press, 1959; *The Question of National Defense,* Random House, 1959, 2nd edition, 1961.

A New Look at Economic Time Series Analysis, Econometric Research Program, Princeton University, 1961; *The Command and Control Structure,* Econometric Research Program, Princeton University, 1962; *On the Accuracy of National Income and Growth Statistics,* Econometric Research Program, Princeton University, 1962; (with Clive W.J. Granger) *Spectral Analysis of New York Stock Market Prices,* Econometric Research Program, Princeton University, 1962; *Spieltheorie und Wirtschaftswissenschaft,* R. Oldenbourg, 1963; *The Element of Time in Value Theory: Perfect Foresight and Economic Equilibrium,* Econometric Research Program, Princeton University, 1963; *Limits to the Uses of Mathematics in Economics,* Econometric Research Program, Princeton University, 1963; *Pareto Optimum and Economic Organi-*

zation, Econometric Research Program, Princeton University, 1964; (with Klaus Knorr) *Science and Defense: Some Critical Thoughts on Military Research and Development*, Center of International Studies, Woodrow Wilson School of Public and International Affairs, Princeton University, 1965; *Nature's Attitude and Rational Behavior*, Econometric Research Program, Princeton University, 1966; (with Klaus-Peter Heiss) *General Report on the Economics of the Peaceful Uses of Underground Nuclear Explosions*, Mathematica, 1967; (with Knorr) *Political Conjecture in Military Planning*, Economic Research Program, Princeton University, 1968; (with Granger) *Predictability of Stock Market Prices*, Heath, 1970.

Contributor to technical journals. Co-editor, *Naval Research Logistics Quarterly*, 1954—, *Zeitschrift fuer Nationaloekonomie*, 1956—, *Information and Control*, 1957—, *Zeitschrift fuer Wahrscheinlichkeits Theorie*, 1962—, and *International Journal for Game Theory*, 1971—.

* * *

MORGENTHAU, Hans Joachim 1904-

PERSONAL: Born February 17, 1904, in Coburg, Germany; came to United States in 1937, naturalized in 1943; son of Ludwig and Frieda (Bachmann) Morgenthau; married Irma Thormann, June 3, 1935; children: Matthew, Susanna. *Education* University of Berlin, student; received degree (magna cum laude) from University of Munich, 1927; University of Frankfort, J.U.D. (summa cum laude), 1929. *Home:* 5825 South Dorchester Ave., Chicago, Ill. 60637. *Office:* University of Chicago, Chicago, Ill. 60637.

CAREER: Admitted to bar in Germany, 1927; University of Frankfort, Frankfort, Germany, assistant to law faculty, 1931; Labor Law Court, Frankfort, Germany, acting president, 1931-33; University of Geneva, Geneva, Switzerland, instructor in political science, 1932-35; Institute of International and Economic Studies, Madrid, Spain, professor, 1935-36; Brooklyn College (now Brooklyn College of the City University of New York), Brooklyn, N.Y., instructor in government, 1937-39; University of Kansas City, Kansas City, Mo., assistant professor of law, history, and political science, 1939-43; admitted to Missouri bar, 1943; University of Chicago, Chicago, Ill., visiting associate professor of political science, 1943-45, associate professor, 1945-49, professor of political science and modern history, 1949-63, Albert A. Michelson Distinguished Service Professor of Political Sciences and Modern History, 1963—, director of Center for Study of American Foreign and Military Policy, 1950—. City College of the City University of New York, New York, N.Y., Leonard Davis Distinguished Professor of Political Science, 1968—. Visiting professor at University of California, Berkeley, 1949, Harvard University, 1951, 1959, 1960-61, Northwestern University, 1954, Columbia University and Yale University, 1956-57; lecturer at Armed Forces Staff College and service war colleges. Institute for Advanced Study, Princeton, N.J., member, 1958-59; Washington Center for Foreign Policy Research, associate, 1958-60. U.S. Department of State, consultant, 1949, 1951, 1963—. Senior research fellow, Council on Foreign Relations, 1966.

MEMBER: American Academy of Arts and Sciences, American Philosophical Society, American Political Science Association, American Association of University Professors, Spanish Institute of Political Science (honorary member), P.E.N., Quadrangle Club (Chicago). *Awards, honors:* LL.D. degrees from Clark University, Ripon College, both 1962, Alma College, 1965, and University of Denver, 1971; Litt.D., Western Reserve University (now Case Western Reserve University), 1965.

WRITINGS: Die Internationale Rechtspflege ihr Wesen und ihre Grenzen, Noske, 1929; *La Notion du "politique" et la theorie des differends internationaux*, Librarie du Recueil Sirey, 1933; *La Realite des normes, en particulier des normes du droit international*, Librarie Felix Alcan, 1934; (editor) *Peace, Security and the United Nations*, University of Chicago Press, 1946; *Scientific Man versus Power Politics*, University of Chicago Press, 1946; *Politics Among Nations*, Knopf, 1948, 4th edition, 1967; (editor with Kenneth W. Thompson) *Principles and Problems of International Politics*, Knopf, 1950; *In Defense of the National Interest*, Knopf, 1951 (published in England as *American Foreign Policy: A Critical Examination*, Methuen, 1952); (editor) *Germany and the Future of Europe*, University of Chicago Press, 1951; *Dilemmas of Politics*, University of Chicago Press, 1958 (also see below); *The Purpose of American Politics*, Knopf, 1960, 2nd edition, with new introduction, Viking, 1964; *The Crisis of American Foreign Policy* (lecture series), [Storrs, Conn.], 1960; *The Tragedy of German-Jewish Liberalism*, Leo Baeck Institute, 1961; *Politics in the Twentieth Century*, three volumes, University of Chicago Press, 1962, abridged edition, 1971 (parts of this work were published as *Dilemmas of Politics*); *The Restoration of American Politics*, University of Chicago Press, 1962; *The Decline of Democratic Politics*, University of Chicago Press, 1962; *The Impasse of American Foreign Policy*, University of Chicago Press, 1962; *Vietnam and the United States*, Public Affairs Press, 1965; *The Crisis of Communism*, Center for the Study of U.S. Foreign Policy, University of Cincinnati, 1965; (editor and author of introduction) *The Crossroad Papers: A Look Into the American Future*, Norton, 1965; (author of foreword) Arnold S. Kaufman, *The Radical Liberal: New Man in American Politics*, Atherton, 1968; (with Thompson and Jerald C. Brauer) *U.S. Policy in the Far East: Ideology, Superstition and Religion*, Council on Religion and International Affairs, 1968; *A New Foreign Policy for the United States*, Praeger, 1969; *Truth and Power: Essays of a Decade, 1960-1970*, Praeger, 1970; (with Lloyd C. Gardner and Arthur Schlesinger, Jr.) *The Origins of the Cold War*, Ginn-Blaisdell, 1970; (with Lincoln Palmer Bloomfield and others) *The Power to Keep Peace: Today and in a World Without War*, Center for International Studies, Massachusetts Institute of Technology, 1971; *Science: Servant or Master*, New American Library, 1972. Contributor to political science, law, and philosophy journals, and to numerous other periodicals. Contributor to *Encyclopaedia Britannica*.

BIOGRAPHICAL/CRITICAL SOURCES: Christian Century, January 30, 1963; *New Republic*, March 23, 1963, May 6, 1969, October 31, 1970; *Saturday Review*, April 6, 1963, May 10, 1969, February 27, 1971; *Economist*, June 15, 1963; *Commentary*, June, 1963, May, 1969; *Times Literary Supplement*, April 23, 1964, June 19, 1969; *Canadian Forum*, May, 1964; *New York Times*, February 24, 1969; *Book World*, March 2, 1969; *New York Times Book Review*, August 3, 1969; *Choice*, November, 1969.

* * *

MORLAN, John E(dmund) 1930-

PERSONAL: Born October 12, 1930, in Abilene, Tex.; son of Grover Cleveland (a professor) and Alma (Adams) Morlan; married second wife, Gwen Tama Higashihara (a teacher), August 25, 1970; children: (first marriage) Charles, Tom. *Education:* Abilene Christian College, B.S., M.Ed., 1955; Texas Technological College, Ed.D., 1959. *Home:* 3837 Underwood, San Jose, Calif. 95117. *Office:* School of Education, San Jose State College, San Jose, Calif. 95114.

CAREER: Lubbock public schools, Lubbock, Tex., teacher and coach, 1955-58; Texas Technological College, Lubbock, instructor in educational psychology, 1958-59; San Jose State College, San Jose, Calif., 1959—, associate professor of education and director of Orient-Pacific Comparative Education Workshops. Consultant to school systems. *Military service:* U.S. Air Force, judo instructor, 1953-54. *Member:* National Education Association, National Science Teachers Association, National Aviation Education Council, American Association of University Professors, Association of California State College Professors, Phi Delta Kappa, Kappa Delta Pi.

WRITINGS: Preparation of Inexpensive Teaching Materials, Chandler Publishing, 1963, 2nd edition, 1972; (with Richard F. Thaw) *Experiences and Demonstrations in Elementary Physical Science,* W.C. Brown, 1964; (with others) *Teaching the Disadvantaged Child,* Oxford University Press, 1968; *Ayudas Audiovisuales,* Agency for International Development, 1968. Contributor to educational journals in science and audiovisual fields.

WORK IN PROGRESS: Classroom Learning Centers; Instructional Media; funded and sponsored research into teacher-prepared multi-sensory teaching materials.

AVOCATIONAL INTERESTS: Singing, fishing, photography, painting, archaeology.

* * *

MORPURGO, J(ack) E(ric) 1918-

PERSONAL: Born April 26, 1918, in Tottenham, Middlesex, England; son of Mark (a linguist) and Nancy (Cook) Morpurgo; married Catherine Noel Kippe Cammaerts (an actress); children: Pieter, Michael, Mark, Katharine. *Education:* Attended Christ's Hospital in England, and University of New Brunswick in Canada; College of William and Mary, B.A., 1938; Institute of Historical Research, London, England, graduate study. *Home:* Cliff Cottage, 51 Cliff Rd., Leeds 6, England. *Office:* School of English, University of Leeds, Leeds LS2 9JT, England.

CAREER: Penguin Books Ltd., London, England, editor, 1945-47; Nuffield Foundation, London, England, assistant director, 1950-54; National Book League, London, England, director-general, 1955-69; University of Leeds, Leeds, England, professor of American literature, 1970—. Visiting professor, Michigan State University, 1949; visiting professor of American Studies, University of Geneva, 1968-70. Has appeared on more than one thousand television and radio programs, including "Transatlantic Quiz" and his own series, "Notes From America" and "Transatlantic Mirror." UNESCO Seminar on Reading Materials, director in Rangoon, India, 1957, Madras, India, 1959. Governor, British and Foreign Schools Society; British National Bibliography executive; chairman of Pestalozzi Children's Village Trust; member, Commonwealth Studies Committee; Great Britain—U.S.S.R. Association executive. *Military service:* British Army, Royal Artillery, 1939-45; regimental and staff officer in India, Middle East, Greece, Italy, later served in War Office; mentioned in dispatches.

MEMBER: Society of Bookmen, Phi Beta Kappa, Arts Club, Reform Club, Pilgrims. *Awards, honors:* Honorary fellow and L.H.D., College of William and Mary, 1949; Litt.D., Ricker College, 1962; D.Lit., Elmira College, 1964.

WRITINGS: (Editor) *Charles Lamb and Elia,* Penguin, 1948; *American Excursion,* Cresset, 1949; (editor and author of introduction) Christopher Marlow, *Edward the Second,* Falcon Books, 1949; (editor and author of introduction and notes) *The Autobiography of Leigh Hunt,* Chanticleer, 1949; (editor) *Life Under the Stuarts,* British Book Centre, 1950; (editor and author of introduction) *The Humorous Verses of Lewis Carroll,* Grey Walls Press, 1950; (contributor) *The Impact of America on European Culture,* Beacon Press, 1951; (editor) Edward John Trelawny, *The Last Days of Shelley and Byron,* Philosophical Library, 1952; (editor) *John Keats: A Selection of His Poetry,* Penguin, 1953; (with Russell B. Nye) *A History of the United States,* two volumes, Penguin, 1955, 3rd edition, 1970; (with Kenneth Pelmear) *Rugby Football: An Anthology,* Allen & Unwin, 1958; *Paper Backs Across Frontiers,* Bowater Paper Corp., c.1960; (compiler with Compton Mackenzie) *Greece, Ancient and Modern: An Annotated Reading List,* National Book League (London), 1961; *The Road to Athens,* Eyre & Spottiswoode, 1963; (author of introduction) James Fennimore Cooper, *The Spy,* Oxford University Press, 1963; (author of introduction) William Cobbett, *A Year's Residence in the United States of America,* Centaur Press, 1964; (editor and author of introduction) Martin Huerlimann, *Venice,* Viking, 1964; *Book and Journal Services for Doctors and Nurses,* Nuffield Provincial Hospitals Trust, 1966; *Barnes Wallis: A Biography,* St. Martin's, 1972. Writer of radio and television programs. Contributor to periodicals in many countries. Formerly editor of *Penguin Parade* and general editor of "Pelican Histories."

WORK IN PROGRESS: The Amiable Spy, life of John Andre; *History of the College of William and Mary.*

SIDELIGHTS: A History of the United States has been translated into German, Portuguese, French, and Bengali. *Avocational interests:* History, especially American and British military history, and travel.

* * *

MORRIS, Harry (Caesar) 1924-

PERSONAL: Born August 9, 1924, in New York, N.Y.; son of Joseph Charles (a salesman) and Gertrude (Ascheim) Morris; married Nancy Anderson (a teacher), January 20, 1949; children: Leslie Scot (daughter), Christopher Bruce. *Education:* University of Miami, Coral Gables, Fla., B.A., 1949, M.A., 1950; University of Minnesota, Ph.D., 1957. *Home address:* Route 2, Box 104, Tallahassee, Fla. 32301. *Office:* Department of English, Florida State University, Tallahassee, Fla. 32306.

CAREER: Tulane University, New Orleans, La., assistant professor of English, 1956-61; Florida State University, Tallahassee, associate professor, 1961-67, professor of English, 1967—. *Military service:* U.S. Naval Air Corps, 1943-45. *Member:* Modern Language Association of America, Renaissance Society of America, South Atlantic Modern Language Association.

WRITINGS: (Editor with Irving Ribner) *Poetry: A Critical and Historical Introduction,* Scott, Foresman, 1962; *Richard Barnfield: Colin's Child,* Research Council, Florida State University, 1963; *The Sorrowful City* (verse), University of Florida Press, 1965; *Birth and Copulation and Death* (verse), Florida State University Press, 1969; *The Snake Hunter* (verse), University of Georgia Press, 1970. Poetry anthologized in *The Golden Year: The Poetry Society of America Anthology,* edited by Melville Cane and others, Fine Editions, 1960. Contributor of more than one hundred poems to *Prairie Schooner, Antioch Review, Sewanee Review, Kenyon Review, New Republic,* and other literary periodicals, and about twenty articles to professional and literary journals.

WORK IN PROGRESS: The Hamlet Poems, verse, completion expected in 1974; *Shakespeare and the Nature of Evil,* a critical study of several Shakespeare plays, 1975.

AVOCATIONAL INTERESTS: Study of snakes and other reptiliana.

MORRIS, Ira (Victor) 1903-

PERSONAL: Born November 11, 1903, in Chicago, Ill.; son of Ira Nelson and Constance Lily (Rothschild) Morris; married Edita de Toll (a writer), February, 1925; children: Ivan. *Education:* Attended Milton Academy; Harvard University, B.A., 1925; Heidelberg University, graduate work, 1925-26. *Home address:* Nesles, par Rozay-en-Brie, France. *Agent:* Ivan van Auw, Harold Ober Associates, 40 East 49th St., New York, N.Y. 10017.

CAREER: Employee of a newspaper publishing firm, New York, N.Y., 1926-28, book publishing firms in New York, N.Y., and London, England, 1928-34; free-lance writer, 1934—. *Member:* P.E.N.

WRITINGS: (Translator with Edward Fachs) Otto Peitsch, *The Devil's Net,* Cecil Palmer, 1929; *Covering Two Years,* Reynal, 1933; *Marching Orders,* Macmillan, 1938; *Liberty Street* (Literary Guild selection), Harper, 1945; *The Tree Within,* Doubleday, 1948; *The Chicago Story,* Doubleday, 1952; *The Bombay Meeting,* Doubleday, 1958; *The Paper Wall,* Chatto & Windus, 1960, Knopf, 1961; *The Road to Spain,* Dobson, 1965, Monthly Review Press, 1966; *La Borgia,* Chatto & Windus, 1967; *Such a Pretty Village,* Chatto & Windus, 1970. Represented in several anthologies, including O'Brien's *Best American Short Stories.* Contributor of short stories to popular magazines.

BIOGRAPHICAL/CRITICAL SOURCES: Spectator, September 22, 1967; *Times Literary Supplement,* September 14, 1969.†

*   *   *

MORRIS, Ivan Ira Esme 1925-

PERSONAL: Born November 29, 1925, in London, England; son of Ira Victor (a writer) and Edit (de Toll) Morris; married Nobuko Uenishi, 1956. *Education:* Harvard University, B.A., 1946; University of London, Ph.D., 1951, D.Lit., 1964. *Religion:* Church of England. *Home:* 173 Riverside Dr., New York, N.Y. 10024. *Agent:* Georges Borchhardt, 145 East 52nd St., New York, N.Y. 10022. *Office:* Columbia University, New York, N.Y. 10027.

CAREER: British Broadcasting Corp., London, England, news editor, 1951-52; British Foreign Office, London, England, senior research assistant, 1953-56; Columbia University, New York, N.Y., associate professor, 1960-66, professor of Japanese history, 1966—, chairman of department of East Asian languages and cultures, 1966-69. Member of executive committee, Amnesty International, London, England; general secretary, Amnesty International in United States. *Military service:* U.S. Navy; became lieutenant j.g. *Member:* Royal Asiatic Society, Royal Institute of International Affairs, Association of Teachers of Japanese (chairman, 1962—), Asiatic Society of Japan. *Awards, honors:* D.Lit., University of London, 1964; Duff Cooper Award, 1965, for *The World of the Shining Prince.*

WRITINGS: Nationalism and the Right Wing in Japan: A Study of Post-War Trends, Oxford University Press, 1960; *Japan,* Cambridge University Press, 1960; *The World of the Shining Prince: Court Life in Ancient Japan,* Knopf, 1964; *Selected List of Bungo and Other Forms Found in Japanese Literature Until c.1330,* privately printed, 1965; *Dictionary of Selected Forms in Classical Japanese Literature,* Columbia University Press, 1966, *Corrigenda, Addenda, Substituenda,* 1970; *The Riverside Puzzles,* Walker & Co., 1969 (published in England as *The Pillow Book Puzzles,* Bodley Head, 1969); *The Lonely Monk and Other Puzzles,* Bodley Head, 1970, Little, Brown, 1971; (with Herbert Paul Varley and wife,

Nobuko Morris) *Samurai,* Delacorte, 1971; *The Tale of Genji Scroll,* Kodansha International, 1971.

Translator: Ooka Shohei, *Fires of the Plain,* Knopf, 1957; Yukio Mishima, *The Temple of the Golden Pavilion,* Knopf, 1959; Jiro Osaragi, *The Journey,* Knopf, 1960; *As I Crossed a Bridge of Dreams: Recollections of a Woman in Eleventh Century Japan,* Dial, 1971.

Editor: (With Paul C. Blum) *Comprehensive Index: A Classified List Followed by Author and Subject Indexes, of Papers Appearing in the Transactions, 1872-1957,* Asiatic Society of Japan, 1958, Tuttle, 1959; (and translator with others, and author of introduction) *Modern Japanese Stories,* Tuttle, 1961; (and translator) Saikaku Ihara, *The Life of an Amorous Woman, and Other Writings,* New Directions, 1963; (and translator) Masao Maruyama, *Thought and Behaviour in Modern Japanese Politics,* Oxford University Press, 1963; (and author of introduction) *Japan 1931-1945: Militarism, Fascism, Japanism?,* Heath, 1963; (and translator) *The Pillow Book of Sei Shonagon,* two volumes, Columbia University Press, 1967; (and author of preface) *Madly Singing in the Mountains: An Appreciation and Anthology of Arthur Waley,* Walker & Co., 1970. Drama critic, *Vogue.*

WORK IN PROGRESS: Japan in the Seventeenth Century; Heroic Failures in Japanese History; a book about the life and work of Muryaki Shikabu.

AVOCATIONAL INTERESTS: Chess and playing the tenor recorder.

BIOGRAPHICAL/CRITICAL SOURCES: Observer Review, December 10, 1967; *Listener,* December 14, 1967, November 26, 1970; *Punch,* January 24, 1968; *Virginia Quarterly Review,* summer, 1968; *Hudson Review,* autumn, 1968; *Christian Science Monitor,* July 14, 1970; *New York Times,* June 11, 1971.

*   *   *

MORRIS, Leon (Lamb) 1914-

PERSONAL: Born March 15, 1914, in Lithgow, New South Wales, Australia; son of George Coleman and Ivy (Lamb) Morris; married Mildred Dann, January 4, 1941. *Education:* University of Sydney, B.S., 1934; Australian College of Theology, Licentiate in Theology (first class), 1938; University of London, B.D. (first class), 1943, Master of Theology, 1946; Cambridge University, Ph.D., 1952. *Home and office:* Ridley College, Parkville N.2, Victora, Australia.

CAREER: Clergyman, Church of England, Ridley College, Melbourne, Australia, vice-principal, 1945-60; Cambridge University, Cambridge, England, warden of Tyndale House, 1961-63; Ridley College, Melbourne, Australia, principal, 1964—. *Member:* Studiorum Novi Testamenti Societas.

WRITINGS: The Apostolic Preaching of the Cross, Eerdmans, 1955, 3rd edition, 1965; *The Wages of Sin: An Examination of the New Testament Teaching on Death,* Tyndale Press, 1955; *The Epistles to Paul to the Thessalonians: An Introduction and Commentary,* Tyndale Press, 1956, Eerdmans, 1957; *The Story of the Cross: A Devotional Study of St. Matthew, Chapters 26-28,* Eerdmans, 1957; *The First Epistle of Paul to the Corinthians: An Introduction and Commentary,* Eerdmans, 1958; *The Lord From Heaven: A Study of the New Testament Teaching on the Deity and Humanity of Jesus Christ,* Eerdmans, 1958; *The First and Second Epistles to the Thessalonians,* Eerdmans, 1959.

Spirit of the Living God, Inter-Varsity Press, 1960; *The Story of the Christ Child: A Devotional Study of the Nativity Stories in St. Luke and St. Matthew,* Marshall, Morgan & Scott, 1960, Eerdmans, 1961; *The Biblical*

Doctrine of Judgment, Eerdmans, 1960; The Dead Sea Scrolls and St. John's Gospel, The Bookroom, 1960; Christian Worship, Church Pastoral Aid Society, 1962; Good Enough?, Inter-Varsity Fellowship, 1962; Ministers of God, Inter-Varsity Press, 1964; The Abolition of Religion: A Study in Religionless Christianity, Inter-Varsity Press, 1964; The New Testament and the Jewish Lectionaries, Tyndale Press, 1964; The Cross in the New Testament, Eerdmans, 1965; Glory in the Cross: A Study in Atonement, Hodder & Stoughton, 1966; (with Arthur E. Cundall) Judges [and] Ruth (the former by Cundall, the latter by Morris), Inter-Varsity Press, 1968; The Revelation of St. John: An Introduction and Commentary, Eerdmans, 1969; Studies in the Fourth Gospel, Eerdmans, 1969; Bible Study Books: Timothy-James, Scripture Union, 1969.

This is the Testimony, Ridley College, 1970; Gospel of John, Eerdmans, 1971 (published in England as The Gospel According to John: The English Text with Introduction, Exposition, and Notes, Marshall, Morgan & Scott, 1972); Apocalyptic, Eerdmans 1972. General editor, "Great Doctrines of the Bible," Inter-Varsity Fellowship, 1960—. Contributor of articles to religious journals.

WORK IN PROGRESS: Commentary on Luke's Gospel.

* * *

MORRIS, Terry Lesser   1914-

PERSONAL: Born February 19, 1914, in New York, N.Y.; daughter of Samuel and Lena (Weissmann) Lesser; married Eugene I. Morris (an attorney), March 29, 1934; children: Richard. Education: Hunter College (now Hunter College of the City University of New York), B.A., 1933, M.A., 1937. Home and office: 200 Central Park S., New York, N.Y. 10019.

CAREER: New York high schools, New York, N.Y., teacher of English, 1937-43; Battle Creek Enquirer and News, Battle Creek, Mich., feature writer, 1943-44; Radio Station WKZO, Kalamazoo, Mich., script writer, 1944-45; New York University, New York, N.Y., lecturer on magazine article writing, 1958-59; free-lance writer. Member: Society of Magazine Writers (vice-president, 1961), Tom Dooley Foundation (New York chapter), Hadassah.

WRITINGS: No Hiding Place (novel), Knopf, 1945; (editor with Peter Farb and Mort Weisinger) Prose by Professionals: The Inside Story of the Magazine Article Writer's Craft, Doubleday, 1961; Doctor America: The Story of Tom Dooley, Hawthorn, 1963; Shalom, Golda (biography of Golda Meir), Hawthorn, 1971. Short story anthologized in Cross-Sections, 1947, Simon & Schuster, 1947. Author of more than fifty magazine features and short stories in national magazines.

* * *

MORRIS, William E(dgar)   1926-

PERSONAL: Born August 16, 1926, in Wilmington, Del.; son of Edgar A. and Virginia (Genn) Morris; married Florence Louise Medd, September 5, 1947; children: Jane Louise, Nancy Virginia. Education: University of Delaware, B.A., 1950, M.A., 1953; University of North Carolina at Chapel Hill, Ph.D., 1957. Religion: Presbyterian. Home: 5 Ransom Rd., Athens, Ohio. Office: University of South Florida, Tampa, Fla.

CAREER: University of North Carolina at Chapel Hill, part-time instructor, 1951-55; Duke University, Durham, N.C., instructor in English, 1955-57; Ohio University, Athens, assistant professor of English, 1957-64; University of South Florida, Tampa, assistant professor of English, 1964—. Military service: U.S. Navy, 1945-46. Member: Modern Language Association of America, Milton Society of America, American Association of University Pro-

fessors (local secretary, 1962-63), National Council of Teachers of English, Conference on College Composition and Communication, Dickens Society.

WRITINGS: (Editor with Robert F. McDonnell) Modern America Through Foreign Eyes, Heath, 1959; (editor with Richard Lettis and McConnell) Stephen Crane's The Red Badge of Courage: Text and Criticism, Harcourt, 1960; (editor with Lettis) A Wuthering Heights Handbook, Odyssey, 1961; (editor with Lettis) The Hungarian Revolt: October 23-November 4, 1956, Scribner, 1961; (editor with McDonnell) Form and Focus, Harcourt, 1961; (editor with Clifford A. Nault, Jr.) Portraits of an Artist: A Casebook on James Joyces A Portrait of the Artist as a Young Man, Odyssey, 1962; (editor with Lettis and McDonnell) Huck Finn and His Critics, Macmillan, 1962; (editor with Lettis) Assessing Great Expectations: Materials for Analysis, Chandler Publishing, 1963; (editor) Form and Focus 2: A Rhetorical Reader, Harcourt, 1964; (editor) The American Heritage Dictionary of the English Language, Houghton, 1969. Contributor of articles to professional journals. Assistant editor, Abstracts of English Studies, 1961-63.

WORK IN PROGRESS: The English Funeral Sermon of the 7th Century; Fiction/Drama/Poetry, for Scott, Foresman; The World of Ebenezer Scrooge; Assignments in Composition; A Fiction Handbook; work on Jeremy Taylor.

* * *

MORRIS, Wright   1910-

PERSONAL: Born January 6, 1910, in Central City, Neb.; son of William Henry and Ethel Grace (Osborn) Morris; married Mary E. Finfrock, December 21, 1934 (divorced, 1961); married Josephine Kantor, 1961. Education: Attended Pomona College, 1930-33. Home: 341 Laurel Way, Mill Valley, Calif. 94941. Office: California State University, 1600 Holloway Ave., San Francisco, Calif. 94132.

CAREER: Lecturer at Haverford College, Princeton University, Sarah Lawrence College, Swarthmore College, University of Utah, and other institutions; California State University, San Francisco (formerly San Francisco State College), professor, 1962—. Awards, honors: Guggenheim fellowship in photography, 1942, 1946, in literature, 1954; National Book Award, 1957, for The Field of Vision; National Institute Grant in Literature, 1960; honorary degrees from Westminster College and University of Nebraska, 1968; National Book Awards fiction judge, 1969. Member: National Institute of Arts and Letters.

WRITINGS: My Uncle Dudley (novel), Harcourt, 1942; The Man Who Was There (novel), Scribner, 1945; The Inhabitants (reminiscences; with photographs by Morris), Scribner, 1946; The Home Place (fiction; with photographs by Morris), Scribner, 1948; The World in the Attic (novel), Scribner, 1949; Man and Boy (novel), Knopf, 1951; The Works of Love (novel), Knopf, 1952 (also see below); The Deep Sleep (novel), Scribner, 1953; The Huge Season (novel), Viking, 1954; The Field of Vision (novel), Harcourt, 1956 (also see below); Love Among the Cannibals (novel), Harcourt, 1957; (contributor) The Living Novel: A Symposium, edited by Granville Hicks, Macmillan, 1957; The Territory Ahead (criticism), Harcourt, 1958, reissued as The Territory Ahead: Critical Interpretations in American Literature, Atheneum, 1963; Ceremony in Lone Tree (novel), Atheneum, 1960; (editor) The Mississippi River Reader, Doubleday-Anchor, 1962; What a Way to Go (novel), Atheneum, 1962; Cause for Wonder (novel), Atheneum, 1963; (author of afterword) Richard H. Dana, Two Years before the Mast, New American Library, 1964; (editor) Samuel L. Clemens, The Tragedy of Pudd'nhead Wilson, New

American Library, 1964; *One Day* (novel), Atheneum, 1965; *In Orbit* (novel), New American Library, 1967; *A Bill of Rites, a Bill of Wrongs, a Bill of Goods* (essays), New American Library, 1968; *God's Country and My People* (reminiscences; with photographs by Morris), Harper, 1968; *Green Grass, Blue Sky, White House*, Black Sparrow Press, 1970; *Wright Morris: A Reader* (novels, short stories, and criticism; includes *The Works of Love* and *The Field of Vision*), introduction by Granville Hicks, Harper, 1970; *Fire Sermon* (novel), Harper, 1971; *War Games*, Black Sparrow Press, 1972; *Love Affair: A Venetian Journal*, Harper, 1972. Contributor to *Harper's Bazaar, New York Times Magazine, Kenyon Review, Atlantic Monthly, Holiday, Vogue, Esquire, and* other publications.

SIDELIGHTS: "I began to invent the Midwest out of my experience," says Wright Morris of his early writing, "then I began to elaborate on it. The slowness of time, the quality of life, the Protestant background." He feels he found out somewhat late in life that he had to create his own synthesis of raw experience, using his imagination in order to transform it into something "more real than life" itself. Morris' early experimental volumes of photographs and text bear out his stated quest for the synthesis and re-creation of raw experience. They are "an attempt to walk back and forth between words and pictures" in order to recapture the American past, particularly that of the Midwestern Nebraska farm country. Chester Eisinger, in *Fiction of the Forties*, says of *The Inhabitants* that Morris, "like so many of his contemporaries, wishes to discover himself by discovering his country.... The quest for the real America and the real American in Morris' work involves the stripping away of nostalgia, of sentimentality, of the optimistic myth of success and progress that has maimed the American psyche." Morris uses both photographs and text to capture the texture and significance of objects we often see, but rarely notice: "Whether he is looking at the living room in the home place on a Sunday afternoon or at the beach in Southern California day after tomorrow, he can produce new meanings out of what would otherwise for most of us remain drab bits of evidence for this or that thesis about our troubled culture."

His work is most often compared with Sherwood Anderson's, a comparison that does not displease Morris: "There are things in Anderson which touch me deeply. Reading him, I sometimes think I was plagiarized before I was born." Eisinger writes: "Morris reminds one of Sherwood Anderson in his belief that the passional life of Americans has been muted or buried, that it must be opened and expressed if people are to avoid destruction. . . . Anderson watched America emerging from a rural, small-town civilization into full-fledged industrialism. He regarded the scene much as Morris does the degeneration of the frontier and the over-powering presence of the city. In both writers the American character shows itself as lonely and inarticulate, with sensitivity inhibited or disguised and channeled toward inanimate objects instead of human beings." Eisinger observes that Morris's disenchantment with the American spirit and character is similar to the critical attitude of many other writers in the forties. "Like them, he is engaged in a reappraisal of the American experience, because, as he says, 'Reappraisal is repossession'. What drives Morris is the need to repossess by understanding the past. . . ."

The "brutal severance of past and present," which Morris sees in American life, becomes one of his major themes. In *The Landscape of Nightmare*, Jonathan Baumbach suggests other important motifs: the prohibitive isolation of individuals; the unlived life; the continuous male-female power struggle in which the female, "more instinctively predatory, usually emerges victorious"; the narcosis of nostalgia; the "self-unmade man"; the whimsical nature of the universe. Morris' characters seem to be particularly vulnerable to circumstance; as one of them says in *In Orbit*, "Things just happen. No reason, no reason, just a happening." Morris's characters are usually dissatisfied, but rarely conscious of the cause. Their limited awareness (they "always seemed a little flat. Their souls . . . are like topographical replicas of those central plains they often inhabit"), coupled with the frequent intervention of a malevolently disinterested universe, prevents them from being redeemed, and they continue to lead their lives of quiet desperation.

"Though Morris never takes his eyes off the berserk elements in the American character, the style he uses to describe disorder, chance, and contingency is the most perfectly controlled style in the United States," notes David Madden. "Everything style has been trained over the centuries to do, Morris makes it do in his novels." His technical mastery of the novel is virtually undisputed, although some critics point out that he is at times too masterful, too controlled, too literary. Arthur Edelstein writes in the *National Observer* that Morris's "extraordinary control dilutes his sense of life, attracting attention more to his technical mastery than to the plight of his characters. But though some of the book does not go deeper than the merely virtuosic, such virtuosity is itself impressive." Baumbach suggests, however, that Morris' style may be appreciated for more than just its virtuosity: "[His] novels are written as if perceived by a slow-motion camera. In all but *The Huge Season, Love among the Cannibals*, and *What a Way to Go*, almost nothing happens, but what does is lingered over, seen in photographic close-up, illuminating the patterned grain of experience. The rhythms of his writing are deliberate, inhibited, drugged, at times hardly perceptible, evoking the slow pulse beat of the atrophied life he renders."

Wright Morris is probably "the least well-known and most widely appreciated" author in America today. He is often compared to other writers—Hemingway, Anderson, Saroyan, Nathanael West, D.H. Lawrence—but rarely used as a standard himself. Morris observes that his relative lack of recognition exists partly because the Midwestern novelist, unlike the Southern or urban novelist, cannot count on a factional audience. John Aldridge suggests other reasons that prevent Morris from being widely read: although his novels deal with American life, he does not march in the parade of fashionable issues such as sex, war, the bomb, race, domestic unrest, except on rare occasions; and, unlike some other writers, he "has never been the darling of any influential literary establishment. . . . He has therefore lacked a coterie of publicists who could advertise him in the right magazines." Another critic offers that "his are books that must be chewed to release their savor, and American readers are not so much chewers as biters and swallowers." Baumbach condenses his recognition of Morris's novels thus: "Although [his] universe is nihilistic, his theme impotence, his characters fools and madmen, he renders experience with great richness of detail and evocation, bringing it to life to expose its essential deadness. If his view of reality is limited, it is no more limited than Hemingway's; it is only less simple, less readily appealing. Though in recent years Morris has received a fair amount of critical approbation, he is still under valued. He may see life through a narrower window than the greatest writers, but he sees its incompleteness distinctly and he sees it whole."

The film rights to *Love among the Cannibals* were acquired by Gabriel Katza Co. in 1969.

BIOGRAPHICAL/CRITICAL SOURCES: New York Times Book Review, August 28, 1949, June 10, 1951, February 5, 1967, January 11, 1970, September 26, 1971;

New York Herald Tribune Book Review, June 3, 1951; *Saturday Review,* October 25, 1958, July 9, 1960, September 22, 1962, February 20, 1965, August 21, 1971, March 16, 1968; *Critique,* winter, 1961-62 (special issue on Morris), spring, 1962, Volume X, number 2; Chester E. Eisinger, *Fiction of the Forties,* University of Chicago Press, 1963; David Madden, *Wright Morris,* Twayne, 1964; Jonathan Baumbach, *The Landscape of Nightmare: Studies in the Contemporary American Novel,* New York University Press, 1965; *Reporter,* April 8, 1965; *Critic,* April, 1965; *Camera,* April, 1966; *Book Week,* February 19, 1967; *National Observer,* March 20, 1967; *Commonweal,* April 7, 1967; *New York Review of Books,* May 4, 1967; Thomas McCormack, *Afterwords: Novelists on Their Novels,* Harper, 1968; Leon Howard, *Wright Morris* (pamphlet), University of Minnesota Press, 1968; *Nation,* April 8, 1968, March 23, 1970; *Partisan Review,* winter, 1968; *New Yorker,* October 18, 1969; *New York Times,* January 5, 1970; *New Republic,* January 10, 1970, October 30, 1971; *Life,* August 27, 1971; *Time,* October 18, 1971.†

*　　*　　*

MORRISON, Lillian   1917-

PERSONAL: Born October 27, 1917, in Jersey City, N.J.; daughter of William and Rebecca (Nehamkin) Morrison. *Education:* Rutgers University, B.S., 1938; Columbia University, B.S. in L.S., 1942. *Office:* New York Public Library, 8 East 40th St., New York, N.Y. 10016.

CAREER: New York Public Library, New York, N.Y., young adult librarian, 1942-47, in charge of work with vocational high schools, 1947-52, assistant coordinator of young adult services, 1952-69, coordinator of young adult services, 1969—. Summer library school instructor, Rutgers University, 1961; lecturer on library school faculty, Columbia University, 1962, 1963. *Member:* American Library Association, Authors League, New York Library Association, Phi Beta Kappa.

WRITINGS: The Ghosts of Jersey City, and Other Poems, Crowell, 1967; (with Jean Boudin) *Miranda's Music* (poems), Crowell, 1968.

Compiler; all published by Crowell: *Yours Till Niagara Falls,* 1950; *Black Within and Red Without: A Book of Riddles,* 1953; *A Diller, a Dollar: Rhymes and Sayings for the Ten O'Clock Scholar,* 1955; *Touch Blue: Signs and Souls, Love Charms and Chants, Auguries and Old Beliefs, in Rhyme,* 1958; *Remember Me When This You See: A New Collection of Autograph Verses,* 1961; *Sprints and Distances: Sports in Poetry and the Poetry in Sport,* 1965; (with William Cole) *Poems from Ireland,* 1972; (with William J. Smith) *Poems from Italy,* 1972. General editor, "Poems of the World" series, Crowell. Contributor of poems to *Prairie Schooner, Sports Illustrated, Atlantic,* and *Poetry Northwest.*

WORK IN PROGRESS: New poems.

AVOCATIONAL INTERESTS: Folk rhymes, outdoor sports, jazz, the dance, and films.

BIOGRAPHICAL/CRITICAL SOURCES: New York Times, September 9, 1967; *Virginia Quarterly Review,* autumn, 1967; *New York Times Book Review,* September 29, 1968; Lee Bennett Hopkins, *Books Are By People,* Citation, 1969.

*　　*　　*

MORRISON, Velma Ford   1909-
　　(Hildegarde Ford)

PERSONAL: Born April 30, 1909, in Madrid, Iowa; daughter of William Bruce and Hildegarde Maria (Berg) Ford; married Hugh Pritchard Morrison (president of Pioneer Hi-Bred Corn Co. of Illinois), November 8, 1930; children: Hugh Pritchard, Jr., Mary (Mrs. James Anderson), Sarah (Mrs. Douglas Criner), John. *Education:* Studied at Drake University. *Home and office:* Route 5, Princeton, Ill. 61356.

CAREER: Elementary teacher in Iowa schools, 1928-33, organizing "opportunity rooms" for teaching physically and mentally handicapped children, 1929-30; Morrison Book Co. (publishers specializing in children's books), Princeton, Ill., president and manager, 1953—. American Cancer Society, Bureau County chairman, 1955-58, member of Illinois board of directors, 1959—, district lay director, 1959—; member of county board of directors, Camp Fire Girls, 1950-60. *Member:* Woman's National Book Association, Phi Mu, Woman's Club (Princeton, Ill.; president, 1940-45).

WRITINGS: "My Book" series, five volumes, Morrison Book Co., 1953-54; *Bow Wow,* Morrison Book Co., 1955; *Meow Meow,* Morrison Book Co., 1955; *My Go to Bed Book,* Morrison Book Co., 1955, revised edition, 1956; *Baby's Animal Book,* Morrison Book Co., 1957; *Pat Little Puppy,* Morrison Book Co., 1958; *Herbie,* Morrison Book Co., 1961, revised edition, Harvey House, 1969; *Twinkle, Little Star,* Morrison Book Co., 1961; *Baby's Book,* Morrison Book Co., 1962; *Scrambola,* Harvey House, 1970.

WORK IN PROGRESS: Biographical novel about a noted scientist.

*　　*　　*

MORRISSEY, Leonard E., Jr.   1925-

PERSONAL: Born July 22, 1925, in Salem, Mass.; son of Leonard E. and Margaret (McCarthy) Morrissey; married Winifred C. White, June 22, 1946; children: James, Thomas, Peter, William, Michael. *Education:* Dartmouth College, student, 1943-44, M.B.A., 1948; University of Rochester, B.S. in Mechanical Engineering, 1946. *Politics:* Republican. *Religion:* Roman Catholic. *Home:* 36 Occom Ridge, Hanover, N.H. 03755. *Office:* Amos Tuck School of Business Administration, Dartmouth College, Hanover, N.H. 03755.

CAREER: Dartmouth College, Hanover, N.H., instructor in economics, 1948-51, assistant professor, Amos Tuck School of Business Administration, 1951-57, associate professor, 1957-63, professor of accounting, 1963—. Part-time private practice as certified public accountant, Hanover, N.H., 1954—. Town of Hanover, member of finance committee, 1954-57, auditor, 1960-65; auditor, Hanover School District, 1956-58. *Military service:* U.S. Navy, 1943-46; became lieutenant j.g. *Member:* American Accounting Association, American Association of University Professors (chapter secretary-treasurer, 1963-64). *Awards, honors:* Elijah Watt Sells Award, American Institute of Certified Public Accountants for highest grades in United States on uniform certified public accountant examinations, 1954.

WRITINGS: The Variable Annuity: Will It Yield More Dollars for Retirement, Amos Tuck School of Business Administration, Dartmouth College, 1956; *The Many Sides of Depreciation,* Amos Tuck School of Business Administration, Dartmouth College, 1960; *Contemporary Accounting Problems: Text and Cases,* Prentice-Hall, 1963. Contributor to professional journals.

WORK IN PROGRESS: Current accounting problems.

*　　*　　*

MORSE, H(enry) Clifton IV   1924-
　　(Clifton Fourth)

PERSONAL: Born September 3, 1924, in Chicago, Ill.; son of H. Clifton III and Augusta (Metz) Morse. *Educa-*

tion: Attended University of Alabama; Brown University, M.B.A. *Home:* 336 Wellington, Chicago, Ill. 60657. *Office:* Morse/Marketing, Inc., 203 North Wabash Ave., Chicago, Ill. 60601.

CAREER: Ford Motor Co., Aircraft Engine Division, assistant to general manager, five years; Morse/Marketing, Inc. (publishing and creative packaging firm), president, ten years; Hughes Aircraft Co., staff planner, director of systems and procedures in electronics production. *Military service:* U.S. Navy, 1942-45; became warrant officer, Supply Corps; awarded Presidential citation; U.S. Naval Reserve, supply officer, aviation, 1945—. *Member:* Operations Research Society of America, National Office Management Society, Association of Management Consultants. *Awards, honors:* International Industrial Management award for cost reduction reporting; awarded television Emmy, 1950, for "Worldly Williams" series.

WRITINGS: Operations Research for Non-Technical Management, FoMoCo, 1957; (with David M. Cox) *Numerically Controlled Machine Tools: Implications for Management,* Cox & Cox, 1958; (with E.E. Wyatt) *Cost Reduction Guide for Manufacturing Management: A Planned Approach to a Continuing Company-Wide Cost Reduction Program,* Wyatt & Morse, 1961; (with Cox) *Numerically Controlled Machine Tools: The Breakthrough of Autofacturing,* American Data Processing, 1965.

WORK IN PROGRESS: An organization-function guide for industry; *Morsels,* a humor book.

*   *   *

MORSE, Samuel French   1916-

PERSONAL: Born June 4, 1916, in Salem, Mass.; son of Carl French Abner (a banker) and Alice (Pickering) Morse; married Jane Crowell (a teacher), November 23, 1950; children: Samuel Crowell. *Education:* Dartmouth College, A.B. (cum laude), 1936; Harvard University, A.M., 1938; Boston University, Ph.D., 1952. *Home:* Box 3, Hancock Point, Me. 04640. *Office:* Northeastern University, Huntington Ave., Boston, Mass., 02115.

CAREER: Harvard University, Cambridge, Mass., 1938-42, began as teaching assistant, became instructor in English; University of Maine, Orono, instructor in English, 1946-49; Trinity College, Hartford, Conn., 1951-58, began as instructor, became associate professor of English; Mount Holyoke College, South Hadley, Mass., associate professor of English, 1958-62; Northeastern University, Boston, Mass., 1962-68, began as associate professor, became professor and director of graduate study in English. Cummington School of the Arts, director, 1946-47. *Military service:* U.S. Army Air Forces, Historical Division, 1943-46; became sergeant. *Member:* New England College English Association (president, 1963-64), New England Poetry Club (vice-president, 1963-68), Phi Beta Kappa, Grolier Club. *Awards, honors:* Emily Clark Balch Prize for poems published in *Virginia Quarterly Review;* American Philosophical Society grant, 1957; Golden Rose Trophy of New England Poetry Club, 1957; Arthur Davison Ficke Memorial Award of Poetry Society of America, 1959, 1961, 1964, 1966; American Council of Learned Societies fellowship, 1960-61.

WRITINGS: Time of Year: A First Book of Poems, introduction by Wallace Stevens, Cummington, 1944; *A Checklist of the Published Writings of Wallace Stevens, 1898-1954,* Yale University Library, 1954, 2nd edition, with Joseph Reddell and Jackson Bryer, published as *Wallace Stevens Checklist and Bibliography of Stevens Criticism,* A. Swallow, 1963; *The Scattered Causes* (poems), A. Swallow, 1955; (editor and author of introduction) Wallace Stevens, *Opus Posthumous* (plays, poems, prose), Knopf, 1957; (editor and author of intro-

duction) Wallace Stevens, *Poems, A Selection,* Vintage, 1959; *The Changes* (poems), A. Swallow, 1964; *All in a Suitcase* (juvenile), Little, Brown, 1966; *Sea Sums* (juvenile), Little, Brown, 1970; *Wallace Stevens: Poetry as Life,* (critical and biographical study), Pegasus, 1970. Contributor to periodicals.

SIDELIGHTS: Characterized as a New England poet, Morse employs a formal attitude in describing the natural environment of that region. Critics are mixed in their reaction to his approach. Milton Hindus believes that "Morse's faults as a poet stem not from the mask he has used to cover his sensitivity . . . but from the weakness of the original poetic impulse which has made it easy for him occasionally to fall into other men's ways of seeing things and speaking of them. . . ." Mark McCloskey, on the other hand, approves of Morse's means of expression. "[He] often shows a fine skill in the use of structural imagery. . . . By the use of 'forms' like the sonnet and villanelle, Mr. Morse uncovers for himself and orders for us his emotive insights, and provides the rhythmical emphasis necessary to convey them. . . . The themes of Mr. Morse's poems are intensely human, stressing how the humor, now the nostalgia, at times the anguish, at others the longing in human experience. The phenomenon of childhood, the subtleties of friendship, the human relevance of geography, often concern him. The imagined journeys of the spirit in search of ontological meaning are his abiding and most significant themes, in terms of which he achieves and communicates dazzling insights." Ruth Lechlitner adds: "Mr. Morse owes the essential flavor of his realism to Thoreau, his studies of men and creatures are framed by the particularities and necessities of place and season. His observations are so exact, so acutely compressed, that they demand the reader's close attention; there is no horizontal landscape prettiness, but a kind of blunt, vertical integrity that strikes down to the essential ore."

AVOCATIONAL INTERESTS: Gardening, conservation, natural history.

BIOGRAPHICAL/CRITICAL SOURCES: New York Times, April 23, 1944, April 15, 1956, July 22, 1970; *Poetry,* September, 1944, November, 1965; *Saturday Review,* May 12, 1956; *Commonweal,* March 19, 1965, November 11, 1966; *New York Times Book Review,* April 18, 1965, October 30, 1966, May 24, 1970; *Horn Book,* October, 1966; *Book Week,* October 9, 1966, December 4, 1966; *Library Journal,* October 15, 1966, May 15, 1970; *Christian Science Monitor,* November 3, 1966; *America,* November 5, 1966; *Atlantic,* December, 1966; *Southern Review,* winter, 1970; *Journal of American Literature,* winter, 1972.

*   *   *

MORTON, A(rthur) L(eslie)   1903-

PERSONAL: Born July 4, 1903, in Hengrave, Bury Saint Edmunds, Suffolk, England; son of Arthur Spence (a farmer) and Mary Hannah (Lampray) Morton; married Vivien Joyce Jackson; children: Nicholas Dion. *Education:* Peterhouse College, Cambridge, B.A. (honors), 1924. *Politics:* Communist. *Home:* Old Chapel, Clare, Suffolk, England.

CAREER: Teacher, bookseller, and journalist. *Military service:* British Army, Royal Artillery, 1941-45; became lance bombardier. *Member:* P.E.N.

WRITINGS: A People's History of England, Random House, 1938, revised edition, Seven Seas, 1965, International Publishers, 1968; *Language of Men* (essays), Cobbett Press, 1945; *The Story of the English Revolution,* Communist Party of Great Britain, 1948; *The English Utopia,* Lawrence & Wishart, 1952; *Get Out!,* East Anglia District Committee, Communist Party, 1953; (with

George Tate) *The British Labour Movement, 1770-1920: A Political History*, Lawrence & Wishart, 1956, International Publishers, 1957; *The Everlasting Gospel: A Study in the Sources of William Blake*, Lawrence & Wishart, 1958; *The Matter of Britain: The Arthurian Cycle and the Development of Feudal Society*, Deutscher Verlag Der Wissenschaften, 1960; *The Life and Ideas of Robert Owen*, Lawrence & Wishart, 1962, Monthly Review Press, 1963, revised edition, International Publishers, 1969; *Socialism in Britain*, Lawrence & Wishart, 1963; *Shakespeare's Idea of History* (pamphlet), Communist Party of Great Britain, 1964; *The Arts and the People*, Lawrence & Wishart, 1965; *The Matter of Britain: Essays in a Living Culture*, Lawrence & Wishart, 1966; *The World of the Ranters: Religious Radicalism in the English Revolution*, Lawrence & Wishart, 1970; (editor) *Political Writings of William Morris*, Lawrence & Wishart, 1971. Contributor to *Criterion, Daily Worker, Left Review, La Pensee, Marxism Today*, and other journals.

* * *

MOSES, W(illiam) R(obert)   1911-

PERSONAL: Born December 24, 1911, in Alexandria, Minn.; son of William John Barr (a newspaperman) and Annette (Peacock) Moses; married Elizabeth B. Petway, April 3, 1935; children: Edwin P. *Education:* Attended University of Tennessee, 1928-29; Vanderbilt University, B.A., 1932, M.A., 1933, Ph.D., 1939. *Politics:* Independent. *Home:* 314 Denison Ave., Manhattan, Kan. 66502. *Office:* Department of English, Kansas State University, Manhattan, Kan. 66502.

CAREER: Hendrix College, Conway, Ark., instructor in English, 1935-36; Washington State University, Pullman, instructor in English, 1936-39; University of Illinois, Urbana, instructor in English, 1939-42; U.S. Department of the Navy, Washington, D.C., civilian employee, 1946-50; Kansas State University, Manhattan, 1950—, began as assistant professor, now professor of English. Visiting professor of English, University of Saskatchewan, 1966-67. *Military service:* U.S. Naval Reserve, active duty, 1942-46; became lieutenant commander. *Member:* American Association of University Professors. *Awards, honors:* Fellowship from Fund for the Advancement of Education, 1952-53.

WRITINGS: (With others) *Five Young American Poets*, New Directions, 1940; *Identities* (poetry) Wesleyan University Press, 1965; *The Metaphysical Conceit in the Poems of John Donne* (based on Ph.D. thesis), Folcroft, 1970. Contributor of poems and essays (especially on William Faulkner) to numerous magazines. Co-editor, *Accent*, 1940-42; editor, *Kansas Magazine*, 1955-67.

WORK IN PROGRESS: Additional poems and essays.

SIDELIGHTS: Of his collection of poetry Moses writes: "In broadest terms, my book celebrates sacred objects. Naturally the things honored are in some sense imperfect or disharmonious—comic or tragic or simply ironic; nevertheless, they exist, and they are wonderful."

BIOGRAPHICAL/CRITICAL   SOURCES: Books Abroad, spring, 1967.

* * *

MOSLEY, Jean Bell   1913-

PERSONAL: Born September 21, 1913, in Elvins, Mo.; daughter of Wilson Leroy (a mining contractor) and Myrtle (Casey) Bell; married Edward Price Mosley (a printing-pressman), April 11, 1936; children: Stephen Price. *Education:* Southeast Missouri State College, B.S. in Education, 1937. *Religion:* Methodist. *Home and office:* 703 East Rodney, Cape Girardeau, Mo. 63701.

CAREER: Elementary school teacher, Graniteville, Mo., 1934-36; secretary in insurance agency, Cape Girardeau, Mo., 1938-44; free-lance writer, 1947—. *Member:* Missouri State Writers Guild (president, 1955-56), Missouri Federation of Women's Clubs (president of Quest Club, 1958-60), Cape Girardeau Writers Guild (president, 1951-52), PEO (chapter chaplain, 1958-59), Phi Theta Kappa, Kappa Delta Phi, Sigma Tau Delta (honorary), Beta Sigma Phi (honorary). *Awards, honors:* Missouri State Writers Guild award for *The Mockingbird Piano*.

WRITINGS: The Mockingbird Piano, Westminster, 1953; *Wide Meadows*, Caxton, 1960; *Famous Women of the New Testament*, Doubleday, 1960; *Animals of the Bible*, Doubleday, 1962; *Queen Esther*, Doubleday, 1963; *The Crosses at Zarin*, Broadman, 1967. Contributor to *Family Edition Bible* and anthologies. Author of eight booklets for Doubleday's "Know-Your-Bible Program." Co-author of column now appearing in seven southeast Missouri weeklies. Contributor of over three hundred stories and articles to *Saturday Evening Post, Ladies' Home Journal, Woman's Day, Farm Journal, Reader's Digest, Progressive Farmer, Writer*, and other magazines and journals in Europe, Australia, and Canada.

WORK IN PROGRESS: Goin' A Ways with Someone.

BIOGRAPHICAL/CRITICAL   SOURCES: St. Louis Globe-Democrat, May 6, 1964; *St. Louis Post Dispatch*, August 24, 1954.

* * *

MOSSE, Werner E(ugen Emil)   1918-

PERSONAL: Born November 5, 1918, in Berlin, Germany; son of Rudolf S. and Dora (Loewe) Mosse. *Education:* Attended St. Paul's School, London, England; Corpus Christi College, Cambridge, B.A., 1939, M.A., 1942, Ph.D., 1950. *Home:* Dawn Cottage, Ashwellthorpe, Norwich, Norfolk, England. *Office:* School of European Studies, University of East Anglia, Norwich, England.

CAREER: Corpus Christi College, Cambridge University, Cambridge, England, research fellow, 1946-48; School of Slavonic and East European Studies, University of London, London, England, lecturer in modern Russian history, 1948-52; University of Glasgow, Glasgow, Scotland, senior lecturer in East European history, 1952-64; School of European Studies, University of East Anglia, Norwich, England, professor of European history, 1964—. *Military service:* British Army, 1941-46; became captain.

WRITINGS: The European Power and the German Question 1848-1871, Cambridge University Press, 1958; *Alexander II and the Modernization of Russia*, Macmillan (New York), 1958, new revised edition, Collier, 1962; *The Rise and Fall of the Crimean System, 1855-1871: The Story of a Peace Settlement*, Macmillan (London), 1963, St. Martin's, 1964; (editor and contributor) *Entscheidungsjahr zur Judenfrage in der Endphase der Weimarer Republik*, J.C.B. Mohr, 1965, 2nd edition, revised and enlarged, 1966; (editor) *Deutsches Judentum in Krieg und Revolution 1916-1923*, J.C.B. Mohr, 1971.

WORK IN PROGRESS: Prosperity and War: Europe, 1849-1873.

* * *

MOSSIKER, Frances (Sanger)   1906-

PERSONAL: Born April 9, 1906, in Dallas, Tex.; daughter of Elihu (a merchant) and Evelyn (Beekman) Sanger; married Jacob Mossiker (in investment field), October 15, 1934. *Education:* Attended Smith College; Barnard College, B.A., 1927; graduate study at the Sorbonne, University of Paris.

CAREER: Book reviewer, Radio Station WFAA, Dallas, Tex., 1933; conductor of "Woman's World" program, Radio Station KGKO, Fort Worth, Tex., 1934; conductor of radio series on decorative arts for Neiman-Marcus Co. over WFAA, Dallas, Tex., 1933-34. Chairman of radio committee, Dallas Red Cross, World War II. Member: Phi Beta Kappa. Awards, honors: Carr P. Collins nonfiction award, Texas Institute of Letters for The Queen's Necklace, 1961, and for Napoleon and Josephine, 1964.

WRITINGS: The Queen's Necklace, Simon & Schuster, 1961; Napoleon and Josephine: The Biography of a Marriage (Literary Guild selection), Simon & Schuster, 1964; The Affair of the Poisons: Louis XIV, Madame du Montespan, and One of the World's Great Unsolved Mysteries, Knopf, 1969; More Than a Queen: The Life of Josephine Bonaparte, Knopf, 1971. Writer of radio scripts.

WORK IN PROGRESS: Research on another French historical project.

SIDELIGHTS: In a review of The Affair of the Poisons, the New Yorker reviewer states: "Mrs. Mossiker deals with one of those episodes when history really approaches melodrama, and she writes in both genres very well. In one impressive respect she goes far beyond melodrama: she has a great understanding of the character of seventeenth-century individuals—people very different from modern men and women, but, thanks to the author, comprehensible and, though scarcely likeable, engrossing."

BIOGRAPHICAL/CRITICAL SOURCES: New York Times Book Review, October 26, 1969; New Yorker, January 31, 1970; Observer Review, June 7, 1970; New York Review of Books, July 23, 1970; Books and Bookmen, August, 1970.

*   *   *

MOTZ, Lloyd   1909-

PERSONAL: Born in Susquehanna, Pa.; married; children: Robin Owen, Julie. Education: College of City of New York (now City College of City University of New York), B.S. (magna cum laude), 1930; University of Gottingen, Naumberg Fellow, 1929; Columbia University, Ph.D., 1936. Home: 815 West 181st St., New York, N.Y. 10033. Office: Columbia University, Box 57 Pupin, New York, N.Y. 10027.

CAREER: College of City of New York, New York, N.Y., instructor in physics, 1931-40; Columbia University, New York, N.Y., professor of astronomy, 1940—; Polytechnic Institute of Brooklyn, Brooklyn, N.Y., adjunct professor of physics, 1960—. Member: American Physical Society (fellow), American Astronomical Society, American Association for the Advancement of Science, American Federation of Scientists, Royal Astronomical Society (fellow), New York Academy of Sciences (president, 1970), Phi Beta Kappa (chapter secretary). Awards, honors: First prize for essay, Gravity Research Foundation, 1960.

WRITINGS: What Is Astronomy All About, Alumni Press, 1953; History of Time, Gerrault-Perroux, 1957; This Is Astronomy, Archer House, 1958; This Is Outer Space, Archer House, 1960; (editor) Astronomy, A to Z (based on Astronomie by Karl Stumpff), Grosset, 1964; (with Anneta Duveen) Essentials of Astronomy, Wadsworth, 1966; (editor with Henry Abraham Boorse) The World of the Atom, two volumes, Basic Books, 1966; (editor) Enrico Fermi, Molecules, Crystals and Quantum Statistics, Benjamin, 1966; Astrophysics and Stellar Structure, Ginn, 1970. Author of introductions to Dover reprints of books of famous astronomers and physicists.

WORK IN PROGRESS: A book on astronomy, for Harcourt; A College Text in Physics, for Ginn; Concepts of Physical Science.

AVOCATIONAL INTERESTS: Music, tennis, chess, folk dancing.

*   *   *

MOULD, Daphne D(esiree) C(harlotte) Pochin   1920-

PERSONAL: Born November 15, 1920, in Salisbury, Wiltshire, England; daughter of Walter (a teacher) and Marguerite (Steer) Mould. Education: University of Edinburgh, B.Sc. (first class honors in geology), 1943, Ph.D., 1946. Politics: Left of center. Religion: Orthodox. Home and office: Aherla House, Aherla, County Cork, Ireland.

CAREER: Full-time author and free-lance journalist, residing in Scotland, 1939-51, Ireland, 1951—. Broadcaster, Radio Eireann. Member: Munster Aero Club.

WRITINGS: The Roads from the Isles: A Study of the North-West Highland Tracks, Oliver & Boyd, 1950; (with Allan C. Macdougall) Let's See Barra and Tiree, William S. Thomson, 1951; Let's See Inverness and Loch Ness William S. Thomson, 1951; Scotland of the Saints, British Book Centre, 1952; West-Over-Sea: An Account of Life in the Outer Hebrides Set Against the Legendary and Historical Background, Oliver & Boyd, 1953; Ireland of the Saints, Batsford, 1953, British Book Centre, 1954; The Rock of Truth (autobiography), Sheed (New York), 1953; The Mountains of Ireland, Batsford, 1955, McBride, 1956; Irish Pilgrimage, M.H. Gill, 1955, Devin, 1957; The Celtic Saints, Macmillan, 1956 (published in England as The Celtic Saints, Our Heritage, Clonmore & Reynolds, 1956; The Resurrection of Aylesford: An Outline Sketch of the Story of the White Friars and of Aylesford Priory, St. Albert's Press, 1956; The Irish Dominicans: The Priar Preachers in the History of Catholic Ireland, Dominican Publications, 1957; Peter's Boat: A Convert's Experience of Catholic Living, Clonmore & Reynolds, 1959; The Lord Is Risen: The Liturgy of Paschal Time, Catholic Truth Society of Ireland, 1959; The Angels of God, Clonmore & Reynolds, 1961, published in America as The Angels of God: Their Rightful Place in the World, Devin, 1963; The Life of Saint Peter Thomas, Scapular Press, 1961; The Second Vatican Council, Catholic Truth Society of Ireland, 1963; The Irish Saints: Short Biographies of the Principal Irish Saints from the Time of St. Patrick to That of St. Laurence O'Toole, Clonmore & Reynolds, 1964; St. Brigid, Clonmore & Reynolds, 1964. Author of small booklets and pamphlets. Contributor of articles to U.S. Catholic, Blackwood's Magazine, Countryman, Irish Times, and other periodicals.

WORK IN PROGRESS: Currently engaged in flying and photographing Ireland from the air, for a series of articles on this theme, and possibly later, a full-length book.

AVOCATIONAL INTERESTS: Flying, motoring, mountaineering, riding, and foreign travel.

*   *   *

MOULTON, William G(amwell)   1914-

PERSONAL: Born February 5, 1914, in Providence, R.I.; son of David Potter and Lillian May (Gamwell) Moulton; married Jenni Karding, July 12, 1938; children: Elizabeth Potter, Susan Karding. Education: Princeton University, A.B., 1935; University of Berlin, graduate study, 1935-36; Yale University, Ph.D., 1941. Home: 37 Heather Lane, Princeton, N.J. 08540. Office: 230 East Pyne Buildings, Princeton University, Princeton, N.J. 08540.

CAREER: Yale University, New Haven, Conn., instructor in German, 1937-41, assistant professor of German,

1941-47; Cornell University, Ithaca, N.Y., associate professor, 1947-49, professor of linguistics, 1949-60; Princeton University, Princeton, N.J., professor of linguistics, 1960—. *Military service:* U.S. Army, 1945-46; became captain. *Member:* Linguistic Society, Maatschappij der Nederlandse Letterkunde, Modern Language Association of America, American Association of Teachers of German, Linguistic Circle of New York. *Awards, honors:* Fulbright research grant to Netherlands, 1953-54; American Council of Learned Societies fellow, 1958-59; Guggenheim fellowship, 1964-65.

WRITINGS: Swiss German Dialect and Romance Patois, Linguistic Society of America, 1941; (with wife, Jenni Karding Moulton) *Spoken German, Basic Course,* two volumes, Linguistic Society of America, 1944; (author of introduction) Frances Adkins Hall, *Sounds and Letters,* Linguistica, 1956; *The Sounds of English and German,* University of Chicago Press, 1962; *A Linguistic Guide to Language Learning,* Modern Language Association, 1966, 2nd edition, 1970. Contributor of articles to professional journals.

BIOGRAPHICAL/CRITICAL SOURCES: PMLA, December, 1962.

* * *

MOW, Anna Beahm 1893-

PERSONAL: Born July 31, 1893, in Daleville, Va.; daughter of I.N.H. and Mary (Butcher) Beahm; married Baxter Merrill Mow, 1921; children: Lois (Mrs. Ernest Snavely) Joseph, Merrill. *Education:* Manchester College, B.A., 1918; Bethany Theological Seminary, B.D., 1921, M.R.E., 1941, M.Th. *Home:* 1318 Varnell Ave. N.E., Roanoke, Va. 24012.

CAREER: Church of the Brethren; General Missions Board, Elgin, Ill., missionary in India, 1923-40; Bethany Theological Seminary, Oak Brook, Ill., associate professor of Christian education, 1940-58, retired, 1958; now lecturer, leader of retreats and institutes. *Member:* Friends of the Middle East. *Awards, honors:* D.D., Bethany Theological Seminary, 1959; Alumni Award, Manchester College, 1963.

WRITINGS: Say "Yes" to Life!, Zondervan, 1961; *Your Child from Birth to Rebirth: How to Educate a Child to Be Ready for Life with God,* Zondervan, 1963; *Going Steady with God: Your Life with God Every Day of the Year,* Zondervan, 1965; *Your Teen-ager and You,* Zondervan, 1967; *So Who's Afraid of Birthdays: For Those Over Sixty and Those Who Expect to Be,* Lippincott, 1969; *The Secret of Married Love: A Christian Approach,* Lippincott, 1970. Contributor to church papers.

BIOGRAPHICAL/CRITICAL SOURCES: Inez Long, *Faces Among the Faithful,* Brethren Press, 1962.

* * *

MUDD, Stuart 1893-

PERSONAL: Born September 23, 1893, in St. Louis, Mo.; son of Harvey Gilmer (a surgeon) and Margaret De la Plaux (Clark) Mudd; married Emily Borie Hartshorne (a professor of family study in psychiatry at University of Pennsylvania), September 12, 1922; children: Emily Borie (Mrs. James Mitchell), Stuart Harvey, Margaret Clark, John Hodgen. *Education:* Princeton University, B.S., 1916; Washington University, St. Louis, Mo., M.A., 1918; Harvard University, M.D., 1920. *Religion:* Episcopal. *Home:* 734 Millbrook Lane, Haverford, Pa. 19041. *Office:* U.S. Veterans Administration Hospital, Philadelphia, Pa. 19104.

CAREER: Harvard University, Cambridge, Mass., research fellow, 1920-23; Rockefeller Institute, New York, N.Y., associate, 1923-25; University of Pennsylvania, Phil-

adelphia, associate in pathology at Henry Phipps Institute, 1925-31, assistant professor of experimental pathology, 1925-31, associate professor of bacteriology, 1931-34, professor of bacteriology, 1934-51, professor of microbiology, 1951-59, professor emeritus, 1959—; U.S. Veterans Administration Hospital, Philadelphia, Pa., chief of microbiologic research program, 1959—.

MEMBER: International Association of Microbiological Societies (vice-president, 1953-58; president, 1958-62), World Academy of Art and Science (charter member; vice-president, 1962—), American Public Health Association (fellow), American Association for Advancement of Science (fellow), American Human Serum Association (president, 1940-41), Physiological Society, American Association of Pathologists and Bacteriologists, American Association of Immunologists, Society for Experimental Pathology, Society for Experimental Biology and Medicine, Society of American Bacteriologists (president, 1945), Harvey Society, Histochemical Society (president, 1952), Royal Society of Medicine (affiliate), Societe d'Encouragement au Progres France (commander), New York Academy of Science (fellow), Biochemical Foundation of Franklin Institute (member of scientific council), College of Physicians of Philadelphia (fellow), Consejo Superior de Investigaciones Scientificas Madrid, Phi Beta Kappa, Sigma Xi, Alpha Omega Alpha, Princeton Club (Philadelphia), Cosmos Club (Washington, D.C.), Merion Cricket Club. *Awards, honors:* Guggenheim Honor Cup Award, 1944; John Fleming Medal, American Institute of Geonomy and Natural Resources, 1967.

WRITINGS: (With E.J. Czarnetzky, Horace Pettit, and David Lackman) *Labile Bacterial Antigens and Methods of Preparing and Preserving Them,* U.S. Government Printing Office, 1937; (with Czarnetzky, Earl W. Flosdorf, and C.H. Shaw) *A Low Temperature Ball Mill for the Liberation of Labile Cellular Products,* U.S. Government Printing Office, 1937; (editor with William Thalhimer) *Blood Substitutes and Blood Transfusion,* C.C Thomas, 1942; (with Miriam Eleanor Herdegen) *Persistence of Antigens at the Site of Inoculation of Vaccine Emulsified in Oil,* [Philadelphia], 1947; (editor) *The Population Crisis and the Use of World Resources,* Indiana University Press, 1964, abridged and revised edition (with Larry K.Y. Ng) published as *The Population Crisis: Implications and Plans for Action, 1965;* (editor) *Conflict Resolution and World Education,* W. Junk (The Hague), 1966, Indiana University Press, 1967; (editor) *Infectious Agents and Host Reactions,* Saunders, 1970. Contributor of about two hundred articles to scientific journals. Former associate editor, *Journal of Bacteriology, Journal of Immunology, American Journal of Public Health,* and *Journal of Histochemistry and Cytochemistry;* chairman of editorial committee, World Academy of Art and Science.†

* * *

MUELLER, Barbara R(uth) 1925-

PERSONAL: Surname pronounced Miller; born September 10, 1925, in Milwaukee, Wis.; daughter of Edward Philip (a hotel manager) and Winifred (Moffott) Mueller. *Education:* University of Wisconsin, student, 1943-46. *Religion:* Lutheran. *Home and office:* 225 South Fischer Ave., Jefferson, Wis. 53549.

CAREER: Barbara R. Mueller Hobby Feature Service, Jefferson, Wis., conductor, 1960—, doing research, writing, editing, layout, exhibitions, lectures in philately, numismatics, paper and political Americana, photographica, collectibles. *Member:* American Philatelic Society, American Numismatic Society, American Numismatic Association, American Philatelic Congress, National Recreation and Park Association, International Platform Association, Royal Philatelic Society (London), Collectors Club (New

York). *Awards, honors:* McCoy Award, American Philatelic Congress, 1955, and Luff Award, American Philatelic Society, 1956, for distinguished philatelic research.

WRITINGS: Common Sense Philately, Van Nostrand, 1956; *United States Postage Stamps: How to Collect, Understand and Enjoy Them,* Van Nostrand, 1958; *Postage Stamps and Christianity,* Concordia, 1964. Contributor to *Milwaukee Journal, This Day, Collier's Encyclopedia,* and to philatelic, numismatic, and antique magazines. Editor, *Essay-Proof Journal* and *Paper Money.*

WORK IN PROGRESS: A book on the history and lore of world paper money.

* * *

MUIR, Barbara K (enrick Gowing) 1908-
(Barbara Kaye)

PERSONAL: Born August 4, 1908, in Saxmundham, Suffolk, England; daughter of Sidney David (a writer) and Muriel Y. (Kenrick) Gowing; married Percy H. Muir (an antiquarian bookseller), February 6, 1936; children: Helen Lisl, David Charles. *Education:* Educated in private schools. *Politics:* Right-wing Liberal. *Home:* Scriveners, Blakeney, Holt, Norfolk, England. *Agent:* John Johnson, 10 Suffield House, 79 Davies St., London W.1, England.

CAREER: Amalgamated Press, London, England, member of editorial staff, 1927-30; representative of cosmetic manufacturers, 1935-37; author. Councillor, Dunmow Rural District Council, 1961-70. *Member:* P.E.N. (English Centre), National Book League.

WRITINGS—Under pseudonym Barbara Kaye, except as indicated: *Call It Kindness,* Hurst & Blackett, 1942; *Home Fires Burning,* Hurst & Blackett, 1943; *Folly's Fabric,* Hurst & Blackett, 1944; *No Leisure to Repent,* Hurst & Blackett, 1945; *Pleasant Burden,* Hurst & Blackett, 1947; *The Gentleys,* Hurst & Blackett, 1948; *Black Market Green,* Hurst & Blackett, 1950; *In Whose Custody?,* Hurst & Blackett, 1951; *Festival at Froke,* Gryphon, 1951; *Champion's Mead,* Hurst & Blackett, 1951; *Rebellion on the Green,* Hurst & Blackett, 1953; *Neighbourly Relations,* Hurst & Blackett, 1954; *London-Lychford Return,* Hurst & Blackett, 1955; *Minus Two,* Pall Mall, 1961; (under own name) *Live and Learn: The Story of Denman College,* National Federation on Women's Institutes, 1970. Contributor to *Housewife, News Chronicle, Home and Country,* and British Broadcasting Corp. "Women's Hour." Women's page editor, *Essex Weekly News,* 1960-63.

* * *

MUIR, Percival H (orace) 1894-
(Percy H. Muir)

PERSONAL: Born December 17, 1894, in London, England; son of Charles Henry and Annie (Hancock) Muir; married Barbara Kenrick Gowing (an author, writing under pseudonym Barbara Kaye), 1935; children: Helen Muir Tulberg, David. *Education:* Attended public schools in England. *Politics:* "Left-wing conservative." *Home:* Scriveners, Blakeney, Holt, Norfolk, England.

CAREER: After varied career as businessman, lecturer, journalist, and actor, set up own antiquarian bookshop in London, 1923; Dulau & Co., Ltd. (antiquarian bookshop and publisher), London, England, member of board, 1925-29, director, 1927-29; Elkin Mathews Ltd. (antiquarian booksellers) Blakeney, Norfolk, England, director, 1930—, managing director, 1939—. *Military service:* London Scottish Regiment, 1914-1916. *Member:* International League of Antiquarian Booksellers (president, 1948-50; honorary president, 1950—), Antiquarian Book-

sellers Association (president, 1945-47), National Book League (honorary life member); bibliographical societies of London, Cambridge, Oxford; fellow of Royal Horticultural Society; Bath Club, Garrick Club.

WRITINGS: Points, 1874-1930: Being Extracts from a Bibliographer's Note-Book, Constable, 1931; *Points: Second Series, 1866-1934,* Bowker, 1934; (contributor) John W. Carter, editor, *New Paths in Book Collecting,* Constable, 1934; *Book-Collecting as a Hobby: In a Series of Letters to Everyman,* Gramol, 1944, 2nd edition, 1945, Knopf, 1947; *Book-Collecting: More Letters to Everyman,* Cassell, 1949; (joint author, and editor) *Talks on Book-Collecting* (delivered under the authority of Antiquarian Booksellers' Association at National Book League, winter, 1948-49), Cassell, 1952; *English Children's quarian Booksellers' Association at National Book Club of California* (San Francisco), 1955; *Minding My Own Business,* Chatto, 1956; *Private Presses* (paper read at opening of exhibition, "Books from British Private Presses," May 17 1965), [Amsterdam], 1966; (editor) A.F. Johnson, *Selected Essays on Books and Printing,* Abner Schram, 1970; *Victorian Illustrated Books,* Praeger, 1971.

Compiler: (With B. Van Thal) Bibliographies of the first editions of books by Aldous Huxley and by T.F. Powys, published by Dulau & Co., 1927, Folcroft, 1970; bibliographies of the first editions of books by Arthur Annesley Ronald Firbank (1886-1926), Maurice Henry Hewlett (1861-1923), and George Eliot (1819-1880), all first published as special issues of *Bookman's Journal,* 1927; *Children's Books of Yesterday* (catalog of an exhibition held in London during May, 1946), foreword by John Masefield, Cambridge University Press, 1946, new edition, revised and enlarged, Singing Tree Press, 1970; (and editor, with John W. Carter) *Printing and the Mind of Man,* (catalog of Eleventh Printing Machinery and Allied Trades Exhibition in London, summer, 1963), Holt, 1967.

Translator: Paul Adolf Hirsch, *Some Early Mozart Editions,* reprinted from *Music Review* [London], 1940; (and editor) *The Good Housekeeping Book of Fairy Stories,* Gramol, 1946; Charles Perrault, *The Sleeping Beauty in the Wood,* Limited Editions Club (New York), 1949; Madame Leprince de Beaumont, *Beauty and the Beast,* Knopf, 1968.

Also editor of Washington Irving's *Alhambra Tales,* Peter Lunn (London), 1946. Contributor of articles to *Colophon, Library,* and various bibliographical journals, including *Bookman's Journal.* Author of column, "Notes on Sales," in *Times Literary Supplement,* 1940-45, and of series, "Further Reminiscences," in *Book Collector,* 1956—. Founder and member of editorial board of *Book Collector.*

BIOGRAPHICAL/CRITICAL SOURCES: Times Literary Supplement, June 22, 1967; *Christian Century,* August 2, 1967.

* * *

MULFORD, David Campbell 1937-

PERSONAL: Born June 27, 1937, in Rockford, Ill.; son of Robert L. and Theo (Mollenhauer) Mulford; married second wife, Barbara Baker, May 26, 1970; children: (first marriage) R. Ian, Edward M. *Education:* Lawrence College, B.A., 1959; Oxford University, graduate study, 1959-60; University of Cape Town, graduate study, 1960; Boston University, M.A., 1962; St. Antony's College, Oxford, D.Phil., 1966.

AWARDS, HONORS: Rotary International fellow to Cape Town, 1960; Woodrow Wilson fellow, 1961-62; grant from Department of Technical Co-operation, London, England, for research in Northern Rhodesia, 1962; Ford Foundation foreign area fellowship, 1963-65; White

House fellow, 1966; Council on Foreign Relations fellowship, 1970.

WRITINGS: The Northern Rhodesia General Election, 1962, Oxford University Press, 1964; *Zambia: The Politics of Independence, 1957-1964,* Oxford University Press, 1967. Contributor to *Africa Report.*

BIOGRAPHICAL/CRITICAL SOURCES: Spectator, January 19, 1968.

* * *

MULISCH, Harry   1927-

PERSONAL: Born July 29, 1927, in Haarlem, Holland; son of Kurt and Alice (Schwarz) Mulisch. *Home:* 103 Leidsekade, Amsterdam, Netherlands. *Agent:* De Bezige Bij, Van Miereveldstract 1, Amsterdam, Holland.

CAREER: Writer all of adult life. Participant in writer's congresses in Finland, Scotland, Romania, Germany. *Awards, honors:* Reina Prinsen Geerligs Prize, 1951, for *Archibald Strohalm;* Bijenkorf Literatuur Prize, 1957, for *Het zwarte Licht;* Anne Frank Prize, 1957; Visser Neerlandia Prize, 1960, for *Tanchelijn;* Athos Prize, 1961.

WRITINGS—All published by De Bezige Bij, except as indicated: *Archibald Strohalm* (novel), 1952; *Chantage op het leven* (two stories), 1953; *Di Diamant* (novel), 1954; *Het Mirakel: Episodes van troost en liederlijkheid uit het leven van der heer Tiennoppen,* De Arbeiderspers, 1956; *Het Zwarte licht* (novel), 1956; *De Versierde mens* (stories), 1957; *Manifesten* (aphorisms), Heinisz, 1958; *Het Stenen bruidsbed* (novel), 1959, translation by Adrienne Dixon published as *The Stone Bridal Bed,* Abelard, 1962; *Tanchelijn, kroniek van een ketter* (play), 1960; *De Knop* (one-act play), 1960; *Voer voor psychologen* (autobiographical), 1961; *Wenken voor de bescherming van uiw gezin en uzelf, tijdens de jongste dag,* 1961; *De Zaak 40/61: Een Reportage* (about Eichmann Trial), 1962; *The Discovery of Moscou* (semi-fiction), 1964; *De Sprong der paarden en de zoete zee,* Meulenhoff, 1964; *Nol Gregoor in gesprek met Harry Mulisch,* 1965; *Bericht aan de rattenkoning* (about Provo), 1966; *Wenken voor de jongste dag* (political), 1967; *Het Woord bij de daad: Getuigenis van de revolutie op Cuba,* 1968; *Israel is zelf een mens: Onzukelijke notities uit de zaak 40/61,* Bakker, 1969; *Paralipomena orphica* (autobiographical), 1970; *De Verteller* (novel), 1970. Founder editor, *Randstad* (literary quarterly).

SIDELIGHTS: Three of Mulisch's books have appeared in foreign translations; *Het Stenen bruidsbed,* which was published in five countries, has gone into nineteen printings, *Het Zwarte licht* into fifteen printings, and all the other books into from three to ten printings. He has traveled in India, Japan, and the U.S.

* * *

MULKERNE, Donald James Dennis   1921-

PERSONAL: Born October 14, 1921, in New Bedford, Mass.; son of James Henry (with U.S. Post Office Department) and Margaret V. (a city auditor) Mulkerne; married Doris D. Driscoll (a registered nurse), June 9, 1946; children: Susan Neville, Donald J.D., Jr., Michelle, Mary Colleen, Brian Patrick, Joanne, Donna Marie. *Education:* Boston University, B.S.E., 1946, M.Ed., 1948; Columbia University, Ed.D., 1950. *Home:* 79 Jordan Blvd., Delmar, N.Y. 12054.

CAREER: Rockland High School, Rockland, Mass., teacher, 1946-48; State University of New York at Albany, 1950—, now professor of business education, chairman of department of administrative services, 1963—. Visiting professor at Columbia University, 1950, College of St. Rose, 1957, Russell Sage College, 1957-63, Catholic University of America, 1958, 1962, Boston University,

1966. Former member, Institute for Certifying Secretaries of National Secretaries Association International. Consultant to Civil Service Employees Association, Young Men's Christian Association, Chamber of Commerce, National Secretaries Association, National Association of Educational Secretaries, Association for the Blind, and Grain League Federation. *Military service:* U.S. Army, Infantry, World War II, served in France and Germany; became first lieutenant; received Bronze Star, Purple Heart, Combat Infantryman's Badge, European theater ribbon with three battle stars.

MEMBER: American Management Association, Association for Systems Management, National Business Education Association, Administrative Management Society (treasurer and member of board of directors, 1963-64; president of Albany chapter, 1966-67), National Secretaries Association International (honorary), Eastern Business Teachers Association, Phi Delta Kappa, Kappa Delta Pi, Pi Omega Pi, Delta Pi Epsilon, Delta Sigma Pi. *Awards, honors:* Bellringer award, Administrative Management Society, Albany chapter, 1966.

WRITINGS: (Contributor) John L. Rowe, editor, *Curriculum Patterns in Business Education,* New York University Bookstore, 1956; (with Sidney E. Ekblaw) *Economic and Social Geography,* McGraw, 1958; (contributor) Estelle L. Popham and others, editors, *Evaluation of Pupils in Business Education,* New York University Bookstore, 1960; (with Gilbert Kahn) *The Term Paper: Step by Step,* Doubleday, 1964; (with Kahn) *How Do You Spell It?,* Doubleday, 1965; (with Harry Huffman and Allien Russon) *Office Procedures and Administration,* McGraw, 1965; (with others) *Selected Readings in Business and Office Occupations,* National Business Education Association, 1967; (with Margaret Andrews) *Civil Service Texts for Typists,* McGraw, 1969; *Typing the Term Paper,* McGraw, 1972. Contributor of articles on business education to *Journal of Business Education, Balance Sheet, Secretary, Business Teacher,* and other professional journals.

WORK IN PROGRESS: Office Management, Systems and Data Processing.

AVOCATIONAL INTERESTS: Reading biography and U.S. military history, visiting U.S. historical locations, especially those associated with early Indian life, pioneer settlement, and the Civil War (frequent speaker on the topic of the assassination of Abraham Lincoln).

* * *

MULLEN, Thomas J (ames)   1934-

PERSONAL: Born August 2, 1934, in Montmorenci, Ind.; son of Albert Edwin (a farmer) and Berniece (Weidlich) Mullen; married Nancy Kortepeter, September 1, 1957; children: Sarah Lee, Martha Ann, Bret Duane, Ruth Elizabeth. *Education:* Earlham College, A.B., 1956; Yale University, B.D., 1959. *Politics:* Independent. *Religion:* Quaker. *Home:* 233 College Ave., Richmond, Ind. 47374.

CAREER: First Congregational Church, Madison, Conn., assistant pastor, 1956-59; Friends Meeting, New Castle, Ind., pastor, 1959-66; Earlham College, Richmond, Ind., dean of students, 1967-70, lecturer in religion and associate dean of School of Religion, 1970—. Member of board on vocations and ministry, Friends United Meeting; member of human relations committee, American Friends Service Committee; member, Friends Committee on National Legislation. Member, National Board of Yokefellow Associates; member of board of trustees, Earlham College, 1970—.

WRITINGS: The Renewal of the Ministry, Abingdon, 1963; *The Ghetto of Indifference,* Abingdon, 1966; *The*

Dialogue Gap, Abingdon, 1969; *Birthdays, Holidays and Other Disasters,* Abingdon, 1971. Contributor of articles to *Religion in Life, Pulpit, Quaker Life, Together,* and *Friends Journal.*

BIOGRAPHICAL/CRITICAL SOURCES: *Encounter,* spring, 1969.

*   *   *

MULVIHILL, Edward Robert   1917-

PERSONAL: Born May 20, 1917, in Boulder, Colo.; son of Edward Robert (a postmaster) and Vida E. (Abair) Mulvihill; married Eleanor Pittenger, December 20, 1939; children: Michael N., W. Dennis, Patricia E. *Education:* University of Colorado, B.A., 1938; University of Wisconsin, M.A., 1939, Ph.D., 1942. *Politics:* Democrat. *Religion:* Roman Catholic. *Home:* 5619L Mendota Dr., Madison, Wis. 53704.

CAREER: Federal Bureau of Investigation, Washington, D.C., special agent, 1942-46; University of Wisconsin, Madison, assistant professor, 1946-48, associate professor, 1948-58, professor of Spanish, 1958—, chairman of department of Spanish and Portuguese, 1952—, associate dean, College of Letters and Science. *Member:* Modern Language Association of America, Association of Teachers of Spanish and Portuguese, Wisconsin Association of Modern Foreign Language Teachers (president, 1954, 1958), Phi Beta Kappa. *Awards, honors:* Ford Foundation faculty fellowship, 1953-54; Order of Vasco Nunez de Balboa (Panama); Order of Isabel la Catolica (Spain).

WRITINGS—Editor with Roberto G. Sanchez: Carmen Laforet, *Nada,* Oxford University Press, 1958; Jose M. Sanchez-Silva, *Marcelino, pan y vino,* Oxford University Press, 1960; Julian Marias, *Modos de vivir,* Oxford University Press, 1964; Benito Perez Galdas, *Miau,* Oxford University Press, 1970. Contributor to journals.

WORK IN PROGRESS: Writing on the contemporary Spanish novel.

SIDELIGHTS: Mulvihill lived in Panama, 1945-46, in Spain, 1953-54.

*   *   *

MUNROE, (Macfarlane) Hugh
  (Jason, Ben Wyvis)

PERSONAL: Born in Glasgow, Scotland; son of George Michele (a riveter) and Margaret (Robinson) Munro; married Elizabeth Baird, September 16, 1939; children: Sally, Margaret, George. *Education:* Educated in Scottish schools. *Politics:* "Suspicious of 'em all." *Religion:* Christian. *Home:* Ealasaid, Eglinton St., Saltcoats, Ayrshire, Scotland. *Agent:* Curtis Brown Ltd., 60 East 56th St., New York, N.Y. 10022.

CAREER: Left school at fourteen and worked as newsboy, farm hand, in shipyards and factories before becoming a free-lance writer. *Member:* National Union of Journalists, Society of Authors, P.E.N., Crime Writers Association, Writers Guild of Great Britain.

WRITINGS: *Who Told Clutha,* Washburn, 1958; *Clutha Plays a Hunch,* Washburn, 1959; *A Clue for Clutha,* Macdonald & Co., 1960; *The Clydesiders,* Macdonald & Co., 1961; *Tribal Town,* Macdonald & Co., 1964; *Clutha and the Lady,* R. Hale, 1973. Short story anthologized in *A Pride of Felons,* edited by The Gordons and others, Macmillan, 1963. Contributor of articles, short stories, and adventure serials for boys to magazines, and of short stories to radio programs. Author of plays for amateur drama festivals. Editor, *Scottish Bagpipe Magazine.*

WORK IN PROGRESS: Another "Clutha" novel, for R. Hale; a full-length play; television scripts; short stories.

SIDELIGHTS: Munro writes: "I have been beating a typewriter ever since my youth, turning out articles and short stories—and also adventure serials for boys' weeklies—but only within the last five years have I attempted novel writing.... In a rather misspent youth my chief interests were chasing girls, playing soccer, playing the Highland bag-pipes and dancing, including Highland dancing. Nowadays fiction writing leaves little time for anything other than an occasional game of chess.... If ever I write a novel about modern Scottish people good enough to be acceptable by ordinary people throughout the world I'll be content."

To new writers he offers this advice: "Although only fools despise the tools of Education, if your heart sings and the words come unbidden into your brain you will write tho' all the Devils of Syntax dare you. Believe in yourself and the urge within you. And then—with one eye on contemporary styles and markets—sweat and grind it out according to your own vision."

BIOGRAPHICAL/CRITICAL SOURCES: *Daily Mail* (London), November 24, 1961; *Sunday Times* (London), November 26, 1961; *John O'London's,* December 21, 1961; *Punch,* December 27, 1961; *Books and Bookmen,* January, 1962.

*   *   *

MUNSON, Mary Lou (Easley)   1935-
  (Lou Munson)

PERSONAL: Born September 30, 1935, in Copley, Ohio; daughter of Henry Austin (a tool and die maker) and Mary Rose (Khemptzow) Easley; married Glenn W. Munson (managing editor of Pyramid Publishing Co.), May 18, 1957 (divorced January, 1966); married Ernest S. Schwartz, September 1, 1967; children: (first marriage) David Frank. *Education:* Kent State University, student, 1953-55. *Politics:* Democrat. *Home:* 340 East 80th St., New York, N.Y. 10021. *Agent:* Jay Garon-Brooke Associates, 415 Central Park W., 17D, New York, N.Y. 10025. *Office:* 331 Madison Ave., New York, N.Y. 10017.

CAREER: Elementary school teacher in Baltimore, Md., 1957-59; *Packaging Magazine,* New York, N.Y., eastern editor, 1965-66; P.R. Rieber, New York, N.Y., public relations writer, 1966—. Secretary-coordinator, Randall's Island Jazz Festival, New York, N.Y., one year. *Member:* Public Relations Society of America, Advertising Women of New York.

WRITINGS—All adapted under name Lou Munson, except as indicated; all published for U.S. Information Agency, except as indicated: *West to the Pacific,* 1963; *Henry Ford,* 1964; *Carbon-14,* 1964; *Science Dates the Past,* 1964; (under name Mary Lou Munson) *Practical Etiquette for Modern Man: Your Questions Answered,* Taplinger, 1964; *Lee De Forest, Electronics Pioneer,* 1965; *Teenagers Want to Know,* 1966.

WORK IN PROGRESS: A revision of *Meet the Vowel Family,* a phonics reader.

*   *   *

MUNTHE, Frances   1915-
  (Frances Cowen; pseudonym, Frances Minto-Cowen)

PERSONAL: Born December 27, 1915, in Oxford, England; daughter of Joseph and Helen (Ainscough) Cowen; married Heinrich Gesle Munthe, November, 1936 (deceased); children: Mary. *Education:* Attended schools in England, 1920-33. *Politics:* Conservative. *Religion:* Roman Catholic. *Home:* 6c Lake Rd., Wimbledon, London S.W.19, England. *Agent:* J.F. Gibson's Literary Agency, 17 Southampton Pl., London WC1A 2AJ, England.

Office: Royal Literary Fund, 11 Ludgate Hill, London E.C.4, England.

CAREER: Writer, whose first book was published when she was seventeen. Former employee of T. A. Blackwell, Publisher, Oxford, England; member of staff, Air Raid Precautions, Dartmouth, England, 1940-44; Royal Literary Fund, London, England, assistant secretary, 1955-66. *Member:* P.E.N., Society of Authors, Crime Writers Association.

WRITINGS—All under name Frances Cowen: *The Little Heiress,* Gresham, 1961; *The Balcony,* Gresham, 1962; *A Step in the Dark,* Gresham, 1962; *The Desperate Holiday,* Gresham, 1962; *The Elusive Quest,* Gresham, 1965; *The Bitter Reason,* Gresham, 1966; *Scented Danger,* Gresham, 1966; *The One Between,* R. Hale, 1967; *The Gentle Obsession,* R. Hale, 1968; *The Daylight Fear,* R. Hale, 1969; *The Fractured Silence,* R. Hale, 1969; *The Shadow of Polperro,* R. Hale, 1969; *Edge of Terror,* R. Hale, 1970; *The Hands of Carvello,* R. Hale, 1970; *The Nightmare Ends,* R. Hale, 1970; *Lake of Darkness,* R. Hale, 1971; *The Unforgiving Moment,* R. Hale, 1971.

Juveniles: *In the Clutch of the Green Hand,* Thomas Nelson, 1929; *The Wings That Failed,* Collins, 1931, abridged edition published as *The Plot That Failed,* 1933; *The Milhurst Mystery,* Blackie & Son, 1933; *The Conspiracy of Silence,* Sheldon Press, 1935; *The Perilous Adventure,* Queensway Press, 1936; *Children's Book of Pantomimes,* Cassell, 1936; *Laddies' Way,* Lutterworth, 1939, new edition, 1955; *The Girl Who Knew Too Much,* Lutterworth, 1940; *Mystery Tower,* Lutterworth, 1945; *Honor Bound,* Lutterworth, 1946; *Castle in Wales,* Schofield & Sims, 1947; *The Secret of Arrivol,* Schofield & Sims, 1947; *Mystery at the Walled House,* Lutterworth, 1951; *The Little Countess,* Thames Publishing Co., 1954; *The Riddle of the Rocks,* Lutterworth, 1956; *Clover Cottage,* Blackie & Son, 1958; *The Secret of Grange Farm,* Children's Press, 1961; *The Secret of the Loch,* Children's Press, 1963. Contributor to anthologies, including O'Brien's *Best Short Stories.* Contributor to *Good Housekeeping, Woman's Weekly, Oxford Times,* and to other periodicals and newspapers. Former staff member, *Little Folks.*

WORK IN PROGRESS: Research among documents of Royal Literary Fund, which dates from 1793; bondwoman novel of the Twenties.

SIDELIGHTS: Mrs. Munthe writes to *CA:* "[I am] definately [a] Francophile. [My] travel in France [is] especially in the Savoy when I can. My present aim is to write a suspense novel as good as your American authors Quintin, Ransome, etc. [I] have done a great deal of hack work since I was widowed, but was encouraged by Sir High Walpole when I was young as most promising. [My] interests [are] chiefly my daughter . . . who . . . now writes herself far better than I. Hobbies: music, good television, politics, and my small cat family."

BIOGRAPHICAL/CRITICAL SOURCES: Good Housekeeping, July, 1960.†

* * *

MURRAY, W(illiam) H(utchison) 1913-

PERSONAL: Born March 18, 1913, in Liverpool, England; son of William Hutchison (H.M. inspector of mines) and Helen Robertson (Dunnachie) Murray; married Anne Burnet Clark, December 1, 1960. *Education:* Studied at Glasgow Academy. *Home:* Lockwood, Loch Goil, Argyll, Scotland.

CAREER: Mountaineer. Leader of Scottish expedition to Garhwal, 1950; deputy leader of Everest expedition, 1951; leader of British expedition to Northwest Nepal, 1953. Adviser on mountainous properties, National Trust for Scotland; member, Countryside Commission for Scotland; chairman, Scottish Countryside Activities Council. *Military service:* British Army, Highland Light Infantry, 1940-46; prisoner in Germany, 1942-45; became captain. *Member:* P.E.N., Society of Authors, Scottish Mountaineering Club (president, 1962), Alpine Club. *Awards, honors:* Mungo Park Medal, Royal Scottish Geographical Society for exploratory work in the Indian and Nepali Himalayas; Order of the British Empire.

WRITINGS: Mountaineering in Scotland, Dent, 1947, Macmillan, 1948, new edition, Dent, 1962; (editor) *Rock Climbs in Glencoe and Ardgour,* Scottish Mountaineering Club, 1949, 2nd edition published as *Climbers' Guide to Glencoe and Ardgour,* 1959; *Undiscovered Scotland: Climbs on Rock, Snow and Ice,* Macmillan, 1951; *The Scottish Himalayan Expedition,* Dent, 1951, Macmillan, 1952; *The Story of Everest,* Dent, 1953; *Highlands in Colour,* Heinman, 1954; (contributor) James R. Ullman, *The Age of Mountaineering,* Collins, 1956; *Appointment in Tibet* (novel), Putnam, 1959 (published in England as *Five Frontiers,* Dent, 1959); *The Spurs of Troodos,* Dent, 1960; (with others) *Scotland's Splendour,* Collins, 1960; *Maelstrom,* Secker & Warburg, 1962; *Highland Landscape: A Survey,* Aberdeen University Press, 1962; (with J.E.B. Wright) *The Craft of Climbing,* Kaye & Ward, 1964; *The Hebrides,* A.S. Barnes, 1966; *Dark Rose the Phoenix,* McKay, 1965; *The Companion Guide to the West Highlands of Scotland: The Seaboard from Kintyre to Cape Wrath,* Collins, 1968, 2nd edition published as *The West Highlands of Scotland: The Seaboard from Kintyre to Cape Wrath,* 1969.

WORK IN PROGRESS: A study of the Hebrides and Scottish Islands.

SIDELIGHTS: The Story of Everest has been translated into nine languages. Mountaineering expeditions and other travels have taken Murray into twenty countries in Asia, Middle East, Europe, North Africa. Sailing is his other recreation.

* * *

MURSTEIN, Bernard I(rving) 1929-

PERSONAL: Born April 29, 1929, in Vilna, Lithuania; son of Leon (a taxi fleet owner) and Martha (Schalach) Murstein; married Nelly Kashy (a professor and chairman of department of French and Italian, Connecticut College), August 27, 1954; children: S. Danielle, Colette Anne. *Education:* City College of New York (now City College of City University of New York), B.S.S., 1950; University of Miami, Miami, Fla., M.S. 1951; University of Texas, Ph.D., 1955. *Politics:* Liberal-independent. *Religion:* Hebrew. *Home:* 11 Winchester Rd., New London, Conn. 06320. *Office:* Department of Psychology, Connecticut College, New London, Conn. 06320.

CAREER: University of Texas, M.D. Anderson Hospital, Austin, Hogg Foundation research fellow, 1955-56; Louisiana State University, Baton Rouge, assistant professor of psychology and director of psychology clinic, 1956-58; University of Portland, Portland, Ore., associate professor of psychology and coordinator of research, 1958-60; National Institute of Mental Health, Portland, Ore., director of research and principal investigator at Interfaith Counseling Center, 1960-62; University of Connecticut, Storrs, associate professor of family relations, 1962-63; Connecticut College, New London, associate professor, 1963-65, professor of psychology, 1965—. Principal investigator, National Institute of Mental Health, 1964-68. Fulbright professor, Universite de Louvain, 1968-69.

MEMBER: American Psychological Association (fellow), Society for Projective Techniques (fellow), National Council on Family Relations, Eastern Psychological

Association. *Awards, honors:* U.S. Public Health Service fellowship, 1954; National Institute of Mental Health research grants, 1960-63, 1964-68.

WRITINGS: Theory and Research in Projective Techniques, Emphasizing the Thematic Apperception Test, Wiley, 1963; (editor) *Handbook of Projective Techniques,* Basic Books, 1965; *Theories of Attraction and Love,* Springer Publishing, 1971.

* * *

MUSCATINE, Doris (Corn)   1926-

PERSONAL: Born January 14, 1926, in New York, N.Y.; daughter of Joseph F. and Lillian Charm (Charnofsky) Corn; married Charles Muscatine (a professor of English at University of California), July 21, 1945; children: Jeffrey, Alison. *Education:* Bennington College, B.A., 1947. *Home:* 2812 Buena Vista Way, Berkeley, Calif. 94708. *Agent:* Carl D. Brandt, Brandt & Brandt, 101 Park Ave., New York, N.Y. 10017.

CAREER: Worker in grass-roots Democratic party politics in California and member of Democratic State Central Committee, 1958-59. *Member:* California Historical Society, Mechanics Institute.

WRITINGS: A Cook's Tour of San Francisco: The Best Restaurants and Their Recipes, Scribner, 1963, revised edition, 1969; *A Cook's Tour of Rome,* Scribner, 1964. Contributor to magazines.

WORK IN PROGRESS: A book on the social history of San Francisco, for Scribner.

* * *

MUUSS, Rolf E (duard Helmut)   1924-

PERSONAL: Born September 26, 1924, in Tating, Germany; son of Rudolf (a minister) and Else (Osterwald) Muuss; married Gertrude L. Kremser, December 22, 1953; children: Michael J., Gretchen E. *Education:* Paedagogische Hochschule Flensburg-Muerwik, teaching diploma, 1951; attended University of Hamburg, 1951, Central Missouri State College, 1951-52, Columbia University, 1952; Western Maryland College, M.Ed., 1954; University of Illinois, Ph.D., 1957. *Religion:* Lutheran. *Home:* 1540 Pickett Rd., Lutherville, Md. 21093. *Office:* Goucher College, Towson, Md. 21204.

CAREER: Teacher or substitute principal in public schools in Morsum, Germany, 1945-46, Hamburg, Germany, 1951, Luengerau, Germany, 1952-53; Child Study Center for Emotionally Disturbed Children, Baltimore, Md., houseparent, 1953; State University of Iowa, Iowa City, research assistant professor at the Child Welfare Research Station, 1957-59; Goucher College, Towson, Md., associate professor of education and child development, 1959-64, professor of education, 1964—. Research associate, Johns Hopkins University, 1962-63; lecturer at other universities. Teaching consultant, Sheppard and Enoch Pratt Hospital, 1969—. Member of advisory board, EDU/CARE, Inc. Certified psychologist, state of Maryland. *Military service:* German Air Force, pilot, 1942-45. *Member:* American Psychological Association (fellow), Society for Research in Child Development Eastern Psychological Association, Maryland Psychological Association, Baltimore Association of Consulting Psychologists (vice-president, 1970-71), Phi Delta Kappa, Kappa Delta Pi (chapter vice-president, 1956-57).

WRITINGS: First for Classroom Discipline Problems, Holt, 1962; *Theories of Adolescence,* Random House, 1962, 2nd edition, 1968; (editor) *Adolescent Behavior and Society: A Book of Readings,* Random House, 1971. Contributor of articles to professional and academic journals in the United States and Germany.

WORK IN PROGRESS: Adolescent Behavior and Society, a general textbook, for Random House.

* * *

MYERS, John H (olmes)   1915-

PERSONAL: Born January 17, 1915, in Chicago, Ill.; son of Henry B. (a salesman) and Jessie (Dudman) Myers; married Elisabeth Perkins (a writer), August 24, 1940; children: Thomas P. *Education:* Northwestern University, B.S.C., 1937, M.B.A., 1938, Ph.D., 1943. *Politics:* Republican. *Religion:* Methodist. *Home address:* R.R. 12, Box 211, Bloomington, Ind. 47401. *Office:* Graduate School of Business, Indiana University, Bloomington, Ind. 47401.

CAREER: Arthur Andersen & Co. (certified public accountants), Chicago, Ill., accountant, 1938-39; University of Buffalo, Buffalo, N.Y., 1939-45, began as instructor, became associate professor; Northwestern University, Chicago and Evanston, Ill., 1945-68, began as assistant professor, became professor of accounting and chairman of accounting department; Indiana University, Bloomington, professor of accounting and chairman of the department, 1968—. *Member:* American Accounting Association (director of research, 1963-64), American Institute of Certified Public Accountants, Illinois Society of Certified Public Accountants, Indiana Association of Certified Public Accountants.

WRITINGS: Statistical Presentation, Littlefield, 1950; (with Ernest Coulter Davies) *Audit Practice Cases,* Ronald, 1953; *Reporting of Leases in Financial Statements,* American Institute of Certified Public Accountants, 1962; *Auditing Cases,* Northwestern University Press, 1964; *Instructor's Manual for Auditing Cases,* Northwestern University Press, 1964; (with Erwin Esser Nemmers) *Business Research: Text and Cases,* McGraw, 1966. Contributor of articles to professional journals.

* * *

MYRDAL, (Karl) Gunnar   1898-

PERSONAL: Born December 6, 1898, in Gustafs, Sweden; son of Karl Adolf and Sofia (Matsdotter) Peterson; married Alva Reimer, October 8, 1924; children: Jan, Sissela Bok, Kaj Foelster. *Education:* University of Stockholm, law graduate, 1923, Juris Dr. in Economics, 1927. *Politics:* Swedish Social Democratic Labour Party. *Home:* Vaesterlanggatan 31, Stockholm, Sweden. *Office:* University of Stockholm, Sveavaegen 166, 19th floor, Stockholm, Sweden.

CAREER: Began career as practicing lawyer in Sweden; University of Stockholm, Stockholm, Sweden, docent in political economy, 1927; Post-Graduate Institute of International Studies, Geneva, Switzerland, associate professor, 1930-31; University of Stockholm, acting professor, 1931-32, Lars Hierta Professor of Political Economy and Financial Science, 1933-50, professor of international economy, 1960—. Social Democrat member of Swedish Senate, 1935-38, 1944-47; Minister of Commerce in Swedish cabinet, 1945-47; member of board of directors of The Central Bank of Sweden and member of government committees on housing, population, agriculture. Executive secretary, United Nations Economic Commission for Europe, 1947-57. Director of study of American Negro problem for Carnegie Corp. of New York, 1938-42; research director of Asian Study for Twentieth Century Fund, 1957-68. Visiting Robert Lazarus Professor of Population Studies, Ohio State University, 1967.

MEMBER: Royal Academy of Science (Sweden), Econometric Society (fellow), American Economic Association (honorary), Americans for Democratic Action (honorary). *Awards, honors:* Rockefeller fellow in United States, 1929-30; Carnegie Grant, 1938; (with wife,

Alva Myrdal) West Germany's Peace Prize, 1970, for literature and public service. Honorary degrees: LL.D., Harvard University, 1938, University of Leeds, 1957, Yale University, 1959, Brandeis University, 1962, Howard University, 1962, University of Edinburgh, 1964, Swarthmore College, 1964, Sir George Williams University, 1967, University of Michigan, 1967, Lehigh University, 1967, Atlanta University, 1970; Dr. Litt., Fisk University, 1947, Upsala College, 1969; J.D., University of Nancy, 1950; L.H.D., Columbia University, 1954, New School for Social Research, 1956, Wayne State University, 1963; Dr. Soc. Sc., University of Birmingham, 1961, University of Louisville, 1968; D.D., Lincoln University, 1964; Fil.dr., Stockholm University, 1966, Oslo University, 1969; D.C.L., Temple University, 1968; Dr. sociologie, Jyvaeskylae University, 1969; D.Sc., Dartmouth College, 1971.

WRITINGS: Prisbildningsproblemet och foeraenderligheten, Almquist & Wiksells, 1927; *The Cost of Living in Sweden, 1830-1890,* King, 1933; (with Une Ahren) *Undersoekning roerande behovet av en utvidgning av bostadsstatisiken jaemte vissa daermed foerbundna bostadspolitiska fraagor,* I. Marcus, 1933; *Konjunktur och offentlig hushaallning, en utredning,* Kooperative forbundet, 1933; (with wife, Alva Myrdal) *Kris i befolkningsfraagen,* A. Bonnier, 1934, English version published as *Nation and Family: The Swedish Experiment in Democratic Family and Population Policy,* Harper, 1941; *Jordbrukspolitiken under omlaeggning,* Kooperativa forbundet, 1938; *Monetary Equilibrium,* W. Hodge & Co., 1939.

Population: A Problem for Democracy, Harvard University Press, 1940; *Amerika mitt i vaerlden,* Kooperativa forbundet, 1943; (with Richard Sterner and Arnold Rose) *An American Dilemma: The Negro Problem and Modern Democracy,* 2 volumes, Harper, 1944, 10th edition, 1962, condensation by Arnold Rose, with foreword by Myrdal, published as *The Negro in America,* Harper, 1948; *Varning foer fredsoptimism,* A. Bonnier, 1944.

The Political Element in the Development of Economic Theory, translated from the German by Paul Streeten, Routledge & Kegan Paul, 1953, Harvard University Press, 1954, new edition, 1961; *An International Economy, Problems and Prospects,* Harper, 1956, new edition, 1969; *Vaerldsekonomin,* Tidens, 1956; *Development and Underdevelopment,* [Cairo], 1956, (revised edition published in England as *Economic Theory and Under-Developed Regions,* Duckworth, 1957), revised edition published in America as *Rich Lands and Poor: The Road to World Prosperity,* Harper, 1958; *Value in Social Theory: A Selection of Essays on Methodology,* edited by Streeten, Harper, 1958.

Beyond the Welfare State: Economic Planning and Its International Implications, Yale University Press, 1960; *Problemet Sverige Hjaelper,* Raben & Sjoegren, 1961; (with Tord Ekstroem and Roland Palsson) *Vi och Vaesteuropa,* Raben & Sjoegren, 1962; *Challenge to Affluence,* Random House, 1963, revised edition, Vintage, 1965; *Vaar onda vaerld,* Raben & Sjoegren, 1964; *Asian Drama: An Inquiry into the Poverty of Nations,* 3 volumes, Random House, 1968, abridged edition, Pantheon, 1971, selections published as *An Approach to the Asian Drama, Methodological and Theoretical,* Vintage, 1970; *Objectivity in Social Research,* Pantheon, 1969; *The Challenge of World Poverty: A World Anti-Poverty Program in Outline,* Pantheon, 1970.

Also author of monographs and lectures, including: *De internationella forhandlingarna i Washington om ekonomiska efterkrigsproblem,* Svenska Bankforeningen, 1944; *The Reconstruction of World Trade and Swedish Trade Policy,* [Stockholm], 1947; *Psychological Impediments to*

Effective International Cooperation, Association Press, 1952; *Realities and Illusions in Regard to Inter-Governmental Organizations,* Oxford University Press, 1955; *The Research Work of the Secretariat of the Economic Commission for Europe,* [London], 1956; *Economic Nationalism and Internationalism,* Australian Institute of International Affairs, 1957; *The Intergovernmental Organizations and the Role of Their Secretariats,* [Stockholm], 1969.

BIOGRAPHICAL/CRITICAL SOURCES: Newsweek, May 20, 1963; *New York Times,* October 4, 1967, July 17, 1970; *New York Times Book Review,* March 24, 1968, July 19, 1970; *New Republic,* May 4, 1968; *Book World,* June 9, 1968; *Virginia Quarterly Review,* summer, 1968; *Listener,* October 17, 1968; *Commentary,* December, 1968; *Spectator,* January 10, 1969; *New Yorker,* February 15, 1969; *Nation,* November 24, 1969.

* * *

NAGEL, Paul C(hester) 1926-

PERSONAL: Born August 14, 1926, in Independence, Mo.; son of Paul Conrad (a mechanic) and Freda (Sabrowsky) Nagel; married Joan R. Peterson, March 19, 1948; children: Eric John, Jefferson, Steven Paul. *Education:* University of Minnesota, BA., 1948, M.A., 1949, Ph.D., 1952. *Politics:* Democrat. *Home:* 1011 South Glenwood Ave., Columbia, Mo. 65201.

CAREER: Augustana College, Sioux Falls, S.D., assistant professor of history, 1953-54; Eastern Kentucky University, Richmond, associate professor of history, 1954-61; University of Kentucky, Lexington, associate professor of history, 1961-65; professor and dean, College of Arts and Sciences, 1965-69; University of Missouri, Columbia, professor of history and Special Assistant to President for Academic Affairs, 1969—. Visiting professor at Amherst College, 1957-58, Vanderbilt University, 1959, University of Minnesota, 1964. *Member:* American Historical Association, Organization of American Historians, Southern Historical Association.

WRITINGS: One Nation Indivisible: The Union in American Thought, 1776-1861, Oxford University Press, 1964; *This Sacred Trust: American Nationality, 1798-1898,* Oxford University Press, 1971. Contributor to *American Quarterly, Journal of Southern History, Midwest Review, Virginia Magazine of History and Biography,* other historical journals.

* * *

NANDAKUMAR, Prema 1939- (Aswin)

PERSONAL: Born February, 1939, in Kodaganallur, Tinnevelly, Madras, India; daughter of K.R. Srinivasa (a university professor) and Padmasani Iyengar; married M.S. Nandakumar (an engineer), August, 1958; children: Ahana (daughter). *Education:* Attended Vizag Tutorial College, 1950-52, Madras A.V.N. College, 1952-54; Andhra University, B.A. (first class honors), 1957, M.A., 1958, Ph.D., 1961. *Religion:* Hindu. *Home:* T/3H, Andhra University Campus, Visakhapatnam-3, India.

MEMBER: All-India P.E.N. Centre.

WRITINGS: (Translator from Tamil, and author of introduction and notes) *Bharati in English Verse,* Porunai Publishers, 1958; *A Study of "Savitri",* Sri Aurobindo Ashram, 1962; *Subramania Bharati,* Rao & Raghavan, 1964; *The Glory and the Good: Essays on Literature,* Asia Publishing House, 1965; (with K.R. Srinivasa Iyengar) *An Introduction to the Study of English Literature,* Asia Publishing House, 1967. Regular contributor of reviews and articles to newspapers and magazines.

WORK IN PROGRESS: Savitri, a verse drama; comparative study of Dante and Sri Aurobindo; a study of Indian writing in English.

NANNES, Caspar Harold 1906-

PERSONAL: Born May 15, 1906, in Fall River, Mass.; son of Max and Minnie (Silverstein) Nannes. *Education:* Rutgers University, A.B., 1931, A.M., 1932; University of Pennsylvania, Ph.D., 1948. *Home:* 4200 Cathedral Ave. N.W., Washington, D.C. 20016. *Office: Washington Star,* 225 Virginia Ave. S.E., Washington, D.C. 20003.

CAREER: Rutgers University, New Brunswick, N.J., graduate assistant, English department, 1931-35; University of Illinois, Champaign, teaching assistant, 1935-38; Rutgers University, English instructor, 1938-42; *Washington Star,* Washington, D.C., reporter, 1943—. *Member:* Religious Newswriters Association (president, 1956-58), Modern Language Association, Phi Beta Kappa, Middle Atlantic Lawn Tennis Association (vice-president, 1952-56), Edgemoor Club, National Press Club, Rutgers Club of Washington (president, 1943-63). *Awards, honors:* Rutgers Alumni Trustees Award, 1959; National Religious Publicity Board award, 1963; R.S. Reynolds award, Presbyterian Church of the United States, 1964; D.Litt., Rutgers University, 1966.

WRITINGS: Politics in the American Drama, Catholic University of America Press, 1960; *The National Presbyterian Church and Center* (history), National Presbyterian Church and Center, 1970. Contributor to periodicals.

SIDELIGHTS: Nannes has made numerous radio and television appearances. *Avocational interests:* Tennis.

*   *   *

NASATIR, A(braham) P(hineas) 1904-

PERSONAL: Born November 24, 1904, in Santa Ana, Calif.; son of Morris (a businessman) and Sarah Esther (Hurwitz) Nasatir; married Ida Hirsch (a high school teacher), September 8, 1929. *Education:* University of California, Berkeley, A.B., 1921, M.A., 1922, Ph.D., 1926. *Home:* 3340 North Mountain View Dr. E., San Diego, Calif. 92116. *Office:* San Diego State College, San Diego, Calif. 92115.

CAREER: State University of Iowa, Iowa City, instructor in history, 1926-27; San Diego State College, San Diego, Calif., assistant professor, 1927-30, associate professor, 1930-34, professor of history, 1934—. Lecturer at University of Chile, 1959-60; Walter L. Fleming Lecturer, Louisiana State University in New Orleans, 1970. Vice-consul for Paraguay, 1936-51, vice-consul for Ecuador, 1941-43; secretary, Consular Corps, 1940-50. United Jewish Federation, member of board of directors and former president. *Member:* American Historical Association (president, Pacific Coast branch, 1963-64), Pacific Coast Council on Latin American Studies (chairman, 1963-64), American Association of University Professors, Western Historical Association, Louisiana Historical Association, Missouri Historical Society, Missouri State Historical Society, California Historical Society, San Diego Historical Society (board of directors), Phi Alpha Theta (international president, 1968-71). *Awards, honors:* Social Science Research Council fellow for study in archives of France and Spain, 1930-31; Fulbright scholar in France, 1950-51; Huntington Library fellow, summer, 1952; California State College System Trustees Distinguished Professor, 1966; L.H.D., University of Judaism, 1969.

WRITINGS: The French in the California Gold Rush, American Society of French Legion of Honor, 1934; (editor and translator) Jacques Antoine Moerenhout, *Inside Story of the Gold Rush,* California Historical Society, 1935; *French Activities in California: An Archival Calendar-Guide,* Stanford University Press, 1945; (editor and author of narrative introduction) *Before Lewis and Clark: Documents Illustrating the History of the Missouri, 1785-1804,* two volumes, St. Louis Historical Documents Foundation, 1952; (with Helen Miller Bailey) *Latin America: The Development of Its Civilization,* Prentice-Hall, 1960, 2nd edition, 1968; (with Leo Shpall) *The Texel Affair* (originally published in *American Jewish Historical Quarterly*), Marstin Press, c.1963; (editor) *A French Journalist in the California Gold Rush: The Letters of Etienne Derbec,* Talisman, 1964; (editor and author of notes) Walter Bond Douglas, *Manuel Lisa,* Argosy-Antiquarian, 1964; (author of preface and notes) John C. Luttig, *Journal of a Fur-Trading Expedition on the Upper Missouri, 1812-1813,* edited by Stella M. Drumm, Argosy-Antiquarian, 1964; (with Gary E. Monell) *French Consuls in the United States,* Library of Congress, 1967; (with Noel Loomis) *Pedro Vial and the Roads to Santa Fe,* University of Oklahoma Press, 1967; *Spanish War Vessels on the Mississippi, 1792-1796,* Yale University Press, 1968; (with James R. Mills) *Commerce and Contraband in New Orleans During the French and Indian War,* American Jewish Archives, 1968.

WORK IN PROGRESS: Anglo Spanish Rivalry on the Upper Mississippi, 1796-1804; the Fleming Lectures at Louisiana State University, 1970, *Frontiers of Spanish Louisiana,* to be published in book form.

*   *   *

NATCHEZ, Gladys W. 1915-

PERSONAL: Born November 13, 1915, in New York, N.Y.; son of Sidney and Hortense (Stern) Worms; married Benjamin Natchez, August 8, 1939; children: Peter, Daniel, Meryl. *Education:* Columbia University, M.A., 1939; New York University, Ph.D., 1958; Adelphi University, postdoctoral certificate in psychoanalysis and psychotherapy, 1968. *Home:* 55 East 87th St., New York, N.Y. 10028.

CAREER: College of the City of New York (now City College of the City University of New York), New York, N.Y., lecturer, 1956-63, assistant professor of education, 1963-67, associate professor of education, 1967—. Private practice in psychotherapy and remedial reading. *Member:* International Reading Association, American Orthopsychiatry Association, American Psychological Association, American Academy of Psychotherapists.

WRITINGS: Personality Patterns and Oral Reading, New York University Press, 1959; (with Florence Roswell) *Reading Disability, Diagnosis and Treatment,* Basic Books, 1964, 2nd edition, 1971; (editor) *Children with Reading Problems: Classic and Contemporary Issues in Reading Disability—Selected Readings,* Basic Books, 1968. Contributor to *Journal of Educational Research.*

BIOGRAPHICAL/CRITICAL SOURCES: Saturday Review, September 21, 1968.

*   *   *

NAUDE, (Aletta) Adele da Fonseca-Wollheim 1910-

PERSONAL: Born August 14, 1910, in Pretoria, Transvaal, South Africa; daughter of Henri Jacques (a farmer) and Maria (Watney) da Fonseca-Wollheim; married David Francois Hugo Naude, December 14, 1935; children: Adele Marie. *Education:* Attended Rustenburg Girls' High School, Cape Town, South Africa; University of Cape Town, B.A., 1930. *Home:* 2 Scott Rd., Claremont, Cape Town, South Africa.

CAREER: Secretary, translator, and free-lance journalist, Cape Town, South Africa, 1930-35; academic assistant to registrar, University of Cape Town, Cape Town, South Africa, and free-lance journalist, 1936-37; *Naweek* (Afrikaans weekly), and *Spotlight* (English weekly),

Capetown, South Africa, editor of women's pages, 1947-50; scriptwriter, broadcaster, and free-lance journalist, 1940—. *Member:* Cape Town P.E.N. Club (secretary).

*WRITINGS: Verhale mit die Griekse legendes (*juvenile), Oxford University Press, 1949; *Koning Arthur en sy ridders* (juvenile), Oxford University Press, 1950; *Pity the Spring* (poems), A.A. Balkema, 1953; *No Longer at Ease* (poems), A.A. Balkema, 1956; *Gentlemen's Relish: Dishes with a Difference*, privately printed, 1956; *Strooihoed en sonbril*, Human & Rousseau, 1965; *Only a Setting Forth* (poems), Human & Rousseau, 1965; *Tousandale aan my Voete* (essays), Human & Rousseau, 1968; *Gregory Kaapse Pikkewyn* (title means "The Story of the Jackass Penguin"), David Philip, 1972; *With Groote Schuur for Playground* (autobiography), David Philip, 1973; *Time and Memory* (poems), Maskew Miller, 1973. Author of four books of short stories for children, in Afrikaans. Scriptwriter for South African Broadcasting Corp. Regular contributor to literary journals and newspapers in South Africa.

WORK IN PROGRESS: A book of essays in English.

AVOCATIONAL INTERESTS: Music, gardening, sports (tennis in particular), architecture, art.

* * *

NAYLOR, Margot Ailsa (Lodge)   1907-

PERSONAL: Born September 28, 1907, in London, England; daughter of Thomas and Isobel (Scott) Lodge; married Guy Naylor (a barrister), August 16, 1906; children: Caroline (Mrs. Geoffrey Allen Clarke). *Education:* Studied at Girton College, Cambridge University, 1926-27, London School of Economics, University of London, 1948-52. *Politics:* Conservative. *Religion:* Agnostic. *Home:* 107 New Kings Rd., London S.W.6, England. *Office:* Daily Mail City Office, 14 Finsbury Circus, London E.C.2, England.

CAREER: Cabinet Office Secretariat, London, England, principal, 1942-45; Civil Service Commission, Final Selection Board, London, England, permanent woman member, 1948-50; *Investor's Chronicle*, special staff writer, 1954-61; *Statist*, investment editor, 1961-63; *Observer*, London, England, financial editor, 1963-67; free-lance financial journalist, 1967—.

WRITINGS: (With Ralph Harris and Arthur Seldon) *Hire Purchase in a Free Society*, Hutchinson, 1958, 3rd edition, 1961; *Profits Under Pressure*, Newman Neame, 1963; *Your Money: A Guide to Individual Investment*, Barrie & Rockliff, 1965; *How to Reduce Your Tax Bill*, Allen & Unwin, 1968, 2nd edition, 1969; (editor) *Financial Times Yearbook [1969]: Business Information*, Longmans, Green, 1969; *The Truth About Life Assurance*, Allen & Unwin, 1971; (editor) *Financial Times Yearbook [1971]: Business Information on 25 Leading Industrial Countries*, Volume 2, St. Martin's, 1971. Contributor to woman's page, *Daily Telegraph*, 1961-62.

BIOGRAPHICAL/CRITICAL SOURCES: Harper's Bazaar, November, 1963.

* * *

NEEDHAM, (Noel) Joseph (Terence Montgomery)   1900-

PERSONAL: Born December 9, 1900, in London, England; son of Joseph (a physician) and Alicia Adelaide (Montgomery) Needham; married Dorothy Mary Moyle, September 13, 1924. *Education:* Attended Oundle School; Cambridge University, M.A., Ph.D., Sc.D. *Home:* Master's Lodge, Gonville and Caius College, Cambridge, England.

CAREER: Cambridge University, Cambridge, England, university demonstrator in biochemistry, 1928-33, Sir

William Dunn Reader in Biochemistry, 1933-66, emeritus, 1966—, fellow of Gonville and Caius College, 1924-66, president of Gonville and Caius College, 1959-66, Master of the College, 1966—. Visiting professor at Stanford University, 1929, University of Lyon, 1951; distinguished lecturer at Yale University, Cornell University, and Oberlin College, 1935, Royal College of Physicians (London), 1935-36, Oxford University, 1936-37, universities in Poland, 1937, University of California and Johns Hopkins University, 1950, University of London, 1950, Colombo, Singapore, Peking, and Jaipur Universities, 1958; Wilkins Lecturer, Royal Society, London, 1958; Wilde Lecturer, University of Manchester, 1959; Earl Grey Lecturer, University of Newcastle Upon Tyne, 1960; Myers Lecturer, Royal Anthropological Society, London, 1964; lecturer, Harveian Society, London, 1970; Rapkine Lecturer, Pasteur Institute, Paris, France, 1970; Fremantle Lecturer, Balliol College, Oxford, 1971; Bernal Lecturer, Birkbeck College, London, 1971. Adviser to Chinese National Resources Commission and military services, 1942-46; director of department of Natural Sciences, UNESCO, 1946-48; chairman of Ceylon Government University Policy Commission, 1958.

MEMBER: Royal Society (London; fellow), International Academy of History of Science, International Academy of History of Medicine, National Academy of China (foreign member), Sigma Xi (honorary). *Awards, honors:* D.Sc. from Universities of Brussels and Norwich; Order of the Brilliant Star (China); Sir William Jones Medallist, Asiatic Society of Bengal, 1963; Leonardo da Vinci Medallist, Society for the History of Technology, 1969; George Sarton Medallist, Society for the History of Science, 1969.

WRITINGS: (Editor and contributor) *Science, Religion and Reality*, Macmillan, 1925, reissued with introductory essay by George Sarton, Braziller, 1955; *Man a Machine: In Answer to a Romantical and Unscientific Treatise Written by Sig. Eugenio Rignano and Entitled "Man Not a Machine"*, Kegan Paul, 1927, Norton, 1928; *Materialism and Religion*, Benn, 1929; *The Sceptical Biologist* (ten essays), Chatto & Windus, 1929, Norton, 1930; *Chemical Embryology*, three volumes, Cambridge University Press, 1931, Hafner, 1963; *The Great Amphibium: Four Lectures on the Position of Religion in a World Dominated by Science* (first lecture originally published in *Nineteenth Century*, second in *Journal of Philosophical Studies* and *Cambridge Review*, and fourth in *Criterion*), S.C.M. Press, 1931, Scribner, 1932; *A History of Embryology* (originally published as part 2 of *Chemical Embryology*), Cambridge University Press, 1934, 2nd edition (with Arthur Hughes), Abelard, 1959; (editor with John Lewis and others) *Christianity and the Social Revolution*, Gollancz, 1935, Scribner, 1936; *Order and Life*, Yale University Press, 1936, new edition, M.I.T. Press, 1968; (translator) Jean Rostand, *Adventures Before Birth*, Gollancz, 1936; (editor with David E. Green) *Perspectives in Biochemistry* (31 essays), Cambridge University Press, 1937; *Integrative Levels: A Revaluation of the Idea of Progress* (lecture), Clarendon Press, 1937; (editor with Walter Pagel) *Background to Modern Science* (ten lectures), Macmillan, 1938; (author of foreword) Marcel Prenant, *Biology and Marxism*, translated by C. Desmond Greaves, International Publishers, 1938.

(Editor) *The Teacher of Nations: Addresses and Essays in Commemoration of the Visit to England of the Great Czech Educationalist Jan Amos Komensky, Comenius, 1641-1941, by Eduard Benes, J.L. Paton, Henry Morris, and Others*, Cambridge University Press, 1942; (editor, with Jane Sykes Davies, and contributor) *Science in Soviet Russia, by Seven British Scientists*, C.A. Watts, 1942; *Biochemistry and Morphogenesis*, Macmillan, 1942; *Time: The Refreshing River* (essays and addresses, 1932-

1942), Macmillan, 1943; *Chinese Science,* Pilot Press (London), 1945; *History Is On Our Side: A Contribution to Political Religion and Scientific Faith,* Allen & Unwin, 1946, Macmillan, 1947; (editor with wife, Dorothy Needham) *Science Outpost: Papers, 1942-1946,* Pilot Press, 1948; (editor with E.H.F. Baldwin) *Hopkins and Biochemistry, 1861-1947,* Heffer, 1949; (author of foreword) Zdenek Hrdlicka, *Contemporary Chinese Woodcuts,* Fore Publications and Collet's Holdings, 1950; *Science and Civilisation in China,* Cambridge University Press, Volume 1: *Introductory Orientations,* 1954, Volume 2: *History of Scientific Thought,* 1956, Volume 3: *Mathematics and the Sciences of the Heavens and the Earth,* 1959, Volume 4: *Physics and Physical Technology,* Part 1: *Physics,* 1962, Part 2: *Mechanical Engineering,* 1965, Part 3: *Engineering and Nautics,* 1970; *The Development of Iron and Steel Technology in China,* published for the Newcomen Society by Heffer, 1958.

(With Wang Ling and Derek J. de Solla Price) *Heavenly Clockwork: The Great Astronomical Clocks of Medieval China,* Cambridge University Press and Antiquarian Horological Society, 1960; *The Grand Titration: Science and Society in East and West,* Allen & Unwin, 1969; *Within the Four Seas: The Dialogue of East and West,* Allen & Unwin, 1969; *Clerks and Craftsmen in China and the West: Lectures and Addresses on the History of Science and Technology,* Cambridge University Press, 1970; (editor and author of introduction) *The Chemistry of Life: Eight Lectures on the History of Biochemistry,* Cambridge University Press, 1970.

Short books and monologues: *The Nazi Attack on International Science,* C.A. Watts, 1941; *Some Thoughts About China,* China Society, 1946; *Science and Society in Ancient China,* C.A. Watts, 1947; *Science and International Relations,* Basil Blackwell, 1948, C.C Thomas, 1949; *Human Law and the Laws of Nature in China and the West,* Oxford University Press, 1951; *Chinese Astronomy and the Jesuit Mission: An Encounter of Cultures,* China Society, 1958; *Classical Chinese Contributions to Mechanical Engineering,* King's College, 1961; *Time and Eastern Man,* Royal Anthropological Institute, 1965.

Contributor of papers to biological, philosophical, and sinological journals. General editor, with Dorothy Needham, of *Sheldon Books of Popular Science,* Sheldon Press, 1931 and 1934.

WORK IN PROGRESS: Further volumes in *Science and Civilisation in China.*

SIDELIGHTS: Needham's seven-volume encyclopedia, *Science and Civilisation in China,* has been called a "mastery enterprise" and "one of the most ambitious and successful historical research projects by a single author in modern times." "Almost no other don in this country," said Dennis J. Duncanson of *Spectator,* "has such thick Chinese mud on his boots . . . his erudition can never fail to command an instant hearing." Leaning heavily on the research assistance of Wang Ling, the series is a prodigious chronicling of the scientific and technical achievements of the Chinese from ancient times to the present day, with hundreds of illustrations, charts, tables, and diagrams. Kenneth Rexroth said of part 2 of Volume 4 of the series: "What Needham does superlatively is convey, as life itself conveys, the all-pervasive flavor, color and tone of a culture different in obvious but ultimately unanalyzable ways from ours. Not exhaustively analyzable in theory, that is, but in this book so elegantly analyzed in terms of an immense structure of very simple and most concrete facts."

BIOGRAPHICAL/CRITICAL SOURCES: Library Journal, January 15, 1960, May 1, 1960; *American Historical Review,* April, 1960; *Times Literary Supplement,* July 8, 1960, February 10, 1966; *Pacific Affairs,* spring, 1961; *New Statesman,* July 20, 1962, November 4, 1966, July 10, 1970; *Nation,* March 14, 1966; *Spectator,* June 28, 1969, October 4, 1969; *Science,* May 8, 1970.

* * *

NEHRLING, Arno H. 1886-

PERSONAL: Born July 25, 1886, in Freistadt, Mo.; son of Henry (a plantsman and ornithologist) and Sophia (Schoff) Nehrling; married Irene Dahlberg (an author), September 18, 1923; children: A. Herbert, Jr., Dorothy Irene (Mrs. Warren P. Higgins). *Education:* Washington University, S. Louis, Mo., B.S., 1909. *Politics:* Republican. *Religion:* Protestant. *Home:* 3 Carey Rd., Needham Heights, Mass. 02194.

CAREER: Massachusetts Agricultural College (now University of Massachusetts), Amherst, professor and head of department of floriculture, 1913-17; McDonald Floral Co., Crawfordsville, Ind., president, 1917-21; Cornell University, Ithaca, N.Y., professor of floriculture, 1921-27; Hill Floral Products Co., Richmond, Ind., sales manager, 1927-33; Massachusetts Horticultural Society, Boston, director of exhibitions, 1933-65, director of publications and executive secretary, 1947-63; retired, 1965—.

MEMBER: Society of American Florists (national president, 1937-38), American Horticultural Society (director; vice-president, 1954-56), Chrysanthemum Society of America (secretary, 1930-37; vice-president, 1940-41, president, 1942—), North American Lily Society (founder and director; president, 1954-55), American Tulip Society (director), American Rose Society (registration committee), Horticultural Club of Boston (president, 1955-58), Pi Alpha Xi, Alpha Gamma Rho, Kappa Sigma. *Awards, honors:* Distinguished achievement citation and plaque, Associated Bulb Growers of Holland, 1954; Arthur Hoyt Scott Garden and Horticultural Award, Swarthmore College, 1957; American Horticultural Council citation, 1958; horticulturist of the year, University of Massachusetts, 1958; Gold Medal of Men's Garden Clubs of America, 1956, of Massachusetts Horticultural Society, 1959, of Horticultural Society of New York, 1962; Horticultural Hall of Fame, 1964.

WRITINGS—All with wife, Irene Dahlberg Nehrling: *An Easy Guide to House Plants,* Hearthside, 1958; *Gardening, Forcing, Conditioning and Drying for Flower Arrangements,* Hearthside, 1958, revised edition published as *Flower Growing for Flower Arrangement,* Jenkins, 1964, 3rd edition, Hearthside, 1969; *Peonies, Outdoors and In,* Hearthside, 1960; *Propagating House Plants for Amateur and Commercial Use,* Hearthside, 1962; *The Picture Book of Perennials,* Hearthside, 1964; *The Picture Book of Annuals,* Hearthside, 1966; *Easy Gardening with Drought-Resistant Plants,* Hearthside, 1968; *Propagating House Plants: New—How to Grow Herbs and Vegetables Indoors,* Hearthside, 1971. Contributor of articles on floriculture to national magazines. Writer of question and answer column, *Richmond Palladium,* 1927-33, and writer of bulletins on horticultural subjects. Guest editor, with Irene Dahlberg Nehrling, of *Summer Flowers for Continuing Bloom* (quarterly published by Brooklyn Botanic Garden), spring, 1968.

* * *

NEHRLING, Irene Dahlberg 1900-

PERSONAL: Born August 24, 1900, in Curtiss, Wis.; daughter of Oke A. (a merchant) and Eleonora (Jensen) Dahlberg; married Arno H. Nehrling (former executive secretary and director of exhibitions and publications, Massachusetts Horticultural Society), September 18, 1923; children: A. Herbert, Jr., Dorothy Irene (Mrs. Warren P. Higgins). *Education:* University of Minnesota, B.S., 1921. *Politics:* Republican. *Religion:* Protestant. *Home:* 3 Carey Rd., Needham Heights, Mass. 02194.

CAREER: Cornell University, Ithaca, N.Y., instructor, 1921-24, assistant professor of home economics and head of department of institutional management, 1924-27; free-lance writer of articles on food, 1927-50; writer on horticultural subjects, 1950—.

WRITINGS—All with husband, Arno H. Nehrling: An Easy Guide to House Plants, Hearthside, 1958; Gardening, Forcing, Conditioning and Drying for Flower Arrangements, Hearthside, 1958, revised edition published as Flower Growing for Flower Arrangement, Jenkins, 1964, 3rd edition, Hearthside, 1969; Peonies, Outdoors and In, Hearthside, 1960; Propagating House Plants for Amateur and Commercial Use, Hearthside, 1962; The Picture Book of Perennials, Hearthside, 1964; The Picture Book of Annuals, Hearthside, 1966; Easy Gardening with Drought-Resistant Plants, Hearthside, 1968; Propagating House Plants: New—How to Grow Herbs and Vegetables Indoors, Hearthside, 1971. Contributor to New Butterick Cook-Book, by Helena Judson, Dodd, 1924. Contributor of articles on food to Delineator and other home magazines, 1921-27, and to Christian Science Monitor during World War II. Associate editor and contributor, American Cookery, during World War II. Guest editor, with Arno H. Nehrling, of Summer Flowers for Continuing Bloom (quarterly published by Brooklyn Botanic Garden), spring, 1968.

* * *

NEIL, William 1909-

PERSONAL: Born June 13, 1909, in Glasgow, Scotland; son of William MacLaren and Jean C. (Hutchison) Neil; married Effie L. Park, December 18, 1936; children: Graham MacLaren, Lindsay Douglas. Education: Attended Glasgow Academy, 1918-26; University of Glasgow, M.A., 1929, B.D., 1932, Ph.D., 1936; University of Heidelberg, postgraduate study, 1932-33. Home: Hugh Stewart Hall, University Park, Nottingham, England.

CAREER: Clergyman, Church of Scotland (Presbyterian). Minister at Bridge of Allan, Scotland, 1937-46; University of Aberdeen, Aberdeen, Scotland, head of department of biblical studies, 1946-53; University of Nottingham, Nottingham, England, warden of Hugh Stewart Hall and reader in biblical studies, 1953—. Military service: British Army, chaplain, 1940-45; mentioned in dispatches. Member: Societas Novi Testamenti Studiorum, Association of University Teachers (chairman of Nottingham branch, 1961-62), University Wardens Conference (chairman, 1962-65), Nottingham Scottish Association (president, 1964-65), Rotary International. Awards, honors: D.D. from University of Glasgow, 1961.

WRITINGS: The Epistle of Paul to the Thessalonians (Moffat New Testament commentary), Harper, 1950, also published as Thessalonians, Hodder & Stoughton, 1950; The Rediscovery of the Bible, Hodder & Stoughton, 1954, Harper, 1955; The Epistle to the Hebrews: Introduction and Commentary, Macmillan, 1955, reissued as The Epistle to the Hebrews: Ritual and Reality, S.C.M. Press, 1968; (translator) Werner Keller, The Bible as History: A Confirmation of the Book of Books, Morrow, 1956 (published in England as The Bible as History: Archaeology Confirms the Book of Books, Hodder & Stoughton, 1956); The Plain Man Looks at the Bible, Collins, 1956, revised edition published as Modern Man Looks at the Bible, Association Press, 1958; St. Paul's Epistles to the Thessalonians: Introduction and Commentary (Torch Bible commentary), Allenson, 1957; (translator) Paul Bruin, Jesus Lived Here, photographs by Philipp Giegel, Morrow, 1958; (editor) The Bible Companion: A Complete Pictorial and Reference Guide to the People, Places, Events, Background, and Faith of the Bible, McGraw, 1960; One Volume Bible Commentary, Hodder &

Stoughton, 1962, published in America as Harper's Bible Commentary, Harper, 1963; (translator) Werner Keller, The Bible as History in Pictures, Morrow, 1964; Prophets of Israel, Volume 2: Jeremiah and Ezekiel, Abingdon, 1964; (editor) Robert Davidson, Old Testament, Hodder & Stoughton, 1964; (editor) F.W. Dillistone, Christian Faith, Hodder & Stoughton, 1964; The Life and Teaching of Jesus, Lippincott, 1965; The Bible Today ("Lift Up Your Hearts" series), B.B.C. Publications, 1965; Apostle Extraordinary: The Life and Letters of Saint Paul, Religious Education Press, 1966; (with Eric Newton) 2000 Years of Christian Art, Harper, 1966; (with Newton) The Christian Faith in Art, Hodder & Stoughton, 1966; The Letter of Paul to the Galatians, Cambridge University Press, 1967; The Truth About Jesus, Hodder & Stoughton, 1968; (editor) F.R. Barry, The Atonement, Hodder & Stoughton, 1968; The Truth About the Early Church, Hodder & Stoughton, 1970; The Bible Story, Abingdon, 1971.

Contributor to Cambridge History of the Bible, Interpreter's Dictionary of the Bible, and Peake's Commentary. General editor of "Knowing Christianity" series, Lippincott, 1964—.

WORK IN PROGRESS: Acts (New Century Bible), to be published by Oliphants; commentaries in Universal Bible.

* * *

NEILL, Stephen Charles 1900-

PERSONAL: Born December 31, 1900, in Edinburgh, Scotland; son of Charles (a physician and minister) and Margaret (Monro) Neill. Education: Trinity College, Cambridge, M.A. (first class honors), 1926. Politics: "Indignant and resentful Conservative." Home: Hofweg 89, 2 Hamburg 22, Germany. Office: University of Hamburg, Von-Melle-Park 6, Hamburg 13, Germany.

CAREER: Ordained to ministry of Anglican Church, 1926. Cambridge University, Cambridge, England, fellow, 1924-38, member of theological faculty, 1944-47; missionary in South India, 1924-44, and Bishop of Tinnevelly, 1939-45; World Council of Churches, Geneva, Switzerland, associate general secretary, 1948-51; World Christian Books, London, England, editor, 1952-62, director, 1962—; University of Hamburg, Hamburg, Germany, professor of missions and ecumenical theology, 1962—. Bampton Lecturer at Oxford University, 1964. Awards, honors: D.D. from Trinity College, University of Toronto, 1950, Culver-Stockton College, 1953, University of Glasgow, 1961; Th.D. from University of Hamburg, 1957; Litt.D. from St. Paul's University, Tokyo, 1960.

WRITINGS: How Readest Thou?: A Simple Introduction to the New Testament, S.C.M. Press, 1925; (editor) The Gospel According to St. John, Macmillan, 1930; Out of Bondage: Christ and the Indian Villager, Edinburgh House, 1930; Annals of an Indian Parish, Church Missionary Society, 1934; Builders of the Indian Church: Present Problems in the Light of the Past, Edinburgh House, 1934; The Remaking of Men in India, Church Missionary Society, 1934; Beliefs (lectures given at Kodaikanal Missionary Conference, 1937), Christian Literature Society for India, 1939.

Foundation Beliefs (lectures given at Kodaikanal Missionary Conference, 1941), Christian Literature Society for India, 1941; The Wrath and the Peace of God, and Other Studies (addresses given at Nilgiri Missionary Convention, 1942), 2nd edition, Christian Literature Society for India, 1944; (with others) Towards a United Church, 1945-94, Edinburgh House, 1947; (editor and author of preliminary chapter) The Ministry of the Church (re e v o various authors of The Apostolic Ministry, edited by K.E. Kirk; originally published in The

Record), Canterbury Press, 1947; *Christ: His Church and His World,* Eyre & Spottiswoode, 1948; *The Cross Over Asia,* Canterbury Press, 1948; *The Breakdown of the Family* (lecture), Oxford University Press, 1949; *A Christian Approach to Psychology* (pamphlet), Guild of Pastoral Psychology, 1949; *Our Relationship with the Indigenous Church,* Conference of Missionaries of the Church Missionary Society, 1949; *Who Was Jesus of Nazareth?,* Mowbray, 1950; *Christian Partnership,* Allenson, 1952; *The Christian Society,* Nisbet, 1952, Harper, 1953; *Fulfill Thy Ministry,* Harper, 1952; *On the Ministry,* S.C.M. Press, 1952; *Towards Church Union, 1937-1952: A Survey of Approaches to Closer Union Among Churches,* Allenson, 1952; (editor with Ruth Rouse) *A History of the Ecumenical Movement, 1517-1948,* Westminster, 1954, 2nd edition, with revised bibliography, 1967; *Under Three Flags,* Friendship, 1954; *The Christians' God,* published for United Society for Christian Literature by Lutterworth, 1954, Association Press, 1955 (also published in *New Power to Witness*—see below); *The Christian Character,* Association Press, 1955, also published as *The Difference in Being a Christian* ("Reflection Book" edition), Association Press, 1960; *Christian Faith To-day,* Penguin, 1955; (translator) Wilhelm Andersen, *Towards a Theology of Mission: A Study of the Encounter Between the Missionary Enterprise and the Church and Its Theology,* S.C.M. Press, 1955; (translator) Eduard Lohse, *Mark's Witness to Jesus Christ,* Association Press, 1955; *Who is Jesus Christ?,* published for United Society for Christian Literature by Lutterworth, 1956, Association Press, 1957; *The Cross in the Church* (four lectures), published for the London Missionary Society by Independent Press, 1957; (editor and contributor) *New Power to Witness* (four volumes in one; includes *The Christians' God* by Neill), Association Press, c.1957; *Seeing the Bible Whole,* Bible Reading Fellowship, 1957; *The Unfinished Task,* Edinburgh House, 1957; *Anglicanism,* Penguin (Harmondsworth), 1958, 3rd edition, Penguin (Baltimore), 1965; *La Doctrina Christiana de la santidad* (originally written in English as the Carnahan Lectures, 1958), La Aurora (Buenos Aires), 1958, published in English as *Christian Holiness,* Harper, 1960; *Paul to the Galatians,* Association Press, 1958; (translator) Giovanni Miegge, *Visible and Invisible: Christian Affirmations in a Secular Age,* Mowbray, 1958, also published as *Christian Affirmations in a Secular Age,* Oxford University Press, 1958; *Creative Tension* (Duff Lectures, 1958), Edinburgh House, 1959; *A Genuinely Human Existence: Towards a Christian Psychology,* Doubleday, 1959.

Brothers of the Faith, Abingdon, 1960; *Men of Unity,* S.C.M. Press, 1960; *What is Man?,* published for United Society for Christian Literature by Lutterworth, 1960, published in America as *Man in God's Purpose,* Association Press, 1961; (translator) Giovanni Miegge, *Gospel and Myth in the Thought of Rudolf Bultmann,* John Knox, 1960; *Christian Faith and Other Faiths: The Christian Dialogue with Other Religions* (Moorehouse Lectures, 1960), Oxford University Press, 1961, 2nd edition, 1970; (editor) *Twentieth Century Christianity: A Survey of Modern Religious Trends by Leading Churchmen,* Collins, 1961, revised edition, Doubleday, 1963; (compiler and translator) Joannes Chrysostomus, *Chrysostom and His Message: A Selection from the Sermons of St. John Chrysostom,* Lutterworth, 1962, Association Press, c.1963; *The Eternal Dimension,* Epworth, 1963; (editor with Hans-Ruedi Weber) *The Layman in Christian History: A Project of the Department on the Laity of the World Council of Churches,* Westminster Press, 1963; *Paul to the Colossians,* published for United Society for Christian Literature by Lutterworth, 1963, Association Press, 1964; *A History of Christian Missions* (The Pelican History of the Church, Volume 6), Penguin,

1964; *The Interpretation of the New Testament, 1861-1961* (Firth Lectures, 1962), Oxford University Press, 1964, reissued with corrections, 1966; *Outreach of the Church* ("Lift Up Your Hearts" series), BBC Publications, 1965; *Colonialism and Christian Missions,* McGraw, 1966; (editor with John Goodwin and Arthur Dowle) *Concise Dictionary of the Bible,* two volumes, Lutterworth, 1966; (editor with Goodwin and Dowle) *The Modern Reader's Dictionary of the Bible,* Association Press, 1966; *Rome and the Ecumenical Movement* (Peter Ainslie Memorial Lecture, No. 18), Rhodes University, 1967; *The Church and Christian Union* (Bampton Lectures, 1964), Oxford University Press, 1968; *Ecumenism Light and Shade* (Gallagher Memorial Lectures, 1967), Ryerson, 1969; *One Increasing Purpose: Lenten Meditations,* Bible Reading Fellowship, 1969; *Bible Words and Christian Meanings,* S.P.C.K., 1970; *Call to Mission,* Fortress, 1970; *The Story of the Christian Church in India and Pakistan,* Eerdmans, 1970; *What We Know About Jesus,* Lutterworth, 1970, Eerdmans, 1972; (editor with Goodwin and Gerald Anderson) *Concise Dictionary of the Christian World Mission,* Lutterworth, 1971.

Also author of *Report of a Survey of Theological Education in East and West Africa, with Special Reference to the Training of the Ordained Ministry,* International Missionary Council, 1950-54. Editor of chapters and author of commentaries for various editions of the New Testament, including I Corinthians and I and II Thessalonians. Member of editorial board, World Christian Books, Lutterworth, 1954—.

SIDELIGHTS: Neill told *CA* that he, "when young, liked writing and disliked preaching, then had much preaching and little time for writing; now when old, like preaching and dislike writing, have little preaching to do and endless writing." A world leader on the ecumenical movement, Bishop Neill has "given a large part of his life to campaigning for reunion," as a reviewer for *Times Literary Supplement* noted. He speaks and preaches fluently in French, German, and Tamil, less readily in Spanish and Italian, and can read most western European languages. He has been around the world twice, preaching on all continents.

BIOGRAPHICAL/CRITICAL SOURCES: Library Journal, February 1, 1959; *Times Literary Supplement,* February 5, 1960, June 11, 1964, June 27, 1968; *Saturday Review,* April 21, 1962; *Journal of Religion,* October, 1962; *Christian Century,* February 8, 1967, May 10, 1967; *Commonweal,* February 17, 1967; *Political Science Quarterly,* September, 1967.

*   *   *

NELSON, J(ohn) Robert 1920-

PERSONAL: Born August 21, 1920, in Winona Lake, Ind.; son of William John (a businessman) and Agnes D. (Soderborg) Nelson; married Dorothy Patricia Mercer (a health educator), August 18, 1945; children: Eric Mercer, William John. *Education:* DePauw University, A.B., 1941; Yale University, B.D., 1944; University of Zurich, D.Theol., 1951. *Politics:* Democrat. *Home:* 480 Jamaicaway, Boston, Mass. 02130. *Office:* 745 Commonwealth Ave., Boston, Mass. 02215.

CAREER: Ordained minister in Methodist Church, 1944; Wesley Foundation, director at Chapel Hill, N.C., 1946-48, associate director in Urbana, Ill., 1950-51; United Student Christian Council, New York, N.Y., study secretary, 1951-53; World Council of Churches, Commission on Faith and Order, Geneva, Switzerland, executive secretary, 1953-57; Vanderbilt University, Nashville, Tenn., professor of theology and dean of Divinity School, 1957-60; Princeton Theological Seminary, Princeton, N.J., visiting professor of ecumenics, 1960-61; United Theological

College and Leonard Theological College, India, visiting professor of theology, 1961-62; Oberlin College, Graduate School of Theology, Oberlin, Ohio, Fairchild Professor of Theology, 1962-65; Boston University, School of Theology, Boston, Mass., professor of systematic theology, 1965—. Member of Commission on Faith and Order, National Council of Churches, 1959—; chairman of Commission on Faith and Order, World Council of Churches, 1967—. Visiting professor, Pontifical Gregorian University, Rome, Italy. Southern Methodist University, Peyton Lecturer, 1961. Delegate to church conferences in India, 1961, Canada, 1963, Sweden, 1968; lecturer on Christian unity in thirty-two countries. *Military service:* U.S. Naval Reserve, chaplain, 1944-46; served with Marines on Guam, and in Japan and China; became lieutenant.

MEMBER: American Theological Society, American Academy of Arts and Sciences (fellow), Societe Europeenne de Culture, North American Academy of Ecumenists (president), Phi Beta Kappa, Beta Theta Pi. *Awards, honors:* LL.D., Wilberforce University, 1954; L.H.D., De Pauw University, 1960; D.D., Ohio Wesleyan University 1964; D.H.L., Loyola University, 1969.

WRITINGS: The Realm of Redemption: Studies in the Doctrine of the Nature of the Church in Contemporary Protestant Theology, Epworth, 1951, 4th edition, 1957; (editor) *The Christian Student and the Church,* Association Press, 1952; (editor) *The Christian Student and the University,* Association Press, 1952; (editor) *The Christian Student and the World Struggle,* Association Press, 1952; (editor) *Christian Unity in North America* (symposium), Bethany Press, 1958; *A Theology to Match the Church's Opportunity,* Vanderbilt University Press, 1958; *One Lord, One Church,* Association Press, 1958, revised edition published as *Overcoming Christian Divisions,* 1962; *Criterion for the Church,* Abingdon, 1963; (with John E. Skoglund) *Fifty Years of Faith and Order: An Interpretation of the Faith and Order Movement in Contemporary Protestantism,* Committee for Inter-Seminary Movement of National Student Christian Federation, 1963; *Let Us Pray for Unity,* Upper Room (Nashville), 1963; *Crisis in Unity and Witness,* Westminster Press, 1968; *Church Union in Focus: Guide for Adult Group Study,* United Church Press, 1968; (editor) *No Man is Alien,* E.J. Brill, 1971.

Contributor: Marvin Halverson and Arthur A. Cohen, editors, *Handbook of Christian Theology: Definition Essays on Concepts and Movements of Thought,* Meridian, 1958; Robert McAfee Brown and David H. Scott, editors, *Challenge to Reunion,* McGraw, 1963. Contributor of articles to journals. Editor-at-large, *Christian Century;* contributing editor, *Engage.*

WORK IN PROGRESS: Writing on medical ethics: science and theology; story of modern Christian unity movement.

SIDELIGHTS: One Lord, One Church has been translated into five languages. Nelson speaks German, Italian, and French, and has traveled in forty-four countries. In 1968 he was the first non-Catholic to teach at Pontifical Gregorian University in Rome.

* * *

NELSON, James G(raham) 1929-

PERSONAL: Born December 20, 1929, in Covington, Ky.; son of Robert Elgin and Bess (Jones) Nelson. *Education:* University of Kentucky, B.A., 1952; Columbia University, M.A., 1955, Ph.D., 1961. *Home:* One Horseshoe Bend, Madison, Wis. 53705. *Office:* 6195 Helen White Hall, University of Wisconsin, Madison, Wis. 53706.

CAREER: Columbia University, New York, N.Y., lecturer in English, 1958-61; University of Wisconsin,

Madison, instructor, 1961-62, assistant professor, 1963-64, associate professor, 1964-69, professor of English, 1969—. *Military service:* U.S. Air Force, 1952-54; became captain. *Member:* Modern Language Association of America, Milton Society of America. *Awards, honors:* Guggenheim fellow, 1965-66.

WRITINGS: The Sublime Puritan: Milton and the Victorians, University of Wisconsin Press, 1963; *Sir William Watson,* Twayne, 1966; *The Early Nineties: A View from the Bodley Head,* Harvard University Press, 1971. Member of editorial board and contributor, *Victorian Poetry.*

WORK IN PROGRESS: "Milton and the Nineteenth Century," for *The Milton Encyclopedia,* to be published by University of Wisconsin Press; a study, *Poetic Theory and Practice in England: 1865-1900.*

* * *

NELSON, Marion Harvey 1925-

PERSONAL: Born November 1, 1925, in Shreveport, La.; son of Robert Hood (in insurance) and Ina Lee (Crawford) Nelson; married Mary Louise Tremain, February 8, 1948 (divorced, 1966); married Ann Schukar, February 24, 1968; children: (first marriage) Marianne, Mark T., Paul T., John A. *Education:* Centenary College, premedical student, three years; Tulane University, M.D., 1951; Dallas Theological Seminary, additional study, two years. *Religion:* Protestant. *Home:* 8218 Park Lane #202, Dallas, Tex. 75231.

CAREER: General practice of medicine in Brookville, Ohio, 1951-55, in Dallas, Tex., 1955-59; psychiatric training at Austin State Hospital, Austin, Tex., 1960, and Parkland Memorial Hospital, Dallas, Tex., 1961-62; practice of psychiatry in Dallas, Tex., 1963-67; Waco Veterans Administration Hospital, Waco, Tex., staff psychiatrist, 1967-71. Consulting psychiatrist for Gainesville State Reform School for Girls, Gainesville, Tex. *Military service:* U.S. Army Air Forces, 1944-45. *Member:* American Psychiatric Association, American Medical Association, Christian Medical Society, Texas Medical Association, Dallas County Medical Society, Dallas Neuropsychiatric Society.

WRITINGS: Why Christians Crack Up: The Causes of and Remedies for Nervous Trouble in Christians, Moody, 1960, revised edition, 1967; *How to Know God's Will,* Moody, 1963.

AVOCATIONAL INTERESTS: Study of Greek New Testament; playing the guitar.

* * *

NEMMERS, Erwin Esser 1916-

PERSONAL: Born October 6, 1916, in Milwaukee, Wis.; son of Erwin Plein (an attorney) and Mechthild (Esser) Nemmers. *Education:* Marquette University, A.B., 1938; University of Chicago, A.M., 1939; Harvard University, LL.B., 1941; University of Wisconsin, Ph.D., 1953, S.J.D., 1956. *Religion:* Catholic. *Home:* 710 North Lake Shore Dr., Chicago, Ill. 60611. *Office:* Northwestern University, 339 East Chicago Ave., Chicago, Ill. 60611.

CAREER: Admitted to bar of Wisconsin, 1941, of Illinois, 1961, of U.S. Supreme Court, 1962; associate of Miller, Mack & Fairchild, 1942; special attorney for Wisconsin Telephone Co. and Ladish Co., 1946-47; Marquette University, Milwaukee, Wis., assistant professor of economics, 1946-52; University of Wisconsin, Madison, lecturer in economics, 1952-56; Milton College, Milton, Wis., associate professor of economics, 1956-57; Northwestern University, Evanston, Ill., professor of business administration, 1957—. Certified public accountant in Wisconsin, 1951. M.L. Nemmers Publishing Co., Milwaukee, Wis., partner, 1942—; RTE Corp., Waukesha, Wis., general counsel, 1947—; U.S. Controls Corp., Milwaukee, Wis., secretary, director, and general counsel, 1969—. Consultant, W.A. Sheaffer Pen Co., Bliss & Laughlin Industries, Peoples Gas, Light & Coke Co., Investors Diversified Services, Inc., Cummins Engine Co., International Minerals & Chemical Co., Utility Equipment Co. *Military service:* U.S. Army Air Forces, 1942-45.

MEMBER: American Economic Association, American Finance Association, Beta Gamma Sigma, Alpha Kappa Psi.

WRITINGS: Breviloquium of Bonaventure, Herder, 1946; *Twenty Centuries of Catholic Church Music,* Bruce, 1949; *Hobson and Underconsumption,* Kelley & Millmann, 1956; (with Cornelius C. Janzen) *Dictionary of Economics and Business,* Littlefield, 1959, revised edition, 1966; *Managerial Economics: Text and Cases,* Wiley, 1962; *Cases in Finance,* Allyn & Bacon, 1964; (with John H. Myers) *Business Research: Text and Cases,* McGraw, 1966; (with Adolph E. Grunewald) *Basic Managerial Finance,* Holt, 1970.

WORK IN PROGRESS: A book, *Steel Job Shop Simulation.*

* * *

NETTIS, Joseph   1928-

PERSONAL: Born September 6, 1928, in Philadelphia, Pa.; son of Morris Abraham and Nellie (Clusman) Nettis; married Betty Seidel (a photographer); children: Lynne, Milton, Jennifer. *Education:* University of Pennsylvania, student, 1947; Philadelphia Museum College of Art, diploma, 1953. *Politics:* Democrat. *Home and office:* 2305 Green St., Philadelphia, Pa. 19130.

CAREER: Free-lance photographer and writer in Philadelphia, Pa., 1953—. *Member:* American Society of Magazine Photographers. *Awards, honors:* Art Directors Award.

WRITINGS—All self-illustrated photo books: *A Spanish Summer,* Ziff-Davis Publishing Co., 1960; *Man and His Religions,* United Church Press, 1963; *Philadelphia Discovered,* Greater Philadelphia Magazine, 1964; *Traveling with Your Camera: Creative 35 mm. Photography,* Chilton, 1965.

SIDELIGHTS: Nettis has pursued his interest in people and how they live in Japan, India, Egypt, Israel, Russia, and in the countries of Europe. He has exhibited his photographs at the Philadelphia Museum of Art. His future plans include work in motion pictures.

* * *

NEUBAUER, William Arthur   1916-
(William Arthur, Christine Bennett, Norman Bligh, Ralph Carter, Joan Garrison, Jan Hathaway, Rebecca Marsh, Norma Newcomb, Gordon Semple)

PERSONAL: Born April 1, 1916, in Maspeth, N.Y.; son of Joseph A. and Madeline (Mulhern) Neubauer; married Elice Popham, 1949. *Home:* Route 1, Box 187, Boulder Creek, Calif.

CAREER: Professional writer, primarily of romantic novels for adults and teen-agers, 1935—. U.S. Naval Missile Center, Point Magu, Calif., technical editor, 1956-59; other technical editing as free lance. *Member:* Redwood Garden Club (president, 1962-64).

WRITINGS—All published by Arcadia, except as indicated: *Heart and Soul,* Gramercy, 1945; *The Nice Long Vacation,* 1949; *A Heart to Serve,* 1950; *The Spring Returns,* 1950; *The City of Gold,* 1951; *Watch for Romance,* 1951; *The Voice of Love,* 1952; *Beneath These Trees,* 1953; *Cabin in the Redwoods,* 1953; *Where Love Dwells,* 1953; *Dream's End,* 1954; *A Man to Marry,* 1954; *Sweet Summer Love,* 1954; *Angel Mountain,* 1955; *The City Sparrow,* 1955; *The Loyal Heart,* 1955; *Doorway to Dreams,* 1956; *The Impetuous Heart,* 1956; *Day to Love,* 1957; *Nurse March,* 1957; *Be Welcome Love,* 1958; *When the Heart Chooses,* 1958; *Assignment: Romance,* 1959; *Love Remains,* 1959; *Blue Waters,* 1960; *Old Covered Bridge,* 1960; *Duel of Hearts,* 1961; *River Song,* 1961; *Beckoning Star,* 1962; *Sweetheart of the Air,* 1963; *Wing of the Blue Air,* 1963; *Police Nurse,* 1964; *The Trouble in Ward J,* 1964; *The Golden Heel,* 1965; *The High Country Dreamer,* 1965; *The Roses of Goose Bay,* 1965; *Love Came Along,* 1966; *This Darkling Love,* 1966; *Girl of Big Mountain,* 1967; *Summer on the Shore,* 1967.

Under pseudonym William Arthur—All published by Phoenix: *She Didn't Care,* 1944; *Convention Girl,* 1945; *Landlady,* 1945; *Love Business,* 1946; *Marriage Later,* 1946; *Lesson in Passion,* 1947; *Burlesque Girl,* 1948; *Redhead,* 1948; *Sinner Take All,* 1948; *Naughty Mary,* 1950.

Under pseudonym Christine Bennett—All published by Arcadia: *Wind in the Sage,* 1962; *Gloria's Ghost,* 1963; *Girl of Black Island,* 1964.

Under pseudonym Ralph Carter—All published by Phoenix: *Ask for Sally,* 1944; *Strictly a Wolf,* 1944; *Blond Venus,* 1945; *Scandalous,* 1945; *A Little Sin,* 1946; *The Shadows of Lust,* 1946; *Night Club Lady,* 1947; *Profane,* 1947; *Quick to Passion,* 1948; *Anybody's Girl,* 1949; *The Quiet Passion,* 1949; *Stand-in for Passion,* 1950.

Under pseudonym Joan Garrison—All published by Arcadia, except as indicated: *A Star to Hold,* Gramercy, 1944; *Dear Nurse,* Gramercy, 1945; *Cinderella Girl,* Gramercy, 1945; *It Was Only a Dream,* Gramercy, 1945; *Wait for Love,* Gramercy, 1945; *Lady Mary,* Gramercy, 1946; *The Old Sweet Song,* Gramercy, 1947; *When the Moon Laughs,* Gramercy, 1948; *Sparkling Windows,* 1948; *Dear Cathy,* 1949; *Portrait in Pastels,* 1950; *The Worthy Heart,* 1953; *Nurse Greer,* 1954; *Mary's Garden,* 1955; *But Love Wants All,* 1955; *Cry of the Wild Goose,* 1955; *Harvest Time,* 1956; *The Library of Love,* 1956; *This Remembered Glory,* 1956; *This Way for Love,* 1957; *Golden Summer,* 1959; *Beyond the Hills,* 1960; *Come Walk with Love,* 1960; *The Heart Knows Best,* 1960; *Magic Web,* 1961; *Brave the Wild Sea,* 1961; *The Loving Heart,* 1962; *This Valued Heart,* 1962; *Ticket to Romance,* 1962; *Blue Herons,* 1963; *The Dream Seeker,* 1963; *Abby Found Him,* 1964; *Snatch a Dream,* 1964; *The Castle on the Lake,* 1965; *Salute to Glory,* 1965; *This Side of Illusion,* 1965; *A Love Named Dan,* 1966; *Rehabilitation Nurse,* 1966; *Love's Sweet Confusion,* 1967; *Run, Heart, Run,* 1967.

Under pseudonym Jan Hathaway—All published by Arcadia: *Junior Nurse,* 1962; *Treasure of the Redwoods,* 1962; *The Coming of Eagles,* 1963; *The Key of Gold,* 1963; *Robynn's Way,* 1963.

Under pseudonym Rebecca Marsh—All published by Arcadia, except as indicated: *Forever After,* Gramercy, 1946; *Girl of My Dreams,* 1947; *Hearts on Holiday,* Gramercy, 1947; *Older Sister,* Gramercy, 1947; *Portrait of Dorothy,* 1948; *The Road Leads Home,* 1948; *The Wind Blows Fair,* Gramercy, 1948; *Sweet Alice,* 1949; *Twilight Star,* 1951; *The Way of a Heart,* 1951; *A Home for Mary,* 1952; *Assistant Angel,* 1954; *The Girl for Him,* 1954; *Summer in Vermont,* 1955; *The Willow Tree,* 1955; *But Love Remains,* 1956; *Girl in Love,* 1956; *Hill Top House,* 1956; *When Love Wakes,* 1959; *Always in Her Heart,* 1960; *Lady Detective,* 1960; *Tiger in her Heart,* 1960; *Library Lady,* 1961; *Maverick Heart,* 1961; *The Walks of Dreams,* 1961; *Nurse Annette,* 1962; *Nurse of Ward B,* 1963; *Remembered Heritage,* 1963; *Some-*

body's Sweetheart, 1964; Nurse Anne's Emergency, 1965; Prelude to Glory, 1965; The Quiet Corner, 1965; Recovery Room Nurse, 1965; Footsteps to Romance, 1966; Million Dollar Nurse, 1966; Redwood Valley Romance, 1967; Trial by Love, 1968.

Under pseudonym Norma Newcomb—All published by Arcadia, except as indicated: An Angel in Love, Gramercy, 1944; A Girl from the Eastern Shore, Gramercy, 1944; A Small Town Girl, Gramercy, 1945; Your Stewardess, Gramercy, 1945; Home is the Heart, Gramercy, 1946; Maybe It's Love, Phoenix, 1946; The Wonderful Summer, Gramercy, 1946; The Heart Story, Gramercy, 1947; The Man That I Marry, Gramercy, 1947; Castle of Dreams, 1948; Doctor's Assistant, 1948; His Good Angel, Gramercy, 1948; Ever to Love, 1949; Princess of Moonlight, 1949; Always a Sister, 1950; A Heart for Elaine, 1952; The Bells of Love, 1953; The Stars of Love, 1953; The Heart Knows Why, 1954; Doctor Charlton, 1955; The Wise Heart, 1955; Brownstone Angel, 1956; The Problem Heart, 1956; Roses are for Love, 1958; Design by Joan, 1959; Dr. Jayne's Escapist Daughter, Foulsham, 1959; Bright Stars of Wyoming, 1960; Love Comes Riding, 1960; Angel of the Hills, 1961; Memo to a Heart, 1961; The Questing Heart, 1962; A Singing Heart, 1962; A Bend in the River, 1963; Eve's Hour, 1963; Forest Creek, 1963; The Green Bench, 1964; The Large Land, 1964; The Girl and the Eagle, 1965; Sparkles in the Water, 1965; This Love to Hold, 1966; The Jade Shamrock, 1967; A Nurse to Marry, 1967.

Under pseudonym Gordon Semple—All published by Phoenix: Nice and Naughty, 1944; Bad Company, 1945; Cue for Passion, 1945; The Way of Passion, 1946; Price of Passion, 1947; Time Lover, 1949; Time for Passion, 1950; Sensuous, 1950.

Ghostwriter of books for doctors and missionaries, and of articles in medical and engineering journals. Editor, Thomas H. Forde, The Principles and Practice of Oral Dynamics dental textbook), 1964.

SIDELIGHTS: Neubauer draws on his own life for background when his light romances concern nurses and hospitals. He grew up in a hospital for crippled children, had thirty operations in the process. Sold his first book at nineteen; has averaged about fourteen books a year for a number of years, many of them reprinted in paperbacks. Avocational interests: Gardening, mathematics, chess.†

* * *

NEUSTADT, Richard Elliott 1919-

PERSONAL: Born June 26, 1919, in New York, N.Y.; son of Richard Mitchells and Elizabeth (Neufeld) Neustadt; married Bertha Frances Cummings, December 21, 1945; children: Richard Mitchells, Elizabeth Ann. Education: University of California, Berkeley, A.B., 1939; Harvard University, M.A., 1941, Ph.D., 1951. Politics: Democrat. Home: 10 Traill St., Cambridge, Mass. 02138. Office: Harvard University, Cambridge, Mass. 02138.

CAREER: U.S. Office of Price Administration, Washington, D.C., assistant economist, 1942; U.S. Bureau of the Budget, Washington, D.C., assistant to the director, 1946-49; special assistant in the White House, 1950-53; Cornell University, Ithaca, N.Y., assistant professor of public administration, 1953-54; Columbia University, New York, N.Y., 1954-64, began as associate professor, became professor of government, and head of department; Harvard University, Cambridge, Mass., associated dean of John Fitzgerald Kennedy School of Government, 1965—, director, Institute of Politics, 1966—. Visiting professor at Princeton University, 1957; Nuffield College, Oxford University, visiting scholar, 1960-61, associate

member, 1965—. Member of the advisory board, Commission on Money and Credit, 1960-61; consultant to the President, 1961-66, and to the director of the Bureau of the Budget, 1961-70, to the Office of the Secretary of State and to the Senate Subcommittee on National Security Staffing and Operations, 1962—, to the Atomic Energy Commission, 1962-68, to Rand Corp., 1964—. Military service: U.S. Naval Reserve, 1942-46; became lieutenant s.g. Member: American Academy of Arts and Sciences (fellow), Council on Foreign Relations, Institute of Strategic Studies, American Philosophical Society, American Political Science Association, American Association of University professors, National Capital Democratic Club, Cosmos Club (Washington), Harvard Club (New York). Awards, honors: Woodrow Wilson Foundation Award of American Political Science Association, 1961.

WRITINGS: Presidential Power, Wiley, 1960, reissued with an afterword on J.F.K., 1968; The Presidency and Legislation: The Growth of Central Clearance (originally published in American Political Science Review, September, 1954), Bobbs-Merrill, 1962; (contributor) The Secretary of State and the Ambassador, Praeger, 1964; (contributor) David B. Truman, editor, The Congress and America's Future, Prentice-Hall, 1965; Alliance Politics, Columbia University Press, 1970; (co-author of afterword) Robert F. Kennedy, Thirteen Days: A Memoir of the Cuban Missile Crisis, Norton, 1971. Contributor to U.S. News and World Report, Reporter, Law and Contemporary Problems, and other journals.

BIOGRAPHICAL/CRITICAL SOURCES: New York Times, May 24, 1970; Library Journal, July, 1970.†

* * *

NEWELL, Gordon 1913-

PERSONAL: Born January 31, 1913, in Olympia, Wash.; son of Roy Edward (a general contractor) and Eugenia C. (Story) Newell; married Bonita H. Murray, October 13, 1941; children: Judith Lynn, Jacqueline. Education: St. Martin's College, Olympia, Wash., student, 1932-34; Central Washington State College, teaching certificate, 1935; University of Washington, Seattle, student, 1937. Politics: Democrat. Religion: Protestant. Address: Route 3, Box 361-A, Olympia, Wash. 98206.

CAREER: Washington State public schools, teacher, coach, and principal, 1935-40; Washington State Highway Department Patrol, Public relations director, 1946-51; Seattle (Wash.) Department of Parks, assistant superintendent and public relations director, 1953-59; free-lance writer, 1959—. Commissioner, Port of Seattle, 1960-63. Military service: U.S. Army, 1940-46, 1951-53; became captain; received Bronze Star, Army Commendation, five battle stars. Member: Puget Sound Maritime Press Association, Puget Sound Maritime Historical Society. Awards, honors: Seattle Historical Society Award of Merit for Northwest Literature, for S.O.S. North Pacific.

WRITINGS: Ships of the Inland Sea, Binfords, 1951; S.O.S. North Pacific, Binfords, 1955; Who's Who at the Zoo: A Guide to the Zoological Gardens, Superior, 1956; Totem Tales of Old Seattle, Superior, 1956; Pacific Tugboats, Superior, 1957; Pacific Steamboats, Bonanza, 1958; Pacific Coastal Liners, Superior, 1959; (with Joe Williamson) Pacific Lumber Ships, Bonanza, c.1960; Paddlewheel Pirate, Dutton, 1960; Ocean Liners of the 20th Century, Superior, 1963; (editor) The H.W. McCurdy Marine History of the Pacific Northwest, Superior, 1966; (with H.W. McCurdy) Don't Leave Any Holidays, pirvately printed, c.1967; The Green Years: The Development of Transportation, Trade, and Finance in the Puget Sound

Region from 1886 to 1969 as Recalled by Joshua Green,
Superior, c.1969; (with Allan E. Smith) *Mighty Mo, the
U.S.S. Missouri: A Biography of the Last Battleship,* Su-
perior, 1969; *Sea Rogues' Gallery,* Superior, 1971. Con-
tributor to *True, Blue Book, Adventure, Ships and the
Sea, Skipper.*

SIDELIGHTS: Newell's writing headquarters is a sev-
enty-foot tugboat permanently moored at his home on
Puget Sound.

*   *   *

NEWHALL, Beaumont   1908-

PERSONAL: Born June 23, 1908, in Lynn, Mass.; son of
Herbert William (a physician) and Alice Lilia (Davis)
Newhall; married Nancy Wynne Parker (now a writer).
Education: Harvard University, A.B., 1930, A.M., 1931;
postgraduate study at Institut d'Art et d'Archeologie, Uni-
versity of Paris, 1933, and Courtauld Institute of Art,
University of London, 1934. *Office:* Department of Art,
University of New Mexico, Albuquerque, N.M. 87106.

CAREER: Philadelphia Art Museum, Philadelphia, Pa.,
lecturer, 1931-32; Metropolitan Museum of Art, New
York, N.Y., assistant, department of decorative arts,
1932-33; Museum of Modern Art, New York, N.Y., librarian, 1935-42, curator of photography, 1940-42, 1945-
46; George Eastman House, Rochester, N.Y., curator,
1948-58, director, 1958-71, trustee, 1962—. Lecturer at
Black Mountain College, 1946, 1947, 1948, at University
of Rochester, 1954-55, at Rochester Institute of Technology, 1956-68, and at Salzburg Seminar in American
Studies, Salzburg, Austria, 1958, 1959; visiting professor
of art, State University of New York at Buffalo, 1969-71,
University of New Mexico, 1971—. Rochester Civic Music Association, director, 1962-71. *Military service:* U.S.
Army Air Forces, 1942-45; became major. *Member:*
Royal Photographic Society of Great Britain (honorary
fellow), Professional Photographers of America (honorary master of photography), Deutsche Gesellschaft fuer
Photographie (honorary). *Awards, honors:* Guggenheim
fellow, 1947; Progress Medal, Photographic Society of
America; Kulturpreis, Deutsche Gesellschaft fuer Photo-
grahie, 1970.

WRITINGS: *Photography: A Short Critical History*
(originally written as illustrated catalog of an exhibition,
"Photography, 1839-1937"), published for Museum of
Modern Art (New York) by Spiral Press, 1938, revised
edition published as *The History of Photography, from
1839 to the Present Day,* Museum of Modern Art, 1949,
4th edition, revised and enlarged, 1964; (contributor)
Herbert Bayer, Walter Gropius, and Ilse Gropius, editors,
Bauhaus, 1919-1928, Museum of Modern Art, 1938; (editor) *On Photography: A Source Book of Photo History
in Facsimile,* Century House, 1956; (editor and author of
introduction with wife, Nancy Newhall) *Masters of Photography,* Braziller, 1958; *The Daguerreotype in America,*
Duell, 1961, revised edition, New York Graphic Society,
1968; (author of introduction) *Photographs* (by Henri
Cartier-Bresson), J. Cape, 1963; *Frederick H. Evans,*
Eastman House, 1964; (with Nancy Newhall) *T.H.
O'Sullivan, Photographer: With an Appreciation by Ansel
Adams,* Eastman House, 1966; *Latent Image: The Dis-
covery of Photography,* Doubleday, 1967; (editor) *Doro-
thea Lange Looks at the American Country Woman,*
Ritchie, 1968; *Airborne Camera: The World from the
Air and Outer Space,* Hastings House, 1969.

WORK IN PROGRESS: *Photo Eye of the 20's,* for the
Museum of Modern Art.

AVOCATIONAL INTERESTS: Gastronomy—historical,
theoretical, and practical.

NEWMAN, Jacob   1914-

PERSONAL: Born July 29, 1914, in Bratislava,
Czechoslovakia; son of William (a businessman) and
Nettie (Bick) Newman; married Zelda Myburg, 1952;
children: Nahum, Avron, Gabriel, Hillel. *Education:* Ye-
shiva College of Bratislava, B.D., 1936; University of
Manchester, M.A., 1945; University of Pretoria, D.Litt.,
1953. *Home:* 10 Oliver Rd., Sea Point, Cape Town,
South Africa.

CAREER: Rabbi. Minister of religion, Petrzalka,
Czechoslovakia, 1936-39, Cumberland/West Moreland,
England, 1939-42; educational welfare officer, Manchester, England, 1942-45; University of Liverpool, Liverpool,
England, researcher and lecturer in juvenile delinquency,
1945-46; rabbi in East Croydon, England, 1947-51; national rabbi in Republic of South Africa, 1951-57; rabbi
in Johannesburg, Republic of South Africa, 1957-70; University of Pretoria, Pretoria, Republic of South Africa,
professor of post-biblical Jewish literature, 1958-70;
rabbi, Green and Sea Point Hebrew Congregations, Cape
Town, Republic of South Africa, 1970—; University of
Cape Town, Cape Town, legation lecturer in religious
studies, 1970—. Ministers' Training College, Johannesburg, Republic of South Africa, director, 1962—. Governor of Midrashic Research Committee, 1945-48, of Jewish
Studies Fund, 1959—. *Member:* South African Ministers
Association (chairman, 1956-60; vice-president, 1962-63;
president, 1963-70).

WRITINGS: *Semikhah* (Ordination), Manchester Uni-
versity Press, 1950; *With Ink in the Book* (short stories),
L. Rubin, 1955; *Speak Unto the Children of Israel: Sermons for Every Sabbath and Festival of the Year for
Jewish Children,* Bloch Publishing, 1955; *A Guide to
Judaism for the Young,* South African Ministers' Associa-
tion, 1956; *Judaism in the Home,* South African Minis-
ters' Association, 1957; (editor and translator) Moses ben
Nahman, *The Commentary of Nahmanides on Genesis,
Chapters 1-6,* E.J. Brill, 1960; *The Eternal Quest: Ser-
mons for High Holy Days, Festivals and Special Sab-
baths,* Bloch Publishing, 1965; *Towards Light,* Jewish
Publication Committee, 1968; *Halachic Sources, from the
Beginning to the Ninth Century,* E.J. Brill, 1969; *Ma'yan
Ya'akov,* Mass Jerusalem, 1971. Editor, with I. Goss, of
Lessons in Jewish Heritage and *Lessons in Jewish His-
tory,* 1955. Contributor of articles to periodicals in South
Africa and abroad.

SIDELIGHTS: Newman is competent in German, Hebrew, Hungarian, Slav, and Arabic languages, and has
lectured in various countries throughout the world.

*   *   *

NEWMAN, L(eonard) Hugh   1909-

PERSONAL: Born February 3, 1909, in Bexley, Kent,
England; son of Leonard Woods (a lepidopterist) and
Amy Blanche (Greenwood) Newman; married Moira
Angela Hjordis Savonius (a horticultural journalist and
broadcaster), January 6, 1938; children: Marjatta April
Gillian, Leonard Perran Vincent, Brian Philip Johannes.
Education: Educated in schools in England. *Politics:*
Right-wing Conservative. *Religion:* Church of England.
Residence: Betsoms, Westerham, Kent, England.

CAREER: Butterfly Farm Ltd., Bexley, Kent, England,
managing director, 1932-68; now markets color transparencies for wildlife photographers through Natural History
Photographic Agency. British Broadcasting Corp. program, "Nature Parliament," resident member, fourteen
years; Natural History Photographic Agency, The
Studios, Betsoms, Westerham, Kent, England, owner and
director, 1959-69. Consultant on films. Royal Horticultural Society of London (fellow).

WRITINGS: *Wings in the Sun,* E.J. Arnold, 1939; *Talking of Butterflies, Moths, and Other Fascinating Insects,* Littlebury, 1946; *Butterfly Haunts,* Chapman & Hall, 1948; *British Moths and Their Haunts* (Country Book Club selection), Edmund Ward, 1949; *Butterflies on the Wing,* Edmund Ward, 1949; (with Walter J.C. Murray) *Stand and Stare,* Staples, 1950; *Moths on the Wing,* Edmund Ward, 1950; (contributor) Charles J. Kaberry, editor, *The Collector's Handbook,* Oxford University Press, 1951; *Linger and Look,* Staples, 1952; (with Murray) *Nature's Way: Questions and Answers on Animal Behaviour,* Country Life, 1952; *Transformations of Butterflies and Moths,* Ward, Lock, 1952; (with Peter Scott and James M.M. Fisher) *Nature Parliament: A Book of the Broadcasts by L.H. Newman, Peter Scott, and J. Fisher,* edited by Fisher, Dent, 1952; (with Eugene F. Linssen) *The Observer's Book of Common British Insects and Spiders* (includes sections on trichoptera and lepidoptera by Newman), Warne, 1953, revised edition, 1964; *How's Your Pet?,* Phoenix House, 1953, revised edition, Parrish, 1967; *Butterfly Farmer* (Scientific Book Club and Country Book Club selection), Phoenix House, 1953, revised and enlarged edition published as *Living with Butterflies,* J. Baker, 1967; *Garden and Woodland Butterflies,* Brockhampton Press, 1954; *Butterflies of the Fields and Lanes, Hills and Heathland,* Brockhampton Press, 1954; (with Murray) *Wander and Watch,* Staples, 1954; *The Fascinating World of Butterflies* (adapted from *Les Plus beaux papillons,* by Charles Ferdinand), Doubleday, 1958 (published in England as *Butterflies of Day and Night: A Book of Beautiful Butterflies and Magnificent Moths,* Rathbone, 1958); *Instructions to Young Naturalists,* Volume 2: *Insects,* Museum Press, 1958, Sportshelf, 1958; *Pets for Pleasure and Profit,* Museum Press, 1958, Sportshelf, 1958; *Looking at Butterflies,* Collins, 1959; (author of introduction) V.J. Stanek, *The World of Nature,* 2nd edition, Hamlyn, 1964; *Hawk-Moths of Great Britain and Europe,* Cassell, 1965; *Man and Insects* (Aldus edition, edited by Alec Lawrie), Aldus Books, 1965, published in *America as Man and Insects: Insect Allies and Enemies,* published for the American Museum of Natural History by Natural History Press, 1967; (with wife, Moira Savonius) *Create a Butterfly Garden,* J. Baker, 1967; *Ants from Close Up,* photographs by Stephen Dalton and others, Crowell, 1967; *The Complete British Butterflies in Colour,* illustrated by Ernest Mansell, M. Joseph, 1968. Contributor to (London) *Times* and other newspapers and periodicals.

WORK IN PROGRESS: *Handbook of British Butterflies,* for Collins.

SIDELIGHTS: Newman told *CA* he has "traveled extensively in Europe to study the habits, courtship, and migration of butterflies, particularly the species *Nymphalis antiopa,* known in the United States as the Mourning Cloak butterfly and in England as the Camberwell Beauty. I have bred this butterfly in captivity and released live specimens in several suitable country localities, but so far have been unsuccessful in establishing the species as a native butterfly to Great Britain. I discovered that the great majority of these butterflies seen in England do not fly across the North Sea or English Channel, but travel as stowaways on timber shipped in the holds of boats."

According to a reviewer for the *Times Literary Supplement,* at one time Newman, as a butterfly farmer, supplied living butterflies for the Festival of Britain and occasionally for the film industry.

AVOCATIONAL INTERESTS: Raising orchids and pelargoniums in greenhouses at his country house in Kent, photographing wild flowers in color; foreign travel.

BIOGRAPHICAL/CRITICAL SOURCES: *Christian Science Monitor,* May 4, 1967; *Times Literary Supplement,* July 27, 1967.

*   *   *

NEWMAN, Peter C(harles)   1929-

PERSONAL: Born May 10, 1929, in Vienna, Austria; moved to Canada, 1940, naturalized Canadian citizen 1945; son of Oskar and Wanda (Newman) Newman; married Christina McCall (a free-lance writer), October 27, 1959; children: Ashley (daughter). *Education:* University of Toronto, B.A., 1950, M.Com., 1953. *Home:* 26 Rachael, Toronto, Ontario, Canada. *Office:* 481 University Ave., Toronto 101, Ontario, Canada.

CAREER: *Financial Post,* Toronto, Ontario, assistant editor, 1953-57; *Maclean's Magazine,* Toronto, Ontario, assistant editor, 1957-59, Ottawa editor, 1959-63, national affairs editor, 1963-64; *Toronto Daily Star,* Toronto, Ontario, Ottawa editor, 1964-69, editor-in-chief, 1969-71; *Maclean's Magazine,* editor, 1971—. Visiting associate professor of political science, McMaster University, 1970—. *Military service:* Royal Canadian Navy; became lieutenant. *Member:* International Press Institute (deputy chairman for Canada, 1970-72), Canadian Authors Association, National Press Club (Canada), Rideau Club (Ottawa). *Awards, honors:* National Newspaper Award for feature writing, 1964; Wilderness Award, Canadian Broadcasting Assoc., 1967.

WRITINGS: *Flame of Power: Intimate Profiles of Canada's Greatest Businessmen,* Longmans, Green, 1960; *Renegade in Power: The Diefenbacker Years,* McClelland, 1963, Bobbs-Merrill, 1964; *The Distemper of Our Times: Canadian Politics in Transition, 1963-1968,* McClelland, 1968, published in America as *A Nation Divided: Canada and the Coming of Pierre Trudeau,* Knopf, 1969. Contributor of more than 500 articles on various aspects of Canadian politics and economics to magazines, newspapers, and journals.

WORK IN PROGRESS: A series of books on Canadian economic, social, and political problems.

BIOGRAPHICAL/CRITICAL SOURCES: *Saturday Night,* November, 1968; *Canadian Forum,* December, 1968; *Book World,* September 28, 1969; *New York Times Book Review,* November 23, 1969; *National Review,* March 10, 1970.

*   *   *

NEWSON, Elizabeth (Palmer)   1929-

PERSONAL: Born April 8, 1929, in London, England; daughter of Richard (an educator) and Mary (Davies) Palmer; married John Newson (a university teacher and researcher in psychology), July 5, 1951; children: Roger, Carey, Joanna. *Education:* Attended Clifton High School for Girls and Mary Datchelor School; University College, London, B.A. (with honors), 1951; University of Nottingham, Ph.D., 1955. *Home:* 36 Orston Dr., Wollaton Park, Nottingham, England. *Office:* Psychology Department, University of Nottingham, Nottingham, England.

CAREER: University of Nottingham, Nottingham, England, instructor and researcher in psychology department, 1951—. *Member:* British Psychological Society (associate member).

WRITINGS: *Discrimination of Line Figures in Pre-School Children,* University of Nottingham, 1955; (with husband, John Newson) *Infant Care in an Urban Community,* Allen & Unwin, 1963, reissued as *Patterns of Infant Care in an Urban Community,* Penguin, 1965; (with J. Newson) *Four Years Old in an Urban Community,* Aldine, 1968; (with Sheila Hewett) *The Family and the*

Handicapped Child, Aldine-Atherton, 1970. Contributor to professional journals.

WORK IN PROGRESS: Long-term research project on child-rearing methods in Britain; studies on design of toys for remediation of handicaps, and use of "toy libraries" for parent-child support with handicaps.

* * *

NEWSON, John 1925-

PERSONAL: Born December 10, 1925, in London, England; son of Frederick W. (a structural engineer) and Dorothy (Noyes) Newson; married Elizabeth Palmer (now a teacher and researcher in psychology), July 5, 1951; children: Roger, Carey, Joanna. *Education:* Attended Bancrofts School; South West Essex Technical College, B.Sc.; University College, London, B.Sc., 1951; University of Nottingham, Ph.D., 1956. *Home:* 36 Orston Dr., Wollaton Park, Nottingham, England. *Office:* Psychology Department, University of Nottingham, Nottingham, England.

CAREER: University of Nottingham, Nottingham, England, teaching and research in psychology department, 1951—. *Military service:* National Service; commissioned. *Member:* British Psychological Society (associate member).

WRITINGS: Lightness Constancy, University of Nottingham, 1956; (with wife, Elizabeth Newson) *Infant Care in an Urban Community,* Aldine, 1963, reissued as *Patterns of Infant Care in an Urban Community,* Penguin, 1965; (with E. Newson) *Four Years Old in an Urban Community,* Aldine, 1968; (with Sheila Hewett and E. Newson) *The Family and the Handicapped Child,* Allen & Unwin, 1970; (with Michael Matthews) *The Language of Basic Statistics,* Longmans, Green, 1971, International Publications Service, 1972. Contributor to psychology and medical journals.

WORK IN PROGRESS: Long-term research project on child-rearing methods in Britain; a book on eleven-year-olds and their relationships with their mothers, and on parents' moral and disciplinary attitudes; a book entitled *Play and Playthings for the Handicapped Child.*

SIDELIGHTS: Newson told *CA:* "The basis of our main research is the assumption that parents know more about their children than anyone else, and that this knowledge can be tapped by the use of appropriate techniques."

BIOGRAPHICAL/CRITICAL SOURCES: Nursery World, January 9, 1964.

* * *

NEWTON, Norman (Lewis) 1929-

PERSONAL: Born July 9, 1929, in Vancouver, British Columbia, Canada; son of Herbert Ernest and Florence (Middleditch) Newton; married Beryl Constable, November 17, 1962; children: Elizabeth Louise. *Education:* Mainly self-educated. *Politics:* No party affiliation. *Religion:* Church of the New Jerusalem (Swedenborgian). *Agent:* Christy & Moore Ltd., 52 Floral St., Covent Garden, London W.C.2, England.

CAREER: Worked as deck hand, laborer, actor, radio announcer, clerk, copywriter, ambulance dispatcher; Canadian Broadcasting Co., 1960—, currently radio producer (drama and music) in studios in Vancouver, British Columbia. Occasional director of stage plays. *Awards, honors:* Canada Foundation grant of $4,000, awarded on basis of work submitted, 1959.

WRITINGS: The House of Gods (novel), P. Owen, 1961; *The One True Man* (novel), P. Owen, 1963; *The*

Big Stuffed Hand of Friendship (novel), P. Owen, 1969; *Thomas Gage in Spanish America* (biography), Barnes & Noble, 1969; *Fire in the Raven's Nest,* Ingluvin Publications, 1972.

Three-act plays: "The Abdication," produced by Off-Broadway group; "The Deaths of Gardeners," produced at Poets Theatre, Cambridge, Mass.; "The Lion and the Unicorn," produced by University of Toronto Alumni Theatrical Group. Also author of a one-act play, "The Rehearsal." Author of other plays for Canadian Broadcasting Co., including a translation of Moliere's "Le Misanthrope." Contributor of criticism and verse to periodicals, including *Essays in Criticism, Listener, Lines, Contemporary Verse, Canadian Forum,* and *Canadian Literature.*

WORK IN PROGRESS: Verse; a novel.

SIDELIGHTS: Newton had these comments for *CA:* "Pleasures: family life, listening to old Indians telling stories and singing songs, sailing, walking by the sea. Chief fears: nuclear war, the Americanisation of Canada, the slow disappearance from daily life of emotional colour, virtue and a sense of the noble. Art I enjoy most: poetic drama; the poetry of Yeats, Roy Campbell and Keats; Tsimshian mythology; Purcell's 'The Faery Queen.' Random dislikes: in literature, those who confuse pornography with candour and formlessness with vigour; in music, the theory and practice of the twelve-tone composers; the psychoanalytical approach to mythology. Random enthusiasms: the philosophy of Ramon Llull; *The Book of Changes.* Chief unrealised ambition: to direct a season of Elizabethan and Jacobean plays. Major non-literary interest: music. Minor disappointment: discovering that I was not a very good actor."

BIOGRAPHICAL/CRITICAL SOURCES: Spectator, March 28, 1969.

* * *

NICHOLS, Jeannette Paddock

PERSONAL: Born in Rochelle, Ill.; daughter of Hosea Cornish Savery and Janette (Styles) Paddock; married Roy Franklin Nichols (now Dean of Graduate School and vice-provost of University of Pennsylvania), 1920. *Education:* Knox College, A.B., 1913, Columbia University, A.M., 1919, Ph.D., 1923. *Home:* The Fairfax, Apt. 811, Philadelphia, Pa. 19104. *Office:* History Department, 215 Duhring Wing, University of Pennsylvania, Philadelphia, Pa. 19104.

CAREER: Columbia University, New York, N.Y., extension division instructor in history, 1919-21; Wesleyan College, Macon, Ga., visiting professor, 1922-23; University of Pennsylvania, Philadelphia, research associate, 1950—, associate professor of history, 1957-61, chairman of graduate group in economic history, 1961-63. University of Birmingham, Birmingham, England, visiting lecturer, 1948. U.S. Treasury Department, consultant, 1945. Lecturer in Far East; International Federation of University Women, conductor of sessions on international relations in Toronto, Canada, 1947, Zurich, Switzerland, 1950, London, England, 1953. *Member:* American Historical Association, American Association of University Women, Middle States Council for Social Studies (president, 1956-57), Organization of American Historians, (council, 1950-53, editorial board, 1953-56), League of Women Voters, Phi Beta Kappa, Pi Gamma Mu, Phi Alpha Theta. *Awards, honors:* LL.D. from Knox College.

WRITINGS: Alaska: A History of Its Administration, Exploitation, and Industrial Development During Its First Half Century Under the Rule of the United States, Arthur H. Clark, 1924; (contributor) *Kull's History of New Jersey,* American Historical Society, 1930; *James Styles of Kingston, New York, and George Stuart of School-craft, Michigan: Their Descendants and Allied Families, with an Historical Narrative,* privately printed, 1936; (with husband, Roy F. Nichlos) *The Growth of American Democracy: Social, Economic, Political,* Appleton, 1939; (editor with James G. Randall) *Democracy in the Middle West, 1840-1940* (essays), Appleton, 1941; (with R.F. Nichols) *The Republic of the United States: A History,* Appleton, 1942; *Twentieth Century United States: A History,* Appleton, 1943; (with M. Wolf and A.C. Bining) *History in the High School and Social Studies in the Elementary School,* Middle States Council for Social Studies, 1944. Contributor to *Dictionary of American Biography.* Contributor of articles to scholarly journals in United States and Great Britain.

WORK IN PROGRESS: The Brothers Sherman; American Monetary Diplomacy.

SIDELIGHTS: Miss Paddock has traveled frequently in Europe, throughout North America, in North Africa, Hawaii, and the Far East, and around the world.

* * *

NICHOLS, John (Treadwell) 1940-

PERSONAL: Born July 23, 1940, in Berkeley, Calif.; son of David G. (a psycho-linguist) and Esther G. Nichols. *Education:* Hamilton College, B.A., 1962. *Home:* 438 West Broadway, New York, N.Y. 10012. *Agent:* Curtis-Brown Ltd., 575 Madison Ave., New York, N.Y., 10022.

CAREER: Has held various jobs, including that of blues singer in a Greenwich Village cafe, firefighter in Chiricuahua Mountains of Arizona, dishwasher in Hartford, Conn.; along with a friend, went into the humorous greeting card business, doing the drawing for "Jest-No" cards in 1962, "a total disaster," he says; after graduating from college, went to Barcelona, Spain, and spent three months teaching English in the American Institute; spent some time as a short order cook.

WRITINGS: The Sterile Cuckoo (novel), McKay, 1965; *The Wizard of Loneliness,* (novel), Putnam, 1966.

SIDELIGHTS: Nichols writes to *CA:* "I'm not a particularly great thinker; rather a looker, a describer, you might say. Ideas, both critical and creative, have turned me off up to now; too many of them are floating around nowadays being used right and left to build comfy little nests into which intellectual eggs can be neatly laid. I have a great horror of books that are vast, wordy, and often well written, that pretend to a serious artistic purpose, which, so far as I can see, is to annihilate communication. (Sort of like the last three sentences, maybe.) Nothing, however, really seems to torment me: I rage against just about everything in the world today from Religion to Politics to cutting off heads in Viet-Nam to painting such and such a colored stripe up Fifth Avenue for both the Irish and the Italians, to rich people and poor people, to automated egg laying (see above) and hoity-toity bridge players, but my rage always seems to be humorous, seldom biting, and very surface.... I worry about being a little too peaceful about life, but I don't complain. I once had a motorcycle, and the very first day I drove it (with a friend seated behind me) over a sidewalk at 40 miles per hour, then up and over a retaining wall, and we landed in a small park in the middle of a kid's sandbox which fortunately didn't have any kids in it. Neither I nor my friend nor my motorcycle received more than a minor scratch. See what I mean?"

Maggie Rennert, in a *Book Week* review of *The Wizard of Loneliness,* writes: "Mr. Nichols, whose first novel, *The Sterile Cuckoo,* written when he was 24, evoked much critical praise, is that reviewer's delight: the promising young beginner who makes good on it. Nothing of

the tyro, except perhaps his energy, marks this new book: it might have been written by a good novelist of any age who was skilled at transmuting what he has known into what can be known by others and who happened also to have a gift for comic invention and a sure feeling for the rhythm of event and discovery."

Nichols was once a fairly good athlete: a cross-country runner, a hockey player, and a low-hurdler, and co-captained the Hamilton College hockey team in his senior year. He now enjoys ice skating. He has lived in Spain (where he studied bullfighting), France, Mexico, and Guatemala; speaks Spanish and French "colorfully." *The Sterile Cuckoo* was filmed by Paramount in 1969; *The Wizard of Loneliness* has been sold to Tandem Productions for filming.

BIOGRAPHICAL/CRITICAL SOURCES: Book Week, January 24, 1965, February 20, 1966; *Saturday Review,* February 26, 1966; *Harper's,* March, 1966; *New York Times Book Review,* March 6, 1966.

* * *

NICHOLS, Sue

PERSONAL: Born in Birmingham, Ala.; daughter of Charles Martin (an engineer) and Lucile (Robinson) Nichols. *Education:* University of Pittsburgh, B.A., 1947; Biblical Seminary in New York (now called New York Theological Seminary), M.R.E., 1956. *Religion:* Presbyterian. *Home:* 219 Ridgefield Ct., Nashville, Tenn. 37205. *Office:* Presbyterian Board of World Missions, Box 330, Nashville, Tenn. 37202.

CAREER: Presbyterian Board of World Missions, Nashville, Tenn., associate in information services, 1966—. *Member:* Altrusa Club of Nashville.

WRITINGS: Words on Target: For Better Christian Communication, John Knox, 1963; (co-author) *The Church in Mission to a World in Crisis: Teacher's Text,* Covenant Life Curriculum, 1971.

* * *

NICHOLSON, Joyce Thorpe 1919-

PERSONAL: Born June 1, 1919, in Melbourne, Australia; daughter of Daniel Wrixon (a publisher) and Miriam (Schenk) Thorpe; married George Harvey Nicholson (a lawyer) May 7, 1943; children: Peter, Hilary (daughter), Wendy, Michael. *Education:* Attended Methodist Ladies' College; University of Melbourne, B.A., 1941. *Politics:* Liberal. *Religion:* Protestant. *Home:* 26 Fordholm Rd., Hawthorn, Melbourne, Australia.

CAREER: Writer. D.W. Thorpe Publishing Ltd., director. Executive display convenor, Children's Book Council, 1956-60. *Member:* Fellowship of Australian Writers, Victorian Women Graduates; P.E.N. and Lyceum Club (both Melbourne).

WRITINGS: How to Play Solo by "Ace High," Gordon & Gotch, 1947; *Adventure at Gulls' Point,* Epworth, 1955; (compiler) *Successful Parties and Social Evenings,* Epworth, 1956; (compiler) *Games, Competitions and Quizzes for Social Evenings and Parties,* Epworth, 1956; (compiler) *The Children's Party and Games Book,* Epworth, 1956; *Gulls' Point and Pineapple,* Epworth, 1957; *Our First Overlander,* Shakespeare Head Press, 1957; *Man Against Mutiny: The Story of Captain Bligh,* Lutterworth, 1961; *Kerri and Honey,* Angus & Robertson, 1963, Sportshelf, 1965; *Cranky, the Baby Australian Camel,* Angus & Robertson, 1963; *A Mortar-board for Priscilla* (novel), Children's Library Guild of Australia, 1963, Ginn, 1966; *Andy's Kangaroo,* Angus & Robertson, 1964; *Ringtail the Possum,* Lansdowne, 1965, Ginn, 1966; *Sir Charles and the Lyrebird,* Lansdowne, 1966; *Yap the*

Penguin, Lansdowne, 1967; *Woop the Wombat*, Lansdowne, 1968. Author of radio and television scripts. Australian books editor for *Ideas* (Australian booksellers' trade journal); editor; *Australian Books in Print*, D.W. Thorpe, 1970-71.

WORK IN PROGRESS Thesis for M.A. degree, with eventual publication as a book on social history of Australia in the nineteen twenties; *The Convict Girl*, a novel.

*   *   *

NICHOLSON, Norman (Cornthwaite) 1914-

PERSONAL: Born January 8, 1914, in Millom, Cumberland, England; son of Joseph (an outfitter) and Edith (Cornthwaite) Nicholson; married Yvonne Gardner (now a teacher), July 5, 1956. *Education:* Attended schools in Millom, Cumberland, England. *Religion:* Church of England. *Home:* 14 St. George's Ter., Millom, Cumberland, England. *Agent:* David Higham Associates Ltd., 5-8, Lower John St., Golden Square, London W.1 R-3PE, England.

CAREER: Author. Public lecturer and broadcaster on modern poetry, the English Lake District, and other subjects. *Member:* Royal Society of Literature, P.E.N. *Awards, honors:* Heinemann Prize, 1945, for *Five Rivers*, University of Manchester, 1959; Cholmondeley Award for Poetry, 1967.

WRITINGS: (Editor) *An Anthology of Religious Verse, Designed for the Times*, Penguin, 1942; (with John Hall and Keith Douglas) *Selected Poems*, Staples, 1943; *Man and Literature* (criticism), S.C.M. Press, 1943; *Five Rivers* (poetry), Faber, 1944, Dutton, 1945; *The Fire of the Lord* (novel), Nicholson & Watson, 1944, Dutton, 1946, *The Old Man of the Mountains* (three-act verse play; first produced Off-Broadway at Mercury Theatre, 1945), Faber, 1946, revised edition, Macmillan, 1950; *The Green Shore* (novel), Nicholson & Watson, 1947; *Rock Face* (poetry), Faber, 1948; *Cumberland and Westmorland*, R. Hale, 1949; (compiler and author of introduction) *Wordsworth: An Introduction and a Selection by Norman Nicholson*, Transatlantic, 1949; *H.G. Wells* (criticism), Arthur Barker, 1950, Alan Swallow, 1951; *Prophesy to the Wind* (verse play in four scenes and prologue), Faber, 1950, Macmillan, 1951; *William Cowper* (criticism), Lehmann, 1951; (compiler and author of introduction) William Cowper, *Poems*, Grey Walls Press, 1951; *The Pot Geranium* (poetry), Faber, 1954; *A Match for the Devil* (verse play in four scenes), Faber, 1955; *The Lakers: Adventures of the First Tourists*, R. Hale, 1955, Dufour, 1964; *Provincial Pleasures* (on life in a small industrial town), R. Hale, 1959; *Birth by Drowning* (verse play), Faber, 1960; *William Cowper* (pamphlet of criticism), published for the British Council by Longmans, Green, 1960; *Portrait of the Lakes* (topography), R. Hale, 1963, Dufour, 1965; *Enjoying it All*, Waltham Forest Books, 1964; (with others) *Writers on Themselves* (radio talks), introduction by Herbert Read, British Broadcasting Corp., 1964; *Selected Poems*, Faber, 1966; *No Star on the Way Back: Ballads and Carols*, Manchester Institute of Contemporary Arts, 1967; *Greater Lakeland* (topography), R. Hale, 1969, International Publications Service, 1970. Also author of a television Christmas play, "No Star on the Way Back," 1963. Contributor to *Times Literary Supplement, Church Times, Stand*, and other periodicals.

SIDELIGHTS: Nicholson told *CA:* "I have spent all my life in the house where I was born and in the town where both my parents were born before me. Millom is a small industrial town . . . and most of my poetry takes its imagery from my immediate surroundings—mines, town, the coast, the mountains."

NICHOLSON, Norman L(eon) 1919-

PERSONAL: Born October 14, 1919, in Barking, Essex, England; son of Albert Leon and Dorothy Nicholson; married Helen Smith (a musician), August 15, 1947; children: Charles. *Education:* University of Western Ontario, B.A., 1943, M.Sc., 1947; University of Ottawa, Ph.D., 1951. *Religion:* Anglican. *Office:* Department of Geography, University of Western Ontario, London, Ontario, Canada.

CAREER: Canadian Department of Mines and Technical Surveys, Geographical Branch, Ottawa, Ontario, geographer, 1949-54, director, 1954-64; University of Western Ontario, London, professor of geography, 1964—, dean of University College, 1967-69. Chairman of Canadian Permanent Committee on Geographical Names, and of Canadian section of Pan American Institute of Geography and History. *Military service:* Royal Air Force, 1943-46; became flying officer. *Member:* Royal Canadian Geographical Society (fellow; director), Royal Geographical Society (fellow), American Geographical Society (fellow), Canadian Association of Geographers, Association of American Geographers.

WRITINGS: The Boundaries of Canada, Its Provinces and Territories, Queen's Printer (Canada), 1954; (contributor) Gordon East and A.E.F. Moodie, editors, *The Changing World: Studies in Political Geography*, World Book, 1956; (editor) *Atlas of Canada*, Queen's Printer (Canada), 1958; (contributor) *The World in Which We Live and Work*, de Haan, 1962; *Canada in the American Community*, Van Nostrand, 1963; (contributor) R. R. Krueger and others, editors, *Regional and Resource Planning in Canada*, Holt, 1963; (contributor) John Warkentin, editor, *Canada: A Geographical Interpretation*, Methuen, 1968; (contributor) C.A. Fisher, editor, *Essays in Political Geography*, Methuen, 1968. Contributor of more than one hundred articles and reviews to geographical journals. Editor, Canadian Association of Geographers, 1951-60.

BIOGRAPHICAL/CRITICAL SOURCES: Times Literary Supplement, December 25, 1969.

*   *   *

NICOLL, (John Ramsay) Allardyce 1894-

PERSONAL: Born June 28, 1894, in Glasgow, Scotland; son of David Binny and Elsie (Allardyce) Nicoll; married Josephine Calina (died, 1962); married Maria Dubno, December 21, 1963. *Education:* University of Glasgow, M.A. (first class honors). *Home:* Wind's Acre, Colwall, Malvern, Worcestershire, England.

CAREER: Began teaching at Loughborough College, Loughborough, England; University of London, London, England, began as lecturer, later professor of English language and literature, 1924-34; Yale University, New Haven, Conn., professor of history of drama and dramatic criticism and chairman of department of drama, 1934-45; served with British Embassy, Washington, D.C., during part of World War II, returning to England in 1945; University of Birmingham, Birmingham, England, professor of English language and literature, 1945-61, now professor emeritus. Shakespeare Institute, Stratford-upon-Avon, director, 1951-61. Visiting professor at Harvard University and University of Chicago; Mellon Visiting Professor of English at University of Pittsburgh, 1963-64, 1965, 1967, 1969. Life trustee, Shakespeare Birthplaces Trust.

MEMBER: Society for Theatre Research (president), Modern Language Association of America (honorary), Accademia Ligure di Scienze e Lettere (honorary), Century Club. *Awards, honors:* D. es L. from University of Toulouse and University of Montpellier; D.Litt. from

University of Durham and University of Glasgow; D.H.L. from Brandeis University.

WRITINGS: *Dryden as an Adapter of Shakespeare*, Oxford University Press, 1922; *William Blake and His Poetry*, Harrap, 1922; *A History of Restoration Drama, 1660-1700*, Macmillan, 1923, third edition, Cambridge University Press, 1940; *Dryden and His Poetry*, Harrap, 1923; *An Introduction to Dramatic Theory*, Harrap, 1923, revised edition published in America as *The Theory of Drama*, Crowell, 1931; (contributor) *Studies in the First Folio*, Shakespeare Association (London), 1924; *British Drama: An Historical Survey from the Beginnings to the Present Time*, Crowell, 1925, fifth edition, Barnes & Noble, 1963; *A History of Early Eighteenth Century Drama, 1700-1750*, Macmillan, 1925; (editor and author of introduction and notes) Edward Sharpham, *Cupid's Whirligig*, Golden Cockerel Press, 1926; (author of introduction) Lodowick Carlell, *The Fool Would Be a Favourit*, Golden Cockerel Press, 1926; (author of introduction) Carlell, *The Tragedy of Osmond the Great Turk*, Golden Cockerel Press, 1926; *Studies in Shakespeare*, L. & V. Woolf, 1927, Harcourt, 1928; *A History of Late Eighteenth Century Drama, 1750-1800*, Macmillan, 1927; (editor with Josephine Nicoll) Raphael Holinshed, compiler, *Holinshed's Chronicles as Used in Shakespeare's Plays*, Dutton, 1927; (editor) *Lesser English Comedies of the Eighteenth Century*, Oxford University Press, 1927; *The Development of the Theatre: A Study of Theatrical Art from the Beginnings to the Present Day*, Harcourt, 1927, 5th edition, 1967; *The English Stage*, Benn's Sixpenny Library, 1928, revised edition published as *The English Theatre: A Short History*, Nelson, 1936; (editor) *Readings from British Drama: Extracts from British and Irish Plays*, Crowell, 1929; (editor) Cyril Tourneur, *Works*, Argus, 1929.

A History of Early Nineteenth Century Drama, 1800-1850, Macmillan, 1930; *What to Read on English Drama*, Leeds Public Libraries, 1930; *Masks, Mimes and Miracles: Studies in the Popular Theatre*, Harcourt, 1931; (contributor) Lee Simonson, editor, *Theatre Art*, Norton, 1934; (contributor) George Malcolm Young, *Early Victorian England, 1850-1865*, Oxford University Press, 1934; *Film and Theatre*, Crowell, 1936, reprinted, Arno, 1972; *Stuart Masques and the Renaissance Stage*, Harrap, 1937, Harcourt, 1938.

(Editor with Theodore Cloak) Dionysus Lardner Boucicault, *Forbidden Fruit and Other Plays*, Princeton University Press, 1940; *A History of Late Nineteenth Century Drama, 1850-1900*, Macmillan, 1947; *World Drama from Aeschylus to Anouilh*, Harrap, 1949, Harcourt, 1950.

A History of English Drama, 1660-1900, six volumes, Cambridge University Press, 1952-59, includes 4th edition of *Restoration Drama*, 3rd edition of *Early Eighteenth Century Drama*, 2nd edition of *Late Eighteenth Century Drama*, 2nd edition of *Early Nineteenth Century Drama*, 2nd edition of *Late Nineteenth Century Drama*, and a catalogue of plays produced or printed in England from 1660-1900; *Cooperation in Shakespearean Scholarship*, British Academy Annual Shakespeare Lecture (London), 1952; *Shakespeare: An Introduction*, Oxford University Press, 1953; (editor and author of introduction and notes) *Chapman's Homer: The Iliad, the Odyssey and the Lesser Homerica*, Pantheon, 1956, 2nd edition, Princeton University Press, 1967; (editor and author of introduction) *The Elizabethans*, Cambridge University Press, 1957; (translator) Barnard W. Hewitt, editor, *Renaissance Stage; Documents of Serlio, Sabbattini and Furtennbach*, University of Miami Press, 1959.

"Tragical-comical-historical-pastoral": Elizabethan Dramatic Nomenclature, John Rylands Library, 1960;

(contributor) Richard Hosley, editor, *Essays on Shakespeare and Elizabethan Drama*, University of Missouri Press, 1962; *The Theatre and Dramatic Theory*, Barnes & Noble, 1962; *The World of Harlequin: A Critical Study of the Commedia Dell'Arte*, Cambridge University Press, 1963; (editor) *Shakespeare in His Own Age*, Cambridge University Press, 1964; *English Drama: A Modern Viewpoint*, Barnes & Noble, 1968; *English Drama, 1900-1930: The Beginnings of the Modern Period*, Cambridge University Press, 1973.

Editor, *The London Series of English Texts*, London University Press, 1925—. Editor, *Shakespeare Survey* (annual), 1948-65. Contributor to learned journals and to magazines and newspapers.

SIDELIGHTS: Characterized by G.N. Nettleton as "the accurate annalist of the stage rather than the acute analyst of its drama," Nicoll has after five decades of research into the theatre, established an outstanding reputation as a scholar and researcher. R. Aldington once called his work "genuine pioneering. He has made clear a whole set of dramatic writers who were hidden in the fog of one's ignorance...." E.L. Tinker has referred to *The Development of the Theatre* as "entirely authoritative and ... the sole work in the English language that summarizes the complete history of the theatre from its beginning to its present."

In addition to being scholarly and accurate, Nicoll's work has also been praised for the enjoyable manner in which it is presented. "He mingles the scholar and the producer," Bonamy Dobree once wrote. "Professor Nicoll examines the 'why' of certain things.... It is a refreshing approach, and he makes many illuminating discoveries." Gordon Gould referred to *The Elizabethans Introduced* as "a rich panorama of the most fascinating period in English history, arranged by a man whose interest in its personalities is untarnished by academic dullness...."

BIOGRAPHICAL/CRITICAL SOURCES: *Nation and Athenaeum*, February 26, 1927, March 17, 1928; *Saturday Review*, October 22, 1927; *New York Times*, September 26, 1937, May 18, 1947; *Chicago Sunday Tribune*, March 17, 1957; *Times Literary Supplement*, September 19, 1968.

*   *   *

NICOLLE, Jacques Maurice Raoul 1901-

PERSONAL: Born December 19, 1901, in Rouen, France; son of Maurice Charles (a microbiologist) and Valentine (Rose) Nicolle. *Education:* College de Normandie, Baccalaureat es Sciences, 1920; Universite de Paris, Diplome d'Etudes Superieures de Physique, 1940, Doctorat es Sciences, 1955. *Religion:* Roman Catholic. *Home:* 24, rue Tournefort, Paris 5, France. *Office:* College de France 11, Place Marcelin-Berthelot, Paris 5, France.

CAREER: Universite de Paris, Paris, France, chercheur, Faculte des Sciences, 1936-40; College de France, Paris, assistant, Laboratoire de Physique Experimentale, 1940-58, sous-directeur, Ecole des Hautes Etudes (biochimie generale), 1959-62, professor and directeur, Laboratoire de Biochimie des Isomeres, 1963—. Lecturer throughout Europe. *Wartime service:* Detache a la Recherche Scientifique de l'Armee; combattant volontaire de la Resistance, 1940-44. *Member:* Societe Francaise de Physique, Academie des Sciences et Lettres (Rouen), Gesellschaft fuer Physiologische Chemie (Wuppertal). *Awards, honors:* Laureat de l'Academie Francaise, laureat de l'Academie des Sciences de Paris, laureat de l'Academie de Medecine de Paris, laureat de l'Academie d'Agriculture de France.

WRITINGS: (Editor) *Textes de Louis Pasteur*, Raison d'Etre, 1947; *La Symetrie et ses applications*, Albin

Michel, 1950; *Naissance d'une Allemagne democratique,* Editions Sociales, 1951; *Louis Pasteur: Un Maitre de l'enquete scientifique,* La Colombe, 1953, translation published in America as *Louis Pasteur: The Story of His Major Discoveries,* Basic Books, 1961 (published in England as *Louis Pasteur: A Master of Scientific Enquiry,* Hutchinson, 1961); *La Symetrie dans la nature et les travaux des hommes* (lecture), Palais de la Decouverte, 1954; *La Republique democratique allemande, par un temoin,* Editions de Minuit, 1956; *La Symetrie,* Presses Universitaires de France, 1957, 2nd edition, 1965; *Une Application de la symetrie a la lutte contre les microbes* (lecture), Palais de la Decouverte, 1957; *Maurice Nicolle, un homme de la Renaissance a notre epoque,* La Colombe, 1957; (with Pierre Lepine) *Cavendish,* Seghers, 1964; (editor) *Roentgen* (selected texts of Wilhelm Conrad Roentgen, including bibliography), Seghers, 1965; (editor) *Palissy* (selected texts of Bernard Palissy, including bibliography), Seghers, 1966; *W.C. Roentgen et l'ere des rayons* X (lecture), Palais de la Decouverte, 1967; *Bernard Palissy, le savant* (lecture), Palais de la Decouverte, 1968; (with Maurice Morisset) *Pour comprendre aujourd'hui rites et symboles de l'Eglise,* Beauchesne, 1968; *Sir Henry Cavendish: L'Homme qui a pese la terre* (lecture), Palais de la Decouverte, 1969; *Pasteur: Sa Vie, sa methode, ses decouvertes,* Gerard, 1969; (editor) *Leonard de Vinci* (selected texts), Seghers, 1970; *Structure moleculaire et proprietes biologiques,* Flammarion, 1972.

Recording: "Scenes de la vie de Pasteur," in *Encyclopedie sonore,* Hachette, 1959. Contributor to *Encyclopedie francaise, Encyclopedia Universalis, Encyclopedia Mondadori,* and *Encyclopaedia Britannica.*

SIDELIGHTS: Nicolle wrote to *CA:* "Following the major example of Louis Pasteur and Pierre Curie, I have devoted considerable time and research to the problem of symmetry in science, and I have extended it to the arts." His father, Maurice Nicolle, was a pupil of Louis Pasteur and founded the Bacteriological Institute of Constantinople in 1893; his uncle, Charles Nicolle, also a microbiologist, was awarded the Nobel Prize in medicine and physiology in 1928 and founded the Institut Pasteur of Tunis in 1903.

Nicolle has submitted about forty *Notes* on his personal work in physics and biochemistry to the Academie des Sciences de Paris. His books have been translated into German, Rumanian, Spanish, and Japanese.

* * *

NICOLSON, Marjorie Hope   1894-

PERSONAL: Born February 18, 1894, in Yonkers, N.Y.; daughter of Charles Butler (a newspaper editor) and Lissie Hope (Morris) Nicolson. *Education:* University of Michigan, A.B., 1914, A.M., 1918; Yale University, Ph.D., 1920; Johns Hopkins University, postdoctoral study, 1923-26. *Home:* Butler Hall, 400 West 119th St., New York, N.Y. 10027.

CAREER: University of Minnesota, Minneapolis, began as instructor, became assistant professor of English, 1920-23; Goucher College, Baltimore, Md., assistant professor, 1923-26; Smith College, Northampton, Mass., associate professor of English, 1927-28, professor and dean, 1928-41; Columbia University, New York, N.Y., professor, 1941-62, chairman of department of English and comparative literature, 1954-62; Claremont Graduate School, Claremont, Calif., visiting professor, 1962-63; Institute for Advanced Study, Princeton, N.J., member, 1963-68. John Simon Guggenheim Foundation, member of committee on awards, 1930-37, of advisory board, 1937-66. Lecturer at colleges and universities.

MEMBER: Modern Language Association of America (vice-president, 1937-38; president, 1962-63), Renaissance Society of America, History of Science Society, United Chapters of Phi Beta Kappa (senator, 1937-62; vice-president, 1937-40; president, 1940-46). *Awards, honors:* Guggenheim fellow, 1926-27; Rose Crawshay Prize of British Academy, 1937, for *Newton Demands the Muse: Newton's Optiks and the Eighteenth Century Poets;* Distinguished Scholar Award ($10,000) from American Council of Learned Societies, 1962; recipient of sixteen honorary degrees from various institutions.

WRITINGS: *The Art of Description,* F.S. Crofts, 1925; *Conway Letters,* Yale University Press, 1930; *The Microscope and English Imagination,* Department of Modern Languages, Smith College, 1935; *A World in the Moon: A Study of the Changing Attitude Toward the Moon in the Seventeenth and Eighteenth Centuries,* Department of Modern Languages, Smith College, 1936; (editor and author of introduction) *A Voyage to Cacklogallinia, with a Description of the Religion, Policy, Customs and Manners of That Country,* by Captain Samuel Brunt (reproduced from 1727 edition), published for Facsimile Text Society by Columbia University Press, 1940; *Newton Demands the Muse: Newton's Optiks and the Eighteenth Century Poets,* Princeton University Press, 1946; *Voyages to the Moon* (sequel to *A World in the Moon),* Macmillan, 1948; *The Breaking of the Circle: Studies in the Effect of the "New Science" Upon Seventeenth Century Poetry,* Northwestern University Press, 1950, revised edition, Columbia University Press, 1960; *Science and Imagination,* Cornell University Press, 1956; *Mountain Gloom and Mountain Glory: The Development of the Aesthetics of the Infinite,* Cornell University Press, 1959; (editor) *Milton: Major Poems,* Bantam, 1962; *Reason and Imagination: Studies in the History of Ideas, 1600-1800* (volume of essays), privately printed, 1962; *John Milton: A Reader's Guide to His Poetry,* Farrar, Straus, 1963; *The Battle of the Books* (convocation address), Brown University Press, 1964; *Pepys' Diary and the New Science* (expanded version of 48th Page-Barbour lectures, University of Virginia, 1965), University Press of Virginia, 1965; (editor) Thomas Shadwell, *The Virtuoso,* University of Nebraska Press, 1966; *Books Are Not Dead Things* (address), College of William and Mary, 1966; (with G.S. Rousseau) *"This Long Disease, My Life": Alexander Pope and the Sciences,* Princeton University Press, 1968. Contributor to periodicals. Editor, *Journal of History of Ideas.*

WORK IN PROGRESS: Writing on the impact of science and philosophy upon literary imagination; research on the development of atomism, particularly from the Renaissance through the eighteenth century.

AVOCATIONAL INTERESTS: Puzzles, especially crossword puzzles.

* * *

NIEBURG, H(arold) L.   1927-

PERSONAL: Born November 26, 1927, in Philadelphia, Pa.; son of Samuel James (a policeman) and Emma (Dubinsky) Nieburg; married Janet McLay Withey, January 27 1958; children: Elizabeth Ann, Patricia, William, Margaret Ellen. *Education:* University of Chicago, Ph.B., 1947, A.M., 1952, Ph.D., 1961. *Home address:* RD#2, Rockwell Rd., Vestal, N.Y. 13850. *Office:* State University of New York at Binghamton, Binghamton, N.Y. 13901.

CAREER: Illinois State University, Normal, assistant professor of political science, 1956-59; University of Chicago, Chicago, Ill., associate director, Center for Government Programs, 1959-61; Case Institute of Technology (now case Western Reserve University), Cleveland, Ohio, assistant professor of political science, 1961-63; University of Wisconsin, Milwaukee, associate professor, 1963-

65, professor of political science, 1965-70; State University of New York at Binghamton, professor of political science, 1970—. *Member:* American Political Science Association, American Civil Liberties Union, American Association of University Professors, Midwest Political Science Conference. *Awards, honors:* Danforth Foundation grant, 1960-61; Rockefeller Foundation grant, 1962-63.

WRITINGS: Nuclear Secrecy and Foreign Policy, Public Affairs Press, 1964; *In the Name of Science,* Quadrangle, 1966, revised edition, 1970; *Political Violence: The Behavioral Process,* St. Martin's, 1969; *Culture Storm: Politics and the Ritual Order,* St. Martin's, 1972. Contributor of more than fifty articles and reviews to *Science, New York Times, Nation, Bulletin of the Atomic Scientists, American Political Science Review, World Politics,* and other professional journals.

BIOGRAPHICAL/CRITICAL SOURCES: Virginia Quarterly Review, autumn, 1967; *New York Times Book Review,* October 26, 1969; *Commonweal,* January 23, 1970; *Christian Century,* January 28, 1970.

* * *

NIELSEN, Niels Christian, Jr. 1921-

PERSONAL: Born June 2, 1921, in Long Beach, Calif.; son of Niels Hansen (a merchant) and Frances (Nofziger) Nielsen; married Erika Kreuth (now a professor of Germanics), May 10, 1958; children: Camilla Regina, Niels Albrecht. *Education:* University of Southern California, student, 1938-40; George Pepperdine College, B.A., 1942; Yale University, B.D., 1946, Ph.D., 1951. *Politics:* Democrat. *Religion:* Methodist. *Home:* 2424 Swift, Houston, Tex. 77025. *Office:* Department of Religious Studies, Rice University, Houston, Tex. 77001.

CAREER: Rice University, Houston, Tex. 1951—, professor of philosophy and religious thought, 1959—, chairman, Department of Religious Studies, 1968—. Ordained local elder of Methodist Church. *Member:* Society for Religion in Higher Education (fellow), American Academy of Religion, American Society for Study of World Religions, American Philosophical Association, Society for Scientific Study of Religion, American Association of University Professors, Metaphysical Society of America, Union for Study of Great Religions (chapter president), Southwest Philosophical Conference (president, 1960), Southern Society for Philosophy of Religion.

WRITINGS: Geistige Landerkunde, USA, Glock & Lutz, 1960; *A Layman Looks at World Religions,* Bethany Press, 1962; *God in Education: A New Opportunity for American Schools,* Sheed & Ward, 1966. Also author of pamphlet, *Religion and Philosophy in Contemporary Japan,* Rice Institute, 1957. Contributor to *America, Churchman, Monist,* and other religious journals.

WORK IN PROGRESS: A short book, *Protestant Catholicism: The Dutch and Other Models;* a book on world religions, historical and commentary.

* * *

NIKLAUS, Robert 1910-

PERSONAL: Born July 18, 1910, in London, England; son of Jean Rodolphe (a minister) and Elizabeth (Weber) Niklaus; married Thelma E.F. Jones (an author), July 25, 1936 (died, 1970); children: Paul Louis, John Robert, Celia Hedli. *Education:* University of Lille, B. es L., 1930; University of London, B.A., 1931, Ph.D., 1934. *Home:* 17 Elm Grove Rd., Topsham, Devonshire, England.

CAREER: Toynbee Hall, London, England, senior tutor in French, 1931-32; University College, University of London, London, England, assistant lecturer in French,

1934-38; University of Manchester, Manchester, England, began as assistant lecturer, became lecturer in French, 1938-52; University of Exeter, Exeter, England, professor of French, 1952—, dean of Faculty of Arts, 1959-62. University of California, Berkeley, visiting professor of French, 1963-64. Ministry of Education, member of postgraduate state studentships awards committee, 1956-61. *Member:* Association of University Teachers of Great Britain (president, 1954-55), International Association of University Professors and Lecturers (president, 1960-64), Modern Humanities Research Association (executive committee, 1956-70), Modern Language Association (United Kingdom), Society for French Studies (president, 1968-70), Manchester Film Society (president, 1950-52), Exeter Film Society (president, 1960-62). *Awards, honors:* Honorary doctorate from University of Rennes, 1964.

WRITINGS: Jean Moreas, poete lyrique, Presses Universitaires de France, 1936; (with John Sinclair Wood) *French Prose Composition: Extracts from Modern and Contemporary Writers for Translation into French,* Duckworth, 1936; *The Year's Work in Modern Language Studies,* Volumes VII-XIII, Cambridge University Press, 1937-52; (with Wood) *French Unseens: Extracts from Contemporary French Writers for Translation into English,* Duckworth, 1940; *Les Pensees philosophiques de Diderot,* Manchester University Press and John Rylands Library, 1941; *Diderot and Drama,* University College of the South West of England, 1953; (with C.E. Loveman) *Modern Method French Course,* Thomas Nelson, Volume IV, 1958, Volume V, 1959; (author of introduction) Jean-Jacques Rousseau, *Les Confessions,* two volumes, Dent, 1960; *The Mind of Diderot: An Enquiry into the Nature of Diderot's Understanding and Thought,* Edizioni di Filosofia, 1963; *Le Barbier de Seville by Beaumarchais: Critical Analysis,* edited by W.G. Moore, Barron's, 1966, hardcover edition published as *Beaumarchais: Le Barbier de Seville,* Edward Arnold, 1968; *A Literary History of France,* Volume III, *The Eighteenth Century, 1715-1789,* Barnes & Noble, 1970.

Editor: (And author of introduction and notes) Jean-Jacques Rousseau, *Les Reveries du promeneur solitaire,* Manchester University Press, 1942, 4th edition, 1961; (and author of introduction, notes, and bibliography) Denis Diderot, *Pensees philosophiques,* critical edition, E. Droz & F. Giard, 1950, 2nd edition, 1957; Diderot, *Lettre sur les aveugles,* critical edition, E. Droz & F. Giard, 1951, 2nd edition, 1963; (and author of introduction with wife, Thelma Niklaus) Pierre Carlet de Chamblain de Marivaux, *Arlequin poli par l'amour,* University of London Press, 1959. General editor, "Textes francais classiques et modernes," twenty-four volumes to date, University of London Press, 1958—.

Contributor to *Diderot Studies,* Volumes IV and VI, *Encyclopaedia Britannica, Chambers' Encyclopaedia,* and *Encyclopedia of Philosophy.* Contributor of reviews and articles to professional journals.

BIOGRAPHICAL/CRITICAL SOURCES: Virginia Quarterly Review, winter, 1971.

* * *

NIKLAUS, Thelma (Jones) 1912-

PERSONAL: Born April 29, 1912, in London, England; daughter of Morgan and Florence (Bowles) Jones; married Robert Niklaus (a professor), July 25, 1936; children: Paul Louis, John Robert, Celia Hedli. *Education:* Studied in France, 1930-31; University College, London, B.A. (with honors), 1934; University of London, Diploma A in Pedagogy, 1935. *Home:* 17 Elm Grove Rd., Topsham, Devonshire, England. *Agent:* Richmond Towers & Benson Ltd., 14 Essex St., London W.C.2,

England; Monica McCall, Inc., 667 Madison Ave., New York, N.Y. 10021.

CAREER: Battle Abbey, Sussex, England, teacher of French, 1935-36; Langham Home (for Basque refugee children), Colchester, Essex, England, supervisor, 1936-38; lecturer in French, University of Nottingham and Workers' Educational Association, Nottingham, England, 1938-52. *Member:* P.E.N., Bronte Society.

WRITINGS: (With Peter Cotes) *The Little Fellow: The Life and Work of Charles Spencer Chaplin*, foreword by W. Somerset Maugham, Philosophical Library, 1951, revised edition, Bodley Head, 1952; *Harlequin; or, The Rise and Fall of a Bergamask Rogue* (biography), Braziller, 1956 (published in England as *Harlequin Phoenix; or, The Rise and Fall of a Bergamask Rogue*, Bodley Head, 1956); *Tamahine* (novel), John Lane, 1957; (editor and author of introduction with husband, Robert Niklaus) Pierre Carlet de Chamblain de Marivaux, *Arlequin poli par l'amour*, University of London Press, 1959; *Lexy* (novel), P. Davies, 1962.

Translator from French: Paul Jacques Bonzon, *The Orphans of Simitra*, University of London Press, 1957; Paul Jacques Bonzon, *The Gold Cross of Santa Anna*, University of London Press, 1961; Monique Peyrouton de Ladebat, *The Village that Slept*, Bodley Head, 1963.

WORK IN PROGRESS: *The Last Knight*, a children's book; a novel; short stories; research on the childhood of the Bronte sisters, and on the origins of drama.

SIDELIGHTS: *Tamahine* was made into a motion picture in 1964 by Metro-Goldwyn-Mayer. *Avocational interests:* Theater, cinema, travel, collecting dolls and dollhouses.†

* * *

NILES, Gwendolyn   1914-

PERSONAL: Born March 11, 1914, in Sanilac County, Mich.; daughter of Lynn A. (a teacher) and Hazel (Schwarzentraub) Niles. *Education:* Eastern Michigan University, B.A., 1940; University of Michigan, M.A., 1946. *Religion:* Protestant. *Home:* 706 Pipestone, Benton Harbor, Mich. 49022. *Office:* Lake Michigan College, Benton Harbor, Mich. 49022.

CAREER: Teacher in Livingston County (Mich.) schools, 1934-41; high school teacher of English at Pickford, Mich., 1941-43, Plymouth, Mich., 1943-47; Community College (now Lake Michigan College), Benton Harbor, Mich., instructor in English, 1947—. *Member:* American Association of University Women (creative writing chairman, 1950-54), Michigan Poetry Society (president, 1960-64). *Awards, honors:* Three awards in American Association of University Women writing project; four awards in Michigan State Poetry Contests.

WRITINGS—All poetry: *A Changing Sky*, Banner Press, 1945; *The Singing of the Days*, Banner Press, 1962; *The Silence of the Rose*, Branden Press, 1970. Contributor of articles to *Peninsula Poets*, and poems to newspapers and literary periodicals.

WORK IN PROGRESS: Another collection of poetry.

* * *

NITCHIE, George W(ilson)   1921-

PERSONAL: Born May 19, 1921, in Chicago, Ill.; son of Francis Raymond (a minister) and Anna (Wilson) Nitchie; married Laura Margaret Woodard, 1947; children: Katherine Margaret, Rebecca Woodard, Judith Anna. *Education:* Middlebury College, A.B., 1943; Columbia University, M.A., 1947, Ph.D., 1958. *Home:* 50 Pleasantview Ave., Weymouth, Mass. 02131. *Office:* Simmons College, 300 The Fenway, Boston, Mass. 02115.

CAREER: Simmons College, Boston, Mass., 1947—, began as instructor, now professor of English. *Military service:* U.S. Army Air Forces, 1943-45; became staff sergeant; received Asiatic-Pacific Theater and Philippine Liberation Medals. *Member:* American Association of University Professors.

WRITINGS: Seven Poems, Simmons College Press, 1959; *Human Values in the Poetry of Robert Frost: A Study of a Poet's Convictions*, Duke University Press, 1960; (contributor) James M. Cox, editor, *Robert Frost: A Collection of Critical Essays*, Prentice-Hall, 1962; *Marianne Moore: An Introduction to the Poetry*, Columbia University Press, 1969.

Contributor of poems and reviews to *American Literature, Southern Review, Shenandoah, Massachusetts Review*, and other journals.

BIOGRAPHICAL/CRITICAL SOURCES: New Leader, April 16, 1970.

* * *

NITYANANDAN, P(erumpilavil) M(adhava Menon)   1926-

PERSONAL: Born November 4, 1926, in Palghat, Kerala, India; son of Madhava Menon K(ozhikode) V(eetil) and Padmavathi (Perumpilavil); married a physician, 1956; children: Aswath, Nirupama. *Education:* Engineering College, Guindy, Madras, B.E. Mechanical, 1947. *Home:* 2A, Sir C.V. Raman Rd., Madras 18, Madras, India. *Office:* Gears India, B-1, Industrial Estate, Guindy, Madras, India.

CAREER: Government of State of Madras, Technical Education Department, Madras, India, lecturer, 1948-55; Mahindra & Mahindra Ltd., Bombay, India, assistant works manager, 1955-58; Gears India, Madras, India, partner, 1958—. Indian Standards Institute, member of subcommittee for gearing, National Productivity Council, member. *Member:* Madras Cricket Club.

WRITINGS: The Long, Long Days (novel) Asia Publishing House, 1960. Contributor of short stories and humorous pieces to *Illustrated Weekly of India*.

SIDELIGHTS: Nityanandan's particular interest in writing is in humorous pieces and science fiction. He enjoys music, is a proficient amateur performer on the flute, and also likes tennis.

* * *

NIXON, Joan Lowery   1927-

PERSONAL: Born February 3, 1927, in Los Angeles, Calif.; daughter of Joseph Michael and Margaret (Meyer) Lowery; married Hershell H. Nixon (now a petroleum geologist), August 6, 1949; children: Kathleen Mary, Maureen Louise, Joseph Michael, Eileen Marie. *Education:* University of Southern California, A.B., 1947. *Religion:* Roman Catholic. *Home:* 800 North "F" St., Midland, Tex. 79701. *Agent:* Ellen Levine, Curtis Brown, Ltd., 60 East 56th St., New York, N.Y. 10022.

CAREER: Elementary teacher in Los Angeles, Calif., 1947-50; Midland College, Midland, Tex., instructor in creative writing, 1971. Member of committee, Summer Writers Conference, University of Houston. *Member:* Authors Guild, Authors League, Houston Writers Workshop, Pasadena Writers Club, Kappa Delta Alumnae Association.

WRITINGS—All published by Criterion: *Mystery of Hurricane Castle*, 1964, *Mystery of the Grinning Idol*, 1965, *Mystery of the Hidden Cockatoo*, 1966, *Mystery of the Haunted Woods*, 1967, *Mystery of the Secret Stowaway*, 1968, *Delbert, the Plainclothes Detective*, 1971.

Contributor of fiction and non-ficion to juvenile and adult magazines. Columnist, *Houston Post.*

WORK IN PROGRESS: An adult historical novel about West Texas; a pre-school book; a juvenile mystery novel.

*　　*　　*

NKETIA, J(oseph) H(anson) Kwabena　1921-

PERSONAL: Born June 22, 1921, in Mampong Ashanti, Gold Coast (now Ghana), West Africa; son of Kwasi and Akua (Adoma) Yeboa; married Lily Agyeman-Dua, January 6, 1951; children: Akosua Adoma, Kwabena Yeboa, Nana Nyako, Kwame Gyima. *Education:* School of Oriental and African Studies, London, certificate in phonetics, 1946, attended Birkbeck College, 1946-49; Trinity College of Music, London, B.A., 1949; further study at Columbia University, 1958-59, Juilliard School of Music, and Northwestern University, 1959. *Office:* University of Ghana, Legon, Ghana, West Africa.

CAREER: Presbyterian Training College, Akropong, Akwapim, Ghana, West Africa, teacher, 1942-44, 1949-52, acting principal, 1952; University of London, School of Oriental and African Studies, London, England, assistant, 1946-49; University College of Ghana (now University of Ghana), Legon, Ghana, West Africa, research fellow in African studies, 1952-59, senior research fellow, 1959-61, associate professor, Institute of African Studies, 1962, professor, 1963—. *Member:* International Folk Music Council (executive board member), International Music Council, Society of Ethnomusicology, African Music Society, Ghana Academy of Sciences, Historical Society of Ghana, Ghana Music Society (president), Royal Anthropological Institute (honorary fellow). *Awards, honors:* Cowell Award, African Music Society, 1958; Rockefeller Foundation fellowship, 1958-59; Ford Foundation travel and study award, 1961.

WRITINGS: The Writing of Twi: Asante Spelling, Scottish Mission Book Depot (Accra, Ghana), 1955; *Funeral Dirges of the Akan People,* Negro Universities Press, 1955; *African Music in Ghana: A Survey of Traditional Forms,* Longmans, Green, 1962, published in America as *African Music in Ghana,* Northwestern University Press, 1963; *Folk Songs of Ghana,* Oxford University Press, 1962; *Drumming in Akan Communities of Ghana* (monograph), Humanities, 1963; *Ghana: Music, Dance, and Drama: A Review of the Performing Arts of Ghana,* Ghana Information Services, 1965; *Our Drums and Drummers,* Ghana Publishing House, 1968, Panther House, 1970; *Creating a Wider Interest in Traditional Music: The Place of Traditional Music in the Musical Life of Ghana,* Institute of African Studies, University of Ghana, c.1969; *Papers in African Studies, No. 3,* Panther House, 1970; *Ethnomusicology in Ghana,* Panther House, 1971.

Books in Twi: *Akanfoo nnwom bi* (collection of Akan songs), Oxford University Press, 1949; *Akanfoo anansesem, Dhoma I* (Akan folk tales, part one), Oxford University Press, 1949, 2nd edition, 1953; *Mframa mu akwantuo ho mpaninsem* (title means "The Story of Flying"), Presbyterian Book Depot (Accra), 1950; (with C.A. Akrofi) *Kan me hwe* (Asante reader), Part 1, Part 2 (Akyem-Asante version), and Part 3 (Asante version, edited by W.M. and I.S. Beveridge), Longmans, Green, 1950-51; *Ananwoma: Agoro bi* (play), Oxford University Press, 1951; *Bo yadee ano* (title means "Preventing Diseases"), Presbyterian Book Depot, 1951; *Kwabena amoa* (story), Oxford University Press, 1952; *Ayaresa ho mpaninsem* (title means "The Story of Healing"), Presbyterian Book Depot, 1952; *Anwonsem, 1944-1949* (poems), Methodist Book Depot (Cape Coast), 1952; (editor of Asante version) D.M. Galbraith, *Kan me hwe 4* (Asante reader 4), Longmans, Green, 1952; *Akwansosem bi* (nar-

rative poems), Presbyterian Book Depot, 1953; *Adee,* Macmillan, 1953; *Woko a na wohunu* (story), Macmillan, 1953; *Semode* (stories), Kumasi Presbyterian Book Depot, 1953; (editor of Asante version) W.M. Beveridge, *Kan me hwe 5* (Asante reader 5), Longmans, Green, 1953; *Kookoo ho mpaninsem* (title means "The Story of Cocoa"), Bureau of Ghana Languages (Accra), 1959.

Contributor to *African Affairs, African Music, Pax Roman, Journal of the International Folk Music Council, Black Orpheus, New World Writing, The Ghanaian, Atlantic, Current Trends in Linguistics,* and other publications.

*　　*　　*

NOAD, Frederick (McNeill)　1929-

PERSONAL: Born August 8, 1929, in Blankenberg, Belgium; naturalized U.S. citizen, 1968; son of Colin Kenneth (in Indian Army) and Eileen (McNeill) Noad; married Marilyn Stuart, June 2, 1960. *Education:* Brasenose College, Oxford, M.A., 1954. *Home:* 8569 Walnut Dr., Los Angeles, Calif. 90046.

CAREER: Player and teacher of the concert guitar; University of Redlands, Redlands, Calif., member of music faculty, 1963—. Initiated guitar instruction series, "Playing the Guitar," networked on national educational television, 1966. *Military service:* British Army, 1948-50; became second lieutenant. *Member:* American Guitar Society, Oxford Society.

WRITINGS: The Collier Quick and Easy Guide to Playing the Guitar: A Self-Instruction Guide to Technique and Theory, Collier, 1963, revised edition, 1972; *Solo Guitar Playing,* Collier, 1968; *The Guitar Songbook,* Collier, 1969; *Graded Guitar,* Collier, 1971; *The Guitar Anthology,* volume I: *Renaissance Songs, Solos, and Duets,* World Publishing, 1972.

WORK IN PROGRESS: Classical Guitar for Classroom Use, grades one through four, to be published by Collier; and *The Guitar Encyclopedia,* to be published by Macmillan.

SIDELIGHTS: Noad spent an entire year in Spain researching the aspects of the guitar and guitar-making. *Avocational interests:* Sports, particularly skiing; travel.

*　　*　　*

NOALL, Roger　1935-

PERSONAL: Born April 1, 1935, in Brigham City, Utah; son of Albert E. (an educator) and Mabel (an educator; maiden surname Sorensen) Noall; married Judith Stelter, March 16, 1962 (divorced 1967); children: Brennan Courtney, Tyler Grey. *Education:* University of Utah, B.S., 1955; Harvard University, LL.B., 1958; New York University, LL.M., 1959. *Office:* One Chase Manhattan Plaza, New York, N.Y. 10005.

CAREER: Officer for Bunge Corp. and partner in a law firm, New York, N.Y. Lecturer, Practising Law Institute, Syracuse Tax Institute, Tennessee Tax Institute.

WRITINGS: (With Stanley Weithorn) *Penalty Taxes on Accumulated Earnings and Personal Holding Companies,* Practising Law Institute, 1963; (with Weithorn) *The Accumulated Earnings Tax,* Practising Law Institute, 1968. Also author of series on corporate acquisitions, Bureau of National Affairs, 1963-70. Contributor to legal and tax law journals.

*　　*　　*

NOBLE, John Wesley　1913-

PERSONAL: Born August 23, 1913, in Oregon City, Ore.; son of Emory James (a lawyer) and Grace (Marshall) Noble; married Jeanne Carabin, August 7, 1938; children: John Wesley II, Robert E. *Education:* College of Marin, A.A., 1935; University of California, A.B., 1937. *Politics:* Republican. *Religion:* Protestant. *Home:* 5477 Masonic Ave., Oakland, Calif. 94618. *Agent:* Kenneth Littauer, Littauer & Wilkinson, 500 Fifth Ave., New York, N.Y., 10036.

CAREER: San Rafael Independent, San Rafael, Calif., sports writer, 1934-35; cable spinner on San Francisco-Oakland bridge, 1935; *Oakland Tribune,* Oakland, Calif., successively reporter, rewrite man, columnist, assistant city editor, 1935-48; free-lance writer, 1948—. Harolds Club, Reno, Nev., copywriter, 1960-63. Annual California Writers Conference, founding general manager. *Member:* Authors Guild of Authors League of America, Society of Magazine Writers, California Writers Club (president, 1955-56), San Francisco Press Club.

WRITINGS: (With Bernard Averbuch) *Never Plead Guilty: The Story of Jake Ehrlich,* Farrar, Straus, 1955; (with Harold S. Smith) *I Want to Quit Winners,* Prentice-Hall, 1961; *Its Name Was M.U.D.: The Story of Water As It Has Affected the Urban Complex on the Eastern Shore of San Francisco Bay,* East Bay Municipal Utility District, 1970.

As ghost writer for Jack LaLanne: *The Jack LaLanne Way to Vibrant Good Health,* Prentice-Hall, 1960; *Foods for Glamour,* Prentice-Hall, 1961; *Abundant Health and Vitality After 40,* Prentice-Hall, 1962. Contributor of articles and short stories to more than thirty periodicals in United States and abroad, including *Saturday Evening Post, Holiday, Reader's Digest, Collier's, Coronet, Field and Stream, Look, Your Life, Westways, American Legion, Boys' Life, True, Nation's Business.*

SIDELIGHTS: Noble has traveled in Mexico, Canada, England, France, Africa, and throughout United States for background of stories on cities, geography, and nature.

* * *

NOCHLIN, Linda Weinberg 1931-

PERSONAL: Born January 30, 1931, in Brooklyn, N.Y.; daughter of Jules and Elka (Heller) Weinberg; married Philip Nochlin, December 20, 1953 (deceased); children: Jessica. *Education:* Vassar College, B.A., 1951; Columbia University, M.A., 1952; New York University, Ph.D., 1963. *Politics:* Democrat. *Religion:* Jewish. *Home:* Vail Rd., Poughkeepsie, N.Y. 12603. *Office:* Vassar College, Poughkeepsie, N.Y. 12601.

CAREER: Vassar College, Poughkeepsie, N.Y., assistant professor of art history, 1952—. *Member:* College Art Association, Phi Beta Kappa. *Awards, honors:* Fulbright fellow; Fels fellow.

WRITINGS: Mathis at Colmar: A Visual Confrontation, Red Dust, 1963; (editor) *Impressionism and Post-Impressionism, 1874-1904: Sources and Documents,* Prentice-Hall, 1966; *Realism and Tradition in Art, 1848-1900: Sources and Documents,* Prentice-Hall, 1966; *Realism,* Penguin, 1971.†

* * *

NOLTE, M(ervin) Chester 1911-

PERSONAL: Born April 1, 1911, in Adel, Iowa; son of Chester Harrison and Macel (Bullington) Nolte; married Gwenneth Earhart; children: Harriet (Mrs. Wayne Wolford), James E. *Education:* Simpson College, B.A., 1937; Drake University, M.S., 1948; University of Denver, Ed.D., 1958. *Politics:* Republican. *Religion:* Methodist. *Home:* 1708 South Downing, Denver, Colo. 80210. *Office:* University of Denver, Denver, Colo. 80210.

CAREER: Rural school teacher in Iowa, 1930-34, in Sioux Rapids, Iowa, 1939-42; superintendent of schools,

Van Cleve, Iowa, 1945-50; superintendent of Washington County High School System, Akron, Colo., 1950-53; superintendent of schools, Gunnison, Colo., 1953-56; Western State College of Colorado, Gunnison, professor, 1953-56; University of Denver, Denver, Colo., associate professor, 1956-69, professor of educational administration, 1969—. *Member:* National Education Association, American Association of School Administrators, National Organization on Legal Problems of Education (board of directors), Tax Education and Finance Committee (state chairman, 1964), Phi Delta Kappa, Colorado Education Association.

WRITINGS: (With John Phillip Linn) *School Law for Teachers,* Interstate, 1963; (with Robert J. Simpson) *Education and the Law in Colorado,* W.H. Anderson, 1966; (editor) *An Introduction to School Administration: Selected Readings,* Macmillan, 1966; (with Linn) *Background Materials on Collective Bargaining for Teachers: A Conference Guide,* Education Commission of the States, 1968; *Guide to School Law,* Parker Publishing, 1969; (compiler) *Bibliography of School Law Dissertations, 1952-1968,* ERIC Clearinghouse on Educational Administration, 1969; *Status and Scope of Collective Bargaining in Public Education,* ERIC Clearinghouse on Educational Administration, 1970; (editor) *Law and the School Superintendent,* W.H. Anderson, 1971; *School Law in Action: One Hundred One Key Decisions with Guidelines for School Administration,* Parker Publishing, 1971; (contributor) *Encyclopaedia of Education,* Macmillan, 1971. Writer of series of articles on school law for *American School Board Journal,* 1963—.

* * *

NORDNESS, Lee 1924-

PERSONAL: Born December 24, 1924, in Olympia, Wash.; son of Elmer and Thelma (Tygum) Nordness. *Education:* Studied at University of Washington, Seattle, 1940-43, Stanford University, 1943-44; Upsala University, Fil.Kand., 1948. *Home:* 140 East 81st St., New York, N.Y. 10028. *Office:* Nordness Gallery, 236 East 75th St., New York, N.Y. 10021.

CAREER: Nordness Gallery, New York, N.Y., director, 1958—. Initiated and directed "Art: USA" exhibit in Madison Square Garden, 1958, New York Coliseum, 1959; acquired exhibit, now the Johnson Collection, 1962. Art authority on television programs, including "Open End" and "Today."

WRITINGS: (Editor) Allen S. Weller, *ART:USA:NOW,* two volumes, Bucher, 1962; *OBJECTS:USA,* Viking, 1970.

* * *

NORRIS, Hoke 1913-

PERSONAL: Born October 8, 1913, in Holly Springs, N.C.; son of Cadvin Hugh (a clergyman) and Mabel Viola (Smith) Norris; married Edna Dees, August 1, 1941; children: Marion Dees. *Education:* Wake Forest College, A.B. (cum laude), 1934; University of North Carolina, graduate study, 1946; Harvard University, Nieman fellow, 1950-51; University of Chicago, Ford Foundation mass media fellow, 1960-61. *Politics:* Democrat. *Home:* 1701 North Park Ave., Chicago, Ill. 60614. *Office:* Chicago Public Library, Michigan Ave. and Randolph St., Chicago, Ill. 60602.

CAREER: Reporter or editor for *Elizabeth City Daily Advance,* Elizabeth City, N.C., 1934-36, *News and Observer* and Associated Press, Raleigh, N.C., 1936-42, *Winston-Salem Journal and Sentinel,* Winston-Salem, N.C., 1947-55; *Sun-Times,* Chicago, Ill., reporter and literary editor, 1955-58; *Chicago Daily News,* Chicago, Ill., member of editorial board, 1968-70; Chicago Public Library, Chicago, Ill., director of public information, 1971—. Publicity director, Lost Colony, Manteo, N.C., 1946-47; instructor in creative writing, University of Chicago, 1959-60, University of Wisconsin, 1971-72. Lecturer. *Military service:* U.S. Army and U.S. Army Air Forces, 1942-46; served as Combat Intelligence officer in Southwest Pacific; became captain. *Member:* Authors League, American Newspaper Guild, Chicago Press Club, Harvard Club.

WRITINGS: All the Kingdoms of Earth (novel), Simon & Schuster, 1956; (editor and contributor) *We Dissent,* St. Martin's, 1962; *It's Not Far But I Don't Know the Way* (novel), Swallow Press, 1969. Contributor of numerous short stories and literary criticism to magazines.

BIOGRAPHICAL/CRITICAL SOURCES: Virginia Quarterly Review, spring, 1970.

* * *

NORRIS, John 1925-

PERSONAL: Born March 3, 1925, in Kelowna, British Columbia, Canada; son of Thomas G. (a judge of appeals court) and Jean (Denovan) Norris; married Barbara Casey, September 15, 1947; children: Thomas. *Education:* University of British Columbia, B.A., 1948, M.A., 1949; Northwestern University, Ph.D., 1955. *Politics:* New Democrat (Socialist). *Home:* 4588 Angus Dr., Vancouver, British Columbia, Canada. *Office:* Department of History, University of British Columbia, Vancouver, British Columbia, Canada 00610.

CAREER: University of British Columbia, Vancouver, professor of history, 1953—. *Military service:* British Navy, 1942-46; awarded Distinguished Service Cross; became acting lieutenant, Royal Naval Volunteer Reserve.

WRITINGS: Shelburne and Reform, St. Martin's, 1963; *Strangers Entertained,* Government of British Columbia, 1971. Contributor of articles to historical journals.

WORK IN PROGRESS: Mobilization of the British Economy for War, 1792-1815; Population, Pestilence, and the Poor Law.†

* * *

NORTHCOTT, (William) Cecil 1902-
(Mary Miller, Arthur Temple)

PERSONAL: Born April 5, 1902, in Buckfast, Devonshire, England; son of William Ashplant and Mary (Nance) Northcott; married Jessie Morton, 1930; children: one son, one daughter. *Education:* Cambridge University, B.A., 1927, M.A., 1930; School of Oriental and African Studies, London, Ph.D., 1961. *Home:* 34 Millington Rd., Cambridge, England.

CAREER: Congregational minister. Began career as social worker in London, England; *Granta,* Cambridge, England, joint proprietor and editor, 1927-28; assistant minister in St. Helens, England, 1929-32, minister in Darwen, Lancashire, England, 1932-35; London Missionary Society, London, England, home secretary and literary superintendent, 1935-50; United Council for Missionary Education (Edinburgh House Press), London, general secretary and editor, 1950-52; United Society for Christian Literature, London, editorial secretary, 1952—; Lutterworth Press, London, editor, 1952—. British Information, Services, representative in United States, 1944. Danforth Foundation lecturer in United States, 1961. Delegate to World Conferences in Europe, India, United States. Lecturer in colleges and seminaries in America. *Awards, honors:* Leverhulme Research Award, 1958.

WRITINGS: (With Harold Cooper and Brooke Crutchley) *Hey Daily Diddle* (burlesque of daily press), Laurie,

1928; *Southward Ho!: An Adventure and an Enterprise in the South Pacific Ocean* (on history of the Christian missions), Livingstone Press, 1935; *Guinea Gold: The London Missionary Society at Work in the Territory of Papua,* Livingstone Press, 1936; *Who Claims the World?: An Attempt to Present the Case for the Christian Missionary Enterprise,* Edinburgh House Press, 1938; *John Williams Sails On* (biography), Hodder & Stoughton, 1939, revised edition, Livingstone Press, 1948; *Change Here for Britain: The Revolution That is Happening,* S.C.M. Press, 1942; *Thirty Heroes from the 150 Years Story of the London Missionary Society, 1795-1945,* Livingstone Press, 1944; *Glorious Company: One Hundred and Fifty Years Life and Work of the London Missionary Society, 1795-1945,* Livingstone Press, 1945; *No Strangers Here: Meditations on the Gospel and the Church in the World,* James Clarke, 1945; *Whose Dominion?,* Livingstone Press, 1946; (with Joyce Reason) *Six Missionaries in Africa: Robert Moffat, David Livingstone, James Stewart, Alexander Mackay, Mary Slessor, and Robert Cook,* Oxford University Press, 1947, 2nd edition, 1956; *Answer from Amsterdam: Congregationalism and the World Church,* Pilgrim Press, 1948; *Freedom of Religion: A Commentary on "A Charter of Religious Freedom," Issued by the Joint Committee on Religious Liberty,* Edinburgh House Press, 1948; *Religious Liberty,* S.C.M. Press, 1948, Macmillan, 1949; *Venturers of Faith,* Edward Arnold, 1950; (editor) *The Church Across the Ages* (series of broadcast talks), Epworth, 1952; *For Britain's Children: The Story of the Sunday Schools, and of the National Sunday School Union, 1803-1953,* National Sunday School Union, 1952; *Voice Out of Africa,* Edinburgh House Press, 1952; *Forest Doctor: The Story of Albert Schweitzer,* Lutterworth, 1955, Roy, 1957; *Hymns We Love: Stories of the Hundred Most Popular Hymns,* Westminster Press, 1955; (editor) *Stories of Faith and Fame,* Lutterworth, 1955; *Livingstone in Africa,* Association Press, 1957; *Star Over Gobi: The Story of Mildred Cable,* Lutterworth, 1957, Christian Literature Crusade, 1960; *Robert Moffat: Pioneer in Africa, 1817-1870,* Lutterworth, 1961, Harper, 1962; (editor and compiler) *The Bible Speaks About Faith: Daily Readings from the Authorised or King James Version and the New English Bible,* Association Press, 1963; *Christianity in Africa,* Westminster Press, 1963; *Bible Encyclopedia for Children,* Westminster Press, 1964; *Hymns in Christian Worship: The Use of Hymns in the Life of the Church,* John Knox, 1964; *South Seas Sailor: The Story of John Williams and His Ships,* Christian Literature Crusade, 1965; *People of the Bible,* Westminster Press, 1967.

Booklets: *What God is Doing About It,* Livingstone Press, 1935; *My Friends the Cannibals: John H. Holmes of Papua,* Edinburgh House Press, 1937; *Hero of the Hottentots: John Vanderkemp,* Edinburgh House Press, 1939; *All God's Chillun: William Wilberforce,* Edinburgh House Press, 1940; *Send Me Among Savages: James Chalmers, 1841-1901,* Edinburgh House Press, 1941; *Towards a New Order,* Edinburgh House Press, 1941; *Give Us Books,* Edinburgh House Press, 1943; *I'll Hit It Hard!,* Edinburgh House Press, 1943; *A Triumph of Voluntary Giving,* Livingstone Press, 1945; *John Calvin,* Lutterworth, 1946; *Christian World Mission,* published for United Society for Christian Literature by Lutterworth, 1952; *Evanston World Assembly: A Concise Interpretation,* Lutterworth, 1954; *A Modern Epiphany* (broadcast on BBC's "Lift Up Your Hearts" series), Independent Press, 1955.

Juveniles, under pseudonym Mary Miller: *The Greatest Gift: Picture Stories of Jesus* ("Picture Stories of the Old Testament," 1-8), Lutterworth, 1953, Revell, 1954; *The Great Promise* ("Picture Stories of the Old Testament," 9-16), Lutterworth, 1954; *The Bible Treasury: Picture Stories from the Bible* (includes *The Greatest Gift* and

The Great Promise), Lutterworth, 1957; *Jesus, the Good Shepherd*, Lutterworth, 1964; *Jesus, the Saviour*, Lutterworth, 1964; *Great Stories of the Bible* (retold), Broadman, 1969; *The Greatest Name of All*, Broadman, 1969; *Children's Prayers and Praises*, Augsberg, 1972.

Editor, *Congregational Monthly*, 1953-58. Editor-at-large, *Christian Century*, 1945-70; church's correspondent, London *Daily Telegraph*, 1967—.

AVOCATIONAL INTERESTS: Walking; travel in Africa and the United States.

*   *   *

NORTHRUP, Herbert Roof   1918-

PERSONAL: Born March 6, 1918, in Irvinton, N.J.; married Eleanor Pearson, June 3, 1944; children: James Pearson, Nancy Warren, Jonathan Peter, David Oliver, Philip Wilson. *Education:* Duke University, A.B., 1939; Harvard University, A.M., 1941, Ph.D., 1942. *Home:* 517 Thornbury Rd., Haverford, Pa. 19041. *Office:* Wharton School of Finance and Commerce. University of Pennsylvania, Philadelphia, Pa. 19104.

CAREER: Cornell University, Ithaca, N.Y., instructor in economics, 1942-43; National War Labor Board, (Detroit, Mich., and New York regions), economist and senior hearing officer, 1943-45; Columbia University, New York, N.Y., assistant professor of industrial relations, 1945-49; National Industrial Conference Board, researcher and consultant on labor economics, 1949-52; Ebasco Services, Inc., industrial relations consultant, 1952-55; Penn-Texas Corp., New York, N.Y., vice-president, industrial relations, 1955-58; General Electric Co., employee relations consultant, 1958-61; University of Pennsylvania, Wharton School of Finance and Commerce, Philadelphia, professor of industry, 1961—, department chairman, 1964-69, director, Industrial Research Unit, 1965—, chairman, Labor Relations Council, 1968—. Visiting professor, New York University, University of California, Berkeley, and Columbia Business School, summers, 1945-49, 1951. *Member:* American Economic Association, Industrial Relations Research Association, Phi Beta Kappa, Harvard Club (New York, N.Y.), Rotunda Club (Richmond, Va.).

WRITINGS: Organized Labor and the Negro, Harper, 1944; *Will Negroes Get Jobs Now?*, Public Affairs Committee, 1945; *Labor Adjustment Machinery*, American Enterprise Association, 1946; *Unionization of Professional Engineers and Chemists*, Industrial Relations Counselors, 1946; (with Gordon Bloom) *Economics of Labor and Industrial Relations*, Blakiston, 1950, 2nd edition published as *Economics of Labor Relations*, Irwin, 1954, 6th edition, 1969; (with Herbert R. Brinberg) *Economics of the Work Week*, National Industrial Conference Board, 1950; *Strike Controls in Essential Industries*, National Industrial Conference Board, 1951; *Shift Problems and Practices*, National Industrial Conference Board, 1951; *Suggestion Systems*, National Industrial Conference Board, 1953, 2nd edition, 1959; (with Gordon Bloom) *Government and Labor: The Role of Government in Union-Management Relations*, Irwin, 1963; (editor with Bloom and Richard L. Rowan) *Readings in Labor Economics*, Irwin, 1963; *Boulwarism: The Labor Relations Policies of the General Electric Company, Their Implications for Public Policy and Management Action*, Bureau of Industrial Relations, University of Michigan, 1964; (editor with Clyde Edward Dankert and F.C. Mann) *Hours of Work*, Harper, 1965; (editor with Rowan) *The Negro and Employment Opportunity: Problems and Practices*, Bureau of Industrial Relations, University of Michigan, 1965; *Compulsory Arbitration and Government Intervention in Labor Disputes: An Analysis of Experience*, Labor Policy Association, 1966; (with

Gordon R. Storholm and others) *Restrictive Labor Practices in the Supermarket Industry*, Wharton School of Finance and Commerce, Industrial Research Unit, University of Pennsylvania, 1967; (editor with Rowan) *Readings in Labor Economics and Labor Relations*, Irwin, 1968; (with Rowan and others) *Negro Employment in Basic Industry: A Study of Racial Policies in Six Industries*, Wharton School of Finance and Commerce, Industrial Research Unit, University of Pennsylvania, 1970; (with Rowan and others) *Negro Employment in Southern Industry: A Study of Racial Policies in Five Industries*, Wharton School of Finance and Commerce, Industrial Research Unit, University of Pennsylvania, 1970.
Racial Policies of American Industry Reports, all published by Wharton School of Finance and Commerce, Industrial Research Unit, University of Pennsylvania: *The Negro in the Automobile Industry*, 1968; *The Negro in the Aerospace Industry*, 1968; (with Alan B. Batchelder) *The Negro in the Rubber Tire Industry*, 1969; *The Negro in the Paper Industry*, 1970; (with Robert I. Ash) *The Negro in the Tobacco Industry*, 1970; (with Armand J. Thieblot and William N. Chernish) *The Negro in the Air Transport Industry*, 1971. Contributor of over 150 articles to business, professional, and popular journals.

*   *   *

NORTON, Hugh S(tanton)   1921-

PERSONAL: Born September 18, 1921, in Delta, Colo.; son of C.A. and Olive (Stanton) Norton; married Miriam Jarmon, December 17, 1949; children: Pamela, John. *Education:* Westminster College, Salt Lake City, Utah, student, 1940-42; George Washington University, A.B., 1947, A.M., 1948, Ph.D., 1956. *Politics:* Republican. *Religion:* Presbyterian. *Home:* 3335 Overcreek Rd., Columbia, S.C. 29206. *Office:* Department of Economics, University of South Carolina, Columbia, S.C. 29208.

CAREER: University of Maryland, College Park, instructor in economics, 1949-54; U.S. Department of Agriculture, Washington, D.C., transportation economist, 1954-57; University of Tennessee, Knoxville, professor of transportation, 1960-66; University of South Carolina, Columbia, Johnson Professor and chairman, Department of Economics, 1966—. Consultant to Tennessee Valley Authority and other organizations. *Military service:* U.S. Army, Signal Corps, 1942-45. *Member:* American Economic Association, American Association of University Professors, American Society of Traffic and Transportation. *Awards, honors:* Russell Award for creative research, 1969.

WRITINGS: Modern Transportation Economics, C.E. Merrill, 1963, 2nd edition, 1971; *Economic Policy: Government and Business*, C.E. Merrill, 1966; *National Transportation Policy: Formation and Implementation*, McCutchan, 1967; *The Role of the Economist in Government: A Study of Economic Advice Since 1920*, McCutchan, 1969; *The Professional Economist: His Role in Business and Industry*, College of Business Administration, University of South Carolina, 1969; *The World of the Economist*, University of South Carolina Press, 1973; *The Employment Act of 1946, 1946-1972*, University of South Carolina, in press. Contributor of articles to transportation economic, and utilities journals.

*   *   *

NORTON, Olive (Claydon)   1913-
(Hilary Neal, Bess Norton, Kate Norway)

PERSONAL: Born January 13, 1913 in England; daughter of Frank Joseph (in art) and Amy (Thickbroom) Claydon; married George Norton (now an ophthalmic optician), March 25, 1938; children: Euan George, Alix Elizabeth, Mary-Ann, Priscilla. *Education:* Studied at King Edward's School, Birmingham, England, Birmingham Children's Hospital, and Manchester Royal Infirmary. *Politics:* Liberal. *Home:* 1 Holly Lane, Four Oaks, Warwickshire, England. *Agent:* Laurence Pollinger Ltd., 18 Maddox St., London W.1, England.

CAREER: Nursing posts, 1930-36; writer, 1954—. Sister in charge of Civil Defense first aid post, Nottingham, England, World War II. Citizens' Advice Bureau, counselor. *Member:* Romantic Novelists' Association.

WRITINGS: Bob-a-Job Pony, Heinemann, 1961; (editor with Meyer Howard Abrams and others) *The Norton Anthology of English Literature,* two volumes, Norton, 1962; *A School of Liars,* Cassell, 1966; *Now Lying Dead,* Cassell, 1967; *Dead on Prediction,* Cassell, 1970; *The Corpse-Bird Cries,* Cassell, 1971.

Under pseudonym Kate Norway—All published by Mills & Boone: *Sister Brookes of Byng's,* 1957, *The Morning Star,* 1959, *Junior Pro,* 1959, *Nurse Elliott's Diary,* 1960, *Waterfront Hospital,* 1961, *The White Jacket,* 1961, *Goodbye, Johnny,* 1962, *The Night People,* 1963, *Nurse in Print,* 1963, *The Seven Sleepers,* 1964, *A Professional Secret,* 1964, *The Lambs,* 1965, *The Nightingale Touch,* 1966, *Be My Guest,* 1966, *Merlin's Keep,* 1966, *A Nourishing Life,* 1967, *The Faithful Failure,* 1968, *Dedication Jones,* 1969, Pocket Books, 1971, *To Care Always,* 1970, *Reluctant Nightingale,* 1970, *Paper Halo,* 1970, Pocket Books, 1971, *The Dutiful Tradition,* 1971.

Under pseudonym Bess Norton—All published by Mills & Boone: *The Quiet One,* 1959, *Night Duty at Duke's,* 1960, *The Red Chalet,* 1960, *The Summer Change,* 1961, *The Waiting Room,* 1961, *A Nurse is Born,* 1962, *The Green Light,* 1963, *The Monday Man,* 1963, *St. Luke's Little Summer,* 1964, *A Miracle at Joe's,* 1965, *St. Julian's Day,* 1965, *What We're Here For,* 1966, *Night's Daughters,* 1966, *The Night is Kind,* 1967.

Under pseudonym Hilary Neal—All published by Mills & Boone: *Factory Nurse,* 1961, *Tread Softly, Nurse,* 1962, *Star Patient: A Third-Year Nurse and a Pop-Singing Teen-Agers Idol,* 1963, *Love Letter,* 1963, *Houseman's Sister,* 1964, *Nurse Off Camera,* 1964, *Mr. Sister,* 1965, *The Team,* 1965, *A Simple Duty,* 1966.

Regular columnist, *Birmingham News,* 1954-59; contributor of short stories and articles to English periodicals. Author of "Rose," a radio play, 1962.

SIDELIGHTS: Mrs. Norton usually writes three "hospital romances" and two crime novels a year. Her books have been published in Canada, and translated into Dutch. *Avocational interests:* Motoring, chess, very difficult crossword puzzles, weekending in a Welsh village.

*   *   *

NOSTRAND, Howard Lee   1910-

PERSONAL: Born November 16, 1910, in New York, N.Y.; son of Elijah H. and Ida (Maeder) Nostrand; married Frances Anne Levering, June 23, 1933 (divorced, 1967); married Frances Brewer Creore, August 9, 1967; children: (first marriage) David, Richard, Robert. *Education:* Amherst College, A.B., 1932; Harvard University, A.M., 1933; University of Paris, Ph.D., 1934. *Office:* Department of Romance Languages and Literature, University of Washington, Seattle, Wash. 98105.

CAREER: University of Buffalo, Buffalo, N.Y., instructor, 1934-36; U.S. Naval Academy, Annapolis, Md., instructor, 1936-38; Brown University, Providence, R.I., assistant professor of French, 1938-39; University of Washington, Seattle, professor of Romance languages and literature, 1939—, chairman of department, 1939-64, director of National Defense Education Act Institute for Modern Language Teachers, 1959. Cultural Relations attache, U.S. Embassy, Lima, Peru, 1944-47; temporary staff associate for national conference on role of colleges and universities in international understanding, American Council on Education, 1949. Member of advisory committee for New Media Program, U.S. Office of Education, 1958-60; member of Humanities Advisory Committee, World Book Encyclopedia, 1964—.

MEMBER: Modern Language Association of America (member of advisory board, Educational Research Information Center, 1966-71), American Association of Teachers of French (vice-president, 1956-58; president, 1960-62), National Council for Accreditation of Teacher Education (member of coordinating board, 1968—), National Education Association (member of commission on teacher education and professional standards, 1963-67, chairman, 1966-67), Phi Beta Kappa (president of Washington Alpha, 1967-68). *Awards, honors:* Order of the Sun (Peru), 1947; Officer d'Academie (France), 1950; Guggenheim fellow, 1953-54; Chevalier, Legion d'Honneur, 1962.

WRITINGS: Le Theatre antique et a l'antique en France de 1840 a 1900, Droz, 1934; (with Homer B. Winchell) *French Phonetics Course,* U.S. Naval Academy, 1937; (translator, editor, and author of introduction) Jose Ortega y Gasset, *Mission of the University,* Princeton University Press, 1944; *The Cultural Attache,* Hazen Foundation, 1947; *Dos problemas de educacion cultural,* Lima, 1947; *Dieciseis problemas y doce recursos de las relaciones culturales,* National University of Trujillo Press, 1947; (editor with Francis J. Brown) *The Role of Colleges and Universities in International Understanding,* American Council on Education, 1949; *Viewer's Guide to College French,* Department of Romance Languages and Literature, University of Washington, 1957; *Final Report of the Director on the National Defense Education Act Summer Session Institute for Elementary-School and Secondary-School Teachers of French, German, Russian, and Spanish,* University of Washington Press, 1959; (editor with others, and author of introduction) *Research on Language Teaching: An Annotated International Bibliography for 1945-1961,* University of Washington Press, 1962, 2nd edition, revised and enlarged, published as *Research on Language Teaching: An Annotated International Bibliography, 1945-64,* 1966; *The University and Human Understanding,* [Seattle], 1965.

Contributor: J.B. Harrison and others, contributors, *If Men Want Peace,* Macmillan, 1946; Julian Harris, editor, *The Humanities: An Appraisal,* University of Wisconsin Press, 1950; *Symbols and Values: An Initial Study,* Conference on Science, Philosophy, and Religion in Their Relation to the Democratic Way of Life (1952), 1954; *Effective Practices in a Program of General Education,* W.C. Brown, 1954; *Analysis of the Modern Cultural Crisis,* University of Washington Press, 1960; *Experiment in Determining Cultural Content, and Survey of Language-Teaching Research,* Department of Romance Languages and Literature, University of Washington, 1964; *Background Data for the Teaching of French,* Department of Romance Languages and Literature, University of Washington, 1967. Contributor to fifth *Review of Foreign Language Education,* American Council on the teaching of Foreign Languages, 1973; contributor of more than fifty articles, and reports to yearbooks and professional journals.

*   *   *

NOURSE, Joan Thellusson   1921-

PERSONAL: Born February 17, 1921, in New York, N.Y.; daughter of Charles F. (a school principal) and Mary (a teacher; maiden surname Fitz-Patrick) Thellusson; married Philip E. Nourse (now a teacher), February 6, 1954; children: William P., Kathleen. *Education:* Manhattanville College of the Sacred Heart, B.A., 1942; Fordham University, M.A., 1944, Ph.D., 1948. *Politics:* Democrat. *Religion:* Roman Catholic. *Home:* 780 Riverside Dr., New York, N.Y. 10032.

CAREER: Hunter College (now Hunter College of the City University of New York), New York, N.Y., instructor in English, 1949-53; Seton Hall University, Paterson, N.J., 1959—, began as associate professor, now professor of English. Professional reviewer and lecturer on drama, 1952—, including radio interview show on current plays, "Personal Appearance," WFUV-TV, 1952-53. *Member:* National Council of Teachers of English, Modern Language Association of America, Catholic Institute of the Press, Outer Circle Theatre Critics Organization.

WRITINGS: (Editor with Aloysius A. Norton) *A Christian Approach to Western Literature: An Anthology,* Newman, 1961; (with Norton) *Literary Craftsmanship,* Seton Hall University Press, 1962; (with husband, Philip E. Nourse) *The Happy Faculty* (3-act comedy; first produced Off-Broadway at Blackfriars' Theatre, April 18, 1967), Blackfriars' Guild, 1967; "Lib Comes High" (a comedy), first produced at Blackfriars' Theatre, October 26, 1971.

"Monarch Notes and Study Guides," all published by Monarch: *Review Notes and Study Guide to Cather's "My Antonia," and Other Major Novels,* 1964; *Arthur Miller's "Death of a Salesman," and "All My Sons,"* 1965; *Arthur Miller's "The Crucible," "A Memory of two Mondays," "A View from the Bridge," "After the Fall," and "Incident at Vichy,"* 1965; *George Bernard Shaw's "Major Barbara,"* 1965. Drama critic of *Catholic News,* 1952—, also currently drama critic of *Long Island Catholic, Advocate, Monitor, Catholic Transcript, Tablet, Catholic Universe Bulletin,* and *Evangelist;* drama and records editor, *Report,* 1963-66; columnist, "The Family Goes," in *Catholic News,* 1962-66.

*   *   *

NOWLAN, Alden (Albert) 1933-

PERSONAL: Born January 25, 1933, near Windsor, Nova Scotia, Canada; son of Freeman and Grace (Reese) Nowlan; married Claudine Orser; children: John Alden. *Education:* Dropped out of public school in Nova Scotia after 37 days in fifth grade. *Home:* 676 Windsor St., Fredericton, New Brunswick, Canada.

CAREER: Newspaper reporter in New Brunswick, 1952-65; *Telegraph-Journal,* Saint John, New Brunswick, night news editor, 1965-67; University of New Brunswick, Fredericton, writer in residence, 1968-72, honorary research associate, School of Graduate Studies, 1972—. *Awards, honors:* Canada Council fellowship, 1961; Canada Council Special Award, 1967; Governor-General's Award for Poetry (Canada), 1967, for *Bread, Wine and Salt;* Guggenheim fellow in poetry, 1967-68; President's Medal, University of Western Ontario, 1970, for best short story published in Canada in 1970; D.Litt., University of New Brunswick, 1970.

WRITINGS: The Rose and the Puritan, University of New Brunswick Press, 1958; *A Darkness in the Earth,* E.V. Griffith, 1959; *Wind in a Rocky Country,* Emblem Books, 1960; *Under the Ice,* Ryerson, 1961; *The Things Which Are,* Contact Press, 1962; *Bread, Wine and Salt* (poems), Clarke, Irwin, 1967; *Miracle at Indian River* (stories), Clarke, Irwin, 1968; *A Black Plastic Button and a Yellow Yoyo* (poems), privately printed, 1968; *The Mysterious Naked Man* (poems), Clarke, Irwin, 1969; *Playing the Jesus Game: Selected Poems,* introduction by Robert Bly, New/Books, 1970; *Between Tears and Laughter* (poems), Clarke, Irwin, 1971.

Poetry and short stories anthologized in *Best Poems of 1958: Borestone Mountain Poetry Awards,* 1959, *Poetry: 62,* edited by Eli Mandel, Ryerson, 1962, *Fire and Sleet and Candlelight,* edited by August Derleth, Arkham, 1962, *Love Where the Nights Are Long,* edited by Irving Layton, McClelland & Stewart, 1962, *The First Five Years,* edited by Robert Weaver, Oxford University Press (Toronto), 1962, *Five New Brunswick Poets,* edited by Fred Cogswell, Fiddlehead, 1962, *A Book of Canadian Stories,* edited by Desmond Pacey, Ryerson, 1962, *Best Poems of 1962: Borestone Mountain Poetry Awards,* 1963, *Modern Canadian Stories,* edited by Giose Rimanelli and Roberto Ruberto, Ryerson, 1966, *Penguin Book of Canadian Verse,* 1967, *Oxford Book of Canadian Verse,* 1968, *How Do I Love Thee: Sixty Poets of Canada (and Quebec) Select and Introduce Their Favourite Poems from Their Own Work,* edited by John Robert Colombo, M.G. Hurtig (Edmonton), 1970, and other collections.

SIDELIGHTS: Born in a Nova Scotian lumbering community, Nowlan left school at the age of twelve to cut pulp, peel pulp, and cut pit-props; he later worked as a bush-clearer for the Nova Scotia Department of Highways and as night watchman in a sawmill, before landing in Hartland, New Brunswick as a journalist on a weekly newspaper. At one time he even managed a hillbilly band, called "George Shaw and The Green Valley Ranch Boys"; Nowlan respects the sincerity of country music and the people who sing it.

Eldon Garnet mentions Nowlan in an essay on Canadian poets as strongly influenced by the wilderness of their homeland: "Our country—and, therefore, our poetry—are haunted by the ghost of the wilderness, the land. . . . Our myth is . . . a historical picture representing a tradition of isolation, frustration and exile. It is a landscape myth—a myth whose body has only recently reached maturity with the development of the modern Canadian city, with the physical separation of the poet from the land. . . . The poet confronted with a violent environment, the frontier, the wilderness, takes on the identity of the isolated wanderer. He becomes a physically and socially isolated figure." Nowlan describes his personal background, in a 1969 interview with the editors of *Fiddlehead,* as "19th Century, a pioneer environment: no electric light or telephones, nothing like that. . . . That country around Stanley wasn't like the Annapolis Valley; the soil was too poor for farming. The people there were mostly pulp-cutters. A great feeling of insecurity all the time. . . . Those people took religion very seriously but it wasn't something they were preoccupied with. It was an emotional thing. My grandmother believed in Heaven and Hell, in angels and Christ—but in witches and ghosts, too. . . . They weren't concerned really with the moral aspects of religion."

Nowlan said in the interview that he started writing at the age of eleven, partly because of a somewhat Biblical "desire to be a prophet. . . . It would have been more natural for me to become a country and western singer or a boxer. This writing was a very secret thing with me, very private." Born of Irish parents, Nowlan feels "very Irish. Goethe talks of love as an elective affinity; I think of myself as an elective Irishman. And of course a feeling of loyalty to a race enables you to project yourself into the infinite past. . . . I suppose I think of myself as Irish because that's the way everybody close to me thinks. My father's people came from Newtown-Barry, County Wexford, in the early 1800's. . . . Those people I grew up among were probably more Irish than the Irish themselves."

Many reviewers have mentioned the "strong regional quality" of Nowlan's poetry (although he once told Edward Ives he "didn't want to be known as a regionalist"). Anne Greer, writer of a thesis on his work, has said: "Irving Layton once asked Alden Nowlan why all Maritime poets were so big; Nowlan replied, half-seriously, that the little ones were all killed off before they were twelve. For a Nova Scotian there is a grim satisfaction in the discovery that the Annapolis Valley, in spite of itself, has produced a weed of such strength that it has resisted all the time-proven attempts to eradicate its kind." After meeting Nowlan in 1967 she wrote: "He is very big. The second thing one notices is his laugh. What one takes away is an impression of great wisdom."

Nowlan readily admits he prefers writing poems to short stories: "With the poems it's a direct emotional release, whereas with the stories there's a lot of hard-bone labour involved." "Mr. Nowlan is, of course, a splendid poet," writes Ernest Buckler in a review of *Miracle at Indian River.* "And all these stories show the poet's touch. But not in the usual way.... No gingerbreads of self-consciously fine phrases, no puffballs of fancy irrelevance. And when he shifts from poetry to prose, the poetic gift does not translate into lint; it is simply that extra eye which sees through things to the core." Louis Dudek classes Nowlan with that group of poets who "seem to write directly from poetic impulse, whatever that is, or from feeling and perception, as though deliberate and conscious complexity was the reverse of poetry, and significance must emerge in the creative process from spontaneity alone." Perhaps the most important tribute to Nowlan's talent comes from Fred Cogswell, who encouraged him to continue writing when they first met in 1958. Reviewing *Bread, Wine and Salt,* for which Nowlan won the Governor-General's Award for Poetry in 1967, Cogswell admires "the transparent fluidity of his presentation. Whether he writes of the inhabitants of Hainesville (Hartland), for whom he feels such ambivalence, his friends, or his own personal feelings and predicament, thought and form merge and change so beautifully and organically that one is not conscious of a seam between them."

BIOGRAPHICAL/CRITICAL SOURCES: Fiddlehead, spring, 1968, August-October, 1969; *Canadian Forum,* September, 1968; *Saturday Night,* February, 1970.

* * *

NURSE, Peter H(arold) 1926-

PERSONAL: Born July 28, 1926, in London, England; son of Harold Samuel and Maude (Glazebrook) Nurse; married Joan Hampshire, June 22, 1951; children: Stephan, Jonathan, Katharine. *Education:* Magdalen College, Oxford, B.A., 1950, M.A., 1954. *Home:* 53 Osborne Pk., Belfast, North Ireland. *Agent:* R. Gibson, 12 Elmwood Ave., Belfast, Northern Ireland.

CAREER: Ecole Normale Superieure, Sorbonne, University of Paris, Paris, France, lecturer, 1950-51; Queen's Univeristy, Belfast, Northern Ireland, senior lecturer, 1952—. *Military service:* Royal Navy, 1944-47. *Member:* Alliance Francaise (Northern Ireland; president, 1959-62). *Awards, honors:* Chevalier, L'Ordre des Palmes Academiques, 1963.

WRITINGS—Editor and author of introduction and notes: Jean Bonaventure des Periers, *Le Cymbalum mundi,* Manchester University Press, 1958; Jean Baptiste de Moliere, *L'Ecole des maris,* Harrap, 1959; Pierre Corneille, *Horace,* Harrap, 1963; Jules Romains, *Un Grand honnete homme,* Harrap, 1963; Jean Baptiste de Moliere, *Le Malade imaginaire,* Oxford University Press, 1965; Marie Madeleine La Fayette, *La Princess de Cleves,* Harrap, 1970.

(Editor) *The Art of Criticism: Essays in French Literary Analysis,* Edinburgh University Press, 1969, Aldine, 1970; *Classical Voices: Studies of Corneille, Racine, Moliere, Mme. de Lafayette,* Harrap, 1971. Contributor to professional journals in Great Britain and France.†

NYE, F(rancis) Ivan 1918-

PERSONAL: Born April 27, 1918, in Prospect, Ore.; son of Nelson M. and Clarice (Paul) Nye; married Esther Miller (now a teacher); children: Beverly Irene, Lloyd Nathan, Betty Jean (Mrs. Clyde Morrison). *Education:* Willamette University, A.B., 1946; Washington State University, M.A., 1947; Michigan State University, Ph.D., 1952. *Politics:* Democrat. *Religion:* Congregational. *Home:* 701 Skyline Dr., Pullman, Wash. 99163. *Office:* Washington State University, Pullman, Wash. 99163.

CAREER: The Ohio State University, Columbus, assistant professor of rural sociology, 1948-50; University of Missouri, Columbia, assistant professor of rural sociology, 1950-52; Bucknell University, Lewisburg, Pa., associate professor of sociology, 1952-54; Florida State University, Tallahassee, professor of sociology, 1960-63; Washington State University, Pullman, 1954-60, 1963—, began as assistant professor, now professor of sociology. *Member:* American Sociological Association, American Association for the Advancement of Science, Rural Sociological Society, National Council on Family Relations, Pacific Sociological Association.

WRITINGS: Family Relationships and Delinquent Behavior, Wiley, 1958; (editor with Lois Wladis Hoffman) *The Employed Mother in America,* Rand McNally, 1963; (editor with Felix M. Berardo) *Emerging Conceptual Frameworks in Family Analysis,* Macmillan, 1966. Editor, *Marriage and Family Living* (quarterly journal of National Council on Family Relations), 1960-64.

* * *

NYGREN, Anders T(heodor) S(amuel) 1890-

PERSONAL: Born November 15, 1890, in Gothenburg, Sweden; son of Samuel (a headmaster) and Anna Maria (Lundstrom) Nygren; married Irmgard Brandin, July 4, 1921; children: Anna-Elisabeth (Mrs. Henrik Ljungman), Irmgard (Mrs. Gunnar Ljungman), Gotthard, Ingemar. *Education:* University of Lund, Teol.Kand., 1912, Teol. lic., 1921, Teol.Dr., 1923. *Home:* Helgonavagen 10, Lund, Sweden.

CAREER: Ordained minister, Church of Sweden, 1912; pastor in Diocese of Gothenburg, Sweden, 1912-20; University of Lund, Lund, Sweden, assistant professor of philosophy of religion, 1921-24, professor of systematic theology, 1924-48, bishop of Diocese of Lund, 1948-58. Visiting professor at University of Minnesota, 1961, University of Chicago Divinity School, 1962. Ecumenical Institute, Evanston, Ill., research scholar 1961-62. World Council of Churches, member of central committee, 1948-54, chairman of Faith and Order Commission on Christ and the Church, 1953-63. Lutheran World Federation, president, 1947-52, member of Theological Commission, 1952-57.

AWARDS: HONORS: D.D. from eight universities or colleges in Hungary, United States, Scotland, Germany, Canada, Finland, including Aberdeen University, University of Heidelberg, University of Helsinki, Knox College, and University of Toronto.

WRITINGS: Religioost apriori, Gleerup (Lund), 1921; *Det bestaaende i kristendomen,* Gleerup, 1922, translation published with *Foersoningen en Gudsgaerning* as *Essence of Christianity: Two Essays* (see below); *Dogmatikens vetenskapliga grundlaeggning med saerskild haensyn till den Kant-Schleiermacherska problemstaellningen,* Gleerup, 1922; *Filosofisk och kristen etik,* Gleerup, 1923; *Etiska Grundfragor,* Gleerup, 1926; *Den kristna kaerlekstanken genom tiderna,* Svenska Kyrkans Diakonistyrelses Bokfoerlag (Stockholm), Part 1, 1930, Part 2, 1936, new edition published as *Eros och Agape,* SKDB, 1966, translation of Part 1 by A.G. Hebert published in America as *Agape and Eros: A Study of the Christian Idea of Love*, Macmillan, 1932, translation of Part 2 by Philip S. Watson published in America as *Agape and Eros: The History of the Christian Idea of Love*, two volumes, Macmillan, 1938-39, also published as three volumes in one, revised and in part retranslated by Philip S. Watson, as *Agape and Eros*, Westminster Press, 1953; *Foersoningen en Gudsgaerning*, Gleerup, 1932, 2nd edition, Sveriges Kristliga Studentroerelses Bokfoerlag (Stockholm), 1956, translation by Philip S. Watson published with *Det bestaaende i kristendomen* as *Essence of Christianity: Two Essays* (see below); *Urkristendom och Reformation*, [Lund], 1932; *The Church Controversy in Germany: The Position of the Evangelical Church in the Third Empire* (several chapters originally published in Swedish in *Svensk Teologisk Kvartalskrift* [*Swedish Theological Quarterly*], 1933), translated by G.C. Richards, S.C.M. Press, 1934; *Filosofi och motivforskning*, Svenska Kyrkans Diakonistyrelses Bokfoerlag, 1940; *Pauli brev till romarna*, Svenska Kyrkans Diakonistyrelses Bokfoerlag, 1944, translation by Carl C. Rasmussen published in America as *Commentary on Romans*, Muhlenberg Press, 1949, 4th edition of German translation by wife, Irmgard Nygren, published as *Der Roemerbrief*, Vandenhoeck & Ruprecht (Goettingen), 1965; *Herdabrev till Lunds stift*, Svenska Kyrkans Diakonistylrelses Bokfoerlag, 1949, translation by L.J. Trinterud published in America as *The Gospel of God*, Westminster Press, 1951.

(Editor with others) *This is the Church*, translated from the Swedish by Carl C. Rasmussen, Muhlenberg Press, 1952; *Kristus och hans kyrka*, Svenska Kyrkans Diakonistyrelses Bokfoerlag, 1955, translation by Alan Carlsten published in America as *Christ and His Church*, Westminster Press, 1956; *Evangelium: Fridens budskap*, Svenska Kyrkans Diakonistyrelses Bokfoerlag, 1956; *Tjaenare och foervaltare: Naagra tankar om praestens kall*, Svenska Kyrkans Diakonistyrelses Bokfoerlag, 1957; *En levande Gusdtjaenst: Nyckel till den svenska hoegmaessans mening*, Svenska Kyrkans Diakonistyrelses Bokfoerlag, 1957; *Augustin und Luther: Zwei Studien ueber den Sinn der augustinischen Theologie*, Evangelische Verlagsanstalt (Berlin), 1958; *Essense of Christianity: Two Essays* (includes translations of *Det bestaaende i kristendomen* and *Foersoningen en Gudsgaerning*), translated by Philip S. Watson, Epworth, 1960, published in America as *Essence of Christianity*, Muhlenberg Press, 1961; *The Significance of the Bible for the Church*, translated from the Swedish by Carl C. Rasmussen, Fortress, 1963; *Tro och vetande*, Luther-Agricola-Saellskapet (Helsinki), 1970; *Meaning and Method in Philosophy and Theology*, edited and translated from the Swedish by Philip S. Watson, Fortress, 1971. Contributor of articles and essays to journals.

SIDELIGHTS: Many of Nygren's books have been published in English, German, Japanese, Chinese, Dutch, Italian, Spanish, Finnish, Danish, and French. Most of his writings have been translated into German by his wife, Irmgard Nygren.

BIOGRAPHICAL/CRITICAL SOURCES: World Lutheranism of Today: A Tribute to Anders Nygren, 15 November, 1950 (in English, German, and French), Svenska Kyrkans Diakonistyrelses Bokfoerlag, 1950; Hans Magnus Nystedt, *Plikt och kaerlek: Studier i Anders Nygrens etik*, [Stockholm] 1951; Gustaf Fredrik Wingreen, *Theology in Conflict: Nygren, Barth, Bultmann*, translated by Eric H. Wahlstrom, Oliver & Boyd, 1958; William Alexander Johnson, *On Religion: A Study of Theological Method in Schleiermacher and Nygren*, E.J. Brill, 1964, Humanities, 1966; Charles W. Kegley, editor, *The Philosophy and Theology of Anders Nygren* (essays), Southern Illinois University Press, 1970.

OAKLEY, Eric Gilbert 1916-
(Peter Capon, Paul Gregson, Grapho)

PERSONAL: Born November 17, 1916, in Kent, England; son of T. Gilbert (chief consultant, Pelman Institute) and Aimee Oakley; married Margery Jones, December 30, 1939; children: Christianna. *Education:* Attended schools in London, England. *Politics:* Conservative. *Religion:* Roman Catholic.

CAREER: Writer, 1953—. *Here's Health* (monthly), editor, 1956-62; *Delicatessen* (monthly), managing editor, 1961-62; *Model Girl and Boy* and *Top Model Mirror*, London, England, publisher, 1962—; *Fitness*, production editor, 1964. *Military service:* British Army, 1940-46; *Member:* Society of Authors.

WRITINGS: Humanalysis Makes Life Easier, privately printed, 1932; (under pseudonym Grapho) *Character Reading from Handwriting*, McKay, 1943, enlarged edition, Foulsham, 1963; *Success Through Self-Analysis*, Health for All Publishing Co., 1954, published in America as *Self-Confidence Through Self-Analysis*, Wilshire, 1957; *Nature Cure Plan for Nerves*, Press Books, 1957; *Phial and Error in Pursuit of Cure*, Daniel Co., 1957. *Your Mind Matters*, Health Science Press, 1960; *How to Cultivate Confidence and Promote Personality*, A. Thomas, 1961; *All About You: Your Birthday Star and Life Guide*, Foulsham, 1961; *Better Health from Health Foods and Herbs*, Parrish, 1962; *Project Telstar: The Amazing History of The World's First Communications Satellite*, Foulsham, 1963; *Analyse Yourself and Solve Your Personal Problems*, New English Library, 1963; (under pseudonym Peter Capon) *The Power of Words*, New English Library, 1963; (under pseudonym Paul Gregson) *Making Friends: The Key to Success*, New English Library, 1963, new edition, 1968; *Successful Salesman to Sales Manager*, Foulsham, 1963; *Sane and Sensual Sex*, Walton Press, 1964; *Man into Woman: The Amazing Account of a Male's Change into Female*, Walton Press, 1964; *Secrets of Self-Hypnosis*, A. Thomas, 1964, Fell, 1965; *Public Speaking*, A. Thomas, 1964; *The History of the Rod, and Other Corporal Punishments*, Walton Press, 1965; *Astrology and Sex: How the Stars Control Your Life*, Walton Press, 1965; (under pseudonym Peter Capon) *The Sex Jungle*, Walton Press, 1965; *Orgies of Torture and Brutality: A Historical Study*, Walton Press, 1965; *Sex and Sadism Through the Ages*, Walton Press, 1966; *Solo Sex: The Problems of the Sexually Lonely*, Canova Press, 1969.

Contributor of horoscopes to *News of the World, Sunday Despatch, Yorkshire Evening Post;* contributor of articles to *Psychology, Health for All, Spiritual Healer*, and other periodicals.†

*   *   *

OATES, Stephen B. 1936-

PERSONAL: Born January 5, 1936, in Pampa, Tex.; son of Steve T. and Florence (Baer) Oates. *Education:* University of Texas at Austin, B.A. (magna cum laude), 1958, M.A., 1960, Ph.D., 1968. *Office:* University of Massachusetts, Amherst, Mass. 01002.

CAREER: Arlington State College (now University of Texas at Arlington), Arlington, instructor, 1964-67, assistant professor of history, 1967-68; University of Massachusetts, Amherst, assistant professor, 1968-70, associate professor, 1970-71, professor of history, 1971—. *Member:* Phi Beta Kappa.

WRITINGS: Confederate Cavalry West of the River, University of Texas Press, 1961; (editor) *Rip Ford's Texas*, University of Texas Press, 1963; (editor) *The Republic of Texas*, American West, 1968; *Visions of Glory: Texans on the Southwestern Frontier*, University of Oklahoma Press, 1970; *To Purge This Land With Blood: A Biography of John Brown,* Harper, 1970; *Portrait of America,* two volumes, Houghton, 1973. Contributor to magazines and historical journals.

WORK IN PROGRESS: A life of Abraham Lincoln, intended as a sequel to John Brown, to be published by Harper.

BIOGRAPHICAL/CRITICAL SOURCES: Newsweek, July 6, 1970; *Best Sellers,* August 15, 1970; *Nation,* March 29, 1971.

*   *   *

O'BRADY, Frederic Michel Maurice   1903-

PERSONAL: Original surname, Abel; born December 11, 1903, in Budapest, Hungary, became French citizen, 1947; son of Jules (expert on cereals and grain) and Anne (Kwaschnofski) Abel; married Edna Lockwood; married Colette Fleuriot, December 13, 1960. *Education:* Attended secondary schools in Germany, Hungary, and Switzerland; attended University of Munich, 1922, University of Liverpool, 1929. *Religion:* Roman Catholic. *Address:* 245 East Pyne, Princeton University, Princeton, N.J. 08540.

CAREER: Connected with the performing arts, 1919-62, in six European countries and the U.S. Danced in Ballets Russe troupe. Appeared in theatre in such plays and musical comedies as "14 juillet" (by Romain Rolland), "Ubu enchaine," "Ninotchka," "The Unthinking Lobster" (by Orson Welles), "Andalousie," "La Plume de ma tante"; member of group "Masses," which was concerned with theatre for workers and spoken choruses, 1932. Worked with Blattner and Temporal in puppet shows. Made debut as motion picture extra in "Drole de drame" (of Marcel Carne), 1937, and appeared in other films including "Blanc comme neige," "Les Amants de Verone," "C'est arrive a Paris," "Foreign Intrigue," "Mr. Arkadin." Has performed on radio and television. Also has been a commercial representative, translator, pianist, stage manager, journalist, language and economics teacher. Trinity-Pawling School, Pawling, N.Y., French teacher and drama coach, 1963-65; Princeton University, Princeton, N.J., instructor in French, 1965—. *Military service:* French Foreign Legion, 1939-40. *Member:* Syndicat Francais des Acteurs (former vice-president), Actors' Equity. *Awards, honors:* French Cross of "merite artistique," 1949.

WRITINGS: Exterieurs a Venise (novel), preface by Orson Welles, Gallimard, 1950; *Le Ciel d'en face* (novel), Gallimard, 1954; *Romarin pour le souvenir* (novel), Correa, 1958; *All Told* (autobiography), Simon & Schuster, 1964 (published in England as *All Told: The Memoirs of a Multiple Man,* Bodley Head, 1964); *There's Always a Throgmorton* (novel), Simon & Schuster, 1970.

Musical works: "L'Objet aime" (eleven-minute opera; text by Alfred Jarry), performed at Paris World Exhibition, 1937; "Rendez-vous a la Trinite" (musical comedy), produced on French television, 1951; "Le Mecene" (one-act opera), produced on French television, 1952; "L'Homme oublie," "Yolande," "Le Generique" (three one-act operas), broadcast on French radio, 1954; "Concertino en sol" (for two trumpets and strings), 1954; "Fait divers" (oratorio), broadcast on French radio, 1956. Also composer of incidental music to Cyril Connolly's English version of Jarry's "Ubu cocu," New York, 1963.

WORK IN PROGRESS: A sequel in French to *All Told,* entitled *Apres Tout;* a book on French playwright Bernstein; a book in English on schools, mainly on foreign language teaching; *Pompeii and Circumstance,* in Latin.

BIOGRAPHICAL/CRITICAL SOURCES: Andre-Charles Gervais, *Marionnettes et marionettistes de France,* Bordas, 1946; Bessy and Chardans, *Dictionnaire du cinema et de la television,* Pauvert, 1966; Ian Cameron, *The Heavies,* Praeger, 1969.

*   *   *

O'BRIEN, Vincent   1916-

PERSONAL: Born January 24, 1916, in Airdrie, Lanarkshire, Scotland; son of A. (an engineer) and Mary (Quinn) O'Brien; married J. Lucille, 1950. *Education:* Loyola College, Montreal, Quebec, student, 1927-35; University of Montreal, B.A. (summa cum laude); McGill University, M.A. (magna cum laude). *Politics:* Liberal. *Religion:* Roman Catholic. *Home:* 272 Circle Rd., Ile Bigras, Laval des Iles, Laval County, Quebec, Canada. *Agent:* Harvey-Unna Ltd., 14 Beaumont Mews, Marylebone, High St., London WIN 3LP, England; and Frank Cooper Associates, Hollywood, Calif.

CAREER: Advertising Associates Ltd., Montreal, Quebec, partner and vice-president, 1955—. Research consultant and originator of teleplays series on historical figures for National Film Board of Canada. Curator, Societe Historique des Deux Montagnes. *Military service:* Canadian Army, served in North Africa and Europe, World War II; became major; received Military Cross (Great Britain), Croix de Guerre. *Member:* Canadian Authors Association, Authors Guild of Authors League of America, Montreal Historical Society, Lake of Two Mountains Historical Society. *Awards, honors:* Concours Litteraire award ($3,000) of Province of Quebec, 1963, for *The White Cockade;* laureate of province of Quebec, 1963.

WRITINGS: The White Cockade (historical novel; Reader's Club selection), Abelard, 1963; *History of Seigneurial Families in St. Eustache,* La Victoire, 1963. Author of research manuscripts for motion pictures on Lord Elgin, Sir George Etienne Cartier, and David Thompson published by National Film Board, 1960-62.

WORK IN PROGRESS: A biography of Sieur d'Iberville; *The Raid,* a mystery story; *The Other Americans,* second historical novel in trilogy started in *The White Cockade;* scripts for two movies, "The Outlaw," the story of Donald Morrison, and "The Year of Jubilo"; research for four more mystery novels based on the hero of *The Raid.*†

*   *   *

O'CLERY, Helen (Gallagher)   1910-

PERSONAL: Born November 1, 1910, in Stranorlar, County Donegal, Ireland; daughter of Henry Thomas (a crown solicitor) and Eileen (Cullen) Gallagher; married Dermot O'Clery (a civil engineer), April 4, 1936; children: Ann, Henry, Peter, Edward, Elizabeth. *Education:* Attended convent school in France, 1927-28; St. Vincent's, Dublin, Ireland, R.G.N., 1932; Trinity College, University of Dublin, C.S.M.M.G., 1936. *Politics:* Fianna Fail. *Religion:* Catholic. *Home:* Oakfield, Brighton Rd., Foxrock, County Dublin, Ireland.

CAREER: St. Vincent's Hospital, Dublin, Ireland, theater sister, 1930-33; Adelaide Hospital, Dublin, Ireland, physiotherapist, 1934-36. *Member:* Society of Authors, Chartered Society of Physiotherapists, British Book League, Trinity College Association, Royal Irish Automobile Club, Kildare Street Club.

WRITINGS: Sparks Fly, Collins, 1948; *Spring Show,* Collins, 1949; *Swiss Adventure,* Collins, 1951; *The Mystery of Black Sod Point* (Junior Literary Guild selection), F. Watts, 1959; *The Mystery of the Phantom Ship,* F. Watts, 1961; *Mysterious Waterway,* Allen Figgis, 1963;

(editor) *The Ireland Reader*, F. Watts, 1963; (editor) *The Mermaid Reader, and of Mermen, Nixies, Water-Nymphs, Sea Sirens, Sea Serpents, Sprites, and Kindred Creatures of the Deep*, F. Watts, 1964; (editor) *Queens, Queens, Queens*, F. Watts, 1965; *Rebel Sea Queen: The Story of Grace O'Malley*, F. Watts, 1965; *The Pegasus Book of Ireland*, Dobson, 1967; *The Pegasus Book of Egypt*, Dobson, 1968; *The Pegasus Book of the Nile*, Dobson, 1970; *The Pegasus Story of Atlantis*, Dobson, 1971.

WORK IN PROGRESS: Anthologies of historical characters, for F. Watts.

SIDELIGHTS: Mrs. O'Clery began to write for children because she wanted to make history more readable for the young. But her first three books (about Irish historical characters) remain unpublished. "Recently," she adds, "I have been trying to get back, by devious routes, to historical writing." Several of her books were illustrated by her daughter, Ann.

*   *   *

O'CONNOR, Philip Marie Constant Bancroft 1916-

PERSONAL: Born September 8, 1916, in Leighton-Buzzard, Buckinghamshire, England; son of Joseph Bernard (a surgeon) and W. Xavier (Rodyk-Thompson) O'Connor; married Anne Nicolle Gaillard-D'Andel, June, 1963; children: Max, Sarah, Peter, John, Allaye, Patric. *Education:* Attended schools in France and England. *Politics:* "One world." *Religion:* Taoist. *Home:* 2 Bryn Hyfryd, Croesor, Penrhyndeudraeth, Merioneth, North Wales. *Agent:* A.P. Watt & Son, 26-28 Bedford Row, London WCIR 4HL, England.

CAREER: Former librarian in London, England; now full-time writer.

WRITINGS: Memoirs of a Public Baby, introduction by Stephen Spender, Faber, 1958, London House, 1963; *The Lower View*, Faber, 1960; *Steiner's Tour*, Olympia Press (Paris), 1960; *Living in Croesor* (autobiography), Hutchinson, 1962; *Britain in the Sixties: Vagrancy, Ethos and Actuality*, Penguin, 1963; *Selected Poems, 1936/1966*, J. Cape, 1968; *Journal*, edited by John Berger, J. Cape, 1969. Author of features and a documentary for British Broadcasting Corp. Represented in anthologies, including *Treasury of Modern Poetry*, edited by A.S. Collins, Scribner, 1946, *Penguin Book of Comic and Curious Verse*, Penguin, 1952, and *Poetry of the Thirties*, edited by Robin Skelton, Penguin, 1964. Contributor of articles and reviews to *Times Literary Supplement, Observer, Antioch Review, Esquire, Statesman, Transatlantic Review*, and other periodicals. Editor, *Seven*, 1942.

WORK IN PROGRESS: London Character: Steiner's Personality, for J. Calder; collected pieces, aphorisms, and stories.

SIDELIGHTS: "I began as a poet (aged twenty). Painted (badly) two years. Interested (hopelessly) in kind of theater—much admire Brecht. Believe ideological vacancy of this age makes almost insuperable difficulties for writers; dislike, but indulge in, avant-garde writing; consider English literary circus to be achieving insignificance; consider American writing (some) in better health than ours—we've left the earth and only return in vulgarity; exception, Sillitoe; youth may help."

BIOGRAPHICAL/CRITICAL SOURCES: London Magazine, June, 1968.†

*   *   *

O'CONNOR, Ulick   1928-

PERSONAL: Born October 12, 1928, in Dublin, Ireland; son of Matthew P. (dean of Royal College of Surgeons, Ireland) and Eileen (Murphy) Harris-O'Connor. *Education:* National University of Ireland, B.A.; King's Inns, Dublin, Barrister-at-Law; Loyola University, New Orleans, La., Diploma in Dramatic Literature. *Religion:* Roman Catholic. *Home and office:* 15 Fairfield Park, Rathgar, Dublin, Ireland. *Agent:* (books) Max Wilkinson Associates, Shelter Island, N.Y. 11964; (lectures) Keedick Lecture Bureau, Inc., 475 Fifth Ave., New York, N.Y. 10017.

CAREER: Practicing barrister, specializing in criminal law, Dublin, Ireland. *Sunday Independent*, Dublin, Ireland, columnist, four years; *Observer*, London, England, formerly sports correspondent; *Times*, London, England, drama critic. Amateur magician. Participant in television programs on Telefis Eireann, British Broadcasting Corp., National Broadcasting Co., "Johnny Carson Show," "Today Show," and other programs. Lecturer on Irish literary renaissance in Stockholm, Paris, and Rome; lecturer and reader at poetry recitals at women's clubs and colleges in U.S., 1965—. Has done two-man show with Sarah Churchill, daughter of Sir Winston. *Member:* Wanderer's Club and Pipers Club (both Dublin).

WRITINGS: Poems, Sceptre Press, 1957; *The Gresham Hotel, 1865-1965*, Guy & Co., c.1964; *James Joyce and Oliver St. John Gogarty: A Famous Friendship*, Texas Quarterly, 1960; *The Times I've Seen: Oliver St. John Gogarty—A Biography*, Obolensky, 1964 (published in England as *Oliver St. John Gogarty: A Poet and His Times*, J. Cape, 1964); *Sputnik and Other Poems*, Devin, 1967; *Travels with Ulick*, Mercier Press, 1967; (editor) *The Joyce We Knew: Memoirs by Eugene Sheehy and Others*, Mercier Press, 1967; *Brendan Behan* (biography), Hamish Hamilton, 1970, published in America as *Brendan*, Prentice-Hall, 1971; (editor) *The Yeats We Knew*, British Book Center, 1971. Also author of a play, "The Dark Lovers," about Swift and Stella, first produced in Dublin, 1968, and later adapted for radio, and two recordings, "An Evening with Oliver Gogarty," and "Poems of the Insurrection," both Mercier Press. Contributor to *Spectator, Listener, Theatre Arts*, and other periodicals. Columnist, *Sunday Mirror*.

WORK IN PROGRESS: One-man show on Brendan Behan.

SIDELIGHTS: O'Connor was the British universities boxing champion in 1950, and held the Irish native record in pole vault, 1951-55.

BIOGRAPHICAL/CRITICAL SOURCES: Observer Review, July 26, 1970; *New York Times*, August 31, 1970; *Plays and Players*, October, 1970; *Variety*, June 9, 1971.

*   *   *

O'CONNOR, William P., Jr.   1916-

PERSONAL: Born September 24, 1916, in New York, N.Y.; son of William Peter (a stockbroker) and Kathryn (Callan) O'Connor; married Dorothy Campbell; children: William P. III, Diane E., Deborah D. *Education:* Attended Portsmouth Priory School, 1929-34; Harvard University, A.B., 1938, M.B.A., 1940. *Politics:* Republican. *Religion:* Roman Catholic. *Home:* 16 Chestnut Ave., Larchmont, N.Y. 10538.

CAREER: American Stock Exchange, New York, N.Y., member, 1946-58; McDonnell & Co., New York, partner and officer, 1948-62; Moore & Schley (now Moore & Schley, Cameron & Co.), New York, partner, 1963—. Mamaroneck-Larchmont Student Aid Fund, president, 1962-64; Larchmont Civic Association, president; Boy Scout leader. *Military service:* U.S. Army, Field Artillery, 1942-46; became captain; received Silver Star and Purple Heart. *Member:* New York Society of Financial Analysts.

WRITINGS: Techniques for Maximum Market Profits: A Guide to Preselecting Growth Stocks, Prentice-Hall, 1964; The Fourteen-Point Method for Beating the Market, Regnery, 1972.

WORK IN PROGRESS: Preservation and Creation of Personal Capital, completed and awaiting publication.

* * *

ODELL, M(ary) E(lise)

PERSONAL: Born in England; daughter of Charles Herbert (a schoolmaster) and Cecilia (Riding) Odell. Education: St. Anne's College, Oxford, B.A. (honors in geography), 1938, M.A., 1949. Religion: Roman Catholic. Home: 276 Woolwick Rd., London S.W.2, England.

CAREER: Bexley Technical High School for Girls, Bexley, Kent, England, schoolmistress in charge of geography, 1942—. Borough magistrate, 1951—; former member of borough council; member of local education committee, 1948—. Member: Royal Geographical Association, National Union of Teachers.

WRITINGS: Jesus in the Holy Land, University of London Press, 1960; Preparing the Way, Hawthorn, 1963; Jesus in His Church, University of London Press, 1964.

WORK IN PROGRESS: Commentaries on the Gospels, with the view of making them intelligible to the less educated.

AVOCATIONAL INTERESTS: Music, literature, and cookery.

* * *

ODEN, Thomas C(lark) 1931-

PERSONAL: Born October 21, 1931, in Altus, Okla.; son of Waldo T. (an attorney) and Lily (Clark) Oden; married Edrita Pokorny, August 10, 1952; children: Clark, Edward, Laura. Education: University of Oklahoma, B.A. (honors), 1953; Southern Methodist University, Perkins School of Theology, B.D. (highest honors), 1956; Yale University, M.A., 1958, Ph.D., 1960. Politics: Democrat. Home: 6 Loantaka Terrace, Madison, N.J. 07940. Office: Theological School, Drew University, Madison, N.J. 07940.

CAREER: Ordained to Methodist ministry, 1956; Yale University, New Haven, Conn., assistant instructor in religion, 1957-58; Southern Methodist University, Perkins School of Theology, Dallas, Tex., visiting lecturer, 1958-60; Phillips University, Graduate Seminary, Enid, Okla., 1960-70, began as associate professor, became professor of theology and ethics; Drew University, Theological School, Madison, N.J., professor of theology and ethics, 1970—. American Society of Christian Social Ethics, Society for Religion in Higher Education, Phi Beta Kappa, Phi Eta Sigma.

WRITINGS: The Crisis of the World and the Word of God, Methodist Student Movement, 1962; Radical Obedience: The Ethics of Rudolf Bultmann, with a Response by Rudolf Bultmann, Westminster, 1964; The Community of Celebration: Toward an Ecclesiology for a Renewing Student Movement, Methodist Student Movement, 1964; Kerygma and Counseling: Toward a Covenant Ontology for Secular Psychotherapy, Westminster, 1966; Contemporary Theology and Psychotherapy, Westminster, 1967; The Structure of Awareness, Abingdon, 1969; The Promise of Barth: The Ethics of Freedom, Lippincott, 1969; Beyond Revolution: A Response to the Underground Church, Westminster, 1970; The Intensive Group Experience: The New Pietism, Westminster, 1972. Contributor of articles to religious periodicals.

WORK IN PROGRESS: Contractual Pedagogy; a critique of the Human Potential Movement; Growth Groups and Christian Community—An Historical and Contemporary Appraisal.

BIOGRAPHICAL/CRITICAL SOURCES: Encounter, autumn, 1967; Christian Century, February 14, 1968.

* * *

OGAN, George F. 1912-
(Lee Castle and M.G. Ogan, joint pseudonyms)

PERSONAL: Born February 1, 1912, in Kirkwood, Mo.; son of George B. and Effie I. (Keefer) Ogan; married Margaret Nettles (a teacher and writer). Education: University of Rochester, B.A. Residence: Columbia, La. Agent: Larry Sternig, 2407 North 44th St., Milwaukee, Wis. 53210.

CAREER: Teacher in Caldwell Parish School System, Columbia, La. Writer.

WRITINGS—With wife, Margaret Ogan; all published by Funk, except as noted: Devil Drivers, 1961, A Place for Ingrid, 1962, Backyard Winner, 1963, Pancake Special, 1965, The Green Galloper, 1966, Goofy Foot, 1967, Choicy, 1968, Number One Son (Dorothy Canfield Fisher Children's Book Award reading list selection, 1970), 1969, Water Rat, 1970, Desert Road Racer (Bound-to-Stay-Bound Book Club selection), Westminster, 1970; Big Iron, Westminster, 1972.

Contributor with wife, Margaret Ogan, under joint pseudonyms Lee Castle and M.G. Ogan, and separately, of short stories to Argosy, Adventure, Alfred Hitchcock Mystery Magazine, Mike Shayne Mystery Magazine, Zane Grey Western Magazine, New York Daily News, Boys Life, Tan Confessions, Toronto Star, Gent, and to magazines in Canada, Denmark, Sweden, Great Britain, Australia, Spain, South Africa, and other foreign countries. Stories anthologized in six Lantern Press anthologies and a Dell anthology of motorcycle stories.

* * *

OGAN, Margaret E. (Nettles) 1923-
(Lee Castle and M.G. Ogan, joint pseudonyms)

PERSONAL: Born April 27, 1923, in Columbia, La.; daughter of Samuel B. and Turah E. (Hamilton) Nettles; married George Ogan (a teacher and writer). Education: Privately tutored; graduate study at California universities. Residence: Columbia, La. Agent: Larry Sternig, 2407 North 44th St., Milwaukee, Wis. 53210.

CAREER: Teacher in public schools in Columbia, La. Author.

WRITINGS—With husband, George Ogan; all published by Funk, except as noted: Devil Drivers, 1961, A Place for Ingrid, 1962, Backyard Winner, 1963, Goofy Foot, 1967, Pancake Special, 1965, The Green Galloper, 1966, Goofy Foot, 1967, Choicy, 1968, Number One Son (Dorothy Canfield Fisher Children's Book Award reading list selection, 1970), 1969, Water Rat, 1970, Desert Road Racer (Bound-to-Stay-Bound Book Club selection), Westminster, 1970; Big Iron, Westminster, 1972.

Contributor with husband, George Ogan, under joint pseudonyms Lee Castle and M.G. Ogan, and separately, of short stories to Argosy, Adventure, Alfred Hitchcock Mystery Magazine, Mike Shayne Mystery Magazine, Zane Grey Western Magazine, New York Daily News, Boys Life, Tan Confessions, Toronto Star, Gent, and to magazines in Canada, Denmark, Sweden, Great Britain, Australia, Spain, South Africa, and other foreign countries. Stories anthologized in six Lantern Press anthologies and a Dell anthology of motorcycle stories.

SIDELIGHTS: The Ogans travel extensively in order to obtain background material for their youth books and short stories. Most of their books are fast-paced adventure stories about auto racing or water sports: swimming, sailing, surfing.

* * *

OGDEN, Daniel M(iller), Jr.   1922-

PERSONAL: Born April 28, 1922, in Clarksburg, W.Va.; son of Daniel Miller (a merchant) and Mary Elizabeth (Maphis) Ogden; married Valeria Juan Munson, December 28, 1946; children: Janeth Lee (Mrs. Jefferson Martin), Patricia Jo, Daniel Munson. *Education:* Washington State University, B.A. (with highest honors), 1944; University of Chicago, M.A., 1947, Ph.D., 1949. *Politics:* Democrat. *Religion:* Unitarian. *Home:* 1812 Seminole Dr., Fort Collins, Colo. 80521. *Office:* College of Humanities and Social Sciences, Colorado State University, Fort Collins, Colo. 80521.

CAREER: Washington State University, Pullman, instructor, 1949-52, assistant professor, 1952-57, associate professor of political science, 1957-61; U.S. Department of the Interior, Washington, D.C., staff assistant, Resources Program Staff, 1961-64, assistant director, Bureau of Outdoor Recreation, 1964-67, Director of Budget, 1967-68; Colorado State University, Fort Collins, dean, College of Humanities and Social Sciences, 1968—. U.S. Senate Committee on Interstate and Foreign Commerce, professional staff member, 1956-57; Democratic National Committee, special consultant to chairman, 1960-61. Washington State Democratic Central Committee, committeeman, 1952-56. *Military service:* U.S. Army, 1943-46; served in European theater; became staff sergeant; received two battle stars. *Member:* American Political Science Association, Western Political Science Association (executive council, 1961-63), Pacific Northwest Political Science Association (secretary-treasurer, 1953-56), Phi Beta Kappa (former chapter president), Pi Sigma Alpha, Phi Kappa Phi.

WRITINGS: (Contributor) *Presidential Nominating Politics in 1952*, Volume V, *The West*, Johns Hopkins Press, 1954; (with Hugh A. Bone) *Washington Politics*, New York University Press, 1960; (with Claudius O. Johnson and others) *American National Government*, 5th edition, Crowell, 1960, 7th edition, 1970; (with Johnson and others) *American State and Local Government*, 3rd edition, Crowell, 1961, 5th edition, 1971; (with Arthur L. Peterson) *Electing the President, 1964*, Chandler Publishing, 1964, revised edition published as *Electing the President, 1968; Basic Elements of the Politics of Water Resources Development* (speech), Colorado State University, 1970. Writer of research studies and reports, and contributor to political science journals. Editor, *Official Proceedings of the Democratic National Convention, 1956.*

* * *

OGLESBY, Richard E(dward)   1931-

PERSONAL: Born March 27, 1931, in Waukegan, Ill.; son of Harold W. and Hedwig (Staranowicz) Oglesby; married Eugenia Basquin, May 11, 1957; children: Susan Deborah. *Education:* Northwestern University, B.S., 1953, M.A., 1957, Ph.D., 1962. *Home:* 925 Calle Cortita Rd., Santa Barbara, Calif. 93109. *Office:* University of California, Santa Barbara, Calif. 92706.

CAREER: Eastern Illinois University, Charleston, assistant professor of history, 1961-65; University of California, Santa Barbara, assistant professor, 1965-69, associate professor of history, 1969—. *Military service:* U.S. Army, Counter Intelligence Corps, 1953-55; became sergeant. *Member:* American Historical Association, Western History Association, Organization of American Historians, Missouri Historical Society, Montana Historical Society.

WRITINGS: Manuel Lisa and the Opening of the Missouri Fur Trade, University of Oklahoma Press, 1963; (editor) Manuel Lisa, *The American West, an Appraisal*, Museum of New Mexico Press, 1963.

WORK IN PROGRESS: A history of the modern West.

AVOCATIONAL INTERESTS: Travel.

* * *

OGNALL, Leopold Horace   1908-
(Harry Carmichael, Hartley Howard)

PERSONAL: Born June 20, 1908, in Montreal, Quebec; son of Harry Henry and Elizabeth (Jacobson) Ognall; married Cecilia Sumroy, July 5, 1932; children: Harry Henry, Michael John, Margaret Rose. *Education:* Attended Rutherglen Academy, Glasgow, Scotland. *Religion:* Jewish. *Home:* 18 Avondale Court, Shadwell Lane, Leeds 17, Yorkshire, England. *Agent:* A.D. Peters, 10 Buckingham St., Adelphi, London WC2N 6BU, England.

CAREER: Before becoming full-time writer, worked in father's business, then as newspaper reporter and editor of local weekly, correspondence manager in mail order firm, ten years, efficiency engineer for British government, four years. *Member:* Society of Authors (North of England committee), P.E.N., Crime Writers Association, Yorkshire Medico-Legal Society.

WRITINGS—Under pseudonym Harry Carmichael: *The Vanishing Trick*, Collins, 1952; *Death Leaves a Diary*, Collins, 1952; *Deadly Nightcap*, Collins, 1953; *School for Murder*, Collins, 1953; *Why Kill Johnny?*, Collins, 1954; *Death Counts Three*, Collins, 1954; *Noose for a Lady*, Collins, 1955; *Money for Murder*, Collins, 1955; *The Screaming Rabbit*, Simon & Schuster, 1955; *The Dead of the Night*, Collins, 1956; *Justice Enough*, Collins, 1956; *Emergency Exit*, Collins, 1957; *Put Out That Star*, Collins, 1957; *Into Thin Air*, Collins, 1957, Doubleday, 1958; *James Knowland: Deceased*, Collins, 1958; *A Question of Time*, Collins, 1958; *Or Be He Dead*, Doubleday, 1958; *Stranglehold*, Collins, 1959; *Marked Man*, Doubleday, 1959; *The Seeds of Hate*, Collins, 1959.

Requiem for Charles, Collins, 1960; *Alibi*, Collins, 1961, Macmillan, 1962; *Confession*, Collins, 1961; *The Late Unlamented*, Doubleday, 1961; *The Link*, Collins, 1962; *Of Unsound Mind*, Doubleday, 1962; *Vendetta*, Macmillan, 1963; *Flashback*, Collins, 1964; *Safe Secret*, Collins, 1964, Macmillan, 1965; *Post Mortem*, Collins, 1965, Doubleday, 1966; *Suicide Clause*, Collins, 1966; *The Condemned*, Collins, 1967; *Murder by Proxy*, Collins, 1967; *A Slightly Bitter Taste*, Collins, 1968.

Death Trap, Collins, 1970, McCall Publishing, 1971; *Remote Control*, Collins, 1970, McCall Publishing, 1971; *The Quiet Woman*, Collins, 1971, Saturday Review Press, 1972; *Most Deadly Hate*, Collins, 1971, Saturday Review Press, 1972; *Naked to the Grave*, Collins, 1972, Saturday Review Press, 1973; *Too Late for Tears*, Collins, 1973.

Under pseudonym Hartley Howard; all published by Collins: *The Last Appointment*, 1951, *The Last Vanity*, 1951, *The Last Deception*, 1951, *Death of Cecilia*, 1952, *Bowman Strikes Again*, 1953, *The Other Side of the Door*, 1953, *Bowman at a Venture*, 1954, *Bowman on Broadway*, 1954, *No Target for Bowman*, 1955, *Sleep for the Wicked*, 1955, *A Hearse for Cinderella*, 1956, *The Bowman Touch*, 1956, *The Long Night*, 1957, *Key to the Morgue*, 1957, *Sleep My Pretty One*, 1958, *The Big Snatch*, 1958, *Deadline*, 1959, *The Armitage Secret*, 1959, *Extortion*, 1960, *Fall Guy*, 1960, *I'm No Hero*, 1961, *Time Bomb*, 1961, *Double Finesse*, 1962, *Count-down*, 1962, *The Stretton Case*, 1963, *Department K*, 1964, *Out of the Fire*, 1965, *Portrait of a Beautiful Harlot*, 1966, *Counterfeit*, 1966, *Routine Investigation*, 1967, *The Eye of the Hurricane*, 1968, *The Secret of Simon Cornell*,

1969, *Cry on My Shoulder*, 1970, *Room 37*, 1970, *Million Dollar Snapshot*, 1971, *Murder One*, 1971, *Epitaph for Joanna*, 1972, *Nice Day for a Funeral*, 1972.

WORK IN PROGRESS: Four new books each year.

SIDELIGHTS: Ognall says he has been described as a fiction factory, social phenomenon, and by various other terms, but with ninety titles (English and foreign) behind him, he enthusiastically writes on. Commenting, "I would prefer to earn my living as a writer [rather] than in any other sphere, irrespective of financial return. My family read my books and occasionally admit that they enjoy them." His elder son is a barrister, the younger one a doctor, the daughter, married to a doctor.

A total of sixty Ognall books have been published in nine foreign languages in Europe and South America; many books have been serialized in newspapers and magazines in Britain, North Africa, and Scandinavia. *Department K* was filmed by Columbia in 1968 as "Assignment K"; *A Slightly Bitter Taste* was produced as a television play.

AVOCATIONAL INTERESTS: Beer, books, and Beethoven.

BIOGRAPHICAL/CRITICAL SOURCES: Best Sellers, January 15, 1971; *Saturday Review*, February 27, 1971.

* * *

O'HARA, Frank 1926-1966

PERSONAL: Born June 27, 1926, in Baltimore, Md. *Education:* Harvard University, A.B., 1950; University of Michigan, M.A., 1951. *Politics:* "Depends, independent I guess." *Religion:* None. *Office:* The Museum of Modern Art, 11 West 53rd St., New York, N.Y.

CAREER: The Museum of Modern Art, New York, N.Y., staff member, 1952-53; *Art News*, New York, N.Y., editorial associate, 1953-55; The Museum of Modern Art, organizer of circulating exhibitions, 1955-60, assistant curator, department of painting and sculpture exhibitions, 1960-66. Poet-playwright-in-residence at Poet's Theatre, Cambridge, Mass., 1955; apprentice in stagecraft, Brattle Theatre, Cambridge, Mass. *Military service:* U.S. Navy, 1944-46. *Awards, honors:* Hopwood Award for poetry, 1951; co-winner, National Book Award, 1972, for *The Collected Poems of Frank O'Hara*.

WRITINGS: A City Winter, and Other Poems, Tibor de Nagy Gallery Editions, 1952; *Meditations in an Emergency* (poems), M. Alcover (Spain), 1956, Grove, 1957, 2nd edition, 1967; *Jackson Pollock*, (monograph), Braziller, 1959; *Hartigan and Rivers with O'Hara* (an exhibition of pictures, with poems by Frank O'Hara), Tibor de Nagy Gallery Editions, 1959; *Second Avenue* (poems), Totem-Corinth Press, 1960; *Odes* (poems; with serigraphs by Michael Goldberg), Tiber Press, 1960, 2nd edition, Poets Press, 1969; *Awake in Spain* (play; produced at The Living Theatre, 1960), American Theatre for Poets, 1960; *New Spanish Painting and Sculpture: Rafael Canogar and Others* (exhibition catalog), Doubleday, for Museum of Modern Art, New York, 1960; *An Exhibition of Oil Paintings by Frankenthaler* (exhibition catalog), Jewish Museum of the Jewish Theological Seminary of America, 1960; *The General's Return from One Place to Another* (play; produced at Present Stages, New York, N.Y., 1964), [New York], 1962; *Franz Kline* (exhibition catalog), [Turin], 1963; *Lunch Poems*, City Lights, 1964; *Love's Labor* (play; produced at The Living Theatre, New York, N.Y., 1960), American Theatre for Poets, 1964; *Arshile Gorky* (exhibition catalog), Hermes (Bonn), 1964; *Featuring Frank O'Hara*, [Buffalo], 1964; *Robert Motherwell: With Selections from the Artist's Writings* (exhibition catalog), Doubleday, for Museum of Modern Art, New York, 1965; *Love Poems (Tentative Title)*, Tibor de Nagy Gallery Editions, 1965; *David Smith, 1907-1965, At the Tate Gallery* (exhibition catalog), [London], 1966; *Nakian* (exhibition catalog), Doubleday, for Museum of Modern Art, New York, 1966; *In Memory of My Feelings: A Selection of Poems*, edited by Bill Berkson, Museum of Modern Art, 1967; *Two Pieces* (poems), Long Hair Books (London), 1969; *Oranges* (poems), Angel Hair Books (New York), 1970; *The Collected Poems of Frank O'Hara*, edited by Donald M. Allen, Knopf, 1971. Unpublished plays: "Try! Try!," first produced at The Poets Theatre, Cambridge, Mass., 1951; "Change Your Bedding," first produced at The Poets Theatre, 1952; "The Houses at Fallen Hanging," produced at the Living Theatre, 1956. Writer of dialogue for films. Represented in anthologies, including *New American Poetry*, edited by Donald M. Allen, Grove, 1960. Contributor of poems to *Accent, Partisan Review, New World Writing*, and other periodicals, and of criticism to *Folder, Evergreen Review*, and *Kulchur*.

SIDELIGHTS: O'Hara was described by Paul Carroll as "the first and ... the best of the poets of the impure." Bill Berkson has written of his work: O'Hara has the ability, and the power, to use in a poem whatever occurred to him at the moment, without reflection. It is not that he lacked selectivity or discrimination, but rather that his poems grew out of a process of natural selection—discrimination conjoining civility of attention—so that any particle of experience quick enough to get fixed in his busy consciousness earned its point of relevance." O'Hara himself had said: "I don't think of fame or posterity (as Keats so grandly and genuinely did), nor do I care about clarifying experiences for anyone or bettering (other than accidentally) anyone's state or social relation, nor am I for any particular technical development in the American language simply because I find it necessary. What is happening to me, allowing for lies and exaggerations which I try to avoid, goes into my poems. I don't think my experiences are clarified or made beautiful for myself or anyone else, they are just there in whatever form I can find them. What is clear to me in my work is probably obscure to others, and vice versa. ... It may be that poetry makes life's nebulous events tangible to me and restores their detail; or conversely, that poetry brings forth the intangible quality of incidents which are all too concrete and circumstantial. Or each on specific occasions, or both all the time." O'Hara, one of the members of "The New York School" of poets, collaborated in creative relationships with "New York School Second Generation" painters in "poem painting." When he was killed in an auto accident, his family and friends established the Frank O'Hara Foundation for Poetry and Art to recognize and assist poets, with eventual corresponding support for artists. *In Memory of My Feelings* is a limited edition volume, the proceeds of which will go to the Foundation for grants-in-aid to young writers.

BIOGRAPHICAL/CRITICAL SOURCES: Donald M. Allen, *New American Poetry*, Grove, 1960; *New York Times*, July 27, 1966, January 19, 1968, August 11, 1968; *Village Voice*, July 28, 1966, April 20, 1967; *Time*, August 5, 1966; *Newsweek*, August 8, 1966; *Antiquarian Bookman*, September 5-12, 1966; *Art and Literature*, spring, 1967; *National Observer*, July 10, 1967; *Newsweek*, January 22, 1968; *New York Times Book Review*, February 11, 1968; Paul Carroll, *The Poem in Its Skin*, Follett, 1968.

(Died July 25, 1966)

* * *

OLDHAM, Frank 1903-

PERSONAL: Born March 17, 1903, in Leicester, England; son of Charles and Edith Sarah (Hopkins) Oldham; married Dorothy Annie Ball, August 30, 1930; children: Laurence, Frances Jane. *Education:* Attended Alderman Newton Boys' School; King's College, London, B.Sc., 1925; St. John's College, Cambridge, B.A., 1927, M.A., 1930, F.Inst.P., 1942. *Home:* 19 Dingle Rd., Boscombe, Hampshire, England.

CAREER: Manchester Grammar School, Manchester, England, senior physics master, 1927-33; Hinckley Grammar School, Leicester, England, headmaster, 1933-63. Police Authority, Leicestershire, member; justice of the peace, 1943; Hinckley Magistrates, chairman, 1951-63. *Member:* Institute of Physics and Physical Society (fellow), Science Masters' Association, Association for Science Education, Rotary Club (past president).

WRITINGS: Thomas Young, Philosopher and Physician, Edward Arnold, 1933; (with Eric Langton) *General Physics, with Some Astronomy,* University of London Press, 1938, 4th edition, 1948; (with Alexander Wood) *Thomas Young, Natural Philosopher, 1773-1829,* Cambridge University Press, 1954; (with Langton) *Physics for Today,* University of London Press, 1962, International Publications Service, 1963; *Becoming Comprehensive: Case Histories,* Pergamon, 1970.

AVOCATIONAL INTERESTS: Horticulture, music; the Welsh countryside, particularly Merioneth.

*　　*　　*

OLDHAM, W(illiam) Dale 1903-

PERSONAL: Born March 30, 1903, in Ripley, Okla.; son of William Harrison (a minister, Church of God) and Myrtle (Elmore) Oldham; married Pauline Edith Brown, August 26, 1924; children: Douglas Reed Oldham. *Education:* Anderson College and Theological Seminary, B.Th., 1938; United Theological Seminary, Dayton, Ohio, B.D., 1941. *Politics:* Normally Republican. *Home:* Star Route, Box 666, Eustis, Fla. 32726.

CAREER: Church of God (headquarters in Anderson, Ind.), pastor in Akron, Ind., 1928-31, Lima, Ohio, 1931-34, Dayton, Ohio, 1934-45, Anderson, Ind., 1945-62; now retired. Speaker on denomination's international weekly radio program, "Christian Brotherhood Hour," emanating from Anderson, Ind., 1947-68, executive director of denomination's Radio and Television Commission, 1961-68. Warner Press, Inc. (denominational), Anderson, Ind., chairman of directors, 1947-71, president of board, 1947-58. *Member:* Kiwanis. *Awards, honors:* D.D., Anderson College and Theological Seminary, 1945.

WRITINGS—All collections of sermons published by Warner Press: *Christ is the Answer,* 1945, *What Christ Can Do,* 1947, *The Compassionate Christ,* 1949, *Messages of Christian Brotherhood,* 1951, *The Enduring Word: A Book of Doctrinal Sermons,* 1952, *Living Close to God,* 1957, *Give Me Tomorrow,* 1964, *Just Across the Street: How to Be a Growing Christian,* 1968.

WORK IN PROGRESS: An autobiography.

SIDELIGHTS: Oldham has made seven speaking trips into the West Indies, 1948-69, seven trips to Europe, 1950-70, and two to Japan. *Avocational interests:* Photography; sports, including hunting, fishing, swimming, golf, hiking.

*　　*　　*

OLECK, Howard L(eoner) 1911-

PERSONAL: Born January 6, 1911, in New York, N.Y.; son of Richard and Yvette (Leoner) Oleck; married Helen Eugenie Gemeiner, December, 1941; children: Anabel, Joan. *Education:* University of Iowa, B.A., 1933; New York Law School, J.D., 1938. *Politics:* Democrat. *Home:* 25 Murwood Dr., Moreland Hills, Ohio 44022.

Office: Cleveland State University, College of Law, 1240 Ontario St., Cleveland, Ohio 44113.

CAREER: Lawyer; admitted to New York Bar, 1938, Ohio Bar, 1957, and to Federal Bar; practice of law in New York, N.Y., 1938-47; New York Law School, New York, associate professor of law, 1947-56; Cleveland State University, College of Law (formerly Cleveland-Marshall Law School of Baldwin-Wallace College), Cleveland, Ohio, 1956—, began as professor of law and associate dean, became dean, now Distinguished Professor of Law. Foreign Language Press Association, New York, N.Y., reporter and advertising man, 1930-33; U.S. Manufacturers Directory Corp., New York, assistant to president, 1933-38. Consultant, Congressional Study of Foundations, 1962. *Military service:* U.S. Army, 1942-45; served with Armored Forces in Europe, later War Department historian and editor; became major; received Purple Heart, four battle stars, Croix de Mouvement Nationale Belge, Medaille Militaire, and other awards.

MEMBER: American Bar Association, American Judicature Society, Law-Science Academy of America, League of Ohio Law Schools (president, 1963-64), Ohio State Bar Association, Cleveland Bar Association, New York City Bar Association, Scribes (director, 1970—), Free and Accepted Masons, Phi Alpha Delta. *Awards, honors:* LL.D., Baldwin-Wallace College, 1963.

WRITINGS: Creditors' Rights, Harmon, 1948; *Creditors' Rights and Remedies,* Harmon, 1949; *Debtor-Creditor Law: A Treatise,* Central Book Co., 1953; *Negligence Investigation Manual: A Handbook for Attorneys, Insurance Adjusters, Private Investigators, and All Interested in the Art of Investigation,* Central Book Co., 1953; *Negligence Forms of Pleading: State-Federal,* Central Book Co., 1954, supplement, 1957; *New York Corporations: State, Federal, Administrative and Private Law, Regulations and Procedures, with Forms, Tables, and Checklists* (includes revisions and supplements by Joseph H. Wishod), two volumes, Slater, 1954; *Digest of all States' Negligence Laws,* Markham's Negligence Counsel, 1955; *Damages to Persons and Property, Illustrated and Annotated,* Central Book Co., 1955, 3rd edition, 1961; *Non-Profit Corporations and Associations: Organization, Management, and Dissolution,* Prentice-Hall, 1956, 2nd edition published as *Non-Profit Corporations, Organizations, and Associations,* 1965; (Volumes 2-6 with assistance of Winifred Knorr) *Modern Corporation Law,* Volume 1: *Organizing the Corporation,* Volume 2: *Management of the Corporation,* Volume 3: *Shareholders and Third Parties,* Volume 4: *Consolidation, Insolvency, and Dissolution,* Volume 5: *Forms,* Volume 6: *Combined General Index,* Bobbs-Merrill, 1958-60, also published in one-volume students' edition, 1960; *Facts and Fictions About Evening Law Schools,* Cleveland-Marshall Law School of Baldwin-Wallace College, 1962; *Research and Writing for the Professional Market: The Financial Aspects,* Cleveland-Marshall Law School of Baldwin-Wallace College, 1966; *Law for Living,* Professional Books Service, 1967; *A Singular Fury: A Sam Benedict Mystery,* World Publishing, 1968; *Primer on Legal Writing for Cleveland State Law Review and for Legal Writing Classes* (pamphlet), College of Law, Cleveland State University, 1969; *Law for Everyone: Everyday Answers to Questions and Problems of Law for the Layman,* Association Press, 1971.

Editor: (With others) *Directors' and Officers' Encyclopedic Manual,* Prentice-Hall, 1955; *Encyclopedia of Negligence,* two volumes, Central Book Co., 1962; *Cases on Damages,* Bobbs-Merrill, 1962; (compiler) *Heroic Battles of World War II,* Belmont Books, 1962; (compiler) *Eye Witness World War II Battles,* Belmont Books, 1963. Editor of *Negligence and Compensation Service,* a bi-weekly, bound annually, Central Book Co., 1955-67, and compiler of special editions, 1956, 1957. Contributor, under own name and various pseudonyms, of more than 300 articles, stories, and monographs to books, professional journals, and magazines. Assistant to editor, *New York Law Journal*, 1946-53; faculty editor, *Cleveland State Law Review*, 1956—; law columnist, *Cleveland Plain Dealer*, 1959—. Advisory editor, *Annotated Connecticut Insurance Statutes, 1960, Indexed*, 1960, and *New Jersey Insurance Statutes, 1962, Indexed*, 1962, both published by National Insurance Law Service.

WORK IN PROGRESS: Revising *Non-Profit Corporations, Organizations, and Associations* for third edition.

BIOGRAPHICAL/CRITICAL SOURCES: New York Times Book Review, December 29, 1968; *Variety*, February 5, 1969.

* * *

OLIVER, E(dward) J(ames) 1911-

PERSONAL: Born March 3, 1911, in London, England. *Education:* Christ Church, Oxford, B.A., 1932. *Address:* c/o Collier Books, 866 Third Ave., New York, N.Y. 10022.

CAREER: Author. *Military service:* British Army, Field Security, 1940-42.

WRITINGS: Not Long to Wait, Longmans, Green, 1948; *The Clown*, J. Cape, 1951; *Coventry Patmore*, Sheed, 1956; *Gibbon and Rome*, Sheed, 1958; *Balzac the European*, Sheed, 1959; *Hypocrisy and Humour*, Sheed, 1960; *Honore de Balzac*, Macmillan, 1964.

WORK IN PROGRESS: Europe's Place in the World.

* * *

OLSON, Philip G(ilbert) 1934-

PERSONAL: Born February 16, 1934, in Racine, Wis.; son of Arthur L. (a businessman) and Rachel (Gilbert) Olson; married Mary Jill Smalley, July 23, 1955; children: Elizabeth, John, Patricia, Charles. *Education:* University of Arizona, B.A., 1954, M.A., 1956; London School of Economics, London, postgraduate study, 1954; Purdue University, Ph.D., 1959. *Office:* Department of Sociology, University of Missouri, Kansas City, Mo. 64110.

CAREER: Purdue University, Lafayette, Ind., instructor, 1957-59; University of Connecticut, Storrs, assistant professor of sociology, 1959-61; Clark University, Worcester, Mass., assistant professor, 1961-64, associate professor of sociology and chairman of department, 1964-69; University of Missouri, Kansas City, professor of sociology, and chairman of department, 1969—. *Member:* American Sociological Association, American Anthropological Association, American Association of University Professors (chapter president, 1963-64), Sigma Xi, Alpha Kappa Delta.

WRITINGS: (With Thomas McCleneghan) *Douglas, Arizona* (monograph), Bureau of Business Research, University of Arizona, 1957; *Job Mobility and Migration in a High Income Rural Community* (monograph), Agricultural Experiment Station, Purdue University, 1960; (editor) *America as a Mass Society: Changing Community and Identity*, Free Press, 1963; *The Study of Modern Society: Perspectives from Classic Sociology*, Random House, 1970. Contributor of articles to *Traffic Quarterly* and *Human Organization.*

WORK IN PROGRESS: A book on the American community, with Art Gallaher, Jr.

* * *

OPPENHEIMER, Joel (Lester) 1930-

PERSONAL: Born February 18, 1930, in Yonkers, N.Y.; son of Leopold (a retailer) and Kate (Rosenwasser) Oppenheimer; married Rena Furlong, June 5, 1952 (divorced June 4, 1960), married Helen Bukberg, June 5, 1966; children: (first marriage) Nicholas Patrick, Daniel Eben; (second marriage) Nathaniel Ezra, Lemuel Shandy, Davin. *Education:* Attended Cornell University, 1947-48, University of Chicago, 1948-49, Black Mountain College, 1950-53. *Politics:* "Non-practicing anarcho-syndicalism." *Religion:* "Non-practicing orthodox Jew." *Home:* 463 West St., New York, N.Y. *Agent:* Karen Hitzig, Wender & Assoc., 30 East 60th St., New York, N.Y.

CAREER: Has worked as printer-typographer-advertising production man in Washington, D.C., Provincetown, Massachusetts, and Rochester, New Hampshire; Arrow Typographic Service, Inc., New York, N.Y., production manager, 1964—. City College of the City University of New York, New York, N.Y., currently poet-in-residence.

WRITINGS: The Dancer (poems), Jargon, 1952; *The Dutiful Son* (poems), J. Williams (London), 1956, Jargon, 1957, Totem, 1961; *The Love Bit and Other Poems*, Totem Press, 1962; (with John Keys, Taylor Mead, Al Fowler, Ed Sanders, and John Harriman) *Poems for Marilyn*, [New York], 1962; *The Great American Desert* (playscript), Grove, 1966; *A Treatise*, Brownstone Press, 1966; *Sirvantes on a Sad Occurrence: A Poem*, Perishable Press, 1967; *In Time: Poems, 1962-1968*, Bobbs-Merrill, 1969; *The Wrong Season* (comment), Bobbs-Merrill, 1973; *On Occasion* (poems), Bobbs-Merrill, in press.

Three plays, *The Great American Desert*, "Like a Hill," and "Miss Right," have been produced "off-off-Broadway." Contributor to little magazines. Editor, *Kulchur 5.*

WORK IN PROGRESS: Four books of verse, *Friends and Lovers, Desert Victory, Clutch,* and *Shooting the Moon;* four plays, "The Interview," "The Hog Ranch," "Two Worms in the Apple," "Tristram Shandy"; research on war and Western man.

AVOCATIONAL INTERESTS: Printing and typography, military history; does "very little traveling."

BIOGRAPHICAL/CRITICAL SOURCES: Poetry, August, 1963; *Library Journal*, October 15, 1969; *Book World*, February 15, 1970; *Nation*, July 20, 1970.

* * *

ORMOND, (Willard) Clyde 1906-

PERSONAL: Born March 19, 1906, in Rigby, Idaho; son of Enos (a farmer) and Nellie (Rolfe) Ormond; married Lucille Anderson (a teacher), October 15, 1926; children: Gerald Clyde, Nikki Lou (Mrs. John Nelson). *Education:* Attended Brigham Young University, 1924-26, Ricks College, summers 1926-27, and Chicago Art Institute, 1930. *Home address:* Route 2, Box 70-A, Rigby, Idaho 83442.

CAREER: Teacher and principal in public schools at Clark, Idaho, and Ririe, Idaho, 1926-38; free-lance writer, 1938—. Musician in professional dance band, 1929-38; inventor, holding three patents; one-time licensed boxer; photographer, illustrating own books and articles. Western Securities, Inc., director, 1954—. *Member:* National Rifle Association of America (life).

WRITINGS: Hunting in the Northwest, Knopf, 1948; *Hunting Our Biggest Game*, Stackpole, 1956; *Hunting Our Medium Size Game*, Stackpole, 1958; *Bear!*, Stackpole, 1961; *Complete Book of Hunting*, Harper, 1962, revised edition, 1972; *Complete Book of Outdoor Lore*, Harper, 1964; *Small Game Hunting*, Popular Science, 1967; *Outdoorsman's Handbook*, edited by Henry Gross, Dutton, 1970. Contributor of outdoor column, "Roamin' East Idaho," *Post-Register*, 1943—; contributor of several hundred articles to outdoor and gun magazines. Contributing editor, *American Rifleman*, 1958-65.

ORMSBY, Virginia H(aire)

PERSONAL: Born in Atlanta, Ga.; daughter of Robert Lee and Juliet (Milmow) Haire; children: Eric Linn, Alan Robert. *Education:* Atlanta Art Institute, completed three-year course, 1936; Oglethorpe University, A.B., 1939. *Politics:* Democrat. *Religion:* Protestant. *Home:* 1336 Obispo Ave., Coral Gables, Fla. 33134.

CAREER: Elementary school teacher, on and off, in southern states and Idaho, 1939-48, in Miami, Fla., 1949—; now a teacher at George Washington Carver Elementary School in Miami. Writer and illustrator; lecturer-cartoonist. *Member:* National Education Association, Classroom Teachers Association, Delta Kappa Gamma. *Awards, honors:* Delta Kappa Gamma certificate of achievement in field of literature, 1960; National Education Association journal writing award, 1964, 1965, 1966.

WRITINGS—Self-illustrated juveniles, all published by Lippincott: *Here We Go*, 1955, *It's Saturday*, 1956, *Twenty-One Children*, 1957, *The Little Country Schoolhouse*, 1958, *Cunning Is Better Than Strong*, 1960, *Long Lonesome Train Whistle*, 1961, *The Right-Handed Horse*, 1963, *The Big Banyan Tree*, 1964, *What's Wrong with Julio?* (Spanish-English picture book), 1965, *Twenty-One Children Plus Ten*, 1971. Also author of *Mountain Magic for Rosy*, illustrated by Paul E. Kennedy, Crown, 1969. Contributor of articles to *Today's Education* and of fictionalized experience stories to a National Education Association anthology. Cartoonist in local Florida newspaper.

*   *   *

ORR, J(ames) Edwin 1912-

PERSONAL: Born January 15, 1912, in Belfast, Ireland; son of William Stewart (a jeweler) and Rose (Wright) Orr; married Ivy Carol Carlson, January 15, 1937; children: Carolyn A. (Mrs. Larry Booth), Alan Carlson, David Carlson. *Education:* Attended College of Technology, Belfast, Ireland, and six graduate schools, received Th.B., B.D.; Northwestern University, M.A., 1942; Northern Baptist Theological Seminary, Th.D, 1943; Oxford University, Ph.D., 1948. *Home:* 11451 Berwick St., Los Angeles, Calif. 90049.

CAREER: Baptist minister; lecturer and author, 1933-42; International Christian Leadership, Washington, D.C., chaplain of mission to the academic community, lecturing in universities and colleges throughout world, 1947—. *Military service:* U.S. Army Air Forces, chaplain, 1943-46; became major. *Member:* Royal Geographical Society (fellow), American Geographical Society (fellow), Royal Historical Society (fellow), American Historical Association, Royal Society of Literature (fellow), American Scientific Affiliation.

WRITINGS—All published by Marshall, Morgan & Scott, except as indicated: *Can God-?* 1934, *Prove Me Now!*, 1935, *The Promise is to You*, 1935, *Times of Refreshing*, 1935, *This is the Victory*, 1935, *All Your Need*, 1936, *If Ye Abide*, 1936, *Such Things Happen*, 1937, *The Church Must First Repent*, 1937, *Telling Australia*, 1939, *Through Blood and Fire in China*, 1939.

Always . . . Abounding, 1940: *I Saw No Tears*, 1948; *Second Evangelical Awakening* (historical), Christian Literature Crusade, 1949; *Full Surrender*, Christian Literature Crusade, 1951; *Good News in Bad Times*, Zondervan, 1953; *Inside Story of the Hollywood Christian Group*, Zondervan, 1955.

Faith That Makes Sense (apologetics), 1961, Judson. 1962; *The Light of Nations: Evangelical Renewal and Advance in the Nineteenth Century*, Eerdmans, 1966; *Campus Aflame*, Regal Books (Glendale, Calif.), 1972.

WORK IN PROGRESS: A textbook of popular apologetics; a history of Christian growth in the past six centuries.

SIDELIGHTS: Orr has traveled in 140 countries; his writings have been translated into a dozen European and Asiatic languages.

BIOGRAPHICAL/CRITICAL SOURCES: Charles Murray Albertyn, *The Messenger of Revival: The Contribution of Dr. J. Edwin Orr to Evangelical Christianity in the Mid-Twentieth Century*, privately printed, 1960; A.H. Appasamy, *Write the Vision!: Edwin Orr's Thirty Years of Adventurous Service*, Marshall, Morgan & Scott, 1964.

*   *   *

OSBORNE, Dorothy (Gladys) Yeo 1917- (Gladys Arthur)

PERSONAL: Born December 19, 1917, in London, England; daughter of Arthur Thomas and Nellie Elizabeth (Adams) Yeo; married Gerald Victor Osborne (a railway signalman); children: David Philip. *Education:* Attended schools in London, England. *Home:* Station House, Newton-St.-Cyres, Exeter, Devonshire, England.

CAREER: Professional artist. *Member:* Royal Society of Arts, Royal Society for Prevention of Cruelty to Animals, British Pets Club.

WRITINGS—All youth books: *The Other Side of the Mountain*, Victory Press, 1957; *Lin and the Legend*, Pickering & Inglis, 1957; *Kanoka of the Pirates*, Pickering & Inglis, 1958; *The Secret of Old White Horn*, Pickering & Inglis, 1960; *Ann, Jerry and the Knights Valiant*, Victory Press, 1960; *Trouble at Keemaha Falls*, Pickering & Inglis, 1962. Contributor to *Christian Herald, Adventurers, Discoverers, Animal Ways, Busy Bees*, and other journals.

WORK IN PROGRESS: Research into sea serpent mystery, particularly Lochness, monster of old world, and Ogopogo, of the new world; research into religions of the world; a book for adults on "forming your own art group" (having done so in her own village, "a famous English beauty spot").

*   *   *

OSMUNSON, Robert Lee 1924-

PERSONAL: Born March 14, 1924, in Oakland, Calif.; son of Earl Ripley (a clergyman) and Dorothy (Fessenden) Osmunson; married Rosemarie White (a teacher), August 13, 1945; children: Marilyn Ruth Osmunson Hergert, Willard Earl. *Education:* Pacific Union College, B.A.; University of Nebraska, M.A.; University of Southern California, Ed.D. *Home:* 5435 Sierra Vista Ave., La Sierra, Riverside, Calif. 92505. *Office:* Loma Linda University, Riverside, Calif. 92505.

CAREER: Seventh-day Adventist Church, pastor and minister in Kansas, 1945-48; Union College Academy, Lincoln, Neb., instructor in religion, 1948-50; Seventh-day Adventist Church, youth director and educational superintendent of Nebraska Conference, 1950-52; Forest Lake Academy, Orlando, Fla., principal 1953-55; Seventh-day Adventist Church, youth director and educational superintendent of East African Union, 1955-60, youth director of Southern Africa Division, 1960-62, of Ohio Conference, 1963-64; Loma Linda University–La Sierra Campus (formerly La Sierra College), Riverside, Calif., director of admissions and student recruitment, 1964-68, Associate Dean of Admission and Director of Student Recruitment, 1968—. Private pilot.

WRITINGS: *Crash Landing*, Pacific Press, 1963; *With God You Win: A Devotional and Inspirational Guide for Early-Teens and Near-Teens*, Review & Herald, 1968. Contributor to youth journals, religious periodicals, and to *School and Society*.

WORK IN PROGRESS: A devotional book for youth.

SIDELIGHTS: Osmunson grew up in India where he lived for fourteen years, and has spent a total of seven years in Africa.

* * *

OSSMAN, David (H.) 1936-

PERSONAL: Born December 6, 1936, in Santa Monica, Calif.; son of Ernest H. (a management consultant) and Jordan (Cope) Ossman; married Bettine Kinney, June 8, 1958; children: Alizon, Devin. *Education:* Pomona College, student, 1954-56; Columbia University, B.F.A. (cum laude), 1958, graduate study, 1958-59. *Office:* KPFK— Pacifica Radio, Los Angeles, Calif. 90038.

CAREER: WBAI—Pacifica Radio, New York, N.Y., production and programming, 1960-61; KPFK—Pacifica Radio, Los Angeles, Calif., 1961—, director of literature and drama programming. *Member:* National Association of Broadcast Employees and Technicians.

WRITINGS: An Offering ... Without Incense, privately printed, 1954; *The Sullen Art: Interviews with Modern American Poets,* Corinth Books, 1963; *Set in a Landscape: Poems and Sequences, 1960-1964,* El Carno Emplumado, 1966; (translator) Pablo Neruda, *The Early Poems,* New Rivers Press, 1969. Author of radio documentaries, including "American Poetry," 1961, "Henry David Thoreau," 1962, "Brecht in Hollywood,' 1963, "The Lie That Always Told the Truth" (biography of Cocteau), 1963. Contributor to *Nation, Nomad, Between Worlds,* and other poetry periodicals.

WORK IN PROGRESS: Research on Indians of Southern California.

* * *

OUTLAND, Charles 1910-

PERSONAL: Born August 30, 1910, in Santa Paula, Calif.; son of Elmer Garfield (a rancher) and Stella (Faulkner) Outland; married Harriet Roberts (a nurse), August 1, 1933 (divorced 1966); children: Richard, Barbara. *Education:* Attended Whittier College and Boston University. *Politics:* Republican. *Religion:* Protestant. *Home:* 314 C Palm Ave., Santa Paula, Calif. 93060.

CAREER: Independent rancher, Santa Paula, Calif., 1933—. *Military service:* U.S. Naval Reserve, 1936-40.

WRITINGS: Man-Made Disaster: The Story of St. Francis Dam, Its Place in Southern California's Water System, Its Failure and the Tragedy of March 12 and 13, 1928, in the Santa Clara River Valley, Arthur H. Clark, 1963; (editor) George Washington Faulkner, *Ho for California: The Faulkner Letters, 1875-1876,* privately printed, 1964; *Mines, Murders, and Grizzlies: Tales of California's Ventura Back Country,* Ventura County Historical Society, 1969. Editor, *Ventura County Historical Society Quarterly,* 1955-64.

WORK IN PROGRESS: Local California research.

AVOCATIONAL INTERESTS: History of the American West, and California.

* * *

OWEN, Alan Robert George 1919-

PERSONAL: Born July 4, 1919, in Bristol, England; son of Edward (a sea captain) and Sarah (Olds) Owen; married Iris May Pepper, January 9, 1952; children: Robin. *Education:* Trinity College, Cambridge, M.A., 1945, Ph.D., 1948. *Politics:* Labour Party. *Religion:* Methodist. *Home:* 4 Luard Close, Cambridge, England. *Office:* Trinity College, Cambridge, England.

CAREER: Cambridge University, Cambridge, England, lecturer in genetics, 1950—, fellow and lecturer of Trinity College. During World War II did radar research work for Admiralty Signal Establishment. *Member:* Genetical Society. *Awards, honors:* First place in International Treatise Competition of Parapsychology Foundation, 1964, for *Can We Explain the Poltergeist?*

WRITINGS: Can We Explain the Poltergeist?, Garrett-Helix, 1964; *Hysteria, Hypnosis and Healing: The Work of J.-M. Charcot,* Dobson, 1971, Garrett-Helix, 1972; (with V. Arunachalam) *Polymorphisms with Linked Loci,* Chapman & Hall, 1971; (with Victor Sims) *Science and the Spook: Eight Strange Cases of Haunting,* Garrett-Helix, 1971. Contributor to *International Journal of Parapsychology,* and to genetics journals.

WORK IN PROGRESS: Research in mathematical genetics and statistics; studies in the history of occultism and in parapsychology.

AVOCATIONAL INTERESTS: Antiquarian topics and philosophy.

* * *

OWEN, John E. 1919-

PERSONAL: Born January 17, 1919, in Manchester, England; came to U.S., 1938; naturalized, 1947; son of William and Lena (Henderson) Owen; married Garnet Hamrick (a free-lance writer), July 7, 1944. *Education:* Attended Manchester Grammar School in England; Duke University, B.A., 1943; University of Southern California, M.A., 1946, Ph.D., 1949; additional study at Boston University and Tufts University, 1944, London School of Economics and Political Science, London, 1952. *Office:* Department of Sociology, Arizona State University, Tempe, Ariz. 85281.

CAREER: Ohio University, Athens, assistant professor of sociology, 1949-51; University of Helsinki, Helsinki, Finland, Smith-Mundt professor of sociology, 1951-52; University of Maryland Overseas Program, U.S. Air Force, lecturer in sociology and economics in England and Wales, 1952-53; Florida Southern College, Lakeland, associate professor, 1953-56, professor of sociology, 1956-58; University of Dacca, Dacca, East Pakistan, Fulbright lecturer in sociology, 1958-59, UNESCO adviser, 1960-63, acting head of sociology department, 1961-63; Wisconsin State College, Superior, associate professor of sociology, 1959-60; Pomona College, Claremont, Calif., visiting associate professor of sociology, 1963-64; Arizona State University, Tempe, associate professor, 1964-68, professor of sociology, 1968—. Visiting summer professor at other universities in United States and Canada. *Member:* American Sociological Association (fellow), Pacific Sociological Association, Phi Beta Kappa, Alpha Kappa Delta, Pi Gamma Mu.

WRITINGS: (Contributor) *Introduction to Sociology,* Stackpole, 1952; (contributor) *The Frontiers of Social Science, Essays in Honor of Radhakamal Mukerjee,* edited by Baljit Singh, Macmillan (London), 1958; (contributor) *Contemporary Sociology,* edited by J.S. Roucek, Philosophical Library, 1958; (editor) *Sociology in East Pakistan,* Asiatic Society of Pakistan, 1962. Contributor of more than 160 articles to American and foreign journals, including *New Leader, Christian Century, British Weekly, Calcutta Statesman,* and *Indian Journal of Social Work.*

WORK IN PROGRESS: History of social thought; studies on philosophical aspects of the social sciences, and on the sociology of religion.

AVOCATIONAL INTERESTS: Music, books, travel.

* * *

OWENS, William A. 1905-

PERSONAL: Born November 2, 1905, in Blossom, Tex.; son of Charles and Jessie Ann (Chennault) Owens; married Ann Slater Wood, December 23, 1946; children: Jessie Ann, David Edward. *Education:* Southern Methodist University, B.A., 1932, M.A., 1933; University of Texas, postgraduate study, 1936; State University of Iowa, Ph.D., 1941; Columbia University, postdoctoral study, 1945-46. *Politics:* Independent. *Religion:* Episcopalian. *Home:* South Blvd., Nyack, N.Y. 10960. *Office:* Summer Session Office, Columbia University, Broadway and 116th St., New York, N.Y. 10027.

CAREER: The Agricultural and Mechanical College of Texas (now Texas A & M University), College Station, started as instructor, 1937, became associate professor of English, 1941-47; Columbia University, New York, N.Y., associate professor and director of summer session, 1947-66, professor of English, 1966—, dean of summer session, 1969—. Director of research for folk materials, University of Texas, 1941. *Military service:* U.S. Army, 1942-45; served in Counter Intelligence Corps; became second lieutenant; received Legion of Merit. *Member:* American Association of University Professors, Modern Language Association of America, Texas Institute of Letters. *Awards, honors:* Texas Institute of Letters Award, 1966, for *This Stubborn Soil.*

WRITINGS: Swing and Turn: Texas Play-Party Games, Tardy Publishing, 1936; (compiler) *Texas Folk Songs,* musical arrangements by Willa Mae Kelly Koehn, Texas Folklore Society, 1950; *Slave Mutiny: The Revolt on the Schooner Amistad,* John Day, 1953, reissued as *Black Mutiny: The Revolt on the Schooner Amistad,* Pilgrim Press, 1968; *Walking on Borrowed Land* (novel), Bobbs-Merrill, 1954; *Fever in the Earth,* Putnam, 1958; *Pocantico Hills, 1609-1959,* Sleepy Hollow Restorations, 1960; (editor) *Energy and Man,* Appleton, 1960; *Look to the River,* Atheneum, 1963; *This Stubborn Soil* (autobiography), Scribner, 1966 (published in England as *This Stubborn Soil: A Frontier Boyhood,* Faber, 1967); *Three Friends: Roy Bedichek, J. Frank Dobie, Walter Prescott Webb,* Doubleday, 1969; (with Mody C. Boatright) *Tales from the Derrick Floor: A People's History of the Oil Industry,* Doubleday, 1970; *A Season of Weathering* (autobiography), Scribner, 1973.

BIOGRAPHICAL/CRITICAL SOURCES: Listener, November 30, 1967.

*   *   *

PACHMUSS, Temira 1927-

PERSONAL: Surname is pronounced *Pock*-muss; born December 24, 1927, in Skamja, Estonia. *Education:* University of Melbourne, B.A. (with honors), 1954; M.A., 1955; University of Washington, Seattle, Ph.D., 1959. *Religion:* Russian Orthodox. *Home:* 902 South Lincoln, Urbana, Ill. 61801. *Office:* University of Illinois, Urbana, Ill. 61801.

CAREER: University of Michigan, Ann Arbor, instructor in Slavic languages and literatures, 1958-59; University of Colorado, Boulder, instructor in Slavic languages and literatures, 1959-60; University of Illinois, Urbana, instructor, 1960-61, assistant professor, 1961-64, associate professor, 1964-68, professor of Slavic languages and literatures, 1968—. *Member:* American Association for the Advancement of Slavic Studies, American Association of Teachers of Slavic and East European Languages, National Slavic Honor Society (honorary), Estonian Learned Society in America, International Dostoevsky Society, Phi Kappa Phi.

WRITINGS: F.M. Dostoevsky: Dualism and Synthesis of the Human Soul, Southern Illinois University Press, 1963; *Zinaida Hippius: An Intellectual Profile,* Southern Illinois University Press, 1971; (editor) *Intellect and Ideas in Action: Selected Correspondence of Zinaida Hippius,* Wilhelm Fink Verlag, 1972; (editor) *Collected Poetical*

Works Zinaida Hippius, two volumes, Wilhelm Fink Verlag, 1972; (translator and editor) *Selected Works of Zinaida Hippius,* University of Illinois Press, 1972. Contributor of articles on Russian, English, American, French, and German literature to professional journals in Canada, England, United States, German, Australia, and France.

SIDELIGHTS: Pachmuss has done research in Europe, 1962, 1964-72.

*   *   *

PACHTER, Henry M(aximilian) 1907-
(Henry Rabasseire)

PERSONAL: Surname originally Paechter; born February 22, 1907, in Berlin, Germany; came to United States in 1941, naturalized in 1948; son of Fritz E. (a printer) and Helene (Streisand) Paechter; married Hedwig Roesler (a secretary); children: Renee Vera. *Education:* University of Berlin, Ph.D., 1930. *Home:* 310 West 106th St., New York, N.Y. 10025.

CAREER: Lived in France, 1933-41, doing research and teaching; *Deutsche Zeitung,* Cologne, Germany, foreign correspondent, 1948-64; New School for Social Research, New York, N.Y., 1952-68, became professor of history and chairman of the department; City College of City University of New York, New York, N.Y., professor of history, 1968—. *Member:* American Association of University Professors, Renaissance Society, American Historical Association, Foreign Press Association, United Nations Correspondents Association. *Awards, honors:* Guggenheim fellow, 1951; National Endowment for the Arts award, 1967, for essay "J.F.K. as an Equestrian Statue."

WRITINGS: (Under pseudonym Henri Rabasseire) *Espagne Creuset Politique,* Editions Fustier, 1938; (contributor) Ladislas Farago, editor, *The Axis Grand Strategy: Blueprints for the Total War,* Farrar & Rinehart, 1942; (with Karl O. Paetel and Berta Hellman) *Nazi-Deutsch: German-English Dictionary of New German Terms,* Office of Economic Research, 1943, reissued as *Nazi-Deutsch: A Glossary of Contemporary German Usage,* Ungar, 1944; (with others) *German Radio Propaganda,* Cornell University Press, 1944; *Paracelsus: Magic into Science,* Henry Schuman, 1951; (contributor) Maurice Baumont, editor, *The Third Reich,* Praeger, 1955; *Collision Course: The Cuban Missile Crisis and Coexistence,* Praeger, 1963; *Weltmacht Russland: Aussenpolitische Strategie in drei Jahrhunderten,* Stalling, 1968, revised edition published as *Weltmacht Russland: Tradition u. Revolution in d. Sowjetpolitik,* Deutscher-Taschenbuch Verlag, 1970; (contributor) *American Literary Anthology,* Farrar, Straus, 1968; (with Robert Boyers) *The Legacy of the German Refugee Intellectuals,* Skidmore College, 1969; *Decline and Greatness of Europe in the Twentieth Century,* Praeger, 1971. Contributor of articles to *World Politics, Problems of Communism, Social Research, Journal of the History of Medicine, History and Theory, Wort und Wahrheit, Aussenpolitik, Der Monat,* and other publications. Co-editor, *Dissent.*

*   *   *

PACKARD, Vance (Oakley) 1914-

PERSONAL: Born May 22, 1914, in Granville Summit, Pa.; son of Philip Joseph (a farm supervisor) and Mabel (Case) Packard; married Mamie Virginia Mathews (an artist), November 25, 1938; children: Vance Philip, Randall Mathew, Cynthia Ann. *Education:* Pennsylvania State College (now Pennsylvania State University), B.S., 1936; Columbia University, M.A., 1937. *Politics:* "My own." *Religion:* Congregational. *Home:* 4 Mill Rd., New Canaan, Conn. 06840.

CAREER: Centre Daily Times, State College, Pa., reporter, 1936; *Boston Record,* Boston, Mass., columnist,

1937-38; Associated Press Feature Service, New York, N.Y., writer, editor, 1938-42; *American Magazine*, editor and staff writer, 1942-56; *Collier's* magazine, staff writer, 1956. Lecturer at Columbia University, 1941-44, at New York University, 1945-57. Member of planning commission, New Canaan, Conn., 1954-56. *Member:* Authors Guild, Society of Magazine Writers, American Sociological Association (associate), Silvermine Guild Artists (director), National Council of Churches, National Right to Privacy Committee (co-chairman). *Awards, honors:* Distinguished Alumni awards, Pennsylvania State University, 1961; Outstanding Alumni Award, Columbia University Graduate School of Journalism, 1963.

WRITINGS: (With Clifford Rose Adams) *How to Pick a Mate: The Guide to a Happy Marriage*, Dutton, 1946, reissued as *How to Pick a Mate: A Guidebook to Love, Sex and Marriage*, Blue Ribbon Books (Toronto), 1947; *Animal IQ: The Human Side of Animals*, Dial, 1950, revised edition published as *The Human Side of Animals*, Pocket Books, 1961; *The Hidden Persuaders*, McKay, 1957; *Books and Culture as Status Symbols: Comments at the 1959 ABA Convention* (booklet), McKay, 1959; *The Status Seekers: An Exploration of Class Behavior in America and the Hidden Barriers That Affect You, Your Community, Your Future*, McKay, 1959; *Do Your Dreams Match Your Talents?* (booklet), Science Research Associates, 1960; *The Waste Makers*, McKay, 1960; *The Pyramid Climbers*, McGraw, 1962; (with others) *Your Goals and You: A Guidance Handbook* (booklet), Science Research Associates, 1962; *The Naked Society* (excerpt, "Invasion of Privacy," published in *Atlantic*, February, 1964; excerpt, "Right to Privacy," published in *Atlantic*, March, 1964), McKay, 1964; *The Sexual Wilderness: The Contemporary Upheaval in Male-Female Relationships* (excerpts, "Sex on the Campus," published in *McCall's*, August, 1968, and September, 1968; excerpt, "Some Contemporary Styles in Wedlock," published in *PTA Magazine*, October, 1968), McKay, 1968 (published in England as *The Sexual Wilderness: The Upheaval in Male-Female Relationships, the Break-Up of Traditional Morality, New Trends in Sexual Behaviour Among the Young*, Pan Books, 1970); *A Nation of Strangers* (advance excerpts published in *Ladies' Home Journal*, September and November, 1972), McKay, 1972.

Contributor to various periodicals, including *Atlantic*, *Saturday Review*, *Saturday Evening Post*, and *New York Times Magazine*.

SIDELIGHTS: Packard's interest is primarily "what is happening to the individual in the face of the new kinds of pressures generated by our violently changing world." William Barrett has called him "a blend of amateur sociologist and crusading journalist, [who] has had his knuckles rapped by the professors of sociology: but his real value has been not as a scientist but as a publicist alerting the public conscience to some of our worst social habits." In a review of *The Status Seekers*, a writer for *Social Education* demonstrated "little sympathy for those academic specialists who complain that Vance Packard is 'a mere popularizer' and who dismiss his work as of little importance. Certainly, Packard writes for the general public, and his book . . . does not attempt to burrow through esoteric intellectual tunnels. On the other hand, it should be recognized that he has made a real contribution to society by familiarizing thousands of readers with the important findings of E. Digby Baltzell, August Hollingshead, Bevode McCall, Liston Pope, W. Lloyd Warner, and other highly reputable scholars."

"Packard has the exciting role of a double agent," Gerald Carson wrote in his review of *The Status Seekers*. "He writes social science, while being a sly satirist, too." Kingsley Amis called this "account of the American class system. . .rich with detail and anecdote, absorbing to

read. . .[and] written with a kind of sprightly pessimism both rare and engaging." Also engaging to the general reading public, Packard's first three major works (*The Hidden Persuaders, The Status Seekers*, and *The Waste Makers*), all published between 1957 and 1960, were national best sellers, as is *A Nation of Strangers*. By September of 1972, his first six books of social criticism (from *The Hidden Persuaders* to *The Sexual Wilderness*) together had sold 750,000 copies in hardcover and 4,000,-000 in paperback.

In his review of *The Hidden Persuaders*, a study of the effective use of motivational research in advertising and public relations, A.C. Spectorsky wrote: "Wisely, Mr. Packard, who is a writer and teacher, does not attempt didactic answers. He reveals the MR men themselves in the act of agonized self-appraisal (a rare posture), and comes up with a few personal, tentative answers, but some basic questions remain unresolved. And that is one of the strengths of this fascinating book—it is frightening, entertaining and thought-stimulating to boot." Charles Winick said the book "is certainly of value in opening to fuller public view an important area in American life which deserves closer scrutiny than it has been getting."

A kind of modern muckraker, Packard is sometimes accused of obscuring the facts with sensationalism. John Brooks writes: "Spying and snooping are in themselves distasteful topics: but there are some ways in which *The Naked Society* is more distasteful than it needs to be, and one of its least attractive aspects is its author's occasional tendency to adopt methods hardly more responsible than those he condemns in others." In contrast, F.H. Guidry believes "Mr. Packard is experienced enough to sustain a mood of mild indignation and to avoid shrill hysterics. He also manages to pay out his impressive accumulation of facts, statistics, and anecdotes in an economical, entertaining style." Melvin Maddocks observes: "It is the Fact—the juicy, solemnly enumerated statistic—that gives Packard his courage to rush in where analysts fear to tread, and stay to moralize where most moralizers long since have mumbled themselves into silence."

The editors of *Publishers Weekly* consider Packard "as pleasantly low-key as they come. If Mr. Packard has a 'hard sell' cell in his body it certainly doesn't come through in an interview. Talking. . .recently about the research he did for *The Sexual Wilderness* and some of the findings he uncovered, he was objective, candid, very much the reporter, not the polemicist." This book required four and a half years of research, during which Packard designed a questionnaire which went to 21 different U.S. colleges and to students in Canada, England, Germany, Italy, and Norway. Packard himself visited ten foreign countries and interviewed hundreds of people in the compilation of information for his book, assisted by members of his family. "The word 'sexual' in the title," according to the *Publishers Weekly* article, "definitely does not refer solely to the physical aspects of sex, but to courtship and marriage and life adjustment seen in the context of the total male-female relationship." A frequent criticism of the survey is that it is a bewildering, often dull collection of statistics which have little or no import, in contrast to his earlier studies which "were nothing if not stimulating," as John Atkins has remarked. Both Atkins and George Krupp believe Packard "has attempted too much in this book." "His earlier books, which became best sellers," writes Krupp, "were reasonably circumscribed. With *The Sexual Wilderness*, however, he has staked out an area of inquiry so vast—involving sociological, psychological, and moral considerations—that it would tax the resources of any writer, no matter how broad his range of knowledge . . . Nowhere in [the book] does the author deal with the central issues concerning sexual life." James J. Conlin notes that "what is most debatable is the assumption that the college population may be representative of the entire young generation." However, he concludes that "this work is the best compiled by Vance Packard, that it will stimulate debate and thought, and that its chief deficiency is its neglect of an objective moral framework."

A Nation of Strangers, Packard's latest and one of the most successful of his analyses of the American scene, deals with the high mobility of Americans and the ominous consequences this may have on their society. Granville Hicks maintains "there is a lot of material in scholarly books and learned journals that might change the way we live if we got hold of it, and Packard not only summarizes and interprets this material but underlines its revolutionary implications." A writer for *Time* refers to the preface of *A Nation of Strangers,* where "Packard reveals that his concern about mobility springs from his own experiences. As a child in Troy, Pa., he knew everybody within four miles of his father's dairy farm. When Packard was nine, his father made a great leap—115 miles—to become farm supervisor at Pennsylvania State College. . . .The uprooting was traumatic, especially for his father." Now, removed from relatives and long-time neighbors, Packard "no longer feels the sense of community he craves." Harriet Van Horne says in her review: "In moving about so much, we are, Packard believes, destroying the traditional patterns that have made us a vigorous nation for 200 years. We are begetting a race of 'don't care' transients, drifters, job-hoppers, and unhappy wives who feel alienated wherever they go. . . . It disturbs Packard that so many of our transient citizens come from the ranks of the talented and the ambitious, for these are the very people who could provide community leadership, if only they'd remain long enough in one community."

In amassing data for his study, Packard spent four years reading, traveling, and interviewing hundreds of sources in 24 states. The resultant book implies that some of America's greatest problems—loneliness and crime included—may be attributable to high mobility, rootlessness, and the loss of community feeling. The *Time* writer concludes that Packard's books have been "criticized by some sociologists as unscientific. But Packard does not claim to be a scientist; he calls himself an observer and synthesizer. As such, he has sometimes been ahead of scientists in diagnosing the nation's ills, and he has often managed to influence those who do not read scholarly works. *The Waste Makers* and *The Naked Society,* for instance, did much to spur the protection of consumers and of the right of privacy. Similarly, perhaps, *A Nation of Strangers* may succeed in alerting the country to the hazards of mobility."

Packard recently donated his manuscripts and papers to the Pattee Library of Pennsylvania State University.

BIOGRAPHICAL/CRITICAL SOURCES: New York Times, April 28, 1957; *Christian Science Monitor,* April 30, 1957, March 19, 1964; *Chicago Sunday Tribune,* May 3, 1959; *Social Education,* October, 1959; *Spectator,* February 5, 1960; *Newsweek,* October 3, 1960; *Management Review,* November, 1960; *Saturday Review,* November 5, 1960, September 14, 1968, September 9, 1972; *New Yorker,* November 12, 1960; *Nation,* January 28, 1961; *Publishers Weekly,* January 6, 1964, August 5, 1968, April 24, 1972; *New York Times Book Review,* March 15, 1964, October 13, 1968, September 10, 1972; *Atlantic,* April, 1964; *Best Sellers,* September 1, 1968; *Life,* September 13, 1968; *New Statesman,* November 8, 1968; *Books and Bookmen,* January, 1969; *Today's Health Magazine,* June, 1972; *Library Journal,* August, 1972; *Time,* September 11, 1972.

PACKER, David W(illiam)   1937-

PERSONAL: Born November 25, 1937, in St. Louis, Mo.; son of William Harold and Leotta May Packer; married Susan P. Thompson, June 11, 1960. *Education:* Massachusetts Institute of Technology, S.B. in Electrical Engineering and S.B. in Humanities and Engineering, 1960, S.M., 1963. *Home:* 31 Great Rd., Bedford, Mass. 01730. *Office:* Digital Equipment Corp., Maynard, Mass. 01745.

CAREER: Massachusetts Institute of Technology, Cambridge, research associate in industrial management, 1963-64; Digital Equipment Corp., Maynard, Mass., staff assistant, 1964—. *Military service:* U.S. Army Reserve; became first lieutenant. *Member:* Institute of Management Science.

WRITINGS: Resource Acquisition in Corporate Growth, M.I.T. Press, 1964; (with Ole C. Nord) *Management Science: A Primer for Managers,* Management Science Associates, 1964.

*   *   *

PAGE, Harry Robert   1915-

PERSONAL: Born March 22, 1915, in Milwaukee, Wis.; son of Harry Allen and Lydia B. (Rosendahl) Page; married Jeanne Tompkins, April 1, 1945; children: Patricia Jeanne, Margaret Berenice. *Education:* Michigan State University, A.B., 1941; Harvard University, M.B.A., 1950; American University, Ph.D., 1966. *Religion:* Congregationalist. *Home:* 3612 North Glebe Rd., Arlington, Va. 22207. *Office:* Department of Business Administration, George Washington University, Washington, D.C. 20006.

CAREER: U.S. Air Force, career service, 1941-61; became colonel; received Legion of Merit, Air Medal, Army Commendation Medal, Air Force Commendation Medal, Purple Heart, Department of Defense Staff Badge for service with Joint Chiefs of Staff; George Washington University, Washington, D.C., 1961—, now professor of business administration. Leader of seminars on church financial management offered by American University in conjunction with Wesley Theological Seminary. Treasurer and member of board of directors, Council of Churches of Greater Washington. Consultant to Brookings Institution. *Member:* Air Force Association, American Management Association, Society for Advancement of Management, American Finance Association, Harvard Business School Association, Alpha Kappa Psi, Pi Sigma Alpha.

WRITINGS: Church Budget Development, Prentice-Hall, 1964; *Federal Contribution to Management,* Praeger, 1971. Contributor of several articles on military management subjects to *Military Review.*

*   *   *

PANKHURST, Richard (Keir Pethick)   1927-

PERSONAL: Born December 3, 1927, in London, England. *Education:* London School of Economics, University of London, B.Sc., 1949, Ph.D., 1952. *Home:* P.O.B. 1896, Addis Ababa, Ethiopia.

CAREER: Haile Sellassie I University, Addis Ababa, Ethiopia, professor, 1957—; Institute of Ethiopian Studies, Addis Ababa, Ethiopia, director, 1963—.

WRITINGS: (With Sylvia Pankhurst) *Ethiopia and Eritrea: The Last Phase of the Reunion Struggle, 1941-1952,* Lalibela House Press, 1954; *William Thompson: Britain's Pioneer Socialist, Feminist, and Cooperator,* C.A. Watts, 1954; *Kenya: The History of Two Nations,* Independent Publishing Co., 1954; *The Saint Simonians, Mill and Carlyle: A Preface to Modern Thought,* Sidgwick & Jackson, 1957; *An Introduction to the Economic History of Ethiopia from Early Times to 1800,* Lalibela House Press,

1961; (editor with S. Chojnacki and William A. Shack) *Register of Current Research on Ethiopia and the Horn of Africa*, Haile Sellassie I University, 1963; *Some Historic Journeys in Ethiopia*, Oxford University Press, 1964; *The Great Ethiopian Famine of 1888-1892: A New Assessment*, Haile Sellassie I University, 1964; (editor) *Travellers in Ethiopia*, Oxford University Press, 1965; *State and Land in Ethiopian History*, Institute of Ethiopian Studies and Faculty of Law, Haile Sellassie I University, 1966; (editor) *The Ethiopian Royal Chronicles*, Oxford University Press, 1967; *An Introduction to the History of the Ethiopian Army*, Imperial Ethiopian Air Force, 1967; *Primitive Money, Money and Banking in Ethiopia*, [Addis Ababa], 1967; *A Brief Note on the Economic History of Ethiopia from 1800 to 1935*, Haile Sellassie I University 1967; *Economic History of Ethiopia, 1800-1935*, Haile Sellassie I University Press, 1968; *The Penetration and Implications of Fire-Arms in Ethiopia Prior to the Nineteenth Century*, Haile Sellassie I University, 1968; (with Geoffrey Last) *A History of Ethiopia in Pictures*, Oxford University Press, 1969.

* * *

PARISEAU, Earl J (oseph) 1928-

PERSONAL: Born August 14, 1928, in Methuen, Mass.; son of Cyril E. and Susan (Gourdeau) Pariseau; married Joyce L. Womack (a legal secretary), August 12, 1960. *Education:* University of Florida, B.A., 1957; Mexico City College, graduate study, 1958; American University, M.A., 1959. *Home:* 5515 Margate St., Springfield, Va. 22151. *Office:* Latin American, Spanish and Portuguese Division, Library of Congress, Washington, D.C.

CAREER: Worked in Florida as branch manager for wholesale medical supply firm, 1950-52; Library of Congress, Washington, D.C., assistant to editor, *World List of Future International Meetings*, 1959-61, with Hispanic Foundation, 1961—, assistant director of foundation, 1964-66, field director of Brazil office, 1966-68, acting chief of Latin American, Spanish and Portuguese Division, 1971—. *Military service:* U.S. Army, 1952-54. *Member:* Association of Latin American Studies (treasurer, Inter-American Council, 1963—), Latin American Studies Association, Society for International Development, International Propellor Club, American Historical Association, Conference on Latin American History, Delta Sigma Pi, Phi Alpha Theta, University of Florida Alumni Club.

WRITINGS: (Editor) *Handbook of Latin American Studies*, University of Florida Press, 1961-65; *Cuba: A Select List of Reference and Research Tools*, Hispanic Foundation, Library of Congress, 1966; (editor) *Cuban Acquisitions and Bibliography*, Library of Congress, 1970; *Latin America: An Acquisitions Guide for Colleges and Public Libraries*, University of Florida Press, 1973.

* * *

PARNABY, Owen Wilfred 1921-

PERSONAL: Born April 18, 1921, in Beaconsfield, Tasmania, Australia; son of Percy Oliver (a clergyman) and Nellie (Chancellor) Parnaby; married Joy E. Mills, May 22, 1948; children: Margaret Rachel. *Education:* Attended Wesley College, Melbourne, Australia, 1935-38, Queen's College, University of Melbourne, 1945-48, and Balliol College, Oxford, 1950-53. *Religion:* Methodist. *Home:* 76a Aberdeen Rd., Takapuna, Auckland, New Zealand. *Office:* University of Auckland, P.O. Box 2175, Auckland, New Zealand.

CAREER: University of Melbourne, Melbourne, Australia, tutor in history, 1948-49; University of Auckland, Auckland, New Zealand, lecturer, 1953-56, senior lecturer, 1957-63, associate professor of history, 1964—. Lay preacher and executive officer in Methodist Church. *Member:* Polynesian Society (Wellington), Auckland Institute and Museum. *Awards, honors:* Carnegie Commonwealth fellow, 1961.

WRITINGS: Britain and the Labor Trade in the Southwest Pacific, Duke University Press, 1964. Contributor of articles to professional journals.

WORK IN PROGRESS: History of Fiji.

SIDELIGHTS: Parnaby traveled in Europe for study, 1950-52, and in United States, 1961-62. *Avocational interests:* Walking, music, and cricket.

* * *

PARTINGTON, Susan Trowbridge 1924-

PERSONAL: Born October 21, 1924, in Milwaukee, Wis.; daughter of John Calvin and Elsa (Gumz) Trowbridge; married James H.M. Partington, 1954; children: Marshall Trowbridge, Bartholomew James. *Education:* Attended University of Wisconsin, two years, and University of Washington, one year. *Religion:* Presbyterian. *Home:* Southfield Point, Stamford, Conn. 06902.

CAREER: American Red Cross, Home Service worker, 1946-47; Abraham & Straus, Brooklyn, N.Y., fashion and beauty programs director, 1948-52; John Robert Powers Enterprises, New York, N.Y., creative director, 1952-55; free-lance fashion and beauty consultant-writer, New York, N.Y., 1955—. Licensed insurance broker in New York State. Board member, Youth Consultation Service of New York. Director of Connecticut branch, Humane Society of United States.

WRITINGS: (With John Robert Powers) *The John Robert Powers Way to Teenage Beauty, Charm and Popularity*, Prentice-Hall, 1962; *Beauty and Charm the Model's Way: A Guide for Teenage Girls*, Hawthorn, 1969. Ghost writer of several books. Contributor of feature articles to *Westchester Magazine*, 1970-71.

SIDELIGHTS: Mrs. Partington has toured Europe, Mexico, United States, and Canada, and kept house on three tropical islands—Jamaica, Bermuda, and Puerto Rico. *Avocational interests:* Interior decorating, raising standard poodles.

* * *

PASCAL, David 1918-

PERSONAL: Born August 16, 1918, in New York, N.Y.; son of Boucour and Carolina (Finor) Pascal; married first wife, Mary K.; married second wife, Theresa P. Auerbach (a biologist), August 24, 1962; children: (first marriage) Jeffrey B. *Education:* Attended American Artists School, 1937-38. *Residence:* New York, N.Y. *Office:* 60 West Eighth St., New York, N.Y. 10011.

CAREER: Free-lance author, cartoonist, and illustrator, 1941—. Instructor, School of Visual Arts, New York, N.Y., 1955-58; lecturer at museums, schools, and congresses in New York, France, Italy, Brazil, and Argentina. Participant in overseas tours sponsored by U.S. Department of Defense, 1957, 1958, 1961. Exhibited work in one-man shows at Librarie Le Kiosque, Paris, 1965, Musee des Arts Decoratifs, 1967, Graham Gallery, New York, N.Y., 1973, and Museu de Arte, Sao Paulo, Brazil. Drawings have appeared in *New Yorker, Harper's, Saturday Review, New York Times, New York Herald Tribune, Punch, Ski, Look*, and other magazines in United States, and other countries. Chairman of cartoon shows given by National Cartoonists Society in New York Veterans Hospital; American organizer of First International Congress of Comics, 1972. *Wartime service:* U.S Merchant Marine, 1940-45.

MEMBER: International Comics Organization (American representative, 1970—), Immagine (Italy; American representative, 1970—), National Cartoonists Society (foreign affairs secretary, 1963—), Magazine Cartoonists Guild. Awards, honors: Second prize, Dattero D'Oro, in sixteenth Salone Internazionale Dell Umorismo, Bordighera, Italy, 1963; illustrator's award, National Cartoonists Society, 1969; Phenix award, Paris, 1971; Critics award, Eighth International Congress of Comics and Phenix award, 1972, both for Comics: The Art of the Comic Strip.

WRITINGS: (Illustrator) The Art of Interior Decorating, text by Eddie Frederics, Chilton, 1963; (illustrator) Ivan Andreevich Krylov, 15 Fables of Krylov, Macmillan, 1965; (self-illustrated) The Silly Knight, Funk, 1967; (illustrator) Jerzy Stanislaw Lec, More Unkempt Thoughts, Funk, 1969; (illustrator) Charles Issawi, Laws of Social Motion, Hawthorn, 1972; (editor with Walter Herdeg) Comics: The Art of the Comic Strip, Graphis Press (Zurich), 1972.

WORK IN PROGRESS: A children's book.

AVOCATIONAL INTERESTS: Tai-chi, swimming, and skiing.

* * *

PATKA, Frederick 1922-

PERSONAL: Born April 17, 1922, in Tonciu, Rumania; became U.S. citizen, 1961; son of Francisco (a judge) and Emma (Hartwig) Patka; married, wife's name, Annita, December 22, 1949; children: Christine, Andrew. Education: Gregorian University, Rome, Italy, Ph.B. (summa cum laude), 1944, Ph.M. (summa cum laude), 1945, Ph.D. (magna cum laude), 1946. Home: 17 Ellicott Rd., Philadelphia, Pa. 19114. Office: Holy Family College, Torrsdale, Philadelphia, Pa. 19114.

CAREER: Colegio Sao Paulo, Sao Paulo, Brazil, professor of philosophy, 1948-50; Liceu Eduardo Prado, Sao Paulo, professor of philosophy and Latin, 1948-55; University of Sao Paulo, Sao Paulo, professor of descriptive, rational, and juvenile psychology, 1950-55, professor of ethics, sociology and social psychology, 1952-55; Instituto Brasileiro de Filosofia, Soa Paulo, professor, 1952-55; LaSalle College, Philadelphia, Pa., assistant professor of psychology and modern languages, 1955-61; Holy Family College, Torresdale, Philadelphia, Pa., associate professor and chairman of philosophy department, 1959—; Chestnut Hill College, Philadelphia, lecturer in philosophy and modern languages, 1961—. Fember: American Philosophical Association, American Association of University Professors, American Catholic Philosophical Association. Awards, honors: Chevalier d'Honneur de L'Ordre Imperial des Chevaliers de Constantin le Grand (Spain).

WRITINGS: Hogyan Tanuljunk Idegen Nyelveket? (title means "How to Learn Foreign Languages?"), A. Gazeta Hungara, 1950; Dicionario Portugues-Hungaro, A. Gazeta Hungara, 1954; Gyakorlati Portugal Nyelvkonyv (grammar and handbook of Portuguese language and conversation), Editora Guia Fiscal, 1954; Dicionario Hungaro-Portugues, Livraria Brody, 1958; (editor) Existentialist Thinkers and Thought, Philosophical Library, 1962; Value and Existence: Studies in Philosophic Anthropology, Philosophical Library, 1964; The Clowns: Modern Adults in Their World of Make-Believe, Magi Books, 1964; (translator) St. Thomas' Commentaries on St. Paul's Epistles to the Thessalonians, Magi Books, 1964. Contributor to professional journals. Editorial staff member, Revista Brasileira de Filosofia, 1952-55; founder and editor, Magyar Szemle (Hungarian review), 1954-55.

WORK IN PROGRESS: Human Types in History; A Non-Freudian Interpretation of the Narcissus Myth; The Ten Commandments in Reverse; Fair Play for Man; a revision of the philosophy curriculum in colleges from an axiological point of view.

SIDELIGHTS: Patka is competent in Italian, Spanish, Portuguese, Rumanian, French, German, Hungarian, and Latin.

* * *

PATTERSON, Sheila Caffyn 1918-

PERSONAL: Born March 30, 1918; daughter of Thomas Percy (a company director) and Edith (Saville) Caffyn; married Tadeusz Horko (a journalist), May 7, 1955; children: Clarissa. Education: Attended Roedean School; St. Hugh's College, Oxford, M.A., 1943; University of Cape Town, advanced study, 1948-50; London School of Economics, London, Ph.D. Religion: Church of England. Home: 55 Wilbury Ave., Hove, Sussex, England. Office: Community Relations Commission, London, England.

CAREER: Polish Government in Exile, Ministry of Information, London, England, translator and editor, 1941-45; University of Edinburgh, Edinburgh, Scotland, research assistant, department of social anthropology, 1955-58; Institute of Race Relations, London, England, editor and research consultant, 1959-68; Centre for Multi-Racial Studies, University of Sussex, Sussex, England, research fellow in charge of fieldwork in Barbados and St. Vincent, 1969-71, University College, University of London, London, England, honorary research fellow, 1972—. Member: Royal Institute of International Affairs, Royal Anthropological Institute, British Sociological Association, Association of Social Anthropologists, Institute of Race Relations, Translators Association, Lansdowne Club, Oxford and Cambridge Club.

WRITINGS: Colour and Culture in South Africa, Routledge & Kegan Paul, 1953, Kraus Reprint Co., 1969; The Last Trek: A Study of the Boer People and the Afrikaner Nation, Routledge & Kegan Paul, 1957; Dark Strangers: A Sociological Study of the Absorption of a Recent West Indian Migrant Group, Tavistock Publications, 1963, Indiana University Press, 1964; (contributor) London: Aspects of Change, Routledge & Kegan Paul, 1963; (translator) Stanislaw Ossowski, Class Structure in the Social Consciousness, Routledge & Kegan Paul, 1963; (editor) Immigrants in London: Report of a Study Group, London National Council of Social Service, 1964; Immigrants in Industry, Oxford University Press for Institute of Race Relations, 1968; Immigration and Race Relations in Britain, 1960-1967, Oxford University Press for Institute of Race Relations, 1969; (translator) Zygmunt Bauman, Between Class and Elite, Manchester University Press, 1972. Contributor to New Society, Political Quarterly, Polish Review, and other periodicals. Editor, News Community (quarterly journal of Community Relations Commission).

WORK IN PROGRESS: A survey of the social aspects of mixed marriages, for Allen Lane and Penguin; a social history of immigration to Britain since 1840, for Routledge & Kegan Paul.

AVOCATIONAL INTERESTS: Travel, food and wine, painting, swimming, and reading detective stories and science fiction.

* * *

PAULSSON, Thomas A(lfred) 1923-

PERSONAL: Born March 26, 1923, in Stockholm, Sweden; son of Gregor and Ester (Wagner) Paulsson; married Eva S. Insulander (a housing consultant), December 21, 1954; children: Patrick G., Rebecka, Blenda. Education: University of Uppsala, B.A., 1946, M.A., 1951; University of Stockholm, Ph.D., 1959; additional study at London School of Economics, London. *Home:* 39 Fogelvagen, Marsta, Sweden. *Office:* Sveriges Radio, P.O. Box 955, Stockholm 1, Sweden.

CAREER: National Museum, Stockholm, Sweden, assistant, 1951-53; National Swedish Association of Architects, Stockholm, public relations officer, 1953-54; independent research in town planning and housing conditions, 1954-61; City Museum, Norrkoping, Sweden, assistant, 1961-63; now with Swedish Broadcasting Corporation. Professional photographer. *Military service:* Swedish Army, 1942-43, 1951, 1962. *Member:* Sallskapet Minerva, Juvenalorden.

WRITINGS: Ny Arkitektur, Almqvist & Wiksell, 1957; *Scandinavian Architecture: Buildings and Society in Denmark, Finland, Norway, and Sweden from the Iron Age Until Today,* Hill & Wang, 1958; *Ny Stad,* Almqvist & Wiksell, 1958; (with wife, Eva S. Paulsson and Jan Stehouwer) *Konsten att bo,* Raben & Sjogren, 1960; *Stadfoer alla: Eller ingen?,* Natur och Kultur, 1969. Contributor to Swedish journals.

WORK IN PROGRESS: Research on housing conditions and living habits in the home and surrounding area, in collaboration with Eva S. Paulsson.

AVOCATIONAL INTERESTS: Golf.

* * *

PAUW, Berthold Adolf 1924-

PERSONAL: Surname rhymes with "grow;" born August 26, 1924, in Madzi Moyo Mission, Fort Jameson, Northern Rhodesia; son of Christoffel Petrus (a missionary) and Esther (Bremer) Pauw; married Rachie J. Van Schalkwyk, April 4, 1951; children: Christoff Karl, Madeleine, Ockert Gerbrandt, Jacobus Cornelis Holtz, Berthold Aris. *Education:* University of Stellenbosch, M.A., B.D.; University of Cape Town, Ph.D.; additional study at University of Leiden, 1951-52. *Office:* University of South Africa, 263 Skinner St., Pretoria, South Africa.

CAREER: Minister of Dutch Reformed Church at Kimberley and Warrenton, Cape Province, South Africa, 1950-57; Institute of Social and Economic Research, Rhodes University, Grahamstown, South Africa, research officer and research fellow, 1958-64; University of South Africa, Pretoria, lecturer, 1964-67, senior lecturer, 1967-68, professor of anthropology, 1968—. Field work in social anthropology in Taung Reserve, Transkei, East London, and Port Elizabeth.

WRITINGS: Religion in a Tswana Chiefdom, Oxford University Press, 1960; *Xhosa in Town,* Volume II: *The Second Generation: A Study of the Family Among Urbanized Bantu in East London,* edited by Philip Mayer, Oxford University Press (Cape Town), 1963; (contributor) Victor E.W. Hayward, editor, *African Independent Church Movements,* Edinburgh House Press, 1963; (with others) *African Systems of Thought,* Oxford University Press (London), 1965; (contributor) W.D. Hammond-Tooke, editor, *The Bantu-Speaking Peoples of South Africa,* Routledge & Kegan Paul, in press. Contributor to *African Studies* and *Standard Encyclopaedia of Southern Africa.*

WORK IN PROGRESS: A book on Christianity among rural and urban Xhosa-speaking peoples of Transkei and Eastern Cape Province, South Africa.

SIDELIGHTS: Pauw is competent in South African languages Afrikaans, Xhosa, and Tswana.

* * *

PAYNE, Bruce 1911-

PERSONAL: Born February 6, 1911, in Bakersfield, Calif.; son of James Bruce and Erma Frances (Deacon) Payne; married Edna Winifred Jessop, June 5, 1935; children: John Bruce, Christopher, Geoffrey. *Education:* University of California, Berkeley, B.S., 1933; Harvard University, M.B.A., 1935. *Religion:* Christian Scientist. *Home:* Thomas Rd., Westport, Conn. 06880. *Office:* Bruce Payne & Associates, Time & Life Building, Rockefeller Center, New York, N.Y. 10020.

CAREER: Republic Steel Corp., Cleveland, Ohio, industrial engineer, 1935-38; Nation City Bank of Cleveland, Cleveland, Ohio, industrial consultant, 1938-40; Dyer Engineers, Inc., Cleveland, Ohio, vice-president and director, 1940-46; Bruce Payne & Associates, Inc. (management consultants), New York, N.Y., president and director, 1946—; Payne Computer Services, New York, N.Y., president and director, 1969—. Member of executive board, Brazilian Institute at New York University; member of executive committee, Action Committee for International Development; Council for International Progress in Management, director, 1951-55, vice-president, 1955-58, vice-president of foundation, 1958—. Lecturer at universities and colleges. Trustee, Fairfield Country Day School, 1951-61.

MEMBER: English-Speaking Union, American Management Association, Society for the Advancement of Management (director, 1946-50; national treasurer, 1950-52; executive vice-president, 1952-53; president, 1953-54; director-at-large, 1955), Chief Executives Forum, Newcomen Society, Harvard Business School Association (president, 1950-51), Economic Club, Harvard Club, Fairfield County Hunt Club, Pequot Yacht Club.

WRITINGS: Planning for Company Growth: The Executive's Guide to Effective Long Range Planning, McGraw, 1963; (with David D. Sweet) *Office Operations Improvement: How to Cut Costs and Improve Morale,* American Management Association, 1967. Contributor of articles to *Christian Science Monitor* and to professional journals.†

* * *

PAYNE, Ernest A (lexander) 1902-

PERSONAL: Born February 19, 1902, in London, England; son of Alexander William and Mary Catherine (Griffiths) Payne; married Winifred Mary Davies, October 28, 1930; children: Elizabeth Ann (Mrs. Antony Fergus Prain). *Education:* King's College, London, B.A., 1921; Regent's Park College, B.D., 1925; Mansfield College, Oxford, B.Litt., 1927, M.A., 1944; University of Marburg, graduate study, 1927-28. *Home:* Elm Cottage, Pitsford, Northampton, England. *Office:* 4 Southampton Row, London W.C.1, England.

CAREER: Ordained to Baptist ministry, 1928, with first pastorate in Bugbrooke, Northampton, England, 1928-32; Baptist Missionary Society, London, England, young people's secretary and editor, 1932-40; Regent's Park College, Oxford, England, senior tutor, 1940-51; Oxford University, Oxford, lecturer in comparative literature and history of modern missions, 1946-51; Baptist Union of Great Britain and Ireland, London, England, general secretary, 1951-67; World Council of Churches, vice-chairman of Central Committee, 1954-68, president, 1968—. British Council of Churches, vice-president, 1960, chairman of executive committee, 1962-71; vice-president, Baptist World Alliance, 1965—. Examiner in Oxford University, Universities of Wales, Edinburgh, and Bristol. Director, Baptist Insurance Co. Ltd.

MEMBER: Baptist Historical Society (president), United Society for Christian Literature (vice-president), Athenaeum Club (London). *Awards, honors:* D.D., University of St. Andrews, 1951; LL.D., McMaster University, 1961; Grand Medaille d'argent de la cite de Paris, 1962; Companion of Honour, 1968.

WRITINGS: The Saktas: An Introductory and Comparative Study, H. Milford, 1933; Freedom in Jamaica: Some Chapters in the Story of the Baptist Missionary Society, Carey Press, 1933; The First Generation: Early Leaders of the Baptist Missionary Society in England and India, Carey Press, 1936; Marianne Lewis and Elizabeth Sale: Pioneers of Missionary Work Among Women, Carey Press, 1937; The Great Succession: Leaders of the Baptist Missionary Society During the Nineteenth Century, Carey Press, 1938, 2nd edition, 1946; Henry Wyatt of Shansi, 1895-1938, Carey Press, 1939, 2nd edition, 1946.

The Church Awakes: The Story of the Modern Missionary Movement, Livingston Press, 1942; (with Katleen Margaret Shuttleworth) Missionaries All: A Pageant of British History, Carey Press, 1942; Before the Start: Steps Towards the Founding of the L.M.S., Livingstone Press, 1942; (editor) Studies in History and Religion, Lutterworth, 1942; The Free Church Tradition in the Life of England, S.C.M. Press, 1944, new, revised edition, Hodder & Stoughton, 1965; The Fellowship of Believers: Baptist Thought and Practice Yesterday and Today, Carey Kingsgate Press, 1944, enlarged edition, 1952; South-East from Serampore: More Chapters in the Story of the Baptist Missionary Society, Carey Kingsgate Press, 1945; Henry Wheeler Robinson, Scholar, Teacher, Principal: A Memoir, Nisbet, 1946; College Street Church, Northampton, 1697-1947, Carey Kingsgate Press, 1947; The Baptist Movement in the Reformation and Onwards, Carey Kingsgate Press, 1947; (translator) Karl Barth, The Teaching of the Church Regarding Baptism, S.C.M. Press, 1948; The Anabaptists of the 16th Century and Their Influence in the Modern World, Carey Kingsgate Press, 1949; The Bible in English, Epworth, 1949.

The Baptists of Berkshire: Through Three Centuries, Carey Kingsgate Press, 1951; The Excellent Mr. Burls, Carey Kingsgate Press, 1951; The Free Churches and Episcopacy, Carey Kingsgate Press, 1952; The Free Churches and the State, Carey Kingsgate Press, 1952; The Baptist Union and Its Headquarters: A Descriptive Record, Carey Kingsgate Press, 1953; James Henry Rushbrooke, 1870-1947: A Baptist Greatheart, Carey Kingsgate Press, 1954; The Baptists of the World And Their Overseas Missions, Carey Kingsgate Press, 1955; The Growth of the World Church: The Story of the Modern Missionary Movement, Macmillan, 1955; The Meaning and Practice of Ordination Among Baptists, Carey Kingsgate Press, 1957; (with David G. Moses) Why Integration?: An Explanation of the Proposal Before the World Council of Churches and the International Missionary Council, Edinburgh House Press, 1957; (translator) Johannes Schneider, Baptism and Church in the New Testament, Carey Kingsgate Press, 1957; (contributor) G.R. Elton, editor, New Cambridge Modern History, Cambridge University Press, 1958; The Baptist Union: A Short History, Attic Press, 1959.

(Compiler with Stephen F. Winward) Orders and Prayers for Church Worship: A Manual for Ministers, Carey Kingsgate Press, 2nd edition, 1962, published in America (with Winward and James W. Cox) as Minister's Worship Manual: Orders and Prayers for Worship, World Publishing, 1969; (author of introduction) William Carey, An Inquiry into the Obligation of Christians to Use Means for the Conversion of the Heathens, Carey Kingsgate Press, 1961; Roger Williams (1603-1683), Independent Press, 1961; (with Norman S. Moon) Baptists and 1662, Carey Kingsgate Press, 1962; Veteran Warrior: Memoir of B. Grey Griffith, Carey Kingsgate Press, 1962; (contributor) G.F. Nuttall and Owen Chadwick, editors, From Uniformity to Unity, 1662-1962, S.P.C.K., 1962; (contributor) R.J.W. Bevan, editor, The Churches and Christian Unity, Oxford University Press, 1963; Baptists

and Church Relations, Baptist Union of Great Britain and Ireland, 1964; Free, Churchmen, Unrepentant and Repentant, and Other Papers, Carey Kingsgate Press, 1965; Thomas Helwys and the First Baptist Church in England, 2nd edition, Baptist Union of Great Britain and Ireland, 1966; (contributor) A.M. Motter, editor, Preaching on Pentecost and Christian Unity, Fortress, 1966; Some Recent Happenings in the Roman Church, Baptist Union, 1966.

The World Council of Churches 1948-69, Baptist Union, 1970; Violence, Non-Violence and Human Rights, Baptist Union, 1971; Thirty Years of the British Council of Churches 1942-72, British Council of Churches, 1972; (contributor) R.H. Fischer, editor, A Palette for a Portrait: Franklin Clark Fry, Lutheran Quarterly, 1972; The Free Churches: Today's Challenges, Free Church Federal Council, 1973. Contributor to festschriften honoring Martin Nemoeller and W.A. Visser't Hooft, to Dictionary of National Biography, and to Upper Room Disciplines. Editor, Baptist Quarterly, 1944-50.

SIDELIGHTS: Payne has traveled extensively in Europe, including the Iron Curtain countries, and in Australia, and North and South America.

*   *   *

PEABODY, Robert Lee   1931-

PERSONAL: Born December 23, 1931, in Seattle, Wash., son of Keith R. and Pearl (Starr) Peabody; married Judith Erken, August 16, 1958; children: Susan Lee, Nancy Lynn, Jennifer Jane. Education: University of Washington, Seattle, B.A., 1954, M.A., 1956; Stanford University, Ph.D., 1960. Home: 4416 Windom Place N.W., Washington, D.C. 20016. Office: Department of Political Science, Johns Hopkins University, Baltimore, Md. 21218.

CAREER: Brookings Institution, Washington, D.C., fellow, 1960-61; Johns Hopkins University, Baltimore, Md., assistant professor, 1961-64, associate professor, 1965-68, professor of political science, 1969—. Associate director, New York Times—Simulmatics Corp. Election Project, 1962, and American Political Science Association Study of Congress, 1965—. Military service: U.S. Army Reserve, 1949-57. Member: American Political Science Association, American Association of University Professors, American Association for the Advancement of Science, American Society for Public Administration (president, Stanford chapter, 1958, member of council, Maryland chapter, 1962-63).

WRITINGS: Job Opportunities in State and Local Government, Bureau of Government Research and Services, University of Washington, 1956; (with William J. Gore) The Functions of a Political Campaign: A Case Study, [Salt Lake City], 1958; Seattle Seeks a Tax, University of Alabama Press, 1959; (editor with Nelson W. Polsby) New Perspectives on the House of Representatives, Rand McNally, 1963, 2nd edition, 1969; Organizational Authority: Superior-Subordinate Relationships in Three Public Service Organizations, Atherton, 1964; The Ford-Halleck Minority Leadership Contest, McGraw, 1965; (with Ralph K. Huitt) Congress: Two Decades of Analysis, Harper, 1969; To Enact a Law: Congress and Campaign Financing, Praeger, 1972.

WORK IN PROGRESS: Congressional leadership change.

AVOCATIONAL INTERESTS: Golf and tennis.

*   *   *

PEARCE, William M(artin)   1913-

PERSONAL: Born March 11, 1913, in Plainview, Tex.; son of Will Martin (a minister) and Annie (Bates) Pearce; married Frances Elizabeth Campbell, September 6, 1939; children: William M. III, Richard C. Education:

Kemper Military School, A.A., 1932; Southern Methodist University, A.B., 1935; University of Texas, Ph.D., 1949. *Religion:* Methodist. *Home:* 2244 Winton Ter. W., Forth Worth, Tex. 76109. *Office:* Texas Wesleyan College, Fort Worth, Tex. 76105.

CAREER: Texas Technological College (now Texas Tech University), Lubbock, instructor, 1938-42, 1946-47, assistant professor, 1949-53, associate professor, 1953-55, professor of history and head of department, 1955-61, vice-president for academic affairs, 1960-68, director of Archaeological Field School in Glorieta, N.M., 1948, Valley of Mexico, 1949; Texas Wesleyan College, Fort Worth, president, 1968—. Part-time instructor, University of Texas, 1947-49. Member of board of directors of Lubbock Chamber of Commerce and United Fund of Lubbock. *Military service:* U.S. Army, 1942-45; became lieutenant; received Bronze Star and Purple Heart, U.S. Army Reserve, 1945—; now lieutenant colonel. *Member:* American Historical Association, Organization of American Historians, Western History Association, Panhandle-Plains History Society (director), Texas History Association, Phi Kappa Phi, Phi Alpha Theta, Phi Kappa Alpha, Rotary International, Fort Worth Club.

WRITINGS: The Matador Land and Cattle Company, University of Oklahoma Press, 1964.†

*   *   *

PEARL, Richard M(axwell)   1913-

PERSONAL: Born May 4, 1913, in New York, N.Y.; son of Morse (an accountant and businessman) and Etta (Stocker) Pearl; married Mignon Wardell (a writer and artist), June 13, 1941. *Education:* University of Colorado, B.A., 1939, M.A., 1940; Harvard University, M.A., 1946. *Politics:* Republican. *Religion:* Unitarian. *Home:* 624 North Cascade Ave., Colorado Springs, Colo. 80302. *Agent:* Paul R. Reynolds, Inc., 599 Fifth Ave., New York, N.Y. 10017. *Office:* Department of Geology, Colorado College, Colorado Springs, Colo. 80903.

CAREER: University of Colorado, Boulder, instructor in geology, 1940; operator of mineral supply business, Denver, Colo., 1941; Remington Arms Co., Denver, Colo., process engineer, 1941-42; Shell Oil Co., Tulsa, Okla., geologist, 1944; Colorado College, Colorado Springs, 1946—, now professor of geology. Visiting professor, Phoenix College, 1956; extension division professor at three Colorado universities. Adviser in mineralogy and gemology, Denver Public Library, 1949-52.

MEMBER: American Association for the Advancement of Science (fellow), American Geographical Society (fellow), Gemological Institute of America (certified gemologist), National Association of Geology Teachers (president, Southwest section, 1962-63), American Federation of Mineralogical Societies (co-founder; president, 1948-49), Research Society of America (president, Colorado Springs chapter, 1965-66), Meteoritical Society (fellow), distinction; Gemmological Association of Australia (distinction), Gemmological Association of Great Britain (fellow with honorary vice-president), Canadian Gemmological Association (honorary), Gesellschaft der Freunde der Mineralogie (honorary vice-president), Rocky Mountain Federation of Mineralogical Societies (founder; president, 1941-42), Historical Society of the Pikes Peak Region (president, 1954, 1966), Council on Abandoned Military Posts, Colorado Mineral Society (co-founder; president, 1948-50), Colorado Authors' League (vice-president, 1968-69), Phi Beta Kappa, Sigma Xi, Delta Epsilon, Sigma Gamma Epsilon. *Awards, honors:* Books named among *Library Journal's* one hundred best scientific and technical books, 1951, 1961, 1964; Colorado Authors' League Top Hand awards for best juvenile non-fiction, 1964, 1967, for best adult non-fiction, 1965.

WRITINGS: Nature as Sculptor: A Geologic Interpretation of Colorado Scenery, Colorado Museum of Natural History, 1941, revised edition, 1956; (with Henry Carl Dake) *The Art of Gem Cutting,* 3rd edition, Mineralogist Publishing, 1945; *Mineral Collectors Handbook,* Mineral Book Co., 1947; *Popular Gemology,* Wiley, 1948, revised edition, 1965; *Guide to Geologic Literature,* McGraw, 1951; *Colorado Gem Trails,* Sage Books, 1951; *America's Mountain: Pike's Peak and the Pikes Peak Region,* Mineral Book Co., 1954, revised edition, Sage Books, 1964; *How to Know the Minerals and Rocks,* McGraw, 1955; *Rocks and Minerals,* Barnes & Noble, 1956, new edition published as *An Introduction to the Mineral Kingdom,* Blandford, 1966; *Colorado Gem Trails and Mineral Guide,* Sage Books, 1958, 3rd edition, Swallow Press, 1972; *1001 Questions Answered About the Mineral Kingdom,* Dodd, 1959, revised edition, 1968.

Geology: An Introduction to Principles of Physical and Historical Geology, Barnes & Noble, 1960, 3rd revised edition, 1966; *Wonders of Rocks and Minerals,* Dodd, 1961; *Successful Mineral Collecting and Prospecting,* McGraw, 1961; *1001 Questions Answered About Earth Science,* Dodd, 1962, reissued as *1001 Answers to Questions About Earth Science,* Grosset, 1965, revised edition published under original title, Dodd, 1969: *Wonders of Gems,* Dodd, 1963; *American Gem Trails,* McGraw, 1964; *Gems, Minerals, Crystals and Ores: The Collector's Encyclopedia,* Odyssey, 1964; *Colorado Rocks, Minerals, Fossils,* Sage Books, 1964, revised edition published as *Exploring Rocks, Minerals, Fossils in Colorado,* 1969; *The Wonder World of Metals,* Harper, 1966; *Gem Identification Simplified,* Maxwell Publishing, 1968; *Geology Simplified: Keynotes,* Barnes & Noble, 1968; *Seven Keys to the Rocky Mountains,* Maxwell Publishing, 1968; *Cleaning and Preserving Minerals,* Maxwell Publishing, 1971; *Handbook for Prospectors,* McGraw, 1972.

Contributor to eight encyclopedias and yearbooks and four anthologies. Writer of scientific and non-technical articles and columns in periodicals in United States and England; contributor to newspapers. Member of editorial board, *Achat* (Hamburg, Germany), 1948-50; geologic consultant *Colorado Wonderland,* 1951-56; editor-in-chief, *Earth Science,* 1947, 1967-68, 1972—.

WORK IN PROGRESS: Books on earth science, history, travel, and related subjects, with writing projected for several years ahead.

SIDELIGHTS: Pearl's books have been translated into French, Persian, Russian, and Japanese.

*   *   *

PEASE, Jane H(anna)   1929-

PERSONAL: Born November 26, 1929, in Waukegan, Ill.; daughter of Leslie P. (a lawyer) and Olive (a teacher; maiden name, Coleman) Hanna; married William H. Pease (a history professor), June 9, 1950. *Education:* Smith College, A.B. (magna cum laude), 1951; University of Rochester, A.M., 1957, Ph.D., 1969; Western Reserve University, M.S. in L.S., 1958. *Home:* 40 East Summer St., Bangor, Me. 04401. *Office:* Department of History, University of Maine, Orono, Me. 04473.

CAREER: University of Rochester, Rush Rhees Library, Rochester, N.Y., assistant to archivist, 1951-55; Emma Willard School, Troy, N.Y., teacher of history, 1955-57, 1958-64, chairman of the department, 1963-64; University of Alberta, Calgary, sessional lecturer and instructor in history, 1964-66; University of Maine, Orono, instructor, 1966-67, assistant professor, 1969-72, associate professor of history, 1972—. *Member:* American Historical Association, Organization of American Historians, American Association of University Professors (president, Orono chapter, 1970-71), Southern Historical Association, New

England Historical Association (member of executive committee, 1972-74). *Awards, honors:* Grants from American Council of Learned Societies, American Philosophical Society, and University of Maine Coe Fund.

WRITINGS: (With husband, William H. Pease) *Black Utopia: Negro Communal Experiments in America,* State Historical Society of Wisconsin, 1963; (editor with William H. Pease) *The Antislavery Argument,* Bobbs-Merrill, 1965; (with William H. Pease) *Austin Steward: Twenty-two Years a Slave and Forty Years a Freeman,* Addison-Wesley, 1969; (contributor) Martin L. Kilson, Nathan Huggins, and Daniel M. Fox, editors, *Key Issues in the Afro-American Experience,* Harcourt, 1971; (with William H. Pease) *Bound with Them in Chains: An Essay in Antislavery History,* Greenwood Press, 1972. Contributor of articles to *Journal of American History, Journal of Southern History, Civil War History, Journal of Negro History,* and other publications.

WORK IN PROGRESS: With William H. Pease, a study of ante-bellum and Northern free black abolitionist and civil rights activity, for Atheneum; a biography of Abby Kelley Foster, completion expected in 1973; a comparative study of Boston, Mass., and Charleston, S.C.

SIDELIGHTS: Ms. Pease is concerned with women's rights and women's history. She has traveled in Western Europe and Great Britain.

*   *   *

PEASE, William H(enry) 1924-

PERSONAL: Born August 31, 1924, in Winchendon, Mass.; son of Clarence A.G. (a manufacturer) and Arline (Brooks) Pease; married Jane Hanna (a professor), June 9, 1950. *Education:* Williams College, B.A. (cum laude), 1947; University of Wisconsin, M.A., 1948; University of Rochester, Ph.D., 1955. *Home:* 40 East Summer St., Bangor, Me. 04401. *Office:* Department of History, University of Maine, Bangor, Me. 04473.

CAREER: Mount Hermon School, Mount Hermon, Mass., teacher of history and English, 1948-51; Rensselaer Polytechnic Institute, Troy, N.Y., instructor, 1955-56, assistant professor, 1956-58, associate professor of history, 1958-64; University of Alberta, Calgary, associate professor of history 1964-66; University of Maine, Orono, associate professor, 1966-68, professor of history, 1968—. Visiting assistant professor of history at Case Institute of Technology, 1957-58; Fulbright lecturer at International People's College, Elsinore, Denmark, 1961-62. *Military service:* U.S. Army, 1943-46. *Member:* American Historical Association, American Studies Association, Organization of American Historians, Canadian Historical Association, New England Historical Association, Phi Beta Kappa. *Awards, honors:* Grants-in-aid from American Council of Learned Societies, American Philosophical Society; research grants from Rensselaer Polytechnic Institute, University of Calgary, and University of Maine.

WRITINGS: (With wife, Jane H. Pease) *Black Utopia: Negro Communal Experiments in America,* State Historical Society of Wisconsin, 1963; (editor with Jane H. Pease) *The Antislavery Argument,* Bobbs-Merrill, 1965; (with Jane H. Pease) *Austin Steward: Twenty-two Years a Slave and Forty Years a Freeman,* Addison-Wesley, 1969; (contributor) Martin L. Kilson, Nathan Huggins, and Daniel M. Fox, editors, *Key Issues in the Afro-American Experience,* Harcourt, 1971; (with Jane H. Pease) *Bound with Them in Slavery: An Essay in Antislavery History,* Greenwood Press, 1972. Contributor to *Journal of American History, Civil War History, Canadian Historical Review, Midwest Quarterly,* and other publications.

WORK IN PROGRESS: With Jane H. Pease, a study of antebellum and Northern free black abolitionist and civil

rights activity, for Atheneum; with Jane H. Pease, a comparative study of Boston, Mass., and Charleston S.C.; a biography of Samuel Joseph May.

SIDELIGHTS: Pease has traveled and lived in Canada and Denmark and has also traveled in Western Europe, Scandinavia, and Great Britain.

PECKHAM, Howard Henry 1910-

PERSONAL: Born July 13, 1910, in Lowell, Mich.; son of H. Algernon (a manufacturer) and Harriet May (Wilson) Peckham; married Dorothy Koth, July 28, 1936; children: Stephen, Angela. *Education:* Olivet College, student, 1927-29; University of Michigan, A.B., 1931, M.A., 1933. *Politics:* Independent. *Religion:* Presbyterian. *Home:* 2108 Vinewood Blvd., Ann Arbor, Mich. 48104. *Office:* Clements Library, University of Michigan, Ann Arbor, Mich. 48105.

CAREER: Grand Rapids Press, editorial writer, 1935; University of Michigan, Ann Arbor, curator of manuscripts, Clements Library of American History, 1936-44, lecturer in library, science, 1942-46; Indiana Historical Bureau, Indianapolis, director, 1945-53; University of Michigan, Ann Arbor, director of Clements Library and professor of history, 1953—. *Member:* Society of American Archivists (fellow; founding member; member of council), American Association for State and Local History (president, 54-56), American Antiquarian Society, American Historical Association, Bibliographical Society of America, Mississippi Valley, Historical Association, Rotary Club.

WRITINGS: (Contributor) *Old Fort Michilimackinac,* William L. Clements Library, University of Michigan, 1938; (editor with R.G. Adams) *Lexington to Fallen Timbers, 1775-1794,* University of Michigan, 1942; (with Colton Storm) *Invitation to Book Collecting: Its Pleasures and Practices,* Bowker, 1947; *Pontiac and the Indian Uprising,* Princeton University Press, 1947, 2nd edition, University of Chicago Press, 1961; *William Henry Harrison, Young Tippecanoe* (juvenile), Bobbs-Merrill, 1951; *Pontiac's Siege of Detroit,* edited by Joe Norris, Wayne University Press, 1951; (with Donald F. Carmony) *A Brief History of Indiana,* Indiana Historical Bureau, 1946, 4th edition, 1953; *Captured by Indians: True Tales of Pioneer Survivors,* Rutgers University Press, 1954; *Nathanael Green, Independent Boy* (juvenile), Bobbs-Merrill, 1956; *The War for Independence, a Military History,* University of Chicago Press, 1959; (author of introduction) Robert Rogers, *Journals,* Corinth Books, 1961; *Pontiac, Young Ottawa Leader* (juvenile), Bobbs-Merrill, 1963; *Why the British Lost the American Revolution,* Allen County-Fort Wayne Historical Society, 1963; *The Colonial Wars 1689-1762,* University of Chicago Press, 1964; *Life in Detroit Under Pontiac's Siege,* Wayne State University Press, 1964; *The Making of the University of Michigan, 1817-1967,* University of Michigan Press, 1967; *Education in Early America: A Guide to an Exhibition in the Clements Library to Commemorate the Sesquicentennial Observance of the Founding of the University of Michigan,* University of Michigan, 1967.

Editor: George Groghan, *Journal of His Trip to Detroit in 1767,* University of Michigan Press, 1939; (with Lloyd A. Brown) *Revolutionary War Journals of Henry Dearborn,* Caxton Club (Chicago), 1939; *Guide to the Manuscript Collections in the William L. Clements Library,* University of Michigan Press, 1942; (with Shirley A. Snyder) *Letters from Fighting Hoosiers,* Indiana War History Commission, 1948; (with Cecil K. Byrd) *A Bibliography of Indiana Imprints, 1804-1853,* Indiana Historical Bureau, 1955; *Rare Book Libraries and Collections,* University of Illinois Library School, c.1957; *A List of Michigan Regiments of the Civil War in Which the Com-*

panies Came from Particular Towns, Michigan Civil War Centennial Observance Commission, 1961; *Memoirs of the Life of John Adlum,* Caxton Club, 1968. Editor, *Indiana Historical Bulletin,* 1945-53; associate editor, *American Heritage,* 1949-54.

WORK IN PROGRESS: A bibliography of Michigan territory imprints.

* * *

PEDLEY, Robin 1914-

PERSONAL: Born August 11, 1914, in Grinton, Richmond, Yorkshire, England; son of Edward (a stone mason) and Martha Jane (Hird) Pedley; married Jeanne Lesley Hitching, July 4, 1951; children: William Godwin, Judith Demain. *Education:* University of Durham, B.A., 1935, diploma in teaching, 1936, M.A., 1938, Ph.D., 1939. *Politics:* Labour. *Office:* School of Education, University of Southampton, Highfield, Southampton 509 5NH, England.

CAREER: Crossley and Porter Schools, Halifax, England, senior history master, 1943-46; College of St. Mark and St. John, Chelsea, England, lecturer in education, 1946-47; University of Leicester, Leicester, England, senior lecturer in education, 1947-63; University of Exeter, Exeter, England, director of university institute of education, 1963-71.

WRITINGS: (With others) *Comprehensive Schools Today,* Councils and Education Press, 1955; *Comprehensive Education: A New Approach,* Gollancz, 1956; *The Comprehensive School,* Penguin, 1963, revised edition, 1969; *The Comprehensive University,* University of Exeter, 1969. Contributor to numerous periodicals. Editor, *Forum,* 1958-63.

BIOGRAPHICAL/CRITICAL SOURCES: Books and Bookmen, January, 1970.

* * *

PEEL, H(azel) M(ary) 1930-
(Hayman)

PERSONAL: Born May 26, 1930, in London, England; daughter of Ernest Leslie Charles (a security policeman) and Elizabeth (Bullen) Wallis; married Roy Peel (a patent's clerk), October 24, 1953; *Education:* Attended Alderman Newton's Girls' School, Leicester, England; left school at fourteen. *Politics:* "Usually vote Conservative." *Religion:* Church of England.

CAREER: Worked as telephonist, 1944; became learner groom, 1945, went to work in riding stables for two winters, working in riding schools during the summers; began working for private stables, 1946, gaining experience with point to point race horses, show jumpers, and show hacks; left stable jobs in 1950 to hitchhike around Europe, touring France, Belgium, Holland, and Luxembourg; worked as car cleaner in London, 1950; did office work, 1950-52; left for Australia, 1952; worked as clerk for Australian Navy for three months in 1952; worked in factories, cafes, and offices, Brisbane, Queensland, Australia, 1952-53; Bristol Siddeley Engines Ltd., Bristol, England, typist, 1953-57; full-time writer, 1957—. *Member:* Society of Authors.

WRITINGS: Fury, Son of the Wilds, Watts, 1959; *Pilot, the Hunter,* Watts, 1962; *Pilot, the Chaser,* Watts, 1964; *Show Jumper,* Watts, 1965 (published in England as *Easter, the Showjumper,* Harrap, 1965); *Jago,* Harrap, 1966; *Night Storm, the Flat Racer,* Harrap, 1966; *Dido and Rogue,* Harrap, 1967; *Gay Darius,* Harrap, 1968; *Untamed!,* Harrap, 1969. Also author of three unperformed television plays: "Zero Hour 11.00," "Five Hours to Dawn," and "The Choice."

WORK IN PROGRESS: To Jenny with Hate; a technical horse book for children, *Pocket Dictionary of the Horse.*

SIDELIGHTS: Mrs. Peel writes: "[I am] very keen on all sports. I ride actively all through the winter on a friend's hunter. . . . Like swimming, though no good at diving. . . . While in London became a member of the Budokwai judo society, attaining a blue belt. In Australia, formed own judo club where practised with women and men. Graded under Japanese Kodokan rules brown or first kyu." Due to leg trouble, she is no longer active in judo.

An avid reader, she usually reads six books per week, "ranging from contemporary authors to old classic favourites and some non-fiction books." She collects stamps, likes good television, and Wagner. She loves outdoor life: "My idea of a holiday," she writes, "[is] lounging on a hot beach and plunging into the sea at will." She dislikes parties.

Fury, Son of the Wilds, which was written three times, has been translated into Danish, Dutch, and Portuguese.

BIOGRAPHICAL/CRITICAL SOURCES: Times Literary Supplement, June 26, 1969.†

* * *

PEEPLES, Edwin A(ugustus, Jr.) 1915-

PERSONAL: Born March 2, 1915, in Atlanta, Ga.; son of Edwin Augustus (a cotton broker) and Robyn (Young) Peeples; married Malvine Ogle, March 17, 1945; children: Edwin A. III, Charles Lewis, Christopher Cabaniss. *Education:* Georgia Institute of Technology, B.S. in General Engineering, 1936. *Religion:* Episcopal. *Home:* Vixen Hill, R.D. 2, Phoenixville, Pa. 19460. *Agent:* Paul R. Reynolds, Inc., 599 Fifth Ave., New York, N.Y. 10017. *Office:* Vixen Hill, R.D. 2, Phoenixville, Pa. 19460.

CAREER: James A. Greene, Advertising, Atlanta, Ga., copyriter, 1936-38; Sudite Chemical Manufacturing Corp., Atlanta, Ga., president and general manager, 1938-42; U.S. Army, Ordnance Department, Philadelphia, Pa., civilian associate engineer, 1942-45; *Fortune,* New York, N.Y., member of editorial staff, 1945; Franklin Institute Laboratories for Research and Development, Philadelphia, Pa., research editor, 1946-50; U.S. Army, Corps of Engineers, Philadelphia, Pa., chief procurement officer, 1950-55; Gray & Rogers, Inc. (advertising and public relations), Philadelphia, Pa., senior vice-president, director, and member of executive committee, 1955-72. Technical copy consultant, McClain-Dorville Advertising, 1948-50. Lecturer on writing and public relations at Charles Morris Price School, Drexel Library School, and Annenberg School of Communications of University of Pennsylvania. Member of steering committee, Children's Reading Round Table, Philadelphia Public Library, 1965—; incorporator, Tax Action Committee, Chester County, 1972. *Member:* Authors Guild of Authors League of America, Association of Industrial Advertisers, Eastern Industrial Advertisers, Phi Gamma Delta, Midday Club (Philadelphia, Pa.)

WRITINGS: Fantasy on an Empty Stage (one-act play with music), Baker's Plays, 1941; *Swing Low* (novel), Houghton, 1945; *A Professional Storywriter's Handbook,* Doubleday, 1960; *Blue Boy* (juvenile), Houghton, 1964; *A Hole in the Hill* (juvenile), Thomas Nelson, 1969. Also author of "Gilbert," a novel, as yet unpublished. Writer of radio scripts for "Chamber Music Society of Lower Basin Street," 1942, and scripts for Jane Cowl's daily comment program, 1946. Contributor of short novel and stories to *Cosmopolitan,* short stories and articles to magazines and trade journals, including *Good House-*

keeping, Collier's, Esquire, Saturday Evening Post, Sports Illustrated, Family Circle, Writer's Digest, and *Writer.*

WORK IN PROGRESS: *Fitzgerald: Posthumous.*

AVOCATIONAL INTERESTS: Managing a sixty-five acre farm he owns, gardening, household repairs and painting, philately, numismatics, reading, playing piano and singing, and dramatic readings.

*   *   *

PEGRAM, Marjorie Anne (Dykes) 1925-

PERSONAL: Born July 26, 1925, in Omaha, Neb.; daughter of James Ralph and Frances Laura (Bollard) Dykes; married William Daniel Pegram (a college coach), December 23, 1947; children: William Daniel III, David Ashley, Robert James, Laura Bethel. *Education:* College of William and Mary, A.B., 1947. *Politics:* Republican. *Religion:* Presbyterian. *Home address:* Box 91, Hampden-Sydney, Va. 23943.

CAREER: Teacher in Roanoke and Hopewall, Va., 1948-51, 1959.

WRITINGS: *When Tomorrow Comes,* Zondervan, 1963. Contributor of articles and short stories to magazines.

WORK IN PROGRESS: A biography.

AVOCATIONAL INTERESTS: Singing (in church choir and as soprano soloist), working with college youth in Bible study.

*   *   *

PELZ, Lotte A(uguste) Hensl 1924-

PERSONAL: Surname is pronounced Pelts; born April 6, 1924, in Vienna, Austria; daughter of Anton (a cabinetmaker) and Else (Stern) Hensl; married Werner Pelz (a writer), October 30, 1944; children: Peter. *Education:* Studied at University of London, 1943-44, at Teachers' Training College, Cheltenham, England, 1946-47. *Politics:* "Radical, anarchic, and kibbutzian." *Home:* Bryn Coch, Llanfachreth, Dolgellau, North Wales. *Agent:* Mrs. D. Greenep, 1 Frognal, London N.W. 3, England.

CAREER: Charwoman, factory hand, and library assistant prior to 1944; teacher at various periods, 1944-61.

WRITINGS: (With husband, Werner Pelz) *God Is No More,* Gollancz, 1963, Lippincott, 1964; (with Werner Pelz) *True Deceivers,* Collins, 1966, Westminster, 1967; (with Werner Pelz) *I Am Adolf Hitler,* S.C.M. Press, 1969, John Knox, 1971. Contributor of short stories and articles to *Guardian* and *Ambit.*

WORK IN PROGRESS: A book of haikus.

*   *   *

PELZ, Werner 1921-

PERSONAL: Surname is pronounced Pelts; born September, 25, 1921, in Berlin, Germany; son of Ludwig (a cinema owner) and Regina (Kallmann) Pelz; married Lotte Hensl (a writer), October 30, 1944; children: Peter. *Education:* University of London, B.A., 1949; Lincoln Theological College, student, 1950-51; University of Bristol, Ph.D., 1973. *Politics:* "Strictly Utopian." *Religion:* "Against it." *Home:* Bryn Coch, Llanfachreth, Dolgellau, North Wales. *Agent:* Mrs. D. Greenep, 1 Frognal, London N.W. 3, England.

CAREER: Farm worker and gardener in Yorkshire and Gloucestershire, England, 1939-45; curate and vicar in Lancashire, England, 1951-63. Extramural lecturer at University of Manchester, 1960-63. Lecturer of Workers' Educational Association.

WRITINGS: *Irreligious Reflections on the Christian Church,* S.C.M. Press, 1959; (with wife, Lotte Pelz) *God*

Is No More, Gollancz, 1963, Lippincott, 1964; *Seduced by Hope,* Independent Press, 1963; *Crowning Absurdity,* BBC Publications, 1963; *Distant Strains of Triumph,* Gollancz, 1964; *Fruitful Dust,* BBC Publications, 1964; (with Lotte Pelz) *True Deceivers,* Collins, 1966, Westminster, 1967; (with Lotte Pelz) *I Am Adolf Hitler,* S.C.M. Press, 1969, John Knox, 1971. Contributor of articles and short stories to *Guardian, Listener,* and other periodicals.

WORK IN PROGRESS: The problem of understanding in sociology.

SIDELIGHTS: "I and my wife suffer from prophetic, poetic, and philosophical proclivities. We always want to write something which is beautiful, profound and revolutionary at the same time.... We hope to continue the autobiographical reflections started in *Distant Strains of Triumph.* [I] want to write a Chehovian-Dostoievskian-original novel."

*   *   *

PENDOWER, Jacques 1899-
   (Kathleen Carstairs, Tom Curtis, Penn Dower, T.C.H. Jacobs, Lex Pender, Marilyn Pender, Anne Penn)

PERSONAL: Born December 30, 1899, in Plymouth, Devonshire, England; son of Robert (an artist) and Mary Pendower; married Muriel Newbury, June 1, 1925; children: one son. *Education:* Attended Grammar School in Plymouth, Devonshire, England. *Home:* 44 Hill Crescent, Bexley, Kent, England.

CAREER: Former investigating officer (revenue); full-time author, 1950—. *Military service:* British Army, Infantry, 1918-21; became second lieutenant. *Member:* Crime Writers Association (founding member; chairman, 1960-61), Press Club, Radio and Television Guild, Society of Authors, Bexley Rotary Club.

WRITINGS—All published by R. Hale, unless otherwise noted: *Hunted Woman,* Ward, Lock, 1955; *The Dark Avenue,* Ward, Lock, 1955; *Mission in Tunis,* 1958, Paperback Library, 1967; *The Long Shadow,* 1959; *The Double Diamond,* 1959; *Anxious Lady,* 1960; *The Widow from Spain,* 1961, published in America as *Betrayed,* Paperback Library, 1967; *Death on the Moor,* 1962; *The Perfect Wife,* 1962; *Operation Carlo,* 1963; *Sinister Talent,* 1964; *Master Spy,* 1964; *Spy Business,* 1965; *Out of This World,* 1966; *Traitor's Island,* 1967; *Try Anything Once,* 1967; *A Trap for Fools,* 1968; *The Golden Statuette,* 1969; *Diamonds for Danger,* 1970; *She Came by Night,* 1971; *Cause for Alarm,* 1971.

Under pseudonym T.C.H. Jacobs: *The Terror of Torlands,* Stanley Paul, 1930; *The Bronkhorst Case,* Stanley Paul, 1931, published in America as *Documents of Murder,* Macaulay, 1933; *Scorpion's Trail,* Stanley Paul, 1932, Macaulay, 1934; *The Kestrel House Mystery,* Stanley Paul, 1932, Macaulay, 1933; *Sinister Quest,* Stanley Paul, 1934, Macaulay, 1936; *The 13th Chime,* Stanley Paul, 1935, Macaulay, 1936; *Silent Terror,* Stanley Paul, 1936, Macaulay, 1937; *Appointment with the Hangman,* Macaulay, 1936; *The Laughing Men,* Hodder & Stoughton, 1937; *Identity Unknown,* Stanley Paul, 1938; *Traitor Spy,* Stanley Paul, 1939; *Brother Spy,* Stanley Paul, 1941; *The Broken Knife,* Stanley Paul, 1941; *Grensen Murder Case,* Stanley Paul, 1943; *Reward for Treason,* Stanley Paul, 1944; *The Black Box,* Stanley Paul, 1946; *The Curse of Khatra,* Stanley Paul, 1947; *With What Motive?,* Stanley Paul, 1948; *Dangerous Fortune,* Stanley Paul, 1949; *The Red Eyes of Kali,* Stanley Paul, 1950; *Lock the Door, Mademoiselle,* Stanley Paul, 1951; *Blood and Sun-Tan,* Stanley Paul, 1952; *Lady, What's Your Game?,* Stanley Paul, 1952; *No Sleep for Elsa,* Stanley Paul, 1953; *The Woman Who Waited,* Stanley Paul, 1954; *Good Night,*

Sailor, Stanley Paul, 1954; *Results of an Accident,* Stanley Paul, 1955; *Cavalcade of Murder,* Stanley Paul, 1955; *Death in the Mews,* Stanley Paul, 1955; *Pageant of Murder,* Stanley Paul, 1956; *Aspects of Murder,* Stanley Paul, 1956; *Cause for Suspicion,* Stanley Paul, 1956; *Broken Alibi,* Roy Publishers, 1957; *Deadly Race,* John Long, 1958; *Black Trinity,* John Long, 1959; *Women Are Like That,* R. Hale, 1960; *Let Him Stay Dead,* R. Hale, 1961; *The Tattooed Man,* R. Hale, 1961; *Target for Terror,* R. Hale, 1961; *The Red Net,* R. Hale, 1962; *Murder Market,* R. Hale, 1962; *The Secret Power,* R. Hale, 1963; *Danger Money,* R. Hale, 1963; *The Elusive Monsieur Drago,* R. Hale, 1964; *Final Payment,* R. Hale, 1965; *Ashes in the Cellar,* R. Hale, 1966; *Sweet Poison,* R. Hale, 1966; *Death of a Scoundrel,* R. Hale, 1967; *Wild Week-End,* R. Hale, 1967; *House of Horror,* R. Hale, 1969; *The Black Devil,* R. Hale, 1969; *Security Risk,* R. Hale, 1972.

Under pseudonym Penn Dower; all published by John Long, unless otherwise indicated: *Lone Star Ranger,* 1952; *Bret Malone, Texas Marshal,* 1953; *Gunsmoke Over Alba,* 1953; *Texas Stranger,* 1954; *Indian Moon,* 1954; *Malone Rides In,* 1955; *Two-Gun Marshal,* 1956; *Desperate Venture,* 1956; *Guns in Vengeance,* 1957; *Frontier Marshal,* 1958; *Bandit Brothers,* Four Square Books, 1964.

Under pseudonym Tom Curtis: *Bandit Gold,* Stanley Paul, 1953; *Gunman's Glory,* Stanley Paul, 1954; *Trail End,* Stanley Paul, 1954; *Frontier Mission,* Stanley Paul, 1955; *Border Justice,* Stanley Paul, 1955; *Ride and Seek,* Stanley Paul, 1957; *Phantom Marshal,* John Long, 1957; *Gun Business,* John Long, 1958; *Lone Star Law,* John Long, 1959.

Under pseudonym Kathleen Carstairs: *It Began in Spain,* John Gresham, 1960; *Third Time Lucky,* John Gresham, 1962; *Shadows of Love,* John Gresham, 1966.

Under pseudonym Marilyn Pender: *The Devouring Flame,* John Gresham, 1960; *A Question of Loyalty,* John Gresham, 1961; *The Golden Vision,* John Gresham, 1962; *Rebel Nurse,* John Gresham, 1962; *Dangerous Love,* John Gresham, 1966.

Under pseudonym Anne Penn: *Dangerous Delusion,* John Gresham, 1960; *Prove Your Love,* John Gresham, 1961; *Mystery Patient,* John Gresham, 1966.

Contributor of short stories, serials, and articles to newspapers and magazines; author of radio plays for British Broadcasting Corp.

SIDELIGHTS: Pendower's novels have been translated into every western European language. *Avocational interests:* Driving a fast car, golf, and rifle shooting.

* * *

PEPE, John Frank 1920-

PERSONAL: Surname is pronounced Pep; born January 15, 1920, in Watertown, N.Y.; son of Louis and Rose (Condino) Pepe. *Education:* Maren Elwood College, Hollywood, Calif., student, three years. *Politics:* Democrat. *Religion:* Roman Catholic. *Home:* 216 Cedar St., Watertown, N.Y. 13601.

CAREER: Varied career includes jobs as printer's apprentice, railroad section hand, aircraft assembler, postal clerk, disk jockey, and mutual funds salesman; also freelance writer, 1947—, in Hollywood, Calif., 1946-57, now in Watertown, N.Y. *Military service:* U.S. Army, 1942-46.

WRITINGS: The Alabaster Bambino (novel), Paisano, 1963. Former radio writer for Red Skelton and Steve Allen and gagwriter for several cartoonists. Contributor of short stories, humor fillers, and sketches to magazines.

WORK IN PROGRESS: A novel tentatively titled *The Apple Orchard Commandos,* based on wartime experience.

AVOCATIONAL INTERESTS: Painting, music, and the theatre.

* * *

PEPITONE, Albert (Davison) 1923-

PERSONAL: Born January 22, 1923, in Brooklyn, N.Y.; son of Albert and Mabel (Davison) Pepitone; married Emmy A. Berger (an assistant professor of education and child development at Bryn Mawr College), October 3, 1949; children: Leslie, Jessica, Andrea, Victor. *Education:* New York University, A.B., 1942; Yale University, M.A., 1943; University of Michigan, Ph.D., 1949. *Office:* Department of Psychology, University of Pennsylvania, 3815 Walnut St., Philadelphia, Pa. 19604.

CAREER: University of Michigan, Ann Arbor, project director, Institute for Social Research, 1949-51; University of Pennsylvania, Philadelphia, assistant professor, 1951-57, associate professor, 1957-64, professor of psychology, 1964—. Visiting professor at University of Wisconsin and Haverford College, 1959; Fulbright research professor in Netherlands, 1960-61, and at National Institute of Psychology, Rome, Italy, 1968. Consultant to Veterans Administration. *Military service:* U.S. Army Air Forces, 1943-46. *Member:* American Psychological Association, Society for the Psychological Study of Social Issues, Sigma Xi.

WRITINGS: Attraction and Hostility: An Experimental Analysis of Interpersonal and Self-Evaluation, Atherton, 1964.

Contributor: Alexander Paul Hare and others, editors, *Small Groups: Studies in Social Interaction,* Knopf, 1955; Frank Joseph McGuigan and A.D. Calvin, editors, *Current Studies in Psychology,* Appleton, 1958; Renato Tagiuri and Luigi Petrullo, editors, *Person Perception and Interpersonal Behavior,* Stanford University Press, 1958; Dorwin Cartwright and A.F. Zander, editors, *Group Dynamics: Research and Theory,* 2nd edition, Row, Peterson & Co., 1960; Norman F. Washburne, editor, *Decisions, Values, and Groups,* Pergamon, 1962; Neil Joseph Smelser and W.T. Smelser, editors, *Personality and Social Systems,* Wiley, 1963; William Edgar Vinacke and others, editors, *Dimensions of Social Psychology,* Scott, Foresman, 1964; Harold Milton Proshansky and Bernard Seidenberg, editors, *Basic Studies in Psychology,* Holt, 1965. Contributor of numerous research papers to professional journals.

WORK IN PROGRESS: A textbook in social psychology; laboratory experiments on competitiveness, persistence, social perception, altruism, violence, and aggression.

* * *

PERCIVAL, Alicia C(onstance) 1903-

PERSONAL: Born May 13, 1903, in London, England; daughter of Philip Edward (a civil servant in India) and Sylvia (Baines) Percival. *Education:* Attended Sherborne School for Girls; St. Hugh's College, Oxford, B.A., 1925, M.A., 1929, Diploma in Education, 1936; University of London, Ph.D. *Home:* 21 Maunsel St., Westminster, London S.W.1, England. *Agent:* A.P. Watt & Sons, 10 Norfolk St., London W.C. 2, England.

CAREER: Bromley High School, Bromley, Kent, England, teacher of English and classics, 1932-36; Madras Women's Christian College, Madras, India, professor of English, 1937; University College of Hull, Kingston upon Hull, England, lecturer in education, 1938-40; British Council lecturer in Middle East, 1941-43; Forest Training College, London, England, 1945-50, began as vice-principal, became principal; Trent Park College, Barnet, Hertfordshire, England, principal lecturer in education, 1950-66. British Red Cross and United Nations Relief and Rehabilitation Administration representative in Italy, 1944. Onetime member of British Broadcasting Corporation Choral Society, Bach Choir, and Third Programme Listeners' Research Panel. *Member:* English Association (member of executive committee), National Library for the Blind (member of executive committee), Secondary Technical Universities Insurance Society (former member of committee of management), Folklore Society (honorary librarian, 1966—). *Awards, honors:* Poetry Society silver medal.

WRITINGS: Samplers (poems), Basil Blackwell, 1933; (adapter) Shakespeare, *Julius Caesar,* Thomas Nelson, 1938; *The English Miss: Ideas, Methods, and Personalities in the Education of and Upbringing of Girls During the Last Hundred Years,* Harrap, 1939; (with Margaret Mare) *Victorian Best-Seller: The World of Charlotte M. Yonge,* Harrap, 1947; *Youth Will Be Led: The Story of the Voluntary Youth Organizations,* Collins, 1951; *The Origins of the Headmasters' Conference,* J. Murray, 1969; (with E.L. Percival) *The Percival Book,* privately printed, 1970. Contributor of reviews and articles to educational journals.

WORK IN PROGRESS: Research into English public schools and the men who made them; a book, *Very Superior Men.*

*   *   *

PEREIRA, Harold Bertram   1890-
(Hussaini Muhammad Askari, Mabel Yeates)

PERSONAL: Born May 31, 1890, in Calcutta, India; son of Henry Thomas (a civil servant) and Mary Francella (Goncalvez) Pereira; married Mabel May Yeates, December 21, 1921. *Education:* University of Calcutta, B.A. *Religion:* Roman Catholic. *Home and office:* 22 Thornton Ave., London S.W. 2, England.

CAREER: Reuters Ltd., general reporter in Calcutta, India, 1911-13; *Statesman,* general reporter in London, England, and Calcutta, India, 1914-28; *Times of India,* general reporter in London, England, 1928-30; free-lance writer on travel, civil aviation, heraldry, 1930—. Marketing consultant, Arthur H. Wheeler. Special officer, Calcutta Police, 1921-24. *Military service:* Indian Auxiliary Force, 1907-17. *Member:* Institute of Journalists (fellow; secretary of free-lance section; member of council, 1961-71), Heraldry Society (fellow; member of council, 1953-71).

WRITINGS: (Under pseudonym Hussaini Muhammad Askari) *The Food of Kings,* Charles Stembridge & Co., 1936; *The Armorial Bearings of the Princes of India,* Batsford, 1938; *The Colour of Chivalry,* Imperial Chemical Industries, 1950; (compiler) *Aircraft Badges and Markings,* Adlard Coles, 1955, De Graff, 1956; (with H. Stanford London) *Royal Beasts,* Heraldry Society, 1956; *Playing Cards of the World,* Walsall Publishing Co., 1967; *The Arab Horse,* Walsall Publishing Co., 1969; *Historic Seals,* Walsall Publishing Co., 1971. Former editor, *Empress, Indian Film Gazette.*

WORK IN PROGRESS: Saracenic Heraldry; Diocesan Arms (illustrations); a manuscript of Persian *Rubiyyat of Omar Khayyam; Stained Glass in Europe.*

SIDELIGHTS: Pereira is competent in Hindi, Urdu, Latin, and some European languages; he reads and writes Old English Court Hand, required for research in medieval history before the late seventeenth century; he has done hundreds of drawings of heraldic achievements, and a number of heraldic wood carvings. *Avocational in-* *terests:* Hindu astronomy, Brahminism, yoga, Islamic culture, Saracenic art (especially surface ornament, faience niello, and Bidri work on metal), collects specimens of Persian penmanship.

*   *   *

PERETZ, Don   1922-

PERSONAL: Born October 31, 1922, in Baltimore, Md.; son of Haym Victor (a social worker) and Josephine (Lasser) Peretz; married Janet Bentson, August, 1962; children: Debora Dawn, Jonathan Lief. *Education:* University of Minnesota, B.A., 1944; Columbia University, M.A., 1952, Ph.D., 1955. *Home:* 209 Pennsylvania Ave., Binghamton, N.Y. 13903. *Agent:* Bertha Klausner, International Literary Agency, Inc., 71 Park Ave., New York, N.Y. 10016. *Office:* Department of Political Science, State University of New York at Binghamton, Binghamton, N.Y. 13901.

CAREER: National Broadcasting Co., New York, N.Y., foreign correspondent, 1947-48; United Nations, New York, N.Y., representative for American Friends Service Committee, 1949, foreign correspondent for *United Nations World,* 1949-50; U.S. Department of State, Middle East media evaluator for Voice of America, 1952, research analyst, 1954-56; American Jewish Committee, consultant on Middle East, 1956-58; Long Island University, Brooklyn, N.Y., and Vassar College, Poughkeepsie, N.Y., lecturer on Middle East, 1959-62; New York State Education Department, State University of New York, Albany, associate director, Office of Foreign Area Studies, 1962-67; State University of New York at Binghamton, professor of political science and director of South West Asia/North Africa Program, 1967—. Lecturer, Williams College, 1964-65. Advisor to assistant secretary of state for Near East and South Asia, 1967-69. *Military service:* U.S. Army, 1943-46. *Member:* American Historical Association, American Academy of Political and Social Science, American Political Science Association, Council on Foreign Relations, Middle East Institute, Overseas Press Club, Middle East Studies Association, Institute for Strategic Studies. *Awards, honors:* Ford Foundation grant, 1952-54; Rockefeller Foundation grant, 1962-63.

WRITINGS: Egyptian Jews Today, American Jewish Committee, 1956; *Israel and the Palestine Arabs,* Middle East Institute, 1958; *Education in the Middle East: A Selected and Annotated Reading Guide,* Office of Foreign Area Studies, New York State Education Department, 1963; *The Middle East Today,* Holt, 1963, revised edition, 1971; (with Hugo Jaeckel) *The Middle East,* Scholastic Book Services, 1964, revised edition, 1967; (editor) *The Middle East: Selected Readings,* Houghton, 1968, hardcover edition, 1969; (with E. Wilson and R. Ward) *A Palestine Entity: Special Study Number One,* Middle East Institute, 1970; *The Middle East: Regional Study* (textbook; grades seven through twelve), Houghton, 1972.

Contributor: Benjamin Revlin and J.S. Szyliowicz, editors, *The Contemporary Middle East: Tradition and Innovation,* Random House, 1965; Jack Howell Thompson and R.D. Reischauer, editors, *Modernization of the Arab World,* Van Nostrand, 1966; John W. Halderman, editor, *The Middle East Crisis: Test of International Law,* Oceana, 1969; Irene Gendzier, editor, *A Middle East Reader,* Pegasus, 1969; Landrum Bolling, editor, *Search for Peace in the Middle East,* Fawcett, 1970. Contributor to *Reporter, New Republic, Foreign Affairs, United Nations World, Middle East Journal, Christian Century, Commonweal, New Leader, Jewish Social Studies, International Journal, Vital Issues,* and other journals.

PERKINS, James Oliver Newton 1924-

PERSONAL: Born July 11, 1924, in Bedford, England; son of Arthur Harry and Daisy (Newton) Perkins; married Ruth Williams, January 15, 1955; children: Caroline. *Education:* Attended Bedford School, Bedford, England; St. Catharine's College. Cambridge, B.A., 1948, M.A., 1950, Ph.D., 1953. *Home:* 18 Riddle St., Bentleigh, Melbourne 3204, Victoria, Australia.

CAREER: Economist, London, England, member of editorial staff, 1952-53; Australian National University, Canberra, research fellow, 1953-56; University of Melbourne, Melbourne, Australia, 1957—, began as lecturer, became senior lecturer and reader, now professor of economics. Simon fellow, University of Manchester, 1961-62. *Military service:* British Army, 1943-47; became captain. *Member:* International Economic Association (member of council, 1964—), Economic Society of Australia and New Zealand.

WRITINGS: Sterling and Regional Payments Systems, Melbourne University Press, 1956; *Britain and Australia: Economic Relationships in the 1950's,* Melbourne University Press, 1962; *Anti-Cyclical Policy in Australia, 1960-64,* Melbourne University Press, 1965, 2nd edition published as *Anti-Cyclical Policy in Australia, 1960-66,* Melbourne University Press, 1967; (contributor) Alan Howard Boxer, editor, *Aspects of the Australian Economy,* Cambridge University Press, 1966, 2nd edition, 1969; (with others) *Effects of U.K. Direct Investment Overseas: An Interim Report,* Cambridge University Press, 1967; *The Sterling Area, the Commonwealth, and World Economic Growth,* Cambridge University Press, 1967, 2nd edition, 1970; *Australia in the World Economy,* Sun Books, 1968, 2nd edition, 1971; *International Policy for the World Economy,* Praeger, 1969; *World Monetary Reform and Its Implications for Australia,* University of Queensland Press, 1969; (contributor) Isaiah A. Litvak and Christopher J. Maule, editors, *Foreign Investment: The Experience of Host Countries,* Praeger, 1970; (with J.E. Sullivan) *Banks and the Capital Market: An Australian Study,* Melbourne University Press, 1970; *Pattern of Australia's International Payments,* Thomas Nelson, 1971; *Macro-Economic Policy in Australia,* Melbourne University Press, 1971. Contributor of articles to economic and banking periodicals.

WORK IN PROGRESS: Editing and contributing to a study of macroeconomic policy in Australia, Canada, New Zealand, and South Africa; contributing to a book-length study of the Australian economy.

*   *   *

PERRY, Thomas Whipple 1925-

PERSONAL: Born August 18, 1925, in Elmira, N.Y.; son of Charles Walker (in insurance) and Genevieve (Pettee) Perry; married Guest Washburn, June 19, 1951; children: Sarah, Annah Taft, Charles. *Education:* Attended Culver Military Academy, 1940-43; Harvard University, A.B., 1950, A.M., 1953, Ph.D., 1957. *Politics:* Democrat. *Religion:* Protestant. *Home:* 64 Russell Ave., Watertown, Mass. 02172. *Office:* Department of History, Boston College, Chestnut Hill, Mass. 02167.

CAREER: Massachusetts Institute of Technology, Cambridge, 1957-64, began as instructor, became assistant professor of history; Boston College, Boston, Mass., associate professor of history, 1964—. *Member,* Watertown Town Meeting. *Military service:* U.S. Army, 1943-46; became first lieutenant. *Member:* American Historical Association, Conference on British Studies, St. Lucia Archaeological and Historical Society, Phi Beta Kappa.

WRITINGS: Public Opinion, Propaganda and Politics in 18th Century England: A Study of the Jew Bill of 1753, Harvard University Press, 1962. Contributor of articles and reviews to professional journals.

WORK IN PROGRESS: Articles on eighteenth-century English politics.

*   *   *

PETERS, William 1921-

PERSONAL: Born July 30, 1921, in San Francisco, Calif.; son of William Ernest (an advertising executive) and Dorothy (Wright) Peters; married Mercy Ann Miller, October 12, 1942 (divorced, 1968); married Muriel M. Neff, August 30, 1968; children: (first marriage) Suzanne P. O'Leary, Geoffrey W., Jennifer, Gretchen. *Education:* Northwestern University, B.S., 1947. *Politics:* Democrat. *Home address:* R.D. 1, Old West Lake Rd., Montauk, N.Y. 11954. *Agent:* Curtis Brown Ltd., 60 East 56th St., New York, N.Y. 10022.

CAREER: J. Walter Thompson Co., Chicago, Ill., account executive in public relations, 1947-51; *Ladies' Home Journal,* Philadelphia, Pa., member of fiction staff, 1951-52; *Women's Home Companion,* New York, N.Y., article editor, 1952-53; free-lance writer, Pelham, N.Y., 1953-62; Columbia Broadcasting System News, New York, N.Y., producer of "CBS Reports," 1962-66; free-lance writer, director, and television producer, 1966—, including "After the Years: the Court and the Schools" for Columbia Broadcasting System, May 13, 1964, and Eastern segment of "Africa," for American Broadcasting Co., September 10, 1967. Consultant on race relations, 1959—. Founder and member of board of directors, North Shore Human Relations Council, 1947-51; Pelham Committee on Human Relations, founder and vice-chairman, 1963-65, chairman, 1965-66. *Military service:* U.S. Army Air Corps, pilot, 1942-45; became captain; received Air Medal with two oak-leaf clusters and Distinguished Flying Cross.

MEMBER: Society of Magazine Writers, Writers Guild of America, East, Directors Guild of America. *Awards, honors:* Two special citations, Benjamin Franklin Magazine awards, Howard W. Blakeslee Award, National Brotherhood Award, and Lincoln University award, for magazine articles; George Foster Peabody Awards, 1963, 1967, 1970, for television documentaries; Golden Gavel Award, American Bar Association, 1963; National School Bell Award, National Education Association, 1964; Christopher Award, *Saturday Review* television award, Catholic Broadcast Association's Gabriel Award, and honorable mention at Monte Carlo Television Festival, all for documentary, "The Eye of the Storm."

WRITINGS: American Memorial Hospital, Reims, France: A History, privately printed by American Memorial Hospital, 1955; *Passport to Friendship: The Story of the Experiment in International Living,* foreword by Pearl S. Buck, Lippincott, 1957; *The Southern Temper,* foreword by Harry Golden, Doubleday, 1959; (with Mrs. Medgar Evers) *For Us, the Living,* Doubleday, 1967; *A Class Divided,* Doubleday, 1971.

Television documentaries: "Mississippi and the 15th Amendment," produced by Columbia Broadcasting System for "CBS Reports," September 26, 1962; "Storm Over the Supreme Court," produced by Columbia Broadcasting System for "CBS Reports," Part II, March 13, 1963, Part III, June 19, 1963; "The Priest and the Politician," produced by Columbia Broadcasting System for "CBS Reports," September 18, 1963; "Filibuster: Birth Struggle of a Law," produced by Columbia Broadcasting System for "CBS Reports," March 18, 1964; "Segregation: Northern Style," produced by Columbia Broadcasting System for "CBS Reports," December 9, 1964; "Southern Accents—Northern Ghettos," produced by

American Broadcasting Co. News, July 6, 1967; "The Eye of the Storm," produced by American Broadcasting Co. News, May 11, 1970; "An Echo of Anger," produced by American Broadcasting Co. News, August 16, 1972. Contributor to *Good Housekeeping, Interracial Review, Ladies' Home Journal, Look, McCall's, New Republic, Reader's Digest, Redbook, Reporter, Saturday Evening Post, Saturday Review, Sports Illustrated,* and *This Week.*

*   *   *

PETERSEN, Sigurd Damskov 1904-

PERSONAL: Born January 29, 1904, in Kenmare, N.D.; son of P.C.K. and Petrea (Damskov) Petersen; married Dorothy Hofstrom, 1933; children: Delores Jorgensen, Verla Cramer, David. *Education:* Studied at St. Olaf College, 1924-25, Dana College, 1925-26, Trinity Seminary, Blair, Neb., 1926-27, 1928-29, Chicago Lutheran Seminary, 1927-28. *Home:* 707 North Hazel, Glenwood, Iowa 51534.

CAREER: Parish pastor in the Lutheran Church, 1929-54; Parsons State Hospital and Training Center, Parsons, Kan., psychiatric chaplain, 1955-63; Glenwood State Hospital School, Glenwood, Iowa, chaplain, 1963-68. Accredited by National Lutheran Council as chaplain supervisor. Staff member, Faribault Summer School of Religious Education, Faribault, Minn., 1961.

WRITINGS: Retarded Children: God's Children, Westminster, 1960; (contributor) Charles F. Kemp, editor, *Pastoral Preaching,* Bethany Press, 1963; (contributor) Robert L. Noland, editor, *Counseling Parents of the Mentally Retarded,* C.C Thomas, 1970. Also author of a manuscript, "The Mentally Retarded: Part of Humanity," as yet unpublished. Contributor to religious journals.

SIDELIGHTS: In preparation for his work with retarded children, Petersen took a nine-month course in psychiatry at a Topeka, Kan., hospital. He is convinced that religion has much common ground with that branch of medicine.

BIOGRAPHICAL/CRITICAL SOURCES: Sunday Digest, Elgin, Ill., August 25, 1957.

*   *   *

PETERSON, Arthur L(aVerne) 1926-

PERSONAL: Born June 27, 1926, in Glyndon, Minn.; son of J. Martin (a minister) and Hilda C. (Moline) Peterson; married Connie Harr, June 14, 1952; children: J. Martin II, Rebecca Ruth, Donna Harr, Ingrid Bliss. *Education:* Yale University, A.B., 1947; University of Southern California, M.S.P.A., 1948; graduate study at Lawrence University, Marquette University, and University of Chicago; University of Minnesota, Ph.D., 1962. *Politics:* Republican. *Religion:* Congregational. *Home:* 124 Oak Hill Ave., Delaware, Ohio 43015. *Office:* Department of Politics and Government, Ohio Wesleyan University, Delaware, Ohio 43015.

CAREER: Wisconsin State College (now Wisconsin State University), Eau Claire, instructor, 1954-58, assistant professor of political science, 1958-60; Republican National Committee, Washington, D.C., assistant to chairman, 1960-61; Ohio Wesleyan University, Delaware, associate professor, 1961-65, professor of political science, 1970—, chairman of the department, 1970—. President, Thunderbird Graduate School of International Management, 1966-70. Member, Wisconsin State Legislature, 1951-55. Chairman, Ohio Civil Rights Commission, 1962—. Chief administrative assistant to the chairman, Republican National Committee, 1965-66. *Military service:* U.S. Navy, 1944-46; U.S. Marine Corps, 1951-52, became captain. *Member:* American Academy of Political and Social Science, American Political Science Association.

WRITINGS: (With Daniel Ogden) *Electing the President: 1964,* Chandler Publishing, 1964, revised edition published as *Electing the President,* 1968. Contributor to political journals.

WORK IN PROGRESS: The Blissful Years: A Brief Recapitulation of the Rebuilding of the Republican Party, 1965-1968.

AVOCATIONAL INTERESTS: Athletics, sailing, flying, and music.

*   *   *

PETERSON, Theodore (Bernard) 1918-

PERSONAL: Born June 8, 1918, in Albert Lea, Minn.; son of Theodore B. and Emilie (Jensen) Peterson; married Helen Clegg, September 13, 1946; children: Thane Eric, Kristin, Megan, Daniel Alan. *Education:* University of Minnesota, B.A. (cum laude), 1941; Kansas State University of Agriculture and Applied Science, M.S., 1948; University of Illinois, Ph.D., 1955. *Religion:* Nonsectarian. *Home:* 103 East George Huff Dr., Urbana, Ill. 61801. *Office:* 119 Gregory Hall, University of Illinois, Urbana, Ill. 61801.

CAREER: Kansas State College of Agriculture and Applied Science (now Kansas State University of Agriculture and Applied Science), Manhattan, 1945-48, began as instructor, became assistant professor of journalism; University of Illinois, Urbana, instructor, 1948-55, associate professor, 1955-57, professor of journalism and communications and dean of College of Communications, 1957—. Former consultant in communications to U.S. Department of Defense and UNESCO; consultant to Engineering College Magazines of America, 1956-57. Editor of manuscripts for American Medical Writers Association, 1952-57. *Military service:* U.S. Army, Quartermaster and Ordnance, 1941-45; served in England with Eighth Air Force; became staff sergeant.

MEMBER: American Association of Schools and Departments of Journalism (president, 1964-65), Association for Education in Journalism (president, 1963; member of executive committee, 1962-64; member of council on communications research, 1958-64; chairman of council on magazine journalism, 1964), Magazine Publishers Association (member of education committee), American Association of University Professors, Kappa Tau Alpha, Alpha Delta Sigma. *Awards, honors:* Sigma Delta Chi award for distinguished research about journalism, 1956, for *Magazines in the Twentieth Century;* co-recipient, Kappa Tau Alpha award, 1956, for *Four Theories of the Press.*

WRITINGS: Writing Nonfiction for Magazines, Educational Publishers, 1949; (with Frederick S. Siebert and Wilbur Schramm) *Four Theories of the Press: The Authoritarian, Libertarian, Social Responsibility, and Soviet Communist Concepts of What the Press Should Be and Do,* University of Illinois Press, 1956; *Magazines in the Twentieth Century,* University of Illinois Press, 1956, 2nd edition, 1964; (with Jay W. Jensen and William L. Rivers) *The Mass Media and Modern Society,* Holt, 1965, 2nd revised edition, 1971. Contributor of chapters to several books. Annual contributor to *Collier's Encyclopedia Yearbook;* contributor of articles to *Antioch Review, Christian Century, Challenge,* and to *Journalism Quarterly* and other professional periodicals.

WORK IN PROGRESS: Continuing research on the contemporary American magazine.

*   *   *

PETERSON, Wilferd Arlan 1900-

PERSONAL: Born August 21, 1900, in Whitehall, Mich.; son of Peter Hans and Elsie Marie (Gilbert) Peterson;

married Ruth Irene Rector, June 21, 1921; children: Lilian Grace (Mrs. Gordon Albert Thorpe). *Education:* Attended business college in Muskegon, Mich., and took special courses at Michigan State University and University of Michigan. *Politics:* Republican. *Religion:* Liberal Protestant. *Home:* 1721 Woodward Ave. S.E., Grand Rapids, Mich. 49506.

CAREER: Jaqua Co. (advertising agency), Grand Rapids, Mich., 1928-65, began as copywriter, became vice-president, creative director, and secretary of board of directors; full-time writer and lecturer, 1965—. *Member:* Rotary International (Grand Rapids). *Awards, honors:* Silver Medal award from *Printers' Ink,* Advertising Federation of America, and the Advertising Club of Grand Rapids in honor of being named Advertising Man of the Year, 1963; George Washington Medal, Freedoms Foundation, 1958.

WRITINGS—All published by Simon & Schuster, except as indicated: *The Art of Getting Along: Inspiration for Triumphant Daily Living,* Harmony Press, 1949; *Twenty-three Essays on the Art of Living,* 1961; *The New Book of the Art of Living: A New Series of Twenty-seven Essays,* 1963; *More About the Art of Living: A Third Book of Twenty-five New Essays,* 1966; *Adventures in the Art of Living: A Fourth Book of New Essays,* 1968; *The Art of Living in the World Today: A Search for a Way of Life for These Times,* 1969. Author of monthly page in *Science and Mind;* contributor to *Reader's Digest* and *Unity.* Former editor of twenty-five industrial house magazines; member of editorial board, *Science and Mind.*

WORK IN PROGRESS: Another book, as yet untitled, for Simon & Schuster.

SIDELIGHTS: A long-playing record has been made of twelve essays from his books; the essays have also been adapted for greeting cards, booklets, and an annual "Art of Living" calender by Hallmark, Inc.

BIOGRAPHICAL/CRITICAL SOURCES: Good Business, October, 1956; *This Week,* November, 1961.

* * *

PETRAKIS, Harry Mark 1923-

PERSONAL: Born June 5, 1923, in St. Louis, Mo.; son of Mark E. (an Eastern Orthodox priest) and Stella (Christoulakis) Petrakis; married Diane Perparos, September 30, 1945; children: Mark, John, Dean. *Education:* Attended University of Illinois, 1940-41. *Politics:* "Radical Democrat." *Home and office:* 80 East Rd., Dune Acres, Chesterton, Ind. 46304.

CAREER: Has worked as laborer, steelworker, real estate salesman, speechwriter, and sales correspondent. Currently teaching modern American literature at Columbia College, Chicago, Ill., and workshop classes in the novel and the short story, Winnetka and Highland Park, Ill. Taught fiction techniques at Indiana University Writer's Conference, 1964-65; lecturer for W. Colston Leigh, Inc., New York, N.Y. Member, Indiana University Writer's Conference, 1964-65, 1970; McGuffey Lecturer, Ohio University, winter, 1971. *Member:* Writer's Guild of America—West, Author's Guild, P.E.N. *Awards, honors:* Atlantic First Award, 1957, and Benjamin Franklin Citation, 1957, both for short stories; awards from Friends of American Writers, Society of Midland Authors, and Friends of Literature, all 1964, for *The Odyssey of Kostas Volakis;* nominations for National Book award in fiction: 1965, *Pericles on 31st Street,* and 1966, *A Dream of Kings.*

WRITINGS: Lion at My Heart (novel), Atlantic-Little, Brown, 1959; *The Odyssey of Kostas Volakis* (novel), McKay, 1963; *Pericles on 31st Street* (stories), Quadrangle, 1965; *The Founder's Touch* (biography of Paul Galvin of Motorola, Inc.), McGraw, 1965 (novel; Literary Guild Selection), *A Dream of Kings,* McKay, 1966; *The Waves of Night* (short stories), McKay, 1969; *Stelmark: A Family Recollection* (autobiography) McKay, 1970. Writer of script for film adaptation of *Dream of Kings,* released, 1970. Represented in anthology, Elizabeth Janeway, *The Writer's World,* McGraw, 1969. Contributor of short stories to *Atlantic, Harper's Bazaar, Saturday Evening Post,* and other publications. Has adapted some of his short stories for television and has done some film work.

WORK IN PROGRESS: A novel about a Greek gambler; short stories, travel pieces, and articles.

SIDELIGHTS: Petrakis wrote to *CA:* "Perhaps the greatest influence in my work at present is the philosophy and writings of the Cretan, Nikos Kazantzakis, born and raised on the island from which my father and mother came."

Critics and reviewers remark this deep influence. "For years," wrote Samuel I. Bellman, "Harry Mark Petrakis has been interpreting the Greek-American 'experience' to an increasingly wide audience. . . . His story collection, *The Waves of Night,* contains a colorful assortment of the moods and concepts that have been traditionally, and sometimes erroneously, associated with the Greek approach to life. Because the stories are low-keyed and Petrakis's literary style, like his artistic aim, is extremely simple and unpretentious, the basic spirit affliction in these tales come through all the more forcefully. Petrakis's vision is a tragic one, redeemed only occasionally by a brief wild exultation, suggesting Kazantzakis's Zorba the Greek. He writes in fact, like an unaffected, present-day Sophocles out of Chicago." Louis T. Grant, too, says: "Perhaps the spirit of Nikos Kazantzakis, the great Greek writer from Crete, survives in the work of Petrakis." He feels that the characters of Petrakis, although members of a unique subculture, nevertheless say much to many of us about the experiences of life: "The minority experience, as Petrakis presents it, is more universal than might be supposed; for each of us, to twist a common phrase, is a minority of one. The Greeks who people Petrakis's stories are a distinguished and essential part of the great melting pot of American fiction."

* * *

PETRIE, Paul J(ames) 1928-

PERSONAL: Born July 1, 1928, in Detroit, Mich.; son of Louis Stuart (a stereotyper) and Mary (Squire) Petrie; married Sylvia Spencer, August 21, 1954; children: Philip Stuart, Emily Ruth, Lisa Evelyn. *Education:* Wayne State University, B.A., 1950, M.A., 1951; State University of Iowa, Ph.D., 1957. *Politics:* Independent. *Home:* 66 Dendron Rd., Peace Dale, R.I. 02879. *Office:* English Department, University of Rhode Island, Kingston, R.I. 02881.

CAREER: University of Rhode Island, Kingston, instructor, 1959-62 assistant professor, 1962-66, associate professor, 1966-69, professor of English, 1969—. *Military service:* U.S. Army, 1951-53. *Member:* American Association of University Professors.

WRITINGS—Poetry: *Confessions of a Non-Conformist* (pamphlet), Hillside Press, 1963; *The Race with Time and the Devil,* Golden Quill, 1965; *The Leader: For Martin Luther King, Jr.* (pamphlet), Hellcoal Press, 1968; *From Under the Hill of Night,* Vanderbilt University Press, 1969. Poetry is anthologized in *Borestone Mountain Poetry Awards, 1959, 1961, 1967,* edited by Lionel Stevenson and others, Pacific Books, 1960, 1962, 1968, and *Midland,* edited by Paul Engle and others, Random House, 1961. Contributor of two hundred poems to fifty journals, including *Atlantic, Commonweal, Massachusetts Review, Michigan Quarterly, Nation, New Republic, New Yorker,* and other publications.

WORK IN PROGRESS: Three books of poetry, *The Academy of Goodbye, Between Two Worlds,* and *Light From the Furnace Rising.*

SIDELIGHTS: Petrie writes: "My whole approach to poetry, both thematic and technical, is governed by a hatred of dogmatic theorizing, and since the twentieth century represents the very apotheosis of theorizing, a paradise for half-baked creeds and counter-creeds, I find myself in a 'school' of one. If there is a critical notion which I find appealing, it is that there is nothing that cannot be said in poetry and that there is no limitation on the way it can or should be said. A poem need not be 'new' or 'old', in 'free verse' or 'meter', 'understated' or 'overstated'—all that it must be is a good poem."

He adds: "As for my own work, I would describe it as lyrical, relatively emotional, dramatic in its inclusion of opposites with a stronger current of movement than is common in verse today, and perhaps an over-indulgence in the doctrine of statement through images. My major strengths are rhythm and organization; my major weaknesses are a lack of exact detail and firm diction. I have a personal notion of the poem as an act of praise (be it positive or negative in theme and tone), and I tend to regard poetry as a semi-religious vocation, but I do not demand that others share these attitudes and I can think of excellent poems which would stretch these terms to the breaking point. The poems will remain; the theory will go."

Petrie's area of major vocational interest is English Romantic poetry. He traveled to Spain and France, 1957-58, and to England and Italy, 1966-67.

AVOCATIONAL INTERESTS: Classical music, tennis.

* * *

PETTERSON, Henry William 1922-

PERSONAL: Born April 29, 1922, in Astoria, Ore.; son of Wilhelm Gustav (in lumber industry) and Fanny Maria (Pentilla) Petterson; married Meryl Mae Sattelmeier, August 21, 1949; children: Norman, Marie. *Education:* University of Washington, Seattle, B.A., 1950, M.F.A., 1951, secondary teachers certificate, 1952. *Home:* 2414 71st St., S.E. Mercer Island, Wash. 98040.

CAREER: Seattle Public Schools, Seattle, Wash., teacher of art, 1950-57, director of art, 1958—; professional painter, Northwest United States, 1951—. Visiting lecturer, Central Washington State University, 1960, Seattle University, 1962, 1963, 1964, University of California, Los Angeles, 1965, University of Washington, 1966, and University of British Columbia, 1971. Has had one-man shows in Edmonds, Upper Preston, and Seattle, Wash., participated in group shows at Seattle World's Fair and University of Arizona, and been represented in exhibitions in Seattle, Tacoma, New York, and at other locations. Regional chairman, Scholastic Art Awards Competition. *Military service:* U.S. Naval Reserve, 1942-46.

MEMBER: National Education Association, National Art Education Association, Pacific Arts Association, Northwest Water Color Society, Washington Education Association, Washington Art Teachers Association, Puget Sound Art Co-ordinators Association, Puget Sound Group of Northwest Painters, Seattle Art Teachers Association, Administrators and Supervisors League (Seattle). *Awards, honors:* Changing Scenes award, Seattle Museum of History of Industry, 1960; Craftsmen Press award, Frye Museum of Seattle, 1962; West Coast Oil Exhibition award, Frye Museum of Seattle, 1963.

WRITINGS: (With Ray Gerring) *Exploring with Paint,* Reinhold, 1964; "Eye, Mind and Hand" (16 mm film), 1967; *Creating Form in Clay,* Reinhold, 1968; "Design in Finland (16 mm film), 1970.

* * *

PEVSNER, Nikolaus (Bernhard Leon) 1902-

PERSONAL: Born January 30, 1902, in Leipzig, Germany; son of Hugo and Anna Pevsner; married Carola Kurlbaum, 1923 (died, 1963); children: Thomas, Dietrich, Uta Hodgson. *Education:* Attended Universities of Leipzig, Berlin, Frankfurt, and Munich; Ph.D., 1924. *Home:* 2 Wildwood Ter., North End, London N.W.3, England. *Office:* 18 Gower St., London W.C.1, England.

CAREER: Dresden Gallery, Dresden Germany, assistant keeper, 1924-28; University of Goettingen, Goettingen, Germany, lecturer in history of art and architecture, 1929-33; Cambridge University, Cambridge, England, Slade Professor Fine Art, 1949-55, fellow of St. John's College, 1950-55, honorary fellow, 1967—; Birbeck College, University of London, London, England, professor of history of art, 1945-68, emeritus professor, 1955—. Reith Lecturer, British Broadcasting Corp., 1968-69; Slade Professor of Fine Art, University of Oxford, 1968-69; lecturer on tours in Canada, South Africa, Australia, and New Zealand. British commissioner, Council of Europe Exhibition, 1961. Art Editor, Penguin Books. Member, Royal Fine Art Commission, Historical Building Council, National Advisory Council for Art Education, National Council for Diplomas in Art and Design, and Advisory Board for Redundant Churches.

MEMBER: Royal Institute of British Architects (honorary associate), Society of Antiquaries (fellow), American Academy of Arts and Sciences (honorary), Academia de Belle Art (Venice; honorary academician), Royal College of Art (honorary associate), Victorian Society (chairman), British Council (member of arts panel), William Morris Society, Akademie der Wissenschaften Goettingen (honorary fellow). *Awards, honors:* Commander, Order of the British Empire, 1953; Howland Prize, Yale University, 1963; Royal Gold medal for architecture, 1967; knighted, 1969; doctorates from University of Leicester, University of York, University of Leeds, Oxford University, University of East Anglia, and University of Zagreb.

WRITINGS: Italian Painting from the End of the Renaissance to the End of the Rococo, Atheneum, 1927-30; *The Baroque Architecture of Leipzig,* W. Jess, 1928; *Pioneers of the Modern Movement from William Morris to Walter Gropius,* Faber, 1936, 2nd edition published as *Pioneers of Modern Design,* Museum of Modern Art, 1949, 2nd edition, revised, Penguin, 1960; *An Inquiry into Industrial Art in England,* Cambridge University Press, 1937; (with S. Sitwell and A. Ayscough) *German Baroque Sculpture,* Duckworth, 1938.

Academies of Art, Past and Present, Macmillan, 1940; *An Outline of European Architecture,* Penguin, 1942, Scribner, 1948, 7th edition, Penguin, 1963; *The Leaves of Southwell,* Penguin, 1945; *Visual Pleasures from Everyday Things: An Attempt to Establish Criteria by Which the Aesthetic Qualities of Design Can Be Judged,* Batsford, 1946; *Matthew Digby Wyatt,* Cambridge University Press, 1950; *Charles R. Mackintosh,* Il Balcone (Milan), 1950; *High Victorian Design,* Architectural Press, 1951; *The Englishness of English Art,* British Broadcasting Corp., 1955, expanded and annotated edition, Praeger, 1956; (author of foreword and postscript) Michael Farr, *Design in British Industry: A Mid-Century Survey,* Cambridge University Press, 1955; (with Michael Meier) *Grunewald,* Abrams, 1958.

Christopher Wren, 1632-1723, Universe Books, 1960; *The Planning of the Elizabethan County House,* Birbeck College, 1961; (with others) *The Sources of Modern Art,* Thames & Hudson, 1962, reissued as *The Sources of Modern Architecture and Design,* Praeger, 1968; *The Choir of Lincoln Cathedral: An Interpretation,* Oxford University Press, 1963; (contributor) Peter Ferriday, editor, *Victorian Architecture,* J. Cape, 1963; (author of introduction) *Maxwell Fry,* Monks Hall Museum, 1964; (author of foreword) Nicholas Taylor, *Cambridge New Architecture: A Guide to the Post-War Buildings,* privately printed, 1964; (author of text) *Art Nouveau in Britain* (catalogue of an exhibition), London, 1965; (editor with John Fleming and Hugh Honour) *The Penguin Dictionary of Architecture,* Penguin, 1966; *Studies in Art, Architecture and Design,* two volumes, Walker & Co., 1968; *Ruskin and Viollet-le-Duc: Englishness and Frenchness in the Appreciation of Gothic Architecture,* Thames & Hudson, 1969; *Robert Willis,* Smith College, 1970.

"The Buildings of England" series; all published by Penguin: *Cornwall,* 1951, 2nd edition, 1970, *Nottinghamshire,* 1951, *Middlesex,* 1952, *South Devon,* 1952, *London,* 1952, 2nd edition, 1962, *Hertfordshire,* 1953, *Derbyshire,* 1953, *North Devon,* 1954, *County Durham,* 1954, *Cambridgeshire,* 1954, 2nd edition, 1969, *Essex,* 1954, 2nd edition, 1965, *Cities of London and Westminster,* 1957 *Northumberland,* 1957, *North Somerset and Bristol,* 1958, *South and West Somerset,* 1958, *Shropshire,* 1958, *Yorkshire: The West Riding,* 1959, 2nd edition, 1968, *Leicestershire and Rutland,* 1959, *Buckinghamshire,* 1960, *Suffolk,* 1961, *Northamptonshire,* 1962, (with Ian Nairn) *Surrey,* 1962, *North-East Norfolk and Norwich,* 1962, *North-West and South Norfolk,* 1962, *Herefordshire,* 1963, (with Derek Simpson) *Wiltshire,* 1963, (with John Harris) *Lincolnshire,* 1964, (with Nairn) *Sussex,* 1965, *Yorkshire: The North Riding,* 1966, *Berkshire,* 1966, (with Alexander Wedgwood) *Warwickshire,* 1966, (with David Lloyd) *Hampshire and the Isle of Wight,* 1967, *Bedfordshire and the County of Huntington and Peterborough,* 1968, *Worcestershire,* 1968, *Lancashire,* 1969. Editor, "Pelican History of Art," Penguin, 1953-66. Member of editorial board, *Architectural Review.*

WORK IN PROGRESS: Additional volumes of "The Buildings of England" series.

* * *

PHILIPP, Elliot Elias 1915-
(Philip Embey, Medicus II, Victor Tempest,

PERSONAL: Born July 20, 1915, in London, England; son of Oscar Isaac (a metallurgist) and Clarisse (Weil) Philipp; married Lucy Ruth Hackenbroch, March 22, 1939; children: Anne Susan, Alan Henry. *Education:* Attended St. Paul's School, London, England; St. John's College, Cambridge, B.A., 1936, M.A., 1942, M.B. and B.Ch., 1947; Middlesex Hospital, London, England, M.R.C.O.G., 1947; F.R.C.S., 1951, F.R.C.O.G. 1962. *Politics:* Liberal. *Religion:* Jewish. *Home:* 27 Harley House, London N.W. 1, England. *Office:* 94 Harley St., London W. 1, England.

CAREER: Consultant obstetrician and gynecologist in London, England, 1952—. *Military service:* Royal Air Force Volunteer Reserve; became squadron leader; twice mentioned in dispatches. *Member:* International Psycho-prophylactic Society, Royal Society of Medicine, French Society for Pscyho-prophylactics, French Society of Gynaecologists.

WRITINGS: (Under pseudonym Victor Tempest) *Near the Sun: The Impressions of a Medical Officer of Bomber Command,* Crabtree Press, 1946; (editor with E.W. Walls and H.J.B. Atkins) John Hilton, *Rest and Pain,* G.

Bell, 1950; (editor under pseudonym Medicus II) John Paterson MacLaren, *Know Your Body,* revised edition, Thorsons, 1955; (under pseudonym Philip Embey) *Woman's Change of Life,* Thorsons, 1956; *From Sterility to Fertility: A Guide to the Causes and Cure of Childlessness,* Philosophical Library, 1957; *Obstetrics and Gynaecology Combined for Students,* H.K. Lewis, 1962, 2nd edition, 1970; (with Eva Crisp) *Midwifery for Nurses,* H.K. Lewis, 1962, 2nd edition, 1964; (with K.L. Gearing) *The Student Nurse in the Operating Theatre,* E. & S. Livingstone, 1964; (with Erna Wright) *Easy Childbirth,* British Medical Association, 1964; (editor with Josephine Barnes and Michael Newton) *Scientific Foundations of Obstetrics and Gynaecology,* F.A. Davis, 1970. Medical correspondent, *News Chronicle* (London), 1947-56; regular contributor to *Family Doctor,* 1948-63, *Sunday Times,* 1958-60.

* * *

PHILIPSON, Susan Sacher 1934-
PERSONAL: Born December 12, 1934, in New York, N.Y.; daughter of Harry (a lawyer) and Tolbie (Snyderman) Sacher; married Morris Philipson (an editor and writer), April 26, 1961; children: Nicholas. *Education:* University of Michigan, B.A., 1956. *Residence:* New York, N.Y.

CAREER: Copy editor for Random House, Inc., Alfred A. Knopf, Inc., and Doubleday & Co., Inc., New York, N.Y., 1956-62; free-lance editor, New York, N.Y., 1962—.

WRITINGS: A Lion for Niccolby, Pantheon, 1963. Regular contributor to *Library Journal,* 1956-57.

WORK IN PROGRESS: Adaptations of Moorish legends and Swedish fairy tales.

BIOGRAPHICAL/CRITICAL SOURCES: Mademoiselle, March, 1963.

* * *

PHILLIPS, Claude S., Jr. 1923-
PERSONAL: Born April 1, 1923, in Greene County, Pa.; son of Claude Smalling (a coal miner) and Louise Phillips; married Marguerite Deal, February 3, 1945; children: Robert Hal, Teresa Ann, David Howard. *Education:* Lee College, Cleveland, Tenn., student, 1943-45; University of Tennessee, B.A., 1947, M.A., 1950; Duke University, Ph.D., 1954. *Home:* 856 Farrell Ave., Kalamazoo, Mich. 49007. *Office:* Department of Political Science, Western Michigan University, Kalamazoo, Mich. 49001.

CAREER: Western Michigan University, Kalamazoo, associate professor, 1957-65, professor of political science, 1965—, director of Institute of Regional Studies, 1959—. Associate research fellow, University of Ibadan, Ibadan, Nigeria, 1961-62. *Member:* American Political Science Association, American Society of International Law, African Studies Association, Phi Beta Kappa. *Awards, honors:* Fulbright Scholar to India, 1961.

WRITINGS: The Development of Nigerian Foreign Policy, Northwestern University Press, 1964; (contributor) David R. Deener, editor, *De Lege pactorum,* Duke University Press, 1970. Contributor of articles to professional journals.

WORK IN PROGRESS: The Non-Western World, a social science approach; *New States in International Politics.*

* * *

PHILLIPS, (Pressly) Craig 1922-
PERSONAL: Born May 23, 1922, in Buffalo, N.Y.; son of Pressly Craig (a journalist) and A. Grace (Vergith)

Phillips; married Fanny Bradford Lee (a biologist), October 26, 1956. *Education:* Attended St. Petersburg Junior College, 1946-47, John G. Stetson University, 1948, Harvard University, summer, 1949, and University of Miami, Coral Gables, Fla., 1949-50. *Home:* 112 Carlyn Towers, 4390 Lorcom Lane, Arlington, Va. 22207. *Agent:* Oliver G. Swan, Paul R. Reynolds & Son, 599 Fifth Ave., New York, N.Y. 10017. *Office:* U.S. National Fisheries Center and Aquarium, U.S. Department of the Interior, Washington, D.C. 20242.

CAREER: Marine Studios, Marineland, Fla., assistant to curator and member of staff of collecting department, 1946-47; University of Miami, Coral Gables, Fla., research associate, Institute of Marine Science, 1951-54; Miami Seaquarium, Miami, Fla., curator, 1954-59. Research consultant to Florida Atlantic University, 1964—; consultant to Florida State Flood Control Board on experimental use of manatees to control water hyacinths and other nuisance vegetation in Florida canals. Illustrator of other books besides his own. Appeared weekly on television program, "Let's Go Fishing," Miami, Fla., 1957-59. *Military service:* U.S. Navy, 1942-46; became pharmacists mate second class. *Member:* National Society of Ichthyologists and Herpetologists.

WRITINGS—All self-illustrated: (With Winfield Brady) *Sea Pests,* University of Miami Press, 1944; *The Captive Sea: Life Behind the Scenes of the Great Modern Oceanariums,* Chilton, 1964; *The World of Penguins,* Chilton, c.1965. Illustrator of fish for *Webster's International Dictionary,* 1960, and of articles in *National Geographic.*

SIDELIGHTS: Phillips and his wife collect wild mushrooms, orchids, minerals, and gems, and have had a fifteen-foot Indian Rock python as a pet for almost ten years (the python currently is on loan to the National Zoo). They have tried some forty local species of mushrooms (without ill effect); they have twenty species of Florida orchids, plus some outstate varieties, in their greenhouse. From time to time the pet python has been joined by other boas and pythons and rare lizards.

* * *

PHIPPS, Grace May Palk 1901-

PERSONAL: Born August 5, 1901, in Christchurch, New Zealand; daughter of Richard (a farmer) and Janet (Reeve) Palk; married Thomas Henry Phipps (a manufacturers' representative), December 15, 1926; children: James Roger, Margaret Jill Phipps Saunders, Carolyn Phipps Cowlishaw. *Education:* Attended Canterbury College School of Art. *Religion:* Methodist. *Home:* 229 Wairakei Rd., Bryndwr, Christchurch 5, New Zealand.

CAREER: Writer. *Awards, honors:* Donovan Cup of New Zealand Women Writers' Society.

WRITINGS: Marriage with Eve, Jenkins, 1955; *The Women of the Family,* Jenkins, 1956; *The Life for Louise,* Jenkins, 1957; *Concerning Eve,* Jenkins, 1959; *The Young Wife,* Jenkins, 1962; *A Nurse Like Kate,* Jenkins, 1963; *Two Sisters in Love,* R. Hale, 1966; *Doctor on the Scene,* R. Hale, 1967; *The Tenderhearted Nurse,* R. Hale, 1968; *No Wife for a Parson,* R. Hale, 1969; *Marriage While You Wait,* R. Hale, 1970; *The Bridal Boutique,* R. Hale, 1971; *And Be My Love,* R. Hale, 1972; *The Doctor's Three Daughters,* R. Hale, in press. Contributor of approximately one hundred short stories to magazines. Writer of radio scripts for Australian and New Zealand Broadcasting Commissions.

WORK IN PROGRESS: Another novel.

AVOCATIONAL INTERESTS: Gardening and baking bread.

PHLEGER, Marjorie Tempel

PERSONAL: Born in Glendale, Calif.; daughter of Charles Homer (a telephone company executive) and Flora (Morrell) Temple; married Fred B. Phleger (a professor), October 23, 1933; children: Charles Frederick, Audrey Anne (Mrs. Scott McElmury). *Education:* University of Southern California, B.S., 1929, general secondary teacher's certificate, 1930; Smith College, M.A., 1948. *Politics:* Republican. *Religion:* Protestant. *Home:* 8593 La Jolla Shores Dr., La Jolla, Calif. 92037.

CAREER: Bishop's School for Girls, La Jolla, Calif., drama instructor and play director, 1952-56; *San Diego Union,* San Diego, Calif., society columnist, 1954-57; La Valencia Hotel, La Jolla, Calif., public relations director, 1957-60; *La Jolla Light,* La Jolla, Calif., columnist, 1957-60. Member of woman's executive committee, La Jolla Summer Playhouse, 1955-63; chairman of publicity committee, La Jolla Town Council, 1957-59; member of San Diego County executive committee, Los Angeles Philharmonic Orchestra, 1961-62. *Member:* Opera Guild, Old Globe Theatre, Smith College Club (all San Diego); Delta Delta Delta (traveling inspector in New England, 1933-34).

WRITINGS: Pilot Down, Presumed Dead, Harper, 1963; (with husband, Fred Phleger) *You Will Live Under the Sea,* Beginner Books, 1966; (with Fred Phleger) *Off to the Races,* Beginner Books, 1968.

SIDELIGHTS: Mrs. Phleger writes: "I love animals, both domestic and wild, and am vitally concerned about present and future wildlife preservation.

"Extensive private plane travel in Baja, California, and other parts of Mexico inspired some story ideas. I am interested in having my readers learn something from my stories, hence research for authenticity of geographic locations, environment and habits of the people involved; also, of course, [I work for] historical accuracy. Travels with my science professor husband have included visits and work in most of the countries of the world.

"My daughter is among the top [women] bicyclists in the world—thus the idea for *Off to the Races.*"

AVOCATIONAL INTERESTS: Travel and horseback riding.

* * *

PIAZZA, Ben Daniel 1934-

PERSONAL: Born July 30, 1934, in Little Rock, Ark.; son of Charles Di (a shoemaker) and Elfrieda (Spillman Piazza; married Dolores Dorn-Heft. *Education:* Princeton University, B.A., 1955; studied at Actor's Studio. *Home:* 1230 Park Ave., New York, N.Y. *Agent:* William Morris Agency, 1740 Broadway, New York, N.Y.

CAREER: Actor on stage, screen, and television; began Broadway career in 1958; toured South America with American Repertory Co., 1961; worked in Theatre of the Absurd, 1962. *Member:* Actors' Equity Association, American Federation of Television and Radio Artists, Screen Actors Guild. *Awards, honors:* Theatre World Award, 1959, for his performance in "Kataki."

WRITINGS: The Exact and Very Strange Truth, Farrar, Straus, 1964. Author of two one-act plays, "Lime Green" and "Khakhi Blue," first produced Off-Broadway at Provincetown Playhouse, March, 1969.

WORK IN PROGRESS: A book of short stories.

SIDELIGHTS: Mr. Piazza's extensive stage career has included performances in "Sweet Bird of Youth," "Who's Afraid of Virginia Woolf," "The Zoo Story," "I Am a Camera," and "Endgame."†

PICKREL, Paul (Murphy) 1917-

PERSONAL: Born February 2, 1917, in Gilson, Ill.; son of Clayton and Inez (Murphy) Pickrel. *Education:* Knox College, A.B., 1938; Yale University, M.A., 1942, Ph.D., 1944. *Office:* Wright Hall, Smith College, Northampton, Mass. 10160.

CAREER: Lafayette College, Easton, Pa., instructor in English, 1941-42; Yale University, New Haven, Conn., began as instructor, became assistant professor of English, 1942-49, lecturer in English and managing editor and book review editor of *Yale Review,* 1949-66; *Harper's* (magazine), New York, N.Y., chief book reviewer, 1954-60; Smith College, Northampton, Mass., professor of English, 1966—.

WRITINGS: The Moving Stairs (novel), Harper, 1949; (author of introduction) Charles Dickens, *A Tale of Two Cities,* Houghton, 1962; (author of introduction) Jane Austen, *Pride and Prejudice,* Houghton, 1963. Contributor of book reviews to *Commentary, New York Herald Tribune,* and *Book Week.*

* * *

PIERSON, G(eorge) W(ilson) 1904-

PERSONAL: Born October 22, 1904, in New York, N.Y.; son of Charles Wheeler and Elizabeth G. (Groesbeck) Pierson; married Laetitia Verdery (a landscape gardener), September 10, 1936; children: Norah, Laetitia Deems. *Education:* Attended St. Bernard's School and Groton School; Yale University, A.B., 1926, Ph.D., 1933. *Religion:* Congregational. *Home:* 176 Ives St., Mount Carmel, Conn. 06518. *Office:* 1691 Yale Station, New Haven, Conn. 06020.

CAREER: Yale University, New Haven, Conn., instructor in English, 1926-27, instructor in history, 1929-30, 1933-36, assistant professor of history, 1936-39, associate professor, 1939-44, professor, 1944-46, chairman of history department, 1956-62, Larned Professor of History, 1946—, director, Division of Humanities, 1964-70. Fellow, Davenport College, Yale University (executive fellow, 1938-45; chairman, 1946). *Member:* American Historical Association (delegate to American Council of Learned Societies, 1963—), American Studies Association, Society for French Historical Studies, Organization of American Historians, Century Association, National Golf Links. *Awards, honors:* Guggenheim fellow, 1955-56.

WRITINGS: Tocqueville and Beaumont in America, Oxford University Press, 1938, abridged edition published as *Tocqueville in America,* edited by Dudley C. Lunt, Doubleday, 1959, hardcover edition, Peter Smith, 1960; *Memorandum of the History of the Georgica Association, 1880-1948, with Particular Attention to Land Covenants Within the Settlement Area,* privately printed, 1949; (contributor) Margaret Clapp, editor, *The Modern University,* Cornell University Press, 1950; *Yale College: An Educational History, 1871-1921,* Yale University Press, 1952; *Yale: The University College, 1921-1937,* Yale University Press, 1955; *The Bringing of the Mill (1942-1943): A Documentary History from Wartime in Wainscott,* [New Haven], 1962; *The Education of American Leaders: Comparative Contributions of U.S. Colleges and Universities,* Praeger, 1969; *The Moving American,* Knopf, 1973. Contributor of critical essays on American frontier, regionalism, and American mobility to historical and scholarly journals.

WORK IN PROGRESS: A book of essays on American frontier and regionalism; further studies of Yale history.

SIDELIGHTS: As a graduate student Pierson was given what he terms the "happy opportunity" of studying the American voyage and experiences of Alexis de Tocqueville through his unpublished letters and diaries. "Became persuaded that the frontier hypothesis of Frederick Jackson Turner was too narrow, nationalistic, and confusing—and so was led to a critical reappraisal. In 1933 [I] began to try to teach a course on the foreign relations of American civilization, and have been trying to teach it ever since, most inadequately, because of the want of literature on the subject and my other preoccupations.... In recent years [I] have become fascinated by the restlessness and mobility of the American experience, which I see as a major factor in our history and an important influence on our national character."

* * *

PIERCE, John Leonard, Jr. 1921-
(John Bramlett)

PERSONAL: Born March 8, 1921, in Coblenz, Germany; son of John Leonard (an army general) and Kate Bodine (Stone) Pierce; married Anne Heathers, October 18, 1962 (separated). *Education:* University of the South, student, 1938-39; Auburn University, B.S. in Journalism, 1942; graduate study at Columbia University, 1946-48, at Sorbonne, University of Paris, 1949-50. *Politics:* "Vote for the man." *Religion:* Episcopalian. *Home and office:* 164 Perry St., New York, N.Y. 10014. *Agent:* Sterling Lord Agency, 660 Madison Ave., New York, N.Y. 10021.

CAREER: Writer, also working at a number of other jobs to support self while writing. Interim work has included stevadoring, clerical posts, jobs with railroads and an oil company. *Military service:* U.S. Army, Artillery, 1942-46, 1950-52; received Silver Star and Army Commendation Medal.

WRITINGS: The Map on the Ceiling, Macmillan, 1964; (under pseudonym John Bramlett) *A Place I Don't Go,* Fawcett, 1964. Contributor of technical articles to Texas oil journals, and of short stories to magazines.

WORK IN PROGRESS: A novel about the peace-time American Army of the twenties and thirties.

AVOCATIONAL INTERESTS: Sports and music.

* * *

PIERSON, John H(erman) G(roesbeck) 1906-

PERSONAL: Born March 28, 1906, in New York, N.Y.; son of Charles W. (a lawyer) and Elizabeth (Groesbeck) Pierson; married Sherleigh Glad (a writer), June 16, 1948; children: (by previous marriage) Elizabeth G. (Mrs. Theodore Wood Friend III), John T.R., James MacDonald Fowler. *Education:* Attended Groton School, 1919-23; Yale University, B.A., 1927, Ph.D., 1938. *Politics:* Democrat. *Home:* 22 Pilot Rock Lane, Riverside, Conn. 06878. *Office:* United Nations, New York, N.Y. 10017.

CAREER: Consolidated Gas Co. of New York, New York, N.Y., assistant to vice-president, 1929-33; Yale University, New Haven, Conn., instructor in economics, 1933-38; U.S. Government, Washington, D.C., variously division chief, economic adviser, special assistant, in Department of Labor, 1941-48, economic adviser to Economic Cooperation Administration, then policy adviser to Mutual Security Agency, 1949-53; United Nations, director of research and planning for Economic Commission for Asia and the Far East, Bangkok, Thailand, 1955-59, special consultant and adviser to undersecretary for economic and social affairs, New York, N.Y., 1959—. *Member:* American Economic Association, American Statistical Association, National Planning Association, Regional Plan Association (New York), Asia Society. *Awards, honors:* Pabst Postwar Employment award for essay on full employment.

WRITINGS: The Mutineers: A Modern Episode, privately printed, 1929; *Full Employment,* Yale University

Press, 1941; *Employment After the War*, Bureau of Labor Statistics, U.S. Department of Labor, 1943; *Full Employment and Free Enterprise*, Public Affairs, 1947; *Insuring Full Employment: A United States Policy for Domestic Prosperity and World Development*, Viking, 1964; *Essays on Full Employment, 1942-1972*, Scarecrow, 1972. Contributor of articles to journals.

*   *   *

PIKE, E(dgar) Royston   1896-

PERSONAL: Born April 9, 1896, in Enfield, Middlesex, England; married Winifred Bower, June 4, 1921. *Education:* Attended Enfield Grammar School. *Religion:* "Liberal thinker." *Home:* 14 Hinchley Dr., Esher, Surrey, England.

CAREER: Amalgamated Press Inc., London, England, associate editor, encyclopedia department, 1932-44; Hutchinson & Co. Ltd. (publishers), London, editor-in-chief, 1944-48; *World Digest*, editor, 1950-60; free-lance writer, 1961—. Esher Urban District Council, member, 1935-68, former chairman. *Military service:* British Army, Machine Gun Corps, 1914-19; became second lieutenant.

WRITINGS: The Story of the Crusades: A Popular Account, C.A. Watts, 1927; *Temple Bells; or, The Faiths of Many Lands*, C.A. Watts, 1930; *Slayers of Superstition*, C.A. Watts, 1931, Kennikat, 1970; *Political Parties and Policies*, Pitman, 1924, 3rd edition, revised, 1948.

Ethics of the Great Religions, C.A. Watts, 1948; *Round the Year with the World's Religions*, C.A. Watts, H. Schuman, 1951; *Encyclopaedia of Religion and Religions*, Allen & Unwin, 1951, Meridian, 1958; (editor of English edition and author of preface) Eva Ingersoll, editor, *The Life and Letters of Robert Ingersoll*, C.A. Watts, 1952; *Jehovah's Witnesses: Who They Are and What They Do*, Philosophical Library, 1954.

Finding Out About the Babylonians, Muller, 1961, Sportshelf, 1965; *Ancient Persia*, Weidenfeld & Nicolson, 1961; *Ancient India*, Weidenfeld & Nicolson, 1961; *Mohammed: Founder of the Religion of Islam*, Weidenfeld & Nicolson, 1962, Roy, 1964, 2nd edition published as *Mohammed: Prophet of the Religion of Islam*, Weidenfeld & Nicolson, 1968, Praeger, 1969; *Lands of the Bible*, Weidenfeld & Nicolson, 1962, Sportshelf, 1966; *The True Book About Charles Darwin*, Muller, 1962; *Finding Out About the Minoans*, Muller, 1962; *Finding Out About the Assyrians*, Muller, 1963, Sportshelf, 1965; *Pioneers of Social Change*, Barrie & Rockliff, 1963; *Finding Out About the Etruscans*, Muller, 1964; *Adam Smith: Founder of the Science of Economics*, Weidenfeld & Nicolson, 1965, Hawthorn, 1966; *Love in Ancient Rome*, Muller, 1965, Humanities, 1966; (with Walter Hugh Jordan) *Finding Out About the Aztecs*, Muller, 1965; *Hard Times: Human Documents of the Industrial Revolution*, Praeger, 1966 (published in England as *Human Documents of the Industrial Revolution in Britain*, Allen & Unwin, 1966); *Republican Rome*, John Day, 1966; *The World's Strangest Customs*, Odhams, 1966, published in America as *The Strange Ways of Man: Rites and Ritual and Incredible Origins*, Hart Publishing, 1967; *Golden Times: Human Documents of the Victorian Age*, Praeger, 1967 (published in England as *Human Documents of the Victorian Golden Age, 1850-1875*, Allen & Unwin, 1967); *Britain's Prime Ministers: From Walpole to Wilson*, Odhams, 1968, Transatlantic, 1970; *Human Documents of the Age of the Forsytes*, Allen & Unwin, 1969, published in America as *Busy Times: Human Documents of the Age of the Forsytes*, Praeger, 1970; *Human Documents of the Lloyd George Era*, St. Mar'in's, 1972; (editor) *Golden Times: Human Documents of the Victorian Age*, Schocken, 1972 (published in England as *Human Documents of the Victorian Golden Age*). Editor, "Exploring the Past" series, Muller, "Pathfinder Biographies" series, Weidenfeld & Nicolson, 1962—, and "Creators of the Modern World," Arthur Barker, 1964—.

WORK IN PROGRESS: Another volume in the "Human Documents" series, entitled *Human Documents of Adam Smith's Time: Britain on the Eve of the Industrial Revolution*, for Weidenfeld & Nicolson; a completely revised edition *of Encyclopaedia of Religion and Religions*, for Allen & Unwin.

SIDELIGHTS: Pike's books have appeared in French, Portuguese, and Mexican editions.

BIOGRAPHICAL/CRITICAL SOURCES: Times Literary Supplement, March 2, 1967, August 31, 1967; *Observer Review*, August 6, 1967; *Best Sellers*, April 1, 1969; *Library Journal*, May 18, 1970, October 7, 1970.

*   *   *

PILDITCH, James (George Christopher)   1929-

PERSONAL: Born August 7, 1929, in London, England; son of Frederick Henry (a company director) and Marie Therese (Priest) Pilditch; married Mollie Christine Jeffery, December 24, 1952; children: Charlotte, Susanna. *Education:* Attended University of Reading. *Home:* 10 Cheniston Gardens, London W.8, England. *Office:* Allied Industrial Designers, 9 Clifford St., London W.1, England.

CAREER: Maclean Hunter Publishing Co., Toronto, Ontario, managing editor, 1955-58; Tom Nash Associates, Toronto, Ontario, general manager, 1958-59; Allied Industrial Designers, London, England, chairman, 1961—. *Military service:* British Army, 1949-51. *Member:* Institute of Directors, Institute of Packaging.

WRITINGS: The Silent Salesman: How to Develop Packaging That Sells, Business Publications, 1961; (with Douglas Scott) *The Business of Product Design*, Business Publications, 1965; *Communication by Design: A Study in Corporate Identity*, McGraw, 1970. Contributor of articles to journals in United States, Canada and Europe. Editor, *Marketing, Canadian Packaging*, and *Institute of Packaging Journal*.

WORK IN PROGRESS: Short stories.†

*   *   *

PILLIN, William   1910-

PERSONAL: Born December 10, 1910, in Alexandrowsk, Russia; son of Elconon (a pharmacist) and Anna (Naiditch) Pillin; married Polia (an artist), 1934; children: Boris. *Education:* Attended Lewis Institute of Chicago, Northwestern University, and University of Chicago. *Politics:* Democrat. *Religion:* None. *Home:* 4913 Melrose Ave., Los Angeles, Calif. 90029.

CAREER: Ceramic craftsman and poet. *Awards, honors:* Jeannette Sewell Davis prize, *Poetry* magazine.

WRITINGS—All poetry: Poems, Press of J.A. Decker, 1939; *Theory of Silence*, George Yamada, 1949; *Dance Without Shoes*, Golden Quill Press, 1956; *Passage After Midnight*, Inferno Press, 1958; *Pavanne for a Fading Memory*, A. Swallow, 1964; *Everything Falling*, Kayak Press, in press. Poetry has appeared in over 100 magazines, including *Poetry, Nation, New Republic, Literary Review*, and *Southwest Review*.

WORK IN PROGRESS: More poems.

SIDELIGHTS: Pillin is mainly interested in music and reading. He writes to *CA:* "As a poet I cannot say I am in sympathy with any of the Anglo-American currents of the past 50 years or more. I like Dylan Thomas and Yeats rather more than any poet now writing. My tradition is more related to European poetry and I think I've been more influenced by Rilke, Lorca and Neruda, than by any English or American poet.

"I believe that poetry is an intensely personal gesture and dislike all manifestoes, sects or cults connected with writing. Each poet must go his own way, can learn little from another. I dislike all conceptual critical presuppositions in relation to poetry."

BIOGRAPHICAL/CRITICAL SOURCES: Inferno, number 8; *Poetry,* May, 1959; *Saturday Review,* July 4, 1964.

* * *

PILO, Giuseppe Maria 1929-

PERSONAL: Born June 16, 1929, in Mogliano Veneto, Italy; son of Giovanni and Adele (Rosseti) Pilo; married Flavia Casagranda (a teacher of art history), September 21, 1955. *Education:* University of Padua, Laurea in Lettere, Storia dell'Arte Moderna, 1954, Diploma di Perfezionamento in Storia dell'Arte Veneta, 1957; Institut Universitaire Catholique, Paris, Diplome de Langue et Civilisation Francaise, 1957; University of Rome, Libera Docenza in Storia dell'Arte Medioevale e Moderna, 1962. *Religion:* Catholic. *Home and office:* Via Museo, 4 Bassano del Grappa, Italy.

CAREER: Liceo classico "Cavanis," Venice, Italy, teacher, 1954-60; Musei Civici d'Arte e di Storia, Venice, assistant, 1955-60; Museo Civico, Biblioteca e Archivo, Bassano del Grappa, Italy, director, 1960—; University of Padua, Padua, Italy, libero docente, 1963—. Ispettore alle antichita, monumenti, opere d'arte della Provincia di Vincenza; ispettore bibliografico per il mandamento di Bassano. *Member:* Ateneo Veneto (socio corrispondente).

WRITINGS: (Author of text) *Disegni del Museo Civico di Bassano da Carpoaccio a Canova* (catalogue of an exhibition), Neri Pozza, 1956; *Ritratti di Carlo Goldoni* (catalogue), Zanetti, 1957; *Francesco Zugo,* Neri Pozza, 1958; (author of text with Pietro Zampetti and Giovanni Mariacher) *La Pittura del seicento a Venezia* (catalogue of an exhibition), Alfieri, 1959.

(Author of text) *Xilografie di Alberto Duerer* (catalogue of an exhibition), Bassano del Grappa, 1960; *Carponi,* Alfieri, 1961; *Canaletto,* Barnes & Noble, 1962; (author of text) *Incisioni di Giulio Carpioni* (catalogue of an exhibition), Bassano del Grappa, 1962; *Marco Ricci,* Alfieri, 1963; (author of text) *Disegni di Giacomo Quarenghi e dei Gaidon* (catalogue of an exhibition), Bassano del Grappa, 1964; (author of text) *Luciano Mingiuzzi* (catalogue of an exhibition), Bassano del Grappa, 1964; (author of text) *Dipinti del XVI al XVIII secola restaurati* (catalogue of an exhibition), Bassano del Grappa, 1965; (with Carlo Conzelli) *I Pittori del seicento veneto,* R. Sandron, 1967.

(Author of text) *Michelangelo Grigoletti e il suo tempo,* Electra, 1971. Contributor to art periodicals. Editor, *Arte Figurativa.*

WORK IN PROGRESS: Pittura italiana del Seicento e Settecento.

AVOCATIONAL INTERESTS: Symphonic-choral music (e.g. oratorios, cantatas), seventeenth to nineteenth centuries, Naval history, and the French language.

* * *

PINDER, John H(umphrey) M(urray)

PERSONAL: Born in London, England; son of Harold Senhouse (a soldier) and Lilian Edith (Murray) Pinder. *Education:* King's College, Cambridge, honors degree in economics, 1949. *Home:* 26 Bloomfield Ter., London S.W. 1, England. *Office:* Political and Economic Planning, 12 Upper Belgrave St., London S.W. 1, England.

CAREER: Federal Union (voluntary organization promoting international federation), London, England, press officer, 1950-52; Economist Intelligence Unit (economic and market research), London, England, began as head of international research and international operations, became director in charge of research, 1952-64; Political and Economic Planning (research institute), London, England, director, 1964—. Member of executive committee of trustees, Federal Trust, 1960—. *Military service:* British Army, West African Artillery, 1943-47; became lieutenant. *Member:* Federal Union (London; chairman of executive committee, 1956-59), Brooks's Club (London).

WRITINGS: U.N. Reform: Proposals for the Charter Amendment, Federal Union, 1953; *Britain and the Common Market,* Cresset, 1961; *Europe Against De Gaulle,* Praeger, 1963; *The Commonwealth and the Trend Towards World and Regional Economic Systems,* Federation of Commonwealth Chambers of Commerce, 1968; (with Ray Pryce) *Europe After De Gaulle: Towards the United States of Europe,* Penguin, 1969.

* * *

PINKNEY, David H(enry) 1914-

PERSONAL: Born July 2, 1914, in Elyria, Ohio; son of David Henry (an engineer) and Zaida Margaret (Fulmer) Pinkney; married Helen Reisinger; children: Janet, David. *Education:* Oberlin College, A.B., 1936; Harvard University, A.M., 1937, Ph.D., 1941. *Politics:* Democrat. *Religion:* Episcopalian. *Home:* 3812 48th Ave. N.E., Seattle, Wash. 98105. *Office:* 208 D Smith Hall, University of Washington, Seattle, Wash. 98105.

CAREER: U.S. Office of Strategic Services, Washington, D.C., and London, England, research analyst, 1941-43; U.S. Department of State, Washington, D.C., research analyst 1946; University of Missouri, Columbia, assistant professor, 1946-51, associate professor, 1951-57, professor of history, 1957-66; University of Washington, Seattle, professor of history, 1966—. *Military service:* U.S. Naval Reserve, 1943-46; became lieutenant junior grade. *Member:* American Association of University Professors, American Historical Association (secretary, modern European history section, 1961-66), Society for French Historical Studies (secretary-treasurer, 1956-63), Societe d'Histoire Moderne, Societe de l'Histoire de Paris et de l'Ile-de-France. *Awards, honors:* Fellowship, Fund for the Advancement of Education, 1954-55; Guggenheim fellowship, 1960-61; Social Science Research Council faculty fellowship, 1965.

WRITINGS: Napoleon III and the Rebuilding of Paris, Princeton University Press, 1958; (editor and contributor with Theodore Ropp) *A Festschrift for Frederick B. Artz,* Duke University Press, 1964; (editor and author of introduction) *Napoleon: Historical Enigma,* Heath, 1969; *The French Revolution of 1830,* Princeton University Press, 1972. Contributor of articles to professional journals. Member of board of editiors, *Journal of Modern History,* 1955-58, *French Historical Studies,* 1958—; editor, *French Historical Studies,* 1966—.

WORK IN PROGRESS: Studies of France under the July Monarchy.

* * *

PINKOWSKI, Edward 1916-

PERSONAL: Born August 12, 1916, in Holyoke, Mass.; son of Felix Andrew and Aniala Barbara (Sobiek) Pinkowski; married Connie Rosiello, September 26, 1943; children: James, Jack. *Education:* Attended New York University; graduated from Newspaper Institute of America, 1939, and Antonelli School of Photography, 1949. *Home:* 127 North 20th St., Philadelphia, Pa. 19103.

CAREER: Anthracite Tri-District News, Hazleton, Pa., columnist, 1939-50; South Side Press, Bridgeport, Pa., editor and publisher, 1950-52; free-lance writer and photographer, 1946—. Military service: U.S. Navy, 1942-46; associate editor, Our Navy Magazine, 1945-46.

WRITINGS: Lattimer Massacre, Sunshine Press, 1950; History of Bridgeport, Pa., South Side Press, 1951, revised and enlarged edition, 1962; Washington's Officers Slept Here, Sunshine Press, 1953; Forgotten Fathers, Sunshine Press, 1953; Chester County Place Names, Sunshine Press, 1955, 2nd edition, 1962; James Gay: Lost Bard of Pennsylvania, Pennsylvania Folklore Society, 1962; John Siney: The Miners' Martyr, Sunshine Press, 1963; Anthony Sadowski: Polish Pioneer, Sadowski Memorial Committee, 1966.

WORK IN PROGRESS: Montgomery County Place Names; Wayne County Place Names; and Poles in Pennsylvania.

*   *   *

PIRONE, Pascal P(ompey)   1907-

PERSONAL: Born October 7, 1907, in Mount Vernon, N.Y.; son of Dominic (a fruit merchant) and Mary (Sirignano) Pirone; married Loretta Kelly, December 21, 1933; children: Thomas, John, Mary, Joseph. Education: Cornell University, B.S., 1929, Ph.D., 1933. Politics: Republican. Religion: Roman Catholic. Home: 1522 Dwight Pl., Bronx, N.Y. 10465.

CAREER: Cornell University, Ithaca, N.Y., assistant professor, 1934-38; Rutgers University, New Brunswick, N.J., associate professor, 1938-47; New York Botanical Garden, New York, N.Y., plant pathologist, 1947—. Consultant on landscape maintenance for United Nations Headquarters, New York, N.Y., and for several corporations. Member: American Phytopathological Society, American Association for the Advancement of Science (fellow), Sigma Xi.

WRITINGS: Maintenance of Shade and Ornamental Trees, Oxford University Press, 1941, 3rd edition published as Tree Maintenance, 1959, 4th edition, 1972; Modern Gardening: A Complete Guide to the Agricultural Uses of Modern Chemistry's Miracle Drugs, Simon & Schuster, 1952, reissued as Complete Guide to Modern Gardening, Hart Publishing, 1967; What's New in Gardening, Hanover House, 1956; (with Bernard O. Dodge and Harold W. Rickett) Diseases and Pests of Ornamental Plants, 3rd edition (Pirone was not associated with earlier editions), Ronald, 1960, 4th edition (as sole author), 1970; (with Michael Rapuano and Brooks E. Wigginton) Open Space in Urban Design, [Cleveland], 1964.

*   *   *

PITZ, Henry C(larence)   1895-

PERSONAL: Born June 16, 1895, in Philadelphia, Pa.; son of Henry William (a manufacturer) and Anna (Stiffel) Pitz; married Molly Wheeler Wood, June 10, 1935; children: Julia Leaming (Mrs. Edward Handy), Henry William II. Education: Studied at Philadelphia Museum College of Art, 1914-18, and Spring Garden Institute, Philadelphia, 1917, 1920. Politics: Independent. Religion: Episcopalian. Home: 3 Cornelia Pl., Philadelphia, Pa. 19118.

CAREER: Artist and illustrator, 1920—. Philadelphia Museum College of Art, Philadelphia, Pa., director of department of illustration and decoration, 1937-60, now professor emeritus. Pennsylvania Academy of Fine Arts, Philadelphia, instructor in water colors, 1939-46; American Artist, New York, N.Y., associate editor, 1942—. Visiting lecturer in fine arts, University of Pennsylvania; visiting instructor, Cleveland Institute of Art; visiting lec-

turer, University of Utah, 1971. Work exhibited in national and international exhibitions; represented in permanent collections in museums, schools, and libraries throughout United States, including Library of Congress, Philadelphia Museum of Art, Cleveland Museum of Art, Los Angeles Museum; painted three murals for Government Building, Century of Progress, Chicago, and National Gallery, Washington, D.C. Official artist, N.A.S.A. Space Project and U.S. Environmental Agency. Military service: U.S. Army, American Expeditionary Forces, 1918-19.

MEMBER: National Academy of Design (academician), American Water Color Society (director), Society of Illustrators (life member), Philadelphia Art Alliance (vice-president, 1938-61; director), Philadelphia Sketch Club (vice-president, 1938-40; president, 1940-42), Philadelphia Water Color Club (director), Newcomen Society, Audubon Artists, Salmagundi Club (New York), Franklin Inn Club (Philadelphia). Awards, honors: Bronze Medal, International Print Exhibition, 1932; Bronze Medal, Paris International Exposition, 1938; Hans Obst Prize, American Water Color Society Annual, 1952; Obrig Prize, National Academy, 1953, 1956; Alumni Gold Medal, Philadelphia Museum College of Art, 1956, Silver Star Cluster, 1957; National Academy Prize for Water Color, 1962; Philadelphia Athenaeum Literary Award, 1969; D.lett., Ursinus College, 1971; more than thirty other awards, 1932—.

WRITINGS: (Author and illustrator with Edward Warwick) Early American Costume, Century Co., 1929, revised edition (with Warwick and Alexander Wyckoff) published as Early American Dress: The Colonial and Revolutionary Periods, Benjamin Blom, 1965; (editor) A Treasury of American Book Illustration, Watson-Guptill and American Studio Books, 1947; The Practice of Illustration, Watson-Guptill, 1947; Pen, Brush and Ink, edited by Arthur L. Guptill, Watson-Guptill, 1949; (editor) Norman Kent and Others, Watercolor Methods, Watson-Guptill, 1955; Drawing Trees, Watson-Guptill, 1956, revised and enlarged edition published as How to Draw Trees, 1972; Ink Drawing Techniques, Watson-Guptill, 1957; Sketching with the Felt-Tip Pen: A New Artist's Tool, Studio Publications, 1959; (editor and reviser) Arthur L. Guptil, Drawing with Pen and Ink, revised edition, Reinhold, 1961; Illustrating Children's Books: History, Technique, Production, Watson-Guptill, 1963; Drawing Outdoors, edited by Susan E. Meyer, Watson-Guptill, 1965; How to Use the Figure in Painting and Illustration, Watson-Guptill and Reinhold, 1965; The Brandywine Tradition, Houghton, 1969; Charcoal Drawing, Watson-Guptill, 1971; (editor and author of introduction) Frederic Remington: 175 Drawings and Illustrations, Dover, 1972. (Contributor) Greek and Roman Civilization, New American Library, in press. Writer of more than one hundred articles for Encyclopaedia Britannica, and for American Artist, Horn Book, Studio, Print, American Heritage, and other periodicals.

Illustrator: John Bennett, Master Skylark, Century Co., 1922; Conan Doyle, Micah Clarke, Harper, 1922; Robert Shackleton, The Book of Washington, Penn Publishing, 1923; Allen French, The Story of Rolf and the Vikings Bow, Little, 1924; Bertha Evangeline Bush, A Prairie Rose, Little, Brown, 1925; Francis S. Drake, Indian History for Young Folks, Harper, 1927; Ula Echols, Knights of Charlemagne, Longmans, Green, 1928; John Buchan, Prester John, Houghton, 1928; Robert Leighton, Olaf, the Glorious, Macmillan, 1929.

Robert W. Chambers, Cardigan, Harper, 1930; Rodrigo Diaz De Bivar (El Cid) The Tale of the Warrior Lord (translated by Merriam Sherwood), Longmans, Green, 1930; Washington Irving, Voyages of Columbus, Macmillan, 1931; The Story of Beowulf (retold by Strafford

Riggs), Appleton, 1933; Ernest P. Mitchell, *Deep Water: The Autobiography of a Sea Captain,* Little, Brown, 1933; Charles J. Finger, *Dog at His Heel,* Winston, 1936; Geoffrey Household, *Spanish Cave,* Little, Brown, 1936; Daniel Defoe, *The Life and Strange Surprising Adventures of Robinson Crusoe* (edition adapted for young readers by Edward L. Thorndike), Appleton, 1937; Paul L. Anderson, *Pugnax the Gladiator,* Appleton, 1939.

Elizabeth Jane Coatsworth, *You Shall Have a Carriage,* Macmillan, 1941; Phyllis Reid Fenner, compiler, *There Was a Horse: Folktales from Many Lands,* Knopf, 1941: Albert L. Stillman, *Jungle Haven,* Winston, 1942; Sydney Greenbie, *Three Island Nations: Cuba, Haiti, Dominican Republic,* Row, Peterson, 1942; Frederic A. Krummer, *For Flag and Freedom,* Morrow, 1942; Phyllis Reid Fenner, editor, *Time to Laugh: Funny Tales from Here and There,* Knopf, 1942; Patricia F. Ross, *In Mexico They Say,* Knopf, 1942; Albert L. Stillman, *Jungle Haven,* Winston, 1942; Catherine Cate Coblentz, *Falcon of Eric the Red,* Longmans, Green, 1942; Robert Davis, *Hudson Bay Express,* Holiday House, 1942; Hope Brister, *Cunning Fox and Other Tales,* Knopf, 1943; Charles J. Finger, *High Waters in Arkansas,* Grosset, 1943: Phyllis Reid Fenner, compiler, *Giants and Witches, and a Dragon or Two,* Knopf, 1943; Phyllis Reid Fenner, compiler, *Princesses and Peasant Boys: Tales of Enchantment,* Knopf, 1944; Mildred A. Jordan, *Shoo-fly Pie,* Knopf, 1944; Mary Regina Walsh, *Molly, the Rogue,* Knopf, 1944; Mildred A. Jordan, *Apple in the Attic: A Pennsylvania Legend,* Grosset, 1944; David Loring MacKaye and J.J.G. MacKaye, under pseudonym Loring MacKaye, *Twenty-Fifth Mission,* Longmans, Green, 1944; William W. Theisen and G.L. Bond, compilers, *Living Literature for Supplementary Reading,* five books, Macmillan, 1945-48; Phyllis Reid Fenner, compiler, *Adventure, Rare and Magical,* Knopf, 1945; Rosita Torr Forbes, *Henry Morgan: Pirate,* McKay, 1946 (published in England as *Henry Morgan: Pirate and Pioneer,* Cassell, 1948); Andre Maurois, *Washington: The Life of a Great Patriot* (translated by Eileen Lane Kinney), Oxford University Press, 1946; David W. Moore, *The End of Long John Silver,* Crowell, 1946; Mary Regina Walsh, *The Mullinger Heifer,* Knopf, 1946; Elizabeth Hough Sechrist, editor, *One Thousand Poems for Children* (based on the selections of Roger Ingpen), new edition, Macrae Smith, 1946; Charlie May Simon, *Joe Mason, Apprentice to Audubon,* Dutton, 1946; Phyllis Reid Fenner, compiler, *Demons and Dervishes: Tales with More-than-Oriental Splendor,* Knopf, 1946; Mildred Houghton Comfort, *Children of the Mayflower,* Beckley-Cardy, 1947; Phyllis Reid Fenner, compiler, *Fools and Funny Fellows: More "Time to Laugh" Tales,* Knopf, 1947; David Loring MacKaye and J.J.G. MacKaye, under pseudonym Loring MacKaye, *John of America,* Longmans, Green, 1947; Kathleen Monypenny, *Young Traveler in Australia,* Phoenix House, 1948, Dutton, 1954; Phyllis Reid Fenner, *With Might and Main,* Knopf, 1948; Charlie May Simon, *Royal Road,* Dutton, 1948; Mildred Houghton Comfort, *Children of the Colonies,* Beckley-Cardy, 1948; Enid LaM. Meadowcraft, *By Secret Railway,* Crowell, 1948; Margaret Carver Leighton, *Judith of France,* Houghton, 1948; Georgii Skrebitskii, *White Bird's Island* (translated from the Russian by Zina Voynow), Knopf, 1948; Phyllis Reid Fenner, compiler, *With Might and Main: Stories of Skill and Wit,* Knopf, 1948; Jeanette Eaton, *That Lively Man, Ben Franklin,* Morrow, 1948; Mary Regina Walsh, *The Widow Woman and Her Goat,* Knopf, 1949; David W. Moore, *End of Black Dog,* Crowell, 1949; Jan Juta, *Look Out for the Ostriches: Tales of South Africa,* Knopf, 1949; Sir Thomas Malory, *Book of King Arthur and His Noble Knights* (stories from *Morte d'Arthur* selected by Mary Macleod), Lippincott, 1949.

Mrs. Stockton V. Banks, *Washington Adventure,* Whittlesey House, 1950; David W. Moore, *Scarlet Jib,* Crowell, 1950; David W. Moore, *Sacramento Sam,* Crowell, 1951; Phyllis Reid Fenner, compiler, *Magic Hoofs: Horse Stories from Many Lands,* Knopf, 1951; Opal Wheeler, *Hans Andersen: Son of Denmark,* Dutton, 1951; Elizabeth Hall Janeway, *Vikings,* Random House, 1951; Nathan Reinherz, *Quest of the Sage's Stone,* Crowell, 1951; Jakob Ludwig Grimm and Wilhelm Karl Grimm, "What Happened to Hansel and Gretel" in *Evergreen Tales,* Limited Editions Club, 1952; Armstrong Sperry, *River of the West,* Winston, 1952; Mabel Watts, *Over the Hills to Ballypog,* Aladdin Books, 1954; Robert Louis Stevenson, *Treasure Island,* Doubleday, 1954; Jules Verne, *Mysterious Island,* World Publishing, 1957; Catherine Owens Peare, *William Penn,* Lippincott, 1957.

Henry Frith, *King Arthur and His Knights,* Doubleday, 1963; James Fenimore Cooper, *The Spy,* Limited Editions Club, 1963; Thomas Fall, *Edge of Manhood,* Dial, 1964; Thomas Fall, *Wild Boy,* Dial, 1965.

His illustrations have appeared in *Scribner's, Cosmopolitan, Harper's, Saturday Evening Post, Gourmet, Jack and Jill, Reader's Digest,* and other national magazines.

WORK IN PROGRESS: Life and Work of Howard Pyle, for Clarkson Potter.

SIDELIGHTS: Many of the books Pitz illustrated were also published in England and Canada, and a number of them have been reprinted.

BIOGRAPHICAL/CRITICAL SOURCES: Forty Illustrators, Watson-Guptill, 1946; Richard Ellis, *Book Illustration,* Kingsport Press, 1952; Norman Kent, *Watercolor Methods,* Watson-Guptill, 1955; David Bland, *A History of Book Illustration,* World Publishing, 1958; *Illustrators of Children's Books: 1946-1956,* Horn Book, 1958, supplement, *1957-1966,* 1968; Diana Klemin, *The Illustrated Book,* C.N. Potter, 1970.

* * *

PIZER, Donald 1929-

PERSONAL: Born April 5, 1929, in New York, N.Y.; son of Morris and Helen (Rosenfeld) Pizer. *Education:* University of California, Los Angeles, B.A., 1951, M.A., 1952, Ph.D., 1955. *Home:* 2128 Palmer Ave., New Orleans, La. 70115. *Office:* Newcomb College, Tulane University, New Orleans, La. 70118.

CAREER: Tulane University Graduate School and Newcomb College, New Orleans, La., assistant professor, 1957-61, associate professor, 1961-64, professor of English, 1964—. Fulbright lecturer, University of Hamburg, 1967-68. *Military service:* U.S. Army, 1955-57. *Member:* Modern Language Association of America, American Studies Association. *Awards, honors:* Guggenheim fellow, 1963.

WRITINGS: Hamlin Garland's Early Work and Career, University of California Press, 1960; *Evolutionary Ethical Dualism in Frank Norris' Vandiver and the Brute and McTeague,* Modern Language Association of America, 1961; (editor) Frank Norris, *Literary Criticism,* University of Texas Press, 1964; *Realism and Naturalism in Nineteenth-Century American Literature,* Southern Illinois University Press, 1966; *The Novels of Frank Norris,* Indiana University Press, 1966; (editor) Hamlin Garland, *Diaries,* Huntington Library, 1968; (editor with Ray B. Browne) *Themes and Directions in American Literature: Essays in Honor of Leon Howard,* Purdue University Studies, 1969; (editor and author of introduction) Hamlin Garland, *The Rose of Dutcher's Coolly,* University of Nebraska Press, 1970; (editor) Theodore Dreiser, *Sister Carrie,* Norton, 1970; (editor) *American Thought and*

Writing: The 1890's, Houghton, 1972. Contributor to professional journals.

BIOGRAPHICAL/CRITICAL SOURCES: *New York Review of Books,* May 18, 1967; *Books Abroad,* spring, 1967; *South Atlantic Quarterly,* spring, 1969.

* * *

PLATH, David W(illiam) 1930-

PERSONAL: Born December 8, 1930, in Elgin, Ill.; son of Ernest Karl (a furniture retailer) and Laura (Baumgardt) Plath; married Marilyn Ann Lusher, August 25, 1956; children: Mark Ernest, Gail Christine. *Education:* Northwestern University, B.S., 1952; graduate study at Sophia University, Tokyo, Japan, 1954-55, University of Michigan, summer, 1956; Harvard University, M.A., 1959, Ph.D., 1962. *Office:* Department of Anthropology, University of Illinois, Urbana, Ill. 61801.

CAREER: University of California, Berkeley, lecturer in anthropology, 1961-63; State University of Iowa (now University of Iowa), Iowa City, assistant professor, 1963-64, associate professor of anthropology, 1964-66; University of Illinois, Urbana, associate professor, 1966-69, professor of anthropology and Asian studies, 1969—, head of department of anthropology, 1970—. Field research in Japan, 1959-61, 1965; field director for International Honors Program, International School of America, 1969-70. *Military service:* U.S. Naval Reserve, active duty, 1952-55; became lieutenant junior grade. *Member:* American Anthropological Association, Association for Asian Studies.

WRITINGS: *The After Hours: Modern Japan and the Search for Enjoyment,* University of California Press, 1964; (with Yoshie Sugihara) *Sensei and His People: The Building of a Japanese Commune,* University of California Press, 1969; (editor) *Aware of Utopia,* University of Illinois Press, 1971. Contributor of articles and reviews to *Journal of American Folklore, Japan Quarterly, American Anthropologist,* and other professional journals.

WORK IN PROGRESS: Studies of adult socialization, especially in present-day Japan.

BIOGRAPHICAL/CRITICAL SOURCES: *New York Review of Books,* September 25, 1969.

* * *

PLOTZ, Helen Ratnoff 1913-

PERSONAL: Born March 20, 1913, in New York, N.Y.; daughter of Hyman (a physician) and Ethel (Davis) Ratnoff; married Milton Plotz (a physician), September 4, 1933 (deceased); children: Elizabeth (Mrs. R.J. Wagman), Paul, Sarah (Mrs. Roy L. Jacobs), John. *Education:* Vassar College, A.B., 1933. *Politics:* Democrat. *Religion:* Jewish. *Home:* 80 Westminster Rd., Brooklyn, N.Y. 11218.

WRITINGS—Compiler; all published by Crowell: *Imagination's Other Place: Poems of Science and Mathematics,* 1955; *Untune the Sky: Poems of Dance and Music,* 1957; *Emily Dickinson, Poems,* 1964; *The Earth Is the Lord's: Poems of the Spirit,* 1965; *Poems from the German,* 1967; *The Marvelous Light: Poets and Poetry,* 1970. Contributor of a chapter to *Children's Bookshelf,* Bantam, and of articles to magazines.

BIOGRAPHICAL/CRITICAL SOURCES: *New York Times Book Review,* November 9, 1967; *Best Sellers,* December 1, 1967.

* * *

PODHORETZ, Norman 1930-

PERSONAL: Surname accented on second syllable; born January 16, 1930, in Brooklyn, N.Y.; son of Julius (a milkman) and Helen P. (Woliner) Podhoretz; married Midge Rosenthal Decter (a writer), October 21, 1956; children: Rachel, Naomi (stepdaughters); Ruth, John. *Education:* Columbia University, A.B., 1950; Jewish Theological Seminary, B.H.L., 1950; Cambridge University, B.A., 1952, M.A., 1957. *Politics:* Democrat. *Religion:* Jewish. *Home:* 924 West End Ave., New York, N.Y. 10025. *Agent:* Candida Donadio, 111 West 57th St., New York, N.Y. 10019. *Office: Commentary,* 165 East 56th St., New York, N.Y. 10022.

CAREER: *Commentary* magazine, New York, N.Y., assistant editor, 1955, associate editor, 1956-58, editor-in-chief, 1960—; Looking Glass Library, New York, N.Y., editor-in-chief, 1958-60. Member of University Seminar of American Civilization, Columbia University, 1958. *Military service:* U.S. Army, 1953-55. *Awards, honors:* L.H.D., Hamilton College, 1969.

WRITINGS: *Doings and Undoings: The Fifties and After in American Writing,* Farrar, Straus, 1964; (editor) *The Commentary Reader: Two Decades of Articles and Stories,* introduced by Alfred Kazin, Atheneum, 1966; *Making It* (autobiography; chapter one originally published in *Harper's,* December, 1967), Random House, 1968.

Contributor: Chandler Brossard, editor, *Scene Before You: A New Approach to American Culture,* Rinehart, 1955; Leslie Fiedler, editor, *Art of the Essay,* Crowell, 1958; Harry W. Rudman and Irving Rosenthal, editors, *A Contemporary Reader: Essays for Today and Tommorrow,* Ronald, 1961; William Phillips and Philip Rhav, editors, *Partisan Review Anthology,* Holt, 1962; Charles Norman, editor, *Poets and Poetry,* Collier, 1962; Joseph J. Waldmeir, editor, *Recent American Fiction: Some Critical Views,* Houghton, 1963; Richard Kostelanetz, editor, *On Contemporary Literature: An Anthology of Critical Essays on the Major Movements and Writers of Contemporary Literature,* Avon, 1964; Bradford Daniel, editor, *Black, White and Gray: Twenty-one Points of View on the Race Question,* Sheed, 1964; John Gassner and Ralph G. Allen, editors, *Theatre and Drama in the Making,* Houghton, 1964; Robert Penn Warren, editor, *Faulkner: A Collection of Critical Essays,* Prentice-Hall, 1966. Contributor to *Commentary, Partisan Review, New Yorker, Show, Esquire, Harper's, New Republic,* and other periodicals.

WORK IN PROGRESS: A book about the resurgence of radical activism in 1960's in America, for Simon & Schuster.

SIDELIGHTS: Renata Adler describes Podhoretz as "one of those writers for little journals who have of late been assimilated almost en bloc into the magazines of broader circulation, and his adjustment, as a thirties' liberal, to the sixties is a highly pragmatic, even a classic one. The rebel whose cause has succeeded traditionally develops a concern with personal power, and the title of Mr. Podhoretz's collection of critical essays, *Doings and Undoings,* implies a faith in the power of the critic to affect, or even determine, the fate of authors and literary works. . . ."

Podhoretz does indeed see his position as a critic as one extending beyond the bounds of merely praising or rejecting books. In his work he attempts, he says, "to relate an aesthetic judgement of the book to some social or cultural or literary issue outside the book itself—the strengths and deficiencies of the work being assumed to mean something more than that the author was operating at the top of his bent here and nodding, as even Homer occasionally does, there. This made it possible for me to use the book review . . . as a vehicle for all my ideas about the subject in question: to show off, in short, how much I knew about this, that, and the other thing." His contemporaries vary in their reaction to his work. Norman Mailer believes that this approach can be a rewarding one. "Podhoretz like many an intellectual before him could use as his *cogito, ergo sum:* I cerebrate, therefore I see. No matter how sensuous the nature, sense experience in such men tends to become the raw material for the processing mills of new hypotheses. That is a superb way to do a kind of literary criticism, perhaps the best kind of literary criticism for which we can ask, since a work confronted by no critical hypothesis can merely be admired or despised, and thereby open questions of taste, but it cannot improve our mind by allowing us to consider simultaneously the work in question and the critical approach...The value of a hypothesis is that it can be tested, tested by the evidence of the work, tested by how much it fails to explain, tested indeed by the fact that it will remain as the best working hypothesis until a better one comes along to replace it. That is the most energetic kind of criticism, probably the most creative, and when done well, certainly the most stimulating to any reader who like Podhoretz lives in large part for the joy of cerebration. And Podhoretz is probably as good as any critic in America at this kind of writing. Indeed his only serious competitors might be Steven Marcus, John Aldridge and Irving Howe."

Rust Hills, however, believes that Podhoretz's polemical approach is destructive and self-congratulatory. "His celebrated assaults on modern novels seem often to be related (both as cause and effect) to his conviction that fiction is somehow in decline in our time. In this he much resembles many others of the pack of angry critics we have so much with us today. They vie with one another to find witty, vicious phrases with which to destroy. They work ferociously and maliciously at picking away at the great reputations and sticking pins in any little minor reputation that seems to them to be getting inflated. They pull down reputations at such a rate that soon there aren't any recognizably major writers left for them to attempt to destroy; then they look around victoriously and crow: 'The Novel is dead! This is the Age of Criticism!' "

It is because he takes his work seriously, Podhoretz counters, that he is often harsh in his reviews; he suggests that to treat criticism lightly is to underrate those works it considers. "All these reviewers inhabit much the same intellectual milieu, and what they have in common, apart from talent and intelligence, is an attitude toward books and an idea about the proper way to discuss them. This attitude might be characterized as one of great suspiciousness: A book is assumed to be guilty until it proves itself innocent—and not many do.... The major premise behind such suspiciousness is that books are enormously important events, far too important to be confronted lightly, and certainly too important to permit of charitable indulgence."

BIOGRAPHICAL/CRITICAL SOURCES: Saturday Review, March 14, 1964, June 11, 1966, January 13, 1968; *Nation,* March 23, 1964, February 5, 1968; *Book Week,* March 29, 1964, June 22, 1966; *New York Times Book Review,* March 29, 1964, April 7, 1966, February 5, 1967, January 7, 1968, June 2, 1968; *New York Herald Tribune,* March 29, 1964; *Christian Century,* April 1, 1964; *Commonweal,* April 17, 1964, February 16, 1968; *Christian Science Monitor,* April 23, 1964, June 23, 1966, January 11, 1968; *New York Review of Books,* April 30, 1964, February 1, 1968; *New Yorker,* July 4, 1964; *Virginia Quarterly Review,* summer, 1964, spring, 1968; *Village Voice,* September 10, 1964; *Yale Review,* October, 1964; *Harper's,* October, 1965, December, 1967; D.J. Enright, *Conspirators and Poets,* Dufour, 1966; *Library Journal,* June 1, 1966, January 1, 1968; Richard Kostelanetz, editor, *The Young American Writers,* Funk, 1967;

National Observer, January 8, 1967; *Prairie Schooner,* spring, 1967; *Minnesota Review,* volume VII, number 3, 1967; *New York Times,* January 5, 1968; *Washington Post,* January 6, 1968; *Book World,* January 7, 1968; *Newsweek,* January 9, 1968; *Life,* January 12, 1968; *Time,* January 19, 1968; *New Republic,* January 27, 1968; *New Leader,* January 29, 1968; *Esquire,* February, 1968, April, 1968; *America,* February 3, 1968; *National Review,* February 27, 1968; *Reporter,* March 7, 1968; *Atlantic,* April, 1968; *Carleton Miscellany,* spring, 1968; *Partisan Review,* spring, 1968; *Listener,* August 29, 1968; October 24, 1968; *Times Literary Supplement,* August 29, 1968; *New Statesman,* August 30, 1968; *Kenyon Review,* Volume XXX, number 2, 1968; *Observer Review,* September 1, 1968, September 15, 1968; *Punch,* September 11, 1968; *Books and Bookmen,* November, 1968; *Playboy,* December, 1968.

* * *

POHLMANN, Lillian (Grenfell) 1902-

PERSONAL: Born March 31, 1902, in Grass Valley, Calif.; daughter of William Albert and Myrtle (Massie) Grenfell; married second husband, George Russell Pohlmann, May 16, 1947; children: (previous marriage) Iris Twigg MacInnes, Hal Grenfell Twigg. *Education:* Special courses at Universities of California, Colorado, and Mexico, and at Free University, Amsterdam, Netherlands. *Home:* 388 Hillside Ave., Mill Valley, Calif. 94941.

WRITINGS: Myrtle Albertina's Secret, Coward, 1956; *Myrtle Albertina's Song,* Coward, 1958; *Calypso Holiday,* Coward, 1959; *Owls and Answers* (Junior Literary Guild selection), Westminster, 1964; *The Summer of the White Reindeer,* Westminster, 1965; *Love Can Say No,* Westminster, 1966; *Wolfskin,* Norton, 1968; *Sing Loose,* Westminster, 1968; *The Bethlehem Mouse,* Stone Educational Publications, 1970.

BIOGRAPHICAL/CRITICAL SOURCES: Book World, November 3, 1968.

* * *

POLACH, Jaroslav G(eorge) 1914-

PERSONAL: Surname is pronounced *Po*-lash; born April 20, 1914, in Ostrava, Czechoslovakia; son of Francis (an administrative officer) and Marie (Pach) Polach; married Eva B. Mocek (an assistant librarian), February 8, 1963. *Education:* Masaryk University, Doctor of Law, 1938; School for Economic Studies, Prague, Czechoslovakia, additional study, 1947-48; American University, M.A. in Economics, 1958, Ph.D., 1962; George Washington University, Master of Comparative Law, 1959. *Religion:* Protestant. *Home:* 225 Panorama Dr., Oxon Hill, Md. 20021. *Office:* Economic Advisory Group, Internal Revenue Service, Department of the Treasury, Washington, D.C. 20225.

CAREER: Law clerk in Ostrava, Czechoslovakia, 1938-39; Czechoslovak Special Mission (of government in exile), Budapest, Hungary, secretary to head of mission, 1939-41; Continental Steel Co., Prague, Czechoslovakia, head of legal department and general counsel for international matters; Ferromet (nationalized steel works), Prague, Czechoslovakia, head of legal and administrative department and general counsel for international matters, 1946-48; U.S. government, Washington, D.C., international economist and legal analyst, 1948-60; Resources for the Future, Washington, D.C., economist, 1961-70; Economic Advisory Group, Internal Revenue Service, Department of the Treasury, economist, 1970—. Lecturer. *Military service:* Czechoslovak Forces in the West, 1941-45, flying with Royal Air Force (British); became younger captain; received Military Cross, Medal for Bravery. *Member:* International Social Science Association, American Economic Association, American Society of International Law, Comparative Economics Association, American Association for the Advancement of Slavic Studies, Society for the Study of Soviet-type Economics, American Statistical Association, Czechoslovak Society for Arts and Sciences in America (member of executive board, 1960—).

WRITINGS: (Editor) A. Heidrich, *International Political Causes of the Czechoslovak Tragedies of 1938 and 1948,* Czechoslovak Society of Arts and Sciences in America, 1962; *Euratom: Its Background, Issues, and Economic Implications,* Oceana, 1964; *Economic Development in the Countries of Eastern Europe,* Joint Economic Committee, U.S. Congress, 1970.

Contributor: Miloslav Rechcigl, editor, *The Czechoslovak Contribution to World Culture,* Mouton & Co., 1965; Richard Alton Tybout, editor, *Economics of Research and Development,* Ohio State University Press, 1965; *Reader of the American Journal of Comparative Law,* Oceana, 1966; Miloslav Rechcigl, editor, *Czechoslovakia Past and Present,* two volumes, Humanities, 1968. Contributor of articles in field of atomic energy and European atomic integration to professional journals in United States and Europe.

WORK IN PROGRESS: Research on the international energy situation, historical statistics, balance, and outlook; economic developments in the Soviet bloc.

SIDELIGHTS: Polach speaks Czechoslovak, French, German, and Polish, and reads Russian. *Avocational interests:* Theatre, music, books, chess, and tennis.

*   *   *

POLS, Edward   1919-

PERSONAL: Born February 1, 1919, in Newark, N.J.; married Eileen Sinnott, October 17, 1942; children: Adrian, Cynthia, Elizabeth, Alison, Edward Benedict, Mary. *Education:* Harvard University, A.B. (magna cum laude), 1940, A.M., 1947, Ph.D., 1949. *Office:* Department of Philosophy, Bowdoin College, Brunswick, Me. 04011.

CAREER: Harvard University, Cambridge, Mass., assistant in philosophy, 1947-48; Princeton University, Princeton, N.J., instructor in philosophy, 1948-49; Bowdoin College, Brunswick, Me., professor of philosophy and chairman of the department, 1949—. *Military service:* U.S. Army; became first lieutenant; awarded Bronze Star. *Member:* American Philosophical Association, Metaphysical Society of America.

WRITINGS: The Recognition of Reason, Southern Illinois University Press, 1963; *Whitehead's Metaphysics: A Critical Examination of "Process and Reality,"* Southern Illinois University Press, 1967.

Contributor: Frank Thilly, *A History of Philosophy,* edited by Ledger Wood, Holt, 1951; Erwin A. Glikes and Paul Schwaber, editors, *Of Poetry and Power: Poems Occasioned by the Presidency and by the Death of John F. Kennedy,* Basic Books, 1964; Thomas Anderson Langford and W.H. Poteat, editors, *Intellect and Hope: Essays in the Thought of Michael Polanyi,* Duke University Press, 1968; Marjorie Grene, editor, *The Anatomy of Knowledge,* University of Massachusetts Press, 1969. Contributor to professional journals and other periodicals.

WORK IN PROGRESS: Various philosophical articles; a book on the nature of personal agency and freedom, with particular reference to the mind-body problem.

POMPER, Gerald M(arvin)   1935-

PERSONAL: Born April 2, 1935, in New York, N.Y.; son of Moe Joseph (a storekeeper) and Celia (Cohen) Pomper; married Marlene Michels (a teacher), January 20, 1957; children: Marc, David, Miles. *Education:* Columbia University, A.B., 1955; Princeton University, M.A., 1957, Ph.D., 1959. *Office:* Department of Political Science, Livingston College, Rutgers University, New Brunswick, N.J. 08903.

CAREER: College of City of New York (now City College of the City University of New York), New York, N.Y., assistant professor of political science, 1959-62; Rutgers University, New Brunswick, N.J., assistant professor, 1962-64, associate professor, 1964-69, professor of political science, 1969—. *Member:* American Political Science Association, American Association of University Professors, Phi Beta Kappa. *Awards, honors:* National Convention Faculty fellowship; Fulbright fellowship.

WRITINGS: Cases in State and Local Government, Prentice-Hall, 1961; *Nominating the President: The Politics of Convention Choice,* Northwestern University Press, 1963, enlarged edition, 1966; (editor with Donald G. Herzberg) *American Party Politics: Essays and Readings,* Holt, 1966; *Elections in America: Control and Influence in Democratic Politics,* Dodd, 1968; (editor and contributor) *Performance of American Government,* Free Press, 1972. Contributor of articles to professional journals.

WORK IN PROGRESS: Research on ethnic voting.

*   *   *

PONSOT, Marie Birmingham

PERSONAL: Born in New York, N.Y.; daughter of William and Marie (Candee) Birmingham; married Claude Ponsot (an artist), December 16, 1948; children: Monique, Denis, Antoine, William, Christopher, Matthew, Gregory. *Education:* St. Joseph's College for Women, Brooklyn, N.Y., B.A., 1940; Columbia University, M.A., 1941; University of Paris, postgraduate study, 1948-49. *Religion:* Roman Catholic. *Home:* 8329 169th St., Jamaica, N.Y. 11432.

CAREER: Thomas Y. Crowell Co. (publishers), New York, N.Y., juvenile production manager, 1947; UNESCO, archivist in Paris, France, 1948-50; translator and adapter of children's classics and other works, and poet, 1957—. Lecturer, SEEK Program, Queens College of City University of New York, 1966—. *Member:* Writers Guild of America, Liturgical Arts Society. *Awards, honors:* Eunice Tietjens Memorial Award, 1960, for poems in *Poetry* (magazine); Gold Bell Awards for best religious television program, 1962, and for best religious radio program, 1963, both for "The Death of Judas."

WRITINGS: True Minds, City Lights, 1956.

Translations or adaptations: *Snow White and Other Stories from Grimm,* Grosset, 1957; *Fables of La Fontaine,* Grosset, 1957; *Cinderella and Other Stories of Charles Perrault,* Grosset, 1957; *The Fairy Tale Book,* Simon and Schuster, 1958; *Once Upon a Time Stories,* Grosset, 1959, new edition, 1965; *My First Picture Encyclopedia,* Grosset, 1959; M. Badouy, *Old One Toe,* Harcourt, 1959; *Chinese Fairy Tales,* Golden Press, 1960; M. Badouy, *Bruno, King of the Mountain,* Harcourt, 1960; *Russian Fairy Tales,* Golden Press, 1961; M. Badouy, *Mick and the "P-105,"* Harcourt, 1961; *Tales of India,* Golden Press, 1961; *The Snow Queen,* Golden Press, 1961; Andree Clair, *Bemba,* Harcourt, 1962; *Selected Tales and Fables of La Fontaine,* Signet Books, 1965; Louis Untermeyer, *Pour toi,* French & European Publications, 1966.

Translations and adaptations for television: Paul Claudel, "The Death of Judas" (also adapted for radio); Diego Fabbri, "The Sign of Fire"; Claudel, "Pilate's Point of View."

Poetry anthologized in *Between Two Cities,* Doubleday, and published in *Inferno,* and *Poetry;* critical articles and reviews have appeared in several other periodicals.

WORK IN PROGRESS: A metrical translation of the poetry of the twelfth-century Anglo-Norman, Marie de France; a book of her own poetry.

SIDELIGHTS: Mrs. Ponsot has lived in Europe and North Africa.†

* * *

POPPLEWELL, Jack 1911-

PERSONAL: Born March 22, 1911, in Leeds, Yorkshire, England; son of Walter (a farmer) and Beatrice (Hudson) Popplewell; married Betty Bryant, July 2, 1941; children: Juliet, Vanessa. *Education:* Attended grammar school in England. *Home:* Swifts, Spotted Cow Lane, Buxted, Sussex, England. *Agent:* Christopher Mann, 140 Park Lane, London W1Y 4BU, England; William Morris Agency, 1350 Avenue of the Americas, New York, N.Y. 10019; and Eric Glass Ltd., 28 Berkeley Sq., London W1X 6HD, England.

CAREER: Composer, lyric writer, and playwright. *Member:* Song Writers Guild of Britain, Performing Rights Society of Great Britain, League of Dramatists (London).

WRITINGS—Plays: Blind Alley (three-act; first produced on West End at Queen's Theatre, 1952), Samuel French, 1956; *Dead on Nine* (three-act; first produced on West End at Westminster Theatre, 1955), Samuel French, 1956; *Breakfast in Bed* (three-act; first produced in B ad-ford, England, at Prince's Theatre, 1957), Evans Brothers, 1957, Dramatists Play Service, 1963; *Dear Delinquent* (three-act; first produced on West End at Westminster Theatre, June 5, 1957), Dramatists Play Service, 1958; *The Vanity Case* (three-act; first produced in Oldham, England, at Repertory Theatre, 1957), Evans Brothers, 1957; *The Last Word* (three-act; first produced in Edinburgh at Lyceum Theatre, March 24, 1958), Samuel French, 1960; *A Day in the Life of—* (two-act; first produced on West End at Savoy Theatre, October 1, 1958), Evans Brothers, 1959; *And Suddenly It's Spring* (three-act; first produced on West End at Duke of York's Theatre, November 4, 1959), Samuel French, 1960; *Hocus Pocus* (two-act; first produced in Eastbourne, England, at Devonshire Park Theatre, 1961), Dramatists Play Service, 1961; *Careful Rapture* (one-act), Samuel French, 1962; *Policy for Murder* (three-act; first produced on West End at Duke of York's Theatre, 1962), Samuel French, 1963; *Busybody* (three-act; first produced on West End at Duke of York's Theatre, 1964), Samuel French, 1965; (adapter) Francois Campaux, *Every Other Evening* (three-act; first produced on West End at Phoenix Theatre, November, 1964), Samuel French, 1965; *Dear Children* (three-act; first produced in Vienna at Josefstadt Theatre, 1962), Samuel French, 1967; *Mother's Day Out,* Samuel French, 1967; "Mississippi" (two-act), first produced in Copenhagen at Apollo Theatre, 1969; *Darling, I'm Home* (two-act; first produced in Johannesburg at Civic Theatre, June 22, 1972), Samuel French, 1972; *High Infidelity* (two-act; first produced at Richmond Theatre, October, 1972), Samuel French, 1972; *Dead Easy* (first produced at Coventry Theatre, October, 1972, produced in London, May, 1973), Samuel French, in press.

Television plays: "Dead on Nine" (based on his stage play), first networked by A.T.V.; "Along Came a Spider," first networked by A.T.V., 1963; "Born Every Minute," first networked by British Broadcasting Corp., 1972.

Screenplays: "Tread Softly, Stranger" (adapted from his stage play *Blind Alley*), 1953

Composer and lyric writer of popular songs, including "My Girl's an Irish Girl," "One Love," "If I Should Fall in Love Again," "No More," "Song of Paradise," published in England by Peter Maurice and in United States by Leeds Music Corp. and Shapiro, Bernstein.

SIDELIGHTS: Popplewell's songs have been recorded by Bing Crosby, Gracie Fields, and other popular vocalists. His television plays have been produced in England and in Hollywood. "Busybody" has been filmed in Denmark as "Mor (d) Skab," 1969.

BIOGRAPHICAL/CRITICAL SOURCES: Quarterly *Theatre Review,* winter, 1967.

* * *

PORTER, Elias H(ull) 1914-

PERSONAL: Born January 29, 1914, in Medford, Ore.; son of Elias Hull (a physician) and Josephine (Perry) Porter; married second wife, Sara Elizabeth Maloney; children: (first marriage) Nicholas A., Frances J. *Education:* University of Oregon, B.A., 1935, M.A., 1936, M.S., 1938; Ohio State University, Ph.D., 1941. *Home address:* P.O. Box 361, Pacific Palisades, Calif. 90272.

CAREER: Diplomate in clinical psychology, American Board of Examiners in Professional Psychology; certified psychologist and licensed counselor, state of California. Oregon State Public Welfare Commission, Portland, merit system supervisor, 1941-43; University of Chicago, Chicago, Ill., research associate in psychology, 1946-53; RAND Corp., Santa Monica, Calif., senior human factors scientist, Systems Development Division, 1955-57; System Development Corp., Santa Monica, Calif., senior human factors scientist, 1957-64; private practice as clinical and consulting psychologist, 1964-66; Technomics, Inc., Santa Monica, Calif., senior system scientist, 1966-70; consultant to management, 1970—. University extension teacher, 1964—. *Military service:* U.S. Navy, classification officer; became lieutenant. *Member:* American Psychological Association, Western Psychological Association, Los Angeles County Psychological Association, Phi Delta Kappa, Sigma Xi.

WRITINGS: An Introduction to Therapeutic Counseling, Houghton, 1950; *Manpower Development: The System Training Concept,* Harper, 1964.

Contributor: E.G. Williamson, editor, *Trends in Student Personnel Work,* University of Minnesota Press, 1949; Stanley W. Standal and R.J. Corsini, editors, *Critical Incidents in Psychotherapy,* Prentice-Hall, 1959; Robert Mills Gagne, editor, *Psychological Principles in System Development,* Holt, 1962. Contributor to *Personal Counselor, Harvard Business Review,* and to psychological journals.

WORK IN PROGRESS: The System in General System Theory.

* * *

PORTER, Hal 1911-

PERSONAL: Born February 16, 1911, in Albert Park, Victoria, Australia; son of Harold Owen (an engineer) and Ida Violet (Ruff) Porter; married Olivia Parnham, 1939 (divorced, 1943). *Education:* Attended schools in Kensington and Bairnsdale, Victoria, Australia. *Politics:* Liberal-Country Party (Conservative). *Religion:* Church of England. *Home:* Glen Avon, Garvoc, Victoria, Australia.

CAREER: Schoolmaster in Williamstown, Australia, 1927-37, Adelaide, South Australia, 1940-45, Hobart, Tasmania, 1946, Sydney, New South Wales, 1948, Ballaarat, Victoria, 1948-49; George Hotel, St. Kilda, Victoria, Australia, manager, 1949; Independents' School, Nijimura, Japan, schoolmaster, 1949-50; Theatre Royal, Hobart, Tasmania, producer, actor, and costume and set designer, 1951-52; Bairnsdale Municipal Library, Bairnsdale, Victoria, chief librarian, 1953-57; Shepparton Regional Library, Shepparton, Victoria, chief regional librarian, 1958-61; now free-lance writer. Australian representative, Edinburgh Festival, 1962. Lecturer at Japanese universities under aegis of Australian Department of External Affairs, 1967; lecturer at Ca Foscari University, 1972.

AWARDS, HONORS: Short story prize, Sydney Sesquicentenary Literary Competitions, 1938; Commonwealth Literary Fund fellowships, 1956, 1960, 1964, 1968, 1972; Short story prizes, Sydney Journalists' Club award, 1957, 1959; Commonwealth Literary Fund grants, 1958, 1960; Adelaide Festival of Arts short story prize, 1962, nonfiction award, 1966, novel award, 1968, Captain Cook Award, 1970; Encyclopaedia Britannica award, 1967.

WRITINGS: Short Stories, Adelaide Advertiser, 1943; The Hexagon (poetry), Angus & Robertson, 1956; (editor) Australian Poetry, 1957, Angus & Robertson, 1958; A Handful of Pennies (novel), Angus & Robertson, 1958; The Tilted Cross (novel), Faber, 1961, revised edition, 1971; A Bachelor's Children (short stories), Angus & Robertson, 1962; (editor) Coast to Coast: Australian Stories 1961-62, Angus & Robertson, 1962; The Watcher on the Cast-Iron Balcony (autobiography), Faber, 1963, Transatlantic, 1964; Stars of Australian Stage and Screen, Rigby (Adelaide), 1964, Tri-Ocean, 1965; The Cats of Venice (short stories), Angus & Robertson, 1965, Tri-Ocean, 1966; The Paper Chase (autobiography), Angus & Robertson, 1966; The Actors, an Image of the New Japan, Angus & Robertson, 1968; Elijah's Ravens: Poems, Angus & Robertson, 1968; Mr. Butterfry and Other Tales of New Japan (short stories), Angus & Robertson, 1970; Selected Stories, Angus & Robertson, 1971; The Right Thing (novel), Rigby, 1971; In an Australian Country Graveyard (poetry), Angus & Robertson, 1972.

Plays: The Tower (three-act; first produced in London at Hampstead Theatre, June, 1962), published in Three Australian Plays, edited by H.G. Kippox, Penguin, 1963; The Professor (three-act; first produced on West End at Royal Court Theatre, May, 1965), Faber, 1966; Eden House (three-act; first produced in Melbourne at St. Martin's Theatre, March 26, 1969; produced as "Home on the Pig's Back" in London at Richmond Theatre, February 28, 1972), Angus & Robertson, 1969; Parker (three-act; first produced in Ballarat at National Theatre, February, 1972), Angus & Robertson, 1971.

Television plays—All networked by Australian Broadcasting Commission: "The Tower" (based on stage play), 1964; "The Forger," 1965; "Eden House" (based on stage play), 1971; "Parker" (based on stage play), 1972. Author of other television plays for Australian Broadcasting Commission. Contributor of stories and articles to magazines and journals, including Southerly, Vogue, Quadrant, Flame, Australian Letters, London Magazine, Meanjin Quarterly, and Texas University.

WORK IN PROGRESS: Three novellas.

SIDELIGHTS: Porter writes to CA: "[I] have traveled extensively in the Old World and the East. [I am] particularly fascinated by Japan—intend to live there for several years. [I] have lived in London, Edinburgh, Athens, Venice, and Paris for months at a time, and in other places for shorter periods. [I] have no desire to see South Africa, U.S.A., Canada, or New Zealand. Collect Japanese prints—especially Hokusai. [I] grow old-fash-ioned roses, but am a particularly perfervid all-round gardener. (I live on cattle property and grow all the flowers from English calendars.) [I] abhor organized sport either as participant or watcher.

He comments on his writings thus: "For an Australian who wants to make Australians clear to the rest of the world, I have had to be both florid and patient, both baroque and meticulous, both cruelly careful and gaudy. There has been the need to superimpose the more sardonic and sophisticated and forthright image on the false image which is still fashionable in the works of such poseurs as Sidney Nolan (with his nineteenth-century lies) and Patrick White (with his fictitious, un-Australian suburbia)." Generally, he refuses to comment on the work of other Australians, feeling that "that sort of bloody work can be left to writers manque, log-rollers, et al, to the sorts of people who write for the sorts of people who read what is written for them. In a sense I [also] write only for those who read me—there are so many kinds of public. [But] I should die of mortification if a Morris West fan were to become a fan of mine."

BIOGRAPHICAL/CRITICAL SOURCES: Times Literary Supplement, May 4, 1967; Books and Bookmen, July, 1967; Variety, April 16, 1969; Stage, March 2, 1972.

*   *   *

PORTER, Richard C(orbin)   1931-

PERSONAL: Born August 1, 1931, in Hartford, Conn.; son of George F. (a teacher) and Marion (Corbin) Porter; married June 11, 1960, wife's maiden name, Burke; children: John F., Jennifer. Education: Williams College, B.A., 1953; Yale University, M.A., 1954, Ph.D., 1957. Office: Department of Economics, University of Michigan, Ann Arbor, Mich. 48104.

CAREER: University of Michigan, Ann Arbor, member of department of economics. Member: American Economic Association.

WRITINGS: Liquidity and Lending: The Volume of Bank Credit in Pakistan (monograph), Institute of Development Economics, 1963; (with John J. Arena) Review Guide and Workbook, Irwin, 1963; (with Barbara Knapp) Future Aid Requirements of Jordan, [Washington, D.C.], c.1965; The Effectiveness of Tax Exemption in Colombia, Development Advisory Service, Center for International Affairs, Harvard University, 1968; Some Trends of Post-War Primary Product Trends, Center for Research on Economic Development, University of Michigan, 1969.

*   *   *

POSY, Arnold   1894-

PERSONAL: Born March 21, 1894, in Mogilev, Russia; son of Mordecai (a rabbi) and Miriam (Lazaref) Posy; married Bella Shapiro, 1929; children: Manuel, Deena Posy Metzger. Education: Attended high school and rabbinical seminary in Mogilev, Russia. Home: 7617 De Longpre Ave., Los Angeles, Calif. 90046.

CAREER: Editor of Jewish Express (daily), London, England, 1916-20, Aufbrau (quarterly), Chicago, Ill., 1928, Milwaukee Jewish Voice (weekly), Milwaukee, Wis., 1930-33, Oifkum (monthly), New York, N.Y., 1934-42, Yiddishe Shriftn, (quarterly), New York, N.Y., 1942-45, American Jewish Life (monthly), New York, N.Y., 1950-52, American Jewish Home (published irregularly), Brooklyn, N.Y., 1952-65, and Heshbon (quarterly), Los Angeles, Calif., 1965—. Teacher of Hebrew.

WRITINGS: Der Binstok, L.M. Stein (Chicago), 1927; Shalit un Tamare (novel), Goldbeil (Vilno), 1929; Der Oyfshtand fun di kinder (drama; title means "the rebellion of the teenagers"), Botomsky (Vilno), 1930;

Trukene beyner, M. Jankovitz, 1932; *Joash* (drama), Central Publishing Co. (Warsaw), 1932; *Hakenkreitz* (drama), Posy-Shoulson Press, 1935; *Yosef* (dramatic poem), M. Ceshinsky (Chicago), 1939; *The Nazi Bible of Hate and The Present War*, American Goodwill Association, 1939; *Seven One-Act Plays*, Yiddishe Shriftn, 1940; *Israeli Tales and Legends* (short stories), Bloch Publishing, 1948, revised edition, J. David, 1966; *Holiday Night Dreams* (short stories), Bloch Publishing, 1953; *Messiah's Chains* (novel), translated by Joseph Leftwich, Bloch Publishing, 1963; *Mystic Trends in Judaism*, J. David, 1966; *Ecology and Man in Eternity*, Goldene Keit, 1971.

WORK IN PROGRESS: A book of essays, monographs on the Hebrew-Yiddish poets, Bialik, Peretz, and Leivik, and *Dawn*, a novel, all for J.L. Peretz Publishing (Tel Aviv).

* * *

POTTEBAUM, Gerald A. 1934-

PERSONAL: Born June 23, 1934, in Teutopolis, Ill.; son of William J. and Johanna (Winkleman) Pottebaum; married Cheryl Ann Shay, August 7, 1956; children: Julie Ann, Cecilia Marie, David Andrew. *Education:* University of Notre Dame, B.A., 1956. *Religion:* Roman Catholic. *Office:* George A. Pflaum, Publisher, Inc., 38 West Fifth St., Dayton, Ohio 45402.

CAREER: U.S. Navy, motion picture script writer and director, 1956-58, editor, 1958-59; Fides Publishers, Inc., Notre Dame, Ind., director of sales promotion and production, 1959-62; George A. Pflaum, Publisher, Inc., Dayton, Ohio, editor, 1962—.

WRITINGS: God Made the World, Pflaum Press, 1963; *How the Animals Got Their Names*, Pflaum Press, 1963; *God's Big Promise*, Pflaum Press, 1963; *They Disobeyed*, Pflaum Press, 1963; *The Story of Christmas*, Pflaum Press, 1963; *The Little Grain of Wheat*, Pflaum Press, 1964; *He Obeyed*, Pflaum Press, 1964; *The Easter Lamb*, Pflaum Press, 1964; (with Joyce Winkel) *1029 Private Prayers for Worldly Christians*, Pflaum Press, 1968; *The Festival of Art*, Augsburg, 1971; *99 Plus One*, Augsburg, 1971; (compiler) *Hello/Goodbye*, St. Mary's College Press, 1972; *Love Is. . .*, St. Mary's College Press, 1972; *Wonderings*, St. Mary's College Press, 1972. Managing editor, *Perspectives Magazine*, 1959-62.

WORK IN PROGRESS: Five books, *The Good Samaritan, The King and the Servant, The Prodigal Son, The Three Wise Men*, and *Little Tissue;* research on Scripture, liturgy, fine arts, and communications.

AVOCATIONAL INTERESTS: Watercolor painting.

BIOGRAPHICAL/CRITICAL SOURCES: Ave Maria Magazine, February, 1963; *Catholic Journalist*, March, 1964.

* * *

PRATT, J(oseph) Gaither 1910-

PERSONAL: Born August 31, 1910, in Winston-Salem, N.C.; son of Joseph Monroe (a farmer) and Mattie (Hauser) Pratt; married Nellie Ruth Pratt (a nurse administrator), June 14, 1936; children: John Herman, Vernon Gaither, Joseph Marion, Ellen Wilson. *Education:* Duke University, A.B., 1931, M.A., 1933, Ph.D., 1936. *Office address:* Box 152, University of Virginia Hospital, Charlottesville, Va. 22204.

CAREER: Duke University, Durham, N.C., research associate in Parapsychology Laboratory, 1937-63; University of Virginia, Charlottesville, research associate, 1964-65, assistant professor, 1966-70, associate professor of neurology and psychiatry, 1970—. President, Psychical

Research Foundation, Inc. Principal investigator for homing pigeon project, U.S. Office of Naval Research, 1953-58. *Military service:* U.S. Naval Reserve, 1944-46. *Member:* American Association for the Advancement of Science, American Psychological Association, Parapsychological Association (member of council, 1959-62, 1964—; president, 1960), Southern Society for Philosophy and Psychology, Phi Beta Kappa, Omicron Delta Kappa, Tau Kappa Alpha, Sigma Xi.

WRITINGS: Towards a Method of Evaluating Mediumistic Material, Boston Society for Psychic Research, 1936; (editor with Charles Edward Stuart) *Handbook for Testing Extrasensory Perception*, Farrar & Rinehart, 1937; (with Joseph Banks Rhine, Burke M. Smith, Joseph A. Greenwood and Stuart) *Extrasensory Perception After Sixty Years: A Critical Appraisal of the Research in Extrasensory Perception*, Holt, 1940; (with Rhine) *Parapsychology, Frontier Science of the Mind: A Survey of the Field, the Methods, and the Facts of ESP and PK Research*, C.C Thomas, 1957, revised edition, 1962; *Parapsychology: An Insider's View of ESP*, Doubleday, 1964; *On the Evaluation of Verbal Material in Parapsychology* (monograph), Parapsychology Foundation, 1969. Contributor of about one hundred scientific articles and reviews to psychological and biological journals. Editor, *Journal of Parapsychology*, 1942-63.

WORK IN PROGRESS: A book on extrasensory perception research in Russia and around the world.

* * *

PRELINGER, Ernst 1926-

PERSONAL: Born September 7, 1926, in Vienna, Austria; son of Heinrich (a physicist) and Magda (Jaeger) Prelinger; married Dorothy Racies, July 22, 1950; children: Richard, Elizabeth, Jane, Polly. *Education:* University of Vienna, Ph.D., 1948. *Politics:* Independent. *Religion:* Protestant. *Home:* 211 St. Ronan St., New Haven, Conn. 06511. *Office:* Yale University, 435 College St., New Haven, Conn. 06520.

CAREER: Federal Employment Service, Vienna, Austria, clinical psychologist, 1948-50; University of Pittsburgh, Pittsburgh, Pa., instructor in psychology, 1950-51; Brooklyn College, Brooklyn, N.Y., instructor in psychology, 1951-52; Yale University, New Haven, Conn., clinical psychologist in Department of University Health and assistant clinical professor of psychiatry, 1956—. *Military service:* U.S. Army, Medical Specialist Corps, 1952-56; clinical psychologist at Walter Reed Hospital; became captain. *Member:* American Psychological Association.

WRITINGS: (With Evelyn G. Pitcher) *Children Tell Stories: An Analysis of Fantasy*, International Universities Press, 1963; (with Carl N. Zimet) *An Egopsychological Approach to Character Assessment*, Free Press, 1964. Contributor of chapters to books. Also contributor to professional journals.

WORK IN PROGRESS: Studies in Identity; research in the formation of ego identity in young adults.

AVOCATIONAL INTERESTS: Sailing and mountain climbing.

* * *

PRESS, John Bryant 1920-

PERSONAL: Born January 11, 1920, in Norwich, Norfolk, England; son of Edward Kenneth and Gladys (Cooper) Press; married Janet Crompton, December 20, 1947; children: Rogert Crompton, Sara Miranda Judith. *Education:* Corpus Christi College, Cambridge, B.A., 1942, M.A., 1946. *Religion:* Church of England. *Home:* 8 Bracondale Ct., Norwich, Norfolk, England. *Office:* British Council, 65 Davies St., London W. 1, England.

CAREER: British Council, lecturer in Athens and Salonika, Greece, 1946-50, administrator in Madras and Colombo, 1950-52, in Birmingham, England, 1952-54, in Cambridge, England, 1955-63, in London, England, 1963-66, in Paris, France, 1966—. George Elliston Poetry Foundation Lecturer, University of Cincinnati, 1962. *Military service:* Royal Artillery, 1940-45; became captain. *Member:* Royal Society of Literature (fellow). *Awards, honors:* Heinemann Award of Royal Society of Literature for *The Chequer'd Shade.*

WRITINGS: The Fire and the Fountain: An Essay on Poetry, Oxford University Press, 1955, 2nd edition, Barnes & Noble, 1966; *Uncertainties, and Other Poems,* Oxford University Press, 1956; (compiler) *Poetic Heritage: A Sunday Times Anthology of English Verse from the 16th to the 20th Century,* Deutsch, 1957; *The Chequer'd Shade: Reflections on Obscurity in Poetry,* Oxford University Press, 1958; *Andrew Marvell,* Longmans, Green, 1958, revised edition, 1966; *Guy Fawkes Night, and Other Poems,* Oxford University Press, 1959; *Robert Herrick,* Longmans, Green, 1961; *Ice-Storm in Cincinnati,* [Cincinnati], 1962; *Rule and Energy: Trends in British Poetry Since the Second World War,* Oxford University Press, 1963 (editor) *The Teaching of English Overseas,* Methuen, 1963; (editor) Francis Turner Palgrave, *The Golden Treasury of the Best Songs and Lyrical Poems in the English Language,* Volume V, Oxford University Press, 1964; (editor) *Commonwealth Literature: Unity and Diversity in a Common Culture,* Barnes & Noble, 1965; *Louis MacNeice,* Longmans, Green, 1965; *A Map of Modern English Verse,* Oxford University Press, 1969; *The Lengthening Shadows,* Oxford University Press, 1971. Author of English libretto for film production of Bartok's "Bluebeard's Castle." Editor, "Poetic Heritage" for Sunday Times.

WORK IN PROGRESS: A collection of poetry.

SIDELIGHTS: Press has lived and traveled in East Africa, Greece, India, Pakistan, and France.

BIOGRAPHICAL/CRITICAL SOURCES: Howard Nemerov, *Poetry and Fiction: Essays,* Rutgers University Press, 1963.

*   *   *

PRETTYMAN, E(lijah) Barrett, Jr.   1925-

PERSONAL: Born June 1, 1925, in Washington, D.C.; son of E. Barrett (a judge, U.S. Court of Appeals) and Lucy (Hill) Prettyman; married Evelyn Walter Savage, June 24, 1950; children: E. Barrett III, Jill Savage. *Education:* Attended St. Albans School, Washington, D.C.; Yale University, B.A., 1949; University of Virginia, LL.B., 1953. *Politics:* Democrat. *Religion:* Methodist. *Home:* 3708 Bradley Lane, Chevy Chase, Md. 20015. *Office:* 815 Connecticut Ave., Washington, D.C. 20016.

CAREER: Providence Journal, Providence, R.I., reporter, 1949-50; law clerk for Supreme Court Justices Jackson, Frankfurter, and Harlan, 1953-55; Hogan & Hartson (law firm), Washington, D.C., associate, 1955-63; special assistant to the U.S. Attorney General, 1963; special assistant to the White House, 1963-64; Hogan and Hartson, Washington, D.C., partner, 1964—. *Military service:* U.S. Army, 1943-45. *Awards, honors:* Mystery Writers of America award for best factual crime book of the year, and Scribes Award for book best expressing to lay readers the aims of the legal profession, both for *Death and the Supreme Court,* 1961.

WRITINGS: (Editor with others) Justice Robert H. Jackson, *The Supreme Court in the American System of Government,* Harvard University Press, 1955; *Death and the Supreme Court,* Harcourt, 1961; (contributor)

Charles Herman Pritchett and A.F. Westin, editors, *The Third Branch of Government: 8 Cases in Constitutional Politics,* Harcourt, 1963.

*   *   *

PRICE, Archibald Grenfell   1892-

PERSONAL: Born January 28, 1892, in Adelaide, South Australia; son of Archibald Henry (a bank manager) and Elizabeth Jane (Harris) Price; married Kitty Pauline Hayward; children: Pauline Elizabeth Price Lewis, Charles Archibald, Kenneth B. *Education:* Magdalen College, Oxford University, B.A., 1914, diploma in education, 1915, M.A., 1919. *Home:* 32 Edwin Ter., Gilberton, South Australia. *Office:* National Library of Australia, Canberra, Australian Capital Territory.

CAREER: University of Adelaide, Adelaide, South Australia, a founder and master of St. Mark's College, 1925-57, member of university council, 1925-62; National Library of Australia, Canberra, first chairman of council, 1959—. Chairman of Emergency Committee of South Australia, 1930-31; member of House of Representatives of Commonwealth Parliament, 1941-43; chairman, advisory board of Commonwealth Literary Fund, 1954—. *Member:* Royal Geographical Society (fellow), American Geographical Society (fellow). *Awards, honors:* Companion of Order of St. Michael and St. George, 1933; Knight Bachelor, 1962; D.Litt., University of Adelaide, 1930.

WRITINGS: The Foundation and Settlement of South Australia 1829-1845: A Study of the Colonization Movement, F.W. Preece, 1924; (with Laurence Dudley Stamp) *The World: A General Geography,* Australian edition, Longmans, Green, 1928, 5th edition, 1939; *Founders and Pioneers of South Australia: Life Studies of Edward Gibbon Wakefield,* F.W. Preece, 1929; *The History and Problems of Northern Territory,* F.W. Preece, 1930; *The Menace of Inflation,* F.W. Preece, 1931; *Progress of Communism,* F.W. Preece, 1931; (contributor) John H. Rose, A.P. Newton, E.A. Benias, and others, editors, *The Cambridge History of the British Empire,* Australian volume, Cambridge University Press, 1933; *Libraries in South Australia,* F. Trigg, 1937; *White Settlers in the Tropics,* American Geographical Society, 1939.

What of Our Aborigines?, Rigby (Adelaide), 1943; *Australia Comes of Age: A Study of Growth to Nationhood and of External Relations,* Georgian Press, 1945; *The Collegiate School of St. Peter 1847-1947,* Collegiate School of St. Peter (Adelaide), 1947; *White Settlers and Native Peoples: An Historical Study of Racial Contacts Between English-Speaking Whites and Aboriginal Peoples in the United States, Canada, Australia and New Zealand,* Georgian Press, 1950, Greenwood Press, 1972; (editor) *The Explorations of Captain James Cook in the Pacific,* Limited Editions Club, 1957, revised edition, Angus & Robertson, 1969; (editor) *The Humanities in Australia: A Survey with Special Reference to the Universities,* Angus & Robertson, 1959; *The Winning of Australian Antarctica: Mawson's B.A.N.Z.A.R.E. Voyages, 1929-31,* Angus & Robertson, 1962; *The Western Invasions of the Pacific and Its Continents: A Study of Moving Frontiers and Changing Landscapes, 1513-1958,* Clarendon Press, 1963; *The Importance of Disease in History,* Libraries Board of South Australia, 1964; *The Challenge of New Guinea: Australian Aid to Papuan Progress,* Angus & Robertson, 1965, Tri-Ocean, 1966; *A History of St. Mark's College, University of Adelaide and the Foundation of the Residential College Movement,* Council of St. Marks College, 1968; *The Skies Remember: The Story of Ron and Keir Smith,* Angus & Robertson, 1969. Contributor to other books and journals.

WORK IN PROGRESS: Historical Geography of Australia and Its Territories.

PRICE, Charles 1925-

PERSONAL: Born September 26, 1925, in Philadelphia, Pa.; son of Charles and Helen (Bohlin) Price. Education: Attended Colgate University; College of the Holy Cross, Worcester, Mass., B.S. Home: 5 East 78th St., New York, N.Y. 10021. Agent: Littauer & Wilkinson, 500 Fifth Ave., New York, N.Y. 10036.

CAREER: Golf, New York, N.Y., editor, 1959-61; TV-Filmways, Inc.-Shell Oil, associate producer for "Wonderful World of Golf," 1962; free-lance writer, 1962—. Military service: U.S. Navy, 1944-46.

WRITINGS: (Editor) Golf Magazine's Pro Pointers and Stroke Savers, Harper, 1960; The World of Golf: A Panorama of Six Centuries of the Game's History, Random House, 1962; (editor) The American Golfer (anthology), Random House, 1964; (with Albert Averbach) The Verdicts Were Just: Eight Famous Lawyers Present Their Most Memorable Cases, Lawyers Cooperative Publishing Co., 1967; (with the editors of Sports Illustrated) Sports Illustrated Book of Golf, Lippincott, 1970, revised edition published as Sports Illustrated Golf, 1972. Contributor of more than three hundred articles to Saturday Evening Post, Cosmopolitan, Saturday Review, Sports Illustrated, Argosy, Newsweek, and other magazines.

* * *

PRICE, Roger 1921-

PERSONAL: Born March 6, 1921, in Charleston, W. Va.; son of Roger T. (a coal operator) and Mary (Presley) Price; divorced; children: Roger Taylor III, Sandi Hope. Education: Attended University of Michigan, 1937, and American Academy of Art, Chicago, Ill., 1939. Home: 5319 Fulton Ave., Van Nuys, Calif. 91401. Office: 410 North La Cienega Blvd., Los Angeles, Calif. 90048.

CAREER: Price/Stern/Sloan (publishers), Inc., Los Angeles, Calif., partner. Television and club comedian and actor; writer.

WRITINGS: In One Head and Out the Other, Simon & Schuster, 1951; Droodles, Simon & Schuster, 1953; The Rich Sardine, and Other New Droodles, Simon & Schuster, 1954; Oodles of Droodles, Simon & Schuster, 1955; I'm for Me First: The Secret Handbook to the Me First Party, Ballantine, 1956; (with Leonard Stern) Mad Libs, Price, Stern, 1958; Son of Mad Libs, Price, Stern, 1959; J.G., the Upright Ape (novel), Lyle Stuart, 1960; (with Stern) What Not to Name the Baby, Price, Stern, 1960; Sooper Mod Libs, Price, Stern, 1961; Non-Quotes, Price, Stern, 1961, revised edition, 1972; The Compleat Droodles: An Art Book That Fights Back, Price, Stern, 1964; Snoop, Price, Stern, 1964; (compiler and illustrator) Edward Gibbon, The Decline and Fall, Random House, 1967; The Last Little Dragon, Harper, 1969; Zap!, Random House, 1969; The Great Roob Revolution, Random House, 1970. Contributor of short stories to Collier's, Playboy, Sports Illustrated, Mad, and other periodicals, and writer of syndicated newspaper feature, "Droodles," for five years.

WORK IN PROGRESS: Television scripts.

SIDELIGHTS: In a review of The Great Roob Revolution, Roderick MacLeish writes: "Mr. Price must be a man of good taste that gurgles from the pores of the American character. His rage is, at the same time, his greatest strength and his greatest weakness. It prods him into hilarious contempt for various strata of the American middle class. But the same rage drives Mr. Price into an absolutism, into an attempt to classify nearly everybody in one of three categor[ies] of his great Roob Theory. A good theory it is, too, but its uses are limited."

BIOGRAPHICAL/CRITICAL SOURCES: Carleton Miscellany, winter, 1968; Washington Post, June 4, 1970.

* * *

PRICE, Victor 1930-

PERSONAL: Born April 10, 1930, in Newcastle, Northern Ireland; son of John (a business executive) and Doreen (Purdy) Price; married Colette Rodot, October 20, 1956; children: Martin John, Eric Michael. Education: Queen's University, Belfast, Northern Ireland, B.A. (honors in modern languages), 1951. Home: 18 Cambridge Park, Twickenham, Middlesex, England. Agent: Curtis Brown Ltd., 575 Madison Ave., New York, N.Y. 10022.

CAREER: Teacher at Lurgan College, Lurgan, Northern Ireland, 1952-54; Oberschule, St. Peter, Nordsee, Germany, 1954-55, and Annadale Grammar School, Belfast, Northern Ireland, 1955-56; British Broadcasting Corp., Belfast, Northern Ireland, announcer, 1956-59; Radio Hong Kong, features producer, 1960-63; British Broadcasting Corp., London, England, script writer for External Services, 1963-64, senior producer for North American and Pacific Service, 1964-65, Greek programme organizer, 1965-66, assistant program editor, 1966-71, general program editor, 1971—.

WRITINGS: The Death of Achilles (novel), Doubleday, 1963; The Other Kingdom (novel), Doubleday, 1964; Caliban's Wooing (novel), Heinemann, 1966; (translator) The Plays of Buechner, Oxford University Press, 1971.

WORK IN PROGRESS: "Ignatius," a play commissioned by the Royal Court Theatre; a novel set in Hong Kong; translations of Tucholsky.

* * *

PRIESTLEY, J(ohn) B(oynton) 1894-
(Peter Goldsmith)

PERSONAL: Born September 13, 1894, in Bradford, Yorkshire, England; son of Jonathan (a schoolmaster) Priestley; married Patricia Tempest (died, 1925); married Mary Holland Wyndham Lewis (marriage dissolved, 1952); married Jacquetta Hawkes (an archaeologist and writer); children: (first marriage) two daughters; (second marriage) two daughters, one son. Education: Trinity Hall, Cambridge, M.A. Home: Kissing Tree House, Alvestan, Stratford-upon-Avon, England. Agent: A.D. Peters, 10 Buckingham St., Adelphi, London W.C.2, England.

CAREER: British author who began writing for newspapers in England at the age of sixteen, and has been writing in one medium or another ever since. Became critic, reviewer, and essayist for various periodicals in London in 1922. Began career as dramatist with production of first play in 1932; has since had plays produced in London and throughout world. Director of Mask Theatre, 1938-39. Lecturer on a U.S. tour in 1937; has spent several winters in Arizona. Has written for stage, screen, radio, and television, acted in advisory capacity on film scripts in Hollywood and England, and, during World War II, broadcast "Postscripts," a series of BBC radio talks. President of Screenwriters' Association, London, 1944-45. United Kingdom delegate to two UNESCO conferences, 1946-47, one of originators of Campaign for Nuclear Disarmament (CND). Chairman of International Theatre Conferences at Paris, 1947, and Prague, 1948, British Theatre Conference, 1948, and International Theatre Institute, 1949. Member of National Theatre Board, 1966-67; former chairman of council on London Philharmonic Orchestra, and a director of New Statesman and Nation. Military service: British Army, Infantry, 1914-19; became commissioned officer; wounded three times. Member: Saville Club (London). Awards, honors:

James Tait Black prize for fiction, 1930, for *The Good Companions;* Ellen Terry Award for best play of 1947, for *The Linden Tree;* LL.D. from St. Andrews University; D.Litt. from Universities of Colorado, Birmingham, and Bradford.

WRITINGS—Novels: *Adam in Moonshine,* Harper, 1927; *Benighted,* Heinemann, 1927, published in America as *The Old Dark House,* Harper, 1928; *The Good Companions,* Harper, 1929, reissued with introduction by Kendall B. Taft, 1930; (with Hugh Walpole) *Farthing Hall* (humorous romance), Macmillan, 1929; *Angel Pavement,* Harper, 1930, reissued with foreword by Sinclair Lewis, Readers Club Press (New York), 1942; *The Town Major of Miraucourt,* Heinemann, 1930; *Faraway,* Harper, 1932; *Albert Goes Through,* Harper, 1933; (with Gerald W. Bullett) *I'll Tell You Everything,* Macmillan, 1933; *Wonder Hero,* Harper, 1933; *They Walk in the City: The Lovers in the Stone Forest,* Harper, 1936, reprinted, Greenwood Press, 1972; *The Doomsday Men: An Adventure,* Harper, 1938; *Let the People Sing,* Heinemann, 1939, Harper, 1940; *Black-Out in Gretley: A Story of and for Wartime,* Harper, 1942; *Daylight on Saturday,* Harper, 1943 (published in England as *Daylight on Saturday: A Novel About an Aircraft Factory,* Heinemann, 1943); *Three Men in New Suits,* Harper, 1945; *Bright Day,* Harper, 1946, reissued with new introduction by Priestley, Dutton, 1966; *Jenny Villiers: A Story of the Theatre,* Harper, 1947; *Festival,* Harper, 1951 (published in England as *Festival at Farbridge,* Heinemann, 1951); *Low Notes on a High Level,* Harper, 1954 (published in England as *Low Notes on a High Level: A Frolic,* Heinemann, 1954); *The Magicians,* Harper, 1954; *Saturn Over the Water: An Account of His Adventures in London, New York, South America, and Australia by Tim Bedford, Painter; Edited with Some Preliminary and Concluding Remarks by Henry Sulgrave; and Here Presented to the Reading Public,* Doubleday, 1961; *The Thirty-First of June: A Tale of True Love, Enterprise, and Progress, in the Arthurian and Ad-Atomic Ages,* Heinemann, 1961, Doubleday, 1962; *The Shapes of Sleep: A Topical Tale,* Doubleday, 1962; *Sir Michael and Sir George: A Tale of COSMA and DISCUS and the New Elizabethans,* Heinemann, 1964, published in America as *Sir Michael and Sir George: A Comedy of the New Elizabethans,* Little, Brown, 1966; *It's an Old Country,* Little, Brown, 1967; *The Image Men,* Heinemann, Volume 1: *Out of Town,* 1968, reissued as separate publication by Penguin, 1969, Volume 2: *London End,* 1968, reissued as separate publication by Penguin, 1969, entire book also published as single-volume edition, *The Image Men,* by Little, Brown, 1969.

Plays: *Dangerous Corner* (three-act; first produced on West End at Lyric Theatre, May 17, 1932; produced in New York at Empire Theatre, October 27, 1932), Heinemann, 1932, Samuel French (acting edition), 1932, novelization by Ruth Holland published by Hamish Hamilton, 1934; *The Roundabout* (three-act comedy; first produced in 1933), Samuel French, 1933; *Eden End* (three-act; first produced on West End at Duchess Theatre, September 13, 1934; produced Off-Broadway at Masque Theatre, October 21, 1935), Heinemann, 1934, Samuel French (acting edition), 1935, reprinted, Greenwood Press, 1972; *Laburnum Grove* (three-act "immoral comedy"; first produced on West End at Duchess Theatre, November 28, 1933; produced on Broadway at Booth Theatre, January 14, 1935), Heinemann, 1934, Samuel French (acting edition), 1935, novelization by Ruth Holland published by Heinemann, 1936, play retold by L.W. Taylor, published by Oxford University Press, 1941; *Cornelius* ("a business affair in three transactions"; first produced on West End at Duchess Theatre, March 20, 1935), Heinemann, 1935, Samuel French (acting edition), 1936; *Duet in Floodlight* (comedy; first produced on

West End, under Priestley's direction, at Appollo Theatre, June 4, 1935), Heinemann, 1935; (with Edward Knoblock) *The Good Companions* (two-act; based on Priestley's novel of the same title; first produced on West End at His Majesty's Theatre, May 14, 1931; produced in New York at Forty-Fourth Street Theatre, October 1, 1931), Samuel French, 1935; *Bees on the Boat Deck* (two-act farcical tragedy; first produced on West End at Lyric Theatre, May 5, 1936), Heinemann, 1936, acting edition, 1936; (under pseudonym Peter Goldsmith, with George Billam) *Spring Tide* (three-act; first produced on West End at Duchess Theatre, July 15, 1936), Heinemann, 1936; *I Have Been Here Before* (three-act; first produced in London at Royalty Theatre, September 22, 1937; produced in New York at Guild Theatre, October 13, 1938), Heinemann, 1937, Harper, 1938, Samuel French (acting edition), 1939; *Mystery at Greenfingers* ("comedy of detection"; first produced in 1938) Samuel French, 1937; *People at Sea* (three-act; first produced on West End at Duchess Theatre, July 15, 1936), Heinemann, 1937, Samuel French (acting edition), 1938; *Time and the Conways* (three-act; first produced on West End at Duchess Theatre, August 26, 1937; produced in New York at Ritz Theatre, January 3, 1938), Heinemann, 1937, Harper, 1938, Samuel French (acting edition), 1939, reissued with introduction by Irene Hentschel, Heinemann, 1950, reissued with introduction and notes by E.R. Wood, 1964, reprinted, Penguin, 1971; *When We Are Married* (three-act Yorkshire farcical comedy; first produced on West End at St. Martin's Theatre, October 11, 1938; produced on Broadway at Lyceum Theatre, December 25, 1939), Heinemann, 1938, Samuel French (acting edition), 1940; *Johnson Over Jordan [and] All About It* (the former a three-act morality play, first produced on West End at New Theatre, February 22, 1939; the latter an essay), Harper, 1939, play published separately by Samuel French (acting edition), 1941; *Desert Highway* (two-act, with an interlude; first produced on Broadway at The Playhouse, February 10, 1944), Heinemann, 1944, Samuel French (acting edition), 1944; *They Came to a City* (two-act; first produced on West End at Globe Theatre, April 21, 1943), Samuel French, 1944; *How Are They at Home/* (two-act topical comedy; first produced on West End at Apollo Theatre, May 4, 1944), Samuel French, 1945; *Good-Night Children* (comedy; first produced on West End at New Theatre, February 5, 1942), published in *Three Comedies,* Heinemann, 1945; *An Inspector Calls* (three-act; first produced on West End at New Theatre, October 1, 1946; produced on Broadway at Booth Theatre, October 21, 1947), Heinemann, 1947, Dramatists Play Service (acting edition), 1948, reissued with introduction by Edward Rudolf Wood, Heinemann, 1965, programmed tutorial on the play, by R. Basey, published by Teaching Programmes (Bristol), 1966, also published with *The Linden Tree* (see below); *The Long Mirror* (three-act; first produced in Edinburgh at Gateway Theatre, November 6, 1945), Samuel French, 1947; *Music at Night* (three-act; first produced on West End at Westminster Theatre, October 10, 1939), Samuel French, 1947; *The Rose and the Crown* (one-act; first produced in 1947), Samuel French, 1947; *The Golden Fleece* (three-act comedy; first produced in 1948), Samuel French, 1948; (with Doris Zinkeisen) *The High Toby* (play for "toy theatre"; first produced in 1948), Penguin (Harmondsworth), 1948; *The Linden Tree* (two-act; first produced on West End at Duchess Theatre, August 15, 1947; produced on Broadway at Music Box Theatre, March 2, 1948), Heinemann, 1948, Samuel French (acting edition), 1948, also published with *An Inspector Calls* (see above); *Ever Since Paradise* (three-act; first produced in London at Winter Garden Theatre, June 4, 1947), Samuel French, 1949; *Home is Tomorrow* (two-act; first produced on West End at Cambridge Theatre,

November 4, 1948), Heinemann, 1949, Samuel French (acting edition), 1950; (with Arthur Bliss) *The Olympians* (three-act opera, with libretto by Priestley, score by Bliss; first produced in London at Covent Garden Theatre, September 29, 1949), Novello, 1949, bilingual edition (German and English), 1950; *Bright Shadow* (three-act "play of detection"; first produced in Palmer's Green at Intimate Theatre, April 10, 1950), Samuel French, 1950; *Summer Day's Dream* (two-act; first produced on West End at St. Martin's Theatre, September 8, 1949), Samuel French, 1950; (with wife, Jacquetta Hawkes) *Dragon's Mouth* (dramatic quartet in two parts; first produced in London at Winter Garden Theatre, May 13, 1952; produced Off-Broadway at Cherry Lane Theatre, November 16, 1955), Harper, 1952; *Mother's Day* (one-act comedy; first produced in 1953), Samuel French, 1953; *Private Rooms* (one-act comedy "in the Viennese style"; first produced in 1953), Samuel French, 1953; *Treasure on Pelican* (three-act; first produced in London at Golder's Green Hippodrome, February 25, 1952), Evans Brothers (acting edition), 1953; *Try It Again* (one-act) Samuel French, 1953; *A Glass of iBtter* (one-act; first produced in 1954), Samuel French, 1954; *The Scandalous Affair of Mr. Kettle and Mrs. Moon* (three-act comedy; first produced on West End at Duchess Theatre, September 1, 1955), Samuel French, 1956; *The Glass Cage* (two-act; written for Crest Theatre, Toronto; first produced on West End at Piccadilly Theatre, April 26, 1957), Kingswood House (Toronto), 1957, Samuel French (acting edition), 1958; (with Iris Murdoch) *A Severed Head* (three-act; adaptation of novel by Murdoch, with same title; first produced on West End at Old Vic Theatre, 1963), Chatto & Windus, 1964, Samuel French (acting edition), 1964.

Unpublished plays: (With Jacquetta Hawkes) "The White Countess," first produced on West End at Saville Theatre, March 24, 1954; "The Golden Entry," first produced in 1955; "These Our Actors," first produced in 1956; "Take the Fool Away," first produced in 1956; "The Pavilion of Masks," first produced in 1963. Also author of several screenplays, including "The Foreman Went to France," "Britain at Bay," "Priestley's Postscripts," "Battle for Music," "They Came to a City" (based on his play), "Last Holiday," and "An Inspector Calls" (based on his play). Also author of television series, "You Know What People Are," of the program, "Lost City," in which he appeared, and of a television play "Anyone for Tennis?," produced by BBC-TV in 1968. Author of an original narrative on which the United Artists film, "Somewhere in France," produced in 1943, was based.

Essays: *Papers from Lilliput*, Bowes, 1922; *I for One*, John Lane, 1923, Books for Libraries, 1967; *Talking*, Harper, 1926; *J.B. Priestley* (selected essays), Harrap, 1926; *Open House*, Harper, 1927; *Apes and Angels*, Methuen, 1928; *Selected Essays*, edited by G.A. Sheldon, A. & C. Black, 1928; *The Balconinny, and Other Essays*, Methuen, 1929, published in America as *The Balconinny*, Harper, 1930; *Self-Selected Essays*, Harper, 1932; "Some Reflections of a Popular Novelist," published in *Essays and Studies by Members of the English Association*, [Oxford], 1933; *The Secret Dream: An Essay on Britain, America and Russia* (based on radio broadcasts, 1946), Turnstile Press, 1946; *Delight*, Harper, 1949; *All About Ourselves, and Other Essays*, selected and introduced by Eric Gillett, Heinemann, 1956; *Thoughts in the Wilderness*, Harper, 1957; *Essays of Five Decades*, selected, with a preface, by Susan Cooper, Little, Brown, 1968.

Other books: *The Chapman of Rhymes* (poems), Alexander Moring (London), 1918; *Brief Diversions* (tales, travesties and epigrams), Bowes, 1922; *Figures in Modern Literature*, Dodd, 1924; *The English Comic Charac-* ters, Dodd, 1925, new edition, Bodley Head, 1963, Dufour, 1964, reprinted, Phaeton, 1972; *Fools and Philosophers: A Gallery of Comic Figures from English Literature*, John Lane, 1925; *George Meredith*, Macmillan, 1926, reprinted, Scholarly Press, 1970; *Thomas Love Peacock*, Macmillan, 1927, new edition, with an introduction by J.I.M. Stewart, St. Martin's, 1966, reprinted, Scholarly Press, 1970; *The English Novel*, Benn, 1927, new illustrated edition, revised, Thomas Nelson, 1935, reprinted, Scholarly Press, 1971; *Too Many People, and Other Reflections*, Harper, 1928; *English Humour*, Longmans, Green, 1929; *English Journey: Being a Rambling but Truthful Account of What One Man Saw and Heard and Felt and Thought During a Journey Through England During the Autumn of the Year 1933*, Harper, 1934, selections by H.W. Haeusermann published as teaching edition, A. Francke (Bern), 1938; *Midnight on the Desert: Being an Excursion into Autobiography During a Winter in America, 1935-36*, Harper, 1937 (published in England as *Midnight on the Desert: A Chapter of Autobiography*, Heinemann, 1937); (with others) *First "Mercury" Story Book*, Longmans, Green, 1939; *Rain Upon Godshill: A Further Chapter of Autobiography*, Harper, 1939; *Britain Speaks* (based on a series of radio talks to America, May 5 to September 24, 1940), Harper, 1940; *Postscripts* (originally radio broadcasts), Heinemann, 1940, published in America as *All England Listened: The Wartime Broadcasts of J.B. Priestley*, introduction by Eric Sevareid, Chilmark, 1967; *Out of the People*, Harper, 1941; *Britain at War*, Harper, 1942; with Philip Gibbs and others) *The English Spirit*, edited and introduced by Anthony Weymouth, Allen & Unwin, 1942; *British Women Go to War*, photographs by P.G. Hennell, Collins, 1943; *Russian Journey*, Writers Group of the Society for Cultural Relations with the U.S.S.R., 1946; *Theatre Outlook*, Nicholson & Watson, 1947; *Going Up* (stories and sketches), Pan Books, 1950; *The Other Place, and Other Stories of the Same Sort* (includes "The Other Place," "The Grey Ones," "Uncle Phil on TV," "Guest of Honour," "Look After the Strange Girl," "The Statues," "The Leadington Incident," "Mr. Strenberry's Tale," and "Night Sequence"), Harper, 1953; (with Jacquetta Hawkes) *Journey Down a Rainbow* (travel sketches), Harper, 1955; *The Art of the Dramatist* (lecture with appendices and discursive notes), Heinemann (Melbourne), 1957; *Topside; or, The Future of England* (dialogue), Heinemann, 1958; *The Wonderful World of the Theatre*, edited by David Lambert, designed by Germano Facetti, Garden City Books, 1959 (published in England as *The Story of Theatre*, Rathbone, 1959), revised and enlarged edition, Doubleday, 1969; *Literature and Western Man: Criticism and Comment of Five Centuries of Western Literature*, Harper, 1960; *William Hazlitt*, published for the British Book Council and the National Book League by Longmans, Green, 1960; *Charles Dickens: A Pictorial Biography*, Thames & Hudson, 1961, Viking, 1962, reissued as *Charles Dickens and His World*, 1969; *Margin Released: A Writer's Reminiscences and Reflections*, Harper, 1962; *Man and Time*, Doubleday, 1964; *The Moments, and Other Pieces*, Heinemann, 1966; *Salt is Leaving*, Pan Books, 1966; *Trumpets Over the Sea: Being a Rambling and Egotistical Account of the London Symphony Orchestra's Engagement at Daytona Beach, Florida, in July-August, 1967*, Heinemann, 1968; *The Prince of Pleasure and His Regency, 1811-20*, Harper, 1969; *Anton Chekhov*, International Textbook, 1970, A.S. Barnes, 1970; *The Edwardians*, Harper, 1970; *Snoggle* (juvenile fiction), Harcourt, 1972; *Victoria's Heyday*, Harper, 1972; *Over the Long High Wall: Some Reflections and Speculations on Life, Death and Time;* Heinemann, 1972.

Editor: (And author of introduction) Thomas Moore, *Tom Moore's Diary* (selections), Cambridge University

Press, 1925, Scholarly Press, 1971; (and author of introduction and notes) *Essayists Past and Present: A Selection of English Essays,* Dial, 1925; (and compiler) *The Book of Bodley Head Verse,* Dodd, 1926; *These Diversions* (essay series), six volumes, Jarrolds, 1926-28; *Our Nation's Heritage* (country anthology), Dent, 1939; (and compiler and author of introduction) Charles Dickens, *Scenes of London Life from "Sketches by Boz"* (selections), Pan Books, 1947; (and author of introduction) *Best of Leacock,* McClelland & Stewart, 1957 (published in England as *The Bodley Head Leacock,* Bodley Head, 1957); (with O.B. Davis) *Four English Novels* (includes *Pride and Prejudice,* by Jane Austen, *Pickwick Papers,* by Charles Dickens, *Return of the Native,* by Thomas Hardy, and *Secret Sharer,* by Joseph Conrad), Harcourt, 1960; (with Davis) *Four English Biographies* (includes *Shakespeare of London,* by Marchette Chute, *The Life of Samuel Johnson,* by James Boswell, *Queen Victoria,* by Lytton Strachey, and *The Edge of Day: Boyhood in the West of England,* by Laurie Lee), Harcourt, 1961; (with Josephine Spear) *Adventures in English Literature,* Laureate edition, Harcourt, 1963.

Author of introduction: Florence Maris Turner, editor, *The Diary of Thomas Turner of East Heathly, 1754-65,* John Lane, 1925; Laurence Sterne, *The Life and Opinions of Tristram Shandy,* Dodd, 1928; Mary Priestley, editor, *Selections from "The Female Spectator",* John Lane, 1929; Henry Fielding, *The History of the Adventures of Joseph Andrews and His Friend, Abraham Adams,* Dodd, 1929; Henry Fielding, *Tom Jones,* Limited Editions Club (New York), 1931; *The Beauty of Britain: A Pictorial Survey,* Batsford, 1935, revised edition, 1962; (author of foreword) Ivor Brown, *The Heart of England,* Scribner, 1935, 3rd edition, Batsford, 1951; Alain Rene Le Sage, *The Adventures of Gil Blas,* as translated from the French by Tobias Smollett, Oxford University Press, 1937; *The Neglected Child and His Family* (welfare report), Oxford University Press, 1948; *The Bodley Head Scott Fitzgerald,* Bodley Head, 1958; Anthony Trollope, *An Autobiography,* Collins, 1962; (author of prologue and epilogue) Richard Herncastle, *Lost Empires,* Little, Brown, 1965; *Everyman Anthology of Excerpts Grave and Gay,* Dutton, 1966; John Cowper Powys, *Autobiography,* new edition, Macdonald, 1967.

Omnibus volumes: *The Works of J.B. Priestley,* Heinemann, 1931; *Four-in-Hand* (includes *Adam in Moonshine, Laburnum Grove, The Roundabout,* and short stories and essays), Heinemann, 1934; *Three Plays and a Preface* (includes *Dangerous Corner, Eden End,* and *Cornelius*), Harper, 1935; *Two Time Plays* (includes *Time and the Conways* and *I Have Been Here Before*), Heinemann, 1938; *Three Plays* (includes *Music at Night, The Long Mirror,* and *They Came to a City*), Heinemann, 1943; *Four Plays* (includes *Music at Night, The Long Mirror, They Came to a City,* and *Desert Highway*), Harper, 1944; *Three Comedies* (includes *Good-Night, Children, The Golden Fleece,* and *How Are They at Home?*), Heinemann, 1945; *Three Time Plays* (includes *Dangerous Corner, Time and the Conways,* and *I Have Been Here Before*), Pan Books, 1947; *The Linden Tree* [and] *An Inspector Calls,* Harper, 1948; *Plays,* three volumes, Heinemann, 1948-50, Harper, 1950-52, Volume I also published separately as *Seven Plays,* Harper, 1950; *Adam in Moonshine* [and] *Benighted,* college edition, Heinemann, 1951; *The Priestley Companion* (selections), introduction by Ivor Brown, Penguin (Harmondsworth), 1951; *The World of J.B. Priestley,* selected and introduced by Donald G. MacRae, Heinemann, 1967; *When We Are Married, and Other Plays* (includes *When We Are Married, Bees on the Boat Deck, Ever Since Paradise,* and *Mr. Kettle and Mrs. Moon*), Penguin, 1969.

Booklets: *The Man-Power Story,* H.M.S.O., 1943; *Here Are Your Answers,* Common Wealth, 1944; *The New Citizen* (speech delivered on January 6, 1944), Council for Education in World Citizenship (London), 1944; *Letter to a Returning Serviceman,* Home & Van Thal, 1945; *The Arts Under Socialism* [and] *What the Government Should Do for the Arts Here and Now* (the former a lecture given to the Fabian Society, the latter a postscript), Turnstile Press, 1947; *The Writer in a Changing Society* (a Herman Ould memorial lecture), Hand and Flower Press (Aldington), 1956.

Contributor of essays, articles, sketches, reviews, and short stories to numerous periodicals and newspapers. Plays anthologized in *Six Plays of Today,* Heinemann, 1939, *Famous Plays of Today,* Gollancz, 1953, *English One-Act Plays of Today,* edited by Donald Fitzjohn, Oxford University Press, 1962, and other anthologies.

SIDELIGHTS: "At 72," wrote a *Time* reviewer of *It's An Old Country* in 1967, "J.B. Priestley is a British institution: a word-factory who has turned out 29 volumes of assorted nonfiction and 24 novels. Yet each successive effort manages to offer a number of odd little surprises. The first in this novel is that a man of Priestley's age should be at all interested in examining Swinging Britain; the second is that his study makes such jolly good entertainment." Entertainment and humor are Priestley's forte; called "Jolly Jack" by a number of British critics, he is frequently compared to Dickens (although Priestley dislikes the comparison) because of the "robust humour" of his style and the hosts of minor characters which crowd his novels. David Williams, John K. Hutchens, and Eric Rhode, among others, have commented on Priestley's "Dickensian" streak. "In many respects," Frederick T. Wood has written, "Mr. Priestley is the Dickens of the modern age. He epitomizes the spirit of the average Englishman of the twentieth century as Dickens did of the nineteenth; his stories, too, have the same air of free, hearty humour, the same spontaneity and inconsequentiality. . . . He writes with an understanding and a sympathy that speaks a depth of experience and a wide contact with humanity."

In spite of his prolific output, Priestley, according to John Gale, has described himself as a lazy man. "I'm a professional writer, and I write," he told Gale recently. "I'm not a freak. Those who think writers shouldn't write are the freaks. One shouldn't start comparing oneself to better men, but think of the amount that Shakespeare wrote, or Dickens, or Tolstoy. Only in this age people don't write." Priestley has lamented the lack of attention recently given fiction in general, and the novel in particular. In a 1967 *New Statesman* article he wrote: "[The novel's] place has been taken in the literary pages (such as they are), in the bookshops, the library lists, the literate sector of the public mind, by ghost-written memoirs, biographies, tarted-up history and sodden slabs of sociology. . . . I have no dislike of facts. I rather enjoy them, and have spent many a cheerful hour just pottering about among statistics laid out like new towns. Every conscientious writer, I feel, should occasionally explore the figures and facts. But no genuine creative writer will ever imagine that here will be found the truth about people. . . .It is good fiction, so largely ignored now, that brings us so much closer to the real facts."

Colin Wilson wrote recently that, after reading *The Edwardians,* "I found myself wondering again why it is that Priestley is so generally underrated. . . .Intelligence is not a word that critics associate with Priestley; they've got him typed as a pipe-smoking Yorkshireman with a slow, deliberate voice. In fact, the sheer range of his interests means that he can usually say something fresh and penetrating on almost any subject. If he was thirty years younger, he could do as Norman Mailer has done, and make a new reputation as a journalist social-commentator." Once labeled "an old-fashioned English radical" in a newspaper profile, Priestley is a master of the farce and of social satire. He pokes fun at modern academia, communications, and what David Williams calls "our sales-promotion world" in *The Image Men,* his most recent novel. Robert Cromie of *Book World* remarks that this book is "a thing to read and enjoy, a volume to restore your slipping faith in the comic novel, a genre which I, at least, was beginning to fear was on the verge of becoming the literary equivalent of the passenger pigeon." John Braine calls the book "a romp, an excursion into jollity, an unashamed piece of escapism. It's the kind of entertainment which I for one relish more and more, and I hope that Mr. Priestley wasn't serious when he said it would be his last novel."

If it should turn out to be his last novel, Priestley will be ending an era he started in 1927 with *Adam in Moonshine.* "In 1929," he notes, "I helped to popularize the long novel by publishing *The Good Companions,* which had an enormous success both in England and America, and was followed by the almost equally successful *Angel Pavement.*" The latter, a best-seller when it appeared in the United States in 1930, was reissued in 1967, testimony to the durability and authenticity of Priestley's characterization of the common man. His "very sure skill in the portrayal of dramatic types," as Benjamin Ifor Evans has observed, carried him easily into drama, a career begun in 1932 with the West End production of his first play, *Dangerous Corner.* Since then Priestley has written over fifty plays (for various media), run his own producing company in London, and staged more than thirty plays, many of them his own. Evans wrote that "Priestley's range as a dramatist was unusual. . . . To all [his skills] was added in a number of the plays a rare, imaginative overtone. It was as if amid all the boldly drawn characters and the Yorkshire fun a sensitive and metaphysical mind was operating. . . . Priestley showed . . . a considerable command of the theatre as a technical instrument." Priestley maintains that he was strongly influenced by the time-theories of J.W. Dunne's *Experiment with Time* and *Serial Universe,* an interest evident in his earlier plays, especially *Time and the Conways* and *I Have Been Here Before.* Frederick Lumley, in a survey of twentieth century drama since Ibsen and Shaw, expressed the belief that the pre-war "time" plays were the product of the first of three distinct periods through which Priestley has moved as a playwright. Lumley notes: "The second period belongs to his adherence to the Labour Party and the ardent faith he once had for Socialist utopias and ideals. Finally there is the 'in wilderness' period of disillusionment, when he realised that the City he wrote about was no longer to be reached through party politics, and, viewed from the wilderness, his common sense told him it was no longer practical. After being for so long a man who knew all the answers he has become a man of doubts; he still has his pipe in his mouth but it has gone out. . . . Priestley is a playwright who has attempted to break out of the conventions of the naturalistic drama, tending sometimes towards a modified form of expressionism, at other times breaking up the illusion of the box-realism deliberately, as in *Ever Since Paradise.* He would fly if he could, but he has not the power of poetry to sweep him over and beyond the immediate present. His blunt Yorkshire idiom and common-sense outlook make this alien to his character. Although an idealist, he is most successful when he realises his limitations; an intelligent thinker, he has not a serious mind. But he has a flare for the theatre, is masterly in his technique, generally topical, and a writer to whom good humour comes naturally."

Priestley himself attests to the fact that "murderous thoughts don't visit me." He agrees with Lumley and Alan Trachtenberg that he "can't manage any real thinking. . . . If I have written more than most authors, this is not because I have been exceptionally industrious—I am in fact rather lazy—but because I can concentrate quickly on my work. On the other hand, I have never thought constructively. My mind moves in a series of intuitive flashes. Whenever I have sat down to work out a complicated plot, let us say, nothing has happened and I found myself wandering away from the notebook—I buy notebooks but never make proper use of them—to clean some pipes or search for a book. Then an idea jumps into my mind while I am shaving or in the bath."

In addition to the novelist, the dramatist, and the journalist in Priestley, "there is yet another side," as Richard Church has said. "He is a master in the art of the essay . . .[and] a sound literary critic. He bases his judgment on his wide reading, as a conscious estimate, and on a native fairness and compassionate common-sense, as an unconscious estimate." ("I think of myself as eighteenth century," Priestley told Harvey Breit in 1951. "Writers wrote everything then, essays, novels, plays, there was a variety, a professionalism.") Dudley Carew of *Time and Tide* agrees with Church that Priestley "has used the medium of the essay to write some of the best critical appreciations that have appeared in this century." To those who are familiar with Priestley the essayist, Carew asserts, "it is. . .his likeness, the impression that he himself, through his essays, has given us, which springs to the mind whenever his name or his work is mentioned. That is the broad figure with the pipe and the survival of the Bruddersford accent, inconspicuously dressed. . .one who speaks his own mind and who, like the bluff, representative Englishman this all so misleadingly seems to add up to, enjoys a good grumble." In a review of *Essays of Five Decades,* a selection covering his entire writing career, Trachtenberg comments on the duality of Priestley's nature as expressed in his essays, in which "the inner life . . . [protests] against the drabness and conformity of increasingly organized modern life, including the beneficent bureaucracies of socialism. These simultaneous wishes, for social order and for personal anarchy, are the coordinates of Priestley's world, and their interplay might very well lay him down as a sentimentalist (a frequent accusation), or a bit of an old-fashioned grouch." Malcolm Muggeridge believes "it was an excellent notion to publish a selection of Mr. Priestley's essays covering the whole of his writing life. This is not just because he is a highly accomplished essayist—I should say about the most accomplished of our time—but also because the selection provides a sort of conspectus of him and his work." David McCord calls the collection "a comfortable book, a book to be at home in. There is a sense of Old Stability stalking through it."

Priestley's plays have been performed all over the world, in many different languages. Several have been made into motion pictures, including *The Old Dark House,* produced by Universal in 1932 and Columbia in 1963, *The Good Companions,* filmed in 1933 by Fox and in 1943 by Associated British-Pathe, *Dangerous Corner,* filmed by Radio Pictures in 1934, *An Inspector Calls,* a 1954 Associated Artists Production, and *The Severed Head,* adapted by Iris Murdoch and filmed in 1970 by Winkast, and adapted by Frederic Raphael and produced for Columbia in 1971 by Alan Ladd, Jr. In February of 1972 Leslie Sands produced and narrated an anthology of Priestley's dramatic works, entitled "J.B. Priestley's Open House," at the Phoenix Theatre on the West End.

A Theatre Guild radio production of *Laburnum Grove* was broadcast on April 25, 1948, and a television adaptation by Edward Mabley was produced on CBS in 1949. *Counterfeit,* adapted for television by Ellen Violett, was produced on CBS for U.S. Steel Hour on August 31, 1955.

AVOCATIONAL INTERESTS: Painting, listening to music, photography.

BIOGRAPHICAL/CRITICAL SOURCES: Denys Val Baker, editor, *Writers of Today,* Sidgwick & Jackson, 1946; Rex Pogson, *J.B. Priestley and the Theatre,* Triangle Press, 1947; *New York Times Magazine,* January 4, 1948; Benjamin Ifor Evans, *English Literature Between the Wars,* 2nd edition, Methuen, 1949; *New York Times Book Review,* May 30, 1954, October 27, 1968; Harvey Breit, *The Writer Observed,* World Publishing, 1956; *Time and Tide,* May 22, 1956; David Hughes, *J.B. Priestley: An Informal Study of His Work,* Hart-Davis, 1958; *John O'London's Weekly* (incorporated with *Time and Tide,* 1954), February 18, 1960; Ladislau Loeb, *Mensch und Gesellschaft bei J.B. Priestley,* Francke Verlag, 1962; *J.B. Priestley: An Exhibition of Manuscripts and Books,* Humanities Research Center, University of Texas, 1962; Gareth Lloyd Evans, *J.B. Priestley: The Dramatist,* Heinemann, 1964; Frederick Lumley, *New Trends in 20th Century Drama,* Oxford University Press, 1967; *New Statesman,* January 6, 1967, February 24, 1967, May 5, 1967; *Time,* May 19, 1967; *Times Literary Supplement,* February 22, 1968; *Book World,* October 6, 1968, May 11, 1969; *Nation,* November 18, 1968; *Punch,* November 20, 1968, October 20, 1970; *Observer Review,* February 16, 1969, September 14, 1969; *National Review,* June 3, 1969; Susan Cooper, *J.B. Priestley: Portrait of an Author,* Harper, 1971; *Stage,* September 9, 1971, February 24, 1972.

*   *   *

PRING-MILL, Robert D(uguid) F(orrest)   1924-
(Robert Duguid)

PERSONAL: Born September 11, 1924, near London; England; son of Richard and Nellie (Duguid) Pring-Mill; married Maria Brigitte Heinsheimer, 1950; children: Francis, Monica Montserrat. *Education:* Colegio de Montesion, student; Oxford University, M.A., 1953; Maioricensis Schola Lullistica, Magister, 1957. *Home:* 51 Hamilton Rd., Oxford, England. *Agent:* International Copyright Bureau, 26 Charing Cross Rd., London WC2H ODG, England. *Office:* New College, Oxford, England.

CAREER: Oxford University, Oxford, England; lecturer in Spanish, 1952—. Regular broadcaster on Spanish and Latin-American Services of British Broadcasting Corp. *Military service:* British Army, Black Watch Regiment, 1943-47; became captain; mentioned in dispatches. *Member:* Sociedad Arqueologica Luliana, Maioricensis Schola Lullistica, Oxford University Mediaeval Society (president, 1959-60), Modern Humanities Research Association, Association Espanola para la Filosofia Medieval (founder member).

WRITINGS: (Compiler with C.A. Jones) *Advanced Spanish Unknowns,* Harrap, 1958; (compiler with Jones) *Advanced Spanish Unseens,* Harrap, 1958; (editor) *Lope de Vega: Five Plays,* Hill & Wang, 1961; *El Microcosmos Lul-lia,* Dolphin Book Co., 1962; *Ramon Llull y el numero primitivo de las dignidades en el "Arte general,"* Dolphin Book Co., 1963; (author of introduction) Pablo Neruda, *The Heights of Macchu Picchu,* Farrar, Straus, 1968; (author of introductory note) Ramon Lull, *Quattuor libri principiorum,* S.R. Publishers, 1969. English editor of *Romantistsches Jahrbuch* and *Estudios Lulianos.*

WORK IN PROGRESS: A study of Fernando de Herrera's *Anotaciones;* translation of Calderonian *Autos sacramentales.*

PRITCHARD, John Paul   1902-

PERSONAL: Born February 8, 1902, in White Lake, N.Y.; son of John Henderson (a clergyman) and Jane Margaret (DuBois) Pritchard; married Ruth Belle Smith, August 19, 1926; children: John Paul, Jr. *Education:* Cornell University, B.A., 1922, Ph.D., 1925. *Religion:* United Presbyterian. *Home:* 1119 West Brooks St., Norman, Okla. 73069. *Office:* Department of English, University of Oklahoma, Norman, Okla. 73069.

CAREER: Catawba College, Salisbury, N.C., professor of ancient languages, 1925-28; Washington and Jefferson College, Washington, Pa., professor of classics, 1928-44, dean of freshman, 1930-32; University of Oklahoma, Norman, professor of English, 1944—, chairman of department, 1945-49. Visiting professor at Duke University, 1948, University of Arkansas, 1961. *Member:* Modern Language Association of America, Phi Beta Kappa.

WRITINGS: Return to the Fountains: Some Classical Sources of American Criticism, Duke University Press, 1942; *Criticism in America,* University of Oklahoma Press, 1956; *The Literary Wise Men of Gotham: Criticism in New York, 1815-1860,* Louisiana State University Press, 1963; (editor and translator) Auguste Boeckh, *On Interpretation and Criticism,* University of Oklahoma Press, 1968; *A Literary Approach to the New Testament,* University of Oklahoma Press, 1972. Contributor of about twenty-five research articles to learned periodicals and of more than one hundred book reviews to magazines and newspapers.

*   *   *

PROCTOR, Samuel   1919-

PERSONAL: Born March 29, 1919, in Jacksonville, Fla.; son of Jack (a merchant) and Celia (Schneider) Proctor; married Bessie Rubin, September 8, 1948; children: Mark Julian, Alan Lowell. *Education:* University of Florida, B.A., 1941, M.A., 1942, Ph.D., 1958; post-graduate study at University of North Carolina, 1948, Emory University, 1949. *Politics:* Democrat. *Religion:* Jewish. *Home:* 2235 Northwest Ninth Pl., Gainesville, Fla. 32601.

CAREER: University of Florida, Gainesville, instructor in history and social science, 1946-48, assistant professor, 1948-57, associate professor, 1957-63, professor of social sciences and history, 1963—. Visiting professor of history at Jacksonville University, summers of 1963-66. Director Oral History Program, 1968—. Member of publications committee, St. Augustine Quadricentennial Commission. Consultant for the Hall of Fame Commission (Florida Public Relations Association), Florida Library and Historical Commission, Florida Civil War Centennial Commission; historical consultant to Silver Springs, Florida Board of Parks and Historic Memorials, Florida State Museum, Florida Division of Archives, History and Records Management, and Historic Pensacola Preservation Board. Member and chairman of publications and research committee, Florida American Revolution Bicentennial Commission. *Military service:* U.S. Army, 1943-46. *Member:* American Association for State and Local History (member of regional awards committee and National American Revolution Bicentennial publications committee), National Oral History Association (member of council), Southern Historical Association, Florida Historical Society (member of board of directors).

WRITINGS: Napoleon Bonaparte Broward: Florida's Fighting Democrat, University of Florida Press, 1950; (contributor) *Future Role and Scope of the University of Florida,* University of Florida, 1962; (editor and author of introduction) *Dickison and His Men: Reminiscences of the War in Florida,* University of Florida Press, 1962; *Florida Commemorates the Civil War Centennial, 1961-1965: A Manual for the Observance of the Civil War in* the Counties and Cities of the State of Florida (pamphlet), Florida Civil War Centennial Commission, 1962; Florida a Hundred Years Ago, Florida Civil War Centennial Commission, 1965; (contributor) In Search of Gulf Coast Colonial History, Historic Pensacola Preservation Board, 1970; (editor) Florida Historic Preservation Planning, Florida Division of Archives, History and Records, 1971; (editor) Eighteenth Century Florida and Its Borderlands, University of Florida Press, 1971.

Contributor of more than seventy articles and feature stories to Jacksonville Journal, Southern Jewish Weekly, Mid-America, Canadian Mining Journal, Southern Observer, Social Science, Caribbean Quarterly, Civil War Times Illustrated, St. Petersburg Times Sunday Magazine, Florida Historical Quarterly, regional and national historical journals, and to encyclopedias. Editor, Florida Historical Quarterly, and author of column "Florida a Hundred Years Ago," written for Florida Civil War Centennial Commission and appearing in newspapers in the state.

WORK IN PROGRESS: editing A Documentary History of Florida, 1821-1971, for University of Florida Press; editing William Stork's An Account of East-Florida, Mickler's Floridiana; editing Floridiana Facsimile Series, University of Florida Press; editing "Florida Bicentennial Monograph" series, University of Florida Press.

* * *

PRODAN, Mario 1911-

PERSONAL: Born April 30, 1911, in Istanbul, Turkey; now an Italian citizen; son of Giovanni and Marika (von Gorog) Prodan; married Cecilia Pollock, January 18, 1941; children: Michela, Claudia, Luca, Andrea. Education: Educated in schools in Italy, Austria, and China; studied Chinese language, art, and philosophy under private tutors. Religion: Catholic. Home: Via di Porto Custello 60, Tarquinia, Italy. Agent: Agenzia Letteraria Internazionale, 3, Corso Matteotti, Milan, Italy.

CAREER: Independent dealer in Chinese antiques in Peking, China, prior to 1948, in Rome, Italy, 1948-73. Member: Peking Polo Club.

WRITINGS: Certain Ming Ivories, Poplar Island Press, 1943; The Faun Endures (novel), Pantheon, 1957; Liuto d'argento (short stories), Aldo Martello, 1957; Chinese Art: An Introduction, Pantheon, 1958; new edition published as An Introduction to Chinese Art, Spring Books, 1966. David at Noon (novel), Pantheon, 1958; The Art of the Tang Potter, Viking, 1961. Contributor of articles to Encyclopedia of Art, McGraw; contributor of short stories to Harper's and to other magazines.

WORK IN PROGRESS: A novel set in Hongkong, A View from the Peak; research on Jesuits in China.

SIDELIGHTS: Prodan speaks, reads, and writes Italian, English, German, French, and Mandarin; he also knows some Russian and modern Greek. Chinese Art and The Art of the Tang Potter have been published in Italy, France, Germany, Holland, and Sweden.

* * *

PRONKO, N(icholas) Henry 1908-

PERSONAL: Born February 28, 1908, in McKees Rocks, Pa.; son of Michael John and Dorothy (Smarsh) Pronko; married Geraldine Allbritten, December 16, 1953. Education: George Washington University, A.B. (with distinction), 1939; Indiana University, M.A., 1941, Ph.D., 1944. Home: 525 Longford Lane, Wichita, Kan. 67206. Office: Department of Psychology, Wichita State University, Wichita, Kan. 67208.

CAREER: Indiana University, Bloomington, instructor in psychology, 1943-45; College of the City of New York

(now City College of the City University of New York), New York, N.Y., assistant professor of psychology, 1946-47; Wichita State University, Wichita, Kan., professor of psychology, 1947—. Lecturer at Shrivenham American University in England, 1945-46, at Biarritz American University in France, 1946; Fulbright lecturer at Istanbul University, 1952-53; visiting professor at Cracow University, 1959, at Technion (Israel Institute of Technology), 1963. Member: American Psychological Association (fellow), American Society of Clinical Hypnosis (fellow), American Association for the Advancement of Science, Midwestern Psychological Association (fellow), Kansas Psychological Association (fellow), Kansas Society for Clinical Hypnosis (fellow), Phi Beta Kappa, Sigma Xi. Awards, honors: Grant from Inter-University Committee on Travel Grants to visit universities in Soviet Union, 1956.

WRITINGS: (With J. W. Bowles, Jr.) Empirical Foundations of Psychology, Rinehart, 1951; (with Frederic W. Snyder) Vision with Spatial Inversion, University of Wichita Press, 1952; (with G.Y. Kenyon) Meprobamate and Laboratory-Induced Anxiety, Southern Universities Press, 1959; Textbook of Abnormal Psychology, Williams & Wilkins, 1963; (with R. Ebert and G. Greenberg) Critical Review of Theories of Perception, New York International Press, 1963; Panorama of Psychology, Brooks-Cole, 1969. Contributor of more than sixty articles and reviews to professional journals.

* * *

PROUT, W(illiam) Leslie 1922-

PERSONAL: Born May 16, 1922 in England; son of Charles Henry and Gertrude Annie Prout; married Rosslyn Joyce Knowles, July 22, 1944. Education: Attended school in Dartmouth, England. Politics: Labour. Home: 9 Crowther's Hill, Dartmouth, South Devon, England.

WRITINGS: Think It Over: A Quantity of Quizzes, Questions, Quips, Quandries, Queries and Quests for the Quiet Quarter-Hour, Warne, 1957; Think Again: Puzzles and Problems to Please and Perplex, Warne, 1958. Contributor of puzzle features to Reveille, Junior Mirror, Picturegoer.

WORK IN PROGRESS: Comedy script writing.

* * *

PROUTY, Olive Higgins

PERSONAL: Born in Worcester, Mass.; daughter of Milton Prince (an educator and manufacturer) and Katherine (Chapin) Higgins; married Lewis I. Prouty (a manufacturer), January 7, 1907 (died, 1951); children: Jane Chapin (Mrs. William Mason Smith), Richard, Anne (deceased), Olivia (deceased), Ann. Education: Smith College, B.L., 1904; Radcliffe College, graduate study, 1908. Politics: Republican. Religion: Unitarian. Home: 393 Walnut St., Brookline, Mass. 02147. Agent: Harold Ober Associates, Inc., 40 East 49th St., New York, N.Y. 10017.

CAREER: Author.

WRITINGS: Bobbie, General Manager, Frederick Stokes, 1913; The Fifth Wheel, Frederick Stokes, 1916; Star in the Window, Frederick Stokes, 1918; Good Sports (short stories), Frederick Stokes, 1919; Conflict, Houghton, 1919; Stella Dallas, Houghton, 1923; White Fawn, Houghton, 1931; Lisa Vale, Houghton, 1938; Now Voyager, Houghton, 1941; Home Port, Houghton, 1947; Fabia, Houghton, 1951; Pencil Shavings: Memoirs, privately printed, 1961. Contributor of short stories to magazines.

SIDELIGHTS: "Stella Dallas" was produced by Samuel Goldwyn as a silent film and later as a talkie; it was the basis of a weekly radio serial that ran for fifteen years. *Now Voyager* was also filmed, starring Bette Davis.†

*   *   *

PUDNEY, John (Sleigh)   1909-

PERSONAL: Born January 19, 1909, in Langley, Buckinghamshire, England; son of Harry William and Mabel (Sleigh) Pudney; married Crystal Herbert, 1934 (marriage dissolved, 1955); married Monica Grant Forbes Curtis, 1955; children: (first marriage) Charlotte, Jeremy, Teresa. *Education:* Educated at Gresham's School. *Religion:* Church of England. *Home:* 4 Macartney House, Chesterfield Walk, Greenwich Park, London S.E. 10, England. *Agent:* David Higham Associates Ltd., 76 Dean St., London W. 1, England; and Christopher Mann Ltd., 140 Park Lane, London W1Y 4BU, England.

CAREER: Author. British Broadcasting Corp., London, England, writer-producer, 1934-38; *News Chronicle*, London, columnist and feature writer, 1938-39; Evans Brothers Ltd. (publishers), London, executive director, 1950-53; Putnam & Co. Ltd. (publishers), London, director, 1953-63. *Military service:* Royal Air Force, World War II.

WRITINGS: Spring Encounter, Methuen, 1933; *Open the Sky* (poems), Boriswood, 1934, Doubleday, Doran, 1935; *And Lastly the Fireworks* (stories), Broiswood, 1935; *Jacobson's Ladder* (novel), Longmans, Green, 1938; *Uncle Arthur, and Other Stories*, Longmans, Green, 1939.

Dispersal Point, and Other Air Poems, John Lane, 1942; *The Green Grass Grew All Around*, John Lane, 1942; *Beyond This Disregard* (poems), John Lane, 1943; *South of Forty* (poems), John Lane, 1943; *Who Only England Know: Log of a War-time Journey of Unintentional Discovery of Fellow Countrymen*, John Lane, 1943; (editor with Henry Treece) *Air Force Poetry*, John Lane, 1944; *Almanack of Hope: Sonnets*, John Lane, 1944; *Flight Above Cloud*, Harper, 1944; *Ten Summers: Poems 1933-43*, John Lane, 1944; *World Still There*, Hollis & Carter, 1945; *Edna's Fruit Hat, and Other Stories*, Harper, 1946 (published in England as *It Breathed Down My Neck*, John Lane, 1946); *Selected Poems*, Bodley Head, 1947; *Low Life: Verses*, Bodley Head, 1947; *Estuary: A Romance*, Bodley Head, 1947; *The Europeans: Fourteen Tales of the Continent*, Bodley Head, 1948; *Laboratory of the Air: An Account of the Royal Aircraft Establishment of the Ministry of Supply, Farnborough*, H.M.S.O., 1948; *Commemorations* (poems), Bodley Head, 1948; *Shuffley Wanderers: An Entertainment*, Bodley Head, 1948; (editor) *Pick of Today's Short Stories*, Odhams, 1949-52, Putnam & Co., 1953-63.

The Accomplice (novel), Bodley Head, 1950; *Saturday Adventure: A Story for Boys*, Bodley Head, 1950; *Hero of a Summer's Day*, Bodley Head, 1951; *Music on the South Bank: An Appreciation of the Royal Festival Hall*, Parrish, 1951; *Sunday Adventure*, John Lane, 1951; *His Majesty, King George VI: A Study*, Hutchinson, 1952; *Monday Adventure: The Secrets of Blackmead Abbey*, Evans Brothers, 1952; *The Net*, M. Joseph, 1952; *A Ring for Luck*, M. Joseph, 1953; (author of text) *The Queen's People*, photographs by Izis Bidermanas, Harvill, 1953; *Sixpenny Songs*, Bodley Head, 1953; *The Thomas Cook Story*, M. Joseph, 1953; *Tuesday Adventure: A Story for Boys and Girls*, Evans Brothers, 1953; (editor) *Popular Poetry*, News of the World, 1953; *The Smallest Room*, M. Joseph, 1954, Hastings House, 1955, revised edition, M. Joseph, 1959; *Wednesday Adventure*, Evans Brothers, 1954; *Six Great Aviators: A.V. Roe, Alcock and Brown, Lindbergh, Kingsford-Smith, Saint-Exupery, Neville Duke*, Hamish Hamilton, 1955; *Thursday Adventure: The Stolen Airliner*, Evans Brothers, 1955; *Friday Adventure*, Evans Brothers, 1956; (editor) *The Book of Leisure*, Odhams,

1957, Transatlantic, 1958; *Collected Poems*, Putnam & Co., 1957; *The Grandfather Clock*, Hamish Hamilton, 1957; *Trespass in the Sun*, M. Joseph, 1957; *Crossing the Road*, Hamish Hamilton, 1958; *The Seven Skies: A Study of the B.O.A.C. and Its Forerunners Since 1919*, Putnam & Co., 1959; *The Trampoline*, M. Joseph, 1959.

A Pride of Unicorns: Richard and David Atcherley of the R.A.F., Oldbourne, 1960; *Bristol Fashion: Some Accounts of the Earlier Days of Bristol Aviation*, Putnam & Co., 1960; *Home and Away: An Autobiographical Gambit*, M. Joseph, 1960; *Spring Adventure*, Evans Brothers, 1961; *Thin Air*, M. Joseph, 1961; *The Hartwarp Dump*, Hamish Hamilton, 1962; *Summer Adventure*, Evans Brothers, 1962; *The Hartwarp Light Railway*, Hamish Hamilton, 1962; *The Hartwarp Circus*, Hamish Hamilton, 1963; *The Hartwarp Balloon*, Hamish Hamilton, 1963; (compiler) *The Harp Book of Toasts*, Harp Lager, 1963; *The Hartwarp Bakehouse*, Hamish Hamilton, 1964; *Autumn Adventure*, Evans Brothers, 1964; *The Camel Fighter*, Hamish Hamilton, 1964; *The Hartwarp Explosion*, Hamish Hamilton, 1965; *Winter Adventure*, Evans Brothers, 1965; (author of introduction) *The Batsford Colour Book of London*, Batsford, 1965, Sportshelf, 1966; *Tunnel to the Sky*, Hamish Hamilton, 1965; *Spill Out: Poems and Ballads*, Dent, 1967; *The Golden Age of Steam*, Hamish Hamilton, 1967; (editor with Norman Hidden and Michael Johnson) *Writers' Workshop*, Writers' Workshop, 1967; *The Hartwarp Jets*, Hamish Hamilton, 1967; (editor) *Flight and Flying*, David White, 1968; *Suez: De Lesseps' Canal*, Dent, 1968, Praeger, 1969; *Spandrels: Poems and Ballads*, Dent, 1969.

Take This Orange (poems and ballads), Dent, 1971; *The Long Time Growing Up* (novel), Dent, 1971; *A Draught of Contentment*, New English Library, 1971.

WORK IN PROGRESS: Crossing the River, a survey of the bridges, tunnels, and ferries across the Thames tideway, for Dent.

BIOGRAPHICAL/CRITICAL SOURCES: Times Literary Supplement, October 5, 1967; *Books and Bookmen*, April, 1968.

*   *   *

PUNDEFF, Marin   1921-

PERSONAL: Born in Sofia, Bulgaria, November 7, 1921; now U.S. citizen; married, 1947; children: Christina, Michael. *Education:* University of Southern California, B.A., 1949, Ph.D., 1958; George Washington University, M.A., 1955. *Politics:* Democrat. *Religion:* Eastern Orthodox. *Home:* 8029 Lurline Ave., Canoga Park, Calif. 91306. *Office:* San Fernando Valley State College, Northridge, Calif. 91324.

CAREER: With consular office, Bulgarian Political Mission to U.S., 1945-47; Library of Congress, Washington, D.C., legal analyst in East European law, 1950-55; Los Angeles State College, Los Angeles, Calif., assistant director in charge of library, International Communications Library Project, 1957-58; San Fernando Valley State College, Northridge, Calif., 1958—, now professor of history. Consultant to Slavic and Central European Division, Library of Congress. *Member:* American Historical Association, American Association for the Advancement of Slavic Studies, American Association of University Professors, Sudosteuropa-Gesellschaft (Munich).

WRITINGS: (Editor and translator) *Communist History: Its Theory and Practice*, College Bookstore, San Fernando Valley State College, 1962, reissued as *History in the U.S.S.R.: Selected Readings*, Chandler Publishing, 1967; (compiler) *Recent Publications on Communism: A Bibliography of Non-Periodical Literature, 1957-1962*, Research Institute on Communist Strategy and Propaganda,

University of Southern California, 1962; *Bulgaria: A Bibliographic Guide,* Slavic and Central European Division, Reference Department, Library of Congress, 1965, Arno, 1969.

Contributor: Vladimir Gsovski and Kazimierz Grzybowski, editors, *Government, Law and Courts in the Soviet Union and Eastern Europe,* two volumes, Praeger, 1959; Stephen A. Fischer-Galati, editor, *Eastern Europe in the Sixties,* Praeger, 1963; Peter Frigyes Sugar and I.J. Lederer, editors, *Nationalism in Eastern Europe,* University of Washington Press, 1969. Contributor to *American Historical Review, American Journal of International Law, Slavic Review, Revue des Etudes Slaves, East European Quarterly,* and other publications.

SIDELIGHTS: Pundeff is competent in French, German, Italian, Russian, and Bulgarian.

* * *

PUSEY, Merlo John 1902-

PERSONAL: Born February 3, 1902, in Woodruff, Utah; son of John Sidney and Nellie (Quibell) Pusey; married Dorothy Richards, 1928; children: C. Richards, David R., John R. *Education:* University of Utah, A.B. *Home address:* Route 2, Dickerson, Md. 20753. *Office: Washington Post,* 1515 L St., Washington, D.C. 20005.

CAREER: *Deseret News,* Salt Lake City, Utah, reporter and assistant editor, 1922-28; *Washington Post,* Washington, D.C., editorial writer, 1928—, associate editor, 1946. Part-time instructor in journalism, George Washington University, 1939-42. Occasional expert for majority, U.S. Senate Finance Committee, 1931-33. *Member:* American Political Science Association, American Association for the Advancement of Science. *Awards, honors:* D. Litt., Brigham Young University; Pulitzer Prize for biography, 1952, for *Charles Evans Hughes;* Bancroft Award, 1952; Tamiment Institute Award, 1952; Distinguished Alumni award, University of Utah, 1958; American Bar Association Gavel Award, 1960.

WRITINGS: *The District Crisis,* privately printed, 1937; *The Supreme Court Crisis,* Macmillan, 1937; *Big Government: Can We Control It?,* Harper, 1945; *Charles Evans Hughes* (authorized biography), two volumes, Macmillan, 1951; *Eisenhower, the President,* Macmillan, 1956; *The Way We Go to War,* Houghton, 1969; *The U.S.A. Astride the Globe,* Houghton, 1971.

Contributor: Allison Dunham and Philip B. Kurland, editors, *Mr. Justice,* University of Chicago Press, 1956; James Morgan, *Our Presidents: Brief Biographies of Our Chief Magistrates from Washington to Eisenhower,* 2nd edition, Macmillan, 1958; Allan Nevins, editor, *Times of Trial,* Knopf, 1958. Contributor to most of the national magazines.

SIDELIGHTS: In a review of *The Way We Go to War,* Senator J. William Fulbright praises Pusey's work, stating that Pusey uses "direct and pungent prose reminiscent of the best pamphleteering of our own Revolutionary days," and describes the book as "journalism at its provocative best."

BIOGRAPHICAL/CRITICAL SOURCES: *Washington Post,* May 20, 1969; *New York Times Book Review,* November 16, 1969.

* * *

PUTNAM, Arnold Oscar 1922-

PERSONAL: Born September 24, 1922, in Springfield, Vt.; son of Solon James (a businessman) and Stella K. (Rice) Putnam; married Dorothy A. Slater, August 4, 1945; children: Timothy, Pamela, Tyler. *Education:* Lehigh University, B.S. in Industrial Engineering, 1943;

Massachusetts Institute of Technology, M.S., 1947. *Politics:* Independent. *Religion:* Protestant. *Home:* 16 Plimpton Rd., West Newton, Mass. 02165.

CAREER: Registered professional engineer. Rath & Strong, Inc. (management consultants), Boston, Mass., 1950—, now vice-president and director. *Military service:* U.S. Army, Ordnance, World War II; became captain; received Bronze Star, European Theatre Medal, and five battle stars. *Member:* American Management Association, American Production and Inventory Control Society.

WRITINGS: (With E. Robert Barlow and Gabriel N. Stilian) *Unified Operations Management: A Practical Approach to the Total Systems Concept,* McGraw, 1963. Contributor of articles to professional journals.

WORK IN PROGRESS: A book, *Competitive Management During a Transition to the Computer Age.*

* * *

PUTZEL, Max 1910-

PERSONAL: Born April 5, 1910, in Denver, Colo.; son of Henry V. and Helen (Renard) Putzel; married second wife, Marion Richardson; children: nine. *Education:* Yale University, A.B., 1932, Ph.D., 1958; Washington University, St. Louis, Mo., A.M., 1953. *Politics:* Democrat. *Religion:* Episcopalian. *Home:* Chaplin, Conn. 06235. *Office:* Box U-25, University of Connecticut, U-6, Storrs, Conn. 06235.

CAREER: *St. Louis Post-Dispatch,* St. Louis, Mo., staff writer and drama editor, 1934-38; *Common Sense* (magazine), New York, N.Y., associate editor, 1939-42; Duell, Sloan & Pearce, Inc., New York, N.Y., associate editor, 1939-42; special correspondent in Europe, 1937-38; Office of Inter-American Affairs, administrative aide, 1942-45; farmer in Missouri, 1946-54; Washington University, St. Louis, Mo., instructor, 1952-55; University of Connecticut, Storrs, assistant professor, 1957-64, assistant dean of graduate school, 1963-70, associate professor of English, 1964—. *Member:* Modern Language Association of America, English Institute, Graduates Club (New Haven).

WRITINGS: *The Man in the Mirror: William Marion Reedy and His Magazine,* Harvard University Press, 1963; (editor and author of introduction and notes) Sir Philip Sidney, *Astrophil and Stella,* Doubleday, 1967.

Contributor: John Paul Runden, editor, *Melville's Benito Cereno: A Text for Guided Research,* Heath, 1965; Seymour Lee Gross, editor, *A Benito Cereno Handbook,* Wadsworth, 1965.

WORK IN PROGRESS: Articles on Melville, Hawthorne, and Faulkner for a symposium on the Gothic in American literature.

* * *

QUASTEN, Johannes 1900-

PERSONAL: Born May 3, 1900, in Homberg, Germany; came to United States in 1938, naturalized in 1944; son of Wilhelm and Sibilla (Schmitz) Quasten. *Education:* University of Muenster, Dr. Theol., 1927; Pontifical Institute of Christian Archaeology, Rome, postdoctoral study, 1927-29. *Home and office:* Catholic University of America, Washington, D.C. 20017.

CAREER: Ordained to Roman Catholic priesthood, 1926; University of Muenster, Muenster, Westphalia, Germany, assistant professor of ancient church history and Christian archaeology, 1931-37; Catholic University of America, Washington, D.C., associate professor, 1938-41, Eugene Kelley Professor of Ecclesiastical History, 1941-70, professor emeritus, 1970—, dean of faculty of theology, 1945-49. Honorary professor, University of

Freiburg, 1970. Member, Pontificia Commissio de Sacra Liturgia Praeparatoria Concilii Vaticani II. *Member:* North American Patristic Society (honorary), American Theological Association, Catholic Commission on Intellectual and Cultural Affairs, Association Internationale d'Etudes Patristiques, Catholic Theological Society of America, Catholic Historical Association, American Benedictine Academy, Henry Bradshaw Society (London; vice-president), Oxford Historical Society, Ildefons Herwegen Institute for Liturgical Research (honorary). *Awards, honors:* Cardinal Spellman Award, Theological Society of America, 1960.

WRITINGS: Musik und Gesang in den Kulten der heidnischen Antike und christlichen Fruehzeit, Aschendorff, 1930, 2nd revised edition, 1973; *Expositio antiquae liturgiae gallicanae,* Aschendorff, 1934; *Monumenta eucharistica et liturgica,* seven volumes, Hanstein, 1935-37; *The Beginnings of Patristic Literature,* Newman, 1950; *The Ante-Nicene Literature after Irenaeus,* Newman, 1953; *Initiation aux peres de l'eglise,* three volumes, Editions ·du Cerf, 1955, 1957, 1962; *The Golden Age of Greek Patristic Literature,* Newman, 1960; *Patrologia I: Hasta el concilio de Nicea,* Editorial Catolica, 1961, revised edition, 1968; *The Golden Age of Latin Patristic Literature,* Newman, 1960; *Patrologia II: La Literature patristica griega,* revised edition, Editorial Catolica, 1972.

Contributor: *Heilige Ueberlieferung: Festgabe I. Herwegen,* Aschendorff, 1938; *Pisciculi: Festschrift F.J. Doelger,* Aschendorff 1939; *Miscellanea Giovanni Mercati,* Bibliotheca Apost Vaticana, 1946; *Paschatis Sollemnia: Festschrift J.A. Jungmann,* Herder Verlag, 1959. Also contributor to *Miscellanea Liturgica C. Mohlberg,* 1948; *Melanges J. De Gellinck,* 1951; *Festgabe Georg Schrieber,* 1953; *Memorial Gustave Bardy,* 1956; *Festgabe Berthold Altaner,* 1958; *Liturgie, Gestalt und Vollzug: Festschrift Joseph Pascher,* 1963; *Miscellanea Giacomo Lecaro,* 1966.

Founder and editor of *Studies in Christian Antiquity,* twenty volumes, 1941—, and *Ancient Christian Writers,* forty volumes, 1946—. Co-editor of *Volkskundliche Quellen,* 1935—, *Stromata patristica et mediaevalia,* 1950—, *Vom christlichen mysterium,* Patmos, 1951, and *Liturgiewissenschaftliche Quellen und Forschungen,* fifty-five volumes, 1956—. Contributor to *Encyclopaedia Britannica, Twentieth Century Encyclopedia of Religious Knowledge, Encyclopedia of Literature, Reallexikon fuer Antike und Christentum, New Catholic Encyclopedia, Lexikon fuer Theologie und Kirche, Religion in Geschichte und Gegenwart,* and *Sacramentum Mundi.* Contributor of more than one hundred and fifty articles on historical, theological, liturgical, and archaeological subjects to professional journals in United States, Italy, Germany, Austria, Belgium, France, and Holland. Member of editorial board, *Viator, Medieval and Renaissance Studies,* 1970—.

WORK IN PROGRESS: The Golden Age of Latin Patristic Literature.

SIDELIGHTS: Quasten has travelled widely in America, Europe and North Africa, to archaeological excavations, libraries, and universities.

BIOGRAPHICAL/CRITICAL SOURCES: P. Granfield, editor, *Theologians at Work,* Macmillan, 1967; P. Granfield and J.A. Jungmann, editors, *Kyriakon: Festschrift Johannes Quasten,* Aschendorff, 1970; *Kuerschners Deutscher Gelehrten-Kalender,* Walter de Gruyter, 1971.

*   *   *

QUIGG, Philip W.   1920-

PERSONAL: Born October 30, 1920, in New York, N.Y.; son of Murray Townsend (a lawyer) and Eleanor (Wisner) Quigg. *Education:* Princeton University, A.B. (with high honors), 1943. *Office: Foreign Affairs,* 58 East 68th St., New York, N.Y. 10021.

CAREER: Macy Newspapers, Westchester County, N.Y., reporter, 1946-47; Princeton University, Princeton, N.J., editorial administrator, 1947-51, editor of *Princeton Alumni Weekly,* 1951-55; *Foreign Affairs,* New York, N.Y., editor 1955—. *Military service:* U.S. Army, Military Intelligence, 1943-46; became master sergeant. *Member:* Council on Foreign Relations, Lotos Club. *Awards, honors:* Sibley Award of American Alumni Council, 1953, for best alumni magazine of the year.

WRITINGS: (Editor) *Africa: A Foreign Affairs Reader,* Praeger, 1964; *South Africa: Problems and Prospects,* Council on Religion and International Affairs, 1965; *America, the Dutiful: An Assessment of U.S. Foreign Policy,* Simon & Schuster, 1971. Contributor of articles on international affairs to periodicals.

*   *   *

QUIN, Ann (Marie)   1936-1973

PERSONAL: Born March 17, 1936, in Brighton, Sussex, England; daughter of Nicholas Montague (former opera singer) and Ann (Reid) Quin. *Education:* Convent of the Blessed Sacrament, Brighton, Sussex. *Politics:* None. *Religion:* None. *Address:* c/o Calder & Boyars Ltd., 18 Brewer St., London W.1, England.

CAREER: Secretary to foreign rights manager, Hutchinson & Co., London, England, two and one half years; manuscript reader for New Authors, Ltd., 1956-58; Royal College of Art, London, secretary to Professor Corel Weight, 1960-62. *Member:* L.A.M.D.A. Theatre Club, P.E.N., Academy Cinema Club. *Awards, honors:* Harkness Commonwealth fellowship, 1965; D.H. Lawrence fellowship.

WRITINGS: Berg (novel), J. Calder, 1964, Scribner, 1965; *Three* (novel), Scribner, 1966; *Passages* (novel), Calder & Boyars, 1969; *Tripticks,* illustrated by Carol Annand, Calder & Boyers, 1972.

SIDELIGHTS: Miss Quin wrote to *CA:* "Interested very much in philosophy and psychology which have been periodically studied on my own. Painting also. Francis Bacon a great influence on my work as a writer, together with the nouvelle vague movement in the cinema."

BIOGRAPHICAL/CRITICAL SOURCES: Times Literary Supplement, June 25, 1964; *New York Times Book Review,* October 31, 1965, October 9, 1966; *Choice,* July, 1967; *Poetry,* August, 1968; *London Magazine,* June, 1969.

(Died, 1973)

*   *   *

QUINN, Francis X.   1932-

PERSONAL: Born June 9, 1932, in Dunmore, Pa.; son of Frank T. (a coal miner) and Alice (Maher) Quinn. *Education:* Fordham University, A.B., 1957, M.A., 1958; Woodstock College, S.T.B., 1964. *Agent:* J. William Echenrode, Box 182, Westminster, Md. 21157.

CAREER: Ordained Roman Catholic priest, member of Society of Jesus, 1963. Georgetown Preparatory School, Garrett Park, Md., teacher, 1957-60; Georgetown University, Washington, D.C., lecturer in social ethics, 1962—. Director of Institute of Social Ethics, Catholic University of America, Washington, D.C. *Awards, honors:* Teacher of Year award from Freedoms Foundation, 1959.

WRITINGS: (Editor) *The Ethical Aftermath of Automation,* Newman, 1962; (editor) *Ethics, Advertising, and Responsibility,* Canterbury, 1963; (editor) *Population Ethics,* Corpus Publications, 1968. Contributor of articles to *Social Order* and *Social Justice Review*. Editor, "Ethical Aftermath" series, Woodstock College.

WORK IN PROGRESS: Poverty Amidst Plenty; and *The Ethical Aftermath of Population Explosion.*

BIOGRAPHICAL/CRITICAL SOURCES: Scranton Times, February 8, 1962.

* * *

QUINTANILLA, Maria Aline Griffith y Dexter, Condesa de 1921-
(Countess of Romanones)

PERSONAL: Born May 22, 1921, in Pearl River, N.Y.; daughter of William F. (in real estate) and Marie (Dexter) Griffith; married Luis Figueroa y Perez de Guzman el Bueno (an artist); children: Alvaro, Luis, Miguel. *Education:* College of Mont St. Vincent, B.A. *Religion:* Catholic. *Home:* Castellon de la Plana 23, Madrid 6, Spain. *Agent:* Julian Bach, Jr., 3 East 48th St., New York, N.Y. 10017.

CAREER: Worked for the office of Strategic Services in wartime Spain. Now Spanish representative of *Vogue* magazine. President of school for poor children in Madrid, Spain; director of Cancer Fund of Spain. *Awards, honors:* Lazo de Dama of Isobel; decoration of the Venezuelan Institute of Hispanic Culture.

WRITINGS: The Story of Pascualete, J. Murray, 1963, published in America as *The Earth Rests Lightly,* Holt, 1964. Contributor to *Estudios Extremenos.*

WORK IN PROGRESS: Book on espionage in Spain during World War II; a historical biography on the half-sister of Isobel the Catholic.

BIOGRAPHICAL/CRITICAL SOURCES: New York Herald Tribune, May 25, 1964; *Life,* October 2, 1964; *New York Times,* December 4, 1964.

* * *

RAFFEL, Burton 1928-

PERSONAL: Surname is pronounced Raf-*fel;* born April 27, 1928; son of Harry L. (a lawyer) and Rose (Karr) Raffel; children: Brian, Blake (deceased), Stefan, Kezia, Shifra. *Education:* Brooklyn College (now Brooklyn College of the City University of New York), B.A., 1948; Ohio State University, M.A., 1949; Yale University, J.D., 1958. *Home:* 337 Albany Ave., Toronto, Ontario, Canada. *Agent:* Hy Cohen, Robert Lantz-Candida Donadio Literary Agency, Inc., 111 West 57th St., New York, N.Y. 10019. *Office:* Humanities Division, York University, Downsview, Ontario, Canada.

CAREER: Brooklyn College (now Brooklyn College of the City University of New York), Brooklyn, N.Y., fellow and lecturer, Department of English, 1950-51; Ford Foundation English Language Teaching Program, Makassar, Indonesia, instructor to Indonesian teachers of English, 1953-55; Milbank, Tweed, Hadley & McCloy (attorneys), New York, N.Y., attorney, 1958-60; Foundation Library Center, New York, N.Y., editor of *Foundation News,* 1960-63; State University of New York at Stony Brook, instructor, 1964-65, assistant professor of English, 1965-66; State University of New York at Buffalo, associate professor of English, 1966-68; University of Texas, Austin, visiting professor, 1969-70, professor of English and classics, and chairman of graduate program in comparative literature, 1970-71; Ontario College of Art, Toronto, senior tutor (dean), 1971-72. Visiting professor of English, Haifa University, Haifa, Israel, 1968-69; visiting professor of humanities, York University, Toronto, Ontario, 1972-73. *Awards, honors:* Two American Philosophical Society grants for a study of modern Indonesian poetry, 1964.

WRITINGS: (With Robert Creeley, Joseph Slotkin, and Matthew Carney) *Short Story 3,* Scribner, 1960; *The Development of Modern Indonesian Poetry,* State University of New York Press, 1967; *Mia Poems,* October House, 1968; *The Forked Tongue: A Study of the Translation Process,* Mouton & Co., 1971; *Introduction to Poetry,* New American Library, 1971; *Why Re-Create?,* National Humanities Faculty (Concord, Mass.), in press.

Translator: (And author of introduction) *Poems from the Old English,* University of Nebraska Press, 1960, 2nd edition, 1964; (and author of introduction) *Beowulf,* New American Library, 1963, reissued with an afterword by Raffel, University of Massachusetts Press, 1971; (with Nurdin Salam) *Chairil Anwar: Selected Poems,* New Directions, 1963; (and editor) *An Anthology of Modern Indonesian Poetry,* University of California Press, 1964, revised edition, State University of New York Press, 1968; (and editor and author of introduction) *From the Vietnamese: 10 Centuries of Poetry,* October House, 1968, (and editor and author of introduction) *The Complete Poetry and Prose of Chairil Anwar,* State University of New York Press, 1970; (and author of introduction) *Sir Gawain and the Green Knight,* New American Library, 1970; (and compiler and author of introduction and notes) *Russian Poetry Under the Tsars: An Anthology,* State University of New York Press, 1971; (and editor) *Poems: An Anthology,* New American Library, 1971; (with Alla Burago) *Selected Works of Nikolai S. Gumilev,* State University of New York Press, 1972; (with Burago) *Complete Poetry of Osip Emilievitch Mandelstam,* State University of New York Press, in press; (and author of introduction) *Lyrics from the Greek,* Coach House Press, in press; *Selected Odes, Epodes, Satires, and Epistles of Horace,* New American Library, in press; (and author of introduction) *Horace: Ars Poetica,* State University of New York Press, in press; (with Harry Aveling, and author of introduction) *Selected Poetry of W.S. Rendra,* Oxford University Press (Kuala Lumpur), in press. Contributor of articles, short stories, poetry, and criticism to *Hudson Review, Virginia Quarterly Review, London Magazine, Prairie Schooner, Saturday Review, Yale Review, Historian, Fantasy and Science Fiction,* and other literary reviews; contributor of articles to legal journals.

WORK IN PROGRESS: A novel, *Emmaline,* a book of poems, *Four Humors,* and a translation from the Catalan, *La Pell de Brau,* by Salvador Espriu, all completed and awaiting publication; two novels, *The True Adventures of Gawain, Knight of the Round Table,* and *Zikaron* (title means "Remember"); a bibliographical handbook, *Guide to Paperback Translations in the Humanities,* for the National Humanities Faculty; translations, with Alla Burago, of *Selected Poems of Alexander Pushkin,* and *Complete Poetry of Anna Akhmatova;* translation, with Noam Flinker, of *Selected Poems of Yehuda Amichai;* translation of *Selected Poems of Heinrich Heine;* editing and writing introduction for *Selected Works of A.E. Housman,* to be published by New American Library.

SIDELIGHTS: Raffel told *CA:* "In the next ten years or so, I propose to translate Dante and maybe Propertius; to write much more fiction, and perhaps more poetry (though I now feel much more at home with prose); to turn out an edition of Wordsworth's *Poem to Coleridge*—better known as *The Prelude*—which will scandalize scholars and please students and their teachers; and to do such other writing as comes my way. I am still waiting for the composer with whom I can do an opera."

Raffel has recorded, with Robert P. Creed, "Lyrics from the Old English," for Folkways Records.

BIOGRAPHICAL/CRITICAL SOURCES: New Leader, April 14, 1969; *Virginia Quarterly Review,* summer, 1969; *Books Abroad,* winter, 1969.

* * *

RAGO, Louis J (oseph von) 1924-
(Louis [Joseph] von Rago)

PERSONAL: Born March 17, 1924, in Budapest, Hungary; came to United States in 1947, naturalized in 1953; married Viorica S. Tymczuk, December 31, 1969; children: Tommy, Vicky, Lou, Larry, Hermine-Angela. *Education:* Hunfalvy College, University of Budapest, B.B.A., 1942, graduate work, 1942-43; Munich Institute of Technology, M.S., 1945; University of Chicago, M.B.A., 1950; University of Munich, Ph.D. (magna cum laude), 1954. *Home:* 2 Normandy, Champaign, Ill. 61802. *Office:* Commerce West, University of Illinois, Urbana, Ill. 61803.

CAREER: U.S. Army, civilian employee in European theater, 1945-46; University of Toledo, Toledo, Ohio, instructor in management, 1949-50; University of Notre Dame, Notre Dame, Ind., assistant professor of management, 1951-52; Marquette University, Milwaukee, Wis., assistant professor of management, 1952-54; University of Rhode Island, Kingston, associate professor of management, 1954-55; Duquesne University, Pittsburgh, Pa., professor of management, 1955-64; University of Illinois, Urbana, associate professor of industrial management, 1964—. Free-lance management consultant. Visiting professor, Valparaiso University, summer, 1951, University of Karlsruhe, summer, 1968. *Member:* American Management Association, Academy of Management, Society for the Advancement of Management, American Association of University Professors, Beta Gamma Sigma.

WRITINGS: Industrial Management (lecture series), University of Munich, 1954; *Kostensenkung durch Rationalisierung in U.S.A.: Management, Rationalisierung, Kostensenkung,* Carl Hanser Verlag, 1958; *Production Analysis and Control,* International Textbook Co., 1963; *Guide to Case and Project Analysis,* International Textbook Co., 1964; *Casebook in Production Management,* International Textbook Co., 1967; *Operations Research in der Productions praxis,* Gabler Verlag, 1970; *Mathematische Modelle der Programmierung,* Max Gehlen Verlag, 1971. Contributor of more than fifty articles on management, production, industrial engineering, and operations research to foreign and domestic journals.

WORK IN PROGRESS: International Plant Management.

SIDELIGHTS: Rago was a member of the all-American water polo team, 1950-51.

* * *

RAISTRICK, Arthur 1896-

PERSONAL: Born August 16, 1896, in Saltaire, Yorkshire, England; son of George (an engineer) and Minnie (Bell) Raistrick; married Sarah Elizabeth Chapman, April, 1929. *Education:* Attended Bradford Grammar School; University of Leeds, B.Sc. in C.E., 1922, M.Sc. in C.E., 1923, B.Sc. in Geology (with honors), 1923, Ph.D., 1925. *Politics:* Socialist. *Religion:* Quaker. *Home:* Home Croft, Linton near Skipton, Yorkshire, England.

CAREER: Workers' Educational Association, North of England, tutor-lecturer, 1921-63; University of Durham, Durham, England, tutor in university extra-mural department, and lecturer and reader in applied geology in department of mining and civil engineering, 1929-56; University of Leeds, Leeds, England, tutor in university extra-mural department, 1956—. National Parks committee, member of Yorkshire Dales group, 1955—, and of national standing committee. *Member:* Institute of Mining Engineers, Geological Society, Newcomen Society, Yorkshire Naturalists Union (former president), Yorkshire Archaeological Society (council member), Yorkshire Geological Society (council member), Ramblers' Association (president, northern section; national vice-president). *Awards, honors:* Lyell Award of Geological Society; Clough Medal of Edinburgh Geological Society for work on coal.

WRITINGS: Two Centuries of Industrial Welfare: The London (Quaker) Lead Company, 1692-1905, Friends' Historical Society, 1938; (with C.E. Marshall) *The Nature and Origin of Coal and Coal Seams,* English Universities Press, 1939; *Teach Yourself Geology,* English Universities Press, 1943, Roy, 1956; *The Story of the Pennine Walls,* Dalesman Publishing Co., 1946; *Malhamdale,* Dalesman Publishing Co., 1946; *Malham and Malham Moor,* Dalesman Publishing Co., 1947; *Grassington and Upper Wharfedale,* Dalesman Publishing Co., 1948; *Silver and Lead: The Story of a Quaker Mining Experiment,* Friends' Home Service Committee, 1948; *The Story of Bolton Priory,* Dalesman Publishing Co., 1949; (with J.L. Illingworth) *The Face of North-West Yorkshire,* Dalesman Publishing Co., 1949, 2nd edition published as *The Face of North-West Yorkshire. Geology and Natural Vegetation,* 1967; *Quakers in Science and Industry: Being an Account of the Quaker Contributions to Science and Industry During the 17th and 18th Centuries,* Bannisdale Press, 1950, reissued with new introduction, Augustus M. Kelley, 1968; *Dynasty of Iron Founders: The Darbys and Coalbrookdale,* Longmans, Green, 1953, Augustus M. Kelley, 1970; *The Calamine Mines, Malham, Yorks,* University of Durham Philosophical Society, 1954; *Mines and Miners of Swaledale,* Dalesman Publishing Co., 1955; *The Romans in Yorkshire,* Dalesman Publishing Co., 1960; *Yorkshire and the North-East,* Oliver & Boyd, 1963; *Prehistoric Yorkshire,* Dalesman Publishing Co., 1964; *A History of Lead Mining in the Pennines,* Longmans, Green, 1965; *Vikings, Angles and Danes in Yorkshire,* Dalesman Publishing Co., 1966; (editor and contributor) *North York Moors,* H.M.S.O., 1966; (editor and author of introduction) Charles Hatchett, *The Hatchett Diary: A Tour Through the Counties of England and Scotland in 1796, Visiting Their Mines and Manufactories,* Barton, 1967; *The Pennine Dales,* Eyre & Spottiswoode, 1968; *Old Yorkshire Dales,* Augustus M. Kelley, 1968; *Ice Age in Yorkshire,* Dalesman Publishing Co., 1968; *Yorkshire Maps and Map-Makers,* Dalesman Publishing Co., 1969; *West Riding of Yorkshire,* Hodder & Stoughton, 1970; (editor) *A Century's Progress: Yorkshire Industry and Commerce,* Brenton Publishing, 1971; *Industrial Archaeology: An Historical Survey,* Barnes & Noble, 1972.

Contributor: George Sweeting, editor, *The Geology of the Yorkshire Dales,* Geologists' Association (London), 1933; George Sweeting, editor, *The Geology of the Country Around Harrogate,* Geologists' Association, 1938; H.M. Abrahams, editor, *Britain's National Parks,* Country Life, 1959, Transatlantic, 1959; Kenneth Hudson, *Industrial Archaeology: An Introduction,* J. Baker, 1963. Contributor of more than one hundred research papers on geology, mining, and archaeology to technical journals.

AVOCATIONAL INTERESTS: Rambling, youth hostelry, and natural and industrial history in the north of England.†

RAMGE, Sebastian Victor 1930-

PERSONAL: Surname is pronounced Ram-gee; born May 21, 1930, in Milwaukee, Wis.; son of Victor Herbert and Ottilia (Hausler) Ramge. Education: Attended Christian Brothers College, Memphis, Tenn.; Mount Carmel College, Washington, D.C., M.A.; Institute of Spirituality, Rome, Italy, postgraduate study. Home address: Rt. 5, Box 87, Ridge Rd., Covington, Ga. 30209. Office address: P.O. Box 792, Altoona, Pa. 16603.

CAREER: Roman Catholic priest, member of Discalced Carmelite Order; previously teacher of spiritual theology in Washington, D.C., and of Latin, French, and German at St. Joseph Seminary, Peterborough, N.H.; Spiritual Life (quarterly), editor, 1961-66; worked in Israel, 1966-67, and in Kuwait, 1969; Pennsylvania State University, Altoona, Catholic chaplin, 1970—. Former director of a halfway house for rehabilitation of teenage boys. Vice-postulator for canonization cause of Pope Blessed Innocent XI. Member: Middle East Institute, American Academy of Religion, Monarchist League, Forum for Contemporary History, Georgia Historical Society, All-state Travel Club.

WRITINGS: St. Florian Parish, [Milwaukee], 1961; An Introduction to the Writings of St. Teresa, Regnery, 1963; (translator) Albinus Marchetti, Spirituality and the States of Life, Spiritual Life, 1963; (translator from the French) Father Gabriel, From Sacred Heart to Trinity, Spiritual Life, 1965. Contributor to New Catholic Encyclopedia and Encyclopedia Hebraica, and of articles and book reviews to other publications. Translator of Italian, French, German, and Latin works.

WORK IN PROGRESS: A biography of Pope Blessed Innocent XI (1611-1689); various research projects.

SIDELIGHTS: Ramge is competent in Latin, French, German, Italian, and Spanish, and has some facility in Hebrew, Greek, and Arabic.

* * *

RAMQUIST, Grace (Bess) Chapman 1907-

PERSONAL: Born October 8, 1907, in Durant, Okla.; daughter of James Blaine (a minister) and Maud (Frederick) Chapman; married A.E. Ramquist (a publisher's representative), December 25, 1929 (deceased); children: Gloria Ramquist Willingham, John Thomas. Education: William Jewell College, B.A., 1927; graduate study at University of Kansas and Central Missouri State College. Politics: Republican. Religion: Church of the Nazarene. Home: 6555 Holmes St., Kansas City, Mo. 64131.

CAREER: Lillenas Publishing Co., Kansas City, Mo., program editor, 1943—; Zondervan Publishing House, Grand Rapids, Mich., program editor, 1952—; kindergarten teacher in Stilwell, Kan., 1960-64, Kansas City, Mo., 1964—. Member: Missouri State Teachers Association, Kansas City Education Association.

WRITINGS: Skits and Readings for Church and School, Zondervan, Book One, 1946, Book Two, 1954, Book Three, 1957 (compiler) The Wit and Wisdom of J.B. Chapman, Unusual Stories Dr. Chapman Told, Zondervan, 1948; And Many Believed (missal study book), Nazarene Publishing, 1951; Let Us Adore Him (Christmas service), Lillenas, 1952; Teen-Age Etiquette, Zondervan, 1953; The Conqueror (Easter service), Lillenas, 1953; The King is Coming (Easter service), Lillenas, 1955; The Boy of Old Illinois, Beacon Hill, 1956; The Boy with the Stammering Tongue, Beacon Hill, 1957; The Boy Who Made Right Choices, Beacon Hill, 1958; The Boy Who Wanted to Preach, Beacon Hill, 1959; (compiler) Choice Readings for Banquets and Other Occasions, Zondervan, 1959; The Boy with the Singing Heart, Beacon Hill, 1960; The Boy with Many Problems, Beacon Hill, 1961; (compiler) Mother-Daughter Banquets, Zondervan, 1961; The Boy Who Moved West, Beacon Hill, 1962; No Respector of Persons (missal study book), Nazarene Publishing, 1962; The Boy Who Loved School, Beacon Hill, 1963; (compiler) Complete Christmas Programs, Zondervan, Volume I, 1964, Volume II, 1968, Volume III, 1970, Volume IV, 1972; We Seek Only Jesus (Easter service), Lillenas, 1969; Under the Banyan Tree, Nazarene Publishing, 1969. Compiler of forty-five program handbooks for Christmas, Easter, and for other special days and age groups published by Lillenas, 1943-64.

WORK IN PROGRESS: Compiling Volume IV of Complete Christmas Programs.

* * *

RAND, Willard J., Jr. 1913-

PERSONAL: Born January 30, 1913, in North Anson, Me.; son of Willard J. (a farmer) and Bessie (Spaulding) Rand; married, wife's name, Rowena, June 14, 1934; children: Dawn Rosalie Rand Ramm, Joanne Rowena Rand Butler, Carl. Education: Bates College, A.B., 1934; Boston University School of Theology, M.A., 1938, S.T.B., 1939. Home: 5455 North Bond St., Fresno, Calif. 93710.

CAREER: Methodist minister with Maine Annual Conference, 1933-43, California-Nevada Annual Conference, 1943—. Chairman, Christian Vocations Commission, Northern California-Nevada Council of Churches; member of program staff, California-Nevada Methodist Conference, 1959-68. Minister of Education, First United Methodist Church, 1968-70.

WRITINGS: Call and Response: An Enlistment Guide for Church Occupations, Abingdon, 1964; Building the Team, Abingdon, 1970. Contributor to church publications.

* * *

RANDAL, Vera 1922-

PERSONAL: Born May 20, 1922; children: Jonathan Michaels, Ann Randal. Education: Connecticut College, B.A., 1943. Agent: Marie Rodell, 141 East 55th St., New York, N.Y. 10022.

AWARDS, HONORS: Mabel Louise Robertson Award, Columbia University, 1959, for a section of The Inner Room.

WRITINGS: The Inner Room, Knopf, 1964; You Get Used to a Place, Putnam, 1972. Short stories anthologized in The Best American Short Stories, 1964, edited by Martha Foley and David Burnett, Houghton, 1964, and Prize Stories, 1966: The O'Henry Awards, edited by Richard Poirier and William Abrahams, Doubleday, 1966.

WORK IN PROGRESS: A novel about a day in a small private school, tentatively titled The Day a Boy Died.

SIDELIGHTS: Segments of The Inner Room, on which the author spent eight years, on and off, appeared in the New Yorker and Saturday Evening Post.

* * *

RANDALL, Francis Ballard 1931-

PERSONAL: Born December 17, 1931, in New York, N.Y.; son of John Herman, Jr. (a philosopher) and Mercedes (Moritz) Randall; married Laura Rosenbaum (an economist), June 11, 1957. Education: Amherst College, B.A., 1952; Columbia University, M.A., 1954, Ph.D., 1960. Politics: "Ecological." Religion: Infidel. Home: 425 Riverside Dr., New York, N.Y. 10025. Office: Sarah Lawrence College, Bronxville, N.Y. 10708.

CAREER: Amherst College, Amherst, Mass., instructor in history, 1956-59; Columbia University, New York,

1959-61, began as instructor, became assistant professor of history; Sarah Lawrence College, Bronxville, N.Y., member of social science and humanities faculties, 1961—. Visiting professor, Columbia University, 1967-68. Freedom Rider, 1961. *Member:* American Historical Association, American Association of University Professors, American Association for the Advancement of Slavic Studies, Phi Beta Kappa, Chi Phi, Delta Sigma Rho.

WRITINGS: (Editor and author of introduction) Sir Bernard Pares, *Russia: Between Reform and Revolution,* Schocken, 1962; (with John S. Curtiss and others) *Essays in Russian and Soviet History,* Columbia University Press, 1963; (editor and author of introduction) Thomas Hobbes, *Leviathan,* Washington Square Press, 1964; *Stalin's Russia: An Historical Reconsideration,* Free Press, 1965; *N.G. Chernyskevskii,* Twayne, 1967; (editor) *Problems in Russian History,* Pitman, 1971; *Vissarion Belinskii,* Twayne, 1971. Contributor of articles on Russian history, communism, and American race relations to learned journals and journals of opinion.

WORK IN PROGRESS: Chorasmia and the Communists.

BIOGRAPHICAL/CRITICAL SOURCES: Books Abroad, summer, 1968.

*   *   *

RANIS, Gustav   1929-

PERSONAL: Born October 24, 1929, in Darmstadt, Germany; came to U.S., 1943, naturalized, 1952; son of Max (a lawyer) and Bettina (Goldschmidt) Ranis; married Ray Lee Finkelstein (a college teacher), June 15, 1958; children: Michael, Bruce, Alan Jonathan. *Education:* Brandeis University, B.A., 1952; Yale University, M.A., 1953; Ph.D., 1956. *Home:* 7 Mulberry Rd., Woodbridge, Conn. 06525. *Office:* Economic Growth Center, Yale University, 52 Hillhouse Ave., New Haven, Conn. 06520.

CAREER: Ford Foundation, research economist concerned with India, 1957-58, in Pakistan, 1958-59; Institute of Development Economics, Karachi, Pakistan, joint director of research, 1959-61; Yale University, New Haven, Conn., associate professor, 1961-64, professor of economics, 1964-65, associate director of Economic Growth Center, 1961-64; Agency for International Development, assistant administrator, 1965-67, member of advisory committee on economic development to administrator, 165-67; Economic Growth Center, Yale University, director, 1967—. Consultant to Office of Secretary of Treasury, 1957, to subcommittee on Japan, Committee for Economic Development, 1961, to Ford Foundation, 1962. Trustee, Brandeis University, 1968—. *Member:* American Economic Association, Phi Beta Kappa.

WRITINGS: (With John H.C. Fei) *A Study of Planning Methodology with Special Reference to Pakistan's Second Five-Year Plan,* Institute of Development Economics (Karachi), 1960; *Industrial Efficiency and Economic Growth: A Case Study of Karachi,* Institute of Development Economics, 1961; *Urban Consumer Expenditure and the Consumption Function,* Institute of Development Economics, 1961; (with Fei) *Development of the Labor Surplus Economy: Theory and Policy,* Irwin, 1964; (editor and author of introduction) *The United States and the Developing Economies,* Norton, 1964, revised edition, 1973; (with Joan M. Nelson) *Measures to Ensure the Effective Use of Aid,* Office of Program Coordination, Agency for International Development, 1966; (editor) *Government and Economic Development,* Yale University Press, 1971; (editor) *The Gap Between Rich and Poor Nations,* St. Martin's, 1972.

WORK IN PROGRESS: A study of employment, income distribution, and growth in a number of developing countries.

*   *   *

RANSOM, Harry Howe   1922-

PERSONAL: Born May 14, 1922, in Nashville, Tenn.; son of John Bostick, Jr. (in insurance) and Marie Litton (Howe) Ransom; married Nancy Alderman, February 25, 1929; children: Jenny A., Katherine M., William H.H. *Education:* Vanderbilt University, B.A., 1943; Princeton University, M.A., 1948, Ph.D., 1954. *Home:* 511 Belle Meade Blvd., Nashville, Tenn. 37025. *Office:* Department of Political Science, Vanderbilt University, Nashville, Tenn. 37203.

CAREER: Princeton University, Princeton, N.J., part-time instructor in politics, 1947-48; Vassar College, Poughkeepsie, N.Y., instructor in political science, 1948-52; Michigan State University, East Lansing, assistant professor of political science, 1955; Harvard University, Cambridge, Mass., research associate, 1955-61; Vanderbilt University, Nashville, Tenn., associate professor, 1961-64, professor of political science, 1964—, chairman of the department, 1969—. *Military service:* U.S. Army, 1943-45; U.S. Army Reserve, 1947-56; became first lieutenant. *Member:* American Political Science Association, American Association of University Professors, Institute for Strategic Studies (London), Southern Political Science Association. *Awards, honors:* American Political Science Association Congressional fellowship, 1953-54; Rockefeller Foundation research grant, 1964-65.

WRITINGS: Central Intelligence and National Security, Harvard University Press, 1958, revised and enlarged edition published as *The Intelligence Establishment,* 1970; *Can American Democracy Survive Cold War?,* Doubleday, 1963; (editor) *An American Foreign Policy Reader,* Crowell, 1965. Contributor of articles to political science, international affairs, and military journals, and to various encyclopedias.

WORK IN PROGRESS: A study of the impact of technology on presidential decision making of foreign and defense policy in the United States.

BIOGRAPHICAL/CRITICAL SOURCES: New York Review of Books, January 1, 1970; *Virginia Quarterly Review,* winter, 1971.

*   *   *

RANSOM, Jay Ellis   1914-
(Henry T. Adams)

PERSONAL: Born April 12, 1914, in Missoula, Mont.; son of Jay George (a doctor and bookbinder) and Lucy Sophia (a teacher; maiden name, Adams) Ransom; married Barbara Elizabeth Callarman, July 31, 1936; married second wife, Wilhelmina Johanna Buitelaar (an artist and writer), December 28, 1960; children: (first marriage) Jay Frederick, Alix-Gay (Mrs. Leroy Harper); (second marriage) Scott Pieter, Lisa Johanna (adopted), Stuart Cornelis. *Education:* University of Washington, B.A. (honors), 1935, graduate study, 1936-41; additional graduate study at University of California, 1943-48, and Northrop Institute, 1950-51. *Politics:* "Nominal Republican." *Religion:* Presbyterian. *Home and office address:* P.O. Box 616, Etna, Calif. 96027. *Agent:* Ann Elmo Agency, Inc., 52 Vanderbilt Ave., New York, N.Y. 10017.

CAREER: Free-lance writer, 1927-36; U.S. Office of Indian Affairs, Nikolski, Umnak Island, and Stevens Village, Alaska, teacher and community worker, 1936-40; high school and college teacher in Washington, Nevada, and California, 1942-49; Northrop Aircraft, Inc., Hawthorne, Calif., senior technical writer and editor, 1950-52;

Enterprise-Courier, Oregon City, Ore., farm editor and editorial writer, 1955-56; Valley College, Los Angeles, Calif., chemistry instructor, 1956-57; Aerojet-General Corp., Azusa, Calif., senior technical editor, 1957-59; American Electronics, Inc., El Monte, Calif., publications supervisor and chief technical writer and editor, 1959-60; Hercules Powder Co., Salt Lake City, Utah, chief technical writer, 1962; *Siskiyou Daily News,* Yreka, Calif., city and wire editor, 1965; *Press-Courier,* Oxnard, Calif., photojournalist and Sunday magazine feature specialist, 1966-67; Genge Industries, Inc., Oxnard, Calif., chief technical writer and editor, 1967-70; free-lance writer. Extension Division leader in social sciences and communications, University of California, Los Angeles, 1966-68; teacher of science in secondary schools in Adelaide, South Australia, and MacKay, Queensland, Australia, 1968. Occasional editorial consultant on scientific and technical documentation, 1950-70. Research assistant and assistant director of anthropological/archaeological expedition to central Aleutian Islands, 1954. West Coast Director for Institute for Regional Exploration, 1954-68.

MEMBER: American Anthropological Association, American Folklore Society, Linguistic Society of America, Pi Gamma Mu, Phi Delta Kappa, Explorers. *Awards, honors:* American Council of Learned Societies grant-in-aid of research in American Indian linguistics, 1945.

WRITINGS: (Contributor) Dean F. Sherman, editor, *Alaska Cavalcade,* Alaska Life Publishing Co., 1943; *High Tension* (biography), privately printed, 1953; *Arizona Gem Trails and the Colorado Desert of California: A Field Guide for the Gem Hunter, the Mineral Collector, the Uranium Hunter,* Mineralogist Publishing Co., 1955; *Petrified Forest Trails: A Guide to the Petrified Forests of America,* Mineralogist Publishing Co., 1955; *The Rock-Hunter's Range Guide: How and Where to Find Minerals and Gem Stones in the United States,* Harper, 1962; *Fossils in America: Their Nature, Origin Identification and Classification, and a Range Guide to Collecting Sites,* Harper, 1964; *A Range Guide to Mines and Minerals: How and Where to Find Valuable Ores and Minerals in the United States,* Harper, 1964; *A Complete Field Guide to American Wildlife* (Book-of-the Month Club selection), Western edition, Harper, 1971.

Poetry anthologized in *Full Sails,* edited by Vincent Hill, [Aberdeen, Wash.], 1931, *Younger Poets,* edited by Nellie B. Sergeant, Appleton, 1932, and *The World's Fair Anthology of Verse,* edited by Paul E. Carter, Exposition, 1939. Contributor of more than four hundred photo-illustrated feature articles in one hundred magazines, including *Better Homes and Gardens, Pageant, American Forests, Catholic Digest, Field and Stream,* and *American West;* contributor of some thirty scientific papers to research quarterlies, including *American Anthropologist, Southwest Journal of Anthropology, Journal of American Folklore,* and *Phi Delta Kappan;* author of approximately one hundred classified scientific and technical papers in missile and aerospace industry company publications; contributor of more than three thousand feature articles, spot news, editorials, photo stories, and business analyses to newspapers.

WORK IN PROGRESS: Gem Stones and Minerals of America, for Harper; research for other books in archaeology, space exploration, and natural history.

SIDELIGHTS: Ransom speaks, reads, writes, or translates Aleut-Eskimo and various American Indian languages of the Pacific Northwest; he has reading facility (mainly scientific) in German, Dutch, French, Spanish, Latin, Italian, and Russian, with some speaking knowledge of German and Spanish; he is also acquainted with Greek, Uigur, Turkish, and Samoyed morphologies. *Avocational interests:* Wilderness exploration by canoe and backpack, field archaeology and anthropology, geology, paleontology, mineralogy, history of the American West, travel, and photography.

* * *

RANUM, Orest Allen 1933-

PERSONAL: Born February 18, 1933, in Lyle, Minn.; son of Luther George (a carpenter) and Nada (Chaffee) Ranum; married Patricia McGroder, July 4, 1955; children: Kristin Helena, Marcus James Aymar. *Education:* Macalester College, A.B., 1955; University of Minnesota, M.A., 1957, Ph.D., 1960. *Home:* 208 Ridgewood Rd., Baltimore, Md. 21210.

CAREER: University of Strasbourg, Strasbourg, France, lecturer, 1959-60; University of Southern California, Los Angeles, assistant professor of history, 1960-61; Columbia University, New York, N.Y., assistant professor, 1961-64, associate professor of history, 1964-69; Johns Hopkins University, Baltimore, Md., professor of history, 1969—. *Member:* American Historical Association, French Historical Society. *Awards, honors:* Guggenheim fellow, 1968-69.

WRITINGS: Richelieu and the Councillors of Louis XIII: A Study of the Secretaries of State and Superintendents of Finance in the Ministry of Richelieu, 1635-1642, Oxford University Press, 1963; *Paris in the Age of Absolutism: An Essay,* Wiley, 1968; (editor) *Searching for Modern Times: Discussion Problems and Readings,* two volumes, Dodd, 1969; (editor with wife, Patricia Ranum) *The Century of Louis XIV,* Harper, 1972; (editor with Patricia Ranum) *Popular Attitudes Toward Birth Control in Pre-Industrial France and England,* Harper, in press. Contributor of articles and reviews to journals.

WORK IN PROGRESS: Royal historiographers of seventeenth-century France.

SIDELIGHTS: In a review of *Paris in the Age of Absolutism,* J.H. Plumb writes: "The story of Paris's growth, of its transmogrification from a small, largely mediaeval, highly clustered town into a city of Roman grandeur worthy of the Sun King, is told with admirable scholarship by Professor Ranum. His range is enviably wide. Most historians fight shy of literary matters, but Corneille, Racine and Moliere have no terrors for him: His sensitivity and knowledge of music, architecture and painting are equally great. He is as much at home with the complexity of the Parisian constitution as its tax system and economic life. Above all, he is a social historian with a keen sense of the importance of religion as well as politics. And in consequence he has written one of the best histories of an epoch in the life of a great city that I know."

BIOGRAPHICAL/CRITICAL SOURCES: Saturday Review, February 22, 1969; *Spectator,* March 21, 1969.

* * *

RANZ, James 1921-
(Jim Ranz)

PERSONAL: Born July 21, 1921, in Atlanta, Neb.; son of Joe and Louie (Fulk) Ranz; married Delores Christensen, August 2, 1942; children: Jo Ann Ranz Cuthbertson, John Martin, Thomas Jay. *Education:* Nebraska State Teachers College, Kearney, B.S., 1942; University of Michigan, A.M.L.S., 1948; University of Illinois, Ph.D., 1960. *Politics:* Democrat. *Religion:* Roman Catholic. *Home:* 2509 Park, Laramie, Wyo. 82070. *Office:* Department of Library Science, University of Wyoming, Laramie, Wyo. 82070.

CAREER: University of Illinois, Urbana, library cataloger, 1948-51; University of Virginia, Charlottesville, library department head, 1951-53; University of Illinois,

Urbana, library administrative assistant, 1953-55; University of Wyoming, Laramie, director of libraries, 1955-62; University of British Columbia, Vancouver, university librarian, 1962-63; University of Wyoming, dean of academic affairs, 1964-70, vice-president for academic affairs, 1970—. *Military service:* U.S. Army, Infantry, 1942-46; became staff sergeant. *Member:* American Library Association, Wyoming Library Association (president, 1949).

WRITINGS: (under name Jim Ranz) *The Printed Book Catalogue in American Libraries, 1723-1900,* American Library Association, 1964. Contributor to library journals.

WORK IN PROGRESS: A study of bibliographical control of printed materials; curricular study in universities.

* * *

RASKIN, Edith Lefkowitz 1908-

PERSONAL: Born October 17, 1908, in New York, N.Y.; daughter of Maximillian (in real estate) and Sara (Brown) Lefkowitz; married Joseph Raskin (an artist), October 30, 1936. *Education:* Hunter College, B.A., 1930; Cornell University, graduate study, 1939-40; New York University, M.A., 1941; American Museum of Natural History, postgraduate courses. *Home:* 59 West 71st St., New York, N.Y. 10023.

CAREER: New York City Board of Education, New York, N.Y., teacher of science, 1930-37, biology laboratory teacher, 1937—. *Member:* United Federation of Teachers, Authors Guild.

WRITINGS: (With Sylvia S. Greenberg) *Home-Made Zoo,* McKay, 1952; *Many Worlds: Seen and Unseen,* McKay, 1954; *Watchers, Pursuers and Masqueraders: Animals and Their Vision,* McGraw, 1964; *The Pyramid of Living Things,* McGraw, 1967; *The Fantastic Cactus, Indoors and in Nature,* Lothrop, 1968; (with husband, Joseph Raskin) *Indian Tales,* Random House, 1969; *World Food,* McGraw, 1971; (with Joseph Raskin) *Tales Our Settlers Told,* Lothrop, 1971.

WORK IN PROGRESS: Moments in Eternity, a history of science.

SIDELIGHTS: Many Worlds was translated into Arabic and Persian. *Avocational interests:* Plastic arts, theatre, opera, hiking, swimming, and watching baseball.

BIOGRAPHICAL/CRITICAL SOURCES: Best Sellers, March 1, 1968; *Book World,* October 12, 1969.

* * *

RATERMANIS, J(anis) B(ernhards) 1904-

PERSONAL: Born June 30, 1904, in Latvia; son of Fricis and Charlote (Grins) Ratermanis; married Mary Maculans, 1942; children: Aristids, Leonids. *Education:* Lycee de Tourcoing, baccalaureat, 1925; University of Lille, licence es lettres, 1928; University of Latvia, master, 1932, doctor of philology and philosophy, 1943. *Religion:* Lutheran. *Home:* 2376 Ron Way, San Diego, Calif. 92123.

CAREER: French Lycee of Riga, Riga, Latvia, teacher, 1929-39; University of Latvia, Riga, Latvia, began as assistant professor, became professor, 1934-44; French Institute of Mainz, Mainz, Federal Republic of Germany, professor, 1945-49; State University of Iowa, Iowa City, professor of Romance languages, 1950-72. *Member:* Modern Language Association of America, American Association of University Professors, American Association of Teachers of French.

WRITINGS: Etude sur le style de Baudelaire, Art & Science, 1949; *Etude sur le comique dans le theatre de*

Marivaux, Droz, 1961; (with W.R. Irwin) *The Comic Style of Beaumarchais,* University of Washington Press, 1961; *Elements de Syntaxe,* two volumes, State University of Iowa, 1963; (editor) Marivaux, *Le Jeu de l'amour et du hasard,* Prentice-Hall, 1967; (editor) Beaumarchais, *Le Mariage de Figaro; ou La Folle journee,* Prentice-Hall, 1968; *Studies on Voltaire and the Eighteenth Century,* Volume LXIII: *Le Mariage de Figaro,* Institute et Musee Voltaire, (Geneva), 1968; *Essai sur les formes verbales dans les tragedies de Racine,* Nizet (Paris), 1972. Contributor of articles, mostly on French stylistics, to periodicals.

* * *

RATHMELL, J(ohn) C. A. 1935-

PERSONAL: Born November 6, 1935, in Leeds, England; married Mirjana Stojanovic (an architectural assistant), August 3, 1963. *Education:* Jesus College, Cambridge, B.A., 1959, M.A., 1962, Ph.D., 1964; Harvard University, graduate student, 1959-60. *Home:* 9 Beaumont Crescent, Cambridge, England. *Agent:* Jan Van Loewen Ltd., 81-83 Shaftesbury Ave., London W.C.1, England.

CAREER: Cambridge University, Cambridge, England, fellow of Christ's College and director of studies in English, 1961—, university lecturer, 1963—. *Awards, honors:* Frank Knox Memorial Fellow, 1959-60.

WRITINGS: (Editor) *The Psalms of Sir Philip Sidney and the Countess of Pembroke,* Doubleday and New York University Press, 1963.

WORK IN PROGRESS: A critical work on Sidney, Jonson, and the non-metaphysical poets, 1580-1640; a reappraisal of Ruskin's *Modern Painters* and its influence.†

* * *

RAUSCHER, Donald J. 1921-

PERSONAL: Born March 5, 1921, in New York, N.Y., son of John and Helen (Duguid) Rauscher; married Justine C. ShirCliff (a teacher), August 14, 1954; children: Mary Cecile, Frances Helen. *Education:* Manhattan School of Music, B.Mus., M.Mus., postgraduate diploma. *Home:* 2500 Johnson Ave., Riverdale, N.Y. 10463. *Office:* Department of Theory, Manhattan School of Music, 120 Claremont Ave., New York, N.Y. 10027.

CAREER: Manhattan School of Music, New York, N.Y., college registrar and music teacher, 1952—. *Military service:* U.S. Army, 321st Army Service Forces Band, 1942-46.

WRITINGS: Orchestration: Scores and Scoring, Free Press, 1963; (with wife, Justine ShirCliff Rauscher, and Stephen Jay) *Chromatic Harmony,* Free Press, 1965. Arranger and orchestrator for Macmillan's music series of school texts.

RAVITZ, Abe Carl 1927-

PERSONAL: Born May 20, 1927, in New York, N.Y.; son of Abe Carl (a taxi driver) and Minerva (Rosenfield) Ravitz; married Esther Cantor, July 16, 1947; children: Lee Hal, Eric Alan, Nelsa Kay, Seth Benjamin. *Education:* College of City of New York (now City College of the City University of New York), B.A., 1949; New York University, M.A., 1950, Ph.D., 1955. *Politics:* Democrat. *Religion:* Hebrew. *Home:* 1863 East Cyrene Dr., Carson, Calif. 90746. *Office:* Department of English, California State College, Dominguez Hills, Calif. 90747.

CAREER: Pennsylvania State University, University Park, assistant professor of English, 1953-58; Hiram College, Hiram, Ohio, professor of English, 1958-66; California State College, Dominguez Hills, professor of English and chairman of department, 1966—. *Military service:* U.S. Army, 1946-47. *Member:* Modern Language Association, American Studies Association.

WRITINGS: Clarence Darrow and the American Literary Tradition, Western Reserve University Press, 1962; (editor with James N. Primm) *The Haywood Case: Materials for Analysis,* Chandler, 1963; *David Graham Phillips* (biography), Twayne, 1966; (compiler) *The American Disinherited: A Profile in Fiction,* Dickenson, 1970; *The Disinherited: Plays,* Dickenson, 1973. Contributor of articles to professional journals.

WORK IN PROGRESS: A biography of Alfred Henry Lewis.

*　　*　　*

RAWLINS, Winifred 1907-

PERSONAL: Born January 20, 1907, in London, England; now a U.S. citizen; daughter of Thomas Griffin (an export merchant) and Kate (Gibson) Rawlins. *Education:* "Informal and unconventional." *Politics:* Liberal-radical, nonviolent. *Religion:* Society of Friends (Quakers). *Home:* 505 Glenwood Ave., Moylan, Pa. 19065.

CAREER: Has worked at various jobs, including migrant farm work and administrative positions; currently director of a home for the aged.

WRITINGS—All poetry: *The Inner Islands,* Pendle Hill, 1953; *Winter Solstice,* Island Press, 1952; *Before No High Altars,* Exposition, 1955; *Fire Within,* Golden Quill, 1959; *Russian Pictures,* Golden Quill, 1961; *Dreaming Is Now,* Golden Quill, 1963; *The Small Land,* Golden Quill, 1966; *Man is a Tender Plant,* Golden Quill, 1969. Contributor of poems to periodicals and to several anthologies.

WORK IN PROGRESS: More poetry.

SIDELIGHTS: Ms. Rawlins has served two prison sentences for her anti-war activities. She has studied French, German, Spanish, Italian, and Russian, and has traveled in twenty-one countries. She has written poetry since the age of seven, and writes that music and dancing, which she has also studied, have greatly influenced her poetry.

*　　*　　*

RAWLS, Eugene S. 1927-

PERSONAL: Born January 7, 1927, in New York, N.Y.; son of Louis and Elsie (Shakofsky) Rosenblum. *Education:* University of Miami, Coral Gables, Fla., A.B., 1948. *Office:* American Institute of Yoga, 987 Southwest 34th Ave., Miami, Fla. 33135.

CAREER: American Institute of Yoga, Miami, Fla., founder, and director, 1958—. Founder, American Karma Yoga Society, 1962. Lecturer on yoga and Buddhism.

WRITINGS: A Handbook of Yoga for Modern Living, Pyramid Books, 1964; (with Eve Diskin) *Yoga for Beauty and Health,* Parker Publishing, 1967.

WORK IN PROGRESS: A book on yoga philosophy; *The Six Systems of Indian Philosophy,* a college-level textbook.

*　　*　　*

RAY, David 1932-

PERSONAL: Born May 20, 1932, in Sapulpa, Okla.; son of Dowell Adolphus and Katherine (Jennings) Ray; married, wife's name, Judy; children: Winifred, Wesley, Samuel, Sapphina. *Education:* University of Chicago, B.A., 1952, M.A., 1957. *Office:* Department of English, University of Missouri at Kansas City, Kansas City, Mo. 64110.

CAREER: Instructor in English, Wright Junior College, Chicago, Ill., 1957-58, Northern Illinois University,

DeKalb, 1958-60, Cornell University, Ithaca, N.Y., 1960-64; Reed College, Portland, Ore., assistant professor of literature and humanities, 1964-66; Bowling Green State University, Bowling Green, Ohio, associate professor of English, 1971-72; University of Missouri at Kansas City, associate professor of English, 1972—. Lecturer at Writers Workshop, University of Iowa, 1969-70. *Member:* Modern Language Association of America. *Awards, honors:* Academy of American Poets honorable mention, 1955, 1956; *New Republic* Young Writers award, 1958; Kossuth Award, Hungarian Freedom Fighters; Woursell fellowship (University of Vienna), 1966-71.

WRITINGS: (Editor) *The Chicago Review Anthology,* University of Chicago Press, 1959; *X-Rays, a Book of Poems,* Cornell University Press, 1965; (editor) *From the Hungarian Revolution A Collection of Poems,* Cornell University Press, 1966, (editor with Robert Bly) *A Poetry Reading Against the Vietnam War,* American Writers Against the Vietnam War, 1966; *Dragging the Main, and Other Poems,* Cornell University Press, 1968. Poetry represented in several anthologies, including *New Poets of England and America,* edited by Donald Hall and Robert Pack, Meridian, 1962, *Of Poetry and Power: Poems Occasioned by the Presidency and by the Death of John F. Kennedy,* edited by Erwin A Glikes and Paul Schwaber, Basic Books, 1964, *Where Is Vietnam?: American Poets Respond,* edited by Walter Lowenfels, Doubleday-Anchor, 1967, *The Voice That Is Great Within Us,* edited by Hayden Carruth, Bantam, 1970, and *The Creative Voice,* edited by Ken Lawless, Holt, 1971. Contributor of poetry, fiction, criticism, and reviews to more than twenty magazines and journals, including *Nation, New Republic, Reporter, Poetry* (Chicago), *Accent, Critic, Odyssey, Paris Review, Chelsea, London Magazine, Saturday Review, New American Review, Yale Review, Quarterly Review of Literature,* and *Atlantic. Chicago Review,* editor, 1956-57, advisory editor, 1963—; associate editor, *Epoch,* 1960-64; editor, *New Letters,* 1971—.

WORK IN PROGRESS: The Blue Duck and Other Poems; fiction.

SIDELIGHTS: The *Chicago Review* said of *X-Rays:* "No book was ever better titled, for in piece after deeply personal piece there is the feel of the x-ray, an excoriated quality. The volume must be one of the most honest—to the point of violent self-deprecation—to appear in a long time, but if Ray is rarely generous to himself he can be to others. Which is astonishing when one considers the thwarters peopling his poems. 'Deathlace' is a very powerful piece about, presumably, the carbon monoxide that poisons the air. What happens is that this becomes a remarkably apt metaphor, used a number of times, for the many things that poison the life of our times."

Elliott Coleman, writing in *Nation,* regards *Dragging The Main* as "a dragnet of a book, catching what is priceless." He calls Ray "a free poet [whose] freedom is a very exacting freedom . . . because he is an explorer."

Robert D. Spector cites *Dragging the Main* for its "sad, tender and angry poems in which the emotion is never forced, the language always appropriate to the feeling. Ray can capture with equal ease a father's response to the birth of his son, or that peculiar blend of melancholy and delight when one observes a child's innocence. His range is great and his quiet humor, including self-mockery, is not the least appealing of his virtues."

BIOGRAPHICAL/CRITICAL SOURCES: Saturday Review, March 15, 1969; *Nation,* March 17, 1969; *Chicago Review,* volume 18, number 2, 1965.

REA, Frederick B(eatty)   1908-

PERSONAL: Born May 31, 1908, in Dublin, Eire; son of William (a draper) and Rebecca (Johnston) Rea; married Kathleen Lawson, August 9, 1937; children: Francis, Sheila. Education: Attended Wesley College, Dublin, Eire; University of Dublin, B.A. (first honors), 1929, diploma in education (first honors), 1930, B.D., 1934; other study at Edgehill Theological College. Home: Wesley Manse, Princes Rd., Belvedere, Salisbury, Rhodesia.

CAREER: Waddilove Training Institution, Southern Rhodesia, director of teacher training, 1937-39; minister of Methodist churches in Bulawayo, and Salisbury, Southern Rhodesia, 1947-56; Epworth Theological College, Salisbury, Rhodesia, principal, 1956-64; Methodist Church, Salisbury, Rhodesia, superintendent minister, 1965—. Chairman, Salisbury Conference on Alcoholism, 1956-57, 1962-63, Rhodesia Christian Conference, 1970—. Military service: Royal Air Force, 1940-42. British Army, chaplain, 1943-45; served in Egypt and Italy; became captain; received Order of British Empire. Member: Capricorn Africa Society (chairman, 1960-63).

WRITINGS: (With others) Ireland To-Day, S.C.M. Press, 1937; Alcoholism, Its Psychology and Cure, Philosophical Library, 1956; (contributor) Lincoln Williams, Tomorrow Will Be Sober, Harper, 1960; (editor) Southern Rhodesia—the Price of Freedom: A Series of Essays by Nine Rhodesians on the Present Political Impasse, Stuart Manning, 1964; We Would see Jesus: An Outline of Theology, privately printed, 1970.

*   *   *

RECORD, Cy Wilson   1916-

PERSONAL: Born January 28, 1916, in Fort Worth, Tex.; son of William Franklin and Ann (Stricklin) Record; married Jane Cassels (an economist), July 24, 1938; children: Jeffrey. Education: University of Texas, student, 1936-39; Roosevelt University, B.A., 1941; University of California, Berkeley, M.A., 1949, Ph.D., 1953. Home: 2397 Hillside Lane, Lake Oswego, Ore. 97034. Office: Department of Sociology, Portland State University, Portland, Ore. 97207.

CAREER: University of Alabama, Tuscaloosa, assistant professor of economics, 1946-47; San Francisco State College, San Francisco, Calif., assistant professor of sociology, 1950-51; Sacramento State College, Sacramento, Calif., assistant professor, 1953-55, associate professor of sociology and chairman of the department, 1958-64; Southern Illinois University, Carbondale, professor of sociology, 1964-65; Portland State University, Portland, Ore., professor of sociology, 1965—. Visiting professor, University of California, Los Angeles, 1956, Berkeley, 1958. Military service: U.S. Air Force, 1943-46. U.S. Air Force Reserve, 1946-49. Member: American Sociological Association, American Studies Association, Society for the Study of Social Problems, American Historical Association, Western History Association, Pacific Sociological Association.

WRITINGS: The Negro and the Communist Party, University of North Carolina Press, 1951. (Editor with wife, Jane Cassels Record) Little Rock: USA, Chandler Publishing, 1960; Discrimination-Fact, P. Chacon, c.1962; Minority Groups and Intergroup Relations in the San Francisco Bay Area, Institute of Government Studies, University of California (Berkeley), 1963; Race and Radicalism: The NAACP and the Communist Party in Conflict, Cornell University Press, 1964. Contributor of more than one hundred articles and reviews to professional journals.

WORK IN PROGRESS: Research for books on counselling and guidance of racial and ethnic minorities in public schools, the role of intellectuals in racial movements, impact of black studies movement on the social sciences, and social problems and social movements.

*   *   *

REDFERN, George B.   1910-

PERSONAL: Born May 24, 1910, in Clarksville, Ohio; son of Robert E. (a carpenter) and Edna (Thompson) Redfern; married Rosanne Reardon, July 6, 1935; children: Anne Redfern. Education: Wilmington College, A.B., 1933; University of Cincinnati, Ed.M., 1939, Ed.D., 1958. Home: 8111 Lewinsville Rd., McLean, Va. 22101. Office: 1801 North Moore St., Arlington, Va. 22209.

CAREER: Wilmington College, Wilmington, Ohio, assistant to president, 1945-46; high school principal in Wilmington, Ohio, 1947-49, in Mariemont, Ohio, 1949-52; Cincinnati (Ohio) public schools, personnel administrator, 1952-59, assistant superintendent, 1959-66; University of Cincinnati, Cincinnati, Ohio, instructor in personnel administration, 1955-66; American Association of School Administrators, Arlington, Va., associate secretary, 1966—. Military service: U.S. Naval Reserve, 1943-46; became lieutenant commander. Member: National Education Association, American Association of School Administrators, National Association of School Personnel Administrators, Ohio Education Association, Ohio Association of School Administrators.

WRITINGS: How to Appraise Teaching Performance, School Management Institute, 1963, revised edition published as How to Appraise Teaching: A Performance Objectives Approach, 1972; Improving Principal-Faculty Relationships, Prentice-Hall, 1966. Contributor to national education journals.

*   *   *

REED, A(lfred) H(amish)   1875-

PERSONAL: Born December 30, 1875, in Hayes, Middlesex, England; son of James William and Elisabeth (Wild) Reed; married Isabel Fisher, January 29, 1899. Education: Attended schools in London, England, and in New Zealand. Religion: Methodist. Home: 153 Glenpark Ave., Dunedin, New Zealand.

CAREER: Was Kauri gumdigger in his teens; worked for New Zealand Typewriter Co., Auckland, 1895-97, opened and operated branch in Dunedin, 1897-1907; with wife Isabel, established mail-order business in religious education materials, 1907, joined by nephew A.W. Reed, 1925, established branch in Wellington, 1932, and extended activities into publishng general New Zealand books; business incorporated as A.H. Reed Ltd., 1941, but all publications bear the imprint, A.H. & A.W. Reed; with active management of business in nephew's hands, A.H. Reed has lived in Dunedin, New Zealand, writing, and traveling afoot around the country, 1941—. Founder of Alfred and Isabel and Marian Reed Trust, 1938; donor of Alfred and Isabel Reed collection of English Bible and its antecedents, Dickensiana, other rare material, to City of Dunedin. Patron of Youth Hostels Association and of Dickens Fellowship (Dunedin). Military service: New Zealand Army, World War I; became sergeant. Awards, honors: Member, Order of British Empire, 1948, Commander, 1962.

WRITINGS—All published by A.H. & A.W. Reed, except as indicated: (Editor) Early Maoriland Adventures of J.W. Stack, 1935; (editor) More Maoriland Adventures of J.W. Stack, 1936; (editor) Further Maoriland Adventures of J.W. and E. Stack, 1938; Marsden of Maoriland: Pioneer and Peacemaker, 1938; (with A.W. Reed) Two Maoriland Adventurers, Marsden and Selwyn (contains

Samuel Marsden, Greatheart of Maoriland by A.H. Reed and *George Augustus Selwyn* by A.W. Reed), Pickering & Inglis, 1939; *Samuel Marsden, Greatheart of Maoriland,* 1939; *Isabel Reed, Her Book,* 1940; (editor with A.W. Reed) *Castaways on the Aucklands,* 1943; (with A.W. and Marian Reed) *The Isabel Reed Bible Story Book,* 1944; *The Story of New Zealand,* 1945, Roy Publishers, 1955, 11th edition, A.H. & A.W. Reed, 1965; *Farthest East: Afoot in Maoriland Byways,* 1946; *The Story of Otago, Age of Adventure,* 1947; *The Gumdigger: The Story of Kauri Gum,* 1948; *The Story of Canterbury, Last Wakefield Settlement,* 1949; (with Alfred Eccles) *John Jones of Otago, Whaler, Coloniser, Shipowner, Merchant,* 1949.

(With A.W. Reed) *Farthest West, Afloat and Afoot,* 1950; *Maori Place Names and Their Meanings,* 1950; *Everybody's Story of New Zealand,* 1950, 3rd edition, 1954; (editor with A.W. Reed) *Captain Cook in New Zealand,* Heinman, 1951, 2nd edition, A.H. & A.W. Reed, 1969; *Coromandel Holiday,* 1952; *The Story of the Kauri,* 1953, 3rd edition published as *The New Story of the Kauri,* 1964; *Farthest South,* 1953; *The Four Corners of New Zealand* (contains *Farthest East, Farthest North, Farthest West,* and *Farthest South*), 1954, 3rd edition, 1959; *The Story of Early Dunedin,* 1956; *The Story of Northland,* 1956; (with A.W. Reed) *The House of Reed: Fifty Years of New Zealand Publishing 1907-1957,* 1957; *The Story of Hawke's Bay,* 1958; *Walks in Maoriland Byways,* Heinman, 1958; *Heroes of Peace and War in Early New Zealand,* 1959; *From North Cape to Bluff, on Foot at Eighty-five,* 1961; *From East Cape to Egmont, on Foot at Eighty-six,* 1962; *Marlborough Journey,* 1963; *The Friendly Road: On Foot Through Otago, Canterbury, Westland, and the Haast,* 1964; *Nelson Pilgrimage,* 1965; *Sydney Melbourne Footslogger,* Tri-Ocean, 1966; *An Autobiography,* 1967, Tri-Ocean, 1968; (editor) *With Anthony Trollope in New Zealand,* 1969.

Short books and pamphlets; all published by A.H. & A.W. Reed, except as indicated: (With A.W. Reed) *First New Zealand Christmases: Tasman, 1642; Cook, 1769; Marsden, 1814,* 1933; (editor) James West Stack, *White Boy Among the Maoris in the Forties,* 1934; *My Little Book of Prayer,* 1939; (with Marian Reed) *Heaven's Morning Breaks: An Anthology of the After Life,* 1939, 2nd edition, 1957; (editor) *A Little Book of Inward Peace,* 1940; *Prayers for the Home Front and Front Line,* 1941; *My Book of Prayer,* 1942; *Battle-Ax of the Beach,* 1942; (with Marian Reed) *Old Testament Heroes, and Other Stories,* 1943; (with A.W. Reed) *Paul and His Friends,* 1943; *Kings and Princes,* 1943; *Jesus of Galilee,* 1943, *Joseph, Slave and Ruler,* 1943; *The King of Love,* 1943; *Bible Games and Puzzles,* 1944; *A Song of Praise for Maoriland,* 1944; *My Book of Prayer and Maoriland Hymns,* 1944; (with A.W. Reed) *Orange Book,* 1945; (with A.W. Reed), *Red Book,* 1945; (with A.W. Reed) *Blue Book for Girls and Boys,* 1945; *Great Barrier, Isle of Enchantment,* 1946; *New World Atlas,* 3rd edition, 1948, 5th edition, 1951.

Larnach and His Castle, 1950, 6th edition, 1957; (editor and author of introduction) Charles Dickins, *From the Black Rocks, on Friday; and, A Gold Digger's Notes,* 1950; (editor) *Bathgate Expeditions from New Zealand's Commercial Capital of the Sixties,* 1952; *The Kauri,* 1953; *Walks Around Dunedin,* 1954; (compiler) *Early Dunedin in Pictures,* 1956; *A XV Century Ms. of the Wyclif-Purvey Gospels: An Introduction to the Dunedin Public Library's Copy,* 1956; *Joseph William Mellor: Dunedin Boy Who Became the World's Greatest Authority on Inorganic Chemistry,* 1957; (editor) *Gabriel's Gully and Dunedin in 1861,* 1957; *The English Bible and Its Antecedents,* 1957; *The Story of the English Bible,* 1958; *The Story of a Kauri Park,* 1959; *Florence Night-*

ingale, 1960; *Historic Bay of Islands,* 1960; *The Milford Track,* Tri-Ocean; (author of introduction) Brian McPherson, compiler, *Charles Dickens, 1812-1870,* 1965; *New Zealand's Forest King, the Kauri,* 1967; *Rare Books and Manuscripts: The Story of the Dunedin Public Library's Alfred and Isabel Reed Collection,* 1968.

SIDELIGHTS: One of Reed's books is an account of an eight hundred-mile walk in New Zealand; he still walks ten miles at a stretch, and climbed Mount Egmont at eighty and eighty-six, Tongariro at eighty-two, Ruapehu at eighty-three, and Ngauruhoe at eighty-five.

*   *   *

REED, A(lexander) W(yclif)   1908-
(Harlequin)

PERSONAL: Born March 7, 1908, in Auckland, New Zealand; son of Alexander John (a clergyman) and Julia (Carter) Reed; married Chrissy Margaretta Hindle, March 10, 1932; children: Wyclif Alfred, John Matthew, Selwyn Thomas, Heather Mary. *Education:* Attended Auckland Grammar School and Mount Albert Grammar School, both in New Zealand. *Home:* 22 Fairview Crescent, Kelburn, Wellington, New Zealand. *Office:* A.H. & A.W. Reed, 182 Wakefield St., Wellington, New Zealand.

CAREER: A.H. & A.W. Reed (publishers), Auckland and Wellington, New Zealand, and Sydney, Australia, managing director, 1933—, chairman of directors, 1959-71. Managing director, Cuisenaire Co. of New Zealand Ltd., Wellington. *Member:* Polynesian Society, P.E.N. (New Zealand Center). *Awards, honors:* Esther Glen Medal for best children's book of year in New Zealand, 1946, for *Myths and Legends of Maoriland.*

WRITINGS—All published by A.H. & A.W. Reed, except as noted: *The Coming of the Maori to Ao-Tea-Roa,* 1934; *The Maori and His First Printed Books,* 1935; *The Wreck of the Osprey,* 1937; *George Augustus Selwyn, Pioneer Bishop of New Zealand,* Pickering & Inglis, 1939, also published in *Two Maoriland Adventurers, Marsden and Selwyn,* Pickering & Inglis, 1939; (with Rudall C. Hayward) *Rewi's Last Stand* (based on Hayward's film scenario), 1939; *Map Reading Simplified,* 1942; *The Book of Christmas,* 1943; *The Adventures of Matchbox Max,* 1943; *Poppa Passes: The Adventures of the Vegetable People in Garden Land,* 1943; *Maui: Legends of the Demigod of Polynesia,* 1943; *Far Round the World,* Independent Press, 1944; *Blue Book for Boys and Girls,* 1945; *Orange Book,* 1945; *Red Book,* 1945; *Stories Jesus Told for Today,* 1945; *My Own Big Book of Bible Stories,* 1946; *The Author-Publisher Relationship,* published for P.E.N., 1946; *Myths and Legends of Maoriland,* 1946, 3rd edition, revised and enlarged, 1961; (with John Reed) *New Zealand Little Folk's Library,* 1947; *Reeds' New World Atlas,* 1947, 5th edition, revised and enlarged, 1951; (illustrator) *Make Your Own Atlas,* 1947; (with J.H. Richards) *New Zealand Christmas Annual,* 1947; (with W.P. Carman) *Conquest Annual,* 1947; *Native Birds,* 1948; *Eastern Village Model Book,* 2nd edition, 1948; *Reeds' Concise Maori Dictionary,* 1948, 3rd edition, revised and enlarged, 1964; *Wonder Tales of Maoriland,* 1948, 2nd edition, 1954; *Bible Stories,* 1949; *Native Plants,* 1949; *Progressive Lessons* (12 teacher's manuals), 1949-51; *Maori Place Names and Their Meanings,* 1950; *Reeds' Bible Story Atlas,* 1951; *More Birds,* 1951; *How the Maoris Lived,* 1952; *Reeds' Atlas of New Zealand,* 1952; *The Story of New Zealand Place Names,* 1952; *The Impact of Christianity on the Maori People,* 1955; *Auckland, City of the Seas,* 1955; *Living in a Maori Village: Rata and Hine at Home,* 1956; *How the White Men Came to New Zealand,* 1956; *How the Maoris Came,* 1956; *Maori Tales of Long Ago,* 1956; *Games the Maoris Played,* 1958; (with J. Halket Miller) *Roads in New Zealand,* 1958; *Pastoral Farming in New*

Zealand, 1958; *Legends of Rotorua and the Hot Lakes*, 1958; *The Islands of the Pacific*, 1959; *Kelburn Presbyterian Church, 1909-1959*, 1959; *A Dictionary of Maori Place Names*, 1961, reissued as *Lilliput Maori Place Names*, 1962; *A Boys' and Girls' History of New Zealand*, 1961; *Legends of Maoriland*, Book 1: *Stories of Fishes*, Book 2: *Nature Stories*, Book 3: *Stories of Fairies*, 1962; (with others) *An Illustrated Encyclopaedia of Maori Life*, 1963, abridged edition published as *Concise Maori Encyclopedia*, 1964; (with Aileen E. Brougham) *Maori Proverbs*, 1963, reissued as *Reeds' Lilliput Maori Proverbs*, 1964; *Treasury of Maori Folklore*, 1963; *Maori Fables and Legendary Tales*, 1964; *Aboriginal Words of Australia*, 1965; *Myths and Legends of Australia*, 1965; *Books Are My Business: The Life of a Publisher*, Educational Explorers, 1966; (with Inez Hames) *Myths and Legends of Fiji and Rotuma*, 1967, Tri-Ocean, 1968; *The House of Reed, 1957-1967*, 1968; *North Island Settlers*, 1968; *South Island Settlers*, 1968; *The Story of the Waikato River*, 1968; *The Growth of Transport in New Zealand*, 1968; *Power from the Earth*, 1968; *Map Book of the Pacific Islands*, 1968; *The Story of the Pacific*, 1968; *The Islands of the Pacific*, 1968; *An Illustrated Encyclopedia of Aboriginal Life*, 1969; *Let's Look at New Zealand*, 1969; *Place Names of New South Wales: Their Origins and Meanings*, 1969; *Family Life in New Zealand*, five books, 1969; *How the Aborigines Lived*, 1970; *Captain Cook in Australia*, 1970; *Little Stories of the Maori People*, six books, 1970; *The Evolution of the Maori People*, 1970; *Workers of New Zealand*, 1970; *New Zealand: The First Hundred Years*, 1970; *New Zealand: The Second Hundred Years*, 1970; *How New Zealand is Governed*, 1970; *Maori Carving*, 1970; *The First Settlement (Australia)*, 1970; *The Discovery of Australia*, 1970; *Maori Fairy Tales*, 1970; *The Maori Language*, 1970; *Before the Treaty of Waitangi*, 1971; *Sidelights on New Zealand History*, 1971; *Great Events in New Zealand History*, 1971; *Fighting in the Forties*, 1971; *Maori Words for Today*, 1971; *Fighting in the Sixties*, 1972; *Builders of New Zealand*, 1972; *Maori Legends*, 1972; *The Exploration of New South Wales*, 1972; *Exploring the Coasts of Australia*, 1972; *How Gold was Discovered in Australia*, 1972; *It Happened Today in New Zealand*, 1973; *Place Names of Australia*, 1973; *Litter and Pollution in New Zealand*, 1973.

With A.H. Reed—All published by A.H. & A.W. Reed: *First New Zealand Christmases*, 1933, 3rd edition, 1934; *Farthest West: Afoot and Afloat*, 1950; *The House of Reed: Fifty Years of New Zealand Publishing, 1907-1957*, 1957.

Under pseudonym Harlequin—All published by A.H. & A.W. Reed: *More Fun at Your Party*, 1941; *Party Night Again*, 1947; *Harlequin's Third Book of Party Games*, 1948.

Editor—All published by A.H. & A.W. Reed: John White, *Revenge: A Love-Tale of the Mount Eden Tribe*, 1940; (with A.H. Reed) *Castaways on the Auckland*, 1943; (with A.H. Reed) *Captain Cook on New Zealand* (extracts from Cook's journal), 1951, 2nd edition, 1969; *Aboriginal Fables and Legendary Tales*, 1965; *Maori Picture Dictionary*, Tri-Ocean, 1965; *Favourite Maori Legends*, 1965; *Aboriginal Place Names and Their Meanings*, 1967; *Fairy Tales from the Pacific Islands* (retold), 1969, Transatlantic, 1971; *The Mischievous Crow: Stories of the Aborigines* (retold), 1969.

Also author of *Social Studies Readers*, eight volumes, Warne, 1967. Writer of religious and educational booklets; editor of educational books and series.

WORK IN PROGRESS: Several books: *A Dictionary of New Zealand Historical Allusions*, *A Chronology of New Zealand History*, *Myths and Legends of Polynesia*, *Myths and Legends of Hawaii*, *Let's Learn a Little Maori*, *The Biggest Fish in the World*, *Teacher's Manual on Citizenship*, *Citizenship: A Readabout Book*, *Citizenship: A Thinkabout Book*, *The Story of the Old Testament*, *Son of the Most High and His Followers* (a layman's paraphrase of the Gospels and Acts in chronological sequence); editing *An Anthology of Twentieth Century Christian Poetry*.

SIDELIGHTS: Reed describes himself as "a New Zealand publisher for thirty years, interested in all aspects of New Zealand life and literature, particularly in primary school and religious education, and in the Maori people of New Zealand. The interest in Polynesian culture and folklore is now extended to Australia and the whole Polynesian area."

* * *

REED, Nelson A.   1926-

PERSONAL: Born April 6, 1926, in St. Louis, Mo.; son of B.E. and Anna (Addington) Reed; married Juliette Deconinck (a teacher), August 11, 1952; children: Nelson F. *Education:* Pennsylvania Academy of Fine Arts, student, 1945-49; Washington University, B.F.A., 1950. *Home:* 5045 Lindell Blvd., St. Louis, Mo. 63108.

CAREER: Reed Rubber Co., St. Louis, Mo., secretary, 1950-65, vice-president, 1965—. Research associate, Washington University, 1965—. *Military service:* U.S. Army, 1944-45; received Bronze Star and Purple Heart with cluster. *Awards, honors:* Page One Civic award, St. Louis Newspaper Guild, 1966.

WRITINGS: The Caste War of Yucatan, Stanford University Press, 1964; (contributor) Melvin L. Fowler, editor, *Explorations into Cahokia Archaeology*, Illinois Archeological Survey, 1969.

WORK IN PROGRESS: An outline survey of Cahokia.

SIDELIGHTS: Reed's interest in archaeology, anthropology, and history has led to extensive travels in Central America, particularly Mayan areas, exploration of the Ix Can River, underwater salvage work in Lake Peten, Guatemala, and work at the Cahokia Mounds near St. Louis, Mo.

* * *

REES, David   1928-

PERSONAL: Born October 15, 1928, in Swansea, Wales. *Education:* University College of Swansea, University of Wales, B.A. (honors), 1952. *Address:* c/o 103 Vivian Rd., Sketty, Swansea, Wales.

CAREER: Writer; joined *Spectator*, London, England, 1963, literary editor, 1964-67.

WRITINGS: Korea: The Limited War, St. Martin's, 1964; *The Age of Containment: The Cold War, 1945-1965*, St. Martin's, 1967; *The New Pressures from North Korea*, Current Affairs Research Services Center (London), 1970; *North Korea's Growth as a Subversive Centre*, Institute for the Study of Conflict (London), 1972; *Harry Dexter White: A Study in Paradox*, Coward, 1973. Contributor to various journals.

AVOCATIONAL INTERESTS: Walking.

BIOGRAPHICAL/CRITICAL SOURCES: Christian Science Monitor, October 19, 1967.

* * *

REESE, Heloise (Bowles)   1919-
   (Heloise)

PERSONAL: Born May 4, 1919, in Forth Worth, Tex.; daughter of Charles Louis and Amelia (Harrison) Bowles; married; children: Louis D., Ponce Kiah. *Education:*

Graduated from Felt and Tarrent Business College, Draughn's Business College, 1939; attended Texas School of Fine Arts, 1938. Residence: San Antonio, Tex. *Address:* c/o King Features Syndicate, 235 East 45th St., New York, N.Y. 10017.

CAREER: Honolulu Advertiser, Honolulu, Hawaii, columnist, 1959-62; King Features Syndicate, New York, N.Y., writer of "Hints from Heloise" column appearing in more than 600 papers, and in numerous foreign languages, 1961—. *Member:* Order of the Eastern Star, Lady Shriners. *Awards, honors:* Writer's award, Headliners Club (Austin, Tex.), 1964; first woman recipient of Silver Banshee award for outstanding columnist, Actors and Writers Professional Organization, 1964; San Antonio Press Club award for outstanding service; National Institute of Rug Cleaning recognition for distinguished service.

WRITINGS: Heloise's Housekeeping Hints, Prentice-Hall, 1962; *Heloise's Kitchen Hints,* Prentice-Hall, 1963; *Heloise All Around the House,* Prentice-Hall, 1965; *Heloise's Work and Money Savers,* Prentice-Hall, 1967; *Heloise's Hints for the Working Woman,* Prentice-Hall, 1970.

SIDELIGHTS: Heloise had never written a column before the day she walked into the *Advertiser's* office, not even knowing how to type, and got the job on a 30-day trial basis. She now manages a permanent staff of five housewives who sort and file the average 5,000 letters a week and type correspondence. One of the best-selling authors in the United States, she puts most of her (estimated) $100,000-a-year income into office expenses, trust funds, and charities.

She admits that a short time before she began her column she did not even know how to clean a toilet. Now she says she's almost embarrassed to admit that her column prevents her from doing all her housework, and necessitates a part-time maid. According to an article in *Life,* "Heloise's proudest achievement of all is not a hint or a column but a song, 'There Are No Phones to Heaven.' 'It took me eight years to get it copyrighted,' she sighs,' and I'll never do another.' Its unarguable message is that we should all tell people we appreciate them *now,* before they pass beyond the reach of area codes and direct distance dialing.... But Heloise's most notable contribution to the American household is her work with nylon net. As she herself demurely admits, 'Before I came along there was no such thing as nylon net pompons on the market.' "

Quite literally a colorful person, she uses hair spray to change the color of her hair at least once a day. She says: "I just can't abide a dreary look, and when I wear a blue dress and blue shoes, why *I'm* going to have blue hair."

AVOCATIONAL INTERESTS: Painting, and playing the electric organ.

BIOGRAPHICAL SOURCES: Time, June 23, 1961; *Newsweek,* April 16, 1962; *American Weekly,* May 27, 1962; *Saturday Evening Post,* March 2, 1963; *Editor and Publisher,* October 31, 1964; *Life,* April 21, 1967.

* * *

REESE, M(ax) M(eredith) 1910-

PERSONAL: Born in August, 1910, in Epsom, Surrey, England; married Clare Campbell, 1950; children: two sons. *Education:* Attended Haileybury College; Merton College, Oxford, M.A. (first class honors in history), 1932. *Home:* 7 Mowatt Rd., Grayshott, Hindhead, Surrey, England.

CAREER: Formerly a teacher, now an author, lecturer, and journalist. *Member:* Rotary Club (Haslemere).

WRITINGS: The Tudors and Stuarts, Longmans, Green (New York), 1940; *Shakespeare: His World and His Work,* St. Martin's, 1953; *The Cease of Majesty: A Study of Shakespeare's History Plays,* Edward Arnold, 1961, St. Martin's, 1962; *William Shakespeare* (juvenile), Edward Arnold, 1963, St. Martin's, 1964; (editor) Shakespeare, *King Henry IV, Part I,* Edward Arnold, 1964; (editor) Shakespeare, *King Henry V,* Edward Arnold, 1966; (editor) *Elizabethan Verse Romances,* Humanities, 1968; (editor) Shakespeare, *As You Like It,* Thomas Nelson, 1969; (editor) Shakespeare, *A Midsummer Night's Dream,* Thomas Nelson, 1970; (editor) Edward Gibbon, *Gibbon's Autobiography,* Routledge & Kegan Paul, 1971; *Documents for History Revision,* Edward Arnold, 1971. Contributor to *Nelson's Dictionary of World History.*

AVOCATIONAL INTERESTS: Cricket, detective stories.

* * *

REESE, Trevor Richard 1929-

PERSONAL: Born July 18, 1929, in Birmingham, England; son of David Richard and Caroline (Pagett) Reese; married Hilary Ethel Charker, January 6, 1961. *Education:* Attended King Edward's School, Birmingham, England, 1941-47; University of Sheffield, B.A., 1952; University of London, Ph.D., 1955. *Office:* Institute of Commonwealth Studies, University of London, London, England.

CAREER: Newcastle University College, Newcastle, New South Wales, Australia, lecturer in history, 1956-59; University of Sydney, Sydney, New South Wales, Australia, senior lecturer in history, 1960-62; University of Hull, Hull, Yorkshire, England, Leverhulme Fellow in Institute of Commonwealth Studies, Commonwealth Studies, 1962-64; University of London, London, England, lecturer, 1964-66, senior lecturer, 1966-68, reader in commonwealth studies, 1968—. *Member:* Royal Institute of International Affairs, Royal Historical Society, Royal Commonwealth Society.

WRITINGS: Colonial Georgia: A Study in British Imperial Policy in the Eighteenth Century, University of Georgia Press, 1963; *Australia in the Twentieth Century: A Political History,* Praeger, 1964 (published in England as *Australia in the Twentieth Century: A Short Political Guide,* Pall Mall, 1964); *The History of the Royal Commonwealth Society, 1868-1968,* Oxford University Press, 1968; *Frederica, Colonial Fort and Town: Its Place in History,* Fort Frederica Association, 1969; *Australia, New Zealand, and the United States: A Survey of International Relations, 1941-1968,* Oxford University Press, 1969. Contributor of articles on British imperial history to academic journals in America, Great Britain, and Australia. Assistant editor, *Journal of Commonwealth Political Studies,* 1965—; editor, *Imperial Studies,* 1970—.

WORK IN PROGRESS: Research in Commonwealth history in the twentieth century, history of Australian external affairs, and American colonial history.

* * *

**REID, J(ohn) C(owie) 1916-
(Caliban)**

PERSONAL: Born January 4, 1916, in Auckland, New Zealand; son of John Thomas (a railwayman) and Olive (Cowie) Reid; married Joyce Helena Burnet, January 4, 1939; children: Christopher, Bernard, Piers, Gerard, Miriam, Godfrey, Nicholas. *Education:* Sacred Heart College, Auckland, New Zealand, student, 1929-31; University of Auckland, M.A., 1939; University of New Zealand, Litt.D., 1957. *Religion:* Roman Catholic. *Home:* 23 Church Crescent, Panmure, Auckland, New Zealand.

Office: University of Auckland, Princes St., Auckland, New Zealand.

CAREER: Post-primary teacher in Auckland, New Zealand, 1940-42, 1946-47; University of Auckland, Auckland, New Zealand, lecturer, 1948-53, senior lecturer, 1954-60, associate professor, 1961-67, professor of English, 1968—. Fulbright scholar at University of Wisconsin, 1953; visiting professor at Aarhus University and University of Toulouse, 1969. Lecturer for Adult Education Service in New Zealand, 1940-62, and at Air Force Administrative School, 1950-57. Radio writer and broadcaster, 1946—; permanent chairman of "Critics," a bi-weekly radio program, 1950-59; own bi-weekly television program, "Comment" (a critical review of the arts in Auckland), 1963-67. President of New Zealand Film Institute, 1949-50; member, New Zealand Literary Fund Committee, 1965-70, and New Zealand Arts Council, 1968; Chairman, Auckland Theatre Trust, 1966—. *Military service:* New Zealand Army, senior administration officer, Auckland District Army Education and Welfare Service, 1942-46; became first lieutenant.

MEMBER: P.E.N. (New Zealand branch), Australian Universities Language and Literature Association, Australian Association of American Studies, Association of University Teachers, New Zealand Recorded Music Society (life; president, 1950-51), Cookery and Food Association (New Zealand division), Auckland English Association (president, 1959-60), Auckland Film Society (founding member; president, 1950-51), Auckland Wine and Food Society. *Awards, honors:* National Association of Educational Broadcasters award (United States) for scripts for radio play series produced at University of Wisconsin, 1958, and presented throughout America.

WRITINGS: Gerard Manley Hopkins, Priest and Poet: A Centennial Tribute, Catholic Supplies, 1944; *The Secret Years* (verse), Griffin Press, 1945; (under pseudonym Caliban) *Live Rounds: Verses of Army Life,* Griffin Press, 1945; *Creative Writing in New Zealand, a Brief Critical History,* Whitcombe & Tombs, 1946; *Catholics and the Films,* Whitcombe & Tombs, 1949; (author of critical history) *Writing in Auckland: A Selection Over a Century,* Free Public Library and Municipal Art Gallery (Auckland), 1955; *The Mind and Art of Coventry Patmore,* Macmillan (New York), 1957; *Francis Thompson, Man and Poet,* Routledge & Kegan Paul, 1959; Newman Press, 1960.

(Editor) *The Kiwi Laughs: An Anthology of New Zealand Prose Humour,* A.H. & A.W. Reed, 1961; (contributor) A.L. McLeod, editor, *The Commonwealth Pen,* Cornell University Press, 1961; *The Hidden World of Charles Dickens* (Macmillan Brown Memorial Lectures), University of Auckland, 1962; *Thomas Hood,* Routledge & Kegan Paul, 1963; (compiler) *A Book of New Zealand* (anthology of prose and poetry), Collins, 1964; (editor) *Forty Short Short Stories,* Edward Arnold, 1965; (editor and author of introduction) William Law, *A Serious Call to a Devout and Holy Life,* Collins, 1965; *New Zealanders at War in Fiction,* New Zealand Publishing Society, 1966; (editor) Shakespeare, *The Tempest,* Edward Arnold, 1967; *Charles Dickens: Little Dorrit,* Edward Arnold, 1967; *New Zealand Non-Fiction: A Survey with Notes for Discussion,* New Zealand University Press, 1968; *Bucks and Bruisers: Pierce Egan and Regency England,* Routledge & Kegan Paul, 1971; (with G.A. Wilkes) *The Literature of Australia and New Zealand,* Pennsylvania University Press, 1971.

Author of pamphlets and booklets, and of radio scripts, including several biographical and literary series. General editor, "New Zealand Fiction" series, Auckland University Press, 1970—. Contributor to *Encyclopaedia Britannica, New Zealand Encyclopaedia,* and *New Catholic En-*cyclopedia. Writer of weekly literary article in *New Zealand Tablet,* Dunedin, 1944-52, 1954-61, weekly radio review in *New Zealand Listener,* Wellington, 1949-52, 1954-61, regular film review column in *Auckland Star,* 1954-61. Other articles and reviews have been published in *Downside Review* (England), *Aristo* (Netherlands), *Renascence* and *Victorian Studies* (United States), and in periodicals in Australia and New Zealand. Founder and editor, *View* (monthly journal of current affairs), 1938-42; editor, *Guerilla* (soldier's monthly), 1942-45.

WORK IN PROGRESS: A Social History of the English Novel 1785-1835, completion expected in 1975.

SIDELIGHTS: Reid collected material for his first major nineteenth-century study (on Coventry Patmore) when he was in the United States in 1953, and researched his book on Thomas Hood during a sabbatical year in Britain and continental Europe in 1962. While in England he also assisted at Cambridge University with the editing of one of the volumes in the Pilgrim edition of the letters of Charles Dickens.

While Reid's major professional interest is the Victorian period he also has published several studies of contemporary French and German writers, and is vitally interested in New Zealand writing, which, he says, "has reached a very significant stage of development since World War II." He has been partly instrumental in arranging a series of individual studies on New Zealand writers to be published by Twayne under the general editorship of Joseph Jones of the University of Texas.

Outside the university, Reid's interests lie in radio, film, and the theatre. Spare-time occupations: Reading, listening to music, golf, and sleeping.

* * *

REISNER, Robert George 1921-

PERSONAL: Born January 18, 1921, in Brooklyn, N.Y.; son of Irving (a dentist) and Bessie (Shure) Reisner. *Education:* Brooklyn College, B.A., 1948; Pratt Institute, B.L.S., 1949. *Home:* 135 West 16th St., New York, N.Y. 10011. *Agent:* Max Gartenberg, 45 West 45th St., New York, N.Y. 10036.

CAREER: Former art reference librarian at Art Institute, Chicago, Ill., Newark (N.J.) Public Library, other institutions; Institute of Jazz Studies, New York, N.Y., curator and librarian, 1952—. Instructor in jazz history, Brooklyn College, City University of New York, 1953-61; instructor in graffiti, New School for Social Research.

WRITINGS: Fakes and Forgeries in the Fine Arts: A Bibliography, Special Libraries Association, 1950; (compiler) *The Literature of Jazz, a Preliminary Bibliography,* New York Public Library, 1954, 2nd edition, 1959; (with Hal Kapplow) *Captions Courageous; or, Comments from the Gallery,* Abelard, 1958; *More Captions Courageous,* Abelard, 1959; (editor) *Beat Jokes, Bop Humor and Cool Cartoons,* Citadel, 1960; (with Bill Adler) *Western on Wry,* Citadel, 1960; *The Brave Ghouls,* Bobbs-Merrill, 1960; *The Jazz Titans,* Doubleday, 1960; (with Igor Cassini) *Igor Cassini's Blue Book of Social Cats,* Citadel, 1962; *Bird: The Legend of Charlie Parker,* Citadel, 1962; (with Adler) *What Goes on Here?,* Citadel, 1963; *Show Me the Good Parts: The Reader's Guide to Sex in Literature,* Citadel, 1964; *Kosher Kaptions* (in Yiddish), J.W. Publications, 1964; *Great Wall Writings,* Grove, 1967; (compiler) *Graffiti: Selected Scrawls from Bathroom Walls,* Canyon Books, 1968; *Graffiti: 2000 Years of Wall Writing,* Cowles, 1971; *Great Erotic Scenes from Literature,* Playboy Press, 1972. Columnist, *Village Voice;* contributor of articles to *Esquire, Playboy, Down Beat, Cavalier,* and other men's magazines.

REMINI, Robert Vincent 1921-

PERSONAL: Born July 17, 1921; son of William Francis and Lauretta (Tierney) Remini; married Ruth T. Kuhner; children: Elizabeth Mary, Joan Marie, Robert William. *Education:* Fordham University, B.S., 1943; Columbia University, M.A., 1947, Ph.D., 1951. *Office address:* Department of History, University of Illinois, Box 4348, Chicago, Ill. 60680.

CAREER: Fordham University, New York, N.Y., instructor, 1947-51, assistant professor, 1951-59, associate professor of American history, 1959-65; University of Illinois, Chicago Circle Campus, professor of history, 1965—, chairman of department, 1965-66, 1967-71. Visiting lecturer, Columbia University, 1959-60. *Military service:* U.S. Navy, 1943-46; became lieutenant. *Member:* American Historical Association, Organization of American Historians, American Association of University Professors. *Awards, honors:* Grant-in-aid, American Council of Learned Societies, 1960; Encaenia Award, Fordham University, 1963; grant-in-aid, American Philosophical Society, 1964.

WRITINGS: Martin Van Buren and the Making of the Democratic Party, Columbia University Press, 1959; *The Election of Andrew Jackson,* Lippincott, 1963; (editor and author of introduction and notes) D.R. Fox, *The Decline of Aristocracy in the Politics of New York, 1801-1840,* Harper, 1965; *Andrew Jackson* (biography), Twayne, 1966; (editor and author of introduction) James Parton, *The Presidency of Andrew Jackson,* Harper, 1967; *Andrew Jackson and the Bank War: A Study in the Growth of Presidential Power,* Norton, 1967; (editor) *The Age of Jackson,* University of South Carolina Press, 1972. Special editor, Crowell-Collier Educational Corp.

WORK IN PROGRESS: A biography of Martin Van Buren.

AVOCATIONAL INTERESTS: Travel, music.

*   *   *

RENDINA, Laura (Jones) Cooper 1902-

PERSONAL: Born November 9, 1902, in Northampton, Mass.; daughter of Edward Lincoln and Emma (Burckes) Jones; widowed; children: (first marriage) Eveleth (Mrs. John C. Cowles), David, Judith (Mrs. Charles M. Chamberlain); (second marriage) Laura (Mrs. James Eadens), Mario. *Education:* Attended Smith College, two years, and Yale Art School. *Politics:* Independent. *Religion:* Unitarian. *Home:* 606 Calle del Otono, Sarasota, Fla. 33581.

CAREER: Writer, mainly of books for young people.

WRITINGS—All published by Little, Brown: *Roommates* (Junior Literary Guild selection), 1948, *Debbie Jones,* 1950, *Summer for Two,* 1952, *My Love for One,* 1955, *Lolly Touchberry,* 1957, *Trudi,* 1959, *World of Their Own* (Junior Literary Guild selection), 1963, *Destination Capri* (Junior Literary Guild selection), 1968. Contributor of short stories to *Ladies' Home Journal* and *Seventeen.*

WORK IN PROGRESS: A juvenile novel about the unicorn.

SIDELIGHTS: Mrs. Rendina has lived in Europe, principally in Italy, at intervals. *Avocational interests:* Working with youth groups.

BIOGRAPHICAL/CRITICAL SOURCES: Best Sellers, November 1, 1968.

*   *   *

REUSS, Henry S(choellkopf) 1912-

PERSONAL: Surname rhymes with "choice"; born February 22, 1912, in Milwaukee, Wis.; son of Gustav (a banker) and Paula (Schoellkopf) Reuss; married Margaret Magrath, October 24, 1942; children: Christopher, Michael, Jacqueline, Ann. *Education:* Cornell University, B.A., 1933; Harvard University, LL.B., 1936. *Politics:* Democrat. *Religion:* Episcopalian. *Home:* 2400 East Bradford Ave., Milwaukee, Wis. 53211.

CAREER: Admitted to Wisconsin bar, 1936; practicing lawyer in Milwaukee, Wis., 1936-55; U.S. House of Representatives, Washington, D.C., congressman for Fifth Wisconsin District, 1955—. Assistant general counsel, Office of Price Administration, Washington, D.C., 1941-42; member of advisory committee, National Resources Board, 1948-52; deputy general counsel, Marshall Plan, Paris, France, 1949. Alumni overseer, *Harvard Law Review,* 1956-60. *Military service:* U.S. Army, Infantry, 1943-45; became captain; received Bronze Star. U.S. Army Reserve, retired as lieutenant colonel, 1964.

WRITINGS: The Task for 1962: A Free World Community, U.S. Government Printing Office, 1961; *The Critical Decade: An Economic Policy for America and the Free World,* with an introduction by Hubert H. Humphrey, McGraw, 1964; (with Robert Ellsworth) *Off Dead Center: Some Proposals to Strengthen Free World Economic Cooperation,* U.S. Government Printing Office, 1965; (with Paul A. Fino) *Food for Progress in Latin America,* U.S. Government Printing Office, 1967; *Revenue-Sharing: Crutch or Catalyst for State and Local Governments?,* Praeger, 1970. Contributor of articles to magazines.

*   *   *

REWALD, John 1912-

PERSONAL: Born May 12, 1912, in Berlin, Germany; came to United States in 1941, naturalized in 1947; son of Bruno A. and Pauline (Feinstein) Rewald; married Estelle Haimovici, 1939 (divorced); married Alice Leglise-Bellony, 1956; children: (first marriage) Paul. *Education:* Studied at University of Hamburg, 1931, University of Frankfort, 1932; Sorbonne, University of Paris, Ph.D., 1936. *Home:* 1075 Park Ave., New York, N.Y. 10028.

CAREER: Art historian; curator of private collection of John Hay Whitney. University of Chicago, Chicago, Ill., professor of art history, 1964-71; City University of New York, New York, N.Y., professor of art history, 1971—. Visiting professor, Princeton University, 1961.

WRITINGS: Cezanne et Zola, Editions A. Sedrowski (Paris), 1936, revised and enlarged edition published as *Cezanne, sa vie, son oeuvre, son amitie pour Zola,* A. Michel (Paris), 1939, translation by Margaret H. Liebman published as *Paul Cezanne: A Biography,* Simon & Schuster, 1948, 2nd edition, Schocken, 1968 (published in England as *The Ordeal of Paul Cezanne,* Phoenix House, 1950, 2nd edition published as *Paul Cezanne,* Spring Books, 1958); (editor) *Paul Cezanne, Correspondance,* B. Grasset (Paris), 1937, translation by Marguerite Kay published as *Paul Cezanne Letters,* Wittenborn, 1941, 3rd edition, Cassirer (Oxford); 1946; *Gauguin,* French and European Publications (New York), 1938; *Camille Pissaro au Musee du Louvre,* Editions Marion, 1939, published in England as *Camille Pissarro at the Musee du Louvre,* Collins, 1946; *Maillol,* translation by P. Montagu, Hyperion Press, 1939.

(Editor with Lucien Pissarro) *Camille Pissarro: Letters to His Son Lucien* (originally written in French, but first published in English), translation by Lionel Abel, Pantheon, 1943, French edition, A. Michel, 1950; (editor) *The Woodcuts of Aristide Maillol: A Complete Catalogue,* Pantheon, 1943; *Georges Seurat* (originally written in French, but first published in English), translation by Lionel Abel, Wittenborn, 1943, 2nd edition, revised, 1946, enlarged French edition, A. Michel, 1958; (editor) *Paul Gauguin: Letters to Ambroise Vollard and Andre Fontainas*, Grabhorn, 1943; (editor) *Degas: Works in Sculpture: A Complete Catalogue* (originally written in French, but published in English), translation by John Coleman and Noel Moulton, Pantheon, 1944; *The History of Impressionism*, Museum of Modern Art, 1946, revised and enlarged edition, 1962; (editor) *Renoir Drawings*, H. Bittner, 1946, new edition, Yoseloff, 1958; *Edouard Manet Pastels*, Cassirer, 1947; (contributor) *Nineteenth Century French Drawings*, California Palace of the Legion of Honor, 1947; *Pierre Bonnard*, Museum of Modern Art, 1948.

(Editor) *Paul Cezanne, Carnet de dessins*, Quatre Chemins-Editart (Paris), 1951; *Les Fauves* (catalogue of an exhibition), Museum of Modern Art, 1952; *Post-Impressionism from Van Gogh to Gauguin*, Museum of Modern Art, 1956, 2nd edition, revised, 1962; *Sculture ed incisioni su legno de Reder* (originally written in English, but first published in Italian), Sansoni (Florence), 1957; (editor) *Gauguin Drawings*, Yoseloff, 1958; (author of introduction) Henri-Edmond Cross, *Carnet de dessins*, Berggruen (Paris), 1959; (with Henri Dorra) *Seurat, l'oeuvre peint, biographie et catalogue critique*, Les Beaux-Arts (Paris), 1959.

Cezanne, Geoffroy et Gasquet, Quatre Chemins-Editart, 1960; (contributor) *Redon and Others*, Museum of Modern Art, 1961; (author of foreword) *Paul Gauguin, A Sketchbook*, Hammer Galleries, 1962; Camille Pissarro, Abrams, 1963; (author of memoir) *Morandi*, Loeb Gallery, 1967; *Giacomo Manzu*, Verlag Galerie Welz (Salzburg), 1966, American edition, New York Graphic Society, 1967; (author of preface) J. Salomon, *Vuillard*, Gallimard, 1968.

WORK IN PROGRESS: Paul Cezanne, catalogue raisonne, for New York Graphic Society.

SIDELIGHTS: Rewald's books have been published in French, German, Italian, Spanish, Czech, Russian, and Japanese editions.

*   *   *

REYNOLDS, Barbara   1914-

PERSONAL: Born June 13, 1914, in Bristol, Gloucestershire, England; daughter of Alfred Charles (a composer) and Barbara (a singer; maiden name, Florac) Reynolds; married Lewis Thorpe (a professor of French at University of Nottingham), September 5, 1939; children: Adrian Charles, Kerstin. *Education:* Attended schools in Detroit, Mich., 1922-26, Chicago, Ill., 1926-27, St. Paul's Girls' School, London, England, 1927-32; University College, University of London, B.A. (honors in French), 1935, B.A. (honors in Italian), 1936, Ph.D., 1948; Cambridge University, M.A., 1940. *Religion:* Church of England. *Office:* Italian Department, University of Nottingham, Nottingham NG7 2RD, England.

CAREER: London School of Economics, University of London, London, England, assistant lecturer in Italian, 1937-40; Cambridge University, Cambridge, England, lecturer in Italian, 1940-62; University of Nottingham, Nottingham, England, lecturer in Italian and warden of a hall of residence, 1963-69, reader in Italian studies, 1969—. Member of council of senate, Cambridge University, 1960-62; governor, Nottingham Bluecoat School. *Member:* Society for Italian Studies (honorary secretary, 1946-52; member of executive committee, 1946-62), British and Foreign Bible Society (member of general committee), Translators' Association, Authors' Society, P.E.N. *Awards, honors:* Silver Cultural medal, 1964, for services to Italian culture; Edmund Gardner prize, 1964, for original Italian scholarship.

WRITINGS: (Editor and author of introduction and notes with K.T. Butler) *Tredici novelle moderne*, Macmillan (New York), 1947, 2nd edition, Cambridge University Press, 1959; *The Linguistic Writings of Alessandro Manzoni: A Textual and Chronological Reconstruction*, Heffer, 1950; (editor) M.A. Orr, *Dante and the Early Astronomers*, 2nd edition, Wingate, 1956; (general editor and chef contributor) *The Cambridge Italian Dictionary*, Volume I, Cambridge University Press, 1962; (translator with Dorothy L. Sayers) Dante, *The Comedy of Dante Alighieri, the Florentine*, three volumes, Basic Books, 1962; (with husband, Lewis Thorpe) *Guido Farina*, Valdonega, 1967; (translator) Dante, *La Vita nuova: Poems of Youth*, Penguin, 1969. Contributor of reviews of Italian books to *Birmingham Post*, and of reviews and articles to *Times* (London), *Times Literary Supplement*, and to learned journals.

WORK IN PROGRESS: Editing *Cambridge Italian Dictionary*, Volume II, and *Concise Italian Dictionary*, both for Cambridge University Press; *Italy, A Companion to Italian Studies*, for Methuen; a critical edition of Manzoni's *Linguistic Writings*, for Lemonnier; a translation of Ariosto's *Orlando Furioso*, for Penguin.

SIDELIGHTS: Miss Reynolds concludes, after thirty-four years of full-time academic career, that "the pursuit of knowledge for its own sake has been indulged in too much in universities. What is needed now is the pursuit of understanding."

*   *   *

REYNOLDS, Charles O.   1921-

PERSONAL: Born April 25, 1921, in Philadelphia, Pa.; son of O.C. and O.E. (Miller) Reynolds. *Education:* Attended Temple University, three years. *Religion:* Protestant. *Office:* Lukens Steel Co., Strode Ave., Coatesville, Pa. 19320.

CAREER: Atlantic Refining Co., Philadelphia, Pa., supervisor, 1950-55; self-employed in own personnel agency, Philadelphia, Pa., 1955-57; W.A. Clark Mortgage Co., Philadelphia, Pa., staff assistant to treasurer, 1957-61; Lukens Steel Co., Coatesville, Pa., senior systems analyst, 1961—; Paramount Publishing Co., Coatesville, Pa., president, 1961—. *Military service:* U.S. Navy, 1942-45; served in four Pacific invasions; became acting chief petty officer. U.S. Naval Reserve, communications instructor, 1946-50, 1955-59. *Member:* National Office Management Association (director, six years), Data Processing Association, American Legion.

WRITINGS: The Modern Programmer, Pyramid Publishing Co., 1960; *Programming the 1401 Systems: Card, Ramac and Tape*, Pyramid Publishing Co., 1961; *The System Behind 1401 Programming*, Pyramid Publishing Co., 1962; *Work Simplification for Everyone*, Pyramid Publishing Co., 1962; *The Modern Systems Analyst*, Pyramid Publishing Co., 1963. Contributor of articles to data processing and other business publications. Editor of journals of National Office Management Association and Data Processing Association.

WORK IN PROGRESS: Over the Side, story of World War II in the Pacific; *The Sixth Key*, mystery adventure; *Faith, Hope, but no Charity*, mystery adventure; "Curtis Boys," an adventure series for boys; *Power and the Plague*.

AVOCATIONAL INTERESTS: Photography, and printing and developing film and slides.

BIOGRAPHICAL/CRITICAL SOURCES: American Data Processing Magazine, 1962.

REYNOLDS, John 1901-

PERSONAL: Born May 16, 1901, in Sydney, Australia; son of Henry and Frances Edith (Rule) Reynolds; married Isabelle Alice Greayer, July 9, 1928; children: David Greayer, Mary Greayer (Mrs. Rex Turner), Henry, Judith Ann. Education: Attended Friend's School, Hobart High School, and Hobart Technical College. Home: 10 Knocklofty Ter., West Hobart, Tasmania, Australia.

CAREER: Electrolytic Zinc Co. of Australasia, Hobart, Australia, metallurgist, 1924-39; Government of Tasmania, Hobart, senior officer, 1938-55; Tasmanian Grain Elevators Board, Hobart, manager, 1956-61, chairman, 1961-66; director of mining companies, 1968—. Member: Tasmanian Fellowship of Australian Writers (president, 1953, 1959-60, 1967-69), Australian Institute of International Affairs (president, Tasmanian branch, 1962-63), Tasmanian Historical Research Association (president, 1969). Awards, honors: Commonwealth Literary Fund award, 1944.

WRITINGS: The Discovery of Tasmania, Tasmanian Government Printer, 1942; Edmund Barton, P.D. & Ione Perkins, 1948; Rt. Hon. Sir Edward Nicholas Coventry Braddon, 1829-1904 (pamphlet), Queen Victoria Museum, 1952; (with Frank Green and W.A. Townsley) Centenary of Responsible Government (1856-1956), Tasmanian Government Printer, 1956; Launceston: History of an Australian City, Macmillan of Australia, 1969; Windmills and Watermills, Praeger, 1970. Contributor of biographical articles to Australian and British newspapers and periodicals.

WORK IN PROGRESS: A Short History of Australian Mining; Americans in Australia 1788-Today (provisional title).

*   *   *

REYNOLDS, Timothy (Robin) 1936-

PERSONAL: Born July 18, 1936, in Vicksburg, Miss.; son of Earle Landry (an anthropologist) and Barbara (Leonard) Reynolds; married Mary Kay Crawford, 1961; children: Anthony Felix. Education: Attended Antioch College, 1953-56; University of Wisconsin, B.A., 1961; Tufts University, M.A., 1962.

CAREER: Writer. Military service: U.S. Army language school, 1956-58.

WRITINGS: Ryoanji: Poems, Harcourt, 1964; Catfish Goodbye: Poems, Anubis Press, 1966; Slocum (poems), Unicorn Press (Santa Barbara), 1967; (author of book and lyrics) "Peace" (musical play based on a play by Aristophanes; music by Al Carmines), first produced Off-Broadway at Astor Place Theatre, January 27, 1969.

WORK IN PROGRESS: Compiling collection, Halflife, Poems 1962-64; also working on "some untenable plays."

SIDELIGHTS: Reynolds has varying degrees of fluency in French, German, Russian, Latin, and Greek.

BIOGRAPHICAL/CRITICAL SOURCES: Cue, February 8, 1969; Variety, February 12, 1969.

*   *   *

RHODES, Anthony (Richard Ewart) 1916-

PERSONAL: Born September 24, 1916, in Plymouth, Devon, England; son of George E. (a colonel) and Dorothy Rhodes; married Rosaleen Forbes. Education: Attended Rugby School, 1930-35, Royal Military Academy, 1935-37; Trinity College, Cambridge, M.A., 1939; University of Geneva, licence es lettres, 1952. Home: 40 Lower Belgrave St., London S.W.1, England. Agent: Anthony Sheil, 47 Dean St., London W.1, England; and Julian Bach, 3 East 48th St., New York, N.Y. 10017.

CAREER: British Army, Royal Engineers, 1936-46; became captain; University of Geneva, Geneva, Switzerland, assistant professor of English literature, 1946-52; Eton College, Windsor, England, assistant master, 1952-53; author. Member: P.E.N., Travellers Club, Pall Mall Club.

WRITINGS: Sword of Bone, Faber, 1942, Harcourt, 1943; The Uniform (novel), Laurie, 1949; A Sabine Journey: To Rome in Holy Year, Putnam (London), 1952; A Ball in Venice (novel), Arthur Barker, 1953; The General's Summer-House (novel), Arthur Barker, 1954; The Dalmatian Coast, Evans Brothers, 1955; Where the Turk Trod: A Journey to Sarajevo with a Slavonic Mussulman, Weidenfeld & Nicolson, 1956; The Poet as Superman: A Life of Gabriele d'Annunzio, Weidenfeld & Nicolson, 1959, published in America as D'Annunzio, the Poet as Superman, McDowell, Oblensky, 1960; The Prophet's Carpet, Weidenfeld & Nicolson, 1961; (editor) Raphael Rupert, A Hidden World, World Publishing, 1963; Louis Renault: A Biography, Cassell, 1969, Harcourt, 1970; Art Treasures of Eastern Europe, Putnam, 1972.

Translator: Roger Nimier, The Blue Hussar, MacGibbon & Kee, 1952; Felicien Marceau, By Invitation Only, Arthur Barker, 1955; Marthe Bibesco, Marcel Proust at the Ball, Weidenfeld & Nicolson, 1956; Jean Francois Revel, As For Italy, Dial, 1959; C. Lorques-Lapouge, The Old Masters: Byzantine, Gothic, Renaissance, Baroque, Crown, 1963; Valentino Crivellato, Tiepolo, Norton, 1962; Hitler's War Directions, Sidgwick & Jackson, 1964; Giulio Carlo Argan, The Europe of the Capitals, 1600-1700, Skira, 1965; (and editor) Pietro Quaroni, Diplomatic Bags: An Ambassador's Memoirs, David White, 1966; Walter Scheidig, Unfamiliar Masterpieces of Painting in East German Collections, October House, 1966; Helmut Radamacher, Masters of German Poster Art, Verlag fuer Kunst & Wissenschaft, 1966; Robert Boulanger and Hatice Nesrin, Egyptian Painting and the Ancient East, Heron House, 1967. Contributor to Listener, Encounter, Sunday Times (London), Daily Telegraph, and other periodicals and newspapers.

WORK IN PROGRESS: The Vatican in the Age of the Dictators, for Holt.

AVOCATIONAL INTERESTS: Astronomy, dendrology.

BIOGRAPHICAL/CRITICAL SOURCES: Books and Bookmen, December, 1961; Observer Review, July 20, 1969; New York Times Book Review, February 22, 1970.

*   *   *

RICE, David Talbot 1903-

*   *   *

PERSONAL: Born July 11, 1903, in Rugby, England; son of Henry Charles Talbot and Cecil Mary (Lloyd) Rice; married Tamara Abelson, 1927; children: Elizabeth Talbot, Nina Talbot, Nicholas Talbot. Education: Attended Eton College; Christ Church, Oxford, B.A., 1925, B.Sc., 1927, M.A., 1928, D.Litt., 1939. Home: 20 Nelson St., Edinburgh 3, Scotland. Office: University of Edinburgh, Edinburgh, Scotland.

CAREER: Courtauld Institute of Art, University of London, London, England, lecturer in Byzantine and Near Eastern art, 1932-34; University of Edinburgh, Edinburgh, Scotland, professor of fine art, 1934—, vice-principal, 1967—. National Gallery of Scotland, trustee. Military service: British Army, Intelligence Corps, 1939-45; became lieutenant colonel; received Order of British Empire. Member: Society of Antiquaries, United University Club (London), Arts Club (Edinburgh), Royal Scottish Academy (honorary). Awards, honors: Commander, Order of the British Empire, 1969.

WRITINGS—Appear under surnames Rice and Talbot Rice: (With Stanley Casson, G.F. Hudson, and A.H.M. Jones) *Preliminary Report Upon the Excavations Carried Out in the Hippodrome of Constantinople in 1927*, British Academy, 1928; (with Casson, Hudson, and B. Gray) *Second Report Upon the Excavations Carried Out in and Near the Hippodrome of Constantinople in 1928*, British Academy, 1929; *Byzantine Glazed Pottery*, Oxford University Press, 1930; (with Robert Byron) *The Birth of Western Painting: A History of Colour Form and Iconography*, Routledge & Sons, 1930, Knopf, 1931; (translator with wife, Tamara Talbot Rice) *Caravan Cities*, Oxford University Press, 1932; *The Scope of Art History*, Oliver & Boyd, 1934; *Byzantine Art*, Clarendon Press, 1935, 2nd revised edition, Penguin, 1962; (editor) *Russian Art*, Gurney & Jackson, 1935; (with Gabriel Millet) *Byzantine Painting at Trebizond*, Allen & Unwin, 1936; (with chapters by Rupert Gunnis and Tamara Talbot Rice) *The Icons of Cyprus*, Allen & Unwin, 1937, Verry, 1964; *The Beginnings of Russian Icon Painting*, Oxford University Press, 1938; *The Background of Art*, Thomas Nelson, 1939.

The Byzantine Element in Late Saxon Art, Oxford University Press, 1947; *Russian Icons*, Penguin, 1947; *Byzantine Painting and Developments in the West Before A.D. 1200*, Transatlantic, 1948; (reviser) William Richard Lethaby, *Medieval Art, From the Peace of the Church to the Eve of the Renaissance, 312-1350*, 3rd edition, Thomas Nelson, 1949, Philosophical Library, 1950; *English Art, 871-1100*, Oxford University Press, 1952; *Teach Yourself to Study Art*, Roy, 1955; (author of preface) *Yugoslavia: Medieval Frescoes*, New York Graphic Society, 1955; *The Beginnings of Christian Art*, Hodder & Stoughton, 1957, Abingdon, 1958; (compiler) *The University Portraits*, Edinburgh University Press, 1957; *Masterpieces of Byzantine Art*, Edinburgh University Press, 1958; (editor) *The Great Palace of the Byzantine Emperors, Second Report*, Edinburgh University Press, 1958; *The Art of Byzantium, Text and Notes*, Abrams, 1959; (editor) *Byzantine Icons*, Faber, 1959.

The Byzantines, Praeger, 1962, revised edition, 1966; *The Art of the Byzantine Era*, Praeger, 1963; *Byzantine Frescoes from Yugoslav Churches*, New American Library, 1963; (reviser) Konrad Onasch, *Icons*, Faber, 1963; (editor) Victor Beyer, *Stained Glass Windows*, Oliver & Boyd, 1964; (reviser) Frederich Moebius and Helga Moebius, *Mediaeval Churches in Germany: Saxony, Thuringia, Brandenburg, and Mecklenburg*, Edition Leipzig, 1964, Boston Book and Art Shop, 1965; *Constantinople from Byzantium to Istanbul*, Stein & Day, 1965 (published in England as *Constantinople: Byzantium—Istanbul*, Elek, 1965); (editor) *The Dawn of European Civilization: The Dark Ages*, McGraw, 1965 (published in England as *The Making of European Civilization: The Dark Ages*, Thames & Hudson, 1965; *Islamic Art*, Praeger, 1965; *The Twelfth Century Renaissance in Byzantine Art*, University of Hull Publications, 1965; (reviser) Liana Castelfranchi Vegas, *International Gothic Art in Italy*, Verlag fuer Kunst & Wissenschaft, 1966; (reviser) *Munich*, Verlag fuer Kunst & Wissenschaft, 1967, A.S. Barnes, 1969; *A Concise History of Painting from Prehistory to the Thirteenth Century*, Thames & Hudson, 1967, Praeger, 1968; *Byzantine Painting: The Last Phase*, Dial, 1968; (editor) *The Church of Hagia Sophia at Trebizond*, Aldine, 1968; (with Tamara Talbot Rice) *Icons: The Natasha Allen Collection*, National Gallery of Ireland, 1968; (reviser) *Stockholm*, A.S. Barnes, 1969; *Islamic Painting: A Survey*, Edinburgh University Press, 1971. Editor with W.G. Constable, "Courtauld Institute Publications on Near Eastern Art," University of London, 1936— ; general editor, "Realms of Art" series, Oliver & Boyd, 1963— .

AVOCATIONAL INTERESTS: Travel and country life.

RICE, Desmond Charles   1924-
(Desmond Meiring)

PERSONAL: Born May 29, 1924, in Kenya; son of H.P. (a colonel, British Colonial Police) and Violet (Allport) Rice; married Magda Heilig, May 5, 1957. *Education:* Attended Cheltenham College, 1937-40, University of Cape Town, 1940-41, 1946-48, and Oxford University, 1948-50. *Politics:* "Practical liberal by conviction." *Religion:* Born Roman Catholic, now neutral. *Home:* No. 6 Appartment, Edificio Tamanacito, Sector Les Naranjos, Los Mercedes, Caracas, Venezuela. *Agent:* Curtis Brown Ltd., 60 East 56th St., New York, N.Y. 10022, and 13 King St., Covent Garden, London W.C. 2, England. *Office:* Compania Shell de Venezuela, Apartado 1074, Caracas, Venezuela.

CAREER: Assistant inspector of Kenya police, Nairobi, Kenya, 1941-42; *Cape Times*, Cape Town, South Africa, reporter, 1951; Shell Oil Co., executive in South Africa, 1951-54, Israel, 1955-57, Tanganyika, 1957-59, Laos and Indochina, 1959-60, Thailand, 1960-61, Venezuela, 1962—. *Military service:* South African Army, 1943-46; gunner in Sixth Armoured Division; served with British Eighth Army and American Fifth Army in Italy. *Member:* Ski Club of Great Britain.

WRITINGS—All under pseudonym Desmond Meiring: *The Man With No Shadow*, Hodder & Stoughton, 1962; *The Brinkman*, Hodder & Stoughton, 1964, Houghton, 1965; *A Square Called Silence*, Houghton, 1966.

WORK IN PROGRESS: A novel set in Caracas.

SIDELIGHTS: Rice is fluent in French and Spanish, speaks fair to good Italian, modern Hebrew, Kiswahili, and Afrikaans, and some German, Mandarin, and Thai.†

*   *   *

RICE, Dorothy Mary   1913-
(Dorothy Borne, Dorothy Vicary)

PERSONAL: Born April 26, 1913, in Dublin, Ireland; daughter of Samuel (a barrister-at-law) and Kathleen (Dixon) Rice. *Education:* Studied at Convent of the Sacred Heart, Armagh, Northern Ireland; Queen's University, Belfast, Northern Ireland, B.A., 1934. *Home:* 9 Pembridge Villas, London W. 11, England. *Agent:* C.V. Jackson, 91 Church St., London N. 9, England. *Office:* Powell Duffryn Ltd., London, England.

CAREER: Secretary, now with Powell Duffryn Ltd., London, England. Author of children's books.

WRITINGS—All published by Blackie & Son: *Hugh Nameless*, 1950, *The Boy on the Boat-Train*, 1952, *A Secret at Sprayle*, 1955, *The Gale in the Wall*, 1959.

Under pseudonym Dorothy Vicary—All published by Blackie & Son: *Lucy Brown's Schooldays*, 1937, *Niece of the Headmistress*, 1939, *Good for Gracie!*, 1938, *Blackie's Girl's School Story Onmibus*, 1956.

Under pseudonym Dorothy Borne: *A House with a Secret*, Thomas Nelson, 1963; *Ringer's Roost*, Thomas Nelson, 1964.

AVOCATIONAL INTERESTS: Pottery, theater, travel, ballroom dancing.

*   *   *

RICE, William C(arroll)   1911-

PERSONAL: Born September 12, 1911, in Mountain Home, Ark.; son of William C. (a farmer) and Mary (Holt) Rice; married Veta N. Douthit, May 28, 1933; children: Janet Carol, Richard David. *Education:* Warrensburg Conservatory of Music, Warrensburg, Mo., diploma 1931; Warrensburg State Teachers College, B.S.,

1932; Northwestern University, M. Mus. Ed., 1941; State University of Iowa, Ph.D., 1953. *Politics:* Independent. *Religion:* Protestant. *Home:* 805 Orange St., Baldwin, Kan. 66006.

CAREER: High school teacher in Middletown, Mo., 1932-34; music teacher in public schools in Nevada, Mo., 1934-37, and in St. Joseph, Mo., 1937-39; Baker University, Baldwin, Kan., head of department of music, 1939—. Assistant field, director and field director, American National Red Cross, 1943-45. *Member:* Music Teachers National Association, National Association of Teachers of Singing, Hymn Society of America, National Fellowship of Methodist Musicians (president, 1958-61), Choristers Guild, Pi Kappa Lambda.

WRITINGS: (With Austin C. Lovelace) *Music and Worship in the Church,* Abingdon, 1960; *Basic Principles of Singing,* Abingdon, 1961; (with Madeline D. Ingram) *Vocal Technique for Children and Youth,* Abingdon, 1962; *A Concise History of Church Music,* Abingdon, 1964. Contributor of articles to *Music Ministry, Music Educators Journal,* and other periodicals in music education, religious education, and related fields.

AVOCATIONAL INTERESTS: Gardening, woodworking, and general carpentry.

* * *

RICH, Adrienne Cecile   1929-

PERSONAL: Born May 16, 1929, in Baltimore, Md.; daughter of Arnold Rice (a physician) and Helen Jones) Rich; married Alfred H. Conrad (an economist), June 26, 1953 (died, 1970); children: David, Paul, Jacob. *Education:* Attended Roland Park Country School, Baltimore, Md., 1938-47; Radcliffe College, A.B. (cum laude), 1951.

CAREER: Poet. Conducted workshop at YM-YWHA Poetry Center, 1966-67; Columbia University, Graduate School of the Arts, New York, N.Y., adjunct professor in writing division, 1967-69; City College of the City University of New York, New York, N.Y., lecturer in SEEK English program, 1968-70, instructor in creative writing program, 1970-71, assistant professor of English, 1971-72. Visiting poet, Swarthmore College, 1966-68; Fannie Hurst Visiting Professor of Creative Literature, Brandeis University, 1972-73. *Member:* Phi Beta Kappa. *Awards, honors:* Yale Series of Younger Poets award, 1951, for *A Change of World;* Guggenheim fellowships, 1952 and 1961; Ridgely Torrence Memorial Award of the Poetry Society of America, 1955; Grace Thayer Bradley award, Friends of Literature (Chicago), 1956, for *The Diamond Cutters;* Phi Beta Kappa Poet, College of William and Mary, 1960, Swarthmore College, 1965, Harvard University, 1966; National Institute of Arts and Letters award for poetry, 1961; Amy Lowell travelling fellowship, 1962; Bollingen Foundation translation grant, 1962; Bess Hokin Prize of *Poetry* magazine, 1963; Litt.D., Wheaton College, 1967; National Translation Center grant, 1968; Eunice Tietjens Memorial Prize of *Poetry* magazine, 1968; National Endowment for the Arts grant, 1970, for poems in *American Literary Anthology: 3;* Shelley Memorial Award of Poetry Society of America, 1971.

WRITINGS—All poetry: *A Change of World* (foreword by W.H. Auden), Yale University Press, 1951; *Poems,* Oxford University Poetry Society, 1952; *The Diamond Cutters and Other Poems,* Harper, 1955; *Snapshots of a Daughter-in-Law: Poems, 1954-62,* Harper, 1962; *Focus,* [Cambridge, Mass.], 1966; *Necessities of Life* (as an epilogue, includes her translations of poetry from the Dutch), Norton, 1966; *Selected Poems,* Chatto & Windus, 1966; *Leaflets: Poems, 1965-1968,* Norton, 1969; *The Will*

to Change: Poems, 1968-1970, Norton, 1971; *Diving Into the Wreck,* Norton, 1973.

Contributor: Anthony Ostroff, editor, *The Poet As Critic,* Little, Brown, 1965; Janine Hensley, editor, *The Works of Anne Bradstreet,* Harvard University Press, 1967; Robert Lowell, Peter Taylor, and Robert Penn Warren, editors, *Randall Jarrell, 1914-1965,* Farrar, Straus, 1967.

Translator: Mark Insingel, *Reflections,* Red Dust, 1973. Contributor of translations: Olga Carlisle, editor, *Poets on Street Corners: Portraits of 15 Russian Poets,* Random House, 1968; Irving Howe and Eliezer Greenberg, editors, *A Treasury of Yiddish Poetry,* Holt, 1969; Aijaz Ahmad, editor, *Selected Poems of Mirza Ghalib,* Columbia University Press, 1971.

Represented in anthologies, including among others, *Contemporary American Poetry,* edited by Donald Hall, Penguin, 1962; *New Poets of England and America,* Meridian, 1962; *A Controversy of Poets,* edited by P. Leary and Robert Kelly, Doubleday, 1965; *Poems of Our Moment,* edited by John Hollander, Pegasus, 1968; *The Contemporary American Poets: American Poetry Since 1940,* edited by Mark Strand, New American Library, 1969; *The Voice That is Great Within Us: American Poetry of the Twentieth Century,* Bantam, 1970; *A Little Treasury of Modern Poetry, English and American,* edited by Oscar Williams, Scribner, 1970; *American Literary Anthology: 3,* edited by George Plimpton and Peter Ardery, Viking, 1970.

Contributor of reviews and critical articles to *Poetry, Nation, New York Review of Books, Partisan Review, Paris Review,* and other publications. Columnist, *American Poetry Review.*

WORK IN PROGRESS: Contributing to forthcoming volume in Harvard English Studies, for Harvard University Press.

SIDELIGHTS: "Adrienne Rich has grown steadily more interesting from book to book and now in her fourth work, *Necessities of Life,* this advance, tortuous and sometimes tortured as it has been, is an arrival, a poised and intact completion," wrote Robert Lowell. "The whole book," he said, "gives an impression of having the continuity and force of a single stream of contemplation. . . the hovering, miragelike landscape and goal, once seen so distantly and dimly, becomes solid. One feels the leisure, rest and elbowroom, and trusts every cadence, image and reflection. Nothing has been put in to startle, nothing has been left out because of caution. The only limits are the necessary, inevitable limits of a trained mind." Philip Booth said: "She has been better than 'good' for several books now; 'good,' 'fine,' 'excellent'—what does it matter? *Leaflets* proves that she has grown well beyond any such carefully-scaled critical adjectives. The poems speak for themselves, for her, and for us. Insofar as their language reflects clear light from dark sources, as they feel deeply a world of which they are fully mindful, it need only be said that these are some of the best poems now being written in America." Saying that "none of the 'young poets' of the 50s has grown with greater or more consistent grace than Adrienne Rich," Booth concludes: " . . . these are finally poems of nothing less than the greatest of revolutions: of being reborn to new vision, new feeling, new senses of both the changing world and one's changing self."

BIOGRAPHICAL/CRITICAL SOURCES: Christian Science Monitor, January 3, 1963, July 24, 1969; *Saturday Review,* June 6, 1963; *New York Times Book Review,* July 17, 1966, May 23, 1971; *Poetry,* January, 1967; *New Statesman,* November 3, 1967; *Times Literary Supplement,* November 23, 1967; *Listener,* November 30, 1967; *Chicago Review,* December, 1969; *Poetry,* March, 1970; *New York Review of Books,* May 7, 1970.

RICH, Alan 1924-

PERSONAL: Born June 17, 1924, in Boston, Mass.; son of Edward and Helen (Hirshberg) Rich. *Education:* Harvard University, B.A., 1945; University of California, Berkeley, M.A., 1952, postgraduate study, 1952-57. *Politics:* Democrat. *Religion:* Jewish. *Home:* 113 River Rd., Grand View-on-Hudson, N.Y. 10960. *Agent:* Theron Raines, 244 Madison Ave., New York, N.Y. 10016. *Office:* 207 East 32nd St., New York, N.Y. 10016.

CAREER: Boston Herald, Boston, Mass., assistant music critic, 1944-45; *New York Sun*, New York, N.Y., assistant music critic, 1947-48; University of California, Berkeley, instructor in music, 1950-58; Alfred Hertz Memorial traveling fellow in music, Vienna, Austria, 1952-53; Pacifica Foundation, Berkeley, Calif., music and program director, FM radio, 1953-60; *New York Times*, New York, N.Y., associate music critic, 1961-63; *New York Herald Tribune*, New York, N.Y., chief music critic, 1963-66; *New York World Journal Tribune*, New York, N.Y., music critic and editor, 1966-67; *Time*, New York, N.Y., contributing editor, 1967-68; *New York*, New York, N.Y., music critic and arts editor, 1968—. *Member:* American Musicological Society, New York Music Critics Circle (secretary, 1961-63; chairman, 1963-64). *Awards, honors:* Deems Taylor Awards of American Society of Composers, Authors and Publishers: award for article, "The Metropolitan Opera vs. the Public" (published in *New York,* December 1, 1969), and first prize for books, 1970, for *Music: Mirror of the Arts.*

WRITINGS: Careers and Opportunities in Music, Dutton, 1964; *Music: Mirror of the Arts,* Praeger, 1969. Contributor to *Thompson's Encyclopedia of Music and Musicians,* and *Grolier's Encyclopedia Yearbook.* Contributor of articles on music to *Musical Quarterly, American Record Guide, High Fidelity, American Judaism,* other periodicals. Author of television script for "Voice of Firestone."

AVOCATIONAL INTERESTS: Gardening, microscopy, old movies, and new plays.

*   *   *

RICHARDS, Dennis (George) 1910-

PERSONAL: Born September 10, 1910, in London, England; son of George and Frances Amelia (Gosland) Richards; married Barbara Smethurst, January 6, 1940; children: Theresa, Caroline, Helena, Penelope. *Education:* Trinity Hall, Cambridge, B.A. (first class honors), 1931, M.A., 1935. *Home:* 16 Broadlands Rd., London N.6, England; and 8 Chichester Ter., Brighton, Sussex, England.

CAREER: Manchester Grammar School, Manchester, England, assistant master, 1931-39; Bradfield College, Berkshire, England, senior history and English master, 1939-41; Air Ministry, London, England, senior narrator, later official historian in Historical Section, 1942-49, principal of administration in Department of Permanent Secretary, 1949-50; Morley College (adult education), London, England, principal, 1950-65; University of Sussex, Falmer, Brighton, England, Longmans fellow, 1965-68. External examiner in history, Redland College, University of Bristol, 1961-64. *Military service:* Royal Air Force, 1941-42; became honorary squadron leader. *Member:* International P.E.N. (member of executive committee, English center, 1961—), Society of Authors, Institute of Strategic Studies, Historical Association, Arts Club of London (member of executive committee, 1961-64). *Awards, honors:* C.P. Robertson Memorial Trophy for best work of the year on Royal Air Force, 1954, for *Royal Air Force, 1939-1945.*

WRITINGS: An Illustrated History of Modern Europe, 1789-1938, Longmans, Green, 1938, 5th edition, 1950, revised and enlarged edition (with J.E. Cruikshank) published in Canada as *The Modern Age,* Longmans, Green, 1955; (with Joseph Wray Hunt) *An Illustrated History of Modern Britain,* Longmans, Green, 1950, 2nd edition, 1965; *Royal Air Force, 1939-1945,* H.M.S.O., Volume I: *The Fight at Odds,* 1953, Volume II: (with H. St. George Saunders) *The Fight Avails,* 1954, Volume III: (with Saunders) *The Fight Is Won,* 1954; *Offspring of 'the Vic': A History of Morley College,* Routledge & Kegan Paul, 1958; *Britain Under the Tudors and Stuarts,* Longmans, Green, 1958; (with Anthony Quick) *Britain, 1714-1851,* Longmans, Green, 1961; (with James A. Bolton) *Britain and the Ancient World,* Longmans, Green, 1963; (with Quick) *Britain 1851-1945,* Longmans, Green, 1967; (with Quick) *Twentieth Century Britain,* Longmans, Green, 1968; (with A. Ellis) *Medieval Britain,* Longmans, Green, 1971. General editor, "A History of Britain," 1958—.

WORK IN PROGRESS: A revised and expanded edition of *An Illustrated History of Modern Europe.*

*   *   *

RICHARDSON, Gayle E(lwin) 1911-

PERSONAL: Born April 10, 1911, in East Orange, N.J.; son of Glenn Ellison (a civil engineer) and Gabrielle (Clyne) Richardson; married Marian Sward, June 5, 1937; children: William B. *Education:* University of Michigan, A.B., 1932; studied at John Marshall Law School, 1934-35, Northwestern University, 1935-36, and Universiy of Minnesota, 1940-41. *Politics:* Conservative independent. *Religion:* Methodist. *Home:* 5367 Graceland Ave., Indianapolis, Ind. 46208. *Office:* 800 Board of Trade, Indianapolis, Ind. 46204.

CAREER: Underwriting, sales, and administrative positions in property and casualty insurance field, 1936-42; Jamestown Mutual Insurance Co., Jamestown, N.Y., actuary, 1942-43; American States Insurance Co., Indianapolis, Ind., assistant secretary, 1943-44; General Insurance Co. of America, Indianapolis, Ind., state manager, 1947-56; insurance consultant and agent and registered securities representative, Indianapolis, Ind., 1957—. Lecturer, Indiana University, Indianapolis Division, 1952-67. For ninety weeks moderator and director of insurance television program, "Behind Your Policy," 1962-63. *Member:* Society of Chartered Property and Casualty Underwriters (chapter president, 1956; member of board of annals), National Association of Life Underwriters, Society of Chartered Life Underwriters, American Risk and Insurance Association, Life Underwriters Training Council, Indiana Association of Life Underwriters. *Awards, honors:* National Quality Award in Life Insurance, 1960-65.

WRITINGS: Behind the Fine Print, David-Stewart, 1961, reissued as *Who Pays?: The Complete Story About an Important Part of Our Lives Few of Us Understand; The Insurance Policies We Buy to Protect Ourselves Against Catastrophes Such as Automobile Accidents, Illnesses, and Long-Term Idleness Due to Casualties of Any Kind,* Capital City Publishers, 1961, reissued as *Who Pays? When ... Your House Burns? Your Car Is Damaged? You Cannot Work?,* E.C. Seale, 1962. Contributor to *Rough Notes* and other periodicals.

BIOGRAPHICAL/CRITICAL SOURCES: Indiana Bar Association Journal, August, 1962; *Indianapolis Times,* January 21, 1962; *United States Review,* March 3, 1962; *Indianapolis News,* March 7, 1962; *U.S. Investor,* April 17, 1962; *American Bar Association Journal,* September, 1963.

RICHARDSON, Ivor Lloyd Morgan 1930-

PERSONAL: Born May 24, 1930, in Ashburton, New Zealand; son of William T. and M.K. (Lloyd) Richardson; married Jane Krchma, June 25, 1955; children: Helen Marie, Megan Lloyd, Sarah. *Education:* Canterbury University College, LL.B.; University of Michigan, LL.M., S.J.D. *Home:* 29 Duthie St., Wellington W. 3, New Zealand. *Office:* Crown Law Office, Wellington, New Zealand.

CAREER: Macalister Bros. (lawyers), Invercargill, New Zealand, partner, 1957-63; Crown Law Office, Wellington, New Zealand, crown counsel, 1963—. Lecturer in law, Victoria University of Wellington. *Member:* Phi Delta Phi.

WRITINGS: Emancipation of Minors (originally published in *Current Trends in State Legislation,* 1955-56), Legislative Research Center, University of Michigan, 1957; (with W. H. Dunn) *Sir Robert Stout* (biography), A.H. & A.W. Reed, 1961; *Religion and the Law,* Sweet & Maxwell, 1962; *Attitudes to Income Tax Avoidance,* Victoria University of Wellington, 1967; (editor) *Essays on the Estate and Gift Duties Act, 1968,* Sweet & Maxwell, 1969; (reviser with others) E.C. Adams, *Adams and Richardson's Law of Estate and Gift Duties,* 4th edition, Butterworths, 1970. Contributor of articles to American, Canadian, Australian, and New Zealand legal periodicals.†

* * *

RICHEY, Dorothy Hilliard

PERSONAL: Born in Norphlet, Ark.; daughter of Albert and Ruth (Gremillion) Hilliard; married Noyes Richey (a chief chemist), April 12, 1947; children: Noyes, Jr., Dorothy Ruth, Kenneth Albert, Jeanne Elizabeth, William Henry. *Education:* University of Southwestern Louisiana, B.A., 1947; McNeese State College, graduate study, 1948. *Address:* P.O. Box 5201, Beaumont, Tex. 77706.

CAREER: Muller Co., Lake Charles, La., radio director and fashion coordinator, 1948-50; television performer in Lake Charles, La., 1953-56; staff and free-lance columnist in Houston, Tex. and Miami, Fla.; writer of fiction and nonfiction for network radio and television, 1948—, lecturer, 1953—; Station KLVI, Beaumont, Tex., star of daily radio program. Writer of syndicated column, "How to Be Rich and Beautiful." Instructor in writing for television in night classes, Lamar State College, Beaumont, Tex., 1963. President, Richey-Bosch Associates. *Member:* American Association of University Women, American Women in Radio and TV (chapter vice-president), Women's Symphony League (Beaumont), Theta Sigma Phi. *Awards, honors:* Golden Mike award, 1968.

WRITINGS: Road to San Jacinto (juvenile), Naylor, 1961. Author, with Patricia Bosch, of *How to Be Rich and Beautiful,* 1968. Contributor to magazines, including *Good Housekeeping.* Writer of radio and television scripts. Also writes under pseudonym.

WORK IN PROGRESS: Two books of fiction, *Class of '39,* and *Wives' Seminar;* mystery novels.†

* * *

RICHMOND, H(ugh) M(acrae) 1932-

PERSONAL: Born March 20, 1932, in Burton, England; son of Ronald Jackson (a bank manager) and Isabella (Macrae) Richmond; married Velma Bourgeois (a professor), August 9, 1958; children: Elizabeth, Claire. *Education:* Emmanuel College, Cambridge, B.A., 1954; Wadham College, Oxford, D.Phil., 1957. *Religion:* Roman Catholic. *Office:* Department of English, University of California, Berkeley, Calif. 94720.

CAREER: Lycee Jean Perrin, Lyon, France, assistant in English, 1954-55; University of California, Berkeley, in-structor, 1957-59, assistant professor, 1959-63, associate professor, 1963-68, professor of English, 1968—. *Military service:* British Army, Royal Artillery, 1950-51; became lieutenant. *Member:* Modern Language Association of America, Renaissance Society of America, Comparative Literature Association. *Awards, honors:* American Council of Learned Societies fellow for study of European landscape poetry, 1964.

WRITINGS: The School of Love: The Evolution of the Stuart Love Lyric, Princeton University Press, 1964; *Shakespeare's Political Plays,* Random House, 1967; (editor) Shakespeare, *King Henry IV, Part I,* Bobbs-Merrill, 1967; *Shakespeare's Sexual Comedy: A Mirror for Lovers,* Bobbs-Merrill, 1971; (editor) Shakespeare, *King Henry VIII,* W.C. Brown, 1971. Contributor of articles to *Comparative Literature, Shakespeare Quarterly, Modern Philology, South Atlantic Quarterly,* and other publications.

WORK IN PROGRESS: The Christian Revolutionary: John Milton; a book about European landscape poetry; studying interdisciplinary methods in literature and the fine arts.

* * *

RICKS, Christopher (Bruce) 1933-

PERSONAL: Born September 18, 1933, in London, England; son of James Bruce and Gabrielle (Roszak) Ricks; married Kirsten Jensen, September 15, 1956; children: David, Julia, Laura, William. *Education:* Attended Balliol College, Oxford, 1953-56. *Politics:* Labour Party supporter. *Religion:* Atheist. *Home:* 134 Queens Rd., Bristol, England. *Office:* Dept. of English, University of Bristol, Bristol, England.

CAREER: Worcester College, Oxford, England, fellow and tutor, and University Lecturer in English Literature, Oxford University, 1958-68; University of Bristol, Bristol, England, professor of English, 1968—. *Military service:* British Army, 1951-53; lieutenant, The Green Howards. *Member:* Tennyson Society (vice-president).

WRITINGS: (Editor and author of introduction with Harry Carter) Edward Rowe Mores, *Dissertation Upon English Typographical Founders and Foundries,* Oxford University Press, 1962; *Milton's Grand Style,* Oxford University Press, 1963; (editor and author of introduction) *Poems and Critics: An Anthology of Poetry and Criticism from Shakespeare to Hardy,* Collins, 1966, Harper, 1972; *Tennyson's Methods of Composition,* Oxford University Press, 1966; (editor) *A.E. Housman: A Collection of Critical Essays,* Prentice-Hall, 1968; (editor) *The Poems of Tennyson,* Longmans, Green, 1969, Atheneum, 1971; (editor) *Twentieth Century Interpretations of Arthur Ransome,* Prentice-Hall, 1968; (editor) John Milton, *Paradise Lost, and Paradise Regained,* New American Library, 1968; (editor and author of introduction) Elizabeth Barrett Browning and Robert Browning, *The Brownings: Letters and Poetry,* Doubleday, 1970; (editor) *English Poetry and Prose 1540-1674,* Barrie & Jenkins, 1970; (editor) *English Drama to 1710,* Barrie & Jenkins, 1971; (editor and author of introduction) *Selected Criticisms of Matthew Arnold,* New American Library, 1972; *Tennyson: A Biographical and Critical Study,* Macmillan, 1972. General editor of Penguin *Critical Anthologies* and Penguin *English Poets.* Co-editor, *Essays in Criticism;* contributor of regular reviews to *The Listener, Sunday Times* (London), and *New York Review of Books;* contributor to learned journals.

WORK IN PROGRESS: A study of the publishers Faber and Faber.

RIDDEL, Joseph N(eill) 1931-

PERSONAL: Born September 11, 1931, in Grantsville, W. Va.; son of James F. and Selma (Stump) Riddel; married Virginia Lee Johnson, April 19, 1963; children: Kevin Joe, Valerie Anne, Vanessa Lee. *Education:* Glenville College, A.B., 1953; University of Wisconsin, M.S., 1956, Ph.D., 1960. *Politics:* Democrat. *Home:* 76 Meadowbrook, Williamsville, N.Y. 14221. *Office:* Department of English, State University of New York at Buffalo, Buffalo, N.Y. 14214.

CAREER: Duke University, Durham, N.C., assistant professor of English, 1960-65; State University of New York at Buffalo, associate professor, 1965-68, professor of English, 1968—. Visiting professor and researcher, University of Rhode Island, summer, 1964; visiting assistant professor, University of California, Riverside, 1964-65; visiting professor, University of California, Los Angeles, summer, 1971. Member, Joint-Awards Council, State University of New York Research Foundation. *Military service:* U.S. Army, 1953-55. *Member:* Modern Language Association of America, American Association of University Professors. *Awards, honors:* Explicator prize for best book of explication and text, 1965, for *The Clairvoyant Eye.*

WRITINGS: (With Samuel French Morse and Jackson Bryer) *Wallace Stevens Checklist and Bibliography of Stevens Criticism,* A. Swallow, 1963; *The Clairvoyant Eye: The Poetry and Poetics of Wallace Stevens,* Louisiana State University Press, 1965; *C. Day Lewis,* Twayne, 1971. Contributor of essays to books of literary criticism and to professional journals.

WORK IN PROGRESS: A book on the poetics of William Carlos Williams; a book on American poetics, from Poe to post-modernism.

BIOGRAPHICAL/CRITICAL SOURCES: Criticism, spring, 1967; *Yale Review,* spring, 1967.

*　　*　　*

RIDDLE, Donald H(usted) 1921-

PERSONAL: Born January 22, 1921, in Brooklyn, N.Y.; son of William Ewing (an accountant) and Ruth (Husted) Riddle; married Leah D. Gallagher (a teacher), June 20, 1942; children: Susan L., Judith L. *Education:* Princeton University, A.B., 1949, Ph.D., 1956. *Politics:* Democrat. *Home:* 45 East 89th St., New York, N.Y. 10028. *Office:* John Jay College of Criminal Justice of the City University of New York, 315 Park Ave. S., New York, N.Y. 10010.

CAREER: Princeton University, Princeton, N.J., instructor in politics, 1950-52; Hamilton College, Clinton, N.Y., assistant professor of government, 1952-58; Rutgers University, Eagleton Institute of Politics, New Brunswick, N.J., associate professor, 1958-64, professor of political science, 1964-65; John Jay College of Criminal Justice of the City University of New York, New York, N.Y., dean of faculty, 1965-68, president, 1968—. Consultant to Connecticut Committee on State Government Organization, 1949, U.S. Department of Interior, 1950, New York State Committee on Constitutional Revision, 1957-58. Member of staff of U.S. Senator Paul Douglas, 1956. Member of Princeton Township Board of Education, 1963—. *Military service:* U.S. Army Air Forces, 1942-46; became first lieutenant. *Member:* American Association of University Professors, American Studies Association, American Political Science Association, Phi Beta Kappa.

WRITINGS: The Truman Committee: A Study in Congressional Responsibility, Rutgers University Press, 1964; (editor with Jack Allen and Robert E. Cleary and contributor) *The Promise and Problems of American Dem-*

ocracy, McGraw, 1964, 2nd edition published as *Contemporary Issues in American Democracy,* 1969; (editor) *American Society in Action: Readings for The Problems and Promise of American Democracy,* McGraw, 1965; (editor with Cleary) *Political Science in the Social Studies,* National Council for the Social Studies, 1966. Contributor of articles to *Nation, Public Opinion Quarterly,* and *Chicago Jewish Forum.*

SIDELIGHTS: Riddle made two trips to South America in 1963 and 1964, for research on a report (with Douglas A. Chalmers) to Agency for International Development on urban leadership in Latin America; he has also traveled to Japan and Europe.

*　　*　　*

RIDGE, Antonia (Florence)

PERSONAL: Born in Amsterdam, Holland. *Education:* Educated in schools in Holland, England, and France. *Home:* 5 Cranbrook Dr., Esher, Surrey, England.

CAREER: Author of books, plays, and songs; writes and broadcasts for British Broadcasting Corp., especially on "Woman's Hour." *Member:* Woman's Press Club of London Ltd., Radio Writers Association, Song Writers Guild of Great Britain Ltd., Writers' Guild of Great Britain, French Society of Authors. *Awards, honors:* Citoyenne d'Honneur, Town of St. Etienne, 1967; gold medal and Diplome d'Honneur, Meilleurs Ouvriers de France, 1967; Best Radio Drama Script award, Writers' Guild of Great Britain, 1969, for "The Little French Clock."

WRITINGS: The Handy Elephant, and Other Stories, Faber, 1946; *Rom-Bom-Bom, and Other Stories,* Faber, 1946; *Hurrah for Muggins, and Other Stories,* Faber, 1947; *Endless and Company,* Faber, 1948; *Galloping Fred,* Faber, 1950; *Leave It to the Brooks,* National Magazine Co., 1950; *Jan and His Clogs,* Roy, 1951; *Family Album,* Harper, 1952; *Puppet Plays for Children,* Transatlantic, 1953; *Cousin Jan,* Faber, 1954; *Six Radio Plays,* E.J. Arnold, 1954; *By Special Request,* Faber, 1958; *Jan Klaassen Cures the King,* Faber, 1952, reissued as *The Poppenkast; or, How Jan Klaassen Cured the Sick King,* 1958, reissued as *How Jan Klaassen Cured the King: A Play for Children,* 1969; *Grandma Went to Russia,* Faber, 1959; *Never Run from the Lion, and Another Story,* Faber, 1958, Walck, 1959; (editor) Dorothy McCall, *A String of Beads,* Faber, 1961, Transatlantic, 1962; (with Mies Bouhuys) *The Little Red Pony,* Harrap, 1960, Bobbs-Merrill, 1962; *The Thirteenth Child,* Faber, 1962, published in America as *The Royal Pawn,* Appleton, 1963; (with Bouhuys) *Hurrah for a Dutch Birthday,* Faber, 1964; *For Love of a Rose,* Faber, 1965; (translator and adapter) Norbert Casteret, *Mission Underground,* Harrap, 1968; (with Bouhuys) *Melodia: A Story from Holland,* Faber, 1969; "The Little French Clock" (radio play), first broadcast by British Broadcasting Corp., 1969.

Writing for British Broadcasting Corp. programs includes talks, stories, and serials, radio and television plays for adults and children, history scripts for schools programs, talks broadcast to France on "Ici Londres." Also writer of plays for Hogarth Puppets, songs, English lyrics of songs and "Stories-in-Song" for Obernkirchen Children's Choir, including English words for "The Happy Wanderer." Contributor of articles and stories to *Woman's Journal, Woman, My Home, Argosy* (England), *Good Housekeeping, Woman's Mirror,* and *Woman's Weekly.*

SIDELIGHTS: A film, "Das Schone Abenteur," is an adaptation of the German edition of *Family Album;* radio and television plays for adults and children are regularly repeated in France, Germany, Italy, Switzerland, Yugoslavia, Belgium, the Scandinavian countries, and

Greece; books have been translated into several languages and serialized in European magazines and newspapers.

BIOGRAPHICAL/CRITICAL SOURCES: Times Literary Supplement, January 12, 1967, October 16, 1969.

* * *

RIEBER, Alfred J(oseph) 1931-

PERSONAL: Born October 1, 1931, in Mount Vernon, N.Y.; son of John J. and Albertina (George) Rieber; married Edith Finton, October 16, 1954. Education: Colgate University, B.A., 1953; Columbia University, M.A., Certificate of Russian Institute, 1954, Ph.D., 1959. Home: 353 Lindsey Dr., Berwyn, Pa. 19312.

CAREER: Northwestern University, Evanston, Ill., 1959-65, became associate professor of history; University of Pennsylvania, Philadelphia, 1965—, now professor of history and chairman of the department. Military service: U.S. Army Reserve, Military Intelligence, 1953-59. Member: American Association for the Advancement of Slavic Studies, American Historical Association, Slavic Conference, Phi Beta Kappa. Awards, honors: Woodrow Wilson fellow, 1953-54; Ford Foundation scholar, 1954-55; Ford Foundation fellow in Paris, 1955-56; Columbia University traveling fellow at Moscow University in first year of American student exchange with the Soviet Union, 1958-59; American Philosophical Society grant, 1963; Guggenheim fellow, 1965; American Council of Learned Societies fellow, 1966; Harbison Award for distinguished teaching, Danforth Foundation, 1968.

WRITINGS: Stalin and the French Communist Party, 1941-1947, Columbia University Press, 1962; (with Robert C. Nelson) A Study of the USSR and Communism: An Historical Approach, Scott, Foresman, 1962; (editor with Nelson) The USSR and Communism: Source Readings and Interpretations, Scott, Foresman, 1964; (editor and author of historical essay) The Politics of Autocracy: Letters of Alexander II to Prince A.I. Bariatinskii, 1857-1864, Mouton & Co., 1966. Contributor to Journal of Modern History.

WORK IN PROGRESS: Railroad politics and modernization in nineteenth-century Russia.

* * *

RIGSBY, Howard 1909-
(Vechel Howard)

PERSONAL: Born November 12, 1909, in Denver, Colo.; son of Vechel and Jean (Howard) Rigsby; divorced; children: Charity (Mrs. Richard Crane), Judith (Mrs. John MacCormack). Education: Studied at San Mateo Junior College, 1928-29, San Jose State College (now California State University at San Jose), 1930, and University of Nevada, 1930-31. Agent: Paul R. Reynolds, Inc., 599 Fifth Ave., New York, N.Y. 10017.

CAREER: Professional writer. Editor of Argosy, 1938. Military service: U.S. Army, Signal Corps, 1942-46; became captain; received Army Commendation Ribbon. Member: Mystery Writers of America (member of national board of directors, 1959), Dramatists Guild and Writers Guild of Authors League of America. Awards, honors: Lucinda was named by the New York Times as one of the ten best mysteries of 1954; poetry prize, Monterey Peninsula Herald, 1964, for Kennedy eulogy, "Seven Gray Horses."

WRITINGS: Voyage to Leandro, Harper, 1939; Kill and Tell, Morrow, 1951; Murder for the Holidays, Morrow, 1951; Rage in Texas, Gold Medal Books, 1953; As a Man Falls, Fawcett, 1954; Lucinda, Gold Medal Books, 1954; The Lone Gun, Fawcett, 1955; The Reluctant Gun, Gold Medal Books, 1957; The Avenger, Crowell, 1957, reissued as Naked to My Pride, Popular Library, 1958;

Clash of Shadows, Lippincott, 1959; A Time for Passion, Dell, 1960; The Tulip Tree, Doubleday, 1963; Calliope Reef, Doubleday, 1967.

Under pseudonym Vechel Howard—All published by Gold Medal Books: Sundown at Crazy Horse, 1957, reissued as The Last Sunset, 1961; Tall in the West, 1958; Murder on Her Mind, 1959; Murder with Love, 1959; Stage to Painted Creek, 1959.

Author with Dorothy Heyward of the play, "South Pacific," which ran on Broadway, 1943-44; writer of television scripts for "Rawhide" series. Short stories have appeared in Saturday Evening Post, McCall's, Ladies' Home Journal, Collier's, American, Blue Book, Argosy, other magazines.

WORK IN PROGRESS: A novel, Point Esperanza.

SIDELIGHTS: Rigsby writes verse and westerns for recreation (also reads and plays tennis) and says he has no major interest outside of writing. The writing has been done in Mexico, Paris, and all over the United States; currently he divides his time between Carmel and New York. His book, Sundown at Crazy Horse, was made into the Universal picture, "The Last Sunset," starring Kirk Douglas and Rock Hudson, in 1961. He wrote the book for two musicals, "neither of which quite made it to Broadway." The Heyward-Rigsby play, "South Pacific," antedated the musical of the same name by six years.

* * *

RIHA, Thomas 1929-

PERSONAL: Born April 17, 1929, in Prague, Czechoslovakia; son of Viktor and Ruth Ann (Kress) Riha. Education: University of California, Berkeley, B.A., 1951, M.A., 1957; Harvard University, Ph.D., 1962. Office: University of Chicago, Chicago, Ill. 60637.

CAREER: University of Chicago, Chicago, Ill., assistant professor of history, 1962—. Military service: U.S. Army, 1953-55. Member: American Association of University Professors, American Association for the Advancement of Slavic Studies, Phi Beta Kappa.

WRITINGS: (Compiler) Readings in Russian Civilization, three volumes, University of Chicago Press, 1960, 2nd edition, revised, 1969; (editor and author of introduction) Readings in Russian Civilization, University of Chicago Press, 1964, 2nd edition, revised, 1969; A Russian European: Paul Miliukov in Russian Politics, 1900-1917, University of Notre Dame Press, 1969.

WORK IN PROGRESS: Editing, with Alfred J. Rieber, Readings in Russian Cultural and Intellectual History.

* * *

RILEY, E(dward) C(alverley) 1923-

PERSONAL: Born October 5, 1923, in Mexico City, Mexico; son of British nationals, Herbert R. (an engineer) and Dulcie (Jones) Riley. Education: Attended Clifton College, 1933-41; Queen's College, Oxford, M.A., 1947; University of Dublin, M.A., 1952. Religion: Church of England. Office: Department of Hispanic Studies, David Hume Tower, George Square, Edinburgh, Scotland.

CAREER: Research in Madrid, Spain, 1948-49; Trinity College, Dublin, Ireland, university lecturer, 1952, reader in Spanish and head of department, 1957, fellow, 1957-65, professor, 1965; University of Edinburgh, Edinburgh, Scotland, professor, 1970—. Visiting professor, Dartmouth College, 1965-66. Military service: Royal Naval Volunteer reserve, 1943-45; became sub-lieutenant. Member: Modern Humanities Research Association, Association of Hispanists of Great Britain and Ireland.

WRITINGS: (Contributor) F.W. Pierce, editor, *Hispanic Studies in Honour of I. Gonzalez Llubers,* Dolphin Book Co., 1959; *Cervantes's Theory of the Novel,* Clarendon Press, 1962; (contributor) *Homenaje a Damaso Alonso,* Volume III, [Madrid], 1963; *Homenaje a W. Fichter,* 1971; (co-editor and contributor) *Suma Cervantina,* [London], 1973. Contributor of articles to professional journals.

WORK IN PROGRESS: A general study, *Cervantes,* for a series on European writers in preparation by Cambridge University Press.

AVOCATIONAL INTERESTS: Cinematography, science fiction.

* * *

RIMMER, Robert H.   1917-

PERSONAL: Born March 14, 1917, in Dorchester, Mass.; son of Frank H. and Blanche (Rochefort) Rimmer; married Erma Richards; children: Robert H., Jr., Stephen King. *Education:* Bates College, B.A., 1939; Harvard University, M.A., 1941. *Politics:* Independent. *Home:* 92 Narragansett Rd., Quincy, Mass. 02169.

CAREER: Relief Printing Corp., Boston, Mass., president, 1945—; Rimmer Engraving Corp., Boston, Mass., president. *Military service:* U.S. Army, Finance Department, 1943-45; became first lieutenant.

WRITINGS: That Girl from Boston, Challenge Press, 1962; *The Rebellion of Yale Marratt,* Challenge Press, 1964; *The Harrad Experiment,* Sherbourne, 1966; *The Zolotov Affair,* Sherbourne, 1967; *Proposition Thirty-One,* New American Library, 1968; (compiler) *The Harrad Letters to Robert H. Rimmer,* New American Library, 1969; *You and I . . . Searching for Tommorrow: The Second Book of Letters to Robert Rimmer Plus Marriage 2000, a Participation,* New American Library, 1971; *Thursday, My Love,* New American Library, 1972.

BIOGRAPHICAL/CRITICAL SOURCES: New York Times Book Review, December 8, 1968.

* * *

RINGER, Barbara Alice   1925-

PERSONAL: Born May 29, 1925, in Lafayette, Ind.; daughter of William Raimond (a lawyer) and Gladys (a lawyer; maiden name, Wells) Ringer. *Education:* George Washington University, A.B. (with distinction), 1945, M.A., 1947; Columbia University, LL.B., 1949. *Home:* 5102 Fairglen Lane, Chevy Chase, Md. 20015.

CAREER: Admitted to practice, U.S. District Court, U.S. Court of Appeals, and U.S. Supreme Court. Library of Congress, Copyright Office, Washington, D.C., copyright examiner, 1949-51, head of renewal and assignment section, 1951-56, assistant chief of examining division, 1956-60, chief of examining division, 1960-63, assistant register of copyrights for examining, 1963-66, assistant register of copyrights, 1966—. Adjunct professor of law, George Washington University, 1962—. *Member:* American Bar Association, Federal Bar Association, Copyright Society of the U.S.A., American Association of University Women, District of Columbia Bar Association, Phi Beta Kappa, Phi Pi Epsilon, Pi Gamma Mu, Alpha Lambda Delta. *Awards, honors:* Library of Congress Superior Accomplishment award, 1951, Superior Service award, 1958; William A. Jump Meritorious Award for exemplary achievement in public administration, 1958.

WRITINGS: (Editor) *Bibliography of Design Protection,* U.S. Copyright Office, 1955, supplement (with William Strauss, Borge Varmer, and Caruther G. Berger), 1959; *The Unauthorized Duplication of Sound Recordings,* U.S. Copyright Office, 1958; *Renewal of Copyright,* U.S. Copyright Office, 1960; (with others) *Notice of Copyright,* House of Representatives Judiciary Committee, 1960; (with Paul Gitlin) *Copyrights,* Practising Law Institute, 1963, revised edition, 1965. Contributor to *Encyclopedia Americana, Encyclopedia of Patent Practice, Copyright Society Bulletin,* and *Revue Internationale de Droit d'Auteur.*

WORK IN PROGRESS: Drafting a bill for general revision of the copyright law.

* * *

RISCHIN, Moses   1925-

PERSONAL: Born October 16, 1925, in New York, N.Y.; son of Meer (a physician) and Rachel (Nelson) Rischin; married Ruth S. Solomon (a specialist in Russian literature); children: Sarah Elizabeth, Abigail Sophia, Rebecca Martha Mira. *Education:* Brooklyn College, A.B., 1947; Harvard University, A.M., 1948, Ph.D., 1957. *Politics:* Democrat. *Religion:* Jewish. *Home:* 350 Arballo Dr., San Francisco, Calif. 94132. *Office:* History Department, San Francisco State College, 1600 Holloway Ave., San Francisco, Calif. 94132.

CAREER: Lecturer at Brooklyn College, Brooklyn, N.Y., 1949-53, instructor at Brandeis University, Waltham, Mass., 1953-54, and lecturer at New School for Social Research, New York, N.Y., 1955-58; American Jewish Committee Institute of Human Relations, New York, N.Y., research associate, 1956-58; Long Island University, Brooklyn, N.Y., assistant professor of history, 1958-59; Radcliffe College, Cambridge, Mass., assistant editor, *Notable American Women,* 1959-60; University of California, Los Angeles, lecturer, 1962-64; San Francisco State College, San Francisco, Calif., 1964—, now professor of history. Fulbright-Hays lecturer, University of Uppsala, 1969. Consultant to Center for the Study of Democratic Institutions, American Jewish Committee, and American Association for Jewish Education.

MEMBER: American Historical Association, American Studies Association, American Jewish Historical Society, Organization of American Historians. *Awards, honors:* Grants-in-aid from American Philosophical Society and American Council of Learned Societies; Tercentenary Fellow in American Jewish History; *The Promised City* was nominated for Pulitzer Prize and received the first non-fiction award of Jewish Book Council of America, 1963; fellowships from American Council of Learned Societies and Guggenheim Foundation.

WRITINGS: An Inventory of American Jewish History, foreword by Oscar Handlin, Harvard University Press, 1954; *Our Own Kind: Voting by Race, Creed or National Origin,* Center for the Study of Democratic Institutions, 1960; *The Promised City: New York's Jews, 1870-1914,* Harvard University Press, 1962, revised edition, Harper, 1970; (contributor) *Documentary History of the Jews in the United States, 1790-1840,* three volumes, Columbia University Press, 1963; (editor) *The American Gospel of Success: Individualism and Beyond,* Quadrangle, 1965; (editor and author of introduction) Hutchins Hapgood, *The Spirit of the Ghetto,* Harvard University Press, 1967; (editor with Samuel J. Hurwitz) *A Liberal Between Two Worlds: Essays of Solomon F. Bloom,* Public Affairs Press, 1968; *Immigration and the American Tradition,* Bobbs-Merrill, 1970; (contributor) Charles Wollenberg, editor, *Ethnic Conflict in California,* Tinnon-Brown, 1970; *Abraham Cahan* (biography), Harper, 1972.

WORK IN PROGRESS: American Immigration, publication by Dial expected in 1975.

RITCHIE, C(icero) T(heodore) 1914-

PERSONAL: Born April 9, 1914, in Halifax, Nova Scotia, Canada; son of Cicero Theodore (a clerk) and Ellen Elizabeth (Manson) Ritchie; married Hazel Robertson, September 5, 1938. *Education:* Dalhousie University, B.Sc., 1938. *Residence:* 37 Henry St., Kentville, Nova Scotia, Canada.

CAREER: Self-employed consulting geologist in Toronto, Ontario for fifteen years, and Kentville, Nova Scotia for three years. *Member:* Canadian Authors Association, Association of Professional Engineers of the Province of Ontario, Board of Trade of Metropolitan Toronto.

WRITINGS: The Willing Maid (historical novel), Abelard, 1957; *Black Angels* (historical novel), Abelard, 1959; *Lady in Bondage* (historical novel), Ace Books, 1960; *The First Canadian: The Story of Champlain,* Macmillan (Canada), 1961, St. Martin's, 1962; *Runner of the Woods: The Story of Young Radisson,* Macmillan (Canada), 1963, St. Martin's, 1964. Contributor to *Encyclopaedia Britannica.*

WORK IN PROGRESS: Preliminary research on many subjects in search for worthwhile story.

*   *   *

RITTERBUSH, Philip C. 1936-

PERSONAL: Born August 9, 1936, in Orange, N.J.; son of Leonard Charles and Anne (Allman) Ritterbush. *Education:* Yale University, B.A., 1958; Oxford University, D.Phil., 1961. *Politics:* Democrat. *Home:* 1527 31st St. N.W., Washington, D.C. 20007. *Office:* Organization Response, Suite 1111, 1329 E St. N.W., Washington, D.C. 20001.

CAREER: U.S. Senate, Washington, D.C., legislative assistant to Senator Tom McIntyre of New Hampshire, 1962-64; Smithsonian Institution, Washington, D.C., staff assistant to the secretary, 1964-67, director of academic programs, 1968-70; Organization Response, Washington, D.C., chairman, 1970—. Lecturer in history of science and medicine, Yale University, 1962. *Awards, honors:* Rhodes scholar, 1958.

WRITINGS: Overtures to Biology: The Speculations of Eighteenth-Century Naturalists, Yale University Press, 1964; *Education and Federal Science Establishment,* [Washington, D.C.], 1964; *The Art of Organic Forms,* Smithsonian Institution Press, 1968; (with others) *Essays on Organic Form,* Routledge & Kegan Paul, 1971; *Talent Waste: Institutional Malfunction in the Market for Skilled Manpower,* Acropolis Books, 1972; (editor) *The Learning Machine: The Impact of Communications Technology on Higher Education and Research,* Acropolis, 1972.

WORK IN PROGRESS: Studying the cultural influences of science.

*   *   *

RIVOIRE, Jean 1929-

PERSONAL: Born December 10, 1929, in Nice, France; son of Georges and Suzanne (Tomasini) Rivoire; married Annie Gaillard, 1966; children Emmanuelle, Christophe. *Education:* Attended Ecole Superieure d'Electricite, Paris, France, 1948-50, Universite de Paris, 1952-55, Ecole Pratique des Hautes-Etudes, Paris, 1957-58. *Religion:* Roman Catholic. *Home:* 23 Rue de Civry, Paris 16, France.

CAREER: French Oceanographic Campaigns, engineer, 1952; with Electricite de France, Paris, 1953-55; Credit Lyonnais, Paris, industrial adviser, 1955-70, secretary general, 1970—. *Military service:* French Navy, 1950-52; became lieutenant. *Member:* International Institute of Space Law.

WRITINGS: (With Pierre de Latil) *A la recherche du monde marin,* Plon, 1954, translation by Edward Fitzgerald published as *Man and the Underwater World,* Putnam, 1956; (with Jacques Guillerme) *Traite de plongee,* Dunad, 1955; (with Daniel F. Dollfus) *A propos de . . . Euratom,* Les Productions de Paris, 1959; (with de Latil) *Tresors engloutis,* Plon, 1959, translation by Denise Folliot published as *Sunken Treasure,* Hill & Wang, 1962; *How to Introduce the Law into the Space* (second colloquium on the law of outer space), Springer-Verlag, 1960; (with de Latil) *Le Professeur Auguste Piccard,* Seghers, 1962.

WORK IN POGRESS: Economic studies.

*   *   *

ROBB, James H(arding) 1920-

PERSONAL: Born April 28, 1920, in Gisborne, New Zealand; son of H(erbert) Frank (a farmer) and Muriel (Harding) Robb; married Margaret Storkey (a teacher), February 8, 1946; children: Murray James, Elizabeth Joan, Alan Douglas, Jennifer Margaret. *Education:* Victoria University of Wellington, B.A., 1943, M.A., 1947; University of London, B.Sc. in Econ., 1948, Ph.D., 1951. *Religion:* Presbyterian. *Home:* 15 Connaught Ter., Wellington 2, New Zealand. *Office:* Victoria University of Wellington, P.O. Box 196, Wellington, New Zealand.

CAREER: Victoria University of Wellington, New Zealand, junior lecturer in psychology, 1947; Family Discussion Bureau (casework agency), London, England, caseworker, 1949-50; Tavistock Institute of Human Relations, London, England, research associate, 1950-54; Victoria University of Wellington, lecturer, 1954-58, senior lecturer, 1959-64, associate professor, 1965-66, professor of sociology, 1966-70, head of department of social administration and sociology, 1971—. Member, New Zealand government advisory committee on marriage guidance, 1959—. *Military service:* Royal New Zealand Air Force, navigator, served with Transport and Bomber Commands, Royal Air Force, 1942-46; became flight lieutenant. *Member:* Royal Society of Medicine, British Sociological Association, Sociological Association of Australia and New Zealand (vice-president, 1963-66, president, 1967), New Zealand Family Planning Association (vice-president, 1958—), Wellington Mental Health Association (chairman, 1962-65).

WRITINGS: Working-Class Anti-Semite: A Psychological Study in a London Borough, Tavistock Publications, 1954; (with others) *Social Casework in Marital Problems,* Tavistock Publications, 1955; (with Anthony Somerset) *Report to Masterton: Results of a Social Survey,* Masterton Printing Co., 1957; (contributor) Elizabeth Bott, *Family and Social Network,* Tavistock Publications, 1958; (contributor) J.L. Roberts, editor, *Decentralisation in New Zealand Government Administration,* Oxford University Press, 1962; *Social Science and Social Welfare* (address), Victoria University of Wellington, 1966; (with others) *The City of Porirua: The Results of a Social Survey,* Victoria University of Wellington, 1969; (contributor) *Health Administration in New Zealand,* New Zealand Institute of Public Administration, 1969. Contributor of articles to professional journals.

WORK IN PROGRESS: A sociological study of New Zealand social welfare services.

*   *   *

ROBB, Nesca A(deline) 1905-

PERSONAL: Born May 27, 1905, in Belfast, Northern Ireland; daughter of Charles (a merchant) and Agnes M. (Arnold) Robb. *Education:* Somerville College, Oxford, B.A. (first class honors in modern languages), 1927, D.Phil., 1932. *Politics:* Conservative. *Religion:* Church of

Ireland. *Home:* 10 Raglan Rd., Bangor, County Down, Northern Ireland.

CAREER: Somerville College, Oxford University, Oxford, England, coach in modern languages, 1934-38; Italian Institute, London, England, senior English teacher, 1938-39; Womens' Employment Federation, London, England, advisory officer, 1940-45; writer, Bangor, Northern Ireland, 1945—. Life member, Committee of National Trust; life governor, Richmond Lodge School. Member of advisory council, British Broadcasting Corp., 1960-63. *Member:* International P.E.N. (chairman of Belfast Centre, 1951-52, 1961-62), Royal Society of Literature (fellow), Netherlands Society of Literature (fellow), Soroptimist Club (Bangor; president, 1947-49).

WRITINGS: Neoplatonism of the Italian Renaissance, Macmillan (New York), 1935; (editor with others) Dorothy Margaret Eastwood, *The Revival of Pascal: A Study of His Relation to Modern French Thought,* Oxford University Press, 1936; *Poems,* Basil Blackwell, 1939; *An Ulsterwoman in England, 1924-1941,* Cambridge University Press, 1942; *Four in Exile,* Hutchinson, 1948, published in America as *Four in Exile: Critical Essays on Leopardi, Hans, C. Andersen, Christina Rosetti, A.E. Housman,* Kennikat, 1968; (editor with Sam Hanna Bell and John Hewitt) *The Arts in Ulster,* Harrap, 1951; "Prisoner of State" (radio play), 1954; *William of Orange: A Personal Portrait,* Volume I: *1650-1673,* Heinemann, 1962, St. Martin's, 1963, Volume II: *1674-1702,* St. Martin's, 1966; *Richmond Lodge School: A History,* William Mullan & Son, 1969; *Ards Eclogues* (verse), William Mullan & Son, 1969. Contributor to professional journals.

SIDELIGHTS: Miss Robb is competent in Italian and French, and has some knowledge of Dutch, Spanish, and German. *Avocational interests:* Reading (anything from theology to detective stories), music, visual arts, nature and human nature, cats, cookery, and travel.

*   *   *

ROBBE-GRILLET, Alain   1922-

PERSONAL: Born August 18, 1922, in Brest, France; son of Gaston (an engineer) and Yvonne (Canu) Robbe-Grillet; married Catherine Rstakian, October 23, 1957. *Education:* Institut National Agronomique, ingenieur agronome. *Religion:* Anti-religious. *Home:* 18 Boulevard Maillot, Neuilly-sur-Seine, France. *Agent:* Georges Borchardt, 100 West 55th St., New York, N.Y. 10019. *Office:* Editions de Minuit, 7 rue Bernard-Palissy, Paris 6e, France.

CAREER: Institut National des Statistiques, Paris, France, charge de mission, 1945-50; engineer with the Institut des Fruits et Agrumes Coloniaux in Morocco, French Guinea, Martinique, and Guadeloupe, 1949-51; Editions de Minuit, Paris, France, literary advisor, 1954—. *Awards, honors:* Feneon Prize, 1954, for *Les Gommes;* Prix des Critiques, 1955, for *Le Voyeur;* Prix Louis Delluc, 1963, for *L'Immortelle.*

WRITINGS: Les Gommes (novel), Editions de Minuit, 1953, translation by Richard Howard published as *The Erasers,* Grove, 1964, edited by J.S. Wood, Prentice-Hall, 1970; *Le Voyeur* (novel), Editions de Minuit, 1955, translation by Howard published as *The Voyeur,* Grove, 1958, published under original French title, edited and with an introduction by Oreste F. Pucciani, Ginn-Blaisdell, 1970; *La Jalousie* (novel), Editions de Minuit, 1957, translation by Howard published as *Jealousy,* Grove, 1959 (also see below), and as *Jealousy: Rhythmic Themes by Alain Robbe-Grillet* (limited edition; with pen and ink drawings by Michele Forgeois), Allen Press, 1971, published under original French title, edited by Germaine Bree and Eric Schoenfeld, Macmillan, 1963

(published in England under original French title, edited by B.G. Garnham, Methuen, 1969); *Dans le labyrinthe* (novel), Editions de Minuit, 1959, translation by Howard published as *In the Labyrinth,* Grove, 1960 (also see below), (translation by Christine Brooke-Rose published in England by Calder & Boyars, 1967), also published as *Dans le labyrinthe* [and] *Dans les couloirs du Metropolitain* [and] *Le Chambre secrete,* with an essay on Robbe-Grillet by Gerard Genette, Union Generale D'Editions, 1964; *L'Annee derniere a Marienbad: cine-roman* (screenplay; with photo extracts from the film by Alain Resnais produced in 1961), Editions de Minuit, 1961, translation by Howard published as *Last Year at Marienbad,* Grove, 1962 (published in England as *Last Year at Marienbad: A Cine-Novel,* J. Calder, 1962); *Instantanes* (short stories), Editions de Minuit, 1962, translation by Bruce Morissette published as *Snapshots,* Grove, 1968, new edition, 1972 (also see below); *L'Immortelle: cine-roman* (screenplay; with photo extracts from the film produced in 1963), Editions de Minuit, 1963, translation by A.M. Sheridan Smith published as *The Immortal One,* Calder & Boyars, 1971; *Pour un nouveau roman* (essays), Editions de Minuit, 1963, new edition, Gallimard, 1970, translation by Barbara Wright of both books published as *Snapshots* [and] *Towards a New Novel,* Calder & Boyars, 1965, translation by Howard published in America as *For a New Novel: Essays on Fiction,* Grove, 1966; *La Maison de Rendez-vous* (novel), Editions de Minuit, 1965, translation by Howard published under original French title, Grove, 1966 (translation by Sheridan Smith published in England as *The House of Assignation: A Novel,* Calder & Boyars, 1970); *Two Novels* (contains *Jealousy* and *In the Labyrinth;* with introductory essays by Morrissette and Roland Barthes), translated by Howard, Grove, 1965; *Projet pour une revolution a New York* (novel), Editions de Minuit, 1970, translation by Howard published as *Project for a Revolution in New York,* Grove, 1972; (with David Hamilton) *Reves de jeunes filles,* Montel, 1971, published in America as *Dreams of a Young Girl,* Morrow, 1971 (translation by Elizabeth Walter published in England as *Dreams of Young Girls,* Collins, 1971); (with Hamilton) *Les Demoiselles d'Hamilton,* Laffont, 1972. Contributor to *L'Express, Evergreen Review, New Statesman, Nouvelle Revue Francaise, Critique* (Paris), and *Revue de Paris.* Author of screenplays for "Trans-Europ Express," produced in 1967, "L'Homme qui ment," 1968, and "L'Eden et apres," 1970.

WORK IN PROGRESS: A novel; two films, "Le Jeu avec le feu," and "Le Retour de Franck."

SIDELIGHTS: As the acknowledged leader and spokesman of the New Novelists in France, Robbe-Grillet has denounced those who talk of the novelist's social responsibility; for him the novel is not a tool and probably has little effect on society. "For us," he writes, "literature is not a means of expression, but a search. And it does not even know for what it searches." "[But] we prefer our searches, our doubts, our contradictions, our joy of having yet invented something."

Balzac's "sacrosanct psychological tradition" has come under his attack. For the New Novelists, phenomenology has replaced traditional psychology; personality has been rendered indefinable and fluid; and objective description has become the primary goal. Moral judgments are avoided: "The world is neither significant nor absurd," says Robbe-Grillet. "It simply *is.*" Furthermore, "our concept of the world around us is now only fragmentary, temporary, contradictory even, and always disputable. How can a work of art presume to illustrate a preordained concept, whatever it might be?"

His preoccupation with inanimate objects has led to charges, notably by Francois Mauriac, of a dehumanized literature. Moreover, confusion for many readers results from the lack of distinction between a seen object and one that is imagined; reality for Robbe-Grillet is always flowing from one state to another. Descriptions are repeated with slight variations. Hence, charges of obscurity and tedium.

Robbe-Grillet's style is to a great extent borrowed from the cinema. According to critic Peter Cortland this style "concentrates on distorted visual images because it is representing mental life, which is of necessity different from the physical 'life,' or arrangement, of things in the material world. . . ." John Weightman believes Robbe-Grillet wants his books to have "the solidity and independent existence of a statue or a picture, which resists any anecdotal or intellectual summary." Robbe-Grillet once noted: "It seems that the conventions of photography (its two-dimensional character, black and white coloring, the limitations of the frame, the differences in scale according to the type of shot) help to free us from our own conventions."

Robbe-Grillet has directed four films based on his screenplays: "L'Immortelle," produced in 1963, "Trans-Europ Express," 1966, "L'Homme qui ment," 1968, and "L'Eden et apres," 1970.

BIOGRAPHICAL/CRITICAL SOURCES—Books: Claude Mauriac, The New Literature, Braziller, 1959; Laurent Le Sage, The French New Novel, Pennsylvania State University Press, 1962; John Cruickshank, editor, The Novelist as Philosopher, Oxford University Press, 1962; Ben Frank Stoltzfus, Alain Robbe-Grillet and the New French Novel, Southern Illinois University Press, 1964; Henry T. Moore, French Literature Since World War II, Southern Illinois University Press, 1966; Henri Peyre, French Novelists of Today, Oxford University Press, 1967; J. Sturrock, The French New Novel, Oxford University Press, 1969; G.H. Szanto, Narrative Consciousness, University of Texas Press, 1972.

Periodicals: Critique (Paris), August, 1954, September-October, 1955, July, 1959; Les Temps Modernes, June, 1957, July, 1960; Evergreen Review, II, 5, 1956, III, 10, 1959; Nation, April 25, 1959; Yale French Studies, 24, summer, 1959; New York Times Book Review, November 22, 1959; Wisconsin Studies in Contemporary Literature, I, 3, 1960; Nouvelle Revue Francaise, November, 1960; Spectator, December 16, 1960; New Statesman, February 17, 1961; Modern Language Notes, May, 1962, May, 1963; Time, July 20, 1962; PMLA, September, 1962; Modern Language Quarterly, September, 1962; Vogue, January 1, 1963; Film Quarterly, fall, 1963; Critique: Studies in Modern Fiction, winter, 1963-64; Listener, February 15, 1968; New York Times Book Review, May 28, 1972; New York Review of Books, June 1, 1972; Huson Review, winter, 1972-73.†

* * *

ROBERT, Marika Barna

PERSONAL: Born in Kosice, Czechoslovakia; daughter of Arnold (a gynecologist) and Olga (Prince) Barna; marriage to first husband, surname Robert, ended in divorce; married George Sereny (an internist), June, 1964. Education: Educated in schools in Czechoslovakia and Hungary. Home: 50 Hillsboro Ave., Apt. 2403, Toronto, Ontario, Canada.

CAREER: Unable to speak English on arrival in Canada in 1952, so occupations ranged from weighing bananas to operating a cash register in a supermarket; later became filing clerk and then a bookkeeper; free-lance writer, mainly for Canadian magazines, 1960—, now travel editor of Toronto Life.

WRITINGS: A Stranger and Afraid (novel), Doubleday, 1964. Contributor to Macleans', Chatelane, Toronto Star Weekly, and other Canadian publications.

WORK IN PROGRESS: A second novel.

SIDELIGHTS: Mrs. Robert is competent in Czech, Slovak, Hungarian, and German, and knows some French and Spanish.

* * *

ROBERTIELLO, Richard C. 1923-

PERSONAL: Born June 20, 1923, in Brooklyn, N.Y.; son of Attilio and Eleanor (Candela) Robertiello; married Carla Rizzotti, March 11, 1950; children: Elizabeth, Robert. Education: Harvard University, B.A., 1943; Columbia University, M.D., 1946. Home and office: 49 East 78th St., New York, N.Y. 10021.

CAREER: Practicing psychiatrist and psychoanalyst. Long Island Consultation Service, Forest Hills, N.Y., director of psychiatric services, 1953—; New York Eye and Ear Infirmary, New York, attending psychiatrist, 1955—; Manhattan General Hospital, New York, N.Y., associate attending psychiatrist, 1955—; Community Guidance Service, New York, N.Y., supervising psychiatrist, 1956—. Military service: U.S. Army, 1943-46, 1948-50; became captain. Member: American Psychiatric Association (fellow), Academy of Psychoanalysis (fellow), Society of Medical Psychoanalysts, National Psychological Association for Psychoanalysis, American Medical Association.

WRITINGS: Voyage from Lesbos: The Psychoanalysis of a Female Homosexual, Citadel, 1959; A Handbook of Emotional Illness and Treatment: A Contemporary Guide, with Case Histories, Argonaut, 1961, revised edition, 1962; (with Bertram Pollens and David B. Friedman) The Analyst's Role, Citadel, 1963; Sexual Fulfillment and Self-Affirmation, Argonaut, 1964.

WORK IN PROGRESS: A book on the psychology of the women's liberation movement.

AVOCATIONAL INTERESTS: Travel, tennis, bridge, and art.

* * *

ROBERTS, Bruce (Stuart) 1930-

PERSONAL: Born February 4, 1930, in Mount Vernon, N.Y.; son of Charles Wesley (a business executive) and Marion (McNally) Roberts; married Nancy Correll (a writer), February 27, 1957; children: Nancy Lee, David Correll. Education: New York University, B.S., 1951; University of Florida, graduate study, 1954. Religion: Presbyterian. Home: 6624 Sunview Dr., Charlotte, N.C. 28210; and Maxton, N.C. 28364.

CAREER: Tampa Tribune, Tampa, Fla., reporter, 1954-55; editor and publisher of weekly newspapers, Lumberton Post, Lumberton, N.C., and Scottish Chief, Maxton, N.C., 1956-58; Charlotte Observer, Charlotte, N.C., staff photographer, 1959-61; director of photography for Wilmington, Del., newspapers, 1962-63; free-lance photographer for magazines and books, 1963—. Director, Carolina Illustrated, Inc. (photographic service). Military service: U.S. Air Force, 1951-53. Member: American Society of Magazine Photographers, National Press Photographers Association, Sigma Delta Chi. Awards, honors: Named Southern Photographer of the Year, 1959, 1961; first place awards in National Press Photographers Association news pictures competition, 1959, 1960, 1961; Where Time Stood Still chosen by the New York Times editorial board as one of the outstanding books of 1970.

WRITINGS: Harper's Ferry in Pictures, with photographs by Roberts, McNally of Charlotte, 1960; (editor) The Face of North Carolina, McNally & Loftin, 1962;

(with wife, Nancy Roberts) *Where Time Stood Still: A Portrait of Appalachia,* photographs by Bruce Roberts, Crowell-Collier, 1970; (with Nancy Roberts) *This Haunted Land,* photographs by Bruce Roberts, McNally & Loftin, 1970; *The California Gold Rush,* photographs by Roberts, McNally & Loftin, 1971.

Photographer: Nancy Roberts, *An Illustrated Guide to Ghosts and Mysterious Occurrences in the Old North State,* Heritage House, 1959; Nancy Roberts, *Ghosts of the Carolinas,* McNally & Loftin, 1962; David Stick, *The Cape Hatteras Seashore,* MacNally & Loftin, 1964; Frances Griffin, *Old Salem in Pictures,* McNally & Loftin, 1966; Nancy Roberts, *David,* John Knox, 1968; Malcolm Boyd and Eric Sevareid, *You Can't Kill the Dream* (contains *Reflections* by Boyd and *The American Dream* by Sevareid), John Knox, 1968; Nancy Roberts, *A Week in Robert's World: The South,* Crowell-Collier, 1969; Nancy Roberts, *Sense of Discovery: The Mountain,* John Knox, 1969; Joel Rothman, *At Last to Ocean: The Story of the Endless Cycle of Water,* Crowell-Collier, 1971.

BIOGRAPHICAL/CRITICAL SOURCES: William Powell, *North Carolina Lives,* Historical Record Association, 1962; *U.S. Camera,* May, 1962; *Editor and Publisher,* March 2, 1963.

*   *   *

ROBERTS, Daniel (Frank) 1922-

PERSONAL: Born November 14, 1922, in Paris, France; son of Charles Raoul and Marie-Antoinette (Bonnami) Roberts; married Geraldine Anne McGwire, 1954. *Education:* Attended private schools in Paris, France. *Home:* Orchard Cottage, Elsdon, West Hill, Ottery St. Mary, Devonshire, England.

CAREER Went into French Maquis at sixteen, serving for four years; sometime worker on farms, in forestry, and as photographer in London, England; teacher in preparatory schools in England for twelve-years before giving up academic career to write full time. *Member:* Society of Assistant Teachers in Preparatory Schools.

WRITINGS: Francois et l'armee secrete, House of Grant, 1957; *La Ligue des chamois,* Cambridge University Press, 1960; *La Chapelle sous la glace,* Cambridge University Press, 1961; (compiler) Romain Rolland, *L'Enfance de Jean Christophe,* Cambridge University Press, 1961; *Marmot Valley,* Oxford University Press, 1962; *Nibbleneat* (juvenile), Oxford University Press, 1963; (editor with Rona Laurie) *Anthology of Prose and Play Scenes for Students of Speech and Drama,* 8th edition, Guildhall School of Music and Drama, 1963; *Calixte,* Oxford University Press, 1964. Contributor of short stories and articles to French and English magazines and educational journals.

WORK IN PROGRESS: Story, with Paris background.

SIDELIGHTS: Roberts is a British citizen by birth, but grew up with French as his first language. *Avocational interests:* Skiing, photography, wildlife.

*   *   *

ROBERTS, Frances C(abaniss) 1916-

PERSONAL: Born December 19, 1916, in Gainesville, Ala.; daughter of Richard H. and Mary (Watson) Roberts. *Education:* Livingston State College, B.S., 1937; University of Alabama, M.A., 1940, Ph.D., 1956. *Politics:* Democrat. *Religion:* Episcopalian. *Home:* 603 Randolph Ave. S.E., Huntsville, Ala. 35801. *Office:* University of Alabama in Huntsville, Box 1247, Huntsville, Ala. 35807.

CAREER: Huntsville (Ala.) Public Schools, teacher, 1937-52; University of Alabama, Huntsville, instructor,

1953-56, assistant professor, 1956-59, associate professor, 1959-61, professor of history, 1961—. Trustee of Burritt Museum and Huntsville Civic Symphony. *Member:* Southern Historical Association, Alabama Historical Association.

WRITINGS: (With Charles G. Summersell) *Exploring Alabama,* Colonial Press, 1961; (reviser with Viola Ayer) Frank L. Owsley, John Craig Stewart, and Gordon T. Chappell, *Know Alabama: An Elementary History,* 2nd edition, Colonial Press, 1961; *Highlights of Huntsville History,* Huntsville Public Library, 1962; (with Sarah Huff Fisk) *Shadows on the Wall: The Life and Works of Howard Weeden,* Colonial Press, 1962; (with Coleman Ransone) *Civics for Alabama Schools,* Colonial Press, 1963, 2nd edition, Viewpoint Publications, 1970.

WORK IN PROGRESS: A History of Public Land Disposal in Alabama; The Huntsville Story: A History of an Alabama City.

*   *   *

ROBERTS, Nancy Correll 1924-

PERSONAL: Born May 30, 1924, in South Milwaukee, Wis.; daughter of Milton Lee (a chemist) and Maud (MacRae) Correll; married Bruce Stuart Roberts (a free-lance photographer), February 27, 1957; children: Nancey Lee, David Correll. *Education:* University of North Carolina, B.A., 1947. *Religion:* Presbyterian. *Home:* 6624 Sunview Dr., Charlotte, N.C. 28210; and Maxton, N.C. 28364.

CAREER: Scottish Chief, Maxton, N.C., editor and publisher, 1954-57. Town commissioner of Maxton, N.C., 1952-56. President, Maxton Development Corp., 1954-55. *Awards, honors: Where Time Stood Still* was picked as one of the outstanding children's books of 1970 by *New York Times* editorial board.

WRITINGS—All with photographs by husband, Bruce Roberts: *An Illustrated Guide to Ghosts and Mysterious Occurrences in the Old North State,* Heritage House, 1959; *Ghosts of the Carolinas,* McNally & Loftin, 1962; *David,* John Knox, 1968; *Sense of Discovery: The Mountain,* John Knox, 1969; *A Week in Robert's World: The South,* Crowell-Collier, 1969; (with Bruce Roberts) *Where Time Stood Still: A Portrait of Appalachia,* Crowell-Collier, 1970; (with Bruce Roberts) *This Haunted Land,* McNally & Loftin, 1970.

BIOGRAPHICAL/CRITICAL SOURCES: New York Times Book Review, November 9, 1969.

*   *   *

ROBERTSON, Arthur Henry 1913-

PERSONAL: Born November 9, 1913, in London, England; son of William Beveridge and Ethel (Camp) Robertson; married July 18, 1942; children: Caroline, Richard. *Education:* Attended Harrow School; Oxford University, B.A., 1935, B.C.L., 1937; Harvard University, LL.M., 1938, S.J.D., 1939. *Home:* 35 Boulevard Tauler, Strasbourg, France. *Office:* Council of Europe, Strasbourg, France.

CAREER: Barrister-at-law, Middle Temple, London, England; British Embassy, Lisbon, Portugal, first secretary, 1940-42; British War Office, London, England, civil assistant, 1942-44; United Nations Relief and Rehabilitation Administration, Washington, D.C., assistant general counsel, 1944-46; Grafica Editora Brasileira, Rio de Janeiro, Brazil, managing director, 1946-49; United Nations International Children's Emergency Fund, Paris, France, deputy director, 1949-50; Council of Europe, Strasbourg, France, various staff posts, 1950—. Lecturer at Hague Academy of International Law and University of Strasbourg; visiting lecturer at University of Manchester.

Public lecturer in Europe and America, mostly on movement for European unity.

WRITINGS: Characterization in the Conflict of Laws, Harvard University Press, 1940; The Council of Europe: Its Structure, Functions, and Achievements, Stevens, 1956, Praeger, 1957, 2nd edition, Praeger, 1961; (editor with B. Landheer) European Yearbook 1955, Heinman, 1957; European Institutions: Co-Operation, Integration, Unification, Praeger, 1959, 2nd edition, 1966; The Law of International Institutions in Europe, Being an Account of Some Recent Developments in the Field of International Law, Oceana, 1961; Human Rights in Europe, Oceana, 1963; Constitutional Developments in the Council of Europe, Institut de'Etudes Europeennes, 1964; Human Rights in Perspective: An Historical Introduction, [Strasbourg], 1956; (editor) Human Rights in National and International Law, Oceana, 1968; Human Rights in the World, Humanities, 1972.

* * *

ROBERTSON, Colin 1906-

PERSONAL: Born May 1, 1906, in Hull, Yorkshire, England; son of William Henry and Kale Louisa (Bottomley) Robertson; married Janet Turner Hutchison, December 19, 1942. Education: Attended schools in Chelsea, London, and Bradford, England. Home: Flat 6, St. Christophers, 23, Sutherland Ave., Bexhill-on-Sea, Sussex, England.

CAREER: Author, mainly of detective novels, 1934—. Ministry of Information, Scotland, senior press censor, 1944-45. Member: Crime Writers Association (founder-member, 1953; member of committee, 1953-61, 1968-71), Society of Authors, Press Club.

WRITINGS—All published by Ward, Lock, except as shown: The Yellow Strangler, 1934, Hillman-Curl, 1938; Painted Faces, 1935; Night Shadows, 1935; The Black Onyx Ring, Mellifont Press, 1936; Devil or Saint?, 1936; The Marble Tomb Mystery, 1936; House of Intrigue. 1937; The Fake, 1937; White Menace, 1938; The Stalking Stranger, 1939; The Temple of Dawn, 1939.

All published by Ward, Lock, except as shown: Soho Spy, 1940; Ghost Fingers, 1941; The Amazing Corpse, 1942; Zero Hour, 1942; Alibi in Black, 1944; Explosion!, 1945; Without Motive, Pendulum Publications, 1946; Two Must Die, 1946; The Dark Knight, 1946; The Devil's Lady, 1947; Knave's Castle, 1948; Calling Peter Gayleigh, 1948; Sweet Justice, 1949; Death Wears Red Shoes, 1949.

All published by Ward, Lock, except as shown: Dusky Limelight, 1951; Peter Gayleigh Flies High, 1951; Demon's Moon, 1951; The Tiger's Claws, 1951; North for Danger, W.H. Allen, 1952; Lady, Take Care, W.H. Allen, 1952; No Trial—No Error, W.H. Allen, 1953; Smugglers' Moon, 1954; You Can Keep the Corpse, 1955; Venetian Mask, 1956; The Eastlake Affair, John Long, 1957; Murder in the Morning, John Long, 1957; Who Rides a Tiger, John Long, 1958; The Golden Triangle, R. Hale, 1959; The Threatening Shadows, R. Hale, 1959.

All published by R. Hale, except as shown: Night Trap, 1960; Murder Sits Pretty, 1961; Time to Kill, 1961; Dark Money, 1962; Conflict of Shadows, 1963; The Frightened Widow, 1963; Dead on Time, 1964; Sinister Moonlight, 1965; Clash of Steel, 1965; Killer's Mask, 1966; The Judas Spies, 1966; Double Take, 1967; Pirate of the Pacific, Bantam, 1967; Twice Dead, 1968; Project X, 1968; The Devil's Cloak, 1969; A Lonely Place to Die, 1969; The Green Diamonds, 1970.

Three-act plays: "A Man of Parts," "The Stalking Stranger," "Murder in the Morning."

One-act plays: "Bride for Sale," "She Came at Night," "Unfinished Business," "The Trickster," "Easy Money."

Contributor of short stories to Evening News (London), and more than two hundred others to periodicals in Europe, the Middle East, and Far East.

SIDELIGHTS: Robertson prepares a detailed synopsis before beginning a detective novel, then, when writing is underway, works mornings and evenings five days a week. Murder in the Morning has appeared in various foreign translations, including Japanese, and was adapted as a play by Radio Francaise and for Polish television. Some of his other books and stories have been translated for publication in most European countries and also appear in large print editions. Avocational interests: Psychology and science.

* * *

ROBERTSON, Don 1929-

PERSONAL: Born March 21, 1929, in Cleveland, Ohio; son of Carl Trowbridge (associate editor, Cleveland Plain Dealer) and Josephine (Wuebben) Robertson; married Shari Kah, August 31, 1963. Education: Attended Harvard University, 1948-49, Western Reserve University, 1953-57. Politics: Democrat. Agent: Max Gartenberg, 45 West 45th St., New York, N.Y. 10036. Office: Cleveland Plain Dealer, 1801 Superior N.E., Cleveland, Ohio 44114.

CAREER: Cleveland Plain Dealer, Cleveland, Ohio, reporter, 1949-52, 1953-55, copy editor, 1955-57; Cleveland News, Cleveland, Ohio, reporter, 1957-59; executive assistant to the Attorney General of Ohio, 1959-60; Cleveland Plain Dealer, Cleveland, Ohio, reporter, 1963—. Military service: U.S. Army, 1946-48. Member: American Newspaper Guild. Awards, honors: Putnam Award ($10,000), 1964, for A Flag Full of Stars.

WRITINGS—All novels: The Three Days, Prentice-Hall, 1959; By Antietam Creek, Prentice-Hall, 1960; The River and the Wilderness, Doubleday, 1962 (published in England as Games Without Rules, Barrie & Rockliff, 1962); A Flag Full of Stars, Putnam, 1964; The Greatest Thing Since Sliced Bread (first in a trilogy), Putnam, 1965; The Sum and Total of Now (2nd in the trilogy), Putnam, 1966; Paradise Falls, Putnam, 1968; (with Marion Steele) The Halls of Yearning: An Indictment of Formal Education—A Manifesto of Student Liberation, [Lakewood, Calif.], 1969, Canfield Press, 1971; The Greatest Thing That Almost Happened (last in the trilogy), Putnam, 1970.

SIDELIGHTS: There is a consensus among reviewers of Robertson's novels that he is skillful in drawing minor characters, who often "outshine the major ones," according to R.F. Cayton. A Flag Full of Stars, a fictional account of the three days of the 1948 election in its impact on various peoples' lives, received mixed reviews. "Mr. Robertson is a Cleveland reporter," wrote Cayton for Library Journal, "and, logically, the best parts of his fourth novel are the city room scenes and the clearest character is an editor. Other characters. . .are fictional stereotypes."

With The Greatest Thing Since Sliced Bread, in which he also used a multiple point-of-view approach, Robertson created a personality in nine-year-old Morris who may take a decisive place in American boyhood fiction. "Morris Bird III and every step he takes," says Haskel Frankel, "are completely, wonderfully alive. Mr. Robertson remembers and vividly recalls everything that makes boyhood heaven and hell in one package." Cayton observes that Robertson, in The Sum and Total of Now, "has expert control of his subject matter. . .he doesn't permit the adult outlook to mar any of Morris' story as he did in the earlier book." Morris reaches the ripe age of seventeen in the last book of the trilogy, which "seems a less original work than *Sliced Bread*" to John Phillipson, writing for *Best Sellers*. "For me it has clear echoes of J.D. Salinger. . .[and] Holden Caulfield. Ellison's Owen Harrison Harding, Farrell's Danny O'Neil (a boy whose talent will one day lift him from a slum environment) and perhaps even John Gunther's son could enter into the composition of this fictional character. . . . Morris Bird III is believable and his story is touching."

Joel Katz has acquired an option on *Paradise Falls*, which he plans to make into a one-hour television series.

Robertson told *CA:* "I like model trains, John O'Hara, the Democratic Party, baseball, bridge, books, and most newspapermen below the rank of city editor."

BIOGRAPHICAL/CRITICAL SOURCES: *Saturday Review*, August 7, 1965; *New York Times Book Review*, March 3, 1968; *Best Sellers*, December 1, 1970.

*   *   *

ROBERTSON, James (Irvin), Jr. 1930-

PERSONAL: Born July 18, 1930, in Danville, Va.; son of J. Irvin (a banker) and Mae (Kympton) Robertson; married Elzabeth Green, June 1, 1952; children: Beth, Jim, Howard. *Education:* Randolph-Macon College, B.A.; Emory University, M.A., Ph.D. *Religion:* Episcopalian. *Home:* 405 Stonegate Dr. N.W., Blacksburg, Va. 24060. *Office:* Department of History, Virginia Polytechnic Institute and State University, Blacksburg, Va. 24061.

CAREER: University of Iowa, Iowa City, editor of *Civil War History,* 1959-61; George Washington University, Washington, D.C., associate professorial lecturer, 1962-65; University of Montana, Missoula, associate professor of history, 1965-67; Virginia Polytechnic Institute and State University, Blacksburg, professor of history, 1967—, chairman of the department, 1969—. Executive director, U.S. Civil War Centennial Commission, 1961-65. Member of board of directors of Jefferson Davis Papers Association and U.S. Grant Association. Certified high school football official, Mason-Dixon Intercollegiate Conference and Commonwealth of Virginia.

MEMBER: American Historical Association, Organization of American Historians, Southern Historical Association, Virginia Historical Society (member of board of directors). *Awards, honors:* Harry S. Truman Historical award; Mrs. Simon Baruch University award; Bennett Memorial Historical award of Randolph-Macon College; centennial medallion, U.S. Civil War Centennial Commission.

WRITINGS: (Editor and author of foreword) Sarah Dawson, *A Confederate Girl's Diary,* Indiana University Press, 1960; (editor and author of introduction and notes) *From Manassas to Appomattox: Memoirs of the Civil War in America,* Indiana University Press, 1960; *Virginia, 1861-1865: Iron Gate to the Confederacy* (booklet), Virginia Civil War Commission, 1961; (editor and author of introduction and notes) Walter Herron Taylor, *Four Years with General Lee,* Indiana University Press, 1962; (editor) Dolly Sumner Burge, *Diary,* University of Georgia Press, 1962; *The Stonewall Brigade,* Louisiana State University Press, 1963; *The Civil War: A Student Handbook,* U.S. Civil War Centennial Commission, 1963; *The Sack of Lawrence: What Price Glory?,* World Co. (Lawrence, Kan.), 1963; (compiler) *Civil War History: Cumulative Index, 1955-1959,* Volumes I-V, State University of Iowa, 1963; (editor) John H. Worsham, *One of Jackson's Foot Cavalry,* McCowat-Mercer, 1965; (editor) *The Civil War Letters of General Robert McAllister,* Rutgers University Press, 1965; (editor with Allan Nevins and Bell I. Wiley) *Civil War Books: A Critical Bibliography,* two volumes, Louisiana State University Press, 1967-69; *The Concise Illustrated History of the Civil War,* Stackpole, 1971; (editor) *Four Years in the Stonewall Brigade,* Morningside Bookshop, 1972. Contributor of more than forty articles on American history to periodicals. Member of board of editors, *Civil War History, Lincoln Herald,* and *American History Illustrated.*

WORK IN PROGRESS: *The North to Posterity,* publication by Knopf expected in 1974.

*   *   *

ROBERTSON, Keith (Carlton) 1914-
(Carlton Keith)

PERSONAL: Born May 9, 1914, in Dows, Iowa; son of Myron Clifford (a merchant) and Harriet (Hughes) Robertson; married Elisabeth Hexter (a bookseller), November 2, 1946; children: Christina Harriet, Hope Elisabeth, Jeffry Keith. *Education:* U.S. Naval Academy, B.S., 1937. *Politics:* Republican. *Religion:* Protestant. *Home:* Booknoll Farm, Hopewell, N.J. 08524. *Agent:* Brandt & Brandt, 101 Park Ave., New York, N.Y. 10017.

CAREER: U.S. Navy, radioman on battleship, 1931-33, officer, serving mainly aboard destroyers in the Atlantic and Pacific, 1941-45; now captain, U.S. Naval Reserve. Civilian refrigeration engineer, 1937-41; employee of publishing firm, 1945-47; free-lance writer, 1947-58; Bay Ridge Specialty Co., Inc. (manufacturer of ceramics), Trenton, N.J., president, 1958-69. Trustee, Hopewell Museum. *Awards, honors:* Pacific Northwest Library Association's "Young Reader's Choice" award, 1969, for *Henry Reed's Baby Sitting Service.*

WRITINGS: *Ticktock and Jim,* Winston, 1948 (published in England as *Watch for a Pony,* Heinemann, 1949); *Ticktock and Jim, Deputy Sheriffs,* Winston, 1949; *The Dog Next Door,* Viking, 1950; *The Missing Brother,* Viking, 1950; *The Lonesome Sorrel,* Winston, 1952; *The Mystery of Burnt Hill,* Viking, 1952; *Mascot of the Melroy,* Viking, 1953; *Outlaws of the Sourland,* Viking, 1953; *Three Stuffed Owls,* Viking, 1954; *The Wreck of the Saginaw,* Viking, 1954; *Ice to India,* Viking, 1955; *The Phantom Rider,* Viking, 1955; *The Pilgrim Goose,* Viking, 1956; *The Pinto Deer,* Viking, 1956; *The Crow and the Castle,* Viking, 1957; *Henry Reed, Inc.,* Viking, 1958; *If Wishes Were Horses,* Harper, 1958; *The Navy: From Civilian to Sailor,* Viking, 1958; *Henry Reed's Journey,* Viking, 1963; *Henry Reed's Baby-Sitting Service,* Viking, 1966; *The Year of the Jeep,* Viking 1968; *New Jersey,* Coward, 1969; *The Money Machine,* Viking, 1969; *Henry Reed's Big Show,* Viking, 1970.

Under pseudonym Carlton Keith: *The Diamond-Studded Typewriter,* Macmillan, 1958, reissued as *A Gem of a Murder,* Dell, 1959; *Missing, Presumed Dead,* Doubleday, 1961; *Rich Uncle,* Doubleday, 1963; *The Hiding Place,* Doubleday, 1965; *The Crayfish Dinner,* Doubleday, 1966 (published in England as *The Elusive Epicure,* R. Hale, 1968); *A Taste of Sangria,* Doubleday, 1968 (published in England as *The Missing Book-keeper,* R. Hale, 1969).

WORK IN PROGRESS: A mystery story for adults; a juvenile.

BIOGRAPHICAL/CRITICAL SOURCES: *New York Times Book Review,* July 28, 1968; *Horn Book,* April, 1971.

*   *   *

ROBERTSON, Olivia (Melian) 1917-

PERSONAL: Born April 13, 1917; daughter of Manning and Nora K. (Parsons) Robertson. *Education:* Studied at Grosvenor School of Modern Art, London, England. *Politics:* Liberal. *Religion:* "Universalist and Spiritualist."

Home: Huntington Castle, Clonegal, Ferns, Eire. *Agent:* Curtis Brown Ltd., 13 King St., London W.C.2, England.

CAREER: Artist, with work exhibited in Dublin, Ireland, 1939, 1956. Currently helping organize Huntington Castle Centre for Meditation and Study. *Military service:* Voluntary Aid Detachment, nurse, 1940. *Member:* Overseas League, P.E.N.

WRITINGS—All self-illustrated: *St. Malachy's Court,* P. Davies, 1946, Odyssey, 1947; *Field of the Stranger* (Book Society choice in England), Random House, 1948; *The Golden Eye,* P. Davies, 1949; *Miranda Speaks,* P. Davies, 1950; *It's an Old Irish Custom,* Vanguard, 1953; *Dublin Phoenix,* J. Cape, 1957.

WORK IN PROGRESS: A book on metaphysics; drafting courses in comparative religious and esoteric studies for meditation center.

BIOGRAPHICAL/CRITICAL SOURCES: Book Society Magazine, February, 1963.

* * *

ROBINSON, Joan Violet 1903-

PERSONAL: Born October 31, 1903; daughter of Major General Sir Frederick Maurice; married E.A.G. Robinson, 1926; children: two daughters. *Education:* Attended St. Paul's Girls' School, London, England; Girton College, Cambridge, economics tripos, 1925. *Home:* 62 Grange Rd., Cambridge, England.

CAREER: Cambridge University, Cambridge, England, assistant lecturer, 1931-37, university lecturer, 1937-49, reader, 1949-64, professor of economics, 1965-71. *Member:* British Academy (fellow).

WRITINGS: The Economics of Imperfect Competition, Macmillan, 1933, 2nd edition, St. Martin's, 1969; *Essays in the Theory of Employment,* Macmillan, 1937, 2nd edition, Basil Blackwell, 1947, Macmillan, 1948; *Introduction to the Theory of Employment,* Macmillan, 1937, 2nd edition, St. Martin's, 1969; *An Essay on Marxian Economics,* Macmillan, 1942, 2nd edition, St. Martin's, 1967; (with others) *Can Planning be Democratic?: A Collection of Essays Prepared for the Fabian Society,* G. Routledge & Sons, 1944; *Collected Economic Papers,* Volume I, Basil Blackwell, 1951, Volume II, Basil Blackwell, 1960, Volume III, Humanities, 1966, Volume IV, Humanities, 1972; *The Rate of Interest, and Other Essays,* Macmillan, 1952; *The Accumulation of Capital,* Irwin, 1956, 3rd edition, Macmillan, 1969; *Exercises in Economic Analysis,* Macmillan, 1960, St. Martin's, 1961; *Essays in the Theory of Economic Growth,* Macmillan, 1962, St. Martin's, 1963; *Economic Philosophy,* Aldine, 1962; *Economics: An Awkward Corner,* Allen & Unwin, 1966, Pantheon, 1967; (compiler) *The Cultural Revolution in China,* Penguin, 1969; *Freedom and Necessity: An Introduction to the Study of Society,* Pantheon, 1970; *Economic Heresies: Some Old-Fashioned Questions in Economic Theory,* Basic Books, 1971; (contributor) Rendigs Fels, editor, *The Second Crisis of Economic Theory, and Other Selected Papers,* foreword by John Kenneth Galbraith, General Learning Press, 1972.

Essay booklets: *Economics Is a Serious Subject,* Heffer, 1932; *Private Enterprise or Public Control,* English Universities Press, 1942; *The Problem of Full Employment: An Outline for Study Circles,* Workers Educational Association, 1943, revised edition, 1949; *The Future of Industry,* Muller, 1943; *Conference Sketch Book: Moscow, April, 1952,* Heffer, 1952; *On Re-Reading Marx,* Students' Bookshops, 1953; *Letters from a Visitor to China,* Students' Bookshops, 1954; *Marx, Marshall, and Keynes,* Delhi School of Economics, University of Delhi, 1955; (with Sol Adler) *China: An Economic Perspective,* foreword by Harold Wilson, Fabian International Bureau,

1958; (with R. Frisch) *Draft of a Multilateral Trade Clearing Agency,* Institute of Economics, University of Oslo, 1962; *Notes from China,* Monthly Review Press, 1964; *The New Mercantilism: An Inaugural Lecture,* Cambridge University Press, 1966. Contributor to economics journals.

* * *

ROBINSON, Sister Marian Dolores 1916-
(Sister Marian Dolores)

PERSONAL: Born November 23, 1916, in Astoria, Ore.; daughter of James Joseph and Mathilda (Carlson) Robinson. *Education:* Marylhurst College, B.A., 1937; Loyola University, Chicago, Ill., M.A., 1944, Ph.D., 1947; postdoctoral study at University of Chicago, 1947, Columbia University, 1954, University of Louvain, 1955-56, and Sorbonne, University of Paris, 1963-65. *Office:* Marylhurst College, Marylhurst, Ore. 97036.

CAREER: Roman Catholic religious. Holy Names College, Spokane, Wash., professor of psychology, 1948; Marylhurst College, Marylhurst, Ore., chairman of department of psychology, 1948-59; University of Windsor, Windsor, Ontario, professor of psychology and dean of women 1959-63; Marylhurst College, Marylhurst, Ore., professor of psychology and chairman of the department, 1965—; Tektronix, Inc., Beaverton, Ore., professor of psychology, 1965—. Professor at Summer sessions, Catholic University of America, 1960-63. *Member:* International Catholic Association for Medical Psychology (assistant secretary-general, 1969—), World Federation for Mental Health (sponsoring member, U.S. Committee), American Psychological Association, American Philosophical Association, American Association of Existential Psychology and Psychiatry, American Catholic Psychological Association, American Catholic Philosophical Association, American Association for the Advancement of Science, Canadian Psychological Association, Western Psychological Association, Oregon Psychological Association (secretary-treasurer, 1953-55), Portland Psychological Association (president, 1970-71), Delta Epsilon Sigma, Pi Gamma Mu, Psi Chi. *Awards, honors:* Fulbright research scholar, Louvain, Belgium, 1955-56; Fulbright cultural award, 1956; University of Detroit research grant, 1963-64.

WRITINGS: (Contributor) Raymond J. Steimel, *Psychological Counseling of Adolescents,* Catholic University of America Press, 1962; *Creative Personality in Religious Life,* Sheed, 1963. Also author of monograph, "Perceptual Research—A Whole with Many Parts." Contributor to education, philosophy, and psychology journals.

WORK IN PROGRESS: Phenomenological Studies in Psychology.

AVOCATIONAL INTERESTS: Music, art, communications.

* * *

ROBINSON, Robert 1927-

PERSONAL: Born December 17, 1927, in Liverpool, England; son of Ernest Redfern (an accountant) and Johanna (Hogan) Robinson; married Josephine Richard, August 28, 1958; children: Nicholas Robert, Lucy Annabel. *Education:* Exeter College, Oxford, M.A. *Home:* 16 Cheyne Row, Chelsea, London, England; and Laurel Cottage, Buckland St. Mary, Somerset, England. *Agent:* Curtis Brown Ltd., 13 King St., Covent Garden, London W.C.2, England.

CAREER: Formerly columnist with *Sunday Times,* London, England, and film critic for *Sunday Telegraph,* London, England; British Broadcasting Corp., London, England, anchorman on various series involving entertainment and the arts.

WRITINGS: *Landscape with Dead Dons,* Rinehart, 1956; *Inside Robert Robinson,* Penguin, 1965; *The Conspiracy,* Hodder & Stoughton, 1968.

*   *   *

RODAHL, Kaare   1917-

PERSONAL: Born August 17, 1917, in Bronnoysund, Norway; son of Anton (a writer) and Tora (Oppsahl) Rodahl; married Joan Hunter, 1946; children: Anton, Kari. *Education:* University of Oslo, M.D., 1948, Dr. med., 1950. *Home:* 1143 Maplecrest Cir., Gladwyne, Pa. *Office:* Division of Research, Lankenau Hospital, Philadelphia, Pa. 19151.

CAREER: U.S. Air Force Aeromedical Laboratory, Dayton, Ohio, special consultant, 1949; Arctic Aeromedical Laboratory, Ladd Air Force Base, Fairbanks, Alaska, chief of department of physiology, 1950-52, director of research, 1954-57; Lankenau Hospital, Philadelphia, Pa., director of research, 1957—. Member of numerous Arctic expeditions. Chairman of panel on biology and medicine of Committee on Polar Research, National Academy of Sciences. Member, Lower Merion (Pa.) Township Board of Health, 1963-64. *Member:* Authors Guild, medical and professional societies in United States and Norway.

WRITINGS: *Tre aar som fallskjermhopper* (title means "Three Years as a Paratrooper"), Gyldendal, 1945; *The Ice Capped Island, Greenland,* Blackie & Son, 1946; *Et aar under breen* (title means "One Year Below the Ice Cap"), Gyldendal, 1946; *Nytt land under vingene* (title means "New Land Under the Wings"), Gyldendal, 1947; *The Toxic Effect of Polar Bear Liver,* I Kommisjon hos J. Dybwad, 1949; *Vitamin Sources in Arctic Regions,* I Kommisjon hos J. Dybwad, 1949; *Hyperviatminosis A: A Study of the Effect of Excess of Vitamin A in Experimental Animals,* I Kommisjon hos J. Dybwad, 1950; *North: The Nature and Drama of the Polar World,* Harper, 1953; *T-3* (title means "Target Three"), Gyldendal, 1954; *Studies on the Blood and Blood Pressure in the Eskimo and the Significances of Ketosis under Arctic Conditions,* I Kommisjon hos Broeggers Boktr. Forlag, 1954; *Eskimo Metabolism:* A Study of Racial Factors in Basal Metabolism, I Kommisjon hos Broeggers Boktr. Forlag, 1954; *Smilets folk,* Gyldendal, 1957; *Human Acclimatization to Cold,* Arctic Aeromedical Laboratory, Ladd Air Force Base, 1957; *Nutritional Requirements under Arctic Conditions,* Norsk Polarinstitutt, 1960; *The Last of the Few* (autobiography), Harper, 1963 (published in England as *Between Two Worlds: A Doctor's Log-Book of Life Amongst the Alaskan Eskimos,* Heinemann, 1964); *Be Fit for Life: A Practical Guide to Physical Well-Being,* Harper, 1966; (with Per Olof Astrand) *Textbook of Work Physiology,* McGraw, 1970.

Editor, with Bela Issekutz, of proceedings of conferences held at Lankenau Hospital: *Bone as a Tissue,* McGraw, 1960; (with Steven M. Horvath) *Muscle as a Tissue,* McGraw, 1962; *Fat as a Tissue,* McGraw, 1964; *Nerve as a Tissue,* Harper, 1966. Contributor to scientific journals.

WORK IN PROGRESS: Popular science account of the functions of the human body at work.

AVOCATIONAL INTERESTS: Sports.

*   *   *

RODGERS, Betty June (Flint)   1921-

PERSONAL: Born February 10, 1921, in Pike, N.Y.; daughter of Darwin Watson (a businessman) and Jessie (Ackerman) Flint; married Charles Woodrow Rodgers (a businessman), July 8, 1948; children: Brian, Rich-

ard. *Education:* Houghton College, B.A., 1942; Geneseo State University, graduate student, 1942-43. *Politics:* Republican. *Religion:* Presbyterian. *Home:* 2416 Atlantic Blvd., Vero eBach, Fla. 32960. *Agent:* Curtis Brown, Ltd., 60 East 56th St., New York, N.Y. 10022. *Office:* 1028 20th Place, Vero Beach, Fla. 32960.

CAREER: Teacher of English, various high schools in New York State, 1942-46; *Idaho Daily Statesman,* Boise, reporter, 1946-47; KIDO (radio station), Boise, Idaho, writer, 1947-48; Indian River County Library, Vero Beach, Fla., director, 1968—. *Member:* Alpha Delta Kappa.

WRITINGS: *The Walker House Mystery,* Bobbs-Merrill, 1964; (compiler with Pascal Covici, Jr., and Lorraine Fowler) *Literate Discourse: Essays at S.M.U.,* Wadsworth, 1966.

WORK IN PROGRESS: Juvenile mystery.

AVOCATIONAL INTERESTS: Swimming, boating, gardening, and outdoor living.

*   *   *

RODGERS, Frank P(eter)   1924-

PERSONAL: Born December 15, 1924, in Utica, N.Y.; son of Frank P. (owner of photoengraving plant) and Emma (Graneis) Rodgers; married Jayne E. Shields; children: Christine Ann, Nancy Jayne. *Education:* University of Buffalo (now State University of New York at Buffalo), B.A., 1946, Ed.D., 1959; University of Rochester, Ed.M., 1951. *Home:* 269 Heritage Dr., Rochester, N.Y. 14615. *Office:* Pfaudler Permutit, Inc., 1100 Midtown Tower Building, Rochester, N.Y. 14604.

CAREER: Rochester Institute of Technology, Rochester, N.Y., associate director of Counseling Center, 1953-64; Pfaudler Permutit, Inc., Rochester, N.Y., manpower planning manager, 1964—. Part-time private practice as psychologist, 1959-64. Consultant to Wetterings & Agnew (executive placement firm), 1962-64. *Member:* American Psychological Association, Genesee Valley Psychological Association.

WRITINGS: (With L. Lipsett and M. Kentner) *Personnel Selection and Recruitment,* Allyn & Bacon, 1964.

WORK IN PROGRESS: Research into personality characteristics of management personnel and early identification of leadership potential.†

*   *   *

RODLI, Agnes Sylvia   1921-

PERSONAL: Born October 3, 1921, in Portland, Ore.; daughter of Conrad E. (a commercial fisherman) and Helga (Odde) Rodli. *Education:* Attended Bethany Bible College, Santa Cruz, Calif., and University of Alaska. *Religion:* Assemblies of God. *Home:* Box 88, North Pole, Alaska. 99705.

CAREER: Assemblies of God missionary to northern California Indians and in Alaska, 1945—. Teacher in public schools at Nikolai, Alaska, 1948-51, and North Pole, Alaska, 1957-58.

WRITINGS: *North of Heaven: A Teaching Ministry Among the Alaskan Indians,* Moody, 1963.

WORK IN PROGRESS: Studies of Alaska natives, their present and future.

*   *   *

ROE, F(rederick) Gordon   1894-
(Criticus, Winslow Rhode, Uncle Gordon)

PERSONAL: Born September 24, 1894, in Chelsea, London, England; son of Fred (an artist, author, and authority on old oak) and Letitia Mabel (Lee) Roe; married Eleanor Beatrice Grundy, March 30, 1921; children: Frances (Mrs. Michael Maynard). *Education:* Studied at Westminster School, 1908-12, then under privat*e* tutor; art studies under father and at Chelsea School of Art. *Religion:* Church of England. *Home:* 19 Vallance Rd., Alexandra Park, London N.22 4UD, England.

CAREER: Connoisseur, London, England, inquiry manager, 1913, became modern art critic, later assistant editor and editor, 1919-33, temporary assistant to editor, 1947; sometime art critic for *Daily Mail* and *Artist,* both London, and house editor in book department of Odhams Press Ltd., London. Director, Connoisseur Ltd., 1931-34. *Military service:* Royal Field Artillery, gunner, 1917-19. *Member:* Society of Antiquaries of London (fellow), Royal Historical Society (fellow), Royal Society of Arts (fellow), Society of Authors, Walpole Society, Pewter Society (honorary), Arms and Armour Society (corresponding member).

WRITINGS: Henry Bright of the Norwich School, Walker's Galleries, 1920; *Charles Bentley, Member of the "Old Water-Colour" Society,* Walker's Galleries, 1921; *Dictator of the Royal Academy,* Walker's Galleries, 1921; *David Cox,* F.A. Stokes, 1924; *Sporting Prints of the Eighteenth and Early Nineteenth Centuries,* Harcourt, 1927; *The Fatal Bargain,* March Brown, 1933; *Coronation Cavalcade,* P.R. Gawthorn, 1937; *Life and Times of King Edward VIII,* P.R. Gawthorn, 1937; (with C. Reginald Grundy) *A Catalogue of the Pictures and Drawings in the Collection of Frederick John Nettlefold,* Volumes III-IV, privately printed, 1937-38; *Sketch Portrait of Francis Wheatley,* privately printed, 1938.

(With William Gaunt) *Etty and the Nude: The Art and Life of William Etty,* F. Lewis, 1943, Transatlantic, 1944; *The Nude from Cranach to Etty and Beyond,* F. Lewis, 1944, Transatlantic, 1946; *The Bronze Cross, a Tribute to Those Who Won the Supreme Award for Valour in the Years 1940-45,* P.R. Gawthorn, 1945; *English Period Furniture, an Introductory Guide,* Tiranti, 1946; *Cox the Master: The Life and Art of David Cox (1783-1859),* F. Lewis, 1946; *Rowlandson: The Life and Art of a British Genius,* F. Lewis, 1946, Studio Publications, 1947; *Sea Painters of Britain,* two volumes, F. Lewis, 1947-48; *Old English Furniture from Tudor to Regency,* National Magazine Co., 1948; (under pseudonym Uncle Gordon) *Clarence Below the Basement* (juvenile), Vawser & Wiles, 1948; *English Cottage Furniture,* Phoenix House, 1949, published in America as *Antique English Cottage Furniture,* M. McBride Co., 1950, 3rd edition, revised and enlarged, published under original title, Phoenix House 1961, Roy, 1962; *Britain's Birthright,* P.R. Gawthorn, 1950; *Victorian Furniture,* Roy, 1952; *Windsor Chairs,* Pitman, 1953; *The Victorian Child,* Phoenix House, 1959.

(With John Raymond Fawcett Thompson) *The British Museum's Pictures,* Connoisseur, 1961; *The Georgian Child,* Phoenix House, 1961, Hillary, 1966; *Home Furnishing with Antiques,* Hastings House, 1965; *Victorian Corners: The Style and Taste of an Era,* Allen & Unwin, 1968, Praeger, 1969; *Women in Profile: A Study in Silhouette,* John Baker, 1970. Contributor to *Daily Mail Ideal Home Book, Empire Youth Annual, Old Water Colour Society Club Annual,* and to periodicals, including *Antique Collector, Antiques* (New York), *Apollo, Artist, British Racehouse, Connoisseur, Journal of the Arms and Armour Society,* and *Journal of the Royal Society of Arts.*

WORK IN PROGRESS: A Catalogue Raisonne.

SIDELIGHTS: The Victorian Child has been issued in Braille. *Avocational Interests:* Genealogy, visiting museums, browsing in second-hand bookshops and small antique shops.

ROELKER, Nancy Lyman 1915-

PERSONAL: Born June 15, 1915, in Warwick, R.I.; daughter of William Greene (a historian) and Anna (Koues) Roelker. *Education:* Radcliffe College, A.B., 1936; Harvard University, A.M., 1937, Ph.D., 1953. *Politics:* Independent. *Home:* 19 Ware St., Cambridge, Mass. 02138. *Office:* Department of History, Boston University, Boston, Mass. 02215.

CAREER: Teacher of European history at Concord Academy, Concord, Mass., 1937-41, at Winsor School, Boston, Mass., 1941-63; Tufts University, Medford, Mass., assistant professor, 1963-65, associate professor, 1965-69, professor of European history 1969-71; Boston University, Boston, Mass., professor of European history, 1971—. *Member:* American Academy of Arts and Sciences, American Historical Association, Society for French Historical Studies, Renaissance Society of America, Societe de l'Histoire de Protestantisme Francais, New England History Teachers Association, Huguenot Society of London, Phi Beta Kappa. *Awards, honors:* Research grant from American Philosophical Society, 1960, 1970; Guggenheim fellow, 1965-66; recipient of Distinguished Achievement medal, Radcliffe Graduate Society, 1970.

WRITINGS: (Translator and editor) Pierre de L'Estoile, *The Paris of Henry of Navarre,* Harvard University Press, 1958; (contributing editor and translator) *In Search of France,* Harvard University Press, 1963; (editor and translator) Jean-Batiste Duroselle, *From Wilson to Roosevelt: American Foreign Policy, 1913-1945,* Harvard University Press, 1963; (editor) Raymond Aron, *The Great Debate: Theories of Nuclear Strategy,* Doubleday, 1965; *Queen of Navarre: Jeanne d'Albret, 1529-1572,* Harvard University Press, 1968; (editor and translator) *Correspondence of Jeanne d'Albret, 1541-1572,* Librarie Droz (Geneva), in press. Translator and editor from the French and Italian, including articles for *Daedalus.* Contributor to *Renaissance News* and *Transactions* of the Huguenot Society of South Carolina.

*   *   *

ROER, Berniece Marie

PERSONAL: Born in Elsinore, Mo.; daughter of William C. and Edna (Casteel) Raymer; married George L. Roer, August 13, 1938 (died June 7, 1964); children: George W., Michael L. *Education:* Educated in Illinois public schools. *Home:* 7809 Kenridge Lane, St. Louis, Mo. 63119.

CAREER: Free-lance writer of articles and short stories; lecturer; teacher of adult evening course in creative writing; workshop leader at writers' conferences. *Member:* Missouri Writers' Guild (former board member), St. Louis Writers Guild (president, 1960).

WRITINGS: How to Write Articles, For Those Who Feel That Writing, too, Is a Ministry, Bethany Press, 1963. Contributor of articles and short stories to *Writer, St. Louis Post-Dispatch, Optimist International, Christian Science Monitor,* and other periodicals.

WORK IN PROGRESS: A three-act play for high school students.

BIOGRAPHICAL/CRITICAL SOURCES: St. Louis Post-Dispatch, July 26, 1963.

*   *   *

ROGERS, Cyril H(arold) 1907-

PERSONAL: Born November 21, 1907, in Cambridge, England. *Education:* Attended high school and technical schools in Cambridge, England. *Home:* The Old Yard, Abington, Cambridge, England.

WRITINGS: Budgerigars, and How to Breed Cinnamonwings, Bird Fancy (London), 1934, 4th edition published as *Budgerigars and How to Breed Them*, Poultry World, c.1945, 5th edition, All Pets Magazine, 1951, 9th edition, Iliffe, 1962; *Budgerigars*, W. & G. Foyle, 1952, published in America as *Care and Breeding of Budgies (Shell Parrakeets)*, Dover, 1953; *Canaries*, W. & G. Foyle, 1953; *Parrots*, W. & G. Foyle, 1953; *Foreign Birds*, W. & G. Foyle, 1954; *The A to Z of Budgerigars: All You Need to Know About Breeding, Colours, Diseases, Exhibiting, Feeding, Societies, Talking*, Parrish, 1961; *Zebra Finches*, Iliffe, 1964; (editor) Abram Rutgers *Budgerigars in Colour: Their Care and Breeding*, Blandford, 1967; *Pet Library's Parrot Guide*, Pet Library, 1969; *Pet Library's Parakeet Guide*, Pet Library, 1970, published in America as *Parakeet Guide*, Doubleday, 1971; *Pet Birds*, Paul Hamlyn, 1970. Contributor to *Cage and Aviary Birds*, *Birds Illustrated*, and *All Pets*, and to other journals in Great Britain, Germany, South Africa, Australia, and New Zealand.

* * *

ROGERS, David C(harles) D(rummond) 1931-

PERSONAL: Born November 30, 1931, in Boston, Mass.; son of Eric Malcolm (a professor) and Janet (Drummond) Rogers; divorced; children: Jane French Drummond, Elizabeth Burgin. *Education:* Harvard University, A.B., 1954, M.B.A., 1956, D.B.A., 1956. *Politics:* Independent. *Religion:* Unitarian. *Home:* Harvard Towers, Apartment 1009, Harvard St., Cambridge, Mass. 02146.

CAREER: Harvard University, School of Business Administration, Boston, Mass., research assistant, 1956-57, doctoral research fellow, 1957-58, assistant professor, 1958-64, associate professor of business administration, 1964—. Member of senior faculty of Graduate School of Sales Management and Marketing, Sales and Marketing Executives—International, 1960—. Director, H.A. Johnson Co., Boston, Mass.

WRITINGS: (With Stanley S. Miller and others) *Manufacturing Policy: A Casebook of Major Production Problems in Six Selected Industries*, revised edition, Irwin, 1964, 3rd edition (with Wickham Skinner and others) published in separate volumes on the furniture industry, 1968, electronics, 1968, plastics, 1968, oil, 1970, and steel, 1970; *Accounting for Managers: The Non-Accountant's Guide to the Language of Business*, Associated Business Programmes (London), 1971.

WORK IN PROGRESS: A book, text and cases, on corporate long-range planning.

* * *

ROGERS, W(illiam) G(arland) 1896-

PERSONAL: Born February 29, 1896, in Chicopee Falls, Mass.; son of Burt Teale (a businessman) and Nancy (Bean) Rogers; married Mildred Weston (a writer), October 5, 1934. *Education:* Amherst College, B.A., 1920; Universiy of Pittsburgh, graduate study, 1927-29. *Home and office:* Greenwood Farm, RFD Box 209, Gallitzin, Pa. 16641. *Agent:* Dorothy Markinko, McIntosh & Otis, Inc., 18 East 41st St., New York, N.Y. 10017.

CAREER: Teacher in Massachusetts and Pennsylvania schools, 1921-30; *Springfield Union*, Springfield, Mass., reporter and art editor, 1931-43; Associated Press, New York, N.Y., arts editor, 1943-61; writer and book reviewer. Member of National Book Awards fiction juries, two years, of National Book Awards advisory committee, three years. *Military service:* U.S. Army, ambulance driver attached to French Army, 1917-19; received Croix de Guerre. *Member:* P.E.N., Phi Beta Kappa, Alpha Delta Phi.

WRITINGS: *Fluent French for Beginners*, Benjamin H. Sanborn, 1927; *Life Goes On* (novel), Liveright, 1929; (editor) *Le Voyage de M. Perrichon*, Oxford Book Co., 1930; *When This You See Remember Me: Gertrude Stein in Person*, Rinehart, 1948; (with Mildred Weston) *Carnival Crossroads: The Story of Times Square*, Doubleday, 1960; *A Picture Is a Picture: A Look at Modern Painting*, Harcourt, 1964; *Wise Men Fish Here: The Story of Frances Steloff and the Gotham Book Mart*, Harcourt, 1965; *What's Up in Architecture: A Look at Modern Building*, Harcourt, 1965; *Ladies Bountiful*, Harcourt, 1968; *Mightier Than the Sword: Cartoons, Caricature, Social Comment*, Harcourt, 1968; *Carl Sandburg, Yes: Poet, Historian, Novelist, Songster*, Harcourt, 1970. Reviewer for *New York Times Book Review*, Saturday Review Syndicate, and other publications.

SIDELIGHTS: Rogers writes: "I live at the top of the Allegheny Mountains in the middle of one hundred acres where it's quiet except for the barking of our collie. And when I'm not here, away from things, I like to be in the middle of things—principally in the middle of Paris."

BIOGRAPHICAL/CRITICAL SOURCES: Amherst College Biographical Record, 1963; *Young Readers' Review*, April, 1966; *Best Sellers*, April 1, 1968, January 1, 1970, February 15, 1971; *Spectator*, August 30, 1968; *Punch*, September 11, 1968; *Observer Review*, September 29, 1968.

* * *

ROLLINS, Charlemae Hill 1897-

PERSONAL: Born June 20, 1897, in Yazoo City, Miss.; daughter of Allen G. and Birdie (Tucker) Hill; married Joseph Walter Rollins, April 8, 1918; children: Joseph Walter, Jr. *Education:* Western University, graduate, 1915; summer study, Columbia University, 1932, and University of Chicago, 1934-36. *Religion:* African Methodist-Episcopal. *Home:* 500 East 33rd St., Chicago, Ill. 60616.

CAREER: Chicago, Ill., Public Library, 1927—, children's librarian at George C. Hall Branch, 1932—. Roosevelt University, Chicago, Ill., instructor in children's literature, 1949—. Summer instructor at Fisk University, 1950, Morgan State College, 1953-54. *Member:* American Library Association (member of Newbery-Caldecott award committee, 1949-50; president, childrens services division, 1957-58), National Association for the Advancement of Colored People, National Council of Teachers of English, Illinois Library Association (chairman, children's section, 1954-55), Phi Delta Kappa (honorary). *Awards, honors:* American Brotherhood Award, National Conference of Christians and Jews, 1952; Library Letter Award, American Library Association, 1953; Grolier Society Award, 1955; woman of the year of Zeta Phi Beta, 1956; Good American Award of the Chicago Committee of One-hundred, 1962; Negro Centennial Awards, 1963; Children's Reading Round Table Award, 1963; Constance Lindsay Skinner Award, Women's National Book Association, 1970; Coretta Scott King Award, 1971.

WRITINGS: *We Build Together*, National Council of Teachers of English, 1943, 3rd edition, revised, 1967; *The Magic World of Books*, Science Research Associates, 1954; (editor) *Call of Adventure*, Crowell Collier, 1962; (compiler) *Christmas Gif': An Anthology of Christmas Poems, Songs, and Stories, Written By and About Negroes*, Follett, 1963; *They Showed the Way: Forty American Negro Leaders*, Crowell, 1964; *Famous American Negro Poets*, Dodd, 1965; *Famous Negro Entertainers of Stage, Screen, and TV*, Dodd, 1967; *Black Troubadour: Langston Hughes*, Rand McNally, 1970. Contributor to *American Childhood*, *Illinois Libraries*, *Junior Libraries*.

other journals. Member of editorial board of *The World Book Encyclopedia* and of *American Educator.*

BIOGRAPHICAL/CRITICAL SOURCES: *New York Times Book Review,* May 9, 1965.

* * *

ROLLINS Wayne G(ilbert) 1929-

PERSONAL: Born August 24, 1929, in Detroit, Mich.; son of Arthur Gilchrist and Ethel (Kamin) Rollins; married Donnalou Myerholtz, August 30, 1953; children: Michael Wayne, Thomas Lawrence, David Mark. *Education:* Capital University, B.A., 1951; Yale Divinity School, B.D., 1954, Yale University, M.A., 1956, Ph.D., 1960. *Politics:* Democrat. *Office:* Hartford Seminary Foundation, Hartford, Conn. 06105.

CAREER: Ordained minister in United Church of Christ (Congregational); Princeton University, Princeton, N.J., instructor in religion, 1958-59; Wellesley College, Wellesley, Mass., assistant professor of Biblical history, 1959-66; Hartford Seminary Foundation, Hartford, Conn., associate professor of biblical studies, 1966—. Visiting professor, Colgate-Rochester Divinity School, 1968; visiting lecturer, Yale University, 1968-69. Member of board of preachers, Wellesley College. *Member:* American Academy of Religion, Societas Novi Testamenti Studiorum, American Association of University Professors, American School of Oriental Research, Society of Biblical Literature and Exegesis.

WRITINGS: *The Gospels: Portraits of Christ,* Westminster, 1964. Contributor of reviews and articles to religious journals.

WORK IN PROGRESS: *Commentary on Colossians,* for Salem Press; research for a book tentatively titled *Slaves and Freedmen in the New Testament and Early Church.*

AVOCATIONAL INTERESTS: Swimming, singing, bicycle excursions, carpentry, skiing, and tennis.

* * *

ROMANOFF, Alexis Lawrence 1892-

PERSONAL: Born 1892 in St. Petersburg, Russia; son of Lawrence Mercury and Dorothy (Kondratieff) Romanoff; married Anastasia J. Sayenko, 1928. *Education:* Studied in Russia at St. Petersburg Academy of Fine Arts, 1912-14, and Tomsk University, 1918-19; Cornell University, B.S., 1925, M.S., 1926, Ph.D., 1928. *Home:* Belleayre Apartments, 700 Stewart Ave., Ithaca, N.Y. 14850.

CAREER: Cornell University, Ithaca, N.Y., research instructor and research assistant professor, 1928-43, associate professor, 1943-48, professor of chemical embryology, 1948-1960, now professor emeritus. Research fellow, Harvard University, 1939-40, Yale University, 1940-41; research associate in biophysics, University of Florida, 1942. Public speaker. Board member, Cornell University Religious Work. *Military service:* Russian Army, Engineer Corps, 1915-17; became lieutenant. *Member:* American Association for the Advancement of Science (fellow), American Chemical Society, American Physiological Society, American Society of Zoologists, Poultry Science Association (fellow), Society for Experimental Biology and Medicine, New York Academy of Science (fellow), Rotary Club (Ithaca, N.Y.). *Awards, honors:* Borden Award and gold medal, 1950, for his investigations in avian embryology.

WRITINGS: *Biochemistry and Biophysics of the Developing Hen's Egg I: Influence of Humidity,* Cornell University, 1930; *Study of Artificial Incubation of Game Birds,* Agricultural Experiment Station, Cornell University, 1934; *Technical Publications on Experimental Avian Embryology,* Agricultural Experiment Station, Cornell University, 1939; (compiler) *Popular Publications in the Field of Poultry Industry,* Agricultural Experiment Station, Cornell University, 1942; (with wife, Anastasia J. Romanoff) *The Avian Egg,* Wiley, 1949; *The Avian Embryo: Structural and Functional Development,* Macmillan, 1960; *The University Campus, a Place of Creative Thought, Work, and Play,* Cayuga Press, 1960; *Ithaca, the Site of Cornell University, a Center of Beauty and Intellect,* Cayuga Press, 1962; *Profiles of American Heritage: The Living Spirit of the Union,* Cayuga Press, 1963; *Reflective Poems: From an Album of Lyrics 1950-1960,* Cayuga Press, 1964; (with Anastasia J. Romanoff) *Biochemistry of the Avian Embryo,* Interscience, 1967; *A Solemn Promise: A Biography in Verse,* two volumes, Cayuga Press, 1967; (with Anastasia Romanoff) *Pathogenesis of the Avian Embryo; Causes of Malformations and Prenatal Death,* Wiley, 1972. Contributor of more than 125 articles to scientific and professional journals.

SIDELIGHTS: Romanoff is interested in painting, poetic writing, mechanical inventions (he has obtained several U.S. patents), and color movies. He illustrated technical books for publishers, 1923-28, and his own books.

BIOGRAPHICAL/CRITICAL SOURCES: . *Saturday Evening Post,* November 25, 1950; *Reader's Digest,* February, 1951; *New Yorker,* June 20, 1953, June 27, 1953; Eugene Kinkead, *Spider, Egg, and Microcosm,* Knopf, 1955; *Science Digest,* March, 1956.

* * *

ROMERSTEIN, Herbert 1931-

PERSONAL: Born August 19, 1931, in New York, N.Y.; son of Philip and Rose (Alpert) Romerstein; married Patricia Cole, 1962; children: Shari. *Education:* Attended Brooklyn College (now Brooklyn College of the City University of New York), 1950-51, 1954-55, and Queen's College (now Queen's College of the City University of New York), 1956. *Politics:* Republican. *Religion:* Jewish. *Address:* c/o Bookmailer, Inc., P.O. Box 101, New York, N.Y. 10016.

CAREER: New York State Commission on Charities, investigator of Communist summer camps, 1954-56; consultant on communism to federal and state agencies, 1954—. Attended Communist youth festivals in Austria, 1959, Finland, 1962, and Afro-Scandinavian Youth Congress in Norway, 1962. *Military service:* U.S. Army, 1952-55; received United Nations Korea Medal and U.S. Korea Medal with two battle stars. *Awards, honors:* Americanism award and medal, Veterans of Foreign Wars of New Jersey, 1961.

WRITINGS: *Communism and Your Child,* Bookmailer, 1962; *The Communist International Youth and Student Apparatus* (monograph), U.S. Senate Subcommittee, 1963. Contributor to *National Review, Washington World,* and *U.S.A.;* author of pamphlet on communism and religion.

WORK IN PROGRESS: A book on Communist-Nazi relations; research in Soviet espionage for possible publication.

* * *

ROOTS, Ivan Alan 1921-

PERSONAL: Born March 3, 1921, in Maidstone, Kent, England; son of Frank Herbert and Ellen (Snashfold) Roots; married Tegwyn Kathleen Williams, August 27, 1947; children: Gerrard Emlyn, Catherine Tegwen. *Education:* Balliol College, Oxford, B.A., 1941, M.A., 1945. *Home:* 4 Roundhill Close, Exeter, Devon, England. *Office:* Department of History, University of Exeter, Exeter, Devon, England.

CAREER: University College of South Wales and Monmouthshire, Cardiff, Wales, lecturer in history, 1946-61, senior lecturer, 1961-67; University of Exeter, Exeter, England, professor of history, 1967-71, professor of modern history, 1971—. Visiting lecturer at Lafayette College, Easton, Pa., 1960-61. Military service: British Army, 1941-46; became captain. Member: Royal Historical Society (fellow), Ecclesiastical History Society, P.E.N., Society of Authors, Economic History Society, Historical Association, Glamorgan Local History Society (member of council, 1958-67). Awards, honors: Leverhulme research grant, 1955; Fulbright award, 1960.

WRITINGS: (Editor with D.H. Pennington) The Committee at Stafford, 1643-45, University of Manchester Press, 1957; (editor with S.B. Chrimes) English Constitutional History: A Select Bibliography, Routledge & Kegan Paul for the Historical Association, 1958; Commonwealth and Protectorate: The English Civil War and Its Aftermath, Schocken, 1966 (published in England as The Great Rebellion: 1642-1660, Batsford, 1966, 3rd edition, 1972); Conflicts in Tudor and Stuart England: A Selection of Arts from History Today, Oliver & Boyd, 1967; Late Troubles in England, University of Exeter, 1969; (editor) Cromwell: A Profile, Hill & Wang, 1973.

Contributor: G. Nann and A. Nitschke, editors, Propylaen-Weltgeschichte, Volume VII, Ullstein, 1964; E.W. Ives, editor, The English Revolution, 1600-1660, Edward Arnold, 1968, Barnes & Noble, 1969; R.H. Parry, editor, The English Civil War and After, 1642-1658, University of California Press, 1970; G.E. Aylmer, editor, The Interregnum: The Quest for Settlement, 1646-1660, Shoe String, 1972; (author of introduction) J.T. Ruh, editor, The Diary of Thomas Burton, four volumes, Johnson Reprint, 1973. Writer of scripts for British Broadcasting Corp. Third Program, and other radio and television broadcast services. Contributor of articles and reviews to Listener, Observer, Daily Telegraph, and to professional journals. Member of editorial board, The English Revolution, Cornmarket Press.

WORK IN PROGRESS: Editing English Historical Documents, 1603-1660; The Stuart Age, for Longmans, Green's "History of England"; studies of parliamentary history of the Protectorate.

BIOGRAPHICAL/CRITICAL SOURCES: New York Review of Books, January 4, 1968.

*   *   *

ROSELIEP, Raymond   1917-

PERSONAL: Surname is pronounced Rose-leap; born August 11, 1917, in Farley, Iowa; son of John Albert (a caterer) and Anna Elizabeth (Anderson) Roseliep. Education: Loras College, B.A., 1939; Catholic University of America, M.A., 1948; University of Notre Dame, Ph.D., 1954. Home and office: Holy Family Hall, 3340 Windsor Extension, Dubuque, Iowa 52001.

CAREER: Ordained Roman Catholic priest, 1943; assistant pastor of church in Gilbertville, Iowa, 1943-45; Witness, Dubuque, Iowa, managing editor, 1945-46; Loras College, Dubuque, Iowa, instructor, 1946-48, assistant professor, 1948-60, associate professor of English, 1960-66; Holy Family Hall, Dubuque, Iowa, resident chaplain, 1966—. Poet-in-residence, Georgetown University, summer, 1964. Poet, and reader of poetry at colleges and universities.

MEMBER: Poetry Society of America, Modern Language Association of America, National Council of Teachers of English, Catholic Press Association, Catholic Poetry Society of America, Modern Poetry Association, State Historical Society of Iowa, Notre Dame English Association, Delta Epsilon Sigma. Awards, honors:

Named to Gallery of Living Catholic Authors, 1957; Kenneth F. Montgomery Poetry Award, Society of Midland Authors, 1968; other poetry prizes from Carolina Quarterly, Writer's Digest, Leigh Hanes Memorial Poetry Contest, Modern Haiku, and Yankee.

WRITINGS: The Linen Bands (poetry), Newman, 1961; The Small Rain (poetry), Newman, 1963; Love Makes the Air Light (poetry), Norton, 1965. Poetry anthologized in many volumes, including Fire and Sleet and Candlelight: New Poems of the Macabre, edited by August Derleth, Arkham, 1961, Of Poetry and Power: Poems Occasioned by the Presidency and by the Death of John F. Kennedy, edited by Erwin A. Glikes and Paul Schwaber, Basic Books, 1964, Out of the War Shadow, edited by Denise Levertov, War Resisters League, 1967, and Inside Outer Space, edited by Robert Vas Dias, Doubleday, 1970. Contributor of poems to more than one hundred and fifty periodicals and newspapers, including Transatlantic Review, Tablet (London), Poetry, Dubliner, Midwest Quarterly, Critic, Nation, Commonweal, Minnesota Review, College English, New York Times, Sign, America, English Journal, University Bookman, Prairie Schooner, and Modern Age. Poetry editor, Sponsa Regis (publicaton of Benedictine Order), 1959-66.

WORK IN PROGRESS: Two books of poems, Tip the Earth and O Western Wind: A Book of Haiku.

SIDELIGHTS: Samuel French Morse comments: "Father Roseliep writes not in competition with his contemporaries nor with a compulsion for acceptance or success, but with a kind of eclectic freedom that sometimes produces remarkably attractive results. One does not think of such poems as 'important' or 'impressive'; but one likes some of them very much, and finds them durable."

Roseliep recorded his poems for modern poetry collections at Harvard University and Fenn College. Avocational interests: Reading—the moderns in poetry, criticism, mystical theology, art, fiction, drama, and the comic strips, "Peanuts" and "Pogo."

BIOGRAPHICAL/CRITICAL SOURCES: Sister Mary Therese, editor, I Sing of a Maiden, Macmillan, 1947; Mutiny, spring, 1961, fall-winter, 1961-62; Four Quarters, May, 1961; Critic, April-May, 1962; Today, October, 1963; Lamp, February, 1964; Contemporary Literature, winter, 1968.

*   *   *

ROSEN, Sidney   1916-

PERSONAL: Born June 5, 1916, in Boston, Mass.; son of Morris and Jennie (Kibrick) Rosen; married Dorothy S. Schack, March 8, 1944; children: David. Education: University of Massachusetts, A.B., 1939; Harvard University, M.A., 1952, Ph.D., 1955. Religion: Judaism. Home: 1417 Mayfair Rd., Champaign, Ill. 61820. Office: Division of General Studies, University of Illinois, Urbana, Ill. 61801.

CAREER: Brandeis University, Waltham, Mass., 1951-58, began as teaching fellow, became assistant professor of physics; University of Illinois, Urbana, 1958—, began as visiting associate professor of science education, now professor of physical science. Ford Foundation, consultant in science at University of Antioquia, Medellin, Colombia, 1963-64; consulting editor for Harcourt, Brace & World, Inc., Encyclopaedia Britannica Films, Inc., and for Science Research Associates. Military service: U.S. Army Air Forces, 1941-46; became sergeant. Member: American Association for the Advancement of Science (fellow), American Association of Physics Teachers, National Science Teachers Association, National Association for Research in Science Teaching, Association for the Education of Teachers of Science, Association for General and Liberal Studies, Authors Guild, Phi Delta Kappa. *Awards, honors:* Clara Ingram Judson Memorial Prize for children's literature by a midwest author, 1969, for *Wizard of the Dome.*

WRITINGS: *Galileo and the Magic Numbers,* Little, Brown, 1958; *Doctor Paracelsus,* Little, Brown, 1959; *The Harmonious World of Johann Kepler,* Little, Brown, 1962; (with Robert Siegfried and John M. Dennison) *Concepts in Physical Science,* Harper, 1965; *Wizard of the Dome: R. Buckminster Fuller, Designer for the Future,* Little, Brown, 1969. Contributor of articles to *World Book Encyclopedia* and to educational and scientific journals. Member of editorial board and book review editor of *Journal of Research in Science Teaching.*

WORK IN PROGRESS: A 2nd edition of *Concepts in Physical Science;* a children's book on scientific thinking; an experimental program in the training of elementary school science teachers.

SIDELIGHTS: Rosen writes: "I became interested in writing for young people through my wife's influence—she was a children's librarian at the time. Since the history of science was one of my doctoral fields of interest, I decided to write biographies of great scientists of the Renaissance. Here was an opportunity to convey to young people the excitement of scientific discovery, the sense of science as a human activity, and the flavor of a period when individuals began to question accepted authority in the quest for scientific truths. I suppose that I was trying to counter the tendency for history to be taught as a past, dead thing by making the Renaissance come alive for my readers.

"As a teacher, I am continually concerned with the need to keep reminding our young people that they are individuals, capable of independent thought and action, who must be prepared to deal with the constant changes that occur in a technological society."

BIOGRAPHICAL/CRITICAL SOURCES: *Saturday Review,* February 21, 1970.

*   *   *

ROSENFELD, Sam   1920-

PERSONAL: Born November 30, 1920, in New York, N.Y.; son of Benjamin and Helen (Fagelman) Rosenfeld; married Hilda Garfinkle (a school nurse-teacher), May 8, 1948; children: Bonnie, Caren, Daniel. *Education:* College of the City of New York (now City College of the City University of New York), B.S., 1941; New York University, M.A., 1953. *Politics:* Independent. *Religion:* Hebrew. *Home:* 1006 Dartmouth Lane, Woodmere, Long Island, N.Y. 11598. *Agent:* Evelyn L. Singer Agency, 41 West 96th St., New York, N.Y. 10025.

CAREER: U.S. Army Air Corps, Wright Field, Ohio, chemist until 1954; G.W. Hewlett High School, Hewlett, N.Y., science teacher, 1954—. *Military service:* U.S. Army Air Forces, 1944-46; became second lieutenant. *Member:* National Education Association, New York State Teachers Association.

WRITINGS: *Scientific Magic,* Lothrop, 1959; *Thirty Days to a Higher IQ for Your Child,* Crown, 1961; *The Magic of Electricity: 100 Experiments with Batteries,* Lothrop, 1963; *Science Experiments with Water,* Harvey House, 1965; *Ask Me A Question About the Earth,* Harvey House, 1966; *Ask Me a Question About the Heavens,* Harvey House, 1966; *Ask Me A Question About the Weather,* Harvey House, 1966; *The Story of Coins,* Harvey House, 1968; *Science Experiments with Air,* Harvey House, 1969; *Ask Me a Question About the Atom,* Harvey House, 1969; *A Drop of Water,* Harvey House, 1970; *Ask Me a Question About Rockets, Satellites, and Space Stations,* Harvey House, 1971; *Science Experiments for the Space Age,* Harvey House, 1972.

WORK IN PROGRESS: A science book for juveniles; a novel.

AVOCATIONAL INTERESTS: Gardening, oil painting.

BIOGRAPHICAL/CRITICAL SOURCES: *Horn Book,* April, 1971.

*   *   *

ROSENTHAL, Eric   1905-

PERSONAL: Born July 10, 1905, in Cape Town, South Africa; son of Richard (a mining agent) and Hedwig (De Beer) Rosenthal; married Jeannette Marguerite Bradley, December 18, 1934; children: Elizabeth (Mrs. Clive Rogers), Richard, Gerald, Alison. *Education:* St. John's College, Johannesburg, South Africa, graduate, 1921; University of the Witwatersrand, qualified as attorney, 1926. *Home:* White Horses, 48 Hillside Rd., Fish Hoek, South Africa. *Agent:* Curtis Brown Ltd., 13 King St., Covent Garden, London W.C.3, England. *Office:* P.O. Box 3800, Cape Town, South Africa.

CAREER: Practiced law in Johannesburg, South Africa, 1926-39; special war work, 1939-44; industrial and commercial historian, specializing in research work on southern Africa, particularly company and commodity histories for large corporations, Cape Town, South Africa, 1946—. Free-lance journalist for newspapers in South Africa, Great Britain, and United States, 1925—. Publicity manager of Empire Exhibition, Johannesburg, 1935-36, of South African Jewish War Appeal, 1944-45. Member of South African national and international radio quiz teams, 1947—. *Member:* South African Association for the Advancement of Science, South African P.E.N., Trident Building Society of Cape Town (local director), Owl Club (Cape Town; president, 1965—), Rotary Club of Cape of Good Hope.

WRITINGS: *From Drury Lane to Mecca, Being an Account of the Strange Life and Adventures of Hedley Churchward (Also Known as Mahmoud Mobarek Churchward), an English Convert to Islam,* Low, 1931; *Old-Time Survivals in South Africa,* Government Printer (Pretoria), 1936; *Stars and Stripes in Africa: Being a History of American Achievements in Africa,* G. Routledge & Sons, 1938, revised edition, Tri-Ocean, 1968.

The Fall of Italian East Africa, Hutchinson, 1941; *Fortress on Sand: An Account of the Siege of Tobruk,* Hutchinson, 1943; *General Dan Pienaar, His Life and His Battles,* Afrikaanse Pers, 1943, 2nd edition, Unie-Volkspers Beperk (Cape Town), 1943; *Japan's Bid for Africa: Including the Story of the Madagascar Campaign,* Central News Agency (Johannesburg), 1944; *General De Wet, a Biography,* Unie-Volkspers Beperk, 1946, 2nd edition, Simondium Publishers (Cape Town), 1968; *Gold Bricks and Mortar: 60 Years of Johannesburg History,* Printing House (Johannesburg), 1946; *South Africa's Own: Happy Hours for Boys and Girls,* verses by Juliet Koenig, Newman Art Publishing Co. (Johannesburg), 1946; *Eric Rosenthal's South African Quiz Book,* Howard Timmins, 1948, 2nd edition, 1955; (compiler with Allister Macmillan) *Homes of the Golden City,* Hortors (Cape Town), 1948; (compiler) *The South African Saturday Book: A Treasury of Writing and Pictures of South Africa, Old and New, Homely and Extraordinary,* Hutchinson, 1948; *African Switzerland: Basutoland of To-day,* Hutchinson, 1949; *They Walk by Night: True South African Ghost Stories and Tales of the Supernormal,* Howard Timmins, 1949, enlarged edition published as *They Walk in the Night: True South African Ghost Stories and Tales of the Supernormal,* 1965.

(Editor) *The City of Cape Town Official Guide*, R. Beerman Publishers (Cape Town), 1950; *Shovel and Sieve*, Howard Timmins, 1950; *South African Jews in World War II*, South African Jewish Board of Deputies, 1950; *Here Are Diamonds*, R. Hale, 1950; *The Hinges Creaked: True Stories of South African Treasure Lost and Found*, Howard Timmins, 1951; *Shelter from the Spray*, Allen & Unwin, 1952; *Other Men's Millions*, Howard Timmins, 1953; (author of introduction) Dorothea Bleek, compiler, *Cave Artists of South Africa*, A.A. Balkema (Cape Town), 1953; *Cutlass and Yardarm*, Howard Timmins, 1955; (compiler) *The Story of Poppe, Schunhoff and Guttery*, Galvin & Sales (Cape Town), 1956; (editor) *The Story of Table Mountain: The Table Mountain Aerial Cableway Official Souvenir Guide*, W.J. Flesch, 1956, 2nd edition, 1961; *Today's News Today: The Story of the Argus Company*, condensed by L.E. Neame, Argus Printing and Publishing Co. (Johannesburg), 1956; *The Changing Years: A History of the Cape Province Municipal Association*, Cape Province Municipal Association, 1957; *River of Diamonds*, Bailey Bros. & Swinfen, 1957; *The Way I Saw It*, Howard Timmins, 1957; *The Cape of Good Hope Triangular Stamp and Its Story*, A.A. Balkema, 1957; (with Albert Jackson) *Trader on the Veld*, A.A. Balkema, 1958; *One Hundred Years of Victoria West, 1859-1959*, [Victoria West], 1959; *Apology Refused*, Bailey Bros. & Swinfen, 1959.

The Taeuber & Corssen Story, privately printed, 1960; (editor, translator, and author of introduction) *The Matabeleland Travel Letters of Marie Lippert, 1891*, Friends of the South African Public Library, 1960; (author of text) Heinrich Egersdoerfer, *An Old-Time Sketch Book: 'N Outydse sketsboek* (in English and Afrikaans), Nasionale Boekhandel (Cape Town), 1960; (editor) *Warne-Juta Rand-Cent Ready Reckoner* (in English and Afrikaans), Warne, 1960; *Tankards and Tradition*, Howard Timmins, 1961; *The Story of the Cape Jewish Orphanage*, [Capetown], 1961; (editor) *Encyclopedia of Southern Africa*, Warne, 1960, 6th edition, 1973; *Alphabetic Index to the Biographical Notices in "South Africa," 1892-1928*, Johannesburg Public Library, 1963; *Schooners and Skyscrapers*, Howard Timmins, 1963; *Manne en maatskappye: Die Geskiedenis van die eerste afrikaanse sakemanne* (in Afrikaans), Human & Rousseau (Cape Town), 1963; *The William Atkinson Story*, Howard Timmins, 1963; *South African Surnames*, Howard Timmins, 1965; (compiler) *South African Dictionary of National Biography*, Warne (London), 1966; *300 Years of the Castle at Cape Town*, H.M. Joynt, 1966; *Vesting van die Suide: Bastion of the South* (in English and Afrikaans), H.M. Joynt, 1966; *On 'Change Through the Years: A History of Share Dealing in South Africa*, Flesch Financial Publications, 1968; *A History of Fish Hoek, Cape*, Fish Hoek Chamber of Commerce, 1968; *Cape Directory 1800*, Howard Timmins, 1969; (with Eliezer Blum) *Runner and Mailcoach: Postal History and Stamps of Southern Africa*, Purnell (Cape Town), 1969, Tri-Ocean, 1972.

Gold! Gold! Gold!: The Johannesburg Gold Rush, Macmillan, 1970; *South Africa's Oil Search Down the Years*, Howard Timmins, 1970.

Pamphlets: (Editor) *Eclipse Postal District Guide and Pocket Dictionary of Johannesburg*, Central News Agency, 1940; *Life in America*, African Bookman (Cape Town), 1945; *The Gateway to South Africa*, South African Railways, 1947; *South Africa in a Nutshell*, South African Information Department (London), 1948; *South African Diplomats Abroad*, South African Institute of International Affairs (Johannesburg), 1949; *Our Royal Visitors*, Stewart Printing Co. (Cape Town), 1949; *Bantu Journalism in South Africa*, Society of the Friends of Africa (Johannesburg), 1949; (editor) *South African Tables and General Information, Including Weights and Measures in Use in South Africa*, Central News Agency, 1949.

Tea in Our Land Through Three Centuries, Tea Bureau of South Africa (Johannesburg), 1950; *How to Look After Your Money*, Longmans, Green, 1950; *Royal Automobile Club of South Africa—Golden Jubilee*, Royal Automobile Club (Cape Town), 1952; *Three Hundred Years of Men's Clothing in South Africa*, Monatic Alba Co. (Wynberg), 1952; *History of the Rand Water Board*, privately printed, 1953; *Johannesburg's New Randles*, privately printed, 1953; *G.E.C. in South Africa*, privately printed, 1953; *History of Johannesburg Building Society*, privately printed, 1953; *Fifty Years of Furnishing: The Story of Bradlows*, Hortors, 1953; *History of John Marcus & Co.*, privately printed, 1954; *Sixty Years of Haddon & Sly*, privately printed, 1954; *History of Federal Insurance Corporation of South Africa*, privately printed, 1954; *Insurance City*, privately printed, 1955; *200 Years of Greatrex*, privately printed, 1955; *Golden Jubilee of the Carlton Hotel*, privately printed, 1956; *History of General Estate & Orphan Chambers*, privately printed, 1956; *History of Lamson Paragon Over Fifty Years*, privately printed, 1956; *History of Phoenix Assurance Co.*, privately printed, 1956; *One Hundred Years of Northern Assurance Co.*, privately printed, 1956; (compiler with Hal Nattrass) *1856-1956, a Century of Service: The Story of Henwoods, Their First Hundred Years*, Knox Printing Co. (Durban), 1956; *Fifty Years of Holmes Service*, privately printed, 1957; *History of the Western Province Agricultural Society*, Western Province Agricultural Society (Cape Town), 1958; *History of R. & H. Morris (Pty) Ltd.*, privately printed, 1958; (compiler with Ena Cloete) *Index to J.W. Matthews' "Incwadi Yami; or, Twenty Years Personal Experience in South Africa,"* Johannesburg Public Library, 1958; (compiler with Cloete) *Index to John Angove's "In the Early Days: The Reminiscences of Pioneer Life on the South Africa Diamond Field,"* Johannesburg Public Library, 1958; (with Cloete) *Index to Barbara Isabella Buchanan's "Natal Memories,"* Johannesburg Public Library, 1958; (compiler with Cloete) *Index to Barbara Buchanan's "Pioneer Days in Natal,"* Johannesburg Public Library, 1958; *History of Liverpool, London & Globe Insurance Company*, privately printed, 1959.

History of Industrial Development Corporation of South Africa, privately printed, 1960; (with J.P. Hutchings) *Shopfitters Cavalcade, Being Half-a-Century of the History of Fredk. Sage & Co. in Southern Africa*, Johannesburg, 1960; *160 Years of Cape Town Printing*, Cape Town Association of Printing House Craftsman, 1960; *History of Lever Brothers in South Africa*, privately printed, 1961; *History of Duly & Co.*, privately printed, 1961; *History of Union Steel Corporation (South Africa) Ltd.*, privately printed, 1961; *As Pioneers Still, 1911-1961: An Appreciation of Lever Brothers Contribution to South Africa*, Hayne & Gibson (Durban), 1961; *Natal Navigation & Estate Company—Golden Jubilee*, privately printed, 1962; *History of Mobil in South Africa*, privately printed, 1962; *History of Goodyear in South Africa*, privately printed, 1963; *British United—50 Years in South Africa*, privately printed, 1963; *History of Dunswart Iron & Steel Works*, privately printed, 1963; *Fifty Years of the Cape Town Orchestra, 1914-1964*, [Cape Town], c.1963; *History of Chemico (Pty) Ltd.*, privately printed, 1964; *From Barter to Barclays*, Barclays Bank, 1968.

125 Years of Music in South Africa—Darter's Jubilee, privately printed, 1970; *The Thesen Centenary*, privately printed, 1970; *Trends in South African Publishing*, English Studies in Africa (Johannesburg), 1970; *Portland Cement in South Africa*, Portland Cement Institute (Johannesburg), 1971.

Contributor to *Encyclopaedia Britannica.* Assistant editor, *South African Mining Journal,* 1936-37; editor, *Guinness Book of Records* (South African edition), 1967—.

WORK IN PROGRESS: Continuous research on histories of industries and commodities in southern Africa.

* * *

ROSS, Alan 1922-

PERSONAL: Born May 6, 1922, in Calcutta, India; married Jennifer Fry, 1949; children: Jonathan. *Education:* Educated at Haileybury College, and at St. John's College, Oxford. *Home:* Clayton Manor, near Hassocks, Sussex, England.

CAREER: With British Council, 1947-50; *Observer,* London, England, member of staff, 1950-71; *London Magazine,* London, England, editor, 1961—. Managing director, Alan Ross Ltd. (publishers). *Military service:* Royal Navy, Intelligence, 1942-46. *Member:* Garrick Club. *Awards, honors:* Atlantic Award for Literature, Rockefeller Foundation, 1947.

WRITINGS: Time Was Away, a Notebook in Corsica, Lehmann, 1948; *The Forties: A Period Piece,* Weidenfeld & Nicolson, 1950; *The Gulf of Pleasure,* Weidenfeld & Nicolson, 1951; *The Bandit on the Billiard Table: A Journey Through Sardinia,* Verschoyle, 1954, revised edition published as *South to Sardinia,* Hamish Hamilton, 1960; *Australia 55: A Journal of the M.C.C. Tour,* with photographs by Ross, M. Joseph, 1955; *Cape Summer, and the Australians in England,* Hamish Hamilton, 1957; *The Onion Man* (juvenile), Hamish Hamilton, 1959; *Through the Caribbean: The M.C.C. Tour of the West Indies 1959-1960,* Hamish Hamilton, 1960; *Danger on Glass Island* (juvenile), Hamish Hamilton, 1960; *The West Indies at Lord's,* Eyre & Spottiswoode, 1963; *Australia 63,* Eyre & Spottiswoode, 1963; *The Wreck of Moni* (juvenile), Alan Ross, 1965; *A Castle in Sicily* (juvenile), Alan Ross, 1966; (author of introduction) Hugo Williams, compiler, *London Magazine Poems, 1961-66,* Alan Ross, 1966.

Poetry: *The Derelict Day: Poems in Germany,* Lehmann, 1947; *Poetry, 1945-1950,* Longmans, Green, 1951; *Something of the Sea: Poems, 1942-1952,* Verschoyle, 1954, Houghton, 1955; *To Whom It May Concern: Poems 1952-57,* Hamish Hamilton, 1958; *African Negatives,* Eyre & Spottiswoode, 1962, Dufour, 1964; *North from Sicily: Poems in Italy, 1961-64,* Eyre & Spottiswoode, 1965; *Poems, 1942-67,* Eyre & Spottiswoode, 1967; *Tropical Ice,* Covent Garden Press, 1972.

Editor: (And author of introduction) John Gay, *Poems,* Grey Walls Press, 1950; (with wife, Jennifer Ross) F. Scott Fitzgerald, *Borrowed Time* (short stories), Grey Walls Press, 1951; (and author of foreword) *Abroad: Travel Stories,* Faber, 1957; *The Cricketer's Companion,* Eyre & Spottiswoode, 1960; *Stories from the London Magazine,* Volume I, Eyre & Spottiswoode, 1964, Volumes II-V published as *London Magazine Stories,* London Magazine Editions, 1967-70.

Translator: Philippe Diole, *The Undersea Adventure,* Messner, 1953; Pierre Gaisseau, *The Sacred Forest,* Weidenfeld & Nicolson, 1954; Philippe Diole, *Gates of the Sea,* Messner, 1955 (published in England as *The Seas of Sicily,* Sidgwick & Jackson, 1955).

Poetry anthologized in *Anthology of Contemporary Verse,* edited by Margaret June O'Donnell, Blackie & Son, 1953, *An Anthology of Modern Verse, 1940-1960,* edited by Elizabeth Jannings, Methuen, 1961, and *Poetry of the Forties,* edited by Robin Skelton, Penguin, 1968. Contributor to *New Statesman, Spectator, New Yorker,* and other periodicals.

WORK IN PROGRESS: A book of poems.

SIDELIGHTS: Reviewing *Poems 1942-67,* Martin Dodsworth writes that Ross "is largely a descriptive poet. His landscapes are not at all symbolic, but stand for themselves, for the real world we all inhabit. . . . His poetry springs from a need to lay claim to the world, as though he were in fact excluded from it. He hopes to possess the countries he has visited by describing them, and he hopes by possessing them to find a place there for himself. . . .But the poems work by letting you feel that it is impossible for them to contain all that there is to say, by suggesting a world that is at once substantial and elusive."

AVOCATIONAL INTERESTS: Cricket, travel, racing, and contemporary art.

BIOGRAPHICAL/CRITICAL SOURCES: New Statesman, December 1, 1967; *Punch,* February 7, 1968; *Times Literary Supplement,* January 18, 1968, January 23, 1969; *Listener,* February 1, 1968; *Observer,* February 11, 1968.

* * *

ROSS, Alan Strode Campbell 1907-

PERSONAL: Born February 1, 1907, at Brecon, Wales; son of Archibald Campbell Carne (a land agent) and Millicent Strode (Cobham) Ross; married Elizabeth Stefanyja Olszewska (a lexicographer), December 12, 1932; children: Alan Waclaw Padmint. *Education:* Attended Malvern College and Christ College; Balliol College, Oxford, M.A. (first class honors), 1929. *Office:* University of Birmingham, Birmingham, England.

CAREER: University of Leeds, Leeds, England, assistant lecturer, 1929-35, lecturer in English language, 1936-46; University of Birmingham, Birmingham, England, lecturer, 1946, reader, 1947, professor of English language, 1948-50, professor of linguistics, 1951—. Seconded to British Foreign Office, 1940-45. *Member:* English Place-Name Society, Philological Society, Viking Society for Northern Research, Suomalais-Ugrilainen Seura (foreign corresponding member), Worshipful Company of Grocers (liveryman), Brecknock Society, *Awards, honors:* M.A., University of Birmingham.

WRITINGS: (Editor with Bruce Dickins) *The Dream of the Rood,* Methuen, 1934, 4th edition revised, 1963, Appleton, 1966; *Studies in the Accidence of the Lindisfarne Gospels,* Titus Wilson, 1937; *The "Numeral-signs" of the Mohenjo-daro Script* (memoirs of the Archaeological Survey of India), Manager of Publications (Delhi), 1938; *The Terfinnas and Beormas of Ohthere,* Titus Wilson, 1940; *The Essentials of Anglo-Saxon Grammar,* Heffer, 1948; *Tables for Old English Sound-Changes,* Heffer, 1951; *Ginger, a Loan-Word Study,* Basil Blackwell, 1952, (contributor) Nancy Mitford, editor, *Noblesse Oblige: An Inquiry into the Identifiable Characteristics of the English Aristocracy,* Harper, 1956; (editor with others) *The Lindisfarne Gospels,* Urs Graf, 1957-60; *Etymology, with Special Reference to English,* Essential Books, 1958; *Aldrediana I: Three Suffixes,* Moderna Spraak, 1959.

The Essentials of German Grammar, Mason Publications, 1963; *The Essentials of Anglo-Saxon Grammar, with Tables for Sound-Changes* (contains *The Essentials of Anglo-Saxon Grammar* and *Tables for Old English Sound Changes*), Heffer, 1963; *The Essentials of English Grammar,* Mason Publications, 1964; (with A.W. Moverley) *The Pitcairnese Language,* Deutsch, 1964; (translator with N.F.C. Owen) I.I. Revzin, *Models of Language,* Methuen, 1966; (editor) *Arts v. Science: A Collection of Essays,* Methuen, 1967, Barnes & Noble, 1968; (editor) *What Are U?,* Deutsch, 1969; (editor with T.J. Brown, F. Wormald, and E.A. Stanley) *The Durham Ritual,* Rosenkilde & Bagger, 1969; *How to Pronounce It,* Hamish Hamilton, 1970. Contributor to more than fifty journals, magazines, and newspapers in England, Europe, and in United States, including *Economic History Review, Folk-*

lore, Geographical Journal, Mathematical Gazette, Speculum, Times Literary Supplement, Holiday, Times (London), *Observer, Guardian,* and *Washington Post.*

WORK IN PROGRESS: A volume of essays; editing and contributing to *The Indoeuropean Numerals;* co-editing the Anglo-Saxon gloss to *The Lindisfarne Gospels;* commentary on the Anglo-Saxon gloss to *The Durham Ritual.*

SIDELIGHTS: Ross participated in a Lapland expedition under the auspices of the Royal Geographical Society. He has some knowledge of German, Dutch, Swedish, Danish, Norwegian, French, Spanish, Welsh, Russian, Czech, Hungarian, Finnish, Estonian, Lappish, and Tahitian languages. *Avocational interests:* Croquet, land-rovering, philately, playing patience.

BIOGRAPHICAL/CRITICAL SOURCES: Uusi Suomi, May 4, 1937; *Diario de la Marina* (Cuba), April 17, 1955; *Sunday Times,* August 12, 1956; *Aftenposten,* August 9, 1957; *TV Times,* June 6, 1958; *Birmingham Post,* September 21, 1961; *Times Literary Supplement,* November 9, 1967; *Bookseller,* December 12, 1970.

*　　*　　*

ROSS, James Frederick Stanley 1886-

PERSONAL: Born January 2, 1886, in London, England; son of James William (a manufacturer's agent) and Ellen Ann (Edwards) Ross; married Emily Jones, December 24, 1913; children: Emily Vivian, Ann Auriol (Mrs. John Dennis Bonney). *Education:* University of London, B.Sc., 1913, B.Sc. Engineering (first class honors), 1926, Ph.D., 1931. *Home:* 3 Conyers Ave., Birkdale, Southport, Lancashire, England.

CAREER: Civil engineer, London, England, 1903-15; lecturer in engineering, Barrow and Loughborough, England, 1919-24; Stockport College for Further Education, Stockport, England, principal, 1924-28; Wigan and District Mining and Technical College, Wigan, England, principal, 1928-50; full-time writer and lecturer, 1950—. Liberal International, member of British group, chairman of Liberal Education Committee (London), 1956-59, president of Southport Liberal Association, 1959—; vice-president, Electoral Reform Society; member, Hansard Society for Parliamentary Government. Chairman, Union of Lancashire and Cheshire Institutes, 1946-47. *Military service:* Royal Engineers, 1915-19; served three years in France and Belgium; became captain; mentioned in dispatches, decorated Military Cross, Chevalier of the Order of the Crown (Belgium); later captain in Regular Army Reserve of Officers. *Member:* International P.E.N., Association of Principals of Technical Institutions (president, 1945-46; now honorary member), Society of Authors, International Political Science Association.

WRITINGS: An Introduction to the Principles of Mechanics, Harcourt, 1923; *The Gyroscopic Stabilization of Land Vehicles,* Edward Arnold, 1933; *Time Is Not Old, and Other Verses,* Basil Blackwell, 1941; *Parliamentary Representation,* Eyre & Spottiswoode, 1943, Yale University Press, 1944, 2nd edition, enlarged, Eyre & Spottiswoode, 1948; *The Achievement of Representative Democracy,* Bowes, 1952; *Election and Electors: Studies in Democratic Representation,* Essential Books, 1955; *The Irish Election System: What It Is and How It Works,* Pall Mall, 1959. Contributor to *Education in Lancashire, The British Party System, Chambers's Encyclopaedia,* and other books. Contributor of poetry to *Time and Tide* and *Fortnightly Review,* of articles to *Spectator, Pilot Papers, Contemporary Review, Guardian,* and political and educational journals.

WORK IN PROGRESS: A book, *The Irish Parliamentary System.*

AVOCATIONAL INTERESTS: Psephology, history, poetry, statistics, and walking.†

*　　*　　*

ROSS, Lillian 1927-

PERSONAL: Born June 8, 1927, in Syracuse, N.Y.; daughter of Louis and Edna (Rosenson) Ross; children: Erik Jeremy. *Office: c/o New Yorker* Magazine, 25 West 43rd St., New York, N.Y. 10036.

CAREER: New Yorker, New York, N.Y., 1948—, staff writer, 1949—; work for *New Yorker* includes fiction ("Profiles" and "Reporter at Large" pieces), and stories in "The Talk of the Town."

WRITINGS: Picture (account of the making of the film "The Red Badge of Courage," originally published in the *New Yorker;* also included in *Reporting* [see below]), Rinehart, 1952; *Portrait of Hemingway* (originally published as a "Profile" in *New Yorker,* May 13, 1950; also included in *Reporting* [see below]), Simon & Schuster, 1961; (with sister, Helen Ross) *The Player: A Profile of an Art* (interviews), Simon & Schuster, 1962; *Vertical and Horizontal* (short stories), Simon & Schuster, 1963; *Reporting* (articles originally published in *New Yorker,* including "The Yellow Bus," "Symbol of All We Possess," "The Big Stone," "Terrific," "El Unico matador," "Portrait of Hemingway," and "Picture"), Simon & Schuster, 1964; *Adlai Stevenson,* Lippincott, 1966; *Talk Stories* (sixty stories first published in "The Talk of the Town" section of *New Yorker,* 1958-1965), Simon & Schuster, 1966; *Reporting Two,* Simon & Schuster, 1969.

WORK IN PROGRESS: Screenplay of *Vertical and Horizontal,* for Paramount Pictures.

SIDELIGHTS: Some reviewers have referred approvingly to the dust jacket copy on *Reporting* for its description of her work. It reads, in part: "Over the years, the reporters of the *New Yorker* have, among them, produced a new literary tradition: reporting as an art. None of them has done more to develop that art than Miss Ross.... She creates the illusion that the reporter has vanished altogether and that life is transferring itself, with startling immediacy, to paper. In her "Profile" of Ernest Hemingway, she employs very much the same method to form an entire portrait in terms of narrative—a minute-by-minute account of what Hemingway did, and how he looked and talked (with friends and family), in a few hours of his life . . ."

In other of her stories in *Reporting,* "Miss Ross again writes narratives, but here a new element is present—dramatic development. . . . The result, in effect, is fact in the form of fiction—'factual short stories.' In *Picture,* her famous account of the making of the film 'The Red Badge of Courage,' still another element is added—the dramatic interplay of a large group of characters—to produce the first reportorial piece ever to be written in the form of a novel."

Concerning the Hemingway profile which appeared in the *New Yorker* in 1950, Miss Ross told *CA* that it is not true—some published reports to the contrary—that the piece drew a large volume of unfavorable mail and other comment. "The overwhelming reaction when it was first published was one of great enthusiasm and appreciation. Some people did not like it and said so; hence the 'controversy.' " (It remained a controversial piece into the sixties, with attacks by such critics as Irving Howe, although Hemingway himself read the article before it was published, made a few corrections, and supported Miss Ross when criticism of it appeared.)

"The Profile was written out of affection and admiration and knowledge," Miss Ross has commented, "and was intended to describe as precisely as possible how Hemingway looked and sounded when he was in action, talking, between books—to give a picture of the man as he was, in his uniqueness, and with his vitality and his enormous spirit of fun intact, rather than of the man as somebody sitting in judgment on him, however well-meaning, might wish him to be."

J. F. Fixx of *Saturday Review* has called Miss Ross's *Reporting* "a vivid and valuable example of the journalist's art and deserves to be recommended to any reporter interested in a postgraduate course in his craft." Robert Manning said of the book: "Depending on the way the reader feels about her subject matter, Lillian Ross. . .is a contemporary journalistic equivalent of Goya the court painter, a tape recorder with a pulsebeat or an only slightly benign reincarnation of Jack the Ripper.... With an Ampex ear, a scalpel for her palette knife and a cool, clear head for structure and style, [she] stands back from the situations she has chosen to chronicle or the subjects (one is strongly tempted to call them victims) who have somehow been beguiled into sitting for her."

Marya Mannes calls Miss Ross an excellent reporter who "knows how to record the revealing phrase, the defining gesture. [In *Talk Stories*] she allows these to make their own comment, withholding hers. Because of this, and because of their vitality and humor, the stories have stood as miniature documentaries of cosmopolitan life peculiar to the *New Yorker's* best tradition." According to Irving Wallace, "she is the mistress of selective listening and viewing, of capturing the one moment that entirely illumines the scene, of fastening on the one quote that Tells All. She is a brilliant interpreter of what she hears and observes. And she is the possessor of a unique writing style—spare, direct, objective, fast—a style that disarms, seemingly only full of wonder, but one that can suddenly, almost sneakily, nail a personality naked to a page."

Miss Ross is not related, incidentally, to Harold W. Ross, founder of the *New Yorker*.

BIOGRAPHICAL/CRITICAL SOURCES: New Republic, August 7, 1961; *Saturday Review*, May 25, 1963, March 14, 1964; *New York Times Book Review*, June 2, 1963, May 15, 1966; *Book Week*, March 15, 1964, May 1, 1966; *Time*, May 9, 1964.

* * *

ROSSET, B(enjamin) C(harles) 1910- (Ozy)

PERSONAL: Born June 7, 1910, in Russia. *Home:* Robin Hill, Loch Gowna, County Cavan, Ireland.

CAREER: Rosset simply says, "Shady"; U.S. Merchant Marine, 1933-41; writer in Ireland, 1959—. *Military service:* U.S. Army, 1943-44. *Member:* Shaw Society of America.

WRITINGS: (Under pseudonym Ozy) *The War Against Bernard Shaw*, White Plume Publishing Co., 1957; *Shaw of Dublin: The Formative Years*, Pennsylvania State University Press, 1964.

* * *

ROSSOFF, Martin 1910-

PERSONAL: Born August 12, 1910; son of Max (a businessman) and Jennie (Steinhart) Rossoff; married Annie Rosenblum (a high school library teacher), December 23, 1939; children: Margaret, Simon. *Education:* New York University, A.B., 1932; Columbia University, A.M., 1933, B.S. in L.S., 1938. *Home:* 1561 East Ninth St., Brooklyn, N.Y. 10030.

CAREER: New York City (N.Y.) secondary schools, teacher of Latin and French, 1934-41; Lafayette High School, Brooklyn, N.Y., library assistant, 1941-47; James Madison High School, Brooklyn, N.Y., teacher of library and head librarian, 1947—. Lecturer in library education, Queens College (now Queen's College of the City University of New York), 1956. *Military service:* U.S. Army 1943-45. *Member:* United Federation of Teachers, American Recorder Society, New York Library Association, New York City School Librarians Association (treasurer, 1953-55), Phi Beta Kappa.

WRITINGS: Using Your High School Library, Wilson, 1952, 2nd edition, revised, 1964; *The Library in High School Teaching*, Wilson, 1955, revised edition, 1961; *The School Library and Educational Change*, Libraries Unlimited, 1971.

* * *

ROTH, Cecil 1899-1970

PERSONAL: Born March 5, 1899, in London, England; son of Joseph (a merchant) and Etty (Jacobs) Roth; married Irene Rosalind Davis, 1928. *Education:* Oxford University, B.A., 1923, M.A., B.Litt., and D.Phil., all 1924. *Home:* 21, Rehov Balfour, Jerusalem, Israel. *Office:* Oriental Institute, Oxford, England.

CAREER: Research in Florence, Italy, 1922-24; freelance writer, journalist, and lecturer (mainly on U.S. tours), 1924-38; Oxford University, Oxford, England, first reader in Jewish studies, 1939-64, reader emeritus, 1964-70. Visiting professor, Columbia University, 1958. *Military service:* British Army, Infantry, 1917-19. *Member:* Royal Historical Society (fellow), Royal Society of Literature (fellow), Academia Colombaria (Florence; corresponding member), Deputazione di storia patria (Venice; corresponding member), Jewish Historical Society of England (president, 1936-45, 1956-57?), American Jewish Historical Society (corresponding member), Arts Club (London).

WRITINGS: (Author of introduction and notes) Mordecai Dato, *Un Hymne sabbatique de XVIe siecle en judeo-italien*, Societe des Etudes Juives, 1925; *The Last Florentine Republic*, Methuen, 1925, Russell & Russell, 1968; *Iscariot* (novel), Mandrake Press, 1929; (translator and author of introduction and notes) *The Casale Pilgrim: A Sixteenth-Century Illustrated Guide to the Holy Places*, Soncino Press, 1929.

Venice, Jewish Publication Society of America, 1930; (editor, translator, and author of introduction and notes) *The Haggadah: A New Critical Edition*, Soncino Press, 1930; *Archives of the United Synagogue: Report and Catalogue*, United Synagogue (London), 1930; *Roberto Ridolfi e la ana congiura*, [Florence], 1930; (author of additional chapters) Katie Magnus, *Outlines of Jewish History*, Myers & Co., 1931; *A Jewish Book of Days*, Bloch Publishing, 1931, revised edition published as *The Jewish Book of Days: A Day-by-Day Almanac of Events from the Settlement of the Jews in Europe to the Balfour Declaration*, Hermon Press, 1966; (reviser) Israel Abrahams, *Jewish Life in the Middle Ages*, new edition, Edward Goldston, 1932; (editor with Roberto Ridolfi) Donato Giannotti, *Lettere a Piero Vettori*, Vallecchi, 1932; *Records of the Western Synagogue, 1761-1932*, Edward Goldston, 1932; *The First Jew in Hampstead*, Jewish Museum, 1932; *A History of the Marranos*, Jewish Publication Society, 1932, 3rd edition, Harper, 1966; *The Nephew of the Almighty: An Experimental Account of the Life and Aftermath of Richard Brothers*, Edward Goldston, 1933; *The Jewish Museum*, Jewish Museum (London), 1933; (editor) Lucien Wolf, *Essays in Jewish History*, Jewish Historical Society of England, 1934; *A Life of Menasseh ben Israel, Rabbi, Printer, and Diplomat*, Jewish Publication Society, 1934; *Mediaeval Lincoln*

Jewry and Its Synagogue, Jewish Historical Society of England, 1934; (editor and author of introduction) Pope Clement XIV, *The Ritual Murder Libel and the Jew,* Woburn Press, 1935; (editor) Sir Richard Worsley, *La Caduta della Serenissima nei dispacci del residente inglese a Venezia,* [Venice], 1935; *A Bird's Eye View of Jewish History,* Union of American Hebrew Congregations, 1935, revised edition published as *A Short History of the Jewish People,* Jewish Publication Society, 1953, 2nd revised edition published as *A History of the Jews,* Schocken, 1961, 3rd revised edition published as *A Short History of the Jewish People,* Hartmore, 1969, 4th revised edition published as *A History of the Jews: From Earliest Times Through the Six Day War,* Schocken, 1970 (published in England as *A Short History of the Jewish People, 1600 B.C.-A.D. 1935,* Macmillan, 1936, 3rd revised edition, East & West Library, 1969); (contributor of essay) Isaak da Costa, *Noble Families Among the Sephardic Jews,* Oxford University Press, 1936; *The Challenge to Jewish History: Some Jewish Contributions to English Life* (address), Jewish Historical Society of England, 1936; (editor with S. Levy) *Jewish Year Book, 1933-40,* Jewish Chronicle, 1937-40; *The Spanish Inquisition,* R. Hale, 1937, Norton, 1964; *The Hebrew Press in London,* privately printed, 1937; *The Evolution of Anglo-Jewish Literature,* Edward Goldston, 1937; *Roberto Dudley duca de Northumberland Fiorentino,* [Florence], 1937; (reviser) Joseph Hacobs and Lucien Wolf, editors, *Magno bibliotheca anglo-judaica: A Bibliographical Guide to Anglo-Jewish History,* Jewish Historical Society of England, 1937; (editor) *Anglo-Jewish Letters 1158-1917,* Soncino Press, 1938; *The Jew as European* (address), Jewish Historical Society of England, 1938; *The Jewish Contribution to Civilization,* Macmillan (London), 1938, Harper, 1940, 3rd edition, East & West Library, 1956; *The Magnificent Rothschilds,* R. Hale, 1939, Pyramid Books, 1962.

(Editor and translator) Arthur Szyk, *The Haggadah,* Beaconsfield Press, 1940, Bloch Publishing, c.1951; *A History of the Jews in England,* Oxford University Press, 1941, 3rd edition, 1964; *The Sassoon Dynasty,* R. Hale, 1941; (editor with L. Epstein and E. Levine) *Essays in Honour of the Very Rev. Dr. J.H. Hertz* (in English and Hebrew), Edward Goldston, 1942; *Ancient Aliyot,* Scopus Publishing Co., 1942; *The Jews in the Defense of Britain, Thirteenth to Nineteenth Centuries* (address), Jewish Historical Society of England, 1943; *The History of the Jews of Italy,* Jewish Publication Society, 1946; *The House of Nasi: Dona Gracia,* Jewish Publication Society, 1948; *The House of Nasi: The Duke of Naxos,* Jewish Publication Society, 1948; (editor) *Jewish Religion,* Hutchinson University Library, 1948; *The Intellectual Activities of Medieval English Jewry,* Oxford University Press, 1949; *England in Jewish History* (lecture), Jewish Historical Society of England, 1949.

The Record of European Jewry, Muller, 1950; *The Rise of Provincial Jewry: The Early History of the Jewish Communities in the English Countryside, 1740-1840,* Jewish Monthly, 1950; *The Great Synagogue, London 1690-1940,* Edward Goldston, 1950; *The Jews of Medieval Oxford,* Clarendon Press, 1951; *Benjamin Disraeli, Earl of Beaconsfield,* Philosophical Library, 1952; *Personalities and Events in Jewish History,* Jewish Publication Society, 1954; *Two Cradles of Jewish Liberty: The New World and the Mother Country,* Anglo-Jewish Association, 1954; (editor with Z. Efron) *Ha-Omanut hayehudit,* Massadah Publishing Co., 1956-57, translation published as *Jewish Art: An Illustrated History,* McGraw, 1961, revised edition, Graphic, 1971; *The Kennicott Bible,* Bodleian Library, 1957; *The Historical Background of the Dead Sea Scrolls,* Basil Blackwell, 1958, Philosophical Library, 1959, reissued as *The Dead Sea Scrolls: A New Historical Approach,* Norton, 1965: *The Aberdeen Codex of the Hebrew Bible,* Oliver & Boyd, 1958; (editor) *The Standard Jewish Encyclopedia,* Massadah Publishing Co., 1958, Doubleday, 1959, 4th edition, revised, published as *The New Standard Jewish Encyclopedia,* Doubleday, 1970; *The Jews in the Renaissance,* Jewish Publication Society of America, 1959.

The Marrano Typography in England, Bibliographical Society (London), 1960; *On the Study of American Jewish History,* American Jewish Archives, 1963; (author of text and introduction) *The Sarajevo Haggadah,* Harcourt, 1963; *Essays and Portraits in Anglo-Jewish History,* Jewish Publication Society, 1963; (translator and author of introduction and historical notes) *Haggadah for Passover,* illustrations by Ben Shahn, Little, Brown, 1965; *Der Anteil der Juden an der politischen Geschichte des Abendlandes* (originally written in English, but published in German), translation by Karl Grosshans, Niedersaechsiche Landeszentrale fuer Politische Bildung (Hanover), 1965; (editor) *The Dark Ages: Jews in Christian Europe, 711-1096,* Rutgers University Press, 1966; (with Max Wurmbrand) *The Jewish People: 4000 Years of Survival,* Thames & Hudson, 1966, Shengold, 1967; *Jewish Historical Society of England: Remember the Days,* Jewish Historical Society of England, 1966; *Gleanings: Essays in Jewish History, Letters, and Art,* Hermon Press, 1967. Contributor to many newspapers and periodicals in journalistic days, and of several hundred articles to scholarly periodicals and encyclopedias since. Editor-in-Chief, *Encyclopedia Judaica.*

SIDELIGHTS: David Daiches writes: "[After the publication of *The Last Florentine Republic* in 1925, Roth] began to bring together his historical research and his Jewish interests and knowledge to produce a series of works which give him a unique place in Jewish historiography. He has always been a practicing Orthodox Jew, and he has had the advantages of Jewish and Hebrew learning that a living Orthodox tradition on good terms with a healthy secular culture can provide. Indeed, I am tempted to believe that Cecil Roth is a product of a phase of Anglo-Jewish history now fast declining, a phase in which it was possible to combine Orthodoxy, secular scholarship, and Jewish learning known from within and regarded as a natural part of one's personal heritage. It is this inwardness with, for example, the history of Jewish liturgy or the structure of Jewish community life in different ages that enables him to read a medieval or Renaissance Hebrew manuscript with an easiness about its terms of reference, an almost effortless familiarity with the hinterland of language and custom and cultural behavior that lies behind the words of a given document. That he has the languages—Hebrew, Italian, Spanish, Portuguese, German—goes without saying. More significant is the fact that he has a kind of commitment to the material with which he is dealing that gives a certain tone, a certain authority, an air of what might be called domestication in the material, which exists side-by-side with the historian's objectivity in the establishment of facts and even a dryness in the handling of subjects calculated to make Jewish blood pressure rise. . . . Superstition, confusion, ignorance, plain silliness, on the part of Jewish religious leaders in the past are recorded with quiet exactness; but underneath there is the implication that the writer can do this because he knows what the true Jewish tradition is, is confident of its survival, and himself adheres to it." *Avocational interests:* Collecting (Roth was a recognized expert in Jewish art).

BIOGRAPHICAL/CRITICAL SOURCES: *Times Literary Supplement,* October 5, 1967; *Commentary,* June, 1968; *Washington Post,* June 22, 1970.

(Died June 21, 1970)

ROTH, June (Spiewak) 1926-

PERSONAL: Born February 16, 1926, in Haverstraw, N.Y.; daughter of Harry I, and Ida (Glazer) Spiewak; married Frederick Roth (a sales executive), July 7, 1945; children: Nancy (Mrs. Thomas Bjorkman), Robert. Education: Pennsylvania State University, student, 1942-44; Tobe-Coburn School for ashion Careers, graduate, 1945. Religion: Jewish. Home and office: 1057 Oakland Ct., Teaneck, N.J. 07666. Agent: Toni Mendez, 140 East 56th St., New York, N.Y. 10022.

CAREER: Merchandising jobs in New York, N.Y., 1944-45; Fred Roth Associates, New York, N.Y., public relations, 1959-62. Has made numerous television appearances. Member: International Platform Association, Authors League of America, National Council of Jewish Women (branch chairman, Teaneck, 1955; branch vice-president, 1956). Awards, honors: Julia Coburn special award, 1970.

WRITINGS: The Freeze and Please Home Freezer Cookbook, Fell, 1963; The Rich and Delicious Low Calorie Figure Slimming Cookbook, Fell, 1964; June Roth's Thousand Calorie Cookbook, Arco, 1968; How to Use Sugar and Lose Weight, Universal Information, Inc., 1969; Fast and Fancy Cookbook, Fawcett, 1969; How to Cook Like a Jewish Mother, Essandess, 1969; Take Good Care of My Son, Cookbook for Brides, Essandess, 1969; The Indoor/Outdoor Barbecue Book, Simon & Schuster, 1970; Pick of the Pantry Cookbook, Simon & Schuster, 1970; June Roth's Let's Have a Brunch Cookbook, Essandess, 1971; The Good and Easy House-keeping Book, Essandess, 1971; The On-Your-Own Cookbook, Dial, 1971; Healthier Jewish Cookery the Unsaturated Fat Way, Arco, 1972; Elegant Desserts, Dodd, 1973; The All in the Family Cookbook, Popular Library, in press; The Working Mother's Cookbook, Western Publishing, in press.

WORK IN PROGRESS: Old Fashioned Candy Making Cookbook, completion expected in 1974; Elegant Appetizers, 1975.

AVOCATIONAL INTERESTS: Bridge, collecting antiques, and gardening.

*   *   *

ROTH, Sister Mary Augustine 1926-

PERSONAL: Born January 16, 1926, in Minneapolis, Minn.; daughter of John Albert and Anne (Boies) Roth. Education: University of Minnesota, B.A., 1947, M.A., 1948; Catholic University of America, Ph.D., 1961. Politics: Republican. Home: 1330 Elmhurst Dr., N.E., Cedar Rapids, Iowa 52402. Office: Mount Mercy College, Cedar Rapids, Iowa 52402.

CAREER: Roman Catholic nun; entered Congregation of the Sisters of Mercy, 1949; Mount Mercy College, Cedar Rapids, Iowa, instructor in English, 1948-56; Sacred Heart High School, Oelwein, Iowa, English teacher, 1956-57; Mount Mercy College, Cedar Rapids, Iowa, academic dean, 1961-63, chairman of English department, 1961—. Member: Modern Language Association of America.

WRITINGS: (Editor and author of critical commentary) Coventry Patmore, Essay on English Metrical Law: A Critical Edition with a Commentary, Catholic University of America Press, 1961.

*   *   *

ROTHA, Paul 1907-

PERSONAL: Born June 3, 1907, in London, England. Education: Attended Highgate School; Slade School of Art, student, 1923-25. Home: Lantern Cottage, Oxshott, Surrey, England. Agent: John Farquharson Ltd., 15 Red Lion Sq., London W.C.1, England; Eric L'Epine Smith, 7 Vigo St., London W.1, England.

CAREER: Began as painter, designer, book illustrator, 1925; Connoisseur, London, England, art critic, 1927-28; entered film industry as property man for British International Pictures Ltd., 1928; became film producer, writer, and director, specializing in documentaries, 1932—; managing director of Paul Rotha Productions Ltd., 1941—. Produced first films for Empire Marketing Board, later formed Strand Films for documentaries; made one hundred documentaries for British Ministry of Information in World War II, seventy-five on British life and international subjects for British Broadcasting Corp. as head of documentary film department, 1953-55. Isotype Institute, member of board, 1959—. Film adviser to British delegation at UNESCO Conference, Paris, France, 1946. Rockefeller Foundation fellow in United States, 1937-38, lecturer on documentary films, 1953-54; lecturer in Australia under UNESCO auspices, 1958. British Film Academy, chairman, 1952.

MEMBER: Federation of Documentary Film Units (chairman, 1945-48), British Film Insitute, Association of Cine-Technicians. Awards, honors: International Theatre Design Award at Paris Exhibition, 1925; Gold Medals at Venice Film Festival, 1934, Brussels Film Festival, 1935; British Film Academy awards for "The World Is Rich," 1947, and "World Without End," 1953; other film awards at Cork and Leipzig.

WRITINGS: (Illustrator) Arthur F. Wallis, Tales of the Norsemen, J. Cape, 1928; (illustrator) Frank Herbert Doughty, A Book of Seamen, J. Cape, 1929; The Film Till Now, J. Cape, 1930, 3rd edition (with Richard Griffith), Twayne, 1960, new edition, Spring Books, 1967; Celluloid: The Film Today, Longmans, Green, 1931; Documentary Film, Faber, 1936, Norton, 1939, 3rd edition (with Sinclair Road and Richard Griffith), Faber, 1952; Movie Parade, Studio Publications, 1936, 2nd edition (with Rober Manvell) published as Movie Parade, 1889-1949: A Pictorial Survey of World Cinema, 1950; (with Eric Mowbray Knight) World of Plenty: The Book of the Film, Nicholson & Watson, 1945; (photographic editor) Michael Young and Theodor Prager, There's Work For All, Nicholson & Watson, 1945; (with Ivor Montagu and others) Eisenstein, 1898-1948, [London], 1948; (editor) Portrait of a Flying Yorkshireman: Letters from Eric Knight to Paul Rotha, Chapman & Hall, 1952; (editor) Television in the Making, Hastings House, 1956; Rotha on the Film, Essential Books, 1958; (researcher with Basil Wright) Arthur Calder-Marshall, The Innocent Eye (biography of Robert J. Flaherty), W.H. Allen, 1963, Harcourt, 1966.

Documentary films—Writer and director: "Contact," 1932; "Shipyard," 1934; "Face of Britain," 135; "New Worlds for Old," 1939; "The Fourth Estate," 1940; "World of Plenty," 1943; "Land of Promise," 1945; "A City Speaks," 1946; "The World is Rich," 1947; "World without End," 1953; "Cradle of Genius," 1958; "The Life of Adolf Hitler," 1960-62. Also writer of film scripts "Children of the City," "Today We Live," Future's in the Air," and "Nightshift."

Feature films—Writer and director: "No Resting Place," 1950; "Cat and Mouse," 1958; "The Silent Raid," 1962. Also author of "The Phantom Fiend."

Founded Documentary News Letter, 1939. Contributor of articles to New Statesman, Spectator, Reader's Digest, Times (London), New York Times, and other publications.

WORK IN PROGRESS: Film script of Abe Brower's Dutch novel, The Golden Whip; autobiography, for

Faber; editor-in-chief, *World Encyclopedia of Film,* for Focal Press.

SIDELIGHTS: *The Film Till Now* is considered one of the definitive works on the cinema as an art form. *Avocational interests:* Gardening.

* * *

ROTHENBERG, Lillian 1922-

PERSONAL: Born April 19, 1922, in New York, N.Y.; daughter of Ezakiel Jack and Anna (Rappaport) Rothenberg. *Education:* Hunter College (now Hunter College of the City University of New York), B.A., 1943, professional certificate in guidance practice and administration, 1953; Columbia University, M.A., 1945. *Religion:* Jewish. *Home:* 31-74 29th St., Long Island City, New York, N.Y. 11106.

CAREER: Long Lane School, Middletown, Conn., teacher, 1943-44; New York City Board of Education, New York, N.Y., elementary school teacher, 1945-50, resource consultant on five-school study, 1951-53, guidance-reading counselor on guidance-reading project, 1955-57, licensed guidance counselor in elementary school early identification and prevention program, 1959-63, guidance counselor in More Effective School Program, 1963—. *Member:* American Personnel and Guidance Association, American Orthopsychiatric Association, New York City Association of Educational and Vocational Guidance Counselors.

WRITINGS: (With Ruth Liebers) *Stevie Finds a Way,* Abingdon, 1958; (with Liebers) *Hector Goes to School,* Abingdon, 1963. Contributor of children's stories to *Humpty Dumpty* and to Bobbs-Merrill and Scott, Foresman supplementary readers. Contributor to *Exceptional Children* and *School Counselor.*

SIDELIGHTS: Miss Rothenberg has traveled extensively, including study tours of Europe, 1950, the Far East, 1959, the world and the Soviet Union, 1963. *Avocational interests:* Sculpture and etching.

* * *

ROTHSCHILD, Joseph 1931-

PERSONAL: Born April 5, 1931, in Fulda, Germany; son of Meinhold and Henrietta (Loewenstein) Rothschild; married Ruth Nachmansohn (an art historian), July 19, 1959; children: Nina, Gerson. *Education:* Columbia University, A.B. (highest honors), 1951, A.M. 1952; Oxford University, D.Phil, 1955. *Religion:* Jewish. *Home:* 445 Riverside Dr., New York, N.Y. 10027. *Office:* Department of Government, Columbia University, New York, N.Y. 10027.

CAREER: Columbia University, New York, N.Y., instructor, 1955-58, assistant professor, 1958-62, associate professor, 1962-68, professor of government, 1968—. *Member:* American Political Science Association, American Association for the Advancement of Slavic Studies, American Civil Liberties Union, Phi Beta Kappa. *Awards, honors:* American Council of Learned Societies, fellow, 1963-64; Guggenheim fellow, 1967-68.

WRITINGS: The Communist Party of Bulgaria: Origins and Development, 1883-1936, Columbia University Press, 1959; (editor) *Introduction to Contemporary Civilization in the West,* 3rd edition, Columbia University Press, 1960; (editor) *Chapters in Western Civilization,* two volumes, 3rd edition, Columbia University Press, 1961; *Communist Eastern Europe,* Walker, 1964; *Pilsudski's Coup d'Etat,* Columbia University Press, 1966. Contributor to *Grolier Encyclopedia, Jefferson Encyclopedia,* and to professional journals.

WORK IN PROGRESS: East central European history.

ROUCEK, Joseph S(labney) 1902-

PERSONAL: Born 1902, in Prague, Czechoslovakia; son of Joseph (a merchant) and Pavla (Nebeska) Roucek; married Bozena Slabey, January 10, 1928. *Education:* Attended Prague Commercial Academy and University of Prague; Occidental College, B.A., 1925; New York University, Ph.D., 1928, M.A., 1937. *Politics:* Republican. *Religion:* Roman Catholic. *Home:* 395 Lakeside Dr., Bridgeport, Conn. 06606.

CAREER: Came to United States on a scholarship, 1921, and supported himself while studying as a concert pianist, lecturer, vaudeville entertainer and actor in silent films; began teaching career at Centenary Junior College (now Centenary College for Women), Hackettstown, N.J., 1929-33; member of faculty of Pennsylvania State College (now Pennsylvania State University), 1933-35, New York University, New York, N.Y., 1935-39, Hofstra College (now Hofstra University), Hempstead, N.Y., 1939-48; University of Bridgeport, Bridgeport, Conn., 1948-67, became professor and chairman of departments of political science and sociology; Queensborough Community College, Bayside, N.Y., professor of social science, 1967-72. Visiting professor of sociology, political science, or education at other colleges and universities in United States, Canada, and Puerto Rico, 1940-54; lecturer at European universities, 1955, 1958. Author and editor.

MEMBER: American Sociological Association, American Political Science Association, American Association of University Professors, Delta Tau Kappa (president). *Awards, honors:* Knight, Order of the Star (Rumania); Knight Commander, Order of the Crown (Yugoslavia).

WRITINGS: The Minority Principle as a Problem of Political Science, Orbis (Prague), 1928; *The Working of the Minorities System under the League of Nations,* Orbis, 1929; *Contemporary Roumania and Her Problems: A Study in Modern Nationalism,* Stanford University Press, 1932, reprinted, Arno, 1971; *The Poles in the United States of America,* Baltic Institute (Gdynia), 1937; *The Politics of the Balkans,* McGraw, 1939, revised edition published as *Balkan Politics: International Relations in No Man's Land,* Stanford University Press, 1948, reprinted, Greenwood Press, 1971; *American Lithuanians,* Lithuanian Alliance of America, 1940; *Foreign Politics and Our Minority Groups,* privately printed, 1941; *Methods of Meeting Domination: The Czecho-Slovaks,* privately printed, 1941; (with Yaroslav J. Chyz) *Ukranian Sociology: Its Development to 1914,* privately printed, 1941; *World War II: A Survey of Recent Literature,* privately printed, 1941; *Axis Psychological Strategy against the United States,* privately printed, 1942; *American Japanese: Pearl Harbor and World War II,* privately printed, 1943; *Die Tschechen und Slowaken in der Vereinigten Staaten,* Publikatiensstelle (Stuttgart), 1943, published in America as *The Czechs and Slovaks in America,* Lerner, 1967; *Aspirations for a Greater Democracy,* privately printed, 1943; *Free Movements of Horthy's Eckhardt and Austria's Otto,* privately printed, 1943; (with Patricia S. Pinkham) *American Slavs: A Bibliography,* New York City Bureau for Intercultural Education, 1944; *Group Tensions in the Modern World,* privately printed, 1945; *Recent Literature on Central-eastern Europe,* privately printed, 1945; *Geopolitics of the Balkans,* privately printed, 1946; *War as a Symptom of Social Crisis,* privately printed, 1946; *American Bulgarians,* privately printed, 1947; *Sociological Foundations of Education,* privately printed, c.1950; *Regionalism and Separation,* edited by Feliks Gross, privately printed, c.1950; (with Roland L. Warren) *Sociology: An Introduction,* Littlefield, 1951, 2nd edition, 1965; *Development of Educational Sociology: History and Trends in America and Abroad,* privately printed, 1956; *School, Society and Sociology: A Survey of the Social and Sociological Aspects of Education The-*

ories and Experiments, [Bridgeport], 1956; *Political Sociology and Public Administration in the U.S.A.*, c.1957; *American Ethnic and Religious Minorities in American Politics* (originally published in *Il Politico*, University of Pavia, 1959), A. Giuffre (Milan), 1959; *The Status and Role of American and Continental Professors: A Comparison of Two Educational Traditions* (originally published in *Journal of Higher Education*, May, 1959), n.p., 1959; *Some Sociological Aspects of Diplomacy*, [Bridgeport], 1960; *The Vote of the American Minorities in President Kennedy's 1960 Election*, privately printed, 1961; (with Kenneth V. Lottich and Theodore H.E. Chen) *Behind the Iron Curtain: The Soviet Satellite States—East European Nationalism and Education*, Caxton, 1964.

Editor: (With Francis J. Brown) *Our Racial and National Minorities: Their History, Contributions, and Present Problems*, Prentice-Hall, 1937, revised edition published as *One America: The History, Contributions, and Present Problems of Our Racial and National Minorities*, 1945, 3rd edition, 1952; (with Brown and Charles Hodges) *Contemporary World Politics: An Introduction to the Problems of International Relations*, Wiley, 1939, revised edition, 1940; *Contemporary Europe: A Study of National, International, Economic, and Cultural Trends*, Van Nostrand, 1941, 2nd edition, 1947; (with Roy V. Peel) *Introduction to Politics*, Crowell, 1941; (and contributor) *Sociological Foundations of Education: A Textbook in Educational Sociology*, Crowell, 1942; *A Challenge to Peacemakers*, American Academy of Political and Social Science, 1944; (with Alice Hero and Jean Downey) *The Immigrant in Fiction and Biography*, Bureau for Intercultural Education, 1945; (and contributor) *Central-eastern Europe: Crucible of World Wars*, Prentice-Hall, 1946; (with others) *Governments and Politics Abroad*, Funk, 1947, 2nd edition, 1948; (and contributor) *Social Control*, Van Nostrand, 1947, 2nd edition, 1956; *Slavonic Encyclopaedia*, Philosophical Library, 1949; *Moscow's European Satellites*, American Academy of Political and Social Science (Philadelphia), 1950; (with George B. Huszar and contributor) *Introduction to Political Science*, Crowell, 1950; (with Arthur Henry Moehlman) *Comparative Education*, Dryden Press, 1951; *Soviet and Russian Educational Imperialism*, [Wilberforce], 1955-56; *Contemporary Sociology*, Philosophical Library, 1958, abridged edition published as *Readings in American Sociology*, Littlefield, 1961; *Juvenile Delinquency*, Philosophical Library, 1958; (with Howard Boone Jacobson) *Automation and Society*, Philosophical Library, 1959; *The Challenge of Science Education*, Philosophical Library, 1959, reprinted, Books for Libraries, 1971; *Contemporary Political Ideologies*, Philosophical Library, 1961; (contributing editor) Howard Boone Jacobson, editor, *A Mass Communications Dictionary: A Reference Work of Common Terminologies for Press, Print, Broadcast, Film, Advertising, and Communications Research*, Philosophical Library, 1961; *Sociology of Crime*, Philosophical Library, 1961; *The Unusual Child*, Philosophical Library, 1962; *Classics in Political Science*, Philosophical Library, 1963; *The Difficult Child*, Philosophical Library, 1964; *Programmed Teaching: A Symposium on Automation Education*, Philosophical Library, 1965, revised edition, 1968; *The Teaching of History*, Philosophical Library, 1967; *The Study of Foreign Language*, Philosophical Library, 1968; *The Slow Learner*, Philosophical Library, 1969; (with Thomas P. Kiernan) *The Negro Impact on Western Civilization*, Philosophical Library, 1970.

Contributor: Harry Elmer Barnes, Howard Becker, and Frances Bennett Becker, editors, *Contemporary Social Theory*, Appleton, 1940; Robert H. Kerner, editor, *Czechoslovakia: Twenty Years of Independence*, University of California Press, 1940, reissued as *Czecho-slovakia*, 1948; Thorsten Kalijarvi and others, *Modern World Politics*, Crowell, 1942, 3rd edition, 1954; George T. Renner, editor, *Global Geography*, Crowell, 1944; Georges Gurvitch and Wilbert E. Moore, editors, *Twentieth Century Sociology*, Philosophical Library, 1945; Feliks Gross, editor, *European Ideologies: A Survey of Twentieth Century Political Ideas*, Philosophical Library, 1948; *World Political Geography*, Crowell, 1948, 2nd edition, 1954; Robert J. Kerner, editor, *Yugoslavia*, University of California Press (Berkeley), 1949; James H.S. Bossard and others, editors, *Introduction to Sociology*, Stackpole, 1952; (and editor) *Contemporary Social Science*, two volumes, Stackpole, 1953; Matthew A. Fitzsimons, Alfred G. Pundt, and Charles E. Nowell, editors, *The Development of Historiography*, Stackpole, 1954; *Social Problems*, Crowell, 1955; Howard R. Anderson and others, editors, *Making of Modern America*, Houghton, 1956, 3rd edition, 1968; Richard Edmund Gross and L.D. Zeleny, editors, *Educating Citizens for Democracy: Curriculum and Instruction in Secondary Social Studies*, Oxford University Press, 1958; Carlton E. Beck, editor, *Perspectives on World Education*, W.C. Brown, 1960; Richard E. Gross, editor, *The Heritage of American Education*, Allyn & Bacon, 1962; Jorge Xifra Heras, editor, *La Prensa*, Internacional de Prensa (Barcelona), 1963; Miloslav Rechcigl, Jr., editor, *The Czechoslovakian Contribution to World Culture*, Mouton & Co. (The Hague), 1964; Jorge Xifra Heras, editor, *Prensa convivencia internacional*, Institute de Ciencias Sociales, Deputacion Provincial de Barcelona, 1964; Irving Louis Horwitz, editor, *Historia y elementas de la sociologia del conocimiento*, Volume II, Editorial Universitaria del Buenos Aires, 1964; Michael O'Leary, Jr., editor, *Readings in Cultural Anthropology*, Selected Academic Readings, Inc., 1965; George Z.F. Bereday and Joseph A. Lauwerys, editors, *The World Book of Education, 1965-1966*, Harcourt, 1965-66; *Anuario de la academia de doctores del distrito universitario de Barcelona*, [Barcelona], 1966; Jonathon C. McLendon, editor, *Social Foundations of Education: Current Readings from the Behavioral Sciences*, Macmillan, 1966; Harold Full, editor, *Controversy in American Education: An Anthology of Crucial Issues*, Macmillan, 1967; Kewal Metwani, editor, *A Critique of Empiricism in Sociology*, Allied Publishers Private Limited (Bombay), 1967; Miloslav Rechcigl, Jr., editor, *Czechoslovakia: Past and Present*, Mouton & Co., 1968; John Kesa, editor, *The Home of the Learned Man: A Symposium on the Immigrant Scholar in America*, College & University Press (New Haven), 1968; Renatus Hartogs and Eric Artzt, editors, *Violence: Causes and Solutions*, Dell, 1970.

Contributor to *Encyclopedia Americana*, *Collier's Encyclopedia*, *People's Encyclopedia*, *Encyclopaedia International*, and to *The Annals of the American Academy of Political and Social Science*. Author of articles and book reviews appearing in more than fifty journals and newspapers.

Member of editorial board of *American Journal of Economics and Sociology* and *United Asia*; American editor of *Indian Sociological Bulletin*, *Indian Journal of Social Research*, and *Journal of Education*, all published in India, and *Il Politico*, published in Italy.

WORK IN PROGRESS: Recent Trends in American Education.

BIOGRAPHICAL/CRITICAL SOURCES: Foreign Affairs, October, 1932; *Books*, October 2, 1932; *Times Literary Supplement*, September 1, 1932, October 23, 1959; *Annals of the American Academy of Political and Social Science*, March, 1933, September, 1939, September, 1946, September, 1948, March, 1950; *American Historical Review*, April, 1933, October, 1946, January, 1949, January, 1950; *American Political Science Review*, April, 1933,

December, 1939, October, 1946, December, 1946, October, 1947, September, 1961; *Christian Science Monitor,* July 15, 1939; *Saturday Review of Literature,* July 15, 1939; *Commonweal,* November 3, 1939, December 20, 1946, August 12, 1949; *Book Week,* May 26, 1942, June 2, 1946; *American Sociological Review,* December, 1942, April, 1948, December, 1961, February, 1962; *Social Forces,* December, 1942, December, 1959, October, 1962, *New Yorker,* May 18, 1946; *Current History,* September, 1946; *Political Science Quarterly,* September, 1946, December, 1948; *Social Education,* October, 1946; *Social Studies,* January, 1948, November, 1959; *Library Journal,* July, 1949, September 1, 1958, November 15, 1958, February 1, 1966, July, 1967, January 15, 1970; *Christian Century,* August 24, 1949, December 10, 1958, June 28, 1961, October 4, 1961; *New Statesman,* October 1, 1949; *Spectator,* April 24, 1959, *Choice,* July, 1966, January, 1968, May, 1970.

*   *   *

ROUNER, Arthur A(cy), Jr. 1929-

PERSONAL: Born May 21, 1929, in Boston Mass.; son of Arthur Acy (a minister) and Elizabeth (Stephens) Rouner; married Mary Sunderland Safford, 1950; children: John Newell, Kristen Safford, Thomasin Sunderland, Mary Elizabeth, Arthur Andrew. *Education:* Attended Choate School; Harvard University, A.B., 1951; New College, University of Edinburgh, graduate study, 1952-53; Union Theological Seminary, New York, N.Y., B.D., 1954. *Politics:* Democrat. *Home:* 4526 Drexel Ave., Edina, Minneapolis, Minn. 55424. *Office:* Colonial Church of Edina, 5532 Wooddale Ave., Minneapolis, Minn. 55424.

CAREER: Minister of Congregational churches in Williamsburg, Mass., 1954-59, Newton, Mass., 1959-62; Colonial Church of Edina, Minneapolis, Minn., minister, 1962—. Lecturer at Andover-Newton Theological School, 1961-62; exchange preacher in Scotland and England, 1962. Member of board of directors, Project Concern. *Member:* Monday Club (Boston), Cambridge Boat Club, Minneapolis Rowing Club, Rotary International.

WRITINGS: When a Man Prays, Revell, 1953; *The Congregational Way of Life,* Prentice-Hall, 1960; *Master of Men,* Denison, 1966; *Salvation for the Nation* (sermon), Colonial Church of Edina, 1967; *The Free Church Today: New Life for the Whole Church,* Association Press, 1968; *Someone's Praying Lord,* Prentice-Hall, 1970; *Satan in Suburbia,* Prentice-Hall, 1971. Contributor to *Christian Herald, Christianity Today, United Church Herald, Union Seminary Quarterly Review,* and other religious periodicals.

*   *   *

ROUSE, (Benjamin) Irving, (Jr.) 1913-

PERSONAL: Born August 29, 1913, in Rochester, N.Y.; son of Benjamin Irving (a nurseryman) and Louise (Bohachek) Rouse; married Mary Uta Mikami (a teacher), June 24, 1939; children: Peter, David. *Education:* Yale University, B.S. 1934, Ph.D., 1938. *Home:* 12 Ridgewood Ter., North Haven, Conn. 06473. *Office:* Department of Anthropology, Yale University, 51 Hillhouse Ave., New Haven, Conn. 06520.

CAREER: Yale University, New Haven, Conn., instructor, 1939-43, assistant professor, 1943-48, associate professor, 1948-54, professor of anthropology, 1954-70, Charles J. MacCurdy Professor of Anthropology, 1970—, director of graduate studies in anthropology, 1953-57, 1969-72, chairman of the department of anthropology, 1957-63, director of undergraduate studies in archaeology, 1967-70, chairman of archaeology program, 1970—. Peabody Museum of Natural History, assistant curator,

1938-47, associate curator of anthropology, 1947-54, research associate in anthropology, 1954-62. Consultant and assistant editor for Caribbean archaeology, Hispanic Foundation, Library of Congress, 1951-63. Archaeological field research in Haiti, Puerto Rico, Cuba, Florida, Trinidad, Venezuela, Martinique, Massachusetts, St. Lucia, New York, Antigua, Guadeloupe, Bahamas, and Dominican Republic. *Military service:* U.S. Naval Reserves, 1934-40.

MEMBER: National Academy of Sciences, American Anthropological Association (member of executive board, 1950-53, president, 1967-68), Society for American Archaeology (editor, 1946-50; president, 1952-53), American Association for the Advancement of Science, American Academy of Arts and Sciences, American Ethnological Society (vice-president, 1957-58), Association for Field Archaeology (member of executive committee, 1971—), Council for Old World Archaeology (trustee, 1955-62; assistant editor for West Africa, 1955-61), National Science Foundation, Royal Anthropological Institute, National Research Council, Eastern States Archaeological Federation (director of publications, 1938-40; director of research, 1940-46; president, 1946-50), Archaeological Society of Connecticut (secretary-treasurer, 1934-38; secretary, 1952-56), Florida Anthropological Society (member of executive board, 1958-60), Sigma Xi. *Awards, honors:* Carnegie Foundation grant, 1939; Medella Commemorativa del Vuelo Panamericano pro Faro a Colon, Cuban Government, 1945; A. Cressy Morrison Prize in Natural Science, New York Academy of Science, 1948, for *Porto Rican Prehistory;* Social Science Research Council grant, 1958; Viking Fund medal and award in anthropology, 1960; National Science Foundation grant, 1962-63; Guggenheim fellow, 1963-64.

WRITINGS: Prehistory in Haiti: A Study in Method, Yale University Press, 1939; *Culture of the Ft. Liberte Region, Haiti,* Yale University Press, 1941; *Archaeology of the Maniabon Hills, Cuba,* Yale University Press, 1942; (editor with Raymond Kennedy) *Bibliography of Indonesian Peoples and Cultures,* Yale University Press, 1946; (editor with John M. Goggin) *An Anthropological Survey of the Eastern Seaboard,* Eastern States Archaeological Federation, 1947.

(Editor) Wendell Clark Bennett, *Gallinazo Group, Viru Valley, Peru,* Yale University Press, 1950; *A Survey of Indian River Archaeology, Florida,* Yale University Press, 1951; *Porto Rican Prehistory: Excavations in the Interior, South and East, Chronological Implications,* New York Academy of Sciences, 1952; *Porto Rican Prehistory: Introduction—Excavations in the West and North,* New York Academy of Science, 1952; (editor) John M. Goggin, *Space and Perspective in Northern St. Johns Archaeology, Florida,* Yale University Press, 1952; (editor) Wendell Clark Bennett, *Excavations at Wari, Ayachucho, Peru,* Yale University Press, 1953; (editor with Loren C. Eiseley, Sol Tax, and Carl F. Voegelin) *An Appraisal of Anthropology Today,* University of Chicago Press, 1953; *Guianas: Indigenous Period,* Instituto Panamericano de Geografia e Historia, 1953; (editor) J.A. Bullbrook, *On the Excavation of a Shell Mound at Palo Seco, Trinidad, B.W.I.,* Yale University Press, 1954; (with J.M. Cruxent) *An Archaeological Chronology of Venezuela,* two volumes, Pan American Union, 1958, 1959.

(With Douglas S. Byers) *A Re-examination of the Guida Farm,* Archaeological Society of Connecticut, 1960; (with Cruxent) *Venezuelan Archaeology,* Yale University Press, 1963; (editor with Charles H. Fairbanks and William C. Sturtevant) *Indian and Spanish: Selected Writings by John M. Goggin,* University of Miami Press, 1964; (author of foreword) Rev. D. Jesse, *The Amerindians in St. Lucia,* new and enlarged edition, St. Lucia Archaeological and Historical Society, 1968; (editor) John M. Goggin,

Spanish Majolica in the New World: Types of the Sixteenth to the Eighteenth Century, Yale University Publications in Anthropology, 1968; *Introduction to Prehistory: A Systematic Approach,* McGraw, 1972.

Contributor: John W. Griffin, editor, *The Florida Indian and His Neighbors,* A.J. Hanna, 1949; Robert Wauchope, editor, *Seminars in Archaeology: 1955,* Society for American Archaeology, 1956; G.R. Willey, editor, *Prehistoric Settlement Patterns in the New World,* American Anthropological Association, 1956; Charles H. Fairbanks, editor, *Florida Anthropology,* Florida Anthropological Society Publications, 1958; Raymond H. Thompson, editor, *Migrations in New World Culture History,* University of Arizona, 1958; Sidney W. Mintz, compiler, *Papers in Caribbean Anthropology,* Department of Anthropology, Yale University, 1960; *Essays in Pre-Columbian Art and Archaeology,* Harvard University Press, 1961; Robert John Braidwood and G.R. Willey, editors, *Courses Towards Urban Life: Archaeological Considerations of Some Cultural Alternatives,* Aldine, 1962; A.V. Kidder, *An Introduction to the Study of Southwestern Archaeology,* revised edition, Yale University Press, 1962; Sol Tax, editor, *Anthropology Today: Selections,* University of Chicago Press, 1962; Ward H. Goodenough, editor, *Explorations in Cultural Anthropology: Essays in Honor of George Peter Murdock,* McGraw, 1964; Jesse D. Jennings and Edward Norbeck, editors, *Prehistoric Man in the New World,* University of Chicago Press, 1964; Frederick R. Matson, editor, *Ceramics and Man,* Aldine, 1965; Joseph R. Caldwell, editor, *New Roads to Yesterday,* Basic Books, 1966; Gordon F. Ekholm and Gordon R. Willey, editors, *Handbook of Middle American Indians,* University of Texas Press, 1967; Carroll L. Riley and Walter W. Taylor, editors, *American Historical Anthropology: Essays in Honor of Leslie Spier,* Southern Illinois University Press, 1967; Kwang-chih Chang, editor, *Prehistory, Typology, and the Study of Society,* National Press, 1968; Brian Regan, editor, *Introductory Readings in Archaeology,* Little, Brown, 1970. Contributor to *Encyclopaedia Britannica, American Anthropologist, American Antiquity, Southwestern Journal of Anthropology, New Century Cyclopedia of Names, Encyclopedia Americana, Handbook of Latin American Studies,* and other publications. Editor, *Bulletin* of the Archaeological Society of Connecticut, 1938-50, *Bulletin* of the Eastern States Archaeological Federation, 1938-40, *American Antiquity,* 1946-50, "Yale University Publications in Anthropology," 1950-63, *Radiocarbon,* 1962—; assistant editor, *Handbook of Latin American Studies,* 1951-63; regional editor, *COWA: Survey and Bibliography,* 1955-61; associate editor, *American Anthropologist,* 1960-62.

WORK IN PROGRESS: African and Western Prehistory and *World Prehistory,* both for McGraw; a monograph on the prehistory of the island of Trinidad, West Indies; several additional research projects in the West Indies.

*   *   *

ROWAN, Richard Lamar   1931-

PERSONAL: Born July 10, 1931, in Guntersville, Ala.; son of Leon Virgle and Willie Mae (Williamson) Rowan; married Marilyn Walker, August 3, 1963; children: John Richard, Jennifer Walker. *Education:* Birmingham-Southern College, A.B., 1953; Auburn University, graduate study, 1956-57; University of North Carolina, Ph.D., 1961. *Politics:* Democrat. *Religion:* Episcopalian. *Home:* 113 Blackthorn Rd., Wallingford, Pa. 19086. *Office:* Wharton School of Finance and Commerce, University of Pennsylvania, Philadelphia, Pa. 19104.

CAREER: University of North Carolina, Chapel Hill, instructor in economics, 1957, 1959; University pf Pennsyl-

vania, Wharton School of Finance and Commerce, Philadelphia, lecturer, 1961-62, assistant professor, 1962-66, associate professor of industry, 1966—. *Military service:* U.S. Army, instructor at Transportation School, 1953-56. *Member:* American Economic Association, Industrial Relations Research Association (secretary, Philadelphia chapter, 1963-64), Southern Economic Association.

WRITINGS: (With Lowell De Witt Ashby) *The Island Economy: A Numerical Illustration of the National Income and Product Accounts of the United States Department of Commerce,* School of Business Administration, University of North Carolina, 1959; (editor with G.F. Bloom and H.R. Northrup) *Readings in Labor Economics,* Irwin, 1963, revised edition, 1972; (contributor) *Hours of Work,* Harper, 1965; (editor with Northrup) *The Negro and Employment Opportunity: Problems and Practices,* Bureau of Industrial Relations, Graduate School of Business Administration, University of Michigan, 1965; (contributor) Arthur Max Ross and Herbert Hill, editors, *Employment, Race and Poverty,* Harcourt, 1967; (editor with Northrup) *Readings in Labor Economics and Labor Relations,* Irwin, 1968; *The Negro in the Steel Industry,* Industrial Research Unit, Wharton School of Finance and Commerce, University of Pennsylvania, 1968; *The Negro in the Textile Industry,* Industrial Research Unit, Wharton School of Finance and Commerce, University of Pennsylvania, 1970; (editor with Northrup) *The Negro in Basic Industry,* Industrial Research Unit, Wharton School of Finance and Commerce, University of Pennsylvania, 1970; (editor with Northrup) *The Negro in Southern Industry,* Industrial Research Unit, Wharton School of Finance and Commerce, University of Pennsylvania, 1971. Contributor to *Labor Law Journal, Journal of Business,* and *Industrial and Labor Relations Review.*

*   *   *

ROWAT, Donald C(ameron)   1921-

PERSONAL: Born 1921, in Somerset, Manitoba, Canada; married Frances Louise Coleman, 1948; children: two. *Education:* University of Toronto, B.A., 1943; Columbia University, M.A., 1946, Ph.D., 1950. *Office:* Carleton University, Ottawa, Ontario, Canada.

CAREER: Canadian Department of Finance, Ottawa, Ontario, research assistant, 1943-44; Canadian Department of National Health and Welfare, Ottawa, Ontario, administrative officer, 1944-45; North Texas State College (now North Texas State University), Denton, lecturer in political science, 1947; Dalhousie University, Halifax, Nova Scotia, director of research, Institute of Public Affairs, and lecturer in political science, 1947-49; University of British Columbia, Vancouver, lecturer in political science, 1949-50; Carleton University, Ottawa, Ontario, assistant professor, 1950-53, associate professor of political science, 1953-58; United Nations, Technical Assistance Administration, expert in public administration in Ethiopia, 1956-57; Carleton University, Ottawa, Ontario, acting director of School of Public Administration, 1957-58, professor of political science, 1958—, department chairman, 1962-65, supervisor of gradaute studies in political science, 1965-66. Member, Commission on Relations Between Universities and Governments, 1968-69. *Member:* Canadian Association of University Teachers (member of executive committee, 1965-67). *Awards, honors:* Canada Council senior research fellowships, 1960-61, 1967-68.

WRITINGS; The Reorganization of Provincial-Municipal Relations in Nova Scotia, Department of Municipal Affairs (Halifax), 1949; *The Public Service of Canada,* Queen's Printer, 1953; *Your Local Government: A Sketch of the Municipal System in Canada,* Macmillan, 1955; *Comparison of Governing Bodies of Canadian Uni-*

versities, School of Public Administration, Carleton College, 1955; *Ottawa's Future Development and Needs*, City Corporation (Ottawa), 1956; *Administrative Directory of the Imperial Ethiopian Government*, Imperial Ethiopian Institute of Public Administration, 1957; *Cases on Administration*, School of Public Administration, Carleton University, 1959, 2nd edition, 1960; (editor) *Basic Issues in Public Administration*, Macmillan, 1961; (editor) *The Ombudsman, Citizen's Defender*, Allen & Unwin, 1965, 2nd edition, 1968; *The Proposal of a Federation Territory for Canada's Capital*, Advisory Committee on Confederation, 1967; (contributor) Stanley V. Anderson, editor, *Ombudsmen for American Government?*, Prentice-Hall, 1968; (contributor) N.H. Lithwick and Gilles Paquet, editors, *Urban Studies: A Canadian Perspective*, Methuen (Toronto), 1968; (contributor) L. Sabourin, editor, *Le Systeme politique du Canada*, Editions de l'Universite d' Ottawa, 1968; *The Canadian Municipal System: Essays on the Improvement of Local Government*, McClelland & Stewart, 1969; (with Rene Hurtubise) *The University, Society and Government*, University of Ottawa Press, 1970; (editor with Hurtubise) *Studies on the University, Society and Government*, two volumes, Commission on the Relations Between Universities and Governments, 1970.

*   *   *

ROWEN, Herbert H(arvey)   1916-

PERSONAL: Born October 22, 1916, in Brooklyn, N.Y.; son of Joseph M. (a teacher) and Sarah (Gordon) Rowen; married Mildred Ringel, June 28, 1940; children: Douglas, Amy, Marthe. *Education:* City College of New York (now City College of the City University of New York), B.S.S., 1936; Columbia University, M.A., 1948, Ph.D., 1951. *Home:* 3 Lemore Cir., Rocky Hill, N.J. 08553. *Office:* Department of History, Rutgers University, New Brunswick, N.J. 08903.

CAREER: Converters Paper Co.. Newark, N.J., assistant to manager, 1938-42; Random House, Inc., New York, N.Y., editorial assistant, *American College Dictionary*, 1946; Brandeis University, Waltham, Mass., instructor in history, 1950-53; State University of Iowa, Iowa City, Iowa, assistant professor, 1953-57; Elmira College, Elmira, N.Y., associate professor, 1957-60; University of Wisconsin, Milwaukee, professor, 1960-64; Rutgers University, New Brunswick, N.J., professor of history, 1964—. Visiting associate professor, University of California, Berkeley, 1959-60. Consulting editor, Free Press. *Military service:* U.S. Army, Signal Corps, 1942-45. *Member:* International Commission for History of Representative and Parliamentary Institutions, American Historical Association, Societe d'Histoire Moderne, Society for French Historical Studies, Nederlands Historisch Genootschap, Phi Beta Kappa. *Awards, honors:* Folger Shakespeare Library grant-in-aid, 1956; Newberry Library fellowship, 1957; Guggenheim fellowship, 1961-62.

WRITINGS: (Translator) Hans Kohn. editor, *German History: Some New German Views*, Beacon Press, 1954; (editor) Simon Nicolas Arnauld de Pomponne, *Pomponne's "Relation de mon ambassade en Hollande" 1669-1671*, Kemink & Zoon, 1955; *The Ambassador Prepares for War: The Dutch Embassy of Arnauld de Pomponne, 1669-1671*, Batsford, 1957; *A History of Early Modern Europe, 1500-1815*, Holt, 1960; (editor) *From Absolutism to Revolution, 1648-1848*, Macmillan, 1963, 2nd edition, 1968; (translator) Jacques Leon Godechat, *France and the Atlantic Revolution of the Eighteenth Century, 1770-1799*, Free Press, 1965; (with Bryce Lyon and Theodore S. Hamerow) *A History of the Western World*, Rand McNally, 1969; (editor) *The Low Countries in Early Modern Times*, Harner, 1972; (translator) Johan Huizinga, *Essays on America*, Harper, 1972. Contributor of

articles and reviews to historical journals. General editor, "Free Press Sources of Western Civilization," 1964-65.

WORK IN PROGRESS: Biography of Johan de Witt, Dutch statesman, 1625-72, publication expected in 1974; a study of Amsterdam in the seventeenth century; a study of the institution of dynastic monarchy in early modern Europe.

SIDELIGHTS: Rowen is fluent in French and Dutch, and reads German, Italian, and Russian. He has traveled in Europe and resided in The Netherlands, 1961-62.

*   *   *

ROWEN, Hobart   1918-

PERSONAL: Born July 31, 1918, in Burlington, Vt.; son of Moses G. and Sarah (Rosenberg) Rowen; married Alice B. Stadler, August 5, 1941; children: Judith Diane, James Everett, Daniel Jared. *Education:* City University of New York, B.S., 1938. *Home:* 5701 Warwick Pl., Somerset, Chevy Chase, Md. 20015. *Agent:* Donald Mac-Campbell, Inc., 12 East 41st St., New York, N.Y. 10017. *Office:* Newsweek, Inc., 1750 Pennsylvania Ave. N.W., Washington, D.C. 20006.

CAREER: Journal of Commerce, reporter and correspondent in New York, N.Y., and Washington, D.C., 1938-42; War Production Board, Washington, D.C., information staff member, 1942-44; *Newsweek*, member of Washington Bureau, 1944—, editor of "Business Trends," 1954—. Business-financial editor, *Town Councilman*, Somerset, Md., 1948—; member of board of directors, National Council on the Aging, 1964. *Member:* National Press Club (Washington, D.C.), Sigma Delta Chi (vice-president, Washington professional chapter, 1959; president, 1960). *Awards, honors:* Sigma Delta Chi National Magazine Reporting Award, 1961, for *Harper's* article, "America's Most Powerful Club"; Loeb Magazine Award for *Newsweek* article, "Spotlight on Gold," 1961.

WRITINGS: The Free Enterprisers: Kennedy, Johnson and the Business Establishment, Putnam, 1964. Contributor to *Harper's, New Republic, Saturday Evening Post*, and other magazines; syndicated columnist for North American Newspaper Alliance, 1960-63.

WORK IN PROGRESS: A book dealing with the national political scene, for Putnam.

*   *   *

ROY, Ewell Paul   1929-
(Victor Bonnette, Ernest Lemoine)

PERSONAL: Born March 25, 1929, in Hessmer, La.; son of Paul Ferrier and Conelia (Bonnette) Roy; married Ina Guillory, February 17, 1947; children: Dean Paul. *Education:* Louisiana State University and Agricultural and Mechanical College, B.S., 1949, graduate study, 1949-55, received M.S. and Ph.D.; University of Minnesota, postgraduate study, 1953. *Religion:* Roman Catholic. *Home:* 1435 West Chimes St., Baton Rouge, La. 70802. *Office:* Department of Agricultural Economics, 239 Agricultural Administration Bldg., Louisiana State University, University Station, Baton Rouge, La. 70803.

CAREER: Louisiana State University, Baton Rouge, research and teaching, 1950-55; U.S. Department of Agriculture, Baton Rouge, La., research economist, 1956; Louisiana State University, Baton Rouge, 1957—, now professor of agricultural economics. President, Campus Federal Credit Union, 1955-62; secretary, Louisiana Council of Farmer Co-ops, 1960—. Chairman, Greater Baton Rouge Diabetic Association, 1964—. *Member:* American Farm Economic Association, American Institute of Cooperation (chairman of research and extension program committee, 1964-65; member of board of trustees, 1969—), Louisiana Poultry and Egg Workers Association (president, 1960-62).

WRITINGS: Contract Farming, U.S.A., Interstate, 1963: *Cooperatives: Today and Tomorrow,* Interstate, 1964, 2nd edition, 1969; *Exploring Agribusiness,* Interstate, 1967; *Collective Bargaining in Agriculture,* Interstate, 1970; *Economics: Applications to Agriculture and Agribusiness,* Interstate, 1971. Contributor of more than three hundred articles to some fifty trade journals; author or co-author of forty-three Louisiana Agricultural Experiment Station Bulletins, other circulars, and reports.

WORK IN PROGRESS: Research on contract farming, farmers' cooperatives, collective bargaining, and agribusiness management and operations.

* * *

RUBINSTEIN, Alvin Zachary 1927-

PERSONAL: Born April 23, 1927, in New York, N.Y.; son of Max (a storekeeper) and Sylvia (Stone) Rubinstein; married Frankie Kimmelman (a teacher), November 12, 1960. *Education:* College of City of New York (now City College of the City University of New York), B.B.A., 1949; University of Pennsylvania M.A., 1950, Ph.D., 1954. *Office:* Department of Political Science, University of Pennsylvania, Philadelphia, Pa. 19104.

CAREER: University of Pennsylvania, Philadelphia, lecturer, 1957-59, assistant professor, 1959-61, associate professor, 1961-66, professor of political science, 1966—, chairman of graduate program in international relations, 1966-70, Director, Anspach Institute of Foreign Affairs, 1968-70. *Military service:* U.S. Naval Reserve, 1945-47, 1954-56; became lieutenant. *Member:* American Political Science Association, Association of Asian Studies, American Association for Advancement of Slavic Studies. *Awards, honors:* Ford Foundation international relations fellowship, 1956-57; grants from Inter-University Committee on Travel Grants (for Soviet Union), 1957, American Philosophical Society, 1958, 1959, 1968, Rockefeller Foundation, 1961-62, National Science Foundation, 1970-71, and Bavaria Foundation, 1970-71; Guggenheim fellowship, 1965-66.

WRITINGS: (Editor and author of introduction and notes) *The Foreign Policy of the Soviet Union,* Random House, 1960, 2nd edition, 1966; (editor with Garold W. Thumm) *The Challenge of Politics: Ideas and Issues,* Prentice-Hall, 1962, 3rd edition, 1970; *The Soviets in International Organizations: Changing Policy Toward Developing Countries, 1953-1963,* Princeton University Press, 1964; *Communist Political Systems,* Prentice-Hall, 1966; (with Peter A.M. Berton) *Soviet Works on Southeast Asia: A Bibliography of Non-Periodical Literature, 1946-1965,* University of Southern California Press, 1967; *Yugoslavia and the Nonaligned World,* Princeton University Press, 1970; (editor with George Ginsburgs) *Soviet and American Policies in the United Nations,* New York University Press, 1971. Contributor of articles to *American Political Science Review, Reporter, Journal of Asian Studies, Orbis, Bulletin of the Atomic Scientist, Survey,* and other journals. Member of board of editors, *Current History.*

WORK IN PROGRESS: Studies of Soviet foreign policy in the Third World.

* * *

RUCKER, Bryce W(ilson) 1921-

PERSONAL: Born October 16, 1921, in Chelyan W. Va.; son of Cary (a railroad engineer) and Grace A. (Calvert) Rucker; married Betty B. Derrickson, September 14, 1944; children: Bryce Calvert, Linda Sue. *Education:* West Virginia Institute of Technology, student, 1939-41:

University of Kentucky, A.B., 1947; University of Wisconsin, M.S., 1949; University of Missouri, Ph.D., 1959. *Politics:* Democrat. *Religion:* Christian. *Home:* 1009 Emerald Lane, Carbondale, Ill. 62901. *Office:* Department of Journalism, Southern Illinois University, Carbondale, Ill. 62901.

CAREER: Raleigh Register, Beckley, W.Va., 1947-48, 1952, began as reporter, became news editor; University of Texas, Austin, assistant professor of journalism, 1949-50, 1956; Southwest Texas State College, San Marcos, assistant professor of journalism, 1950-56; University of Missouri, Columbia, foreign student adviser, 1956-58, assistant professor, 1958-62, associate professor of journalism, 1962-63; Southern Illinois University, Carbondale, assistant professor, 1963-67, professor of journalism, 1967—, director of graduate studies in journalism, 1963-70, director of journalism research, 1963—. *Military service:* U.S. Army, 1942-46; received Combat Infantryman Medal, European Theater Medal, Asiatic-Pacific Theater Medal. *Member:* Association for Education in Journalism, Sigma Delta Chi, Kappa Tau Alpha. *Awards, honors:* Outstanding faculty award, Southern Illinois University, 1968.

WRITINGS: (With others) *Modern Journalism,* Pitman, 1962; (editor) *Twentieth Century Reporting at Its Best,* Iowa State University Press, 1964; *The First Freedom,* Southern Illinois University Press, 1968. Contributor to *Texas Outlook* and *Journalism Quarterly.*

WORK IN PROGRESS: Biography of a former F.C.C. commissioner; conducting attitude and behavioral studies on a variety of subjects.

BIOGRAPHICAL/CRITICAL SOURCES: Raleigh Register, May 4, 1964; *Nation,* June 24, 1968; *New York Times Book Review,* November 17, 1968; *Christian Century,* February 19, 1969; *Virginia Quarterly Review,* Spring, 1969.

* * *

RUDOLPH, Frederick 1920-

PERSONAL: Born June 19, 1920, in Baltimore Md.; son of Charles Frederick and Jennie (Swope) Rudolph; married Dorothy Dannenbaum, June 18, 1949, children: Marta, Lisa. *Education:* Williams College, B.A., 1942; Yale University, M.A., 1949, Ph.D., 1953. *Home:* Ide Rd., Williamstown, Mass. 02167. *Office:* Department of History, Williams College, Williamstown, Mass. 01267.

CAREER: Williams College, Williamstown, Mass., instructor, 1946-47, 1951-53, assistant professor, 1953-58, associate professor, 1958-61, professor of history, 1961-64, Mark Hopkins Professor of History, 1964—, director of program in American studies, 1969—. Visiting lecturer in history and education, Harvard University, 1960, 1961. Member, commission of future of higher education, American Council on Education, 1964-66. *Military service:* U.S. Army, 1942-46; became captain. *Member:* American Historical Association, American Studies Association, American Association of University Professors, Berkshire County Historical Society (vice-president, 1962-66; president, 1966-68). *Awards, honors:* John Addison Porter Prize, 1953, for *Mark Hopkins and the Log,* Yale University; Guggenheim fellowship for studies in history of higher education, 1958-59, 1968-69.

WRITINGS: Mark Hopkins and the Log: Williams College, 1836-1872, Yale University Press, 1956; *The American College and University: A History,* Knopf, 1962; (editor) *Essay on Education in the Early Republic: Benjamin Rush, Noah Webster, Robert Coram, Simeon Doggett, Samuel Harrison Smith, Amable-Louis-Rose de Lafitte du Courteil, Samuel Knox,* Harvard University Press, 1965; *Threshold, 1965: Ideas for a New Univer-*

sity, Ball State University, c.1966. Contributor of articles to *Holiday, Mademoiselle*, and to professional journals.

WORK IN PROGRESS: Williams College 1872-1961.

*   *   *

RUNDELL, Walter, Jr. 1928-

PERSONAL: Born November 2, 1928, in Austin, Tex.; son of Walter (a college dean) and Olive (Spillar) Rundell; married Deanna A. Boyd, June 12, 1959; children: Shelley Elizabeth, David Walter, Jennifer Diane. *Education:* Lee College, student, 1946-48; University of Texas, B.J. and B.S. (high honors), 1951; American University, M.A., 1955, Ph.D., 1957. *Politics:* Democrat. *Religion:* Methodist. *Home:* 413 Ash Ave., Ames, Iowa 50010. *Office:* Department of History, Iowa State University, Ames, Iowa 50010.

CAREER: U.S. Army, 1951-57; historical officer in Office of the Chief of Finance, Washington, D.C., 1954-57; became first lieutenant; Del Mar College, Corpus Christi, Tex., instructor in history, 1957-58; Texas Woman's University, Denton, assistant professor of history, 1958-61; American Historical Association, Washington, D.C., assistant executive secretary, 1961-65, director, Survey on the Use of Original Sources in Graduate History Training, 1965-67; University of Oklahoma, Norman, professor of history, 1967-69; Iowa State University, Ames, professor of history and chairman of the department, 1969—. Professorial lecturer, American University, 1962-64, and University of Maryland, 1963-64; visiting professor, Columbia University, 1968, and Emory University, 1970.

MEMBER: American Studies Association, American Historical Association, National Council for Social Studies, Organization of American Historians, Society of American Archivists, American Association of University Professors, Western History Association (member of council, 1962-65), Southern Historical Association, U.S. Capitol Historical Society (honorary member of board of trustees, 1962-65), Potomac Corral of Westerners (chuckwrangler and program chairman, 1962-63). *Awards, honors:* Waldo Gifford Leland award of Society of American Archivists, 1971, for *In Pursuit of American History: Research and Training in the United States.*

WRITINGS: (With others) *Probing the American West*, Museum of New Mexico Press, 1962; *Black Market Money: The Collapse of U.S. Military Currency Control in World War II*, Louisiana State University Press, 1964; (editor) *List of Doctoral Dissertations in History in Progress or Completed at Colleges and Universities in the United States Since 1961*, American Historical Association, 1964; (contributor) Trevor Nevitt Dupuy, editor, *Holidays: Days of Significance for All Americans*, Watts, 1965; (contributor) Dagmar Horna Perman, editor, *Bibliography and the Historian*, American Bibliographical Center-Clio Press, 1968; (with others) *Reflections of Western Historians*, University of Arizona Press, 1969; *In Pursuit of American History: Research and Training in the United States*, University of Oklahoma Press, 1970; (with others) *In Search of Gulf Coast Colonial History*, Historic Pensacola Preservation Board, 1970; *Walter Prescott Webb*, Steck, 1971; (contributor) *Handbook of Texas*, Texas State Historical Association, in press. Contributor of articles to *Social Studies, American West, Pacific Historical Review, Arizona and the West, Military Affairs, New York History, Business History Review, Western Pennsylvania Historical Magazine, Social Education, American Archivist, Historian, Journal of Southern History*, and other journals. Editor of series of pamphlets for high school teachers published by Service Center for Teachers of History; member of executive board, *Social Education*, 1962—.

WORK IN PROGRESS: A book on the West as conceived by the artist (composers, writers, and painters).

SIDELIGHTS: Rundell originally intended to be a music critic (majoring in musical literature as well as journalism), but switched to the history field after military assignment as an historian. "Writing," he says, "is the common thread in this switch of vocational aims."

*   *   *

RUSSELL, John David 1928-

PERSONAL: Born December 12, 1928, in Chicago, Ill.; son of John David (a coach) and Charlotte (Graf) Russell; married Mary Elizabeth Need, 1954; children: David, Ryan. *Education:* Colgate University, A.B., 1951; University of Washington, M.A., 1956; Rutgers University, Ph.D., 1959. *Home:* 3112 Landfall Lane, Annapolis, Md. 21403. *Office:* Department of English, University of Maryland, College Park, Md. 20740.

CAREER: Pace College, New York, N.Y., instructor, 1956-57; University of South Carolina, Columbia, 1958-69, began as assistant professor, became professor of English; University of Maryland, College Park, professor of English, 1969—. Fulbright professor, University of Brazil, 1966-67. *Military service:* U.S. Navy, 1952-55; became lieutenant. *Member:* South Atlantic Modern Language Association. *Awards honors: Explicator* Prize, 1961, for *Henry Green: Nine Novels and An Unpacked Bag;* Russell Award, University of South Carolina, 1962, for creative research.

WRITINGS: Henry Green: Nine Novels and An Unpacked Bag, Rutgers University Press, 1960; (editor with Ashley Brown) *Satire: A Critical Anthology*, World Publishing, 1967; *Anthony Powell: A Quintet, Sextet, and War*, Indiana University Press, 1970. Contributor to *Explicator, Kenyon Review*, and *Wisconsin Studies in Contemporary Literature.*

WORK IN PROGRESS: Style in Modern British Fiction, Completion expected in 1974.

*   *   *

RUSSELL, John L(owry), Jr. 1921-

PERSONAL: Born November 19, 1921; son of John L. (an author and lecturer) and Alice (Belle) Russell; married Anne Arnone. *Education:* Bates College, A.B., 1948; University of Pennsylvania, graduate study, 1949; University of Miami, Coral Gables, Fla., B.Ed., 1952, graduate study, 1953. *Home address:* P.O. Box 1141, Coral Gables, Fla. 33134. *Office:* 1367 Southwest 37th St., Miami, Fla. 33145.

CAREER: University of Miami, Coral Gables, Fla., staff counselor and assistant dean, 1949-52; Dade Country Public Schools, Dade County, Fla., teacher, 1952-55; full-time writer, 1955—. *Military service:* U.S. Army Air Forces, 1942-45; member of B-25 bomber crew; Japanese prisoner of war, 1944; received Purple Heart, Presidential citation, two battle stars.

WRITINGS: Destination: Space, Popular Mechanics Press, 1959, revised edition, 1960; *Science Year*, Popular Mechanics Press, 1959. Contributor of over two thousand articles to two hundred magazines, including *Science Digest, Farming, Grade Teacher, American Mercury, National Enquirer*, and *American Banker.*

WORK IN PROGRESS: Articles for magazines.

*   *   *

RUTGERS van der LOEFF-BASENAU, An(na) 1910-

PERSONAL: Born March 15, 1910, in Amsterdam, The Netherlands; daughter of Jacob F. (a doctor of medicine) and Nora (Goemans) Basenau; married Michael Rutgers van der Loeff (an electrical engineer), September 18, 1934; children: Paul, Frits and Romee (twins, boy and girl; Romee is now Mrs. R. J. Velthuys), Lucy. *Education:* Barlaeus Gymnasium, Amsterdam, graduated, 1929; studied classical languages at University of Amsterdam, two years. *Home:* Vossiusstraat 31, Amsterdam, Netherlands. *Agent:* Robert Harben, 3 Church Vale, London N.2, England.

CAREER: Writer and translator. *Member:* Dutch Association of Writers, P.E.N. *Awards, honors:* Prijs voor het Beste Kinderboek (Dutch prize for the best children's book), 1955, for *Lawines razen;* second Dutch prize, Atlantic competition, 1958, for *Je bent te goed, Giacomo;* honor book award, *New York Herald Tribune* Children's Spring Book Festival, 1958, *New York Times Book Review* "One Hundred Outstanding Books" list, 1958, and Junior Book Award, Boys' Clubs of America, 1959, all for *Avalanche;* first prize for best information book, German governmental competition for juveniles, 1959, for *Amerika;* first prize for literary work in the sphere of travel, 1961, for *Gideons reizen.*

WRITINGS—Juveniles; all Dutch editions published by Ploegsma, unless otherwise indicated: *De Kinderkaravaan,* 1949, 5th edition, 1958, translation by Roy Edwards published in England as *Children on the Oregon Trail,* University of London Press, 1961, published in America as *Oregon at Last!,* Morrow, 1962; *Rossy, dat krantenkind,* 1952, translation by Edward Fitzgerald published as *Rossy, This Newspaper Child,* University of London Press, 1964; *Lawines razen,* 1954, 5th edition, 1959, translation by Dora Round published as *Avalanche!,* University of London Press, 1957, Morrow, 1958; *Jimmy en Ricky,* 1955; *Het licht in je ogen* (title means "The Light in Your Eyes"), Arbeiderspers, 1956; *Konijne-Japie* (title means "Rabbit-Jack"), 1957; *Ze verdrinken ons dorp,* 1957, translation by Roy Edwards published as *They're Drowning Our Village,* University of London Press, 1959, F. Watts, 1960; *Het verloren koffertje* (title means "The Lost Handbag"), 1958; *Dat zijn M-brigadiers* (title means "The Milk-Brigade"), 1959; *Gideons reizen* (title means "The Voyages of Gideon"), 1960; *Elfstedentocht,* c.1960, translation by Henrietta Anthony published as *Great Day in Holland: The Skating Race,* Abelard, 1965; *Het wilde land [en] Iedersland,* Samsom, 1961, translation by Elizabeth Meijer published as *Everybody's Land,* University of London Press, 1964; *Vlucht, Wassilis, vlucht!,* 1962, translation by George Mocniak published as *Vassilis on the Run,* University of London Press, 1965, Follett, 1969; *Steffos en zijn paaslam,* Samsom, 1963, translation by Elizabeth Meijer published as *Steffos and His Easter Lamb,* Brockhampton Press, 1969; *Bevrijdingsspel 1813,* Wolters, 1963.

Adult books; all Dutch editions published by Ploegsma, unless otherwise indicated: *Van een dorp, een jongen en een orgel* (title means "A Village, a Boy, and an Organ"), 1946; *Zweden, droom em werklijkheid* (title means "Sweden, Dream and Reality"), 1938; *Amerika: Pioniers en hun kleinzoons,* R. van Goor, 1951, 3rd edition published as *Amerikaans avontuur,* 1966; *Anna Menander,* R. van Goor, 1951; *Mens of wolf?* (title means "Man or Wolf?"), 1951, 7th edition, E. Querido, 1964; *Vader, de kinderen en ik* (title means "Father, the Children, and I"), Strengholt, 1953; *Drie studentenliederen,* Universitaire Pers Leiden, 1953; *Een kans op geluk* (title means "In Pursuit of Happiness"), 1953; *Je bent te goed, Giacomo* (title means "You Are Too Good, Giacomo"), 1957; *Alleen Tegen alles* (title means "Alone Against All"), 1962; *Vlucht in de poolnacht,* Samsom, c.1966, translation by Marieke Clarke published as *Flight from the Polar Night,* Brockhampton Press, 1968; *Vals spoor in Waterland,* 1967; *Het uur van de Scapinezen,* 1968; *Donald,* E. Querido, 1969; *Wrak onder water,* 1970; *Gewoon in het ongewone,* 1971. Translator of about fifty books into Dutch from Scandinavian languages, English, and German.

WORK IN PROGRESS: Jacht op de vlinder (title means "The Chase for the Butterfly"), and *Als je zou durven ...* ("If You Had the Courage ..."), both for Ploegsma.

SIDELIGHTS: The author's works have been translated into many different languages, including Finnish, Indonesian, Hebrew, Japanese, Portuguese, and Czech. *Avocational interests:* Gardening, handicrafts, cycling, horseback riding.†

*   *   *

RUTSALA, Vern   1934-

PERSONAL: Born February 5, 1934, in McCall, Idaho; son of Ray Edwin (a salesman) and Virginia (Brady) Rutsala; married Joan Colby, April 6, 1957; children: Matthew, David, Kirsten. *Education:* Reed College, B.A., 1956; State University of Iowa, M.F.A., 1960. *Office:* English Department, Lewis and Clark College, Portland, Ore. 92719.

CAREER: Lewis and Clark College, Portland, Ore., 1961—, now associate professor of English. Visiting professor, University of Minnesota, 1968-69, Bowling Green University, 1970. *Military service:* U.S. Army, 1956-58.

WRITINGS: The Window: Poems, Wesleyan University Press, 1964; *Small Songs: A Sequence* (poems), Stone Wall Press, 1969; *The Harmful State,* Best Cellar Press, 1971. Poetry anthologized in *West of Boston,* edited by G. Stevenson, Qara Press, 1959, *Midland,* edited by Paul Engle and others, Random House, 1961, *Where Is Vietnam?: American Poets Respond,* edited by Walter Lowenfels, Doubleday-Anchor, 1967, and *Out of the War Shadow,* edited by Denise Levertov, War Resisters League, 1967. Contributor to *Paris Review, Nation, Midland, Poetry, New American Review,* and other publications. Poetry editor, *December,* 1959-62.

WORK IN PROGRESS: Poetry and fiction.

SIDELIGHTS: In a review of *The Window,* Norman Friedman comments: "Vern Rutsala . . . seems to me to have one of the keenest poetic senses of contemporary society that I can remember since Cummings, Auden, the earlier Karl Shapiro, and a few of Simpson's poems, coupled with one of the most natural yet elevated styles of any of the in-between poets discussed so far

Friedman continues: ". . . The book as a whole gathers momentum, as situation after situation is assimilated, familiar image after familiar image is turned over like a rock to reveal the squirming horror beneath, until gradually we sense a full and various picture being formed, in mosaic-like fashion, of all our lives. Rutsala deals card after card, surprise after surprise, building up unbearably to a remorseless climax, until not a corner is left for us to hide in, nothing is spared—not a toothbrush, a family album, a mantlepiece clock, a visit from relatives, a souvenir ashtray, a flushing of the toilet, a garden hose— nothing escapes his bright and curious gaze. The result is an incredible illumination of the things that are so ordinary that we have forgotten them, so close that we haven't seen them; these poems suddenly bring them back to sight and mind and focus, revealing to us what we thought we already knew but never quite understood."

BIOGRAPHICAL/CRITICAL SOURCES: Chicago Review, June, 1967.

RUTT, Richard 1925-
(Ro Tae-yong)

PERSONAL: Born August 27, 1925, in Langford, Bedfordshire, England; son of Cecil (a local government officer) and Mary (Turner) Rutt; married Joan Mary Ford, 1969. Education: Kelham Theological College, student 1942-51; Pembroke College, Cambridge, B.A., 1954, M.A., 1958. Home: 194 Drove Rd., Biggleswade, Bedfordshire, England. Postal address: Anglican Church, P.O. Box 22, Taejon, Korea. Office: 88-1 Sonhwa 2 Dong, Taejon, Korea.

CAREER: Ordained priest, Church of England, 1952, consecrated bishop, 1966; St. George's Church, Cambridge, England, curate, 1952-54; Anglican Diocese of Korea, 1954—, parish priest in Korean village, 1956-59, warden of St. Bede's Student Center, Seoul, 1959-64, rector of Diocesan Seminary, Seoul, 1964-66, bishop of Taejon, 1968—. Military service: Royal Naval Volunteer Reserve, 1943-46; became sublieutenant. Member: Royal Asiatic Society (councilor, Korea branch, 1955—). Awards, honors: Tasan Award, 1964, for foreign writings on Seoul, Korea.

WRITINGS: The Church Serves Korea, Society for the Propagation of the Gospel in Foreign Parts, 1956; An Introduction to the Sijo, a Form of Short Korean Poem, Korean Branch of the Royal Asiatic Society, 1958; Korea: Answers to Your Questions About the Korean People, Their Customs, Politics and Religion, Korean Mission, Church of England, 1959; (editor) Church Music and Hymnbook (in Korean), Anglican Church (Seoul), 1962; Contribution of Literature and the Arts to Korean Modernization, [Seoul], 1963; Korean Notes and Days: Notes From the Diary of a Country Priest, Tuttle, 1964; P'ungnyu Han'guk (essays in Korean), Sin T'aeyang Co. (Seoul), 1964; The Bamboo Grove: An Introduction to Sijo, University of California Press, 1971; (editor and annotator) J.S. Gale, History of the Korean People, Royal Asiatic Society, 1971; (translator) The Nine Cloud Dream, Asia Society, in press; (translator) Ch'unhyang ka, Asia Society, in press. Contributor of articles in both English and Korean to newspapers and periodicals in Korea and elsewhere, including regular articles in daily press on customs and literature.

WORK IN PROGRESS: Translating an anthology of verse written in Chinese by Korean writers.

*   *   *

RUTZEBECK, Hjalmar 1889-

PERSONAL: Born April 17, 1889, in Copenhagen, Denmark; son of Hans Julius and Martha (Von Voelkel) Rutzebeck; married Henri Etta (a placement officer), December 22, 1937; children: John David, Mary Ingrid Rutzebeck Kellogg, Lief Hjalmar, Diana Margaret Rutzebeck Tillion. Education: Studied at Feilberg's Private School, Copenhagen, Denmark. Politics: Democrat. Religion: Quaker. Home: 10538 Art St., Sunland, Calif. 91040.

CAREER: Went to sea as a youth; homesteader and fisherman in Alaska, 1913-22; successively structural iron foreman, real estate salesman, produce peddler, and personnel officer for Unemployed Exchange Association, in vicinity of San Francisco, Calif., 1922-34; administrative work with Works Progress Administration, Washington, D.C., 1934, Los Angeles County Department of Rehabilitation, Los Angeles, Calif., 1935-37, Cooperative Hydroponics, Fort Lauderdale, Fla., 1937-38, State of California Relief Administration, 1938-39. Presently a tax practitioner in Los Angeles. Member of board of directors, Los Angeles branch of Urban League, 1942-45. Military service: U.S. Army, Infantry, 1910-13.

WRITINGS: Alaska Man's Luck: A Romance of Fact, Boni & Liveright, 1920; My Alaskan Idyll, Boni & Liveright, 1922; Reciprocal Economy: Self-Help, Cooperative Technique and Management, J. F. Rowney Press, c.1933, 3rd edition, revised, 1935; Common Sense in Idealism: "The Only Way to Prosperity with Freedom," Builders of a Better America, Inc., 1938; Hell's Paradise, Humphries, 1947; Mad Sea: The Life and Loves of a Windjammer Sailor, Greenberg, 1956; Sailor with a Gun, Pageant, 1957 (published in England as The Wind Is Free, Redman, 1957); Gate to Paradise, Exposition, 1967; Men of Iron, Exposition, 1967; Bait, Novel Books, 1967; Chantey Man, R. Greenfield Co., 1969. Also author of Under a Third Party Platform, and The Principles of Government. Contributor of short stories and novelettes to magazines. Editor, Paradise Progress Review, 1926-29, Oakland World, 1933, Key, 1936-37.

WORK IN PROGRESS: From Little Acorns Grow; Pandora's Box.

BIOGRAPHICAL/CRITICAL SOURCES: Politiken (Copenhagen), June 9, 1963.

*   *   *

RYAN, Leonard Eames 1930-

PERSONAL: Born July 8, 1930, in Albion, N.Y.; son of Bernard (an attorney and judge) and Harriet (Fitts) Ryan; married Carol Lois Boggs, July 2, 1963. Education: Kent School, graduate, 1948; University of Pennsylvania, A.B., 1954; New York University, 1962. Politics: Democrat. Home: 34 West 12th St. New York, N.Y. 10011. Ageny: Margot Johnson Agency, 405 East 54th St., New York, N.Y. 10022.

CAREER: Admitted to New York Bar, Bars of U.S. District Court and U.S. Court of Appeals for the District of Columbia; Upper Darby News, Upper Darby, Pa., reporter, 1954-55; Associated Press, newsman in Pittsburgh, Pa., Philadelphia, Pa., Harrisburg, Pa., and New York, N.Y., 1955-62; New York Times, New York, N.Y., reporter, 1962-63; private practice of law, New York, N.Y., 1964-66; U.S. Department of Justice, Washington, D.C., trial attorney with civil rights division, 1966-68; Ford Foundation, New York, N.Y., program officer in Office of Government and Law, 1968—.Military service: U.S. Army Reserve, 1950-57. Member: American Judicature Society, Delta Phi, St. Elmo Club (Philadelphia).

WRITINGS: (With Bernard Ryan, Jr.) So You Want to Go Into Journalism, Harper, 1963.

*   *   *

RYRIE, Charles C(aldwell) 1925-

PERSONAL: Born March 2, 1925, in St. Louis, Mo.; son of John Alexander and Elizabeth (Caldwell) Ryrie; married Anne Belden, June 27, 1959; children: Elizabeth, Bruce, Carolyn. Education: Haverford College, A.B., 1946; Dallas Theological Seminary, Th.M., 1947, Th.D., 1949; University of Edinburgh, Ph.D., 1954. Home: 6719 Velasco Ave., Dallas, Tex. 75214.

CAREER: Ordained Baptist minister, 1947; Midwest Bible and Missionary Institute, St. Louis, Mo., instructor, 1947; Westmont College, Santa Barbara, Calif., associate professor, 1948-49, professor of Greek and Bible, 1949-53, dean of men, 1950-51, chairman of Division of Biblical Studies and Philosophy, 1950-53; Dallas Theological Seminary, Dallas, Texas., assistant professor, 1954-57, associate professor of systematic theology, 1957-58; Philadelphia College of Bible, Philadelphia, Pa., president, 1958-62; Dallas Theological Seminary, dean of doctoral studies and professor of systematic theology, 1962—. Director, Mosher Steel Co., Dallas and Houston. Director,

Word of Life Fellowship; member of executive council, Central American Mission, Dallas. Visiting professor, Dallas Theological Seminary, 1953-54. *Member:* National Institute of Religion, Evangelical Theological Society, Society of Biblical Literature, Phi Beta Kappa.

WRITINGS: Easy-to-Get Object Lessons, Zondervan, 1949; *The Basis of the Premillennial Faith,* Loizeaux Brothers, 1953; *Neo-Orthodoxy: What It Is and What It Does,* Moody, 1956; *The Place of Women in the Church,* Macmillan, 1958; *Biblical Theology of the New Testament,* Moody, 1959; *The Thessalonian Epistles,* Moody, 1959; *The Acts of the Apostles,* Moody, 1961; *The Grace of God,* Moody, 1963; *Dispensationalism Today,* Moody, 1965; *The Holy Spirit,* Moody, 1965; *Patterns for Christian Youth,* Moody, 1966; *Revelation,* Moody, 1968; *Balancing the Christian Life,* Moody, 1969; *The Bible and Tomorrow's News: A New Look at Prophecy,* Scripture Press, 1969; *The Bible of the Middle Way,* Brite Divinity School, Texas Christian University, 1969; *Easy Object Lessons,* Moody, 1970; *A Survey of Bible Doctrine,* Moody, 1972.

* * *

SABINI, John Anthony 1921-
(John Anthony)

PERSONAL: Born February 25, 1921, in Fort Sill, Okla.; son of Dominic Joseph (an Army officer) and Frances (Horan) Sabini; married Susan Wingfield, December 27, 1951 (deceased); children: Jemima Sophy. *Education:* Swarthmore College, B.A., 1942; graduate study at School of Advanced International Studies, 1947-48, Institut de Hautes Etudes Internationales, 1947-48. *Home address:* P.O. Box 1348 Beirut, Lebanon. *Agent:* London International Press Ltd., 3-4 Ludgate Circus Building, London E.C.4, England. *Office address:* c/o Trans-Arabian Pipe Line Co., P.O. Box 1348, Beirut, Lebanon.

CAREER: U.S. Department of State, career foreign service in Tunis, 1949-54, in Washington, D.C., 1954-55, in Jerusalem, 1955-57; Trans-Arabian Pipe Line Co., employee in Saudia Arabia, 1958-60, in Beirut, Lebanon, 1960—. *Military service:* U.S. Marine Corps, 1942-47; became major; received Purple Heart and Navy Cross.

WRITINGS: About Tunisia, Bles, 1961; *Tunisia: A Personal View of a Timeless Land,* Scribner, 1962. Contributor of travel articles to *New York Times.*

WORK IN PROGRESS: Novel on Middle East.

AVOCATIONAL INTERESTS: History, archaeology, and travel.†

* * *

SAHGAL, Nayantara (Pandit) 1927-

PERSONAL: Born May 10, 1927, in Allahabad, Uttar Pradesh, India; daughter of Ranjit Sitaram (in law and politics) and Vijaya Lakshmi (Nehru) Pandit; married Gautam Sahgal (in industry), January 2, 1949 (divorced March 2, 1967); children: Nonika, Ranjit, Gita. *Education:* Attended schools in India; Wellesley College, B.A., 1947. *Religion:* Hindu. *Residence:* New Delhi, India.

CAREER: Free-lance writer. Lecturer on U.S. tours, 1962, 1963; exchange lecturer, Southern Methodist University, 1973; participant in seminar at University of London, 1974. *Member:* India International Centre (New Delhi).

WRITINGS: Prison and Chocolate Cake, Knopf, 1954; *A Time to Be Happy* (Book Society choice), Knopf, 1958; *From Fear Set Free,* Gollancz, 1962, Norton, 1963; *This Time of Morning,* Gollancz, 1965, Norton, 1966; *Storm in Chandigarh,* Norton, 1969; *Freedom Movement in India,* National Council of Educational Research and Training (India), 1970; *The Day in Shadow,* Norton, 1971. Contributor to *Atlantic, Statesman,* and to newspapers and magazines in India.

WORK IN PROGRESS: A book with tentative title *Indira Gandhi: Her Emergence and Style;* a collection of short stories.

SIDELIGHTS: In a review of *Storm in Chandigarh,* Martin Levin writes: "Mrs. Sahgal creates a realistic climate in which the lives of her young marrieds move along, with the imminent threat of political violence giving the humdrum an added sharpness. And she pursues ideas with a subtle intelligence that never interferes with the vital sweep of action." *Avocational interests:* Cross-country walks, European and Indian classical music, theatre, and good contemporary novels.

BIOGRAPHICAL/CRITICAL SOURCES: Village Voice, May 15, 1969; *Times Literary Supplement,* June 26, 1969; *Books Abroad,* summer, 1969; *London Magazine,* September, 1970.

* * *

St. CLAIR, Robert James 1925-

PERSONAL: Born August 6, 1925, in Brooklyn, N.Y.; son of Raymond Joseph and Anne M. (Wasson) St. Clair; married Ruth Marshall, August 19, 1951; children: Paul Raymond, Charles James. *Education:* Brooklyn College (now Brooklyn College of the City University of New York), A.B., 1947; Biblical Seminary in New York, S.T.B., 1951; University of Cincinnati, M.A., 1956; Southern Methodist University, S.T.M., 1968; Chicago Theological Seminary, Rel.D., 1968. *Politics:* Democrat. *Home:* 2912 Mystic Lane, Springfield, Ohio 45503. *Office:* Hamma School of Theology, Wittenberg University, Springfield, Ohio 45501.

CAREER: Minister, United Presbyterian Church; now associate professor of practical theology, Hamma School of Theology, Wittenberg University, Springfield, Ohio.

WRITINGS: Neurotics in the Church, Revell, 1963; *The Adventure of Being You,* Revell, 1966. Contributor to *Christianity Today, Journal of Pastoral Care,* and other religious journals.

WORK IN PROGRESS: A Book on the phenomenological approach to theology, entitled *Meanings on Fire.*

* * *

SAISSELIN, Remy G (ilbert) 1925-

PERSONAL: Born August 17, 1925, in Moutier, Jura Bernois, Switzerland; son of Paul A. and Jeanne L. (Nydegger) Saisselin; married Nicole M. Fischer, May 31, 1955; children: Anne Francoise, Juliette Carole, Peter Hugh. *Education:* Queens College (now Queens College of City University of New York), B.A., 1951; University of Wisconsin, M.A. in history, 1952, M.A. in French, 1953, Ph.D., 1957. *Office:* Department of Fine Arts, University of Rochester, River Campus, Rochester, N.Y. 14627.

CAREER: Western Reserve University (now Case Western Reserve University), Cleveland, Ohio, assistant professor of French, 1956-59; Cleveland Museum of Art, Cleveland, Ohio, assistant curator for research; now member of faculty of fine arts, University of Rochester, Rochester, N.Y. *Military service:* U.S. Army, Infantry, 1944-46. *Member:* Phi Beta Kappa.

WRITINGS: Style, Truth, and the Portrait, Cleveland Museum of Art, 1963; *Taste in Eighteenth Century France: Critical Reflections on the Origins of Aesthetics; or, An Apology for Amateurs,* Syracuse University Press, 1965; *The Rule of Reason and the Ruses of the Heart: A*

Philosophical Dictionary of Classical French Criticism, Critics, and Aesthetic Issues, Press of Case Western Reserve University, 1970; *The Transformation of Art into Culture: From Pascal to Diderot,* Institut et Musee Voltaire (Geneva), 1970; *Le Dix-Huiteme siecle: Gout, lumieres, nature,* Prentice-Hall, 1972. Contributor of articles on French literature, aesthetic theory, and art criticism to journals, including *Theatre Annual, Prairie Schooner, French Review, Personalist,* and *Apollo.* Assistant editor, *Journal of Aesthetics and Art Criticism,* 1959-62.

WORK IN PROGRESS: A book entitled *Still Life;* a book on eighteenth-century French painting and imagination.

AVOCATIONAL INTERESTS: Collecting seventeenth and eighteen-century French and British books, mostly on criticism and artistic thought.

*   *   *

SALE, Richard (Bernard) 1911-
(John St. John)

PERSONAL: Born December 17, 1911, in New York, N.Y.; son of Richard Bernard and Frances (Topinka) Sale; married second wife, Mary Anita Loos (an author), December 17, 1946 (divorced); children: Lindsey (Mrs. Keith Tucker), Richard Townsend, Edward Clifford. *Education:* Washington and Lee University, student, 1930-33. *Politics:* Independent. *Religion:* Christian. *Home:* 405 North Star Lane, Newport Beach, Calif. 92660. *Agent:* Paul R. Reynolds & Son, 599 Fifth Ave., New York, N.Y. 10017.

CAREER: Free-lance writer for magazines, 1930-44; writer for Paramount Pictures, Hollywood, Calif., 1944; writer-director for Republic Pictures, Studio City, Calif., 1945-48, 20th Century-Fox, Beverly Hills, Calif., 1948-52, British Lion, London, England, 1953-54, United Artists, New York, N.Y., and Europe, 1954, Columbia Pictures, Hollywood, Calif., 1956; television writer, director, producer for Columbia Broadcasting System, 1958-59. Composer of music for several motion pictures. *Member:* Authors League of America, Writers Guild of America, Directors Guild of America, Academy of Motion Picture Arts and Sciences, National Academy of Television Arts, Delta Upsilon, Sigma Delta Chi, Balboa Angling Club, Shark Island Yacht Club.

WRITINGS: Not Too Narrow, Not Too Deep, Simon & Schuster, 1936; *Is a Ship Burning?,* Cassell, 1937, Dodd, 1938; *Cardinal Rock,* Cassell, 1940; *Lazarus No. 7,* Simon & Schuster, 1942 (published in England as *Death Looks In,* Cassell, 1943); *Sailor Take Warning,* Wells Gardner, 1942; *Passing Strange: A Story of Birth and Burial,* Simon & Schuster, 1942, reissued as *Passing Strange: A Mystery of Birth and Burial,* Quinn, 1943; *Destination Unknown,* World's Work, 1943, published in America as *Death at Sea,* Popular Library, 1948; *Benefit Performance,* Simon & Schuster, 1946; *The Oscar,* Simon & Schuster, 1963; *For the President's Eyes Only,* Simon & Schuster, 1971; *Square-Shooters,* Simon & Schuster, 1972.

Contributor of 350 short stories and serials to *New Yorker, Saturday Evening Post, Country Gentleman, Scribner's, Liberty, Blue Book, Good Housekeeping, Esquire, Coronet, Argosy, Detective Fiction Weekly, Adventure, Maclean's,* and to pulp magazines, 1930-44, co-author with wife of thirty-four screenplays, including "Suddenly," "A Ticket to Tomahawk," "Mr. Belvedere Goes to College," "Abandon Ship," and "Torpedo Run."

Writer of three segments, and co-author with wife, Mary Loos, of twenty-two other segments of "Yancy Derringer" television series, 1958-59. Yachting editor and

contributor of other articles to *Orange County Illustrated,* Newport Beach, Calif., 1963—.

SIDELIGHTS: Sale has made films in England, Spain, and France. He now lives on an island in Newport Bay, Calif., fishes marlin, hunts (with rifle) shark and killer whale, and has spent more than two thousand hours at sea in all weathers.

The Oscar was filmed by Avco Embassy in 1966.

*   *   *

SALISBURY, Robert H(olt) 1930-

PERSONAL: Born April 29, 1930, in Elmhurst, Ill.; son of Robert Holt (an architect) and Beulah (Hammer) Salisbury; married Rose Marie Cipriani, June 19, 1953; children: Susan Marie, Robert Holt, Matthew Gary. *Education:* Washington and Lee University, A.B., 1951; University of Illinois, M.A., 1952, Ph.D., 1955. *Politics:* Democrat. *Religion:* Methodist. *Home:* 337 Westgate, University City, Mo. 63130. *Office:* Washington University, St. Louis, Mo. 63130.

CAREER: Washington University, St. Louis, Mo., instructor, 1955-57, assistant professor, 1957-60, associate professor, 1960-65, professor of political science, 1965—, chairman of department, 1966—. Consultant to National Institutes of Health. *Member:* American Political Science Association (member of executive council), Midwest Political Science Association, Missouri Political Science Association (president, 1964-65), Pi Sigma Alpha.

WRITINGS: (With others) *Functions and Policies of American Government: Big Democracy in Action,* edited by Jack W. Peltason and James MacGregor Burns, Prentice-Hall, 1958; (with Thomas H. Eliot and William N. Chambers) *American Government: Readings and Politics for Analysis,* Dodd, 1959; (editor and author of introduction with Chambers) *Democracy in the Mid-Twentieth Century: Problems and Prospects,* Washington University Press, 1960, reissued as *Democracy Today: Problems and Prospects,* Collier, 1962; (contributor) Joseph Walter Towle, editor, *Ethics and Standards in American Business,* Houghton, 1963; (with Nicholas A. Masters and Eliot) *State Politics and the Public Schools: An Exploratory Analysis,* Knopf, 1964; *Governmental Reorganization: Prospects for Action* (report), Greater Hartford Chamber of Commerce, 1964; (contributor) Herbert Jacob and K.N. Vines, *Politics in the American States: A Comparative Analysis,* Little, Brown, 1965; (contributor) Austin Ranney, editor, *Political Sciences and Public Policy,* Markham, 1968; (editor, author of introduction, and contributor) *Interest Group Politics in America,* Harper, 1970.

Contributor of articles to *American Political Science Review, Harvard Educational Review, Journal of Politics, Current Affairs Bulletin, Midwest Journal of Political Science,* and other periodicals.

WORK IN PROGRESS: Urban Politics and Education; Agricultural Politics in the United States; research on interest groups; policy analysis.

AVOCATIONAL INTERESTS: Listening to music, reading history, and acquiring art objects.

*   *   *

SALOUTOS, Theodore 1910-

PERSONAL: Surname pronounced Sah-*loo*-tus; born August 3, 1910, in Milwaukee, Wis.; son of Peter and Demetra (Perdikis) Saloutos; married Florence L. Scwefel, September 12, 1940; children: Bonnie Louis (Mrs. Martin Gilbert), Peter. *Education:* Milwaukee State Teachers College, B.Ed., 1933; University of Wisconsin, studied law, summers 1934-36, M.Phil., 1938, Ph.D., 1940. *Pol-*

itics: Democrat. *Religion:* Greek Orthodox. *Home:* 3745 Wade St., Los Angeles, Calif. 90066. *Office:* 405 Hilgard Ave., Los Angeles, Calif. 90066.

CAREER: University of Wisconsin, Madison, extension division instructor in history, 1941-43; Oberlin College, Oberlin, Ohio, visiting lecturer, 1943-45; University of California, Los Angeles, 1945—, started as lecturer, now professor of history and chairman of department. Fulbright research scholar at University of Athens, 1952-53, 1966-67; Fulbright professor at University of Freiburg, 1959-60; visiting professor, University of Hawaii, 1968. *Member:* American Historical Association (executive committee, Pacific Coast branch), Economic History Association, Agricultural History Society (former president; chairman of nominating committee), Business History Association, Economic History Society of Great Britain, Organization of American Historians (executive committee, 1969-72), Hellenic University Club of Southern California (president, 1961-63, 1969—), Mar Vista Democratic Club (president 1961-63). *Awards, honors:* Guggenheim fellow, 1967.

WRITINGS: (With John D. Hicks) *Agricultural Discontent in the Middle West, 1900-1939,* University of Wisconsin Press, 1951, revised and enlarged edition published as *Twentieth Century Populism: Agricultural Discontent in the Middle West, 1900-1939,* Peter Smith, 1964; *They Remember America: The Story of the Repatriated Greek-Americans,* University of California Press, 1956; *Farmer Movements in the South, 1865-1933,* University of California Press, 1960; *The Greeks in the United States,* Harvard University Press, 1964; *The Greeks in America: A Students' Guide to Localized History,* Teachers College Press, 1967; (compiler *Populism: Reaction or Reform?,* Holt, 1968. Contributor to *Encyclopaedia Britannica* and *Dictionary of American Biography.* Contributor of articles to *Argonaut, Los Angeles Times, Greek Heritage, Santa Monica Evening Outlook,* and numerous professional periodicals. Member of editorial board, *Journal of American History,* 1967-70, and *Agricultural History.*

WORK IN PROGRESS: The New Deal and Agriculture.

*   *   *

SALVADORI-PALEOTTI, Massimo   1908-
(Massimo Salvadori, Max William Salvadori)

PERSONAL: Born June 16, 1908, in London, England; came to United States in 1939; son of Count Guglielmo (a professor of philosophy) and Cynthia (Galletti di Cadilhac) Salvadori-Paleotti; married Joyce Woodforde Pawle, May 7, 1934; children: Cynthia, Clement L. *Education:* University of Geneva, Lic. es Sc. Soc., 1929; University of Rome, Dr. Sc., 1930. *Politics:* Liberal. *Religion:* Agnostic. *Home:* 36 Ward Ave., Northampton, Mass. 00160. *Office:* Department of History, Smith College, Northampton, Mass. 01060.

CAREER: Institute of Foreign Trade, Rome, Italy, economic analyst, 1931-32; sentenced to five years internment in concentration camp in Italy, for anti-fascist activities, 1932; upon release a year later went first to England, where he lectured, and then to Kenya, East Africa, 1933-36; University of Geneva, Geneva, Switzerland, privatdocent of economics, 1937-39; St. Lawrence University, Canton, N.Y., assistant professor of sociology, 1939-41; Bennington College, Bennington, Vt., professor of social sciences, 1945-62; Smith College, Northampton, Mass., professor of history, 1947-64, Dwight W. Morrow Professor of History, 1964—. Director of division of political sciences, UNESCO, Paris, France, 1948-49; political analyst in information service, North Atlantic Treaty Organization, Paris, France, 1952-53; with ENI (Italian Fuel Authority), 1956-57; director of School for Freedom, Liberal International, 1955-63. *Military service:* British Army, 1943-45; became lieutenant colonel; received Military Cross and Distinguished Service Order. *Member:* Society for Italian Historical Studies, American Historical Association, Liberal International, Special Forces Club (London). *Awards, honors:* Litt.D., American International College, 1959.

WRITINGS—All under name Massimo Salvadori: *L-'Unita del Mediterraneo,* Saturnia, 1931; *La Penetrazione demografica europea in Africa,* Fratelli Bocca, 1932; *La Colonisation europeenne au Kenya,* Larose Editeurs, 1938; *Problemi de liberta,* G. Laterza, 1949.

Las Ciencias sociales del siglo XX en Italia, Instituto de Investigaciones Sociales, Universidad Nacional (Mexico), 1950; *Resistenza ed azione: Ricordi di un liberale,* G. Laterza, 1951, translation by Giacinta Salvadori-Paleotti published as *The Labour and the Wounds: A Personal Chronicle of One Man's Fight for Freedom,* Pall Mall, 1958; (with Michele Cantarella) *Italy [and] Italy's Post-war Foreign Policy* (the former by Salvadori, the latter by Salvadori and Cantarella), Foreign Policy Association, 1951; *The Rise of Modern Communism: A Brief History of the Communist Movement in the Twentieth Century,* Holt, 1952, 2nd revised edition, 1973; *American Capitalism,* Liberal International, 1954, 2nd edition published as *American Capitalism: A Liberal View,* Pall Mall, 1956; *Brief History of the Patriot Movement in Italy, 1943-1945,* Parola del Popolo, 1954; *A Liberal's Answer to Communism,* Liberal International, 1954; *American Capitalism* (pamphlet), U.S. Department of State, 1956; *Croce, Sforza, de Gasperi, e il publico americano,* Edizioni Panorama, 1956; *Excerpts from a Lecture on American Capitalism,* Ethyl Corp., 1956; *Liberal Democracy,* Doubleday, 1957 (published in England as *Liberal Democracy: An Essay on Liberty,* Pall Mall, 1958); *NATO: A Twentieth-Century Community of Nations,* Van Nostrand, 1957; *Education for Liberty: A Few Considerations* (pamphlet), Pall Mall, 1957; *The Economics of Freedom: American Capitalism Today,* Doubleday, 1959; *Liberty and Progress: Some Considerations* (pamphlet), Pall Mall, 1959.

Prospettive americane, Opere Nuove, 1960; *Western Roots in Europe: An Aid to the Educated Traveller,* Pall Mall, 1961, Roy, 1962; *Cavour and the Unification of Italy,* Van Nostrand, 1961; *La Resistenza nell'Anconetano e nel Piceno,* Opere Nuove, 1962; *Gli Stati Unitida Roosevelt a Kennedy: Breve storia della nazione americana dal 12 April 1945 al 22 Novembre 1963,* Edizioni Scientifiche Italiane, 1964; *Italy,* Prentice-Hall, 1965.

"A Stone of Stumbling": The Debate on Democracy Between the Second and Third Internationals, 1919-1922, Smith College, 1970; *A Pictorial History of the Italian People,* Crown, 1972.

Editor: *La Science politique contemporaine,* UNESCO, 1950; *Contemporary Social Science: The Eastern Hemisphere,* Stackpole, 1954; *Lettere de Giacinta Salvadori,* Segreti, 1953; (and author of introduction) *Locke and Liberty: Selections from the Works of John Locke,* Pall Mall, 1960; *The American Economic System: An Anthology of Writings Concerning the American Democracy,* Bobbs-Merrill, 1963; *Modern Socialism,* Walker & Co., 1968; *European Liberalism,* Wiley and Interscience, 1972.

WORK IN PROGRESS: Liberalism: An Essay; a book on the role of liberty in Europe, 1748-1961.

*   *   *

SAMACHSON, Dorothy (Mirkin)   1914-

PERSONAL: Surname pronounced *Sam*-ak-son; born August 22, 1914, in New York, N.Y.; daughter of Harry and Menya (Friedman) Mirkin; married Joseph Samachson (an associate clinical professor of oral biology) December 12, 1937; children: Michael, Miriam (Mrs. David A. Berkley). *Education:* Hunter College (now Hunter College of the City University of New York), student, 1932-34. *Religion:* Jewish. *Home and Office:* 185 North Marion St., Oak Park, Ill. 60301.

CAREER: Pianist and accompanist for dancers, singers, and instrumentalists, New York, N.Y., 1936-62; piano teacher, Oak Park, Ill., 1962—. *Member:* American Federation of Musicians.

WRITINGS: Let's Meet the Ballet, Henry Schuman, 1951.

With husband, Joseph Samachson: *Let's Meet the Theatre,* Abelard, 1954; *The Dramatic Story of the Theatre,* Abelard, 1955; *Good Digging: The Story of Archaeology* (Junior Literary Guild selection), Rand McNally, 1960; *The Fabulous World of Opera* (Junior Literary Guild selection), Rand McNally, 1962; *Rome,* Rand McNally, 1964; *Masters of Music: Their Works, Their Lives, Their Times,* Doubleday, 1967; *The First Artists,* Doubleday, 1970; *The Russian Ballet and Three of Its Masterpieces,* Lothrop, 1971. Dance reviewer for *Chicago Daily News,* 1970—.

* * *

SAMHABER, Ernst Marzell 1901-

PERSONAL: Born April 28, 1901, in Valparaiso, Chile; son of August Stenger and Therese (Marzell) Samhaber; married Ilse Pruhlen, May 22, 1947. *Education:* University of Munich, Dr. phil., and Referendarirus iuris. *Religion:* Roman Catholic. *Home:* Oberstrasse 81, Hamburg, Germany.

CAREER: August Samhaber & Co. (tanneries), Santiago, Chile, partner, 1923-32; professor of ancient history in Santiago, 1928; Iberoamerikanisches Institut, Berlin, Germany, chief of Chile section, 1928-31; *Deutsche Zukunft,* Berlin, Germany, editor, 1937-41; *Die Zeit,* Hamburg, Germany, editor, 1946; with Institute of Economy, Santiago, Chile, 1949-50; *Europakurier,* Hamburg, Germany, editor, 1950-51; Technische Universitat, Berlin, Germany, teacher of sociology, 1957-61. *Member:* Lions Club (Hamburg).

WRITINGS: Die rohstoffrage in wirtschaft und politik, Schaffstein, 1939; *Suedamerika: Gesicht-geistgeschichte,* Govert, 1939; *Wie werden kriege finanziert?,* Gloeckner, 1940; *Die neuen wirtschaftsformer, 1914-1940,* Paul Neff, 1941; *Der Magier des Kredits: Glueck und Unglueck des John Law of Lauriston,* Bruckmann, 1941; *Spanisch-Suedamerika,* Deutscher Verlag, 1941; *Ueberwindung der Krise: Englands Problem heute,* Claassen & Goverts, 1948; *Die neue Welt: Wandlungen in Suedamerika—Eine Fibel,* Badischer Verlag, 1949; *125 Jahre Hamburger Sparcasse von 1827, 1827-1952,* [Hamburg], 1952; *Geschichte der Vereinigten Staaten von Nordamerika: Werden der Weltmacht,* Bruckmann, 1954; *Suedamerika von heute: Ein Kontinent wird new entdeckt,* Scherz & Goverts, 1954; *Kleine Geschichte Suedamerikas,* Scheffler, 1954; *Knaurs Geschichte der Entdeckungsreisen: Die Grossen Fahrten ins Unbekannte,* Th. Knaur Nachf., 1955; (with Otto A. Freidrich) *Hundert Jahre Weltwirtschaft im Spiegel eines Unternehmens,* Klemm, 1956; *Kaufleute wandeln die Welt,* Scheffler, 1960, translation by E. Osers published as *Merchants Make History: How Trade Has Influenced the Course of History Throughout the World,* Harrap, 1963, John Day, 1964; *Welt von heute, Welt von morgen: Eine Soziologie der Konjunktur,* Scheffler, 1961; *Das Geld: Eine Kulturgeschichte,* Keysersche Verlagsbuchhandlung, 1964; *Suedamerika und der Kommunismus,* [Hannover], 1964; *Geschichte Europas,*

DuMont Schauberg, 1967; *Wirtschaft verstaendlich gemacht,* Scheffler, 1968; *Die grossen Erfindungen,* Ueberreuter, 1971.

WORK IN PROGRESS: Das verpfuschte Gesichtesbild: Weltgeschichte.

* * *

SAMPSON, Ronald Victor 1918-

PERSONAL: Born November 12, 1918, in St. Helens, Lancashire, England; son of Leonard and Emily (Middlehurst) Sampson; married Ruth W. Blundell, January 9, 1943; children: Eroica Jill, Elizabeth Eve. *Education:* Attended Cowley School, St. Helens, England; Keble College, Oxford, B.A., 1947, M.A., 1947; Nuffield College, Oxford, D.Phil, 1951. *Politics:* For unilateral disarmament. *Home:* "Beechcroft," Hinton Charterhouse, Bath, Somerset, England.

CAREER: John Hay Whitney visting fellow to United States, 1951-52; University of Bristol, Bristol, England, lecturer in politics, 1953—.

WRITINGS: Progress in the Age of Reason: The Seventeenth Century to the Present Day, Harvard University Press, 1956; (contributor) Philip Appleman, William A. Madden, and Michael Wolff, editors, *1859: Entering an Age of Crisis,* Indiana University Press, 1959; *Equality and Power,* Heinemann, 1965, published in America as *The Psychology of Power,* Pantheon, 1966.

* * *

SAMUELS, Gertrude

PERSONAL: Daughter of Sam and Sarah Samuels; children: Paul. *Education:* Attended George Washington University. *Office:* New York Times, New York, N.Y. 10036.

CAREER: Staff member of *New York Post, Newsweek,* and *Time* prior to 1943; *New York Times,* New York, N.Y., staff writer for Sunday department, 1943—, staff writer and photographer, 1947—. Special United Nations observer for United Nations Children's Fund in eight European countries, 1948. War correspondent in Korea, 1952. *Member:* Authors Guild, Dramatists Guild, American Newspaper Guild, American Society of Magazine Photographers, Actors Studio, Playwrights Unit (New York). *Award, honors:* Front Page Awards of American Newspaper Guild for articles on Little Rock crisis and drug addiction; George Polk Award of Long Island University for articles on school desegregation; citation from Overseas Press Club for international reporting; various photography awards.

WRITINGS: Report on Israel, Herzl Press, 1960; *B-G, Fighter of Goliaths: The Story of David Ben-Gurion,* photos by Samuels, Crowell, 1961; *The People vs. Baby: A Documentary Novel,* Doubleday, 1967; *The Secret of Gonen,* photos by Samuels, Avon, 1969. Author of several plays, including "The Corrupters," 1969, "The Plant That Talked Back" and "Judah The Maccabee and Me," the latter two produced in New York at Lambs Club Theatre, January 26, 1970. *New York Times* articles anthologized in school texts and other books; "The Corrupters," included in *The Best Short Plays, 1969,* edited by Stanley Richards, Chilton, 1969. Contributor of articles and pictures to *Nation, National Geographic, Saturday Evening Post,* and *Harper's.*

WORK IN PROGRESS: A full-length play, *The Assignment.*

BIOGRAPHICAL/CRITICAL SOURCES: U.S. Camera, January, 1961; *New York Times Book Review,* May 7, 1967; *Variety,* February 14, 1970.

SANCHEZ, Jose M(ariano) 1932-

PERSONAL: Born November 1, 1932, in Santa Fe, N.M.; son of Manuel A. and Amalia (Sena) Sanchez; married Carol Mahan, November 17, 1956; children: Clara Manuel, Maria, Leonora, Rodrigo. *Education:* St. Louis University, B.S., 1954, A.M., 1957; University of New Mexico, Ph.D., 1961. *Office:* Department of History, St. Louis University, St. Louis, Mo. 63103.

CAREER: St. Louis University, St. Louis, Mo., assistant professor, 1962-69, professor of history, 1969—, chairman of department, 1971—. *Military service:* U.S. Army, 1954-56. *Member:* American Historical Association, Catholic Historical Association.

WRITINGS: Reform and Reaction: The Politico-Religious Background of the Spanish Civil War, University of North Carolina Press, 1964. Associate editor, *Great Events: Modern European History,* Salem Press-McGraw, 1971. Contributor of articles to *Church History* and *Catholic Historical Review;* book reviewer for *St. Louis Globe-Democrat, America,* and *Catholic Historical Review.*

WORK IN PROGRESS: Anticlericalism: A Brief History.

* * *

SANDERS, Joan Allred 1924-

PERSONAL: Born August 28, 1924, in Three Forks, Mont.; daughter of M. Thatcher (a professor of speech and drama) and Pearl (Oberhansley) Allred; married Raymond T. Sanders (an associate professor of cellular physiology), August 10, 1947; children: Raymond Craig. *Education:* Weber Junior College, A.A., 1944; Leland Stanford Junior University, student, 1947; University of Utah, B.A. (cum laude), 1948. *Politics:* "Variable." *Home:* 815 Canyon Rd., Logan, Utah 84321. *Agent:* Curtis Brown Ltd., 60 East 56th St., New York, N.Y. 10022.

CAREER: Former library and teaching assistant; freelance writer.

WRITINGS: La Petite: The Life of Louise de la Valliere, Houghton, 1959 (published in England as *The Devoted Mistress: A Life of Louise de la Valliere,* Longmans, 1959); *The Marquis,* Houghton, 1963; *The Nature of Witches,* Houghton, 1964; (with Geoffrey F. Hall) *D'Artagnan: The Ultimate Musketeer,* Houghton, 1964; *Baneful Sorceress; or, The Countess Bewitched,* Houghton, 1969. Contributor of short stories to *Saturday Evening Post, Canadian Home Journal, Canadian Liberty,* of plays to *Plays Magazine,* and of verse to *Scholastic, Utah Sings,* and *Inland.*

SIDELIGHTS: Mrs. Sanders lived in Uppsala, Sweden, where her husband held a postdoctoral fellowship for two years.

BIOGRAPHICAL/CRITICAL SOURCES: Best Sellers, November 1, 1969.

* * *

SANDERS, Leonard 1929-
(Dan Thomas)

PERSONAL: Born January 15, 1929, in Denver, Colo.; son of Leonard M. (a purchasing agent) and Jacqueline (Thomas) Sanders; married Florine Cooter (a freelance writer), August 21, 1956. *Education:* Attended University of Oklahoma. *Home:* 4200 Clayton Rd. West, Fort Worth, Tex. 76116. *Agent:* Oliver Swan, Paul R. Reynolds & Son, 599 Fifth Ave., New York, N.Y. 10017. *Office:* Fort Worth Star-Telegram, 400 West Seventh St., Fort Worth, Tex. 76102.

CAREER: Newspaperman in Wichita Falls, Tex., and Oklahoma City, Norman, and Enid, Okla., *Fort Worth Star-Telegram,* Fort Worth, Tex., fine arts editor, 1958—. *Military service:* U.S. Naval Reserve, two years sea duty.

WRITINGS: Four-Year Hitch, Ace Books, 1961; *The Wooden Horseshoe,* Doubleday, 1964; (under pseudonym Dan Thomas) *The Seed* (science fiction), Ballantine, 1968. Contributor of articles to *True* and other magazines.

WORK IN PROGRESS: A novel; a nonfiction book on unexplored aspects of Southwest history.

* * *

SANDERS, Norman (Joseph) 1929-

PERSONAL: Born April 22, 1929, in Birkenhead, England; son of Henry and Elizabeth (Jordon) Sanders; married Marjorie Cooper (a university teacher), July 30, 1951. *Education:* University of Birmingham, Birmingham, England, diploma in education and B.A. (honors), 1951; Shakespeare Institute, Stratford on Avon, England, Ph.D., 1957. *Home:* 7113 Deane Hill Dr., Knoxville, Tenn. 37919. *Office:* English Department, University of Tennessee, Knoxville, Tenn. 37916.

CAREER: University of Alabama, Tuscaloosa, assistant professor of English, 1957-58; Shakespeare Institute, Stratford on Avon, England, fellow, 1958-62; University of Tennessee, Knoxville, associate professor, 1962-65, professor of English, 1965—. Secretary and assistant to editor of *Shakespeare Survey,* 1958-63. *Military service:* British Army, Educational Corps, 1951-53. *Member:* Modern Language Association of America, Shakespeare Association of America, Renaissance Society of America, Modern Humanities Research Association, International Association of Professors of English, South Atlantic Modern Language Association, Southeastern Renaissance Conference, Bibliographical Society of Virginia, Malone Society. *Awards, honors:* Fulbright award, 1957.

WRITINGS: (Editor with Alwin Thaler) *Shakespearean Essays,* University of Tennessee Press, 1964; (editor) Shakespeare, *Julius Caesar,* Penguin, 1967; (contributor) *A Book of Masques: In Honour of Allardyce Nicoll,* Cambridge University Press, 1967; *The Taming of the Shrew: A Scene-by-Scene Analysis with Critical Commentary,* American R.D.M., 1967; (editor) Shakespeare, *The Two Gentlemen of Verona,* Penguin, 1968; (contributor) K.L. Knickerbocker and H.W. Reninger, editors, *Interpreting Literature: Preliminaries to Literary Judgment,* 4th edition, Holt, 1969; (editor) Robert Greene, *The Scottish History of James IV,* Methuen, 1970; (editor) Shakespeare, *Richard II,* W.C. Brown, 1970. Contributor of articles to literary journals.

WORK IN PROGRESS: Editing Shakespeare's *Henry VI, Part 1;* editing the plays of John Marston.

SIDELIGHTS: Sanders teaches from September through May each year, and spends the remaining months at Stratford on Avon and in France. *Avocational interests:* Theatre and caricature.

* * *

SANDERS, Thomas Griffin 1932-

PERSONAL: Born April 18, 1932, in Mineola, N.Y.; son of Samuel Edwin (a businessman) and Sarah (Griffin) Sanders; married Louise Chesebro, July 17, 1961; children: Dorcas Rebekah, Charles William. *Education:* Duke University, A.B., 1952; studied at Union Theological Seminary, New York, N.Y., 1952-53, and University of Copenhagen, 1953-54; Columbia University, Ph.D., 1958. *Politics:* Democrat. *Religion:* Protestant. *Home:* 401 Benefit St., Providence, R.I. 02903.

CAREER: Sweet Briar College, Sweet Briar, Va., assistant professor of religion, 1957-59; Brown University, Providence, R.I., assistant professor of religious studies, 1959—. Member: Society for the Scientific Study of Religion, Religious Research Association, National Association of Biblical Instructors, Phi Beta Kappa.

WRITINGS: Protestant Concepts of Church and State: Historical Backgrounds and Approaches for the Future, Holt, 1964; Catholic Innovation in a Changing Latin America, Centro Intercultural de Documentacion (Cuernavaca, Mexico), 1969. „

WORK IN PROGRESS: A book relating a Protestant ethic to problems of church and state; a study of Roman Catholic thought and action in respect to Latin American church-state and social problems.

AVOCATIONAL INTERESTS: Long-distance running.

*   *   *

SANDERSON, Milton W(illiam)   1910-

PERSONAL: Born July 29, 1910, in Pittsburg, Kan.; son of William Calvin and Flora (McKinley) Sanderson; divorced; children: Steven Carl. Education: University of Kansas, A.B., 1932, M.A., 1933, Ph.D., 1937; additional study at University of Michigan Biological Station, 1935, 1936. Residence: Urbana, Ill. Agent: Ruth Cantor, 120 West 12th St., New York, N.Y. 10036. Office: Illinois Natural History Survey, Urbana, Ill. 61801.

CAREER: University of Arkansas, Fayetteville, instructor and assistant entomologist, 1937-42; Illinois Natural History Survey, Urbana, Ill., primarily engaged in research on beetles, 1942—, as assistant entomologist, 1942-47, associate taxonomist, 1947-54, taxonomist in charge of identification service, 1955—. Discoverer of many species of insects new to science. University of Illinois, Urbana, consultant for graduate students, 1942—. Member: Entomological Society of America (fellow), Coleopterists Society, American Entomological Society, Association of Economic Entomologists, Society of Systematic Zoology, Society for Study of Evolution, American Association for Advancement of Science (fellow), Illinois State Academy of Science (chairman of zoology section, grants committees), Arkansas Academy of Sciences, Kansas Entomological Society, Entomological Society of Washington, Sigma Xi, Phi Sigma. Awards, honors: National Science Foundation grant for scientific investigation in West Indies, 1958-62.

WRITINGS: A Monographic Revision of the North American Species of Stenelmis, University of Kansas Press, 1938; The Phyllophaga of Hispaniola, Museum of Comparative Zoology, Harvard University, 1951; (with Melville Harrison Hatch and others) Beetles of the Pacific Northwest, Volume II, Staphyliniformia, University of Washington Press, 1957; (co-author) Ward and Whipple's Freshwater Biology, Wiley, 1959; (with John Mark Kingsolver) A Selected Bibliography of Insect-Vascular Plant Associations in the United States and Canada, Illinois Natural History Survey, 1962, reissued as A Selected Bibliography of Insect-Vascular Plant Associational Studies, Agricultural Research Service, U.S. Department of Agriculture, 1967; (with James Sterling Ayars) Butterflies, Skippers, and Moths, Whitman Publishing, 1964. Scientific editor for film, "How to Collect Insects," produced by Illinois Natural History Survey in 1960. Contributor to professional journals, and to Proceedings of California Academy of Sciences, 1965. Editor of coleoptera section, Biological Abstracts; contributing editor, Coleopterists Bulletin; member of editorial board, Entomological Society of America.

WORK IN PROGRESS: Maybeetles of West Indies, completion expected in 1975.

SANDERSON, Sabina W(arren)   1931-
(Marion Fawcett)

PERSONAL: Born August 19, 1931, in Upland, Pa.; daughter of Richard and Sabina (Grzybowski) Warren; married Ivan Terence Sanderson (a writer and editor), May 4, 1972. Education: Attended University of Delaware, 1949-52. Address: R.D.1, Ivan Rd., Columbia, N.J. 07832.

CAREER: Hahnemann Medical College and Hospital, Philadelphia, Pa., secretary in pediatric department, 1953-59; J.B. Lippincott Co. (publishing firm), Philadelphia, Pa., associate editor, medical book publishing division, 1959-65; American Philosophical Society Library, Philadelphia, Pa., secretarial assistant, 1965-68; Society for Investigation of the Unexplained, Columbia, N.J., executive secretary, assistant to the director, 1968—.

WRITINGS: An Index to Films in Review: 1950-1959, National Board of Review of Motion Pictures, 1961, 1960-64 supplement, 1966. Contributor to Films in Review and to professional journals. Executive editor, Pursuit.

WORK IN PROGRESS: A panoramic outline history of the world.

SIDELIGHTS: Miss Fawcett is competent in French and a smattering of about five other languages. Avocational interests: Evolution (geological, zoological, sociological), natural sciences, Chinese art, cats, and tangible unexplaineds.

*   *   *

SARRAUTE, Nathalie   1902-

PERSONAL: Born July 18, 1902, in Ivanovo, Russia; daughter of Ilya (a chemist) and Pauline (a writer; maiden name, Chatounovsky) Tcherniak; married Raymond Sarraute (a barrister), July 28, 1925; children: Claude (Mrs. L.F. Revel), Anne (Mrs. Sacha Vierny), Dominique. Education: Sorbonne, University of Paris, licence d'anglais, license en droit, 1925; attended Oxford University, 1921. Home: 12 Avenue Pierre I de Serbie, Paris 16, France. Agent: Renee Spodheim Associates, 698 West End Ave., New York 25, N.Y.

CAREER: Member of French Bar, 1926-1941; full time writer, 1941—. Awards, honors: International Publishers Prize ($10,000), 1964, for The Golden Fruits.

WRITINGS: Tropismes, Denoel, 1939, translation by Maria Jolas published as Tropisms, Braziller, 1967 (also see below); Portrait d'un Inconnu (novel), with preface by Jean-Paul Sartre, Robert Marin, 1948, translation by Jolas published as Portrait of a Man Unknown, Braziller, 1958; Martereau (novel), Gallimard, 1953, translation by Jolas published as Martereau, Braziller, 1959; L'Ere du Soupcon (essays), Gallimard, 1956, translation by Jolas published as The Age of Suspicion, Braziller, 1963 (published in England as Tropisms [and] The Age of Suspicion, Calder, 1964); Le Planetarium (novel), Gallimard, 1959, translation by Jolas published as The Planetarium, Braziller, 1960; Les Fruits d'Or (novel), Gallimard, 1963, translation by Jolas published as The Golden Fruits, Braziller, 1964; Le Silence, suivi de Le Mensonge, Gallimard, 1967, translation by Jolas published in England as Silence: and the Lie, Calder, 1969; Entre la vie et la mort (novel), Gallimard, 1968, translation by Jolas published as Between Life and Death, Braziller, 1969; Isma; ou, Cequi s'appelle rien. Suivi de Le silence et Le mensonge, Gallimard, 1970; Vous les entendez?, Gallimard, 1972, translation by Jolas published as Do You Hear Them?, Braziller, 1973. Contributor to Times Literary Supplement, Books and Bookmen, Temps Modernes, Nouvelle Revue Francaise.

SIDELIGHTS: Believing that the existing novel, in the tradition of Balzac and Stendhal, was dead, Mme. Sarraute began writing her *Tropismes* during the winter of 1932-33. Today many would agree with Claude Mauriac who calls her "the only living author who has created anything new after Proust." Her *nouveaux romans,* she says, are "based on the quest of an unknown reality." Critic Henri Peyre disparages her effort, calling it "an honest, pedestrian, and fumbling search for authenticity. But good intentions count scantly in literature." By suppressing plot and leaving her characters for the most part anonymous, she is freed from the conventions of fiction to concentrate on people's movements, often nebulous movements, "those hidden dramatic actions, those tropisms." Her characters are not characters in the usual sense, but rather what Jean-Paul Sartre refers to as "a continual coming and going between the particular and the general." In his preface to *Portrait of a Man Unknown,* Sartre writes: "Nathalie Sarraute seeks to safeguard her sincerity as a storyteller. She takes her characters neither from within nor from without, for the reason that we are, both for ourselves and for others, entirely within and without at the same time."

Mme. Sarraute believes that the contemporary reader is ever suspicious of what the author has to offer. Hence, the author must be suspicious of his own approach. In *The Age of Suspicion* she writes: "As regards the character, he [the author] realizes that it is nothing other than a crude label which he himself makes use of, without real conviction and by way of convenience, for the purpose of orienting, very approximately, his own behavior. So he is wary of the abrupt, spectacular types of action that model the character with a few resounding whacks; he is also wary of plot, which winds itself round the character like wrappings, giving it, along with an appearance of cohesiveness and life, mummylike stiffness."

"When the sensation is strong enough," she once said, "form follows." Her masterful style is what Sartre accurately calls "stumbling, groping, ... with its honesty and numerous misgivings, a style that approaches the object with reverent precautions, withdraws from it suddenly out of a sort of modesty, or through timidity before its complexity, then, when all is said and done, suddenly presents us with the drooling monster, almost without having touched it, through the magic of an image." Her narrative is akin to ripples on water, reflecting and blurring the currents underneath, resulting in what she calls "soudings [which] are psychology itself, presented in the condensed form of images, in the choice of words, of repetitions of rhythms which show rather than comment upon or define the real content which they symbolize." She once observed that "the language has not yet been discovered that can explain at a single stroke what one perceives in a blink of the eye...."

Mme. Sarraute is fluent in Russian, English and German.

BIOGRAPHICAL/CRITICAL SOURCES: Critique (Paris), January, 1954, August-September, 1956; *The Contemporary French Novel,* by Henri Peyre, Oxford University Press, 1955; *Yale French Studies,* winter, 1955-56, summer, 1959, spring-summer, 1961; the Jean-Paul Sartre introduction to *Portrait of a Man Unknown,* Braziller, 1958; *Revue de Paris,* June, 1958; *The New Literature,* by Claude Mauriac, Braziller, 1959; *Lettres Nouvelles,* April 29, 1959; *French Review,* December, 1959; *Times Literary Supplement,* January 1, 1960, January 30, 1964; *Modern Fiction Studies,* winter, 1960-61; *The French New Novel,* by Laurent Le Sage, Pennsylvania State University Press, 1962; *Critique: Studies in Modern Fiction,* winter, 1963-64; Richard Kostelanetz, editor, *On Contemporary Literature,* Avon, 1964; *New York Times Book Review,* February 9, 1964, May 21,

1967, May 18, 1969; *New York Review of Books,* March 5, 1964, July 31, 1969; Harry T. Moore, *French Literature Since World War II,* Southern Illinois University Press, 1966; Henri Peyre, *French Novelists of Today,* Oxford University Press, 1967; *Saturday Review,* May 6, 1967, May 24, 1969; *Christian Science Monitor,* July 15, 1969; *New Yorker,* November 22, 1969; *New York Times,* July 24, 1970.†

*   *   *

SARTRE, Jean-Paul 1905-

PERSONAL: Born June 21, 1905, in Paris, France; son of Jean-Baptiste (a naval officer) and Anne-Marie (Schweitzer) Sartre. *Education:* Attended Lycee Henri IV, Lycee de la Rochelle, Lycee Louis-le-Grand; Ecole Normale Superieure, agrege de philosophie, 1930; further study in Egypt, Italy, Greece, and in Germany under Edmund Husserl and Martin Heidegger. *Politics:* Communistic, not Party member. *Religion:* Atheist. *Home:* 42 rue Bonaparte, Paris 6e, France. *Office:* Les Temps modernes, 30 rue de l'Universite, Paris 7, France.

CAREER: Professeur of philosophy at Lycee du Havre, 1931-32, 1934-36, Institut Francais, Berlin, 1933-34, Lycee de Laon, 1936-37, Lycee Pasteur, 1937-39, Lycee Condorcet, 1941-44; full-time writer, 1944—. Founded *Les Temps modernes,* 1945, editor, 1945—. Visiting lecturer at Harvard, Columbia, Yale, and Princeton Universities. *Military service:* Meteorological Corps, 1929-31; French Army, 1939-40; prisoner of war in Germany for nine months, 1940-41. Served in Resistance Movement, 1941-44, wrote for its underground newspapers, *Combat,* and *Les Lettres Francaises.* One of founders of the French Rally of Revolutionary Democrats. *Member:* American Academy of Arts and Sciences. *Awards, honors:* French Popular Novel Prize, 1940, for *La Nausee;* French Legion d'honneur, 1945 (refused); New York Drama Critics Award for the best foreign play of the season, 1947, for *No Exit;* French Grand Novel Prize, 1950, for *La Nausee;* Omegna Prize (Italy), 1960, for total body of work; named Honorary Fellow, Modern Language Association of America; Nobel Prize for Literature ($53,-000), 1964 (refused).

WRITINGS—Philosophy: *L'imagination,* [Paris], 1936, 4th edition, Presses universitaires de France, 1956, translation by Forrest Williams published as *Imagination: A Psychological Critique,* University of Michigan Press, 1962; *Esquisse d'une theorie des emotions, of a Theory,* Philosophical Library, 1948 (translation by Bernard Frechtman published as *The Emotions: Outline of a Theory,* Philosophical Library, 1948, (translation by Philip Mairet published in England as *Sketch for a Theory of the Emotions,* Methuen, 1962); *L'imaginaire: Psychologie phenomenologique de l'imagination,* Gallimard, 1940, translation published as *The Psychology of Imagination,* Rider & Co., 1950; *L'etre et le neant: Essai d'ontologie phenomenologique,* Gallimard, 1943, translation by Hazel E. Barnes published as *Being and Nothingness: An Essay on Phenomenological Ontology,* Philosophical Library, 1956, abridged edition, Citadel, 1964; *L'existentialisme est un humanisme,* Nagel, 1946, translation by Frechtman published as *Existentialism,* Philosophical Library, 1947, reprinted, Kraus, 1965, (translation by Mairet published in England as *Existentialism and Humanism,* Methuen, 1948); *Existential Psychoanalysis* (selections from Barnes's translation of *Being and Nothingness),* Philosophical Library, 1953; *Existentialism and Human Emotions* (selections from *Existentialism* and *Being and Nothingness),* Philosophical Library, 1957; *La Transcendance de l'ego: Esquisse d'une description phenomenologique* (first published in *Recherches Philosophique),* translation by Forrest Williams and Robert Kirkpatrick published as *Transcendence of the*

Ego: An Existentialist Theory of Consciousness, Noonday, 1957, published under original title, J. Vrin, 1965; *Critique de la raison dialectique, precede de Question de methode,* Gallimard, 1960; (with others) *Marxisme et Existentialisme,* Plon, 1962; *Jean-Paul Sartre: Choix de textes,* edited by J. Sebille, Nathan, 1962, 2nd edition, 1966; *Essays in Aesthetics,* selected and translated by Wade Baskin, Philosophical Library, 1963; *Question de Methode* (first published as prefatory essay in *Critique de la raison dialectique, precede de Question de Method*), translation by Barnes published as *Search for a Method ,* Knopf, 1963 (published in England as *The Problem of Method,* Methuen, 1964), published under original title, Gallimard, 1967; *The Philosophy of Jean-Paul Sartre,* (translations from extracts of his work), edited by Robert Denoon Cummings, Random House, 1966; *Of Human Freedom,* edited by Baskin, Philosophical Library, 1967; *Essays in Existentialism,* selected and edited with a foreword by Baskin, Citadel, 1967; *The Wisdom of Jean-Paul Sartre* (selections from Barnes's translation of *Being and Nothingness*), Philosophical Library, 1968; *Textes choisis,* edited by Marc Beigbeder and Gerard Deledalle, Bordes, 1968.

Fiction: *La Nausee,* Gallimard, 1938, translation by Lloyd Alexander published as *Nausea,* New Directions, 1949 (published in England as *The Diary of Antoine Requentin,* J. Lehmann, 1949), new edition with illustrations by Walter Spitzer, Editions Lidis, 1964, new translation by Robert Baldick, Penguin, 1965; *Le Mur,* edition with preface by Jean-Louis Curtis, published as *The Wall, and Other Stories,* New Directions, 1948, new edition, with preface by Jean-Louis, published as *Le Mur,* Editions Rencontre, 1965, new edition with illustrations by Spitzer, Editions Lidis, 1965; *Les Chemins de la liberte:* Volume I: *L'age de raison,* Gallimard, 1945, new edition with illustrations by Spitzer, Editions Lidis, 1965, Volume II: *Le Sursis,* Gallimard, 1945, Volume III: *La Mort dans l'ame,* Gallimard, 1949, translation published as *The Roads of Freedom:* Volume I: *The Age of Reason,* translated by Eric Sutton, Knopf, 1947, new edition with introduction by Henri Peyre, Bantam, 1968, Volume II: *The Reprieve,* translated by Sutton, Knopf, 1947, Volume III: *Iron in the Soul,* translated by Gerard Hopkins, Hamish Hamilton, 1950, published in America as *Troubled Sleep,* Knopf, 1951; *Intimacy, and Other Stories,* translated by Alexander, Berkley Publishing Corp., 1956.

Plays: *Les Mouches,* Gallimard, 1943, new edition edited by Robert J. North, Harrap, 1963, new edition edited by F.C. St. Aubyn and Robert G. Marshall, Harper, 1963; *Huis-clos,* Gallimard, 1945, new edition edited by Jacques Hardre and George B. Daniel, Appleton, 1962; *Les Mouches* and *Huis-clos,* translation by Stuart Gilbert published as *The Flies* [and] *In Camera,* Hamish Hamilton, 1946, published in America as *No Exit,* [and] *The Flies,* Knopf, 1947; *Morts sans sepulture,* Marguerat, 1946; *La Putain respectueuse,* Nagel, 1946, translation published as *The Respectful Prostitute: Art and Action,* Twice a Year Press, 1949; *Theatre* (includes *Les Mouches, Huis-clos, Mort sans sepulture* and *La Putain respectueuse*), Gallimard, 1947; *Les jeux sont faits* (screenplay), Nagel, 1947, translation by Louise Varese published as *The Chips Are Down,* Lear, 1948, published as *Les jeux sont faits,* edited by Mary Elizabeth Storer, Appleton, 1952; *Les Mains sales,* Gallimard, 1948, published in England as *Les Mains sales: Piece en sept tableaux,* edited by Geoffrey Brereton, Methuen, 1963; *L'engrenage* (scenario), Nagel, 1948, translation by Mervyn Savill published as *In the Mesh,* A. Dakers, 1954; *Three Plays,* translation by Lionel Abel of *Morts sans sepulture (The Victors), Les Main sales (Dirty Hands),* and *La Putain respectuese (The Respectable*

Prostitute), Knopf, 1949, translation by Kitty Black, Hamish Hamilton, 1949; *Crime passionnel,* first published in 1949, translation by Black published as *Crime Passionnel,* Methuen, 1961; *Le Diable et le bon Dieu,* Gallimard, 1951, translation by Black published as *Lucifer and the Lord,* Hamish Hamilton, 1953, published in America as *The Devil and the Good Lord, and Two Other Plays,* Knopf, 1960; (adapter) Alexander Dumas, *Kean,* Gallimard, 1954; *No Exit, and Three Other Plays,* including *The Flies, Dirty Hands,* and *The Respectful Prostitute,* Vintage, 1956; *Nekrassov,* Gallimard, 1956, translation by Sylvia and George Leeson, published as *Nekrassov: A Farce,* Hamish Hamilton, 1956; *Les Sequestres d'Altona,* Gallimard, 1960, translation by S. and G. Leeson published as *Loser Wins,* Hamish Hamilton, 1960, published in America as *The Condemned of Altona,* Knopf, 1961, published as *Les Sequestres d'Altona,* edited and with an introduction by Philip Thody, University of London Press, 1965; *Three Plays: Crime Passionnel, Men Without Shadows, The Respectable Prostitute,* translated by Black, Hamish Hamilton, 1960; *Bariona,* Anjou-Copies, 1962, 2nd edition, E. Marescot, 1967; *Altona, Man Without Shadows, The Flies,* translation by S. and G. Leeson of *Les Sequestres d'Altona,* by Black of *Morts sans Sepulture,* and by Gilbert of *Les Mouches,* Penguin, 1962; *Black Orphee* (translation of "Orphee Noir" by S.W. Allen), Gallimard, 1963; *La Putain respectueuse, piece an un acte et deux tableaux: Suivi de Morts sans sepulture, piece en deux actes et quatre tableaux,* Gallimard, 1963; (adapter) Euripides, *The Trojan Women,* translated by Ronald Duncan, Knopf, 1967; *La Putain respectueuse, Le Diable et le Bon Dieu,* [Paris], 1968; *Three Plays,* includes *Kean: Or Disorder and Genius, Nekrassov, a Farce,* and *The Trojan Women,* Penguin, 1969; *Les Mains sales* (extracts) with analysis and notes by Gaston Meyer, Edition Bordas, 1971. Also author of "Les Sorceres de Salem" (screenplay), adapted from Arthur Miller's *The Crucible.*

Literary criticism and political writings: *Reflexions sur la question juive,* P. Morihien, 1947, translation by George J. Becker published as *Anti-Semite and Jew,* Schocken, 1948 (translation by Erik de Mauney published in England as *Portrait of the Anti-Semite,* Secker & Warburg, 1948); *Baudelaire: Precede d'une note de Michel Leiris,* Gallimard, 1947, translation by Martin Turnell published as *Baudelaire,* Horizon (London), 1949, New Directions, 1950; *Situations 1,* Gallimard, 1947; *Situations II,* Gallimard, 1948; *Qu'est-ce que le litterature?,* Gallimard, 1948 (first published in *Situations II*), translation by Frechtman published as *What Is Literature?,* Philosophical Library, 1949, also published as *Literature and Existentialism,* Citadel, 1962; *Situations III,* Gallimard, 1949; (with David Rousset and Gerard Rosenthal) *Entretiens sur la politique,* Gallimard, 1949; *Saint Genet, comedien et martyr,* Gallimard, 1952, translation by Frechtman published as *Saint Genet, Actor and Martyr,* Braziller, 1963; *Literary and Philosophical Essays* (excerpts from *Situations I* and *III*), translated by Annette Michelson, Criterion, 1955; *Literary Essays* (excerpts from *Situations I* and *III*), translated by Michelson, Philosophical Library, 1957; *Sartre on Cuba,* Ballantine, 1961; *Colonialisme et neo-colonialisme* (also included in *Situations V*), Gallimard, 1964; *Situations IV,* Gallimard, 1964, translation by Benita Eisler published as *Situations,* Braziller, 1965; *Situations V,* Gallimard, 1964; *Situations VI,* Gallimard, 1966; (contributor) Aime Cesaire, *Das politische Denken Lumumbas,* Verlag Klaus Wagenbach, 1966; *Situations VII,* Gallimard, 1967; *On Genocide,* with a summary of the evidence and the judgments of the International War Crimes Tribunal by Arlette el Kaim-Sartre, Beacon, 1968; *The Ghost of Stalin,* translated by Martha H. Fletcher and John R. Kleinschmidt, Braziller, 1968, (translation by Irene

Clephane published in England as *The Spectre of Stalin,* Hamish Hamilton, 1969); *Les Communistes et la paix* (first published in *Situations VI),* Gallimard, 1964, transation by Fletcher and Kleinschmidt, with "A Reply to Claude Lefort" translated by Philip R. Berk, published as *The Communists and Peace,* Braziller, 1968, translation by Clephane, Hamish Hamilton, 1969; *El Inteectual frente a la revolution,* Ediciones Hombre Nuevo, 1969; *Les Communistes ont peur de la revolution,* J. Didier, 1969; (with Vladimir Dedijer) *War Crimes in Vietnam,* Bertrand Russell Peace Foundation, 1971; *L'idiot de la famille,* Gallimard, 1971.

Contributor: *L'existentialisme, grand debat,* Editions Atlas, 1948; Leopold S. Senghor, editor, *Anthologie de la nouvelle poesie negre et malgache de langue francaise,* Presses Universitaires de France, 1948, 2nd edition, 1969.

Author of foreword, preface, or introduction: *Baudelaire: Ecrits intimes: Fusees, Mon coeur mis a nu, carnet, correspondance,* Editions du Point du jour, n.d.; Nathalie Sarraute, *Portrait d'un Inconnu,* Robert Marin, 1948; *Descartes, 1596-1650,* [Paris], 1946; Jean Genet, *Thief's Journal,* Olympia Press, 1954; Henri Cartier-Bresson, *D'une Chine a l'autre,* Thames & Hudson, 1956; Genet, *The Maids,* Grove Press, 1956; Henri Alleg (pseudonym of H. Salem), *The Question,* J. Calder, 1958; Andre Gorz, *Traitor,* J. Calder, 1960; Frantz Fanon, *Les Damnes de la Terre,* [Paris], 1961; Robert Lapoujade, *Peintures sur le theme des Emeutes: Triptyque sur la torture,* Gallerie Pierre Domec, 1961; Ronald D. Laing, *Reason & Violence: A Decade of Sartre's Philosophy, 1950-1960,* Tavistock Publications (London), 1964; Genet, *Our Lady of the Flowers,* Anthony Blond, 1964; George Michel, *La Promenade du dimanche,* Gallimard, 1967, adaptation by Jean Benedetti published as *The Sunday Walk,* Methuen Playscripts, 1968; Paul Nizan, *Aden-Arabie,* 2nd edition, MR Press (New York), 1968; Andre Puig, *L'Inacheve,* Gallimard, 1970; Antonin Liehm, editor, *Trois Generations,* Gallimard, 1970.

Other: (Editor) *L'Affaire Henri Martin,* Gallimard, 1953; *Sartre par lui-meme,* edited by Francis Jeanson, [Paris], 1955; (author of text) Andre Masson, *Vingt deux dessins sur le theme du desir,* F. Mourtot, 1961; *Les Mots* (autobiography), Gallimard, 1963, translation by Frechtman published as *The Words,* Braziller, 1964 (translation by Clephane published in England as *Words,* Hamish Hamilton, 1964); *J-P Sartre: Huis-clos, La nausee, Les Sequestres d'Altona, Reflexions sur la question juive, Critique de la raison dialectique, Kean,* edited by Kenneth Douglas and Joseph H. McMahon, originally published in 1963, reprinted, Kraus, 1968; *Sartre por Sartre,* edited by Juan Jose Sebreli, Jorge Alvarez, 1968; (editor with Bertrand Russell) *Das Vietnam Tribunal,* Rowohlt Verlag, 1970; *Gott ohne Gott,* including *Bariona* and a dialogue with Sartre, edited by Gotthold Hasenhuttl, Graz Verlag (Austria), 1972; author of unpublished play, "All the Treasures of the Earth," translated by Black. Contributor to numerous periodicals. Has adapted some of his plays for the screen.

WORK IN PROGRESS: Further volumes of autobiography.

SIDELIGHTS: When the Nobel Prize for Literature was announced on October 22, 1964, the chairman of the Swedish Academy's Nobel Committee hailed Jean-Paul Sartre as "the father of existentialist doctrine, which became this generation's intellectual self-defense." The accompanying announcement read that the man so honored was the first to freely reject the prize and the $53,000 that goes with it. In a statement in Paris, Sartre explained his position: "A writer who takes political, social, or literary positions must act only with the means that are his. Those means are the written word. A writer must not accept official awards because he would be adding the influence of the institution that crowned his work to the power of his pen. That is not fair to the reader. It is not the same thing," he continued, "if I sign Jean-Paul Sartre or if I sign Jean-Paul Sartre, Nobel Prize winner." His French contemporaries approved the Nobel Committee's choice; Marcel Jouhandeau remarked: "The most beautiful thing was to refuse. One grows by what one refuses."

Sartre has distinguished himself as perhaps *the* leading intellectual in the world today, an accomplished philosopher, novelist, playwright, essayist, anti-Freudian psychologist, lecturer, and conversationalist, all the while involved in a search for an intellectual reconciliation with the dominant forces of his time. The *New Statesman and Nation* wrote in 1956: "The Vatican has placed his works on the Index; yet Gabriel Marcel, himself a militant Catholic, regarded him as the greatest of French thinkers. The State Department found his novels subversive; but *Les Mains Sales* was the most effective counter-revolutionary play of the entire cold war. Sartre has been vilified by the Communists in Paris and feted by them in Vienna. No great philosopher ever had fewer disciples, but no other could claim the intellectual conquest of an entire generation." Another Nobel Prize winner, Albert Camus, once said that the prophets of France today are "Marx, Jean-Paul Sartre, and Jesus Christ. And in that order."

Sartre originally considered himself a phenomenologist, and he and his work were first labeled "existentialist" by Gabriel Marcel. His philosophy in part affirms that man is the sum of his acts, that any meaning the world may have must be given it by the individual, that one's life is significant only in relation to the lives of others, that consciousness is achieved only through anguish, that man, "condemned to be free," has the responsibility of free choice, and that man must heroically persist against odds.

Existentialism asserts that man is no more than an inanimate object until he chooses a course of action. From such a doctine of action it follows that man must take sides in issues; he must become engaged. Sartre himself, without becoming a Communist, chose the Soviet side in the early fifties, chose opposition to the Soviet Union during the Hungarian revolt, and, more recently, independence for Algeria, a choice which twice led to the bombing of his apartment by right-wing terrorists.

Sartre believes one must write as one must act—for one's own time. He at one time believed that literature could produce social change, though he now doubts it. He acknowledges the difficulties of communication between people, and in his own writing strives for lucidity. His works are the products of an orginal mind. Henri Peyre, in *The Contemporary French Novel,* writes: "First of all, his mastery of the language is extraordinary. . . . Metaphors are scarce, but they are precise, convincing, and sharply delineated. . . . Sartre's mastery is conspicuous in some of his dialogues, in an interior monologue purified of much of the irrelevancy and insignificance of the genre, and in his unorthodox use of the spoken language. . . . His language welcomes slang, profanity, and obscenity." Jacques Guicharneaud believes that "in literature his effort is very influential even among those who disagree with him. He brought a new approach to human beings and objects outside of the classic manner of literary expression." Of his own fictional creations Sartre says: "Every one of my characters, after having done anything, may still do anything whatever. . . . I never calculate whether the act is credible according to previous ones, but I take the situation and a freedom chained in situation." On the negative side, he has been criticized for his attachment to melodrama that is evident in his works. The *New York Times Book Review* notes that "His grandfather deplored his taste for bad literature, both as a reader and a writer. His doubtful taste persists even today, he admits; he still prefers to read detective novels rather than Wittgenstein."

In 1967 Sartre, with Bertrand Russell and others, participated in an international war crimes tribunal which resulted in their indictment of the United States for atrocities in the Vietnam War.

Sartre's plays have been produced numerous times throughout the Western world. By 1970, *The Respectful Prostitute* had been performed well over a thousand times in Munich alone since its revival there in 1967. "Intimacy Behind Closed Doors," based on his short story, was staged in Italy in 1969. Vernon Dobtcheff's translation of *The Flies* was performed in London in 1968, and *Kean* was first performed in England, at the Oxford Playhouse, from a translation by Frank Hauser, in 1970. An adaptation of the play *Les Mains Sales*, by D. Taradash, was produced in America under the title "Red Gloves." The play *L'Engrenage* was adapted for the screen and filmed in 1948. In 1968, The *Condemned of Altona* was made into a film directed by Vittorio de Sica. Screenrights to *The Devil and the Good Lord* were purchased in 1970. The trilogy, *The Roads to Freedom*, was made into a thirteen part television dramatization and shown on the BBC in 1970.

BIOGRAPHICAL/CRITICAL SOURCES—Articles: *Orbis Litterarum*, VI, 1948, pages 209-72, VII, 1949, pages 61-141; *New Statesman and Nation*, June 30, 1956; *London Magazine*, November, 1960; *Tulane Drama Review*, spring, 1961; *Times Literary Supplement*, April 2, 1964; *Newsweek*, October 5, 1964; *New York Times Book Review*, October 11, 1964; *New York Times*, October 23, 1964; *Prairie Schooner*, winter, 1965-66; *New Republic*, June 11, 1968.

Books: *Literature of the Graveyard: Jean-Paul Sartre, Francois Mauriac, Andre Malraux, Arthur Koestler*, by Roger Garaudy, International Publishers, 1948; Edmund Wilson, *Classics and Commercials*, Farrar, Straus, 1950; *The Psychology of Sartre*, by P.J.R. Dempsey, Newman Press, 1951; *Critique of Jean-Paul Sartre's Ontology*, by M. Natanson, University of Nebraska, 1951; *Sartre*, by R. M. Alberes, Editions Universitaires, 1953; *Sartre: His Philosophy and Psychoanalysis*, by S. Stern, Liberal Arts, 1953; *Sartre: Romantic Rationalist*, by Iris Murdoch, Yale University Press, 1953; *The Playwright as Thinker*, by Eric Bentley, Noonday, 1955; *The Contemporary French Novel*, by Henri Peyre, Oxford University Press, 1955; *Sartre par lui-meme*, by Francis Jeanson, Editions du Seuil, 1955; *Journey Through Dread*, by A. Ussher, Devin-Adair, 1955; *Stages on Sartre's Way, 1938-1952*, by R.J. Champigny, Indiana University Press, 1959; *Sartre*, by S. U. Zuidema, Presbyterian and Reformed, 1960; *Les Ecrivains en personne*, by Madeleine Chapsal, Julliard, 1960; *Jean-Paul Sartre*, by P. Thody, Hamish Hamilton, 1960; *Jean-Paul Sartre: To Freedom Condemned*, Philosophical Library, 1960; *Jean-Paul Sartre*, N.N. Greene, University of Michigan Press, 1960; *Jean-Paul Sartre: A Philosopher Without Faith*, by R. Marill, Philosophical Library, 1961; Toby Cole, editor, *Playwrights on Playwriting*, Hill & Wang, 1961; *The Philosophy of Existentialism*, by Gabriel Marcel, translated by Manya Harari, Citadel, 1961; *Sartre*, by F.R. Jameson, Yale University Press, 1961; *Sartre: A Collection of Critical Essays*, edited by E.G. Kern, Prentice-Hall, 1962; *Jean-Paul Sartre*, by M.W. Cranston, Peter Smith, 1963; Richard Kostelanetz, editor, *On Contemporary Literature*, Avon, 1964; Travis Bogard and William I. Oliver, editors, *Modern Drama: Essays in Criticism*, Oxford University Press (New York), 1965; Frederick Lumley, *New Trends in 20th Century Drama*,

Oxford University Press, 1966; Harry T. Moore, *French Literature Since World War II*, Southern University Press, 1966; Henri Peyre, *French Novelists of Today*, Oxford University Press (New York), 1967; Dorothy McCall, *The Theatre of Jean-Paul Sartre*, Columbia University Press, 1971; Joseph H. McMahon, *Human Beings: The World of Jean-Paul Sartre*, University of Chicago Press, 1971.†

*   *   *

SATIN, Joseph (Henry) 1922-

PERSONAL: Born December 16, 1922, in Philadelphia, Pa.; son of Philip Reuben (a salesman) and Harriet (Price) Satin; married Selma Rosen (an artist), January 13, 1946; children: Mark, Diane. *Education:* Temple University, student, 1938-41, B.S., 1946; Columbia University, A.M., 1948, Ph.D., 1952. *Office:* Midwestern University, Wichita Falls, Tex. 76308.

CAREER: Midwestern University, Wichita Falls, Tex., chairman of English department, 1963—. *Military service:* U.S. Army, 1942-46; served in European theater; received five battle stars. *Member:* National Council of Teachers of English (executive council, College Conference on Composition and Communication), Modern Language Association of America, South-Central Renaissance Conference (program chairman), Texas Teachers of College English (executive council).

WRITINGS: Shakespeare and His Sources, Houghton, 1966; *The Humanities Handbook*, two volumes, Holt, 1969; *The Humane Heritage of Africa*, Chandler Publishing, in press.

Editor—All published by Houghton: *Ideas in Context*, 1958; *The 1950's: America's Placid Decade*, 1960; *Reading Literature, Part 1: Non-Fiction Prose, Part 2: Prose Fiction, Part 3: Drama, Part 4: Poetry*, 1964; *Reading Literature: Stories, Plays and Poems*, 1968. Contributor of short stories and articles to *This Week, Harper's Bazaar, Beyond, Negro Digest, Glamour, Toronto Star, Discourse*, and *Forum*.

WORK IN PROGRESS: Co-authoring *The Humane Heritage of the Far East*, and *The Humane Heritage of Latin America*, both for Chandler Publishing.

*   *   *

SAURO, Regina Calderone 1924-

PERSONAL: Born September 8, 1924, in Altoona, Pa.; daughter of Augustine R. and Clory (Martini) Calderone; married Thomas Joseph Sauro (a school maintenance man), June 5, 1944. *Education:* Attended public schools in Niagara Falls, N.Y. *Home:* 1529 LaSalle Ave., Niagara Falls, N.Y. 14301.

CAREER: Private secretary for ten years in Niagara Falls, N.Y., and Los Angeles, Calif. Free-lance writer, mainly for primary grades.

WRITINGS: The Too-Long Trunk, Lantern Press, 1964.

Contributor: *Jack and Jill Treasury*, Wonder Books, 1957; *Stories from Jack and Jill*, Wonder Books, 1960; *Read-Aloud Stories from Child Life*, Wonder Books, 1960; *The Old Woman's Flower Garden, A Fair Trade*, and *A Summer Picnic*, Science Research Associates, 1961; *My English Book 3*, Sadlier, 1962. Contributor of some four hundred stories, poems, and plays to juvenile publications.

WORK IN PROGRESS: Research on Bolivia and Peru for stories on Indians.

AVOCATIONAL INTERESTS: Doing crossword puzzles, collecting shells, drawing, reading, motoring trips.

SAVAGE, (Leonard) George (Gimson) 1909-

PERSONAL: Born August 31, 1909, in London, England. *Politics:* "Anti-Socialism in any form." *Religion:* Agnostic. *Home:* Humphreys, Guestling, Sussex, England. *Agent:* Curtis Brown Ltd., 13 King St., Covent Garden, London WC2E 8HU, England.

CAREER: Art consultant to several private collectors and to publishers of art books.

WRITINGS: Ceramics for the Collector: An Introduction to Pottery and Porcelain, Macmillan, 1949; *18th-Century English Porcelain,* Macmillan, 1952, new edition, Spring Books, 1966; *Porcelain Through the Ages,* Penguin, 1954, 2nd edition, 1963; *The Art and Antique Restorer's Handbook: A Dictionary of Materials and Processes Used in the Restoration and Perservation of All Kind of Works of Art,* Philosophical Library, 1954, revised edition, Praeger, 1962; *18th-Century German Porcelain,* Macmillan, 1958, 2nd edition, Spring Books, 1967; *Pottery Through the Ages,* Penguin, 1959; *The Antique Collectors' Handbook,* Dover, 1959, revised edition, Spring Books, 1968, Praeger, 1969; *Seventeenth and Eighteenth Century French Porcelain,* Barrie & Rockliff, 1960, Macmillan, 1961; *English Pottery and Porcelain,* Universe Books, 1961; (editor) *International Art Sales,* two volumes, Crown, 1961-62; (editor and author of introduction) *The American Birds of Dorothy Doughty,* Worcester Royal Porcelain Co., 1962; *Fakes, Forgeries, and Reproduction: A Handbook for the Collector,* Barrie & Rockliff, 1963, published in America as *Fakes, Forgeries, and Reproductions: A Handbook for the Art Dealer and Collector,* Praeger, 1964; *Chinese Jade: A Concise Introduction,* Cory, Adams & Mackay, 1964, October House, 1965; *Glass,* Putnam, 1965; *A Concise History of Interior Decoration,* Thames & Hudson, 1966, Grosset, 1969; (translator) Pierre Verlet, *The Eighteenth Century in French: Society, Decoration, Furniture,* Tuttle, 1967 (published in England as *French Furniture and Interior Decoration of the 18th Century,* Barrie & Rockliff, 1967); *A Concise History of Bronzes,* Thames & Hudson, 1968, Praeger, 1969; *The Story of Royal Worcester and the Dyson Perrins Museum,* Pitkin Pictorials, 1968; *French Decorative Art, 1638-1793,* Praeger, 1969; *The Market in Art,* Institute of Economic Affairs, 1969; *Dictionary of Antiques,* Praeger, 1970. Contributor to *Encyclopaedia Britannica* and *Encyclopaedia of Visual Arts.* Regular contributor of articles to *Studio,* and occasional contributor to other art journals.

* * *

SAVAGE, Mildred (Spitz) 1919-
(Jane Barrie)

PERSONAL: Born in New London, Conn.; married Bernard L. Savage; children: Susan Jean, Michael Donald. *Education:* Wellesley College, B.A.; Yale University, special student in Law School, 1971-72. *Home:* 235 Harland Rd., Norwich, Conn. 06360.

CAREER: Author. Lecturer, Writers Conference, Pennsylvania State Teacher's College, 1960, Pennsylvania State University, 1961, John Jay College, 1970, 1971. *Awards, honors:* Edgar Allan Poe award for "Best Fact-Crime Book," 1970.

WRITINGS: (Under pseudonym Jane Barrie) *The Lumberyard and Mrs. Barrie,* Holt, 1952; *Parrish* (Literary Guild selection), Simon & Schuster, 1958; *In Vivo* (Literary Guild selection), Simon & Schuster, 1964; *A Great Fall: A Murder and Its Consequences,* Simon & Schuster, 1970.

SIDELIGHTS: In line with Mrs. Savage's first two novels, *A Great Fall: A Murder and Its Consequences* resembles fiction at first glance; it turns out to be a compelling nonfiction murder novel. As a reviewer for *Library Journal* said: "The circumstances surrounding a murder are seldom clear, even if that murder is witnessed. In the case of the murder of Connecticut housewife Dorothy Thompsen in June 1965, the confusion was exacerbated not only by lack of witnesses, but also by the intrusion of personal conflicts among state police officers, the state's attorney's office, and the defense during the subsequent trials, and by the demands of the *Miranda* decision which, although handed down after the murder, affected the admissibility of evidence in the trials. Novelist Savage . . . has succeeded admirably in recreating the confusion and complexity of the case." A *National Observer* writer called the book "stunning," but considered it "flawed . . . by Mrs. Savage's passionate commitment. Her characters—and she is dealing with real people, remember—are drawn black or white. Her comments are invariably sympathetic to the defense."

Fred Powledge seems to want "very badly an ending that explains everything—a death-bed confession, a last chapter in which Harry Solberg [the murder suspect] says, 'Well, it's over now, and this is what happened.' That, of course, is where fact-crime and its fictional equivalent part company. What really matters is that Miss Savage *does* ask the important questions. The most important of those, which she asks well, is 'Which do we want: justice or jurisprudence?'" In a review for the *New York Times* entitled "Too Real to Believe, Too False to Forget," Christopher Lehmann-Haupt writes: "It is really much too much—for art. But the sheer profusion of clumsiness in *A Great Fall*—the impossible combination of drama and dreary detail, of cliche and passion, of form and chaos, of skilled narrative and the narrator's heavy-handed intrusion, of the ordinary and the barely credible, of small-town life and the major issues of the present day—make this book impossible to stop reading and even more difficult to forget when it is over."

Reviewers of Mrs. Savage's first novel, *Parrish,* called her "a new Edna Ferber"; the book has since been published in nine foreign countries and produced as a motion picture by Warner Brothers in 1961.

BIOGRAPHICAL/CRITICAL SOURCES: Library Journal, July, 1958, February 1, 1970; *Chicago Sunday Tribune,* October 19, 1958; *New York Times,* October 26, 1958, February 11, 1970; *Book Week,* May 31, 1964; *New York Times Book Review,* July 5, 1964, March 1, 1970; *Best Sellers,* March 15, 1970; *National Observer,* April 27, 1970.

* * *

SAVERY, Constance (Winifred) 1897-

PERSONAL: Born October 31, 1897; daughter of John Manly (a clergyman) and Constance Eleanor (Harbord) Savery. *Education:* Attended King Edward VI High School, Birmingham, England; Somerville College, Oxford, M.A. (with honors), 1927. *Religion:* Church of England. *Home:* Trevalfry, Halesworth Rd., Reydon, Southwold, Suffolk, England.

CAREER: Author, mainly of junior novels and children's stories. *Member:* Society of Authors. *Awards, honors: Junior Scholastic Magazine* Gold Seal Award for *The Good Ship Red Lily.*

WRITINGS: Forbidden Doors, Harrap, 1929, published in America as *Tenthragon,* Alfred H. King, 1930; *Nicolas Chooses White May,* Nelson, 1930; *There was a Key: Stories for Girls,* Brown, Son & Ferguson, 1930; *Pippin's House: An East Anglian Story,* Longmans, Green, 1931; *Yellow Gates: A Boy's Story,* Pickering & Inglis, 1935, reissued as *Peter of Yellow Gates,* Pickering & Inglis, 1945; *Danny and the Alabaster Box,* Zondervan, 1937; *Moonshine in Candle Street,* Longmans, Green, 1937;

Green Emeralds for the King: A Story of the Civil War, Harrap, 1938, published in America as *Emeralds for the King*, Longmans, Green, 1945.

She Went Alone: Mary Bird of Persia, Livingston Press, 1942; *Enemy Brothers*, Longmans, Green, 1943; *The Good Ship Red Lily*, Longmans, Green, 1944, revised edition published as *Flight to Freedom*, Children's Special Service Mission, 1958; *Blue Fields*, Victory Press, 1947; *Dark House on the Moss*, Longmans, Green, 1948; *Bishop Guy Bullen, 1896-1937*, Church Book Room Press, 1948; *Up a Winding Stair*, Victory Press, 1949.

Three Houses in Beverley Road, Lutterworth, 1950; *Redhead at School*, Lutterworth, 1951; *Scarlet Plume*, Victory Press, 1953; *Meg Plays Fair*, Lutterworth, 1953; *Young Elizabeth Green*, Lutterworth, 1954; *Five Wonders for Wyn*, Lutterworth, 1955; *Welcome, Santza*, Longmans, Green, 1956; *Tabby Kitten*, Lutterworth, 1956; *Four Lost Lambs*, Lutterworth, 1957; *Thistledown Tony*, Victory Press, 1957; *The Boy from Brittany*, Pickering & Inglis, 1957; *In Apple Alley*, Lutterworth, 1958; *To the City of Gold*, Lutterworth, 1958; *Magic in my Shoes* (Junior Literary Guild selection), Longmans, Green, 1958; *The Sea Urchins*, Lutterworth, 1959.

Rebel Jacqueline, Lutterworth, 1960; *The Reb and the Redcoats* (Junior Literary Guild selection), McKay, 1961; *All Because of Sixpence*, Lutterworth, 1961; *The White Kitling*, Lutterworth, 1962; *The Royal Caravan*, Lutterworth, 1963; *Breton Holiday*, Lutterworth, 1963; *Joric and the Dragon*, Lutterworth, 1964; *The Sea Queen*, Lutterworth, 1965; *Please Buy My Pearls*, Lutterworth, 1965; *The Golden Cap*, Lutterworth, 1966; *The Strawberry Feast*, Lutterworth, 1967; *The Silver Angel*, Lutterworth, 1968; *Lavender's Tree*, Lutterworth, 1969; *Gilly's Tower*, Lutterworth, 1969; *The Sapphire Ring*, Lutterworth, 1969.

The City of Flowers, Lutterworth, 1970. Contributor of articles and short stories to periodicals.

WORK IN PROGRESS: A novel.

SIDELIGHTS: Three of Miss Savery's four sisters also are writers. She has a working knowledge of Latin, Greek, and French, and a smattering of several other languages. Some of her books have been published in German and Swedish, and some short stories have been broadcast on radio. The Library Science Department of the University of Southern Mississippi has made a collection of some of her American published books together with typescripts, proofs, and illustrations for their children's library collection. *Avocational interests:* Church architecture and history, archaeology, astronomy, geology, conchology, botany.

*   *   *

SAVORY, Alan Forsyth   1905-

PERSONAL: Born January 11, 1905, in Blicking, Norfolk, England; son of Frank Foley (a farmer) and Catherin (Leeds) Savory; married Eleanor .Doris Kuhr, August 18, 1956. *Education:* Attended Ipswich School, Suffolk, England. *Religion:* Church of England. *Home:* Riverdale, Strumpshaw Rd., Brundall, Norfolk, England.

CAREER: Writer, mainly for periodicals, 1928—; photographer, fur and duck farmer, and rose grower. *Military service:* Royal Air Force, Air-Sea Rescue Service, 1941-45. *Member:* National Book League, Wildfowlers Association of Great Britain and Ireland, Institute of Advanced Drivers, Farmers Club, Norfolk Club, Norwich Anglers, Overseas Club, Royal Automobile Association.

WRITINGS: Norfolk Fowler, Bles, 1953; *Lazy Rivers*, Bles, 1956; *Thunder in the Air*, Bles, 1960. Contributor of articles to *Shooting Times, Country Life, Field*, and other outdoor magazines.

WORK IN PROGRESS: Articles; editing 16mm film of African trip.

SIDELIGHTS: Savory traveled extensively in Africa, 1956-57.

*   *   *

SAWYER, P(eter) H(ayes)   1928-

PERSONAL: Born June 25, 1928, in Oxford, England; son of William and Grace (Woodbridge) Sawyer; married Ruth Howard, 1955; children: Richard, Catherine, Dorothy, John. *Education:* Jesus College, Oxford, B.A., 1951. *Home:* 4 Headingley Terrace, Leeds 6, England.

CAREER: University of Edinburgh, Edinburgh, Scotland, assistant lecturer in history, 1953-56; University of Leeds, Leeds, England, assistant lecturer in history, 1956-57; University of Birmingham, Birmingham, England, lecturer in history, 1957-64; University of Leeds, Leeds, England, lecturer in history, 1964-67, reader in medieval history, 1967-70, professor of medieval history, 1970—.

WRITINGS: Early English Manuscripts in Facsimile: Textus Roffensis, Rosenkilde & Bagger, Part I, Volume 7, 1957, Part II, Volume 11, 1962; *The Age of the Vikings*, Edward Arnold, 1962, St. Martins, 1963, 2nd edition, Edward Arnold, 1971, St. Martins, 1972; *Anglo-Saxon Charters: An Annotated List and Bibliography*, Royal Historical Society, 1968.

WORK IN PROGRESS: Editing the pre-Conquest charters of Burton Abbey; a general study of the Vikings; a book on Anglo-Saxon England; and a book on early medieval towns in Europe.

BIOGRAPHICAL/CRITICAL SOURCES: Times Literary Supplement, May 9, 1968.

*   *   *

SAYEGH, Fayez A(bdullah)   1922-

PERSONAL: Surname is pronounced *Sigh*-egg; born January 11, 1922, in Kharaba, Syria; son of Abdullah Yusif (a minister) and Afifi (Batronie) Sayegh; married Arlene-Faye Briem, August 23, 1960. *Education:* American University of Beirut, B.A., 1941, M.A., 1945; Georgetown University, Ph.D., 1949. *Politics:* Arab Nationalist. *Religion:* Presbyterian. *Office:* Department of Political Studies, American University of Beirut, Beirut, Lebanon.

CAREER: Embassy of Lebanon, Washington, D.C., research officer, 1949-50; United Nations, New York, N.Y., adviser to Lebanon delegation, 1949-50, program officer in Radio Division, 1950-52, social affairs officer, 1952-55, counselor to Yemen delegation and deputy, later acting director, of Arab States delegation, 1955-59; Stanford University, Stanford, Calif., visiting associate professor of political science and philosophy, 1960-62; Macalester College, St. Paul, Minn., Barclay Acheson Professor of International Studies, 1962-63; St. Antony's College, Oxford University, Oxford, England, research under grant, 1963-64; American University of Beirut, Beirut, Lebanon, associate professor of political studies, 1964—. Visiting lecturer in political science at Yale University, 1955; lecturer on tours in Africa, Middle East, United Kingdom, and in more than 120 colleges and universities throughout the United States. President of Palestine Arab Congress, Beirut, Lebanon, 1959; honorary adviser to U.S. Organization for Medical and Education Needs in the Middle East, 1960—.

MEMBER: Middle East Institute, Institute of American-Arab Affairs (honorary chairman, 1960—), American Friends of the Middle East (guest membership). *Awards, honors:* Commander, Order of the Cedars (Lebanon), 1959.

WRITINGS—In Arabic: *Al-Ba'th al-qawmi* (title means "The Road to National Dignity"), Al-Wajib Press (Beirut), 1946; *The Sectarian Problem*, Al-Wajib Press, 1947; *Nida al-a'maq* (title means "The Call from the Depths"), Al-Fikr Press (Beirut), 1947; *Ila ayn?*, Al-Kitab Press (Beirut), 1947; *National Socialism Versus Freedom of Thought*, Ak-Kitab Press, 1948; *Risalat al-mufakkir al-arabi* (title means "The Mission of the Arab Intellectual"), Al-Kofah Press (Beirut), 1955; *Mashru' Hammarshuld wa-qadiyat al-laji in* (title means "The Hammarskjold Plan and the Palestine Refugees"), Al-Fajr Press (Beirut), 1959. Also author of *Hafnab min dabab*, *Al-Isti'mar al-sahyuni*, and *Al-Diblumasiyah al-sahyuniyah.*

In English: *The Palestine Refugees*, AMARA Press, 1952; *Understanding the Arab Mind*, Organization of Arab Students in the United States (New York), 1953; *The Arab-Israeli Conflict*, Arab Information Center (New York), 1956; *Arab Property in Israeli-Controlled Territories: Israeli Measures for the Disposal of Arab Property*, Arab Information Center, 1956; *Notes on the Suez Canal Controversy*, Arab Information Center, 1956; *Turmoil in the Middle East: Anglo-French-Israeli Aggression in Egypt*, Arab Information Center, 1956; *The Record of Israel at the United Nations*, Arab Information Center, 1957; (contributor) *New Look at the Middle East*, Middle East Institute, 1957; *Communism in Israel*, Arab Information Center, 1958; *Arab Unity: Hope and Fulfillment*, Devin, 1958; (contributor) William Sands, editor, *The Arab Nation: Paths and Obstacles to Fulfillment*, Middle East Institute, 1961; (editor, contributor, and author of introduction) *The Dynamics of Neutralism in the Arab World: A Symposium*, Chandler Publishing, 1964; (contributor) J.H. Proctor, editor, *Islam and International Relations*, Praeger, 1964; *The United Nations and the Palestine Question, April 1947-April 1965*, Palestine Liberation Organization, 1965; *Zionist Colonialism in Palestine* (monograph), Research Center, Palestine Liberation Organization, 1965; (contributor) Benjamin Rivlin and J.S. Szyliowicz, editors, *The Contemporary Middle East: Tradition and Innovation*, Random House, 1965; (contributor) *St. Antony's Papers*, Number 17, Oxford University Press, 1965; *Discrimination in Education Against the Arabs in Israel*, Palestine Liberation Organization, 1966; *Dr. Fayez Sayegh Presents Arab Viewpoint on the "David Susskind" Show*, Permanent Mission of the State of Kuwait to the United Nations, c.1967; *Do Jews Have a "Divine Right" to Palestine?*, Research Center, Palestine Liberation Organization, 1967; *Do You Know?: Twenty Basic Facts About the Palestine Problem*, Palestine Liberation Organizaton, 1968.

Palestine, Israel and Peace, Research Center, Palestine Liberation Organization, 1970.

Contributor of articles in English to *Current History*, *Social Science*, *America*, *Annals of the American Academy of Political and Social Science*, *Isis* (England), *Middle East Forum* (Lebanon), *International Review* (India), and more than fifteen other journals; contributor of articles in Arabic to thirteen periodicals in the Middle East. Editor-in-chief of *Al-Nahda* (Arabic daily), and *Ath-Thaqafa* (Arabic bi-monthly), 1945-47. Columnist, "For the Record," *Brooklyn Caravan*, 1957-61.

SIDELIGHTS: Sayegh's magazine articles in English have been translated for German, Spanish, and Arabic periodicals.†

*   *   *

SAYRE, J(ohn) Woodrow   1913-

PERSONAL: Born March 18, 1913, in Clarksburg, W.Va.; married Nell Shircliff (a teacher), July 31, 1938; children: Martha Sayre Garman, Daniel F. *Education:* Fairmont State College, B.A., 1938; Marshall University, graduate study, 1940; University of Pittsburgh, M.A., 1946; postgraduate study at State University of New York at Buffalo, 1948, Syracuse University, 1956-59. *Home:* Babcock Lake, Petersburg, N.Y. 12138.

CAREER: Worked in industry, 1938-42; high school teacher, 1942-55; State University of New York School of Industrial and Labor Relations at Cornell University, Ithaca, assistant professor, 1955-60; Syracuse University, Syracuse, N.Y., assistant professor of education, 1960-65; New York State Council on Economic Education, executive director, 1960—; State University of New York at Albany, associate professor of economics, 1965—. Consultant to New York State Education Department and to various New York school systems. *Member:* American Economic Association, American Association of University Professors, National Council for the Social Studies, New York State Council for the Social Studies (director), Air Force Association.

WRITINGS: *Assimilation of Swedes in Jamestown, N.Y.*, University of Pittsburgh Press, 1946; (with Leo John Alilunas) *Youth Faces American Citizenship: A Problems of Democracy Text*, Lippincott, 1956, 4th edition, 1970; (with Robert E. Rowland) *Labor and the Government: Changing Government Policies Toward Labor Unions*, New York State School of Industrial and Labor Relations, Cornell University, 1956, revised edition, 1961; (with Edith Stull) *Taxation*, F. Watts, 1963; *Paperbound Books in Economics: An Annotated Bibliography*, New York State Council on Economic Education, 1964; *A Pilot Study of the Use of Instructional Materials in Introductory Courses in the State University of New York*, New York State Council on Economic Education, 1968. Author of several pamphlets and filmstrips.

WORK IN PROGRESS: Survey of economics taught in New York colleges and secondary schools; a high school economics text.

*   *   *

SAYRE, Kenneth Malcolm   1928-

PERSONAL: Born August 13, 1928, in Scottsbluff, Neb.; son of Harry Malcolm (a railroad agent) and Mildred (Potts) Sayre; married Lucille M. Shea, August 18, 1958; children: Gregory, Christopher, Jeffrey. *Education:* Grinnell College, B.A., 1952; Harvard University, M.A., 1954, Ph.D., 1958. *Office:* Department of Philosophy, University of Notre Dame, Notre Dame, Ind. 46556.

CAREER: Harvard University, Graduate School of Arts and Sciences, Cambridge, Mass., assistant dean, 1953-56; Massachusetts Institute of Technology, Lincoln Laboratory, Lexington, Mass., systems analyst, 1956-58; University of Notre Dame, Notre Dame, Ind., instructor in philosophy, 1958-60, assistant professor, 1960-66, associate professor of philosophy, 1966—. Director, Philosophic Institute for Artificial Intelligence; consultant in human factors research. *Military service:* U.S. Navy, 1946-48. *Member:* American Philosophical Association.

WRITINGS: (Editor with Frederick James Crosson) *The Modeling of Mind: Computers and Intelligence*, University of Notre Dame Press, 1963; *Recognition: A Study in the Philosophy of Artificial Intelligence*, University of Notre Dame Press, 1965; (editor with Crosson) *Philosophy and Cybernetics* (essays), University of Notre Dame Press, 1967; *Plato's Analytic Method*, University of Chicago Press, 1969; *Consciousness: A Philosophic Study of Minds and Machines*, Random House, 1969. Contributor to *Mind*, *Inquiry Methods*, *Notre Dame Journal of Formal Logic*, and other periodicals.

SAYRE, Robert F(reeman)   1933-

PERSONAL: Born November 6, 1933, in Columbus, Ohio; son of Harrison M. (a publisher) and Mary Elizabeth (White) Sayre; married Constance Mitchell, July 8, 1961; children: Gordon, Nathan, Laura. *Education:* Wesleyan University, B.A., 1955; Yale University, Ph.D., 1962. *Politics:* Democrat. *Home:* 1033 Woodlawn, Iowa City, Iowa 52240.

CAREER: Wesleyan University, Middletown, Conn., instructor in English, 1960; University of Illinois, Urbana, instructor in English, 1961-63; Lund University, Lund, Sweden, Fulbright lecturer in American literature, 1963-64, research docent in American literature, 1964-65; University of Iowa, Iowa City, associate professor of English, 1966—. *Military service:* U.S. Navy, seaman, 1955-57.

WRITINGS: The Examined Self: Benjamin Franklin, Henry Adams and Henry James, Princeton University Press, 1964; (contributor of essay) *Adventures, Rhymes, and Designs* (of Vachel Lindsay), Eakins, 1968. Contributor to *Journal of English and Germanic Philology, Yale Review, Texas Studies in Literature and Language, Nation, College English, Chicago Review,* and *Moderna Spraak.*

WORK IN PROGRESS: A study of relationships between personality and utopias; a history of American autobiography.

*   *   *

SCANLAN, James P(atrick)   1927-

PERSONAL: Born February 22, 1927, in Chicago, Ill.; son of Gilbert Francis (a manufacturer) and Helen (Meyers) Scanlan; married Marilyn Morrison, June 12, 1948. *Education:* University of Chicago, B.A., 1948, M.A., 1950, Ph.D., 1956; postdoctoral study at University of California, Berkeley, 1960-61, at University of Moscow, 1964-65. *Office:* Department of Philosophy, Ohio State University, Columbus, Ohio 43210.

CAREER: Institute for Philosophical Research, San Francisco, Calif., research fellow, 1953-55; Case Institute of Technology, Cleveland, Ohio, instructor in humanities, 1955-56; Goucher College, Baltimore, Md., instructor, 1956-59, assistant professor, 1959-64, associate professor of philosophy, 1964-68; University of Kansas, Lawrence, professor of philosophy and chairman of Slavic and Soviet area studies, 1968-70; Ohio State University, Columbus, professor of philosophy, 1971—. University of Moscow, Moscow, Russia, participant in cultural exchange program and researcher, 1964-65, 1969. *Military service:* U.S. Marine Corps, 1944-45. *Member:* American Philosophical Association, American Association for the Advancement of Slavic Studies, Phi Beta Kappa. *Awards, honors:* Ford Foundation foreign area training fellowship, University of California, 1960-61.

WRITINGS: (Editor with James M. Edie, Mary-Barbara Zeldin, and George L. Kline) *Russian Philosophy,* three volumes, Quadrangle, 1965; (editor, author of introduction, and translator) Peter Lavrov, *Historical Letters,* University of California Press, 1967. Contributor to *Ethics, Review of Politics, Bucknell Review, Choice, Slavic Review, Russian Review,* and *Baltimore Sun.* Member of editorial board, *Encyclopedia of Philosophy,* published by Macmillan.

WORK IN PROGRESS: Translations from the Russian of Michael Gershenzon's *History of "Young Russia",* and Gustav Shpet's *Appearance and Meaning;* research for books on Russian aesthetic theory and socialist realism.

SCHAAP, Richard J(ay)   1934-

PERSONAL: Born September 27, 1934, in New York, N.Y.; son of Maurice William and Leah (Lerner) Schaap; married Barbara Barron, June 20, 1956; children: Renee, Beth, Michelle. *Education:* Cornell University, B.S., 1955; Columbia University, M.S. in Journalism, 1956. *Agent:* Sterling Lord Agency, 660 Madison Ave., New York, N.Y. 10021.

CAREER: Newsweek, New York, N.Y., 1956-63, successively sports editor, general editor, and senior editor; *New York Herald Tribune,* New York, N.Y., city editor, 1964, columnist, 1964-66; *New York World Journal Tribune,* New York, N.Y., columnist, 1966-67. *Member:* Magazine Sportswriters Association (former president), American Newspaper Guild, Sigma Delta Chi, Phi Sigma Delta.

WRITINGS: Mickey Mantle: The Indispensable Yankee, Macfadden, 1961; *Paul Hornung: Pro Football's Golden Boy,* Macfadden, 1962; *An Illustrated History of the Olympics,* Knopf, 1963, 2nd edition, revised and enlarged, 1967; *Turned On: The Friede-Crenshaw Case,* New American Library, 1967; *R.F.K.,* New American Library, 1967; (editor) *Instant Replay: The Green Bay Diary of Jerry Kramer,* World Publishing, 1968; (with Paul D. Zimmerman) *The Year the Mets Lost Last Place,* World Publishing, 1969; (author of introductory essay) *Jack Johnson Is a Dandy: An Autobiography,* Chelsea House, 1969; (editor) Jerry Kramer, *Farewell to Football,* World Publishing, 1969; (with Joe Namath) *I Can't Wait Until Tomorrow . . . 'Cause I Get Better-Looking Every Day,* Random House, 1969; (with Tom Seaver) *The Perfect Game: Tom and the Mets,* Dutton, 1970; *The Masters: The Winning of a Golf Classic,* Random House, 1970; (editor) *Pro: Frank Beard on the Golf Tour,* World Publishing, 1970. Contributor of articles to *Saturday Evening Post, True, Argosy, Sports Illustrated,* and other magazines.

WORK IN PROGRESS: A novel, for McGraw.

CAREER: St. Louis University, St. Louis, Mo., instructor in modern languages, 1946-50; De Paul University, Chicago, Ill., 1952-58, began as instructor, became assistant professor of history; Loyola University, Chicago, Ill., assistant professor, 1958-61, associate professor of history, 1961-66; St. Joseph's College, Philadelphia, Pa.,

BIOGRAPHICAL/CRITICAL SOURCES: Best Sellers, March 15, 1967; *Saturday Review,* October 12, 1968; *Time,* November 22, 1968; *Variety,* February 5, 1969; *Newsweek,* December 8, 1969.†

*   *   *

SCHALL, James V(incent)   1928-

PERSONAL: Born January 20, 1928, in Pocahontas, Iowa; son of Lawrence Nicholas and Mary (Johnson) Schall. *Education:* Gonzaga University, B.A., 1954, M.A., 1955; Georgetown University, Ph.D., 1960; University of Santa Clara, M.S.T., 1964; Oude Abdij, Drongen, Belgium, Jesuit studies, 1964-65. *Politics:* Democrat.

CAREER: University of San Francisco, San Francisco, Calif., instructor in political science, 1955-56; ordained Roman Catholic priest, member of California Province of Society of Jesus, 1963. *Military service:* U.S. Army, 1946-47.

WRITINGS: (With Donald J. Wolf) *American Society and Politics,* Allyn & Bacon, 1964; (editor with Wolf) *Current Trends in Theology,* Doubleday, 1965; *Redeeming the Time,* Sheed, 1968; *Human Dignity and Human Numbers,* Alba, 1971. Contributor of articles to *Commonweal, World Justice, New Scholasticism, Catholic World, America, Social Order, Modern Age, Worship, Thomist,* and to journals of political science.

WORK IN PROGRESS: Co-editor of a theology series, "Contemporary Catholic Theology," for Doubleday; co-editor of The Worship of a Family, for Paulist Press.

BIOGRAPHICAL/CRITICAL SOURCES: Encounter, autumn, 1968.

*   *   *

SCHAPPER, Beatrice 1906-1974

PERSONAL: Born January 22, 1906, in Pittsburgh, Pa.; daughter of Morris and Sadie (Friedman) Aronson; married Henry J. Schapper (president of own agency), September 6, 1928. Education: University of Wisconsin, B.A., 1928. Home: 1080 Fifth Ave., #6B, New York, N.Y. 10028. Office: Henry Schapper Agency, 101 Park Ave., New York, N.Y. 10017.

CAREER: Pittsburgh Post-Gazette, Pittsburgh, Pa., promotion manager, 1928-32; Meyer Jonasson's, Pittsburgh, Pa., promotion manager, 1934-36; owner of public relations agency, Pittsburgh, Pa., 1936-39; free-lance writer. College of City of New York (now City College of the City University of New York), founder and leader of magazine article workshop, 1947-54; New York University, New York, N.Y., 1958-74, began as lecturer at magazine article workshop, then associate professor, leader of "Dialogues with Editors" series, 1964. U.S. Treasury Department, consultant on periodicals. Member: Society of Magazine Writers (founder member; secretary, 1957), Overseas Press Club.

WRITINGS: (Contributor) Prose by Professionals, Doubleday, 1961; (contributor) A Treasury of Tips for Writers, Writer's Digest, 1965; (editor) Writing the Magazine Article: From Idea to Printed Page, Writer's Digest, 1970. Contributor to Glamour, Pageant, Reader's Digest, Good Housekeeping, Redbook, Today's Health, and other periodicals.

AVOCATIONAL INTERESTS: Volunteer work in infants' wards at Mt. Sinai Hospital in New York where she and her husband initiated a project to supply rocking chairs as an old-fashioned supplement to modern hospital treatment.

BIOGRAPHICAL/CRITICAL SOURCES: New York World-Telegram and Sun, February 5, 1960.

(Died January 27, 1974)

*   *   *

SCHARLEMANN, Robert Paul 1929-

PERSONAL: Born April 4, 1929, in Lake City, Minn.; son of Ernst K. and Johanna (Harre) Scharlemann. Education: Northwestern College, student, 1946-49; Concordia College, B.A., 1952, B.D., 1955; University of Heidelberg, Dr.Theol., 1957. Politics: Democrat. Office: Gilmore Hall 310, University of Iowa, Iowa City, Iowa 52240.

CAREER: Lutheran minister. Valparaiso University, Valparaiso, Ind., instructor in philosophy, 1957-59; pastor in Ferrin-Carlyle, Ill., 1960-62; in Durham, N.C., 1962-63; University of Southern California, Los Angeles, assistant professor of theology, Graduate School of Religion, 1963-66; University of Iowa, Iowa City, Iowa, professor of religion, 1966—. Member: American Academy of Religion, Lutheran Academy for Scholarship, Society for the Scientific Study of Religion, Paul-Tillich-Gesellschaft. Awards, honors: Postdoctoral research fellowship, Yale University.

WRITINGS: Communism and the Christian Faith, Concordia, 1963; Thomas Aquinas and John Gerhard: Theological Controversy and Construction in Medieval and Protestant Scholasticism, Yale University Press, 1964; Reflection and Doubt in the Thought of Paul Tillich, Yale University Press, 1969. Contributor to periodicals. Associate editor of Dialog (theology journal).

BIOGRAPHICAL/CRITICAL SOURCES: Library Journal, January 1, 1970.

*   *   *

SCHECHTER, Alan H(enry) 1936-

PERSONAL: Born March 2, 1936, in Brooklyn, N.Y.; son of Henry H. (a teacher) and Mildred (Cohen) Schechter; married Alison Rhoads (a college administrator), August 30, 1958; children: Kathryn Alison, Andrew Rhoads, Stephen Alan. Education: Amherst College, B.A., 1957; Columbia University, Ph.D., 1965; graduate study at University of Leiden, 1960-61. Politics: Democrat. Home: 71 Denton Rd., Wellesley, Mass. 02181. Office: Department of Political Science, Wellesley College, Wellesley, Mass. 02181.

CAREER: Wellesley College, Wellesley, Mass., instructor, 1962-64, assistant professor, 1964-70, associate professor of political science, 1970—, chairman of department, 1970—. Member: American Political Science Association, Academy of Political Science. Awards, honors: University scholar, Columbia University; U.S. Steel Foundation fellow; Fulbright scholar; Ford Foundation fellow; Huber Foundation fellow; National Endowment for the Humanities fellow.

WRITINGS: Interpretation of Ambiguous Documents by International Administrative Tribunals, Praeger, 1964; Contemporary Constitutional Issues, McGraw, 1972. Contributor of numerous articles to professional journals.

WORK IN PROGRESS: A study of housing discrimination in the United States.

AVOCATIONAL INTERESTS: Reading, music, theatre; sports, particularly skiing, tennis, sailing.

*   *   *

SCHEEL, J(oergen) D(itlev) 1918-

PERSONAL: Born November 16, 1918, in Denmark; son of Poul (a diplomat) and Esther (Fabricius) Scheel; married Else Jenk, July 2, 1946; children: Joergen Ulrich, Birgitte. Education: University of Copenhagen, Law Degree (first class honors), 1943. Office: Royal Danish Embassy, Tunis, Tunisia.

CAREER: Danish Foreign Service, 1943—, serving as secretary of Legation at Berne, Switzerland, 1948-50, first secretary of Embassy at London, England, 1953-57, consul general at Montreal, Quebec, Canada, 1961-70, ambassador to Tunisia, Algeria, and Libya, 1970—, in Copenhagen at other intervals. Member: Institute of Advanced Motorists, other motoring clubs.

WRITINGS: Koerekunst (title means "The Art of Driving"), Thaning & Appel, 1958; Bilkundskab (title means "Car Craft"), Thaning & Appel, 1959; (with Henry Bohnstedt-Petersen) Fra grunden af (of Henry Bohnstedt-Petersen), Bohnstedt-Petersen, 1959; Beroemte Biler, Politiken, 1962, translation by D. Cook-Radmore published in America as Cars of the World in Color, Dutton, 1963, 3rd edition, 1967 (published in England as Cars of the World, Methuen, 1964); Rivulins of the Old World, photographs by Scheel, T.F.H. Publications, 1968. Contributor of articles on automotive subjects to periodicals; former motoring columnist for a Danish newspaper.

WORK IN PROGRESS: Lesser known historic and technical problems connected with the better automobiles.

*   *   *

SCHLEBECKER, John T(homas) 1923-

PERSONAL: Surname is pronounced Shlay-becker; born February 8, 1923, in Fort Wayne, Ind.; son of Erwin Charles (a railroad man) and Emma Catherine (Wiseman) Schlebecker; married Ruth Barbara Atwater,

March 20, 1922; children: Susan, Ann Terry, Mark Geoffrey, David John, John Peter. *Education:* Hiram College, B.A., 1949; Harvard University, M.A., 1951; University of Wisconsin, Ph.D., 1954. *Office:* Division of Agriculture and Mining, Smithsonian Institution, Washington, D.C. 20560.

CAREER: Montana State University, Missoula, assistant professor of history, 1954-56; Iowa State University, Ames, associate professor of history, 1956-65; Smithsonian Institution, Washington, D.C., curator, Agriculture and Mining, 1965—. *Military service:* U.S. Marine Corps, 1942-46; became gunnery sergeant. *Member:* Agricultural History Society, British Agricultural History Society, American Economic History Society, Organization of American Historians. *Awards, honors:* James L. Sellers award, Nebraska Historical Society, 1968.

WRITINGS: (With Andrew W. Hopkins) *A History of Dairy Journalism in the United States, 1810-1950,* University of Wisconsin Press, 1957; (contributor) *Probing the American West,* Museum of New Mexico Press, 1962; *Cattle Raising on the Plains, 1900-1961,* University of Nebraska Press, 1963; *A History of American Dairying,* Rand McNally, 1967; *Living Historical Farms: A Walk Into the Past,* Smithsonian Institution, 1968; *A Bibliography of Books and Pamphlets on the History of Agriculture in the United States, 1607-1967,* published for the Smithsonian Institution by American Biographical Center-Clio Press, 1969.

WORK IN PROGRESS: History of American Agriculture, under grant from the American Philosophical Society; agriculture during the American Revolution, 1774-1783.

*   *   *

SCHLEICHER, Charles P.   1907-

PERSONAL: Born January 15, 1907, in Marysville, Ind.; son of Charles P. (a teacher) and Emma (Watt) Schleicher; married Marion E. Putnam, December 23, 1934; children: Karyn Ann, Cheryl Lynne. *Education:* University of the Pacific, A.B., 1928; University of Hawaii, M.A., 1931; Stanford University, Ph.D., 1936. *Politics:* Democrat. *Religion:* Protestant. *Home:* 2685 Columbia, Eugene, Ore. 97403. *Office:* University of Oregon, Eugene, Ore. 97403.

CAREER: College of the Sequoias, Visalia, Calif., instructor in social science, 1934-37; Eastern Washington College, Cheney, instructor in history and political science, 1937-39; University of Utah, Salt Lake City, began as instructor, became professor of political science, 1939-47; U.S. War Department, Washington, D.C., Chief of Report Development and Review Section of Civilian Personnel Division, 1943-45; U.S. Department of State, Washington, D.C., Central Secretariat, 1945-46; University of Oregon, Eugene, professor of political science, 1947—, Associate Director of Institute of International Studies and Overseas Administration. Fulbright Professor of International Relations in India at Allahabad University, 1954-55, Delhi University, 1962-63, Indian School of International Studies, 1966-67. U.S. Educational Foundation in India, Acting Director, 1962-63. *Member:* American Political Science Association, International Studies Association (vice-president, 1961-62), Association for Asian Studies.

WRITINGS: (With G. Homer Durham) *Utah: The State and Its Government,* Oxford Book Co., 1943; *Introduction to International Relations,* Prentice-Hall, 1954; *The Role of the United Nations in Disarmament, 1960-1975* (research report), Technical Military Planning Operation, General Electric Co., 1960; *International Relations: Cooperation and Conflict,* Prentice-Hall, 1962; *The Administration of Indian Foreign Policy Through the United Nations,* edited by Robert W. Gregg, Oceana, 1969.*

WORK IN PROGRESS: International Behavior: Analysis and Operations—A Project in Real-Nation Gaming; The Interrelationships of Personnel and Institutions at the Local Level in Indian Community Development.

*   *   *

SCHMANDT, Raymond H(enry, Jr.)   1925-

PERSONAL: Born September 20, 1925, in Indianapolis, Ind.; son of Raymond Henry (an insurance broker) and Estelle (Overman) Schmandt; married Elizabeth Convy, June 9, 1949; children: Christopher Martin, Stephen John. *Education:* St. Louis University, A.B., 1947, M.A., 1949; attended Washington University, 1949; University of Michigan, M.A. in German literature, and Ph.D. in history, 1952. *Politics:* Democrat. *Religion:* Roman Catholic. *Home:* 2216 George's Lane, Philadelphia, Pa. 19131. *Office:* Department of History, St. Joseph's College, Philadelphia, Pa. 19131.

professor of history, 1966—. *Military service:* Missouri National Guard, 1948-50; became sergeant. *Member:* American Historical Association, American Catholic Historical Association, Mediaeval Academy of America, American Society of Church History, American Association of University Professors (chapter president, 1957-58, 1962-64, 1972-74), Verein fuer Reformationsgeschichte, American Catholic Historical Society Philadelphia.

WRITINGS: (With Thomas P. Neill) *History of the Catholic Church,* Bruce, 1957, 2nd edition, 1965; (editor) Joseph Gill, *Eugenius IV, Pope of Christian Union,* Newman, 1961; (with Edward T. Gargan and others) *Leo XIII and the Modern World,* Sheed, 1961; (with Dwight Follett and others) *Europe and Asia,* Follett, 1963; (editor) E.G. Weltin, *The Ancient Popes,* Newman, 1964; *The Crusades: Origin of an Ecumenical Problem,* University of St. Thomas, 1967. General editor of "The Popes Through History" series for Newman. Contributor of articles to encyclopedias and historical journals. Editor, *Records of the American Catholic Historical Society of Philadelphia,* 1968—.

WORK IN PROGRESS: Gregory the Great, Founder of the Medieval Papacy, for Newman.

SIDELIGHTS: Schmandt prefers to write biography because of a personal fascination with the human element in history, believing that "all too often, historians concentrate on forces, trends, ideas and movements, and forget that fundamentally individual people lie behind all these factors and ultimately give them the shape they bear."

*   *   *

SCHMEISER, Douglas Albert   1934-

PERSONAL: Born May 22, 1934, in Bruno, Saskatchewan, Canada; son of Charles A. and Elsie (Hazelwanter) Schmeiser; married Ellen Catherine Rupich (a lawyer), June 9, 1956; children: Mary Ellen, Douglas Charles, Robert Peter, James Paul. *Education:* University of Saskatchewan, B.A. (with distinction), 1954, LL.B. (with great distinction), 1956; University of Michigan, LL.M., 1958, S.J.D., 1963. *Politics:* Liberal. *Religion:* Roman Catholic. *Home:* 1309 13th St. East, Saskatoon, Saskatchewan, Canada. *Office:* College of Law, University of Saskatchewan, Saskatoon, Saskatchewan, Canada.

CAREER: University of Saskatchewan, Saskatoon, special lecturer in law, 1956-57; private practice of law, Saskatoon, Saskatchewan, 1958-61; University of Saskatchewan, associate professor of law, 1961—. Former vice-president, Catholic Charities Council of Canada; former president, Catholic Welfare Society; vice-president, Saskatoon United Appeal; trustee, Saskatoon Separate School

Board. Former secretary, Saskatoon Liberal Association. *Member:* Canadian Bar Association, Canadian Association of University Teachers, Law Society of Saskatchewan, John Howard Society of Saskatchewan (former director; now director of Saskatoon branch), Saskatoon Bar Association (director).

WRITINGS: Civil Liberties in Canada, Oxford University Press, 1964; *Cases and Comments on Criminal Law,* University of Saskatchewan Press, 1964.

WORK IN PROGRESS: Casebook on Canadian Civil Liberties.

* * *

SCHMIDT, Dana Adams 1915-

PERSONAL: Born September 6, 1915, in Bay Village, Ohio; son of Edward (a businessman) and Margaret (Adams) Schmidt; married Tatiana Constantinidis, October 27, 1947; children: Dana, Jr. *Education:* Attended Chillon College, Villeneuve, Switzerland, 1930-31; Western Reserve Academy, Hudson, Ohio, 1932-33; Pomona College, B.A., 1937; Columbia University, M.S. in Journalism, 1938. *Religion:* Protestant. *Home:* 2208 King Pl. N.W., Washington, D.C. 20007.

CAREER: Foreign correspondent for United Press, Berlin, Balkans, Middle East, North Africa, and France, 1938-44, including service as war correspondent with American, British, and French forces; *New York Times,* New York, N.Y., 1944—, foreign correspondent in France, Germany, Greece, Israel, and Czechoslovakia, with Washington bureau, 1953-61, based in Lebanon, 1961-65, London, 1965-68, Lebanon, 1968-70, Washington, 1970—. *Member:* Overseas Press Club (New York); National Press Club and Overseas Writers (both Washington, D.C.). *Awards, honors:* Croix de Guerre (France) for work as war correspondent; George Polk Award of Overseas Press Club, 1963, for *New York Times* stories on his visit to the Kurds of northern Iraq.

WRITINGS: Anatomy of a Satellite (on Czechoslovakia), Little, Brown, 1952; *Journey Among Brave Men* (on the Kurds), foreword by William O. Douglas, Little, Brown, 1964; *Yemen: The Unknown War,* Holt, 1968.

WORK IN PROGRESS: A book about Israel and the Arab states.

BIOGRAPHICAL/CRITICAL SOURCES: Observer Review, March 17, 1968; *Spectator,* March 22, 1968; *Book World,* September 29, 1968.

* * *

SCHMIDT, Helmut Dan 1915-

PERSONAL: Born March 9, 1915, in Beuthen, Germany; son of Anselm (a lawyer) and Elfriede (Riesenfeld) Schmidt. *Education:* Hebrew University, Jerusalem, M.A., 1941; University of London, B.A. (with honors), 1943; Oxford University, B.Litt., 1952. *Politics:* "Depend on issue." *Home:* Carmel College, Wallingford, Berkshire, England.

CAREER: Carmel College, Wallingford, Berkshire, England, director of social studies, 1952—. *Military service:* British Army, Royal Engineers, 1943-46; served in Egypt and Italy; became sergeant.

WRITINGS: (With J. Toury) *Toldot Heamin Bazeman Hehadash* (textbook of modern history, 1756-1939), three volumes, Yavnah, 1957; (with Richard Koebner) *Imperialism,* Cambridge University Press, 1964. Contributor to historical and political science journals.

WORK IN PROGRESS: Problems of Understanding.

SCHMIDT, Werner Felix 1923-

PERSONAL: Born October 1, 1923, in Evanston, Ill.; son of Werner B. (an artist) and Margaret (an author; maiden name, Chase) Schmidt; married Mary Jane Lodge; children: four. *Education:* Yale University, B.A., 1945; Stanford University, M.D., 1950. *Office:* 105 Taylor Blvd., Millbrae, Calif. 94030.

CAREER: Physician in general practice. *Military service:* U.S. Army, Medical Corps; became captain.

WRITINGS: The Forests of Adventure, Atlantic-Little, Brown, 1963.

WORK IN PROGRESS: A novel.

* * *

SCHMOKEL, Wolfe W(illiam) 1933-

PERSONAL: Born July 25, 1933, in Waldenburg, Germany; son of Guenther W. and Charlotte (Gramm) Schmokel; married Mary Varian Douglas, July 12, 1958; children: Sylvia, Frederick, Marcus. *Education:* University of Maryland, B.A., 1957; Yale University, M.A., 1958, Ph.D., 1962. *Religion:* Lutheran. *Home address:* R.F.D. 2, Rt. 15, Essex Junction, Vt. 05452. *Office:* Department of History, University of Vermont, Burlington, Vt. 05401.

CAREER: University of Maryland, Overseas Program, lecturer in history, 1958-59; Orange County Community College, Middletown, N.Y., lecturer in history, 1961-62; University of Vermont, Burlington, assistant professor of history, 1962—. *Military service:* U.S. Army, 1952-57. *Member:* American Historical Association, American Association of University Professors, African Studies Association. *Awards, honors:* National Defense Education Administration, postdoctoral language fellowship, 1964-65.

WRITINGS: Dream of Empire: German Colonialism, 1919-1945, Yale University Press, 1964; (contributor) Prosser Gifford and William Roger Louis, editors, *Britain and Germany in Africa: Imperial Rivalry and Colonial Rule,* Yale University Press, 1967; (contributor) Robert I. Rotberg, editor, *Africa and Its Explorers: Motives, Methods, and Impact,* Harvard University Press, 1970. Contributor of articles and reviews to *Current History, Africa Report,* and *American Historical Review.*

WORK IN PROGRESS: A biography of Gustav Nachtigal.

* * *

SCHOENBERG, Wilfred Paul 1915-

PERSONAL: Born January 5, 1915, in Uniontown, Wash.; son of James Jacob Arthur and Magdalene (Heitstuman) Schoenberg. *Education:* Attended Gonzaga Preparatory School; Gonzaga University, B.A., 1945, M.A., 1946. *Politics:* Independent. *Religion:* Roman Catholic. *Home:* 1211 Euclid Ave., Spokane, Wash. 99221. *Office:* Oregon Province Archives, Crosby Library, Gonzaga University, Spokane, Wash. 99202.

CAREER: Roman Catholic priest, member of Society of Jesus, Oregon Province, 1939—. Oregon Province Archives, Spokane, Wash., archivist, 1946—; Gonzaga Preparatory School, Spokane, Wash., counselor, 1954—.

WRITINGS: (Editor with John Patrick Leary) *Better a Day,* Macmillan, 1951; (editor with Leary) *I Lift My Lamp,* Newman, 1955; *Garlic for Pegasus: The Life of Brother Benito de Goes of the Society of Jesus,* Newman, 1955; *Jesuit Mission Presses in the Pacific Northwest: A History and Bibliography of Imprints, 1876-1899,* Champoeg Press, 1957; *Jesuits in Oregon, 1844-1959,* Oregon-Jesuit, 1959; *Jesuits in Montana, 1840-1960,* Oregon-Jesuit, 1960; *Father Dave: David Plante McAstocker, S.J.,* Bruce, 1960; *A Chronicle of the Catholic History of* the Pacific Northwest, 1743-1960, Gonzaga Preparatory School, 1962; Gonzaga University: Seventy-Five Years, 1887-1962, Gonzaga University, 1963; Crosby Library, Gonzaga University's Unique Crosby Memorial, Gonzaga University, 1963. Contributor of articles to Ave Maria, and other religious journals.

WORK IN PROGRESS: Jesuits in Alaska; a bibliography of Jesuit historical sources in the Pacific Northwest; other works on the ecclesiastical history of the Northwest.

BIOGRAPHICAL/CRITICAL SOURCES: Oregon-Jesuit, June, 1951.

*   *   *

SCHOFIELD, William   1921-

PERSONAL: Born April 19, 1921, in Springfield, Mass.; son of William and Angie Mae (St. John) Schofield; married Geraldine Bryan (a college teacher), January 11, 1946; children: Bryan St. John, Gwen Star. Education: Springfield College, Springfield, Mass., B.S., 1942; University of Minnesota, M.A., 1946, Ph.D., 1948. Religion: Protestant. Home: 1441 East River Rd., Minneapolis, Minn. 55414. Office address: Box 393, University Hospital, Minneapolis, Minn. 55455.

CAREER: University of Minnesota, Minneapolis, Medical School, instructor, 1947-48, assistant professor, 1948-51, associate professor, 1951-59, professor of psychology, 1959—. Visiting professor, University of Washington, 1960, University of Colorado, 1965. Consultant to Minneapolis Public Schools, Hennepin County General Hospital, and Veterans Administration Hospital, Minneapolis. Member, Minnesota Governor's Committee on Penal Reform, 1952; member of medical policy advisory committee, Minnesota Department of Public Welfare, 1960-68; member of mental health services research review committee, National Institute of Mental Health, 1969—; member, National Advisory Committee to Department of Mental Health and Behavioral Sciences of the Veterans Administration, 1970—. Military service: U.S. Army Air Forces, 1943-46. Member: American Association for the Advancement of Science (fellow), American Psychological Association (fellow; secretary-treasurer of clinical division), American Association of University Professors, American Association of Medical Colleges, Midwestern Psychological Association, Minnesota Psychological Association (executive secretary, 1956-61), Sigma Xi, Pi Gamma Mu, St. Croix Yacht Club. Awards, honors: Award for distinguished service, Minnesota Psychological Association.

WRITINGS: Changes in Response to the Minnesota Multiphasic Inventory Following Certain Therapies (monograph), American Psychological Association, 1950; Psychotherapy: The Purchase of Friendship, Prentice-Hall, 1964. Contributor to Humanitas, and to other psychological journals. Associate editor, Psychological Abstracts, 1961-62.

WORK IN PROGRESS: Collaborating with P.E. Meehl, B.C. Glueck, and Dean J. Clyde on a study of results of a research project supported by Ford Foundation and National Institute of Mental Health.

*   *   *

SCHOLES, Robert (Edward)   1929-

PERSONAL: Surname is pronounced Skolz; born May 19, 1929, in Brooklyn, N.Y.; son of Herbert J. (a businessman) and Leila (Emalle) Scholes; married Joan Grace Carter (a secretary), January 6, 1951 (died, 1971); married Jo Ann S. Putnam, January 30, 1972; children: (first marriage) Christine, Peter. Education: Yale University, A.B., 1950; Cornell University, M.A., 1956,

Ph.D., 1959. Politics: Democrat. Religion: Ex-Catholic. Office: Brown University, Providence, R.I. 02912.

CAREER: University of Virginia, Charlottesville, instructor, later assistant professor of English, 1959-63; University of Wisconsin, Madison, visiting fellow at Humanities Institute, 1963-64; State University of Iowa, Iowa City, associate professor, 1964-66, professor of English, 1966-70; Brown University, Providence, R.I., professor of English, 1970—. Military service: U.S. Naval Reserve, 1951-55; became lieutenant. Member: Modern Language Association of America, William Morris Society, Yale Club of New York.

WRITINGS: The Cornell Joyce Collection: A Catalogue, Cornell University Press, 1961; (editor) Approaches to the Novel: Materials for a Poetics, Chandler Publishing, 1961, revised edition, 1966; (editor) Learners and Discerners: A Newer Criticism (discussions of modern literature by Harry Levin and others), University Press of Virginia, 1964; (editor with Richard M. Kain) The Workshop of Daedalus: James Joyce and the Raw Materials for "A Portrait of the Artist as a Young Man", Northwestern University Press, 1965; (with Robert L. Kellogg) The Nature of Narrative, Oxford University Press, 1966; (editor with Richard Eelman) James Joyce, Dubliners, Viking, 1966; The Fabulators, Oxford University Press, 1967; Elements of Fiction, Oxford University Press, 1968; (editor with A. Walton Litz) James Joyce, Dubliners (Viking critical edition), Viking, 1969; Elements of Poetry, Oxford University Press, 1969; (with Carl H. Klaus) Elements of the Essay, Oxford University Press, 1969; (editor) Poetic Theory/Poetic Practice, Midwest Modern Language Association, 1969; (editor) The Philosopher-Critic, University of Tulsa, 1970; (editor) Some Modern Writers: Essays and Fiction by Conrad, Dinesen, Lawrence, Orwell, Faulkner, and Ellison, Oxford University Press, 1971; (with Klaus) Elements of Drama, Oxford University Press, 1971; Elements of Writing, Oxford University Press, 1972. Contributor of numerous articles and book reviews to learned journals, literary magazines, and weekly reviews.

WORK IN PROGRESS: A critical study of James Joyce.

SIDELIGHTS: To quote their own introduction, Scholes and Kellogg are attacking "our veneration of the novel as a literary form" in The Nature of Narrative. Dorrit Cohn of Indiana University writes that the book "aims to re-educate us to a more liberal view of the narrative genre by studying the diversity of its forms from the Homeric epic to the post-novel. . . . The authors' vast erudition is impressive; so are the apparent ease with which they range over the literature of twenty-five centuries and the considerable yield of their comparative readings of specific texts."

Writing for South Atlantic Quarterly, Morris Beja calls The Fabulators "a valuable book. . . a sort of gloss on the study" written with Kellogg. Centrally concerned with the relation between fiction and reality, Scholes evaluates Durrell, Hawkes, Southern, Iris Murdoch, Vonnegut, and Barth in terms of their "fabulation," by which he means a "more verbal . . . more fictional . . . less realistic and more artistic kind of narrative" than the traditional novel. "Clearly, Mr. Scholes is writing about an important development in contemporary fiction," notes a writer for New York Times Book Review, "but his case for these writers is weakened by his excessive enthusiasms." Bernard Bergonzi believes Scholes "is entitled to his admirations, but in trying to establish them I think he says some silly things about the realistic tradition whose demise he is celebrating. . . . Mr. Scholes, in his enthusiasm for post-realistic fabulation, sells short the realistic tradition." In an especially acerb article on "the pretentious nonsense passing for profundity" published today, Motive critic James

P. Degnan faults Scholes for feeling "compelled to pretend that he is 1) providing us with some kind of special 'literary equipment' . . . ; and 2) that *The Fabulators* documents the death of 'realism' and demonstrates that the 'fabulators,' e.g., Durrell, Hawkes, Southern and the bunch, have replaced the 'realists.' " In contrast, Irving Malin ends his review of the book with the statement that "these flaws—or my prejudices?—are minor. They do not hide the fact that *The Fabulators* is an important, engaging, and useful book which enables us to 'judge and appreciate' the real achievements of contemporary writers."

BIOGRAPHICAL/CRITICAL SOURCES: Kenyon Review, January, 1967; *New York Times Book Review,* October 29, 1967; *Western Humanities Review,* winter, 1968; *Motive,* March, 1968; *Virginia Quarterly Review,* spring, 1968; *Hudson Review,* summer, 1968; *South Atlantic Quarterly,* summer, 1968; *Canadian Forum,* December, 1968; *Comparative Literature,* spring, 1969.

*   *   *

SCHOLL, John 1922

PERSONAL: Born August 7, 1922, in Maquoketa, Iowa; son of Albert and Aileen (Weber) Scholl. *Education:* Graduated from Harlan (Iowa) High School, 1940; attended summer session, Yale University, 1948. *Residence:* Maquoketa, Iowa 52060. *Agent:* Joan Foley, Foley Agency, 34 East 38th St., New York, N.Y. 10016.

CAREER: Newspaper reporter or copy editor in Harlan, Iowa, 1940-41, Davenport, Iowa, 1941-43, Dubuque, Iowa, 1945-46, Maquoketa, Iowa, 1946-47, Salt Lake City, Utah, 1947-48, 1949, Milwaukee, Wis., 1952, Memphis, Tenn., 1958-59, Detroit, Mich., 1960; executive editor of three newspapers in Bartlesville, Okla., 1948-49; free-lance writer, general, 1950-51, 1953-58, of fiction, 1960—. Contracted as writer for television series, Ted Corday, New York, N.Y. *Military service:* U.S. Army, 1943-45; served as correspondent for *Stars and Stripes,* Europe; received Silver Battle Star, Presidential Citation, World War II Victory medals. *Member:* Authors Guild of Authors League of America. *Awards, honors:* State Sigma Delta Chi Prize, Iowa, 1947; MacDowell Memorial Literary Fellowship, 1961.

WRITINGS: The Changing of the Guard, Simon & Schuster, 1963. Also author of an unpublished novel, *The Lemmings of Euphoria,* 1965; poem, "Mayerling," anthologized in *Lyrical Iowa* twentieth annual.

WORK IN PROGRESS: A novella, *The Box;* a roman-fleuve, *The Age of Apathy.*

SIDELIGHTS: The Changing of the Guard was nominated for the Pulitzer Prize in Fiction in 1963, and also for the Hamlin Garland Award, 1964, which is given for the best first book written by an Iowan. Scholl's manuscripts are catalogued at Creighton University in Omaha, Neb.

*   *   *

SCHONFIELD, Hugh J(oseph) 1901-
(Hegesippus)

PERSONAL: Born May 17, 1901, in London, England; son of William and Florence (Joseph) Schonfield; married Helene Muriel Cohn, 1927; children: Marian Singer, Joyce Netter, Audrey Sandbank. *Education:* Studied at St. Paul's School, London, England, University of Glasgow, and King's College, London. *Home:* 35 Hyde Park Sq., London W.2, England. *Agent:* Mark Paterson, 42 Canonbury Sq., London N.1, England.

CAREER: Worked in advertising, 1927-34, in publishing field, 1934-46; author, editor, and translator. President, International Arbitration League, 1955-60; founder and first president, Commonwealth of World Citizens, 1959-63; trustee, World Service Trust. *Member:* P.E.N., Old Pauline Club, Society of Authors. *Awards, honors:* Nominated for Nobel Peace Prize; Doctor of Sacred Literature, St. John's University (Madras Province, India), 1955.

WRITINGS: (Translator) *An Old Hebrew Text of St. Matthew's Gospel,* Scribner, 1927; *The Lost "Book of the Nativity of John": A Study in Messianic Folklore and Christian Origins,* T. & T. Clark, 1929; *The New Hebrew Typography,* Denis Archer, 1932; (under pseudonym Hegesippus) *The Speech That Moved the World,* Search Publishing, 1932; *The History of Jewish Christianity from the First to the Twentieth Century,* Duckworth, 1936; *Richard Burton, Explorer,* Herbert Joseph, 1936; *Ferdinand de Lesseps,* Herbert Joseph, 1937; *According to the Hebrews: A New Translation of the Toldoth Jeshu,* Duckworth, 1937; *Jesus: A Biography,* Duckworth, 1939, 2nd edition, 1948; *The Suez Canal,* Penguin, 1939.

The Divine Plan of World Government, privately printed, 1940; *Italy and Suez,* Hutchinson, 1940; *The Holy Nation and Its Mission* (pamphlet), Society for the Constitution of a Holy Nation, 1940; *Judaism and World Order,* Secker & Warburg, 1943; *By What Authority?: The Question of Our Time, and the Answer,* Herbert Joseph, 1945; *The Jew of Tarsus: An Unorthodox Portrait of Paul,* Macdonald & Co., 1946, Macmillan (New York), 1947; *Saints Against Caesar: The Rise and Reactions of the First Christian Community,* Macdonald & Co., 1948; *The Suez Canal in World Affairs,* Constellation Books, 1952, Philosophical Library, 1953, revised edition published as *The Suez Canal in Peace and War, 1869-1969,* University of Miami Press, 1969; *Egypt: Cross-Road on a World Highway* (pamphlet), Peace News, 1953; *Secrets of the Dead Sea Scrolls: Studies Towards Their Solution,* Vallentine, Mitchell, 1956, Yoseloff, 1957; *The Bible Was Right: New Light on the New Testament,* Muller, 1958, published in America as *The Bible Was Right: An Astonishing Examination of the New Testament,* New American Library, 1959.

A History of Biblical Literature, New American Library, 1962; *A Popular Dictionary of Judaism,* Arco, 1962, Citadel, 1966; *The Passover Plot: New Light on the History of Jesus,* Hutchinson, 1965, Geis, 1966; *Readers' A to Z Bible Companion,* New American Library, 1967; *Those Incredible Christians,* Geis, 1968 (published in England as *Those Incredible Christians: A New Look at the Early Church,* Hutchinson, 1968); *The Politics of God,* Hutchinson, 1970, Regnery, 1971.

Editor: *Letters to Frederick Tennyson,* L. & Virginia Woolf, 1930; K. De Proszynski, *Authentic Photography of Christ,* Search Publishing, 1932; Lewis Carroll, *For the Train: Five Poems and a Tale,* Search Publishing, 1932; (with E.J.L. Garstin) *Jesus Christ Nineteen Centuries After,* Search Publishing, 1933; *The Book of British Industries,* Denis Archer, 1933; *Great Explorations,* Herbert Joseph, 1937; (and author of introduction) *Readings from the Apocryphal Gospels,* Thomas Nelson, 1940; *The Treaty of Versailles,* Peace Books, 1940; (and author of introduction) Woodrow Wilson, *This Man Was Right: Woodrow Wilson Speaks Again,* W.H. Allen, 1943; (and translator) *The Authentic New Testament,* Dobson, 1955, New American Library, 1958; (and translator) *The Song of Songs,* New American Library, 1959. Contributor of articles on Biblical subjects to *Evening News* (London).

WORK IN PROGRESS: The Pentecost Revolution, a study of Christian beginnings in the light of Jewish history, 36-66 A.D.

SIDELIGHTS: Schonfield's book, *The Passover Plot,* caused something of a sensation among theologians and scholars of the New Testament and became a best seller. Hypothesizing that Christ planned his own crucifixion to comply with prophetic intimations, but did not anticipate that his survival of the ordeal would be frustrated by the lance of a Roman soldier, Schonfield suggests that Christ saw himself as the Messiah, but not as the Divine Son of God. Some critics support Schonfield's theory while others dismiss it as groundless. Samuel Sandmel, a hostile critic, writes: "Schonfield's imaginative reconstruction is devoid of a scintilla of proof, and rests on dubious inferences from passages in the Gospels whose historical reliability he himself has antecedently rejected on page after page. In my view, the book should be dismissed as the mere curiousity it is." Schonfield argues, however, that his thesis has strong evidential support, presenting "a realistic rather than idealized picture" of Christ.

He adds: "I don't want it to be regarded as the work of an academic intellectual or of intellectual ingenuity. No, to me Jesus shows that we must have faith in the future and recognize the work to be done. Jesus is the example of the man who makes dreams come true. We must realize that nothing is beyond our capacity. I hope my book will help to equip us with the will-power to enact our faith into reality. My gospel is one of confidence and action. I derive this from Jesus in no small measure."

BIOGRAPHICAL/CRITICAL SOURCES: America, September 10, 1966; Book Week, September 18, 1966; Saturday Review, December 3, 1966; Village Voice, January 26, 1967; Commonweal, April 28, 1967; Punch, March 20, 1968; Books and Bookmen, April, 1968; Observer Review, May 5, 1968; New York Times Book Review, July 20, 1968; New Republic, September 21, 1968.

*   *   *

SCHUBERT, Delwyn George   1919-

PERSONAL: Born October 16, 1919, in Manitowoc, Wis.; son of Norman John (a teacher) and Violet (Holsen) Schubert; married Beatrice-Ann Gehrung (a writer and lecturer), June 26, 1948 (died, 1965); children: Patrice-Ann, Heidi-Dell, Norman. Education: Wisconsin State College, Oshkosh, B.S. (with honors), 1941; University of Wisconsin, M.S., 1947; Northwestern University, Ph.D., 1949; University of California, Los Angeles, postdoctoral study, 1949-50. Home: 1967 Micheltorena St., Los Angeles, Calif. 90039. Office: California State College at Los Angeles, 5151 State College Dr., Los Angeles, Calif. 90032.

CAREER: California State College at Los Angeles, Los Angeles, Calif., 1949-59, 1961—, became professor of education, reading clinic director, 1965—; U.S. Air Force Schools, director of elementary education, Europe, Asia, and Africa, 1959-61. Conductor of reading improvement courses for American Bankers Institute and for industry. California Optometric Association, member of advisory education committee, southern section; Los Angeles College of Optometry, trustee. Military service: U.S. Army, Signal Corps, cryptographer, 1942-46; received three battle stars. Member: International Reading Association, American Academy of Optometry, California International Reading Association, Association of California State College Professors.

WRITINGS: The Doctor Eyes the Poor Reader, C.C Thomas, 1957; (with Theodore L. Torgerson) Improving Reading in the Elementary School: A Handbook Emphasizing Individualized Correction, W.C. Brown, 1963, 2nd edition published as Improving Reading Through Individualized Correction, 1968, 3rd edition published as Improving the Reading Program, 1972; (with Torgerson) A Dictionary of Terms and Concepts in Reading, C.C Thomas, 1964, 2nd edition, 1969; (contributor) Morris V. Jones, editor, Special Education Programs Within the United States, C.C Thomas, 1968; (editor) Readings in Reading: Practice, Theory, Research, Crowell, 1968; (contributor) Early Experience and Visual Information Processing in Perceptual and Reading Disorders, National Academy of Sciences (Washington, D.C.), 1970; Reading Games That Teach, Creative Teaching Press, 1970. Contributor of more than seventy research studies and articles to education journals; writer of three filmstrip scripts for BSA Educational Media, Santa Monica, Calif.

WORK IN PROGRESS: Reading and the Atypical Child.

AVOCATIONAL INTERESTS: Music (plays violin and collects records), ping-pong, reading.

*   *   *

SCHULLER, Robert Harold   1926-

PERSONAL: Born September 16, 1926, in Alton, Iowa; son of Anthony (a farmer) and Jennie (Beltman) Schuller; married Arvella DeHaan, June 15, 1950; children: Sheila, Robert, Jeanne Anne. Education: Hope College, B.A., 1947; Western Seminary, B.D., 1950. Home: 520 Memory Lane, Santa Ana, Calif. 92706.

CAREER: Minister, Reformed Church in America. Garden Grove Community Drive-In Church, Garden Grove, Calif., founder, pastor, 1955—. President of Robert Schuller Institute for Successful Church Leadership; president of Robert Schuller Televangelism Assoc., Inc. Reformed Church in America, member of board of education. Member: Pi Kappa Delta. Awards, honors: George Washington Honor Medal of Freedoms Foundation, 1962; LL.D., Azusa Pacific College, 1970.

WRITINGS: God's Way to the Good Life, Eerdmans, 1963; Your Future is Your Friend: An Inspirational Pilgrimage Through the Twenty-Third Psalm, Eerdmans, 1964; Move Ahead with Possibility Thinking, introduction by Norman Vincent Peale, Doubleday, 1967; Self-Love: The Dynamic Force of Success, introduction by Norman Vincent Peale, Hawthorn, 1969; Power Ideas for a Happy Family, Revell, 1972.

SIDELIGHTS: In collaboration with architect Richard Neutra, Schuller designed his own church, the first walk-in, drive-in church of its kind, in the mid-1950's. Avocational interests: Architecture.

*   *   *

SCHULTZ, Vernon B (urdette)   1924-

PERSONAL: Born August 15, 1924, in Tampico, Ill.; son of Ernest Albert (a farmer) and Edith (Eshelman) Schultz. Education: North Central College, Naperville, Ill., B.A.; University of Arizona, M.A. Religion: Presbyterian. Home address: P.O. Box 127, Morenci, Ariz. 85540.

CAREER: Goodyear Tire & Rubber Co., Akron, Ohio, time clerk, 1942-45; English and Latin teacher in Wonewoc, Wis., 1950-51, New Troy, Mich., 1951-53, Casa Grande, Ariz., 1953-54; Morenci High School, Morenci, Ariz., English and political science teacher, 1954—. Member: National Education Association, Arizona Education Association, Arizona English Teachers' Association, Lions International (president, Morenci club, 1960-61).

WRITINGS: Southwestern Town: The Story of Willcox, Arizona, University of Arizona Press, 1964.

AVOCATIONAL INTERESTS: Exchanging recorded tapes, mainly with persons in foreign countries.

SCHULZ, Charles M(onroe) 1922-

PERSONAL: Born November 26, 1922, in Minneapolis, Minn.; son of Carl (a barber) and Dena (Halverson) Schulz; married Joyce Halverson, April 18, 1949; children: Meredith, Charles Monroe, Craig, Amy, Jill. *Education:* Studied cartooning in an art school after graduation in 1940 from public high school in St. Paul, Minn. *Home:* 2162 Coffee Lane, Sebastopol, Calif. 95472. *Office:* c/o United Feature Syndicate, Daily News Building, New York, N.Y. 10017.

CAREER: Cartoonist, *St. Paul Pioneer Press* and *Saturday Evening Post*, 1948-49; creator of syndicated comic strip, "Peanuts," 1950. *Military service:* U.S. Army, served with Twentieth Armored Division in Europe, 1943-45; became staff sergeant. *Awards, honors:* Reuben award as outstanding cartoonist of the year, National Cartoonists' Society, 1955 and 1964; Yale award as outstanding humorist of the year, 1956; School Bell award, National Education Association, 1960; L.H.D., Anderson College, 1963; Peabody award and Emmy award, both 1966, for CBS cartoon special, "A Charlie Brown Christmas"; D.H.L., St. Mary's College of California, 1969.

WRITINGS—Cartoon books with captions, many collected from newspaper work: *Peanuts*, Rinehart, 1952; *More Peanuts*, Rinehart, 1954, selections from Volume 1 published as *Wonderful World of Peanuts*, Fawcett, 1963, selections from Volume 2 published as *Hey, Peanuts!*, Fawcett, 1963; *Good Grief, More Peanuts!*, Rinehart, 1956, selections from Volume 1 published as *Good Grief, Charlie Brown!*, Fawcett, 1963, selections from Volume 2 published as *For the Love of Peanuts*, Fawcett, 1963; *Good Ol' Charlie Brown*, Rinehart, 1957, selections from Volume 1 published as *Fun with Peanuts*, Fawcett, 1964, selections from Volume 2 published as *Here Comes Charlie Brown*, Fawcett, 1964; *Snoopy*, Rinehart, 1958, selections from Volume 1 published as *Here Comes Snoopy*, Fawcett, 1966, selections from Volume 2 published as *Good Ol' Snoopy*, Fawcett, 1958; *Young Pillars*, Warner Press, 1958; *But We Love You, Charlie Brown*, Rinehart, 1959, selections from Volume 1 published as *We're On Your Side, Charlie Brown*, Fawcett, 1966, selections from Volume 2 published as *You Are Too Much, Charlie Brown*, Fawcett, 1966; *Peanuts Revisited: Favorites Old and New*, Rinehart, 1959; *You're Out of Your Mind, Charlie Brown!*, Rinehart, 1959, selections from Volume 1 published as *Very Funny, Charlie Brown!*, Fawcett, 1965, selections from Volume 2 published as *What Next, Charlie Brown/*, Fawcett, 1965.

Go Fly a Kite, Charlie Brown, Holt, 1960, selections from Volume 1 published as *You're a Winner, Charlie Brown*, Fawcett, 1967, selections from Volume 2 published as *Let's Face It, Charlie Brown*, Fawcett, 1967; *Peanuts Every Sunday*, Holt, 1961, selections from Volume 1 published as *Who Do You Think You Are, Charlie Brown?*, Fawcett, 1968, selections from Volume 2 published as *You're My Hero, Charlie Brown*, Fawcett, 1968; *"Teen-ager" is Not a Disease*, Warner Press, 1961; *Happiness is a Warm Puppy*, Determined Productions, 1962; *It's a Dog's Life, Charlie Brown*, Holt, 1962, selections from Volume 1 published as *This is Your Life, Charlie Brown*, Fawcett, 1968, selections from Volume 2 published as *Slide, Charlie Brown, Slide*, Fawcett, 1968; *Snoopy, Come Home*, Holt, 1962, selections published as *We Love You, Snoopy*, Fawcett, 1970; *You Can't Win, Charlie Brown*, Holt, 1962, selections from Volume 1 published as *All This and Snoopy, Too*, Fawcett, 1969, selections from Volume 2 published as *Here's to You, Charlie Brown*, Fawcett, 1969; *Peanuts Project Book*, Determined Productions, 1963; *Security is a Thumb and a Blanket*, Determined Productions, 1963; *You Can Do It, Charlie Brown*, Holt, 1963, selections from Volume 1 published as *Nobody's Perfect, Charlie Brown*, Fawcett,

1969, selections from Volume 2 published as *You're a Brave Man, Charlie Brown*, Fawcett, 1969; *As You Like It, Charlie Brown*, Holt, 1964; *Christmas is Together-Time*, Determined Productions, 1964; *I Need All the Friends I Can Get*, Determined Productions, 1964; *We're Right Behind You, Charlie Brown*, Holt, 1964, Volume 1 reissued as *Peanuts for Everybody*, Fawcett, 1970, selections from Volume 2 published as *You've Done It Again, Charlie Brown*, Fawcett, 1970; *What Was Bugging Ol' Pharaoh?*, Warner Press, 1964; *A Charlie Brown Christmas* (adapted from the television production), World Publishing, 1965; *Love is Walking Hand in Hand*, Determined Productions, 1965; *Sunday's Fun Day, Charlie Brown*, Holt, 1965, Volume 1 reissued as *It's for You, Snoopy*, Fawcett, 1971, Volume 2 reissued as *Have It Your Way, Charlie Brown*, Fawcett, 1971; *You Need Help, Charlie Brown*, Holt, 1965, selections from Volume 1 published as *You're Not for Real, Snoopy*, Fawcett, 1971, selections from Volume 2 published as *You're a Pal, Snoopy*, Fawcett, 1972; *Charlie Brown's All-Stars* (adapted from the television production), World Publishing, 1966; *Home Is on Top of a Doghouse*, Determined Productions, 1966; *Snoopy and the Red Baron*, Holt, 1966; *The Unsinkable Charlie Brown* Holt, 1966, selections from Volume 1 published as *What Now, Charlie Brown?*, Fawcett, 1972, selections from Volume 2 published as *You're Something Special, Snoopy!*, Fawcett, 1972; *You're Something Else, Charlie Brown*, Holt, 1966; *Happiness is a Sad Song*, Determined Productions, 1967; *It's the Great Pumpkin, Charlie Brown* (adapted from the television production), World Publishing, 1967; *Teen-Agers, Unite!*, Bantam, 1967; *You'll Flip, Charlie Brown*, Holt, 1967, selections published as *You've Got a Friend, Charlie Brown*, Fawcett, 1972; *He's Your Dog, Charlie Brown!* (adapted from the television production), World Publishing, 1968; *Peanuts Treasury*, foreword by Johnny Hart, Holt, 1968; *Suppertime!*, Determined Productions, 1968; *You're in Love, Charlie Brown* (adapted from the television production), World Publishing, 1968; *You're You, Charlie Brown*, Holt, 1968; *A Boy Named Charlie Brown* (adapted from the film production), Holt, 1969; *Charlie Brown's Yearbook* (includes *He's Your Dog, Charlie Brown!*, *It's the Great Pumpkin, Charlie Brown*, *You're in Love, Charlie Brown*, and *Charlie Brown's All-Stars*), World Publishing, 1969; *You've Had It, Charlie Brown*, Holt, 1969; *Peanuts Cook Book*, recipes by June Dutton, Determined Productions, 1969; *Peanuts School Year Date Book, 1969-1970*, Determined Productions, 1969; *Snoopy and His Sopwith Camel*, Holt, 1969.

For Five Cents, Determined Productions, 1970; *It Was a Short Summer, Charlie Brown* (adapted from the television production), World Publishing, 1970; *It Really Doesn't Take Much to Make a Dad Happy*, Determined Productions, 1970; *Peanuts Classics*, Holt, 1970; *Peanuts Date Book 1972*, Determined Productions, 1970; *Peanuts Lunch Bag Cook Book* (including recipes by June Dutton), Determined Productions, 1970; *Snoopy and "It Was a Dark and Stormy Night"*, Holt, 1970; *It's Fun to Lie Here and Listen to the Sounds of the Night*, Determined Productions, 1970; *You're Out of Sight, Charlie Brown*, Holt, 1970; *Winning May Not Be Everything, But Losing Isn't Anything!*, Determined Productions, 1970; *You're the Greatest, Charlie Brown*, Fawcett, 1971; *You've Come a Long Way, Charlie Brown*, Holt, 1971; *Play It Again, Charlie Brown* (adapted from the television production), World Publishing, 1971; *You're Elected, Charlie Brown*, World Publishing, 1972; *Ha Ha, Herman Charlie Brown*, Holt, 1972; *Snoopy's Grand Slam*, Holt, 1972; *The Snoopy, Come Home Movie Book* (adapted from the film production), Holt, 1972; *Snoopy's Secret Life*, Hallmark, 1972; *The Peanuts Philosophers*, Hallmark, 1972; *Love a la Peanuts*, Hallmark, 1972; *It's Good to Have a Friend*, Hallmark, 1972. Also author, with Kenneth F. Hall, of a child study, *Two-by-Fours: A*

Sort of Serious Book About Small Children, Warner Press, 1965; (author of foreword) Morrie Turner, *Nipper,* Westminster, 1970.

Teleplays—26-minute animated cartoons, produced for CBS-TV: "A Charlie Brown Christmas," December 9, 1965; "Charlie Brown's All-Stars," June 8, 1966; "It's the Great Pumpkin, Charlie Brown," October 27, 1966; "You're in Love, Charlie Brown," June 12, 1967; "He's Your Dog, Charlie Brown!," February 14, 1968; "It Was a Short Summer, Charlie Brown," September 27, 1969; "Play It Again, Charlie Brown," March 28, 1971. Also writer of screenplays for "A Boy Named Charlie Brown," 1969, and "Snoopy, Come Home," 1972, both feature-length animated films produced for National General Pictures.

Illustrator: Art Linkletter, *Kids Say the Darndest Things,* Prentice-Hall, 1957; Art Linkletter, *Kids Still Say the Darndest Things,* Geis, 1961; Bill Adler, compiler, *Dear President Johnson,* Morrow, 1964; Fritz Ridenour, editor, *I'm a Good Man, But . . . ,* Regal Books (Glendale, Calif.), 1969.

SIDELIGHTS: "Sparky" Schulz maintains that the only thing he "really ever wanted to be was a cartoonist." A great admirer of Roy Crane, George Herriman, Al Capp, and Milt Caniff in his youth, he had a hard time selling his own comic strip at first; United Feature Syndicate finally bought it in 1950 and named it "Peanuts." "I was very upset with the title . . . and still am," recalls Schulz, who wanted to name the strip "Li'l Folks." "Peanuts" started in eight newspapers with a $90-a-month income; according to Schulz, "it took a long time to develop . . . in fact, the next twenty years saw a basic evolution of the strip." According to the public, however, the strip was a success right from the beginning. Schulz is the only cartoonist ever. to have won the Reuben award (the cartoonist's equivalent of the "Oscar," designed by and named after Rube Goldberg) twice, in 1955 and again in 1964. In a 1969 *Saturday Review* article entitled "The Not-So-Peanuts World of Charles M. Schulz," John Tebbel wrote that "the total income from the strip, including that of its twenty-one licensed subsidiaries, has been estimated at [up to] $50,000,000 a year," and that "Peanuts" has "audiences in more than 1,000 newspapers in the U.S. and Canada, and more than 100 others in forty-one foreign countries. Charlie Brown and his friends speak in twelve languages around the world."

"Peanuts" has in fact become the most popular comic strip of all time. As Lee Mendelson points out in his biography of Schulz, "Charlie Brown has become *the* symbol of mid century America . . . because [he is] a basic reflection of his time," the "Mr. Anxious" of the age, "our greatest seeker of identity in the 1950's and 1960's." Schulz contends that there really is no specific "philosophy" behind the strip, and that his "chief purpose is to get the strips done in time to get down to the post office by five o'clock when it closes." Like many cartoonists, he works in a studio within walking distance of his home in Sebastapol, California. Unlike many cartoonists, Schulz does all the work for the strip himself because, as Tebbel has said, " 'Peanuts' is so much a projection of the Schulz personality that it is inconceivable that anyone else could do it. . . . In the hierarchy of immortal comic strips—"Blondie," "Little Orphan Annie," "Andy Gump," "L'il Abner," "Krazy Kat"—Schulz has created something unique, more successful than all the others, but paradoxically more fragile. Perhaps it is because the strip is so personal that it elicits an unprecedented identification and affection from its vast readership." Commenting on the universality of the appeal of Charlie Brown, the perpetual loser, Schulz says: "It has always seemed to me that the strip has a rather bitter feeling to it, and it certainly deals in defeat. . . . It is interesting to put . . . adult fears and anxieties into the conversations of the children in 'Peauts.' " Schulz draws material for the strip from his own childhood memories, and from his experiences in raising five children. The populaity of the strip "cuts across every kind of classification," writes Tebbel, "for all kinds of special reasons. Schroeder, the Beethoven-loving character who is usually seen playing the piano when he isn't playing baseball, appeals to people who had never heard of Beethoven before. The little tyrant Lucy is seen by the small fry as a dliciously contrary girl, and by some adults as the typically abrasive female in American life. Linus, with his security blanket, seems to speak to everyone who would like to have a blanket of his own in troubled times. And Snoopy, the beagle who has Van Goghs hanging in his doghouse and a World War I aviator's helmet on his head, is the kind of fantasy dog everyone would like to own."

Schulz added an extra dimension to Charlie Brown with his introduction to television in 1965, and his associates, Lee Mendelson and Bill Melendez, plan to produce a new special every year. "Peanuts" subsidiaries manufacture everything from clothing, toys, stationery, and cosmetics to furniture, lunch boxes, and Charlie Brown baseballs, and dozens of new applications for licenses roll in every day. Reprints of "Peanuts," handled by seven different publishers at last count, have passed the 50,000,000 mark; Tebbel notes that Charlie Brown and his friends have even "emerged as modern evangelists" in Robert L. Short's two books, *The Gospel According to Peanuts,* published by John Knox in 1965, and *The Parables of Peanuts,* Harper, 1968. The hit musical, "You're a Good Man, Charlie Brown," adapted by Clark Gesner from the comic strip, was first produced Off-Broadway at Theatre 80 St. Marks, March 7, 1967, and has since played all over the world. The book of the same title, including music, lyrics, and adaptation by Gesner, was published by Random House in 1967, and an original cast recording of the music from the play was released by M-G-M Records the same year. A documentary on Schulz, produced by Mendelson and Melendez, was broadcast by CBS-TV in 1969. Schulz, Mendelson, and Warren Lockhart formed Snoopy Company in 1970 to create and develop a 300-acre Charlie Brown amusement park, probably on the Coast, to be opened in 1974. Snoopy has been adopted by NASA as a promotional device, and, notes Tebbel, "Snoopy emblems are now worn by more than 800 members of the manned space flight team as rewards for outstanding work." As everyone knows, the ubiquitous beagle made international history as the official name of the LEM (Lunar Excursion Module) of the Apollo 10 manned flight to the moon in 1969. Great Pumpkin sightings are reported almost as often as UFO's, and Schroeder and his toy piano have been immortalized in the stained glass window of the Westminster Presbyterian Church in Buffalo, New York, along with Bach, Martin Luther, Duke Ellington, and Dr. Albert Schweitzer. And all because, as Tebbel concludes, "everyone sees something different, and something of himself, in Charlie Brown and his friends. He's everybody's boy."

AVOCATIONAL INTERESTS: Outdoor sports, especially ice hockey and golf.

BIOGRAPHICAL/CRITICAL SOURCES: Saturday Evening Post, January 12, 1957, April 25, 1964; *Look,* July 22, 1958; Carmen Richards, *Minnesota Writers,* Denison, 1961; *Newsweek,* March 6, 1961; *Seventeen,* January, 1962; *Time,* April 9, 1965, January 5, 1970; *Village Voice,* March 16, 1967; *Life,* March 17, 1967; *New Yorker,* March 18, 1967; *New York Times Magazine,* April 16, 1967; *Redbook,* December, 1967; *Punch,*

February 7, 1968; *Christian Science Monitor,* November 29, 1968, November 11, 1970; *Saturday Review,* April 12, 1969; *New York Times,* May 26, 1969, June 2, 1971; *Valuator,* spring, 1969; *U.S. Catholic,* July, 1969; *Business World,* December 20, 1969; Lee Mendelson (with Schulz), *Charlie Brown and Charlie Schulz,* World Publishing, 1970; *Washington Post,* April 4, 1970.

*   *   *

SCHURR, Cathleen

PERSONAL: Born in London, England; daughter of Henry William and Elsa (Von Halle) Schurr; married Joseph Skelly, 1941; children: Christopher. *Education:* University of Michigan, B.A. *Agent:* Phyllis Jackson, Ashley Steiner-Famous Artists, Inc., 555 Madison Ave., New York, N.Y. 10022.

CAREER: Free-lance writer and public relations consultant, 1939—.

WRITINGS: The Shy Little Kitten, Simon & Schuster, 1946; *The Long and the Short of It,* Vanguard, 1950; *Naturally Yours: A Personal Experience with Natural Childbirth* (adult non-fiction), Holt, 1953; *Dark Encounter* (adult mystery), Holt, 1955; *Cats Have Kittens, Do Gloves Have Mittens?,* Knopf, 1962. Contributor to national magazines.

AVOCATIONAL INTERESTS: Theatre, cooking, tennis, birds.

*   *   *

SCHWAB, Arnold T.   1922-

PERSONAL: Born January 5, 1922, in Los Angeles, Calif.; son of Samuel B. and Sarah (Pinsker) Schwab. *Education:* University of California, Los Angeles, A.B., 1943; Harvard University, A.M., 1947, Ph.D., 1951. *Home:* 302 Winnipeg Pl., #7, Long Beach, Calif. 90814.

CAREER: University of California, Los Angeles, instructor in English, 1952-54; University of Michigan, Ann Arbor, instructor in English, 1954-55; *Wisdom* (magazine), Beverly Hills, Calif., research director, 1956-57; United Service Organizations—Jewish Welfare Board, Los Angeles, Calif., club director, 1957-60; Long Beach State College, Long Beach, Calif., assistant professor, 1961-69, professor of English, 1969—. *Military service:* U.S. Navy, 1943-46; served in Pacific theater, became lieutenant j.g. *Member:* Modern Language Association of America, College English Association of Southern California, Phi Beta Kappa. *Awards, honors:* Sheldon fellow, Harvard University, 1951-52; James D. Phelan Award for Literature, and Silver Medal of Commonwealth Club of California, 1964, both for *James Gibbons Huneker, Critic of the Seven Arts.*

WRITINGS: James Gibbons Huneker, Critic of the Seven Arts, Stanford University Press, 1963. Contributor of articles on James Huneker and Joseph Conrad to scholarly periodicals.

WORK IN PROGRESS: A study of Huneker and Edward MacDowell, completed and awaiting publication; editing a collection of unreprinted essays by James Huneker on Americans in the arts; editing Huneker's complete letters.

SIDELIGHTS: Schwab worked fifteen years on his first book; views "with admiration those [teaching] scholars who turn out books at more frequent intervals." *Avocational interests:* Music (especially operatic), bridge, tennis (captained university tennis team in 1943).

BIOGRAPHICAL/CRITICAL SOURCES: Long Beach Independent Press-Telegram, September 22, 1963.

SCHWEBELL, Gertrude C(lorius)

PERSONAL: Surname is pronounced *Shva*-bell. Born in Diller, Neb.; daughter of Otto H.S. (a minister) and Gretchen (Schumacher) Clorius; married John R. Schwebell (an assistant manager), July 5, 1928. *Education:* Attended University of Rostock (Germany), two years. *Home:* 549 Riverside Dr., New York, N.Y. 10027.

MEMBER: American Translators Association, Pen and Brush Club, Verband Deutscher Uebersetzer Literarischer und Wissenschaftlicher Werke, Query, Japan Society.

WRITINGS: (Adapter) *Where Magic Reigns: German Fairy Tales Since Grimm* (retold), Stephen Daye Press, 1957; (editor and translator) *Contemporary German Poetry: An Anthology,* New Directions, 1964; (author of German text) William Carlos Williams, *New Places/Neue Orte,* English and German edition, Blaeschke, 1966; *Die Geburt des modernen Japan* (history), Rauch (Dusseldorf), 1970; (adapter) Freidrich de la Motte Fouque, *Undine,* Simon & Schuster, 1971. Contributor of articles to *New Standard Encyclopedia, Yearbooks,* 1966, 1967, 1968, 1970, and to *Encyclopedia of World Literature,* Ungar, 1967, 1969, 1970, 1971. Contributor of English and German poems to periodicals in the United States, Canada, Germany, and Japan; represented in anthologies in the United States and Germany; short stories and articles have been published in the United States and Germany.

WORK IN PROGRESS: A book, tentatively titled *New York: Short Stories.*

BIOGRAPHICAL/CRITICAL SOURCES: Poetry, February, 1968.

*   *   *

SCHWEITZER, Arthur   1905-

PERSONAL: Born November 27, 1905, in Pirmasens, Germany; son of Heinrich (a shoe manufacturer) and Louise (Haarlos) Schweitzer; married Elfriede Zimmerman, October 27, 1937; children: Linda, Eric. *Education:* University of Berlin, student, 1932-33; University of Basel, Dr.rer.pol., 1936; postgraduate study at Harvard University, Columbia University, University of Chicago, 1937-39. *Office:* Indiana University, Bloomington, Ind. 47401.

CAREER: Indiana University, Bloomington, associate professor, 1947-51, professor of economics, 1951—. Fulbright lecturer, 1961-62. *Member:* American Economic Association, Association of Comparative Economics (vice-president, 1964; president, 1965), Economic History Association. *Awards, honors:* Rockefeller fellow, 1937-39; Ford Foundation fellow, 1958-59; Rockefeller research fellow, 1966-67.

WRITINGS: Spiethoffs Konjunkturlehre (title means "Spiethoff's Business Cycle Theory"), Helbing & Lichtenhahn, 1938; (co-author) *Third Reich,* edited by Baumont and Fried, [London], 1954; (co-author) *Hamburger Jahrbuch fur Wirtschafts und Gesellschaftspolitik,* Mohr-Verlag, 1962; *Big Business in the Third Reich,* Indiana University Press, 1964; *Nazifizierung des Mittelstandes,* Enke Verlag, 1970. Contributor of more than fifty articles to professional journals.

WORK IN PROGRESS: Charisma, Ideology, and Violence, an application and further development of Max Weber's socio-political theory to modern rightist movements, especially Nazis and neo-Nazis; *State Directed Capitalism,* a book on the second phase of Nazi economy.

SCHWERNER, Armand 1927-

PERSONAL: Born May 11, 1927, in Antwerp, Belgium; son of Elie (in manufacturing) and Sarah (Bartnowski) Schwerner; married Doloris Holmes (an art ecologist), January 13, 1961; children: Adam, Ari. *Education:* Attended Cornell University, 1945-47, Universite de Geneve, 1947-48; Columbia University, B.S., 1950, M.A., 1964. *Religion:* Jewish. *Home:* 30 Catlin Ave., Staten Island, N.Y. 10304. *Office:* Staten Island Community College, City University of New York, 715 Ocean Ter., Staten Island, N.Y. 10301.

CAREER: Eron Preparatory School, New York, N.Y., teacher, 1955-59; Barnard School for Boys, Riverdale, N.Y., instructor in English and French, 1959-64; Long Island University, New York, N.Y., instructor in English, 1963-64; Staten Island Community College of City University of New York, Staten Island, N.Y., associate professor of English and speech, 1964—. *Military service:* U.S. Navy, 1945-46. *Awards, honors:* Two research fellowships from State University of New York; research fellowship from City University of New York.

WRITINGS: The Lightfall (poems), Hawks Well Press, 1963; (with Donald M. Kaplan) *The Domesday Dictionary,* Simon & Schuster, 1963; (project editor) *A Farewell to Arms: A Critical Commentary,* American R.D.M., 1963; (project editor with Jerome Neibrief) *A Critical Commentary: The Sound and the Fury,* American R.D.M., 1964; *(if personal)* (poems), Black Sparrow Press, 1968; *The Tablets, I-VIII* (poems), Cummington, 1968; *Seaweed* (poems), Black Sparrow Press, 1969; *The Tablets, I-XIV* (poems), Grossman, 1971.

Monarch Notes and Study Guides, all published by Monarch: *John Steinbeck's "The Red Pony," and "The Pearl",* 1965, *John Steinbeck's "Of Mice and Men",* 1965, *Dos Passos' "U.S.A.," and Other Works,* 1966, *Andre Gide's "The Immoralist," "Strait is the Gate," and Other Works: A Critical Commentary,* 1966.

Poetry anthologized in *New Directions Annual 19,* edited by James McLaughlin, New Directions, 1966; *Conditions of Man,* edited by Dale E. Bonnette and Willoughby H. Johnson, Houghton, 1968; *Technicians of the Sacred: A Range of Poetries from Africa, America, Asia, and Oceania,* edited by Jerome Rothenberg, Doubleday, 1968; *The East Side Scene,* edited by Allen De Loach, University Press at Buffalo, 1968; *A Treasury of Yiddish Poetry,* edited by Irving Howe and Eliezer Greenberg, Holt, 1969; *Inside Outer Space: New Poems of the Space Age,* edited by Robert Vas Dias, Doubleday-Anchor, 1970; *Possibilities of Poetry: An Anthology of American Contemporaries,* edited by Richard Kostelanetz, Dell, 1970; *A Caterpillar Anthology,* edited by Clayton Eshleman, Doubleday, 1971; *Art Work, No Commercial Value, 9 oz.,* edited by Jerry G. Bowles, Grossman, 1971; *The New Open Poetry,* edited by Gross and Quasha, Simon & Schuster, 1971; *Breakthrough,* edited by Richard Kostelanetz, Holt, 1971; *This Book is a Movie: An Exhibition of Language Art,* edited by Jerry G. Bowles and Tony Russell, Dell, 1972; and *Shaking the Pumpkin: Traditional Poetry of the North American Indians,* edited by Jerome Rothenberg, Doubleday, 1972.

Contributor to *Nation, Beloit Poetry Review, Trobar, Accent, West Wind, Nomad,* and other literary publications, and to professional journals. Co-publisher, Hawk's Well Press, 1961-62.

WORK IN PROGRESS: Workings and adaptations from American Indian, Yiddish, and French.

AVOCATIONAL INTERESTS: Playing the clarinet.

BIOGRAPHICAL/CRITICAL SOURCES: Virginia Quarterly Review, summer, 1969.

SCIGLIANO, Robert (G.) 1925-

PERSONAL: Surname is pronounced *Sig-lee-ah-*no; born February 15, 1925, in Boston, Mass.; son of Alma A. (Mazzei) Scigliano and stepfather Patrick F. Russo (a plumber); married June Buerge (a teacher), September 1, 1949; children: Eric, Brian, Claire, John. *Education:* University of California, Los Angeles, B.A., 1950, M.A., 1952; University of Chicago, Ph.D., 1957. *Office:* Political Science Department, Boston College, Chestnut Hill, Mass. 02167.

CAREER: Michigan State University, East Lansing, instructor, 1953-56, assistant professor, 1956-59, associate professor, 1959-63, professor of political science, 1963-66; State University of New York at Buffalo, professor of political science, 1966-70; Boston College, Chestnut Hill, Mass., professor of political science, 1970—. *Military service:* U.S. Navy, 1942-46. *Member:* American Political Science Association (life).

WRITINGS: Michigan Legislative Report, Governmental Research Bureau, Michigan State University, 1955; *Michigan One-Man Grand Jury,* Governmental Research Bureau, Michigan State University, 1957; (editor) *The Courts,* Little, Brown, 1962; *South Vietnam: Nation Under Stress,* Houghton, 1963; (with G.H. Fox) *Technical Assistance in Vietnam: The Michigan State University Experience,* Praeger, 1965; *The Supreme Court and the Presidency,* Free Press, 1971. Contributor of articles to scholarly journals.

* * *

SCOBIE, James R(alston) 1929-

PERSONAL: Born June 16, 1929, in Valparaiso, Chile; son of Jordan Ralston (an educator and banker) and Freda (Johnson) Scobie; married Patricia Beauchamp, November 1, 1957 (died, 1965); married Ingrid Ellen Winther, June 14, 1967; children: (first marriage) William Ralston, Clare Beauchamp; (second marriage) Kirsten Winther. *Education:* Princeton University, A.B., 1950; Harvard University, M.A., 1951, Ph.D., 1954. *Home:* 516 Hamilton Court, Bloomington, Ind. 47401. *Office:* Department of History, Indiana University, Bloomington, Ind. 47401.

CAREER: University of California, Berkeley, instructor, 1957-59, assistant professor of history, 1960-62, 1963-64; Indiana University, Bloomington, associate professor, 1964-65, professor of history, 1965—, director of Latin American studies, 1965-68, chairman of history department, 1970—. U.S. national alternate, Pan American Institute of Geography and History, 1968—. Visiting scholar of Latin American studies, Columbia University, 1962-63. *Military service:* U.S. Army, 1954-57; became first lieutenant. *Member:* American Historical Association, Conference on Latin American History, Latin American Studies Association, Academia Nacional de la Historia (Argentina; corresponding member), Pacific Coast Council on Latin American Studies, World Affairs Council of Northern California, Phi Beta Kappa. *Awards, honors:* Social Science Research Council faculty fellowship, 1959-60; Organization of American States scholarship, 1959-60; Guggenheim fellowship, 1967-68.

WRITINGS: (Editor with Palmira Bollo Cabrios) *Correspondencia Mitre-Elizalde,* University of Buenos Aires Press, 1960; *Disolucion de un triunvirato,* Seminario de Historia Argentina, 1960; *Argentina: A City and a Nation,* Oxford University Press, 1964, 2nd edition, 1971; *Revolution on the Pampas: A Social History of Argentina Wheat, 1860-1910* (monograph), University of Texas Press, 1964; (editor and author of introduction with Dale Morgan) *Three Years in California: William Perkins' Journal of Life at Sonora, 1849-52,* University of California Press, 1964; *La lucha por la consolidacion de la nacionalidad argentina, 1852-1862,* Hachette, 1964. Contributing editor, *Handbook of Latin American Studies,* 1966—; member of board of editors, *Hispanic American History Review,* 1966-72; advisory editor, *Latin American Research Review,* 1967-69.

WORK IN PROGRESS: The City of Buenos Aires: Plaza to Suburb, 1870-1910, for Oxford University Press.

SIDELIGHTS: Scobie's travels have been focused on Argentina and Brazil, with research in South America, 1949, 1952-54, 1959-60, 1961, 1965, 1968-69, 1973; he has made other trips to Germany, 1955-57, and to Mexico, 1958.

*   *   *

SCOTT, John Anthony 1916-

PERSONAL: Born January 20, 1916, in London, England; became U.S. citizen, 1943; son of Philip (a dentist) and Nora (Mort de Bois) Scott; married Maria Malleville Haller (a teacher), August 27, 1940; children: Elizabeth (Mrs. Jean-Paul Jannot), John Wardlaw, Robert Alan. *Education:* Attended St. Paul's School, London, England; Trinity College, Oxford, B.A. (first class honors), 1937, M.A., 1945; Columbia University, B.A., 1947, Ph.D., 1950. *Politics:* Reform Democrat. *Home:* 3900 Manhattan College Pkwy., New York, N.Y. 10471.

CAREER: Amherst College, Amherst, Mass., instructor in European history, 1948-51; Fieldston School, New York, N.Y., instructor in U.S. history and chairman of department, 1951-67; Rutgers University, Newark, N.J., visiting professor of legal history, 1967—. Instructor at Seminar on American Culture, Cooperstown, N.Y., 1963; sometime ballad singer at Old Sturbridge Village. Aided in organization of Prayer Pilgrimage to Washington, 1957, and two youth marches for integrated schools, 1958, 1959; New York metropolitan coordinator for March on Washington for Equal Rights and Jobs, August, 1963. *Military service:* U.S. Army, Armored Forces and Intelligence, 1942-45; served in Europe; became staff sergeant; received Field Citation. *Member:* American Historical Association, National Association of Independent Schools, Association for the Study of Negro Life and History, Authors Guild of Authors League of America, American Society for Legal History. *Awards, honors:* M.A. from Oxford University, 1945.

WRITINGS: (Co-editor) *Introduction to Contemporary Civilization in the West,* Columbia University Press, 1946; *Republican Ideas and the Liberal Tradition in France, 1870-1914,* Columbia University Press, 1951; (editor) Frances Anne Kemble, *Journal of a Residence on a Georgian Plantation in 1838-1839,* Knopf, 1961; (editor) *Living Documents in American History,* Washington Square Press, Volume I: *From Earliest Colonial Times to the Civil War,* 1964, Volume II: *From Reconstruction to the Outbreak of World War I,* 1968; (editor, translator, and contributor) *The Defense of Gracchus Babeuf Before the High Court of Vendome,* Gehenna Press, 1964; (editor) Thomas More, *Utopia,* Washington Square Press, 1965; *The Ballad of America: The History of the United States in Song and Story,* Bantam, 1966, hardcover edition, Grosset, 1967; *Settlers on the Eastern Shore, 1607-1750,* Knopf, 1967; (editor and author of introduction) Frank Moore, compiler, *The Diary of the American Revolution, 1775-1781,* abridged edition, Washington Square Press, 1967; (editor) James M. McPherson, *Marching Toward Freedom: The Negro in the Civil War, 1861-1865,* Knopf, 1968; *The Trumpet of a Prophecy: Revolutionary America, 1763-1783,* Knopf, 1969. Contributor of articles to *Teaching and Learning, New York Folklore Quarterly, Activist, Journal of Negro History, Country Dancer, History Notes, Sing Out,* and

to other folklore and educational journals. General editor, "The Living History Library," Knopf, 1965—.

Recordings for Heirloom Records: (Writer of script and producer) "The New Deal Through Its Songs and Ballads," "Irish Immigration Through Its Songs and Ballads," "The Negro People Through Their Songs and Ballads," "New England Whaling Through Its Songs and Ballads," "New York City Through Its Songs and Ballads," and "The Story of the Cowboy Through His Songs and Ballads"; (writer and performer with Gene Bonyun and Bill Bonyun) "The American Revolution Through Its Songs and Ballads"; (writer with Bill Bonyun) "The Civil War Through Its Songs and Ballads."

WORK IN PROGRESS: Social Science and Survival, to be published by Bantam; biographies of Joseph P. Bradley and Frances Anne Kemble.

SIDELIGHTS: Calling textbooks "mere dry husks of facts," Scott insists that his students learn history directly from original sources, and supplies them with mimeographed copies of documents that are ordinarily seen only by scholars. He writes: "Documents are the life blood of history.... Historical documentation for me includes national song, the so-called 'folk music' that is a profound embodiment of American historical experience from the beginning to the present. No small part of my researches has been in the digging out of old and forgotten songs dealing with the great events and conflicts of the past." He has been known to strum a guitar and sing obscure colonial tunes for his classes.

AVOCATIONAL INTERESTS: Tennis, swimming, bicycle riding, ice skating, and traveling. ("At various times I have travelled on foot or by bike in France, Germany, Greece, Austria, and Yugoslavia.... I have been in almost every state of the Union.")

BIOGRAPHICAL/CRITICAL SOURCES: Time, June 1, 1962; *Best Sellers,* December 1, 1967; *New York Times Book Review,* February 25, 1968; *Best Sellers,* June 1, 1970; *Library Journal,* June 15, 1970.

*   *   *

SCOTT, Nathan A(lexander), Jr. 1925-

PERSONAL: Born April 24, 1925, in Cleveland, Ohio; son of Nathan A. (a lawyer) and Maggie (Martin) Scott; married Charlotte Hanley (an economist), December 21, 1946; children: Nathan A. III, Leslie Kristin. *Education:* Wayne State University, student, 1940-41; University of Michigan B.A., 1944; Union Theological Seminary, New York, N.Y., B.D., 1946; Columbia University, Ph.D., 1949. *Home:* 5517 S. Kimbark Ave., Chicago, Ill. 60637.

CAREER: Virginia Union University, Richmond, dean of chapel, 1946-47; Howard University, Washington, D.C., instructor, 1948-50, assistant professor, 1950-53, associate professor of humanities, 1953-55, director of general education program in humanities, 1953-55; University of Chicago, Divinity School, Chicago, Ill., assistant professor, 1955-58, associate professor, 1958-64, Shailer Mathews Professor of Theology and Literature, 1964—; ordained priest in Episcopal Church, 1960. Adjunct professor, University of Michigan, 1969; Walter and Mary Tuohy visiting professor, John Carroll University, 1970. Canon theologian, Cathedral of St. James, Chicago, Ill. Trustee of Seabury-Western Theological Seminary, Episcopal Radio-TV Foundation, Society for the Arts, Religion, and Contemporary Culture, and Chicago Historical Society.

MEMBER: Society for Religion in Higher Education (Kent fellow), American Philosophical Association, Modern Language Association of America, American Academy of Religion, *Awards, honors:* Litt.D., Ripon

College, 1965, St. Mary's College, 1969; L.H.D., Wittenberg University, 1965; D.D., Philadelphia Divinity School, 1967; S.T.D., General Theological Seminary, 1968; fellow of School of Letters, Indiana University.

WRITINGS: Rehearsals of Discomposure: Alienation and Reconciliation in Modern Literature, King's Crown Press, 1952; (editor) *The Tragic Vision and the Christian Faith,* Association Press, 1957; *Modern Literature and the Religious Frontier,* Harper, 1958; *The Broken Center: A Definition of the Crisis of Values in Modern Literature* (lecture), National Council of the Protestant Episcopal Church, 1959.

Albert Camus, Hillary, 1962, 2nd revised edition, Bowes, 1969; *Reinhold Niebuhr* (pamphlet), University of Minnesota Press, 1963; (editor) *The New Orpheus: Essays Toward a Christian Poetic,* Sheed, 1964; (editor) *The Climate of Faith in Modern Literature,* Seabury, 1964; *Samuel Beckett,* Hillary, 1965, 2nd revised edition, Bowes, 1969; (editor) *Forms of Extremity in the Modern Novel,* John Knox, 1965; (editor) *Four Ways of Modern Poetry,* John Knox, 1965; (editor) *Man in the Modern Theatre,* John Knox, 1965; *The Broken Center: Studies in the Theological Horizon of Modern Literature,* Yale University Press, 1966; *Ernest Hemingway: A Critical Essay,* Eerdmans, 1966; (editor) *The Modern Vision of Death,* John Knox, 1967; (editor) *Adversity and Grace: Studies in Recent American Literature,* University of Chicago Press, 1968; *Craters of the Spirit: Studies in the Modern Novel,* Corpus Publications, 1968; *The Unquiet Vision: Mirrors of Man in Existentialism,* World Publishing, 1969; *Negative Capability: Studies in the New Literature and the Religious Situation,* Yale University Press, 1969.

The Wild Prayer of Longing: Poetry and the Sacred, Yale University Press, 1971; *Nathanael West,* Eerdmans, 1971.

Contributor: Rollo May, editor, *Symbolism in Religion and Literature,* Braziller, 1960; Robert O. Evans, editor, *Graham Greene: Some Critical Considerations,* University of Kentucky Press, 1963; Melvin J. Friedman and Lewis A. Lawson, editors, *The Added Dimension: The Mind and Art of Flannery O'Connor,* Fordham University Press, 1966; William V. Spanos, editor, *Existentialism,* Crowell, 1966; Edward Cell, editor, *Religion and Contemporary Western Culture,* Abingdon Press, 1967; Donald B. Gibson, *Five Black Writers: Essays on Wright, Ellison, Baldwin, Hughes, and LeRoi Jones,* New York University Press, 1970; Howard Hunter, editor, *Humanities, Religion, and the Arts Tomorrow,* Holt, 1972. Book review editor, *Christian Scholar,* 1960—; co-editor, *Journal of Religion,* 1963—.

BIOGRAPHICAL/CRITICAL SOURCES: Contemporary Literature, spring, 1968; *Comparative Literature,* spring, 1968; *Virginia Quarterly Review,* autumn, 1968; *Christian Century,* February 19, 1969, May 6, 1970; *Georgia Review,* summer, 1969; *Books Abroad,* winter, 1970.

*   *   *

SCOTT, Tom   1918-

PERSONAL: Born June 6, 1918, in Glasgow, Scotland; son of William Kerr (a boiler-maker and builder) and Catherine (Newell Baillie) Scott; married Heather Fretwell, 1963; children: one son, twin daughters. *Education:* Attended Madras College, St. Andrews University; Edinburgh University, M.A. (with honors in English literature and language), Ph.D. *Politics:* Non-party socialist and Scottish Nationalist. *Religion:* Humanist. *Home:* 12 St. Vincent St., Edinburgh, Midlothian, Scotland.

CAREER: Writer. *Military service:* Royal Army Pay Corps, 1939-44; served in Africa; became sergeant. *Member:* Traverse Theatre Club (Edinburgh). *Awards, honors:* Atlantic Award (Rockefeller Trust), 1950; Carnegie Senior Scholarship and Fellowship.

WRITINGS: Seeven Poems o Maister Francis Villon, Pound Press, 1953; *An Ode til New Jerusalem,* MacDonald, 1956; *The Ship and Ither Poems,* Oxford University Press, 1963; *A Possible Solution to the Scotch Problem* (pamphlet), MacDonald, 1963; *Dunbar: A Critical Exposition of the Poems,* Barnes & Noble, 1966; (editor with John MacQueen) *The Oxford Book of Scottish Verse,* Clarendon Press, 1966; (editor 'and author of introduction and notes) *Late Medieval Scots Poetry: A Selection from the Makars and Their Heirs Down to 1610,* Barnes & Noble, 1967; *At the Shrine o the Unkent Sodger: A Poem for Recitation,* Akros Publications, 1968; (adapter) *Tales of King Robert the Bruce* (juvenile; freely adapted from "The Brus" of John Barbour, 14th Century), Pergamon, 1969; (editor, author of introduction, and contributor) *The Penguin Book of Scottish Verse,* Penguin, 1970; (editor) *Poetry of the Scots,* Pergamon, 1970. Contributor to *New World Writing, Poetry, Botteghe Oscure,* and other journals. Editor, "Scottish Literature" series, Pergamon.

WORK IN PROGRESS: A book on middle Scots poets, for Heinemann; more poems.

SIDELIGHTS: Scott writes: "My aim is to contribute to Scottish literature as much as I can within my limitations. I write in the Modern Scots language for verse, standard English for prose, and sometimes a mixture of the two. I belong to and support the Scottish Renaissance group of Scottish writers led by Hugh MacDiarmid. This movement, although strongly national-centered, is," he asserts, "much more international in outlook than any other British group." Scott has traveled in France, Italy, Sicily, Belgium, Germany, Austria, Greece, Yugoslavia, and Nigeria, and has a reading knowledge of French, Italian, Anglo-Saxon, Middle English, and Middle Scots.

BIOGRAPHICAL/CRITICAL SOURCES: Babette Deutsch, *Poetry in Our Time,* 2nd edition, Doubleday-Anchor, 1963; *Times Literary Supplement,* January 12, 1967, June 26, 1969; *Listener,* March 9, 1967; *Poetry,* March, 1968, October, 1968.

*   *   *

SCOWCROFT, Richard P(ingree)   1916-

PERSONAL: Surname is pronounced *Sko*-croft; born June 26, 1916, in Ogden, Utah; son of Heber (a businessman) and Ida (Pingree) Scowcroft; married Anne M. Kendall, July 16, 1948; children: Richard Mark, Roger Kendall, Philip Henry. *Education:* University of Utah, B.A., 1937; Harvard University, M.A., 1941, Ph.D., 1946. *Agent:* Russell & Volkening, Inc., 551 Fifth Ave., Room 1414, New York, N.Y. 10017. *Office:* Department of English, Stanford University, Stanford, Calif. 94305.

CAREER: Harvard University, Cambridge, Mass., Briggs-Copeland Instructor, 1946-47; Stanford University, Stanford, Calif., assistant professor, 1947-50, associate professor, 1950-57, professor of English literature, 1957—.

WRITINGS—All novels: Children of the Covenant, Houghton, 1945; *First Family,* Houghton, 1950; *A View of the Bay,* Houghton, 1955; *Wherever She Goes,* Lippincott, 1967; *The Ordeal of Dudley Dean,* Lippincott, 1969.

(Editor with Wallace Stegner and Boris Ilyin) *The Writer's Art* (short stories), Heath, 1950; (editor with Stegner and Nancy Packer): *Twenty Years of Stanford Short Stories,* Stanford University Press, 1966; *Stanford Short Stories, 1968,* Stanford University Press, 1968.

WORK IN PROGRESS: A novel, *Back to Fire Mountain,* publication by Little, Brown expected in 1973.

BIOGRAPHICAL/CRITICAL SOURCES: New York Times Book Review, December 18, 1966, February 9, 1969, July 20, 1969; *Library Journal,* July, 1969.

* * *

SCUDDER, Mildred Lee 1908-
(Mildred Lee)

PERSONAL: Born February 19, 1908, in Blockton, Ala.; daughter of Dallas Powell and Aeolian (Spear) Lee; married James Henry Hurstwood Scudder (a lands acquisition agent), May 10, 1947; children: Barbara Lee Schimpff DuLac, Robert Donald Schimpff, Jane Powell. *Education:* Attended Bessie Tift College, 1925-26; additional study at Troy Normal College, Columbia University, New York University, and University of New Hampshire. *Religion:* United Liberal. *Home:* 1361 52nd Ave. N., St. Petersburg, Fla. 33703.

CAREER: Free-lance writer. Member, St. Petersburg Council on Human Relations.

WRITINGS—All under name Mildred Lee: *The Invisible Sun,* Westminster, 1946; *The Rock and Willow,* Lothrop, 1963; *Honor Sands,* Lothrop, 1966; *The Skating Rink,* Seabury, 1969; *The Bride of the Lamb,* Seabury, 1970; *Fog,* Seabury, 1972. Contributor of short stories to *Ladies' Home Journal, Redbook,* and *Tanager.*

WORK IN PROGRESS: A novel for teenagers with working title *The Years Between.*

* * *

SCULLARD, Howard Hayes 1903-

PERSONAL: Born February 9, 1903, in Bedford, England; son of Herbert Hayes (a minister and professor), and Barbara Louise (Dodds) Scullard. *Education:* Attended Highgate School; St. John's College, Cambridge, B.A., 1926; University of London, Ph.D., 1930. *Home:* 6 Foscote Rd., Hendon, London N.W. 4, England.

CAREER: New College, University of London, London, England, classical tutor, 1926-35; King's College, University of London, reader, 1935-59, professor of ancient history, 1959-70, professor emeritus, 1970—. Governor, New College. *Member:* British Academy (fellow; council, 1962—), Society of Antiquaries (fellow), Society for the Promotion of Roman Studies (vice-president), Royal Numismatic Society (council member, various periods). *Awards, honors:* Thirlwall Prize, 1929, for *Scipio Africanus in the Second Punic War.*

WRITINGS: Scipio Africanus in the Second Punic War (essay), Cambridge University Press, 1930; *A History of the Roman World from 753 to 146 B.C.,* Methuen, 1935, Macmillan, 1939, 3rd edition, Barnes & Noble, 1961; (editor with H.E. Butler) *Livy, Book XXX,* Methuen, 1939, 6th edition, 1954; (joint editor and contributor) *The Oxford Classical Dictionary,* Clarendon Press, 1949, 2nd edition (with N.G.L. Hammond), 1970; *Roman Politics, 220-150 B.C.,* Clarendon Press, 1951; (reviser) Frank B. Marsh, *A History of the Roman World from 146 to 30 B.C.,* 2nd edition, Methuen, 1953, 3rd edition, revised, Barnes & Noble, 1961; *From the Gracchi to Nero: A History of Rome from 133 B.C. to A.D. 68,* Praeger, 1959, 3rd edition, Barnes & Noble, 1970; (editor with A.A.M. van der Heyden) *Atlas of the Classical World,* Thomas Nelson, 1960; (revised with W.S. Maguinnes) John C. Stobart, *The Grandeur That Was Rome,* 4th edition, Sidgwick & Jackson, 1961, Praeger, 1969; (editor with van der Heyden) *Shorter Atlas of the Classical World,* Thomas Nelson (Edinburgh), 1962, Dutton, 1966; (contributor) Thomas Allen Dorey, editor, *Cicero,* Basic Books, 1965; *The Etruscan Cities and Rome,* Cornell University Press, 1967; *Scipio Africanus, Soldier and Politician,* Cornell University Press, 1970. Contributor of articles to *Encyclopaedia Britannica,* and of articles and reviews to professional journals. General editor, "Aspects of Greek and Roman Life" series, Cornell University Press, 1967—.

AVOCATIONAL INTERESTS: Golf.

BIOGRAPHICAL/CRITICAL SOURCES: Times Literary Supplement, September 28, 1967; *Library Journal,* July, 1970.

* * *

SEAGER, Ralph William 1911-

PERSONAL: Born November 3, 1911, in Geneva, N.Y.; son of William Thomas and Ellen (Nichols) Seager; married Ruth Lovejoy (a high school cafeteria manager), December 11, 1932; children: William, Douglas, Keith. *Education:* University of California, Berkeley, special courses, 1950-51. *Religion:* Baptist. *Home and office:* 311 Keuka St., Penn Yan, N.Y. 14527.

CAREER: District manager and claims adjuster for insurance companies, Penn Yan, N.Y., 1932-37; physiotherapist for Bernarr MacFadden, Dansville, N.Y., 1937-38; U.S. Post Office, Penn Yan, N.Y., clerk, 1938-67; Keuka College, Keuka Park, N.Y., lecturer in creative verse, 1960-67. Director of poetry workshops at writers conferences, St. David's, Pa., 1958, 1963, Green Lake, Wis., 1963, at Judson College, Elgin, Ill., 1966, 1967, 1968, and 1969, and at East Dover, Vt., 1970. Lecturer at colleges and high schools. *Military service:* U.S. Navy, 1944-45; served in South Pacific theater. *Member:* Poetry Society of America. *Awards, honors:* University of New Hampshire Writers' Conference, first prize in verse, 1954, second prize in non-fiction, 1956; Wake-Brook House award, 1958, for *Beyond the Green Gate;* D.Litt. from Keuka College, 1970.

WRITINGS—All poetry, except as otherwise noted: *Songs from a Willow Whistle,* Wake-Brook, 1956; *Beyond the Green Gate,* Wake-Brook, 1958; (with E. Merrill Root) *Writing Poetry* (nonfiction), Christian Authors' Guild, 1958; *Christmas Chimes in Rhyme,* Judson, 1962; *The Sound of an Echo* (prose), Wake-Brook, 1963; *Cup, Flagon, and Fountain,* Wake-Brook, 1965; *A Choice of Dreams,* Partridge Press, 1970. Consulting editor, *Time of Singing.* Poems have appeared in *Ladies' Home Journal, Saturday Evening Post, Good Housekeeping, McCall's, New York Times, New York Herald Tribune,* poetry journals.

WORK IN PROGRESS: Another book of verse.

SIDELIGHTS: Seager told *CA:* "Man has inherited three essential 'thirsts': His thirst for environment, or whatever it is that makes him homesick; his thirst for companionship—he does not want to go it alone; his thirst to know who it is he means when he says 'Our Father.' " Seager states: "The purpose of the poet is to share the common life with common man, but to share it uncommonly." There is a collection of Seager's manuscripts at Syracuse University. *Avocational interests:* Photography, music, nature.

BIOGRAPHICAL/CRITICAL SOURCES: Baptist Leader, November, 1961; *Lutheran Standard,* March 26, 1963; *Finger Lakes Chronicle,* October, 1965.

* * *

SEAMANDS, John Thompson 1916-

PERSONAL: Born November 15, 1916, in Cleveland, Ohio; son of Earl Arnett (a missionary to India) and Yvonne (Shields) Seamands; married Ruth Childers (a writer), June 5, 1938; children: Sylvia Ruth, Sheila Ellen,

Sandra Joan, Linda Helen. *Education:* Graduated from Kodaikanal High School in India, 1953; Asbury College, B.A., 1938; Asbury Theological Seminary, B.D., 1940, D.D., 1954; Kennedy School of Missions, Hartford, Conn., student, 1945-46; University of Kentucky, M.A., 1946; Serampore University, India, Th.D., 1970. *Home:* 407 Talbott Dr., Wilmore, Ky. 40390. *Office:* Asbury Theological Seminary, Wilmore, Ky. 40390.

CAREER: Methodist minister. Missionary to India, 1941-60; Asbury Theological Seminary, Wilmore, Ky., professor of Christian missions, 1961—. South India Annual Conference of Methodism in India, member, 1940—. *Member:* Theta Phi. *Awards, honors:* D.D., Asbury Theological Seminary, 1954.

WRITINGS: Shuddhikarana (Sanctification), Mysore Publishing House, 1953; *Vesha Bakthi athava Vishesha Bakthi* (True and False Devotion), Mysore Publishing House, 1957; *The Supreme Task of the Church: Sermons on the Mission of the Church,* Eerdmans, 1964; *Pioneers of the Younger Churches,* Abingdon, 1967; *On Tiptoe with Joy,* Nazarene Publishing, 1967; *On Tiptoe with Love,* Nazarene Publishing, in press. Writer of column, "Into All the World," for *Herald* (bi-weekly religious magazine).

SIDELIGHTS: Seamands speaks German, Hindi, and Kanarese; his first two books were written in Kanarese.

*   *   *

SEARLE, Humphrey   1915-

PERSONAL: Born August 26, 1915, in Oxford, England; son of Humphrey Frederic (a civil servant) and May (Schlich) Searle; married Margaret Lesley Gillen Gray, August 26, 1949 (died, 1957); married Fiona Elizabeth Anne Nicholson (an actress), November 5, 1960. *Education:* New College, Oxford, M.A., 1937; studied at Royal College of Music, London, and New Vienna Conservatorium of Music; studied composition with Anton Webern in Vienna. *Home:* 44 Ordnance Hill, London N.W. 8, England. *Agent:* London Management, 235/241 Regent St., London W1A 2JT, England.

CAREER: Composer. British Broadcasting Corp., London, England, member of music department, 1938-40, producer, 1946-48; International Society for Contemporary Music, general secretary, 1947-49; Sadler's Wells and Royal Ballet, London, England, musical adviser, 1951-57; Stanford University, Stanford, Calif., composer in residence, 1964-65; Royal College of Music, London, England, professor of composition, 1965—. Guest composer, Aspen Music Festival, 1967. *Military service:* British Army, Gloster Regiment, Intelligence Corps and General List, 1940-46; became captain. *Member:* Royal Musical Association, Composers' Guild of Great Britain (council), Society for the Promotion of New Music, Liszt Society (honorary secretary, 1950-62). *Awards, honors:* UNESCO Radio Critics' Award for opera, "The Diary of a Madman," 1960; Commander, Order of British Empire, 1968; fellow, Royal College of Music (London), 1969.

WRITINGS: Twentieth Century Counterpoint: A Guide for Students, Williams & Norgate, 1954, De Graff, 1955; *The Music of Liszt* (includes biographical survey and catalogue of works), De Graff, 1954, 2nd edition, Dover, 1966; (editor) Arnold Schoenberg, *Structural Functions of Harmony,* Norton, 1954; (translator) Josef Rufer, *Composition with Twelve Notes Related Only to One Another,* Macmillan, 1954; *Ballet Music: An Introduction,* Cassell, 1958, revised edition, Dover, 1972; (translator with Edith Temple Roberts) Hans Heinz Stuckenschmidt, *Arnold Schoenberg,* J. Calder, 1959, Grove, 1960; (translator with Roberts) Friedrich Wildgans, *Anton Webern,* J. Calder, 1966; (editor and translator) Hector Berlioz:

A Selection from His Letters, Harcourt, 1966; (translator) Walter Kolneder, *Anton Webern: An Introduction to His Works,* University of California Press, 1968; (with Robert Layton) *Twentieth Century Composers,* Weidenfeld & Nicholson, Volume III, *Britain, Scandinavia, and the Netherlands,* 1972.

Music: *Put Away the Flutes* (score for high voice with the accompaniment of flute, oboe, and string quartet), A. Lengnick, 1948; *Passacaglietta in Nomine Arnold Schoenberg, for String Quartet,* A. Lengnick, 1950. Composer of five symphonies; three operas, "The Diary of a Madman" after Gogol, "The Photo of the Colonel" after Ionesco, and "Hamlet" after Shakespeare; three ballets, "Noctambules," "The Great Peacock," "Dualities"; trilogy for speakers, chorus and orchestra on texts of Edith Sitwell and James Joyce, "Gold Coast Customs," "The Riverrun," "The Shadow of Cain"; "Poem for 22 Strings"; sinfonietta for nine instruments; Zodiac Variations for chamber orchestra; choral music for "Jerusalem" (cantata after Blake); piano sonata, chamber music, songs, incidental music for stage, radio, television, and films.

Contributor to *Grove's Dictionary of Music, Chambers's Encyclopaedia, Dictionary of National Biography, Proceedings of Royal Musical Association,* and *Encyclopaedia Britannica.*

BIOGRAPHICAL/CRITICAL SOURCES: Musical Times, September, 1955, June, 1964, August, 1968, April, 1969; *Listener,* November 29, 1962, May 1, 1969; *Musik in Geschichte und Gegenwart,* Kassel, 1964.

*   *   *

SEARLE, Ronald (William Fordham)   1920-

PERSONAL: Born March 3, 1920, in Cambridge, England; son of William James and Nellie (Hunt) Searle. *Education:* Studied at Cambridge School of Art, Cambridge, England. *Agent:* Hope Leresche & Steele, 11 Jubilee Pl., Chelsea, London S.W. 3, England; and John Locke Studio, 15 East 76th St., New York, N.Y. 10021.

CAREER: Artist, with one-man shows at galleries in London, England, 1947, 1948, 1950, 1954, 1957, and 1968, in New York, 1959, 1963, and 1969, in Kunsthalle, Bremen, Germany, 1965, in Paris, France, 1966, 1967, 1968, 1969, and 1971, in Munich, Germany, 1967, 1968, 1969, 1970, and 1971. Perpetua Books, London, England, editorial director, 1951-62; *Punch,* London, England, member of editorial board. *Military service:* British Army, Royal Engineers, 1939-46; Japanese prisoner of war, 1942-45. *Member:* Alliance Graphique Internationale, Society of Industrial Artists (fellow), Garrick Club (London). *Awards, honors:* Film, "On the Twelfth Day," nominated for Academy Award, American Academy of Motion Picture Arts and Sciences, 1954; five awards, including Stratford (Ontario) Festival award, International Film Festival award, and Art Directors Club of Los Angeles medal, for film "Energetically Yours," 1958-59; Art Directors Club of Philadelphia award, 1959; Reuben Award, National Cartoonists Society of America, 1960; III Biennale, Tolentino, Italy, gold medal, 1965; Prix de la Critique Belge, 1968; Prix d'Humour, Festival d'Avignon, 1971; Medal of the City of Avignon, 1971; Grand Prix de l'Humour Noir, 1971; Prix Internationale Charles Huard, 1972.

WRITINGS: Forty Drawings, foreword by Frank Kendon, Cambridge University Press, 1946, Macmillan, 1947; *Le Nouveau ballet anglaise,* Editions Montbrun, 1947; *Hurrah for St. Trinian's!, and Other Lapses,* foreword by D.B. Wyndham Lewis, Macdonald & Co., 1948; *The Female Approach, with Masculine Sidelights,* foreword by Max Beerbohm, Macdonald & Co., 1949; *Back to the Slaughterhouse and Other Ugly Moments,* Macdonald

& Co., 1951; *Weil noch das Laempchen glueht,* Diogenes, 1952; *Souls in Torment,* preface and short dirge by C. Day Lewis, Perpetua, 1953; *Medisances,* Editions Neuf, 1953; *The Female Approach,* foreword by Malcolm Muggeridge, Knopf, 1954; *The Rake's Progress,* Perpetua, 1955, new edition published as *The Rake's Progress: Some Immoral Tales,* Dobson, 1968; *Merry England,* Perpetua, 1956, Knopf, 1957; (editor and author of introduction) *The Biting Eye of Andre Francois,* Perpetua, 1960; *The Penguin Ronald Searle,* Penguin, 1960; (editor) Henri Perruchot, *Toulouse-Lautrec: A Definitive Biography,* translated by Humphrey Hare, Perpetua, 1960, World Publishing, 1961; (editor) Henri Perruchot, *Cezanne: A Definitive Biography,* translated by Humphrey Hare, Perpetua, 1961, World Publishing, 1962; *Which Way Did He Go?,* Perpetua, 1961, World Publishing, 1962; *From Frozen North to Filthy Lucre: With Remarks by Groucho Marx and Commentaries by Jane Clapperton,* Viking, 1964; *Searle in the Sixties,* Penguin, 1964; *Pardong M'sieur: Paris et autres,* Denoel, 1965; *Searle's Cats,* Dobson, 1967, Greene, 1968; *The Square Egg,* Greene, 1968; *Take One Toad: A Book of Ancient Remedies,* Dobson, 1968; *Hello—Where Did All the People Go?,* Weidenfeld & Nicolson, 1969, Greene, 1970; *Hommage a Toulouse-Lautrec,* introduction by Roland Topor, Edition Empreinte, 1969, published in England as *The Second Coming of Toulouse-Lautrec,* Weidenfeld & Nicolson, 1970; *Filles de Hambourg,* J.-J. Pauvert, 1969, published in England as *Secret Sketchbook: The Back Streets of Hamburg,* Weidenfeld & Nicolson, 1970; *The Addict,* Greene, 1971.

Books in collaboration: (With Kaye Webb) *Paris Sketchbook,* Saturn Press, 1950, revised edition, Perpetua, 1957, Braziller, 1958; (with D.B. Wyndham Lewis, under pseudonym Timothy Shy) *The Terror of St. Trinian's; or, Angela's Prince Charming,* Parrish, 1952; (with Geoffrey Willans) *Down with Skool!: A Guide to School Life for Tiny Pupils and Their Parents,* Parrish, 1953, Vanguard, 1954; (with Webb) *Looking at London, and People Worth Meeting,* News Chronicle (London), 1953; (with Willans) *How to Be Topp: A Guide to Sukcess for Tiny Pupils, Including All There Is to Kno About Space,* Parrish, 1954, Vanguard, 1955; (with Willans) *Whizz for Atomms: A Guide to Survival in the 20th Century for Fellow Pupils, Their Doting Maters, Pompous Paters and Any Others Who Are Interested,* Parrish, 1956, published in America as *Molesworth's Guide to the Atomic Age,* Vanguard, 1957; (with Willans) *The Dog's Ear Book, with Four Lugubrious Verses,* Parrish, 1958, Crowell, 1960; (with Alex Atkinson) *The Big City; or, The New Mayhew,* Perpetua, 1958, Braziller, 1959; (with Willans) *The Compleet Molesworth* (includes *Down with Skool!, How to Be Topp, Whizz for Atomms,* and *Back in the Jug Agane),* Parrish, 1959; (with Atkinson) *USA for Beginners,* Perpetua, 1959, published in America as *By Rocking Chair Across America,* Funk, 1959; (with Willans) *Back in the Jug Agane,* Parrish, 1959, published in America as *Molesworth Back in the Jug Agane,* Vanguard, 1960; (with Atkinson) *Russia for Beginners: By Rocking Chair Across Russia,* Perpetua, 1960, published in America as *By Rocking Chair Across Russia,* World Publishing, 1960; (with Webb) *Refugees 1960,* Penguin, 1960; (with Atkinson) *Escape from the Amazon!,* Perpetua, 1964; (with Heinz Huber) *Anatomie eines Adlers,* Desch, 1966, translation by Constantine Fitz Gibbon published in America as *Haven't We Met Before Somewhere?: Germany from the Inside and Out,* Viking, 1966; (with Kildare Dobbs) *The Great Fur Opera: Annals of the Hudson's Bay Company, 1670-1970,* Greene, 1970.

Illustrator: W. Henry Brown, *Co-operation in a University Town,* Co-operative Printing Society, 1939; Ronald Hastain, *White Coolie,* Hodder & Stoughton, 1947; Douglas Goldring, *Life Interests,* Macdonald & Co., 1948; W.E. Stanton Hope, *Tanker Fleet,* Anglo-Saxon Petroleum Co., 1948; Gillian Olivier, *Turn But a Stone,* Hodder & Stoughton, 1949; Audrey Hilton, *This England 1946-1949,* Turnstile Press, 1949; *Meet Yourself on Sunday* (compiled by staff of Mass-Observation), Naldrett Press, 1949; *Meet Yourself at the Doctor's* (compiled by staff of Mass-Observation), Naldrett Press, 1949; Patrick Gordon Campbell, *A Long Drink of Cold Water,* Falcon Press, 1949; Noel Langley, *The Inconstant Moon,* Arthur Barker, 1949; Patrick Gordon Campbell, *An Irishman's Diary,* Cassell, 1950; Patrick Gordon Campbell, *A Short Trot with a Cultured Mind,* Falcon Press, 1950; Oliver Philpott, *Stolen Journey,* Hodder & Stoughton, 1950; Russell Braddon, *The Piddingtons,* Laurie, 1950; Patrick Gordon Campbell, *Life in Thin Slices,* Falcon Press, 1951; Harry Hearson and John Courtenay Trewin, *An Evening at the Larches,* Elek, 1951; Russell Braddon, *The Naked Island* (includes drawings made in Changi prison camps by Searle), Laurie, 1952; Winifred Ellis, *London—So Help Me!,* Macdonald & Co., 1952; William Cowper, *The Diverting History of John Gilpin,* Chiswick Press, 1952; Frank Carpenter, *Six Animal Plays,* Methuen, 1953; Denys Parsons, *It Must Be True,* Macdonald & Co., 1953; Richard Haydn, *The Journal of Edwin Carp,* Hamish Hamilton, 1954; Patrick Gordon Campbell, *Patrick Campbell's Omnibus,* Hulton Press, 1954; Geoffrey Gorer, *Modern Types,* Cresset Press, 1955; Reuben Ship, *The Investigator: A Narrative in Dialogue,* Sidgwick & Jackson, 1956; Kaye Webb, compiler, *The St. Trinian's Story: The Whole Ghastly Dossier,* Perpetua, 1959, London House & Maxwell, 1959; Christopher Fry, *Phoenix Too Frequent: A Comedy,* Oxford University Press, 1959; *Anger of Achilles: Homer's Iliad,* translated by Robert Graves, Doubleday, 1959; Ted Patrick and Silas Spitzer, *Great Restaurants of America,* Lippincott, 1960; Charles Dickens, *A Christmas Carol,* Perpetua, 1961, World Publishing, 1961; Charles Dickens, *Great Expectations,* abridged edition, edited by Doris Dickens, Norton, 1962; Charles Dickens, *Oliver Twist,* abridged edition, edited by Doris Dickens, Norton, 1962; James Thurber, *The Thirteen Clocks and The Wonderful O,* Penguin, 1962; Allen Andrews and William Richardson, *Those Magnificent Men in Their Flying Machines; or, How I Flew from London to Paris in 25 Hours, 11 Minutes,* Norton, 1965; Rudolf Erich Raspe and others, *The Adventures of Baron Munchausen,* Pantheon, 1969; Jack Davies, Ken Annakin, and Allen Andrews, *Those Daring Young Men in Their Jaunty Jalopies: Monte Carlo or Bust!,* Putnam, 1969 (published in England as *Monte Carlo or Bust!: Those Daring Young Men in Their Jaunty Jalopies,* Dobson, 1969); Leslie Bricusse, *Scrooge* (juvenile), Aurora Publications, 1970.

Films designed: "John Gilpin," British Film Institute, 1951; "On the Twelfth Day," Bahamian Films, 1954; "Energetically Yours," Esso, 1957; "Germany," Sueddeutscher Rundfunk Television, 1960; "The King's Breakfast," Montague Productions, 1963. Also author of television script, "Toulouse-Lautrec," networked by the British Broadcasting Corp. in 1961. Designer of animation sequences for the films, "Those Magnificent Men in Their Flying Machines," 20th Century-Fox, 1964, "Monte Carlo or Bust," Paramount, 1968, and "Scrooge," Cinema Center Films, 1970.

Contributor to *Encyclopaedia Britannica,* and to *Holiday, Life, Fortune, New Yorker,* and other periodicals.

BIOGRAPHICAL/CRITICAL SOURCES: Graphis, Number 23, 1948, Number 80, 1958, Number 109, 1963; *American Artist,* September, 1955; *Publimondial,* Number 76, December, 1955, Number 82, 1956; *Elseviers Weekblad,* May 18, 1957; *Texas Quarterly,* Number 4, 1960; *Gebrauschgraphic,* December, 1961; *Das Schoenste,*

July, 1962; *Studio,* March, 1963; *Idea,* Number 78, 1966; *Les Nouvelles Litteraires,* December, 1966; *Les Lettres Francaises,* December 22, 1966, November 15, 1967; *La Quinzaine Litteraire,* December, 1967; *Library Journal,* June 1, 1969; *Cartoonist Profiles,* fall, 1969; *Le Monde,* January 3, 1970; *Opus,* January, 1972.

*   *   *

SEASOLTZ, R(obert) Kevin   1930-

PERSONAL: Born December 29, 1930, in Johnstown, Pa.; son of Walter Joseph and Alice (Hackett) Seasoltz. *Education:* Duquesne University, student, 1948-50; St. Mary's Seminary College, Baltimore, Md., A.B., 1952; Catholic University of America, S.T.L., 1956, J.C.D., 1961; Lateran University, Rome, Italy, J.C.L., 1958. *Home:* St. Anselm's Abbey, Washington, D.C. 20017. *Office:* Department of Religion, Catholic University of America, Washington, D.C. 20017.

CAREER: Roman Catholic priest, member of Order of St. Benedict; Catholic University of America, Washington, D.C., instructor in religious education, 1962—. *Member:* Catholic Theological Society of America.

WRITINGS: The House of God—Sacred Art and Architecture, Herder & Herder, 1963; *The New Liturgy: A Documentation, 1903-1965,* Herder & Herder, 1966†

*   *   *

SEBEOK, Thomas A(lbert)   1920-

PERSONAL: Surname is pronounced *See*-bee-oak; born November 9, 1920, in Budapest, Hungary; came to U.S., 1937; naturalized, 1944; son of Derso (a lawyer and economist) and Veronica (Perlman) Sebeok; married Eleanor Lawton (a lecturer), September 11, 1947; children: Veronica C. *Education:* University of Chicago, B.A., 1941, graduate study, 1941-42; University of North Carolina, graduate study, 1942; Princeton University, M.A., 1943, Ph.D., 1945. *Home:* 1104 Covenanter Dr., Bloomington, Ind. 47401. *Office:* Research Center for the Language Sciences, Indiana University, Bloomington, Ind. 47401.

CAREER: Indiana University, Bloomington, 1943—, started as instructor, now Distinguished Professor of Linguistics, 1967—, and professor of anthropology, of Uralic and Altaic studies, and chairman of Research Center for the Language Sciences. Visiting professor at University of Puerto Rico, 1949, University of New Mexico, 1953-54, University of Michigan, 1958, University of Vienna, 1963, University of Besancon, 1965, University of Hamburg, 1966, University of Bucharest, 1967, 1969, University of Colorado, 1969, Stanford University, 1971, University of South Florida, 1972. Visiting scholar at University of Arizona, 1958-59. Assistant director of Linguistic Institute (Linguistic Society of America), summer of 1952, 1953, associate director, 1958, director, 1964; director of publications, Research Center in Anthropology, Folklore, and Linguistics, 1956-65; former director, Air Force Language Training Program. Panel member for linguistics, National Endowment for the Humanities, 1966—.

MEMBER: American Anthropological Association (fellow; delegate to American Council of Learned Societies, 1960—), American Association for the Advancement of Science (council), National Academy of Science-National Research Council, American Folklore Society (fellow), Modern Language Association of America, Linguistic Society of America (secretary-treasurer, 1969—), Social Science Research Council, American Association for Machine Translation and Computational Linguistics (executive board), Animal Behavior Society (executive board), International Association for Semiotic Studies (executive committee), Central States Anthropological Society

(former president), Finno-Ugric Society (Helsinki; fellow), Societe Linguistique de Paris, Sigma Xi, Cosmos Club (Washington, D.C.), Princeton Club and Explorers Club (both New York). *Awards, honors:* American-Scandinavian Foundation fellow, 1947; American Philosophical Society fellowships, 1952-53, 1954-55, 1955-56, 1960; Newberry Library fellow, 1955; Guggenheim fellow, 1958-59; fellow, Center for Advanced Study in the Behavioral Sciences, 1960-61, 1966-67, and 1971; grants from Wenner-Gren Foundation for Anthropological Research, 1948, 1958, 1960, Social Science Research Council, 1958, Inter-University Committee on Travel Grants, 1958, National Science Foundation, 1958-60, 1964-66, American Council of Learned Societies, 1960, Farfield Foundation, 1960, American-Scandinavian Foundation, 1960; Fulbright grantee in Germany, 1966; senior postdoctoral research fellow, National Science Foundation, 1966-67.

WRITINGS: Spoken Hungarian: Basic Course, published for U.S. Armed Forces Institute by Linguistic Society of America, 1944, reissued as *Spoken Hungarian,* with twenty-five records, Holt, 1945, also issued by U.S. War Department with *Guide's Manual for Spoken Hungarian,* 1945, 2nd edition, privately printed, 1949; *Finnish and Hungarian Case Systems: Their Form and Function,* Acta Instituti Hungarici Universitatis Holmiensis, 1946; *Spoken Finnish,* with twenty-five records, Holt, 1947, revised and enlarged edition (with Meri K. Lehtinen) published as *Basic Course in Finnish,* Indiana University Press, 1963; *Data on Nakedness and Related Traits in Hungary* (originally published in *Journal of American Folklore,* Number 61, 1948), privately printed, 1949; (editor and contributor with C.F. Voegelin) *Results of the Conference of Anthropologists and Linguists,* Indiana University Press, 1953; (editor and contributor with Charles E. Osgood) *Psycholinguistics: A Survey of Theory and Research Problems,* Indiana University Press, 1954, 2nd edition (with "A Survey of Psycholinguistic Research, 1954-1964," by A. Richard Diebold, and "The Psycholinguists," by George A. Miller), 1965; (editor) *Myth: A Symposium,* American Folklore Society, 1955, 2nd edition, Indiana University Press, 1965; (editor, author of introduction, and contributor) *Style in Language,* M.I.T. Press, 1960; (co-editor and contributor) *American Studies in Uralic Linguistics,* Indiana University Press, 1960; (editor with A.S. Hayes and M.C. Bateson) *Approaches to Semiotics: Cultural Anthropology, Education, Linguistics, Psychiatry, Psychology,* Mouton, 1964; (editor) *Portraits of Linguists: A Biographical Source Book for the History of Western Linguistics, 1746-1963,* Volume 1: *From Sir William Jones to Karl Brugmann,* Volume 2: *From Edward Sievers to Benjamin Lee Whorf,* Indiana University Press, 1966; (editor and author of preface and introduction) *Selected Writings of Gyula Laziczius,* Humanities, 1966; *Animal Communication: Techniques of Study and Results of Research,* Indiana University Press, 1968; (editor with Alexandra Ramsay) *Approaches to Animal Communication,* Mouton, 1969, Humanities, 1970; *Perspectives in Zoosemiotics,* Mouton, 1972.

"Studies in Cheremis" series: (Editor and contributor) Volume 1: *Folklore,* Indiana University Press, 1952; (with Frances J. Ingemann) Volume 2: *The Supernatural,* American Anthropological Association, 1956; (editor with Alo Raun) Volume 3: *The First Cheremis Grammar,* Newberry Library, 1956; (author of preface) Eeva K. Minn, Volume 4: *Derivation,* Indiana University Press, 1956; Volume 5: *The Cheremis,* Human Relations Area File Press, 1955; (with Paul G. Brewster) Volume 6: *Games,* Indiana University Press, 1958; (author of preface) Bruno Nettl, Volume 7: *Musical Style,* Indiana University Press, 1960; (with Valdis J. Zeps) Volume 8: *Concordance and Thesaurus of Cheremis Poetic Language,*

Mouton, 1961; (with Ingemann) Volume 9: *An Eastern Cheremis Manual: Phonology, Grammar, Texts, and Glossary,* Indiana University Press, 1961.

"Current Trends in Linguistics" series, all published by Humanities—Editor and author of introductions: Volume 1: *Soviet and East European Linguistics,* 1963, Volume 2: *Linguistics in East Asia and Southeast Asia,* 1967, Volume 3: *Theoretical Foundations,* 1967, Volume 4: *Ibero-American and Caribbean Linguistics,* 1967, Volume 5: *Linguistics in South Asia,* 1968, Volume 6: *Linguistics in South West Asia and North Africa,* 1971, Volume 7: *Linguistics in Sub-Saharan Africa,* 1972, Volume 8: *Linguistics in Oceania,* 1972, Volume 9: *Linguistics in Western Europe,* 1973, Volume 10: *Linguistics in North America,* 1973, Volume 11: *Diachronic, Areal, and Typological Linguistics,* in press, Volume 12: *Linguistics and Adjacent Arts and Sciences,* in press, Volume 13: *Historiography of Linguistics,* in press, Volume 14: *Index to Volumes 1-12,* in press.

Contributor: *Studies in Folklore in Honor of Distinguished Service Professor Stith Thompson,* Indiana University Press, 1957; Ithiel da Sola Pool, editor, *Trends in Content Analysis,* University of Illinois Press, 1959; Paul L. Garvin, editor, *Natural Language and the Computer,* McGraw, 1963; Dell Hymes, editor, *Language in Culture and Society: A Reader in Linguistics and Anthropology,* Harper, 1964; Dell Hymes, editor, *The Use of Computers in Anthropology,* Humanities, 1965; Stuart A. Altmann, editor, *Social Communication Among Primates,* University of Chicago Press, 1967; *To Honor Roman Jakobson,* Mouton, 1967, Humanities, 1968; P. Maranda and J. Pouillon, editors, *Festschrift for Claude Levi-Strauss,* Mouton, 1967; *The Finns in North America: A Social Symposium,* Michigan State University Press, 1968; *Linguaggi nella societa e nella techica,* Edizioni di Communita, 1970; P. Guiraud and P. Kuntz, editors, *La Stylistique,* Klincksieck, 1970; J. Kristera, J. Rey-Debore, and D.J. Umiker, editors, *Essays in Semiotics/Essais de Semiotique,* Mouton, 1971; *Les Dictionnaires du Savoir moderne: La Communication,* CEPL, 1972.

Principal investigator and director of preparation of sixteen Uralic monographs for Chief of Psychological Warfare, U.S. Army, 1954-55. Consultant in linguistics for *Language: Anthropology and Communication,* by Alexandra Ramsay, University of Georgia Press, 1968. Contributor of hundreds of articles to folklore, anthropology, and linguistic journals, including *Acta Linguistica, American Speech, Anthropos, Behavioral Science, Beitraege zur Linguistik und Informations-verarbeitung, Ceskoslovenska Psychologie* (Czech), *Explorers Journal, Hoosier Folklore, International Journal of American Linguistics, Journal de la Societe des Americanistes de Paris, Journal of the American Oriental Society, Language, Lingua, Magyar Nyelvoer* (Hungarian), *Memoires de la Societe Finno-Ougrienne, Modern Language Journal, Nyelvtudomanyi Koezlemenyek* (Hungarian), *Quarterly Journal of Speech, Roman Philology, Science, Slavonic and East European Review, Southwestern Journal of Anthropology, Studia Filozaficzne* (Polish), *Studies in Linguistics,* and *Virittaejae* (Finnish). Contributor to *Encyclopaedia Britannica, Collier's Encyclopedia,* and *International Encyclopedia of the Social Sciences.*

Associate editor of Indiana University Publications in Anthropology and Linguistics, 1953-65, and editor of Indiana University "Russian and East European" series, 1956-61, "Folklore" series, 1957-65, and "Uralic and Altaic" series, 1960-69. Editor-in-chief, *Semiotica,* and "Approaches to Semiotics" series, 1968—; editor of *Journal of American Folklore* and American Folklore Society "Memoir" series, 1954-58, and of *Ural-Altaische Jahrbuecher,* 1962—; associate editor of *American Anthropologist,* 1960-62, *Computing Reviews,* 1963, *Journal of the Folklore Institute,* 1964—, *Journal of Communication* (linguistics), 1965—, *Recherches Semiologiques-Semiotic Studies, Social Science Information* (International Social Science Council of UNESCO), 1967—; member of editorial council, American Anthropological Association, 1954-58; consulting editor (linguistics), *The New Century Cyclopedia of Names,* 1954, and *Etudes Finno-Ougriennes,* 1965—; member of editorial committee of *Slavic and East European Journal,* 1957—; member of editorial board of *Journal of Verbal Learning and Verbal Behavior,* 1962—.

WORK IN PROGRESS: Editing *Structuralism Around the World,* for Mouton; two books to be published by Mouton, *Semiotics: A Survey of the State of the Art,* and *Zoosemiotics.*

BIOGRAPHICAL/CRITICAL SOURCES: Library Journal, January 1, 1967, February 1, 1969; *Times Literary Supplement,* March 2, 1967; *Choice,* November, 1967; *Science,* May 9, 1969.

* * *

SEBESTYEN, Gyorgy 1930-

PERSONAL: Born October 30, 1930, in Budapest, Hungary; son of Sandor and Rozsa (Fischer) Sebestyen; divorced; children: Julia, Piroska, Anna. *Education:* University Eotvos Lorand, Budapest, Ph.D. (ethnology). *Religion:* Roman Catholic. *Home:* Ennsgasse 7, Vienna, Austria.

CAREER: Madach Theatre, Budapest, Hungary, lecturer, 1948-49; Hunnia Film Studio, Budapest, Hungary, lecturer, 1949-50; *Szinhaz es Filmuveszet* (journal), Budapest, Hungary, editor, 1950-52; *Magyar Nemzet* (newspaper), Budapest, Hungary, cultural editor, 1952-55; *Magyar Hirado* (newspaper), Vienna, Austria, chief editor, 1957-61. Austrian correspondent for Radio Bremen, *Duesseldorfer Nachrichten.*

WRITINGS: (Editor) *Roppenj szikra* (lyric poetry anthology), Minsz (Budapest), 1948; (editor) *Orosz nepmesek* (folklore anthology), Ifjusagi-Konyv Kiado (Budapest), 1949; *Die Tueren schliessen sich* (novel; translation from the Hungarian of "Kilincs nelkueli ajtok"), translated by Lena Dur, Desch (Munich), 1957, translation by Peter White published as *Moment of Triumph,* Harcourt, 1958 (published in England as *The Doors Are Closing,* Angus & Robertson, 1958); *Der Mann im Sattel; oder, Ein langer Sonntag* (novel), Desch, 1961; *Die Schule der Verfuehrung* (novel), Desch, 1964; *Floetenspieler und Phantome* (guide book), Desch, 1965; *Lob der Venusbrust, und andere Leckereien,* Forum, 1966; *Anatomie eines Sieges* (essay), Zsolnay, 1967; *Beispiele,* Kremayr & Scheriau, 1967; *Thennberg; oder, Versuch einer Heimkehr* (novel), Desch, 1969; *Ungarn,* (essay), Schroll, 1970. Short stories have appeared in *Frankfurter Allgemeine Zeitung, Die Welt* (Hamburg), *Presse* (Vienna), and other publications.

SIDELIGHTS: Sebestyen's German novels have been translated into Dutch and Italian. *Avocational interests:* cooking and women.

* * *

SEDWICK, B(enjamin) Frank 1924-

PERSONAL: Born April 7, 1924, in Baltimore, Md.; son of B. Frank (a civil engineer) and Louise (a teacher; maiden name, Lambert) Sedwick; married Alice E. Magdeburger, June 4, 1949; children: Eric, Lyn, Coralie, Daniel. *Education:* Duke University, A.B., 1945; Stanford University, M.A., 1947; University of Southern California, Ph.D., 1953. *Politics:* Unaffiliated. *Home:* 2033 Cove Trail, Maitland, Fla. 32751. *Office:* Rollins College, Winter Park, Fla. 32789.

CAREER: Instructor in Spanish and Italian at University of Maryland, College Park, 1947-49, U.S. Naval Academy, Annapolis, 1951-53; University of Wisconsin, Milwaukee, assistant professor, 1953-58; Ohio Wesleyan University, Delaware, associate professor, 1958-61, professor of Spanish, 1961-63, chairman of Department of Spanish and Italian, 1958-63; Rollins College, Winter Park, Fla., professor of Spanish and Head of Department of Foreign Languages, 1963—, Director of Rollins Overseas Programs (in Spain and Colombia). *Military service:* U.S. Navy, 1942-45; became lieutenant. *Member:* Modern Language Association, American Association of Teachers of Spanish and Portuguese. *Awards, honors:* American Philosophical Society research grant, for *The Tragedy of Manuel Azana and the Fate of the Spanish Republic.*

WRITINGS: Puken aueuen fosun ingnes; ngeni chon sukunun chuk (first English grammar written in language of Truk), U.S. Navy, 1946; (editor) Miguel de Unamuno, *Otro [y] Raquel Encadenada* (two comedies; textbook), Las Americas, 1960; (editor with C.R. Linsalata) Azana Martinez, *La Forja de los suenos* (textbook), Houghton, 1963; *A History of the "Useless Precaution" Plot in Spanish and French Literature,* University of North Carolina Press, 1964; *The Tragedy of Manuel Azana and the Fate of the Spanish Republic,* Ohio State University Press, 1964; (editor with Robert Hatton) Enrique Rodriguez Larreta, *La Gloria de Don Ramiro: Una Vida en Tiempos de Filipe Segundo* (textbook), Heath, 1966; (editor with Elizabeth van Orman) *Selecciones de Madariaga* (textbook), Prentice-Hall, 1969; *Conversation in Spanish: Points of Departure* (textbook), American Book Co., 1969; (with Peter Bonnell) *Conversation in French: Points of Departure,* American Book Co., 1969; (with Bonnell) *Conversation in German: Points of Departure,* American Book Co., 1969. Contributor to *Encyclopedia of World Literature in the Twentieth Century, Hispania, Studies in Philology, Modern Language Quarterly, Italica, Philological Quarterly,* other professional journals; also contributor of feature stories to *Metropolitan Opera News,* 1957—.

* * *

SEIFERT, Harvey (J.D.) 1911-

PERSONAL: Born September 25, 1911, in Posey County, Ind.; son of Daniel Frederick (a bookkeeper) and Elfrieda (Ehrhardt) Seifert; married Lois Olive Cummings, August 6, 1942; children: Carolyn, Mary Lois, Linda Jean. *Education:* Evansville College, A.B., 1932; Boston University, M.A., 1934, S.T.B., 1935, Ph.D., 1940; London School of Economics and Political Science, University of London, postgraduate study, 1935-36. *Religion:* Methodist. *Office:* School of Theology at Claremont, Claremont, Calif. 91711.

CAREER: Adrian College, Adrian, Mich., professor of sociology, 1942-45; University of Southern California, Los Angeles, professor of social ethics, 1945-56; School of Theology at Claremont, Claremont, Calif., professor of social ethics, 1956—. *Member:* American Sociological Association, Society for the Study of Social Problems, Religious Research Association, American Society of Christian Social Ethics.

WRITINGS: Fellowships of Concern: A Manual on the Cell Group Process, Abingdon, 1949; *The Church in Community Action,* Abingdon, 1952; *Ethical Resources for International Relations,* Westminster, 1964; *Conquest by Suffering: The Process and Prospects of Non-Violent Resistance,* Westminster, 1965; *Power Where the Action Is,* Westminster, 1968; (with Howard J. Clinebell) *Personal Growth and Social Change: A Guide for Ministers and Laymen as Change Agents,* Westminster, 1969; *Eth-*

ical Resources for Political and Economic Decision, Westminster, 1972. Also author of *Decision-Making in World Affairs,* Division of Peace and World Order, Methodist Church. Contributor of articles to professional periodicals.

* * *

SELSAM, Millicent Ellis 1912-

PERSONAL: Born May 30, 1912, in Brooklyn, N.Y.; daughter of Israel and Ida (Abrams) Ellis; married Howard B. Selsam (an author), September 1, 1936; children: Robert. *Education:* Brooklyn College (now Brooklyn College of the City University of New York), B.A., 1932; Columbia University, M.A., 1934. *Home:* 100 West 94th St., New York, N.Y. 10025.

CAREER: New York City Public Schools, New York, N.Y., high school teacher, 1935-45; author of books for young people. *Member:* American Association for the Advancement of Science (fellow), American Nature Study Society, Authors Guild. *Awards, honors:* Gold medal award, Boys' Clubs of America, 1962, for *Stars, Mosquitoes and Crocodiles;* Eva L. Gordon Award, American Nature Study Society, 1964; Thomas A. Edison Award for best juvenile science book of the year, 1965, for *Biography of an Atom;* certificate, Boys' Clubs of America Junior Book Awards, 1966-67, for *Benny's Animals, and How He Put Them in Order.*

WRITINGS: Egg to Chick, International Publishers, 1946, revised edition, Harper, 1970; *Hidden Animals,* International Publishers, 1947, revised edition, Harper, 1969; *Play With Plants,* Morrow, 1949. *Play With Trees,* Morrow, 1950; *Play With Vines,* Morrow, 1951; *Play With Leaves and Flowers,* Morrow, 1952; *All About Eggs, and How They Change into Animals,* W.R. Scott, 1952; *Microbes at Work,* Morrow, 1953; *All Kinds of Babies and How They Grow,* W.R. Scott, 1953; *A Time for Sleep: How the Animals Rest,* W.R. Scott, 1953; *How the Animals Eat,* W.R. Scott, 1955; *The Plants We Eat,* Morrow, 1955; (with Betty Morrow) *See Through the Sea,* Harper, 1955; *See Through the Forest,* Harper, 1956; *Exploring the Animal Kingdom,* Garden City Books, 1957; *Play With Seeds,* Morrow, 1957; *See Through the Jungle,* Harper, 1957; *See Through the Lake,* Harper, 1958; (editor) Betty Morrow, *See Up the Mountain,* Harper, 1958; *Nature Detective;* W.R. Scott, 1958, reissued as *How to Be a Nature Detective,* Harper, 1966; *Plants That Heal,* Morrow, 1959; *Things to Do with Seeds,* Chatto & Windus, 1959; *Seeds and More Seeds,* Harper, 1959; (editor) Charles Darwin, *Voyage of the Beagle,* Harper, 1959; *Birth of an Island,* Harper, 1959.

How to Grow House Plants, Morrow, 1960; *Plenty of Fish,* Harper, 1960; *Around the World with Darwin,* Harper, 1960; *Tony's Birds,* Harper, 1961; *See Along the Shore,* Harper, 1961; *The Science Book of Seeds,* Science Material Center, 1961; *Underwater Zoos,* Morrow, 1961; *The Language of Animals,* Morrow, 1962; (editor) Alexander Freiherr von Humboldt, *Stars, Mosquitoes, and Crocodiles,* [His] *American Travels,* Harper, 1962; *The Quest of Captain Cook,* Doubleday, 1962; *Terry and the Caterpillars,* Harper, 1962; *Plants that Move,* Morrow, 1962; *How Animals Live Together,* Morrow, 1963; *Greg's Microscope,* Harper, 1963; *You and the World Around You,* Doubleday, 1963; *The Doubleday First Guide to Wildflowers,* Doubleday, 1964; *The Courtship of Animals,* Morrow, 1964; *Birth of a Forest,* Harper, 1964; *Let's Get Turtles,* Harper, 1965; (with Jacob Bronowski) *Biography of an Atom,* Harper, 1965; *Animals as Parents,* Morrow, 1965; *Benny's Animals, and How He put Them in Order,* Harper, 1966; *When an Animal Grows,* Harper, 1966; *The Bug That Laid the Golden Eggs,* Harper, 1967; *How Animals Tell Time,* Morrow, 1967; *Milkweed,* Morrow, 1967; *Questions and Answers about Ants,* Four

Winds Press, 1967; *Maple Tree*, Morrow, 1968; (with George Schaller) *The Tiger: Its Life in the Wild*, Harper, 1969; *Peanut*, Morrow, 1969.

The Tomato and Other Fruit Vegetables, Morrow, 1970; *Egg to Chick*, Harper, 1970; *The Carrot and Other Root Vegetables*, Morrow, 1971; *More Potatoes*, Harper, 1972; *Is This a Baby Dinosaur and Other Science Puzzles*, Harper, 1972; *Vegetables from Stems and Leaves*, Morrow, 1972; *How Puppies Grow*, Four Winds, 1972; *A First Look at Leaves*, Walker & Co., 1972, *A First Look at Fish*, Walker & Co., 1972.

SIDELIGHTS: "I have certain childlike qualities," Mrs. Selsam has said. "I love to investigate everything and get great pleasure from growing plants indoors and out. I have always loved to know the why of everything. Science is dynamic and exciting, and it has changed the world."

She adds: "To write about science for children an author needs to know science, to know children, and to know how to write—particularly to understand how to communicate with children on their level. Good science books should communicate some of the excitement of discovery—and the triumph that goes with the solution of scientific problems."

Mrs. Selsam evidently communicates her own enthusiasm through her work; most critics of children's literature acknowledge her to be one of the best writers in her field. Lee Bennett Hopkins writes: "Her books are always simply written, easy to understand, and filled with beautiful prose and scientific facts; they make one want to delve further into the areas she has explored." Millicent Taylor agrees, and adds: "[Her] nature books are remarkable for their accuracy and [are] always interesting. She never talks down to children, but has a gift for channeling their natural curiosity about their fellow creatures into the beginnings of scholarly investigation. Her prose is consistently beautiful, with poetic rhythms and literary tempos. . . ."

Her books have been translated into Dutch, Swedish, Danish, German, Urdu, Arabic, Japanese, Greek, Italian, and several African languages.

AVOCATIONAL INTERESTS: Collecting specimens of marine life for aquarium on Fire Island, swimming, plants, dancing, painting, making various objects out of glass bottles, polishing beach stones.

BIOGRAPHICAL/CRITICAL SOURCES: Horn Book, October 1962, June, 1963, June, 1965, October, 1967; *Library Journal*, October 15, 1962, December 15, 1962, May 15, 1963, October 15, 1963, June 15, 1964, April 15, 1965, May 15, 1966, May 15, 1967, October 15, 1967, January 15, 1968, November 15, 1968, June 15, 1970; *Saturday Review*, January 19, 1963, April 22, 1967, November 9, 1968; *Christian Science Monitor*, May 9, 1963, November 14, 1963, November 5, 1964, December 21, 1967; *New York Times Book Review*, May 12, 1963, November 10, 1963, July 5, 1964, May 9, 1965, November 7, 1965, May 8, 1966, November 5, 1967, April 20, 1969, November 9, 1969, May 9, 1970; *Natural History*, December, 1963, November, 1967; *Book Week*, November 1, 1964, May 16, 1965, May 7, 1967; *Fire Island News*, May 28, 1966; *Young Reader's Review*, October, 1966, May, 1967, November, 1967; *Book World*, November 3, 1968, May 4, 1969; Lee Bennett Hopkins, *Books Are by People*, Citation, 1969; *Times Literary Supplement*, June 26, 1969.

*   *   *

SELVIN, Hanan C(harles)   1921-

PERSONAL: Born September 19, 1921, in New York, N.Y.; son of Herman B. and Minnie (Mirken) Selvin;

married Rhoda Hurwitt, 1952; children: Barbara, Albert. *Education:* Columbia University, A.B., 1942, Ph.D., 1956. *Home:* 32 Hawkins Rd., Stony Brook, N.Y. 11790. *Office:* State University of New York at Stony Brook, Stony Brook, N.Y. 11790.

CAREER: Columbia University, New York, N.Y., research associate and lecturer, 1948-56; University of California, Berkeley, 1956-64, became associate professor of sociology; University of Rochester, Rochester, N.Y., professor of sociology, department chairman, 1964-67; State University of New York at Stony Brook, professor, 1967—, chairman of Department of Sociology, 1967-70. *Military service:* U.S. Army Air Forces, 1943-46; became first lieutenant. *Member:* American Sociological Association, American Association for Public Opinion Research, Eastern Sociological Society (president, 1970). *Awards, honors:* National Science Foundation senior post-doctoral fellow in London and Paris, 1963-64; co-winner of C. Wright Mills Award, Society for the Study of Social Problems, 1967.

WRITINGS: The Effects of Leadership, Free Press, 1960; (with Travis Hirschi) *The Methodological Adequacy of Delinquency Research: Discussion Draft*, Survey Research Center, University of California, 1962; (with Hirschi) *Delinquency Research: An Appraisal of Analytic Methods*, Free Press, 1967.

*   *   *

SETHNA, Minocher Jehangirji   1911-

PERSONAL: Born November 1, 1911, in Bombay, India; son of Jehangirji Minocher (a veterinary surgeon) and Ratanbai (Khambatta) Sethna; married Khorshed Jamshedji Anklesaria (principal of a girls' high school), January, 1950; children: Jehangir Minocher (son). *Education:* Wilson College, B.A., 1931; Middle Temple, London, England, Barrister-at-Law, 1935; University of Bombay, Ph.D., 1947. *Home:* Sethna House, 251 Tardeo Rd., Bombay 7, Mahrashtra, India. *Office:* University of Bombay, Fuller Rd., Bombay 32BR, Mahrashtra, India.

CAREER: Admitted to Bombay High Court bar, 1935. Practiced law in Bombay, India, as High Court advocate, 1936-52; Government Law College, Bombay, India, professor of law, 1953-60; University of Bombay, Bombay, India, professor of jurisprudence, 1960—. Legal adviser and consultant in company law to several firms, 1940-52. Indian School of Synthetic Jurisprudence, president and founder, 1955—. Legal Aid Society, Bombay, legal adviser to the indigent, 1940-45.

WRITINGS: Indian Company Law, with a Full Text of the Indian Companies Act, 1913, as Amended Up to Date, privately printed, 1938, 5th edition, revised and enlarged, Standard Accountancy Publications (Bombay), 1951, students' edition, with special chapters on banking and insurance companies, Educational Publishers (Bombay), 1959, 7th edition published as *Indian Company Law, with a Full Text of the Indian Companies Act, 1956, as Amended Up to Date*, Lakhani Book Depot (Bombay), 1967; *Civil Wrongs and Their Legal Remedies*, Taraporevala Sons (Bombay), 1939, 2nd revised and enlarged edition, 1950; *Mercantile Law*, privately printed, 1949, 2nd edition published as *Mercantile Law, Including Industrial Law*, Standard Accountancy Publications, 1951, 6th edition, Lakhani Book Depot, 1970; *Society and the Criminal, with Special Reference to the Problems of Crime and Its Prevention, the Personality of the Criminal, Prison Reform and Juvenile Delinquency in India*, Leaders' Press (Bombay), 1952, 3rd edition, revised and enlarged, Tripathi (Bombay), 1971; *Jurisprudence*, Lakhani Book Depot, 1956, 3rd edition, revised and enlarged, Lakhani Book Depot, 1972, Abacus Press, 1972; (contributor) Ralph A. Newman, editor, *Essays in Honor of Roscoe Pound,* Bobbs-Merrill, 1962; (editor) *Contributions to Synthetic Jurisprudence,* Oceana, 1962; (editor) *Progress of Law, Containing Research Papers, Case Comments, and Book Reviews,* Tripathi, 1962; *The Essentials of an Ideal Legal System* (monograph), University of Bombay, 1968; *Law and Morality* (monograph), University of Bombay, 1969; *Photography,* Lakhani Book Depot, 1970; *Art of Living* (Practical Code based on Universal Truths, including those of Oriental philosophies), Lakhani Book Depot, 1972, Abacus Press, 1972.

Contributor of articles on law and philosophical topics to *Bombay Law Reporter, Indian Advocate, Supreme Court Journal, Journal of Mahrashtra State Bar Council,* and to other periodicals and newspapers. Associate editor, *NACCA Law Journal.*

WORK IN PROGRESS: Research in social legislation, international law, criminology jurisprudence, equity, and photographic evidence.

AVOCATIONAL INTERESTS: Art, philosophy, religions of the world, nature, and photography.

*   *   *

SETTON, Kenneth M(eyer)   1914-

PERSONAL: Born June 17, 1914, in New Bedford, Mass.; son of Ezra (a businessman) and Louise (Crossley) Setton; married Josephine W. Swift, September 11, 1941 (died, 1967); married Margaret T. Henry, January 4, 1969; children: (first marriage) George Whitney Fletcher. *Education:* Boston University, B.A., 1936, Litt.D., 1957; Columbia University, M.A., 1938, Ph.D., 1941; also studied at University of Chicago, 1936, and Harvard University, 1939-40. *Office:* Institute for Advanced Study, Princeton, N.J. 08540.

CAREER: Boston University, Boston, Mass., instructor in classics and history, 1940-43; University of Manitoba, Winnipeg, Canada, associate professor, 1943-45; professor of history and head of department, 1945-50; University of Pennsylvania, Philadelphia, associate professor of medieval history, 1950-53, H.C. Lea Professor of Medieval History, 1953-54, 1955-63, Curator of Lea Library, 1951-54, Director of Libraries, 1955-65, university professor and Lea Professor of History, 1963-65; Columbia University, New York, N.Y., professor of medieval history, 1954-55; University of Wisconsin, Madison, W.F. Vilas Research Professor of History and Director, Institute for Research in the Humanities, 1965-68; Institute for Advanced Study, Princeton, N.J., professor of history, 1968—. Bryn Mawr College, visiting lecturer, 1952-53; American School of Classical Studies, Athens, Greece, research fellow, 1960-61; acting director, Gennadius Library, Athens, Greece, 1960-61; member of Board of Scholars, Dumbarton Oaks, 1960—.

MEMBER: American Philosophical Society (vice-president, 1966-69), Mediaeval Academy of America (fellow; president, 1971-72), American Academy of Arts and Sciences (fellow), American Historical Association, Society of Macedonian Studies (Greece; honorary fellow), Institute of Catalan Studies (Spain; corresponding member), Wistar Association. *Awards, honors:* Guggenheim fellowships, to Greece, 1949, to Italy, 1950; John Frederick Lewis Prize, American Philosophical Society, 1957, for essay, "The Byzantine Background to the Italian Renaissance"; Litt.D., Boston University, 1957.

WRITINGS: Christian Attitude Towards the Emperor in the Fourth Century, Especially as Shown in Addresses to the Emperor, Columbia University Press, 1941; *Catalan Domination of Athens, 1311-1388,* Mediaeval Academy of America, 1948; (editor with Henry R. Winkler) *Great Problems in European Civilization,* Prentice-Hall, 1954, 2nd edition, 1966; (contributor) John Hine Mundy and

others, editors, *Essays in Medieval Life and Thought,* Columbia University Press, 1955; (editor-in-chief) *A History of the Crusades,* University of Pennsylvania Press, Volume I (with M.W. Baldwin): *The First Hundred Years,* 1955, 2nd edition, 1958, Volume II (with R.L. Wolff and H.W. Hazard): *The Later Crusades, 1189-1311,* 1962, 2nd edition of two-volume set, University of Wisconsin Press, 1969; (author of introduction and bibliography) Henry Osborn Taylor, *Classical Heritage of the Middle Ages,* Harper, 1958; (contributor) *Guide to Historical Literature,* American Historical Association, 1961; (with others) *The Age of Chivalry,* National Geographic Society, 1969; (with others) *The Renaissance: Maker of Modern Man,* National Geographic Society, 1970. Contributor to learned journals, including *Speculum, American Historical Review, American Journal of Philology, Balkan Studies,* and *Proceedings* of the American Philosophical Society.

WORK IN PROGRESS: The Papacy, Italy, and the Levant, 1204-1571, three volumes; *Byzantium and the Italian Renaissance; Athens in the Middle Ages;* two or three chapters for Volumes III-IV of *History of the Crusades,* to be published by University of Wisconsin Press; editing some correspondence of the Florentine family of the Acciajuoli; various articles for publication in periodicals.

*   *   *

SEUFERT, Karl Rolf   1923-

PERSONAL: Born December 1, 1923, in Frankfurt am Main, Germany; married Christine Hoelzer, July 13, 1952; children: Elizabeth, Rudolf. *Religion:* Roman Catholic. *Home:* 22 Adam von Itzsteinstrasse, Hallgarten, Rheingau, Hessen, Germany.

CAREER: Teacher of German, history, and geography in German schools. *Awards, honors:* Friedrich Gerstaecker Award for best historical adventure book published in Germany during two-year period, 1962, for *Caravan in Peril.*

WRITINGS: Die Karawane der weissen Maenner, Verlag Herder, 1961, translation by Stella Humphries published as *Caravan in Peril,* Pantheon, 1963; *Die Tuerme von Mekka* (title means "The Towers of Mecca", Verlag Herder, 1963, 3rd edition, 1966; *Die vergessenen Buddhas* (title means "The Forgotten Buddhas"; stories about China before Mao Tse-tung), Verlag Herder, 1965; *Das Jahr in der Steppe* (title means "The Year in the Steppe"; novel), Verlag Herder, 1967; *Einmal China und zurueck* (stories about Red China), Signal-Verlag (Baden-Baden), 1971; *Huegel der Goetter und Koenige* (title means "Hill of Gods and Kings"; history of Henry Austen Layard's discovery of the Old Orient), Arena-Verlag (Wuerzburg), 1971; *Explorers, Travellers, Adventurers* (history of the exploration of Africa), Verlag Herder, 1971.

WORK IN PROGRESS: A novel, primarily for young people, about the travel of French explorer Evariste Huc from China to Lhasa, *Reise durch das Schneeland* (title means "Journey Through the Snowland").

*   *   *

SEWARD, William W(ard), Jr.   1913-
  (Leigh Rives)

PERSONAL: Born February 2, 1913, in Surry, Va.; son of William Ward (a physician) and Elizabeth (Gwaltney) Seward; married Virginia Leigh Widgeon, December 27, 1941; children: Jenny Rives, Leigh Ward (daughter). *Education:* University of Richmond, A.B., 1934, A.M., 1935; Duke University, graduate fellow, 1938-39, 1940-41. *Politics:* Democrat. *Religion:* Methodist. *Home:* 1421 Daniel Ave., Lochhaven, Norfolk, Va. 23505. *Office:* Old Dominion University, Norfolk, Va. 23508.

CAREER: Teacher of English in public schools, 1935-38; University of Richmond, Richmond, Va., instructor in English, 1939-40; Greenbrier Military School, Greenbrier, W.Va., head of department of English, 1941-42; Tift College, Forsyth, Ga., professor and head of department of English, 1942-45; Old Dominion College (now Old Dominion University), Norfolk, Va., professor of English, 1945—, head of department, 1947-61. University of Virginia, Charlottesville, lecturer in contemporary fiction, 1952-54. *Member:* National Council of Teachers of English, Modern Language Association of America, American Association of University Professors, Poetry Society of America, Mystery Writers of America, Poetry Society of Virginia (president, 1952-55; advisory board, 1955—), Phi Beta Kappa, Pi Delta Epsilon, Kappa Alpha, Norfolk Executives Club, Norfolk Yacht and Country Club, Princess Ann Country Club.

WRITINGS: The Quarrels of Alexander Pope (monograph), University of Richmond, 1935; (editor) William Wager, *The Longer Thou Livest, the More Fool Thou Art,* Duke University Press, 1939; *Literature and War,* Baylor University Press, 1942; *Skirts of the Dead Night* (novel), Bookman Associates, 1950; (author of foreword) Barbara Whitney, *Descent of the White Bird,* Fine Editions, 1955; (member of editorial board) *Lyric Virginia Today,* Dietz, 1956; *Contrasts in Modern Writers: Some Aspects of British and American Fiction Since Mid-Century* (essays; majority originally published in *Norfolk Virginian Pilot*), Fell, 1963; *My Friend Ernest Hemingway: An Affectionate Reminiscence,* A.S. Barnes, 1969. Member of book review staff, *Norfolk Virginian Pilot,* 1950—; book editor, radio station WMTI-FM, Norfolk, Va., 1956-58.

WORK IN PROGRESS: A work on William Lisle Bowles.

AVOCATIONAL INTERESTS: Nature and outdoor life, farming, reading.

*   *   *

SEYMOUR, Charles, Jr. 1912-

PERSONAL: Born February 26, 1912, in New Haven, Conn.; son of Charles (a historian and president of Yale University) and Gladys (Watkins) Seymour; married Charlotte Ball, May 4, 1940; children: Charlotte Elizabeth, (Mrs. Thomas E. Lovejoy III), Charles. *Education:* Attended Choate School, 1925-30; King's College, Cambridge University, student, 1930-31; Yale University, B.A., 1935, Ph.D., 1938; additional study at Sorbonne, University of Paris. *Home:* 145 Cliff St., New Haven, Conn. 06512. *Office:* 203 Art Gallery, Box 2009, Yale University, New Haven, Conn. 06520.

CAREER: Yale University, New Haven, Conn., instructor in history and history of art, 1938-39; National Gallery of Art, Washington, D.C., curator of sculpture, 1939-42, assistant chief curator, 1945-49; Yale University, associate professor and curator of Renaissance art, 1949-54, professor and curator of Renaissance art, 1954—, chairman of department of history of art, 1956-59. Visiting lecturer at Johns Hopkins University, American University, University of Colorado, Oberlin College; visiting Mellon Professor in Art History, University of Pittsburg, 1965. Served in Military Intelligence Division, U.S. War Department, 1943-45. *Member:* Renaissance Society of America (director, 1962—), College Art Association (director, 1940-42, 1958-61), Committee for the Rescue of Italian Art. *Awards, honors:* Guggenheim fellow, 1954-55.

WRITINGS: Notre Dame of Noyon in the Twelfth Century: A Study in the Early Development of Gothic Architecture, Yale University Press, 1939, Norton, 1968; *Masterpieces of Sculpture from the National Gallery of Art,* Coward, 1949; *Tradition and Experiment in Modern Sculpture,* American University Press, 1950; (author of introduction) *Ten Contemporary Italian Sculptors, April 25 through June 1, 1958* (catalogue of exhibition), Museum of Fine Arts (Houston), 1958; (author of introduction and commentary) *The Rabinowitz Collection of European Paintings,* Yale University Art Gallery, 1961; (author of commentary) *Art Treasures for America: An Anthology of Paintings and Sculpture in the Samuel H. Kress Collection,* Phaidon, 1961; *Sculpture in Italy, 1400-1500,* Penguin, 1966; *Michelangelo's David: A Search for Identity,* University of Pittsburgh Press, 1967; *Early Italian Paintings in the Yale University Art Gallery: A Catalogue,* published for Yale University Art Gallery by Yale University Press, 1970; *The Sculpture of Verrocchio,* New York Graphic Society, 1971; (editor) *Michelangelo: The Sistine Ceiling,* Norton, 1971; *Jacopo Della Quercia: Sculptor,* Yale University Press, 1973. Contributor of articles to art journals. Editor of catalogues of National Gallery of Art and Yale University Art Gallery.

WORK IN PROGRESS: A book on Jacopo della Quercia.

BIOGRAPHICAL/CRITICAL SOURCES: Yale Review, summer, 1967.

*   *   *

SEYMOUR, William Kean 1887-

PERSONAL: Born September 27, 1887, in London, England; son of William and Jane (Kean) Seymour; married Beatrice Mary Stapleton; married second wife, Rosalind Herschel Wade (a novelist); children: Philip Herschel Kean, Gerald William Herschel Kean. *Education:* King's College, London, extension course in English literature, 1911-14. *Home and office:* White Cottage, Old Alresford, Hampshire, England.

CAREER: Midland Bank Ltd., London, England various positions, 1908-47, including managership of branch bank in Chelsea, 1928-47. Lecturer, most recently on tour of Denmark, appearing jointly with author-wife. British representative at Biennial International Congress on Poetry, 1963. President of Guildford and West Surrey Centre, 1962—. *Military service:* Royal Naval Air Service, 1917, Royal Air Force, 1918. *Member:* Royal Society of Literature (fellow), Poetry Society (London; vice-president, 1947—; chairman of general council, 1961-64), P.E.N. (honorary treasurer, 1932-37), West Country Writers' Association. *Awards, honors:* Presidential Gold Medal for Poetry (Philippines), as Distinguished Anglo-Irish Poet, 1968; D.Litt., Free University of Asia, Karachi, 1968.

WRITINGS: The Street of Dreams (poems), John G. Wilson, 1914; *To Verhaeren, and Other Poems,* John G. Wilson, 1917; *Twenty-Three Poems,* C. Palmer & Hayward, 1918; (editor with Cecil Palmer) *Air Pie: The Royal Air Force Annual* (poetry and humor), C. Palmer & Hayward, 1919; *Swords and Flutes* (poems), T. Fisher Unwin, 1919; (editor) *A Miscellany of British Poetry, 1919,* two volumes, Harcourt, 1919, 2nd edition published in England as *A Miscellany of Poetry, 1919,* C. Palmer & Hayward, 1920; (editor) *A Miscellany of Poetry, 1920-1922,* John G. Wilson, 1922; *A Jackdaw in Georgia: A Book of Polite Parodies and Imitations of Contemporaries and Others,* John G. Wilson, 1923; *Caesar Remembers, and Other Poems,* T. Seltzer, 1923, Boni, 1923; *Captain Gunn* (parody of "The Cowled Ape; or, Pretty Polly's Pride," by E.H. Visiak), L.C.C. Camberwell School of Arts, 1926; *Parrot Pie: Parodies and Imitations of Contemporaries,* Harrap, 1927; *Time Stands, and Other Poems,* Gollancz, 1935; *Chinese Crackers,* Boriswood, 1938; *The Little Cages* (novel), R. Hale, 1944; *Collected Poems,* R. Hale, 1946; *Friends of the Swallow* (novel), Jenkins,

1953; *Burns into English: Renderings of Selected Dialect Poems of Robert Burns,* Wingate, 1954, Philosophical Library, 1955; *The Secret Kingdom* (novel), Jenkins, 1954; *Names and Faces* (novel), Jenkins, 1956; *The First Childermas* (verse play), Signet Press, 1959; (editor with John Smith) *The Pattern of Poetry: The Poetry Society Verse-Speaking Anthology,* Burke Publishing, 1963, F. Watts, 1967; *Jonathan Swift: The Enigma of a Genius* (biographical pamphlet), Moor Park College, 1967; (compiler with Swift) *Happy Christmas* (poems), Westminster, 1968; (editor) *Silver Jubilee: Poems Contributed by Members of the Guildford and West Surrey Centre of the Poetry Society to Celebrate Its Twenty-Fifth Anniversary,* Guildford and West Surrey Centre of the Poetry Society, 1969; *The Cats of Rome: New and Selected Poems,* Linden Press, 1970.

Contributor of articles and reviews to *Contemporary Review* and *Poetry Review.*

WORK IN PROGRESS: A new collection of own poems; a novel.

BIOGRAPHICAL/CRITICAL SOURCES: Times Literary Supplement, October 5, 1967; *New York Times Book Review,* December 1, 1968; *Punch,* December 11, 1968.

*   *   *

SHAMBURGER, (Alice) Page

PERSONAL: Born in Aberdeen, N.C.; daughter of Frank Dudley (an oil distributor) and Alice (Page) Shamburger. *Education:* Graduate of St. Mary's School and Junior College, Raleigh, N.C., 1945, Marjorie Webster College, 1947. *Religion:* Methodist. *Home and office:* 500 Carolina St., Aberdeen, N.C. 28315.

CAREER: Cross Country News (aviation newspaper), Fort Worth, Tex., eastern editor, 1954-66. *Air Progress* (magazine) New York, N.Y., contributing editor, 1966—. Mid-South Horse Show Association, secretary, 1957—. *Member:* 99's International Organization of Licensed Women Pilots (executive board; governor of Southeast Section, 1969-71), Aircraft Owners and Pilots Association, National Pilots Association, National Aeronautics Association, Aviation/Space Writers Association, Air Force Association, Air Force Historical Foundation, Wingfoot Lighter-Than-Air Society, American Aviation Historical Society, Moore County Hounds.

WRITINGS: Tracks Across the Sky: The Story of the Pioneers of the U.S. Air Mail, Lippincott, 1964; *Classic Monoplanes,* Sports Car Press, 1966.

With Joe Christy: *Aces and Planes of World War I,* Sports Car Press, 1968; *Command the Horizon: A Pictorial History of Aviation,* A.S. Barnes, 1968; *Summon the Stars,* A.S. Barnes, 1970; *The Curtiss Hawk Fighters,* Sports Car Press, 1971.

Writer of radio and television scripts. Contributor of articles to *Ford Times, Chronicle of the Horse, AOPA Pilot, Professional Pilot, Rotor & Wing, Boston Globe,* and *Sports Afield.*

SIDELIGHTS: Miss Shamburger holds a commercial pilots license for aircraft and helicopters; she flies her own plane, a Beechcraft Bonanza, in doing research for articles and books. *Avocational interests:* Horseback riding, particularly fox hunting.

*   *   *

SHANE, Harold Gray   1914-

PERSONAL: Born August 11, 1914, in Milwaukee, Wis.; son of Ben L. and Grace (Gray) Shane; married Ruth Marion Williams, September 1, 1938 (died, 1964); married June Grant Mulry, 1965; children: (first marriage) Michael Stewart Williams, Patricia Mills, Susan Hatker,

Ann Gray. *Education:* University of Wisconsin, student, 1931-33; Milwaukee State Teachers College, B.E., 1935; Ohio State University, M.A., 1939, Ph.D., 1943. *Religion:* Presbyterian. *Home:* 1416 Sare Rd., Bloomington, Ind. 47401. *Office:* Education Building, Indiana University, Bloomington, Ind. 47401.

CAREER: Elementary school teacher and principal in Cincinnati and Toledo, Ohio, 1935-40; Ohio State Department of Education, Columbus, state supervisor of elementary education, 1942-43; Ohio State University, Columbus, assistant professor, 1943-46; Winnetka (Ill.) Public Schools, superintendent, 1946-49; Northwestern University, Evanston, Ill., professor of elementary education and school administration, 1949-59; Indiana University, Bloomington, dean of School of Education, 1959-65, professor of education, 1965—. Visiting professor at University of Hawaii, summer, 1959; visiting lecturer at other universities; consultant to local school systems in twenty-two states. Member of board of directors of Center for Applied Research in Education, 1961—, of CARE, 1962. Winnetka (Ill.) Public Library, trustee, 1950-57, president, 1951-54. *Military service:* U.S. Navy, line officer, 1944-46.

MEMBER: National Education Association (vice-president, department of elementary school principals, 1939-43), Association for Supervision and Curriculum Development, Association for Childhood Education, John Dewey Society (board of directors, 1954-58, 1959-62; vice-president, 1957-58), National Society for Study of Education, National Council for Research in English, American Educational Research Association, Comparative Education Society, Center for Applied Research in Education, Indiana State Teachers Association, Indiana Schoolmen's Association, American Association of University Professors, American Association of School Administrators, Phi Delta Kappa, Kappa Delta Pi, Beta Phi Theta. *Awards, honors: The American Elementary School,* 1953, and *Creative School Administration in Elementary and Junior High Schools,* 1954, each chosen as outstanding education book of year in Enoch Pratt Memorial Library poll; Pi Lambda Theta "Best Book" award, 1971, for *Guiding Human Development.*

WRITINGS: (Editor) *Nutrition for Health,* Ohio State Department of Education, 1943; (editor) *A Handbook of Inexpensive Resources for the Ohio Elementary Teacher,* Ohio Education Association, 1943; (with Marie Quick) *Working with the Child from Two to Six,* Ohio State Department of Education, 1943; *Living and Learning with the Children of Ohio,* Ohio State Department of Education, 1944; (with others) *The Language Arts in the Ohio Elementary Schools,* Ohio State Department of Education, 1944; (with wife, Ruth Shane) *The New Baby,* Simon & Shuster, 1948, 3rd edition, 1954, school edition, 1950; (contributor) *Basic Reading Instruction in Elementary and High Schools,* University of Chicago Press, 1948.

(With E.T. McSwain) *Evaluation and the Elementary Curriculum,* Holt, 1951, revised edition, 1958; (contributor) *Promoting Growth toward Maturity in Interpreting What Is Read,* University of Chicago Press, 1951; (with F.K. Ferris and E. Keener) "The Good English Series," grades 3-8, six books, Laidlaw Brothers, 1952, revised, 1957; (contributor) *Dealing with Fear and Tension,* Association for Childhood Education, 1952; (chairman and editor) *The American Elementary School* (13th yearbook of John Dewey Society), Harper, 1953; (with Wilbur A. Yauch) *Creative School Administration in Elementary and Junior High Schools,* Holt, 1954; (with R. Shane) *The Twins: The Story of Two Little Girls Who Look Alike,* Simon & Shuster, 1955; *Research Helps in Teaching the Language Arts,* Association for Supervision and Curriculum Development, 1955; *Grade Level and*

Curriculum Chart, F. Watts, 1956, revised edition, 1957; (contributor) *Social Education of Young Children,* National Council for Social Studies, 1956; (with John R. Lee) *An Evaluative Audit of the Educational Program: An Evaluation and Survey Instrument for the Comprehensive Appraisal of Elementary and Secondary Schools,* revised edition, Field Service and Survey Division, School of Education, Northwestern University, 1959; (with Arnold Gesell, Benjamin Spock, Henry S. Commager, and others) *Guiding Children as They Grow,* National Congress of Parents and Teachers, 1959.

(With Mary Reddin and Margaret Gillespie) *Beginning Language Arts Instruction with Children,* C.E. Merrill, 1961; (contributor) Ellen Lewis Buell, editor *A Treasury of Little Golden Books* (anthology), Golden Books, 1960; (with York, Ferris, and Keener) "Using Good English Series," grades 2-12, seven books, Laidlaw Brothers, 1961-62, revised edition of books 7 and 8, 1964; (author of foreword) Charlotte Huck and D.A. Young, *Children's Literature in the Elementary School,* Holt, 1961; (contributor) Leonard Freedman and C.P. Cotter, editors, *Issues of the Sixties,* Wadsworth, 1961; (contributor) Nelson B. Henry, editor, *Individualizing Instruction,* University of Chicago Press, 1962; (with June Grant Mulry, Reddin, and Gillespie) *Improving Language Arts Instruction in the Elementary School,* C.E. Merrill, 1962; (author of foreword) M.E. Bonney and Richard Hampleman, *Personal-Social Evaluation Techniques,* Library of Education, 1962; (with Mulry) *Improving Language Arts Instruction Through Research,* Association for Supervision and Curriculum Development, 1963; (with others) *Becoming an Educator,* Houghton, 1963; (with others) *Critical Incidents in Teaching,* edited by R.J. Corsini and D.D. Howard, Prentice-Hall, 1964; *Our Professional Heritage: Foundations and Principles of Education,* Instructional Systems in Teacher Education, 1966; (senior author) *English,* Books II, III, IV, and V, Laidlaw Brothers, 1967; (with John H. Harris and Georgene Lestina) *Practice for English,* grades 3-6, four practice books, Laidlaw Brothers, 1967; *Linguistics and the Classroom Teacher: Some Implications for Instruction in the Mother Tongue,* Association for Supervision and Curriculum Development, 1967; (with others) *The Arts, the Humanities, and the School Library,* American Association of School Librarians, 1967; (contributor) *Reading Instruction,* Millikin University, 1968; (contributor) *Curriculum Imperative: Survival of Self in Society,* Department of Secondary Education, University of Nebraska, 1968; (with Dean F. Berkley, Donald C. Manlove, and Michael Chiappetta) *A Visit to English and Scottish Schools [and] English Instruction in U.K. Secondary Schools [and] The Case for Comparative Education* (the first by Berkley and Manlove, the second by Shane, the third by Chiappetta), School of Education, Indiana University, 1968; (with others) *New Approaches to Language and Composition,* Books 7 and 8, Laidlaw Brothers, 1969; (editor and contributor) *The United States and International Education: 68th Yearbook,* Part I, published for the National Society for the Study of Education by University of Chicago Press, 1969.

(Contributor) Albert H. Marckwardt, editor, *Linguistics in School Programs: 69th Yearbook,* published for the National Society for the Study of Education by University of Chicago Press, 1970; (with June Grant Shane, Robert Gibson, and Paul Munger) *Guiding Human Development: The Counselor and Teacher in the Elementary School,* Charles A. Jones Publishing, 1971; (contributor) Robert McClure, editor, *The Curriculum: Past, Present and in Perspective—70th Yearbook,* Part II, published for the National Society for the Study of Education by University of Chicago Press, 1971; (with Robert H. Anderson) *As the Twig Is Bent: Readings in Early Childhood Education,* Houghton, 1971; (compiler with James Walden and Ronald Green) *Interpreting Language Arts Research for the Teacher,* Association for Supervision and Curriculum Development, 1971; (contributor) Ira Gordon, editor, *Early Childhood Education: 71st Yearbook,* Part II, published for the National Society for the Study of Education by University of Chicago Press, 1972; (editor and contributor with John I. Goodlad) *The Elementary School in American Society: 72nd Yearbook,* Part II, published for the National Society for the Study of Education by University of Chicago Press, 1973; (contributor) Robert H. Anderson, editor, *Education in Anticipation of Tomorrow,* Charles A. Jones, 1973.

Reader series with Kathleen Hester, all published by Laidlaw Brothers: *Tales to Read,* 1960, *Stories to Remember,* 1960, *Storyland Favorites,* 1960, *Doorways to Adventure,* 1960; *Magic and Laughter,* 1962, *Words with Wings,* 1963, *Courage and Adventure,* 1963.

Primary urban readers with Kathleen Hester and Barbara Mason, all published by Laidlaw Brothers: *Happy Days in the City, All Around the City, Good Times in the City, [and] Adventures in the City,* 1967, expanded edition, 1968.

Middle school series with Kathleen Hester and Barbara Mason, all published by Laidlaw Brothers: *Friends from Many Lands, Adventures in Living and Make-Believe, [and] Doorways to Life and Wonder,* 1970.

Film scripts: (With June Grant Shane) "Linguistic Backgrounds of English," Society for Visual Education, Group 1, six filmstrips, 1967, Group 2, six filmstrips, 1969; "Words That Name and Do" (16mm motion picture), Coronet Films, 1969; "Words That Add Meaning" (16mm motion picture), Coronet Films, 1969; (with J.G. Shane) "Understanding Your Language," Group 1, six filmstrips, Society for Visual Education, 1971.

Booklets: *The Solar System,* American Education Press, 1939; *The Magic of Electricity,* American Education Press, 1939; (with others) *A Wartime Focus for Ohio Elementary Schools,* Ohio Department of Education, 1943; (contributor) *Ohio Schools in Wartime,* Ohio State Department of Education, 1943; (editor) *Books and Materials for Curriculum Workers: An Annual Bibliography,* Association for Supervision and Curriculum Development, 1953; *Oral Aspects of Reading,* University of Chicago Press, 1955; (with others) *Elementary Education in the Chicago Public Schools,* School of Education, Northwestern University, 1959; (with Hollis L. Caswell) *College of Education Semicentennial Addresses,* Kent State University, 1960; (with others) *Motivation,* Department of Elementary-Kindergarten-Nursery Education, National Education Association, 1968.

Writer of fourteen U.S. Navy textbooks and manuals, including *Skill in the Surf: A Landing Boat Manual,* and *The Power Boat Book.* Also author or editor of numerous educational and administrative reports to universities, school systems, and government agencies. Contributor to *Encyclopedia of Educational Research, American Educator Encyclopedia, World Topics Yearbook,* and to yearbooks of educational organization; also contributor of short stories and articles to *Collier's, Cheshire, Weird Tales,* and of more than 150 articles to educational journals.

Member of editorial board of *Childhood Education,* 1947-49, *Phi Delta Kappa Magazine,* 1961, (advisory) *Childcraft,* 1964; member of publications committee of Association for Supervision and Curriculum Development, 1950-55, John Dewey Society, 1959—. Educational consultant and editor, filmstrip series, "Hero Legends of Many Lands," Society for Visual Education, 1956. Consultant for other educational films.

WORK IN PROGRESS: Five books, and twelve filmstrips.

SHANKLE, Ralph O(tis)   1933-

PERSONAL: Born April 5, 1933, in High Point, N.C.; son of Spencer W. (in real estate) and Susan Jane (Poore) Shankle; divorced; children: Gary L., Kim Lauren. *Education:* College of William and Mary, A.B., 1958. *Home address:* P.O. Box 33062, Houston, Tex. 77033. *Agent:* Littauer & Wilkinson, 500 Fifth Ave., New York, N.Y. 10036.

CAREER: National Aeronautics and Space Administration (NASA; formerly National Advisory Council for Aeronautics), member of public information staff at Langley Research Center, Langley Field, Va., 1958-61, public information specialist at Manned Spacecraft Center, Houston, Tex., 1962—. Wrote press kits for Mercury manned orbital space flights; worked actual flights at Cape Kennedy (Glenn and Cooper), Bermuda (Carpenter), and Houston (Schirra). *Military service:* U.S. Air Force, 1951-55; member of B-29 test flight crew at David-Monthan Air Force Base, Ariz., during Korean War.

WRITINGS: The Twins of Space: The Story of the Gemini Program, Lippincott, 1964.

WORK IN PROGRESS: Two Westerns; four books on space, two of them for boys; other fiction.

AVOCATIONAL INTERESTS: Painting in oils, playing folk songs on guitar.

* * *

SHANNON, Edgar F(inley), Jr.   1918-

PERSONAL: Born June 4, 1918, in Lexington, Va.; son of Edgar Finley and Mary Eleanor (Duncan) Shannon; married Eleanor Bosworth, February 11, 1956; children: Eleanor Bosworth, Elizabeth Anderson, Lois McCain. *Education:* Washington and Lee University, A.B., 1939, Duke University, A.M., 1941; Harvard University, A.M., 1947; Oxford University, Rhodes Scholar, 1947-50, D.Phil., 1949. *Politics:* Democrat. *Religion:* Presbyterian. *Home:* Carr's Hill, University of Virginia, Charlottesville, Va. 22204. *Office:* Pavilion VIII, East Lawn, University of Virginia, Charlottesville, Va. 22204.

CAREER: Harvard University, Cambridge, Mass., associate professor of naval science and tactics, 1946, instructor in English, 1950-52, assistant professor, 1952-56; University of Virginia, Charlottesville, associate professor, 1956-59, professor of English and president of university, 1959—. *Military service:* U.S. Navy, 1941-46; U.S. Naval Reserve, 1946—; became captain, 1960; received Bronze Star. *Member:* Modern Language Association of America, State Universities Association (president), Association of State Universities and Land-Grant Colleges (president; chairman, executive committee), Council of Southern Universities (president), Southern Association of Colleges and Schools, Association of Virginia Colleges (president), Society of the Cincinnati, Tennyson Society (honorary vice-president), Phi Beta Kappa, Omicron Delta Kappa, Phi Eta Sigma, Raven Society (University of Virginia), Bibliographical Society of the University of Virginia, The Signet (Harvard), Authors Club (London). *Awards, honors:* Guggenheim fellow, 1953-54; Fulbright research fellowship, 1953-54.

WRITINGS: Tennyson and the Reviewers: A Study of His Literary Reputation and of the Influence of the Critics Upon His Poetry, 1827-1851, Harvard University Press, 1952; *Lockwood's Dreams and the Exegesis of Wuthering Heights* (originally published in *Nineteenth-Century Fiction,* September, 1959), University of California Press, 1959; *Chaucer and the Roman Poets,* Russell, 1964; *The University of Virginia: A Century and a Half of Innovation,* Newcomen Society in North America, 1969. Contributor of articles to professional journals and to *Papers* of the Bibliographical Society of America.

WORK IN PROGRESS: Research in nineteenth-century English literature; editing a complete collection of Tennyson's letters.

* * *

SHANNON, William V(incent)   1927-

PERSONAL: Born August 24, 1927, in Worcester, Mass.; son of Patrick Joseph (a carpenter) and Nora Agnes (McNamara) Shannon; married Elizabeth McNelly, August 5, 1961; children: Liam Anthony, Christopher Andrew. *Education:* Clark University, A.B., 1947; Harvard University, A.M., 1948. *Religion:* Roman Catholic. *Home:* 3821 Gramercy St. N.W., Washington, D.C. 20016.

CAREER: Free-lance writer in Washington, D.C., 1949-51; *New York Post,* New York, N.Y., Washington correspondent, 1951-57; columnist for *New York Post* and other newspapers, 1957-64; member of *New York Times* editorial board, 1964—. *Member:* National Press Club, Overseas Writers, Phi Beta Kappa. *Awards, honors:* Page One Award, New York Newspaper Guild, 1951; fellowship, Center for Study of Democratic Institutions, 1961-62; Litt.D., Clark University, 1964; Edward J. Meeman Award, Scripps Howard Foundation, 1968; fellowship, Alicia Patterson Fund, 1969-70.

WRITINGS: (Contributor) Robert S. Allen, editor, *Our Sovereign State,* Vanguard, 1949; (with Robert S. Allen) *The Truman Merry-Go-Round,* Vanguard, 1950; *The American Irish,* Macmillan, 1963, revised edition, 1966; *The Heir Apparent: Robert Kennedy and the Struggle for Power,* Macmillan, 1967.

WORK IN PROGRESS: A book, *The Way England Is Now,* for World Publishing.

SIDELIGHTS: The Heir Apparent: Robert Kennedy and the Struggle for Power was one of several books on Kennedy written during a turbulent pre-presidential election year. In a *New York Times* review published in September of 1967, Eliot Fremont-Smith wrote: "Of the 22 books—by latest count—that have been or are being written about Robert Kennedy, *The Heir Apparent* is doubtless one of the most honest and balanced." A reviewer for *Time* agreed, calling the book "more compelling than its predecessors. Shannon is a native of Massachusetts, a Harvard graduate, an Irish Catholic and a liberal Democrat—the perfect candidate, it would seem, to write an admiring or even adoring book about Bobby. The surprise is that *The Heir Apparent* is often severely critical. But it is always dispassionate in its analysis and at times sympathetic." Frank Getlein quarreled with Shannon's conclusion that Bobby, four years after John Kennedy's assassination, " 'has raised himself to a position of independent national political power,' " while admiring the record as "meticulously laid out and penetratingly examined by Mr. Shannon." Edwin Tetlow of *Christian Science Monitor* was less equivocating in his praise: "[The book] is a thoroughly professional assessment by one of the country's most knowledgeable and careful political commentators—one who has watched the crusades and the skulduggeries intently for many years."

BIOGRAPHICAL/CRITICAL SOURCES: New York Times, September 23, 1967; *Christian Science Monitor,* September 28, 1967; *Time,* October 6, 1967; *Book World,* October 22, 1967; *Commonweal,* February 2, 1968.

* * *

SHAPIRO, Henry D(avid)   1937-

PERSONAL: Born May 7, 1937, in New York, N.Y.; son of Lawrence Milton (a physician) and Estelle V. (Srebnik) Shapiro; married Nancy Wynne Kasdin, July 14, 1963; children: Lawrence Milton, Elliot Hart, Matthew Joseph. *Education:* Columbia University, A.B., 1958; Cornell University, M.A., 1960; Rutgers University, Ph.D., 1966. *Religion:* Jewish. *Office:* Department of History, University of Cincinnati, Cincinnati, Ohio 45221.

CAREER: Rutgers University, New Brunswick, N.J., assistant instructor in history, 1960-62; Manhattan School of Music, New York, N.Y., lecturer in history of science, 1963; Ohio State University, Columbus, instructor in history, 1963-66; University of Cincinnati, Cincinnati, Ohio, assistant professor of history, 1966—. *Member:* American Historical Association, American Studies Association, American Association of University Professors. *Awards, honors:* Moses Coit Tyler Prize, Cornell University, 1961, for *Confiscation of Confederate Property in the North.*

WRITINGS: Confiscation of Confederate Property in the North, Cornell University Press, 1962; (editor and author of introductions with Zane L. Miller) *Physician to the West: Selected Writings of Daniel Drake on Science and Society,* University Press of Kentucky, 1970; (author of introduction) John C. Campbell, *The Southern Highlander and His Homeland,* University Press of Kentucky, 1969.

WORK IN PROGRESS: Two books, *A Strange Land and Peculiar People: The Discovery of Appalachia, 1870-1920,* and *The Search for an American Folk Tradition, 1910-1941;* general research into the idea of culture in America.

* * *

SHAPLEN, Robert M. 1917-

PERSONAL: Born March 22, 1917, in Philadelphia, Pa.; son of Joseph (a journalist) and Sonia (Modell) Shaplen; married third wife, June Herman (an editor), March 31, 1962; children: Peter, Kate. *Education:* University of Wisconsin, B.A. (with honors), 1937; Columbia University, M.S. in Journalism, 1938. *Politics:* Democrat. *Home:* Repulse Bay Towers, B-5, 119-A Repulse Bay Rd., Hong Kong. *Agent:* Brandt & Brandt, 101 Park Ave., New York, N.Y. 10017. *Office:* New Yorker, 25 West 43rd St., New York, N.Y. 10036.

CAREER: New York Herald Tribune, New York, N.Y., reporter and rewrite man, 1937-43; *Newsweek,* former war correspondent in Pacific, and chief of Far East bureau, 1945-47; staff member, *Fortune,* 1948-50; *Colliers,* 1950-51; columnist abroad for fifteen American newspapers, 1950-51. *New Yorker,* staff-writer, 1952—, Far Eastern Correspondent, 1962—. *Member:* Harvard Club (New York). *Awards, honors:* Nieman fellowship, 1947-48; Overseas Press Club Awards for both *The Lost Revolution* and *Time Out of Hand.*

WRITINGS: A Corner of the World (fiction), Knopf, 1949, reissued as *The Love-Making of Max-Robert,* New American Library, 1950; *Free Love and Heavenly Sinners: The Story of the Great Henry Ward Beecher Scandal,* Knopf, 1954; *A Forest of Tigers* (fiction), Knopf, 1956; *Kreuger, Genius and Swindler,* introduction by John Kenneth Galbraith, Knopf, 1960; *Toward the Well-Being of Mankind: Fifty Years of the Rockefeller Foundation,* edited by Arthur Bernon Tourtellot, Doubleday, 1964; *The Lost Revolution: The Story of Twenty Years of Neglected Opportunities in Viet Nam and of America's Failure to Foster Democracy There,* Harper, 1965, revised edition published as *The Lost Revolution: The U.S. in Vietnam, 1946-1966,* 1966 (published in England as *The Lost Revolution: Vietnam, 1945-1965,* Deutsch, 1966); *Letter from South Vietnam* (originally published in *New Yorker,* March 12, 1966), American Friends of Viet Nam, c.1966; *Time Out of Hand: Revolution and Reaction in Southeast Asia,* Harper, 1969, revised edition, 1970; *The Road from War: Vietnam, 1965-1970,* Harper, 1970. Contributor of stories and arti-

cles to *Reporter, Yale Review, Foreign Affairs,* and other periodicals; author of television scripts for "Twentieth Century."

SIDELIGHTS: In a review of *Time Out of Hand,* Southeast Asia specialist Louis Kraar wrote of Shaplen: "The *New Yorker*'s man in Asia and a correspondent with more than two decades of experience in the East, Shaplen is nothing less than the best-informed, most thorough journalist covering the area. He shuns slick stereotypes and grand theoretical designs to approach each country in terms of its own historical forces, culture, leaders, and basic aspirations.... He thoroughly connects the happenings that make 'news' with the more fundamental influences that largely shape Southeast Asian events." Joel Blocker of *Newsweek* called Shaplen "one of the most thoughtful and knowledgeable American journalists in Southeast Asia during the '60's, [who] specializes in failed revolutions. His earlier, already classic *The Lost Revolution* carefully documented how first French and later U.S. mistakes effectively thwarted the emergence of a true, nationalist movement in South Vietnam and in the process allowed that country's revolution to be pre-empted by the Communists. Shaplen's new book [*Time Out of Hand*], based in good part on a series of richly detailed Letters to the *New Yorker* over the past several years, ranges far wider, covering ten countries and a quarter of a billion people. Yet his theme is essentially the same: the failures and frustrations of anti-colonial revolution."

William P. Bundy calls "the real Bob Shaplen . . . a fluent writer and electric talker."

A cautious and objective reporter whose "even-handedness is legendary among his colleagues," according to Geoffrey Wolff, Shaplen has maintained an anti-Communist stance and a consistent belief in America's good intentions. However, his latest book on Southeast Asia, *The Road from War,* shows there are limits to even "Shaplen's patience." As Wolff notes, "it must be understood that Shaplen, ... who believes in exhausting rival arguments before he decides, . . . has given up hope slowly and with palpable reluctance." Concluding his review of *The Road from War,* a writer for *Library Journal* writes: "Whatever the final judgment on Shaplen's personal position, his unflagging devotion to his reportorial tasks have made his dispatches classics of Vietnam war journalism."

BIOGRAPHICAL/CRITICAL SOURCES: Library Journal, June 15, 1964, September 1, 1970; *New York Times Book Review,* October 31, 1965, May 18, 1969; *Atlantic,* November, 1965; *Book Week,* November 7, 1965; *New Leader,* May 26, 1969; *Newsweek,* July 14, 1969, September 28, 1970; *Saturday Review,* July 26, 1969; *Commonweal,* October 3, 1969; *Washington Post,* November 4, 1970; *Newsday,* October 26, 1970.

* * *

SHARLIN, Harold I (ssadore) 1925-

PERSONAL: Born July 8, 1925, in Trenton, N.J.; son of Solomon S. and Jennie (Kaplan) Sharlin; married Tiby Mintz, June 27, 1948; children: Allan, Joshua, Shifra. *Education:* Drexel Institute of Technology, B.S. in E.E., 1948; Columbia University, M.A., 1953; University of Pennsylvania, Ph.D., 1958. *Home:* 2214 Storm St., Ames, Iowa 50012. *Office:* Department of History, Iowa State University, Ames, Iowa 50010.

CAREER: Drexel Institute of Technology, Philadelphia, Pa., instructor in electrical engineering, 1952-56; Polytechnic Institute of Brooklyn, Brooklyn, N.Y., associate professor of history and economics, 1956-62; Iowa State University, Ames, associate professor of history, 1962—. *Military service:* U.S. Navy, 1944-46. *Member:* American

Historical Association, History of Science Society (council, 1970—), American Association of University Professors, Organization of American Historians, American Association for the Advancement of Science, Society for History of Technology (advisory council, 1970—), Phi Alpha Theta, Phi Kappa Phi. *Awards, honors:* Iowa State University Research Foundation grant, 1965-66; American Philosophical Society research grants, 1965, 1966, 1968; fellow, Woodrow Wilson International Center for Scholars, 1970-71.

Writings: The Making of the Electrical Age: From the Telegraph to Automation, Abelard, 1964; *The Convergent Century: The Unification of Science in the Nineteenth Century,* Abelard, 1966; *Kelvin: A Biography of William Thomson,* Macmillan (London), in press. Member of editorial board, *Annals of Science,* 1969—.

WORK IN PROGRESS: Writing on the influence of nineteenth century science and technology on American scholarship and on popular beliefs.

BIOGRAPHICAL/CRITICAL SOURCES: Times Literary Supplement, February 23, 1967.

*　　　*　　　*

SHARP, Aaron John 1904-

PERSONAL: Born July 29, 1904, in Plain City, Ohio; son of Prentice Daniel and Maude Katherine (Herriott) Sharp; married Cora Evelyn Bunch (a mathematics teacher), July 25, 1929; children: Rosa Elizabeth (Mrs. Odis Chambers), Maude Katharine (Mrs. E.C. Clebsch), Mary Martha (Mrs. R.L. McFarland), Fred P., Jennie Lou (Mrs. Peter Haskell). *Education:* Ohio Wesleyan University, A.B., 1927; University of Oklahoma, M.S., 1929; Ohio State University, Ph.D., 1938. *Politics:* Independent. *Religion:* Unitarian. *Home:* 1201 Tobler Rd., Knoxville, Tenn. 37919. *Office:* Department of Botany, Universiy of Tennessee, Knoxville, Tenn. 37916.

CAREER: University of Tennessee, Knoxville, instructor, 1929-37, assistant professor, 1937-40, associate professor, 1940-46, professor of botany, 1946-65, Distinguished Service Professor, 1965—, curator of herbarium, 1949-68, associate curator, 1968—, head of department of botany, 1951-61. Instructor in summer school, University of West Virginia, 1939-41; Cecil Billington Lecturer, Cranbrook Institute of Science, 1947; visiting professor, Stanford University, 1951, University of Michigan Biological Station, summers, 1959-64, University of Minnesota Biological Station, summer, 1971, and University of Montana Biological Station, summer, 1972; visiting lecturer, American Institute of Biological Sciences, 1967-70. Great Smoky Mountains National Park, botanist technician, summer, 1934, ranger-naturalist, summers, 1939-41; Highlands Biological Laboratories, trustee, 1934-38, 1948-64, member of board of managers, 1946-52. Honorary member, HaHori Botanical Laboratory, Nichinang, Japan, 1956—. Consultant, Union Carbide Nuclear Corp. and National Park Service.

MEMBER: International Society of Phytomorphologists, International Association for Plant Taxonomy, International Society of Tropical Foresters, American Association for the Advancement of Science (fellow; vice-president and chairman of botanical science section, 1963), American Bryological Society (president, 1935), American Institute of Biological Sciences, American Phycological Society, American Society of Naturalists, American Society of Plant Taxonomists (president, 1961), Botanical Society of America (council member, 1954; treasurer, 1957-62; vice-president, 1963; president, 1965), Ecological Society of America (council member, 1954-55; vice-president, 1959), Nature Conservancy (member of board of governors, 1955-61), Society for the Study of Evolution, American Fern Society, Wilderness Society, Sociedad Botanica de Mexico, Sociedad Mexicana de Historia Natural, Association of Southeastern Biologists (vice-president, 1956), New England Botany Club, Southern Appalachian Botanical Club (president, 1946-47), Great Smoky Mountains Conservation Association (director), Tennessee Academy of Science (executive committee member, 1943-44; vice-president, 1952; president, 1953), Phi Beta Kappa, Sigma Xi, Phi Epsilon Phi, Phi Kappa Phi, Phi Sigma, Sigma Delta Pi, Explorers Club, Torrey Botanical Club. *Awards, honors:* Guggenheim fellow in Mexico and Guatemala, 1944-46; D.Sc., Ohio Wesleyan University, 1952; Meritorious teaching award, Association of Southeastern Biologists, 1972; merit award, Botanical Society of America, 1972.

WRITINGS: *Relationships Between the Floras of California and Southeastern United States,* Natural History Museum, Stanford University, 1951; *Great Smoky Mountains Wildflowers,* University of Tennessee Press, 1962, 3rd edition (with Carlos Clinton Campbell), 1970. Contributor to *Encyclopaedia Britannica. Bryologist,* associate editor, 1938-42, 1945-53, acting editor, 1943-44; associate editor, *Castanea,* 1947-70, *Journal* of the HaHori Botanical Laboratory, 1962.

WORK IN PROGRESS: *Ferns of the Great Smoky Mountains; An Introduction to Bryology; Manual of Mexican Mosses.*

*　　　*　　　*

SHARP, Harold S(pencer) 1909-

PERSONAL: Born December 23, 1909, in Alameda, Calif.; son of Harold Gibbons (a civil engineer) and Mary (Spencer) Sharp; married Marjorie Barnhill Zehr, June 27, 1958. *Education:* Indiana University, B.S. in B.A. (with distinction), 1954, M.S. in L.S., 1957. *Home:* 2110 Springfield Ave., Fort Wayne, Ind. 46805.

CAREER: Rosenberg Bros. & Co., San Francisco, Calif., contract administrator, 1928-42; U.S. Army, Quartermaster Corps, 1942-52; Farnsworth Electronics Co., Fort Wayne, Ind., chief librarian, 1957-59; General Motors Corp., A.C. Spark Plug Division, Milwaukee, Wis., technical librarian, 1959-63; Lockheed-Georgia Co., Marietta, Ga., engineering information analyst, 1963-64; free-lance library consultant, Berkeley, Calif., 1964-65; University of Hawaii, Honolulu, professor of library science and head of general reference, 1965-68; Indiana State University, Terre Haute, professor of library science, 1968-72. Library consultant sponsored by Special Libraries Association. *Member:* Special Libraries Association (Wisconsin chapter, secretary, 1960-62; vice-president, program chairman, and president-elect, 1962-63), Beta Gamma Sigma, Beta Phi Mu.

WRITINGS: *The House of a Million Wonders* (booklet), Employee Relations, Inc., 1961; *How to Use Your Library,* Consolidated Book Service, 1963; (editor) *Readings in Special Librarianship,* Scarecrow, 1963, revised edition, 1973; (editor) *Readings in Information Retrieval,* Scarecrow, 1964; (editor with wife, Marjorie Z. Sharp) *Index to Characters in the Performing Arts,* Scarecrow, Volume I: *Non-Musical Plays,* 1966, Volume II: *Operas, and Other Musical Productions,* 1969, Volume III: *Ballets A-Z and Symbols,* 1972, Volume IV: *Radio and Television,* 1973; (editor) *Handbook of Pseudonyms and Personal Nicknames,* Scarecrow, 1972. Contributor of articles on business management and library science to more than twenty-five technical periodicals.

WORK IN PROGRESS: First supplement to *Handbook of Pseudonyms and Personal Nicknames,* publication by Scarecrow expected in 1974; *Handbook of Geographical Nicknames,* Scarecrow, 1974.

SIDELIGHTS: "[I] play piano (once organized and conducted a college dance orchestra); [I] collect jazz records and have approximately five thousand collector's items. [I] don't care a bit for outdoor life, sports clothes, or open cars, but do like cats, flying, and having two or three books going at once."

* * *

SHEA, John Gerald 1906-
(Jack Fitzgerald)

PERSONAL: Born June 7, 1906, in Rye, N.Y.; son of John G. and Margaret (Fitzgerald) Shea; married C. Vada Tracy, March 20, 1930; children: John Frederick, Gerald Curtis. Education: Attended State University of New York, 1926-30; graduate study at New York University, Columbia University, Whitewater College. Religion: Catholic. Home: 102 Milbank Ave., Greenwich, Conn. 06830.

CAREER: Professional writer, 1944—. Chance Vought Aircraft, aviation editor, publication section, 1944-45. Writer and designer of advertising, books, other publications.

WRITINGS: (With Paul N. Wenger) Colonial Furniture, Bruce, 1934; (with Wenger) Provincial Furniture, Bruce, 1936; Woodworking for Everybody, International Textbook Co., 1944, 4th edition, Van Nostrand, 1970; Your Professional Office, Hamilton Advertising, 1947; Plywood Working for Everybody, Van Nostrand, 1963; Colonial Furniture Making for Everybody, Van Nostrand, 1964; Contemporary Furniture Making for Everybody, Van Nostrand, 1965; The American Shakers and Their Furniture, with Measured Drawings of Museum Classics, Van Nostrand, 1971. Building and design editor, Medical Economics, 1946-47; book editor, Family Handyman, 1955. Contributor of articles to American Home, Better Homes and Gardens, Living, Popular Mechanics, Science and Mechanics, Mechanix Illustrated, Motor Boating, Rudder, Canadian Boating, and other magazines.

WORK IN PROGRESS: Country Furniture of America, for Van Nostrand; How Scheduled Air Transportation Originated: Transport in the Sky—A Pictorial History of U.S. Scheduled Air Transportation.

AVOCATIONAL INTERESTS: Travel, power boating, aviation.

* * *

SHEEHY, Eugene P(aul) 1922-

PERSONAL: Born October 10, 1922, in Elbow Lake, Minn.; son of Thomas J. (a farmer) and Roxy (Vincent) Sheehy. Education: St. John's University, Collegeville, Minn., B.A., 1950; University of Minnesota, M.A., 1951, B.S. in L.S., 1952. Religion: Roman Catholic. Home: 185 West End Ave., New York, N.Y. 10023.

CAREER: Georgetown University, Washington, D.C., reference librarian, 1952-53; Columbia University, New York, N.Y., senior reference assistant in library, 1953-64, head of Reference Department, 1965—. Military service: U.S. Marine Corps, 1942-46; became sergeant. Member: American Library Association.

WRITINGS—Compiler with Kenneth A. Lohf: Joseph Conrad at Mid-Century: Editions and Studies, 1895-1955, University of Minnesota Press, 1957; The Achievement of Marianne Moore: A Bibliography, 1907-1957, New York Public Library, 1958; Yvor Winters: A Bibliography, A. Swallow, 1959; Frank Norris: A Bibliography, Talisman, 1959; Sherwood Anderson: A Bibliography, Talisman, 1960; An Index to "The Little Review," 1914-1929, New York Public Library, 1961. Editor, with Lohf, of Index to Little Magazines, 1953-63.

Contributor: Ulick O'Connor, editor, The Joyce We Knew, Mercier Press, 1967. Also author of Supplement I (1965-66), 1968, and Supplement II (1967-68), 1970, to Constance M. Winchell's Guide to Reference Books, 8th edition, published by the American Library Association. Editor of semi-annual column, "Selected Reference Books," in College and Research Libraries, 1963—.

* * *

SHEFTER, Harry 1910-

PERSONAL: Born July 16, 1910, in New York, N.Y.; son of Aaron (a decorator) and Sonia (Afremov) Shefter; married Evelyn Palevsky (a clinical psychologist), December 15, 1937; children: Barbara J., Sharon Ann. Education: College of City of New York (now City College of City University of New York), B.A., 1931, M.S., 1932; postgraduate study at New York University. Home: 182 Robert Dr., New Rochelle, N.Y. 10804. Agent: Harold Matson Co., Inc., 22 East 40th St., New York, N.Y. 10016.

CAREER: William Howard Taft High School, New York, N.Y., vice-principal, 1937—; New York University, New York, N.Y. associate professor of English, 1945—. Supervising editor for supplements and teacher's manuals in "Readers Enrichment Series," Pocket Books, Inc., 1963—. Vice-president, Knolls Cooperative, Riverdale, N.Y. Member: National Council of Teachers of English, English Teachers Association (executive board member, 1946-48), Administrative Assistants Association (New York; vice-president).

WRITINGS: Six Minutes a Day to Perfect Spelling, Pocket Books, 1954; Short Cuts to Effective English, Pocket Books, 1955; Faster Reading Self-Taught, Pocket Books, 1958; Shefter's Guide to Better Compositions, Washington Square Press, 1960; How to Get Higher Marks in School, Washington Square Press, 1961; How to Prepare Talks and Oral Reports, Washington Square Press, 1963; (editor) Great Adventures of Sherlock Holmes, Washington Square Press, 1972. Contributor to professional journals.†

* * *

SHEPARD, Ernest Howard 1879-

PERSONAL: Born December 10, 1879, in St. John's Wood, London, England; son of Henry Dunkin (an architect) and Jessie (Lee) Shepard (grandaughter of William Lee, watercolor painter); married Florence Chaplin, September, 1904 (died, 1927); married Norah Radcliffe Mary Carroll, 1944; children: Mary Eleanor (illustrator of the Mary Poppins books), Graham Howard (killed in World War II while serving with the Royal Navy). Education: Attended St. Paul's School, London, 1892-94; Heatherleys Art School, 1896, Royal Academy Schools, 1897-1902. Home and Office: Woodmancote-Lodsworth, Petworth, Sussex, England.

CAREER: Has exhibited his work in many galleries since 1901. Began drawing for Punch magazine, 1907, joined the round table, 1921, Punch political cartoonist, 1940-45, and afterwards until his retirement in 1959. Military service: Royal Artillery, 1915-19; became major; awarded military cross. Member: Art Worker's Guild, National Art Collections Fund, Artists General Benevolent Institution, Savage Club.

WRITINGS—All self-illustrated: Fun and Fantasy (drawings), Methuen, 1927; (compiler) Edward V. Lucas, As the Bee Sucks, Methuen, 1937; Drawn from Memory (autobiography), Lippincott, 1957; Drawn from Life (autobiography), Methuen, 1961, Dutton, 1962; Pooh, His Art Gallery (drawings), Dutton, 1962; Ben and Brock (juvenile), Methuen, 1965, Doubleday, 1966; Betsy and Joe (juvenile), Methuen, 1966, Dutton, 1967.

Illustrator—All books by A.A. Milne: *When We Were Very Young* (poems), Dutton, 1924, new edition, Methuen, 1934, Dutton, 1935, edition with foreward by Sir James Pitman, Dutton, 1966; *The King's Breakfast*, Dutton, 1925; *Fourteen Songs from "When We Were Very Young,"* Dutton, 1925; *Teddy Bear, and Other Songs from "When We Were Very Young,"* music by H. Fraser Simson, Dutton, 1926; *Winnie-the-Pooh*, Dutton, 1926, new edition, Methuen, 1934, Dutton, 1935, edition with foreword by Sir James Pitman, Dutton, 1966; *Now We Are Six* (poems), Dutton, 1927, new edition, Dutton, 1934; *The House at Pooh Corner*, Dutton, 1928, new edition, Methuen, 1934, Dutton, 1935; *The Christopher Robin Story Book* (from *When We Were Very Young, Now We Are Six, Winnie-the-Pooh,* and *The House at Pooh Corner*), Dutton, 1929; *The Very Young Calendar, 1930* (verses), Dutton 1929; *The Christopher Robin Calendar*, Methuen, 1929; *When I Was Very Young*, Fountain Press (N.Y.), 1930; *Tales of Pooh* (selections from *Winnie-the-Pooh* and *The House at Pooh Corner*), Methuen, 1930; *The Christopher Robin Verses (When We Were Very Young* and *Now We Are Six*), Dutton, 1932; *Songs from "Now We Are Six,"* Dutton, c. 1935; *The Christopher Robin Birthday Book*, Methuen, 1930, Dutton, 1931; *More "Very Young" Songs*, Dutton, 1937; *The Hums of Pooh*, Dutton, 1937; *Sneezles, and Other Selections*, Dutton, 1947; *Old Sailor, and Other Selections*, Dutton, 1947; *Introducing Winnie-the-Pooh, and Other Selections*, Dutton, 1947, Garden City Publishing, 1950; *Year In, Year Out*, Dutton, 1952; *The World of Pooh* (includes *Winnie-the-Pooh* and *The House at Pooh Corner;* with new illustrations in full color), Dutton, 1957; *The World of Christopher Robin* (includes *When We Were Very Young* and *Now We Are Six;* with new illustrations in full color), Dutton, 1958; *Pooh's Library* (four volumes contain: *Now We Are Six, Winnie-the-Pooh, When We Were Very Young,* and *The House at Pooh Corner*), Dutton, 1961; *The Pooh Song Book* (containing *The Hums of Pooh, The King's Breakfast,* and *Fourteen Songs from "When We Were Very Young"*), Dutton, 1961; *Pooh's Birthday Book*, Dutton, 1963; *The Pooh Story Book* (with decorations and illustrations in full color), Dutton, 1965; *The Christopher Robin Book of Verse* (selections from *When We Were Very Young* and *Now We Are Six,* with decorations and illustrations in full color), Dutton, 1967 (published in England as *The Christopher Robin Verse Book*, Methuen, 1969); *Pooh's Pot O'Honey*, Dutton, 1968.

Illustrator—All books by Laurence Housman: *Victoria Regina*, J. Cape, 1934, Scribner, 1935; *Golden Sovereign* (play), Scribner, 1937, J. Cape, 1940; *We Are Not Amused* and *Happy and Glorious* (play), J. Cape, 1939; *Bedchamber Plot* (play), J. Cape, 1939; *Suitable Suitors* (play), J. Cape, 1939; *Stable Government* (play), J. Cape, 1939; *Promotion Cometh* (play), J. Cape, 1939; *Primrose Way* (play), J. Cape, 1939; *Great Relief* (play), J. Cape, 1939; *Go-Between* (play), J. Cape, 1939; *Firelighters* (play), J. Cape, 1939; *Enter Prince* (play), J. Cape, 1939; *Comforter* (play), J. Cape, 1939; *Gracious Majesty* (scenes from the life of Queen Victoria), J. Cape, 1941, Scribner, 1942.

Illustrator: Edward Verrall Lucas, *Book of Children's Verse*, Doubleday, c. 1925; Lucas, *Playtime and Company*, Doubleday, 1925; Samuel Pepys, *Everybody's Pepys*, abridged and edited by O.F. Morshead, G. Bell, 1926, Harcourt, 1931; Charles Dickens, *The Holly-tree, and Other Christmas Stories*, Scribner, 1926; Eva Violet Isaacs (Marchioness of Reading), *The Little One's Log*, Partridge (London), 1927; Georgette Agnew, *Let's Pretend* (poems), Putnam, 1927; Lucas, *Mr. Punch's County Songs*, Methuen, 1928; Kenneth Grahame, *The Golden Age* (limited autographed edition), John Lane, 1928,

Dodd, 1929, edition with new illustrations, 1954; Anthony Armstrong (pseudonym of Anthony Armstrong Willis), *Livestock in Barracks*, Methuen, 1929; James Boswell, *Everybody's Boswell*, abridged and edited by F.V. Morley, Harcourt, 1930; Grahame, *Dream Days*, new edition, John Lane, 1930, Dodd, 1931, edition with new illustrations, Dodd, 1954; Grahame, *The Wind in the Willows* (first edition published in 1908 without Shepard illustrations), Methuen, 1931, Scribner, 1933, new edition, Scribner, 1953, edition with new plates in color, Methuen, 1959, Scribner, 1960; John Drinkwater, *Christmas Poems*, Sidgwick & Jackson, 1931; Jan Struther (pseudonym of Joyce Maxtone Graham), *Sycamore Square* (verse), Methuen, 1932; Richard Jeffries, *Bevis*, new·edition, P. Smith, 1932; Boswell, *The Great Cham·(Dr. Johnson)*, G. Bell, 1933; *Everybody's Lamb*, abridged and edited by A.C. Ward, G. Bell, 1933; Patrick R. Chalmers, *The Cricket in the Cage* (verse), Macmillan, 1933; Struther, *The Modern Struwelpeter*, Methuen, 1936; John Collings Squire, editor, *Cheddar Gorge*, Collins, 1937, Macmillan (New York), 1938; Grahame, *Reluctant Dragon* (previously published as chapter in *Dream Days*), Holiday House, 1938; Grahame, *Bertie's Escapade* (first published in *First Whisper of the Wind in the Willows*), Lippincott, 1945; Eleanor Farjeon, *Silver Curlew*, Oxford University Press, 1953, Viking, 1954; Juliana Ewing, *Brownies, and Other Stories*, Dutton, 1954; Mary Louisa Molesworth, *Cuckoo Clock*, Dutton, 1954; E. and Herbert Farjeon, *Glass Slipper*, Oxford University Press, 1955, Viking, 1956; Susan Colling, *Frogmorton,·* Collins, 1955, Knopf, 1956; Roger L. Green, editor, *Modern Fairy Stories*, Dutton, 1955; George MacDonald, *At the Back of the North Wind*, Dutton, 1956; Hans Christian Andersen, *Fairy Tales*, translated by L.W. Kingsland, Oxford University Press, 1961, Walck, 1962; Emile Victor Rieu, *The Flattered Flying Fish, and Other Poems*, Dutton, 1962; Virginia H. Ellison, *The Pooh Cook Book*, Dutton, 1969; Ellison, *The Pooh Party Book*, Dutton, 1971; and others. Has done drawings for magazines.

SIDELIGHTS: Shepard began to draw as a boy, to illustrate his sister's stories. He relates: "Some of my early efforts at drawing were shown, with a certain pride, by my father to his artist friends. Father had quite decided that I should be an artist when I grew up, though I myself considered an artist's life to be a dull one and looked for something more adventurous."

"During the 1920s, E.H. Shepard illustrated all the Milne's famous children's books," wrote Robert Cowley. "Those little figures of Pooh and Piglet and Eeyore, the Old Grey Donkey, seemed much too real to have been drawn by any human hand, but in fact it was Shepard who did them, almost fifty years ago.... Milne created an imaginary world in Ashdown Forest for his little boy [whose name was that of his own son] and made him the central character in it. But Shepard modeled the Christopher Robin of the drawings after his own son, Graham. Pooh looks like Graham's Teddy bear, whose name was Growler.... Shepard also made countless sketches of the toy animals belonging to the real Christopher Robin—Eeyore, Kanga, Tigger, and Piglet."

Shepard did not ask for a share of the royalties on the books he illustrated until he did *The Wind in the Willows;* he sold many of his original drawings for income in his early years, drawings which now bring large sums at auction. Until recently he owned almost 300 drawings and sketches which he gave to the Victoria and Albert Museum in London. He has kept only six tiny original drawings of Piglet, which he will leave to his great-grandchildren. "Winnie the Pooh and the Honey Tree," based on Shepard's illustrations, was filmed by Walt Disney Productions in 1965.

AVOCATIONAL INTERESTS: Gardening.

BIOGRAPHICAL/CRITICAL SOURCES: Times Literary Supplement, January 12, 1962; Christian Science Monitor, March 21, 1963, May 5, 1966; McCalls, August, 1970.

*   *

SHEPS, Cecil G(eorge)   1913-

PERSONAL: Born July 24, 1913, in Winnipeg, Manitoba, Canada; came to United States in 1946, naturalized in 1956; married Mindel Cherniack (now a professor of biostatistics), May 29, 1937; children: Samuel Barry. Education: University of Manitoba, M.D., 1936; Yale University, M.P.H., 1947. Home address: Rt. 6, Arboretum Dr., Chapel Hill, N.C. 27514. Office: 104 South Bldg., University of North Carolina at Chapel Hill, N.C. 27514.

CAREER: Public health and medical care administration with army and in private practice in Canada, 1938-46; Beth Israel Hospital, Boston, Mass., general director, 1953-60; Harvard University, Boston, Mass., clinical professor of preventive medicine, 1958-60; University of Pittsburgh, Graduate School of Public Health, Pittsburgh, Pa., professor of medical and hospital administration, 1960-65; Mount Sinai School of Medicine, New York, N.Y., professor of community medicine and general director, Beth Israel Medical Center, 1965-68; University of North Carolina at Chapel Hill, professor of social medicine and director of Health Services Research Center, 1969—, vice chancellor of Health Sciences, 1971—. Welfare Administration of U.S. Department of Health, Education, and Welfare, consultant on medical affairs, 1964—. U.S. Public Health Service, member of national advisory community health committee. Member: American Public Health Association (fellow), American Association of Medical Colleges, Gerontological Society, Association of Teachers of Preventive Medicine.

WRITINGS: (With Eugene E. Taylor) Needed Research in Health and Medical Care: A Bio-Social Approach, University of North Carolina Press, 1954; (with Floyd Hunter and R.C. Shaffer) Community Organization: Action and Inaction, University of North Carolina Press, 1956; (contributor) Wilma Donahue and Clark Tibbits, editors, The New Frontiers of Aging, University of Michigan Press, 1957; (editor with S.J. Axelrod, F. Goldmann, and J.N. Muller) Readings in Medical Care, University of North Carolina Press, 1958; (editor with G.A. Wolf and C. Jacobsen) Medical Education and Medical Care: Interactions and Prospects, Association of American Medical Colleges, 1961; (with others) Study of Affiliations Between Medical Schools and Teaching Hospitals, Association of American Medical Colleges, 1962; (with others) Guide to Surveying Clinic Procedures, Public Health Service, 1964; (contributor) Medical Education and Practice: Relationships and Responsibilities in a Changing Society, Association of American Medical Colleges, c.1965; (senior author) Medical Schools and Hospitals: Interdependence for Education and Service, Association of American Medical Colleges, 1965.

Also contributor to symposia, proceedings, and published reports, including: Venereal Disease Control Seminar, Health Publications Institute, 1950; Planning, American Society of Planning Officials, 1952; The Past, Present and Future of Schools of Public Health, School of Public Health, University of North Carolina, 1963; Evaluation of Neighborhood Health Centers: A Plan for Implementation, Clearinghouse for Federal Scientific and Technical Information, 1968. Contributor of more than eighty articles to Public Health Reports, Nursing Outlook, Progressive Architecture, New England Journal of Medicine, and other medical and public health journals.

SHERIDAN, John V.   1915-

PERSONAL: Born December 19, 1915, in Longford, Ireland; son of Farrell (a farmer) and Brigid (Kiernan) Sheridan. Education: Attended St. John's College, Waterford, Ireland. Office: Catholic Information Center, Los Angeles, Calif.

CAREER: Ordained Roman Catholic priest, April, 1943; Our Lady Chapel, Los Angeles, Calif., chaplain, 1951-65; assistant pastor in several parishes, including Cathedral of St. Vibiana; Catholic Information Center, Los Angeles, Calif., director, 1951-65. Radio television, and platform lecturer.

WRITINGS: Questions and Answers on the Catholic Faith, foreword by James Francis Cardinal McIntyre, Hawthorn, 1963.

Pamphlets: "I Believe in God," "The Rosary," "The Liturgy," "Christ in the Home," "Christ in the School," "Christ in the Office," "The Lesson of President Kennedy's Death," "The Sacred Liturgy," "You Are the Church." Editor of weekly column in Our Sunday Visitor, "Ask Me a Question." Contributor of numerous articles to religious and secular periodicals.

WORK IN PROGRESS: Compiling certain of his articles in book form; a book on the contemporary developments in theology.

AVOCATIONAL INTERESTS: Golf; collecting old books and family heirlooms.

*   *   *

SHERLOCK, John   1932-

PERSONAL: Born July 14, 1932, in Manchester, England. Education: University of California, Berkeley, B.A., 1956; Columbia University, M.S., 1957; Oxford University, postgraduate study, 1959-60. Agent: Paul R. Reynolds & Son, 588 Fifth Ave., New York, N.Y. 10017.

CAREER: International Business Machines, New York, N.Y., staff writer, 1957; King Publications, San Francisco, Calif., managing editor, 1957-59; New York Herald Tribune, New York, N.Y., assistant to columnist Joe Hyams, 1960-63; free-lance writer, 1963—. Military service: Royal Air Force, 1950-52.

WRITINGS: The Ordeal of Major Grigsby (novel), Morrow, 1964, reissued as The Last Grenade, Dell, 1970; The Instant Saint, Morrow, 1965. Contributor to British and American magazines, including Saturday Evening Post, TV Guide, This Week, Today, and Travel.

WORK IN PROGRESS: A novel.

SIDELIGHTS: Josef Shaftel produced motion pictures of The Ordeal of Major Grigsby, entitled "The Last Grenade," and The Instant Saint in 1969, and has applied for film rights to Sherlock's third novel, as yet unpublished. Avocational interests: Travel, skin diving, gliding, collecting and drinking wines, experimenting in foods, and (especially) "just sitting around dusty old squares in southern Europe and waiting for something to happen (it usually does)."

BIOGRAPHICAL/CRITICAL SOURCES: Times Literary Supplement, July 7, 1966.

*   *   *

SHERMAN, Diane (Finn)   1928-

PERSONAL: Born December 6, 1928, in Boston, Mass.; daughter of Henry M. (a retailer) and Bess (Golding) Finn; married Matthew Sherman, June 26, 1949; children: Jane, Lisa, Adam. Education: Mount Holyoke College, B.A., 1950. Home address: Old Bedford Rd., R.F.D. #2, Lincoln, Mass. 01773. Agent: Dorothy Markinko,

McIntosh & Otis, 18 East 41st St., New York, N.Y. 10017.

CAREER: Free-lance writer, mainly for children.

WRITINGS: Little Skater, Rand McNally, 1959; *My Counting Book,* Rand McNally, 1960; *Myrtle Turtle,* Rand McNally, 1961; *Jumping Jack,* Rand McNally, 1962; (with Shirlee Newman) *About the People Who Run Your City,* Melmont, 1963; (with Newman) *About Canals,* Melmont, 1964; *You and the Oceans,* Childrens Press, 1965; *Nancy Plays Nurse,* Rand McNally, 1965; *The Boy from Abilene: The Story of Dwight D. Eisenhower,* Westminster, 1968. Contributor of stories, articles, poems, and plays to *Child Life* and other children's magazines; contributor of science articles to adult magazines.

WORK IN PROGRESS: A picture book; a book for older children; writing on science.

* * *

SHERTZER, Bruce E(ldon)   1928-

PERSONAL: Born January 11, 1928, in Bloomfield, Ind. son of Edwin F. and Lois B. (Fitzpatrick) Shertzer; married Carol M. Rice, November 24, 1948; children: Sarah, Mark. *Education:* Indiana University, B.S., 1952, M.S., 1953, Ed.D., 1958. *Religion:* Methodist. *Home:* 1620 Western Dr., West Lafayette, Ind. 47906. *Office:* Department of Education, Purdue University, Lafayette, Ind. 46207.

CAREER: Martinsville (Indiana) Metropolitan School District, counselor and teacher, 1951-52, director of testing and guidance, 1954-56; Indiana State Department of Public Instruction, director of division of guidance and pupil instruction, 1956-58; North Central Association Superior Student Project, associate director, 1958-60; Purdue University, Lafayette, Ind., assistant professor, 1960-62, associate professor, 1962-65, professor of education, 1965—, chairman, Counseling and Personnel Services. Visiting professor of educational psychology, University of Hawaii, 1967; Fulbright senior lecturer, University of Reading, 1967-68. *Military service:* U.S. Army, 1946-48; became sergeant. *Member:* American Personnel and Guidance Association (chairman, constitution committee, 1963-64), Association for Counselor Education and Supervision (president, 1970-71), Indiana Personnel and Guidance Association (president, 1963). *Awards, honors:* Counselor Educator of the Year Award, Indiana Personnel and Guidance Association, 1969.

WRITINGS: (Editor) *Working with Superior Students: Theories and Practices,* Science-Research Associates, 1960; (with William Van Hoose) *Guidance in Elementary Schools,* Department of Public Instruction, State of Indiana, 1961; (editor with others) *Counseling: Selected Readings,* C.E. Merrill, 1962; (with Herman J. Peters) *Guidance: Program Development and Management,* C.E. Merrill, 1963, 2nd edition, 1969; (with Harry S. Belman) *My Career Guidebook,* Bruce, 1963, 2nd edition, 1970; (with Richard Knowles) *Teacher's Guide to Group Vocational Guidance,* Bellman Publishing, 1964, 2nd edition, 1971; (with Peters) *Guidance: Techniques for Individual Appraisal and Development,* Macmillan, 1965; (with Shelley C. Stone) *Fundamentals of Guidance,* Houghton, 1966, 2nd edition, 1971; (with Stone) *Fundamentals of Counseling,* Houghton, 1968; (editor with Stone) *Introduction to Guidance: Selected Readings,* Houghton, 1970; *Careers in Counseling and Guidance,* Houghton, 1972. Editor with Stone of "Guidance Monograph" series, forty-eight volumes, Houghton, 1968. Contributor of articles to *Personnel and Guidance Journal, Theory Into Practice, School Counselor, Vocational Guidance Quarterly, Counselor Education and Supervision,* and other professional journals.

WORK IN PROGRESS: High school text and materials on career development, for Houghton; research on high school counselors' predictive ability.

* * *

SHEWELL-COOPER, Wilfred Edward

PERSONAL: Born September 15, in Waltham Abbey, Essex, England; son of Edward (a colonel, British Army) and Mabel Alice (Read) Shewell-Cooper; married Irene Ramsay (a company director); children: Caerveth Ramsay George, Jeremy Gervase Edward. *Education:* Attended Monkton Combe School, and Diocesan College (South Africa); Wye College, London, C.D.H., 1922. *Religion:* Church of England. *Home:* Arkley Manor, Arkley, South Hertfordshire, England. *Office:* International Horticultural Advisory Bureau Ltd., Abbey House, Saffron Walden, Essex, England.

CAREER: County horticultural advisor, Warwickshire and, later, Cheshire, England, 1924-32; Swanley Horticultural College, Kent, England, superintendent and chief horticultural lecturer, 1932-38; British Army, Southeast and Eastern Commands, horticultural adviser with rank of colonel, 1940-49; Thaxted Horticultural College, Essex, England, principal, 1950-60; International Horticultural Advisory Bureau Ltd., Hertfordshire, England, general director, 1960—. Lecturer; conductor of regular television program from gardens of his home. President of International Mission to Miners; president, Farmers Christian Postal Service; Good Gardens Institute, honorary director; Good Gardeners Association, director. *Member:* Linnean Society (fellow), Royal Horticultural Society (fellow), Royal Society of Teachers, British Association of Consultants (founder), Protestant Reformation Society (president), Campaigners (clans' chief). *Awards, honors*—Civilian: Chevalier du Merite Agricole (France), 1955; fellow of Horticultural College, University of Vienna; Commandeur du Merite (France), 1964. Military: Order of the British Empire, Army commendation.

WRITINGS: The Garden (based on broadcast talks given on "The Northern Garden"), Benn, 1933; *Modern Flower Growing for Profit,* Benn, 1934, 3rd edition, 1947; (editor) Thomas Smith, *The Profitable Culture of Vegetables for Market Gardeners, Small Holders, and Others,* 2nd edition, revised, Longmans, Green, 1937; *The Vegetable Garden,* English Universities Press, 1937, 2nd edition published as *The A.B.C. of Vegetable Gardening* (see below); *The Garden Pool,* Epworth, 1938; *Home, Window and Roof Gardening,* Epworth, 1938, revised edition, Crosby Lockwood, 1951; *Up-to-Date Fruit Growing,* English Universities Press, 1938, reissued as *The A.B.C. of Fruit Growing* (see below); *Grow Your Own Food Supply,* English Universities Press, 1939; *Rock Gardens: Their Construction, Planting and Maintenance,* Epworth, 1939; *The Scout's Book of Gardening,* Scout Book Club, 1939; *The Amateur Greenhouse,* Gifford, 1940; (with wife, Irene Ramsay Shewell-Cooper) *Cook What You Grow* (sequel to *Grow Your Own Food Supply*), English Universities Press, 1940; *Doctoring the Garden,* Gifford, 1941; *Continuous Cloche Gardening: A Handbook on Growing Crops Under Cloches,* English Universities Press, 1941; *Land Girl: A Handbook for the Women's Land Army,* English Universities Press, 1941; *Bulb Growing Inside and Out,* Gifford, 1943; *Eating Without Heating: A New Conception of Salad Growing,* Gifford, 1943; *Soil Humus and Health,* Gifford, 1944; *Continuous Tomato Growing: Growing Tomatoes Under Continuous Cloches,* Intensive Gardening Press, 1945; *The Gardeners' Standby* (reference book), Gifford, 1947; *Roses and How to Grow Them,* Gifford, 1947; (reviser and author of introduction) J.F.C. Dix and Walter Roozen, editors, *Flowers in Colour,* revised edition, Oxford University Press, 1948; *Gardening* ("Reason Why" series), Jenkins, 1948; *Continuous Flower Growing,* Gifford, 1948; *The Book of* the Dahlia, Gifford, 1949; The Book of the Tomato, Gifford, 1949; Modern Glasshouse Flowers for Profit, Benn 1949; (reviser) John Clark Newsham, The Horticultural Notebook: A Manual for the Use of Horticultural Advisers, Gardeners, Nurserymen, Students, and All Horticulturists, 4th edition, revised, Anglobooks, 1950; The Complete Gardener, Collins, 1950, 10th edition, revised, 1971; Fruit Growing, Cooking and Preserving, Wingate, 1951; Modern Market Gardening for Profit, Benn, 1951; Chrysanthemum Growing, Wingate, 1952; Vegetable Growing and Cooking, Wingate, 1952; The Royal Gardeners, King George VI and His Queen, Cassell, 1952; A Gardener's Diary, English Universities Press, 1953; Enjoy Your Gardening, Evans Brothers, 1954; The Complete Fruit Grower, Faber, 1954; Born Gardeners, Evans Brothers, 1955; The Chrysanthemum Pocket Book, Evans Brothers, 1955; The Complete Vegetable Grower, Faber, 1955, 2nd edition, 1966; Pot Plants, Museum Press, 1955; The Rhododendron and Azalea Pocket Book, Benn, 1955; The Complete Illustrated Gardener, Educational Book Co., 1957; Gardening ("Junior Teach Yourself" book), English Universities Press, 1957, Sportshelf, 1958, revised edition, Brockhampton Press, 1965; Your Weekend in the Garden, Stanley Paul, 1958; (editor) The Fundamentals of Gardening, Seeley Service, 1958; George, Market Gardener: A Career Book, Chatto & Windus, 1959; The Complete Flower Grower, Faber, 1960; (editor with others) Alpine and Rock Gardening, Seeley Service, 1961; Plants and Fruits of the Bible, Darton, Longman & Todd, 1962; Cut-Work Gardening, Elliot Right Way Books, 1963; Vegetable Fare: Recipes for Cooking Vegetables So As to 'Add Variety and Spice to Life, Mowbray, 1963; Town and City Gardening, Percival Marshall, 1964; Weekend Gardening; or, Week by Week in the Garden, English Universities Press, 1967, International Publications Service, 1970; Healthy Soil, Healthy People, Australian Broadcasting Commission, 1969; Mini-Work Gardening, English Universities Press, 1970; Cut Flowers for the House, Collins, 1970; The Compost Gardening Book, David & Charles, 1971; The Beginners Pot Plant Book, Gifford, 1971, published in America as How to Grow Potted Plants, Drake Publications, San Francisco, 1972.

"The A.B.C." series, published by English Universities Press: The A.B.C. of Gardening, 1935, 3rd edition, 1957, Sportshelf, 1958; . . . of Vegetable Gardening, revised edition, 1947, 3rd edition, revised, 1958, International Publications Service, 1970; . . . of Flower Growing, 1947, Sportshelf, 1958; . . . of Fruit Growing, 1947, International Publications Service, 1970; . . . of the Greenhouse, 1947, revised edition, 1966, International Publications Service, 1970; . . . of Bulbs and Corms, 1948, 2nd edition, 1956; . . . of the Rock Garden and Pool (combination of Rock Gardens: Their Construction, Planting and Maintenance, and The Garden Pool), 1949; . . . of Garden Pests and Diseases, 1950, 3rd edition, 1957, Sportshelf, 1958; . . . of Cloche Gardening, 1952, International Publications Service, 1970; . . . of Flowering Shrubs, 1953, International Publications Service, 1970; . . . Guide to Garden Flowers, 1955, International Publications Service, 1970; . . . of the Herbaceous Border, 1955; . . . of Cacti and Succulents, 1957, Sportshelf, 1957; . . . of Roses, 1957, Sportshelf, 1957, revised edition, English Universities Press, 1968; . . . of Pot Plants, 1958, Sportshelf, 1958; . . . of Soils, Including Manuring, Composts, and Lawns, 1959, Sportshelf, 1959; . . . of Carnations and Pinks, 1960, International Publications Service, 1970; . . . of Dahlias, 1961, International Publications Service, 1970; . . . of Herbs, Salads and Tomatoes, 1961; . . . of Pruning, Including Hard Fruits, Soft Fruits, and Shrubs, 1963, International Publications Service, 1970; . . . of Chrysanthemums, 1964, International Publications Service, 1970; The New Gardener's A.B.C., 1965.

"Shewell-Cooper's Guide" series, published by English Universities Press: Shewell-Cooper's Guide to Roses, 1952, . . . to Salads and Herbs, 1952, . . . to Soil Humus and Manuring, 1952, . . . to Carnations, 1953, . . . to Dahlias, 1953, . . . to Pruning Fruit Trees and Shrubs, 1953, . . . to Tomatoes, 1953. Regular contributor of articles to over fifty newspapers, journals, and magazines in Great Britain, including Evening News.

WORK IN PROGRESS: Experiments in the demonstration gardens at Arkley Manor; horticultural experiments, or organic lines, in flowers, fruits, vegetables, and greenhouse planning.

*   *   *

SHIPLEY, Nan(cy) (Sommerville)

PERSONAL: Born in Glasgow, Scotland; brought to Canada as infant; daughter of Robert and Mary (MacDonald) Sommerville; married George Harold Shipley (divorced); children: Norma Ellen. Education: Attended public schools, adult university night classes, and business school. Home: 308, 1650 Pembina Hwy., Winnipeg 19, Manitoba, Canada. Agent: James Reach, Samuel French, Inc., 25 West 45th St., New York, N.Y. 10036.

CAREER: Clerk in railway office prior to marriage; now free-lance writer. Indian and Metis Friendship Centre, Winnipeg, Manitoba, Canada, associate, 1959—, instituting first sale and display of Manitoba Indian handicrafts in Winnipeg, Manitoba. Writing instructor at University of Manitoba, Winnipeg. Member: Authors Guild, Canadian Authors' Association, Women's Canadian Press Association, Business and Professional Women's Association. Awards, honors: Manitoba Woman of the Year, 1964.

WRITINGS: Anna and the Indians (life of Anna Jane Gaudin), Ryerson, 1955; Frances and the Crees, Ryerson, 1957; The Scarlet Lily, Fell, 1959; Whistle on the Wind, Fell, 1961; Return to the River, Fell, 1964; The Railway Builders, Ryerson, 1965; The James Evans Story, Ryerson, 1966; Almighty Voice and the Red Coats, Burns & MacEachern, 1967; Road to the Forks: A History of the Community of Fort Garry, Stovel-Advocate Press, 1969. Scriptwriter for thirteen-week television series on crafts and customs of early Indians, 1963. Contributor of some 300 articles and 200 short stories to magazines in Canada, United States, and England.

WORK IN PROGRESS: A history of the first white woman in Western Canada, 1804; short material of lesser scope.

SIDELIGHTS: Mrs. Shipley's books have been published in Germany and Holland, and Whistle on the Wind has been issued in Braille. Avocational interests: Collecting Indian legends (which she may someday publish) and Canadian railway memorabilia, and preservation and encouragement of native art.

*   *   *

SHIRER, William L(awrence) 1904-

PERSONAL: Surname pronounced Shy-rer; born February 23, 1904, in Chicago, Ill.; son of Seward Smith (a lawyer) and Josephine (Tanner) Shirer; married Theresa Stiberitz, January 30, 1931; children: Eileen Inga Shirer Dyk, Linda Elizabeth. Education: Coe College, B.A., 1925; College de France, Paris, courses in European history, 1925-27. Politics: Independent. Religion: Presbyterian. Agent: Paul Reynolds, 599 Fifth Ave., New York, N.Y. 10017.

CAREER: Chicago Tribune, Paris edition, reporter, 1925-26, foreign correspondent, 1926-29, chief of Central European bureau, Vienna, 1929-32; with New York Herald, Paris edition, 1934; Universal News Service, foreign correspondent, 1935-37; Columbia Broadcasting System, became continental representative, 1937, war correspondent, 1939-45, commentator, 1945-47; Mutual Network, commentator, 1947-49; full-time writer, 1950—. Columnist for *New York Herald Tribune* and its syndicate, 1942-48. *Member:* Council on Foreign Relations, Foreign Policy Association, Authors Guild (former president), P.E.N., Phi Beta Kappa, Tau Kappa Epsilon, Century Club. *Awards, honors:* Litt. D., Coe College, 1941; Chevalier, Legion d'Honneur; George Foster Peabody award, 1947; Wendell Willkie One World award, 1948; National Book Award, 1961, for *The Rise and Fall of the Third Reich.*

WRITINGS: Berlin Diary: The Journal of a Foreign Correspondent, 1934-1941 (Book-of-the-Month Club selection), Knopf, 1941; *End of a Berlin Diary,* Knopf, 1947; *The Traitor* (novel), Farrar, Straus, 1950; *Midcentury Journey: The Western World Through Its Years of Conflict* (Literary Guild selection), Farrar, Straus, 1952; *Stranger Come Home* (novel), Little, Brown, 1954; *The Challenge of Scandinavia: Norway, Sweden, Denmark, and Finland in Our Time,* Little, Brown, 1955; *The Consul's Wife* (novel), Little, Brown, 1956; *The Rise and Fall of the Third Reich: A History of Nazi Germany* (Book-of-the-Month Club selection), Simon & Schuster, 1960; *The Rise and Fall of Adolf Hitler,* Random House, 1961 (published in England as *All About the Rise and Fall of Adolf Hitler,* W. H. Allen, 1962); *The Sinking of the Bismarck,* Random House, 1962 (published in England as *All About the Sinking of the Bismarck,* W.H. Allen, 1963); *The Collapse of the Third Republic: An Inquiry into the Fall of France in 1940* (Book-of-the-Month Club selection), Simon & Schuster, 1969. Contributor to *Harper's, Atlantic, Reader's Digest, Look,* and other publications.

SIDELIGHTS: Berlin Diary, and *The Rise and Fall of the Third Reich* have appeared in numerous foreign-language editions. The latter also achieved the distinction of being the first ten-dollar book ever to head the American best-seller list. In connection with *The Collapse of the Third Republic,* Edwin Tetlow has said: "Mr. Shirer simply must be our world's most painstaking and careful journalist-historian...." *Avocational interests:* Walking, skiing, theater and ballet, symphonic and chamber music, novels and history; plays accordian and piano.

BIOGRAPHICAL/CRITICAL SOURCES:. Newsweek, January 23, 1961; *Christian Century,* December 12, 1962; *New York Times Book Review,* November 9, 1969; *Christian Science Monitor,* December 4, 1969; *Virginia Quarterly Review,* spring, 1970; *Times Literary Supplement,* April 23, 1970.†

*   *   *

SHORT, Wayne   1926-

PERSONAL: Born August 16, 1926, in Nadaburg, Ariz.; son of Walter Lucien (a commercial fisherman) and Grace (Price) Short; married Barbara Martin, April 15, 1954; children: Luke, Mark, Michael, Lafe, Patrick. *Education:* Attended schools in Alaska. *Home:* Warm Springs Bay, Baranof, Alaska 99822. *Agent:* Paul R. Reynolds & Son, 599 Fifth Ave., New York, N.Y. 10017.

CAREER: Sometime trapper, bounty hunter, and skipper of cannery tender; now commercial fisherman on own vessel in Alaskan waters.

WRITINGS: The Cheechakoes, Random House, 1964; *This Raw Land* (nonfiction), Random House, 1968. Contributor of short stories to *Argosy* and *Climax,* and of outdoors articles to *Sports Afield.*

WORK IN PROGRESS: A novel, *The Sixty-Niners.*

BIOGRAPHICAL/CRITICAL SOURCES: Best Sellers, June 15, 1968.

*   *   *

SHULEVITZ, Uri   1935-

PERSONAL: Born February 27, 1935, in Warsaw, Poland; came to United States in 1959; naturalized during 1960's; son of Abraham and Szandla (Hermanstat) Shulevitz; married Helene Weiss (an artist), June 11, 1961 (divorced). *Education:* Teacher's College, Israel, Teacher's Degree, 1956; Tel-Aviv Art Institute, evening student, 1953-55; Brooklyn Museum Art School, student, 1959-61. *Religion:* Jewish. *Home:* 133 West 3rd St., New York, N.Y. 10012.

CAREER: Kibbutz Ein-Geddi (collective farm), Israel, member, 1957-58; art director of youth magazine in Israel, 1958-59; illustrator of children's books. Art instructor at School of Visual Arts, New York, N.Y., 1967-68, Pratt Institute, Brooklyn, N.Y., 1970-71, New School for Social Research, New York, N.Y., 1970—. *Military Service:* Israeli Army, 1956-59. *Member:* Authors Guild. *Awards, honors:* Children's Book Awards, American Institute of Graphic Arts, 1963-64, 1965-66, 1967-68; certificate of merit, Society of Illustrators (New York), 1965; International Biennali of Illustrations, Bratislava, Czechoslovakia, 1969; Caldecott Medal, 1969, for *The Fool of the World and the Flying Ship;* selected for inclusion in American Booksellers 1969 Gift to the Nation from the Library of the White House; bronze medal, International Book Exhibition (Leipzig), 1970, for *Rain Rain Rivers.*

WRITINGS—Self illustrated: *The Moon in My Room,* Harper, 1963; *One Monday Morning,* Scribner, 1967; *Rain Rain Rivers,* Farrar, Straus, 1969.

Illustrator: Charlotte Zolotow, *A Rose, A Bridge, and a Wild Black Horse,* Harper, 1964; Mary Stolz, *The Mystery of the Woods,* Harper, 1964; H.R. Hays and Daniel Hays, *Charley Sang a Song,* Harper, 1964; Sulamith Ish-Kishor, *The Carpet of Solomon,* Pantheon, 1964; Jack Sendak, *The Second Witch,* Harper, 1965; Molly Cone, *Who Knows Ten?,* Union of American Hebrew Congregations, 1965; Brothers Grimm, *The Twelve Dancing Princesses,* Scribner, 1966; Mary Stolz, *Maximilian's World,* Harper, 1966; Jean Russell Larson, *The Silkspinners,* Scribner, 1967; Dorothy Nathan, *The Month Brothers,* Dutton, 1967; Jan Wahl, *Runaway Jonah, and Other Tales,* Macmillan, 1968; Arthur Ransome, adapter, *The Fool of the World and the Flying Ship,* Farrar, Straus, 1968; Jan Wahl, *The Wonderful Kite,* Delacorte, 1971; Elizabeth Shub, adapter, *Oh What a Noise!* (text adapted from "A Big Noise" by William Brighty Rands), Macmillan, 1971. Designer, with Tom Spain, of film "One Monday Morning." Contributor to *Horn Book* (magazine).

WORK IN PROGRESS: Soldier and Czar in the Forest, A Russian tale, to be published by Farrar, Straus.

SIDELIGHTS: "Drawing has always been with me," Shulevitz once said. "The encouragement of my parents, who were both talented, probably contributed to my early interest in drawing. . . . Realizing the excess of words in our culture, I followed an Oriental tradition, trying to say more with fewer words. *The Moon in My Room* contains very brief text and suggestive rather than descriptive illustrations, that have the purpose of awakening the child's imagination, leaving him free space to add to his own."

"As far as technique goes: it is best when it is an *organic extension of the content.* This is the way I approach it. Therefore the variety of methods I have used in different books. I am also constantly searching for a new way of illustrating. I use a lot of pen and ink and watercolor. I have used colored inks and tempera in full color illustrations. In some black and white ones, I have also scratched with a razor blade the pen and ink line and then reworked for a long time to achieve a certain effect as in an etching (*The Carpet of Solomon, The Month Brothers, Runaway Jonah*). I have used a Japanese reed pen (*Maximilian's World*) and a Chinese brush (*The Silkspinners*)."

Shulevitz commented in his Caldecott Award acceptance speech: "There is no real distinction between 'art' and illustration, between old art and new art. There is only good art and bad art. While teaching, I have observed that one of the main reasons why students do poor illustration is that they maintain the distinction between 'art' and illustration.

"As a child I loved Rembrandt. I still do. His etchings are sublime illustrations. I have seen a landscape drawing of his at the Fogg Museum that looks like a Chinese painting. In Rembrandt the distinction between East and West, between child and adult, fades away. He was wise. But again, in his day many considered him a fool."

In the future Shulevitz will direct more films of his books for Weston Woods, Conn.

AVOCATIONAL INTERESTS: Art, music, old tales and parables of eastern traditions.

BIOGRAPHICAL/CRITICAL SOURCES: The Villager, October 3, 1963; *New York Herald Tribune,* October 6, 1963; *Chicago Tribune,* November 10, 1963; *Christian Science Monitor,* November 19, 1963; *Buffalo Evening News,* January 18, 1964; *Book Week* (children's section), May 7, 1967; *Graphis* (Zurich), Number 131, 1967; *Horn Book,* 1968; *School Library Journal,* May, 1969; *Horn Book,* August, 1969, December, 1969, June, 1971; *New York Times,* December 8, 1969; *New York Times Book Review,* September 21, 1969, September 19, 1970; Selma G. Lanes, *Down the Rabbit Hole,* Atheneum, 1971.

* * *

SHUMAN, Samuel I(rving) 1925-

PERSONAL: Born August 7, 1925, in Fall River, Mass.; son of Max (a realtor) and Fannie (Pearlmutter) Shuman; married Maria Barbetsea, March 22, 1964. *Education:* University of Pennsylvania, A.B., 1947, A.M., 1948, Ph.D., 1951; University of Michigan, J.D., 1954; Harvard University, S.J.D., 1959. *Office:* Law School, Wayne State University, Detroit, Mich. 48202.

CAREER: University of Pennsylvania, Philadelphia, instructor in philosophy, 1949-51; University of Michigan, Ann Arbor, legal researcher, 1953-55; Wayne State University, Detroit, Mich., assistant professor, 1954-55, associate professor, 1955-57, professor of law, 1957—; C. N. Davidson & Co. (securities brokers), Detroit, Mich., partner, 1957—. University of Rome, Rome, Italy, visiting professor of law, 1963-64; spent six months each year in Italy, Germany, and Greece, 1960-65; Franklin Lecturer, 1969. *Military service:* U.S. Army, 1944. *Member:* American Law Institute, American Philosophical Society, International Association for Legal and Political Philosophy, American Association for Legal and Political Philosophy, American Society of International Law, American Judicature Society. *Awards, honors:* Probus Club Award for contribution to humanities, 1963.

WRITINGS: Broadcasting and Telecasting of Judicial and Legislative Proceedings, University of Michigan Press, 1956; *Legal Positivism: Its Scope and Limitations,* Wayne State University Press, 1963; (translator with Norbert D. West) *The Austrian Penal Act, 1852 and 1945 as Amended to 1965,* Fred B. Rothman, 1966; (compiler and author of introduction) *The Future of*

Federalism: The Law Center Dedication Lecture Series, Wayne State University Press, 1968; (editor with Gray L. Dorsey) *Validation of New Forms of Social Organization,* Steiner Verlag GMBH (Weisbaden), 1968; (compiler and contributor) *Law and Disorder: The Legitimation of Direct Action as an Instrument of Social Policy* (lectures), Wayne State University Press, 1971; (general editor with West) *American Law: An Introductory Survey of Some Principles—Cases and Text,* Wayne State University Press, 1971. American editor, *Archives of Legal and Social Philosophy.*

WORK IN PROGRESS: Philosophical Jurisprudence: An Introduction to Some of the Problems.

* * *

SHUMWAY, George (Alfred, Jr.) 1928-

PERSONAL: Born December 19, 1928, in New York, N.Y.; son of George Alfred (YMCA researcher) and Orpha V. (Johnson) Shumway; married Anne E. Revelle, June 8, 1951; children: Loren, Mark, Holly, Caroly, Eric. *Education:* Middlebury College, A.B., 1951; Massachusetts Institute of Technology, B.S., 1951, M.S., 1951; University of California Scripps Institution of Oceanography, Ph.D., 1959. *Home and Office:* R.D. 7, York, Pa. 18702.

CAREER: U.S. Navy Electronics Laboratory, San Diego, Calif., oceanographer, 1951-62; George Shumway, Publisher, York, Pa., president, 1962—. *Member:* Geological Society of America (fellow), Sigma Xi.

WRITINGS: (With Howard C. Frey) *Conestoga Wagon, 1750-1850: Freight Carrier for 100 Years of America's Westward Expansion,* Shumway, 1962, 3rd edition, 1968; *Longrifles of Note, Pennsylvania,* Shumway, 1968; (reviser and editor) William Buchele, *Recreating the Kentucky Rifle,* Shumway, 1970; *Charrette at York, Pa., April 1970,* Shumway, 1971; *Arms Makers of Philadelphia,* Shumway, 1971. Contributor to scientific journals.

* * *

SIEGEL, Dorothy (Schainman) 1932-

PERSONAL: Born February 3, 1932, in New York, N.Y.; daughter of Phillip Pincus and Anne (Keats) Schainman; married Jerome Siegel (a civil engineer), February 11, 1953; children: David Mark, Irene Rachel. *Education:* University of California, Los Angeles, A.A., 1951, B.A., 1953. *Politics:* Independent. *Home:* 168-20 127th Ave., Jamaica, N.Y. 11434.

CAREER: Music Corporation of America, Los Angeles, Calif., secretary, 1953-55; Myer P. Beck, Public Relations, New York, N.Y., secretary, 1956-58; *Good Housekeeping,* New York, an assistant editor and staff writer, 1959-60. *Member:* Society of Magazine Writers.

WRITINGS: Checklist for a Perfect Home, Dolphin Books, 1964; (with Maury Colow) *The Big Town for Teens,* Teen Calendar, 1964.

AVOCATIONAL INTERESTS: Travel (spent nine months in western Europe, 1955), reading, the theatre, music, ballet, and the arts.

* * *

SILBER, Irwin 1925-

PERSONAL: Born October 17, 1925, in New York, N.Y.; son of Bernard and Matilda (Gettinger) Silber; married Sylvia Kahn (a singer), September 15, 1950; children: Joshua, Fred, Nina. *Education:* Brooklyn College (now Brooklyn College of City University of New York), B.A., 1945. *Politics:* Independent. *Agent:* Jeanne Hale, 31 West Tenth St., New York, N.Y. 10011. *Office:* Sing Out!, 165 West 46th St., New York, N.Y. 10036.

CAREER: Sing Out! (folk song magazine), New York, N.Y., editor, 1950—; Oak Publications, New York, N.Y., president, 1959—.

WRITINGS: (Editor) *Lift Every Voice: The Second People's Song Book* (introduction by Paul Robeson), Oak, 1957; (editor) *Reprints from People's Songs,* Oak, 1961; (editor) *Hootenanny Song Book,* Consolidated Music, 1963; (editor) *Soldier Songs and Home-Front Ballads of the Civil War,* Oak, 1964; (editor with Ethel Raim) *The Bells of Rhymney, and Other Songs and Stories from the Singing of Pete Seeger,* Oak, 1964; (editor) *Songs of the Great American West,* Macmillan, 1967; (editor with Barbara Dane) *The Vietnam Songbook,* Guardian Publications, 1969; *The Cultural Revolution: A Marxist Analysis,* Times Change Press, 1970; (editor) *Voices of National Liberation: The Revolutionary Ideology of the Third World,* Central Book Co., 1970; (editor) *Songs America Voted By,* Stackpole, 1971; (editor) *Words to One Thousand Songs,* Oak, 1972.

AVOCATIONAL INTERESTS: Tennis, golf, and bridge.

*   *   *

SILBERMAN, Charles Eliot 1925-

PERSONAL: Born January 31, 1925, in Des Moines, Iowa; son of Seppy Israel (a businessman) and Cel (Levy) Silberman; married Arlene Propper (a free-lance writer), September 12, 1948; children: David, Richard, Jeffrey, Steven. *Education:* Columbia University, A.B., 1946, graduate study, 1946-49. *Politics:* Democrat. *Religion:* Jewish. *Home:* 110 Stuyvesant Plaza, Mt. Vernon, N.Y. 10552. *Office:* 30 Park Ave., Mt. Vernon, N.Y. 10550.

CAREER: City College of New York (now City College of the City University of New York), New York, N.Y., tutor in economics, 1946-48; Columbia University, New York, instructor in economics, 1949-53, lecturer in economics, 1955—; *Fortune* Magazine, New York, associate editor, 1954-61, member of board of editors, 1961-71; director, Study of Law and Justice (project funded by Ford Foundation), Mt. Vernon, N.Y., 1972—. Director, Carnegie Study of the Education of Educators, 1966-69. *Military service:* U.S. Naval Reserve, 1943-46; became lieutenant j.g. *Member:* American Economic Association, National Association of Business Economists (fellow). *Awards, honors:* Field Foundation fellow, 1971-72; L.H.D., Kenyon College, 1972.

WRITINGS: (Contributor) *Markets of the Sixties,* Harper, 1960, also published as *America in the Sixties: The Economy and the Society,* Harper, 1960; *Crisis in Black and White,* Random House, 1964; (with others) *The Myths of Automation* (seven articles originally published in *Fortune*), Harper, 1966; *Crisis in the Classroom: The Remaking of American Education* (originally published as serial in *Atlantic* entitled "Murder in the Schoolroom," June-August, 1970), Random House, 1970. Contributor to *Fortune, Atlantic, Commentary,* and *Harper's.*

SIDELIGHTS: Crisis in the Classroom was the result of a three-and-one-half-year, $300,000 study of the education of educators contracted by the Carnegie Corporation of New York. It first appeared as a serial in *Atlantic* entitled "Murder in the Schoolroom," and was "received with pretty general cries of hosanna," according to Samuel McCracken of *Commentary.* McCracken notes: "*Crisis in the Classroom* deserves much of its reputation: it does contain a great deal of striking report, and of recent critics of the school Silberman is among the more judicious. But the book is not the massively complete statement some of its supporters have made of it. And—in common with most critiques—it is longer on diagnosis than on

prescription. Although it will probably provide underpinning for disparate and indeed conflicting schools of reform (some of them distinctly unhelpful), its possible misuse will render it no less useful to the discerning reader."

Christopher Lehmann-Haupt calls *Crisis in the Classroom* "profoundly worthwhile reading ... in part just because of its dryness." He points out that "the shelves have been crammed these past years with passionate and poetic books on our educational wasteland" by Paul Goodman, George Dennison, Herbert Kohl, et al, and that what is needed is a comprehensive, dispassionate evaluation of the situation. "Mr. Silberman has sailed up the shallow creek of American education, surveyed the landscape, and pronounced it joyless, mindless, barren." Although Silberman fails to provide his own definition of the purpose of education, Lehmann-Haupt writes, "suddenly one's mind is awake, because Silberman has put it all in perspective and condemned it for what it is—meaninglessness." Silberman himself believes "this mindlessness—the failure or refusal to think seriously about educational purpose, the reluctance to question established practice—is not the monopoly of the public school; it is diffused remarkably evenly throughout the entire educational system, and indeed the entire society."

BIOGRAPHICAL/CRITICAL SOURCES: Commonweal, January 27, 1967; *Christian Science Monitor,* March 18, 1967; *Atlantic,* June, 1970; *New York Times,* October 8, 1970; *New Leader,* December 14, 1970; *Commentary,* March, 1971.

*   *   *

SILCOCK, Thomas H(enry) 1910-

PERSONAL: Born April 17, 1910, in Chengtu, West China; son of Harry T. (a missionary) and Margaret (Standing) Silcock. *Education:* University College, London, student, 1928-29; Jesus College, Oxford, B.A. (first class honors), 1933, M.A. and D.Phil., 1936. *Politics:* Labour. *Religion:* Society of Friends. *Home:* 22 Lindsey St., Epping, Essex, England.

CAREER: Raffles College, Singapore, professor of economics, 1938-49; University of Malaya, Singapore, professor of economics, 1949-60, emeritus professor, 1960—. Senior research fellow, Institute of Commonwealth Studies, University of London, London, England, 1960-62, 1963-64; visiting professor, Australian National University, Canberra, 1962, 1964—. Consultant, United Nations Economic Commission for Asia and Far East, 1954. President, Singapore Council for Adult Education, 1955-57; vice-president, Federation of Malaya Adult Education Association, 1956-58. *Member:* Royal Economic Society (life,) Royal Statistical Society (life), Malayan Economic Society (life; president, 1956-57).

WRITINGS: Dilemma in Malaya, Fabian Publications and Gollancz, 1949; (with Ungku Abdul Aziz) *Nationalism in Malaya,* International Secretariat, Institute of Pacific Relations, 1950; *The Economy of Malaya: An Essay in Colonial Political Economy,* Donald Moore, 1954, 2nd revised edition, 1960; *Fiscal Survey of Report of Sarawak,* Government Printing Office (Sarawak), 1956; *The Commonwealth Economy in Southeast Asia,* Duke University Press, 1959; *Towards a Malayan Nation,* Donald Moore for Eastern Universities Press, 1961, Cellar Book Shops, 1962; (editor) *Readings in Malayan Economics,* Donald Moore for Eastern Universities Press, 1961, Cellar Book Shops, 1962; (with Marcel Bouchard and Lucien Massart) *Academic Standards and the New Universities of South-East Asia, The Universities in France: Freedom and Autonomy, [and] The Belgian Universities* (the first by Silcock, the second by Bouchard, the third by Massart), Committee on Science and Freedom (Manchester), 1961; (editor with E.K. Fisk) *The Political Economy of Independent Malaya: A Case Study in Development,* University of California Press, 1963; *Southeast Asian University: A Comparative Account of Some Development Problems, 1964;* (editor) *Thailand: Social and Economic Studies in Development,* Australian National University Press, 1967, Duke University Press, 1968; *Proud and Serene: Sketches from Thailand,* Australian National University Press, 1968; *The Economic Development of Thai Agriculture,* Cornell University Press, 1970; *Tradeways,* Currawong Publishing Co., 1971.

Contributor: William Holland, editor, *Asian Nationalism and the West,* Macmillan, 1953; *Teaching of Social Sciences in South Asia,* UNESCO, 1954; Brinley Thomas, editor, *Economics of International Migration,* St. Martin's, 1958; C.B. Hoover, editor, *Economic Systems of the Commonwealth,* Duke University Press, 1962; *Social Research and Rural Development in Southeast Asia,* UNESCO, 1963. Contributor to economics journals.

SIDELIGHTS: Silcock is fluent in Thai and Malay languages.

* * *

SILLITOE, Alan 1928-

PERSONAL: Born March 4, 1928, in Nottingham, England; son of Christopher (a tannery laborer) and Sylvina (Burton) Sillitoe; married Ruth Esther Fainlight (American-born poet), November 19, 1959; children: David Nimrod, Susan (adopted). *Education:* Left school at fourteen. *Residence:* 21 The Street, Wittersham, Kent, England.

CAREER: Worked in a bicycle plant, in a plywood mill, and as a capstan-lathe operator. *Military service:* Royal Air Force, radio operator in Malaya, 1946-49. *Awards, honors:* Author's Club prize, 1958, for· *Saturday Night and Sunday Morning;* Hawthornden Prize for Literature, 1959, for *Loneliness of the Long-Distance Runner.*

WRITINGS: Without Beer or Bread (poems), Outpost Publications (London), 1957; *Saturday Night and Sunday Morning* (novel), W.H. Allen, 1958, Knopf, 1959, revised edition with an introduction by the author and commentary and notes by David Craig, Longmans, Green, 1968; *The Loneliness of the Long-Distance Runner* (stories), W.H. Allen, 1959, Knopf, 1960 (also see below); *The Rats, and Other Poems,* W.H. Allen, 1960; *The General* (novel), W.H. Allen, 1960, Knopf, 1961; *Key to the Door* (novel), W.H. Allen, 1961, Knopf, 1962; *The Ragman's Daughter* (stories), W.H. Allen, 1963, Knopf, 1964; *Road to Volgograd,* Knopf, 1964; (author of introduction) Arnold Bennett, *Riceyman Steps,* Pan Books, 1964; (author of introduction) Arnold Bennett, *The Old Wives' Tale,* Pan Books, 1964; *A Falling Out of Love, and Other Poems,* W.H. Allen, 1964; *The Death of William Posters* (novel), Knopf, 1965; (translator and adapter from the Spanish of Lope de Vega, with wife, Ruth Fainlight) *All Citizens Are Soldiers* (two-act play; first produced in London, 1967), Macmillan, 1969, Dufour, 1970; *A Tree on Fire* (novel), Macmillan, 1967, Doubleday, 1968; *The City Adventures of Marmalade Jim,* Macmillan, 1967; (with Theodore Dreiser) *The Loneliness of the Long-Distance Runner* [*by*] *Alan Sillitoe; Sanctuary* [*by*] *Theodore Dreiser; and Related Poems,* edited by Roy Bentley, Book Society of Canada, 1967; *Shaman, and Other Poems,* Turret Books, 1968; *Guzman Go Home, and Other Stories,* Macmillan, 1968, Doubleday, 1969; *A Sillitoe Selection* (stories), Longmans, Green, 1968; *Love in the Environs of Voronezh, and Other Poems,* Macmillan, 1968, Doubleday, 1969; "This Foreign Field" (play), first produced in London, 1970; *A Start in Life* (novel), W.H. Allen, 1970, Scribner, 1971; *Travels in Nihilon,* W.H. Allen, 1971, Scribner, 1972; (with Ruth Fainlight and Ted Hughes) *Poems* [*by*] *Ruth Fainlight, Ted Hughes, Alan Sillitoe,* Rainbow Press, 1971.

Film scripts: "Saturday Night and Sunday Morning," 1960, "The Loneliness of the Long-Distance Runner," 1961, "The Ragman's Daughter," 1971, all adapted by the author from his own books; "Che Guevara," 1968.

WORK IN PROGRESS: Raw Material (non-fiction).

SIDELIGHTS: With the publication of *Saturday Night and Sunday Morning* some critics saw the breaking of new ground. Anthony West observed: "For the first time, English working-class life is treated . . . as a normal aspect of the human condition and as natural subject matter for a writer. . . ." Martin Price wrote: "Sillitoe never ignores the poverty and boredom, the aimlessness and narrowness; but he can present as well the laughter and adventure. . . ."

Sillitoe's talent seems great enough to withstand any labeling as "the writer of the working class." John Rosselli in *The Reporter* observed that Sillitoe's rebellion is so profound as to be directed "not just against the circumstances of life in Britain today but against all organized society, almost against life itself; yet the author's own attitude is not easy to make out. He is impersonal, a strong but anonymous voice."

Allen R. Penner writes: "Insofar as Sillitoe's works are dominated by any one theme, that theme is rebellion. In many of his novels and short stories he presents his heroes, who, with few exceptions, are members of the laboring class, rebelling against those mainstays of proletarian literature of the 1930's, oppressive management and conservative politicians. To those who regard the subjects as anachronistic in the present decade, Sillitoe might assert, as he did in an essay on contemporary British social conditions, 'In England there are half a million people out of work, and ten times that number living in real poverty, what I would call below the telly-line, as well as below the bread-line. The gap between the very poor and the normal rich is wider than it has ever been.' "

Sillitoe began to write in Malaya during the war—"several hundred poems (destroyed), a few short stories (destroyed), and the 100,000 word first draft of a novel in seventeen days (also destroyed)." After the war, the discovery that he was tubercular brought the conviction that he would not again be "part of the lusty, boozy factory life he liked," according to Kenneth Allsop, and gave him the necessary impetus to continue writing. For one year, Sillitoe and his wife lived in a cottage near Mentone, in France, on the tiny amount of disability pension left after fares were paid. They moved to Majorca, where the living was cheaper, and stayed six years. Allsop recounts how Sillitoe scrapped nine full-length novels, "almost followed into the fire by the tenth, the one entitled *Saturday Night and Sunday Morning,*" and reports that Sillitoe said, "All those early stories had been wrong. It was meeting Robert Graves while Ruth and I were living on two quid a week in Majorca that helped me to find my true voice. I'd nervously shown Graves my poems and he was encouraging. But when he read some prose—a fantasy idea—he said, 'That's all very well, but why not write about Nottingham? That's what you know.' "

Sillitoe told Allsop: "I don't really understand what made me a writer—that's a mystical thing that can't be analysed. A feel part of a common fountain that's supplied from all sections of society. The beautiful thing for someone with my background is that if I'd wanted to be a doctor or a lawyer there'd have been real difficulties. But if you want to be a writer—there's the pen and paper, and you just write. There's no obstacle between you and writing except talent—and if you don't know what talent is, there's no obstacle at all."

The General was filmed by Universal in 1968, with the title "Counterpoint."

BIOGRAPHICAL/CRITICAL SOURCES: New Republic, August 12, 1959; Yale Review, September, 1959; New Yorker, September 5, 1959; Saturday Review, September 5, 1959; Reporter, November 10, 1960; Howard Nemerov, Poetry and Fiction, Rutgers University Press, 1963; Critique, spring, 1963; Wilson Library Bulletin, October, 1963; New York Review of Books, March 5, 1964; Commonweal, March 27, 1964; Books and Bookmen, November, 1967, June, 1969; New York Times Book Review, September 22, 1968; Nation, January 27, 1969; Contemporary Literature, spring, 1969.

*   *   *

SILVER, James W(esley)   1907-

PERSONAL: Born June 28, 1907, in Rochester, N.Y.; son of Henry Dayton and Elizabeth Julia (Squier) Silver; married Margaret Thompson, December 31, 1935; children: James William, Virginia Elizabeth Silver Little, Margaret Gail. Education: University of North Carolina, A.B., 1927; Peabody College, M.A., 1929; Vanderbilt University, Ph.D., 1935. Politics: Democrat (national). Home: 7015B North 56th St., Tampa, Fla. 33610.

CAREER: Southwestern College, Winfield, Kans., associate professor of history, 1935-36; University of Mississippi, University, assistant professor, 1936-42, associate professor, 1942-46, professor of history, 1946-65, department chairman, 1946-57; University of Notre Dame, South Bend, Ind., professor of history, 1965-69; University of South Florida, Tampa, professor of history, 1969—. Summer lecturer, Emory University, Harvard University, University of Virginia, University of Missouri, University of Notre Dame. Member, State Historical Commission of Mississippi, 1948-57; member, board of directors, Forest History Foundation. Wartime service: With American Red Cross in Pacific area, 1945. Member: American Academy of Arts and Sciences, American Historical Association, Organization of American Historians, Southern Historical Association (president, 1963; executive committee member), Forest History Society, Phi Beta Kappa, Omicron Delta Kappa, Pi Gamma Mu, Tau Kappa Alpha, Rotary International. Awards, honors: Fulbright scholar, Aberdeen, Scotland, 1949-50; Ford fellow, Harvard University, 1951-52; Anisfield-Wolfe Race Relations Award, 1965.

WRITINGS: Edmund Pendleton Gaines: Frontier General, Louisiana State University Press, 1949; Confederate Morale and Church Propaganda, Confederate Publishing, 1957; (editor) Robert A. Moore, A Life for the Confederacy, McCowat-Mercer, 1959; Mississippi in the Confederacy: As Seen in Retrospect, Louisiana State University Press, 1961; Mississippi: The Closed Society, Harcourt, 1964, new, enlarged edition, 1966. Member of board of editors, Journal of Mississippi History, 1947-48, Journal of Southern History, 1952-56, Mississippi Valley Historical Review, 1963—. Contributor to professional journals.

WORK IN PROGRESS: A book on Southern leadership, 1820-65; a book on William Faulkner and the race problem.

SILVERMAN, Al   1926-

PERSONAL: Born April 12, 1926, in Lynn, Mass.; son of Henry and Minnie (Damsky) Silverman; married Rosa Magaro, September 9, 1951; children: Thomas, Brian, Matthew. Education: Boston University, B.S., 1949. Home: 311 Rosedale Ave., White Plains, N.Y. 10605. Office: Macfadden-Bartell Corp., 205 East 42nd St., New York, N.Y. 10017.

CAREER: Sport, New York, N.Y., associate editor, 1951-52; True, New York, sports editor, 1952-54; Argosy, New York, assistant editor, 1954-55; free-lance writer for magazines, 1955-60; Macfadden-Bartell Corp., New York, editor-in-chief of Sport, 1960—. Member: Society of Magazine Writers.

WRITINGS: Warren Spahn, Immortal Southpaw, Bartholomew House, 1961; (with Phil Rizzuto) The "Miracle" New York Yankees, Coward, 1962; (editor) The World of Sport: The Best from Sport Magazine, Holt, 1962; Mickey Mantle, Mister Yankee, Putnam, 1963; Heroes of the World Series, Putnam, 1964; (editor) John F. Kennedy Memorial Album, Macfadden, 1964; (editor) Churchill: A Memorial Album, Macfadden, 1965; (with Paul Hornung) Football and the Single Man, Doubleday, 1965; Sports Titans of the 20th Century, Putnam, 1965; (editor) The Specialist in Pro Football (articles originally published in Sport, fall, 1962), Random House, 1966; (with Frank Robinson) My Life is Baseball, Doubleday, 1968; More Sports Titans of the 20th Century, Putnam, 1968; Joe DiMaggio: The Golden Year, 1941, Prentice-Hall, 1969; (with Gale Sayers) I Am Third, Viking, 1970; (editor) Best of Sport, Viking, 1971.

BIOGRAPHICAL/CRITICAL SOURCES: Book World, May 12, 1968; New York Times, May 31, 1968; Saturday Review, January 23, 1971.

*   *   *

SILVERMAN, Alvin Michaels   1912-

PERSONAL: Born January 16, 1912, in Louisville, Ky.; son of Alvin A. (a newspaperman) and May (Michaels) Silverman; married Phyllis Israel (an artist), November 22, 1936; children: Sue Frances, Lora, Jane. Education: Attended Western Reserve University, 1930-33. Religion: Jewish. Home: 4740 Connecticut Ave. N.W., Washington, D.C. 20008.

CAREER: Cleveland Plain Dealer, Cleveland, Ohio, 1930-65, began as sportswriter, later legislative correspondent in Columbus, editorial columnist, and day city editor, 1930-57, chief of Washington Bureau, 1957-65; Pearl-Silverman Agency, Public Relations Consultants, Washington, D.C., president, 1965—. Member: Overseas Writers, White House Correspondents Association, National Press Club, Zeta Beta Tau, Sigma Delta Chi, Federal City Club, Gridiron Club. Awards, honors: Awards from Cleveland Newspaper Guild, Cleveland Press Club, Ohio Legislative Correspondents Association, and Ohio Press Club for articles and columns.

WRITINGS: The American Newspaper, Robert B. Luce, 1964.

WORK IN PROGRESS: The Wit of LBJ.

AVOCATIONAL INTERESTS: Golf.

*   *   *

SIMCKES, L(azarre) S(eymour)   1937-

PERSONAL: Surname is pronounced Sim-kiss; born October 4, 1937, in Saratoga Springs, N.Y.; son of Herbert Isaac (a rabbi) and Fayette (Resnikoff) Simckes. Education: Hayim Greenberg Teachers Institute, Jerusalem, Israel, student, 1957-58; Hebrew Teachers College, B.J.E., 1958; Harvard University, A.B. (magna cum laude),

1959, Ph.D., 1968. Stanford University, A.M., 1961. *Home:* 32 Gorham St., Cambridge, Mass. 02138. *Agent:* Sterling Lord Agency, 660 Madison Ave., New York, N.Y. 10021.

CAREER: Harvard University, Cambridge, Mass., teaching fellow, 1962-64, assistant professor, Graduate School of Education, 1968-70; Jewish Theological Seminary, New York, N.Y., writing-research fellow, 1964; Vassar College, Poughkeepsie, N.Y., assistant professor of English, 1965-66. *Member:* Phi Beta Kappa. *Awards, honors:* Writing grants from National Foundation on Arts and Humanities, 1967-68, and Littauer Foundation, 1970-71.

WRITINGS: Seven Days of Mourning (novel), Random House, 1963; (translator from Hebrew) Haim Gouri, *The Chocolate Deal,* Holt, 1968; (translator from Hebrew) Yoram Kaniuk, *Adam Resurrected,* Atheneum, 1971. Also author of two-act drama, "Seven days of Mourning," first produced Off-Broadway at Circle in the Square, December 16, 1969, and of a dramatic reading, "Ten Best Martyrs of the Year," first produced in Cambridge, Mass., at Harvard University, November, 1971. Author of film script, "The Last Temptation," based on *The Last Temptation of Christ* by Nikos Kazantzakis, to be produced by Sidney Lumet Productions.

Short stories anthologized in *Stanford Short Stories, 1962,* Stanford University Press, 1962, *My Name Aloud,* edited by H.U. Ribalow, Yoseloff, 1969, and *American Literary Anthology,* Harper, 1971. Essay included in *Writers as Teachers: Teachers as Writers,* edited by Jonathan Baumbach, Holt, 1970. Contributor to *Massachusetts Review* and other periodicals; contributor of short story to *Fiction,* spring, 1972.

WORK IN PROGRESS: A novel, *The Comatose Kids; or, The Stupor of Love,* completed and awaiting publication; short stories.

SIDELIGHTS: "I got an exciting feeling of disorientation each time a new character in 'Seven Days of Mourning' began to speak," wrote David De Porte of *Village Voice* after seeing the play. "From a play about a Jewish family on the Lower East Side, I had expected at best authenticity, warmth perhaps, comfortable humor, hadn't known that L.S. Simckes loves words, loves people, and that he has a command of words, an understanding of people unrivaled by any other new writer represented on or Off-Broadway this year." In contrast, Marilyn Stasio wrote: "Playwright Seymour Simckes has turned what is essentially a provocative dramatic thesis into a turgid, pretentious, and enervating drama. Building on the observation that conditions of extreme poverty maim men's souls and turn them into emotional cripples, Simckes has created a Jewish family of grotesques. . . . The tedium seems to be inherent in the script. Simckes belabors his points with verbose, repetitive rhetoric, while offering little dramatic action to reward our patience." *New York Times* critic Clive Barnes called it "a dark play, at times very funny, at times abrasive. . . . The story itself is perfectly clear, but the writing has a quality of fantastication, of wild exaggeration, that gives the play its unique character. Of course, the writing, the whole theme of struggle, guilt and redemption, presumably comes from the Yiddish tradition. . . . I read it three days ago, I saw it two days ago and it still haunts and puzzles me. And the more I think of it the more it worries my heart."

AVOCATIONAL INTERESTS: Rabbinic literature, sketching, chess, ping-pong, acting, tennis.

BIOGRAPHICAL/CRITICAL SOURCES: New York Times, December 17, 1969; *Village Voice,* December 25, 1969; *Cue,* December 27, 1969; *New Yorker,* December 27, 1969; *Variety,* October 15, 1969; *New York Magazine,* January 12, 1970.

*　　*　　*

SIMMONS, Ozzie Gordon 1919-

PERSONAL: Born October 9, 1919, in Winnipeg, Manitoba, Canada; son of Max and Rose (Goldstone) Simmons; married Charlotte Sonenklar, December 9, 1942; children: Gregor, Lauren, Paula. *Education:* Northwestern University, B.S., 1941; Harvard University, M.A., 1948, Ph.D., 1952. *Home:* 320 East 43rd St., New York, N.Y. 10017. *Office:* Ford Foundation, V. Subercaseaux 121, Santiago, Chile.

CAREER: Smithsonian Institution, Institute of Social Anthropology, Washington, D.C., director in Peru, 1949-52; Institute of Inter-American Affairs, Santiago, Chile, consulting anthropologist, 1953; Harvard University, School of Public Health, Boston, Mass., associate professor of anthropology, 1953-61; University of Colorado, Boulder, professor of sociology and director of Institute of Behavioral Science, 1961-68; Ford Foundation, Santiago, Chile, program advisor, 1968—. University of San Marcos, Lima, Peru, visiting professor, 1949-52; Brandeis University, senior faculty associate in research, 1961—; National Institutes of Health, member of health services research study section, 1961—. Consultant to National Institute of Mental Health, Veterans Administration. *Military service:* U.S. Air Force, 1942-46; became captain.

MEMBER: American Sociological Association (fellow; executive council, section on medical sociology, 1961-64), American Anthropological Association (fellow), Society for Applied Anthropology (fellow), American Association for Advancement of Science (fellow), Phi Beta Kappa. *Awards, honors:* Co-winner of Hofheimer Prize of American Psychiatric Association for outstanding creative research in human behavior, 1963, for *The Mental Patient Comes Home.*

WRITINGS: Social Status and Public Health, Social Science Research Council, 1958; *After Hospitalization: The Mental Patient and His Family,* Hogg Foundation for Mental Health, 1960; (with Howard E. Freeman) *The Mental Patient Comes Home,* Wiley, 1963; (with Helen MacGill Hughes) *Work and Mental Illness: Eight Case Studies,* Wiley, 1965. Contributor of more than thirty articles to professional journals. Associate editor, *American Sociological Review,* 1959-62; associate editor, *Journal of Health and Human Behavior,* 1959-70.

WORK IN PROGRESS: A book on alcohol use in Peruvian peasant society, to be published by Cornell University Press.

*　　*　　*

SIMON, Leonard 1922-

PERSONAL: Born August 16, 1922, in New York, N.Y.; son of Barney and Rose (Zuckerman) Simon; married Shirley Telefus, July 8, 1945; children: Stephen Marc, Ann Lee. *Education:* College of City of New York (now City College of the City University of New York), B.S., 1947; Columbia University, M.A., 1956. *Home:* 86 Howe Court, Woodmere, N.Y. 11598. *Office:* Bureau of Curriculum Research, 130 West 55th St., New York, N.Y. 10019.

CAREER: New York City (N.Y.) Board of Education, Bureau of Curriculum Research, 1959—, started as curriculum coordinator for junior high schools, became acting assistant director. Editor, Film-Strip-of-Month-Club. *Military service:* U.S. Army, 1942-45; became staff sergeant; received Bronze Star. *Member:* National Council of Teachers of Mathematics (chairman, film committee),

Association of Mathematics Teachers of New York State, Association of Mathematics Teachers of New York City.

WRITINGS: (with Jeanne Bendick) *The Day the Numbers Disappeared,* McGraw, 1963; (with Kenneth E. Brown and others) *General Mathematics,* books one and two, Laidlaw Brothers, 1963; *Counting Lightly,* Holt, 1964; *Stretching Numbers,* Holt, 1964; (with others) *Mathematics: Patterns and Structures,* grades 1-8, Holt, 1966; *Introduction to High School Mathematics,* Laidlaw Brothers, 1970; *Applying High School Mathematics,* Laidlaw Brothers, 1970.

AVOCATIONAL INTERESTS: Motoring throughout United States.

*   *   *

SIMON, William   1927-

PERSONAL: Born April 7, 1927, in Brooklyn, N.Y.; son of Irving J. and Shirley (Joseph) Simon; married Rona Hament, May 23, 1953; children: Anne, Barbara, Steven. *Education:* Roanoke College, student, 1942; New York University, B.A., 1949. *Home:* 148 Schuyler Rd., Allendale, N.J. 07401.

CAREER: National Brake Block Corp., Woodside, N.Y., sales manager, 1950-63; Brassbestos Mfg. Corp., Paterson, N.J., president, 1963—. *Military service:* U.S. Army Air Forces, 1943; became sergeant.

WRITINGS: Effective Card Magic, edited by Jean Hugard, Lewis Tannen, 1952; *Sleightly Sensational,* Lewis Tannen, 1954; *Mathematical Magic,* Scribner, 1964.

WORK IN PROGRESS: More Mathematical Magic, additional material on unusual applications of mathematical principles.

*   *   *

SIMONS, Katherine Drayton Mayrant   1892-
(Drayton Mayrant, Kadra Maysi)

PERSONAL: Born 1892, in Charleston, S.C.; daughter of Sedgwick Lewis and Kate Drayton (Mayrant) Simons. *Education:* Attended Misses Sass School, Charleston, S.C., and Brownfield Academy; Converse College, B.L., 1910. *Home:* 26 Gibbes St., Charleston, S.C. 29401.

CAREER: Summerville High School, Summerville, S.C., French teacher, four years; tutor in French, German, and Latin; author. *Wartime service:* American and French Red Cross worker, World War I; U.S. Army Air Forces radar warning worker, World War II. *Member:* South Carolina Historical Society, Poetry Society of South Carolina (president), Huguenot Society of South Carolina. *Awards, honors:* D.Litt. from Converse College.

WRITINGS: (Under pseudonym Kadra Maysi) *The Patteran* (poems), State Co., 1925; *Stories of Charleston Harbor,* State Co., 1930.

Under name Drayton Mayrant: *A Sword from Galway* (novel), Appleton, 1948; *The Running Thread* (novel), Appleton, 1949; *First the Blade* (novel), Appleton, 1950; *White Horse Leaping* (poems), University of South Carolina Press, 1951; *Courage Is Not Given* (novel), Appleton, 1952; *The Red Doe* (novel), Appleton, 1953; *Always a River* (novel), Appleton, 1956; *Lamp in Jerusalem* (novel), Appleton, 1957; *The Land Beyond the Tempest* (novel), Coward, 1960. Also author of several plays. Contributor of short stories, articles, poetry to *Saturday Evening Post, New York Times,* and other periodicals and newspapers.

WORK IN PROGRESS: A novel on the lost Scots colony of Stuart Town.

BIOGRAPHICAL/CRITICAL SOURCES: News and Courier (Charleston, S.C.), July 23, 1961.†

SIMONSON, Lee   1888-1967

PERSONAL: Born June 26, 1888, in New York, N.Y.; son of Sali and Augusta (Goldenberg) Simonson; married Helen Strauss, 1916 (divorced, 1926); married Carolyn Hancock, 1927 (deceased); children: Joan (Jody), Karl. *Education:* Harvard University, A.B. (magna cum laude), 1908; private study of painting in France, 1908-12. *Politics:* Democrat. *Religion:* Agnostic. *Home and office:* 411 East 50th St., New York, N.Y. 10022.

CAREER: Washington Square Players, New York, N.Y., scenic designer, 1915-17; founder and director of Theatre Guild, Inc., Garrick Theatre, and Guild Theatre, New York, N.Y., during period 1919-40; Metropolitan Museum of Art, New York, N.Y., costume instructor, consultant, and Gillender Lecturer, 1944-45. Scenery designer for Broadway productions of "Liliom," "Peer Gynt," "Back to Methuselah," "Heartbreak House," "Elizabeth the Queen," "Idiot's Delight," "Amphytrion 38," and other shows, and for "The Ring of the Niebelungen," Metropolitan Opera Association, 1949. Consultant to university theatres at University of Wisconsin, 1939, University of Indiana, 1940, Hunter College (now Hunter College of City University of New York), 1940, Rosary College, 1948. Critic and lecturer. *Military service:* U.S. Army, Corps of Interpreters, 1918; became second lieutenant. *Member:* Harvard Club. *Awards, honors:* Ford Foundation fellowship, 1961-62.

WRITINGS: Minor Prophecies, Harcourt, 1927; *The Stage is Set,* Harcourt, 1932, revised edition, Theatre Arts, 1963; (with Fedor Kommissarzhevskii) *Settings and Costumes of the Modern Stage,* Studio Publications, 1933; (editor and author of introduction) *Theatre Art,* Norton, 1934; *Part of a Lifetime,* Duell, Sloan & Pearce, 1943, 2nd edition, 1962; *Untended Grove,* Duell, Sloan & Pearce, 1946; *The Art of Scenic Design,* Harper, 1950. Contributor of articles to *Encyclopedia Britannica* and *New Republic.* Editor, *Creative Art,* 1928-29.

(Died January 23, 1967)

*   *   *

SIMPSON, D(avid) P(enistan)   1917-

PERSONAL: Born October 3, 1917, in Canterbury, Kent, England; son of Bertram Fitzgerald (a bishop, Church of England) and Ethel (Penistan) Simpson; married Dorothy Frances Thompson, November 11, 1943; children: John Graham, Bridget Mary, Elizabeth Frances. *Education:* Educated at Eton College, 1931-36; Christ Church, Oxford University, 1936-40. *Religion:* Church of England. *Home:* Jourdelays Pl., Eton College, Windsor, Berkshire, England.

CAREER: Eton College, Windsor, Berkshire, England, assistant master, teaching Latin, Greek, English, divinity, 1946—, formerly head of classical department, currently house master. *Military service:* British Army, General Star officer, World War II; became major.

WRITINGS: (Editor) *Cassell's New Latin-English, English-Latin Dictionary,* Cassell, 1959, Funk, 1960, 3rd edition, Cassell, 1964; (editor) *Cassell's New Compact Latin-English, English-Latin Dictionary,* Cassell, 1963, Funk, 1964; *First Principles of Latin Prose,* Longmans, Green, 1965; (with P.H. Vellacott) *Writing in Latin: Style and Idiom for Advanced Latin Prose,* Longmans, Green, 1970.

*   *   *

SIMPSON, Harold Brown   1917-

PERSONAL: Born April 3, 1917, in Hindsboro, Ill.; son of Harry Leon (a salesman) and Louise (Brown) Simpson; married Lorraine C. Hennings (a professor at Baylor University); children: Jeffrey, Harold Brown, Jr.,

Gregory, Georganna, Deborah. *Education:* University of Illinois, B.S., 1940, M.S. and M.A., 1950; other study at Harvard University, 1944-45, University of Alabama, 1946-47, George Washington University, 1952; Texas Christian University, Ph.D., 1969. *Politics:* Independent voter. *Religion:* Protestant. *Home:* 2624 Austin Ave., Waco, Tex. 76710.

CAREER: U.S. Air Force, career service, 1941-63, retiring as colonel; Hill Junior College, Hillsboro, Tex., instructor in history, 1963—. Public lecturer on Civil War and Texas history. *Member:* U.S. Naval Institute, Air Force Association, Company of Military Historians (fellow), Civil War Round Table (president, Wiesbaden, Germany, 1955-58, Montgomery, Ala., 1958-59, Waco, Tex., 1960-61), Texas Junior College Teachers Association, Illinois Historical Society, Texas State Historical Society, West Texas Historical Society. *Awards, honors*—Military: Asiatic-Pacific Ribbon with three battle stars, Presidential Unit Citation with two oak-leaf clusters, Commendation Ribbon with one oak-leaf cluster. Literary: Award of merit from American Association of State and Local History and from Civil War Centennial Commission of Texas, both for *Gaines' Mill to Appomattox.*

WRITINGS: Brawling Brass: North and South, Texian Press, 1960; *Gaines' Mill to Appomattox: Waco and McLennan County in Hood's Texas Brigade,* Texian Press, 1963; (editor) Todd, *First Texas Regiment,* Texian Press, 1964; (editor and author of biography) James B. Robertson, *Touched with Valor: Civil War Papers and Casualty Reports of Hood's Texas Brigade,* Hill Junior College Press, 1964; (editor) Benjamin M. Seaton, *The Bugle Blows Softly: The Confederate Diary,* Texian Press, 1965; (editor) *Hood's Texas Brigade in Poetry and Song,* Hill Junior College Press, 1968; *Red Granite for Gray Heroes: The Monuments to Hood's Texas Brigade on Eastern Battlefields,* Hill Junior College Press, 1969. Contributor of articles to *Armed Forces Management* and *Texas Military History.* Book review editor and editorial board member, *Texana.*

AVOCATIONAL INTERESTS: Sports and collecting books on military history.†

* * *

SIMPSON, John L(iddle)

PERSONAL: Born in Kalimpong, India; son of James and Mary (Scotland) Simpson; married Ursula Vaughan Rigby, April 27, 1959. *Education:* Attended George Watson's College; University of Edinburgh, M.A., 1934. *Home:* 52 Ashley Gardens, Westminster, London S.W. 1, England. *Office:* Foreign and Commonwealth Office, London S.W. 1, England.

CAREER: Barrister-at-law, Middle Temple, London, England, 1937; Control Commission for Germany, and Control Office for Germany and Austria, member of staff, 1945-47; Foreign Office (now Foreign and Commonwealth Office) London, England, member of legal staff, 1947-51, legal counselor, 1954-59; United Kingdom Mission to United Nations, New York, N.Y., legal adviser, 1959-61; Foreign Office, legal counselor, 1961-68, deputy legal adviser, 1968—. *Military service:* British Army, 1939-45; became lieutenant colonel, General Staff. *Member:* British Institute of International and Comparative Law. *Awards, honors:* Companion of the Most Distinguished Order of St. Michael and St. George; D.Litt., University of Edinburgh, 1951.

WRITINGS: (With Maurice E. Bathurst) *Germany and the North Atlantic Community: A Legal Survey,* Praeger, 1956; (with Hazel Fox) *International Arbitration: Law and Practice,* Praeger, 1959. Contributor of articles to professional journals in England and the United States.

SIMPSON, Richard L(ee)   1929-

PERSONAL: Born February 2, 1929, in Washington, D.C.; son of Donald Dake (a building contractor) and Lottie (Lee) Simpson; married Ida Ann Harper (a sociologist at Duke University), July 10, 1955; children: Robert Donald and Frank Daniel (twins). *Education:* University of North Carolina, A.B., 1950, Ph.D., 1956; Cornell University, M.A., 1952. *Home:* 604 Brookview Rd., Chapel Hill, N.C. 27514. *Office:* Department of Sociology, University of North Carolina, Chapel Hill, N.C. 27514.

CAREER: Pennsylvania State University, University Park, instructor in sociology, 1956-57; Northwestern University, Evanston, Ill., assistant professor of sociology, 1957-58; University of North Carolina, Chapel Hill, 1958—, began as assistant professor, now professor of sociology. *Member:* American Sociological Association, Southern Sociological Society (president, 1971-72).

WRITINGS: (With Paul E. Wehr) *Cumberland County Library-Community Survey: A Study of Factors Affecting the Use of Library Services in Cumberland County, North Carolina,* Institute for Research in Social Science, University of North Carolina, 1960; (with David R. Norsworthy, H. Max Miller, and John R. Earle) *Occupational Choice and Mobility in the Urbanizing Piedmont of North Carolina,* Institute for Research in Social Science, University of North Carolina, 1960; *Attendants in American Mental Hospitals,* Institute for Research in Social Science, University of North Carolina, 1961; (editor with wife, Ida Harper Simpson) *Social Organization and Behavior: A Reader in General Sociology,* Wiley, 1964; (editor with Herman Turk) *Institutions and Social Exchange: The Sociologies of Talcott Pearsons and George C. Homans,* Bobbs-Merrill, 1971. Contributor to sociology journals. *Social Forces,* associate editor, 1958-69, 1972—, book review editor, 1964-69, editor, 1969-72; associate editor, *American Sociologist,* 1967-70.

WORK IN PROGRESS: A research project on professionalism among school teachers sponsored by U.S. Office of Education, to be reported in a book.

* * *

SINCLAIR, Andrew Annandale   1935-

PERSONAL: Born January 21, 1935, in Oxford, England; son of Stanley Charles and Hilary (Nash-Webber) Sinclair; married Mirando Seymour, October 18, 1972. *Education:* Attended Eton College, 1948-53; Trinity College, Cambridge, B.A. (double first honors in history), 1958; Churchill College, Cambridge, Ph.D., 1963. *Home:* 15 Hanover Terrace, London N.W.1, England. *Agent:* Elaine Greene, 31 Newington Green, London N.16, England. *Office:* Lorrimer Publishing, 47 Dean St., London, W.1, England.

CAREER: Commonwealth fellow, 1959-61; Churchill College, Cambridge University, Cambridge, England, director of historical studies, 1961-63; American Council of Learned Societies, New York, N.Y., fellow, 1963-65; University College, University of London, London, England, lecturer in American history, 1965-67; Lorrimer Publishing, London, managing director, 1967—; Timon Films, managing director, 1969—. *Military service:* British Army, Coldstream Guards, 1953-55; became lieutenant. *Member:* A.C.T.T., Royal Society of Literature (fellow). *Awards, honors:* Somerset Maugham Literary Prize, 1967.

WRITINGS: The Breaking of Bumbo, Simon & Schuster, 1959; *My Friend Judas,* Faber, 1959, Simon & Schuster, 1961; *The Project,* Simon & Schuster, 1960; *Prohibition: The Era of Excess,* introduction by Richard Hofstadter, Atlantic-Little, Brown, 1962, reissued as *The Era of*

Excess: A Social History of the Prohibition Movement, Harper, 1964; *The Paradise Bum,* Atheneum, 1963 (published in England as *The Hallelujah Bum,* Faber, 1963); *The Raker,* Atheneum, 1964; *The Available Man: The Life Behind the Masks of Warren Gamaliel Harding,* Macmillan, 1965; *The Better Half: The Emancipation of the American Woman,* Harper, 1965, reissued as *The Emancipation of the American Woman,* 1966; *A Concise History of the United States,* Viking, 1967; *Gog,* Macmillan, 1967; (translator) *Selections from Greek Anthology,* Weidenfeld & Nicolson, 1967, Macmillan, 1968; (author of introduction) Homer, *The Iliad,* translation by W.H.D. Rouse, Heron Books, 1969; *The Last of the Best: The Aristocracy of Europe in the Twentieth Century,* Macmillan, 1969; *Che Guevara,* Viking, 1970 (published in England as *Guevara,* Fontana, 1970); *Magog,* Harper, 1972.

Plays: "My Friend Judas" (adapted from his book), first produced in London at Arts Theatre, October, 1959; (adapter) Dylan Thomas, *Adventures in the Skin Trade* (first produced at Hampstead Theatre Club, March 7, 1965; produced in Washington, D.C. at Washington Theatre Club, February 25, 1970), Dent, 1967, New Directions, 1968.

Screenplays: "Before Winter Comes" (based on *The Interpreter,* a short story by Frederick L. Keefe), Columbia, 1969; (and director) "The Breaking of Bumbo" (based on his novel), Associated British Pictures Corp., 1970; "The Voyage of the Beagle," CBS Films, 1970; "Wasn't This What You Came to See?," Timon Films, 1971; (and director) "Under Milk Wood" (based on the play by Dylan Thomas), Timon Films, 1971. Also author of television scripts. Contributor to *Atlantic, Harper's, Observer, Guardian, Spectator, New Statesman,* and other periodicals and newspapers.

WORK IN PROGRESS: Writing and directing two films, "The Carrycot," for Impact Films, and "Bryon's Evil," for Timon Films.

SIDELIGHTS: Sinclair writes: "I travel much, liking it only in retrospect. I collect old oak, old friends, and the grotesqueries of life; my interests are radical, and my hope is to overcome the fear of death."

Sinclair's novel, *Gog,* received both high praise and harsh criticism. Frank McGuinness believes that it is "a picaresque tale with perhaps more satirical pretensions than the author's talent for ribald and extravagant inventiveness can finally support.... The truth is that if the novel is not without distinction as a study of a mind hovering between sanity and madness, its satirical aims are lost in a welter of scholarly clowning, crude farce, and the sort of glib cynicism that is so often mistaken for cold, hard-headed intellectualism." J.D. Scott states that although Sinclair "has too much talent to fail to make an impression, . . . the impression is confused by too much frenetic action, and softened by long lapses into flat, sometimes merely clever, sometimes merely banal prose.... Like some great Gothic folly seen through the mist, it fails to communicate its meaning."

Other critics, like Philip Callow, are impressed both with the book's style and content. "The book sears and scalds, it's the vision of a cold, planetary eye, and somehow it all founders in the end, goes mad like a cancer and finally smashes in a blind fury of destruction. I'm still reeling. I think there's genius in it." The *Time* reviewer appreciates Sinclair's "great verbal felicity," adding: "He can, in the manner of James Joyce in his celebrated parody of all English prose since the Venerable Bede, catch the tone of class and time." Rachel Trickett describes the novel as one "based on a mixture of traditional genres, the allegory, the romance, and the picaresque tale . . . at once realistic and a fantasy, didactic and mythical, precise and comprehensive.... The love of life and compulsive literary energy are what makes *Gog* so impressive a book. . . . [It] is more ambitious in bringing together a whole sequence of episodes and a whole context of myth and literature. Confusion and carelessness are its worst faults, but its inclusiveness is also its strength. Self-indulgent and undisciplined, it nevertheless shows a clumsy but powerful genius which can only leave one astonished, occasionally repelled, but consistently grateful for so much imaginative vigor and breadth."

BIOGRAPHICAL/CRITICAL SOURCES: New York Times Book Review, January 22, 1967, September 10, 1967, October 8, 1967; *Books and Bookmen,* May, 1967, June, 1967; *London Magazine,* June, 1967; *Times Literary Supplement,* June 8, 1967, July 13, 1967; *New Statesman,* June 9, 1967; *Observer Review,* June 11, 1967, January 11, 1970; *Drama,* summer, 1967; *Time,* September 1, 1967; *Book World,* September 24, 1967; *Best Sellers,* October 1, 1967; *Hudson Review,* winter, 1967; *Listener,* April 4, 1968; *Yale Review,* spring, 1968; *Variety,* January 15, 1969; *Spectator,* April 25, 1969; *Punch,* January 20, 1970.

*   *   *

SINGH, G(han) Shyam   1926-

PERSONAL: Born December 20, 1926, in Jaipur, Rajasthan, India; son of Kaloo and Gulab (Kunwar) Singh. *Education:* Studied at Rajasthan University, 1944-50, B.A., M.A., Ph.D.; Birkbeck College, University of London, Ph.D., 1962; Milan State University, Dott.Lett.; University of Bologna, Dott.Lett. in Italian. *Office:* Bocconi University, Via Sarfatti, 25 Milan, Italy.

CAREER: Aligarh University, Aligarh, India, lecturer in English, 1954-56; Institute of Middle East and Far East Studies, Milan, Italy, lecturer in Indian languages and literature, 1958—; Universita Commerciale Luigi Bocconi, Milan, Italy, reader in English, 1962—. Anglo-American Centre, Mullsjo, Sweden, summer lecturer in English, 1958—.

WRITINGS: Pessimism in Swinburne's Early Poetry (monograph), Raleigh Literary Society, Muslim University (Aligarh), 1956; *Leopardi and the Theory of Poetry,* University Press of Kentucky, 1964; (compiler and author of introduction) Frank Raymond Leavis, *Essaer,* translated by Aake Nylinder, Seelig (Stockholm), 1966; (compiler and author of introduction) *Contemporary Italian Verse,* London Magazine Editions, 1967; *Leopardi e l'Inghilterra,* Le Monnier, 1968; (translator from Italian) Eugenio Montale, *The Butterfly of Dinard,* London Magazine Editions, 1970, University Press of Kentucky, 1971. Contributor to *Italian Studies* (Cambridge, England), and to *English Miscellany, Letterature Comparate,* and *Osservatore Letterario e Politico* (all Italy).

WORK IN PROGRESS: History of Modern Indian Literature, for publication by Nuova Accademia, Milan.

BIOGRAPHICAL/CRITICAL SOURCES: Times Literary Supplement, October 17, 1968; *London Magazine,* September, 1970.

*   *   *

SINGH, Khushwant   1915-

PERSONAL: Born February 2, 1915, in Punjab, India; son of Sobha (a builder) and Veera (Bai) Singh; married; children: two sons, Rahul and Mala. *Education:* Government College, Lahore, India, B.A., 1934; Inner Temple, London, England, barrister-at-law, 1938; Kings College, London, LL.B., 1938. *Religion:* Sikh. *Home:* 1A, Janpath, New Delhi, India.

CAREER: Lawyer in practice before the high court, Lahore, India, 1940-47; Indian Government, press attache in Ottawa, Ontario, Canada, and London, England, 1947-52; UNESCO, Paris, France, mass communications staff member, 1954-56; Planning Commission, Delhi, India, editor, 1956-58; free-lance writer. Regular broadcaster at various times for Air India, British Broadcasting Corp., and Canadian Broadcasting Corp.

WRITINGS: The Mark of Vishnu, and Other Stories, Saturn Press, 1950; (editor with Peter Russell) A Note on G.V. Desani's "All About H. Hatterr and Hali", Szeben, 1952; The Sikhs, Allen & Unwin, 1953; Mano Majra, Grove, 1956, also published as Train to Pakistan, Chatto & Windus, 1956, Grove, 1961; The Unending Trail, privately printed, 1957; The Voice of God, and Other Stories, Jaico Publishing House (Bombay), 1957; (translator and author of introduction) Jupji, the Sikh Prayer, Royal India, Pakistan and Ceylon Society (London), c.1958; I Shall Not Hear the Nightingale, Grove, 1959; The Sikhs Today: Their Religion, History, Culture, Customs and Way of Life, Orient Longmans, 1959, revised edition, 1964; (translator) Umrao Jan Ada, Orient Longmans, 1961; The Fall of the Kingdom of the Punjab, Orient Longmans, 1962; Ranjit Singh, Maharajah of the Punjab, 1780-1839, Hillary, 1962; A History of the Sikhs, Princeton University Press, Volume 1: 1469-1839, 1963, Volume 2: 1839-1964, 1966; (editor with Jaya Thadani) Land of the Five Rivers, Jaico Publishing House, 1965; Not Wanted in Pakistan, Rajkamal Prakashan (Delhi), 1965; (with Suneet Vir Singh) Homage to Guru Gobind Singh, Jaico Publishing House, 1966, Orientalia, 1971; (with Satindra Singh) Ghadar, 1915: India's First Armed Revolution, R & K Publishing House (New Delhi), 1966; (editor) Sita Ram Kohli, Sunset of the Sikh Empire, Orient Longmans, 1967; A Bride for the Sahib, and Other Stories, Hind Pocket Books (Delhi), 1967; (translator) Rajindar Singh Bedi, I Take This Woman, Hind Pocket Books, 1967; (with Arun Joshi) Shri Ram: A Biography, Asia Publishing House, 1968; (translator) Hymns of Guru Nanak, Orient Longmans, 1969; Khushwant Singh's India, India Book House, 1970. Contributor to Harper's, New York Times, Guardian, Observer, Times Literary Supplement, and to newspapers in India. Editor, Illustrated Weekly of India (Bombay).

WORK IN PROGRESS: Delhi, a novel.

AVOCATIONAL INTERESTS: Long walks, birds and trees, wine and women.

*   *   *

SITWELL, Dame Edith   1887-1964

PERSONAL: Born September 7, 1887, in Scarborough, England; daughter of Sir George and Lady Ida Emily Augusta (Denison) Sitwell. Education: Privately educated. Religion: Roman Catholic convert, 1955.

CAREER: Writer. Visiting professor, Institute of Contemporary Arts, 1957. Member: Royal Society of Literature (fellow; vice-president, 1958), American Institute of Arts and Letters (honorary associate). Awards, honors: Benson medal, Royal Society of Literature, 1934; created Dame, Commander Order of the British Empire, 1954 (the first poet to be so honored); William Foyle Poetry Prize, 1958, for Collected Poems; with Robert Lowell and W.H. Auden, shared Guiness Poetry Award, 1959; Litt.D., University of Leeds, 1948; D.Litt., University of Durham, 1948, Oxford University, 1951, University of Sheffield, 1955, University of Hull, 1963.

WRITINGS: The Mother and Other Poems, Basil Blackwell, 1915; (with Osbert Sitwell) Twentieth Century Harlequinade and Other Poems, Basil Blackwell, 1916; Clowns' Houses (poems), Longmans, Green, 1918.

The Wooden Pegasus (poems), Basil Blackwell, 1920; Facade (poems), Favil Press, 1922, new edition with introduction by Jack Lindsay, Duckworth, 1950; Bucolic Comedies (poems), Duckworth, 1923; The Sleeping Beauty (poems), Duckworth, 1924; (with Osbert and Sacheverell Sitwell) Poor Young People (poems), Fleuron, 1925; (author of introduction) Ann Taylor, Meddlesome Matty and Other Poems for Infant Minds, John Lane, 1925; Poetry and Criticism, L. and V. Woolf, 1925, Holt, 1926, Folcroft Press, 1969; Troy Park (poems), Duckworth, 1925; Elegy on Dead Fashion, Duckworth, 1926; Twelve Poems, E. Benn, 1926; Rustic Elegies, Knopf, 1927; Popular Song (poems), Faber and Gwyer, 1928; Five Poems, Duckworth, 1928; Gold Coast Customs (poems), Duckworth, 1929.

Alexander Pope, Cosmopolitan Book Corp., 1930; The Collected Poems of Edith Sitwell, Duckworth, 1930, Vanguard, 1968; (editor) The Pleasures of Poetry: A Critical Anthology, three volumes, Duckworth, 1930-32, Norton, 1934; Children's Tales from the Russian Ballet, [London], 1930; Epithalamium, Duckworth, 1931; Jane Barston, 1719-1746, Faber, 1931; In Spring (poems), privately printed, 1931; Bath, Faber, 1932, new edition, 1948; (author of introductory essay to translation by Helen Rootham) Rimbaud, Prose Poems from Les Illuminations, Faber, 1932; Five Variations on a Theme, Duckworth, 1933; The English Eccentrics, Houghton, 1933, new edition, Vanguard, 1957, abridged edition, Arrow Books, 1960; Aspects of Modern Poetry, Duckworth, 1934; Selected Poems, Duckworth, 1936; Some Recent Developments in English Literature, University of Sydney, 1936; Victoria of England, Houghton, 1936, revised edition, Faber, 1949; (author of introductory essay) Sacheverell Sitwell, Collected Poems, Duckworth, 1936; I Live Under a Black Sun (novel), Gollancz, 1937, Doubleday, Doran, 1938, new edition, Lehmann, 1948; (with Osbert and Sacheverell Sitwell) Trio: Dissertations on Some Aspects of National Genius, Macmillan, 1938.

(Editor) Edith Sitwell's Anthology, Gollancz, 1940; Poems New and Old, Faber, 1940; (editor) Look! The Sun, Gollancz, 1941; English Women, Collins, 1942; Street Songs, Macmillan, 1942; A Poet's Notebook, Macmillan, 1943, Little, Brown, 1950; Green Song and Other Poems, Macmillan, 1944, Vanguard, 1946; (compiler) Planet and Glow-Worm: A Book for the Sleepless, Macmillan, 1944; The Song of the Cold (poems), Macmillan, 1945, Vanguard, 1948; Fanfare for Elizabeth, Macmillan, 1946; The Shadow of Cain (blank verse), Lehmann, 1947; A Notebook on William Sheakespeare, Macmillan, 1948, Beacon, 1961; The Canticle of the Rose: Selected Poems, 1920-1947, Macmillan, 1949, Vanguard, 1949; (author of foreword) Charles Henri Ford, Sleep in a Nest of Flames, New Directions, 1949.

(Compiler) A Book of the Winter (poems and prose), Macmillan, 1950, Vanguard, 1951; Poor Men's Music, Fore Publications, 1950; (editor) The American Genius, Lehmann, 1951; Facade: An Entertainment With Poems by Edith Sitwell, with music by William Turner Walton (performed in 1922), Oxford University Press, 1951; (compiler) A Book of Flowers, Macmillan, 1952; Gardeners and Astronomers: New Poems, Vanguard, 1953; Collected Poems, Vanguard, 1954; (editor) The Atlantic Book of British and American Poetry, Little, Brown, 1958; (author of introduction) Jose Garcia Villa, Selected Poems and New, McDowell, Oblensky, 1958.

(Editor) Algernon Charles Swinburne, Swinburne: A Selection, Harcourt, 1960, Edith Sitwell (poems), Vista Books, 1960, The Queens and the Hive, Little, Brown, 1962; The Outcasts (poems), Macmillan, 1962; Music and Ceremonies (poems), Vanguard, 1963; Taken Care Of (autobiography), Atheneum, 1965; Selected Poems, chosen and with an introduction by John Lehmann, Macmillan, 1965; *Selected Letters, 1919-1964,* edited by John Lehmann and Derek Parker, Macmillan, 1970, Vanguard, 1971; Editor of *Wheels,* an annual anthology of modern verse, 1916-21.

SIDELIGHTS: In the introduction to *The Canticle of the Rose* Dame Edith wrote: "At the time I began to write, a change in the direction, imagery and rhythms in poetry had become necessary, owing to the rhythmical flaccidity, the verbal deadness, the dead and expected patterns, of some of the poetry immediately preceding us." Her early work was often experimental, creating melody, using striking conceits, new rhythms, and confusing private allusions. Her efforts at change were resisted, but, as the *New Statesman* observed, "losing every battle, she won the campaign," and emerged the high priestess of twentieth-century poetry.

The Times (London) wrote in 1955 that "she writes for the sake of sound, of color, and from an awareness of God and regard for man." She believed that "Poetry is the deification of reality, and one of its purposes is to show that the dimensions of man are, as Sir Arthur Eddington said, 'half way between those of an atom and a star.'" An admiring critic, John Lehmann, admits that "her tendency has always been rather to overwork her symbolism; by a certain overfluid quality in her imagination to make the use of the symbols sometimes appear confused and indiscriminate." This Baroque quality has its admirers, however. Babette Deutsch in *Poetry in Our Time* writes: ". . . like the medieval hangings that kept the cold away from secular kings and princes of the Church, the finest of [Dame Edith's] poems have a luxurious beauty that serves to grace the bareness, to diminish the chill of this bare, cold age."

The *New Statesman* has said that her place in poetry is "roughly commensurate with that of Christina Rossetti in the previous century," and insists on the primacy of her personality. The sister of Osbert and Sacheverell was indeed not to be trifled with. Says Sacheverell: "She was always determined to be remarkable and she has succeeded." The *New Statesman* described her thus: ". . . great rings load the fingers, the hands are fastidiously displayed, the eye-sockets have been thumbed by a master, the eyes themselves haunt, disdain, trouble indifference, and the fashions are century-old with a telling simplification." At times, and perhaps not unintentionally, she looked like a Tudor monarch. The author of a study of Elizabeth I, she once remarked: "I've always had a great affinity for Queen Elizabeth. We were born on the same day of the month and about the same hour of the day and I was extremely like her when I was young." Dame Edith always insisted that she was no eccentric: "It's just that I am more alive than most people."

Her outspoken manner and rebellion against accepted modes of behavior led to encounters with such as Wyndham Lewis and Geoffrey Grigson. When *Facade* was first performed in London in 1922, the response of the audience and of critics was derisive and indignant. Dame Edith recalled: "I had to hide behind the curtain. An old lady was waiting to beat me with an umbrella." (In 1949 the work was enthusiastically received in New York.) She remained wonderfully candid. On a recent visit to America she revealed that her most serious objection to certain Beat poets was that they smelled bad, and found she liked the late Marilyn Monroe, "largely because she was ill treated. She was like a sad ghost."

True to her image, she never mastered a typewriter, and was able to write, she said, only in bed. "Every woman," she once remarked, "no matter what the circumstances, should have a day a week in bed." She shunned the strenuous life, saying, "I detest walking more than anything else in the world."

AVOCATIONAL INTERESTS: Music, silence, reading.

BIOGRAPHICAL/CRITICAL SOURCES: R.L. Megroz, *The Three Sitwells,* Doran, 1927, reprinted, Kennikat, 1969; J.G. Villa, *Celebrations for Edith Sitwell,* New Directions, 1948; John Lehmann, *Edith Sitwell,* Longmans, Green, 1952; *Triad of Genius,* Part 1, British Book Centre, 1954; *New Statesman and Nation,* January 23, 1954; Louise Bogan, *Selected Criticism,* Noonday, 1955; Babette Deutsch, *Poetry in Our Time,* Columbia University Press, 1956; *Vogue,* July, 1960; *A Marianne Moore Reader,* Viking, 1961; Richard Fifoot, *A Bibliography of Edith, Osbert, and Sacheverell Sitwell,* Hart-Davis, 1963; *Life,* January 4, 1963; *New York Times,* December 10, 1964; *Time,* December 18, 1964; *Observer,* April 4, 1965; *New Republic,* April 24, 1965; *Nation,* June 7, 1965; Ralph J. Mills, Jr., *Edith Sitwell: A Critical Essay,* Eerdmans, 1966, *Encounter,* May, 1966; Elizabeth Salter, *The Last Years of a Rebel: A Memoir of Edith Sitwell,* Houghton, 1967; *Criticism,* winter, 1967; J.D. Brophy, *Edith Sitwell,* Southern Illinois University Press, 1968; John Lehmann, *A Nest of Tigers: The Sitwells in Their Times,* Little, Brown, 1968; *London Magazine,* September, 1970.

(Died December 9, 1964)

*   *   *

SKINNER, B(urrhus) F(rederic) 1904-

PERSONAL: Born March 20, 1904, in Susquehanna, Pa.; son of William Arthur and Grace (Burrhus) Skinner; married Yvonne Blue, November 1, 1936; children: Julie (Mrs. Ernest Vargas), Deborah. *Education:* Hamilton College, A.B., 1929; Harvard University, M.A., 1930, Ph.D., 1931. *Home:* 13 Old Dee Rd., Cambridge 38, Mass. *Office:* William James Hall, Harvard University, Cambridge 38, Mass.

CAREER: Harvard University, Cambridge, Mass., research fellow, National Research Council, 1931-32, junior fellow in Harvard Society of Fellows, 1933-36; University of Minnesota, Minneapolis, instructor in psychology, 1936-37, assistant professor of psychology, 1937-39, associate professor, 1939-45; Indiana University, Bloomington, professor of psychology, department chairman, 1945-48; Harvard University, Cambridge, Mass., William James Lecturer, 1947, professor of psychology, 1948-57, Edgar Pierce Professor of Psychology, 1958—. Frequent participant in lecture series and seminars. Conducted war research for the Office of Scientific Research and Development, 1942-43. *Member:* American Psychological Association, American Association for the Advancement of Science, Society of Experimental Psychologists, National Academy of Sciences, American Philosophical Society, American Academy of Arts and Sciences. Swedish Psychological Society, Phi Beta Kappa, Sigma Xi. *Awards, honors:* Howard Crosby Warren medal, 1942; Guggenheim fellow, 1944-45; career grant from the National Institute of Mental Health; award for distinguished scientific contribution from American Psychological Association, 1958; National Medal of Science, 1968; Gold Medal from the American Psychological Association, 1971; Joseph P. Kennedy, Jr. Foundation Award, 1971. Honorary degrees from a dozen universities and colleges, including Sc.D., University of Chicago, 1967, University of Exeter (England), 1969, McGill University, 1970; Litt.D., Ripon College, 1961; LH.D., Rockford College, 1971; L.L.D., Ohio Wesleyan University, 1971.

WRITINGS: (Editor with William A. Skinner) *A Digest of Decisions of the Anthracite Board of Conciliation,* [Scranton], 1928; *Behavior of Organisms: An Experimental Analysis,* Appleton, 1938; (with others) *Current Trends in Psychology* (lectures), University of Pittsburgh Press, 1947; *Walden Two* (novel), Macmillan, 1948, with a new preface by the author, Macmillan (London), 1969; *Science and Human Behavior,* Macmillan, 1953; (editor with Peter B. Dews) *Techniques for the Study of Behavioral Effects of Drugs,* Annals of the New York Academy of Sciences, 1956; (with C.B. Ferster) *Schedules of Reinforcement,* Appleton, 1957; *Verbal Behavior,* Appleton, 1957; *Cumulative Record: A Selection of Papers,* Appleton, 1959, enlarged edition, 1961, 3rd edition, 1972; (with James G. Holland) *The Analysis of Behavior: A Program for Self-Instruction,* McGraw, 1961; *Teaching Machines,* Freeman, 1961; (with others) *Understanding Maps: A Programmed Text,* Allyn, 1964; (with Sue-Ann Krakower) *Handwriting with Write and See* (patented method of teaching writing), six volumes in eight, Lyons & Carnahan, 1968; *The Technology of Teaching,* Appleton, 1968; *Earth Resources* (textbook), Prentice-Hall, 1969; *Contingencies of Reinforcement: A Theoretical Analysis,* Appleton, 1969; (with Arnold J. Toynbee and others) *On the Future of Art* (lectures), Viking, 1970; *Beyond Freedom and Dignity,* Knopf, 1971.

WORK IN PROGRESS: An autobiography.

SIDELIGHTS: Burrhus Frederic Skinner, named by American university professors as the most influential figure in modern psychology, became a controversial author with his novel, *Walden Two.* The Utopian society described in *Walden Two,* based on scientific control of behavior, alarmed humanists, who pointed out that a benevolent dictator is still a dictator. A "behaviorist"— that is, a psychologist who believes in the study of behavior through measurable data, not by "idle speculation" about the inner mind—Skinner has, according to Berkley Rice, turned "the study of behavior into an objective science." Skinner advocates using his theory of "operant conditioning" to control human behavior in order to ensure the survival of the human race. *Beyond Freedom and Dignity,* his plea for a planned society, evoked even greater response and stronger reactions than his earlier works. It was "the year's most controversial book," said *Time,* who also listed it as one of the best.

Skinner's impact has been no less controversial in other, widely divergent areas. As inventor of the teaching machine and "father" of programmed instruction, he has, according to some, "revolutionized teaching;" according to others, he has "mechanized education." His widely publicized "aircrib," a glass-sided, atmosphere-controlled baby-tender, was often confused, by a horrified public, with his "Skinner box," which was solely a laboratory device for experiments with animals. His theories have been applied with apparent success not only to psychotic patients, but in corporation management.

Walden Two, which has sold nearly a half-million copies, has inspired several small, experimental communities, as well as, in 1966, a National Walden Two Conference. Skinner's lectures and seminars can be heard on three phonorecords produced by the Center for the Study of Democratic Institutions.

AVOCATIONAL INTERESTS: Listening to music; playing the piano.

BIOGRAPHICAL/CRITICAL SOURCES: Newsweek, October 19, 1959; *Business Week,* September 17, 1960; *New York Times Magazine,* September 25, 1960; *Time,* March 24, 1961; *Science News Letter,* October 21, 1961; *Harper's,* April, 1963; *Saturday Review,* September 21, 1968; *New York Times Magazine,* March 17, 1968; *New Republic,* November 21, 1970; Peter B. Dews, editor, *Festschrift for B.F. Skinner,* Appleton, 1970; *Washington Post,* September 23, 1971; *Atlantic,* October, 1971; *Life,* October 22, 1971; *Time,* January 3, 1972; *Business Week,* December 2, 1972.

SKLAR, Richard L(awrence) 1930-

PERSONAL: Born March 22, 1930, in New York, N.Y.; son of Kalman (an attorney) and Sophie L. Sklar; married Eva Molineux, July 14, 1962; children: Judith Anne, Katherine Elizabeth. *Education:* University of Utah, B.A., 1952; Princeton University, Ph.D., 1961. *Office:* Department of Political Science, University of California, Los Angeles, Calif. 90024.

CAREER: Brandeis University, Waltham, Mass., assistant professor of politics, 1961-63; University of Ibadan, Ibadan, Nigeria, lecturer in political science, 1963-65; University of Zambia, Lusaka, senior lecturer in political science, 1966-68; University of California, Los Angeles, professor of political science, 1969—. *Military service:* U.S. Army, 1952-54.

WRITINGS: Nigerian Political Parties: Power in an Emergent African Nation, Princeton University Press, 1963; (with C.S. Whitaker, Jr.) *The Federal Republic of Nigeria,* African Studies Center, University of California (Los Angeles), 1966.

Contributor: J.S. Coleman and C.G. Rosbery, Jr., editors, *Political Parties and National Integration in Tropical Africa,* University of California Press, 1964; G.M. Carter, editor, *National Unity and Regionalism in Eight African States,* Cornell University Press, 1966; G.M. Carter, editor, *Politics in Africa: Seven Cases,* Harcourt, 1966; R. Melson and H. Wolpe, editors, *Nigeria: Modernization and the Politics of Communalism,* Michigan State University Press, 1971.

WORK IN PROGRESS: The political influence of multinational corporations in Zambia.

*   *   *

SKOGLUND, John Egnar 1912-

PERSONAL: Born April 1, 1912, in San Diego, Calif.; son of Gustaf (a carpenter) and Amanda (Wetterskog) Skoglund; married Daisy W. Nelson, November 4, 1934; children: Jean (Mrs. Robert Abbe), Joy (Mrs. Eldon Ernst), Linda (Mrs. David Renne), Mary Louise, John Eric, Jeana, Gabrielle. *Education:* University of California, Berkeley, A.B., 1933; Berkeley Baptist Divinity School, M.A., 1935, B.D., 1936; Yale University, Ph.D., 1939. *Politics:* Democrat-Independent. *Home:* 51 Woodmont Rd., Rochester, N.Y., 14620. *Office:* 1100 South Goodman St., Rochester, N.Y. 14620.

CAREER: Ordained Baptist minister, 1936; pastor in Yalesville, Conn., 1936-38; Central Baptist Seminary, Kansas City, Kans., professor of Christian theology, 1938-40; Berkeley Baptist Divinity School, Berkeley, Calif., professor of Christian theology, 1940-47; American Baptist Foreign Mission Society, Valley Forge, Pa., foreign secretary, 1947-54; pastor in Seattle, Wash., 1954-58; Colgate Rochester Divinity School, Rochester, N.Y., Cornelius Woelfkin Professor of Preaching, 1958—. Visiting professor, United Theological College, Bangalore, India, 1973. Member of Faith and Order Commission, World Council of Churches, 1955—; chairman of board of managers, American Baptist Foreign Mission Society, 1956-64; member of executive council, Societas Liturgica, 1969—. *Member:* American Homiletical Society.

WRITINGS: The Spirit Tree, Judson, 1951; *They Reach for Life,* Friendship, 1955; *Come and See,* Judson, 1956; *I Believe,* Judson, 1957; *To the Whole Creation: The Church Is Mission,* Judson, 1962; *In the Beginning,* Judson, 1963; (with J.R. Nelson) *Fifty Years of Faith and Order: An Interpretation of Faith and Order Movement,* Bethany Press, 1964; (editor) *Worship and Renewal,* Colgate Rochester Press, 1964; *Worship in the Free Churches,* Judson, 1965; (editor) *Worship in a*

Secular Age, Colgate Rochester Press, 1967; *A Manual of Worship,* Judson, 1968; *The Baptists,* Judson, 1968. Editor, *Foundations,* 1969—.

WORK IN PROGRESS: A Study of Religious Communication in India; Localization of Worship in Indian Churches; a manual of contemporary worship materials.

SIDELIGHTS: Skoglund's travels in interests of missions and ecumenicity have taken him to Far East five times, and to Africa and Europe.

*   *   *

SLATOFF, Walter J(acob)   1922-

PERSONAL: Born March 1, 1922, in New York, N.Y.; son of Ellis and Jeanette (Armstrong) Slatoff; married Jane Metzger, 1946; children: Joan, Donald. *Education:* Columbia University, B.A., 1943; University of Michigan, M.A., 1950, Ph.D., 1955. *Home:* 23 Renwick Heights Rd., Ithaca, N.Y. 14850. *Office:* Department of English, Cornell University, Ithaca, N.Y. 14850.

CAREER: Cornell University, Ithaca, N.Y., instructor, 1955-58, assistant professor, 1958-61, associate professor, 1961-66, professor of English, 1966—. *Military service:* U.S. Army, 1943-46. *Member:* National Council of Teachers of English, American Association of University Professors.

WRITINGS: Quest for Failure: A Study of William Faulkner, Cornell University Press, 1960; *With Respect to Readers: Dimensions of Literary Response,* Cornell University Press, 1970. Associate editor of *Epoch* Magazine.

*   *   *

SLAVIN, Arthur Joseph   1933-

PERSONAL: Born February 15, 1933, in Brooklyn, N.Y.; son of David (a cab driver) and Mildred (Eisner) Slavin; married Camille Marie LeBlanc (a registered nurse), June 19, 1954; married second wife, Inger-Johanne Espe, November 30, 1968; children: (first marriage) Ruth, Aaron, Rebecca, Laura. *Education:* New York University, student, 1950-51; Louisiana State University, A.B. (magna cum laude), 1958; University of North Carolina, Ph.D., 1962. *Politics:* Independent Socialist. *Office:* University of California at Los Angeles, Los Angeles, Calif. 90024.

CAREER: Bucknell University, Lewisburg, Pa., assistant professor of history, 1961-65; University of California, Los Angeles, assistant professor, 1965-66, associate professor of history, 1966—. Louisiana State University, Baton Rouge, visiting assistant professor of history, 1963-64. *Military service:* U.S. Air Force, 1951-55. *Member:* American Historical Association, International Commission for the History of Parliamentary and Representative Institutions, Renaissance Society of America, Conference on British Studies, other organizations. *Awards, honors:* Woodrow Wilson fellow, 1958-59; Southern Teaching Fellowship Foundation fellow, 1958-61; grants-in-aid, American Philosophical Society, 1965, American Council of Learned Societies, 1966 and 1969; Folger Library, fellow, 1965, senior research fellow, 1970-71; fellow, University of California Humanities Institute, 1966 and 1968; Guggenheim fellow, 1967-68.

WRITINGS: Politics and Profit: A Study of Sir Ralph Sadler, 1507-1547, Cambridge University Press, 1966; *The Precarious Balance: England, 1450-1640,* Random House, in press.

Editor: (And author of introduction) *The New Monarchies and Representative Assemblies: Medieval Constitutionalism or Modern Absolutism?,* Heath, 1964; (and author of introduction) *Henry VIII and the English Reformation,* Heath, 1968; *Humanism, Reform and Reformation in England,* Wiley, 1969; (with Eugene C. Black) *Thomas Cromwell on Church and Commonwealth: Selected Letters, 1523-1540,* Harper, 1969; *Tudor Men and Institutions: Studies in English Law and Government,* Louisiana State University, in press. Contributor of numerous articles to scholarly journals in England and America.

WORK IN PROGRESS: A book about Lord Chancellor Thomas Wriothesley, as a sequel to the Sadler study, *Politics and Power;* a study of Thomas Cromwell and the revolution of the 1530's in England, to be published by Knopf; editing (as general editor) the Random House-Knopf "History of England," in ten volumes; a book on the civilization of the West.

AVOCATIONAL INTERESTS: Collecting graphics and recordings of baroque, classical, and modern music.

BIOGRAPHICAL/CRITICAL SOURCES: Times Literary Supplement, February 23, 1967.

*   *   *

SLOCUM, Robert Bigney   1922-

PERSONAL: Born April 6, 1922, in Brockton, Mass.; son of George Wheaton (a welting manufacturer) and Florence (Huestis) Slocum; married Christine Stanfield, August 23, 1953; children: Robert S., Kathryn. *Education:* Boston University, B.A., 1946; Columbia University, M.A., 1947; Simmons College, B.S. in L.S., 1949. *Politics:* Democrat. *Religion:* Presbyterian. *Home:* 92 West Main St., Dryden, N.Y. 13053. *Office:* Cornell University Libraries, Ithaca, N.Y. 14850.

CAREER: U.S. Library of Congress, Washington, D.C., librarian internee, 1949-50; Simmons College Library, Boston, Mass., assistant to director, 1950-51; University of Illinois Library, Urbana, cataloger (instructor), 1951-54; Cornell University Library (now Cornell University Libraries), Ithaca, N.Y., associate catalog librarian, 1954—. *Military service:* U.S. Army, 1942-45; served in Europe. *Member:* American Historical Association, American Library Association, American Association of University Professors.

WRITINGS: (Editor) *Manual of Procedures, Cornell University Library Catalog Department,* Cornell University Library, 1959, 2nd edition published as *Manual of Cataloging Procedures, Cornell University Libraries,* Cornell University Libraries, 1969; *Sample Catalog Cards: Illustrating Solutions to Problems in Descriptive Cataloging,* Scarecrow, 1962, 2nd revised edition (with Lois Hacker) published as *Sample Cataloging Forms: Illustrations of Solutions to Problems in Descriptive Cataloging,* 1968; *Biographical Dictionaries and Related Works,* Gale, 1967; *Biographical Dictionaries and Related Works Supplement,* Gale, 1972. Contributor to professional journals.

SIDELIGHTS: Slocum reads German, Russian, French, Spanish, Italian, and some Latin, Portuguese, Dutch, Slavic, and Scandinavian languages. He calls himself a "movie buff."

AVOCATIONAL INTERESTS: Camping, hiking, sports.

*   *   *

SMITH, Alfred G(oud)   1921-

PERSONAL: Born August 20, 1921, in The Hague, Netherlands; son of William Goud and Joan (Wraslouski) Smith; married Britta Helen Bonazzi, May 30, 1946. *Education:* University of Michigan, A.B., 1943; University of Wisconsin, M.A., 1947, Ph.D., 1956. *Home:* 540 Kingswood Ave., Eugene, Ore. 97405. *Office:* Department of Anthropology, University of Oregon, Eugene, Ore. 97403.

CAREER: U.S. Government, Far East analyst in Office of Strategic Services, 1943-45, in Department of State, 1945-46; University of Wisconsin, Madison, 1946-50, began as acting instructor, became instructor; Trust Territory of Pacific Islands, Micronesia, supervisor of linguistics, 1950-53; Antioch College, Yellow Springs, Ohio, assistant professor of anthropology, 1953-56; Emory University, Atlanta, Ga., 1956-62, began as assistant professor, became associate professor of anthropology; University of Oregon, Eugene, 1962—, began as associate professor, became professor of anthropology and professor of community service and public affairs. Consultant, to Georgia Department of Public Health, 1957-59 and to Peace Corps, Job Corps, Agency for International Development, and industry, 1966—. Military service: U.S. Army, 1942-45; became first lieutenant. Member: American Anthropological Association (fellow), American Association for the Advancement of Science (fellow), Linguistic Society of America, International Communication Association.

WRITINGS: Unannotated Bibliography of Kore, Amok, and Latah, with Primary Emphasis on Southeast Asia (Excluding the Philippines), Emory University, 1957; (editor) Communication and Culture: Readings in the Codes of Human Interaction, Holt, 1966; Communication and Status: The Dynamics of a Research Center (monograph), Center for the Advanced Study of Educational Administration, University of Oregon, 1966; (contributor) Communication: Concepts and Perspectives, Thayer, 1967; Perspectives on Communication, Larsen & Dance, 1968; Managerial Control Through Communication, Vardaman & Halterman, 1968. Language books, all published by Department of Education, Trust Territory of Pacific Islands: Gamwoelhaelhi ishilh Weleeya (guide to Woleai spelling), 1951, reissued in Selected Micronesian Publications (see below); Ki luwn specl Kosray (Kusaien phonemics, orthography, and toponymy), 1951, reissued in Selected Micronesian Publications (see below); Wahween jibehhleh kajin Marshall (guide to Marshallese spelling), 1951, reissued in Selected Micronesian Publications (see below); Selected Micronesian Publications, Volume 1: Gamwoelhaelhi ishilh Weleeya: Guide to Woleai Spelling, Volume 2: Ki luwn specl Kosray: Kusaien Phonemics, Orthography, and Toponymy, Volume 3: Wahween jibehhleh kajin Marshall: Guide to Marshallese Spelling, Volume 4: A Guide to Trukese Spelling, Volume 5: A Tentative Guide to Writing Kapingamarangian: Ngangahihi o Kapingi, Volume 6: Pinoaw koa pii sukuul: A Yapese Reader, Volume 7: When Wone Played Ronkiti: English Reader for Ponapeans, 1961. Contributor of articles to anthropological journals.

WORK IN PROGRESS: A book, The Communicators.

BIOGRAPHICAL/CRITICAL SOURCES: R. Jean Hills, A Secondary Analysis of "Communication and Status: The Dynamics of a Research Center", Center for Advanced Study of Educational Administration, University of Oregon, 1966.

*   *   *

SMITH, Anthony John Francis 1926-

PERSONAL: Born March 30, 1926, in Maidenhead, England; son of Hubert J.F. (a land agent) and Diana (Watkin) Smith; married Barbara Dorothy Newman (a journalist and economist), September 1, 1956. Education: Attended Blundell's School; Balliol College, Oxford, M.A., 1951. Home: 7 Elsworthy Ter., London N.W. 3, England. Agent: Curtis Brown Ltd., 13 King St., London W.C. 2, England.

CAREER: Guardian, Manchester, England, reporter, 1953, 1956-57; Drum, West Africa, general manager, 1954-55; Daily Telegraph, London, England, science edi-

tor, 1957-63; now free-lance writer. Broadcasts include some four hundred radio programs, twenty on television. Military service: Royal Air Force, four years. Member: Association of British Science Writers.

WRITINGS: Blind White Fish in Persia, Dutton, 1953; Sea Never Dry, Allen & Unwin, 1958; High Street Africa, Allen & Unwin, 1961; Jambo: African Balloon Safari, Dutton, 1963 (published in England as Throw Out Two Hands, Allen & Unwin, 1963); The Body, Walker, 1968, 2nd edition, Allen & Unwin, 1970; The Seasons: Life and Its Rhythms, Harcourt, 1970 (published in England as The Seasons: Rhythms of Life, Cycles of Change, Weidenfeld & Nicolson, 1970); The Dangerous Sort: The Story of a Balloon, Allen & Unwin, 1970. Contributor of articles to magazines, including Saturday Evening Post and New Scientist. Writer of commentary for television films, notably "Balloon Over Africa" series.

SIDELIGHTS: Smith has traveled widely in about forty countries, and uses his experiences abroad as background for his books.

Kestrel Productions produced a film version of The Body in 1969.

BIOGRAPHICAL/CRITICAL SOURCES: Book World, June 16, 1968; New York Times Book Review, October 20, 1968.

*   *   *

SMITH, Dean E(llis) 1923-

PERSONAL: Born April 3, 1923, in Salina, Kans.; son of L.L. (a hardware dealer) and Kathryn O. (Combs) Smith; married Betty Clark, June 17, 1947; children: Kathy, Karen, Clark, Kelly. Education: Arizona State University, B.S., 1947. Politics: Republican. Religion: Methodist. Home: 6737 East Monte Vista Rd., Scottsdale, Ariz. 85257. Agent: Donald MacCampbell, Inc., 12 East 41st St., New York, N.Y. 10017. Office: Arizona State University, Tempe, Ariz. 85281.

CAREER: Former newspaperman, editor, free-lance writer; Arizona State University, Tempe, director of publications, 1959—. Military service: U.S. Air Force Reserve, 1943—, currently reserve liaison officer for U.S. Air Force Academy, with rank of major. Member: American College Public Relations Association, Phoenix Press Box Association (president, 1957).

WRITINGS: (with Rob Wood) Barry Goldwater: The Biography of a Conservative, Avon, 1961; Conservatism, Avon, 1963; (editor) Grady Grammage Memorial Auditorium, Bureau of Publications, Arizona State University, 1964. Contributor to Arizona Republic.

WORK IN PROGRESS: The Babbitts of Arizona, history of a leading business and ranching family.

AVOCATIONAL INTERESTS: Sports and history.

*   *   *

SMITH, Donald Eugene 1927-

PERSONAL: Born September 1, 1927, in Phoenixville, Pa.; son of George J. and Anna (Loux) Smith; married Violet Ramanjulu, July 1, 1950. Education: Eastern Baptist Theological Seminary, B.A., Th.B., 1951, B.D., 1953; University of Pennsylvania, M.A., 1953, Ph.D., 1956. Home: 740 Red Oak Ter., Wayne, Pa. 19087. Office: Department of Political Science, University of Pennsylvania, Philadelphia, Pa. 19104.

CAREER: University of Pennsylvania, Philadelphia, instructor in political science, 1955-56; University of Rhode Island, Kingston, instructor, 1956-57, assistant professor, 1957-62, associate professor of political science, 1962-64; University of Pennsylvania, Philadelphia, associate professor of political science, 1964—. Council on Religion and International Affairs, director of research project, "Religion and the State in Southern Asia," with Carnegie Corporation grant. *Member:* American Political Science Association, Association for Asian Studies. *Awards, honors:* Fulbright fellowship to India, 1954-55; senior research grant in India, 1960-61; Social Science Research Council grant for research in Latin America, 1968; senior specialist grant, East-West Center, Hawaii, 1969-70.

WRITINGS: Nehru and Democracy: The Political Thought of an Asian Democrat, Orient Longmans (Bombay), 1958; *India as a Secular State,* Princeton University Press, 1963; *Religion and Politics in Burma,* Princeton University Press, 1965; (editor and contributor) *South Asian Politics and Religion,* Princeton University Press, 1966; *Religion and Political Development: An Analytic Study,* Little, Brown, 1970; (editor and author of introductory notes) *Religion, Politics, and Social Change in the Third World: A Sourcebook,* Free Press, 1971.

* * *

SMITH, Frank Seymour 1898-

PERSONAL: Born November 22, 1898, in London, England; married Marjorie Harris (a writer under pseudonym Elena Fearn); children: Martin Seymour-Smith. *Education:* Birkbeck College, London, student, 1919; Library Association, diploma (with honors), 1928. *Home:* Rose Cottage, 43 St. Johns Rd., Bexhill, Sussex, England. *Office:* Head Office, W.H. Smith & Son Ltd., Strand House, London W.C. 2, England.

CAREER: Borough of Finchley, Middlesex, England, chief librarian, 1937-49; W.H. Smith & Son Ltd. (booksellers), London, England, editor and bibliographer, 1950—. British Ministry of Food, officer for Finchley, Middlesex, England, 1939-43. Book selector for UNESCO, 1945-46; broadcaster of series of book talks for British Services abroad, 1951-61. Cultural lecturer for British Foreign Office, 1949. *Military service:* Royal Air Force, 1917-19; became cadet sergeant. *Member:* Society of Authors and Art Theatre Club (both London).

WRITINGS: The Classics in Translation: An Annotated Guide to the Best Translations of the Greek and Latin Classics into English, Scribner, 1930, B. Franklin, 1968; *The English Classics,* National Book League, 1941; *An English Library: An Annotated List of 1300 Classics,* published for National Book League by Cambridge University Press, 1943, 4th edition published as *An English Library: an Annotated List of Classics and Standard Books,* 1950, 5th edition, revised and enlarged, published as *An English Library: A Bookman's Guide,* Deutsch, 1963; *Pamphlet Bibliographies: A Reader's Guide,* published for National Book League by Cambridge University Press, 1948; *What Shall I Read Next?: A Personal Selection of Twentieth-Century English Books,* published for National Book League by Cambridge University Press, 1953; *Know-How Books: An Annotated Bibliography of Do It Yourself Books for the Handyman and of Introductions to Science, Art, History and Literature for the Beginner and Home Student,* Thames & Hudson, 1956, Bowker, 1957; *Bibliography in the Bookshop,* Deutsch, 1964, revised edition, 1971; *Progress in Library Science,* Butterworth & Co., 1966; (with Frederick Thomas Bell) *Library Bookselling: A History and Handbook of Current Practice,* Deutsch, 1966; *A Treasury of Wit and Wisdom,* John Baker, 1966; *The Writer in the Market Place: A Symposium,* Clive Bingley, 1969; *Build Your Own Library,* Wolfe Publishing, 1970. Also author of project book, *Write Your Own Novel,* c.1970. Contributor of articles to *British Book News, Aryan Path,* and to trade periodicals. Editor of library reports, and of *Book Window,* 1952-57.

SIDELIGHTS: Smith told *CA* he is a "Philhellene; and next to that a Francophile (ante De Gaulle era); all vacations have been spent in Greece and France, in that order. . . . Enjoy footpath walking, which one can still get in Greece and Sussex; enjoy good conversation in clubs and British pubs, but this is now disappearing—many people will talk, but few know how to converse; enjoy good wine . . . loathe noise and crowds, that is why I live in Sussex by the sea in an old cottage."

* * *

SMITH, G(eorge) E(verard) Kidder 1913-

PERSONAL: Born October 1, 1913, in Birmingham, Ala.; son of F. Hopkinson (a certified public accountant) and Anne (Kidder) Smith; married Dorothea F. Wilder, August 22, 1942; children: G.E. Kidder, Jr., Hopkinson K. *Education:* Princeton University, A.B., 1935, M.F.A., 1938. *Politics:* Independent. *Religion:* Episcopalian. *Home and office:* 163 East 81st St., New York, N.Y. 10028.

CAREER: Architect, Princeton Expedition to Antioch, Syria, 1938; designer and camofleur for Army bases in Caribbean, 1940-42; architect in private practice, 1946—. Critic at Yale University School of Architecture, 1948-49; visiting professor at Massachusetts Institute of Technology, 1955-56; visiting lecturer at universities and museums throughout the United States. His photographs appear in collection of Museum of Modern Art; organizer of exhibits on architecture in this country and abroad. Member of commission on architecture, National Council of Churches. *Military service:* U.S. Naval Reserve, Bureau of Yards and Docks, 1942-46; became lieutenant.

MEMBER: International Institute of Arts and Letters (Switzerland; life fellow), American Institute of Architects (fellow), American Association of Architectural Bibliographers, Society of Architectural Historians, College Art Association, Association of Collegiate Schools of Architecture, Municipal Art Society, Century Association, Princeton Club, Church Club, Badminton Club, Cooperstown Country Club. *Awards, honors:* American-Scandinavian Foundation fellow, 1939-40; Order of Southern Cross from Brazilian Government, 1943, for *Brazil Builds;* Guggenheim fellow, 1946-47; President's fellow of Brown University, 1949-50; Fulbright fellow (research) in Italy, 1950-51, in India, 1965-66; ENIT Gold medal for best book of the year on Italy from Italian Government, 1956, for *Italy Builds;* A.W. Brunner fellow, 1959-60; Gold medal for architectural photography, American Institute of Architects, 1963; Graham Foundation for Advancement of the Arts and National Council on the Arts joint fellowship, 1967-69. National Council on the Arts fellow, 1970-71; Ford Foundation grant, 1971-72.

WRITINGS: (With P.L. Goodwin) *Brazil Builds,* Museum of Modern Art, 1943; *Switzerland Builds,* Albert Bonnier, 1950; *Sweden Builds,* Albert Bonnier, 1950, revised edition, Reinhold, 1957; *Italy Builds,* Reinhold, 1955; *The New Architecture of Europe,* Meridian, 1961; *The New Churches of Europe,* Holt, 1964. Contributor of articles to architectural journals, and to *Encyclopaedia Britannica* and *New Catholic Encyclopedia.*

* * *

SMITH, Godfrey 1926-

PERSONAL: Born May 12, 1926, in London, England; son of Reginald Montague Smith; married Mary Schoenfeld, June 23, 1951; children: Deborah, Amanda, Candida. *Education:* Worcester College, Oxford, M.A. *Politics:* Radical. *Religion:* Agnostic. *Home:* 6 Abbey Gardens, London N.W.8, England. *Agent:* Curtis Brown Ltd.,

13 King St., Covent Garden, London W.C.2, England
Office: Sunday Times, London W.C.1, England.

CAREER: Sunday Times, London, England, 1951—, editor of Sunday Times Magazine, 1965—. Military service: Royal Air Force, 1944-47. Member: Oxford Union Society (president, 1950); Savile Club and Map Collectors Circle (both London).

WRITINGS—All novels: The Flaw in the Crystal, Putnam, 1954; The Friends, Gollancz, 1957, Stein & Day, 1968; The Business of Loving (Book Society choice), Gollancz, 1961, Stein & Day, 1968; The Network, Hodder & Stoughton, 1965. Contributor to New York Times.

WORK IN PROGRESS: A novel, Leila, for Hodder & Stoughton.

BIOGRAPHICAL/CRITICAL SOURCES: Christian Science Monitor, February 1, 1968; New York Times Book Review, September 29, 1968; Best Sellers, November 1, 1968.

*   *   *

SMITH, John H(azel) 1928-

PERSONAL: Born January 9, 1928, in Harrisburg, Ill.; son of Hartley Wilkins (a coal miner) and Pearl (Hazel) Smith; married Mary Jean Fox, August 18, 1951; children: Janet Ann, Kevin Thomas, David Ian. Education: University of Illinois, A.B., 1949, M.A., 1951, Ph.D., 1957. Religion: Roman Catholic. Home: 122 Concord St., Newton Lower Falls, Mass. 02162. Office: 209 Rabb, Brandeis University, Waltham, Mass. 02154.

CAREER: Wayne State University, Detroit, Mich., instructor in English, 1957-61; Marquette University, Milwaukee, Wis., assistant professor, 1961-64, associate professor of English, 1964-66; Brandeis University, Waltham, Mass., visiting associate professor, 1965-66, associate professor, 1966-70, professor of English, 1970—. University of Illinois, Urbana, visiting professor, 1969. Member: Renaissance Society of America, Shakespeare Association, Malone Society, American Association of University Professors (chapter president, 1964-65). Awards, honors: Huntington Library fellow, 1964; John Simon Guggenheim fellow, 1966-67; American Council of Learned Societies grant, 1969.

WRITINGS: (translator and author of critical study) A Humanist's "Trew Imitation": Thomas Watson's Absalom, University of Illinois Press, 1964; The Comedy of Errors: A Scene-by-Scene Analysis with Critical Commentary, American R.D.M. Corp., 1966; (editor) George Chapman, The Gentleman Usher, University of Nebraska Press, 1970.

WORK IN PROGRESS: Editing George Chapman's The Revenge of Bussy D'Ambois; editing and translating Two Latin Comedies by John Foxe the Martyrologist, to be published by Cornell University Press and Renaissance Society of America.

*   *   *

SMITH, R(ichard) A(lbert) N(ewton) 1908-

PERSONAL: Born April 4, 1908, in Glasgow, Scotland; son of Richard Staines and Myra (Newton) Smith; married Ellen Paterson Hanley, July 27, 1932; children: Eric Murray, Norma Myra Smith Kenmure, Alan Ian Scott. Education: Scottish College of Commerce, diploma, 1928; Jordanhill Teachers' Training College, Glasgow, Scotland, teacher's technical certificate, 1928. Politics: Independent. Religion: Protestant. Home: Lynton, Riverside Rd., Eaglesham, Glasgow, Scotland.

CAREER: Shawlands Academy, Glasgow, Scotland, principal of commerce department, 1952—; Scottish Instructional Films Ltd., Eaglesham, Glasgow, Scotland,

managing director, 1937—; examiner and assessor in bookkeeping, Glasgow Corp. Further Education Department, 1947—. Justice of the peace, Renfrewshire; councilor, Renfrewshire First District Council, 1949—; Renfrewshire County councilor, 1955—. Vice-chairman, Eaglesham Joint Restoration Committee, 1955—.

WRITINGS: Modern Typewriting, Gregg, 1948, revised edition, Cassell, 1955; The Loop Film, Current Affairs, 1953. Author and producer of sports coaching films.

WORK IN PROGRESS: A testbook on bookkeeping for ordinary, higher, and advanced levels, for Scottish Education Department examinations.†

*   *   *

SMITH, Robert Dickie 1928-

PERSONAL: Born August 13, 1928, in Framingham, Mass.; son of Richard E. and Doris (Dickie) Smith. Education: Harvard University, A.B., 1949; St. John's Seminary, Brighton, Mass., seminarian, 1950-56. Home: 43 Sycamore Rd., South Weymouth, Mass. 02190.

CAREER: Chatham (Mass.) High School, mathematics teacher, 1949-50; ordained Roman Catholic priest, 1956; St. Catherine of Siena Parish, Charlestown, Mass., assistant pastor, 1956—.

WRITINGS: The Mark of Holiness, Newman, 1961; Comparative Miracles, Herder, 1965.

WORK IN PROGRESS: Christian Elegance, an explanation of Christian spirituality "in terms of the word elegance, rather than tired ones like perfection or sanctity"; Jane Austen and the Christian Novel, a study of "the art of writing that rarest of art forms: the Christian novel."

*   *   *

SMYTH, R(obert) L(eslie) 1922-

PERSONAL: Born December 31, 1922, in Belfast, Northern Ireland; son of Samuel (a medical practitioner) and Mary (Thompson) Smyth; married Mary E. Pyper (a social worker), September, 1951; children: Moya Cathleen, Sean Michael. Education: Queen's University, Belfast, Northern Ireland, B.(Com.) Sc., (with honors), 1951. Politics: Labour. Home: 17 Ranger Rd., Mount Yokine, Perth, West Australia.

CAREER: Queen's University, Belfast, Northern Ireland, assistant lecturer in economics, 1951-52; University of Hull, Hull, England, lecturer in economics, 1952-59; University of Keele, Keele, England, lecturer in economics, 1960-63; University of Western Australia, Nedlands, senior lecturer in commerce, 1964—. Member: British Association for Advancement of Science (recorder, economics section, 1960-64).

WRITINGS: The Distribution of Fruit and Vegetables, Duckworth, 1959; Economics: Reader's Guide, published for National Book League by Cambridge University Press, 1960; (editor) Essays in Economic Method (selected papers), Duckworth, 1962, Fernhill, 1962; (editor) Essays in the Economics of Socialism and Capitalism (selected papers), Duckworth, 1964, Fernhill, 1964; (editor) Economic Growth in Western Australia, Economic Society of Australia and New Zealand, Western Australia Branch, 1964; (with D.H. Briggs) Distribution of Groceries: Economic Aspects of the Distribution of Groceries with Special Reference to Western Australia, University of Western Australia Press, 1967; (with D.J. Machin) The Changing Structure of the British Pottery Industry, 1935-1968, Department of Economics, University of Keele, c.1969; (compiler) Essays in Modern Economic Development (selected papers), Duckworth, 1969, Fernhill, 1970; (with Hugh Macdiarmid) Exports of Pottery from the United Kingdom, 1948-68, University of Keele Library, 1970. Contributor to economics journals.

Consultant economic editor, *World Encyclopedia,* Commonwealth edition.

WORK IN PROGRESS: Investigating aspects of Australian economy.

AVOCATIONAL INTERESTS: Pre-1935 jazz records; painting landscapes in oils with a breadknife.

*   *   *

SMYTHE, Hugh H(eyne)   1913-

PERSONAL: Born August 19, 1913, in Pittsburgh, Pa.; son of William Henry and Mary Elizabeth (Barnhardt) Smythe; married Mabel Hancock Murphy, 1939; children: Karen Pamela. *Education:* Virginia State College, A.B., 1936; Atlanta University, M.A., 1937; Fisk University, special fellow, 1937-38, graduate study, 1938-39; University of Chicago, graduate study, 1940; Northwestern University, Ph.D., 1945; Columbia University, postgraduate study, 1950-51. *Home:* 345 Eighth Avenue, New York, N.Y. 10001. *Office:* Department of Sociology, Brooklyn College of the City University of New York, Brooklyn, N.Y. 11210.

CAREER: Instructor, administrative assistant, and researcher at various colleges and organizations in Atlanta, Ga., and Nashville, Tenn., 1937-42; Morris Brown College, Atlanta, Ga., professor, 1944; Negro Land Grant Colleges project for cooperative social studies, assistant coordinator, 1944; Tennessee State College (now Tennessee Agricultural and Industrial State University), Nashville, professor, 1945-46; W.B. Graham & Associates (public relations and advertising), New York, N.Y., director of research, 1949-50; National Association for the Advancement of Colored People, New York, assistant director, department of special research, national office, 1947-49; Yamaguchi National University, Yamaguchi, Japan, visiting professor, 1951-53; Brooklyn College (now Brooklyn College of the City University of New York), Brooklyn, N.Y., associate professor, 1953-60, professor of sociology, 1962-63; special lecturer for Foreign Service Institute of U.S. State Department, 1960-65, for Special Forces, U.S. Army, Fort Bragg, N.C., 1964; examiner on New York State Civil Service Commission Panel of Examiners, 1961-65; senior adviser to several United Nations committees, New York, N.Y., 1961-62; senior U.S. adviser to National Research Council of Thailand, and Fulbright professor at Chulalongkorn University, Bangkok, Thailand, 1963-64; U.S. Ambassador to Syria, 1965-67; U.S. Ambassador to Malta, 1967-69; Brooklyn College of the City University of New York, professor in sociology department, 1969—. Director of research, New York State Commission Against Discrimination, 1956; chief consultant, Youth in Action, Poverty Program in Brooklyn, N.Y., 1965. Consultant to many organizations; trustee, Luther College. *Military service:* U.S. Army, 1943.

MEMBER: American Anthropological Association (fellow), Society for Applied Anthropology (fellow), United Nations Association of U.S.A. (member of board of directors, 1970), United Service Organization (member of board of directors and executive committee, 1971—), American Foreign Service Association (life member), Atlantic Council, Institute of Race Relations of Great Britain, American Civil Liberties Union, National Association for the Advancement of Colored People, National Urban League, Committee for Democratic Institutions, American Association of University Professors, Holy Land Center (board member), Near East Foundation (member of board and executive committee, 1971—), Middle East Institute, Arab-Israeli Research and Relations Project of the Fund for Peace (member of board and executive committee, 1971—), Eastern Sociological Society, Association for Asian Studies, American Associa-

tion of Teachers of Chinese Language and Culture, Siam Society, Washington Task Force on Africa, African Studies Association (fellow; board member, 1962-65), African-American Scholars Council (board member), American Committee on Africa (executive board member, 1954-65), African Student Aid Fund (secretary, 1970—), Operation Crossroads Africa (vice-chairman, board member, and executive committee member, 1957—), Museum of African Art (Washington, D.C.; board member, 1963—), Sigma Xi, Iota Sigma Lambda, Alpha Pi Zeta, Alpha Kappa Delta, Alpha Phi Alpha, Malta-U.S. Alumni Association.

AWARDS, HONORS: Scholarships or fellowships from Harriet M. Strong Foundation, 1935-37, Atlanta University, 1936-37, 1942, Ford Foundation, 1957-58; Rosenwald fellow, 1939-41; grants from American Council of Learned Societies, 1940 and 1962, American Friends Service Committee, 1950, Social Science Research Council, 1960; British Colonial Office award, 1948; Distinguished Alumni Award, Virginia State College, 1958; Delta Tau Kappa International Social Science Society award for distinguished work in the field of social science, 1967; diploma, International Institute JVEK, Germany, for contributions to better human relations and world peace, 1968; Knight of the Grand Cross of the Royal Crown of Crete, 1968; LL.D., Virginia State College, 1968; Knight of the Grand Cross of the Sovereign Military Order of Saint Agatha, 1969.

WRITINGS: (With W.E.B. DuBois) *Negro Land Grant Colleges Social Study Project: A Report,* Atlanta University, 1944; (with Michael M. Davis) *Providing Adequate Health Service to Negroes* (pamphlet), Committee on Medical Economics, 1949; (with wife, Mabel M. Smythe) *The New Nigerian Elite,* Stanford University Press, 1960; (with M.M. Smythe) *Subgroups of the New Nigerian Elite,* Duquesne University Press, 1960; (with Lester D. Crow and Walter I. Murray) *Educating the Culturally Disadvantaged Child: Principles and Programs,* McKay, 1966.

Contributor: Joseph S. Roucek and others, editors, *Contemporary Social Science,* Volume II, Stackpole, 1954; James H. Robinson, editor, *Love of this Land: Progress of the Negro in the United States,* Christian Education Press, 1954; Joseph S. Roucek, editor, *Social Control,* Van Nostrand, 1956; Joseph S. Roucek, editor, *Contemporary Sociology,* Philosophical Library, 1958; J.A. Davis, editor, *Africa as Seen by American Negroes,* Presence Africaine (Paris), 1958; Anne O'H. Williamson, editor, *Dawn in the Dark Continent: Politics, Problems, Promises,* Central State College, 1960; *Afrika Heute* (edited by staff of Deutschen Afrika Gesellschaft), Verlag Deutscher Wirtschaftsdienst (Frankfurt), 1960; Joseph S. Roucek, editor, *Readings in Contemporary American Sociology,* Littlefield, 1961; J.H. Durston and N.J. Meiklejohn, editors, *International Cooperation and Problems of Transfer and Adaptation,* Agency for International Development, 1963; H.N. Weiler, editor, *Education and Politics in Nigeria,* Verlag Rombach (Freiburg), 1964; S.L. Wormley and L.H. Fenderson, editors, *Many Shades of Black,* Morrow, 1969; Helen MacGill Hughes, editor, *Racial and Ethnic Relations,* Allyn & Bacon, 1970; Michael Curtis, editor, *The Middle East: People and Politics,* Transaction Books, 1971; C.A.O. van Nieuwenhuijze, *Development: The Western View,* Mouton, 1972. Contributor of hundreds of articles to professional journals and general publications, principally on African and Asian countries, especially Japan. United Nations correspondent for *Eastern World* and *Africa Trade and Development;* member of editorial board of *Africa Today, Journal of Human Relations,* and *Sociological Abstracts.*

WORK IN PROGRESS: A study of second and third generation elites in contemporary Africa; continuing research on: world minorities and race relations in world perspective; the foreign policy of new African nations; African leadership with special emphasis on East Africa; the educational foundation of modern African politicians; general problems related to African affairs; problems of the Middle East; intergroup conflict in Israel; racism in the U.S.A. and its impact on American foreign policy; Japanese-American relations; institutionalism and social change in the developing nations; urbanization and its effect on under-developed areas of the world; developments in Southeast Asia; examination of U.S. foreign policies and programs on the international scene.

SIDELIGHTS: Smythe was a member of the United States Delegation to the 16th session of the United Nations General Assembly, and to various commissions of the United Nations. He has done much research in the field of race relations and international affairs, has given many lectures both in universities and elsewhere, and has spoken on radio and television.

* * *

SNAPE, H(enry) Currie 1902-

PERSONAL: Born May 16, 1902, in Swinton, Lancashire, England; son of Walter Bertram (a manufacturing stationer) and Eliza Dorning (Wilson) Snape; married Joyce Mary Cuthbertson, July 31, 1934; children: Anne Currie, John Michael Walter. *Education:* Shrewsbury School, student, 1917-20; Corpus Christi College, Oxford, B.A., 1924, M.A., 1931, Diploma in Theology, 1932; Cambridge University, Certificate in Education, 1944. *Politics:* Independent. *Home:* Corner House, Bampton, Oxford, England.

CAREER: Clergyman, Church of England; vicar of Whalley, Lancashire, England, 1951-67. *Member:* Author's Club (London).

WRITINGS: (Translator from the French) Maurice Goguel, *The Birth of Christianity,* Allen & Unwin, 1953; (translator) M. Goguel, *The Primitive Church,* Macmillan, 1964. Contributor of articles and reviews to *Modern Churchman, Hibbert Journal, Harvard Theological Review,* and *Numen.* Assistant editor, *Modern Churchman.*

AVOCATIONAL INTERESTS: Music and travel.

* * *

SNELLGROVE, L(aurence) E(rnest) 1928-

PERSONAL: Born February 2, 1928, in Woolwich, London, England; son of Ernest George and Emily (Wren) Snellgrove; married Jean Hall, April 5, 1951; children: Peter Laurence. *Education:* Culham College, teacher's certificate, associate of College of Preceptor, 1953. *Religion:* Church of England. *Home:* 2 Hackenden Close, East Grinstead, Sussex, England.

CAREER: Assistant master at Rose Hill School, Oxford, England, 1950-53, Cheshunt County Secondary School, Hertfordshire, England, 1953-55, Yaxley School, Huntingdonshire, England, 1955-57; Caterham Valley County Secondary School, Surrey, England, head of history department, 1957-66; de Stafford Comprehensive School, Caterham, Surrey, head of history department, 1966—. *Military service:* Royal Air Force, 1945-48; became leading aircraftsman. *Member:* National Association of Schoolmasters, Society of Local Yokels (chairman, 1951-52).

WRITINGS: From Kitty Hawk to Outer Space, Longmans, Green, 1960; *From Steam Carts to Minicars,* Longmans, Green, 1961; *From Coracles to Cunarders,* Longmans, Green, 1962; *From 'Rocket' to Railcar,* Longmans, Green, 1963; *Suffragettes and Votes for Women,* Longmans, Green, 1964; *Franco and the Spanish Civil War,* Longmans, Green, 1965, McGraw, 1968; *The Modern World Since 1870,* Longmans, Green, 1968; (with Richard J. Cootes) *The Ancient World,* Longmans, Green, 1970. Occasional contributor of articles to *Times Educational Supplement,* and *New Schoolmaster.*

WORK IN PROGRESS: A book on European-British history, 1453-1725, *The Early Modern Age.*

AVOCATIONAL INTERESTS: Music, theatre, tennis, swimming, and sitting in deckchair during short English summer.

* * *

SNOW, Edward Rowe 1902-

PERSONAL: Born August 22, 1902; son of Edward Sumpter and Alice (Rowe) Snow; married Anna-Myrle Haegg, July 8, 1932; children: Dorothy Caroline. *Education:* Harvard University, B.A., 1932; Boston University, M.A., 1939. *Politics:* Republican. *Religion:* Congregationalist. *Home:* 550 Summer St., Marshfield, Mass. 02050. *Office:* Patriot Ledger, Temple St., Quincy, Mass. 02169.

CAREER: High school teacher in Winthrop, Mass., 1932-36; free-lance writer, 1946—. Daily columnist, *Patriot Ledger,* Quincy, Mass., 1957—. Lecturer, making more than five thousand appearances in New England and eastern states; television and radio speaker, mainly on Boston stations. *Military service:* U.S. Air Force, 12th Bomber Command; wounded in 1942; became first lieutenant. *Member:* Explorers Club, Boston Marine Society. *Awards, honors:* Boys' Clubs of America Junior Book award, 1953, for *True Tales of Buried Treasure.*

WRITINGS: Castle Island, Andover Press, 1935; *The Islands of Boston Harbor,* Andover Press, 1935, revised edition published as *The Islands of Boston Harbor, 1630-1971,* Dodd, 1971; *The Story of Minot's Light,* Yankee Publishing, 1940; *Historic Fort Warren,* Yankee Publishing, 1941; *Sailing Down Boston Bay,* Yankee Publishing, 1941; *The Rise and Fall of the Boston Market,* Yankee Publishing, 1942; *Great Storms and Famous Shipwrecks of the New England Coast,* Yankee Publishing, 1943; *Pirates and Buccaneers of the Atlantic Coast,* Yankee Publishing, 1944; *The Romance of Boston Bay,* Yankee Publishing, 1944; *Winthrop by the Sea,* Boston Printing, 1945; *Famous New England Lighthouses,* Yankee Publishing, 1945; *Cruising the Massachusetts Coast,* Yankee Publishing, 1945; *A Pilgrim Returns to Cape Cod,* Yankee Publishing, 1946; *Searching for Treasure,* Yankee Publishing, 1947; *South Shore to Cape Cod by Canoe,* Yankee Publishing, 1948; *Mysteries and Adventures Along the Atlantic Coast,* Dodd, 1948; *True Adventure Tales,* Yankee Publishing, from Nova Scotia to Cape Hatteras, Dodd, 1949.

Secrets of the North Atlantic Islands, Dodd, 1950; *A Century of the Boston Y.M.C.U.,* privately printed, 1951; *The Mayflower, Plymouth Rock and the Pilgrims,* Dodd, 1951; *True Tales of Buried Treasure,* Dodd, 1951, revised edition, 1960; *Forgotten Sea Tragedies,* Dodd, 1952; *Great Gales and Dire Disasters,* Dodd, 1952; *True Tales of Pirates and Their Gold,* Dodd, 1953; *Amazing Sea Stories Never Told Before,* Dodd, 1954; *Famous Lighthouses of America,* Dodd, 1955; *Lighthouse Date Book,* Dodd, 1956; *The Vengeful Sea,* Dodd, 1956; *New England Sea Drama,* 1956; *Legends of the New England* 1949; *Exploring the Rim,* Dodd, 1949; *Strange Tales Coast,* Dodd, 1957; *Great Sea Rescues, and Tales of Survival,* Dodd, 1958; *Beacons of New England,* Dodd, 1958; *Exploring Boston Bay,* Dodd, 1959; *Piracy, Mutiny, and Murder,* Dodd, 1959; *Down Massachusetts Bay,* Dodd, 1959.

New England Sea Tragedies, Dodd, 1960; *Nautical Engagement Calender* Dodd, 1960; *New England Coast in Maps and Stories,* Dodd, 1961; *Mysterious Tales of the New England Coast,* Dodd, 1961 (published in England as *Tales of the Atlantic Coast,* Redman, 1963); *Women of the Sea,* Dodd, 1962; *True Tales of Terrible Shipwrecks,* Dodd, 1963; *Unsolved Mysteries of Sea and Shore,* Dodd, 1963; *The Fury of the Sea,* Dodd, 1964; *Astounding Tales of the Sea,* Dodd, 1965; *Tales of Sea and Shore,* Dodd, 1966; *Incredible Mysteries and Legends of the Sea,* Dodd, 1967; *Fantastic Folklore and Fact: New England Tales of Land and Sea,* Dodd, 1968; *True Tales and Curious Legends: Dramatic Stories from the Yankee Past,* Dodd, 1969; *Great Atlantic Adventures,* Dodd, 1970; *Ghost, Gales and Gold,* Dodd, 1972.

WORK IN PROGRESS: The Story of Casco Bay; Romantic, Chronological, and Mysterious Boston.

BIOGRAPHICAL/CRITICAL SOURCES: Best Sellers, January 1, 1970.†

* * *

SNOW, Philip Albert 1915-

PERSONAL: Born August 7, 1915, in Leicester, England; son of William Edward (an organist) and Ada Sophia (Robinson) Snow; married Mary Anne Harris, May 2, 1940; children: Stephanie Dale Vuikamba. *Education:* Christ's College, Cambridge University, B.A., 1937, M.A., 1940. *Home:* Horton House, 6 Hillmorton Rd., Rugby, Warwickshire, England. *Office:* The Bursary, Barby Rd., Rugby, Warwickshire, England.

CAREER: Government of Fiji and Western Pacific, served variously as administrator, magistrate, and assistant colonial secretary, 1938-52; Rugby School, Warwickshire, England, bursar, 1952—; Justice of the Peace, Warwickshire, 1967—. Civil defence officer, Lautoka, Fiji, 1942; Fiji government liaison officer, U.S. and New Zealand military forces, 1942-44. Permanent representative, Fiji on International Cricket Conference, 1965—. Examiner for Cambridge and Oxford Universities on Pacific subjects. *Member:* Public Schools Bursars' Association of Great Britain, North Ireland, and Commonwealth (chairman, 1961-64), Royal Anthropological Institute (fellow), Marylebone Cricket Club. *Awards, honors:* Foreign Specialist award, U.S. Government, 1964, for *Visit to Schools and Universities in U.S.A. and Canada.*

WRITINGS: Civil Defence Services, Fiji Government Printer, 1942; (editor) *Fiji Civil Service Journal,* Fiji Government Printer, 1945; *Cricket in the Fiji Islands,* Whitcombe & Tombs, 1948; *Rock Carvings in Fiji,* Fiji Society, 1953; (contributor) *Cricket Heroes,* Phoenix Books, 1959; *Visit to Schools and Universities in U.S.A. and Canada,* Public Schools Bursars' Association of Great Britain, 1964; (contributor) E.W. Swanton and Michael Melford, editors, *The World of Cricket,* M. Joseph, 1966; (editor, author of introduction, and contributor) *Best Stories of the South Seas,* Faber, 1967; *A Bibliography of Fiji, Tonga, and Rotuma,* University of Miami Press, 1969; (author of introduction) George Palmer, *Kidnapping in the South Seas,* Fernhill, 1972; (author of introduction) B.C. Seeman, *Viti,* Dawsons of Pall Mall, 1972. Contributor to *The Far East and Australasia,* Europa, 1972, and to *Dictionary of National Biography.* Contributor of articles on the Pacific to *American Anthropologist, Journal of Polynesian Society, Discovery, Journal de la Societe des Oceanistes, Field, Sunday Times, Go, Daily Telegraph, Times Literary Supplement, Geographical Journal, Journal of Royal Anthropological Institute.*

SIDELIGHTS: The Hon. Philip Snow is the brother of C.P. Snow, the author and scholar, whose wife, Pamela Hansford Johnson, is also a writer. In 1948 he captained

the Fiji cricket team touring New Zealand, and organized celebrations for the 400th anniversary of Rugby School and visit from Queen Elizabeth and Prince Philip, in 1967.

BIOGRAPHICAL/CRITICAL SOURCES: J.W. Goldman, *Cricketers and the Law,* Hodgson, 1958; *School and College,* July, 1962; E.W. Swanton and Michael Melford, editors, *The World of Cricket,* M. Joseph, 1966.

* * *

SNOW, (Charles) Wilbert 1884-

PERSONAL: Born April 6, 1884, on White Head Island, St. George, Me.; son of Forrest Alvin (member of the Coast Guard) and Catherine (Quinn) Snow; married Jeannette Simmons, February 23, 1921; children: Charles W., Jr., John Forrest, Nicholas, Stephen (deceased), Gregory. *Education:* Bowdoin College, A.B., 1907; Columbia University, A.M., 1910. *Politics:* Democrat. *Religion:* Episcopalian. *Home:* 473 Newfield St., Middletown, Conn. 06457. *Office:* Wesleyan Station, Middletown, Conn. 06457.

CAREER: Instructor in English, New York University, New York, N.Y., 1907-08, Bowdoin College, Brunswick, Me., 1908-09, Williams College, Williamstown, Mass., 1909-10; reindeer agent and Eskimo teacher on Seward Peninsula, Alaska, 1911-12; University of Utah, Salt Lake City, instructor in English, 1913-15; Indiana University, Bloomington, instructor, 1916-18, assistant professor of English, 1919-21; Reed College, Portland, Ore., acting professor of English, 1918-19; Wesleyan University, Middletown, Conn., assistant professor, 1921-26, associate professor, 1926-29, professor of English, 1929—; lieutenant-governor of Connecticut, 1945-46, governor, 1946-47. State department lecturer in Europe and Near East, 1951-52. Member of Middletown, Conn., school board, and Democratic Town Committee. *Military service:* U.S. Army, Artillery, World War I; captain, U.S. Army Reserve. *Member:* Modern Language Association of America, Phi Beta Kappa, Beta Theta Pi. *Awards, honors:* M.A., Bowdoin College, 1925; LL.D., Wesleyan University, 1945; Litt.D., Marietta College, 1946; Doctor of Fine Arts, Nassau College; Doctor of Humane Letters, University of Maine.

WRITINGS—All poetry: Maine Coast, Harcourt, 1923; *Inner Harbor: More Maine Coast Poems,* Harcourt, 1926; *Down East,* Gotham, 1932; *Selected Poems,* Valentine Mitchell, 1936; *Before the Wind,* Gotham, 1938; *Maine Tides,* Holt, 1940; *Sonnets to Steve, and Other Poems,* Exposition, 1957; *Spruce Head: Selections from* [His] *Poetry,* Seth Low 1958; *The Collected Poems of Wilbert Snow,* Wesleyan University Press, 1963, second edition, 1973; *Autobiography,* Wesleyan University Press, 1973.

WORK IN PROGRESS: Two more books of poems; a book of prose.

SIDELIGHTS: As a poet involved with the mood and life of the Maine coast, Snow is acknowledged by many critics to be adept in conveying certain sensory experiences particular to that region of America. R.P.T. Coffin states that "Snow's substance is compounded of seeing many small bits of gear and weather and human nature day by day which add up to the amazing total of a science, and even a song, of living still to be found along the Maine seacoast." Coffin also believes that Snow's imagery is even more "impressive" because the poet sees his subjects "in perspective, at a good distance." John Fandel is impressed with the various forms Snow employs, "from the long story in verse to the brief lyric of a single image." Fandal adds: "In all, he sustains the form strictly, surely. One is aware of his force and his fine feeling. The vigor of his plain spoken awareness of life comes through directly."

Some critics believe that Snow's work deserves attention greater than that usually bestowed upon a strictly regional poet. Percy Hutchinson sees in Snow's writing a distinctively American quality which reflects the essential mood and experience of the nation's heritage. "Wilbert Snow . . . has advanced American poetry by making it more richly American without sacrifice of universality," Hutchinson maintains. "Though radios and automobiles, even if second-hand ones, transform outwardly the erstwhile humble centers of the world over, the sturdy, humble essentials of living still prevail, and will prevail, whatever changes may come. It is these essentials which Mr. Snow realizes in his poems. He tempts one to alter Keats and say simplicity is truth, truth simplicity."

BIOGRAPHICAL/CRITICAL SOURCES: New York Tribune, May 6, 1923; *Independent*, May 12, 1923; *Nation*, May 23, 1923, November 10, 1926; *Dial*, July, 1923; *Bookman*, August, 1923; *Freeman*, September 5, 1923; *Outlook*, November 24, 1926; *Saturday Review*, December 11, 1926, November 5, 1932, July 4, 1936, May 6, 1939; *Books*, November 20, 1932, February 12, 1939; *New York Times*, August 2, 1936, January 15, 1939; *Christian Science Monitor*, August 19, 1936; *Library Journal*, March 1, 1964; *Commonweal*, May 8, 1964.

* * *

SNYDER, Rachel 1924-

PERSONAL: Born February 12, 1924, in Topeka, Kan.; daughter of Otis F. (an agricultural inspector and researcher) and Lela (Retter) Snyder. *Education:* Washburn University, A.B., 1945. *Home:* 4200 Oxford Rd., Prairie Village, Kan. 66208. *Office: Flower and Garden,* 4251 Pennsylvania, Kansas City, Mo. 64111.

CAREER: Topeka Daily Capital, Topeka, Kan., reporter, 1943-46; UN Food and Agriculture Organization, Washington, D.C., informational writer, 1948-50; *Workbasket,* Kansas City, Mo., assistant editor, 1952-56; *Flower and Garden,* Kansas City, Mo., editor, 1956—. *Member:* Garden Writers Association of America (director, 1968), American Penstemon Society (Midwest chairman, 1962, 1963), American Horticultural Society, Theta Sigma Phi, Garden Center Association of Greater Kansas City (secretary, 1961-66; director), Kansas City Astronomy Club. *Awards, honors:* American Seed Trade Association award for garden writing, 1967.

WRITINGS: (Editor) *The Complete Book for Gardeners,* Van Nostrand, 1964.

AVOCATIONAL INTERESTS: Birds, wild flowers, and other phases of natural history, and photography.

* * *

SNYDER, Zilpha Keatley 1927-

PERSONAL: Born May 11, 1927, in Lemoore, Calif.; daughter of William Solon (a rancher and driller) and Dessa J. (Jepson) Keatley; married Larry Alan Snyder (a dean), June 18, 1950; children: Susan, Douglas, Ben (foster child). *Education:* Whittier College, B.A.; additional study at University of California, Berkeley. *Politics:* Democrat. *Religion:* Episcopalian. *Home:* 21 Hawthorne Ave., Larkspur, Calif. 94939.

CAREER: Public school teacher in California, New York, Washington, and Alaska, nine years; University of California, Berkeley, master teacher and demonstrator for education classes, 1959-61.

WRITINGS—All published by Atheneum: *Season of Ponies,* 1964, *The Velvet Room,* 1965, *Black and Blue Magic,* 1966, *The Egypt Game,* 1967, *Eyes in the Fish Bowl,* 1968, *Today Is Saturday* (poems), 1969, *The Changeling,* 1970, *The Headless Cupid,* 1971, *The Witches of Worm,* 1972.

SIDELIGHTS: "My teaching experience and my own children have been invaluable sources of inspiration and incentive. My own kids have also served constantly as both guinea pigs and critics and they have been very patient and conscientious in both roles."

BIOGRAPHICAL/CRITICAL SOURCES: New York Times Book Review, May 9, 1965, July 23, 1967, May 26, 1968; *Young Readers' Review,* May, 1966, May, 1967, May, 1968, October, 1969; *Book World,* December 3, 1967; *Christian Science Monitor,* February 29, 1968.†

* * *

SOFEN, Edward 1919-

PERSONAL: Born October 5, 1919, in Brooklyn, N.Y.; son of Gabriel and Gertrude (Lewin) Sofen; married Annette Tobb. *Education:* Brooklyn College (now Brooklyn College of the City University of New York) A.B. (cum laude), 1943; Columbia University, A.M., 1946, Ph.D., 1963. *Home:* 6781 S.W. 75th Ter., South Miami, Fla. 33143. *Office:* Department of Politics and Public Affairs, University of Miami, Coral Gables, Fla. 33124.

CAREER: University of Miami, Coral Gables, Fla., instructor, 1947-49, assistant professor, 1949-55, associate professor, 1955-64, professor of government, 1964—, also associate director of Center for Urban Studies. Consultant, Prince George's County Government Commission, 1966, Local Government Studies Commission, Metropolitan Dade County, 1971; associate of Ford Foundation research team, University of Miami, 1957-59; faculty fellow attached to office of mayor of San Diego, 1964-65. *Member:* Omicron Delta Kappa, Phi Kappa Alpha, Pi Sigma Alpha, Iron Arrow.

WRITINGS: Comparative Services and Expenditures in Dade County, University of Miami, 1960; *Comparative Basic Costs of Home Ownership in Dade County,* University of Miami, 1960; (with Thomas J. Wood) *Municipal Finance in Dade County,* University of Miami, 1961; *A Report on Politics in Greater Miami,* two volumes, Joint Center for Urban Studies of Massachusetts Institute of Technology and Harvard University, 1961; *The Miami Metropolitan Experiment,* Indiana University Press, 1963, revised edition published as *The Miami Metropolitan Experiment: A Metropolitan Action Study,* Doubleday-Anchor, 1966; (contributor) *Psycho-Social Dynamics in Greater Miami,* Center for Advanced International Studies, University of Miami, 1968. Contributor of articles and papers to *American Political Science Review, Midwest Journal of Political Science, University of Miami Law Quarterly, Wayne Law Review, Maryland Law Review, National Civic Review, Public Management,* and to *City Reports of the Joint Center for Urban Studies of MIT and Harvard University.*

* * *

SOHN, David A. 1929-

PERSONAL: Born November 28, 1929, in Columbus, Ind.; son of Albert Edward and Margaret (Crittenden) Sohn; married Elizabeth Manning, October 15, 1954; children: Matthew, Elizabeth, Jennifer, Andrew. *Education:* Wabash College, A.B., 1950; Indiana University, A.M., 1952. *Home:* 2333 Ridge Ave., Evanston, Ill. 60201.

CAREER: Middlesex Junior High School, Darien, Conn., instructor in English, 1952-67; School District 65, Evanston, Ill., curriculum consultant in language arts, 1968—. Yale University, New Haven, Conn., assistant supervisor of study skills, Study Skills Office, 1957-66. Bantam Books, Inc., chairman of board of consultants to Learning Units Division, and chief consultant in education. *Member:* International Reading Association, National Council of Teachers of English, National Education Association, National Reading Conference, College Reading Association, New England Reading Association, Connecticut Education Association.

WRITINGS—"Bantam Learning Unit Series": *How to Read, Study and Enjoy the Short Story*, 1963; *The Art of the Short Story*, 1963; (with Norman Fedde) *Improving Study Skills*, 1963; (with Nathan Lipofsky) *Focus on Youth: The Road to Maturity*, 1963; (with Lipofsky) *Youth and Challenge: Problems of Growing Up*, 1963; *Youth and Cars: Simulating Reading*, 1963; (with Gordon Hall) *The Civil War: Perspectives*, 1963; (with Lipofsky) *Success in Reading: A Remedial Program*, 1964; (with Fedde) *Readings for the College-Bound Student: Backgrounds in Human Action in Science and Social Studies*, 1964; (with Fedde) *Readings for the College-Bound Student: Backgrounds in Literature*, 1964.

Other books: (Editor with Alexander Butman and Donald Reis, and contributor) *Paperbacks in the Schools*, Bantam, 1963; (editor) *Great Tales of Horror by Poe*, Bantam, 1964; (editor with Alfred DeGrazia) *Programs, Teachers, and Machines*, Bantam, 1964; (editor with A. DeGrazia) *Revolution in Teaching: New Theory, Technology, and Curricula*, Bantam, 1964; (with Hart Day Leavitt) *Stop, Look and Write!*, Bantam, 1964; (editor) *Ten Top Stories*, Bantam, 1964; (editor) *Peppermint: Prize Winning Student Writing from the Scholastic Writing Awards*, Scholastic Book Services, 1965; (editor) *Ten Modern American Short Stories*, Bantam, 1965; (editor with Leavitt) *The Writer's Eye*, Bantam, 1966; (with Ralph Staiger) *New Directions in Reading*, Bantam, 1967; (with Richard Tyre) *Frost: The Poet and His Poetry*, Holt, 1967, special revised edition, 1969; *Film Study and the English Teacher*, Indiana University Audio-Visual Center, 1968; (editor with Melinda Stucker) *Film Study in the School: Grades Kindergarten through 8* (curriculum report), American Film Institute, 1968; *Pictures for Writing: A Visual Approach to Composition*, Bantam, 1969; *Film: The Creative Eye*, Pflaum, 1970. Also author of film, "Autumn: Frost Country," Pyramid Films, 1969, and filmstrip, "Come to Your Senses: A Filmstrip Series on Observation," Scholastic, 1970. Contributor to professional periodicals.

*   *   *

SOLBERG, Richard W.   1917-

PERSONAL: Born May 25, 1917, in Minneapolis, Minn.; son of Carl K. (a clergyman) and Sina (Varland) Solberg; married June Joanne Nelson, August 18, 1942; children: David, John, Mary, Daniel, Lois. *Education:* St. Olaf College, B.A., 1938; University of Wisconsin, M.A., 1939; Luther Theological Seminary, St. Paul, Minn., B.Th., 1943; University of Chicago, Ph.D., 1952. *Politics:* Democrat. *Home:* 21 Evergreen Dr., Greenville, Pa. 16125. *Office:* Thiel College, Greenville, Pa. 16125.

CAREER: Ordained minister of Lutheran church. St. Olaf College, Northfield, Minn., instructor in history, 1940-41; pastor in Ingleside, Ill., 1943-45; Augustana College, Sioux Falls, S.D., started as assistant professor, 1945, associate professor of history, 1948-53; Lutheran World Federation, Geneva, Switzerland, senior representative in Germany, 1953-56; Augustana College, professor of history and chairman of department, 1956-64; Thiel College, Greenville, Pa., vice-president for Academic Affairs, 1964—. El Colegio de Mexico, Organization of American States Professor, 1963. U.S. High Commission in Germany, adviser on religious affairs, 1949-50. Script adviser for film, "Question 7," 1959-60. *Member:* American Historical Association, Norwegian-American Histori-

cal Association, Organization of American Historians. *Awards, honors:* Officer's Cross, Order of Merit, Federal Republic of Germany, 1956; Johan Hinrich Wichern Award of Inner Mission of Evangelical Church of Germany, 1956; faculty research grant, Social Science Research Council, 1959.

WRITINGS: As Between Brothers: The Story of Lutheran Response to World Need, Augsburg, 1957; *Also Sind Wir Viele Ein Leib*, Lutherisches Verlagshaus, 1960; *God and Caesar in East Germany: The Conflicts of Church and State in East Germany Since 1945*, Macmillan, 1961. Contributor of articles and reviews to religious periodicals in Germany and United States. Contributing editor, *Dialog*.

AVOCATIONAL INTERESTS: Color photography.

*   *   *

SOLOMON, Daniel   1933-

PERSONAL: Born May 11, 1933, in Chicago, Ill.; son of Isadore Albert and Esther (Aaron) Solomon; married Jean Anne Soerens, April 19, 1963; children: Nicholas Jay, Paula Kay. *Education:* Antioch College, B.A., 1956; University of Michigan, M.A., 1956, Ph.D., 1960. *Home:* 8206 Bondage Dr., Gaithersburg, Md. 20760.

CAREER: Center for the Study of Liberal Education for Adults, Chicago, Ill., research associate, 1959-63; Institute for Juvenile Research, Chicago, Ill., senior research associate, 1963-71; Montgomery County (Md.) Public Schools, social psychologist, 1971—. *Member:* Society for the Psychological Study of Social Issues, Society for Research in Child Development, American Educational Research Association, American Psychological Association.

WRITINGS: (With Harry L. Miller) *Exploration in Teaching Styles: Report of Preliminary Investigations and Development of Categories*, Center for the Study of Liberal Education for Adults, 1961; (with William Bezdek and Larry Rosenberg) *Teaching Styles and Learning*, Center for the Study of Liberal Education for Adults, 1963; (editor and author of introduction) *The Continuing Learner*, Center for Study of Liberal Education for Adults, 1964; *The Judgment of Appropriateness as an Intervening Variable*, Research Program in Child Development, Institute for Juvenile Research, 1965. Contributor of articles and reviews to twenty psychology and educational journals.

WORK IN PROGRESS: Research on situational generality of striving dispositions, and effects of varying educational environments.

*   *   *

SOLOTAROFF, Theodore   1928-

PERSONAL: Born October 9, 1928, in Elizabeth, N.J.; son of Ben (a contractor) and Rose (Weiss) Solotaroff; married Lynn Friedman, 1950 (divorced); married Shirley Fingerhood (a lawyer), 1965 (divorced); married Ghislaine Boulanger, 1972; children: (first marriage) Paul, Ivan; (second marriage) Jason; (third marriage) Isaac. *Education:* University of Michigan, B.A., 1952; University of Chicago, M.A., 1956. *Politics:* Independent. *Religion:* Jewish. *Home:* 210 West 78th St., New York, N.Y. 10024.

CAREER: Commentary (magazine), New York, N.Y., associate editor, 1960-66; *New York Herald Tribune*, New York, N.Y., editor of *Book Week*, 1966; New American Library and Simon & Schuster, Inc., New York, N.Y. editor of *New American Review*, 1966-72; Bantam Books, Inc., New York, N.Y., editor of *The American Review*, 1972—. *Military service:* U.S. Navy, 1946-48. *Member:* Phi Beta Kappa. *Awards, honors:* Avery Hopwood Awards in fiction and criticism, University of Michigan.

WRITINGS: (Editor) Isaac Rosenfeld, *An Age of Enormity,* World Publishing, 1962; (editor and author of introduction) *Writers and Issues,* New American Library, 1969; *The Red Hot Vacuum, and Other Pieces on the Writing of the Sixties,* Atheneum, 1970. Contributor of reviews to *Esquire, Book Week, Commentary, New Republic,* and *New York Times Book Review.*

WORK IN PROGRESS: An autobiography.

SIDELIGHTS: "If *New American Review* has a single signature, it is one of complex and aggressive honesty," wrote Geoffrey Wolff after the publication of issue No. 5 in January, 1969. Reviving a tradition of paperback-as-literary-magazine popular in the 1950's, *New American Review,* according to Wolff, "continues to thrive, continues to discover and print poems, essays, stories and fragments of novels that are among the best work of our time, much of it by heretofore unknown writers." Eric Oatman of *Village Voice* reacted differently: "My gut reaction to the first two issues of *New American Review* was tempered rage. . . . In retrospect, I suppose I should have anticipated the lack-luster competence of the first issue, with its fiction seldom rising above the level of 'good writing,' with its intelligently carpentered, spiritless verse, and with its essays, virtuoso performances by Concerned Men, extremely pleasant to read but too gracefully conceived and executed to trigger any permanent alteration of vision. It was a satisfactory arrangement: nothing hallowed got too bruised, and the writers got paid." Most critic reaction has been enthusiastic, however, as this characteristic statement from Margot Hentoff would indicate: *"New American Review* has become a kind of outpost of literary civilization, a place where writers write well, and where diverse voices speak more thoughtfully than they might in other places. Looking back at past issues, one is impressed by how much good writing first appeared in *NAR;* two of the best sections of *Portnoy's Complaint;* part of Kate Millett's *Sexual Politics;* some wonderfully wild and original stories by Donald Barthelme and Robert Coover.... Solotaroff has said that he wanted to create a national, not a New York City, magazine and he has indeed succeeded. Almost any other magazine has been directed to readers of a particular generation, place, class, or state of mind. *NAR* has been able to cut across these lines and to remain responsive to what is happening in America—all of it."

Solotaroff's latest book, *The Red Hot Vacuum, and Other Pieces on the Writing of the Sixties,* is a collection of essays and reviews. Reviewing the book for *Library Journal,* one critic believes Solotaroff "displays a rare skill in evoking the spirit and elucidating the ideas of a literary work. Although he is able to discuss with great intelligence and insight a variety of contemporary foreign and American authors, it is clear that Solotaroff is best equipped to explain the writings of Jewish Americans. . . . I was particularly impressed by the last essay, in which Solotaroff ingeniously weaves details of his off-and-on 13-year friendship with [Philip] Roth into a discussion of *Portnoy's Complaint* and earlier works. Highly recommended for all modern literature collections."

BIOGRAPHICAL/CRITICAL SOURCES: New York Times Book Review, September 17, 1967; *Book World,* September 24, 1967; *Christian Century,* November 29, 1967; *Village Voice,* February 29, 1968; *Saturday Review,* October 5, 1968; *Washington Post,* January 23, 1969; *Library Journal,* October 7, 1970; *Newsweek,* November 16, 1970; *Antioch Review,* fall-winter, 1970-71; *New York Times,* December 4, 1970; *New York,* May 17, 1971.

SOMAN, Shirley 1922-
(Shirley Camper)

PERSONAL: Born March 7, 1922, in Boston, Mass.; married second husband, Robert O. Soman (a manufacturer), November 10, 1962; children: (first marriage) Frederic D. Camper, Francie Camper. *Education:* University of Wisconsin, B.A., 1945; Smith College, M.S.S., 1946. *Home:* 40 West 77th St., New York, N.Y. 10024.

CAREER: My Baby and *Shaw's Market News,* New York, N.Y., associate editor, 1952-53; New York City (N.Y.) Board of Education, Bureau of Child Guidance, social work and public relations, 1956-57; Family Service Association of America, New York, N.Y., editor and consultant, 1957-63. Public relations work, editor, and social worker for other social agencies and hospitals; free-lance consultant and writer. Associated Film Consultants, currently vice-president. *Member:* Society of Magazine Writers, National Council on Family Relations, Authors League of America, American Medical Writers Association, National Association of Social Workers, National Conference on Social Welfare, American Historical Association, Oral History Association.

*WRITINGS—*Under name Shirley Camper: *How to Get Along with Your Child,* Belmont Books, 1962. Child care columnist for *Redbook,* 1960-62; book columnist for newspaper syndicate. Contributor to *Reader's Digest, McCall's, Cosmopolitan,* and other magazines.

WORK IN PROGRESS: A book on social welfare history; a book on children and youth.

* * *

SOMERVILLE, (James) Hugh (Miller) 1922-

PERSONAL: Original name, James Hugh Miller; name legally changed in 1930; born November 10, 1922, in Singapore; son of James Somerville (a merchant and soldier) and Joan Mary (Underhill) Miller. *Education:* Attended Royal Naval College at Dartmouth, England. *Religion:* Roman Catholic. *Home:* Beeches Farm, Crowborough, Sussex, England.

CAREER: Sunday Times, London, England, yachting correspondent, 1953—; *Yachtsman,* London, associate editor, 1949-58, editor, 1958—. *Military service:* Royal Navy, 1939-49; became lieutenant; received Distinguished Service Cross. *Member:* Institute of Journalists.

WRITINGS: Yacht Racing Rules Simplified, Adlard Coles, 1955, 3rd edition, revised, De Graff, 1959; *Yacht and Dinghy Racing: Tactics, Tuning and Handling,* De Graff, 1957, 2nd edition, revised, 1961; *Sceptre: The Seventeenth Challenger,* Cassell, 1958. Founder with Adlard Coles, *Dinghy Year Book.*

* * *

SOMMER, Robert 1929-

PERSONAL: Born April 26, 1929, in New York, N.Y.; son of Robert M. and Margaret Sommer; married Dorothy Twente, 1957 (divorced); children: Ted, Kenneth, Margaret. *Education:* University of Kansas, Ph.D., 1956. *Office:* University of California, Davis, Calif.

CAREER: University of Alberta, Edmonton, assistant professor, 1961-63; University of California, Davis, 1963—, began as associate professor, became professor.

WRITINGS: Expertland, Doubleday, 1963; *The Ecology of Study Areas* (research report), University of California, 1968; *Personal Space: The Behavioral Basis of Design,* Prentice-Hall, 1969.

SOPER, Eileen A(lice)   1905-

PERSONAL: Born 1905, in Enfield, Middlesex, England; daughter of George (a fellow, Royal Society of Painter-Etchers and Engravers) and Ada Soper. *Education:* Educated privately; studied art under her father. *Home:* Wildings, Harmer Green, Welwyn, Hertfordshire, England.

CAREER: Artist, doing engraving, book illustrating, child and animal portraiture, and wild life painting in water color; writer. *Member:* Society of Wild Life Artists, British Trust for Ornithology, Royal Society for the Protection of Birds, Mammal Society of the British Isles.

WRITINGS—All self-illustrated: *Happy Rabbit* (juvenile), Macmillan, 1947; *Dormouse Awake* (juvenile), Macmillan, 1948; *Songs on the Wind*, Museum Press, 1948; *Sail Away Shrew* (juvenile), Macmillan, 1949; *When Badgers Wake*, Routledge & Kegan Paul, 1955; *Wild Encounters*, Routledge & Kegan Paul, 1957; *Wanderers of the Field*, Routledge & Kegan Paul, 1959, Sportshelf, 1960, excerpt published as *New Tracks*, Routledge & Kegan Paul, 1966; *Wild Favours*, Hutchinson, 1963; *From Nesting Into Flight*, Routledge & Kegan Paul, 1966; *Well-Worn Paths*, Routledge & Kegan Paul, 1966; *Muntjac: A Study of These Small Elusive Asiatic Deer Which Colonized an English Garden*, Longmans, Green, 1969.

Illustrator: Elizabeth Gould, *Country Days*, Blackie & Son, 1944; Elizabeth Gould, *Farm Holidays*, Blackie & Son, 1944; Elizabeth Gould, *Happy Days on the Farm*, Blackie & Son, 1944; Enid Blyton, *Stories and Notes to Enid Blyton Nature Plates*, Macmillan, 1949. Contributor of articles, illustrations, and poetry to *Christian Science Monitor*, *Country Life*, *Sunday Times*, and other periodicals and newspapers, and of sketches to British Broadcasting Corp. natural history unit programs, "Look" and "Animal Magic."

AVOCATIONAL INTERESTS: Natural history, wild life preservation, gardening, and the countryside.

*   *   *

SORAUF, Francis Joseph   1928-
(Frank J. Sorauf)

PERSONAL: Surname is pronounced *Sor*-uf; born May 31, 1928, in Grand Rapids, Mich.; son of Francis Joseph (a chemical engineer) and Mary (Norton) Sorauf. *Education:* University of Wisconsin, B.A., 1950, M.A., 1952, Ph.D., 1953; Harvard University, graduate study, 1950-51. *Home:* 3506 Edmund Blvd., Minneapolis, Minn. 55406.

CAREER: Pennsylvania State University, State College, 1953-60, began as instructor, became assistant professor of political science; University of Arizona, Tucson, associate professor of political science, 1960-61; University of Minnesota, Minneapolis, associate professor, 1961-65, professor of political science, 1965—, chairman of department, 1966-69. Johns Hopkins Center, Bologna, Italy, Fulbright lecturer, 1964-65. *Member:* American Political Science Association, American Association of University Professors, American Civil Liberties Union, Phi Beta Kappa. *Awards, honors:* Atherton Press Prize, American Political Science Association, 1963, for best scholarly manuscript, *Party and Representation*.

WRITINGS—Under name Frank J. Sorauf: *Party and Representation: Legislative Politics in Pennsylvania*, Atherton, 1963; *Political Parties in the American System*, Little, Brown, 1964; *Political Science: An Informal Overview*, Merrill, 1965; *Perspectives on Political Science*, Merrill, 1966; (contributor) William Nisbet Chambers and Walter Dean Burnham, editors, *The American Party Systems: Stages of Political Development*, Oxford University Press, 1967; *Party Politics in America*, Little, Brown, 1968. Contributor to political science journals, including *American Political Science Review*, *Journal of Politics*, *Midwest Journal of Political Science*, and *Public Administration Review*.

WORK IN PROGRESS: A study of the litigating of constitutional issues in the area of separation between church and state in the United States.

*   *   *

SOREL, Edward   1929-

PERSONAL: Born March 26, 1929, in New York, N.Y.; son of Morris (a salesman) and Rebecca (Kleinberg) Schwartz; married Elaine Rothenberg, July 1, 1956; married Nancy Caldwell (a writer), May 29, 1965; children: Madeline, Leo, Jenny, Katherine. *Education:* Cooper Union College, diploma, 1951. *Agent:* Sterling Lord Agency, 75 East 55th St., New York, N.Y. 10019.

CAREER: Staff artist at one time for *Esquire*, CBS Television Promotion, and Push Pin Studios; now free-lance illustrator and writer. *Awards, honors:* New York Herald Tribune first prize for illustration in children's books, 1961, for *Gwendolyn, the Miracle Hen*, by Nancy Sherman; various awards for artwork from Society of Illustrators, American Institute of Graphic Arts, and Art Directors Club of New York.

WRITINGS—All self-illustrated: *How to be President*, Grove, 1960; *Moon Missing*, Simon & Schuster, 1962; *Sorel's World's Fair*, New York, 1964, McGraw, 1964; *Making the World Safe for Hypocrisy*, Swallow Press, 1972.

Illustrator: Warren Miller, *King Carlo of Capri*, Harcourt, 1958; Warren Miller, *The Goings-On at Little Wishful*, Little, Brown, 1959; Warren Miller, *Pablo Paints a Picture*, Little, Brown, 1959; Nancy Sherman, *Gwendolyn, the Miracle Hen*, Golden Press, 1961; Nancy Sherman, *Gwendolyn and the Weather Cock*, Golden Press, 1963; William Cole, *What's Good for a Five-Year-Old?*, Holt, 1969; Joy Cowley, *The Duck in the Gun*, Doubleday, 1969; Nancy Caldwell Sorel, *Word People*, American Heritage Press, 1970. Contributor to *Show*, *Playboy*, *Horizon*, *Monocle*, *New York*, *Atlantic*, *Ramparts*, and *The Realist*.

BIOGRAPHICAL/CRITICAL SOURCES: American Artist, May, 1960; *Graphis*, January, 1963; *New York*, May 25, 1960; *Atlantic*, February, 1971.

*   *   *

SORRELLS, Dorothy C.

PERSONAL: Born in Washington D.C.; daughter of Will Emory (a cotton broker) and Olive (Carty) Sorrells. *Education:* Rice University, B.A.; University of Houston, M.A.; also studied at Wesleyan College, Macon, Ga., and National University of Mexico. *Religion:* Methodist. *Home:* 2154 Dryden Rd., Houston, Tex. 77025.

CAREER: Houston Independent School District, Houston, Tex., began as teacher, became principal, 1950-62, director for elementary schools, 1962—. *Member:* Association for Childhood Education, National Council of Teachers of Mathematics, National Council for Geographic Education, International Reading Association, American Malacological Union, National Wildlife Federation, Texas State Teachers Association, Texas Elementary Principals and Supervisors Association, Harris County Heritage Society, Houston Association of School Administrators.

WRITINGS: The Little Shell Hunter, Steck, 1961. Contributor to trade magazines.

WORK IN PROGRESS: Three juveniles, *The Beachcomber Dog; Island Adventures; The Little Shell Hunter in the Bahamas.*

AVOCATIONAL INTERESTS: Conchology, photography, beachcombing, camping, hiking, and reading biography and travel books.†

* * *

SOUKUP, James R (udolph) 1928-

PERSONAL: Born November 3, 1928, in Madison, Ill.; son of Rudolph Anton and Mary (Stajdl) Soukup; married Margaret Belle Grigsby (an elementary schoolteacher), March 26, 1951; children: James Evans, Susan Jane, Jeffrey Allan. *Education:* Wayne State University, B.A., 1950; University of Minnesota, M.A., 1952; University of Michigan, Ph.D., 1957. *Politics:* Democrat. *Religion:* Methodist. *Home:* 9 University Park, Fredonia, N.Y. 14063. *Office:* Department of Political Science, State University of New York College at Fredonia, Fredonia, N.Y. 14063.

CAREER: University of Texas, Austin, instructor, 1956-60, assistant professor, 1961-64, associate professor of history, 1964-70, associate director, Center for Asian Studies, 1965-70. State University of New York College at Fredonia, professor of political science and chairman of department, 1970—. Member of screening committee selecting Japanese and American exchange college students, 1962-63. *Member:* American Political Science Association, Association for Asian Studies, Midwest Conference on Asian Agairs (director of Texas activities). *Awards, honors:* Fulbright research scholar in Japan, 1961-62, 1967-68.

WRITINGS: (With Clifton McCleskey and Harry Holloway) *Party and Factional Division in Texas,* University of Texas Press, 1964. Contributor of articles to *Journal of Politics, Asian Survey,* and *Orient/West.*

WORK IN PROGRESS: *Japanese Aid and Diplomacy in Southeast Asia.*

* * *

SOUTHALL, Ivan (Francis) 1921-

PERSONAL: Born June 8, 1921, in Canterbury, Victoria, Australia; son of Francis Gordon (in insurance) and Rachel Elizabeth (Voutier) Southall; married Joyce Blackburn, September 8, 1945; children: Andrew John, Roberta Joy, Elizabeth Rose, Melissa Frances. *Education:* Melbourne Technical College, part-time student, 1937-41. *Politics:* Independent. *Religion:* Methodist. *Home:* 10 Lawrence Ct., The Patch, Victoria 3792, Australia.

CAREER: Herald and Weekly Times, Melbourne, Victoria, Australia, process engraver, 1936-41, 1947; free-lance author, 1948—. Community Youth Organization (Victoria), past president; Knoxbrooke Training Centre for the Intellectually Handicapped (Victoria), Foundation President. *Military service:* Royal Australian Air Force, pilot, 1941-44, war historian, 1945-46; became flight lieutenant; received Distinguished Flying Cross. *Member:* Australian Society of Authors. *Awards, honors:* Australian Children's Book of the Year awards, for *Ash Road,* 1966, *To the Wild Sky,* 1968, *Bread and Honey,* 1971; Australian Picture Book of the Year award, 1969, for *Sly Old Wardrobe;* Japanese Government's Children's Welfare and Culture Encouragement award, 1969, for *Ash Road.*

WRITINGS: *Out of the Dawn* (short stories), privately printed, 1942; *The Weaver from Meltham* (biography of Godfrey Hirst), Whitcombe & Tombs, 1950; *The Story of The Hermitage: The First Fifty Years of the Geelong Church of England Girls' Grammar School,* F.W. Cheshire, 1956; *They Shall Not Pass Unseen,* Angus & Robertson, 1956; *A Tale of Box Hill: Day of the Forest,* Box Hill City Council, 1957; *Bluey Truscott: Squadron Leader Keith William Truscott,* Angus & Robertson, 1958; *Softly Tread the Brave: A Triumph Over Terror, Devilry, and Death by Mine Disposal Officer John Stuart Mould and Hugh Randall Syme,* Angus & Robertson, 1960; *Journey into Mystery: A Story of the Explorers Burke and Wills,* Lansdowne Press, 1961, Sportshelf, 1961; *Woomera,* Angus & Robertson, 1962, International Publications Service, 1962; *Hills End,* Angus & Robertson, 1962, St. Martins, 1963; *Parson on the Track: Bush Brothers in the Australian Outback,* Lansdowne Press, 1962; *Lawrence Hargrave,* Oxford University Press, 1964; *Indonesia Face to Face,* Lansdowne Press, 1964, Sportshelf, 1965; *Rockets in the Desert: The Story of Woomera,* Angus & Robertson, 1965; *Indonesian Journey,* Lansdowne Press, 1965, George Newnes, 1966, International Publications Service, 1970; *Ash Road,* Angus & Robertson, 1965, St. Martins, 1966; *The Challenge—Is the Church Obsolete?: An Australian Response to the Challenge of Modern Society,* Lansdowne Press and Australian Council of Churches, 1966, Sportshelf, 1966; *To the Wild Sky,* St. Martins, 1967; *The Fox Hole,* St. Martins, 1967; *The Sword of Esau: Bible Stories Retold,* Angus & Robertson, 1967, St. Martins, 1968; *Let the Balloon Go,* St. Martins, 1968; *Bushfire!,* Angus & Robertson, 1968; *The Curse of Cain: Bible Stories Retold,* St. Martins, 1968; *Sly Old Wardrobe* (picture book), drawings by Ted Greenwood, Angus & Robertson, 1968, St. Martins, 1969; *Finn's Folly,* St. Martins, 1969; *Chinaman's Reef is Ours,* St. Martins, 1970; *Bread and Honey,* St. Martins, 1970, reissued as *Walk a Mile and Get Nowhere,* Prentice-Hall, 1970; *Josh,* Macmillan, 1972.

"Simon Black" series for boys: *Meet Simon Black,* Angus & Robertson, 1950; *Simon Black in Peril,* Angus & Robertson, 1951; *. . . in Coastal Command,* Anglobooks, 1953; *. . . in Space,* Anglobooks, 1953; *. . . in China,* Angus & Robertson, 1954; *. . . and the Spacemen,* Angus & Robertson, 1955; *. . . in the Antarctic,* Angus & Robertson, 1956; *. . . Takes Over: The Strange Tale of Operation Greenleaf,* Angus & Robertson, 1959; *. . . at Sea: The Fateful Maiden Voyage of A.P.M.I. Arion,* Angus & Robertson, 1962.

Short novels—All published by Horwitz: *Third Pilot, Flight to Gibraltar, Mediterranean Black, Sortie in Cyrenaica, Mission to Greece, Atlantic Pursuit,* 1959-61. Contributor of articles, essays, and short stories to Australian, New Zealand, European, and American press and journals.

WORK IN PROGRESS: *Flowers Coming Up All Around,* a short novel, to be published by Methuen.

SIDELIGHTS: Southall told CA: "As a lad the death of my father cut my education short and professionally, for good or bad, I am self-trained. I have seen writing as my vocation since childhood and have applied myself almost ruthlessly to this end but have enjoyed, indeed loved, every minute of it. And there are so many stories I want to write, that I'm impatient to write, that already life looks as if it might be too short."

Southall's books have been translated into Norwegian, Swedish, Danish, Finnish, French, Dutch, German, Italian, Polish, Yugoslav, Japanese, and Afrikaans.

BIOGRAPHICAL/CRITICAL SOURCES: John Hetherington, *Forty-Two Faces,* F.W. Cheshire, 1962, Angus & Robertson, 1963; *Christian Science Monitor,* May 4, 1967; *Times Literary Supplement,* May 25, 1967; *New York Times Book Review,* November 19, 1967, December 15, 1968; *Books and Bookmen,* December, 1967, August, 1968, November, 1968; *Book World,* August 4, 1968; *New Statesman,* November, 1968; *Horn Book,* February, 1970, April, 1971; *Library Journal,* July, 1970, October 15, 1970; *Books,* November, 1970; John Rowe Townsend, *A Sense of Story,* Lippincott, 1971.

SOUTHERN, Richard William   1912-

PERSONAL: Born February 8, 1912, in Newcastle upon Tyne, England; son of Matthew Henry (a merchant) and Eleanor (Sharp) Southern; married Sheila Cobley, June 2, 1944; children: Andrew Henry, Peter Campbell David. *Education:* Balliol College, Oxford University, M.A., 1936. *Religion:* Church of England. *Home and office:* President's Lodgings, St. John's College, Oxford, England.

CAREER: Oxford University, Oxford, England, research fellow, Exeter College, 1933-37, fellow and tutor, Balliol College, 1937-61, fellow and Chichele Professor of Modern History, All Souls College, 1961-69, president, St. John's College, 1969—. *Military service:* British Army, 1940-45; became major. *Member:* British Academy (fellow). *Awards, honors:* D.Litt. from Universities of Glasgow, Durham, and Cambridge.

WRITINGS: The Making of the Middle Ages, Yale University Press, 1953; *The Shape and Substance of Academic History* (inaugural lecture given at University of Oxford, November 2, 1961), Clarendon Press, 1961; *Western Views of Islam in the Middle Ages,* Harvard University Press, 1962; (editor, translator, and author of introduction and notes) Eadmer, *The Life of St. Anselm, Archbishop of Canterbury,* Thomas Nelson, 1962; *St. Anselm and His Biographer: A Study of Monastic Life and Thought, 1059-c.1130,* Cambridge University Press, 1963; (compiler) *Essays in Medieval History: Selected from the Transactions of the Royal Historical Society on the Occasion of Its Centenary,* Macmillan, 1968; (editor) *Memorials of St. Anselm,* Oxford University Press, 1969; *Medieval Humanism and Other Studies,* Harper, 1970; *Western Society and the Church in the Middle Ages,* Penguin, 1970.

WORK IN PROGRESS: A history of the medieval church.

*   *   *

SPAULL, Hebe (Fanny Lily)   1893-

PERSONAL: Born March 4, 1893, in London, England; daughter of Barnard and Fanny Spaull. *Religion:* Congregationalist. *Home:* 9 Elm Grove, London N.W. 2, England.

CAREER: Sub-editor for Amalgamated Press, 1913; press officer for Food Economy Department, British Ministry of Food, and for Voluntary Aid Detachment, Red Cross Society, 1914-18; publications officer of World's Young Women's Christian Association; assistant press officer for League of Nations Union, 1922-39; free-lance writer and lecturer, 1946—. *Member:* National Union of Journalists (London), United Nations Association (chairman of Cricklewood Branch).

WRITINGS: Fighting Death, and Other Plays, League of Nations Union, 1922; *The Fight for Peace: Stories of the Work of the League of Nations,* G. Bell, 1923, 4th edition, 1930; *Women Peace-Makers,* Harrap, 1924; *Champions of Peace,* Allen & Unwin, 1926; *Peeps at the League of Nations,* A. & C. Black, 1927, Macmillan, 1928; (with Simon S. Sherman) *The United World,* Dutton, 1929, 3rd edition, Dent, 1947; *Peeps at Roumania,* Macmillan, 1930; *Peeps at the Baltic States: Latvia, Lithuania, and Estonia,* Macmillan, 1931; *Pioneering for Peace,* Macmillan, 1931; *The World's Weapons,* Nicholson & Watson, 1932; *The Youth of Russia Today,* Nicholson & Watson, 1933; *The Adventures of Anai and Jok: A Tale of Two Little Slaves,* Evans Brothers, 1933; *How the World is Governed: A Study in World Civics,* Hogarth, 1933; *World Problems of To-day Explained for Boys and Girls,* S.C.M. Press, 1935; *The World Since You Were Born: A Junior History of Recent Years,* Macmillan, 1935, 3rd edition, 1939; *People, Parliament and King,* United Society for Christian Literature, 1945; *The United Nations and Their Problems,* Lutterworth, 1946; (with D.H. Kay) *The Co-operative Movement at Home and Abroad,* Macmillan, 1947; *The ABC of Civics: A Dictionary of Terms Used in Connection with Parliament, Local Authorities, Courts of Law, Diplomacy, and the United Nations,* Staples Press, 1949, enlarged and revised edition published as *The New ABC of Civics: A Dictionary of Terms Used in Connection with Parliament, Local Authorities, Courts of Law, Diplomacy, and the United Nations,* Barrie & Rockliff, 1957, 4th edition, enlarged, 1971; *The World Since 1945,* Barrie & Rockliff, 1960, revised edition, 1961; *The World Unites Against Want,* Barrie & Rockliff, 1961; *Peoples of the World,* Ward, Lock, 1961; *Africa: Continent on the Move,* Barrie & Rockliff, 1962; *The World's Changed Face Since 1954,* Barrie & Rockliff, 1964; *The Co-operative Movement in the World Today,* Barrie & Rockliff, 1965; *The Agencies of the United Nations: A Survey of Economic and Social Achievements,* Ampersand, 1967; *New Place Names of the World,* Ward, Lock, 1970.

"Rockliff Picture Book" series, all published by Barrie & Rockliff: *This is the United Nations,* 1951, 5th edition, revised and enlarged, 1965, *This is Morocco,* 1953, *This is Yugoslavia,* 1953, *This is the Saar,* 1954, *This is the British West Indies,* 1955, *The Changing Face of the World: How Modern Man is Changing the Physical World,* 1955.

"Life in Other Lands" series, all published by S.C.M. Press: *France,* 1937, *United States of America,* 1937, *Czechoslovakia,* 1937, *Union of Soviet Socialist Republics,* 1938. Also author of "World-Friendship" series, National Sunday School Union, 1929. Major contributor to *Wonder Book Encyclopaedia;* contributor of articles to *New World, New Commonwealth,* and other periodicals.

WORK IN PROGRESS: An enlarged edition of *New Place Names of the World.*

SIDELIGHTS: Miss Spaull has traveled in many parts of the world gathering material for writing, lecturing, and broadcasting; most recently, she visited Africa in 1961, the Caribbean in 1962, Singapore and Malaya in 1963, Pakistan and India in 1964, and Japan in 1965 and 1970. Her books have been recommended by the Council for Education in World Citizenship and by the United Nations Association.

*   *   *

SPECTOR, Shushannah   1903-

PERSONAL: Born February 15, 1903, in Russia; came to United States in 1923, naturalized in 1925; daughter of Elkana (a rabbi) and Fuida Spector; married Louis Greenberg (died, 1963). *Education:* Attended Israel Seminar Teachers Institute. *Religion:* Hebrew. *Home:* Helen Mar Hotel, 2421 Lake Pancoast Dr., Miami Beach, Fla. 33140. *Office:* 23rd St. and Pine Tree Dr., Miami Beach, Fla. 33140.

CAREER: Hebrew Academy of Greater Miami, Miami, Fla., teacher, 1951—; Dade Junior College, Miami, Fla., teacher of Hebrew, 1965—. Radio announcer, WEVD, New York, N.Y., 1950, WPBB, Miami Beach, Fla., 1951—. *Member:* Hebrew Teachers and Educators Alliance of Greater Miami (secretary). *Awards, honors:* Selected Hebrew Teacher of the Year by National Federation of Hebrew Teachers and Principals, 1965.

WRITINGS: (With Joseph Zeitlin) *Hebrew Made Easy,* Liveright, 1950; (with Rosabelle Edlin) *My Jewish Kitchen: The Momale's Ta'am Cookbook,* Liveright, 1964; *The Seder That Almost Wasn't,* Shengold, 1967; *Five Young Heroes of Israel,* Shengold, 1970. Also author of *A Hand Book for Israel.*

WORK IN PROGRESS: Double Fun in Reading, stories in both English and Hebrew; an English translation of *Hilory Mindlin.*†

* * *

SPECTOR, Stanley 1924-

PERSONAL: Born June 10, 1924, in New York, N.Y. *Education:* College of the City of New York (now City College of the City University of New York), B.S., 1945; School of Oriental and African Studies, University of London, graduate study, 1950-51; University of Washington, Seattle, Ph.D., 1953. *Office address:* Box 111, Washington University, St. Louis, Mo. 63130.

CAREER: University of Washington, Seattle, instructor in Far Eastern history, 1951-52; University of California, Los Angeles, lecturer in history, 1953; Chung Cheng Chung Hsueh, Singapore, lecturer in history, 1954; Washington University, St. Louis, Mo., assistant professor of Far Eastern affairs, 1955-58, associate professor of Chinese history, 1959—, chairman, committee on Asian studies, chairman of department of Chinese and Japanese, 1964—. Visiting professor of Chinese and Japanese history at Columbia University, 1962. National Committee on Undergraduate Training in Oriental Studies, chairman, 1961-62; Midwest Conference on Asian Affairs, program chairman and member of executive committee, 1962. Canadian Institute of International Affairs, lecturer on two trans-Canada tours; lecturer on radio and television in Malaya, United States.

MEMBER: Association for Asian Studies (committee on undergraduate education, 1963—). *Awards, honors:* Social Science Research Council fellow in London, England, 1950-51, award for Malaya and Singapore, 1958-59; Ford Foundation fellow, Southeast Asia, 1953-55.

WRITINGS: (With C.L. Chang) *Guide to the Memorials of Seven Leading Officials of 19th-Century China.* University of Washington Press, 1955; (contributor) Morton Fried, editor, *Colloquium on Overseas Chinese,* Institute of Pacific Relations, 1959; *Li Hung-chang and the Huai Army,* University of Washington Press, 1964; (with Ed Ritter and Helen Ritter) *Our Oriental Americans,* McGraw, 1965. Contributor of articles and reviews to *Nation, World Politics, New Leader, Nanyang Hsueh Pao, Pacific Affairs,* and other professional journals.

WORK IN PROGRESS: Research in modern and contemporary Chinese history; development of Chinese language teaching materials and curricula; development of Asian area and language programs; integration of China and Asian area research within the behavioral sciences.

* * *

SPENCER, John (Walter) 1922-

PERSONAL: Born September 24, 1922, in England; son of Walter Spencer; married Eileen Hatwell, November 19, 1944. *Education:* Attended Culford School; Oxford University, B.A. (honors in English language and literature), 1949, M.A., 1956. *Home:* White Cottage, Cattal, York, England. *Office:* School of English, University of Leeds, England.

CAREER: Lund University, Lund, Sweden, university lecturer in English, 1949-52; University of Edinburgh, Edinburgh, Scotland, lecturer in phonetics, 1955-56; English Language Institute, Allahabad, India, associate professor of phonetics, 1956-58; Punjab University, Lahore, Pakistan, reader in phonetics, 1958-59; University of Ibadan, Ibadan, Nigeria, head of department of phonetics, 1959-62; University of Leeds, Leeds, England, currently senior lecturer in modern English. *Member:* Linguistic Society of America, International Phonetics Association, Philological Society (Great Britain), International African Institute, African Studies Association (United Kingdom), Royal Overseas League.

WRITINGS: (With C.S. Bhandari and D. Ram) *Read and Tell,* eight books, Orient Longmans, 1957-58; (with Bhandari and Ram) *Read and Learn,* two books, Orient Longmans, 1958-59; (with Bhandari and Ram) *An English Pronouncing Vocabulary,* Orient Longmans, 1959; *Workers for Humanity,* Harrap, 1962; (with L.F. Brosnahan) *Language and Society,* Ibadan University Press, 1962; (editor and contributor) *Language in Africa: Papers,* Cambridge University Press, 1963; (with M. Gregory and N.E. Enkvist) *Linguistics and Style,* Oxford University Press, 1964; (editor with Maurice Wollman) *Modern Poems for the Commonwealth,* Harrap, 1966; (editor and contributor) *The English Language in West Africa,* Longmans, Green, 1971. Contributor of reviews, articles, and occasional poetry to learned journals. Co-editor, *Journal of West African Languages* and of *West African Language Monographs,* published by Cambridge University Press.

WORK IN PROGRESS: Writing on stylistics, and on language problems in the new states of Africa and Asia.

* * *

SPENDER, Stephen (Harold) 1909-

PERSONAL: Born February 28, 1909, in London, England; son of Edward Harold (a journalist and lecturer) and Violet Hilda (Schuster) Spender; married Agnes Marie Pearn, 1936 (divorced); married Natasha Litvin (a pianist), 1941; children: Matthew Francis, Elizabeth. *Education:* Attended University College, Oxford University, 1928-30. *Home:* 15 Loudoun Rd., London N.W.8, England.

CAREER: In his teens, supported self by printing chemists' labels on his hand press, later printed books for friends; *Horizon Magazine,* co-editor, 1939-41; UNESCO, counselor in Section of Letters, 1947; *Encounter,* London, England, co-editor, 1953-67. Holder of Elliston Chair of Poetry, University of Cincinnati, 1953; Beckman Professor, University of California, 1959; visiting lecturer, Northwestern University, 1963; consultant in poetry in English, Library of Congress, Washington, D.C., and Clark lecturer, Cambridge University, 1965-66; Mellon lecturer, Washington, D.C., 1968; visiting lecturer, University of Connecticut, 1968-70; Cliffe lecturer, London University, 1969. *Wartime service:* National Fire Service, fireman, 1941-44.

MEMBER: American Academy of Arts and Letters (honorary), National Institute of Arts and Letters (honorary), Phi Beta Kappa (Harvard University; honorary member), Savile Club, Garrick Club. *Awards, honors:* Commander of the British Empire, 1962; D.Litt., University of Montpelier; fellow, Institute of Advanced Studies, Wesleyan University, 1967.

WRITINGS: The Destructive Element: A Study of Modern Writers and Beliefs (literary criticism), J. Cape, 1935, Albert Saifer, 1953; *The Burning Cactus* (short stories; includes "The Dead Island," "The Cousins," "The Burning Cactus," "Two Deaths," and "By the Lake"), Faber, 1936; *Forward from Liberalism* (essay), Random House, 1937; *Trial of a Judge: A Tragedy in Five Acts,* Random House, 1938; *The New Realism: A Discussion* (lecture), Hogarth, 1939, Folcroft, 1969; *The Backward Son* (novel), Hogarth, 1940; *Life and the Poet* (essay), Secker & Warburg, 1942, Folcroft, 1969; (with William Samson and James Gordon) *Jim Braidy: The Story of Britain's Firemen,* Lindsay Drummond, 1943; *Citizens in War, and After,* Harrap, 1945; (author of introduction and notes) *Botticelli* (10 reproductions), Faber, 1945, Pitman, 1948; *European Witness,* Reynal & Hitchcock,

1946; *Poetry Since 1939,* published for the British Council by Longmans, Green, 1946, reissued in two volumes, Phoenix House, 1948, Lansdowne Press, 1969; (author of introduction) Patrice de la Tour du Pin, *The Dedicated Life in Poetry* [and] *The Correspondence of Laurent de Cayeux,* Harvill Press, 1948; (contributor) Richard Crossman, editor, *The God That Failed: Six Studies in Communism,* Harper, 1950; *World Within World* (autobiography), Harcourt, 1951; *Shelley* (essay), published for the British Council and the National Book League by Longmans, Green, 1952; *Learning Laughter,* Weidenfeld & Nicolson, 1952, Harcourt, 1953; *The Creative Element: A Study of Vision, Despair and Orthodoxy Among Some Modern Writers,* Hamish Hamilton, 1953; *The Making of a Poem* (essays), Hamish Hamilton, 1955, Norton, 1962; *Engaged in Writing* [and] *The Fool and the Princess* (short stories), Farrar, Straus, 1958; *The Imagination of the Modern World,* U.S. Government Printing Office, 1962; *The Struggle of the Modern,* University of California Press, 1963; (author of libretto, with Nicolas Nabokov) *Rasputin's End* (opera), Ricordi (Milan), 1963; (author of texts, with Patrick Leigh Fermor) Nikolaos Chatzeky-riakos-Ghikas, *Ghika: Paintings, Drawings, Sculpture,* Lund Humphries, 1964, Boston Book and Art Shop, 1965; *The Magic Flute* (juvenile; based on the opera by Mozart), retold by Spender, illustrated by Beni Montresor, Putnam, 1966; *Chaos and Control in Poetry* (lecture given at Library of Congress, October 11, 1965), U.S. Government Printing Office, 1966; *The Year of the Young Rebels* (essays), Random House, 1969.

Poetry: *Nine Experiments: Being Poems Written at the Age of Eighteen,* privately printed 1928; *Twenty Poems,* Basil Blackwell, 1930; *Poems,* Faber, 1933, Random House, 1934, 2nd edition, Faber, 1934; *Perhaps* (limited edition), privately printed, 1933; *Poem* (limited edition), privately printed, 1934; *Vienna,* Faber, 1934, Random House, 1935; *The Still Centre,* Faber, 1939; *Selected Poems,* Faber, 1940; *Ruins and Visions: Poems, 1934-1942,* Random House, 1942; *Poems of Dedication,* Faber, 1946, Random House, 1947; *Returning to Vienna, 1947: Nine Sketches,* Banyan Press, 1947; *The Edge of Being,* Random House, 1949; *Sirmione Peninsula,* Faber, 1954; *Collected Poems, 1928-1953,* Random House, 1955; *Inscriptions,* Poetry Book Society, 1958; *Selected Poems* Random House, 1964; *The Generous Days,* D.R. Godine, 1969.

Poems anthologized in *Modern British Poetry,* 5th edition, edited by Louis Untermeyer, Harcourt, 1942, *Chief Modern Poets of England and America,* 3rd edition, edited by Gerald DeWitt Sanders and John Herbert Nelson, Macmillan, 1943, *Anthology of Famous English and American Poetry,* edited by William Rose Benet and Conrad Potter Aiken, Modern Library, 1945, *A Little Treasury of British Poetry: The Chief Poets from 1500 to 1950,* edited by Oscar Williams, Scribner, 1951, *Poetry for Pleasure,* Doubleday, 1960, *Modern Love Poems,* edited by D.J. Klemer, Doubleday, 1961, *A Poetry Sampler,* edited by Donald Hall, F. Watts, 1962, *An Anthology of Commonwealth Verse,* edited by Margaret Jane O'Donnell, Blackie, 1963, *Poetry in English,* edited by Warren Taylor and Donald Hall, Macmillan, 1963, *Poems on Poetry: The Mirror's Garland,* edited by Robert Wallace and James G. Taaffe, Dutton, 1965, and other collections.

Editor: W.H. Auden, *Poems,* privately printed, 1928; *Oxford Poetry, 1927-32,* Basil Blackwell, Volume 3 (with Louis MacNeice), 1929, Volume 4 (with Bernard Spencer), 1930; (with John Lehmann, and author of introduction) *Poems for Spain,* Hogarth, 1939; *Spiritual Exercises: To Cecil Day Lewis* (poems), privately printed, 1943; (and author of introduction) *A Choice of*

English Romantic Poetry, Dial, 1947; (and author of introduction) Walt Whitman, *Selected Poems,* Grey Walls Press, 1950; Martin Huerlimann, *Europe in Photographs,* Thames & Hudson, 1951; (with Elizabeth Jennings and Dannie Abse) *New Poems 1956: An Anthology,* M. Joseph, 1956; (and author of introduction) *Great Writings of Goethe,* New American Library, 1958; (and author of introduction) *Great German Short Stories,* Dell, 1960; (and author of introduction) Arnold Joseph Toynbee and others, *The Writer's Dilemma* (essays originally published in *Times Literary Supplement* as "Limits of Control"), Oxford University Press (London), 1961; (with Irving Kristol and Melvin J. Lasky) *Encounters: An Anthology from the First Ten Years of "Encounter" Magazine,* Basic Books, 1963; (with Donald Hall) *The Concise Encyclopedia of English and American Poets and Poetry,* Hawthorn, 1963, 2nd edition, revised, Hutchinson, 1970; (compiler and author of introduction) *A Choice of Shelley's Verse,* Faber, 1971.

Translator: (And author of introduction and commentary, with J.B. Leishman) Rainer Maria Rilke, *Duino Elegies* (includes German text), Norton, 1939, 4th edition, revised, Hogarth, 1963; (with Hugh Hunt) Ernst Toller, *Pastor Hall* (three-act play), J. Lane, 1939, also published with *Blind Man's Buff* (see below); (with Hunt) Ernst Toller and Denis Johnson, *Pastor Hall* [and] *Blind Man's Buff* (two plays; the former by Toller, the latter by Toller and Johnson), Random House, 1939; (with Goronwy Rees) Georg Buechner, *Danton's Death,* Faber, 1939; (with J.L. Gili) Federico Garcia Lorca, *Poems,* Oxford University Press, 1939; (with Gili) *Selected Poems of Federico Garcia Lorca,* Hogarth, 1943; (with Frances Cornford) Paul Eluard, *Le Dur desir de durer,* Grey Falcon Press, 1950; (and author of introduction) Rainer Maria Rilke, *The Life of the Virgin Mary* (includes German text), Philosophical Library, 1951; (with Frances Fawcett) Frank Wedekind, *Five Tragedies of Sex,* Vision Press, 1952; (and adaptor) Johann Christoph Friedrich von Schiller, *Mary Stuart* (play; first produced on Broadway at Vivian Beaumont Theatre, November 11, 1971), Faber, 1959.

SIDELIGHTS: During the thirties it was Spender, along with W.H. Auden, Louis MacNeice, and C. Day Lewis, who formed the so-called Oxford Group which influenced both poetry and politics. The members' differences were more striking than their similarities, and Spender was the most romantic and lyrical. M.L. Rosenthal observes in *The Modern Poets* that Spender, "the most delicate lyricist of the group, has an almost Shelleyan ethereality and passion for fraternal love and beauty." Babette Deutsch once said of him: "The locus of his vision of felicity was what seemed to him, as it had to Shelley, a compassable future. His romanticism was fed, and occasionally poisoned, by German sources as well, and his later work was to show other influences, including that of Edith Sitwell, but from the outset his work differed clearly from that of his confreres." Discussing post-war literature in *The Angry Decade,* Kenneth Allsop locates Spender among "those for whom Connolly's 'gardens of the West' have closed, and who are indeed in a state of sad solitude. I mean the Sitwells, the Ivy Compton-Burnetts, the Henry Greens, the Stephen Spenders and the John Lehmanns. Rather like ... the survivors of the old *literati,* the candelabra-and-wine *rentier* writers have taken the Fifties on sufferance. Wincing with distaste, mournful and puzzled, they have withdrawn to a remote and musty fantasy life among their woodland temples. Their considerable talent is absorbed into the construction of elaborate, private languages, elegiac remembrance of things past, reveries that are passed like an empty parcel around an ever diminishing circle. Their writing becomes more and more heavily wrought with convoluted scroll-work, or more and more allusive, quivering with *nuance,* gauzy with conversational subtleties that taper off into the raising of an eyebrow."

Commenting on his later poetry, Howard Nemerov does "not see any very considerable development. There is usually a greater calm, there is a technical command which can make a very attractive poem in a subdued mode, ... and there are brief flashes of intensity finely handled.... But Spender remains an uneven poet, either wildly soaring or noncommittally flat.... He is a splendid phrase-maker, master of the noble gesture, of which examples will easily occur to his readers. His dramatic stance and sweeping motions initiate poetically his ideal heroes, 'Beholders of the promised dawn of truth,/ The explorers of immense and simple lines.' " Less interested in technique than are most poets, "his subjects frequently are as screens, behind which he awaits the moment for breaking rhapsodically out...." R.K. Burns makes this statement: "Mr. Spender is a major spokes-man for the Romantic movement in contemporary poetry, and has been characterized often as an eloquent singer of glowing sentiment. Though most critics view sadly his work of later years, it remains a poetry of human dimensions: a combination of unexaggerated emotion, and delicate, extraordinary writing. For this, he is a major poet."

Spender recently told an American audience that American poetry today is "more interesting" than contemporary British poetry. "Modern poetry—in the English language," he wrote in an article for *Saturday Review,* "might almost be called an American invention." He analyzes American influences on British poetry, noting "the interesting possibility that the English did not *listen* to their own language spoken so much as the Americans do because, until recently at any rate, English, spoken or written, had a standard of correctitude deriving from class.... If there is a new English in England it will be different from American, and may result in a new English poetry as independent of the American as America has become of England."

Of late, his critical essays have been more favorably received than his poetry. John Berryman said in a review of *The Making of a Poem:* "Candor has long been known as one of Spender's chief notes, both as a writer and as a man, and it looks forth at us, tranquil and friendly, everywhere in this collection of his recent criticism." Spender himself once said that his writing suffers "from an excess of ideas and a weak sense of form." Rosenthal mentioned this in his review of *The Making of a Poem:* "Spender's reluctance to affirm has something impersonal behind it, the same thing that is behind [his] poetic development since the war. In the title-essay he treats his own work in [this] same way. Though it is the warmest, most mellow of the pieces, he depreciates his own abilities and sometimes even his own phrasing. This essay on his methods of work is one of the best things of its kind for young poets and indeed for anyone interested in the psychology of composition."

In his youth, while trying to reconcile his ideals with himself and his world, Spender turned to Communism, hoping to be "on the side of history." As a writer for *New Statesman and Nation* expressed it, "Communism had appealed to Spender because he believed that the individual could and should matter; that his task was no longer to interpret history but to change it." He actually joined the British Communist Party for only a few weeks during the winter of 1936-37. The disillusionment that followed the dimunition of his individualism is recorded in the *The God That Failed.* Because of his own youthful dedication to "personal self-realization," Spender was deeply interested in the international student revolts of 1968. *The Year of the Young Rebels* has received wide acclaim as a definitive account of the student rebellions at Columbia, Paris, Prague, and Berlin. Political columnist Jack Newfield called it a "gentle, wise book.... Spender ... can see the personalities, confrontations and dreams of the young Left in larger than just its surface political dimension." He believes this is because of Spender's own experiences: "His essay in the collection *The God That Failed* convinced me personally, more than anything else written on the subject, of the futility of Communist dogma, of the illegitimacy of the Communist notion of the end justifying the means. Later he was duped by the C.I.A., while he was co-editor of *Encounter.* He has survived these two potentially embittering experiences still a gentle radical, still a fine poet with a modernist sensibility, still a good man living in a bad time." A writer for *Times Literary Supplement* called *The Year of the Young Rebels* "probably the best book yet on student revolt—sensitive, carefully written, well informed and thoughtful.... With a poet's insight into human motives, together with a natural sympathy for young rebels that springs from his own unrepudiated activities of the 1930's, Mr. Spender is very well equipped to give [the student revolt] its due." Spender believes "the power of the universities lies ... essentially in their position as centers of a life more disinterested, more democratic, more critical than that of the society. The problem for the present generation of students is to exercise this power—the power of criticism—within the limits of what is possible, without destroying the university.... The grievances and demands of the students [at Nanterre] ... express their total rejection of the depersonalizing forces of modern society.... They were confident that just because they were a different generation they would avoid the mistakes of young people in the thirties who fell into the traps of Fascism or of Communism. I am not so sure."

BIOGRAPHICAL/CRITICAL SOURCES: *New Statesman and Nation,* February 20, 1954; Louise Bogan, *Selected Criticism,* Noonday, 1955; Babette Deutsch, *Poetry in Our Time,* Columbia University Press, 1956; *Nation,* December 13, 1958; Louis Untermeyer, *Lives of the Poets,* Simon & Schuster, 1959; *Saturday Review,* May 19, 1962, September 22, 1962, April 23, 1966; Howard Nemerov, *Poetry and Fiction: Essays,* Rutgers University Press, 1963; *New York Times Book Review,* April 28, 1963, May 11, 1969; *New Republic,* June 29, 1963; M.L. Rosenthal, *The Modern Poets,* Oxford University Press, 1965; *New York Times Magazine,* March 30, 1969; *Spectator,* April 18, 1969; *Times Literary Supplement,* May 22, 1969; *Book World,* June 22, 1969; *Time,* July 4, 1969; *Christian Science Monitor,* August 28, 1969; *Partisan Review,* Number 1, 1970.†

*   *   *

SPICE, Marjorie Davis 1924-

PERSONAL: Born October 12, 1924, in Irvine, Ky.; daughter of E. Scott (a railroad switchman) and Elizabeth (Wilson) Davis; married Byron L. Spice, June 24, 1947; children: Ronald, Byron, Jr., Elizabeth, Susan. *Education:* Transylvania University, A.B., 1947. *Religion:* Disciples of Christ. *Home:* 23 North Hawthorne Lane, Indianapolis, Ind. 46219.

CAREER: United Christian Missionary Society, Indianapolis, Ind., missionary, 1949-62, working for many years in Mexico and Paraguay; currently teaching English at Howe High School, Indianapolis, Ind.

WRITINGS: *Marica of Paraguay,* Bethany, 1961; *Junior Teacher's Guide to Accompany "The Mysterious Mr. Cobb",* Friendship, 1967. Contributor to *Jack and Jill, Junior World,* and *Bethany Guide.*

SPIEGEL, Joseph   1928-

PERSONAL: Born October 27, 1928, in New York, N.Y.; son of Felix (a salesman) and Ida (Kantrowitz) Spiegel; married wife, Doris, May 28, 1953; children: Terry Leeann, Amy Ellen, Tamy Jo, Felice B. *Education:* University of Louisville, A.B., 1950, M.A., 1951; Columbia University, Ph.D., 1960. *Office:* MITRE Corp., Bedford, Mass. 01730.

CAREER: MITRE Corp., Bedford, Mass., subdepartment head, System Design Laboratory Institute, 1959—. *Military service:* U.S. Army, 1953-55. *Member:* American Association for Advancement of Science, American Psychological Association, Society for Psychological Study of Social Issues, Institute of Electrical and Electronics Engineers.

WRITINGS: (Editor with Edward M. Bennett and James W. Degan) *Human Factors in Technology,* McGraw, 1963; (editor with Bennett and Degan) *Military Information Systems: The Design of Computer-Aided Systems for Command,* Praeger, 1964.

WORK IN PROGRESS: Editing, with Bennett and Degan, *Fundamentals of Information System Science and Engineering,* for McGraw.

*   *   *

SPIEGELBERG, Herbert   1904-

PERSONAL: Born May 18, 1904, in Strasbourg, France; became U.S. citizen, 1944; son of Wilhelm (an Egyptologist) and Elisabeth (von Recklinghausen) Spiegelberg; married Eldora Haskell, July 6, 1944; children: Gwen Elisabeth, Lynne Sylvia. *Education:* Attended University of Heidelberg, 1922-24, University of Freiburg, 1924-25; University of Munich, Ph.D., 1928. *Home:* 7200 Pershing Ave., St. Louis, Mo. 63130.

CAREER: Swarthmore College, Swarthmore, Pa., instructor, research associate, 1938-41; Lawrence College, Appleton, Wis., began as instructor, became professor of philosophy, 1941-63; Washington University, St. Louis, Mo., professor of philosophy, 1963-71, professor emeritus, 1971—. Visiting professor, University of Michigan, 1951-52, University of Southern California, 1960; Fulbright lecturer, University of Munich, 1961-62. *Member:* American Philosophical Association, American Association of University Professors, Phi Beta Kappa (honorary).

WRITINGS: Gesetz und Sittengesetz: Strukturanalytische und historische vorstudien zu einer gesetzesfreien ethik, Max Niehans, 1935; *Antirelativismus: Kritik des relativismus und skeptizismus der werte und des sollens,* Max Niehans, 1935; *The Phenomenological Movement: A Historical Introduction,* two volumes, Nijhoff, 1960, Humanities, 1966, 2nd edition, Nijhoff, 1965, Humanities, 1969, Chapter XIV published separately as *The Essentials of the Phenomenological Method,* Humanities, 1965; (author of introduction) Alexander Pfaender, *Phaenomenologie des Wollens: Eine psychologische Analyse—Motive und Motivation,* J.A. Barth, 1963; *Alexander Pfaender's Phaenomenologie, nebst einem Anhang: Texte zur phaenomenologischen Philosophie aus dem Nachlass,* Nijhoff, 1963; (editor with Bayard Quincy Morgan, and author of introduction) *The Socratic Enigma: A Collection of Testimonies Through Twenty-Four Centuries,* Bobbs-Merrill, 1964; (translator and author of introduction and supplementary essays) Alexander Pfaender, *Phenomenology of Willing and Motivation and Other Phaenomenologica,* Northwestern University Press, 1967; *Phenomenology in Psychology and Psychiatry: A Historical Introduction,* Northwestern University Press, 1972. Contributor to professional journals.

WORK IN PROGRESS: Essays in Phenomenology.

SPIEGLER, Charles G.   1911-

PERSONAL: Born March 14, 1911, in New York, N.Y.; son of George and Lena (Gang) Spiegler; married Evelyn Weiser (now executive secretary of Manhattan chapter, United Nations Association of the U.S.A.), December, 1948; children: George Benjamin. *Education:* College of the City of New York (now City College of the City University of New York), B.A., 1932; postgraduate study. *Politics:* Liberal. *Religion:* Jewish. *Home:* 67-65 Fleet St., Forest Hills 75, N.Y. 11375.

CAREER: College of the City of New York (now City College of the City University · of New York), New York, N.Y., speech examiner, 1933-36, evening school lecturer in English composition, 1946—; New York City (N.Y.) Board of Education, teacher of English and speech, 1934-54, chairman of academic subjects, 1954—. Hunter College of the City University of New York, member of staff of Project English under U.S. Office of Education grant, 1963-64. *Reader's Digest,* writer-editor on education editions, 1957-60; Scott, Foresman and Co., consultant on bibliography of children's books. *Member:* English Teachers Association, English Association (chairman), Education Writers Association, International Reading Association (president, Manhattan chapter, 1957; member of national commission on lifetime reading, 1963), Kappa Delta Phi.

WRITINGS: (With Martin Hamburger) *If You're Not Going to College,* Science Research Associates, 1959; (with Helen Derrick and Wilbur Schramm) *Adventures for Americans,* Harcourt, 1962, 3rd edition, 1969; (editor) *Courage Under Fire,* C.E. Merrill, 1967; (editor) *Against the Odds,* C.E. Merrill, 1967; (with William B. Reiner) *What To Do After High School,* Science Research Associates, 1971. Contributor of articles to *New York Times Magazine, This Week, Parents', Chicago Jewish Forum, T.V. Guide, Scholastic,* and other journals. New York adviser, *English Record.* Writer of film script, "Museum: Classroom Unlimited," for New York City Board of Education.

WORK IN PROGRESS: With Alex McKay and John MacKenzie, a series of textbooks aimed at motivating youngsters to write, for Addison-Wesley.

AVOCATIONAL INTERESTS: Tennis, reading, the theatre.

*   *   *

SPIRO, Jack D.   1933-

PERSONAL: Born March 4, 1933, in New Orleans, La.; son of Harry and Rebecca (Cohen) Spiro; married Marilyn S. Loevy; children: Hillary Ann, David K. *Education:* Tulane University, B.A., 1953; Hebrew Union College-Jewish Institute of Religion, B.H.L., 1953, M.A., 1958, D.H.L., 1962. *Home:* 7 Bernard Rd., East Brunswick, N.J. 08816. *Office:* 222 Livingston Ave., New Brunswick, N.J. 08902.

CAREER: Temple Anshe Emeth, New Brunswick, N. J., rabbi, 1962—. *Military service:* U.S. Air Force, Chaplains Corps, 1958-61; became captain. *Member:* Academy of Religion and Mental Health, Central Conference of American Rabbis, B'nai B'rith, Phi Alpha Theta.

WRITINGS: (With Sylvan Schwartzman) *The Living Bible,* Union of American Hebrew Congregations, 1962; *A Time to Mourn: Judaism and the Psychology of Bereavement,* Bloch Publishing, 1967; (editor) Albert Vorspan, *Jewish Values and Social Crisis: A Casebook for Social Action,* Union of American Hebrew Congregations, 1968. Contributor to religious periodicals.†

SPRINKEL, Beryl W(ayne)   1923-

PERSONAL: Born November 20, 1923, in Richmond, Mo.; son of Clarence (a farmer) and Emma (Schooley) Sprinkel; married Esther Pollard, September 7, 1947; married second wife, Barbara Pipher, May 31, 1970; children: (first marriage) Dennis Wayne, Gary Lynn, Kevin Glenn; stepchildren: Debra Pipher, Pamela Pipher. *Education:* Northwest Missouri State College, student, 1941-43; University of Oregon, student, 1943-44; University of Missouri, B.S., 1947; University of Chicago, M.B.A., 1948, Ph.D., 1952. *Politics:* Republican. *Religion:* Baptist. *Home:* 1705 Brookwood Dr., Flossmoor, Ill. 60422. *Office:* Harris Bank, 111 West Monroe, Chicago 90, Ill. 60603.

CAREER: University of Missouri, Columbia, instructor in economics, 1948-49; University of Chicago, Chicago, Ill., instructor in economics, 1950-52; Harris Trust and Savings Bank, Chicago, Ill., 1952—, now director of research. Occasional consultant to U.S. Treasury, other government fiscal agencies. Homewood-Flossmore Board of Education, member, 1957-65, president, 1959-60. Member of Board of Directors, U.S. Chamber of Commerce; member of board economists, *Time* magazine. *Military service:* U.S. Army, 1943-45. *Member:* American Economic Association, National Association of Business Economists, American Statistical Association (president, Chicago chapter). *Awards, honors:* University of Chicago citation for public service, 1964.

WRITINGS: Money and Stock Prices, Irwin, 1964; *Money and Markets: A Monetarist View,* Dow-Jones-Irwin, 1971. Economic editor of *Financial Analyst Journal;* contributor of articles to professional journals.

AVOCATIONAL INTERESTS: Singing, lecturing.

*   *   *

SPULBER, Nicolas   1915-

PERSONAL: Born January 1, 1915, in Rumania; son of John (a contractor) and Ana Spulber; married Pauline, August 5, 1950; children: Daniel. *Education:* New School for Social Research, M.A., 1950, Ph.D. (magna cum laude), 1952. *Office:* Indiana University, Bloomington, Ind. 47401.

CAREER: Massachusetts Institute of Technology, Cambridge, research associate of Center for International Studies, 1952-54; Indiana University, Bloomington, lecturer, 1954-55, associate professor, 1955-61, acting chairman of Institute of East European Studies, 1956-57, 1958-59, professor of economics, 1961—. City University of New York, visiting professor, 1963-64. *Member:* American Economic Association, Royal Economic Society.

WRITINGS: (Editor with Norman J.G. Pounds) *Resources and Planning in Eastern Europe,* Indiana University Press, 1957; (editor with Vratislav Busek) *Czechoslovakia,* Praeger, 1957; *The Economics of Communist Eastern Europe,* M.I.T. Press, 1957; (editor) *Study of the Soviet Economy,* Indiana University Press, 1961; *The Soviet Economy: Structure, Principles, Problems,* Norton, 1962, revised edition, 1969; (editor) *Foundations of Soviet Strategy for Economic Growth: Soviet Essays, 1924-1930,* translated by Robert M. Hankin and others, Indiana University Press, 1964; *The State and Economic Development in Eastern Europe,* Random House, 1966; *Socialist Management and Planning: Topics in Comparative Socialist Economics,* Indiana University Press, 1971.

SIDELIGHTS: Spulber speaks French, Spanish, Italian, Russian, German, and Rumanian.

SQUIRE, Norman   1907-

PERSONAL: Born May 9, 1907, in Southsea, Hampshire, England; son of John Henry (a musician) and Mary (Cooper) Squire; married Olivia Walker, September 20, 1947. *Education:* Attended schools in England. *Politics:* Anti-Conservative. *Home:* 51 Neville Ct., London N.W.8, England.

CAREER: Started as errand boy in department store, London, England, at age of thirteen, later salesman; dancer and cabaret artist, 1930-40. *Military service:* British Army, 1940-46; became lieutenant; mentioned in dispatches. *Member:* Imperial Society of Teachers of Dancing (life; fellow), Lederer's Bridge Club (secretary), Dorset Bridge Club (secretary).

WRITINGS: The Theory of Bidding, Duckworth, 1957; *A Guide to Bridge Conventions,* Duckworth, 1958; (with M. Harrison-Gray) *Winning Points at Match-Point Bridge,* Faber, 1959; *Bidding at Bridge,* Penguin, 1964; *The Laws of Kalooki,* Crockford, 1964; *How to Win at Roulette,* Pelham Books, 1968, Gamblers Book Club, 1972; *Beginner's Guide to Bridge,* Drake Publishers, 1971. Contributor of articles to bridge journals throughout the world, and of a regular column to *Express and Star* and *Bombay Sunday Standard.* Competition editor, *Bridge,* 1948-64.

WORK IN PROGRESS: Advanced Roulette.

*   *   *

STACEY, Roy   1919-

PERSONAL: Born December 9, 1919, in London, England; son of Frederick Robert and Edith Mabel (Rance) Stacey; married Daphne Dall (an artist), March 19, 1955; children: Anthony Neil, Jacqueline Diana. *Education:* Attended Merchant Taylors' School. *Home:* 9 Houndsden Rd., London N.21, England.

CAREER: Stock Exchange, London, England, broker, 1937-41; Vawsar & Wiles (publishers), London, editor, 1945-50; Stacey Publications, London, managing editor and proprietor, 1950—. Director, L.R. Stacey & Co. Ltd. (property company). *Military service:* Royal Air Force, 1941-45. *Member:* Institute of Journalists.

WRITINGS: Small Man's Guide to Profitable Investing, S.E.S., 1946; *Running an Amateur Society,* Jenkins, 1955; *Choosing a Play,* Jenkins, 1961. Editor, "Amateur Stage Handbooks" series, Stacey Publications. Editor, *Amateur Stage;* assistant editor, *Commonwealth Review* and *Creative Drama.*

WORK IN PROGRESS: A survey of drama for *Junior Year Book* published by Everybody's Publications.

AVOCATIONAL INTERESTS: Playing t e n n i s and watching football.†

*   *   *

STACEY, Thomas Charles Gerrard   1930-
(Tom Stacey)

PERSONAL: Born January 11, 1930, in Bletchingley, England; son of David Henry and Gwen (Part) Stacey; married Caroline Clay (a sculptress), January 5, 1952; children: Emma, Mathilda, Isabella, Samuel, Tomasina. *Education:* Educated at Eton College. *Politics:* Conservative. *Religion:* Anglican. *Home:* Stonegate Link, Stonegate, Sussex, England. *Office:* Tom Stacey Ltd., 28 Maiden Lane, London W.2, England.

CAREER: Hulton Press, London, England, writer and foreign correspondent, 1952-54; *Daily Express,* London, foreign and diplomatic correspondent, 1954, 1956-60; *Montreal Star,* Montreal, Quebec, correspondent, 1955-56; *Sunday Times,* London, England, chief roving correspondent, 1960-65; *Evening Standard,* London, columnist, 1965-67; Correspondents World Wide, London, managing director, 1967—; Tom Stacey Ltd., London, managing director, 1969—. Prospective Parliamentary candidate, North Hammersmith, 1960-64, Dover, 1965-67, Putney, 1971—. Crossed Africa overland, 1954-55, and made anthropoligical study of Bakonjo tribe of Ruwenzori Mountains; undertook mission for Uganda Government to settle rebellion of same tribe, 1963; public lecturer on foreign affairs. Governor, Christopher Wren School, 1960-68, Wandsworth School, 1972—. *Military service:* Scots Guards, served in Malaya, 1949-50; became second lieutenant. *Member:* Royal Geographical Society (fellow), White's Club, Beefsteak Club, Marylebone Cricket Club. *Awards, honors:* John Llewellyn Rhys Memorial Prize, 1954, for *The Hostile Sun;* Granada award for journalism, 1961.

WRITINGS: The Hostile Sun, Duckworth, 1953; *The Brothers M.,* Secker & Warburg, 1960; *Summons to Ruwenzori,* Secker & Warburg, 1965; (editor) *Today's World: A Map Notebook of World Affairs,* Collins, 1968; *Immigration and Enoch Powell,* Stacey Publications, 1970.

Contributor: Peter Chambers and Amy Landreth, editors, *Called Up,* Wingate, 1955; *Where Monsoons Meet,* Harrap, 1957; Colin Legum, editor, *Africa: A Handbook to the Continent,* Praeger, 1961; *Encore,* M. Joseph, 1962; R.W. Mack, editor, *Race, Class, and Power,* American Book Co., 1963; *Encore 2,* M. Joseph, 1963. Editor-in-chief, *Chambers's Encyclopaedia Yearbook,* 1969—.

SIDELIGHTS: Stacey's travels cover a million miles, and 106 countries; world political figures he has interviewed include Khrushchev in the Kremlin, 1963.

BIOGRAPHICAL/CRITICAL SOURCES: Time, May 12, 1961; *Time and Tide,* September, 1972.

* * *

STALLWORTHY, Jon (Howie) 1935-

PERSONAL: Born January 18, 1935, in London, England; son of John Arthur (a surgeon) and Margaret (Howie) Stallworthy; married Gillian Waldock, June 25, 1960. *Education:* Student at Rugby School, 1948-53; Magdalen College, Oxford, B.A., 1958, B. Litt., 1961. *Religion:* Church of England. *Home:* Shotover Edge, Headington, Oxford, England. *Office:* Oxford University Press, Ely House, 37 Dover St., London W.1, England.

CAREER: Oxford University Press, London, England, editor, 1959—. *Military service:* British Army, Oxfordshire and Buckinghamshire Light Infantry, 1953-55; became lieutenant. *Awards, honors:* Newdigate Prize for English verse, 1958.

WRITINGS: The Earthly Paradise (poem), privately printed, 1958; *The Astronomy of Love* (poems), Oxford University Press, 1961; *Between the Lines: W.B. Yeats's Poetry in the Making,* Clarendon Press, 1963; *Out of Bounds* (poems), Oxford University Press, 1963; *Vision and Revision in Yeats's Last Poems,* Clarendon Press, 1963; *The Almond Tree* (poem), Turret Books, 1967; (editor) *Yeats: Last Poems* (collection of critical essays), Macmillan (London), 1968; *Root and Branch* (poems), Oxford University Press, 1969; *Positives* (poem), Dolmen Press, 1969. Contributor of poems and articles to periodicals, including *New York Times, London Magazine, Critical Quarterly, Review of English Studies, Times Literary Supplement, Review of English Literature.* Editor of *Workshop,* summer, 1968.

SIDELIGHTS: Stallworthy has traveled in France, Italy, Spain, Nigeria, India, Pakistan, Nepal, America, Mexico, Australia, New Zealand, and Greece.

BIOGRAPHICAL/CRITICAL SOURCES: Punch, February 26, 1969; *New Statesman,* February 8, 1969; *Virginia Quarterly Review,* autumn, 1969; *Books and Bookmen,* June, 1969; *London Magazine,* October, 1969.

* * *

STANDER, Siegfried 1935-

PERSONAL: Born August 26, 1935, in Rietbron, South Africa; son of Adam and Janet (Derbyshire) Stander; married Jo Heydenreich (a medical practitioner), May 1, 1957; children: Andre, Karen. *Education:* University of South Africa, extra-mural student, 1952-54. *Home:* Cliff Cottage, P.O. Box 23, Plettenberg Bay, South Africa. *Agent:* A.M. Heath & Co. Lt., 35 Dover St., London W.1, England.

CAREER: E.P. Newspapers Ltd., Port Elizabeth, South Africa, reporter, 1955-58, copyreader, 1960-62, columnist, 1963-67; farmer in Bechuanaland, South Africa, 1959; "The Cape Argus," Cape Town, South Africa, copyreader, 1967-69; full-time writer, 1969—. *Member:* P.E.N. (South Africa branch). *Awards, honors:* Central News Agency Literary Award, 1961, for *This Desert Place;* Central News Agency Literary Award, 1968, for *The Horse.*

WRITINGS—All novels: This Desert Place, Gollancz, 1961; *The Emptiness of the Plains,* Gollancz, 1963; *Strangers,* Gollancz, 1965; *The Journeys of Josephine* (juvenile), Gollancz, 1968; *The Horse,* Gollancz, World Publishing, 1969; (contributor) *Wine Country,* Buren (Cape Town), 1970.

WORK IN PROGRESS: A novel, tentatively titled *The Fortress.*

BIOGRAPHICAL/CRITICAL SOURCES: Johannesburg Star, October 26, 1961; *South African Panorama,* May, 1962; *Observer Review,* August 11, 1968; *Books and Bookmen,* September, 1968; *Best Sellers,* March 1, 1969.

* * *

STANFORD, Ann 1916-

PERSONAL: Born November 25, 1916, in La Habra, Calif.; daughter of Bruce (an oil well tools dealer) and Rose (Corrigan) Stanford; married Ronald Arthur White (an architect), September 18, 1942; children: Rosanna (Mrs. William Norton, Jr.), Patricia Jane, Susan Lora, Bruce. *Education:* Stanford University, B.A., 1938; University of California, Los Angeles, M.A. (journalism), 1958, M.A. (English), 1961, Ph.D., 1962. *Politics:* Democrat. *Religion:* Protestant. *Agent:* Patience Ross, A.M. Heath & Co. Ltd., 35 Dover St., London W. 1, England. *Office:* San Fernando Valley State College, Northridge, Calif. 91324.

CAREER: University of California, Los Angeles, Foreign Press Awards, executive secretary, 1957-58, acting instructor in journalism, 1958-59, extension division instructor, poetry workshop, 1960-61; San Fernando Valley State College, Northridge, Calif., assistant professor, 1962-66, associate professor, 1966-68, professor of English, 1968—. Editorial consultant, Los Angeles County council on inservice education, 1958-59; consultant to UCLA department of journalism, 1961-64; poetry critic, Pacific Coast Writers Conference, 1964-66, 1968; poetry juror, James D. Phelan Awards in Literature, 1966. *Member:* Modern Language Association, P.E.N., National Council of Teachers of English, Philological Association of the Pacific Coast, California Writers Guild, Wilderness Society, Defenders of Wildlife, Save-the-Redwoods League, Phi Beta Kappa. *Awards, honors:* James D. Phelan fellowship in literature, 1938-39; Yaddo fellowship, 1957, 1967; Commonwealth Club of California silver medal in poetry, 1959, for *Magellan;* University of Redlands, Browning prizes, first award for manuscript of *Magellan;* Borestone Mountain Poetry Awards, first prize for "Pandora," in *Best Poems of 1960;* National Endowment for the Arts grant, 1967; Shelley Memorial Award, Poetry Society of America, 1969.

WRITINGS: In Narrow Bound, Alan Swallow, 1943; *The White Bird,* Alan Swallow, 1949; *Magellan: A Poem to be Read by Several Voices,* Talisman Press, 1958; *The Weathercock* (originally published as a poetry folio, Talisman Press, 1956), Viking, 1966; *The Descent,* Viking, 1970; (editor and translator) *The Bhagavad Gita: A New Verse Translation,* Herder, 1970.

Also author of an unpublished libretto, "The Lucky Dollar," score by Ernest Kanitz. Poems anthologized in *Twelve Poets of the Pacific,* edited by Yvor Winters, Alan Swallow, 1937, Borestone Mountain Poetry Awards *Best Poems of 1959, ... of 1960, ... of 1963, ... of 1964, ... of 1965, ... of 1966, ... of 1968, ... of 1969,* and *A Western Sampler: Nine Contemporary Poets,* Talisman Press, 1963. Contributor of poetry and articles to *Modern Verse, New Mexico Quarterly Review, Sewanee Review, Arizona Quarterly, California English Journal, Recurrence, PS, Variegation, Talisman, Yankee, University of Kansas City Review, Poetry, Western Humanities Review, Hudson Review, Approach, New Yorker, Southern Review, Coastlines, Massachusetts Review, New York Times Book Review,* and *Atlantic* Editor, *Uclan Review,* 1961-64; co-editor and co-founder, San Fernando Valley State College Renaissance Editions, 1968—; member of editorial board, *Early American Literature,* 1971—; poetry reviewer, *Los Angeles Times.*

WORK IN PROGRESS: A new collection of poems; a study of Ann Bradstreet's work.

SIDELIGHTS: Miss Stanford has recorded her poems for the Library of Congress.

BIOGRAPHICAL/CRITICAL SOURCES: Los Angeles Times, June 16, 1960; *La Habra Review,* July 14, 1960; *UCLA Alumni Magazine,* April, 1962; *Fine Arts,* December, 1962; *New Leader,* March 27, 1967; *Prairie Schooner,* winter, 1968-69; *Virginia Quarterly Review,* winter, 1971.

* * *

STANFORD, Derek 1918-

PERSONAL: Born October 11, 1918, in Middlesex, England; son of Richard James and Ada Stanford; married Margaret Holdsworth (poet, under name Margaret Philips). *Education:* Attended Upper Latymer School, London, England. *Politics:* Liberal Constitutionalist. *Religion:* Anglican. *Home:* 46 Lulworth Ave., Lampton, Hounslow, Middlesex, England.

CAREER: City Literary Institute, Holborn, London, England, lecturer in literature and creative writing; North Foreland Lodge, Basingstoke, Hampshire, England, teacher of history of art; teacher in adult education center. *Military service:* British Army, 1940-45. *Member:* Royal Society of Literature (fellow).

WRITINGS: (With John Bayliss) *A Romantic Miscellany* (verse), Fortune Press, 1946; *Music for Statues* (verse), Routledge & Kegan Paul, 1948; *The Freedom of Poetry: Studies in Contemporary Verse,* Falcon Press, 1948; *Christopher Fry: An Appreciation,* Nevill, 1951; *Christopher Fry Album,* Nevill, 1952; (with Muriel Spark) *Emily Bronte: Her Life and Work,* P. Owen, 1953, London House, 1960; *Dylan Thomas: A Literary Study,* Citadel, 1954; *Christopher Fry,* Longmans, Green, for British Council, 1954; revised edition, 1962; (with Ada Harrison) *Anne Bronte: Her Life and Work,* Day, 1959; *Movements in English Poetry, 1900-1958* (monograph), Centaur Press, 1959, reprinted, Folcraft, 1969; *John Betjeman: A Study,* Neville Spearman, 1961;

Muriel Spark: A Biographical and Critical Study, Centaur Press, 1963; *Stephen Spender, Louis MacNeice, Cecil Day Lewis: A Critical Essay,* Eerdmans, 1969.

Editor, and author of introduction: *Thackeray's English Humorists,* Grey Walls Press, 1949; (with Spark) *Tribute to Wordsworth* (symposium), Wingate, 1950, Kennikat, 1970; (with Spark) *My Best Mary: Letters of Mary Wollstonecraft Shelley,* Wingate, 1953, Folcraft, 1972; (with Spark) *Letters of John Henry Newman,* Newman, 1957; *Francois de Salignao de La Mothe Fenelon, Letters to Men and Women,* Newman, 1957; (editor and translator with others) *Balzac: Conjugal Life,* Neville Spearman, 1958; *The Body of Love: An Anthology of Erotic Verse from Chaucer to Lawrence,* Anthony Blond, 1965; *Writings of the Nineties: From Wilde to Beerbohm,* Dent, 1970, Dutton, 1971.

Editor: *Poets of the Nineties,* Verry, 1965; *Prose of This Century,* Thomas Nelson, 1966; *The Arts of Sport and Recreation,* Thomas Nelson, 1967; *Aubrey Beardsley's Erotic Universe,* New English Library, 1967; *Short Stories of the Nineties,* John Baker, 1968, Roy, 1969; *Landmarks: An Anthology of Drama, 1945 to the Present,* Thomas Nelson, 1969; *Critics of the Nineties,* John Baker, 1970, Roy, 1971; *Witticisms of Oscar Wilde,* John Baker, 1971.

Verse appears in: Kenneth Rexroth, editor, *New British Poets,* New Directions, 1949; J.W. Robertshaw, editor, *Towards the Sun,* Collins, 1950; B. Gardner, editor, *Terrible Rain,* Methuen, 1966.

Contributor of articles on painters to "New Road" anthologies, Grey Walls Press. Contributor to literary periodicals in many countries, including *Observer, Month, Times Literary Supplement, Critic* (United States), *Commonweal* (United States), *Meanjin* (Australia), *Kroniek van Kunst en Kulture* (Netherlands). Fiction reviewer, *The Scotsman;* poetry critic, *Books and Bookmen;* art and literary correspondent, *Statesman.*

AVOCATIONAL INTERESTS: The visual arts, philosophy, religion.†

* * *

STANLEY-JONES, D(ouglas) 1905-

PERSONAL: Born February 2, 1905, in Cornwall, England; son of Herbert and Florence Eliza (Parry) Stanley-Jones; married Irene Katherine Fox (a registered nurse), February 29, 1936; children: Rosemarie, Kenneth, Geoffrey, Jillian. *Education:* Attended Whitgift Trinity School, 1916; St. Bartholomew's Hospital Medical College, University of London, B.Sc. (with honors in physiology), M.B., and B.S. *Home:* Buckshead, Townshend, Hayle, Cornwall, England.

CAREER: Fellow, Royal College of Surgeons; fellow, Royal Society of Medicine; director, Full Circle Foundation for Education and Research, Hayle, Cornwall.

WRITINGS: (With wife, Katherine Stanley-Jones) *Structural Psychology: De humani mentis fabrica,* Wright & Sons, 1957, Pergamon, 1960; (with K. Stanley-Jones) *The Kybernetics of Natural Systems: A Study in Patterns of Control,* Pergamon, 1960; *Electrical and Mechanical Oscillations: An Introduction,* Free Press, 1961; *Biological Origin of Love and Hate,* Academic Press, 1970; *The Role of Positive Feedback,* Gordon & Breach, 1970; *The Kybernetics of Mind and Brain,* C.C Thomas, 1970. Contributor to *Nature, British Medical Journal, American Naturalist, Psychoanalytic Review, Journal of Nervous and Mental Diseases,* and other professional journals.

WORK IN PROGRESS: Research on mind and brain, with special reference to emotional blocking of learning in children.

STANLEY-WRENCH, Margaret 1916-

PERSONAL: Born May 29, 1916, in New Barnet, Hertfordshire, England; daughter of William (an engineer and journalist) and Mollie Kennedy (an author and journalist; maiden name Gibbs) Stanley-Wrench. *Education:* Sommerville College, Oxford, B.A. (honours), 1939, M.A., 1942. *Religion:* Church of England. *Home:* Flat 3, Wilberforce House, 15 Northside, Clapham Common, London S.W.4, England. *Office:* St. Gabriels Teachers Training College, Cormont Rd., London, S.E.5, England.

CAREER: Home Office, Whitehall, London, England, administrative assistant, 1940-47; free-lance journalist, author, and poet, 1947-59; St. Gabriel's Teachers Training College, London, England, lecturer in English, 1959—. *Member:* P.E.N. (London), British Federation of University Women. *Awards, honors:* Newdigate Prize, 1937; Greenwood Poetry Prize, 1957.

WRITINGS: The Man in the Moon (poem), Basil Blackwell, 1937; *News Real, and Other Poems,* Macmillan (London), 1938; *The Rival Riding Schools,* Lutterworth, 1952; *The Splendid Burden* (plays in verse), Edinburgh House Press, 1954; *How Much for a Pony?,* Lutterworth, 1955; *Harlequin's Revenge* (plays for puppets), Centaur Press, 1955; *A Tale for the Fall of the Year, and Other Poems,* Linden Press, 1959; *The Story of Thomas More,* Methuen, 1961, published in America as *The Conscience of the King,* Hawthorn, 1962; *Teller of Tales,* Hawthorn, 1965 (published in England as *Chaucer: Teller of Tales,* World's Work, 1967); (translator and author of notes and introduction) Chaucer, *Troilus and Criseyde,* Centaur Press, 1965; *The Silver King: Edward the Confessor, the Last Great Anglo-Saxon Ruler,* Hawthorn, 1966. Poems included in many anthologies, including *Welcome Christmas,* edited by A.T. Eaton, Viking, 1955, *Four Feet and Two,* Penguin, *New Voices,* Horizon, *New Poems, 1958: A P.E.N. Anthology,* edited by Bonamy Dobree and others, M. Joseph, 1958, *Transatlantic,* 1959, and *New Poems, 1961: A P.E.N. Anthology of Contemporary Poetry,* edited by William Plomer and others, Hutchinson, 1961.

WORK IN PROGRESS: Poems, *The Beasts of Love.*

AVOCATIONAL INTERESTS: Cooking, especially inventing new recipes, gardening, entertaining friends, exploring London, and travel, especially to Italy.

* * *

STANTON, Gerald B(arry) 1918-

PERSONAL: Born April 22, 1918, in Cambridge, England; son of Percival (an importer) and Maidie (Richardson) Stanton; married Marry Elizabeth Engstrom (a guidance counselor), August 4, 1946; children: Kenneth Paul, Sharon Elizabeth, Richard Allen, Elaine Christine. *Education:* St. Petersburg Junior College, St. Petersburg, Fla., student, 1936-37; Wheaton College, Wheaton, Ill., B.Sc., 1940; Wheaton Theological Seminary, student, 1940-41; Dallas Theological Seminary, Th.M. (magna cum laude), 1945, Th.D. (magna cum laude), 1952. *Politics:* Republican. *Home:* 1392 Southwest Fourth Ct., Boca Raton, Fla. 33432. *Office:* Christian World Foundation, P.O. Box A, Boca Raton, Fla. 33432.

CAREER: Baptist minister. Bible conference speaker, 1945-50; head of Bible department at Biola College and professor of systematic theology at Talbot Theological Seminary, both Los Angeles, Calif., 1952-61; Christian World Foundation, Boca Raton, Fla., executive director, and staff teacher, Bibletown U.S.A., 1962—. *Member:* Evangelical Theological Society.

WRITINGS: Kept From the Hour: A Systematic Study of the Rapture in Bible Prophecy, Zondervan, 1956, 2nd edition published as *Kept from the Hour: Biblical Evidence for the Pretribulational Return of Christ,* Marshall, Morgan, & Scott, 1964; *Christian Foundations,* privately printed, 1956, 2nd edition, 1964; *The Great Words of the Gospel,* privately printed, 1960; *What is God Like?,* privately printed, 1963. Member of revision committee, *The Fundamentals for Today,* Kregal. Contributor to *Dictionary of Theology,* Baker Book. Columnist, "Theologically Thinking," *King's Business,* 1952-61; contributor of articles to religious journals. Member of editorial board, *King's Business,* 1952-61.

WORK IN PROGRESS: Prophetic Highways.

* * *

STARK, Irwin 1912-

PERSONAL: Born November 17, 1912, in Passaic, N.J.; son of Samuel and Rose (Friedman) Stark; married Alice Fox (a teacher), June 13, 1936; children: Evan Davd, Joyce. *Education:* College of City of New York (now City College of City University of New York), B.A., 1935, M.S., 1940. *Religion:* Jewish. *Home:* 2 Louisiana Ave., Bronxville, N.Y. 10708. *Agent:* Theron Raines, 244 Madison Ave., New York, N.Y. 10016. *Office:* City College of City University of New York, 139th at Convent Ave., New York, N.Y. 10031.

CAREER: City College of City University of New York, New York, N.Y., 1952—, began as assistant professor, now professor of English. Member of board of directors, Bronxville Gardens Cooperative Apartments. *Member:* American Association of University Professors. *Awards, honors:* First prize ($2,000) in short story division, Five Arts Award, for "The Bridge."

WRITINGS: The Invisible Island (novel), Viking, 1948; (editor with Irving Malin) *Breakthrough: A Treasury of Contemporary American-Jewish Literature,* McGraw, 1964; *Subpoena,* New American Library, 1966. Short stories anthologized in *Best American Short Stories,* edited by Martha Foley, Houghton, 1946, 1947. Contributor of short stories, poetry, and articles to magazines.

WORK IN PROGRESS: A novel.

* * *

STEANE, J(ohn) B(arry) 1928-

PERSONAL: Born April 12, 1928, in Coventry, Warwickshire, England; son of William John and Winifred (Gaskin) Steane. *Education:* Educated at King Henry VIII School, Coventry, England, 1934-46, Jesus College, Cambridge, 1948-52. *Office:* Merchant Taylors' School, Northwood, Middlesex, England.

CAREER: Merchant Taylors' School, Northwood, Middlesex, England, assistant master of English, 1952—. Director, Coventry Cathedral special choir, 1948-52; director, Cassiobury Singers, 1960—.

WRITINGS: Marlowe: A Critical Study, Cambridge University Press, 1964; *Tennyson,* Evans Brothers, 1966, Arco, 1969.

Editor: Thomas Dekker, *The Shoemaker's Holiday,* Cambridge University Press, 1965; Ben Jonson, *The Alchemist,* Cambridge University Press, 1967; Christopher Marlowe, *The Complete Plays,* Penguin, 1969; Thomas Nashe, *Selected Writings,* Penguin, in press. Contributor to *Record Collector.*

AVOCATIONAL INTERESTS: Music, early recordings.

* * *

STEARNS, Martha Genung 1886-

PERSONAL: Born March 18, 1886, in Amherst, Mass.; daughter of John Franklin (a college professor) and

Florence Mabel (Sprague) Genung; married Foster Stearns (New Hampshire representative, U.S. Congress, and diplomat), June 22, 1905 (deceased). *Education:* Privately educated at home and abroad. *Politics:* Republican. *Religion:* Roman Catholic. *Home:* Exeter Inn, Exeter, N.H. 03833.

MEMBER: Herb Society of America, Colonial Dames of America, New Hampshire League of Arts and Crafts, Boston Society of Arts and Crafts.

WRITINGS: (Editor) *The Transplanting,* Houghton, 1928; *Homespun and Blue: A Study of American Crewel Embroidery,* Scribner, 1940, 2nd edition, 1963; *Needle in Hand,* Washburn, 1950; *Herbs and Herb Cookery Through the Years,* Old Sturbridge Village, 1965. Contributor of articles on art and handicraft to magazines. Editor, *Herb Society of America Newsletter.*

SIDELIGHTS: Mrs. Stearns has lived in Turkey, Italy, and France.†

* * *

STECKLER, Phyllis B. (Schwartzbard)   1933-

PERSONAL: Born May 15, 1933, in New York, N.Y.; daughter of Irwin Henry (a retailer) and Bertha (Fellner) Schwartzbard; married Stuart J. Steckler (a retailer), June 3, 1956; children: Randall Ian, Sharon Royce. *Education:* Hunter College (now Hunter College of the City University of New York), B.A., 1954; New York University, M.A., 1958. *Religion:* Jewish. *Residence:* Atlantic Beach, N.Y. *Office:* CCM Information Corp., 909 Third Ave., New York, N.Y. 10022.

CAREER: R.R. Bowker Co. (publishers), New York, N.Y., editor, 1954-69; CCM Information Corp. (subsidiary of Crowell Collier and Macmillan, Inc.), New York, N.Y., project director, 1969—.

WRITINGS—Editor: (With Sidney Gross) *How to Run a Paperback Bookshop,* Bowker, 1963; (with Max Russell) *The College Blue Book,* 10 volumes, 13th edition, CCM Information Corp., 1969; (with Russell) *The Blue Book of Occupational Education,* CCM Information Corp., 1971; (with Ben Faden) *Computer Programs Directory,* CCM Information Corp., 1971. Contributor to *Encyclopaedia Britannica Yearbook.*

* * *

STEEL, Edward M(arvin), Jr.   1918-

PERSONAL: Born November 11, 1918, in Nashville, Tenn.; son of Edward Marvin (a clergyman) and Judith (Wilkes) Steel; married Barbara Manley, June 24, 1956; children: Philip. *Education:* Harvard University, A.B., 1940; University of North Carolina, M.A., 1950, Ph.D., 1953. *Home:* 412 Hill St., Morgantown, W.Va. 26505. *Office:* Department of History, West Virginia University, Morgantown, W.Va. 26505.

CAREER: Virginia Polytechnic Institute, Blacksburg, instructor in English, 1946-48; Millsaps College, Jackson, Miss., assistant professor of history, 1952-53; Limestone College, Gaffney, S.C., associate professor of history, 1953-56; West Virginia University, Morgantown, 1956—, began as assistant professor, now professor of history. *Military service:* U.S. Army Air Forces, 1942-46; became captain; received Purple Heart and Air Medal. *Member:* American Historical Association, Organization of American Historians, Southern Historical Association.

WRITINGS: T. Butler King of Georgia, University of Georgia Press, 1964. Contributor to *Georgia Historical Quarterly, Journal of American History,* and *Journal of Mississippi History.*

WORK IN PROGRESS: A biographical study of Mary Harris Jones.

STEEL, Ronald (Lewis)   1931-

PERSONAL: Born March 25, 1931, in Morris, Ill. *Education:* Northwestern University, B.A., 1953; Sorbonne, University of Paris, graduate student, 1953; Harvard University, M.A., 1955. *Agent:* International Famous Agency, 1301 Avenue of the Americas, New York, N.Y. 10019.

CAREER: U.S. Foreign Service, vice-consul, 1957-58; Scholastic Magazines, New York, N.Y., editor, 1959-62; writer. Visiting fellow, Jonathan Edwards College, Yale University, 1970-71, 1971-72, 1972-73. *Military service:* U.S. Army, 1954-56. *Awards, honors:* Fellow, American Political Science Association, 1962-63; Sidney Hillman Award for best non-fiction book, 1967, for *Pax Americana.*

WRITINGS: The End of Alliance: America and the Future of Europe, Viking, 1964; (with G.H.T. Kimble) *Tropical Africa Today,* McGraw, 1966; *Pax Americana,* Viking, 1967, revised edition, with introduction by D.W. Brogan, 1968, 3rd edition, revised, 1970; *Imperialists and Other Heroes: A Chronicle of the American Empire,* Random House, 1971.

Editor: *Federal Aid to Education,* Wilson, 1961; *U.S. Foreign Trade Policy,* Wilson, 1962; *Italy,* Wilson, 1963; *New Light on Juvenile Delinquency,* Wilson, 1967; *North Africa,* Wilson, 1967. Regular contributor to *New York Review of Books* and *Book World;* contributor of articles to *Atlantic, Harper's, Commentary, Foreign Policy, World View, New Leader,* and *Commonweal.*

WORK IN PROGRESS: A biography of Walter Lippmann.

BIOGRAPHICAL/CRITICAL SOURCES: New York Times Book Review, July 16, 1967; *Book Week,* July 16, 1967; *Newsweek,* July 24, 1967; *Times Literary Supplement,* August 3, 1967; *Commonweal,* October 27, 1967; *Punch,* February 28, 1968.

* * *

STEELE, Arthur R(obert)   1916-

PERSONAL: Born October 28, 1916, in Oakland, Calif.; son of Will Arthur and Mary Louise (Waterman) Steele; married Elizabeth Mae Smith (an assistant professor of English), December 22, 1947. *Education:* University of California, Berkeley, A.B., 1937; University of New Mexico, M.A., 1950; National University of Mexico, summer graduate study, 1948; Duke University, Ph.D., 1957. *Home:* 3219 Cheltenham Rd., Toledo, Ohio 43606. *Office:* University of Toledo, Toledo, Ohio 43606.

CAREER: Employed in San Francisco, Calif., by California Packing Corp. 1937-41, Southern Pacific Railroad, 1945-47; State University of New York, College for Teachers, Buffalo, assistant professor of history, 1957; University of Toledo, Toledo, Ohio, began as instructor, 1957, professor of history, 1964—. *Military service:* U.S. Army, 1941-45; became technical sergeant. *Member:* American Historical Association (Conference on Latin American History), Midwest Council for Latin American Studies, Ohio Academy of History, Phi Beta Kappa, Phi Kappa Phi, Phi Alpha Theta, Sigma Delta Pi. *Awards, honors:* Doherty Foundation fellowship to Latin America, 1951-52.

WRITINGS: Flowers for the King: The Expedition of Ruiz and Pavon and the Flora of Peru, Duke University Press, 1964.

* * *

STEIN, Aaron Marc   1906-
(George Bagby, Hampton Stone)

PERSONAL: Born November 15, 1906, in New York, N.Y.; son of Max and Fannie (Blumberg) Stein. *Educa-*

tion: Princeton University, A.B., 1927. *Home:* 1070 Park Ave., New York, N..Y. 10028.

CAREER: New York Evening Post, New York, N.Y., reporter, critic, columnist, 1927-38; Time, Inc., New York, N.Y., an editor, 1938; U.S. Office of War Information, Washington, D.C., propaganda analyst, 1942-43; freelance writer. *Military service:* U.S. Army, three years. *Member:* Princeton Club (New York).

WRITINGS—All published for the Crime Club by Doubleday, unless otherwise indicated: *Spirals,* Covici, Friede, 1930, *Her Body Speaks,* Covici, Friede, 1931, *The Sun is a Witness,* 1940, *Up to No Good,* 1941, *Only the Guilty,* 1942, *The Case of the Absent-Minded Professor,* 1943, *... And High Water,* 1946, *We Saw Him Die,* 1947, *Death Takes A Paying Guest,* 1947, *The Cradle and the Grave,* 1948, *The Second Burial,* 1949, *Days of Misfortune,* 1949, *Three—With Blood,* 1950, *Frightened Amazon,* 1950, *Shoot Me Dacent,* 1951, *Pistols For Two,* 1951, *Mask for Murder,* 1952, *The Dead Thing in the Pool,* 1952, *Death Meets 400 Rabbits,* 1953, *Moonmilk and Murder,* 1955, *Sitting Up Dead,* 1958, *Never Need an Enemy,* 1959, *Home and Murder,* 1962, *Blood on the Stars,* 1964, *I Fear the Greeks,* 1966 (published in England as *Executioner's Rest,* R. Hale, 1967), *Deadly Delight,* 1967, *Snare Andalucian,* 1968 (published in England as *Faces of Death,* R. Hale, 1968), *Kill is a Four-Letter Word,* 1968, *Alp Murder,* 1970, *The Finger,* 1973, *Lock and Key,* 1973.

Under pseudonym George Bagby—All published for the Crime Club by Doubleday, unless otherwise indicated: *Bachelor's Wife,* Covici, Friede, 1932, *Murder at the Piano,* Covici, Friede, 1935, *Ring Around a Murder,* Covici, Friede, 1936, *Murder Half-Baked,* Covici, Friede, 1937, *Murder on the Nose,* 1938, *Bird Walking Weather: An Inspector Schmidt Story,* 1939, *The Corpse With the Purple Thighs,* 1939, *The Corpse Wore a Wig,* 1940, *Here Comes the Corpse,* 1941, *Red is for Killing,* 1941, *Murder Calling "50": An Inspector Schmidt Story,* 1942, *Dead on Arrival,* 1946, *The Original Carcase,* 1946, *The Twin Killing,* 1947, *The Starting Gun,* 1948, *In Cold Blood,* 1948, *Drop Dead,* 1949, *Coffin Corner,* 1949, *Blood Will Tell,* 1950, *Death Ain't Commercial,* 1951, *Scared to Death,* 1952, *The Corpse With Sticky Fingers,* 1952, *Give the Little Corpse a Great Big Hand,* 1953, *Dead Drunk,* 1953, *The Body in the Basket,* 1954, *A Dirty Way to Die,* 1955, *Dead Storage,* 1956, *Cop Killer,* 1956, *Dead Wrong,* 1957, *The Three-Time Losers,* 1958, *The Real Gone Goose,* 1959, *Evil Genius,* 1961, *Murder's Little Helper,* 1963, *Mysteriouser and Mysteriouser,* 1965, (published in England as *Murder in Wonderland,* Hammond, 1965), *Dirty Pool,* 1966 (published in England as *Bait for a Killer,* Hammond, 1967), *Corpse Candle,* 1967, *Another Day, Another Death,* 1968, *Honest, Reliable Corpse,* 1969, *Killer Boy Was Here,* 1970.

Under pseudonym Hampton Stone—All "Inner Sanctum" mysteries, published by Simon & Schuster: *The Corpse in the Corner Saloon,* 1948, *The Girl With the Hole in Her Head,* 1949, *The Needle That Wouldn't Hold Still,* 1950, *The Murder That Wouldn't Stay Solved,* 1951, *The Corpse That Refused to Stay Dead,* 1952, *The Corpse Who Had Too Many Friends,* 1953, *The Man Who Had Too Much to Lose,* 1955, *The Strangler Who Couldn't Let Go,* 1956, *The Girl Who Kept Knocking Them Dead,* 1957, *The Man Who Was Three Jumps Ahead,* 1959, *The Man Who Looked Death in the Eye,* 1961, *The Babe With the Twistable Arm,* 1962, *The Real Serendipitous Kill,* 1964, *The Kid Was Last Seen Hanging Ten,* 1966, *The Funniest Killer in Town,* 1967, *The Corpse Was No Bargain At All,* 1968, *The Swinger Who Swung by the Neck,* 1970, *The Kid Who Came Home With a Corpse,* 1971.

WORK IN PROGRESS: A Stein novel; a Stone novel, *The Corpse Was a Mother's Day Gift.*

AVOCATIONAL INTERESTS: Archeology, painting.

BIOGRAPHICAL/CRITICAL SOURCES: New York Times Book Review, March 26, 1967, January 7, 1968, April 14, 1968, August 11, 1968, December 29, 1968; *Book World,* September 8, 1968.

*   *   *

STEINER, Gary A(lbert)   1931-

PERSONAL: Born August 3, 1931, in Vienna, Austria; son of Walter S. and Herma (Rosenberg) Steiner; married Faith Hudson, June 20, 1953; children: Linda. *Education:* University of Chicago, B.A., 1951, M.A., 1954, Ph.D., 1957. *Home:* 420 Briarwood, Highland Park, Ill. 60035. *Office:* Graduate School of Business, Haskell S26, University of Chicago, Chicago, Ill. 60637.

CAREER: Director of research in an advertising agency, 1956-58; Graduate School of Business, University of Chicago, Chicago, Ill., assistant professor of behavioral science, 1958-61, associate professor, 1961-64, professor of psychology, 1964—. Visiting research consultant and national television study director, Bureau of Applied Social Research, Columbia University, 1959-61; visiting professor at Instituto Superiore per Imprenditori E Dirigenti D'Azienda, Sicily, 1961, at Stanford University, 1964. Consultant to Elrick and Lavidge, Inc., 1958—, Columbia Broadcasting System Television Network, 1962—, WBBM-TV, Chicago, Ill., 1962—. *Member:* American Psychological Association, Phi Beta Kappa, Sigma Xi.

WRITINGS: The People Look at Television: A Study of Audience Attitudes, Knopf, 1963; (with Bernard Berelson) *Human Behavior: An Inventory of Scientific Findings,* Harcourt, 1964, abridged edition, 1967; (editor and author of introduction) *The Creative Organization,* University of Chicago Press, 1965. Contributor to professional periodicals.

WORK IN PROGRESS: A companion casebook for *Human Behavior,* with Bernard Berelson; a study of audience attitude toward non-program elements in television broadcasting.

AVOCATIONAL INTERESTS: Skiing, flying, and sailing.†

*   *   *

STEINER, Paul   1921-

PERSONAL: Born in 1921, in Germany; son of Otto (a banker) and Bertha (Sulmann) Steiner. *Education:* New York University, B.S., 1947. *Residence:* New York, N.Y.

CAREER: Coronet, New York, N.Y., features editor, 1947-53, humor editor, 1963. North American Newspaper Alliance, New York, N.Y., columnist and feature writer, 1958—; Women's News Service, New York, N.Y., correspondent, 1959—; Bell-McClure Syndicate's Pop Scene Service, New York, N.Y., feature writer, interviewer, 1967—. *Military service:* U.S. Army, World War II. *Member:* Alpha Delta Sigma, Psi Chi Omega. *Awards, honors:* Beaux Arts awards, 1968, for satire, 1969, for press, and 1970, for columnist.

WRITINGS: Israel Laughs: A Collection of Humor from the Jewish State, Bloch, 1950; *Women and Children First,* Bantam, 1955; *Bedtime Laughs,* Lion Press, 1956; *Bottoms Up,* edited by Charles Preston, Dell, 1957; *Bedside Bachelor,* Lion Press, 1957; *Useless Information: How to Know More and More About Less and Less,* Citadel, 1959; *How to be Offensive to Practically Everybody,* Citadel, 1960; *Sex After Six,* Hillman, 1961; *More Useless Information* (companion volume to *Useless In-*

formation), Citadel, 1962; *Useless Facts of History*, Abelard, 1964; *175 Little Known Facts About John F. Kennedy*, Citadel, 1964; *Useless Facts About Women*, Abelard, 1965; (editor) Adlai E. Stevenson, *The Stevenson Wit and Wisdom*, Pyramid, 1965; *1001 Tips for Teens*, Pyramid, 1967.

Contributor of features, quizzes and short humor to *This Week, TV Guide, Redbook, Show Business Illustrated, Reader's Digest, New York Times Magazine, Pageant, Argosy, Maclean's, Teen World, Cavalier, Variety, Critic's Guide, Bravo, Military Life, Cat Fancy, Dog Fancy*, and other magazines and newspapers. Columnist, "Working Rules" and "Picket Lines" in *Partners;* "New York Pro and Con" in *Promenade;* "The Wheel of Fortune" in *Fate;* "Israel Laughs" in *American Zionist;* "Where in the World" in *Travel Weekly;* "Theatre Talk" in *Playbill;* "Places to Go" in *Signature;* "Musically Speaking" in *Ascap Today;* "Notes and Quotes" in *Escapade;* "Raw & Recent" in *Caper;* "Odds & Ends" in *True Love.*

AVOCATIONAL INTERESTS: Stamp collecting, ancient relics, art.

* * *

STEINLE, John G. 1916-

PERSONAL: Born November 8, 1916, in Montana; son of Frank J. and Ada (de Lorimier) Steinle; married Joan E. Sinnott; children: Susan, Elizabeth, Gretchen, Jacqulynn, Abbe Anne. *Education:* University of Southern California, M.A., 1939; City College of Law, St. Louis, Mo., LL.B., 1941; University of Syracuse, M.S., 1947. *Religion:* Catholic. *Home:* 6660 North St.Andrews, Tucson, Ariz. 85718. *Office:* 61 Hilton Avenue., Garden City, New York, N.Y. 11530.

CAREER: Social Security Commission, St. Louis, Mo., medical and institutional director, 1937-39; St. Louis City Infirmary, St. Louis, Mo., superintendent, 1940-43; U.S. Public Health Service, section chief in Hospital Facilities Division, Washington, D.C., 1947-49; hospital program director, New York, N.Y., 1949-53; Cresap, McCormick, & Paget (management engineering firm), director of hospital studies, 1953-56; John G. Steinle and Associates (management consultants), Garden City, N.Y., president, 1956—. Columbia University, New York, N.Y., lecturer in School of Administrative Medicine, 1952-58. Adelphi College, former trustee. *Military service:* U.S. Army, 1943-45. *Member:* Academy of Hospital Counselors (vice-president), American Institute of Architects, Association of American Medical Colleges, Association of Hospital Planners.

WRITINGS: (With Ivan C. Belknap) *The Community and Its Hospitals: A Comparative Analysis*, Syracuse University Press, 1963. Consulting editor, *Hospital Topics*, 1956—.

* * *

**STEPHENS, Henrietta Henkle
(Henrietta Buckmaster)**

PERSONAL: Daughter of Rae D. (an editor) and Pearl (Wintermute) Henkle; married Peter John Stephens. *Education:* Attended Friends Seminary, New York, N.Y., and Brearley School. *Politics:* Liberal. *Religion:* Christian Science. *Agent:* Russell & Volkening, Inc., 551 Fifth Ave., New York 17, N.Y.

CAREER: Writer. *Awards, honors:* Ohioana Award in fiction for *Deep River*, 1945; Guggenheim fellowship.

WRITINGS—All under pseudonym Henrietta Buckmaster: *Tomorrow is Another Day*, R.D. Henkle, 1934; *His End Was His Beginning*, Henkle-Yewdale House, 1936; *Let My People Go: The Story of the Underground Rail-road and the Growth of the Abolition Movement*, Harper, 1941 (published in England as *Out of the House of Bondage: The Story of the Famous Underground Railroad of the American Negro Slaves*, Gollancz, 1943); *Deep River*, Harcourt, 1944; *Fire in the Heart*, Harcourt, 1948; *Bread from Heaven*, Random House, 1952; *And Walk in Love: A Novel Based on the Life of the Apostle Paul*, Random House, 1956; *All the Living: A Novel of One Year in the Life of William Shakespeare*, Random House, 1962; *Paul, a Man Who Changed the World* (biography), McGraw, 1965; *Freedom Bound*, Macmillan, 1965; *The Lion in the Stone* (novel), Harcourt, 1968.

Children's books, all under pseudonym Henrietta Buckmaster: *Lucy and Loki*, Scribner, 1958; *Flight to Freedom: The Story of the Underground Railroad*, Crowell, 1958; *Walter Raleigh, Man of Two Worlds*, Random House, 1964; *The Seminole Wars*, Collier, 1966; *Women Who Shaped History*, Collier, 1966; *Rebel Congressmen*, Scholastic Book Services, 1971.

SIDELIGHTS: A writer for *Young Readers' Review* acclaimed Miss Buckmaster's "candor and frankness regarding the often degrading behavior of the American government and its agents" during *The Seminole Wars*. "Though some historians may object because certain perfidious deeds have not been included, the author's selection of incidents and details is quite sufficient to establish the pattern of behavior.... A young person will better be able to appreciate our accomplishments after reading such an honest account of our past, for he can then understand that despite the base, cruel, heartless actions we are capable of, we have adopted a different code of behavior."

Although it is written in novel form, Robert Scholes regards *The Lion in the Stone* as "a political tract in fictional form, arguing the case for subordination of national interests to an international authority.... [The book] meets some of our fears and aspirations head-on.... As an introduction to the U.N. it is clearly superior to most textbooks, because it is committed as well as informed, and has sufficient hardness of head to justify its softness of heart."

Krishna Shah and Norman Muller (Norm-Krish Productions) have purchased film rights to *The Lion in the Stone.*

BIOGRAPHICAL/CRITICAL SOURCES: Young Readers' Review, April, 1966; *Christian Science Monitor*, May 5, 1966, June 6, 1968; *Best Sellers*, July 1, 1968; *New York Times Book Review*, July 14, 1968; *Variety*, August 19, 1970.

* * *

STERLING, Dorothy 1913-

PERSONAL: Born November 23, 1913, in New York, N.Y.; daughter of Joseph (a lawyer) and Elsie (Darmstadter) Dannenberg; married Philip Sterling (a writer) May 14, 1937; children: Peter, Anne. *Education:* Attended Wellesley College, student; Barnard College, B.A., 1934. *Politics:* Independent. *Home and office address:* Box 463, South Wellfleet, Mass. 02663.

CAREER: Architectural Forum, New York, N.Y., secretary, 1936-41; *Life*, New York, N.Y., researcher, 1941-49; free-lance writer. Democratic county committeewoman. *Member:* Authors Guild, National Association for Advancement of Colored People. *Awards, honors:* Nancy Bloch Award for children's book which best fosters intercultural understanding, 1958, for *Captain of the Planter*, and 1959, for *Mary Jane.*

WRITINGS: Sophie and Her Puppies (Junior Literary Guild selection), Doubleday, 1951; *The Cub Scout Mystery*, Doubleday, 1952; *Billy Goes Exploring* (Junior Literary Guild selection), Doubleday, 1953; *Trees and Their Story* (Junior Literary Guild selection), Doubleday, 1953; *United Nations, N.Y.*, Doubleday, 1953, revised edition, 1961; *Insects and the Homes They Build*, Doubleday, 1954; *Freedom Train: The Story of Harriet Tubman*, Doubleday, 1954; *The Story of Mosses, Ferns, and Mushrooms*, Doubleday, 1955; *Wall Street: The Story of the Stock Exchange*, Doubleday, 1955; (with husband, Philip Sterling) *Polio Pioneers: The Story of the Fight Against Polio*, Doubleday, 1955; *The Brownie Scout Mystery*, Doubleday, 1955; *The Story of Caves* (a Literary Guild selection), Doubleday, 1956; *The Silver Spoon Mystery* (Junior Literary Guild selection), Doubleday, 1958; *Captain of the Planter: The Story of Robert Smalls*, Doubleday, 1958; (with Donald Gross) *Tender Warriors*, Hill & Wang, 1958; *Mary Jane*, Doubleday, 1959; *Secret of the Old Post-Box*, Doubleday, 1960; *Creatures of the Night*, Doubleday, 1960; *Caterpillars*, Doubleday, 1961; *Ellen's Blue Jays*, Doubleday, 1961; *Forever Free: The Story of the Emancipation Proclamation*, Doubleday, 1963; *Spring's Here!*, Doubleday, 1964; *Lucretia Mott, Gentle Warrior*, Doubleday, 1964; (with Benjamin Quarles) *Lift Every Voice: The Lives of Booker T. Washington, W.E.B. Du Bois, Mary Church Terrell, and James Weldon Johnson*, Doubleday, 1965; *Fall is Here!*, published for American Museum of Natural History by Natural History Press, 1966; *The Outer Lands: A Natural History Guide to Cape Cod, Martha's Vineyard, Nantucket, Block Island, and Long Island*, published for American Museum of Natural History by Natural History Press, 1967; *Tear Down the Walls!: A History of the American Civil Rights Movement*, Doubleday, 1968; *The Making of an Afro-American: Martin Robison Delany, 1812-1885*, Doubleday, 1971; *It Started in Montgomery: A Picture History of the Civil Rights Movement*, Scholastic Book Services, 1972; (editor) *Speak Out in Thundertones: Letters and Other Writings of Black Northerners, 1787-1865*, Doubleday, 1973. Contributor of nature articles to *Book of Knowledge*. Editorial consultant for Perspective Books, series of biographies of notable black men and women, published by Doubleday; consulting editor for Firebird Books, Scholastic; editorial consultant on black history for Beacon Press.

WORK IN PROGRESS: Editing a second volume of letters and other writings by blacks to cover period from 1865-1905.

SIDELIGHTS: Mrs. Sterling's writing interests fall into two fields. One of these is the stimulation of interest in science, particularly biology, in children of elementary-school age, and the other is exploration of little known aspects of American history, especially the story of the American Negro and his fight for equality. She has also written a number of fiction books for children.

In a review of *Tear Down The Walls!* for *Negro Digest*, Nikki Giovanni called [Dorothy Sterling's] "treatment of the civil rights movement . . . one of the more understanding ones for youngsters. . . . She tells our story with such compassion and understanding that it is difficult to believe she is non-Black." *Mary Jane*, a fictional account of school integration, won the Nancy Bloch Award in 1959, in addition to the Community-Woodward School's award for promotion of "one worldness" among children, and an honorable mention from the Child Study Association of America.

BIOGRAPHICAL/CRITICAL SOURCES: Best Sellers, October 1, 1968, June 15, 1971; *Negro Digest*, January, 1969.

*   *   *

STERN, Karl   1906-

PERSONAL: Born April 8, 1906, in Cham, Bavaria, Germany; Canadian citizen; son of Adolf and Ida (Rosenbaum) Stern; married Liselotte von Baeyer, 1936; children: Anthony, Katherine Stern Skorzewska, Michael. *Education:* Attended University of Munich and University of Berlin; University of Frankfurt, M.D., 1930. *Home:* 3800 Grey Ave., Montreal 28, Quebec, Canada.

CAREER: Served medical internship and residency in Germany, and trained in psychoanalysis as Rockefeller fellow at German Research Institute for Psychiatry, 1932-36; National Hospital for Nervous Diseases, London, England, work under research grant, 1936-39; McGill University, Montreal, Quebec, lecturer in neuropathology, 1940-44, assistant professor of psychiatry, 1944-52; University of Ottawa, Ottawa, Ontario, professor of psychiatry, 1952—; University of Montreal, Montreal, Quebec, associate professor of psychiatry, 1955—; St. Mary's Hospital, Montreal, Quebec, psychiatrist-in-chief, 1958-68. Canadian representative, UNESCO Institute for Education, 1951-59. *Member:* Canadian Psychiatric Association, American Psychiatric Association, American Association of Neuropathologists, P.E.N. *Awards, honors:* Christopher Award, 1951, 1954; Canadian Newman Award, 1961.

WRITINGS: The Pillar of Fire, Harcourt, 1951; *The Third Revolution*, Harcourt, 1954; *Through Dooms of Love*, Farrar, Straus, 1960; *The Flight from Woman*, Farrar, Straus, 1965. Contributor of more than sixty articles to scientific journals.

SIDELIGHTS: Stern is interested in philosophy and music.

*   *   *

STERNER, R. Eugene   1912-

PERSONAL: Born July 7, 1912, in Clarion County, Pa.; son of J.C. and Mae (Ashbaugh) Sterner; married Mildred Rabberman (a clerical worker), August 19, 1935; children: Sylvia Waneta Sterner Wilson, Kathy Sue, Peggy Loree. *Education:* Anderson College, student, 1933-36; Louisiana Polytechnic Institute, B.A., 1941; Alabama Polytechnic Institute (now Auburn University) graduate study, 1942-43; Bonebrake Theological Seminary, theological study, 1947-49. *Politics:* Republican. *Home:* 420 Stuart Circle, Anderson, Ind. 46012. *Office address:* Church of God, 1303 East 5th St., Box 2420, Anderson, Ind. 46012.

CAREER: Minister, Church of God; pastor of churches in Pennsylvania, Louisiana, Alabama, and Ohio, 1936-53, and director of youth work in ten southeastern states, 1944-45; Church of God, Anderson, Ind., director of Radio and Television Commission, 1953-62, director of Church Service, 1962—, member of Missionary Board and of commissions on race, social concerns, revision and planning, and world service. *Member:* Kiwanis Club (member of board of directors, Anderson).

WRITINGS: Toward a Christian Fellowship, Warner Press, 1957; *We Reach Our Hands in Fellowship*, Warner Press, 1960; *You Have a Ministry*. Warner Press, 1963; *Being the Community of Christian Love*, Warner Press, 1971; *Where Are You Going, Jesus?*, Warner Press, 1971. Author of series of twelve booklets, "Steps Toward Vital Christian Living," Warner, 1955. Contributor to *Vital Christianity* (denominational weekly), and to church school quarterlies.

WORK IN PROGRESS: A manual, *The Local Church at Work.†*

*   *   *

STERNSHER, Bernard   1925-

PERSONAL: Born March 3, 1925, in Fall River, Mass.; son of Nathan (a lawyer) and Eleanor (Bernard) Sternsher; married Carol Yvonne Edwards (a photophysicist),

August 26, 1961; children: Daniel, David. *Education:* University of Alabama, B.A., 1949; Boston University, A.M., 1950, Ph.D., 1957. *Politics:* Democrat. *Home:* 430 Edgewood Dr., Perrysburg, Ohio 43551.

CAREER: Westtown School, Westtown, Pa., master, 1955-56; Rochester Institute of Technology, Rochester, N.Y., assistant professor of history, 1956-61; Fairleigh Dickinson University, Madison, N.J., assistant professor of history, 1961-62; Seton Hall University, South Orange, N.J., associate professor, 1962-64, professor of history, 1964-69; Bowling Green State University, Bowling Green, Ohio, professor of history, 1969—. Democratic county committeeman, Rochester, N.Y., 1958-61. *Military service:* U.S. Coast Guard Reserve, 1943-46; one of survivors of crew of U.S.S. "Jackson," lost off Cape Hatteras in hurricane, 1944; served in Philippines, 1945-46; became sonarman third class. *Member:* American Historical Association, American Studies Association, American Association of University Professors, Organization of American Historians, Phi Beta Kappa. *Awards, honors:* Phi Alpha Theta prize, 1966, for *Rexford Tugwell and the New Deal.*

WRITINGS: Rexford Tugwell and the New Deal, Rutgers University Press, 1964; (editor and contributor) *The New Deal: Doctrines and Democracy,* Allyn & Bacon, 1966; (editor and author of commentary) *The Negro in Depression and War: Prelude to Revolution, 1930-1945,* Quadrangle, 1969; (editor) *Hitting Home: The Great Depression in Town and Country,* Quadrangle, 1970. Contributor of articles and reviews to *American Quarterly, Antioch Review, Labor History, Pacific Historical Review,* and other journals.

WORK IN PROGRESS: United States Historiography since World War II: The Rise and Confinement of the Consensus View; and *The American Trotskyites: A Case Study in Radical Politics.*

AVOCATIONAL INTERESTS: Watching football and baseball, woodworking, the theatre.

* * *

STESSIN, Lawrence 1911-

PERSONAL: Born July 23, 1911, in New York, N.Y.; son of Hyman and Eva (Lipchine) Stessin; married Dorothy Kaden, 1937. *Education:* Columbia University, M.A., 1950; New York University, Ph.D., 1957. *Home:* 70 East 10th St., New York, N.Y. 10003. *Office:* Hofstra College, Hempstead, N.Y. 11050.

CAREER: New York Times, New York, N.Y., writer, 1934-41; *Forbes,* New York, N.Y., an editor, 1941-51; Row Features, New York, N.Y., owner, 1951-57; Hofstra College, Hempstead, N.Y., professor of management, 1958—. U.S. State Department, mission chief in Middle East for International Cooperation Administration executive development program, 1956-59. *Member:* American Association of University Professors, National Academy of Management, Overseas Press Club.

WRITINGS: Employee Discipline, Bureau of National Affairs, 1960; *The Practice of Personnel and Industrial Relations: A Casebook,* Pitman, 1964; (with Ira Wit) *The Disloyal Employee,* Man & Manager, Inc., 1967. Contributor of articles to *Personnel Management Review, Reader's Digest, New York Times Magazine.* Contributing editor, *Dun's Review and Modern Industry.*

AVOCATIONAL INTERESTS: Golf.

* * *

STEVENS, Clifford 1926-

PERSONAL: Born March 27, 1926, in Brattleboro, Vt.; son of Clarence Frederick and Agnes (Murray) Stevens.

Education: Attended high school at Boys Town, Neb., 1942-44; studied at Creighton University, 1945-46, 1959-60, New Melleray Abbey Seminary, 1946-52, Conception Seminary, 1954-56. *Home:* Boys Town, Neb. 68010.

CAREER: Worked in a California shipyard one year before studying for the priesthood; ordained Roman Catholic priest in Omaha, Neb., 1956; parish priest in Omaha Diocese, 1956-61; U.S. Air Force, chaplain, 1961-69, stationed in California, in Alaska (as chaplain to men at remote radar sites), at Holloman Air Force Base, N.M., in Itazuke, Japan; Institute of Man and Science, Rensselaerville, N.Y., 1969.

WRITINGS: Flame Out of Dorset (historical novel), Doubleday, 1964; *Father Flanagan: Builder of Boys,* Kenedy, 1968; *Astro-Theology,* Divine Word Publications, 1969. Author of play, "Vitoria," produced at New Mexico State University, 1964. Contributor to *Catholic World, American Benedictine Review,* and other denominational publications. Executive editor, *Priest* Magazine, 1969; editor and publisher, *Schema XIII* (journal for the priest in the modern world).

WORK IN PROGRESS: Canticle of the Sun, a biographical study of St. Thomas Aquinas; a contemporary novel, *The Vatican Murder;* a juvenile biography of Michizane Sugawara, Japanese statesman and scholar, *Plum Blossom;* a narrative poem set in Japan, *Takashima; Edward Joseph Flanagan,* a full-length biography of the founder of Boys Town, Neb.

SIDELIGHTS: In a feature story in the *Anchorage News,* Chaplain Stevens is quoted as saying that "my real purpose is to corner the market on green cheese," another way of stating that his career objective is to get into space. This aim was born of a ride with X15-pilot Robert M. White in an F104 in 1962. Later he co-authored an article, "An Astronaut's View of God," with White. Several other of his magazine articles have been on the aerospace-religious theme.

BIOGRAPHICAL SOURCES: Anchorage Daily News, Anchorage, Alaska, May 4, 1963; *El Paso Times,* El Paso, Tex., February 16, 1964; *Aerospace Historian,* autumn, 1968; *Religious News Service,* December 30, 1969.

* * *

STEVENS, Denis William 1922-

PERSONAL: Born March 2, 1922, in High Wycombe, Buckinghamshire, England; son of William James and Edith (Driver) Stevens; married Sheila Holloway, June 25, 1949; children: Anthony Vincent, Daphne Elizabeth, Michael David. *Education:* Jesus College, Oxford, M.A., 1947, post-graduate study, 1947-49. *Home:* 25 Claremont Ave., New York, N.Y. 10027. *Office:* Department of Music, Columbia University, New York, N.Y. 10027.

CAREER: Philharmonia Orchestra, London, England, violinist, 1949; British Broadcasting Corp., London, England, producer, Music Division, 1949-54; Ambrosian Singers, London, England, conductor, 1952—; Columbia University, New York, N.Y., professor of musicology, 1964—. Visiting professor at Cornell University, Columbia University, University of California, Berkeley; Distinguished Visiting Professor at Pennsylvania State University, 1962-66. Consultant in musicology, British Broadcasting Corp., artistic director, Accademia Monteverdiana. Lecturer and conductor of principal international festivals. *Military service:* Royal Air Force, 1942-46; served in India and Burma. *Member:* Royal Academy of Music (honorary), Society of Antiquaries (fellow), American Musicological Society, Plainsong and Medieval Music Society, International Musicological Society, Societe Francaise de Musicologie, Worshipful Company of Musicians Medieval Academy of America.

WRITINGS: The Mulliner Book: A Commentary, Stainer & Bell, 1952; *Tudor Church Music,* Merlin Press, 1955, 2nd edition, Norton, 1966; *Thomas Tomkins, 1572-1656,* St. Martin's, 1957; (editor) *A History of Song,* Hutchinson, 1960, Norton, 1961, revised edition, 1970; (with Edward Greenfield and Ivan March) *Stereo Record Guide,* Long Playing Record Library, Volume I, 1960, Volume II, 1961, Volume III, 1963; (editor with Alec Robertson) *The Pelican History of Music,* Penguin, Volume I: *Ancient Forms to Polyphony,* 1960, Volume II: *Renaissance and Baroque,* 1963, Volume III (by Hugh Ottaway and Arthur Hutchins): *Classical and Romantic,* 1968; *Penguin Book of English Madrigals for Four Voices,* Penguin, 1967; (author of foreword) Francois Lesure, *Music and Art in Society,* Pennsylvania State University Press, 1968; *Second Penguin Book of English Madrigals,* Penguin, 1970.

Editor—Music series, published by Pennsylvania State University Press: George F. Handel, *Look Down Harmonious Saint,* 1963, Richard Dering, *Cries of London,* 1964, Claudio Monteverdi, *Hor Che'l Ciel e la Terra,* 1964, Thomas Roseingrave, *Compositions for Organ and Harpsichord,* 1964, Giuseppe Tartini, *Violin Concerto in D,* 1971, Giovanni Gabrieli, *In Ecclesiis,* 1972. Contributor of articles to encyclopedias, dictionaries, popular magazines, and scholarly journals. Associate editor of Sir George Grove's *Dictionary of Music and Musicians,* 5th edition, St. Martin's, 1954; music critic, *Gramophone,* 1954-64.

WORK IN PROGRESS: Studies on fourteenth-century English music, Monteverdi, and Italian church music.

AVOCATIONAL INTERESTS: Travel and photography.

BIOGRAPHICAL/CRITICAL SOURCES: Times Literary Supplement, September 21, 1967.

*   *   *

STEVENSON, George J(ames)   1924-

PERSONAL: Born September 19, 1924, in Van Buren, Ark.; son of Oscar (a locomotive engineer) and Mabel (French) Stevenson; married Joyce Ellen Bledsoe, June 27, 1948; children: Laura Ellen, George James, Jr. *Education:* University of Arkansas, B.S., 1948, M.A., 1949; Vanderbilt University, Ph.D., 1954. *Politics:* Democrat. *Religion:* Episcopalian. *Home:* P.O. Drawer S, Emory, Va. 24327.

CAREER: Emory and Henry College, Emory, Va., professor of history, 1952—, chairman of department of history and political science. University of Virginia Extension Division, instructor. *Military service:* U.S. Army, Infantry, 1943-45; became sergeant; received Bronze Star and Purple Heart. *Member:* American Studies Association, American Association of University Professors, Southern Historical Association, Organization of American Historians, Southwest Virginia Historical Society, Historical Society of Washington County (Va.), Pi Kappa Alpha, Pi Gamma Mu, Phi Alpha Theta, Pi Sigma Alpha.

WRITINGS: Increase in Excellence: A History of Emory and Henry College, 1863-1963, Appleton, 1963. Contributor to *Emory and Henry Review.* Editor, publications of the Historical Society of Washington County, Virginia (collected edition, 1964).

WORK IN PROGRESS: The Brotherhood of Locomotive Engineers and Its Leaders, 1863-1920; editing the autobiography of Richard N. Price.

*   *   *

STEWART, James S(tuart)   1896-

PERSONAL: Born July 21, 1896, in Dundee, Scotland; son of William and Katharine (Duke) Stewart; married Rosamund Anne Barron, September 29, 1931; children: Robert J., John F. *Education:* University of St. Andrews, M.A., 1917, B.D., 1921; also studied at New College, University of Edinburgh, and at University of Bonn. *Home:* 6 Crawfurd Rd., Edinburgh 9, Scotland.

CAREER: Clergyman, Church of Scotland. Minister in Auchterarder, Perthshire, Scotland, 1924-28, in Aberdeen, Scotland, 1928-35, in Edinburgh, Scotland, 1935-46; University of Edinburgh, Edinburgh, Scotland, professor of New Testament, 1947-66. Lyman Beecher Lecturer at Yale University; Stone Lecturer at Princeton University; Hoyt Lecturer at Union Theological Seminary, New York, N.Y.; moderator, General Assembly of Church of Scotland, 1963-64. Chaplain to Her Majesty The Queen in Scotland. *Military service:* Royal Engineers, 1917-18. *Awards, honors:* D.D. from University of St. Andrews, 1945.

WRITINGS: (Editor of English translation with H.R. Mackintosh) F.D.E. Schleiermacher, *The Christian Faith,* T. & T. Clark, 1928; *The Life and Teaching of Jesus Christ,* Church of Scotland, 1932, Abingdon, 1958; *A Man in Christ: The Vital Elements of St. Paul's Religion,* Hodder & Stoughton, 1935, Harper, 1963; *The Gates of New Life,* T. & T. Clark, 1937, Scribner, 1938; *The Strong Name,* T. & T. Clark, 1940, Scribner, 1941; *Heralds of God,* Hodder & Stoughton, 1946, Scribner, 1947, new edition published as *Preaching,* English Universities Press, 1955; *A Faith to Proclaim,* Scribner, 1953; *Exposition and Encounter: Preaching in the Context of Worship,* Berean Press, 1956; *Thine is the Kingdom,* St. Andrew Press, 1956, Scribner, 1957; *The Wind of the Spirit,* Hodder & Stoughton, 1968, Abingdon, 1969; *River of Life,* Abingdon, 1972.

*   *   *

STEWART, John B(enjamin)   1924-

PERSONAL: Born November 19, 1924, in Antigonish, Nova Scotia; son of George Harvie (a farmer) and Mary Elizabeth (MacGregor) Stewart. *Education:* Acadia University, B.A. (honors), 1945, M.A., 1946; Columbia University, Ph.D., 1953. *Politics:* Liberal. *Religion:* Baptist. *Home:* Bayfield, Antigonish County, Nova Scotia, Canada.

CAREER: Columbia University, New York, N.Y., instructor in public law, 1950-53; Barnard College, New York, N.Y., assistant professor of government, 1953-59; St. Francis Xavier University, Antigonish, Nova Scotia, professor of political science, 1959-62; elected to Canadian House of Commons, 1962, 1963, Parliamentary Secretary for External Affairs, 1963-64, vice-chairman of Canadian delegation to United Nations, 1963, Parliamentary secretary to Secretary of State, 1964—. Consultant, Rockefeller Foundation, 1953-55.

WRITINGS: The Moral and Political Philosophy of David Hume, Columbia University Press, 1963.†

*   *   *

STEWART, Katharine Jeanne (Dark)   1914-

PERSONAL: Born August 29, 1914, in Reading, England; daughter of Richard (a teacher) and Hilda (Carter) Dark; married S.C. Stewart (a civil servant), June 22, 1945; children: Hilda Grace. *Education:* Attended schools in France and St. George's School, Edinburgh, Scotland; University of Edinburgh, M.A. (honors), 1937. *Politics:* Liberal. *Religion:* Protestant. *Home:* Schoolhouse, Abriachan, by Inverness, Scotland. *Agent:* A.M. Heath & Co. Ltd., 35 Dover St., London WIX 4EB, England.

CAREER: War-time civil servant in Edinburgh, Scotland, and London, England, 1940-45; crofter (small farmer) in

Scottish Highlands, 1950-60; teacher of French, Inverness, Scotland, 1960—. *Member:* Scottish Secondary Teacher's Association, British Federation of University Women, Gaelic Society of Inverness.

WRITINGS: A Croft in the Hills, Oliver & Boyd, 1960; *A Chanter in the Glen,* Thomas Nelson, 1963; *Mairi's Island* (juvenile), Thomas Nelson, 1964; *A Dream in the Sea,* Thomas Nelson, 1966; *Silver in the Peat,* Oliver & Boyd, 1966. Contributor of short stories and articles to *Scots, Scotland's Magazine,* and *English Digest,* a monthly column to *Weekly Scotsman,* and twenty-five short stories to British Broadcasting Corp. Home and Overseas Service.

WORK IN PROGRESS: A children's book.

AVOCATIONAL INTERESTS: The arts and travel in the remoter parts of the Highlands by van and tent, and in France.†

*   *   *

STEWART, Robert Neil   1891-

PERSONAL: Born August 8, 1891, in Edinburgh, Scotland; son of John Charles and Anna (Babington) Stewart; married Georgette Hambachidze, April 20, 1937; chidren: Nino, Danali. *Education:* Attended Harrow School and Royal Military College (now Academy) at Sandhurst. *Home:* Kinlochmoidart, Fort William, Scotland.

CAREER: British Army, 1911-21, 1939-45, retired as major general. Served in France, 1914-16, the Balkans, 1916-18, Caucasia, 1918-19, Great Britain, 1939-45. *Awards, honors*—Military: Order of British Empire, Military Cross (twice), Legion d'Honneur, Order of the Falcon (Iceland).

WRITINGS: Experiment in Angling, and Some Essays, Northern Chronicle Office, 1947; *Casting Around,* Thomas Nelson, 1948; *Rivers of Iceland,* Icelandic Government, 1950; *Running Silver,* W. & R. Chambers, 1952; *Open Spaces,* Thomas Nelson, 1953; *Boys' Book of Angling,* W. & R. Chambers, 1955; *Boys' Book of Boats,* W. & R. Chambers, 1956; *Dogs of the Northern Trails,* W. & R. Chambers, 1956; *Boys' Book of the Deep Sea,* W. & R. Chambers, 1957; *Boys' Book of the Jungle,* W. & R. Chambers, 1958; *Boys' Book of the Yukon,* W. & R. Chambers, 1959; *Unsung Trails,* W. & R. Chambers, 1960; (with Moray MacLaren) *Fishing as We Find It,* Stanley Paul, 1960; *Salmons and Trout: Their Habits and Haunts,* W. & R. Chambers, 1963; *A Living from Lobsters,* Fishing News, 1971.

WORK IN PROGRESS: A book on the hunting instinct.†

*   *   *

STILL, C. Henry   1920-

PERSONAL: Born January 29, 1920, in Stockport, Iowa; son of Perry A. (a farmer) and Mary A. (Wallingford) Still; married Charlene Dorothy Draker, August 21, 1941; children: Gary, Santha, Peter, Stephen, Richard, Francis. *Education:* University of Iowa, A.B. in Journalism, 1942. *Politics:* Democrat. *Religion:* Catholic. *Home:* 1931 Montgomery Rd., Thousand Oaks, Calif. 91360. *Agent:* Anita Diamant, The Writer's Workshop, Inc., 51 East 42nd St., New York, N.Y. 10017.

CAREER: Newspaper man in San Francisco, Calif., 1946-47, in Iowa City, Iowa, 1947-52; *Rocky Mountain News,* Denver, Colo., assistant city editor, 1952-56, city editor, 1956-60; Martin Co., news bureau manager, Denver, Colo., 1960, public relations director, Baltimore, Md., 1960-62; Martin Marietta Corp., New York, N.Y.,

news director, 1962-63; Northrop Ventura Corp. (aerospace), Newbury Park, Calif., public relations manager, 1963-67, assistant director of public relations, 1967-70; full-time author, 1970—. Planning commissioner, Thousand Oaks, Calif., one year. *Military service:* U.S. Naval Reserve, 1942-45; gunnery officer aboard U.S.S. "Idaho"; received eight battle stars and Unit Commendation for service in Pacific. *Member:* Authors League, American Institute of Aeronautics and Astronautics, Public Relations Society of America, Aviation/Space Writers Association, National Press Club, Overseas Press Club, Air Force Association, Rotary Club, Sigma Delta Chi.

WRITINGS: To Ride the Wind (biography), Messner, 1964; *Will the Human Race Survive?,* Hawthorn, 1966; *The Dirty Animal* Hawthorn, 1967; *Man: The Next 30 Years,* Hawthorn, 1968; (with Francis Wise) *Youth and Drugs: Prevention, Detection and Cure,* Association Press, 1970; *In Quest of Quiet: Meeting the Menace of Noise Pollution—Call to Citizen Action,* Stackpole, 1970; (contributor) *As We Live and Breathe,* National Geographic Society, 1971; *Of Times, Tides, and Inner Clocks: Making the Most of What Man Knows About the Biological Rhythms of Life,* Stackpole, 1972. Contributor of 18 articles to *Minneapolis Tribune* "Science Reading Series"; contributor of a dozen science fiction stories to *Amazing, Fantastic, If,* and *Imagination,* of factual articles to *Country Gentleman* and other magazines.

WORK IN PROGRESS: Another book dealing with genetics and biological time clocks.

SIDELIGHTS: Still wrote: "I like mountain climbing, fishing, boating, gardening, and almost anything which helps me avoid getting any serious work done. Primarily, I'm a nut on the subject of space travel, and since the age of eleven, when I read my first science fiction story, I've prayed that I'd live long enough to see the first manned landing on the moon. It happened."

Still told *CA* that his "basic motivation stems from the awareness that interrelated scientific developments are seldom transmitted to the public in integrated form. Therefore, my attempt is to translate and indicate significance of new trends, particularly in the realms of natural resources, ecology, population, and environmental degradation."

*   *   *

STILSON, Max   1919-

PERSONAL: Born May 10, 1919, in Freeport, Ill.; son of Jesse Madison (a physician) and Edna (Wilson) Stilson; married Jean Cox, February 24, 1946; children: Patricia, Nancy, Delores. *Education:* Moody Bible Institute, student, 1947-51. *Religion:* Baptist. *Home:* 3238 East Moreland St., Phoenix, Ariz. 85008.

CAREER: With Merchant Police Patrol, Phoenix, Ariz., 1953—. *Military service:* U.S. Army, 18th Field Hospital, 1942-45.

WRITINGS: Bible Number Quiz, W.A. Wilde, 1957; *Bible Number Quiz Number Two,* W.A. Wilde, 1957; *Who, What, Where Bible Quizzes,* W.A. Wilde, 1959; *Snappy Bible Quizzes,* Zondervan, 1961; *The Day We Met Christ,* Zondervan, 1961; *How to Deal with Jehovah's Witnesses,* Zondervan, 1962; *How to Deal with Roman Catholics,* Zondervan, 1963; *Major Religions of the World,* Zondervan, 1964; *How to Deal with Mormons,* Zondervan, 1965.

WORK IN PROGRESS: Research into various religions of the world, and in field of sex as related to sexual fulfillment in marriage.

AVOCATIONAL INTERESTS: Sports.†

STINETORF, Louise (Allender)   1900-

PERSONAL: Born February 4, 1900, in Ward Township, Ind.; daughter of Samuel Grove and Ida Elnora (Burton) Allender; married Roscoe Stinetorf, 1919 (divorced 1937); married Henry Loel Wilson (a pharmacist; died 1955). *Education:* Earlham College, A.B., 1925; Temple University, M.A., 1941; additional study at Pendle Hill, University of Puebla, Hebrew University of Jerusalem, and Bryn Mawr College. *Politics:* Republican. *Religion:* Quaker. *Home:* 2305 Harbor Point Dr., Celina, Ohio 45822.

CAREER: Former teacher, now retired. Also worked in public relations and served as missionary for two years.

WRITINGS: Children of North Africa, Lippincott, 1943; *Children of South Africa,* Lippincott, 1945; *White Witch Doctor,* Westminster, 1950; *Beyond the Hungry Country,* Lippincott, 1954; *Elephant Outlaw,* Lippincott, 1956; *Musa, the Shoemaker,* Lippincott, 1959; *La China Poblana,* Bobbs-Merrill, 1960; *The Shepherd of Abu Kush,* John Day, 1963; *Children of Africa,* Lippincott, 1964; *A Charm for Paco's Mother,* John Day, 1965; *Manuel and the Pearl,* John Day, 1966; *The Treasure of Tolmec,* John Day, 1967; *Tomas and the Hermit,* John Day, 1968; *The Bears of Sansur,* John Day, 1969; *Sultanie the Beautiful,* John Day, in press. Also author of serials, some two hundred short stories, and several hundred poems.

AVOCATIONAL INTERESTS: Gardening, bird study, nature study hikes, art needle work, collecting antique pocket perfume flasks.

*   *   *

STIRLING, Betty Rutledge   1923-

PERSONAL: Born February 18, 1923, in Costa Mesa, Calif.; daughter of Elmer Elwood and Doris (Keck) Rutledge; married James H. Stirling August 23, 1942; children: Rose Marie, Paul Malcolm, Isabel Ann, Eric Leroy, Ralph Lloyd. *Education:* La Sierra College, A.S., 1941; San Jose State College, B.A., 1957; University of California, Berkeley, M.A., 1959, Ph.D., 1963. *Politics:* Republican. *Religion:* Seventh-Day Adventist. *Home:* 210 Pettis Ave., Mountain View, Calif. 94040. *Office:* Department of Sociology, San Jose State College, San Jose, Calif. 95114.

CAREER: Free-lance writer and editor, 1948—; San Jose State College, San Jose, Calif., assistant professor of sociology, 1962—. University of California Medical Center, San Francisco, lecturer in sociology, 1962. *Member:* American Sociological Association, American Association of University Professors, Society for Study of Social Problems, Pacific Sociological Association, Phi Kappa Phi, Kappa Tau Alpha.

WRITINGS—All published by Pacific Press Publishing Association, unless otherwise indicated: *Brush Valley Adventure,* 1952, *Polly's D-Day,* 1953, *Redwood Pioneer,* Follett, 1955, *Julie Otis, Student Nurse,* 1956, *This is How It Happened,* 1956, *Neil and Pam, Teachers of Tomorrow,* 1958, *This is Where They Went,* 1959, *Mission to the Navajo,* 1961, *Ned of the Navajos,* 1962. Contributor of articles, stories, and verse to home, nature, religious, and children's journals.

WORK IN PROGRESS: Research and monograph on relationship of employment of married women to popular attitudes and social structure.

*   *   *

STODDARD, Edward G.   1923-

PERSONAL: Born November 26, 1923, in Peking, China; son of Ross Emory (a minister) and Georgia (Luccock) Stoddard; children: Mark, Eric, Judith. *Education:* University of Chicago, Ph.B, 1947. *Politics:* Democrat. *Home:* 210 East 11th St., New York, N.Y. 10003. *Agent:* Lurton Blassingame, 60 East 42nd St., New York, N.Y. 10017. *Office:* Doubleday & Co., Inc., 277 Park Ave., New York, N.Y. 10017.

CAREER: Doubleday & Co., Inc., New York, N.Y., director of advertising, book clubs division, 1964-68, president, Doubleday Advertising Co., Inc., 1968—.

WRITINGS: The First Book of Magic (juvenile), Watts, 1953, revised edition, 1970; *The First Book of Television* (juvenile), Watts, 1955, revised edition, 1970; *The Story of Power* (juvenile), Garden City Books, 1956; *The Real Book of Electronics* (juvenile), Garden City Books, 1956; *The Story of Engines* (adapted from *The Story of Power*), Doubleday, 1959; *Speed Mathematics Simplified* (adult), Dial, 1962; *An Alternate Text of Advertising Effectiveness* (business), Doubleday, 1970.

*   *   *

STOIKO, Michael   1919-

PERSONAL: Born April 10, 1919, in New York, N.Y.; son of John and Pauline (Szumma) Stoiko; married Margaret Jane Hoehn, December 1, 1951; children: Jane Dallas, Michael Austin, Patty Houston. *Education:* Polytechnic Institute of Brooklyn, B.A.E., 1951. *Home:* 1218 Wine Spring Lane, Towson, Md. 21204. *Office:* Martin-Marietta Co., Middle River, Md. 21220.

CAREER: Wright Aeronauticals, Woodbridge, N.J., development test engineer on Sapphire Jet, 1950-51; General Electric Co., Schenectady, N.Y., missile systems designer on Project Hermes, 1951-53; Martin-Marietta Co., Middle River, Md., 1954—, was field test engineer on Viking rocket, contributor to design study of Vanguard booster, project engineer on Nova launch vehicle, now technical director on Project Gemini. *Military service:* U.S. Marine Corps, Aviation, 1940-45; became master sergeant. *Member:* American Institute of Aeronautics and Astronautics, British Interplanetary Society (fellow), American Rocket Society, National Wildlife Federation.

WRITINGS: (With Donald Cox) *Spacepower: What It Means to You,* Winston, 1958; (with Cox) *Man in the Universe,* Winston, 1959; (with Cox) *Rocketry Through the Ages,* Winston, 1959; *Project Gemini: A Step to the Moon,* Holt, 1964; *Soviet Rocketry: Past, Present, and Future,* Holt, 1970. Contributor to technical journals in United States, Mexico, and England.

WORK IN PROGRESS: A college text, *Rocket Booster Design;* adult nonfiction on space sciences.†

*   *   *

STOKELY, James R(orex), Jr.   1913-

PERSONAL: Born October 8, 1913, in Newport, Tenn.; son of James Rorex (a canner) and Janie May (Jones) Stokely; married Wilma Dykeman (a writer), October 12, 1940; children: Dykeman Cole, James Rorex III. *Education:* University of Tennessee, B.S., 1934. *Politics:* Independent. *Home:* 405 Clifton Heights, Newport, Tenn. 37821.

CAREER: Stokely Apple Orchard, owner and manager, Newport, Tenn., 1940-53, Asheville, N.C., 1944-53. *Member:* Authors Guild, Southern Historical Association, Newport Kiwanis Club. *Awards, honors:* Co-winner with wife of Sidney Hillman Foundation Award ($500), 1958, for *Neither Black nor White.*

WRITINGS: (With wife, Wilma Dykeman) *Neither Black nor White,* Rinehart, 1957; (with Wilma Dykeman) *Seeds of Southern Change: The Life of Will*

Alexander, University of Chicago Press, 1962; (contributor) *We Dissent* (symposium), St. Martin's, 1962; (with Wilma Dykeman) *The Border States: Ky., N.C., Tenn., Va., W.Va.,* Time-Life, 1968. Contributor of articles to *New York Times Magazine, Progressive, Nation, Commentary,* and *New Republic,* of poems to *Carolina Israelite, New South, Nation,* and *Atlantic Monthly,* and of book reviews to *Chattanooga Times,* and *Chicago Tribune.*

WORK IN PROGRESS: A book of poems.

*   *   *

STONE, Betty E.   1926-

PERSONAL: Born June 14, 1926, in Meriden, Conn.; daughter of Raymond Charles and Vera G. (Root) Stone. *Education:* William Jewell College, A.B.; Hartford Seminary Foundation, B.D. *Home:* 2 Summer St., Nahant, Mass. 01908. *Office:* United Church Press, 14 Beacon St., Boston, Mass. 02108.

CAREER: Minister of United Church of Christ; Lake Region Parish, Barton, Vt., associate minister, 1953-56; New Hampshire Congregational-Christian Conference, minister of Christian education, 1956-61; United Church of Christ, Division of Christian Education, United Church Press, Boston, Mass., editor of *Children's Religion,* 1961—.

WRITINGS: Lenton Devotions for Young People, Pilgrim, 1959; (compiler) *Here Begins the Gospel,* United Church Press, 1963; *Ministry of Christian Education Movement,* United Church Press, 1966. Columnist, "Special Delivery," in *Children's Religion;* contributor of articles to *Church School Worker, Power,* and other church periodicals. Author of Japanese haiku poetry.†

*   *   *

STONE, Eugenia   1879-
(Gene Stone)

PERSONAL: Born May 11, 1879, in Gold Hill, Nev.; daughter of William Hamilton (an attorney) and Cassaline (Mara) Stone. *Education:* Studied at University of California and University of Southern California. *Politics:* Democrat. *Home:* 294 North Raymond Ave., Pasadena, Calif. 91103.

CAREER: Onetime teacher in public schools in Nevada and California; Railroad and Public Service Commission of Nevada, assistant secretary, 1913-19; free-lance writer, mostly of books for young people, 1920—.

WRITINGS: (Under name Gene Stone) *Sagebrush Stories,* Crowell, Volume I: *Jane and the Owl,* 1920, Volume II: *The Adventures of Jane,* 1921; (under name Gene Stone) *Cousin Nancy,* Crowell, 1920; (under name Gene Stone) *The Story of Thomas Jefferson,* Barse & Hopkins, 1922; *Big Wheels Rolling,* Caxton, 1942; *Freemen Shall Stand,* Thomas Nelson, 1944; *Robin Hood's Arrow,* Wilcox & Follett, 1948; *Secret of the Bog,* Holiday House, 1948; *Page Boy for King Arthur,* Wilcox & Follett, 1949, reissued as *Page Boy of Camelot,* Scholastic Book Services, 1972; *Sagebrush Filly* (Junior Literary Guild selection), Knopf, 1950; *Squire for King Arthur,* Wilcox & Follett, 1955; *Magpie Hill,* Watts, 1958; *Tall Sails to Jamestown,* Macrae Smith, 1967.

WORK IN PROGRESS: Wild Marjoram, a historical novel; *Swimmer in the Rain;* "Panorama," a dramatic poem; "The Sorcerer," an epic poem based on Chinese ancient love story and comedy.

BIOGRAPHICAL/CRITICAL SOURCES: Young Wings, February, 1951.†

STONE, Peter H.   1930-

PERSONAL: Born February 27, 1930, in Los Angeles, Calif.; son of John (a motion picture producer) and Hilda (a film writer; maiden surname Hess) Stone; married Mary O'Hanley, February 17, 1961. *Education:* Bard College, B.A., 1951; Yale University, M.F.A., 1953. *Home:* 1161 York Ave., New York, N.Y. 10021; and Stony Hill Rd., Amagansett, N.Y. 11930.

CAREER: Playwright, and film and television scenarist. *Member:* Dramatists Guild of Authors League of America, Writers Guild of America. *Awards, honors:* Emmy Award of National Academy of Television Arts and Sciences, 1962, for "The Defenders"; Writers Guild of America nomination, 1962, for television play, "The Benefactors"; Writers Guild of America nomination for best comedy film, 1963, for "Charade," and 1964, for "Father Goose"; Mystery Writers of America award for best mystery film, 1963, for "Charade"; Academy Award for best original story and screenplay, 1964, for "Father Goose"; Tony Award for best musical, 1969, Drama Desk Award for best musical book writer, 1969, New York Drama Critics Circle Award, and *Plays & Players* award for new musical, 1970, all for "1776."

WRITINGS—Books for Musicals: "Kean," first produced on Broadway at Broadway Theatre, November 2, 1961; "Skyscraper," first produced on Broadway at Lunt-Fontanne Theatre, November 13, 1965; "Two by Two" (based on play by Clifford Odets, "The Flowering Peach"), first produced on Broadway at Imperial Theatre, November 10, 1970; "1776," first produced in New Haven at Shubert Theatre, February 10, 1969, produced on Broadway at Forty-Sixth Street Theatre, March 16, 1969; "Sugar" (based on film "Some Like It Hot") first produced on Broadway at Majestic Theatre, April 9, 1972. Also author of play, "Friend of the Family," first produced in St. Louis, Mo., at Crystal Palace, December 9, 1948.

Books: *Charade,* Gold Medal Books, 1963; *1776,* Viking, 1970.

Screenplays: (And author of film script) "Charade," Universal, 1963; "Father Goose," Universal, 1964; "Mirage," Universal, 1965; "Arabesque," Universal, 1966; (with Frank Tarloff) "The Secret War of Harry Frigg," Universal, 1968; "Jigsaw" (based on novel by Howard Fast, *Fallen Angel*), Universal, 1968; "Sweet Charity" (based on play book by Neil Simon), Universal, 1969; "Skin Game," Warner Bros., 1971; "1776," Jack Warner and Columbia, 1972. Also author of television scripts for "Studio One," networked by CBS in 1956, "Brenner," CBS, 1959, "Witness," CBS, 1961, "Asphalt Jungle," ABC, 1961, "The Defenders," CBS, 1961-62, "Espionage," NBC, 1963, and of script for musical special, "Androcles and the Lion," networked by NBC in 1968.

BIOGRAPHICAL/CRITICAL SOURCES: Variety, February 19, 1969; *Cue,* March 22, 1969; *Time,* March 28, 1969; *New York Times,* November 11, 1970; *New York,* November 23, 1970; *Life,* December 18, 1970.

*   *   *

STORM, Hester G(lory), pseudonym   1903-

PERSONAL: Born August 15, 1903, in Madison, Wis.; *Education:* University of Colorado, B.A., 1926; attended Cosmopolitan Conservatory, Chicago, 1930-31. *Politics:* Liberal Democrat. *Religion:* "Quite a bit, but no church." *Address:* c/o City Lights Book, 621 Columbus Ave., San Francisco, Calif. 94111.

CAREER: Held many odd jobs, including private tutor, music teacher, factory worker, peddler, and domestic worker. Editorial writer for *Chinese World* (bilingual newspaper), San Francisco, Calif., 1962-63.

WRITINGS: Bop for Laotzu and Other American Versions of Chinese Poetry, Golden Mountain, 1962; *Wrongside-Up Rainbow* (poetry), Alan Swallow, 1964; *Fugue,* Pommel Press, 1966. Poems have appeared in *Archer, Wormwood Review, Parnassus 1963,* and other publications.

WORK IN PROGRESS: Poems, proposed title, *Endless Toccato.*

SIDELIGHTS: Miss Storm writes to *CA:* "I am very fond of children—especially unhappy ones. [I] have a passion for teaching. [I] love to play the piano and to listen to chamber music. I used to be quite a hiker. There's nothing finer than climbing a good mountain."†

*   *   *

STOVALL, Floyd 1896-

PERSONAL: Born July 7, 1896, in Temple, Tex.; son of Jonathan B. (a farmer) and Henrietta (Hock) Stovall; married Maude Lambert. *Education:* University of Texas, B.A., 1923, M.A., 1924, Ph.D., 1927. *Home:* 1631 Bruce Ave., Charlottesville, Va. 22903. *Office:* Department of English, University of Virginia, Charlottesville, Va. 22204.

CAREER: University of Texas, Austin, instructor in English, 1924-25, assistant professor, 1927-34; North Texas State University, Denton, head of English department, 1935-49, dean of College of Arts and Sciences, 1945-49; University of North Carolina, Chapel Hill, professor of English, 1949-55; University of Virginia, Charlottesville, Edgar Allan Poe Professor of English, 1955-67, chairman of department, 1956-61; retired, 1967. *Member:* Modern Language Association of America (chairman, literature and society group, 1948-49; chairman, American literature section, 1951-52), Phi Beta Kappa, Colonnade Club, Farmington Country Club.

WRITINGS: Desire and Restraint in Shelley, Duke University Press, 1932; (editor and author of introduction and notes) *Walt Whitman: Representative Selections,* American Book Co., 1934; *American Idealism,* University of Oklahoma Press, 1943; (editor with Leo Hughes and Haldeen Braddy) *Reading Around the World,* Macmillan, 1946; (with Harry H. Clark and others) *Transitions in American Literary History,* Duke University Press, 1948; (editor) *The Development of American Literary Criticism,* University of North Carolina Press, 1955; (editor, and author with Jay B. Hubbell and others) *Eight American Authors: A Review of Research and Criticism,* Modern Language Association of America, 1956; (editor) *Whitman's Prose Works, 1892,* variorum edition, New York University Press, Volume I: *Specimen Days,* 1963, Volume II: *Collect and Other Prose,* 1964; (contributor) Norman Foerster and R.P. Falk, editors, *Eight American Writers* (anthology), Norton, 1963; (editor and author of introduction and notes) *The Poems of Edgar Allan Poe,* University Press of Virginia, 1965; *Edgar Poe the Poet: Essays New and Old on the Man and His Work,* University Press of Virginia, 1969. Contributor of articles on American and English literature of Romantic period to scholarly journals. Member of editorial board, *American Literature,* 1959-63.

WORK IN PROGRESS: A book on the foreground of *Leaves of Grass,* studies in the reading and other experience that shaped Whitman's poems.

AVOCATIONAL INTERESTS: Golf.

STOWE, David M. 1919-

PERSONAL: Born March 30, 1919, in Council Bluffs, Iowa; son of Ernest L. (a postal clerk) and Florence (Metz) Stowe; married Virginia Ware, November 25, 1943; children: Nancy, Elizabeth, Priscilla, David. *Education:* University of California, Los Angeles, B.A., 1940; Pacific School of Religion, B.D., 1943, Th.D., 1953; Yale University, postdoctoral study at Institute of Chinese Studies, 1945-46. *Politics:* Independent. *Home:* 54 Magnolia Ave., Tenafly, N.J. 07670. *Office:* National Council of Churches, 475 Riverside Dr., Room 678, New York, N.Y. 10027.

CAREER: First Congregational Church, Berkeley, Calif., associate minister, 1943-45, 1951-53; missionary and university professor in Peking, China, 1947-50; Carleton College, Northfield, Minn., chaplain and chairman of department of religion, 1953-56; American Board of Commissioners for Foreign Missions, Boston, Mass., and United Church Board for World Ministries, New York, N.Y., educational secretary, 1956-62; professor of theology in Beirut, Lebanon, 1962-63; National Council of Churches, Division of Foreign Missions, New York, N.Y., executive secretary, 1963-64, associate general secretary for overseas ministries, 1965-70, member of general board; United Church Board for World Ministries, New York, N.Y., executive vice-president, 1970—. *Member:* Society for Religion in Higher Education, Society for the Scientific Study of Religion, Theological Education Fund and Division of World Mission and Evangelism of World Council of Churches, Phi Beta Kappa, Pi Gamma Mu, Blue Key.

WRITINGS: The Church's Mission in the World, United Church Press, 1963; *When Faith Meets Faith,* Friendship, 1963, revised edition, 1967; *Partners with Almighty,* United Church Press, 1966; *The Worldwide Mission of the Church: A Coursebook for Leaders of Adults,* United Church Press, 1966; (contributor) W.J. Richardson, editor, *China and Christian Responsibility,* Maryknoll Publications, 1968; (contributor) James P. Cotter, editor, *The Word in the Third World,* Corpus Instrumentorum, 1968; (contributor) N.A. Horner, editor, *Protestant Crosscurrents in Mission,* Abingdon, 1968; *Ecumenicity and Evangelism,* Eerdmans, 1970. Contributor of articles to *Christian Century, United Church Herald,* and *Social Action.*

*   *   *

STRAND, Kenneth A(lbert) 1927-

PERSONAL: Born September 18, 1927, in Tacoma, Wash.; son of Jens Albrigt and Bertha (Odegaard) Strand; married Lois Marie Lutz (now a high school teacher), June 1, 1952. *Education:* Emmanuel Missionary College, B.A., 1952; University of Michigan, M.A., 1955, Ph.D., 1958. *Office:* Andrews University, Berrien Springs, Mich. 49104.

CAREER: Emmanuel Missionary College (now undergraduate college of Andrews University), Berrien Springs, Mich., associate professor of religion, 1959-62; Andrews University Theological Seminary, Berrien Springs, Mich., associate professor, 1962-66, professor of church history, 1966—. *Member:* Renaissance Society of America, American Society for Reformation Research, American Historical Association, American Society of Church History, American Association of University Professors, Society of Biblical Literature, Phi Beta Kappa.

WRITINGS: A Reformation Paradox: The Condemned New Testament of the Rostock Brethren of the Common Life, Ann Arbor Publishers, 1960; *Reformation Bibles in the Crossfire: The Story of Jerome Emser, His Anti-Lutheran Critique and His Catholic Bible Version,* Ann Arbor Publishers, 1961; (editor) *The Reformation and Other Topics Presented to Honor Albert Hyma,* Ann Arbor Publishers, 1962, 2nd edition, 1964; *German Bibles*

Before Luther: The Story of Fourteen High-German Editions, Eerdmans, 1966; Early Low-German Bibles: The Story of Four Pre-Lutheran Editions, Eerdmans, 1967; Three Essays on Early Church History with Emphasis on the Roman Province of Asia, Braun-Brumfield, 1967; (editor) Essays on the Northern Renaissance, Ann Arbor Publishers, 1968; (editor) Essays on Luther, Ann Arbor Publishers, 1969; Brief Introduction to the Ancient Near East: A Panorama of the Old Testament World, Braun-Brumfield, 1969; The Open Gates of Heaven: A Brief Introduction to Literary Analysis of the Book of Revelation, Braun-Brumfield, 1970.

Compiler—All published by Ann Arbor Publishers: Woodcuts from the Earliest Lutheran and Emserian New Testaments, 1962, Reformation Bible Pictures: Woodcuts from Early Lutheran and Emserian New Testaments, 1963, Woodcuts to the Apocalypse in Duerer's Time, 1966, Woodcuts to the Apocalypse from the Early 16th Century, 1969, Duerer's Apocalypse: The 1498 German and 1511 Latin Texts in Facsimile Plus Samples of Duerer's Woodcuts and Graeff's Copies, 1969. Contributor to scholarly journals, including Journal of Biblical Literature, New Testament Studies, Archive for Reformation History, and Renaissance Quarterly. Associate editor, Andrews University Seminary Studies.

WORK IN PROGRESS: Studies on phases of Reformation history.

* * *

STRATFORD, Philip 1927-

PERSONAL: Born October 13, 1927, in Chatham, Ontario; son of Reginald Killmaster (a research chemist) and Phyllis (Coate) Stratford; married Jacqueline de Puthod, September 26, 1952; children: John-Paul, Catherine, Christopher, Peter, Anne. Education: Attended Trinity College School, Port Hope, Ontario; University of Western Ontario, B.A., 1950; University of Paris, D. Univ. Paris, 1954. Home: 799 Hellmuth Ave., London, Ontario, Canada.

CAREER: University of Windsor, Windsor, Ontario, lecturer in English, 1954-56; University of Western Ontario, London, associate professor of English, 1956—. Visiting professor at University of Montreal, 1964-65.

WRITINGS: Faith and Fiction: Creative Process in Greene and Mauriac, University of Notre Dame Press, 1964; (translator) Jean Le Moyne, Convergence: Essays from Canada, Ryerson, 1966; Marie-Claire Blais, Forum House, 1971. Contributor to Kenyon Review, Canadian Forum, Tamarack Review, and Saturday Night.

AVOCATIONAL INTERESTS: Theatre, art, cooking, French, antique velocipedes, and snails.†

* * *

STRAUSS, Gerald 1922-

PERSONAL: Born May 3, 1922, in Frankfurt, Germany; married Alice Fellows; children: Victoria, Konrad. Education: Boston University, B.A., 1949; Columbia University, M.A., 1950, Ph.D., 1957. Office: Indiana University, Bloomington, Ind. 47401.

CAREER: Phillips Exeter Academy, instructor in history, 1951-57; University of Alabama, University, assistant professor of history, 1957-59; Indiana University, Bloomington, 1959—, began as assistant professor, now associate professor of history. Awards, honors: Fulbright fellow; Guggenheim fellow; awards from American Council of Learned Societies and Akademischer Austauschdienst.

WRITINGS: Sixteenth-Century Germany: Its Topography and Topographers, University of Wisconsin Press, 1959; Historian in an Age of Crisis: The Life and Work of Johannes Aventinus, 1477-1534, Harvard University Press, 1963; Nuremberg in the Sixteenth Century, Wiley, 1967; (editor and translator) Manifestations of Discontent in Germany on the Eve of the Reformation (collection of documents), Indiana University Press, 1971.

* * *

STRAUSZ-HUPE, Robert 1903-

PERSONAL: Born March 25, 1903, in Vienna, Austria; came to United States in 1923, naturalized in 1938; son of Rudolf and Doris (Hedwig) Strausz-Hupe; married Eleanor de Graff Cuyler, April 26, 1938. Education: University of Pennsylvania, M.A., 1943, Ph.D., 1946. Religion: Lutheran. Home: White Horse Farms, Newtown Square, Pa. 19073.

CAREER: Investment banker, 1927-37; Current History, associate editor, 1939-41; University of Pennsylvania, Philadelphia, special lecturer, 1940-46, associate professor, 1946-52, professor of political science, 1952—, director of Foreign Policy Research Institute, 1955-69. U.S. ambassador to Ceylon, 1970-72, to Belgium, 1972—. Lecturer, U.S. Air War College, 1953. Consultant, U.S. Department of the Army. Military service: U.S. Army, World War II, now lieutenant colonel (retired). Member: American Political Science Association, Council on Foreign Relations, Royal Geographical Society (fellow), Merion Cricket Club (Haverford, Pa.), Rittenhouse Club (Philadelphia, Pa.), Cosmos Club (Washington, D.C.), The Brook (New York, N.Y.).

WRITINGS: The Russian-German Riddle, University of Pennsylvania Press, 1940; Axis America, Putnam, 1941; Geopolitics, Putnam, 1942; The Balance of Tomorrow, Putnam, 1945; (with S.T. Possony) International Relations in the Age of the Conflict Between Democracy and Dictatorship, McGraw, 1950, 2nd edition, 1954; The Estrangement of Western Man, Gollancz, 1952; The Zone of Indifference, Putnam, 1952; The United States and the Western Alliance, Foreign Policy Research Institute, University of Pennsylvania, 1956; (editor with Alvin J. Cottrell and James E. Daugherty) American-Asian Tensions, Praeger, 1956; (editor with Possony) Air Power and National Security, American Academy of Political and Social Science, 1956; Power and Community, Praeger, 1956; (editor with Hary Hazard) The Idea of Colonialism, Praeger, 1958; (with others) Protracted Conflict, Harper, 1959; (with William R. Kitner and Possony) A Forward Strategy for America, Harper, 1961; (with Dougherty and Kitner) Building the Atlantic World, Harper, 1963; In My Time (autobiography), Norton, 1965; (with others) New Directions in U.S. Foreign Policy: A Symposium, Foreign Policy Association, 1969. Contributor to report of U.S. House of Representatives Committee on Un-American Activities, Communist Strategy of Protracted Conflict, U.S. Goverment Printing Office, 1958.

* * *

STROMMEN, Merton P. 1919-

PERSONAL: Born March 31, 1919, in Calumet, Mich.; married Irene Huglen; children: Peter, Timothy, James, John, David. Education: Normal School, Lamberton, Minn., teacher's certificate, 1937; Augsburg College and Theological Seminary, B.A., 1942, B.Th., 1944; attended University of Minnesota, 1940-41, 1951-53, M.A., 1955, Ph.D., 1960. Home: 7005 Garfield Ave., Minneapolis, Minn. 55423.

CAREER: Lutheran minister; country school teacher, 1937-38; pastor in Mora, Minn., 1942-47, and at Augsburg College, Minneapolis, Minn., 1947-56; Lutheran Church Youth Research, Minneapolis, Minn., executive director, 1958—. Youth director, Lutheran Free Church,

1944-61. *Member:* American Psychological Association, American Personnel Guidance Association, Clergyman of American Lutheran Church, Minnesota Psychological Association. *Awards, honors:* Preus Award of Lutheran Brotherhood, 1956.

WRITINGS: A Comparison of Youth and Adult Reactions to Lutheran Youth Problems and Sources of Assistance, Lutheran Youth Research, 1960; *Profiles of Church Youth: Report of a Four-Year Study of 3,000 Lutheran High School Youth,* Concordia, 1963; (editor) *Research on Religious Development: A Comprehensive Handbook,* Hawthorn, 1971; (with others) *A Study of Generations,* Augsburg, 1972. Also author of two published choral compositions, "Sun Arises Now," and "At the Foot of the Cross."

WORK IN PROGRESS: Editing "Christian Youth" series, for Thomas Nelson.

AVOCATIONAL INTERESTS: Music, especially choral directing and piano.

*　　*　　*

STROVER, Dorothea
(Dorothea Tinne, E.D. Tinne)

PERSONAL: Daughter of Theodore and Grace (Lane) Tinne; married Strover (now a retired colonel); children: Alexine, Christian. *Education:* Attended art schools in London, England, three years, and in Amsterdam, Netherlands, one year. *Politics:* Conservative. *Religion:* Church of England. *Home:* High Wray, Lodge Hill Rd., Farnham, Surrey, England.

CAREER: Art teacher in schools, 1940-45, and in own studio. *Member:* Royal Horticultural Society (fellow), Society of Wild-life Artists (founder member). *Awards, honors:* Member of the Order of the British Empire, 1971.

WRITINGS: The Lure of Lakeland, Warne, 1946; *Cheeky and Coy,* Oxford University Press, 1948; *Signposts to the Wild,* G. Bell, 1957; *Adventurous Holidays,* Peter Skelton, 1964; *Love and Laughter,* Farnham Publishing Co., 1970. Contributor of articles on natural history to magazines.

AVOCATIONAL INTERESTS: Gardening; all branches of natural history, with special interest in deer.

*　　*　　*

STRYKER, Sheldon　1924-

PERSONAL: Born May 26, 1924, in St. Paul, Minn.; son of Max and Rose (Moskovitz) Stryker; married Alyce Agranoff, September 7, 1947; children: Robin Sue, Jeffery, David, Michael, Mark. *Education:* University of Minnesota, B.A. (summa cum laude), 1948, M.A., 1950, Ph.D., 1955. *Office:* Indiana University, Bloomington, Ind. 47401.

CAREER: Indiana University, Bloomington, instructor in sociology, 1951-56, assistant professor, 1956-60, associate professor, 1960-64, professor of sociology, 1964—, Director, Institute of Social Research, 1965-70, chairman, Department of Sociology, 1969—. *Military service:* U.S. Army, 1943-46; received Purple Heart. *Member:* American Sociological Association, Society for Study of Social Problems, Ohio Valley Sociological Society. *Awards, honors:* Postdoctoral fellowship, Social Science Research Council; Fulbright research scholar, Italy, 1966-67.

WRITINGS: (With Theodore Caplow and Samuel Wallace) *The Urban Ambience,* Bedminster, 1964; (with Michael Schwartz) *Deviance, Selves, and Others,* American Sociological Association, 1971. Associate editor, *Social Problems;* editor, *Sociometry,* 1966-69.

WORK IN PROGRESS: Determinants of Political Trust; Role Socialization.

STURMEY, S(tanley) G(eorge)　1924-

PERSONAL: Born May 5, 1924, in England; son of William John and Winifred (LeHuquet) Sturmey; married Evelyn Ann Staniforth, 1955. *Education:* University of Adelaide, Master of Economics, 1951; University of Manchester, Ph.D., 1954. *Home:* Westrigg, Haverbreaks, Lancaster, England.

CAREER: University College, University of London, London, England, assistant lecturer in political economy, later lecturer, and reader, 1954-63; University of Lancaster, Lancaster, England, professor of economics, 1963—. *Military service:* Royal Australian Air Force, 1942-46.

WRITINGS: The Economic Development of Radio, Duckworth, 1958; *Income and Economic Welfare,* Longmans, Green, 1959; *British Shipping and World Competition,* Athlone Press, 1962; (with D. W. Pearce) *Economic Analysis: An Introductory Text,* McGraw, 1966. Contributor of articles to learned journals.

AVOCATIONAL INTERESTS: Gardening, music, fell walking, tennis; collecting maritime books and pictures.

*　　*　　*

STURMTHAL, Adolf F(ox)　1903-

PERSONAL: Born September 10, 1903, in Vienna, Austria; came to United States in 1938; son of Leo (an accountant) and Anna (Fuchs) Sturmthal; married Hattie Ross, June 25, 1940; children: Joan Frances, Anne Lenore, Suzanne Lois. *Education:* University of Vienna, Doctor Rerum Politicarum, 1925. *Home:* 61 Greencroft, Champaign, Ill. 61820. *Office:* Institute of Labor and Industrial Relations, University of Illinois, 504 East Armory Ave., Champaign, Ill. 61820.

CAREER: International Information (news and article agency), Zurich, Switzerland, and Brussels, Belgium, 1926-37, began as editor, became editor-in-chief; American University, Washington, D.C., lecturer on international relations, 1939-40; Bard College, Annandale-on-Hudson, N.Y., professor of economics, 1940-55; Roosevelt University, Chicago, Ill., Philip Murray Professor, 1955-60; University of Illinois, Champaign, Ill., professor of labor and industrial relations, 1960—. Visiting professor at Cornell University, 1952-54, Columbia University, 1958-59, Yale University, 1962-63. Lecturer in United States, Canada, Europe. Consultant to RAND Corp., Foreign Economic Administration, Mutual Security Agency, International Business Machines Corp., and U.S. Department of Labor. *Member:* Industrial Relations Research Association, American Political Science Association, American Economic Association.

WRITINGS: Die Schweiz in der Zeitenwende (title means "Switzerland at the Crossroads"), Bruckereigenossenschaff Aarau, 1935; *Die grosse Krise* (title means "The Great Depression"), Verlag Oprecht Auerich, 1937; *The Tragedy of European Labor, 1918-1939,* Columbia University Press, 1943, 2nd edition, 1951; *A Survey of Literature on Postwar Reconstruction,* 2nd edition, New York University Press, 1944; *Portrait der amerikanischen Gewerkschaften,* Wiener Volksbuchhandlung, 1951; *Labour and World Affairs,* Canadian Institute of International Affairs, 1951; *Unity and Diversity in European Labor,* Free Press, 1953; (editor) *Contemporary Collective Bargaining in Seven Countries,* Institute of International Industrial and Labor Relations, Cornell University, 1957; *Collective Bargaining in France,* Institute of International Industrial and Labor Relations, Cornell University, 1957; *An Essay on Comparative Collective Bargaining,* Institute of International Industrial and Labor Relations, Cornell University, 1957; *The Workers' Councils in Poland,* University of Illinois, 1961; *Amerikanische Forschungsarbeiten ueber Automation und*

Arbeitsbeziehungen, Bund-Verlag, 1962; *Der Einfluss der Lohnpolitik uuf Produktvitaet und Preisnieveau,* Bund-Verlag, 1963; *Workers Councils: A Study of Workplace Organizations on Both Sides of the Iron Curtain,* Harvard University Press, 1964; (with W.H. Franke) *Current Manpower Problems: An Introductory Survey,* Institute of Labor and Industrial Relations, University of Illinois, 1964; (editor) *White Collar Trade Unions: Contemporary Developments in Industrialized Societies,* University of Illinois Press, 1966; *A Study of Methods for Forecasting Employment,* Institute of Industrial Relations, University of Illinois, 1967; *Comparative Labor Movement: Ideological Roots and Institutional Development,* Wadsworth, 1972.

Contributor: *Foundations for World Organizations,* Conference on Science, Philosophy and Religion, 1952; Neil W. Chamberlain and others, editors, *A Decade of Industrial Relations and Research, 1946-1956,* Harper for Industrial Relations Research Associates, 1958; Emile Benoit and Kenneth E. Boulding, editors, *Disarmament and the Economy,* Harper, 1963. Author or co-author of pamphlets and reports on labor topics, including a study for the U.S. Senate. Editor, "Studies in International Labor," Cornell University Press, 1956-57. Contributor to *Encyclopedia Americana,* 1951, *International Labor Directory and Handbook,* 1955, and *Encyclopedia of the Social Sciences.* Contributor of about forty articles to *Forum, World Politics, Labor and Nation, Droit* Social (Paris), *Wirtschaftsdienst* (Germany), *New Leader, Managemento* (Japan), and other journals.

WORK IN PROGRESS: The Recovery of Western Europe.

SIDELIGHTS: Sturmthal speaks and writes German and French, handles Italian and Spanish fairly well, and is acquainted with some Slavic languages. *Avocational interests:* Travel, skiing, hiking, swimming, and reading detective stories.

* * *

SUBILIA, Vittorio 1911-

PERSONAL: Born August 5, 1911, in Turin, Italy; son of Marco (a painter) and Adele (Pecoraro) Subilia; married Berta Baldoni, November 12, 1936. *Education:* Facolta Valdese di Teologia, Lic. Theol., 1937. *Religion:* Waldensian Church. *Home:* Via Pietro Cossa 42, Rome, Italy. *Office:* Facolta Valdese di Teologia, Via Pietro Cossa 42, Rome, Italy.

CAREER: Waldensian Church, pastor, 1937-50; Facolta Valdese di Teologia (Waldensian Theological Seminary), Rome, Italy, professor of theology (systematics), 1950—; former dean of theological faculty. Director of Waldensian Ecumenical Committee. *Military service:* Italian Army, Alpine troops, 1935-36, 1940; became captain. *Member:* Italian Association for the History of Religions. *Awards, honors:* Dr. Theol., Faculte de Theologie Protestante, Paris, 1956.

WRITINGS: Il Movimento Ecumenico, Centro Evangelico di Cultura, 1948; *Gesu nella piu antica tradizione cristiana,* Claudiana, 1954; *Il Problema del male,* Claudiana, 1959; (co-author) *Ginevra e l'Italia,* Sansoni, 1959; *Il Problema del cattolicesimo,* Claudiana, 1962, translation published as *The Problem of Catholicism,* Westminster, 1964; *Cattolicesimo e presenza protestante in Italia,* Claudiana, 1965; *La Nuova cattolicita del cattolicesimo,* Claudiana, 1967; *Tempo di confessione e di rivoluzione,* Claudiana, 1968; *I Tempi di Dio,* Claudiana, 1971; *L'Evangelo della contestazione,* Paideia, 1971. Editor, *Protestantesimo;* contributor to other religious periodicals.

WORK IN PROGRESS: La Questione di Dio nella problematica teologica contemporanea.

AVOCATIONAL INTERESTS: Philosophy, history, politics, and Alpinism.

* * *

SUELFLOW, August R(obert) 1922-

PERSONAL: Born September 5, 1922, in Rochfield, Wis.; son of August Henry (a telephone executive) and Selma (Kressin) Suelflow; married Gladys I. Gierach, June 16, 1946; children: August Mark, Kathryn Lynn. *Education:* Attended Concordia College, Milwaukee, Wis.; Concordia Seminary, St. Louis, Mo., B.A., 1942, B.D., 1946, S.T.M., 1947; Washington University, St. Louis, Mo., postgraduate study, 1947; Concordia Seminary, Springfield, Ill., D.D., 1967. *Home:* 7249 Northmoor Dr., St. Louis, Mo. 63105. *Office:* Concordia Historical Institute, 801 De Mun Ave., St. Louis, Mo. 63105.

CAREER: Lutheran historian and archivist. Concordia Historical Institute, St. Louis, Mo., assistant curator, 1947-48; Lutheran Church—Missouri Synod, St. Louis, Mo., position director of department of archives and history, 1948—, research director of synodical survey, 1960-62. Assistant pastor of churches in Richmond Heights, Mo., 1948-56, Olivette, Mo., 1956-58; Mount Olive Lutheran Church, St. Louis, Mo., assistant pastor, 1959—, interim pastor, 1963—. Concordia Seminary, St. Louis, Mo., guest lecturer, 1952—; Washington University, St. Louis, Mo., instructor, 1967—. *Member:* American Historical Association, Society of American Archivists (committee chairman), American Microform Academy (board of trustees), American Society of Church History, American Society for Reformation Research, American Records Management Association, Organization of American Historians, Lutheran Historical Conference (president), Lutheran Academy for Scholarship.

WRITINGS: The Heart of Missouri: A History of the Western District of the Lutheran Church, Missouri Synod, 1854-1954, Concordia, 1954; (contributor and departmental consultant) *Lutheran Cyclopedia,* Concordia, 1954; (with Roy A. Suelflow) *The History of Trinity,* Friestadt, 1954; *Moving Frontiers,* Concordia, 1964; (editor) *The Encyclopedia of the Lutheran Church,* Augsburg, 1965. Contributor to religious periodicals. Associate editor, *Concordia Historical Institute Quarterly,* 1950—. Editor, *Directory of Religious Historical Depositories in America,* 1963, *Microfilm Index and Bibliography,* 1966, *A Preliminary Guide to Church Records Repositories,* 1969.

WORK IN PROGRESS: Polity and Government in the Lutheran Church—Missouri Synod; Movements Toward Lutheran Union in America.

* * *

SUGGS, Robert Carl 1932-

PERSONAL: Born February 24, 1932, in Portchester, N.Y.; son of Middleton O. and Almira (Barnes) Suggs; married Rachel Brown, September 7, 1951; children: Wayne J., Donald K., Jennifer L. *Education:* Columbia University, B.A. (with highest honors), 1955, M.A., 1956, Ph.D., 1959. *Politics:* Independent. *Home:* 8705 Bradgate Rd., Alexandria, Va. 22308. *Office:* Institute for International Studies, U.S. Office of Education, Washington, D.C. 20202.

CAREER: American Museum of Natural History, New York, N.Y., research assistant, 1956-59; Martin Co., Baltimore, Md., senior engineer, 1959-60; Dunlap and Associates, Inc., Stamford-Darien, Conn., senior anthropologist, 1960-64; Tech OPS/CORG, Fort Belvoir, Va., senior staff analyst, 1964-66; Kaman Systems Center, Bethesda, Md., senior scientist, 1966-69; U.S. Army Combat Developments Command, Fort Bragg, N.C., OPS analyst, 1969-70; U.S. Office of Education, Washington, D.C., chief, Language and Area Centers Branch, 1970—. Led two American Museum expeditions to Marquesas Islands, 1956, 1957-58; other archaeological investigations in Connecticut and New York. *Military service:* U.S. Marine Corps, 1950-52. *Member:* American Association for the Advancement of Science, American Ordnance Association, Aircraft Owners and Pilots Association, Phi Beta Kappa, Delta Phi Alpha. *Awards, honors:* Fellowship, American Association for the Advancement of Science; research grant, Human Ecology Fund, 1962.

WRITINGS: Island Civilizations of Polynesia, New American Library, 1960; *The Hidden Worlds of Polynesia: The Chronicle of an Archaeological Expedition to Nuku Hiva in the Marquesas Islands,* Harcourt, 1962; *Modern Discoveries in Archaeology,* Crowell, 1962; *Lords of the Blue Pacific,* New York Graphic Society, 1962; *Survival Handbook,* Macmillan, 1962; *Alexander the Great, Scientist-King,* Macmillan, 1964; *The Archaeology of San Francisco,* Crowell, 1965; *The Archaeology of New York,* Crowell, 1966; *Marquesan Sexual Behavior,* Harcourt, 1966; (editor with Donald S. Marshall) *Human Sexual Behavior: Variations Across the Ethnographic Spectrum,* Basic Books, 1971. Also author of *Excavation at the Marylander's Burial Site, Brooklyn,* National Park Service, 1957. Contributor of articles to professional journals. Former regional editor, *Asian Perspectives.*

SIDELIGHTS: Suggs speaks German, French, Marquesan, Tahitian, and reads Spanish. He holds a 2nd degree black belt in karate, and is a private pilot.

BIOGRAPHICAL/CRITICAL SOURCES: Baltimore Sun, February 14, 1960; *Saturday Evening Post,* January, 1961; *Bridgeport Sunday Post,* April 15, 1962; *Times Literary Supplement,* January 19, 1967.

* * *

SUHR, Elmer George 1902-

PERSONAL: Born October 18, 1902, in Rochester, N.Y.; son of Louis and Mary (Binder) Suhr; married Helen G. Kruger, 1941. *Education:* Wittenberg College, A.B., 1923; Johns Hopkins University, A.M., 1925, Ph.D., 1926. *Home:* 31 Rand Pl., Pittsford, N.Y. 14534. *Office:* University of Rochester, Rochester, N.Y. 14627.

CAREER: University of Missouri, Columbia, assistant professor of history of art, 1926-29; Wagner College, Staten Island, N.Y., professor of Greek and history of art, 1929-34; Wittenberg College, Springfield, Ohio, Patterson Assistant Professor of Latin, 1937-42; University of Rochester, Rochester, N.Y., associate professor of classics, 1946—. *Member:* Archaeological Institute of America (secretary of Rochester branch), Phi Beta Kappa.

WRITINGS: Sculptured Portraits of Greek Statesmen, with a Special Study of Alexander the Great, Johns Hopkins Press, 1931; *Two Currents in the Thought Stream of Europe: A History of Opposing Points of View,* Johns Hopkins Press, 1942; *Theme and Variations: A Mental Autobiography,* John W. Luce, 1944; *Venus de Milo, the Spinner: The Link Between a Famous Art Mystery and Ancient Fertility Symbols,* Exposition, 1958; *The Ancient Mind and Its Heritage,* foreword by Van L. Johnson, Exposition, Volume I: *Exploring the Primitive, Egyptian, and Mesopotamian Cultures,* 1959, Volume II: *Exploring the Hebrew, Hindu, Greek, and Chinese Cultures,* 1960; *The Magic Mirror,* Helios, 1966; *Before Olympos: A Study of the Aniconic Origins of Poseidon, Hermes and Eros,* Helios, 1967; *The Spinning Aphrodite: The Evolution of the Goddess from Earliest Pre-Hellenic Symbolism Through Late Classical Times,* Helios, 1969;

The Mask, the Unicorn and the Messiah, Helios, 1970; *Prisoners of Love,* Helios, 1971. Contributor to *American Journal of Archaeology* and other professional journals.

* * *

SUSSMAN, Marvin B(ernard) 1918-

PERSONAL: Born October 27, 1918, in New York, N.Y.; son of M. Lewis and Gertrude (Clar) Sussman; married Ruth Annette Strahler, August 15, 1942. *Education:* New York University, B.A., 1941; George Williams College, M.S., 1943; Yale University, M.A., 1947, Ph.D., 1951. *Politics:* Republican. *Religion:* Unitarian-Quaker. *Home:* 2837 East Overlook Rd., Cleveland Heights, Ohio 44118. *Office:* Sociological Research Building, 11027 Magnolia Dr., Cleveland, Ohio 44106.

CAREER: Union College, Schenectady, N.Y., assistant professor of sociology, 1951-54; University of Chicago, Chicago, Ill., visiting assistant professor of sociology, 1954-55; Western Reserve University (now Case Western Reserve University), Cleveland, Ohio, professor of sociology and head of department, 1955—. U.S. Department of Health, Education, and Welfare, consultant to Social Security Administration research and development program, and member of research study section of Welfare and Vocational Rehabilitation administrations. *Member:* American Sociological Association (fellow), American Public Health Association (fellow), Sociological Research Association, Society for the Study of Social Problems (president, 1962-63), American Statistical Association, American Anthropological Association, Society for Applied Anthropology, Ohio Valley Sociological Society (president, 1962-63), Ohio Council on Family Relations (president, 1962-63), Groves Conference on Marriage and the Family (president, 1969—).

WRITINGS: (Editor) *Sourcebook in Marriage and the Family,* Houghton, 1955, 3rd edition, 1968; (with W. Bock, W. Lawson, and R. Yankower) *Social Class and Maternal Health,* New York State Health Department Publications, 1958; (editor) *Community Structure and Analysis,* Crowell, 1959; (with R. Clyde White) *Hough, Cleveland Ohio: A Study of Social Life and Change,* Western Reserve University Press, 1959; (co-author) *Tuberculosis and Rehabilitation,* Department of Sociology, Western Reserve University, 1964; (editor) *Sociology and Rehabilitation,* American Sociological Association, 1966; (with others) *The Walking Patient: A Study in Outpatient Care,* Press of Case Western Reserve University, 1967; (with others) *The Family and Inheritance,* Russell Sage, 1970. Author of some fifty articles in professional journals. Editor, *Journal of Marriage and Family,* 1964-69.

WORK IN PROGRESS: A book, *Social Problems of the Family;* co-authoring two books, *Sociology of Rehabilitation* and *Divorce and Remarriage.*

AVOCATIONAL INTERESTS: Painting, sailing, watch repairing.

* * *

SUTHERLAND, Donald W(ayne) 1931-

PERSONAL: Born January 24, 1931, in Sioux Falls, S.D.; son of Donald Wayne (a builder) and Kathleen (Bickert) Sutherland; married Janet Meager, July 27, 1957; married Judith Lynne Cleveland, December 17, 1961; children: Anne, Jean, Kathleen. *Education:* Swarthmore College, B.A., 1953; Oxford University, D.Phil., 1957. *Religion:* Lutheran. *Home:* 81 Richmond Park Rd., East Sheen, London S.W.14, England.

CAREER: State University of Iowa, Iowa City, assistant professor of history, 1958—. *Military service:* U.S. Army, 1956-58. *Member:* American Historical Association,

Medieval Academy of America, Conference of British Studies, Royal Historical Association.

WRITINGS: Quo Warranto Proceedings in the Reign of Edward I, 1278-1294, Clarendon Press, 1963.

WORK IN PROGRESS: An investigation of the concepts of seisin and conquest in medieval thought.

* * *

SWAIM, Alice Mackenzie 1911-

PERSONAL: Born June 5, 1911, in Aberdeen, Scotland; came to United States, 1928; naturalized, 1939; daughter of Donald Campbell (a professor at Princeton Theological Seminary) and Alice (Murray) Mackenzie; married William Thomas Swaim, Jr. (a minister, administrator of Presbyterian Homes of Central Pennsylvania), December 27, 1932; children: Elizabeth Anne, Kathleen Mackenzie. *Education:* Attended Chatham College, 1928-30; Wilson College, A.B., 1932. *Religion:* Presbyterian. *Home:* 322 North 2nd St., Apt. 1606, Harrisburg, Pa. 17101.

CAREER: Poet. Judge of poetry contests. *Member:* Poetry Society of America, National Federation of State Poetry Societies, American Poetry League (vice-president, 1964-67, 1967-70), Society of North American Poets, National Writers Club, Amateur Press Association, Centro Studi e Scambi (international executive committee, 1964), Pennsylvania Poetry Society (chapter vice-president, 1963), Poetry Society of New Hampshire, Clan Mackenzie Organization, Dillsburg Fine Arts Club, Kimport Doll Talk Club. *Awards, honors:* Anna Hempstead Branch Lyric award, 1959; first prize, New York Writers Guild Contest, 1959; silver medal Esternaux award, 1959; Borestone Mountain Poetry Awards, 1960; Henry Seidel Canby Award, 1962; $500 award for best book published by Pageant Press in 1960, for *Crickets Are Crying Autumn;* American Poetry League award; medal of merit Studie Scambi, Italy, 1965; prizes in Jesse Stuart Contest, 1970, and Clover International Contest, 1970; poetry awards from thirty other groups.

WRITINGS—Books of poetry: Let the Deep Song Rise, Blue River Press, 1952; *Up To the Stars,* Allan Swallow, 1954; *Poetry Calendar,* privately printed, 1956; *Sunshine in a Thimble,* Telegraph Press, 1958; *Crickets Are Crying Autumn,* Pageant, 1960; *The Gentle Dragon,* Golden Quill, 1962; *Beyond a Dancing Star,* privately printed, 1967; *Beyond My Catnip Garden,* Golden Quill, 1970.

Books—All privately printed: *Pennsylvania Profile,* 1966, *Scented Honeysuckle Days,* 1966, *Here on the Threshold,* 1966. Writer of thirteen published brochures of poems, including *Paws, Tails and Whiskers,* 1967. Author of some 1700 poems published in more than 200 periodicals and newspapers in twelve countries.

WORK IN PROGRESS: A Nosegay of Remembrances, poetry.

AVOCATIONAL INTERESTS: Collecting foreign dolls (has more than four hundred), coin collecting, gardening, handicrafts, reading.

BIOGRAPHICAL/CRITICAL SOURCES: Wilson College Alumnae Bulletin, winter issue, 1963.

* * *

SWAIN, Raymond Charles 1912-

PERSONAL: Born March 15, 1912, in Danbury, N.H.; son of Owen Albert and Etta Luella (Brock) Swain; married Jennie Belle Guyette, July 1, 1960. *Education:* Butler Hospital School of Nursing, R.N., 1932; George Washington University, B.S., 1949. *Politics:* Democrat. *Religion:* Catholic. *Home:* Fourth St., Bristol, N.H.

03222. *Agent:* Alex Jackinson, 55 West 42nd St., New York, N.Y. 10036.

CAREER: Riverside Nursing Home, Lebanon, N.H., owner, 1935-42; Rockingham County Home and Hospital, Brentwood, N.H., supervisor, 1951-61; retired to farming, writing, and private duty nursing, 1961—. Founder and director, New Hampshire Writers' Conference. *Military service:* U.S. Navy, Medical Corps, 1942-45; received Bronze Star and Purple Heart. *Member:* Poetry Society of America, Poetry Fellowship of Maine, Terre Haute Poet's Study Club, American Legion, Veterans of Foreign Wars, Disabled American Veterans, Poetry Society of New Hampshire (founder and president). *Awards, honors:* National Stephen Vincent Benet Narrative Poetry Awards, 1968.

WRITINGS: Home Songs (poems), Pegasus Press, 1939; *Out of Darkness* (poems), Golden Quill, 1963; *A Breath of Maine: Portrait of Robert P. Tristram Coffin,* Branden Press, 1967. Contributor of articles to *Down East* and *Profile,* poetry to *American Weave, Christian Science Monitor,* and other periodicals.

WORK IN PROGRESS: A novel, *The Man Who Stole Heaven.*

AVOCATIONAL INTERESTS: Fishing.

BIOGRAPHICAL/CRITICAL SOURCES: Manchester Union Leader, Manchester, N.H., January, 1964; *Poetry Society of America Bulletin,* February, 1964.

* * *

SWANN, Francis 1913-

PERSONAL: Born July 16, 1913, in Annapolis, Md.; son of S. Donovan and Rita (Harrell) Swann; married Jean Scriven, January 15, 1944; children: Richard. *Education:* Studied at Princeton University, 1931, and Johns Hopkins University, 1932-33. *Religion:* Protestant. *Home:* 32 West 72nd St., New York, N.Y. 10023. *Agent:* Robert Mills, 156 East 52nd St., New York, N.Y. 10022.

CAREER: Has worked as actor, musician, and stage director; author, principally of motion picture scripts. *Military service:* U.S. Naval Reserve, 1943-45; became lieutenant junior grade. *Member:* Dramatists Guild of America, Authors League of America, Writers Guild of America.

WRITINGS—Novels: The Brass Key, Simon & Schuster, 1964; *Greenwood,* Lancer Books, 1965; *Royal Street,* Lancer Books, 1966; *Hermit Island,* Lancer Books, 1967; *You'll Hang My Love,* Lancer Books, 1967; *Hacienda Triste,* Lancer Books, 1968; *House of Terror,* Lancer Books, 1968; *Day of Dark Memory,* Avon, 1970; *Angelica,* Lancer Books, 1973; *Hellgate Plantation,* Lancer Books, 1973. Also author of "One Rooster Is Enough," as yet unpublished.

Plays: *Out of the Frying Pan* (first produced in Baltimore at Hilltop Theatre, September, 1940; produced on Broadway at Windsor Theatre, February 11, 1941), Samuel French, 1942; "It's in the Air," first produced in Los Angeles at Belasco Theatre, August, 1945; (with Victor Clement) "Bad Angel," first produced in West Los Angeles at Phoenix Theatre, 1949; "Whatever Happened," first produced in Baltimore at Hilltop Theatre, September, 1956; "Prior to Broadway," first produced in Baltimore at Hilltop Theatre, September, 1958; (contributor) "Follies of 1910," first produced in New York at Carnegie Playhouse, January 12, 1960; (and director) "Paradise Island" (musical), first produced in Jones Beach, N.Y., at Marine Theatre, 1961; "No Vacancy," first produced in Baltimore, Md. at Vagabond Theatre; "Be My Guest"; (author of book) *Into the Fire* (musical; first produced in Somers Point, N.J., at Gateway Theatre, August, 1961), Samuel French, 1963;

(author of libretto) "Rehearsal Call" (opera), first produced in New York at Julliard School of Music, February 11, 1962.

Screenplays: (With Sam Hellman, Richard Weil and James V. Kern) "Shine on Harvest Moon" (musical comedy), Warner Brothers, 1944; (with Edmund Joseph) "Make Your Own Bed," Warner Brothers, 1944; "A Very Rich Man," Warner Brothers, 1944; (with Eugene Conrad and I.A.L. Diamond) "Love and Learn," Warner Brothers, 1946; (contributor of additional dialogue) "That Way with Women" (based on Idle Hands, a short story by Earl Derr Biggers), Warner Brothers, 1946; (with Agnes Christine Johnson and Leonard Lee) "The Time, the Place and the Girl," Warner Brothers, 1946; "The Gay Intruders," 20th Century-Fox, 1948; "Jungle Patrol," 20th Century-Fox, 1948; "Roy Rogers," Republic, 1949; "Miss Grant Takes Richmond," Columbia, 1949; (contributor of additional dialogue) "Cover-Up," United Artists, 1949; "Mrs. Mike," United Artists, 1949; (with Richard English) "711 Ocean Drive," Columbia, 1950; (with Bradford Ropes) "Belle of Old Mexico," Republic, 1950; (with Samuel Newman) "Tarzan's Peril," RKO, 1951; (with James Gunn) "The Barefoot Mailman" (based on a novel by Theodore Pratt), Columbia, 1951; (contributor of additional dialogue) "One Big Affair," United Artists, 1952; "Adventures of Haji Baba," Walter Wanger, 1952; "Force of Impulse," Sutton, 1961; "Instant Love," Paul Simon, 1964.

WORK IN PROGRESS: Where Is Penelope?, a novel.

SIDELIGHTS: Out of the Frying Pan was filmed by United Artists in 1942 as "Young and Willing." Avocational interests: Golf and fishing.

*　　*　　*

SWEET, Franklyn Haley 1916-

PERSONAL: Born August 19, 1916, in Madison, Wis.; son of Benjamin Franklin (an engineer) and Camilla (Haley) Sweet; married Melba Cameron, December 22, 1936; children: Richard Franklyn. Education: University of Alabama, B.S., 1938, M.S., 1948; University of Texas, Ph.D., 1962. Religion: Catholic. Residence: Mobile, Ala. Office: University of South Alabama, 307 Gillard Dr., Mobile, Ala. 36688.

CAREER: Certified public accountant, state of Alabama, 1944; Sears, Roebuck & Co., Atlanta Ga., auditor, 1938-42; public accountant, Dothan, Ala., 1942-46; University of Alabama, Tuscaloosa, assistant professor of accounting, 1946-48; Spring Hill College, Mobile, Ala., professor of accounting, 1948-64, chairman of department of commerce, 1954-64; Kent State University, Kent, Ohio, professor of accounting and department chairman 1964-66; University of South Alabama, Mobile, professor of accounting, and director of professiorial accounting studies, 1966-67, interim dean of academic affairs, 1967-68, dean of administration, 1968-71, vice-president for administration, 1971—.

Partner, Wiik, Reimer & Sweet (certified Public accountants). Military service: U.S. Navy, 1945. Member: American Institute of Certified Public Accountants, American Accounting Association, Alabama Society of Certified Public Accountants, Beta Alpha Psi, Beta Gamma Sigma.

WRITINGS: (Contributor) Leo Schloss, editor, Accounting Teachers Guide, South-Western, 1953; (contributor) Principles of Accounting, Pitman, 1959; Strategic Planning: A Conceptual Model, Bureau of Business Research, University of Texas, 1963.

SWING, Thomas Kaehao 1930-

PERSONAL: Born September 20, 1930, in Jungin, Korea; came to United States, 1954. Education: Yale University, B.A., 1958, law student, 1958-59, graduate student, 1959-64. Religion: Roman Catholic. Home: 1554 Yale Station, New Haven, Conn. 06520.

CAREER: Yale University, New Haven, Conn., lecturer in philosophy, 1963—. Military service: Republic of Korea Army, 1950-53; became captain.

WRITINGS: The Fragile Leaves of the Sybil (Dante's master plan), Newman, 1961; Kant's Transcendental Logic, Yale University Press, 1969.

WORK IN PROGRESS: A book on Hegel's dialectical logic, 1966.

*　　*　　*

SWINYARD, Alfred W (ilbur) 1915-

PERSONAL: Born June 13, 1915, in Logan, Utah; son of William and Bertha (Halverson) Swinyard; married June Hanson, June 1, 1941; children: Alfred, Suzanne. Education: Utah State University, B.S., 1937; Harvard University, M.B.A., 1939; Syracuse University, Ph.D., 1955. Office: 422 Business Administration Building, University of Michigan, Ann Arbor, Mich. 48104.

CAREER: Utah State University, Logan, 1939-46, began as instructor, became assistant professor; Syracuse University, College of Business Administration, Syracuse, N.Y., professor of marketing and chairman of department, 1946-57, assistant director of Business and Economic Research Center, 1946-51, director, 1953-56; Booz, Allen & Hamilton (management consultants), Chicago, Ill., director of management research, 1957-62; University of Michigan, Graduate School of Business Administration, Ann Arbor, professor of business administration, and director of Bureau of Business Research, 1962-71, associate dean, 1968—. Marketing consultant to Esso Standard Oil Co., 1951-52, and other companies. Ann Arbor Chamber of Commerce, member of board of directors, 1963-65. Military service: U.S. Army, 1941-46; became lieutenant colonel; received Bronze Star. Member: American Economic Association, American Marketing Association (vice-president, central New York chapter, 1954, president, 1956), Associated University Bureaus of Business and Economic Research (member of executive committee, 1965-68; vice-president, 1968-69; president, 1969-70), Beta Gamma Sigma, Alpha Kappa Psi.

WRITINGS: (With Sidney C. Sufrin) Let's Look at the Record, Syracuse University Press, 1949; (with others) Business Stability and Opportunities for Growth in Metropolitan Syracuse, Committee for Economic Development, 1954; Metropolitan Syracuse Appliance Dealer Survey, Business Research Center, Syracuse University, 1954; (with Sufrin) Research and Development in Commercial Laboratories and Non-Profit Institutes, National Science Foundation, 1955; (with Floyd A. Bond and Dick A. Leabo) Preparation for Business Leadership, Bureau of Business Research, University of Michigan, 1964; (editor) Industrial Development Fundamentals, Bureau of Business Research, University of Michigan, 1965; (with W.G. Moller, Jr.) The Ann Arbor Retail Market: Its Structure and Prospects, Bureau of Business Research, University of Michigan, 1966; (with Moller) The In-House Reproduction Industry: Some Growth Characteristics and Problems, Bureau of Business Research, University of Michigan, 1966; (with others) State Economic Development: Status and Appraisal, Bureau of Business Research, University of Michigan, 1967. Author or co-author of thirty-five articles in trade magazines and professional journals.

WORK IN PROGRESS: Research on evolving competition in concentrated industries and executive succession.

SWOMLEY, John M., Jr. 1915-

PERSONAL: Born May 31, 1915, in Harrisburg, Pa.; son of John M. (a realtor) and Florence (Forsyth) Swomley; married Marjie L. Carpenter, August 4, 1957; children: Kathryn Elizabeth, Joanna Ruth, John Gregory. Education: Dickinson College, A.B., 1936; Boston University, M.A., 1939, S.T.B., 1940; University of Colorado, Ph.D., 1958. Home: 1095 South Shore Dr., Kansas City, Mo. 64151. Office: St. Paul School of Theology, 5123 Truman Rd., Kansas City, Mo. 64127.

CAREER: Ordained Methodist minister, 1956; Fellowship of Reconciliation, Nyack, N.Y., youth secretary, later associate secretary, 1940-44; National Council against Conscription, Washington, D.C., executive director, 1944-52; Fellowship of Reconciliation, executive secretary, 1953-60; St. Paul School of Theology, Kansas City, Mo., professor of social ethics, 1960—. National Council of Churches, member of committee on civil and religious liberty. Lecturer on tour in Great Britain, 1950; visiting professor of social ethics, Facultad Evangelica de Teologia, Buenos Aires, Argentina, 1969. Member: American Political Science Association, American Society for Christian Social Ethics, American Civil Liberties Union (member of national board; president, Western Mo. Branch, 1969—), United Methodist Peace Fellowship (national president), Phi Beta Kappa, Tau Kappa Alpha.

WRITINGS: (Contributor) Peace and Power, Parthenon Press, 1960; The Military Establishment, foreword by George McGovern, Beacon, 1964; Religion, the State, and the Schools, Pegasus, 1968; American Empire: The Political Ethics of 20th Century Conquest, Macmillan, 1970; Liberation Ethics, Macmillan, 1972.

Monographs: Militarism in Education, National Council Against Conscription, 1949; America, Russia and the Bomb, National Council Against Conscription, 1950; Church, State and Education, National Council of Churches, 1964. Editor, Conscription News, 1944-52; contributing editor, Fellowship; contributor of numerous articles to Christian Century, Nation, and Progressive.

BIOGRAPHICAL/CRITICAL SOURCES: Saturday Review, May 17, 1969; Christian Century, February 24, 1971.

* * *

SWOR, Chester E (ugene) 1907-

PERSONAL: Born July 8, 1907, in Harrison County, Miss. Education: Mississippi College, B.A., 1929; University of North Carolina, M.A., 1934; Columbia University, professional diploma in guidance, 1944; New York University, special study. Religion: Baptist. Home and office: 902 Whitworth, Jackson, Miss. 39202.

CAREER: Delta Junior College, Moorhead, Miss., teacher, 1929-30; Mississippi College, Clinton, dean of men and assistant professor of English, 1930-42; religious lecturer and counselor, 1942—. Awards, honors: L.H.D. from Baylor University, 1945; LL.D. from Mississippi College, 1962; Litt.D. from William Carey College; HH.D. from Blue Mountain College; Alumnus of the Year, Mississippi College, 1967.

WRITINGS: Very Truly Yours, Broadman, 1954; If We Dared!, Broadman, 1961; (with Jerry Merriman) The Teen-Age Slant, Broadman, 1963; Neither Down Nor Out, Broadman, 1966; (with Merriman) Youth at Bat, Revell, 1968; (with Merriman) To Enrich Each Day, Revell, 1969; The Parent Slant, Broadman, 1971.

WORK IN PROGRESS: Cap and Gown, a book for high school graduates; College Confusions!, a book for college students who are confused by strange values; Whimsy, a book of humorous messages.

SIDELIGHTS: Very Truly Yours has been published in Spanish and Chinese.

* * *

SYME, (Neville) Ronald 1913-

PERSONAL: Born March 13, 1913, in Lancashire, England; son of David Godfrey and Ida Florence (Kerr) Syme; married Marama Amoa, February 12, 1960; children: Florence Tia te Pa Tua. Education: Attended Durham School in England, 1924-26, Collegiate School, Wanganui, New Zealand, 1926-29. Politics: Conservative. Home: Rarotonga, Cook Islands, South Pacific Ocean.

CAREER: British Merchant Service, cadet and officer, 1930-34, gunner, 1939-40; press reporter and foreign correspondent, 1934-39; John Westhouse & Peter Lunn Ltd., London, England, assistant editor, 1946-48; British Road Federation, London, public relations officer, 1948-50. Military service: British Army, Intelligence Corps, 1940-45; became major. Member: Authors Society (England). Awards, honors: Boys' Clubs of America medallist award, 1951, for Bay of the North.

WRITINGS—Nonfiction; all published by Morrow, except as indicated: Full Fathom Five, Peter Lunn, 1946; Hakluyt's Sea Stories, Heinemann, 1948.

Bay of the North, 1950; A Roman Post-Mortem: An Inquest on the Fall of the Roman Republic, Australasian Medical Publishing Co., 1950; The Story of British Roads, British Road Federation, 1951; Cortes of Mexico, 1951 (published in England as Cortez, Conqueror of Mexico, Hodder & Stoughton, 1952); Champlain of the St. Lawrence, 1952; Columbus, Finder of the New World, 1952; La Salle of the Mississippi, 1952; The Story of Britain's Highways, Pitman, 1952; Magellan, First Around the World, 1953; The Windward Islands, Pitman, 1953; John Smith of Virginia, 1954, new edition, University of London Press, 1965; The Story of New Zealand, Pitman, 1954; Henry Hudson, 1955 (published in England as Hudson of the Valley, Hodder & Stoughton, 1955); The Cook Islands, Pitman, 1955; Balboa, Finder of the Pacific, 1956; De Soto, Finder of the Mississippi, 1957; Tacitus, Clarendon Press, 1958; The Man Who Discovered the Amazon, 1958; Cartier, Finder of the St. Lawrence, 1958; Colonial Elites: Rome, Spain, and the Americas, Oxford University Press, 1958; On Foot to the Arctic: The Story of Samuel Hearne, 1959 (published in England as Trail to the North, Hodder & Stoughton, 1959); Vasco Da Gamma, Sailor Towards the Sunrise, 1959.

The Roman Revolution, Oxford University Press, 1960; Captain Cook, Pacific Explorer, 1960; Francis Drake, Sailor of the Unknown Seas, 1961; Walter Raleigh, 1962; The Young Nelson, Parrish, 1962, Roy, 1963; First Man to Cross America: The Story of Cabeza de Vaca, 1962; African Traveler: The Story of Mary Kingsley, 1962; Francisco Pizarro: Finder of Peru, 1963; Invaders and Invasions, Batsford, 1964, Norton, 1965; Nigerian Pioneer: The Story of Mary Slessor, 1964; Alexander Mackenzie, Canadian Explorer, 1964; Sir Henry Morgan, Buccaneer, 1965; Quesada of Colombia, 1966; William Penn, Founder of Pennsylvania, 1966; Francisco Coronado and the Seven Cities of Gold, 1967; Garibaldi, the Man Who Made a Nation, 1967; Bolivar the Liberator, 1968; Captain John Paul Jones, America's Fighting Seaman, 1968; Amerigo Vespucci, Scientist and Sailor, 1969; Frontenac of New France, 1969.

Benedict Arnold: Traitor of the Revolution, 1970; Vancouver: Explorer of the Pacific Coast, 1970; Toussaint: The Black Liberator, 1971; (with Werner Forman) The Travels of Captain Cook, McGraw, 1971; Zapata: Mexican Rebel, 1971; John Cabot and His Son Sebastian, 1972; Juarez, the Founder of Modern Mexico, 1972.

Fiction; all published by Hodder & Stoughton, except as indicated: *That Must Be Julian*, Peter Lunn, 1947; *Julian's River War*, Heinemann, 1949; *Ben of the Barrier*, Evans Brothers, 1949; *I, Mungo Park*, Burke Publishing, 1951; *I, Captain Anson: My Voyage Around the World*, Burke Publishing, 1952; *The Settlers of Carriacou*, 1953; *I, Gordon of Khartoum*, Burke Publishing, 1953; *Gipsy Michael*, 1954; *They Came to an Island*, 1955; *Isle of Revolt*, 1956; *Ice Fighter*, 1956; *The Amateur Company*, 1957; *The Great Canoe*, 1957; *The Forest Fighters*, 1958; *River of No Return*, 1958; *The Spaniards Came at Dawn*, 1959; *Trail to the North*, 1959; *Thunder Knoll*, 1960; *The Mountainy Men*, 1961; *Coast of Danger*, 1961; *Nose-Cap Astray*, 1962; *Two Passengers for Spanish Fork*, 1963; *Switch Points as Kamlin*, 1964; *The Dunes and the Diamonds*, 1964; *The Missing Witness*, 1965; *The Saving of the Fair East Wind*, Dent, 1967.

SIDELIGHTS: Syme writes: "I've lived in queer little Polynesian islands where no tourists or sight-seeing liners ever go. I've paddled outrigger canoes into deep water beyond the reef and caught fish which were so large that they towed the canoe for a considerable distance. Perhaps the fact that I speak Polynesian tongue has helped me to live closer to the Islanders than most Europeans ever get. A thatched cottage not far from the lagoon has also revealed to me that one can get along very nicely without a telephone, car, television, daily newspapers and the monthly gas bill.

"I'm now stationed semi-permanently in Rarotonga which means that I have a comfortable small cottage here where I can at least unload some of the hundreds of ancient books which for years have been accompanying me around the world. I built the place so as to have a dumping-ground for such Excess Baggage and simultaneously provide myself with a retreat for old age!

"I have visited most of the world, including the West Indies, Mexico, Brazil, Canada, United States, most European countries, and many in Africa. I speak French, Italian, Arabic, and Maori. Plus, of course, some English! I think too many authors make the mistake of living ... where a high cost of living necessitates a high rate of literary productivity.... Nowadays I write a couple of books a year—more or less—and go fishing the rest of the time. Moreover, I now have infinitely more leisure for historical study, on which my books (U.S.A.) are largely based.... Polynesiana is my outstanding interest and perhaps more than a hobby."

BIOGRAPHICAL/CRITICAL SOURCES: May Hill Arbuthnot, *Children and Books*, 3rd edition, Scott, Foresman, 1964; *The Children's Bookshelf*, Child Study Association of America and Bantam, 1965; *Books for Children, 1960-1965*, American Library Association, 1966; *New York Times Book Review*, March 16, 1969.†

* * *

SYRKIN, Marie 1899-

PERSONAL: Born March 22, 1899, in Bern, Switzerland; daughter of Nachman and Batya (Osnos) Syrkin; married Charles Reznikoff (a writer), 1930; children: David Bodansky. *Education:* Cornell University, B.A., 1920, M.A., 1922. *Politics:* Socialist Zionist. *Religion:* Jewish. *Agent:* Curtis Brown Ltd., 60 East 56th St., New York, N.Y. 10022. *Home:* 180 West End Ave., New York, N.Y. 10023. *Office:* Brandeis University, Waltham, Mass. 02154.

CAREER: Former teacher in New York City high schools. Brandeis University, Waltham, Mass., 1950—, began as associate professor, became professor of English, professor emeritus, 1966—; *Jewish Frontier*, New York, N.Y., editor, 1950-72; Herzl Press, New York, N.Y.,

editor, 1971—. *Member:* American Association of University Professors. *Awards, honors:* Hayim Greenberg Prize for *Way of Valor.*

WRITINGS: The Communists and the Arab Problem (pamphlet), League for Labor Palestine, c.1936; *Why a Jewish Commonwealth?*, Political and Education Committee of Hadassah, c.1944; *Your School, Your Children: A Teacher Looks at What's Wrong with Our Schools*, L.B. Fischer, 1944; *Blessed Is the Match: The Story of Jewish Resistance*, Knopf, 1947; *Way of Valor: A Biography of Golda Myerson*, Sharon Books, 1955; *Nachman Syrkin, Socialist Zionist: A Biographical Memoir*, Herzl, 1961; *Golda Meir, Woman with a Cause*, Putnam, 1963, revised edition published as *Golda Meir, Israel's Leader*, 1969; (editor and author of introduction) *Hayim Greenberg Anthology*, Wayne State University Press, 1968. Translator of poetry for anthologies. Editor, *Jewish Frontier* (monthly).

BIOGRAPHICAL/CRITICAL SOURCES: Commentary, September, 1969.

* * *

SYROP, Konrad 1914-

PERSONAL: Born August 9, 1914, in Vienna, Austria; son of Juliusz and Helen Syrop; married Sara Joelson (a doctor), April 6, 1940; children: Helen Ann, Mary Jane, Barbara Joan, Alan Nigel. *Education:* University of Cracow, student; University of Warsaw, Bachelor of Law, 1936; Sorbonne, University of Paris, Certificate de Droit, 1936. *Home:* 10 Hayes Rd., Bromley, Kent, England. *Agent:* Bolt and Watson, Chandos House, Palmer St., London W.1, England. *Office:* British Broadcasting Corp. London S.W.1, England.

CAREER: Kurjer Polski (daily newspaper), Warsaw, Poland, leader writer, 1935-37, London correspondent, 1938-39; British Broadcasting Corp., London, England, 1939—, announcer and translator, 1939-40, producer, war correspondent, and scriptwriter, 1941-45, assistant head of European Productions, 1946-56, head of External Services Productions, 1956-68, programme editor, (General) Talks and Features, 1968-71, head of Central European Service, 1971—. *Military service:* British Army, 1942-43.

WRITINGS: Spring in October: The Polish Revolution of 1956, Weidenfeld & Nicolson, 1957, published in America as *Spring in October: The Story of the Polish Revolution, 1956*, Praeger, 1958; *Poland: Between the Hammer and the Anvil*, R. Hale, 1968.

Translator: Jerzy Andrzejewski, *The Inquisitors*, Knopf, 1960; Slawomir Mrozek, *The Elephant*, Macdonald & Co., 1962, Grove, 1963; Slawomir Mrozek, *The Ugupu Bird*, Macdonald & Co., 1965. Contributor to *Guardian* and other English and Polish newspapers and journals, and to *Chambers's Encyclopaedia;* writer of radio features.

* * *

SZCZESNIAK, Boleslaw (B.) 1908-

PERSONAL: Born March 31, 1908, in Poland; now U.S. citizen; son of Nicholas and Tekla (Andrzejewicz) Szczesniak; married Natalia Walendziak; children: Leszek, Andrew, Jacek (sons). *Education:* Oriental Institute, University of Warsaw, Dipl. M.A., 1935; Waseda University, postgraduate study, 1938-42; University of Ottawa, Ph.D., 1950. *Office:* Department of History, University of Notre Dame, Notre Dame, Ind. 46556.

CAREER: Rikkyo University, Tokyo, Japan, lecturer in European history, 1938-42; University of London, London, England, lecturer in Japanese history, during the forties; University of Notre Dame, Notre Dame, Ind., assistant professor, 1948-51, associate professor, 1952-56, professor of history, 1956—. *Member:* American Oriental Society (president, Middle West branch, 1963-64), American Association for the Advancement of Slavic Studies, Royal Asiatic Society, Japanese Palaeological Society, Hakluyt Society. *Awards, honors:* Awards and grants-in-aid from American Philosophical Society, Social Science Research Council, and Ford Foundation.

WRITINGS: (Editor, translator, and author of introductory essay) *The Russian Revolution and Religion,* University of Notre Dame Press, 1959; (editor) George Preble, *The Opening of Japan: A Diary of Discovery in the Far East, 1853-1856,* University of Oklahoma Press, 1962; *The Russian Central Asia,* University of Notre Dame Press, 1964; *The Knights Hospitallers in Poland and Lithuania,* Mouton & Co., 1969. Author of more than one hundred research papers and articles, mainly on relationships between the Far East and the Western world, including history of Russia.

WORK IN PROGRESS: A book, *United States Expedition to Korea, 1871.*

AVOCATIONAL INTERESTS: Collecting manuscripts.

* * *

SZULC, Tad 1926-

PERSONAL: Born July 25, 1926, in Warsaw, Poland; son of Seweryn and Janina (Baruch) Szulc; married Marianne Carr, July 8, 1948; children: Nicole, Anthony. *Home:* 4515 29th St. N.W., Washington, D.C. 20008. *Agent:* Brandt & Brandt, 101 Park Ave., New York, N.Y. 10017. *Office: New York Times,* 1920 L St. N.W., Washington, D.C. 20036.

CAREER: New York Times, New York, N.Y., 1953—, formerly correspondent in Southeast Asia, Latin America, Spain, Eastern Europe, and the Middle East, now with Washington Bureau. Lecturer on foreign affairs, at universities, government seminars, for Peace Corps, and on radio and television. *Member:* National Press Club and Overseas Writers (both Washington, D.C.), Overseas Press Club (New York). *Awards, honors:* Maria Moors Cabot Gold Medal ($1,000 award) of Columbia University for advancement of international friendship in the Americas, 1959; Overseas Press Club Citation, 1965; Sigma Delta Distinguished Service Award, 1968.

WRITINGS: Twilight of the Tyrants, Holt, 1959; *New Trends in Latin America,* Foreign Policy Association, 1960; (with Karl E. Meyer) *The Cuban Invasion: The Chronicle of a Disaster,* Praeger, 1962; *The Winds of Revolution: Latin America Today and Tomorrow,* Praeger, 1963, 2nd edition, revised, 1965; *Latin America,* Encyclopaedia Britannica, 1965; *The Dominican Diary,* Delacorte, 1965; *The Bombs of Palomares,* Viking, 1967; *Czechoslovakia Since World War II,* Viking, 1971; (editor) *The United States and the Caribbean* (American Assembly series), Prentice-Hall, 1971. Contributor to *Look, Venture, New Yorker,* and other magazines and newspapers.

WORK IN PROGRESS: Reportage books on Spain and U.S.A.

BIOGRAPHICAL/CRITICAL SOURCES: New York Times Book Review, April 23, 1967; *Listener,* May 18, 1967; *Christian Science Monitor,* June 12, 1967; *New Leader,* July 3, 1967, May 3, 1971; *Saturday Review,* January 30, 1971.

* * *

TALLON, Robert 1940-

PERSONAL: Born September 21, 1940, in New York, N.Y.; son of Charles A. and Anne E. Tallon. *Education:*

Attended Art school for two years, college for three years, and studied voice at Metropolitan Opera Studios for two years. *Home:* 94-25 57th Ave., Elmhurst, Long Island, New York, N.Y.

CAREER: Artist in oil, watercolor, and mixed mediums, with four one-man shows in New York, N.Y. *Military service:* U.S. Army.

WRITINGS: Conversations: Cries, Croaks, and Calls, Holt, 1963; (illustrator) Ruth Leslie Smith, *Hurry!, Dinner Is at Six,* Bobbs-Merrill, 1969; (self-illustrated) *A.B.C. . . .* (in English and Spanish), Lion Press, 1970; (self-illustrated) *The Thing in Dolores' Piano,* Bobbs-Merrill, 1970; *Zoophabets,* Bobbs-Merrill, in press.

WORK IN PROGRESS: A movie script.

BIOGRAPHICAL/CRITICAL SOURCES: Library Journal, September, 1970.

* * *

TAMBURINE, Jean 1930-

PERSONAL: Born February 20, 1930, in Meriden, Conn.; daughter of Paul D. and Helen (Marks) Tamburine; married Eugene E. Bertolli (vice-president of design, Napier Co.), April 21, 1956; children: E. Robert, Lisa Marie. *Education:* Studied at Art Students League and Traphagen School of Fashion, New York, N.Y., 1948-50. *Religion:* Roman Catholic. *Home:* 73 Reynolds Dr., Meriden, Conn. 06450.

CAREER: Designer and publisher of greeting cards, 1945; Norcross, Inc., New York, N.Y., designer, 1948-50; Rust Craft, Boston, Mass., designer, 1954-55; free-lance artist, 1950—, illustrating more than thirty books. Paintings reproduced in annual Christmas card collection of American Artists Group. Lecturer. *Member:* Connecticut Governor's Commission to Study the Arts. *Member:* International Platform Association, Authors Guild, Allied Artists of America, Women's National Book Association, Catholic Fine Arts Society, North Shore Arts Association, Meriden Arts and Crafts Association.

WRITINGS—Self-illustrated: (With Jackie Peller) *The Three Little Pigs and Little Red Riding Hood,* Grosset, 1954; (editor with Jackie Peller) *Treasure Book of Favorite Nursery Tales,* Grosset, 1954; *Almost Big Enough,* Abingdon, 1963; *I Think I Will Go to the Hospital,* Abingdon, 1965; *How Now, Brown Cow,* Abingdon, 1967.

Illustrator: May Justus, *Peter Pocket and His Pickle Pup,* Holt 1953; *Little Red Riding Hood,* Wonder Books, 1954; Helen Hilles, *Moving Day,* Lippincott, 1954; May Justus, *Surprise for Peter Pocket,* Holt, 1955; May Justus, *Use Your Head, Hildy,* Holt, 1956; May Justus, *Peddler's Pack,* Holt, 1957; May Justus, *Big Log Mountain,* Holt, 1958; May Justus, *Barney, Bring Your Banjo,* Holt, 1959; May Justus, *The Right House for Rowdy,* Holt, 1960; May Justus, *Winds a'Blowing,* Abingdon, 1961; May Justus, *Smoky Mountain Sampler: Stories,* Abingdon, 1962; Gina Bell, *Who Wants Willy Wells,* Abingdon, 1965; John Stanley, *It's Nice to Be Little,* Rand McNally, 1965; Mary Sue White, *See Me Grow,* Abingdon, 1966; May Justus, *The Complete Peddler's Pack: Games, Songs, Rhymes, and Riddles From Mountain Folklore,* University of Tennessee Press, 1967; Helen Guittard, *Something Was Missing,* Follett, 1969; Marjorie Barrows, *Scamper,* Rand McNally, 1970. Contributor to *Woman's Day.*

WORK IN PROGRESS: Illustrating two books for children; writing and illustrating a fourth book for Abingdon.

BIOGRAPHICAL/CRITICAL SOURCES: Meriden Record, July 10, 1963, July 23, 1963; *Hartford Courant,* August 11, 1963; *Elementary English,* November, 1966.

TANNENBAUM, Frank 1893-1969

PERSONAL: Born March 4, 1893, in Austria; came to United States in 1905; son of Abraham Wolf and Anna (Wilder) Tannenbaum; married Esther Abramson, June 1, 1917 (divorced 1928); married Jane Belo, May 22, 1940 (died 1968). *Education:* Columbia University, B.A., 1921; New School for Social Research, fellow, 1922; Robert Brookings Graduate School in Economic and Political Science, Ph.D., 1927.

CAREER: Newspaper correspondent in Mexico, 1922-24; surveyed land and agricultural conditions in Mexico for Institute of Economics, Washington, D.C., 1925-27, economic and social conditions in Puerto Rico for Institute of Economics, 1928-30, rural education in Mexico for Mexican government, 1931; wrote National Commission on Law Observance and Law Enforcement report on penal institutions, 1932; Columbia University, New York, N.Y., lecturer, 1935-37, associate professor, 1937-45, professor of Latin American history, 1945-61, professor emeritus and director of University Seminars, 1961-69. Visiting instructor, Cornell University, 1932; visiting lecturer, Yale University, 1934, Escuela do Aetus Eotublios, Sao Paulo, Brazil, 1946, San Marcos, Lima, Peru, 1957; visiting professor of history, Hofstra University, 1965-67; distinguished visiting professor of history, Fairleigh Dickinson University, 1967-68. Member of staff, President's Commission on Prison Industries, 1934, National Commission on Law Observance and Law Enforcement; member, Commission on Cultural Relations with Latin America.

MEMBER: National Academy of History (Venezuela; corresponding member), Instituto Drago de Cultura Americana (Argentina; corresponding member), Instituto Geographico e Historico da Bahia (Brazil; corresponding member), Academy of Political Science, American Historical Society, Economic History Association, Hispanic Society of America, Inter-American Round Table, International Rescue Committee, Latin American Studies Association, Society of American Historians, American Economic Association, American History Association, American Geographical Society (fellow), Council on Foreign Relations, Asia Society, Bolivarian Society of the U.S., Center of Inter-American Relations, Committee for the Americas, American Association of University Professors, American Civil Liberties Union, American Council for Emigres in the Professions, American Society of Criminology, National Association for the Advancement of Colored People, Overseas Press Club of America, Dissenters, International Association of Machinists, Society of Older Graduates of Columbia University, Phi Beta Kappa, Columbia University Club. *Awards, honors:* National Mexican Order of Aguila Azteca, 1933; Mark Van Doren Award, 1961; Bolivian Order del Condor de Los Andes, 1963; Bolton Prize, 1963; honorary professor, John F. Kennedy University of Argentina.

WRITINGS: Life in an Army Training Camp, American Union Against Militarism, 1919; *The Labor Movement: Its Conservative Functions and Social Consequences,* Putnam, 1921, Arno, 1969; *Wall Shadows: A Study in American Prisons,* Putnam, 1922; *Darker Phases of the South,* Putnam, 1924, Negro Universities Press, 1969; *The Mexican Agrarian Revolution,* Macmillan, 1929, Archon, 1968; *Peace by Revolution: An Interpretation of Mexico,* Columbia University Press, 1933, reissued as *Peace by Revolution: Mexico After 1910,* 1966; *Osborne of Sing Sing,* introduction by Franklin D. Roosevelt, University of North Carolina Press, 1933; *Whither Latin America?: An Introduction to Its Economic and Social Problems,* Crowell, 1934; *Crime and the Community,* Ginn, 1938; *Slave and Citizen, the Negro in the Americas,* Knopf, 1947; *Mexico, the Struggle for Peace and Bread,* Knopf, 1950; *A Philosophy of Labor,* Knopf, 1951 (published in

England as *The True Society, a Philosophy of Labour,* J. Cape, 1964); *The American Tradition in Foreign Policy,* University of Oklahoma Press, 1955; *Ten Keys to Latin America,* Knopf, 1962; (editor and contributor) *A Community of Scholars: The University Seminars at Columbia,* Praeger, 1965; *The Balance of Power in Society, and Other Essays,* Macmillan, 1969.

BIOGRAPHICAL/CRITICAL SOURCES: New York Times, June 2, 1969.

(Died June 1, 1969)

*   *.   *

TANYZER, Harold Joseph 1929-

PERSONAL: Surname is pronounced *Tan*-ih-zer; born August 16, 1929, in New Haven, Conn.; son of Joseph and Rose (Weinberg) Tanyzer. *Education:* New Haven State Teachers College, B.S., 1951; University of Connecticut, M.A., 1955, professional diploma in education, 1957, Ph.D., 1962. *Home:* 75 Knightsbridge Rd., Great Neck, N.Y. 11020. *Office:* Department of Reading, Hofstra University, 1000 Fulton Ave., Hempstead, N.Y. 11550.

CAREER: Taught elementary school, Southington, Conn., three years; Southern Connecticut State College, New Haven, demonstration elementary teacher, three years; Hofstra University, Hempstead, N.Y., professor of reading and education, 1957—. Member, professional advisory board, Maimonides Institute for Exceptional Children. *Member:* International Reading Association, American Educational Research Association, National Council of Teachers of English, National Conference on Research in English, National Society for the Study of Education, Scholars-in-Residence, Nassau Board of Cooperative Educational Services and The Education Council, Nassau-Suffolk School Library Association, Nassau Reading Council.

WRITINGS: (With Albert J. Mazurkiewicz) *Early-to-Read i.t.a. Program,* i.t.a. Publications, 1963, revised edition, 1966; (with others) *Growing with Language* (primary language arts series consisting of 10 readers and 10 laboratory manuals), i.t.a. Publications, 1967; (with Mazurkiewicz) *Easy-to-Read Sequence,* i.t.a. Publications, 1971; *Series I Newsbook in Reading Instruction,* Multimedia Education, 1971; (editor with Jean Karl) *Reading, Children's Books, and Our Pluralistic Society,* International Reading Association, 1972; (with George Riemer) *Balloons: A Child's First Writing Book,* Creative Writing Service, 1973.

Research studies: (With Harvey Alpert) *Effectiveness of Three Different Basal Reading Systems on First-Grade Reading Achievement,* Hofstra University, 1965; (with Alpert and L. Sandel) *Beginning Reading: The Effectiveness of i.t.a. and T.O.,* Hofstra University and The Education Council, annually, 1965-68.

Growing with Language Program, published by i.t.a. Publications—With Albert J. Mazurkiewicz: *Reference: Reading to Find Out,* 1967, *Words: Their Structure,* 1967, *Thinking and Understanding,* 1967, *Writing and Perception,* 1968, *Punctuation and Capitalization,* 1969.

Contributor: *Today's Challenges in the Teaching of Reading,* Southern California Intermediate Council, International Reading Association, 1965; *A Decade of Innovations: Approaches to Beginning Reading,* International Reading Association, 1968; J.R. Block, editor, *i.t.a. as a Language Arts Medium,* Pitman, 1968; Sir James Pitman and John St. John, *Alphabets and Reading,* Pitman, 1969. Consultant on film, "The Forty Sounds of English: The Story of i.t.a.," Bransby Films, 1963; contributor to professional publications.

WORK IN PROGRESS: A Parent's Guide to the Initial Teaching Alphabet; Problems in the Teaching of Children's Literature.

SIDELIGHTS: Tanyzer is one of the American pioneers in introducing the initial teaching alphabet into the public schools of the United States. His Early-to-Read i.t.a. Program includes twelve readers, teacher's guides, workbooks, and vocabulary cards.

* * *

TARN, Nathaniel 1928-

PERSONAL: Born June 29, 1928, in Paris, France; married; children: two. Education: Cambridge University, B.A. (honors), 1948, M.A., 1952; studied at the Sorbonne, University of Paris, 1949-51; University of Chicago, M.A., 1952, Ph.D., 1957. Address: c/o Nan Talese, Random House, 201 East 50th St., New York, N.Y. 10022.

CAREER: Writer; has been employed as an anthropologist in Guatemala and Burma; taught at University of Chicago and University of London, and lectured at other universities, 1952-67; now professor of comparative literature, Livingston College, Rutgers University, New Brunswick, N.J. Visiting professor, State University of New York College at Buffalo and Princeton University, 1969-70. General editor, Cape Editions, and founder-director, Cape-Goliard Press with Jonathan Cape, 1967-69. Awards, honors: Guinness Prize for poetry, 1963.

WRITINGS: Old Savage/Young City (poems), J. Cape, 1964, Random House, 1965; (with Richard Murphy and Jon Silkin) Penguin Modern Poets No. Seven: Richard Murphy, Jon Silkin, Nathaniel Tarn, Penguin, 1965; (translator) Pablo Neruda, The Heights of Macchu Picchu, J. Cape, 1966, Farrar, Straus, 1967; Where Babylon Ends, J. Cape, 1968, Grossman, 1968; (editor and co-translator) Con Cuba: An Anthology of Cuban Poetry of the Last Sixty Years, Grossman, 1969; The Beautiful Contradictions, J. Cape, 1969, Random House, 1970; October (poems), Trigram Press, 1969; (translator) Victor Segalen, Stelae, Unicorn Press, 1969; (editor) Pablo Neruda, Selected Poems, J. Cape, 1970, Delacorte, 1972; A Nowhere for Vallejo, Random House, 1971; Lyrics for the Bride of God: Section: The Artemision, Tree Books, 1972. Represented in several anthologies, including The Pattern of Poetry, edited by W. Kean Seymour, Burke Publishing, 1963, Young Commonwealth Poets '65, edited by Peter Ludwig Brent, Heinemann, 1965, New Poems 1965: A P.E.N. Anthology of Contemporary Poetry, edited by Cicely Veronica Wedgwood, Hutchinson, 1966, The Penguin Book of Modern Verse Translation, edited by George Steiner, Penguin, 1966, Poems Addressed to Hugh MacDiarmid, edited by Duncan Glen, Akros Publications, 1967, Music and Sweet Poetry: A Verse Anthology, edited by John Bishop, Baker Publishers, 1968, Frontier of Going: Anthology of Space Poetry, edited by John Fairfax, Panther Books, 1969, British Poetry Today, edited by Edward Lucie-Smith, Penguin, 1971, Shaking the Pumpkin, edited by Jerome Rothenberg, Doubleday, 1972, and America: A Prophecy, edited by Jerome Rothenberg and George Quasha, Random House, 1973. Contributor to Agenda, Ambit, Poetry Review, Times Literary Supplement, Observer, Spectator, Listener, Outposts, Solstice, Tribune, Stand, Akzente, Nouvelle Revue Francaise, Plamen, Unicorn Folios, Transatlantic Review, El Corno Emplumado, Io, Chicago Review, and other publications.

WORK IN PROGRESS: Translations of Antonin Artaud, Andre Breton, Alfred Jarry, Pierre Reverdy, Charles Cros, and of Maya Texts and Queredo; studies in relations between poetry and science, especially information theory.

TATON, Rene 1915-

PERSONAL: Born April 4, 1915, in L'Echelle, Ardennes, France; son of Andre and Therese (Launoy) Taton; married Juliette Battesti (a history professor), August 21, 1945; children: Annie, Nicole. Education: Attended Ecole normale superieure de Saint-Cloud; Faculte des sciences de Paris, agregation de mathematiques, 1941, doctorat es-lettres, 1951. Home: 64 rue Gay-Lussac, Paris V, France. Office: Centre Alexandre Koyre, 12 rue Colbert, Paris II, France.

CAREER: Professeur agrege de mathematiques, Orleans, France, 1941-46, Suresnes, France, 1951-53; Centre national de la recherche scientifique, Paris, France, 1946-51, 1953—, directeur de recherche, 1964—; Ecole des Hautes Etudes, Paris, France, charge de conferences, 1958, professor, 1964—. Directeur, Centre Alexandre Koyre, Paris, France. Military service: French Army, anti-aircraft defense, 1939-40.

MEMBER: International Union of the History and Philosophy of Science (general secretary, 1955-71), Academie Internationale d'Histoire des Sciences (membre effectif), Societe Mathematique de France, Association Francaise pour l'Avancement des Sciences, Association des Ecrivains Scientifiques de France. Awards, honors: Prix Cavailles, 1951; Prix Pelliot, 1953; Laureat de l'Institut, 1955.

WRITINGS: Pour continuer le calcul integral, G. Doin, 1943; Histoire du calcul, Presses Universitaires de France, 1946, 5th edition, 1969; Le Calcul mecanique, Presses Universitaires de France, 1949, 2nd edition (with Jean-Paul Flad), 1963; Gaspard Monge, Birkhaeuser (Basel), 1950; L'Oeuvre mathematique de G. Desargues, Presses Universitaires de France, 1951; L'Oeuvre scientifique de F. Monge, Presses Universitaires de France, 1951; La Geometrie projective en France de Desargues a Poncelet, University of Paris, 1951; L'Histoire de la geometrie descriptive, Les Conferences du Palais de la Decouverte, 1954; Causalites et accidents de la decouverte scientifique: Illustration de quelques stapes caracteristiques de l'evolution des sciences, Masson, 1955, translation by A.J. Pomerans published as Reason and Chance in Scientific Discovery, Philosophical Library, 1957; Le Calcul mental, Presses Universitaires de France, 1957, 5th edition, 1970; (with Albert Flocon) La Perspective, Presses Universitaires de France, 1963, 2nd edition, 1970; Les Origines de l'Academie Royale des Sciences, Palais de la Decouverte, 1966.

Editor: (With Marie-Elisa Cohen) Eugene Boris Uvarov and D.R. Chapman, Dictionnaire des sciences: Mathematiques, mecanique, cosmographie, physique, chimie, Presses Universitaires de France, 1956; Histoire generale des sciences, Presses Universitaires de France, Volume I: La Science antique et medievale: Des origines a 1450, 1957, Volume II: La Science moderne: De 1450 a 1800, 1958, Volume III: La Science contemporaine: Le XIXe siecle, 1961, Volume IV: La Science contemporaine: Le XXe siecle, 1964, translation by A.J. Pomerans published as History of Science, Volume I: Ancient and Medieval Science from Prehistory to A.D. 1450, Thames & Hudson, 1963, published in America as Ancient and Medieval Science from the Beginnings to 1450, Basic Books, 1964, Volume II: The Beginnings of Modern Science From 1450 to 1800, Basic Books, 1964, Volume III: Science in the Nineteenth Century, Basic Books, 1965, Volume IV: Science in the Twentieth Century, Basic Books, 1966 (series title published in England as A General History of the Sciences, Thames & Hudson, 1963-66); Oeuvres completes d'Augustin Cauchy, Gauthier-Villars, Volume II, 1958, Volume XV, 1973; Enseignement et diffusion des sciences en France au XVIIIe siecle, Hermann, 1964.

Co-editor, *Revue d'Histoire des Sciences et de Leurs Applications*, 1948—.

WORK IN PROGRESS: Conducting research on the history of mathematics in the seventeenth century, history of geometry in the nineteenth century, and the sciences and the French Revolution.

* * *

TAYLOR, Jack W(ilson) 1915-

PERSONAL: Born June 19, 1915, in Huntingdon, Pa.; son of Seibert A. and Agnes (Wilson) Taylor; married Elleanora Shingler, May 19, 1945; children: Jane M., Margaret K. Bowman (stepdaughter). *Education:* Juniata College, B.A., 1937; Pennsylvania State College (now Pennsylvania State University), M.S., 1944. *Office:* Cumberland Engineering Co., Inc., Providence, R.I. 02904.

CAREER: Professional musician in Huntingdon, Pa., 1934-41; Piper Aircraft Corp., Lock Haven, Pa., industrial engineer, 1941-44; Owens-Corning Fiberglas Corp., Huntingdon, Pa., training supervisor, 1944-50; Packaging Corp. of America, Rittman, Ohio, director of management development, 1950-63; Cumberland Engineering Co., Inc., Providence, R.I., personnel director, 1964—. Consultant on management development to business and industry, 1963—. *Member:* American Management Association, American Society of Training Directors.

WRITINGS: How to Create New Ideas, Prentice-Hall, 1961; *How to Select and Develop Leaders,* McGraw, 1962; *Twelve Basic Ideas About People,* Management Center of Cambridge, 1969.

AVOCATIONAL INTERESTS: Flying (licensed aircraft pilot).

* * *

TAYLOR, John Vernon 1914-

PERSONAL: Born September 11, 1914, in Cambridge, England; son of Ralph Strickland (a bishop) and Irene (Garrett) Taylor; married Margaret Wright, October 5, 1940; children: Joanna, Peter, Veronica. *Education:* Attended St. Lawrence College, Ramsgate, England; Trinity College, Cambridge, M.A., 1938; St. Catherine's College, Oxford, B.A., 1938; Institute of Education, University of London, Dip.Ed., 1943. *Home:* 4 The Orchard, Blackheath, London S.E.3, England. *Office:* Church Missionary Society, 157 Waterloo Rd., London S.E.1, England.

CAREER: Curate in London, England, 1938-40, in St. Helens, England, 1940-43; Bishop Tucker Theological College, Mukono, Uganda, warden, 1944-54; International Missionary Council, London, England, research worker, 1955-59; Church Missionary Society, London, England, Africa secretary, 1959-63; general secretary, 1963—. *Member:* Royal Commonwealth Society. *Awards, honors:* D.D., Wycliffe College, Toronto, Ontario, 1964.

WRITINGS: Were You There?: An African Presentation of the Passion Story, Highway Press, 1950; *Man in the Midst,* Highway Press, 1955, published in America as *In Perilous Paths,* Seabury Press, 1957; *Courts of the Lord's House: A Guide to the Holy Communion,* Lutterworth Press, 1955, 2nd edition, Daystar Press, 1966; *Christianity and Politics in Africa,* Penguin, 1957; (author of introduction) *Afrikanische Passion: The Passion in Africa,* Kaiser Verlag, 1957; *The Growth of the Church in Buganda: An Attempt at Understanding,* S.C.M. Press, 1958; *Black and White,* S.C.M. Press, 1958; *Processes of Growth in an African Church* (pamphlet), S.C.M. Press, 1958; (with Dorothea Lehmann) *Christians of the Copperbelt: The Growth of the Church in Northern Rhodesia,* S.C.M. Press, 1961; *The Primal Vision: Christian Presence Amid African Religion,* S.C.M. Press, 1963, Fortress, 1964; *For All the World: The Christian Mission in*

the Modern Age, Westminster, 1966; *Change of Address: Selections From the C.M.S. Newsletters,* Hodder & Stoughton, 1968. Author of scripts for British Broadcasting Corp. Schools Department. Contributor of articles to religious journals.

WORK IN PROGRESS: Research on African religion and the idea of the Immanent God, and on the sociology of church growth.

BIOGRAPHICAL/CRITICAL SOURCES: West Africa, July, 1963.

* * *

TEC, Nechama 1931-

PERSONAL: Born May 15, 1931, in Lublin, Poland; daughter of Roman (a businessman) and Esther (Hachamoff) Bawnik; married Leon Tec (a child psychiatrist), February, 1950; children: Leora, Roland. *Education:* Columbia University, B.S., 1954, M.A., 1955, Ph.D., 1963. *Home:* 11 Rockyfield Rd., Westport, Conn. 06880.

CAREER: New York State Department of Mental Hygiene, New York, N.Y., research sociologist in biometrics, 1956-57; Columbia University, New York, N.Y., lecturer in School of General Studies, 1957-60; Douglass College, New Brunswick, N.J., instructor in sociology, 1959-60; Columbia University, New York, N.Y., lecturer in sociology, 1968—, Mid-Fairfield Child Guidance Center, Norwalk, Conn., research director, 1968—. *Member:* American Sociological Association, Phi Beta Kappa.

WRITINGS: Gambling in Sweden, Bedminster, 1964. Contributor to *Journal of Social Problems, Journal of Social Science and Medicine,* and *Journal of Marriage and Family.*

WORK IN PROGRESS: A research report dealing with suburban teenagers and illegal drugs.

* * *

TEN HOOR, Elvie Marie (Mortensen) 1900-

PERSONAL: Born October 23, 1900, in Watseka, Ill.; daughter of John (a merchant) and Emma (Kemnitz) Mortensen; married Perry John Ten Hoor (an attorney), October 11, 1917; children: Gloria Jean (Mrs. George Scofield), Perry John, Jr. *Education:* Studied at Art Institute of Chicago and at Famous Artists School, Westport, Conn. *Home and office:* 6740 Oglesby Ave., Chicago, Ill. 60649.

CAREER: Artist and former art teacher. *Member:* Artists' Equity Association, Inc., Alumni of School of the Art Institute of Chicago (board), All-Illinois Society of the Fine Arts, North Shore Art League, Chicago Society of Artists, Inc., Renaissance Society (University of Chicago), Sigma Kappa (chapter president, 1964-66). *Awards, honors:* Prize for outstanding work from Dunes Art Foundation of Indiana, 1958, and additional prizes in 1959, 1961, 1962, 1963; Margaret R. Dingle Award for most original work, 1961.

WRITINGS: (With Dona Z. Meilach) *Collage and Found Art,* Reinhold, 1964; (with Meilach) *Collage and Assemblages,* Crown, 1973.

BIOGRAPHICAL/CRITICAL SOURCES: Sigma Kappa Triangle, Autumn, 1960.

* * *

TENNANT, Nora Jackson 1915-
(Nora Jackson)

PERSONAL: Born July 7, 1915, in London, England; daughter of Herbert E. (an educator) and Lillie (Hainsworth) Jackson; married John Geoffrey Tennant (an estimator engineer), July 27, 1957. *Education:* Willesden

County School, London, England, teachers certificate, 1935; Furzedown Training College, London, England, associate of College of Preceptors, 1938. *Religion:* Methodist. *Home:* 58 Hill Rd., Pinner, Middlesex, England.

CAREER: Headstone School, Harrow, England, head of geography department, 1942-57; Netherton Secondary Modern School, Dudley, England, senior mistress, 1957-60; Vauxhall Manor School, London, England, head of geography department, 1960-67; Langley County Secondary School, Langley, near Slough, Buckinghamshire, England, deputy head, 1967—. *Member:* Royal Society of Teachers, Royal Geographical Society (fellow), National Union of Teachers, Pinner Horticultural Society.

WRITINGS—All with Philip Penn under name Nora Jackson: "Groundwork Geographies" series, published by Philip & Son: Book 1: *British Isles,* 1959, 5th edition, 1968, Book 2: *Europe,* 1959, 4th edition, 1968, Book 3: *The Southern Continents,* 1959, 6th edition, 1971, Book 4: *North America and Asia,* 1960, 2nd edition, 1961; *A Groundwork of Physical Geography,* Philip & Son, 1963; *A Dictionary of Natural Resources and Their Principal Uses,* Pergamon, 1966, 2nd edition, 1969; *A Groundwork of World Wealth,* Philip & Son, 1966. Contributor to *World Book Encyclopedia.*

WORK IN PROGRESS: A Geology for Schools, for Heinemann.

AVOCATIONAL INTERESTS: Gardening, especially roses; walking in the country and by the sea, reading thrillers, color photography, and people.

* * *

TESTER, Sylvia (Root) 1939-

PERSONAL: Born October 6, 1939; daughter of Orrin (an editor) and Thelma (Aldridge) Root; married N. Eugene Tester (a teacher), July 18, 1959; children: Rachael Anne, Julia Linette. *Education:* Attended Cincinnati Bible College for two years. *Religion:* Christian. *Office:* David C. Cook Publishing Co., Elgin, Ill. 60120.

CAREER: Standard Publishing Co., Cincinnati, Ohio, assistant editor, 1959-60; David C. Cook Publishing Co., Elgin, Ill., 1963-68, school products editor, 1968—.

WRITINGS: The Life of Jesus in Pictures, Standard Publishing, 1962; *Jesus Is Born,* Standard Publishing, 1963; *Jesus Lives,* Standard Publishing, 1963; *Gifts for Baby Jesus,* David Cook, 1963; *Let Me Help,* David Cook, 1963; *Where Are You Going Today?,* Standard Publishing, 1964; *Baby Jesus,* Standard Publishing, 1964; *Happy Sunday Morning,* Standard Publishing, 1964; *God's Children Help,* David Cook, 1964; (with Betty Freedy Larsen) *The Birth of Jesus,* David Cook, 1964; *But I Can't See Him,* David Cook, 1966; *Teachers' Manual for Health and Cleanliness,* David Cook, 1966; *Plants and Seeds* (teaching pictures), David Cook, 1967; *My Friend, the Doctor,* David Cook, 1967; *My Friend, the Policeman,* David Cook, 1967; *My Friend, the Fireman,* David Cook, 1968; *Teachers' Manual for Moods and Emotions,* David Cook, 1970; *Teachers' Manual for Creative Adventures,* David Cook, 1972. Also author of "Purple Shadow on a Cold Wind," "Melinda," and "Ugly Brunhilda," as yet unpublished.

WORK IN PROGRESS: Fire Child.

* * *

THOMAS, Gordon 1933-
(Tom Gordon, Brian James, Robert Street)

PERSONAL: Born February 21, 1933, in Carmarthon, South Wales; son of Gwyn (a painter) and Linda (Griffiths) Thomas; married Anne Nightingale (a British Broadcasting Corp. television reporter), June 17, 1962; children: Alexander Iuan. *Education:* Attended schools in South Africa and Bedford Modern School in England. *Home and office:* 5 Arundel Ter., Brighton 7, Sussex, England. *Agent:* Stella Jonckheere, 28 Maida Ave., London W.1, England.

CAREER: The People, London, England, feature writer, 1953-54; *Daily Express,* London, England, feature writer, 1954-1959; *Today,* London, England, record reviewer, 1959-61; *Evening Argus,* London, England, literary editor, 1961—; runs public relations company, Gordon Thomas Associates Ltd. Consultant public relations officer to Canary Islands. *Member:* Screenwriters Guild.

WRITINGS: (With Scotty Young) *Descent into Danger,* Wingate, 1954; *Thames Number One,* Wingate, 1955; *Physician Extraordinary,* Wingate, 1956; (with Michael Blondini) *Bed of Nails: The Story of the Amazing Blondini,* Wingate, 1955; *The Camp on Blood Island,* Hamish Hamilton, 1958; (with Ronald Hutchinson) *Turn by the Window: The Trial and Imprisonment in Japan of Signalman Graham Nicholls,* Cassell, 1959; *Torpedo Run,* Hamish Hamilton, 1959; *Midnight Trader,* Harrap, 1959; *The Jack Spot Story,* Wingate, 1962; *Miracle of Surgery,* Hamish Hamilton, 1962; *The National Health Service,* Panther Books, 1964; (with Max Morgan Witts) *The Day the World Ended,* Stein & Day, 1969; (with Ian Donald Hudson) *The Parents' Home Doctor,* revised edition, Arco, 1969; (with Hudson) *What To Do Until the Doctor Comes,* Auerbach, 1970; *An Overall Study of the Work of Norma Redpath and in Particular the Years 1960-1970,* Rudy Komon Gallery, 1970; (with Witts) *The San Francisco Earthquake,* Stein & Day, 1971.

Under pseudonym Brian James: *Cookabundy Bridge, and Other Stories,* Angus & Robertson, 1946; *The Advancement of Spencer Button* (novel), Angus & Robertson, 1950; *The Bunzip of Barney's Elbow* (short stories), Angus & Robertson, 1956; (compiler) *Selected Australian Stories* (anthology), Oxford University Press, 1959; (compiler and author of introduction) *Australian Short Stories,* second series, Oxford University Press, 1963; *Hopeton High* (novel), Angus & Robertson, 1963; *Orchards,* Oxford University Press, 1963; *The Big Burn* (short stories), Angus & Robertson, 1965; *England vs. Scotland,* Pelham, 1969.

Film scripts: "The Rotherham Candidate"; "Two Weeks in a New Town"; "The Third Bed"; "Two Bob Short." Writer of "Paperback Parade," a syndicated pocketbook review column.

WORK IN PROGRESS: "The Set Up," a television series for British Broadcasting Corp.

BIOGRAPHICAL/CRITICAL SOURCES: New York Times, April 15, 1969; *Times Literary Supplement,* July 24, 1969.†

* * *

THOMAS, Graham Stuart 1909-

PERSONAL: Born April 3, 1909, in Cambridge, England; son of William Richard and Lilian (Hays) Thomas. *Education:* Horticultural training at Cambridge University Botanic Garden with botanical courses in the University. *Home:* Briar Cottage, West End, Woking, Surrey, England.

CAREER: T. Hilling & Co. Ltd. (wholesale nurserymen) Chobham, Woking, Surrey, England, 1931-56, began as foreman, became manager; Sunningdale Nurseries, Windlesham, Surrey, England, manager, 1956-68, associate director, 1968—. Gardens adviser, National Trust, 1955—. Artist and illustrator; photographer; lecturer on horticultural subjects. *Member:* Royal Horticultural Society (fellow), British Pteridological Society, Northern Horticultural Society (fellow). *Awards, honors:* Veitch Memorial

Medal, Royal Horticultural Society, 1966; Victoria Medal of Honour, Royal Horticultural Society, 1968.

WRITINGS: The Old Shrub Roses, Phoenix House, 1955, Branford, 1956, 4th edition, Phoenix House, 1963; *Sheffield Park Gardens, Sussex: A Property of the National Trust* (pamphlet), Country Life, 1956; *The Manual of Shrub Roses: A Concise Account of the Wild Species, the Old French and the New Hybrid Roses,* Sunningdale Nurseries, 1957, 3rd edition, 1962; (self-illustrated) *Colour in the Winter Garden,* Branford, 1957, revised edition, 1967; *The Modern Florilegium,* Sunningdale Nurseries, 1958; (self-illustrated) *Shrub Roses of Today,* Phoenix House, 1962, St. Martin's, 1963; *Tintenhull House, Somerset: A Property of the National Trust* (pamphlet), Country Life, 1963; (contributor) Peter Hunt, editor, *Shell Gardens Book,* Phoenix House, 1964; (self-illustrated) *Climbing Roses, Old and New,* Phoenix House, 1965, St. Martin's 1966; (self-illustrated) *Plants for Ground Cover,* Dent, 1970. Contributor of illustrated articles to horticultural journals.

WORK IN PROGRESS: A book on herbaceous plants, for Dent.

SIDELIGHTS: Thomas originated the term "shrub rose"; he has spent much time propagating and naming roses almost lost to cultivation. *Avocational interests:* Music and singing.

*   *   *

THOMAS, Hugh Swynnerton 1931-

PERSONAL: Born October 21, 1931, in Windsor, England; son of Hugh Whitelegge (a colonial servant) and Margery (Swynnerton) Thomas; married Vanessa Jebb, 1962; children: Inigo, Isambard, Isabella. *Education:* Cambridge University, first class degree in history, 1953; attended the Sorbonne, University of Paris, 1954. *Politics:* Labour. *Home:* 29 Ladbroke Grove, London W.11, England.

CAREER: With Foreign Office, 1954-57, acting as secretary of United Kingdom delegation to UN disarmament sub-committee; lecturer in politics and government, Royal Military Academy, Sandhurst, England, 1957; prospective Labour Party candidate, Ruislip-Northwood, 1957-58; worked as disarmament adviser to United Nations Association, London, 1960-61; University of Reading, Reading, England, professor of history, 1966—. *Member:* Reform Club, Beefsteak Club. *Awards, honors:* Somerset Maugham Prize, 1962.

WRITINGS: Disarmament: The Way Ahead (pamphlet), Fabian Society, 1957; *The World's Game* (novel), Eyre & Spottiswoode, 1957; *The Oxygen Age* (novel), Eyre & Spottiswoode, 1958; (editor) *The Establishment* (symposium), C.N. Potter, 1959; *Death of a Conference: An Account of the Negotiations for General Disarmament, 1960,* United Nations Association of Great Britain and Northern Ireland, 1960; *The Spanish Civil War,* Harper, 1961, revised edition, Penguin and Eyre & Spottiswoode, 1965; *The Story of Sandhurst,* Hutchinson, 1961; *Suez,* Harper, 1967 (published in English as *The Suez Affair,* Weidenfeld & Nicolson, 1967, 2nd edition, revised, Penguin, 1970); (editor and contributor) *Crisis in the Civil Service* (essays), Anthony Blond, 1968; *Cuba: The Pursuit of Freedom,* Harper, 1971 (published in England as *Cuba; or, The Pursuit of Freedom,* Eyre & Spottiswoode, 1971); (author of introduction and notes) Esmond Romilly, *Boadilla,* new edition, Macdonald & Co., 1971; (editor and author of introduction) Jose Antonio Primo de Rivera, *Selected Writings,* J. Cape, 1972; *Goya: The Third of May, 1808,* Allen & Unwin, 1972, Viking, 1973; *Europe: The Radical Challenge,* Harper, 1973. Contributor to *New Statesman.*

SIDELIGHTS: Sir Charles Petrie wrote that Thomas, in *The Suez Affair,* "discusses the latest crisis in the long series of misunderstandings between London and Cairo. For obvious reasons he has had to be extremely circumspect in what he says, and his narrative necessarily contains a good deal of conjecture, but it is a real contribution to history, and it will be surprising if many of his surmises do not prove to stand the test of time." In her review, Elizabeth Monroe said that "Hugh Thomas is well known, through his good book on the Spanish Civil War, for his ability to sort out a muddle. His book on Suez has the merit of being splendidly written, clear and brief." She faults him for less than complete documentation in his account of the Suez crisis, but concludes that "one must be thankful to a contemporary historian of his quality for readiness to stick his neck out, because evidence better than this may never materialise."

Petrie remarked that "the Suez Affair was the last essay, barring Gibraltar, in British Imperialism." Thomas's account of "this tragic confusion," in the words of a reviewer for *Times Literary Supplement,* "has that gripping quality usually associated with Greek tragedy: even though one knows what the end is going to be, one still hopes against hope up to the eleventh hour that it may be averted. This quality is inherent in the drama, but it takes a true historian to bring it out."

Writing on *Cuba; or, The Pursuit of Freedom,* a columnist for *Bookseller* notes the "sheer bulk of the undertaking." Contending that "Castroism can be more fully understood in the light of Cuban history," Thomas spent ten years researching and writing this analysis of the causes of the Cuban revolution. According to the *Bookseller* writer, several critics were dismayed by the extreme length of the book (1,700 pages), but "there were no complaints from Norman Lewis, who told *Sunday Times* readers that this enormous book testified to rare scholarship and terrific industry, presented in a highly readable style, frequently embellished with delicate irony and wit."

BIOGRAPHICAL/CRITICAL SOURCES: Observer Review, April 30, 1967; *Times Literary Supplement,* April 27, 1967; *Books and Bookmen,* May, 1967; *New Statesman,* May 5, 1967; *Illustrated London News,* May 6, 1967; *Punch,* May 10, 1967; *Book Week,* July 2, 1967; *New York Times Book Review,* July 30, 1967; *New York Review of Books,* August 24, 1967; *Spectator,* March 8, 1968; *Bookseller,* January 30, 1971.

*   *   *

THOMAS, Mack 1928-

PERSONAL: Born September 17, 1928, in West, Tex.; son of Mack Finis (a laborer) and Leaughty (Chennault) Thomas; married Anne Amelia Holgate, February 28, 1964; children (previous marriage) Louann. *Education:* Attended Austin College, 1950-51. *Religion:* None. *Residence:* New York, N.Y. *Agent:* Sterling Lord Agency, 660 Madison Ave., New York, N.Y. 10021.

CAREER: Sold insurance, pitched a season of professional baseball, played tenor sax with a jazz group in a Negro hotel in Dallas, Tex.; modeled suits and coats for a clothing manufacturer in Kansas City; designed and sold a chromeplated bug deflector for automobiles; rode freight trains for a time, hung around hobo jungles, and spent a few months around the Indian reservations in New Mexico and Arizona; taught dancing for Arthur Murray in Denver, Colo.; owned and operated a diaper service for a year before becoming a disc jockey; played tenor sax in San Francisco; started for Cleveland to manage a dance studio, but changed his mind and went to New York and Europe; travelled in France, Spain, and Germany, then returned to San Francisco; on his way back to Paris he stopped in Dallas and was placed under arrest for the possession of narcotics; served part of a 22-year prison term in the Texas State Prison, 1958-63, on parole since October, 1963. *Military service:* U.S. Army Air Forces, 1946-49.

WRITINGS: Gumbo (novel), Grove, 1965; *The Total Beast* (novel), Simon & Schuster, 1970. Short stories have appeared in *Evergreen Review, Kulchur, Cosmopolitan, Saturday Evening Post,* and *Wild Dog;* poems in *Junge Amerikanische Lyrik* (German anthology).

SIDELIGHTS: Thomas told *CA:* "I am interested in the way the thought process channels material toward conclusions implicit in the process but irrelevant to the material. I play jazz tenor sax and understand music as a language. If I played better than I write, it would make me sad. My back aches in damp weather. I am losing my teeth. I expect to write a play someday."†

*   *   *

THOMAS, Owen Clark 1922-

PERSONAL: Born October 11, 1922, in New York, N.Y.; son of Harrison Cook and Frances (Arnold) Thomas; married Bernice Louise Lippitt, 1951; children: Aaron B., Addison L., Owen C., Jr. *Education:* Hamilton College, A.B., 1944; Cornell University, graduate student, 1943-44; Episcopal Theological School, B.D., 1949; Columbia University, Ph.D., 1956. *Home:* 10 St. John's Rd., Cambridge, Mass. 02138. *Office:* Episcopal Theological School, 99 Brattle St., Cambridge, Mass. 02138.

CAREER: Episcopal Diocese of New York, New York, N.Y., director of college work, 1951-52; Episcopal Theological School, Cambridge, Mass., instructor, 1952-56, assistant professor, 1956-62, associate professor, 1962-65, professor of theology, 1965—. Research at Cambridge University, University of Basel, and Graduate Theological Union, Berkeley, Calif. *Military service:* U.S. Navy, 1944-45; became ensign. *Member:* Society for Religion in Higher Education (fellow), Hazen Theological Discussion Group, Phi Beta Kappa.

WRITINGS: William Temple's Philosophy of Religion, Seabury, 1961; (translator) Adolphe Monod, *Farewell to His Friends and to His Church,* Banner of Truth, 1962; *Science Challenges Faith,* Seabury, 1967; (editor) *Attitudes Toward Other Religions: Some Christian Interpretations,* Harper, 1969; *Introduction to Theology,* Greeno & Hadden, 1973. Contributor of articles to *Anglican Theological Review, Religion in Life,* and to other publications.

WORK IN PROGRESS: The use of the case method in the teaching of systematic theology; the purposes and functions of theological reflection.

*   *   *

THOMETZ, Carol Estes 1938-

PERSONAL: Born May 30, 1938, in Fort Worth, Tex.; daughter of Joe Ewing (a federal judge) and Carroll (Cox) Estes; married Michael C. Thometz (a banker), June 27, 1959 (divorced); married David H. Gelfand (a research biochemist), April 28, 1967; children: (second marriage) Duskie Lynn. *Education:* Stanford University, A.B., 1959; University of California, Berkeley, graduate study, 1959-60; Southern Methodist University, M.A., 1961; University of California, San Diego, Ph.D. candidate, 1970—. *Home:* 1717 Westminster Dr., Cardiff, Calif. 92007.

CAREER: Stanford University, Palo Alto, Calif., research assistant in sociology, 1961-62; Brandeis University, Waltham, Mass., assistant study director, 1962-63, research associate, 1964-66; Simmons College, Boston, Mass., research director, 1963-64; U.S. Department of

Health, Education and Welfare, research consultant on aging programs, 1966-70; San Diego State College, San Diego, Calif., assistant professor of social work, 1967-70. *Member:* American Sociological Association, Alpha Kappa Delta. *Awards, honors:* Theta Sigma Phi (Dallas chapter) Matrix award, 1964, for *The Decision-Makers: The Power Structure of Dallas.*

WRITINGS: The Decision-Makers: The Power Structure of Dallas, Southern Methodist University Press, 1963; *A Study Relating to the Agency for Protective Services in San Diego,* Administration on Aging, U.S. Department of Health, Education and Welfare, 1970.

WORK IN PROGRESS: Research on programs and planning for the elderly.

BIOGRAPHICAL/CRITICAL SOURCES: Dallas Times Herald, December 30, 1963; *Longview News,* January 28, 1964.

*   *   *

THOMPSON, Denys 1907-

PERSONAL: Born February 15, 1907, in Darlington, England; son of Arthur Stanley (a clergyman) and Emma Jane (Courthope) Thompson; children: Sarah, Edward. *Education:* Attended St. John's School, Leatherhead, England; St. John's College, Cambridge, M.A. *Home:* 6 Storeys Way, Cambridge CB3, ODT, England.

CAREER: Gresham's School, Holt, Norfolk, England, senior English master, 1930-42; Yeovil School, Somerset, England, headmaster, 1944-62. Lecturer in England and abroad.

WRITINGS: (With F.R. Leavis) *Culture and Environment: The Training of Critical Awareness,* Chatto & Windus, 1933, Hillary, c.1957; *Reading and Discrimination,* Chatto & Windus, 1934, revised edition, 1954; *Between the Lines; or, How to Read a Newspaper,* Muller, 1939; *Voice of Civilisation: An Enquiry into Advertising,* Muller, 1943, 2nd edition, 1944; *The Importance of Leisure,* Bureau of Current Affairs, 1949; (with Raymond O'Malley) *English for the Living,* Methuen, Part 1, 1949, Part 2, 1952; *Practice in Reading: Examples for Comprehension and Expression,* Chatto & Windus, 1953; (with O'Malley) *English One,* Heinemann, 1955; (with O'Malley) *English Two,* Heinemann, 1955; *The English Language Paper: A Handbook for Candidates,* Chatto & Windus, 1956, new and revised edition, 1970; (with O'Malley) *English Three,* Heinemann, 1956; (with O'Malley) *English Four,* Heinemann, 1958; (with O'Malley); *English Five,* Heinemann, 1960; "Your English" series, Heinemann, Volume I, 1962, Volumes II-V (with R.J. Harris); 1962-65; (with O'Malley) *Precis and Comprehension: A Year's Work for Ordinary Level,* Heinemann, 1964, revised edition published as *Comprehension and Summary,* 1970; (with Michael Morland) *English for the Individual: Programmed Instruction in English Usage and Punctuation,* Heinemann, 1967.

Editor: (With James Reeves) *The Quality of Education: Methods and Purposes in the Secondary Curriculum,* Muller, 1947; Angus Graham, *The Golden Grindstone: The Adventures of George M. Mitchell,* Heinemann, 1951; *Science in Perspective: Passages of Contemporary Writing,* J. Murray, 1953, Transatlantic, 1966; (with O'Malley) *Rhyme and Reason: An Anthology,* Chatto & Windus, 1957; *Society in Focus: An Approach to General Studies,* Hutchinson, 1961; (with O'Malley) *The Key of the Kingdom* (poetry anthology), four volumes, Chatto & Windus, 1961-63; (with Brian Jackson) *English in Education: A Selection of Articles on the Teaching of English at Different Levels from Infant School to University,* Chatto & Windus, 1962, Dufour, 1964; *Discrimination and Popular Culture,* Penguin, 1964; (with

O'Malley) *The Bough on the Tree,* Watts, 1968; (with O'Malley) *The Egg in the Nest,* Watts, 1968; (with O'Malley) *The Nest on the Twig,* Watts, 1968; (with O'Malley) *The Twig on the Bough,* Watts, 1968; Jack London, *Love of Life, and Other Stories,* Chatto & Windus, 1968; *Directions in the Teaching of English,* Cambridge University Press, 1969; (and author of introduction and commentary) *Matthew Arnold: Selected Poems and Prose,* Barnes & Noble, 1971. General editor, "The Queen's Classics," Chatto & Windus, 1954—.

WORK IN PROGRESS: Textbooks; books on the relationship of men and animals, and on the function of poetry, from its earliest days.

SIDELIGHTS: Thompson's main interest is the teaching of English, and especially "education against the mass media and other products of the affluent society."

*   *   *

THOMPSON, Kenneth W (infred)   1921-

PERSONAL: Born August 29, 1921, in Des Moines, Iowa; son of Thor Carlyle and Agnes (Rorbeck) Thompson; married Lucille Elizabeth Bergquist, February 4, 1948; children: Kenneth Carlyle, Paul Andrew, James David. *Education:* Augustana College, Sioux Falls, S.D., A.B., 1943; University of Chicago, M.A., 1948, Ph.D., 1950. *Home:* 66 Carthage Rd., Scarsdale, N.Y. 10583. *Office:* Rockefeller Foundation, 111 West 50th St., New York, N.Y. 10028.

CAREER: Northwestern University, Evanston, Ill., 1948-51, began as instructor, became assistant professor of political science; University of Chicago, Chicago, Ill., assistant professor of political science; 1951-53; Northwestern University, associate professor and chairman of international relations committee, 1953-55; Rockefeller Foundation, New York, N.Y., consultant in international relations, 1953-55, assistant director for social sciences, 1955-57, associate director for social sciences, 1957-60, director for social sciences, 1960-61, vice-president, 1961—. Member of board of trustees, Union Theological Seminary. *Military service:* U.S. Army; Infantry officer, Intelligence, 1943-45; Counter-Intelligence, 1944-46. *Member:* American Academy of Arts and Sciences, American Political Science Association, Council on Foreign Relations, Institute of Current World Affairs, Century Association.

WRITINGS: (Editor with Hans J. Morgenthau) *Principles and Problems of International Politics: Selected Readings,* Knopf, 1950; (with Karl de Schweinitz) *Man and Modern Society: Conflict and Choice in the Industrial Era,* Holt, 1953; *Ethics and National Purpose* (pamphlet) Church Peace Union, 1957; *Christian Ethics and the Dilemmas of Foreign Policy,* Duke University Press, 1959; *Political Realism and the Crisis of World Politics: An American Approach to Foreign Policy,* Princeton University Press, 1960; (with Ivo D. Duchacek) *Conflict and Cooperation Among Nations,* Holt, 1960; *American Diplomacy and Emergent Patterns,* New York University Press, 1962; (editor, contributor, and author of introduction with Joseph E. Black) *Foreign Policies in a World of Change,* Harper, 1963; *The Moral Issue in Statecraft: Twentieth Century Approaches and Problems,* Louisiana State University Press, 1966; (with Morgenthau and Jerald C. Brauer) *U.S. Policy in the Far East: Ideology, Religion and Superstition,* Council on Religion and International Affairs, 1968; *Foreign Assistance: A View from the Private Sector,* University of Notre Dame Press, 1972.

Contributor: Roy C. Macridis, editor, *Foreign Policy in World Politics,* Prentice-Hall, 1958, 3rd edition, 1967; George W. Keeton and Georg Schwarzenberger, editors, *The Year Book of World Affairs, 1959,* Praeger, 1959;

John C. Bennett, editor, *Nuclear Weapons and the Conflict of Conscience,* Scribner, 1962; Horace V. Harrison, editor, *The Role of Theory in International Relations,* Van Nostrand, 1964; Norman J. Padelford and Leland M. Goodrich, editors, *The United Nations in the Balance: Accomplishments and Prospects,* Praeger, 1965; Boyd R. Keenan, editor, *Science and the University,* Columbia University Press, 1966; *Alternatives for Balancing World Food Production and Needs,* Iowa State University Press, 1967; Paul J. Braisted, editor, *Cultural Affairs and Foreign Relations,* revised edition, Columbia Books, 1968; Abdul A. Said, editor, *Theory of International Relations: The Crisis of Relevance,* Prentice-Hall, 1968; Victor E. Amend and Leo T. Hendrick, editors, *Readings from Left to Right,* Free Press, 1970; Edward LeRoy Long, Jr. and Robert T. Handy, editors, *Theology and Church in Times of Change,* Westminster, 1970; M.S. Rahan, editor, *Studies in Politics: National and International,* Vikas Publications (New Delhi), 1971; Jean-Claude Casanova, editor, *Science et conscience de la societe,* Calmann-Levy (Paris), 1971; Albert Lepawsky, editor, *The Search for World Order,* Appleton, 1971; Stephen D. Kertesz, editor, *The Task of Universities in a Changing World,* University of Notre Dame Press, 1971. Contributor of articles in fields of foreign policy, international organization, and the philosophy of international relations to periodicals. Member of board of editors, *International Organization,* 1956—, *Dialog,* 1961—; *Christianity and Crisis,* contributing editor, 1956—, member of board of editors, 1963—.

BIOGRAPHICAL/CRITICAL SOURCES: Virginia Quarterly Review, summer, 1967; *Christian Century,* December 13, 1967.

*   *   *

THOMPSON, Lawrence Sidney   1916-

PERSONAL: Born December 21, 1916, in Raleigh, N.C.; son of Lawrence Sidney (a businessman) and Elizabeth Luraa (Jones) Thompson; married Algernon Smith Dickson, September 21, 1950 (died July 17, 1962); married Ellen Marshall, May 23, 1968; children: (first marriage) Sarah Elizabeth, Mary Lawrence, Richard Dickson. *Education:* University of North Carolina, A.B., 1934, Ph.D., 1938; University of Chicago, A.M., 1935; University of Uppsala, graduate study, 1938-39; University of Michigan, A.B. in L.S., 1940. *Politics:* Southern Democrat. *Religion:* Presbyterian. *Home:* 225 Culpepper, Lexington, Ky. 40502. *Office:* Department of Classics, University of Kentucky, Lexington, Ky. 40506.

CAREER: Iowa State College Library, Ames, assistant reference librarian, 1940-42; Federal Bureau of Investigation, special agent with assignments in North and South America, 1942-45; U.S. Department of Agriculture Library, Washington, D.C., bibliographer, 1945-46; Western Michigan College (now Western Michigan University), Kalamazoo, librarian, 1946-48; University of Kentucky, Lexington, director of libraries, 1948-65, professor of classics, 1948—. President, Erasmus Press, Inc. (microform publishing firm), 1965—. Adviser on library matters to Turkish Ministry of Education, 1951-52, and to Caribbean Commission, 1955. *Member:* Bibliographical Society of America, Mediaeval Academy of America, Sociedad de Bibliofilos Argentinos, Kentucky Folklore Society (president, 1963-64), Los Cien Bibliofilos de Barcelona, Grolier Club (New York), Caxton Club (Chicago), Lexington Rotary Club, Filson Club (Louisville).

WRITINGS: Notes on Bibliokleptomania, New York Public Library, 1944, reissued as *Bibliokleptomania,* Peacock Press, 1968; (translator) Albert Predeek, *A History of Libraries in Great Britian and North America,* American Library Association, 1947; (with Algernon D.

Thompson) *The Kentucky Novel,* University of Kentucky Press, 1953; *Wilhelm Waiblinger in Italy,* University of North Carolina Press, 1953; *Kurze Geschichte der Handbuchbinderei in den Vereinigten Staaten von Amerika* (title means "a short history of handbookbinding in the United States"), M. Hettler, 1955; (with Elbert A. Thompson) *Fine Binding in America: The Story of the Club Bindery,* Beta Phi Mu (Urbana), 1956; *Kentucky Tradition,* Shoe String, 1956; *Boktryckarkonstens uppkomst in Foerenta Staterna* (title means "the origins of printing in the United States"), Gibers, 1956.

Printing in Colonial Spanish America, Archon Books, 1962; *A Bibliography of French Plays on Microcards,* Shoe String, 1967; *A Bibliography of American Doctoral Dissertations in Classical Studies and Related Fields,* Shoe String, 1968; *A Bibliography of Spanish Plays on Microcards,* Shoe String, 1968; *Bibliologia Comica; or, Humorous Aspects of the Caparisoning and Conservation of Books,* Shoe String, 1969; (compiler) *The Southern Black, Slave and Free: A Bibliography of Anti- and Pro-Slavery Books and Pamphlets, and of Social and Economic Conditions in the Southern States from the Beginnings to 1950,* Whitston Publishing Co., 1970; *Essays in Hispanic Bibliography,* Shoe String, 1970; *Pictorial History of Kentucky,* University of Kentucky Press, 1971; *Books in our Time,* McGrath, 1972; *Bibliography of French Revolutionary Pamphlets in Microform,* Whitston Publishing Co., in press; *A Decade of Bibliographical Scholarship,* Whitston Publishing Co., in press.

Pamphlets: *Bibliopegia Fantastica,* New York Public Library, 1947; *Folklore of the Chapel,* Society of Typographic Arts, 1950; *University of Kentucky Library Ranks High,* University of Kentucky Library, 1956; *Margaret Cooper Gay, 5 January 1900-9 September 1957,* University of Kentucky Library, 1958; *Uncle Remus in Syracuse,* Ross County Historical Society, 1959; *Some Kentucky Snake Superstitions,* Ohio Valley Folk Research Project, Ross County Historical Society, 1959; *Hoppy-Toads: At Home with Hoppy-Toads in the Ohio Valley,* Ohio Valley Folk Research Project, Ross County Historical Society, 1959.

A Few Notes on the Folklore of Tobacco, Ohio Valley Folk Research Project, Ross County Historical Society, 1960; *Johann Peter Zenger and Freedom of the Press in America,* Ohio Valley Folk Research Project, Ross County Historical Society, 1961; *The Water of Life in the Ohio Valley,* Ohio Valley Folk Research Project, Ross County Historical Society, 1961; *Prolegomena to Boreal Bibliophily,* University of Kentucky Library, 1961; *Mr. Beadle and the Folklorists,* Ohio Valley Folk Research Project, Ross County Historical Society, 1961; *Bee Lore in the Ohio Valley,* Ohio Valley Folk Research Project, Ross County Historical Society, 1961; *The Owl in the Ohio Valley,* Ohio Valley Folk Research Project, Ross County Historical Society, 1961; *Popular Ideas About the Future World in the Ohio Valley,* Ohio Valley Folk Research Project, Ross County Historical Society, 1962; *Legends of the Battlefield,* Ohio Valley Folk Research Project, Ross County Historical Society, 1962; *The Moon in the Ohio Valley,* Ohio Valley Folk Research Project, Ross County Historical Society, 1962; *Folklore of the Needle in the Ohio Valley,* Ohio Valley Folk Research Project, Ross County Historical Society, 1963; *Some Notes on the Folklore of Tobacco and Smoking,* University of Kentucky Library, 1964; *Who Killed Bibliography?,* Peacock Press, 1965; *The Incurable Mania,* Peacock Press, 1966.

Contributor of articles on literary, historical, and bibliographical subjects to professional journals in United States and Scandinavia. Contributing editor and member of editorial board, *Papers* of the Bibliographical Society of America, *Biblos* (Vienna), *Germanic Notes, Kentucky Folklore Record,* and *South Atlantic Bulletin.*

AVOCATIONAL INTERESTS: Collector of European private press books and fine printing, sample pages of early books.

BIOGRAPHICAL/CRITICAL SOURCES: Books Abroad, autumn, 1967.

* * *

THOMPSON, Richard   1924-

PERSONAL: Born October 9, 1924, in London, England; son of R. Thurlow (a journalist) and V. Kathleen (Lowe) Thompson; married Jennifer Wood, May 9, 1953; children: Jane, Jeremy, Susan, Sara, Timothy, Rachel, Bridget. *Education:* Canterbury University College, University of New Zealand, M.A., 1945. *Religion:* Anglican. *Home:* 435 Port Hills Rd., Christchurch 2, New Zealand. *Office:* Department of Psychology and Sociology, University of Canterbury, Christchurch, New Zealand.

CAREER: University of Otago, Dunedin, New Zealand, assistant lecturer, department of philosophy, 1946; University of Canterbury, Christchurch, New Zealand, lecturer, department of psychology and sociology, 1947—, reader, 1960-66, counselor for overseas students. Councillor, Heathcota County Council, 1968—. Member of Christchurch Regional Planning Authority. *Member:* British Psychological Society, American Sociological Association, Religious Research Association, Society for the Scientific Study of Religion.

WRITINGS: The Church's Understanding of Itself: A Study of Four Birmingham Parishes, S.C.M. Press, 1957; *Training for the Ministry,* University of Canterbury, 1958; *Race Relations in New Zealand: A Review of the Literature,* New Zealand Council of Churches, 1963; *Race and Sport,* published for Institute of Race Relations by Oxford University Press, 1964; *Race Discrimination in New Zealand-South African Sports Tours: A Bibliography,* Department of Psychology and Sociology, University of Canterbury, 1966, revised edition, 1972; *Race Discrimination in Sport: A New Zealand Controversy,* National Council of Churches, 1969; *Town Planning Reports,* Department of Psychology and Sociology, University of Canterbury, Number 1, 1969, Number 2, 1971. Contributor to *Race, Journal of the Polynesian Society, Theology, Revue de Criminologie et de Droit Penal Compare,* and other periodicals.

WORK IN PROGRESS: A study of the factors moulding the churches of New Zealand; *Sport, Race, and Politics: New Zealand and South Africa,* an account of continuing controversy over race discrimination in New Zealand's reciprocal sports tours with South Africa.

* * *

THOMPSON, Willa   1916-

PERSONAL: Born April 27, 1916, in Boston, Mass.; daughter of Frank V. (superintendent of Boston public schools) and Blanche (Wingate) Thompson; married second husband, Kenneth D. Amidon (self-employed), January 26, 1962; children: (first marriage) Eugenie (Mrs. Rene Scholtes), Antoinette (Mrs. Roger Schock), Helen, Laddie. *Education:* Studied at University of Munich, 1936, Smith College, 1938; Massachusetts Institute of Technology, and Harvard University, special courses, 1959-64. *Home:* 28 Hancock St., Auburndale, Mass. 02166. *Agent:* Alex Jackinson, 11 West 42nd St., New York, N.Y. 10036. *Office:* Massachusetts Institute of Technology, 3-463, Cambridge, Mass. 02139.

CAREER: Supreme Headquarters, Allied Expeditionary Forces, member of staff, Radio Luxembourg, 1944-45;

American Hospital of Paris, Paris, France, administrative work, 1955-57; Massachusetts Institute of Technology, Cambridge, executive secretary, National Magnet Laboratory, 1959—.

WRITINGS: *Garden Without Flowers* (fiction), Beacon Press, 1957. Contributor of poetry to magazines.

WORK IN PROGRESS: *When Spring Comes*, non-fiction; *Paris sans Amour*, fiction; a fiction book about an American hospital in Paris.

SIDELIGHTS: Miss Thompson lived in Luxembourg for fifteen years; she speaks French, German, Luxembourg dialect, Spanish, some Russian. *Avocational interests:* All sports, fishing.

* * *

THOMSON, Betty Flanders 1913-

PERSONAL: Born May 10, 1913, in Cleveland, Ohio; daughter of James Bewick and Bess (Whitmore) Thomson. *Education:* Mount Holyoke College, B.A., 1935, M.A., 1938; Columbia University, Ph.D., 1942. *Home:* 10 Dunbar Rd., Quakerhill, Conn. 06375. *Office:* Connecticut College, New London, Conn. 06320.

CAREER: University of Vermont, Burlington, instructor in botany, 1941-43; Connecticut College, New London, 1943—, began as instructor, now professor of botany. *Member:* Botanical Society of America, Ecological Society of America, American Association for Advancement of Science (fellow), Wilderness Society, Sigma Xi. *Awards, honors:* Faculty fellowship, National Science Foundation, 1958-59.

WRITINGS: (With G.S. Avery, R.M. Addoms, and E.B. Johnson) *Hormones and Horticulture*, McGraw, 1947; *The Changing Face of New England*, Macmillan, 1958. Contributor of a number of scientific research papers on plant growth and development to *American Journal of Botany* and other professional journals.

WORK IN PROGRESS: A book on landscape of the Midwest.

* * *

THOMSON, C(harles) Leslie 1914-

PERSONAL: Born April 19, 1914, in Edinburgh, Scotland; son of James Charles and Jessie (Hood) Thomson; married Olive Homer Lane, January 3, 1942; children: Douglas, Alan, Joanna. *Education:* Edinburgh Academy, student, 1921-31; University of Edinburgh, B.Sc., 1938; Edinburgh School of Natural Therapeutics, diploma, 1938. *Home:* Kingston, Liberton, Edinburgh 16, Scotland.

CAREER: Kingston Clinic, Edinburgh, Ltd., Edinburgh, Scotland, director, 1938—. *Member:* Incorporated Society of Registered Naturopaths.

WRITINGS: (Illustrator) James Charles Thomson, *Constipation and Our Civilisation*, Thorsons, 1943, revised edition published as *Intestinal Fitness: A Complete Revision of James C. Thomson's Constipation and Our Civilisation*, 1962; *Colour Transparencies: Exposure, Processing and Viewing*, Focal Press, 1948; *To See and to Hear*, Thorsons, 1949; *How to Use Colour Film*, Focal Press, 1950, 7th edition published as *How to Make Colour Films*, 1970; (with B.T. Fraser) *Honest Bread, and That Which Is Not*, Thorsons, 1950; *All About Taking Colour*, Focal Press, 1952, reissued as *All About Taking Colour with Your Camera*, 1958; *Colour Transparencies: Latest Information* (pamphlet), Focal Press, 1954; *Build Your Own Stereo Equipment: Notes on Making and Using Stereo Equipment*, Rayelle Publications, 1954; *Cine Stereo for Amateurs*, Fountain Press, 1955; *Your Sight: Care and Improvement by Natural Methods*, Thorsons, 1956; *Colour Films: The Technique of Working with Colour Materials*, Focal Press, 1958, 5th edition, 1971; *All About Colour with Ferraniacolor in Your Camera*, Focal Press, 1958; *All About Processing Reversal Colour*, Focal Press, 1959, *Successful Colour Photography*, Focal Press, 1959; 3rd edition, 1963; *How to Choose and Use Colour Films*, Focal Press, 1963, 2nd edition, Amphoto, 1969; (with James Charles Thomson) *Healthy Hair: Care and Restoration by Natural Methods*, revised and enlarged edition, Thorsons, 1967, Arc Books, 1969. Contributor to British photographic periodicals. Editor and publisher, *Kingston Health Chronicle*, 1960—.

WORK IN PROGRESS: Natural methods of health attainment; color photography.

* * *

THOMSON, (George) Ian F(alconer) 1912-

PERSONAL: Born September 2, 1912, in Canton, South China; son of George Dornin (a missionary) and Margaret (Everall) Thomson; married Bridget de Courcy; married second wife, Mary Josephine Lambart Dixon, February 22, 1952; children: Margaret (Mrs. Michael Paine), Richard Ian. *Education:* Attended Shrewsbury School; Balliol College, Oxford University, B.A., 1934, M.A. 1938; Westcott House, Cambridge, theological student. *Politics:* Liberal. *Religion:* Church of England. *Address:* 8 Ladbroke Ter., London W.11, England. *Office:* St. Michael's House, 2 Elizabeth St., London S.W.1, England.

CAREER: Ordained deacon, Church of England, 1936, priest, 1937. Hertford College, Oxford University, Oxford, England, chaplain, tutor, junior dean, and dean of degrees, 1937-42; rector of Hilgay, Norfolk, England, and secretary of examinations committee of Church of England, 1946-52; Maidstone Grammar School, Maidstone, England, senior divinity master, 1951-62; St. Paul's College, Cheltenham, England, chaplain and senior lecturer in religious education, 1962-66; director of research program, Edinburgh House, 1966-68; director of Bible Reading Fellowship, 1968—. Visiting lecturer, McMaster University, Hamilton, Ontario, Canada, 1964. Rowing correspondent for *Observer*, 1938-65, reporting international regattas, including Olympic Games, 1948, 1960, European championships, 1957, 1963, world championships, 1962. Member of commonwealth committee, Liberal Party, 1960-61. *Military service:* Royal Air Force, pilot, 1932-36, chaplain, 1942-46; became wing commander; glider instructor, 1952-60. *Member:* Vincent's Club (Oxford), Leander Club (Henley-on-Thames), Royal Air Force Club (Piccadilly). *Awards, honors:* Ellerton Theological Essay Prize, Westcott House, 1963; holder of five silver medals for rowing.

WRITINGS: *The Oxford Pastorate: The First Half Century*, Canterbury Press, 1946; *An Experiment in Worship*, S.C.M. Press, 1951; *The Rise of Modern Asia*, J. Murray, 1957, Pitman, 1958; *Changing Patterns in South Asia*, Barrie & Rockliff, 1961, Roy, 1962; *Two Hundred School Assemblies*, Mowbray, 1966; *Laymen Abroad in Christian Mission*, Conference of British Missionary Societies, 1967. Contributor of articles to *Times Literary Supplement* and *Quarterly Review*. Editor, *Word for the World*, Books 1-4, British Reading Fellowship, 1970-71.

WORK IN PROGRESS: Biblical exposition and editorial work for British Reading Fellowship, as director and editor-in-chief.

* * *

THOMSON, George Malcolm 1899-
(Aeneas MacDonald)

PERSONAL: Born August 2, 1899, in Leith, Scotland; son of Charles (a journalist) and Mary (Eason) Thomson; married Else Fredrikke Ellefsen, 1926 (died 1957); married Diana Robertson, 1963; children: (first marriage) Ann Berit Malcolm (Mrs. Max Ettlinger), Peter George Malcolm. *Education:* Attended Daniel Stewart's College; University of Edinburgh, M.A., B.Com., 1923. *Religion:* Presbyterian. *Home:* 46 Well Walk, London N.W.3, England. *Agent:* David Higham Associates Ltd., 76 Dean St., London W.1, England.

CAREER: Beaverbrook Organization, London, England, journalist for *Daily Express* and *Evening Standard,* 1931—. Temporary civil servant with British Ministry of Aircraft Production, Ministry of Supply, and Office of Lord Privy Seal during World War II. *Military service:* Royal Field Artillery, 1918; became second lieutenant. *Member:* Garrick Club (London).

WRITINGS: An Epistle to Roderick Watson Kerr (verse), Porpoise Press, 1926; *Caledonia; or, The Future of the Scots,* Dutton, 1927; *The Re-Discovery of Scotland,* Kegan Paul, 1928; *A Short History of Scotland from Earliest Times to the Outbreak of the Great War,* Kegan Paul, 1930; (under pseudonym Aeneas Macdonald) *Whiskey,* Henry & Longwell, 1930, expanded edition, Duffield & Green, 1934; *The Lambeth Conference,* Faber, 1930; *The Kingdom of Scotland Restored,* Humphrey Toulmin, 1930; *Will the Scottish Church Survive?* (pamphlet), Porpoise Press, 1930; *Scotland, That Distressed Area,* Porpoise Press, 1935; *Crisis in Zanat* (novel), Faber, 1942; *The Twelve Days: 24 July to 4 August 1914,* Putnam, 1964; *The Robbers Passing By,* Hutchinson, 1966; *The Crime of Mary Stuart,* Dutton, 1967; *Vote of Censure,* Stein & Day, 1968; *A Kind of Justice: Two Studies in Treason,* Hutchinson, 1970; *Sir Francis Drake,* Morrow, 1972.

AVOCATIONAL INTERESTS: Painting.

BIOGRAPHICAL/CRITICAL SOURCES: Times Literary Supplement, March 16, 1967; *Library Journal,* June 1, 1968; *Observer Review,* August 16, 1970.

*   *   *

THORN, William E.   1923-

PERSONAL: Born February 27, 1923, in McAlister, Okla.; son of Floyd B. (a minister) and Irma (Roller) Thorn; married Jessie D. Holder, August 20, 1947; children: Jenny Lynn, Martha Jane, Rebecca, Kay. *Education:* Hardin-Simmons University, B.A., 1948; Southwestern Baptist Theological Seminary, B.D. *Address:* Metropolitan Baptist Church, 525 West Douglas, Wichita, Kan. 67213.

CAREER: Baptist minister; formerly pastor of Calvary Baptist Church, Lubbock, Tex.; currently pastor of Metropolitan Baptist Church, Wichita, Kan. *Military service:* U.S. Navy, 1942-45.

WRITINGS: A Bit of Honey: After-Dinner Addresses of Inspiration, Wit, and Humor, Zondervan, 1964.

WORK IN PROGRESS: A biography of L.R. Millican; *Wake Up, Make Up and Go.*

*   *   *

THORNTON, John Leonard   1913-

PERSONAL: Born September 4, 1913, in Edgware, Middlesex, England; married Vera Hannah Sharpe, June 26, 1937; children: John, Ann, David. *Education:* University College, University of London, part-time librarianship student, 1930-34. *Home:* 120 Grasmere Ave., Wembley, Middlesex, England. *Office:* Medical College Library, St. Bartholomew's Hospital, West Smithfield, London E.C. 1, England.

CAREER: Staff member at University College Library, London, England, 1929-34, Wellcome Historical Medical Library, London, 1934-37; St. Bartholomew's Hospital Medical College, London, librarian, 1938—. Consultant librarian, Royal College of Obstetricians and Gynaecologists, 1961—. *Military service:* Royal Signals, 1942-46. *Member:* Library Association, Society of Indexers, Osler Club.

WRITINGS: Cataloguing in Special Libraries—A Survey of Methods, Grafton & Co., 1938; *Special Library Methods: An Introduction to Special Librarianship,* Grafton & Co., 1940; *The Chronology of Librarianship: An Introduction to the History of Libraries and Book-Collecting,* Grafton & Co., 1941; (editor) *A Mirror for Librarians: Selected Readings in the History of Librarianship,* Grafton & Co., 1948; *Medical Books: A Study of Bibliography and the Book Trade in Relation to the Medical Sciences,* Grafton & Co., 1949, 2nd revised edition, Deutsch, 1966.

John Abernethy: A Biography, privately printed, 1953; (with R.I.J. Tully) *Scientific Books, Libraries and Collectors: A Study of Bibliography and the Book Trade in Relation to Science,* Library Association, 1954, 3rd edition, 1971; (editor) *Classics of Librarianship, Further Selected Readings in the History of Librarianship,* Library Association, 1957; (compiler with Audrey J. Monk and Elaine S. Brooke) *A Select Bibliography of Medical Biography,* Library Association, 1961, 2nd edition, 1970; *Medical Librarianship: Principles and Practices,* Philosophical Library, 1963; (compiler) *Selected Readings in the History of Librarianship* (contains *A Mirror for Librarians* and *Classics of Librarianship*), Library Association, 1966; (contributor) Robert Thomas Bottle and H.V. Wyatt, editors, *The Use of Biological Literature,* Butterworth & Co., 1966, Shoe String, 1967; (author of introduction and biographical sketch) James Hobson Aveling, *English Midwives: Their History and Prospects,* Elliott, 1967; (editor) *Short-Title Catalogue of Books Printed Before 1857 in the Library of the Royal College of Obstetricians and Gynaecologists,* 2nd edition, Library Association, 1968; (contributor) Robert Thomas Bottle, editor, *The Use of Chemical Literature,* 2nd edition, Archon Books, 1969; (contributor) G. Norman Knight, editor, *Training in Indexing: A Course of the Society of Indexers,* M.I.T. Press, 1969. Contributor of articles to *Encyclopaedia Britannica, Britannica Book of the Year,* and to librarianship and medical history journals. Editor, *Indexer,* 1959-63.

WORK IN PROGRESS: A history of St. Bartholomew's Hospital Medical College; a life of Sir Archibald Garrod.

*   *   *

THORNTON, Martin (Stuart Farrin)   1915-

PERSONAL: Born November 11, 1915, in Hockley, Essex, England; son of Alfred Augustus (a chartered patent agent) and Ida (Farrin) Thornton; married Monica Anne Ritson; children: one daughter. *Education:* Dulwich College, student, 1930-34; King's College, London, A.K.C., 1946; Christ's College, Cambridge, B.A., 1951, M.A., 1955; General Theological Seminary, S.T.D., 1966. *Home:* Trinity Cottage, Loders, Dorsetshire, England.

CAREER: Clerk in holy orders, Church of England. Sub-warden of St. Deiniol's Library (founded by Gladstone), Hawarden, Chester, England, 1960-70; visiting lecturer in ascetical theology, General Theological Seminary, New York, N.Y., 1960, 1965, Philadelphia Divinity School, 1970.

WRITINGS: Rural Synthesis: The Religious Basis of Rural Culture, Skeffington & Sons, 1948; *Pastoral Theology: A Reorientation,* S.P.C.K., 1956, 2nd edition, 1961; *Christian Proficiency,* Morehouse, 1959; *Essays in Pastoral Reconstruction,* S.P.C.K., 1960, published in America as *Feed My Lambs: Essays in Pastoral*

Reconstruction, Seabury, 1961; *Margery Kempe,* S.P.C.K., 1960; *The Purple Headed Mountain,* Morehouse, 1962; *English Spirituality,* S.P.C.K., 1963; *The Rock and the River: An Encounter Between Traditional Spirituality and Modern Thought,* Morehouse, 1965; *The Function of Theology,* Seabury, 1968; *Prayer: A New Encounter,* Morehouse, 1973. Contributor of articles to religious journals in United States and England. Editor, *Vision,* 1953-57; editor, Library of Practical Theology, 1966—.

AVOCATIONAL INTERESTS: Gardening, cooking, country life.

* * *

THORNTON, Thomas Perry   1931-

PERSONAL: Born March 4, 1931, in Pittsburgh, Pa.; son of Thomas Anthony (a naval officer and lawyer) and Catherine (Bredendiek) Thornton; married Karin Lore Stuebben, June 27, 1953; children: Thomas Anthony III, Nalini Peter. *Education:* Haverford College, B.A., 1950; University of Tubingen, graduate study, 1950-51; Johns Hopkins University, Ph.D., 1953. *Religion:* Roman Catholic. *Home:* 5064 Sedgwick St. N.W., Washington, D.C. 20016.

CAREER: Johns Hopkins University, Baltimore, Md., lecturer in German, 1952-53, 1954-55; U.S. Information Agency, cultural affairs officer in India, 1955-58; U.S. Department of the Navy, Washington, D.C., analyst, 1958-60, 1961-63; Princeton University, Princeton, N.J., research associate in politics, 1960-61; U.S. Department of State, Washington, D.C., chief of research on South Asia, 1963-69, member of planning and coordination Staff, 1969—. *Military service:* U.S. Naval Reserve; active duty, 1953-55; now commander. *Member:* Association for Asian Studies, Modern Language Association of America.

WRITINGS: (Editor) *Grobianische Tischzuchten,* Erich Schmidt, 1957; (editor) *Hofische Tischzuchten,* Erich Schmidt, 1957; (editor and author of introduction) *The Third World in Soviet Perspective: Studies by Soviet Writers on the Developing Areas,* Princeton University Press, 1964; (editor with Cyril E. Black) *Communism and Revolution: The Strategic Uses of Political Violence,* Princeton University Press, 1964. Contributor to *Journal of English and Germanic Philology, Military Review, Journal of Asian Studies, World Politics,* and to other journals.

WORK IN PROGRESS: Research on Soviet international relations; research on Rosa Luxemburg; a study of theological elements in medieval German literature.

* * *

THORPE, E(ustace) G(eorge)   1916-

PERSONAL: Born December 25, 1916, in Loscoe, Derbyshire, England; son of Walter Alfred (a coal miner and farmer) and Ivy (Burton) Thorpe; married Freda Davies (a schoolmistress), December 29, 1940; children: Judith Ann, Margaret Jane. *Education:* Borough Road College, B.A. (University of London). *Home:* 4 Manor Dr., St. Albans, Hertfordshire, England.

CAREER: Schoolmaster, Middlesex, England, 1938-39, 1946-54; Margaret Wix School, St. Albans, England, headmaster, 1954—. *Military service;* British Army, Duke of Cornwall's Light Infantry, 1939-45.

WRITINGS: Chance Intruder (novel), R. Hale, 1952; *Out of Darkness* (novel), R. Hale, 1953; *Endless Road* (novel), R. Hale, 1954; *Sad Little Star* (juvenile), University of London Press, 1958; *Dobbo* (juvenile), University of London Press, 1958; *Young Ruffles* (juvenile), University of London Press, 1958; *Complete English,* Books 1-4, Heinemann, 1962-63. *Junior Dictionary,*

Heinemann, 1967, illustrated edition, McGraw, 1970; *Correct English,* Heinemann (India), 1971. Writer of seven short stories for British Broadcasting Corp. radio.

WORK IN PROGRESS: Introductory Book to Complete English.

AVOCATIONAL INTERESTS: Travel.

* * *

THORPE, Lewis (Guy Melville)   1913-

PERSONAL: Born November 5, 1913, in Croydon, Surrey, England; son of Lewis (a civil servant) and Jessie Emily (Melville) Thorpe; married Barbara Reynolds (an author), September 5, 1939; children: Adrian Charles, Kerstin. *Education:* University of London, diploma of French phonetics, 1934, B.A. (honours), 1935, teaching diploma, 1936, Ph.D., 1948; University of Lille, Licence es-Lettres, 1939; University of Paris, Docteur de l'Universite, 1957. *Politics:* Conservative. *Religion:* Anglican. *Home:* 26 Parkside, Wollaton Vale, Nottingham NG8 2NN, England. *Office:* University of Nottingham, Nottingham NG7 2RD, England.

CAREER: County School for Boys, Hove, England, senior modern language master, 1936-39; Technical College, Brighton, England, lecturer in medieval French language and literature, 1937-39; University College, Nottingham, England, lecturer in Romance linguistics, 1946-54; University of Nottingham, Nottingham, England, reader in medieval French, 1955-57, professor of French language and literature, head of department, 1958—. *Military service:* British Army, 1940-46; served in North Africa, Italy, Greece, Austria; became lieutenant colonel; mentioned in dispatches. *Member:* International Arthurian Society (honorary secretary of British branch, 1951-66; president of British branch, 1966—; international secretary, 1966—), International Association of Arts and Letters (fellow), Associazione degli Scrittori Veneti (fellow), Royal Society of Arts (fellow), Royal Historical Society (fellow), Association of University Teachers of French in Great Britain (honorary treasurer, 1951-52; secretary, 1953-55; president, 1956).

WRITINGS: (Compiler) *La France guerriere, une anthologie,* Penguin, 1945; (editor) *Le Roman de Laurin, fils de Marques le Senechal,* Bowes, 1950, text edition, Heffer, 1960; *The Study of French in a Modern University* (lecture), University of Nottingham, 1959; (translator and author of introduction) Geoffrey of Monmouth, *The History of Kings of Britain,* Penguin, 1966; (with Barbara Reynolds) *Guido Farina, Pittore de Verona, 1896-1957,* Valdonega, 1967; (compiler, translator, and author of introduction) *Two Lives of Charlemagne,* Penguin, 1969; *Einhard the Frank: The Life of Charlemagne,* Folio Society, 1970; (translator) Gregory of Tours, *Historia Francorum,* Penguin, 1972. Contributor of more than sixty research articles and ninety reviews to scholarly publications, including *Modern Language Review, Scriptorium, Erasmus,* and *Oxford Magazine.* Founder and editor, *Nottingham Mediaeval Studies* (annual journal), 1957—, and *Nottingham French Studies* (semi-annual journal), 1962—; editor, *Bibliographical Bulletin of the International Arthurian Society,* 1967—.

WORK IN PROGRESS: Collaborating with T.H.L. Parker on an edition of sixty-seven recently discovered sermons by John Calvin, completion expected in 1973.

* * *

THRAPP, Dan Lincoln   1913-

PERSONAL: Born June 26, 1913, in West Chicago, Ill.; son of Frank H. and Grace (Romig) Thrapp; married Margaret Statler Sproat (a singer and voice teacher), December 5, 1952 (died March 10, 1965); children:

Linda, Richard. *Education:* Attended University of Wisconsin, 1930-31, University of Illinois, 1935-37; University of Missouri, B.J., 1938. *Religion:* Methodist. *Home:* 11529 Starlight Ave., Whittier, Calif. 90601. *Office:* Los Angeles Times, Los Angeles, Calif. 90053.

CAREER: United Press, foreign correspondent in Argentina, 1940-42, London, England, 1946-48, Greece, 1948, Italy, 1948-49, Africa, 1949; *Los Angeles Times,* Los Angeles, Calif., religion editor, 1951-57, assistant city editor, 1957-60, religion editor, 1960—. *Military service:* U.S. Army. Infantry, 1943-46; became captain; served in Burma and China; received four battle stars, breast order Yun Hui (China). *Member:* Religious Newswriters Association (member of executive committee), Wilderness Society, Sigma Delta Chi, Sierra Club. *Awards, honors:* D.H.L., Chapman College, 1969.

WRITINGS: Al Sieber, Chief of Scouts, University of Oklahoma Press, 1964; *The Conquest of Apacheria,* University of Oklahoma Press, 1967; (contributor) Ray Brandes, editor, *Brand Book Number One: The San Diego Corral of the Westerners,* [San Diego], 1968; (contributor) William F. Kimes, editor *The Westerners Brand Book No. 13,* Los Angeles Corral, [Los Angeles], 1969; (contributor) Ray Brandes, editor, *Troopers West: Military and Indian Affairs on the American Frontier,* Frontier Heritage Press, 1970; *Victorio,* University of Oklahoma Press, 1971; *General Crook and the Sierra Madre Adventure,* University of Oklahoma Press, 1972.

WORK IN PROGRESS: Christian, a novel.

* * *

THROWER, Percy John 1913-

PERSONAL: Born January 30, 1913, in Winslow, Buckinghamshire, England; son of Harry (a gardener) and Beatrice (Dunnett) Thrower; married Constance Margaret Cook, September 9, 1939; children: Margaret Ina, Susan Constance, Ann Elizabeth. *Education:* Educated in English schools; received Royal Horticultural Society's certificates in general horticulture, 1938, 1939, 1941, and national diploma in horticulture, 1945. *Religion:* Anglican. *Home:* Quarry Lodge, Shrewsbury, Shropshire, England. *Office:* Borough of Shrewsbury, Parks Superintendent's Office, The Quarry, Shrewsbury, Shropshire, England.

CAREER: Apprentice gardener, 1927-31; journeyman gardener at Royal Gardens, Windsor, England, 1931-36, City Parks Department, Leeds, England, 1936-38; County Borough of Derby, Derbyshire, England, journeyman gardener, later assistant parks superintendent, 1938-45; Borough of Shrewsbury, Shropshire, England, parks superintendent, 1945—. British Broadcasting Corp., speaker on more than six hundred radio gardening programs, 1947—, and more than five hundred television "Gardening Club" programs, 1951—. Lecturer on horticulture. *Member:* Institute of Parks Administration, Royal Horticultural Society. *Awards, honors:* Associateship of honor of Royal Horticultural Society for distinguished work in horticulture, 1963.

WRITINGS: In the Flower Garden with Percy Thrower, Collingridge, 1957; *Gardening and Garden Tools,* Spear & Jackson, 1958; *In Your Garden with Percy Thrower,* Collingridge, 1959; *Percy Thrower's Picture Book of Gardening,* Collingridge, 1961; *Percy Thrower's Encyclopaedia of Gardening,* Collingridge, 1962, Transatlantic, 1963; *In Your Greenhouse with Percy Thrower,* Transatlantic, 1963; *Roses,* Collingridge, 1964; *Garden Flowers,* Collingridge, 1965; *Guide to Colour in Your Garden,* Collingridge, 1966; *Bulbs, Corms and Tubers for Garden, Greenhouse and Home,* Collingridge, 1966; *Practical Guide to Roses,* Pearson, 1966; *Percy Thrower's Garden Notebook,* George Newnes, 1966; *Dahlias and Chrysanthemums,* Collingridge, 1967; *Trees and Shrubs,* Collingridge, 1968; *Everyday Gardening in Colour,* Paul Hamlyn, 1969. Contributor to *Amateur Gardening, Woman's Own, Sunday Express* (London).

* * *

THUILLIER, Jacques 1928-

PERSONAL: Surname is pronounced Twee-lee-*ay*; born March 18, 1928, in Vaucouleurs, Meuse, France; son of Andre (professeur) and Berthe (Caritey) Thuillier. *Education:* Ecole normale superieure, Paris, France, agrege de l'Universite, 1954; pensionnaire at Fondation Primoli, Rome, Italy, 1955, and Foundation Thiers, Paris, France, 1956. *Religion:* Catholic. *Home:* 129, rue de la Pompe, Paris, France.

CAREER: Centre national de la recherche scientifique, Paris, France, attache de recherches, 1956-59; Universite de Paris (Sorbonne), Paris, France, assistant d'histoire de l'art, 1959-62; Universite de Dijon, Dijon, France, faculte des lettres, charge d'enseignement, 1962-70; Sorbonne, University of Paris, Paris, maitre de conference d'histoire de l'art moderne a l'Institut d'Art et d'Archeologie, 1970—. *Member:* Comite International d'Histoire de l'Art (secretaire scientifique). *Awards, honors:* Chevalier de l'Ordre des arts et lettres.

WRITINGS: (With Jennifer Montagu) *Catalogue de l'Exposition Charles Le Brun,* Palais de Versailles, 1963; (with Albert Chatelet) *La Peinture francaise, de Fouquet a Poussin,* Skira, 1963, translation by Stuart Gilbert published as *French Painting from Fouquet to Poussin,* Skira, 1963; (with Chatelet) *La Peinture francaise de Le Nain a Fragonard,* Skira, 1964, translation by James Emmons published as *French Painting, from Le Nain to Fragonard,* Skira, 1964; *Fragonard: Etude biographique et critique,* Skira, 1967, translation by Robert Allen published as *Fragonard: Biographical and Critical Study,* World Publishing, 1967; *Le Storie di Maria de' Medici di Rubens al Lussemburgo,* Rizzoli, 1967, revised edition published in French as *Rubens, La Galerie Medicis au Palais du Luxembourg,* Rizzoil-Laffont, 1969, translation by Robert Erich Wolf published as *Rubens' Life of Marie de' Medici,* Abrams, 1970; *Nicolas Poussin,* Edizioni par il Club de' Libro, 1969. Contributor of articles to professional journals.

WORK IN PROGRESS: La litterature d'art en France au XVIIe siecle; la peinture parisienne sous Richelieu et Mazarin; with Pierre Rosenberg, Laurent de la Hyre, biographie et catalogue critiques.

SIDELIGHTS: Thuillier told *CA* that his work is concerned with "bringing back to light fields now unknown in the art and thought of the seventeenth century."

BIOGRAPHICAL/CRITICAL SOURCES: Time, December 14, 1970.

* * *

THUM, Marcella

PERSONAL: Born in St. Louis, Mo.; daughter of Frank and Louise (Holle) Thum. *Education:* Washington University, St. Louis, Mo., B.A., 1948; University of California, Berkeley, B.L.S., 1954. *Politics:* Democrat. *Religion:* Protestant. *Home:* 6716 Smiley Ave., St. Louis, Mo. 63139. *Agent:* Lurton Blassingame, 60 East 42nd St., New York, N.Y. 10017.

CAREER: Advertising copywriter in St. Louis, Mo., 1948-49; U.S. Army, Public Information Office, civilian writer on Okinawa, 1949-50, with historical division in Heidelberg and Karlsruhe, Germany, 1951-53; U.S. Air Force, civilian librarian in Korea, at Scott Air Force Base, Ill., and at Schofield Barracks and Hickam Air

Force Base, Hawaii, 1954-60; Affton Senior High School, Affton, Mo., school librarian, 1962-67; Meramec Community College, Kirkwood, Mo., reference librarian, 1968—. *Member:* American Library Association, Missouri Writer's Guild, St. Louis Writer's Guild. *Awards, honors:* Dodd, Mead Librarian and Teacher Prize Competition award, 1964, for *Mystery at Crane's Landing;* "Edgar" award for best juvenile mystery, Mystery Writers of America, 1964, for *Mystery at Crane's Landing;* Missouri Writer's Guild award for best juvenile, 1966, for *Treasure of Crazy Quilt Farm.*

WRITINGS: Mystery at Crane's Landing, Dodd, 1964; *Treasure of Crazy Quilt Farm,* Watts, 1965; *Anne of the Sandwich Islands,* Dodd, 1967; *Librarian with Wings,* Dodd, 1967; *Secret of the Sunken Treasure,* Dodd, 1969; (with Gladys Thum) *The Persuaders: Propaganda in War and Peace,* Atheneum, 1972. Contributor to *Young Miss* and other magazines for girls.

WORK IN PROGRESS: A novel and a nonfiction book for young adults.

AVOCATIONAL INTERESTS: Gardening, antiques, and visiting places of historical interest in the United States.

* * *

TIBBLE, Anne   1912-
(Anne Northgrave)

PERSONAL: Born January 29, 1912, in Rounton Grange, England; married J.W. Tibble (professor of education), 1930; children: Hilary, Robin. *Education:* University of Leeds, B.A. (honors in English), 1930, diploma in education, 1931. *Politics:* Labour. *Religion:* Christian. *Home:* Clare Cottage, Guilsborough, Northamptonshire, England.

CAREER: Teacher, Orkney Islands, off coast of Scotland, 1932-33, later at City of Hull (England) School for Cripples. *Member:* P.E.N.

WRITINGS: (Under name Anne Northgrave) *The Apple Reddens* (novel), Collins, 1942; *Gertrude Bell,* A. & C. Black, 1957; *With Gordon in the Sudan,* Muller, 1960; *African-English Literature: A Short Survey and Anthology of Prose and Poetry up to 1965,* October House, 1965; *The Story of English Literature: A Critical Survey,* P. Owen, 1970, Humanities, 1971; *Labyrinth* (poems), Oriel Press, 1972; *Greenhorn: A Twentieth Century Childhood,* Routledge & Kegan Paul, 1973.

With husband, J.W. Tibble: *John Clare: A Life,* Cobden-Sanderson, 1932, revised edition, M. Joseph, 1972; (editors) *The Letters of John Clare,* Routledge & Kegan Paul, 1951; (editors) *The Prose of John Clare,* Routledge & Kegan Paul, 1951; *John Clare: His Life and Poetry,* Heinemann, 1956; *Helen Keller,* A. & C. Black, 1957, Putnam, 1958; (editors) John Clare, *Selected Poems,* Dutton, 1965.

SIDELIGHTS: Helen Keller has been translated into Swedish, Assamese, and Bengali.

* * *

TILLINGHAST, Pardon E(lisha)   1920-

PERSONAL: Born April 19, 1920, in Providence, R.I.; son of Frederick W. (a lawyer) and Helen (Darling) Tillinghast; married Ellen Chafee, October 6, 1945 (died, 1972); children: Peggy, Nancy, Elizabeth. *Education:* Williams College, student, 1938-41; Brown University, B.A., 1942; University of Oklahoma, graduate study, 1944-45; Harvard University, M.A., 1947, Ph.D., 1952. *Religion:* Episcopalian. *Home:* 6 Adirondack View, Middlebury, Vt. 05753. *Office:* Department of History, Middlebury College, Middlebury, Vt. 05753.

CAREER: Middlebury College, Middlebury, Vt., 1947—, now professor of history. *Military service:* U.S. Navy, 1942-46. *Member:* American Historical Association, Renaissance Society of America, Conference on British Studies, Historical Association (England).

WRITINGS: (Editor) *Approaches to History: Selections in the Philosophy of History from the Greeks to Hegel,* Prentice-Hall, 1963; *The Specious Past: Historians and Others,* Addison-Wesley, 1972.

WORK IN PROGRESS: Research on Nicholas of Cusa and the late medieval church.

* * *

TIPPLE, John Ord   1916-

PERSONAL: Born July 20, 1916, in Pueblo, Colo.; son of Albert Benjamin (a pharmacist) and Francis Bell (Karrick) Tipple; married Catherine Owens, 1948 (divorced, 1958); married Edith Harrison Dickinson, 1961; children: Jonathan, Nicole, Clare, Jocelyn. *Education:* University of Colorado, B.A., 1938; Stanford University, M.A., 1954, Ph.D., 1958. *Home:* 2810 East Valley Rd., Santa Barbara, Calif. 93108. *Office:* California State College, 5151 State College Dr., Los Angeles, Calif. 90032.

CAREER: Stanford University, Stanford, Calif., instructor in history, 1953-56; California State College at Los Angeles, assistant professor, 1956-60, associate professor, 1960-63, professor of history, 1963—. *Military service:* U.S. Naval Reserve, 1942-46; became lieutenant. *Member:* American Studies Association, Organization of American Historians.

WRITINGS: Andrew Carnegie/Henry George: The Problems of Progress, Howard Allen, 1960; *A. Hamilton/Th. Jefferson: The New Order,* Howard Allen, 1961; (contributor) H. Wayne Morgan, editor, *The Gilded Age,* Syracuse University Press, 1963, revised edition, 1970; (compiler) *Crisis of the American Dream: A History of American Social Thought 1920-1940,* Pegasus, 1968; (compiler) *The Capitalist Revolution: A History of American Social Thought 1890-1919,* Pegasus, 1970; (contributor) Sidney Fine and Gerald Brown, editors, *The American Past,* Macmillan, 1970.

WORK IN PROGRESS: Editing *The Great Money Machine: A History of American Social Thought 1865-1890,* for Pegasus.

* * *

TOCH, Henry   1923-

PERSONAL: Born August 15, 1923; son of L. and Alice (Muller) Toch; married Margit Schwarz (a social worker), April 3, 1957. *Education:* London School of Economics and Political Science, University of London, B.Com. (with second class honors), 1950. *Politics:* Labour Party. *Religion:* Jewish. *Home:* "Candida," 49 Hawkshead Lane, North Mymms, Hertfordshire, England. *Office:* City of London Polytechnic, Moorgate, London E.C.2, England.

CAREER: Tailor for various firms, London, England, 1939-44; British Inland Revenue, London, England, H.M. inspector of taxes, 1949-56; Hertfordshire County Council, St. Albans, England, teacher, 1956-57; City of London Polytechnic, London, England, senior lecturer, 1957—. Free-lance tax consultant. Examiner in economics, University of London; examiner in taxation, Association of Certified Accountants. Parliamentary Labour candidate, Poole, Dorsetshire, England, 1962, 1964, and Rutland and Stamford, 1970. *Military service:* British Army, served in Italy and Germany, 1944-48; became sergeant; awarded Italy Star. *Member:* Association of Teachers in Technical Institutes, Josephine Butler Society (treasurer).

WRITINGS: How to Pay Less Income Tax, Museum Press, 1959, 3rd edition, 1966; Tax Saving for the Business Man, Museum Press, 1961, 2nd edition, 1966; British Political and Social Institutions, Pitman, 1962; Income Tax: Including Corporation Tax and Capital Gains Tax, Macdonald & Evans, 1966, 4th edition, 1970. Contributor of articles to Journal of Business Law.

WORK IN PROGRESS: Economics for Professional Students, for Macdonald & Evans; a textbook in income tax.

*   *   *

TODD, John M(urray)   1918-
(John Fox)

PERSONAL: Born May 27, 1918, in Liverpool, England; son of Murray and Elizabeth (Brancker) Todd; married Patricia Calnan (a chiropodist), May 3, 1953; children: Zia, Fabian, Stephany. Education: Attended Wellington College, Berkshire, England; Corpus Christi College, Cambridge, B.A. (honors), 1939, certificate of education, 1940. Religion: Roman Catholic. Home: Doulting Manor, Shepton Mallet, Somerset, England. Agent: A.M. Heath & Co. Ltd., 35 Dover St., London W.1, England. Office: Darton, Longman & Todd Ltd., 85 Gloucester Rd., London S.W.7, England.

CAREER: Free-lance journalist, 1940-56; Longmans, Green & Co. Ltd., London, England, editor of Roman Catholic books, 1956-59; Darton, Longman & Todd Ltd., London, director, 1959—; Search Press, London, director, 1970—. Member, Shepton Mallet Rural District Council, 1952-67. Military service: Conscientious objector, World War II.

WRITINGS: We Are Men: A Book for the Catholic Layman, Sheed, 1955; Catholicism and the Ecumenical Movement, Longmans, Green, 1956; John Wesley and the Catholic Church, Macmillan, 1958; African Mission: A Historical Study of the Society of African Missions Whose Priests Have Worked on the Coast of West Africa and Inland, in Liberia, the Ivory Coast, Ghana, Togoland, Dahomey and Nigeria, and in Egypt, Since 1856, Macmillan, 1962; Martin Luther: A Biographical Study, Newman, 1964; (contributor) M. de la Bedoyere, Objections to Roman Catholicism, Constable, 1964, Lippincott, 1965; The Laity: The People of God, Darton, Longman & Todd, 1965, Paulist Press, 1967; (contributor) M. de la Bedoyere, The Future of Catholic Christianity, Lippincott, 1966; Reformation, Doubleday, 1971.

Editor: (Under pseudonym John Fox) Christian Letters on Sex and Marriage, Longmans, Green, 1955; The Springs of Morality: A Catholic Symposium, Macmillan (New York), 1956; The Arts, Artists, and Thinkers, an Inquiry into the Place of the Arts in Human Life: A Symposium, Longmans, Green ·(New York), 1958; Work: Christian Thought and Practice: A Symposium, Helicon, 1960; Problems of Authority, Helicon, 1962. Contributor to religious journals, mostly Catholic. Consultant editor, Search.

*   *   *

TOLEDANO, Ralph de   1916-

PERSONAL: Surname is pronounced Toe-leh-dah-no; born August 17, 1916, in International Zone, Tangier, Morocco; married Nora Romaine, July 6, 1938 (divorced, 1968); children: James Edward, Paul Christopher. Education: Fieldston School, student, 1928-34; Columbia University, B.A., 1938; Cornell University, language studies, 1943-44. Politics: Republican. Office: 1052A National Press Building, Washington, D.C. 20004.

CAREER: During earlier career in New York, N.Y., was associate editor of New Leader, 1941-43, editor of Standard, 1946, managing editor of Plain Talk 1946-47, publicity director of Dress Joint Board of International Ladies' Garment Workers' Union, 1947-48; Newsweek, New York, N.Y., assistant editor, 1948, associate editor, 1949, national reports editor, 1950-60, Washington correspondent, 1956-60; King Features Syndicate, New York, N.Y., syndicated columnist 1960—; National News-Research, Inc., Washington, D.C., president, 1960—; National Review, New York, N.Y., associate editor, 1960—. Former radio and television commentator. Publisher, Anthem Books. Military service: U.S. Army 1943-46 became staff sergeant. Member: Sigma Delta Chi, National Press Club, Dutch Treat Club, Capitol Hill Club. Awards, honors: Philolexian Prize for Poetry, Columbia College (twice); Freedoms Foundation Award (twice).

WRITINGS: (Editor) Frontiers of Jazz, Oliver Durrell, 1947, 2nd edition, Ungar, 1962; (with Victor Lasky) Seeds of Treason: The True Story of the Hiss-Chambers Tragedy, Funk, 1950, revised and updated edition, Regnery, 1962; Spies, Dupes and Diplomats, Duell, Sloan & Pearce, 1952, new edition, Arlington House, 1967; Day of Reckoning (novel), Holt, 1955; Nixon, Holt, 1956, revised and expanded edition, Duell, Sloan & Pearce, 1960; Lament for a Generation, foreword by Richard Nixon, Farrar, Straus, 1960; The Greatest Plot in History, Duell, Sloan & Pearce, 1963; The Winning Side: The Case for Goldwater Republicanism, Putnam, 1963, revised and updated edition, Macfadden, 1964; (editor with Karl Hess) The Conservative Papers, Anchor, 1964; R.F.K., the Man Who Would Be President, Putnam, 1967; America, I Love You, National Press, 1968; One Man Alone: Richard Nixon, Funk, 1969; (with Philip V. Brennan, Jr.) Claude Kirk—Man and Myth, Pyramid Publications, 1970; (author of introduction) William F. Buckley, Jr., editor, Odyssey of a Friend, Putnam, 1970; Little Cesar, Anthem Books, 1971. Contributor to Commentary, American Scholar, Commonweal, Collier's, American Mercury, Coronet, Saturday Review, New York Herald Tribune, Chicago Tribune, and other periodicals and newspapers.

WORK IN PROGRESS: Books on Whittaker Chambers and White House internal politics; a collection of poems.

SIDELIGHTS: Toledano, a music critic and political writer who turns out about three hundred thousand words a year, says, "Writing is hard work. ... My advice to my own children has always been 'stay out of this profession; there are better ways to make a living.' But this kind of advice won't keep out those who really want to write. And they don't ask for advice."

BIOGRAPHICAL/CRITICAL SOURCES: National Review, May 2, 1967, October 22, 1968, January 13, 1970, June 29, 1971; Time, May 19, 1967; New York Review of Books, June 1, 1967; New York Times Book Review, November 23, 1969; New York Times, December 12, 1969; Library Journal, November 1, 1970.

*   *   *

TOMLINSON, T(homas) B(rian)   1925-

PERSONAL: Born October 22, 1925, in Perth, Western Australia; son of John (a packer) and Mary (Smith) Tomlinson; married Mary O'Keefe (a university lecturer in English literature), October 25, 1954; children: Michael Antony. Education: University of Western Australia, B.A. and LL.B., 1948; Cambridge University, M.A., 1952. Politics: Labour. Office: Department of English, University of Melbourne, Parkville, Victoria, Australia 3052.

CAREER: University of Western Australia, Perth, lecturer in English, 1952; University of Melbourne, Melbourne, Victoria, Australia, lecturer in English, 1953-63; University of Sydney, Sydney, New South Wales, Australia, senior lecturer in English, 1964-66, University of Melbourne, Melbourne, Victoria, Australia, reader in English, 1967—.

WRITINGS: A Study of Elizabethan and Jacobean Tragedy, Cambridge University Press, 1964. Regular contributor to, and managing editor of, *Melbourne Critical Review.* Also contributor to other literary periodicals.

WORK IN PROGRESS: The nineteenth and twentieth century English novel and society.

SIDELIGHTS: Tomlinson spent several years visiting England and the continent on each of three trips there. Other interests: Mainly music.

*   *   *

TOMPKINS, Peter 1919-

PERSONAL: Born April 29, 1919; son of Laurence (a sculptor) and Mary (Arthur) Tompkins; married Jerree Lee Talbot Smith, April 3, 1945; children: Elektra Robin, Timothy Christopher, Ptolemy Christian. *Education:* Attended Stowe School, Buckinghamshire, England, and Harvard University; additional study at Sorbonne, University of Paris. *Home:* 318 A St. N.E., Washington, D.C. 20002. *Agent:* Florence Strauss Day, 24 Fifth Ave., New York, N.Y. 10021. *Office:* 18 East 77th St., New York, N.Y. 10021.

CAREER: Left Harvard University to become war correspondent, 1939-41; worked for *New York Herald Tribune* Rome Bureau; was Mutual Broadcasting System's representative for Italy, and National Broadcasting Co. correspondent in Greece. Author. *Wartime service:* U.S. Office of Strategic Services. *Member:* National Press Club (Washington, D.C.).

WRITINGS: (Editor and author of introduction) George Bernard Shaw, *To a Young Actress: The Letters of Bernard Shaw to Molly Tompkins,* C.N. Potter, 1960; (editor) *Shaw and Molly Tompkins in Their Own Words,* Anthony Blond, 1961, C.N. Potter, 1962; *A Spy in Rome,* Simon & Schuster, 1962; *The Eunuch and the Virgin, a Study of Curious Customs,* C.N. Potter, 1963; *The Murder of Admiral Darlan, a Study in Conspiracy,* Simon & Schuster, 1965; *Italy Betrayed,* Simon & Schuster, 1966; *Secrets of the Great Pyramid,* Harper, 1971. Author of some twenty film and television scripts. Contributor to *New Yorker, New Republic, Esquire, London Sunday Times, Times of India,* and Associated Press.

*   *   *

TONG, Te-kong 1920-

PERSONAL: Born August 24, 1920, in Hofei, Anhwei, China; now a U.S. citizen; son of Mon-fu and Jo-hsia (Liu) Tong; married Sharon Chao-wen Woo, December 22, 1957; children: Ray Kuang-yi, June Kuang-pei. *Education:* National Central University, Chungking, China, B.A., 1943; Columbia University, M.A., 1952, Ph.D., 1959. *Home:* Apartment 7F, 100 La Salle St., New York, N.Y. 10027. *Office:* 619 Kent Hall, Columbia University, New York, N.Y. 10027.

CAREER: Chinese Navy Monthly, staff writer, 1941-43; *Anhwei Daily,* editorial writer, 1943-47; Anhwei University, Li-huang and Hofei, China, instructor in history, 1945-47; research assistant on Chinese history project jointly sponsored by Columbia University, New York, N.Y., and University of Washington, Seattle, Wash., 1955-57; Columbia University, research associate, Chinese and oral history projects of East Asian Institute, 1958-62, assistant professor, 1963-67, curator, Chinese collection, East Asian Library, 1963-70, adjunct associate professor of Chinese history, 1968—. Lecturer in Asian history,

Brooklyn College, 1961-62. *Member:* American Historical Association, Association for Asian Studies. *Awards, honors:* Social Science Research Council grant, 1963-65.

WRITINGS: United States Diplomacy in China, 1844-60, University of Washington Press, 1964; (compiler) *Modern China, 1912-1949: A Bibliographical Study,* East Asian Library, Columbia University, 1965. Editor, *Bulletin of National Defense,* 1947-48; chief editor, *China Life Semi-Monthly,* 1955-56; editor, *World Forum Monthly, 1959-62.* Also author of books in Chinese.

WORK IN PROGRESS: A book on modern China.

SIDELIGHTS: Tong writes fiction, essays, and poetry in Chinese.

*   *   *

TOOLEY, R(onald) Vere 1898-

PERSONAL: Born September 29, 1898; son of William James and Annie Edwards (Sutton) Tooley; married Winefred Flora Read; children: Michael Vere, Ann Frances Tooley Plested. *Education:* Attended City of London School.

MILITARY SERVICE: British Army, Queen's Westminister Rifles, 1916-19.

WRITINGS: Some English Books with Coloured Plates: Their Points, Collations and Values—Art, Sport, Caricature, Topography and Travel, First Half of the Nineteenth Century, Ingpen & Grant, 1935, Gale, 1971, revised edition published as *English Books with Coloured Plates, 1790 to 1860: A Bibliographical Account of the Most Important Books Illustrated by English Artists in Colour Aquatint and Color Lithography,* Boston Book & Art Shop, 1954; *Maps and Map-Makers,* Batsford, 1949, 2nd edition, Crown, 1952, 4th edition, Batsford, 1970; *Collector's Guide to Maps of the African Continent and Southern Africa,* Carta Press, 1969; (author of introduction) *Blaeuu's Atlas of England, Scotland, Wales, and Ireland,* British Book Centre, 1971.

"Map Collectors'" series; all published by Map Collectors' Circle: *Early Antarctica: A Glance at the Beginnings of Cartographic Representation of the South Polar Regions,* 1963; *Early Maps and Views of the Cape of Good Hope,* 1963; *Geographical Oddities; or, Curious, Ingenious, and Imaginary Maps and Miscellaneous Plates Published in Atlases,* 1963; *Leo Belgicus: An Illustrated List of Variants,* 1963; *The Printed Maps of Tasmania: A Chronological List from 1777-1900 with Alphabetical Index,* 1963; *California as an Island: A Geographical Misconception,* 1964; (compiler) *One Hundred Foreign Maps of Australia, 1773-1887,* 1964; *A Dictionary of Mapmakers, Including Cartographers, Geographers, Publishers, Engravers, Etc., from Earliest Times to 1900,* 1965; *Early Maps of Australia, the Dutch Period,* 1965; *The Printed Maps of the Continent of Africa and Regional Maps South of the Tropic of Cancer, 1500-1900,* 1966; *French Mapping of the Americas: The De l'Isle, Buache, Dezauche Succession (1700-1830),* 1967; (with R.A. Skelton) *The Marine Surveys of James Cook in North America, 1758-1768, Particularly the Survey of Newfoundland: A Bibliography of Printed Charts and Sailing-Directions,* 1967; *Maps of Africa, a Selection of Printed Maps from the Sixteenth to the Nineteenth Centuries,* 1968; *The Printed Maps of New South Wales 1773-1873,* 1968; *The Printed Maps of Antigua, 1689-1889,* 1969; *Printed Maps of Australia, Being a Catalogue of a Collection,* 1970; *The Printed Maps of Dominica and Grenada,* 1970; *Printed Maps of Southern Africa and Its Parts: Catalogue of a Collection,* 1970.

Contributor of maps to *Italian Atlases of the XVI Century,* 1939. Founder and editor, *Map Collectors' Circle,* 1963—.†

TORBET, Robert G(eorge) 1912-

PERSONAL: Born December 25, 1912, in Spokane, Wash.; son of A.M. and Alberta (Harpel) Torbet. Education: Wheaton College, Wheaton, Ill., B.A., 1934; Eastern Baptist Theological Seminary, B.D., 1937; University of Pennsylvania, M.A., 1937, Ph.D., 1944. Home: 1810 Rittenhouse Sq. S., Philadelphia, Pa. 19103. Office: American Baptist Churches in U.S.A., Valley Forge, Pa. 19481.

CAREER: Ordained a Baptist minister, 1936. Eastern Baptist Theological Seminary, Philadelphia, Pa., professor of history and church history, 1937-51; American Baptist Board of Education and Publication, Valley Forge, Pa., editor and director of educational services, 1951-58, now member of board of managers; Central Baptist Theological Seminary, Kansas City, Kan., dean and professor of church history, 1958-66; American Baptist Convention, Valley Forge, Pa., president, 1965-66, executive director, Division of Cooperative Christianity, 1967-72; American Baptist Churches in U.S.A., ecumenical officer, 1973—. Member: American Society of Church History, American Baptist Historical Society (member of board of managers, 1950-59).

WRITINGS: A Social History of the Philadelphia Baptist Association, 1707-1940, Westbrook Publishers, 1940; A History of the Baptists, Judson, 1950, revised edition, 1963; The Baptist Ministry: Then and Now, Judson, 1953; (reviser) Henry K. Rowe, The Baptist Witness, revised edition, Judson, 1953; Venture of Faith: The Story of the American Baptist Foreign Mission Society and the Woman's American Baptist Foreign Mission Society, 1814-1954, Judson, 1955; The Baptist Story, Judson, 1957; The Protestant Reformation, Judson, for the Cooperative Publication Association, 1961; (with Henry R. Bowler) Reuben E. Nelson: Free Churchman, Judson, 1961; (editor) Focal Points in the History of American Baptists, American Baptist Convention, 1963; (with Samuel Hill) Baptists: North and South, Judson, 1964; Ecumenism: Free Church Dilemma, Judson, 1968. Contributor of chapter to The American Church of the Protestant Heritage, edited by Vergilius Ferm, Philosophical Library, 1953. Also contributor to Encyclopaedia Britannica.

*   *   *

TORBETT, Harvey Douglas Louis 1921-
(Henry Dee, Isis)

PERSONAL: Born January 26, 1921, in Hammersmith, London, England; son of Reginald Napoleon and Minnie (Banner) Torbett; married Olive Duckworth, July 17, 1948; children: Neil, Martin, Joan, Diana, Kenneth and Lucinda (twins). Education: Wandsworth College, teacher's certificate, 1949. Religion: Methodist. Home: 9 Langley Rd., Welling, Kent, England. Agent: Carl Routledge, Charles Lavell Ltd., Mowbray House, Norfolk St., London W.C.2, England.

CAREER: Kent Education Committee, Kent, England, librarian, 1946-48; London County Council, London, England, schoolmaster in remedial education, 1949—. Military service: Royal Navy, 1941-46; became lieutenant.

WRITINGS: Towpath Tours, Fishing Gazette, 1960; Techniques of Ledgering, Thorsons, 1960; The Angler's Freshwater Fishes, Putnam, 1961; Coarse Fishing, Museum Press, 1961; Swimming and Diving, Foulsham, 1961; (reviser) John Bickerdyke, Angling for Coarse Fish, revised edition, Thorsons, 1962; (reviser) John Bickerdyke, Angling in Salt Water, 7th edition, Thorsons, 1962; Sea Fishing, Museum Press, 1964, Sportshelf, 1964. The Handbook for Fishermen, Hamlyn, 1964, new edi-

tion, 1967. Contributor of scripts and commentaries to London Schools Film Unit. Angling correspondent, British Broadcasting Corp; columnist, Angler's Mail.

AVOCATIONAL INTERESTS: Amateur film making, angling, natural history, and youth work.†

*   *   *

TORRANCE, Thomas F(orsyth) 1913-

PERSONAL: Born August 30, 1913, in Chengtu, Szechwan, China; son of Thomas (a missionary) and Annie Elizabeth (Sharp) Torrance; married Margaret Edith Spear, October, 1946; children: Thomas Spear, Iain Richard, Alison Meta Elizabeth. Education: Attended Canadian School, Chengtu, China, 1921-27; Bellshill Academy, Scotland, 1927-31; University of Edinburgh, M.A., 1934, B.D., 1937; University of Basel, graduate study, 1937-38, D.Theol., 1946; Oriel College, Oxford, graduate study, 1939-40. Home: 37 Braid Farm Rd., Edinburgh, Scotland EH10 6LE. Office: New College, The Mound, Edinburgh 1, Scotland.

CAREER: Clergyman of Church of Scotland. Auburn Community College, Auburn, N.Y., professor of theology, 1938-39; ordained minister of Alyth Barony Parish, 1940; minister of Beechgrove Church, Aberdeen, Scotland, 1947; University of Edinburgh, Edinburgh, Scotland, professor of church history, 1950-52, professor of Christian dogmatics, 1952—. Hewett Lecturer, New York, N.Y. and Boston, Mass., 1959; has worked for ten years in ecumenical movement. Military service: Chaplain, 1943-45; made member of Order of British Empire. Member: Academie Internationale des Sciences Religieuses (president, 1972—), Societe Internationale pour l'Etude de la Philosophie Medievale, Society for Study of Theology (founder member; honorary president, 1966-68), Scottish Church Theology Society (former president), Church Service Society of Church of Scotland (honorary president, 1970-71); Societe de l'Histoire du Protestantisme Francais (foreign member, 1968—). Awards, honors: D.D., Presbyterian College, Montreal, 1950, St. Andrews University, 1960; D.Theol., University of Paris, 1959, University of Geneva, 1959, University of Oslo, 1961; D.Litt., University of Edinburgh, 1970; Cross of St. Mark (first class), 1970; Collins Biennial Religious Book Award, 1970, for Theological Science.

WRITINGS: The Modern Theological Debate, Inter-Varsity Fellowship of Evangelical Unions, 1941; The Doctrine of Grace in the Apostolic Fathers, Oliver & Boyd, 1948, Eerdmans, 1959; Calvin's Doctrine of Man, Lutterworth, 1949, 2nd edition, Eerdmans, 1957; Royal Priesthood, Oliver & Boyd, 1955; Kingdom and Church: A Study in the Theology of the Reformation, Essential Books, 1956; When Christ Comes and Comes Again, Eerdmans, 1957; (author of historical notes and introduction) John Calvin, Tracts and Treatises on the Reformation of the Church, three volumes, Oliver & Boyd, 1958; The Apocalypse Today, James Clarke and Eerdmans, 1959; Conflict and Agreement in the Church, Lutterworth, Volume I, 1959, Volume II, 1960; Karl Barth: An Introduction to His Early Theology, 1910-1931, S.C.M. Press, 1962; (author of introduction) Karl Barth, Theology and Church: Shorter Writings, 1920-1928, S.C.M. Press, 1962; Theology in Reconstruction, S.C.M. Press, 1965, Eerdmans, 1966; Space, Time and Incarnation, Oxford University Press, 1969; (with Piet Frans Fransen) Intelligent Theology, Franciscan Herald Press, 196Ω; Theological Science, Oxford University Press, 1969; God and Rationality, Oxford University Press, 1971; Newton, Einstein, and Scientific Theology (Keese Lecture for 1971), University of Tennessee at Chattanooga, 1971.

Editor: (With G.W. Bromiley) Karl Barth, *Church Dogmatics,* Volumes 1-4, T. & T. Clark, 1956-69; (and translator) Robert Bruce, *The Mystery of the Lord's Supper* (sermons), James Clarke, 1958; (with D.W. Torrance) John Calvin, *New Testament Commentaries,* Oliver & Boyd, 1959-63; (and translator and author of introduction) *The School of Faith: The Catechisms of the Reformed Church,* Harper, 1959; (with R.S. Wright) Henry J. Wotherspoon and J.M. Kirkpatrick, *A Manual of Church Doctrine According to the Church of Scotland,* 2nd edition, revised and enlarged, Oxford University Press, 1960; John Calvin, *The Epistles of Paul the Apostle to the Galatians, Ephesians, Philippians and Colossians,* Oliver & Boyd, 1965; (with D.W. Torrance) John Calvin, *Acts of the Apostles,* 1-18, St. Andrew Press, 1965-66; William Manson, *Jesus and the Christian,* Eerdmans, 1967; (with D.W. Torrance) *Calvin's Commentary on the Harmony of the Gospels,* three volumes, St. Andrew Press, 1972. Founder-editor with J.K.S. Reid, *Scottish Journal of Theology,* 1948—.

WORK IN PROGRESS: A three-volume work on Hermeneutics: *The Hermeneutics of the Fathers, The Hermeneutics of the Mediaevals and the Reformers,* and *The Hermeneutics of the Moderns; God and the World; Integration and Interpretation in Natural and Theological Science, Christianity and Social Change, Christian Dogmatics,* in three volumes.

AVOCATIONAL INTERESTS: Golf, fishing.

*   *   *

TORREY, Gordon H(oward) 1919-

PERSONAL: Born December 4, 1919, in Eugene, Ore.; son of Raymond Albert and Minnie (Marsh) Torrey; married Ann Indseth (now in real estate). *Education:* University of Oregon, B.S., 1942, M.A., 1952; Harvard University, graduate student, 1942; University of Michigan, Ph.D., 1956. *Religion:* Methodist. *Home:* 3065 Porter St. N.W., Washington, D.C. 20008.

CAREER: U.S. government, Washington, D.C., Middle East consultant, 1956—. *Military service:* U.S. Army, 1942-43. *Member:* American Historical Association, Middle East Institute, American Philatelic Society, Royal Philatelic Society (fellow), Society of Philatelic Americans, Washington Philatelic Society (president, 1962-64).

WRITINGS: (Contributor) Sidney N. Fisher, editor, *The Military in the Middle East,* Ohio State University Press, 1963; *Syrian Politics and the Military, 1945-1958,* Ohio State University Press, 1964. Contributor to *International Affairs,* and to philatelic journals.

WORK IN PROGRESS: A history of the Ba'th party.

SIDELIGHTS: Torrey speaks French, Arabic, and reads German, Italian, and Spanish. He lived in Syria, 1953-54.

*   *   *

TOTTEN, George Oakley III 1922-

PERSONAL: Born July 21, 1922, in Washington, D.C.; son of George Oakley, Jr. (an architect) and Vicken (a sculptress; maiden name, von Post) Totten: married Astrid Maria Anderson (a professor and researcher in social psychology), June 26, 1948; children: Vicken Yuriko, Linnea Catherine. *Education:* Choate School diploma, 1940; Columbia University, A.B., 1946, A.M., 1949; Yale University, M.A., 1950, Ph.D., 1954. *Home address:* Greenleaf Ranch, P.O. Box 88, Topanga, Calif. 90290. *Office:* Department of Political Science, School of Politics and International Relations, University of Southern California, Los Angeles, Calif. 90007.

CAREER: East Asian Institute, Columbia University, New York, N.Y., lecturer in government, 1954-55;

Fletcher School of Law and Diplomacy, Tufts University, Medford, Mass., research associate in Far Eastern affairs, 1955-58; Massachusetts Institute of Technology, Cambridge, assistant professor of political science, 1958-59; Boston University, Boston, Mass., assistant professor of history and government, 1959-61; University of Rhode Island, Kingston, associate professor of political science, 1961-64; University of Southern California, Los Angeles, associate professor, 1965-68, professor of political science, 1968—. Visiting associate professor, Eastern Michigan University, 1965, Sophia University, Tokyo, 1967. Chairman, Columbia University Seminar on Japan, 1962-63; co-ordinator, Visiting Asian Professors Program, University of Rhode Island, 1962-64; director, California Private Universities and Colleges Year-in-Japan Program at Waseda University, Tokyo, 1968—, resident director and professor, 1971-72. Producer, "The Open Shoji on Japan," biweekly radio program for KPFK-FM, Los Angeles, 1968-69. *Military service:* U.S. Army, Military Intelligence, 1942-46; became first lieutenant.

MEMBER: American Historical Association, American Political Science Association, Japanese Political Science Association, Association for Asian Studies (member, program committee, 1968-69), Society for Asian and Comparative Philosophy, World Association of World Federalists, World Federalists—USA (chapter vice-president, 1965), American Civil Liberties Union (member of chapter executive board, 1963-65), American Association of University Professors.

WRITINGS: Studies on Japan's Social Democratic Parties, Yale University Press, Volume I: *The Social Democratic Movement in Prewar Japan,* 1966, Volume II: (with Alan B. Cole and Cecil H. Uyehara) *Socialist Partes in Postwar Japan,* 1966.

Editor: (With Hattie Kawahara Colton and Kenneth E. Colton) *Japan Since Recovery of Independence: The Annals,* American Academy of Political and Social Science, 1956; *Democracy in Prewar Japan: Groundwork or Facade?,* Heath, 1965; (and contributor with Willard A. Beling) *Developing Nations: Quest for a Model,* Van Nostrand, 1970.

Contributor: Ryusaku Tsunoda, William T. de Bary, and Donald Keene, compilers, *Sources of the Japanese Tradition,* Columbia University Press, 1958; Cecil H. Uyehara, compiler, *Left-Wing Social Movements in Japan: An Annotated Bibliography,* Tuttle, 1959; Joseph Dunner, compiler, *The Dictionary of Political Science,* Philosophical Library, 1964; George De Vos and Hiroshi Wagatsuma, editors, *Japan's Invisible Race: Caste in Culture and Personality,* University of California Press, 1966; Ronald P. Dore, editor, *Aspects of Social Change in Modern Japan,* Princeton University Press, 1967; Klaus Pretzer and Klaus W. Bender, editors, *One World Only: The Ethical and Social Demands of World Religions for a Modern Society,* Friedrich Ebert Stiftung (Tokyo), 1969; Henry S. Albinski, editor, *Asian Political Processes,* Allyn & Bacon, 1971; Bernard S. Silberman and Harry Hartoonian, editors, *Dimensions in Crisis: Japan in Midpassage,* Princeton University Press, 1973. Contributor of articles on Japan and reviews to historical and other learned journals. Member of editorial advisory board, *Journal of Asian Studies,* 1965-67.

WORK IN PROGRESS: A book, *Japanese Socialist and Communist Local and Agrarian Policies;* editing *The Russian Impact on Japan; Literature and Social Thought: Two Essays by Nobori Shomu and Akamatsu Katsumaro,* with Paul Langer and Peter Berton; editing and translating *Chung-kuo li-tai cheng-chih teh-shih,* by Chien Mu; compiling *Asian Political Philosophy.*

SIDELIGHTS: The Totten family is bilingual, using Swedish and English at home. In addition, Dr. Totten is competent in Japanese, Chinese, and French, and manages in German and Russian for research purposes. *Avocational interests:* Designing, building, and decorating homes.

BIOGRAPHICAL/CRITICAL SOURCES: New Statesman, July 28, 1967.

* * *

TOULMIN, Stephen Edelston 1922-

PERSONAL: Born March 25, 1922, in London, England; son of Geoffrey Edelston (a company secretary) and Doris (Holman) Toulmin; married June Goodfield (a documentary film director), July 25, 1960. *Education:* Cambridge University, B.A., 1943, M.A., 1946, Ph.D., 1948; King's College, Cambridge, research student, 1947-51. *Home:* Tile Barn, Alfriston, Polegate, Sussex, England. *Agent:* A.P. Watt & Son, 26-28 Bedford Row, London W.C.1, England. *Office:* Department of Philosophy, Michigan State University, East Lansing, Mich. 48823.

CAREER: British Ministry of Aircraft Production (research establishment), junior scientific officer, 1942-45; Oxford University, Oxford, England, lecturer in philosophy of science, 1949-55; University of Leeds, Leeds, England, professor of philosophy, 1955-59; Nuffield Foundation, London, England, director of Unit for History of Ideas, 1960-65; Brandeis University, Waltham, Mass., professor of philosophy, 1965-69; Michigan State University, East Lansing, professor of philosophy, 1969—. Visiting professor of philosophy at New York University and Columbia University, 1959-60.

WRITINGS: An Examination of the Place of Reason in Ethics, Cambridge University Press, 1950; *The Philosophy of Science: An Introduction,* Rinehart, 1953; (contributor) Alasdair Macintyre, editor, *Metaphysical Beliefs: Three Essays,* Allenson, 1957, 2nd edition, Schocken, 1970; *The Uses of Argument,* Cambridge University Press, 1958.

Foresight and Understanding: An Enquiry into the Aims of Science, foreword by Jacques Barzun, Indiana University Press, 1961; (contributor) Hedley Howell Rhys, editor, *Seventeenth-Century Science and the Arts,* Princeton University Press, 1961; (with wife, June Goodfield) *The Ancestry of Science,* Volume I: *The Fabric of the Heavens: The Development of Astronomy and Dynamics,* Hutchinson, 1961, Harper, 1962, Volume II: *The Architecture of Matter,* Hutchinson, 1962, Harper, 1963, Volume III: *The Discovery of Time,* Harper, 1965; (author of introduction and commentary) Kurt Otto-Wasow, *The Riviera,* Viking, 1961; *Night Sky at Rhodes,* Methuen, 1963, Harcourt, 1964.

(Editor) *Physical Reality: Philosophical Essays on Twentieth Century Physics,* Harper, 1970; *Human Understanding,* Princeton University Press, Volume I: *Concepts: Their Collective Use and Evolution,* 1972. Author of scripts with June Goodfield for documentary films, "Earth and Sky," 1959, "The God Within," 1963. Contributor to learned journals.

* * *

TRACY, Clarence 1908-

PERSONAL: Born May 9, 1908, in Dixie, Ontario; son of Frederick (a professor) and Charlotte (Haines) Tracy; married Minerva Jacox, August 20, 1940; children: Prudence, Nicholas, Sarah. *Education:* University of Toronto, B.A., 1930; Yale University, Ph.D., 1935. *Office:* Department of English, Acadia University, Wolfville, Nova Scotia, Canada.

CAREER: Queen's University, Kingston, Ontario, lecturer, 1930-31; Cornell University, Ithaca, N.Y., instructor in English, 1934-36; University of Alberta, Edmonton, began as lecturer, became assistant professor of English, 1936-47; University of New Brunswick, Fredericton, associate professor of English, 1947-50; University of Saskatchewan, Saskatoon, professor of English, 1950-64, dean of residence and head of department of English, 1964-66; University of British Columbia, Vancouver, professor of English, 1966-68; Acadia University, Wolfville, Nova Scotia, professor of English and head of the department, 1968—.

MEMBER: International Association of University Professors of English, Modern Language Association of America, Humanities Association of Canada (president, 1954-56), Canadian Association of University Teachers of English, American Society for Eighteenth-Century Studies, Royal Society of Canada (fellow). *Awards, honors:* Canadian government senior overseas fellowship, 1957-58.

WRITINGS: The Artificial Bastard: A Biography of Richard Savage, Harvard University Press, 1953; (editor and author of notes and commentaries) *Poetical Works of Richard Savage,* Cambridge University Press, 1962; (editor and author of introduction) Richard Graves, *The Spiritual Quixote, or The Summer's Ramble of Mr. Geoffrey Wildgoose: A Comic Romance,* Oxford University Press, 1967; (editor) *Browning's Mind and Art: Essays,* Oliver & Boyd, 1968, Barnes & Noble, 1970; (editor) Samuel Johnson, *Life of Savage,* Clarendon Press, 1971.

WORK IN PROGRESS: An illustrated edition of Alexander Pope's *Rape of the Lock.*

* * *

TRACY, L(ee) Jack 1926-

PERSONAL: Born July 27, 1926, in Minneapolis, Minn.; son of Palister and Mary (Tkach) Tracy; married Eleanor Struve, February 9, 1950; children: Michael, Christine, Timothy. *Education:* University of Minnesota, B.A., 1949. *Politics:* Democrat (usually). *Home:* 4632 Van Noord, Sherman Oaks, Calif. 91403. *Office:* Mercury Records, 1800 North Argyle, Hollywood, Calif. 90028.

CAREER: Down Beat, managing editor, 1952-53; Maher Publications, executive editor, 1954-58; Mercury Records, director of artists and repertoire in Chicago, Ill., 1958-62, in Hollywood, Calif., 1962—. Columbia College, Chicago, Ill., lecturer, 1955-58. *Military service:* U.S. Navy, 1944-46. *Member:* National Academy of Recording Arts and Sciences, Broadcast Music, Inc. (professional songwriters' association), Sigma Delta Chi.

WRITINGS: (With Leonard Feather) *Laughter from the Hip,* Horizon, 1963. Contributor to *Encyclopaedia Britannica, American People's Encyclopedia.*

WORK IN PROGRESS: A second book on the light and amusing aspects of popular music and its practitioners.

AVOCATIONAL INTERESTS: Politics, literature (especially O'Hara, Nathaniel West, John Updike, Norman Mailer, and other contentious sorts), sports—watching baseball and football, playing golf.†

* * *

TRANTER, Nigel (Godwin) 1909-
(Nye Tredgold)

PERSONAL: Born November 23, 1909, in Glasgow, Scotland; son of Gilbert Tredgold (an insurance official) and Eleanor Anne (Cass) Tranter; married May Jean Campbell Grieve; children: Frances May (Mrs. Robert Baker), Philip Nigel Lakin (died 1966). *Education:* Studied at George Heriot's School, Edinburgh, Scotland.

Politics: Liberal. *Religion:* Scottish Episcopal Church. *Home:* Quarry House, Aberlady, East Lothian, Scotland.

CAREER: Accountant and inspector in family insurance company, Edinburgh, Scotland, 1929-39; full-time writer, 1946—. Broadcast on own historical program, "Towers of Strength," carried by Scottish Television, Border Television, and other programs on British Broadcasting Corp. Public lecturer. Chairman, National Forth Road Bridge Committee. *Military service:* British Army, Royal Artillery, World War II; become lieutenant. *Member:* Society of Authors (Scottish chairman), National Book League (member of Scottish committee), P.E.N. (former Scottish president), Berwick and East Lothian Liberal Association (president), East Lothian Wildfowlers Association (president), East Lothian St. Andrew Society (chairman), Fawside Castle Preservation Committee (former chairman). *Awards, honors:* Knight Commander of Order of St. Lazarus of Jerusalem; M.A., University of Edinburgh.

WRITINGS—Novels: *Trespass,* Moray Press, 1937; *Mammon's Daughter,* Ward, Lock, 1939; *Harsh Heritage,* Ward, Lock, 1939.

Eagle's Feathers, Ward, Lock, 1941; *Watershed,* Ward, Lock, 1941; *The Gilded Fleece,* Ward, Lock, 1942; *Delayed Action,* Ward, Lock, 1944; *Tinker's Pride,* Ward, Lock, 1945; *Man's Estate,* Ward, Lock, 1946; *Flight of Dutchmen,* Ward, Lock, 1947; *Island Twilight,* Ward, Lock, 1947; *Root and Branch,* Ward, Lock, 1948; *Colours Flying,* Ward, Lock, 1948; *The Chosen Course,* Ward, Lock, 1949.

Fair Game, Ward, Lock, 1950; *High Spirits,* Collins, 1950; *The Freebooters,* Ward, Lock, 1950; *Tidewrack,* Ward, Lock, 1951; *Fast and Loose,* Ward, Lock, 1951; *Bridal Path,* Ward, Lock, 1952; *Cheviot Chase,* Ward, Lock, 1952; *Ducks and Drakes,* Ward, Lock, 1953; *The Queen's Grace,* Ward, Lock, 1953; *Rum Week,* Ward, Lock, 1954; *The Night Riders,* Ward, Lock, 1954; *There Are Worse Jungles,* Ward, Lock, 1955; *Rio D'Oro,* Ward, Lock, 1955; *The Long Coffin,* Ward, Lock, 1956; *MacGregor's Gathering,* Hodder & Stoughton, 1957; *The Enduring Flame,* Hodder & Stoughton, 1957; *Balefire,* Hodder & Stoughton, 1958; *The Stone,* Hodder & Stoughton, 1958, Putnam, 1959; *The Man Behind the Curtain,* Hodder & Stoughton, 1959; *The Clansman,* Hodder & Stoughton, 1959.

Spanish Galleon, Hodder & Stoughton, 1960; *The Flockmasters,* Hodder & Stoughton, 1960; *Kettle of Fish,* Hodder & Stoughton, 1961; *The Master of Gray,* Hodder & Stoughton, 1961; *A Drug on the Market,* Hodder & Stoughton, 1962; *Gold for Prince Charlie,* Hodder & Stoughton, 1962; *The Courtesan,* Hodder & Stoughton, 1963; *Chain of Destiny,* Hodder & Stoughton, 1964; *Past Master,* Hodder & Stoughton, 1965; *A Stake in the Kingdom,* Hodder & Stoughton, 1966; *Lion Let Loose,* Hodder & Stoughton, 1967; *Cable from Kabul,* Hodder & Stoughton, 1968; *Black Douglas,* Hodder & Stoughton, 1968; *Robert the Bruce: The Steps to the Empty Throne,* Hodder & Stoughton, 1969, St. Martin's, 1972.

Robert the Bruce: The Path of the Hero King, Hodder & Stoughton, 1970; *Robert the Bruce: The Price of the King's Peace,* Hodder & Stoughton, 1971.

Juvenile action: *Spaniards' Isle,* Brockhampton Press, 1958; *Border Riding,* Brockhampton Press, 1959; *Nestor the Monster,* Brockhampton Press, 1960; *Birds of a Feather,* Brockhampton Press, 1961; *The Deer Poachers,* Blackie & Son, 1961; *Something Very Fishy,* Collins, 1962; *Give a Dog a Bad Name,* Collins, 1963, Platt, 1964; *Silver Island,* Thomas Nelson, 1964; *Smoke Across the Highlands,* Platt, 1964; *Pursuit,* Collins, 1965; *Fire and High Water,* Collins, 1967; *Tinker Tess,* Dobson, 1967; *To the Rescue,* Dobson, 1968.

Westerns under pseudonym Nye Tredgold: *Thirsty Range,* Ward, Lock, 1949; *Heartbreak Valley,* Ward, Lock, 1950; *The Big Corral,* Ward, Lock, 1952; *Trail Herd,* Ward, Lock, 1952; *Desert Doublecross,* Ward, Lock, 1953; *Cloven Hooves,* Ward, Lock, 1954; *Dynamite Trail,* Ward, Lock, 1955; *Rancher Renegade,* Ward, Lock, 1956; *Trailing Trouble,* Ward, Lock, 1958; *Bloodstone Trail,* Ward, Lock, 1958.

Nonfiction: *The Fortalices and Early Mansions of Southern Scotland, 1400-1650,* Moray Press, 1935; *The Fortified House in Scotland,* Volume I: *South-East Scotland,* Oliver & Boyd, 1962, Volume II: *Central Scotland,* Oliver & Boyd, 1963, Volume III: *Southwest Scotland,* Oliver & Boyd, 1965, Volume IV: *Aberdeenshire, Angus and Kincardineshire,* Oliver & Boyd, 1966, Volume V: *North and West Scotland and Miscellaneous,* W. & R. Chambers, 1970; *The Pegasus Book of Scotland,* Dobson, 1964; *Outlaw of the Highland: Rob Roy,* Dobson, 1965; *Land of the Scots,* Weybright, 1968; (editor) Philip Tranter, *No Tigers in the Hindu Kush,* Hodder & Stoughton, 1968; *The Queen's Scotland,* Hodder & Stoughton, Volume I: *The Heartland, Clackmannanshire, Perthshire, and Stirlingshire,* 1971. Contributor of articles to all major Scottish magazines and newspapers.

WORK IN PROGRESS: A trilogy of novels on the great Marquis of Montrose; Volume II of *The Queen's Scotland,* for Hodder & Stoughton; *Portrait of the Borders,* for R. Hale.

SIDELIGHTS: Tranter set his sights on Scottish history, antiquities, and domestic architecture at an early age, and after writing almost forty novels, set about chronicling a historical nonfiction series, *The Fortified House in Scotland.* Of his novels, two recent ones, *The Master of Gray,* and its sequel, *The Courtesan,* have been his most successful; a number of others have been serialized in Great Britain and overseas, and translated for foreign editions. *Bridal Path* was made into a film of the same name; two other books, one adult novel and one juvenile, have been sold to film producers.

Tranter describes himself as a moderate nationalist concerned with such internal matters as better roads in the Highlands, and with the larger problem of personal freedom and public rights.

BIOGRAPHICAL/CRITICAL SOURCES: Best Sellers, May 1, 1969; *Books and Bookmen,* December, 1969; *Observer Review,* May 17, 1970.

*   *   *

TREADGOLD, Donald W(arren) 1922-

PERSONAL: Born November 24, 1922, in Silverton, Ore.; son of Frederic Vere (a lumberman) and Mina (Hubbs) Treadgold; married Alva Adele Granquist, August 24, 1947; children: Warren Templeton, Laura Margaret, Catherine Mina. *Education:* University of Oregon, B.A. (with honors), 1943; Harvard University, M.A., 1947; Oxford University, D.Phil., 1950. *Home:* 4507 52nd Ave. N.E., Seattle, Wash. 98105. *Office:* Department of English, University of Washington, Seattle, Wash. 98105.

CAREER: University of Washington, Seattle, assistant professor, 1949-55, associate professor, 1955-59, professor of Russian history, 1959—, chairman of Department of History, 1972—, and chairman of Russian and East European Seminar. Visiting professor, National Taiwan University, Taipei, 1959; exchange professor, Institute of History, U.S.S.R. Academy of Sciences, Mocwow, 1965; research professor, Toyo Bunko, Tokyo, 1968. Chairman of Region XIV, Wilson Fellowship Foundation, 1957-60; consultant, Ford Foundation, 1960-61. Chairman, joint committee on Slavic studies of American Council of

Learned Societies and Social Science Research Council. *Military service:* U.S. Army, 1943-46; became captain; received Bronze Star Medal. *Member:* American Historical Association, American Association for the Advancement of Slavic Studies, American Association of Rhodes Scholars, Phi Beta Kappa. *Awards, honors:* Rhodes Scholar, 1947; Ford fellowship, 1954; Rockefeller grants, 1959, 1961; Guggenheim fellow, 1964-65; Harbison Award for Distinguished Teaching, 1967.

WRITINGS: Lenin and His Rivals, Praeger, 1955; *The Great Siberian Migration,* Princeton University Press, 1957; *Twentieth Century Russia,* Rand McNally, 1959, 3rd edition, 1972; (editor) *The Development of the U.S.S.R.,* University of Washington Press, 1964; (editor) *Soviet and Chinese Communism,* University of Washington Press, 1967; *The West in Russia and China,* Cambridge University Press, Volume I: *Russia, 1472-1917,* 1973, Volume II: *China, 1582-1949,* 1973. Contributor to *New Republic, New Leader, National Review, Problems of Communism,* and other journals. Managing editor, *Slavic Review,* 1961-65, 1968—.

*   *   *

TREBACH, Arnold S. 1928-

PERSONAL: Born May 15, 1928, in Lowell, Mass.; son of Morris (a merchant) and Vina (Sandler) Trebach; married Shirley Zuckerman, February 6, 1954; children: David, Paul. *Education:* Calvin Coolidge College, A.A., 1948; Portia Law School, LL.B., 1951; Princeton University, M.A., 1956, Ph.D., 1958. *Politics:* Independent Democrat. *Religion:* Hebrew. *Home:* 555 Everett Ave., Chicago, Ill. 60637. *Office:* National Defender Project, National Legal Aid and Defender Association, American Bar Center, Chicago, Ill. 60637.

CAREER: Admitted to Massachusetts Bar, 1951; practicing attorney in Boston, Mass., 1951-52; University of Tennessee, Knoxville, assistant professor of political science, 1957-60; U.S. Commission on Civil Rights, Washington, D.C., chief of Administration of Justice Section, 1960-63; National Legal Aid and Defender Association, American Bar Center, Chicago, Ill., administrator of National Defender Project, supported by Ford Foundation grant, 1963-64; Howard University, Washington, D.C., director of Law and Human Rights Program, 1964—. Investigator, Administrative Office of the Courts of New Jersey, 1955. *Military service:* U.S. Army, 1952-54; became sergeant. *Member:* International Political Science Association, American Bar Association (member of committee on defense of indigent persons), American Political Science Association.

WRITINGS: (Contributor) *Equal Justice for the Accused* (report of Special Committee to Study Defender Systems), Doubleday, 1959; *The Rationing of Justice: Constitutional Rights and the Criminal Process,* Rutgers University Press, 1964. Principal author of *Justice* Reports of U.S. Commission on Civil Rights, 1961, 1963. Contributor to law reviews.†

*   *   *

TREE, Michael (John) 1926-

PERSONAL: Born December 6, 1926, in Harrow, Middlesex, England; son of Wilfred Charles and Amy Monica (Bradford) Tree; married Margaret June Patrick, November 17, 1956; children: Matthew Patrick. *Education:* Attended Haberdashers' Aske's School; Brasenose College, Oxford, M.A., 1953. *Religion:* Church of England. *Home:* 1 Guildhouse St., London S.W.1, England. *Office:* Council of Industrial Design, 28 Haymarket, London S.W.1, England.

CAREER: Pond's Extract Co., Longon, England, member of staff of export section, 1951-53; Webster & Bennett

Ltd. (machine toolmakers), Coventry, England, assistant sales manager, 1953-55; Architectural Association School of Architecture, London, England, bursar, 1955-61; Council of Industrial Design, London, England, head of information division, 1962—. *Member:* Architectural Association (vice-president, 1970).

WRITINGS: Contend No More (novel), J. Cape, 1958; (with Michael Patrick) *A Career in Architecture,* Museum Press, 1961, Sportshelf, 1964; *Those Weaker Glories* (novel), Hodder & Stoughton, 1962; *The Semi-Detached Affair* (novel), Hodder & Stoughton, 1964. Contributor of articles to *Design* and other publications.

WORK IN PROGRESS: A novel.

AVOCATIONAL INTERESTS: Arts, literature, and religion.

BIOGRAPHICAL/CRITICAL SOURCES: Design, December, 1961; *Church Times,* March, 1962.

*   *   *

TREGONNING, Kennedy Gordon 1923-

PERSONAL: Born June 13, 1923, in Perth, Australia; son of Donald Rupert and Florence (Agar) Tregonning; married Judith Manford, January 26, 1950; children: Jennifer, Joanna, Susan, Margaret, Fiona. *Education:* University of Adelaide, B.A., 1949; New College, Oxford, B.Litt., 1953; University of Malaya, Ph.D., 1957. *Politics:* Liberal. *Religion:* Christian. *Home:* Hale School, Perth, Western Australia.

CAREER: West Australian (newspaper), Perth, reporter, 1950-51; University of Adelaide, Adelaide, Australia, assistant lecturer, 1951; University of Malaya, Singapore, lecturer, 1954-67, Raffles Professor of History, 1958-67; Hale School, Perth, Western Australia, headmaster, 1967—. *Military service:* Royal Australian Air Force, 1941-45, served with Bomber Command in Great Britain, 1944-45. *Member:* International Association of Historians of Asia (secretary-general), Royal Asiatic Society, Australian Board of Literary Review. *Awards, honors:* Carnegie fellow, 1963.

WRITINGS: World History for Malayans, from Earliest Times to 1511, University of London Press, 1957; *Under Chartered Company Rule: North Borneo, 1881-1946,* University of Malaya Press, 1958, 2nd edition published as *A History of Modern Sabah (North Borneo, 1881-1963),* Oxford University Press, 1965; *Twenty Great Men of Asia, 1500 B.C.-A.D. 1500,* University of London Press, 1959; *Straits Tin: A Brief Account of the First Seventy-Five Years of The Straits Trading Company Ltd., 1887-1962,* Straits Times Press, 1962; *The Claim for North Borneo by the Philippines,* W.A. Spradbrow, 1962; (editor) *Papers on Malayan History,* Journal of Southeast Asian History, 1962; (editor) *Malaysian Historical Sources* (essays), Department of History, University of Singapore, 1962; *Singapore in Malaysia: A Brief Study of Its Industrial Potential,* J.M. Sassoon, 1963; *Malaysia,* published for the Australian Institute of International Affairs by F.W. Cheshire, 1964, revised edition published as *Malaysia and Singapore,* 1966; *A History of Modern Malaya,* University of London Press, 1964, McKay, 1967; *The British in Malaya: The First Forty Years, 1786-1826,* published for the Association for Asian Studies by University of Arizona Press, 1965; *Home Port Singapore: A History of Straits Steamship Compamy Limited, 1890-1965,* published for Straits Steamship Co. by Oxford University Press, 1967; *Southeast Asia: A Critical Bibliography,* University of Arizona Press, 1969. Editor, *Journal of Southeast Asian History.*

WORK IN PROGRESS: A biography of Tau Cheng Lock, Malaysia's greatest Chinese.

AVOCATIONAL INTERESTS: Ocean cruising.

*　　*　　*

TREVELYAN, Julian O(tto) 1910-

PERSONAL: Born February 20, 1910, in Dorking, England; son of Robert Calverley (an author) and Elizabeth Trevelyan; married Ursula Darwin, July 20, 1934 (divorced, 1950); married Adye Mary Fedden, March 20, 1951; children: (first marriage) Philip Erasmus. *Education:* Studied at Bedales School, 1923-28, Trinity College, Cambridge, 1928-30, and Atelier 17, Paris, France, 1931-34. *Politics:* Socialist. *Home:* Durham Wharf, Hammersmith Ter., London W.6, England. *Agent:* Curtis Brown Ltd., 13 King St., London W.C. 2, England.

CAREER: British painter; work exhibited at one-man shows at Lefevre Galleries, 1935-48, Zwemmer Galleries, 1955-67, and at other galleries and museums. Engraving tutor, Royal College of Art, 1955-63. *Military service:* British Army, Royal Engineers, 1940-43; became captain.

WRITINGS: Indigo Days (autobiography), MacGibbon, & Kee, 1957; *The Artist and His World,* Gollancz, 1960; *Etching: Modern Methods of Intaglio Printmaking,* Studio Books, 1963, Watson-Guptill, 1964; (illustrator) Anne Bronte, *The Tenant of Wildfell Hall,* Folio Society, 1966.

AVOCATIONAL INTERESTS: Sailing on the Thames.

*　　*　　*

TRILLING, Lionel 1905-

PERSONAL: Born July 4, 1905, in New York, N.Y.; son of David W. (a businessman) and Fannie (Cohen) Trilling; married Diana Rubin (a writer), June 12, 1929; children: James Lionel. *Education:* Columbia University, B.A., 1925, M.A., 1926, Ph.D., 1938. *Office:* Hamilton Hall, Columbia University, New York, N.Y. 10027.

CAREER: University of Wisconsin, Madison, instructor in English, 1926-27; Hunter College (now Hunter College of the City University of New York), New York, N.Y., instructor in English, 1927-30; Columbia University, New York, N.Y., instructor, 1931-39, assistant professor, 1939-45, associate professor, 1945-48, professor of English, 1948-65, George Edward Woodberry Professor of Literature and Criticism, 1965-70. With John Crowe Ransom and F.O. Mattheissen, helped to organize Kenyon School of Letters at Kenyon College, George Eastman Visiting Professor, Oxford University, 1963-65; Charles Eliot Norton Professor of Poetry, Harvard University, 1969-70. *Member:* American Academy of Arts and Sciences, National Institute of Arts and Letters, Phi Beta Kappa, Athenaeum Club (London), Century Club (New York). *Awards, honors:* Senior fellow, Kenyon School of Letters (now Indiana University School of Letters); D.Litt., Trinity College (Hartford, Conn.), Harvard University, 1962, Case Western Reserve University, 1968; L.H.D., Northwestern University, 1964; Mark Van Doren Award from the student body of Columbia College, 1966; Brandeis University Creative arts award, 1967-68.

WRITINGS: Matthew Arnold, Norton, 1939, 2nd edition, Columbia University Press, 1949; *E.M. Forster,* New Directions, 1943, revised edition, 1965 (published in England as *E.M. Forster: A Study,* Hogarth, 1944); *The Middle of the Journey* (novel), Viking, 1947; (editor and author of introduction) *The Portable Matthew Arnold,* Viking, 1949 (published in England as *The Essential Matthew Arnold,* Chatto & Windus, 1969); *The Liberal Imagination: Essays on Literature and Society,* Viking,

1950; (author of introduction) Leo Tolstoy, *Anna Karenina,* Cambridge University Press, 1951; (editor and author of introduction) John Keats, *Selected Letters,* Farrar, Straus, 1951; *The Opposing Self: Nine Essays in Criticism,* Viking, 1955; *Freud and the Crisis of Our Culture,* Beacon Press, 1955; (editor and author of introduction) John O'Hara, *Selected Short Stories,* Modern Library, 1956; *A Gathering of Fugitives* (essays), Beacon Press, 1956; (author of introduction) Isaak Babel, *The Collected Stories,* Criterion, 1957; (editor) Ernest Jones, *The Life and Works of Sigmund Freud,* Basic Books, 1961; *The Scholar's Caution and the Scholar's Courage,* [Ithaca], 1962; (author of introduction) Saul Bellow, *The Adventures of Augie March,* Modern Library, 1965; *Beyond Culture: Essays on Literature and Learning,* Viking, 1965; *The Experience of Literature: A Reader with Commentaries,* Doubleday, 1967, text edition, Holt, 1967; (editor and author of introduction) *Literary Criticism: An Introductory Reader,* Holt, 1970.

Contributor: Malcolm Cowley, editor, *After the Genteel Tradition: American Writers, 1910-1930,* Norton, 1937, revised edition, Southern Illinois University Press, 1964; Morton Dauwen Zabel, editor, *Literary Opinion in America,* Harper, 1973, 3rd revised edition, 1962; Margaret Denny and William H. Gilman, editors, *The American Writer and the European Tradition,* University of Minnesota Press, 1950; Chandler Brossard, editor, *The Scene Before You: A New Approach to American Culture,* Rinehart, 1955; Irving Howe, editor, *Modern Literary Criticism,* Beacon Press, 1958; Harold Beaver, editor, *American Critical Essays: Twentieth Century,* Oxford University Press, 1959; Meyer Howard Abrams, editor, *English Romantic Poets: Modern Essays in Criticism,* Oxford University Press, 1960; Sylvan Barnet, Morton Berman, and William Burto, editors, *The Study of Literature: A Handbook of Critical Essays and Terms,* Little, Brown, 1960; Alfred Kazin, editor, *The Open Form: Essays for Our Time,* Harcourt, 1961; Frederick J. Hoffman, editor, *The Great Gatsby: A Study,* Scribner, 1962; Northrup Frye, editor, *Romanticism Reconsidered: Selected Papers from the English Institute,* Columbia University Press, 1963; Carroll Camden, editor, *Literary Views: Critical and Historical Essays,* University of Chicago Press, 1964; Norman Podhoretz, editor, *The Commentary Reader: Two Decades of Articles and Stories,* Atheneum, 1966.

Work represented in many anthologies, including *The Stature of Theodore Dreiser: A Critical Survey of His Life and His Work,* edited by Alfred Kazin and Charles Shapiro, Indiana University Press, 1955, *Literature in America,* edited by Philip Rahv, Meridian Books, 1957, *The Art of the Essay,* edited by Leslie Fiedler, Crowell, 1958, 2nd edition, 1969, *Hemingway and His Critics: An International Anthology,* edited by Carlos Baker, Hill & Wang, 1961, and *Modern British Fiction: Essays in Criticism,* edited by Mark Schorer, Oxford University Press, 1961. Member of editorial board of *Partisan Review* and *Kenyon Review.* Contributor to *Menorah Journal, New York Evening Post, Nation, New Republic, New York Times Book Review, New Yorker, Commentary, Poetry,* and other periodicals.

SIDELIGHTS: Described by Morton Dauwen Zabel as "the best critical intelligence now discernible in America," Trilling is distinguished among his peers by a philosophical framework which is the core and purpose of his literary criticism. In his role as a critic he avoids the process of simple evaluation by set standards; rather he strives to elucidate and extend the various implications he perceives in the books and writers which he considers. Perry Miller elucidates: "Mr. Trilling dares to bring scholarship into criticism; and therefore he is one of the few critics in this country who can write limpidly, humanely, undogmatically about any and every book that interests him, and who can be interested in any and every kind. While he takes care not to confuse the effects of a book upon himself with the book itself, he is not afraid to entertain relativity; he boldly sets forth a writer's intention, unperturbed by the cry of 'fallacy!' So he is constantly instructive, eminently readable, always refreshing." David Daiches suggests that this course provides Trilling's most inspired, though sometimes slightly labored, work. "Mr. Trilling likes to move out and consider the implications, the relevance for culture, for civilization, for the thinking man today, of each particular literary phenomenon which he contemplates, and this expansion of the context gives him both his moments of greatest perception and his moments of disconcerting generalization. . . . It is civilization, we feel, that he really wants to talk about, and though, of course, all discourse about literature is and should be ultimately discourse about civilization, we sometimes feel that Mr. Trilling is stretching and forcing his literary material to allow himself to move over quickly to the larger issues."

Tony Tanner describes this cultural concern as Trilling's "underlying question—what does this writer tell us of the self and its potentialities, its duties, its sufferings in a world of conditioning circumstances?" In Trilling's philosophy that question can be satisfactorily resolved in only one way: by the individual's realization "that one may live a real life apart from the group, that one may exist as an actual person not only at the centre of society but on its margins, that one's values may be none the less real and valuable because they do not prevail and are rejected and submerged, that as a person one has not ceased to exist because one has 'failed.'"

Trilling's rejection of established culture as the arbiter of taste becomes evident in his judgments of literature. He regards each piece of writing in its own context. Through this disregard of immutable standards, he challenges the reader, in Milton Wilson's words, "to revise and reorganize his own values, he shows us (to use his own terms) the work of art functioning as subject as well as object, with an existence of its own beyond our partial comprehensions." George Whicher also perceives this approach: "As a conscious liberal Mr. Trilling is reluctant to commit himself to any single critical attitude. He cherishes a freedom to experiment, to use a combination of methods and a diversity of standards as tools at his disposal. . . ." This literary attitude is apparent in Trilling's political and social views. "I'm a great skeptic on the question of social truth," he once remarked to a student. "I think people respond to somebody's ideas because they serve a special purpose." Tanner illustrates this stance in describing Trilling's approach to ideologies. "The lazy or frightened mind seeks the refuge of ideology ('ideology is not the product of thought'): those capable of 'the energy of the encompassing mind' will persist in uncertainty, if only out of respect for everything that cannot be finally known about ourselves and our world."

His theory of the individual versus cultural domination leads many of Trilling's evaluators to describe him as a moralist. It is his distinctive method of criticism which, as John Wain maintains, limits the readership capable of appreciating Trilling's work. "This is, in fact, real criticism, which can only be addressed to those who are directly on a level with the critic himself; they need not have read exactly the same books, but he has to assume that they have the same quality of interest in the subject as he has. Professor Trilling is a master of this procedure, for all that his tone is not conversational or intimate, but rather Arnoldian, without sharing Arnold's tendency to nag or preach. And, far more than Arnold, he has the true critic's gift of describing *exactly* the thing he is talking about. . . . His criticism, at bottom, is not technical, nor aesthetic, but moral. What makes a great book great, for him, is the spiritual and moral health it embodies." In Ben Ray Redman's judgment this unusual perception of moral value leads to a somewhat limited view of political reality. "He is parochial, I think, when he declares that 'it is the plain facts that there are no conservative or reactionary ideas in general circulation.' . . . What he is really saying here is that he cannot believe in the genuineness of any political ideas save those to which he can himself subscribe. . . ."

Such reservations about Trilling are relatively few, however, for his admirers see in him qualities scarce in the contemporary literary world. "The peculiar value of Trilling's work," Tanner maintains, "is that he brings to the problem an unusual wisdom and patience; his reading of literature has prepared him for shades and paradoxes which simply madden hastier, cruder minds." John Henry Raleigh agrees, comparing Trilling with the literary figure who was both the subject of Trilling's first published work, and, some believe, an unconscious model for his career. "His particular blend of literary sensibility, learning, historical orientation and a civilized, urbane and ironical prose style is all too rare, and getting rarer. What he has tried to do in his career as a whole, as I understand it, is to perform in twentieth-century America the two roles that Matthew Arnold performed in nineteenth-century England: the conservor of what was valuable from the past and the proponent of the free play of the critical intelligence on the present."

BIOGRAPHICAL/CRITICAL SOURCES—Books: John Peale Bishop, *Collected Essays*, edited by Edmund Wilson, Scribner, 1948; Harry Redcay Warfel, *American Novelists of Today*, American Book Co., 1951; R.P. Blackmur, *The Lion and the Honeycomb: Essays in Solicitude and Critique*, Harcourt, 1955; John Henry Raleigh, *Matthew Arnold and American Culture*, University of California Press (Berkeley), 1957; Morton Dauwen Zabel, *Craft and Character: Texts, Method and Vocation in Modern Fiction*, Viking, 1957; Charles Feidelson, Jr. and Paul Brodtkorb, Jr., editors, *Interpretations of American Literature*, Oxford University Press, 1959; Louis Benjamin Fraiberg, *Psychoanalysis and American Literary Criticism*, Wayne State University Press, 1960; Robert Warshow, *The Immediate Experience: Movies, Comics, Theatre and Other Aspects of Popular Culture*, Doubleday, 1962; Chester E. Eisinger, *Fiction of the Forties*, University of Chicago Press, 1963; Joseph Frank, *The Widening Gyre: Crisis and Mastery in Modern Literature*, Rutgers University Press, 1963; Martin Green, *Science and the Shabby Curate of Poetry*, Longmans, 1964, Norton, 1965; Gordon Milne, *The American Political Novel*, University of Oklahoma Press, 1966.

Articles: *New Yorker*, January 21, 1939, August 14, 1943, October 12, 1947, January 21, 1956; *Saturday Review of Literature*, January 28, 1939, August 28, 1943, October 11, 1947; *New York Times*, January 29, 1939, August 15, 1943, October 12, 1947, February 13, 1955, November 4, 1956, October 26, 1965, April 11, 1968; *Books*, February 5, 1939; *Times Literary Supplement*, March 11, 1939, August 26, 1955; *New Statesman*, March 11, 1939, August 13, 1955; *Nation*, March 11, 1939, August 7, 1943, October 18, 1947, March 5, 1955, August 13, 1955, October 19, 1970; *Manchester Guardian*, March 12, 1939, August 23, 1955; *New Republic*, March 22, 1939, September 6, 1943, November 9, 1956; *New York Herald Tribune*, April 9, 1950, April 3, 1955; *Saturday Review*, April 15, 1950, February 12, 1955, February 14, 1958, November 6, 1965; *Spectator*, April 28, 1939, July 29, 1955; *Commonweal*, September 24, 1943, November 14, 1947, March 9, 1956; *New York Herald Tribune Book Review*, October 12, 1947; *Time*, October 20, 1947;

Atlantic, June, 1950; *New York Times Book Review,* February 13, 1955, November 14, 1965, December 31, 1967; *Newsweek,* July 27, 1959; *New York Review of Books,* December 9, 1965; *Encounter,* August, 1966; *Partisan Review,* summer, 1966; *Best Sellers,* September 1, 1967; *Book World,* September 24, 1967; *Commentary,* April, 1968; *Poetry,* December, 1968.

* * *

TRIMBLE, William Raleigh 1913-

PERSONAL: Born December 26, 1913, in Portland, Ore.; son of William Alfred and Catherine Mercedes (Rowe) Trimble. *Education:* Reed College, B.A., 1937; University of Chicago, M.A., 1944; Harvard University, Ph.D., 1950. *Religion:* Roman Catholic. *Home:* 880 Lake Shore Dr., Chicago, Ill. 60611. *Office:* Department of History, Loyola University, 820 North Michigan Ave., Chicago, Ill. 60611.

CAREER: Loyola University, Chicago, Ill., assistant professor, 1955-63, associate professor, 1963-67, professor of English history, 1967—. *Member:* American Historical Association, Mediaeval Academy of America, American Association of University Professors.

WRITINGS: The Catholic Laity in Elizabethan England, 1558-1603, Belknap Press, 1964. Contributor of articles and reviews to historical journals.

WORK IN PROGRESS: A book on the origins of international law in England, 1590-1713.

* * *

TRIMMER, Ellen McKay 1915-

PERSONAL: Born March 5, 1915, in London, Ontario, Canada; daughter of Donald Alexander (a building contractor) and Evelyn (Simpson) McKay; married Vincent D. Trimmer (a clergyman), July 6, 1940; children: David D., Ruth Ellen. *Education:* London College of Bible and Missions, London, Ontario, Canada, graduate, 1939. *Religion:* Baptist. *Home:* 25 Widdicombe Hill, Apt. 809, Weston, Ontario, Canada. *Office:* Ontario Probation Services, 4198 Dundee St. W., Toronto 18, Ontario, Canada.

CAREER: Christian education lecturer in United States and Canada, 1940-62; Ontario Probation Services, Toronto, Ontario, probation officer, 1962—. Sessional lecturer, Ontario Bible College, 1965-70. *Member:* Christian Writers Association of Canada (executive member, 1960-62, 1963-64), Probation Officers of Ontario.

WRITINGS: The Characters of Christmas Meet Christ, Moody, 1955; *The Three Gifts of Christmas,* Moody, 1956; *The "Fear Nots" of Christmas,* Waterloo Music Co., 1957; *Christmas Wonders,* Waterloo Music Co., 1958; *Christmas Pathways,* Moody, 1960; *The Gates of Christmas,* Moody, 1960; *Garments of the Saviour,* Moody, 1960; *Home for Christmas,* Moody, 1961; *Tiny Tales and Tunes,* Moody, 1963; *The Cup,* Zondervan, 1963; *You and Yours: Building Inter-Personal Relationships,* Moody, 1972. Contributor to *Chatelaine* and to religious periodicals.

WORK IN PROGRESS: The Preacher Takes a Wife, completion expected in 1973.

SIDELIGHTS: Some of Mrs. Trimmer's Christmas books have been translated into French, German, Spanish, and Tagalog. *Avocational interests:* Classical music.

BIOGRAPHICAL/CRITICAL SOURCES: Canadian Press, October 28, 1961; *Toronto Globe and Mail,* February 29, 1964; *Toronto Telegram,* July, 1969; *Toronto Star,* October 17, 1970.

TRIMMER, Eric J. 1923-
(Eric Jameson)

PERSONAL: Born June 11, 1923; married Marjorie Rudge, 1947; children: Jane Elizabeth, Christopher James. *Education:* King's College, University of London, M.B.B.S., Westminster Hospital, London, England, M.R.C.S. and L.R.C.P., 1947. *Religion:* Church of England. *Home:* Wellswood, Parkview Rd., Pinner Hill, Middlesex, England. *Agent:* Curtis Brown Ltd., 13 King St., Covent Garden W.C.2, England.

CAREER: General practitioner, Pinner, Middlesex, England, 1950—; medical journalist, 1953—. Medical advisor, Internation Publishing Corp., Reader's Digest, 1967—. *Military service:* Royal Air Force, Medical Branch; served as flight lieutenant. *Member:* Royal Society of Medicine (fellow; member of council, section of history of medicine), British Medical Association, Faculty of Medical History, Worshipful Society of Apothecaries (liveryman), Hunterian Society (fellow), Royal College of General Practitioners, Royal Society of Health.

WRITINGS: (Under pseudonym Eric Jameson) *The Natural History of Quackery,* M. Joseph, 1961; *The Young Man's Guide to Medicine,* Hamish Hamilton, 1962; *Look at the Body,* Hamish Hamilton, 1962; *Look at Doctors,* Hamish Hamilton, 1963; *Teach Your Child About Health Care and First Aid,* Pearson, 1964; *Live Long and Stay Young: An Essay on Positive Health and Rejuvenation,* Allen & Unwin, 1965; *I Swear and Vow: The Story of Medicine,* Anthony Blond, 1966; *Before Birth: Fact and Fantasy,* MacGibbon & Kee, 1966; *Femina: What Every Woman Should Know About Her Body,* Stein & Day, 1966 (published in England as *Femina: A Manual of Sex Hygiene,* MacGibbon & Kee, 1966; *Rejuvenation: The History of an Idea,* R. Hale, 1967, A.S. Barnes, 1970; *Understanding Anxiety,* Allen & Unwin, 1970. Contributor of articles to professional journals and to *Sunday Times, Homes and Gardens, Woman's Mirror, English Digest, You Magazine,* and other periodicals and newspapers.

BIOGRAPHICAL/CRITICAL SOURCES: Homes and Gardens, August, 1963.

* * *

TRINQUIER, Roger Paul 1908-

PERSONAL: Born March 20, 1908, in La Beaume, Hautes-Alpes, France; son of Seraphin (a farmer) and Angeline (Gauthier) Trinquier; married Simone Fabry (a university science assistant), July 27, 1953; children: Richard. *Education:* Attended Ecole Normale, Ecole Militaire d'Infanterie et Chars. *Politics:* Anti-Gaullist. *Religion:* Catholic. *Home:* 36 rue des Plantes, Paris XIV, France.

CAREER: French Army, lieutenant in Indochina (chief of frontier post in Tonkin), 1934-37, capitaine in China (guard of French Embassy in Peking, adjutant to the colonel in Shanghai), 1938-45, commandant and lieutenant-colonel in Indochina, 1946-54, colonel in Algeria, 1956-60, in Katanga, 1961, retired as colonel, 1961; now a farmer. *Member:* Association Nationale des Parachutistes (president), Association pour le Reforme des Structures de l'Etat (president), Repatries d'Algerie (member, board of directors). *Awards, honors:* Commandeur, Legion d'Honneur; Croix de Guerre with 14 citations; Blessure de Guerre.

WRITINGS: La Guerre moderne, La Table Ronde, 1961, translation by Daniel Lee published as *Modern Warfare: A French View of Counterinsurgency,* Praeger, 1964; *Le Coup d'etat du 13 mai,* Esprit Nouveau, 1962; (with Jacques Duchemin and Jacques Le Bailly) *Notre guerre au Katanga,* Pensee Moderne, 1963; *L'Etat nouveau: La*

Solution de l'avenir, Nouvelles Editions Latines, 1964; *La Bataille pour l'election du president de la Republique,* Independant, 1964; *Guerre, subversion, revolution,* R. Laffont, 1968.

WORK IN PROGRESS: Chine et Indochine, 1934-1946.

SIDELIGHTS: Trinquier writes that he has been deeply engaged in the anti-communist and anti-Gaullist struggle in France and he left the army so that he could be completely free. He is often attacked by the French communist press. His views are set forth by Bernard Fall in the preface to *Modern Warfare.*

*   *   *

TROCCHI, Alexander 1925-
(Frances Lengel)

PERSONAL: Surname rhymes with *rocky;* born July 30, 1925, in Glasgow, Scotland; son of Alfredo Luigi (a musician) and Annie Jack (Robertson) Trocchi; married Lyn Hicks, August 13, 1956; children: Mark Alexander. *Education:* Attended University of Glasgow, 1942-43, 1946-50, received M.A. (with honors).

CAREER: Founding participant in Project Sigma, an international cultural engineering project, London, England. Visiting lecturer in sculpture, St. Martin's School of Art, London, England. Painter and sculptor. *Military service:* Royal Navy, 1943-46.

WRITINGS: (Contributor) *New World Writing,* [New York], 1953; *Cain's Book,* Grove, 1960; *The Outsiders* (contains *Young Adam* and stories), New American Library, 1961; (editor with Terry Southern & Richard Seaver) *Writers in Revolt,* Berkeley, 1963; (with N. Rawson, S. Belles, and D. Mercer) *New Writers, No. 3* (includes *Four Stories* by Trocchi, *Texts* by Rawson, *Four Poems* by Belles, and *Long Crawl Through Time* by Mercer) J. Calder, 1965, Transatlantic, 1967; *Thongs,* introduction by Robert Creeley, Brandon House, 1967; *What Frank Harris Did Not Say: Being the Tumultous, Apocryphal 5th Volume of "My Life and Loves," as Embellished by Alexander Trocchi, with an Apolgetic Preface by Maurice Girodias* (originally published as spurious fifth volume of Frank Harris's *My Life and Loves,* Olympia, c.1958, reissued, New English Library, 1966), Travellers Companion, 1968.

Under pseudonym Frances Lengel: *Young Adam,* Olympia (Paris), 1954; *Helen and Desire,* Olympia, 1954, revised edition published under own name, Brandon House, 1967; *The Carnal Days of Helen Seferis,* Olympia, 1954, revised edition published under own name, Brandon House, 1967; *White Thighs,* Olympia, 1955, revised edition published under own name, Brandon House, 1967; *School for Sin,* Olympia, 1955, revised edition published under own name as *School for Wives,* Brandon House, 1967. Editor of *Merlin, The Paris Quarterly,* 1952-55, and *The Moving Times.* Contributor to *Botteghe Oscure, Points, Paris Review, Evergreen Review, City Lights Journal,* and other periodicals.

WORK IN PROGRESS: With William Burroughs and R.D. Laing, M.D., editing *Drugs and the Creative Process,* for Heinemann; *The Long Book,* a contemporary fiction for J. Calder, and Grove; doing translations from the French.

SIDELIGHTS: Barry Farrell once noted that "Trocchi's double misfortune is to be the world's second most famous junkie" (William Burroughs is the first). Since the early 1960's Trocchi has been involved with Project Sigma, a plan he originated to organize Underground forces on a worldwide basis. "We're coming along at a perfect time," he told Farrell in 1967. "Society is declining in its energies, falling off from its old mastery. It is now completely unable to control the quality of people's lives, and

there is great discomfort in conventional circles everywhere. People don't know how to cope with the kind of life we're approaching. What Sigma has put together is a thin veneer of people all over the world, people who up to now haven't realized their vital contemporaneousness."

Samuel Beckett has called Trocchi's work "visual writing" which projects the transcendent element in experience by focusing on that which is immediate. *Cain's Book,* which the *New York Times* failed to review, is a novel concerned with drug addiction. Mel R. Sabre in *The Village Voice* has said that the book, in a larger sense, "concerns the disciplines of a uniquely perceptive mind driving toward absolute awareness. . . . What has proved so startling to other writers is not Trocchi's attitude to junk, but rather his intensely poetic effort ('poetic' not in the sense of euphony, but in the more profound, traditional sense) to penetrate those areas of experience generally considered inaccessible to language." Sabre adds: "There is much to be said about [*Cain's Book*] and not all commendatory. But the book will be read, now and in the future, because it says so much and says it well."

In a review of *The Outsiders,* Robert Sage sees Trocchi's characters thus: "Not quite existentialists, not quite beatniks, they are, however, shabby individuals who live without plans or ideals, and who prowl around on the fringes of society." In contrast to other authors using similar characters, Trocchi, according to Sage, "not only has remarkable (albeit rather unsavory) stories to tell, but his manner of telling them is the original and studied one of a man who takes pride in writing well."

BIOGRAPHICAL/CRITICAL SOURCES: Village Voice, September 1, 1960; *New York Herald Tribune* (Paris edition), March 11-12, 1961; *New York Times Book Review,* March 12, 1961; *Gambit* (University of Edinburgh), 1962; *Kulchur 7,* autumn, 1962; *Life,* February 17, 1967; *Book World,* December 17, 1967.

*   *   *

TRUMBULL, Robert 1912-

PERSONAL: Born May 26, 1912, in Chicago, Ill.; son of Oliver Morton (an actor) and Sydney (Farmer) Trumbull; married Jean Magnier Musson, September 30, 1934; children: Suzanne, Joan, Stephanie. *Education:* Attended University of Washington, Seattle, 1930-33. *Home:* 39, 2-chome, Sendagaya, Shibuya-ku, Tokyo, Japan. *Agent:* N.S. Bienstock, 850 Seventh Ave., New York, N.Y. 10019. *Office: New York Times,* 229 West 43rd St., New York, N.Y. 10036.

CAREER: Honolulu Advertiser, Honolulu, Hawaii, began as reporter, became city editor, 1933-43; *New York Times,* New York, N.Y., war correspondent in Pacific theater, 1941-45; foreign correspondent in Japan, Philippine Islands, South and Southeast Asia, 1945-54, chief of Tokyo Bureau, 1954-61, 1964-68, chief correspondent in China-Southeast Asia, 1961-63, correspondent in Australia, New Zealand, Pacific Islands. Former member of Fulbright Commissions in India and Japan. *Member:* Press associations in several countries, Overseas Press Club of America, Authors Guild of Authors League of America, Phi Sigma Kappa, Sigma Delta Chi. *Awards, honors:* Commendation and Asiatic-Pacific Theater ribbon from U.S. Navy for work as war correspondent; English-Speaking Union Better Understanding Award, 1951; Overseas Press Club award, 1964, for *The Scrutable East.*

WRITINGS: (With Jerry Chong) *Sol Pluvius' Hawaiian Communiques* (book of cartoons from *Honolulu Advertiser*), Honolulu Advertiser, 1942; *The Raft* (Book-of-the-Month Club selection), Henry Holt, 1942; *Silversides,* Henry Holt, 1945; *India Since Independence,* Foreign

Policy Association, 1954; *As I See India,* Sloane, 1956; *Nine Who Survived Hiroshima and Nagasaki,* Dutton, 1957; *Paradise in Trust,* Sloane, 1959; *The Scrutable East: A Correspondent's Report on Southeast Asia,* McKay, 1964; (editor) *This is Communist China,* McKay, 1968. Contributor of articles on Asian and Pacific affairs to *Encyclopedia Americana,* and to various periodicals, including *Holiday, Reader's Digest, Saturday Review, New York Times Magazine, Mademoiselle,* and *Collier's.*

WORK IN PROGRESS: An untitled memoir and critique of the South Pacific.

AVOCATIONAL INTERESTS: Swimming.

BIOGRAPHICAL/CRITICAL SOURCES: New York Times Book Review, December 15, 1968; *Saturday Review,* March 15, 1969.

* * *

TUCKER, William E(dward)   1932-

PERSONAL: Born June 22, 1932, in Charlotte, N.C.; son of Cecil Edward and Ethel (Godley) Tucker; married Ruby Jean Jones, April 8, 1955; children: Janet Sue, William Edward, Jr., Gordon Vance. *Education:* Atlantic Christian College, A.B., 1953; Texas Christian University, B.D., 1956; Yale University, M.A., 1958, Ph.D., 1960. *Politics:* Democrat. *Religion:* Christian Church (Disciples of Christ). *Home:* 2712 Harlanwood Dr., Fort Worth, Tex. 76109. *Office:* Brite Divinity School, Texas Christian University, Fort Worth, Tex. 76129.

CAREER: Atlantic Christian College, Wilson, N.C., associate professor, 1959-63, professor of religion, 1963-66, chairman of department of religion and philosophy, 1962-66; Brite Divinity School, Texas Christian University, Fort Worth, associate professor and assistant dean, 1966-69, professor of church history and associate dean, 1969-71, dean, 1971—. *Member:* American Society of Church History, Disciples of Christ Historical Society (member of board of trustees), American Academy of Religion.

WRITINGS: J.H. Garrison and Disciples of Christ, Bethany Press, 1964.

* * *

TURNER, Amedee E.   1929-

PERSONAL: Born March 26, 1929, in London, England; son of Frederick William (a corporation secretary) and Ruth (Hempson) Turner; married Deborah Dudley Owen, December 31, 1960; children: Philippa Anne, Amedee Andrew. *Education:* Attended Dauntsey's School, 1942-47, and Christ Church, Oxford, 1948-51. *Politics:* Conservative and Unionist. *Religion:* Church of England. *Home:* 3 Montrose Pl., London S.W.1, England. *Office:* 1 Essex Ct., Temple, London E.C.4, England.

CAREER: Practicing barrister-at-law, London, England, 1954-57; Kenyon & Kenyon (patent attorneys), New York, N.Y., associate, 1957-60; practicing barrister-at-law, London, England, 1960—. Honorary secretary of patent bar subcommittee, Bar Council of London, 1963—. Conservative Parliamentary candidate for Norwich North, 1964, 1966, 1970. *Member:* New York Patent Law Association (associate). *Awards, honors:* Kentucky Colonel, 1961.

WRITINGS: The Law of Trade Secrets, Fred B. Rothman, 1962, 1st supplement, 1968.

* * *

TURNER, Henry Andrew, Jr.   1919-

PERSONAL: Born January 2, 1919; in King City; Mo.; son of Henry Andrew and Bessie (Claxton) Turner; married Mary Margaret Tilton, 1943; children: John Andrew, Nancy Ellen, Stephen Heald. *Education:* Northwest Missouri State College, B.S., 1939; University of Missouri, M.A., 1941; University of Chicago, Ph.D., 1950. *Home:* 955 Camino Medio, Santa Barbara, Calif. 93110. *Office:* Department of Political Science, University of California, Santa Barbara, University, Calif. 93108.

CAREER: Wentworth Military Academy, Lexington, Mo., instructor, 1940-41; Iowa State College, Ames, instructor, 1945-46; University of California, Santa Barbara, University, Calif., 1948—, began as instructor, became professor of political science, chairman of the department, 1960-65. *Military service:* U.S. Navy, 1942-45, became lieutenant. *Member:* American Political Science Association, Western Political Science Association, Southern California Political Science Association.

WRITINGS: (Editor) *Politics in the United States: Readings in Political Parties and Pressure Groups,* McGraw, 1955; (with John A. Vieg) *The Government and Politics of California,* McGraw, 1960, 4th edition, 1971; *American Democracy: State and Local Government,* Harper, 1968, 2nd edition, 1970; (with others) *American Democracy in World Perspective,* 2nd edition, Harper, 1970. Contributor of articles to political and professional journals.

* * *

TURNER, John Frayn   1923-

PERSONAL: Born August 9, 1923, in Portsmouth, England; son of George Francis and Daisy Louise (Frayn) Turner; married Joyce Isabelle Howson, August 9, 1945; children: Francesca Lynn. *Education:* Educated in English schools. *Home:* 9 Southbury, Lawn Rd., Guildford, Surrey, England. *Agent:* London Authors, 8 Upper Brook St., London W.1, England. *Office:* Royal Air Force, Publicity Branch, Adastral House, Theobalds Rd., London W.C.1, England.

CAREER: Ideal Home, London, England, feature writer, 1951-55; *House Beautiful,* London, editor, 1956-57; *News Chronicle,* London, columnist, 1958-59; *Weekend Magazine,* London, feature writer, 1962-63; Royal Air Force, Publicity Branch, London, editor, 1963—. *Military service:* Royal Navy.

WRITINGS: Service Most Silent: The Navy's Fight Against Enemy Mines, Harrap, 1955; *V.C.s of the Royal Navy,* Harrap, 1956; *Prisoners at Large,* Staples Press, 1957; *Periscope Patrol: The Saga of Malta Submarines,* Harrap, 1957; *Hovering Angels: The Record of the Royal Navy's Helicopters,* Harrap, 1957; *Invasion '44: The Full Story of D-Day in Normandy,* Putnam, 1959; *Battle Stations: The U.S. Navy's War,* Putnam, 1960; *V.C.s of the Air,* Harrap, 1960; *Highly Explosive: The Exploits of Major "Bill" Hartley, M.B.E., G.M. of Bomb Disposal,* Harrap, 1961; *The Blinding Flash: The Remarkable Story of Ken Revis and His Struggle to Overcome Blindness,* Harrap, 1962; *V.C.s of the Army, 1939-1951,* Harrap, 1962; *A Girl Called Johnnie: Three Weeks in an Open Boat,* Harrap, 1963; *Famous Air Battles,* Arthur Barker, 1963. Contributor to newspapers and magazines.

WORK IN PROGRESS: Collaborating with Douglas Bader on Bader's autobiography.

* * *

TURNGREN, Annette
(A. T. Hopkins)

PERSONAL: Born in Montrose, Minn.; daughter of John O. and Sarah (Norberg) Turngren. *Education:* University of Minnesota, B.S. *Politics:* Democrat. *Religion:* Protestant. *Residence:* New York, N.Y.

CAREER: Former school teacher; associate editor of magazine for teen-age girls, 1944-51; editorial positions with other magazines, and in juvenile department of book publisher, 1951-56; later employed by *New York Times,* New York, N.Y. Free-lance writer, mainly for young people.

WRITINGS: Flaxen Braids, Thomas Nelson, 1937; *The Copper Kettle,* Thomas Nelson, 1939; *Canyon of No Sunset,* Thomas Nelson, 1942; *Mystery Rides the River,* Thomas Nelson, 1943; *The Mystery of the Hidden Village* (Junior Literary Guild selection), Thomas Nelson, 1951; *Choosing the Right College,* Harper, 1952; *Great Artists,* Abelard, 1953; (under pseudonym A.T. Hopkins) *Have a Lovely Funeral,* Rinehart, 1954; *Steamboat's Coming,* Longmans, Green, 1955; *Mystery Walks the Campus,* Funk, 1956; *Mystery Haunts the Fair,* Funk, 1959; *Mystery Clouds the Canyon,* Funk, 1961; *Mystery of the Water Witch,* Random House, 1964; *Mystery Enters the Hospital,* Funk, 1965; *Mystery Plays a Golden Flute,* Funk, 1969.

WORK IN PROGRESS: A boys' book with American Revolution background.

* * *

TURVILLE-PETRE, Edward Oswald Gabriel 1908-

PERSONAL: Petre is pronounced like Peter; born March 25, 1908, in Leicestershire, England; son of O.H.P. (a lieutenant colonel, British Army) and Margaret Lucy (Cave) Turville-Petre; married Joan Elizabeth Blomfield (a university tutor); children: Thorlac, Merlin, Brendan. *Education:* Educated at Ampleforth College, 1921-26, Christ Church, Oxford, 1927-32, 1964. *Home:* The Court, Old Headington, Oxford, England. *Office:* The University, Oxford, England.

CAREER: University of Iceland, Reykjavik, lecturer in English, 1936-38; Oxford University, Oxford, England, reader in ancient Icelandic literature, 1941-53, professor, 1953—, student of Christ Church, 1964—. Honorary lecturer in modern Icelandic, University of Leeds, 1935-50; visiting professor, University of Melbourne, 1965. Served in Foreign Office and in Faroe Islands during World War II. *Member:* Viking Society for Northern Research (joint honorary secretary, 1938—; president, 1940-45); British Academy (fellow, 1973—). *Awards, honors:* Knight of the Order of the Falcon (Iceland), 1958, Knight Commander, 1963; D.Phil., University of Iceland, 1961.

WRITINGS: (Editor) *Viga-Glums Saga,* Oxford University Press, 1940, 2nd edition, 1960; (translator with E.S. Olszewska) *The Life of Gudmund the Good, Bishop of Holar,* Viking Society for Northern Research, 1942; *The Heroic Age of Scandinavia,* Hutchinson, 1953, 2nd edition, in press; *Origins of Icelandic Literature,* Clarendon Press, 1953; *Hervarar Saga ok Heiofreks konungs,* Viking Society for Northern Research, 1958; *Um Oofinsdyrkun a Islandi* (title means "The Cult of Odinn in Iceland"), 1958; *Myth and Religion of the North: The Religion of Ancient Scandinavia,* Holt, 1964; *Haraldr the Hard-Ruler and His Poets* (lecture), published for University College, London, by H.K. Lewis, 1968. Also author of *Nine Norse Studies,* 1972. Contributor to *Folklore, Saga-Book* of Viking Society for Northern Research, *Medieval Studies, Modern Language Review,* other professional journals. General editor of text series, Viking Society for Northern Research, 1953.

WORK IN PROGRESS: The Poetry of the Scalds.

SIDELIGHTS: Turville-Petre speaks Icelandic fluently, as well as Swedish, Norwegian, Faroese, German, and some French.

TUSIANI, Joseph 1924-

PERSONAL: Born January 14, 1924, in Foggia, Italy; came to United States in 1947, naturalized in 1956; son of Michael and Maria (Pisone) Tusiani. *Education:* University of Naples, Ph.D. (summa cum laude), 1947. *Religion:* Catholic. *Home:* 553 East 188th St., New York, N.Y. 10458. *Office:* Herbert H. Lehman College of the City University of New York, Bronx, N.Y. 10468.

CAREER: Liceo Classico, San Severo, Italy, taught Latin and Greek, 1944-47; Hunter College (now Hunter College of the City University of New York), New York, N.Y., lecturer in Italian, 1950-63; New York University, New York, N.Y., lecturer in Italian literature, 1956-63; College of Mount Saint Vincent, Riverdale, N.Y., chairman of Italian department, 1948-71; Herbert H. Lehman College of the City University of New York, Bronx, N.Y., instructor in Italian literature, 1971—. *Member:* Poetry Society of America (vice-president, 1958-68), Catholic Poetry Society of America (director, 1956-69), P.E.N., Dante Society of America, American Association of University Professors. *Awards, honors:* Greenwood Prize, Poetry Society of England, 1956; silver medal for Latin poetry (Rome), 1962; Alice Fay di Castagnola Award, Poetry Society of America, 1968; *Spirit* gold medal of Catholic Poetry Society of America, 1969; outstanding teacher award, College of Mount Saint Vincent, 1969; Litt.D., College of Mount Saint Vincent, 1971.

WRITINGS: (Translator and author of introduction and notes) *The Complete Poems of Michelangelo,* Noonday, 1960; *Rind and All, Fifty Poems,* Monastine Press, 1962; (translator and author of introduction and notes) *Lust and Liberty: The Poems of Machiavelli,* Obolensky, 1963; *The Fifth Season: Poems,* Obolensky, 1964; *Envoy from Heaven* (novel), Obolensky, 1965; *Dante's Inferno, as Told for Young People,* Obolensky, 1965; *Dante's Purgatoria, as Told for Young People,* Obolensky, 1966; (translator and author of introduction) Torquato Tasso, *Jerusalem Delivered,* Fairleigh Dickinson University Press, 1970; (translator and author of introduction) Boccaccio, *Nymphs of Fiesole,* Fairleigh Dickinson University Press, 1971; *Italian Poets of the Renaissance,* Baroque Press, 1971; (editor and translator) *From Marino to Marinetti,* Baroque Press, 1972.

In Italian: *Flora* (poetry), Caputo, 1947; *Amore e morte* (poetry), Caputo, 1948; *Peccato e luce* (poetry), Venetian Press, 1949; *La Poesia amorosa di Emily Dickinson,* Venetian, 1950; *Dante in Licenza* (novel), Nigrizia, 1951; *Wordsworthiana,* Venetian Press, 1952; *Poesia missionaria in Inghilterra ed America: Storia critica ed antologica,* Nigrizia, 1952; *Sonettisti Americani,* introduction by Frances Winwar, Clemente Publishing Co., 1954; *L'Italia nell' opera di Frances Winwar,* [Chicago], 1956; *Lo Speco celeste* (poetry), Editrice Circanna, 1956; *Odi Sacre* (poetry), Editrice Circanna, 1959; *Influenza cristiana nella poesia Negro-Americana,* Nigrizia, 1971.

In Latin: *Melos Cordis* (poems), Venetian Press, 1959; (editor) *Viva Camena* (verse anthology), Artemis (Stuttgart), 1961.

Contributor of essays and reviews to *Modern Language Journal, Italica, Italian Quarterly, British Miscellany, La Fiera Letteraria, Literary Review, Spirit, Catholic World,* and *La Parola de Popolo,* and of poetry to *New Yorker, New York Times, Poetry* (London), *Voices, Yale Literary Magazine,* and other publications. Associate editor, *Spirit,* 1960-69.

WORK IN PROGRESS: The Creation of the World, the first English translation of Tasso's *Mondo Creato,* for Baroque Press; *Dante's Minor Poems,* for Baroque Press.

SIDELIGHTS: In his youth Tusiani considered being a painter, then a composer; he passed, he says, "through all the forms of creative restlessness" before realizing that he sought to be a writer. As a child he remembers serving at Mass with Padre Pio, the Italian stigmatic. He arrived in America at the age of twenty-three, with the ability to read, but not speak, the English language. He had mastered the words, but found that was not adequate. He writes: "One must arrive at the point where mastery becomes creative atmosphere. I comforted myself with the thought that poetry had no linguistic barriers and that a poet. . .could write in any idiom he has mastered, for language is but a goblet bearing the wine, the ineffable essence which gives universality to his thought and feeling." His major area of interest is the Renaissance. He told CA that "perhaps [Italian poet Conte Giacomo] Leopardi has influenced me most. He was the literary god of my childhood. I am considering a verse translation of all his poetry."

AVOCATIONAL INTERESTS: Music and painting.

*   *   *

TUTUOLA, Amos 1920-

PERSONAL: Born 1920, in Abeokuta, Nigeria; son of Charles (a cocoa farmer) and Esther (Aina) Tutuola; married Alake Victoria, 1947; children: Olubunmi, Oluyinka, Erinola. *Education:* Attended schools in Nigeria. *Religion:* Christian. *Home:* Ago-Odo, West Nigeria. *Office:* Nigerian Broadcasting Corp., Ibadan, Nigeria, West Africa.

CAREER: Employed by Nigerian Government Labor Department, Lagos, and by Nigerian Broadcasting Corp., Ibadan, Nigeria. Free-lance writer. *Military service:* Royal Air Force, 1943-45; served as metal worker in Nigeria. *Member:* Mbari Club (Nigerian authors; founder).

WRITINGS: The Palm-Wine Drinkard and His Dead Palm-Wine Tapster in the Dead's Town, Faber, 1952, Grove, 1953; *My Life in the Bush of Ghosts,* Grove, 1954; *Simbi and the Satyr of the Dark Jungle,* Faber, 1955; *The Brave African Huntress,* Grove, 1958; *The Feather Woman of the Jungle,* Faber, 1962; *Ajaiyi and His Inherited Poverty,* Faber, 1967. Writer of short stories for radio.

SIDELIGHTS: Tutuola was the first Nigerian novelist to win international acclaim, with publication in 1952 of his now-famous *The Palm-Wine Drinkard and His Dead Palm-Wine Tapster in the Dead's Town.* Bernth Lindfors wrote that "critics outside Nigeria were enthusiastic, finding the story full of 'weird and wonderful surprises' and the author's language 'naive,' 'quaint' and 'amusing.' Dylan Thomas called it a 'brief, thronged, grisly and bewitching story, written in young English,' a 'tall devilish story.' Underlying much of this criticism was the notion that *The Palm-Wine Drinkard* was a highly original work written by an untutored but extraordinarily imaginative native genius. In Nigeria the response of the critics was quite different. Many educated Nigerians looked down upon Tutuola and fretted that his imperfect control of English would come to be regarded by the outside world as typical of Nigerian speech and writing. Some tried to discredit [the novel] by asserting that Tutuola had borrowed far more than he had created. . . . In Nigerian criticism the emphasis fell on Tutuola's lack of originality." It is Lindfors' contention in his essay that *The Palm-Wine Drinkard* is indeed "largely derived from oral tradition," while it is also the work of a unique and fertile imagination. "By keeping one foot in the old world and one in the new while translating oral art into literary art, Tutuola bridges two traditions. Herein lies his originality."

In a review of *Ajaiyi and His Inherited Poverty,* a writer for *Times Literary Supplement* deplores the fact that "even now, apparently, this extraordinary writer is treated with little respect by his fellow-countrymen. There is a feeling among the bourgeoisie that European appreciation for his work is merely patronizing, and that his publishers ought to 'correct' his English, like schoolmasters.... Part of the delightfulness of his work stems from the beauty of a working-class man asserting himself, his own instinctive taste operating on scraps of the colonizers' literature and on old African tales and proverbs, criticizing and blending his sources into a unity. Always the voice is that of a man with little schooling who talks marvellously."

Desmond Macnamara believes there is merit to Tutuola's work because it "can charm and beguile people who couldn't tell a Yoruba carving from an Ife bronze. I get an impression from Africans that they prefer a more modern image for their various countries and I can see their point. But I continue to hope vainly for a tolerant coexistence between fearful monsters and oil refineries."

Tutuola appears in a National Educational Television film entitled "African Writers of Today." Kola Ogunmola has written a play in Yoruba entitled *Omuli,* based on *The Palm-Wine Drinkard,* and published by West African Book Publishers.

BIOGRAPHICAL/CRITICAL SOURCES: Observer, July 6, 1952; Melville J. Herskovits and Francis S. Herskovits, *Dahomean Narrative: A Cross-Cultural Analysis,* Northwestern University Press, 1958; *Critique,* fall-winter, 1960-61, fall-winter, 1967-68; Gerald Moore, *Seven African Writers,* Oxford University Press, 1962; *Bulletin* of the Association for African Literature in English, March, 1966; *Presence Africaine,* 3rd trimestre, 1967; *New Statesman,* December 8, 1967; *Listener,* December 14, 1967; *Times Literary Supplement,* January 18, 1968; *Books Abroad,* summer, 1968.

*   *   *

TYLER, Anne 1941-

PERSONAL: Born October 25, 1941, in Minneapolis, Minn.; daughter of Lloyd Parry (a chemist) and Phyllis (Mahon) Tyler; married Taghi Modarressi (a psychiatrist), May 3, 1963; *Children:* Tezh, Mitra. *Education:* Duke University, B.A., 1961; Columbia University, graduate study in Russian, 1961-62. *Religion:* Quaker. *Home:* 4314 Roland Ave., Baltimore, Md. 21210. *Agent:* Diarmuid Russell, 551 Fifth Ave., New York 17, N.Y.

CAREER: Duke University Library, Durham, N.C., Russian bibliographer, 1962-63; McGill University Law Library, Montreal, Quebec, Canada, assistant to the librarian. *Member:* Authors' Guild, Phi Beta Kappa. *Awards, honors: Mademoiselle* award for writing, 1966.

WRITINGS: If Morning Ever Comes, Knopf, 1964; *The Tin Can Tree;* Knopf, 1965; *A Slipping Down Life,* Knopf, 1970; *The Clock Winder,* Knopf, 1972; *A Help to the Family,* Knopf, 1972. Contributor of short stories to *Post, Seventeen, Critic, Antioch Review,* and *Southern Review.*

SIDELIGHTS: The Clock Winder, according to *Book Week,* "seems . . . to have many of the virtues that we associate with 'southern' writing—an easy, almost confidential directness, fine skill at quick characterization, a sure eye for atmosphere, and a special nostalgic humor—and none of its liabilities. . . ."

Miss Tyler, who spent her childhood in a Utopian community in North Carolina, expects her permanent residence to be Iran, her husband's country. She speaks Persian fluently.

Film rights to *A Slipping Down Life* were acquired by Paul Newman in 1970, with Miss Tyler signed to adapt it.

BIOGRAPHICAL/CRITICAL SOURCES: *Best Sellers,* May 1, 1970; *Book Week,* May 14, 1972; *New York Times Book Review,* May 21, 1972.

* * *

TYLER, Hamilton A(lden) 1917-

PERSONAL: Born October 20, 1917, in Fresno, Calif.; son of John Gripper (a fig culturist) and Hazel (Hamilton) Tyler; married Mary Campbell (a school teacher), April 11, 1942; children: Brenda. *Education:* Attended University of California, Berkeley, intermittently, 1935-41. *Home:* 8450 West Dry Creek Rd., Healdsburg, Calif. 95448.

CAREER: Dairy, poultry, and fruit farmer in Placer and Sonoma Counties, Calif., 1942—, with exception of five years spent as landscaper.

WRITINGS: *Pueblo Gods and Myths,* University of Oklahoma Press, 1964; *Organic Gardening Without Poisons,* Van Nostrand, 1970. Also author of *Pueblo Animals and Myths* and *Pueblo Birds and Myths,* as yet unpublished.

WORK IN PROGRESS: *Gourmet Gardening.*

SIDELIGHTS: "My interest is in harvesting the scattered fruits of scholarship and in presenting this material for the intelligent non-specialist.... The fields which I find most exciting are those in the shadowy areas where mythology, philosophy, and religion overlap, or cast oblique lights upon one another."

* * *

UNGER, Irwin 1927-

PERSONAL: Born May 2, 1927, in Brooklyn, N.Y.; son of Elias C. (a garment worker) and Mary (Roth) Unger; married Bernate Spaet, February 12, 1956 (divorced 1970); married Debi Irene Marcus, June, 1970; children: (first marriage) Brooke David, Miles Jeremy, Paul Joshua; (step children) Anthony Allen, Elizabeth Sarah. *Education:* College of City of New York (now City College of City University of New York), B.S.S., 1948; Columbia University, M.A., 1949, Ph.D., 1959; University of Washington, Seattle, postgraduate study, 1949-51. *Politics:* Democrat. *Religion:* Jewish. *Home:* 305 West 13th St., New York, N.Y. 10014.

CAREER: Columbia University, New York, N.Y., instructor in history, 1956-58; Long Beach State College, Long Beach, Calif., assistant professor of history, 1959-62; University of California, Davis, assistant professor, 1962-63, associate professor of history, 1964-65; New York University, New York, N.Y., professor of history, 1966—. *Military service:* U.S. Army, 1952-54. *Member:* American Historical Association, Economic History Association, Organization of American Historians.

WRITINGS: *The Greenback Era: A Social and Political History of American Finance, 1865-1879,* Princeton University Press, 1964; (editor) *Populism: Nostalgic or Progressive?,* Rand McNally, 1964; (editor) *Essays on the Civil War and Reconstruction,* Holt, 1970; (editor with David M. Reimers) *The Slavery Experience in America,* Holt, 1970; (editor) *Beyond Liberalism: The New Left Views American History,* Xerox College Publications, 1971; (editor with others) *The American Past: A Social Record, 1607-Present,* Xerox College Publications, 1971; (editor with others) *The Course of American History: Interpretive Readings, 1607-Present,* Xerox Publications, 1971.

WORK IN PROGRESS: A biography of Salmon P. Chase, Lincoln's secretary of treasury, for Oxford University Press, completion expected in 1975.

UNGER, Maurice Albert 1917- (Al Munger)

PERSONAL: Born June 18, 1917, in Brooklyn, N.Y.; son of Harry and Augusta (Hoormann) Unger; married Ruth Mann, 1945 (divorced 1965); children: H. Stephen, Douglas, John. *Education:* Duke University, A.B., 1940, LL.B., 1946, J.D., 1970; Harvard University, graduate study in business administration, 1941. *Home:* 1304 South Terry St., Longmont, Colo. 80501. *Office:* School of Business, University of Colorado, Boulder, Colo. 80302.

CAREER: Private practice of law, Patchogue, N.Y., 1946-50; National Technological Institute, New York, N.Y., instructor in real estate, 1950-51; University of Idaho, Moscow, assistant professor of real estate, 1951-56; University of Massachusetts, Amherst, associate professor of finance, 1956-57; University of Florida, Gainesville, associate professor of real estate, 1957-62; University of Colorado, Boulder, 1962-65, became professor of real estate. *Military service:* U.S. Navy, 1941-45; became lieutenant. *Member:* New York Bar Association, American Society of Appraisers, American Finance Association, American Arbitration Association (panel member), Rocky Mountain Charolais Association, Rocky Mountain Business Law Association.

WRITINGS: *Questions and Answers for the Real Estate Broker's and Salesmen's Examinations,* Oceana, 1951, 3rd edition, revised by Oceana editorial staff, 1966; *Real Estate: Principles and Practices,* South-Western, 1954, 4th edition, 1969; *The Green Fuse* (novel), Pageant, 1954; (with Harold A. Wolf) *Personal Finance,* Allyn & Bacon, 1964, 3rd edition, 1972; *Elements of Business Law,* Prentice-Hall, 1968; *Introduction to Business Law,* Prentice-Hall, 1971. Contributor of articles to popular magazines and to professional periodicals.

* * *

UNGERMANN, Kenneth Armistead 1916-

PERSONAL: Born October 23, 1916, in Birmingham, Ala.; son of Charles Henry (a businessman) and Elizabeth G. (Armistead) Ungermann; married Judith B. Ponsonby, December 20, 1951; children: Greig, Brett, Michael. *Education:* Philips Academy, Andover, Mass., student, 1931-32; attended high school in Bronxville, N.Y. *Home:* 3022 Sullivan Rd., Sebastopol, Calif. 95472.

CAREER: Ungermann Chevrolet (dealership), Oyster Bay, N.Y., proprietor, 1938-42; American Field Service, subsection leader in North Africa, 1941-42; El Mesquital (guest ranch), Tucson, Ariz., owner, 1945-48; International News Service, staff correspondent, 1950-55, three years of that time in Paris, France; *Florida Business Letter,* Miami, managing editor, 1955-57; moved to Alaska in 1958, sold radio advertising for six months, then took up 160-acre homestead, cleared land and built house; later fished for salmon commercially in Bristol Bay. *Military service:* U.S. Air Force, 1942-45; flew thirty-two missions as bomber pilot in Europe; became captain; received Distinguished Flying Cross, Air Medal with three oak-leaf clusters.

WRITINGS: *The Race to Nome: The Story of the Heroic Alaskan Dog Teams That Rushed Diphtheria Serum to Stricken Nome in 1925,* edited by Walter Lord, Harper, 1963.

AVOCATIONAL INTERESTS: Sailing (crewed in ocean races to Nassau and Havana) and dachshunds.

* * *

UNSTEAD, R(obert) J(ohn) 1915-

PERSONAL: Born November 21, 1915, Deal, Kent, England; son of Charles Edmond and Elizabeth (Nightingale) Unstead; married Florence Margaret Thomas (her husband's secretary), March 15, 1917; children: Judith, Mary, Susan. *Education:* Goldsmiths' College, University of London, student, 1934-36. *Religion:* Church of England *Home:* "Reedlands," Lakeside, Thorpeness, Suffolk, England.

CAREER: Schoolmaster in St. Albans, England, 1936-46; headmaster in Letchworth, England, 1947-57; self-employed author, 1957—. Director, R.J. Unstead Publications Ltd. *Military service:* Royal Air Force, 1940-46; became flight lieutenant. *Member:* Society of Authors and National Book League (both London).

WRITINGS—All published by A. & C. Black, except as indicated: *Cavemen to Vikings,* 1953; *The Middle Ages,* 1953; *Tudors and Stuarts,* 1954; "English for Every Day" series, three books, 1954; *Queen Anne to Elizabeth II,* 1955; *Looking at History: Britain from Cavemen to the Present Day* (contains *Cavemen to Vikings, The Middle Ages, Tudors and Stuarts,* and *Queen Anne to Elizabeth II),* 1955, Macmillan (New York), 1956, 3rd edition, A. & C. Black, 1966; *People in History,* Book I: *From Caractacus to Alfred,* 1955, Book II: *From William the Conqueror to William Caxton,* 1955, Book III: *Great Tudors and Stuarts,* 1956, Book IV: *Great People of Modern Times,* 1956, published in America in one volume as *People in History: From Caractacus to Alexander Fleming,* Macmillan, 1957; *Teaching History in the Junior School,* 1956, 3rd edition, 1963; *A History of Houses,* 1958; *Travel by Road Through the Ages,* 1958, 2nd edition, 1969; *Looking at Ancient History,* 1959, Macmillan (New York), 1960.

(Editor with William Worthy, and contributor) *Black's Children's Encyclopaedia,* 1961; *Monasteries,* Dufour, 1961, 2nd edition, A. & C. Black, 1970; *Some Kings and Queens,* Odhams, 1962, Follett, 1967; *England: A History,* Book I: *The Medieval Scene, 787-1485,* 1962, Book II: *Crown and Parliament, 1485-1688,* 1962, Book III: *The Rise of Great Britain: 1688-1837,* 1963, Book IV: *The Century of Change, 1837-Today,* 1963; *Royal Adventurers,* Odhams, 1963, Follett, 1967; *Men and Women in History,* Book I: *Heroes and Saints,* 1964, Book II: *Princes and Rebels,* 1964, Book III: *Discoverers and Adventurers,* 1965, Book IV: *Great Leaders,* 1966; *Early Times: A First History from Cave-men to the Middle Ages,* 1965; *Britain in the Twentieth Century,* 1966; *Kings and Queens in World History* (contains *Some Kings and Queens* and *Royal Adventurers),* Odhams, 1966; *The Story of Britain,* 1969, Thomas Nelson (New York), 1970; (with W.F. Henderson) *Homes in Australia,* 1969.

British Castles, Crowell, 1970 (published in England as *Castles,* A. & C. Black, 1970); *My World,* Herder, 1970; *Transport in Australia,* 1970; *Pioneer Home Life in Australia,* 1971; *Living in a Medieval City,* 1971; *Living in a Castle,* 1971; *Living in a Medieval Village,* 1971; *Living in a Crusader Land,* 1971. General editor, "Looking at Geography" series, five books, A. & C. Black, 1957-60, and "Black's Junior Reference Books," twenty titles, A. & C. Black, 1958-63.

WORK IN PROGRESS: A History of the English-Speaking Peoples, eight books, for Macdonald & Co.

BIOGRAPHICAL/CRITICAL SOURCES: Best Sellers, February 15, 1971.

*   *   *

UNWIN, David S(torr)   1918-
  (David Severn)

PERSONAL: Born December 3, 1918, in London, England; son of Sir Stanley (a publisher) and Alice Mary (Storr) Unwin; married Periwinkle Herbert, July 31, 1945; children: Phyllida Mary and Richard Corydon (twins). *Education:* Attended schools in England and Germany. *Politics:* Liberal. *Home:* St. Michaels, Helions Bumpstead, Haverhill, Suffolk, England. *Office:* George Allen & Unwin Ltd., 40 Museum St., London W.C.1, England.

CAREER: League of Nations Secretariat, Geneva, Switzerland, editorial assistant, 1938-39; Allen & Unwin Ltd. (publishers), London, England, art editor, 1940-43. Publisher's reader for Allen & Unwin and other firms. *Member:* Authors Society, P.E.N., Screenwriters Guild. *Awards, honors:* Authors Club First Novel award, 1955, for *The Governor's Wife.*

WRITINGS—Adult novels: *The Governor's Wife,* M. Joseph, 1954, Dutton, 1955; *A View of the Heath,* M. Joseph, 1956.

Juveniles, under pseudonym David Severn: *Rick Afire!,* John Lane, 1942, Houghton, 1946; *A Cabin for Crusoe,* John Lane, 1943; *Wagon for Five,* John Lane, 1944, Houghton, 1947; *A Hermit in the Hills,* John Lane, 1945; *Forest Holiday,* John Lane, 1946; *Ponies and Poachers,* John Lane, 1947; *Bill Badger and the Pine Martens,* Bodley Head, 1947; *Wily Fox and the Baby Show,* Bodley Head, 1947; *The Cruise of the Maiden Castle,* Bodley Head, 1948, Macmillan (New York), 1949; *Bill Badger and the Bathing Pool,* Bodley Head, 1948; *Wily Fox and the Christmas Party,* Bodley Head, 1948; *Treasure for Three,* Bodley Head, 1949, Macmillan (New York), 1950; *Dream Gold,* Bodley Head, 1949, Viking, 1952.

Wily Fox and the Missing Fireworks, Bodley Head, 1950; *Bill Badger and the Buried Treasure,* Bodley Head, 1950; *Crazy Castle,* Bodley Head, 1951, Macmillan (New York), 1952; *Burglars and Bandicoots,* Bodley Head, 1952, Macmillan (New York), 1953; *My Foreign Correspondent Through Africa,* Meiklejohn, 1951; *Drumbeats!,* Bodley Head, 1953; *Blaze of Broadfurror Farm,* Bodley Head, 1955; *Walnut Tree Meadow,* Bodley Head, 1955; *The Green-Eyed Gryphon,* Hamish Hamilton, 1958; *The Future Took Us,* Bodley Head, 1958; *Foxy-Boy,* Bodley Head, 1959, published in America as *The Wild Valley,* Dutton, 1963; *Three at Sea,* Bodley Head, 1959.

Jeff Dickson: Cowhand, J. Cape, 1963; *Clouds Over the Alberhorn,* Hamish Hamilton, 1963. Co-editor, *My Foreign Correspondent,* 1947—.

WORK IN PROGRESS: The Girl in the Grove, a novel for adolescents; *The Wishing Bone,* a fantasy for children.

SIDELIGHTS: "I write, very largely, from personal experience and tend to dovetail my fictional plots into known topography, climate, local conditions. . . . My books for children, which I began to write in my early twenties, are for the most part conceived out of a love for the English countryside. Many are set in specific locations: Cornwall, Wales, the New Forest. Some are straightforward holiday adventure stories; others are not—and I am perhaps happiest when, as often happens, my tales edge over into fantasy."

*   *   *

URBANEK, Mae Bobb   1903-

PERSONAL: Born September 10, 1903, in Denver, Colo.; daughter of Boyd Byron and Sarah (Hotze) Bobb; married Jerry Urbanek (a rancher), December 15, 1928. *Education:* Northwestern University, B.S., 1927. *Politics:* Democrat. *Home:* Lusk, Wyo. 82225.

CAREER: Rancher at Lusk, Wyo., 1928—; free-lance writer. *Member:* Wyoming Federation of Garden Clubs (president, 1959-61), Wyoming Press Women (president, 1963-65), Rebekah Lodge, Alpha Gamma Delta, Deita Kappa Gamma (honorary member).

WRITINGS: The Uncovered Wagon, Sage Books, 1958; Songs of the Sage, Big Mountain Press, 1962; The Second Man, Sage Books, 1962; Wyoming Wonderland, Sage Books, 1964; Wyoming Place Names, Johnson Publishing Co. (Colo.), 1967; Almost Up Devil's Tower, Johnson Publishing Co. (Colo.), 1968; Memoirs of Andrew McMaster, Lusk Herald, 1969; Know Wyoming, Johnson Publishing Co. (Colo.), 1969. Writer of three brochures on Wyoming, published by Lusk Herald. Editor, Paintbrush (publication of Wyoming Federation of Garden Clubs).

WORK IN PROGRESS: Chief Washakie, a novel about life in Jackson Hole, Wyoming.

AVOCATIONAL INTERESTS: Developing an experimental garden, and sawing and polishing rocks for garden structures; photography, cooking, dogs, and wilderness trips.

* * *

URQUHART, Fred(erick Barrows) 1912-

PERSONAL: Born July 12, 1912, in Edinburgh, Scotland; son of Frederick Burrows and Agnes (Harrower) Urquhart. Education: Attended village and secondary schools in Scotland. Home: Spring Garden Cottage, Fairwarp, Uckfield, Sussex, England. Agent: Frank Rudman, 41 Clerkenwell Green, London E.C.1, England. Office: c/o Cassell & Co. Ltd., 35 Red Lion Sq., London W.C.1, England.

CAREER: Left school at fifteen and worked in a bookshop, Edinburgh, Scotland, 1927-34, starting to write in this period; first story published, 1936, first novel, 1938; reader for literary agency in London, England, 1947-51, for Metro-Goldwyn-Mayer, 1951-54; Cassell & Co. Ltd., London, reader, 1951—. Occasional reader for other publishers. Awards, honors: Tom Gallon Award of Society of Authors, 1951-52, for story, "The Ploughing Match."

WRITINGS: Time Will Knit, Duckworth, 1938, Penguin (New York), 1943; I Fell for a Sailor, and Other Stories, Duckworth, 1940; The Clouds Are Big with Mercy: Short Stories, William Mclellan, 1946; Selected Stories, Maurice Fridberg, 1946; The Last G.I. Bride Wore Tartan, Serif Books, 1947; (editor with Maurice Lindsay) No Scottish Twilight: New Scottish Short Stories, William Mclellan, 1947; The Ferret Was Abraham's Daughter, Methuen, 1949; The Year of the Short Corn, and Other Stories, Methuen, 1949.

The Last Sister, and Other Stories, Methuen, 1950; Jezebel's Dust, Methuen, 1951; The Laundry Girl and the Pole: Selected Stories, Arco Publications, 1955; (editor) W.S.C., a Cartoon Biography, Cassell, 1955; (editor) Scottish Short Stories, 3rd revised edition, Faber, 1957, (editor) Great True War Adventures, Arco Publications, 1957; (editor) Men at War, the Best War Stories of All Time, Arco Publications, 1957; (editor) The Cassell Miscellany (1848-1958), Cassell, 1958; (editor) Great True Escape Stories, Arco Publications, 1958; (author of text) Kenneth Scowen, Scotland in Color, Viking, 1961; The Collected Stories of Fred Urquhart, Hart-Davis, Volume I: The Dying Stallion, 1967, Volume II: The Ploughing Match, 1968.

Represented in many anthologies, including Best Stories of 1938, edited by Edward J.H. O'Brien, Houghton, 1938, Horizon Stories, edited by Cyril Connolly, Faber, 1945, Story: The Fiction of the Forties, edited by Whit Burnett and Hallie Burnett, Dutton, 1950, Modern English Short Stories, edited by Derek Hudson, Oxford University Press, 1956, Pick of Today's Stories, edited by John Pudney, Putnam, 1960, Scottish Short Stories, edited by J.M. Reid, Oxford University Press, 1963, The Language of Love, edited by Michael Rheta Martin, Bantam, 1964,

Thy Neighbour's Wife, edited by James Turner, Cassell, 1964, The Fourth Ghost Book, edited by James Turner, Barrie & Rockliff, 1965, Unlikely Ghosts, edited by James Turner, Taplinger, 1969, and Penguin Book of Scottish Short Stories, edited by J.F. Hendry, Penguin, 1970. Contributor of about one hundred short stories to London Magazine, London Mercury, Adelphi, Horizon, Life and Letters, Spectator, New Statesman, Story, Harper's Bazaar, and other periodicals. Book reviewer for Time and Tide, Books of the Month, Sunday Telegraph, Oxford Mail, and other periodicals and newspapers.

WORK IN PROGRESS: A novel; short stories.

BIOGRAPHICAL/CRITICAL SOURCES: Listener, December 14, 1967; Punch, June 5, 1968; London Magazine, September, 1968.

* * *

UTECHIN, S(ergei) V(asilievich) 1921-

PERSONAL: Surname is pronounced U-te-kin; born December 18, 1921, in Tenki, Russia; married Patricia Rathbone, June 4, 1951; children: Nicholas. Education: University of Moscow, student, 1939-41; University of Kiel, Dr. Phil., 1949; Oxford University, B. Litt., 1954. Home: 14 St. Anne's Rd., Headington, Oxford, England. Office: St. Antony's College, Oxford, England.

CAREER: London School of Economics and Political Science, London, England, senior research officer in Soviet studies; St. Antony's College, Oxford University, Oxford, England, research fellow.

WRITINGS: Education and Social Mobility in the U.S.S.R., St. Antony's College, 1955; Everyman's Concise Encyclopaedia of Russia, Dutton, 1961, reissued as A Concise Encyclopaedia of Russia, 1964; (translator with wife, Patricia Utechin, and editor and author of introduction and notes) Vladimir Lenin, "What Is to Be Done?," Oxford University Press, 1963; Russian Political Thought: A Concise History, Praeger, 1964. Contributor to Survey, Soviet Studies, Problems of Communism, Russian Review, and other journals.†

* * *

UTT, Richard H. 1923-

PERSONAL: Born April 29, 1923, in Stoneham, Mass.; son of Charles D. (a professor of English) and Miriam (Clark) Utt; married Gwendolyn Woodward, July 6, 1947; children: Charles, Jeannette, David, Lynn. Education: Pacific Union College, B.A., 1945; Andrews University, M.A., 1958; University of California, Berkeley, postgraduate study in journalism, 1967. Home: 1325 Isabelle Ave., Mountain View, Calif. 94040.

CAREER: Seventh-day Adventists, foreign missionary in Panama and Costa Rica, 1948-57; Signs of the Times, Assistant editor, 1958-61; Pacific Press Publishing Association, Mountain View, Calif., book editor, 1961—. Awards, honors: Second prize ($350) for article in Liberty's Mr. Freedom Contest.

WRITINGS—All published by Pacific Press Publishing Association: A Century of Miracles, 1963, Quiz Time With Your Bible, 1965, Harris and the Pines, 1967, The Builders, 1970; (editor) Creation: Nature's Design and Designer, 1971. Contributor of about three hundred short stories and articles to religious magazines, 1946—.

* * *

VACZEK, Louis 1913-
(Peter Hardin)

PERSONAL: Born November 26, 1913, in Szeged, Hungary; son of Louis (a diplomat) and Jane (Szvoboda) Vaczek; married Katharine Pfeiffer (divorced); married

Barbara Chipman (divorced); children: (first marriage) Nicolas, Adam. *Education:* McGill University, B.Sc., 1935. *Politics:* Democrat. *Home:* 516 Oakdale, Chicago, Ill. 60657. *Office:* Encyclopaedia Britannica, 425 North Michigan Ave., Chicago, Ill. 60611.

CAREER: Employed as an engineer in Middle East, and as a lecturer and science editor, New York, N.Y., and Chicago, Ill. *Military service:* Royal Canadian Air Force, pilot, 1942-45.

WRITINGS: River and Empty Sea, Houghton, 1950; (under pseudonym Peter Hardin) *The Frightened Dove,* Scribner, 1951; (under pseudonym Peter Hardin) *The Hidden Grave,* Harper, 1955; (under pseudonym Peter Hardin) *The Golden Calf,* Sloane, 1956; *The Troubador,* Sloane, 1960. Also translator from the Hungarian of Imre Madacs' *Tragedy of Man. The Enjoyment of Chemistry,* Viking, 1964.

WORK IN PROGRESS: Two novels; a science book.

AVOCATIONAL INTERESTS: Sculpture.

*   *   *

Van ALSTYNE, Richard W(arner)   1900-

PERSONAL: Born August 19, 1900, in Sandusky, Ohio; son of Pierre L. (a businessman) and Anna E. (Paine) Van Alstyne; married Margaret Ware, March 29, 1930; children: Richard Ware, William Warner. *Education:* Harvard University, B.A., 1922; University of Southern California, M.A., 1924; Stanford University, Ph.D., 1928. *Home:* 1214 South Tuxedo, Stockton, Calif. 95204. *Office:* Callison College, University of the Pacific, Stockton, Calif. 95204.

CAREER: Chico State College, Chico, Calif., 1928-45, began as assistant professor, became professor; University of Southern California, Los Angeles, professor of American international history, 1945-65, professor emeritus, 1965—; Callison College, University of the Pacific, Stockton, Calif., Distinguished Professor of History, 1967—. University of London, London, England, Commonwealth Fund Lecturer, 1956, Fulbright fellow and honorary research associate, 1960-61. Visiting professor at Fletcher School of Law and Diplomacy, 1950; summer visiting professor at University of Washington, Seattle, 1948, University of Michigan, 1950, University of British Columbia, 1956, Queen's University, Kingston, Ontario, 1958; fellow, Henry E. Huntington Library and Art Gallery, 1965-66; external examiner, University of Toronto, 1969. *Military service:* U.S. Army, 1918.

MEMBER: American Historical Association (vice-president, Pacific Coast branch, 1962-63; president, 1963-64), Organization of American Historians, Athenaeum Club, (London). *Awards, honors:* Appointed Officier d'Academie by French Ministry of Education, 1938; research grants from American Philosophical Society and University of Southern California.

WRITINGS: American Diplomacy in Action, Stanford University Press, 1944, 3rd edition, Peter Smith, 1968; *American Crisis Diplomacy: The Quest for Collective Security, 1918-1952,* Stanford University Press, 1952; *The American Empire: Its Historical Pattern and Evolution,* Routledge & Kegan Paul, for the Historical Association, 1960, also published in *From Metternich to Hitler,* edited by W.N. Medlicott, Routledge & Kegan Paul, 1963; *The Rising American Empire,* Oxford University Press, 1960; *Empire and Independence: The International History of the American Revolution,* Wiley, 1965; *Genesis of American Nationalism,* Blaisdell, 1970; (contributor) William Williams, editor, *From Colony to Empire: Essays in the History of American Foreign Relations,*

Wiley, 1972; *The United States and East Asia,* Norton, 1973. Contributor to *International Affairs* (London), *Queen's Quarterly* (Canada), *Pacific Historical Review,* other journals. Member of board of editors, *Mississippi Valley Historical Review,* 1949-52; managing editor, *World Affairs Quarterly,* 1956-60.

WORK IN PROGRESS: A book on the decline of the American Empire.

AVOCATIONAL INTERESTS: Gardening, mountain hiking, camping.

*   *   *

Van BRIGGLE, Margaret F(rances) Jessup   1917-
(Frances Jessup)

PERSONAL: Born January 7, 1917, in Decatur County, Ind.; daughter of Frank Eldo and Myrtle (Patrick) Jessup; married Vard Lester Van Briggle (an ordained minister), October 14, 1933; children: Nancy Jean (Mrs. Donald Paul Shook). *Education:* Studied piano at Franklin Pilgrim College, practical nursing at Chicago School of Nursing. *Religion:* Protestant. *Home:* 303 Jackson St., Greensburg, Ind. 47240.

CAREER: Jessup Nursing Homes, Greensburg and Westport, Ind., administrator, 1962—. *Awards, honors:* Franklin Pilgrim College Alumni Association award for distinguished service as Christian layman, 1956.

WRITINGS: Wild Olive, West Publishing, 1950; *Eternal Heritage,* Beacon Hill Press, 1955; *The High Place,* Zondervan, 1964. Contributor of monthly feature article to *Pilgrim Youth News* for six years, and of more than twenty-five short stories to religious periodicals.

WORK IN PROGRESS: The Colonel, based on author's grandfather's life as country auctioneer; a novel about life of woman doctor in West Virginia mountains.

*   *   *

VANCE, Eleanor Graham   1908-

PERSONAL: Born October 16, 1908, in Pittsburgh, Pa.; daughter of J. Paul and Margaret (Hargrave) Graham; married W. Silas Vance (a professor), November 22, 1945; children: Eleanor Margaret (Mrs. John Raders), Dale Lines. *Education:* Westminster College, New Wilmington, Pa., B.A., 1930; Northwestern University, M.A. in Journalism, 1931; additional study at University of Pittsburgh, Columbia University, and Middlebury College. *Home and office:* 109 Austin Blvd., Edinburg, Tex. 78539.

CAREER: Akron Typesetting Co., Akron, Ohio, proofreader, 1931-32; Pittsburgh Public Schools, Pittsburgh, Pa., teacher, 1933-37, 1939-43, organized home teaching of handicapped children, 1935-37; Colonial Williamsburg, Williamsburg, Va., member of research department, 1944-45; Northwestern State College, Alva, Okla., teacher, 1954-55. Free-lance writer, 1931—; professional lecturer on literary and educational subjects, 1935—. Staff member for writers' conferences at West Texas State College, University of Oklahoma, Nebraska Wesleyan University. *Member:* Chi Omega, Delta Kappa Gamma (honorary). *Awards, honors:* Award of Merit of Northwestern University Alumni Association, 1938, for organizing home teaching of handicapped children in Pittsburgh; Litt.D., Westminster College, 1952; Achievement Award of Westminster College Alumni Association, 1956; George Washington Medal, Freedoms Foundation, 1958, for poem, "Jamestown".

WRITINGS: Christmas in Old England (operetta), Silver Burdett, 1938; *For These Moments* (poems), Stephen Daye Press, 1939; *A Musical Calendar,* Silver Burdett,

1940; *Canciones Pan-Americanas* (Latin-American folk-songs), Silver Burdett, 1942; (author of introduction) Arthur Guiterman, *Brave Laughter,* Dutton, 1943; *Henry the Helicopter,* Albert Whitman, 1945; (adapter) *Famous Fairy Tales,* Wonder Books, 1946; (adapter) *Favorite Nursery Tales,* Wonder Books, 1946; (adapter) *Bedtime Stories,* Wonder Books, 1946; (adapter) *The Tall Book of Fairy Tales Retold,* Harper, 1947; (adapter) Anna Sewell, *Black Beauty,* Random House, 1949.

Store in Your Heart (poems), Bookman Associates, 1950; (adapter) *Adventures of Robin Hood,* Random House, 1953; (compiler) *A Puffin Book of Verse,* Penguin, 1953; *The Story of Tweets, a Cat,* Twayne, 1956; *It Happens Every Day* (poems), Golden Quill, 1962; *Jonathan,* Follett, 1966; *Treasured Memories of Our Baby,* Gibson, 1970; *Little and Big* (poems), Follett, 1971. Contributor of poems and articles to *Good Housekeeping, Saturday Evening Post, New Yorker, Ladies' Home Journal, Saturday Review, Parents', New York Times, New York Herald Tribune,* and to children's magazines.

WORK IN PROGRESS: Children's books; a biography of Benito Juarez, for Hill and Wang; a book of activities for adults to enjoy with children.

SIDELIGHTS: "One of my pet peeves is all the theorizing that is done about children's literature. Children like a good story, and that is all there is to it.... I mourn the fact that verse is disappearing from our general magazines. When I read poetry to an audience they respond warmly, so I know people haven't suddenly stopped liking poetry." *Avocational interests:* Reading, music, swimming; travel and eating in foreign countries.

*   *   *

van den BERGHE, Pierre L.   1933-

PERSONAL: Born January 30, 1933, in Elisabethville, Congo; son of Louis (a medical doctor) and Denise (Caullery) van den Berghe; married Irmgard Niehuis, January 21, 1956; children: Eric, Oliver. *Education:* Stanford University, B.A., 1952, M.A., 1953; Sorbonne, University of Paris, postgraduate study, 1956-57; Harvard University, M.A., 1959, Ph.D., 1960. *Office:* Department of Sociology, University of Washington, Seattle, Wash. 98105.

CAREER: University of Natal, Durban, South Africa, lecturer in sociology, 1960-61; Sorbonne, University of Paris, Paris, France, lecturer in sociology, 1962; Wesleyan University, Middletown, Conn., assistant professor of sociology, 1962-63; State University of New York, Buffalo, associate professor of sociology, 1963-65; University of Washington, Seattle, professor of sociology, 1965—. *Military service:* U.S. Army, Medical Corps, 1954-56. *Member:* American Sociological Association, American Anthropological Association, African Studies Association. *Awards, honors:* Ford Foundation fellowship.

WRITINGS: (with Edna Miller) *Caneville: The Social Structure of a South African Town,* Wesleyan University Press, 1964; *South Africa, a Study in Conflict,* Wesleyan University Press, 1965; (editor) *Africa: Social Problems of Change and Conflict,* Chandler Publishing, 1965; *Race and Racism: A Comparative Perspective,* Wiley, 1967; (with Benjamin N. Colby) *Ixil County: A Plural Society in Highland Guatemala,* University of California Press, 1969; *Academic Gamesmanship: How to Make a Ph.D. Pay,* Abelard, 1970; *Race and Ethnicity: Essays in Comparative Sociology,* Basic Books, 1970; (editor) *Intergroup Relations: Sociological Perspective,* Basic Books, 1972; *Power and Privilege in an African University,* Schenkman, 1972.

SIDELIGHTS: Van den Berghe is fluent in French, German, and English; he reads Spanish, Portuguese, Dutch and Afrikaans. He has done field work in Mexico and South Africa.

BIOGRAPHICAL/CRITICAL SOURCES: Best Sellers, January 1, 1971.

*   *   *

VAN DEUSEN, Dayton G (roff)   1914-

PERSONAL: Born May 20, 1914, in Claverack, N.Y.; son of Robert J. (a Lutheran pastor) and Nettie (Groff) Van Deusen; married Margaret Van Raden, 1953. *Education:* Hartwick College, A.B., 1935; Hartwick Seminary, B.D., 1938; Union Seminary and Columbia University, S.T.M., 1956; clinical training at North Carolina Baptist Hospital, South Carolina State Hospital, Luther Theological Seminary, 1952, 1953-54, 1961.

CAREER: Minden and Manheim Lutheran Churches, Little Falls, N.Y., pastor, 1938-40; Gilead Lutheran Church, Troy, N.Y., pastor, 1940-51; Nebraska, Lutheran Social Service, Omaha, institutional chaplain, 1954-56; National Lutheran Council, Chicago, Ill., chaplaincy consultant, division of welfare, 1957-61; Lutheran General Hospital, Park Ridge, Ill., research fellow, 1961-62; Winnebago State Hospital & Lutheran Welfare Services of Wisconsin and Upper Michigan, hospital chaplain, 1962—. Hartwick College Board of Trustees, alumni representative, 1946-51, secretary, 1948-51. *Military service:* U.S. Army, 1943-46; became captain; served as infantry chaplain in Pacific Theater; awarded Bronze Star, Silver Star. *Member:* Lutheran Hospital Association, National Lutheran Social Welfare Conference, American Protestant Hospital Association, Association of Mental Hospital Chaplains, Conference of Lutheran Clinical Pastoral Educators, Wisconsin-Upper Michigan Synod of United Lutheran Church in America.

WRITINGS: (Contributor) *The Clergy and Psychiatry,* Nebraska Psychiatric Institute, 1957; *Redemptive Counseling: Relating Psychotherapy to the Personal Meanings in Redemption,* John Knox, 1960; (contributor) C.F. Kemp, editor, *Pastoral Preaching,* Bethany, 1963. Contributor to professional journals.

WORK IN PROGRESS: Research on religious attitudes and depression.

AVOCATIONAL INTERESTS: Fishing, travel, music, and bowling.

*   *   *

VAN DUYN, Mona   1921-

PERSONAL: Surname is pronounced "van dine"; born May 9, 1921, in Waterloo, Iowa; daughter of Earl George (a businessman) and Lora (Kramer) Van Duyn; married Jarvis A. Thurston (now a professor of English), August 31, 1943. *Education:* Iowa State Teachers College (now University of Northern Iowa), B.A., 1942; State University of Iowa, M.A., 1943, also further graduate work. *Politics:* Independent. *Religion:* None. *Home:* 7505 Teasdale Ave., St. Louis, Mo. 63130.

CAREER: State University of Iowa, Iowa City, instructor in English, 1945; University of Louisville, Louisville, Ky., instructor in English, 1946-50; University College, Washington University, St. Louis, Mo., lecturer in English, 1950-67. *Awards, honors:* Eunice Tietjens memorial prize, 1956, for "Three Valentines to the Wide World"; Helen Bullis Prize, *Poetry Northwest,* 1966; National Endowment for the Arts grant, 1966-67; Harriet Monroe Memorial Prize, 1968; Hart Crane Memorial Award, American Weave Press, 1968; first prize, Borestone Mountain Awards, 1968; Bollingen Prize, 1970; National Book Award for Poetry, 1971, for *To See, To Take;* D.Lett., Washington University, 1971, Cornell College, 1972; Guggenheim fellowship, 1972-73.

WRITINGS: Valentines to the Wide World (poems), Cummington, 1959; *A Time of Bees* (poems), University of North Carolina Press, 1964; *To See, To Take* (poems), Atheneum, 1970; *Bedtime Stories* (poems), Ceres, 1972. Anthologized in *The New Pocket Anthology of American Verse,* edited by Oscar Williams, Pocket Books, 1957, *Midland,* edited by Paul Engle, Random House, 1961, and *The Honey and the Gall,* edited by Chad Walsh, Macmillan, 1967.

Editor, *Perspective,* 1947—; poetry advisor, *College English,* 1955-57. Contributor of poems, short stories, critical articles, and reviews to *Kenyon Review, College English, Critique, American Prefaces, Western Review, Southern Review, Quarterly Review of Literature, Chelsea, Poetry Bag, Kayak, New American Review, New Republic, New Yorker, Epoch, Sewanee Review, Poetry, Perspective, Transatlantic Review,* and many other periodicals.

SIDELIGHTS: In 1965, James Dickey described Mona Van Duyn as "one of the best woman-poets around." Since that time, she seems to have shrugged off the qualifier, and has been increasingly accepted as a significant writer. H.C. Burke states that her "poems have in their free and varied syllabics an organic soundness at which we marvel." Of her latest volume of poems, *To See, To Take,* David Kalstone writes: "Like Scheherazade's stories they are accomplished, never ragged; and their restlessness, their driven quality, is apparent not in any hysteria or lapse in technique; but only in the felt necessity to continue to activity." The *Virginia Quarterly Review* reviewer believes that Miss Van Duyn's work has long merited critical attention. "Yet there are few poets whose dedication to the art [of poetry] is more intense, whose craftsmanship is more meticulous, whose verbal effects are more stunning, and whose visions are more intrinsically meaningful and wonderful."

In her acceptance speech for the 1971 National Book Award for Poetry, Miss Van Duyn aptly describes her own work in clarifying her intentions in writing poetry. "Poetry honors the formed use of language particularly, being concerned with both its sound and its meaning, and a poet spends his life's best effort in shaping these into a patterned experience which will combine an awareness of earlier patternings with the unique resonance of his own voice. He tries to do so in such a way that the experience may be shared with other people. This effort assumes a caring about other human beings, a caring which is a form of love."

AVOCATIONAL INTERESTS: Miss Van Duyn told *CA:* "I am interested in flower and vegetable gardening, dogs, D.N.A., Mexico City, cooking, fishing, sewing, the poem, the short story, the novel, the causes and cures of mental illness, old movies, myself, and other human beings, particularly my friends."

BIOGRAPHICAL/CRITICAL SOURCES: Library Journal, May 1, 1964, March 15, 1970; *New York Review of Books,* April 8, 1965; *Virginia Quarterly Review,* spring, 1965; *Poetry,* July, 1965; *New York Times Book Review,* November 21, 1965, August 2, 1970; *New York Times,* January 11, 1971.

* * *

Van PROOSDY, Cornelis 1919-

PERSONAL: Born November 5, 1919, in Amsterdam, Netherlands; married Elzina G. Hartzema (a pharmacologist), 1945. *Education:* University of Amsterdam, student, 1938-45, M.D., 1957. *Home:* Loosdrechtse Bos 5, Hilversum, Netherlands.

CAREER: Physician; specialist in internal diseases and geriatrics at Zonnestraal Hospital, Hilversum, Netherlands. *Member:* Several Dutch medical societies.

WRITINGS: Roken: Een Individueel—en Sociaalgeneeskundige Studie, Elsevier, 1957, translation by M.E. Hollander published in America as *Smoking: Its Influence on the Individual and Its Role in Social Medicine,* 1960. Contributor of articles to the Dutch medical press.†

* * *

Van STOCKUM, Hilda 1908-

PERSONAL: Born February 9, 1908, in Rotterdam, Netherlands; daughter of Abraham John and Olga Emily (Boissevain) van Stockum; married Ervin Ross Marlin (senior director of office of high Commissioner for Refugees), June 27, 1932; children: Olga, Brigid (Mrs. Benjamin Oakley), Randal, Sheila (Mrs. Shane O'Neill), John, Elisabeth. *Education:* Educated at art schools in Netherlands, France, and Ireland; also studied at Corcoran School of Art, Washington, D.C., 1936-37, and Thomas More Institute, Montreal, Quebec, 1959-61. *Politics:* Democrat. *Religion:* Roman Catholic.

CAREER: Author and illustrator of children's books; painter specializing in portraits and still life. *Member:* P.E.N., Authors' Club (Montreal).

WRITINGS—All self-illustrated, except as otherwise noted: *A Day on Skates: The Story of a Dutch Picnic,* foreword by Edna St. Vincent Millay, Harper, 1934; *The Cottage at Bantry Bay,* Viking, 1938; *Francie on the Run,* Viking, 1939; *Kersti and St. Nicholas,* Viking, 1940; *Pegeen,* Viking, 1941; *Andries,* Viking, 1942; *Gerrit and the Organ,* Viking, 1943; *The Mitchells,* Viking, 1945; *Canadian Summer,* Viking, 1948; *The Angels' Alphabet,* Viking, 1950; *Patsy and the Pup,* Viking, 1951; *King Oberon's Forest,* illustrations by daughter, Brigid Marlin, Viking, 1957; *Friendly Gables,* Viking, 1960; *Little Old Bear,* Viking, 1962; *The Winged Watchman,* Farrar, Straus, 1962; *Jeremy Bear,* Constable, 1963; *Bennie and the New Baby,* Constable, 1964; *New Baby Is Lost,* Constable, 1964; *Mogo's Flute,* illustrations by Robin Jacques, Viking, 1966; *Penengro,* Farrar, Straus, 1972.

Translator: (And illustrator) Rudolf Voorhoeve, *Tilio, a Boy of Papua,* Lippincott, 1937; J.M. Selleger-Elout, *Marian and Marion,* Viking, 1949; C.E. Pothast-Gimberg, *Corso the Donkey,* Constable, 1962.

Illustrator: Sjoukje Troelstra, *Afke's Ten,* Lippincott, 1936; Catherine C. Coblentz, *Beggar's Penny,* Longmans, Green, 1943; Catherine C. Coblentz, *Bells of Leyden Sing,* Longmans, Green, 1944; Louisa May Alcott, *Little Women,* World Publishing, 1946; Mary M. Dodge, *Hans Brinker; or, The Silver Skates,* World Publishing, 1946; May L. Becker, editor, *Book of Bible Stories,* World Publishing, 1948; Katherine D. Christ, *Willow Brook Farm,* Heath, 1948; Louisa May Alcott, *Little Men,* World Publishing, 1950. Contributor to *Horn Book, Canadian Banker,* and *Parents' Magazine.*

WORK IN PROGRESS: A book on Africa for children; memoirs of life with children; a fairy story set in Ireland; translating a Dutch book on rescuing children from the Nazis.

BIOGRAPHICAL/CRITICAL SOURCES: Horn Book, Christmas edition, 1944.

* * *

VAN WORMER, Joseph Edward 1913-
(Joe Van Wormer)

PERSONAL: Born June 15, 1913, in West Plains, Mo.; son of Allan and Vivian (Bohrer) Van Wormer; married Helen Williams, August 24, 1935; children: Alison (Mrs.

Keith Miles), Jill (Mrs. Allan Skorpen). *Education:* University of Missouri, student, 1930-33; Draughons Business College (Springfield, Mo.), student, 1933-35. *Home address:* Route 1, Box 537, Salem, Ore. 97304.

CAREER: Certified public accountant, Seattle, Wash., 1938-40, Portland, Ore., 1941-43, Bend, Ore., 1944-49; writer-photographer, Bend, Ore., 1949—. *Member:* Outdoor Writers Association of America.

WRITINGS: The World of the Bobcat, Lippincott, 1963; *The World of the Coyote,* Lippincott, 1964; (illustrator) A.J. Ricci, *Understanding and Training Horses,* Lippincott, 1964; *The World of the Black Bear,* Lippincott, 1966; *The World of the Canada Goose,* Lippincott, 1968; *The World of the Pronghorn,* Lippincott, 1969; *The World of the American Elk,* Lippincott, 1969; *The World of the Moose,* Lippincott, 1972; *The World of the Swan,* Lippincott, 1972. Contributor of articles to many national magazines, including *Life, Look, Sports Illustrated, Outdoor Life, True, Field and Stream.*

* * *

VARNADO, Jewel Goodgame 1915-

PERSONAL: Born November 3, 1915, in Collins, Miss.; daughter of John Gordon (a railroad construction foreman) and Mary Etta (Evans) Goodgame; married Lathan A. Varnado (deceased); children: Ray Varnado Clarke, Lathan A., Jr., Sandra Jean Draper. *Education:* Florida State University, A.B., M.A., postgraduate work. *Politics:* Democrat. *Religion:* Baptist. *Home:* 4304 Colonial Ave., Jacksonville, Fla. 32210.

CAREER: Teacher in Jacksonville, Fla., fourteen years. *Member:* National Education Association, Teachers Reading Council, Florida Educational Association, Duval County Classroom Teachers Association.

WRITINGS: Strait Ahead, Vantage, 1956; *English: Practice for Mastery,* Steck, 1961; *English: Practice for Mastery,* Books 1-4, Steck, 1962; *English Workbook for Adult Education,* Steck, 1964; *English Essentials: A Refresher Course,* Steck, 1964; *Basic Science for Living,* two volumes, Steck, 1965-66; (with Philip J. Gearing) *English Lessons for Adults: A Basic Course,* Harcourt, 1967. Author of children's stories.

WORK IN PROGRESS: Books for teen-agers; workbooks for adult education in science, literature, and social studies; children's stories.†

* * *

VAUGHN, Sister Ann Carol 1922-

PERSONAL: Born August 17, 1922, in Detroit, Mich.; daughter of Cornelius Aloyious (a Detroit fireman) and Beatrice (Eaton) Vaughn. *Education:* Siena Heights College, B.A., 1945; Loyola University, Chicago, Ill., M.A., 1950; Providence College, theology certificate, 1957; Michigan State University, Ph.D., 1957; Northwestern University, postdoctoral study. *Address:* Siena Heights College, Adrian, Mich. 49221.

CAREER: Roman Catholic nun, member of Dominican Order; name in religion, Sister Ann Carol. Teacher in elementary and secondary schools, 1942-62; Siena Heights College, Adrian, Mich., instructor in English, 1963—. *Member:* National Council of Teachers of English (associate chairman of two national meetings), Modern Language Association of America, Catholic Poetry Society of America, Michigan English Association, Notre Dame English Association, Chicago Archdiocesan English Association (founder; coordinating chairman, 1961-63).

WRITINGS—Editor: *Beginnings of American Literature,* Macmillan, 1961, revised edition, 1964; *Early Christian Writers,* Macmillan. Writer of book reviews and articles on teaching English.

WORK IN PROGRESS: Second revision of *Beginnings of American Literature;* an English project on composition, with books for grades seven to fourteen.†

* * *

VAUGHAN WILLIAMS, Ursula Lock 1911-

PERSONAL: Born March 15, 1911, in Valletta, Malta; daughter of Sir Robert Ferguson (an army officer) and Beryl (Penton) Lock; married Michael Forrester Wood (an army officer), May 24, 1933 (died, 1942); married Ralph Vaughan Williams (a composer), February 7, 1953 (died, 1958). *Education:* Attended private schools in England and Brussels, Belgium. *Home:* 69 Gloucester Crescent, London N.W.1, England.

CAREER: Activities, besides writing, have been connected largely with music. Member of committee of Musicians Benevolent Fund and trustee of National Folk Music Library and Butterworth Trust. Chairman of trustees, British Music Information Centre; member of governing body, Royal Academy of Music.

WRITINGS—Verse, under name Ursula Wood: *No Other Choice,* Basil Blackwell, 1941; *Fall of Leaf,* Basil Blackwell, 1943; *Need for Speech,* Basil Blackwell, 1948; *Wandering Pilgrimage,* Hand & Flower Press, 1952; *Silence and Music,* Essential Books, 1959.

Other books: (Translator, under name Ursula Wood) Engel Lund, *A Second Book of Folk Songs,* C. Fischer, 1947; (editor with Imogen Holst) Ralph Vaughan Williams and Gustav Holst, *Heirs and Rebels: Letters Written to Each Other and Occasional Writings on Music,* Oxford University Press, 1959; (editor with Holst) *A Yacre of Land: 16 Folk-songs from the Manuscript Collection of Ralph Vaughan Williams,* Oxford University Press, 1961; (author of preface) Ralph Vaughan Williams, *National Music and Other Essays,* Oxford University Press, 1963; *R.V.W.: A Biography of Ralph Vaughan Williams,* Oxford University Press, 1964; *Metamorphoses* (novel), Duckworth, 1966; *Set to Partners,* Duckworth, 1968.

Author of words for musical compositions: Ralph Vaughan Williams, *The Songs of Light: A Cantata for Chorus and Orchestra,* Oxford University Press, 1951; Ralph Vaughan Williams, *The Bridal Day,* Oxford University Press, 1956; Elizabeth Maconchy, "The Sofa" (one-act opera), 1959; Ralph Vaughan Williams, *Four Last Songs: For Medium Voice and Piano,* Oxford University Press, 1960; Charles Camileri, *Melita* (opera), Novello, 1968; David Barlow, "David and Bathsheba", 1969; Malcolm Williamson, *The Brilliant and the Dark: An Operatic Sequence,* Weinberger, 1969; Anthony Scott, *The Icy Mirror,* Weinberger, 1972; Anthony Scott, *Ode to Music,* Weinberger, 1972; Anthony Scott, "Serenade," 1972.

WORK IN PROGRESS: A pictorial biography of Ralph Vaughan Williams, with John Lunn.

AVOCATIONAL INTERESTS: The theatre and travel.

* * *

VAUSSARD, Maurice (Rene Jean Arthur Andre) 1888-

PERSONAL: Born September 8, 1888, in Ramburelles, Somme, France; son of Leon and Nelly (Delattre) Vaussard; married Madeleine Drouet, February 6, 1919. *Education:* Institution Sainte-Croix, Neuilly-sur-Seine, France, Licence es-lettres, 1908; Sorbonne, Universite de Paris, Diplome d'etudes superieures d'italien, 1909; attended University of Pisa. *Home:* 1, rue de Fleurus, Paris VI, France.

CAREER: Institut francais de Milan, Milan, Italy, sous-directeur, 1916-18; Ecole des Roches, Verneuil-sur-Avre, France, professor and "chef de maison," 1929-33; College de Normandie, Cleres, Seine-Maritime, France, directeur, 1934-38. Charge de conferences a l'Ecole pratique des hautes etudes, Paris, 1960. *Member:* Societe d'Histoire Moderne, Societe des Gens de Lettres (Paris). *Awards, honors:* Academie Francaise, Prix Barthou; Grand Prix du Rayonnement Francais; Prix Paul-Michel Perret; Prix Drouyn de Lluys; Academie des Sciences Morales et Politiques, Chevalier de la Legion d'Honneur; Commandeur du Merite de la Republique Italienne.

WRITINGS: (Editor) *Enquete sur le nationalisme: Reponses de Emile Baumann—Mgr. Batiffol—Hilaire Belloc,* Spes, 1924; *Histoire de l'Italie contemporaine, 1870-1946,* Hachette, 1950; *Histoire de la democratie chretienne,* Volume I: *France, Belgique, Italie,* Editions du Seuil, 1956; *La Vie quotidienne en Italie au XVIIIe siecle,* Hachette, 1959, translation by Michael Heron published as *Daily Life in Eighteenth Century Italy,* Allen & Unwin, 1962, Macmillan, 1963; *Jansenisme et gallicanisme aux origines religieuses, de Risorgimento,* Letouzey et Ane, 1959; *De Petrarque a Mussolini: Evolution du sentiment nationaliste italien,* Armand Colin, 1961; *Lettres a l'abbe Gregoire de l'ex-jesuite M.-J. Dufraisse, eveque constitutionnel du Cher,* Letouzey & Ane, 1962; *Correspondance Scipione de'Ricci-Henri Gregoire (1796-1807),* Marcel Didier, 1963; *La Fin du pouvoir emporel des papes,* Spes, 1964; *La Conjuration du grand conseil fasciste contre Mussolini,* Duca, 1965; *La Vie quotidienne a la naissance en fascisme,* Hachette, 1971. Contributor to periodicals and newspapers, including *Le Monde, L'Aube, Le Correspondant, Revue des Deux Mondes, Vita e Pensiero.* Has made numerous translations from Italian into French, including *Les Archives secretes du comte Ciano.*

*   *   *

VERDERY, John D(uane) 1917-

PERSONAL: Born March 4, 1917, in Berkeley, Calif.; son of Marion Jackson (in construction business) and Eleanor (Simonds) Verdery; married Suzanne Aldrich, June 17, 1942; children: Joan, Daniel, Donald, Benjamin. *Education:* Princeton University, B.A., 1939; Union Theological Seminary, student, 1939-41; Episcopal Theological School, B.D., 1942. *Home:* Wooster School, Danbury, Conn. 06810. *Agent:* Malcolm Reiss, Paul R. Reynolds & Son, 599 Fifth Ave., New York, N.Y. 10017.

CAREER: Ordained Episcopalian priest, 1942; Wooster School, Danbury, Conn., headmaster, 1943—. Trustee of Harvey School and Palm Beach Day School. *Member:* National Association of Episcopal Schools (treasurer), Headmasters Association, Century Club (New York). *Awards, honors:* D.D., Hobart College, 1959; Litt.D., Princeton University, 1963.

WRITINGS: Dedication of Window to Sarah Weston Angier, Stinehour Press, 1963; *It's Better to Believe,* M. Evans, 1964.

WORK IN PROGRESS: How to Stay Sane Over Thirty.

SIDELIGHTS: Verdery lived in France, 1963-64.

*   *   *

VICKERS, John 1916-

PERSONAL: Born December 7, 1916, in London, England; son of John Eliot Harrison and Rosa May (Whiting) Vickers; married Jean Watson (a dress designer), March, 1943; married Hazel Madeline Rushworth-Lund, December 21, 1960 (deceased); married Norma Maria Campbell (a teacher), May, 1967; children: (first marriage) Jonathan, Sarah; (stepchildren) Michael Healy, Timothy Healy. *Education:* Attended schools in London,

England. *Politics:* Basic Socialist. *Home and office:* 54 Kenway Rd., Earl's Court Village, London S.W.5, England. *Agent:* Rosica Colin, 4 Hereford Sq., London S.W.7, England.

CAREER: John Vickers Studio (artists, photographers, and marketing presentation consultants), London, England, principal, 1938—. Lecturer, Ealing School of Photography, 1968—. Consultant on graphic arts problems to Attwood Statistics Ltd. and Television Audience Measurement Ltd., 1957-60, and on color film surveys to Consumers' Association, 1962, 1965, 1967. Official photographer, Old Vic and other theater companies, 1942-58. *Military service:* British Army, Royal Artillery, 1939-42. *Member:* Institute of British Photographers (associate, 1950; fellow, 1957), Royal Society of Arts (fellow), Physical Society (color group).

WRITINGS: The Old Vic in Photographs, Saturn Press, 1947; (illustrator) Ralph Hill, *Orchestra in the South,* Southern Press, 1948; *Making and Printing Colour Negatives,* Fountain Press, 1959, Morgan & Morgan, 1964, 2nd edition, Fountain Press, 1971. Translator of works of Charles Dorat and Jean Tardieu. Contributor of articles to *Focal Encyclopedia of Photography* and to photography magazines.

AVOCATIONAL INTERESTS: Cooking.

*   *   *

VIDGER, Leonard P(erry) 1920-

PERSONAL: Born January 25, 1920, in Fargo, N.D.; son of Harry (a farmer) and May Eliza (Reynolds) Vidger; married Alice Esther Lorentzen (an elementary teacher); children: Karen Mae, Donald Leonard. *Education:* Studied at Dakota Business College, Fargo, N.D., 1937-38, Greenville College, 1945-47; Seattle Pacific College, B.A., 1948; University of Washington, Seattle, M.B.A., 1950; D.B.A., 1960; University of Southern California, M.S., 1954; additional study at New York University. *Politics:* Republican. *Religion:* Protestant. *Home:* 6500 Franklin St., Lincoln, Neb. 68506. *Office:* Department of Finance, University of Nebraska, Lincoln, Neb. 68508.

CAREER: Office and accounting positions in Minnesota, 1938-40; Stoudt Motor Co., Washpeton, N.D., chief accountant, 1940-41; Albert T. Bacon & Co. (certified public accountants), Chicago, Ill., senior accountant, 1946-47; Seattle Pacific College, Seattle, Wash., instructor in economics and business administration and college controller, 1953-54; San Francisco State College, San Francisco, Calif., assistant professor, 1955-60, associate professor, 1960-65, professor of business and director of Real Estate Research Program, 1965-70; University of Nebraska, Lincoln, professor of finance, 1970—. Visiting professor of accounting, University of Idaho, 1954-55. *Military service:* U.S. Naval Reserve, 1942-46, 1948—; on active duty 1942-46, 1951-53; currently holds rank of commander, Supply Corps. *Member:* American Accounting Association, American Finance Association, American Real Estate and Urban Economics Association, Financial Management Association, Regional Science Association, Rho Epsilon, Beta Gamma Sigma. *Awards, honors:* Summer college-business exchange fellowships, Foundation for Economic Education, 1954, 1957, 1960, 1966; faculty fellowship, Mortgage Bankers Association of America, 1970.

WRITINGS: (With others) *Washington State Statistical Abstract,* University of Washington Press, 1952; *Selected Cases and Problems in Real Estate,* Wadsworth, 1963; *Suggested Solutions to Selected Cases and Problems in Real Estate,* Wadsworth, 1963; *Residential Property in San Francisco: A Study of Price Movements and Trends in Financing, 1960-64,* Real Estate Research Program,

San Francisco State College, 1966; *San Francisco Housing Markets: A Study of Price Movements in 1958-1967, with Projections to 1975,* Real Estate Research Program, San Francisco State College, 1969. Contributor to business and academic journals.

WORK IN PROGRESS: Real Estate Mortgages as Investments for Individuals; research on variable interest rates in mortgages and on the San Francisco housing market, 1958-70.

AVOCATIONAL INTERESTS: Reading, mathematics, swimming, horseback riding, hiking, and hunting.

* * *

VILLAREJO, Mary (Holan) 1915-

PERSONAL: Surname is pronounced Villa-*ray*-ho; born January 30, 1915, in Milwaukee, Wis.; daughter of Vincent Charles (a tool-maker) and Frances (Marshalek) Holan; married Oscar M. Villarejo (a college professor), March, 1945. *Education:* Milwaukee State Teachers College (now University of Wisconsin, Milwaukee Campus), B.E. in Art Education, 1937; also studied at Corcoran Art School, Washington, D.C., and Art Students League, New York, N.Y. *Politics:* Democrat. *Religion:* Roman Catholic. *Home:* 4213 Jenifer St. N.W., Washington, D.C. 20015. *Agent:* Marion Vannett Ridgway, 299 Madison Ave., New York, N.Y. 10017.

CAREER: U.S. Central Intelligence Agency and Office of Strategic Services, Washington, D.C., cartographic draftsman, 1942-49; Norcross, Inc. (greeting cards), New York, N.Y., letterer, 1949-50; Time, Inc., New York, N.Y., staff artist, and staff artist for *Architectural Forum* and *House and Home,* 1950-53; Larry Smith & Co. (real estate consultants), Washington, D.C., art director, 1968—.

WRITINGS—Juveniles, all self-illustrated: *The Tiger Hunt,* Knopf, 1959; *The Art Fair,* Knopf, 1960; (illustrator) Ann Nolan Clark, *A Santo for Pasqualita,* Viking, 1960; *Fuzzy the Tiger,* Knopf, 1962; *The Famous Blue Gnu of Colonel Kachoo,* Knopf, 1964.

* * *

VINSON, J(ohn) Chal(mers) 1919-

PERSONAL: Born August 27, 1919, in Luebo, Belgian Congo (now Republic of Congo); son of Thomas Chalmers (a missionary) and Nan (Wharton) Vinson; married Almira Johnson, July 25, 1942; children: John Chalmers, Douglas C. *Education:* Davidson College, A.B., 1941; University of Georgia, M.A., 1944, M.F.A., 1947; Duke University, Ph.D., 1949. *Politics:* Democrat. *Religion:* Methodist. *Home:* Greenwood Dr., Athens, Ga. 30601. *Office:* Department of History, University of Georgia, Athens, Ga. 30601.

CAREER: University of Georgia, Athens, 1943—, now professor of American diplomatic history. William E. Borah Outlawry of War Foundation Lecturer, 1963. *Member:* Organization of American Historians, Southern Historical Association, Phi Kappa Phi. *Awards, honors:* Guggenheim fellow, 1957-58.

WRITINGS: The Parchment Peace: The United States Senate and the Washington Conference, 1921-22, University of Georgia Press, 1955; *William E. Borah and the Outlawry of War,* University of Georgia Press, 1957; *Isolation and Security,* edited by Alexander DeConde, Duke University Press, 1957; *Referendum for Isolation: Defeat of Article Ten of the League of Nations Covenant,* University of Georgia Press, 1961; *An Uncertain Tradition,* edited by Normand Grasbner, McGraw, 1961; (with Marian C. McKenna, Claudius O. Johnson, and Frank Church) *Senator William E. Borah: His Contribution to Peace,* University of Idaho, 1964; *Thomas Nast,*

Political Cartoonist, University of Georgia Press, 1967. Contributor of articles to historical journals.

WORK IN PROGRESS: The United States, Australia and Pacific Security; The United States Senate and American Foreign Policy, 1931-41.

AVOCATIONAL INTERESTS: Oil painting, wood carving, furniture refinishing, collecting antiques.

BIOGRAPHICAL/CRITICAL SOURCES: Georgia Review, spring, 1969.

* * *

VIORST, Milton 1930-

PERSONAL: Born February 18, 1930, in Paterson, N.J.; son of Louis and Betty (Levine) Viorst; married Judith Stahl (a poet and syndicated humorist), January 30, 1960; children: Anthony Jacob, Nicholas Nathan, Alexander Noah. *Education:* Rutgers University, B.D., 1951; Harvard University, M.A., 1954; Columbia University, M.S., 1955; postgraduate study at University of Lyon. *Home:* 1725 Q St., Washington, D.C. 20009.

CAREER: New York Post, Washington correspondent, 1961-64; *Washington Star,* Washington, D.C., syndicated political columnist, 1964—; free-lance writer. *Military service:* U.S. Air Force, Intelligence, 1952-54; became first lieutenant.

WRITINGS: Liberalism: A Guide to Its Past, Present and Future in American Politics, introduction by Hubert H. Humphrey, Avon, 1963; *Hostile Allies: F.D.R. and Charles de Gaulle,* Macmillan, 1965; *The Great Documents of Western Civilization,* Chilton, 1965; *Fall from Grace: The Republican Party and the Puritan Ethic,* New American Library, 1968; (with wife, Judith Viorst) *The Washington, D.C. Underground Gourmet,* Simon & Schuster, 1970; (with Clinton P. Anderson) *Outsider in the Senate: Senator Clinton Anderson's Memoirs,* World Publishing, 1970; *Hustlers and Heroes,* Simon & Schuster, 1971. Contributor to *Harper's, Nation, Esquire, New York Times Magazine,* and *Figaro Citteraire.*

BIOGRAPHICAL/CRITICAL SOURCES: Book World, May 19, 1968; *Newsweek,* May 20, 1968; *Washington Post,* May 21, 1968; *New York Review of Books,* June 20, 1968; *New York Times Book Review,* August 4, 1968; *Christian Science Monitor,* September 14, 1968; *New York,* January 19, 1970.

* * *

VISSER 'T HOOFT, Willem Adolf 1900-

PERSONAL: Born September 20, 1900, in Haarlem, The Netherlands; son of Hendrik Philip and Jacoba (Lieftinck) Visser 't Hooft; married Henriette Boddaert, 1924 (died, 1968); children: Anna Johanna Visser 't Hooft Musacchio, Hendrik Philip, Cornelis. *Education:* Leiden University, theological doctorate, 1928. *Home:* 13 chemin des Voirons, Chene-Bougeries, Geneva, Switzerland. *Office:* 150, Route de Ferney, 1211, Geneva 20, Switzerland.

CAREER: Ordained pastor, Netherlands Reformed Church and Protestant Church of Geneva. World's Alliance of Young Men's Christian Association, Geneva, Switzerland, secretary, 1924-31; World's Student Christian Federation, Geneva, Switzerland, general secretary, 1931-38; World Council of Churches, Geneva, Switzerland, general secretary, 1938-66, honorary president, 1968; Honorary professor, Budapest University, 1946, Theological Academy, Moscow, U.S.S.R., 1964. Honorary fellow, Hebrew University, 1972. Lecturer, radio and television speaker.

AWARDS, HONORS: Medal of gratitude, Netherlands Government, 1946; Commander of Order of Dutch Lion, 1948; Grand Cross in Order of Merit, Federal Republic of Germany, 1957; Officer of the Legion of Honor of France, 1959; van de Wateler Peace Prize, 1962; great silver medal, City of Paris, 1962; Cross of Great Commander of Holy Sepulchre, 1963; Peace prize, Booksellers and Publishers Association, German Federal Republic, 1966; Sonning Prize, Copenhagen, 1967; Order of Prince of Cilicia, 1967; honorary commander, Order of St. John, 1968. *Degrees:* D.D. from Aberdeen University, 1939, Princeton University, 1950, Trinity College (Toronto, Ontario), 1950, University of Geneva, 1951, Yale Divinity School, 1954, Oberlin College, 1954, Oxford University, 1955, Harvard University, 1958, St. Paul's University (Tokyo, Japan), 1959, Faculte Libre de Theologie Protestante (Paris), 1963, Kirchliche Hochschule (Berlin), 1964, Brown University, 1965, Zurich Theological Faculty, 1966, University of Louvain, 1967.

WRITINGS: The Background of the Social Gospel in America, H.D. Tjeenk Willink & Sons, 1928, Bethany Press, 1963; (editor) *A Traffic in Knowledge,* S.C.M. Press, 1931; *Anglo-Catholicism and Orthodoxy: A Protestant View,* S.C.M. Press, 1933; *None Other Gods,* introduction by Reinhold Niebuhr, Harper, 1937; (with J.H. Oldham) *The Church and Its Function in Society,* Willett, Clark & Co., 1937.

Die Mission als oekumenische Tat, Basler Missionsbuchhandlung, 1941; *Misere et grandeur de l'eglise,* Labor et Fides, 1943, translation by Dorothy Mackie and Hugh Martin published as *The Wretchedness and Greatness of the Church,* S.C.M. Press, 1944; (editor) *Hollaendische kirchendokumente: Der Kampf der hollaendischen Kirche um die Geltung der goettlichen Gebote im Staatsleben,* Evangelischer Verlag, 1944, translation by Tilly Weinstock published as *The Struggle of the Dutch Church for the Maintenance of the Commandments of God in the Life of the State,* S.C.M. Press, 1944, American Committee for the World Council of Churches, 1945; *Rembrandt et la Bible,* Delachaux et Niestle, 1947, translation by K. Gregor Smith published as *Rembrandt and the Gospel,* revised edition, S.C.M. Press, 1957, Westminster, 1958; (editor) *Man's Disorder and God's Design,* Volume V: *The First Assembly of the World Council of Churches: Official Report,* S.C.M. Press, 1948-49, Harper, 1949; *The Kingship of Christ: An Interpretation of Recent European Theology,* Harper, 1948.

The Ecumenical Movement and the Racial Problem, UNESCO (Paris), 1954; *The Meaning of Ecumenical,* S.C.M. Press, 1954; *Our Ecumenical Task in the Light of History,* John Knox House Association, 1955; *The Renewal of the Church,* S.C.M. Press, 1956, Westminster, 1957; *Rembrandt et nous,* Berger-Levrault, 1956; *Die Sammlung der zerstreuten Kinder Gottes,* Evangelischer Missionsverlag, 1956; *The Pressure of Our Common Calling,* Doubleday, 1959.

(Editor) *The New Delhi Report: The Third Assembly of the World Council of Churches, 1961,* S.C.M. Press, 1962; (editor) *New Delhi Speaks About Christian Witness, Service and Unity: The Message, Appeal, and Section Reports,* Association Press, 1962; *No Other Name: The Choice Between Syncretism and Christian Universalism,* Westminster Press, 1963; (with Jacques Freymond) *The International Civil Servant and Today's World,* Foyer John Knox Association, 1965; (author of foreword) Robert C. Mackie and others, *Layman Extraordinary: John R. Mott, 1865-1955,* Association Press, 1965; (with Guenter Jacob) *Dietrich Bonhoeffer 1945-1965,* Lettner-Verlag, 1965; *Oekumenische Bilanz,* Evangelischer Missionsverlag, 1966; *Hauptschriften,* translation by Werner Simpfendoerfer, edited by Hans Juergen Schultz, Kreuz-Verlag, Volume I: *Die Ganze Kirche fuer die ganze Welt,* 1967, Volume II: *Oekumenischer Aufbruch,* 1967; (with Augustin Bea) *Friede zwischen Christen,* Herder (Geneva), 1966, translation by Judith Moses published as *Peace Among Christians,* Association Press, 1967; *Christians for the Future,* British Broadcasting Corp., 1967; *Leren Leven met de oecumene,* G.F. Callenbach, 1968; *Die Welt war meine Gemeinde* (autobiography), Piper Verlag, 1972. Editor, *Ecumenical Review,* 1948-66.

BIOGRAPHICAL/CRITICAL SOURCES: Time, December 8, 1961.

*   *   *

VLASIC, Ivan Albert   1926-

PERSONAL: Born July 29, 1926, in Gorizia, Italy; son of Jovan (a lawyer) and Ljerka Vlasic; married Katherine C. Parker, November 17, 1956; children: Edward Parker, John Barry. *Education:* University of Zagreb, B.C.L., 1949; McGill University, LL.M., 1955; Yale University, LL.M., 1958, J.S.D., 1961. *Religion:* United Church of Canada. *Home:* 669 Warwick, Dr., Baie d'Urfe, Quebec, Canada. *Office:* McGill University, 3644 Peel, Montreal, Quebec, Canada.

CAREER: University of Zagreb, Zagreb, Yugoslavia, assistant professor of law, 1950-53; University of Florida, Gainesville, assistant professor of law, 1958-59; Ottawa University, Ottawa, Ontario, assistant professor of law, 1962-63; McGill University, Montreal, Quebec, Canada, associate professor, 1963-69, professor of law, 1969—. *Member:* International Law Association, American Society of International Law, Quebec Civil Liberties Union.

WRITINGS: (With M.S. McDougal and H.D. Lasswell) *Law and Public Order of Space,* Yale University Press, 1963; (editor) John Cobb Cooper, *Explorations in Aerospace Law: Selected Essays,* McGill University Press, 1968. Contributor to law journals.

*   *   *

VOIGT, Milton   1924-

PERSONAL: Born March 19, 1924, in Milwaukee, Wis.; son of Arthur W. (a realtor) and Esther (Bartelt) Voigt; married Leta Jean Slack, July 29, 1947; children: John Gregory, James, Andrew. *Education:* University of Wisconsin, Ph.B., 1948; University of California, M.A., 1950; University of Minnesota, Ph.D., 1960. *Home:* 1376 Princeton Ave., Salt Lake City, Utah 84105. *Office:* Department of English, University of Utah, Salt Lake City, Utah 84112.

CAREER: University of Idaho, Moscow, instructor in English, 1952-55; University of Kentucky, Lexington, instructor in English, 1956-60; University of Utah, Salt Lake City, assistant professor, 1960-64, associate professor, 1964-68, professor of English, 1968—, associate dean of College of Letters and Science, 1965-66, acting dean, 1966-67, dean, 1967-70, chairman of department of English, 1971—. *Military service:* U.S. Army Air Forces, 1943-45; became second lieutenant. *Member:* American Association of University Professors, Modern Language Association of America.

WRITINGS: Swift and the Twentieth Century, Wayne State University Press, 1964.

*   *   *

von der MEHDEN, Fred R.   1927-

PERSONAL: Born December 1, 1927, in San Francisco, Calif.; son of Fred and Margaret (de Valasco) von der Mehden; married Audrey Whitehead, December 27, 1954; children: Laura W., Victoria M. *Education:* University of Pacific, B.A., 1948; Claremont Graduate School, M.A., 1950; University of California, Berkeley, Ph.D., 1957. *Home:* 12530 Mossycup Dr., Houston, Tex. 77024. *Office:* Rice University, Houston, Tex. 77001.

CAREER: University of Wisconsin, Madison, 1957-68, became professor of political science and chairman of East Asian studies; Rice University, Houston, Tex., Albert Thomas Professor of Political Science, 1968—. Member: Association for Asian Studies, Bibliothek van Land-Tall-en Volkenkunde. Awards, honors: Fulbright research grant for Burma, 1959-60; Ford Foundation grant for Southeast Asia, 1963.

WRITINGS: Religion and Nationalism in Southeast Asia, University of Wisconsin Press, 1963; Politics of the Developing Nations, Prentice-Hall, 1964, 2nd edition, revised, 1969; (with Charles W. Anderson and Crawford Young) Issues of Political Development, Prentice-Hall, 1967; (co-editor) Local Authority and Administration in Thailand, AACT, 1970; (contributor) The Military in Five Developing Nations, CRESS, 1970; Comparative Political Violence, Prentice-Hall, 1972. Contributor to Studies on Asia, 1961 and 1964; also contributor to Antioch Review, Asian Survey, Pacific Affairs, other journals.

WORK IN PROGRESS: Writing on the legacy of colonialism and nationalism in Southeast Asia; research on political ramifications of income distribution in Malaysia.

SIDELIGHTS: Von der Mehden reads Burmese as well as some European languages, and has done field research in Thailand, Burma, and Malaysia.

BIOGRAPHICAL/CRITICAL SOURCES: New Leader, November 4, 1968.

* * *

Von LAUE, Theodore Herman 1916-

PERSONAL: Surname rhymes with flower; born June 22, 1916, in Frankfurt am Main, Germany; son of Max and Magda (Milkau) Von Laue; married Hildegard Hunt (a teacher); children: Christopher, Madeleine, Esther. Education: University of Freiburg, student, 1936-37; Princeton University, A.B., 1939, Ph.D., 1944; Columbia University, Certificate of Russian Institute, 1948. Politics: Independent. Religion: Society of Friends. Office: History Department, Clark University, Worcester, Mass. 01610.

CAREER: Princeton University, Princeton, N.J., instructor in history, 1943-45, 1947; University of Pennsylvania, Philadelphia, instructor in history, 1948-49; Swarthmore College, Swarthmore, Pa., assistant professor of history, 1949-52; Bryn Mawr College, Bryn Mawr, Pa., lecturer in history, 1952-54; University of California, Riverside, 1954-64, began as assistant professor, became professor of history; Washington University, St. Louis, Mo., professor of history, 1964-70; Clark University, Worcester, Mass., professor of history, 1970—. Military service: U.S. Army, Medical corps. Member: American Historical Association, American Association for the Advancement of Slavic Studies, Economic History Association, American Association of University Professors. Awards, honors: Fulbright scholar in Finland, 1954-55; Guggenheim fellow, 1962-63.

WRITINGS: Leopold Ranke, the Formative Years, Princeton University Press, 1950; Sergei Witte and the Industrialization of Russia, Columbia University Press, 1963; Why Lenin? Why Stalin? A Reappraisal of the Russian Revolution, 1900-1930, Lippincott, 1964; The Great Powers, Leopold Ranke, the Formative Years, University of Chicago Press, 1964; The Global City: Freedom, Power, and Necessity in the Age of World Revolution, Lippincott, 1969. Contributor of articles and reviews to German and American scholarly journals, and articles to cooperative volumes on Russia.

WORK IN PROGRESS: Research on the westernization of the Gold Coast-Ghana; global perspectives for contemporary history.

BIOGRAPHICAL/CRITICAL SOURCES: New Leader, June 27, 1969.

* * *

VOSS, Earl H. 1922-

PERSONAL: Born February 25, 1922, in LaCrosse, Wis.; son of Arthur H. and Lilah B. (Major) Voss; married Marie F. Coughlin, October 26, 1947; children: Stephen, Philip, Martha. Home: 8109 Ainsworth Ave., Springfield, Va. 22152.

CAREER: Washington Star, Washington, D.C., diplomatic correspondent, 1951-64; with American Enterprise Institute for Public Policy Research, 1964-70; research director for Senator Robert P. Griffin. Military service: U.S. Army; became technical sergeant.

WRITINGS: Nuclear Ambush: The Test-Ban Trap, Regnery, 1963.

* * *

VROOM, Victor H(arold) 1932-

PERSONAL: Born August 9, 1932, in Montreal, Quebec; son of Harold H. (an electrical engineer) and Avice (Brown) Vroom; married Ann Workman (a clinical psychologist), June 12, 1956; children: Derek. Education: McGill University, B.Sc., 1953, M.Sc., 1955; University of Michigan, Ph.D., 1958. Home: 610 Foxhurst Dr., Pittsburgh, Pa. 15238.

CAREER: University of Michigan, Ann Arbor, lecturer in psychology, 1955-60; University of Pennsylvania, Philadelphia, assistant professor of psychology, 1960-63; Carnegie Institute of Technology, Pittsburgh, Pa., associate professor of industrial administration and psychology, 1963—. Former professional musician, playing saxophone and clarinet. Member: International Congress of Applied Psychology, American Psychological Association, Society for the Psychological Study of Social Issues, Eastern Psychological Association. Awards, honors: Ford Foundation faculty fellowship.

WRITINGS: Some Personality Determinants of the Effects of Participation, Prentice-Hall, 1960; Work and Motivation, Wiley, 1964; Motivation in Management, American Foundation for Management Research, 1965; (editor and author of foreword) Methods of Organizational Research, University of Pittsburgh Press, 1967; (editor with Edward L. Deci) Management and Motivation: Selected Readings, Penguin, 1970. Contributor of chapters to books and articles to psychological journals. Consulting editor, Wadsworth Publishing Co.

WORK IN PROGRESS: Research on individual motivation and organizational behavior.

AVOCATIONAL INTERESTS: Gardening.†

* * *

WADE, Mason 1913-

PERSONAL: Born July 3, 1913, in New York, N.Y.; son of Alfred B. (a merchant) and Helena (Mein) Wade. Education: Harvard University, student 1931-35. Home: R.F.D. 2, Windsor, Vt. 05089.

CAREER: Publisher's editor and free-lance writer, New York, N.Y., 1935-43; Guggenheim fellow in Canadian history, 1943-45; research under Rockefeller grant, 1946-47, Carnegie Corp. grant, 1948-49; U.S. Embassy, Ottawa, Ontario, public affairs officer, 1951-53; University of Rochester, Rochester, N.Y., associate professor of history, 1955-61, professor, 1961-65, director of Canadian studies program, 1955-65; University of Western Ontario, London, professor of history and chairman of department, Middlesex College, 1965-66, senior professor of history, 1966-72. Lecturer at summer session, Laval University,

1946-49, University of British Columbia, 1954; Gray Lecturer at University of Toronto, 1954; visiting fellow at Institute of Canadian Studies, Carleton University, 1963.

MEMBER: American Historical Association (chairman, American section, joint committee of American and Canadian Historical Associations, 1963-64), Canadian Historical Association (council, 1955-58; vice-president, 1963-64; president, 1964-65), Canadian Political Science Association, Canadian Association of Geographers, Arctic Institute, New York State Historical Association. *Awards, honors:* M.A. from McGill University, 1953; LL.D. from University of New Brunswick, 1957; Litt.D. from University of Ottawa, 1963; Lieutenant Governor of Quebec Medal, 1957; Canada Council grants, 1958, 1959, 1963.

WRITINGS: Margaret Fuller, Whetstone of Genius, Viking, 1940; (editor) *Selected Writings of Margaret Fuller,* Viking, 1941; *Francis Parkman, Heroic Historian,* Viking, 1942; (editor) *The Oregon Trail,* Limited Editions Club, 1943; *The French-Canadian Outlook: A Brief Account of the Unknown North Americans,* Viking, 1946, reissued with a new introduction by Wade, McClelland & Stewart, 1964; (editor) *The Journals of Francis Parkman,* two volumes, Harper, 1947; (contributor) Tom Twitty, *Canada, a Great Small Power,* Foreign Policy Association, 1954; *The French Canadians, 1760-1945,* two volumes, Macmillan, 1955, revised edition published as *The French Canadians, 1760-1967,* 1968; (editor) *Canadian Dualism: Studies of French-English Relations,* University of Toronto Press, 1960; (editor) *Regionalism in the Canadian Community, 1867-1967: Canadian Historical Association Centennial Seminars,* University of Toronto Press, 1969; (editor) *The International Megalopolis,* University of Toronto Press, 1969.

WORK IN PROGRESS: Research in Canadian-American relations, French Canada, interaction between the Acadians, the New Englanders, and the early British immigrants in the Maritime Provinces, 1755.

BIOGRAPHICAL/CRITICAL SOURCES: Library Journal, March 15, 1970.

* * *

WADSWORTH, Frank W (hittemore) 1919-

PERSONAL: Born June 14, 1919, in New York, N.Y.; son of Prescott Kingsley (an engineer and rancher) and Elizabeth B. Whittemore; married Roxalene H. Nevin, October 22, 1943; children: Susan Browning, Roxalene Elizabeth. *Education:* Princeton University, A.B., 1946, M.A., 1948, Ph.D., 1951. *Home:* Bailiwick Rd., Greenwich, Conn. 06830. *Office:* State University of New York at Purchase, Purchase, N.Y. 10577.

CAREER: Princeton University, Princeton, N.J., instructor in English, 1949-50; University of California, Los Angeles, began as assistant professor, became associate professor of English, 1950-61; University of Pittsburgh, Pittsburgh, Pa., professor of English and dean of Division of Humanities, 1962-67; State University of New York at Purchase, professor of English and academic vice-president, 1967—. Woodrow Wilson National Fellowship Foundation, national representative and consultant, 1957-61. *Military service:* U.S. Naval Reserve, naval aviator; became lieutenant j.g. *Member:* Modern Language Association of America, American Society for Theatre Research, Malone Society. *Awards, honors:* Woodrow Wilson fellow, 1946-47; Folger Shakespeare Library fellow, 1961; Guggenheim fellow, 1961-62.

WRITINGS: The Poacher From Stratford: A Partial Account of the Controversy Over the Authorship of Shakespeare's Plays, University of California Press, 1958; (contributor) Alfred Harbage, editor, *The Complete Pelican Shakespeare,* Penguin, 1969. Contributor of articles and reviews to professional journals and other periodicals.

WORK IN PROGRESS: Research in nineteenth-century revivals of non-Shakespearean Elizabethan plays.

* * *

WAGNER, Linda Welshimer 1936-

PERSONAL: Born August 18, 1936, in St. Marys, Ohio; daughter of Sam A. (a merchant) and Esther (Scheffler) Welshimer; married Paul V. Wagner (with International Business Machines), January 22, 1957; children: Paul Douglas, Thomas Anderson, Andrea Townsend. *Education:* Bowling Green State University, B.A. (magna cum laude), 1957, B.S. (magna cum laude), 1957, M.A., 1959, licentiate, 1961, Ph.D., 1963. *Politics:* Undecided. *Religion:* Methodist. *Office:* Morrill Hall, Michigan State University, East Lansing, Mich. 48823.

CAREER: High school teacher for three years; Bowling Green State University, Bowling Green, Ohio, instructor in English, 1960-64; Wayne State University, Detroit, Mich., assistant professor of English, 1966-68; Michigan State University, East Lansing, associate professor of English, 1968—. *Member:* Modern Language Association of America, American Association of University Professors, Delta Gamma, Detroit Women Writers.

WRITINGS: The Poems of William Carlos Williams: A Critical Study, Wesleyan University Press, 1964; *Denise Levertov,* Twayne, 1967; *Intaglios: Poems,* South & West, 1967; *The Prose of William Carlos Williams,* Wesleyan University Press, 1970; *Phyllis McGinley,* Twayne, 1970. Contributor of over 130 essays and poems to scholarly and poetry periodicals, including *Kenyon Review, Shakespeare Quarterly,* and *Minnesota Review.*

WORK IN PROGRESS: A volume of collected poems; a critical study of Faulkner, Hemingway, Dos Passos, and Stein.

BIOGRAPHICAL/CRITICAL SOURCES: Library Journal, November 1, 1970.

* * *

WAHL, Paul (Francis) 1922-

PERSONAL: Born January 17, 1922, in Union City, N.J.; son of Frank Joseph (a gunsmith) and Anne (Frechen) Wahl. *Education:* Attended parochial and public schools in Bogota, N.J. *Home address:* P.O. Box 6, Bogota, N.J. 07603.

CAREER: Free-lance writer and photographer. Wahl Arms Co., Bogota, N.J., partner, 1948-68; Wahl Co. (medalists), Bogota N.J., owner, 1962-68, and designer of commemorative medals, including Saint Sebastian, Gatling Gun Centennial, Ulysses S. Grant, and Robert E. Lee. *Member:* American Society of Magazine Photographers, Authors Guild of Authors League of America, Aviation/Space Writers Association, National Association of Science Writers, Outdoor Writers Association of America, Society of Magazine Writers.

WRITINGS: The Gun Trader's Guide, Greenberg, 1953, revised 3rd edition published as *Gun Value Guide,* Modern Guide Publications, 1962, revised 4th edition published as *Shooter's Bible: Gun Trader's Guide,* Shooter's Bible, Inc., 1964, revised 5th edition, 1968; *Single Lens Reflex Guide,* Chilton, 1959, revised 2nd edition, 1960; *Subminiature Technique,* Chilton, 1960; *Press/View Camera Technique,* Chilton, 1962; *The Candid Photographer,* Chilton, 1963; *Carbine Handbook: The Complete Manual and Guide to U.S. Carbine, cal. .30, M1,* Arco, 1964; (with Donald R. Toppel) *The Gatling Gun,* Arco, 1965. Compiler and publisher of *Arms Trade Yearbook,* 1955. Contributor to popular magazines.

WAHL, Thomas (Peter) 1931-
(Father Caedmon)

PERSONAL: Born November 23, 1931, in St. Cloud, Minn.; son of Arthur Lewis (a contractor) and Romana (Seberger) Wahl. *Education:* St. John's University, Collegeville, Minn., B.A., 1954; Catholic University of America, Licentiate in Theology, 1959; Pontifical Biblical Institute, Licentiate in Scripture, 1967; Union Theological Seminary, New York, N.Y., student, 1969—. *Home:* St. John's Abbey, Collegeville, Minn. 56321. *Office:* St. John's University, Collegeville, Minn. 56321.

CAREER: Saint John's Abbey, Collegeville, Minn., Roman Catholic monk, 1951—; ordained priest, 1958; St. Bernard's Parish, St. Paul, Minn., assistant pastor, 1959-61; St. Boniface Parish, Minneapolis, Minn. assistant pastor, 1961-64; St. John's University, Collegeville, Minn., instructor in theology, 1967—.

WRITINGS: (Under name Father Caedmon) *How Jesus Came,* North Central Publishing, 1959; (editor) *Library Index to Biblical Journals,* St. John's University Press, 1971. Regular anonymous contributor to *Worship,* 1955-58.

WORK IN PROGRESS: Judith, Esther (Old Testament reading guides), for Liturgical Press.

AVOCATIONAL INTERESTS: Vegetable gardening, mushroom hunting, "and such odd things."

* * *

WAITE, P(eter) B(usby) 1922-

PERSONAL: Born July 12, 1922, in Toronto, Ontario, Canada; son of Cyril and Mary (Craig) Waite; married Masha Gropuzzo, August 22, 1958; children: Alice Nina, Anya Mary. *Education:* University of British Columbia, B.A. (with honors), 1948, M.A., 1950; University of Toronto, Ph.D., 1954. *Home:* 53 Laurentide Dr., Halifax, Nova Scotia, Canada. *Office:* Dalhousie University, Halifax, Nova Scotia, Canada.

CAREER: Dalhousie University, Halifax, Nova Scotia, lecturer, 1951-54, assistant professor, 1955-59, associate professor, 1960-62, professor of history, 1962—, head of department, 1960-68. University of Western Ontario, London, Ontario, senior professor, 1963-64. *Military service:* Royal Canadian Navy, 1941-45. *Member:* Canadian Historical Association (member of council, 1960-63; president, 1968-69), Historic Sites and Monuments Board of Canada, Nova Scotia Historical Society, Champlain Society.

WRITINGS: The Life and Times of Confederation, 1864-1867: Politics, Newspapers, and the Union of British North America, University of Toronto Press, 1962, 2nd edition, 1967; (editor) *The Confederation Debates in the Province of Canada, 1865,* McClelland & Stewart, 1963; *The Charlottetown Conference, 1864* (booklet), Canadian Historical Association, 1963; (editor) *Canadian Historical Documents Series,* Volume 2: *Pre-Confederation,* Prentice-Hall of Canada, 1965; *Canada, 1874-1896,* McClelland & Stewart, 1971; *Confederation: Canadian Studies,* Holt, 1972. Editor, Canada, House of Commons, *Debates, 1867-8,* 1968, Canada, Senate, *Debates, 1867-68,* 1968, Canada, House of Commons and Senate, *Debates, 1869,* 1971.

WORK IN PROGRESS: Early Travellers in the Atlantic Colonies, 1700-1867, to be published by Macmillan of Canada; a book on Canadian history through the present, for Holt of Canada.

* * *

WAITE, Robert G(eorge) L(eeson) 1919-

PERSONAL: Born February 18, 1919, in Cartwright, Newfoundland, Canada; came to United States, 1929, naturalized, 1943; son of George Lloyd and Alice (Carter) Waite; married Anne Barnett (a school nurse), September 6, 1943; children: Geoffrey C.W., Peter B.G. *Education:* Macalester College, B.A., 1941; University of Minnesota, M.A., 1945; Harvard University, A.M., 1947, Ph.D., 1949; University of Munich, postdoctoral study, 1954-55. *Religion:* Congregational. *Home:* Talcott Rd., Williamstown, Mass. 01267. *Office:* Department of History, Williams College, Williamstown, Mass. 01267.

CAREER: Williams College, Williamstown, Mass., assistant professor, 1949-53, associate professor, 1953-58, professor, 1958-60, Brown Professor of History, 1960—, chairman of department, 1968—. John Hay Institute in the Humanities, staff member of summer institutes at Williams College, 1959-60, Colorado College, 1963, University of Oregon, 1963. Member of Regional School Committee, 1961-66; director, Education Professions Development Act, Summer History Institute, 1969. *Military service:* U.S. Army, 1942-45. *Member:* American Historical Association, Central European Study Group, Harvard Club, Williams Club. *Awards, honors:* Guggenheim fellow, 1954-55; American Council of Learned Societies grant, 1966-68.

WRITINGS: Vanguard of Nazism: The Free Corps Movement in Post-War Germany, 1918-1923, Harvard University Press, 1952; (translator with Harlan P. Hanson) Erich Eyck, *A History of the Weimar Republic,* Harvard University Press, Volume I: *From the Collapse of the Empire to Hindenburg's Election,* 1962, Volume II: *From the Locarno Conference to Hitler's Seizure of Power,* 1963; (editor) *Hitler and Nazi Germany,* Holt, 1965. Also author of *Instructions for Writing Papers and Theses in History and in American History and Literature,* Williams College, 1957. Contributor to *World Book,* 1958, *Collier's Encyclopedia,* 1964. Member of editorial board, *Journal of Modern History,* 1958-61.

WORK IN PROGRESS: A psychoanalytical study of Adolf Hitler.

AVOCATIONAL INTERESTS: Mountain climbing, church activity, secondary education.

* * *

WALDMEIR, Joseph John 1923-

PERSONAL: Born December 12, 1923, in Detroit, Mich.; son of Joseph John and Helen (Nielsen) Waldmeir; married Margaret A. Petrisko, January 25, 1947; children: John Christian. *Education:* Wayne State University, B.A., 1948; University of Michigan, M.A., 1949; Michigan State University, Ph.D., 1959. *Politics:* Democrat. *Religion:* Roman Catholic. *Home:* 1377 Biscayne Way, Haslett, Mich. 48840.

CAREER: University of Detroit, Detroit, Mich., instructor in English, 1950-54; Michigan State University, East Lansing, instructor in English, 1956-57, assistant professor of American thought and language, 1958-65, professor of English, 1966—. University of Helsinki, Helsinki, Finland, Fulbright professor of American literature, 1963-64; University of Copenhagen, Copenhagen, Denmark, Fulbright professor, 1967-68. *Military service:* U.S. Army, 1943-45; became sergeant. *Member:* Modern Language Association of America, American Studies Association, Michigan Academy of Science, Arts, and Letters, Canadian Association for American Studies. *Awards, honors:* University College Book Award, 1961, for manuscript on World War II fiction.

WRITINGS: (Editor and contributor) *Recent American Fiction: Some Critical Views,* Houghton, 1963; *American Novels of the Second World War,* Humanities, 1969. Contributor: Henry M. Christman, editor, *A View of the Nation,* Grove, 1960; Robert P. Weeks, editor, *Hemingway,* Prentice-Hall, 1962; Carlos Baker, editor, *Ernest*

Hemingway: Critiques of Four Major Novels, Scribner, 1962. Contributor of poetry, reviews, and articles to *Nation, Books Abroad, Wisconsin Studies,* and *Modern Fiction Studies.*

WORK IN PROGRESS: Research on contemporary literature for a collection of essays.

* * *

WALDRON-SHAH, Diane Lynn   1936-
(D'Lynn Waldron)

PERSONAL: Born October 22, 1936, in New Jersey. *Education:* Attended Texas Christian University, 1954-55; Boston University, A.A., 1963; Washington University, St. Louis, Mo., Ford Foundation special master's degree program, 1964—. *Agent:* Theron Raines, 244 Madison Ave., New York, N.Y. 10016.

CAREER: Sun Press, Shaker Heights, Ohio, foreign correspondent, sketch artist, and photographer in Asia and Arab countries, 1957-58; free-lance writer in Polynesia and London, England, 1959; *Cleveland Press-News,* Cleveland, Ohio, foreign correspondent, sketch artist, and photographer in Africa, including Congo, 1960; free-lance writer and artist in Asia, 1961. Lecturer on Asian and African affairs, British Broadcasting Corp., Hong Kong, 1961, and on American television.

WRITINGS—Under name D'Lynn Waldron: (Self-illustrated) *Further Than at Home,* Harper, 1959; *Far From Home,* Redman, 1962.

WORK IN PROGRESS: The Last of the White Man's Days, a book on conditions in the Congo just before independence.

BIOGRAPHICAL/CRITICAL SOURCES: Newsweek, December 29, 1958, January 12, 1959.

* * *

WALKER, Brooks R.   1935-

PERSONAL: Born January 2, 1935, in Gunnison, Colo.; son of Robert H. and Letha (Brooks) Walker; married Sandra Fraser, March 5, 1956; children: John, Robert, Kate. *Education:* University of Colorado, B.A., 1956; Harvard University, S.T.B., 1959. *Religion:* Unitarian Universalist. *Home:* 40 Brook Manor Rd., Pleasantville, N.Y. 10570.

CAREER: North Shore Unitarian Society, Plandome, N.Y., assistant minister, 1959-60; Emerson Unitarian Church, Canoga Park, Calif., minister, 1960-65; Unitarian Fellowship of Northern Westchester, Mt. Kisco, N.Y., minister, 1965—. Member of advisory committee, department of social responsibility, Unitarian Universalist Association; member of steering committee, Town Meeting for Democracy, Los Angeles, 1962; member, Advisory Committee for KPFK, 1963—. *Member:* American Association for the United Nations (president, 1963-64), Unitarian Universalist Ministers Association, American Civil Liberties Union, National Association for the Advancement of Colored People, Southwest Liberal Religious Educators Association, Southern California Friends of Free Radio (chairman), Southern California State Council of the United Nations Association. *Awards, honors:* John Haynes Holmes-Arthur L. Weatherly Award, Unitarian Universalist Fellowship for Social Justice, 1964.

WRITINGS: The Christian Fright Peddlers, Doubleday, 1964; *The New Immorality,* Doubleday, 1968. Contributor to *Crane Review, Frontier, Liberal Context, Christian Advocate,* and other journals.

WORK IN PROGRESS: Research on the contribution of Ralph Waldo Emerson to American democratic idealism.

BIOGRAPHICAL/CRITICAL SOURCES: Christian Century, January 8, 1969.†

* * *

WALKER, David Maxwell   1920-

PERSONAL: Born April 9, 1920, in Glasgow, Scotland; son of James Mitchell (a bank manager) and Mary (Irvine) Walker; married Margaret Knox, September 1, 1954. *Education:* University of Glasgow, M.A., 1946, LL.B., 1948; University of Edinburgh, Ph.D., 1952, LL.D., 1960; University of London, LL.B., 1957. *Home:* 1 Beaumont Gate, Glasgow W. 2, Scotland. *Office:* University of Glasgow, Glasgow W. 2, Scotland.

CAREER: Advocate of the Scottish Bar, 1948—; barrister-at-law, Middle Temple, London, England, 1957—; Queen's Counsel, Scotland, 1958—. In practice at Scottish Bar, 1948-53; University of London, London, England, researcher, 1953-54; University of Glasgow, Glasgow, Scotland, professor of jurisprudence, 1954-58, Regius Professor of Law, 1958—. *Military service:* British and Indian Armies, 1939-46; served overseas in India, North Africa, Italy. *Awards, honors:* LL.D., University of London, 1968.

WRITINGS: The Law of Damages in Scotland, Green & Son, 1955; *The Scottish Legal System: An Introduction to the Study of Scots Law,* Green & Son, 1959, 3rd edition, 1969; *The Law of Delict in Scotland,* two volumes, Green & Son, 1966; *Principles of Scottish Private Law,* two volumes, Oxford University Press, 1970. Contributor of articles to legal journals.

WORK IN PROGRESS: A book, *Law of Civil Remedies in Scotland,* expected completion in 1975.

* * *

WALKER, Donald Smith   1918-

PERSONAL: Born April 6, 1918, in Ashton, Lancashire, England; son of Thomas and Kate (Smith) Walker; married Caterina Fabris, 1946. *Education:* St. Catharine's College, Cambridge, B.A., 1939, M.A. (in absentia), 1942. *Home:* 66 The Rise, Ponteland, Newcastle upon Tyne, England.

CAREER: Schoolmaster. *Military service:* British Army, six years during World War II, five years in Territorial Army; became lieutenant.

WRITINGS: A Geography of Italy, Dutton, 1958, 2nd edition, Methuen, 1967; *The Mediterranean Lands,* Methuen, 1960, 3rd edition, Barnes & Noble, 1965.

* * *

WALKER, Gerald   1928-

PERSONAL: Born April 16, 1928, in New York, N.Y.; son of Max Joseph (an accountant and lawyer) and Anne (Furman) Walker; married Greta Markson (a singer, writer, and actress), December 14, 1956; children: David Joseph. *Education:* New York University, B.S. 1950. *Home:* 145 West 86th St., New York, N.Y. 10024. *Agent:* Theron Raines, 244 Madison Ave., New York, N.Y. 10016. *Office: New York Times Magazine,* 229 West 43rd St., New York, N.Y. 10036.

CAREER: Theatrical publicity work in Corning, Rochester, and New York, N.Y., 1953-55; *Coronet,* New York, N.Y., assistant advertising promotion manager, 1956-58; free-lance magazine writer, New York, N.Y., 1956-63; *New York Times Magazine,* New York, N.Y., assistant articles editor, 1963—. *Awards, honors:* Certificate of recognition from National Conference of Christians and Jews for magazine article; grant from Philip M. Stern Family Fund, Washington, D.C., for article.

WRITINGS: (Co-author) *The Consumers Union Report on Smoking and the Public Interest,* Consumers Union, 1963; *Cruising* (novel), Stein & Day, 1970. Editor, *Best Magazine Articles* (annual), Crown, 1966, 1967, and 1968.

SIDELIGHTS: Robert Weiner is producing a motion picture of *Cruising.*

BIOGRAPHICAL/CRITICAL SOURCES: New York Times Book Review, June 4, 1967, September 15, 1968; *New York Times,* November 11, 1967; *Saturday Review,* October 12, 1968; *Variety,* August 12, 1970.

* * *

WALKER, Mack 1929-

PERSONAL: Born June 6, 1929, in Springfield, Mass.; son of Gilbert J. (a schoolteacher) and Lavinia (Mack) Walker; married Irma J. Wiesinger, March 27, 1954; children: Barbara B., Gilbert C. *Education:* Bowdoin College, A.B., 1950; Harvard University, Ph.D., 1959. *Home:* 743 Snyder Hill Rd., Ithaca, N.Y. 14850. *Office:* Department of History, Cornell University, Ithaca, N.Y. 14850.

CAREER: Rhode Island School of Design, Providence, instructor in history, 1957-59; Harvard University, Cambridge, Mass., instructor, 1959-62, assistant professor of history, 1962-66; Cornell University, Ithaca, N.Y., associate professor, 1966-72, professor of history, 1972—. *Military service:* U.S. Army; became sergeant.

WRITINGS: Germany and the Emigration, 1816-1885, Harvard University Press, 1964; (editor) *Metternich's Europe,* Walker & Co., 1968; (editor) *Plombieres: Secret Diplomacy and the Rebirth of Italy,* Oxford University Press, 1968; *German Home Towns, Community, State, and General Estate, 1648-1871,* Cornell University Press, 1971.

WORK IN PROGRESS: Research in German political and social history in eighteenth and nineteenth centuries.

* * *

WALKER, Richard Louis 1922-

PERSONAL: Born April 13, 1922, in Bellefonte, Pa.; son of Robert Shortlidge and Genevieve (Bible) Walker; married Celeno Kenly, March 29, 1945; children: Geoffrey Kenly, Dorothy Anne, Stephen Bradly. *Education:* Drew University, B.A. (cum laude), 1944; University of Pennsylvania, graduate study; Yale University, M.A., 1947, Ph.D., 1950. *Home:* 700 Springlake Rd., Columbia, S.C. 29206. *Office:* Institute and Department of International Studies, University of South Carolina, Columbia, S.C. 29208.

CAREER: Yale University, New Haven, Conn., assistant professor of history, 1950-57; University of South Carolina, Columbia, chairman of department of international studies, 1957—, James F. Byrnes Professor of International Relations, 1959—, director of Institute of International Studies, 1961—. Visiting professor at National Taiwan University, 1954-55, University of Washington, 1959, 1965; faculty lecturer at National War College, 1960-61; visiting Fulbright research scholar, Academia Sinica, Taiwan, 1965-66; visiting lecturer for Foreign Service Institute, U.S. Department of State, 1971; lecturer at other U.S. service colleges, at Nan Yang University, and in Australia, Japan, and elsewhere in Asia. Keynote speaker for U.S. delegation at SEATO Seminar, Philippines, 1957; U.S. delegate to XXVth International Congress of Orientalists, Moscow, 1960. Director, Aid Chinese Refugee Intellectuals, 1952-70, American Bureau for Medical Aid to China, 1955—, American-Asian Educational Exchange, 1957—; member of academic advisory board, Center for Strategic and International Studies, Georgetown University, 1968—; member of academic board, Charles Edison Memorial Youth Fund, 1972—; member of advisory council, U.S. Army Institute for Military Assistance, 1972—; member of board of directors, University of Carolina Educational Foundation, 1958—, National Committee on U.S.-China Relations, 1969—, National Council of Community World Affairs Organizations. Consultant, Rockefeller Brothers, 1956-57, American Bar Association, 1961—. *Military service:* U.S. Army, 1942-46; Chinese interpreter, Intelligence, General MacArthur's headquarters. U.S. Army Reserve, 1946-53.

MEMBER: Association for Asian Studies, American Historical Association, American Political Science Association, American Association of University Professors, Institute for American Strategy, International Studies Association, American Emergency Committee for Tibetan Refugees, Aurelian Honor Society, Pi Gamma Mu, Omicron Delta Kappa, Forest Lake Club, Torch Club, Summit Club. *Awards, honors:* Drew University Alumni award for achievement in the arts, 1958; distinguished service award, Air University, 1970.

WRITINGS: Western Language Periodicals on China, Far Eastern Publications, Yale University, 1949; *The Multi-State System of Ancient China,* Shoe String, 1953; *China Under Communism: The First Five Years,* Yale University Press, 1955; (editor) *China and the West: Cultural Collision,* Far Eastern Publications, Yale University, 1956; *The Continuing Struggle; Communist China and the Free World,* Athene Press, 1958; *Communist China: Power and Prospects,* American-Asian Cultural Exchange, 1958; (with Eustace Seligman) *Should the U.S. Change Its China Policy?,* Foreign Policy Association, 1958; (editor) *Letters from Communes,* New Leader, 1959; (with George Curry) *American Secretaries of State and Their Diplomacy,* Volume XIV: *E.R. Stettinius, Jr.* [and] *James F. Byrnes* (the former by Walker, the latter by Curry), Cooper Square, 1965; *The China Danger,* American Bar Association, 1966; *Ancient China and Its Influence in Modern Times,* F. Watts, 1969; *The Human Cost of Communism in China,* U.S. Government Printing Office, 1971; *The Republic of China and Asian Security,* Center of Asian Studies, St. John's University, c.1971; *Prospects in the Pacific: Peace Development and Security in the 1970's,* Heldref, 1972. Contributor to *Collier's Yearbook, World Book,* and to more than thirty symposium volumes; contributor of more than one hundred articles and reviews to *New York Times Book Review, New Leader, America, Problems of Communism, Journal of Asian Studies,* and to historical, political, and sociological journals.

WORK IN PROGRESS: A book on early Japan; *New Pacific Balance; United States and Security in the Pacific;* co-authoring a work on Korea in the 1970's.

* * *

WALKER, Warren S(tanley) 1921-

PERSONAL: Born March 19, 1921, in Brooklyn, N.Y.; son of Harold S. and Althea (Loescher) Walker; married Barbara Kerlin (a writer), December 9, 1943; children: Brian, Theresa. *Education:* State University of New York at Albany, A.B., 1947, M.A., 1948; Cornell University, Ph.D., 1951. *Office:* Texas Tech University, Lubbock, Tex. 79409.

CAREER: Blackburn College, Carlinville, Ill., began as faculty member, became chairman of English department, 1951-59; Parsons College, Fairfield, Iowa, professor and dean, 1959-64; Texas Technological College (now Texas Tech University), Lubbock, professor of English, 1964—. Fulbright lecturer in American literature at University of Ankara, Ankara, Turkey, 1961-62. Visiting summer professor at State University of New York at Albany, 1957, State University College at Cortland, 1959.

Fairfield (Iowa) Community Fund, director, 1963-64. *Military service:* U.S. Army Air Forces, 1942-45; served in Italy. *Member:* Modern Language Association of America, American Folklore Society, American Association of University Professors, National Council of Teachers of English, New York Folklore Society, Middle East Studies Association.

WRITINGS: James Fenimore Cooper: An Introduction and Interpretation, Barnes & Noble, 1962; (with Ahmet Uysal) *Tales Alive in Turkey,* Harvard University Press, 1966.

Editor: *Whatever Makes Papa Laugh: A Folklore Sheaf Honoring Harold W. Thompson,* New York Folklore Society, 1958; (and author of introduction) James Fenimore Cooper, *The Spy,* Hafner, 1960; (with wife, Barbara K. Walker) *Nigerian Folk Tales* (as told by Olawale Idewu and Omotayo Adu), Rutgers University Press, 1961; *Twentieth-Century Short Story Explication: Interpretations, 1900-1960 Inclusive, of Short Fiction Since 1800,* Shoe String, 1961, Supplement I, 1963, Supplement II, 1965, 2nd edition, 1968, Supplement I (to 2nd edition), 1970; (with B.K. Walker) *The Erie Canal: Gateway to Empire,* Heath, 1963; (and author of introduction) James Fenimore Cooper, *The Red Rover,* University of Nebraska Press, 1963; *Prose Lyrics: A Collection of Familiar Essays,* Odyssey, 1964; (and author of introduction) James Fenimore Cooper, *The Sea Lions,* University of Nebraska Press, 1965; *Leatherstocking and the Critics,* Scott, Foresman, 1965; (with Ahmet Uysal) *Turkish Folktales,* Folkways Records, 1965.

Contributor: Clay Perry, *Underground Empire: Wonders and Tales of New York Caves,* S. Daye, 1948; Mary Cunningham, editor, *James Fenimore Cooper: A Reappraisal,* New York Historical Association, 1954. Contributor of more than twenty articles and reviews to professional and folklore journals. Member of editorial board, Center for Editions of American Authors, Cooper Edition.

WORK IN PROGRESS: The third edition of *Twentieth-Century Short Story Explication;* with Faruk Suemer and Ahmet Uysal, *The Book of Dede Korkut: A Turkish Oral Epic.*

SIDELIGHTS: Walker spends summers at his home, self-built with hand tools, on an island in Georgian Bay, writing, fishing, boating and swimming. He reads French and German, has some facility in spoken Turkish.

*   *   *

WALKER, William Edward 1925-

PERSONAL: Born May 20, 1925, in Meridian, Miss.; son of Magnes William and Perlene (Branning) Walker. *Education:* University of South Carolina, A.B., 1947; Columbia University, M.A., 1948; Harvard University, postgraduate study, 1951; Vanderbilt University, Ph.D., 1957. *Politics:* Independent. *Office:* University of Bridgeport, Bridgeport, Conn. 06602.

CAREER: Darlington School for Boys, Rome, Ga., English teacher, 1948-52; College of William and Mary, Williamsburg, Va., instructor in English, 1953-55; Vanderbilt University, Nashville, Tenn., instructor in English, 1957-58; Converse College, Spartanburg, S.C., dean, 1958-60; Memphis State University, Memphis, Tenn., assistant professor of English, 1960-63; New Haven College, West Haven, Conn., chairman of department of English and Humanities, 1963-64; University of Bridgeport, Bridgeport, Conn., began as instructor, became associate professor of English and Assistant Dean for Undergraduate Affairs, College of Arts and Sciences, 1964—. *Military service:* U.S. Naval Reserve, 1945-46; served in Pacific theater. *Member:* Modern Language Association of Amer-

ica, National Council of Teachers of English, American Association of University Professors, Conference on College Composition and Communication, Phi Beta Kappa, Phi Delta Kappa.

WRITINGS: (Editor and contributor with Robert L. Welker) *Reality and Myth: Essays in American Literature in Memory of Richmond Croom Beatty,* Vanderbilt University Press, 1964. Contributor of poetry to *New Republic,* and of articles to scholarly and popular periodicals, including *Salt Water Sportsman.*

WORK IN PROGRESS: A novel; a volume of poetry; articles on Coleridge and John Esten Cooke.

AVOCATIONAL INTERESTS: Tennis, deep sea fishing, boating.

*   *   *

WALLACE, Ronald S(tewart) 1911-

PERSONAL: Born April 16, 1911, in Edinburgh, Scotland; son of Robert George and Rachel (Sellar) Wallace; married Mary Torrance, July 28, 1937; children: David Stewart, Mary Elizabeth, Heather Margaret. *Education:* University of Edinburgh, M.A. and B.Sc., 1933, Ph.D., 1960. *Home:* 5 Polwarth Grove, Edinburgh, Scotland.

CAREER: Minister, Church of Scotland, serving at Brora, 1936-37; Crosshill, Ayrshire, 1937-40; Glasgow, 1940-50, Lanark, 1950-57; Lothian Road Parish Church, Edinburgh, minister, 1957—.

WRITINGS: Calvin's Doctrine of the Word and Sacrament, Oliver & Boyd, 1953, Eerdmans, 1957; *Many Things in Parables,* Oliver & Boyd, 1955, Harper, 1956; *Elijah and Elisha: Expositions From the Book of Kings,* Eerdmans, 1957; *Calvin's Doctrine of the Christian Life,* Eerdmans, 1959; (translator) Albert Marie-Schmidt, *Calvin and the Calvinistic Tradition,* Harper, 1960; *The Gospel Miracles: Studies in Matthew, Mark and Luke,* Eerdmans, 1960; *Many Things in Miracles* [and] *The Gospel Miracles,* two volumes in one, Eerdmans, 1963; *Words of Triumph: The Words from the Cross and Their Application Today,* John Knox, 1964; *The Ten Commandments: A Study of Ethical Freedom,* Eerdmans, 1965. Contributor to Baker's *Dictionary of Theology* and *I.V.F. Bible Dictionary.* Contributor of books reviews to *Expository Times.*

WORK IN PROGRESS: A Pelican paperback on John Calvin.†

*   *   *

WALLACE, Sarah Leslie 1914-

PERSONAL: Born October 28, 1914, in Kansas City, Mo.; daughter of Leslie Linn and Mary Louise (Shortall) Wallace. *Education:* College of St. Catherine, St. Paul, Minn., B.A., 1935, B.S. in L.S., 1936. *Religion:* Catholic. *Home:* 8705 Jones Mill Rd., Chevy Chase, Md. (Washington, D.C.) 20015. *Office:* Library of Congress, Washington, D.C. 20540.

CAREER: Minneapolis (Minn.) Public Library, successively reference, publicity, and administrative assistant, 1936-54; administrative assistant in charge of public relations and research, 1954-57; public relations officer, 1958-63; College of St. Catherine, St. Paul, Minn., instructor, 1944-60; Library of Congress, Washington, D.C., publications officer, 1963—. Broadcaster on weekly television show, "Library Showcase," WCCO, Minneapolis, Minn., ten years. *Member:* American Library Association (membership chairman, 1962—; vice-chairman of public relations section, 1963-64, chairman of public relations section, 1964—), Minnesota Library Association, Maryland Library Association, District of Columbia Library Association, Kappa Gamma Pi, Delta Phi Lambda.

Awards, honors: First Jeanne d'Arc Award for civic achievement from Minneapolis Junior Catholic League, 1963.

WRITINGS: (Self-illustrated) *Patrons are People: How to Be a Model Librarian,* American Library Association, 1945, 2nd edition, 1956; (self-illustrated) *Promotion Ideas for Public Libraries,* American Library Association, 1953; *Definition: Library,* American Library Association, 1961; (editor) *Friends of the Library: Organization and Activities,* American Library Association, 1962; *So You Want to be a Librarian,* Harper, 1963. Contributor of essays, stories, puppet plays, and articles to professional journals. Editor, *Quarterly Journal of the Library of Congress.*

* * *

WALLACH, Ira 1913-

PERSONAL: Born January 22, 1913, in New York, N.Y.; son of Morris David (a dentist) and Rose (Simcovitz) Wallach; married Devera Sievers (an actress), January 25, 1941 (divorced, 1970); married Lillian W. Opatoshu, June 4, 1970; children: (first marriage) Leah. *Education:* Attended Cornell University, 1930. *Politics:* Independent. *Religion:* None. *Home:* 345 West 58th St., New York, N.Y. 10019. *Agent:* Flora Roberts, Inc., 116 East 59th St., New York, N.Y. 10022.

CAREER: Full-time writer and dramatist. *Military service:* U.S. Army; served in Pacific theater more than two years in World War II; became sergeant. *Member:* Writers Guild of America, West, Screen Writers Guild, Dramatists Guild, Authors Guild, P.E.N., Aircraft Owners and Pilots Association. *Awards, honors:* Writers Guild of Great Britain award for best British comedy screenplay, 1968, for "Hot Millions."

WRITINGS: (Translator with Angel Flores) Rafael Alberti, *A Spectre is Haunting Europe: Poems of Revolutionary Spain,* Critics Group, 1936; *The Horn and the Roses: A Novel Based on the Life of Peter-Paul Rubens,* Boni & Gaer, 1947; *How to be Deliriously Happy (The Foible Gompkin Method),* Henry Schuman, 1950; *Hopalong-Freud, and Other Modern Literary Characters,* (essays) Henry Schuman, 1951; *Hopalong-Freud Rides Again* (essays), Henry Schuman, 1952; (and illustrator) *Gutenberg's Folly: The Literary Debris of Mitchel Hackney,* Abelard, 1954; *How to Pick a Wedlock: A Pocket Guide to Bliss,* McGraw, 1956; *Muscle Beach,* Little, Brown, 1959; *The Absence of a Cello* (novel), Little, Brown, 1960; *Hopalong-Freud, and Other Parodies* (selected essays from *Hopalong-Freud, and Other Modern Literary Characters* and *Hopalong-Freud Rides Again),* Dover, 1966.

Plays: "Horatio" (musical), first produced in Dallas, Tex., at Margo Jones Theatre, March 8, 1954; (author of sketches) *Phoenix '55* (musical revue; first produced Off-Broadway at Phoenix Theatre, April 23, 1955), Samuel French, 1957; (author of lyrics) "Sticks and Stones" (musical revue), first produced in New Hope, Pa., at Bucks County Playhouse, summer, 1956; (contributor of a sketch) "Surprise Party," one-night benefit performance Off-Broadway at Phoenix Theatre, 1957; (author of lyrics and book for musical adaptation) "Mistress of the Inn," first produced in New Hope, Pa., at Bucks County Playhouse, summer, 1957; (with Abram S. Ginnes) *Drink to Me Only* (three-act comedy; first produced on Broadway at Fifty-Fourth Street Theatre, October 8, 1958), Samuel French, 1958; (author of sketches and lyrics) "Dig We Must," first produced in East Hampton, N.Y., at John Drew Theatre, July 4, 1959; (author of lyrics for musical adaptation) "Petticoat Fever," first produced in New Hope, Pa., at Bucks County Playhouse, summer, 1960; (adaptor of book) "Hit the Deck," first produced in Jones Beach, N.Y., at Marine Theatre, summer, 1960;

"Smiling, the Boy Fell Dead" (musical), first produced Off-Broadway at Cherry Lane Theatre, April 9, 1961; *The Absence of a Cello* (three-act comedy; adapted from his novel; first produced in New Hope, Pa., at Bucks County Playhouse, summer, 1963; produced on Broadway at Ambassador Theatre, September 21, 1964; produced on West End at St. Martin's Theatre as "Out of the Question," October 15, 1968), Dramatists Play Service, 1965. Also author of a play, "Grisdale," as yet neither published nor produced, and of the book for musical comedy, "April's Fool," to be produced in 1973.

Screenplays: "Boys Night Out," Filmways and M-G-M, 1962; (with George J.W. Goodman) "The Wheeler Dealers" (based on the novel by Goodman), Filmways and M-G-M, 1963; (with George Kirgo) "Don't Make Waves" (based on Wallach's novel, *Muscle Beach),* M-G-M, 1967; (with Peter Ustinov) "Hot Millions," M-G-M, 1968.

WORK IN PROGRESS: A play, "Beer Island"; a screenplay, "April in the Wind," to be produced by Andrea de Penta; a novel, *Grady,* completed and awaiting publication.

SIDELIGHTS: Wallach told *CA:* "I have been to Europe a few times, and to the Near East. I have been to Los Angeles too many times. I enjoy working and I never give much thought to my motivations."

In a review of the St. Martin's production of "Out of the Question," Jeremy Kingston called the comedy "a curious mixture of good and banal, as though one person wrote most of it and somebody else came along and adorned it. Again and again, just when the plot is forfeiting our respect, an excellent and surprising line jolts us back into high humour. Odder than this: the author's name may be defiantly Jewish-American but his mockery of American big business attitudes is so very English in tone that I occupied an idle moment in the second interval trying to discover in the words 'Ira Wallach' an anagram of 'Hugh and Margaret Williams.' It is their style of comedy exactly."

"Hot Millions" was one of the Academy Award nominees of 1968 for best story and screenplay written directly for the screen.

Wallach writes: "My favorite recreation is light plane flying. I have also descended to golf, having given up tennis because of a bad back."

BIOGRAPHICAL/CRITICAL SOURCES: Observer Review, October 20, 1968; *Punch,* October 23, 1968; *Show Business,* January 4, 1969.

* * *

WALLER, George Macgregor 1919-

PERSONAL: Born June 7, 1919, in Detroit, Michigan; son of George and Marguerite (Rowland) Waller; married Martha Stifler, 1943; children: Susan, Marguerite, Elizabeth, Donald, Richard. *Education:* Amherst College, B.A., 1941; Columbia University, M.A., 1947, Ph.D., 1953. *Religion:* Presbyterian. *Home:* 1701 West 51st St., Indianapolis, Ind. 46208. *Office:* Butler University, Indianapolis, Ind. 46208.

CAREER: Detroit Edison Company, Detroit, Mich., employee in commercial office, 1941-43; Amherst College, Amherst, Mass., instructor, 1948-52; State Historical Society of Wisconsin, Madison, chief, American History Research Center, 1952-54; Butler University, Indianapolis, Ind., professor and head of department of history, political science, and geography, 1954—. *Military service:* U.S. Navy, 1943-46; became lieutenant commander.

MEMBER: American Historical Association, American Studies Association, Organization of American Historians,

American Association of University Professors, Indiana Historical Society, Indiana Museum Society (president), Indiana Academy of Social Sciences, Indianapolis Council on World Affairs, Phi Beta Kappa, Phi Kappa Phi, Indianapolis Literary Club. *Awards, honors:* Fulbright Senior Scholar, University of Southampton, England, 1961-62; Holcomb Faculty Award, Butler University, 1960.

WRITINGS: (Editor) *Puritanism in Early America,* Heath, 1950; (editor and author of introduction) *Pearl Harbor: Roosevelt and the Coming of the War,* Heath, 1953, revised edition, 1965: *Samuel Vetch, Colonial Enterpriser,* University of North Carolina Press, 1960.

* * *

WALLS, H(enry) J(ames) 1907-

PERSONAL: Born December 24, 1907, in Edinburgh, Scotland; son of William and Elizabeth (Maclellan) Walls; married Constance Mary Butler, May 18, 1940; children: Robert, Ann. *Education:* University of Edinburgh, B.Sc. (first class honors in chemistry), 1930, Ph.D., 1933; research at University of Munich, 1930-32, University of Bristol, 1934-35. *Politics:* Radical. *Home:* 65 Marmora Rd., London S.E. 22, England.

CAREER: Imperial Chemical Industries Ltd., research chemist, Nobel Division, 1935-36; Metropolitan Police Laboratory, London, England, scientific officer, 1936-46; Home Officer Forensic Science Laboratory, chief chemist at Bristol, England, 1946-58, director at Newcastle upon Tyne, England, 1958-64; Metropolitan Police Laboratory, director, 1964-68; retired, 1968. *Member:* British Academy of Forensic Sciences (founder member, 1959; president, 1965-66), Forensic Science Society of Great Britain.

WRITINGS: Photo-Technique: Fundamentals and Equipment, Focal Press, 1954, 2nd edition published as *Camera Techniques: Fundamentals and Equipment,* 1960, 3rd revised edition, 1964; *How Photography Works,* Macmillan, 1959; *Forensic Science: An Introduction to the Science of Crime Detection,* Praeger, 1968; (with Alistair R. Brownlie) *Drink, Drugs and Driving,* Sweet & Maxwell, 1970. Contributor of scientific papers to professional journals.

WORK IN PROGRESS: Reminiscences of 30 years in forensic science.

AVOCATIONAL INTERESTS: Theatre, the arts, and other people.

* * *

WALSH, James (Jerome) 1924-

PERSONAL: Born May 23, 1924, in Seattle, Wash.; son of John Jerome and Agnes (Counihan) Walsh; married Carol Jean Paton (a librarian), September 16, 1946; children: John Jerome, James Paton. *Education:* Reed College, B.A., 1949; Oxford University, B.A., 1951, M.A., 1956; Columbia University, Ph.D., 1960. *Politics:* Democrat. *Home:* 50 Haverstraw Rd., Suffern, N.Y. 10901. *Office:* 715 Philosophy Hall, Columbia University, New York, N.Y. 10027.

CAREER: Columbia University, New York, N.Y., lecturer, 1954-55, instructor, 1955-60, assistant professor, 1960-63, associate professor and director of Graduate Studies, 1963-66, professor of philosophy and chairman of department, 1967—. Adviser, "College Bowl" television program. Democratic committeeman, 1963-66. *Military service:* U.S. Army, 1942-45; became staff sergeant; received Purple Heart. *Awards, honors:* Stanwood Cockey Lodge publication prize for *Aristotle's Conception of Moral Weakness;* American Council of Learned Societies research fellowship; Guggenheim fellowship.

WRITINGS: (With Sidney Morgenbesser) *Free Will* (anthology), Prentice-Hall, 1962; *Aristotle's Conception of Moral Weakness,* Columbia University Press, 1963; (editor with Henry L. Shapiro) *Aristotle's Ethics: Issues and Interpretations* (anthology), Wadsworth, 1967; (editor with Arthur Hyman) *Philosophy in the Middle Ages: The Christian, Islamic, and Jewish Traditions,* Harper, 1967. Editor, *Journal of Philosophy,* 1964—.

WORK IN PROGRESS: Studies in the moral philosophy of Jean Buridan and later nominalists.

* * *

WALTARI, Mika (Toimi) 1908- (Nauticus, M. Ritvala)

PERSONAL: Born September 19, 1908, in Helsinki, Finland; son of Toimi Armas and Olga Maria (Johansson) Waltari; married Marjatta Lukkonen, 1931; children: Satu (Mrs. Esko Elstela). *Education:* Helsinki University, M.A., 1929. *Home:* Tunturikatu 13, Helsinki 10, Finland.

CAREER: Maaseudun Talevaisuus, literary critic, 1932-42; *Suomen Kuvalehti* (weekly illustrated magazine), editor, 1936-38; Finnish State Information Bureau, member of staff, editorial office, 1939-44. Literary critic on Finnish radio, 1937-38. Member, Academy of Finland, 1957—. *Member:* Finnish Author's Society, P.E.N. (Finland). *Awards, honors:* State literary prizes, 1934, 1935, 1950, 1954; Pro Finlandia medal, 1952; Commander of the Finnish Lion, 1960.

WRITINGS—All published by Soederstroem (Helsinki), except as indicated: *Kuolleen silmaet* (short stories), H. Schildt, 1926; *Sinun ristisi juureen* (poems), 1927; *Suuri illusioni,* 1928; *Dshinnistanin prinssi* (fairy tales), 1929; *Muukalaislegioona* (poems), 1929.

Jaettilaeset ovat kuolleet (short stories and plays), 1930; *Appelsiininsiemen* (novel), 1931; *Siellae missae miehiae tehdaeaen,* 1931, *Kiinalainen kissa ja muita satuja* (fairy tales), 1932; *Mies ja haave* (novel), 1933; (editor) *Nuoret runoilijat, 1934,* 1934; *Sielu ja liekki* (novel), 1934; *Aiotko kirjailijaksi?,* 1935; *Palava nuoruus* (novel), 1935; *Surun ja ilon Kaupunki,* 1936; *Akhnaton, auringosta syntynyt* (play), Suomalaisen Kirjallisuuden Seura (Helsinki), 1973; *Kuriton sukupolvi* (three-act comedy), 1937; *Vieras mies tuli taloon* (novel), 1937, translation by Naomi Walford published as *A Stranger Came to the Farm,* Putnam, 1952; (under pseudonym M. Ritvala) *Ihmeellinen Joosef eli elaemae on seikkailu,* 1938; *Jaelkinaeytoes* (novel), 1938; *Haemeenlinnan Kaunotar* (play), Karisto (Haemeenlinna) 1939; *Kuka murhasi rouva Skrofin* (novel), Otava (Helsinki), 1939.

Antero ei enaeae palaa (novella), 1940; *Komisario Palmun erehdys* (novel), 1940; *Maa on ikuinen* (play), 1941; *Tulevaisuuden tiellae* (play), 1941; (under pseudonym Nauticus) *Totuus virosta: Latviasta ja lietnasta,* Balticum (Malmoe), 1941; *Neuvostovakoilun varjossa,* Otava, 1942; *Hyvin Larkittu—puoleksi tehty,* Valtioneuvooton Tuotantokonitoa (Helsinki), 1942; *Isaestae poikaan* (novel), 1942; *Kaarina Maununtyaer* (novel), 1942; *Novelleja* (short stories), 1943, translation by Lily Leino, Alan Beesley, and Paul Sjoeblom published as *The Tree of Dreams and Other Stories,* Putnam, 1965; *Paracelsus Baselissa* (five-act play), 1943; *Fine van Brooklyn,* 1943; *Rakkaus vainoaikaan* (novel), 1943; *Ei koskaan huomispaeivaeae,* 1944; *Tanssi yli hautojen* (novel), 1944; *Runoja, 1925-1945* (poems), 1945; *Sinuhe egyptilaeinen* (novel), 1945, translation by Naomi Walford published as *The Egyptian,* Putnam, 1949 (published in England as *Sinuhe the Egyptian,* Putnam, 1949); *Noita palaa elaemaeaen* (play), 1947; *Portti pimeaeaen* (play), 1947; *Elaemaen rikkaus* (three-act play), 1947; *Laehdin Istanbuliin* (title means "I Left for Istanbul"), 1947; *KultaKutri* (novella), 1948; *Mikael Karvajalka* (novel),

1948, translation by Naomi Walford published as *The Adventurer*, Putnam, 1950 (published in England as *Michael the Finn*, Putnam, 1950); *Mikael Hakin* (novel), 1949, translation by Naomi Walford published as *The Wanderer*, Putnam, 1951; *Neljae paeivaenlaskua*, 1949, translation by Alan Beesley published as *A Nail Merchant at Nightfall*, Putnam, 1954.

Johannes angelos (novel), 1952, translation by Naomi Walford published as *The Dark Angel*, Putnam, 1953; *Leikkaus* (play), 1952; *Kuun maisema*, 1953, translation by Naomi Walford published as *Moonscape, and Other Stories*, Putnam, 1954; *Turms, kuolematon* (novel), 1955, translation by Lily Leino published as *The Etruscan*, Putnam, 1956 (translation from the Swedish by Evelyn Ramsden published in England as *The Etruscan*, Putnam, 1957); *Vallaton Waltari*, 1957; *Feliks onnellinen* (novel), 1958, translation by Alan Blair published as *The Tongue of Fire*, Putnam, 1958; *Valtakunnan salsisuus* (novel), 1959, translation by Naomi Walford published as *The Secret of the Kingdom*, Putnam, 1961.

Koiranheisipuu (novella), 1961; *Greetings from Finland* (travel book; in English, German, and Swedish), 1961; *Taehdet kertovat, komisario Palmu!* (novel), 1962; *Keisari ja senaattori* (play), Karisto, 1963; *Ihmiskunna viholliset* (novel), 1964, translation by Joan Tate published as *The Roman*, Putnam, 1966; *Pienoisromaanit* (novellas), 1966; *Poeytaelaatikko* (poems), 1967.

SIDELIGHTS: The Egyptian was a best seller in the U.S. and was filmed by 20th Century-Fox in 1954.

* * *

WALTER, Eugene 1927-

PERSONAL: Born November 30, 1927, in Mobile, Ala.; son of Eugene and Muriel (Sabina) Walter. *Education:* Attended Spring Hill College, University of Alabama (Mobile extension), Museum of Modern Art (New York City), New York University, New School for Social Research, Alliance Francaise, Institut Brittanique de la Sorbonne, Instituto Dante Alighieri. *Agent:* William Morris Agency, 1350 Avenue of the Americas, New York, N.Y. 10019.

CAREER: Associate editor of *Botteghe Oscure*, 1950-59, *Paris Review*, 1951-60, *Folder*, 1951-54, *Whetstone*, 1953-58, *Intro Bulletin*, 1957-58, *Wormwood Review*, 1957-58, *Transatlantic Review*, 1959—. Also prizewinning scenic designer for more than 60 stage productions in New York area. Actor, who once toured his own marionette theater to schools and prisons in Gulf Coast region, and has played character parts, including leads, in 47 films, chiefly Italian; musician, who has played recorder with Ancient Instruments Society in Alabama, and was a founder and the first manager of the Mobile Symphony Orchestra. *Military service:* U.S. Army Airways Communications System, cryptographer, 1942-46. *Member:* The Willoughby Institute (secretary-treasurer). *Awards, honors:* Lippincott Fiction Prize, 1954, for *The Untidy Pilgrim*; Sewanee-Rockefeller fellowship, 1956, for *Monkey Poems*; O. Henry citation, 1959, for story, "I Love You Batty Sisters."

WRITINGS: (Self-illustrated) *Jennie, the Watercress Girl*, Willoughby Institute (Rome), 1947; *Monkey Poems*, Editions Finisterre, 1953, Noonday Press, 1954; *The Untidy Pilgrim* (novel), Lippincott, 1954; (author of text) Gwen Barnard, *The Shapes of the River: The London Thames*, Gaberbocchus Press, 1955; *Singerie Songerie: A Masque on the Subject of Lyric Mode* (ballet-opera), Willoughby Institute, 1958; *Love You Good* (novel), Julliard, 1963, published in America as *Love You Good, See You Later*, Scribner, 1964; *Fellini Satyricon* (English shooting script for film), Ballantine, 1970; *American Cooking: Southern Style*, Time-Life, 1971. Author of

ballad, "What is a Youth?," in Zefferelli film, "Romeo and Juliet." Contributor of stories, poems, and articles to *Ladies' Home Journal, Transatlantic Review, Harper's, Harper's Bazaar, Gourmet* and other periodicals, and to several anthologies.

WORK IN PROGRESS: Books of short stories, poems, and literary recollections; a novel; a cookbook; and translations.

* * *

WALVOORD, John F(lipse) 1910-

PERSONAL: Born May 1, 1910, in Sheboygan, Wis.; son of John Garrett and Mary (Flipse) Walvoord; married Geraldine Lundgren, June 28, 1939; children: John Edward, James Randall, Timothy Peter, Paul David. *Education:* Wheaton College, Wheaton, Ill., A.B., 1931; Dallas Theological Seminary, Th.B., 1934, Th.M., 1934; Th.D., 1936; Texas Christian University, A.M., 1945. *Home:* 1302 El Patio Dr., Dallas, Tex. 75218.

CAREER: Minister, Independent Fundamental Churches of America. Dallas Theological Seminary, Dallas, Tex., registrar, 1935-45, associate professor of systematic theology, 1936-52, professor, 1952—, assistant to the president, 1945-52, president, 1952—. *Member:* Evangelical Theological Society (president, 1954). *Awards, honors:* D.D. from Wheaton College, Wheaton, Ill., 1960.

WRITINGS: The Doctrine of the Holy Spirit: A Study in Pneumatology, Dallas Theological Seminary, 1943, revised edition published as *The Holy Spirit: A Comprehensive Study of the Person and Work of the Holy Spirit*, Van Kampen Press, 1954, 3rd edition, Dunham, 1958; *The Return of the Lord*, Dunham, 1955; *The Thessalonian Epistles*, Dunham, 1956; *The Rapture Question*, Dunham, 1957; (editor) *Inspiration and Interpretation*, Eerdmans, 1957; *The Millennial Kingdom*, Dunham, 1959; *To Live Is Christ: An Exposition of the Epistle of Paul to the Philippians*, Dunham, 1961; *Israel in Prophecy*, Zondervan, 1962; (editor) *Truth for Today: Bibliotheca Sacra Reader, Commemorating Thirty Years of Publication by Dallas Theological Seminary, 1934-1963*, Moody, 1963; *The Church in Prophecy*, Zondervan, 1964; *The Revelation of Jesus Christ: A Commentary*, Moody, 1966; *The Nations in Prophecy*, Zondervan, 1967; *Jesus Christ Our Lord*, Moody, 1969; *Daniel, the Key to Prophetic Revelation: A Commentary*, Moody, 1971; *Philippians: Joy and Peace*, Moody, 1971. Contributor of essays to books on prophecy and articles to religious magazines. Editor of *Bibliotheca Sacra*, 1952—.

* * *

WARD, Elizabeth Honor (Shedden) 1926-
(Ward S. Leslie)

PERSONAL: Born April 12, 1926, in Birmingham, England; daughter of Leslie Herbert (a chartered accountant) and Phebe Eliza (Line) Shedden; married Alan Howard Ward (a professor of physics, University of Zambia), September 23, 1950; children: Kristina Mary, Sheena Lesley, James Howard, Thomas Boulton. *Education:* Attended King Edward VI School, Birmingham, England, 1937-44; University of Birmingham, B.Sc. (with honors in physics), 1947, diploma in education, 1948. *Religion:* Evangelical Christian (Methodist). *Address:* c/o Professor Alan Ward, Natural Sciences, University of Zambia, P.O. Box 2379, Lusaka, Zambia.

CAREER: Sutton Coldfield High School for Girls, Warwickshire, England, physics teacher, 1948-50; University of Ghana, Legon, demonstrator in physics, 1951-55. West African Examinations Council, part-time examiner in physics, 1951-63. *Member:* Institute of Physics (associate), Zambia Association for Science Education.

WRITINGS: *Touchdown to Adventure,* Children's Special Service Mission, 1955; *Senior Physics for Tropical Secondary Schools,* Books 1 and 2, Nelson, 1966. Also author of booklets, *What is a Christian?* and *What is Christian Marriage?,* and co-author of *Newtown Families,* all published by Africa Christian Press.

WORK IN PROGRESS: Revising *Senior Physics for Tropical Secondary Schools,* for a new edition in S.I. units, to be published by Nelson; a juvenile, *The Story of Creation.*

*   *   *

WARD, William Ernest Frank   1900-

PERSONAL: Born December 24, 1900, in London, England; son of William Henry (an accountant) and Selina Agnes (Bowes) Ward; married Sylvia Grace Vallance, September 11, 1926. *Education:* Dulwich College, student, 1917-19; Lincoln College, Oxford, B.A., 1922, B.Litt., 1923, M.A., 1927; Ridley Hall, student, 1923-24, received Cambridge University certificate in education. *Religion:* Christian. *Home:* 59 Beresford Rd., Cheam, Sutton, Surrey, England.

CAREER: Achimota College, Gold Coast, West Africa, master, 1924-40; director of education, Mauritius (formerly Ile de France), 1940-45; Colonial Office, London, England, deputy education adviser, 1945-55. Member of British delegation to UNESCO and United Nations conferences. *Member:* Historical Association. *Awards, honors:* Companion of the Order of St. Michael and St. George, 1945.

WRITINGS: *Longmans' African Histories,* Longmans, Green, Book 1: *Africa Before the White Man Came,* 1934, Book 2: *Africa and European Trade,* 1939; *British History for Overseas Students,* Longmans, Green, 1934; *A Short History of the Gold Coast,* Longmans, Green, 1935, 7th edition published as *A Short History of Ghana,* 1957; *Music: A Handbook for African-Teachers,* Longmans, Green, 1939; *A History of the Gold Coast,* Allen & Unwin, 1948, revised 2nd edition published as *A History of Ghana,* 1958, Praeger, 1963, revised 4th edition, Allen & Unwin, 1967; (editor) *African Education: A Study of Educational Policy and Practice in British Tropical Africa,* Oxford University Press, 1953; *Educating Young Nations,* Essential Books, 1959; *A History of Africa,* Allen & Unwin, Book 1: *The Old Kingdoms of the Sudan; Nigeria Before the British Came; South Africa,* 1960, International Publications Service, 1961, new edition, Allen & Unwin, 1966, Book 2: *Egypt and the Sudan, Uganda, Kenya, Tanganyika,* 1963, new edition, 1966, Book 3: *Central Africa,* 1969; (editor and author of introduction) William W. Claridge, *A History of the Gold Coast and Ashanti,* 2nd edition, Cass, 1964; *Fraser of Trinity and Achimota,* Ghana Universities Press, 1965; *Government in West Africa,* Allen & Unwin, 1965; (editor and author of introduction) Thomas Edward Bowdich, *Mission from Cape Coast Castle to Ashantee,* 3rd edition, Cass, 1966; (editor and author of introduction) Joseph Dupuis, *Journal of a Residence in Ashantee,* 2nd edition, Cass, 1966; *Emergent Africa,* Allen & Unwin, 1967, International Publications Service, 1967; (editor and author of introduction) F.C.B.D. Fuller, *A Vanished Dynasty: Ashanti,* 2nd edition, Barnes & Noble, 1968; *The Royal Navy and the Slavers: The Suppression of the Atlantic Slave Trade,* Pantheon, 1969; (with L.W. White) *East Africa: A Century of Change,* Allen & Unwin, in press.

AVOCATIONAL INTERESTS: Music, walking, gardening, natural history, and travel.

BIOGRAPHICAL/CRITICAL SOURCES: *Book World,* June 29, 1969.

WARD-THOMAS, Evelyn Bridget Patricia Stephens   1928-
(Evelyn Anthony, Anthony Evelyn)

PERSONAL: Born July 3, 1928, in London, England; daughter of Henry Christian (an inventor) and Elizabeth (Sharkey) Stephens; married Michael Ward-Thomas (director of a diamond mining company), April 16, 1955; children: Susan Ileana Mary, Anthony Christian, Ewan Fitzgerald, Katharine Maria, Christian Rupert Francis. *Education:* Attended Convent of Sacred Heart, Roehampton, London, England. *Religion:* Roman Catholic. *Home:* Horham Hall, Thaxted, Essex, England; and 21 Cadogan Sq., London, S.W.1, England. *Agent:* A. P. Watt & Son, 26-28 Bedford Row, London WCIR 4HI, England. *Office:* Anthony Enterprises Ltd., 21 Cadogan Sq., London S.W.1, England.

CAREER: Author, 1952—.

WRITINGS—Under pseudonym Evelyn Anthony: *Rebel Princess,* Crowell, 1953 (published in England as *Imperial Highness,* Museum Press, 1953); *Royal Intrigue,* Crowell, 1954 (published in England as *Curse Not the King,* Museum Press, 1954); *Far Flies the Eagle,* Crowell, 1955; *Anne Boleyn* (Literary Guild and Dollar Book Club selections), Crowell, 1957; *Victoria and Albert* (Literary Guild selection), Crowell, 1958 (published in England as *Victoria,* Museum Press, 1959); *All the Queen's Men,* Crowell, 1960 (published in England as *Elizabeth,* Museum Press, 1960); *Charles the King,* Doubleday, 1961; *Clandara,* Doubleday, 1963; *The Heiress,* Doubleday, 1964; *The French Bride,* Doubleday, 1964; *Valentina,* Doubleday, 1966; *The Legend,* Hutchinson, 1967, Coward, 1969; *The Rendezvous,* Coward, 1968; *The Cardinal and the Queen,* Coward, 1968 (published in England as *Anne of Austria,* Hurst & Blackett, 1968); *The Assassin,* Coward, 1970; *The Tamarind Seed,* Coward, 1971; *The Poellenberg Inheritance,* Coward, 1972. Contributor of short stories to British magazines under pseudonym Anthony Evelyn.

WORK IN PROGRESS: A novel on Clive of India.

SIDELIGHTS: Mrs. Ward-Thomas reversed her original pseudonym used in magazine writing ("thought man's name more acceptable") when her first historical novel was published. Her first three novels form a trilogy based on Catherine the Great, her son, Paul I, and his son, Alexander I. She classifies her first seven novels as "animated history"—based on real people with endeavor to give a new slant on their contemporary relations and motives. She began writing pure historical fiction with *Clandara* and its sequel, *The Heiress.* She believes that the market "for animated historical fiction seems to be in temporary (I hope) doldrums."

About her literary and private life, the novelist says: "Have five children under seven and therefore have to write in a pretty noisy and confused atmosphere as like to look after them myself, rather than employ a nannie. Loathe house work or cooking and therefore employ two servants. Have six peacocks in my country home and don't mind the noise. Write for money, which is always useful."

She admits to a veneration for Napoleon, but does not feel competent to undertake a major work on him yet; she contents herself with collecting his personal papers, porcelain service, and other personal possessions. She also likes to entertain.

*   *   *

WARE, Timothy (Richard)   1934-

PERSONAL: Born September 11, 1934, in Bath, Somerset, England; son of Richard Fenwick and Evereld (Edwardes) Ware. *Education:* Attended Westminster

School, London, England, 1947-52; Magdalen College, Oxford, B.A., 1956; M.A., 1959. *Religion:* Eastern Orthodox. *Home:* Old Bridge, Kelvedon, Essex, England.

CAREER: Westminster Under School, London, England, classics master, 1958-59; Magdalen College, Oxford University, Oxford, England, researcher in church history, 1960-63; Russian Orthodox Church Outside of Russia, Montreal, Quebec, church publishing and other work for the archbishop, 1963-64. Jane Eliza Proctor visiting fellow, Princeton University, 1959-60. Church warden of the Orthodox Chapel, Shrine of Our Lady of Walsingham, Norfolk, England, 1961—; mission secretary of Orthodox Youth Association of Great Britain, 1961-63.

WRITINGS: The Orthodox Church, Penguin, 1963, revised edition, 1964; *Eustratios Argenti: A Study of the Greek Church under Turkish Rule,* Clarendon Press, 1964, Oxford University Press (New York), 1965; (author of introduction) Khariton, editor, *The Art of Prayer: An Orthodox Anthology,* Faber, 1966.

WORK IN PROGRESS: A Short Treasury of Orthodox Devotion, publication expected by J. Clarke; research on the early history of Christian monasticism in Egypt and Palestine in the fourth and fifth centuries; translations of the Orthodox Church service books from Greek into English.

SIDELIGHTS: Ware has travelled to, and been a member of, expeditions to Greece, Jerusalem, the Dead Sea, and monasteries of the Judaean wilderness.†

*   *   *

WARKENTIN, John 1928-

PERSONAL: Born March 3, 1928, at Lowe Farm, Manitoba, Canada; son of Isaac J. (a teacher) and Mary Warkentin; married Germaine Clinton, December 26, 1956; children: Juliet. *Education:* University of Manitoba, B.Sc., 1948; University of Toronto, M.A., 1954, Ph.D., 1961. *Office:* Department of Geography, York University, 2275 Bayview Ave., Toronto 12, Ontario, Canada.

CAREER: University of Manitoba, Winnipeg, Manitoba, Canada, teacher, 1959-63; York University, Toronto, Ontario, Canada, associate professor, 1963-68, professor of geography, 1968—. *Member:* Canadian Association of Geographers, American Association of Geographers, Canadian Historical Association, Champlain Society.

WRITINGS: (Editor) *The Western Interior of Canada: A Record of Geographical Discovery, 1612-1917,* McClelland & Stewart, 1964; (editor) *Canada: A Geographical Interpretation,* Methuen, 1968; (with Richard I. Ruggles) *Manitoba Historical Atlas: A Selection of Facsimile Maps, Plans and Sketches from 1612 to 1969,* Historical and Scientific Society of Manitoba, 1970.

WORK IN PROGRESS: Research into regional geography of western Canada and history of the scientific, exploration of Canada.

*   *   *

WARNER, Robert M(ark) 1927-

PERSONAL: Born June 28, 1927, in Montrose, Colo.; son of Mark Thomas (a clergyman) and Bertha (Rich) Warner; married Jane Bullock, August 21, 1954; children: Mark Steven, Jennifer Jane. *Education:* University of Denver, student, 1945; Muskingum College, A.B., 1949; University of Michigan, M.A., 1952, Ph.D., 1958. *Religion:* Presbyterian. *Home:* 1821 Coronada Dr., Ann Arbor, Mich. 48103. *Office:* Michigan Historical Collections, 160 Rackham Building, Ann Arbor, Mich.

CAREER: Michigan Historical Collections, Ann Arbor, assistant director, 1961-66, director, 1966—; University of

Michigan, Ann Arbor, 1961—, began as lecturer, currently associate professor of history. Ann Arbor Historical Commission, member, 1966—. *Military service:* U.S. Army, 1950-52; became sergeant. *Member:* American Historical Association, Society of American Archivists, American Association for State and Local History, Organization of American Historians, Historical Society of Michigan (trustee, 1961-67, 1970—; secretary-treasurer, 1970—), Michigan Academy of Science, Arts, and Letters.

WRITINGS: Guide to Manuscripts in the Michigan Historical Collections of the University of Michigan, Michigan Historical Collections, 1963; *Profile of a Profession: A History of the Michigan State Dental Association,* Wayne State University Press, 1964; (with Ruth B.A. Bordin) *The Modern Manuscript Library,* Scarecrow, 1966; *Chase Salmon Osborn, 1860-1949,* University of Michigan, 1969.

*   *   *

WARSHOFSKY, Fred 1931-

PERSONAL: Born February 14, 1931, in Brooklyn, N.Y.; son of Jack and Mariam (Silverstein) Warshofsky; married Carol Barbara Masnik, June 7, 1959; children: Marian Kay, Beth Marla, Amy Ruth. *Education:* New York University, B.A., 1952; Columbia University, graduate study, 1963-64. *Agent:* Theron Raines, 244 Madison Ave., New York, N.Y. 10016.

CAREER: Free-lance magazine writer, 1957-63; *Parade,* New York, N.Y., science and medical editor, 1963-66; CBS News, New York, N.Y., science editor and writer of "21st Century" series, 1966-69. *Military service:* U.S. Navy, 1953-56; became lieutenant. *Member:* American Association for the Advancement of Science Writing, Writers Guild of America, National Association of Science Writers. *Awards, honors:* National Kidney Foundation award, 1965; Emmy awards, National Academy of Television Arts and Sciences, both 1968, for "21st Century" and "Who Shall Play God?"; Albert Lasker award, 1968, for "Man-Made Man"; special commendation, American Medical Association, 1969; Dumont-UCLA International Journalism Award, 1970.

WRITINGS: War Under the Waves, Pyramid Books, 1962; *Epidemic Detectives,* Scholastic Book Services, 1963; *The Rebuilt Man: The Story of Spare-Parts Surgery,* Crowell, 1965; (with S. Smith Stevens) *Sound and Hearing,* Time, Inc., 1965; *Target Moon,* Four Winds, 1966; (with Edward Edelson) *Poisons in the Air,* Pocket Books, 1966; *The Twenty-First Century: The Control of Life,* Viking, 1969; *The Twenty-First Century: The New Age of Exploration,* Viking, 1969.

Television documentaries—All produced by CBS for "The 21st Century," except as indicated: "The Communications Explosion," January 29, 1967; "To the Moon," February 5, 1967; "A Trip from Chicago," February 19, 1967; "Mystery of Life," February 26, 1967; "The Remarkable Schoolhouse," March 5, 1967; "At Home, 2001," March 12, 1967; "Mars and Beyond," March 19, 1967; "Man-Made Man," March 26, 1967; "The Deep Frontier," April 2, 1967; "Autos, Autos Everywhere," April 9, 1967; "Cities of the Future," April 16, 1967; "The Class of '01," April 23, 1967; "Conquering the Sea," April 30, 1967; "Standing Room Only," May 7, 1967; "The Mighty Atom," May 14, 1967; "The Futurists," May 21, 1967; "The Laser: A Light Fantastic," September 10, 1967; "Atomic Medicine," September 17, 1967; "The Computer Revolution," Part I, September 24, 1967; "The Computer Revolution," Part II, October 1, 1967; "The Four-Day Week," October 15, 1967; "Bats, Birds and Bionics," October 22, 1967; "Miracle of the Mind," October 29, 1967; "New Weapons Against Crime," January 28, 1968;

"Medical Electronics," February 4, 1968; "Now You See It," February 11, 1968; "From Cradle to Classroom," Part I, February 18, 1968; "From Cradle to Classroom," Part II, February 25, 1968; "Jonas Salk: Science of Life," March 3, 1968; "How Do Things Look?," March 10, 1968; "Fighting Fear with Fear," March 15, 1968; "Can We Live to Be 100?," March 24, 1968; "Industries of the Future," March 31, 1968; "The Shape of Films to Come," April 1, 1968; "The Human Heart," April 7, 1968; "Anatomy of a Shoot," April 12, 1968; "The Weird World of Robots," September 15, 1968; "Can We Control the Weather?," September 22, 1968; "The Good Revolution," September 29, 1968; "An Incredible Voyage," October 13, 1968; "Games Futurists Play," October 20, 1968; "Surviving in Space," October 27, 1968; "Eye in the Sky," produced by CTV, 1970. Also author of other scripts for "The 21st Century," produced in 1969, and for "The Great American Dream Machine," NET, 1971. Contributor to national magazines, including *Saturday Evening Post, Reader's Digest,* and *Pageant.*

*   *   *

WARTH, Robert D(ouglas)   1921-

PERSONAL: Born December 16, 1921, in Houston, Tex.; son of Robert Douglas (an industrial engineer) and Virginia (Adams) Warth; married Lillian Eleanor Terry (a librarian), September 18, 1945. *Education:* University of Kentucky, B.S., 1943; University of Chicago, M.A., 1945, Ph.D., 1949. *Home:* 640 West Cooper Dr., Lexington, Ky. 40502.

CAREER: University of Tennessee, Knoxville, instructor in history, 1950-51; Rutgers University, Newark, N.J., began as instructor, became assistant professor of history, 1951-58; Grolier Society, New York, N.Y., editor, 1960-64; Hunter College (now Hunter College of the City University of New York), Bronx, N.Y., lecturer in history 1962-63; Staten Island Community College, Staten Island, N.Y., associate professor of history, 1964-68; University of Kentucky, Lexington, professor of history, 1968—. University of Kentucky, summer instructor in history, 1949; Paine College, visiting professor, 1960. *Military service:* U.S. Army, 1943-44. *Member:* American Historical Association, American Association for the Advancement of Slavic Studies, American Association of University Professors. *Awards, honors:* New Jersey Author Award, 1963, for *Soviet Russia in World Politics,* and 1969, for *Joseph Stalin.*

WRITINGS: The Allies and the Russian Revolution: From the Fall of the Monarchy to the Peace of Brest-Litovsk, Duke University Press, 1954; *Soviet Russia in World Politics,* Twayne, 1963; *Joseph Stalin,* Twayne, 1969. Contributor to *Antioch Review, South Atlantic Quarterly, Nation, Russian Review,* and historical journals.

WORK IN PROGRESS: A biography of Lenin, to be published by Twayne.

AVOCATIONAL INTERESTS: Tennis, chess.

*   *   *

WASHINGTON, Joseph R(eed) Jr.   1930-

PERSONAL: Born October 30, 1930, in Iowa City, Iowa; son of Joseph R. (a minister) and Susie (Duncan) Washington; married Sophia May Holland, June 28, 1952; children: Bryan Reed, David Eugene. *Education:* University of Wisconsin, B.A., 1952; Andover Newton Theological School, B.D., 1957, advanced study, 1957-58; Boston University School of Theology, Th.D., 1961. *Office:* Department of Religious Studies, University of Virginia, Charlottesville, Va. 22903.

CAREER: Ordained to ministry of Baptist Church, 1957; now Methodist minister; assistant minister of Baptist church in Woburn, Mass., 1954-56; minister of Congregational church in West Newfield, Me., and of Methodist church in Newfield, Me., 1956-57; First Baptist Church, Brookline, Mass., minister to students, 1957-58; Boston University, Boston, Mass., associate Protestant chaplain, 1958-61; Dillard University, New Orleans, La., dean of chapel and assistant professor of religion and philosophy, 1961-63; Dickinson College, Carlisle, Pa., chaplain and assistant professor of religion and philosophy, 1963-66; Albion College, Albion, Mich., associate professor of religion and dean of the chapel, 1966-69; Beloit College, Beloit, Wis., professor of religious studies and sociology and dean of the chapel, 1969-70; University of Virginia, Charlottesville, professor of religious studies and chairman of department of Afro-American studies, 1970—. *Military service:* U.S. Army, Corps of Military Police 1952-54; served in Korea; became first lieutenant. *Member:* American Society of Christian Ethics, American Academy of Religion, National Association of College and University Chaplains (treasurer, 1963-66; vice-president, 1969-70), National Association of Biblical Instructors, Society for the Scientific Study of Religion, National Association for the Advancement of Colored People (former president, Carlisle, Pa.). *Awards, honors:* D.D., University of Vermont, 1969.

WRITINGS: Black Religion: The Negro and Christianity in the United States, Beacon Press, 1964; *The Politics of God,* Beacon Press, 1967; *Black and White Power Subreption,* Beacon Press, 1969; *Marriage in Black and White,* Beacon Press, 1970; *Black Sects and Cults,* Doubleday, 1972. Contributor of articles on racial and religious issues to *Central Christian Advocate, Motive, Theology Today, Religious Education,* and *Foundations.*

BIOGRAPHICAL/CRITICAL SOURCES: Christian Century, May 3, 1967, June 16, 1971.

*   *   *

WASSERMANN, Selma (Ginsberg)   1929-

PERSONAL: Born July 25, 1929, in New York, N.Y.; daughter of Julius and Mae (Goldstein) Ginsberg; married Jack Wassermann, 1950; children: Paula. *Education:* City College of New York (now City College of City University of New York), B.S., in Education, 1950, M.S. in Education, 1957; New York University, Ed.D., 1962. *Home:* 6006 Eagleridge Dr., West Vancouver, British Columbia, Canada. *Office:* Department of Education, Simon Fraser University, Burnaby 2, British Columbia, Canada.

CAREER: Columbus School, San Francisco, Calif., teacher, 1950-51; Abbey Lane School, Levittown, N.Y., teacher, 1952-56; Lee Road School, Levittown, N.Y., reading specialist, 1956-59, teacher, 1960-61; Hofstra University, Hempstead, N.Y., instructor, 1961-62; Newark State College, Union, N.J., associate professor, 1962-65, professor of education and assistant coordinator of curriculum and instruction, 1965-66; Simon Fraser University, Burnaby, British Columbia, associate professor of education, 1966—. Lecturer and consultant in Cumberland County, N.J., and Baltimore County, Md. *Member:* Association for Supervision and Curriculum Development, American Association of University Professors, Canadian Association of University Professors, American Education Research Association.

WRITINGS: (With husband, Jack Wasserman) *Guide for Improvement of Reading and Thinking,* Benefic, 1962.

With Jack Wasserman, "Sailor Jack" series; all published by Benefic: *Sailor Jack,* 1960, *Sailor Jack's New Friend,* 1960, . . .*and Bluebell,* 1960, . . .*and the Target Ship,*

1960, . . .and Bluebell's Dive, 1961, . . .and Eddy, 1961, . . .and Homer Pots, 1961, . . .Goes North, 1961, . . .and the Ball Game, 1962, . . .and the Jet Plane, 1962.

With Jack Wasserman, "Moonbeam" series, published by Benefic: Moonbeam, 1965, Moonbeam at the Rocket Port, 1965, . . .Is Caught, 1965, . . .and the Captain, 1965, . . .and Dan Star, 1966, . . .and Sunny, 1967, . . .Finds a Moon Stone, 1967, . . .Is Lost, 1970.†

* * *

WASSERSTROM, (Jacob) William 1922-

PERSONAL: Born October 14, 1922, in Brooklyn, N.Y.; son of Isaiah (a businessman) and Nellie (Bergknopf) Wasserstrom; married Rose Friedenberg (a college ceramics teacher), December 17, 1944; children: Robert, John Andrews, James. Education: Bucknell University, A.B., 1946; Columbia University, M.A., 1947, Ph.D., 1951. Home: 102 Brockton Lane, Dewitt, N.Y. 13214. Office: Syracuse University, Syracuse, N.Y. 13210.

CAREER: Adelphi University, Garden City, N.Y., instructor in English, 1951-52; Swarthmore College, Swarthmore, Pa., assistant professor of English, 1952-54; University of Rochester, Rochester, N.Y., assistant professor of English, 1954-60; Syracuse University, Syracuse, N.Y., began as associate professor, became professor of English, 1960—. Visiting professor, Cornell University, 1965; Fulbright Professor of American Literature, University of Pisa and University of Bologna, Italy, 1965-66; NATO Visiting Professor of American literature, University of Venice, Italy, 1971. Member: American Association of University Professors, Modern Language Association.

WRITINGS: Heiress of All the Ages: Sex and Sentiment in the Genteel Tradition, University of Minnesota Press, 1959; (editor) The Time of The Dial, Syracuse University Press, 1963; (editor) A Dial Miscellany, Syracuse University Press, 1963; (editor and author of introduction) Civil Liberties and the Arts: Selections from "Twice a Year," 1938-48, Syracuse University Press, 1964; (editor and author of introduction) The Modern Short Novel, Holt, 1965; The Genius of American Fiction, Allyn & Bacon, 1970; The Legacy of Van Wyck Brooks: A Study of Maladies and Motives, Southern Illinois University Press, 1971. Contributor of articles to Yale Review, Sewanee Review, American Quarterly, Psychoanalysis, Nation, Prairie Schooner, Psychiatric Opinion, Virginia Quarterly Review, and other journals. Member of board of editors, Literature and Psychology and Hartford Studies in Literature.

WORK IN PROGRESS: Energy and Genius: Henry Adams and American Thought, completion expected in 1974.

AVOCATIONAL INTERESTS: Travel, tennis.

BIOGRAPHICAL/CRITICAL SOURCES: Saturday Review, December 21, 1963.

* * *

WATKINS, A(rthur) M(artin) 1924-

PERSONAL: Born August 6, 1924, in New York, N.Y.; son of Harry (a builder) and Hilda (Bergen) Watkins; married Joyce M. Orr, August 20, 1949; children: David M., Anne Elizabeth, Mary Ellen. Education: Drexel Institute of Technology, B.S. in Mechanical Engineering, 1944. Home and office: 855 River Rd., Piermont, N.Y. 10968.

CAREER: Air-conditioning engineer, 1947-51; associate editor, House and Home magazine, Dewitt, 1952-57; free-lance writer, 1957—. Military service: U.S. Navy, 1944-46. Member: Society of Magazine Writers, Authors League.

WRITINGS: How to Judge a House Before You Build or Buy, All About Houses, Inc., 1960; Building or Buying the High-Quality House at the Lowest Cost, Doubleday, 1962; The Complete Book of Home Remodeling, Improvement and Repair: A Handbook for the Owner Who Wants to Do It Right—But Not Do It Himself, Doubleday, 1963; How to Avoid the Ten Biggest Home-Buying Traps, Meredith, 1968; The Home-Owner's Survival Kit: How to Beat the High Cost of Owning and Operating Your Home, Hawthorn, 1971. Contributor to American Home, Better Homes and Gardens, Family Circle, Harper's, Redbook, and other magazines.

* * *

WATKINS-PITCHFORD, Denys James 1905-
(BB, Michael Traherne)

PERSONAL: Born July 25, 1905, in Lamport, Northamptonshire, England; son of Walter and Edith Elizabeth (Wilson) Watkins-Pitchford; married Cecily Mary Adnitt, August 10, 1939; children: Angela June, Robin John (deceased). Education: Privately educated; Royal College of Art, A.R.C.A. Home: The Round House, Sudborough, Kettering, England. Agent: David Higham Associates Ltd., 76 Dean St., London W.1, England.

CAREER: Rugby School, Warwickshire, England, art master, 1934-49; retired to devote full time to writing and illustrating. Illustrator of other books besides his own. Military service: Royal Horse Artillery territorial army, 1925-29; King's Prize, 1928; Home Guard, World War II; became captain. Member: Royal Society of Arts (fellow). Awards, honors: British Library Association Carnegie Medal, for The Little Grey Men, as outstanding children's book of the year.

WRITINGS—Under pseudonym BB; all self-illustrated under own name: The Sportsman's Bedside Book, Eyre & Spottiswoode, 1937; Wild Lone: The Story of a Pytchley Fox, Eyre & Spottiswoode, 1938; Manka, the Sky Gipsy: The Story of a Wild Goose, Scribner, 1939 (published in England as Sky Gipsy: The Story of a Wild Goose, Eyre & Spottiswoode, 1939); The Countryman's Bedside Book, Eyre & Spottiswoode, 1941; The Idle Countryman, Eyre & Spottiswoode, 1943; Brendon Chase, Hollis & Carter, 1944, Scribner, 1945; (compiler) The Fisherman's Bedside Book, Eyre & Spottiswoode, 1945, Scribner, 1946, 2nd edition, Eyre & Spottiswoode, 1955; The Wayfaring Tree, Hollis & Carter, 1946; The Shooting Man's Bedside Book, Scribner, 1946; A Stream in Your Garden: How the Amateur May Install Running Water in Rock Gardens, and the Construction of Pools, Eyre & Spottiswoode, 1948; (under pseudonym Michael Traherne) Be Quiet and Go A-Angling, Lutterworth, 1949; Confessions of a Carp Fisher, Eyre & Spottiswoode, 1950, 2nd edition, revised, Witherby, 1970; Tide's Ending, Scribner, 1950; Letters from Compton Deverell, Eyre & Spottiswoode, 1950, new edition, 1954; Dark Estuary, Hollis & Carter, 1953; (contributor) 5 More: Stories, Basil Blackwell, 1957; Alexander, Basil Blackwell, 1958; A Carp Water (Wood Pool) and How to Fish It, Putnam (London), 1958; The Autumn Road to the Isles, Nicholas Kaye, 1959; The White Road Westwards, Nicholas Kaye, 1961; September Road to Caithness and the Western Sea, Nicholas Kaye, 1962; The Summer Road to Wales, Nicholas Kaye, 1964; A Summer on the Nene, Kaye & Ward, 1967; At the Back o' Ben Dee, Benn, 1968; The Whopper, Benn, 1969. Contributor to Country Life, Field, and Shooting Times.

Juveniles—Under pseudonym BB; all self-illustrated under own name: The Little Grey Men: A Story for the Young in Heart, Eyre & Spottiswoode, 1942, Scribner, 1949, 3rd edition, Eyre & Spottiswoode, 1952; Down the Bright Stream, Eyre & Spottiswoode, 1948; Meeting Hill: BB's Fairy Book, Hollis & Carter, 1948; The Wind in the

Wood, Hollis & Carter, 1952; *The Forest of Boland Light Railway,* Eyre & Spottiswoode, 1955, published in America as *The Forest of the Railway,* Dodd, 1957; *Monty Woodpig's Caravan,* Edmund Ward, 1957; *Ben the Bullfinch,* Hamish Hamilton, 1957; *Wandering Wind,* Hamish Hamilton, 1957; *Monty Woodpig and His Bubblebuzz Car,* Edmund Ward, 1958; *Mr. Bumstead,* Eyre & Spottiswoode, 1958; *The Wizard of Boland,* Edmund Ward, 1959; *Bill Badger's Winter Cruise,* Hamish Hamilton, 1959; *Bill Badger and the Pirates,* Hamish Hamilton, 1960; *Bill Badger's Finest Hour,* Hamish Hamilton, 1961; *The Badgers of Bearshanks,* Benn, 1961; *Bill Badger's Whispering Reeds Adventure,* Hamish Hamilton, 1962; *Lepus, the Brown Hare,* Benn, 1962; *Bill Badger's Big Mistake,* Hamish Hamilton, 1963; *The Pegasus of the Countryside,* Dobson, 1964; *Bill Badger and the Big Store Robbery,* Hamish Hamilton, 1967; *Bill Badger's Voyage to the World's End,* Kaye & Ward, 1969; *The Tyger Tray,* Methuen, 1971.

Illustrator: Hesketh V. Prichard, *Sport in Wildest Britain,* Philip Allan, 1936; Robert G. Walmsley, *Winged Company: Sudies in Birdwatching,* Eyre & Spottiswoode, 1940; Clarence H. Warren, *England is a Village,* Eyre & Spottiswoode, 1940, Dutton, 1941; Eric Benfield, *Southern English,* Eyre & Spottiswoode, 1942; L.T.C. Rolt, *Narrow Boat,* Eyre & Spottiswoode, 1944; Brian Vesey-Fitzgerald, *It's My Delight,* Eyre & Spottiswoode, 1947; Arthur Applin, *Philandering Angler,* Hurst & Blackett, 1948; J.B. Drought, *A Sportsman Looks at Eire,* Hutchinson, 1949; Arthur G. Street, *Landmarks,* Eyre & Spottiswoode, 1949; Gerald D. Adams, *Red Vagabond: The Story of a Fox,* Batchworth, 1951; Mabel C. Carey, editor, *Fairy Tales of Long Ago,* Dutton, 1952; Arthur B.W. Richards, *Vix: The Story of a Fox Cub,* Benn, 1960; Henry Stuart Tegner, *Beasts of the North Country, from Whales to Shrews,* Galley Press, 1961; Andrew Lang, *Prince Prigio and Prince Ricardo,* Dent, 1961; Arthur B.W. Richards, *Birds of the Lonely Lake,* Benn, 1961; Arthur B.W. Richards, *The Cabin in the Woods,* Friday Press, 1963; A.R. Channel, *Rogue Elephant,* Macrae Smith, 1963; Norah A. Burke, *King Todd: The True Story of a Wild Badger,* Putnam (London), 1963; Frances Browne, *Granny's Wonderful Chair,* Dutton, 1963; Arthur B.W. Richards, *The Wild White Swan,* Friday Press, 1965; Henry Stuart Tegner, *To Do with Birds,* Jenkins, 1965; George Macdonald, *The Lost Princess: A Double Story,* Dutton, 1965; A.R. Channel, *Jungle Rescue,* S.G. Phillips, 1968.

SIDELIGHTS: Watkins-Pitchford's books have been translated for publication in Germany, Holland, Yugoslavia, and Israel.

* * *

WATNEY, John B(asil) 1915-
(Anthony Roberts)

PERSONAL: Born January 13, 1915, in London, England; son of Basil Gilbey (an architect) and Margit (Dietrichsen) Watney; married Antoinette Pratt-Barlow (a painter), November 6, 1948; children: Marcus John Andrew. *Education:* University of Poitiers, Bachelier es Lettres, 1933; Wadham College, Oxford, B.A., 1947. *Religion:* Church of England. *Home:* Flat 36, 5 Elm Park Gardens, London SWIO 9QQ, England. *Agent:* c/o Hope Leresche & Steele Literary Agents, 11 Jubilee Place, London S.W.3, England. *Office:* Queens Gate Place Tutors, 17 Queens Gate Place, London SW7 5NY, England.

CAREER: Journalist, reporter, columnist, London, England, 1947-54; Imperial Chemical Industries, London, publicity executive, 1954-61; Invalid Childrens Aid Association, London, assistant general secretary, 1963-70; Queens Gate Place Tutors, London, director, 1970—. *Military service:* British Army, 1939-46; became captain.

Member: Society of Authors, Institute of Journalists, P.E.N., Chelsea Arts Club.

WRITINGS: The Enemy Within, Hodder & Stoughton, 1946; *The Unexpected Angel,* Collins, 1949; *Common Love,* Putnam, 1954; *Leopard with a Thin Skin,* J. Cape, 1959; *The Quarrelling Room,* J. Cape, 1960; *The Glass Facade,* J. Cape, 1963; *He Also Served,* Hamish Hamilton, 1971. Contributor to *New Yorker* and to British magazines and newspapers.

Under pseudonym Anthony Roberts; all published by J. Gifford: *Sunstroke,* 1943, *Scheme for One,* and *The Five Houses.*

WORK IN PROGRESS: A thriller; a historical work on beer; a biography; *Clive of India.*

* * *

WATSON, William 1917-

PERSONAL: Born January 5, 1917, in Clydebank, Scotland; son of Thomas and Jessie (Brockett) Watson; married Pamela Matthews, February 8, 1949; children: Hamish Brockett, Calum Macfarlane, Angus Clark. *Education:* Jesus College, Cambridge, B.A., 1948, M.Sc., 1950; University of Manchester, Ph.D., 1953. *Home:* 1847 Rolling Hills, Norman, Okla. 73069. *Office:* University of Oklahoma, Norman, Okla. 73069.

CAREER: Medical Research Council, London, England, research anthropologist, 1948-51; Rhodes-Livingstone Institute for Social Research, Lusaka, Northern Rhodesia, research officer, 1951-56; University of Manchester, Manchester, England, senior lecturer in sociology, 1956-63; University of Virginia, Charlottesville, visiting professor of sociology, 1963-64, professor of sociology, 1964-69; University of Oklahoma, Norman, professor of sociology and chairman of department, 1969—. Medical Research Council, Social Medicine Research Unit, consultant sociologist, 1959-63. British Ministry of Education, member of Youth Service Development Council, 1960-63. *Military service:* Royal Air Force, 1938-45; became flight lieutenant; received Distinguished Flying Cross. *Member:* Association of Social Anthropologists, Royal Anthropological Institute, British Sociological Association, International African Institute, African Studies Association, Association of University Teachers.

WRITINGS: Tribal Cohesion in a Money Economy, Manchester University Press, 1958, Humanities, 1964; (with M.W. Susser) *Sociology in Medicine,* Oxford University Press, 1962; *The Youth Service and Education in Britain,* UNESCO Youth Institute, 1962. Contributor of articles to learned journals, newspapers, and magazines.

WORK IN PROGRESS: Preparing research work in socio-medical field for publication.

* * *

WATZLAWICK, Paul 1921-

PERSONAL: Surname is accented on first syllable: born July 25, 1921, in Villach, Austria; son of Paul (a bank manager) and Emy (Casari) Watzlawick. *Education:* University of Venice (Ca Foscari), Italy, Ph.D., 1949; C.G. Jung Institute for Analytical Psychology, Zurich, Switzerland, analyst's diploma, 1954. *Office:* Mental Research Institute, 555 Middlefield Rd., Palo Alto, Calif. 94301.

CAREER: Training analyst accredited with C.G. Jung Institute for Analytical Psychology. Psychotherapist in private practice, 1954—. University of El Salvador, San Salvador, professor of abnormal psychology and psychotherapy in Medical School and department of psychology, 1957-59; Temple University, Medical Center, Philadelphia, Pa., research associate at Institute for Study of

Psychotherapy, 1960; Mental Research Institute, Palo Alto, Calif., research associate, 1960—; Stanford University, Palo Alto, Calif., clinical instructor in psychiatry department, 1967—. *Member:* International Association for Analytical Psychology, American Psychological Association.

WRITINGS: An Anthology of Human Communication (text and tapes), Science and Behavior Books, 1964; (with Janet Helmick Beavin and Don D. Jackson) *Pragmatics of Human Communication: A Study of Interactional Patterns, Pathologies, and Paradoxes,* Norton, 1967; (contributor) H.-G. Gadamer, editor, *Neue Anthropologie,* Volume 5, Georg Thieme Verlag, 1971. Contributor of articles to professional journals.

WORK IN PROGRESS: Study of behavioral effects of human communication, especially in psychotherapy.

*   *   *

WEAVER, John D(owning) 1912-

PERSONAL: Born February 4, 1912, in Washington, D.C.; son of Henry Byrne (official reporter of House of Representatives), and Beatrice (Petty) Weaver; married Harriett Sherwood, May 28, 1937. *Education:* Georgetown University, student, 1928-29; College of William and Mary, A.B., 1932; George Washington University, A.M., 1933. *Home:* 9933 Beverly Grove Dr., Beverly Hills, Calif. 90210. *Agent:* Harold Ober Associates, 40 East 49th St., New York, N.Y. 10017.

CAREER: Worked for various Federal agencies, including the National Recovery Administration, Washington, D.C., and Richmond, Va., 1933-35; *Kansas City Star,* reporter, feature writer, book reviewer, and copy editor, 1935-40; free-lance writer, 1940—. West coast editor, *Holiday,* 1964—. *Military service:* U.S. Army, Signal Corps, 1943-46.

WRITINGS: Wind Before Rain, Macmillan, 1942; *Another Such Victory,* Viking, 1948; *As I Live and Breathe,* Rinehart, 1959; *Tad Lincoln, Mischief-Maker in the White House,* Dodd, 1963; *The Great Experiment: An Intimate View of the Everyday Workings of the Federal Government,* Little, Brown, 1965; *Warren: The Man, the Court, the Era,* Little, Brown, 1967; *The Brownsville Raid: The Story of America's "Black Dreyfus Affair",* Norton, 1970. Contributor of articles and short stories to magazines, including *Harper's, Atlantic Monthly, Collier's,* and *Holiday.*

BIOGRAPHICAL/CRITICAL SOURCES: New York Times Book Review, September 24, 1967; *Book World,* October 1, 1967; *Times Literary Supplement,* January 18, 1968; *Punch,* January 24, 1968.

*   *   *

WEAVER, Robert C(lifton) 1907-

PERSONAL: Born December 29, 1907, in Washington, D.C.; son of Mortimer G. (a government clerk) and Florence (Freeman) Weaver; married Ella V. Haith (a college professor), July 18, 1935; children: Robert, Jr. (deceased). *Education:* Harvard University, B.S., 1929, M.A., 1931, Ph.D., 1934. *Politics:* Democrat. *Home:* 215 East 86th St., New York, N.Y. 10021. *Office:* Department of Urban Affairs, Hunter College of the City University of New York, 790 Madison Ave., New York, N.Y. 10021.

CAREER: U.S. Government, Washington, D.C., adviser on Negro affairs for U.S. Department of Interior, 1933-37, special assistant to administrator of U.S. Housing Authority, 1937-40, administrative assistant for War Planning Board, 1940-42; J.H. Whitney Foundation, New York, N.Y., director of opportunity fellowships, 1949-54; State of New York, New York, deputy commissioner of housing, 1955, rent control administrator, 1955-58; Ford Foundation, New York, N.Y., consultant, 1959-60; Housing and Redevelopment Board, New York, N.Y., vice-chairman, 1960-61; U.S. Government, Washington, D.C., administrator, Housing and Home Finance Agency, 1961-66, secretary of Housing and Urban Development, 1966-68; City University of New York, New York, N.Y., president of Bernard M. Baruch College of Business and Public Administration, 1969-70, Distinguished Professor of Urban Affairs at Hunter College, 1970—. Visiting professor, Columbia University, 1947, New York University, 1947-49. Trustee, Bowery Savings Bank and Metropolitan Life Insurance Co. Member, Comptroller General's Consultant Panel. Former chairman, National Association for the Advancement of Colored People. *Member:* National Academy of Public Administration, Committee for Economic Development, National Research Council (member of research advisory board), American Academy of Arts and Sciences (fellow), Royal Society for the Encouragement of Arts, Manufacture and Commerce (Benjamin Franklin Fellow). *Awards, honors:* LL.D., Harvard University, Howard University, Morehouse College, Amherst College, Boston College, Rutgers University, University of Michigan, Southern Illinois University, Columbia University, Unversity of Pennsylvania; L.H.D., Temple University, Pratt Institute; D.C.L., University of Illinois; D.S.S., Duquesne University; fifteen other honorary degrees; Springarn Medal, National Association for the Advancement of Colored People, 1962; Albert Einstein Commemorative Award, 1968.

WRITINGS: Hemmed In: ABC's of Race Restrictive Housing Covenants, American Council on Race Relations, 1945; *Negro Labor: A National Problem,* Harcourt, 1946; *The Negro Ghetto,* Harcourt, 1948; *The Future of the American City,* Ohio State University, 1962; *The Urban Complex: Human Values in Urban Life,* Doubleday, 1964; *Housing for Senior Citizens: A Progress Report,* Office of the Administrator, Housing and Home Finance Agency, 1964; *Dilemmas of Urban America,* Harvard University Press, 1965; *Cities in Crisis* (address), Urban America, 1968; (with William E. Zisch and Paul H. Douglas) *The Urban Environment: How It Can Be Improved,* New York University Press, 1969.

Contributor: *The Urban Negro Worker in the United States, 1925-1936,* two volumes, U.S. Government Printing Office, 1938-39; Leonard J. Diehl, editor, *The Urban Condition,* Basic Books, 1963; Margaret S. Gordon, editor, *Poverty in America,* Chandler Publishing, 1965; *The Metropolitan Future: California and the Challenge of Growth,* University of California Press, 1965; Joseph Tucker, editor, *Our Changing Cities,* Public Affairs Press, 1966; *Essays in Urban Economics,* Real Estate Research Program, University of California (Los Angeles), 1966; *New Towns: A New Dimension in Urbanism,* International City Managers Association, 1966; Leo Schnore and Henry Fagan, editors, *Urban Research and Policy Planning,* Sage Publications, 1967; *Urban Development: Its Implications for Social Welfare,* Columbia University Press, 1967; *Planning of Metropolitan Areas and New Towns,* United Nations, 1967; Jeffrey Y. Hadden, Louis H. Masotti, and Calvin J. Farrow, editors, *Metropolis in Crisis,* Peacock Press, 1967; Samuel I. Shuman, editor, *The Future of Federalism,* Wayne State University Press, 1968; Walter J. Ong, editor, *Knowledge and the Future of Man,* Holt, 1968; Edward W. Mill, editor, *Politics and Progress: Readings in American Government,* Silver Burdett, 1971; *Improving Management for More Effective Government,* U.S. Government Printing Office, 1972; Marion Clawson and Harvey Perloff, editors, *Modernizing Urban Land Policy,* Johns Hopkins Press, 1973. Also contributor to *Encyclopaedia Britannica,* 1968, and of some one hundred and thirty articles to periodicals.

BIOGRAPHICAL/CRITICAL SOURCES: Look, April 11, 1961; New York Times Magazine, May 14, 1961; Saturday Evening Post, December 22, 1962.

* * *

WEBB, Ruth Enid Borlase Morris 1926-
(Ruth Morris)

PERSONAL: Born August 24, 1926, in Queenscliff, Victoria, Australia; daughter of Basil Moorhouse (a major general) and Audrey (Cogan) Morris; married Geoffrey Heywood Webb (a grazier), October 5, 1961; children: Cecily (stepchild), Peter, Russell. Education: University of Melbourne, B.A., 1947. Politics: Australian Liberal. Religion: Anglican. Home: Coonawarra, Morven, via Culcairn, New South Wales, Australia.

CAREER: Kent County Council, Kent, England, teacher, 1949-50; St. Catherine's Girl's School, Melbourne, Australia, teacher, 1951; Commonwealth Public Service, Melbourne, Australia, typist, 1953-54; Hector Crawford Radio Productions, Melbourne, Australia, production executive, 1954-56. Member: Holbrook Pony Club.

WRITINGS: The Runaway, Rigby, 1961, published in America as Runaway Girl, Random House, 1962. Editor of scripts for domestic-type radio drama, and scriptwriter for radio.

AVOCATIONAL INTERESTS: Country pursuits, including fishing, riding, growing trees, and watching baby animals and birds.

* * *

WEBER, Francis J. 1933-

PERSONAL: Born January 22, 1933, in Indianapolis, Ind.; son of Frank J. (a plumbing company executive) and Katherine E. (Thompson) Weber. Education: Los Angeles College, A.A., 1953; St. John's College, Camarillo, Calif., B.A., 1955; St. John's Seminary, Camarillo, Calif., seminarian, 1955-59; Catholic University of America, M.A., 1962; American University, Certificate in Archival Administration, 1962. Home: 454 South Mansfield Ave., Los Angeles, Calif. 90036. Office: 1531 West Ninth St., Los Angeles, Calif. 90015.

CAREER: Ordained a Roman Catholic priest in 1959. Archdiocese of Los Angeles, Los Angeles, Calif., archivist, 1962—; Queen of Angels Seminary, San Fernando, Calif., professor of history, 1962-72; Saint Catherine's Military School, Anaheim, Calif., chaplain, 1972—. (Calif.) State Department of Parks and Recreation, member of California History Plan Committee, 1970—. Member: American Catholic Historical Society, Society of American Archivists, American Catholic Historical Association, Hispanic American Historical Society, Historical Society of Southern California, California Historical Society, Zamorano Club. Awards, honors: Grant-in-aid from American Association for State and Local History, 1968; merit award from Rounce and Coffin Club, 1969, for The Missions and Missionaries of Baja California: An Historical Perspective.

WRITINGS: A Biographical Sketch of Right Reverend Francisco Garcia Diego y Moreno, O.F.M., First Bishop of the Californias, 1785-1846, Borromeo Guild, 1961; A Historiographical Sketch of Pioneer Catholicism in the Californias: Missions and Missionaries, California Historical Publications, 1961; A Biographical Sketch of Right Reverend Joseph Sadoc Alemany, O.P., Bishop of Monterey, 1850-1853, California Historical Publications, 1961; Saint Victor's Church: A Pictorial History of Pioneer Catholicism in West Hollywood, [Los Angeles], 1961; Bishop Amat at the Vatican Council, Saint John's University, 1962; California's Reluctant Prelate: The Life and Times of Right Reverend Thaddeus Amat, C.M.

(1811-1878), Dawson's Book Shop, 1964; (editor) The Spiritual Diary of Raphael Cardinal Merry del Val, Exposition, 1964; (editor) Documents of California Catholic History, 1784-1963, Dawson's Book Shop, 1965; George Thomas Montgomery, California Churchman, Westernlore, 1966; A Guide to Saint John's Seminary, Camarillo, California, Westernlore, 1966; (compiler) Sacerdotal Necrology for the Archdiocese of Los Angeles, 1840-1965, Chancery Archives, Archdiocese of Los Angeles, 1966; A Select Guide to California Catholic History, Westernlore, 1966; Francis Mora, Last of the Catalans, Westernlore, 1967; Readings in California Catholic History, Westernlore, 1967; A Bibliography of California Bibliographies, Ritchie, 1968; El Pueblo de Nuestra Senora de Los Angeles: An Inquiry into Early Appellations, Plantin Press, 1968; (editor) Francisco Orozco y Jimenez: An Apologia Pro Vita Sua, privately printed, 1968; Mission San Fernando, Westernlore, 1968; The Missions and Missionaries of Baja California: An Historical Perspective, Dawson's Book Shop, 1968; Up 65 Years to Larchmont, Bela Blau, 1969; A Bibliophilic Odyssey: The Story of the Bibliotheca Montereyensis-Angelorum Dioceseos, Westernlore, 1969; Christ on Wilshire Boulevard: Saint Basil's Catholic Church, Westernlore, 1969; Thomas James Conaty, Pastor, Educator, Bishop, Westernlore, 1969; The United States versus Mexico: The Final Settlement of the Pious Fund, foreword by Earl Warren, Historical Society of Southern California, 1969; What Happened to Junipero Serra?, Bela Blau, 1969; Catholic Footprints in California, Hogarth Press, 1970; The Founding of the Pueblo de Nuestra Senora de Los Angeles: A Study in Historiography, Plantin Press, 1970; A Letter of Junipero Serra to the Reverend Father Preacher Fray Francisco de Lasuen: A Bicentennial Discovery, Godine, 1970; A Select Los Angeles Bibliography, 1872-1970, Dawson's Book Shop, 1971; An Earthquake Memoir, Dawson's Book Shop, 1971; (with Doyce B. Nunis, Jr.) Maynard H. Geiger, O.F.M., Franciscan Historian: A 70th Birthday Tribute, Dawson's Book Shop, 1971; (translator) Turning the Tide: A Letter Written by Fray Junipero Serra, Godine, 1971; Francisco Garcia Diego, California's Transitional Bishop, Dawson's Book Shop, 1972; A Selected Bibliographical Guide to California History, Dawson's Book Shop, 1972; Hollywood's "Padre of the Films", Dawson's Book Shop, 1972; A Select Bibliography: The California Missions, 1765-1972, Dawson's Book Shop, 1972; The California Missions as Others Saw Them, Dawson's Book Shop, 1972. Writer of syndicated newspaper column, "California's Catholic Heritage." Contributor of more than fifty articles and reviews to religious and historical periodicals, including American Ecclesiastical Review, Hispanic American Historical Review, Catholic Digest, American Archivist, and California Librarian.

WORK IN PROGRESS: "The Catholic Church in California" series, with seven projected volumes.

* * *

WEBER, Gerard Peter 1918-

PERSONAL: Born May 8, 1918, in Chicago, Ill.; son of Jacob George and Marie (Henrici) Weber. Education: Quigley Preparatory Seminary, seminarian, 1932-37; St. Mary of the Lake Seminary, M.A., S.T.L. Home: 331 East 71st St., Chicago, Ill. 60619.

CAREER: Roman Catholic priest. Foundation for Adult Catechetical Teaching Aids, Chicago, Ill., vice-president, 1962—.

WRITINGS—All with James J. Killgallon: Life in Christ: Instructions in the Catholic Faith, Adult Catechetical Teaching Aids, 1958; The God Who Loves Us: A Program of Instructions Originally Prepared for Use in the Archdiocese of Chicago, Liturgical Press,

1962, reissued as *The God Who Loves Us: Encounter in the Sunday Gospels,* Sheed & Ward, 1963; *The Love of Neighbor,* Alba, 1964; *Our Love for God,* privately printed, 1964; *Beyond the Commandments,* Herder, 1964, revised edition, 1968; *Liturgical Sermons,* Alba, 1964; *Love One Another: Sermon Outlines for Sundays and Holydays,* Alba, 1965; *Witness to the World: Homilies on the Sunday Gospels,* Alba, 1965; *Praise the Lord: Homilies on the Sunday Gospels,* Alba, 1966; *To Be Church: Source Material for Homilies on the Sunday Scripture Readings,* Alba, 1967. Also author, with Sister Mary Michael O'Shaughnessy and others, of *The Child and the Christian Mystery: Essays on the Philosophy of Elementary School Religious Education,* Benziger, 1965. Contributor of articles to magazines. Co-editor of *Word and Worship;* editor of a series of eight books in the Catholic religion for use in Catholic grade schools.

*   *   *

WEDDLE, Ethel Harshbarger   1897-

PERSONAL: Born September 6, 1897, in Girard, Ill.; daughter of Isaac Joseph (a farmer-preacher) and Martha (Brubaker) Harshbarger; married Lemon Talmage Weddle (a farmer), November 19, 1919; children: Edgar (deceased), Marzetta (Mrs. Oscar Rutherford, Jr.), Lois (Mrs. Henry L. Tipton), Leroy. *Education:* La Verne College, drama student, 1913-14; Illinois State Library extension courses in librarianship and writing. *Politics:* Republican. *Religion:* Protestant. *Home address:* R.F.D. 1, Girard, Ill. 62640.

CAREER: Girard Township Library, Girard, Ill., chief librarian, 1947—. *Member:* Illinois State Historical Society, Macoupin County Historical Society, American Legion Auxiliary (Girard; historian, 1952—), Girard Woman's Club (president, 1947-49; secretary, 1963-66).

WRITINGS: Pleasant Hill, Brethren Publishing, 1956; (contributor) *Ginn Basic Reader,* Ginn, 1957; *Walter Chrysler, Boy Machinist,* Bobbs-Merrill, 1960; (contributor) *Brethren Trail Blazers,* Brethren Press, 1960; *Joel Chandler Harris, Young Storyteller,* Bobbs-Merrill, 1964; *Alvin C. York, Young Marksman,* Bobbs-Merrill, 1967; *A Brubaker Genealogy: The Descendants of Henry Brubaker, 1775-1848, of Salem, Virginia,* Brethren Press, 1970. Contributor of stories to periodicals and Sunday school papers, including *American Childhood* and *Children's Activities.*

WORK IN PROGRESS: A human interest novel of central Illinois; an historical novel of southern Illinois, 1802-30; a book chronicling the growth of rural education in Illinois to 1912.

AVOCATIONAL INTERESTS: Book reviews, public speaking, dramatics, gardening, painting.

*   *   *

WEDDLE, Robert S(amuel)   1921-

PERSONAL: Born June 5, 1921, near Bonham, Tex.; son of Charles Leonard (a farmer) and Montee (Nelms) Weddle; married Nan Avis Williamson (a teacher), October 27, 1943; children: Timothy Robert, Teresa Weddle Rainwater. *Education:* Texas Technological College, B.A., 1947. *Politics:* Democrat. *Religion:* Methodist. *Home:* 1602 Glenvalley Dr., Austin, Tex. 78723. *Office:* 730 Littlefield Bldg., Austin, Tex. 78701.

CAREER: Avalanche-Journal (daily newspaper), Lubbock, Tex., reporter, 1942-43, 1946-47; United Press, Dallas, Tex., newswriter, columnist, and night manager, 1947-49; Texas A. & M. University, College Station, information assistant, 1950-52; *Democrat* (daily newspaper), Sherman, Tex., sports editor and city editor, 1952-56; *Menard News,* Menard, Tex., editor and publisher,

1956-67; University of Texas Press, Austin, production manager, 1967-70; public information director, Texas Criminal Justice Council, 1970—. Menard County Hospital Advisory Committee, member, 1957-58; Chamber of Commerce, Menard, Tex., director, 1957-59; Menard County Historical Society, president, 1963-64. *Military service:* U.S. Naval Reserve, 1943-46; became lieutenant j.g. *Member:* Texas Old Missions Restoration Association, Texas State Historical Association (fellow), West Texas Historical Association. *Awards, honors:* Amon G. Carter Award, Texas Institute of Letters, for year's best book on Southwestern history, 1968, for *San Juan Bautista.*

WRITINGS: The San Saba Mission: Spanish Pivot in Texas, University of Texas Press, 1964; *San Juan Bautista: Gateway to Spanish Texas,* University of Texas Press, 1968; *Wilderness Manhunt: The Spanish Search for La Salle,* University of Texas Press, 1972.

AVOCATIONAL INTERESTS: Photography, Southwestern history.

BIOGRAPHICAL/CRITICAL SOURCES: Youth's Instructor, Volume 108, nos. 21-25.

*   *   *

WEIGHTMAN, J(ohn) G(eorge)   1915-

PERSONAL: Born November 29, 1915, in Callerton, England; son of Lancelot (a coal miner) and Emily (Robson) Weightman; married Jessie Doreen Wade (a translator), June 10, 1940; children: Jane Isabel, Gavin Alan. *Education:* King's College, Durham, B.A. (honors in French), 1938; University of Poitiers, graduate study, 1937, 1939; University of London, Ph.D., 1955. *Politics:* Labour. *Religion:* Agnostic. *Home:* 13 Weech Rd., London N.W.6, England. *Office:* Westfield College, University of London, Hampstead, London N.W.3, England.

CAREER: British Broadcasting Corp., London, England, translator and announcer in French, later program organizer, 1939-50; King's College, University of London, London, lecturer in French, 1950-63; Westfield College, University of London, reader in French, 1963—. *Member:* L'Alliance Francaise (council member), P.E.N.

WRITINGS: (Translator) Alice Jahier, *Inoubliable France,* Sylvan Press, 1944; (editor and translator) *French Writing on English Soil,* Sylvan Press, 1945; *On Language and Writing,* Sylvan Press, 1947; (translator) Werner Bischof, *Japan,* Sylvan Press, 1954; (translator) Henri de Montherlant, *Selected Essays,* Weidenfeld & Nicolson, 1960; (contributor) John Cruickshank, editor, *The Novelist as Philosopher,* Oxford University Press, 1962; (translator with wife, Doreen Weightman) Roger Bordier, *The Golden Plain,* Gollancz, 1963; (translator with Doreen Weightman) Claude Levi-Strauss, *The Raw and the Cooked: Introduction to a Science of Mythology,* Volume I, Harper, 1970. Author of essays on French subjects, English literature, and sociological topics. Regular contributor to *Observer, Encounter,* and *Times Literary Supplement;* also contributor to *Nation, Commentary,* and *New York Review of Books.* Editor, *Twentieth Century,* 1955-56.

BIOGRAPHICAL/CRITICAL SOURCES: Harper's November, 1965.†

*   *   *

WEINBERG, Gerhard L(udwig)   1928-

PERSONAL: Born January 1, 1928, in Hanover, Germany; son of Max B. (an accountant) and Kathe (Grunebaum) Weinberg; married Wilma Jeffrey, March 29, 1958. *Education:* New York College for Teachers (now State University of New York at Albany), B.A., 1948; University of Chicago, M.A., 1949, Ph.D., 1951.

Politics: Democratic. *Religion:* Jewish. *Home:* 1400 Linwood Ave., Ann Arbor, Mich. 48103. *Office:* Department of History, University of Michigan, Ann Arbor, Mich. 48104.

CAREER: Columbia University, research analyst in war documentation project in Alexandria, Va., 1951-54; University of Chicago, Chicago, Ill., lecturer in modern European history, 1954-55; University of Kentucky, Lexington, began as visiting lecturer, became assistant professor of modern European history, 1955-56, 1957-59; American Historical Association, Alexandria, Va., director of microfilm project, 1956-57; University of Michigan, Ann Arbor, associate professor, 1959-63, professor of modern European history, 1963—. American Historical Association, consultant on German documents microfilming, 1957-60. Ann Arbor City Democratic party, chairman, 1961-63; Democratic State Central Committee of Michigan, member, 1963-67. *Military Service:* U.S. Army, 1946-47. *Member:* American Historical Association. *Awards, honors:* Rockefeller Foundation and Social Science Research Council fellow 1962-63; American Council of Learned Societies fellow, 1965-66; George Louis Beer Prize from American Historical Association, 1972, for *The Foreign Policy of Hitler's Germany.*

WRITINGS: (With others) *Guide to Captured German Documents,* Maxwell Air Force Base, 1952; *Germany and the Soviet Union, 1939-41,* E.J. Brill, 1954, Humanities, 1972; (editor) *Hitlers Zweites Buch: Ein Dokument aus dem Jahre 1928,* Deutsche Verlags-Anstalt, 1961; (with John Armstrong and others) *Soviet Partisans in World War II,* University of Wisconsin Press, 1964; *The Foreign Policy of Hitler's Germany, 1933-36: Diplomatic Revolution in Europe,* University of Chicago Press, 1969. Writer of guides to German records for National Archives. Contributor of articles and reviews to professional journals.

WORK IN PROGRESS: A two-volume history of German foreign policy in Hitler period, completion of second volume covering years 1937-39.

*   *   *

WEINGARTEN, Violet (Brown)   1915-

PERSONAL: Born February 23, 1915, in San Francisco, Calif.; daughter of William (a businessman) and Elvira (Fleischman) Brown; married Victor Weingarten (a public relations executive); children: Jan, Kathy. *Education:* Cornell University, student, 1931-35. *Home:* Croton Lake Rd., Mount Kisco, N.Y. 10549.

CAREER: Brooklyn Eagle, Brooklyn, N.Y., began as reporter, became department editor, 1937-49; Associated Press, district reporter, 1942-45. Victor Weingarten Public Relations, Inc., vice-president. *Member:* Authors Guild, P.E.N., Phi Beta Kappa.

WRITINGS: You Can Take Them with You: A Guide to Traveling with Children in Europe, Dutton, 1961; *The Mother Who Works Outside the Home,* Child Study Association of America, 1961; *The Nile, Lifeline of Egypt,* Garrard, 1964; *Life at the Bottom,* Citizens' Committee for Children of New York, c.1965; *The Jordan, River of the Promised Land,* Garrard, 1967; *Mrs. Beneker,* Simon & Schuster, 1968; *The Ganges, Sacred River of India,* Garrard, 1969; *A Loving Wife,* Knopf, 1969; *A Woman of Feeling,* Knopf, 1972. Also author of films, "The Deep Well," 1959, and "Debbie," 1961. Contributor of stories to *Atlantic Monthly, Ladies' Home Journal,* and *Saturday Evening Post.*

SIDELIGHTS: "The Deep Well" was a U.S. entry at the Venice and Edinburgh film festivals; "Debbie" won the American Film Festival Blue Ribbon award. Rastar Productions and Columbia are co-producing a motion picture of *Mrs. Beneker.*

BIOGRAPHICAL/CRITICAL SOURCES: Best Sellers, February 15, 1968; *Atlantic,* March, 1968, September, 1969; *New York Times Book Review,* August 24, 1969; *Saturday Review,* September 27, 1969.

*   *   *

WEINSTEIN, Arnold   1927-

PERSONAL: Born June 10, 1927, in New York, N.Y.; son of Samuel and Ada (Goldstein) Weinstein. *Education:* Attended University of London, 1949-50; Hunter College (now Hunter College of the City University of New York), B.A., 1951; Harvard University, M.A., 1953; attended University of Florence, 1958-60. *Home:* 156 West 13th St., New York, N.Y. 10011. *Agent:* International Famous Agency, 1301 Avenue of the Americas, New York, N.Y. 10019.

CAREER: Has been instructor in English at New York University, taught creative writing at University of Southern California, and English at Rutgers University; currently teaching creative writing at New School for Social Research, New York, N.Y. Director of drama workshop at Wagner College, summer writers conference, 1963—. *Military service:* U.S. Navy, 1944-46. *Member:* Phi Beta Kappa.

WRITINGS: Poems, [Rome,] 1960; (with others) *Pardon Me, Sir, But Is My Eye Hurting Your Elbow?* (screenplays), Geis, 1968.

Plays: *Red Eye of Love* (comedy; first produced Off-Broadway at Living Theatre, June 12, 1961), Grove, 1962; (author of English book and lyrics) Francis Thorne, "Fortuna" (musical), first produced in New York at Hardman Playhouse, January 3, 1962; "The 25¢ White Cap" (one-act), first produced Off-Broadway at Maidman Playhouse, March, 1963; (author of libretto) "Dynamite Tonight" (musical), first produced Off-Broadway at York Playhouse, March 15, 1964; produced Off-Broadway at Martinique Theatre, 1967; (with William Balcom) "Greatshot" (musical), first produced in New Haven at Yale Repertory Theatre, May 9, 1969. Has made numerous translations of poems and plays. Contributor to *New Directions 16* (anthology), 1957. Contributor to *Poetry, Encounter, Harper's Bazaar, Saturday Review, New Directions,* and other publications.

WORK IN PROGRESS: A collection of poems; two new plays.

SIDELIGHTS: Weinstein is competent in Latin, Greek, and Italian, less so in French and Spanish. *Red Eye of Love* has been translated into 15 languages.

BIOGRAPHICAL/CRITICAL SOURCES: Pierre Dommergues, *Les Ecrivains americains d'aujourd'hui,* Presses Universitaires de France, 1965; *New Leader,* April 10, 1967; *Show Business,* March 22, 1969; *Variety,* May 14, 1969; *Cue,* May 24, 1969.†

*   *   *

WEISGARD, Leonard Joseph   1916-
(Adam Green)

PERSONAL: Born December 13, 1916, in New Haven, Conn.; son of Samuel H. and Fanny (Cohen) Weisgard; married Phyllis Monnot (a designer and film-maker), February 22, 1952; children: Abigail, Christina, Ethan. *Education:* Attended Pratt Institute and New School for Social Research. *Residence:* Roxbury, Conn. 06783; temporarily living in Denmark.

CAREER: Artist, illustrator of some twenty books, freelance writer. R.H. Macy (department store), New York, N.Y., muralist, 1947-48; art director of *Childcraft,* Marshall Field Enterprises, Chicago, Ill., and art instructor in Roxbury, Conn., 1959-60, 1964; lecturer, Danbury State

College, Danbury, Conn., 1962, University of Arkansas, Fayetteville, 1963. United Nations Childrens Emergency Fund, member of art committee, 1953—. Roxbury (Conn.) School Board, chairman, 1959-63. *Member:* American Institute of Graphic Arts. *Awards, honors:* Caldecott Medal for the best illustrated book for children, 1947, for *The Little Island;* other awards from American Institute of Graphic Arts, Society of Illustrators.

WRITINGS—All self-illustrated: *Suki, the Siamese Pussy,* Thomas Nelson, 1937; *Cinderella* (retold), Garden City Publishing Co., 1939; *Whose Little Bird Am I?,* Crowell, 1944; (with Esther W. Reno) *Pick the Vegetables,* Lothrop, 1944; *Would You Like to Be a Monkey?,* Crowell, 1945; *Down Huckleberry Hill,* Scribner, 1947; *Pelican Here, Pelican There,* Scribner, 1948; (under pseudonym Adam Green) *The Funny Bunny Factory,* Grosset, 1950; *Who Dreams of Cheese?,* Scribner, 1950; *The Clean Pig,* Scribner, 1952; *Down Huckleberry Hill,* Scribner, 1947; *Let's Play,* World Publishing, 1951; *Let's Play Train,* Treasure Books, 1953; *My First Picture Book,* Grosset, 1953; *Silly Willy Nilly,* Scribner, 1953; *Just Like Me,* Treasure Books, 1954; *The Most Beautiful Tree in the World,* Wonder Books, 1956; *Mr. Peaceable Paints,* Scribner, 1956; *Treasures to See: A Museum Picture-Book,* Harcourt, 1956; *The Athenians in the Classical Period,* Coward, 1963; *The First Farmers in the New Stone Age,* Coward, 1966; *The Plymouth Thanksgiving,* Doubleday, 1967; *The Beginnings of Cities: Re-creation in Pictures and Text of Mesopotamian Life from Farming to Early City Building,* Coward, 1968.

Illustrator: Irmengarde Eberle, *Through the Harbor, from Everywhere,* Bobbs-Merrill, 1938; Esther W. Reno, *Pup Called Cinderella,* Bobbs-Merrill, 1939; Dorothy Clark, *Little Joe,* Lothrop, 1940; Julia Louise Reynolds, compiler, *Under the Greenwood Tree* (selected songs from Shakespeare's plays), Oxford University Press, 1940; Frances Cavanah, *Pedro of Santa Fe,* McKay, 1941; Frances Cavanah, *Louis of New Orleans,* McKay, 1941; Lavinia R. Davis and Marjorie Fischer, compilers, *Grab Bag: Stories for Each and Every One,* Doubleday, 1941; Mordecai M. Kaplan, *The New Haggadah,* Behrman, 1942; Lavinia R. Davis, *Americans Every One,* Doubleday, 1942; Marion Lacey, *Picture Book of Musical Instruments,* Lothrop, 1942; Maria Cristina Chambers, *The Water-Carrier's Secrets,* Oxford University Press, 1942; Elaine Wayne, *Bucky Bear, Who Would Not Take His Nap,* Lothrop, 1944; Elizabeth Howard, *Dorinda,* Lothrop, 1944; Gweneira Maureen Williams, *Timid Timothy, the Kitten Who Learned to Be Brave,* W.R. Scott, 1944; Nettie King, *Susie is a Kitten,* Garden City Publishing Co., 1945; Charlotte E. Jackson, *Round the Afternoon,* Dodd, 1946; Alvin R. Tresselt, *Rain Drop Splash,* Lothrop, 1946; Johanna Spyri, *Heidi,* World Publishing, 1946; Morrell Gipson, *City Country ABC,* Garden City Publishing Co., 1946; Clelia Delafield, *Mrs. Mallard's Ducklings,* Lothrop, 1946; Vivian Breck, *High Trail,* Doubleday, 1948; Alice I. Hazeltine and Elva S. Smith, compilers, *Just for Fun,* Lothrop, 1948; Lewis Carroll, *Alice's Adventures in Wonderland* [*and*] *Through the Looking Glass,* Harper, 1949; Clement Clarke Moore, *The Night Before Christmas,* Grosset, 1949; Alvin R. Tresselt, *The Little Lost Squirrel,* Grosset, 1950; Alice I. Hazeltine and Elva S. Smith, editors, *Stories of Love,* Lothrop, 1951; *The Family Mother Goose,* Harper, 1951; Kathryn Jackson, *Pantaloon,* Simon & Schuster, 1951; Kathryn Jackson, *Little Eskimo,* Simon & Schuster, 1952; Kathryn Jackson, *Wheels,* Simon & Schuster, 1952; Charlotte Zolotow, *Indian, Indian,* Simon & Schuster, 1952; Margueritte Harmon Bro, *Three, and Domingo,* Doubleday, 1953; Florence M. Fitch, *A Book About God,* Lothrop, 1953; Jakob Ludwig Karl and W.K. Grimm, *Grimms' Fairy Tales,* Garden City Publish-

ing Co., 1954; Evelyn Andreas, editor, *The Big Treasure Book of Nursery Tales, Retold,* Grosset, 1954; Jonathan Swift, *Gulliver's Travels* (edited for young readers), Doubleday, 1954; Alice Dalgliesh, *The Courage of Sarah Noble,* Scribner, 1954; L. Frank Baum, *The New Wizard of Oz,* Doubleday, 1955; Marjorie K. Rawlings, *Secret River,* Scribner, 1955; *The Big Book of Train Stories,* Grosset, 1955; Wilma P. Hays, *Pilgrim Thanksgiving,* Coward, 1955; Charles and Mary Lamb, *Tales from Shakespeare,* Doubleday, 1955; Beatrix Potter, *Peter Rabbit,* Grosset, 1955, revised edition, 1962; Florence M. Fitch, *The Child Jesus,* Lothrop, 1955; Hans Christian Andersen, *Fairy Tales,* Doubleday, 1956; Wilma P. Hays, *The Story of Valentine,* Coward, 1956; *Baby's Playthings,* McLoughlin, 1956; Miriam S. Potter, *Mrs. Goose's Green Trailer,* Wonder Books, 1956; Miriam Schlein, *Something for Now, Something for Later,* Harper, 1956; Samuel S. Vaughan, *Who Ever Heard of Kangaroo Eggs?,* Doubleday, 1957; Helen Ferris, editor, *Favorite Poems Old and New,* Doubleday, 1957; Alvin R. Tresselt, *Rabbit Story,* Lothrop, 1957; Isabel and Frederick Eberstadt, *Where Did Tuffy Hide?,* Little, Brown, 1957; Alf Evers, *Abner's. Cabin,* F. Watts, 1957; Hyman Chanover and Evelyn Zusman, *My Book of Prayer: Sabbath and Weekdays,* United Synagogue of America, 1957; Edric A. Weld and William Sydnor, *The Son of God: Readings from the Gospel According to St. Mark, with Background Information,* Seabury, 1957; Ruth Franchere, *Willa: The Story of Willa Cather's Growing Up,* Crowell, 1958; Patricia Miles Martin, *Sylvester Jones and the Voice in the Forest,* Lothrop, 1958; Gerald Ames and Rose Wyler, *First Days of the World,* Harper, 1958 (also published with *The First People in the World*—see below); Gerald Ames and Rose Wyler, *The First People in the World,* Harper, 1958 (also published with *First Days of the World*—see below); Hyman Chanover and Evelyn Zusman, *My Book of Prayer: Holidays and Holy Days,* United Synagogue of America, 1959; John D. Barnard and others, *The Macmillan Science-Life Series,* Macmillan, Books 1-6, 1959, Books 7-8, 1960; Clyde R. Bulla, *The Valentine Cat,* Crowell, 1959; Robert Nathan, *The Snowflake and the Starfish,* Knopf, 1959; Alice Dalgliesh, *Adam and the Golden Cock,* Scribner, 1959; Elizabeth A. Campbell, *Nails to Nickles: Story of American Coins Old and New,* Little, Brown, 1960; Isabel and Frederick Eberstadt, *Who is at the Door?,* Little, Brown, 1960; Sylvia Berger Redman, *Do You Want to Hear a Secret?,* Lothrop, 1960; Nora Kramer, editor, *Cozy Hour Storybook,* Random House, 1960; May Garelick, *Where Does the Butterfly Go When It Rains?,* W.R. Scott, 1961; Patricia M. Martin, *The Raccoon and Mrs. McGinnis,* Putnam, 1961; Virginia Haviland, editor, *Favorite Fairy Tales Told in Norway, Retold from Norse Folklore,* Little, Brown, 1961; James Otis, *Toby Tyler; or, Ten Weeks with a Circus,* Doubleday, 1961; Mary Le Duc O'Neill, *Hailstones and Halibut Bones: Adventure in Color,* Doubleday, 1961; Claudia Lewis, *When I Go to the Moon,* Macmillan, 1961; Margaret Bevans, editor, *McCall's Read Me a Story Book,* Putnam, 1961; Isabel and Frederick Eberstadt, *What Is for My Birthday?,* Little, Brown, 1961; Lee Pape, *The First Doll in the World,* Lothrop, 1961; Bernice Frankel, *Half-as-Big and the Tiger,* F. Watts, 1961; Millicent E. Selsam, *See Along the Shore,* Harper, 1961; Peggy Parish, *Good Hunting Little Indian,* W.R. Scott, 1962; Aileen Fisher, *Like Nothing At All,* Crowell, 1962; Eve Titus, *The Mouse and the Lion,* Parents' Magazine Press, 1962; Faith McNulty, *When a Boy Wakes Up in the Morning,* Knopf, 1962; Johanna Johnston, *Penguin's Way,* Doubleday, 1962; Hila Colman, *Watch That Watch,* Morrow, 1962; Adelaide Holl, *Sir Kevin of Devon,* Lothrop, 1963; Lois Duncan, *Giving Away Suzanne,* Dodd, 1963; Elizabeth A. Campbell, *Fins and Tails,* Little, Brown, 1963; Faith McNulty, *When a Boy Goes to Bed at Night,* Knopf, 1963; Marguerite

Vance, *The Beloved Friend*, Colonial Williamsburg, 1963; Hila Colman, *Peter's Brownstone House*, Morrow, 1963; Maxine W. Kumin, *The Beach Before Breakfast*, Putnam, 1964; E. La Monte Meadowcroft, *Scarab for Luck*, Crowell, 1964; Christopher Fry, *The Boat That Mooed*, Macmillan, 1965; Wilma P. Hays, *The French Are Coming*, Colonial Williamsburg, 1965; Johanna Johnston, *Whale's Way*, Doubleday, 1965; Clyde R. Bulla, *White Bird*, Crowell, 1966; Vivian Laubach Thompson, editor, *Hawaiian Myths of Earth, Sea, and Sky*, Holiday House, 1966; Phyllis McGinley, *A Wreath of Christmas Legends*, Macmillan, 1967; Berniece Freschet, *The Little Woodcock*, Scribner, 1967; Mary L. Ellis, *Jesus Christ, Son of God*, John Knox, 1967; Frances Burnett, *The Lost Prince*, Lippincott, 1967; Jean Todd Freeman, *Cynthia and the Unicorn*, Norton, 1967; Doris Orgel, *On the Sand Dune*, Harper, 1968; Mary Perrine, *Salt Boy*, Houghton, 1968; Mary K. Phelan, *Midnight Alarm: The Story of Paul Revere's Ride*, Crowell, 1968; Doris Johnson, *Su An*, Follett, 1968; Gerald Ames and Rose Wyler, *How Things Began* (includes *The First People in the World*, and *First Days of the World*), Blackie & Son, 1969; Scott O'Dell, *Journey to Jericho*, Houghton, 1969; S.S. Warburg, *Growing Time*, Houghton, 1969; May Garelick, *Look at the Moon*, W.R. Scott, 1969; May Garelick, *What Makes a Bird a Bird?*, Follett, 1969; Judith Masefield, *Shepherdess of France: Remembrances of Jeanne d'Arc*, Coward, 1969; Mary Perrine, *Nannabah's Friend*, Houghton, 1970; Mark Twain, *Tom Sawyer*, American Education Publications, 1970; Rudyard Kipling, *The Elephant's Child*, Walker & Co., 1971; Charlotte Zolotow, *Wake Up and Goodnight*, Harper, 1971; Jean Slaughter, *And It Came to Pass*, Macmillan, 1971; Irma S. Black, *Doctor Proctor and Mrs. Merriwether*, Albert Whitman, 1971; Konstantin Paustovsky, *The Magic Ringlet*, Addison-Wesley, 1971.

Illustrator of books by Margaret Wise Brown: *The Noisy Book*, W.R. Scott, 1939; *The Country Noisy Book*, Harper, 1940; *Comical Tragedy or Tragical Comedy of Punch and Judy* (adapted by Brown), W.R. Scott, 1940; *The Seashore Noisy Book*, Harper, 1941, new edition, 1951; *The Poodle and the Sheep*, Dutton, 1941; *The Indoor Noisy Book*, Harper, 1942; *Night and Day*, Harper, 1942; *Little Chicken*, Harper, 1943; *The Noisy Bird Book* (includes some reproductions from Audubon), W.R. Scott, 1943; *The City Noisy Book*, W. R. Scott, 1946; *The Golden Egg Book*, Simon & Schuster, 1947; *The Important Book*, Harper, 1949; *Dark Wood of the Golden Birds*, Harper, 1950; *The Quiet Noisy Book*, Harper 1950; *The Summer Noisy Book*, Harper, 1951; *Pussy Willow*, Simon & Schuster, 1951; *Noon Balloon*, Harper, 1952; *The Golden Bunny, and Seventeen Other Stories and Poems*, Simon & Schuster, 1953; *Nibble, Nibble: Poems for Children*, W.R. Scott, 1959.

Illustrator of books by Golden MacDonald (pseudonym of Margaret Wise Brown)—All published by Doubleday: *Big Dog, Little Dog*, 1943; *Red Light, Green Light*, 1944; *Little Lost Lamb*, 1945; *The Little Island*, 1946, *Little Frightened Tiger*, 1953, *Whistle for the Train*, 1956.

Illustrator of books by Sesyle Joslin—All published by Harcourt: *Brave Baby Elephant*, 1960, *Baby Elephant's Trunk*, 1961, *Baby Elephant and the Secret Wishes*, 1962, *Senor Baby Elephant, the Pirate*, 1962, *Baby Elephant Goes to China*, 1963, *Baby Elephant's Baby Book*, 1964.

SIDELIGHTS: Weisgard has said he "came to write books because I felt the urge and need to and was most unhappy with the books I was forced to read in schools. Sadly many of them today are still not much better. Why must school texts be so discouraging for children so that many of them would rather not learn to read nor even discover the excitement of books? . . . Young children have imagination but as they grow older they are forced to lose their lustre due to these unimaginative people who are somehow involved with children. . . . Books for me have always, for as long as I can recall, been a source of real magic in this wildly confusing world. Books have opened doors and spread wide vistas of excitement and hope for me and I want so very much for young people everywhere to experience this same potential breadth and hope. From my European grandparents I was given a love and respect for the printed word and I try desperately to bring a sense of real truth and honesty in the work I do in picture and word form, trying to overcome the falseness of sentiment and artificiality that so much of our world is hidden by."

Weisgard uses a full range of colors and media for his illustrations: water color, gouache, poster paint, crayon, chalk, and pen and ink. He dislikes working with the acetate surface of color separations, would rather "work on sidewalk or wood or plaster." In *Books Are by People*, he comments "on the development of his own books, their ideas, and their styles. 'Books sometimes have grown from the moment of shaving, a moment of pain, a time of listening to children, from out of a dark tunnel, a groping into the past, or a stretching into the future, from amorphic places of the blackness of despair, or the joyousness of the bursting heart. And sometimes, even from the noise of a subway train.' "

AVOCATIONAL INTERESTS: Early American folk art, the theatre and the dance, education, lecturing on creativity and the need for school libraries.

BIOGRAPHICAL/CRITICAL SOURCES: C.L. Meigs and others, *A Critical History of Children's Literature*, Macmillan, 1953; *Junior Reviewers*, October, 1956; B.E. Mahony and E.W. Field, editors, *Caldecott Medal Books: 1938-1957*, Horn Book, 1957; *Horn Book*, June, 1958, April, 1960; Charlotte S. Huck and D.A. Young, *Children's Literature in the Elementary School*, Holt, 1961; May Hill Arbuthnot, *Children and Books*, 3rd edition, Scott, Foresman, 1964; *The Children's Bookshelf*, Child Study Association of America, Bantam, 1965; Lee Kingman, editor, *Newbery and Caldecott Medal Books: 1956-1965*, Horn Book, 1965; Diana Klemin, *The Art of Art for Children's Books*, Clarkson Potter, 1966; Lee Bennett Hopkins, *Books Are By People*, Citation Press, 1969; *Commonweal*, May 21, 1971.

*   *   *

WEISINGER, Mort 1915-

PERSONAL: Born April 25, 1915, in New York, N.Y.; son of Hyman and Anna (Bernfeld) Weisinger; married Thelma Rudnick, September 27, 1944; children: Joyce Carol, Hendrie Davis. *Education:* New York University, B.S., 1938. *Religion:* Hebrew. *Home:* 9 Henhawk Rd., Great Neck, N.Y. 11024. *Agent:* Lurton Blassingame, 60 East 42nd St., New York, N.Y. 10017. *Office:* National Periodical Publications, Inc., 575 Lexington Ave., New York, N.Y. 10022.

CAREER: College Humor, New York, N.Y., associate editor, 1939-40; *Superman* Magazines, New York, N.Y., editor, 1940-63; "Superman" television series, Hollywood, Calif., story editor, 1948-63. Lecturer on nonfiction writing, New York University, Columbia University, and New School for Social Research; instructor in nonfiction writing course for adults, Great Neck, N.Y. *Military service:* U.S. Army Air Force, stationed at Yale University with public relations staff, 1942-45; became staff sergeant. *Member:* National Multiple Sclerosis Society (member, public relations committee), National Myasthenia Gravis Foundation, Society of Magazine Writers (treasurer, 1949-52, 1961-62), Society of American Business News Writers.

WRITINGS: Atomic Survival, P. & G. Publishing, 1951; *1,001 Valuable Things You Can Get Free*, Bantam, 1955,

6th edition, 1965; (editor with Terry Morris and Peter Farb) *Prose by Professionals*, Doubleday, 1961; *Bonanza U.S.A.*, Bantam, 1966; *The Contest*, World Publishing, 1970; (with Arthur Henley) *The Complete Alibi Handbook*, Citadel, 1972. Contributor of more than 300 articles to *Saturday Evening Post, Reader's Digest, This Week, Cosmopolitan, Redbook, True, Holiday, Family Circle, Better Homes and Gardens, Argosy, Colliers, Science Digest, Esquire*, and other publications.

WORK IN PROGRESS: Two books, *1,001 Ways to Win a Bet*, and *"God Spoke to Me."*

SIDELIGHTS: The film rights to *The Contest* have been purchased by Columbia.

BIOGRAPHICAL/CRITICAL SOURCES: Cosmopolitan, June, 1959; *Best Sellers*, December 1, 1970.†

* * *

WEISMAN, Herman M.   1916-

PERSONAL: Born December 21, 1916, in Visk, Russia; son of Abraham and Reva (Gailerman) Weisman; married Margaret Cohen; children: Harlan, Lise, Abbi. *Education:* University of Minnesota, B.A., 1939; New York University, M.A., 1948; University of Denver, Ph.D., 1950. *Religion:* Jewish. *Home:* 1300 Springfield Dr., Fort Collins, Colo. 80521.

CAREER: Colorado State University, Fort Collins, 1957—, now professor and chairman of department of technical journalism and executive director of Center for Research Communications. Consultant in communications, National Institute of Child Health and Human Development. *Military service:* U.S. Army, 1942-46; became captain; received two battle stars. *Member:* Society of Technical Writers and Publishers (secretary), National Society for the Study of Communication, American Association for Education in Journalism, American Documentation Institute, American Business Writing Association, National Business Publications, Speech Communication Association of America, American Council of Learned Societies (regional associate), Colorado Press Association, Sigma Xi, Sigma Delta Chi.

WRITINGS: Basic Technical Writing, C.E. Merrill, 1962, 2nd edition, 1968; *Technical Report Writing*, C.E. Merrill, 1966; *Technical Correspondence: A Handbook and Reference Source for the Technical Professional*, Wiley, 1968; (with Gertrude B. Sherwood) *Annotated Accession List of Data Compilations of the Office of Standard Reference Data*, U.S. Government Printing Office, 1970; *Information Systems, Services and Centers*, Becker & Hayes, 1972. Editor of *Proceedings of Institute of Technical and Industrial Communications*, 1958-63, Colorado State University Press, 1958-63. Contributor of more than thirty articles to communication and technical journals.

WORK IN PROGRESS: Theory and Process of Communications, a synthesis of "state-of-the-art" of communication theory and process.†

* * *

WEISS, Theodore (Russell)   1916-

PERSONAL: Born December 16, 1916, in Reading, Pa.; son of Nathan (a businessman) and Mollie (Weinberg) Weiss; married Renee Karol (a violinist, editor, and author of children's books), July 6, 1941. *Education:* Muhlenberg College, A.B., 1938; Columbia University, M.A., 1940, further study, 1940-41. *Politics:* Independent. *Office:* Creative Arts Program, 185 Nassau St., Princeton, N.Y. 08540.

CAREER: Maryland University, Washington D.C., instructor in English, summer, 1941; University of North Carolina, Chapel Hill, instructor in English, 1942-44; Yale University, New Haven, Conn., instructor in English, 1944-46; Bard College, Annandale-on-Hudson, N.Y., assistant professor, 1947-52, associate professor, 1952-55, professor of English, 1955—; Princeton University, Princeton, N.J., poet-in-residence, 1966-67, professor of English and creative writing, 1967—. Visiting professor of poetry, Massachusetts Institute of Technology, 1961-62. Juror for poetry, National Book Awards, 1967. *Member:* P.E.N., Bollingen Committee. *Awards, honors:* Wallace Stevens Award, 1956, for "House of Fire"; Ford fellowship, 1953-54; honorary fellow, Ezra Stiles College, Yale University; National Foundation of Arts and Letters grant in poetry, 1967-68; D.Litt., Muhlenberg College, 1968.

WRITINGS—Books of poetry: *The Catch*, Twayne, 1951; *Outlanders*, Macmillan, 1960; *Gunsight*, New York University Press, 1962; *The Medium*, Macmillan, 1965; *The Last Day and the First*, Macmillan, 1968; *The World Before Us: Poems 1950-1970*, Macmillan, 1970.

Other publications: (Editor) *Selections from the Note-Books of Gerard Manley Hopkins*, New Directions, 1945; (contributor) Angel Flores, editor, *The Kafka Problem*, New Directions, 1946; *The Breath of Clowns and Kings: Shakespeare's Early Comedies and Histories*, Atheneum, 1971. Contributor of poems, articles, and reviews to anthologies, literary quarterlies, and other periodicals. Article anthologized in *Accent Anthology: Selections from "Accent", a Quarterly of New Literature, 1940-1945*, edited by Kerker Quinn and Charles Shattuck, Harcourt, 1946. Editor and publisher, *Quarterly Review of Literature*, 1943—; member of poetry board, Wesleyan University Press, 1964-69.

WORK IN PROGRESS: A volume on Shakespeare's tragedies; a poetic play; a new volume of poems.

SIDELIGHTS: "Coming to New York in 1938 from a town in Pennsylvania to study literature at Columbia University released in me a spate of what I then believed to be poetry," Weiss wrote in an essay for *Poets on Poetry*. He described his "rapidly growing admiration for Homer" and eventual attraction to the narrative poem, which "reflects my desire to pass beyond the lyrical. The dramatic monologue as developed by Browning has long attracted me in the conviction that poetry can and must renew its older, larger interests in people and a world past the poet's self-preoccupation." He said that his second book of poetry, *Outlanders*, "in contradistinction to *The Catch*, emphasizes the basic American sense of going out, the various ways of meeting the dilemmas of our day. This pioneering spirit, however, has brought in its train a feeling of uprootedness, of being lost in the boundless desert of time and space. Gradually the book organized itself around the theme of the homelessness of our time; I found it brilliantly exampled in America itself, this continent with its extraordinary mixture of savage climates and landscapes, its vastness, frightening indeed to men usually fled from smaller, man-sized worlds. Against the desperate modern struggle to subdue nature through technology I posed a number of worthies, outlanders like Thoreau and the nineteenth century American painter Albert Ryder, who were, in their personal stands, heroic replies to, if not solutions of, the outrages unleashed."

Hayden Carruth, a contemporary and friend of "Ted Weiss," finds himself "eating Proust's madeleine" on the first page of *The World Before Us: Poems 1950-1970*. Speaking of Weiss's earlier poems, Carruth is "cast back on waves of sensuous language to the exact feeling of literature in our youth a quarter-century ago," and "can think of no better poet than Weiss with whom to celebrate our nostalgia." He states that "a poem by Weiss is indelibly his own. . . . The shape of Weiss's poetry on the page, its coiling, spiraling movement up and down, corresponds to the way his language winds ever back on itself in the search for more precise discriminations of feeling, moral and aesthetic judgment and descriptive rightness. It is civilized poetry, in both the ordinary meaning of polish and refinement and in the higher meaning of eagerness to discover, reaffirm, and transfigure its own primitivism." F.H. Griffin Taylor comments on Weiss's words "which are honeyed, and so affectionately played with that they seem to have a life of their own. . . . Amused or serious, Mr. Weiss charms without recourse to sorcery. His poems speak of a world that is whole, however beleaguered. He is never smug and there is nothing coy or sham in what he says. As befits one who has the capacity to wonder, he has courage and gaiety: so that one reads as quickly as possible his whole book [in this case, *The Medium*] with delight."

In *A Controversy of Poets* Weiss himself wrote: "I am concerned in a proudly snippety time with the sustained poem, one that is more than merely personal and lyrical and happily fragmented. It is easy to go with the time or to cry out against it; but to do something with it, to take it by surprise, to make more of it (as poets usually have) than it can do itself—might that not still occupy poets? And let it be poetry, rather than the poor poet and his predicaments."

Weiss's poetry has been recorded for the Yale Series of Recorded Poets, Lamont Library of Harvard University, the Library of Congress, and The Voice of America.

BIOGRAPHICAL/CRITICAL SOURCES: New York Times, October 28, 1951; Western Review, spring, 1952; Poetry, February, 1953, July, 1963, July, 1969, April, 1972; The Fat Abbot, summer-fall, 1961; Sewanee Review, spring, 1961, spring, 1969; New Republic, November 16, 1963; Reporter, September 12, 1963; Minnesota Review, spring, 1963; Nation, June 29, 1963, January 4, 1971; Paris Leary and Robert Kelly, editors, A Controversy of Poets, Doubleday, 1965; Howard Nemerov, editor, Poets on Poetry, Basic Books, 1966; M.L. Rosenthal, The New Poets: American and British Poetry since World War II, Oxford University Press, 1967; Richard Howard, Alone with America: Essays on the Art of Poetry in the U.S. since 1950, Atheneum, 1969. Saturday Review, March 15, 1969; Virginia Quarterly Review, winter, 1969; Yale Review, autumn, 1971; Crazy Horse, March, 1972.

*   *   *

WELCH, Ann Courtenay Edmonds   1917-
(Ann C. Douglas, Ann C. Edmonds)

PERSONAL: Born May 20, 1917, in London, England; daughter of Courtenay Harold Wish (an engineer) and Edith Maud (Austin) Edmonds; married Graham Douglas, 1939 (divorced, 1950), married Lorne Elphinstone Welch (an engineer), June 25, 1953; children: Vivien Ann Douglas, Elizabeth Ann Douglas, Janet. Education: Attended a private school in England. Home: 14 Upper Old Park Lane, Farnham, Surrey, England.

CAREER: Pilot, and holder of British womens national glider goal flight record of 328 miles (1961); manager of British team in World Gliding Championships, 1948-68; chairman of organizing committee for England's National Gliding Championships, 1948-63, and for World Gliding Championships, 1965; vice-president, Commission Internationale Vol a Voile, 1971; lecturer on gliding. Artist and illustrator. Military service: Air Transport Auxiliary, ferry pilot, World War II; became first officer. Member: British Gliding Association (executive), Royal Aeronautical Society (associate fellow). Awards, honors: Member of Order of the British Empire, 1953, Officer of the Brit-

ish Empire, 1966; Royal Aero Club silver medal, 1958; FAI Bronze Medal, 1969.

WRITINGS—Under name Ann C. Edmonds: (Editor with Norman Macmillan) Let Experts Tell You—How We Fly, published for the Guild of Air Pilots and Air Navigators of the British Empire by Virtue, 1939; Silent Flight, Country Life, 1939; (under name Ann Courtenay Edmonds) Come Gliding with Me, Muller, 1955, Soccer, 1956.

Under name Ann C. Douglas: Cloud Reading for Pilots, Transatlantic, 1943, reissued under name Ann Courtenay Edmonds, J. Murray, 1950; (with P.A. Wills and A.E. Slater) Gliding and Advanced Soaring, J. Murray, 1947, Transatlantic, 1949.

Under name Ann Courtenay Welch: (With husband, Lorne Welch) Manual for Elementary Flying Instruction in Two-Seater Gliders, British Gliding Association, 1952, 2nd edition, revised, published as Flying Training in Gliders, 1956; (with L. Welch and F.G. Irving) The Soaring Pilot, J. Murray, 1955, Pitman, 1956, 3rd edition published as The New Soaring Pilot, J. Murray, 1968; Go Gliding, (illustrated by Gabor Denes), Faber, 1960; Glider Flying, Constable, 1963; John Goes Gliding (juvenile novel), J. Cape, 1964; The Woolacombe Bird (historical novel for young people), J. Cape, 1964, World Publishing, 1965: (with L. Welch) The Story of Gliding, J. Murray, 1965; Weather for Pilots, J. Murray, in press.

WORK IN PROGRESS: World Gliding Championships-Guidelines.

SIDELIGHTS: As manager of a British gliding team or international commission representative, Mrs. Welch has been to world championships in Switzerland, Sweden, Spain, France, Poland, Germany, Argentina, Yugoslavia, and the United States. She has illustrated many of her own books, and intends to spend her retiring years ocean sailing. Avocational interests: Skiing, scuba diving, photography, modern houses, and sailing with her grandchildren.

*   *   *

WELKER, Robert L(ouis)   1924-

PERSONAL: Born June 26, 1924, in Clarksville, Tenn.; son of George Thomas (an engineer) and Emma (Wickham) Welker. Education: Attended Austin Peay State College, 1941-42, University of Connecticut, 1942-43; Peabody College for Teachers, B.A., 1948; Vanderbilt University, M.A., 1952, Ph.D., 1958. Religion: Protestant. Home: 600 Franklin St., Huntsville, Ala. 35801. Office: P.O. Box 1247, West Station, University of Alabama, Huntsville, Ala. 35807.

CAREER: Vanderbilt University, Nashville, Tenn., assistant professor of English, 1958-64; University of Alabama, Huntsville, associate professor, 1964-66, professor of English, 1966—. Public lecturer on Shakespeare, Chaucer, and fourteenth-century costume. Military service: U.S. Army, Combat Engineers, 1942-46; served in European theater.

WRITINGS: (Editor with William E. Walker, and contributor) Reality and Myth: Essays in American Literature in Memory of Richmond Croom Beatty, Vanderbilt University Press, 1964; (editor with Herschel Gower) The Sense of Fiction, Prentice-Hall, 1966. Assistant editor, Poem, 1967—.

WORK IN PROGRESS: A biography of Evelyn Scott, tentatively titled No Escape in Living; a critical study of the work of Evelyn Scott; editing the unpublished novels, poetry, and letters of Evelyn Scott; a collection of essays on Shakespeare.

SIDELIGHTS: Welker is a semi-professional ceramic sculptor.

BIOGRAPHICAL/CRITICAL SOURCES: Nashville Tennessean Magazine, March 26, 1961; *Friends,* April, 1963.

* * *

WELLBORN, Fred W(ilmot)   1894-

PERSONAL: Born October 14, 1894, in Trinity, N.C.; son of Robert Clark (a farmer) and Mary (Von Canon) Wellborn; married Lois Small, August 29, 1929; children: Bruce, Jennifer, Virginia (Mrs. Robert Keating). *Education:* Baker University, B.A., 1918; attended Harvard University, 1920-21; Kansas University, M.A., 1923; University of Wisconsin, Ph.D., 1926. *Religion:* Episcopalian. *Home:* Route 1, Olney, Md. 20832.

CAREER: Iowa State College, Cedar Falls, member of history department, 1926-46; University of Maryland, College Park, professor of history, 1946-65, professor emeritus, 1965—. *Member:* Organization of American Historians (member of executive committee, 1946-49).

WRITINGS: The Growth of American Nationality, 1492-1865, Macmillan, 1943; *Diplomatic History of the United States,* Littlefield, Adams, 1961, revised edition, 1970.

* * *

WELLWARTH, George E(manuel)   1932-

PERSONAL: Born June 6, 1932, in Vienna, Austria; son of Erwin (a theater owner) and Martha (Sobotka) Wellwarth; married Marcia Cobourn (a teacher of Romance languages), November 9, 1963. *Education:* New York University, B.A. (summa cum laude), 1953; Columbia University, M.A., 1954; University of Chicago, Ph.D., 1957. *Agent:* Kurt Hellmer, 52 Vanderbilt Ave., New York, N.Y. 10017. *Office:* Theatre Department, State University of New York at Binghamton, Binghamton, N.Y. 13901.

CAREER: Wilson Junior College, Chicago, Ill., instructor in English, 1955-58; University of Chicago, Chicago, Ill., lecturer in English, 1958; College of City of New York (now City College of the City University of New York), New York, N.Y., instructor in English, 1959-60; Staten Island Community College, Staten Island, N.Y., assistant professor, 1960-63, associate professor of English, 1963-64; Pennsylvania State University, University Park, assistant professor of English, 1964-70; State University of New York at Binghamton, Binghamton, N.Y., professor of theatre and comparative literature, 1970—. Onetime professional actor in Chicago, Ill., San Diego, Calif., and in off-Broadway theaters, New York, N.Y. *Member:* Modern Language Association of America, American Educational Theatre Association, American Comparative Literature Association, Phi Beta Kappa.

WRITINGS: The Theatre of Protest and Paradox: Developments in the Avant-Garde Drama, New York University Press, 1964, 2nd edition, revised, 1971; (editor and translator with Michael Benedikt) *Modern French Theatre: An Anthology of Plays—The Avant-Garde, Dada, and Surrealism,* Dutton, 1964 (published in England as *Modern French Plays: An Anthology from Jarry to Ionesco,* Faber, 1965); (translator) Siegfried Melchinger, *The Concise Encyclopedia of Modern Drama,* foreword by Eric Bentley, Horizon Press, 1964; (editor and translator with Benedikt) *Postwar German Theatre: An Anthology of Plays,* Dutton, 1967; (editor with Benedikt) *Modern Spanish Theatre: An Anthology of Plays,* Dutton, 1968; (editor) *The New Wave Spanish Drama: An Anthology,* New York University Press, 1970; *German Drama Between the Wars,* Dutton, 1971. Translator of plays of Jean Tardieu, produced Off-Broadway, January,

1962. Contributor of twenty-seven articles to learned journals. Co-editor and co-founder, *Modern International Drama Magazine.*

WORK IN PROGRESS: A study of the relationship between dramatic form and subject matter and political and social conditions; *The Spanish Underground Drama,* a critical study to be published by Pennsylvania State University Press.

SIDELIGHTS: Wellwarth has traveled and observed theatre in all countries of western Europe except Finland; he is fluent in French and German.

BIOGRAPHICAL/CRITICAL SOURCES: Nation, September 4, 1967; *Poetry,* February, 1969; *Books Abroad,* spring, 1971.

* * *

WELTY, Eudora   1909-

PERSONAL: Born April 13, 1909, in Jackson, Miss.; daughter of Christian Webb (an insurance company president) and Chestina (Andrews) Welty. *Education:* Attended Mississippi State College for Women, 1926-27; University of Wisconsin, B.A., 1929; attended Columbia University School of Advertising, 1930-31. *Home:* 1119 Pinehurst St., Jackson, Miss. 39202.

CAREER: Worked for newspapers and radio stations in Mississippi during early depression years, and as a publicity agent for the state office of the Works Progress Administration (WPA). Was briefly a member of the *New York Times Book Review* staff, in New York City. Honorary consultant in American letters, Library of Congress, 1958—. *Member:* National Institute of Arts and Letters. *Awards, honors:* Guggenheim fellowship, 1942; O. Henry award, 1942, 1943; National Institute of Arts and Letters grant in literature, 1944, Gold Medal for fiction, 1972; William Dean Howells medal of American Academy of Arts and Letters, 1955, for *The Ponder Heart,* elected to membership, 1971; Edward McDowell Medal, 1970; National Book Awards nomination in fiction, 1971, for *Losing Battles;* Pulitzer Prize in fiction, 1973, for *The Optimist's Daughter.*

WRITINGS: A Curtain of Green (stories; with an introduction by Katherine Anne Porter), Doubleday, 1941; *The Robber Bridegroom* (novella) Doubleday, 1942; *The Wide Net, and Other Stories,* Harcourt, 1943; *Delta Wedding* (novel), Harcourt, 1946; *Music From Spain,* Levee Press, 1948; *Short Stories* (address delivered at University of Washington), Harcourt, 1949; *The Golden Apples* (connected stories), Harcourt, 1949; *Selected Stories* (containing all of *A Curtain of Green* and *The Wide Net, and Other Stories;* with an introduction by Katherine Anne Porter), Modern Library, 1953; *The Ponder Heart* (novel), Harcourt, 1954; *The Bride of the Innisfallen, and Other Stories,* Harcourt, 1955; *Place in Fiction* (lectures for Conference on American Studies in Cambridge, England), House of Books, 1957; *John Rood* (catalog of sculpture exhibition), [New York], 1958; *Three Papers on Fiction* (addresses), Smith College, 1962; *The Shoe Bird* (juvenile), Harcourt, 1964; *Thirteen Stories* (selected and with an introduction by Ruth M. Vande Kieft), Harcourt, 1965; *A Sweet Devouring* (nonfiction), Albondocani Press, 1969; *Losing Battles* (novel), Random House, 1970; *A Flock of Guinea Hens Seen from a Car* (poem), Albondocani Press, 1970; *One Time, One Place: Mississippi in the Depression; A Snapshot Album,* Random House, 1971; *The Optimist's Daughter* (novella; first published in *New Yorker,* 1969), Random House, 1972. Contributor to *Southern Review, Atlantic, Harper's, Manuscript, New Yorker,* and other periodicals.

SIDELIGHTS: Perhaps the most notable American regionalist today, Miss Welty writes a unique fiction. William Peden calls it "conscious ambiguity"; Diana Trilling, "self-conscious contriving." Miss Welty's work is highly imaginative, yet her fantasies are distinguished by what Katherine Anne Porter calls "the waking faculty of daylight reason recollecting and recording the crazy logic of the dream."

The *National Observer* suggested recently that she "may have her best days as a writer behind her," but added, "it is also past time to admit the high excellence of her craft." Her writing is feminine in the sense of being intuitive, fragile, as well as hypersensitive. But, as the *National Observer* noted, she has "a man's knowledge of the world," ever aware of man's brutality.

Alun R. Jones writes that she has "the storyteller's gift of compelling attention . . . [and] the unfailing ability to maintain what she has called 'believability.'" Extraordinarily able to sustain a mood, ever conscious of "mythical and imaginative reality impinging on and informing the trivial and the banal," she structures her prose "like poetry with an intuited center."

Miss Welty believes that, in her words, "each novel written stands as something of a feat. . . . First ask, what was the heart's desire? Not the creating of an illusion, but the restoring of one; something brought off. . . . We ask only that it be magic. Good action grants this boon, bad denies it. And performance is what the novelists would like to give . . . a fresh performance, . . . out of respect, love, and fearlessness for all that may be tried, to command the best skill."

Briefly, during her early career, Eudora Welty used a pseudonym. Walter Clemons recalls the story: "A lesser-known episode of her career is her stint as a staff member of *The [New York] Times Book Review*, which she joined at the invitation of the editor, Robert Van Gelder, who had admired her first book and interviewed her in 1942. She was good at her job, according to a colleague of those wartime days: 'Although the only battlefields Eudora had probably ever seen,' he wrote recently, 'were at Vicksburg and Shiloh, she turned out splendid reviews of World War II battlefield reports from North Africa, Europe and the South Pacific. When a churlish *Times* Sunday editor suggested that a lady reviewer from the Deep South might not be the most authoritative critic for the accounts of World War II's far-flung campaigns, she switched to a pseudonym, Michael Ravenna.' Michael Ravenna's sage judgments came to be quoted prominently in publishers' ads and invitations from radio networks for Mr. Ravenna to appear on their programs had to be politely declined on grounds that he had been called away to the battlefronts." The *Ponder Heart* was adapted for Broadway in 1956, and a stage presentation, in 1971, "The Wanderers," was based on Miss Welty's stories.

BIOGRAPHICAL/CRITICAL SOURCES: Alexander Cowie, *American Writers Today*, Radiojaenst, 1956; *Bulletin of Bibliography*, January, 1956, January 1960, January, 1963, September, 1963; R.M. Vande Kieft, *Eudora Welty*, Twayne, 1962; *The Creative Present*, edited by Nona Balakian and Charles Simmons, Doubleday, 1963; *Contemporary American Novelists*, edited by Harry T. Moore, Southern Illinois University Press, 1964; *Critique*, winter, 1964-65; Louise Y. Gossett, *Violence in Recent Southern Fiction*, Duke University Press, 1965; Alfred Appel, Jr., *A Season of Dreams: The Fiction of Eudora Welty*, Louisiana State University Press, 1965; *Shenandoah*, spring, 1969; *New York Times Book Review*, April 12, 1970; *Contemporary Literary Criticism*, edited by Carolyn Riley, Gale, 1973.

WENKART, Henny 1928-
(Henni Wenkart)

PERSONAL: Born July 5, 1928, in Vienna, Austria; daughter of Herman (a lawyer) and Rose (Stein) Wenkart; married Henry David Epstein (an engineer); children: Jonathan, Heitzi, Ari. *Education:* Pembroke College, A.B., 1949; Columbia University, M.S., 1950; Radcliffe College, M.A., 1957; Harvard University, Ph.D., 1970. *Religion:* Jewish. *Home:* 4 Shady Hill Sq., Cambridge, Mass. 02138.

CAREER: Harvard University, Cambridge, Mass., teaching fellow in general education, 1958-62; Wenkart Publishing Co., Cambridge, Mass., publisher, 1960—. *Member:* Phi Beta Kappa.

WRITINGS—All published by Wenkart: *At a Zoo*, 1960, *The Man in the Moon*, 1961, *Fun at Camp*, 1961, *Get Off the Desk*, 1962, *The Big Puppet Mix-Up*, 1962, *Teaching Jonny's Sister to Read*, 1963. Former assistant editor, *Schools and Better Living*.

WORK IN PROGRESS: Editing Santayana's *Philosophy of Matter and of Mind; Liberated Housekeeping*.

BIOGRAPHICAL/CRITICAL SOURCES: Time, March 8, 1962; *Vogue*, August, 1963; *New York Times*, November 2, 1963; *Chicago Tribune*, November 12, 1963; *New York Daily News*, December 8, 1963.

*   *   *

WENTZ, Frederick K(uhlman) 1921-

PERSONAL: Born January 21, 1921, in Gettysburg, Pa.; son of Abdel Ross (a seminary professor) and Mary Edna (Kuhlman) Wentz; married Marian Jean Benson, January 20, 1951; children: Lisa Jean, Theodore Valentine, Melanie Kuhlman. *Education:* Gettysburg College, B.A., 1942; Gettysburg Lutheran Seminary, B.D., 1945; attended University of Southern California, 1946-47; Yale University, Ph.D., 1954. *Politics:* Democrat. *Home:* 272 North Broadmoor, Springfield, Ohio 45504. *Office:* Hamma School of Theology, Springfield, Ohio.

CAREER: Ordained a Lutheran clergyman, 1945. Grace Lutheran Church, Culver City, Calif., pastor and mission organizer, 1945-48; Hartwick College, Oneonta, N.Y., chaplain and assistant professor of religion, 1951-53; Lutheran Southern Seminary, Columbia, S.C., professor of church history, 1953-56; Gettysburg Lutheran Seminary, Gettysburg, Pa., professor of historical theology, 1956-66; Hamma School of Theology, Springfield, Ohio, president and professor of church history, 1966—. National Lutheran Council, archivist-researcher, 1964-65. *Member:* American Society of Church History, Phi Sigma Kappa, Phi Beta Kappa. *Awards, honors:* D.Litt., Thiel College, 1967; D.D., Hartwick College, 1972.

WRITINGS: The Times Test the Church, Muhlenberg, 1956; *The Layman's Role Today*, Doubleday, 1963; *Lutherans and Other Denominations*, edited by Philip R. Hoh, Fortress, 1964; (editor) S.S. Schmucker, *Fraternal Appeal to the American Churches, with a Plan for Catholic Union on Apostolic Principles*, Fortress, 1965; (editor) *My Job and Faith: Twelve Christians Report on Their Work Worlds*, Abingdon, 1967; *Lutherans in Concert: The Story of the National Lutheran Council, 1918-1966*, Augsburg, 1968; *Set Free for Others*, Friendship, 1969. Contributor to *Lutheran, Lutheran World, Church History, Religion in Life, Christian Century, International Journal of Religious Education, Interpretation*, and other periodicals. Editor, *Lutheran Quarterly*, 1966-70.

*   *   *

WERLICH, Robert 1924-

PERSONAL: Born January 23, 1924, in Paris, France; son of McCeney (a U.S. diplomat) and Gladys (Hinckley) Werlich; married Nancy Shanklin (an artist), August 1, 1951; children: Nancy O., Eleanora O. *Education:* Attended U.S. Merchant Marine Academy, 1943-44, and George Washington University, 1945-46. *Home:* 3218 O St. N.W., Washington D.C. 20007.

CAREER: Did government work prior to becoming a writer; Quaker Press, Washington, D.C., president, 1960—. *Military service:* U.S. Merchant Marine, 1943-45; became lieutenant commander.

WRITINGS: "Beast" Butler: The Incredible Career of Major General Benjamin Franklin Butler, Quaker Press, 1962; (editor) *Catalogue of United States, Canadian and Confederate Currency,* Quaker Press, 1963, reissued as *Fully Illustrated Catalogue of United States, Canadian and Confederate Currency,* 1965; *Orders and Decorations of All Nations: Ancient and Modern, Civil and Military,* Quaker Press, 1965; *Russian Orders, Decorations and Medals, Including Those of Imperial Russia, the Provisional Government, and the Soviet Union,* Quaker Press, 1968; (translator) S. Andolenko, *Badges of Imperial Russia, Including Military, Civil, and Religious,* Quaker Press, 1971; *Carpetbaggers and Scalawags,* Quaker Press, 1971.

* * *

WERRY, Richard R. 1916-

PERSONAL: Born March 22, 1916, in Pittsburgh, Pa.; son of Thomas H. (a manufacturer) and Myrtle (Ivory) Werry; married Kathryn Simon (a teacher), 1939; married second wife, Laura Sarko, 1969; children: (first marriage) Richard R., Jr., Margaret Jean, Thomas H. *Education:* University of Pittsburgh, B.A., 1937, A.M., 1939; graduate study, Columbia University, 1939-40. *Home:* 1252 Pierce, Birmingham, Mich. 48009. *Agent:* McIntosh & Otis, Inc., 18 East 41st St., New York, N.Y. 10017. *Office:* English Department, Wayne State University, Detroit, Mich. 48202.

CAREER: Wayne State University, Detroit, Mich., 1946—, began as instructor, now associate professor of English. Member of board of directors, Colorado Tungsten Corp. *Military service:* U.S. Navy, 1943-46. *Member:* Modern Language Association of America.

WRITINGS: Frozen Tears (poems), Dorrance, 1947; *Where Town Begins* (novel), Greenberg, 1951; *Hammer Me Home* (novel), Dodd, 1955. Book reviewer for *Detroit News,* 1968—. Contributor of articles and short stories to periodicals.

WORK IN PROGRESS: A novel, *The Thinkmobile.*

* * *

WESSON, Robert G(ale) 1920-

PERSONAL: Born March 11, 1920, in Washington, D.C.; son of Laurence G. (a chemist) and Elizabeth (Matthews) Wesson; married Deborah Tarsier, April 24, 1958; children: Laura Helen, Carol Ann, Richard M., Eric A. *Education:* University of Arizona, A.B., 1940; Fletcher School of Law and Diplomacy, M.A., 1941; Columbia University, postgraduate study, 1946-47, Ph.D., 1961. *Home:* 984 Memorial Dr., Cambridge, Mass. 02138.

CAREER: Self-employed in private business, Costa Rica and Brazil, 1948-58; Bates College, Lewiston, Me., visiting assistant professor, 1961-62, 1963-64; University of California, Santa Barbara, Calif., assistant professor, 1964-66, associate professor of political science, 1966—.

WRITINGS: Soviet Communes, Rutgers University Press, 1963; *The American Problem: The Cold War in Perspective,* Abelard, 1963; *The Imperial Order,* University of California Press, 1967; *Soviet Foreign Policy in Perspec-*

tive, Dorsey, 1969; *The Soviet Russian State,* Wiley, 1972; *The Soviet State: An Aging Revolution,* Wiley, 1972. Contributor to *Current History* and *Soviet Studies.*

* * *

WEST, Jessamyn 1907-

PERSONAL: Born 1907, in Indiana; married H.M. McPherson. *Education:* Whittier College, A.B.; attended University of California; studied in England. *Religion:* Quaker. *Home:* 2480 3rd Ave., Napa, Calif. 94558.

CAREER: Writer. Taught at writers conferences at Breadloaf, Indiana University, University of Notre Dame, University of Colorado, University of Utah, University of Washington, Stanford University. *Awards, honors:* Honorary doctorates from Whittier College, Mills College, Swarthmore College, Indiana University, and Western College for Women; Indiana Authors' Day Award, 1956, for *Love, Death and the Ladies' Drill Team;* Thormod Monsen Award, 1958, for *To See the Dream.*

WRITINGS—All published by Harcourt, except as indicated: *The Friendly Persuasion,* 1945; *A Mirror for the Sky* (opera libretto), 1948; *The Witch Diggers,* 1951; *Cress Delahanty,* 1953; *Little Men,* Ballantine, 1954, republished as *The Chile Kings,* 1967; *Love, Death and the Ladies Drill Team* (stories), 1955 (published in England as *Learn to Say Goodbye,* Hodder & Stoughton, 1956); *To See the Dream,* 1957; *Love is Not What You Think,* 1959; *South of the Angels,* 1960, reprinted, Fawcett, 1963; (editor) *The Quaker Reader,* Viking, 1962; *A Matter of Time,* 1966; *Leafy Rivers,* 1967; *Except for Me and Thee: A Companion to The Friendly Persuasion,* 1969; *Crimson Ramblers of the World, Farewell,* 1970; *Hide & Seek: A Continuing Journey,* 1973. Wrote movie scripts for "Friendly Persuasion," "The Big Country," "Lucy Crown," "Stolen Hours." Contributor to *New Yorker, Good Housekeeping, Harper's, Redbook, Reader's Digest,* and other publications. Included in various editions of *Best American Short Stories,* edited by Martha Foley and David Burnett.

WORK IN PROGRESS: "I am constantly writing—with more in mind to do than time will ever permit—novels, stories, articles."

SIDELIGHTS: Miss West, who describes the four cornerstones of her life as "family, words on paper (this means books and writing), the world of nature (weeds, wind, buzzards, clouds), and privacy," recently spent several months in a house trailer specifically to be by herself; *Hide & Seek,* a book of reflections and recollections of her life, is the result.

In 1969, Allied Artists acquired the film rights to *Except for Me and Thee.* The play, "The Rise and Fall of Practically Nobody," based on Miss West's story "Public Address System," was optioned for an off-Broadway production by Otto Preminger in 1970.

BIOGRAPHICAL/CRITICAL SOURCES: New York Times Book Review, May 11, 1969, January 10, 1971; *Harper's,* July, 1969; A.S. Shivers, *Jessamyn West,* Twayne, 1972.†

* * *

WESTING, John Howard 1911-

PERSONAL: Born August 5, 1911, in New Era, Mich.; son of John and Cora (Haan) Westing; married Margaret Anderson, September 1, 1939; children: Janet Powell, Mary Margaret. *Education:* Calvin College, B.A., 1932; University of Michigan, M.B.A., 1935, Ph.D., 1942. *Religion:* Protestant. *Home:* 1107 Wellesley Rd., Madison, Wis. 53705.

CAREER: American Sugar Refining Co., assistant manager of raw sugar and customs department, 1935-38; U.S. Government, associate director of food rationing division, Office of Price Administration, 1941-43, chief of food allocations division, Foreign Economic Administration, 1944-45, chief of business practices division, office of International Trade Policy, Department of Commerce, 1945-46; University of Michigan, Ann Arbor, associate professor of business administration, 1947-49; University of Wisconsin, Graduate School of Business, Madison, professor of marketing, 1949-68, associate dean, 1955-68. Military service: U.S. Naval Reserve, 1943-44; became lieutenant. Member: American Marketing Association, American Economics Association, National Association of Purchasing Agents, National Sales Executives International, Rotary International.

WRITINGS: (Editor) Readings in Marketing, Prentice-Hall, 1953; (with I.V. Fine and others) Industrial Purchasing: Buying for Industry and Budgetary Institutions, Wiley, 1955, 3rd edition, with Fine and Gary J. Zenz, published as Purchasing Management: Materials in Motion, 1969; The Area of Effectiveness of a Selected VHF Television Station: A Case Study Based on WBAY-TV, Bureau of Business Research and Service, University of Wisconsin, Madison, 1955; (with Dudley M. Phelps) Marketing Management, Irwin, 1960, 3rd edition, revised, 1968; (editor with Gerald S. Albaum) Modern Marketing Thought, Macmillan, 1964, 2nd edition, revised, 1969.

WORK IN PROGRESS: Revisions of books.

*   *   *

WETHERELL-PEPPER, Joan Alexander   1920-
(Joan Alexander, Joan Pepper)

PERSONAL: Born July 21, 1920, in Southborough, Kent, England; daughter of Henry Lethbridge (a major general) and Dorothy Blanche (Long) Alexander; married M.I. Gregson, July 14, 1938 (divorced, 1945); married Denis Wetherell-Pepper (a civil servant), February 19, 1946 (died, 1968); children: (first marriage) Jocelyn, Marcia; (second marriage) Colin. Education: Attended St. Mary's School, Calne, England, La Vicomtesse de Seze Cour, Cheverney, Blois, France, and Fay Compton's School of Dramatic Art. Politics: Tory. Religion: Church of England. Home: 33 Grove Rd., London, Barnes S.W.1, England. Agent: E.P.S. Lewin, 7 Chelsea Embankment, London S.W.3, England.

CAREER: Writer. Military service: Voluntary Air Detachment, Fifteenth Scottish Hospital, 1939-40; Women's Royal Naval Service, 1941-45; became third officer. Member: P.E.N., New Arts Theatre, Hurlingham Country Club.

WRITINGS—Under name Joan Pepper; all published by Cassell: Fly Away Paul, 1954, The Choice and the Circumstance, 1956, Carola, 1957, Lewis's Wife, 1959.

Under name Joan Alexander: Thy People, My People, J. Cape, 1967; Where Have All the Flowers Gone?, Heinemann, 1969; Strange Loyalty, Heinemann, 1969; Bitter Wind, Heinemann, 1970.

Contributor of articles to Argosy, Cosmopolitan, Candida, London Mystery Magazine, and Homes & Gardens; contributor of scripts to British Broadcasting Corp.

WORK IN PROGRESS: The Sky Has Died, a novel on the building of a motorway.

SIDELIGHTS: Where Have All the Flowers Gone was sold to Twickenham Associates for filming.

*   *   *

WETMORE, William T.   1930-

PERSONAL: Born November 29, 1930, in Boston, Mass.; son of William Thomson and Joan (Deery) Wet-

more; married Margaret Kiser, December 21, 1957; children: Charles Delevan, Michael Finley, Joan Dixon. Education: Harvard College, B.A., 1954. Politics: Independent. Religion: Episcopalian. Home: Flint Hill Rd., Amenia, N.Y. 12501. Agent: Bob Mills, 156 East 52nd St., New York, N.Y. 10022.

CAREER: Middletown Times Herald, Middletown, N.Y., assistant city editor, 1954-56; Frenkel de Venezuela (insurance brokerage), Caracas, Venezuela, manager, 1957-60; writer, 1960—. Military service: U.S. Marine Corps, 1948-49.

WRITINGS: All the Right People, Doubleday, 1964; A Matter of Blue Chips, Doubleday, 1965; House of Flesh, Little, Brown, 1968; Here Comes Jamie, Little, Brown, 1970.

WORK IN PROGRESS: A fifth novel, Inside Outside; a series of short novels, The Beekman Chronicles.

BIOGRAPHICAL/CRITICAL SOURCES: New York Times Book Review, May 5, 1968, May 24, 1970; Library Journal, May 15, 1970.

*   *   *

WETTER, Gustav A(ndreas)   1911-

PERSONAL: Born May 4, 1911, in Moedling, Austria; son of Johann and Agathe (Follner) Wetter. Education: Pontifical Gregorian University, doctorate in philosophy, 1932, license in theology, 1936; Pontifical Institute of Oriental Studies, doctorate, 1941. Home: Piazza Pilotta, 4, 00187 Rome, Italy.

CAREER: Roman Catholic priest, member of Society of Jesus (Jesuits), 1936—. Pontifical Institute of Oriental Studies, Rome, Italy, professor of history of Russian philosophy, 1943—; Pontifical Gregorian University, Rome, professor of Russian and Marxist philosophy, 1954—, director of Center for Marxist Studies, 1970—. Pontifical Russian College, Rome, vice-rector, 1947-49, rector, 1949-54.

WRITINGS: Il Materialismo dialettico sovietico, 2nd edition, G. Einaudi, 1948, translation from German edition by Peter Heath published as Dialectical Materialism: A Historical and Systematic Survey of Philosophy in the Soviet Union, Routledge & Kegan Paul, 1958, Praeger, 1959, 5th German edition, under title Der dialektische Materialismus: Seine Geschichte und sein System in der Sowjetunion, Herder, 1960; Ordnung ohne Freiheit: Der dialektische Materialismus, Butzon & Bercker, 1956; Philosophie und Naturwissenschaft in der Sowjetunion, Rowohlt, 1958; Der dialektische Materialismus und das Problem der Entstehung des Lebens: Zur Theorie von A.I. Oparin, A. Pustet, 1958; Die sowjetische Konzeption der Koexistenz, Bundeszentrale fuer Heimatdienst, 1959; (with Dominikus Thalhammer) Die Kirche in der Zeit, E. Russ, 1959; Sowjetideologie heute, Volume I: Dialektischer und historischer Materialismus, Fischer Buecherei, 1962, translation by Peter Heath published as Soviet Ideology Today, Praeger, 1966 (published in England as Soviet Ideology Today: Dialectical and Historical Materialism, Heinemann, 1966); Die Umkehrung Hegels: Grundzuege und Urspruenge der Sowjetphilosophie, Verlag Wissenschaft und Politik, 1963; Kommunismus und Religion: Kirche in der Sowjetunion, Butzon & Bercker, 1964; (editor) Kampf des Glaubens: Dokumente aus der Sowjetunion, Verlag des Schweizerischen Ost-Instituts, 1967.

*   *   *

WEYL, Nathaniel   1910-

PERSONAL: Surname is pronounced "wile"; born July 20, 1910, in New York, N.Y.; son of Walter Edward (an economist and writer) and Bertha (Poole) Weyl; married

Sylvia Castleton (a writer), February 13, 1937; children: Jonathan Vanderpoel and Walter Castleton (twins). *Education:* Attended Friends Seminary, New York, N.Y., 1916-27, and Haverford College, 1927-28; Columbia University, B.Sc., 1931, graduate study, 1931-33; additional study at London School of Economics and Poli ical Science, London, 1931-32, and Washington School of Psychiatry, 1950-51. *Politics:* Republican. *Religion:* Episcopalian. *Home and office:* 4201 South Ocean Blvd., Delray Beach, Fla. 33444.

CAREER: U.S. Government, Washington, D.C., economist with Agricultural Adjustment Administration, 1933-34, and Federal Reserve System, 1940-41, special assistant, Board of Economic Warfare, 1941-43, member of policy staff, Office of International Trade, Department of Commerce, 1946-47; Commission on Refugee Settlement, Paramaribo, Surinam (Netherlands Guiana), economist, 1948; self-employed writer in Washington, D.C., and Delray Beach, Fla., 1949—. Jose Marti Journalistic Award, chairman of jury, 1966; president, International Foundation for Gifted Children. *Military service:* U.S. Army, 1943-45; received Bronze Star and four battle stars. *Member:* American Political Science Association, Academy of Political Science, Mensa (Palm Beach County secretary), National Academy of Sciences (India), Phi Beta Kappa. *Awards, honors:* Award of merit from American Academy of Public Affairs of Los Angeles County, 1962, for *Red Star Over Cuba.*

WRITINGS: (With wife, Sylvia Weyl) *The Reconquest of Mexico,* Oxford University Press, 1939; (contributor) *Concerning Latin American Culture* (symposium), Columbia University Press, 1940; *Treason: The Story of Disloyalty and Betrayal in American History,* Public Affairs Press, 1950; (contributor) Glenn Edwin Hoover, editor, *Twentieth Century Economic Thought,* Philosophical Library, 1950; *The Battle Against Disloyalty,* Crowell Collier, 1951; *The Negro in American Civilization,* Public Affairs Press, 1960; *Red Star Over Cuba: The Russian Assault on the Western Hemisphere,* Devin, 1960, 3rd revised edition, 1962; (with John Martino) *I Was Castro's Prisoner,* Devin, 1963; (with Stefan T. Possony) *The Geography of Intellect,* Regnery, 1963; *The Creative Elite in America,* Public Affairs Press, 1966; *The Jew in American Politics,* Arlington House, 1968; *Traitors' End: The Rise and Fall of the Communist Movement in Southern Africa,* Arlington House, 1970; (with William Marina) *American Statesmen on Slavery and the Negro,* Arlington House, 1971.

Contributor of articles and reviews to various periodicals, including *National Review, Catholic Digest, U.S. News & World Report, Mankind Quarterly, Perspectives in Biology and Medicine,* and *Ideas.*

WORK IN PROGRESS: With William Marina, *Integration: The Dream That Failed;* a novel concerning Ireland under the Tudors.

SIDELIGHTS: Red Star Over Cuba has been published in three Spanish editions and one German edition, 1961-65. Weyl has traveled overseas (often by freighter) about twenty times to pursue archaeological and political interests. *Avocational interests:* Ethnology, anthropology, chess, yachting, and tennis.

BIOGRAPHICAL/CRITICAL SOURCES: National Review, May 16, 1967, May 7, 1968, May 19, 1970.

* * *

WEZEMAN, Frederick Hartog 1915-

PERSONAL: Born May 1, 1915, in Oak Park, Ill.; son of Paul Henry (a medical doctor) and Jacoba (Hartog) Wezeman; married Marjorie Vaughn, August 11, 1960; children: Christine, Peter. *Education:* Lewis Institute

(Chicago, Ill.), B.S., 1937; Chicago Teachers College, M.E., 1940; University of Chicago, B.L.S., 1946. *Religion:* Methodist. *Home:* 114 Mt. Vernon Dr., Iowa City, Iowa 52240. *Office:* University of Iowa Library School, Iowa City, Iowa 52240.

CAREER: Racine Public Library, Racine, Wis., director, 1947-53; Oak Park Public Library, Oak Park, Ill., director, 1953-55; University of Minnesota, Minneapolis, associate professor, Library School, 1955—. Has made numerous library surveys in Minnesota, Iowa, Montana, Wisconsin, Oklahoma, and Michigan; has planned and moderated conferences, institutes, and meetings; has addressed library, church, and similar groups. University of Minnesota, member, executive board, and chairman, personnel committee, Wesley Foundation. *Military service:* U.S. Naval Reserve, 1940-42; became specialist second class. *Member:* American Library Association (life member), Canadian Library Association (life member), Minnesota Library Association, American Association of University Professors, American Civil Liberties Union, Minneapolis Public Library Friends (president, 1963-64), Iowa Library Association.

WRITINGS: (Contributor) Alfred Stefferud, editor, *Wonderful World of Books,* Houghton, 1953; (with Raymond H. Shove, Blanche E. Moen, and Harold G. Russell) *The Use of Books and Libraries,* 10th edition, University of Minnesota Press, 1963. Also author of numerous library surveys. Contributor of articles and reviews to professional journals.

BIOGRAPHICAL/CRITICAL SOURCES: New York Times, November 11, 1962.

* * *

WHALEN, Philip 1923-

PERSONAL: Born October 20, 1923, in Portland, Ore.; son of Glenn Henry and Phyllis (Bush) Whalen. *Education:* Reed College, B.A., 1951. *Home:* 123 Beaver St., San Francisco, Calif. 94114.

CAREER: Writer; part-time lecturer and instructor. *Military service:* U.S. Army Air Forces, 1943-46. *Awards, honors:* Poets Foundation award, 1962; V.K. Ratcliff Award, 1964; American Academy of Arts and Letters grant-in-aid, 1965; Committee on Poetry grant, 1968, 1970, 1971.

WRITINGS: Three Satires (poems), privately printed, 1951; *Self Portrait from Another Direction* (a poem), Auerhahn Press, 1959; *Memoirs of an Interglacial Age* (poems), Auerhahn Press, 1960; *Like I Say* (poems), Totem Press, 1960; *Hymnus ad Patrem Sinensis* (broadside), Four Seasons Foundation, 1963; *Three Mornings* (broadside), Four Seasons Foundation, 1964; *Monday in the Evening* (poems), Pezzoli (Milan), 1964; *Goddess* (broadside), Auerhahn Press, 1964; *Every Day* (poems), Coyote's Journal, 1965; *Highgrade: Doodles, Poems,* Coyote Books, 1966; *T/o* (poems), 1967; *The Invention of the Letter: A Beastly Morality Being an Illuminated Moral History, for the Edification of Younger Readers,* Carp & Whitefish Press, 1967; *You Didn't Even Try* (novel), Coyote Books, 1967; *Intransit: The Philip Whalen Issue* (poems), Toad Press, 1967; *On Bear's Head* (poems), Harcourt and Coyote Books, 1969; *Severance Pay* (poems), Four Seasons Foundation, 1970; *Imaginary Speeches for a Brazen Head* (novel), Black Sparrow Press, 1971.

Represented in several anthologies, including *A New Folder: Americans,* edited by Wallace Fowlie, Folder Press, 1959, *The New American Poetry, 1945-1960,* edited by Donald M. Allen, Grove, 1960, *Junge Amerikanische Lyrik,* edited by Gregory Corso, Carl Hanser Verlag (Munich), 1961, and *A Casebook on the Beat,* edited by

Thomas Parkinson, Crowell, 1961. Contributor to *Northwest Review, Chicago Review, Evergreen Review, Black Mountain Review, Yugen Paris Review, Angel Hair, Noose, Coyote's Journal, Wild Dog,* and *Cambridge Review.*

SIDELIGHTS: Paul Carroll describes Philip Whalen as "the laureate of the day after the Seven Days of Creation, the prosaic everyday, the world of Monday at 10 a.m.: the poet of the drawing room to which Alice returns after her adventures behind the looking-glass. . . . And the interesting possibility is, it seems to me, that the more one reads Mr. Whalen—even the punk and Lenten poems—the more one can participate in his special vision that the routines and newspaper and streets and books of Monday are as poetical as the glory of the creation that began one week before when the spirit of God moved over the waters." To Neil Millar, Whalen sees the world through "an original dreamy, sharp mind, . . . speaking in the world's images and his own and often, like modern music, in silences."

David Kherdian believes that Whalen departs from many of his contemporaries in that he "is not concerned with revolutons and social panaceas. If he sees the big man at all he sees him in the small situation: tripping over a pebble on his journey to deliver a rose. Out of themes that are often seemingly mundane and prosaic he creates poetry of significance because his vision is peculiarly his own and because the clarity of his intelligence is capable of grasping and arresting meaning in seemingly ephemeral and unimportant subjects. He has an ear for conversatonal language that reveals those absurd convictions which render him immune to any belief in sweeping changes. For Whalen, social responsibility means friendship in a field of limited reactions." Whatever Whalen's intentions may be, critics and poets like Kenneth Rexroth continue to admire both the man and his writing. "Whalen is a greatly learned man, more in the mainstream of international avant-garde literature than almost anybody else of his generation, a man of profound insights and the most delicate discriminations. It all seems so effortless, you never notice until it has stolen up and captivated you, the highly wrought music of his verse. . . ."

BIOGRAPHICAL/CRITICAL SOURCES: David Kherdian, *Six Poets of the San Francisco Renaissance,* Giligia Press, 1965; *New York Times Book Review,* August 31, 1969; *Saturday Review,* September 6, 1969; *Christian Science Monitor,* December 18, 1969; *Poetry,* February, 1971.

*   *   *

WHELPTON, (George) Eric   1894-
(Richard Lyte, John Parry)

PERSONAL: Born March 21, 1894, in Le Havre, France; son of George (a minister) and Georgina (Holmes) Whelpton; married Barbara Crocker (a painter and author), December 22, 1943; children: Peter. *Education:* Attended The Leys School, Cambridge; Hertford College, Oxford, B.A. (with honors). *Politics:* Conservative. *Religion:* Church of England. *Home:* West Watch, Trader's Passage, Rye, Sussex, England. *Agent:* Winant, Towers Ltd., 1 Furnival St., London EC4, England.

CAREER: Italian Mail, Florence, Italy, editor, 1922-26; King's College School, London, England, director of modern studies, 1926-42; with British Foreign Service, 1944-45. Broadcaster on international affairs in English, French, and German for British Broadcasting Corp.; also broadcaster for Canadian Broadcasting Corp., Columbia Broadcasting System, Radio Paris, Radio Diffusions Parisiennes, other radio stations in North Africa, Germany,

Austria, and Italy. *Military service:* British Army, Infantry, World War I; became captain; General Staff, Intelligence Corps, World War II; became major. *Member:* Authors Club (London). *Awards, honors:* Knight of Italian Order of Merit.

WRITINGS: The Book of Dublin, Rockliff, 1948; *Paris Today, with a Gazetteer of Places of Interest and Entertainment,* Rockliff, 1948, Macmillan, 1950, revised edition, Rockliff, 1956; *By Italian Shores: Genoa to Naples,* Evans Brothers, 1950; (translator) Jean Belin, *Secrets of the Surete,* Putnam, 1950 (published in England as *My Work at the Surete,* Harrap, 1950); *The Balearics: Majorca, Minorca, Ibiza,* R. Hale, 1952; *Delmatia,* R. Hale, 1954; *The Road to Nice,* R. Hale, 1955; *Paris Cavalcade,* R. Hale, 1959; *Horizon Guide to the Bay of Naples: Ischia, Capri, Sorrento, Positano, Praiano, Amalfi, Vietri sul Mare, and Ravello,* R. Hale, 1963; *Horizon Guide to Sardinia,* R. Hale, 1963; *Southern Spain, with Chapters on the Algarve,* R. Hale, 1964; *A Concise History of Italy,* R. Hale, 1964, Roy, 1965; *The Southern Shores of Spain and Portugal,* R. Hale, 1964; *Normandy and Brittany,* Collins, 1965; *Florence and Tuscany,* R. Hale, 1965, International Publications Service, 1965; *Venice and North-Eastern Italy,* R. Hale, 1965, International Publications Service, 1966; *Gastronomic Guide to Unknown France,* Johnson Publications, 1966, International Publications Service, 1966; *Rand McNally Pocket Guide to Paris,* Rand McNally, 1967 (published in England as *Paris,* Collins, 1967); *Rand McNally Pocket Guide to Rome,* Rand McNally, 1968 (published in England as *Rome,* Collins, 1968); *Italian Lakes and Dolomites,* Collins, 1969; *The Road to Venice,* Shire Publications, 1969, International Publications Service, 1969; *The Road to the Costa Brava,* Shire Publications, 1969, International Publications Service, 1969; *The Road to Rome via Florence,* Shire Publications, 1969, International Publications Service, 1969; *The Road to Provence,* Shire Publications, 1969, International Publications Service, 1969; *The Road to Rome via Genoa,* Shire Publications, 1969, International Publications Service, 1969; *The Road to Salzburg,* Shire Publications, 1969, International Publications Service, 1969; *The Fall, the Reign, and the Eclipse of Rome: History of Europe, 476-1530,* Harrap, 1970; *The Austrians: How They Live and Work,* David & Charles, 1970.

With wife, Barbara Whelpton: *The Intimate Charm of Kensington,* Nicholson & Watson, 1948; *Springtime at St. Hilaire,* Museum Press, 1953; *Grand Tour of Italy,* R. Hale, 1956; *Summer at San Martino,* Hutchinson, 1956; *Calabria and the Aeolian Islands,* R. Hale, 1957, International Publications Service, 1966; *Sicily, Sardinia and Corsica,* R. Hale, 1960; *Greece and the Islands,* R. Hale, 1961, Roy, 1962.

Author of short stories; contributor of articles to *Daily Telegraph* (London), *Monde* (Paris), *Go,* various newspaper syndicates, sometimes writing under pseudonyms Richard Lyte or John Parry.

WORK IN PROGRESS: A history of the Holy Roman Empire; an autobiography.

BIOGRAPHICAL/CRITICAL SOURCES: John O'London's, June 30, 1960.

*   *   *

WHISTLER, Laurence   1912-

PERSONAL: Born January 21, 1912, in Eltham, Kent, England; son of Henry (a building contractor) and Helen (Ward) Whistler; married Jill Furse (an actress), September 12, 1939 (died 1944); married Theresa Furse (an author), August 15, 1950; children: (first marriage) Simon, Caroline; (second marriage) Daniel, Frances. *Education:* Balliol College, Oxford University, B.A. (with

2nd class honors in English literature), 1934. *Religion:* Church of England. *Home:* Little Place, Lyme Regis, Dorsetshire, England.

CAREER: Engraver of glass, chiefly steel-point or drill, 1935—. Poet and author. *Military service:* British Army, 1940-45, serving in Royal Corps of Signals, 1940-41, and Rifle Brigade, 1941-45; became captain. Fellow, Royal Society of Literature, 1960. *Member:* Society of Authors, Glass Circle. *Awards, honors:* Chancellor's English Essay Prize, Oxford University, 1934; Royal Medal for poetry, 1935; Atlantic Award in Literature, 1945; Order of the British Empire, 1955.

WRITINGS: Children of Hertha, and Other Poems, Holywell Press, 1929; *Proletaria, en avant!: A Poem of Socialism,* Alden Press, 1932; *Armed October, and Other Poems,* Cobden-Sanderson, 1932; *Four Walls,* (poems), Heinemann, 1934, Macmillan, 1935; *The Emperor Heart* (poems), Heinemann, 1936, Macmillan, 1937; *Sir John Vanbrugh, Architect and Dramatist, 1664-1726,* Cobden-Sanderson, 1938; Macmillan, 1939; *In Time of Suspense* (poems), Heinemann, 1940; *The Burning Glass,* privately printed, 1941; *Ode to the Sun, and Other Poems,* Heinemann, 1942; *Who Live in Unity* (poems), Heinemann, 1944; *Jill Furse: Her Nature and Her Poems, 1915-1944,* Chiswick Press, 1945; (with brother, Rex Whistler) *Oho!: Certain Two-Faced Individuals Now Exposed by the Bodley Head,* John Lane, 1946; *The Masque of Christmas: Dramatic Joys of the Festival, Old and New,* Curtain Press, 1947; *The English Festivals,* Heinemann, 1947; *Rex Whistler: His Life and His Drawings,* Art & Technics, 1948, Pellegrini & Cudahy, 1949; *The World's Room* (collected poems), Heinemann, 1949; (editor and author of introduction) *Selected Poems of John Keats,* Grey Walls Press, 1950; (editor and author of introduction) *The Koenigsmark Drawings* (by Rex Whistler), Richards Press, 1952; *The Engraved Glass of Laurence Whistler,* Hart-Davis, 1952; *The Kissing Bough: A Christmas Custom,* Heinemann, 1953; *The Imagination of Vanbrugh, and His Fellow Artists,* Art & Technics, 1954; *Stowe: A Guide to the Gardens,* published for Stowe School by Country Life, 1956; *The View from This Window* (poems), Hart-Davis, 1956; *Engraved Glass, 1952-1958,* Hart-Davis, 1959; (with Ronald Fuller) *The Work of Rex Whistler,* Batsford, 1960; *Audible Silence* (poems), Hart-Davis, 1961; *Fingal's Cave* (poem), privately printed, 1963; *The Initials in the Heart,* Houghton, 1964, 2nd edition, revised, Hart-Davis, 1966; *To Celebrate Her Living* (poems), Hart-Davis, 1967; *For Example: Ten Sonnets in Sequence to a New Pattern* (poems originally published in *To Celebrate Her Living*), privately printed, 1969; *Way: Two Affirmations, in Glass and Verse,* Golden Head Press, 1969. Occasional contributor to *Connoisseur, Country Life,* and *Times Literary Supplement.*

WORK IN PROGRESS: A third book on his engravings, *Pictures on Glass.*

SIDELIGHTS: Whistler told *CA* he began the revival of diamond point engraving on glass in Britain in 1935. He engraves goblets, decanters, window-panes, and also large-scale works like office panels and church windows. Primarily a writer of verse, his prose books are chiefly concerned with architecture and with the work of his elder brother, the artist Rex Whistler, killed in action with the Welsh Guards in Normandy in 1944. (Several of Whistler's books of poetry are also illustrated with his brother's artwork.) *The Initials in the Heart* is the story of Laurence Whistler's first marriage; he is now married to Jill Furse's younger sister, Theresa, who is writing a biography of Walter de la Mare.

BIOGRAPHICAL/CRITICAL SOURCES: Punch, July 5, 1967; *Books and Bookmen,* November, 1967.

WHITAKER, Gilbert R(iley), Jr.   1931-

PERSONAL: Born October 8, 1931, in Oklahoma City, Okla.; son of Gilbert Riley (an engineer) and Melodese (Kilpatrick) Whitaker; married Ruth Tonn, December 18, 1953; children: Kathleen, David, Thomas. *Education:* Rice University, B.A., 1953; Southern Methodist University, graduate study, 1956-57; University of Wisconsin, M.S., 1958, Ph.D., 1961. *Office:* Graduate School of Business Administration, Washington University, St. Louis, Mo. 63130.

CAREER: Northwestern University, Evanston, Ill., instructor, 1960-61, assistant professor, 1961-64, associate professor of business economics, 1964-66, part-time member of research staff, Transportation Center, 1963-66; Washington University, St. Louis, Mo., associate professor, 1966-67, professor of business economics, 1967—, associate dean, Graduate School of Business Administration, 1969—. *Military service:* U.S. Navy, 1953-56; became lieutenant. *Member:* American Economic Association, American Statistical Association (vice-president of Chicago chapter, 1963-64). Econometric Society, Institute of Management Science.

WRITINGS: (With Marshall Colberg and Dascomb Forbush) *Business Economics,* 3rd edition, Irwin, 1964, 4th edition, 1970; *The Market for Bank Stock* (monograph), U. S. Government Printing Office, 1964; *A Decision Unit Model of Short-Run Production and Inventory Decisions of Manufacturing Firms* (monograph), Bureau of Business Research, University of Wisconsin, 1966; (contributor) David McConaughy and C. Joseph Clawson, editors, *Business Logistics: Policies and Decisions,* University of Southern California, 1968; (with Roger K. Chisholm) *Forecasting Methods,* Irwin, 1971. Editor, *Parameter* (publication of Chicago chapter of American Statistical Association), 1963-64.

*   *   *

WHITAKER, Urban George, Jr.   1924-

PERSONAL: Born May 19, 1924, in Colony, Kans.; son of Urban George and Gladys (Fackler) Whitaker; married Rebekah Jean Knox, March 18, 1950; children: Susan (Mrs. Jon Wittwer), Bruce Knox, Keith George. *Education:* Occidental College, A.B., 1946; College of Chinese Studies, Peking, China, language study, 1947-48; University of Washington, Seattle, Ph.D., 1954. *Home:* 1590 Greenwood Way, San Bruno, Calif. 94066. *Office:* Department of Undergraduate Studies, California State University, 1600 Holloway Ave., San Francisco, Calif. 94132.

CAREER: California State University (formerly San Francisco State College), San Francisco, chairman, International Relations Department, 1959-60, now professor of international relations, and dean of undergraduate studies. Co-director, International Studies Project, Carnegie Corp., 1958-61; delegate, North Atlantic Treaty Organization conference, Paris, 1960. Ford Foundation fellow, University of Iowa summer conference, 1955; Rockefeller fellow, Columbia University and United Nations, 1960-61. Member of national executive committee, Commission to Study the Organization of Peace, 1964—. Lecturer, radio commentator, and United Nations correspondent. *Military service:* U.S. Navy, 1942-46, 1950-52; became lieutenant; received letter of commendation from the Commander of the Seventh Fleet. *Member:* International Studies Association (secretary, 1961-62), American Association for the United Nations (president, San Francisco chapter, 1961-62; member, national board of directors, 1962-70).

WRITINGS: (editor) *The Foundations of U.S. China Policy,* Pacifica Foundation, 1959; (editor with Frank K.

Sloan) *China and the West,* San Francisco State College, 1959; (editor) *Nationalism and International Progress,* Chandler Publishing, 1960, 2nd edition, 1961; (editor) *Propaganda and International Relations,* Chandler Publishing, 1960, 2nd edition, 1962; (editor) *Democracies and International Relations,* Chandler Publishing, 1961; *Politics and Power, A Text in International Law,* Harper, 1964; (contributor) Franz Michael, *The Taiping Rebellion,* three volumes, University of Washington Press, 1966-71; (with Bruce E. Davis) *The World and Ridgeway, South Carolina,* Institute of International Affairs, University of South Carolina, 1967; (contributor) Abdul Said, editor, *America's World Role in the '70's,* Prentice-Hall, 1970. Contributor of articles to *Western Political Quarterly, Nation, Frontier, Progressive, War/Peace Report,* and other publications.

WORK IN PROGRESS: A textbook on international relations, for C.E. Merrill.

BIOGRAPHICAL/CRITICAL SOURCES: New York Post, July 26, 1961; *Christian Science Monitor,* July 28, 1961.

*   *   *

WHITE, Anne Terry   1896-

PERSONAL: Born February 19, 1896, in Russia; married, 1918; children: Ruth Levitan, Joan Pinkham. *Education:* Brown University, Ph.B., 1918; Stanford University, M.A., 1925. *Home:* 7 Fourth St., Stamford, Conn. 06905.

CAREER: Teacher, social worker, editor of *Young Citizen,* writer for Social Security Board. *Member:* Phi Beta Kappa.

WRITINGS—All juveniles, except as otherwise noted: *Heroes of the Five Books,* Harper, 1937; *Three Children and Shakespeare* (includes readings from *The Merchant of Venice, A Midsummer Night's Dream, Julius Caesar,* and *The Taming of the Shrew*), Harper, 1938; *Lost Worlds: Adventures in Archaeology,* Random House, 1941; *Men Before Adam* (adult book), Random House, 1942; *Prehistoric America,* Random House, 1951; *The First Men in the World,* Random House, 1953, reissued as *All About the First Men in the World,* W.H. Allen, 1959; *George Washington Carver: The Story of a Great American,* Random House, 1953; *Will Shakespeare and the Globe Theater,* Random House, 1955; *Rocks All Around Us* (3rd grade geology), Random House, 1959; *Natural Wonders,* Golden Press, 1960; *The St. Lawrence, Seaway of North America,* Garrard, 1961; *Birds of the World,* Golden Press, 1962; *The False Treaty,* Scholastic, 1970; *Human Cargo: The Story of the Atlantic Slave Trade,* Garrard, 1972; *North to Liberty: The Story of the Underground Railroad,* Garrard, 1972.

"All About" series—All published by Random House: *All About the Stars,* 1954, *All About Our Changing Rocks,* 1955, reissued as *All About Rocks and Minerals,* 1963, *All About Great Rivers of the World,* 1957, *All About Archaeology,* 1959, *All About Mountains and Mountaineering,* 1962.

With Gerald S. Lietz—All published by Garrard: *Windows on the World,* 1965, *Secrets of the Heart and Blood,* 1965, *When Hunger Calls,* 1966, *Built to Survive,* 1966, *Man the Thinker,* 1967.

Adaptor: (And editor with Isidor Schneider) I.G. Ehrenburg, *Storm,* translated by J. Fineberg, Gaer, 1949; Robert Louis Stevenson, *Treasure Island,* Adprint (London), 1955, Simon & Schuster, 1956; J.H. Spyri, *Heidi,* Simon & Schuster, 1956; Mark Twain, *Adventures of Tom Sawyer,* Simon & Schuster, 1956; Mary M. Dodge, *Hans Brinker; or, The Silver Skates,* Simon & Schuster, 1957; *King Arthur and the Knights of the Round Table* (adapted from Sir Thomas Malory's *Morte d'Arthur*), Adprint, 1957; Jonathan Swift, *Gulliver's Travels,* Adprint, 1957; Daniel Defoe, *Robinson Crusoe,* Adprint, 1957, Golden Press, 1960; Hans Christian Andersen, *Fairy Tales,* Simon & Schuster, 1958; Rachel Louise Carson, *The Sea Around Us,* Simon & Schuster, 1958; *Indians and the Old West: The Story of the First Americans* (adapted from *American Heritage* magazine), Simon & Schuster, 1958; *Aladdin and the Wonderful Lamp,* Random House, 1959; *The Golden Treasury of Myths and Legends* (adapted from the world's great classics), deluxe edition, Golden Press, 1959, reissued as *Myths and Legends,* Paul Hamlyn, 1963; Ivan Terence Sanderson, *The Continent We Live On,* Random House, 1962; William Brandon, *The American Indian,* edited by Alvin M. Josephy, introduction by John F. Kennedy, Random House, 1963; *Aesop's Fables* (retold), Random House, 1964; (and editor) Harriet Beecher Stowe, *Uncle Tom's Cabin,* Braziller, 1966; *Ali Baba and the Forty Thieves* [*and*] *Abu Kir and Abu Sir* (two Arabian tales), Garrard, 1968; *Odysseus Comes Home from the Sea* (Homer's *Odyssey* retold), Crowell, 1968; *Sindbad the Seaman* [*and*] *The Ebony Horse* (two Arabian tales), Garrard, 1969; *Of Beasts, Birds, and Men: Fables from Three Lands* (retold), Garrard, 1970; *David the Giantkiller* (retold), Crowell, 1970; *Knights of the Table Round* (retold), Garradd, 1970.

Translator from the Russian: Vladimir Klavdievich Arsenyev, *With Dersu the Hunter: Adventures in the Taiga,* Braziller, 1965; G.A. Skrebitskii, *In the Forest and on the Marsh,* Braziller, 1966; G.A. Skrebitskii, *Forest Echo,* Braziller, 1967; Grigori Fedoseyev, *Pashka of Bear Ravine,* Random House, 1967; Vitali Bianki, *How I Wanted to Pour Salt on a Rabbit's Tail, and Other Stories,* Braziller, 1967; Lev Kassil, *Brother of the Hero,* Braziller, 1968; *Czar of the Water* [*and*] *The Little Humpbacked Horse* (the latter by Petr Pavlovich Ershov), Garrard, 1968; Yuri Kazakov, *Arcturus, the Hunting Hound,* Doubleday, 1968; Vera Panova, *On Faraway Street,* Braziller, 1968; *Six Russian Tales* (includes three stories by Alexander Pushkin), Garrard, 1969; Lev Kassil, *Once in a Lifetime,* Doubleday, 1970.

WORK IN PROGRESS: Patriots of the Plains, to be published by Scholastic; *Black Revolts in the United States,* for Garrard.

BIOGRAPHICAL/CRITICAL SOURCES: Natural History, December, 1963; *New York Times Book Review,* November 3, 1968; *Library Journal,* December 15, 1968.

*   *   *

WHITE, Mary Alice   1920-

PERSONAL: Born March 18, 1920, in Washington, D.C.; daughter of Charles Stanley (a doctor) and Blanche (Strong) White; married Edward N. Kimball, Jr., March 26, 1949; children: Christopher, Katharine. *Education:* Vassar College, B.A., 1941; Columbia University, M.A., 1944, Ph.D., 1948. *Home:* 60 Forest Ave., Rye, N.Y. 10580. *Office:* Department of Psychology, Teachers College, Columbia University, New York, N.Y. 10027.

CAREER: Westchester division of New York Hospital, director department of psychology, 1950-60; Pelham School System, New York, N.Y., psychological consultant, 1956-61; Teachers College, Columbia University, New York, N.Y., associate professor, 1961—. *Member:* American Psychological Association (fellow).

WRITINGS: (With Myron W. Harris) *The School Psychologist,* Harper, 1961; (editor with June B. Charry) *School Disorder, Intelligence, and Social Class,* Teachers College Press, 1966. Contributor of articles to professional journals.

WHITE, Robin 1928-

PERSONAL: Born July 12, 1928, in Kodaikanal, South India; son of Emmons Eaton (a minister) and Ruth Esther (Parker) White; married Marian Lucille Biesterfeld, February 3, 1948; children: Christopher, Parker, Shelley. Education: Yale University, B.A., 1950; Middlebury College, Bread Loaf fellow, 1956; Stanford University, creative writing fellow, 1956-57. Politics: Independent. Religion: Independent. Home: 40 Granada Court, Portola Valley, Calif. 94025. Agent: James Brown Associates, 22 East 60th St., New York, N.Y. 10022.

CAREER: Free-lance writer, 1950—. Awards, honors: Curtis Prize, 1958, for Elephant Hill; Harper Prize; O. Henry Prize.

WRITINGS: House of Many Rooms, Harper, 1958; Elephant Hill, Harper, 1959; Men and Angels, Harper, 1961; Foreign Soil: Tales of South India, Atheneum, 1962; All in Favor Say No, Farrar, Straus, 1964; His Own Kind, Bodley Head, 1967. Contributor to Harper's, New Yorker, Maclean's Magazine, Ladies' Home Journal, Harper's Bazaar, Mademoiselle, Seventeen, New York Times Book Review, Saturday Review, and Writer. Editor-in-chief, Per/se International Quarterly, 1966-69.

WORK IN PROGRESS: A photo-narrative book on the Sierra Nevada.

BIOGRAPHICAL/CRITICAL SOURCES: Times Literary Supplement, May 4, 1967.

* * *

WHITE, Sarah Harriman 1929-

PERSONAL: Born July 6, 1929, in Nevada, Mo.; daughter of Fred Leo and Marie (Inwood) Harriman; married John H. White (a chemist), October 18, 1952; children: Sarah Jeanne, Daniel John, Margaret Anne. Education: Saint Louis University, B.A., 1950. Religion: Roman Catholic. Home: 4009a Shaw Blvd., St. Louis, Mo. 63110.

CAREER: WEW (radio station), St. Louis, Mo., music librarian, 1950-52; Society of Helpers of Holy Souls, bookkeeper-typist, 1955-56; St. Louis University, St. Louis, Mo., 1956-58, began as secretary, became chairman of English department. Member: Catholic Daughters of America, Court Blessed Rose Philippine Duchesne (financial secretary, 1962-1965), St. Margaret's Women's Sodality.

WRITINGS: (With Daniel D. McGarry) Historical Fiction Guide, Scarecrow, 1963; (editor) Guide to Science and Technology in the U.S.S.R., Francis Hodgson, 1971†.

* * *

WHITE, Stanley 1913-
(Felix Krull, Peto, James Peto, James Dillon White)

PERSONAL: Born August 8, 1913, in London, England; son of Ernest Bentley (a civil servant) and Annie May (Rutterford) White; married Olive Joan Coppen, December 4, 1948; children: Anthony Dillon, Christopher Dillon, Jeremy Dillon. Politics: Liberal humanist. Religion: Christian. Home: Watchfield, St. Mary's Rd., Leatherhead, Surrey, England. Office: Standard Life Assurance Co., 3 Abchurch Yard, London E.C.4, England.

CAREER: Standard Life Assurance Co., London, England, regional agency manager, 1930—. Military service: Royal Artillery; became captain. Member: National Book League, P.E.N., Army and Navy Club, Gresham Club.

WRITINGS:—All under pseudonym James Dillon White, except as indicated: Heartbreak Camp, Quality Press,

1949; The Edge of the Forest, Heinemann, 1952; The Spoletta Story, Heinemann, 1952; A Stranger in Town, Heinemann, 1953; The Quiet River, Heinemann, 1953; The Maggie, Heinemann, 1954; Flamingo Lake, Heinemann, 1954; Genevieve, Heinemann, 1955; Night on the Bare Mountain, Heinemann, 1957; Born to Star (biography), Heinemann, 1957; The Tall Ship, Heinemann, 1958; Brave Captain Kelso, Hutchinson, 1959; Captain of Marine, Hutchinson, 1960; The Princess of Persia, Hutchinson, 1961; (under pseudonym Felix Krull) The Village Pub Murders, Ward, Lock, 1962; (under pseudonym James Peto) Iscariot, Jarrolds, 1962; Young Mr. Kelso, W.H. Allen, 1963; The Hound of Heaven, Hutchinson, 1966; Commodore Kelso, Hutchinson, 1967; Summer Has Gone, Hutchinson, 1967; Sweet Evil, Hutchinson, 1968; Kelso of the Paragon, Hutchinson, 1969; The Furzedown Comet, Hutchinson, 1970; Lords of Human Kind, Hutchinson, 1971; The Running Lions, Hutchinson, 1972; A Wind in the Rigging, Hutchinson, 1973. Also author of film script (with Lindsay Galloway), "Fire Over Greece," and of a radio adaptation of The Quiet River. Contributor of a monthly review of light fiction to Smith's Trade News, and of a weekly column, "Inspectors' Table," to Post Magazine and Insurance Monitor.

WORK IN PROGRESS: A novel, The Sassenach.

SIDELIGHTS: White rises at 4:30 a.m. and writes for two hours daily before leaving for office; he revises in evening.

BIOGRAPHICAL/CRITICAL SOURCES: Books and Bookmen, April, 1971.

* * *

WHITEHEAD, Don(ald) F. 1908-

PERSONAL: Born April 8, 1908, in Inman, Va.; son of Harry Ford (a merchant) and Elizabeth (Bond) Whitehead; married Marie Patterson, December 20, 1928; children: Ruth (Mrs. Eugene Y. Neilsen). Education: University of Kentucky, student, 1926-28. Home and office: Northshore Dr., Route 1, Concord, Tenn.

CAREER: Harlan Daily Enterprise, Harlan, Ky., city editor, 1929-33, Knoxville Journal, Knoxville, Tenn., reporter, 1934-35; Associated Press, New York, N.Y., reporter, 1935-42, war correspondent, 1942-45, bureau chief in Hawaii, 1945-48, special correspondent in Washington, D.C., 1948-56; New York Herald Tribune, New York, N.Y., chief of Washington bureau, 1956-57; Knoxville News-Sentinel, Knoxville, Tenn., columnist, 1959—. As war correspondent was attached to British Eighth Army in Egypt, made assault landings with American troops in Sicily, and at Salerno and Anzio, Italy, landed in Normandy with spearheading forces on D Day, remained with First Army until it joined with Russians on the Elbe. Member: Authors Guild, National Press Club, Cherokee Country Club. Awards, honors: U.S. Medal of Freedom, 1945, for war reporting; Pulitzer prize, 1951, for international reporting, and 1953, for national reporting; Sigma Delta Chi award, 1950; George Polk award, 1951; Freedoms Foundation award, 1957; Christopher award, 1957; LL.D., University of Kentucky, 1947.

WRITINGS: The FBI Story: A Report to the People (foreword by J. Edgar Hoover), Random House, 1956, juvenile edition, 1963; Journey Into Crime, Random House, 1960; Border Guard—The Story of the U.S. Customs Service, McGraw, 1963; The Dow Story: The History of the Dow Chemical Company, McGraw, 1968; Attack on Terror: The FBI Against the Ku Klux Klan in Mississippi, Funk, 1970.

WHITFIELD, John Humphreys 1906-
(Gerone Pilio)

PERSONAL: Born October 2, 1906, in Wednesbury, Staffordshire, England; son of John Allen (a costing clerk) and Florence Kate (Organ) Whitfield; married Joan Herrin, April 26, 1936; children: Roderick, Clovis. Education: Magdalen College, Oxford, B.A. (first class honors), 1928 and 1929, M.A., 1932. Home: 2 Woodbourne Rd., Edgbaston, Birmingham 15, England. Office: Department of Italian, University of Birmingham, Birmingham 15, England.

CAREER: King Edward VII School, Sheffield, England, assistant French master, 1930-36; Oxford University, Oxford, England, university lecturer in Italian, 1936-46; University of Birmingham, Birmingham, England, Serena Professor of Italian language and literature, 1946—. Awarder to Oxford and Cambridge Schools examination board (in Italian). Member: Society for Italian Studies (chairman), Modern Humanities Research Association, Dante Alighieri Society (president of Birmingham branch), Georgian Group, National Trust, National Art Collections Fund. Awards, honors: Edmund Gardner Prize of University of London for publications, 1953-57, including Giacomo Leopardi, 1954; Cavaliere Ufficiale, Ordine al Merito della Repubblica Italiana, 1960; member, Academy of Arcadia, Rome; Amedeo Maiuri Prize, Rome, 1965.

WRITINGS: Petrarch and the Renascence, Salloch, 1943; Machiavelli, Salloch, 1947; Dante and Virgil, Macmillan, 1949; Giacomo Leopardi, Basil Blackwell, 1954; Barlow Lectures on Dante, 1959, Heffer, 1960; Essays in the Like and Unlike, published for the Society for Italian Studies by Heffer, 1960; A Short History of Italian Literature, Peter Smith, 1960, Barnes & Noble 1964; (editor, translator into English verse, and author of introduction and notes) Giacomo Leopardi, The Canti, Scalabrini, 1962; Discourses on Machiavelli, Heffer, 1969; (editor) Niccolo Machiavelli, Prince (facsimile edition of the Charlecote manuscript), S.R. Publishers, 1969. Contributor of articles and reviews to professional journals in England and on the Continent. Editor, Italian Studies; member of editorial board, Le Parole e le Idee, and Studies in Romanticism.

WORK IN PROGRESS: Research on Italian humanism, Machiavelli, and Italian literature and seventeenth-century France.

*   *   *

WHITMAN, (Evelyn) Ardis

PERSONAL: Born in Little River, Nova Scotia, Canada; daughter of Melburne Burkee (a minister) and Cora (Hennigar) Whitman; married Owen T. Rumsey (a school teacher), June 29, 1927; children: Patricia Marie (Mrs. Richard Brookman), James Elvin. Education: Acadia University, Nova Scotia, Canada, B.A., 1926. Politics: Democrat. Religion: Baptist. Home: 127 Victoria Rd., New Britain, Conn. 06052. Agent: McIntosh & Otis, Inc., 18 East 41st St., New York, N.Y. 10017.

CAREER: Junior high school teacher of English literature, Belmont, Mass., 1926-27. Free-lance writer and public lecturer. Leader in Great Books program, fifteen years. Member: National Council on Family Relations, Authors Guild of Authors League of America, American Association of University Women, Society of Magazine Writers.

WRITINGS: I'm Tired of Grandma!, Bobbs-Merrill, 1949; How To Be a Happy Woman, Appleton, 1952; A New Image of Man, Appleton, 1955. Contributor to Redbook, Woman's Day, Reader's Digest, Ladies' Home Journal, McCall's, and other periodicals.

WORK IN PROGRESS: An untitled book on the relationship of religion and maturity.

*   *   *

WHITNAH, Donald R(obert) 1925-

PERSONAL: Born June 9, 1925, in Canton, Ill.; son of Leon Arthur (in banking and insurance) and Anna (Jackley) Whitnah; married Florentine Egger, August 9, 1947; children: Victoria Ann, Tara Beth. Education: Lincoln College, Lincoln, Ill., A.A., 1949; University of Illinois, B.A., 1951, M.A., 1952, Ph.D., 1957. Religion: Methodist. Home: 1215 Catherine St., Cedar Falls, Iowa 50613. Office: University of Northern Iowa, Cedar Falls, Iowa 50613.

CAREER: U.S. War Department Army Exchange Service, Salzburg, Austria, merchandise control, 1946-47; Lincoln Evening Courier, Lincoln, Ill., reporter, 1948-49; Illinois State Water Survey, Urbana, weather observer and meteorological assistant, 1951-56; State Teachers College (now Valley City State College), Valley City, instructor in history, 1956-59; State College of Iowa (now University of Northern Iowa), Cedar Falls, assistant professor of history, 1959-62, associate professor, 1962-66, professor of history, 1966—, head of department, 1969—, co-director of seminar in Europe, 1963, 1965. Member: American Historical Association, Organization of American Historians, American Association of University Professors (chapter vice-president, 1961-62; chapter president, 1962-63), Phi Kappa Phi, Phi Alpha Theta, Pi Gamma Mu. Awards, honors: Alumni award, Lincoln College, 1962; research grant in Austro-American relations, Lincoln Educational Foundation, 1969—.

WRITINGS: A History of the United States Weather Bureau, University of Illinois Press, 1961; Safer Skyways: Federal Control of Aviation, 1926-1966, Iowa State University Press, 1967.

WORK IN PROGRESS: Austria and the United States: Twentieth-Century Diplomacy.

AVOCATIONAL INTERESTS: Classical music, opera, sports, travel.

*   *   *

WHITNEY, David C(harles) 1921-

PERSONAL: Born March 8, 1921, in Salina, Kan.; son of William R. and Jerusha F. (McCartney) Whitney; married Elizabeth J. West, January 31, 1943; children: Ann G., Katherine W., Jane P., West Martin, Peter A., Lynn McC. Education: University of Kansas, A.B., 1942; attended Columbia University, 1946. Home: 291 Roaring Brook Rd., Chappaqua, N.Y. 10514. Office: UEC Inc., 1501 Broadway, New York, N.Y. 10036.

CAREER: United Press Associations, New York, N.Y., feature writer and overnight news editor, 1945-51; World Book Encyclopedia, Chicago, Ill., assistant managing editor, 1952-54, managing editor, 1954-64, editorial director and vice-president, 1964; Encyclopedia Americana, New York, N.Y., editor-in-chief and vice-president, 1964-65; Cowles Education Corp., New York, N.Y., president and editor, 1965-68; UEC Inc., New York, N.Y., vice-president of educational systems division, 1969—. President, Board of Education, Illinois School District 110, 1956-61; mayor, Deerfield, Ill., 1961-64. Military service: U.S. Naval Reserve, 1942-45; became lieutenant senior grade. Member: Authors Guild, Mayflower Society, Association for Supervision and Curriculum Development of the National Education Association, New York Academy of Sciences, Royal Society of Arts (London; Benjamin Franklin Fellow), Sigma Delta Chi.

WRITINGS: Founders of Freedom in America, J.G. Ferguson, Volume I: Lives of the Men Who Signed the Declaration, of Independence and So Helped to Establish the United States of America, 1964, Volume II: *Lives of the Men Who Signed the Constitution of the United States and So Helped to Establish the United States of America,* 1965; *The American Presidents,* Doubleday, 1967, revised and expanded edition published as *The Graphic Story of the American Presidents,* 1968; *The Trials and Triumphs of Two Dynamic Decades,* edited by Thomas C. Jones, J.G. Ferguson, 1968; *Latin America,* Golden Press, 1968; *U.S.A.,* Golden Press, 1968; (editor with Francine Klagsburn) *Assassination: Robert F. Kennedy, 1925-1968,* United Press International and Cowles, 1968.

Juveniles published by F. Watts: *The First Book of Facts and How to Find Them,* 1966, *Let's Find Out About Addition,* 1966, *Let's Find Out About Milk,* 1967, *The Picture Life of Lyndon Baines Johnson,* 1967, *Blueberry, the Bloodhound,* 1967, *Willie & Winnie & Wilma, the Wicked Witch,* 1967, *Let's Find Out About Subtraction,* 1968, *Let's Find Out About the President of the United States,* 1968, *The Picture Life of Dwight D. Eisenhower,* 1968, *Skippy the Skunk,* 1968, *Ann's Ann-imal,* 1969, *The Easy Book of Multiplication,* 1969, *Limpy the Lion,* 1969, *The Easy Book of Fractions,* 1970, *The Easy Book of Division,* 1970, *The Easy Book of Sets,* 1972. Contributor to *Teachers College Record, Chicago Daily News,* and *Educational Technology.*

*   *   *

WHITNEY, Peter Dwight   1915-

PERSONAL: Born May 7, 1915, in San Francisco, Calif.; son of James Lyman and Elizabeth (Goodrich) Whitney; married Frances Friedman, 1955; children: (prior marriage) James C., Elizabeth A., Stephen C.; (present marriage) Joanna G. *Education:* Yale University, B.A., 1936. *Politics:* Democrat. *Residence:* Inverness, Calif.

CAREER: San Francisco Chronicle, San Francisco, Calif., war and foreign correspondent, 1937-44; *Chicago Sun,* London bureau, foreign correspondent, 1944-46; *London Observer,* Washington and Paris, foreign correspondent, 1946-50; *Washington Post,* Washington, D.C., assistant editor, 1950; Voice of America, New York, N.Y., writer, commentator, 1951; *New York Times,* New York, foreign correspondent, 1953-59; presently writer, photographer, and political public relations man. Executive director of Scenic Roads Association of California; participant in conservation activities in Northern California. *Member:* American Canoe Association (executive committee delegate), Sierra Club, Appalachian Mountain Club.

WRITINGS: White-Water Sport, Ronald, 1960. Contributor to national magazines. Editor, *American White Water.*

SIDELIGHTS: "I am a believer in the idea that conservation, in its broadest sense, is the most important single problem mankind faces; it even includes our ideological conflict with the Soviet Union, in the sense that we are seeking to conserve our planet and our species, as well as our way of life." He is interested in white-water canoeing, Jungian psychology, and conservation. He appears on radio and television on behalf of conservation, and as a news commentator.†

*   *   *

WHITRIDGE, Arnold   1891-

PERSONAL: Born June 29, 1891, in New Rochelle, N.Y.; son of Frederick Wallingford and Lucy (Arnold) Whitridge; married Janetta Alexander, April 25, 1918; children: Janetta (Mrs. John B. Leake), Frederick W., Rhoda (Mrs. Daniel L. Boyd). *Education:* Attended Groton School for five years; Yale University, B.A.,

1913; Oxford University, graduate study, 1913-14; Columbia University, M.A., 1922, Ph.D., 1925. *Politics:* Republican. *Religion:* Episcopalian. *Home:* Hill Top Farm, Salisbury, Conn. 06068.

CAREER: Columbia University, New York, N.Y., assistant professor of English, 1921-32; Yale University, New Haven, Conn., professor in department of history, arts, and letters, and master of Calhoun College, 1932-42. Fulbright professor of American civilization at University of Athens, 1949-51, at University of Bordeaux, 1952. Trustee of Metropolitan Museum of Art and St. Luke's Hospital, both New York, N.Y.; chairman of New York Art Commission; president of Scoville Memorial Library, Salisbury, Conn. *Military service:* British Army, Royal Field Artillery, 1914-17; became lieutenant. U.S. Army, Field Artillery, American Expeditionary Forces, 1917-19; became major. U.S. Army Air Forces, Combat Intelligence, 1942-45; served overseas with Ninth Air Force; became colonel. *Member:* Century Association, Yale Club, University Club (all New York); Athenaeum Club (London), Delta Kappa Epsilon, Scroll and Key. *Awards, honors:* Annual book award of Colonial Dames of America, 1966, for *Rochambeau.*

WRITINGS: Tobias Smollett: A Study of His Miscellaneous Works, privately printed, 1923; (editor) Matthew Arnold, *Unpublished Letters,* Yale University Press, 1923; *Critical Ventures in Modern French Literature,* Scribner, 1924, Books for Libraries, 1967; *Dr. Arnold of Rugby,* Henry Holt, 1928; *Alfred de Vigny,* Oxford University Press, 1933; (editor with J.W. Dodds) *Oxford Anthology of English Prose,* Oxford University Press, 1935; *Men in Crisis: The Revolutions of 1848,* Scribner, 1949; *Simon Bolivar, The Great Liberator,* Random House, 1954; *No Compromise!: The Story of the Fanatics Who Paved the Way to the Civil War,* Farrar, Straus, 1960; *Rochambeau,* Macmillan, 1965.

*   *   *

WHITTEMORE, Charles P(ark)   1921-

PERSONAL: Born September 15, 1921, in Bryn Mawr, Pa.; son of Henry Lawrence (an advertising executive) and Carol (Park) Whittemore. *Education:* Williams College, Williamstown, Mass., B.A., 1943; Columbia University, M.A., 1947, Ph.D., 1957. *Politics:* Democrat. *Religion:* Episcopalian. *Home:* 40 Main, Essex, Conn.

CAREER: South Kent School, South Kent, Conn., head of department of history and director of studies, 1943—. *Military service:* U.S. Army, 1943. *Member:* American Historical Association, Organization of American Historians, St. Anthony Club (New York).

WRITINGS: A General of the Revolution: John Sullivan of New Hampshire, Columbia University Press, 1961; (contributor) George A. Billias, editor, *George Washington's Generals,* Morrow, 1964.

*   *   *

WHITTEMORE, Mildred   1946-

PERSONAL: Born May 25, 1946, in Boston, Mass.; daughter of Carroll Ernest (an ecclesiologist) and Roberta (Cooper) Whittemore. *Education:* Beloit College, student, 1964—. *Religion:* Protestant. *Home:* 265 Commonwealth Ave., Boston, Mass. 02116.

WRITINGS: Hymn Writers of the Christian Church, Whittemore, 1963.

WORK IN PROGRESS: Sporadic research and writing on two novels—a story of medieval England and a fictionalized biography of Vercingetorix, the Gallic chieftain; a science fiction book.

SIDELIGHTS: Miss Whittemore is studying for a degree in anthropology, specializing in Asian and African ethnology. She has been to Europe four times, and plans future study and research abroad.†

* * *

WHITTEMORE, (Edward) Reed (Jr.) 1919-

PERSONAL: Born September 11, 1919, in New Haven, Conn.; son of Edward Reed (a doctor) and Margaret (Carr) Whittemore; married Helen Lundeen, October 3, 1952; children: Catherine, Edward, John, Margaret. Education: Yale University, B.A., 1941; Princeton University, graduate study, 1945-46. Address: 3509 Macomb St. N.W., Washington, D.C. 20016. Office: English Department, University of Maryland, College Park, Md.

CAREER: Furioso (literary quarterly), editor, 1939-53; Carleton College, Northfield, Minn., professor of English, 1947-66, chairman of department, 1962-64, editor, Carleton Miscellany (literary quaterly), 1960-64; University of Maryland, College Park, professor of English, 1967—; New Republic, Washington, D.C., literary editor, 1969—. Library of Congress, Consultant in poetry, 1964-65, honorary consultant in American letters, 1968-71; Bain-Swiggett lecturer, Princeton University, 1967. Consultant to National Institute of Public Affairs, 1966-68; director of Association of Literary Magazines of America. Military service: U.S. Army Air Forces, 1941-45; became major, awarded bronze star. Awards, honors: Harriet Monroe Memorial Prize of Poetry magazine, 1954; Emily Clark Balch Prize of Virginia Quarterly Review, 1962, for "The Music of Driftwood"; National Endowment for the Arts grant, 1968-69; National Council on the Arts Award, 1969, for lifelong contribution to American letters; American Academy of Arts and Letters Award of Merit Medal, 1970; former National Book Awards judge.

WRITINGS—All poetry, except as indicated: Heroes and Heroines, Reynal & Hitchcock, 1946; An American Takes a Walk, University of Minnesota Press, 1956; The Self-Made Man, and Other Poems, Macmillan, 1959; The Boy From Iowa, Macmillan, 1962; The Fascination of the Abomination (poems, stories, and essays), Macmillan, 1963; Little Magazines (pamphlet), University of Minnesota Press, 1963; Return, Alpheus: A Poem for the Literary Elders of Phi Beta Kappa, King & Queen Press (Williamsburg, Va.), 1965; Ways of Misunderstanding Poetry (lecture delivered at Library of Congress, October 12, 1964), U.S. Government Printing Office, 1965; Poems New and Selected, University of Minnesota Press, 1968; From Zero to the Absolute (essays), Crown, 1968; Fifty Poems Fifty, University of Minnesota Press, 1970. Contributor to New Republic, Nation, New Yorker, Saturday Review, Kenyon Review, Esquire, and Yale Review.

SIDELIGHTS: "In so many of Reed Whittemore's poems, the ear is flawless," writes Laurence Lieberman. "His voice is perfectly pitched, immaculate, suave, urbane. There are no slips, no mistakes—if he trips, it is always accidentally-on-purpose, he comes up smiling, and we smile with him, not at him. He is one of our dwindling few tasteful and intelligent satirists. . . . When the good poem starts to unwind to uncoil, it serpentines cunningly, and as the poem rises to a perfect little loop at the finish, and sticks its little forked tongue out at me, I am genuinely tickled and stung." Howard Nemerov believes that Whittemore's work has been neglected: "Its rare candor and integrity of purpose have not been valued as they ought to be, [because Whittemore] is often funny, and . . . he is often literary. People who either have no faculty of independent judgment or perhaps rightly distrust what they do have, are suspicious and even resentful of new poetry which is funny . . .

because they are afraid of being caught admiring something which will turn out to be light verse." Nemerov continues: "To consider Whittemore's poems as a whole is to be convinced of a singleness of purpose, growing in clarity, to which both the humor and the 'literary' quality are essential instruments."

Michael Benedikt says that although "most of those who have written about him think Whittemore is best characterized by mirthfulness, . . . Whittemore is, in fact, a poet of spiritual misery. The particular spiritual misery engaged in his work has to do with the utter emptiness of all the realities—but especially the American reality—around him." Benedikt writes that the finest of Whittemore's poems "have the habit of dealing . . . with the processes of art. There is an exhilarating lack of consideration of art as the burden of some kind of cultural colonist; and a concentration on its actually sustaining pleasures. Among his poems are many in which he attends to the positive and real task of examining the things that he has really been up to."

Whittemore writes in Poets on Poetry: "I think of poetry as a thing of the mind and tend to judge it, at least in part, by the qualities of mind it displays. . . . the properties of mind I most admire are the daytime properties—those that get us to the store or shop and back, and put us on the radio discussing poetry or arguing about communism and democracy. Most of my poems, therefore, tend to deal primarily with the daytime part of the mind, that is, the prosaic part; only occasionally do they deal directly with the nighttime self." Since he writes short poems, he says: "I have been impressed by the insufficiencies of the short-poem art for about twenty-five years; yet I have gone on writing short poems and I suspect that my reputation as a poet, if I have any, is almost entirely based on a few short poems. I find the genre a congenial one in which to deal with my own insufficiencies, among which is my own rational incapacity to work things out, order them logically, on a big scale."

Nemerov cites a statement of Shaw "to the effect that the most serious intellectual concerns might be just 'a mere middle-class business.' " He suggests that poetry might come under this heading, and that this has always been one of Whittemore's concerns. "It is a major virtue in Whittemore's work that he has constantly brought himself face to face with this dilemma; the fineness of the best of his poems has intimately to do with their rejection of the theatrical, oracular, and 'significant,' their refusal to be 'important' and 'deep' by faking up an irrelevant heroism."

BIOGRAPHICAL/CRITICAL SOURCES: New York Times Book Review, June 2, 1963; Saturday Review, June 8, 1963; Howard Nemerov, Poetry and Fiction, Rutgers University Press, 1963; Howard Nemerov, editor, Poets on Poetry, Basic Books, 1966; New Leader, December 4, 1967; Yale Review, winter, 1968; Shenandoah, spring, 1968; Poetry, June, 1968; Antioch Review, spring, 1971.

* * *

WHITTEMORE, Robert Clifton 1921-

PERSONAL: Born February 1, 1921, in Lockport, N.Y.; son of Clifton Houghton (an electrical engineer) and Zelia (Duke) Whittemore; married Dorothy Jane Gordon Lawton (a reference librarian), June 6, 1959; stepchildren: Stanley Allen Lawton, Shirley Anne Lawton. Education: Yale University, B.A., 1949, M.A., 1951, Ph.D., 1953. Politics: Independent. Religion: Episcopalian. Home: 7521 Dominican St., New Orleans, La. 70118. Office: 124 Gibson Hall, Tulane University, 6823 Charles Ave., New Orleans, La. 70118.

CAREER: Yale University, New Haven, Conn., instructor in philosophy, 1951-52; Tulane University, New

Orleans, La., instructor, 1952-54, assistant professor, 1954-58, associate professor, 1958-63, professor of philosophy, 1963—, dean of University College, 1968—. Lecturer on educational television series, "The American Mind," 1961-62. *Miltary service:* U.S. Army Quartermaster and Engineer Corps, 1942-46; became sergeant. *Member:* American Philosophical Association, Metaphysical Society of America, Society for Religion in Higher Education (fellow), Indian Philosophical Congress, Southern Society for Philosophy and Psychology, Southwestern Philosophical Society. *Awards, honors:* Society for Religion in Higher Education fellowship for travel in India, Pakistan, and Ceylon, 1964-65.

WRITINGS: Makers of the American Mind, Morrow, 1964. Contributor of articles to religious and philosophical journals.

WORK IN PROGRESS: \American Conceptions of God, The Frontiers of American Religious Thought 1831-1965; In God We Live: The Compass of Panentheism.

AVOCATIONAL INTERESTS: The study of history.

*   *   *

WHITTINGTON-EGAN, Richard   1924-

PERSONAL: Born October 22, 1924, in Liverpool, England; son of Cyril and Helen Margaret (Barrington) Whittington-Egan. *Education:* Studied under private tutors; read medicine. *Home:* 4 Doughty St., London W.C.1, England. *Office:* Associated Newspapers Ltd., Northcliffe House, London E.C.4, England.

CAREER: Liverpolitan, Liverpool, England, assistant editor, 1950-52; *Liverpool Daily Post and Echo,* Liverpool, free-lance writer and columnist, 1953-56; Associated Newspapers, London, England, staff feature writer, 1958—. Broadcaster. *Military service:* British Army, 1943-46. *Member:* Society for Psychical Research (official investigator), National Union of Journalists (father of the chapel), Instituto Palaeontologia Umana (Florence), Medico-Legal Society, Press Club (London).

WRITINGS: Liverpool Colonnade, Philip, Son & Nephew, 1955; *Liverpool Roundabout,* Philip, Son & Nephew, 1957; *The Quest of the Golden Boy,* Unicorn Press, 1960, Barre, 1962; (with G.T. Smerdon) *A Life of Richard Le Gallienne,* Secker & Warburg, 1960, published in America as *The Life and Letters of Richard Le Gallienne,* Dufour, 1961; *Tales of Liverpool: Murder, Mayhem, Mystery,* Gallery Press, 1967; (contributor) *Treasures of Britain and Ireland,* Drive Publications for Automobile Association, 1968; *Liverpool Soundings,* Gallery Press, 1969; *The Ordeal of Philip Yale Drew: A Real Life Murder Melodrama in Three Acts,* Harrap, 1972. Contributor of articles to *Times, Guardian, Chambers's Journal, Contemporary Review,* and other periodicals, and of book reviews to *Books and Bookmen, New York Times,* and *Tomorrow.*†

*   *   *

WHYTE, William H(ollingsworth)   1917-

PERSONAL: Born October 1, 1917, in West Chester, Pa., son of William H. and Louise (Price) Whyte; married Jenny Bell Bechtel, October, 1964; children: Alexandre (daughter). *Education:* Princeton University, B.A. (cum laude), 1939. *Politics:* Democrat. *Religion:* Episcopalian. *Home:* 175 East 94th St., New York, N.Y. 10028.

CAREER: Fortune Magazine, New York, N.Y., assistant managing editor, 1953-58, writer. Has done extensive work on conservation problems. *Military service:* U.S. Marine Corps, 1941-45; became captain. *Member:* Authors League of America. *Awards, honors:* Benjamin Franklin award, 1954.

WRITINGS: Is Anybody Listening?: How and Why U.S. Business Fumbles When It Talks with Human Beings, Simon & Schuster, 1952; *The Organization Man,* Simon & Schuster, 1956; (editor and contributor) *The Exploding Metropolis,* Doubleday, 1958; *Securing Open Spaces for Urban America: Conservation Easements,* Urban Land Institute, 1959; *Cluster Development,* American Conservation Association, 1964; *The Last Landscape,* Doubleday, 1968. Contributor of articles to *Harper's, Encounter,* and *Life.*

WORK IN PROGRESS: A study on the street life of cities.

BIOGRAPHICAL/CRITICAL SOURCES: Book World, September 8, 1968; *Washington Post,* November 7, 1968; *New York Times Book Review,* November 10, 1968.

*   *   *

WICKES, George   1923-

PERSONAL: Born January 6, 1923, in Antwerp, Belgium; son of Francis C. (an attorney) and Germaine (Attout) Wickes; married second wife, Linda Wells, August 11, 1962; children: Gregory, Geoffrey, Madeleine, Thomas, Jonathan. *Education:* St. Michael's College, University of Toronto, B.A., 1944; Columbia University, M.A., 1949; University of California, Berkeley, Ph.D., 1954. *Office:* English Department, University of Oregon, Eugene, Ore. 97403.

CAREER: Belgian American Educational Foundation, New York, N.Y., assistant secretary, 1947-49; U.S. Educational Foundation in Belgium. Brussels, director, 1952-54; Duke University, Durham, N.C., instructor, 1954-57; Harvey Mudd College and Claremont Graduate School, Claremont, Calif., 1957—, began as assistant professor of English, now associate professor. Fulbright lecturer in France, 1962-63, and summer, 1966; U.S. Information Service lecturer in Europe, 1969-70; visiting professor, University of Rouen, France, 1970, University of Oregon, 1970-71. *Military service:* U.S. Office of Strategic Services, 1943-46; became sergeant.

WRITINGS: Henry Miller (pamphlet), University of Minnesota Press, 1966; *Americans in Paris,* Doubleday, 1969.

Editor: *Lawrence Durrell and Henry Miller: A Private Correspondence,* Dutton, 1963; *Masters of Modern British Fiction,* Macmillan, 1963; *Henry Miller and the Critics,* Southern Illinois University Press, 1963; *Aldous Huxley at UCLA: A Catalogue of the Manuscripts in the Aldous Huxley Collection,* University of California Library, 1964. Contributor to *Paris Review* and *Shenandoah.* Editor of *Claremont Quarterly,* 1963-64; member of editorial board, *Twentieth Century Literature.*

BIOGRAPHICAL/CRITICAL SOURCES: Book World, July 20, 1969; *National Observer,* October 13, 1969; *New York Times Book Review,* November 16, 1969.

*   *   *

WIDICK, B.J.   1910-

PERSONAL: Born October 25, 1910, in Yugoslavia; son of Joseph and Angelina Widick; married 2nd wife, Barbara, December 30, 1966. *Education:* University of Akron, B.A., 1933; Wayne State University, M.A., 1962. *Politics:* Independent. *Home:* 560 Riverside Dr., New York, N.Y. 10027. *Office:* Graduate School of Business, Columbia University, New York, N.Y. 10027.

CAREER: Akron Beacon-Journal, Akron, Ohio, reporter, 1933-36; United Rubber Workers Union, research director, 1937; United Automobile Workers, Detroit, Mich., plant union official, 1947-59, economist on Walter Reuther's research staff, 1960-61; University of Michigan-

Wayne State University Institute of Labor and Industrial Relations, Detroit, Mich., lecturer, 1960-62; Wayne State University, Detroit, Mich., member of adjunct faculty, economics department, 1962, associate professor of economics, 1968-69; Columbia University, Graduate School of Business, New York, N.Y., adjunct professor, 1963; Institute of Labor and Industrial Relations, research associate and economic consultant, 1963—; Columbia University, Graduate School of Business, associate professor, 1969—. Labor Extension Service and United Automobile Workers adult education program, teacher, 1950-60. *Nation,* correspondent, 1958-60. *Military service:* U.S. Army and U.S. Army Air Corps, 1942-45. *Member:* Industrial Relations Research Association (member of advisory council, 1960-61).

WRITINGS: (with Irving Howe) *The UAW and Walter Reuther,* Random House, 1949; *Labor Today: The Triumphs and Failures of Unionism in the United States,* Houghton, 1964; *Detroit: City of Race and Class Violence,* Quadrangle, 1972. Co-author of *A New Focus on Detroit and Michigan's Economy* (monograph), Wayne State University Press, 1963. Contributor of articles to *New Republic, Nation, Virginia Quarterly Review,* and *Monthly Labor Review.*

* * *

WIEGAND, William G (eorge) 1928-

PERSONAL: Surname rhymes with "seaman"; born June 11, 1928, in Detroit, Mich.; son of Jack J. (a clerk) and Kathryn (Diener) Wiegand. *Education:* University of Michigan, A.B., 1949, A.M., 1950; Stanford University, Ph.D., 1960. *Office:* San Francisco State College, San Francisco, Calif. 94132.

CAREER: Harvard University, Cambridge, Mass., Briggs Copland Instructor in English, 1960-62; San Francisco State College, San Francisco, Calif., assistant professor, 1962-66, associate professor of English, 1966—. *Awards, honors:* Mary Roberts Rinehart Award for *At Last, Mr. Tolliver;* Joseph Henry Jackson Award, 1958, for *The Treatment Man.*

WRITINGS: At Last, Mr. Tolliver (novel), Rinehart, 1950; *The Treatment Man* (novel), McGraw, 1959; *The School of Soft Knocks* (novel), Lippincott, 1968; (editor and author of introduction with Richard Kraus) *Students Choice: An Anthology of Short Stories,* Merrill, 1970. Contributor of short stories and articles on Salinger, Arthur Miller, Capote, and Hemingway to *Story, New Republic, New Leader,* and to regional literary reviews.

WORK IN PROGRESS: Novels and short stories.

* * *

WIENPAHL, Paul D (eVelin) 1916-

PERSONAL: Born March 6, 1916, in Rock Springs, Wyo.; son of Paul (a watchmaker) and Constance (De-Velin) Wienpahl; married Janet Elizabeth Ward, June 9, 1942; children: Paul Mark, Jan. *Education:* University of California, B.A., 1937, M.A., 1939, Ph.D., 1946. *Home:* 1489 Tunnel Rd., Santa Barbara, Calif. 93105. *Office:* University of California, Santa Barbara, Calif 93106.

CAREER: University of California, Santa Barbara, assistant professor, 1948-54, associate professor, 1954-64, professor of philosophy, 1964—. *Military service:* U.S. Army, 1942-46; served in European theater; became captain. *Member:* American Philosophical Association, Phi Beta Kappa. *Awards, honors:* Ford faculty fellowship, 1954-55.

WRITINGS: The Matter of Zen: A Brief Account of Zazen, New York University Press, 1964; *Zen Diary,* Har-

per, 1970. Contributor to *Mind, Chicago Review, Journal of Philosophy, Inquiry,* and other periodicals.

WORK IN PROGRESS: The Lifework of Spinoza, a study in metaphysics.

BIOGRAPHICAL/CRITICAL SOURCES: Hal Bridges, *American Mysticism: From William James to Zen,* Harper, 1970.

* * *

WIER, Ester (Alberti) 1910-

PERSONAL: Born October 17, 1910, in Seattle, Wash.; daughter of Robert Armenio (a broker) and Lydea (Harshbarger) Alberti; married Henry Robert Wier (a naval officer, now retired, and a professor of mathematics), October 29, 1934, in Hankow, China; children: David Anthony, Susan (Mrs. John Zoltewicz). *Education:* Attended Southeastern Teachers College, 1929-30, University of California, Los Angeles, 1931-32. *Home:* Apt. 406, 205 A-1-A, Satellite Beach, Fla. 32935.

CAREER: As a Navy wife for thirty years, has lived all over United States, sometimes abroad. Air Force Aid Society, patron member. *Member:* Authors Guild. *Awards, honors: The Loner* was runner-up for Newbery Medal, 1964.

WRITINGS: (With Dorothy Rickey) *The Answer Book on Naval Social Customs,* Stackpole, 1956, 2nd edition, 1957; (with Rickey) *The Answer Book on Air Force Social Customs,* Stackpole, 1957, 2nd edition, 1959; *Army Social Customs,* Stackpole, 1958, 2nd edition, 1960; *What Every Air Force Wife Should Know,* Stackpole, 1958, 3rd revised edition, 1966; *The Loner,* McKay, 1963; *The Gift of the Mountains* (Junior Literary Guild selection), McKay, 1963; *The Rumptydoolers,* Vanguard, 1964; *Easy Does It,* Vanguard, 1965; *The Barrel,* McKay, 1966; *The Wind Chasers,* McKay, 1967; *The Winners,* McKay, 1967; *The Space Hut* (Weekly Reader book selection), Stackpole, 1967; *Action at Paradise Marsh* (Junior Literary Guild selection), Stackpole, 1968; *The Long Year,* McKay, 1969; *The Straggler: Adventures of a Sea Bird* (Junior Literary Guild selection), McKay, 1970; *The White Oak,* McKay, 1971; *The Partners,* McKay, 1972. Contributor of poems, stories, and articles to magazines.

SIDELIGHTS: The Loner, Mrs. Wier's first book for children, was produced as a two-part television movie by Walt Disney Productions. Her materials related to books for juveniles are now included in the Kerlan Collection at the University of Minnesota. Foreign editions of her work include Canadian, Dutch, British, German, Afrikaans, Swedish, and Finnish, and several books have been produced in Braille.

AVOCATIONAL INTERESTS: Travel, animals.

BIOGRAPHICAL/CRITICAL SOURCES: Library Journal, March 15, 1964, May 15, 1969; *New York Times Book Review,* November 6, 1966, January 21, 1968; *Young Readers' Review,* May, 1968; *Books and Bookmen,* September, 1968; *Saturday Review,* January 18, 1969; *Horn Book,* August, 1969, August, 1971.

* * *

WIESE, Kurt 1887-

PERSONAL: Born April 22, 1887, in Minden, Germany; married Gertrude Hansen (a realtor), June 26, 1930. *Education:* Attended high school in Germany. *Religion:* Lutheran. *Home and office:* R.D. #1, Frenchtown, N.J. 08825.

CAREER: Free-lance writer and illustrator of books, including almost four hundred books by other authors. *Member:* Philadelphia Water Color Club. *Awards, honors:* Award at 1937 World's Fair, Paris, France; *New*

York Herald Tribune Children's Spring Book Festival award for *Fish in the Air.*

WRITINGS—All self-illustrated: *Karoo, the Kangaroo,* Coward, 1929; *The Chinese Ink Stick,* Doubleday, 1929; *Liang & Lo,* Doubleday, 1930; *Wallie the Walrus,* Coward, 1930; *Ella, the Elephant,* Coward, 1931; *Joe Buys Nails,* Doubleday, 1931; *The Parrot Dealer,* Coward, 1932; *Buddy the Bear,* Coward, 1936; *Kurt Wiese's Picture Book of Animals* (includes *Ella, the Elephant, Karoo, the Kangaroo,* and *Wallie, the Walrus*), Coward, 1937; *The Rabbits' Revenge,* Coward, 1940; *Little Boy Lost in Brazil,* Dodd, 1942; *You Can Write Chinese,* Viking, 1945; *Fish in the Air,* Viking, 1948; *Happy Easter,* Viking, 1952; *The Dog, the Fox, and the Fleas,* McKay, 1953; *The Cunning Turtle,* Viking, 1956; *The Groundhog and His Shadow,* Viking, 1959; *Rabbit Brothers Circus: One Night Only,* Viking, 1963; *The Thief in the Attic,* Viking, 1965.

Illustrator: Zane Grey, *Don: The Story of a Lion Dog,* Harper, 1928; Carlo Collodi, *Adventures of Pinocchio,* Thomas Nelson, 1928, reissued as *Adventures of Pinocchio: The Story of a Puppet,* 1938; Felix Salten, *Bambi,* Simon & Schuster, 1929; Archer Butler Gilfillan, *Sheep,* Little, Brown, 1929; Harold Kellock, *Down in the Grass,* Coward, 1929; Lawton and Ruth Mackall, *Poodle-Oodle of Doddle Farm,* Stokes, 1929; Dhan Gopal Mukerji, *Hindu Fables, for Little Children,* Dutton, 1929; Augusta Seaman, *Book of Mysteries—Three Baffling Tales: The River Acres Riddle, Cat's Cradle, and The Hexagonal Chest,* Doubleday, 1929.

Felix Salten, *The Hound of Florence,* translated by Huntley Paterson, Simon & Schuster, 1930; Frank Thiess, *Abschied vom paradies,* edited by O.G. Boetzkes, Heath, 1930; Waldemar Bonsels, *The Adventures of Mario,* translated by Whittaker Chambers, Boni, 1930; Zane Grey, *Wolf-Tracker,* Harper, 1930; Alexander C. Jenkins, *Pal: The Story of an Airedale,* Appleton, 1930; Lowell Jackson Thomas, *The Wreck of the Dumaru: A Story of Cannibalism in an Open Boat,* Doubleday, 1930; Hakkon Lie, *Ekorn,* Albert Whitman, 1931, new edition, 1938; Lucy Mitchell, *North America: The Land They Live In for the Children Who Live There,* Macmillan, 1931; Dhan Gopal Mukerji, *Bunny, Hound and Clown,* Dutton, 1931; Rudyard Kipling, *The Jungle Book,* Doubleday, 1932; Margaret Isabel Ross, *Back of Time,* Harper, 1932; Felix Salten, *City Jungle,* Simon & Schuster, 1932; Alice Gall and F.H. Crew, *Wagtail,* Oxford University Press, 1932; Elizabeth Lewis, *Young Fu of the Upper Yangtze,* Winston, 1932; Charlotte Chandler Wyckoff, *Jothy: A Story of the South Indian Jungle,* Longmans, Green, 1933; Helen Bannerman, *The Story of Little Black Sambo,* Garden City Publishing Co., 1933; Marjorie Flack, *Story About Ping,* Viking, 1933; Wendell McKown, *Me an' Pete,* Doubleday, 1934; Lillian Rifkin, *Our Planet, the Earth: Then and Now,* Lothrop, 1934; Arthur Russell Goode, *Snowy for Luck,* Albert Whitman, 1934; Marion Brown, *Alexander: The Tale of a Monkey,* Bobbs-Merrill, 1934; R.L.H. Haig-Brown, *Ki-Yu: A Story of Panthers,* Houghton, 1934 (published in England as *Panther,* J. Cape, 1934); Julius King, *Odie Seeks a Friend,* Coward, 1934; Elizabeth Lewis, *Ho-Ming, Girl of New China,* Winston, 1934; Inis Weed Jones, *Peetie: The Story of a Real Cat,* McBride, 1935; Anna Ratzesberger, *Camel Bells: A Boy of Baghdad,* Albert Whitman, 1935; Mary Hollister, *River Children: A Story of Boat Life in China,* Dodd, 1935; Dorothy Kunhardt, *Little Ones,* Viking, 1935; Ethel J. Eldridge, *Yen-Foh, a Chinese Boy,* Albert Whitman, 1935; Rudyard Kipling, *All the Mowgli Stories,* Doubleday, 1936; Rudyard Kipling, *Great Kipling Stories* (includes life of Kipling by Lowell Thomas), Winston, 1936; Burdette Ross Buckingham, editor, *Attack, and Other Stories,* Ginn, 1936; Burdette Ross Buck-

ingham, editor, *Too Many Bears, and Other Stories,* Ginn, 1936; Ethel J. Eldridge, *Ling, Grandson of Yen-Foh,* Albert Whitman, 1936; Eleanor Fairchild Pease and Beatrice De Melik, *Gay Pippo,* Albert Whitman, 1936; Mary Hollister, *Mulberry Village: A Story of Country Life in China,* Dodd, 1936; Edith Janice Craine, *Ki-Ki, a Circus Trooper,* Albert Whitman, 1937; Alice Gall and F.H. Crew, *Each in His Way: Stories of Famous Animals,* Oxford University Press, 1937; Anna Ratzesberger, *Jasmine: A Story of Present-Day Persia,* Albert Whitman, 1937; Mary Hollister, *Beggars of Dreams,* Dodd, 1937; Elizabeth Lewis, *China Quest,* Winston, 1937; Josephine Sanger Lau, *Cheeky, a Prairie Dog,* Albert Whitman, 1937; Mary Katherine Reely, *Blue Mittens,* Grosset, 1937; Claire Huchet Bishop, *The Five ·Chinese Brothers,* Coward, 1938; Alice Day Pratt, *Animals of a Sagebrush Ranch,* new edition, Rand McNally, 1938; May V. Harris, *Carnival Time at Stroebeck,* Albert Whitman, 1938; Margaret Wise Brown, *The Streamlined Pig,* Harper, 1938; Mable (Chesley) Kahmann, *Jasper, the Gypsy Dog,* Messner, 1938; Alice Lide, *Yinka-Tu, the Yak,* Viking, 1938; Anna Ratzesberger, *Donkey Beads: A Tale of a Persian Donkey,* Albert Whitman, 1938; Jane F. Tompkins, *Moo-Wee, the Musk-Ox,* Stokes, 1938; Aime Felix Tschiffely, *Tale of Two Horses,* Grosett, 1938; Laura Benet, *Hidden Valley,* Dodd, 1938; Irma Black, *Hamlet, a Cocker Spaniel,* Holiday, 1938; Priscilla Holton, *The Blue Junk,* Grosset, 1938; Mary Hollister, *Kee-Kee and Company: A Story of American Children in China,* Dodd, 1938; Marjorie Hayes, *Alice-Albert Elephant,* Little, Brown, 1938; Meindert De Jong, *Dirk's Dog, Bello,* Harper, 1939; Irma Black, *Kip, a Young Rooster,* Holiday, 1939; Mabel Scudder La Rue, *Cats for the Tooseys,* Thomas Nelson, 1939; Marjorie Medary, *Joan and the Deer,* Random House, 1939; Cornelia Spencer, *Three Sisters: The Story of the Soong Family of China,* John Day, 1939; Elizabeth Anne Bond and J.E. Rabin, *Crunch the Squirrel,* Dodd, 1939; Elsie and Morris Glenn, *Amandus, Who Was Much Too Big,* Macrae Smith, 1939; Attilio Gatti, *Saranga, the Pygmy,* Scribner, 1939; Rutherford Montgomery, *The Trial of the Buffalo,* Houghton, 1939; Leila and W.K. Harris, *Blackfellow Bundi, a Native Australian Boy,* Albert Whitman, 1939; Esther Wood, *Silk and Satin Lane,* Longmans, Green, 1939.

Theodore J. Waldeck, *On Safari,* Viking, 1940; William Bridges, *Toco Toucan,* Harper, 1940; Sterling North, *Greased Lightning,* Winston, 1940; Ruth H. Hutchinson, *Blue Butterfly Goes to South America,* Albert Whitman, 1940; Leigh Peck, *Pecos Bill and Lightning,* Houghton, 1940; Marie Ahnighito Stafford, *Little Tooktoo: The Story of Santa Claus' Youngest Reindeer,* Morrow, 1940; Albert Payson Terhune, *Dogs,* Saalfield, 1940; Yu-t'ang Lin, *With Love and Irony,* John Day, 1940; Charlotte E. Jackson, *Tito, the Pig of Guatemala,* Dodd, 1940; Robert Nathan, *Tapiola's Brave Regiment,* Knopf, 1941; Claire Huchet Bishop, *The Ferryman,* Coward, 1941; Meindert De Jong, *Bells of the Harbor,* Harper, 1941; Zenobia Bird, *Muffy: The Tale of a Muskrat,* Albert Whitman, 1941; Maristan Chapman, *The Mystery Dogs of Glen Hazard,* Grosset, 1941; (with Erna Pinner) Felix Salten, *Bambi's Children,* Grosset, 1941; Alice Day Pratt, *Animal Babies,* Beacon Press, 1941; Leo Kanner, *In Defense of Mothers: How to Bring Up Children in Spite of the More Zealous Psychologists,* Dodd, 1941; Theodore J. Waldeck, *The White Panther,* Viking, 1941; West Lathrop, *Juneau, the Sleigh Dog,* Random House, 1942; Sidonie M. Gruenberg, editor, *Favorite Stories Old and New,* Doubleday, 1942, revised and enlarged edition, 1955; Marie Ahnighito Stafford, *Ootah and His Puppy,* Heath, 1942; Mabel Leigh Hunt, *Corn-Belt Billy,* Grosset, 1942; Mirim Isasi and M.B. Denny, *White Stars of Freedom,* Albert Whitman, 1942; Theodore J. Waldeck, *Lions on the Hunt*, Viking, 1942; MacKinlay Cantor, *Angleworms on Toast*, Coward, 1942; Don Lang, *Nibs, the Orphan Deer of the Adirondacks*, Grosset, 1942; Helen Albee Monsell, *Paddy's Christmas*, Knopf, 1942; Elizabeth Lewis, *When the Typhoon Blows*, Winston, 1942; Enid Meadowcroft, *Abraham Lincoln*, Crowell, 1942; JoBesse McElveen Waldeck, *Little Lost Monkey*, Viking, 1942; Theodore J. Waldeck, *Jamba the Elephant*, Viking, 1942; Julius Ernst Lips, *Tents in the Wilderness: The Story of a Labrador Indian Boy*, Stokes, 1942; Cornelia Spencer, *Made in China: The Story of China's Expression*, Knopf, 1943, 2nd edition, revised, 1952; Attilio Gatti, *Adventure in Black and White*, Scribner, 1943; Lorraine and Jerrold Beim, *Igor's Summer: A Story of Our Russian Friends*, Russian War Relief, Inc., 1943; Carl Glick, *Oswald's Pet Dragon*, Coward, 1943; Charlotte E. Jackson, *Roger and the Fishes*, Dodd, 1943; Quail Hawkins, *Puppy for Keeps*, Holiday, 1943; Katherine Pollock, *Sly Mongoose*, Scribner, 1943; Don Lang, *Tramp, the Sheep Dog*, Grosset, 1943; Sterling North, *Midnight and Jeremiah*, Winston, 1943; Thomas Pendleton Robinson, *Mr. Red Squirrel*, Viking, 1943; Agnes Edward Rothery, *Central American Roundabout*, Dodd, 1944; Wu Ch'eng-en, *The Adventures of Monkey* (adapted from translation by Arthur Waley), John Day, 1944; Alfred S. Campbell, *The Wizard and His Magic Powder: Tales of the Channel Islands*, Knopf, 1945; Lucy Mitchell and Dorothy Stall, *Our Country*, Heath, 1945; Grace Winifred McGavran, *Mpengo of the Congo*, Friendship, 1945; Sarah Litchfield, *Hello, Alaska*, Albert Whitman, 1945; Alfred Stuart Campbell, *Channel Islands*, Knopf, 1945; Lavinia Davis, *A Very Special Pet*, Grosset, 1945; Florence Hayes, *The Eskimo Hunter*, Random House, 1945; Warren Hastings Miller, *The Home-Builders*, Winston, 1946; Emily Hahn, *The Picture Story of China*, McKay, 1946; Margaret L. Macpherson, *Australia Calling*, Dodd, 1946; Muriel F. Millen, *Wild West Bill Rides Home*, Albert Whitman, 1946; Marion Cothren, *This is the Moon*, Coward, 1946; Quail Hawkins, *Too Many Dogs*, Holiday, 1946; JoBesse McElveen Waldeck, *Jungle Journey*, Viking, 1946; Jules Verne, *Twenty Thousand Leagues Under the Sea*, World Publishing, 1946; Eleanor Hoffman, *Four Friends*, Macmillan, 1946; M.S. Klutch, *Mr. Two of Everything*, Coward, 1946; Carolyn Treffinger, *Li Lun, Lad of Courage*, Abingdon-Cokesbury, 1947; Miriam Evangeline Mason, *Hoppity*, Macmillan, 1947; Donald Hutter, *Abraham, the Itinerant Mouse*, Dodd, 1947; Elsie and Morris Glenn, *Dumblebum*, Macrae Smith, 1947; Irmengarde Eberle, *A Circus of Our Own*, Dodd, 1948; Inglis Fletcher, *White Leopard: A Tale of the African Bush*, Bobbs-Merrill, 1948; Carol Denison, *What Every Young Rabbit Should Know*, Dodd, 1948; James Hilton, *Lost Horizon*, World Publishing, 1948; Mary Hollister, *Dike Against the Sea*, Friendship, 1948; Charles Stanley Strong, *Ranger, Sea Dog of the Royal Mounted*, Winston, 1948; Elizabeth Hamilton, *Go West, Young Bear*, Coward, 1948; Louise S. Rankin, *Daughter of the Mountains*, Viking, 1948; Marion Conger, *Rosie, the Rhino*, Abingdon-Cokesbury, 1948; Ruth Brindze, *Boating is Fun*, Dodd, 1949; Agnes Hewes, *Anabel's Windows*, Dodd, 1949; Dock Hogue, *Bob Clifton, Elephant Hunter*, Holt, 1949; Mitchell Dawson, *Magic Firecrackers*, Viking, 1949; Betty Heskett MacDonald, *Mrs. Piggle-Wiggle's Magic*, Lippincott, 1949; Jene Barr, *Little Circus Dog*, Albert Whitman, 1949; Hertha Ernestine Pauli, *The Golden Door: A Story of Liberty's Children*, Knopf, 1949; Hertha Ernestine Pauli, *The Most Beautiful House, and Other Stories*, Knopf, 1949; Helen R. Smith, editor, *Laughing Matter*, Scribner, 1949; Jene Barr, *Little Prairie Dog*, Albert Whitman, 1949.

Marguerite Harmon Bro, *Su-Mei's Golden Year*, Doubleday, 1950; Dock Hogue, *Bob Clifton, Jungle Traveler*, Holt, 1950; Margaret Mackay, *The Flowered Donkey*, John Day, 1950; *The Fables of Aesop*, compiled and retold by Joseph Jacobs, Macmillan, 1950; Miriam Macmillan, *Etuk, the Eskimo Hunter*, Dodd, 1950; William N. Hall, *The Walking Hat*, Knopf, 1950; Irene Smith, *Lucky Days for Johnny*, McGraw, 1950; Eleanor Lowenton Clymer, *Tommy's Wonderful Airplane*, Dodd, 1951; Dock Hogue, *Bob Clifton, Congo Crusader*, Holt, 1951; Irene Smith, *Down the Road with Johnny*, McGraw, 1951; John Oldrin, *Round Meadow*, Viking, 1951; Leone Adelson, *The House with Red Sails*, McKay, 1951; Margaret Mackay, *The Poetic Parrot*, John Day, 1951; Freeman Henry Hubbard, *Roundhouse Cat, and Other Railroad Animals*, McGraw, 1951; Albert J. Nevins, *The Adventures of Wu Han of Korea*, Dodd, 1951; Irma Roberts, *The Jungle Twins*, Coward, 1951; Robert Shaffer, *Skeeter: The Story of an Arabian Gazelle*, Dodd, 1952; Albert J. Nevins, *The Adventures of Kenji of Japan*, Dodd, 1952; Heluiz Chandler Washburne and Anauta Blackmore, *Children of the Blizzard*, John Day, 1952; Vernon Bowen, *The Wonderful Adventures of Ting Ling*, McKay, 1952; Charles Stanley Strong, *Ranger's Arctic Patrol*, Winston, 1952; Ethel Daniels Hubbard, *The Moffats*, new edition, Friendship, 1952; Freeman Henry Hubbard, *The Train That Never Came Back, and Other Railroad Stories*, McGraw, 1952; Ann Meyer, *Nibby*, Coward, 1952; Vernon Bowen, *Snow for Christmas*, McKay, 1953; Estelle Barnes Clapp, *Laurie*, Doubleday, 1953; Hester Hawkes, *Ning's Pony*, Coward, 1953; John Parke, *Amos, the Beagle with a Plan*, Pantheon, 1953; Frederick Harvey Pough, *All About Volcanoes and Earthquakes*, Random House, 1953; David Barnard Steinman, *Famous Bridges of the World*, Random House, 1953; Dock Hogue, *Bob Clifton, African Planter*, Holt, 1953; Alice Kelsey, *Many Hands in Many Lands*, Friendship, 1953; Albert J. Nevins, *The Adventures of Pancho of Peru*, Dodd, 1953; Benjamin C. Gruenberg and Leone Adelson, *Your Breakfast and the People Who Made It*, Doubleday, 1954; Albert J. Nevins, *The Adventures of Ramon of Bolivia*, Dodd, 1954; Ethel Lisle Smither, *Stories of Jesus*, Abingdon, 1954; Ethel Lisle Smither, *Early Old Testament Stories*, Abingdon, 1954; Basil Joseph Mathews, *Livingstone, the Pathfinder*, new edition, Friendship, 1955; Esma Booth, *Bright Pathways*, Friendship, 1955; Stringfellow Barr, *Copydog in India*, Viking, 1955; Albert J. Nevins, *The Adventures of Duc of Indochina*, Dodd, 1955; Ethel Lisle Smither, *First to Be Called Christians*, Abingdon, 1955; Roy Chapman Andrews, *Quest of the Snow Leopard*, Viking, 1955; Faith Grigsby Norris and Peter Lumn, *Kim of Korea*, Messner, 1955; Virginia Frances Voight, *Lions in the Barn*, Holiday, 1955; Ethel Lisle Smither, *Later Old Testament Stories*, Abingdon, 1956; Alice Hudson Lewis, *Day After Tomorrow*, Friendship, 1956; Hester Hawkes, *Three Seeds*, Coward, 1956; John Oldrin, *Eight Rings on His Tail: A Round Meadow Story*, Viking, 1956; Virginia Frances Voight, *Rolling Show*, Holiday, 1956; Carol Denison and Jane Cummin, *Where Any Young Cat Might Be*, Dodd, 1956; Hyde Matzdorff, *Limpy: Tale of a Monkey Hero*, John Day, 1957; Vincent Starrett, *Great All-Star Animal League Ball Game*, Dodd, 1957; Anne Terry White, *All About Great Rivers of the World*, Random House, 1957; Johanna ohnston, *Great Gravity, the Cat*, Knopf, 1958; John Beecroft, *Rocco Came In*, Dodd, 1959; Florence Hayes, *Alaskan Hunter*, Houghton, 1959; Elizabeth Coatsworth, *Pika and the Roses*, Pantheon, 1959.

Kathryn Gallant, *The Flute Player of Beppu*, Coward, 1960; John Beecroft, *What? Another Cat!*, Dodd, 1960; Anne M. Halladay, *Cuddle Bear of Piney Forest*, Bethany Press, 1960; Eleanor Lowenton Clymer, *Mr. Piper's Bus*, Dodd, 1961; Ruth Tooze, *Silver from the Sea*, Viking, 1962; Jeanette Guillaume and M.L. Bachmann, *Amat and the Water Buffalo*, Coward, 1962; Claire Huchet Bishop,

Twenty-Two Bears, Viking, 1964; Claire Huchet Bishop, *The Truffle Pig*, Coward, 1971.

Illustrator of books by Walter Rollin Brooks—All published by Knopf, except as otherwise indicated: *More To and Again*, 1930, reissued as *Freddy Goes to the North Pole*, 1951, *Freddy the Detective*, 1932, *The Story of Freginald*, 1935, *The Clockwork Twin*, 1937, *Wiggins for President*, 1939, reissued as *Freddy the Politician*, 1948, *Freddy's Cousin Weedly*, 1940, *Freddy and the Ignormus*, 1941, *Freddy and the Perilous Adventure*, 1942, *Freddy and the Bean Home News*, 1943, *Freddy and Mr. Camphor*, 1944, *Freddy and the Popinjay*, 1945, *Freddy the Pied Piper*, 1946, *Freddy the Magician*, 1947, *Freddy Goes Camping*, 1948, *Freddy Goes to Florida*, 1949 (published in England as *Freddy's First Adventure*, John Lane, 1949), *Freddy the Explorer*, John Lane, 1949, *Freddy Plays Football*, 1949, *Freddy the Cowboy*, 1950, *Freddy Rides Again*, 1951, *Freddy and Freginald*, John Lane, 1952, *Freddy the Pilot*, 1952, *Collected Poems of Freddy the Pig*, 1953, *Freddy and the Spaceship*, 1953, *Freddy and the Men from Mars*, 1954, *Freddy and the Baseball Team from Mars*, 1955, *Freddy and Simon the Dictator*, 1956, *Freddy and the Flying Saucer Plans*, 1957, *Freddy and the Dragon*, 1958.

Illustrator of books by Marguerite Henry—All published by Albert Whitman: *Alaska in Story and Pictures*, 1941, 2nd edition, 1942, *Argentina in Story and Pictures*, 1941, 2nd edition, 1942, *Brazil in Story and Pictures*, 1941, 2nd edition, 1942, *Canada in Story and Pictures*, 1941, 2nd edition, 1942, *Chile in Story and Pictures*, 1941, 2nd edition, 1942, *Mexico in Story and Pictures*, 1941, 2nd edition, 1942, *Panama in Story and Pictures*, 1941, 2nd edition, 1942, *West Indies in Story and Pictures*, 1941, 2nd edition, 1942, *Australia in Story and Pictures*, 1946, *The Bahamas in Story and Pictures*, 1946, *Bermuda in Story and Pictures*, 1946, *British Honduras in Story and Pictures*, 1946, *Dominican Republic in Story and Pictures*, 1946, *Hawaii in Story and Pictures*, 1946, *New Zealand in Story and Pictures*, 1946, *The Virgin Islands in Story and Pictures*, 1946.

Illustrator of books by Philip Duffield Stong—All published by Dodd, except as otherwise noted: *Farm Boy: A Hunt for Indian Treasure*, Doubleday, 1934, *Honk, the Moose*, 1935, *No-Stitch, the Hound*, 1936, *High Water*, 1937, *Young Settler*, 1938, *Cowhand Goes to Town*, 1939, *Captain Kidd's Cow*, 1941, *Missouri Canary*, 1943, *Censored, the Goat*, 1945, *Positive Pete!*, 1947, *Hirum, the Hillbilly*, 1950, *The Prince and the Porker*, 1950, *A Beast Called an Elephant*, 1955, *Mike: The Story of a Young Circus Acrobat*, 1957, *Phil Stong's Big Book* (includes *Farm Boy: A Hunt for Indian Treasure, High Water*, and *No-Stitch, the Hound*), 1961.

Illustrator of books by Jack O'Brien: *Silver Chief, Dog of the North*, Winston, 1932; *Silver Chief to the Rescue*, Winston, 1937; *Corporal Corey, of the Royal Canadian Mounted*, Harrap, 1938; *The King and the Princess*, Follett, 1940; *Valiant, Dog of the Timberline*, E.M. Hale, 1940, Grosset, 1952; *Spike of Swift River*, Winston, 1942; *Return of Silver Chief*, Winston, 1943; *Royal Red*, Winston, 1951; *Silver Chief's Revenge*, Winston, 1954.

Illustrator of books by Lois Donaldson—All published by Albert Whitman: *Costa Rica in Story and Pictures*, 1943, *Nicaragua in Story and Pictures*, 1943, *El Salvador in Story and Pictures*, 1943, *Uruguay in Story and Pictures*, 1943, *Colombia in Story and Pictures*, 1944, *Guiana in Story and Pictures*, 1944, *Newfoundland in Story and Pictures*, 1944, *Paraguay in Story and Pictures*, 1944.

Illustrator of books by Bernadine Bailey—All published by Albert Whitman: *Bolivia in Story and Pictures*, 1942, *Ecuador in Story and Pictures*, 1942, *Greenland in Story and Pictures*, 1942, *Guatemala in Story and Pictures*, 1942, *Honduras in Story and Pictures*, 1942, *Iceland in Story and Pictures*, 1942, *Peru in Story and Pictures*, 1942, *Venezuela in Story and Pictures*, 1942; *Our Nation's Capital, Washington, D.C.*, revised edition, 1967. Also illustrator of "Picture Book" series by Bernadine Bailey, published by Albert Whitman, one for each of the 50 states.

Illustrator of books by Jane F. Tompkins: *Polar Bear Twins*, Stokes, 1937; *Penguin Twins*, Stokes, 1939; *Snowshoe Twins*, Stokes, 1941; *Raccoon Twins*, Stokes, 1942; *Red Squirrel Twins*, Lippincott, 1950; *Black Bear Twins*, Lippincott, 1952; *Porcupine Twins*, Lippincott, 1954; *Otter Twins*, Lippincott, 1955; *Reindeer Twins*, Lippincott, 1956.

SIDELIGHTS: Interested in becoming an artist at an early age (a time when this was "unheard of"), in his teens Wiese was sent from his native Minden to Hamburg to learn the export trade to China. He subsequently worked and traveled to China for six years until the war with Japan erupted. Wiese was captured by the Japanese and handed over to the British; he remained a prisoner for one year in Hong Kong and four years in Australia, where he began writing and drawing for pleasure. He later returned to Germany, visited Brazil for a year and lived there for two, and eventually settled in the United States after his work had become well known.

Wiese works chiefly in color. Early work was done directly on litho plates or frosted glass; the illustrations for his latest book, *The Thief in the Attic*, were done in four-color separations on acetate.

BIOGRAPHICAL/CRITICAL SOURCES: Elementary English, April, 1956.

* * *

WIGGIN, Maurice (Samuel) 1912-

PERSONAL: Born October 21, 1912, in Walshall, England; son of Samuel (an engineer) and Lucy K. (Haycock) Wiggin; married Eveline Ruth Kinsey, July 25, 1936. *Education:* St. Catherine's College, Oxford, B.A. (honors in modern history), 1934. *Politics:* Radical Tory. *Home:* Lower Barnsfold, Tismans Common, Rudgwick, Sussex, England. *Agent:* Curtis Brown Ltd., 13 King St., Covent Garden, London WCZE 8HU, England. *Office:* *Sunday Times*, Thomson House, Grays Inn Rd., London W.C.1, England.

CAREER: Started career as journalist on *Evening Despatch*, Birmingham, England, 1934-39; *Gazette*, Birmingham, editor, 1939; *Daily Express*, London, England, literary editor, 1939-40; *Daily Graphic* and *Sunday Graphic*, London, angling correspondent, 1949-59; television critic, country columnist, reviewer, 1951—. *Military service:* Royal Air Force, 1940-45; became sergeant. *Member:* Institute of Journalists.

WRITINGS: My Court Casebook, Sylvan Press, 1948; *The Passionate Angler*, Sylvan Press, 1949; *Fishing for Beginners*, Phoenix House, 1953, revised edition, 1957; *In Spite of the Price of Hay*, Phoenix House, 1956; *Teach Yourself Fly Fishing*, English Universities Press, 1958; *Troubled Waters*, Hutchinson, 1960; *My Life on Wheels*, John Baker, 1963; (editor) *The Angler's Bedside Book*, Batsford, 1965, Sportshelf, 1967; *Life with Badger*, John Baker, 1967, Taplinger, 1968; *The Memoirs of a Maverick*, Thomas Nelson, 1968; *A Cottage Idyll*, Thomas Nelson, 1969; *Sea Fishing for Beginners*, John Baker, 1970. Contributor to *Time and Tide* and *Bookman;* author of more than six hundred articles on angling.

WORK IN PROGRESS: Critical studies of W. H. Auden and Hilaire Belloc.

AVOCATIONAL INTERESTS: Fishing, (a hobby for forty years), automobiles (owned thirty-four in thirty-one years), motorcycling, photography, sailing, cooking, Bach's music, and poetry of W. H. Auden.

BIOGRAPHICAL/CRITICAL SOURCES: New Statesman, November 29, 1968.†

*   *   *

WIGHTON, Rosemary Neville 1925-

PERSONAL: Born January 6, 1925, in Adelaide, South Australia; daughter of Arthur Seaforth (a lawyer and soldier) and Rose Ada (Kelly) Blackburn; married Dugald Craven Wighton (a medical practitioner), May 22, 1948; children: Helen Craven, Mary Craven, David Blackburn, James Dugald, Henrietta Elizabeth. *Education:* University of Adelaide, B.A. (honors), 1945, postgraduate research, 1946-47. *Home:* 40 Barnard St., North Adelaide, South Australia.

CAREER: University of Adelaide, Adelaide, South Australia, part-time tutor in English literature, 1948-58.

WRITINGS: (Editor) *Kangaroo Tales: A Collection of Australian Stories for Children,* Penguin, 1963; *Early Australian Children's Literature,* Lansdowne Press, 1963. Co-editor, *Australian Book Review* and *Australian Letters.* Reviewer of children's books for Australian Broadcasting Commission.

AVOCATIONAL INTERESTS: Music and fishing and camping in the outback of Australia.†

*   *   *

WILES, John 1924-

PERSONAL: Born September 25, 1924, in Kimberley, South Africa; son of Arthur Edward and Beryl (Cousins) Wiles. *Education:* University of Cape Town, student, 1941. *Home:* 39a St. John's Ave., Putney, London S.W. 15, England.

CAREER: Former stage director in theatre in South Africa; British Broadcasting Corp. Television, London, England, 1957-72, began as story editor, became television producer; Director, National Travelling Boys' Theatre, 1972; free-lance writer, 1972—. *Military service:* British Army, 1941-46; served in Italy. *Member:* Society of Authors, P.E.N., Writers Guild. *Awards, honors:* John Llewelyn Rhys Memorial Prize for Literature, 1955, for *The Moon to Play With.*

WRITINGS: The Moon to Play With, John Day, 1955; *The Try-Out,* Chatto & Windus, 1955; *Scene of the Meeting,* Chatto & Windus, 1956; *Tom Runs a Hotel,* Chatto & Windus, 1957; (with Alan Garrard) *Leap to Life: An Experiment in School and Youth Drama,* Chatto & Windus, 1957, new and revised edition, 1965; *The Asphalt Playground,* Ace Books, 1958; (with Ronald P. Menday) *The Everlasting Childhood: The Predicament of the Backward Boy,* Gollancz, 1959; *The March of the Innocents,* Chatto & Windus, 1964; *A Short Walk Abroad,* Chatto & Windus, 1969; *In Praise of Vengeance* (political novel), 1972. Also author of a screenplay, "White Bird," of four stage plays and numerous television plays.

SIDELIGHTS: Wiles has done experimental work on mime and "physical" drama as a therapeutic medium for maladjusted and delinquent boys, working with mass casts of 150 boys at residential schools.

BIOGRAPHICAL/CRITICAL SOURCES: Times Literary Supplement, July 24, 1969.

WILKINSON, Bertie 1898-

PERSONAL: Born January 21, 1898, in Bingley, Yorkshire, England; son of John (a merchant) and Emily (Petttifer) Wilkinson; married Edith Provost, July 28, 1923; children: John Provost, Ann (Mrs. J.M. Robson). *Education:* University of Manchester, B.A., 1919, M.A., 1920, Ph.D., 1926. *Home:* 66 Woodlawn Ave. W., Toronto, Ontario, Canada. *Office:* Department of History, University of Toronto, Toronto, Ontario, Canada.

CAREER: University of Exeter, Exeter, England, lecturer, 1923-30; Victoria University of Manchester, Manchester, England, special lecturer in constitutional history, 1930-38; University of Toronto, Toronto, Ontario, professor of medieval history and director of graduate center for medieval studies, 1938-69. *Military service:* British Army, 1916-19, Reserve, 1939-45; became captain. *Member:* Mediaeval Academy of America (fellow; vice-president), Canadian Historical Association, American Historical Association, Royal Society of Canada (fellow).

WRITINGS: The Chancery Under Edward III, Manchester University Press, 1929; *The Medieval Council of Exeter,* Manchester University Press, 1931; (contributor) *Essays in Honour of James Tait,* Manchester University Press, 1933; *Studies in the Constitutional History of the Thirteenth and Fourteenth Centuries,* Manchester University Press, 1937, 2nd edition, 1952; *Freemen and the Crisis of 1051* (pamphlet), Manchester University Press, 1938; (contributor) J.F. Willard and W.A. Morris, editors, *The English Government at Work, 1327-37,* Mediaeval Academy of America, 1940; (contributor) R.W. Hunt and others, editors, *Studies in Medieval History Presented to F.M. Powicke,* Oxford University Press, 1947; *The Constitutional History of Medieval England, 1216-1399,* 3 volumes, Longmans, Green, 1948-58; *The Coronation in History* (pamphlet), Philip & Son, 1953; (with D.F. Fishwick and G.E. Cairns) *The Foundations of the West,* Clarke, Irwin, 1963; *Constitutional History of England in the Fifteenth Century, 1399-1485,* Barnes & Noble, 1964; *The Later Middle Ages in England, 1216-1485,* McKay, 1969; *The Creation of Medieval Parliaments,* Wiley, 1972. Contributor of articles and reviews to professional journals.

WORK IN PROGRESS: Angevin England, 1154-1377, for Cambridge University Press.

*   *   *

WILKINSON, (John) Burke 1913-

PERSONAL: Born August 24, 1913, in New York, N.Y.; son of Henry and Edith Lee (Burke) Wilkinson; married Frances Proctor, June 11, 1938; children: Eileen Burke, Charles Proctor. *Education:* Harvard University, B.A. (magna cum laude), 1935; Cambridge University, Lionel Harvard scholar, 1935-36. *Politics:* Independent. *Religion:* Episcopalian. *Home:* 3210 Scott Pl. N.W., Washington, D.C. 20007. *Agent:* Phyllis Jackson, International Famous Agency, 1301 Avenue of the Americas, New York, N.Y. 10019. *Office:* 1518 K St. N.W., Washington, D.C. 20005.

CAREER: Lord & Thomas (advertising agency), New York, N.Y., copywriter, 1936-38; Reynal & Hitchcock (publishers), New York, N.Y., assistant advertising manager, 1938-39; Little, Brown and Co., Boston, Mass., advertising manager, 1939-41; free-lance writer, 1946-50, 1952-54; with U.S. Department of State, Washington, D.C., 1954-58, deputy assistant secretary for public affairs, 1956-58; Supreme Headquarters, Allied Powers, Europe, public affairs adviser, 1958-62; novelist, 1962—. Foreign Students Service Council, director; U.S. Lawn Tennis Hall of Fame, vice-president and director, 1959—.

Military service: U.S. Naval Reserve, 1941-46, 1950-52; became commander; received Navy Commendation Ribbon for work in preparing for Normandy Invasion.

MEMBER: Authors Guild, National Press Club, International Lawn Tennis Club of United States (director), International Lawn Tennis Club of United Kingdom (honorary), International Lawn Tennis Club of France (honorary), Phi Beta Kappa, St. Botolph's Club (Boston). *Awards, honors*: Commendatore, Italian Order of Merit for Italian sections of *By Sea and by Stealth.*

WRITINGS: Proceed at Will, Little, Brown, 1948, *Run, Mongoose,* Little, Brown, 1950, *Last Clear Chance,* Little, Brown, 1954, preceding three volumes reissued in one as *The Adventures of Geoffrey Mildmay: A Trilogy,* Luce, 1969; *By Sea and by Stealth,* (non-fiction), Coward, 1956; *Night of the Short Knives,* Scribner, 1964; *The Helmet of Navarre* (biography of Henri IV), Macmillan, 1965; *Cardinal in Armor: The Story of Richelieu and His Times,* Macmillan, 1966; (editor) *Cry, Spy!: True Stories of 20th Century Spies and Spy Catchers,* Bradbury, 1969; *Young Louis XIV: The Early Years of the Sun King,* Macmillan, 1970; *Cry Sabotage,* Bradbury, 1972; *Francis in All His Glory* (biography of Francis I), Farrar, Straus, 1972. Contributor of articles to magazines and some one hundred reviews to *New York Times Book Review.*

WORK IN PROGRESS: An adventure novel in the Mildmay series; a play.

SIDELIGHTS: Shelby Coffey III calls Wilkinson "a gentleman and the son of a gentleman. . . . With his Foreign Service manners, and his pinstripes and taste for Dubonnet and Scott Fitzgerald, J. Burke Wilkinson seems an unlikely spy novelist. But J. Burke Wilkinson's novels are not the ordinary run of sex *cum* violence *cum* politix novels squatting on the bookstands. Rather, Wilkinson's books give hints of a subtler mind, a fresher style, and an insider's grasp of some of the machinations of power in the Pentagon. . .and the State Department." Coffey mentions that this is hardly surprising, since Wilkinson has worked there. A self-described "in-and-out" author of books since 1948, Wilkinson feels that his brand of fiction profits by first-hand experience, and has drawn heavily on his own activities for "backgrounds and foregrounds." •

Wilkinson has recently published his fourth French historical biography for young people; the first of these biographies, *The Helmet of Navarre,* was selected by the *New York Times Book Review* as one of the twelve best juveniles of 1964. John Ratte enumerated the virtues of this work and *Cardinal in Armor* for a *Book Week* review: "solid narrative structure, clarity and zest of language, sustained dramatic interest. But most distinctive are his confident grasp of the main lines of recent scholarly investigation, and his conviction that matters of social and cultural history, and even of historiographical fashion, can be thoroughly and unapologetically integrated into a narrative which remains engrossing and entertaining."

BIOGRAPHICAL/CRITICAL SOURCES: Book Week, February 26, 1967; *Washington Post,* May 4, 1969, April 5, 1970; *New York Times Book Review,* November 9, 1969, March 8, 1970; *Library Journal,* May 15, 1970.

* * *

WILKINSON, John (Donald) 1929-
(Maximus Ironmaster)

PERSONAL: Born March 28, 1929, in Wimbledon, England; son of Donald Frederick (a priest, Church of England) and Hilda Mary (Smyth) Wilkinson. *Education:* Haileybury and Imperial Service College, student, 1944-

48; Merton College, Oxford, B.A., 1953, M.A., 1956; also studied at Cuddesdon College, 1954-56, and Catholic University of Louvain, 1959-60. *Home:* 15 John Spencer Sq., London N.1, England. *Office address:* St. George's College, P.O. Box 1248, Jerusalem, Israel.

CAREER: Ordained priest, Church of England, 1956; Parish of St. Dunstan and All Saints', Stepney, London, England, assistant priest, 1956-59; Theological College, Ely, England, tutor, 1960; St. Augustine's College, Canterbury, England, assistant lecturer, 1961; St. George's College, Jerusalem, tutor, 1961-63; United Society for the Propagation of the Gospel, London, England, general editor, 1963-69; St. George's College, dean of studies, 1969—. *Military service:* British Army, 1948-49; became second lieutenant.

WRITINGS: No Apology, Darton, Longman & Todd, 1961; *Jerusalem Prayers,* St. George's College, 1962; *Interpretation and Community,* St. Martin's, 1963; *The Stations of the Cross in Jerusalem,* St. George's College, 1963, reissued as *Jerusalem Stations of the Cross,* S.P.C.K., 1967; (editor) *Mutual Responsibility: Questions and Answers,* S.P.C.K., 1964; *The Supper and the Eucharist: A Layman's Guide to Anglican Revision,* Macmillan (London), 1965, St. Martin's, 1966; *Family and Evangelistic Services: An Outline,* Church Information Office, 1967; (editor) *Catholic Anglicans Today,* Darton, Longman & Todd, 1968; *Egeria's Travels,* S.P.C.K., 1971.

* * *

WILKINSON, Rupert Hugh 1936-

PERSONAL: Born May 18, 1936; son of Gerald Hugh (a merchant and manufacturer) and Lorna Mary (Davies) Wilkinson. *Education:* Attended Winchester College, Winchester, England, 1949-54; Harvard University, A.B., 1961; Stanford University, graduate student, and research assistant, 1962-65. *Agent:* Lloyd-George & Coward, 5th Floor, 8 Waterloo Pl., London S.W.1, England.

CAREER: Mayfair Books Ltd., London, England, assistant to publisher, 1961-62; *Military service:* Royal Air Force, 1954-56.

WRITINGS: Gentlemanly Power: British Leadership and the Public School Tradition, Oxford University Press, 1964 (published in England as *The Prefects: British Leadership and the Public School Tradition,* Oxford University Press, 1964); (with T.J.H. Bishop) *Winchester and the Public School Elite: A Statistical Analysis,* Faber, 1967, Humanities, 1968; (editor) *Governing Elites: Studies in Training and Selection,* Oxford University Press, 1969; *The Prevention of Drinking Problems: Alcohol Control and Cultural Influences,* Oxford University Press, 1970; *The Broken Rebel: A Study in Culture, Politics, and Authoritarian Character,* Harper, 1972. Contributor to *Encounter, New Society, New Republic,* and to sociology journals.

WORK IN PROGRESS: The Authoritarians, with Nevitt Sanford; a biography of Cortes; a book on high federal careers in America; editing a symposium on education of the leadership elite in history, for Oxford University Press (New York).

BIOGRAPHICAL/CRITICAL SOURCES: Listener, August 24, 1967.†

* * *

WILLAN, Thomas Stuart 1910-

PERSONAL: Born January 3, 1910, in Hawes, Yorkshire, England; son of Matthew and Jane (Stuart) Willan. *Education:* The Queen's College, Oxford University, B.A., 1931, B. Litt., 1932, M.A., 1934, D.Phil., 1934. *Home:* 3 Raynham Ave., Didsbury, Manchester M20

OBW, England. *Office:* University of Manchester, Manchester, M13 9PL, England.

CAREER: University of Manchester, Manchester, England, assistant lecturer in history, 1935-45, lecturer, 1945-47, senior lecturer, 1947-49, reader in history, 1949-61, professor of economic history, 1961—. *Member:* Royal Historical Society (fellow).

WRITINGS: River Navigation in England, 1600-1750, Oxford University Press, 1936, Augustus M. Kelley, 1965; *The English Coasting Trade, 1600-1750,* Manchester University Press, 1938, reissued with a new preface, Augustus M. Kelley, 1967; (editor with E.W. Crossley) Robert Saxton, *Three Seventeenth-Century Yorkshire Surveys,* Yorkshire Archaeological Society, 1941; (editor) *The Navigation of the Great Ouse Between St. Ives and Bedford in the Seventeenth Century,* Bedfordshire Historical Record Society, 1942; *The Navigation of the River Weaver in the Eighteenth Century,* Chetham Society, 1951; *The Muscovy Merchants of 1555,* Manchester University Press, 1953; *The Early History of the Russia Company, 1553-1603,* Manchester University Press, 1956, Barnes & Noble, 1956; *Studies in Elizabethan Foreign Trade,* Manchester University Press, 1959, Augustus M. Kelley, 1968; (editor) *A Tudor Book of Rates,* Manchester University Press, 1962, Barnes & Noble, 1962; *The Early History of the Don Navigation,* Manchester University Press, 1965, Augustus M. Kelley, 1968; *An Eighteenth-Century Shopkeeper, Abraham Dent of Kirkby Stephen,* Augustus M. Kelley, 1970. Contributor to *Journal of Transport History,* other history journals.

*   *   *

WILLETT, John (William Mills) 1917-

PERSONAL: Born June 24, 1917, in England; son of Herbert William Mills (a master builder) and Mary Amelia (Tizard) Willett; married Anne Priscilla Sainsbury, February 23, 1951; children: two adopted children. *Education:* Winchester College, student, 1930-36; Christ Church, Oxford, M.A., 1939; also studied at Ruskin School of Art and Manchester Municipal College of Art. *Home:* Voltä ˉHouse, Windmill Hill, London N.W. 3, England. *Agent:* Hope, Leresche & Steele, 11 Jubilee Pl., London, S.W. 3, England. *Office:* Printing House Sq., London E.C. 4, England.

CAREER: Guardian, Manchester, England, leader writer, 1948-51; *Times Literary Supplement,* London, England, assistant editor, 1960-67, planning editor, 1969-71. *Military service:* British Army, served in Egypt, North Africa, and Italy, 1939-46; became lieutenant colonel; awarded Order of the British Empire (military).

WRITINGS: Popski: A Life of Vladimir Peniakoff, MacGibbon & Kee, 1954; *The Theatre of Bertolt Brecht: A Study from Eight Aspects,* New Directions, 1959, 3rd revised edition, Methuen, 1967, New Directions, 1968; (translator, editor, and author of notes) *Brecht on Theatre,* Hill & Wang, 1964, reissued as *Brecht on Theatre: The Development of an Aesthetic,* Hill & Wang, 1966; (translator) Bertolt Brecht, *The Messingkauf Dialogues,* Methuen, 1965; (author of introduction) *Max Beckmann, 1884-1950: Paintings, Drawings, and Graphic Work* (catalog of exhibition at Tate Gallery), Arts Council (London), 1965; *Art in a City,* Methuen, 1967, Fernhill, 1968; *Expressionism,* McGraw, 1971; (editor with Ralph Manheim) *Bertolt Brecht: Collected Plays,* Volume I: *1918-1923,* Methuen, 1970, Random House, 1971; (contributor) Alan Bullock, editor, *The Twentieth Century,* McGraw, 1971. Contributor to *Times Literary Supplement* and other journals.

WORK IN PROGRESS: Theatre in the Weimar Republic, to be published by Routledge.

BIOGRAPHICAL/CRITICAL SOURCES: Spectator, May 2, 1970; *Observer Review,* June 11, 1967, May 16, 1971; *London Magazine,* November, 1967.

*   *   *

WILLEY, Basil 1897-

PERSONAL: Born July 25, 1897, in London, England; son of William Herbert and Alice Ann (Le Gros) Willey; married Zelie Murlis Ricks, 1923; children: Maurice, Margaret Willey Hartree, Peter, Lucy Willey Sherlock. *Education:* Educated at University College School, London, England, and Peterhouse, Cambridge University; M.A., first class honors in historical tripos, 1920, in English tripos, 1921. *Home:* 18 Adams Rd., Cambridge, England.

CAREER: Cambridge University, Cambridge, England, lecturer in English, 1923-34, university lecturer, 1934-46, King Edward VII Professor of English literature, 1946-64, professor emeritus, 1964—, fellow of Pembroke College, 1934-64, president of Pembroke College, 1958-64, honorary fellow, 1964—. Visiting professor at Columbia University, 1948-49, Cornell University, 1953, University College, Cardiff, 1971; Ballard Matthews Lecturer, University College of North Wales, 1964; Drew Lecturer; New College, University of London, 1967. *Military service:* British Army, West Yorks Regiment, 1916-18; became lieutenant. *Member:* British Academy (fellow), Royal Society of Literature (fellow), Athenaeum Club. *Awards, honors:* Litt.D. from University of Manchester, 1948.

WRITINGS: Tendencies in Renaissance Literary Theory, Bowes, 1922; *Seventeenth Century Background: Studies in the Thought of the Age in Relation to Poetry,* Chatto & Windus, 1934, Columbia University Press, 1942; *The Eighteenth Century Background: Studies on the Idea of Nature in the Thought of the Period,* Chatto & Windus, 1940, Columbia University Press, 1941; (contributor) *Essays and Studies, 1941,* Oxford University Press, 1942; *Q Tradition: An Inaugural Lecture,* Cambridge University Press, 1946, Macmillan, 1947; *Coleridge on Imagination and Fancy,* Oxford University Press, 1946; (contributor) Sir Ernest Baker, editor, *The Character of England,* Oxford University Press, 1947; (editor) *Essays and Studies by Members of the English Association, 1946,* Oxford University Press, 1947; (contributor) *Ideas and Beliefs of the Victorians: An Historic Revaluation of the Victorian Age,* Sylvan Press, 1949; *Richard Crashaw,* Cambridge University Press, 1949; *Nineteenth Century Studies: Coleridge to Matthew Arnold,* Columbia University Press, 1949; (contributor) *The History of Science: Origins and Results of the Scientific Revolution, a Symposium,* Cohen & West, 1951; (author of introduction) Henry David Thoreau, *Walden,* Norton, 1951; *Christianity, Past and Present,* Cambridge University Press, 1952; (contributor) G.B. Harrison, editor, *Major British Writers,* two volumes, Harcourt, 1953; (contributor) R.E. Davies, editor, *An Approach to Christian Education,* Epworth, 1956; *More Nineteenth Century Studies: A Group of Honest Doubters,* Columbia University Press, 1956; (contributor) *Essays and Studies by Members of the English Association, 1957,* J. Murray, 1957, Transatlantic, 1958; *The Religion of Nature,* Lindsey Press, 1957; (editor) *Essays and Studies by Members of the English Association, 1958,* J. Murray, 1958, Transatlantic, 1959; *Darwin and Butler: Two Versions of Evolution,* Chatto & Windus, 1959, Harcourt, 1960; (contributor) Appleman, Madden, and Wolf, editors, *1859: Entering an Age of Crisis,* Indiana University Press, 1959; (author of introduction) Arthur Quiller-Couch, *Troy Town,* Dent, 1963; *Helen Darbishire, 1881-1961* (originally published in *Proceedings* of the British Academy, 1961), Oxford University Press, 1961; *Eustace Mandeville Wetenhall Tillyard, 1889-1962* (originally published in *Proceedings* of the British Academy, 1963), Oxford University Press, 1965; (author of introduction) Cardinal John H. Newman, *Apologia Pro Vita Sua: Being a History of His Religious Opinions,* Oxford University Press, 1964; *The English Moralists,* Norton, 1964; *Spots of Time: A Retrospect of the Years 1897-1920,* Norton, 1965; *Cambridge and Other Memories,* Chatto & Windus, 1968, Norton, 1969; *Religion Today,* A. & C. Black, 1969; (author of introduction) Mark Rutherford, *Autobiography and Deliverance,* Leicester University Press, 1969; (contributor) *Essays and Studies, 1970,* J. Murray, 1970; *Samuel Taylor Coleridge,* Norton, 1972. Contributor of articles and reviews to professional journals.

AVOCATIONAL INTERESTS: Music and the English countryside.

*   *   *

WILLHELM, Sidney M(clarty) 1934-

PERSONAL: Born October 5, 1934, in Galveston, Tex.; son of Ernest Virgil (an accountant) and Edyth (Harbour) Willhelm. *Education:* University of Texas, B.A., 1957, M.A., 1957, Ph.D., 1961. *Politics:* Democrat. *Office:* Department of Sociology, State University of New York at Buffalo, Buffalo, N.Y. 14214.

CAREER: San Francisco State College, San Francisco, Calif., assistant professor of sociology, 1960-62; State University of New York at Buffalo, Buffalo, assistant professor, 1962-65, associate professor of sociology, 1965—. Visiting associate professor of sociology, McGill University, 1970, University of British Columbia, summer, 1971. *Member:* American Sociological Association, American Association of University Professors, Eastern Sociological Association.

WRITINGS: Urban Zoning and Land-Use Theory, Free Press, 1962; *Who Needs the Negro?,* Schenkman, 1970.

Contributor: Irving Louis Horowitz, editor, *The New Sociology,* Oxford University Press, 1964; Larry T. Reynolds and Janice M. Reynolds, editors, *The Sociology of Sociology,* McKay, 1970; Allan C. Ornstein and others, editors, *Educating the Disadvantaged: School Year 1969-1970,* AMS Press, 1970; Jack Roach and David Colfax, editors, *Radical Sociology,* Basic Books, 1970. Contributor of articles to sociological journals.

WORK IN PROGRESS: Sociological inquiry of academic associations.

*   *   *

WILLIAMS, Dorian 1914-

PERSONAL: Born July 1, 1914, in London, England; son of Vivian D.S. and Violet (Wood) Williams; married Jennifer Neale, April 4, 1957; children: Piers Dorian, Carola Dawn. *Education:* Attended Harrow School. *Home:* Pendley Manor, Tring, Hertfordshire, England. *Agent:* John Farquharson Ltd., 15 Red Lion Sq., London W.C.1, England.

CAREER: Pendley Center of Adult Education, Hertfordshire, England, founder and director, 1945—; British Broadcasting Corp., London, England, commentator, 1951—. Lecturer on communications in industry. Pendley Shakespeare Festival, director and producer, 1949—. Whaddon Chase, master of foxhounds, 1951—. *Awards, honors:* Gold Medal, British Horse Society, 1962.

WRITINGS: Poems for the People, Stockwell, 1943; *Peace Weapon: A Treatise on Education,* Stockwell, 1943; *Clear Round: The Story of Show Jumping,* Hodder & Stoughton, 1957; *Pendley and a Pack of Hounds,* Hodder & Stoughton, 1959; *Horses in Color,* Batsford, 1959, Viking, 1960; (with wife, Jennifer Williams) *Every Child's Book of Riding,* Burke Publishing, 1960; (with J.

Williams) *The Girls' Book of Horses and Riding,* Roy, 1961, 3rd revised edition, Burke Publishing, 1968; (with J. Williams) *Show Pony: A Practical Guide to Pony Care and Showing,* Brockhampton Press, 1961, Dutton, 1965; *Wendy Wins a Pony,* Burke Publishing, 1961; *Wendy Wins Her Spurs,* Burke Publishing, 1962; *Wendy at Wembley,* Burke Publishing, 1963; *A Gallery of Riders,* Burke Publishing, 1963; *Work with Horses as a Career,* Batsford, 1963; *Pony to Jump,* Stephen Greene, 1963; *Learning to Ride,* Collins, 1964; *The Vanguard Book of Ponies and Riding,* Collins, 1966; *Showing Horse Sense,* Arthur Barker, 1967; *Pancho: The Story of a Horse,* Dent, 1967, Walker & Co., 1968; *The Vanguard Book of Horses,* Collins, 1967; (editor) *The Horseman's Companion,* Eyre & Spottiswoode, 1967; *Show Jumping,* Faber, 1968, reissued as *Show Jumper,* A.S. Barnes, 1970; (editor) *My Favourite Horse Stories,* Lutterworth, 1968; *Show Jumping: The Great Ones,* Pelham, 1970, Arco, 1972; *Dorian Williams' World of Show Jumping,* 1970, Purnell, 1970; *Kingdom for a Horse,* Dent, 1971; *The Book of Horses,* Lippincott, 1971.

WORK IN PROGRESS: Great Riding Schools of the World, for Weidenfeld & Nicolson; *Great Moments in Sport: Show Jumping,* to be published by Pelham Books.

BIOGRAPHICAL/CRITICAL SOURCES: Times Literary Supplement, April 13, 1967, May 25, 1967; *Books and Bookmen,* December, 1967.

*   *   *

WILLIAMS, E(rnest) N(eville) 1917-

PERSONAL: Born March 28, 1917, in Leicester, England; son of Albert Ernest and Leah (Hunt) Williams; married Joyce Muriel Court, August 22, 1944. *Education:* Pembroke College, Cambridge, B.A., 1939, M.A., 1943. *Home:* 10 Chatsworth Way, London S.E. 27, England.

CAREER: Instructor in history, Hele's School, Exeter, England, 1944-47; Wallington School, Surrey, England, 1947-51, Emanuel School, London, England, 1951-57; Dulwich College, London, England, head of the history side, 1957—. *Military service:* Royal Artillery, 1940-44; became lieutenant.

WRITINGS: The Eighteenth-Century Constitution, 1688-1815: Documents and Commentary, Cambridge University Press, 1960; *Life in Georgian England,* Putnam, 1962; *A Documentary History of England,* Volume II: *1159-1939,* Penguin, 1966; *The Ancien Regime in Europe: Government and Society in the Major States, 1648-1789,* Harper, 1970. Contributor of articles and reviews to *History Today.*

*   *   *

WILLIAMS, Eric (Ernest) 1911-

PERSONAL: Born July 13, 1911, in London, England; son of Ernest and Mary Elizabeth (Beardmore) Williams; married Sibyl Grain, April 1, 1948. *Education:* Attended Christ's College, London, England. *Home:* "Wherever he and his wife happen to be." *Address:* c/o Union Bank of Switzerland, Bubenbergplatz 3, Bern, Switzerland.

CAREER: Lewis's Ltd., London, England, interior architect, 1932-40, book buyer, 1946-49; London Films, London, England, scriptwriter, 1949; self-employed writer and journalist, 1949. *Military service:* Royal Air Force, 1939-45; became squadron leader; awarded Military Cross for successful escape from a German prison camp in 1943.

WRITINGS: Goon in the Block, J. Cape, 1945; *The Wooden Horse,* Collins, 1949, Harper, 1950; *The Tunnel,* Collins, 1951, Coward, 1952, revised edition, edited for young readers, Collins, 1959, original version reissued as

The Tunnel Escape, Berkley, 1963; (editor) *The Escapers: A Chronicle of Escape in Many Wars, with Eighteen First-Hand Accounts,* Eyre & Spottiswoode, 1953, published in America as *The Book of Famous Escapes: A Chronicle of Escape in Many Wars, with Eighteen First-Hand Accounts,* Norton, 1954; *Complete and Free: A Modern Idyll,* Eyre & Spottiswoode, 1957; *Dragoman Pass: An Adventure in the Balkans,* Coward, 1959; (editor and author of introduction) *Great Escape Stories,* Weidenfeld & Nicolson, 1958, McBride, 1959, reissued as *The Will to be Free: Great Escape Stories,* Thomas Nelson, 1971; *The Borders of Barbarism,* Heinemann, 1961, Coward, 1962; (editor and author of introduction) *More Escapers in War and Peace, with Eighteen First-Hand Accounts,* Collins, 1968; *People: English in Action,* Edward Arnold, 1970; *Great Air Battles,* Pan, 1971. Contributor to film script, "The Wooden Horse," produced by Karda in 1951. Contributor to *Sunday Express* (London).

WORK IN PROGRESS: A political thriller; a book about his yacht.

SIDELIGHTS: Williams' novels have autobiographical elements; *The Wooden Horse* is the story of his escape from a German prison camp, *Dragoman Pass* and *The Borders of Barbarism* are based on an overland expedition he made in Hungary, Roumania, Bulgaria, Yugoslavia. He spent 1962 in Denmark supervising the building of his motorsailer yacht, then sailed for the Mediterranean, whose coasts and islands he is still exploring. He prefers action to writing, but writes because it is his way to freedom and independence. *Avocational interests:* Fishing and shooting, only "for the pot."

* * *

WILLIAMS, George W(alton)   1922-

PERSONAL: Born October 10, 1922, in Charleston, S.C.; son of Ellison Adger and Elizabeth (Dillingham) Williams; married Harriet Porcher Simons, November 28, 1953; children: George, Jr., Ellison Adger II, Harriet. *Education:* Episcopal High School, Alexandria, Va., student, 1939-40; Yale University, student, 1940-43, A.B., 1947; University of Virginia, M.A., 1949, Ph.D., 1957. *Politics:* Non-partisan. *Religion:* Episcopal. *Home:* 6 Sylvan Rd., Durham, N.C. 27701. *Office:* Duke University, Durham, N.C. 27706.

CAREER: Carolina Savings Bank, Charleston, S.C., assistant cashier, 1947-53; Duke University, Durham, N.C., assistant professor, 1957-62, associate professor 1962-65, professor of English, 1965—. Historiographer, Diocese of South Carolina and St. Michael's Church. Charleston, S.C. American Red Cross, former chapter treasurer. Dock Street Theatre, member of board. *Member:* Modern Language Association, Renaissance Society of America, English-Speaking Union, Royal Society of Arts (London; fellow), Bibliographical Society (London), South Atlantic Modern Language Association, Southeastern Renaissance Conference, Carolina Art Association, South Carolina Historical Society, Dalcho Historical Society, Bibliographical Society of University of Virginia, Elizabethan Club (Yale), Phi Beta Kappa, St. Cecilia Society, Carolina Yacht Club.

WRITINGS: St. Michael's, Charleston, 1751-1951, University of South Carolina Press, 1951; (editor) *Catalogue of the Library of the Reverend James Warley Miles,* University Press of Virginia, 1955; (compiler with Carl L. Anderson) *British and American Essays, 1905-1956,* Holt, 1959; (editor with A.K. Davis) *More Traditional Ballads of Virginia,* University of North Carolina Press, 1960; *Early Ministers at St. Michael's,* Dalcho Historical Society, 1962; *Image and Symbol in the Sacred Poetry of Richard Crashaw,* University of South Carolina Press,

1963; (editor) William Shakespeare, *The Most Excellent and Lamentable Tragedie of Romeo and Juliet: A Critical* Edition, Duke University Press, 1964; (editor) Thomas Middleton and William Rowley, *The Changeling,* University of Nebraska Press, 1965; (editor with Robert K. Turner, Jr.) William Shakespeare, *Henry VI,* parts 2 and 3, Penguin, 1966; *The Best Friend* (juvenile), Berg Publishing House, 1968; (editor and author of introduction) *The Complete Poetry of Richard Crashaw,* Doubleday-Anchor, 1970, New York University Press, 1972; (editor with G.B. Evans) *Dering Ms. of Henry IV,* Folger Library, 1971; (editor) *Jacob Eckhard's Choirmaster's Book of 1809,* University of South Carolina Press, 1971.

Writer of monographs for Dalcho Historical Society. Contributor of articles to learned journals. Editor of *Renaissance Papers* (publication of Southeastern Renaissance Conference), 1958-70. Contributing editor, "The Dramatic Works of Beaumont and Fletcher," published by Cambridge University Press, including *The Woman Hater,* and *A King and No King.*

WORK IN PROGRESS: Continuing work for "The Dramatic Works of Beaumont and Fletcher," specifically *Love's Cure,* and *The Chances,* for Cambridge University Press.

* * *

WILLIAMS, Harold S(tannett)   1898-

PERSONAL: Born November 16, 1898, in Melbourne, Australia; son of William Donaldson (a pharmacist) and Helene (Couchmann) Williams; married Gertrude F. McDonald, April 6, 1935; children: Judith Jane (Mrs. J. P. Mason), Carol Ann (Mrs. W.N. Holsworth), Peter John. *Education:* Attended University of Melbourne. *Home:* House #38, James-Yama, Shioya, Tarumi-ku, Kobe, Japan. *Office:* A. Cameron & Co. Ltd., Toyo Building, Number 5-chome Hachiman-Dori, Kobe, Japan.

CAREER: Findlay Richardson & Co. Ltd. (import-export), Kobe, Japan, assistant, 1919-27; Cooper Findlay & Co. Ltd. (import-export), Kobe, Japan, managing director, 1927-49; A. Cameron & Co. Ltd. (import-export), Kobe, Japan, managing director and proprietor, 1949—. *Military service:* Australian Military Forces, 1941-49; became major; received African Star, Pacific Star, Burma Star. *Awards, honors:* International Cultural Award, Hyogo Prefecture, Japan, 1967.

WRITINGS: Tales of the Foreign Settlements in Japan, Tuttle, 1959; *Shades of the Past; or, Indiscreet Tales of Japan,* Tuttle, 1959; *Foreigners in Mikadoland,* Tuttle, 1963; *The Story of Holme Ringer & Co. Ltd. in Western Japan, 1868-1968,* Tuttle, 1968; *The First Hundred Years, 1870-1970,* Kobe Regatta and Athletic Club, 1971. Contributor of historical articles to newspapers in Japan and Australia, and to *Japan Quarterly Review.*

WORK IN PROGRESS: With Hiroshi Naito, *The Kamakura Murders of 1864.*

* * *

WILLIAMS, (John Hargreaves) Harley

PERSONAL: Born in England; son of John and Lilian Williams; married Elizabeth Mackay Pascoe, 1941. *Home:* Cloisters, Temple, London E.C.4, England.

CAREER: Physician, barrister-at-law, and author.

WRITINGS: A Century of Public Health in Britain, 1832-1929, A. & C. Black, 1932; *The Inheritors,* Rich & Cowan, 1939; *Northern Lights and Western Stars,* Rich & Cowan, 1939; *Fingal's Box,* J. Cape, 1941; *At Cape Faithful,* J. Cape, 1943; *Doctors Differ: Five Studies in Contrast—John Elliotson, Hugh Owen Thomas, James Mackenzie, William Macewen, and R.W. Philip,* J. Cape,

1946, Fernhill, 1947; *Men of Stress: Three Dynamic Interpretations—Woodrow Wilson, Andrew Carnegie, William Hesketh Lever,* J. Cape, 1948; *The Healing Touch* (on prominent physicians of the 19th and 20th centuries), J. Cape, 1949, C.C Thomas, 1951; *Between Life and Death* (biographical sketches), J. Cape, 1951; *The Conquest of Fear* (biographical sketches of eminent physicians), J. Cape, 1952; *Don Quixote of the Microscope: An Interpretation of the Spanish Savant, Santiago Ramon y Cajal (1852-1934),* J. Cape, 1954; *A Doctor Looks at Miracles,* Anthony Blond, 1958, Roy, 1959; *Great Biologists,* G. Bell, 1961; (editor) *Stroke Rehabilitation: Conference Transactions,* Chest & Heart Association, 1961; *The Will to Health,* Museum Press, 1962; *British Pioneers in the Study of Heart Disease,* Chest & Heart Association, 1966; *Your Heart,* Cassell, 1970, published in America as *Living With Your Heart,* Regnery, 1971; *Learning to Live with Angina,* Health Horizon, 1970; *Coming to Terms with Chronic Bronchitis,* Health Horizon, 1970. Editor of *Health* (a quarterly journal).

AVOCATIONAL INTERESTS: The arts.

* * *

WILLIAMS, Jonathan (Chamberlain) 1929-

PERSONAL: Born March 8, 1929, in Asheville, N.C.; son of Thomas Benjamin and Georgette (Chamberlain) Williams. *Education:* Attended St. Albans School, Washingon, D.C., 1941-47; studied at Princeton University, 1947-49, Phillips Memorial Gallery, 1949, Atelier 17, 1949-50, and Black Mountain College, intermittently, 1951-56. *Residence:* Highlands, N.C. 28741; and Corn Close, Dentdale, Sedbergh, Yorkshire, England. *Office:* Jargon Society, c/o Penland School, Penland, N.C. 28765; or Jargon Society, c/o Small Publishers' Co., Elm St., Millerton, N.Y. 12546.

CAREER: Jargon Books (a poet's press), Highlands, N.C., founder, executive director, editor, publisher, and designer, 1951—; The Nantahala Foundation, Highlands, N.C., president, 1960—. Aspen Institute for Humanistic Studies, Aspen, Colo., poet-in-residence, summer, 1962, scholar-in-residence, 1967-68; Maryland Institute College of Art, Baltimore, Md., scholar-in-residence, 1968-69; University of Kansas, Lawrence, poet-in-residence, 1971. Visiting poet, Wake Forest University, North Carolina School of the Arts, Salem Academy, Winston-Salem State College, 1973. Has given approximately 750 lectures, readings, and seminars at universities and organizations throughout the world, 1954-73. *Military service:* U.S. Army Medical Corps, 1952-54; conscientious objector. *Member:* Bruckner Society of America, Congress of Racial Equality, Appalachian Trail Conference, Sierra Club, Youth Hostel Association, Society for Individual Rights, Campaign for Homosexual Equality, National Trust of Great Britain, Cast-Iron Lawn-Deer Owners of America (co-founder), Elgar Society, Cottonmouth Heterosexuals for Wallace (costume designer), Carlos Toadvine Trust (secretary), Macon County North Carolina Meshuggah Sound Society (musical director). *Awards, honors:* Guggenheim fellowship for poetry, 1957-58; Longview Foundation grant, 1960, for editing of Jargon Books; Jargon Society grants, 1968, 1969, 1970, for publishing National Endowment for the Arts projects; D.H.L., Maryland Institute College of Art, 1969.

WRITINGS—All poetry unless otherwise indicated: *Garbage Litters the Iron Face of the Sun's Child,* engraving by David Ruff, Jargon, 1951; *Red/Gray,* drawings by Paul Ellsworth, Jargon, 1951; *Four Stoppages: A Configuration,* drawings by Charles Oscar, Jargon, 1953; *The Empire Finals at Verona,* collages and drawings by Fielding Dawson, Jargon, 1959; *Lord! Lord! Lord!,* Jargon, 1959; *Amen/Huzza/Selah,* preface by Louis Zukofsky, photographs by Williams, Jargon, 1960; *Elegies & Cel-*

ebrations, preface by Robert Duncan, photographs by Aaron Siskind and Williams, Jargon, 1962; *In England's Green & (A Garland & A Clyster),* drawings by Philip Van Aver, Auerhahn, 1962; *Emblems for the Little Dells, & Nooks & Corners of Paradise* (reproduction of a page of Samuel Palmer's sketch-book of 1824), Jargon, 1962; *LTGD (Lullabies Twisters Gibbers Drags),* covers by R.B. Kitaj, Jargon (London), 1963, Design Department, Indiana University, 1967; *Lines About Hills Above Lakes,* foreword by John Wain, drawings by Barry Hall, Roman Books, 1964; *Petite Country Concrete Suite,* Fenian Head Centre Press, 1965; *Twelve Jargonelles from the Herbalist's Notebook,* graphic design by Ann Wilkinson, Design Department, Indiana University, 1965; *Ten Jargonelles from the Herbalist's Notebook,* graphic design by Arthur Korant, Graduate Graphic Design Program, University of Illinois, 1966; *Four Jargonelles from the Herbalist's Notebook,* Lowell House Printers, Harvard College, 1966; *Paean to Dvorak, Deemer & McClure,* Dave Haselwood, 1966; *Eight Jargonelles from the Herbalist's Notebook,* graphic design by Dave Ahlsted, Design Department, Indiana University, 1967; *Affilati attrezzi per i giardini di Catullo* (selected poems in English and Italian), translations by Leda Sartini Mussio, drawings by James McGarrell, Roberto Lerici Editori (Milan), 1967, published in America as *Sharp Tools for Catullan Gardens,* introductory note by Guy Davenport, Fine Arts Department, Indiana University, 1968; *Mahler Becomes Politics, Beisbol* (portfolio with silk-screen prints by R.B. Kitaj, with texts in separate book), Marlborough Fine Arts (London), 1967; *50! EPIphytes, -taphs, -tomes, -grams, -thets! 50!,* Poet & Printer (London), 1967; *Les Six Pak* ("disposable six-pak xerox edition"), Aspen Institute, 1967; *A French 75! (Salut Milhaudious),* Dave Haselwood, 1967; *Futura 15: Polycotyledonous Poems,* Edition Hansjoerg Mayer (Stuttgart), 1967; *The Lucidities (Sixteen in Visionary Company),* drawings by John Furnival, Turret Books, 1968; *Descant on Rawthey's Madrigal (Conversations with Basil Bunting),* Gnomon Press, 1968; *Ripostes,* silk-screen print and design by William Katz, Edition Domberger (Stuttgart), 1969; *An Ear in Bartram's Tree: Selected Poems 1957-1967,* introduction by Guy Davenport, University of North Carolina Press, 1969; *On Arriving at the Same Age as Jack Benny,* Finial Press, 1969; *Mahler,* drawings by R.B. Kitaj, Grossman, 1969; *Six Rusticated, Wall-Eyed Poems,* graphic realizations by Dana Atchley, Press of the Maryland Institute of Art, 1969; *The New Architectural Monuments of Baltimore City,* lithographs by John Sparks, typography by Robert Gotsch, Press of the Maryland Institute of Art, 1970; *The Apocryphal, Oracular Yeah-Sayings of Mae West,* lithographs by Raoul Middleman, Press of the Maryland Institute of Art, 1970 (not released); (editor) *Edward Dahlberg: A Tribute* (prose and poetry collection; festschrift for his seventieth birthday), David Lewis, 1970; *Strung Out with Elgar on a Hill,* plates by Peter Bodner, Finial Press, 1971; *Blues & Roots/Rue & Bluets (A Garland for the Appalachians),* photographs by Nicholas Dean, graphic realizations by Dana Atchley, Grossman, 1971; *The Loco Logodaedalist in Situ: Selected Poems 1968-1970,* embellishments by Joe Tilson, Cape Goliard Press, 1971, Grossman, 1972; (with Thomas Meyer) *EPitaph,* typography by Asa Benveniste, [Corn Close], 1972; (with Meyer) *Fruits Confits,* decorations by Ian Gardner, [Corn Close], 1972; *Adventures with a Twelve-Inch Pianist Beyond the Blue Horizon,* photographs by David Colley, Finial Press, 1973; *Pairidaeza* ("a celebration for the garden at Levens Hall"), lithographs by Ian Gardner, typography by Ronald Pearson, Blue Funnel Press, 1973; *Imaginary Postcards (Clints Grikes Gripes Glints),* drawings by Tom Phillips, typography by Asa Benveniste, Trigram Press, 1973; *Much Further Out Than You Thought* ("Stevie Smith in conversation and celebration"), drawings by John Furnival, Turret Books, 1973;

(with Meyer) *Gone Into When* (seven epitaphs), William Katz, 1973; *Selected Essays (Poeticules Criticasters Kitschdiggers & Just-folks)*, edited by Herbert Leibowitz, [New York], 1973.

Poems anthologized in *New Directions in Prose and Poetry*, Volume 16, New Directions, 1957, *The Beat Scene*, edited by Elias Wilentz, Corinth Books, 1960, *The New American Poetry, 1945-1960*, edited by Donald Allen, Grove, 1960, *New Directions in Prose and Poetry*, Volume 17, edited by James Laughlin, New Directions, 1961, *Beat Poets*, Vista Books, 1963, *Erotic Poetry*, edited by William Cole, Random House, 1963, *A Controversy of Poets*, edited by Paris Leary and Robert Kelly, Doubleday-Anchor, 1965, *Poets of North Carolina*, edited by Richard Gaither Walser, University of North Carolina Press, 1965, *The Voice That Is Great Within Us*, edited by Hayden Carruth, Bantam, 1970, and anthologies of concrete poetry edited by Mary Ellen Solt, Stephen Bann, Emmett Williams, Jerry G. Bowles, and Milton Klonsky.

Contributor to *Evergreen Review, Contact, Vogue, Nation, Aperture, Black Mountain Review, Monk's Pond, Kulchur, Origin, Jazz Monthly* (St. Ives), *Poor. Old. Tired. Horse.* (Dunsyre, Lanarkshire), *Vou* (Tokyo), *I Quattro Soli* (Turin), *Cimaise* (Paris), *Art International* (Zurich), *Cultural Affairs, Art in Society, Craft Horizons, Poetry Review* (London), *Parnassus, Prose,* and other periodicals. Member of advisory board, *Foxfire Magazine*.

WORK IN PROGRESS: Corbel & Misericord, with drawings by John Furnival; *I (Also) Remember,* a homage to Joe Brainard; *Letters to the Great Dead,* with details by R.B. Kitaj; *A Man Standing by His Word,* a year of letters; *Elite Elate Poems,* selected poems 1971-1973, to be published in New York and London.

SIDELIGHTS: Williams has described himself as "your friendly Ecological Logodaedalist talking, during what we shall call the Deaf-Ear Explosion." It has been said of him that "he is an intelligent conversationalist who turns his confrontations with all kinds of people into impudent and sparkling poetry. Attention is paid to the value of language and he deals equally successfully with Blakean mysticism or the humor of bawdy Americanisms."

"Perhaps the most obviously striking quality in Williams' work," Ralph J. Mills, Jr. has written, "aside from the erudition and bookishness (which are of the delightful, never the pedantic variety), is the extraordinary acuteness of his ear. As a perpetual traveler, largely a hiker in America and England, he has attuned his sensitive powers of listening to every nuance of speech and sound, and given them back to his readers beautifully articulated." Dan Jaffe said of *An Ear in Bartram's Tree: Selected Poems, 1957-1967:* "Jonathan Williams snags odd bits of information, characteristic gestures, unique speech patterns. His book is eclectic in style and subject; it gives the impression of scholarship without narcissism, muscle without pomposity. On occasion it may be almost private, even cute, at times cluttered with outrageous puns, but these seem the faults of a man whose admiration for terseness and intelligence is so strong he may sometimes sacrifice other virtues." "More than any other poet," wrote Robert Morgan in *Nation,* "Jonathan Williams has used the Objectivist principle, the idea that a poem is first of all a linguistic, phonetic, graphic object. . . .He takes the language eroding right now in our mouths and cultivates it, shapes it, and speaks it to life. For Williams more than anyone I know, poetry is an active art, the language being spoken."

Williams told *CA:* "Like John Clare, I tend to find poems in fields. I believe the two most important concerns of any man, poet and citizen, are social justice and the development of an ecological conscience. My poems are directed accordingly. Robert Creeley once noted, you do not derail a train by standing in front of it, but by placing a small wedge of steel in the proper place. So, with the poem and men's minds."

The purpose behind his numerous lectures is to support Jargon Books. Williams writes: "I am in the position of having no income except what I snare by these readings and the few book sales. This isn't very much, it could not be, but it allows other money to go into book production. It is a consistent juggling act, and, like they say, how is it really possible? Since my image seems often that of 'southern gentlemen and deepcountry publisher,' counting endless amounts of lucre from the slave market, I would like the picture to be apparent. The *modus operandi* is thus more than a private matter: I am able to use the family place, which sits on a mountain in western North Carolina. It is the requisite, occasional sanctuary. Without it, no such hopeless vocational mission as Jargon could persist. I prefer it to institutional sanctuaries; i.e., I don't need a job in teaching or in commercial bookmaking. . . .The poems are constructed with vocal intentions; the books are made to be looked at, etc., and I must act as my own agent. It is simple enough, if not simple at all."

His Jargon venture as both publisher and book designer has been enthusiastically received. Robert Creeley writes that Williams has "persistently published poetry and prose of a demonstrably high order against the criticism and, even worse, the silence of many people indeed." And Donald Hall says: "Jargon designs the best looking books around, and it has also printed a number of the best poets before the publishers in New York knew they were there."

"There are certain kindred spirits at work in the country," Williams explains, "and it is to make coherence of these that Jargon exists. It does not represent an armed camp. The *avant-garde* is never anything but a community of particular sympathy. I have attempted to know it in a number of areas because it is the total locale of America that produces the culture. [Poet Edward] Dahlberg asks whether a civilization can be produced on a landscape vaster than the body of a Titan. It is our business to try."

Concerning his lectures, Williams writes: "It is very rarely that an English Department will sponsor me. This may be because: (1) I do not wear a Confederate uniform; (2) I do not play the Beat/Square Game, or other forms of the old American Pushme/Pullyou, like Brainwashed / Great Unwashed, In/ Out, SF / NYC, Queer / Straight—these are peculiar ways to con people and sell them things; (3) I am involved in an area which is, has been, always will be 'outside the Academy.' It is where all them idiosyncratic, autochthonous injuns live in the thickets of disinterest, etc. And so, Jargon and its poet get confused with some kind of Chaos by some sitting there by the campfires, martinis loaded in readiness. However, there are many ways to get on a campus and I shall not forget an inventive friend who got me to Earlham College on a Tuesday afternoon, under the auspices of the Friday Tea Committee of the Humanities & Social Sciences Division. . . . . I would prefer, frankly, to be sponsored by the Ecology Department, since poetry is a matter of making the viable connections between written things. . . . I dress and behave *only* as one who almost entered the Anglican ministry; viz., let us keep our attention on the poetry and one or two of the major tendencies for writing it, as I see it now in America."

"About my poems—my business is to make them, not to obfuscate or clarify them. A few people have said a few very decent things. James Laughlin writes me that 'nobody who is writing today has a more individual style, or more vitality, or a more salty wit.' I hope, but, like they say, I don't know. Also Hugh Kenner has written well of the poems in (hang on) *The National Review*. Otherwise, it has been 'just friends': Zukofsky, WCW [William Carlos Williams], Creeley, Layton, Levertov, Turnbull, Metcalf, Edelstein, Niedecker. So be it. I am not running in a competition for public office. The poems and the books. . .are made for one person at a time. I hope to keep finding him and her."

An avid hiker "to recover from confinement in the little world of poetry," Williams has hiked 1,408 miles of the Appalachian Trail, and over 5,000 miles in England and America, including Hadrian's Wall, the Pennine Way, the Lake District, North York Moors, Wye River, Offa's Dyke, and the North Cornish and Devon coasts.

Folkways Records recorded Jonathan Williams reading his poems in "Blues & Roots/Rue & Bluets," summer, 1964.

BIOGRAPHICAL/CRITICAL SOURCES: Kenneth Rexroth, *Assays*, New Directions, 1962; *Books at Brown*, Volume 19, John Hay Library of Brown University, 1963; Guy Davenport's introduction to *An Ear in Bartram's Tree*, University of North Carolina Press, 1969; *Library Journal*, June 1, 1969, May 1, 1970; *Saturday Review*, September 6, 1969; *New Statesman*, September 12, 1969; *Virginia Quarterly Review*, autumn, 1969; *Poetry*, February, 1971; *Nation*, August 16, 1971; *New York Times Book Review*, November 21, 1971; *Manchester Guardian*, July 3, 1972; *Studio International*, September, 1972; *Parnassus*, fall/winter, 1972.

*   *   *

WILLIAMS, Wirt Alfred, Jr.   1921-

PERSONAL: Born August 21, 1921, in Goodman, Miss.; son of Wirt Alfred and Nina (Rayner) Williams; married Ann Meredith, April 10, 1954; children: Meredith. *Education:* Mississippi Delta State College, B.A., 1940; Louisiana State University, M.A., 1941; State University of Iowa, Ph.D., 1953. *Politics:* Democrat. *Religion:* Episcopalian. *Residence:* San Juan Capistrano, Calif. *Agent:* Ned Brown, 315 South Beverly Dr., Beverly Hills, Calif. 90212; and Patricia Schartle, 18 East 41st St., New York, N.Y. 10017. *Office:* Department of English, California State University at Los Angeles, 5151 State College Dr., Los Angeles, Calif. 90032.

CAREER: *Shreveport Times*, Shreveport, La., assistant news editor, later news editor, 1941-42, capitol correspondent, 1946; *New Orleans Item*, New Orleans, La., 1946-49, variously reporter, special writer, and city editor; California State College at Los Angeles, professor of English, 1953—. *Military service:* U.S. Navy, 1942-46; served aboard destroyer, 1942-44, landing ship, 1944-46; lieutenant commander in Reserves. *Member:* P.E.N., Philological Association of the Pacific Coast, Association of California State University Professors. *Awards, honors:* Nominated by publisher for Pulitzer Prize in fiction for *The Enemy*, 1951, *Ada Dallas*, 1959; and *The Far Side*, 1972.

WRITINGS: *The Enemy*, Houghton, 1951; *Love in a Windy Space*, Reynal, 1957; *Ada Dallas*, McGraw, 1959; *A Passage of Hawks*, McGraw, 1963; *The Trojans*, Little, Brown, 1966; *The Far Side*, Horizon Press, 1972.

WORK IN PROGRESS: A critical study of Ernest Hemingway; a novel.

SIDELIGHTS: Williams says it was his interest in the works of Ernest Hemingway that drew him to serious fiction writing. In 1952 Hemingway listed *The Enemy* as one of the books he most liked, and later reportedly wrote, "I think Wirt Williams writes as well as anybody

writing." An amateur boxer, Williams was runner-up for the Southern Golden Gloves heavyweight championship, New Orleans, 1947. *Ada Dallas* was filmed as "Ada" by Metro-Goldwyn-Mayer, 1961.

BIOGRAPHICAL/CRITICAL SOURCES: Orange Coast Illustrated, October, 1963; *Punch*, August 9, 1967.

*   *   *

WILLIAMSON, Eugene L. (Jr.)   1930-

PERSONAL: Born April 13, 1930, in Gurley, Ala.; married Mary Stowe; children: two. *Education:* University of Alabama, B.A., 1951; University of Michigan, M.A., 1955, Ph.D., 1960. *Office:* P.O. Box 762, University, Ala. 35486.

CAREER: University of Kentucky, Lexington, instructor in English, 1957-59; University of Alabama, University, assistant professor, 1959-63, associate professor, 1963-68, professor of English, 1968—. *Military service:* U.S. Naval Reserve, 1951-53, 1954—; lieutenant commander.

WRITINGS: *The Liberalism of Thomas Arnold: A Study of His Religious and Political Writings*, University of Alabama Press, 1964. Contributor of articles to scholarship journals, including *PMLA*, *Modern Language Quarterly*, *Studies in English Literature*, and *Journal of English and Germanic Philology*.

WORK IN PROGRESS: Uses of Biblical Phrasing by Five Nineteenth Century Poets; a study of the problem of value in literary criticism.

*   *   *

WILLIAMSON, Geoffrey   1897-
(Alan Hastings)

PERSONAL: Born October 7, 1897, in Hornsey, London, England; son of William and Betsy Ann (Hebron) Williamson; married Margaret Lloyd Roberts, March 12, 1926; children: David Geoffrey. *Education:* Attended Merchant Taylors' School.

CAREER: Odhams Press Ltd., London, England, subeditor and staff writer, 1924-36, staff writer and periodicals feature manager, 1946-58; *John Bull*, London, editor, 1937-45; Aims of Industry Ltd., London, press officer, 1960—. *Military service:* British Army, served in Africa, India, and Mesopotamia, 1916-20; became staff sergeant.

WRITINGS: *The Lovable Outlaw*, Heinemann, 1930; *Grand Trunk Knight*, Hutchinson, 1933; *Changing Greenland*, Sidgwick & Jackson, 1953, Library Publishers, 1954; *Inside Buchmanism*, C. A. Watts, 1954, Philosophical Library, 1955; *Morality Fair*, C. A. Watts, 1955; *Star-Spangled Square: The Saga of Little America in London*, Bles, 1956; *Sky Smuggler*, R. Hale, 1958; *Young Traveller in the Far North*, Phoenix House, 1958; *How to Retire Happily*, Museum Press, 1962; *Wheels Within Wheels: The Story of the Starleys of Coventry*, Bles, 1966; *Exploring Bridges*, Odhams, 1967; *The Ingenious Mr. Gainsborough*, St. Martin's, 1972. Author of short stories, and pamphlets and booklets, including "The Scandal of Death Duties," "How to Get the Best Out of Your Tax Allowances," and "A Tax on Our Future."

WORK IN PROGRESS: A history of polar aviation.

SIDELIGHTS: Williamson was one of four British writers to cover Danish Royal Tour of Greenland, 1952. *Avocational interests:* Trying to paint in oils.

BIOGRAPHICAL/CRITICAL SOURCES: Punch, November 29, 1967.†

WILLIAMSON, William Landram 1920-

PERSONAL: Born August 13, 1920, in Lexington, Ky.; son of Clarence Linden (an attorney) and Eugenia (Dunlap) Williamson; married Daisy Levy, August 18, 1962; children: Andrea Grant Williamson Irizarry. Education: University of Kentucky, 1937-38; University of Wisconsin, B.A. (with honors), 1941; Emory University, B.A. in Library Science, 1942; Columbia University, M.S., 1949; University of Chicago, Ph.D., 1959. Politics: Democrat. Home: 5105 Tomahawk Trail, Madison, Wis. 53705. Office: Library School, University of Wisconsin, Madison, Wis. 53706.

CAREER: Atlanta Public Library, Atlanta, Ga., reference assistant, 1942, 1946; Baylor University, Waco, Tex., assistant librarian, 1947-48, associate librarian and acting university librarian, 1949-51; Columbia University, New York, N.Y., Butler Librarian, 1954-64, on leave as library consultant, Ford-State University of New York Indonesia Project, Bandung, Indonesia, 1960-62, senior lecturer in School of Library Service, 1964; Montclair State College, Upper Montclair, N.J., librarian, professor of library science, 1964-66; University of Wisconsin, Madison, professor in Library School, 1966—. Visiting lecturer, University of Chicago, summer, 1966; visiting professor, University of Hawaii, summer, 1970; university library consultant, Government of Indonesia, summer, 1970. Military service: U.S. Army, troop transport and cargo officer, 1942-46; became first lieutenant. Member: American Library Association, American Association of University Professors (president, Montclair State College chapter, 1966), Wisconsin Library Association, Archons of Colophon.

WRITINGS: William Frederick Poole and the Modern Library Movement, Columbia University Press, 1963; (editor) The Impact of the Public Law 480 Program on Overseas Acquisitions by American Libraries, Library School, University of Wisconsin, Madison, 1968. Contributor to professional journals.

WORK IN PROGRESS: Predecessors of Pollard; Studies in the History of Analytical Bibliography, with publication anticipated in parts in periodical form, and book publication if warranted.

*   *   *

WILLIS, Ted 1918-

PERSONAL: Born January 13, 1918, in Tottenham, Middlesex, England; son of Alfred John (a bus driver) and Maria Harriett (Meek) Willis; married Audrey Mary Hale (a former actress), August 18, 1944; children: John Edward, Sally Ann Hale. Education: Attended Green Elementary School and Downhills Central School. Home: 5 Shepherds Green, Chislehurst, Kent, England. Agent: ALS Management, 67 Brook St., London W.1, England.

CAREER: Left school at fifteen, and worked as office and delivery boy, newsboy, farm helper, and at other casual labor before becoming free-lance journalist; at the end of the war (and after first play was produced) J. B. Priestley guaranteed him a sum of money as support for a year while establishing himself as a writer; free-lance writer of plays for stage, films, and television since. Director of a film production company; member of board of governors, National Film School, London. Military service: British Army, World War II; served in Royal Fusiliers, then as writer of War Office films and Ministry of Information documentaries. Member: Royal Society of Arts (London; fellow), Writers Guild of Great Britain (president, 1959-69). Awards, honors: Berlin Festival Award and London Picture-Goer Award, both for "Woman in a Dressing Gown"; Edinburgh Festival Award for "Story of Achievement"; created Lord Willis of Chislehurst, 1963.

WRITINGS: God Bless the Guv'nor: A Moral Melodrama in Three Acts in Which the Twin Evils of Trades Unionism and Strong Drink Are Exposed, New Theatre Publications, 1945; The Blue Lamp (novel based on his film script), Convoy Publications, 1950; The Lady Purrs: A Farcical Comedy in Three Acts, Baker's Plays, 1950; George Comes Home: A Play in One Act for Women, Samuel French, 1955; (with Richard Gordon) Doctor in the House (three-act comedy, based on the novel by Gordon), Evans Brothers, 1957, Samuel French, 1966; The Devil's Churchyard, Parrish, 1957; Seven Gates to Nowhere, Parrish, 1958; Woman in a Dressing Gown, and Other Television Plays, Barrie & Rockliff, 1959, title play (two-act) published separately as Woman in a Dressing Gown, Evans Brothers, 1964; Hot Summer Night (three-act play), Samuel French, 1959; (with Henry Cecil) Brothers in Law: A Comedy in Three Acts (based on the novel by Cecil), Samuel French, 1959; The Eyes of Youth (two-act play adapted from novel A Dread of Burning, by Rosemary Timperley), Evans Brothers, 1960; (with Charles Hatton under joint pseudonym George Dixon) Dixon of Dock Green: My Life, William Kimber, 1960; The Little Goldmine (one-act television play), Samuel French, 1962; Whatever Happened to Tom Mix?: The Story of One of My Lives, Cassell, 1970.

Other stage plays produced: "Buster," at Arts Theatre, London, England, July, 1943; "No Trees in the Street," 1948; "The Magnificent Moodies," 1952; "Kid Kenyon Rides Again," 1954; "Farewell Yesterday," renamed "The Eyes of Youth," 1959; "Mother" (adapted from the novel by Maxim Gorky), 1961; "Doctor at Sea" (adapted from the novel by Richard Gordon), 1962; "A Slow Roll of Drums," 1964; "A Murder of Crows," 1965; "Queenie" (musical), 1968; "A Fine Day for Murder," 1970; "Dead on Saturday," at the Thorndike, Leatherhead, England, January 26, 1971. Also author of "Yellow Star," "All Change Here," (with Jan Read) "The Blue Lamp," "When in Rome" (musical), and "Duel at Wapping Creek."

Film scripts: "It's Great to be Young," Columbia, 1946; "Holiday Camp," Gainsborough Pictures, 1947; "Good Time Girl," Sydney Box, 1950; "The Blue Lamp," Ealing Studios, 1950; "Burnt Evidence," 1952; "Trouble in Store," Two Cities Films, 1953; "Top of the Form," J. Arthur Rank, 1953; "Up to His Neck," J. Arthur Rank, 1954; "Woman in a Dressing Gown," Godwin-Willis, 1957; "The Young and the Guilty," 1957; "No Trees in the Street," Associated British-Pathe, 1958; "Bitter Harvest," 1960; "Flame in the Streets," Atlantic Pictures Corp., 1962. Also script writer for "The Undefeated," (with Gerard Bryant) "The Huggetts Abroad," "The Wallet," "The Horsemasters," and "Last Bus to Banjo Creek."

Television series: "Patterns of Marriage," British Broadcasting Corp.; "Dixon of Dock Green," British Broadcasting Corp.; "Big City," International Television; "Dial 999" (pilot script); "Lifeline" (pilot script); (with Edward J. Mason) "Days of Vengeance"; "Flower of Evil"; "Outbreak of Murder"; "Sergeant Cork"; "Taxi"; "The Sullavan Brothers"; "Crime of Passion"; "Mrs. Thursday"; "Virgin of the Secret Service."

Television plays: "What Happens to Love"; "The Young and the Guilty"; "Look in Any Window"; "Strictly for the Sparrows"; "Hot Summer Night"; "Scent of Fear"; "The Four Seasons of Rosie Carr" (cycle of four plays).

Also author of pamphlet, Fighting Youth of Russia: The Story of the Young Men and Women of the Soviet Union, Russia Today Society, 1942. Writer of about fifty scripts for War Office films and Ministry of Information documentaries.

SIDELIGHTS: Willis's plays have been performed in many countries around the world. Several books based on film or television scripts by Willis have been published, notably Mabel and Denis Constanduros' *The Huggetts Abroad*, Sampson Low, Marston & Co., 1949, Douglas Enefer's *The Days of Vengeance*, World Distributors, 1961, and John Burke's *Flame in the Streets*, Four Square Books, 1961. In 1969 John Long published *Sergeant Cork's Second Casebook* by Arthur Swinson, a book of stories from the A.T.V. television series featuring Willis's character, Sergeant Cork.

AVOCATIONAL INTERESTS: Tennis, badminton, football, traveling (with special interest in Australia and South America).

BIOGRAPHICAL/CRITICAL SOURCES: Observer Review, October 25, 1970; *The Stage and Television Today*, November 26, 1970.

* * *

WILLSON, A(mos) Leslie, Jr. 1923-

PERSONAL: Born June 14, 1923, in Texhoma, Okla.; son of Amos Leslie (an electrical contractor) and Richie (Hobgood) Willson; married Jeanne Redrow, August 26, 1950; children: Brian La Don, Juliet Lisa, Kevin Redrow. *Education:* University of Texas, B.J., 1947, B.A., 1949, M.A., 1950; Yale University, Ph.D., 1954. *Politics:* Republican. *Religion:* Methodist. *Home:* 4205 Far West Blvd., Austin, Tex. 78731. *Office address:* Department of Germanic Languages, University of Texas, P.O. Box 7939, Austin 78712.

CAREER: Wesleyan University, Middletown, Conn., instructor in German, 1953-54; Northwestern University, Evanston, Ill., instructor in German, 1954-55; University of Texas, Austin, instructor, 1955-58, assistant professor of German, 1958-61; Duke University, Durham, N.C., associate professor of German, 1961-65; Pennsylvania State University, University Park, professor of German, 1965-66; University of Texas at Austin, professor of German, 1966—, chairman of department, 1972—. *Military service:* U.S. Army, Intelligence, 1943-46; became technical sergeant. *Member:* Modern Language Association of America, American Association of Teachers of German, Internationale Vereinigung fuer Germanische Sprach und Literaturwissenschaft, South Atlantic Modern Language Association, Phi Beta Kappa. *Awards, honors:* Fulbright senior research fellowship, 1962-63.

WRITINGS: (Editor and author of introduction) *A Schiller Symposium*, Department of Germanic Languages, University of Texas, 1960; *A Mythical Image: The Ideal of India in German Romanticism*, Duke University Press, 1964; (editor) Herman John Wiegand, *Surveys and Soundings in European Literature*, Princeton University Press, 1966; (editor) Guenter Grass, *Hochwasser*, and *Noch zehn Minuten bis buffalo*, Appleton, 1967; (contributor of translation) Guenther Grass, *Four Plays*, Harcourt, 1967; (editor) Herman J. Weigand, *Faehrten und Funde. Aufsaetze zur deutschen Literatur*, Francke Verlag, 1967; (translator with Ralph Manheim) Guenter Grass, "Uptight" (play), first produced in English at University of Texas at Austin, April 6, 1970; (editor) *A Guenter Grass Symposium*, University of Texas Press, 1971; (translator with Manheim) Guenther Grass, *Max*, Harcourt, 1972; (editor) Martin Walser, *Luegengeschichten*, Harcourt, 1972. Founder and editor of *Dimension: Contemporary Arts and Letters*, 1968—. Contributor of numerous articles to professional periodicals.

WORK IN PROGRESS: Editing two volumes of the letters of Friedrich Schlegel; research in contemporary German literature.

AVOCATIONAL INTERESTS: Modern fiction, drama of the absurd theatre, travel, camping, stamp collecting, and chess.

* * *

WILLY, Margaret (Elizabeth) 1919-

PERSONAL: Born October 25, 1919, in London, England; daughter of Arthur and Mabel (Fisher) Willy. *Education:* Goldsmiths' College, London, diploma in humanities, 1940. *Home:* Brockmere, Wray Park Rd., Reigate, Surrey, England.

CAREER: Copywriter for various publishing houses and book wholesale firms, London, England, 1936-42; lecturer in English literature and the art of writing, British Council, 1950—, City Literary Institute, 1956—, Goldsmiths' College, University of London, 1959—, Stanhope Institute of Adult Education, 1966—, all London, England. Lecturer in Poland, 1963. *Wartime service:* Women's Land Army, 1942-46. *Member:* Royal Society of Literature (fellow), English Association. *Awards, honors:* Atlantic Award in Literature, offered by Rockefeller Institute to young British writers whose careers were interrupted by the war, 1946.

WRITINGS: The Invisible Sun (poems), Chaterson, 1946; *Life Was Their Cry*, (critical biographies), Evans Brothers, 1950; *Every Star a Tongue* (poems), Heinemann, 1951; *The South Hams* (topographical study), R. Hale, 1955; *Three Metaphysical Poets: Richard Crashaw, Henry Vaughan, Thomas Traherne*, published for the British Council by Longmans, Green, 1961, reissued as *Richard Crashaw, Henry Vaughan, Thomas Traherne* ("British Writers and Their Work, No. 4"), University of Nebraska Press, 1964; (editor with Guy Boas) Oliver Goldsmith, *Two Plays of Goldsmith* (includes *She Stoops to Conquer*, edited by Boas, and *The Good Natur'd Man*, edited by Willy), Edward Arnold, 1962; *The English Diarists: Evelyn and Pepys*, published for the British Council and the National Book League by Longmans, Green, 1963; (editor and contributor) *Poems of Today*, fifth series, Macmillan, 1963; *Three Women Diarists: Celia Fiennes, Dorothy Wordsworth, Katherine Mansfield*, published for the British Council and the National Book League by Longmans, Green, 1964; *Lesser Metaphysical Poets*, published for the British Council by Longmans, Green, c.1965; *A Critical Commentary on Emily Bronte's "Wuthering Heights"*, Macmillan, 1966; *Browning's "Men and Women": A Critical Commentary*, Macmillan, 1968; (with others) *Literature and Life: Addresses to the English Association*, Kennikat, 1970; (editor with James Sutherland) *The Metaphysical Poets*, University of South Carolina Press, 1971.

Poetry anthologized in *Images of Tomorrow: An Anthology of Recent Poetry*, edited by J.F.A. Heath-Stubbs, S.C.M. Press, 1953, *An Anthology of Contemporary Verse*, edited by Margaret J. O'Donnell, Blackie & Son, 1953, *New Poems, 1954*, edited by Rex Warner and others, Transatlantic, 1954, *Anthology of Spoken Verse and Prose*, edited by Geoffrey Johnson, Oxford University Press, 1957, *New Poems, 1958*, edited by Bonamy Dobree and others, Transatlantic, 1958, *The School Book of Modern Verse*, edited by Guy Boas, Macmillan, 1962, *The Albermarle Book of Modern Verse for Schools*, edited by Frederick E.S. Finn, J. Murray, 1962, *Commonwealth Poems of Today*, edited by Howard Sergeant, J. Murray, 1967, *Poems from Hospital*, edited by J. Sergeant and Howard Sergeant, Allen & Unwin, 1968, *Without Adam: The Femina Anthology*, edited by M.M. Simpson and J.M. Simpson, Femina, 1968, and *The Voice of Poetry*, edited by Hermann Peschmann, Evans Brothers, 1969. Contributor of articles and poems to *Observer, John O'London's, Adelphi, Books and Bookmen, Country*

Life, Time and Tide, and other journals. Editor, *English* (journal of the English Association), 1954—.

AVOCATIONAL INTERESTS: Music and foreign travel.

* * *

WILSON, Helen Helga (Mayne)

PERSONAL: Born in Zeehan, Tasmania, Australia; daughter of William C. and Florence (Miller) Mayne; married Edward Lionel Wilson (a chartered accountant), 1927; children: Peter, Margaret Wilson Hamersley, Warwick. *Education:* University of Western Australia, B.A. *Home:* 40 Bower St., Manly, 2095, New South Wales, Australia. *Agent:* Babette Johnson, 4a Alfred Rd., Woolwich, 2110, New South Wales, Australia.

CAREER: Free-lance writer. International Federation of University Women, delegate to Economic Commission for Asia and Far East conference, New Delhi, India, 1961. *Member:* Australian Federation of University Women, Fellowship of Australian Writers (executive board). *Awards, honors:* Ten awards for short stories in Australian literary competitions.

WRITINGS: Occasional Verse, 1942-1943, Patersons, 1945; *Quiet, Brat!* (novel), R. Hale, 1958, abridged edition published as *The Flames of Love,* Corgi, 1960; *The Golden Age* (novel), R. Hale, 1960; *Where the Wind's Feet Shine* (novel), R. Hale, 1960; *If Golde Rust* (novel), R. Hale, 1961; *Doctor Under Suspicion* (novel), Horwitz, 1963; *Gateways to Gold* (history), Verry, 1969; *A Show of Colours* (short stories), London Publishing Co. (Perth), 1970; *Westward Gold* (history), Rigby (Adelaide), 1973. Author of serials, articles, radio scripts, and over one hundred short stories. Contributor of short stories to seven anthologies in England, Australia, and America.

WORK IN PROGRESS: A third history of the Western Australia goldfield.

SIDELIGHTS: Mrs. Wilson's short story, "The Skedule," will be made into a motion picture in London, England, by Ted Willis Associates. She has traveled in Europe, the Far East, the Near East, Iran, Turkey, Troy, Gallipoli, and America; her stories have been published in England, America, Denmark, Norway, South Africa, and Australia.

* * *

WILSON, John Boyd 1928-

PERSONAL: Born October 6, 1928, in London, England; son of Percy Edward (a clergyman) and Emily Priscilla Mary (Parker) Wilson; married Sophia McKenna, July 3, 1965. *Education:* Attended Winchester College; New College, Oxford, M.A. and B.A., 1954. *Religion:* Anglican. *Home:* 53, Old High St., Headington, Oxford, England.

CAREER: King's School, Canterbury, England, second master, 1959-62; University of Trinity College, Toronto, Ontario, professor of religious knowledge, 1962-63; University of Sussex, Brighton, England, lecturer in philosophy, 1963-65; Farmington Trust Research Unit, Oxford, England, director 1965-72; Department of Educational Studies, Oxford University, Oxford, lecturer and tutor, 1972—; Warborough Trust Research Unit, director, 1973—.

WRITINGS: Language and the Pursuit of Truth, Cambridge University Press, 1956; *Canoeing Down the Rhone,* Chapman & Hall, 1957; *Language and Christian Belief,* St. Martin's, 1958; *The Truth of Religion,* S.P.C.K., 1958; (with Clive Parsons) *A Basic Latin Vocabulary: The First 1000 Words,* Macmillan, 1960;

Reason and Morals, Cambridge University Press, 1961; *Philosophy and Religion: The Logic of Christian Belief,* Oxford University Press, 1961; *Public Schools and Private Practice,* Allen & Unwin, 1962; (editor) *The Faith of an Artist,* Allen & Unwin, 1962; *Thinking with Concepts,* Cambridge University Press, 1963; (with Max Cary) *A Shorter History of Rome,* St. Martin's, 1963; *Logic and Sexual Morality,* Penguin, 1965; *Equality,* Harcourt, 1966; (with Ludwig Bieler) *History of Roman Literature,* St. Martin's, 1966; *Philosophy: Thinking About Meaning,* Heinemann, 1968; *Education and the Concept of Mental Health,* Humanities, 1969; *Moral Education and the Curriculum,* Pergamon, 1969; *Approach to Religious Education,* Farmington Trust, 1970; *Education in Religion and the Emotions,* Heinemann, 1971, Hillary, 1972; *Religion,* Heinemann, 1972; *Ideals,* Lutterworth, 1972; *Philosophy and Educational Research,* National Foundation for Educational Research, 1973; *The Advancement of Morality,* National Foundation for Educational Research, 1973. Contributor to *Mind, Hibbert Journal,* and *Philosophy.*

WORK IN PROGRESS: Research in the problems in philosophy of education, the problems of moral philosophy, and moral education.

SIDELIGHTS: Wilson is competent in French, Greek, and Latin, and knows some Spanish and German. *Avocational interests:* Travel by water, particularly to the Mediterranean.

BIOGRAPHICAL/CRITICAL SOURCES: Carleton Miscellany, spring, 1967.

* * *

WILSON, Wesley M. 1927-

PERSONAL: Born June 21, 1927, in Mangum, Okla.; son of Frank H. (a farmer) and Fern (McCool) Wilson; married Marjorie H. Montague (a physician), September 7, 1957; children: Larry A., Bruce A. *Education:* Illinois Institute of Technology, B.S., 1953; University of Chicago, M.B.A., 1954; University of Washington, Seattle, Wash., LL.B., 1960. *Politics:* Democrat. *Religion:* Protestant. *Home:* 1403 South First Ave., Yakima, Wash. 98902. *Office:* 321 Miller Bldg., Yakima, Wash. 98901.

CAREER: American Telephone and Telegraph Co., Chicago, Ill., repeaterman, 1948-50; Western Electric Co., Chicago, Ill., equipment engineer, 1952-54; West Coast Telephone Co., Everett, Wash., personnel assistant, 1954-56, personnel director, 1956-57; National Labor Relations Board, Seattle, Wash., attorney, 1960-69; private practice of labor law, 1970—. Donworth & Associates, Seattle, Wash., management consultant, 1957-58; University of Washington, Seattle, Wash., evening school instructor in personnel management, 1958. *Military service:* U.S. Maritime Service, 1945; U.S. Merchant Marine, 1945-46; U.S. Army Signal Corps, 1946-48. *Member:* American Civil Liberties Union, Washington State Bar Association, Seattle-King County Bar Association (secretary, labor law section), Seattle Mountaineers.

WRITINGS: Labor Law Handbook, Bobbs-Merrill, 1963.

WORK IN PROGRESS: Supplementary material for *Labor Law Handbook.*

AVOCATIONAL INTERESTS: Camping, hiking, fishing, boating, skiing.

* * *

WILTZ, John Edward 1930-

PERSONAL: Born August 21, 1930, in Fairfield, Ill.; son of John Franklin (a locomotive engineer) and Lola Daniels) Wiltz; married Susan Wycoff Stark, June 6, 1955; children: Margaret Ellen, John Franklin, Mary Theresia, Catherine Clare, Jennie Annie, Paul Louis,

Thomas Daniels, James Philip. *Education:* Marquette University, student, 1948-50; University of Kentucky, A.B., 1954, M.A., 1955, Ph.D., 1959. *Politics:* Democrat. *Religion:* Roman Catholic. *Home:* 114 Glenwood Ave., West Bloomington, Ind. 47401. *Office:* Department of History, Indiana University, Bloomington, Ind. 47401.

CAREER: Indiana University, Bloomington, lecturer, 1958-59, instructor, 1959-62, assistant professor, 1962-65, associate professor of history, 1965—. Visiting lecturer in history, University of the West Indies, 1965-66; guest professor of history, University of Hamburg, 1970-71. *Military service:* U.S. Army, 1951-53; became sergeant first class. U.S. Army Reserve, 1953-60; became first lieutenant. *Member:* American Historical Association, Organization of American Historians, American Federation of Teachers.

WRITINGS: In Search of Peace: The Senate Munitions Inquiry, 1934-36, Louisiana State University Press, 1963; (with Robert H. Ferrell and Maurice G. Baxter) *The Teaching of American History in High Schools*, Indiana University Press, 1964; *Books in American History: A Basic List for High Schools*, Indiana University Press, 1964; *From Isolation to War, 1931-1941*, Crowell, 1968; *The Search for Identity: Modern American History*, Lippincott, 1973.

WORK IN PROGRESS: A history of the U.S. in the 1960's.

* * *

WINDAL, Floyd W(esley)   1930-

PERSONAL: Born September 23, 1930, in Bradley, Ill.; son of Floyd and Marguerite (Meyer) Windal. *Education:* University of Illinois, B.S., 1952, M.S., 1955, Ph.D., 1959. *Religion:* Christian Scientist. *Home:* 305 St. George Dr., Athens, Ga. 30601. *Office:* Department of Accounting and Business Law, University of Georgia, Athens, Ga. 30602.

CAREER: Arthur Andersen and Co. (certified public accountants), Chicago, Ill., audit staff, 1952; University of Illinois, Urbana, instructor in accountancy, 1956-58; Arthur Andersen and Co., Los Angeles, Calif., member of audit staff, 1958-59; Michigan State University, East Lansing, assistant professor, 1959-63, associate professor, 1963-69, professor of accounting, 1969-72; University of Georgia, Athens, professor of accounting, and head of department of accounting and business law, 1972—. *Military service:* U.S. Army, Quartermaster Corps, 1952-54; became first lieutenant. *Member:* American Accounting Association, American Institute of Certified Public Accountants, National Association of Accountants, Michigan Association of Certified Public Accountants, Georgia Society of Certified Public Accountants.

WRITINGS: The Accounting Concept of Realization, Bureau of Business and Economic Research, Graduate School of Business Administration, Michigan State University, 1961. Contributor to professional journals.

SIDELIGHTS: Windal is very much interested in sports; he participates actively in golf and tennis.

* * *

WINEHOUSE, Irwin   1922-

PERSONAL: Born May 13, 1922, in New York, N.Y.; son of Abraham (a sales executive) and Lena (Dennerstein) Winehouse; married Angelina DeMichael (a model), June 24, 1950. *Education:* Hamilton College, student, 1943; New York University, B.A., 1946. *Home:* 99 Comstock Hill Ave., Silvermine, Norwalk, Conn. 06850. *Office:* Julian Messner, Inc., 8 West 40th St., New York, N.Y. 10018.

CAREER: Free-lance magazine writer in New York, N.Y., 1946-55; television and screen writer, Hollywood, Calif., 1955-62; Julian Messner, Inc. (book publishers), New York, N.Y., director of trade sales and promotion, 1962—. President, Young Moderns, Inc. vice-president, Cathedral Press. *Military service:* U.S. Army, Infantry, 1943-46. *Member:* Writers Guild of America. *Awards, honors:* Wrangler Award from National Cowboy Hall of Fame for outstanding television script of year, 1963, for "John Stetson Story" in Death Valley Days" series.

WRITINGS: The Assemblies of God, Vantage, 1959; *The Duke Snider Story*, Messner, 1964; (with Sam Crowther) *Highway Robbery*, Stein & Day, 1966. Author of more than fifty original television and screen stories, including "Blueprint for Robbery" for Paramount, 1961, and "The Naked Brigade" for Universal-International, 1964. Contributor to magazines.

WORK IN PROGRESS: A biography of Pontiac, the Indian chief; an original screen comedy; a Western film drama based upon the explosive penal system at Huntsville, Tex. during 1870's.†

* * *

WINGATE, John Williams   1899-

PERSONAL: Born February 7, 1899, in Talas, Turkey; son of Henry Knowles (a missionary) and Jane (Smith) Wingate; married Isabel L. Barnum (a professor), June 22, 1925; children: Elaine (Mrs. William K. Gay), John Barnum. *Education:* Carleton College, A.B., 1921; New York University, M.S., 1923, D.C.S., 1931. *Politics:* Republican. *Religion:* Congregationalist. *Home:* 15 East 10th St., New York, N.Y. 10003. *Office:* Baruch College, City University of New York, 17 Lexington Ave., New York, N.Y. 10010.

CAREER: New York University, School of Retailing, New York, N.Y., 1923-45, started as instructor, became professor; Washington University, St. Louis, Mo., professor of retailing, 1945-46; College of City of New York, Baruch School of Business and Public Administration (now Baruch College of the City University of New York), New York, N.Y., professor of business administration, 1946—, chairman of department, 1964-68, director of Evening Division, 1951-54, professor of marketing emeritus, 1968—. National Cancer Foundation, founding member, trustee, and vice-president, 1959-62, president, 1968—. Trustee and chairman of executive committee, American Society for Psychical Research, 1968—; trustee, Housing Development Corp. of Council of Churches of the City of New York. *Member:* American Marketing Association, American Economic Association, American Collegiate Retailing Association (founding member; president, 1955-57), American Association of University Professors, Phi Beta Kappa, Beta Gamma Sigma, Delta Sigma Rho, Eta Mu Pi, Sigma Alpha, Alpha Phi Omega. *Awards, honors:* Elected to first roster of Hall of Fame in Distribution, Boston Conference on Distribution, 1953.

WRITINGS: (With Norris A. Brisco) *Retail Buying*, Prentice-Hall, 1925, sole author of three revised editions, published as *Buying for Retail Stores*, 1937-60, 4th edition, completely revised (with Joseph S. Friedlander), published as *The Management of Retail Buying*, 1963; (with Brisco) *Retail Receiving Practice*, Prentice-Hall, 1925; (with Elmer O. Schaller) *Problems in Retail Merchandising*, Prentice-Hall, 1931, 5th edition (with Schaller and Irving Goldenthal), 1961; *Manual of Retail Terms*, Prentice-Hall, 1931; *Retail Merchandise Control*, Prentice-Hall, 1933; *Retail Buying Under the Robinson-Patman Act*, School of Retailing, New York University, 1937; (with Brisco) *Elements of Retail Merchandising*, Prentice-Hall, 1938, revised and enlarged edition (with

Schaller) published as *Techniques of Retail Merchandising*, 1950, 3rd edition, 1956; (with Schaller and Goldenthal) *A Workbook for Retail Buying and Marketing* (designed to accompany *Buying for Retail Stores*), Prentice-Hall, 1939, 3rd edition, 1954; (with Rea Gillespie Walters) *Fundamentals of Selling: Meeting Consumer Demand*, 4th edition (Wingate was not associated with earlier editions under different titles), South-Western, 1942, 7th edition (with Carroll A. Nolan), 1959, 9th edition, 1969; (with Walters and E.J. Rowse) *Retail Merchandising*, 3rd edition (Wingate was not associated with earlier editions under different titles), South-Western, 1943, 5th edition (with J. Dana Weiner), 1957, 7th edition (with Harland E. Samson), 1968; (editor with Arnold Corbin) *Changing Patterns in Retailing: Readings on Current Trends*, Irwin, 1956; *Management Audit for Small Retailers*, Small Business Administration (Washington, D.C.), 1964; (with Seymour Helfant) *Small Store Planning for Growth*, Small Business Administration, 1966; (with others) *Retail Merchandise Management*, Prentice-Hall, 1972.

Retailing manuals published by School of Retailing, New York University: (with Irving Goldenthal and Norris A. Brisco) *Sixty Questions and Answers in Regard to the New York City Sales Tax, Including the 293 Communities and Subdivisions of the City of New York*, 1935, (editor with Brisco) Nancy H. Bowman, *Successful Fashion Shows*, 1938, (with Selma Annette Kahn) *Merchandising Manual for the Corset Department*, 1939, (with V.S. Putter, Charles Mundy, Jr., and W.H. Howard) *Promoting the Linen, Domestics, and Blanket Department*, c.1945.

Contributor to encyclopedias, yearbooks, and trade journals. Founder and former editor, *Journal of Retailing;* founder and current editor, *New York Retailer*.

AVOCATIONAL INTERESTS: Psychical research.

* * *

WINSBOROUGH, Hal (Liman) H. 1932-

PERSONAL: Born April 13, 1932, in St. Louis, Mo.; son of Hallman P. and Jean (Herrin) Winsborough; married Shirley Hale, 1956; children: William Hale, Edward Hale. *Education:* University of Chicago, A.B., 1952, M.A., 1959, Ph.D., 1961. *Home:* 2218 Hillington Green, Madison, Wis. 53705. *Office:* Center for Demography, University of Wisconsin, Madison, Wis. 53706.

CAREER: University of Chicago, Chicago, Ill., assistant to director of development research, 1954-56, research assistant, 1956-60; Ohio State University, Columbus, assistant professor, 1960-62; Duke University, Durham, N.C., began as assistant professor, became associate professor, 1962-67; University of Wisconsin, Madison, professor, 1967—. *Military service:* U.S. Army, 1952-54; became corporal. *Member:* American Association for the Advancement of Science, American Sociological Association, American Statistical Association, Population Association of America, Regional Science Association.

WRITINGS: Metropolis and Region, Johns Hopkins Press, 1960. Contributor to professional journals.

* * *

WINTERS, John D(avid) 1917-

PERSONAL: Born December 23, 1917, in McCool, Miss.; son of John D. and Estrella (Fancher) Winters; married Frances Locke (a librarian), January 26, 1950. *Education:* Louisiana State University, B.A., 1939, M.A., 1948, Ph.D., 1966; special courses at Rollins College, 1943, Harvard University, 1943-44. *Politics:* Democrat. *Religion:* Methodist. *Office:* History Department, Louisiana Tech University, Box 4761, Tech Station, Ruston, La. 71270.

CAREER: Louisiana Polytechnic Institute (now Louisiana Tech University), Ruston, 1948—, now professor of history. *Military service:* U.S. Army, 1941-45. *Member:* Organization of American Historians, Southern Historical Association, Southwestern Social Sciences Association, Louisiana Historical Association, North Louisiana Historical Association. *Awards, honors:* Award from Louisiana Library Association, 1963, for *The Civil War in Louisiana.*

WRITINGS: The Civil War in Louisiana, Louisiana State University Press, 1963; (with Hodding Carter and Walter Lowrey) *The Rivers and Bayous of Louisiana*, edited by Edwin A. Davis, Louisiana Education Research Association, 1968.

WORK IN PROGRESS: Portrait of a Republican: A Biography of W.C.C. Claiborne, for Louisiana State University Press.

AVOCATIONAL INTERESTS: Skin diving, swimming, oil painting, gardening.

* * *

WINTON, Calhoun 1927-

PERSONAL: Born January 21, 1927, at Fort Benning, Ga.; son of George P. (a colonel, U.S. Army) and Dorothy (Calhoun) Winton; married Elizabeth Myers, June 30, 1948; children: Jefferys Hobart, William Calhoun. *Education:* University of the South, A.B., 1948; Vanderbilt University, M.A., 1950; Princeton University, M.A., 1954, Ph.D., 1955. *Politics:* Democrat. *Religion:* Episcopalian. *Home:* 3600 Chateau Dr., Apt. 142, Columbia, S.C. 29204. *Office:* Department of English, University of South Carolina, Columbia, S.C. 29208.

CAREER: Dartmouth College, Hanover, N.H., instructor in English, 1954-57; University of Virginia, Charlottesville, assistant professor of English, 1957-60; University of Delaware, Newark, Henry F. duPont Winterthur Associate Professor of English and coordinator of Winterthur graduate program, 1960-67; University of South Carolina, Columbia, professor of English and head of department, 1967—. *Military service:* U.S. Naval Reserve, 1943—, on active duty 1943-47, 1950-52; now captain. *Member:* Modern Language Association of America, American Studies Association, English Institute, Johnson Society, Conference on British Studies. *Awards, honors:* Guggenheim fellowship, 1965-66.

WRITINGS: Captain Steele: The Early Career of Richard Steele, Johns Hopkins Press, 1964; (editor) Richard Steele, *The Tender Husband*, University of Nebraska Press, 1967; *Sir Richard Steele, M.P.: The Later Career*, Johns Hopkins Press, 1970. Contributor of critical articles to professional journals.

WORK IN PROGRESS: First volume of a social history of the English novel (Defoe to Smollett), for Routledge & Kegan Paul, completion expected in 1974.

* * *

WINWARD, Stephen Frederick 1911-

PERSONAL: Born February 12, 1911, in Tarporley, Cheshire, England; son of Samuel and Jessie (Walley) Winward; married Marjorie Alice Cropp, July 22, 1939; children: Christopher, David John. *Education:* University of London, B.D.; Oxford University, M.A. *Home:* 88 Trinity Rd., Sutton Coldfield, Warwickshire, England.

CAREER: Baptist minister. Pastor of Highams Park Baptist Church, London, England, 1938-1966, of Sutton Coldfield Baptist Church, Warwickshire, England, 1967—.

WRITINGS: The New Testament Teaching on Baptism, Carey Kingsgate Press, 1952; *Responsive Praises and Prayers for Minister and Congregation*, Hodder &

Stoughton, 1958; (with E.A. Payne) *Orders and Prayers for Church Worship: A Manual for Ministers,* Carey Kingsgate Press, 1960, 3rd edition (with James W. Cox) published as *Minister's Worship Manual: Orders and Prayers for Worship,* World Publishing, 1969; *Teach Yourself to Pray,* Harper, 1961; *The Truth and the Life,* Hodder & Stoughton, 1963; *The Reformation of Our Worship,* Carey Kingsgate Press, 1964, John Knox, 1965; *A Modern ABeCedary for Protestants,* Association Press, 1964; *Responsive Service Book,* Hodder & Stoughton, 1965; *A Guide to the Prophets,* Hodder & Stoughton, 1968, John Knox, 1969; *Your Baptism,* Baptist Union, 1969; *Your Five Senses,* Lakeland Paperbacks, 1971.

With G.C. Robinson: *The Way,* C.S.S.M., 1945; *Here is the Answer,* Marshall, Morgan & Scott, 1949, Judson, 1970; *The Art of Living,* Henry E. Walter, 1951, 3rd edition, 1954; *Colony of Heaven,* Henry E. Walter, 1954; *The King's Business,* C.S.S.M., 1957; *The Christian's Conduct,* C.S.S.M., 1960; *Companions of the Way,* C.S.S.M., 1962; *Our Returning King,* Henry E. Walter, 1962; *In the Holy Land,* Scripture Union and C.S.S.M., 1963, Eerdmans, 1968; (compilers) *Prayers for School Youth Groups, Church Services, and Personal Use,* Scripture Union, 1967. Also author of several pamphlets on religious subjects for Carey Kingsgate Press and *Crusade.*

*   *   *

WISBESKI, Dorothy (Cecilia Gross)   1929-

PERSONAL: Born July 24, 1929, in Elizabeth, N.J.; daughter of Frank (a cabinet and coffin maker) and Katherine (Wojciak) Gross; married Louis Wisbeski (a carpenter), September 11, 1954. *Education:* Newark State College, B.S. in Ed., 1950; Rutgers University, graduate study, 1951-52. *Religion:* Catholic. *Home:* 201 High St., South Bound Brook, N.J. 08880. *Office:* Bound Brook Memorial Library, 108 Hamilton St., Bound Brook, N.J. 08805.

CAREER: Edison Township (N.J.) public schools, teacher, 1950-51; Bound Brook (N.J.) Memorial Library, children's librarian, 1951—. *Member:* National Wildlife Federation, National Catholic Society for Animal Welfare, New York Zoological Society, New Jersey Library Association, Somerset County Dog Obedience Club (training secretary).

WRITINGS: Okee: The Story of an Otter in the House, Farrar, Straus, 1964 (published in England as *An Otter in the House: The Story of Okee,* Methuen, 1965); (compiler with Lura A. Backer) *Tomahawks, Tomatoes, Technology: A New Jersey Tercentenary Bibliography,* Bound Brook Memorial Library, 1964; *The True Story of Okee the Otter* (juvenile), Farrar, Straus, 1967; *Picaro, a Pet Otter,* Hawthorn, 1971.

WORK IN PROGRESS: A picture book, *Tweeter, the Groundhog;* preparing illustrations for Lorna Beer's fantasy, *The Fish That Lived in Mr. Haskell's Brook;* an otter book for young children.

AVOCATIONAL INTERESTS: Animals—wild and domestic, and painting and drawing them; handicrafts.

BIOGRAPHICAL/CRITICAL SOURCES: Bound Brook Chronicle, Bound Brook, N.J., April 2, 1964.†

*   *   *

WISE, Arthur   1923-
(John McArthur)

PERSONAL: Born January 12, 1923, in York, England; son of Arthur (a policeman) and Edith Mary (Hobson) Wise; married Lilian Nanette Gregg (a writer and teacher), September 6, 1947; children: John Christopher, Susan, Julia. *Education:* Attended Bootham School,

1934-39; Central School of Speech and Drama, diploma in speech and drama, 1949; University of London, diploma in dramatic art, 1949; International Phonetics Association, certificate. *Home:* Birchinlea, 453 Strensall Rd., York YO3 8TA, England. *Agent:* Busby and Rose, 76 New Oxford St., London WC1A 1EU, England.

CAREER: Theatre Royal, Leicester, England, actor, 1949; Norfolk Education Committee, Norfolk, England, assistant county drama organizer, 1950-52; College of Housecraft, Leeds, England, lecturer in speech and drama, 1952-54; University of Leeds, Leeds, England, lecturer in speech education, 1953-69. University of Durham, chief examiner of spoken English, 1959-64; University of London, chief examiner of spoken English, 1963-68. Consultant on theatrical weapons, 1950—. Swords of York Ltd., York, England, director, 1963—. *Military service:* Royal Air Force, served as fighter pilot in the United States, Canada, West Africa, Middle East, Corsica, and Italy, 1941-46. *Member:* Society of Teachers of Speech and Drama (council member, 1955-58), Society of Arms and Armour, Society of Authors. *Awards, honors:* Yorkshire Television Award, 1970, for "Go to Work on a Pig."

WRITINGS: (Under pseudonym John McArthur) *Days in the Hay,* Cassell, 1960; *The Little Fishes,* Gollancz, 1961; (under pseudonym John McArthur) *How Now Brown Cow,* Cassell, 1962; *The Death's Head,* Cassell, 1962; *Reading and Talking in English,* Harrap, 1964; *Communication in Speech,* Longmans, Green, 1965, Humanities, 1967; *Spoken English for C.S.E.: A Course in Speech Education for the Secondary School,* Harrap, 1966; *Your Speech,* Longmans, Green, 1966; *Talking Together: A Course in Speech Education for the Primary School,* Harrap, 1968; *Weapons in the Theatre,* Longmans, Green, 1968, Barnes & Noble, 1969; *The Day the Queen Flew to Scotland for the Grouse Shooting,* Cavalier, 1968; *Leatherjacket* (mystery novel), Weidenfeld & Nicolson, 1970; (with Sid Chaplin) *Us Northerners,* Harrap, 1970; *Who Killed Enoch Powell?* (mystery novel), Weidenfeld & Nicolson, 1970, Harper, 1971; (with wife, Nan Wise) *Talking for Management: A Practical Course in Oral Communication,* Pitman, 1971; *The Art and History of Personal Combat,* Hugh Evelyn, 1971, New York Graphic Society, 1972.

Plays: "The Admirable History of St. Ethelstone"; "After the Ball"; "The Museum Keeper's Daughter"; "The Lost Leeds Bus"; "Bingle's Balloon"; "Penny for The Guy"; "Go to Work on a Pig." Contributor to *Times Educational Supplement, Guardian,* and to speech and drama journals.

WORK IN PROGRESS: A History of Stunting, to be published by Constable; *The Naughty Girls.*

SIDELIGHTS: Wise writes that he is "fanatically interested in the use of weapons in the theater." He has visited continental Europe on camping expeditions.

BIOGRAPHICAL/CRITICAL SOURCES: John O'London's, July 14, 1960; *Daily Express,* London, England, October 25, 1961; *Yorkshire Post,* October 14, 1963; *Observer Review,* September 1, 1968; *Drama,* spring, 1969.

*   *   *

WISLER, Gene C(harles)   1920-

PERSONAL: Born July 11, 1920, in Newton, Kan.; son of Charles Smith and Rena (Beck) Wisler; married Helen Jane Boyes, 1944; children: Helen Kay, Carolyn Jeanne. *Education:* Attended College of Idaho, 1938-41, 1946; San Jose State College, A.B.; University of Minnesota, M.A.; University of Southern California, postgraduate student, 1952; University of Oregon, Ed.D. *Religion:* Presbyterian. *Home:* 2530 East Canal Dr., Turlock,

Calif. 95380. *Office:* Stanislaus State College, 800 Monte Vista, Turlock, Calif. 95380.

CAREER: High school teacher, Sonora, Calif., 1947-49; College of Idaho, Caldwell, teacher and administrator, 1950-57; University of Oregon, Eugene, teacher, 1955; San Francisco State College, teacher and administrator, 1957-63; Stanislaus State College, Turlock, Calif., teacher and administrator, 1963—. *Military service:* U.S. Army, Infantry, 1941-45; became technical sergeant. *Member:* Music Educators National Conference (Idaho State chairman of student members, 1953), Association of California State College Professors, California Teachers Association, Phi Delta Kappa, Kiwanis Club.

WRITINGS: Music Fundamentals for the Classroom Teacher, Allyn & Bacon, 1961, 3rd edition, 1971.

* * *

WITTKOFSKI, Joseph Nicholas 1912-

PERSONAL: Born September 9, 1912, in Findlay, Ohio; son of Joseph (a railroad engineer) and Mary Louise (Thiry) Wittkofski; married Laura Filmyer, February 1, 1943; children: Mary Louise, Joseph Filmyer, John Mark, Edward Louis. *Education:* Attended St. Joseph's College, Rensselaer, Ind., 1926-32; St. Gregory Seminary, Cincinnati, Ohio, B.A., 1934; attended Maryknoll Seminary, Ossining, N.Y., 1935-39, University of Illinois, 1939-40; Fordham University, M.S., 1942. *Politics:* Republican. *Home:* 509 Sixth St., Charleroi, Pa. 15022. *Agent:* Daniel S. Mead, 915 Broadway, New York, N.Y. 10010.

CAREER: Ordained a Roman Catholic priest, 1939; received into Episcopal church, 1943. Venard College, Clarks Summit, Pa., instructor in biological sciences, 1940-43; St. Mary's Episcopal Church, Charleroi, Pa., rector, 1944—, director, spiritual healing center and institute of Christian psychotherapy, 1963—; Braid Institute, Pittsburgh, Pa., director of pastoral training, 1959—. Elevated to be Canon to the Ordinary, Diocese of Pittsburgh, 1962. Chaplain, Senate of Pennsylvania, 1959, 1963. *Military service:* U.S. Army, 1940.

MEMBER: Academy of Religion and Mental Health, Society for the Scientific Study of Religion, American Association of Religious Therapists, Institute of Pastoral Care, Spiritual Frontiers Fellowship, Anglican Society, American Church Union, American Legion (Pennsylvania state chaplain, 1955-56), 40 & 8 Society (Pennsylvania state chaplain, 1952-53), United American Mechanics, Charleroi Chamber of Commerce, Charleroi Ministerial Association (president, 1950-56), Old Guard (Philadelphia).

WRITINGS: (Co-author) *Pittsburgh Plan of Religious Education,* Esquire Press, 1948; *The Secret Way,* Morehouse, 1949; *Little Book of Contemplation,* Morehouse, 1950; (with Demas Barnes) *Unity in Faith,* Esquire Press, 1953; *The Pastoral Use of Hypnotic Technique,* Macmillan, 1960.

Contributor: D.W. Soper, editor, *These Found the Way: Thirteen Converts to Protestant Christianity,* Westminster, 1951; J.A. Pike, editor, *Modern Canterbury Pilgrims and Why They Chose the Episcopal Church,* Morehouse, 1956. Contributor of more than four hundred articles, booklets, poems to religious and secular magazines and Forward Movement of Episcopal Church. Editor, *Church News of the Diocese of Pittsburgh,* 1946-48.

WORK IN PROGRESS: Call to Revolution, about degenerate forms of current religion and proposals for a real Christian revolution; *Mystic of Tarsus,* about the spiritual teaching of St. Paul against background of ex-istentialism and new pastoral psychology; *I Can Give You What You Want.*

SIDELIGHTS: Wittkofski is interested in the mission of the church in industrial areas, pastoral consultation and religious therapy, and training clergy in pastoral psychology. In early 1964, he conducted a speaking tour in the province of Ontario, Canada, to challenge the law which prohibits clergymen from practicing hypnotism.†

* * *

WITTON-DAVIES, Carl(yle) 1913-

PERSONAL: Born June 10, 1913, in Bangor, Caernarvonshire, Wales; son of Thomas Witton (a university professor) and Hilda Mabel (Everett) Davies; married Mary Rees (now a part-time teacher), July 2, 1941; children: Bridget, Catherine, Anne, David, Edward Eugene, Frances Faith, Godfrey Giles Gerallt. *Education:* University College of North Wales, B.A., 1934; Exeter College, Oxford, B.A., 1937, M.A., 1940. *Home:* Archdeacon's Lodging, Christ Church, Oxford, England.

CAREER: Anglican clergyman, ordained in Wales, serving as assistant curate of Buckley, 1937-40, subwarden of St. Michael's College, Llandaff, 1940-44, adviser on Judaica to Anglican bishop in Jerusalem, canon of Nazareth, Palestine, 1944-49, dean of St. David's Cathedral, 1950-57; archdeacon of Oxford and canon of Christ Church, 1957—. Examining chaplain to bishop in Jerusalem and bishops of Monmouth, St. David's and Oxford. Chairman of Council of Christians and Jews, 1957—, Clergy Friendly Society, 1959-62. *Awards, honors:* Chaplain, Order of St. John of Jerusalem.

WRITINGS: (Translator) Martin Buber, *Hasidism,* Philosophical Library, 1948; (translator) Martin Buber, *The Prophetic Faith,* Macmillan, 1949; *Journey of a Lifetime,* Arthur Barker, 1962.

Contributor: F.L. Cross, editor, *Oxford Dictionary of the Christian Church,* Oxford University Press, 1957; Jacob Baal-Teshuva, editor, *The Mission of Israel,* Speller, 1963. Contributor of reviews to religious journals.

WORK IN PROGRESS: Writing on Hosea in "World Christian Books."

* * *

**WOJCIECHOWSKA, Maia (Teresa) 1927-
(Maia Larkin, Maia Rodman)**

PERSONAL: Surname is pronounced Voi-che-*hov*-skah; born August 7, 1927, in Warsaw, Poland; came to U.S. in 1942, naturalized, 1950; daughter of Zygmunt (wartime chief-of-staff, Polish Air Force) and Zofia (Rudakowska) Wojciechowska; married Selden Rodman (a writer), December 8, 1950 (divorced, 1957); married Richard Larkin (poet and antique restorer), January 9, 1972; children: (first marriage) Oriana (a daughter). *Education:* Attended schools in Poland, France, and England, Sacred Heart Academy, Los Angeles, Calif., and Immaculate Heart College. *Politics:* "Ethical Anarchist". *Religion:* Roman Catholic. *Home:* 239 East 86th St., New York, N.Y. *Office:* c/o Harcourt Brace & Jovanovich, 750 Third Ave., New York, N.Y. 10017. *Agent:* Jay Sanford, International Famous Agency, 1301 Ave. of the Americas, New York, N.Y. 10019.

CAREER: Has worked at a variety of jobs ("a record of seventy-two jobs in one year"), including undercover detective, restaurant hostess, masseuse, professional tennis player and instructor, ghost writer, translator for Radio Free Europe, and waitress. *Newsweek,* New York, N.Y., copygirl, 1956; *RWDSU Record* (labor newspaper), New York, N.Y., assistant editor, 1957; *American Hairdresser* (trade publication), New York, N.Y., assistant editor, 1958-60; Kurt Hellmer, New York,

N.Y., literary agent, 1960-61; operated her own literary agency, 1960-61; Hawthorn Books, Inc., New York, N.Y., publicity manager, 1960-62. *Awards, honors: New York Herald Tribune* Children's Spring Book Festival Awards honor book, 1964, and Newbery Medal, 1965, both for *Shadow of a Bull.*

WRITINGS: (Under name Maia Rodman) *Market Day for 'Ti Andre* (juvenile), Viking, 1952; (under name Maia Rodman) *The Loved Look: International Hairstyling Guide,* American Hairdresser, 1960; *Shadow of a Bull* (juvenile), Atheneum, 1964; (under name Maia Rodman) *Odyssey of Courage: The Story of Alvar Nunez Cabeza de Vaca* (juvenile biography), Atheneum, 1965; *A Kingdom in a Horse,* Harper, 1965; *The Hollywood Kid* (young adult novel), Harper, 1966; (author of foreword) P.H. Newby, *The Spirit of Jem,* Delacorte, 1967; *A Single Light* (juvenile), Harper, 1968; *Tuned Out* (young adult novel), Harper, 1968; *Hey, What's Wrong With This One?* (juvenile), Harper, 1969; (translator from the Polish) Monika Kotowska, *Bridge to the Other Side,* Doubleday, 1970; *Don't Play Dead Before You Have To,* Harper, 1970; *The Rotten Years,* Doubleday, 1971; *The Life and Death of a Brave Bull,* Harcourt, 1972; *Through the Broken Mirror with Alice* (juvenile; includes parts of *Through the Looking-Glass* by Lewis Carroll), Harcourt, 1972; *Till the Break of Day: Memories* (juvenile), Harcourt, 1972; *Winter Tales from Poland* (juvenile), Doubleday, 1973. Contributor of poetry to anthologies; writer of humorous pieces for *Sports Illustrated,* articles and reviews for other magazines. Translator from the Polish of a play by Slawomir Mrozek, performed Off-Broadway in 1962, and on British Broadcasting Corp. radio in 1963 and 1964.

WORK IN PROGRESS: A novel about Haiti before the Revolution, tentatively titled *Cresting of a Wave;* a collection of short stories, *Future Tense,* "with the common thread: Men's relationship to their God"; a film script; a film adaptation of *A Single Light;* with husband, Richard Larkin, *Instant Creole: A Survival Manual for Haiti.*

SIDELIGHTS: Miss Wojciechowska told *CA* that "having attended 17 different schools in one year alone (in France), there had never been a love affair between me and education. . . . While both of my brothers went through college I pretended I had to work to put them through it. That year (at 18) I held a record 72 different jobs.

"During what seems like an extremely long and adventurous life have parachuted, fought bulls, won a few tennis championships, motorcycle raced, snuck into almost every Broadway theatre in an attempt to stimulate applause even for mediocre plays, bid at numerous auctions and have been caught a few times, jaywalked out of a sense of duty to preserve some right to self determination. . .tried periodically and always unsuccessfully to be 'like everybody else' and at advanced age of 36 fell in love with a horse."

When she was ten years old, her father, a pilot, insisted upon her parachuting from a plane three times, and this was the "beginning of a lifelong affair with fear, fighting it and loving the fight." Many of her personal experiences are recorded in *Till the Break of Day: Memories.* A writer for *Horn Book* said of the autobiography: "Confession may be good for the soul, but confessional writing may not be good reading unless the penitent is blessed, as is the author of this remarkable document, with an understanding of life's absurdities, a sense of the dramatic, and a felicitous talent for precise, vivid description. Because of these qualities, her reminiscences of a turbulent adolescence during the Second World War are both intensely personal and yet recognizable as a universal statement on the tragicomic conditions which are a necessary part of maturation. . . .The book is a dazzling blend of emotional pyrotechnics and disciplined structure. A compelling and sensitive study which adds a new dimension for evaluating the author's previous works."

Shadow of a Bull is about a boy who trains to be a matador but ends up becoming a physician instead. In the opinion of the Newbery Award committee it "epitomizes all humanity's struggle for conquest of fear and knowledge of self." *Tuned Out* is the first-person (fictional) narrative of a sixteen-year-old boy's struggle with his beloved older brother, who has begun experimenting with drugs. A.M. Feagles writes that "nothing is fudged up . . . .The story is vivid enough to need no moralizing." L.P. Scanlon comments on the authenticity of mood: "The author is so skillful that the narrator's own ambivalence and anger is effectively expressed, sometimes through subtle changes in the journal's style. The book offers no pat resolution." "Maia Wojciechowska," wrote Edward Fenton in a review of *A Single Light,* "is obviously on the side of the angels. Her new book is a legend imbued with the desperation of the human need for love . . . . It concludes with a miracle of understanding and regeneration which some readers may find a little too pat."

Miss Wojciechowska is fluent in Polish, French, and Spanish, and understands Russian, Italian, Portuguese, and missal-Latin. She has traveled widely and states that her "heart adopted Andalusia as real country, Poland remains the sentimental one, and America the one out of choice and admiration."

In 1973 she told *CA:* "Having recently married a man 20 years my junior (a sometime poet and a full-time antiques restorer) I feel I have done my bit for women's lib (which I think is a diverting tactic by women who failed as mothers and wives, if not as females). I would love to live in New Mexico, for it is there, in the desert, that I could think most clearly about man's coming of age and becoming god-like. I firmly believe that the bankruptcy of our system—schools, society, family—is but the necessary evolutionary step towards that day when everyone will live in grace, in harmony with nature and in awareness of our destiny to be god-like. I also hope to live long enough to see my daughter, Oriana (a truly marvelous human being endowed, unfortunately, with a rather lousy personality) married and a mother, and belonging to a new generation of people who will value the family as the only important human unit, dispensing with the obsolete slavery to a government which evolved into a wasteful bureaucracy."

BIOGRAPHICAL/CRITICAL SOURCES: New York Times Book Review, March 22, 1964, November 24, 1968; *Horn Book,* June, 1964, December, 1972; *Saturday Review,* March 27, 1965; *Library Journal,* November 15, 1966, May 15, 1969; *Book World,* May 5, 1968; *Commonweal,* November 22, 1968.

* * *

WOLF, John B(aptist) 1907-

PERSONAL: Born July 16, 1907, in Ouray, Colo.; son of John and Anna Mae (Stadter) Wolf; married Theta Holmes (now a professor of psychology); children: John K.F. *Education:* University of Colorado, A.B., 1929, M.A., 1930; Northwestern University, postgraduate study, 1930-31; University of Minnesota, Ph.D., 1933. *Home:* 2440 Lake View, Chicago, Ill. 60614.

CAREER: University of Missouri, Columbia, instructor in history, 1934-37, assistant professor, 1937-43; University of Minnesota, Minneapolis, associate professor of history, 1943-49, professor, 1949-66; University of Illinois, Chicago, professor, 1966—, professorial lecturer, 1967—. Sorbonne, University of Paris, visiting professor, 1950-51.

Member: Societe d'Histoire Moderne, Societe de XVII Siecle, Societe d'Histoire Diplomatique, Society of French History Studies, Societe d'Archeologie Francaise, American Historical Association (chairman, European history section). *Awards, honors:* Fulbright fellow, 1950-51; Guggenheim fellow, 1959-60, 1967-68; Illinois Sesquecentennial prize ($1500) for nonfiction, 1968.

WRITINGS: Diplomatic History of the Bagdad Railroad, New York University Press, 1936, Octagon, 1972; *France, 1815 to Present,* Prentice-Hall, 1940; (reviser) Hutton Webster, *History of Civilization,* Volume 2: *Modern and Contemporary,* Heath, 1947; *The Emergence of the Great Powers, 1685-1715,* Harper, 1951, 2nd edition, 1959; *The Emergence of European Civilization: From the Middle Ages to the Opening of the Nineteenth Century,* Harper, 1959; *France, 1814-1919: The Rise of a Liberal-Democratic Society,* Harper, 1963; *Louis XIV,* Norton, 1968; *Toward a European Balance of Power, 1620-1715,* Rand McNally, 1970; *Early Modern Europe,* Scott, Foresman, 1971.

Contributor: Kenneth M. Setton and H. Winkler, *Great Problems in European Civilization,* 2nd edition, Prentice-Hall, 1966; "European Civilization" series, Columbia University Press. Contributor of articles to professional journals.

WORK IN PROGRESS: The Barbary on the Seventeenth Century.

AVOCATIONAL INTERESTS: Amateur portrait painting, art, fishing, and travel.

BIOGRAPHICAL/CRITICAL SOURCES: New York Times Book Review, March 24, 1968; *New Republic,* May 25, 1968; *New York Review of Books,* June 20, 1968; *Observer Review,* July 7, 1968.

*   *   *

WOLSTEIN, Benjamin   1922-

PERSONAL: Born September 11, 1922, in Woodbine, N.J.; son of David and Rebecca (Rudnick) Wolstein; married Irma Holland (an artist), January 12, 1952. *Education:* Yeshiva College, B.A. (magna cum laude), 1944; Columbia University, M.A., 1947, Ph.D., 1949; W.A. White Institute of Psychiatry, Psychoanalysis and Psychology, certificate, 1958. *Home and office:* 2 West 67th St., New York, N.Y. 10023.

CAREER: Psychoanalyst in private practice, New York, N.Y. New School for Social Research, New York, N.Y., lecturer, 1958—; W.A. White Institute of Psychiatry, Psychoanalysis and Psychology, New York, N.Y., member of faculty, 1960—; Adelphi University, Garden City, N.Y., clinical professor, 1964—. *Member:* American Psychological Association, American Philosophical Association, W.A. White Psychoanalytic Society.

WRITINGS: Experience and Valuation, Kent Associates, 1949; *Transference: Its Structure and Function in Psychoanalytic Therapy,* Grune & Stratton, 1954, 2nd edition, 1964; *Countertransference,* Grune & Stratton, 1959; *Irrational Despair: An Examination of Existential Analysis,* Free Press, 1962; *Freedom to Experience: A Study of Psychological Change from a Psychoanalytic Point of View,* Grune & Stratton, 1965; *Theory of Psychoanalytic Therapy,* Grune & Stratton, 1967; *Human Psyche in Psychoanalysis: The Development of Three Models of Psychoanalytic Therapy,* C.C. Thomas, 1971. Contributor of reviews and papers to professional journals.

WORK IN PROGRESS: The Psychoanalytic Experience.

AVOCATIONAL INTERESTS: History of philosophy and philosophy of science.

WOOD, A(rthur) Skevington   1916-

PERSONAL: Born April 21, 1916, in Ashbourne, Derbyshire, England; son of William Arthur (a school headmaster) and May (Cooper) Wood; married Mary Fearnley, January 1, 1943. *Education:* Attended Wesley Theological College, Leeds, 1936-40; University of London. B.A., 1939; New College, Edinburgh, Ph.D., 1951. *Address:* Ridgeway, Cliff Lane, Calver, Sheffield S30 1XD, England.

CAREER: Methodist circuit minister, 1940-62; Movement for World Evangelization, West Croydon, Surrey, England, lecturer, 1962-70. Cliff College, Derbyshire, England, senior tutor in theology, 1970—. Vice-president, National Young Life Campaign. *Member:* Royal Historical Society (fellow), British Christian Endeavour Union (president, 1959-60), Society for Ecclesiastical History (founder member), Church Historical Society, Wesley Historical Society (life member), Evangelical Alliance, Evangelization Society, Victory Tract Club.

WRITINGS: Thomas Haweis, 1734-1820, S.P.C.K., for Church Historical Society, 1957; *And with Fire: Messages on Revival,* Pickering & Inglis, 1958; *Luther's Principles of Biblical Interpretation,* Tyndale Press, 1960; *The Inextinguishable Blaze: Spiritual Renewal and Advance in the Eighteenth Century,* Eerdmans, 1960; *The Bible Is History,* Bible Testimony Fellowship, 1960; *Paul's Pentecost: Studies in the Life of the Spirit from Romans 8,* Paternoster Press, 1963, published in America as *Life by the Spirit,* Zondervan, 1963; *Designed by Love: Short Studies in the Plan of Salvation,* Christian Endeavour Union, 1963; *Heralds of the Gospel: Message, Method and Motive in Preaching,* Marshall, Morgan & Scott, 1963, published in America as *The Art of Preaching: Message, Method, and Motive in Preaching,* Zondervan, 1964; *Prophecy in the Space Age: Studies in Prophetic Themes,* Zondervan, 1963; *William Grimshaw of Haworth,* Evangelical Library, 1963; *Evangelism: Its Theology and Practice,* Zondervan, 1966; *The Principles of Biblical Interpretation as Enunciated by Irenaeus, Origen, Augustine, Luther, and Calvin,* Zondervan, 1967; *The Burning Heart: John Wesley, Evangelist,* Paternoster Press, 1967, Eerdmans, 1968; *Captive to the Word: Martin Luther, Doctor of Sacred Scripture,* Eerdmans, 1969; *Signs of the Times: Biblical Prophecy and Current Events,* Lakeland Paperbacks, 1970, Baker Book, 1971.

Contributor: Tom Allan, editor, *Crusade in Scotland,* Pickering & Inglis, 1955; G.W. Kirby, editor, *Remember I Am Coming Soon: A Symposium on the Second Advent,* Victory Press, 1964; Stanley Banks, editor, *The Right Way: A Symposium of Teaching on the Way of Holiness,* Oliphants, 1964. Contributor to *Baker's Dictionary of Theology, New Bible Dictionary,* and *Dictionary of World Methodism;* contributor of articles and reviews to numerous religious journals. Contributing editor, *Christianity Today,* and *The Hour.*

WORK IN PROGRESS: Research on the rise of Anglican evangelicalism in the London area.

BIOGRAPHICAL/CRITICAL SOURCES: Encounter, autumn, 1968.

*   *   *

WOOD, E(dward) Rudolf   1907-

PERSONAL: Born February 26, 1907, in Keighley, Yorkshire, England; son of John (a hairdresser) and Kate (Hartley) Wood; married Margaret Bellamy (a playwright), April 27, 1937; children: Margaret Helen, Caroline. *Education:* University of Manchester, B.A. *Politics:* Socialist. *Religion:* Agnostic. *Home:* White House, Much Birch, Hereford, Herefordshire, England.

CAREER: High School for Boys, Hereford, England, deputy headmaster, 1950-67; retired, 1967—. *Military service:* Royal Air Force, education officer, 1941-46; became flight lieutenant; received Czechoslovak Medal of Merit, first class. *Member:* British Drama League.

WRITINGS: (With E.L. Black) *First Year English,* and successive books for second-fifth years, Blackie & Son, 1961-63.

Editor: *Short Historical Plays by Modern Authors,* Macmillan, 1938; (and author of introduction and notes) *Seven Short Plays,* Heinemann, 1956; *Specimens of Contemporary Drama,* Heinemann, 1957; *Contemporary Short Stories,* Blackie & Son, 1958; (and author of introduction) *The Windmill Books of One Act Plays,* six books, Heinemann, 1960-71.

General editor, Heinemann's "Hereford Plays": John Whiting, *Marching Song, Saint's Day,* and *A Penny for a Song;* Robert Bolt, *The Tiger and the Horse,* and *A Man for All Seasons;* John Synge, *Riders to the Sea,* and *The Playboy of the Western World;* R.C. Sherriff, *Journey's End;* J.B. Priestley, *Time and the Conways, An Inspector Calls,* and *When We Are Married;* Harold Brighouse, *Hobson's Choice;* Arthur Miller, *The Crucible, Death of a Salesman,* and *All My Sons;* Tennessee Williams, *The Glass Menagerie;* Robert Ardrey, *Thunder Rock;* Augustus Goetz and Ruth Goetz, *The Heiress;* Harley Granville-Barker, *The Voysey Inheritance;* Willis Hall, *The Long and the Short and the Tall;* Peter Ustinov, *Romanoff and Juliet;* George Farquhar, *The Recruiting Officer;* Brandon Thomas, *Charley's Aunt,* 1960-71.

*   *   *

WOOD, James Playsted   1905-
(Playsted Wood)

PERSONAL: Born December 11, 1905, in Brooklyn, N.Y.; son of William Thomas and Olive Padbury (Hicks) Wood; married Elizabeth Craig (teacher of French, Latin, and Greek), August 14, 1943. *Education:* Columbia University, A.B., 1927, M.A., 1933. *Religion:* Protestant. *Home:* 103 Atwater Rd., Springfield, Mass. 01107.

CAREER: Du Pont Manual Training High School, Louisville, Ky., teacher of English, 1930-37; Amherst College, Amherst, Mass., began as instructor, became assistant professor of English, 1937-46; Curtis Publishing Co., Philadelphia, Pa., assistant to director of research, 1946-62, managing editor, *Jack and Jill,* 1954-55, contributing editor, 1959-64; full-time writer, 1966—. Instructor, Southern Writers Workshop, University of Georgia, 1957-65. *Military service:* U.S. Army Air Forces, served in Office of Chief of Staff, General Marshall, in Pentagon, Washington, D.C., 1943-46; became major; received army commendation medal.

WRITINGS: The Presence of Everett Marsh, Bobbs-Merrill, 1937; *Magazines in the United States: Their Social and Economic Influence,* Ronald, 1949, 3rd edition, revised and enlarged, 1971; (with D.M. Hobart) *Selling Forces,* Ronald, 1952; *The Beckoning Hill,* Longmans, Green, 1952; *An Elephant in the Family,* Thomas Nelson, 1957; *Of Lasting Interest: The Story of the Reader's Digest,* Doubleday, 1958, revised edition, 1967; *The Story of Advertising,* Ronald, 1958; *Advertising and the Soul's Belly: Repetition and Memory in Advertising,* University of Georgia Press, 1961; *The Queen's Most Honorable Pirate,* Harper, 1961; *The Elephant in the Barn,* Harper, 1961; *A Hound, a Bay Horse, and a Turtle-Dove: A Life of Thoreau for the Young Reader,* Pantheon, 1963; *Trust Thyself: A Life of Ralph Waldo Emerson for the Young Reader,* Pantheon, 1964; *The Life and Words of John F. Kennedy: A Thorough Narrative of the Late President's Life,* Doubleday, 1964; *The Man Who Hated Sherlock Holmes: A Life of Sir Arthur Conan Doyle,* Random House, 1965; *Very Wild Animal Stories,* Pantheon, 1965; *The Lantern Bearer: A Life of Robert Louis Stevenson,* Pantheon, 1965; *The Elephant on Ice,* Seabury, 1965; *The Golden Swan,* Seabury, 1965; *The Snark Was a Boojum: A Life of Lewis Carroll,* Pantheon, 1966; *Washington, D.C.,* Seabury, 1966; *What's the Market?: The Story of Stock Exchanges,* Duell, Sloan & Pearce, 1966; *Sunnyside: A Life of Washington Irving,* Pantheon, 1967; *When I Was Jersey,* Pantheon, 1967; *Boston,* Seabury, 1967; *The Man With Two Countries,* Seabury, 1967; *Alaska, the Great Land,* Meredith, 1967; *Spunkwater, Spunkwater!: A Life of Mark Twain,* Pantheon, 1968; *Mr. Jonathan Edwards,* Seabury, 1968; *The Elephant Tells,* Reilly & Lee, 1968; *This Is Advertising,* Crown, 1968; *I Told You So!: A Life of H.G. Wells,* Pantheon, 1969; *The Mammoth Parade,* Pantheon, 1969; *Colonial Massachusetts,* Thomas Nelson, 1969; *The Unpardonable Sin: A Life of Nathaniel Hawthorne,* Pantheon, 1970; *The People of Concord,* Seabury, 1970; *Scotland Yard,* Hawthorn, 1970; *The Admirable Cotton Mather,* Seabury, 1971; *The Curtis Magazines, 1883-1970,* Ronald, 1971; *This Little Pig: The Story of Marketing,* Thomas Nelson, 1971; *New England Academy: Wilbraham to Wilbraham & Monson,* R.L. Dothard Associates, 1971; *Poetry Is,* Houghton, 1972; *Emily Elizabeth Dickinson,* Thomas Nelson, 1972.

Contributor of articles and verse to *Reader's Digest, Ladies' Home Journal, Georgia Review, Saturday Review, Book World, Horn Book, New England Quarterly,* and *American Scholar,* and contributor of hundreds of stories, articles, and poems to *Jack and Jill.* Editor, with Kenneth Roberts, of *One Hundred Years Ago: American Writing of 1847,* Funk, 1947, . . . *of 1848,* 1948.

AVOCATIONAL INTERESTS: Collecting jade, growing hollies, and ice skating.

BIOGRAPHICAL/CRITICAL SOURCES: Book Week, June 25, 1967; *Book World,* March 17, 1968; *Young Readers Review,* October, 1969; *Horn Book,* April, 1971.

*   *   *

WOODBERRY, Joan (Merle)   1921-

PERSONAL: Born February 10, 1921, in Narrabri, New South Wales, Australia; daughter of Robert (an engineer) and Merle (Cain) Woodberry. *Education:* University of Sydney, B.A., 1942, Diploma in Education, 1943; University of Melbourne, B.Ed., 1960. *Home:* 657 Nelson Rd., Mount Nelson, Tasmania, Australia.

CAREER: Teacher and librarian in New South Wales, Australia, 1946-52; British Council, London, England, bursar, 1953-58; Teachers' College, Launceston, Tasmania, Australia, lecturer, 1959-60; Teachers' College, Hobart, Tasmania, warden, lecturer in charge of academic subjects, 1962—. Writer for children. *Member:* Australian Federation of University Women, Australian Society of Authors, Fellowship of Australian Writers, Australian Journalists Association. *Awards, honors:* Australian Children's Book of the Year award, 1962, for *Rafferty Rides a Winner.*

WRITINGS: Rafferty Takes to Fishing, Parrish, 1958; *Floodtide for Rafferty,* Parrish, 1959; *Rafferty Rides a Winner,* Parrish, 1961; *Rafferty Makes a Landfall,* Parrish, 1962; (with R. Iglesias) *Pleasure in English,* Longmans, Green, Book I, 1964, Book II, c.1965; *Come Back Peter,* Rigby, 1968, Crowell, 1972; *Ash Tuesday,* Macmillan, 1969; *Little Black Swan,* Macmillan, 1970. Contributor, *English in Australia,* and *Tasmanian Journal of Education.*

WORK IN PROGRESS: Children's fiction, *My Friend Rafferty,* and *All in the Summer Weather.*

AVOCATIONAL INTERESTS: Water-color painting, gardening.

BIOGRAPHICAL/CRITICAL SOURCES: Times Literary Supplement, October 16, 1969, April 4, 1970.†

*   *   *

WOODBRIDGE, Hensley Charles 1923-

PERSONAL: Born February 6, 1923, in Champaign, Ill.; son of Dudley Warner (a professor) and Ruby Belle (Mendenhall) Woodbridge; married Annie Emma Smith (a teacher), August 28, 1953; children: Ruby Susan.

EDUCATION: College of William and Mary, A.B., 1943; Universidad Nacional Autonoma de Mexico, summer student, 1941, 1945; Harvard University, M.A., 1946; University of Illinois, Ph.D., 1950, M.S. in L.S., 1951. *Politics:* Democrat. *Home:* 1804 West Freeman, Carbondale, Ill. 62901. *Office:* Department of Foreign Languages, Southern Illinois University, Carbondale, Ill. 62901.

CAREER: Mexican correspondent for Worldover Press, 1945; University of Richmond, Va., instructor in French and Spanish, 1946-47; Auburn University, Auburn, Ala., reference librarian, 1951-53; Murray State College (now Murray State University), Murray, Ky., librarian, 1953-65; Southern Illinois University, Carbondale, Latin American bibliographer, associate professor, 1965-71, professor of modern languages, 1971—. *Member:* American Folklore Society, Mediaeval Academy of America, Bibliographical Society of America, American Association of Teachers of Spanish and Portuguese, Instituto de Estudios Madrilenos, Southeastern Library Association, Kentucky Folklore Society, Kentucky Historical Society, Kentucky Library Association, Filson Club.

WRITINGS: (Compiler) *A List of the Catalan, Italian, Portuguese and Rumanian Periodicals in the Library of the University of Illinois,* Library of the University of Illinois, 1949; (With Paul Olson) *A Tentative Bibliography of Hispanic Linguistics,* Department of Spanish and Italian, University of Illinois, 1952; (editor and translator) F.H.A. von Humboldt, *Political Essay on the Kingdom of New Spain,* Book 1, University of Kentucky Library, 1957; (contributor) Harold B. Allen, *Minor Dialect Areas of the Upper Midwest,* University of Alabama Press, 1958; (contributor) *Jesse Stuart: A Bibliography,* Lincoln Memorial University Press, 1960; (with Hunter M. Hancock) *A Bibliography of the Striped Bass or Rockfish Roccus Saxatilis (Walbaum),* Sport Fishing Institute, 1964, revised edition (with William Massmann), 1967; (with Gerald M. Moser) *Ruben Dario y "El Cojo Ilustrado,"* Hispanic Institute, Columbia University, 1964; (compiler with John London and George H. Tweney) *Jack London: A Bibliography,* Talisman Press, 1966, reissued with supplement, Kraus Reprint Co., 1972; (compiler) *Jesse and Jane Stuart: A Bibliography,* Murray State University, 1969. Contributor of reviews, bibliographies, articles, and translations to some two dozen journals in the United States and to periodicals in Great Britain, India, Belgium, Spain, and Mexico. Editor, *Kentucky Library Association Bulletin,* 1959-60, *Kentucky Folklore Record,* 1963-64; contributing editor, *American Book Collector,* 1965—; associate editor, *Hispania,* 1967—; editor and publisher, *Jack London Newsletter,* 1967—; member of editorial board, *Modern Language Journal,* 1971—.

WORK IN PROGRESS: Ruben Dario: Una Bibliografia anotada, selectiva y clasificada, to be published by Universidad Nacional Autonoma de Nicaragua in 1974; with L. S. Thompson, *A History of Printing in Early Spanish America.*

BIOGRAPHICAL/CRITICAL SOURCES: Essay in *Jesse Stuart: A Bibliography,* Lincoln Memorial University Press, 1960; *Times Literary Supplement,* May 11, 1967; *Jack London Newsletter,* May, 1972.

*   *   *

WOODFIELD, William Read 1928-

PERSONAL: Born January 21, 1928; son of William H., Jr. (in real estate) and E. Lylia Woodfield; married Gitta Parker (a writer), December 8, 1957; children: Michael, Nancy Lynn. *Education:* Attended University of California, Berkeley, and Golden Gate College. *Home:* 12336 Rye St., Studio City, Calif. 91604.

CAREER: Free-lance writer and photographer, writing some articles and scripts in collaboration with wife, Gitta Woodfield.

WRITINGS: (With Peter Ustinov) *Ustinov's Diplomats,* Geis, 1959; (with Milton Machlin) *Ninth Life,* Putnam, 1961. Author of motion picture and television scripts, including "Death Valley Days" and "Sea Hunt." Contributor of articles and/or photographs to *Life, Look, Paris Match, Saturday Evening Post, London Daily Mirror, Der Stern, Esquire, Playboy, This Week, Ladies' Home Journal, McCall's,* and other magazines and newspapers.

WORK IN PROGRESS: Editing Jerry Lewis' autobiography; a novel, *Raymond Hoppler's Secret Diary;* collaborating with Gitta Woodfield and John Florea on a television series, "The Outsider."

*   *   *

WOODGATE, Mildred Violet

PERSONAL: Born in Dublin, Eire; daughter of Arthur G.K. and Sylvia (Barton) Woodgate. *Education:* Attended Francis Holland School for Girls, London. *Politics:* Conservative. *Home:* 12 Stanley Rd., Oxford, England.

CAREER: Worked for some years in British Foreign Office, London, England, then as librarian of Bede Library, London. Also worked with youths at Wormwood Scrubbs Prison, London, for fifteen years.

WRITINGS: The World of a Child, Heath, Cranton & Co., 1913; *The Children of Danecourt Park,* Thomas Nelson, 1924; *The Secret of the Sapphire Ring,* Hurst & Blackett, 1930, abridged edition, Mellifont Press, 1946; *Pauline's Lady,* Hurst & Blackett, 1931, abridged edition publishd as *The Mystery of Pauline's Lady,* Mellifont Press, 1945; *The Two Houses on the Cliff,* Hurst & Blackett, 1931, abridged edition, Mellifont Press, 1945; *The Silver Mirror,* Bles, 1935, Mellifont Press, 1945; *Pere Lacordaire, Leader of Youth,* Sands & Co., 1939; *St. Louise de Marillac, Foundress of the Sisters of Charity,* Herder, 1942 (published in Ireland as *Louise de Marillac, the First Sister of Charity,* Browne & Nolan, 1942); *Madame Elizabeth of France, Born at Versailles, May, 1764, Guillotined in Paris, May, 1794,* Browne & Nolan, 1943; *Jacqueline Pascal and Her Brother,* Browne & Nolan, 1944, published in America as *Pascal and His Sister Jacqueline,* Herder, 1945; *The Cross of Twigs,* Mellifont Press, 1945; *The Abbe Edgeworth (1745-1807),* Browne & Nolan, 1945, Longmans, Green (New York), 1946; *Madame Swetchine, 1782-1857,* Browne & Nolan, 1948; *Charles de Condren,* Browne & Nolan, 1949, Newman, 1950; *Father Benson, Founder of the Cowley Fathers,* Bles, 1953; *Father Congreve of Cowley,* S.P.C.K., 1956; *St. Vincent de Paul,* Browne & Nolan, 1958, Newman, 1960; *Francis de Sales,* Newman, 1961; *Junipero Serra, Apostle of California, 1713-1784,* Browne & Nolan, 1965, Newman, 1966. Also author of juvenile biographies of St. Vincent de Paul, St. Dominic, St. Joan of Arc, St. Columba, St. Bernadette, St. Thomas Becket, and St. Thomas More, published by St. Paul Publications, 1966-71. Contributor of articles to *Everybody's, Lady,* and *Irish Ecclesiastical Record.*

WOODS, Joan (LeSueur) 1932-

PERSONAL: Born September 5, 1932, in Phoenix, Ariz.; daughter of LeRoy Afton (a clothing merchant) and Ruby May (a primary music consultant; maiden surname, Kinsey) LeSueur; married Kenneth Ray Woods (a scientist), March 21, 1952 (divorced August 27, 1963); children: Gregory, Victoria, Monica, Cynthia. Education: Student at Brigham Young University, 1950-52, Hunter College (now Hunter College of the City University of New York), 1964-68, Arizona State University, 1968-70, Columbia University, 1970-72, Mozarteum, Salzburg, Austria, and York University, England, 1971. Politics: Republican. Religion: Mormon. Home: 1401 West Pepper Place, Mesa, Ariz. 85201. Agent: Barthold Fles Literary Agency, 507 Fifth Ave., New York, N.Y. 10017.

CAREER: Private teacher of piano since teens, in California, in Mesa, Arizona, Minneapolis, Minn., Cleveland, Ohio, Provo, Utah, and in New York, N.Y., 1956-67; lecturer at public schools, colleges, and professional meetings in Ariz., 1967-72; National Piano Foundation, Chicago, Ill., now clinician, teacher, and writer. Public school consultant for Keyboard Experience Program in Ariz., 1971-72. Idaho Stake of Church of Latter Day Saints, organist, 1948-50; pianist; radio, television, and concert performer, conductor of choruses and women's trio, and orchestra tympani player; composer of songs for children and of piano works; teacher of religion classes in primary grades.

WRITINGS: Maudie's Mush Pots (juvenile), Abingdon, 1963. Contributor of articles on music to periodicals, including Recorder Magazine and Musicgram.

WORK IN PROGRESS: With Joe Rezits, Buying Pianos; with Rezits, research on piano method books; a novel; music article research.

* * *

WOOLLAM, William Gifford 1921-

PERSONAL: Born September 8, 1921, in Glasgow, Scotland; married Frances Miriam Lyness, September 24, 1945; chldren: Pamela Jane. Education: Attended Merchant Taylors' School, London, England, 1933-35, and Nautical College, Pangbourne, England, 1935-38. Religion: Protestant. Home: 7, Bluff Path, The Peak, Hong Kong. Office: Jardine, Matheson & Co. Ltd., 22 Pedder St., Hong Kong.

CAREER: At sea for ten years, earning masters certificate; Jardine, Matheson & Co. Ltd. (ship owners and agents), Hong Kong, assistant, 1949—. Chartered shipbroker. Member: Institute of Chartered Shipbrokers (chairman, Hong Kong), Conway-Worcester-Pangbourne Association of Hong Kong (secretary). Awards, honors: Freeman of City of Glasgow, Scotland.

WRITINGS: Shipping Terms and Abbreviations: Maritime, Insurance, International Trade, Cornell Maritime Press, 1963.†

* * *

WRIGHT, Charles Stevenson 1932-

PERSONAL: Born June 4, 1932, in New Franklin, Mo.; son of Stevenson (a laborer) and Dorthey (Hughes) Wright. Education: Attended public schools in New Franklin and Sedalia, Mo. Religion: Protestant. Home: 118 West 49th St., New York, N.Y. 10019. Agent: Robert Lantz-Candida Donadio Literary Agency, Inc., 111 West 57th St., New York, N.Y. 10019.

CAREER: Free-lance writer. Began his writing career as a teen-ager with a regular column in Kansas City Call, a weekly negro paper in Kansas City, Mo., and received one dollar from this paper for his first published short story; left high school in his junior year, has since studied writing off and on at Lowney Handy's colony in Marshall Ill. Military service: U.S. Army, 1952-54; served in Korea.

WRITINGS: The Messenger, Farrar, Straus, 1963; The Wig: A Mirror Image, Farrar, Straus, 1966. Also author of short stories. Contributor to Village Voice.

WORK IN PROGRESS: Two one-act plays; a nonfiction book (personal reporting and experiences), for Farrar, Straus.

SIDELIGHTS: After reading The Wig, which Martin Shuttleworth called "a loud, frenetic, batty, bitty book," he wrote he "could see why Charles Wright has quite a reputation; a wit of the Lenny Bruce variety." A Books and Bookmen reviewer adds: "Icy comedy can be infinitely more lethal than hysterical drama and Charles Wright makes his point many times, but never in purple, moaning prose. The tone of happy optimism is deceptive until one looks again. . . . Maybe The Wig is slight, a comic raspberry, but within its limits it works."

A writer for New York Times Book Review notes that Wright "got the idea for The Wig by allowing a friend to experiment on his hair, this experiment taking place deep in the fumes of alcohol. As a result of the Wright wig, he will carry a small bald spot to his grave, but a book came out of it so everything seems even. . . .About the antics of [his book] he amiably observed, 'Being black, I thought I would write black humor.' Besides, 'I think it's time to take some of this color matter with a grain of humor.'"

The U.S. Information Agency broadcast The Messenger overseas.

AVOCATIONAL INTERESTS: Jazz, good books, good people, travel.

BIOGRAPHICAL/CRITICAL SOURCES: Ebony, November, 1957; Sepia, December, 1957; New York Times Book Review, February 27, 1966; Punch, February 15, 1967; Times Literary Supplement, March 9, 1967; Books and Bookmen, May, 1967.

* * *

WRIGHT, Christopher 1926-

PERSONAL: Born October 31, 1926, in Chicago, Ill.; son of Quincy (a scholar) and Louise (Leonard) Wright; married Anne Carolyn McCoy (now a biological researcher), September 15, 1956; children: Malcolm Morehead, Diana Sewall. Education: Harvard University, A.B., 1949; Oxford University, graduate study, 1949-51. Home: 21, Claremont Ave., New York, N.Y. 10027.

CAREER: University of Chicago, Chicago, Ill., social sciences research associate in Law School, 1955-58; Columbia University, New York, N.Y., executive director of Columbia University Council for Atomic Age Studies, 1958-66, director, Institute for the Study of Science in Human Affairs, 1966—. Consultant to governmental and other organizations on interactions of science and society. Military service: U.S. Army, assigned to Manhattan Project, World War II.

WRITINGS: (Editor with Robert Gilpin, and contributor) Scientists and National Policy Making, Columbia University Press, 1964. Contributor to International Affairs, Bulletin of the Atomic Scientists, Journal of World History, Political Science Quarterly and to Britannica Yearbook of Science and the Future.

* * *

WRIGHT, David (John Murray) 1920-

PERSONAL: Born February 23, 1920, in Johannesburg, South Africa; son of Gordon Alfred (a stockbroker) and

Jean (Murray) Wright; married Phillipa Reid (an actress), October 6, 1951. *Education:* Attended Northampton School for the Deaf; Oriel College, Oxford, B.A., 1942. *Religion:* Church of England. *Home:* 45 Great Ormond St., London W.C. 1, England. *Agent:* A.D. Peters, 10 Buckingham St., Adelphi, London W.C. 2, England.

CAREER: Sunday Times, London, England, member of staff, 1942-47. Gregory Fellow in Poetry, University of Leeds, 1965-67. *Member:* Royal Society of Literature (fellow, 1967), Caves de France, Mandrake Club. *Awards, honors:* Atlantic Award for Literature, 1950; third Guinness poetry award for "A Thanksgiving," 1958; second Guinness poetry award for "Adam at Evening," 1960.

WRITINGS: Poems, Editions Poetry, 1947; (with John Heath-Stubbs) *The Forsaken Garden,* Lehmann, 1950; (with Heath-Stubbs) *The Faber Book of 20th Century Verse,* Faber, 1953, 2nd revised edition, 1965; *Moral Stories,* Verschoyle, 1954; (translator) *Beowulf,* Penguin, 1957; *Monologue of a Deaf Man* (poems), Deutsch, 1958; (editor) *South African Stories,* Faber, 1960; *Roy Campbell* (biography), published for the British Council by Longmans, Green, 1961; (editor and author of introduction and commentary) *Seven Victorian Poets,* Heinemann, 1964, Barnes & Noble, 1966; (translator into prose) Geoffrey Chaucer, *The Canterbury Tales,* Barrie & Rockliff, 1964, Random House, 1965; *The Mid-Century: English Poetry, 1940-1960,* Penguin, 1964; *Adam at Evening* (poems), Hodder & Stoughton, 1965; (with Patrick Swift) *Algarve,* Barrie & Rockliff, 1965, International Publications Service, 1965, 2nd edition, Barrie & Jenkins, 1971; (with Swift) *Minho and North Portugal: A Portrait and a Guide,* Barrie & Rockliff, 1968; (with Swift) *Lisbon: A Portrait and a Guide,* Barrie & Jenkins, 1971, Scribner, 1972; (compiler and author of introduction) *Longer Contemporary Poems,* Penguin, 1966; (editor and author of introduction) *The Penguin Book of English Romantic Verse,* Penguin, 1968; *Nerve Ends* (poems), Hodder & Stoughton, 1969; *Deafness: A Personal Account,* Allen Lane, 1969, published in America as *Deafness,* Stein & Day, 1970; (editor) Thomas De Quincey, *Recollections of the Lakes and the Lake Poets,* Penguin, 1970. Contributor to *Encounter, London Magazine, Times Literary Supplement, Time and Tide, Listener, New Yorker, Paris Review, Hudson Review.* Co-editor, *Nimbus,* 1956-57, *X* (quarterly review), 1959-62.

AVOCATIONAL INTERESTS: South African history (pursued on travels in Africa).

BIOGRAPHICAL/CRITICAL SOURCES: Poetry, June, 1967; *London Magazine,* October, 1969; *Book World,* March 8, 1970.

*   *   *

WRIGHT, F(rank) J(oseph)   1905-

PERSONAL: Born October 10, 1905, in Cardiff, Glamorganshire, South Wales; *Education:* Cardiff Technical College, student; University of London, B.Sc. (external), 1934, M.Sc., (economics), 1939, B.Com., 1945; Oxford University, diploma in education, 1945. *Home:* 35 Welsford Rd., Eaton Rise, Norwich, Norfolk, England.

CAREER: Norwich City College, Norwich, England, formerly senior lecturer in public administration studies, department of business and management studies; now retired.

WRITINGS: The Elements of Sociology: An Introduction to Social and Political Science, University of London Press, 1942; *Commerce,* English Universities Press, 1944; *Commercial Law,* two volumes, English Universities Press, 1948-50; *Teach Yourself Business Organisation,* English Universities Press, 1949; *The Evolution of Modern Industrial Organisation,* Macdonald & Evans, 1954, 3rd edition, 1967; *The Elements of Modern Industrial Organisation,* Macdonald & Evans, 1958; *An Introduction to Industry and Commerce,* Jordan, 1962, 2nd edition, 1965; *Transfer Values of Private Metropolitan Transit Systems: A Study of Pittsburgh Railways,* Duquesne University Press, 1964; *An Introduction to the Principles of Economics,* Pergamon, 1965; *An Introduction to the Study of Democratic Government,* Barrie & Rockliff, 1967; *British Constitution and Government,* Macdonald & Evans, 1967; *British Social Services,* Macdonald & Evans, 1968; *Basic Sociology,* Macdonald & Evans, 1970.

AVOCATIONAL INTERESTS: European travel, films; music, especially grand opera.

*   *   *

WRIGHT, Gordon   1912-

PERSONAL: Born April 24, 1912, in Lynden, Wash.; son of Parke A. (a superintendent of schools) and Marion (Beaty) Wright; married Louise Aiken, August 17, 1940; children: Eric, Michael, Gregory, Philip, David. *Education:* Whitman College, A.B., 1933; Stanford University, A.M., 1935, Ph.D., 1939; postgraduate study at George Washington University, 1936-37, Universities of Grenoble and Paris, 1937-38. *Politics:* Democrat. *Religion:* Congregational. *Home:* 813 San Francisco Ter., Stanford, Calif. 94305. *Office:* Department of History, Stanford University, Stanford, Calif. 94305.

CAREER: University of Oregon, Eugene, assistant professor of history, 1939-43; U.S. Department of State, country specialist, Washington, D.C., 1943-44, foreign service officer at U.S. Embassy, Paris, France, 1945-47; University of Oregon, associate professor, 1947-49, professor of history, 1949-57, chairman of department, 1951-57; Stanford University, Stanford, Calif., professor of history, 1957-69, William H. Bonsall Professor of History, 1969—, executive head of department, 1959-65, associate dean, School of Humanities and Sciences, 1970—. National War College, member of faculty, 1952; Columbia University, visiting professor, 1954-55; visiting summer professor at other universities. Cultural attache, U.S. Embassy, Paris, France, 1967-69. *Member:* American Historical Association, American Academy of Arts and Sciences, American Association of University Professors, Phi Beta Kappa. *Awards, honors:* Social Science Research Council Fellow, 1950-51; honorary LL.D. from Whitman College; American Council of Learned Societies and Center for Advanced Study in the Behavioral Sciences fellow, 1962-63; decorated by French Government, Commandeur, Ordre des Arts et des Lettres.

WRITINGS: Raymond Poincare and the French Presidency, Stanford University Press, 1942; *The Reshaping of French Democracy,* Reynal & Hitchcock, 1948; (contributor) Max Savelle, editor, *A History of World Civilization,* two volumes, Holt, 1957; (editor with Taylor Cole) *European Political Systems,* 2nd edition, revised (Wright was not associated with earlier editions), Knopf, 1959; *France in Modern Times: 1760 to the Present,* Rand McNally, 1960; (editor with Arthur Mejia, Jr.) *An Age of Controversy: Discussion Problems in Twentieth-Century European History,* Dodd, 1963; *Rural Revolution in France: The Peasantry in the Twentieth Century,* Stanford University Press, 1964; *France in the Twentieth Century* (pamphlet), Service Center for Teachers of History, American Historical Association, 1965; (editor) Jules Michelet, *History of the French Revolution,* translated by Charles Cocks, University of Chicago Press, 1967; *The Ordeal of Total War, 1939-1945,* Harper, 1968. Contributor of articles to professional journals.

BIOGRAPHICAL/CRITICAL SOURCES: Virginia Quarterly Review, winter, 1969.

WRIGHT, (Mary) Helen 1914-

PERSONAL: Born December 20, 1914, in Washington, D.C.; daughter of Frederick E. (a geophysicist) and Kathleen (Finley) Wright; married John F. Hawkins, 1946 (divorced); married Rene Greuter, 1967. *Education:* Bennett Junior College, student, 1932-34; Vassar College, B.A., 1937, M.A., 1939; additional study at University of California. *Home and office:* 6040 Boulevard East, Apt. 20G, West New York, N.J. 07093.

CAREER: Mt. Wilson Observatory, Pasadena, Calif., assistant, 1937; U.S. Naval Observatory, Washington, D.C., junior astronomer, 1942-43. Free-lance writer and editor. *Member:* American Astronomical Society, History of Science Society, International Astronomical Union.

WRITINGS: Sweeper in the Sky: The Life of Maria Mitchell, First Woman Astronomer in America, Macmillan, 1949; *Palomar, the World's Largest Telescope,* Macmillan, 1952 (published in England as *The Great Palomar Telescope,* Faber, 1958); *Explorer of the Universe: A Biography of George Ellery Hale,* Dutton, 1966.

Editor with Harlow Shapley and Samuel Rapport: *A Treasury of Science,* Harper, 1943, 5th edition, revised and enlarged, 1963; *Readings in the Physical Sciences,* Appleton, 1948; *The New Treasury of Science,* Harper, 1965.

Editor with Samuel Rapport: *Great Adventures in Medicine,* Dial, 1952, 2nd edition, revised, 1961; *The Crust of the Earth,* New American Library, 1955; *Great Adventures in Science,* Harper, 1956; *The Great Explorers,* Harper, 1957; *Great Adventures in Nursing,* Harper, 1960; *The Amazing World of Medicine,* Harper, 1961; "Library of Science" series, New York University Press, *Science: Method and Meaning,* 1963, *Archaeology,* 1963, *Engineering,* 1963, *Mathematics,* 1963, *Physics,* 1964, *Astronomy,* 1964, *Anthropology,* 1967, *Biology,* 1967; *Great Undersea Adventures* (anthology), Harper, 1966; *Great Adventures with Wild Animals,* Harper, 1967; (and Hamilton Wright) *To the Moon!,* Meredith, 1968. Also editor, with others, of *The Legacy of George Ellery Hale,* M.I.T. Press, 1971.

AVOCATIONAL INTERESTS: Sculpting.

BIOGRAPHICAL/CRITICAL SOURCES: New York Times Book Review, July 2, 1967.

* * *

WRIGHT, Robert Roy 1917-

PERSONAL: Born December 11, 1917, in Evanston, Ill.; son of Merle Leslie (a teacher) and Alice (Selleck) Wright; married Marian Dorothy Linn, February 19, 1944; children: Robert Henry, David Leslie, Mary-Linn Dorothy. *Education:* De Pauw University, A.B., 1939; Yale University, B.D., 1942. *Home:* 30 Reid Ave., Port Washington, Long Island, N.Y. 11050. *Office:* Association Press, 291 Broadway, New York, N.Y. 10007.

CAREER: Methodist minister. Abingdon Press, New York, N.Y., assistant editor, 1951-65; Friendship Press, New York, N.Y., director of adult publications, 1965-69; Association Press, New York, N.Y., managing editor, 1969—.

WRITINGS: The Church's First Thousand Years, published for the Cooperative Publication Association by Abingdon, 1960; *Seven Themes from the Gospel of John: A Devotional Guide,* Abingdon, 1964.

* * *

WU, Nelson I(kon) 1919-
(Lu-ch'iao)

PERSONAL: Born June 9, 1919, in Peking, China; son of Aitchen K. (author, diplomat, professor) and Lu-yu (Yang) Wu; married Mu-lien Hsueh, December 1, 1951; children: Chao-ming, Chao-ting, Chao-ping, Chao-ying. *Education:* Graduated from Nankai Middle School (Tientsin, China), 1936; National South-west Associated University (Kunming, China), B.A., 1942; attended New School for Social Research, 1946-47; Yale University, M.A., 1949, Ph.D., 1954. *Home:* Yenling Yeyuan, 1530 Notch Road, Cheshire, Conn. 06410; and 6306 Waterman Ave., St. Louis, Mo. 63130. *Office:* Department of Art and Archaeology, Washington University, St. Louis, Mo. 63130.

CAREER: National South-west Associated University, Kunming, China, instructor in literature, 1942-43; San Francisco State College, San Francisco, Calif., assistant professor of history of art, 1954-55; Yale University, New Haven, Conn., Department of the History of Art, instructor, 1955-59, assistant professor, 1959-65, Davenport College, fellow, 1956-65; Washington University, St. Louis, Mo., professor of the history of art and Chinese culture, 1965-68, on leave as research professor, Kyoto University, Japan, 1965-67, Edward Mallinckrodt Distinguished University Professor of the History of Art and Chinese Culture, 1968—, chairman, Department of Art and Archaeology, 1969-70. Trustee, Yale-in-China Association, 1959-65; organized Ashiya Seminar in Japan, 1966-67. *Member:* Elizabethan Club (Yale University). *Awards, honors:* Tsing-hua research fellow, 1954-55; Yale University, Morse fellowship, 1958-59; American Council of Learned Societies fellow, 1958-59; New Haven Festival of Arts award, 1960, for *Wei-yang Ko;* Fulbright research scholar, 1965-67; Guggenheim fellow, 1965-66.

WRITINGS: (Under pseudonym Lu-ch'iao) *Wei-yang Ko* (novel in Chinese; title means "Song Never to End"), Young Sun, 1959, 3rd edition, Commercial Press (Taiwan), 1970; (contributor) *Art and the Craftsman: The Best of the Yale Literary Magazine, 1836-1961,* Southern Illinois University Press, 1962; (contributor) Arthur Frederick Wright and D.C. Twitchett, editors, *Confucian Personalities,* Stanford University Press, 1962; *Chinese and Indian Architecture: The City of Man, the Mountain of God, and the Realm of the Immortals,* Braziller, 1963. Films: "The Flop," 1952; "The Finger Painting of Wu Tzai-yeh," 1956. Contributor to journals in the field of art.

WORK IN PROGRESS: Tung Ch'i-ch'ang (1555-1636) and His Landscape Painting; Art History Sense: Essays on the Study of the History of Art; Come Back to Life in Spring Breeze, on Chinese thought and the modern world; plans to co-author with wife and children a work on life in their gardens; considering possibility of editing and releasing his films on oriental art and architecture taken in Asia in 1958-59.

SIDELIGHTS: Wu held an annual "Yenling Yeyuan Picnic" in his garden in Cheshire, Conn., with art exhibits and poetry, music, drama, and film programs, 1952-65. He has traveled widely in Asia. *Chinese and Indian Architecture* has been published in German and Italian translations. *Avocational interests:* Landscape architecture, painting, and calligraphy.

BIOGRAPHICAL/CRITICAL SOURCES: Herald-Tribune, Sarasota, Fla., February 9, 1964; *Cheshire Herald,* Cheshire, Conn., July 27, 1967; *Yale University Art Gallery Bulletin,* spring, 1968; *St. Louis Post-Dispatch,* June 10, 1968; *St. Louis Globe-Democrat,* November 14, 1970.

* * *

WYATT, Stanley P(orter, Jr.) 1921-

PERSONAL: Born April 20, 1921, in Medford, Mass.; son of Stanley Porter (a banker) and Maud Scott (Norton) Wyatt; married Catherine Jeannette Barber, December 18, 1948; children: Stanley Porter III, Christopher Monroe, Scott Emery. *Education:* Dartmouth College, A.B., 1942; Harvard University, A.M., 1948, Ph.D., 1950. *Religion:* Episcopalian. *Home:* 510 West Michigan Ave., Urbana, Ill. 61801. *Office:* Department of Astronomy, University of Illinois, Urbana, Ill. 61801.

CAREER: University of Michigan, Ann Arbor, instructor in astronomy, 1950-53; University of Illinois, Urbana, assistant professor, 1953-58, associate professor, 1958-61, professor of astronomy, 1961—. *Military service:* U.S. Naval Reserve, 1942-46; served aboard destroyers in Pacific; became lieutenant. *Member:* International Astronomical Union, American Astronomical Society, Phi Beta Kappa.

WRITINGS: Principles of Astronomy, Allyn & Bacon, 1964, 2nd edition, 1971.

With J.M. Atkin and others, books produced in National Science Foundation-University of Illinois Astronomy Program—All published by Harper, 1969: *Charting the Universe, The Universe in Motion, Gravitation, The Message of Starlight, The Life Story of a Star, Galaxies and the Universe.* Contributor to *Astrophysical Journal, Smithsonian Contributions to Astrophysics, Science, Nature, Sky and Telescope,* and *Planetary and Space Science.*

WORK IN PROGRESS: Research in dynamics of interplanetary matter.

AVOCATIONAL INTERESTS: Cape Cod, clams, cooking, doing double-crostics.

*   *   *

WYCKOFF, (Gregory) Jerome 1911-

PERSONAL: Born March 17, 1911, in Jersey City, N.J.; son of George H. (a chemist) and Villette (Waldron) Wyckoff; married Marjorie Elaine Morrison (a music teacher), October 25, 1941; children: Thomas, Alan, Celia. *Education:* Trinity College, Hartford, Conn., B.S., 1931; Columbia University, M.A., 1940; New York University, postgraduate study, 1940. *Politics:* Usually Democratic. *Religion:* Independent. *Home:* 477 Colonial Rd., Ridgewood, N.J. 07450.

CAREER: Senior editor, Western Publishing Co. and Golden Press, New York, N.Y., 1940-67; free-lance editor, author, and earth-science photographer, 1967—. Lecturer on geology. Area chairman, United Negro College Fund, 1949—. *Military service:* U.S. Army, technical editor, 1942-46. *Member:* American Association for the Advancement of Science, League for Conservation Legislation (co-founder), American Association of Variable Star Observers, Wilderness Society, Sierra Club, Adirondack Mountain Club, Wyckoff Association in America, Orpheus Club of Ridgewood (N.J.).

WRITINGS: (Editor) *The Golden Grab Bag of Stories, Poems, and Songs,* Simon & Schuster, 1951; (with Robert Newton Mayall and Margaret Mayall) *The Sky Observer's Guide,* Golden Press, 1959; *The Story of Geology: Our Changing Earth Through the Ages,* Golden Press, 1960, reissued as *Geology: Our Changing Earth Through the Ages,* 1967; *Marvels of the Earth* (adapted from *The Story of Geology*), Golden Press, 1964 (published in England as *Secrets of the Earth,* Hamlyn, 1967); *Rock, Time, and Landforms,* Harper, 1966; *The Adirondack Landscape: Its Geology and Landforms—A Hiker's Guide,* Adirondack Mountain Club, 1967; (co-author) *Pocket Science Guide,* Golden Press, 1967; (with George Adams) *Landforms: A Guide to Rock Scenery,* Golden Press, 1971. Managing editor and contributor, *Harper Encyclopedia of Science,* Harper, 1963 and 1967.

WORK IN PROGRESS: Two juveniles: an earth-science dictionary, and geological story of North America; books on rock scenery of Hudson Highlands and Pleistocene glaciation in northeastern states.

AVOCATIONAL INTERESTS: Conservation, hiking, landscape photography, music, interracial relations.

*   *   *

WYLDER, Robert C(lay) 1921-

PERSONAL: Born January 10, 1921, in Malta, Mont.; son of Robert James (an automobile mechanic) and Myrtle (Monroe) Wylder; married Elizabeth Anne Cutts (a musician), July 1, 1944; children: Martha E., Nancy A., Jamie R. (daughter). *Education:* Montana State University, student, 1939-43, 1946-49, B.A., 1947, M.A., 1949; Western Michigan College (now Western Michigan University), student, 1943; University of Wisconsin, student, 1949-53, Ph.D., 1955. *Politics:* Democrat. *Religion:* Unitarian. *Home:* 1817 Iroquois Ave., Long Beach, Calif. 90815.

CAREER: Long Beach State College (now California State College at Long Beach), Long Beach, Calif., instructor, 1953-55, assistant professor, 1955-59, associate professor, 1959-63, professor of English, 1963—. *Long Beach Independent-Press-Telegram,* drama critic, 1957-63, 1968—. *Military service:* U.S. Marine Corps Reserve, 1943-46; became major.

WRITINGS: (With Kevin G. Burne and Edward H. Jones, Jr.) *Functional English for Writing,* McCutcheon, 1961, revised edition published as *Functional English for Writers,* Scott, Foresman, 1964; (with Mary Joe Purcell) *The Narrative Impulse: Short Stories for Analysis,* Odyssey, 1963; (with Burne and Jones) *RX: Remedies for Writing,* Lippincott, 1964; (with Burne and Jones) *Limits and Latitudes: A Concise English Handbook,* Lippincott, 1965; (with Joan G. Johnson) *Writing Practical English,* Macmillan, 1966; *Writer and Reader: Fact and Form,* Macmillan, 1968; *Functional English for Writers,* Form B, Scott, Foresman, 1969; *English in Action: Improving Language Skills,* Macmillan, 1970; (with Joan Roloff) *There Is No "Away": Readings and Language Activities in Ecology,* Glencoe Press, 1971.

*   *   *

WYLLIE, John (Vectis Carew) 1914-

PERSONAL: Born January 26, 1914, in Guna, Central Province, India; became Canadian citizen; son of Richard John and Muriel (Freeman) Wyllie; married (wife's maiden name Poniatowski), September, 1949; children: Jan. *Education:* Attended Lancing College in England. *Address:* c/o Bank of Montreal, St. Catherine and Drummond, Montreal, Quebec, Canada. *Agent:* David Higham Associates Ltd., 5-8 Lower John St., London, WIR 4HA, England; Harold Ober & Associates, Inc., 40 East 49th St., New York, N.Y. 10017. *Office:* Bois McCay & Associates, 1476 Sherbrooke St., Montreal, Canada.

CAREER: Cadet with British Mercantile Marine, four years; held various production positions with British film industry, five years; administrator for British Red Cross Society, five years; creative director in advertising agencies and television, seven years. Industrial communications consultant. Tree farmer in Vermont. Vice-president, Canadian Society for Emotionally Disturbed Children. *Military service:* Royal Air Force, six years; became squadron leader; Japanese prisoner of war for three years; mentioned in dispatches, received Distinguished Flying Cross.

WRITINGS: The Goodly Seed, Secker & Warburg, 1953, Dutton, 1955, reissued as *Survival,* Transworld Publishers, 1957; *Riot,* Secker & Warburg, 1954, Dutton, 1957; *John-*

ny Purple, Secker & Warburg, 1955, Dutton 1956; *Down Will Come the Sky,* Secker & Warburg, 1961, Dutton, 1962. Writer of a variety of produced documentary films and television scripts. Regular contributor to British Broadcasting Corp., Canadian Broadcasting Corp., and Canadian National Film Board; contributor of book reviews to *Montreal Star* and *Canadian Author and Bookman.*

WORK IN PROGRESS: A novel, tentatively titled *The Invicible Summer.*

SIDELIGHTS: Wyllie has traveled widely in Far East, Middle East, Africa, Europe, South America, Canada, and United States. *Avocational interests:* Reading, amateur sailing.†

*   *   *

WYNES, Charles E.   1929-

PERSONAL: Born August 11, 1929, in Rectortown, Va.; son of Charles Andersen (a farmer) and Mae Dean (Payne) Wynes; married Anna Gibson Winsbro, August 27, 1955; children: Mary Anna. *Education:* Madison College, BS. in Ed., 1952; University of Virginia, M.A., 1957, Ph.D., 1960. *Home:* 859 Cherokee Rd., Winterville, Ga. 30683. *Office:* History Department, University of Georgia, Athens, Ga. 30601.

CAREER: Texas A & M University, College Station, began as instructor, became assistant professor of history, 1958-62; University of Georgia, Athens, assistant professor, 1962-66, associate professor, 1966-70, professor of history, 1970—. *Military service:* U.S. Naval Reserve, 1952—, active duty, 1952-54; now lieutenant commander. *Member:* Southern Historical Association, Organization of American Historians, Western History Association. *Awards, honors:* Research grants from American Philosophical Society, 1960-62, 1965, and from Social Science Research Council, 1964.

WRITINGS: Race Relations in Virginia, 1870-1902, University Press of Virginia, 1961; (editor) Orra Langhorne, *Southern Sketches from Virginia, 1881-1901,* University Press of Virginia, 1964; (editor) *The Negro in the South Since 1865: Selected Essays in American Negro History,* University of Alabama Press, 1965; (editor) *Forgotten Voices: Dissenting Southerners in an Age of Conformity,* Louisiana State University Press, 1967. Contributor of articles to historical journals.

WORK IN PROGRESS: James Wormley: A Biography.

*   *   *

YACINE, Kateb   1929-

PERSONAL: Born August 6, 1929, in Constantine, Algeria; son of Kateb Mohamed and Kateb Jasmina. *Education:* Attended College de Setif during the forties.

CAREER: Reporter for *Alger Republicain* until 1950; now full-time writer.

WRITINGS: Soliloques (poems), 1946; *Abdelkader et l'independance algerienne,* En-Nahda (Algeria), 194?; *Nedjma* (novel), Editions du Seuil, 1956, translation by Richard Howard published as *Nedjma,* Braziller, 1961; *Le Cercle des represailles* (dramatic pieces), Editions du Seuil, 1959; *Le Polygone etoile* (novel), Editions du Seuil, 1966; *L'Homme aux sandales de caoutchouc* (dramatic pieces), Editions du Seuil, 1970. Contributor to *Mercure de France, Esprit,* and other publications.

WORK IN PROGRESS: A drama about Palestine, *Les Pensees de Moh-Zitonh.*

SIDELIGHTS: Yacine is probably the most notable French Algerian writing today. *Nedjma,* a long prose poem reminiscent of Faulkner in the handling of time, has been called by Georges J. Joyaux "undoubtedly the best testimonial to the birth of a new Algeria." Yacine once said: "Nedjma [the girl in the story] is the soul of Algeria, torn apart since its origin and ravaged by too many exclusive passions."

BIOGRAPHICAL/CRITICAL SOURCES: Les Lettres Nouvelles, July-August, 1956, January, 1959, April 29, 1959; *Yale French Studies,* summer, 1959; *French Review,* December, 1960; Laurent Le Sage, *The French New Novel,* Pennsylvania State University Press, 1962.†

*   *   *

YADIN, Yigael   1917-

PERSONAL: Born March 21, 1917, in Jerusalem, Israel; son of Eleazar (an archaeologist) and Chassia (Feinsod) Sukenik; married Carmella Ruppin, December 22, 1941; children: Orly and Littal (daughters). *Education:* Hebrew University, Jerusalem, M.A., 1946, Ph.D., 1955. *Religion:* Jewish. *Home:* 47 Ramban Rd., Jerusalem, Israel. *Office:* Hebrew University, Jerusalem, Israel.

CAREER: Hebrew University, Jerusalem, Israel, professor of archaeology, 1963—. *Military service:* Israel Defence Forces, chief of staff, 1949-52, with rank of lieutenant general.

WRITINGS: New Light on the Dead Sea Scrolls (lecture), American Israel Society, 1954; (editor and author of introduction) *Megilat milkheinet bneior, birnei hoshekh,* Bialik Institute (Jerusalem), 1955, translation by Batya Rabin and Chaim Rabin published as *The Scroll of the War of the Sons of Light Against the Sons of Darkness,* Oxford University Press, 1962; (translator and transcriber with Nahman Avigad) *A Genesis Apocryphon: A Scroll from the Wilderness of Judea,* Magnes Press, 1956; *The Message of the Scrolls,* Simon & Schuster, 1957; *Hazor,* Magnes Press, 1958, Oxford University Press, 1972; (editor with Abe Harman) *Israel,* introduction by David Ben-Gurion, Doubleday, 1958; (editor with Chaim Rabin) *Aspects of the Dead Sea Scrolls,* Oxford Unversity Press, 1958.

(With Yohanan Aharoni, Ruth Amiran, and Trude Dothan) *Hazor II: An Account of the Second Season of Excavations, 1956,* Magnes Press, 1960; *Military and Archaeological Aspects of the Conquest of Canaan in the Book of Joshua,* Department for Education and Culture in the Diaspora of the Jewish Agency, 1960, 3rd edition, Hahevra Leheker Hamikra, 1965; (with Yoshinori Maeda and John Kenneth Galbraith) *The Past Speaks to the Present, Television for Teaching,* [and] *The Language of Economics* (the first by Yadin, the second by Maeda, the third by Galbraith), Granada TV Network (Manchester), 1962; *Torat ha-milhamah be-artsot ha-mikra,* International Publishing Co., 1963, translation by Moshe Pearlman published as *The Art of Warfare in Biblical Lands in the Light of Archaeological Study,* two volumes, McGraw, 1963; *The Finds from the Bar Kokhba Period in the Cave of Letters,* Israel Exploration Society, 1963; (author of introductions and commentary) *The Ben Sira Scroll from Masada,* Israel Exploration Society (Jerusalem), 1965; *The Excavation of Masada, 1963/64, Preliminary Report,* Israel Exploration Society, 1965; (translator) William Foxwell Albright, *Ha-Arkhe'ologyah shel erets yisrae.* (translation of *The Archaeology of Palestine*), Am-Oved, 1965; (with others) *Hazor 3-4: An Account of the Third and Fourth Seasons of Excavations, 1957-58,* Oxford University Press, 1965; *Metsadah,* Ma'ariv & Shikmona, 1966, translation by Moshe Pearlman published as *Masada: Herod's Fortress and the Zealots' Last Stand,* Random House, 1966; *The Story of Masada,* adapted for young readers by Gerald Gottlieb, Random House, 1969; *Tefillin from Qumran,* Israel Exploration Society, 1969.

Bar-Kokhba: The Rediscovery of the Legendary Hero of the Second Jewish Revolt Against Rome, Random House, 1971; *Hazor,* British Academy, 1972.

WORK IN PROGRESS: The Cave of Letters, Volume II.

BIOGRAPHICAL/CRITICAL SOURCES: New York Times, September 28, 1966; *New York Times Book Review,* July 16, 1969; *Best Sellers,* May 1, 1969.

*   *   *

YARMON, Morton 1916-

PERSONAL: Born March 8, 1916, in New York, N.Y.; son of Jacob M. (a merchant) and Mary (Berman) Yarmon; married Betty Myra Gross (a fashion promotion executive), November 7, 1948. *Education:* College of City of New York (now City College of City University of New York), B.S.S., 1934; Columbia University, B.S. in Journalism, 1935. *Politics:* Democrat. *Religion:* Jewish. *Home:* 35 Sutton Pl., New York, N.Y. 10022. *Agent:* Marie F. Rodell, 141 East 55th St., New York, N.Y. 10022. *Office:* American Jewish Committee, 165 East 56th St., New York, N.Y. 10022.

CAREER: New York Herald Tribune, New York, N.Y., assistant to editor, European edition, 1945-46; *New York Times,* New York, N.Y., assistant to foreign editor, 1948-56; Ruder & Finn (public relations), New York, N.Y., director of creative services, 1956-58; *Parade,* New York, N.Y., associate managing editor, 1959-63; American Jewish Committee, New York, N.Y., director of public relations, 1963—. Lecturer in English, College of City of New York. Consultant, U.S. Department of Commerce. *Military service:* U.S. Army, Military Intelligence, 1942-45; became captain. *Member:* Society of Magazine Writers, Overseas Press Club.

WRITINGS: (With Maxwell Lehman) *Opportunities in the Armed Forces,* Viking, 1942, supplement, 1943; (with Lehman) *Complete Guide to Your Civil Service Job,* Harcourt, 1949; (with Lehman) *Every Woman's Guide to Spare-Time Income,* Harcourt, 1950; *Early American Antique Furniture,* Fawcett, 1952; (with N.H. Mager) *Put Your Money to Work for You,* Harper, 1954, reissued as *Make Your Money Work,* Trend Publications, c.1956; (with Lehman) *Jobs After Retirement,* Holt, 1954; (with Irving Rosenthal) *The Art of Writing Made Simple,* Garden City Books, 1956; *Opportunities in Civil Service,* Vocational Guidance Manuals, 1957; *Invest Smartly,* Scribner, 1961; (with Selma G. Hirsh) *AJC Review and Broadcast,* Institute of Human Relations, 1964. Syndicated columnist, Women's News Service; contributor to "Topics of the Times" column, *New York Times.*

*   *   *

YATES, Aubrey J(ames) 1925-

PERSONAL: Born December 16, 1925, in Liverpool, England; married Sylvia Mary Jupp, March 30, 1955; children: Julian, Alison, Stephen. *Education:* University of Liverpool, B.A. (with honors), 1951; University of London, diploma in psychology, 1952, Ph.D., 1954. *Office:* University of Western Australia, Nedlands, Western Australia.

CAREER: Institute of Psychiatry, University of London, London, England, lecturer in psychology, 1954-57; University of New England, Armidale, New South Wales, Australia, 1957-60, began as lecturer, became senior lecturer; University of Western Australia, Nedlands, 1960-65, began as senior lecturer, became reader; University of New England, Armidale, New South Wales, Australia, professor of psychology, 1965-67; University of Western Australia, Nedlands, professor of psychology, 1967—. *Member:* Australian Psychological Society (fellow).

Awards, honors: Senior Fulbright scholar at University of Wisconsin, 1963-64.

WRITINGS: Frustration and Conflict, Wiley, 1962; (editor) *Frustration and Conflict: Enduring Problems in Psychology* (selected readings), Van Nostrand, 1965; *Behavior Therapy,* Wiley, 1970. Contributor of almost fifty scientific papers to psychological journals. Consulting editor, *Behavior Research and Therapy, Behavior Therapy, Journal of Applied Behavior Analysis,* 1973-74, and *Australian Journal of Psychology.*

WORK IN PROGRESS: Research on delayed auditory feedback, dichotic stimulation, and behavior therapy.

*   *   *

YATES, Brock W(endel) 1933-

PERSONAL: Born October 21, 1933, in Buffalo, N.Y.; son of Raymond F. Yates (an author) and Marguerite (Wendel) Yates; married Sally Kingsley, June 13, 1955; children: Brock W., Jr., Daniel H., Claire Anne. *Education:* Hobart College, B.A., 1955. *Politics:* Democrat. *Religion:* Unitarian. *Home:* Castile, N.Y. 14427.

CAREER: Perry Herald, Perry, N.Y., news editor, 1959-63; *Buffalo Courier-Express,* Buffalo, N.Y., correspondent, 1959-63; Wyoming County Community Hospital, Warsaw, N.Y, public relations director, 1960-63; *Car and Driver Magazine,* New York, N.Y., editor, 1964-66, senior editor and columnist, 1966—. Consultant work for several national advertising agencies, 1967—. *Military service:* U.S. Navy, 1955-59, became lieutenant. *Member:* Sports Car Club of America, Automobile Clubs of Western New York (director), Kappa Alpha Society. *Awards, honors:* Co-recipient, *Playboy Magazine* editorial award for satire, 1971.

WRITINGS: (With Raymond F. Yates) *Sports and Racing Cars,* Harper, 1954; *The Indianapolis 500: The Story of the Motor Speedway,* Harper, 1956, revised edition, 1961; *Destroyers and Destroyermen: The Story of Our "Tin Can" Navy,* Harper, 1959; *Famous Indianapolis Cars and Drivers,* Harper, 1960; *Guide to Racing Cars,* Sterling, 1962, revised edition, Bonanza Books, c.1963; (with Rodger Ward) *Rodger Ward's Guide to Good Driving,* Harper, 1963; *Plastic Foam for Arts and Crafts,* Sterling, 1965; (with Don Garlits) *King of the Dragsters: The Story of Big Daddy "Don" Garlits,* Chilton, 1967, enlarged edition, 1970; *Racers and Drivers: The Fastest Men and Cars from Barney Oldfield to Craig Breedlove,* Bobbs-Merrill, 1968; (with Fran Tarkenton) *Broken Patterns: The Education of a Quarterback,* Simon & Schuster, 1971; *Sunday Driver,* Farrar, Straus, 1972. Has done television writing for Triangle Television, Philadelphia. Contributor of articles to *Sports Illustrated, Playboy, True,* and other national magazines, 1967—.

WORK IN PROGRESS: A book for Farrar, Straus.

SIDELIGHTS: Yates holds a competitive driving license with the Sports Car Club of America.

*   *   *

YATES, Norris W(ilson) 1923-

PERSONAL: Born February 22, 1923, in Corvallis, Ore.; son of Willard W. (an entomologist) and Phoebe Mae (Chamberlain) Yates. *Education:* University of Oregon, B.A., 1946; University of Wisconsin, M.A., 1947; New York University, Ph.D., 1953. *Office:* 210 Pearson Hall, Iowa State University, Ames, Iowa 50010.

CAREER: Teacher of English composition and literature prior to 1953; Iowa State University, Ames, 1953—, professor of English, 1963—. *Military service:* U.S. Army, World War II. *Member:* Modern Language Association of America, American Studies Association, Wilderness Society.

WRITINGS: William T. Porter and the "Spirit of the Times": A Study of the Big Bear School of Humor, Louisiana State University Press, 1957; *The American Humorist: Conscience of the Twentieth Century,* Iowa State University Press, 1964, revised edition, Citadel, 1965; *Guenter Grass: A Critical Essay,* Eerdmans, 1967; *Robert Benchley,* Twayne, 1968. Contributor to professional journals.

* * *

YERBY, Frank G(arvin) 1916-

PERSONAL: Born September 5, 1916, in Augusta, Ga.; son of Rufus Garvin (a postal clerk) and Wilhelmina (Smythe) Yerby; married Flora Helen Claire Williams, March 1, 1941 (divorced); married Blanca Calle-Perez (now her husband's secretary, translator, researcher, and "general manager"), July 27, 1956; children: (first marriage) Jacques Loring, Nikki Ethlyn, Faune Ellena, Jan Keith. *Education:* Painc College, A.B., 1937; Fisk University, M.A., 1938; University of Chicago, graduate study, 1939. *Politics:* Independent. *Religion:* Agnostic. *Address:* General Mola 103, Madrid 6, Spain. *Agent:* Owen Laster, William Morris Agency, 1350 Avenue of the Americas, New York, N.Y. 10019.

CAREER: Florida Agricultural and Mechanical College, Tallahassee, instructor in English, 1939-40; Southern University and Agricultural and Mechanical College, Baton Rouge, La., instructor in English, 1940-41; Ford Motor Co., Dearborn, Mich., laboratory technician, 1941-44; Ranger (Fairchild) Aircraft, Jamaica, N.Y., chief inspector, Magnaflux, 1944-45; full time writer, 1945—; resident of Madrid, Spain, since 1955; also lived in France for an extended period earlier in the fifties. *Member:* Author's Guild (New York), Real Sociedad Hipica Espanola (Madrid), Madrid Country Club. *Awards, honors:* O. Henry Memorial Award, 1944, for best first short story, "Health Card."

WRITINGS—All novels; all published by Dial unless otherwise noted: *The Foxes of Harrow,* 1946, *The Vixens,* 1947, *The Golden Hawk,* 1948, *Pride's Castle,* 1949, *Floodtide,* 1950, *A Woman Called Fancy,* 1951, *The Saracen Blade,* 1952, *The Devil's Laughter* 1953, *Bride of Liberty,* Doubleday, 1954, *Benton's Row,* 1954, *The Treasure of Pleasant Valley,* 1955, *Captain Rebel,* 1956, *Fairoaks,* 1957, *The Golden Hawk* [and] *A Woman Called Fancy,* two volumes in one, 1958, *The Serpent and the Staff,* 1958, *Jarrett's Jade,* 1959, *Gillian,* 1960, *The Garfield Honor,* 1961, *Griffin's Way,* 1962, *The Old Gods Laugh: A Modern Romance,* 1964, *An Odor of Sanctity: A Novel of Medieval Moorish Spain,* 1965, *Goat Song: A Novel of Ancient Greece,* 1968, *Judas My Brother: The Story of the Thirteenth Disciple,* 1968, *Speak Now: A Modern Novel,* 1969, *The Dahomean,* 1971, *The Girl from Storyville,* 1972.

Anthologized in *Writing in America,* edited by John Fischer and Robert B. Silvers, Rutgers University Press, 1960, *The Best Short Stories by Negro Writers: An Anthology from 1899 to the Present,* edited by Langston Hughes, Little, Brown, 1967, *Black American Literature: Fiction,* edited by Darwin T. Turner, C.E. Merrill, 1969, *Voices of Man/This Is Just to Say,* edited by Gerald Goff, Addison-Wesley, 1969, *The Poetry of the Negro, 1746-1970,* edited by Arna Bontemps and Langston Hughes, Doubleday, 1970, *Blacklash,* edited by Stewart H. Benedict, Popular Library, 1970, *Understanding Literature,* edited by Elizabeth White, Joan Wofford, and Edward J. Gordon, Ginn, 1970, *Black Literature in America: A Casebook,* edited by Ramay K. Singh and Peter Fellowes, Crowell, 1970, and *Re-Action,* edited by Conn McAuliffe, Boyd & Fraser, 1971. Contributor to *Liberty, Collier's, Harper's, France Soir, Le Meuse, La Laterne, Berlin Zeitung,* and many little magazines.

WORK IN PROGRESS: Arms and the Man, a novel of the French resistance.

SIDELIGHTS: Yerby told CA he finds the popularity of his novels "both incomprehensible and disquieting.... I ... believe that the only excuse for writing is that you love it beyond measure and beyond reason; and that to make any compromise whatsoever for the sake of sales or popularity is to join the world's oldest profession. I believe that a writer should have the guts to starve; and that if he doesn't come close to it most of the time, he'd better take a long, hard look at what he's doing. The reason I believe that is thousands of letters over the years have convinced me that great, perceptive, participating readers are as rare as great writers—no, rarer. And that they're the only kind who count."

Many critics have been unyielding in their charges that Yerby writes with the best seller list in mind. Richard Match once wrote that "Mr. Yerby could be a pretty good novelist if he ever got his mind off the neckline and the cash register." To such accusations, Yerby reasserts his lack of concern with monetary success. "I write only because I have to. What I get out of it financially doesn't come under consideration at all. I write exactly what I feel and think I want to do, but within that framework I try to give pleasure to the reading public."

Yerby's novels are characterized by colorful language, complex plot lines, and a multiplicity of characters. The critics' attitudes toward his work appear to depend on whether they accept his genre of novel as a legitimate piece of fiction in its own right. While Florence Crowther dismisses *Floodtide* as "Pandemonium on a lending-library scale," a *Times Literary Supplement* reviewer states that although "Yerby's style could be called old-fashioned, rather in the manner of Western films. . .it is nevertheless employed by a writer of intelligence and, more surprisingly, a writer of authentic moral nobility." Whereas Wilbur Watson charges that "Mr. Yerby's roaring prose belongs in a cartoon balloon, rather than between the covers of a full-price novel," Arna Bontemps finds in Yerby's writing "a flair for color, an air of easy abandon, the ability to live in the moment and to create characters that live in the moment, a touch of very elementary magic."

For most of his literary career, Yerby has been criticized for failing to deal with racial issues. He countered this criticism by asserting that "the novelist hasn't any right to inflict on the public his private ideas on politics, religion or race. If he wants to preach he should go on the pulpit." Later he stated: "My mother was Scotch-Irish, a grandparent was an Indian; I've far more Irish blood than Negro. I simply insist on remaining a member of the human race. I don't think a writer's output should be dictated by a biological accident. It happens there are many things I know far better than the race problem." He told *CA* that two of his more recent books, *Speak Now* and *The Dahomean,* "have racial themes. But I don't think they preach."

Three of his novels, *The Foxes of Harrow, The Golden Hawk,* and *The Saracen Blade,* have been made, he says, into "horrendously bad motion pictures." *Pride's Castle* has been presented as a television program. Translations of his novels have appeared in 14 languages, including Hebrew and Japanese. He speaks "rapidly, fluently, with total disregard of grammar, and with execrable accent, both French and Spanish," reads Italian and Portuguese, and with more difficulty, German; has fair mastery of medieval Latin, and is beginning to teach himself the rudiments of written Arabic. (He uses these languages in the intensive research that precedes each novel). He has traveled to 41 countries (all of those bordering on the Mediterranean, and most of those on the Caribbean), and to 22 states of the United States.

AVOCATIONAL INTERESTS: Photography, painting (oils), skiing, and electronics (has a house full of functioning transistor radios, interphones, etc. which he built himself); "I used to be a sportscar nut," he writes, "until I cracked up my Jag XK 120 and cured myself of folly; I still make an occasional stab at spearfishing."

BIOGRAPHICAL/CRITICAL SOURCES: New Yorker, February 9, 1946, April 24, 1948; *Book Week,* February 10, 1946, April 27, 1947; *New York Times,* February 10, 1946, May 2, 1948, May 15, 1949, September 10, 1950, May 6, 1951, April 6, 1952, November 15, 1953, December 5, 1954, September 23, 1956, September 8, 1957, October 12, 1958; *Christian Science Monitor,* February 16, 1946, October 15, 1950; *Saturday Review,* February 23, 1946, May 8, 1948, June 18, 1949, September 30, 1950, June 23, 1951, May 10, 1952, October 27, 1956, August 24, 1957; *Weekly Book Review,* February 24, 1946; *New York Herald Tribune Book Review,* May 4, 1947, June 12, 1949, October 22, 1950, July 15, 1951, September 21, 1952, October 4, 1953, November 14, 1954, December 19, 1954, October 14, 1956, September 22, 1957; *Time,* May 5, 1947, September 4, 1950, April 7, 1952, November 23, 1953, November 29, 1954; *San Francisco Chronicle,* May 8, 1949, July 15, 1951, November 1, 1953; *Chicago Sunday Tribune,* August 27, 1950, May 20, 1951, April 6, 1952, November 1, 1953, November 14, 1954, November 28, 1954, September 16, 1956, August 25, 1957, September 21, 1958; *Chicago Sun,* September 5, 1950; Harvey Breit, *The Writer Observed,* World Publishing, 1956; *Times Literary Supplement,* March 27, 1959; *Newsweek,* November 30, 1959; *Best Sellers,* February 15, 1968, January 1, 1969; *Negro Digest,* July, 1968, April, 1969; *New York Times Book Review,* November 10, 1968.

*   *   *

YOST, Charles W(oodruff) 1907-

PERSONAL: Born November 6, 1907, in Watertown, N.Y.; son of Nicholas Doxtater and Gertrude (Cooper) Yost; married Irena Oldakowska, September 8, 1934; children: Nicholas Churchill, Casimir Anthony, Felicity. *Education:* Hotchkiss School, graduate, 1924; Princeton University, A.B., 1928; Ecole des Hautes Etudes Internationales, University of Paris, graduate study, 1928-29. *Politics:* Democrat. *Religion:* Presbyterian. *Home:* 1050 Fifth Ave., New York, N.Y. 10028. *Agent:* Curtis Brown Ltd., 60 East 56th St., New York, N.Y. 10022. *Office:* U.S.-China Committee, 777 United Nations Plaza, New York, N.Y. 10017.

CAREER: U.S. Department of State, Washington, D.C., foreign service officer, 1930-33, 1935—, serving as deputy U.S. representative to United Nations, 1961-66; chief U.S. representative to United Nations, 1969-71; counselor to United Nations Association, 1971; president of National Committee on U.S.-China Relations, United Nations Plaza, New York, N.Y., 1972—. Principal posts also include vice-consul in Alexandria, Egypt, 1931-32, in Warsaw, Poland, 1932-33; secretary-general of U.S. delegation to Potsdam Conference, 1945; diplomatic posts in Thailand, 1945-46, Vienna, Austria, 1948-49, Athens, Greece, 1950-53; deputy U.S. high commissioner for Austria, 1953-54; ambassador to Laos, 1954-56; minister, U.S. Embassy, Paris, France, 1956-57; ambassador to Syria, 1957-58, Morocco, 1958-61. Distinguished Lecturer, School of International Affairs, Columbia University, 1971—; sponsor, Atlantic Council of the United States. *Member:* American Society of International Law, American Academy of Political and Social Sciences,

Council on Foreign Relations (senior fellow, 1966-69), National Planning Association. *Awards, honors:* Rockefeller Public Service Award, 1964; LL.D. from St. Lawrence University, Princeton University, Hamilton College, and University of Louisville.

WRITINGS: The Age of Triumph and Frustration: Modern Dialogues, Speller, 1964; *The Insecurity of Nations: International Relations in the Twentieth Century,* published for the Council on Foreign Relations by Praeger, 1968; *The Pursuit of World Order* (inaugural lecture of World Order Research Institute), Villanova University Press, 1969; *The Conduct and Misconduct of Foreign Affairs,* Random House, 1972.

BIOGRAPHICAL/CRITICAL SOURCES: New York Times, February 9, 1968; *New York Review of Books,* September 12, 1968; *Times Literary Supplement,* June 12, 1969.

*   *   *

YOST, Stanley K. 1924-

PERSONAL: Born April 21, 1924, in Mendota, Ill.; son of Carl John and Nora (Sauressig) Yost; married Barbara J. Heininger, March 29, 1947; children: Beth Ann, Steven Karl, Joel Arthur, Jennifer Alyson. *Education:* Attended University of Illinois. *Politics:* "No party, slight Democratic leanings." *Religion:* Methodist. *Home:* 4443 Elmwood Ave., Royal Oak, Mich. 48073. *Office:* Oakland Mall Shell, 32845 John R St., Madison Heights, Mich. 48071.

CAREER: Formerly a photoengraver, employed by Detroit Colortype Co., Detroit, Mich.; Oakland Mall Shell, Madison Heights, Mich., owner. *Military service:* U.S. Army and U.S. Air Force, 1942-45; became second lieutenant (pilot). *Awards, honors:* Thomas L. McKean Award of Antique Automobile Club, 1964, for auto historical writing.

WRITINGS: The Great Old Cars, Where Are They Now?, Wayside Press, 1960; *They Don't Build Cars Like They Used To,* Wayside Press, 1963. Contributor to *Automobile Quarterly.*

*   *   *

YOUNG, Arthur N(ichols) 1890-

PERSONAL: Born November 21, 1890, in Los Angeles, Calif.; son of William Stewart (a clergyman) and Adele (Nichols) Young; married Nellie May Bailey (an author), June 11, 1915; children: Elizabeth (Mrs. Phil W. Roulac), Allen, William Dwight. *Education:* Occidental College, A.B., 1910; Princeton University, A.M., 1911, Ph.D., 1914; George Washington University, LL.B., 1927. *Religion:* Protestant. *Home:* 985 East California Blvd., Apartment 303, Pasadena, Calif. 91106.

CAREER: Began as college and university teacher of economics; financial adviser, with special reference to currency, central banking, loans, and investments, in China, elsewhere in southeast Asia, Saudi Arabia, and most countries of Latin America, 1918—; economist, then head of economic office, U.S. Department of State, 1922-28; financial adviser to Chinese government, 1929-46, also serving as vice-chairman of United China Relief Coordinating Commission, 1942-45, chairman of American Relief and Red Cross Committees in China, 1943-45, trustee of China Foundation, and member of Chinese delegation to Bretton Woods Conference, 1944; chief of American financial mission, acting director of Point IV program in Saudi Arabia, 1951-52; financial consultant to American foreign aid administrations, 1954, 1957-58, and to Stanford Research Institute, 1962-63. Occidental College, Los Angeles, Calif., trustee, 1950—, lecturer, 1958-59.

MEMBER: American Economic Association, American Guild of Organists, Phi Beta Kappa, Phi Gamma Delta, Cosmos Club (Washington, D.C.), Twilight Club (Pasadena). *Awards, honors:* LL.D., Occidental College, 1937; Order of the Brilliant Jade (China), 1939; Guggenheim fellowship, 1956-58.

WRITINGS: The Single Tax Movement in the United States, Princeton University Press, 1916; *The Possibilities and Limitations of Special Taxation of Land,* National Conference of Social Work, 1917; *Finances of Federal District of Mexico, D.F. May,* 1918; *Spanish Finance and Trade,* U.S. Government Printing Office, 1920; *China's Financial Progress,* Foreign Policy Association, 1938; *China's Economic and Financial Reconstruction,* Carnegie Endowment for International Peace, 1947; *Saudi Arabian Currency and Finance,* Middle East Institute, 1953; *China and the Helping Hand, 1937-1945,* Harvard University Press, 1963; *China's Wartime Finance and Inflation, 1937-1945,* Harvard University Press, 1965; (contributor) Paul K.T. Sih, editor, *The Strenuous Decade: China's Nation-Building Efforts, 1927-1937,* St. John's University Press, 1970; *China's Nation-Building Effort, 1927-1937: The Financial and Economic Record,* Hoover Institution Press, 1971. Author of reports for U.S. and foreign governments; contributor to periodicals.

WORK IN PROGRESS: Writing on experiences in advisory work.

AVOCATIONAL INTERESTS: Music.

*   *   *

YOUNG, Howard Thomas   1926-

PERSONAL: Born March 24, 1926, in Cumberland, Md.; son of Samuel Phillip (a minister) and Sarah Emaline (Frederick) Young; married Carol Margot Osborne, October 7, 1949 (divorced, 1965); married Jennifer Bunker, July 15, 1966; children: (first marriage) Laurie Margaret, Jennifer Anne. *Education:* Westminster College, New Wilmington, Pa., student, 1946-47; Columbia University, B.S. (summa cum laude), 1950, M.A., 1952, Ph.D., 1954. *Home:* 338 Harvard Ave., Claremont, Calif. 91711. *Office:* Department of Modern European Languages, Pomona College, Claremont, Calif. 91711.

CAREER: Columbia University, New York, N.Y., lecturer in Spanish, 1950-54; Pomona College, Claremont, Calif., instructor, 1954-56, assistant professor, 1956-60, associate professor and director of language laboratory, 1960-67, professor of Romance languages and chairman of department of modern European languages, 1967—. Visiting professor of Spanish, University of Massachusetts, 1966; lecturer, University of London, 1968. *Military service:* U.S. Naval Reserve, 1944-46. *Member:* Modern Language Association of America, American Association of Teachers of Spanish, Philosophical Association of the Pacific Coast. *Awards, honors:* Del Ame Foundation grant for study in Spain, 1960; Fulbright lecture grant, 1967-68.

WRITINGS: The Victorious Expression: A Study of Four Contemporary Poets, University of Wisconsin Press, 1964; *Juan Ramon Jimenez,* Columbia University Press, 1967. Contributor of articles and reviews to *New York Times Book Review, New Republic, Books Abroad,* and professional journals.

WORK IN PROGRESS: Juan Ramon Jimenez and English and American Poetry; Juan Ramon Jimenez and Tagore.

SIDELIGHTS: Young has lived and traveled in Spain and South America.

YOUNG, Kenneth   1916-

PERSONAL: Born November 27, 1916, in Middlestown, Yorkshire, England; son of Robert William (an iron-founder) and Alice Jane (Ramsden) Young; married Phyllis Dicker, May 2, 1952; children: Milena, Julian, Christian, Phyllida, Quentin. *Education:* University of Leeds, B.A. (first class honors). *Politics:* Conservative. *Religion:* Church of England. *Home:* Amberfield House, Chart Sutton, Maidstone, Kent, England. *Office: Daily Express,* Fleet St., London E.C.4, England.

CAREER: British Broadcasting Corp., London, England, sub-editor, 1948-49; *Daily Mirror,* London, sub-editor, 1949-50; *Daily Telegraph,* London, book critic and leader writer, 1951-60; *Yorkshire Post,* Leeds, England, editor-in-chief, 1961-65; Beaverbrook Newspapers Ltd., London, England, political and literary adviser, 1965—. Governor, Welbeck College. *Member:* Royal Society of Literature (fellow). *Military service:* Intelligence Corps, 1940-45; served in Algeria, Italy, and Greece; became major. Second secretary, British Foreign Office, 1945-48.

WRITINGS: D.H. Lawrence, Longmans, Green, 1952, revised edition, 1960; *John Dryden: A Critical Biography,* Sylvan Press, 1954, Russell, 1969; *Ford Madox Ford,* Longmans, Green, 1956, revised edition, 1970; (editor) *The Bed Post: A Miscellany of the Yorkshire Post,* Macdonald & Co., 1962; *Arthur James Balfour: The Happy Life of the Politician, Prime Minister, Statesman, and Philosopher, 1848-1930,* G. Bell, 1963; *The Press and the Universities* (lecture), University of Hull 1964; (editor) *The Second Bed Post: A Miscellany of the Yorkshire Post,* Macdonald & Co., 1964; *Churchill and Beaverbrook: A Study in Friendship and Politics,* Eyre & Spottiswoode, 1966, James H. Heineman, 1967; *Rhodesia and Independence: A Study in British Colonial Policy,* James H. Heineman, 1967, new edition, Dent, 1969; *Music's Great Days in the Spas and Watering-Places,* Macmillan, 1968; *Compton Mackenzie,* Longmans, Green, 1968; *The Greek Passion: A Study in People and Politics,* Dent, 1969; *Sir Alec Douglas-Home,* Dent, 1970, Fairleigh Dickinson University Press, 1971. Contributor of articles to *Spectator, Encounter,* and other periodicals. Contributor to British Broadcasting Corp. and Independent Television programs.

WORK IN PROGRESS: Editing journals and letters of Sir Robert Bruce-Lockhart.

AVOCATIONAL INTERESTS: Politics and music.

BIOGRAPHICAL/CRITICAL SOURCES: Times Literary Supplement, March 9, 1967; *New Statesman,* March 31, 1967; *Books and Bookmen,* May, 1967, October, 1969; *Observer Review,* January 19, 1969; *Spectator,* September 27, 1969; *Punch,* October 7, 1970.

*   *   *

YOUNG, Lois Horton   1911-

PERSONAL: Born April 2, 1911, in Hamburg, N.Y.; daughter of Roy Austin (a minister) and Grace (Spencer) Horton; married Carl Edgar Young (a minister), April 25, 1934; children: Mary Lois (Mrs. J. Robert Miller), Margaret Carol (Mrs. Edwin M. Wray), Ruth Elizabeth (Mrs. George A. McGuire), Kathryn Louise. *Education:* Hunter College (now Hunter College of the City University of New York), A.B., 1933; additional study at University of Maryland and at Biblical Seminary. *Religion:* Protestant. *Home:* 303 Windsor Mill Rd., Ext., Baltimore, Md. 21208. *Office:* Milford Mill Kindergarten, 901-915 Milford Mill Rd., Baltimore, Md. 21208.

CAREER: Director of pre-school center, Baltimore, Md., 1942-43; kindergarten teacher in Baltimore, 1945-54;

Milford Mill Church, Baltimore, Md., director of Christian education 1953—; Milford Mill Kindergarten, Baltimore, Md., director, 1954—. *Member:* Childhood Education Association, National Association for Education of Young Children, Phi Sigma Gamma (president, 1932-33). *Awards, honors:* Hymn Society of America award, for Christian education hymns.

WRITINGS: Curriculum Materials for Children's Leader, Otterbein Press, 1937-57; *Kindergarten Teacher's Guides,* six books, Pilgrim Press, 1953-54; *Let's Grow Up,* Pilgrim Press, 1955; *My Bible Story Book,* three books, Judson, 1955; *Kindergarten Teacher's Book,* three books, Judson, 1955; *Kindergarten Superintendent's Book,* Judson, 1956; *Making Christmas Christian,* Christian Education Press, 1957; *God and His World: A Cooperative Vacation School Course for Use with Kindergarten Children* (teacher's book), Otterbein Press, 1958; *God and His World* (pupil's book), Otterbein Press, 1958; *Teaching Kindergarten Children,* Judson, 1959.

Kindergarten Storytime, Judson, 1962; *God's World of Wonder,* Otterbein Press, 1964; *The Little Church That Grew,* Abingdon, 1965; *No Biscuits at All,* Friendship, 1966; *Through Hospital Windows,* Judson, 1966; *For a Child's Day: Thoughts and Verses Selected from the Bible,* Abingdon, 1967; *Whatever Happened on Peony Street?,* Friendship 1968.

This Is Benjamin, Judson, 1970; *Mundi's World,* Judson, 1970; *We Remember Jesus,* Judson, 1970; *What Can You Decide?,* Judson, 1970; *The Brown Shoes,* Judson, 1970; *God Plans for Us to Grow,* Judson, 1970; *Dimensions for Happening,* Judson, 1971. Author of curriculum materials for United Methodist Church; writer of children's songs. Contributor to religious and educational journals.

WORK IN PROGRESS: For Every Branch, a book on theology; *No Can Be a Loving Word; Vermont, a Special Flavor; As a Child Grows;* and *Kavanaugh.*

AVOCATIONAL INTERESTS: Interior decorating and cooking.

* * *

YOUNG, Philip 1918-

PERSONAL: Born May 26, 1918, in Boston, Mass.; son of Roswell Philip (a businessman) and Katharine (Pratt) Young; married Carolyn Anderson (deceased); married Katherine Garner; children: (first marriage) Jeffrey Anderson; (second marriage) Rosalie. *Education:* Amherst College, B.A., 1940; Harvard University, graduate student, 1940-41; University of Iowa, Ph.D., 1948. *Politics:* Democrat. *Home:* 719 Cornwall Rd., State College, Pa. 16801. *Office:* 136 South Burrowes, Pennsylvania State University, University Park, Pa. 16802.

CAREER: New York University, New York, N.Y., 1948-53, began as instructor, became assistant professor of English; Kansas State University, Manhattan, associate professor of English, 1953-59; Pennsylvania State University, University Park, professor of American literature, 1959-65, research professor of English, 1965—. Fellow, Institute for the Arts and Humanistic Studies, 1965—. U.S. Department of State specialist in India, 1957; Fulbright lecturer in France and Italy, 1962-63. *Military service:* U.S. Army, 1942-46; served in European theater; became first lieutenant; received Air Medal, three battle stars. *Member:* Modern Language Association of America. *Awards, honors:* American Council of Learned Societies scholar, 1950-51.

WRITINGS: Ernest Hemingway, Rinehart, 1952, revised edition published as *Ernest Hemingway: A Reconsideration,* Pennsylvania State University Press, 1966; (editor and author of introduction) Nathaniel Hawthorne, *The House of the Seven Gables,* Rinehart, 1957; *Ernest Hemingway* (pamphlet), University of Minnesota Press, 1959; (editor with William White) *By-Line: Ernest Hemingway,* Collins, 1968; (with Charles W. Mann) *The Hemingway Manuscripts: An Inventory,* Pennsylvania State University Press, 1969; *Three Bags Full: Essays in American Fiction,* Harcourt, 1972.

Contributor: Robert P. Weeks, editor, *Hemingway: A Collection of Critical Essays,* Prentice-Hall, 1962; Bernard S. Oldsey and Arthur O. Lewis, Jr., editors, *Visions and Revisions in Modern American Literary Criticism,* Dutton, 1962; Carlos Baker, editor, *Ernest Hemingway: Critiques of Four Major Novels,* Scribner, 1962; James E. Miller, Jr. and Bernice Slote, editors, *Dimensions of the Short Story: A Critical Anthology,* Dodd, 1964; William Van O'Connor, editor, *Seven Modern American Novelists: An Introduction,* University of Minnesota Press, 1964. Contributor to many other collections of criticism.

Contributor of articles on three American writers to *Dictionary of World Literature in Twentieth Century,* and of articles on Hemingway to *Collier's Encyclopedia, Reader's Encyclopedia of American Literature, Encyclopaedia Britannica,* and *Encyclopedia Americana;* contributor of articles on more than seventy authors to *Encyclopedia International,* 1963. Contributor of about twenty articles and thirty reviews to periodicals, including *Sewanee Review, Kenyon Review,* and *Atlantic.*

WORK IN PROGRESS: Essays in American Fiction, for Harcourt; a collection of Hemingway stories, for Scribner.

SIDELIGHTS: Tagged as "the Hemingway man," Young's book on that writer has been published in England, and in German and Spanish translations; his pamphlet on Hemingway has been issued in translation in nine countries, including Japan, Korea, and Lebanon. "I have, however, read some other writers," he says.

BIOGRAPHICAL/CRITICAL SOURCES: Books Abroad, spring, 1967; *Times Literary Supplement,* March 7, 1968; *Listener,* March 14, 1968.

* * *

YOUNG, Scott A (lexander) 1918-

PERSONAL: Born April 14, 1918, in Manitoba, Canada; son of Percy Andrew (a druggist) and Jean (Paterson) Young; married Astrid Carlson (a researcher, writer, bookkeeper), May 20, 1961; children: (previous marriage) Robert, Neil; (present marriage) Dierdre, Astrid. *Agent:* Willis Kingsley Wing, 24 East 38th St., New York, N.Y. 10016. *Office:* Ascot Productions, 17 Rosedale Heights Dr., Toronto, Ontario, Canada.

CAREER: Journalist, 1936-48; free-lance fiction writer, 1948-56; *Toronto Globe and Mail,* Toronto, Ontario, columnist, 1957-69; *Toronto Telegram,* Toronto, Ontario, sports editor and columnist, 1969—. *Military service:* Canadian Navy, World War II. *Awards, honors:* National Newspaper Award, 1958, for sportswriting; Wilderness Medal, 1963, for television documentary, "The Opening of the West."

WRITINGS: Red Shield in Action, Salvation Army, 1948; *Scrubs on Skates* (juvenile), Little, Brown, 1952; *Boy on Defense* (juvenile), Little, Brown, 1953; *The Flood* (novel), McClelland & Stewart, 1956, Transatlantic, 1957; *The Clue of the Dead Duck* (juvenile), Little, Brown, 1962; *A Boy at the Leafs Camp* (juvenile), Little, Brown, 1963; (with wife, Astrid Young) *Big City Office Junior,* Ryerson, 1964; *Sports Stories,* Ryerson, 1965; *The Leafs I Knew,* Ryerson, 1966; (with Astrid Young) *O'Brien,* Ryerson, 1967; *We Won't Be Needing You, Al: Stories of Men and Sports,* Ryerson, 1968; (with Punch

Imlach) *Hockey Is a Battle: Punch Imlach's Own Story,* Crown, 1969. Editor, "Canadian Careers Library," Ryerson. Author of television documentaries. Contributor of about seventy short stories to magazines and anthologies.

BIOGRAPHICAL/CRITICAL SOURCES: Book World, March 1, 1970.

* * *

YOUNGBERG, Norma Ione (Rhoads) 1896- (Leigh Winfield)

PERSONAL: Born May 24, 1896, in Sutherland, Iowa; daughter of Bert (a teacher) and Mary (Rowland) Rhoads; married Gustavus B. Youngberg, December 24, 1916 (died 1944); children: Ruth (Mrs. Jonathan Knittel), Robert, Rhoda (Mrs. Elmo Kincaid), James R., Ina Madge (Mrs. Milton Longway), Gustavus B., Jr. *Education:* Attended San Jose State College. *Politics:* Democrat. *Religion:* Seventh Day Adventist. *Home:* 1635 the Alameda, San Jose, Calif. 95126. *Office:* Winfield-Harmon Agency, 1635 the Alameda, San Jose, Calif. 95126.

CAREER: Public school teacher in Elk Point, S.D., 1914-15; Malayan Union Seminary, Singapore, teacher, 1933-35, 1936-38; Styria Trading Co. Ltd., manager, 1945-51; Casa Bella Sanitarium, manager, 1950-56; San Jose Unified Schools, San Jose, Calif., teacher, 1957—; Los Gatos Union High School, Los Gatos, Calif., teacher, 1962—; Winfield-Harmon Agency, San Jose, Calif., owner and manager, 1961—. *Member:* League of American Pen Women (branch president, 1957), Word Crafters (founder and director, 1957—), Edwin Markham Poetry Society (workshop leader), Chaparral Poets, Robert Frost Chapter.

WRITINGS: Jungle Thorn (juvenile), Southern Publishing, 1951; *Miracle in Borneo* (juvenile), Southern Publishing, 1953; *Miracle of the Song* (juvenile), Morrow, 1955; *The Queen's Gold* (juvenile), Morrow, 1956; *Tiger of Bitter Valley,* Morrow, 1957; *Taught by a Tiger,* Zondervan, 1961; *Ayesha, Beloved of God,* Review & Herald, 1961; *Fire on the Mountain,* Review & Herald, 1962; *Nyla and the White Crocodile,* Review & Herald, 1963; *Singer on the Sand: The True Story of an Occurrence on the Island of Great Sangir, North of the Celebes, More* (with Beth Hill) *Dixie, a Dedicated Doberman,* Pacific than a Hundred Years Ago, Review & Herald, 1964; Press Publishing Association, 1967; (with Eric Kreye) *Under the Blood Banner: The Story of a Hitler Youth,* Pacific Press Publishing Association, 1968; (with G.H. Minchin) *Under Sealed Orders: The Story of Gus Youngberg,* Pacific Press Publishing Association, 1970.

Textbooks: *Story Craft: A Creative Writing Manual for All Who Would Write and Sell for Publication,* Volumes I-III, Winfield-Harmon Agency, 1961-62; *Victory Notes,* Cliff's, 1962; *Lord Jim Notes,* Cliff's, 1962; *Heart of Darkness,* Cliff's, 1964; *Creative Techniques for Christian Writers,* Pacific Press Publishing Association, 1968. Contributor of serials to *Junior Guide* and *Youth's Instructor.*

WORK IN PROGRESS: Under contract to do twelve collections of bedtime stories for "Buckaroo-500" television program.

* * *

YOUNGER, Richard D(avis) 1921-

PERSONAL: Born April 3, 1921, in Jefferson, Wis.; son of George W. (an educator) and Eleanor M. (Davis) Younger. *Education:* Wisconsin State College, B.S., 1943; Marquette University, LL.B., 1948, M.A., 1950; University of Wisconsin, Ph.D., 1953. *Home:* 4045 Linkwood, No. 741, Houston, Tex. 77025.

CAREER: University of Wisconsin, Milwaukee, instructor in history, 1953-54; University of Houston, Houston, Tex., assistant professor, 1954-58, associate professor, 1958-62, professor of history, 1962—. *Military service:* U.S. Army Air Corps, 1943-46. *Member:* American Historical Association, Organization of American Historians, Southern Historical Association, Texas Gulf Coast Historical Association.

WRITINGS: The People's Panel: The Grand Jury in the United States, 1634-1941, Brown University Press, 1963.

* * *

YU, Frederick T.C. 1921-

PERSONAL: Born July 15, 1921, in China; married Alice Chen; children: Frederick, Jr., Jacqueline. *Education:* University of Nanking, B.A., 1944; State University of Iowa, M.A., 1948, Ph.D., 1951. *Religion:* Presbyterian. *Home:* 39 Allison Dr., Englewood Cliffs, N.J. 07632. *Office:* Graduate School of Journalism, Columbia University, New York, N.Y. 10027.

CAREER: Stetson University, Stetson, Fla., assistant professor of journalism, 1954-55; Montana State University, Missoula, 1955-62, began as associate professor, became professor of journalism; Graduate School of Journalism, Columbia University, New York, N.Y., associate professor, 1962-67, professor of journalism, 1967—, associate dean, 1970—. *Member:* American Association for Public Opinion Research, Association for Education in Journalism, Sigma Delta Chi, Kappa Tau Alpha, Phi Kappa Phi.

WRITINGS: The Propaganda Machine in Communist China, with Special Reference to Ideology, Policy, and Regulations, as of 1952, Air Force Personnel and Training Research Center, Air Research and Development Command, 1955; *The Strategy and Tactics of Chinese Communist Propaganda as of 1952,* Air Force Personnel and Training Research Center, Air Research and Development Command, 1955; *Mass Persuasion in Communist China,* Praeger, 1964; (editor) *Behavioral Sciences and the Mass Media,* Russell Sage, 1968.

WORK IN PROGRESS: Research on foreign news in the American press.

* * *

YUNCK, John A(dam) III 1917-

PERSONAL: Born July 8, 1917, in Orange, N.J.; son of John A. (a banker) and Helen Faivre (Davis) Yunck; married Ruth E. Taylor, April 19, 1943; children: Edward R., Thomas P. *Education:* Michigan State University, B.A., 1938, M.A., 1940; New York University, Ph.D., 1953. *Home:* 4536 Indian Hills Dr., Okemos, Mich. 48864. *Office:* Department of English, Michigan State University, East Lansing, Mich. 48823.

CAREER: Michigan State University, East Lansing, 1940—, began as instructor, now professor of English and comparative literature. *Military service:* U.S. Army Air Corps, World War II, 1942-46. U.S. Air Force Reserves, now colonel and military support liaison officer for civil defense in Michigan. *Member:* International Arthurian Society, Modern Language Association of America, Mediaeval Academy of America, American Comparative Literature Association, Midwest Modern Language Association.

WRITINGS: The Lineage of Lady Meed: The Development of Medieval Venality Satire, University of Notre Dame Press, 1963. Contributor to professional and literary journals.

WORK IN PROGRESS: Research into medieval satirical themes, materials, and devices; also research in the origins and social functions of medieval romance.

YURKA, Blanche

PERSONAL: Born in St. Paul, Minn.; daughter of Anton (a teacher) and Caroline (Nowak) Yurka; married Ian Keith (deceased). Education: Studied at Institute of Musical Art (now Julliard School of Music), and at training school of Metropolitan Opera House. Home: 325 East 72nd St., New York, N.Y. 10021.

CAREER: Studied for an operatic career, then turned to acting, appearing in more than sixty roles on Broadway, in stock and on tour, 1909-59. Presented one-woman repertory program on U.S. tours in 1935-38, again in 1959; visited Athens under U.S. International Exchange of Artists to open Greek Drama Festival in "Prometheus Bound," 1957. Director of stage production of "Carry Nation," 1932, and other productions including The Wild Duck, Hedda Gabler, and Lady from the Sea; film roles include "A Tale of Two Cities," 1935, and "Song of Bernadette." Member: American National Theatre and Academy (board), Actors Equity Association (life). Awards, honors: A citation for high acting achievement from Washington Theatre Club; doctorate from Tampa University; recipient of other awards from American National Theatre and Academy.

WRITINGS: Dear Audience: A Guide to Greater Enjoyment of Theatre, Prentice-Hall, 1959; (editor and author of introduction) Three Scandinavian Plays, Washington Square Press, 1962; (editor and author of introduction) Three Classic Greek Plays, Washington Square Press, 1964; Bohemian Girl: Blanche Yurka's Theatrical Life, Ohio University Press, 1970. Co-adapter of "Spring in Autumn" from the Spanish, 1933.

WORK IN PROGRESS: A textbook on acting; an autobiography by her cat "Moukra"; editing a short story by Sarah Bernhardt; Happy Ending, a novel; Sisters, fiction.

AVOCATIONAL INTERESTS: Foreign travel, music, and people.

BIOGRAPHICAL/CRITICAL SOURCES: Best Sellers, July 15, 1970; Variety, August 26, 1970.

*   *   *

ZACK, Arnold M(arshall) 1931-

PERSONAL: Born October 7, 1931, in Lynn, Mass.; son of Samuel George (an attorney) and Bess (Freedman) Zack; married Norma Wilner, August 10, 1969. Education: Tufts University, A.B., 1953; Yale University, LL.B., 1956; Harvard University, M.P.A., 1961, M.A., 1963. Home: 170 West Canton St., Boston, Mass. 02118. Office: 151 Tremont St., Boston, Mass. 02111.

CAREER: Attorney, arbitrator, and manpower consultant in Boston, Mass., 1956—. Lecturer in labor economics, Northeastern University; Fulbright professor, Haile Selassie I University, 1963-64. Consultant to United Nations Congo Operation, U.S. Peace Corps, Department of Labor, Ethiopian Ministry of National Community Development, and to other agencies. Member: National Academy of Arbitrators, African Studies Association (fellow), Industrial Relations Research Association (chapter officer program chairman, 1959 national meeting), Society for International Development.

WRITINGS: Trade Unions and the Development of Middle Level Manpower, University of Ghana, 1962; The New Labor Relations in Ethiopia, Department of Economics, Haile Selassie I University, 1964; Labor Training in Developing Countries: A Challenge in Responsible Democracy, Praeger, 1964.

Contributor: Colin Legum, editor, Africa: A Handbook to the Continent, Praeger, 1962; William Y. Elliot, editor, Education and Training in Developing Countries: The Role of U.S. Foreign Aid, Praeger, 1966; Jeffrey Butler,

editor, Boston University Papers on Africa, Praeger, 1967; Thomas Christensen, editor, Proceedings of Annual Conference of New York University Conference on Labor, 1967, Matthew Bender, 1968; Thomas Christensen, editor, Proceedings of Annual Conference of New York University Conference on Labor, 1970, Matthew Bender, 1971. Contributor of articles to reports and journals.

*   *   *

ZAHN, Gordon C(harles) 1918-

PERSONAL: Born August 7, 1918, in Milwaukee, Wis. Education: College of St. Thomas, St. Paul, Minn., B.A. (summa cum laude), 1949; Catholic University of America, M.A., 1950, Ph.D., 1953; Harvard University, postgraduate student, 1952-53. Politics: Independent Democrat. Religion: Roman Catholic. Home: 780 Boylston, Apt. 26D, Boston, Mass. 02199. Office: Department of Sociology, University of Massachusetts—Boston, 100 Arlington, Boston, Mass. 02199.

CAREER: Loyola University, Chicago, Ill., 1953-67, began as assistant professor, became professor of sociology; University of Massachusetts—Boston, professor of sociology, 1967—. Conscientious objector, World War II. Member of board of directors, National Committee for a Sane Nuclear Policy, American PAX Association, and Fellowship of Reconciliation. Member: American Sociological Association, American Catholic Sociological Society (former president), American Association of University Professors, Eastern Sociological Society, Religious Research Association, Association for the Sociology of Religion Awards, honors: Social Science Research Council fellow, 1952-53; Fulbright fellow (research) in Germany, 1956-57; American Philosophical Society grant for Austria, 1961; Simon Senior Research fellow, University of Manchester, 1964-65; Christopher Award, 1971.

WRITINGS: A Descriptive Study of the Social Backgrounds of Conscientious Objectors in Civilian Public Service During World War II, Catholic University of America Press, 1953; (editor and author of introduction and commentaries) Readings in Sociology, Newman, 1958; (contributor) William J. Nagle, editor, Morality and Modern Warfare: The State of the Question, Helicon, 1960; German Catholics and Hitler's Wars: A Study in Social Control, Sheed, 1962; (contributor) Breakthrough to Peace, New Directions, 1962; An Alternative to War (pamphlet), Council on Religion and International Affairs, 1963; In Solitary Witness: The Life and Death of Franz Jaegerstaetter, Holt, 1964; What Is Society?, Hawthorn, 1964; War, Conscience, and Dissent, Hawthorn, 1967; The Military Chaplaincy: A Study of Role Tension in the Royal Air Force, University of Toronto Press, 1969 (published in England as Chaplains in the RAF: A Study in Role Tension, Manchester University Press, 1969); (contributor) J. Andrews, editor, Paul VI: A Critical Appraisal, Bruce, 1970; (author of introduction) Thomas Merton, Thomas Merton on Peace, McCall Publishing, 1971.

WORK IN PROGRESS: A book on the social history of Catholic CO camps during World War II.

SIDELIGHTS: In Solitary Witness has been the basis for documentaries and dramatizations on BBC radio and American, German, Austrian, Swiss, and Dutch television.

BIOGRAPHICAL/CRITICAL SOURCES: Times Literary Supplement, September 21, 1967; New York Times Book Review, October 8, 1967; Christian Century, January 14, 1970.

ZAMONSKI, Stanley W.   1919-

PERSONAL: Surname was originally Zamojski; born August 7, 1919, in Shenandoah, Pa.; son of Stanley (a coal miner) and Cecilia (Waliszewski) Zamojski. Education: Studied fine arts and writing under private tutors; Wentworth Institute, Boston, Mass., student, two years. Politics: Independent. Home: 10120 West 20th, Lakewood, Colo. 80215. Office: P.O. Box 15312, Lakewood, Colo. 80215.

CAREER: Colorado State Highway Department, right-of-way engineer, 1947-54; free-lance photographer in Denver, Colo., 1954—; has also worked as draftsman, newspaper reporter, cartographer, and advertising man. Member of American Polish Civil War Centennial Committee. Treasurer, Industries for Jefferson County, Colo; member of board of directors, Lakewood Chamber of Commerce. Military service: U.S. Air Force, 1939-46; pilot in Asiatic-Pacific theater; became first lieutenant; received Air Medal with two oak leaf clusters. Member: Western Writers of America, Rocky Mountain Professional Photographers Association, Denver Press Club, Denver Authors League, Polonia Art Society (president, 1962-63), Polish Club of Denver (president, 1957), Westernaires (Denver Posse), Evil Companions, Jefferson County Coin Club, Rocky Mountain Sportsmen, Rocky Mountain Horsemen. Awards, honors: Fifty-nine awards for photography.

WRITINGS: (With Teddy Keller) The Fifty-Niners: A Denver Diary, Sage Books, 1961.

Stories are anthologized in Anthology of Best Original Short Shorts, edited by Robert Oberfirst, Oberfirst Publications, 1955, A Treasury of New Short Fiction, edited by Stewart Bronfeld, National Publishing Co., 1955, and in The Denver Brand, 1957, 1961, 1963. Contributor to True West and Westerners Round-Up.

WORK IN PROGRESS: The 16th Century Golden Era of Poland; The Anthracite Coal Fields of Pennsylvania; Colorado before the Civil War.

BIOGRAPHICAL/CRITICAL SOURCES: Polish American Journal, January 13, 1962; Montana Magazine, January, 1962; Polonia Reporter, March, 1962.

*   *   *

ZARTMAN, I(ra) William   1932-

PERSONAL: Born January 9, 1932, in Allentown, Pa.; son of Ira F. (an administrative physicist) and Edythe Grace (Wenger) Zartman; married Marie-Daniele Harmel, March 26, 1960; Education: Johns Hopkins University, M.A., 1952; University of Copenhagen, diplome, 1953; Yale University, Ph.D., 1956. Politics: Republican. Religion: Lutheran. Home: 110 Bleecker St., Apt. 17E, New York, N.Y. 10012. Office: Department of Politics, New York University, New York, N.Y. 10003.

CAREER: Yale University, New Haven, Conn., instructor in international relations, 1956; University of South Carolina, Columbia, assistant professor, 1960-62, associate professor of international relations, 1963-65; New York University, New York, N.Y., visiting associate professor of U.N. affairs, 1965-66, professor of politics, 1966—, associate director, Center of International Studies, 1967-69, head of Department of Politics, 1970—. Military service: U.S. Navy, 1956-60; became lieutenant commander. Member: African Studies Association, American Political Science Association, U.S. Naval Institute, Middle East Studies Association (executive secretary and treasurer, 1966—).

WRITINGS: The Sahara: Bridge or Barrier?, International Conciliation, 1963; Government and Politics in Northern Africa, Praeger, 1963; Morocco: Problems of New Power, Atherton, 1964; Destiny of a Dynasty: The Search for Institutions in Morocco's Developing Society, University of South Carolina Press, 1964; International Relations in the New Africa, Prentice-Hall, 1966; The Politics of Trade Negotiations Between Africa and the European Community: The Weak Confront the Strong, Princeton University Press, 1971.

Contributor: Jeane J. Kirkpatrick, editor, Strategy of Deception: A Study in Worldwide Communist Tactics, Farrar, Straus, 1963; Benjamin Rivlin and J.S. Szyliowicz, editors, The Contemporary Middle East: Tradition and Innovation, Random House, 1965; William Hubert Lewis, French-Speaking Africa, Walker & Co., 1965; Vernon McKay, editor, African Diplomacy: Studies in the Determinants of Foreign Policy, published for the School of Advanced International Studies, Johns Hopkins University, by Praeger, 1966; Leon Carl Brown, editor, State and Society in Independent North Africa, Middle East Institute, 1966; African Boundaries, Uppsala, 1969; (and editor) Czechoslovakia: Intervention and Impact, New York University Press, 1970; Claude E. Welch, Jr., editor, Soldier and State in Africa: A Comparative Analysis of Military Intervention and Political Change, Northwestern University Press, 1970; Hugh C. Brooks and Yassin El-Ayouty, editors, Refugees South of the Sahara: An African Dilemma, Negro Universities Press, 1970; Conflitti e sviluppo nal Mediterraneo, Instituti di Affari Internazionali, 1970; (and editor) Man, State and Society in the Contemporary Maghrib, Praeger, 1972. Contributor to Colliers Encyclopedia and to political science journals.

WORK IN PROGRESS: Studies of elite circulation, and theory of negotiation.

SIDELIGHTS: Zartman speaks French, Danish, German, Swedish, Norwegian, and Arabic. Avocational interests: Painting, constructing mobiles, designing Christmas cards.

*   *   *

ZEFF, Stephen A(ddam)   1933-

PERSONAL: Born July 26, 1933, in Chicago, Ill.; son of Roy David (an advertising man) and Hazel (Sex) Zeff. Education: University of Colorado, B.S., 1955, M.S., 1957; University of Michigan, M.B.A., 1960, Ph.D., 1962. Office: Graduate School of Business Administration, Tulane University, New Orleans, La. 70118.

CAREER: University of Colorado, Boulder, instructor in accounting, 1955-57; University of Michigan, Ann Arbor, lecturer in accounting, 1960-61; Tulane University, New Orleans, La., assistant professor, 1961-63, associate professor, 1963-67, professor of accounting, 1967—. Arthur Andersen & Co. Lecturer, University of Edinburgh, 1970; honorary senior Fulbright scholar, Monash University, 1972. Member: American Accounting Association, American Economic Association, National Association of Accountants, Financial Executives Institute, British Institute of Management, Australasian Association of University Teachers of Accounting, Beta Alpha Psi, Beta Gamma Sigma. Awards, honors: Certificate of Merit from National Association of Accountants, 1958-59; U.S. Steel Foundation fellow, 1960-61; Wissner Award for Teaching Excellence, 1968-69.

WRITINGS: Uses of Accounting for Small Business, Bureau of Business Research, University of Michigan, 1962; (editor with Thomas F. Keller) Financial Accounting Theory: Issues and Controversies, McGraw, Volume I, 1964, 2nd edition, 1973, Volume II, 1969; (with others) The American Accounting Association: Its First Fifty Years, Prentice-Hall, 1966; (editor) Business Schools and the Challenge of International Business, Graduate School of Business Administration, Tulane University, 1968; (editor with Alfred Rappaport and Peter A. Firmin) Public Reporting by Conglomerates: The

Issues, the Problems, and Some Possible Solutions, Prentice-Hall, 1968; *Forging Accounting Principles in Five Countries: A History and an Analysis of Trends,* Stipes, 1972; *Forging Accounting Principles in Australia,* Australian Society of Accountants, 1973. Contributor of articles to professional and academic periodicals. Book review editor, *Accounting Review,* 1962-66.

WORK IN PROGRESS: A history of the Accounting Principles Board; a biographical study of the late Henry Rand Hatfield of the University of California, Berkeley.

* * *

ZEIGER, Henry A(nthony)   1930-
(James Peterson)

PERSONAL: Born September 6, 1930, in Brooklyn, N.Y.; son of Henry and Helen (Cahill) Zeiger. *Education:* Kenyon College, B.A.; graduate courses at Columbia University, 1952; Yale University, 1955-56. *Politics:* Democrat. *Home:* 91 Joralemon St., Brooklyn, N.Y. 11201.

CAREER: Magazine Management Co., New York, N.Y., managing editor, 1958-60; *New Leader,* New York, N.Y., drama critic, 1968-69; free-lance writer. *Military service:* U.S. Army, 1953-55.

WRITINGS: (Editor and author of commentary) *The Case Against Adolf Eichmann,* New American Library, 1960; *The Seizing of the Santa Maria,* Popular Library, 1961; *Lyndon B. Johnson: Man and President,* Popular Library, 1963; *The Remarkable Henry Cabot Lodge,* Popular Library, 1964; *Ian Fleming: The Spy Who Came in with the Gold,* Duell, Sloan & Pearce, 1965; *Robert F. Kennedy: A Biography* (juvenile), Meredith, 1969; *Inquest!: Ted Kennedy-Mary Jo Kopechne,* Tower, 1970; *Sam the Plumber,* New American Library, 1970; *The Jersey Mob,* New American Library, 1972. Play anthologized in *The Best Short Plays of 1955-1956,* Beacon Press, 1957.

BIOGRAPHICAL/CRITICAL SOURCES: Best Sellers, February 1, 1969.

* * *

ZERNOV, Nicolas   1898-

PERSONAL: Born October 9, 1898, in Moscow, Russia; son of Michael and Sophia (Kesler) Zernov; married Militsa Lavrov, 1927; *Education:* Moscow University, medical student, 1917; Beograd University, B.A. in Theology, 1925; Oxford University, Ph.D., 1932, M.A., 1947, D.D., 1966. *Religion:* Russian Orthodox. *Home:* 4A Northmoor Rd., Oxford, England.

CAREER: Russian Student Christian Movement Outside Russia, general secretary, 1925-35; Fellowship of St. Albans and St. Sergius, secretary, 1935-47; Oxford University, Oxford, England, Spalding Lecturer in Eastern Orthodox Culture, 1947-66. Principal of Catholicate College, South India, 1953-54; visiting professor at Drew University, 1956, at University of Iowa, and at Duke University. Vice-president of Fellowship of St. Albans and St. Sergius; warden of St. Gregory and St. Macrina House, Oxford University. *Member:* Royal Society of Literature (fellow).

WRITINGS: Moscow, the Third Rome, Macmillan, 1937; *St. Sergius, Builder of Russia,* Macmillan, 1939; *The Church of the Eastern Christians,* S.P.C.K., 1942, Macmillan, 1944; *Three Russian Prophets: Khomiakov, Dostoevsky, Soloviev,* S.C.M. Press, 1944; *The Russians and Their Church,* Macmillan, 1945, 3rd edition, S.P.C.K., 1964; (editor) *Manual of Eastern Orthodox Prayers,* Macmillan, 1945.

The Reintegration of the Church: A Study of Intercommunion, S.C.M. Press, 1952, Seabury, 1953; *Vselenskaia tserkov i russkoe pravoslavie,* Y.M.C.A. Press (Paris), 1952; *Ruslands kirke og nordens kirke,* [Copenhagen], 1954; *The Christian East: The Eastern Orthodox Church and Indian Christianity,* Delhi S.P.C.K., 1956; *Eastern Christendom: A Study of the Origins and Development of the Eastern Orthodox Church,* Putnam, 1961; *Il Christianismo orientale milano,* Il Saggiatore, 1962; *Christianismo orientale Madrid,* Ed. Guadarrama, 1962; *Orthodox Encounter: The Christian East and the Ecumenical Movement,* James Clarke, 1962; *The Russian Religious Renaissance of the Twentieth Century,* Darton, Longman & Todd, 1963, Harper, 1964; *Na Perelome* (about three generations of a Moscow family), Y.M.C.A. Press, 1970; *Za Rubegtom* (chronicle of the Zernov family), Y.M.C.A. Press, 1972; *Biographical Index and Bibliography of Works of Russian Emigre Authors on Theology, Religious Philosophy, Church History and Orthodox Culture, 1921-1972,* G.K. Hall, 1973. Contributor of articles and book reviews to professional journals.

* * *

ZOLLA, Elemire   1926-

PERSONAL: Born July 9, 1926, in Turin, Italy; son of Venanzio (a painter) and Blanche (a pianist; maiden name, Smith) Zolla. *Education:* University of Turin, Doctor in jurisprudence, 1954. *Home:* Piazza S. Anselmo 2, Rome, Italy. *Office:* Faculty of Magistero, University of Genoa, Genoa, Italy.

CAREER: University of Rome, Rome, Italy, faculty of letters and philosophy, chairman, American literature, 1959—; La Nuova Italia Editrice, Florence, Italy, director of *Conoscenza Religiosa* (literary and religious studies quarterly), 1969—. Director of Istituto Ticinese Alti Studi (summer institute in symbology and archaeology), Lugano, Switzerland. *Awards, honors:* Premio Strega, opera prima, 1956, for *Minuetto all'inferno;* Premio Crotone, 1959, for *Eclissi dell'intellettuale.*

WRITINGS: Minuetto all'inferno (novel), Einaudi (Turin), 1956; *Eclissi dell'intellettuale* (essays), Bompiani (Milan), 1956, 5th edition, 1965, translation by Raymond Rosenthal published in America as *The Eclipse of the Intellectual,* Funk, 1968; *Cecilia; o, La Disattenzione* (novel), Garzanti, 1961; *Volgarita e dolore* (essays), Bompiani, 1962, 3rd edition, 1966, English translation included in *The Eclipse of the Intellectual; Le origini del trascendentalismo* (essay), Edizioni di Storia e Letteratura (Rome), 1963; *Storia del fantasticare* (essay), Bompiani, 1964; (translator into Spanish) Herman Melville, *Clarel,* Einaudi, 1965; *I Letterati e lo sciamano* (essay on the Indian in American literature), Bompiani, 1968, translation by Raymond Rosenthal published in America, Harcourt, 1973; *Le potenze dell'anima* (essay), Bompiani, 1968; (contributor) Raymond Rosenthal, editor, *McLuhan: Pro and Con* (essays), Funk, 1968; *Che cos'e la tradizione?* (essay), Bompiani, 1971. Also author of *Le Parole e la cosmogonia* (philological study of Indo-European roots), published in special issue on linguistics of *Conoscenza Religiosa,* 1972.

Editor: (With Alberto Moravia) *I Moralisti moderni* (anthology), Garzanti (Milan), 1959; *La Psicanalisi* (anthology), Garzanti, 1960; Emily Dickinson, *Selected Poems and Letters,* U. Mursia (Milan), 1961; *Antologia di Sade,* Longnesi, 1962; *I Mistici* (anthology), Garzanti, 1963. Editor of special issue on American Indians, *Conoscenza Religiosa,* 1970.

Contributor to *Lo Spettatore Italiano, Il Pensiero Critico, Tempo Presente, Questioni, Nuovi Argomenti, Corriere della Sera* (Milan), *La Nacion* (Buenos Aires), *Conoscenza Religiosa.*

WORK IN PROGRESS: A special issue of *Conoscenza Religiosa* for 1973, devoted to the Vedas and Yoga; a book, *Introduction to Alchemy.*

SIDELIGHTS: In a review of *The Eclipse of the Intellectual,* Roger Shattuck writes that Zolla "is concerned not so much with the avant-garde as with the modern." He states that some of his basic concepts show the influence of Croce, Ortega, and Walter Benjamin, but that "beneath lies a slow-burning Catholicism that finally gives a passionate tone to his case against a culture produced by the trauma of the machine." Elaine Bender of *Library Journal* calls the book "a fascinating criticism by a man who seems to be able to generalize in spite of the fragmentation of our culture"; however, F.M. Esfandiary views it as "another example in this long procession of literary self-flagellation." Shattuck mentions Zolla's "stylistic obscurity" and "ambivalence" about modernity, being convinced that "he is in closer touch with the printed record of our lives than with those lives themselves . . . .I hear a man resolutely defending an intellectual position that he knows he will not be able to hold long in the face of forces to which he, more than most, is sensitive."

In a review of *Che cọs' e la tradizione?,* a *Times Literary Supplement* writer states: "Elemire Zolla is a thinker who must be watched; and he is in the prime of life. His deep, polymathic probing of the terms of human existence makes it sensible to compare him with Simone Weil, while some of his conclusions about ultimate mysteries—expressed in signs, symbols and sacraments, the sense of which we have lost—will make us think of the later T.S. Eliot or the *Anathemata* of David Jones. . . . Professor Zolla is far from being a romantic. . . . He writes in the spirit of a poet and artist in rebellion against a delirium of that negation which, according to Aquinas, was a definition of evil; his book should have an echo in the hearts of all those writers who are uneasy about the drift of our civilization"

BIOGRAPHICAL/CRITICAL SOURCES: La Fiera Litteraria, June 17, 1956, November 15, 1959, March 16, 1961; *Paragone,* XII, 1959, VIII, 1961; *Vitae Pensiers,* January, 1969; *Library Journal,* January 1, 1969; *New York Times Book Review,* August 10, 1969; *New York Review of Books,* March 12, 1970; *La Nacion,* April 2, 1971; *Settanta,* April 3, 1971; *Esquire,* May, 1971; *Times Literary Supplement,* October 29, 1971.

* * *

ZUKOFSKY, Louis 1904-

PERSONAL: Born January 23, 1904, in New York, N.Y.; son of Paul and Chana (Pruss) Zukofsky; married Celia Thaew (a composer), August 20, 1939; children: Paul. *Education:* Columbia University, M.A., 1924.

CAREER: University of Wisconsin, Madison, instructor in English, 1930-31; Polytechnic Institute of Brooklyn, Brooklyn, N.Y., 1947-66, began as assistant, became associate professor of English, retired, 1966. Visiting assistant professor, Colgate University, summer, 1947; poet-in-residence, San Francisco State College (now California State University), 1958. *Awards, honors:* Lola Ridge Memorial Award of Poetry Society of America, 1949; Longview Foundation award, 1961; Union League Civic and Arts Foundation Prize of *Poetry* Magazine, 1964; Oscar Blumenthal/Charles Leviton Prize of *Poetry* Magazine, 1966, and National Endowment for the Arts, *American Literary Anthology* awards, 1967 and 1968, both for excerpts from *"A" 13-21* published in *Poetry* Magazine; nominee, 1968, for National Book Awards in poetry.

WRITINGS: (Editor) An *"Objectivists" Anthology,* To Publishers (Le Beausset, France), 1932; (with Rene Tau-

pin) *Le Style Apollinaire* (criticism), [Paris], 1934; *First Half of "A"* 9, privately printed, 1934; *55 Poems,* Press of J.A. Decker, 1941; *Anew,* Press of J.A. Decker, 1946; *A Test of Poetry* (criticism), The Objectivist Press, 1948, Routledge & Kegan Paul, 1952, Jargon/Corinth Books, 1964, *Some Time* (poetry), Jargon Books, 1956; *Barely & Widely,* [New York], 1958; *5 Statements for Poetry,* [San Francisco], 1958; *It Was,* Origin Press (Kyoto), 1959; *"A" 1-12* (poetry; with an essay on poetry by the author and a note by William Carlos Williams), Origin Press, 1959, 2nd edition (with foreword by the author and a note by Robert Creeley), J. Cape, 1966, Doubleday, 1967; *Louis Zukofsky: 16 Once Published* (a selection by his wife, Celia Zukofsky, from *55 Poems, Anew, Some Time, Barely and Widely),* Wild Hawthorn Press (Edinburgh), 1962; *Bottom: on Shakespeare* (criticism), two volumes (Volume II is a musical setting for Shakespeare's "Pericles," by Celia Zukofsky), University of Texas Press, 1963; *I's,* Trobar Books, 1963; *Found Objects,* Blue Grass Books, 1964; *After I's,* Boxwood Press, 1964; *Iyyob,* Turret Books, 1965; *An Unearthing,* [Cambridge, Mass.], 1965; *I Sent Thee Late,* [Cambridge, Mass.], 1965; *Finally a Valentine, a Poem,* Piccolo Press (London), 1965; *All: The Collected Short Poems, 1923-1958,* Norton, 1965; *All: The Collected Short Poems, 1956-1964,* Norton, 1966; *Prepositions* (collected critical essays), Rapp & Whiting, 1967, Horizon, 1968; *Little: A Fragment for Careenagers,* Black Sparrow Press, 1967; *"A" 14,* Turret Books, 1967; *Ferdinand, Including "It Was,"* Grossman, 1968; (translator, with Celia Zukofsky; music by Paul Zukofsky) *Catullus Fragmenta,* Turret Books, 1968; *"A" 13-21* (excerpts first published serially in *Poetry* Magazine), Doubleday, 1969; (translator with Celia Zukofsky) *Catullus,* Grossman, 1969; *Autobiography* (poems set to music by Celia Zukofsky), Grossman, 1970; *Little* (novel), Grossman, 1970; *All the Collected Short Poems, 1923-1964,* Norton, 1971; *"A" 24,* Grossman, 1972; *Arise, Arise* (play; first produced Off-Broadway at Cinematheque Theatre, August, 1965), first published in *Kulture,* 1962, Grossman, 1973. Work included in *American Literary Anthology,* Volume I, edited by John Hawkes, Farrar, Strauss, 1966, and Volume II, edited by George Plimpton and Peter Ardery, Random House, 1968.

WORK IN PROGRESS: "A" 22 and "A" 23.

SIDELIGHTS: Zukofsky's poems have been acclaimed by such fellow-poets as Ezra Pound, Marianne Moore, William Carlos Williams, Robert Duncan, Robert Creeley, and Kenneth Rexroth. Robert Beum has written: ". . . the best of Louis Zukofsky's lyrics will stand with those of Williams. . . . it seems only just to concede Zukofsky himself the credit for having established the propriety of sustained rhyme in the short-lined, speech-cadenced lyric. The one other centrality of Zukofsky's style—one of his dominant styles—enormously successful and from which many of the verslibrists have much to learn, is the experimenting with counterpoint. People whom Williams hasn't convinced that the poet can still sing in the 20th century . . . must by all means reorient their views with a copy of *Some Time.*"

Of one of his works, Zukofsky writes: "To me *Bottom* is: 1) A long poem built on a theme for the variety of its recurrences. The theme is simply that Shakespeare's text thruout favors the clear physical eye against the erring brain, and that this theme has historical implications. 2) A valid skepticism that as 'philosophy of history' (taking in the arts and sciences) my book takes exception to all philosophies from Shakespeare's point of view ('Shakespeare's,' as expressed above and as excused by my preface to the book). 3) A continuation of my work on prosody in my other writings. In this sense my wife's music saves me a lot of words. 4) A poet's autobiography, as involvement of twenty years in a work shows him up, or as in the case of Shakespeare his words show it, are his life."

Guy Davenport calls Zukofsky's long poem "*A*," "one of the most beautiful books in English," and of his translation of Catullus he says it is "a feat so astounding as to seem mad, for the poet has kept the vowels and consonants of the original so closely that the translation when read aloud sounds like the Latin." Davenport describes Zukofsky's poetry as "wonderfully lyrical and wonderfully intelligent." He continues: "His prose, which ranges from long books about Shakespeare to fiction to essays with a good hard idea per half inch of type, is equally good—but equally terse, guileless and uncompromising." "Louis Zukofsky," he writes, "is that peculiarly American phenomenon, the writer too good for any known audience, and, if that weren't enough to keep him solidly within the obscurity of his excellence, a writer so indifferent to fame that he has never lifted a finger in his own interest [although] he has built up a body of work that has influenced practically every poet worth reading today."

BIOGRAPHICAL/CRITICAL SOURCES: Ezra Pound, *Polite Essays*, Faber, 1937; *New York Times Book Review*, July 28, 1957, June 15, 1969, December 6, 1970; *Poetry*, January, 1958; *Black Mountain Review*, number 7; *Kulchur*, numbers 12 and 14; *The Critic*, February-March, 1967; *National Review*, March 25, 1969; *Chicago Panorama*, September 13, 1970; *Saturday Review*, September 5, 1970; *The New York Times*, September 17, 1970; *Agenda*, autumn-winter, 1970, autumn-winter, 1971-72.